Recent Titles in the
Children's and Young Adult Literature Reference Series

Catherine Barr, Series Editor

A to Zoo: Subject Access to Children's Picture Books, Supplement to the
Ninth Edition
Rebecca L. Thomas

A to Zoo: Subject Access to Children's Picture Books, Ninth Edition
Rebecca L. Thomas

Best Books for Children: Preschool Through Grade 6, 10th Edition
Catherine Barr

Best STEM Resources for Nextgen Scientists: The Essential Selection and
User's Guide
Jennifer L. Hopwood

Build It, Make It, Do It, Play It! Subject Access to the Best How-To Guides
for Children and Teens
Catharine R. Bomhold and Terri Elder

Diversity Programming for Digital Youth: Promoting Cultural Competence in the
Children's Library
Jamie Campbell Naidoo

Best Books for High School Readers, Grades 9–12: Third Edition
Catherine Barr

Best Books for Middle School and Junior High Readers, Grades 6–9:
Third Edition
Catherine Barr

Rainbow Family Collections: Selecting and Using Children's Books with Lesbian,
Gay, Bisexual, Transgender, and Queer Content
Jamie Campbell Naidoo

A to Zoo

10th Edition

Rebecca L. Thomas

Subject Access to Children's Picture Books

Children's and Young Adult Literature Reference
Catherine Barr, Series Editor

LIBRARIES UNLIMITED™

An Imprint of ABC-CLIO, LLC

Santa Barbara, California • Denver, Colorado

Library of Congress Cataloging-in-Publication Data is available at www.loc.gov.

ISBN: 978-1-4408-3434-9 (hardcover)
       978-1-4408-3435-6 (ebook)

22 21 20 19 18   1 2 3 4 5

This book is also available as an eBook.

Libraries Unlimited
An Imprint of ABC-CLIO, LLC

ABC-CLIO, LLC
130 Cremona Drive, P.O. Box 1911
Santa Barbara, California 93116-1911
www.abc-clio.com

This book is printed on acid-free paper ∞
Manufactured in the United States of America

Contents

Preface

A to Zoo: Subject Access to Children's Picture Books has been the premier resource for teachers, librarians, parents, and anyone planning programs for young people. It was created by John and Carolyn Lima in the early 1980s and is now one of the most highly regarded reference books in school and public libraries. John and Carolyn Lima's creation has served generations of readers and provides the foundation for future editions and users. Rebecca L. Thomas continues the tradition established by the Limas. Dr. Thomas has a PhD in Early and Middle Childhood Education from the Ohio State University. She retired in 2011 after 35 years as an elementary school librarian in the Shaker Heights City Schools. She has also been a university teacher and author in the field of children's literature.

> "*A to Zoo* continues to be the single best source for locating children's picture books by subject, both for personal use and for supporting programming and curricular needs." – **ARBAonline, October 1, 2014**

The importance of the picture book, long a source of delight and learning for young readers, continues today with the increasing emphasis on early childhood education and on reading, and with the need for supervised childcare for working parents. Teachers, librarians, and parents are finding the picture book an important learning and entertainment tool.

Even with today's computerized library catalogs, choosing the right book for a particular program or need can be time-consuming and frustrating without some guidance. The specialized subjects in *A to Zoo* give librarians, teachers, and parents easy access to books that will meet the needs of their patrons and their programs. Public librarians organizing thematic programs, school librarians and teachers looking for curriculum connections, and parents planning learning experiences for home-schooling or for reading enjoyment will find using *A to Zoo* provides a time-saving, up-to-date resource focused on specific needs and interests. The 10th edition of *A to Zoo: Subject Access to Children's Picture Books* has 19,716 titles cataloged under 1,223 subjects.

Several library collections served as guides in the selection process, including the San Diego Public Library—the collection that served as the original resource for early editions of *A to Zoo*. Also examined was the catalog of the CLEVNET libraries in Ohio, which includes the Cleveland Public Library along with numerous independent libraries in northeastern Ohio, and the collections of the Cuyahoga County Public Library system. School library collections were also explored, including those of the Shaker Heights (Ohio) City schools and other schools in northeastern Ohio. Standard reviewing sources were also consulted, including *School Library Journal* and *Booklist*.

Titles with copyright dates in the 2000s are generally included, while titles with earlier dates have been checked for availability. Out-of-print titles are retained because public and school library collections are largely retrospective. Folktales, poetry, and informational picture books in particular are maintained in many libraries along with books about holidays and seasons. Popular titles from beloved authors and illustrators will still be found here, regardless of the copyright date.

New titles from 2016 and 2017 have been added to this edition along with the titles in the *Supplement to the 9th Edition* (2016). Many sources were consulted to select titles for inclusion, including the library collections mentioned above, along with published reviews and review copies from publishers.

The picture book, as it is broadly defined within the scope of this book, is a fiction or nonfiction title with illustrations occupying as much or more space than the text and with text, vocabulary, or concepts suitable for preschool through grade two. It is noted, however that picture books appeal to a wider audience; adults, older children, and others often find picture books enjoyable, useful, and informative.

HOW TO USE THIS BOOK

A to Zoo can be used to obtain information about children's picture books in two ways: to learn the titles, authors, and illustrators of books on a particular subject, such as "dragons" or "weddings"; or to ascertain the subject (or subjects) when only the title, author and title, or illustrator and title are known. For example, if the title *Marigold bakes a cake* is known, this volume will enable the user to discover that *Marigold bakes a cake* is written by Mike Malbrough, illustrated by the author, published by Philomel in 2017, and that the subject areas are: Activities – baking, cooking. Animals – cats. Behavior – messy. Birds. Character traits – orderliness. Character traits – perfectionism.

For ease and convenience of reference use, *A to Zoo* is divided into five sections:

    Subject Headings
    Subject Guide
    Bibliographic Guide
    Title Index
    Illustrator Index

SUBJECT HEADINGS: This section contains an alphabetical list of the subjects cataloged in this book. The subject headings reflect the established terms used commonly in public libraries, originally based on questions asked by parents and teachers and then modified and adapted by librarians. To facilitate reference use, and because subjects are requested in a variety of terms, the list of subject headings contains numerous cross-references. Subheadings are arranged alphabetically under each general topic, for example:

    Animals (general topic)
    Animals – apes *see* Animals – baboons; Animals – chimpanzees; Animals – gorillas; Animals – monkeys (cross reference)

Animals – babies (subheading)
Animals – badgers (subheading)

SUBJECT GUIDE: This guide to 19,716 picture books for preschool children through second graders is cataloged under 1,223 subjects. The guide reflects the arrangement in the Subject Headings—alphabetical by subject heading and subheading. Many books, of course, relate to more than one subject, and this comprehensive list provides a means of identifying all those books that may contain any information or material on a particular subject.

If, for example, the user wants books on knitting, the Subject Headings section will show that Activities is a subject classification. A look in the Subject Guide reveals that under Activities – knitting there are 20 titles listed alphabetically by author. For ease of access to the extensive list of subjects, many headings are organized in groupings:

Activities	Emotions	Musical instruments
Anatomy	Ethnic groups in the U.S.	Mythical creatures
Animals	Family life	Religion
Behavior	Foreign lands	Reptiles
Birds	Format, unusual	Royalty
Careers	Holidays	Seasons
Character traits	Illness	Senses
Clothing	Indians of North	Sports
Concepts	America	Toys
Disabilities	Insects	Weather

Using the list of Subject Headings, a teacher can examine the general subject Activities and see topics such as driving, flying, hiking, running, traveling, and walking to select books for a program on motion. Or a parent can look through the list of Careers to plan a home-schooling lesson on jobs and work. A librarian might explore the books in Ethnic Groups in the U.S. and find African Americans and then organize programming for Black History Month.

Two of the most-used groupings in the Subject Headings list are Behavior and Character Traits. These two areas contain subheadings such as Behavior – boredom, Behavior – bullying, teasing, Behavior – fighting, arguing, Behavior – sharing, Character traits – helpfulness, Character traits – individuality, Character traits – shyness, and Character traits – vanity. They are the "go to" headings for programs on character development and conduct. Cross-references have been generated for all of the subheadings for Behavior and Character Traits.

BIBLIOGRAPHIC GUIDE: Each book is listed with full bibliographic information. This section is arranged alphabetically by author, or by title when the author is unknown, or by uniform (classic) title. Each entry contains bibliographic information in order: author, title, illustrator, publisher and date of publication, International Standard Book Number (ISBN), and subjects, listed according to the alphabetical classification in the Subject Headings section.

The user can consult the Bibliographic Guide to find complete data on each of the titles listed in the Subject Guide. Turning from the Subject Guide heading of School to consult the Bibliographic Guide, for example, the user will find the following entry:

> **Yousafzai, Malala.** *Malala's magic pencil* ill. by Kerascoët. Little, Brown, 2017. ISBN 978-031631957-7 Subj: Behavior – seeking better things. Character traits – bravery. Character traits – freedom. Foreign lands – Pakistan. School. Violence, nonviolence.

In the case of joint authors, the second author is listed in alphabetical order, followed by the book title and the name of the primary author or main entry. The user can then locate the primary author for complete bibliographic information. For example:

> **Hamilton, Emma Walton.** *The very fairy princess: a spooky, sparkly Halloween* (Andrews, Julie)

Bibliographic information for this title will be found in the Bibliographic Guide section under Andrews, Julie.

Titles for an author who is both a single author and a joint author are interfiled alphabetically. Where the author is not known, the entry is listed alphabetically by title with complete bibliographic information following the same format as given above.

TITLE INDEX: This section contains an alphabetical list of all titles in the book with authors in parentheses where appropriate, followed by the page number of the full listing in the Bibliographic Guide, such as:

> *In the middle of fall* (Henkes, Kevin), 816

For books with the same title, for example, *The Three Bears,* the titles are distinguished by the inclusion of the illustrators name along with the title and the page in the Bibliographic Guide.

> *The three bears*, ill. by Byron Barton (The three bears), 1177
> *The three bears*, ill. by Paul Galdone (The three bears), 1177

Variant titles are included with the relevant page numbers in the Bibliographic Guide. And, in this example, users would also want to check for related books beginning with Goldilocks.

> *The three bears ABC* (Maccarone, Grace), 934
> *The 3 bears and Goldilocks* (The three bears), 1177
> *The Three Bears' Christmas* (Duval, Kathy), 725
> *The Three Bears' Halloween* (Duval, Kathy), 725
> *The three bears holiday rhyme book* (Yolen, Jane), 1242

Ultimately, the Title Index guides the reader to the full bibliographic information in the Bibliographic Guide.

ILLUSTRATOR INDEX: This section contains an alphabetical list of illustrators with titles, author names in parentheses, and the page number of the full listing in the Bibliographic Guide. For example:

> **Lewin, Betsy.** *Click, clack, moo I love you!* (Cronin, Doreen), 690

Titles listed under an illustrator's name appear in alphabetical sequence. When the author is the same as the illustrator the author's name is not repeated.

Acknowledgments

The author wishes to express her thanks for the assistance provided by many people in bringing this book together. Special thanks to Christine McNaull whose knowledge of the database, sorting, and formatting was essential. Series editor Catherine Barr provided guidance and support throughout the process. Thanks also to Barbara Ittner of Libraries Unlimited. My family and friends provided me with time and encouragement to complete this book.

Subject Headings

Main headings, subheadings, and cross-references are arranged alphabetically and provide a quick reference to the subjects used in the Subject Guide section, where author and title names appear under appropriate headings. For more information on how subjects are grouped, see Preface page vii.

ABC books
Aborigines, Australian *see* Australian aborigines
Abused children *see* Child abuse
Accidents
Activities
Activities – babysitting
Activities – baking, cooking
Activities – ballooning
Activities – bargaining *see* Activities – trading
Activities – bartering *see* Activities – trading
Activities – bathing
Activities – cooking *see* Activities – baking, cooking
Activities – dancing
Activities – digging
Activities – drawing
Activities – driving
Activities – eating *see* Food
Activities – flying
Activities – gardening *see* Gardens, gardening
Activities – hiking
Activities – jumping
Activities – kissing *see* Kissing
Activities – knitting
Activities – making things
Activities – painting *see also* Careers – artists
Activities – photographing
Activities – picnicking
Activities – playing
Activities – reading *see* Books, reading
Activities – running
Activities – sewing
Activities – shopping *see* Shopping
Activities – singing
Activities – storytelling
Activities – swapping *see* Activities – trading
Activities – swimming *see* Sports – swimming

Activities – swinging
Activities – talking
Activities – trading
Activities – traveling
Activities – vacationing
Activities – walking
Activities – weaving
Activities – whistling
Activities – wood carving
Activities – working
Activities – writing
Adoption
Aged *see* Old age
Airplanes, airports
Alaska
Aliens
Alphabet books *see* ABC books
Ambition *see* Character traits – ambition
American Indians *see* Indians of Central America; Indians of North America; Indians of South America
Amphibians *see also* Frogs & toads; Reptiles
Amusement parks *see* Parks – amusement
Anatomy
Anatomy – belly buttons *see* Anatomy – navels
Anatomy – brain
Anatomy – ears
Anatomy – eyes
Anatomy – faces
Anatomy – feet
Anatomy – fins
Anatomy – hands
Anatomy – heads
Anatomy – mouths
Anatomy – navels
Anatomy – noses
Anatomy – skeletons
Anatomy – skin
Anatomy – tails
Anatomy – teeth *see* Teeth

Anatomy – thumbs *see* Thumb sucking
Anatomy – toes
Anatomy – tongues
Anatomy – wings
Angels
Animals *see also* Birds; Frogs & toads; Reptiles
Animals – aardvarks
Animals – anteaters
Animals – apes *see* Animals – baboons; Animals – chimpanzees; Animals – gorillas; Animals – monkeys
Animals – armadillos
Animals – babies
Animals – baboons
Animals – badgers
Animals – bandicoots
Animals – bats
Animals – bears
Animals – beavers
Animals – bison *see* Animals – buffaloes
Animals – bonobos
Animals – brush wolves *see* Animals – coyotes
Animals – buffaloes
Animals – bulls, cows
Animals – camels
Animals – caribou *see* Animals – reindeer
Animals – cats
Animals – cheetahs
Animals – chimpanzees
Animals – chipmunks
Animals – coatis
Animals – cougars
Animals – cows *see* Animals – bulls, cows
Animals – coyotes
Animals – dislike of *see* Behavior – animals, dislike of
Animals – deer
Animals – dogs
Animals – dolphins

Animals – donkeys
Animals – elephants
Animals – endangered animals
Animals – ferrets
Animals – foxes
Animals – gazelles
Animals – gerbils
Animals – giraffes
Animals – gnus
Animals – goats
Animals – gorillas
Animals – groundhogs
Animals – guinea pigs
Animals – hamsters
Animals – hedgehogs
Animals – hippopotamuses
Animals – horses, ponies
Animals – hyenas
Animals – jackals
Animals – jaguars
Animals – kangaroos
Animals – kindness to *see*
    Character traits – kindness
    to animals
Animals – koalas
Animals – lemmings
Animals – lemurs
Animals – leopards
Animals – lions
Animals – llamas
Animals – lorises
Animals – manatees
Animals – marsupials
Animals – meerkats
Animals – mice
Animals – migration *see*
    Migration
Animals – moles
Animals – mongooses
Animals – monkeys
Animals – moose
Animals – mountain lions *see*
    Animals – cougars
Animals – mules
Animals – muskoxen
Animals – muskrats
Animals – narwhals
Animals – octopuses *see*
    Octopuses
Animals – opossums *see*
    Animals – possums
Animals – orangutans
Animals – otters
Animals – oxen
Animals – pack rats
Animals – pandas
Animals – panthers *see* Animals
    – leopards
Animals – pigs
Animals – platypuses
Animals – polar bears
Animals – porcupines

Animals – possums
Animals – prairie dogs
Animals – prairie wolves *see*
    Animals – coyotes
Animals – pumas *see* Animals –
    cougars
Animals – rabbits
Animals – raccoons
Animals – rats
Animals – red pandas
Animals – reindeer
Animals – rhinoceros
Animals – salamanders *see*
    Reptiles – salamanders
Animals – sea lions
Animals – seals
Animals – service animals
Animals – sheep
Animals – shrews
Animals – skunks
Animals – sloths
Animals – slugs
Animals – snails
Animals – snow leopards *see*
    Animals – leopards
Animals – squid *see* Squid
Animals – squirrels
Animals – swine *see* Animals –
    pigs
Animals – tapirs
Animals – Tasmanian devils
Animals – tigers
Animals – voles
Animals – wallabies
Animals – walruses
Animals – warthogs
Animals – weasels
Animals – whales
Animals – wolves
Animals – wombats
Animals – woolly mammoths
Animals – worms
Animals – yaks
Animals – zebras
Anti-violence *see* Violence,
    nonviolence
Anxiety *see* Behavior –
    worrying; Emotions – fear
Apartments *see* Homes, houses
Appearance *see* Character traits
    – appearance
Aquariums
Arachnids *see* Spiders
Arguing *see* Behavior – fighting,
    arguing
Arithmetic *see* Counting,
    numbers
Art
Assertiveness *see* Character
    traits – assertiveness
Astrology *see* Zodiac

Astronauts *see* Careers –
    astronauts; Space & space
    ships
Astronomy
Aurora Borealis *see* Northern
    lights
Australian aborigines
Authors *see* Careers – writers
Authors, children *see* Children
    as authors
Automobiles
Autumn *see* Seasons – fall
Award-winning books *see*
    Caldecott award books;
    Caldecott award honor books

Babies, new *see* Family life – new
    sibling
Babies, toddlers *see also* Animals
    – babies
Bad day *see* Behavior – bad day,
    bad mood
Bad mood *see* Behavior – bad
    day, bad mood
Ballerinas *see* Ballet; Careers –
    dancers
Ballet
Balloons *see* Toys – balloons
Balls *see* Toys – balls
Barns
Bayous *see* Swamps
Beaches *see* Sea & seashore –
    beaches
Beasts *see* Monsters
Beauty shops
Bedtime
Bedwetting *see* Behavior –
    bedwetting
Behavior
Behavior – animals, dislike of
Behavior – arguing *see* Behavior
    – fighting, arguing
Behavior – bad day, bad mood
Behavior – bedwetting
Behavior – boasting, showing
    off
Behavior – boredom
Behavior – bossy
Behavior – bullying, teasing
Behavior – carelessness
Behavior – cheating
Behavior – collecting things
Behavior – disbelief
Behavior – dissatisfaction
Behavior – fidgeting
Behavior – fighting, arguing
Behavior – forgetfulness
Behavior – forgiving
Behavior – gossip, rumors
Behavior – greed
Behavior – growing up
Behavior – hiding

Behavior – hiding things
Behavior – hurrying
Behavior – imitation
Behavior – indecision
Behavior – indifference
Behavior – lost
Behavior – lost & found
  possessions
Behavior – lying
Behavior – messy
Behavior – misbehavior
Behavior – mistakes
Behavior – misunderstanding
Behavior – name calling
Behavior – naughty *see* Behavior
  – misbehavior
Behavior – needing someone
Behavior – potty training *see*
  Toilet training
Behavior – promptness,
  tardiness
Behavior – resourcefulness
Behavior – rumors *see* Behavior
  – gossip, rumors
Behavior – running away
Behavior – saving things
Behavior – secrets
Behavior – seeking better
  things
Behavior – sharing
Behavior – showing off *see*
  Behavior – boasting, showing
  off
Behavior – solitude
Behavior – stealing
Behavior – talking to strangers
Behavior – tardiness *see*
  Behavior – promptness,
  tardiness
Behavior – teasing *see* Behavior
  – bullying, teasing
Behavior – toilet training *see*
  Toilet training
Behavior – trickery
Behavior – unnoticed, unseen
Behavior – wishing
Behavior – worrying
Being different *see* Character
  traits – being different
Bereavement *see* Death;
  Emotions – grief
Bible *see* Religion
Bicycling *see* Sports – bicycling
Bigotry *see* Prejudice
Bilingual *see* Foreign languages
Birds
Birds – blackbirds
Birds – bluebirds
Birds – bluejays
Birds – buzzards
Birds – canaries
Birds – cardinals

Birds – chickadees
Birds – chickens, roosters
Birds – cockatoos
Birds – cranes
Birds – crows
Birds – cuckoos
Birds – dodos
Birds – doves
Birds – ducks
Birds – eagles
Birds – falcons
Birds – finches
Birds – flamingos
Birds – geese
Birds – guinea fowl
Birds – hawks
Birds – herons
Birds – hummingbirds
Birds – kestrels
Birds – larks
Birds – loons
Birds – macaws
Birds – magpies
Birds – nightingales
Birds – ostriches
Birds – owls
Birds – parakeets, parrots
Birds – peacocks, peahens
Birds – pelicans
Birds – penguins
Birds – pigeons
Birds – plovers
Birds – ptarmigans
Birds – puffins
Birds – ravens
Birds – roadrunners
Birds – robins
Birds – sandpipers
Birds – seagulls
Birds – sparrows
Birds – storks
Birds – swallows
Birds – swans
Birds – toucans
Birds – turkeys
Birds – vultures
Birds – woodpeckers
Birds – wrens
Birth
Birthdays
Blackouts *see* Power failures
Blindness *see* Disabilities –
  blindness; Senses – sight
Board books *see* Format,
  unusual – board books
Boasting *see* Behavior –
  boasting, showing off
Boats, ships
Bombs *see* Weapons
Boogy man *see* Monsters
Books, reading *see also* Libraries

Boredom *see* Behavior –
  boredom
Bossy *see* Behavior – bossy
Bragging *see* Behavior –
  boasting, showing off
Bravery *see* Character traits –
  bravery
Bridges
Brothers *see* Family life
  – brothers; Family life –
  brothers & sisters; Sibling
  rivalry
Brownies *see* Mythical creatures
  – elves
Bubbles
Bugs *see* Insects
Buildings
Bulldozers *see* Machines
Bullying *see* Behavior –
  bullying, teasing
Burros *see* Animals – donkeys
Buses

Cabs *see* Taxis
Cafés *see* Restaurants
Caldecott award books
Caldecott award honor books
Calendars
Camouflages *see* Disguises
Camping *see* Camps, camping
Camps, camping
Canoes & canoeing
Canyons
Cards *see* Letters, cards
Careers
Careers – acrobats
Careers – actors
Careers – aerialists
Careers – airplane pilots
Careers – architects
Careers – artists *see also*
  Activities – painting; Art
Careers – astronauts
Careers – astronomers
Careers – authors *see* Careers –
  writers
Careers – bakers
Careers – barbers
Careers – beekeepers
Careers – beggars
Careers – blacksmiths
Careers – bookbinders
Careers – bus drivers
Careers – butchers
Careers – carpenters
Careers – cartographers
Careers – chauffeurs
Careers – chefs, cooks
Careers – clergy
Careers – coaches
Careers – composers
Careers – conductors (music)

Careers – construction workers
Careers – cooks *see* Careers – chefs, cooks
Careers – custodians, janitors
Careers – dancers
Careers – dentists
Careers – detectives
Careers – doctors
Careers – doormen
Careers – electricians
Careers – emergency medical technicians
Careers – engineers
Careers – entertainers
Careers – explorers
Careers – farmers
Careers – firefighters
Careers – fishermen
Careers – forest rangers *see* Careers – park rangers
Careers – fortune tellers
Careers – fur traders
Careers – garbage collectors *see* Careers – sanitation workers
Careers – geologists
Careers – handymen
Careers – harpists
Careers – housekeepers
Careers – illustrators
Careers – inventors
Careers – janitors *see* Careers – custodians, janitors
Careers – jockeys
Careers – journalists
Careers – judges
Careers – lawyers
Careers – librarians
Careers – lifeguards
Careers – lumberjacks
Careers – magicians
Careers – mail carriers *see* Careers – postal workers
Careers – mathematicians
Careers – mechanics
Careers – messengers
Careers – meteorologists
Careers – migrant workers
Careers – military
Careers – miners
Careers – motion picture producers
Careers – musicians
Careers – naturalists
Careers – nuns
Careers – nurses
Careers – oceanographers
Careers – opera singers *see* Careers – singers
Careers – opticians, optometrists
Careers – ornithologists

Careers – painters *see* Careers – artists
Careers – paleontologists
Careers – park rangers
Careers – peddlers
Careers – pharmacists
Careers – photographers
Careers – physicians *see* Careers – doctors
Careers – plasterers
Careers – poets
Careers – police officers
Careers – postal workers
Careers – potters
Careers – preachers *see* Careers – clergy
Careers – principals *see* Careers – school principals
Careers – printers
Careers – publishers
Careers – race car drivers
Careers – railroad engineers
Careers – ranchers
Careers – rangers *see* Careers – park rangers
Careers – sailors *see* Careers – military; Sailors
Careers – salespeople
Careers – sanitation workers
Careers – school principals
Careers – scientists
Careers – sculptors
Careers – seamstresses
Careers – shepherds
Careers – sheriffs
Careers – shoe shiners
Careers – shoemakers
Careers – singers
Careers – soldiers *see* Careers – military
Careers – storekeepers
Careers – tailors
Careers – teachers
Careers – toy makers
Careers – train engineers *see* Careers – railroad engineers
Careers – truck drivers
Careers – veterinarians
Careers – waiters, waitresses
Careers – weather reporters *see* Careers – meteorologists
Careers – weavers
Careers – window cleaners
Careers – woodcarvers
Careers – writers
Careers – zookeepers
Carelessness *see* Behavior – carelessness
Caribou *see* Animals – reindeer
Carnivals *see* Fairs, festivals
Carousels *see* Merry-go-rounds
Cars *see* Automobiles

Castles
Caterpillars *see* Insects – butterflies, caterpillars
Cave drawings *see* Petroglyphs
Cave dwellers
Caves
Cell phone *see* Telephone, cell phone
Centipedes *see* Crustaceans – centipedes, millipedes
Chanukah *see* Holidays – Hanukkah
Character traits
Character traits – ambition
Character traits – appearance
Character traits – assertiveness
Character traits – being different
Character traits – bravery
Character traits – cleanliness
Character traits – cleverness
Character traits – clumsiness
Character traits – completing things
Character traits – compromising
Character traits – conceit
Character traits – confidence
Character traits – cooperation
Character traits – courage *see* Character traits – bravery
Character traits – cruelty to animals *see* Character traits – kindness to animals
Character traits – curiosity
Character traits – flattery
Character traits – foolishness
Character traits – fortune *see* Character traits – luck
Character traits – freedom
Character traits – generosity
Character traits – helpfulness
Character traits – honesty
Character traits – hopefulness
Character traits – incentive *see* Character traits – ambition
Character traits – individuality
Character traits – kindness
Character traits – kindness to animals
Character traits – laziness
Character traits – loyalty
Character traits – luck
Character traits – meanness
Character traits – optimism
Character traits – orderliness
Character traits – ostracism *see* Character traits – being different
Character traits – patience, impatience

Character traits – perfectionism
Character traits – perseverance
Character traits – persistence
Character traits – practicality
Character traits – pride
Character traits – questioning
Character traits – responsibility
Character traits – selfishness
Character traits – shyness
Character traits – smallness
Character traits – stubbornness
Character traits – vanity
Character traits – willfulness
Character traits – wisdom
Cheating *see* Behavior – cheating
Cheerleading
Cherubs *see* Angels
Child abuse
Children as authors
Children as illustrators
Children as inventors
Church
Circular tales
Circus
Cities, towns
Cleanliness *see* Character traits – cleanliness
Cleverness *see* Character traits – cleverness
Climate change *see* Ecology
Cloaks *see* Clothing – coats
Clocks, watches
Clothing
Clothing – aprons
Clothing – boots
Clothing – coats
Clothing – costumes
Clothing – dresses
Clothing – gloves, mittens
Clothing – handbags, purses
Clothing – hats
Clothing – kimonos
Clothing – neckties
Clothing – pajamas
Clothing – pants
Clothing – pockets
Clothing – scarves
Clothing – shirts
Clothing – shoes
Clothing – socks
Clothing – suits
Clothing – sweaters
Clothing – underwear
Clowns, jesters
Clubs, gangs
Clumsiness *see* Character traits – clumsiness
Cold *see* Concepts – cold & heat; Weather – cold

Collecting things *see* Behavior – collecting things
Communication
Communities, neighborhoods
Competition *see* Contests; Sibling rivalry; Sports; Sportsmanship
Completing things *see* Character traits – completing things
Compromising *see* Character traits – compromising
Computers *see also* Technology
Conceit *see* Character traits – conceit
Concepts
Concepts – change
Concepts – cold & heat
Concepts – color
Concepts – counting *see* Counting, numbers
Concepts – distance
Concepts – left & right
Concepts – measurement
Concepts – motion
Concepts – opposites
Concepts – patterns
Concepts – perspective
Concepts – self *see* Self-concept
Concepts – shape
Concepts – size
Concepts – speed
Concepts – up & down
Concepts – weight
Confidence *see* Character traits – confidence
Conservation *see* Ecology
Contests
Cooking *see* Activities – baking, cooking
Cooks *see* Careers – bakers; Careers – chefs, cooks
Cooperation *see* Character traits – cooperation
Counting, numbers
Countries, foreign *see* Foreign lands
Country
Courage *see* Character traits – bravery
Cowboys, cowgirls
Cows *see* Animals – bulls, cows
Crafts *see* Activities – making things
Creation
Creatures *see* Monsters; Mythical creatures
Creeks *see* Rivers
Crime
Crocodiles *see* Reptiles – alligators, crocodiles

Cruelty to animals *see* Character traits – kindness to animals
Crustaceans
Crustaceans – centipedes, millipedes
Crustaceans – crabs
Crustaceans – lobsters
Crustaceans – shrimp
Crying *see* Emotions
Cumulative tales
Curiosity *see* Character traits – curiosity
Currency *see* Money
Cycles *see* Activities – bicycling; Motorcycles

Dark *see* Night; Power failures
Darkness – fear *see* Emotions – fear
Dawn *see* Morning
Day
Day care *see* School – nursery
Daydreams *see* Dreams
Days of the week, months of the year
Deafness *see* Anatomy – ears; Disabilities – deafness; Senses – hearing
Death
Demons *see* Devil; Monsters
Department stores *see* Shopping; Stores
Desert
Detective stories *see* Careers – detectives; Mystery stories; Problem solving
Devil
Dictionaries
Diet *see* Food; Health & fitness
Diggers *see* Careers – construction workers; Machines
Diners *see* Restaurants
Dinosaurs
Disabilities
Disabilities – ADD
Disabilities – Asperger's
Disabilities – autism
Disabilities – blindness *see also* Anatomy – eyes
Disabilities – cerebral palsy
Disabilities – deafness *see also* Anatomy – ears
Disabilities – Down syndrome
Disabilities – dyslexia
Disabilities – mental disabilities
Disabilities – physical disabilities
Disabilities – stuttering
Disbelief *see* Behavior – disbelief

Discrimination *see* Prejudice

Diseases *see* Illness

Disguises

Dissatisfaction *see* Behavior – dissatisfaction

Diversity *see* Ethnic groups in the U.S.

Diving *see* Sports – skin diving

Divorce

Down & up *see* Concepts – up & down

Dragons

Dreams *see also* Nightmares

Dwarfs, midgets

Dwellings *see* Buildings; Homes, houses

Dying *see* Death

Ears *see* Anatomy – ears; Disabilities – deafness; Senses – hearing

Earth

Earthquakes

Eating *see* Food

Ecology

Education *see* School

Eggs

Egyptian language *see* Hieroglyphics

Elderly *see* Old age

Elevators, escalators

Emotions

Emotions – anger

Emotions – embarrassment

Emotions – envy, jealousy

Emotions – fear

Emotions – grief

Emotions – happiness

Emotions – hate

Emotions – jealousy *see* Emotions – envy, jealousy

Emotions – loneliness

Emotions – love

Emotions – sadness

Emotions – unhappiness *see* Emotions – happiness; Emotions – sadness

Engineered books *see* Format, unusual – toy & movable books

Entertainment *see* Theater

Entrepreneur *see* Money

Environment *see* Ecology

Eskimos *see also* Indians of North American – Inuit

Ethnic groups in the U.S.

Ethnic groups in the U.S. – African Americans

Ethnic groups in the U.S. – Amish

Ethnic groups in the U.S. – Arab Americans

Ethnic groups in the U.S. – Asian Americans

Ethnic groups in the U.S. – Black Americans *see* Ethnic groups in the U.S. – African Americans

Ethnic groups in the U.S. – Cajuns

Ethnic groups in the U.S. – Cambodian Americans

Ethnic groups in the U.S. – Chinese Americans

Ethnic groups in the U.S. – Cuban Americans

Ethnic groups in the U.S. – Dominican Americans

Ethnic groups in the U.S. – East Indian Americans

Ethnic groups in the U.S. – Filipino Americans

Ethnic groups in the U.S. – French Americans

Ethnic groups in the U.S. – German Americans

Ethnic groups in the U.S. – Greek Americans

Ethnic groups in the U.S. – Guatemalan Americans

Ethnic groups in the U.S. – Haitian Americans

Ethnic groups in the U.S. – Hispanic Americans

Ethnic groups in the U.S. – Hmong Americans

Ethnic groups in the U.S. – Hungarian Americans

Ethnic groups in the U.S. – Irish Americans

Ethnic groups in the U.S. – Italian Americans

Ethnic groups in the U.S. – Jamaican Americans

Ethnic groups in the U.S. – Japanese Americans

Ethnic groups in the U.S. – Jewish Americans *see* Jewish culture

Ethnic groups in the U.S. – Korean Americans

Ethnic groups in the U.S. – Lebanese Americans

Ethnic groups in the U.S. – Mexican Americans

Ethnic groups in the U.S. – Pakistani Americans

Ethnic groups in the U.S. – Puerto Rican Americans

Ethnic groups in the U.S. – Russian Americans

Ethnic groups in the U.S. – Shakers

Ethnic groups in the U.S. – Somali Americans

Ethnic groups in the U.S. – Sudanese Americans

Ethnic groups in the U.S. – Swedish Americans

Ethnic groups in the U.S. – Tibetan Americans

Ethnic groups in the U.S. – Vietnamese Americans

Etiquette

Evening *see* Twilight

Evolution

Exercise *see* Health & fitness – exercise

Experiments *see* Science

Extraterrestrial beings *see* Aliens

Eye glasses *see* Glasses

Eyes *see* Anatomy – eyes; Glasses; Disabilities – blindness; Senses – sight

Fables *see* Folk & fairy tales

Fairies

Fairs, festivals

Fairy tales *see* Folk & fairy tales

Family life

Family life – aunts, uncles

Family life – brothers *see also* Family life; Family life – brothers & sisters; Sibling rivalry

Family life – brothers & sisters

Family life – cousins

Family life – daughters

Family life – fathers

Family life – grandfathers

Family life – grandmothers

Family life – grandparents

Family life – great-grandparents

Family life – mothers

Family life – new sibling

Family life – only child

Family life – parents

Family life – same-sex parents

Family life – single-parent families

Family life – sisters *see also* Family life; Family life – brothers & sisters; Sibling rivalry

Family life – sons

Family life – stepchildren *see* Divorce; Family life – stepfamilies

Family life – stepfamilies

Family life – stepparents *see* Divorce; Family life – stepfamilies

Farms

Feathers

Feeling *see* Senses – touch

Feelings *see* Emotions
Fidgeting *see* Behavior – fidgeting
Fighting *see* Behavior – fighting, arguing
Fingers *see* Anatomy – hands
Finishing things *see* Character traits – completing things
Fire
Fire engines *see* Careers – firefighters; Trucks
Fish
Fish – seahorses
Fish – sharks
Fitness *see* Health & fitness
Flags
Flattery *see* Character traits – flattery
Flowers
Flowers – roses
Fold-out books *see* Format, unusual – toy & movable books
Folk & fairy tales
Folk & fairy tales – pourquoi tales
Food
Foolishness *see* Character traits – foolishness
Foreign lands
Foreign lands – Afghanistan
Foreign lands – Africa
Foreign lands – Antarctic
Foreign lands – Arabia
Foreign lands – Arctic
Foreign lands – Argentina
Foreign lands – Armenia
Foreign lands – Asia
Foreign lands – Australia
Foreign lands – Austria
Foreign lands – Bangladesh
Foreign lands – Bavaria *see* Foreign lands – Austria; Foreign lands – Germany
Foreign lands – Belarus
Foreign lands – Belgium
Foreign lands – Bosnia-Herzegovina
Foreign lands – Brazil
Foreign lands – British Columbia
Foreign lands – Burkina Faso
Foreign lands – Cambodia
Foreign lands – Cameroon
Foreign lands – Canada
Foreign lands – Caribbean Islands
Foreign lands – Central America
Foreign lands – Chad
Foreign lands – Chile
Foreign lands – China
Foreign lands – Colombia

Foreign lands – Congo (Democratic Republic)
Foreign lands – Costa Rica
Foreign lands – Cuba
Foreign lands – Czechoslovakia
Foreign lands – Denmark
Foreign lands – Dominican Republic
Foreign lands – Ecuador
Foreign lands – Egypt
Foreign lands – El Salvador
Foreign lands – England
Foreign lands – Ethiopia
Foreign lands – Europe
Foreign lands – Finland
Foreign lands – France
Foreign lands – French Guiana
Foreign lands – Galapagos Islands
Foreign lands – Gambia
Foreign lands – Germany
Foreign lands – Ghana
Foreign lands – Gilbert Islands *see* Foreign lands – South Sea Islands
Foreign lands – Great Britain
Foreign lands – Greece
Foreign lands – Greenland
Foreign lands – Guatemala
Foreign lands – Haiti
Foreign lands – Himalayas
Foreign lands – Holland
Foreign lands – Honduras
Foreign lands – Hungary
Foreign lands – Iceland
Foreign lands – India
Foreign lands – Indonesia
Foreign lands – Iran
Foreign lands – Iraq
Foreign lands – Ireland
Foreign lands – Israel
Foreign lands – Italy
Foreign lands – Jamaica
Foreign lands – Japan
Foreign lands – Kenya
Foreign lands – Korea
Foreign lands – Korea (North)
Foreign lands – Laos
Foreign lands – Lapland
Foreign lands – Latin America
Foreign lands – Lebanon
Foreign lands – Liberia
Foreign lands – Madagascar
Foreign lands – Malawi
Foreign lands – Malaysia
Foreign lands – Mali
Foreign lands – Martinique
Foreign lands – Mauritania
Foreign lands – Mexico
Foreign lands – Middle East
Foreign lands – Mongolia
Foreign lands – Morocco
Foreign lands – Namibia

Foreign lands – Nepal
Foreign lands – Netherlands *see* Foreign lands – Holland
Foreign lands – Nicaragua
Foreign lands – Nigeria
Foreign lands – Norway
Foreign lands – Pakistan
Foreign lands – Palestine
Foreign lands – Panama
Foreign lands – Persia
Foreign lands – Peru
Foreign lands – Philippines
Foreign lands – Poland
Foreign lands – Puerto Rico
Foreign lands – Romania
Foreign lands – Russia
Foreign lands – Rwanda
Foreign lands – Sahara Desert
Foreign lands – Saudi Arabia
Foreign lands – Scandinavia
Foreign lands – Scotland
Foreign lands – Siam *see* Foreign lands – Thailand
Foreign lands – Somalia
Foreign lands – South Africa
Foreign lands – South America
Foreign lands – South Sea Islands
Foreign lands – Spain
Foreign lands – Sudan
Foreign lands – Sweden
Foreign lands – Switzerland
Foreign lands – Syria
Foreign lands – Taiwan
Foreign lands – Tanzania
Foreign lands – Tasmania
Foreign lands – Thailand
Foreign lands – Tibet
Foreign lands – Trinidad
Foreign lands – Turkey
Foreign lands – Tyrol
Foreign lands – Uganda
Foreign lands – Ukraine
Foreign lands – Uzbekistan
Foreign lands – Venezuela
Foreign lands – Vietnam
Foreign lands – Wales
Foreign lands – West Indies
Foreign lands – Yukon Territory
Foreign lands – Zaire
Foreign lands – Zambia
Foreign lands – Zanzibar
Foreign lands – Zimbabwe
Foreign languages
Forest, woods
Forgetfulness *see* Behavior – forgetfulness
Forgiving *see* Behavior – forgiving
Format, unusual
Format, unusual – board books
Format, unusual – graphic novels

Format, unusual – toy & movable books
Fortune *see* Character traits – luck
Fossils
Foster children, foster homes
Freedom *see* Character traits – freedom
Friendship
Frogs & toads
Frontier life *see* U.S. history – frontier & pioneer life
Furniture
Furniture – beds
Furniture – chairs

Games
Gangs *see* Clubs, gangs
Garage sales, rummage sales
Garbage collectors *see* Careers – sanitation workers
Gardens, gardening
Gender identity
Gender roles
Genealogy
Generosity *see* Character traits – generosity
Geography
Ghosts
Giants
Gifts
Gilbert Islands *see* Foreign lands – South Sea Islands
Glasses *see also* Careers – opticians, optometrists
Global warming *see* Ecology
Gossip *see* Behavior – gossip, rumors
Grammar *see* Language
Graphic novels *see* Format, unusual – graphic novels
Greed *see* Behavior – greed
Grocery stores *see* Shopping; Stores
Growing up *see* Behavior – growing up
Guns *see* Weapons
Gypsies *see* Romani

Habits *see* Thumb sucking
Hair
Handicaps *see* Disabilities
Hares *see* Animals – rabbits
Hawaii
Health & fitness
Health & fitness – exercise
Hearing *see* Anatomy – ears; Disabilities – deafness; Senses – hearing
Heat *see* Concepts – cold & heat
Heavy equipment *see* Machines

Helicopters
Helpfulness *see* Character traits – helpfulness
Hens *see* Birds – chickens, roosters
Hibernation
Hiccups
Hiding *see* Behavior – hiding
Hiding things *see* Behavior – hiding things
Hieroglyphics
Hobby horses *see* Toys – rocking horses
Hogs *see* Animals – pigs
Holidays
Holidays – April Fools' Day
Holidays – Chanukah *see* Holidays – Hanukkah
Holidays – Chinese New Year
Holidays – Christmas
Holidays – Cinco de Mayo
Holidays – Day of the Dead
Holidays – Diwali
Holidays – Earth Day
Holidays – Easter
Holidays – Father's Day
Holidays – Fourth of July
Holidays – Groundhog Day
Holidays – Halloween
Holidays – Hanukkah
Holidays – Independence Day *see* Holidays – Fourth of July
Holidays – Juneteenth
Holidays – Kwanzaa
Holidays – Mardi Gras *see* Mardi Gras
Holidays – Martin Luther King, Jr. Day
Holidays – May Day
Holidays – Memorial Day
Holidays – Mother's Day
Holidays – New Year's
Holidays – Passover
Holidays – Purim
Holidays – Ramadan
Holidays – Rosh Hashanah
Holidays – Rosh Kodesh
Holidays – Seder
Holidays – Shavuot
Holidays – St. Patrick's Day
Holidays – Sukkot
Holidays – Thanksgiving
Holidays – Tu B'Shevat
Holidays – Valentine's Day
Holidays – Yom Kippur
Holocaust
Homeless
Homes, houses
Homework
Homosexuality *see* LGBTQ
Honesty *see* Character traits – honesty

Honey bees *see* Insects – bees
Hope *see* Character traits – hopefulness
Hopefulness *see* Character traits – hopefulness
Horses, rocking *see* Toys – rocking horses
Hospitals
Hot air balloons *see* Activities – ballooning
Hotels
Houses *see* Homes, houses
Hugging
Humorous stories
Hurrying *see* Behavior – hurrying
Hygiene *see* Character traits – cleanliness; Health & fitness

Identity *see* Self-concept
Illness
Illness – AIDS
Illness – alcoholism
Illness – allergies
Illness – Alzheimer's
Illness – asthma
Illness – cancer
Illness – chicken pox
Illness – cold (disease)
Illness – dementia
Illness – diabetes
Illness – epilepsy
Illness – influenza
Illness – mental illness
Illness – poliomyelitis
Illness – tonsillectomy
Imagination
Imagination – imaginary friends
Imitation *see* Behavior – imitation
Immigrants, immigration; *see also* Refugees
Impatience *see* Character traits – patience, impatience
Incentive *see* Character traits – ambition
Indecision *see* Behavior – indecision
Independence Day *see* Holidays – Fourth of July
Indians of Central America – Maya
Indians of Central America – Taino
Indians of North America
Indians of North America – Algonquin
Indians of North America – Aztec
Indians of North America – Blackfoot

Indians of North America –
Cherokee
Indians of North America –
Cheyenne (Sioux)
Indians of North America –
Chippewa
Indians of North America –
Choctaw
Indians of North America –
Chumash
Indians of North America –
Comanche
Indians of North America –
Cree
Indians of North America –
Creek
Indians of North America –
Crow
Indians of North America –
Dakota (Sioux)
Indians of North America –
Goshute
Indians of North America –
Great Basin
Indians of North America –
Great Plains
Indians of North America –
Haida
Indians of North America –
Hopi
Indians of North America –
Huichol
Indians of North America –
Inuit
Indians of North America –
Iroquois
Indians of North America –
Kato
Indians of North America –
Lakota
Indians of North America –
Lakota (Sioux)
Indians of North America –
Lenape
Indians of North America –
Metis
Indians of North America –
Miwok
Indians of North America –
Mohawk
Indians of North America –
Muskogee
Indians of North America –
Narragansett
Indians of North America –
Navajo
Indians of North America –
Nez Perce
Indians of North America –
Ojibwa
Indians of North America –
Papago

Indians of North America –
Passamaquoddy
Indians of North America –
Pawnee
Indians of North America –
Pima
Indians of North America –
Powhatan
Indians of North America –
Pueblo
Indians of North America –
Seminole
Indians of North America –
Seneca
Indians of North America –
Shoshone
Indians of North America –
Siksika
Indians of North America –
Sioux
Indians of North America –
Southwest
Indians of North America –
Suquamish
Indians of North America –
Taino
Indians of North America –
Tewa
Indians of North America –
Tlingit
Indians of North America –
Tsimshian
Indians of North America –
Wampanoag
Indians of North America –
Windigos
Indians of North America –
Zapotec
Indians of North America –
Zuni
Indians of South America
Indians of South America –
Karina
Indians of South America –
Quechua
Indians, American *see* Indians
of Central America; Indians
of North America; Indians of
South America
Indifference *see* Behavior –
indifference
Individuality *see* Character
traits – individuality
Indonesian Archipelago *see*
Foreign lands – South Sea
Islands
Insects
Insects – ants
Insects – bees
Insects – beetles
Insects – butterflies,
caterpillars

Insects – cockroaches
Insects – crickets
Insects – dragonflies
Insects – fireflies
Insects – fleas
Insects – flies
Insects – gnats
Insects – grasshoppers
Insects – ladybugs
Insects – lice
Insects – lightning bugs *see*
Insects – fireflies
Insects – mosquitoes
Insects – moths
Insects – termites
Internet *see* Technology
Interracial marriage *see*
Marriage, interracial
Inventions
Islands

Jackets *see* Clothing – coats
Janitors *see* Careers –
custodians, janitors
Jealousy *see* Emotions – envy,
jealousy
Jesters *see* Clowns, jesters
Jewelry
Jewish culture
Jobs *see* Careers
Jokes *see* Riddles & jokes
Jumping rope *see* Activities –
jumping
Jungle

Kindness *see* Character traits –
kindness
Kindness to animals *see*
Character traits – kindness
to animals
Kissing
Kites
Knights

Lady birds *see* Insects –
ladybugs
Lakes, ponds
Lambs *see* Animals – babies;
Animals – sheep
Language
Language – sign language *see*
Sign language
Languages, foreign *see* Foreign
languages
Laundry
Law *see* Careers – judges;
Careers – lawyers; Careers –
police officers; Crime
Laziness *see* Character traits –
laziness

Legends *see* Folk & fairy tales

Letters, cards

LGBTQ *see also* Gender identity

Libraries *see also* Books, reading

Light, lights

Lighthouses

Lightning bugs *see* Insects – fireflies

Little people

Littleness *see* Character traits – smallness

Lost *see* Behavior – lost

Lost & found possessions *see* Behavior – lost & found possessions

Loyalty *see* Character traits – loyalty

Luck *see* Character traits – luck

Lullabies

Lying *see* Behavior – lying

Machines

Magic

Mail *see* Careers – postal workers; Letters, cards; Post office

Mail carriers *see* Careers – postal workers; Letters, cards

Manners *see* Etiquette

Maps

Mardi Gras

Marionettes *see* Puppets

Markets *see* Stores

Marriage, interracial

Marriages *see* Weddings

Masks

Math *see* Counting, numbers

Mazes

Meanness *see* Character traits – meanness

Mechanical men *see* Robots

Medical technicians *see* Careers – emergency medical technicians

Memories, memory

Merry-go-rounds

Messy *see* Behavior – messy

Metamorphosis

Middle Ages

Migration

Mimes *see* Clowns, jesters

Ministers *see* Careers – clergy

Minorities *see* Ethnic groups in the U.S.

Mirages *see* Optical illusions

Mirrors

Misbehavior *see* Behavior – misbehavior

Missing *see* Behavior – lost

Missions

Mist *see* Weather – fog

Mistakes *see* Behavior – mistakes

Misunderstanding *see* Behavior – misunderstanding

Mittens *see* Clothing – gloves, mittens

Money

Monsters

Months of the year *see* Days of the week, months of the year

Moon

Mopeds *see* Motorcycles

Morning

Mother Goose *see* Nursery rhymes

Motion picture producers *see* Careers – motion picture producers

Motion pictures *see* Theater

Motorcycles

Mountain climbing *see* Sports – mountain climbing

Mountain lions *see* Animals – cougars

Mountains

Moving

Multi-ethnic *see* Ethnic groups in the U.S.

Multiple births – triplets

Multiple births – twins

Mummies

Muppets *see* Puppets

Museums

Music

Musical instruments

Musical instruments – accordions

Musical instruments – bagpipes

Musical instruments – bands

Musical instruments – banjos

Musical instruments – cellos

Musical instruments – drums

Musical instruments – fiddles *see* Musical instruments – violins

Musical instruments – flutes

Musical instruments – guitars

Musical instruments – harmonicas

Musical instruments – harps

Musical instruments – lutes

Musical instruments – orchestras

Musical instruments – pianos

Musical instruments – saxophones

Musical instruments – trombones

Musical instruments – trumpets

Musical instruments – tubas

Musical instruments – violins

Mystery stories

Mythical creatures

Mythical creatures – aliens *see* Aliens

Mythical creatures – elves

Mythical creatures – genies

Mythical creatures – gnomes

Mythical creatures – goblins

Mythical creatures – griffins, gryphons

Mythical creatures – leprechauns

Mythical creatures – lutins

Mythical creatures – mermaids, mermen

Mythical creatures – ogres

Mythical creatures – Pegasus

Mythical creatures – phoenix

Mythical creatures – pixies

Mythical creatures – pooka spirit

Mythical creatures – trolls

Mythical creatures – unicorns

Mythical creatures – werewolves

Mythology *see* Folk & fairy tales

Name calling *see* Behavior – name calling

Names

Napping *see* Sleep

Native Americans *see* Eskimos; Indians of Central America; Indians of North America; Indians of South America

Nature

Naughty *see* Behavior – misbehavior

Neatness *see* Character traits – cleanliness

Needing someone *see* Behavior – needing someone

Negotiation *see* Activities – trading

Neighborhoods *see* Communities, neighborhoods

Netherlands *see* Foreign lands – Holland

Night

Nightmares *see also* Bedtime; Monsters; Mythical creatures – goblins; Night; Sleep

Ninjas *see* Sports – martial arts

No text *see* Wordless

Noise, sounds

Noise, sounds – snoring *see* Sleep – snoring

Nomads

North Pole *see* Foreign lands – Arctic

Northern lights

Noses *see* Anatomy – noses; Senses – smell

Numbers *see* Counting, numbers

Nursery rhymes

Nursery school *see* School – nursery

Nutrition *see* Food; Health & fitness

Occupations *see* Careers

Oceans *see* Sea & seashore

Octopuses

Odors *see* Senses – smell

Oil

Old age

Olympics *see* Sports – Olympics

Opossums *see* Animals – possums

Optical illusions

Optimism *see* Character traits – optimism

Orderliness *see* Character traits – orderliness

Orphans

Outer space *see* Space & space ships

Pageants *see* Theater

Painters *see* Activities – painting; Careers – artists

Panthers *see* Animals – leopards

Paper

Parades

Parks

Parks – amusement

Parrots *see* Birds – parakeets, parrots

Participation

Parties

Patience *see* Character traits – patience, impatience

Peace *see* Violence, nonviolence

Peahens *see* Birds – peacocks, peahens

Pen pals

Perfectionism *see* Character traits – perfectionism

Perseverance *see* Character traits – perseverance

Persistence *see* Character traits – persistence

Petroglyphs

Petroleum *see* Oil

Pets

Physicians *see* Careers – doctors

Picture puzzles

Pilgrims

Pioneer life *see* U.S. history – frontier & pioneer life

Pirates

Planes *see* Airplanes, airports

Planets

Plants

Plays *see* Theater

Pockets *see* Clothing

Poetry

Pollution *see* Ecology

Poltergeists *see* Ghosts

Ponds *see* Lakes, ponds

Ponies *see* Animals – horses, ponies

Poor *see* Homeless; Poverty

Pop-up books *see* Format, unusual – toy & movable books

Porpoises *see* Animals – dolphins

Post office

Potty training *see* Toilet training

Pourquoi tales *see* Folk & fairy tales – pourquoi tales

Poverty

Pow-wows

Power failures

Practicality *see* Character traits – practicality

Prairie wolves *see* Animals – coyotes

Prayers *see* Religion

Preachers *see* Careers – clergy

Pregnancy *see* Birth

Prehistoric man *see* Cave dwellers

Prehistory

Prejudice

Preschool *see* School – nursery

Pretending *see* Imagination

Priests *see* Careers – clergy

Problem solving

Progress

Promptness *see* Behavior – promptness, tardiness

Pumas *see* Animals – cougars

Punctuality *see* Behavior – promptness, tardiness

Puppets

Purses *see* Clothing – handbags, purses

Puzzles *see also* Picture puzzles; Rebuses; Riddles & jokes

Questioning *see* Character traits – questioning

Quicksand *see* Sand

Quilts

Rabbis *see* Careers – clergy

Race relations *see* Prejudice

Racially mixed *see* Ethnic groups in the U.S.

Radios

Railroads *see* Trains

Rain *see* Weather – rain

Rain forest *see* Jungle

Rangers *see* Careers – park rangers

Reading *see* Books, reading

Rebuses

Recycling *see* Behavior – resourcefulness; Ecology

Refugees *see also* Immigrants, immigration

Religion

Religion – Daniel

Religion – David

Religion – Hinduism

Religion – Islam

Religion – Jonah

Religion – Moses

Religion – Nativity

Religion – Noah

Remembering *see* Memories, memory

Repetitive stories *see* Cumulative tales

Reptiles

Reptiles – alligators, crocodiles

Reptiles – chameleons

Reptiles – iguanas

Reptiles – lizards

Reptiles – salamanders

Reptiles – snakes

Reptiles – turtles, tortoises

Resourcefulness *see* Behavior – resourcefulness

Responsibility *see* Character traits – responsibility

Rest *see* Sleep

Restaurants

Rhyming text

Riddles & jokes

Right & left *see* Concepts – left & right

Riots *see* Violence, nonviolence

Rivers

Roads

Robbers *see* Crime

Robots

Rockets *see* Space & space ships

Rocks

Rodeos

Romani

Roosters *see* Birds – chickens, roosters

Royalty

Royalty – emperors

Royalty – khans

Royalty – kings

Royalty – pharaohs

Royalty – princes

Royalty – princesses

Royalty – queens

Royalty – rajahs

Royalty – sultans

Royalty – tsars

Rummage sales *see* Garage sales, rummage sales

Rumors *see* Behavior – gossip, rumors

Running *see* Activities – running; Sports – racing

Running away *see* Behavior – running away

Safety

Sailors *see also* Careers – military

Sand *see also* Sea & seashore – beaches

Sandcastles *see* Sand

Santa Claus

Sasquatch *see* Monsters

Saving things *see* Behavior – saving things

Scarecrows

School

School – field trips

School – first day

School – nursery

School teachers *see* Careers – teachers

Science

Scorpions

Scuba diving *see* Sports – skin diving

Sea & seashore

Sea & seashore – beaches

Sea serpents *see* Monsters; Mythical creatures

Seahorses *see* Fish – seahorses

Seashore *see* Sand; Sea & seashore – beaches

Seasons

Seasons – fall

Seasons – spring

Seasons – summer

Seasons – winter

Secrets *see* Behavior – secrets

Seeds

Seeing *see* Anatomy – eyes; Glasses; Disabilities – blindness; Senses – sight

Seeing eye dogs *see* Animals – service animals

Seeking better things *see* Behavior – seeking better things

Self-concept

Self-esteem *see* Self-concept

Self-image *see* Self-concept

Self-reliance *see* Character traits – confidence

Selfishness *see* Character traits – selfishness

Senses

Senses – hearing

Senses – sight

Senses – smell

Senses – taste

Senses – touch

Sex instruction

Sex roles *see* Gender roles

Shadows

Shaped books *see* Format, unusual

Sharing *see* Behavior – sharing

Shells *see* Sea & seashore

Ships *see* Boats, ships

Shopping

Shops *see* Stores

Showing off *see* Behavior – boasting, showing off

Shows *see* Theater

Shyness *see* Character traits – shyness

Siam *see* Foreign lands – Thailand

Sibling rivalry

Siblings *see* Family life – brothers; Family life – brothers & sisters; Family life – sisters; Family life – stepfamilies; Sibling rivalry

Sickness *see* Health & fitness; Illness

Sight *see* Anatomy – eyes; Glasses; Disabilities – blindness; Senses – sight

Sign language

Signs

Singers *see* Careers – singers

Sioux Indians *see* Indians of North America – Cheyenne (Sioux); Indians of North America – Dakota (Sioux); Indians of North America – Sioux

Sisters *see* Family life – brothers & sisters; Family life – sisters; Sibling rivalry

Skating *see* Sports – ice skating; Sports – hockey; Sports – roller skating

Sky

Slavery

Sleep

Sleep – snoring

Sleepovers

Sleight-of-hand *see* Magic

Smallness *see* Character traits – smallness

Smell *see* Anatomy – noses; Senses – smell

Smiles, smiling *see* Anatomy – faces

Snoring *see* Noise, sounds; Sleep – snoring

Snow *see* Weather – blizzards; Weather – snow

Snow plows *see* Machines

Snowmen

Society Islands *see* Foreign lands – South Sea Islands

Soldiers *see* Careers – military

Soldiers, toy *see* Toys – soldiers

Solitude *see* Behavior – solitude

Songs

Sorcerers *see* Wizards

Sounds *see* Noise, sounds

South Pole *see* Foreign lands – Antarctic

Space & space ships

Spectacles *see* Glasses

Speech *see* Disabilities – stuttering; Language

Spelunking *see* Caves

Spiders

Split page books *see* Format, unusual

Spooks *see* Ghosts; Mythical creatures – goblins

Sports

Sports – archery

Sports – baseball

Sports – basketball

Sports – bicycling

Sports – bowling

Sports – boxing

Sports – camping *see* Camps, camping

Sports – fishing

Sports – football

Sports – golf

Sports – gymnastics

Sports – hiking *see* Activities – hiking

Sports – hockey

Sports – hunting

Sports – ice skating

Sports – karate

Sports – martial arts

Sports – mountain climbing

Sports – Olympics

Sports – racing

Sports – roller skating

Sports – sailing

Sports – skateboarding

Sports – skiing

Sports – skin diving

Sports – sledding

Sports – soccer

Sports – Special Olympics

Sports – surfing

Sports – swimming

Sports – T-ball

Sports – Tae Kwon Do

Sports – tennis

Sports – volleyball

Sports – wrestling
Sportsmanship
Squid
Stage *see* Theater
Starfishes
Stars
Stealing *see* Behavior – stealing; Crime
Steam shovels *see* Machines
Steamrollers *see* Machines
Step families *see* Divorce; Family life – stepfamilies
Stepchildren *see* Divorce; Family life – stepfamilies
Stepparents *see* Divorce; Family life – stepfamilies
Stones *see* Rocks
Stores
Stories in rhyme *see* Rhyming text
Strangers *see* Behavior – talking to strangers
Streams *see* Rivers
Streets *see* Roads
String
Stubbornness *see* Character traits – stubbornness
Submarines *see* Boats, ships
Subway *see* Trains
Sullivan Islands *see* Foreign lands – South Sea Islands
Sun
Superstition
Sustainability *see* Ecology
Swamps
Swapping *see* Activities – trading

Talent shows *see* Theater
Talking to strangers *see* Behavior – talking to strangers
Tall tales
Tardiness *see* Behavior – promptness, tardiness
Tattletale *see* Behavior – gossip, rumors
Taxis
Teasing *see* Behavior – bullying, teasing
Technology
Teddy bears *see* Toys – bears
Teeth
Telephone, cell phone
Television
Telling stories *see* Activities – storytelling
Telling time *see* Clocks, watches; Time
Temper tantrums *see* Emotions – anger

Texas
Textless *see* Wordless
Theater
Therapy animals *see* Animals – service animals
Thieves *see* Crime
Thumb sucking
Thunder *see* Weather – lightning, thunder; Weather – storms
Time
Tin soldiers *see* Toys – soldiers
Toads *see* Frogs & toads
Toddlers *see* Babies, toddlers
Toilet training
Toilets
Tongue twisters
Tools
Tooth fairy *see* Fairies; Teeth
Tortoises *see* Reptiles – turtles, tortoises
Towns *see* Cities, towns
Toy & movable books *see* Format, unusual – toy & movable books
Toys
Toys – balloons
Toys – balls
Toys – bears
Toys – blocks
Toys – dolls
Toys – rocking horses
Toys – soldiers
Toys – teddy bears *see* Toys – bears
Toys – tin soldiers *see* Toys – soldiers
Toys – trains
Toys – wagons
Tractors
Traffic, traffic signs
Train engineers *see* Careers – railroad engineers
Trains
Trains, toy *see* Toys – trains
Transgender *see* Gender identity; LGBTQ
Transportation
Trees
Trickery *see* Behavior – trickery
Tricks *see* Magic
Triplets *see* Multiple births – triplets
Trucks
Tsunamis
TV *see* Television
Twilight
Twins *see* Multiple births – twins

U.S. history

U.S. history – frontier & pioneer life
Umbrellas
Uncles *see* Family life – aunts, uncles
Unhappiness *see* Emotions – happiness; Emotions – sadness
UNICEF
Unnoticed *see* Behavior – unnoticed, unseen
Unseen *see* Behavior – unnoticed, unseen
Unusual format *see* Format, unusual

Vanity *see* Character traits – vanity
Vikings
Violence, nonviolence
Vocabulary *see* Language
Volcanoes

Wagons *see* Toys – wagons
Waiters *see* Careers – waiters, waitresses
Waitresses *see* Careers – waiters, waitresses
War
Washing machines *see* Machines
Watches *see* Clocks, watches
Water
Weapons
Weather
Weather – blizzards
Weather – clouds
Weather – cold
Weather – droughts
Weather – floods
Weather – fog
Weather – hurricanes
Weather – lightning, thunder
Weather – mist *see* Weather – fog
Weather – rain
Weather – rainbows
Weather – sandstorms
Weather – snow
Weather – storms
Weather – thunder *see* Weather – lightning, thunder
Weather – tornadoes
Weather – wind
Weather reporters *see* Careers – meteorologists
Weddings
Weekdays *see* Days of the week, months of the year
West *see* U.S. history – frontier & pioneer life

Wheelchairs *see* Disabilities – physical disabilities

Wheels

Whistles

Wildlife rescue *see* Character traits – kindness to animals

Willfulness *see* Character traits – willfulness

Wisdom *see* Character traits – wisdom

Wishing *see* Behavior – wishing

Witches

Wizards

Woodchucks *see* Animals – groundhogs

Woods *see* Forest, woods

Word games *see* Language

Wordless

Working *see* Activities – working; Careers

World

Worrying *see* Behavior – worrying

Wrecking machines *see* Machines

Writers *see* Careers – writers; Children as authors

Writing letters *see* Letters, cards

Yeti *see* Monsters

Yoga *see* Health & fitness – exercise; Character traits – patience, impatience

Zodiac

Zombies *see* Monsters

Zoos

Subject Guide

This is a subject-arranged guide to picture books. Under appropriate subject headings and subheadings, titles appear alphabetically by author name, or by title when author is unknown. Complete bibliographic information for each title cited will be found in the Bibliographic Guide.

ABC books

Abrams, Pam. *Now I eat my ABC's*
Ada, Alma Flor. *Gathering the sun*
Agee, Jon. *Z goes home*
Alberti, Theresa Jarosz. *Vietnam ABCs*
Alda, Arlene. *Arlene Alda's ABC*
Alko, Selina. *B is for Brooklyn*
Allen, Susan. *Read anything good lately?*
    Used any numbers lately?
Alphamals A-Z
American Museum of Natural History. *ABC insects*
Anno, Mitsumasa. *Anno's alphabet*
Archer, Peggy. *Name that dog!*
Arnosky, Jim. *Mouse letters*
    Mouse numbers and letters
    Mouse writing
Ashley Bryan's ABC of African American poetry
Ashman, Linda. *M is for mischief*
Aylesworth, Jim. *The folks in the valley*
    Little Bitty Mousie
    Old Black Fly
Azarian, Mary. *A gardener's alphabet*
Babypants, Caspar. *Augie to zebra*
Baker, Alan. *Black and White Rabbit's ABC*
Baker, Keith. *LMNO pea-quel*
    LMNO peas
Barrett, Judi. *An excessive alphabet*
Barron, Rex. *Fed up!*
Base, Graeme. *Animalia*
Basher, Simon. *ABC kids*
Baskin, Leonard. *Hosie's alphabet*
Bataille, Marion. *ABC3D*
Bayer, Jane. *A my name is Alice*
Bea, Holly. *My spiritual alphabet book*
Beaton, Clare. *Zoë and her zebra*
Belle, Jennifer. *Animal stackers*
Berenstain, Stan and Jan. *The Berenstains' B book*
Bingham, Kelly. *Z is for Moose*
Blackstone, Stella. *Alligator alphabet*
    Cleo's alphabet book

Bleiman, Andrew. *ABC zooborns!*
Boldt, Mike. *123 versus ABC*
Bottner, Barbara. *An annoying ABC*
Brennan-Nelson, Denise. *J is for jack-o-lantern*
Bridwell, Norman. *Clifford's ABC*
Bronson, Linda. *The circus alphabet*
Brown, Marc. *Arthur's animal adventure*
Brown, Margaret Wise. *Goodnight moon ABC*
    Sleepy ABC, ill. by Karen Katz
    Sleepy ABC, ill. by Esphyr Slobodkina
Bruchac, Joseph. *Many nations*
Bruel, Nick. *Bad Kitty*
    Bad Kitty, scaredy-cat
    Poor puppy
Brunhoff, Laurent de. *B is for Babar*
    Babar's ABC
Bryant, Megan E. *Alphasaurus*
Bunting, Eve. *P is for pirate*
Burnard, Damon. *I spy in the ocean*
Burningham, John. *First steps*
Butler, Dori Hillestad. *F is for firefighting*
C is for caboose
Cabatingan, Erin. *A is for Musk Ox*
Caldicott, Chris. *World food alphabet*
Capucilli, Alyssa Satin. *Mrs. McTats and her houseful of cats*
Carlson, Nancy. *ABC, I like me!*
Carluccio, Maria. *D is for dress up*
Catalanotto, Peter. *Matthew A.B.C.*
Charlip, Remy, et al. *Handtalk*
Chin-Lee, Cynthia. *A is for Asia*
Chung, Hyechong. *K is for Korea*
Clayton, Dallas. *A is for awesome*
Cleary, Beverly. *The hullabaloo ABC*
Cleary, Brian P. *Peanut butter and jellyfishes*
Cline-Ransome, Lesa. *Quilt alphabet*
Compestine, Ying Chang. *D is for dragon dance*
Cooper, Elisha. *Eight, an animal alphabet*
Crane, Carol. *D is for dancing dragon*
Crews, Donald. *We read*
Cronin, Doreen. *Click, clack, quackity-quack*
Crowther, Robert. *Robert Crowther's pop-up dinosaur ABC*
Czekaj, Jef. *A call for a new alphabet*
Day, Nancy Raines. *A is for alliguitar*
Dealey, Erin. *K is for kindergarten*
Delessert, Etienne. *A was an apple pie*
Demarest, Chris L. *All aboard! a traveling alphabet*
    Alpha Bravo Charlie
    Firefighters A to Z

DeRubertis, Barbara. *Alexander Anteater's amazing act*
  Bobby Baboon's banana be-bop
  Corky Cub's crazy caps
  Dilly Dog's dizzy dancing
De Vicq de Cumptich, Roberto. *Bembo's zoo*
DiTerlizzi, Tony. *G is for one gzonk!*
Dodd, Emma. *Dog's ABC*
Domeniconi, David. *M is for masterpiece*
Doodler, Todd H. *The zoo I drew*
Downie, Mary Alice. *A pioneer ABC*
Downing, Johnette. *Amazon alphabet*
Doyle, Charlotte Lackner. *The bouncing, dancing, galloping ABC*
Dragonwagon, Crescent. *All the awake animals are almost asleep*
Dugan, Joanne. *ABC NYC*
Eastman, P. D. *The alphabet book*
Ehlert, Lois. *Eating the alphabet*
Eichenberg, Fritz. *Ape in cape*
Elya, Susan Middleton. *F is for fiesta*
  N is for Navidad
Engelbreit, Mary. *Mary Engelbreit's A merry little Christmas*
Ernst, Lisa Campbell. *The letters are lost!*
Eschbacher, Roger. *Nonsense! He yelled*
Escoffier, Michael. *Take away the A*
Evans, Nate. *Bang! Boom! Roar!*
Falkenstern, Lisa. *Professor Whiskerton presents Steampunk ABC*
Farley, Carol J. *The king's secret*
Faulkenberry, Lauren. *What do animals do on the weekend?*
Feelings, Muriel. *Jambo means hello*
Fisher, Valorie. *Ellsworth's extraordinary electric ears and other amazing alphabet anecdotes*
Fleming, Denise. *Alphabet under construction*
  Shout! shout it out!
Ford, Juwanda G. *K is for Kwanzaa*
Frampton, David. *My beastie book of ABC*
Franceschelli, Christopher. *Alphablock*
Frasier, Debra. *A fabulous fair alphabet*
Freymann, Saxton. *Food for thought*
Fuge, Charles. *Astonishing animal ABC*
Gaiman, Neil. *The dangerous alphabet*
Geisert, Arthur. *Country road ABC*
Gerstein, Mordicai. *The absolutely awful alphabet*
Gillingham, Sara. *Alpha, Bravo, Charlie: the complete book of nautical codes*
Girnis, Margaret. *ABC for you and me*
Golenbock, Peter. *ABCs of baseball*
Green, Dan. *Wild alphabet*
Gross, Benedikt. *ABC: the alphabet from the sky*
Grossman, Bill. *My little sister hugged an ape*
Gutierrez, Elisa. *Letter lunch*
Haas, Jessie. *Appaloosa zebra*
Hague, Kathleen. *Alphabears*
Hall, Michael. *Little i*
Hatanaka, Kellen. *Work: an occupational ABC*
Heder, Thyra. *Fraidyzoo*
Heller, Lora. *Sign language ABC*
Hepworth, Catherine. *ANTics! an alphabetical anthology*
Herzog, Brad. *G is for gold medal*
  R is for race
Hills, Tad. *R is for Rocket*
Hoban, Tana. *A B see!*
  26 letters and 99 cents
Hobbie, Holly. *Toot and Puddle, Puddle's ABC*

Hopkins, Lee Bennett. *Alphathoughts*
  April, bubbles, chocolate
Horowitz, Dave. *Twenty-six pirates*
  Twenty-six princesses
Howell, Will C. *Zoo flakes ABC*
Howland, Naomi. *ABCDrive!*
Hudes, Quiara Alegría. *Welcome to my neighborhood!*
Hughes, Langston. *The sweet and sour animal book*
Hughes, Shirley. *Alfie's ABC*
Hyman, Trina Schart. *A little alphabet*
Inkpen, Mick. *Kipper's A to Z*
Isadora, Rachel. *ABC pop!*
Janovitz, Marilyn. *A, B, see!*
Jocelyn, Marthe. *ABC x 3*
Johnson, Stephen T. *Alphabet city*
  Alphabet school
Johnston, Tony. *P is for piñata*
Jonas, Ann. *Aardvarks, disembark!*
Joubert, Beverly. *African animal alphabet*
Joyce, Susan. *ABC nature riddles*
  ABC school riddles
Joyce, William. *The Numberlys*
Kabakov, Vladimir. *R is for Russia*
Kalman, Maira. *What Pete ate from A-Z*
Katz, Susan B. *ABC, baby me!*
  ABC school's for me!
Kelley, Marty. *Summer stinks*
Kellogg, Steven. *Aster Aardvark's alphabet adventures*
Kirk, David. *Miss Spider's ABC*
Kontis, Alethea. *Alpha oops!*
  AlphaOops!
Krans, Kim. *ABC dream*
Krull, Kathleen. *M is for music*
Kutner, Merrily. *Z is for zombie*
Lauture, Denizé. *Running the road to ABC*
Lawlor, Laurie. *Muddy as a duck puddle and other American similes*
Layne, Steven L. *T is for teachers*
Lester, Mike. *A is for salad*
Levis, Caron. *May I have a word?*
Lewis, J. Patrick. *M is for monster*
Lichtenheld, Tom. *E-mergency!*
Lindbergh, Reeve. *The awful aardvarks go to school*
Lionni, Leo. *The alphabet tree*
Lobel, Anita. *Alison's zinnia*
  Animal antics: A to Z
  Playful pigs from A to Z
Lobel, Arnold. *On Market Street*
London, Jonathan. *Do your ABC's, Little Brown Bear*
Maass, Robert. *A is for autumn*
McArthur, Meher. *An ABC of what art can be*
Maccarone, Grace. *The three bears ABC*
MacDonald, Ross. *Achoo! Bang! Crash!*
MacDonald, Suse. *Alphabatics*
  Edward Lear's A was once an apple pie
McDonnell, Flora. *Flora McDonnell's ABC*
McDonnell, Patrick. *The little red cat who ran away and learned his ABC's (the hard way)*
McGuirk, Leslie. *If rocks could sing*
McLean, Dirk. *Play mas'! a carnival ABC*
McLeod, Bob. *Super hero ABC*
McLimans, David. *Gone wild*
McNamara, Margaret. *Apples A to Z*
Major, Kevin. *Eh to zed?*
Marino, Gianna. *Zoopa*
Markes, Julie. *Sidewalk ABC*
Martin, Bill, Jr.. *Chicka chicka boom boom*
Marzollo, Jean. *Baby's alphabet*
  I spy A to Z

I spy little letters
Massie, Felix. *Dogs in cars*
Medina, Juana. *ABC pasta*
Melmed, Laura Krauss. *Capital! Washington D.C. from A to Z*
 New York, New York!
Merriam, Eve. *Halloween ABC*
Michaels, Pat. *W is for wind*
Milich, Zoran. *The city ABC book*
Minor, Wendell. *Yankee Doodle America*
Miranda, Anne. *Alphabet fiesta*
 Pignic
Mitter, Matt. *ABC: alphabet rhymes*
Mora, Pat. *Marimba!*
Morales, Yuyi. *Just in case: a trickster tale and Spanish alphabet book*
Most, Bernard. *ABC T-Rex*
Moxley, Sheila. *ABCD an alphabet book of cats and dogs*
Mullins, Patricia. *V for vanishing*
Munari, Bruno. *ABC*
Murphy, Liz. *ABC doctor*
Murphy, Mary. *The Alphabet Keeper*
Murray, Alison. *Apple pie ABC*
Musgrove, Margaret. *Ashanti to Zulu*
Napier, Matt. *Z is for zamboni*
Neyer, Andrew. *Letters are for learning*
Nichol, Barbara. *Trunks all aboard*
Nickle, John. *Alphabet explosion!*
O'Connell, Rebecca. *Danny is done with diapers*
O'Connor, Jane. *Fancy Nancy's collection of fancy words*
O'Keefe, Susan Heyboer. *Hungry monster ABC*
Olivera, Ramon. *ABCs on wheels*
 ABCs on wings
Pallotta, Jerry. *The airplane alphabet book*
 The construction alphabet book
 F is for Fenway
 The jet alphabet book
Parker, Marjorie Blain. *A paddling of ducks*
Paul, Ann Whitford. *Eight hands round*
 Everything to spend the night . . . from A to Z
Pearle, Ida. *A child's day*
Pearson, Debora. *Alphabeep*
Pelham, David. *A is for animals*
Pelletier, David. *The graphic alphabet*
Petersham, Maud. *An American ABC*
Pfister, Marcus. *Animal ABC*
 Rainbow fish ABC
Pomeroy, Diana. *Wildflower ABC*
Potter, Beatrix. *Peter Rabbit's ABC*
Raczka, Bob. *3-D ABC*
Raschka, Chris. *Alphabetabum*
 Talk to me about the alphabet
Rash, Andy. *Agent A to Agent Z*
Reed, Lynn Rowe. *Pedro, his perro, and the alphabet sombrero*
Rey, H. A. *Curious George learns the alphabet*
Richardson, Bill. *The alphabet thief*
Riehle, Mary Ann McCabe. *A is for airplane*
Rodriguez, Sonia. *T is for tutu*
Rogalski, Mark. *Tickets to ride*
Rogers, Jacqueline. *Kindergarten ABC*
Rose, Deborah Lee. *Into the A, B, sea*
Rosen, Michael J. *Avalanche*
Rosenberg, Liz. *A big and little alphabet*
Rosenthal, Amy Krouse. *Al Pha's bet*
 Awake beautiful child
Roth, Ruby. *V is for vegan*

Roussen, Jean. *Beautiful birds*
Rumford, James. *Sequoyah*
 There's a monster in the alphabet
Saaf, Donald. *The ABC animal orchestra*
Sabuda, Robert. *The Christmas alphabet*
Sanders, Nancy. *D is for drinking gourd*
Sandved, Kjell Bloch. *The butterfly alphabet*
Schaefer, Carole Lexa. *ABCers*
Schaefer, Lola M. *Homes ABC*
Schafer, Kevin. *Penguins A B C*
Schnur, Steven. *Autumn*
 Spring
 Summer
 Winter
Schoonmaker, Elizabeth. *Square cat ABC*
Scieszka, Jon. *Race from A to Z*
Seeger, Laura Vaccaro. *The hidden alphabet*
 Walter was worried
Sendak, Maurice. *Alligators all around*
Shahan, Sherry. *The jazzy alphabet*
Shannon, George. *Tomorrow's alphabet*
Shapiro, Zachary. *We're all in the same boat*
Shelby, Anne. *Potluck*
Shindler, Ramon. *Found alphabet*
Shoulders, Michael. *The ABC book of American homes*
 D is for drum
 D is for dump truck
Shulman, Mark. *A is for zebra*
 Aa is for Aardvark
Siddals, Mary McKenna. *Compost stew*
Sierra, Judy. *Sleepy little alphabet*
 There's a zoo in room 22
Singh, Rina. *My first book of Hindi words*
Slate, Joseph. *Miss Bindergarten celebrates the last day of kindergarten*
 Miss Bindergarten gets ready for kindergarten
 Miss Bindergarten has a wild day in kindergarten
 Miss Bindergarten stays home from kindergarten
 Miss Bindergarten takes a field trip with kindergarten
Sloat, Teri. *Patty's pumpkin patch*
Smith, Marie. *N is for our nation's capital*
 S is for Smithsonian
 Z is for zookeeper
Sneed, Brad. *Picture a letter*
Sobel, June. *Shiver me letters*
Spirin, Gennady. *A apple pie*
Spradlin, Michael P. *Baseball from A to Z*
Staake, Bob. *My little ABC book*
Stevenson, James. *Grandpa's great city tour*
Stewig, John Warren. *The animals watched*
Stock, Catherine. *Alexander's midnight snack*
Stone, Tanya Lee. *D is for dreidel*
Stutson, Caroline. *Prairie primer A to Z*
Sweet, Melissa. *Carmine*
Tapahonso, Luci. *Navajo ABC*
Teyssèdre, Fabienne. *Joseph wants to read*
Thurlby, Paul. *Paul Thurlby's alphabet*
Todd, Traci. *T is for tugboat*
Troll, Ray. *Sharkabet*
Tryon, Leslie. *Albert's alphabet*
Twohy, Mike. *Oops, pounce, quick, run!*
Ulmer, Wendy. *A isn't for fox*
Vamos, Samantha R. *Alphabet trains*
 Alphabet trucks
Van Allsburg, Chris. *The Z was zapped*
van Lieshout, Maria. *Backseat A-B-see*
Verstraete, Larry. *S is for scientists*

Viano, Hannah. *B is for bear*
Vidrine, Beverly Barras. *Easter Day alphabet*
Viorst, Judith. *The alphabet from Z to A*
Waber, Bernard. *An anteater named Arthur*
Wallace, Nancy Elizabeth. *Alphabet house*
Walters, Eric. *An African alphabet*
Walton, Rick. *So many bunnies*
Watkins, Adam F. *R is for robot*
Watson, Clyde. *Applebet*
Watterson, Carol. *An edible alphabet*
Wells, Rosemary. *Letters and sounds*
   Max's ABC
Werner, Sharon. *Alphasaurs and other prehistoric types*
Wethered, Peggy. *Touchdown Mars!*
White, Teagan. *Adventures with barefoot critters*
Wilbur, Helen L. *Z is for Zeus*
Wilbur, Richard. *The disappearing alphabet*
Williams, Laura E. *ABC kids*
Wilner, Isabel. *A garden alphabet*
Winnie-the-Pooh's A B C
Wishinsky, Frieda. *Where are you, Bear?*
Wood, Audrey. *Alphabet adventure*
   Alphabet rescue
Wormell, Christopher. *The new alphabet of animals*
Yolen, Jane. *All in the woodland early*
Young, Judy. *H is for hook*
Ziefert, Harriet. *ABC dentist*
   Lights on Broadway
Zuckerman, Andrew. *Creature abc*

Aborigines, Australian *see* Australian aborigines

Abused children *see* Child abuse

Accidents

Bauer, Marion Dane. *Uh-oh! a lift-the-flap story*
Bond, Michael. *Paddington Bear goes to the hospital*
Brown, Marc. *D. W. thinks big*
Byous, Shawn. *Because I stubbed my toe*
Dyckman, Ame. *Horrible Bear!*
Hurd, Thacher. *Santa Mouse and the ratdeer*
Lange, Willem. *John and Tom*
Luján, Jorge. *Sky blue accident / Accidente celeste*
Polacco, Patricia. *In Enzo's splendid gardens*
Proimos, James. *The best bike ride ever*
Pulver, Robin. *Axle Annie and the speed grump*
Rand, Gloria. *Baby in a basket*
   Little Flower
Rylant, Cynthia. *Silver packages*
Singer, Marilyn. *Boo hoo boo-boo*
Stower, Adam. *Slam!*
Sykes, Julie. *Careful, Santa*
Timmers, Leo. *Bang*
Tsurumi, Andrea. *Accident!*
Wardlaw, Lee. *The chair where bear sits*
Weller, Frances Ward. *The angel of Mill Street*
Wild, Margaret. *The pocket dogs*
Wood, Audrey. *A cowboy Christmas*

Activities

Adler, David A. *Circles*
Ajmera, Maya. *To be a kid*
Aliki. *All by myself!*
   Overnight at Mary Bloom's

Allard, Harry. *The Stupids step out*
Arquette, Kerry. *What did you do today?*
Asch, Frank. *Like a windy day*
Ashman, Linda. *Henry wants more!*
Barasch, Lynne. *Radio rescue*
Blackstone, Stella. *You and me*
Bowie, C. W. *Busy toes*
Boyd, Lizi. *I love Daddy*
   I love Mommy
Bridges, Margaret Park. *Edna elephant*
Bush, Timothy. *Teddy bear, teddy bear*
Carle, Eric. *From head to toe*
Carlson, Nancy. *Look out kindergarten, here I come!*
Carluccio, Maria. *The sounds around town*
Carr, Jan. *Frozen noses*
Cauley, Lorinda Bryan. *Clap your hands*
Cocca-Leffler, Maryann. *Let it rain*
   Time to say bye-bye
Crews, Nina. *A high, low, near, far, loud, quiet story*
Cronin, Doreen. *Wiggle*
Day, Alexandra. *Carl's sleepy afternoon*
Denim, Sue. *Make way for Dumb Bunnies*
Doyle, Malachy. *Well, a crocodile can!*
Falconer, Ian. *Olivia*
Faulkenberry, Lauren. *What do animals do on the weekend?*
Fitz-Gibbon, Sally. *Two shoes, blue shoes, new shoes!*
Franco, Betsy. *Summer beat*
Friend, Catherine. *Eddie the raccoon*
   Funny Ruby
Gay, Marie-Louise. *Read me a story, Stella*
Gentieu, Penny. *Baby! Talk!*
George, Jean Craighead. *Morning, noon, and night*
Gerstein, Mordicai. *The man who walked between the towers*
Gibbons, Gail. *The missing maple syrup sap mystery*
Gibson, Amy. *By day, by night*
Grindley, Sally. *Mucky Duck*
Haley, Amanda. *It's a baby's world*
Harper, Dan. *Sit, Truman*
Hayles, Marsha. *He saves the day*
Heidbreder, Robert. *Noisy poems for a busy day*
Hennessy, B. G. *Busy Dinah Dinosaur*
Herkert, Barbara. *Birds in your backyard*
Hindley, Judy. *What's in baby's morning*
Hines, Anna Grossnickle. *What can you do in the rain?*
   What can you do in the snow?
   What can you do in the sun?
   What can you do in the wind?
Hooks, Bell. *Be boy buzz*
Hop a little, jump a little!
Hughes, Shirley. *Annie Rose is my little sister*
Johnson, Angela. *Lottie Paris lives here*
Johnson, Doug. *Substitute teacher plans*
Johnson, Paul Brett. *The pig who ran a red light*
Jonas, Ann. *When you were a baby*
Kavanagh, Peter. *I love my mama*
Kerley, Barbara. *The world is waiting for you*
Koller, Jackie French. *Bouncing on the bed*
Kroll, Virginia L. *Boy, you're amazing!*
Lavis, Steve. *Jump!*
Lee, Ho Baek. *While we were out*
Levine, Abby. *Daddies give you horsey rides*
Lionni, Leo. *Let's make rabbits*
McGuirk, Leslie. *Tucker off his rocker*
McPhail, David. *Those can-do pigs*
McQuade, Jacqueline. *Good times with Teddy Bear*
Magliaro, Elaine. *Things to do*

Maitland, Barbara. *My bear and me*
Markes, Julie. *Good thing you're not an octopus!*
Martin, David. *Piggy and Dad*
Matheson, Christie. *Plant the tiny seed*
    Tap the magic tree
Mayo, Margaret. *Stomp, dinosaur, stomp!*
Meyers, Susan. *Everywhere babies*
Mora, Pat. *Join hands!*
Most, Bernard. *A pair of protoceratops*
    A trio of triceratops
Munsch, Robert N. *Up, up, down!*
Murkoff, Heidi Eisenberg. *What to expect at preschool*
Murphy, Mary. *I like it when . . .*
    Some things change
Newman, Lesléa. *Dogs, dogs, dogs*
Nobisso, Josephine. *The moon's lullaby*
Noble, Trinka Hakes. *The day Jimmy's boa ate the wash*
Numeroff, Laura Joffe. *Chimps don't wear glasses*
    If you take a mouse to the movies
    What puppies do best
O'Connor, Jane. *Ready, set, skip!*
O'Mara, Carmel. *Good morning*
    Good night
Ormerod, Jan. *Who's whose?*
Paradis, Susan. *My Daddy*
Pearle, Ida. *A child's day*
Pilkey, Dav. *Make way for Dumb Bunnies*
Pomeroy, Diana. *Wildflower ABC*
Ray, Karen. *Sleep song*
Regan, Lara Jo. *A Winkle in time*
Reinen, Judy. *Bow wow*
    Meow
Roberts, Bethany. *Fourth of July mice*
Rosenberry, Vera. *Run, jump, whiz, splash*
Rotner, Shelley. *What can you do?*
Rylant, Cynthia. *In November*
Samuels, Barbara. *Duncan and Dolores*
Scanlon, Elizabeth Garton. *All the world*
Schindel, John. *Busy penguins*
Schwartz, Amy. *The boys teams*
Senisi, Ellen B. *Hurray for pre-K!*
Seven spunky monkeys
Shields, Carol Diggory. *Day by day a week goes round*
Sif, Birgitta. *Where my feet go*
Silbaugh, Elizabeth. *Raggedy Ann's birthday party book*
Simmons, Jane. *Daisy says, "Here we go round the mulberry bush"*
Simon, Francesca. *Toddler time*
Siomades, Lorianne. *Kangaroo and cricket*
Spetter, Jung-Hee. *Lily and Trooper's winter*
Spinelli, Eileen. *What do angels wear?*
Spinelli, Jerry. *My daddy and me*
Stanley, Mandy. *Bloomer, the dog you can play with*
Stevenson, James. *Rolling Rose*
Stock, Catherine. *Halloween monster*
Tafuri, Nancy. *Do not disturb*
Tirabosco, Tom. *At the same time*
Uff, Caroline. *Lulu's busy day*
Vogel, Vin. *The thing about yetis*
Walsh, Melanie. *Do donkeys dance?*
Warnick, Elsa. *Bedtime*
Wells, Rosemary. *Night sounds, morning colors*
Willis, Jeanne. *Susan laughs*
Winch, John. *Keeping up with Grandma*
Wood, Audrey. *King Bidgood's in the bathtub*
Ziefert, Harriet. *A polar bear can swim*

    Robin, where are you?
    Rockheads
    Toes have wiggles, kids have giggles
Zuckerberg, Randi. *Dot*

Activities – babysitting

Anderson, Peggy Perry. *Time for bed, the babysitter said*
Berenstain, Stan and Jan. *The Berenstain bears and the sitter*
Brown, Marc. *Arthur babysits*
Butler, M. Christina. *The special blankie*
Child, Lauren. *Clarice Bean, guess who's babysitting?*
Christelow, Eileen. *Five little monkeys trick-or-treat*
Day, Alexandra. *Carl's birthday*
    Follow Carl!
    Good dog, Carl
Fox, Mem. *Good night, sleep tight*
Gardner, Sally. *Mama, don't go out tonight*
Harris, Robie H. *Don't forget to come back*
Hughes, Shirley. *Don't want to go!*
Hunter, Dette. *38 ways to entertain your babysitter*
Johnson, Angela. *Shoes like Miss Alice's*
Joyce, William. *George shrinks*
Keller, Holly. *Geraldine and Mrs. Duffy*
Kromhout, Rindert. *Little Donkey and the baby-sitter*
McCourt, Lisa. *Chicken soup for little souls: The never-forgotten doll*
McNiff, Dawn. *Mommy's little monster*
Moss, Miriam. *A babysitter for Billy Bear*
Reagan, Jean. *How to babysit a grandma*
    How to babysit a grandpa
Robbins, Beth. *Tom, Ally, and the baby-sitter*
Schwartz, Amy. *Willie and Uncle Bill*
Sendak, Maurice. *Outside over there*
Stewart, Amber. *No babysitters allowed*
Teague, Mark. *Baby tamer*
Urbanovic, Jackie. *Sitting duck*
Van Laan, Nancy. *Mama rocks, Papa sings*
Viorst, Judith. *The good-bye book*
Ward, Nick. *Don't eat the babysitter!*
Wardlaw, Lee. *Saturday night jamboree*
Wells, Rosemary. *Max's dragon shirt*
    Shy Charles
    Stanley and Rhoda
Weninger, Brigitte. *Davy in the middle*
    Will you mind the baby, Davy?
Winthrop, Elizabeth. *Bear and Mrs. Duck*
    Bear's Christmas surprise

Activities – baking, cooking

Ahlberg, Allan. *Hooray for bread*
Anderson, Brian. *Monster chefs*
Argueta, Jorge. *Arroz con leche / Rice pudding*
    Guacamole
    Salsa
    Sopa de frijoles: un poema para cocinar / Bean soup: a cooking poem
    Tamalitos
Auch, Mary Jane. *The princess and the pizza*
Averbeck, Jim. *The market bowl*
Axelrod, Amy. *Pigs in the pantry*
Bailey, Linda. *Toads on toast*
Bastianich, Lidia. *Nonna tell me a story*
    Nonna's birthday surprise
Beck, Andrea. *Elliot bakes a cake*
Bee, William. *Stanley's diner*

Best, Cari. *Easy as pie*
Blackstone, Stella. *Making minestrone*
Burfoot, Ella. *How to bake a book*
Cartaya, Pablo. *Tina Cocolina*
Cazet, Denys. *The perfect pumpkin pie*
Chavarría-Cháirez, Becky. *Magda's tortillas / Las tortillas de Magada*
Christelow, Eileen. *Don't wake up Mama!*
Coffelt, Nancy. *Aunt Ant leaves through the leaves*
Compestine, Ying Chang. *Boy dumplings*
   The runaway wok
   The story of noodles
Cooper, Helen. *Delicious!*
   A pipkin of pepper
Cousins, Lucy. *Maisy makes gingerbread*
Denise, Anika. *Baking day at Grandma's*
   Pigs love potatoes
dePaola, Tomie. *Pancakes for breakfast*
   The popcorn book
Donohue, Dorothy. *Veggie soup*
Dooley, Norah. *Everybody serves soup*
Dunbar, Joyce. *Pat-a-cake baby*
Edwards, Michelle. *Max makes a cake*
Edwards, Pamela Duncan. *Warthogs in the kitchen*
Elya, Susan Middleton. *Eight animals bake a cake*
Emberley, Ed. *The red hen*
Erdrich, Louise. *The range eternal*
Ericsson, Jennifer A. *Out and about at the bakery*
Ernst, Lisa Campbell. *Little Red Riding Hood: a newfangled prairie tale*
Evans, Lezlie. *The bunnies' picnic*
Everitt, Betsy. *Mean soup*
Falwell, Cathryn. *Feast for ten*
   Rainbow Stew
Fearnley, Jan. *Mr. Wolf and the three bears*
   Mr. Wolf's pancakes
Florence, Tyler. *Tyler makes pancakes!*
   Tyler makes spaghetti!
Fox, Christyan. *Count to ten, PiggyWiggy!*
Gibbons, Gail. *Apples*
   The berry book
   The too-great bread bake book
Glaser, Linda. *Mrs. Greenberg's messy Hanukkah*
Goldin, Barbara Diamond. *Cakes and miracles*
Gourley, Robbin. *Bring me some apples and I'll make you a pie*
Grey, Mini. *Ginger bear*
Hall, Margaret. *Corn*
   Peanuts
Hartland, Jessie. *Bon appetit!*
Hassett, Ann. *Too many frogs!*
Head, Judith. *Mud soup*
Heath, Amy. *Sofie's role*
Heras, Theo. *Baby cakes*
Hill, Eric. *Spot bakes a cake*
Hill, Mary. *Let's make pizza*
   Let's make tacos
Himes, Rachel. *Princess and the peas*
Holub, Joan. *The pizza that we made*
Hopkinson, Deborah. *Fannie in the kitchen*
Howe, James. *Houndsley and Catina*
Hunter, Dette. *38 ways to entertain your babysitter*
   38 ways to entertain your grandparents
Iwai, Melissa. *Pizza day*
   Soup day
Jackson, Kathryn. *Pantaloon*
Jenkins, Emily. *A fine dessert*
Katzler, Eva. *Florentine and Pig*
Kimmel, Eric A. *Jack and the giant barbecue*

Klostermann, Penny Parker. *A cooked-up fairy tale*
Kneen, Maggie. *Chocolate moose*
Krause, Ute. *Oscar and the very hungry dragon*
Kyle, Tracey. *Gazpacho for Nacho*
Laminack, Lester L. *Saturdays and teacakes*
Lewin, Ted. *Big Jimmy's Kum Kau Chinese take out*
Lin, Grace. *Dim sum for everyone*
Lipson, Eden Ross. *Applesauce season*
The little red hen. *The little red hen*, ill. by Byron Barton
   The little red hen, ill. by Emily Bolam
   The little red hen, ill. by Paul Galdone
   Little red hen
   The little red hen, ill. by Jerry Pinkney
   The little red hen, ill. by Kate Slater
   The little red hen, ill. by Annie West
   The little red hen, ill. by Margot Zemach
   The little red hen: an old fable
   The Little Red Hen and the Passover matzah
   The Little Red Hen makes a pizza
Livingston, A. A. *B. Bear and Lolly: catch that cookie!*
Long, Ethan. *Snickerdoodle takes the cake*
Lyons, Kelly Starling. *Tea cakes for Tosh*
McAlister, Caroline. *Holy Molé!*
McElligott, Matthew. *Even aliens need snacks*
McKissack, Patricia C. *Messy Bessey's holidays*
McLaughlin, Lauren. *Mitzi Tulane, preschool detective, in The secret ingredient*
McMullan, Kate. *Bulldog's big day*
Malbrough, Mike. *Marigold bakes a cake*
Malkin, Michele. *Pinky's sweet tooth*
Many, Paul. *The great pancake escape*
Manzano, Sonia. *Miracle on 133rd Street*
Martin, David. *All for pie, pie for all*
Martin, Jacqueline Briggs. *Alice Waters and the trip to delicious*
May, Eleanor. *Albert the muffin-maker*
Meadows, Michelle. *Piggies in the kitchen*
Meddaugh, Susan. *Hog-eye*
Millen, C. M. *Blue bowl down*
Miller, Pat. *The hole story of the doughnut*
Miller, Pat Zietlow. *Sharing the bread*
Mora, Pat. *The bakery lady / La señora de la panadería*
Mother Goose *Pat-a-cake*, ill. by Olga Ivanov
   Pat-a-cake, ill. by Annie Kubler
Mozelle, Shirley. *The bear upstairs*
Muir, Leslie. *The little bitty bakery*
Müller, Birte. *Finn cooks*
Murphy, Stuart J. *A fair bear share*
Murray, Alison. *Apple pie ABC*
Nakagawa, Chihiro. *Who made this cake?*
Nakagawa, Rieko. *Guri and Gura*
   Guri and Gura's special gift
Neuschwander, Cindy. *Pastry school in Paris*
Newman, Lesléa. *A sweet Passover*
Nieminen, Lotta. *Pancakes! an interactive recipe book*
Nolen, Jerdine. *In my momma's kitchen*
Oxenbury, Helen. *It's my birthday*
Parenteau, Shirley. *Bears and a birthday*
Parish, Herman. *Amelia Bedelia's first apple pie*
Park, Frances. *Where on earth is my bagel?*
Park, Linda Sue. *Bee-bim bop!*
Parkhurst, Carolyn. *Cooking with Henry and Elliebelly*
Paschkis, Julie. *Apple cake*
Pelham, David. *Sam's pizza*
Peppa Pig and the vegetable garden
Platt, Cynthia. *A little bit of love*

Priceman, Marjorie. *How to make a cherry pie and see the U.S.A.*
   How to make an apple pie and see the world
Reich, Susanna. *Minette's feast*
Rex, Michael. *The pie is cherry*
Reynolds, Aaron. *Buffalo wings*
   Chicks and salsa
Rice, Eve. *Benny bakes a cake*
Robbins, Ken. *Apples*
Roberts, Bethany. *Cookie angel*
Rodman, Mary Ann. *Surprise soup*
Rosenthal, Amy Krouse. *Cookies*
   One smart cookie: bite-size lessons for the school years and beyond
Rosoff, Meg. *Wild boars cook*
Rossell, Judith. *Ruby and Leonard and the great big surprise*
Rotner, Shelley. *Hold the anchovies!*
Rylant, Cynthia. *The cookie-store cat*
Sanders, Rob. *Cowboy Christmas*
Sanger, Amy Wilson. *First book of sushi*
Schubert, Leda. *The Princess of Borscht*
Shannon, George. *Who put the cookies in the cookie jar?*
Shulman, Lisa. *The moon might be milk*
Simmonds, Posy. *Baker cat*
Smalls, Irene. *My Pop Pop and me*
Smith, Linda. *Mrs. Biddlebox*
Smothers, Ethel Footman. *Auntee Edna*
Speed, Toby. *Brave potatoes*
Staake, Bob. *The donut chef*
Stadler, Alexander. *Beverly Billingsly takes the cake*
Stevens, Jan Romero. *Carlos digs to China / Carlos excava hasta la China*
Stevens, Janet. *Cook-a-doodle-doo!*
Stewig, John Warren. *Making plum jam*
Stowell, Penelope. *The greatest potatoes*
Sylver, Adrienne. *Hot diggity dog*
Teevin, Toni. *What to do? What to do?*
Tegen, Katherine. *Pink cupcake magic*
Thomas, Jan. *Is that wise, Pig?*
Torres, Leyla. *Saturday sancocho*
Ungar, Richard. *Rachel's gift*
Urbanovic, Jackie. *Duck soup*
Vamos, Samantha R. *The cazuela that the farm maiden stirred*
VanHecke, Susan. *An apple pie for dinner*
Wallace, Nancy Elizabeth. *Apples, apples, apples*
Wellington, Monica. *Mr. Cookie Baker*
   Pizza at Sally's
Wells, Rosemary. *Bunny cakes*
   Max's apples
Wheeler, Lisa. *Ugly pie*
Whelan, Gloria. *The boy who wanted to cook*
Wilson, Karma. *Whopper cake*
Wolff, Nancy. *Tallulah in the kitchen*
Yamada, Utako. *The story of Cherry the pig*
Yorinks, Arthur. *Company's going*
Zepeda, Gwendolyn. *Growing up with tamales / Los tamales de Ana*
Zia, F. *Hot, hot roti for Dada-ji*
Zolkower, Edie Stoltz. *Too many cooks*

Activities – ballooning

Adams, Adrienne. *The great Valentine's Day balloon race*
Appelt, Kathi. *Elephants aloft*
Calhoun, Mary. *Hot-air Henry*

Curious George and the hot air balloon
De Beer, Hans. *Little Polar Bear and the big balloon*
Gibbons, Gail. *Flying*
Gordon, Gus. *Somewhere else*
Huneck, Stephen. *Sally's great balloon adventure*
Jahn-Clough, Lisa. *Felicity and Cordelia*
McGrory, Anik. *Mouton's impossible dream*
McPhail, David. *Henry Bear's park*
Migy. *And away we go!*
Moseley, Keith. *Where's the dinosaur?*
Olshan, Matthew. *A voyage in the clouds*
Priceman, Marjorie. *Hot air*
Rawlinson, Julia. *A surprise for Rosie*
Sakai, Komako. *Emily's balloon*
Smith, Matthew Clark. *Lighter than air*
Stead, Philip C. *Sebastian and the balloon*

Activities – bargaining *see* Activities – trading

Activities – bartering *see* Activities – trading

Activities – bathing

Anderson, Derek. *Ten pigs*
Anderson, Peggy Perry. *To the tub*
Andreasen, Dan. *The treasure bath*
Andres, Kristina. *Elephant in the bathtub*
Arnold, Tedd. *No more water in the tub!*
Averbeck, Jim. *Oh no, Little Dragon!*
Barner, Bob. *Animal baths*
Barnett, Mac. *President Taft is stuck in the bath*
Beaumont, Karen. *Dini Dinosaur*
Beck, Andrea. *Elliot's bath*
Bedford, David. *Shaggy Dog and the terrible itch*
Boyd, Colin. *The bath monster*
Brown, Alan James. *Love-a-Duck*
Brown, Margaret Wise. *The dirty little boy*
Browne, Christopher. *Marlo*
Capucilli, Alyssa Satin. *Bathtime for Biscuit*
   Biscuit visits the pumpkin patch
Coffelt, Nancy. *Catch that baby!*
Conrad, Pam. *The Tub People*
DaCosta, Barbara. *Mighty Moby*
Dodds, Dayle Ann. *Pet wash*
Ehrlich, Fred. *Does an elephant take a bath?*
Esbaum, Jill. *Estelle takes a bath*
Feeney, Tatyana. *Small Elephant's bathtime*
Ficocelli, Elizabeth. *Kid tea*
Gehl, Laura. *Peep and Egg: I'm not taking a bath*
Geisert, Arthur. *Hogwash*
Gershator, Phillis. *Time for a bath*
Harper, Jamie. *Splish splash, Baby Bundt*
Jenkins, Steve. *Time for a bath*
Johansen, K. V. *Pippin takes a bath*
Jones, Sylvie. *Who's in the tub?*
Kay, Julia. *Gulliver Snip*
Krosoczka, Jarrett J. *Bubble bath pirates*
Landström, Lena. *A hippo's tale*
Lauber, Patricia. *What you never knew about tubs, toilets and showers*
Lindgren, Barbro. *Sam's bath*
McDonnell, Flora. *I love boats*
Mack, Jeff. *Who needs a bath?*
McNaulty, Stacy. *101 reasons why I'm not taking a bath*
Mahy, Margaret. *The green bath*
Maizes, Sarah. *On my way to the bath*
Messer, Claire. *Grumpy pants*

Mortensen, Lori. *Cowpoke Clyde and Dirty Dawg*
Myers, Tim. *Down at the Dino Wash Deluxe*
Neubecker, Robert. *Beasty bath*
Noonan, Julia. *Bath day*
Palatini, Margie. *Tub-boo-boo*
Pallotta, Jerry. *Dory story*
Parenteau, Shirley. *Bears in the bath*
Patricelli, Leslie. *Tubby*
Pattison, Darcy. *Desert baths*
Pelletier, Andrew T. *The amazing adventures of Bathman!*
Philip, Neil. *The fish is me*
Postgate, Daniel. *Smelly Bill: love stinks*
Puttock, Simon. *Squeaky clean*
Robinson, Michelle. *How to wash a woolly mammoth*
Russo, Marisabina. *Little Bird takes a bath*
Sayre, April Pulley. *Splish! splash! animal baths*
Schotter, Roni. *Captain Bob sets sail*
Segal, John. *Pirates don't take baths*
Shannon, Terry Miller. *Tub toys*
Shyba, Jessica. *Bathtime with Theo and Beau*
Slangerup, Erik Jon. *Dirt Boy*
Smith, Janice Lee. *Jess and the stinky cowboys*
Spinelli, Eileen. *Summerbath, winterbath*
Sykes, Julie. *I don't want to take a bath!*
Teckentrup, Britta. *Big smelly bear*
  Get out of my bath!
Thompson, Kay. *Kay Thompson's Eloise takes a bawth*
Weinert, Matthias. *No bath, no cake!*
Wells, Rosemary. *Max's bath*
Weninger, Brigitte. *"No bath! No way!"*
Westaway, Kylie. *A whale in the bathtub*
Willems, Mo. *The pigeon needs a bath*
Wilson, Karma. *Hogwash!*
Wood, Audrey. *King Bidgood's in the bathtub*
Yoshitake, Shinsuke. *Still stuck*
Zion, Gene. *Harry, the dirty dog*

Activities – cooking *see* Activities – baking, cooking

Activities – dancing

Ackerman, Karen. *Song and dance man*
Allen, Debbie. *Brothers of the knight*
  Dancing in the wings
Andreae, Giles. *Giraffes can't dance*
Andrews, Sylvia. *Dancing in my bones*
Appelt, Kathi. *The Alley Cat's Meow*
  Bats around the clock
Arnosky, Jim. *Rattlesnake dance*
Asch, Frank. *Moondance*
  Moongame
Asher, Sandy. *Stella's dancing days*
Auch, Mary Jane. *Hen lake*
  Peeping Beauty
Axelrod, Amy. *Pigs in the corner*
Backx, Patsy. *Skippy and Jack*
Bansch, Helga. *Brava, Mimi!*
Baryshnikov, Mikhail. *Because . . .*
Bell, Cece. *Sock Monkey boogie-woogie*
Benzwie, Teresa. *Numbers on the move*
Bird, Betsy. *Giant dance party*
Bloom, Suzanne. *Bear can dance!*
Bluemle, Elizabeth. *How do you wokka-wokka?*
Bonwill, Ann. *Naughty toes*
Boynton, Sandra. *Dinosaur dance!*
Bradley, Kimberly Brubaker. *Ballerino Nate*

Brandenberg, Alexa. *Ballerina flying*
Brown, Margaret Wise. *Sailor boy jig*
Burningham, John. *It's a secret!*
Callahan, Sean. *Shannon and the world's tallest leprechaun*
Capucilli, Alyssa Satin. *Katy Duck*
  Katy Duck, big sister
  Katy Duck is a caterpillar
  Tulip loves Rex
Catrow, David. *Monster mash*
Chaconas, Dori. *Dancing with Katya*
Clarke, Jane. *Dancing with the Dinosaurs*
Collins, Pat Lowery. *I am a dancer*
Corey, Shana. *Ballerina bear*
Craig, Lindsey. *Dancing feet!*
Crimi, Carolyn. *Tessa's tip-tapping toes*
Cristaldi, Kathryn. *Baseball ballerina*
  Baseball ballerina strikes out
Cronin, Doreen. *Click, clack, moo I love you!*
Dawavendewa, Gerald. *The butterfly dance*
De Anda, Diane. *Dancing Miranda / Baila, Miranda, baila*
DePalma, Mary Newell. *The Nutcracker doll*
dePaola, Tomie. *Oliver Button is a sissy*
DeRubertis, Barbara. *Dilly Dog's dizzy dancing*
Dunlap, Cirocco. *This book will not be fun*
Durango, Julia. *Cha-cha chimps*
Duval, Kathy. *Take me to your BBQ*
Edwards, Pamela Duncan. *Bravo, Livingstone Mouse!*
  Honk!
Elliott, David. *One little chicken*
Federle, Tim. *Tommy can't stop!*
Feiffer, Jules. *Rupert can dance*
Foges, Clare. *Kitchen disco*
French, Jackie. *Josephine wants to dance*
Gauch, Patricia Lee. *Bravo, Tanya*
  Dance, Tanya
  Presenting Tanya, the Ugly Duckling
  Tanya and Emily in a dance for two
Geras, Adèle. *Giselle*
  The nutcracker
  Sleeping beauty
  Swan Lake
  Time for ballet
Gliori, Debi. *Polar Bolero*
Goble, Paul. *Star boy*
Gollub, Matthew. *Gobble, quack, moon*
Gorbachev, Valeri. *Catty Jane who loved to dance*
Greenberg, Jan. *Ballet for Martha*
Grimm, Jacob and Wilhelm. *Twelve dancing princesses*
  The twelve dancing princesses, ill. by Lucy Corvino
  The twelve dancing princesses, ill. by Kinuko Y. Craft
  The twelve dancing princesses, ill. by Rachel Isadora
  The twelve dancing princesses, ill. by Alison Jay
  The twelve dancing princesses, ill. by Gerald McDermott
  The twelve dancing princesses, ill. by Jane Ray
  The twelve dancing princesses, ill. by Suçie Stevenson
  The twelve princesses
Gruska, Denise. *The only boy in ballet class*
Gunnufson, Charlotte. *Halloween hustle*
Hager, Sarah. *Dancing Matilda*
Hague, Michael. *The nutcracker*
Hallworth, Grace. *Sing me a story*

Hannert, Todd. *Morning dance*
Hanson, Warren. *Bugtown Boogie*
Hayward, Linda. *A day in the life of a dancer*
Headley, Justina Chen. *The patch*
Heidbreder, Robert. *Drumheller dinosaur dance*
Hesse, Karen. *Come on, rain*
Hest, Amy. *Mabel dancing*
Hoffmann, E. T. A. *The nutcracker*, ill. by Renée
 Graef
 The nutcracker, ill. by Alison Jay
 The nutcracker, ill. by Peter Malone
 The nutcracker, ill. by Maurice Sendak
 The nutcracker, ill. by Lisbeth Zwerger
 The Nutcracker and the Mouse King
 The nutcracker ballet
 The Nutcracker in Harlem
Holabird, Katharine. *Angelina and the princess*
 Angelina ballerina
 Angelina dances
 Angelina on stage
 Angelina, star of the show
 Angelina's ballet class
 Christmas in Mouseland
Hudson, Cheryl Willis. *My friend Maya loves to
 dance*
Hueston, M. P. *The all-American jump and jive jig*
Hutchins, Pat. *Barn dance!*
Idle, Molly. *Flora and the flamingo*
 Flora and the peacocks
Isadora, Rachel. *Bea in The Nutcracker*
 Lili at ballet
 Lili on stage
 Not just tutus
Janni, Rebecca. *Every cowgirl needs dancing boots*
Jennings, Sharon. *Priscilla's paw de deux*
Jonas, Ann. *Color dance*
Kajikawa, Kimiko. *Yoshi's feast*
Kinerk, Robert. *Clorinda*
Kirwan, Wednesday. *Baby loves to boogie!*
Kleven, Elisa. *The dancing deer and the foolish hunter*
Knister. *Sophie's dance*
Kohuth, Jane. *Duck sock hop*
Kroll, Virginia L. *Can you dance, Dalila?*
Krosoczka, Jarrett J. *Ollie the purple elephant*
Lasky, Kathryn. *Starring Lucille*
Lee, Jeanne M. *Silent lotus*
Leiner, Katherine. *Mama does the mambo*
Lillegard, Dee. *The Big Bug Ball*
Litwin, Eric. *The Nuts: sing and dance in your polka-
 dot pants*
Loggins, Kenny. *Footloose*
London, Jonathan. *Who bop*
Lynn, Sarah. *Tip-tap pop*
Lyons, Kelly Starling. *One more dino on the floor*
Maccarone, Grace. *Miss Lina's ballerinas and the
 prince*
 Miss Lina's ballerinas and the wicked wish
McElmurry, Jill. *Mario makes a move*
McKissack, Patricia C. *Mirandy and Brother Wind*
Mahy, Margaret. *Mister Whistler*
Manning, Maurie J. *Kitchen dance*
Manson, Ainslie. *Ballerinas don't wear glasses*
Marshall, James. *The Cut-Ups carry on*
 George and Martha encore
 Swine lake
Martin, Bill, Jr.. *Barn dance!*
 Spunky Little Monkey
Mayhew, James. *Ella Bella ballerina and The
 Nutcracker*

Medearis, Angela Shelf. *Dancing with the Indians*
Mills, Judith Christine. *The painted chest*
Mitton, Tony. *Dinosaurumpus*
 Down by the cool of the pool
Murphy, Kelly. *The boll weevil ball*
Newsome, Jill. *Dream dancer*
Paraskevas, Betty. *Marvin, the tap-dancing horse*
Pavlova, Anna. *I dreamed I was a ballerina*
Paxton, Tom. *Engelbert the elephant*
Pinkney, Andrea Davis. *Alvin Ailey*
Pinkwater, Daniel. *Dancing Larry*
Proimos, James. *Waddle! waddle!*
Pulver, Robin. *Alicia's tutu*
Puttock, Simon. *A ladder to the stars*
Quattlebaum, Mary. *Sparks fly high*
Ray, Mary Lyn. *Deer dancer*
Riecherter, Daryn. *The Cambodian dancer*
Rubin, Susan Goldman. *Matisse dance for joy*
Ryder, Joanne. *Big bear ball*
 Dance by the light of the moon
Saab, Julie. *Little Lola saves the show*
Sandall, Ellie. *Everybunny dance!*
Sanders, Rob. *Ruby Rose*
Sauer, Tammi. *Bawk and roll*
 Chicken dance
Schaefer, Carole Lexa. *Dragon dancing*
Schneider, Christine M. *Saxophone Sam and his
 snazzy jazz band*
Schofield-Morrison, Connie. *I got the rhythm*
Schroeder, Alan. *Ragtime Tumpie*
Schumaker, Ward. *Dance!*
Shannon, George. *April showers*
Shields, Carol Diggory. *Saturday night at the
 dinosaur stomp*
Sif, Birgitta. *Frances Dean who loved to dance and
 dance*
Silverman, Erica. *The Hanukkah hop!*
Singer, Marilyn. *Feel the beat*
 Tallulah's tap shoes
 Tallulah's toe shoes
Sís, Peter. *Ballerina*
Smith, Charles R. *Dance with me*
Smith, Cynthia Leitich. *Jingle dancer*
Snyder, Betsy. *I can dance*
Stanley, Mandy. *Lettice the dancing rabbit*
Stanton, Elizabeth Rose. *Peddles*
Stickland, Paul. *Dinosaur stomp!*
Stower, Adam. *Two left feet*
Stroud, Bettye. *Dance y'all*
Stutson, Caroline. *Cats' night out*
Symes, Ruth. *Harriet dancing*
Taylor, Ann. *Baby dance*
Teague, Mark. *The sky is falling!*
Thomas, Joyce Carol. *Shouting*
Thomas, Peggy. *Snow dance*
Thompson, Lauren. *Ballerina dreams*
Thorpe, Kiki. *Time to cha-cha-cha!*
Tricarico, Christine. *Cock-a-doodle dance!*
Tryon, Leslie. *The thumbtack dancer*
Tucker, Lindy. *Porkelia*
Waboose, Jan Bourdeau. *Firedancers*
Walton, Rick. *How can you dance?*
 Noah's square dance
Wardlaw, Lee. *Saturday night jamboree*
Waters, Kate. *Lion dancer*
Welch, Willy. *Dancing with Daddy*
Wensink, Patrick. *Go go gorillas*
Wheeler, Lisa. *Hokey pokey*
Wild, Margaret. *Midnight babies*

Witte, Anna. *Lola's fandango*
Wood, Audrey. *Little Penguin's tale*
Yee, Wong Herbert. *The Officers' Ball*
Young, Amy. *Belinda and the glass slipper*
 Belinda begins ballet
 Belinda in Paris
 Belinda, the ballerina
Zapf, Marlena. *Underpants dance*
Zuill, Andrea. *Dance is for everyone*

Activities – digging

Aliki. *Digging up dinosaurs*
Barnett, Mac. *Sam and Dave dig a hole*
Gay, Marie-Louise. *Roslyn Rutabaga and the biggest hole on earth!*
Gibbons, Gail. *Tunnels*
Hoban, Tana. *Dig, drill, dump, fill*
Jenson-Elliott, Cindy. *Dig in!*
Krauss, Ruth. *A hole is to dig*
Paraskevas, Betty. *Maggie and the Ferocious Beast, the big carrot*
Stevens, Jan Romero. *Carlos digs to China / Carlos excava hasta la China*
Tyler, Jenny. *Big Pig on a dig*

Activities – drawing

Ahlberg, Allan. *The pencil*
Alexander, Martha G. *I'll never share you, Blackboard Bear*
 Max and the dumb flower picture
Baker, Liza. *Dinosaur days*
Banks, Kate. *The eraserheads*
Barnett, Mac. *How this book was made*
Becker, Aaron. *Journey*
 Quest
 Return
Bloom, Becky. *Mice make trouble*
Brecon, Connah. *Paws McDraw*
Browne, Anthony. *The little Bear book*
Carle, Eric. *Draw me a star*
Carlin, Laura. *A world of your own*
Collins, Ross. *Doodleday*
Colón, Raúl. *Draw!*
Davies, Matt. *Ben draws trouble*
Degen, Bruce. *I gotta draw*
Demi. *The girl who drew a phoenix*
Dominguez, Angela. *Knit together*
Dormer, Frank W. *The obstinate pen*
Edwards, Pamela Duncan. *The neat line*
Emberley, Ed. *Ed Emberley's drawing book of trucks and trains*
 Ed Emberley's fingerprint drawing book
Ericsson, Jennifer A. *A piece of chalk*
Falwell, Cathryn. *David's drawing*
Florian, Douglas. *How to draw a dragon*
Freedman, Deborah. *Scribble*
Gerstein, Mordicai. *The first drawing*
Gretz, Susanna. *Riley and Rose in the picture*
Hamsa, Bobbie. *Fast-draw Freddie*
Haring, Kay A. *Keith Haring*
Heap, Sue. *Danny's drawing book*
Hillenbrand, Will. *Louie!*
Hutchins, Hazel. *The sidewalk rescue*
Jagtenberg, Yvonne. *Jack's rabbit*
Johnson, D. B. *Eddie's kingdom*
Kleven, Elisa. *The paper princess*
Kroll, Steven. *Patches*

 Patches lost and found
Larsen, Andrew. *A squiggly story*
Lee, Suzy. *Lines*
Lehrhaupt, Adam. *This is a good story*
Lichtenheld, Tom. *Bridget's beret*
Light, Kelly. *Louise loves art*
Lucas, David. *Something to do*
Ludwig, Trudy. *The invisible boy*
Luyken, Corinna. *The book of mistakes*
McCarty, Peter. *Jeremy draws a monster*
 The monster returns
McDonnell, Patrick. *Art*
McPhail, David. *Andrew draws*
 Beatrix Potter and her paint box
 Drawing lessons from a bear
 Moony B. Finch, fastest draw in the West
Mills, Claudia. *Ziggy's blue-ribbon day*
Moss, Marissa. *Regina's big mistake*
Myers, Christopher. *My pen*
Nikola-Lisa, W. *Can you top that?*
O'Connor, Jane. *Fancy Nancy: aspiring artist*
Ohi, Debbie Ridpath. *Sam and Eva*
Otoshi, Kathryn. *Draw the line*
Pericoli, Matteo. *See the city*
 Tommaso and the missing line
Poydar, Nancy. *Cool Ali*
Priest, Robert H. *The pirate's eye*
Raczka, Bob. *Niko draws a feeling*
Reidy, Jean. *Time out for monsters!*
Rey, Margret. *Billy's picture*
Roslonek, Steve. *The shape song swingalong*
Russell, Natalie. *Lost for words*
Russo, Marisabina. *Under the table*
Saltzberg, Barney. *Andrew drew and drew*
Say, Allen. *Emma's rug*
Sierra, Judy. *Imagine that! how Dr. Seuss wrote The Cat in the Hat*
Stubbs, Lisa. *Lily and Bear*
 Lily and Bear: grumpy feet
Sturm, James. *Gryphons aren't so great*
 Ogres awake!
 Sleepless knight
Tate, Don. *It jes' happened*
Thomson, Bill. *Chalk*
Tierney, Fiona. *Lion's lunch?*
Van Allsburg, Chris. *Bad day at Riverbend*
Wallner, Alexandra. *Beatrix Potter*
Watt, Mélanie. *Chester*
 Chester's back!
 Chester's masterpiece
Williams, Karen Lynn. *A beach tail*
Wilson, April. *April Wilson's magpie magic*
Wing, Natasha. *Go to bed, monster!*
Yates, Louise. *Dog loves drawing*
Zemach, Kaethe. *Ms. McCaw learns to draw*

Activities – driving

Burningham, John. *Motor Miles*
Calmenson, Stephanie. *No honking allowed*
Hatanaka, Kellen. *Drive: a look at roadside opposites*
Pulver, Robin. *Axle Annie and the speed grump*
Timmers, Leo. *Who is driving?*
Wilson, Karma. *Sakes alive!*

Activities – eating *see* Food

Activities – flying

Aardema, Verna. *Jackal's flying lesson*
Allard, Harry. *The Stupids take off*
Bang, Molly. *Goose*
Bently, Peter. *Those magnificent sheep in their flying machine*
Berger, Melvin. *How do airplanes fly?*
Berkeley, Jon. *Chopsticks*
Berne, Jennifer. *Calvin can't fly*
Biddulph, Rob. *Blown away*
Bildner, Phil. *The hallelujah flight*
Blake, Robert J. *Fledgling*
Bloom, Suzanne. *Bear can dance!*
Breen, Steve. *Violet the pilot*
Brill, Calista. *Little Wing learns to fly*
Brown, Tami Lewis. *Soar, Elinor!*
Cave, Kathryn. *The boy who became an eagle*
Church, Caroline Jayne. *Ping Pong Pig*
Clark, Leslie Ann. *Peepsqueak!*
Comden, Betty, et al. *Flying to Neverland with Peter Pan*
Conover, Chris. *The lion's share*
Crews, Donald. *Flying*
De Beer, Hans. *Little Polar Bear and the big balloon*
Demarest, Chris L. *Lindbergh*
    Smokejumpers one to ten
Dollinger, Renate. *The rabbi who flew*
Dominguez, Angela. *Let's go, Hugo!*
Dorros, Arthur. *Abuela*
Dudley, Rebecca. *Hank has a dream*
Edwards, Pamela Duncan. *The Wright brothers*
Fardell, John. *Jeremiah Jellyfish flies high!*
Finn, Isobel. *The very lazy ladybug*
Forler, Nan. *Bird child*
Fuge, Charles. *Three little dinosaurs*
Garland, Michael. *Icarus Swinebuckle*
Gibbons, Gail. *Flying*
Glass, Andrew. *The wondrous whirligig*
Gorbachev, Valeri. *The fool of the world and the flying ship: a Ukrainian folk tale*
Gordon, Gus. *Somewhere else*
Graham, Bob. *Max*
Gregorowski, Christopher. *Fly, eagle, fly!*
Grist, Julie. *Flying, just plane fun*
Heide, Florence Parry. *Princess Hyacinth*
Heller, Nicholas. *Elwood and the witch*
Hodgkins, Fran. *How people learned to fly*
Ichikawa, Satomi. *Come fly with me*
James, Simon. *George flies south*
Jeffers, Oliver. *Up and down*
Jenkins, Steve. *Animals in flight*
Jessell, Tim. *Falcon*
Johnson, Angela. *Wind flyers*
Johnson, Paul Brett. *The cow who wouldn't come down*
Joyce, William. *The fantastic flying books of Mr. Morris Lessmore*
    Santa calls
Judge, Lita. *Flight school*
Kang, A. N. *Papillon goes to the vet*
    The very fluffy kitty, Papillon
Kinerk, Robert. *Clorinda takes flight*
Kleven, Elisa. *The paper princess*
Kotzwinkle, William. *Walter, the farting dog: rough weather ahead*
Kroll, Steven. *Super-dragon*
Lam, Thao. *Skunk on a string*
Lang, Heather. *Fearless flyer*

Lehrhaupt, Adam. *Chicken in space*
Leiter, Richard. *The flying hand of Marco B.*
Lewis, Kim. *Here we go Harry*
Light, Steve. *Zephyr takes flight*
Lindbergh, Reeve. *Nobody owns the sky*
Loux, Lynn C. *The day I could fly*
Lund, Deb. *Dinosoaring*
McCarty, Peter. *Moon plane*
McDermott, Gerald. *Coyote*
McGhee, Alison. *Only a witch can fly*
McGill, Alice. *Way up and over everything*
McKee, David. *Elmer and the wind*
    Elmer takes off
McLellan, Stephanie Simpson. *The chicken cat*
Marcero, Deborah. *Ursa's light*
Meade, Holly. *If I never forever endeavor*
Minshull, Evelyn White. *Eaglet's world*
Modarressi, Mitra. *Owlet's first flight*
Morison, Toby. *Little Louie takes off*
Munsch, Robert N. *Angela's airplane*
Myers, Christopher. *Wings*
O'Malley, Kevin. *Little Buggy*
Paul, Alison. *The plan*
Peet, Bill. *The kweeks of Kookatumdee*
    Merle the high flying squirrel
Pinkney, Brian. *The adventures of sparrowboy*
Pomerantz, Charlotte. *Flap your wings and try*
Previn, Stacey. *Aberdeen*
Priceman, Marjorie. *Princess Picky*
Provensen, Alice. *The glorious flight*
Ransome, Arthur. *The fool of the world and the flying ship*
Rau, Dana Meachen. *Flying*
Ringgold, Faith. *Tar Beach*
Rosen, Michael. *Bear flies high*
Ryan, Candace. *Ewe and Aye*
Ryan, Pam Muñoz. *Amelia and Eleanor go for a ride*
Ryder, Joanne. *Rainbow wings*
Schotter, Roni. *Captain Bob takes flight*
Seibold, J. Otto. *Penguin dreams*
Simont, Marc. *The goose that almost got cooked*
Spinelli, Eileen. *Buzz*
Stanley, Mandy. *Lettice the flying rabbit*
Stevenson, James. *The castaway*
    Grandpa's great city tour
Tarpley, Natasha Anastasia. *Joe-Joe's first flight*
Thompson, Colin. *Falling angels*
Tibo, Gilles. *The cowboy kid*
Vere, Ed. *Max and Bird*
Walter, Mildred Pitts. *Brother to the wind*
Ward, Helen. *The dragon machine*
    The king of the birds
Whitaker, Suzanne George. *The daring Miss Quimby*
Wiesner, David. *Tuesday*
Willard, Nancy. *The flying bed*
Willis, Jeanne. *Fly, chick, fly!*
Winer, Yvonne. *Butterflies fly*
Yolen, Jane. *Wings*
Young, Ed. *Hook*
Zullo, Germano. *Little bird*

Activities – gardening *see* Gardens, gardening

Activities – hiking

Bissonette, Aimée. *North woods girl*
Chin, Jason. *Grand Canyon*

Coyle, Carmela LaVigna. *Do princesses really kiss frogs?*
Curious George goes hiking
Harper, Jamie. *Miss Mingo weathers the storm*
Johnson, D. B. *Henry hikes to Fitchburg*
Katschke, Judy. *Take a hike, Snoopy*
Korngold, Jamie S. *Sadie and the big mountain*
Kwan, James. *Dear Yeti*
Longstreth, Galen Goodwin. *Yes, let's*
Oldland, Nicholas. *Walk on the wild side*
Quattlebaum, Mary. *Jo MacDonald hiked in the woods*
Shaw, Nancy. *Sheep take a hike*

Activities – jumping

Aman, Kimiko. *The fox wish*
Cronin, Doreen. *Bounce*
English, Karen. *Hot day on Abbott Avenue*
Fischer, Scott M. *Jump!*
King, Stephen Michael. *Emily loves to bounce*
Murphy, Stuart J. *Ready, set, hop!*
Scruggs, Afi. *Jump rope magic*
Tabor, Corey R. *Fox and the jumping contest*
Yelchin, Eugene. *Spring hare*

Activities – kissing *see* Kissing

Activities – knitting

Aber, Linda Williams. *Carrie measures up!*
Barnett, Mac. *Extra yarn*
Brosgol, Vera. *Leave me alone!*
Bunge, Daniela. *The scarves*
Campbell, K. G. *Lester's dreadful sweaters*
Clifton-Brown, Holly. *Annie Hoot and the knitting extravaganza*
Dominguez, Angela. *Knit together*
Edwards, Michelle. *A hat for Mrs. Goldman*
Elliott, David. *Knitty Kitty*
Grant, Jacob. *Cat knit*
Hopkinson, Deborah. *Knit your bit*
Martins, Isabel Minhós. *Little lamb, have you any wool?*
Mortimer, Rachael. *The three Billy Goats Fluff*
Murray, Diana. *Ned the knitting pirate*
Pomranz, Craig. *Made by Raffi*
Shannon, Margaret. *The red wolf*
Waterton, Betty. *A bumblebee sweater*
Webster, Sheryl. *Noodle's knitting*
Wild, Margaret. *Mr. Nick's knitting*
Yoon, Salina. *Penguin in love*

Activities – making things

Alter, Anna. *What can you do with an old red shoe?*
Bastin, Marjolein. *Christmas with Vera*
Bright, Rachel. *Love Monster and the perfect present*
Cocca-Leffler, Maryann. *A homemade together Christmas*
Côté, Geneviève. *Mr. King's machine*
Cummings, Phil. *Newspaper hats*
Demas, Corinne. *Valentine surprise*
DiPucchio, Kelly. *Crafty Chloe*
Crafty Chloe: dress-up mess-up
Ehlert, Lois. *Hands*
Rain fish
Fleming, Denise. *Alphabet under construction*
Gibbons, Gail. *How a house is built*

Ginsburg, Mirra. *Clay boy*
Hall, Donald. *Lucy's Christmas*
Hall, Kirsten. *The jacket*
Hoban, Tana. *Construction zone*
Hohn, Nadia L. *Malaika's costume*
Howell, Will C. *Zoo flakes ABC*
Hunter, Dette. *38 ways to entertain your babysitter*
38 ways to entertain your grandparents
Inkpen, Mick. *Wibbly Pig can make a tent*
Jeffers, Oliver. *The great paper caper*
Johnson, Angela. *Those building men*
Johnson, Stephen T. *My little blue robot*
Kenney, Sean. *Cool cars and trucks*
Cool castles
Cool city
Cool creations in 101 pieces
Cool creations in 35 pieces
Kleber, Dori. *More-igami*
Kleven, Elisa. *The apple doll*
Knick knack paddy whack
Kroll, Steven. *Will you be my valentine?*
Lachenmeyer, Nathaniel. *The origami master*
Lin, Grace. *Lissy's friends*
Lloyd, Megan Wagner. *Fort-building time*
Lovell, Patty. *Have fun, Molly Lou Melon*
Lum, Kate. *What! cried Granny*
McCain, Becky R. *Grandmother's dreamcatcher*
McClure, Nikki. *Waiting for high tide*
McDonald, Megan. *It's picture day today!*
Mantchev, Lisa. *Sister day!*
Meshon, Aaron. *Tools rule!*
Messier, Mireille. *The branch*
Michelin, Linda. *Zuzu's wishing cake*
Moffatt, Judith. *Snow shapes*
Moon, Nicola. *Lucy's picture-*
Moss, Marissa. *Knick knack paddywack*
Neitzel, Shirley. *The house I'll build for the wrens*
Potter, Giselle. *This is my dollhouse*
Ransom, Candice F. *The promise quilt*
Ray, Mary Lyn. *Basket moon*
Rinker, Sherri Duskey. *The twelve sleighs of Christmas*
Rockwell, Anne. *What we like*
Rylant, Cynthia. *If you'll be my Valentine*
Smith, Danna. *Balloon trees*
Sturges, Philemon. *I love tools!*
Swinburne, Stephen R. *Swallows in the birdhouse*
Tafuri, Nancy. *Counting to Christmas*
Timmers, Leo. *Franky*
Trice, Linda. *Kenya's art*
Tryon, Leslie. *Albert's alphabet*
Wellington, Monica. *Riki's birdhouse*
Wood, Audrey. *The flying dragon room*
Ziefert, Harriet. *Grandma, it's for you!*
Knick-knack paddywhack

Activities – painting *see also* Careers – artists

Adams, Adrienne. *The Easter egg artists*
Agee, Jon. *The incredible painting of Felix Clousseau*
Arnold, Katya. *Elephants can paint, too!*
Arnold, Tedd. *Vincent paints his house*
Aspinall, Sarah. *Penguins love colors*
Baker, Alan. *Black and White Rabbit's ABC*
White Rabbit's color book
Bang, Molly. *When Sophie's feelings are really, really hurt*
Beaumont, Karen. *I ain't gonna paint no more!*
Bilgrami, Shaheen. *Farmyard painting party*

Jungle art show
Black, Harley. *Magic art class*
Bridges, Shirin Yim. *The Umbrella Queen*
Campoy, F. Isabel. *Maybe something beautiful*
Caple, Kathy. *Worm gets a job*
Carle, Eric. *The artist who painted a blue horse*
Demi. *The boy who painted dragons*
dePaola, Tomie. *The legend of the Indian paintbrush*
Eaton, Maxwell. *The mystery*
Edwards, Pamela Duncan. *Warthogs paint*
Engle, Margarita. *The sky painter*
    Summer birds
Flanagan, Alice K. *The Wilsons, a house-painting
    team*
Freedman, Deborah. *Blue chicken*
Geoghegan, Adrienne. *All your own teeth*
Haseley, Dennis. *Twenty heartbeats*
Hawkes, Kevin. *Remy and Lulu*
Hogrogian, Nonny. *Cool cat*
Hong, Chen Jiang. *The magic horse of Han Gan*
Hurd, Thacher. *Art dog*
Johnson, Angela. *Lily Brown's paintings*
Kelley, True. *Claude Monet*
Knapp, Ruthie. *Who stole Mona Lisa?*
Kulling, Monica. *Grant and Tillie go walking*
Larsen, Andrew. *The imaginary garden*
Lodding, Linda Ravin. *Painting Pepette*
Long, Ethan. *Lion and Tiger and Bear*
Look, Lenore. *Brush of the gods*
MacLachlan, Patricia. *Painting the wind*
McPhail, David. *Beatrix Potter and her paint box*
    Something special
Numeroff, Laura Joffe. *The Jellybeans and the big art
    adventure*
Parker, Marjorie Blain. *Colorful dreamer*
Partridge, Elizabeth. *Pig's eggs*
Pinkwater, Daniel. *The picture of Morty and Ray*
Reynolds, Peter H. *Sky color*
Rhodes-Pitts, Sharifa. *Jake makes a world*
Rolli, Jennifer Hansen. *Claudia and Moth*
Rylant, Cynthia. *All I see*
Seeger, Laura Vaccaro. *One boy*
Segal, Lore Groszmann. *Morris the artist*
Snyder, Carol. *We're painting*
Spier, Peter. *Oh, were they ever happy!*
Sweet, Melissa. *Carmine*
Tafuri, Nancy. *Blue goose*
Tamar, Erika. *The garden of happiness*
Twohy, Mike. *Mouse and Hippo*
Walsh, Ellen Stoll. *Mouse paint*
Walsh, Melanie. *Ned's rainbow*
Wiesner, David. *Art and Max*
Wilhelm, Hans. *Quacky Ducky's Easter fun*
Williams, Karen Lynn. *Painted dreams*
Winter, Jonah. *Just behave, Pablo Picasso!*
Ziefert, Harriet. *Lunchtime for a purple snake*
    My dog thinks I'm a genius

Activities – photographing

Casteel, Seth. *Underwater dogs*
Davis, Jill. *Orangutans are ticklish*
Diesen, Deborah. *Picture day perfection*
Hest, Amy. *Guess who, Baby Duck*
Jenson-Elliott, Cindy. *Antsy Ansel*
Levinson, Riki. *I go with my family to Grandma's*
McPhail, David. *Pig Pig and the magic photo album*
Magruder, Nilah. *How to find a fox*
Perkins, Lynne Rae. *Pictures from our vacation*

Pichon, Liz. *Penguins*
Plourde, Lynn. *School picture day*
Roche, Denis. *The best class picture ever*
Rosenstock, Barb. *Dorothea's eyes*
Scotton, Rob. *Russell and the lost treasure*
Swinburne, Stephen R. *Guess whose shadow?*
Trimble, Marcia. *Hello sun*

Activities – picnicking

Alborough, Jez. *It's the bear*
Asch, Frank. *Sand cake*
Asher, Sandy. *Here comes Gosling!*
Ashforth, Camilla. *Willow on the river*
Bee, William. *Stanley's numbers*
Bertrand, Diane Gonzales. *Uncle Chente's picnic /
    El picnic de Tío Chente*
Bunting, Eve. *A picnic in October*
Burningham, John. *Picnic*
Capucilli, Alyssa Satin. *Biscuit's picnic*
Christelow, Eileen. *Five little monkeys sitting in a tree*
Cronin, B. B. *The lost picnic*
Cronin, Doreen. *Click, clack, quackity-quack*
Crum, Shutta. *Dozens of cousins*
Dubuc, Marianne. *Lucy and company*
Eilenberg, Max. *Squeak's good idea*
Elya, Susan Middleton. *Oh no, gotta go #2*
Ets, Marie Hall. *In the forest*
Evans, Lezlie. *The bunnies' picnic*
Goode, Diane. *The most perfect spot*
Graham, Bob. *Jethro Byrd, fairy child*
    Oscar's half birthday
Granowsky, Alvin. *Can I help?*
Hamilton, Richard. *Polly's picnic*
Harper, Charise Mericle. *Pink me up*
Inkpen, Mick. *Picnic*
Jarrett, Clare. *The best picnic ever*
Kasza, Keiko. *Ready for anything*
Katzler, Eva. *Florentine and Pig*
Keller, Holly. *Henry's Fourth of July*
Kennedy, Jimmy. *The teddy bears' picnic*, ill. by
    Alexandra Day
    The teddy bears' picnic, ill. by Michael Hague
    The teddy bears' picnic, ill. by Prue Theobalds
Kroll, Steven. *It's Groundhog Day!*
Kruusval, Catarina. *Franny's friends*
Landström, Olof. *Boo and Baa in the woods*
Lies, Brian. *Bats at the beach*
Livingston, Irene. *Finklehopper Frog cheers*
Lo, Ginnie. *Auntie Yang's great soybean picnic*
London, Jonathan. *Duck and Hippo lost and found*
    Let's go, Froggy!
Longstreth, Galen Goodwin. *Yes, let's*
McCully, Emily Arnold. *Picnic*
Mack, Jeff. *Good news, bad news*
Mahy, Margaret. *The rattlebang picnic*
Manzano, Sonia. *No dogs allowed*
Miranda, Anne. *Pignic*
Murphy, Mary. *Panda Foo and the new friend*
Murphy, Stuart J. *More or less*
Naylor, Phyllis Reynolds. *Please do feed the bears*
Numeroff, Laura Joffe. *What mommies do best*
Phillipps, J. C. *The Simples love a picnic*
Polacco, Patricia. *Picnic at Mudsock Meadow*
Slade-Robinson, Nikki. *Muddle and Mo's worm
    surprise*
Spetter, Jung-Hee. *Lily and Trooper's spring*
Steig, William. *Toby, who are you?*
Thomas, Jane Resh. *Celebration!*

Vincent, Gabrielle. *Ernest and Celestine's picnic*
Virján, Emma J. *What this story needs is a munch and a crunch*
Wardlaw, Lee. *Red, white, and boom!*
Webster, Christine. *Otter everywhere*
Wells, Rosemary. *Bunny mail*
   McDuff saves the day
Woodson, Jacqueline. *We had a picnic this Sunday past*
Yolen, Jane. *Picnic with Piggins*

Activities – playing

Abbot, Judi. *Train!*
Ahlberg, Janet. *Funnybones*
   Playmates
Ajmera, Maya. *Come out and play*
Alda, Arlene. *Lulu's piano lesson*
Alexander, Martha G. *Blackboard Bear*
Aliki. *Overnight at Mary Bloom's*
   Push button
Alko, Selina. *Every-day dress-up*
Allen, Joy. *Princess Palooza*
Anderson, Peggy Perry. *Joe on the go*
Anglund, Joan Walsh. *The brave cowboy*
Apperley, Dawn. *Flip and Flop*
Arnosky, Jim. *Watching foxes*
Ashburn, Boni. *The fort that Jack built*
Ashman, Linda. *Rain!*
Atteberry, Kevan. *Bunnies!!!*
Ayres, Katherine. *Matthew's truck*
Baguley, Elizabeth. *Meggie moon*
Baillie, Marilyn. *Nose to toes*
Baker, Leslie A. *You bad dog!*
Bang, Molly. *Yellow ball*
Banks, Kate. *Max's dragon*
Barba, Ale. *When your elephant comes to play*
Barclay, Jane. *Going on a journey to the sea*
Beaty, Andrea. *When giants come to play*
Beck, Andrea. *Elliot's shipwreck*
Bently, Peter. *King Jack and the dragon*
Berger, Carin. *Good night! Good night!*
   A perfect day
Berger, Samantha. *Crankenstein*
Bergman, Mara. *Lively Elizabeth!*
Bertier, Anne. *Wednesday*
Best, Cari. *If I could drive, Mama*
   A perfect day for digging
Bloom, Suzanne. *A mighty fine time machine*
   What about Bear?
Border, Terry. *Peanut Butter and Cupcake!*
Bottner, Barbara. *Bootsie Barker bites*
Boyd, Lizi. *Inside outside*
Brenning, Juli. *Maggi and Milo make new friends*
Brimner, Larry Dane. *The big, beautiful, brown box*
Brown, Jo. *Hoppity skip Little Chick*
Brown, Susan Taylor. *Oliver's must-do list*
Bruzzone, Catherine. *Puppy finds a friend / Cachorrito encuentra un amigo*
   Puppy finds a friend / Le petit chien se trouve un ami
Butler, John. *Ten in the meadow*
Buxton, Jane. *The littlest llama*
Cabrera, Jane. *Monkey's play time*
Cader, Lisa Lebowitz. *When I wear my crown*
   When I wear my tiara
Capucilli, Alyssa Satin. *Biscuit wants to play*
   Little spotted cat
Castle, Caroline. *Naughty!*
Cauley, Lorinda Bryan. *Clap your hands*

Chase, Kit. *Charlie's boat*
Chung, Arree. *Ninja!*
Clanton, Ben. *Boo who?*
   Rex wrecks it!
Clarke, Jane. *Gilbert the hero*
Cole, Joanna. *Sharing is fun*
Come and play
Cotten, Cynthia. *Rain play*
Cousins, Lucy. *Doctor Maisy*
Crews, Donald. *Cloudy day/sunny day*
Crews, Nina. *Below*
   Sky-high Guy
   Snowball
Cronin, Doreen. *Bounce*
Crum, Shutta. *Dozens of cousins*
   Uh-oh!
Cuyler, Margery. *Please play safe!*
Day, Alexandra. *Carl goes to daycare*
   Follow Carl!
DeBear, Kirsten. *Be quiet, Marina!*
Dempsey, Kristy. *A hop is up*
DePrisco, Dorothea. *Snowbear's winter day*
Dewan, Ted. *Baby gets the zapper*
   Crispin, the pig who had it all
Dewdney, Anna. *Nelly Gnu and Daddy too*
Doerrfeld, Cori. *Maggie and Wendel*
Doyle, Charlotte Lackner. *The bouncing, dancing, galloping ABC*
Duke, Kate. *One guinea pig is not enough*
Dunbar, Polly. *Where's Tumpty?*
Dunrea, Olivier. *Gideon*
Durand, Hallie. *Mitchell's license*
Eaton, Maxwell. *Superheroes*
Ehrlich, H. M. *Gotcha, Louie!*
Ellery, Amanda. *If I had a dragon*
Escoffier, Michael. *The day I lost my superpowers*
Ets, Marie Hall. *Play with me*
Fitzpatrick, Marie-Louise. *I'm a tiger, too!*
Fleming, Denise. *Maggie and Michael get dressed*
Ford, Miela. *Follow the leader*
   Mom and me
Fosberry, Jennifer. *Isabella*
Friend, David. *With any luck, I'll drive a truck*
Fucile, Tony. *Let's do nothing!*
Fuge, Charles. *I know a rhino*
Gammell, Stephen. *Mudkin*
Gardiner, Lindsey. *Here come Poppy and Max*
   When Poppy and Max grow up
Garland, Sally Anne. *Share*
Gay, Marie-Louise. *Stella, queen of the snow*
George, Jean Craighead. *Snow bear*
Gerber, Carole. *A band of babies*
Gibala-Broxholm, Scott. *Maddie's monster dad*
Gibbons, Gail. *Playgrounds*
Gibson, Amy. *Split! splat!*
Gill, Deirdre. *Outside*
Gomi, Taro. *The great day*
Gorbachev, Valeri. *Big Little Elephant*
   Chicken chickens
Gordon, David. *Extremely cute animals operating heavy machinery*
Gravett, Emily. *Monkey and me*
Gray, Nigel. *Time to play!*
Greenfield, Eloise. *Big friend, little friend*
   The friendly four
   My doll, Keshia
Grindley, Sally. *Can we play too, Piglittle?*
Gudeon, Adam. *Me and Meow*
Gundersheimer, Karen. *Find cat, wear hat*

Gutierrez, Akemi. *The mummy and other adventures of Sam and Alice*

Guy, Ginger Foglesong. *¡Bravo!*

Hale, Christy. *Dreaming up*

Halpern, Julie. *Toby and the snowflakes*

Hannigan, Katherine. *Gwendolyn Grace*

Harper, Charise Mericle. *Mimi and Lulu*

Havill, Juanita. *Jamaica Tag-Along*

Heap, Sue. *What shall we play?*

Heidbreder, Robert. *I wished for a unicorn*

Heide, Iris van der. *The red chalk*

Henkes, Kevin. *Oh!*
A weekend with Wendell

Hest, Amy. *Buster and the baby*

Hill, Eric. *Spot at play*
Spot goes to the beach
Spot goes to the park
Spot sleeps over

Hines, Anna Grossnickle. *I am a backhoe*

Hoffman, Eric. *A dark, dark cave*

Holmes, Janet A. *Me and you*

Hru, Dakari. *Tickle, tickle*

Hubbell, Patricia. *Pots and pans*
Snow happy!

Hudelhoff, Allen H. *Cats and kids*

Hughes, Sarah. *Let's play hopscotch*
Let's play jacks

Hunter, Sally. *Humphrey's corner*

Inkpen, Mick. *Kipper's snowy day*
Swing!
Wibbly Pig can make a tent

Ismail, Yasmeen. *Imagine that!*

Jackson, Richard. *This beautiful day*

Janovitz, Marilyn. *Play baby play!*

Jarrett, Clare. *The best picnic ever*

Jenkins, Emily. *Toys meet snow*

Jocelyn, Marthe. *A day with Nellie*

Joosse, Barbara. *Old Robert and the sea-silly cats*
Sleepover at Gramma's house

Kaneko, Yuki. *Into the snow*

Kasza, Keiko. *Dorothy and Mikey*

Keats, Ezra Jack. *The snowy day*

King, Stephen Michael. *Emily loves to bounce*

Koehler, Fred. *Super Jumbo*

Könnecke, Ole. *Anthony and the girls*

Kraus, Robert. *Come out and play, little mouse*

Kuefler, Joseph. *Rulers of the playground*

Kuhlman, Evan. *Hank's big day*

Kvasnosky, Laura McGee. *Really truly Bingo*

Lacome, Julie. *Ruthie's big old coat*

Lakin, Patricia. *Rainy day*

Lambert, Jonny. *Tiger tiger*

Landström, Lena. *Pom and Pim*
Where is Pim?

Lawler, Janet. *A father's song*

Lee, Michelle. *Play with me!*

Lendler, Ian. *Saturday*

Leslie, Amanda. *Who's that scratching at my door?*

Lewin, Betsy. *Thumpy Feet*

Lewis, Kim. *Floss*
Seymour and Henry

Lewison, Wendy Cheyette. *Mud*

Lia, Simone. *Red's great chase*

Litwin, Eric. *The Nuts: bedtime at the Nut house*
The Nuts: sing and dance in your polka-dot pants

Liwska, Renata. *Red wagon*

Lloyd, Megan Wagner. *Fort-building time*

Lobel, Anita. *Playful pigs from A to Z*

London, Jonathan. *Otters love to play*
Puddles
Sun dance, water dance

Loomis, Christine. *Cowboy bunnies*

Luenn, Nancy. *Otter play*

Lundquist, Mary. *Cat and Bunny*

Lynn, Sarah. *1-2-3 va-va-vroom!*

McAllister, Angela. *Harry's box*

McCarty, Peter. *First snow*

McClintock, Barbara. *Dahlia*

McClure, Nikki. *In*

McClurkan, Rob. *Playdates rule!*

McCully, Emily Arnold. *First snow*

McDonnell, Christine. *Dog wants to play*

McGhee, Alison. *The case of the missing donut*
Percy, dog of destiny

McGuirk, Leslie. *Tucker flips!*

McHenry, E. B. *Poodlena*

Mack, Jeff. *Playtime?*

McKay, Hilary. *Pirates ahoy!*

McKee, David. *Elmer in the snow*

McLean, Janet. *Let's go, baby-o!*

MacLennan, Cathy. *Chicky Chicky Chook Chook*

McLerran, Alice. *Roxaboxen*

McPhail, David. *Emma in charge*
Olivia loves Owl
Pig Pig rides

McQuinn, Anna. *Leo loves baby time*
Lola loves stories

Mallat, Kathy. *Just ducky*
Trouble on the tracks

Marley, Cedella. *Every little thing*

Martin, David. *Peep and Ducky*
Peep and Ducky: rainy day

Merz, Jennifer J. *Playground day*

Meshon, Aaron. *The best days are dog days*

Milgrim, David. *Time to get up, time to go*

Miller, Ruth. *I went to the farm*

Miller, Virginia. *In a minute!*

Mills, Judith Christine. *The painted chest*

Moers, Hermann. *Rufus and Max*

Morgan-Vanroyen, Mary. *Wild Rosie*

Morozumi, Atsuko. *Playing*

Morris, Ann. *Play*

Morrison, Toni. *Peeny butter fudge*

Morstad, Julie. *How to*

Moss, Miriam. *The snow bear*

Munsch, Robert N. *Mud puddle*

Murguia, Bethanie Deeney. *Princess! Fairy!*
Ballerina!
Zoe's jungle

Murkoff, Heidi Eisenberg. *What to expect at a play date*

Murphy, Jill. *All for one*

Naylor, Phyllis Reynolds. *King of the playground*

Neitzel, Shirley. *I'm taking a trip on my train*

Neubecker, Robert. *What little boys are made of*

Newcome, Zita. *Pop-up toddlerobics*

Newman, Lesléa. *A fire engine for Ruthie*

Nikola-Lisa, W. *Bein' with you this way*

Nordling, Lee. *Shehewe*

Ochiltree, Dianne. *Pillow pup*

O'Connor, George. *Ker-splash!*

Ohi, Ruth. *And you can come too*

O'Keefe, Susan Heyboer. *Baby day*

O'Mara, Carmel. *Rainy day*
Sunny day

Onyefulu, Ifeoma. *Omer's favorite place*

Ormerod, Jan. *Miss Mouse's day*

Patricelli, Leslie. *Tubby*

Paul, Ann Whitford. *Hello toes! Hello feet!*
Phelan, Matt. *Druthers*
Pilutti, Deb. *Ten rules of being a superhero*
Portis, Antoinette. *No es una caja / not a box*
   Not a box
   Not a stick
   Princess Super Kitty
Poydar, Nancy. *Snip, snip . . . snow!*
Priest, Robert H. *The old pirate of Central Park*
Pringle, Laurence P. *Octopus hug*
Pritchett, Andy. *Stick!*
Purcell, Rebecca. *Super Chicken*
Rankin, Laura. *My turn!*
Ray, Mary Lyn. *Red rubber boot day*
Rayner, Catherine. *Solomon Crocodile*
Reynolds, Luke. *Bedtime blastoff!*
Rim, Sujean. *Birdie's big-girl shoes*
Ritchie, Alison. *What Bear likes best!*
Rockwell, Anne. *At the beach*
Roddie, Shen. *Toes are to tickle*
Rodman, Mary Ann. *My best friend*
Rogers, Fred. *Making friends*
Roode, Daniel. *Little Bea and the snowy day*
Ross, Michael Elsohn. *Play with me*
Russo, Marisabina. *The big brown box*
Ryan, Pam Muñoz. *Mud is cake*
Rylant, Cynthia. *Brownie and Pearl get dolled up*
   Henny, Penny, Lenny, Denny, and Mike
   Little penguins
Sanders, Rob. *Rodzilla*
Sarah, Linda. *Big friends*
Sarcone-Roach, Julia. *The secret plan*
Sattler, Jennifer. *Pig kahuna pirates!*
Schaefer, Carole Lexa. *ABCers*
   Kids like us
   Snow pumpkin
Schaefer, Lola M. *One busy day*
Scheffler, Axel. *Pip and Posy: the super scooter*
Schertle, Alice. *The adventures of old Bo Bear*
Schoenherr, Ian. *Cat and mouse*
Schwartz, Corey Rosen. *Hop! Plop!*
Schwartz, Roslyn. *The mole sisters and the fairy ring*
Schwarz, Viviane. *There are cats in this book*
Sendak, Maurice. *The sign on Rosie's door*
Sheridan, Sara. *I'm me!*
Shields, Gillian. *Library Lily*
Shirotani, Hideo. *Let's play*
Siddals, Mary McKenna. *I'll play with you*
Silverman, Erica. *Follow the leader*
Simmons, Jane. *Little Fern's first winter*
Simon, Francesca. *Calling all toddlers*
Singer, Marilyn. *A stick is an excellent thing*
Slegers, Liesbet. *Playing*
Sloat, Teri. *Pablo in the snow*
Smalls, Irene. *My Nana and me*
Smith, Lois T. *Carrie and Carl play*
Snyder, Betsy. *I can play*
Soman, David. *The amazing adventures of Bumblebee Boy*
   Ladybug Girl
   Ladybug Girl and Bumblebee Boy
   Ladybug Girl and the best ever playdate
   Ladybug Girl and the big snow
   Ladybug Girl and the Bug Squad
Spetter, Jung-Hee. *Lily and Trooper's fall*
   Lily and Trooper's spring
   Lily and Trooper's summer
Steig, William. *Pete's a pizza*
   Toby, what are you?

Toby, where are you?
Stein, David Ezra. *Monster hug!*
Steptoe, John. *Baby says*
Stevenson, Robert Louis. *Where go the boats?*
Sullivan, Deirdre. *Ming goes to school*
Sullivan, Mary. *Ball*
Sykes, Julie. *Wait for me, Little Tiger*
Teague, Mark. *The pirate jamboree*
Thomas, Jan. *Here comes the big, mean dust bunny!*
Thomas, Shelley Moore. *No, no, kitten!*
Thompson, Lauren. *Little Quack's new friend*
Thomson, Bill. *The typewriter*
Tompert, Ann. *Just a little bit*
Torrey, Richard. *The almost terrible playdate*
Tullet, Herve. *Let's play*
Van Allsburg, Chris. *Zathura*
Van der Meer, Mara. *Can we play?*
Vigna, Judith. *Boot weather*
Waber, Bernard. *Ira sleeps over*
Waddell, Martin. *Snow bears*
   Squeak-a-lot
   Tom Rabbit
Weatherford, Carole Boston. *Jazz baby*
Weeks, Sarah. *Bunny fun*
   Overboard!
Weiss, Ellen. *Playtime for twins*
Wells, Rosemary. *A lion for Lewis*
Wewer, Iris. *My wild sister and me*
White, Kathryn. *The tickle test*
Whybrow, Ian. *Harry and the bucketful of dinosaurs*
Williams, Sherley Anne. *Girls together*
Wilson, Karma. *Horseplay*
Winter, Jeanette. *Cowboy Charlie*
Wishinsky, Frieda. *You're mean, Lily Jean!*
Wohnoutka, Mike. *Little puppy and the big green monster*
Wolff, Nancy. *It's time for school with Tallulah*
Won, Brian. *Hooray for today!*
Wood, Audrey. *The Tickleoctopus*
Wood, Douglas. *Nothing to do*
Woodcock, Fiona. *Hiding Heidi*
Yaccarino, Dan. *Happyland: rainy day*
Yolen, Jane. *Before the storm*
   Dimity Duck
   Romping monsters, stomping monsters
   Soft house
   What to do with a box
Young, Ned. *Zoomer*
Yuly, Toni. *Cat nap*
Yum, Hyewon. *Puddle*
Zehler, Antonia. *Two fine ladies*
   Two fine ladies have a tiff
Ziefert, Harriet. *Mighty Max*

Activities – reading *see* Books, reading

Activities – running

Best, Cari. *My three best friends and me, Zulay*
Cartier, Wesley. *Marco's run*
Golding, Theresa Martin. *Abby's asthma and the big race*
Grant, Brianna K. *We are girls who love to run / Somos chicas y a nosotras nos encanta correr*
Livingston, Irene. *Finklehopper Frog*
Miller, Pat Zietlow. *The quickest kid in Clarksville*
Mitton, Tony. *The Jungle Run*

Activities – sewing

Ashburn, Boni. *I had a favorite dress*
Beck, Andrea. *Elliot's emergency*
Brown, Monica. *Maya's blanket*
Cotten, Cynthia. *Abbie in stitches*
Edwards, Michelle. *Room for the baby*
Fulton, Kristen. *Long may she wave*
Gibbons, Gail. *The quilting bee*
Gordon, Domenica More. *Archie*
Green, Stephanie. *Betsy Ross and the silver thimble*
Heo, Yumi. *Lady Hahn and her seven friends*
Herkert, Barbara. *Sewing stories*
Hopkinson, Deborah. *Sweet Clara and the freedom quilt*
Johnston, Tony. *Levi Strauss gets a bright idea*
    My best friend Bear
Kimmel, Eric A. *Stormy's hat*
Leedahl, Shelley A. *The bone talker*
Luxbacher, Irene. *Mr. Frank*
McDonald, Megan. *The Hinky Pink*
McKee, David. *Elmer and Super El*
Marshall, Linda Elovitz. *Grandma Rose's magic*
Masini, Beatrice. *Here comes the bride*
Paul, Ann Whitford. *The seasons sewn*
Ransom, Candice F. *The promise quilt*
Sabuda, Robert. *The Blizzard's robe*
Shea, Pegi Deitz. *The whispering cloth*
Strauss, Linda Leopold. *The princess gown*
Wallner, Alexandra. *Betsy Ross*
White, Becky. *Betsy Ross*
Ziefert, Harriet. *My forever dress*

Activities – shopping *see* Shopping

Activities – singing

Andrews, Julie. *The very fairy princess sparkles in the snow*
Auch, Mary Jane. *Bantam of the opera*
Barrett, Ron. *Cats got talent*
Barton, Suzanne. *The sleepy songbird*
Bolliger, Max. *The happy troll*
Bonwill, Ann. *The Frazzle family finds a way*
Cave, Kathryn. *Henry's song*
Crimi, Carolyn. *Tessa's tip-tapping toes*
Crow, Kristyn. *The middle-child blues*
Cunnane, Kelly. *Chirchir is singing*
Daly, Niki. *Ruby sings the blues*
D'Arc, Karen Scourby. *My grandmother is a singing Yaya*
dePaola, Tomie. *The song of Francis*
DiCamillo, Kate. *La la la*
Dominguez, Angela. *Sing, don't cry*
Elya, Susan Middleton. *Sophie's trophy*
Gray, Luli. *Ant and Grasshopper*
Howe, James. *Horace and Morris join the chorus (but what about Dolores?)*
Kushner, Tony. *Brundibar*
Litwin, Eric. *The Nuts: sing and dance in your polka-dot pants*
    Pete the Cat: rocking in my school shoes
    Pete the Cat and his four groovy buttons
Ljungkvist, Laura. *Pepi sings a new song*
Lucado, Max. *Alabaster's song*
Martin, Jacqueline Briggs. *Chicken joy on Redbean Road*
Millner, Denene. *Early Sunday morning*
Mitchell, Margaree King. *When Grandmama sings*

Peterson, Jeanne Whitehouse. *My mama sings*
Raposo, Joe. *Sing!*
Schotter, Roni. *Doo-Wop Pop*
Sproule, Gail. *Singing the dark*
Taylor, Ann. *Baby dance*
Van Dusen, Chris. *Hattie and Hudson*
Watts, Leslie Elizabeth. *The Baabaasheep Quartet*
Weaver, Tess. *Opera cat*
Wright, Catherine. *Steamboat Annie and the thousand-pound catfish*

Activities – storytelling

Ahlberg, Allan. *The snail house*
Ahlberg, Janet. *It was a dark and stormy night*
Asher, Sandy. *Chicken story time*
Aska, Warabe. *Tapicero tap tap*
Banks, Kate. *Max's words*
Benton, Jim. *The end (almost)*
Blackstone, Stella. *How big is a pig?*
Bottner, Barbara. *Miss Brooks' Story Nook (where tales are told and ogres are welcome)*
Bouchard, Dave. *The song within my heart*
Brutschy, Jennifer. *Just one more story*
Carlson, Nancy. *Henry's amazing imagination!*
Cazet, Denys. *The octopus*
Davol, Marguerite W. *The snake's tales*
Dominguez, Angela. *Sing, don't cry*
Donaldson, Julia. *The fish who cried wolf*
Dotlich, Rebecca Kai. *One day, the end*
Downey, Lynn. *Matilda's humdinger*
Esenwine, Matt Forrest. *Flashlight night*
Fagan, Cary. *Mr. Zinger's hat*
Fleming, Candace. *Clever Jack takes the cake*
Fox, Mem. *This and that*
Freedman, Deborah. *The Story of Fish and Snail*
Gay, Marie-Louise. *Any questions?*
Gonzalez, Lucia. *The storyteller's candle / La velita de los cuentos*
Grey, Mini. *Toys in space*
Hanlon, Abby. *Ralph tells a story*
Hanson, Regina. *A season for mangoes*
Hest, Amy. *The babies are coming!*
Hughes, Vi. *Aziz, the story teller*
Johnston, Tony. *My abuelita*
Joosse, Barbara. *Grandma calls me Beautiful*
Kasza, Keiko. *Silly Goose's big story*
Kroll, Steven. *The Tyrannosaurus game*
Kurtz, Jane. *In the small, small night*
LaRochelle, David. *The haunted hamburger and other ghostly stories*
    It's a tiger
Lehrhaupt, Adam. *This is a good story*
Lodding, Linda Ravin. *Little red riding sheep*
Luján, Jorge. *Moví la mano / I moved my hand*
Lyon, George Ella. *My friend, the starfinder*
McGhee, Alison. *Tell me a tattoo story*
McKinlay, Meg. *No bears*
McQuinn, Anna. *Leo loves baby time*
    Lola loves stories
Mahoney, Daniel J. *The Saturday escape*
Martin, Rafe. *The storytelling princess*
Mayr, Diane. *Littlebat's Halloween story*
Mortimer, Rachael. *Song for a princess*
Murguia, Bethanie Deeney. *The too-scary story*
Muth, Jon J. *Zen ghosts*
    Zen shorts
    Zen socks
Nash, Scott. *Tuff Fluff*

Nolan, Janet. *The St. Patrick's Day shillelagh*
O'Leary, Sara. *This is Sadie*
O'Malley, Kevin. *Velcome*
Paschkis, Julie. *Mooshka*
Reiser, Lynn. *Little clam*
Rinker, Sherri Duskey. *Big machines*
Robberecht, Thierry. *Sam tells stories*
Roberts, Bethany. *Gramps and the fire dragon*
Rochelle, Belinda. *Jewels*
Rosenthal, Eileen. *I'll save you Bobo!*
Say, Allen. *Kamishibai man*
Schaefer, Carole Lexa. *Down in the woods at sleepytime*
Schwartz, Amy. *Some babies*
Scrimger, Richard. *Eugene's story*
Shannon, David. *Jangles*
Sierra, Judy. *Tell the truth, B. B. Wolf*
Simms, Laura. *Rotten teeth*
Slate, Joseph. *Story time for Little Porcupine*
Spalding, Andrea. *Solomon's tree*
Stead, Philip C. *Bear has a story to tell*
Sullivan, Sarah. *Once upon a baby brother*
Taback, Simms. *Kibitzers and fools*
Tokuda-Hall, Maggie. *Also an octopus*
Turk, Evan. *The storyteller*
Van Leeuwen, Jean. *The tickle stories*
Velasquez, Eric. *Grandma's records*
Virján, Emma J. *What this story needs is a pig in a wig*
Wallen, Ila. *The moon in my room*
Wyeth, Sharon Dennis. *The granddaughter necklace*
Yaccarino, Dan. *I am a story*
Yeh, Kat. *The magic brush*
Yolen, Jane. *Miz Berlin walks*
Zagarenski, Pamela. *The whisper*

Activities – swapping *see* Activities – trading

Activities – swimming *see* Sports – swimming

Activities – swinging

Patricelli, Leslie. *Higher! higher!*
Tusa, Tricia. *Follow me*

Activities – talking

Blackstone, Stella. *Baby talk*
Cruise, Robin. *Bartleby speaks!*
Higgins, Ryan T. *Be quiet!*
Hindley, Judy. *Baby talk*
Jones, Christianne C. *Lacey Walker, nonstop talker*
Meddaugh, Susan. *Martha and Skits*
 Martha blah blah
 Martha calling
 Martha says it with flowers
 Martha speaks
 Martha walks the dog
 Perfectly Martha
Ziefert, Harriet. *Talk, baby!*

Activities – trading

Bram, Elizabeth. *Rufus the writer*
Chorao, Kay. *Pig and Crow*
Dick Whittington and his cat. *Dick Whittington and his cat*
Gardella, Tricia. *Blackberry booties*

Heide, Iris van der. *The red chalk*
Jennings, Sharon. *Franklin makes a deal*
Johnson, Paul Brett. *Bearhide and crow*
Light, Steve. *Swap!*
Lodding, Linda Ravin. *A gift for Mama*
Martin, Jacqueline Briggs. *On Sand Island*
Murphy, Stuart J. *Dinosaur deals*
O'Neill, Alexis. *Estela's swap*
Ormerod, Jan. *The baby swap*
Pham, LeUyen. *A piece of cake*
Pryor, Katherine. *Zora's zucchini*
Steig, Jeanne. *Fleas!*
Suen, Anastasia. *Window music*
Torres, Leyla. *Saturday sancocho*
VanHecke, Susan. *An apple pie for dinner*

Activities – traveling

Aardema, Verna. *Traveling to Tondo*
Alsenas, Linas. *Mrs. Claus takes a vacation*
Arena, Jen. *Lady Liberty's holiday*
Ashman, Linda. *Over the river and through the wood*
Axelrod, Amy. *Pigs on the move*
Aylesworth, Jim. *My sister's rusty bike*
Bailey, Linda. *Stanley at sea*
Baillie, Allan. *Dragonquest*
Banks, Kate. *City cat*
Barnett, Mac. *Oh no! Not again!*
 Places to be
Barracca, Debra. *Maxi, the star*
Bart, Kathleen. *Town Teddy and Country Bear go global*
Bateman, Teresa. *Gus, the pilgrim turkey*
Bauer, Sepp. *The Christmas rose*
Becker, Aaron. *Journey*
 Quest
 Return
Best, Cari. *When Catherine the Great and I were eight!*
Blackstone, Stella. *Bear takes a trip*
Border, Terry. *Merry Christmas, Peanut!*
Brown, Laurie Krasny. *Dinosaurs travel*
Brown, Lisa. *The airport book*
Brown, Marc. *Arthur meets the president*
Brown, Margaret Wise. *North, south, east, west*
Brunhoff, Jean de. *The travels of Babar*
Brunhoff, Laurent de. *Babar's USA*
 Babar's world tour
Brutschy, Jennifer. *Just one more story*
Buitrago, Jairo. *Two white rabbits*
Bunting, Eve. *Ducky*
 Peepers
Burleigh, Robert. *Hit the road, Jack*
Carle, Eric. *Friends*
 The rooster who set out to see the world
 Rooster's off to see the world
Chancellor, Deborah. *Traveling on land*
Clifton-Brown, Holly. *Annie Hoot and the knitting extravaganza*
Cocca-Leffler, Maryann. *Bus route to Boston*
Codell, Esme Raji. *Seed by seed*
Conrad, Donna. *See you soon, Moon*
Cooney, Barbara. *Miss Rumphius*
Cooper, Elisha. *Train*
Cora, Cat. *A suitcase surprise for Mommy*
Cousins, Lucy. *Maisy goes on a plane*
 Maisy goes to London
Coy, John. *Vroomaloom zoom*
Crampton, Gertrude. *Scuffy the tugboat*
Crowley, Ned. *Nanook and Pryce*

Cummings, Pat. *My aunt came back*
Davies, Stephen. *All aboard for the Bobo Road*
Davis, Kenneth C. *Don't know much about the pioneers*
Deacon, Alexis. *A place to call home*
Dickson, Louise. *The vanishing cat*
Diesen, Deborah. *The pout-pout fish, far, far from home*
Docherty, Thomas. *To the beach*
Dunbar, Joyce. *Shoe baby*
Dupre, Kelly. *The raven's gift*
Egan, Tim. *Dodsworth in London*
   Dodsworth in New York
   Dodsworth in Paris
   Dodsworth in Rome
Elissa, Barbara. *The remarkable journey of Josh's kippah*
Eschbacher, Roger. *Road trip*
Evans, Lezlie. *The bunnies' trip*
Evert, Lori. *The Christmas wish*
Faller, Regis. *The adventures of Polo*
   Polo
   Polo and the magician!
Fitzpatrick, Marie-Louise. *You, me and the big blue sea*
Foreman, Michael. *Fortunately, unfortunately*
Fox, Mem. *Possum magic*
Gaiman, Neil. *Instructions*
Gall, Chris. *The littlest train*
Gammell, Stephen. *How about going for a ride*
Gerstein, Mordicai. *How to bicycle to the moon to plant sunflowers*
Gordon, Gus. *Somewhere else*
Gravett, Emily. *Meerkat mail*
Gutman, Anne. *Lisa's airplane trip*
Handford, Martin. *Find Waldo now*
   The great Waldo search
   Where's Waldo?
   Where's Waldo? In Hollywood
   Where's Waldo? The fantastic journey
   Where's Waldo? The wonder book
   Where's Waldo now?
Hawkes, Kevin. *The wicked big toddlah goes to New York*
Helldorfer, M. C. *Hog music*
Hobbie, Holly. *Toot and Puddle*
   Toot and Puddle: wish you were here
   Toot and Puddle, I'll be home for Christmas
   Toot and Puddle, top of the world
Hodgkinson, Leigh. *Boris and the snoozebox*
Holabird, Katharine. *Angelina's Cinderella*
Holmes, Mary Tavener. *A giraffe goes to Paris*
Horowitz, Dave. *Duck, duck, moose*
Howland, Naomi. *ABCDrive!*
Hubbell, Patricia. *My first airplane ride*
Hume, Stephen Eaton. *Red moon follows truck*
Hutchins, Hazel. *Beneath the bridge*
Isadora, Rachel. *Over the green hills*
Jahn-Clough, Lisa. *Felicity and Cordelia*
Jonas, Ann. *Round trip*
Joosse, Barbara. *Sail away Dragon*
Joslin, Mary. *The shore beyond*
Kaczman, James. *A bird and his worm*
Kasparavicius, Kestutis. *The bear family's world tour Christmas*
Kay, Verla. *Covered wagons, bumpy trails*
Kellogg, Steven. *Johnny Appleseed: a tall tale*
Kelly, Mij. *William and the night train*
Kerby, Mona. *Owney, the mail-pouch pooch*

Kimmel, Eric A. *Pumpkinhead*
Kirk, Daniel. *Honk honk! Beep beep!*
Kono, Erin Eitter. *Every color*
Krebs, Laurie. *Off we go to Mexico*
   We're riding on a caravan
   We're sailing down the Nile
   We're sailing to Galapagos
Laden, Nina. *Are we there yet?*
Lawlor, Laurie. *Old Crump*
Lazo, Caroline. *Someday when my cat can talk*
Lester, Alison. *Sophie Scott goes south*
Levitin, Sonia. *Nine for California*
Lin, Grace. *Olvina flies*
Lindbergh, Reeve. *Johnny Appleseed*
Lloyd-Jones, Sally. *Poor Doreen*
London, Jonathan. *Froggy goes to Hawaii*
   Moshi moshi
Long, Matty. *Super Happy Magic Forest*
Loth, Sebastian. *Clementine*
Louis, Catherine. *Liu and the bird*
Luzzati, Emanuele. *Three little owls*
McCarthy, Meghan. *The adventures of Patty and the big red bus*
McCarty, Peter. *Little bunny on the move*
McClintock, Barbara. *Adele and Simon in America*
   Lost and found: Adele and Simon in China
McCourt, Lisa. *I miss you, Stinky Face*
McPhail, David. *Pig Pig returns*
Margolin, H. Ellen. *Goin' to Boston*
Mauner, Claudia. *Zoe Sophia's scrapbook*
Miller, Pat Zietlow. *Wherever you go*
Miller, Sara Swan. *Cat in the bag*
Moss, Miriam. *Matty takes off!*
Munro, Roxie. *The inside-outside book of Texas*
   The inside-outside book of Washington, D.C.
   Mazescapes
Na, Il Sung. *Welcome home, Bear*
Neitzel, Shirley. *The bag I'm taking to Grandma's*
Neubecker, Robert. *Courage of the blue boy*
Norling, Beth. *The stone baby*
Nye, Naomi Shihab. *Come with me*
Ohi, Ruth. *A trip with Grandma*
Ormerod, Jan. *Miss Mouse takes off*
Orona-Ramirez, Kristy. *Kiki's journey*
Pattison, Darcy. *The journey of Oliver K. Woodman*
   Searching for Oliver K. Woodman
Piepmeier, Charlotte. *Lucy's journey to the wild west*
Pinkney, Gloria Jean. *The Sunday outing*
Potter, Giselle. *The year I didn't go to school*
Priceman, Marjorie. *How to make a cherry pie and see the U.S.A.*
   How to make an apple pie and see the world
Ramsey, Calvin Alexander. *Ruth and the Green Book*
Reibstein, Mark. *Wabi Sabi*
Rockwell, Anne. *Whoo! whoo! goes the train*
Rogers, Fred. *Going on an airplane*
Rohmann, Eric. *Pumpkinhead*
Rosen, Michael J. *A drive in the country*
Rubin, Adam. *Those darn squirrels fly south*
Rumford, James. *Chee-lin*
   The Island-below-the-star
Rylant, Cynthia. *The relatives came*
   Tulip sees America
Santat, Dan. *Are we there yet?*
Say, Allen. *Grandfather's journey*
Segal, John. *Alistair and Kip's great adventure*
Seuss, Dr. *I had trouble getting to Solla Sollew*
Siegel, Randy. *Grandma's smile*
Silvano, Wendi. *Just one more*

Sís, Peter. *Robinson*
  Tibet through the red box
Skinner, Daphne. *All aboard!*
Slater, Dashka. *The antlered ship*
Smath, Jerry. *Sammy Salami*
Smith, Maggie. *Counting our way to Maine*
Sorensen, Henri. *New Hope*
Staake, Bob. *The Book of Gold*
Stanley, Diane. *Joining the Boston Tea Party*
  Thanksgiving on Plymouth Plantation
Stead, Philip C. *Jonathan and the big blue boat*
  Sebastian and the balloon
  Special delivery
Steggall, Susan. *Rattle and rap*
Stem, J. David. *Kay Thompson's Eloise in Hollywood*
Steptoe, Javaka. *The Jones family express*
Stevenson, James. *All aboard!*
Stoop, Naoko. *Red Knit Cap Girl to the rescue*
Suen, Anastasia. *Road work ahead*
Swain, Gwenyth. *Johnny Appleseed*
Swanson, Matthew. *Everywhere, wonder*
Thomas, Joyce Carol. *In the land of milk and honey*
Thompson, Emma. *The further tale of Peter Rabbit*
Thompson, Kay. *Kay Thompson's Eloise in Moscow*
Tibo, Gilles. *The grand journey of Mr. Man*
Tonatiuh, Duncan. *Pancho Rabbit and the coyote*
Trimble, Marcia. *Hello sun*
Turner, Ann Warren. *Nettie's trip south*
Uhlberg, Myron. *Lemuel, the fool*
Van Leeuwen, Jean. *Across the wide dark sea*
van Lieshout, Maria. *Backseat A-B-see*
Verburg, Bonnie. *The kiss box*
Waddell, Martin. *Small Bear lost*
Wallace, Ivy. *Pookie*
Walters, Virginia. *Are we there yet, Daddy?*
Waugh, Peter. *The great cannon beach mouse caper*
Wiesmüller, Dieter. *The adventures of Marco and
  Polo*
Wild, Margaret. *Going home*
Willems, Mo. *Knuffle Bunny free*
Willis, Jeanne. *Poles apart*
Wishinsky, Frieda. *What's up, bear?*
Wong, Janet S. *The trip back home*
Wood, Audrey. *Silly Sally*
Wright, Courtni Crump. *Wagon train*
Yolen, Jane. *Johnny Appleseed: the legend and the truth*
Yoon, Salina. *Penguin's big adventure*
Young, Rebecca. *Teacup*
Ziefert, Harriet. *From Kalamazoo to Timbuktu!*
Zullo, Germano. *Line 135*

Activities – vacationing

Adams, Adrienne. *The Easter egg artists*
Alsenas, Linas. *Mrs. Claus takes a vacation*
Arena, Jen. *Lady Liberty's holiday*
Becker, Suzy. *Manny's cows*
Berenstain, Stan and Jan. *The Berenstain bears and
  too much vacation*
Breen, Steve. *The secret of Santa's island*
Brown, Marc. *Arthur's family vacation*
Cali, Davide. *The truth about my unbelievable
  summer . . .*
Chapra, Mimi. *Sparky's bark / El ladrido de Sparky*
Cocca-Leffler, Maryann. *A vacation for Pooch*
Corderoy, Tracey. *Now!*
Cottle, Joan. *Miles away from home*
Cousins, Lucy. *Maisy goes on vacation*
Davies, Jacqueline. *The house takes a vacation*

Day, Alexandra. *Carl's summer vacation*
dePaola, Tomie. *Strega Nona takes a vacation*
Diesen, Deborah. *The pout-pout fish, far, far from
  home*
Dubuc, Marianne. *Mr. Postmouse takes a trip*
Falconer, Ian. *Olivia goes to Venice*
Frazee, Marla. *A couple of boys have the best week ever*
Gutman, Anne. *Gaspard on vacation*
Hundal, Nancy. *Camping*
Jocelyn, Marthe. *Mayfly*
Joyce, William. *Dinosaur Bob*
Kellogg, Steven. *Ralph's secret weapon*
Koch, Ed. *Eddie's little sister makes a splash*
Korda, Lerryn. *It's vacation time*
Laden, Nina. *Clowns on vacation*
Larsen, Andrew. *See you next year*
Latimer, Alex. *Stay! a top dog story*
McPhail, David. *Emma's pet*
  Emma's vacation
Marshall, James. *George and Martha 'round and
  'round*
Maynard, Bill. *Santa's time off*
Meddaugh, Susan. *Martha calling*
Murphy, Stuart J. *The best vacation ever*
Pearlman, Robb. *Groundhog's day off*
Perkins, Lynne Rae. *Pictures from our vacation*
Perret, Delphine. *The Big Bad Wolf goes on vacation*
Pulver, Robin. *Punctuation takes a vacation*
Puttock, Simon. *Goat and Donkey in the great
  outdoors*
Reiss, Mike. *Santa claustrophobia*
Samuels, Barbara. *Aloha, Dolores*
Smath, Jerry. *Sammy Salami*
Soffer, Gilad. *Duck's vacation*
Stephens, Helen. *Ahoyty-toyty*
Stevenson, James. *The castaway*
  The Sea View Hotel
Stock, Catherine. *A porc in New York*
Tafuri, Nancy. *The brass ring*
Teague, Mark. *LaRue across America*
Thomas, Shelley Moore. *A Good Knight's rest*
Van Leeuwen, Jean. *Touch the sky summer*
Yoon, Salina. *Penguin on vacation*
Ziefert, Harriet. *Pushkin minds the bundle*

Activities – walking

Arnosky, Jim. *Crinkleroot's guide to walking in wild
  places*
  Outdoors on foot
Best, Cari. *When we go walking*
Briggs, Raymond. *The puddleman*
Cooper, Elisha. *A good night walk*
Denos, Julia. *Windows*
Devine, Monica. *Carry me, Mama*
Duncan, Lois. *I walk at night*
Edwards, Pamela Duncan. *The worrywarts*
Frazee, Marla. *Walk on!*
George, Lindsay Barrett. *In the woods*
Graham, Bob. *The silver button*
Haughton, Emma. *Rainy day*
Hertz, Grete Janus. *Olie's bedtime walk*
Hill, Eric. *Spot's first walk*
Hoban, Tana. *I walk and read*
Hubbell, Patricia. *Sidewalk trip*
Inches, Alison. *Corduroy's hike*
Johnson, D. B. *Henry hikes to Fitchburg*
  Henry works
Jonas, Ann. *The trek*

Watch William walk
Kimmelman, Leslie. *The Shabbat puppy*
Lam, Maple. *My little sister and me*
Lawson, Jonarno. *Sidewalk flowers*
Lewis, Kim. *One summer day*
London, Jonathan. *Wiggle, waggle*
Luenn, Nancy. *Squish!*
Monroe, Chris. *Cookie, the walker*
Murphy, Patricia J. *Mama, look!*
Pfister, Marcus. *Penguin Pete and Little Tim*
Robert, Nadine. *Toshi's little treasures*
Rockwell, Anne. *Willy can count*
Sattler, Jennifer. *Uh-oh, Dodo!*
Schindler, S. D. *Spike and Ike take a hike*
Shirotani, Hideo. *Let's take a walk / Vamos a caminar*
Showers, Paul. *The listening walk*
Silverman, Erica. *Wake up, city!*
Singer, Marilyn. *Didi and Daddy on the Promenade*
Smalls-Hector, Irene. *Jonathan and his mommy*
Stead, Philip C. *Ideas are all around*
Stevenson, James. *Rolling Rose*
Sullivan, Paula. *Todd's box*
Waber, Bernard. *Lyle walks the dogs*
Walton, Rick. *Girl and Gorilla: out and about*
White, Kathryn. *Ruby's school walk*
Williams, Sue. *I went walking*
Yolen, Jane. *Miz Berlin walks*
Zolotow, Charlotte. *Say it!*

Activities – weaving

Bang, Molly. *Dawn*
Blood, Charles L. *The goat in the rug*
Bodkin, Odds. *The crane wife*
Brill, Marlene Targ. *Margaret Knight, girl inventor*
Castaneda, Omar S. *Abuela's weave*
Francis, Lee DeCora. *Kunu's basket*
Hamilton, Virginia. *The girl who spun gold*
Heyer, Marilee. *The weaving of a dream*
Hurd, Thacher. *The weaver*
Marshall, Linda Elovitz. *Rainbow weaver / Tejedora del arcoíris*
Medearis, Angela Shelf. *Seven spools of thread*
Musgrove, Margaret. *The spider weaver*
Oughton, Jerrie. *The magic weaver of rugs*
Perrow, Angeli. *Many hands*
San Souci, Robert D. *The enchanted tapestry*
    A weave of words
Schubert, Leda. *Feeding the sheep*
Shah, Idries. *Fatima the spinner and the tent*
Tseng, Grace. *White tiger, blue serpent*
Yagawa, Sumiko. *The crane wife*

Activities – whistling

Egielski, Richard. *Three magic balls*
Keats, Ezra Jack. *Whistle for Willie*
Mahy, Margaret. *Mister Whistler*
Spinelli, Jerry. *Mama Seeton's whistle*

Activities – wood carving

Dorros, Arthur. *Julio's magic*
Martín, Hugo C. *Pablo's Christmas*

Activities – working

Ackerman, Karen. *By the dawn's early light*

Aesop. *The ant and the grasshopper*, ill. by Amy Lowry Poole
    The ant and the grasshopper, ill. by Sara Rojo
    The grasshopper and the ants
Altman, Linda Jacobs. *Amelia's road*
Ancona, George. *Mis quehaceres / My chores*
Asim, Jabari. *Daddy goes to work*
Bair, Sheila. *Isabel's car wash*
Ballard, Robin. *My day, your day*
Banks, Kate. *Mama's coming home*
    The night worker
Barton, Byron. *Machines at work*
Batt, Tanya Robyn. *The faerie's gift*
Bloom, Becky. *Crackers*
Bunting, Eve. *A day's work*
Burton, Virginia Lee. *Mike Mulligan and his steam shovel*
Carle, Eric. *Walter the baker*
Cordsen, Carol Foskett. *The milkman*
Dahl, Roald. *The giraffe and the pelly and me*
dePaola, Tomie. *Boss for a day*
Emberley, Rebecca. *The ant and the grasshopper*
Ericsson, Jennifer A. *Home to me, home to you*
Gershator, Phillis. *Sky sweeper*
Gibbons, Gail. *Deadline!*
    Zoo
Gray, Luli. *Ant and Grasshopper*
Haley, Gail E. *Two bad boys*
Hall, Donald. *Ox-cart man*
Hartland, Jessie. *Night shift*
Heide, Florence Parry. *The day of Ahmed's secret*
Hertz, Grete Janus. *Olie's bedtime walk*
Johnson, Angela. *I dream of trains*
Johnson, D. B. *Henry works*
Levine, Arthur A. *Monday is one day*
Lewis, Kim. *Floss*
Look, Lenore. *Love as strong as ginger*
Lum, Kate. *Princesses are not quitters!*
Lyon, George Ella. *Mama is a miner*
McPhail, David. *Pig Pig gets a job*
Markel, Michelle. *Brave girl*
Mills, Judith Christine. *The painted chest*
Morck, Irene. *Old bird*
Morris, Ann. *Work*
Murphy, Stuart J. *Sluggers' car wash*
Paulsen, Gary. *Worksong*
Pedersen, Marika. *Mommy works, Daddy works*
Pilkey, Dav. *The paperboy*
Pryor, Bonnie. *The dream jar*
Purmell, Ann. *Christmas tree farm*
Reichert, Amy. *Take your mama to work today*
Richards, Doyin. *I wonder*
Rotner, Shelley. *Everybody works*
Rylant, Cynthia. *Mr. Griggs' work*
San Souci, Robert D. *The hired hand*
Spinelli, Eileen. *Night shift daddy*
Stolz, Mary. *Zekmet, the stone carver*
Taber, Tory. *Rufus at work*
Waber, Bernard. *Lyle at the office*
Warwick, Dionne. *Little Man*
Wells, Rosemary. *Love waves*
Wheeler, Lisa. *Jam and jelly by Holly and Nellie*
Williams, Sherley Anne. *Working cotton*
Yee, Wong Herbert. *Hamburger Heaven*
Yu, Li-Qiong. *A New Year's reunion*

Activities – writing

Aliki. *Communication*

Arnosky, Jim. *Mouse writing*
Asch, Frank. *The Daily Comet*
Auch, Mary Jane. *The buk buk buk festival*
　The plot chickens
Banks, Kate. *The eraserheads*
Barnett, Mac. *Chloe and the lion*
　How this book was made
Battle-Lavert, Gwendolyn. *Papa's mark*
Best, Cari. *Beatrice spells some lulus and learns to write a letter*
Birdsall, Jeanne. *My favorite pets*
Bram, Elizabeth. *Rufus the writer*
Brown, Marc. *Arthur writes a story*
Brown, Monica. *My name is Gabito / Me llamo Gabito*
Burleigh, Robert. *If you spent a day with Thoreau at Walden pond*
Carlson, Nancy. *Henry's amazing imagination!*
Christelow, Eileen. *The desperate dog writes again*
　Letters from a desperate dog
Cline-Ransome, Lesa. *Words set me free*
Clinton, Catherine. *Phillis's big test*
Crimi, Carolyn. *Dear Tabby*
　Henry and the Crazed Chicken Pirates
Cronin, Doreen. *Click, clack, moo*
　Click, clack, quackity-quack
　Diary of a fly
　Diary of a spider
　Diary of a worm
Danneberg, Julie. *Cowboy Slim*
Darbyshire, Kristen. *Put it on the list!*
de Las Casas, Dianne. *The Little "Read" Hen*
Dormer, Frank W. *The obstinate pen*
Dotlich, Rebecca Kai. *One day, the end*
Dubosarsky, Ursula. *Rex*
Esbaum, Jill. *Stanza*
Farley, Brianne. *Ike's incredible ink*
French, Jackie. *Diary of a baby wombat*
　Diary of a wombat
Gerstein, Mordicai. *A book*
Gorbachev, Valeri. *What's the big idea, Molly?*
Graham, Joan Bransfield. *The poem that will not end*
Hanlon, Abby. *Ralph tells a story*
Heide, Florence Parry. *The day of Ahmed's secret*
Hills, Tad. *Rocket writes a story*
Hobbie, Holly. *Fanny and Annabelle*
Holub, Joan. *Little red writing*
Hopkins, Lee Bennett. *Full moon and star*
Howe, James. *Houndsley and Catina*
Inches, Alison. *Corduroy writes a letter*
Johnson, D. B. *Henry works*
Joyce, William. *Billy's booger*
Kempter, Christa. *Dear Little Lamb*
Kirk, Daniel. *Library mouse*
　Library mouse: a friend's tale
　Library mouse: a museum adventure
　Ten things I love about you
Larsen, Andrew. *A squiggly story*
Leedy, Loreen. *The Furry News*
　Messages in the mailbox
Lehrhaupt, Adam. *This is a good story*
Linch, Tanya. *My duck*
Lionni, Leo. *The alphabet tree*
Long, Ethan. *The book that Zack wrote*
Look, Lenore. *Polka Dot Penguin Pottery*
Louis, Catherine. *Liu and the bird*
McAnulty, Stacy. *Dear Santasaurus*
McElroy, Lisa Tucker. *Meet my grandmother. She's a children's book author*

McNamara, Margaret. *A poem in your pocket*
Matsuoka, Mei. *Footprints in the snow*
Meisel, Paul. *Good night, bat! good morning, squirrel!*
Morgan, Michaela. *Dear bunny*
Muntean, Michaela. *Do not open this book!*
Murphy, Stuart J. *Write on, Carlos!*
Niemann, Christoph. *The pet dragon*
O'Connor, Jane. *Fancy Nancy: poet extraordinaire!*
O'Malley, Kevin. *Once upon a cool motorcycle dude*
　Once upon a royal superbaby
Palatini, Margie. *Under a pig tree*
Pearson, Susan. *Slugs in love*
Pichard, Alexandra. *Pen pals*
Polacco, Patricia. *An A from Miss Keller*
Pulver, Robin. *The case of the incapacitated capitals*
　Thank you, Miss Doover
Puttock, Simon. *Yours truly, Louisa*
Rinker, Sherri Duskey. *Big machines*
Rockwell, Anne. *Father's Day*
Rumford, James. *Silent music*
Rylant, Cynthia. *Best wishes*
Saltzberg, Barney. *Inside this book (are three books)*
Savage, Stephen. *Little Plane learns to write*
Schubert, Leda. *Reading to Peanut*
Scieszka, Jon. *Battle Bunny*
Seabrooke, Brenda. *'Twas the day before Christmas*
Sher, Emil. *Away*
Shipton, Jonathan. *Baby baby blah blah blah!*
Sierra, Judy. *Imagine that! how Dr. Seuss wrote The Cat in the Hat*
Sís, Peter. *Ice cream summer*
Solheim, James. *Born yesterday*
Spinelli, Eileen. *The best story*
Stanton, Melissa. *My pen pal, Santa*
Stead, Philip C. *Ideas are all around*
Stein, David Ezra. *Love, Mouserella*
Stevens, Janet. *Help me, Mr. Mutt!*
Stewart, Sarah. *The journey*
Sullivan, Sarah. *Once upon a baby brother*
Sutton, Jane. *Don't call me Sidney*
Taback, Simms. *Postcards from camp*
Teague, Mark. *Dear Mrs. LaRue*
　Detective LaRue
　LaRue across America
Thomson, Bill. *The typewriter*
Tonatiuh, Duncan. *Dear Primo*
Tullet, Hervé. *Help! we need a title!*
Van Nutt, Julia. *Skyrockets and snickerdoodles*
Wallner, Alexandra. *Lucy Maud Montgomery*
Watt, Mélanie. *Chester*
　Chester's back!
　Chester's masterpiece
Wells, Rosemary. *Yoko writes her name*
Yeh, Kat. *The magic brush*
Yorinks, Arthur. *Homework*
Zwillich, Julie. *Phoebe sounds it out*

Adoption

Bunting, Eve. *Jin Woo*
Carlson, Nancy. *My family is forever*
Clark, Karen Henry. *Sweet moon baby*
Cole, Joanna. *How I was adopted*
Coste, Marion. *Finding Joy*
Curtis, Jamie Lee. *Tell me again about the night I was born*
Czech, Jan M. *An American face*
D'Antonio, Nancy. *Our baby from China*
dePaola, Tomie. *A new Barker in the house*

Dyckman, Ame. *Wolfie the bunny*
Elschner, Geraldine. *Like a wolf*
Foggo, Cheryl. *Dear baobab*
Friedman, Darlene. *Star of the Week: a story of love, adoption, and brownies with sprinkles*
Friedrich, Molly. *You're not my real mother!*
Galindo, Renata. *My new mom and me*
Garden, Nancy. *Molly's family*
Gliori, Debi. *Dragon's extraordinary egg*
Heo, Yumi. *Ten days and nine nights*
Hodge, Deborah. *Emma's story*
Höjer, Dan. *Heart of mine*
Joosse, Barbara. *Nikolai, the only bear*
Kasza, Keiko. *A mother for Choco*
Katz, Karen. *Over the moon*
Keller, Holly. *Horace*
Krishnaswami, Uma. *Bringing Asha home*
Lears, Laurie. *Megan's birthday tree*
Lewis, Rose A. *Every year on your birthday*
   I love you like crazy cakes
   Orange Peel's pocket
Lin, Grace. *The red thread*
López, Susana. *The best family in the world*
Lottridge, Celia Barker. *Berta, a remarkable dog*
McCully, Emily Arnold. *My real family*
McCutcheon, John. *Happy adoption day!*
McDonnell, Christine. *Goyangi means cat*
McLaughlin, Lauren. *Wonderful you*
McMahon, Patricia. *Just add one Chinese sister*
Mora, Pat. *Pablo's tree*
Oelschlager, Vanita. *Made in China*
Okimoto, Jean Davies. *The White Swan express*
Parr, Todd. *We belong together*
Peacock, Carol Antoinette. *Mommy far, Mommy near*
Pettitt, Linda. *Yafi's family*
Rogers, Fred. *Adoption*
Rosenberg, Liz. *We wanted you*
Rotner, Shelley. *I'm adopted!*
Say, Allen. *Allison*
Schreck, Karen Halvorsen. *Lucy's family tree*
Stoeke, Janet Morgan. *Waiting for May*
Sugarman, Brynn Olenberg. *Rebecca's journey home*
Thisdale, François. *Nini*
Thomas, Eliza. *The red blanket*
Tupper Ling, Nancy. *The story I'll tell*
Turner, Ann Warren. *Through moon and stars and night skies*
Williams, Vera B. *Home at last*
Wynne-Jones, Tim. *The boat in the tree*
Xinran, Xue. *Motherbridge of love*
Young, Ed. *My Mei Mei*

Aged *see* Old age

Airplanes, airports

Barton, Byron. *Airplanes*
   Airport
Bently, Peter. *Those magnificent sheep in their flying machine*
Berger, Melvin. *How do airplanes fly?*
Bingham, Caroline. *DK big book of airplanes*
Blechman, Nicholas. *Night light*
Brown, Don. *Ruth Law thrills a nation*
Brown, Lisa. *The airport book*
Bunting, Eve. *Fly away home*
Buzzeo, Toni. *Lighthouse Christmas*

Cousins, Lucy. *Maisy goes on a plane*
Crews, Donald. *Flying*
Demarest, Chris L. *Lindbergh*
Edwards, Pamela Duncan. *The Wright brothers*
Fardell, John. *Jeremiah Jellyfish flies high!*
Flanagan, Alice K. *Flying an agricultural plane with Mr. Miller*
Floca, Brian. *Five trucks*
Ford, Gilbert. *Flying lessons*
Gibbons, Gail. *Flying*
Gordon, David. *The ugly truckling*
Green, Rod. *Giant vehicles*
Grist, Julie. *Flying, just plane fun*
Gutman, Anne. *Lisa's airplane trip*
Hodgkins, Fran. *How people learned to fly*
Hubbell, Patricia. *Airplanes: soaring! diving! turning!*
   My first airplane ride
Ichikawa, Satomi. *Come fly with me*
Joseph, Lynn. *Fly, Bessie, fly*
Lang, Heather. *Fearless flyer*
Lenski, Lois. *The little airplane*
Light, Steve. *Planes go*
Lin, Grace. *Olvina flies*
Lindbergh, Reeve. *Nobody owns the sky*
London, Jonathan. *A plane goes ka-zoom!*
Lund, Deb. *Dinosoaring*
Lyon, George Ella. *Planes fly!*
McCarty, Peter. *Moon plane*
Meadows, Michelle. *Pilot pups*
Munsch, Robert N. *Angela's airplane*
Olivera, Ramon. *ABCs on wings*
Ormerod, Jan. *Miss Mouse takes off*
Pallotta, Jerry. *The airplane alphabet book*
   The jet alphabet book
Paul, Alison. *The plan*
Pearson, Peter. *How to eat an airplane*
Pett, Mark. *The boy and the airplane*
Poletti, Frances. *Miss Todd and her wonderful flying machine*
Provensen, Alice. *The glorious flight*
Raven, Margot Theis. *Mercedes and the chocolate pilot*
Reynolds, Peter H. *I'm here*
Riehle, Mary Ann McCabe. *A is for airplane*
Rockwell, Anne. *Planes*
Rogers, Fred. *Going on an airplane*
Ryan, Pam Muñoz. *Amelia and Eleanor go for a ride*
Savage, Stephen. *Little Plane learns to write*
Schaefer, Lola M. *Airport*
   The Wright brothers
Siebert, Diane. *Plane song*
Spier, Peter. *Bored — nothing to do!*
Stanley, Mandy. *Lettice the flying rabbit*
Sturges, Philemon. *I love planes*
Suen, Anastasia. *Air show*
Van Lieshout, Maria. *Flight 1-2-3*
Wells, Rosemary. *Yoko finds her way*
Williams, Treat. *Air show!*
Yolen, Jane. *My brothers' flying machine*

Alaska

Aillaud, Cindy Lou. *Recess at 20 below*
Blake, Robert J. *Painter and Ugly*
Chamberlin-Calamar, Pat. *Alaska's twelve days of summer*
Claflin, Willy. *The uglified ducky*

Crummel, Susan Stevens. *Ten-Gallon Bart beats the heat*
Gill, Shelley. *Up on Denali*
Guenther, James. *Turnagain, Ptarmigan, where did you go?*
Joosse, Barbara. *Wind-wild dog*
Laverde, Arlene. *Alaska's three pigs*
London, Jonathan. *Little Puffin's first flight*
   Sled dogs run
McCarthy, Meghan. *The incredible life of Balto*
Miller, Debbie S. *A caribou journey*
   River of life
Rand, Gloria. *Baby in a basket*
   Prince William
Schoenherr, John. *Bear*
Seibert, Patricia. *Mush!*
Senshu, Noriko. *Sonny's dream*
Stihler, Chérie B. *The giant cabbage turnip*

Aliens

Agee, Jon. *The other side of town*
Arnold, Tedd. *Green Wilma, frog in space*
Bartram, Simon. *Bob's best-ever friend*
Breathed, Berkeley. *Edwurd Fudwupper fibbed big*
   Mars needs moms!
Corey, Shana. *First graders from Mars: Horus's horrible day*
   First graders from Mars: Nergal and the Great Space Race
   First graders from Mars: Tera, star student
   First graders from Mars: The problem with Pelly
Daywalt, Drew. *BB-8 on the run*
Dolan, Elys. *Nuts in space*
Donovan, Sandy. *Bob the Alien discovers the Dewey Decimal System*
Duffield, Katy S. *Aliens get the sniffles too! ahhh-choo!*
Duval, Kathy. *Take me to your BBQ*
Jeffers, Oliver. *The way back home*
Karas, G. Brian. *Bebe's bad dream*
Kirk, Daniel. *Hush, little alien*
Layton, Neal. *Smile if you're human*
McElligott, Matthew. *Even aliens need snacks*
McNamara, Margaret. *The three little aliens and the big bad robot*
McNaughton, Colin. *Here come the aliens!*
   We're off to look for aliens
McPhail, David. *Tinker and Tom and the Star Baby*
O'Malley, Kevin. *Captain Raptor and the moon mystery*
Pallotta, Jerry. *Twizzlers percentages book*
Passen, Lisa. *Attack of the 50-foot teacher*
Portis, Antoinette. *Best frints in the whole universe*
Porto, Tony. *Blue aliens*
   Get red
Sanders, Rob. *Outer space bedtime race*
Sauer, Tammi. *Your alien*
   Your alien returns
Schories, Pat. *Jack and the night visitors*
   When Jack goes out
Scieszka, Jon. *Baloney, Henry P.*
Shields, Carol Diggory. *Martian rock*
Singer, Marilyn. *The boy who cried alien*
Slack, Michael. *Wazdot?*
Smallcomb, Pam. *Earth to Clunk*
Staub, Leslie. *Time for (Earth) school, Dewey Dew*
Viva, Frank. *A long way away*
Whatley, Bruce. *Captain Pajamas*
Wiesner, David. *Mr. Wuffles!*
Wood, Audrey. *The Christmas adventure of Space Elf Sam*
Yaccarino, Dan. *First day on a strange new planet*
   New pet
Yorinks, Arthur. *Company's going*
Young, Ned. *Zoomer's out-of-this-world Christmas*

Alphabet books *see* ABC books

Ambition *see* Character traits – ambition

American Indians *see* Indians of Central America; Indians of North America; Indians of South America

Amphibians *see also* Frogs & toads; Reptiles

Florian, Douglas. *Lizards, frogs, and polliwogs*

Amusement parks *see* Parks – amusement

Anatomy

Andrews, Sylvia. *Dancing in my bones*
Arnold, Tedd. *More parts*
   Parts
Baker, Keith. *My octopus arms*
Bang, Molly. *All of me!*
Barnett, Mac. *Mustache!*
Bauer, Marion Dane. *If you had a nose like an elephant's trunk*
   Thank you for me!
   Toes, ears, and nose!
Bennett, Artie. *The butt book*
The best part of me
Bilgrami, Shaheen. *Amazing dinosaur discovery*
   Incredible animal discovery
Bottner, Barbara. *Feet go to sleep*
Brown, Laurie Krasny. *What's the big secret?*
Carle, Eric. *From head to toe*
   My very first book of heads and tails
Cole, Joanna. *The magic school bus inside the human body*
Collard, Sneed B. *Beaks!*
Davick, Linda. *I love you, nose! I love you, toes!*
Harper, Charise Mericle. *Henry's heart*
Harrington, Tim. *Nose to toes, you are yummy!*
Harris, Robie H. *Who has what?*
Henderson, Kathy. *Look at you!*
Hickling, Meg. *Boys, girls and body science*
Hindley, Judy. *Eyes, nose, fingers and toes*
Jenkins, Steve. *Actual size*
   Creature features
   Prehistoric actual size
   What do you do with a tail like this?
Kudlinski, Kathleen V. *Boy, were we wrong about the human body!*
McNeil, Kelli. *Sleepy toes*
Maloney, Peter. *His mother's nose*
Martin, Bill, Jr.. *Here are my hands*
Martin, David. *We've all got bellybuttons*
Menchin, Scott. *What if everything had legs?*
Moore, Julianne. *Freckleface Strawberry*
   Freckleface Strawberry: best friends forever
Rotner, Shelley. *The body book*
Saltz, Gail. *Amazing you*

Schwartz, Amy. *A beautiful girl*
Seuling, Barbara. *From head to toe*
Showers, Paul. *A drop of blood*
   Hear your heart
   How you talk
Singer, Marilyn. *The one and only me*
Ward, Jennifer. *Feathers and hair, what animals wear*
Zoboli, Giovanna. *I wish I had . . .*

Anatomy – belly buttons *see* Anatomy – navels

Anatomy – brain

O'Connor, Teddy. *A new brain for Igor*

Anatomy – ears

Genechten, Guido van. *Flop-Ear*
Hartley, Karen, et al. *Hearing in living things*
Harvey, Amanda. *Dog-eared*
McCarthy, Meghan. *Earmuffs for everyone!*
Miles, Elizabeth J. *Ears*
Rowe, Jeannette. *Whose ears?*
Showers, Paul. *Ears are for hearing*
Slegers, Liesbet. *Funny ears*

Anatomy – eyes

Barclay, Eric. *I can see just fine*
Cobb, Vicki. *Open your eyes*
Fielding, Beth. *Animal eyes*
Glaser, Jason. *Pinkeye*
Gordon, Sharon. *Pinkeye*
   Seeing
Hartley, Karen. *Seeing in living things*
Jenkins, Steve. *Eye to eye*
Kostecki-Shaw, Jenny Sue. *My travelin' eye*
Lyon, George Ella. *The pirate of kindergarten*
Priest, Robert H. *The pirate's eye*
Rotner, Shelley. *Whose eye am I?*
Showers, Paul. *Look at your eyes*
Wiesmüller, Dieter. *In the blink of an eye*

Anatomy – faces

Alda, Arlene. *Here a face, there a face*
Cotter, Bill. *Beard in a box*
Ehrlich, Fred. *Does a seal smile?*
Hodgkinson, Leigh. *Smile!*
Miller, Margaret. *Baby faces*
Orloff, Karen Kaufman. *Miles of smiles*
Piven, Hanoch. *Let's make faces*
Rayner, Catherine. *Augustus and his smile*
Rotner, Shelley. *Faces*
Siegel, Randy. *Grandma's smile*

Anatomy – feet

Aliki. *My feet*
Crocker, Nancy. *Betty Lou Blue*
Dempsey, Kristy. *Ten little toes, two small feet*
Ellis, Sarah. *The queen's feet*
Gow, Nancy. *Ten big toes and a prince's nose*
Hayles, Marsha. *Bunion Burt*
Hulbert, Laura. *Who has these feet?*
Konagaya, Kiyomi. *Beach feet*
Mara, Nichole. *So many feet*
O'Connor, George. *Uncle Bigfoot*
O'Hair, Margaret. *Sweet baby feet*

Paul, Ann Whitford. *Hello toes! Hello feet!*
Pearson, Susan. *Hooray for feet!*
Rowe, Jeannette. *Whose feet?*
Slegers, Liesbet. *Funny feet*
Vail, Rachel. *Righty and Lefty*
Walton, Rick. *My two hands, my two feet*
Young, Amy. *Belinda and the glass slipper*
   Belinda begins ballet
   Belinda in Paris
   Belinda, the ballerina

Anatomy – fins

Miles, Elizabeth J. *Wings, fins, and flippers*

Anatomy – hands

Aliki. *My hands*
Bowie, C. W. *Busy fingers*
Clements, Andrew. *The handiest things in the world*
Dempsey, Kristy. *Ten little fingers, two small hands*
Ehlert, Lois. *Hands*
Emberley, Ed. *Ed Emberley's fingerprint drawing book*
Fox, Mem. *Ten little fingers and ten little toes*
Hendra, Sue. *Barry, the fish with fingers*
Kroll, Virginia L. *Hands!*
Lasky, Kathryn. *Mommy's hands*
Mason, Margaret H. *These hands*
Otoshi, Kathryn. *Beautiful hands*
Price, Hope Lynne. *These hands*
Ryder, Joanne. *My father's hands*
Shannon, George. *Hands say love*
Walton, Rick. *My two hands, my two feet*

Anatomy – heads

Kimmel, Eric A. *Pumpkinhead*
Miller, Margaret. *What's on my head?*
Swanson, Diane. *Headgear that hides and plays*

Anatomy – mouths

Brown, Heather. *Chomp!*
Miles, Elizabeth J. *Mouths and teeth*

Anatomy – navels

Batten, Mary. *Who has a belly button?*
Maloney, Peter. *Belly button boy*
Martin, David. *We've all got bellybuttons*
Pringle, Laurence P. *Everybody has a bellybutton*
Willis, Jeanne. *The boy who lost his bellybutton*

Anatomy – noses

Brown, Marc. *Arthur's nose*
Conway, David. *Errol and his extraordinary nose*
Cullen, Lynn. *Little Scraggly Hair*
Eaton, Jason Carter. *The day my runny nose ran away*
Flesher, Vivienne. *Alfred's nose*
Freymann, Saxton. *Dr. Pompo's nose*
Gordon, Sharon. *Smelling*
Gow, Nancy. *Ten big toes and a prince's nose*
Hartley, Karen. *Smelling in living things*
Johnston, Tony. *The badger and the magic fan*
Kipling, Rudyard. *How the elephant got his trunk*
Levine, Deb. *Parker picks*
Lucke, Deb. *Sneezenesia*
May, Robert L. *Rudolph the red-nosed reindeer*

Miles, Elizabeth J. *Noses*
Rowe, Jeannette. *Whose nose?*
Samuels, Jenny. *A nose like a hose*
Schwarz, Viviane. *The adventures of a nose*
Swanson, Diane. *Noses that plow and poke*
Warrick, Karen Clemens. *Who needs that nose?*

Anatomy – skeletons

Ahlberg, Janet. *Funnybones*
Bunting, Eve. *The bones of Fred McFee*
Crow, Kristyn. *Skeleton cat*
Cuyler, Margery. *Bonaparte falls apart*
    Skeleton for dinner
    Skeleton hiccups
Fromental, Jean-Luc. *Bonesville*
Glaser, Byron. *Bonz, inside-out*
Gunnufson, Charlotte. *Halloween hustle*
Heidbreder, Robert. *Black and bittern was night*
Jaramillo, Susie. *Little skeletons / Esqueletitos*
Johansen, K. V. *Pippin and the bones*
Johnston, Tony. *The ghost of Nicholas Greebe*
    Soup bone
Levine, Sara. *Bone by bone*
Lucas, David. *The skeleton pirate*
Morales, Yuyi. *Just in case: a trickster tale and*
    Spanish alphabet book
Pickering, Jimmy. *Skelly the skeleton girl*
Rohmann, Eric. *Bone dog*
San Souci, Robert D. *Cinderella Skeleton*
Schertle, Alice. *The skeleton in the closet*
Stevenson, James. *The most amazing dinosaur*

Anatomy – skin

Ciraolo, Simona. *The lines on Nana's face*
Iyengar, Malathi Michelle. *Tan to tamarind*
McGhee, Alison. *Tell me a tattoo story*
Manushkin, Fran. *Happy in our skin*
Pinkney, Sandra L. *A rainbow all around me*
Rotner, Shelley. *Shades of people*
Showers, Paul. *Your skin and mine*
Swanson, Diane. *Skin that slimes and scares*
Tyler, Michael. *The skin you live in*

Anatomy – tails

Ashman, Linda. *The tale of Wagmore Gently*
Bechtold, Lisze. *Edna's tale*
Duvall, Deborah L. *The opossum's tale*
Feiffer, Kate. *Henry, the dog with no tail*
Fielding, Beth. *Animal tails*
Hatkoff, Craig, et al. *Winter's tail*
Hulbert, Laura. *Who has this tail?*
Kawata, Ken. *Animal tails*
Kleven, Elisa. *A carousel tale*
McDonnell, Patrick. *Wag!*
Milne, A. A. *Eeyore loses a tail*
Sandu, Anca. *Churchill's tale of tails*
Slegers, Liesbet. *Funny tails*
Warrick, Karen Clemens. *If I had a tail*

Anatomy – teeth *see* Teeth

Anatomy – thumbs *see* Thumb sucking

Anatomy – toes

Bowie, C. W. *Busy toes*
Byous, Shawn. *Because I stubbed my toe*
Crum, Shutta. *Who took my hairy toe?*
Dempsey, Kristy. *Ten little toes, two small feet*
Fox, Mem. *Ten little fingers and ten little toes*
Harrington, Tim. *This little piggy*
Hood, Susan. *Tickly toes*
Madison, Alan. *The littlest grape stomper*
Paul, Ann Whitford. *Hello toes! Hello feet!*
Tarpley, Todd. *Ten tiny toes*

Anatomy – tongues

Bonsignore, Joan. *Stick out your tongue*
Hartley, Karen. *Tasting in living things*

Anatomy – wings

Miles, Elizabeth J. *Wings, fins, and flippers*
Myers, Christopher. *Wings*
Tanaka, Shinsuke. *Wings*

Angels

Arrigan, Mary. *Mario's angels*
Clements, Andrew. *Bright Christmas*
Cole, Brock. *Larky Mavis*
dePaola, Tomie. *Angels, angels everywhere*
Durango, Julia. *Angels watching over me*
Greenfield, Eloise. *Angels*
Judd, Naomi. *Naomi Judd's guardian angels*
Kleven, Elisa. *The friendship wish*
Lach, William. *I imagine angels*
Lester, Julius. *What a truly cool world*
    Why heaven is far away
Lucado, Max. *Alabaster's song*
McGhee, Alison. *Star bright*
Magnier, Thierry. *Isabelle and the angel*
Marzollo, Jean. *Snow angel*
Morpurgo, Michael. *On angel wings*
Myers, Walter Dean. *Brown angels*
Norris, Leslie. *Albert and the angels*
Pienkowski, Jan. *Bel and Bub and the baby bird*
    Bel and Bub and the bad snowball
    Bel and Bub and the big brown box
    Bel and Bub and the black hole
Pittman, Helena Clare. *The angel tree*
Randall, Angel. *Snow angels*
Roberts, Bethany. *Cookie angel*
Rylant, Cynthia. *Dog Heaven*
Sloat, Teri. *Hark! The aardvark angels sing*
Spinelli, Eileen. *City angel*
    What do angels wear?
Tazewell, Charles. *The littlest angel*, ill. by Deborah
    Lanino
    The littlest angel, ill. by Paul Micich
    The littlest angel, ill. by Rebecca Thornburgh
Tolan, Stephanie S. *Bartholomew's blessing*
Turner, Ann Warren. *Angel hide and seek*
Vainio, Pirkko. *The Christmas angel*
Wangerin, Walter. *Probity Jones and the Fear Not*
    Angel
Weller, Frances Ward. *The angel of Mill Street*
Williams, Sam. *Angel's Christmas cookies*
    Snowy magic

Animals *see also* Birds; Frogs & toads; Reptiles

Aardema, Verna. *Princess Gorilla and a new kind of water*
  Rabbit makes a monkey of lion
  Traveling to Tondo
  The vingananee and the tree toad
  What's so funny, Ketu?
  Who's in Rabbit's house?
  Why mosquitoes buzz in people's ears
Ada, Alma Flor. *Dear Peter Rabbit*
Adler, Victoria. *Baby, come away*
Adlerman, Daniel. *Africa calling*
Aesop. *Animal fables from Aesop*
  Bat's big game
  Belling the cat and other Aesop fables
  Doctor Coyote
  The donkey in the lion's skin
  Fox tails
  The lion and the mouse and other Aesop fables
  Road signs
Agee, Jon. *Dmitri the astronaut*
  Mr. Putney's quacking dog
Ajmera, Maya. *Animal friends: a global celebration of children and their animals*
Alborough, Jez. *Captain Duck*
  Duck in the truck
  Fix-it Duck
  Hug
  Super Duck
  Tall
  Watch out! Big Bro's coming!
Alda, Arlene. *Sheep, sheep, sheep, help me fall asleep*
Alexander, Cecil Frances. *All creatures great and small*
Alexander, Claire. *Back to front and upside down*
  Lucy and the bully
Alexander, Kwame. *Animal ark*
Aliki. *My visit to the aquarium*
  My visit to the zoo
  Wild and woolly mammoths
Allard, Harry. *Bumps in the night*
Allen, Jonathan. *"I'm not cute!"*
  I'm not reading!
  The little rabbit who liked to say moo
Allen, Pamela. *Who sank the boat?*
Alphamals A-Z
Alter, Anna. *Disappearing Desmond*
American Museum of Natural History. *Spot the animals*
Anastas, Margaret. *A hug for you*
  Mommy's best kisses
Anaya, Rudolfo A. *Roadrunner's dance*
Andersen, Hans Christian. *The emperor's new clothes*
Anderson, Derek. *Story county*
Anderson, Peggy Perry. *Chuck's band*
  Chuck's truck
Anderson, Stephen Axel. *I know the moon*
Andreae, Giles. *Cock-a-doodle-doo!*
  Rumble in the jungle
Anholt, Catherine. *Chimp and Zee's noisy book*
Animal I spy
Animal 123
Apperley, Dawn. *Good night, sleep tight, little bunnies*
  Santa Claus will come tonight
Archer, Micha. *Daniel finds a poem*
Arena, Jen. *Marta! big and small*
Arndt, Michael. *Cat says meow and other animalopoeia*
Arnold, Caroline. *Australian animals*

Arnold, Katya. *The adventures of Snowwoman*
  Let's find it!
  Meow!
Arnold, Marsha Diane. *Lost. found*
  Waiting for snow
Arnold, Tedd. *Vincent paints his house*
Arnosky, Jim. *At this very moment*
  Babies in the bayou
  Crinkleroot's guide to knowing animal habitats
  Crinkleroot's 25 mammals every child should know
  Every autumn comes the bear
  Gobble it up!
  I see animals hiding
  Wild and swampy
  Wild tracks!
Arquette, Kerry. *What did you do today?*
Artell, Mike. *Petite Rouge*
Aruego, José. *We hide, you seek*
  Weird friends
Asch, Frank. *Barnyard lullaby*
  Moonbear's dream
Asher, Sandy. *Here comes Gosling!*
Ashforth, Camilla. *Willow by the sea*
Ashman, Linda. *Castles, caves, and honeycombs*
  Rock-a-bye romp
  William's winter nap
Askani, Tanja. *A friend like you*
Aston, Dianna Hutts. *Loony Little*
  A nest is noisy
Auch, Mary Jane. *The nutquacker*
  Poultrygeist
  Souperchicken
Auld, Mary. *Noah's ark*
Austin, Margot. *A friend for Growl Bear*
Averbeck, Jim. *Except if*
Aylesworth, Jim. *Cock-a-doodle-doo, creak, pop-pop, moo*
  The mitten
  One crow
Azore, Barbara. *Wanda and the wild hair*
Babypants, Caspar. *Augie to zebra*
Baddiel, Ivor. *Cock-a-doodle quack! quack!*
Badescu, Ramona. *Big Rabbit's bad mood*
Bailey, Linda. *The farm team*
Baillie, Marilyn. *Nose to toes*
Baker, Alan. *Gray Rabbit's one, two, three*
Baker, Ken. *Old MacDonald had a dragon*
Banks, Kate. *What's coming for Christmas?*
Bansch, Helga. *At night*
Barasch, Lynne. *First come the zebra*
Barner, Bob. *Animal baths*
  Sea bones
Barnes, Laura T. *Ernest's special Christmas*
Barnett, Mac. *Count the monkeys*
Barrett, Judi. *Animals should definitely not act like people*
  Animals should definitely not wear clothing
  Never take a shark to the dentist and other things not to do
Barretta, Gene. *Dear deer*
Barroux. *Where's the elephant?*
Bartoletti, Susan Campbell. *Naamah and the ark at night*
Barton, Byron. *My bus*
  Zoo animals
Base, Graeme. *Animalia*
  Jungle drums
  The water hole
Bateman, Donna M. *Out on the prairie*

Bateman, Teresa. *Farm flu*
  The frog with the big mouth
Bates, Ivan. *All by myself*
Batten, Mary. *Please don't wake the animals*
  Who has a belly button?
Battut, Eric. *The fox and the hen*
  Little Mouse's big secret
Bauer, Marion Dane. *Frog's best friend*
  If frogs made the weather
  If you had a nose like an elephant's trunk
  If you were born a kitten
  The longest night
  My mother is mine
  Sleep, little one, sleep
  Why do kittens purr?
Bayer, Jane. *A my name is Alice*
Beames, Margaret. *Night cat*
Beaton, Clare. *Clare Beaton's bedtime rhymes*
  Clare Beaton's farmyard rhymes
  How loud is a lion?
  One moose, twenty mice
Beaumont, Karen. *Duck, duck, goose!*
  No sleep for the sheep!
  Who ate all the cookie dough?
  Wild about us!
Beautiful moments in the wild
Beaver steals fire
Beck, Andrea. *Elliot bakes a cake*
  Elliot digs for treasure
  Elliot gets stuck
  Elliot's bath
  Elliot's Christmas surprise
  Elliot's emergency
  Elliot's shipwreck
Becker, Bonny. *An ant's day off*
  Tickly prickly
Becker, Helaine. *Mama likes to mambo*
Beedie, Duncan. *The lumberjack's beard*
Beeke, Jemma. *The Rickety Barn show*
Beeke, Tiphanie. *Roar like a lion!*
Beeny, Emily. *Hector the collector*
Behrens, Janice. *Let's find rain forest animals*
Belle, Jennifer. *Animal stackers*
Benevelli, Alberto. *The colors of the chameleon*
Berger, Melvin. *Brrr! a book about polar animals*
  Dive! a book of deep sea creatures
Bergman, Mara. *Yum yum! What fun!*
Bergstein, Rita M. *Your own big bed*
Berkes, Marianne. *Animalogy*
  Going home: the mystery of animal migration
  Marsh music
  Over in a river
  Over in Australia
  Over in the Arctic
  Over in the forest
  Over in the jungle
  Over on a mountain
Bernhard, Durga. *Earth, sky, wet, dry*
Bernstrom, Daniel. *One day in the eucalyptus,
  eucalyptus tree*
Biddulph, Rob. *Blown away*
Bijsterbosch, Anita. *Whose hat is that?*
Bilgrami, Shaheen. *Amazing dinosaur discovery*
  Farmyard painting party
  Incredible animal discovery
  Jungle art show
Bishop, Poppy. *Bear's house of books*
Black, Harley. *Amazing magic school*

Blackaby, Susan. *Brownie Groundhog and the wintry
  surprise*, ill. by Carmen Segovia
  Brownie Groundhog and the wintry surprise, ill. by
    Carmen Segovia
Blackstone, Stella. *Alligator alphabet*
  How big is a pig?
  Octopus opposites
  Secret seahorse
Blaich, Ute. *The star*
Blake, Quentin. *Fantastic Daisy Artichoke*
Bleiman, Andrew. *ABC zooborns!*
  1-2-3 zooborns!
Bless the beasts
Bloom, Suzanne. *A mighty fine time machine*
  A number slumber
Bock, Lee. *Oh, crumps! / Ay, caramba!*
Bolam, Emily. *Animals talk*
Bond, Felicia. *Big hugs, little hugs*
Bonfield, Chloe. *The perfect tree*
Bonnett-Rampersaud, Louise. *How do you sleep?*
Booth, Tom. *Don't blink!*
Borando, Silvia. *Now you see me, now you don't*
Bosca, Francesca. *The apple king*
Bourgeois, Paulette. *Franklin and Harriet*
  Franklin and the thunderstorm
  Franklin rides a bike
  Franklin's class trip
  Franklin's secret club
Boutignon, Beatrice. *Not all animals are blue*
Boyd, Lizi. *Big bear little chair*
Boyle, Bob. *Hugo and the really, really, really long
  string*
Boynton, Sandra. *Christmas parade*
Bracken, Beth. *The little bully*
Brenner, Barbara A. *One small place by the sea*
Brenner, Emily. *On the first day of grade school*
Brett, Jan. *The animals' Santa*
  Annie and the wild animals
  Armadillo rodeo
  Berlioz the bear
  The hat
  The mitten
  The three little dassies
  The turnip
Brett, Jessica. *Animals on the go*
Brière-Haquet, Alice. *One very big bear*
Bright, Paul. *Quiet!*
Brisson, Pat. *Hobbledy-clop*
Broach, Elise. *Gumption!*
Brooks, Alan. *Frogs jump*
Brooks, Erik. *Slow days, fast friends*
Brown, Heather. *Chomp!*
Brown, James. *Farm*
Brown, Jo. *Where's my mommy?*
Brown, Ken. *What's the time, Grandma Wolf?*
Brown, Lisa. *How to be*
Brown, Marc. *Arthur and the true Francine*
  Arthur goes to camp
  Arthur's animal adventure
  Arthur's April fool
  Arthur's Christmas
  Arthur's eyes
  Arthur's Halloween
  Arthur's perfect Christmas
  Arthur's teacher moves in
  Arthur's teacher trouble
  Arthur's Thanksgiving
  Arthur's tooth
  Arthur's underwear

Arthur's Valentine
The bionic bunny show
Brown, Marcia. *Once a mouse . . .*
Brown, Margaret Wise. *A child's good morning book*
The dirty little boy
The fathers are coming home
The friendly book
The Golden sleepy book
Where have you been?
Brown, Ruth. *Monkey's friends*
Browne, Anthony. *Animal fair*
Browne, Eileen. *Handa's hen*
Bruchac, Joseph. *The great ball game*
Bruss, Deborah. *Book! book! book!*
Bunting, Eve. *Happy birthday, dear duck*
Have you seen my new blue socks?
Hey diddle diddle
Hurry! hurry!
Little Badger's just-about birthday
Night tree
Our library
Swan in love
We were there
Whose shoe?
Burach, Ross. *There's a giraffe in my soup*
Burnard, Damon. *I spy in the jungle*
I spy in the ocean
Burningham, John. *Mr. Gumpy's outing*
The shopping basket
The way to the zoo
Burns, Diane L., et al *Backyard beasties*
Butler, Christina. *One cozy Christmas*
Butler, John. *Bedtime in the jungle*
Can you growl like a bear?
Ten in the den
Ten in the meadow
While you were sleeping
Butler, M. Christina. *Mouse and the moon*
One snowy night
One special Christmas
One winter's day
The smiley snowman
Butterworth, Nick. *One snowy night*
Cabatingan, Erin. *A is for Musk Ox*
Musk Ox counts
Cabrera, Jane. *If you're happy and you know it*
Monkey's play time
Rock-a-bye baby
Row, row, row your boat
Twinkle, twinkle, little star
Callahan, Sean. *A wild Father's Day*
Callery, Sean. *Hide and seek in the jungle*
Calmenson, Stephanie. *Birthday at the Panda Palace*
Jazzmatazz!
Campbell, Rod. *Dear zoo*
Farm animals
Caple, Kathy. *Worm gets a job*
Capucilli, Alyssa Satin. *Biscuit visits the pumpkin patch*
Inside a zoo in the city
Carle, Eric. *The artist who painted a blue horse*
Does a kangaroo have a mother, too?
From head to toe
Hello, red fox
My first peek-a-boo: animals
1, 2, 3 to the zoo
"Slowly, slowly, slowly," said the sloth
10 little rubber ducks
Today is Monday

The very busy spider
Carle, Eric, et al. *What's your favorite animal?*
Carlson, Nancy. *Arnie and the skateboard gang*
Get up and go!
Henry and the bully
How about a hug?
Think happy!
Carlstrom, Nancy White. *The way to Wyatt's house*
Carrick, Carol. *Patrick's dinosaurs*
Carryl, Charles E. *The camel's lament*
Carter, David A. *Old MacDonald had a farm: a pop-up book*
Whoo? Whoo?
Cartwright, Reg. *What we do*
Casanova, Mary. *One-dog canoe*
One-dog sleigh
Casey, Dawn. *The great race: the story of the Chinese zodiac*
Casey, Patricia. *One day at Wood Green Animal Shelter*
Cash, Megan Montague. *I saw the sea and the sea saw me*
Cassie, Brian. *Say it again*
Cave, Kathryn. *Henry's song*
Cazet, Denys. *Never poke a squid*
Never spit on your shoes
Nothing at all
Ceelen, Vicky. *Baby! baby!*
Chaconas, Dori. *Don't slam the door!*
Looking for Easter
Chamberlin-Calamar, Pat. *Alaska's twelve days of summer*
Chapman, Jane. *No more cuddles!*
Very special friends
Chedru, Delphine. *Spot it!*
Chernaik, Judith. *Carnival of the animals: poems inspired by Saint-Saëns' music*
Cherry, Lynne. *The great kapok tree*
Chichester Clark, Emma. *Follow the leader!*
Little Miss Muffet counts to ten
Chicken Little. *Brave Chicken Little*
Chicken Little
Henny Penny, ill. by Emily Bolam
Henny Penny, ill. by Paul Galdone
Henny-Penny, ill. by Jane Wattenberg
Henny Penny, ill. by Sophie Windham
The sky is falling
Chiew, Suzanne. *When you need a friend*
Child, Lauren. *I am not sleepy and I will not go to bed*
Chin, Oliver. *The year of the tiger*
Chitwood, Suzanne Tanner. *Wake up, big barn!*
Chivers, Natalie. *Rhino's great big itch!*
Christelow, Eileen. *Where's the big bad wolf?*
Claire, Céline. *Shelter*
Clark, Leslie Ann. *Peepsqueak!*
Cneut, Carll. *The amazing love story of Mr. Morf*
Cocca-Leffler, Maryann. *Jungle Halloween*
Coffelt, Nancy. *Aunt Ant leaves through the leaves*
Big, bigger, biggest!
Cohen, Caron Lee. *Digger Pig and the turnip*
Cohen, Peter Zachary. *Boris's glasses*
Cohn, Diana. *Dream carver*
Colato Laínez, René. *Señor Pancho had a rancho*
Cole, Henry. *Eddie the bully*
Collard, Sneed B. *Animals asleep*
Making animal babies
Collicott, Sharleen. *Toestomper and the caterpillars*
Colón, Raúl. *Draw!*
Comden, Betty. *What's new at the zoo?*

Conover, Chris. *The lion's share*
Conway, David. *The most important gift of all*
Cooper, Elisha. *Eight, an animal alphabet*
Cooper, Helen. *Delicious!*
    A pipkin of pepper
Corr, Christopher. *Deep in the woods*
Costello, David Hyde. *I can help*
Côté, Geneviève. *With you always, Little Monday*
Cotten, Cynthia. *At the edge of the woods*
Cotton, Katie. *The road home*
Cousins, Lucy. *Doctor Maisy*
    Happy birthday, Maisy
    I'm the best
    Maisy at the fair
    Maisy, Charley, and the wobbly tooth
    Maisy dresses up
    Maisy's amazing big book of learning
    Maisy's bedtime
    Maisy's book of things that go
    Maisy's farm
    Maisy's Halloween
    Maisy's morning on the farm
    Maisy's noisy day
    Maisy's pool
    Noah's ark
Cowan, Charlotte. *Katie caught a cold*
    Peeper has a fever
    Sadie's sore throat
Cowell, Cressida. *What shall we do with the Boo-Hoo Baby?*
Cowley, Joy. *Mrs. Wishy-Washy's Christmas*
Cox, Judy. *Sheep won't sleep*
Coxe, Molly. *Bunny and the beast*
Craig, Lindsey. *Dancing feet!*
    Farmyard beat
Crawford, Laura. *In arctic waters*
Crawford, Sheryl Ann. *The baby who changed the world*
Crimi, Carolyn. *Dear Tabby*
    Don't need friends
Crisp, Marty. *Black and white*
Cronin, Doreen. *Boom Snot Twitty*
    Boom, Snot, Twitty, this way that way
    Click, clack, boo!
    Click, clack, ho! ho! ho!
    Click, clack, moo I love you!
    Click, clack, quackity-quack
    Click, clack, splish, splash
    Click, clack, surprise!
    Dooby dooby moo
    Duck for President
    Giggle, giggle, quack
    Thump, quack, moo
Cruickshank, Margrit. *We're going to feed the ducks*
Crum, Shutta. *The bravest of the brave*
    A family for Old Mill Farm
Cullen, Lynn. *Little Scraggly Hair*
Cummings, Pat. *Ananse and the lizard*
Cummings, Phil. *Boom bah!*
Cummins, Lucy Ruth. *A hungry lion; or, a dwindling assortment of animals*
Cusimano, Maryann K. *You are my wonders*
Cuyler, Margery. *The biggest, best snowman*
    That's good! that's bad!
Czekaj, Jef. *Oink-a-doodle-moo*
Dahl, Michael. *Hippo says "excuse me."*
    One giant splash
    Starry arms
Dahl, Roald. *The enormous crocodile*

    The giraffe and the pelly and me
Dale, Penny. *The boy on the bus*
Dallas-Conte, Juliet. *Cock-a-moo-moo*
Daly, Catherine. *Whiskers*
Daly, Niki. *Next stop — Zanzibar Road!*
    Welcome to Zanzibar Road
Danylyshyn, Greg. *A crash of rhinos*
Davis, Jill. *Orangutans are ticklish*
Davis, Katie. *Who hoots?*
Davis, Lee. *Feeding time*
Day, Alexandra. *Special deliveries*
Day, Trevor. *Youch! it bites!*
Deacon, Alexis. *Slow Loris*
Deady, Kathleen W. *It's time!*
    Out and about at the zoo
Deak, Erzsi. *Pumpkin time!*
deGroat, Diane. *Happy birthday to you, you belong in a zoo*
    Jingle bells, homework smells
    Roses are pink, your feet really stink
    Trick or treat, smell my feet
de Las Casas, Dianne. *The Little "Read" Hen*
Demers, Dominique. *Every single night*
Dempsey, Kristy. *Mini racer*
Denim, Sue. *The Dumb Bunnies go to the zoo*
Dennard, Deborah. *Bullfrog at Magnolia Circle*
    Koala country
Denslow, Sharon Phillips. *In the snow*
DePalma, Mary Newell. *The perfect gift*
dePaola, Tomie. *Bill and Pete to the rescue*
    Jack
    Jingle, the Christmas clown
DePrisco, Dorothea. *Snowbear's winter day*
    Who lives here?
De Regniers, Beatrice Schenk. *May I bring a friend?*
    What did you put in your pocket?
Derrick, Patricia. *Riley the rhinoceros*
Desmoinaux, Christel. *Mrs. Hen's big surprise*
De Vicq de Cumptich, Roberto. *Bembo's zoo*
Díaz, Katacha. *Badger at Sandy Ridge Road*
Dijs, Carla. *Mommy, what if —?*
DiPucchio, Kelly. *What's the magic word?*
DiTerlizzi, Angela. *Say what?*
Dobbins, Jan. *Driving my tractor*
Docherty, Helen. *The Snatchabook*
Dodd, Emma. *Dog's noisy day*
    Meow said the cow
Dodd, Lynley. *Find me a tiger*
Dodds, Dayle Ann. *Pet wash*
Donahue, Shari Faden. *The zebra-striped whale with the polka-dot tail*
Donaldson, Julia. *The Giant Jumperee*
    Room on the broom
    What the ladybug heard
    Where's my mom?
Doner, Kim. *On a road in Africa*
Donnelly, Liza. *A hippo in our yard*
Donohue, Dorothy. *Veggie soup*
Doolittle, Bev. *Reading the wild*
Doray, Malika. *One more Wednesday*
Doremus, Gaetan. *Bear despair*
Dorros, Arthur. *City chicken*
Downey, Lynn. *The flea's sneeze*
    Matilda's humdinger
Downing, Johnette. *Down in Louisiana*
Downs, Mike. *Pig giggles and rabbit rhymes*
Doyle, Malachy. *Well, a crocodile can!*
Dragonwagon, Crescent. *All the awake animals are almost asleep*

Drummond, Ree. *Charlie goes to school*
Du Bois, William Pène. *Bear party*
Dubuc, Marianne. *Animal masquerade*
    The animals' ark
    Lucy and company
Dudley, Rebecca. *Hank finds an egg*
Duke, Kate. *In the rainforest*
Dunbar, Polly. *Hello Tilly*
    Pretty Pru
    Where's Tumpty?
Dunnick, Regan. *Sweet dreams, Douglas*
Dunrea, Olivier. *Bear Noel*
    Me and Annie McPhee
Dupasquier, Philippe. *1 2 3, follow me!*
Du Quette, Keith. *They call me Woolly*
Dutton, Sandra. *Dear Miss Perfect*
Duvoisin, Roger Antoine. *Petunia*
Dyer, Sarah. *Clementine and Mungo*
Dylan, Bob. *Man gave names to all the animals*
Edens, Cooper. *The Animal Mall*
Edwards, Pamela Duncan. *Bravo, Livingstone Mouse!*
    The grumpy morning
    McGillycuddy could
    Ms. Bitsy Bat's kindergarten
    Roar
    Some smug slug
    While the world is sleeping
    The worrywarts
Edwards, Richard. *Good night, Copycub*
Egan, Tim. *Dodsworth in London*
    Dodsworth in New York
    Dodsworth in Paris
    Dodsworth in Rome
    The pink refrigerator
    Serious farm
    The trial of Cardigan Jones
Ehlert, Lois. *Lots of spots*
    Oodles of animals
Ehrlich, Fred. *Does a baboon sleep in a bed?*
    Does a camel cook?
    Does a chimp wear clothes?
    Does a duck have a daddy?
    Does a giraffe drive?
    Does a mouse have a mommy?
    Does a seal smile?
    Does an elephant take a bath?
Ellery, Amanda. *If I were a jungle animal*
Elliott, David. *And here's to you!*
    In the sea
    In the wild
Elliott, Laura Malone. *A string of hearts*
    Thanksgiving Day thanks
Elya, Susan Middleton. *Eight animals bake a cake*
    Eight animals on the town
    No more, por favor
Emberley, Barbara. *One wide river to cross*
Emberley, Ed. *The red hen*
    Thanks, Mom!
    Where's my sweetie pie?
Emberley, Rebecca. *Chicken Little*
    My animals / Mis animales
Emmett, Jonathan. *The best gift of all*
    Bringing down the moon
    No place like home
Erdrich, Liselotte. *Bears make rock soup and other stories*
Ericsson, Jennifer A. *Whoo goes there?*
Eriksson, Eva. *A crash course for Molly*

Ernst, Lisa Campbell. *Wake up, it's Spring!*
Escoffier, Michaël. *Have you seen my trumpet?*
Ets, Marie Hall. *In the forest*
    Just me
    Mister Penny
    Play with me
Eure, Wesley. *A fish out of water*
Evans, Lezlie. *Finding Christmas*
Evert, Lori. *The Christmas wish*
Farber, Norma. *How the hibernators came to Bethlehem*
Fardell, John. *Jeremiah Jellyfish flies high!*
Faulkenberry, Lauren. *What do animals do on the weekend?*
Faulkner, Keith. *Do you have my quack?*
    The giraffe who cock-a-doodle-doo'd
    Jumbled jungle
    The tallest shortest longest greenest brownest animal in the jungle!
Fearnley, Jan. *Arthur and the meanies*
    A perfect day for it
Feiffer, Kate. *Which puppy?*
Felix, Monique. *The rumor*
Fernandes, Eugenie. *Busy little mouse*
    Kitten's winter
Ferri, Giuliano. *Peekaboo*
Ferry, Beth. *Pirate's perfect pet*
Fielding, Beth. *Animal eyes*
    Animal tails
Finn, Isobel. *The very lazy ladybug*
Fischer, Scott M. *Jump!*
Fisher, Aileen Lucia. *Do rabbits have Christmas?*
    Know what I saw?
Fisher, Carolyn. *A twisted tale*
Fitzgerald, Joanne. *Yum! yum!*
Fitzpatrick, Marie-Louise. *I'm a tiger, too!*
FitzSimmons, David. *Curious critters*
    Curious critters, vol. 2
Flack, Marjorie. *Ask Mr. Bear*
Flanagan, Alice K. *Dr. Friedman helps animals*
Fleming, Candace. *Emma's circus*
    Gator gumbo
    Oh, no!
    Who invited you?
Fleming, Denise. *Barnyard banter*
    Count!
    The cow who clucked
    In the small, small pond
    Sleepy, oh so sleepy
    Underground
    Where once there was a wood
Fleming, Meg. *I heart you*
Florian, Douglas. *I love my hat*
    Zoo's who
Flynn, Kitson. *Carrot in my pocket*
Foley, Greg. *Don't worry Bear*
    Good luck Bear
    Purple Little Bird
    Thank you, Bear
Ford, Christine. *Ocean's child*
Foster, John. *Pet poems*
Fox, Mem. *Hattie and the fox*
    Hello, baby!
    Time for bed
    Wombat divine
    Zoo-looking
Frampton, David. *My beastie book of ABC*
Franco, Betsy. *Pond circle*
    A spectacular selection of sea critters

Fraser, Mary Ann. *Where are the night animals?*
Fredericks, Anthony D. *In one tidepool*
Freedman, Claire. *One magical day*
    One magical morning
    Snuggle up, sleepy ones
    Where's your smile, crocodile?
Freeman, Mylo. *Potty*
Freeman, Tor. *Hooray! I'm five today!*
    Olive and the big secret
    Olive and the embarrassing gift
Fries, Claudia. *A pig is moving in*
A frog he would a-wooing go [folk-song] *Frog went a-courtin'*
    Frog went a-courting
    Froggie went a courting
    Froggy went a-courtin'
Fuge, Charles. *Astonishing animal ABC*
    I know a rhino
Galdone, Paul. *Cat goes fiddle-i-fee*
Galko, Francine. *Cave animals*
Gallo, Frank. *Night sounds*
Gamble, Isobel. *Who's that?*
Gannij, Joan. *Hidden hippo*
Garelli, Cristina. *Farm friends clean up*
Garland, Michael. *Last night at the zoo*
Gay, Marie-Louise. *On my island*
    Stella, fairy of the forest
Gehl, Laura. *One big pair of underwear*
Geist, Ken. *Who's who?*
Genechten, Guido van. *Guess what?*
    Guess where?
Geoghegan, Adrienne. *All your own teeth*
George, Jean Craighead. *Morning, noon, and night*
George, Lindsay Barrett. *Around the pond*
    In the garden: who's been here?
    In the woods
    The secret
George, William T. *Christmas at Long Pond*
    Fishing at Long Pond
Geraghty, Paul. *Help me!*
    The hoppameleon
Geras, Adèle. *My wishes for you*
Gerrard, K.A. *My family is a zoo*
Gershator, Phillis. *Moo, moo, brown cow! Have you any milk?*
    When it starts to snow
    Who's awake in springtime?
    Who's in the farmyard?
    Who's in the forest?
Gerstein, Mordicai. *The absolutely awful alphabet*
    Leaving the nest
Gibbons, Gail. *Nature's green umbrella*
    Prehistoric animals
    Say woof!
    Zoo
Gibbs, Edward. *I spy on the farm*
    I spy under the sea
    I spy with my little eye
Gibert, Bruno. *The king is naked!*
Gibson, Ginger Foglesong. *Tiptoe Joe*
Gillham, Bill. *How many sharks in the bath?*
Gilman, Rita Golden. *Mole in a hole*
    Rice is life
Ginsburg, Mirra. *Mushroom in the rain*
Giogas, Valarie. *In my backyard*
Gliori, Debi. *Mr. Bear to the rescue*
Goble, Paul. *The great race of the birds and animals*
Godwin, Laura. *Barnyard prayers*
    Little white dog

Goembel, Ponder. *Animal fair*
Goldin, David. *Go-Go-Go!*
Gollub, Matthew. *Gobble, quack, moon*
    The Jazz Fly
Goodhart, Pippa. *Noah makes a boat*
Goodman, Susan E. *What do you do — at the zoo?*
Gorbachev, Valeri. *Chicken chickens*
    Chicken chickens go to school
    Dragon is coming!
    Molly who flew away
    One rainy day
    Red red red
    What's the big idea, Molly?
    Where is the apple pie?
    Whose hat is it?
Gordon, David. *Extremely cute animals operating heavy machinery*
Gore, Leonid. *The wonderful book*
    Worms for lunch?
Gottfried, Maya. *Our farm*
Graham-Barber, Lynda. *Spy hops and belly flops*
Grahame, Kenneth. *The wind in the willows*
    A wind in the willows Christmas
Grambling, Lois G. *This whole Tooth Fairy thing's nothing but a big rip-off!*
Gravett, Emily. *Little Mouse's big book of beasts*
    Monkey and me
Gray, Kes. *The "Get well soon" book*
Green, Alison. *The fox in the dark*
Green, Dan. *Wild alphabet*
Greene, Rhonda Gowler. *Barnyard song*
    Jamboree day
    Noah and the mighty ark
Grey, Mini. *Three by the sea*
Griessman, Annette. *Like a hundred drums*
Grimes, Nikki. *Minnie's new friend*
Grimm, Jacob and Wilhelm. *Battle of the beasts*
    The Bremen town band
    The Bremen town musicians, ill. by Bill Dickson
    The Bremen town musicians, ill. by Ilse Plume
    The Bremen town musicians, ill. by Bernadette Watts
    The Bremen town musicians, ill. by Lisbeth Zwerger
    Musicians of Bremen
    Musicians of Bremen / Los musicos de Bremner
    Snow White
Grindley, Sally. *Where are my chicks?*
Grobler, Piet. *Hey, frog!*
Grupper, Jonathan. *Destination — Rocky Mountains*
Guarino, Deborah. *Is your mama a llama?*
Gugler, Laurel Dee. *There's a billy goat in the garden*
Haas, Rick de. *Peter and the winter sleepers*
Hacohen, Dean. *Tuck me in!*
    Who's hungry?
Hague, Michael. *Animal friends: a collection of poems for children*
Hall, Michael. *My heart is like a zoo*
    Wonderfall
Hamburg, Jennifer. *A moose that says moooooooooo*
Hamilton, Martha. *The hidden feast*
Hamilton, Richard. *Polly's picnic*
Hamilton, Virginia. *Jaguarundi*
Hargrove, Linda. *Wings across the moon*
Harker, Lesley. *Annie's ark*
Harley, Bill. *Bear's all-night party*
Harper, Jamie. *Miss Mingo and the fire drill*
    Miss Mingo and the first day of school
    Miss Mingo weathers the storm

Harper, Jessica. *A place called Kindergarten*
Harper, Jo. *I could eat you up!*
Harrington, Tim. *Nose to toes, you are yummy!*
Harris, Joel Chandler. *Jump! the adventures of Brer Rabbit*
 Jump again!
Harris, Robie H. *Maybe a bear ate it!*
Harris, Trudy. *The clock struck one*
Harrison, David L. *A perfect home for a family*
Hartley, Karen. *The sixth sense and other special senses*
Hartman, Gail. *As the crow flies*
Hassett, John. *Mouse in the house*
Haughton, Chris. *Goodnight everyone*
Hayashi, Leslie Ann. *Fables from the sea*
Hayles, Marsha. *A pet of a pet*
Hays, Anna Jane. *The pup speaks up*
Hayward, Linda. *The King's chorus*
Heinz, Brian J. *Butternut Hollow Pond*
Helmer, Marilyn. *Three barnyard tales*
 Three tales of three
Henkes, Kevin. *A good day*
 Oh!
 Waiting
Hennessy, B. G. *Corduroy at the zoo*
Henry, Jed. *Cheer up, Mouse!*
Heos, Bridget. *Shell, beak, tusk*
Hewitt, Sally. *All year round*
 Animal homes
 Face to face safari
 Woods and meadows
Hickman, Pamela. *It's moving day!*
Hill, Eric. *Spot at play*
 Spot at the fair
 Spot counts from 1 to 10
 Spot goes to the farm
 Spot on the farm
Hill, Susanna Leonard. *Can't sleep without sheep*
Hillenbrand, Will. *Down by the barn*
 Fiddle-i-fee
Himmelman, John. *Mouse in a meadow*
Hindley, Judy. *Does a cow say boo?*
 Sleepy places
Hines, Anna Grossnickle. *Miss Emma's wild garden*
Hirschi, Ron. *Fall*
 Spring
 Summer
 When morning comes
 When night comes
 Winter
Hiscock, Bruce. *Coyote and badger*
Hissey, Jane. *Jolly snow*
Ho, Minfong. *Brother Rabbit*
 Hush!
Hoban, Tana. *A children's zoo*
 Who are they?
Hoberman, Mary Ann. *"It's simple," said Simon*
Hodgkins, Fran. *Who's been here?*
Hodgkinson, Leigh. *Limelight Larry*
Hofmann-Maniyar, Ariane. *That's NOT how you do it!*
Hogg, Gary. *Beautiful Buehla and the zany zoo makeover*
Holmes, Anita. *Can you find us?*
 Who dug that hole?
Holub, Joan. *Turkeys never gobble*
Hood, Susan. *Spike, the mixed-up monster*
Hooper, Patricia. *Where do you sleep, little one?*
Horácek, Petr. *Animal opposites*

Look out, Suzy Goose
One spotted giraffe
Silly Suzy Goose
Suzy Goose and the Christmas star
When the moon smiled
Horn, Peter. *The best father of all*
Horowitz, Dave. *Buy my hats!*
 Soon, Baboon, soon
Horowitz, Ruth. *Crab moon*
Hort, Lenny. *We're going on a treasure hunt*
 We're going on safari
Horton, Joan. *Hippopotamus stew*
Hosta, Dar. *I love the night*
Howell, Will C. *Zoo flakes ABC*
Hruby, Emily. *Counting in the garden*
Hubbell, Patricia. *Earthmates*
Hughes, Langston. *The sweet and sour animal book*
Hulbert, Laura. *Who has these feet?*
 Who has this tail?
Huling, Jan. *Ol' Bloo's boogie-woogie band and blues ensemble*
Hull, Rod. *Mr. Betts and Mr. Potts*
Huneck, Stephen. *Sally goes to the farm*
Hunter, Anne. *Cricket song*
 Possum and the peeper
 Possum's harvest moon
 What's in the meadow?
 What's in the tide pool?
Hurwitz, Johanna. *Ethan out and about*
Hutchins, Pat. *Barn dance!*
 Little pink pig
 One hunter
 Shrinking mouse
 The surprise party
 Ten red apples
 What game shall we play?
Ichikawa, Satomi. *My little train*
Ikegami, Aiko. *Friends*
Inkpen, Mick. *The great pet sale*
 Kipper's A to Z
 Kipper's book of numbers
 Meow!
 Picnic
 Splosh!
Ipcizade, Catherine. *'Twas the Day before Zoo Day*
Isaacs, Anne. *Pancakes for supper!*
Isadora, Rachel. *Old Mikamba had a farm*
 A South African night
Isop, Laurie. *How do you hug a porcupine?*
Jackson, Richard. *All ears, all eyes*
Jacobs, Joseph. *The three sillies*
Jahn-Clough, Lisa. *On the hill*
Jamieson, Victoria. *Olympig!*
Janovitz, Marilyn. *A, B, see!*
Jarrett, Clare. *The best picnic ever*
Jay, Alison. *Welcome to the zoo*
Jeffers, Oliver. *The great paper caper*
Jenkins, Steve. *Actual size*
 Animals in flight
 Animals upside down
 Big and little
 Biggest, strongest, fastest
 Creature features
 Eye to eye
 Flying frogs and walking fish
 How to clean a hippopotamus
 How to swallow a pig
 I see a kookaburra
 Living color

Move!
Never smile at a monkey
Prehistoric actual size
Slap, squeak, and scatter
Time for a bath
Time to eat
Time to sleep
What do you do when something wants to eat you?
What do you do with a tail like this?
Who am I? an animal guessing game
Jennewein, Lenore. *Chick-o-Saurus Rex*
Jennings, Linda. *Hide and seek birthday treat*
Jennings, Sharon. *Franklin forgives*
   Franklin makes a deal
   Franklin wants a badge
Jocelyn, Marthe. *Eats*
Johnson, Amy Crane. *Cinnamon and the April shower / Canela y el aguacero de abril*
Johnson, Angela. *The girl who wore snakes*
Johnson, D. B. *Four legs bad, two legs good!*
Johnson, Paul Brett. *On top of spaghetti*
Johnston, Tony. *Desert song*
   Winter is coming
Jolivet, Joëlle. *Zoo-ology*
Jonas, Ann. *Aardvarks, disembark!*
   Splash!
   The trek
Jones, Stella J. *The very grumpy day*
Jones, Sylvie. *Who's in the tub?*
Jordan, Mary Ellen. *Lazy Daisy, cranky Frankie*
Jordan, Sandra. *Frog hunt*
Jorgensen, Gail. *Crocodile beat*
   Gotcha!
Joubert, Beverly. *African animal alphabet*
Juan, Ana. *The pet shop revolution*
Judge, Lita. *Red hat*
   Red sled
Kajikawa, Kimiko. *Sweet dreams: how animals sleep*
Kaner, Etta. *And the winner is . . .*
Kang, Anna. *I am (not) scared*
   That's not mine
   You are (not) small
Kangas, Juli. *The surprise visitor*
Kasza, Keiko. *Finders keepers*
   A mother for Choco
   Silly Goose's big story
Kaufmann, Nancy. *Bye, Bye*
Kawata, Ken. *Animal tails*
Keats, Ezra Jack. *Pet show!*
Keller, Emily Snowell. *Sleeping Bunny*
Keller, Holly. *Cecil's garden*
   Help!
   That's mine, Horace
Keller, Laurie. *Do unto otters*
Kellogg, Steven. *Aster Aardvark's alphabet adventures*
   Chicken Little
Kelly, Irene. *Even an octopus needs a home*
Kelly, L. J. R. *Sometimes it's storks*
Kelly, Mij. *Achoo!*
   A bed of your own!
   Friendly Day
   Where's my darling daughter?
Kenah, Katharine. *Predator attack!*
Kennedy, Anne Vittur. *The farmer's away! baa! neigh!*
Kepes, Juliet. *Five little monkeys*
Kherdian, David. *Come back, Moon*
Khing, T. T. *Where is the cake?*
   Where is the cake now?

Kimmel, Eric A. *Anansi and the moss-covered rock*
   Anansi and the talking melon
   I took my frog to the library
Kinerk, Robert. *Clorinda takes flight*
King, Thomas. *Coyote sings to the moon*
Kipling, Rudyard. *The elephant's child*
   How the camel got his hump
   How the elephant got his trunk
   The jungle book
Kirk, Daniel. *The thing about spring*
Klausmeier, Jesse. *Open this little book*
Kleven, Elisa. *Sun bread*
Klise, Kate. *Why do you cry?*
Kohara, Kazuno. *The Midnight Library*
Koponen, Libby. *Mmm . . . let's eat!*
Korda, Lerryn. *Into the wild*
   It's vacation time
Kramer, Jackie Azúa. *The green umbrella*
Kranking, Kathy. *The ocean is . . .*
Krans, Kim. *1, 2, 3 dream*
Krebs, Laurie. *We're roaming in the rainforest*
   We're sailing to Galapagos
Krensky, Stephen. *Mother's Day surprise*
   Noah's bark
Krilanovich, Nadia. *Chicken, chicken, duck!*
   Moon child
Kroll, Steven. *It's Groundhog Day!*
   Jungle bullies
Krosoczka, Jarrett J. *Punk Farm*
   Punk Farm on tour
Kudlinski, Kathleen V. *The sunset switch*
Kumin, Maxine. *Mites to astodons*
Kurtz, Jane. *Do kangaroos wear seat belts?*
LaMarche, Jim. *The raft*
Lambert, Jonny. *The great aaa-ooo!*
Landa, Norbert. *The great monster hunt*
Lang, Suzanne. *Families, families, families!*
Langstaff, John M. *Over in the meadow*
Larios, Julie. *Yellow elephant*
LaRochelle, David. *It's a tiger*
Larson, Bonnie. *When animals were people / Cuando los animales eran personas*
Lass, Bonnie. *Who took the cookies from the cookie jar?*
Latham, Irene. *Dear Wandering Wildebeest*
Latimer, Alex. *Lion vs Rabbit*
   Penguin's hidden talent
Lavis, Steve. *Cock-a-doodle-doo*
   Jump!
   On the farm
Lawler, Janet. *Love is real*
   Ocean counting
Lawrence, John. *This little chick*
Lawrence, Michael. *The caterpillar that roared*
Lawson, JonArno. *Leap!*
Layton, Neal. *Hot, hot, hot*
   Smile if you're human
   The tree
Lê, Minh. *Let me finish!*
Ledwon, Peter. *Midnight math twelve terrific math games*
Lee, Chinlun. *Good dog, Paw*
Lee, Jeanne M. *Toad is the uncle of heaven*
Leedy, Loreen. *Fraction action*
   The Furry News
   The great trash bash
   Missing math
   Mission — addition
   There's a frog in my throat
Leeson, Christine. *Molly and the storm*

Lehrhaupt, Adam. *I will not eat you*
    Please, open this book!
Lenski, Lois. *The Easter Rabbit's parade*
Léonard, Marie. *Tibili, the little boy who didn't want*
    to go to school
Leslie, Amanda. *Alfie and Betty Bug*
    Are chickens stripy?
    Do crocodiles moo?
    Flappy, waggy, wiggly
    Who's that scratching at my door?
Lesser, Carolyn. *What a wonderful day to be a cow*
Lester, Alison. *Noni the pony*
Lester, Helen. *Hooway for Wodney Wat*
    It wasn't my fault
    Wodney Wat's wobot
Lester, Julius. *Ackamarackus*
    Albidaro and the mischievous dream
Levine, Sara. *Bone by bone*
Lewandowski, Frrich. *It's Christmas again*
Lewis, J. Patrick. *Earth and me, our family tree*
    Good mousekeeping
    A hippopotamusn't
    Long was the winter road they traveled
    Tulip at the bat
    What's looking at you, kid?
Lewis, Kevin. *Not inside this house!*
Lewis, Kim. *Here we go Harry*
Lewison, Wendy Cheyette. *"Buzz," said the bee*
    Going to sleep on the farm
Lillegard, Dee. *Tortoise brings the mail*
Limentani, Alison. *How long is a whale?*
    How much does a ladybug weigh?
Lindbergh, Reeve. *The day the goose got loose*
    Midnight farm
    North country spring
Lionni, Leo. *The biggest house in the world*
    Frederick's fables
Lithgow, John. *Carnival of the animals*
    Never play music right next to the zoo
Little Bear's Valentine
Little, Jean. *Pippin the Christmas pig*
Little old lady who swallowed a fly. There was an old
    monkey who swallowed a frog
The little red hen. *The little red hen*, ill. by Byron
    Barton
    The little red hen, ill. by Emily Bolam
    The little red hen, ill. by Paul Galdone
    Little red hen
    The little red hen, ill. by Jerry Pinkney
    The little red hen, ill. by Kate Slater
    The little red hen, ill. by Annie West
    The little red hen, ill. by Margot Zemach
    The little red hen: an old fable
    The Little Red Hen and the Passover matzah
    The Little Red Hen makes a pizza
Litton, Jonthan. *Snip snap*
Livingston, Myra Cohn. *Valentine poems*
Livinson, Nancy Smiler. *North Pole, South Pole*
Liwska, Renata. *Red wagon*
Ljungkvist, Laura. *Follow the line around the world*
    Search and spot: animals!
Lloyd-Jones, Sally. *Being a pig is nice*
    Old MacNoah had an ark
    Time to say goodnight
    The ultimate guide to grandmas and grandpas!
Lobel, Anita. *Animal antics: A to Z*
    Hello, day!
Lobel, Arnold. *Fables*
Lobel, Gillian. *Little Honey Bear and the smiley moon*

Lodge, Jo. *Happy birthday, Moo Moo*
Logelin, Matthew. *Be glad your dad . . . is not an*
    octopus!
Loggins, Kenny. *Footloose*
Logue, Mary. *Sleep like a tiger*
London, Jonathan. *Crunch munch*
    Fireflies, fireflies, light my way
    Froggy plays in the band
    Froggy plays soccer
    Froggy's first Christmas
    Gone again ptarmigan
    Loon Lake
    The owl who became the moon
    What the animals were waiting for
    Who bop
    Wiggle, waggle
Long, Ethan. *In, over, and on (the farm)*
    Snickerdoodle takes the cake
Long, Loren. *Little tree*
Long, Steffanie. *Such a silly baby!*
Loomis, Christine. *Scuba bunnies*
Lottridge, Celia Barker. *Berta, a remarkable dog*
Louise, Tina. *When I grow up*
Low, William. *Daytime nighttime*
Lowell, Susan. *The tortoise and the jackrabbit*
Lumry, Amanda. *Safari in South Africa*
Lunde, Darrin. *Whose poop is that?*
Lyon, George Ella. *Mother to tigers*
    Sleepsong
McBratney, Sam. *Just you and me*
McCall, Francis X. *A huge hog is a big pig*
Maccarone, Grace. *Oink! moo! how do you do?*
McCarthy, Michael. *The story of Noah and the ark*
McCarty, Peter. *Little bunny on the move*
McClements, George. *Dinosaur Woods*
McClintock, Barbara. *The five forms*
MacDonald, Alan. *Wilfred to the rescue*
MacDonald, Elizabeth. *The wolf is coming!*
MacDonald, Margaret Read. *Give up, Gecko!*
    A hen, a chick, and a string guitar
    The squeaky door
McDonald, Megan. *Hen hears gossip*
    When the library lights go out
MacDonald, Suse. *Look whooo's counting*
McDonnell, Christine. *Dog wants to play*
McDonnell, Flora. *Giddy-up! Let's ride!*
    I love animals
    Splash!
McDonnell, Patrick. *Me . . . Jane*
McFarland, Clive. *A bed for Bear*
McFarlane, Sheryl. *On the farm*
McGee, Marni. *The noisy farm*
McGill, Alice. *Sure as sunrise*
McGinley-Nally, Sharon. *The friendly beasts*
McGowan, Jayme. *One bear extraordinaire*
McGrath, Barbara Barbieri. *The little gray bunny*
Mack, Jeff. *Duck in the fridge*
McKee, David. *Elmer and Super El*
    Elmer's special day
Maclear, Kyo. *The wish tree*
MacLennan, Cathy. *Chicky Chicky Chook Chook*
McMullan, Kate. *Mama's kisses*
    Supercat
McNamara, Margaret. *Apples A to Z*
McPhail, David. *Edward in the jungle*
    Farm morning
    The puddle
McQuade, Jacqueline. *At the petting zoo with Teddy*
    Bear

Big babies
Small babies
Snow babies
Maggi, María Elena. *The great canoe*
Mahoney, Daniel J. *The perfect clubhouse*
  The Saturday escape
Mahy, Margaret. *Boom Baby boom, boom*
  The Christmas tree tangle
  17 kings and 42 elephants
  Simply delicious!
  A summery Saturday morning
Maitland, Barbara. *Moo in the morning*
Manceau, Edouard. *Windblown*
Manning, Mick. *Supermom*
Mara, Nichole. *So many feet*
Marino, Gianna. *Night animals*
  One too many
  Zoopa
Markes, Julie. *Good thing you're not an octopus!*
Marshall, James. *Eugene*
Marshall, Janet Perry. *A honey of a day*
Martin, Bill, Jr.. *Baby bear, baby bear, what do you see?*
  Chicken Chuck
  Listen to our world
  Polar bear, polar bear, what do you hear?
Martin, David. *Let's have a tree party!*
  We've all got bellybuttons
Martin, Emily Winfield. *Dream animals*
Martin, Francesca. *Clever Tortoise*
Martin, Rafe. *Will's mammoth*
Martins, Isabel Minhós. *My neighbor is a dog*
Marzollo, Jean. *I spy little animals*
  Mama, Mama
  Papa, Papa
  Pretend you're a cat
  Sun song
  Ten cats have hats
  Ten little Christmas presents
Mathers, Petra. *A cake for Herbie*
Mathews, Judith. *Nathaniel Willy, scared silly*
Mayer, Marianna. *Beauty and the beast*
Mayer, Mercer. *What do you do with a kangaroo?*
Mayo, Margaret. *Roar!*
Meade, Holly. *A place to sleep*
Meadows, Michelle. *Hibernation station*
Meddaugh, Susan. *The best place*
Medina, Juana. *One big salad*
Melmed, Laura Krauss. *I love you as much . . .*
Mena, Pato. *The perfect siesta*
Meng, Cece. *Tough chicks*
Meres, Jonathan. *The big bad rumor*
Merz, Jennifer J. *Playground day*
Meschenmoser, Sebastian. *Waiting for winter*
Messner, Kate. *Over and under the snow*
  Tree of wonder
Metaxas, Eric. *It's time to sleep, my love*
Metzger, Steve. *Waiting for Santa*
Meyers, Susan. *This is the way a baby rides*
Michelson, Richard. *Ten times better*
Migy. *And away we go!*
Miles, Elizabeth J. *Ears*
  Mouths and teeth
  Noses
  Wings, fins, and flippers
Milgrim, David. *Santa Duck*
  Wild feelings
  Young MacDonald
Miller, David. *Just like you and me*
Miller, Edna. *Mousekin's Thanksgiving*

Miller, Margaret. *I love colors*
Miller, Mary Beth. *Handtalk zoo*
Miller, Pat. *Squirrel's New Year's resolution*
  Substitute Groundhog
Miller, Ruth. *I went to the farm*
Minarik, Else Holmelund. *Am I beautiful?*
Minor, Wendell. *Daylight starlight wildlife*
  My farm friends
Miranda, Anne. *Alphabet fiesta*
  To market, to market
Mitchell, Susan K. *The rainforest grew all around*
Mitter, Matt. *ABC: alphabet rhymes*
  Once upon a rhyme
  1, 2, 3, counting rhymes
Mitton, Tony. *All afloat on Noah's boat!*
  Down by the cool of the pool
  Farmer Joe and the music show
  The Jungle Run
Miyakoshi, Akiko. *The tea party in the woods*
Modesitt, Jeanne. *Oh, what a beautiful day!*
Molchadsky, Yael. *The chameleon that saved Noah's ark*
Mollel, Tololwa M. *Rhinos for lunch and elephants for supper*
  To dinner, for dinner
Monfreid, Dorothée de. *The cake*
  Dark night
Montanari, Eva. *The crocodile's true colors*
Montes, Marisa. *Egg-napped!*
Moore, Inga. *A house in the woods*
Moore, Raina. *How do you say good night?*
Mora, Pat. *Delicious hullabaloo / Pachanga deliciosa*
  Listen to the desert / Oye al desierto
  Marimba!
  The race of toad and deer
  The song of Francis and the animals
  Sweet dreams / Dulces suenos
  This big sky
Moran, Alex. *Boots for Beth*
  Come here, tiger
Moreton, Daniel. *La Cucaracha Martina*
Morlock, Lisa. *Track that scat!*
Morozumi, Atsuko. *One gorilla*
Morpurgo, Michael. *Wombat goes walkabout*
Morrow, Tara Jaye. *Mommy loves her baby; Daddy loves his baby*
Moss, Miriam. *Bad hare day*
  This is the tree
Most, Bernard. *Cock-a-doodle-moo!*
  The cow that went oink
Mother Goose. *Hey, diddle, diddle*
  Hey, diddle, diddle [board book]
  Hickory, dickory, dock
Moüy, Iris de. *Naptime*
Mozelle, Shirley. *The pig is in the pantry, the cat is on the shelf*
Munari, Bruno. *Bruno Munari's zoo*
Munsch, Robert N. *Alligator baby*
Murphy, Mary. *Crocopotamus*
  Good night like this
  How kind
  Koala and the flower
  Say hello like this!
Murphy, Stuart J. *Animals on board*
  Freda is found
  Write on, Carlos!
Muth, Jon J. *Mama Lion wins the race*
  The three questions
Myers, Walter Dean. *The story of the three kingdoms*

Na, Il Sung. *A book of sleep*
  Hide and seek
  The opposite zoo
  Snow rabbit, spring rabbit
Nakamura, Katherine Riley. *Song of night*
Nakawaki, Hatsue. *Wait! wait!*
National Wildlife Federation. *My first book of*
  animal opposites
Nelson, Kadir. *Baby Bear*
  If you plant a seed
Nelson, Robert Lyn. *Ocean friends*
Newman, Jeff. *Reginald*
Newman, Lesléa. *Skunk's spring surprise*
Nikola-Lisa, W. *Can you top that?*
Norman, Kim. *If it's snowy and you know it, clap your*
  paws!
  Ten on the sled
Numeroff, Laura Joffe. *The Chicken sisters*
  Chimps don't wear glasses
  The hope tree
  The Jellybeans and the big art adventure
  The Jellybeans and the big book bonanza
  The Jellybeans and the big camp kickoff
  The Jellybeans and the big dance
  What grandmas do best; What grandpas do best
  When sheep sleep
Nygaard, Elizabeth. *Snake alley band*
Odanaka, Barbara. *A crazy day at the Critter Café*
Ohmura, Tomoko. *The long, long line*
Old MacDonald had a farm. *Grandma's nursery*
  rhymes: Old MacDonald
  Old MacDonald
  Old MacDonald had a farm, ill. by Holly Berry
  Old MacDonald had a farm, ill. by Jane Cabrera
  Old MacDonald had a farm, ill. by Carol Jones
  Old MacDonald had a farm, ill. by Tracey
    Campbell Pearson
  Old MacDonald had a farm, ill. by Glen Rounds
  Old MacDonald had a farm, ill. by Jessica
    Souhami
  Old MacDonald had a farm, ill. by Prue
    Theobalds
  Old MacDonald had a truck
  Pete the Cat: Old MacDonald had a farm
Oldland, Nicholas. *Up the creek*
Olson, David J. *The thunderstruck stork*
Olson, Nathan. *Animal patterns*
O'Malley, Kevin. *Animal crackers fly the coop*
Onishi, Satoru. *Who's hiding*
Oram, Hiawyn. *Badger's bad mood*
Orgel, Doris. *The cat's tale*
Ormerod, Jan. *If you're happy and you know it!*
  Ms. MacDonald has a class
  When we went to the zoo
Otto, Carolyn. *What color is camouflage?*
Over in the meadow
Owens, Mary Beth. *Panda whispers*
Oxenbury, Helen. *It's my birthday*
Page, Robin. *How many ways can you catch a fly?*
  Sisters and brothers
Pajalunga, Lorena V. *Yoga for kids*
Palatini, Margie. *Earthquack*
  Moo who?
Paley, Joan. *One more river*
Pallotta, Jerry. *Dory story*
  A giraffe did one
  Ocean counting: odd numbers
  Who will see their shadows this year?
Paquette, Ammi-Joan. *Bunny Bus*

Parachini, Jodie. *This is a serious book*
Park, Linda Sue. *Xander's panda party*
  Yaks yak
Parker, Kim. *Counting in the garden*
Parker, Marjorie Blain. *A paddling of ducks*
  Your kind of mommy
Parker, Victoria. *Bearum scarum*
Partridge, Elizabeth. *Moon glowing*
Patent, Dorothy Hinshaw. *Bold and bright, black-*
  and-white animals
Paterson, Brian. *Zigby camps out*
Patkau, Karen. *Creatures*
Patricelli, Leslie. *Faster! faster!*
Patten, Brian. *The big snuggle-up*
Pattison, Darcy. *Desert baths*
Paul, Ann Whitford. *Fiesta fiasco*
  If animals kissed goodnight
  If animals said I love you
Paul, Ruth. *Hedgehog's magic tricks*
Paxton, Tom. *Going to the zoo*
Peaceful moments in the wild
Pearce, Clemency. *Three little words*
Pearson, Tracey Campbell. *Bob*
  Elephant's story
Peck, Jan. *Way up high in a tall green tree*
Peek, Merle. *Mary wore her red dress and Henry wore*
  his green sneakers
Peet, Bill. *The ant and the elephant*
  Cock-a-doodle Dudley
  Farewell to Shady Glade
  The gnats of knotty pine
  No such things
Pelham, David. *A is for animals*
  Crawlies creep
Perrin, Martine. *Cock-a-doodle who?*
  Look who's there!
Petersen, David. *Snowy Valentine*
Petty, Dev. *I don't want to be a frog*
Pfister, Marcus. *Animal ABC*
  Charlie at the zoo
  Hopper hunts for spring
  How Leo learned to be king
  Just the way you are
Pham, LeUyen. *The bear who wasn't there*
  A piece of cake
Phillips, Mildred. *And the cow said, "moo"!*
Pienkowski, Jan. *Pizza!*
Piers, Helen. *Who's in my bed?*
Pilkey, Dav. *The Moonglow Roll-O-Rama*
Pinder, Eric. *If all the animals came inside*
Pinkney, Jerry. *Noah's ark*
Pinkwater, Daniel. *Rainy morning*
Pitcher, Caroline. *Are you spring?*
Pittau, Francisco. *Out of sight*
Piven, Hanoch. *The perfect purple feather*
Plourde, Lynn. *Only cows allowed!*
Polacco, Patricia. *Mommies say shhh!*
Posada, Mia. *Who was here?*
Potter, Beatrix. *Appley Dapply's nursery rhymes*
  Cecily Parsley's nursery rhymes
  Ginger and Pickles
  More tales from Beatrix Potter
  Peter Rabbit's ABC
  The tale of Peter Rabbit and other stories
  Yours affectionately, Peter Rabbit
Pow, Tom. *Who is the world for?*
Prap, Lila. *Animal lullabies*
  Animals speak
  Daddies

Prelutsky, Jack. *Behold the bold umbrellaphant and other poems*
  Beneath a blue umbrella
  The pack rat's day and other poems
  Stardines swim high across the sky
Price, Kathy. *The Bourbon Street musicians*
Pritchett, Andy. *Stick!*
Provensen, Alice. *The year at Maple Hill Farm*
Puttock, Simon. *The baby that roared*
  Big bad wolf is good
Quattlebaum, Mary. *Jo MacDonald hiked in the woods*
Rankin, Joan. *First day*
  You're somebody special, Walliwigs!
Raschka, Chris. *Moosey Moose*
Rash, Andy. *Are you a horse?*
Rathmann, Peggy. *Good night, Gorilla*
Raye, Rebekah. *The very best bed*
Rayner, Catherine. *Abigail*
Rechner, Amy. *Out and about at the aquarium*
Regan, Dian Curtis. *Barnyard slam*
  The Snow Blew Inn
Reibstein, Mark. *Wabi Sabi*
Reider, Katja. *The big little sneeze*
  Snail started it!
Reidy, Jean. *Busy builders, busy week!*
Reinhart, Matthew. *Animal popposites*
Reiser, Lynn. *Little clam*
Rempt, Fiona. *Snail's birthday wish*
Rex, Michael. *Dunk skunk*
Rey, Margret. *Billy's picture*
Reynolds, Aaron. *Buffalo wings*
Rice, Eve. *Sam who never forgets*
Richards, Dan. *Can one balloon make an elephant fly?*
Riley, Linda Capus. *Elephants swim*
Rinck, Maranke. *I feel a foot!*
Rinker, Sherri Duskey. *Steam train, dream train*
Riphagen, Loes. *Animals home alone*
Robberecht, Thierry. *I can't do anything!*
  Sam's new friend
Robbins, Beth. *Tom's first day at school*
  Tom's new haircut
Roberts, Bethany. *Birthday mice*
  Valentine mice!
Robinson, Fiona. *What animals really like*
Robinson, Michelle. *And the robot went . . .*
  There's a lion in my cornflakes
  What to do if an elephant stands on your foot
Rock, Brian. *The deductive detective*
Rockwell, Anne. *Chip and the karate kick*
  Katie Catz makes a splash
  Morgan plays soccer
Roderick, Stacey. *Ocean animals from head to tail*
Root, Barry. *Gumbrella*
Root, Phyllis. *One duck stuck*
  Toot toot zoom!
Rose, Caroline Starr. *Over in the wetlands*
Rose, Deborah Lee. *Birthday zoo*
  Into the A, B, sea
Rosen, Michael. *How the animals got their colors*
  Tiny little fly
Rosen, Michael J. *With a dog like that, a kid like me . . .*
Rosenberg, Liz. *A big and little alphabet*
Rosenberry, Vera. *Who is in the garden?*
Rosenthal, Betsy R. *An ambush of tigers*
Rosoff, Meg. *Wild boars cook*
Ross, Eileen. *The Halloween showdown*
Ross, Michael Elsohn. *Mama's milk*

  Play with me
Roth, Carol. *All aboard to work — choo-choo!*
  The little school bus
  Will you still love me?
Rotner, Shelley. *Pick a pet*
  Whose eye am I?
Rouillard, Wendy. *Barnaby's bunny*
Rowand, Phyllis. *It is night*
Rowe, Jeannette. *Whose ears?*
  Whose feet?
  Whose nose?
Ruddell, Deborah. *A whiff of pine, a hint of skunk*
Rueda, Claudia. *Let's play in the forest while the wolf is not around*
Rumford, James. *Nine animals and the well*
Ruurs, Margriet. *In my backyard*
Ryan, Candace. *Zoo zoom!*
Ryan, Pam Muñoz. *Armadillos sleep in dugouts*
Ryder, Joanne. *Big bear ball*
  Dance by the light of the moon
  Each living thing
  A fawn in the grass
Rylant, Cynthia. *Life*
  Night in the country
  Puppies and piggies
Saaf, Donald. *The ABC animal orchestra*
Sabuda, Robert. *Beauty and the beast: a pop-up book of the classic fairy tale*
  The movable Mother Goose
Sage, Angie. *Monkeys in the jungle*
St. Pierre, Stephanie. *What the sea saw*
Salley, Coleen. *Epossumondas*
  Epossumondas saves the day
San Souci, Robert D. *Two bear cubs: a Miwok legend from California's Yosemite Valley*
Santore, Charles. *A stowaway on Noah's Ark*
Sassi, Laura. *Goodnight, Ark*
Sauer, Tammi. *Ginny Louise and the school showdown*
  I love cake!
  Me want pet!
  Mr. Duck means business
Saunders, Dave. *So slow!*
Sayre, April Pulley. *Dig, wait, listen*
  Home at last: a song of migration
  If you should hear a honey guide
  If you're hoppy
  Splish! splash! animal baths
Schaefer, Carole Lexa. *Big Little Monkey*
  Cool time song
  Down in the woods at sleepytime
Schaefer, Lola M. *Just one bite*
  Lifetime
Scheffler, Axel. *Axel Scheffler's Flip flap safari*
Schertle, Alice. *Advice for a frog and other poems*
  Button up!
Schindel, John. *What did they see?*
Schindler, S. D. *Spike and Ike take a hike*
Schneider, Josh. *Everybody sleeps (but not Fred)*
Schoenherr, Ian. *Read it, don't eat it!*
Schofield, Jennifer. *Animal babies in grasslands*
  Animal babies in polar lands
  Animal babies in ponds and rivers
  Animal babies in rain forests
Schubert, Ingrid. *There's always room for one more*
Schulman, Janet. *Countdown to spring*
Schultz, Sam. *Animal antics: the beast jokes ever*
Schumaker, Ward. *Dance!*
Schwartz, Amy. *A beautiful girl*
  Starring Miss Darlene

Schwartz, David M. *If you hopped like a frog*
  Where else in the wild?
  Where in the wild
Schwartz, Roslyn. *The mole sisters and the cool breeze*
  The mole sisters and the question
  Tales from Parc la Fontaine
Scieszka, Jon. *Battle Bunny*
Sebe, Masayuki. *One hundred animals on parade!*
Seder, Rufus Butler. *Waddle!*
Seeger, Laura Vaccaro. *Bully*
  I had a rooster
Selkowe, Valrie M. *Happy birthday to me!*
Selsam, Millicent E. *How to be a nature detective*
  Keep looking!
Sendak, Maurice. *Very far away*
Sensel, Joni. *Bears barge in*
Serfozo, Mary. *Whooo's there?*
Seuling, Barbara. *Spring song*
  Winter lullaby
Shahan, Sherry. *Cool cats counting*
Shannon, David. *Duck on a bike*
  Duck on a tractor
Shannon, George. *Rabbit's gift*
  Turkey Tot
Shapiro, Zachary. *We're all in the same boat*
Sharmat, Marjorie Weinman. *The 329th friend*
Sharratt, Nick. *Shark in the park*
Shaskan, Stephen. *A dog is a dog*
Shea, Kitty. *Out and about at the vet clinic*
Sheehy, Shawn. *Welcome to the neighborwood*
Sherry, Kevin. *Turtle Island*
Showers, Paul. *Sleep is for everyone*
Shulman, Lisa. *The moon might be milk*
Shuttlewood, Craig. *Who's in the tree?*
Sidman, Joyce. *Just us two*
  Winter bees and other poems of the cold
Sierra, Judy. *E-I-E-I-O*
  Make way for readers
  Preschool to the rescue
  There's a zoo in room 22
  We love our school!
  Wild about books
  Zoozical
Silvestro, Annie. *Bunny's book club*
Siminovich, Lorena. *Monkey see, look at me!*
Simmons, Jane. *Daisy and the Beastie*
  Daisy says coo!
  Daisy's favorite things
  Daisy's hide-and-seek
  Little Fern's first winter
Simple gifts
Singer, Isaac Bashevis. *Why Noah chose the dove*
Singer, Marilyn. *Creature carnival*
  Fred's bed
  Quiet night
  Turtle in July
Siomades, Lorianne. *Cuckoo can't find you*
  Kangaroo and cricket
  My box of color
Slack, Michael. *Monkey Truck*
Slate, Joseph. *Little Porcupine's Christmas*
  Miss Bindergarten celebrates the last day of kindergarten
  Miss Bindergarten celebrates the 100th day of kindergarten
  Miss Bindergarten gets ready for kindergarten
  Miss Bindergarten has a wild day in kindergarten
  Miss Bindergarten stays home from kindergarten

  Miss Bindergarten takes a field trip with kindergarten
  Who is coming to our house?
Slegers, Liesbet. *Funny ears*
  Funny feet
  Funny tails
Slingsby, Janet. *Hush-a-bye babies*
Sloat, Teri. *Farmer Brown goes round and round*
  Pieces of Christmas
  Rib-ticklers
  There was an old lady who swallowed a trout
  The thing that bothered Farmer Brown
Small, David. *George Washington's cows*
  Imogene's antlers
Smallman, Steve. *Hiccupotamus*
Smath, Jerry. *The animals' Christmas carol*
Smee, Nicola. *Clip-clop*
  Jingle-jingle
Smith, Lane. *It's a book*
  A perfect day
  There is a tribe of kids
Sockabasin, Allen. *Thanks to the animals*
Souhami, Jessica. *Foxy!*
  No dinner!
Soule, Jean Conder. *Never tease a weasel*
Spafford, Suzy. *Witzy's colors*
Spence, Robert, III.. *Clickety clack*
Spier, Peter. *Gobble, growl, grunt*
  Noah's ark
Spinelli, Eileen. *Peace Week in Miss Fox's class*
  Polar bear, arctic hare
  Silly Tilly
Spurling, Margaret. *Bilby moon*
Spurr, Elizabeth. *Two bears beneath the stairs*
Srinivasan, Divya. *Little Owl's night*
Staake, Bob. *My little opposites book*
Stadler, John. *What's so scary?*
Staines, Bill. *All God's critters*
Staub, Leslie. *Bless this house*
Stead, Philip C. *Bear has a story to tell*
  A sick day for Amos McGee
Steig, William. *Sylvester and the magic pebble*
  Toby, what are you?
  Toby, where are you?
  Toby, who are you?
Stein, David Ezra. *The nice book*
Stern, Ellen. *I saw a bullfrog*
Stevens, Janet. *And the dish ran away with the spoon*
  Cook-a-doodle-doo!
  Old bag of bones
Stevenson, Emma. *Hide-and-seek science*
Stevenson, James. *Christmas at Mud Flat*
  Don't make me laugh
  Happy Valentine's Day, Emma!
  Heat wave at Mud Flat
  The most amazing dinosaur
  Mr. Hacker
  National worm day
  No need for Monty
  A village full of valentines
  We can't sleep
  Which one is Whitney?
  Yard sale
Stewart, Melissa. *Beneath the sun*
  Can an aardvark bark?
  Under the snow
  When rain falls
Stewart, Whitney. *Meditation is an open sky*
Stewig, John Warren. *The animals watched*

Stihler, Chérie B. *The giant cabbage turnip*
Sting [Musician]. *Rock steady*
Stock, Catherine. *A porc in New York*
Stockdale, Susan. *Spectacular spots*
Stoeke, Janet Morgan. *Hide and seek*
Stojic, Manya. *Rain*
   Snow
Stoop, Naoko. *Red Knit Cap Girl*
   Red Knit Cap Girl and the reading tree
Straaten, Harmen van. *Duck's tale*
   For me?
Strete, Craig Kee. *How the Indians bought the farm*
Sturm, James. *Sleepless knight*
Surplice, Holly. *Peek-a-boo Bunny*
Sutton, Jane. *Don't call me Sidney*
Swanson, Diane. *Headgear that hides and plays*
   Noses that plow and poke
   Skin that slimes and scares
Sweeney, Jacqueline. *What about Bettie?*
Sweet, Melissa. *Fiddle-i-fee*
Swenson, Jamie A. *Boom! boom! boom!*
   If you were a dog
Swinburne, Stephen R. *Lots and lots of zebra stripes*
   Safe, warm, and snug
   Water for one, water for everyone
Sykes, Julie. *Careful, Santa*
   Dora's chicks
   Dora's eggs
   I don't want to take a bath!
   Smudge
Symes, Sally. *Yawn*
Taback, Simms. *Simms Taback's city animals*
   Simms Taback's farm animals
   Simms Taback's safari animals
Tafuri, Nancy. *All kinds of kisses*
   The barn party
   The big storm
   Counting to Christmas
   Daddy hugs
   Do not disturb
   The donkey's Christmas song
   I love you, little one
   Junglewalk
   Rabbit's morning
   Silly little goose!
   This is the farmer
   Where we sleep
   Who's counting?
Tang, Greg. *Math fables too*
Tankard, Jeremy. *Boo hoo Bird*
   Grumpy Bird
   Me hungry!
Tarlow, Ellen. *Pinwheel days*
Taylor, Eleanor. *Beep, beep, let's go!*
Taylor, Harriet Peck. *Secrets of the stone*
   Ulaq and the northern lights
Taylor, Theodore. *Hello, Arctic!*
Teague, Mark. *The sky is falling!*
Tebbs, Victoria. *Noah's Ark story*
Teckentrup, Britta. *Busy bunny days*
   Get out of my bath!
   The odd one out
   Where's the pair?
Terry, Michael. *Rhino's horns*
Teyssèdre, Fabienne. *Joseph wants to read*
Thimmesh, Catherine. *Friends: true stories of extraordinary animal friendships*
Thomas, Jan. *A birthday for Cow!*
   The doghouse

   Is that wise, Pig?
Thompson, Lauren. *One starry night*
   Wee little lamb
Thomson, Pat. *The squeaky, creaky bed*
Thomson, Sarah L. *Around the neighborhood*
Thornhill, Jan. *I am Josephine (and I am a living thing)*
   The rumor
   Wild in the city
   Winter's coming
Thorpe, Kiki. *A comfy, cozy Thanksgiving*
   Time to cha-cha-cha!
Thurlby, Paul. *Paul Thurlby's wildlife*
Tibi, Marie. *The bear who didn't want to miss Christmas*
Tildes, Phyllis Limbacher. *Animals in camouflage*
   Eye guess
Tillman, Nancy. *The crown on your head*
Timmers, Leo. *Bang*
   Gus's garage
   Who is driving?
Todd, Mark. *Start your engines*
Toft, Kim Michelle. *Neptune's nursery*
   The world that we want
Tolman, Marije. *The tree house*
Tolstoy, Aleksey Nikolayevich. *The enormous turnip*
Tomlinson, Jill. *The owl who was afraid of the dark*
Trapani, Iza. *Baa baa black sheep*
   Row, row, row your boat
   What am I?
Trenc, Milan. *Another night at the museum*
Tresselt, Alvin R. *The mitten: an old Ukrainian folktale*
   Wake up, farm!
Tricarico, Christine. *Cock-a-doodle dance!*
Trumbauer, Lisa. *The great reindeer rebellion*
Tryon, Leslie. *Albert's birthday*
   Albert's Christmas
   Albert's Halloween
   Albert's play
   Patsy says
Tsurumi, Andrea. *Accident!*
Tudor, Tasha. *A tale for Easter*
Tulloch, Shirley. *Who made me?*
Tweet, Jonathan. *Grandmother Fish*
Underwood, Deborah. *The quiet book*
Urban, Linda. *Mouse was mad*
Urbanovic, Jackie. *Duck soup*
Uribe, Verónica. *Buzz buzz buzz*
Vagin, Vladimir. *The enormous carrot*
Vail, Rachel. *Over the moon*
Vamos, Samantha R. *The cazuela that the farm maiden stirred*
Van Fleet, Matthew. *Fuzzy yellow ducklings*
   Heads
   Moo
   One yellow lion
   Spotted yellow frogs
Van Kampen, Vlasta. *It couldn't be worse*
Van Laan, Nancy. *Little Fish lost*
   Moose tales
   Sleep, sleep, sleep
   This is the hat
   A tree for me
   When winter comes: a lullaby
Van Woerkom, Dorothy. *The rat, the ox and the zodiac*
Vaughan, Marcia Kapok. *Snap!*
   Whistling Dixie

Verboven, Agnes. *Ducks like to swim*
Vestergaard, Hope. *Hillside lullaby*
　Potty animals
Viano, Hannah. *B is for bear*
Virján, Emma J. *What this story needs is a pig in a wig*
Voce, Louise. *Over in the meadow*
Votaw, Carol. *Good morning, little polar bear*
　Waking up down under
Vrombaut, An. *Clarabella's teeth*
Waber, Bernard. *Bearsie Bear and the surprise sleepover party*
　Fast food! gulp! gulp!
Waddell, Martin. *Farmer Duck*
　The pig in the pond
　Webster J. Duck
Wadsworth, Ginger. *One tiger growls*
Waldron, Kevin. *Mr. Peek and the misunderstanding at the zoo*
　Panda-monium at Peek Zoo
Wallace, Ivy. *Pookie*
　Pookie believes in Santa Claus
　Pookie puts the world right
Wallen, Ila. *The moon in my room*
Wallner, Alexandra. *Beatrix Potter*
Walsh, Ellen Stoll. *Pip's magic*
Walsh, Joanna. *I love Mom*
　The perfect hug
Walsh, Melanie. *Do donkeys dance?*
　Do lions live on lily pads?
　Do monkeys tweet?
Walter, Virginia. *"Hi, pizza man!"*
Walters, Eric. *The matatu*
Walton, Rick. *Little dogs say "Rough!"*
　Noah's square dance
Wan, Joyce. *Hug you, kiss you, love you*
Wang, Gabrielle. *The race for the Chinese zodiac*
Ward, Helen. *Old shell, new shell*
　The tin forest
Ward, Jennifer. *Feathers and hair, what animals wear*
　Forest bright, forest night
　Way up in the Arctic
Wardlaw, Lee. *The chair where bear sits*
Warhola, James. *If you're happy and you know it: jungle edition*
Warnes, Tim. *Daddy hug*
Warrick, Karen Clemens. *If I had a tail*
　Who needs that nose?
Wayne-von Königslöw, Andrea. *How do you read to a rabbit?*
Weeks, Sarah. *Catfish Kate and the sweet swamp band*
　Crocodile smile
　My somebody special
Wegerif, Gay. *Up close*
Weigelt, Udo. *Bear's last journey*
　Old Beaver
　Who stole the gold?
Weill, Cynthia. *Animal talk: Mexican folk art animal sounds in English and Spanish*
Weinstein, Ellen Slusky. *Everywhere the cow says "Moo!"*
Weiss, Nicki. *Where does the brown bear go?*
Welch, Willy. *Dancing with Daddy*
Welling, Peter J. *Shawn O'Hisser, the last snake in Ireland*
Wellington, Monica. *Bunny's first snowflake*
Wells, Rosemary. *Hazel's amazing mother*
　Miracle melts down
　My kindergarten

　Stella's Starliner
Weninger, Brigitte. *Bye-bye, Binky*
　The elf's hat
　Merry Christmas, Davy!
Wenzel, Brendan. *They all saw a cat*
West, Colin. *One day in the jungle*
West, Judy. *Have you got my purr?*
Westcott, Nadine Bernard. *There's a hole in the bucket*
Wheeler, Lisa. *Babies can sleep anywhere*
　The pet project
Whippo, Walt. *Little white duck*
White, Kathryn. *The tickle test*
White, Teagan. *Adventures with barefoot critters*
Whitfield, Susan. *The animals of the Chinese zodiac*
Whybrow, Ian. *Good night, monster*
　Hello! Is this grandma?
Wick, Walter. *Can you see what I see? cool collections*
　Can you see what I see? Seymour and the juice box boat
Wiesmüller, Dieter. *In the blink of an eye*
Wild, Margaret. *Nighty night*
Wildsmith, Brian. *Goat's trail*
　Jungle party
Wilhelm, Hans. *A hole in the wall*
Willems, Mo. *Naked mole rat gets dressed*
Willey, Margaret. *Clever Beatrice and the best little pony*
Williams, Brenda. *Home for a tiger, home for a bear*
Williams, Linda. *Horse in the pigpen*
Williams, Sue. *I went walking*
　Let's go visiting
Williams, Suzanne. *Old MacDonald in the city*
Willis, Jeanne. *Boa's bad birthday*
　The boy who lost his bellybutton
　Hippospotamus
　That's not funny!
　The wheels on the bus: a read-along sing-along trip to the zoo
Wilner, Isabel. *A garden alphabet*
Wilson, Anna. *Over in the grasslands*
Wilson, Anne. *Noah's ark*
Wilson, Karma. *Animal strike at the zoo, it's true!*
　Bear feels scared
　Bear feels sick
　Bear says thanks
　Bear sees colors
　Bear stays up for Christmas
　Big bear, small mouse
　Mama always comes home
　Moose tracks!
Wilson, Sarah. *Love and kisses*
Winnick, Karen B. *Barn sneeze*
Winters, Kay. *Wolf watch*
Wise, William. *Zany zoo*
Witte, Anna. *The parrot Tico Tango*
Wojtowycz, David. *Animal antics from 1 to 10*
Wolf, Jake. *Daddy, could I have an elephant?*
Wolff, Ferida. *It is the wind*
Wolkstein, Diane. *Little Mouse's painting*
Won, Brian. *Hooray for hat!*
Wood, Audrey. *The full moon at the napping house*
　Little Penguin's tale
　The napping house
　The napping house wakes up
　Silly Sally
Wood, Douglas. *Old Turtle*
　When a dad says "I love you"
Wood, Jakki. *Moo moo, brown cow*

Never say boo to a goose!
Wormell, Christopher. *Blue Rabbit and friends*
   Blue Rabbit and the runaway wheel
   The new alphabet of animals
   Puff, puff, chugga-chugga
Wormell, Mary. *Bernard the angry rooster*
   Hilda Hen's happy birthday
   Why not?
Worth, Valerie. *Pug and other animal poems*
Wright, Maureen. *Barnyard fun*
   Earth Day, birthday!
Yaccarino, Dan. *Deep in the jungle*
   Five little ducks
   Lawn to lawn
   An octopus followed me home
   So big
Yamaguchi, Kristi. *It's a big world, little pig!*
Yarrow, Peter. *Day is done*
Yee, Wong Herbert. *Detective Small in the amazing banana caper*
   Eek! There's a mouse in the house
   Fireman Small
   Fireman Small, fire down below
   Fireman Small to the rescue
   Hamburger Heaven
   Mrs. Brown went to town
   The Officers' Ball
   A small Christmas
   Tracks in the snow
Ying, Jonathan. *Not quite black and white*
Yolen, Jane. *Jane Yolen's Old MacDonald songbook*
   Picnic with Piggins
   Piggins
   Sleep, black bear, sleep
   Welcome to the icehouse
   Welcome to the river of grass
   Welcome to the sea of sand
Yoon, Salina. *Do cows meow?*
   Do crocs kiss?
Yorinks, Arthur. *Quack!*
Young, Ruth. *Who says moo?*
Zahares, Wade. *Big, bad, and a little bit scary*
Zane, Alexander. *The wheels on the race car*
Zelch, Patti R. *Ready, set . . . wait!*
Ziefert, Harriet. *Animal music*
   Be fair, share!
   Beach party!
   A bunny is funny
   I swapped my dog
   A polar bear can swim
   What do ducks dream?
   Wiggle like an octopus
   You and me: we're opposites
Zoboli, Giovanna. *The big book of slumber*
   I wish I had . . .
Zoehfeld, Kathleen Weidner. *What lives in a shell?*
   What's alive?
Zolotow, Charlotte. *Sleepy book*, ill. by Ilse Plume
   Sleepy book, ill. by Stefano Vitale
Zommer, Yuval. *The big blue thing on the hill*
Zuckerman, Andrew. *Creature abc*

Animals – aardvarks

Brown, Marc. *Arthur babysits*
   Arthur goes to school
   Arthur lost and found
   Arthur meets the president
   Arthur tricks the tooth fairy

Arthur turns green
Arthur writes a story
Arthur's animal adventure
Arthur's baby
Arthur's birthday
Arthur's chicken pox
Arthur's computer disaster
Arthur's family vacation
Arthur's first sleepover
Arthur's neighborhood
Arthur's new puppy
Arthur's nose
Arthur's perfect Christmas
Arthur's pet business
Arthur's really helpful word book
Arthur's spookiest Halloween
Arthur's teacher moves in
Arthur's TV trouble
Arthur's underwear
D. W., go to your room!
D. W. rides again!
D. W., the picky eater
D. W. thinks big
D. W.'s library card
D. W.'s lost blankie
Glasses for D. W.
The true Francine
Kellogg, Steven. *Aster Aardvark's alphabet adventures*
Lindbergh, Reeve. *The awful aardvarks go to school*
   The awful aardvarks shop for school
Moodie, Fiona. *Noko and the night monster*
Sloat, Teri. *Hark! The aardvark angels sing*

Animals – anteaters

Bagley, Jessixa. *Before I leave*
Brown, Marc. *D. W. all wet*
   D. W. flips!
DeRubertis, Barbara. *Alexander Anteater's amazing act*
Dewdney, Anna. *Roly Poly pangolin*
Waber, Bernard. *An anteater named Arthur*

Animals – apes *see* Animals – baboons; Animals – chimpanzees; Animals – gorillas; Animals – monkeys

Animals – armadillos

Arnosky, Jim. *Armadillo's orange*
Brett, Jan. *Armadillo rodeo*
Brimner, Larry Dane. *Trick or treat, Old Armadillo*
David, Lawrence. *The land of the hungry armadillos*
Fearnley, Jan. *Milo Armadillo*
Ketteman, Helen. *Armadillo tattletale*
   Armadilly chili
Kipling, Rudyard. *The beginning of the armadillos*
Radunsky, Vladimir. *One: a nice story about an awful braggart*
   Ten
Swinburne, Stephen R. *Armadillo trail*
Waring, Zoe. *No hugs for Porcupine*

Animals – babies

Abercrombie, Barbara. *Bad dog, Dodger*
Alexander, Martha G. *When the new baby comes, I'm moving out*

Aliki. *At Mary Bloom's*
Asch, Frank. *Baby Bird's first nest*
Ashman, Linda. *Babies on the go*
Asper-Smith, Sarah. *I would tuck you in*
Baby animals
Baby animals at the zoo
Baddiel, Ivor. *Cock-a-doodle quack! quack!*
Baillie, Marilyn. *Small wonders*
Bajaj, Varsha. *This is our baby, born today*
Bauer, Marion Dane. *The cutest critter*
   If you were born a kitten
Blomgren, Jennifer. *Where do I sleep?*
Bogue, Gary. *There's an opossum in my backyard*
Bourguignon, Laurence. *Heart in the pocket*
Brenner, Barbara A. *What the elephant told*
Bruzzone, Catherine. *Puppy finds a friend /*
   Cachorrito encuentra un amigo
   Puppy finds a friend / Le petit chien se trouve un ami
Bunting, Eve. *The baby shower*
   Sing a song of piglets
Butler, John. *Hush, little ones*
   Pi-shu, the little panda
   Whose baby am I?
Buzzeo, Toni. *Just like my Papa*
   Stay close to Mama
Cabrera, Jane. *Mommy, carry me please!*
Calmenson, Stephanie. *Perfect puppy*
Capucilli, Alyssa Satin. *Biscuit wants to play*
   Biscuit's new trick
   Biscuit's Valentine's Day
Castle, Caroline. *Naughty!*
Chaconas, Dori. *Christmas mouseling*
Chwast, Seymour. *Harry, I need you!*
Clark, Leslie Ann. *Peepsqueak!*
Clarke, Jane. *Who woke the baby?*
Clements, Andrew. *Slippers at home*
Cole, Babette. *Lady Lupin's book of etiquette*
Collard, Sneed B. *Leaving home*
Cordell, Matthew. *Dream*
   Wish
Costello, Emily. *Realm of the panther*
Cowen-Fletcher, Jane. *Hello, puppy!*
Cronin, Doreen. *Click, clack, peep!*
Davies, Nicola. *Dolphin baby!*
Davis, Kate. *Barnyard babies*
Deady, Kathleen W. *It's time!*
DePrisco, Dorothea. *What will I become?*
Doepker, David. *Animal babies*
   Farm babies
Dowson, Nick. *Tigress*
Doyle, Malachy. *Baby see, baby do!*
Dunrea, Olivier. *Little cub*
Edwards, Nicola. *Goodnight Baxter*
Edwards, Pamela Duncan. *Wake-up kisses*
Ellis, Gerry. *Natumi takes the lead*
Evans, Lezlie. *Who loves the little lamb?*
Falconer, Ian. *Olivia counts*
   Olivia's opposites
Falwell, Cathryn. *Pond babies*
Faulconer, Maria. *A mom for Umande*
Fearnley, Jan. *Just like you*
Fernandes, Eugenie. *Kitten's spring*
Fisher, Aileen Lucia. *You don't look like your mother*
Fisher, Doris. *Happy birthday to whooo?*
Fleming, Denise. *Mama cat has three kittens*
Fraggalosch, Audrey. *Trails above the tree line*
Fraser, Mary Ann. *How animal babies stay safe*
French, Jackie. *Diary of a baby wombat*
French, Vivian. *Growing frogs*

Freymann, Saxton. *Baby food*
Friedman, Mel. *Kitten castle*
Frost, Helen. *Wake up!*
Genechten, Guido van. *Kai-Mook*
Gentle, Victor. *Baby sharks*
George, Jean Craighead. *Look to the north*
Gibson, Ginger Foglesong. *Tiptoe Joe*
Godwin, Laura. *What the baby hears*
Goodhart, Pippa. *Pudgy, a puppy to love*
Gréban, Quentin. *Nestor*
Grindley, Sally. *Little Elephant Thunderfoot*
Guion, Melissa. *Baby penguins everywhere!*
Gulbis, Stephen. *Cowgirl Rosie and her five baby bison*
Halfmann, Janet. *Eggs 1, 2, 3*
Halls, Kelly Milner. *I bought a baby chicken*
Henkes, Kevin. *Kitten's first full moon*
Heos, Bridget. *What to expect when you're expecting hatchlings*
   What to expect when you're expecting joeys
Hewett, Joan. *A flamingo chick grows up*
   A giraffe calf grows up
   A harbor seal pup grows up
   A kangaroo joey grows up
   A koala joey grows up
   A monkey baby grows up
   A penguin chick grows up
   A tiger cub grows up
Hindley, Judy. *The best thing about a puppy*
Holt, Sharon. *Did my mother do that?*
Houran, Lori Haskins. *I will keep you safe and sound*
Howatt, Sandra J. *Sleepyheads*
Hulme, Joy N. *Easter babies*
Hutchins, Hazel. *One dark night*
Jackson, Ellen. *Beastly babies*
James, Betsy. *Tadpoles*
Jenkins, Steve. *My first day*
Johnson, Paul Brett. *The goose who went off in a huff*
Jonovitz, Marilyn. *Maybe, my baby*
Joosse, Barbara. *Higgledy-piggledy chicks*
Judge, Lita. *Born in the wild*
Kajikawa, Kimiko. *Close to you*
Kessler, Cristina. *Jubela*
Kimmelman, Leslie. *The three bully goats*
Kirk, David. *Oh So Tiny bunny*
Kirwan, Wednesday. *Baby loves to boogie!*
Krauss, Ruth. *The growing story*
Kuiper, Nannie. *Bailey the bear cub*
Kunhardt, Katharine. *Let's count the puppies*
Larsen, Mylisa. *If I were a kangaroo*
Lawrence, John. *This little chick*
Levine, Ellen. *Seababy*
Lewis, Kim. *Just like Floss*
   Little Baa
   Little calf
   Little lamb
   Little puppy
Llewellyn, Claire. *Crocodile*
   Duck
London, Jonathan. *Baby whale's journey*
   Little penguin
   Snuggle wuggle
McAllister, Angela. *Little Mist*
McClure, Nikki. *How to be a cat*
McLellan, Stephanie Simpson. *The chicken cat*
McMullan, Kate. *If you were my bunny*
   Supercat
McPhail, David. *Baby Pig Pig talks*
McPike, Elizabeth. *Little bitty friends*

McQuade, Jacqueline. *Big babies*
   Farm babies
   Small babies
   Snow babies
Magloff, Lisa. *Bear*
   Butterfly
   Duckling
   Elephant
   Frog
   Kitten
   Penguin
   Rabbit
Magoon, Scott. *Breathe*
Marciano, John Bemelmans. *Delilah*
Markle, Sandra. *Creepy, crawly baby bugs*
Morton-Shaw, Christine. *Wake up, sleepy bear!*
Murphy, Mary. *A kiss like this*
Murphy, Stuart J. *Pepper's journal*
Murray, Marjorie Dennis. *Little Wolf and the moon*
Nakamura, Katherine Riley. *Song of night*
National Wildlife Federation. *My first book of baby animals*
Nolan, Lucy A. *Jack Quack*
Numeroff, Laura Joffe. *What puppies do best*
Nyeu, Tao. *Bunny days*
O'Hair, Margaret. *My kitten*
Olson, David J. *The thunderstruck stork*
Otto, Carolyn. *Our puppies are growing*
Partis, Joanne. *Stripe*
Pfeffer, Wendy. *Mallard duck at Meadow View Pond*
Porter, Sue. *Parsnip*
Purmell, Ann. *Where wild babies sleep*
Radcliffe, Theresa. *Bashi, elephant baby*
Reasoner, Charles. *Animal babies!*
Robinson, Sue. *I want to play*
Roddie, Shen. *Not now, Mrs. Wolf*
Root, Phyllis. *Flip, flap, fly!*
   Oliver finds his way
Rose, Deborah Lee. *Ocean babies*
Rostoker-Gruber, Karen. *Bandit's surprise*
Ryder, Joanne. *Little panda*
Saltzberg, Barney. *Baby animal kisses*
Schneider, Howie. *Chewy Louie*
Schofield, Jennifer. *Animal babies in grasslands*
   Animal babies in polar lands
   Animal babies in ponds and rivers
   Animal babies in rain forests
Sheneman, Drew. *Nope!*
Shoulders, Michael. *Say Daddy!*
Sidman, Joyce. *Just us two*
Sierra, Judy. *Wild about you!*
Sturges, Philemon. *How do you make a baby smile?*
Swinburne, Stephen R. *Safe, warm, and snug*
Tafolla, Carmen. *Baby Coyote and the old woman / El coyotito y la viejita*
Tafuri, Nancy. *Five little chicks*
   I love you, little one
Talbott, Hudson. *It's all about me-ow*
Tanner, Suzy-Jane. *Tinyflock Nursery School*
Tatham, Betty. *Baby Sea Otter*
   Penguin chick
Thompson, Lauren. *Little Quack*
   Wee little bunny
Volkmann, Roy. *Curious kittens*
Waddell, Martin. *It's quacking time*
Walters, Catherine. *Are you there, Baby Bear?*
Ward, Jennifer. *Somewhere in the ocean*
Wilson, Karma. *What's in the egg, Little Pip?*
   Where is home, Little Pip?

Wormell, Mary. *Why not?*
Yolen, Jane. *Off we go!*
Yuly, Toni. *Night owl*
Zenz, Aaron. *Chuckling ducklings and baby animal friends*
Ziefert, Harriet. *A dozen ducklings lost and found*

Animals – baboons

Bustos, Eduardo. *Going ape!*
Bynum, Janie. *Altoona up north*
DeRubertis, Barbara. *Bobby Baboon's banana be-bop*
Horowitz, Dave. *Soon, Baboon, soon*
Olaleye, Isaac. *Bitter bananas*

Animals – badgers

Bagley, Jessixa. *Laundry day*
Brett, Jan. *Honey, honey — lion!*
Bright, Paul. *Grumpy Badger's Christmas*
Bunting, Eve. *Can you do this, Old Badger?*
   Little Badger, terror of the seven seas
   Little Badger's just-about birthday
Chiew, Suzanne. *When you need a friend*
Díaz, Katacha. *Badger at Sandy Ridge Road*
Grahame, Kenneth. *The wind in the willows*
Gravett, Emily. *Tidy*
Hiscock, Bruce. *Coyote and badger*
Hoban, Russell. *A baby sister for Frances*
   A bargain for Frances
   Bedtime for Frances
   Best friends for Frances
   A birthday for Frances
   Bread and jam for Frances
Isern, Susanna. *The lonely mailman*
Jenkins, Emily. *Tiger and Badger*
Johnston, Tony. *The badger and the magic fan*
Kasza, Keiko. *Badger's fancy meal*
Lester, Helen. *Boris and the worrisome wakies*
Linders, Clara. *The very best door of all*
Menchin, Scott. *What are you waiting for?*
Muller, Robin. *Badger's new house*
Odone, Jamison. *Honey badgers*
Oram, Hiawyn. *Badger's bad mood*
Potter, Beatrix. *The tale of Mr. Tod*
Saunders, Karen. *Baby Badger's wonderful night*
Schuurmans, Hilde. *Sydney won't swim*
Varley, Susan. *Badger's parting gifts*
Wells, Rosemary. *Hazel's amazing mother*
Weninger, Brigitte. *Davy, soccer star!*

Animals – bandicoots

Fox, Mem. *Hunwick's egg*

Animals – bats

Aesop. *Bat's big game*
Appelt, Kathi. *Bats around the clock*
   Bats on parade
Berk, Ari. *Nightsong*
Cannon, Janell. *Stellaluna*
Carr, Matt. *Superbat*
Davies, Nicola. *Bat loves the night*
Dyer, Sarah. *Batty*
Edwards, Pamela Duncan. *Ms. Bitsy Bat's kindergarten*
Gerber, Carole. *Little red bat*
Gibbons, Gail. *Bats*
Jennings, Patrick. *Bat and Rat*

Lies, Brian. *Bats at the ballgame*
  Bats at the beach
  Bats at the library
  Bats in the band
Lunde, Darrin. *Hello, bumblebee bat*
Maestro, Betsy. *Bats*
Markle, Sandra. *Bats: biggest! littlest!*
  Little lost bat
Mayr, Diane. *Littlebat's Halloween story*
Meisel, Paul. *Good night, bat! good morning, squirrel!*
Mitchard, Jacquelyn. *Baby bat's lullaby*
Quackenbush, Robert M. *Batbaby*
Waring, Geoff. *Oscar and the bat*
Wilson, Steve. *Hedgehugs: autumn hide-and-squeak*

Animals – bears

Abbott, Bud. *Who's on first?*
Agee, Jon. *Milo's hat trick*
Alborough, Jez. *Ice cream bear*
  It's the bear
  My friend bear
  Where's my teddy?
Alexander, Martha G. *And my mean old mother will be sorry, Blackboard Bear*
  Blackboard Bear
  I sure am glad to see you, Blackboard Bear
  I'll never share you, Blackboard Bear
  We're in big trouble, Blackboard Bear
  You're a genius, Blackboard Bear
Alter, Anna. *Abigail spells*
Altes, Marta. *My grandpa*
Anglund, Joan Walsh. *The cowboy's Christmas*
Appelt, Kathi. *Where, where is Swamp Bear?*
Apperley, Dawn. *Blossom and Boo*
  Blossom and Boo stay up late
Arnold, Marsha Diane. *Lost. found*
Arnosky, Jim. *Every autumn comes the bear*
Aruego, José. *Splash!*
Asch, Frank. *Bear shadow*
  Bear's bargain
  Good night, Baby Bear
  Goodbye house
  Happy birthday, moon!
  Just like daddy
  Moonbear
  Moonbear's books
  Moonbear's canoe
  Moonbear's dream
  Moonbear's friend
  Moonbear's pet
  Mooncake
  Moondance
  Moongame
  Pizza
  Popcorn
  Sand cake
  Skyfire
Atkinson, Cale. *Explorers of the wild*
Austin, Margot. *A friend for Growl Bear*
Banks, Kate. *The bear in the book*
Bardill, Linard. *The great golden thing*
Barner, Bob. *Bears! bears! bears!*
Barnett, Mac. *Places to be*
Bauer, Marion Dane. *Jason's bears*
The bear
Beaty, Andrea. *Artist Ted*
  Doctor Ted
  Firefighter Ted

Becker, Bonny. *A bedtime for Bear*
  A birthday for Bear
  A Christmas for Bear
  A library book for Bear
  The sniffles for Bear
  A visitor for Bear
Bedford, David. *Big bears can!*
  I've seen Santa!
Beebe, Katy. *Brother Hugo and the bear*
Bentley, Dawn. *Fuzzy bear*
  Fuzzy Bear's potty book
Bentley, Jonathan. *Where is Bear?*
Benton, Jim. *The end (almost)*
Berenstain, Jan. *The Berenstain bears trim the tree*
Berenstain, Stan and Jan. *The bear detectives*
  Bears in the night
  Bears on wheels
  The Berenstain bears and mama's new job
  The Berenstain bears and the bad dream
  The Berenstain bears and the bad habit
  The Berenstain bears and the big road race
  The Berenstain bears and the double dare
  The Berenstain bears and the ghost of the forest
  The Berenstain bears and the messy room
  The Berenstain bears and the missing dinosaur bone
  The Berenstain bears and the missing honey
  The Berenstain bears and the prize pumpkin
  The Berenstain bears and the real Easter eggs
  The Berenstain bears and the sitter
  The Berenstain bears and the slumber party
  The Berenstain bears and the spooky old tree
  The Berenstain bears and the trouble with friends
  The Berenstain bears and the truth
  The Berenstain bears and the week at grandma's
  The Berenstain bears and the wild, wild honey
  The Berenstain bears and too much birthday
  The Berenstain bears and too much junk food
  The Berenstain bears and too much TV
  The Berenstain bears and too much vacation
  The Berenstain bears blaze a trail
  The Berenstain bears' Christmas tree
  The Berenstain bears' counting book
  The Berenstain bears don't pollute anymore
  The Berenstain bears forget their manners
  The Berenstain bears get in a fight
  The Berenstain bears get stage fright
  The Berenstain bears get the gimmies
  The Berenstain bears go out for the team
  The Berenstain bears go to camp
  The Berenstain bears go to school
  The Berenstain bears go to the doctor
  The Berenstain bears in the dark
  The Berenstain bears learn about strangers
  The Berenstain bears meet Santa Bear
  The Berenstain bears' moving day
  The Berenstain bears no girls allowed
  The Berenstain bears on the moon
  The Berenstain bears ready, set, go!
  The Berenstain bears' report card trouble
  The Berenstain bears' science fair
  The Berenstain bears' that stump must go!
  The Berenstain bears trick or treat
  The Berenstain bears' trouble at school
  The Berenstain bears' trouble with money
  The Berenstain bears' trouble with pets
  The Berenstain bears visit the dentist
  The Berenstains' B book
  He bear, she bear
  Inside outside upside down

Glass, Andrew. *Bewildered for three days*
Glicksman, Caroline. *Eric the math bear*
Gliori, Debi. *Can I have a hug?*
　Mr. Bear to the rescue
　Mr. Bear's new baby
Godwin, Jane. *Bear make den*
Goodings, Lennie. *When you grow up*
Goossens, Philippe. *Knock! knock! knock! who's there?*
Gorbachev, Valeri. *Me too!*
Gordon, Gus. *Somewhere else*
Gravett, Emily. *Bear and Hare: share!*
　Bear and Hare: snow!
　Bear and Hare go fishing
　Bear and Hare—where's Bear?
　Orange pear apple bear
Greene, Rhonda Gowler. *Firebears*
Grimm, Jacob and Wilhelm. *As luck would have it*
　Rose Red and the bear prince
Grindley, Sally. *What are friends for?*
　What will I do without you?
Guiberson, Brenda Z. *Moon bear*
Hague, Kathleen. *Calendarbears*
　Ten little bears
Hansen, Felicity. *The first bear*
Harley, Bill. *Bear's all-night party*
Harrison, Joanna. *Grizzly dad*
Haseley, Dennis. *A story for Bear*
Haughton, Chris. *Goodnight everyone*
Hayes, Geoffrey. *Patrick at the circus*
Hayes, Karel. *The summer visitors*
　The winter visitors
Heap, Sue. *Four friends in the garden*
Hegarty, Patricia. *Bug Bear*
Helquist, Brett. *Bedtime for Bear*
Henkes, Kevin. *Old Bear*
Hest, Amy. *Are you sure, Mother Bear?*
　Kiss good night
　When you meet a bear on Broadway
　You can do it, Sam
Higgins, Ryan T. *Hotel Bruce*
　Mother Bruce
Hillenbrand, Will. *All for a dime! a Bear and Mole story*
　Kite day
　Off we go! a Bear and Mole story
　Spring is here
Hirschi, Ron. *Our three bears*
Ho, Jannie. *Bear and Chicken*
Hodgkinson, Leigh. *Goldilocks and just one bear*
Horowitz, Ruth. *Are we still friends?*
Horvath, David. *Bossy bear*
　Just like Bossy Bear
Hudson, Katy. *Bear and Duck*
Imai, Ayano. *Mr. Brown's fantastic hat*
Irwin, Michael. *Bears in my bed*
Ismail, Yasmeen. *Imagine that!*
Itaya, Satoshi. *Buttons and Bo*
Jackson, Gwen. *Lump Lump and the blanket of dreams*
James, Ann. *Bird and Bear*
Janice. *Little Bear marches in the St. Patrick's Day parade*
　Little Bear's Christmas
　Little Bear's Thanksgiving
Jeffers, Oliver. *The great paper caper*
Jennings, Sharon. *Bearcub and Mama*
John, Jory. *Come home already!*
　Goodnight already!
　I love you already!

Johnson, D. B. *Henry builds a cabin*
　Henry climbs a mountain
　Henry works
　Henry's night
Johnson, Mariana Ruiz. *I know a bear*
Jonas, Ann. *Two bear cubs*
Joosse, Barbara. *Nikolai, the only bear*
　Roawr!
Jorgensen, Gail. *Gotcha!*
Jukes, Mavis. *You're a bear*
Kaplanoglou, Mania. *Mama Bear, Little Bear*
Kasparavicius, Kestutis. *The bear family's world tour Christmas*
Kasza, Keiko. *Don't laugh, Joe*
　The mightiest
Katz, Susan B. *ABC school's for me!*
Keller, Holly. *Jacob's tree*
Kempter, Christa. *Wally and Mae*
Ketteman, Helen. *If Beaver had a fever*
Kherdian, David. *Come back, Moon*
Kimmel, Eric A. *Hanukkah bear*
Kinsey-Warnock, Natalie. *The bear that heard crying*
Klassen, Jon. *I want my hat back*
Kolar, Bob. *Big kicks*
Kornell, Max. *Bear with me*
Krauss, Ruth. *Bears*
Kroll, Virginia L. *On the way to kindergarten*
Kuiper, Nannie. *Bailey the bear cub*
Lamb, Albert. *The abandoned lighthouse*
　Sam's winter hat
　Tell me the day backwards
Landa, Norbert. *Little Bear and the wishing tree*
Langreuter, Jutta. *Little Bear and the big fight*
　Little Bear brushes his teeth
　Little Bear goes to kindergarten
　Little Bear won't go to bed
Langsen, Richard C. *When someone in the family drinks too much*
Lansky, Vicki. *It's not your fault, KoKo Bear*
Lasky, Kathryn. *Fourth of July bear*
Lee, Michelle. *Play with me!*
Lewis, Paeony. *I'll always love you*
Lipan, Sabine. *Mom, there's a bear at the door*
Litchfield, David. *The bear and the piano*
Little Bear's Valentine
Liu, Cynthea. *Bike on, Bear!*
Livingston, A. A. *B. Bear and Lolly: catch that cookie!*
　B. Bear and Lolly: off to school
Lobel, Gillian. *Little Honey Bear and the smiley moon*
London, Jonathan. *Count the ways, Little Brown Bear*
　Do your ABC's, Little Brown Bear
　Honey Paw and Lightfoot
Loney, Andrea J. *Bunnybear*
Long, Ethan. *Lion and Tiger and Bear*
Lowell, Susan. *Dusty Locks and the three bears*
Lucas, David. *Something to do*
McBratney, Sam. *There, there*
Maccarone, Grace. *The three bears ABC*
McCloskey, Robert. *Blueberries for Sal*
McCully, Emily Arnold. *My real family*
MacDonald, Alan. *Beware of the bears!*
McFarland, Clive. *A bed for Bear*
McGinness, Suzanne. *My bear Griz*
McGowan, Jayme. *One bear extraordinaire*
Mack, Jeff. *Who needs a bath?*
　Who wants a hug?
McKinlay, Meg. *No bears*
McMullan, Kate. *Papa's song*

McPhail, David. *The bear's toothache*
  Big Brown Bear goes to town
  Big Brown Bear's birthday surprise
  Big Brown Bear's up and down day
  Budgie and Boo
  Drawing lessons from a bear
  Emma in charge
  Emma's pet
  Emma's vacation
  Henry Bear's Christmas
  Henry Bear's park
  I promise
  Lost
  Tinker and Tom and the Star Baby
Magloff, Lisa. *Bear*
Mahoney, Daniel J. *A really good snowman*
Marcero, Deborah. *Ursa's light*
Martin, Bill, Jr.. *Baby bear, baby bear, what do you see?*
  Brown bear, brown bear, what do you see?
Martin, David. *Shh! bears sleeping*
Martin, Emily Winfield. *The littlest family's big day*
Marzollo, Jean. *Little Bear, you're a star!*
Mattick, Lindsay. *Finding Winnie*
Melling, David. *Don't worry, Douglas!*
  Hugless Douglas
Merlin, Christophe. *Under the hood*
Miles, Victoria. *Old Mother Bear*
Miller, Ruth. *The bear on the bed*
Miller, Virginia. *Be gentle!*
  I love you just the way you are
  In a minute!
  On your potty!
  Ten red apples
Minarik, Else Holmelund. *Little Bear's new friend*
Mitton, Tony. *Snowy Bear*
  A very curious bear
Monari, Manuela. *Zero kisses for me!*
Moss, Miriam. *A babysitter for Billy Bear*
  Bare bear
  Matty in a mess!
  Matty takes off!
Mozelle, Shirley. *The bear upstairs*
Murphy, Jill. *Peace at last*
Murphy, Stuart J. *A fair bear share*
Na, Il Sung. *Bird, balloon, Bear*
  Welcome home, Bear
Nash, Ogden. *The adventures of Isabel*, ill. by James Marshall
  The adventures of Isabel, ill. by Bridget Starr Taylor
Nastro, Caroline. *The bear who couldn't sleep*
Naylor, Phyllis Reynolds. *Please do feed the bears*
Nelson, Kadir. *Baby Bear*
Nesbitt, Kenn. *More bears!*
Nolan, Janet. *A Father's Day thank you*
Novak, Matt. *Jazzbo and Googy*
  Jazzbo goes to school
Numeroff, Laura Joffe. *Otis and Sydney and the best birthday ever*
Nyeu, Tao. *Bunny days*
OHora, Zachariah. *The not so quiet library*
O'Keefe, Susan Heyboer. *Baby day*
Oldland, Nicholas. *Big bear hug*
  Walk on the wild side
O'Mara, Carmel. *Good morning*
  Good night
  Rainy day
  Sunny day
Oram, Hiawyn. *Going to Grandpa's*

  Kiss it better
Ørdal, Stina Langlo. *Princess Aasta*
Ormerod, Jan. *Maudie and Bear*
Pamintuan, Macky. *Twelve haunted rooms of Halloween*
Parenteau, Shirley. *Bears and a birthday*
  Bears in a band
  Bears in beds
  Bears in the bath
  Bears in the snow
  Bears on chairs
Parker, Victoria. *Bearum scarum*
Peek, Merle. *Mary wore her red dress and Henry wore his green sneakers*
Peet, Bill. *Big bad Bruce*
Percival, Tom. *Herman's letter*
Peters, Lisa Westberg. *Sleepyhead bear*
Petty, Dini. *The queen, the bear and the bumblebee*
Pfister, Marcus. *Make a wish, Honey Bear!*
Pham, LeUyen. *The bear who wasn't there*
Pilutti, Deb. *Bear and Squirrel are friends . . . yes, really!*
Pinder, Eric. *How to share with a bear*
Pinkwater, Daniel. *Bear and Bunny*
  Bear in love
  Bear's Picture
  Bongo Larry
Pitcher, Caroline. *Are you spring?*
Prasadam-Halls, Smriti. *I love you night and day*
Pringle, Laurence P. *Bear hug*
Rayner, Catherine. *The bear who shared*
Reed, Lynn Rowe. *Bear's big breakfast*
Reider, Katja. *The big little sneeze*
Rim, Sujean. *Chee-Kee*
Ritchie, Alison. *Me and my dad!*
  Me and my mom!
  What Bear likes best!
Robinson, Michelle. *A beginner's guide to bear spotting*
Rock, Brian. *With all my heart*
Rockwell, Anne. *Backyard bear*
  Boats
  First comes spring
  Morgan plays soccer
Roddie, Shen. *Sandbear*
Rodman, Mary Ann. *Surprise soup*
Rogers, Gregory. *The boy, the bear, the baron, the bard*
  Midsummer knight
Root, Phyllis. *Oliver finds his way*
Rosales, Melodye Benson. *Leola and the honeybears*
Rosen, Michael. *Bear flies high*
  Bear's day out
  We're going on a bear hunt
Rouillard, Wendy. *Barnaby's bunny*
Rueda, Claudia. *No*
Russo, Marisabina. *Peter is just a baby*
Ruzzier, Sergio. *Bear and Bee*
  Too busy
Ryder, Joanne. *Bear of my heart*
  Big bear ball
Rylant, Cynthia. *Bear day*
San Souci, Robert D. *Two bear cubs: a Miwok legend from California's Yosemite Valley*
Sarcone-Roach, Julia. *The bear ate your sandwich*
Sayre, April Pulley. *Eat like a bear*
Scheffler, Ursel. *Taking care of Sister Bear*
  Who has time for Little Bear?
Schertle, Alice. *Very hairy bear*
Schoenherr, Ian. *Don't spill the beans!*

Schoenherr, John. *Bear*
Schubert, Ingrid. *Bear's eggs*
Senshu, Noriko. *Sonny's dream*
Shannon, George. *Lizard's song*
Sharmat, Marjorie Weinman. *I'm terrific*
Sherry, Kevin. *Acorns everywhere!*
Shoulders, Michael. *Goodnight Baby Bear*
 Say Daddy!
Skofield, James. *Bear and Bird*
Smallman, Steve. *My dad!*
Smith, Ben Bailey. *I am Bear*
Smith, Lane. *A perfect day*
Soman, David. *Three bears in a boat*
Spelman, Cornelia Maude. *Mama and Daddy Bear's
 divorce*
 When I care about others
 When I feel scared
Sperring, Mark. *How many sleeps 'til my birthday?*
Spohn, Kate. *Snow play*
Stanley, Diane. *Goldie and the three bears*
Starin, Liz. *Splashdance*
Stead, Philip C. *Bear has a story to tell*
Stein, David Ezra. *Leaves*
 Ol' Mama Squirrel
Stevens, Janet. *Tops and bottoms*
Stewart, Amber. *Bedtime for Button*
Stewart, Joel. *Addis Berner Bear forgets*
Stickland, Paul. *Bears*
Stower, Adam. *Silly doggy*
Stubbs, Lisa. *Lily and Bear*
 Lily and Bear: grumpy feet
Tafuri, Nancy. *Mama's little bears*
Taylor, Sean. *A brave bear*
 The grizzly bear with the frizzly hair
 The snowbear
Teckentrup, Britta. *Big smelly bear*
Thorpe, Kiki. *A comfy, cozy Thanksgiving*
 Time to cha-cha-cha!
The three bears *Goatilocks and the three bears*
 Goldilocks
 Goldilocks and the three bears, ill. by Jan Brett
 Goldilocks and the three bears, ill. by Mark
 Buehner
 Goldilocks and the three bears, ill. by Lorinda
 Bryan Cauley
 Goldilocks and the three bears, ill. by Emma
 Chichester Clark
 Goldilocks and the three bears, ill. by Valeri
 Gorbachev
 Goldilocks and the three bears, ill. by Steven
 Guarnaccia
 Goldilocks and the three bears, ill. by David
 McPhail
 Goldilocks and the three bears, ill. by James
 Marshall
 Goldilocks and the three bears, ill. by Gerda Muller
 Goldilocks and the three bears, ill. by Gennady
 Spirin
 Goldilocks and the three bears, ill. by Janet Stevens
 The three bears, ill. by Byron Barton
 The three bears, ill. by Paul Galdone
 The 3 bears and Goldilocks
Tibi, Marie. *The bear who didn't want to miss
 Christmas*
Tolhurst, Marilyn. *Somebody and the three Blairs*
Trapani, Iza. *The bear went over the mountain*
 Row, row, row your boat
Turkle, Brinton. *Deep in the forest*
Vainio, Pirkko. *The best of friends*

Van Buren, David. *I love you as big as the world*
Van Kampen, Vlasta. *Bear tales*
van Lieshout, Maria. *Tumble!*
Van Woerkom, Dorothy. *Becky and the bear*
Verburg, Bonnie. *The kiss box*
Vincent, Gabrielle. *Ernest and Celestine at the circus*
 Ernest and Celestine's picnic
 Merry Christmas, Ernest and Celestine
Waddell, Martin. *Can't you sleep, Little Bear?*
 Good job, Little Bear!
 Let's go home, Little Bear
 Night night Cuddly Bear
 Sleep tight, Little Bear
 Snow bears
 Yum, yum, yummy
Walker, Sally M. *Winnie*
Wallace, John. *Anything for you*
Wallace, Nancy Elizabeth. *Pond walk*
 Rocks! rocks! rocks!
 Seeds! seeds! seeds!
 Shells! shells! shells!
Wallen, Ila. *The moon in my room*
Walters, Catherine. *Are you there, Baby Bear?*
 Play gently, Alfie Bear
 When will it be spring?
Walton, Rick. *The bear came over to my house*
Ward, Lynd. *The biggest bear*
Wardlaw, Lee. *The chair where bear sits*
Wargin, Kathy-jo. *Scare a bear*
Watanabe, Shigeo. *Ice cream is falling!*
 Let's go swimming
 Where's my daddy?
Watts, Frances. *Kisses for Daddy*
Weaver, Jo. *Little One*
Wechterowicz, Przemyslaw. *Hug me, please!*
Weigelt, Udo. *Bear's last journey*
Weinberg, Larry. *The Forgetful Bears help Santa*
Wells, Rosemary. *The bear went over the mountain*
Weston, Carrie. *The new bear at school*
Wheeler, Lisa. *Ugly pie*
Williams, Sam. *Angel's Christmas cookies*
Wilson, Karma. *Bear counts*
 Bear feels scared
 Bear feels sick
 Bear says thanks
 Bear sees colors
 Bear stays up for Christmas
 Bear's loose tooth
Winters, Kay. *The bears go to school*
Winthrop, Elizabeth. *Bear and Mrs. Duck*
 Bear's Christmas surprise
Wolff, Ashley. *Baby Bear counts one*
 Baby Bear sees blue
 Where, oh where, is Baby Bear?
Wood, Audrey. *Oh my baby bear!*
Wright, Cliff. *Bear and ball*
 Bear and kite
Wright, Maureen. *Sleep, Big Bear, sleep!*
 Sneeze, Big Bear, sneeze
Yee, Wong Herbert. *Big black bear*
Yektai, Niki. *Bears at the beach*
 Bears in pairs
Yolen, Jane. *Baby Bear's big dreams*
 Baby Bear's books
 Baby Bear's chairs
 Sister Bear
 The three bears holiday rhyme book
Yoon, Salina. *Bear's big day*
 Found

Stormy night
Zalben, Jane Breskin. *Beni's first Chanukah*
    Beni's first wedding
Zehler, Antonia. *Two fine ladies*
Zoehfeld, Kathleen Weidner. *Apples, apples*

Animals – beavers

Arnosky, Jim. *Beaver pond, moose pond*
Bagley, Jessixa. *Boats for Papa*
Bentley, Dawn. *Busy little beaver*
Cooper, Elisha. *Beaver is lost*
George, William T. *Beaver at Long Pond*
Gibbons, Gail. *Beavers*
Harper, Charise Mericle. *When Randolph turned
    rotten*
Harrison, Hannah E. *My friend Maggie*
Johnson, Amy Crane. *Mason moves away / Mason
    se muda*
Kuiper, Nannie. *Bravo, brave beavers*
Long, Heather. *Max and Milo go to sleep!*
Markle, Sandra. *Build, beaver, build!*
Oldland, Nicholas. *The busy beaver*
    Walk on the wild side
Schubert, Ingrid. *There's always room for one more*
Van Laan, Nancy. *Moose tales*
Weigelt, Udo. *Old Beaver*

Animals – bison *see* Animals – buffaloes

Animals – bonobos

Napoli, Donna Jo. *Bobby the bold*

Animals – brush wolves *see* Animals – coyotes

Animals – buffaloes

Arnosky, Jim. *Grandfather Buffalo*
Baker, Olaf. *Where the buffaloes begin*
Bruchac, Joseph. *Buffalo song*
Fern, Tracey E. *Buffalo music*
George, Jean Craighead. *The buffalo are back*
Goble, Paul. *Her seven brothers*
    The return of the buffaloes
Gulbis, Stephen. *Cowgirl Rosie and her five baby
    bison*
Ravishankar, Anushka. *Elephants never forget!*
Vernick, Audrey. *Is your buffalo ready for
    kindergarten?*
    Teach your buffalo to play drums
Waldman, Neil. *They came from the Bronx*
Wiebe, Rudy. *Hidden buffalo*

Animals – bulls, cows

Aliki. *Milk from cow to carton*
Alsdurf, Phyllis. *It's milking time*
Baehr, Patricia. *Boo Cow*
Becker, Suzy. *Manny's cows*
Borgo, Lacy. *Big Mama's baby*
Bunting, Eve. *The baby shower*
Busch, Miriam. *Raisin, the littlest cow*
Chaconas, Dori. *When cows come home for Christmas*
Chambers, Angela. *How now, cow?*
Climo, Shirley. *The Irish Cinderlad*
Cordsen, Carol Foskett. *Market day*
Cronin, Doreen. *Click, clack, moo*

Cutbill, Andy. *The cow that laid an egg*
    First week at cow school
Ditchfield, Christin. *Cowlick!*
Doyle, Malachy. *Cow*
Drummond, Ree. *Charlie and the new baby*
Duffield, Katy. *Farmer McPeepers and his missing
    milk cows*
Esbaum, Jill. *I am cow, hear me moo!*
Flanagan, Alice K. *Raising cows on the Koebels' farm*
Fleming, Denise. *The cow who clucked*
Fox, Mem. *A particular cow*
Gibbons, Gail. *Yippee-yay!*
Gollub, Matthew. *Gobble, quack, moon*
Gomi, Taro. *Spring is here*
Hamilton, Arlene. *Only a cow*
Helakoski, Leslie. *Fair cow*
Hill, Ros. *Shamoo*
Himmelman, John. *Cows to the rescue*
Hoberman, Mary Ann. *Mrs. O'Leary's cow*
Hume, Lachie. *Clancy the courageous cow*
Hurd, Thacher. *Moo Cow Kaboom!*
Johnson, Paul Brett. *The cow who wouldn't come
    down*
Ketteman, Helen. *Bubba the cowboy prince*
Kinerk, Robert. *Clorinda*
    Clorinda plays baseball!
    Clorinda takes flight
Korchek, Lori. *Adventures of Cow, too*
Kulling, Monica. *Grant and Tillie go walking*
LaRochelle, David. *Moo!*
Leaf, Munro. *The story of Ferdinand the bull*
Lewis, Kim. *Little calf*
Lodge, Jo. *Moo Moo goes to the city*
Lowell, Susan. *Little Red Cowboy Hat*
Macaulay, David. *Black and white*
Merino, Gemma. *The cow who climbed a tree*
Milgrim, David. *Cows can't fly*
Miller, Tim. *Moo Moo in a tutu*
Milway, Katie Smith. *Cappuccina goes to town*
Mortensen, Lori. *Cindy Moo*
Murphy, Andy. *Out and about at the dairy farm*
Neubecker, Robert. *Courage of the blue boy*
Newman, Jeff. *Reginald*
Newman, Marlene. *Myron's magic cow*
Ohi, Ruth. *Chicken, Pig, Cow and the class pet*
    Chicken, Pig, Cow horse around
    Chicken, Pig, Cow's first fight
Palatini, Margie. *Boo-hoo moo*
    Moo who?
Pedersen, Janet. *Millie wants to play*
Peterson, Cris. *Amazing grazing*
    Extra cheese, please!
Plourde, Lynn. *Only cows allowed!*
Raschka, Chris. *Cowy cow*
Root, Phyllis. *Kiss the cow*
Ross, Fiona. *Chilly Milly Moo*
Schertle, Alice. *How now, brown cow?*
Schnitzler, Pattie L. *Widdermaker*
Schuh, Mari C. *Cows on the farm*
Seeger, Laura Vaccaro. *Bully*
Shaffer, Jody Jensen. *Prudence the part-time cow*
Shannon, George. *The Secret Chicken Club*
Smith, Linda. *When Moon fell down*
Souders, Taryn. *Whole-y cow!*
Speed, Toby. *Two cool cows*
Steffensmeier, Alexander. *Millie and the big rescue*
    Millie in the snow
    Millie waits for the mail
Stevens, Janet. *Find a cow now!*

Thomas, Jan. *A birthday for Cow!*
  Is everyone ready for fun?
Weis, Carol. *When the cows got loose*
Wheeler, Lisa. *Sixteen cows*
Willis, Jeanne. *Misery Moo*
Wilson, Karma. *The cow loves cookies*
  Sakes alive!

Animals – camels

Alsenas, Linas. *Peanut*
Carryl, Charles E. *The camel's lament*
Kipling, Rudyard. *How the camel got his hump*
Manuel, Lynn. *Camels always do*
Peet, Bill. *Pamela Camel*
Thury, Frederick. *The last straw*

Animals – caribou *see* Animals – reindeer

Animals – cats

Abley, Mark. *Ghost cat*
Adoff, Arnold. *Daring Dog and Captain Cat*
Aesop. *Belling the cat*
  Town mouse, country mouse
Alexander, Lloyd. *The house Gobbaleen*
  How the cat swallowed thunder
Aliki. *Tabby*
Allenby, Victoria. *Nat the cat can sleep like that*
Almond, David. *Kate, the cat and the moon*
Alter, Anna. *Estelle and Lucy*
Anderson, Airlie. *Cat's colors*
Appelt, Kathi. *The Alley Cat's Meow*
Apple, Margot. *Brave Martha*
Aralan, Haydé. *Milton*
  Milton's Christmas
Arnold, Katya. *Meow!*
Arnold, Marsha Diane. *Metro cat*
Asch, Frank. *Mr. Maxwell's mouse*
  Mrs. Marlowe's mice
Asher, Sandy. *Stella's dancing days*
Austin, Mike. *Countdown with Milo*
Austin, Patricia. *The cat who loved Mozart*
Aylesworth, Jim. *Mother Halverson's new cat*
Baeten, Lieve. *Happy birthday, Little Witch!*
Bailey, Linda. *Stanley's little sister*
Bailey, Mary Bryant. *Jeoffry's Christmas*
Balian, Lorna. *Leprechauns never lie*
Banks, Kate. *City cat*
Barbero, Maria. *The bravest mouse*
Barrett, Ron. *Cats got talent*
Bartoletti, Susan Campbell. *Nobody's nosier than a cat*
Barton, Byron. *My house*
  The wee little woman
Beames, Margaret. *Night cat*
Beaton, Clare. *One moose, twenty mice*
Bechtold, Lisze. *Edna's tale*
Berger, Joe. *My special one and only*
Bergman, Tamar. *Where is?*
Berry, Lynne. *The curious demise of a contrary cat*
The best cat in the world
Bibbel, Mark. *Oh, Harry!*
Birnbaum, Abe. *Green eyes*
Blackstone, Stella. *Cleo and Caspar*
  Cleo in the snow
  Cleo on the move
  Cleo the cat
  Cleo's alphabet book

  Cleo's color book
  Cleo's counting book
  Come here, Cleo
Bloom, Becky. *Crackers*
Bogan, Paulette. *Momma's magical purse*
Borando, Silvia. *Black cat, white cat*
  The cat book
Bowman, Patty. *The amazing Hamweenie*
Boxall, Ed. *Francis the scaredy cat*
Boyer, Cécile. *Woof meow tweet-tweet*
Bradford, Karleen. *You can't rush a cat*
Bramsen, Carin. *Hey, duck!*
  Just a duck?
Brett, Jan. *Annie and the wild animals*
  Comet's nine lives
Brimner, Larry Dane. *Cat on wheels*
Brown, Margaret Wise. *Sneakers, the seaside cat*
Brown, Ruth. *Gracie the lighthouse cat*
  Holly, the true story of a cat
  The tale of two mice
Browne, Anthony. *Little Beauty*
Bruel, Nick. *Bad Kitty*
  A Bad Kitty Christmas
  Bad Kitty, scaredy-cat
  Poor puppy
Bryan, Ashley. *The cat's purr*
Bunting, Eve. *Ghost cat*
  Mouse island
Burningham, John. *It's a secret!*
Busch, Miriam. *Lion, lion*
Butterworth, Nick. *Jasper's beanstalk*
  Jingle bells
Cabrera, Jane. *Kitty's cuddles*
Calhoun, Mary. *Blue-ribbon Henry*
  Cross-country cat
  Henry the Christmas cat
  Henry the sailor cat
  High-wire Henry
  Hot-air Henry
Caple, Kathy. *Hillary to the rescue*
Capucilli, Alyssa Satin. *Biscuit wants to play*
  Happy birthday, Biscuit!
  Little spotted cat
  Mrs. McTats and her houseful of cats
  Only my mom and me
Carle, Eric. *Have you seen my cat?*
Carlson, Nancy. *Arnie and the skateboard gang*
Carmody, Isobelle. *Magic night*
Casanova, Mary. *Some cat!*
Cash, Megan Montague. *What makes the seasons?*
Catalanotto, Peter. *Kitten red, yellow, blue*
Cazet, Denys. *Never spit on your shoes*
Cecka, Melanie. *Violet comes to stay*
  Violet goes to the country
Chan, Ruth. *Georgie's best bad day*
  Where's the party?
Chichester Clark, Emma. *Plenty of love to go around*
  Will and Squill
Chorao, Kay. *Knock at the door and other baby action rhymes*
Christian, Mary Blount. *If not for the calico cat*
Chwast, Seymour. *Harry, I need you!*
Clements, Andrew. *Dolores and the big fire*
Coffey, Maria. *A cat adrift*
Cole, Henry. *Spot, the cat*
Cole, Joanna. *My new kitten*
Collington, Peter. *Clever cat*
Cooper, Elisha. *Big cat, little cat*
  Magic thinks big

Cooper, Helen. *Delicious!*
　A pipkin of pepper
Côté, Geneviève. *Mr. King's machine*
Cox, Judy. *One is a feast for Mouse*
Crawley, Dave. *Cat poems*
Crimi, Carolyn. *Dear Tabby*
　Tessa's tip-tapping toes
Crow, Kristyn. *Skeleton cat*
Crum, Shutta. *Thunder-Boomer!*
Cushman, Doug. *Space cat*
Czekaj, Jef. *Cat secrets*
da Costa, Deborah. *Snow in Jerusalem*
Dahl, Michael. *Nap time for Kitty*
Davis, Anne. *No dogs allowed!*
Davis, David. *Jazz cats*
Day, Nancy Raines. *A kitten's year*
Dean, James. *Pete the Cat: the wheels on the bus*
　Pete the Cat: twinkle, twinkle, little star
　Pete the Cat: Valentine's Day is cool
　Pete the Cat and his magic sunglasses
　Pete the Cat and the bedtime blues
　Pete the Cat and the new guy
Dean, Kim. *Pete the Cat and the missing cupcakes*
Demas, Corinne. *Here comes trouble!*
Desmond, Jenni. *Red cat blue cat*
Dick Whittington and his cat. *Dick Whittington and his cat*, ill. by Marcia Brown
　Dick Whittington and his cat, ill. by Mélisande Potter
Dickson, Louise. *The vanishing cat*
Dodd, Emma. *I don't want a cool cat!*
Donaldson, Julia. *Tabby McTat, the musical cat*
Dormer, Frank W. *Click!*
Downey, Lynn. *Matilda's humdinger*
Doyle, Malachy. *Storm cats*
Duncan, Lois. *I walk at night*
Eaton, Jason Carter. *The catawampus cat*
Egan, Tim. *Roasted peanuts*
Egielski, Richard. *Slim and Jim*
Ehlert, Lois. *Boo to you!*
　Feathers for lunch
　Top cat
Einhorn, Edward. *A very improbable story*
Elliott, David. *Knitty Kitty*
Elschner, Geraldine. *Mark's messy room*
Elsdale, Bob. *Mac side up*
Emberley, Rebecca. *Mice on ice*
Esbaum, Jill. *Tom's tweet*
Ets, Marie Hall. *Mr. T. W. Anthony Woo*
Ewert, Marcus. *Mummy cat*
Faglia, Matteo. *Happy birthday, I'm 3*
Farish, Terry. *The cat who liked potato soup*
Feiffer, Jules. *Rupert can dance*
Fernandes, Eugenie. *Kitten's spring*
　Kitten's winter
Flake, Sharon G. *You are not a cat!*
Fleming, Candace. *Bulldozer helps out*
Fleming, Denise. *Buster*
　Mama cat has three kittens
Fletcher, Ashlee. *My dog, my cat*
Florian, Douglas. *Bow wow meow meow, it's rhyming cats and dogs*
Ford, Bernette. *Ballet Kitty*
Foreman, Michael. *Cat in the manger*
　Friends
Fox, Diane. *The cat, the dog, Little Red, the exploding eggs, the wolf, and Grandma*
Franco, Betsy. *A curious collection of cats*
Freeman, Tor. *Olive and the bad mood*
　Olive and the big secret
French, Vivian. *A present for mom*
Friedman, Laurie. *Ruby Valentine and the sweet surprise*
Friedman, Mel. *Kitten castle*
Friend, Catherine. *The perfect nest*
Fuller, Sandy F. *My cat, coon cat*
Gág, Wanda. *Millions of cats*
Galindo, Renata. *My new mom and me*
Gall, Chris. *Dog vs. Cat*
Gantos, Jack. *Back to school for Rotten Ralph*
　Happy birthday, Rotten Ralph
　The nine lives of Rotten Ralph
　Not so Rotten Ralph
　Rotten Ralph
　Rotten Ralph's rotten Christmas
　Rotten Ralph's rotten romance
　Rotten Ralph's show and tell
　Rotten Ralph's trick or treat
　Wedding bells for Rotten Ralph
　Worse than Rotten Ralph
Gay, Marie-Louise. *Caramba*
　Caramba and Henry
Geras, Adèle. *Sleep tight, Ginger Kitten*
Gerstein, Mordicai. *Minifred goes to school*
　The night world
Ghahremani, Susie. *Stack the cats*
Gibbons, Gail. *Cats*
Giff, Patricia Reilly. *Good luck, Ronald Morgan*
Godwin, Laura. *One moon, two cats*
Going, K. L. *Dog in charge*
Goodwin-Sturges, Judy Sue. *Construction Kitties*
Gorbachev, Valeri. *The best cat*
　Cats are cats
　Catty Jane who hated the rain
　Catty Jane who loved to dance
Graham-Yooll, Liz. *Timothy Tib*
Grant, Jacob. *Cat knit*
Grant, Joan. *Cat and Fish*
Gravdahl, John. *Curious catwalk*
Gravett, Emily. *Matilda's cat*
Gray, Kes. *Frog on a log?*
Greene, Carol. *Where is that cat?*
Gretz, Susanna. *Riley and Rose in the picture*
Grey, Mini. *Space Dog*
Grimes, Nikki. *When Gorilla goes walking*
Grimm, Jacob and Wilhelm. *The fisherman and his wife*
Gudeon, Adam. *Me and Meow*
Hafner, Marylin. *Molly and Emmett's camping adventure*
　Molly and Emmett's surprise garden
Hall, Michael. *Cat tale*
Hamilton, Martha. *Priceless gifts*
Hancocks, Helen. *Penguin in peril*
Harjo, Joy. *The good luck cat*
Harper, Anita. *It's not fair!*
Harper, Charise Mericle. *The best birthday ever!*
　Superlove
Harper, Dan. *Telling time with Big Mama Cat*
Harper, Jessica. *I'm not going to chase the cat today*
Harris, Trudy. *Tally cat keeps track*
Harrison, Hannah E. *Bernice gets carried away*
Harvey, Amanda. *Dog days*
Hassett, John. *The nine lives of Dudley Dog*
Havill, Juanita. *Jamaica is thankful*
Helmer, Diana Star. *The cat who came for tacos*
Helmer, Marilyn. *Three cat and mouse tales*
Henkes, Kevin. *Kitten's first full moon*

When spring comes
Henrichs, Wendy. *I am Tama, lucky cat*
Henry, Steve. *Nobody asked me!*
Hernandez, Leeza. *Cat napped*
Hicks, Barbara Jean. *The secret life of Walter Kitty*
Himmelman, John. *Katie loves the kittens*
Hobbie, Holly. *A cat named Swan*
Hoberman, Mary Ann. *The looking book*
   The two sillies
Hodgkins, Fran. *The cat of Strawberry Hill*
Hodgkinson, Leigh. *Boris and the snoozebox*
   Boris and the wrong shadow
Hogg, Gary. *Look what the cat dragged in!*
Hogrogian, Nonny. *Cool cat*
Holub, Joan. *Cinderdog and the wicked stepcat*
   Scat cats
   Why do cats meow?
Hood, Susan. *Meet Trouble*
Hooper, Meredith. *Celebrity cat*
Horn, Emily. *Excuse me — are you a witch?*
Howe, James. *Houndsley and Catina*
   Houndsley and Catina and the birthday surprise
Hubbell, Patricia. *Wrapping paper romp*
Hudelhoff, Allen H. *Cats and kids*
Hughes, Shirley. *Alfie and the birthday surprise*
Huling, Jan. *Puss in cowboy boots*
Hurd, Thacher. *Cat's pajamas*
Hutchins, Hazel. *One dark night*
Imai, Ayano. *Puss and boots*
Inkpen, Mick. *Meow!*
Jackson, Shelley. *Mimi's Dada Catifesto*
Jacobs, Joseph. *King of the cats*
Jane, Pamela. *Milo and the greatest trick ever*
Janovitz, Marilyn. *We love school!*
Jarka, Jeff. *Love that kitty!*
Jenkins, Emily. *Five creatures*
   Love you when you whine
   Princessland
Jenkins, Steve. *Dogs and cats*
   Perros y gatos / dogs and cats
Jennings, Sharon. *Priscilla's paw de deux*
Jobling, Curtis. *Frankenstein's cat*
Johansen, K. V. *Pippin and Pudding*
Johnson, Paul Brett. *Mr. Persnickety and Cat Lady*
Johnston, Tony. *The cat with seven names*
Jonathan, Langley. *Missing*
Jones, Elizabeth. *Sunshine and Storm*
Jonovitz, Marilyn. *Three little kittens*
Joosse, Barbara. *Nugget and Darling*
   Old Robert and the sea-silly cats
Kang, A. N. *Papillon goes to the vet*
   The very fluffy kitty, Papillon
Keats, Ezra Jack. *Hi, cat!*
   Kitten for a day
Kellogg, Steven. *A rose for Pinkerton*
   Tallyho, Pinkerton!
Khalsa, Dayal Kaur. *Green cat*
Kim, Aram. *Cat on the bus*
   No kimchi for me!
Kirk, Daniel. *Library mouse: a museum adventure*
Kitamura, Satoshi. *Comic adventures of Boots*
   Me and my cat?
Kleven, Elisa. *The wishing ball*
Knapman, Timothy. *Can't catch me!*
Krasnesky, Thad. *That cat can't stay*
Kraus, Robert. *Come out and play, little mouse*
Krauss, Ruth. *And I love you*
Kroll, Steven. *It's April Fools' Day!*
Krosoczka, Jarrett J. *Ollie the purple elephant*

Kuskin, Karla. *So, what's it like to be a cat?*
   Toots the cat
Kwon, Yoon-duck. *My cat copies me*
Lakin, Patricia. *Clarence the copy cat*
Larson, Kirby. *Two Bobbies*
Lawson, Janet. *Audrey and Barbara*
Lazo, Caroline. *Someday when my cat can talk*
Lear, Edward. *The owl and the pussycat*, ill. by Jan Brett
   The owl and the pussycat, ill. by Paul Galdone
   The owl and the pussycat, ill. by Anne Mortimer
Leathers, Philippa. *How to catch a mouse*
Lee . *The lost kitten*
Le Guin, Ursula K. *Cat dreams*
Lent, Blair. *Ruby and Fred*
Leroy, Jean. *Stripes the tiger*
Lewin, Betsy. *Thumpy Feet*
   Where is Tippy Toes?
Lewis, J. Patrick. *Kindergarten cat*
Light, Steve. *Lucky Lazlo*
Lindbergh, Reeve. *Homer the library cat*
Lindgren, Barbro. *Sam's ball*
Litwin, Eric. *Pete the Cat: I love my white shoes*
   Pete the Cat: rocking in my school shoes
   Pete the Cat and his four groovy buttons
   Pete the Cat saves Christmas
Lloyd, Sam. *Doctor Meow's big emergency*
   Mr. Pusskins
   Mr. Pusskins and Little Whiskers
Lobel, Anita. *Nini here and there*
   Nini lost and found
   One lighthouse, one moon
Long, Loren. *Otis and the kittens*
Lord, Janet. *Where is Catkin?*
Lundquist, Mary. *Cat and Bunny*
Luxbacher, Irene. *Mattoo, let's play!*
McAnulty, Stacy. *Mr. Fuzzbuster knows he's the favorite*
McBratney, Sam. *The dark at the top of the stairs*
McCarty, Peter. *Fabian escapes*
   Henry in love
   Hondo and Fabian
McClure, Gillian. *Tom Finger*
McClure, Nikki. *How to be a cat*
McCully, Emily Arnold. *Four hungry kittens*
MacDonald, Margaret Read. *Fat cat*
   Mabela the clever
MacDonald, Maryann. *The Christmas cat*
McDonnell, Christine. *Goyangi means cat*
McDonnell, Patrick. *The gift of nothing*
   Just like Heaven
   The little red cat who ran away and learned his ABC's (the hard way)
   South
   Wag!
McFarland, Lyn Rossiter. *Widget and the puppy*
McGraw, Sheila. *Pussycats everywhere*
McGuinness-Kelly, Tracy-Lee. *Bad Cat puts on his top hat*
McKinlay, Penny. *Flabby Tabby*
MacLachlan, Patricia. *Bittle*
   Cat talk
   Who loves me?
McLaren, Chesley. *Zat cat!*
McLellan, Stephanie Simpson. *The chicken cat*
McMullan, Kate. *Supercat*
   Supercat to the rescue
McPhail, David. *Crash! the cat*
McQuade, Jacqueline. *Good times with Teddy Bear*

McQuinn, Anna. *Lola gets a cat*
Mader, C. Roger. *Lost cat*
  Tiptop cat
Magloff, Lisa. *Kitten*
Mahy, Margaret. *The Christmas tree tangle*
Malbrough, Mike. *Marigold bakes a cake*
Mallat, Kathy. *Trouble on the tracks*
Manley, Curtis. *The summer Nick taught his cats to read*
Manning, Jane. *Cat nights*
Manzano, Sonia. *A box full of kittens*
Marciano, John Bemelmans. *Madeline and the cats of Rome*
Martin, Bill, Jr.. *Kitty Cat, Kitty Cat, are you going to school?*
  Kitty Cat, Kitty Cat, are you going to sleep?
  Kitty Cat, Kitty Cat, are you waking up?
Martin, David. *All for pie, pie for all*
Marzollo, Jean. *Thanksgiving cats*
  Valentine cats
Masurel, Claire. *A cat and a dog*
Meggs, Libby Phillips. *Go home!*
Merriam, Eve. *Where's that cat?*
Meyers, Susan. *Kittens! kittens! kittens!*
Miller, Sara Swan. *Cat in the bag*
Miller, Virginia. *Be gentle!*
  Ten red apples
Minarik, Else Holmelund. *It's spring!*
Monks, Lydia. *The cat barked?*
Monson, A. M. *Wanted . . . best friend*
Montes, Marisa. *Los gatos black on Halloween*
Moore, Inga. *Captain Cat*
Moore, Suzi. *Whoops!*
Mora, Pat. *A birthday basket for Tía*
  Here, kitty, kitty! / ¡Ven, gatita, ven!
Moran, Alex. *Come here, tiger*
  Sam and Jack
Morris, Bob. *Crispin the Terrible*
Morris, Dewi. *Sandy's street*
Morris, Jackie. *I am Cat*
Mortimer, Anne. *Pumpkin cat*
Moss, Miriam. *Matty in a mess!*
  Matty takes off!
Mother Goose. *The three little kittens*
Moxley, Sheila. *ABCD an alphabet book of cats and dogs*
Muncaster, Harriet. *I am a witch's cat*
Murphy, Stuart J. *Pepper's journal*
Murray, Alison. *Princess Penelope and the runaway kitten*
Murray, Andrew. *Have you seen Chester?*
Myers, Tim. *Looking for Luna*
Myron, Vicki. *Dewey*
Napoli, Donna Jo. *Rocky, the cat who barks*
Neal, Christopher Silas. *I won't eat that*
Nelson-Schmidt, Michelle. *Cats, cats!*
Newberry, Clare Turlay. *April's kittens*
  Marshmallow
Newbery, Linda. *Posy*
Newgarden, Mark. *Bow-Wow's nightmare neighbors*
Newman, Lesléa. *Cats, cats, cats*
  Ketzel, the cat who composed
Nishimura, Kae. *Dinah*
Nishizuka, Koko. *The beckoning cat*
Norwich, William D. *Molly and the magic dress*
Numeroff, Laura Joffe. *If you give a cat a cupcake*
Oh, Jiwon. *Cat and mouse*
O'Hair, Margaret. *My kitten*
Olien, Jessica. *Shark Detective!*

Oller, Erika. *The cabbage soup solution*
Olson, Jennifer Gray. *Me and Mr. Fluffernutter*
Oram, Hiawyn. *Just Dog*
Oxley, Jennifer. *The chicken problem*
Page, Gail. *How to be a good cat*
Partridge, Elizabeth. *Big Cat Pepper*
Peacock, Carol Antoinette. *Pilgrim cat*
Peet, Bill. *Jennifer and Josephine*
Pelley, Kathleen T. *Raj the bookstore tiger*
Penner, Fred. *The cat came back*
Perkins, Lynne Rae. *The broken cat*
Perrault, Charles. *Puss in boots*, ill. by Marcia Brown
  Puss in boots, ill. by Lorinda Bryan Cauley
  Puss in boois, ill. by Paul Galdone
  Puss in boots, ill. by Steve Light
  Puss in boots, ill. by Giuliano Lunelli
  Puss in boots, ill. by Fred Marcellino
  Puss in boots, ill. by Bernhard Oberdieck
  Puss in boots, ill. by Jerry Pinkney
  Puss in boots, ill. by Alain Vaës
Peters, Lisa Westberg. *Frankie works the night shift*
Philip, Simon. *I don't know what to call my cat*
Pilkey, Dav. *Dragon's fat cat*
  When cats dream
Pinkney, Jerry. *Three little kittens*
Pinkwater, Daniel. *Beautiful Yetta's Hanukkah kitten*
Pizzoli, Greg. *Templeton gets his wish*
Plecas, Jennifer. *Olive's perfect world*
Polacco, Patricia. *Because of Thursday*
  Mrs. Katz and Tush
  Tikvah means hope
Potter, Alicia. *Miss Hazeltine's Home for Shy and Fearful Cats*
Potter, Beatrix. *The pie and the patty-pan*
  Rolly-polly pudding
  The sly old cat
  The story of Miss Moppet
  The tale of Tom Kitten
Powell-Tuck, Maudie. *The messy book*
Prap, Lila. *Doggy whys*
Preston-Gannon, Frann. *Pepper and Poe*
Priceman, Marjorie. *My nine lives / by Clio*
Pringle, Laurence P. *Naming the cat*
Protopopescu, Orel. *Thelonious Mouse*
Pullman, Philip. *Puss in boots: the adventures of that most enterprising feline*
Pulver, Robin. *Christmas for a kitten*
  Christmas kitten, home at last
Radzinski, Kandy. *Where to sleep*
Raschka, Chris. *John Coltrane's giant steps*
Rathmann, Peggy. *Ruby the copycat*
Reeve, Rosie. *Training Tallulah*
Regan, Dian Curtis. *The Snow Blew Inn*
Reibstein, Mark. *Wabi Sabi*
Reich, Susanna. *Minette's feast*
Reinen, Judy. *Meow*
Reinhardt, Jennifer Black. *Blue Ethel*
Reiser, Lynn. *My cat Tuna*
Reynolds, Marilynn. *A present for Mrs. Kazinski*
Ritz, Karen. *Windows with birds*
Robbins, Beth. *Tom, Ally, and the baby-sitter*
  Tom, Ally, and the new baby
  Tom and Ally visit the doctor
  Tom's afraid of the dark
  Tom's first day at school
  Tom's new haircut
Roberts, Bethany. *Christmas mice*
Robinson, Sue. *I want to play*

Robledo, Honorio. *Nico visits the moon*
Rockwell, Anne. *Katie Catz makes a splash*
    Space vehicles
Rohmann, Eric. *The cinder-eyed cats*
Root, Phyllis. *Lucia and the light*
    Scrawny cat
Rose, Deborah Lee. *All the seasons of the year*
Rosenthal, Eileen. *Bobo the sailor man!*
    I must have Bobo!
    I'll save you Bobo!
Ross, Eileen. *The Halloween showdown*
Rostoker-Gruber, Karen. *Bandit*
    Bandit's surprise
    Ferret fun
Roth, Carol. *Where's my mommy?*
Rubin, Adam. *Those darn squirrels and the cat next door*
Rueda, Claudia. *Is it big or is it little?*
Rylant, Cynthia. *Brownie and Pearl get dolled up*
    Brownie and Pearl go for a spin
    Brownie and Pearl grab a bite
    Brownie and Pearl hit the hay
    Brownie and Pearl make good
    Brownie and Pearl see the sights
    Brownie and Pearl take a dip
    The cookie-store cat
    Moonlight, the Halloween cat
Rymond, Lynda Gene. *Oscar and the mooncats*
Saab, Julie. *Little Lola*
    Little Lola saves the show
Sage, James. *Farmer Smart's fat cat*
Saltzberg, Barney. *I love cats*
Samuels, Barbara. *Aloha, Dolores*
    Dolores meets her match
    Duncan and Dolores
    Happy Valentine's Day, Dolores
    The trucker
Sanderson, Ruth. *A castle full of cats*
    Papa Gatto
San Souci, Robert D. *The white cat*
Santoro, Scott. *Farm-fresh cats*
Sarcone-Roach, Julia. *The secret plan*
Saul, Carol P. *Barn cat*
Say, Allen. *Allison*
Schachner, Judith Byron. *Bits and pieces*
    The Grannyman
    Skippyjon Jones and the big bones
    Skippyjon Jones Cirque de Olé
    Skippyjon Jones class action
    Skippyjon Jones in mummy trouble
    Skippyjon Jones, lost in spice
Schertle, Alice. *I am the cat*
Schoenherr, Ian. *Cat and mouse*
Schoonmaker, Elizabeth. *Square cat*
    Square cat ABC
Schwarz, Viviane. *Is there a dog in this book?*
    There are cats in this book
    There are no cats in this book
Scillian, Devin. *Memoirs of a hamster*
Scotton, Rob. *Love, Splat*
    Merry Christmas, Splat
    Scaredy-cat, Splat!
    Secret Agent Splat!
    Splat and the cool school trip
    Splat says thank you!
    Splat the cat
    Splat the cat: on with the show
    Splish, splash, splat!
Segal, John. *Alistair and Kip's great adventure*

Seki, Sunny. *The tale of the lucky cat*
Shea, Bob. *Cheetah can't lose*
Shireen, Nadia. *Hey, Presto!*
Sidman, Joyce. *Meow ruff*
Siminovich, Lorena. *Alex and Lulu*
Simler, Isabelle. *Plume*
Simmonds, Posy. *Baker cat*
Singleton, Linda Joy. *A cat is better*
Siomades, Lorianne. *Three little kittens*
Skinner, Daphne. *The right place for Albert*
Smath, Jerry. *Sammy Salami*
Smiley, Norene. *That stripy cat*
Smith, Maggie. *Desser, the best ever cat*
So, Meilo. *Gobble, gobble, slip, slop*
Song, Mika. *Tea with Oliver*
Soto, Gary. *Chato and the party animals*
    Chato goes cruisin'
    Chato's kitchen
Spinelli, Eileen. *Callie Cat, ice skater*
    Do you have a cat?
    Hero cat
Spires, Elizabeth. *The big meow*
Stadler, John. *Catilda*
    The cats of Mrs. Calamari
Stainton, Sue. *The chocolate cat*
    I love cats!
    The lighthouse cat
    Santa's snow cat
Steig, William. *Solomon the rusty nail*
Stein, Joel Edward. *A Hanukkah with Mazel*
Stephens, Helen. *I'm too busy*
    What about me?
Stevens, Janet. *My big dog*
Stower, Adam. *Naughty kitty!*
Sturges, Philemon. *Waggers*
Stutson, Caroline. *Cats' night out*
Surovec, Yasmine. *I see Kitty*
Sykes, Julie. *This and that*
Taber, Tory. *Rufus at work*
Talbott, Hudson. *It's all about me-ow*
Tan, Amy. *The Chinese Siamese cat*
Teague, Mark. *Detective LaRue*
    LaRue across America
Teckentrup, Britta. *Grumpy cat*
Thomas, Jan. *Here comes the big, mean dust bunny!*
Thomas, Shelley Moore. *No, no, kitten!*
    Take care, Good Knight
Thomas, Valerie. *Winnie the witch*
    Winnie's midnight dragon
Thompson, Lauren. *How many cats?*
Thornhill, Jan. *Wild in the city*
Tillman, Nancy. *Tumford the terrible*
    Tumford's rude noises
Titus, Eve. *Anatole and the cat*
Townsend, Michael. *Cute and cuter*
Trimmer, Christian. *Simon's new bed*
Trukhan, Ekaterina. *Me and my cat*
Turkle, Brinton. *Do not open*
Turner, Ann Warren. *Pumpkin cat*
Uchida, Yoshiko. *The two foolish cats*
Umansky, Kaye. *I don't like Gloria!*
Underwood, Deborah. *Here comes Santa Cat*
    Here comes teacher cat
    Here comes the Easter Cat
    Here comes the Tooth Fairy Cat
    Here comes Valentine Cat
Ungerer, Tomi. *Flix*
Vagin, Vladimir. *Here comes the cat*
Varon, Sara. *Chicken and Cat*

Chicken and Cat clean up
Verde, Susan. *You and me*
Vere, Ed. *Max and Bird*
   Max the brave
Viorst, Judith. *The tenth good thing about Barney*
Vischer, Frans. *Fuddles*
   Fuddles and Puddles
   A very Fuddles Christmas
Voake, Charlotte. *Ginger*
   Ginger and the mystery visitor
   Pizza kittens
Volkmann, Roy. *Curious kittens*
Waber, Bernard. *Lyle at Christmas*
Waddell, Martin. *A kitten called Moonlight*
   Who do you love?
Wade, Mary Dodson. *No year of the cat*
Wahman, Wendy. *A cat like that*
Waite, Judy. *Mouse, look out!*
   The stray kitten
Walton, Rick. *The remarkable friendship of Mr. Cat
   and Mr. Rat*
Ward, B. J. *Farty Marty*
Ward, Cindy. *Cookie's week*
Wardlaw, Lee. *Won Ton*
   Won Ton and Chopstick
Warhola, James. *Uncle Andy's cats*
Waring, Geoff. *Oscar and the bat*
   Oscar and the cricket
   Oscar and the moth
Warner, Sunny. *The moon quilt*
Washington, Donna L. *A big, spooky house*
Watson, Wendy. *Happy Easter day!*
Watt, Mélanie. *Chester*
   Chester's back!
   Chester's masterpiece
Weaver, Tess. *Cat jumped in!*
   Opera cat
Webb, Holly. *Little puppy lost*
Weeks, Sarah. *Glamourpuss*
   Woof
Wellington, Monica. *Squeaking of art, the mice go to
   the museum*
Wells, Rosemary. *McDuff's wild romp*
   Yoko
   Yoko finds her way
   Yoko learns to read
   Yoko writes her name
   Yoko's paper cranes
   Yoko's show-and-tell
Weninger, Brigitte. *Good night, Nori*
Wenzel, Brendan. *They all saw a cat*
West, Judy. *Have you got my purr?*
Wethered, Peggy. *Touchdown Mars!*
Wheeler, Lisa. *Castaway cats*
Wiesner, David. *Mr. Wuffles!*
Willard, Nancy. *The mouse, the cat and
   Grandmother's hat*
Wilson, Karma. *Hello, Calico!*
   Sleepyhead
Wisnewski, Andrea. *Trio*
Wiviott, Meg. *Benno and the night of broken glass*
Woelfle, Gretchen. *Katje the windmill cat*
Wojtusik, Elizabeth. *Kitty up!*
Wolff, Nancy. *It's time for school with Tallulah*
   Tallulah in the kitchen
Wong, Liz. *Quackers*
Wood, Jakki. *Moo moo, brown cow*
   Never say boo to a goose!
Wormell, Mary. *Why not?*

Yokococo. Matilda and Hans
Yolen, Jane. *The day Tiger Rose said goodbye*
   Soft house
Young, Ed. *Cat and Rat*
   The cat from Hunger Mountain
Yuly, Toni. *Cat nap*
Ziefert, Harriet. *No kiss for Grandpa!*

Animals – cheetahs

Shea, Bob. *Cheetah can't lose*

Animals – chimpanzees

Alborough, Jez. *Hug*
   Yes
Anholt, Catherine. *Chimp and Zee and the big storm*
   Chimp and Zee's noisy book
   Happy birthday, Chimp and Zee
   Monkey around with Chimp and Zee [board book]
Browne, Anthony. *How do you feel?*
   I like books
   One gorilla: a counting book
   Willy and Hugh
   Willy the champ
   Willy the dreamer
   Willy the wimp
   Willy the wizard
   Willy's pictures
   Willy's stories
Bustos, Eduardo. *Going ape!*
Durango, Julia. *Cha-cha chimps*
Durant, Alan. *Brown Bear gets in shape*
Faulkner, Keith. *Charlie Chimp's Christmas*
McDonnell, Patrick. *Me . . . Jane*
Napoli, Donna Jo. *Bobby the bold*
Oram, Hiawyn. *The wrong overcoat*
Watson, Richard Jesse. *The boy who went ape*
Winter, Jeanette. *The watcher*

Animals – chipmunks

Bruchac, Joseph. *How Chipmunk got his stripes*
Gorbachev, Valeri. *Me too!*
Ryder, Joanne. *Chipmunk song*
Sauer, Tammi. *Oh, nuts!*
Stevenson, James. *Wilfred the rat*
Taylor, Jane. *Twinkle, twinkle, little star*
Valentine, Madeline. *I want that nut!*
Vojtech, Anna. *Surprise in the meadow*
Williams, Barbara. *Chester Chipmunk's Thanksgiving*

Animals – coatis

Schindler, S. D. *Spike and Ike take a hike*

Animals – cougars

Costello, Emily. *Realm of the panther*
London, Jonathan. *Panther, shadow of the swamp*
Mora, Pat. *Doña Flor*

Animals – cows *see* Animals – bulls, cows

Animals – coyotes

Aardema, Verna. *Borreguita and the coyote*
Aesop. *Doctor Coyote*
Appelt, Kathi. *When Otis courted Mama*

Arnosky, Jim. *Coyote raid in Cactus Canyon*
Beaumont, Karen. *Duck, duck, goose!*
Beaver steals fire
Czernecki, Stefan. *Huevos rancheros*
Gianferrari, Maria. *Coyote moon*
The gingerbread boy. *The Gingerbread Cowboy*
Goble, Paul. *Iktomi and the ducks*
Hausman, Gerald. *Coyote walks on two legs*
Hiscock, Bruce. *Coyote and badger*
Hopkins, Jackie Mims. *Prairie chicken little*
Johnston, Tony. *The tale of Rabbit and Coyote*
King, Thomas. *Coyote sings to the moon*
Lowell, Susan. *Josefina javelina*
    The three little javelinas
McDermott, Gerald. *Coyote*
Paul, Ann Whitford. *Tortuga in trouble*
Pia Toya
Puttock, Simon. *Little lost cowboy*
Stevens, Janet. *Old bag of bones*
Tafolla, Carmen. *Baby Coyote and the old woman / El coyotito y la viejita*
Taylor, Harriet Peck. *Coyote and the laughing butterflies*
Tonatiuh, Duncan. *Pancho Rabbit and the coyote*

Animals – deer

Arnosky, Jim. *All about deer*
    Deer at the brook
Collins, Pat Lowery. *The deer watch*
Gordon, Gus. *Herman and Rosie*
Kleven, Elisa. *The dancing deer and the foolish hunter*
Marzollo, Jean. *Once upon a springtime*
Puttock, Simon. *The baby that roared*
Ray, Mary Lyn. *Deer dancer*
Scott, Nathan Kumar. *Mangoes and bananas*
    The sacred banana leaf
Slater, Dashka. *The antlered ship*
Soros, Barbara. *Tenzin's deer*
Springett, Martin. *Kate and Pippin*
Townsend, Emily Rose. *Deer*

Animals – dislike of *see* Behavior – animals, dislike of

Animals – dogs

Abercrombie, Barbara. *Bad dog, Dodger*
Abramson, Jill. *Ready or not, here comes Scout*
Adamson, Ged. *Douglas, you need glasses!*
    Shark Dog!
Adderson, Caroline. *Norman, speak!*
Adoff, Arnold. *Daring Dog and Captain Cat*
Aesop. *The dog and the wolf*
    Smog, the city dog
Agee, Jon. *It's only Stanley*
Ahlberg, Jessica. *Fairy tales for Mr. Barker*
Ajmera, Maya. *A kid's best friend*
Alexander, Claire. *Back to front and upside down*
Appelt, Kathi. *Mogie*
Archer, Peggy. *Name that dog!*
Arnold, Katya. *Meow!*
Asare, Meshack. *Sosu's call*
Asch, Frank. *The last puppy*
Ashman, Linda. *Stella, unleashed*
    The tale of Wagmore Gently
Autry, Gene. *Here comes Santa Claus*
Backx, Patsy. *Josie and Mr. Fernandez*

Skippy and Jack
Baek, Matthew J. *Be gentle with the dog, dear*
Bailey, Linda. *Stanley at sea*
    Stanley's beauty contest
    Stanley's little sister
    Stanley's party
    Stanley's wild ride
Baker, Leslie A. *You bad dog!*
Barclay, Eric. *Counting dogs*
Barracca, Debra. *Maxi, the hero*
    Maxi, the star
    A taxi dog Christmas
Barracca, Sal. *The adventures of taxi dog*
Barry, Holly M. *Helen Keller's best friend Belle*
Bartoletti, Susan Campbell. *Nobody's diggier than a dog*
Bateman, Teresa. *Job wanted*
Beaumont, Karen. *Crybaby*
    Doggone dogs!
    Move over, Rover
    Where's my t-r-u-c-k?
Bedford, David. *Shaggy Dog and the terrible itch*
    The way I love you
Bee, William. *Digger Dog*
Beeny, Emily. *Hector the collector*
Beil, Karen Magnuson. *Jack's house*
Bell, Cece. *Itty Bitty*
Belton, Robyn. *Herbert*
Bemelmans, Ludwig. *Madeline's rescue*
Berenstain, Stan and Jan. *The Berenstain bears on the moon*
Bergen, Lara Rice. *Blue's world of words*
Berger, Lou. *Dream dog*
Berry, Lynne. *Pig and Pug*
Birdsall, Jeanne. *Lucky and Squash*
Blabey, Aaron. *Pig the elf*
    Pig the pug
    Pig the winner
Blackstone, Stella. *Cleo and Caspar*
    Cleo in the snow
    Cleo on the move
    An island in the sun
Blades, Ann. *Mary of mile 18*
Blake, Quentin. *Mrs. Armitage*
Blake, Robert J. *Painter and Ugly*
Bliss, Harry. *Bailey*
    Bailey at the museum
Bluemle, Elizabeth. *Dogs on the bed*
    My father the dog
Blumenthal, Deborah. *The blue house dog*
Boase, Susan. *Lucky boy*
Boelts, Maribeth. *Before you were mine*
Bogan, Paulette. *Momma's magical purse*
    Spike in the city
Boldt, Claudia. *Odd dog*
Bowen, Anne. *Scooter in the outside*
Bowles, Paula. *Messy Jesse*
Boyer, Cécile. *Woof meow tweet-tweet*
Bradley, Kimberly Brubaker. *Ballerino Nate*
Braeuner, Shellie. *The great dog wash*
Brecon, Connah. *Paws McDraw*
Breen, Steve. *Pug and Doug*
Brennan, Eileen. *Bad Astrid*
Brenning, Juli. *Maggi and Milo*
    Maggi and Milo make new friends
Brett, Jan. *Comet's nine lives*
    The first dog
    The trouble with trolls
Bridwell, Norman. *Clifford celebrates Hanukkah*

Clifford counts bubbles
Clifford goes to Hollywood
Clifford the champion
Clifford's ABC
Clifford's good deeds
Clifford's Halloween
Clifford's neighborhood
Glow-in-the-dark Halloween
Broach, Elise. *Wet dog!*
Brown, Alison. *Eddie and Dog*
Brown, Marc. *Arthur's new puppy*
   Arthur's pet business
Brown, Margaret Wise. *Sailor boy jig*
Brown, Peter. *Chowder*
Browne, Anthony. *Voices in the park*
Browne, Christopher. *Marlo*
Bruce, Lisa. *Fran's friend*
Bruel, Nick. *Poor puppy*
Bruzzone, Catherine. *Puppy finds a friend /*
      Cachorrito encuentra un amigo
   Puppy finds a friend / Le petit chien se trouve un ami
Buckley, Carol. *Tarra and Bella*
Buehner, Caralyn. *Superdog, the heart of a hero*
Bunge, Daniela. *Cherry time*
Bunting, Eve. *Ghost's hour, spook's hour*
   My dog Jack is fat
Burleigh, Robert. *Good-bye, Sheepie*
Burningham, John. *Motor Miles*
Butler, Kristi T. *Rip's secret spot*
Byrne, Richard. *This book is out of control!*
   This book just ate my dog!
Cabrera, Jane. *Here we go round the mulberry bush*
Calhoun, Mary. *High-wire Henry*
Calmenson, Stephanie. *May I pet your dog?*
   Perfect puppy
Capucilli, Alyssa Satin. *Bathtime for Biscuit*
   Biscuit
   Biscuit finds a friend
   Biscuit gives a gift
   Biscuit goes to school
   Biscuit loves school
   Biscuit wants to play
   Biscuit wins a prize
   Biscuit's big friend
   Biscuit's new trick
   Biscuit's picnic
   Biscuit's Valentine's Day
   Happy birthday, Biscuit!
   Happy Hanukkah, Biscuit
   Hello, Biscuit!
   Merry Christmas, from Biscuit
   Tulip loves Rex
Carbone, Elisa. *Night running*
Carlin, Patricia. *Alfie is not afraid*
Carlson, Nancy. *Harriet and George's Christmas treat*
   Harriet and the garden
   Harriet and the roller coaster
   Harriet and Walt
   Harriet's Halloween candy
Carlstrom, Nancy White. *It's your first day of school,*
      Annie Claire
Carnesi, Monica. *Little dog lost*
Casanova, Mary. *Some cat!*
   Some dog!
Casteel, Seth. *Puppy pool party!*
   Underwater dogs
Caston, Jane. *Will you help Doug find his dog?*
Catalano, Dominic. *Mr. Bassett plays*
Catalanotto, Peter. *Ivan the terrier*

Catusanu, Mircea. *The strange case of the missing sheep*
Cazet, Denys. *The octopus*
Cecil, Randy. *Lucy*
Chall, Marsha Wilson. *Bonaparte*
   One pup's up
   Pick a pup
Chapman, Nancy Kapp. *Doggie dreams*
Chapra, Mimi. *Sparky's bark / El ladrido de Sparky*
Chess, Victoria. *The costume party*
Chichester Clark, Emma. *Love is my favorite thing*
   Melrose and Croc
   Piper
   Plenty of love to go around
Child, Lauren. *Who wants to be a poodle*
Chorao, Kay. *Bad boy, good boy*
Christelow, Eileen. *The desperate dog writes again*
   The five-dog night
   Letters from a desperate dog
   Not until Christmas, Walter!
Chung, Arree. *Out!*
Church, Caroline Jayne. *Digby takes charge*
   Ruff!
Clements, Andrew. *Brave Norman*
   Circus family dog
   Dogku
   Naptime for Slippers
   Slippers at home
   Slippers at School
   Slippers loves to run
   Tara and Tiree, fearless friends
Cneut, Carll. *The amazing love story of Mr. Morf*
Cocca-Leffler, Maryann. *A vacation for Pooch*
Cochran, Bill. *The forever dog*
Coffelt, Nancy. *Fred stays with me!*
   Pug in a truck
Cohen, Miriam. *Jim's dog Muffins*, ill. by Ronald
      Himler
   Jim's dog Muffins, ill. by Lillian Hoban
Cole, Babette. *Lady Lupin's book of etiquette*
   Truelove
Cole, Barbara Hancock. *Anna and Natalie*
Cole, Joanna. *My puppy is born*
Conahan, Carolyn. *The twelve days of Christmas dogs*
Consentino, Ralph. *The story of Honk-Honk-Ashoo*
      and Swella-Bow-Wow
Cooper, Elisha. *Homer*
Cooper, Helen. *Dog biscuit*
Corderoy, Tracey. *Just right for two*
Costain, Meredith. *Daddies are awesome*
Cotterill, Samantha. *No more bows*
Cottle, Joan. *Miles away from home*
Cousins, Lucy. *I'm the best*
Cowen-Fletcher, Jane. *Hello, puppy!*
Crimi, Carolyn. *Don't need friends*
   Pugs in a Bug
   There might be lobsters
Crisp, Marty. *Black and white*
   The most precious gift
Cronin, Doreen. *Bounce*
   Smick!
   Stretch
   Wiggle
Crosby, Jeff. *Wiener Wolf*
Crouse, Livingstone. *Kisses for kindergarten*
Crummel, Susan Stevens. *Sherlock Bones and the*
      missing cheese
   Ten-Gallon Bart
   Ten-Gallon Bart and the Wild West Show

Ten-Gallon Bart beats the heat
Crunk, Tony. *Grandpa's overalls*
Cullen, Lynn. *Little Scraggly Hair*
   The mightiest heart
   Moi and Marie Antoinette
Curious George and the puppies
Cyrus, Kurt. *Motor Dog*
Dalgleish, Sharon. *Working dogs*
Daly, Niki. *Pretty Salma*
Davis, Anne. *No dogs allowed!*
Day, Alexandra. *Carl goes shopping*
   Carl goes to daycare
   Carl's birthday
   Carl's Halloween
   Carl's sleepy afternoon
   Carl's snowy afternoon
   Carl's summer vacation
   The fairy dogfather
   Follow Carl!
   Good dog, Carl
Deady, Kathleen W. *It's time!*
De Beer, Hans. *Oh no, Ono!*
Degen, Bruce. *I gotta draw*
deGroat, Diane. *Homer*
Demas, Corinne. *Always in trouble*
   Here comes trouble!
Demers, Dominique. *Old Thomas and the little fairy*
Dennis, Major Brian. *Nubs*
DePalma, Mary Newell. *Bow-wow wiggle-waggle*
dePaola, Tomie. *Boss for a day*
   Hide-and-seek all week
   Meet the Barkers
   A new Barker in the house
DeRubertis, Barbara. *Dilly Dog's dizzy dancing*
Desimini, Lisa. *Dot the Firedog*
Desrosiers, Sylvie. *Hocus Pocus*
Dewdney, Anna. *Grumpy Gloria*
Dickson, Louise. *The vanishing cat*
DiPucchio, Kelly. *Antoinette*
   Dog days of school
   Gaston
Dodd, Emma. *Dog's ABC*
   Dog's colorful day
   Dog's noisy day
   I don't want a posh dog
Dodd, Lynley. *A dragon in a wagon*
Dodds, Dayle Ann. *The Kettles get new clothes*
   Where's Pup?
Dormer, Frank W. *Click!*
Doyle, Malachy. *Sleepy Pendoodle*
Drummond, Ree. *Charlie and the new baby*
   Charlie goes to school
   Charlie the ranch dog
Dunbar, Polly. *Dog Blue*
Dunnick, Regan. *Sweet dreams, Douglas*
Dylan, Bob. *If not for you*
Edwards, Karl Newsom. *I got a new friend*
Edwards, Nicola. *Goodnight Baxter*
Edwards, Pamela Duncan. *Muldoon*
Egan, Tim. *A mile from Ellington Station*
Ehlert, Lois. *Rrralph*
   Wag a tail
Elliott, Rebecca. *Dalmatian in a digger*
Ellwand, David. *Alfred's camera*
   Alfred's party
Elschner, Geraldine. *Like a wolf*
Esbaum, Jill. *Stanza*
Estefan, Gloria. *Noelle's treasure tale*
Ets, Marie Hall. *Mr. T. W. Anthony Woo*

Faglia, Matteo. *Happy birthday, I'm 2*
Faller, Regis. *The adventures of Polo*
   Polo
   Polo and Lily
   Polo and the dragon
   Polo and the magician!
Falwell, Cathryn. *P.J. and Puppy*
Fearnley, Jan. *The search for the perfect child*
Feiffer, Jules. *Bark, George*
Feiffer, Kate. *Henry, the dog with no tail*
   President Pennybaker
   Which puppy?
Fergus, Maureen. *Buddy and Earl*
   Buddy and Earl and the great big baby
   Buddy and Earl go exploring
   Buddy and Earl go to school
Ferry, Beth. *Land shark*
Figley, Marty Rhodes. *Emily and Carlo*
Fischer, Ellen. *Latke, the lucky dog*
Fleming, Denise. *Buster*
   Buster goes to Cowboy Camp
   Maggie and Michael get dressed
Flesher, Vivienne. *Alfred's nose*
Fletcher, Ashlee. *My dog, my cat*
Florian, Douglas. *Bow wow meow meow, it's rhyming cats and dogs*
Fogliano, Julie. *Old dog baby baby*
Foreman, Jack. *Say hello*
Foreman, Michael. *Mia's story*
   Oh! if only . . .
Fox, Diane. *The cat, the dog, Little Red, the exploding eggs, the wolf, and Grandma*
Fox, Mem. *Nellie Belle*
   Night noises
Franco, Betsy. *A dazzling display of dogs*
Frank, John. *The toughest cowboy, Or, How the Wild West was tamed*
Frasier, Debra. *Spike*
Frazee, Marla. *Boot and Shoe*
French, Jackie. *Pete the sheep-sheep*
Freymann, Saxton. *Dog food*
Fucile, Tony. *Poor Louie*
Fuge, Charles. *Yip! snap! yap!*
Furstinger, Nancy. *Maggie's second chance*
Gal, Susan. *Please take me for a walk*
Galindo, Renata. *My new mom and me*
Gall, Chris. *Dog vs. Cat*
Gallion, Sue Lowell. *Pug and Pig trick-or-treat*
   Pug meets Pig
Gardiner, Lindsey. *Good night, Poppy and Max*
   Here come Poppy and Max
   When Poppy and Max grow up
Gardner, Carol. *Princess Zelda and the frog*
Gay, Marie-Louise. *What are you doing, Sam?*
George, Jean Craighead. *Cliff hanger*
George, Kristine O'Connell. *Little Dog and Duncan*
George, Lindsay Barrett. *Maggie's ball*
   That pup!
Gianferrari, Maria. *Hello goodbye dog*
   Penny and Jelly: the school show
   Penny and Jelly: slumber under the stars
Gibbons, Gail. *Dogs*
Gibson, Amy. *Split! splat!*
Giff, Patricia Reilly. *Good luck, Ronald Morgan*
Giglio, Judy. *The tapping tale*
Gill-Brown, Vanessa. *Rufferella*
Gliori, Debi. *The snow lambs*
Going, K. L. *Dog in charge*
Goldfinger, Jennifer P. *My dog Lyle*

Goode, Diane. *Mama's perfect present*
  The most perfect spot
  Tiger trouble
Goodhart, Pippa. *Pudgy, a puppy to love*
Goodman, Susan E. *It's a dog's life*
Goodrich, Carter. *Mister Bud wears the cone*
  Say hello to Zorro!
  Zorro gets an outfit
Gordon, Domenica More. *Archie*
  Archie's vacation
Gormley, Greg. *Dog in boots*
Gottfried, Maya. *Good dog*
Graham, Bob. *"Let's get a pup!" said Kate*
  "The trouble with dogs," said Dad
Grambling, Lois G. *Big Dog*
Granowsky, Alvin. *At the park*
Gravett, Emily. *Dogs*
Gregory, Nan. *How Smudge came*
Gretz, Susanna. *Riley and Rose in the picture*
Grey, Mini. *Space Dog*
Grogan, John. *Bad dog, Marley!*
  Marley goes to school
  Trick or treat, Marley!
  A very Marley Christmas
Grover, Jan Zita. *A home for Dakota*
Gutman, Anne. *Gaspard and Lisa, friends forever*
  Gaspard and Lisa's Christmas surprise
  Gaspard and Lisa's rainy day
  Gaspard at the seashore
  Gaspard in the hospital
  Gaspard on vacation
  Lisa in New York
  Lisa in the jungle
  Lisa's airplane trip
  Lisa's baby sister
Guy, Ginger Foglesong. *Perros! perros! dogs! dogs!*
Haber, Tiffany Strelitz. *Ollie and Claire*
Hall, Kirsten. *The jacket*
Hall, Marcellus. *Everyone sleeps*
Harper, Charise Mericle. *Henry's heart*
Harper, Dan. *Sit, Truman*
Harper, Jessica. *I'm not going to chase the cat today*
Harper, Lee. *Snow! snow! snow!*
Harrison, David L. *Farmer's garden*
Harrison, Hannah E. *Extraordinary Jane*
Harvey, Amanda. *Dog days*
  Dog-eared
  Dog gone
Hassett, John. *The nine lives of Dudley Dog*
Haughton, Chris. *Oh no, George!*
Hawkes, Kevin. *Remy and Lulu*
Hayes, Sarah. *Dog day*
Hays, Anna Jane. *The pup speaks up*
Heiligman, Deborah. *Cool dog, school dog*
  Fun dog, sun dog
  Snow dog, go dog
Helakoski, Leslie. *Doggone feet!*
Helberg, Berit. *Sniffer and Tinni*
Henkes, Kevin. *Circle dogs*
Henry, Rohan. *The gift box*
Heos, Bridget. *Queen Dog*
Herman, R. A. *Gomer and Little Gomer*
Hernandez, Leeza. *Dog gone!*
Hest, Amy. *Buster and the baby*
  Charley's first night
  The dog who belonged to no one
  My old pal, Oscar
  On the night of the shooting star
  The reader

When Charley met Grampa
Hewitt, Kathryn. *No dogs here!*
Hill, Eric. *Spot at home*
  Spot at play
  Spot at the fair
  Spot bakes a cake
  Spot counts from 1 to 10
  Spot goes to a party
  Spot goes to school
  Spot goes to the beach
  Spot goes to the circus
  Spot goes to the farm
  Spot goes to the park
  Spot looks at colors
  Spot looks at opposites
  Spot looks at shapes
  Spot looks at weather
  Spot on the farm
  Spot sleeps over
  Spot visits his grandparents
  Spot's baby sister
  Spot's big book of words / El libro grande de las
    palabras de Spot
  Spot's first Christmas
  Spot's first Easter
  Spot's first walk
  Spot's first words
  Spot's magical Christmas
Hill, Meggan. *Nico and Lola*
Hills, Tad. *How Rocket learned to read*
  R is for Rocket
  Rocket writes a story
  Rocket's mighty words
Himmelman, John. *Katie and the puppy next door*
  Katie loves the kittens
  Ten little hot dogs
Hindley, Judy. *The best thing about a puppy*
Hines, Anna Grossnickle. *No, no Jack!*
Hoberman, Mary Ann. *One of each*
Hodge, Marie. *Are you sleepy yet, Petey?*
Holt, Kimberly Willis. *Skinny brown dog*
Holub, Joan. *Cinderdog and the wicked stepcat*
  Why do dogs bark?
Hooks, William H. *A dozen dizzy dogs*
Hooper, Meredith. *Dogs' Night*
Hornsey, Chris. *Why do I have to eat off the floor?*
Horvath, James. *Dig, dogs, dig*
  Work, dogs, work
Howard, Arthur. *Cosmo zooms*
  My dream dog
Howe, James. *Houndsley and Catina*
  Houndsley and Catina and the birthday surprise
Hubbell, Patricia. *Shaggy dogs, waggy dogs*
Hume, Stephen Eaton. *Red moon follows truck*
Huneck, Stephen. *Sally gets a job*
  Sally goes to heaven
  Sally goes to the beach
  Sally goes to the farm
  Sally goes to the mountains
  Sally's great balloon adventure
  Sally's snow adventure
Hurd, Thacher. *Art dog*
Hurley, Jorey. *Fetch*
Hutchins, Hazel. *Up dog*
Ichikawa, Satomi. *Come fly with me*
Imai, Ayano. *Chester*
Inkpen, Mick. *Hissss!*
  Honk!
  I will love you anyway

Groovy Joe: ice cream and dinosaurs
Lloyd, David. *Polly Molly Woof Woof*
London, Jonathan. *Froggy gets a doggy*
　Sled dogs run
　What do you love?
Long, Loren. *Otis and the puppy*
Lord, Cynthia. *Hot Rod Hamster*
Lottridge, Celia Barker. *Berta, a remarkable dog*
Loupy, Christophe. *Don't worry, Wags*
　Wiggles
Lupton, David. *Goodbye, Brecken*
Lyon, Tammie. *Olive and Snowflake*
McAllister, Angela. *Harry's box*
McAnulty, Stacy. *Excellent Ed*
McCardie, Amanda. *Our very own dog*
McCarthy, Meghan. *The incredible life of Balto*
McCarty, Peter. *Fabian escapes*
　First snow
　Hondo and Fabian
McCue, Lisa. *Quiet Bunny and Noisy Puppy*
McCully, Emily Arnold. *Strongheart*
MacDonald, Margaret Read. *The great smelly,*
　slobbery small-toothed dog
McDonald, Megan. *Shoe dog*
McDonnell, Christine. *Dog wants to play*
McDonnell, Flora. *Sparky*
McDonnell, Patrick. *The gift of nothing*
　Just like Heaven
　Wag!
McFarland, Lyn Rossiter. *Widget and the puppy*
McGhee, Alison. *Always*
　Percy, dog of destiny
McGuirk, Leslie. *Ho, ho, ho, Tucker!*
　Lucky Tucker
　Tucker flips!
　Tucker off his rocker
　Tucker over the top
　Tucker's spooky Halloween
McHenry, E. B. *Has anyone seen Winnie and Jean?*
　Poodlena
MacLachlan, Patricia. *Bittle*
　Three names
　Who loves me?
McMullan, Kate. *Bulldog's big day*
Macomber, Debbie. *The yippy, yappy Yorkie in the*
　green doggy sweater
McPhail, David. *Bad dog*
　Weezer changes the world
Magoon, Scott. *Hugo and Miles in I've painted*
　everything!
Manuel, Lynn. *The trouble with Tilly Trumble*
Manzano, Sonia. *No dogs allowed*
Marcus, Kimberly. *Scritch-scratch a perfect match*
Marino, Gianna. *A boy, a ball, and a dog*
Martin, Sarah Catherine. *Old Mother Hubbard*
　Old Mother Hubbard and her wonderful dog
Martins, Isabel Minhós. *My neighbor is a dog*
Mason, Adrienne. *Lu and Clancy sound off*
　Lu and Clancy's spy stuff
Massie, Felix. *Dogs in cars*
Masurel, Claire. *A cat and a dog*
　Domino
Mauner, Claudia. *Zoe Sophia's scrapbook*
Mayer, Mercer. *A boy, a dog, a frog and a friend*
　A boy, a dog and a frog
Meadows, Michelle. *Pilot pups*
　Traffic pups
Meddaugh, Susan. *Martha and Skits*
　Martha blah blah

Martha calling
Martha says it with flowers
Martha speaks
Martha walks the dog
Perfectly Martha
The witches' supermarket
Menchin, Scott. *Harry goes to dog school*
Meschenmoser, Sebastian. *Pug Man's 3 wishes*
Meserve, Adria. *No room for Napoleon*
Meshon, Aaron. *The best days are dog days*
Meyers, Susan. *Puppies! puppies! puppies!*
Milgrim, David. *Dog brain*
　My friend Lucky
　Why Benny barks
Mitchell, Hazel. *Toby*
Moers, Hermann. *Rufus and Max*
Monfreid, Dorothée de. *Shhh! I'm sleeping*
Monks, Lydia. *The cat barked?*
Monroe, Chris. *Cookie, the walker*
　Sneaky sheep
Montalván, Luis Carlos. *Tuesday tucks me in*
Moore, Elaine. *Roly-poly puppies*
Moore, Suzi. *Whoops!*
Mortensen, Lori. *Cowpoke Clyde and Dirty Dawg*
Moss, Marissa. *Knick knack paddywack*
Moxley, Sheila. *ABCD an alphabet book of cats and*
　dogs
Murphy, Mary. *Here comes spring, and summer and*
　fall and winter
　I feel happy, and sad, and angry, and glad
　You smell and taste and feel and see and hear
Murphy, Stuart J. *Get up and go!*
　Henry the fourth
Murray, Alison. *Apple pie ABC*
　Hickory dickory dog
　One two that's my shoe!
Murray, Andrew. *Have you seen Chester?*
Myers, Walter Dean. *The blues of Flats Brown*
Mystery manor
Napoli, Donna Jo. *Rocky, the cat who barks*
Nelson, Marilyn. *Snook alone*
Nelson-Schmidt, Michelle. *Dogs, dogs!*
Newberry, Clare Turlay. *Barkis*
Newgarden, Mark. *Bow-Wow bugs a bug*
　Bow-Wow orders lunch
　Bow-Wow's nightmare neighbors
Newman, Lesléa. *Dogs, dogs, dogs*
Nez, John. *One smart Cookie*
Noble, Sheilagh. *More*
Noonan, Julia. *Bath day*
　Breakfast time
Norman, Kim. *Puddle pug*
Norris, Leslie. *Albert and the angels*
North, Sherry. *Champ's story*
Noullet, Georgette. *Bed hog*
Novak, Matt. *The Pillow War*
Numeroff, Laura Joffe. *If you give a dog a donut*
　Sherman Crunchley
　What puppies do best
Ochiltree, Dianne. *Pillow pup*
O'Connor, Jane. *Fancy Nancy and the posh puppy*
　The perfect puppy for me
O'Hair, Margaret. *My pup*
O'Malley, Kevin. *The perfect dog*
Oppel, Kenneth. *The king's taster*
Oram, Hiawyn. *Just Dog*
　My friend Fred
Otto, Carolyn. *Our puppies are growing*
Page, Gail. *Bobo and the new neighbor*

How to be a good cat
Papp, Lisa. *Madeline Finn and the library dog*
Paraskevas, Betty. *Chocolate at the Four Seasons*
Parker, Marjorie Blain. *Jasper's day*
Parr, Todd. *Otto goes to school*
Patricelli, Leslie. *The Patterson puppies and the midnight monster party*
Patton, Julia. *The very very very long dog*
Paul, Ann Whitford. *Hello toes! Hello feet!*
Paul, Ruth. *Bad dog, Flash*
    Go home Flash
Peet, Bill. *The Whingdingdilly*
Perkins, Lynne Rae. *Frank and Lucky get schooled*
    Snow music
Perrow, Angeli. *Lighthouse dog to the rescue*
    Sirius, the dog star
Peters, Bernadette. *Stella is a star!*
Pfister, Marcus. *Snow puppy*
Pickering, Jimmy. *It's fall*
    It's winter
    Skelly the skeleton girl
Piepmeier, Charlotte. *Lucy's journey to the wild west*
Pilkey, Dav. *The Hallo-wiener*
Pinfold, Levi. *Black dog*
Pinkwater, Daniel. *I am the dog*
Pitzer, Susanna. *Not afraid of dogs*
Pizzoli, Greg. *Number one Sam*
Polacco, Patricia. *Remembering Vera*
Postgate, Daniel. *Smelly Bill*
    Smelly Bill: love stinks
Posthuma, Sieb. *Benny*
Potter, Beatrix. *The pie and the patty-pan*
Powell, Consie. *Old dog Cora and the Christmas tree*
Powell-Tuck, Maudie. *The messy book*
Prap, Lila. *Doggy whys*
Pritchett, Andy. *Stick!*
Provensen, Alice. *Murphy in the city*
Radunsky, Vladimir. *You?*
Rankin, Joan. *First day*
Rankin, Laura. *Fluffy and Baron*
Raschka, Chris. *A ball for Daisy*
    Can't sleep
    Daisy gets lost
    Hip Hop Dog
Rathmann, Peggy. *Officer Buckle and Gloria*
Ray, Mary Lyn. *Boom!*
    Goodnight, good dog
    A lucky author has a dog
Reed, Lynn Rowe. *Pedro, his perro, and the alphabet sombrero*
Regan, Dian Curtis. *Space Boy and his dog*
Regan, Lara Jo. *What is Mr. Winkle?*
    A Winkle in time
Reinen, Judy. *Bow wow*
Reiser, Lynn. *Any kind of dog*
    Hardworking puppies
    My dog Truffle
    Two dogs swimming
Rey, Margret. *Pretzel*
Rice, Eve. *Benny bakes a cake*
Richardson, Bill. *Sally Dog Little*
Ries, Lori. *Aggie and Ben*
Roberton, Fiona. *The perfect present*
Rockwell, Anne. *Fire engines*
Rohmann, Eric. *Bone dog*
Rosen, Michael. *Howler*
Rosen, Michael J. *Avalanche*
    The dog who walked with God
    With a dog like that, a kid like me . . .

Rowe, John A. *Moondog*
Rubinger, Ami. *Dog number 1 dog number 10*
Rudge, Leila. *A perfect place for Ted*
Ruelle, Karen Gray. *Bark park*
Russell, Joan Plummer. *Aero and Officer Mike*
Ruzzier, Sergio. *Amandina*
Rylant, Cynthia. *The bookshop dog*
    Dog Heaven
    The great Gracie chase
    Tulip sees America
    We love you, Rosie!
Sadler, Judy Ann. *Sandwiches for Duke*
Saltzberg, Barney. *I love dogs*
Sampson, Michael R. *Caddie, the golf dog*
Samuels, Barbara. *Fred's beds*
San Souci, Robert D. *The Hobyahs*
    The silver charm
Sarcone-Roach, Julia. *The bear ate your sandwich*
Sattler, Jennifer. *Chick 'n' Pug*
    Chick 'n' Pug: the love pug
    A Chick 'n' Pug Christmas
    Chick 'n' Pug meet the Dude
Sayre, April Pulley. *Hush, little puppy*
Schachner, Judith Byron. *Skippyjon Jones and the big bones*
    Skippyjon Jones Cirque de Olé
    Skippyjon Jones class action
    Skippyjon Jones in mummy trouble
    Skippyjon Jones, lost in spice
Schindel, John. *The babies and doggies book*
Schmidt, Karen Lee. *Carl's nose*
Schneider, Christine M. *I'm bored!*
Schneider, Howie. *Chewy Louie*
Schneider, Josh. *Princess Sparkle-Heart gets a makeover*
Schories, Pat. *Jack and the night visitors*
    Jack wants a snack
    When Jack goes out
Schubert, Ingrid. *The umbrella*
Schubert, Leda. *Reading to Peanut*
    Winnie all day long
    Winnie plays ball
Schwartz, Amy. *Oma and Bobo*
Schwarz, Viviane. *Is there a dog in this book?*
Schweninger, Ann. *Autumn days*
Seeber, Dorothea P. *A pup just for me . . . A boy just for me*
Seeger, Laura Vaccaro. *Dog and Bear: three to get ready*
    Dog and Bear: tricks and treats
    Dog and Bear: two friends, three stories
    Dog and Bear: two's company
Segal, John. *Alistair and Kip's great adventure*
Seibert, Patricia. *Mush!*
Serfozo, Mary. *What's what?*
Shannon, David. *Good boy, Fergus!*
Shannon, George. *Tippy-toe chick, go*
Sharmat, Marjorie Weinman. *I'm the best*
Shaskan, Stephen. *A dog is a dog*
Shaw, Nancy. *Sheep go to sleep*
Shields, Carol Diggory. *I wish my brother was a dog*
Shireen, Nadia. *Hey, Presto!*
Shyba, Jessica. *Bathtime with Theo and Beau*
    Naptime with Theo and Beau
Sidman, Joyce. *Meow ruff*
Siminovich, Lorena. *Alex and Lulu*
Simmons, Jane. *Ebb and Flo and the greedy gulls*
    Ebb and Flo and the new friend
    Together

Simon, Charnan. *Big bad Buzz*
Simont, Marc. *The stray dog*
Singer, Marilyn. *Every day's a dog's day*
   What is your dog doing?
Singleton, Linda Joy. *A cat is better*
   Snow dog, sand dog
Sirotich, Erica. *Found dogs*
Slater, Teddy. *Smooch your pooch*
Slonim, David. *Patch*
Smith, Charles R. *Loki and Alex*
Smith, Janice Lee. *Jess and the stinky cowboys*
Smith, Linda. *The inside tree*
Snicket, Lemony. *Thirteen words*
Soman, David. *Ladybug Girl and Bingo*
Sookocheff, Carey. *Solutions for cold feet and other*
   little problems
Soto, Gary. *Chato goes cruisin'*
   Chato's kitchen
Spetter, Jung-Hee. *Lily and Trooper's fall*
   Lily and Trooper's spring
   Lily and Trooper's summer
   Lily and Trooper's winter
Spinelli, Eileen. *Do you have a dog?*
Spires, Ashley. *The most magnificent thing*
Spires, Elizabeth. *The big meow*
Springett, Martin. *Kate and Pippin*
Staake, Bob. *The first pup*
Stadler, John. *The cats of Mrs. Calamari*
Stainton, Sue. *I love dogs!*
Stanley, Mandy. *Bloomer, the dog you can play with*
Stanton, Karen. *Monday, Wednesday, and every other*
   weekend
Steig, William. *Caleb and Kate*
   Tiffky Doofky
Stein, David Ezra. *I'm my own dog*
Stein, Garth. *Enzo's very scary Halloween*
Stephens, Helen. *Fleabag*
   Poochie-poo
   Ruby and the muddy dog
Sterling, Holly. *Hiccups!*
Sternberg, Julie. *Puppy, puppy, puppy*
Stevens, Janet. *Find a cow now!*
   The great fuzz frenzy
   Help me, Mr. Mutt!
   My big dog
Stevenson, James. *Worse than the worst*
Stohner, Anu. *Brave Charlotte*
Sturges, Philemon. *Waggers*
Stuve-Bodeen, Stephanie. *A small brown dog with a*
   wet pink nose
Sullivan, Mary. *Ball*
   Frankie
   Treat
Swaim, Jessica. *The hound from the pound*
Sweeney, Joan. *Suzette and the puppy*
Sweet, Melissa. *Carmine*
   Tupelo rides the rails
Sykes, Julie. *Smudge*
Tafuri, Nancy. *Who's counting?*
Talbott, Hudson. *From wolf to woof*
Tanaka, Shinsuke. *Wings*
Taylor, Alastair. *Swollobog*
Taylor, Eleanor. *Beep, beep, let's go!*
Teague, Mark. *Dear Mrs. LaRue*
   Detective LaRue
   Firehouse!
   Funny farm
   LaRue across America
   LaRue for mayor

Tellis, Annabel. *If my dad were a dog*
Thayer, Jane. *Part-time dog*
   The puppy who wanted a boy
Thomas, Jan. *The doghouse*
Thomas, Jane Resh. *Scaredy dog*
Thompson, Colin. *Unknown*
Thompson, Laurie Ann. *My dog is the best*
Thomson, Bill. *Fossil*
Torrey, Richard. *My dog, Bob*
Townsend, Michael. *Cute and cuter*
Trapani, Iza. *How much is that doggie in the window?*
Trimble, Marcia. *Peppy's shadow*
Trimmer, Christian. *Simon's new bed*
Trukhan, Ekaterina. *Patrick wants a dog!*
Turner, Pamela S. *Hachiko*
Turner, Sandy. *Silent night*
Twohy, Mike. *Oops, pounce, quick, run!*
Uhlberg, Myron. *Mad Dog McGraw*
Umansky, Kaye. *I don't like Gloria!*
Underwood, Deborah. *Here comes Valentine Cat*
Ungerer, Tomi. *Flix*
Urbanovic, Jackie. *Sitting duck*
U'Ren, Andrea. *Pugdog*
Van Allsburg, Chris. *The garden of Abdul Gasazi*
Van Dusen, Chris. *Down to the sea with Mr. Magee*
   Learning to ski with Mr. Magee
Van Leeuwen, Jean. *The strange adventures of Blue*
   Dog
Van Steenwyk, Elizabeth. *First dog Fala*
Vischer, Frans. *Fuddles and Puddles*
Waber, Bernard. *Lyle walks the dogs*
Waddell, Martin. *The Super Hungry Dinosaur*
   We love them
Wahman, Wendy. *Don't lick the dog*
Waite, Judy. *Mouse, look out!*
Waite, Michael P. *Jojofu*
Walton, Rick. *Bertie was a watchdog*
Ward, Helen. *Little Moon Dog*
Ward, Lindsay. *Rosco vs. the baby*
Wardlaw, Lee. *Won Ton and Chopstick*
Watt, Mélanie. *Scaredy Squirrel makes a friend*
Webb, Holly. *Little puppy lost*
Weeks, Sarah. *Glamourpuss*
   Oh my gosh, Mrs. McNosh!
   Woof
Wegman, William. *Flo and Wendell explore*
Weingarten, Gene. *Me and dog*
Weller, Frances Ward. *The angel of Mill Street*
Wells, Rosemary. *Bingo*
   Lucy comes to stay
   McDuff and the baby
   McDuff comes home
   McDuff goes to school
   McDuff moves in
   McDuff saves the day
   McDuff's hide-and-seek
   McDuff's new friend
   McDuff's wild romp
   Otto runs for President
   Otto se presenta para presidente / Otto runs for
   President
Whatley, Bruce. *Captain Pajamas*
Wheeler, Lisa. *The Christmas boot*
White, Ellen Emerson. *Santa paws*
White, Marsha. *Hooper has lost his owner*
Wild, Margaret. *Fox*
   Harry and Hopper
   The pocket dogs
Wildsmith, Brian. *Give a dog a bone*

Wilhelm, Hans. *I'll always love you*
  Schnitzel's first Christmas
Willems, Mo. *City dog, country frog*
  The pigeon wants a puppy!
Williams, Suzanne. *My dog never says please*
Willis, Jeanne. *The boy who lost his bellybutton*
Winters, Kari-Lynn. *Bad pirate*
  Good pirate
Winthrop, Elizabeth. *I'm the Boss!*
Wishinsky, Frieda. *Please, Louise!*
Wohnoutka, Mike. *Little puppy and the big green*
  monster
Wojtusik, Elizabeth. *Kitty up!*
Wolff, Ashley. *When Lucy goes out walking*
Wood, Audrey. *A dog needs a bone*
  It's Duffy time!
Woodruff, Liza. *Emerson barks*
Yaccarino, Dan. *Oswald*
  Unlovable
Yates, Louise. *Dog loves books*
  Dog loves counting
  Dog loves drawing
Yorinks, Arthur. *Harry and Lulu*
  Hey, Al
Young, Ned. *Zoomer*
  Zoomer's out-of-this-world Christmas
  Zoomer's summer snowstorm
Zarins, Kim. *The helpful puppy*
Ziefert, Harriet. *I swapped my dog*
  Knick-knack paddywhack
  Lucy rescued
  Mommy, I want to sleep in your bed!
  Murphy jumps a hurdle
  My dog thinks I'm a genius
  Pushkin meets the bundle
  Pushkin minds the bundle
Zimmerman, Andrea Griffing. *My dog Toby*
Zion, Gene. *Harry, the dirty dog*
  No roses for Harry
Zolotow, Charlotte. *The old dog*
  The poodle who barked at the wind
Zommer, Yuval. *One hundred bones*
  One hundred sausages
Zuill, Andrea. *Wolf camp*

Animals – dolphins

Allen, Judy. *Whales and dolphins*
Arnosky, Jim. *Dolphins on the sand*
Canyon, Christopher. *John Denver's Ancient rhymes*
Davies, Nicola. *Dolphin baby!*
Edgemon, Darcie. *Seamore, the very forgetful porpoise*
Hatkoff, Craig, et al. *Winter's tail*
Nelson, Robert Lyn. *Ocean friends*
Pfeffer, Wendy. *Dolphin talk*
Winton, Tim. *The deep*
Wood, Audrey. *The rainbow bridge*

Animals – donkeys

Aesop. *The donkey in the lion's skin*
Arnosky, Jim. *Little Burro*
Barnes, Laura T. *Ernest and the big itch*
  Ernest's special Christmas
  Teeny tiny Ernest
  Twist and Ernest
Barton, Bob. *Paul Gallico's The small miracle*
Bell, Cece. *I yam a donkey!*
Brown, Monica. *Waiting for the Biblioburro*

Byrd, Robert. *Saint Francis and the Christmas donkey*
Clanton, Ben. *Vote for me!*
Crawford, Sheryl Ann. *The baby who changed the*
  world
Daly, Niki. *Thank you, Jackson*
Ismail, Yasmeen. *I'm a girl!*
Kennedy, Kim. *Hee-Haw-Dini and the Great Zambini*
Kornell, Max. *Me first*
Kromhout, Rindert. *Little Donkey and the baby-sitter*
  Little Donkey and the birthday present
McGee, Marni. *The colt and the king*
Mandell, Muriel. *A donkey reads*
Newton, Jill. *Crash bang donkey!*
Puttock, Simon. *Goat and Donkey in strawberry*
  sunglasses
  Goat and Donkey in the great outdoors
Seim, Donna Marie. *Where is Simon, Sandy?*
Smith, Kathryn. *Little Donkey's Christmas story*
Spang, Günter. *The ox and the Donkey*
Steig, William. *Farmer Palmer's wagon ride*
  Sylvester and the magic pebble
Tafuri, Nancy. *The donkey's Christmas song*
Tarlow, Ellen. *Pinwheel days*
Taylor, Sean. *Crocodiles are the best animals of all*
Van Woerkom, Dorothy. *Abu Ali counts his donkeys*
  Donkey Ysabel
Wildsmith, Brian. *A Christmas story*
  The Easter story
Winter, Jeanette. *Biblioburro*
Young, Ed. *Donkey trouble*
Ziefert, Harriet. *Buzzy had a little lamb*

Animals – elephants

Abbot, Judi. *Train!*
Alsenas, Linas. *Peanut*
Andreasen, Dan. *Saturday with Daddy*
Andres, Kristina. *Elephant in the bathtub*
Appelt, Kathi. *Elephants aloft*
Arnold, Katya. *Elephants can paint, too!*
Ashman, Linda. *Ella who?*
Bachelet, Gilles. *My cat, the silliest cat in the world*
  When the silliest cat was small
Badescu, Ramona. *Pomelo begins to grow*
  Pomelo's opposites
Bajaj, Varsha. *This is our baby, born today*
Banks, Kate. *How to find an elephant*
Barba, Ale. *When your elephant comes to play*
Barclay, Eric. *Hiding Phil*
Barrow, David. *Have you seen Elephant?*
Base, Graeme. *Little elephants*
Bates, Ivan. *All by myself*
Beake, Lesley. *Home now*
Beeler, Selby B. *How many Elephants?*
Blackford, Harriet. *Elephant's story*
Brenner, Barbara A. *What the elephant told*
Bridges, Margaret Park. *Edna elephant*
Brunhoff, Jean de. *Babar and Father Christmas*
  Babar and his children
  Babar the king
  Babar the king [facsimile ed.]
  The story of Babar, the little elephant
  The travels of Babar
Brunhoff, Laurent de. *B is for Babar*
  Babar and the ghost
  Babar and the succotash bird
  Babar and the Wully-Wully
  Babar on Paradise Island
  Babar's ABC

Babar's battle
Babar's birthday surprise
Babar's guide to Paris
Babar's little girl
Babar's Museum of Art
Babar's USA
Babar's world tour
Meet Babar and his family
Buckley, Carol. *Tarra and Bella*
Bunting, Eve. *Tweak tweak*
Burningham, John. *Tug-of-war*
Buzzeo, Toni. *My Bibi always remembers*
   A passion for elephants
Chase, Kit. *Charlie's boat*
   Oliver's tree
Clanton, Ben. *Vote for me!*
Clarke, Jane. *Trumpet*
Conway, David. *Errol and his extraordinary nose*
Cordell, Matthew. *Wish*
Côté, Geneviève. *What elephant?*
Cousins, Lucy. *Maisy makes lemonade*
Cowcher, Helen. *Desert elephants*
Curato, Mike. *Little Elliot, big city*
   Little Elliot, big family
   Little Elliot, big fun
   Little Elliot, fall friends
Daly, Niki. *Next stop — Zanzibar Road!*
   Welcome to Zanzibar Road
D'Amico, Carmela. *Ella sets sail*
   Ella sets the stage
   Ella takes the cake
   Ella, the elegant elephant
Davies, Gill. *Tiny's big wish*
Day, Alexandra. *Frank and Ernest*
   Frank and Ernest on the road
   Frank and Ernest play ball
Dijs, Carla. *Mommy, what if —?*
Dodd, Emma. *Always*
   Cinderelephant
   No matter what
Doerrfeld, Cori. *Maggie and Wendel*
Dunbar, Polly. *Where's Tumpty?*
Eilenberg, Max. *Squeak's good idea*
Ellis, Gerry. *Natumi takes the lead*
Engler, Michael. *Elephantastic!*
Fearnley, Jan. *Arthur and the meanies*
Feeney, Tatyana. *Small Elephant's bathtime*
Fox, Mem. *Baby bedtime*
Genechten, Guido van. *Kai-Mook*
Gibbons, Gail. *Elephants of Africa*
Ginkel, Anne. *I've got an elephant*
Goodhart, Pippa. *Little Nelly's big book*
Goodman, Joan Elizabeth. *Bernard goes to school*
Gorbachev, Valeri. *Big Little Elephant*
Gréban, Quentin. *Nestor*
Grindley, Sally. *Little Elephant Thunderfoot*
Gude, Paul. *When Elephant met Giraffe*
Hänel, Wolfram. *Little elephant's song*
Harrison, Hannah E. *My friend Maggie*
Hart, Christopher. *Merwin, master of disguise*
Henrichs, Wendy. *When Anju loved being an elephant*
Henry, Rohan. *The gift box*
Hillenbrand, Will. *My book box*
Hoberman, Mary Ann. *Miss Mary Mack*
Horáček, Petr. *My elephant*
Hunter, Sally. *Humphrey's bedtime*
   Humphrey's birthday
   Humphrey's Christmas
   Humphrey's corner

Jackson, Kathryn. *The saggy baggy elephant*
Jaramillo, Susie. *Elefantitos / little elephants*
Javaherbin, Mina. *Elephant in the dark*
Johnson, Paul Brett. *The goose who went off in a huff*
Joosse, Barbara. *Sleepover at Gramma's house*
Judge, Lita. *Pennies for elephants*
Kasza, Keiko. *The mightiest*
Kavanagh, Peter. *I love my mama*
Kilaka, John. *True friends*
Kimmel, Eric A. *Anansi and the talking melon*
Kipling, Rudyard. *The elephant's child*
   How the elephant got his trunk
Kitamura, Satoshi. *Pablo the artist*
Kleven, Elisa. *Welcome home, Mouse*
Knapman, Timothy. *Soon*
Koehler, Fred. *How to cheer up Dad*
   Super Jumbo
Kramer, Jackie Azúa. *The green umbrella*
Krosoczka, Jarrett J. *Ollie the purple elephant*
Leslie, Amanda. *Alfie and Betty Bug*
Lester, Helen. *Hurty feelings*
   Tacky in trouble
Levitin, Sonia. *When Elephant goes to a party*
Lewis, Kim. *Good night, Harry*
   Here we go Harry
   Hooray for Harry
   My friend Harry
McClurkan, Rob. *Playdates rule!*
MacDonald, Suse. *Elephants on board*
McDonnell, Flora. *Splash!*
McGrory, Anik. *Kidogo*
McKee, David. *Elmer*
   Elmer again
   Elmer and Butterfly
   Elmer and Grandpa Eldo
   Elmer and Rose
   Elmer and Snake
   Elmer and Super El
   Elmer and the big bird
   Elmer and the flood
   Elmer and the hippos
   Elmer and the kangaroo
   Elmer and the lost teddy
   Elmer and the monster
   Elmer and the race
   Elmer and the whales
   Elmer and the wind
   Elmer and Wilbur
   Elmer in the snow
   Elmer takes off
   Elmer's Christmas
   Elmer's special day
Magloff, Lisa. *Elephant*
Magoon, Scott. *Hugo and Miles in I've painted everything!*
Mantchev, Lisa. *Strictly no elephants*
Marino, Gianna. *Meet me at the moon*
Markle, Sandra. *Thirsty, thirsty elephants*
Melmed, Laura Krauss. *Jumbo's lullaby*
Monroe, Chris. *Monkey with a tool belt and the seaside shenanigans*
Mueller, Doris L. *Small One's adventure*
Muir, Leslie. *The little bitty bakery*
Murphy, Jill. *Mr. Large in charge*
   A piece of cake
   A quiet night in
Na, Il Sung. *Hide and seek*
   The thingamabob
Nichol, Barbara. *Trunks all aboard*

Ormerod, Jan. *When an elephant comes to school*
Oyibo, Papa. *Big brother, little sister*
Paxton, Tom. *Engelbert the elephant*
Pearson, Tracey Campbell. *Elephant's story*
Peet, Bill. *The ant and the elephant*
　Ella
　Encore for Eleanor
Perepeczko, Jenny. *Moses: the true story of an*
　elephant baby
Polacco, Patricia. *Emma Kate*
Prince, April Jones. *Twenty-one elephants and still*
　standing
Radcliffe, Theresa. *Bashi, elephant baby*
Ravishankar, Anushka. *Elephants never forget!*
Robinson, Bruce. *The obvious elephant*
Root, Barry. *Gumbrella*
Rubinger, Ami. *I dream of an elephant*
Samuels, Jenny. *A nose like a hose*
Sarcone-Roach, Julia. *The secret plan*
Schubert, Leda. *Ballet of the elephants*
Schwartz, Amy. *A beautiful girl*
　How to catch an elephant
　Tiny and Hercules
Schwartz, Corey Rosen. *Hop! Plop!*
Seuss, Dr. *Horton hatches the egg*
　Horton hears a Who!
Shields, Gillian. *Elephantantrum!*
Slack, Michael. *Elecopter*
Slobodkina, Esphyr. *Circus caps for sale*
Smith, Maggie. *Paisley*
Stead, Philip C. *Special delivery*
Steig, William. *Doctor De Soto goes to Africa*
Stock, Catherine. *Alexander's midnight snack*
Teckentrup, Britta. *Get out of my bath!*
Tompert, Ann. *Just a little bit*
Turner, Sandy. *Otto's trunk*
van Lieshout, Maria. *Hopper and Wilson*
　Hopper and Wilson fetch a star
Vere, Ed. *Everyone's little*
　The getaway
Wallace, Joseph E. *Big and noisy Simon*
Warnes, Tim. *The great cheese robbery*
Watkins, Rowboat. *Pete with no pants*
Wells, Robert E. *Why do elephants need the sun?*
Westcott, Nadine Bernard. *Peanut butter and jelly*
Wilson-Max, Ken. *Max's starry night*
Wojtowycz, David. *Elephant Joe, Brave Knight!*
Won, Brian. *Hooray for hat!*
Young, Cybèle. *Nancy knows*
Young, Ed. *Seven blind mice*

Animals – endangered animals

Alexander, Kwame. *Animal ark*
Aliki. *My visit to the zoo*
Barry, Frances. *Let's save the animals*
Beard, Alex. *Crocodile's tears*
Beeke, Tiphanie. *Roar like a lion!*
Blackford, Harriet. *Elephant's story*
Butler, John. *Pi-shu, the little panda*
Cline-Ransome, Lesa. *Whale trails, before and now*
Cotton, Katie. *Counting lions*
Coville, Bruce. *The prince of butterflies*
Dewdney, Anna. *Roly Poly pangolin*
George, Jean Craighead. *The buffalo are back*
　The eagles are back
　The wolves are back
Gibbons, Gail. *Giant pandas*
　Grizzly bears

Guiberson, Brenda Z. *Moon bear*
Hamilton, Virginia. *Jaguarundi*
Hatkoff, Craig, et al. *Leo the snow leopard*
　Looking for Miza
Heinz, Brian J. *The wolves*
Jacobs, Francine. *Lonesome George, the giant tortoise*
Jenkins, Martin. *Can we save the tiger?*
Jenkins, Priscilla Belz. *Falcons nest on skyscrapers*
Jenkins, Steve. *Almost gone*
Jonas, Ann. *Aardvarks, disembark!*
Kirk, Daniel. *Rhino in the house*
Lunde, Darrin. *Hello, bumblebee bat*
McCully, Emily Arnold. *Hurry!*
McLimans, David. *Gone wild*
Markle, Sandra. *Family pack*
Martin, Jacqueline Briggs. *The chiru of High Tibet*
Mullins, Patricia. *V for vanishing*
Noonan, Diana. *The crocodile*
Raffi. *Baby beluga*
Schertle, Alice. *Advice for a frog and other poems*
Slade, Suzanne. *What's the difference?*
Thomson, Sarah L. *Tigers*
Weeks, Sarah. *Crocodile smile*

Animals – ferrets

Elsdale, Bob. *Mac side up*
Jenkins, Emily. *Num, num, num!*
　Plonk, plonk, plonk!
　Up, up, up!
Rostoker-Gruber, Karen. *Ferret fun*
Weigelt, Udo. *It wasn't me*

Animals – foxes

Aesop. *Anno's Aesop*
　The donkey in the lion's skin
　The fox and the grapes
　Fox tails
　Three Aesop fox fables
Alborough, Jez. *Six little chicks*
Aman, Kimiko. *The fox wish*
Arnosky, Jim. *Watching foxes*
Auch, Mary Jane. *Peeping Beauty*
Bailey, Linda. *Toads on toast*
Baker, Liza. *I love you because you're you*
Banks, Kate. *Fox*
Battut, Eric. *The fox and the hen*
Bauer, Marion Dane. *Winter dance*
Blackaby, Susan. *Brownie Groundhog and the*
　February Fox
Bloom, Suzanne. *Alone together*
　Bear can dance!
　Fox forgets
　Oh! what a surprise!
　What about Bear?
Bonnet, Rosalinde. *Daddy Honk Honk!*
Bonning, Tony. *Fox tale soup*
Camcam, Princesse. *Fox's garden*
Campoy, F. Isabel. *Rosa Raposa*
Carlstrom, Nancy White. *Mama, will it snow*
　tonight?
Chaucer, Geoffrey. *Chanticleer and the fox*
Chrustowski, Rick. *My Little Fox*
Church, Caroline Jayne. *One smart goose*
Cocca-Leffler, Maryann. *Bravery soup*
Cox, Phil Roxbee. *Fox on a box*
Crum, Shutta. *Fox and Fluff*
Dodd, Emma. *Foxy*

Foxy in love
Dyckman, Ame. *Read the book, lemmings!*
Ehlert, Lois. *Mole's hill*
   Moon rope / Un lazo a la luna
Ernst, Lisa Campbell. *The Gingerbread Girl goes animal crackers*
The fox went out on a chilly night
Ginsburg, Mirra. *Across the stream*
   Mushroom in the rain
Gliori, Debi. *No matter what*
   Stormy weather
Graegin, Stephanie. *Little fox in the forest*
Grindley, Sally. *Silly Goose and Dizzy Duck play hide-and-seek*
   What are friends for?
   What will I do without you?
Hawkins, Emily. *Little snow goose*
Heinz, Brian J. *Red Fox at McCloskey's farm*
Helberg, Berit. *Sniffer and Tinni*
Hindley, Judy. *Do like a duck does*
Hogrogian, Nonny. *One fine day*
Husband, Amy. *The noisy foxes*
Hutchins, Pat. *Rosie's walk*
   Where, oh where, is Rosie's chick?
Jonovitz, Marilyn. *Good morning, Little Fox*
Keller, Holly. *Nosy Rosie*
Keller, John G. *The rubber-legged ducky*
Leedy, Loreen. *Crazy like a fox*
Letourneau, Marie. *Argyle Fox*
Levine, Michelle. *Red foxes*
Liwska, Renata. *Red wagon*
Lobel, Gillian. *Too small for honey cake*
London, Jonathan. *Ice Bear and Little Fox*
McBratney, Sam. *I'll always be your friend*
McCanna, Tim. *Watersong*
McFarland, Clive. *The fox and the wild*
McKissack, Patricia C. *Flossie and the fox*
Magruder, Nilah. *How to find a fox*
Marshall, James. *Wings: a tale of two chickens*
Migy. *And away we go!*
Myers, Tim. *Basho and the fox*
Numeroff, Laura Joffe. *What daddies do best*
Palatini, Margie. *Lousy rotten stinkin' grapes*
   Three French hens
   Zoom Broom
Pauli, Lorenz. *The fox in the library*
Pierce, Christa. *Did you know that I love you?*
Potter, Beatrix. *The tale of Mr. Tod*
Puttock, Simon. *Miss Fox*
Rankin, Joan. *Wow! It's great being a duck*
Rankin, Laura. *Ruthie and the (not so) teeny tiny lie*
   Ruthie and the (not so) very busy day
Rave, Friederike. *Outfoxing the fox*
Rawlinson, Julia. *Fletcher and the falling leaves*
   Fletcher and the snowflake Christmas
   Fletcher and the springtime blossoms
Rodriguez, Béatrice. *The chicken thief*
   Fox and hen together
Root, Phyllis. *Toot toot zoom!*
Salzano, Tammi. *One windy day*
San Souci, Robert D. *The silver charm*
Shapiro, Esmé. *Ooko*
Sharmat, Marjorie Weinman. *The best Valentine in the world*
Slater, Dashka. *The antlered ship*
Smith, Alex T. *Foxy and Egg*
Snitselaar, Nicole. *Little Fox, lost*
Souhami, Jessica. *Foxy!*
Spinelli, Eileen. *Miss Fox's class earns a field trip*

Miss Fox's class gets it wrong
   Miss Fox's class goes green
   Miss Fox's class shapes up
   Peace Week in Miss Fox's class
Steig, William. *Doctor De Soto*
   Roland, the minstrel pig
Stoeke, Janet Morgan. *Oh no! a fox!*
Subramaniam, Manasi. *The fox and the crow*
Tabor, Corey R. *Fox and the jumping contest*
Taylor, Harriet Peck. *Ulaq and the northern lights*
Thompson, Jolene. *Faraway fox*
The three little pigs The three little pigs and the fox
Tolan, Stephanie S. *Bartholomew's blessing*
Tompert, Ann. *Grandfather Tang's story*
   Little Fox goes to the end of the world
Townsend, Emily Rose. *Arctic foxes*
Trukhan, Ekaterina. *Apples for little Fox*
Turnbull, Victoria. *Pandora*
Twohy, Mike. *Outfoxed*
Wahl, Phoebe. *Sonya's chickens*
Walsh, Ellen Stoll. *You silly goose*
Ward, Helen. *The rooster and the fox*
Waring, Richard. *Hungry hen*
Watson, Clyde. *Valentine foxes*
Watt, Mélanie. *Have I got a book for you!*
Weston, Carrie. *If a chicken stayed for supper*
Wild, Margaret. *Fox*
Wilhelm, Hans. *More bunny trouble*
Willems, Mo. *That is not a good idea!*
Williams, Sue. *Dinnertime*
Yerkes, Jennifer. *A funny little bird*

Animals – gazelles

Rex, Adam. *XO, Ox*

Animals – gerbils

Roth, Susan L. *Cinnamon's day out*

Animals – giraffes

Andreae, Giles. *Giraffes can't dance*
Averbeck, Jim. *One word from Sophia*
Bender, Rebecca. *Giraffe meets Bird*
   Not friends
Bergmann, Andy. *The starry giraffe*
Bracken, Beth. *Too shy for show-and-tell*
Burach, Ross. *I am not a chair!*
Buzzeo, Toni. *Stay close to Mama*
Cowan, Charlotte. *Sadie's sore throat*
Cronin, Doreen. *Rescue bunnies*
De Vries, Anke. *Raf*
Dominguez, Angela. *How do you say? / ¿Cómo se dice?*
Flory, Neil. *The short giraffe*
Freedman, Deborah. *Shy*
Gude, Paul. *When Elephant met Giraffe*
Hewett, Joan. *A giraffe calf grows up*
Holmes, Mary Tavener. *A giraffe goes to Paris*
Horowitz, Dave. *A monkey among us*
Lin, Grace. *Okie-dokie, Artichokie*
Litten, Kristyna. *Blue and Bertie*
McEvoy, Anne. *Betsy B. Little*
Ommen, Sylvia van. *The surprise*
O'Neill, Gemma. *Oh dear, Geoffrey!*
Rayner, Catherine. *Abigail*
Rey, H. A. *Cecily G and the nine monkeys*
Rumford, James. *Chee-lin*
St. George, Judith. *Zarafa*

Schulz, Heidi. *Giraffes ruin everything*
Sirett, Dawn. *Happy birthday Sophie!*
Spanyol, Jessica. *Carlo likes counting*
Tourville, Amanda Doering. *A giraffe grows up*
Yuly, Toni. *The Jelly Bean tree*

Animals – gnus

Dewdney, Anna. *Nelly Gnu and Daddy too*

Animals – goats

Alakija, Polly. *Catch that goat!*
Andrews, Julie. *Dumpy to the rescue!*
Asbjørnsen, P. C. *The three billy goats Gruff*, ill. by Stephen Carpenter
   The three billy goats Gruff, ill. by Paul Galdone
   The three billy goats gruff, ill. by Jerry Pinkney
   The three billy goats Gruff, ill. by Glen Rounds
   The three billy goats Gruff, ill. by Janet Stevens
   The three Billygoats Gruff and Mean Calypso Joe
   Who's that tripping over my bridge?
Berry, Lynne. *What floats in a moat?*
Blood, Charles L. *The goat in the rug*
Bunting, Eve. *Mr. Goat's valentine*
Burks, James. *Beep and Bah*
Church, Caroline Jayne. *Little Apple Goat*
Cole, Henry. *Trudy*
Crummel, Susan Stevens. *Ten-Gallon Bart*
Dewdney, Anna. *Llama Llama and the bully goat*
Elschner, Geraldine. *Pashmina the little Christmas goat*
Emberley, Rebecca. *Three cool kids*
Ford, Bernette. *No more biting for Billy Goat!*
Fox, Mem. *Let's count goats!*
Garland, Michael. *King Puck*
Gorbachev, Valeri. *One rainy day*
   That's what friends are for
Grant, Jacob. *Through with the zoo*
Gugler, Laurel Dee. *There's a billy goat in the garden*
Hale, Dean. *Scapegoat*
Helquist, Brett. *Grumpy Goat*
Hoberman, Mary Ann. *Bill Grogan's goat*
Johnston, Tony. *Desert dog*
Keefer, Janice Kulyk. *Anna's goat*
Kimmel, Eric A. *The three cabritos*
Kimmelman, Leslie. *The three bully goats*
Kimura, Yuichi. *One stormy night . . .*
   One sunny day . . .
McBrier, Page. *Beatrice's goat*
Mortimer, Rachael. *The three Billy Goats Fluff*
Nobleman, Marc Tyler. *The chupacabra ate the candelabra*
Palatini, Margie. *The three silly billies*
Polacco, Patricia. *Oh, look!*
Puttock, Simon. *Goat and Donkey in strawberry sunglasses*
   Goat and Donkey in the great outdoors
Rankin, Laura. *My turn!*
Ross, Tony. *Our Kid*
Schrock, Jan West. *Give a goat*
Sharmat, Mitchell. *Gregory, the terrible eater*
Shea, Bob. *Unicorn thinks he's pretty great*
Shepard, Aaron. *One-eye! Two-eyes! Three-eyes!*
Slade-Robinson, Nikki. *Muddle and Mo's worm surprise*
   Muddle and Mo
Taylor, Sean. *Huck runs amuck!*
The three bears *Goatilocks and the three bears*

Waddell, Martin. *Captain Small Pig*
Wildsmith, Brian. *Goat's trail*
Willis, Jeanne. *Troll stinks*
Wolkstein, Diane. *The banza*
Yaccarino, Dan. *Billy and Goat at the state fair*
Young, Amy. *A new friend for Sparkle*
   A unicorn named Sparkle
Ziefert, Harriet. *Pumpkin Pie*

Animals – gorillas

Aardema, Verna. *Princess Gorilla and a new kind of water*
Adams, Sarah. *Gary and Ray*
Anderson, Derek. *Gladys goes out to lunch*
Antony, Steve. *Betty goes bananas*
Applegate, Katherine. *Ivan*
Bottner, Barbara. *Priscilla gorilla*
Browne, Anthony. *Gorilla*
   Little Beauty
   One gorilla: a counting book
   Voices in the park
   Willy and Hugh
   Willy the champ
   Willy the wimp
Bustos, Eduardo. *Going ape!*
Clarke, Jane. *Who woke the baby?*
Cordell, Matthew. *Dream*
Durango, Julia. *Go-go gorillas*
Fairgray, Richard. *Gorillas in our midst*
Faulconer, Maria. *A mom for Umande*
Gibbons, Gail. *Gorillas*
Graves, Keith. *Second banana*
Harvey, Damian. *Just the thing!*
Hatkoff, Craig, et al. *Looking for Miza*
Howe, James. *The day the teacher went bananas*
Layton, Neal. *Smile if you're human*
Lazar, Tara. *Normal Norman*
Mack, Jeff. *Look!*
   Playtime?
Morozumi, Atsuko. *My friend gorilla*
   One gorilla
Norman, Kim. *Still a gorilla!*
OHora, Zachariah. *No fits, Nilson!*
Palatini, Margie. *Ding dong ding dong*
Philip, Simon. *I don't know what to call my cat*
Rex, Michael. *Furious George goes bananas*
Robinson, Michelle. *Ding dong! Gorilla!*
Sattler, Jennifer. *Frankie the blankie*
Shulman, Mark. *Gorilla Garage*
Walton, Rick. *Girl and Gorilla: out and about*
Wensink, Patrick. *Go go gorillas*
Willis, Jeanne. *Gorilla! Gorilla!*

Animals – groundhogs

Bang, Molly. *Goose*
Bell, Cece. *Chuck and Woodchuck*
Biedrzycki, David. *Groundhog's runaway shadow*
Blackaby, Susan. *Brownie Groundhog and the February Fox*
   Brownie Groundhog and the wintry surprise
Cherry, Lynne. *How Groundhog's garden grew*
Cox, Judy. *Go to sleep, Groundhog*
Cuyler, Margery. *Groundhog stays up late*
Freeman, Don. *Gregory's Shadow*
   Groundhog at Evergreen Road
Hill, Susanna Leonard. *April Fool, Phyllis!*
   Punxsutawney Phyllis

Hiskey, Iris. *The secret of the first one up*
Holub, Joan. *Groundhog weather school*
Jenkins, Emily. *A greyhound, a groundhog*
Johnson, Crockett. *Will spring be early or will spring be late?*
Levine, Abby. *Gretchen Groundhog, it's your day!*
Lewin, Betsy. *Groundhog day*
Miller, Pat. *Substitute Groundhog*
Olson, Julie. *Tickle, tickle! itch, twitch!*
Pace, Anne Marie. *Groundhug Day*
Pallotta, Jerry. *Who will see their shadows this year?*
Pearlman, Robb. *Groundhog's day off*
Roberts, Bethany. *Double trouble Groundhog Day*
Swallow, Pamela Curtis. *Groundhog gets a say*
Tompert, Ann. *Nothing sticks like a shadow*
Welling, Peter J. *Andrew McGroundhog and his shady shadow*

Animals – guinea pigs

Berenzy, Alix. *Sammy*
Blumenthal, Deborah. *Charlie hits it big*
Child, Lauren. *I completely know about guinea pigs*
Cuyler, Margery. *Guinea pigs add up*
Duke, Kate. *One guinea pig is not enough*
  Ready for pumpkins
  Twenty is too many
Katz, Susan. *Oh, Theodore!*
Knutson, Barbara. *Love and roast chicken*
Kroll, Steven. *Patches*
  Patches lost and found
Liersch, Anne. *Nell and Fluffy*
McGinty, Alice B. *Eliza's kindergarten pet*
Meade, Holly. *John Willy and Freddy McGee*
Middleton, Charlotte. *Nibbles*
  Nibbles' garden
Ohi, Ruth. *Clara and the Bossy*
  The couch was a castle
  A trip with Grandma
Potter, Beatrix. *The tale of Tuppeny*
Roth, Susan L. *Great big guinea pigs*
Rylant, Cynthia. *Little Whistle*
  Little Whistle's Christmas
  Little Whistle's dinner party
  Little Whistle's medicine
Shannon, Margaret. *Gullible's troubles*
Spelman, Cornelia Maude. *When I feel sad*
  When I feel worried
  When I miss you
Surplice, Holly. *Guinea pig party*
Weigelt, Udo. *Super Guinea Pig to the rescue*
Wells, Rosemary. *Felix stands tall*

Animals – hamsters

Bateman, Teresa. *Hamster Camp*
Bee, William. *Stanley the builder*
  Stanley the farmer
  Stanley the mailman
  Stanley's colors
  Stanley's diner
  Stanley's garage
  Stanley's numbers
  Stanley's opposites
  Stanley's store
Cohen, Peter Zachary. *Boris's glasses*
Deacon, Alexis. *A place to call home*
Eaton, Maxwell. *I'm awake!*
Fraser, Mary Ann. *Pet shop lullaby*

Hill, Susanna Leonard. *Not yet, Rose*
Inkpen, Deborah. *Harriet and the little fat fairy*
Inkpen, Mick. *Kipper and Roly*
Kimmel, Elizabeth Cody. *Glamsters*
Kimmel, Eric A. *The great Texas hamster drive*
Kirk, Daniel. *Bus stop, bus go*
Lord, Cynthia. *Happy birthday, Hamster*
  Hot Rod Hamster
  Hot Rod Hamster: monster truck mania!
Norac, Carl. *Hello, sweetie pie*
  I love to cuddle
  I love you so much
Ohi, Ruth. *Chicken, Pig, Cow and the class pet*
Perl, Erica S. *Ferocious Fluffity*
Rathmann, Peggy. *10 minutes till bedtime*
Reich, Kass. *Up hamster, down hamster*
Rockwell, Anne. *My pet hamster*
Root, Andrew. *Hamsters don't fight fires!*
Rubel, Nicole. *Ham and Pickles*
Saltzberg, Barney. *Crazy hair day*
Scillian, Devin. *Memoirs of a hamster*
Van Allsburg, Chris. *The misadventures of Sweetie Pie*
Walsh, Ellen Stoll. *Hamsters to the rescue*
Weigelt, Udo. *Who stole the gold?*

Animals – hedgehogs

Anderson, Lena. *The hedgehog, the pig, and their little friend*
Bagley, Jessixa. *Before I leave*
Brett, Jan. *Christmas trolls*
  The hat
  Hedgie blasts off!
  Hedgie's surprise
Butler, Christina. *One cozy Christmas*
Butler, M. Christina. *One special Christmas*
  One winter's day
  The special blankie
Dennard, Deborah. *Hedgehog haven*
Dumont, Jean-François. *The chickens build a wall*
Falkenstern, Lisa. *A dragon moves in*
Fergus, Maureen. *Buddy and Earl*
  Buddy and Earl and the great big baby
  Buddy and Earl go exploring
  Buddy and Earl go to school
Grimm, Jacob and Wilhelm. *Hans my hedgehog*
Muir, Leslie. *C.R. Mudgeon*
Paul, Ruth. *Hedgehog's magic tricks*
Petz, Moritz. *Wish you were here*
Pfister, Marcus. *The happy hedgehog*
Poh, Jennifer. *Herbie's big adventure*
Potter, Beatrix. *The tale of Mrs. Tiggy-Winkle*
Sauer, Tammi. *Ginny Louise and the school showdown*
Schindler, S. D. *Spike and Ike take a hike*
Schubert, Ingrid. *Bear's eggs*
Stewart, Paul. *The birthday presents*
  A little bit of winter
  Rabbit's wish
Sutton, Benn. *Hedgehug*
Symes, Ruth. *Harriet dancing*
Wheeler, Lisa. *Hokey pokey*
  Porcupining
Wilson, Steve. *Hedgehugs*
  Hedgehugs: autumn hide-and-squeak
  Hedgehugs and the Hattiepillar
Yeh, Kat. *The friend ship*

Animals – hippopotamuses

Bauer, Marion Dane. *A mama for Owen*
Bonwill, Ann. *I am not a copycat!*
Burningham, John. *Tug-of-war*
Castle, Caroline. *Naughty!*
Coat, Janik. *Hippopposites*
Crow, Kristyn. *Hello, Hippo! Goodbye, Bird!*
Dahl, Michael. *Hippo says "excuse me."*
Fliess, Sue. *Books for me!*
    Shoes for me!
Gorbachev, Valeri. *Big Little Hippo*
Grambling, Lois G. *This whole Tooth Fairy thing's
    nothing but a big rip-off!*
Green, John Patrick. *Hippopotamister*
Hill, Eric. *Spot's baby sister*
Horowitz, Dave. *A monkey among us*
Jenkins, Emily. *Num, num, num!*
    Plonk, plonk, plonk!
    Up, up, up!
Kasza, Keiko. *Dorothy and Mikey*
Landström, Lena. *A hippo's tale*
    The little hippos' adventure
Lester, Helen. *Hurty feelings*
London, Jonathan. *Duck and Hippo in the rainstorm*
    Duck and Hippo lost and found
    Here comes Doctor Hippo
    Here comes firefighter Hippo
    Hippos are huge!
Loomis, Christine. *Hattie hippo*
McKee, David. *Elmer and the hippos*
Marshall, James. *George and Martha*
    George and Martha back in town
    George and Martha encore
    George and Martha one fine day
    George and Martha rise and shine
    George and Martha 'round and 'round
    George and Martha, tons of fun
Meng, Cece. *The wonderful thing about hiccups*
Minarik, Else Holmelund. *Am I beautiful?*
Neugebauer, Charise. *The real winner*
Paxton, Tom. *The jungle baseball game*
Pfister, Marcus. *Bertie*
    Bertie at bedtime
    Happy birthday, Bertie!
    Questions, questions
Plourde, Lynn. *You're doing that in the talent show?!*
    You're wearing that to school?!
Puttock, Simon. *A story for Hippo*
Raschka, Chris. *The blushful hippopotamus*
Rissi, Anica Mrose. *The teacher's pet*
Rox, John. *I want a hippopotamus for Christmas*
Saltzberg, Barney. *Hip, hip, hooray day!*
    The problem with pumpkins
Schwartz, Amy. *Starring Miss Darlene*
Shea, Bob. *Oh, Daddy!*
Shipton, Jonathan. *How to be a happy hippo*
Shum, Benson. *Holly's day at the pool*
Smallman, Steve. *Hiccupotamus*
Stephens, Helen. *Ruby and the noisy hippo*
Twohy, Mike. *Mouse and Hippo*
Waber, Bernard. *Evie and Margie*
Wild, Margaret. *Hush, hush!*
Willis, Jeanne. *Hippospotamus*
Winter, Jeanette. *Mama: a true story, in which a baby
    hippo loses his mama during a tsunami, but finds
    a new home*
Yee, Wong Herbert. *The Officers' Ball*

Animals – horses, ponies

Addy, Sharon Hart. *When wishes were horses*
Ammon, Richard. *Amish horses*
Anderson, Peggy Perry. *We go in a circle*
Angleberger, Tom. *Crankee Doodle*
Armstrong, Jennifer. *Magnus at the fire*
Barnes, Laura T. *Twist and Ernest*
Beaton, Kate. *The princess and the pony*
Bemelmans, Ludwig. *Madeline in London*
Bradley, Kimberly Brubaker. *The perfect pony*
Brett, Jan. *Fritz and the beautiful horses*
Brill, Marlene Targ. *Bronco Charlie and the Pony
    Express*
Bunting, Eve. *Thunder horse*
Cantrell, Charlie. *A friend for Einstein*
Chan, Chin-Yi. *Good luck horse*
Clayton, Elaine. *A blue ribbon for Sugar*
Clement-Davies, David. *Spirit*
Cohen, Caron Lee. *The mud pony*
Collier, Kelly. *A horse named Steve*
Cotten, Cynthia. *Snow ponies*
Cowley, Joy. *Where horses run free*
Darrow, Sharon. *Old Thunder and Miss Raney*
Dockray, Tracy. *The lost and found pony*
Doyle, Malachy. *Horse*
Egan, Tim. *Roasted peanuts*
Ets, Marie Hall. *Mr. Penny's race horse*
Galing, Ed. *Tony*
Goble, Paul. *Adopted by the eagles*
    The gift of the sacred dog
    The girl who loved wild horses
    Mystic horse
Gray, Rita. *The wild little horse*
Haas, Jessie. *Appaloosa zebra*
Hamilton, Arlene. *Only a cow*
Hammerle, Susa. *Let's try horseback riding*
Haseley, Dennis. *Twenty heartbeats*
Havill, Juanita. *Call the horse lucky*
Hayden, Kate. *Horse show*
High, Linda Oatman. *The girl on the high-diving
    horse*
    Winter shoes for Shadow Horse
Hoban, Russell. *Rosie's magic horse*
Hobbie, Holly. *Everything but the horse*
Hoffman, Mary. *Clever Katya*
Hong, Chen Jiang. *The magic horse of Han Gan*
Hubbell, Patricia. *Horses: trotting! prancing! racing!*
Isaacs, Anne. *Dust Devil*
Jeffers, Susan. *My Chincoteague pony*
Jeppson, Ann-Sofie. *Here comes Pontus*
    You're growing up, Pontus
Kay, Verla. *Whatever happened to the Pony Express?*
Kumin, Maxine. *Oh, Harry!*
Lange, Willem. *John and Tom*
Lester, Alison. *Noni the pony*
    Running with the horses
Lester, Julius. *Black cowboy, wild horses*
Lewin, Betsy. *Good night, Knight*
Lewin, Ted. *Horse song*
Libby, Barbara. *I rode the red horse*
London, Jonathan. *Mustang canyon*
Long, Loren. *An Otis Christmas*
McCarthy, Meghan. *Seabiscuit*
McCully, Emily Arnold. *Wonder horse*
McDonnell, Flora. *Giddy-up! Let's ride!*
Martin, Bill, Jr.. *Chicken Chuck*
Morck, Irene. *Old bird*
Mullins, Patricia. *One horse waiting for me*

Murphy, Stuart J. *Same old horse*
Nelson, S. D. *Gift horse*
Numeroff, Laura Joffe. *Ponyella*
Ohi, Ruth. *Chicken, Pig, Cow horse around*
O'Neill, Richard. *Yokki and the Parno Gry*
Otsuka, Yuzo. *Suho's white horse*
Paraskevas, Betty. *Marvin, the tap-dancing horse*
Peet, Bill. *Cowardly Clyde*
Polacco, Patricia. *Mrs. Mack*
Rosenberg, Liz. *The carousel*
Rounds, Glen. *Once we had a horse*
Sanderson, Ruth. *The golden mare, the firebird, and the magic ring*
Schnitzler, Pattie L. *Widdermaker*
Stein, David Ezra. *Cowboy Ned and Andy*
    Ned's new friend
Stockland, Patricia M. *In the horse stall*
Sturm, James. *Gryphons aren't so great*
Tibo, Gilles. *The cowboy kid*
Trollinger, Patsi B. *Perfect timing*
Willey, Margaret. *Clever Beatrice and the best little pony*
Wilson, Karma. *Horseplay*
Winnick, Karen B. *Sybil's night ride*
Yolen, Jane. *Hush, little horsie*
    Sky dogs
Young, Ed. *The lost horse*

Animals – hyenas

Jantzen, Doug. *Henry Hyena, why won't you laugh?*
Kimmel, Eric A. *Anansi and the magic stick*
Prelutsky, Jack. *The mean old mean hyena*
Willis, Jeanne. *That's not funny!*

Animals – jackals

Aardema, Verna. *Jackal's flying lesson*

Animals – jaguars

Campoy, F. Isabel. *Rosa Raposa*
Hamilton, Virginia. *Jaguarundi*
Rabinowitz, Alan. *A boy and a jaguar*
Ryder, Joanne. *Jaguar in the rain forest*
Tourville, Amanda Doering. *A jaguar grows up*

Animals – kangaroos

Beaumont, Karen. *Who ate all the cookie dough?*
Bonnett-Rampersaud, Louise. *Polly Hopper's pouch*
Bourguignon, Laurence. *Heart in the pocket*
Chichester Clark, Emma. *Where are you, Blue Kangaroo?*
Edwards, Pamela Duncan. *McGillycuddy could*
French, Jackie. *Josephine wants to dance*
Hewett, Joan. *A kangaroo joey grows up*
Levitin, Sonia. *When Kangaroo goes to school*
Lithgow, John. *Marsupial Sue*
    Marsupial Sue presents "The Runaway Pancake"
McAllister, Angela. *Mama and Little Joe*
McBratney, Sam. *Yes we can!*
McKee, David. *Elmer and the kangaroo*
Murphy, Stuart J. *Too many kangaroo things to do!*
Numeroff, Laura Joffe. *Nighty-night, Cooper*
Payne, Emmy. *Katy no-pocket*
Stein, David Ezra. *Pouch!*
Vaughan, Marcia Kapok. *Snap!*

Animals – kindness to *see* Character traits – kindness to animals

Animals – koalas

Backker, Vera de. *Coco the koala*
Bright, Rachel. *The koala who could*
Dennard, Deborah. *Koala country*
Dodd, Emma. *Everything*
Du Bois, William Pène. *Bear party*
Ferrell, Sean. *I don't like Koala*
Fox, Mem. *Koala Lou*
Hewett, Joan. *A koala joey grows up*
Markle, Sandra. *Finding home*
Murphy, Mary. *Koala and the flower*
Sutton, Jane. *The trouble with cauliflower*

Animals – lemmings

Briggs, John. *Leaping lemmings!*
Dyckman, Ame. *Read the book, lemmings!*

Animals – lemurs

Browne, Anthony. *One gorilla: a counting book*
Dennard, Deborah. *Lemur landing*
Lester, Helen. *Something might happen*
Preston-Gannon, Frann. *How to lose a lemur*
Ryan, Candace. *Ewe and Aye*
Sandall, Ellie. *Follow me!*

Animals – leopards

Aardema, Verna. *Half-a-ball-of-kenki*
Fox, Mem. *Two little monkeys*
Frampton, David. *The whole night through*
Hatkoff, Craig, et al. *Leo the snow leopard*
Jennings, Linda. *Hide and seek birthday treat*
Keller, Holly. *Brave Horace*
    Horace
Kipling, Rudyard. *How the leopard got his spots*
Landau, Orna. *Leopardpox!*
McAllister, Angela. *Little Mist*
Mollel, Tololwa M. *To dinner, for dinner*
Nagda, Anne Whitehead. *World above the clouds*
Orr, Wendy. *The princess and her panther*
Souhami, Jessica. *The leopard's drum*

Animals – lions

Aardema, Verna. *The lonely lioness and the ostrich chicks*
Aesop. *Androcles and the lion*, ill. by Dennis Nolan
    Androcles and the lion, ill. by Janet Stevens
    Androcles and the lion: and other Aesop fables
    The lion and the mouse, ill. by Lisa McCue
    The lion and the mouse, ill. by Sara Rojo
    The lion and the mouse, ill. by Bernadette Watts
    Mouse and lion
Agee, Jon. *Lion lessons*
Auld, Mary. *Daniel in the lions' den*
Bennett, Barbara. *Lion's precious gift*
Bright, Paul. *Quiet!*
Bright, Rachel. *The lion inside*
Busch, Miriam. *Lion, lion*
Buzzeo, Toni. *Just like my Papa*
Cohen, Caron Lee. *Martin and the giant lions*
Collingridge, Richard. *Lionheart*
Conover, Chris. *The lion's share*

Cummins, Lucy Ruth. *A hungry lion; or, a dwindling assortment of animals*
Cuyler, Margery. *We're going on a lion hunt*
Daugherty, James Henry. *Andy and the lion*
Day, Nancy Raines. *The lion's whiskers*
DiLorenzo, Barbara. *Renato and the lion*
Du Bois, William Pène. *Lion*
Dubuc, Marianne. *The lion and the bird*
Edwards, Pamela Duncan. *Roar*
Foley, Greg. *Willoughby and the lion*
Freeman, Don. *Dandelion*
Gibert, Bruno. *The king is naked!*
Goldsboro, Bobby. *Jonah and the whale; and, Daniel in the lion's den*
Hartman, Bob. *Dinner in the lions' den*
Horácek, Petr. *Silly Suzy Goose*
Ismail, Yasmeen. *Specs for Rex*
Kanevsky, Polly. *Sleepy boy*
Kasza, Keiko. *The mightiest*
Knudsen, Michelle. *Library lion*
Latimer, Alex. *Lion vs Rabbit*
Long, Ethan. *Lion and Tiger and Bear*
McCarthy, Michael. *The story of Daniel in the lions' den*
McElligott, Matthew. *The lion's share*
McPhail, David. *Pig Pig meets the lion*
Markham, Beryl. *The good lion*
Marzollo, Jean. *Daniel in the lion's den*
Muth, Jon J. *Mama Lion wins the race*
Nogales, Jill. *Zebra on the go*
O'Neill, Gemma. *Monty's magnificent mane*
Peet, Bill. *Eli*
  Hubert's hair-raising adventures
  Randy's dandy lions
Pfister, Marcus. *How Leo learned to be king*
Pinkney, Jerry. *The lion and the mouse*
Reynolds, Aaron. *Carnivores*
Richardson, Justin. *Christian, the hugging lion*
Smith, Alex T. *Little Red and the very hungry lion*
Stephens, Helen. *How to hide a lion*
Tierney, Fiona. *Lion's lunch?*
Trimble, Marcia. *Hello sun*
Waber, Bernard. *A lion named Shirley Williamson*
Yaccarino, Dan. *Deep in the jungle*

Animals – llamas

Buxton, Jane. *The littlest llama*
Dewdney, Anna. *Llama Llama and the bully goat*
  Llama Llama Gram and Grandpa
  Llama Llama home with Mama
  Llama Llama mad at Mama
  Llama Llama misses Mama
  Llama, Llama red pajama
  Llama Llama time to share
Dominguez, Angela. *Maria had a little llama/Maria tenia una llama pequena*
Guarino, Deborah. *Is your mama a llama?*
Horowitz, Dave. *Chico the brave*
Livingstone, Star. *Harley*

Animals – lorises

Deacon, Alexis. *Slow Loris*

Animals – manatees

Arnosky, Jim. *All about manatees*
  A manatee morning
  Slow down for manatees

Lithgow, John. *I'm a manatee*

Animals – marsupials

Heos, Bridget. *What to expect when you're expecting joeys*

Animals – meerkats

Gravett, Emily. *Meerkat mail*
Lunde, Darrin. *Meet the meerkat*
O'Neill, Gemma. *Monty's magnificent mane*
Paterson, Brian. *Zigby camps out*
  Zigby hunts for treasure

Animals – mice

Ada, Alma Flor. *Friend frog*
Aesop. *Belling the cat*
  The country mouse and the city mouse
  The lion and the mouse, ill. by Lisa McCue
  The lion and the mouse, ill. by Sara Rojo
  The lion and the mouse, ill. by Bernadette Watts
  Milly and Tilly
  Mouse and lion
  The town mouse and the country mouse, ill. by Lorinda Bryan Cauley
  The town mouse and the country mouse, ill. by Janet Stevens
  The town mouse and the country mouse: an Aesop fable, ill. by Helen Ward
  The town mouse and the country mouse: an Aesop fable, ill. by Bernadette Watts
  Town mouse, country mouse, ill. by Jan Brett
  Town mouse, country mouse, ill. by Carol Jones
Alborough, Jez. *Watch out! Big Bro's coming!*
Alborozo, Gabriel. *The mouse and the moon*
Alexander, Claire. *Monkey and the little one*
Aliki. *At Mary Bloom's*
Alter, Anna. *Estelle and Lucy*
Arnosky, Jim. *Mouse letters*
  Mouse numbers and letters
  Mouse writing
Asch, Frank. *Mr. Maxwell's mouse*
  Mrs. Marlowe's mice
Austin, Mike. *Countdown with Milo*
Aylesworth, Jim. *The completed hickory dickory dock*
  Little Bitty Mousie
  Two terrible frights
Baker, Keith. *Hickory dickory dock*
Balian, Lorna. *Mother's Mother's Day*
Bansch, Helga. *Brava, Mimi!*
Barbero, Maria. *The bravest mouse*
Bardhan-Quallen, Sudipta. *Snoring Beauty*
Barnett, Mac. *The wolf, the duck, and the mouse*
Barringer, William. *Gregory and Alexander*
Bastin, Marjolein. *Christmas with Vera*
Battut, Éric. *Little Mouse's big secret*
Baum, Louis. *The mouse who braved bedtime*
Becker, Bonny. *A bedtime for Bear*
  A birthday for Bear
  A Christmas for Bear
  A library book for Bear
  The sniffles for Bear
  A visitor for Bear
Bedford, David. *Ella's games*
Benjamin, A. H. *Mouse, mole and the falling star*
Berkeley, Jon. *Chopsticks*
Bernheimer, Kate. *The girl who wouldn't brush her hair*

Billingsley, Franny. *Big bad bunny*
Bloom, Becky. *Crackers*
   Mice make trouble
Bond, Felicia. *The Halloween play*
Bonnett-Rampersaud, Louise. *Bubble and Squeak*
Bottner, Barbara. *Wallace's lists*
Braun, Sebastien. *Back to bed, Ed!*
Bright, Rachel. *The lion inside*
   Side by side
Brooks, Nigel. *Country mouse cottage*
   Town mouse house
Brown, Ruth. *The tale of two mice*
Buehner, Caralyn. *Merry Christmas, Mr. Mouse*
Bunting, Eve. *The Mother's Day mice*
   Mouse island
   Whose shoe?
Burton, LeVar. *The rhino who swallowed a storm*
Butler, M. Christina. *Mouse and the moon*
Butterworth, Nick. *Jingle bells*
Bynum, Janie. *Nutmeg and Barley*
Cain, Sheridan. *By the light of the moon*
Calmenson, Stephanie. *Birthday at the Panda Palace*
Carle, Eric. *Do you want to be my friend?*
Carlson, Nancy. *First grade, here I come!*
   Henry and the bully
   Henry and the Valentine surprise
   Henry's 100 days of kindergarten
   I don't like to read!
   Look out kindergarten, here I come!
   Start saving, Henry!
Carlstrom, Nancy White. *I'm not moving, Mama!*
Chaconas, Dori. *Christmas mouseling*
Chapman, Jane. *Very special friends*
Christie, R. Gregory. *Mousetropolis*
Church, Caroline Jayne. *One more hug for Madison Ruff!*
Collicott, Sharleen. *Mildred and Sam*
Collins, Ross. *There's a bear on my chair*
Corderoy, Tracey. *I want my daddy*
   I want my mommy!
   Just right for two
   Monty and Milli
Cousins, Lucy. *Count with Maisy*
   Count with Maisy, cheep, cheep, cheep!
   Doctor Maisy
   Ha ha, Maisy!
   Happy birthday, Maisy
   Happy Easter, Maisy!
   Maisy at the fair
   Maisy at the farm
   Maisy big, Maisy small
   Maisy, Charley, and the wobbly tooth
   Maisy cleans up
   Maisy dresses up
   Maisy goes on a plane
   Maisy goes on vacation
   Maisy goes shopping
   Maisy goes to London
   Maisy goes to preschool
   Maisy goes to the hospital
   Maisy goes to the library
   Maisy goes to the movies
   Maisy goes to the museum
   Maisy learns to swim
   Maisy makes gingerbread
   Maisy makes lemonade
   Maisy plays soccer
   Maisy's amazing big book of learning
   Maisy's amazing big book of words

   Maisy's bedtime
   Maisy's book of things that go
   Maisy's Christmas tree
   Maisy's colors
   Maisy's farm
   Maisy's field day
   Maisy's first clock
   Maisy's Halloween
   Maisy's morning on the farm
   Maisy's noisy day
   Maisy's pirate treasure hunt
   Maisy's pool
   Maisy's rainbow dream
   Maisy's twinkly, crinkly counting book
   Maisy's wonderful weather book
   More fun with Maisy!
   Stop and go, Maisy
   Sweet dreams, Maisy
   With love from Maisy
Cox, Judy. *Cinco de Mouse-o!*
   Haunted house, haunted Mouse
   One is a feast for Mouse
   Snow day for Mouse
Crimi, Carolyn. *Tessa's tip-tapping toes*
Crum, Shutta. *Mouseling's words*
Curato, Mike. *Little Elliot, big city*
   Little Elliot, big family
   Little Elliot, big fun
   Little Elliot, fall friends
Currey, Anna. *Truffle's Christmas*
Dahlie, Elizabeth. *Bernelly and Harriet*
Deedy, Carmen Agra. *Martina the beautiful cockroach*
Demas, Corinne. *Two Christmas mice*
dePaola, Tomie. *Charlie needs a cloak*
Docherty, Helen. *The storybook knight*
Donofrio, Beverly. *Mary and the mouse, the mouse and Mary*
   Where's Mommy?
Doyen, Denise. *Once upon a twice*
Dubuc, Marianne. *Mr. Postmouse takes a trip*
   Mr. Postmouse's rounds
Duke, Kate. *The tale of Pip and Squeak*
Dunlap, Cirocco. *This book will not be fun*
Edwards, Pamela Duncan. *Bravo, Livingstone Mouse!*
Egielski, Richard. *Slim and Jim*
Ehlert, Lois. *Boo to you!*
Eldarova, Sofia. *Builder mouse*
Ellwand, David. *Midas Mouse*
Emberley, Ed. *Thanks, Mom!*
Emberley, Rebecca. *Mice on ice*
Emmett, Jonathan. *I love you always and forever*
Engelbreit, Mary. *Mary Engelbreit's A merry little Christmas*
Esbaum, Jill. *Estelle takes a bath*
Ets, Marie Hall. *Mr. T. W. Anthony Woo*
Falkenstern, Lisa. *Professor Whiskerton presents Steampunk ABC*
Fearnley, Jan. *Just like you*
   Martha in the middle
   Watch out!
Fernandes, Eugenie. *Big week for little mouse*
   Busy little mouse
   Sleepy little mouse
Fleming, Denise. *Alphabet under construction*
   Go, shapes, go!
   Lunch
   Shout! shout it out!

Foley, Greg. *I miss you Mouse*
    Thank you, Bear
Fontes, Justine Korman. *Signs of spring*
Forward, Toby. *Ben's Christmas carol*
Fox, Mem. *This and that*
Fraser, Mary Ann. *I.Q. gets fit*
    I.Q. goes to school
    I.Q. goes to the library
    I.Q., it's time
Frederick, Heather Vogel. *Hide and squeak*
Freedman, Deborah. *By Mouse and Frog*
Fyleman, Rose. *Mice*
Garland, Michael. *Hooray José!*
    How many mice?
Geras, Adèle. *The nutcracker*
Gerritsen, Paula. *Nuts*
Goldsboro, Bobby. *Noah and the ark; and, David and Goliath*
Goodall, John S. *Creepy castle*
Goodhart, Pippa. *Little Nelly's big book*
Gorbachev, Valeri. *Dragon is coming!*
    Molly who flew away
    What's the big idea, Molly?
Gore, Emily. *And Nick*
Gore, Leonid. *Mommy, where are you?*
Gravett, Emily. *Little Mouse's big book of beasts*
    Little Mouse's big book of fears
Grey, Mini. *Hermelin the detective mouse*
    Space Dog
Guest, C. Z. *Tiny green thumbs*
Hague, Michael. *The nutcracker*
Harper, Jessica. *I'm not going to chase the cat today*
Harris, Robie H. *Goodbye, Mousie*
Heling, Kathryn. *Mouse makes magic*
    Mouse's hide-and-seek words
Helmer, Marilyn. *Three cat and mouse tales*
Henkes, Kevin. *Chester's way*
    Chrysanthemum
    El gran día de Lily / Lilly's big day
    Julius, the baby of the world
    Lilly's big day
    Lilly's chocolate heart
    Lilly's purple plastic purse
    Owen
    Sheila Rae, the brave
    Sheila Rae's peppermint stick
    A weekend with Wendell
    Wemberly worried
Henry, Jed. *Cheer up, Mouse!*
    Good night, Mouse!
Higgins, Ryan T. *Be quiet!*
    Hotel Bruce
Hines, Anna Grossnickle. *Whose shoes?*
Hoberman, Mary Ann. *The two sillies*
Hodgkinson, Jo. *A big day for Migs*
Hodgkinson, Leigh. *Boris and the wrong shadow*
Hoffman, Elizabeth Stokes. *Miss Renée's mice*
    Miss Renée's mice go to an exhibition
Hoffmann, E. T. A. *The nutcracker*, ill. by Renée Graef
    The nutcracker, ill. by Alison Jay
    The nutcracker, ill. by Peter Malone
    The nutcracker, ill. by Niroot Puttapipat
    The nutcracker, ill. by Maurice Sendak
    The nutcracker, ill. by Lisbeth Zwerger
    The Nutcracker and the Mouse King
    The nutcracker ballet
    The Nutcracker in Harlem
Holabird, Katharine. *Angelina and Alice*

    Angelina and Henry
    Angelina and the princess
    Angelina and the royal wedding
    Angelina at the fair
    Angelina at the palace
    Angelina ballerina
    Angelina dances
    Angelina ice skates
    Angelina on stage
    Angelina, star of the show
    Angelina's baby sister
    Angelina's ballet class
    Angelina's big city ballet
    Angelina's Christmas
    Angelina's Cinderella
    Angelina's Halloween
    Christmas in Mouseland
    Christmas with Angelina
Holmes, Janet A. *Me and you*
Hood, Susan. *The Tooth Mouse*
Horácek, Petr. *The mouse who reached the sky*
    The mouse who ate the moon
    A surprise for Tiny Mouse
Horowitz, Ruth. *Are we still friends?*
Howe, James. *Horace and Morris but mostly Dolores*
    Horace and Morris join the chorus (but what about Dolores?)
    Horace and Morris say cheese (which makes Dolores sneeze!)
Hucke, Johannes. *Pip in the Grand Hotel*
Hurd, Thacher. *Little Mouse's big Valentine*
    Santa Mouse and the ratdeer
Inkpen, Mick. *Kipper's toybox*
Irving, John. *A sound like someone trying not to make a sound*
Ivimey, John William. *The complete story of the three blind mice*
    Three blind mice
Johnson, Paul Brett. *Mr. Persnickety and Cat Lady*
Johnston, Tony. *First grade, here I come!*
Kangas, Juli. *The surprise visitor*
Keller, Holly. *Help!*
Kelley, True. *Blabber Mouse*
Kellogg, Steven. *The island of the skog*
Kelly, Mark. *Mousetronaut*
    Mousetronaut goes to Mars
Kennedy, Kim. *Hee-Haw-Dini and the Great Zambini*
Kirk, Daniel. *Library mouse*
    Library mouse: a friend's tale
    Library mouse: a museum adventure
    Library mouse: a world to explore
    Library mouse: home sweet home
Kleven, Elisa. *Welcome home, Mouse*
Knapman, Timothy. *Can't catch me!*
Kneen, Maggie. *Chocolate moose*
Knight, Hilary. *A firefly in a fir tree*
Kolanovic, Dubravka. *Everyone needs a friend*
Kraus, Robert. *Another mouse to feed*
    Come out and play, little mouse
    Mouse in love
    Where are you going, little mouse?
    Whose mouse are you?
Kroll, Steven. *The Hanukkah mice*
Krupinski, Loretta. *Christmas in the city*
    Pirate treasure
Lakin, Patricia. *Clarence the copy cat*
Leathers, Philippa. *How to catch a mouse*
Leeson, Christine. *Molly and the storm*
Lionni, Leo. *Alexander and the wind-up mouse*

A busy year
Frederick
Geraldine, the music mouse
The greentail mouse
Matthew's dream
Mr. McMouse
Nicolas, where have you been?
Theodore and the talking mushroom
Tillie and the wall
Lithgow, John. *Mahalia Mouse goes to college*
Long, Ethan. *Me and my big mouse*
Lord, Cynthia. *Hot Rod Hamster*
Low, Joseph. *Mice twice*
Lurie, Susan. *Will you be my friend?*
McBratney, Sam. *The dark at the top of the stairs*
McCully, Emily Arnold. *The Christmas gift*
First snow
Monk camps out
Mouse practice
New baby
Picnic
School
MacDonald, Alan. *Wilfred to the rescue*
MacDonald, Margaret Read. *Fat cat*
Mabela the clever
McFarland, Lyn Rossiter. *Mouse went out to get a snack*
Mack, Jeff. *Good news, bad news*
Mine!
McMillan, Bruce. *Mouse views*
McMullan, Kate. *Supercat to the rescue*
Marino, Gianna. *I am the Mountain Mouse*
Martin, Bill, Jr.. *A beasty story*
Martin, David. *All for pie, pie for all*
Masters, Anthony. *Ricky's rat gang*
May, Eleanor. *Albert is not scared*
Albert the muffin-maker
Albert's amazing snail
The mousier the merrier
Mayer, Mercer. *The little drummer mouse*
Meadows, Michelle. *Itsy-bitsy baby mouse*
Medoff, Francine. *The mouse in the matzah factory*
Merski, P. K. *Roaring, boring, Alice*
Miller, Edna. *Mousekin's Christmas eve*
Mousekin's Easter basket
Mousekin's frosty friend
Mousekin's golden house
Mousekin's Thanksgiving
Modesitt, Jeanne. *Little Mouse's happy birthday*
Molk, Laurel. *Eeny, Meeny, Miney, Mo and Flo!*
Mollel, Tololwa M. *Kitoto the mighty*
Monson, A. M. *Wanted . . . best friend*
Moore, Clement Clarke. *The night before Christmas,* ill. by Rachel Isadora
The night before Christmas, ill. by Barbara Reid
'Twas the night before Christmas
Moore, Suzi. *Whoops!*
Moran, Alex. *Sam and Jack*
Morgan, Michaela. *Brave, brave mouse*
Bunny wishes
Dear bunny
Morgan-Vanroyen, Mary. *Curious Rosie*
Gentle Rosie
Patient Rosie
Sleep tight, little mouse
Wild Rosie
Morrissey, Dean. *The wizard mouse*
Mortensen, Lori. *Mousequerade ball*
Mortimer, Anne. *Pumpkin cat*

Moser, Lisa. *Perfect soup*
Moss, Miriam. *I'll be your friend, Smudge*
It's my turn, Smudge
A new house for Smudge
Muir, Leslie. *The little bitty bakery*
Muller, Robin. *Badger's new house*
Nakagawa, Rieko. *Guri and Gura*
Guri and Gura's special gift
Nikola-Lisa, W. *Magic in the margins*
Nivola, Claire A. *The forest*
Noonan, Julia. *Mouse by mouse*
Numeroff, Laura Joffe. *Happy Valentine's Day, Mouse!*
If you give a mouse a cookie
If you take a mouse to school
If you take a mouse to the movies
Merry Christmas, Mouse!
What mommies do best
Oh, Jiwon. *Cat and mouse*
Olson, Julie. *Tickle, tickle! itch, twitch!*
Ormerod, Jan. *Miss Mouse's day*
Oyibo, Papa. *Big brother, little sister*
Papineau, Lucie. *Lulu's pajamas*
Paraskevas, Betty. *Maggie and the Ferocious Beast, the big carrot*
Maggie and the Ferocious Beast, the big scare
Pauli, Lorenz. *The fox in the library*
Pennypacker, Sara. *Pierre in love*
Petz, Moritz. *Wish you were here*
Pfister, Marcus. *Milo and the magical stones*
Milo and the mysterious island
Pham, LeUyen. *A piece of cake*
Pinkney, Jerry. *The lion and the mouse*
Platt, Cynthia. *A little bit of love*
Plourde, Lynn. *You're doing that in the talent show?!*
You're wearing that to school?!
Pomerantz, Charlotte. *The mousery*
Potter, Beatrix. *The tailor of Gloucester*
The tale of Johnny Town-Mouse
The tale of Mrs. Tittlemouse
The tale of two bad mice
The two bad mice
Previn, Stacey. *Aberdeen*
Protopopescu, Orel. *Thelonious Mouse*
Provencher, Rose-Marie. *Mouse cleaning*
Pryor, Bonnie. *The porcupine mouse*
Puttock, Simon. *Mouse's first night at Moonlight School*
Rand, Gloria. *Prince William*
Randall, Ronne. *The Hanukkah mice*
Rayner, Catherine. *The bear who shared*
Reiser, Lynn. *Two mice in three fables*
Reitman, Andrea. *Mouse in the house*
Reynolds, Peter H. *Sydney's star*
Riddell, Chris. *Wendel's workshop*
Riley, Linnea Asplind. *Mouse mess*
Roberts, Bethany. *Birthday mice*
Christmas mice
Easter mice
Fourth of July mice
Valentine mice!
Rogers, Paul. *Ruby's dinnertime*
Ruby's potty
Rohmann, Eric. *My friend Rabbit*
Rossell, Judith. *Ruby and Leonard and the great big surprise*
Rudy, Maggie. *City mouse, country mouse*
I wish I had a pet
Rueda, Claudia. *Is it big or is it little?*

Ruzzier, Sergio. *Two mice*
Ryan, Pam Muñoz. *Mice and beans*
Ryder, Joanne. *Mouse tail moon*
Sage, James. *Farmer Smart's fat cat*
San Souci, Robert D. *The silver charm*
Santore, Charles. *A stowaway on Noah's Ark*
Scheffler, Axel. *Pip and Posy: the bedtime frog*
  Pip and Posy: the big balloon
  Pip and Posy: the little puddle
  Pip and Posy: the new friend
  Pip and Posy: the scary monster
  Pip and Posy: the snowy day
  Pip and Posy: the super scooter
Schertle, Alice. *Such a little mouse*
Schoenherr, Ian. *Cat and mouse*
  Pip and Squeak
Schoonmaker, Elizabeth. *Square cat ABC*
Schwartz, Amy. *Tiny and Hercules*
Schwartz, Corey Rosen. *Hop! Plop!*
Scotton, Rob. *Splat says thank you!*
  Splat the cat
Shepard, Aaron. *The princess mouse*
Sierra, Judy. *The beautiful butterfly*
  'Twas the fright before Christmas
Sif, Birgitta. *Swish and Squeak's noisy day*
Silvestro, Annie. *Mice skating*
Simmonds, Posy. *Baker cat*
Siomades, Lorianne. *Three little kittens*
Skinner, Daphne. *Albert keeps score*
  The right place for Albert
Slate, Joseph. *Who is coming to our house?*
Smith, Mavis. *'Twas the day after Thanksgiving*
Snell, Gordon. *'Twas the day after Christmas*
Song, Mika. *Tea with Oliver*
Soto, Gary. *Chato's kitchen*
Spinelli, Eileen. *Now it is summer*
  Together at Christmas
Spohn, Kate. *By word of mouse*
Springman, I. C. *More*
Spurling, Margaret. *Bilby moon*
Steig, William. *Doctor De Soto*
  Doctor De Soto goes to Africa
Stein, David Ezra. *Love, Mouserella*
Steptoe, John. *The story of jumping mouse*
Stevenson, James. *All aboard!*
  The castaway
  The Sea View Hotel
  The stowaway
Stills, Caroline. *Mice mischief*
Summers, Kate. *Milly's wedding*
Szekeres, Cyndy. *The mouse that Jack built*
  Toby!
  Toby's please and thank you
Tashiro, Chisato. *Five nice mice*
Taylor, Thomas. *Little Mouse and the big cupcake*
Thomas, Jan. *Pumpkin trouble*
Thompson, Lauren. *Mouse's first Christmas*
  Mouse's first fall
  Mouse's first Halloween
  Mouse's first snow
  Mouse's first spring
  Wee little lamb
Titus, Eve. *Anatole*
  Anatole and the cat
Tolan, Stephanie S. *Bartholomew's blessing*
Tompert, Ann. *A carol for Christmas*
  Just a little bit
  The pied piper of Peru
Trapani, Iza. *Shoo fly!*

Tupera, Tupera. *Polar Bear's underwear*
Twohy, Mike. *Mouse and Hippo*
  Oops, pounce, quick, run!
Underwood, Deborah. *Here comes the Tooth Fairy Cat*
Urban, Linda. *Mouse was mad*
Vagin, Vladimir. *Here comes the cat*
Valentine, Madeline. *I want that nut!*
van Lieshout, Maria. *Hopper and Wilson*
  Hopper and Wilson fetch a star
Vere, Ed. *The getaway*
Vincent, Gabrielle. *Ernest and Celestine at the circus*
  Ernest and Celestine's picnic
  Merry Christmas, Ernest and Celestine
Viva, Frank. *A trip to the bottom of the world with Mouse*
Vulliamy, Clara. *Small*
Waber, Bernard. *Do you see a mouse?*
  The mouse that snored
Waddell, Martin. *Mimi's Christmas*
  Sam Vole and his brothers
  Squeak-a-lot
Wagner, Karen. *Bravo, Mildred and Ed!*
  A friend like Ed
Wahl, Jan. *The field mouse and the dinosaur named Sue*
Waite, Judy. *Mouse, look out!*
Wallace, Nancy Elizabeth. *Look! look! look!*
  Look! look! look! at sculpture
Walsh, Ellen Stoll. *Balancing act*
  Dot and Jabber and the great acorn mystery
  Dot and Jabber and the mystery of the missing stream
  Mouse count
  Mouse magic
  Mouse paint
  Mouse shapes
  Where is Jumper?
  You silly goose
Warnes, Tim. *The great cheese robbery*
Waugh, Peter. *The great cannon beach mouse caper*
Wax, Wendy. *A very mice Christmas*
Webster, Sheryl. *Noodle's knitting*
Weigelt, Udo. *It wasn't me*
Wellington, Monica. *Squeaking of art, the mice go to the museum*
Wells, Rosemary. *Noisy Nora*
  Say hello, Sophie!
  Shy Charles
  Sophie's terrible twos
  Stanley and Rhoda
  Ten kisses for Sophie!
  Time-out for Sophie
  Use your words, Sophie!
Weninger, Brigitte. *Double birthday*
  Miko goes on vacation
  Miko wants a dog
  "Mom, wake up and play!"
  "No bath! No way!"
Willard, Nancy. *The mouse, the cat and Grandmother's hat*
Willems, Mo. *Time to pee*
  Time to say "please"!
Willis, Jeanne. *Cottonball Colin*
  Gorilla! Gorilla!
Wilson, Karma. *Bear counts*
  Mortimer's Christmas manger
  Mortimer's first garden
  Who goes there?
Wisniewski, David. *Sumo Mouse*

Wolkstein, Diane. *Little Mouse's painting*
Wood, Don. *Merry Christmas, big hungry bear*
Yamashita, Haruo. *Seven little mice go to school*
　　Seven little mice have fun on the ice
Yolen, Jane. *Beneath the ghost moon*
Young, Ed. *Mouse match*
　　Seven blind mice
Zalben, Jane Breskin. *Mousterpiece*
Zelinsky, Paul O. *The maid and the mouse and the odd-shaped house*
Ziefert, Harriet. *Messy Bessie*

Animals – migration *see* Migration

Animals – moles

Armo, Nancy. *A friend for Mole*
Bedford, David. *Mole's in love*
Bee, William. *Stanley the farmer*
Benjamin, A. H. *Mouse, mole and the falling star*
Crimi, Carolyn. *Rock 'n' roll Mole*
Delessert, Etienne. *Alert!*
Ehlert, Lois. *Holey Moley*
　　Mole's hill
　　Moon rope / Un lazo a la luna
Emmett, Jonathan. *The best gift of all*
　　Bringing down the moon
　　Diamond in the snow
　　No place like home
Gilman, Rita Golden. *Mole in a hole*
Grahame, Kenneth. *The wind in the willows*
　　A wind in the willows Christmas
Hillenbrand, Jane. *What a treasure!*
Hillenbrand, Will. *All for a dime! a Bear and Mole story*
　　Kite day
　　Off we go! a Bear and Mole story
　　Spring is here
Kuhlmann, Torben. *Moletown*
McAllister, Angela. *Take a kiss to school*
McPhail, David. *Mole music*
Moon, Nicola. *Tick-tock, drip-drop*
Newman, Marjorie. *Mole and the baby bird*
Odone, Jamison. *Mole had everything*
Oram, Hiawyn. *Badger's bad mood*
Pilcher, Steve. *Over there*
Schwartz, Roslyn. *The mole sisters and the cool breeze*
　　The mole sisters and the fairy ring
　　The mole sisters and the piece of moss
　　The mole sisters and the question
　　The mole sisters and the rainy day
Shannon, George. *Heart to heart*
Villeneuve, Anne. *The red scarf*
Yaccarino, Dan. *Morris Mole*

Animals – mongooses

Aardema, Verna. *The lonely lioness and the ostrich chicks*
Kipling, Rudyard. *Rikki-tikki-tavi*, ill. by Lambert Davis
　　Rikki-tikki-tavi, ill. by Jerry Pinkney

Animals – monkeys

Alborough, Jez. *Tall*
Alexander, Claire. *Monkey and the little one*
Auerbach, Adam. *Monkey brother*
Barnett, Mac. *Count the monkeys*

Bell, Cece. *Sock Monkey boogie-woogie*
　　Sock Monkey goes to Hollywood
　　Sock Monkey rides again
Bernstein, Ariel. *I have a balloon*
Black, Michael Ian. *The purple kangaroo*
Blake, Quentin. *Three little monkeys*
Bloom, C. P. *The Monkey goes bananas*
Brown, Marc. *Monkey: not ready for bedtime*
　　Monkey: not ready for kindergarten
　　Monkey: not ready for the baby
Brown, Ruth. *Monkey's friends*
Browne, Anthony. *Animal fair*
　　One gorilla: a counting book
Bustos, Eduardo. *Going ape!*
Bynum, Janie. *Kiki's blankie*
Cabrera, Jane. *Monkey's play time*
Chin, Oliver. *The year of the monkey*
Choldenko, Gennifer. *Putting the monkeys to bed*
Christelow, Eileen. *Don't wake up Mama!*
　　Five little monkeys go shopping
　　Five little monkeys jumping on the bed
　　Five little monkeys reading in bed
　　Five little monkeys sitting in a tree
　　Five little monkeys trick-or-treat
　　Five little monkeys wash the car
　　Five little monkeys with nothing to do
Curious George and the dump truck (1984)
　　Curious George and the dump truck (1999)
Curious George and the hot air balloon
Curious George and the pizza
Curious George and the puppies
Curious George at the fire station
Curious George goes camping
Curious George goes hiking
Curious George goes sledding
Curious George goes to a chocolate factory
Curious George goes to a movie
Curious George goes to the aquarium
Curious George goes to the circus
Curious George in the big city
Curious George in the snow
Curious George makes pancakes
Curious George takes a train
Curious George visits a toy store
Curious George visits the zoo
Curious George's 1 to 10 and back again
DePalma, Mary Newell. *The strange egg*
Diakité, Baba Wagué. *The hatseller and the monkeys*
DiCamillo, Kate. *Great joy*
Dodd, Emma. *More and more*
Donaldson, Julia. *Where's my mom?*
Dunrea, Olivier. *Me and Annie McPhee*
Du Quette, Keith. *Little Monkey lost*
Durant, Alan. *I love you, little monkey*
Elliott, George. *The boy who loved bananas*
Fox, Mem. *Two little monkeys*
Franco, Betsy. *Double play!*
Graves, Keith. *Second banana*
Gravett, Emily. *Monkey and me*
Gréban, Quentin. *Nestor*
Hamburg, Jennifer. *Monkey and Duck quack up!*
Hapka, Cathy. *Margret and H. A. Rey's Merry Christmas, Curious George*
Heck, Ed. *Monkey lost*
Heide, Florence Parry. *The one and only Marigold*
Hewett, Joan. *A monkey baby grows up*
Horowitz, Dave. *A monkey among us*
Jeyaveeran, Ruth. *The road to Mumbai*

Jiang, Ji-li. *The magical Monkey King, mischief in heaven*
Kepes, Juliet. *Five little monkeys*
Koller, Jackie French. *One monkey too many*
Landström, Lena. *A hippo's tale*
LaReau, Kara. *Rocko and Spanky have company*
Lehrhaupt, Adam. *Warning: do not open this book!*
Lin, Grace. *Okie-dokie, Artichokie*
Lunde, Darrin. *Monkey colors*
McDermott, Gerald. *Monkey*
Mangan, Anne. *The monkey who wanted the moon*
Martin, Bill, Jr.. *Spunky Little Monkey*
Martin, David. *Monkey business*
　Monkey trouble
Metzger, Steve. *The dancing clock*
Monroe, Chris. *Monkey with a tool belt and the seaside shenanigans*
Myers, Walter Dean. *Looking for the easy life*
Na, Il Sung. *The opposite zoo*
Oxenbury, Helen. *Tom and Pippo go shopping*
　Tom and Pippo in the garden
　Tom and Pippo on the beach
　Tom and Pippo see the moon
Patricelli, Leslie. *Be quiet, Mike!*
Paxton, Tom. *The jungle baseball game*
Peet, Mal. *Cloud tea monkeys*
Perez, Monica. *Curious George plants a tree*
　Curious George saves his pennies
Phillipps, J. C. *Monkey Ono*
Phillips, Betty Lou. *Emily goes wild*
Price, Ben Joel. *Earth space moon base*
Puttock, Simon. *A story for Hippo*
Regan, Dana. *Monkey see, monkey do*
Rey, H. A. *Cecily G and the nine monkeys*
　Curious George
　Curious George gets a medal
　Curious George learns the alphabet
　Curious George rides a bike
　Curious George takes a job
　The original Curious George
Rey, Margret. *Curious George and the dinosaur*
　Curious George flies a kite
　Curious George goes to an ice cream shop
　Curious George goes to school
　Curious George goes to the dentist
　Curious George goes to the hospital
Rosenthal, Marc. *Archie and the pirates*
San Souci, Robert D. *Pedro and the monkey*
Sayre, April Pulley. *Meet the howlers!*
Schaefer, Carole Lexa. *Big Little Monkey*
Schwartz, Amy. *Oscar*
Scott, Nathan Kumar. *Mangoes and bananas*
Sebe, Masayuki. *One hundred hungry monkeys!*
Sehgal, Kabir. *A bucket of blessings*
Seven spunky monkeys
Sierra, Judy. *Counting crocodiles*
Silvano, Wendi. *Counting coconuts / Contando cocos*
Siminovich, Lorena. *Monkey see, look at me!*
Slack, Michael. *Monkey Truck*
Slobodkina, Esphyr. *Caps for sale*
　Caps for sale and the mindful monkeys
　More caps for sale
Souhami, Jessica. *Rama and the demon king*
Sturm, James. *Birdsong: a story in pictures*
Tekavec, Heather. *Manners are not for monkeys*
Temple, Frances. *Tiger soup*
Teyssèdre, Fabienne. *Joseph wants to read*
Thomson, Sarah L. *Quick, Little Monkey!*
Van Laan, Nancy. *So say the little monkeys*

Vere, Ed. *Banana!*
Wiesmüller, Dieter. *The adventures of Marco and Polo*
Williams, Suzanne. *Ten naughty little monkeys*
Wright, Maureen. *Earth Day, birthday!*
Young, Ed. *Monkey King*

Animals – moose

Allen, Jonathan. *Mucky moose*
Arnosky, Jim. *Beaver pond, moose pond*
Bakos, Lisa. *Too many moose!*
Beck, Andrea. *Elliot bakes a cake*
　Elliot digs for treasure
　Elliot gets stuck
　Elliot's bath
　Elliot's Christmas surprise
　Elliot's emergency
　Elliot's great big lift-the-flap book
　Elliot's noisy night
　Elliot's shipwreck
Bingham, Kelly. *Circle, square, Moose*
　Z is for Moose
Bloxam, Frances. *Antlers forever!*
Bourgeois, Paulette. *Franklin's new friend*
Bunting, Eve. *A turkey for Thanksgiving*
Capucilli, Alyssa Satin. *Biscuit visits the pumpkin patch*
Claflin, Willy. *The uglified ducky*
Egan, Tim. *The trial of Cardigan Jones*
Gannij, Joan. *Elusive moose*
Green, Stephanie. *Not just another moose*
Haseley, Dennis. *The invisible moose*
Horowitz, Dave. *Duck, duck, moose*
Jeffers, Oliver. *This moose belongs to me*
Kneen, Maggie. *Chocolate moose*
Morris, Richard T. *This is a moose*
Murray, Martine. *A moose called Mouse*
Numeroff, Laura Joffe. *If you give a moose a muffin*
Oldland, Nicholas. *Making the moose out of life*
　Walk on the wild side
Pace, Anne Marie. *Groundhug Day*
Palatini, Margie. *Moosetache*
Plourde, Lynn. *Merry Moosey Christmas*
Raschka, Chris. *Moosey Moose*
Rayner, Catherine. *Ernest, the moose who doesn't fit*
Root, Phyllis. *Looking for a moose*
Segal, John. *The lonely moose*
Seuss, Dr. *Thidwick, the big-hearted moose*
Stihler, Chérie B. *The giant cabbage turnip*
Van Laan, Nancy. *Moose tales*
Wilson, Karma. *Moose tracks!*

Animals – mountain lions *see* Animals – cougars

Animals – mules

Bishop, Brett. *Clayton's path*
Edwards, Pamela Duncan. *Rude mule*
Ramsey, Calvin Alexander. *Belle, the last mule at Gee's Bend*
Rawlinson, Julia. *Mule school*
Sharmat, Marjorie Weinman. *Hooray for Father's Day!*

Animals – muskoxen

Cabatingan, Erin. *A is for Musk Ox*

Musk Ox counts

Animals – muskrats

Arnosky, Jim. *Come out, muskrats*
Chaconas, Dori. *Cork and Fuzz: merry merry holly holly*

Animals – narwhals

Mantchev, Lisa. *Someday, narwhal*
Sima, Jessie. *Not quite narwhal*

Animals – octopuses *see* Octopuses

Animals – opossums *see* Animals – possums

Animals – orangutans

Browne, Anthony. *One gorilla: a counting book*
Bustos, Eduardo. *Going ape!*
Daddo, Andrew. *Goodnight, me*
Engle, Margarita. *Orangutanka*

Animals – otters

Bedford, David. *Little Otter's big journey*
Berger, Samantha. *Martha doesn't say sorry*
   Martha doesn't share!
Casanova, Mary. *Utterly otterly day*
   Utterly otterly night
Galvin, Laura Gates. *River Otter at Autumn Lane*
Garton, Sam. *I am Otter*
   Otter goes to school
   Otter in space
   Otter loves Easter!
   Otter loves Halloween
Howe, James. *Otter and odder*
Levine, Ellen. *Seababy*
London, Jonathan. *Ollie's first year*
   Otters love to play
   Pup the sea otter
Luenn, Nancy. *Otter play*
Ohora, Zachariah. *Stop snoring, Bernard!*
Stewart, Amber. *Little by little*
Tatham, Betty. *Baby Sea Otter*
Webster, Christine. *Otter everywhere*

Animals – oxen

Balcziak, Bill. *Paul Bunyan*
Kellogg, Steven. *Paul Bunyan: a tall tale*
Lawlor, Laurie. *Old Crump*
Luckhurst, Matt. *Paul Bunyan and Babe the Blue Ox*
Rex, Adam. *XO, Ox*
Spang, Günter. *The ox and the Donkey*

Animals – pack rats

Kroll, Steven. *Stuff!*
Mariconda, Barbara. *Sort it out!*
Ruzzier, Sergio. *The room of wonders*

Animals – pandas

Antony, Steve. *I'll wait, Mr. Panda*
   Please, Mr. Panda
Baek, Matthew J. *Panda and polar bear*

Briant, Ed. *A day at the beach*
Butler, John. *Pi-shu, the little panda*
Calmenson, Stephanie. *Birthday at the Panda Palace*
Carr, Jan. *Sweet hearts*
Davies, Jacqueline. *Panda pants*
Dillard, Sarah. *First day at Zoo School*
Dowson, Nick. *Tracks of a panda*
Gaiman, Neil. *Chu's day*
   Chu's day at the beach
   Chu's first day of school
Gibbons, Gail. *Giant pandas*
Granfield, Linda. *The legend of the panda*
Henn, Sophy. *Pom Pom Panda gets the grumps*
Jarman, Julia. *Two shy pandas*
Kraus, Robert. *Milton the early riser*
Lambert, Jonny. *The only lonely panda*
Latimer, Miriam. *Dear Panda*
Liwska, Renata. *Little panda*
Manushkin, Fran. *Bamboo for me, bamboo for you!*
Markle, Sandra. *How many baby pandas?*
Morrow, Tara Jaye. *Panda goes to school*
Murphy, Mary. *Panda Foo and the new friend*
Muth, Jon J. *Hi, Koo!*
   Zen ghosts
   Zen shorts
   Zen socks
   Zen ties
Nagda, Anne Whitehead. *A home for panda*
Park, Linda Sue. *Xander's panda party*
Perry, Phyllis J. *Pandas' earthquake escape*
Pignataro, Anna. *Our love grows*
Potter, Alicia. *Mrs. Harkness and the panda*
Ransom, Candice F. *Amanda Panda quits kindergarten*
Rim, Sujean. *Chee-Kee*
Ryder, Joanne. *Little panda*
   Panda kindergarten
Saltzberg, Barney. *Chengdu could not, would not, fall asleep*
Sif, Birgitta. *Where my feet go*
Telchin, Eric. *The Black and White Factory*
Wild, Margaret. *Tom goes to kindergarten*
Yim, Natasha. *Goldy Luck and the three pandas*

Animals – panthers *see* Animals – leopards

Animals – pigs

Addy, Sharon Hart. *Lucky Jake*
Ahlberg, Allan. *Half a pig*
Alexander, Claire. *Small Florence*
Anderson, Derek. *Ten hungry pigs*
   Ten pigs
Anderson, Lena. *The hedgehog, the pig, and their little friend*
Asch, Frank. *Happy birthday, Big Bad Wolf*
   Ziggy Piggy and the three little pigs
Austin, Richard. *Pocket piggies opposites!*
Axelrod, Amy. *Pigs in the corner*
   Pigs in the pantry
   Pigs on a blanket
   Pigs on the ball
   Pigs on the move
   Pigs will be pigs
Bailey, Linda. *Goodnight, sweet pig*
Barba, Ale. *Time out!*
Bardhan-Quallen, Sudipta. *Hampire!*
Bassède, Francine. *A day with the Bellyflops*

Beck, Scott. *A mud pie for mother*
Bendall-Brunello, Tiziana. *I wish I could read!*
Bently, Peter. *The prince and the porker*
Berry, Lynne. *Pig and Pug*
Black, Michael Ian. *A pig parade is a terrible idea*
Bloom, Suzanne. *No place for a pig*
    Piggy Monday
Bond, Felicia. *Poinsettia and her family*
    Poinsettia and the firefighters
Bonnice, Lindsey. *Libby and Pearl: the best of friends*
Boynton, Sandra. *Happy birthday, Little Pookie*
    Little Pookie
    Night-night, Little Pookie
    Spooky Pookie
Branford, Henrietta. *Little Pig Figwort can't get to*
    sleep
Brown, Marc. *Perfect pigs*
Brown, Margaret Wise. *The good little bad little pig*
Bunting, Eve. *Sing a song of piglets*
Burks, James. *Pigs and a blanket*
Bynum, Janie. *Otis*
Carlson, Nancy. *Get up and go!*
    How about a hug?
    Louanne Pig in the mysterious Valentine
Cazet, Denys. *Will you read to me?*
Chataway, Carol. *The perfect pet*
Chorao, Kay. *Pig and Crow*
Christelow, Eileen. *The great pig escape*
    The great pig search
Church, Caroline Jayne. *Ping Pong Pig*
Cocca-Leffler, Maryann. *A homemade together*
    Christmas
Cordell, Matthew. *Trouble gum*
Cort, Ben. *Pigs can't fly!*
Costello, David Hyde. *Little Pig joins the band*
    Little Pig saves the ship
Côté, Geneviève. *Goodnight, you*
    Me and you
    Starring me and you
    Without you
Dahl, Michael. *Pie for piglets*
Dakos, Kalli. *Our principal promised to kiss a pig*
Denise, Anika. *Pigs love potatoes*
Dewan, Ted. *Crispin and the 3 little piglets*
    Crispin, the pig who had it all
Dorros, Arthur. *When the pigs took over*
Dotlich, Rebecca Kai. *Mama loves*
    Papa loves
Downey, Lynn. *The tattletale*
Dunbar, Polly. *Happy Hector*
Eaton, Maxwell. *Best buds*
    The mystery
    Superheroes
Edwards, Pamela Duncan. *Princess Pigtoria and the*
    pea
Egan, Tim. *The experiments of Doctor Vermin*
Elliot, David. *Henry's map*
Elya, Susan Middleton. *Adiós, tricycle*
Emmett, Jonathan. *The princess and the pig*
Ernst, Lisa Campbell. *Sylvia Jean, drama queen*
    Sylvia Jean, scout supreme
Falconer, Ian. *Olivia*
    Olivia and the fairy princesses
    Olivia — and the missing toy
    Olivia counts
    Olivia forms a band
    Olivia goes to Venice
    Olivia saves the circus
    Olivia the spy

    Olivia's opposites
Fine, Howard. *A piggie Christmas*
Folgueira, Rodrigo. *Ribbit!*
Ford, Bernette. *No more pacifier for Piggy!*
Fox, Christyan. *Astronaut PiggyWiggy*
    Count to ten, PiggyWiggy!
    Fire fighter PiggyWiggy
    What color is that, PiggyWiggy?
    What shape is that, PiggyWiggy?
Gal, Susan. *Day by day*
Gallion, Sue Lowell. *Pug and Pig trick-or-treat*
    Pug meets Pig
Garland, Michael. *Icarus Swinebuckle*
Geisert, Arthur. *The giant ball of string*
    The giant seed
    Hogwash
    Ice
    Lights out
    Mystery
    Nursery crimes
    Oops
    Pigaroons
Gibbons, Gail. *Pigs*
Gliori, Debi. *What's the time, Mr. Wolf?*
Gorbachev, Valeri. *One rainy day*
    Pizza-pie snowman
    That's what friends are for
Gravett, Emily. *Wolf won't bite!*
Grindley, Sally. *Can we play too, Piglittle?*
Griswell, Kim T. *Rufus blasts off!*
    Rufus goes to school
    Rufus goes to sea
Guarnaccia, Steven. *The three little pigs: an*
    architectural tale
Harris, Trudy. *Twenty hungry piggies*
Harrison, David L. *Piggy Wiglet*
Heim, Alastair. *Love you too*
Helakoski, Leslie. *Big pigs*
Heller, Nicholas. *Elwood and the witch*
Hillenbrand, Will. *Louie!*
Himmelman, John. *Pigs to the rescue*
Hobbie, Holly. *Toot and Puddle*
    Toot and Puddle: let it snow
    Toot and Puddle: wish you were here
    Toot and Puddle, a present for Toot
    Toot and Puddle, I'll be home for Christmas
    Toot and Puddle, Puddle's ABC
    Toot and Puddle, top of the world
    Toot and Puddle, you are my sunshine
Horning, Sandra. *The giant hug*
Hutchins, Pat. *Little pink pig*
Inkpen, Mick. *Kipper and Roly*
    Kipper's A to Z
    Wibbly Pig can make a tent
    Wibbly Pig is upset
    Wibbly Pig likes bananas
    Wibbly Pig opens his presents
Jacobs, Joseph. *The three sillies*
Jamieson, Victoria. *Olympig!*
Johnson, Angela. *Julius*
Johnson, Paul Brett. *The pig who ran a red light*
Johnston, Tony. *Farmer Mack measures his pig*
Kasza, Keiko. *My lucky birthday*
Katzler, Eva. *Florentine and Pig*
Kaufmann, Nancy. *Bye, Bye*
Keller, Holly. *Geraldine and Mrs. Duffy*
    Geraldine first
    Geraldine's baby brother
    Geraldine's big snow

Santore, Charles. *Three hungry pigs and the wolf who came to dinner*
Sattler, Jennifer. *Pig kahuna*
  Pig kahuna: who's that pig?
  Pig kahuna pirates!
Schroeder, Alan. *Smoky Mountain Rose*
Schuh, Mari C. *Pigs on the farm*
Schwartz, Corey Rosen. *The three ninja pigs*
Scieszka, Jon. *The true story of the three little pigs by A. Wolf, as told to Jon Scieszka*
Segal, John. *Far far away!*
  Pirates don't take baths
Sendak, Maurice. *Bumble-ardy*
Shaw, Natalie. *Olivia plans a tea party*
Sillifant, Alec. *Farmer Ham*
Simon, Charnan. *A greedy little pig*
Smith, Maggie. *Pigs in pajamas*
Snyder, Laurel. *Baxter, the pig who wanted to be kosher*
Spinelli, Eileen. *Princess Pig*
  Six hogs on a scooter
Spurr, Elizabeth. *A pig named Perrier*
Stanton, Elizabeth Rose. *Peddles*
Steig, William. *The amazing bone*
  Farmer Palmer's wagon ride
  Roland, the minstrel pig
  Zeke Pippin
Stein, Mathilde. *Monstersong*
Stockland, Patricia M. *In the pig pen*
Stolz, Mary. *Emmett's pig*
Sturges, Philemon. *This little pirate*
Sutton, Jane. *Don't call me Sidney*
Teague, Mark. *Pigsty*
  The three little pigs and the somewhat bad wolf
Thaler, Mike. *Pig Little*
Thomas, Jan. *Is that wise, Pig?*
  Pumpkin trouble
The three little pigs. *The three little pigs*, ill. by Gavin Bishop
  The three little pigs, ill. by Paul Galdone
  The three little pigs, ill. by Rob Hefferan
  The three little pigs, ill. by Steven Kellogg
  The three little pigs, ill. by David McPhail
  The three little pigs, ill. by James Marshall
  The three little pigs, ill. by Bernadette Watts
  The three little pigs, ill. by Margot Zemach
  The three little pigs / Los tres cerditos
  The three little pigs and the big bad wolf
  The three little pigs and the fox
Thurman, Kathryn K. *A garden for Pig*
Timmers, Leo. *Gus's garage*
Trivizas, Eugenios. *The three little wolves and the big bad pig*
Tryon, Leslie. *Patsy says*
Tucker, Lindy. *Porkelia*
Twohy, Mike. *Poindexter makes a friend*
Tyler, Jenny. *Big Pig on a dig*
Vail, Rachel. *Piggy Bunny*
Van Nutt, Julia. *The mystery of Mineral Gorge*
  Pignapped!
  Pumpkins from the sky?
Virján, Emma J. *What this story needs is a munch and a crunch*
Vischer, Phil. *Sidney and Norman*
Waddell, Martin. *Captain Small Pig*
  The pig in the pond
Waldron, Jan L. *Angel Pig and the hidden Christmas*
  John Pig's Halloween
Walton, Rick. *Pig, pigger, piggest*

Weeks, Sarah. *Ella, of course!*
  I'm a pig
Wells, Rosemary. *The little lame prince*
Weston, Martha. *Tuck in the pool*
  Tuck's haunted house
Whatley, Bruce. *Wait! no paint!*
Whybrow, Ian. *Wish, change, friend*
Wiesner, David. *The three pigs*
Wild, Margaret. *Old Pig*
  Piglet and Granny
  Piglet and Mama
  Piglet and Papa
Wilson, Karma. *Hogwash!*
Wood, Audrey. *Piggy Pie Po*
Wood, Don. *Piggies*
Yamada, Utako. *The story of Cherry the pig*
Yamaguchi, Kristi. *Dream big, little pig!*
  It's a big world, little pig!
Yee, Wong Herbert. *Fireman Small*
  Fireman Small, fire down below
  Fireman Small to the rescue
  Hamburger Heaven
Yolen, Jane. *Picnic with Piggins*
  Piggins

Animals – platypuses

Arnold, Caroline. *A platypus' world*
Clarke, Ginjer L. *Platypus!*
Collard, Sneed B. *A platypus, probably*
Dean, James. *Pete the Cat and the new guy*
Fuge, Charles. *Swim, Little Wombat, swim!*
Riddell, Chris. *Platypus*
  Platypus and the lucky day

Animals – polar bears

Anderson, Derek. *Romeo and Lou blast off*
Baek, Matthew J. *Panda and polar bear*
Banks, Kate. *Pup and bear*
Barroux. *Welcome*
Bedford, David. *Touch the sky, my little bear*
Bergren, Lisa Tawn. *God gave us Easter*
Bloom, Suzanne. *A splendid friend, indeed*
Bogan, Paulette. *Virgil and Owen*
  Virgil and Owen stick together
Brett, Jan. *The three snow bears*
Brière-Haquet, Alice. *One very big bear*
Brooks, Erik. *Polar opposites*
  The practically perfect pajamas
Bushey, Jeanne. *The polar bear's gift*
Cabrera, Jane. *The lonesome polar bear*
Carrick, Carol. *The polar bears are hungry*
Cleminson, Katie. *Magic box*
Collins, Ross. *There's a bear on my chair*
Czekaj, Jef. *Yes, yes, Yaul!*
Davies, Nicola. *Ice bear*
De Beer, Hans. *Little Polar Bear and the big balloon*
  Little Polar Bear and the submarine
  Little Polar Bear and the whales
Dodd, Emma. *Forever*
Floyd, Madeleine. *Cold paws, warm heart*
Ford, Miela. *Follow the leader*
  Mom and me
Genechten, Guido van. *Because you are my friend*
George, Jean Craighead. *The last polar bear*
  Snow bear
Gibbons, Gail. *Polar bears*

Gliori, Debi. *Polar Bolero*
Graber, Janet. *Jacob and the polar bears*
Guiberson, Brenda Z. *Ice bears*
Hatkoff, Isabella, et al. *Knut*
Heder, Thyra. *The bear report*
Just like father
Karas, G. Brian. *Skidamarink*
Kern, Noris. *I love you with all my heart*
Kimmel, Eric A. *Simon and the bear*
Kono, Erin Eitter. *Every color*
Levis, Caron. *Ida, always*
London, Jonathan. *Ice Bear and Little Fox*
Lumry, Amanda. *Polar bear puzzle*
Markle, Sandra. *Waiting for ice*
Mercer, Lynn. *Schubert's snowflakes*
Modugno, Maria. *Santa Claus and the three bears*
Moss, Miriam. *The snow bear*
Murphy, Yannick. *Baby Polar*
Olien, Jessica. *Adrift*
Ørdal, Stina Langlo. *Princess Aasta*
Pinkwater, Daniel. *At the Hotel Larry*
  Bad bear detectives
  Bad bears and a bunny
  Bad bears go visiting
  Bad bears in the big city
  Bongo Larry
  Dancing Larry
  Ice-cream Larry
  Irving and Muktuk
  Sleepover Larry
  Young Larry
Rives. *If I were a polar bear*
Rockhill, Dennis. *Polar slumber / Sueño polar*
Rueda, Claudia. *My little polar bear*
Ryder, Joanne. *A pair of polar bears*
  White bear, ice bear
Stafford, Liliana. *The snow bear*
Steven, Kenneth. *The biggest thing in the world*
Stoop, Naoko. *Red Knit Cap Girl to the rescue*
Thompson, Lauren. *Polar bear morning*
Thomson, Sarah L. *Cub's big world*
  Where do polar bears live?
Townsend, Emily Rose. *Polar bears*
Tupera, Tupera. *Polar Bear's underwear*
Ward, Lindsay. *Please bring balloons*
Wild, Margaret. *Thank you, Santa*
Willis, Jeanne. *Poles apart*
Wilson, Karma. *Mama, why?*
Winter, Jeanette. *Nanuk the ice bear*
Wojtowycz, David. *A cuddle for Claude*
Yoon, Salina. *Penguin's big adventure*

Animals – porcupines

Haines, Mike. *Countdown to bedtime*
LaReau, Kara. *Mr. Prickles*
Lester, Helen. *A porcupine named Fluffy*
Linders, Clara. *The very best door of all*
Moodie, Fiona. *Noko and the night monster*
Pfister, Marcus. *Where is my friend?*
Rowe, John A. *I want a hug*
Schmid, Paul. *Hugs from Pearl*
  Perfectly Percy
Slate, Joseph. *Little Porcupine's Christmas*
  Story time for Little Porcupine
Stevenson, James. *The castaway*
Underwood, Deborah. *A balloon for Isabel*
Waring, Zoe. *No hugs for Porcupine*
Wheeler, Lisa. *Hokey pokey*

  Porcupining
Wilson, Karma. *Sweet Briar goes to camp*

Animals – possums

Bogue, Gary. *There's an opossum in my backyard*
Chaconas, Dori. *Cork and Fuzz: merry merry holly holly*
deGroat, Diane. *Ants in your pants, worms in your plants!*
  Brand-new pencils, brand-new books
  Good night, sleep tight, don't let the bedbugs bite
  Jingle bells, homework smells
  Last one in is a rotten egg!
  Liar, liar, pants on fire
  Lola the elf
  Mother, you're the best! (but Sister, you're a pest!)
Duvall, Deborah L. *The opossum's tale*
Fox, Mem. *Possum magic*
Gallaher, Jason. *Whobert Whover, owl detective*
Hunter, Anne. *Possum and the peeper*
  Possum's harvest moon
Hurd, Thacher. *Mama don't allow*
Kasza, Keiko. *Don't laugh, Joe*
Keller, Holly. *Henry's Fourth of July*
  Henry's happy birthday
Marino, Gianna. *Night animals*
Salley, Coleen. *Epossumondas*
  Epossumondas plays possum
  Epossumondas saves the day
Van Laan, Nancy. *Possum come a-knocking*

Animals – prairie dogs

Stevens, Janet. *The great fuzz frenzy*

Animals – prairie wolves *see* Animals – coyotes

Animals – pumas *see* Animals – cougars

Animals – rabbits

Abbott, Bud. *Who's on first?*
Adams, Adrienne. *The Christmas party*
  The Easter egg artists
  The great Valentine's Day balloon race
Aesop. *The hare and the tortoise*, ill. by Paul Galdone
  The hare and the tortoise, ill. by Carol Jones
  The hare and the tortoise, ill. by Helen Ward
  The hare and the tortoise / La liebre y la tortuga
  Hare and Tortoise
  The race
  Road signs
  The tortoise and the hare, ill. by Jerry Pinkney
  The tortoise and the hare, ill. by Sara Rojo
  The tortoise and the hare: an Aesop fable
Allen, Jonathan. *"I'm not Santa!"*
  The little rabbit who liked to say moo
Amant, Kathleen. *Little Rabbit gets messy*
  On your potty, Little Rabbit
Anderson, Derek. *How the Easter Bunny saved Christmas*
Andros, Camille. *Charlotte the scientist is squished*
Apperley, Dawn. *Blossom and Boo*
  Blossom and Boo stay up late
Araki, Mie. *The magic toolbox*
Arnosky, Jim. *Rabbits and raindrops*

Asher, Sandy. *Too many frogs!*
Atteberry, Kevan. *Bunnies!!!*
   Puddles!!!
Badescu, Ramona. *Big Rabbit's bad mood*
Baguley, Elizabeth. *A long way from home*
Baker, Alan. *Black and White Rabbit's ABC*
   Brown Rabbit's shape book
   Gray Rabbit's one, two, three
   Little Rabbit's first number book
   Little Rabbit's first word book
   White Rabbit's color book
Balian, Lorna. *Humbug rabbit*
Bardill, Linard. *The great golden thing*
Barton, Chris. *That's not Bunny!*
Bate, Lucy. *Little Rabbit's loose tooth*
Battersby, Katherine. *Brave Squish Rabbit*
   Squish Rabbit
Bauer, Marion Dane. *One brown bunny*
Beck, Robert. *A bunny in the ballet*
Becker, John Leonard. *Seven little rabbits*
Berger, Barbara. *Thunder Bunny*
Berger, Carin. *Forever friends*
   Good night! Good night!
Berlin, Irving. *Easter parade*
Bianco, Margery Williams. *The velveteen rabbit*, ill.
   by David Jorgensen
   The velveteen rabbit, ill. by Thea Kliros
   The velveteen rabbit, ill. by Komako Sakai
   The velveteen rabbit, ill. by Gennady Spirin
   The velveteen rabbit: or, How toys became real, ill. by
     Allen Atkinson
   The velveteen rabbit: or, How toys became real, ill. by
     Steve Johnson
Birchall, Mark. *Rabbit's birthday surprise*
   Rabbit's wooly sweater
Blake, Stephanie. *I don't want to go to school!*
Boelts, Maribeth. *Sweet dreams, Little Bunny!*
   You're a brother, Little Bunny!
Bottner, Barbara. *Raymond and Nelda*
Brett, Jan. *The animals' Santa*
   The Easter egg
Brown, Marc. *The bionic bunny show*
Brown, Margaret Wise. *Bunny's noisy book*
   The golden egg book
   Good day, good night
   Goodnight moon
   Goodnight moon ABC
   Goodnight moon 123: a counting book
   My world
   The runaway bunny
Bruchac, James. *Rabbit's snow dance*
Burg, Sarah Emmanuelle. *One more egg*
Burke, Bobby. *Daddy's little girl*
Burleigh, Robert. *Hit the road, Jack*
Burningham, John. *Tug-of-war*
Capucilli, Alyssa Satin. *Only my dad and me*
Carlson, Nancy. *Harriet and George's Christmas treat*
   Loudmouth George and the cornet
   Loudmouth George and the fishing trip
   Loudmouth George and the new neighbors
   Loudmouth George and the sixth-grade bully
   Loudmouth George earns his allowance
Carlstrom, Nancy White. *Mama, will it snow*
   tonight?
Carnesi, Monica. *Sleepover with Beatrice and Bear*
Carrer, Chiara. *Otto Carrotto*
Cate, Annette LeBlanc. *The magic rabbit*
Catrow, David. *Fun in the sun*
Cazet, Denys. *December 24th*

Chaconas, Dori. *Looking for Easter*
Chase, Kit. *Charlie's boat*
   Oliver's tree
Church, Caroline Jayne. *I love my bunny*
Cooper, Helen. *Tatty-Ratty*
Costa, Maria S. *How to find a friend*
Côté, Geneviève. *Goodnight, you*
   Me and you
   Starring me and you
   With you always, Little Monday
   Without you
Cowell, Cressida. *Emily Brown and the Thing*
   That rabbit belongs to Emily Brown
Crimi, Carolyn. *Henry and the Buccaneer Bunnies*
   Henry and the Crazed Chicken Pirates
Cronin, Doreen. *Rescue bunnies*
Crummel, Susan Stevens. *Tumbleweed stew*
Czekaj, Jef. *Hip and Hop, don't stop!*
   Yes, yes, Yaul!
D'Amico, Carmela. *Suki and Mirabella*
   Suki the very loud bunny
Davis, Jacky. *Black Belt Bunny*
Davis, Jon. *Small Blue and the deep dark night*
DeLaporte, Bérengère. *Superfab saves the day*
Denim, Sue. *The Dumb Bunnies*
   The Dumb Bunnies' Easter
   The Dumb Bunnies go to the zoo
   Make way for Dumb Bunnies
Desrosiers, Sylvie. *Hocus Pocus*
   Hocus Pocus takes the train
Dewdney, Anna. *Nobunny's perfect*
Diakité, Baba Wagué. *The magic gourd*
Dierssen, Andreas. *Timid Timmy*
   Timmy's new friend
Dieterlé, Nathalie. *I am the king!*
Dijkstra, Lida. *Cute*
Dodd, Emma. *Love*
Donohue, Dorothy. *Veggie soup*
Dotlich, Rebecca Kai. *The knowing book*
Downard, Barry. *The Race of the Century*
Dubosarsky, Ursula. *The terrible plop*
Durant, Alan. *Big Bad Bunny*
   Brown Bear gets in shape
Dyckman, Ame. *Wolfie the bunny*
Edvall, Lilian. *The rabbit who longed for home*
Empson, Jo. *Rabbityness*
Engle, Margarita. *Tiny rabbit's big wish*
Esbaum, Jill. *Frankenbunny*
Escoffier, Michael. *Rabbit and the Not-So-Big-Bad*
   Wolf
   Sleep tight, Charlie
Evans, Lezlie. *The bunnies' picnic*
   The bunnies' trip
Faglia, Matteo. *Happy birthday, I'm 1*
Falkenstern, Lisa. *A dragon moves in*
Faller, Regis. *Polo and Lily*
Feeney, Tatyana. *Small Bunny's blue blanket*
Fleming, Candace. *Muncha! muncha! muncha!*
   Tippy-tippy-tippy, hide!
   Tippy-tippy-tippy, splash!
Florian, Douglas. *The wonderful habits of rabbits*
Ford, Bernette. *First snow*
   No more bottles for Bunny!
Freedman, Claire. *Follow that bear if you dare!*
   Hushabye Lily
Galbraith, Kathryn O. *Boo, bunny!*
   Two bunny buddies
Garland, Sally Anne. *Share*
Garoche, Camille. *The snow rabbit*

Gay, Marie-Louise. *Roslyn Rutabaga and the biggest hole on earth!*
Genechten, Guido van. *Flop-Ear*
  Ricky and the squirrel
  Ricky is brave
George, Lindsay Barrett. *My bunny and me*
Geras, Adèle. *My wishes for you*
Gershator, Phillis. *Time for a bath*
  Time for a hug
Glaser, Linda. *Hoppy Passover!*
Gliori, Debi. *Flora's blanket*
  Flora's surprise
  The scariest thing of all
Goodhart, Pippa. *My very own space*
Goodman, Joan Elizabeth. *Ballet Bunnies*
Gorbachev, Valeri. *Christopher counting*
  Nicky and the big, bad wolves
  Nicky and the fantastic birthday gift
  Nicky and the rainy day
Gore, Leonid. *Danny's first snow*
Got, Yves. *Sam's big book of words*
  Sam's little sister
Grambling, Lois G. *Here comes T. Rex Cottontail*
Gravett, Emily. *Bear and Hare: share!*
  Bear and Hare: snow!
  Bear and Hare go fishing
  Bear and Hare—where's Bear?
  The rabbit problem
  Wolves
Gretz, Susanna. *Rabbit food*
Griffith, Helen V. *Moonlight*
Grimm, Jacob and Wilhelm. *The rabbit's bride*
Grossman, Virginia. *Ten little rabbits*
Guest, C. Z. *Tiny green thumbs*
Hample, Stoo. *I will kiss you (lots and lots and lots!)*
Harper, Charise Mericle. *Pink me up*
Harry, Rebecca. *Snow Bunny's Christmas wish*
Hayes, Geoffrey. *The bunny's night-light*
Heap, Sue. *Four friends in the garden*
Henkes, Kevin. *Bailey goes camping*
  Little white rabbit
  So happy!
Henry, Steve. *Here is Big Bunny*
Hest, Amy. *On the night of the shooting star*
Heyward, Du Bose. *The country bunny and the little gold shoes*
Hillenbrand, Will. *Snowman's story*
Ho, Minfong. *Brother Rabbit*
Hoban, Tana. *Where is it?*
Holmes, Janet A. *Me and you*
Horse, Harry. *Little Rabbit lost*
  Little Rabbit runaway
  Little Rabbit's new baby
Hubbell, Patricia. *Rabbit moon*
Hughes, Laura. *We're going on an egg hunt*
Hurley, Jorey. *Hop*
Ichikawa, Satomi. *La La Rose*
Ives, Penny. *Rabbit pie*
Jackson, Ellen. *The seven seas*
Jagtenberg, Yvonne. *Jack's rabbit*
Jahn-Clough, Lisa. *Felicity and Cordelia*
Jeram, Anita. *I love my little storybook*
Jin, Susie Lee. *Mine!*
Johnson, Paul Brett. *Little Bunny Foo Foo*
Johnston, Tony. *Little Rabbit goes to sleep*
  The tale of Rabbit and Coyote
Julian, Alison. *Brave as a bunny can be*
Kaplan, Michael B. *Betty Bunny didn't do it*
  Betty Bunny loves chocolate cake

  Betty Bunny loves Easter
  Betty Bunny wants a goal
  Betty Bunny wants everything
Keller, Emily Snowell. *Sleeping Bunny*
Keller, Holly. *Cecil's garden*
  Pearl's new skates
Kempter, Christa. *Wally and Mae*
Kenyon, Tony. *Hyacinth Hop has the hic-hops*
Kirk, Daniel. *Ten thank-you letters*
  Ten things I love about you
Kirk, David. *Little bunny, Biddle bunny*
  Oh So Tiny bunny
Klise, Kate. *Imagine Harry*
  Little Rabbit and the Meanest Mother on Earth
  Little Rabbit and the Night Mare
  Why do you cry?
Knudsen, Michelle. *Big Mean Mike*
Kortepeter, Paul. *Oliver's red toboggan*
Krensky, Stephen. *Milo and the really big bunny*
Krishnaswami, Uma. *Remembering Grandpa*
Kroll, Steven. *The big bunny and the Easter eggs*
  The big bunny and the magic show
Kroll, Virginia L. *Really rabbits*
Krosoczka, Jarrett J. *Naptastrophe!*
Lacome, Julie. *Ruthie's big old coat*
Larsen, Andrew. *Bella and the bunny*
Lasky, Kathryn. *Lunch bunnies*
  Science fair bunnies
  Show and tell bunnies
  Tumble bunnies
Latimer, Alex. *Lion vs Rabbit*
Layne, Steven L. *Love the baby*
Leathers, Philippa. *The black rabbit*
Lee, Ho Baek. *While we were out*
Lester, Helen. *Listen, Buddy*
Lewis, Rob. *Friends*
Light, Steve. *The bunny burrow buyer's book*
Lillegard, Dee. *Balloons, balloons, balloons*
Lionni, Leo. *Let's make rabbits*
Livingston, Irene. *Finklehopper Frog*
  Finklehopper Frog cheers
Lloyd-Jones, Sally. *Bunny's first spring*
Lobe, Mira. *Hoppelpopp and the best bunny*
Lobel, Anita. *Taking care of Mama Rabbit*
  Ten hungry rabbits
Lodding, Linda Ravin. *Painting Pepette*
London, Jonathan. *Jackrabbit*
Loney, Andrea J. *Bunnybear*
Long, Sylvia. *Deck the hall*
Loomis, Christine. *Astro Bunnies*
  Cowboy bunnies
  Scuba bunnies
Lowell, Susan. *The tortoise and the jackrabbit*
Lundquist, Mary. *Cat and Bunny*
Luthardt, Kevin. *You're weird!*
McAllister, Angela. *The little blue rabbit*
  Night-night, little one
McBratney, Sam. *Guess how much I love you*
McCarty, Peter. *Bunny dreams*
  Chloe
  Henry in love
  Little bunny on the move
McCue, Lisa. *Quiet Bunny*
  Quiet Bunny and Noisy Puppy
McCullough, Sharon Pierce. *Bunbun at bedtime*
  Bunbun, the middle one
McDermott, Gerald. *Zomo the rabbit*
MacDonald, Elizabeth. *The wolf is coming!*
MacDonald, Margaret Read. *Conejito*

Schulman, Janet. *A bunny for all seasons*

Schwartz, Amy. *Oscar*

Schweninger, Ann. *Halloween surprises*
   Valentine friends

Scieszka, Jon. *Battle Bunny*

Segal, John. *Carrot soup*

Selkowe, Valrie M. *Happy birthday to me!*

Shannon, George. *Rabbit's gift*

Shields, Gillian. *When the world was waiting for you*

Silvestro, Annie. *Bunny's book club*

Simmons, Jane. *Little Fern's first winter*

Slegers, Liesbet. *Happy Easter!*

Smee, Nicola. *What's the matter, Bunny Blue?*

Smythe, Theresa. *Chester's colorful Easter eggs*

Soto, Gary. *Lucky Luis*

Spelman, Cornelia Maude. *When I feel angry*

Spinelli, Eileen. *A big boy now*

Stadler, John. *Wilson and Miss Lovely*

Stalder, Päivi. *Ernest's first Easter*

Stanley, Mandy. *Lettice the dancing rabbit*
   Lettice the flower girl
   Lettice the flying rabbit

Steig, William. *Solomon the rusty nail*
   Which would you rather be?

Stein, Janet. *This little bunny can bake*

Sterling, Cheryl. *Some bunny to talk to*

Sternberg, Julie. *Bedtime at Bessie and Lil's*

Stevens, Janet. *Tops and bottoms*

Stevenson, James. *Monty*

Stewart, Amber. *I'm big enough*
   No babysitters allowed
   Rabbit ears

Stewart, Paul. *The birthday presents*
   A little bit of winter
   Rabbit's wish

Stiegemeyer, Julie. *Seven little bunnies*

Stills, Caroline. *The house of twelve bunnies*

Surplice, Holly. *Peek-a-boo Bunny*

Szekeres, Cyndy. *I can count 100 bunnies, and so can
   you!*

Tafuri, Nancy. *Rabbit's morning*
   Where did Bunny go?
   Will you be my friend?

Taylor, Sean. *The grizzly bear with the frizzly hair*

Taylor, Shirley. *The cross in the egg*

Teckentrup, Britta. *Busy bunny days*

Tegen, Katherine Brown. *The story of the Easter
   Bunny*

Thomas, Jan. *The Easter Bunny's assistant*

Thompson, Emma. *The further tale of Peter Rabbit*

Thompson, Lauren. *Wee little bunny*

Thornhill, Jan. *The rumor*
   Winter's coming

Tingle, Tim. *When Turtle grew feathers*

Tompert, Ann. *Nothing sticks like a shadow*

Tonatiuh, Duncan. *Pancho Rabbit and the coyote*

Tone, Satoe. *The very big carrot*

Trasler, Janee. *Mimi and Bear in the snow*

Vainio, Pirkko. *The best of friends*

Van Leeuwen, Jean. *Five funny bunnies*

Van Woerkom, Dorothy. *Harry and Shelburt*

Waddell, Martin. *Tom Rabbit*
   We love them

Waechter, Phillip. *Rosie and the nightmares*

Wakeman, Daniel. *Ben's bunny trouble*

Wallace, Ivy. *Pookie*
   Pookie believes in Santa Claus
   Pookie puts the world right

Wallace, John. *Tiny Rabbit goes to a birthday party*

Wallace, Nancy Elizabeth. *Alphabet house*
   Apples, apples, apples
   Count down to clean up
   Fly, monarch! fly!
   Paperwhite
   Planting seeds
   Pumpkin day
   Rabbit's bedtime
   Ready, set, 100th day!
   Recycle every day!
   Snow
   Stars! stars! stars!
   Tell-a-bunny
   The Valentine Express

Walters, Catherine. *The magical snowman*

Walton, Rick. *Bunny school*
   One more bunny
   What do we do with the baby?

Washington, Donna L. *Li'l Rabbit's Kwanzaa*

Watson, Wendy. *Bedtime bunnies*

Watt, Mélanie. *You're finally here!*

Weeks, Sarah. *Bunny fun*
   Overboard!

Weigelt, Udo. *The Easter Bunny's baby*

Weil, Lisl. *The candy egg bunny*

Welch, Willy. *Grumpy Bunnies*

Wellington, Monica. *Bunny's first snowflake*
   Night rabbits

Wells, Rosemary. *Bunny cakes*
   Bunny mail
   Bunny money
   Bunny party
   Carry me!
   Clean-up time
   Emily's first 100 days of school
   First tomato
   Goodnight Max
   The island light
   Love waves
   McDuff's hide-and-seek
   Max and Ruby at the Warthogs' wedding
   Max and Ruby's bedtime book
   Max and Ruby's Midas
   Max and Ruby's treasure hunt
   Max cleans up
   Max counts his chickens
   Max's ABC
   Max's apples
   Max's bath
   Max's bedtime
   Max's birthday
   Max's breakfast
   Max's bunny business
   Max's chocolate chicken
   Max's Christmas
   Max's dragon shirt
   Max's Easter surprise
   Max's first word
   Max's new suit
   Max's ride
   Max's toys
   Max's worm cake
   Morris's disappearing bag
   Moss pillows
   My kindergarten
   Peek-a-boo
   Read to your bunny
   Red boots
   Ruby's beauty shop

Shopping
Weninger, Brigitte. *Davy in the middle*
   Davy loves his mommy
   Davy, soccer star!
   Happy birthday, Davy
   Happy Easter, Davy
   Happy Easter, Davy!
   Merry Christmas, Davy!
   What's the matter, Davy?
   Why are you fighting, Davy?
   Will you mind the baby, Davy?
Whybrow, Ian. *Bella gets her skates on*
Wild, Margaret. *Rosie and Tortoise*
Wilhelm, Hans. *Bunny trouble*
   More bunny trouble
Willems, Mo. *Knuffle Bunny*
   Knuffle Bunny free
   Knuffle Bunny too
Williams, Garth. *Benjamin's treasure*
Williams, Sue. *Dinnertime*
Winget, Susan. *Tucker's four-carrot school day*
Wolf, Winfried. *The Easter bunny*
Wormell, Christopher. *Blue Rabbit and friends*
   Blue Rabbit and the runaway wheel
Wright, Joanna. *Bunnies on ice*
Yelchin, Eugene. *Spring hare*
Ziefert, Harriet. *Bunny's lessons*
Zolotow, Charlotte. *The bunny who found Easter*
   Mr. Rabbit and the lovely present
Zuniga, Elisabeth. *A friend for Bo*

Animals – raccoons

Arnosky, Jim. *Raccoon on his own*
   Raccoons and ripe corn
Bunting, Eve. *Our library*
Castillo, Lauren. *The troublemaker*
Cocca-Leffler, Maryann. *Bravery soup*
DiPucchio, Kelly. *Super Manny stands up!*
Elliott, David. *Hunter's best friend at school*
Elliott, Laura Malone. *Hunter and Stripe and the soccer showdown*
   Hunter's big sister
Friend, Catherine. *Eddie the raccoon*
Glass, Andrew. *Bewildered for three days*
Guest, Elissa Haden. *Harriet's had enough!*
Haines, Mike. *Countdown to bedtime*
Harrison, David L. *A perfect home for a family*
Hubery, Julia. *A friend for all seasons*
Kasza, Keiko. *Ready for anything*
McPhail, David. *Henry Bear's Christmas*
   The Searcher and Old Tree
   Something special
   Waddles
Milord, Susan. *If I could*
Mitchard, Jacquelyn. *Ready, set, school!*
Modarressi, Mitra. *Stay awake, Sally*
   Taking care of Mama
Neugebauer, Charise. *The real winner*
Penn, Audrey. *A bedtime kiss for Chester Raccoon*
   Chester Raccoon and the almost perfect sleepover
   A color game for Chester Raccoon
Percival, Tom. *Herman's letter*
Plant, David J. *Hungry Roscoe*
Rayner, Catherine. *The bear who shared*
Rubin, Adam. *Secret pizza party*
Schachner, Judith Byron. *Dewey Bob*
Sharmat, Marjorie Weinman. *The 329th friend*
Shaw, Hannah. *School for bandits*

Shaw, Nancy. *Raccoon tune*
Wells, Rosemary. *Timothy goes to school*
   Yoko

Animals – rats

Browning, Robert. *The pied piper of Hamelin*, ill. by Mercer Mayer
   The pied piper of Hamelin, ill. by Drahos Zak
Bryan, Ashley. *The cat's purr*
Child, Lauren. *That pesky rat*
Coffey, Maria. *A cat adrift*
Covell, David. *Rat and Roach*
   Rat and Roach rock on!
Crimi, Carolyn. *Don't need friends*
Crow, Kristyn. *Cool Daddy Rat*
Deacon, Alexis. *Cheese belongs to you!*
Donaldson, Julia. *The Highway Rat*
Egielski, Richard. *Slim and Jim*
Emberley, Rebecca. *Three cool kids*
Grahame, Kenneth. *The wind in the willows*
   A wind in the willows Christmas
Hamilton, Martha. *Priceless gifts*
Jennings, Patrick. *Bat and Rat*
Jennings, Sharon. *Priscilla and Rosy*
   Priscilla's paw de deux
Kellogg, Steven. *The Pied Piper's magic*
Kilaka, John. *True friends*
Lester, Helen. *Hooway for Wodney Wat*
   Wodney Wat's wobot
McPhail, David. *Big Brown Bear goes to town*
   Big Brown Bear's birthday surprise
   Big Brown Bear's up and down day
Meddaugh, Susan. *Cinderella's rat*
Moore, Inga. *Captain Cat*
Potter, Beatrix. *The sly old cat*
Stevenson, James. *The most amazing dinosaur*
   Wilfred the rat
Van Woerkom, Dorothy. *The rat, the ox and the zodiac*
Wade, Mary Dodson. *No year of the cat*
Walton, Rick. *Just me and 6,000 rats*
   The remarkable friendship of Mr. Cat and Mr. Rat
Young, Ed. *Cat and Rat*

Animals – red pandas

Green, John Patrick. *Hippopotamister*

Animals – reindeer

Brennan-Nelson, Denise. *Good night, reindeer*
Brett, Jan. *The wild Christmas reindeer*
Killen, Nicola. *The little reindeer*
McCaughrean, Geraldine. *How the reindeer got their antlers*
May, Robert L. *Rudolph shines again*
   Rudolph the red-nosed reindeer
Miller, Debbie S. *A caribou journey*
Moulton, Mark Kimball. *Reindeer Christmas*
Plourde, Lynn. *Merry Moosey Christmas*
Root, Phyllis. *If you want to see a caribou*
Trumbauer, Lisa. *The great reindeer rebellion*

Animals – rhinoceros

Agee, Jon. *My rhinoceros*
Araki, Mie. *The magic toolbox*
Breen, Steve. *A perfect mess*
Brown, Susan Taylor. *Oliver's must-do list*

Brunhoff, Laurent de. *Babar's battle*
Burton, LeVar. *The rhino who swallowed a storm*
Chivers, Natalie. *Rhino's great big itch!*
Coat, Janik. *Rhymoceros*
Corderoy, Tracey. *It's Christmas! Now!*
Derrick, Patricia. *Riley the rhinoceros*
Jones, Stella J. *Glitter*
Kessler, Cristina. *Jubela*
Kirk, Daniel. *Rhino in the house*
Lloyd, Sam. *Chief Rhino to the rescue!*
McCully, Emily Arnold. *Clara*
Mammano, Julie. *Rhinos who play baseball*
   Rhinos who play soccer
   Rhinos who rescue
   Rhinos who surf
Moser, Lisa. *Cowboy Boyd and Mighty Calliope*
Newman, Jeff. *Hippo! No, rhino!*
O'Malley, Kevin. *Bud*
Ross, Tony. *Rita's rhino*
Terry, Michael. *Rhino's horns*

Animals – salamanders *see* Reptiles – salamanders

Animals – sea lions

Schreiber, Georges. *Bambino the clown*
Tafuri, Nancy. *Follow me!*

Animals – seals

Butterworth, Chris. *See what a seal can do*
Cox, Lynne. *Elizabeth, queen of the seas*
Haas, Rick de. *Peter and the seal*
Hewett, Joan. *A harbor seal pup grows up*
Hollenbeck, Kathleen M. *Islands of ice*
Manley, Curtis. *Shawn loves sharks*
Mitton, Tony. *Playful little penguins*
Rotter, Charles. *Seals*
Rumford, James. *Dog-of-the-Sea-Waves*
Seeger, Laura Vaccaro. *What if?*
Townsend, Emily Rose. *Seals*
van Lieshout, Maria. *Splash: a little book about bouncing back*

Animals – service animals

Appelt, Kathi. *Mogie*
Dalgleish, Sharon. *Working dogs*
Gianferrari, Maria. *Hello goodbye dog*
Kovacs, Deborah. *Katie Copley*
Lang, Glenna. *Looking out for Sarah*
Montalván, Luis Carlos. *Tuesday tucks me in*
Papp, Lisa. *Madeline Finn and the library dog*
Russell, Joan Plummer. *Aero and Officer Mike*

Animals – sheep

Aardema, Verna. *Borreguita and the coyote*
Aesop. *The wolf in sheep's clothing*
Alborough, Jez. *The gobble gobble moooooo tractor book*
Alda, Arlene. *Sheep, sheep, sheep, help me fall asleep*
Beaty, Andrea. *Hide and sheep*
Beaumont, Karen. *No sleep for the sheep!*
Belloni, Giulia. *Anything is possible*
Bently, Peter. *The great sheep shenanigans*
   Those magnificent sheep in their flying machine

Birdsall, Jeanne. *My favorite pets*
Brown, Margaret Wise. *Sheep don't count sheep*
Cabrera, Jane. *Baa, baa, black sheep*
Calhoun, Mary. *Henry the Christmas cat*
Carrick, Carol. *Valentine*
Catusanu, Mircea. *The strange case of the missing sheep*
Chin, Oliver. *The year of the sheep*
Church, Caroline Jayne. *Digby takes charge*
Cordell, Matthew. *Another brother*
dePaola, Tomie. *Charlie needs a cloak*
De Sève, Randall. *Mathilda and the orange balloon*
Driscoll, Amanda. *Wally does not want a haircut*
Dumont, Jean-François. *The sheep go on strike*
Edwards, David. *The pen that Pa built*
Elliott, David. *Baabwaa and Wooliam*
Ford, Bernette. *No more blanket for Lambkin!*
Fox, Mem. *Where is the green sheep?*
Fraggalosch, Audrey. *Trails above the tree line*
French, Jackie. *Pete the sheep-sheep*
Friend, Catherine. *Funny Ruby*
Gliori, Debi. *The snow lambs*
Goodings, Christina. *Lost sheep story*
Hale, Sarah Josepha Buell. *Mary had a little lamb,* ill. by Tomie dePaola
   Mary had a little lamb, ill. by Laura Huliska-Beith
   Mary had a little lamb, photos by Bruce McMillan
   Mary had a little lamb, ill. by Salley Mavor
Heap, Sue. *Four friends in the garden*
Helakoski, Leslie. *Woolbur*
Hill, Susanna Leonard. *Can't sleep without sheep*
Hoberman, Mary Ann. *Mary had a little lamb*
Imai, Ayano. *The 108th sheep*
Kelly, Mij. *One more sheep*
Kempter, Christa. *Dear Little Lamb*
Klise, Kate. *Grammy Lamby and the secret handshake*
Landström, Lena. *Boo and Baa have company*
Landström, Olof. *Boo and Baa get wet*
   Boo and Baa in the woods
Lester, Helen. *The sheep in wolf's clothing*
Levine, Gail Carson. *Betsy Red Hoodie*
   Betsy who cried wolf
Lewis, Kim. *Emma's lamb*
   First snow
   Little Baa
   Little lamb
   The shepherd boy
Livingstone, Star. *Harley*
Lobel, Anita. *Lena's sleep sheep*
Lodding, Linda Ravin. *Little red riding sheep*
Lunge-Larsen, Lise. *Noah's mittens*
McCully, Emily Arnold. *My real family*
McGinty, Alice B. *Ten little lambs*
McGrory, Anik. *Mouton's impossible dream*
McQuinn, Anna. *The sleep sheep*
Marciano, John Bemelmans. *Delilah*
Marshall, Linda Elovitz. *The passover lamb*
Martins, Isabel Minhós. *Little lamb, have you any wool?*
Merino, Gemma. *The sheep who hatched an egg*
Monroe, Chris. *Sneaky sheep*
Moses, Will. *Mary and her little lamb*
Numeroff, Laura Joffe. *When sheep sleep*
Olsen, Sylvia. *Yetsa's sweater*
Ommen, Sylvia van. *The surprise*
Peet, Bill. *Buford the little bighorn*
Porter, Sue. *Parsnip*
Puttock, Simon. *Miss Fox*
Rankin, Laura. *My turn!*

Root, Phyllis. *Ten sleepy sheep*
Rothstein, Gloria. *Sheep asleep*
Ryan, Candace. *Ewe and Aye*
Sanders, Scott R. *Warm as wool*
Schroeder, Lisa. *Baby can't sleep*
Schubert, Leda. *Feeding the sheep*
Schuh, Mari C. *Sheep on the farm*
Scotton, Rob. *Russell and the lost treasure*
    Russell the sheep
    Russell's Christmas magic
Shaw, Nancy. *Sheep blast off!*
    Sheep go to sleep
    Sheep in a jeep
    Sheep in a shop
    Sheep on a ship
    Sheep out to eat
    Sheep take a hike
    Sheep trick or treat
Sloat, Teri. *Farmer Brown shears his sheep*
    Pablo in the snow
Smallman, Steve. *The lamb who came for dinner*
Smith, Kathryn. *Little Lamb's Christmas story*
Stickland, Paul. *Bears*
Stockland, Patricia M. *In the sheep pasture*
Stohner, Anu. *Brave Charlotte*
    Brave Charlotte and the wolves
Sundgaard, Arnold. *The lamb and the butterfly*
Tanner, Suzy-Jane. *Tinyflock Nursery School*
Taylor-Butler, Christine. *Lamb's Easter surprise*
Thompson, Lauren. *Wee little lamb*
Trapani, Iza. *Baa baa black sheep*
Twohy, Mike. *Wake up, Rupert!*
Urbigkit, Cat. *A young shepherd*
Watts, Leslie Elizabeth. *The Baabaasheep Quartet*
Weeks, Sarah. *Counting Ovejas*
Wheeler, Lisa. *Wool gathering*
Wiley, Thom. *One sheep, blue sheep*
Willis, Jeanne. *Misery Moo*
Wright, Maureen. *Barnyard fun*
Zalben, Jane Breskin. *Pearl's eight days of Chanukah*
    Pearl's marigolds for grandpa

Animals – shrews

Goodall, John S. *Shrewbettina's birthday*
Macaulay, David. *How machines work: zoo break!*
Pilcher, Steve. *Over there*
Weiss, Ellen. *The taming of Lola*

Animals – skunks

Barnett, Mac. *The skunk*
Crum, Shutta. *The bravest of the brave*
Greenberg, David. *Skunks*
Hillenbrand, Will. *All for a dime! a Bear and Mole story*
Jenkins, Emily. *Skunkdog*
Lam, Thao. *Skunk on a string*
Mack, Jeff. *Who needs a bath?*
    Who wants a hug?
Newman, Lesléa. *Skunk's spring surprise*
Reed, Lynn Rowe. *Please don't upset P.U. Zorilla!*
Schmid, Paul. *A pet for Petunia*
Shaskan, Tricia Speed. *Punk skunks*
Stevens, Jan Romero. *Carlos and the skunk / Carlos y el zorrillo*
Wells, Rosemary. *Fritz and the mess fairy*
Wilson, Karma. *Sweet Briar goes to camp*

Animals – sloths

Berger, Samantha. *Snoozefest at the Nuzzledome*
Carle, Eric. *"Slowly, slowly, slowly," said the sloth*
Lester, Helen. *Score one for the sloths*
Macaulay, David. *How machines work: zoo break!*
Offill, Jenny. *Sparky!*
Preston-Gannon, Frann. *Sloth slept on*
Seibold, J. Otto. *Lost sloth*

Animals – slugs

Cazet, Denys. *Snail and Slug*
Colborn, Mary Palenick. *Rainy day slug*
Edwards, Pamela Duncan. *Some smug slug*
Hendra, Sue. *Norman the slug with the silly shell*
Krosoczka, Jarrett J. *My buddy, Slug*
Pearson, Susan. *How to teach a slug to read*
    Slugs in love
Raschka, Chris. *Sluggy Slug*
Willis, Jeanne. *Slug needs a hug!*

Animals – snails

Ahlberg, Allan. *The snail house*
Allen, Judy. *Are you a snail?*
Base, Graeme. *The legend of the Golden Snail*
Cazet, Denys. *Snail and Slug*
Dorros, Arthur. *When the pigs took over*
Foley, Greg. *Willoughby and the moon*
Freedman, Deborah. *The Story of Fish and Snail*
Leedy, Loreen. *The great graph contest*
Loomis, Christine. *The best Father's Day present ever*
Loth, Sebastian. *Clementine*
McGuirk, Leslie. *Snail boy*
May, Eleanor. *Albert's amazing snail*
Murguia, Bethanie Deeney. *Snippet the early riser*
Murphy, Mary. *Slow snail*
Reider, Katja. *Snail started it!*
Rempt, Fiona. *Snail's birthday wish*
Rosoff, Meg. *Jumpy Jack and Googily*
Saunders, Dave. *So slow!*
Slater, Dashka. *Escargot*
Veit, Barbara. *Who stole my house?*

Animals – snow leopards *see* Animals – leopards

Animals – squid *see* Squid

Animals – squirrels

Apperley, Dawn. *Don't wake the baby*
Blecha, Aaron. *Good morning, Grizzle Grump!*
Bottner, Barbara. *Raymond and Nelda*
Bowers, Tim. *A new home*
Braun, Sebastien. *I love my mommy*
Bynum, Janie. *Nutmeg and Barley*
Cherry, Lynne. *How Groundhog's garden grew*
Chichester Clark, Emma. *Will and Squill*
Cooper, Helen. *Delicious!*
    A pipkin of pepper
Costa, Maria S. *How to find a friend*
Desbordes, Astrid. *Edmond, the moonlit party*
Ehlert, Lois. *Nuts to you!*
Emmett, Jonathan. *Leaf trouble*
Frazee, Marla. *Boot and Shoe*
Freeman, Don. *Earl the squirrel*

One more acorn

Genechten, Guido van. *Ricky and the squirrel*

George, Lindsay Barrett. *That pup!*

Glaser, Linda. *Hello, squirrels!*

Glass, Beth Raisner. *Blue-ribbon dad*

Grindley, Sally. *What will I do without you?*

Guthrie, James. *Last song*

Hall, Pamela. *Miss you like crazy*

Harper, Charise Mericle. *The trouble with normal*

Hawcock, Claire. *Mine, all mine!*

Iwamura, Kazuo. *Bedtime in the forest*
   Hooray for fall!
   Hooray for snow!
   Hooray for spring!
   Hooray for summer!

Kasza, Keiko. *Finders keepers*

Kimmel, Eric A. *Pumpkinhead*

Kroll, Steven. *The squirrels' Thanksgiving*

Lithgow, John. *Micawber*

Lloyd-Jones, Sally. *Just because you're mine*

McClurkan, Rob. *Aw, nuts!*

McElmurry, Jill. *Mario makes a move*

Meisel, Paul. *Good night, bat! good morning, squirrel!*

Miller, Pat. *Squirrel's New Year's resolution*

Muir, Leslie. *C.R. Mudgeon*

Ohi, Debbie Ridpath. *Where are my books?*

OHora, Zachariah. *My cousin Momo*

Peet, Bill. *Merle the high flying squirrel*

Pfister, Marcus. *Hopper's treetop adventure*

Pilutti, Deb. *Bear and Squirrel are friends . . . yes, really!*

Potter, Beatrix. *The tale of Squirrel Nutkin*
   The tale of Timmy Tiptoes

Quackenbush, Robert M. *Batbaby*

Raye, Rebekah. *The very best bed*

Roberts, Bethany. *Rosie to the rescue*

Rose, Nancy. *Merry Christmas, squirrels!*
   The secret life of squirrels

Rubin, Adam. *Those darn squirrels!*
   Those darn squirrels and the cat next door
   Those darn squirrels fly south

Sayre, April Pulley. *Squirrels leap, squirrels sleep*

Shannon, George. *Heart to heart*
   The surprise

Sherry, Kevin. *Acorns everywhere!*

Shore, Diane Z. *Look both ways*

Stein, David Ezra. *Ol' Mama Squirrel*

Stevenson, James. *Wilfred the rat*

Tafuri, Nancy. *The busy little squirrel*

Townsend, Emily Rose. *Squirrels*

Vainio, Pirkko. *Who hid the Easter eggs?*

Walsh, Ellen Stoll. *Dot and Jabber and the great acorn mystery*

Watt, Mélanie. *Scaredy Squirrel*
   Scaredy Squirrel at night
   Scaredy Squirrel at the beach
   Scaredy Squirrel goes camping
   Scaredy Squirrel has a birthday party
   Scaredy Squirrel makes a friend
   Scaredy Squirrel prepares for Christmas
   Scaredy Squirrel prepares for Halloween

White, Alexina B. *Frisky brisky hippity hop*

Animals – swine *see* Animals – pigs

Animals – tapirs

Kim, Hanmin. *Tiptoe tapirs*

Meschenmoser, Sebastian. *Gordon and Tapir*

Russell, Natalie. *Lost for words*

Animals – Tasmanian devils

Blake, Robert J. *Little devils*

Animals – tigers

Asch, Frank. *The Lending Zoo*

Banks, Kate. *Close your eyes*

Bannerman, Helen. *The story of Little Babaji*
   The story of Little Black Sambo (1996)
   The story of Little Black Sambo (1990)
   The story of Little Black Sambo (2003)

Bee, William. *Whatever*

Blackford, Harriet. *Tiger's story*

Brown, Peter. *Mr. Tiger goes wild*

Bunting, Eve. *Riding the tiger*

Chichester Clark, Emma. *Follow the leader!*

Child, Lauren. *Maude*

Chin, Oliver. *The year of the tiger*

Davies, Gill. *Wilbur waited*

Derrick, David G., Jr. *I'm the scariest thing in the jungle!*

Dowson, Nick. *Tigress*

Duncan, Lois. *Song of the circus*

Fore, S. J. *Read to Tiger*
   Tiger can't sleep

Gaiman, Neil. *Cinnamon*

Gliori, Debi. *Where did that baby come from?*

Goode, Diane. *Tiger trouble*

Gorbachev, Valeri. *Cats are cats*

Hewett, Joan. *A tiger cub grows up*

Hoberman, Mary Ann. *"It's simple," said Simon*

Hoffman, Eric. *No fair to tigers / No es justo para los tigres*

Hogrogian, Nonny. *The tiger of Turkestan*

Jenkins, Emily. *Tiger and Badger*

Kraus, Robert. *Leo the late bloomer*
   Little Louie the baby bloomer

Lambert, Jonny. *Tiger tiger*

LaRochelle, David. *It's a tiger*

Leroy, Jean. *Stripes the tiger*

Lester, Julius. *Sam and the tigers*

London, Jonathan. *Little lost tiger*

Long, Ethan. *Lion and Tiger and Bear*

Nagda, Anne Whitehead. *A tiger tale*

O'Brien, Patrick. *Sabertooth*

Partis, Joanne. *Stripe*
   Stripe's naughty sister

Prelutsky, Jack. *The terrible tiger*

Rayner, Catherine. *Augustus and his smile*

Rumford, James. *Tiger and turtle*

Seuss, Dr. *I can lick 30 tigers today and other stories*

Sheth, Kashmira. *Tiger in my soup*

Stewart, Amber. *Too small for my big bed*

Stower, Adam. *Naughty kitty!*

Sykes, Julie. *I don't want to take a bath!*
   Little Tiger's big surprise
   Wait for me, Little Tiger

Temple, Frances. *Tiger soup*

Thomson, Sarah L. *Tigers*

Tseng, Grace. *White tiger, blue serpent*

Turnbull, Victoria. *The sea tiger*

Winters, Kay. *Tiger trail*

Wolkstein, Diane. *The banza*

Xiong, Blia. *Nine-in-one Grr! Grr!*

Yep, Laurence. *Auntie Tiger*

Animals – voles

Bright, Rachel. *Side by side*
Schwartz, Roslyn. *The Vole brothers*

Animals – wallabies

Wild, Margaret. *Bobbie Dazzler*

Animals – walruses

Rotter, Charles. *Walruses*
Savage, Stephen. *Where's Walrus?*
   Where's Walrus? and Penguin?

Animals – warthogs

Base, Graeme. *Jungle drums*
Edwards, Pamela Duncan. *Slop goes the soup*
   Warthogs in a box
   Warthogs in the kitchen
   Warthogs paint
Wallace, Nancy Elizabeth. *Water! water! water!*

Animals – weasels

Dolan, Elys. *Weasels*
George, Jean Craighead. *Frightful's daughter meets the Baron Weasel*
Grant, Rose Marie. *Andiamo, Weasel*
Ruzzier, Sergio. *A letter for Leo*
Shaw, Hannah. *Sneaky Weasel*

Animals – whales

Alexander, Kwame. *Surf's up*
Allen, Judy. *Whales and dolphins*
Auld, Mary. *The story of Jonah*
Barnett, Mac. *Billy Twitters and his big blue whale problem*
Bible. Old Testament. Jonah. *The Book of Jonah*
Burleigh, Robert. *Trapped! a whale's rescue*
Cline-Ransome, Lesa. *Whale trails, before and now*
DaCosta, Barbara. *Mighty Moby*
Davies, Benji. *The storm whale*
   The storm whale in winter
De Beer, Hans. *Little Polar Bear and the whales*
Edwardson, Debby Dahl. *Whale snow*
Ferry, Beth. *A small blue whale*
Fogliano, Julie. *If you want to see a whale*
Gentle, Victor. *Orcas, killer whales*
Gerstein, Mordicai. *The boy and the whale*
Gibbons, Gail. *Whales*
Goldsboro, Bobby. *Jonah and the whale; and, Daniel in the lion's den*
Heinz, Brian J. *Mocha Dick*
Hill, Ros. *Shamoo*
Hodson, Sally. *Granny's clan*
Horácek, Petr. *Puffin Peter*
James, Simon. *Dear Mr. Blueberry*
London, Jonathan. *Baby whale's journey*
Lucas, David. *The skeleton pirate*
   Whale
Lunde, Darrin. *Hello, baby beluga*
McKee, David. *Elmer and the whales*
Magoon, Scott. *Breathe*
Malone, Cheryl Lawton. *Dario and the whale*
Marino, Gianna. *Following Papa's song*
O'Neill, Alexis. *Loud Emily*
Oppel, Kenneth. *Peg and the whale*

Pfister, Marcus. *Rainbow fish and the big blue whale*
Pinkney, Andrea Davis. *Peggony-Po*
Raff, Courtney Granet. *Giant of the sea*
Raffi. *Baby beluga*
Raschka, Chris. *Whaley Whale*
Robinson, Fiona. *Whale shines*
Rylant, Cynthia. *The whales*
Sayre, April Pulley. *Here come the humpbacks!*
Schuch, Steve. *A symphony of whales*
Siberell, Anne. *Whale in the sky*
Sís, Peter. *An ocean world*
Sobol, Richard. *Adelina's whales*
Spinelli, Eileen. *Jonah's whale*
Staake, Bob. *Beachy and me*
Thomson, Sarah L. *Amazing whales*
Tokuda, Wendy. *Humphrey the lost whale*
Van Dusen, Chris. *Down to the sea with Mr. Magee*
Vernick, Audrey. *I won a what?*
Westaway, Kylie. *A whale in the bathtub*
Wood, Audrey. *Little Penguin's tale*
Yolen, Jane. *The stranded whale*

Animals – wolves

Aesop. *The boy who cried wolf*
   The dog and the wolf
   The wolf in sheep's clothing
Allen, Jonathan. *Mucky moose*
Alley, Zoe B. *There's a wolf at the door*
Anderson, Derek. *Ten hungry pigs*
   Ten pigs
Andres, Kristina. *Good Little Wolf*
Armo, Nancy. *A friend for Mole*
Asch, Frank. *Happy birthday, Big Bad Wolf*
   Ziggy Piggy and the three little pigs
Banks, Kate. *Pup and bear*
Barnett, Mac. *The wolf, the duck, and the mouse*
Bedard, Michael. *The wolf of Gubbio*
Belloni, Giulia. *Anything is possible*
Bently, Peter. *The great sheep shenanigans*
Bevis, Mary. *Wolf song*
Blades, Ann. *Mary of mile 18*
Brett, Jan. *The first dog*
Brimner, Larry Dane. *The littlest wolf*
Brown, Ken. *What's the time, Grandma Wolf?*
Brun-Cosme, Nadine. *Big Wolf and Little Wolf*
   Big Wolf and Little Wolf, such a beautiful orange!
Burgess, Mark. *Where teddy bears come from*
Carey, Lorraine. *Cinderella's stepsister and the big bad wolf*
Catusanu, Mircea. *The strange case of the missing sheep*
Chapman, Jared. *Steve, raised by wolves*
Child, Lauren. *Beware of the storybook wolves*
Christelow, Eileen. *Where's the big bad wolf?*
Cohn, Scotti. *One wolf howls*
Conway, David. *The great fairy tale disaster*
Cordell, Matthew. *Wolf in the snow*
Crosby, Jeff. *Wiener Wolf*
Dyckman, Ame. *Wolfie the bunny*
Egan, Tim. *The experiments of Doctor Vermin*
Egielski, Richard. *St. Francis and the wolf*
Elliott, David. *Baabwaa and Wooliam*
Elya, Susan Middleton. *Little Roja Riding Hood*
Ernst, Lisa Campbell. *Little Red Riding Hood: a newfangled prairie tale*
Escoffier, Michael. *Rabbit and the Not-So-Big-Bad Wolf*
Fearnley, Jan. *Mr. Wolf and the three bears*

Mr. Wolf's pancakes
Felix, Monique. *The rumor*
George, Jean Craighead. *Look to the north*
  Nutik and Amaroq play ball
  Nutik, the wolf pup
  The wolves are back
Gliori, Debi. *What's the time, Mr. Wolf?*
Godkin, Celia. *Wolf island*
Gorbachev, Valeri. *Nicky and the big, bad wolves*
Grant, Rose Marie. *Andiamo, Weasel*
Gravett, Emily. *Wolf won't bite!*
  Wolves
Grimm, Jacob and Wilhelm. *Little red cap*
  Little Red Riding Hood, ill. by Célia Chauffrey
  Little Red Riding Hood, ill. by Gwen Connelly
  Little Red Riding Hood, ill. by Trina Schart
    Hyman
  Little Red Riding Hood, ill. by Jerry Pinkney
  Little Red Riding Hood, ill. by Gennady Spirin
  Little Red Riding Hood, ill. by Bernadette Watts
  Little Red Riding Hood, ill. by Andrea Wisnewski
  The story of Little Red Riding Hood
Guarnaccia, Steven. *The three little pigs: an
    architectural tale*
Hartman, Bob. *The wolf who cried boy*
Heapy, Teresa. *Very little Red Riding Hood*
Heinz, Brian J. *The wolves*
Helakoski, Leslie. *Big chickens*
Hennessy, B. G. *The boy who cried wolf*
Jagtenberg, Yvonne. *Jack the wolf*
Judes, Marie-Odile. *Max, the stubborn little wolf*
Kasza, Keiko. *The dog who cried wolf*
  The wolf's chicken stew
Kelly, Mij. *One more sheep*
Kempter, Christa. *Dear Little Lamb*
Kimmel, Eric A. *Little Red Hot*
  The three little tamales
Kimura, Yuichi. *One stormy night . . .*
  One sunny day . . .
Knapman, Timothy. *Time now to dream*
Kolanovic, Dubravka. *Everyone needs a friend*
Koster, Gloria. *Little Red Ruthie*
Krensky, Stephen. *Big bad wolves at school*
Kulka, Joe. *Wolf's coming*
Kvasnosky, Laura McGee. *Little Wolf's first howling*
Lairla, Sergio. *Abel and the wolf*
Lallemand, Orianne. *The wolf who wanted to change
    his color*
Langton, Jane. *Saint Francis and the wolf*
Lazar, Tara. *Little Red Gliding Hood*
Leroy, Jean. *A well-mannered young wolf*
Lester, Helen. *The sheep in wolf's clothing*
  Tacky the penguin
Levine, Gail Carson. *Betsy Red Hoodie*
  Betsy who cried wolf
Lindbergh, Reeve. *Bridget and the gray wolves*
London, Jonathan. *Red wolf country*
  The seasons of Little Wolf
Lowell, Susan. *Little Red Cowboy Hat*
MacDonald, Elizabeth. *The wolf is coming!*
McGee, Marni. *Winston the book wolf*
Machado, Ana Maria. *Wolf wanted*
McNaughton, Colin. *Oomph!*
  Oops!
  Preston's goal!
  Suddenly!
Mallat, Kathy. *Papa pride*
Markle, Sandra. *Family pack*
Marshall, James. *Red Riding Hood*

Swine lake
Matsuoka, Mei. *Footprints in the snow*
Meddaugh, Susan. *The best place*
  Hog-eye
Melling, David. *The Scallywags*
Milhander, Laura Aron. *Not for all the
    hamantaschen in town*
Mortimer, Rachael. *Red Riding Hood and the sweet
    little wolf*
Murphy, Yannick. *Ahwooooooooo!*
Murray, Marjorie Dennis. *Little Wolf and the moon*
Palatini, Margie. *Bad boys get cookie!*
  Bad boys get henpecked!
  Piggie pie
Perret, Delphine. *The Big Bad Wolf and me*
  The Big Bad Wolf goes on vacation
Pichon, Liz. *The three horrid little pigs*
Pinkwater, Daniel. *Wolf Christmas*
Prokofiev, Sergei Sergeievitch. *Peter and the wolf*,
    ill. by Charles Mikolaycak
  Peter and the wolf, ill. by Josef Palecek
  Peter and the wolf, ill. by Chris Raschka
  Peter and the wolf, ill. by Vladimir Vagin
Puttock, Simon. *Big bad wolf is good*
Ramadier, Cédric. *Help! the wolf is coming!*
Ramos, Mario. *I am so handsome*
  I am so strong
Reynolds, Aaron. *Carnivores*
Robberecht, Thierry. *The wolf who fell out of a book*
Rocco, John. *Wolf! wolf!*
Roche, Denis. *Little Pig is capable*
Roddie, Shen. *Not now, Mrs. Wolf*
Ross, Gayle. *How Turtle's back was cracked*
Ross, Tony. *The boy who cried wolf*
Roth, Susan L. *Kanahena*
Rueda, Claudia. *Huff and puff*
  Let's play in the forest while the wolf is not around
Santangelo, Colony Elliott. *Brother Wolf of Gubbio*
Santore, Charles. *Three hungry pigs and the wolf who
    came to dinner*
Schwartz, Corey Rosen. *Ninja Red Riding Hood*
Scieszka, Jon. *The true story of the three little pigs by A.
    Wolf, as told to Jon Scieszka*
Shireen, Nadia. *Good little wolf*
Sierra, Judy. *Mind your manners, B. B. Wolf*
  Tell the truth, B. B. Wolf
Smallman, Steve. *The lamb who came for dinner*
Souhami, Jessica. *No dinner!*
Spinelli, Eileen. *Thanksgiving at the Tappletons'*
Stevenson, Harvey. *Big scary wolf*
Stohner, Anu. *Brave Charlotte and the wolves*
Sweet, Melissa. *Carmine*
Talbott, Hudson. *From wolf to woof*
Teague, Mark. *The three little pigs and the somewhat
    bad wolf*
Teckentrup, Britta. *Little Wolf's song*
The three little pigs. *The three little pigs*, ill. by
    Gavin Bishop
  The three little pigs, ill. by Paul Galdone
  The three little pigs, ill. by Rob Hefferan
  The three little pigs, ill. by Steven Kellogg
  The three little pigs, ill. by David McPhail
  The three little pigs, ill. by James Marshall
  The three little pigs, ill. by Bernadette Watts
  The three little pigs, ill. by Margot Zemach
  The three little pigs / Los tres cerditos
  The three little pigs and the big bad wolf
Trivizas, Eugenios. *The three little wolves and the big
    bad pig*

Ts'o, Pauline. *Whispers of the wolf*
Vozar, David. *Yo, hungry wolf!*
Whatley, Bruce. *Wait! no paint!*
Whybrow, Ian. *Badness for beginners*
Wiesner, David. *The three pigs*
Winters, Kay. *Wolf watch*
Woollvin, Bethan. *Little Red*
Young, Ed. *Lon Po Po*
Yum, Hyewon. *There are no scary wolves*
Zuill, Andrea. *Wolf camp*

Animals – wombats

Arnold, Caroline. *A wombat's world*
Churchill, Vicki. *Sometimes I like to curl up in a ball*
Fox, Mem. *Wombat divine*
French, Jackie. *Christmas wombat*
    Diary of a baby wombat
    Diary of a wombat
Fuge, Charles. *Swim, Little Wombat, swim!*
    Where to, Little Wombat?
Lester, Helen. *Batter up Wombat*
McAllister, Angela. *Found you, Little Wombat!*
Morpurgo, Michael. *Wombat goes walkabout*
Shields, Carol Diggory. *Wombat walkabout*

Animals – woolly mammoths

Elliott, David. *This Orq. (He #1!)*
    This Orq. (He cave boy.)
    This Orq. (He say "ugh!")
Grambling, Lois G. *Can I bring Woolly to the library, Ms. Reeder?*
Hall, Algy Craig. *Mammoth and me*
Manning, Mick. *Woolly mammoth*
Miller, Debbie S. *Woolly mammoth journey*
Robinson, Michelle. *How to wash a woolly mammoth*
Stead, Philip C. *Samson in the snow*
Wheeler, Lisa. *Mammoths on the move*

Animals – worms

Austrian, J. J. *Worm loves Worm*
Bruel, Robert O. *Bob and Otto*
Caple, Kathy. *Worm gets a job*
Cronin, Doreen. *Diary of a worm*
Donaldson, Julia. *Superworm*
French, Vivian. *Yucky worms*
Hemingway, Edward. *Bad apple*
Horácek, Petr. *Jonathan and Martha*
James, Brian. *Supertwins and the sneaky, slimy book worms*
Kaczman, James. *A bird and his worm*
Lackner, Michelle Myers. *Toil in the soil*
Martin, David. *Piggy and Dad go fishing*
Pfeffer, Wendy. *Wiggling worms at work*
Pinczes, Elinor J. *Inchworm and a half*
Raschka, Chris. *Wormy Worm*
Runton, Andy. *Owly and Wormy: bright lights and starry nights!*
    Owly and Wormy: friends all aflutter!
San Souci, Robert D. *Two bear cubs: a Miwok legend from California's Yosemite Valley*
Scanlon, Elizabeth Garton. *Noodle and Lou*
Slade-Robinson, Nikki. *Muddle and Mo's worm surprise*
Wells, Rosemary. *Max's worm cake*

Animals – yaks

Berger, Barbara. *All the way to Lhasa*
Johnston, Tony. *Go track a yak*
Kromhout, Rindert. *Little Donkey and the birthday present*
Stryer, Andrea Stenn. *Kami and the yaks*

Animals – zebras

Bingham, Kelly. *Circle, square, Moose*
    Z is for Moose
Cabatingan, Erin. *A is for Musk Ox*
    Musk Ox counts
Castle, Caroline. *Naughty!*
Gay, Michel. *Zee is not scared*
Miranda, Anne. *Alphabet fiesta*
Nogales, Jill. *Zebra on the go*
Paterson, Brian. *Zigby camps out*
    Zigby dives in
    Zigby hunts for treasure
Peet, Bill. *Zella, Zack, and Zodiac*
Rudolph, Shaina. *All my stripes*
Telchin, Eric. *The Black and White Factory*
Walker, Anna. *I love birthdays*
    I love my dad
    I love my mom

Anti-violence *see* Violence, nonviolence

Anxiety *see* Behavior – worrying; Emotions – fear

Apartments *see* Homes, houses

Appearance *see* Character traits – appearance

Aquariums

Aliki. *My visit to the aquarium*
Buzzeo, Toni. *One cool friend*
Calmenson, Stephanie. *Ollie's class trip*
Curious George goes to the aquarium
Levine, Ellen. *Seababy*
Poydar, Nancy. *Fish school*
Rechner, Amy. *Out and about at the aquarium*
Rylant, Cynthia. *Henny, Penny, Lenny, Denny, and Mike*

Arachnids *see* Spiders

Arguing *see* Behavior – fighting, arguing

Arithmetic *see* Counting, numbers

Art

Agee, Jon. *The incredible painting of Felix Clousseau*
Alexander, Martha G. *Max and the dumb flower picture*
Andrews-Goebel, Nancy. *The pot that Juan built*
Angelou, Maya. *My painted house, my friendly chicken, and me*
Arrigan, Mary. *Mario's angels*
Auch, Mary Jane. *Eggs mark the spot*

Herzog, Brad. *R is for race*
Horácek, Petr. *Beep beep*
Howland, Naomi. *ABCDrive!*
Hubbell, Patricia. *Cars: rushing! honking! zooming!*
Hurd, Thacher. *Sleepy Cadillac*
　　Zoom City
Kenney, Sean. *Cool cars and trucks*
Kirk, Daniel. *Honk honk! Beep beep!*
Kirk, David. *Miss Spider's new car*
Kolar, Bob. *Racer dogs*
LaReau, Kara. *Otto: the boy who loved cars*
LaRochelle, David. *Moo!*
Leiter, Richard. *The flying hand of Marco B.*
Lord, Cynthia. *Hot Rod Hamster*
Lynn, Sarah. *1-2-3 va-va-vroom!*
Maccarone, Grace. *Cars! cars! cars!*
McMullan, Kate. *I'm fast*
Mahy, Margaret. *The rattlebang picnic*
Manzano, Sonia. *No dogs allowed*
Marshall, James. *The Cut-Ups crack up*
Medina, Meg. *Tía Isa wants a car*
Meister, Cari. *Busy, busy city street*
Merlin, Christophe. *Under the hood*
Milusich, Janice. *Off go their engines, off go their
　　lights*
Miranda, Anne. *Beep! beep!*
　　Vroom, chugga, vroom-vroom
Mitton, Tony. *Cool cars*
Murphy, Stuart J. *Beep beep, vroom vroom!*
Nobles, Kristen M. *Drive this book*
Olivera, Ramon. *ABCs on wheels*
Pearson, Debora. *Alphabeep*
Peet, Bill. *Jennifer and Josephine*
Perry, Michael. *Daniel's ride*
Pizzoli, Greg. *Number one Sam*
Rex, Michael. *My race car*
Rockwell, Anne. *Cars*
Root, Phyllis. *Rattletrap car*
　　Toot toot zoom!
Rylant, Cynthia. *Brownie and Pearl go for a spin*
　　Tulip sees America
The scrubbly-bubbly car wash
Sehgal, Kabir. *The wheels on the tuk tuk*
Shulevitz, Uri. *Troto and the trucks*
Shulman, Mark. *Gorilla Garage*
Soto, Gary. *My little car / Mi carrito*
Stanley, Mandy. *On the move*
Steen, Sandra. *Car wash*
Steggall, Susan. *The life of a car*
Stein, Peter. *Cars galore*
Suen, Anastasia. *Red light, green light*
Timmers, Leo. *Who is driving?*
Todd, Mark. *Start your engines*
van Lieshout, Maria. *Backseat A-B-see*
Walters, Virginia. *Are we there yet, Daddy?*
Weston, Mark. *Honda*
Wheeler, Lisa. *Dino-racing*
Zane, Alexander. *The wheels on the race car*

Autumn *see* Seasons – fall

Award-winning books *see* Caldecott award
　　books; Caldecott award honor books

Babies, new *see* Family life – new sibling

Babies, toddlers *see also* Animals – babies

Adler, Victoria. *All of baby nose to toes*
　　Baby, come away
Ahlberg, Janet. *The baby's catalogue*
　　Peek-a-boo!
Ajmera, Maya. *Global baby boys*
　　Global baby girls
Alexander, Martha G. *Nobody asked me if I wanted a
　　baby sister*
Aliki. *Welcome, little baby*
Alko, Selina. *I'm your peanut butter big brother*
Allen, Kathryn Madeline. *I am a baby*
American babies
Andreae, Giles. *There's a house inside my mommy*
Anholt, Catherine. *What makes me happy?*
Anholt, Laurence. *Sophie and the new baby*
Appelt, Kathi. *Brand-new baby blues*
Apperley, Dawn. *Don't wake the baby*
Archer, Peggy. *From dawn to dreams*
Arnosky, Jim. *Babies in the bayou*
Asher, Sandy. *Here comes Gosling!*
Ashman, Linda. *Henry wants more!*
　　Mama's day
　　Rock-a-bye romp
　　When I was king
Aston, Dianna Hutts. *Mama Outside, Mama Inside*
Baek, Matthew J. *Be gentle with the dog, dear*
Baicker, Karen. *Pea pod babies*
Ballard, Robin. *I used to be the baby*
Banks, Kate. *This baby*
Bauer, Marion Dane. *Grandmother's song*
Beaton, Kate. *King Baby*
Beaumont, Karen. *Crybaby*
Bennett, Barbara. *Lion's precious gift*
Bennett, Kelly. *Vampire baby*
Bently, Peter. *A recipe for bedtime*
Bertrand, Lynne. *Granite baby*
Best, Cari. *If I could drive, Mama*
Blackall, Sophie. *The baby tree*
Blackstone, Stella. *Baby talk*
Boelts, Maribeth. *You're a brother, Little Bunny!*
Bonnice, Lindsey. *Libby and Pearl: the best of friends*
Bourgeois, Paulette. *Franklin's baby sister*
Bowen, Anne. *I loved you before you were born*
　　When you visit Grandma and Grandpa
Brantz, Loryn. *Feminist Baby*
Brenner, Barbara A. *What the elephant told*
Broach, Elise. *What the no-good baby is good for*
Brown, Marc. *Arthur's baby*
Brownlow, Mike. *Way out West — with a baby!*
Bunting, Eve. *Baby can*
　　Will it be a baby brother?
Burell, Sarah. *Diamond Jim Dandy and the sheriff*
Burningham, John. *There's going to be a baby*
Calmenson, Stephanie. *Good for you!*
　　Welcome, baby!

Capucilli, Alyssa Satin. *Hush a bye, baby*
Carlstrom, Nancy White. *Before you were born*
Carter, Alden R. *Big brother Dustin*
Ceelen, Vicky. *Baby! baby!*
Charlip, Remy. *Baby hearts and baby flowers*
   Sleepytime rhyme
Chichester Clark, Emma. *Will and Squill*
Chorao, Kay. *Knock at the door and other baby action*
   rhymes
Chung, Arree. *Out!*
Cocca-Leffler, Maryann. *Theo's mood*
   Time to say bye-bye
Cocovini, Abby. *What's inside your tummy, Mommy?*
Coffelt, Nancy. *Catch that baby!*
Cohen, Caron Lee. *Happy to you!*
Cole, Babette. *Truelove*
Cole, Brock. *Larky Mavis*
Cole, Joanna. *How you were born*
   I'm a big brother
   I'm a big sister
   The new baby at your house
   When you were inside mommy
Collicott, Sharleen. *Mildred and Sam*
Cooke, Trish. *So much*
Cowell, Cressida. *What shall we do with the Boo-Hoo*
   Baby?
Creech, Sharon. *Who's that baby?*
Crum, Shutta. *Mine!*
   Uh-oh!
Cuetara, Mittie. *Baby business*
Cullen, Catherine Ann. *Thirsty baby*
Cummings, Pat. *Angel baby*
Curtis, Jamie Lee. *Tell me again about the night I was*
   born
   When I was little
Davies, Gill. *Wilbur waited*
Dempsey, Kristy. *Ten little fingers, two small hands*
   Ten little toes, two small feet
Dempsey, Sheena. *Bye-bye baby brother!*
dePaola, Tomie. *The baby sister*
   Baby's first Christmas
Dewan, Ted. *Baby gets the zapper*
   Crispin and the 3 little piglets
Dickson, Irene. *Blocks*
Diesen, Deborah. *The barefooted, bad-tempered baby*
   brigade
DiPucchio, Kelly. *Littles*
   Zombie in love 2 + 1
DiTerlizzi, Angela. *Baby love*
Dixon, Ann. *Waiting for Noël*
Doerrfeld, Cori. *Penny loves pink*
Douglas, Ann. *Before you were born*
Downes, Belinda. *Baby days*
Doyle, Malachy. *Baby see, baby do!*
Dunbar, Joyce. *Pat-a-cake baby*
   Shoe baby
Dunrea, Olivier. *It's snowing*
Dyer, Jane. *Little Brown Bear and the bundle of joy*
Elkin, Mark. *Samuel's baby*
Elya, Susan Middleton. *Bebé goes shopping*
   Bebé goes to the beach
Enersen, Adele. *Vincent and the night*
   When my baby dreams
English, Karen. *The baby on the way*
Falwell, Cathryn. *We have a baby*
Farrington, Susan. *What I love about you*
Fearnley, Jan. *A special something*
Feiffer, Kate. *But I wanted a baby brother!*
   No go sleep!

Fergus, Maureen. *Buddy and Earl and the great big*
   baby
Fleming, Candace. *Seven hungry babies*
Fogliano, Julie. *Old dog baby baby*
Ford, Bernette. *No more pacifier for Piggy!*
Fox, Mem. *Baby bedtime*
   Hello, baby!
   Ten little fingers and ten little toes
Frasier, Debra. *On the day you were born*
Frazee, Marla. *The boss baby*
   The bossier baby
   Hush, little baby: a folk song with pictures
   Walk on!
Frederick, Heather Vogel. *Babyberry pie*
French, Simon. *Guess the baby*
Fucile, Tony. *Poor Louie*
Gentieu, Penny. *Baby! Talk!*
   Grow! babies!
Gerber, Carole. *A band of babies*
   Tuck-in time
Gershator, Phillis. *This is the day!*
Gillingham, Sara. *Friends*
Gliori, Debi. *Mr. Bear's new baby*
   Penguin post
   Where did that baby come from?
Good, Jason. *Must. push. buttons!*
Graham, Bob. *The silver button*
Grambling, Lois G. *Grandma tells a story*
Green, Jen. *Our new baby*
Greenstein, Elaine. *As big as you*
Grimes, Nikki. *Welcome, Precious*
Gutman, Anne. *Lisa's baby sister*
Hale, Bruce. *Big Bad Baby*
Haley, Amanda. *It's a baby's world*
Hanson, Mary Elizabeth. *The difference between*
   babies and cookies
Harris, Robie H. *Hi, new baby*
   What's in there?
Havill, Juanita. *Just like a baby*
Hawkes, Kevin. *The wicked big toddlah*
   The wicked big toddlah goes to New York
Heiligman, Deborah. *Babies*
Henderson, Kathy. *Baby knows best*
   Look at you!
Heos, Bridget. *Mustache Baby*
   Mustache Baby meets his match
   Queen Dog
Heras, Theo. *Baby cakes*
Hest, Amy. *The babies are coming!*
   Buster and the baby
   Off to school, Baby Duck
   You're the boss, Baby Duck
Hiatt, Fred. *Baby talk*
Hill, Susanna Leonard. *Not yet, Rose*
Hillenbrand, Will. *Fiddle-i-fee*
Hindley, Judy. *Baby talk*
   What's in baby's morning
Hines, Anna Grossnickle. *Big like me*
Höjer, Dan. *Heart of mine*
Holabird, Katharine. *Angelina's baby sister*
Holt, Kimberly Willis. *Waiting for Gregory*
Hood, Susan. *Mission: new baby*
   Tickly toes
Hop a little, jump a little!
Horácek, Petr. *Time for bed*
Horse, Harry. *Little Rabbit's new baby*
Hort, Lenny. *We're going on a treasure hunt*
   We're going on safari
Hru, Dakari. *Tickle, tickle*

Hubbell, Patricia. *Bouncing time*
    Wrapping paper romp
Hughes, Shirley. *Olly and me*
Hughes, Susan. *Up! how families around the world*
    carry their little ones
Hurwitz, Johanna. *Russell's secret*
Hush, little baby
Hutchins, Hazel. *Two so small*
Hutchins, Pat. *Where's the baby?*
Intrater, Roberta Grobel. *Peek-a-boo!*
    Smile!
Isadora, Rachel. *Bea in The Nutcracker*
James, Simon. *Baby Brains and RoboMom*
Janovitz, Marilyn. *Baby, Baby, Baby!*
    Play baby play!
Jenkins, Emily. *That new animal*
Johnston, Tony. *Laugh-out-loud baby*
Kallok, Emma. *Gem*
Katz, Karen. *The babies on the bus*
    Baby loves winter!
    Now I'm big
    Over the moon
    Princess Baby
    Princess Baby, night-night
    Ten tiny babies
    Ten tiny tickles
    Where is baby's mommy?
Katz, Susan B. *ABC, baby me!*
Keane, Claire. *Little big girl*
Keats, Ezra Jack. *Peter's chair*
Keller, Holly. *Geraldine's baby brother*
Kelly, L. J. R. *Sometimes it's storks*
Kirwan, Wednesday. *Baby loves to boogie!*
Kleven, Elisa. *A monster in the house*
Koller, Jackie French. *Baby for sale*
Krensky, Stephen. *I am so brave!*
    We just had a baby
Krishnaswami, Uma. *Bringing Asha home*
Landolf, Diane Wright. *What a good big brother!*
Lasky, Kathryn. *Baby love*
Lawrence, Michael. *Baby loves*
Layne, Steven L. *Love the baby*
Leigh, Heather. *Hey little baby!*
L'Engle, Madeleine. *The other dog*
Lester, J. D. *Mommy calls me Monkeypants*
Lewis, Rose A. *I love you like crazy cakes*
Lindgren, Barbro. *Benny and the binky*
Lloyd-Jones, Sally. *His Royal Highness, King Baby*
    How to be a baby — by me, the big sister
Lobel, Gillian. *Too small for honey cake*
Lohans, Alison. *Waiting for the sun*
Long, Steffanie. *Such a silly baby!*
Look, Lenore. *Henry's first-moon birthday*
Lund, Deb. *Tell me my story, Mama*
Lyon, George Ella. *Sleepsong*
McCarty, Peter. *Baby steps*
McCormick, Wendy. *The night you were born*
MacDonald, Ross. *Bad baby*
McElmurry, Jill. *I'm not a baby!*
Mackall, Dandi Daley. *There's a baby in there!*
Macken, JoAnn Early. *Baby says "moo!"*
MacLachlan, Patricia. *All the places to love*
    Before you came
    Bittle
    You were the first
McLean, Janet. *Let's go, baby-o!*
McMullan, Kate. *If you were my bunny*
    Papa's song
    Rock-a-baby band

    Supercat to the rescue
McNaughton, Colin. *Captain Abdul's little treasure*
McPike, Elizabeth. *Little bitty friends*
    Little sleepyhead
McQuinn, Anna. *Leo can swim*
    Leo loves baby time
    Lola reads to Leo
Mahy, Margaret. *Boom Baby boom, boom*
Making faces: a first book of emotions
Manning, Jane. *My first baby games*
Manzano, Sonia. *A box full of kittens*
Margalith, Joan. *The babies are landing*
Marzollo, Jean. *Baby's alphabet*
    Do you know new?
Melmed, Laura Krauss. *The rainbabies*
Mendes, Valerie. *Look at me, Grandma!*
Meyers, Susan. *Everywhere babies*
    Rock-a-bye room
    This is the way a baby rides
Michels-Gualtieri, Akaela S. *I was born to be a sister*
Milgrim, David. *Best baby ever*
Miller, Margaret. *Baby faces*
    I love colors
    Now I'm big
Milord, Susan. *Love that baby*
Moon, Nicola. *Something special*
Morris, Richard T. *Bye-bye, baby!*
Morrow, Tara Jaye. *Mommy loves her baby; Daddy*
    loves his baby
Moses, Will. *Silent night*
Munsch, Robert N. *Alligator baby*
Murkoff, Heidi Eisenberg. *What to expect when the*
    new baby comes home
Murphy, Jill. *Meltdown!*
Myers, Anna. *Tumbleweed Baby*
Newman, Marjorie. *Just like me*
Nichols, Grace. *Whoa, Baby, whoa!*
North, Sherry. *Because you are my baby*
Novak, Matt. *A wish for you*
Oborne, Martine. *One beautiful baby*
O'Connell, Rebecca. *Baby parade*
    Baby party
O'Hair, Margaret. *Star baby*
    Sweet baby feet
O'Keefe, Susan Heyboer. *Baby day*
Okimoto, Jean Davies. *The White Swan express*
Oliver, Lin. *Little poems for tiny ears*
O'Malley, Kevin. *Once upon a royal superbaby*
Orlean, Susan. *Lazy little loafers*
Osofsky, Audrey. *Dreamcatcher*
Overend, Jenni. *Welcome with love*
Palatini, Margie. *Goldie is mad*
    No nap! yes nap!
Park, Bomi. *First snow*
Patricelli, Leslie. *Baby happy, baby sad*
    Binky
    Blankie
    Fa la la
    Nighty-night
    No no, yes yes
Patz, Nancy. *Babies can't eat kimchee!*
Peddicord, Jane Ann. *That special little baby*
Pinkney, Brian. *Hush, little baby*
Puck. *Babies around the world*
Puttock, Simon. *The baby that roared*
Radunsky, Vladimir. *Ten*
Rand, Gloria. *Baby in a basket*
Reiser, Lynn. *My baby and me*
Reynolds, Marilynn. *The name of the child*

Bad day, bad mood *see* Behavior – bad day, bad mood

Ballerinas *see* Ballet; Careers – dancers

Ballet

Allen, Debbie. *Dancing in the wings*
Auch, Mary Jane. *Hen lake*
    Peeping Beauty
Bansch, Helga. *Brava, Mimi!*
Beck, Robert. *A bunny in the ballet*
Bonwill, Ann. *Naughty toes*
Bradley, Kimberly Brubaker. *Ballerino Nate*
Brandenberg, Alexa. *Ballerina flying*
Capucilli, Alyssa Satin. *My first ballet class*
Chaconas, Dori. *Dancing with Katya*
Copeland, Misty. *Firebird*
Corey, Shana. *Ballerina bear*
Cristaldi, Kathryn. *Baseball ballerina*
    Baseball ballerina strikes out
Crow, Kristyn. *Zombelina*
Dempsey, Kristy. *A dance like starlight*
DePalma, Mary Newell. *The Nutcracker doll*
dePaola, Tomie. *Oliver Button is a sissy*
Edwards, Pamela Duncan. *Honk!*
Ellwood, David. *Cinderlily*
Ferguson, Sarah. *Ballerina Rosie*
The firebird. *The firebird*, ill. by Demi
    The firebird, ill. by Rachel Isadora
    The tale of the firebird
Ford, Bernette. *Ballet Kitty*
French, Jackie. *Josephine wants to dance*
Gauch, Patricia Lee. *Bravo, Tanya*
    Dance, Tanya
    Presenting Tanya, the Ugly Duckling
    Tanya and Emily in a dance for two
Geras, Adèle. *Giselle*
    Little ballet star
    The nutcracker
    Sleeping beauty
    Swan Lake
    Time for ballet
Goodman, Joan Elizabeth. *Ballet Bunnies*
Gorbachev, Valeri. *Catty Jane who loved to dance*
Gravel, Elise. *The cranky ballerina*
Greenberg, Jan. *Ballet for Martha*
Gruska, Denise. *The only boy in ballet class*
Hague, Michael. *The nutcracker*
Hayward, Linda. *A day in the life of a dancer*
Headley, Justina Chen. *The patch*
Hoffmann, E. T. A. *The nutcracker*, ill. by Renée
    Graef
    The nutcracker, ill. by Alison Jay
    The nutcracker, ill. by Peter Malone
    The nutcracker, ill. by Maurice Sendak
    The nutcracker, ill. by Lisbeth Zwerger
    The Nutcracker and the Mouse King
    The nutcracker ballet
Holabird, Katharine. *Angelina and the princess*
    Angelina at the palace
    Angelina ballerina
    Angelina dances
    Angelina on stage
    Angelina's ballet class
    Angelina's big city ballet
    Angelina's Cinderella
    Christmas in Mouseland
Howe, James. *Brontorina*
Isadora, Rachel. *Bea at ballet*
    Bea in The Nutcracker
    Lili at ballet
    Lili on stage
    Not just tutus

Jennings, Sharon. *Priscilla's paw de deux*
Kent, Allegra. *Ballerina gets ready*
    Ballerina swan
Kinerk, Robert. *Clorinda*
Kroll, Virginia L. *Can you dance, Dalila?*
Lasky, Kathryn. *Starring Lucille*
Lowell, Susan. *Josefina javelina*
Maccarone, Grace. *Miss Lina's ballerinas*
    Miss Lina's ballerinas and the prince
    Miss Lina's ballerinas and the wicked wish
McClintock, Barbara. *Emma and Julia love ballet*
McEvoy, Anne. *Betsy B. Little*
MacKay, Elly. *Waltz of the snowflakes*
Manson, Ainslie. *Ballerinas don't wear glasses*
Marshall, James. *Swine lake*
Mayhew, James. *Ella Bella ballerina and A
    Midsummer Night's Dream*
    Ella Bella ballerina and Swan Lake
    Ella Bella ballerina and The Nutcracker
    Ella Bella ballerina and The sleeping beauty
Membrino, Anna. *I want to be a ballerina*
Miller, Tim. *Moo Moo in a tutu*
Mills, Elaine. *Marinetta at the ballet*
Nelson, Marilyn. *Beautiful ballerina*
Newman, Lesléa. *Miss Tutu's star*
Newsome, Jill. *Dream dancer*
Numeroff, Laura Joffe. *The Jellybeans and the big
    dance*
Pace, Anne Marie. *Vampirina ballerina*
    Vampirina ballerina hosts a sleepover
Pavlova, Anna. *I dreamed I was a ballerina*
Pennypacker, Sara. *Pierre in love*
Peters, Bernadette. *Stella is a star!*
Pinkwater, Daniel. *Dancing Larry*
Polacco, Patricia. *Rotten Richie and the ultimate dare*
Pulver, Robin. *Alicia's tutu*
Rodriguez, Sonia. *T is for tutu*
Saab, Julie. *Little Lola saves the show*
Schubert, Leda. *Ballet of the elephants*
Shulman, Lisa. *Over in the meadow at the big ballet*
Singer, Marilyn. *Tallulah's Nutcracker*
    Tallulah's solo
    Tallulah's tap shoes
    Tallulah's toe shoes
    Tallulah's tutu
Sís, Peter. *Ballerina*
Skeers, Linda. *Tutus aren't my style*
Snyder, Laurel. *Swan*
Stanley, Mandy. *Lettice the dancing rabbit*
Thompson, Lauren. *Ballerina dreams*
Weeks, Sarah. *Ella, of course!*
Yolen, Jane. *The firebird*
Young, Amy. *Belinda and the glass slipper*
    Belinda begins ballet
    Belinda in Paris
    Belinda, the ballerina
Zuill, Andrea. *Dance is for everyone*

Balloons *see* Toys – balloons

Balls *see* Toys – balls

Barns

Atwell, Debby. *Barn*
Johnston, Tony. *The barn owls*
Martin, Bill, Jr.. *Barn dance!*
Schubert, Leda. *Here comes Darrell*

Tafuri, Nancy. *The barn party*
Yolen, Jane. *Raising Yoder's barn*

Bayous *see* Swamps

Beaches *see* Sea & seashore – beaches

Beasts *see* Monsters

Beauty shops

Buehner, Caralyn. *The queen of style*
Caseley, Judith. *In style with Grandma Antoinette*
Choung, Euh-hee. *Minji's Salon*
Daly, Niki. *A song for Jamela*
Munsch, Robert N. *Makeup mess*
O'Connor, Jane. *Fancy Nancy: ooh la la! it's beauty day*
Schotter, Roni. *Mama, I'll give you the world*
Wells, Rosemary. *Ruby's beauty shop*

Bedtime

Adams, Diane. *I can do it myself!*
Adler, David A. *It's time to sleep, it's time to dream*
Alborough, Jez. *Yes*
Alda, Arlene. *Sheep, sheep, sheep, help me fall asleep*
Allen, Elanna. *Itsy Mitsy runs away*
Allenby, Victoria. *Nat the cat can sleep like that*
Anderson, Christine. *Bedtime!*
Anderson, Peggy Perry. *Time for bed, the babysitter said*
Appelt, Kathi. *Cowboy dreams*
Apperley, Dawn. *Blossom and Boo stay up late*
    Good night, sleep tight, little bunnies
Apple, Margot. *Brave Martha*
Arnold, Marsha Diane. *Roar of a snore*
Arnold, Tedd. *No jumping on the bed!*
Asch, Frank. *Good night, Baby Bear*
Ashman, Linda. *How to make a night*
    Rock-a-bye romp
    Starry safari
    William's winter nap
Asper-Smith, Sarah. *I would tuck you in*
Averbeck, Jim. *In a blue room*
Aylesworth, Jim. *Teddy bear tears*
Baguley, Elizabeth. *A long way from home*
Bailey, Linda. *Goodnight, sweet pig*
Baker, Ken. *Brave little monster*
Baker, Roberta. *Olive's first sleepover*
Ballard, Robin. *Tonight and tomorrow*
Balmes, Santi. *I will fight monsters for you*
Bang, Molly. *Ten, nine, eight*
Banks, Kate. *The bear in the book*
Bansch, Helga. *At night*
Bardhan-Quallen, Sudipta. *Chicks run wild*
Baring-Gould, S. *Now the day is over*
Barnett, Mac. *Noisy night*
Bauer, Marion Dane. *Sleep, little one, sleep*
Baum, Louis. *The mouse who braved bedtime*
Bea, Holly. *Bless your heart*
Bean, Jonathan. *At night*
Beaton, Clare. *Clare Beaton's bedtime rhymes*
Beaty, Andrea. *Hush, Baby Ghostling*
Beaumont, Karen. *Crybaby*
    Dini Dinosaur
    No sleep for the sheep!

Beck, Andrea. *Elliot's noisy night*
Becker, Bonny. *A bedtime for Bear*
Bentley, Jonathan. *Where is Bear?*
Bently, Peter. *A recipe for bedtime*
Berenstain, Stan and Jan. *Bears in the night*
    The Berenstain bears and the slumber party
Berger, Carin. *Good night! Good night!*
Bergman, Mara. *Musical beds*
    Oliver who would not sleep!
Berkner, Laurie. *Pillowland*
Bertram, Debbie. *My new big-kid bed*
Blackall, Sophie. *Are you awake?*
Bloom, Suzanne. *A number slumber*
Bluemle, Elizabeth. *Dogs on the bed*
Boelts, Maribeth. *Looking for Sleepy*
    Sweet dreams, Little Bunny
Bogan, Paulette. *Goodnight Lulu*
Bolden, Tonya. *Beautiful moon*
Bond, Felicia. *Poinsettia and the firefighters*
Bonnett-Rampersaud, Louise. *Bubble and Squeak*
Bottner, Barbara. *Feet go to sleep*
Boudreau, Hélène. *I dare you not to yawn*
Boynton, Sandra. *Night-night, Little Pookie*
Bradley, Kimberly Brubaker. *Favorite things*
Branford, Henrietta. *Little Pig Figwort can't get to sleep*
Braun, Sebastien. *Back to bed, Ed!*
Brennan-Nelson, Denise. *Good night, reindeer*
Briggs, Kelly Paul. *Lighthouse lullaby*
Bright, Paul. *The bears in the bed and the great big storm*
    There's a bison bouncing on the bed!
Bright, Rachel. *Love Monster and the scary something*
Brisson, Pat. *Star blanket*
Brown, Marc. *Monkey: not ready for bedtime*
Brown, Margaret Wise. *Good day, good night*
    Goodnight moon
    Goodnight moon ABC
    Goodnight moon 123: a counting book
    Sleepy ABC, ill. by Karen Katz
    Sleepy ABC, ill. by Esphyr Slobodkina
Brunelle, Nicholas. *Snow moon*
Burnell, Heather Ayris. *Bedtime monster / ¡A dormir, pequeño monstruo!*
Butler, John. *Bedtime in the jungle*
    Can you growl like a bear?
    While you were sleeping
Cabrera, Jane. *Bear's good night*
    Rock-a-bye baby
    Ten in the bed
Cain, Sheridan. *By the light of the moon*
Camp, Lindsay. *The biggest bed in the world*
Capucilli, Alyssa Satin. *Biscuit*
    Hush a bye, baby
Castle, Caroline. *Naughty!*
Chapman, Jane. *I'm not sleepy!*
Charlip, Remy. *Baby hearts and baby flowers*
Child, Lauren. *I am not sleepy and I will not go to bed*
Choldenko, Gennifer. *Putting the monkeys to bed*
Chriscoe, Sharon. *Race car dreams*
Christelow, Eileen. *Five little monkeys jumping on the bed*
    Five little monkeys reading in bed
Church, Caroline Jayne. *One more hug for Madison*
Cocca-Leffler, Maryann. *Time to say bye-bye*
Cole, Rachael. *City moon*
Cornell, Kevin. *Go to sleep, monster!*
Cousins, Lucy. *Maisy's bedtime*
    Sweet dreams, Maisy

Cowell, Cressida. *Emily Brown and the Thing*
Cox, Judy. *Sheep won't sleep*
Coy, John. *Vroomaloom zoom*
Craig, Lindsey. *Farmyard beat*
Crimi, Carolyn. *Principal Fred won't go to bed*
    Where's my mummy?
Crow, Kristyn. *Bedtime at the swamp*
Crowe, Caroline. *Pirates in pajamas*
Crowther, Kitty. *Scritch scratch scraww plop*
Crum, Shutta. *All on a sleepy night*
Cushman, Doug. *Christmas Eve good night*
    Halloween good night
DaCosta, Barbara. *Mighty Moby*
    Nighttime Ninja
Daddo, Andrew. *Goodnight, me*
Dahl, Michael. *Bedtime for Batman*
    Goodnight baseball
    Goodnight football
Davey, Owen. *Night Knight*
Davies, Jacqueline. *The night is singing*
Dean, James. *Pete the Cat and the bedtime blues*
Delacroix, Sibylle. *Blanche hates the night*
Demers, Dominique. *Every single night*
De Vries, Maggie. *How sleep found Tabitha*
Dewdney, Anna. *Llama, Llama red pajama*
Docherty, Helen. *The Snatchabook*
Dodd, Emma. *Best bear*
Dodds, Dayle Ann. *The prince won't go to bed*
Donaldson, Julia. *One Ted falls out of bed*
Dragonwagon, Crescent. *All the awake animals are almost asleep*
Dunbar, Joyce. *The monster who ate darkness*
Dunnick, Regan. *Sweet dreams, Douglas*
Durand, Hallie. *Mitchell's license*
Durango, Julia. *Dream hop*
Edwards, Nicola. *Goodnight Baxter*
Edwards, Pamela Duncan. *While the world is sleeping*
Edwards, Richard. *Good night, Copycub*
Egielski, Richard. *The sleepless little vampire*
Eilenberg, Max. *Cowboy Kid*
Emberley, Ed. *Go away, big green monster!*
    Nighty night Little Green Monster
Enersen, Adele. *Vincent and the night*
Escoffier, Michaël. *Sleep tight, Charlie*
Fancher, Lou. *Star climbing*
Farrell, Darren. *Thank you, Octopus*
Faulkner, Keith. *The scared little bear*
Fearnley, Jan. *Just like you*
Feder, Sandra. *The moon inside*
Feiffer, Kate. *No go sleep!*
Ferreri, Della Ross. *How will I ever sleep in this bed?*
Flattinger, Hubert. *Stormy night*
Fleming, Candace. *Go sleep in your own bed*
Fleming, Denise. *Sleepy, oh so sleepy*
Ford, Christine. *Ocean's child*
Fore, S. J. *Tiger can't sleep*
Foreman, Michael. *I love you, too!*
Fox, Mem. *Baby bedtime*
    Good night, sleep tight
    Tell me about your day today
    This and that
    Time for bed
    Where the giant sleeps
Fraser, Mary Ann. *Pet shop lullaby*
Frederick, Heather Vogel. *Babyberry pie*
    Hide and squeak
Fredrickson, Lane. *Monster trouble!*
Freedman, Claire. *Beep beep beep: time for sleep!*

    Hushabye Lily
    Night-night, Emily
    Snuggle up, sleepy ones
Gabriel, Ashala. *Night night toes*
Gal, Susan. *Night lights*
Gamble, Isobel. *Who's that?*
Gardiner, Lindsey. *Good night, Poppy and Max*
Gay, Michel. *Zee is not scared*
Geisert, Arthur. *Lights out*
Genechten, Guido van. *No ghost under my bed*
Gerber, Carole. *Tuck-in time*
Geringer, Laura. *Boom boom go away!*
Gershator, Phillis. *Moo, moo, brown cow! Have you any milk?*
    Who's awake in springtime?
Ginsburg, Mirra. *Asleep, asleep*
Glass, Beth Raisner. *Noises at night*
Gliori, Debi. *Flora's blanket*
    Goodnight world
    Polar Bolero
    Stormy weather
Gorbachev, Valeri. *Nicky and the big, bad wolves*
Graff, Lisa. *It is not time for sleeping*
Grant, Holly. *Wee Sister Strange*
Gravett, Emily. *Again!*
Greenstein, Elaine. *Dreaming*
Griffith, Helen V. *Moonlight*
Gurney, John Steven. *Dinosaur train*
Guthrie, James. *Last song*
Hächler, Bruno. *What does my teddy bear do all night?*
Hacohen, Dean. *Tuck me in!*
Hadfield, Chris. *The darkest dark*
Hague, Kathleen. *Good night, fairies*
Haines, Mike. *Countdown to bedtime*
Hall, Marcellus. *Everyone sleeps*
Harby, Melanie. *All aboard for Dreamland!*
Harper, Jamie. *Night night, Baby Bundt*
Harris, Peter. *The night pirates*
Harris, Robie H. *Maybe a bear ate it!*
Harshman, Marc. *All the way to morning*
Haughton, Chris. *Goodnight everyone*
Hayes, Geoffrey. *The bunny's night-light*
Hegarty, Patricia. *Good night farm*
Heller, Nicholas. *This little piggy*
Hemingway, Edward. *Bump in the night*
Henry, Jed. *Good night, Mouse!*
Hest, Amy. *Buster and the baby*
    Kiss good night
    Mabel dancing
Hicks, Barbara Jean. *Jitterbug jam*
Hill, Susanna Leonard. *Can't sleep without sheep*
Hindley, Judy. *Sleepy places*
Hines, Anna Grossnickle. *Rumble thumble boom!*
Hissey, Jane. *Hoot*
Hoban, Russell. *Bedtime for Frances*
Hodge, Marie. *Are you sleepy yet, Petey?*
Hodgkinson, Leigh. *The big monster snorey book*
Holt, Sharon. *Did my mother do that?*
Hoppe, Paul. *The woods*
Horácek, Petr. *Time for bed*
Howatt, Sandra J. *Sleepyheads*
Howland, Naomi. *Princess says goodnight*
Hunter, Anne. *Cricket song*
Hunter, Jana Novotny. *My tail's not tired*
Hunter, Sally. *Humphrey's bedtime*
Hurd, Thacher. *Sleepy Cadillac*
Hutchins, Pat. *Little pink pig*
Imai, Ayano. *The 108th sheep*

Imbody, Amy. *Snug as a bug?*
Inches, Alison. *The stuffed animals get ready for bed*
Irving, John. *A sound like someone trying not to make a sound*
Isadora, Rachel. *I just want to say good night*
 Peekaboo bedtime
Ismail, Yasmeen. *Time for bed, Fred!*
Ives, Penny. *Rabbit pie*
Iwamura, Kazuo. *Bedtime in the forest*
Jackson, Richard. *All ears, all eyes*
Jadoul, Émile. *Good night, Chickie*
Jennings, Sharon. *No monsters here*
Jewel. *Sweet dreams*
 That's what I'd do
John, Jory. *Goodnight already!*
Johnson, D. B. *Henry's night*
Johnson, Lindan Lee. *The dream jar*
Johnston, Tony. *Little Rabbit goes to sleep*
Jonas, Ann. *The quilt*
Joosse, Barbara. *Lovabye Dragon*
 Roawr!
Jordan, Laurie. *Yawning yoga*
Joyce, William. *The Sandman: the story of Sanderson Mansnoozie*
 Sleepy time Olie
Kanevsky, Polly. *Sleepy boy*
Katz, Karen. *Princess Baby, night-night*
Keller, Joy. *Monster trucks*
Kellogg, Steven. *A-hunting we will go!*
Kelly, Mij. *A bed of your own!*
 William and the night train
Kempter, Christa. *When Mama can't sleep*
Ketteman, Helen. *Goodnight, Little Monster*
Kirk, Daniel. *Hush, little alien*
Kloske, Geoffrey. *Once upon a time, the end (asleep in 60 seconds)*
Knapman, Timothy. *Dinosaurs don't have bedtimes!*
Koller, Jackie French. *No such thing*
Kono, Erin Eitter. *Hula lullaby*
Kramer, Andrew. *Pajama pirates*
Krauss, Ruth. *Goodnight, goodnight, sleepyhead*
Krilanovich, Nadia. *Moon child*
Krosoczka, Jarrett J. *Good night, Monkey Boy*
Kurtz, Jane. *In the small, small night*
Lamb, Albert. *Tell me the day backwards*
Landry, Leo. *Space boy*
Langreuter, Jutta. *Little Bear won't go to bed*
LaReau, Kara. *Snowbaby could not sleep*
LaRochelle, David. *The haunted hamburger and other ghostly stories*
Larsen, Mylisa. *How to put your parents to bed*
 If I were a kangaroo
Lester, Helen. *Boris and the worrisome wakies*
Lesynski, Loris. *Night school*
Leuck, Laura. *Goodnight, baby monster*
Levine, Joan. *Topsy-turvy bedtime*
Lewis, Anne Margaret. *Fly blanky fly*
Lewis, Kim. *Good night, Harry*
Lewis, Paeony. *No more yawning!*
Lewis, Rose A. *Sweet dreams*
Lewison, Wendy Cheyette. *Going to sleep on the farm*
Litwin, Eric. *The Nuts: bedtime at the Nut house*
Lloyd-Jones, Sally. *Just because you're mine*
 Time to say goodnight
Lobel, Anita. *Lena's sleep sheep*
Logue, Mary. *Sleep like a tiger*
London, Jonathan. *Froggy goes to bed*
Long, Heather. *Max and Milo go to sleep!*
Long, Kathy. *Christopher sat straight up in bed*

Lum, Kate. *What! cried Granny*
Lundgren, Mary Beth. *Seven scary monsters*
Lyon, George Ella. *Sleepsong*
McAllister, Angela. *Night-night, little one*
McBratney, Sam. *The caterpillow fight*
 The dark at the top of the stairs
 Guess how much I love you
 In the light of the moon and other bedtime stories
McCanna, Tim. *Bitty Bot*
Maccarone, Grace. *A child's good night prayer*
McCarty, Peter. *Bunny dreams*
McCourt, Lisa. *Good night, Princess Pruney Toes*
 I love you, Stinky Face
McCullough, Sharon Pierce. *Bunbun at bedtime*
MacDonald, Margaret Read. *The squeaky door*
 Tuck-me-in tales
McDonnell, Patrick. *Thank you and good night*
McFarland, Clive. *A bed for Bear*
McGee, Marni. *Sleepy me*
Mack, Jeff. *Duck in the fridge*
 Hush little polar bear
 Playtime?
McKellar, Danica. *Goodnight, numbers*
MacLachlan, Patricia. *The moon's almost here*
McMullan, Kate. *If you were my bunny*
 Mama's kisses
McNeil, Kelli. *Sleepy toes*
McPike, Elizabeth. *Little sleepyhead*
McQuinn, Anna. *The sleep sheep*
Maitland, Barbara. *My bear and me*
Maizes, Sarah. *On my way to bed*
Manceau, Edouard. *Tickle monster*
Manning, Maurie J. *Kitchen dance*
Markes, Julie. *Shhhhh! Everybody's sleeping*
Marlow, Layn. *Hurry up and slow down*
Martin, Bill, Jr.. *Kitty Cat, Kitty Cat, are you going to sleep?*
Martin, Emily Winfield. *Dream animals*
Matheis, Mickie. *Bedtime for Boo*
Matheson, Christie. *Touch the brightest star*
Mathews, Judith. *Nathaniel Willy, scared silly*
Mayer, Mercer. *There's a nightmare in my closet*
 There's an alligator under my bed
Meade, Holly. *A place to sleep*
Meadows, Michelle. *Piggies in pajamas*
Melmed, Laura Krauss. *The first song ever sung*
 Jumbo's lullaby
Meng, Cece. *Bedtime is canceled*
 I will not read this book
Meserve, Jessica. *Bedtime without Arthur*
Messer, Claire. *Grumpy pants*
Metaxas, Eric. *It's time to sleep, my love*
Meyers, Susan. *Rock-a-bye room*
Mitchard, Jacquelyn. *Baby bat's lullaby*
Miyakoshi, Akiko. *The way home in the night*
Modarressi, Mitra. *Stay awake, Sally*
Monari, Manuela. *Zero kisses for me!*
Moon, Nicola. *Tick-tock, drip-drop*
Moore, Raina. *How do you say good night?*
Mora, Pat. *Sweet dreams / Dulces suenos*
Morales, Yuyi. *Little night*
Morgan, Mary. *My good night book*
Morgan-Vanroyen, Mary. *Sleep tight, little mouse*
Morozumi, Atsuko. *Time for bed*
Morrissey, Dean. *The crimson comet*
Morton, Lone. *Hurry up, Molly / Apúrate, Molly*
 Hurry up, Molly / Dépêche-toi, Molly
Mühle, Jörg. *Tickle my ears*
Munsch, Robert N. *Mortimer*

Murguia, Bethanie Deeney. *The too-scary story*
Murphy, Jill. *A quiet night in*
Murphy, Mary. *Good night like this*
Murray, Alison. *Little Mouse*
Nakamura, Katherine Riley. *Song of night*
Newman, Lesléa. *Daddy's song*
Nobisso, Josephine. *The moon's lullaby*
Noll, Amanda. *I need my monster*
Numeroff, Laura Joffe. *Nighty-night, Cooper*
    When sheep sleep
Odgers, Sally. *Good night, Truck*
Ohi, Ruth. *Pants off first*
O'Keefe, Susan Heyboer. *Good night, God bless*
Otto, Carolyn. *Dinosaur chase*
Owens, Mary Beth. *Panda whispers*
Papineau, Lucie. *Lulu's pajamas*
Parenteau, Shirley. *Bears in beds*
Patricelli, Leslie. *Nighty-night*
    The Patterson puppies and the midnight monster
        party
Paul, Ann Whitford. *Everything to spend the night*
    . . . from A to Z
    If animals kissed goodnight
Paul, Miranda. *10 little ninjas*
Pearle, Ida. *The moon is going to Addy's house*
Pearson, Susan. *The drowsy hours*
Peck, Jan. *Way up high in a tall green tree*
Peck, Richard. *Monster night at Grandma's house*
Pedersen, Judy. *When night time comes near*
Penn, Audrey. *A bedtime kiss for Chester Raccoon*
Perlman, Willa. *Good night, world*
Pfister, Marcus. *Bertie at bedtime*
    Good night, little rainbow fish
Piers, Helen. *Who's in my bed?*
Pizzoli, Greg. *Good night Owl*
Plourde, Lynn. *Wild child*
Pomerantz, Charlotte. *All asleep*
Porter, Pamela. *Yellow moon, apple moon*
Potter, Giselle. *Tell me what to dream about*
Pow, Tom. *Tell me one thing, Dad*
Prap, Lila. *Daddies*
Pumphrey, Jerome. *Creepy things are scaring me*
Purmell, Ann. *Where wild babies sleep*
Quackenbush, Robert M. *Batbaby*
Ramadier, Cédric. *Shh! this book is sleeping*
Raschka, Chris. *Can't sleep*
Rathmann, Peggy. *10 minutes till bedtime*
Ray, Karen. *Sleep song*
Ray, Mary Lyn. *Go to sleep, little farm*
    Goodnight, good dog
Raye, Rebekah. *The very best bed*
Reidy, Jean. *Light up the night*
Reiser, Lynn. *Little clam*
Rex, Michael. *Goodnight goon*
    You can do anything, Daddy!
Reynolds, Luke. *Bedtime blastoff!*
    If my love were a fire truck
Rice, Eve. *Goodnight, goodnight*
Richardson, Bill. *But if they do*
Richmond, Marianne. *I'm not tired yet!*
Rinker, Sherri Duskey. *Goodnight, goodnight,*
    construction site
Robbins, Beth. *Tom's afraid of the dark*
Robbins, Maria Polushkin. *Mother, Mother, I want*
    another
Roberts, Bethany. *Gramps and the fire dragon*
Rock, Lois. *God bless me, God bless you*
Rockwell, Anne. *Here comes the night*
Rohmann, Eric. *The cinder-eyed cats*

Clara and Asha
Root, Phyllis. *Ten sleepy sheep*
Roques, Dominique. *Sleep tight, Anna Banana!*
Roscoe, Lily. *The night parade*
Rose, Deborah Lee. *Someone's sleepy*
Rosen, Michael. *Send for a superhero!*
Rosenberg, Liz. *Eli's night-light*
Rosenthal, Amy Krouse. *Bedtime for Mommy*
    Little Hoot
Ross, Tony. *I want my light on!*
Roth, Carol. *Ten dirty pigs / Ten clean pigs*
Roth, Susan L. *Night-time numbers*
Rothstein, Gloria. *Sheep asleep*
Rowand, Phyllis. *It is night*
Ruddell, Deborah. *Who said coo?*
Rueda, Claudia. *No*
Rusackas, Francesca. *Daddy all day long*
Russo, Marisabina. *The bunnies are not in their beds*
Rylant, Cynthia. *Brownie and Pearl hit the hay*
    Puppies and piggies
Saltzberg, Barney. *Chengdu could not, would not,*
    fall asleep
    Cornelius P. Mud, are you ready for bed?
Sanders, Rob. *Outer space bedtime race*
Sanromán, Susana. *Señora Reganoña*
Sarcone-Roach, Julia. *The secret plan*
Sartell, Debra. *Time for bed, Baby Ted*
Sassi, Laura. *Goodnight, Ark*
Saudo, Coralie. *My dad is big and strong, but . . .*
Sayles, Elizabeth. *The goldfish yawned*
Sayre, April Pulley. *Hush, little puppy*
Sayres, Brianna Caplan. *Where do diggers sleep at*
    night?
Schaefer, Carole Lexa. *Down in the woods at*
    sleepytime
    Someone says
    Who's there?
Scheffler, Axel. *Pip and Posy: the bedtime frog*
Schertle, Alice. *Goodnight, Hattie, my dearie, my dove*
Schneider, Josh. *Bedtime monsters*
    Everybody sleeps (but not Fred)
Schroeder, Lisa. *Baby can't sleep*
Schubert, Ingrid. *There is a crocodile under my bed*
Schwartz, Amy. *Lucy can't sleep*
    Some babies
Scotton, Rob. *Russell the sheep*
Selig, Josh. *Red and Yellow's noisy night*
Shannon, David. *David gets in trouble*
Shaw, Nancy. *Sheep go to sleep*
Shea, Bob. *Dinosaur vs. bedtime*
    Race you to bed
Shoulders, Michael. *Goodnight Baby Bear*
Showers, Paul. *Sleep is for everyone*
Sierra, Judy. *Sleepy little alphabet*
Silverman, Erica. *Follow the leader*
Simmons, Jane. *The dreamtime fairies*
    Go to sleep, Daisy
Simon, Francesca. *Hello, Moon!*
Slater, Dashka. *Firefighters in the dark*
Slingsby, Janet. *Hush-a-bye babies*
Smee, Nicola. *No bed without Ted*
Smiley, Jane. *Twenty yawns*
Smith, Danna. *Mother Goose's pajama party*
Smith, Shoham. *An after bedtime story*
Snyder, Betsy E. *Sweet dreams lullaby*
Sobel, June. *The goodnight train*
Sperring, Mark. *Max and the won't go to bed show*
    Mermaid dreams
Spinelli, Eileen. *When Mama comes home tonight*

Bedwetting *see* Behavior – bedwetting

Behavior

Donnelly, Jennifer. *Humble pie*
Doyle, Malachy. *Get happy*
   Well, a crocodile can!
Dutton, Sandra. *Dear Miss Perfect*
Edwards, Pamela Duncan. *Rude mule*
Elliott, David. *Hunter's best friend at school*
Ets, Marie Hall. *Play with me*
Falconer, Ian. *Olivia*
   Olivia's opposites
Fearnley, Jan. *The search for the perfect child*
   Watch out!
Fernandes, Eugenie. *Sleepy little mouse*
Gary, Meredith. *Sometimes you get what you want*
Gibbons, Gail. *Bats*
Good, Jason. *Must. push. buttons!*
Graham-Barber, Lynda. *Spy hops and belly flops*
Griffin, Kitty. *The foot-stomping adventures of
   Clementine Sweet*
Gutman, Anne. *Lisa's baby sister*
Harley, Bill. *Dear Santa*
Harper, Jamie. *Don't grown-ups ever have fun?*
Harper, Jessica. *Lizzy's do's and don'ts*
Harris, Robie H. *Don't forget to come back*
Helakoski, Leslie. *Woolbur*
Heos, Bridget. *Mustache Baby*
Hubbard, Woodleigh Marx. *Whoa, jealousy*
Huget, Jennifer LaRue. *Thanks a lot, Emily Post!*
Hutchins, Pat. *Tidy Titch*
James, Betsy. *Tadpoles*
Javernick, Ellen. *What if everybody did that?*
Johnson, Angela. *Lottie Paris lives here*
Johnson, Paul Brett. *The pig who ran a red light*
Kasza, Keiko. *Don't laugh, Joe*
Keller, Holly. *That's mine, Horace*
Keller, Laurie. *Do unto otters*
Kelley, Marty. *The rules*
Kelly, Mij. *Achoo!*
Knowlton, Laurie Lazzaro. *Why cowgirls are such
   sweet talkers*
Kopelke, Lisa. *Excuse me!*
Kroll, Steven. *That makes me mad*
Kroll, Virginia L. *Cristina keeps a promise*
   Good citizen Sarah
   Good neighbor Nicholas
Kurtz, Jane. *Rain romp*
Lester, Helen. *Hurty feelings*
   Me first
   Tacky in trouble
Lester, Julius. *Albidaro and the mischievous dream*
Levine, Deb. *Parker picks*
Levine, Gail Carson. *Forgive me, I meant to do it*
Lloyd-Jones, Sally. *Being a pig is nice*
Lucado, Max. *All you ever need*
McCarthy, Meghan. *George upside down*
MacDonald, Amy. *Quentin Fenton Herter three*
McGee, Marni. *Wake up, me!*
Mahoney, Daniel J. *The Saturday escape*
Marlowe, Sara. *No ordinary apple*
Monster, be good!
Mora, Pat. *Abuelos*
Morgan-Vanroyen, Mary. *Gentle Rosie*
   Wild Rosie
Morstad, Julie. *How to*
Murkoff, Heidi Eisenberg. *What to expect at a play
   date*
Muth, Jon J. *The three questions*
Naylor, Phyllis Reynolds. *Sweet strawberries*
Niner, Holly L. *Mr. Worry*
Parr, Todd. *Do's and don'ts*

Patricelli, Leslie. *No no, yes yes*
Pfister, Marcus. *How Leo learned to be king*
   Milo and the magical stones
Pilkey, Dav. *The Silly Gooses*
Pinkwater, Daniel. *Bad bears and a bunny*
Puttock, Simon. *Big bad wolf is good*
Reider, Katja. *Snail started it!*
Reidy, Jean. *Too pickley!*
Roberts, David. *Dirty Bertie*
Rockliff, Mara. *The Grudge Keeper*
Rosenthal, Amy Krouse. *Christmas cookies*
   Cookies
   *One smart cookie: bite-size lessons for the school years
    and beyond*
   This plus that
Rotner, Shelley. *The A.D.D. book for kids*
Shannon, David. *A bad case of stripes*
   The rain came down
Spelman, Cornelia Maude. *When I feel angry*
Stem, J. David. *Kay Thompson's Eloise in Hollywood*
Stevenson, James. *Don't make me laugh*
Sweetland, Nancy Rose. *Yelly Kelly*
Teague, Mark. *Baby tamer*
Thomas, Joan G. *If Jesus came to my house*
Thompson, Kay. *Kay Thompson's Eloise*
Torrey, Richard. *Because*
Wahl, Jan. *Little Johnny Buttermilk*
Walker, Alice. *Finding the green stone*
Wallace, Joseph E. *Big and noisy Simon*
Wheeler, Lisa. *Old Cricket*
Willis, Jeanne. *Do little mermaids wet their beds*
Winer, Yvonne. *Frogs sing songs*
Wisdom, Jude. *Whatever Wanda wanted*
Yaccarino, Dan. *If I had a robot*
Yolen, Jane. *How do dinosaurs play with their friends?*
   How do dinosaurs say good night?
Ziefert, Harriet. *Bunny's lessons*
Zimmett, Debbie. *Eddie enough*

Behavior – animals, dislike of

Bemelmans, Ludwig. *Madeline and the bad hat*
Pitzer, Susanna. *Not afraid of dogs*
Simon, Charnan. *Big bad Buzz*

Behavior – arguing *see* Behavior – fighting,
   arguing

Behavior – bad day, bad mood

Agee, Jon. *Terrific*
Badescu, Ramona. *Big Rabbit's bad mood*
Bakos, Lisa M. *The wrong side of the bed*
Becker, Shelly. *Even superheroes have bad days*
Berenstain, Stan and Jan. *The Berenstain bears get
   in a fight*
Breznak, Irene. *Sneezy Louise*
Burach, Ross. *I am not a chair!*
Chan, Ruth. *Georgie's best bad day*
Corey, Shana. *First graders from Mars: Horus's
   horrible day*
Dean, James. *Pete the Cat and his magic sunglasses*
Delacroix, Sibylle. *Prickly Jenny*
Everitt, Betsy. *Mean soup*
Freeman, Tor. *Olive and the bad mood*
Friday, Mary Ellen. *It's a bad day*
Gammell, Stephen. *Is that you, winter?*
Giff, Patricia Reilly. *Today was a terrible day*

Gourounas, Jean. *Something's fishy*
Gravel, Elise. *The cranky ballerina*
Grindley, Sally. *The sulky vulture*
Harrison, Hannah E. *Bernice gets carried away*
Harrison, Joanna. *Grizzly dad*
Henkes, Kevin. *A good day*
Henn, Sophy. *Pom Pom Panda gets the grumps*
Higgins, Ryan T. *Hotel Bruce*
    Mother Bruce
Hodgkinson, Leigh. *Smile!*
Holm, Jennifer L. *I'm Grumpy*
Hurd, Thacher. *Santa Mouse and the ratdeer*
Jackson, Ellen. *Sometimes bad things happen*
Jenkins, Emily. *Princessland*
John, Jory. *The bad seed*
    Penguin problems
Jones, Stella J. *The very grumpy day*
Koehler, Fred. *How to cheer up Dad*
Krosoczka, Jarrett J. *Naptastrophe!*
Lombardi, Kristine A. *The grumpy pets*
Lubner, Susan. *Ruthie Bon Bair, do not go to bed with wringing wet hair!*
Mack, Jeff. *Good news, bad news*
Meschenmoser, Sebastian. *Pug Man's 3 wishes*
Messer, Claire. *Grumpy pants*
Miller, Virginia. *I love you just the way you are*
Moss, Miriam. *Smudge's grumpy day*
Murphy, Stuart J. *Probably pistachio*
Oram, Hiawyn. *Badger's bad mood*
    Kiss it better
Palatini, Margie. *Gone with the wand*
Patterson, Rebecca. *My no, no, no day!*
Pippin-Mathur, Courtney. *Maya was grumpy*
Rankin, Laura. *Ruthie and the (not so) very busy day*
Riddell, Chris. *Platypus and the lucky day*
Rockwell, Anne. *No! no! no!*
Rodman, Mary Ann. *First grade stinks!*
Rosen, Michael. *Totally wonderful Miss Plumberry*
Rosenthal, Amy Krouse. *One of those days*
Sattler, Jennifer. *Pig kahuna pirates!*
Shea, Bob. *The happiest book ever*
Slate, Joseph. *Miss Bindergarten has a wild day in kindergarten*
Smallman, Steve. *Scowl*
Snicket, Lemony. *The bad mood and the stick*
Stubbs, Lisa. *Lily and Bear: grumpy feet*
Tankard, Jeremy. *Grumpy Bird*
van Lieshout, Maria. *Splash: a little book about bouncing back*
Viorst, Judith. *Alexander and the terrible, horrible, no good, very bad day*
Wells, Rosemary. *Sophie's terrible twos*
Wight, Tamra. *The three grumpies*
Won, Brian. *Hooray for hat!*
Wormell, Mary. *Bernard the angry rooster*

Behavior – bedwetting

Clarke, Jane. *Dippy's sleepover*
Willis, Jeanne. *Do little mermaids wet their beds*

Behavior – boasting, showing off

Auch, Mary Jane. *Beauty and the beaks*
Bertier, Anne. *Wednesday*
Border, Terry. *Milk goes to school*
Braun, Sebastien. *Toot and Pop!*
Butterworth, Nick. *My dad is awesome*
Carlson, Nancy. *Loudmouth George and the cornet*
    Loudmouth George and the fishing trip
    Loudmouth George and the new neighbors
    Loudmouth George and the sixth-grade bully
Cohen, Deborah Bodin. *Engineer Ari and the Rosh Hashana ride*
Collier, Kelly. *A horse named Steve*
Cousins, Lucy. *I'm the best*
Grimm, Jacob and Wilhelm. *Rumpelstiltskin*, ill. by Paul Galdone
    Rumpelstiltskin, ill. by David Shaw
    Rumpelstiltskin, ill. by Paul O. Zelinsky
Heo, Yumi. *Lady Hahn and her seven friends*
Hodgkinson, Leigh. *Limelight Larry*
Johnston, Tony. *Farmer Mack measures his pig*
Kimmel, Eric A. *Rattlestiltskin*
Knapman, Timothy. *Can't catch me!*
Kulka, Joe. *My crocodile does not bite*
Ludwig, Trudy. *Better than you*
Marino, Gianna. *I am the Mountain Mouse*
Martin, Ann M. *Rachel Parker, kindergarten show-off*
Ross, Gayle. *How Turtle's back was cracked*
Shea, Bob. *Cheetah can't lose*
Singleton, Linda Joy. *A cat is better*
Taylor, Sean. *Crocodiles are the best animals of all*
Van Dusen, Chris. *King Hugo's huge ego*
Wortche, Allison. *Rosie Sprout's time to shine*

Behavior – boredom

Anholt, Catherine. *Come back, Jack!*
Arena, Jen. *Lady Liberty's holiday*
Arqués, Isabel M. *Ken's cloud*
Bagley, Jessixa. *Laundry day*
Black, Michael Ian. *I'm bored*
Brown, Peter. *Mr. Tiger goes wild*
Buehner, Caralyn. *The queen of style*
Christelow, Eileen. *Five little monkeys with nothing to do*
Coh, Smiljana. *Princesses on the run*
Cordell, Matthew. *Trouble gum*
Cuevas, Michelle. *Smoot*
Donovan, Sandy. *Bored Bella learns about fiction and nonfiction*
Dubuc, Marianne. *The animals' ark*
Elschner, Geraldine. *Max's magic seeds*
Fenske, Jonathan. *Barnacle is bored*
Fergus, Maureen. *Buddy and Earl*
Gall, Chris. *There's nothing to do on Mars*
Gay, Marie-Louise. *On my island*
Graves, Keith. *Pet boy*
Gutman, Anne. *Gaspard and Lisa's rainy day*
Haber, Tiffany Strelitz. *Ollie and Claire*
Heide, Florence Parry. *Princess Hyacinth*
Heide, Iris van der. *The red chalk*
Jenkins, Emily. *Princessland*
Knapman, Timothy. *A monster moved in!*
Kvasnosky, Laura McGee. *Really truly Bingo*
Lakin, Patricia. *Rainy day*
Levert, Mireille. *The princess who had almost everything*
McCleery, Peter. *Bob and Joss get lost!*
McKee, David. *Elmer again*
Mantchev, Lisa. *Someday, narwhal*
Murray, Alison. *Princess Penelope and the runaway kitten*
Myer, Andy. *Delia's dull day*
Pennypacker, Sara. *Meet the Dullards*
Petty, Dev. *There's nothing to do!*
Phelan, Matt. *Druthers*

Rosenthal, Marc. *Phooey!*
Santat, Dan. *Are we there yet?*
Schneider, Christine M. *I'm bored!*
Spier, Peter. *Bored — nothing to do!*
Staake, Bob. *Beachy and me*
Stevenson, James. *There's nothing to do!*
Szekeres, Cyndy. *Toby!*
Yolen, Jane. *Soft house*
Yum, Hyewon. *Puddle*

Behavior – bossy

Beaton, Kate. *King Baby*
Bogan, Paulette. *Virgil and Owen*
Choldenko, Gennifer. *Louder, Lili*
D'Amico, Carmela. *Suki and Mirabella*
deGroat, Diane. *Last one in is a rotten egg!*
dePaola, Tomie. *Boss for a day*
  Strega Nona does it again
Escoffier, Michaël. *Me first!*
Frazee, Marla. *The boss baby*
  The bossier baby
Hofmann-Maniyar, Ariane. *That's NOT how you do it!*
Horvath, David. *Bossy bear*
  Just like Bossy Bear
Ohi, Ruth. *Clara and the Bossy*
Palatini, Margie. *Shelly*
Rankin, Laura. *My turn!*
Reynolds, Aaron. *President Squid*
Ritchie, Alison. *Duck says don't!*
Watkins, Rowboat. *Rude cakes*
Zemach, Margot. *Eating up Gladys*

Behavior – bullying, teasing

Alexander, Claire. *Lucy and the bully*
  Small Florence
Alexander, Martha G. *I sure am glad to see you, Blackboard Bear*
Amato, Mary. *The chicken of the family*
Anaya, Rudolfo A. *Roadrunner's dance*
Anderson, Laurie Halse. *The big cheese of Third Street*
Aruego, José. *The last laugh*
Aston, Dianna Hutts. *Not so tall for six*
Bateman, Teresa. *The Bully Blockers Club*
Bottner, Barbara. *Bootsie Barker bites*
Bowles, Paula. *Scary Mary*
Bracken, Beth. *The little bully*
Brennan, Eileen. *Bad Astrid*
Brill, Calista. *Tugboat Bill and the river rescue*
Brooks, Erik. *The practically perfect pajamas*
Brown-Wood, JaNay. *Imani's moon*
Browne, Anthony. *Willy the champ*
Buehner, Caralyn. *Would I ever lie to you?*
Burningham, John. *Tug-of-war*
Calvert, Pam. *Princess Peepers*
Carlson, Nancy. *Henry and the bully*
  Loudmouth George and the sixth-grade bully
Carter, Anne Laurel. *The F team*
Caseley, Judith. *Bully*
Cazet, Denys. *Snail and Slug*
Christelow, Eileen. *Jerome camps out*
Church, Caroline Jayne. *One smart goose*
Cocca-Leffler, Maryann. *Janine*
Cohen, Miriam. *Tough Jim*
Cole, Henry. *Eddie the bully*
Cole, Joanna. *Bully trouble*

Collicott, Sharleen. *Toestomper and the caterpillars*
Cooper, Ilene. *Jake's best thumb*
Couric, Katie. *The brand new kid*
Cristaldi, Kathryn. *Baseball ballerina strikes out*
Crocker, Nancy. *Betty Lou Blue*
Cuyler, Margery. *Bullies never win*
D'Amico, Carmela. *Ella, the elegant elephant*
Davies, Matt. *Ben rides on*
De Kinder, Jan. *Red*
Dewdney, Anna. *Llama Llama and the bully goat*
Diggs, Taye. *Chocolate me!*
Docherty, Thomas. *Big scary monster*
Dolenz, Micky. *Gakky Two-Feet*
Eaton, Maxwell. *Two dumb ducks*
Elliott, David. *This Orq. (He say "ugh!")*
Emberley, Ed. *Ed Emberley's bye-bye, big bad bullybug!*
Fearnley, Jan. *Arthur and the meanies*
Finlay, Lizzie. *Little Croc's purse*
Forler, Nan. *Bird child*
Frankel, Erin. *Dare!*
  Nobody!
  Tough!
  Weird!
Garden, Nancy. *Molly's family*
Gordon, David. *Extremely cute animals operating heavy machinery*
Haber, Tiffany Strelitz. *The monster who lost his mean*
Harrison, Hannah E. *My friend Maggie*
Hassett, John. *The three silly girls Grubb*
Henkes, Kevin. *Chester's way*
High, Linda Oatman. *Tenth Avenue cowboy*
Hilton, Perez. *The boy with pink hair*
Hoffman, Sarah. *Jacob's new dress*
Jantzen, Doug. *Henry Hyena, why won't you laugh?*
Javaherbin, Mina. *Goal!*
Jennewein, Lenore. *Chick-o-Saurus Rex*
Keats, Ezra Jack. *Goggles*
Keller, Holly. *Nosy Rosie*
Kilodavis, Cheryl. *My princess boy*
Kimmelman, Leslie. *The three bully goats*
Kling, Kevin. *Big little brother*
Kliphuis, Christine. *Robbie and Ronnie*
Kroll, Steven. *It's April Fools' Day!*
  Jungle bullies
Kroll, Virginia L. *Ryan respects*
Kushner, Tony. *Brundibar*
Lacombe, Benjamin. *Cherry and Olive*
LaReau, Kara. *Ugly fish*
Latimer, Alex. *Lion vs Rabbit*
Lester, Helen. *Hooway for Wodney Wat*
  Wodney Wat's wobot
Levert, Mireille. *Eddie Longpants*
Levy, Janice. *Thomas the toadily terrible bully*
Lovell, Patty. *Stand tall, Molly Lou Melon*
Lynch, Jane. *Marlene, Marlene, Queen of Mean*
McBratney, Sam. *Yes we can!*
McCain, Becky R. *Nobody knew what to do*
McKee, David. *Elmer and the big bird*
Masters, Anthony. *Ricky's rat gang*
Mayer, Mercer. *Just big enough*
Meddaugh, Susan. *Martha walks the dog*
Montanari, Eva. *Dino bikes*
Moore, Julianne. *Freckleface Strawberry and the dodgeball bully*
Morrison, Toni. *The book of mean people*
Moss, Peggy. *Say something*
Naylor, Phyllis Reynolds. *King of the playground*
Newman, Lesléa. *Sparkle boy*

Nickle, John. *The ant bully*
Nolen, Jerdine. *Plantzilla goes to camp*
O'Connor, George. *Ker-splash!*
O'Neill, Alexis. *The Recess Queen*
Otoshi, Kathryn. *One*
Palacio, R. J. *We're all wonders*
Peet, Bill. *Big bad Bruce*
Pendziwol, Jean E. *The tale of Sir Dragon*
Penn, Audrey. *Kai to the rescue!*
Pfister, Marcus. *The little moon raven*
Pienkowski, Jan. *Bel and Bub and the bad snowball*
Pinkney, Brian. *The adventures of sparrowboy*
Pinkwater, Daniel. *Yo-yo man*
Polacco, Patricia. *Mr. Lincoln's way*
   Rotten Richie and the ultimate dare
Poulin, Andrée. *Pablo finds a treasure*
Ramos, Mario. *I am so strong*
Recorvits, Helen. *Yoon and the jade bracelet*
Reed, Lynn Rowe. *Benny Shark goes to friend school*
Rickards, Lynne. *Pink!*
Robberecht, Thierry. *Stolen smile*
Robbins, Jacqui. *Two of a kind*
Roberts, Justin. *The smallest girl in the smallest grade*
Roche, Denis. *Mim, gym, and June*
Sauer, Tammi. *Cowboy camp*
   Ginny Louise and the school showdown
Schaefer, Lola M. *Frankie Stein starts school*
Schafer, Milton. *That crazy Barb'ra*
Seeger, Laura Vaccaro. *Bully*
Shaw, Hannah. *Sneaky Weasel*
Shipton, Jonathan. *No biting, horrible crocodile!*
Shulevitz, Uri. *Troto and the trucks*
Smith, Stu. *The bubble gum kid*
Sorel, Edward. *The Saturday kid*
Soule, Jean Conder. *Never tease a weasel*
Springstubb, Tricia. *Phoebe and Digger*
Staake, Bob. *Bluebird*
Teckentrup, Britta. *Little Wolf's song*
Tierney, Fiona. *Lion's lunch?*
Waddell, Martin. *Yum, yum, yummy*
Wells, Rosemary. *Felix stands tall*
   Stella's Starliner
   Yoko writes her name
Weninger, Brigitte. *Davy, soccer star!*
Weulersse, Odile. *Nasreddine*
Willis, Jeanne. *Troll stinks*
Winstead, Rosie. *Ruby and Bubbles*
Woodson, Jacqueline. *Each kindness*

Behavior – carelessness

Bergman, Mara. *Lively Elizabeth!*
Brett, Jan. *Comet's nine lives*
Brimner, Larry Dane. *Cat on wheels*
Brunhoff, Laurent de. *Babar's little girl*
dePaola, Tomie. *The quicksand book*
   Strega Nona's magic lessons
Oldland, Nicholas. *The busy beaver*
Whatley, Bruce. *Wait! no paint!*

Behavior – cheating

Bailey, Linda. *The farm team*
Cotter, Bill. *Beard in a box*
Cuyler, Margery. *I repeat, don't cheat!*
Fox, Kathleen. *The pirates of plagiarism*
Havill, Juanita. *Jamaica and the substitute teacher*
McKee, David. *Elmer and the race*
Tabor, Corey R. *Fox and the jumping contest*

Behavior – collecting things

Armstrong-Ellis, Carey. *Prudy's problem and how she solved it*
Banks, Kate. *Max's words*
Beeny, Emily. *Hector the collector*
Best, Cari. *When we go walking*
Blumenthal, Deborah. *Aunt Claire's yellow beehive hair*
Bunting, Eve. *Anna's table*
Corderoy, Tracey. *Just right for two*
Côté, Geneviève. *Mr. King's things*
Delessert, Etienne. *Alert!*
DiPucchio, Kelly. *Alfred Zector, book collector*
Fleischman, Paul. *The matchbox diary*
Gall, Chris. *Awesome Dawson*
Hughes, Ted. *My brother Bert*
Hurst, Carol Otis. *Rocks in his head*
Jocelyn, Marthe. *Hannah's Collections*
Kleven, Elisa. *The puddle pail*
Kroll, Steven. *Stuff!*
McDonald, Megan. *Insects are my life*
McGinty, Alice B. *Eliza's kindergarten surprise*
Major, Kevin. *Aunt Olga's Christmas postcards*
Manuel, Lynn. *The trouble with Tilly Trumble*
Mariconda, Barbara. *Sort it out!*
Palatini, Margie. *Stuff*
Reid, Margarette S. *Lots and lots of coins*
Robert, Nadine. *Toshi's little treasures*
Ruzzier, Sergio. *The room of wonders*
Schachner, Judith Byron. *Dewey Bob*
Slingsby, Janet. *Hetty's 100 hats*
Springman, I. C. *More*
Sullivan, Paula. *Todd's box*
Thompson, Richard. *The night walker*
Tusa, Tricia. *Stay away from the junkyard!*
Wahl, Jan. *The art collector*
Wellington, Monica. *My leaf book*
Wimmer, Sonja. *The word collector*

Behavior – disbelief

Merino, Gemma. *The cow who climbed a tree*
Turner, Ann Warren. *Nettie's trip south*
Waber, Bernard. *Do you see a mouse?*

Behavior – dissatisfaction

Agee, Jon. *Terrific*
Aliki. *The twelve months*
Baguley, Elizabeth. *A long way from home*
Berger, Samantha. *Crankenstein*
Burningham, John. *Motor Miles*
Butterworth, Nick. *Jasper's beanstalk*
Child, Lauren. *Who wants to be a poodle*
Clarkson, Stephanie. *Sleeping Cinderella and other princess mix-ups*
Cronin, Doreen. *Click, clack, moo*
Crosby, Jeff. *Wiener Wolf*
Daywalt, Drew. *The day the crayons quit*
DiPucchio, Kelly. *Dog days of school*
Gallion, Sue Lowell. *Pug meets Pig*
Grindley, Sally. *The sulky vulture*
Heide, Florence Parry. *How to be a hero*
Helquist, Brett. *Grumpy Goat*
Hosford, Kate. *Big birthday*
John, Jory. *Penguin problems*
Keane, Dave. *Who wants a tortoise?*
Keats, Ezra Jack. *Jennie's hat*
Kornell, Max. *Bear with me*

Laminack, Lester L. *Three hens and a peacock*
MacDonald, Margaret Read. *The old woman who lived in a vinegar bottle*
McDonnell, Patrick. *Shine!*
Meddaugh, Susan. *The best place*
Palatini, Margie. *Good as Goldie*
Pearlman, Robb. *Groundhog's day off*
Peet, Bill. *The caboose who got loose*
    The luckiest one of all
    The Whingdingdilly
Petty, Dev. *I don't want to be a frog*
Reynolds, Peter H. *The smallest gift of Christmas*
Rosenthal, Amy Krouse. *It's not fair!*
Roth, Carol. *Little Bunny's sleepless night*
Shea, Bob. *The happiest book ever*
VanSickle, Vikki. *If I had a gryphon*
White, Linda. *Too many pumpkins*
Yaccarino, Dan. *Deep in the jungle*
Young, Ed. *The cat from Hunger Mountain*

Behavior – fidgeting

Carlson, Nancy. *Sit still!*

Behavior – fighting, arguing

Alborough, Jez. *Yes*
Angleberger, Tom. *Crankee Doodle*
Barasch, Lynne. *First come the zebra*
Bedford, David. *Two tough crocs*
Bender, Rebecca. *Not friends*
Bruchac, Joseph. *The great ball game*
Burdett, Lois. *Macbeth for kids*
    Romeo and Juliet for kids
Burg, Sarah Emmanuelle. *Do you still love me?*
Burningham, John. *Mr. Gumpy's outing*
Clanton, Ben. *Vote for me!*
Coh, Smiljana. *The seven princesses*
Côté, Geneviève. *Without you*
Desmond, Jenni. *Red cat blue cat*
Dorros, Alex. *Número uno*
Edwards, Pamela Duncan. *Gigi and Lulu's gigantic fight*
Foster, Travis. *Give me back my book!*
Galbraith, Kathryn O. *Two bunny buddies*
Gretz, Susanna. *Riley and Rose in the picture*
Grimm, Jacob and Wilhelm. *Battle of the beasts*
Gunnufson, Charlotte. *Prince and Pirate*
Harris, Robie H. *The day Leo said I hate you!*
Heo, Yumi. *Lady Hahn and her seven friends*
Horácek, Petr. *Jonathan and Martha*
Jeffers, Oliver. *The Hueys in It wasn't me*
Jenkins, Emily. *Tiger and Badger*
Jin, Susie Lee. *Mine!*
Johnson, D. B. *Eddie's kingdom*
Kang, Anna. *That's not mine*
    You are (not) small
Kaplan, Bruce Eric. *Meaniehead*
Keller, Holly. *Cecil's garden*
Könnecke, Ole. *Anton and the battle*
Kornell, Max. *Me first*
Kortepeter, Paul. *Oliver's red toboggan*
Kuefler, Joseph. *Rulers of the playground*
Lionni, Leo. *It's mine!*
Lyon, George Ella. *No dessert forever!*
McBratney, Sam. *I'm sorry*
McFarland, Lyn Rossiter. *The pirate's parrot*
Mack, Jeff. *Mine!*
Masurel, Claire. *A cat and a dog*

Mayer, Pamela. *The Grandma cure*
Monfreid, Dorothée de. *The cake*
Morrison, Toni. *The book of mean people*
Moüy, Iris de. *Naptime*
Murguia, Bethanie Deeney. *Princess! Fairy! Ballerina!*
Murray, Andrew. *Have you seen Chester?*
Nichols, Lori. *Maple and Willow together*
Novak, Matt. *The Pillow War*
Ohi, Ruth. *Chicken, Pig, Cow's first fight*
O'Malley, Kevin. *Little Buggy runs away*
Otoshi, Kathryn. *Draw the line*
    Two
Pfister, Marcus. *Rainbow fish and the big blue whale*
Ransom, Jeanie Franz. *Don't squeal unless it's a big deal*
Rumford, James. *Tiger and turtle*
Schmid, Paul. *Peanut and Fifi have a ball*
Selig, Josh. *Red and Yellow's noisy night*
Shaskan, Tricia Speed. *Punk skunks*
Soman, David. *The monster next door*
Souhami, Jessica. *Mrs. McCool and the giant Cuhullin*
Strauss, Linda Leopold. *The Elijah door*
Thomas, Louis. *Hug it out!*
Udry, Janice May. *Let's be enemies*
Valentine, Madeline. *I want that nut!*
Van Kampen, Vlasta. *It couldn't be worse*
Van Leeuwen, Jean. *Sorry*
Ward, Lindsay. *Brobarians*
Weninger, Brigitte. *Why are you fighting, Davy?*
White, Kathryn. *When they fight*
Zehler, Antonia. *Two fine ladies have a tiff*
Zolotow, Charlotte. *The quarreling book*

Behavior – forgetfulness

Aliki. *Use your head, dear*
Ashman, Linda. *To the beach!*
Birdseye, Tom. *Soap! soap! don't forget the soap!*
Bloom, Suzanne. *Fox forgets*
Bonwill, Ann. *The Frazzle family finds a way*
Cordsen, Carol Foskett. *Market day*
Cruise, Robin. *Little Mama forgets*
dePaola, Tomie. *Strega Nona*
Edgemon, Darcie. *Seamore, the very forgetful porpoise*
Empson, Jo. *Chimpanzees for tea!*
Fox, Mem. *Wilfrid Gordon McDonald Partridge*
Galdone, Paul. *The magic porridge pot*
Hutchins, Pat. *Don't forget the bacon!*
Lindbergh, Reeve. *My little grandmother often forgets*
Plourde, Lynn. *Pajama day*
Shepherd, Jessica. *Grandma*
Sherry, Kevin. *Acorns everywhere!*
Van Allsburg, Chris. *The stranger*
Weinberg, Larry. *The Forgetful Bears help Santa*
Wolff, Kathy. *What George forgot*
Young, Cybèle. *Nancy knows*

Behavior – forgiving

Bower, Gary. *Ivy's icicle*
Dierssen, Andreas. *Timmy's new friend*
Dyckman, Ame. *Horrible Bear!*
Jennings, Sharon. *Franklin forgives*
Kroll, Virginia L. *Forgiving a friend*
Otoshi, Kathryn. *Draw the line*
Rockliff, Mara. *The Grudge Keeper*
Thompson, Lauren. *The forgiveness garden*

Tsurumi, Andrea. *Accident!*
Tutu, Archbishop Desmond. *Desmond and the very mean word*

Behavior – gossip, rumors

Andersen, Hans Christian. *It's perfectly true!*
Aston, Dianna Hutts. *Loony Little*
Bowen, Anne. *The great math tattle battle*
Chicken Little. *Brave Chicken Little*
   Chicken Little
   Henny Penny, ill. by Emily Bolam
   Henny Penny, ill. by Paul Galdone
   Henny-Penny, ill. by Jane Wattenberg
   Henny Penny, ill. by Sophie Windham
   The sky is falling
Downey, Lynn. *The tattletale*
Emberley, Rebecca. *Chicken Little*
Felix, Monique. *The rumor*
Gorbachev, Valeri. *Dragon is coming!*
Hopkins, Jackie Mims. *Prairie chicken little*
Hutchins, Pat. *The surprise party*
Jones, Christianne C. *Miles McHale, tattletale*
Ketteman, Helen. *Armadillo tattletale*
McDonald, Megan. *Hen hears gossip*
Madonna. *Mr. Peabody's apples*
Meres, Jonathan. *The big bad rumor*
Ransom, Jeanie Franz. *Don't squeal unless it's a big deal*
Rosenberg, Liz. *What James said*
Spinelli, Eileen. *Miss Fox's class gets it wrong*
Waldman, Debby. *A sack full of feathers*
Zolotow, Charlotte. *The hating book*

Behavior – greed

Aardema, Verna. *Sebgugugu the glutton*
Aesop. *The goose that laid the golden egg*
Ahmed, Said Salah. *The lion's share / Qayb Libaax*
Andersen, Hans Christian. *The princess and the pea*
   The woman with the eggs
Bardhan-Quallen, Sudipta. *The Mine-o-saur*
Berenstain, Stan and Jan. *The Berenstain bears get the gimmies*
Bernstrom, Daniel. *One day in the eucalyptus, eucalyptus tree*
Blabey, Aaron. *Pig the elf*
   Pig the winner
Bolliger, Max. *The happy troll*
Brett, Jan. *Honey, honey — lion!*
The brothers gruesome
Buckley, Richard. *The greedy python*
Carlson, Nancy. *Harriet's Halloween candy*
Carr, Jan. *Greedy apostrophe*
Cox, Judy. *One is a feast for Mouse*
David, Lawrence. *The land of the hungry armadillos*
Diakité, Baba Wagué. *The magic gourd*
Donnelly, Jennifer. *Humble pie*
Edwards, Pamela Duncan. *The leprechaun's gold*
Farrell, Darren. *Stop following me, Moon!*
Forward, Toby. *Ben's Christmas carol*
Gerson, Mary-Joan. *Why the sky is far away*
Gregory, Nan. *Pink*
Grimm, Jacob and Wilhelm. *The fisherman and his wife*, ill. by Eleanor Hubbard
   The fisherman and his wife, ill. by Rachel Isadora
   The fisherman and his wife, ill. by Todd Ouren
   The fisherman and the turtle
   The golden goose

Grobler, Piet. *Hey, frog!*
Hamilton, Virginia. *The girl who spun gold*
Hausman, Gerald. *Coyote walks on two legs*
Hawthorne, Nathaniel. *King Midas and the golden touch*
Johnson, Paul Brett. *Bearhide and crow*
Kaplan, Michael B. *Betty Bunny wants everything*
Kasbarian, Lucine. *The greedy sparrow*
Krudop, Walter Lyon. *The man who caught fish*
Lasky, Kathryn. *Pirate Bob*
Lepp, Bil. *The King of Little Things*
Lester, Helen. *All for me and none for all*
Lind, Michael. *Bluebonnet girl*
Lionni, Leo. *The biggest house in the world*
McClurkan, Rob. *Aw, nuts!*
MacDonald, Margaret Read. *Little Rooster's diamond button*
Mangan, Anne. *The monkey who wanted the moon*
Marshall, James. *Yummers too*
Metz, Lorijo. *Floridius Bloom and the planet of Gloom*
Mollel, Tololwa M. *The flying tortoise*
Muth, Jon J. *Zen socks*
Norac, Carl. *Monster, don't eat me!*
Oxenbury, Helen. *Pig tale*
Peet, Bill. *Kermit the hermit*
   The kweeks of Kookatumdee
Reiss, Mike. *The boy who wouldn't share*
Rohmer, Harriet, et al. *The invisible hunters*
Rolli, Jennifer Hansen. *Just one more*
Sanderson, Ruth. *Papa Gatto*
San Souci, Robert D. *The enchanted tapestry*
Sauer, Tammi. *I love cake!*
Schlessinger, Laura. *But I waaannt it!*
Schroeder, Alan. *The stone lion*
Scott, Nathan Kumar. *Mangoes and bananas*
Simon, Charnan. *A greedy little pig*
Smallman, Steve. *The very greedy bee*
Smath, Jerry. *The animals' Christmas carol*
So, Meilo. *Gobble, gobble, slip, slop*
Stanley, Diane. *Rumpelstiltskin's daughter*
Stevens, Janet. *The great fuzz frenzy*
Stewart, Whitney. *A catfish tale*
Stewig, John Warren. *King Midas*
Waddell, Martin. *Yum, yum, yummy*
Wells, Rosemary. *The little lame prince*
   Max and Ruby's Midas
Willard, Nancy. *The flying bed*
Witte, Anna. *The parrot Tico Tango*

Behavior – growing up

Adoff, Jaime. *Small fry*
Aliki. *I'm growing!*
Anholt, Laurence. *Billy and the big new school*
Atkins, Jeannine. *Robin's home*
Badescu, Ramona. *Pomelo begins to grow*
Bailey, Linda. *When Santa was a baby*
Banks, Kate. *Fox*
Beaty, Daniel. *Knock knock*
Bedford, David. *Touch the sky, my little bear*
Bentley, Dawn. *Fuzzy Bear's potty book*
Bergstein, Rita M. *Your own big bed*
Berk, Ari. *Nightsong*
Best, Cari. *Sally Jean, the Bicycle Queen*
Blackford, Harriet. *Tiger's story*
Brimner, Larry Dane. *The littlest wolf*
Brown, Margaret Wise. *Another important book*
Cannon, Janell. *Verdi*
Capucilli, Alyssa Satin. *This bear's birthday*

Carle, Eric. *My very first book of growth*
Carluccio, Maria. *I'm three! Look what I can do*
Chrustowski, Rick. *My Little Fox*
Cohen, Miriam. *Jim meets the thing*
Cole, Joanna. *My big boy potty*
    My big girl potty
Collard, Sneed B. *Leaving home*
Cote, Nancy. *Jackson's blanket*
Cruise, Robin. *Bartleby speaks!*
Curtis, Jamie Lee. *It's hard to be five*
    My brave year of firsts
    When I was little
Davies, Gill. *Tiny's big wish*
Devine, Monica. *Carry me, Mama*
Diesen, Deborah. *Bloom*
Dodd, Emma. *When I grow up*
Dowson, Nick. *Tigress*
Dungy, Tony. *You can do it!*
Emmett, Jonathan. *I love you always and forever*
Ferri, Giuliano. *Little Tad grows up*
Ford, Bernette. *No more bottles for Bunny!*
    No more pacifier for Piggy!
Fox, Mem. *Shoes from grandpa*
Fraggalosch, Audrey. *Grizzly bear family*
Frazee, Marla. *Walk on!*
Freeman, Mylo. *Potty*
Galvin, Laura Gates. *River Otter at Autumn Lane*
Gay, Marie-Louise. *When Stella was very, very small*
Gentieu, Penny. *Grow! babies!*
George, Jean Craighead. *Look to the north*
Gerstein, Mordicai. *Leaving the nest*
Goodings, Lennie. *When you grow up*
Gore, Leonid. *When I grow up*
Greenstein, Elaine. *As big as you*
Groundhog at Evergreen Road
Hänel, Wolfram. *Little elephant's song*
Harper, Charise Mericle. *When I grow up*
Harris, Robie H. *Go! go! Maria!*
Harris, Teresa E. *Summer Jackson*
Heiligman, Deborah. *Babies*
Henkes, Kevin. *Owen*
Hewett, Joan. *A flamingo chick grows up*
    A giraffe calf grows up
    A harbor seal pup grows up
    A kangaroo joey grows up
    A koala joey grows up
    A monkey baby grows up
    A penguin chick grows up
    A tiger cub grows up
Hines, Anna Grossnickle. *Big like me*
Hoffman, Don. *Billy is a big boy*
Horn, Peter. *When I grow up . . .*
Howard, Arthur. *When I was five*
Jadoul, Emile. *All by myself!*
James, Simon. *George flies south*
Jeppson, Ann-Sofie. *You're growing up, Pontus*
Johnson, Marion. *Caillou, new shoes*
Jonas, Ann. *When you were a baby*
Jorgensen, Richard. *Reading with Dad*
Joslin, Mary. *The shore beyond*
Joyce, William. *Big time Olie*
Karon, Jan. *The trellis and the seed*
Katz, Karen. *Now I'm big*
Keller, Holly. *Jacob's tree*
Kelly, Luke. *Blanket and bear, a remarkable pair*
Kelly, Scott. *My journey to the stars*
Kerley, Barbara. *The world is waiting for you*
Kipling, Rudyard. *The jungle book*
Kirk, Daniel. *Bigger*

Kraus, Robert. *Leo the late bloomer*
Krauss, Ruth. *The growing story*
Krensky, Stephen. *I am so brave!*
Kroll, Virginia L. *On the way to kindergarten*
Kuiper, Nannie. *Bailey the bear cub*
Laden, Nina. *Once upon a memory*
Lane, Adam J. B. *Stop thief!*
Lewison, Wendy Cheyette. *The princess and the potty*
Lindgren, Barbro. *Sam's potty*
London, Jonathan. *Pup the sea otter*
Louise, Tina. *When I grow up*
McCarty, Peter. *Baby steps*
MacDonald, Amy. *Cousin Ruth's tooth*
McElmurry, Jill. *I'm not a baby!*
McGhee, Alison. *Bye-bye, crib*
    Little boy
    Someday
McPhail, David. *Pig Pig grows up*
Magloff, Lisa. *Bear*
    Butterfly
    Duckling
    Elephant
    Frog
    Kitten
    Penguin
    Rabbit
Mayer, Marianna. *The prince and the pauper*
Mayer, Mercer. *Bun Bun's birthday*
    Just big enough
Meddaugh, Susan. *Martha and Skits*
Milgrim, David. *How you got so smart*
Miller, Virginia. *On your potty!*
Minor, Florence. *How to be a bigger bunny*
Minshull, Evelyn White. *Eaglet's world*
Monnier, Miriam. *Just right*
Morgan, Richard. *Zoo poo*
Moss, Thylias. *I want to be*
Mueller, Doris L. *Small One's adventure*
Munsch, Robert N. *Andrew's loose tooth*
    I have to go!
Murguia, Bethanie Deeney. *I feel five!*
My potty book for boys
My potty book for girls
Nelson, S. D. *Gift horse*
Nicholls, Judith. *Billywise*
Otto, Carolyn. *Our puppies are growing*
Oud, Pauline. *Ian's new potty*
Parker, Marjorie Blain. *Mama's little duckling*
    When dads don't grow up
Patz, Nancy. *Babies can't eat kimchee!*
Pearson, Debora. *Leo's tree*
    Sophie's wheels
Petty, Dev. *I don't want to be big*
Pfeffer, Wendy. *Mallard duck at Meadow View Pond*
Piggy and Bear in their underwear
Pignataro, Anna. *Our love grows*
Pinkwater, Daniel. *Young Larry*
Plourde, Lynn. *Bella's fall coat*
Poh, Jennifer. *Herbie's big adventure*
Rockwell, Anne. *Growing like me*
Rogers, Fred. *Going to the potty*
Rogers, Paul. *Ruby's dinnertime*
    Ruby's potty
Rueda, Claudia. *My little polar bear*
Sattler, Jennifer. *Frankie the blankie*
Schlessinger, Laura. *Dr. Laura Schlessinger's*
    Growing up is hard
Schwartz, Amy. *Begin at the beginning*
    Things I learned in second grade

Sears, William, M.D., et al.. *You can go to the potty*
Senior, Olive. *Birthday suit*
Senshu, Noriko. *Sonny's dream*
Shapiro, Lawrence E. *It's time to give up your pacifier*
Shavick, Andrea. *You'll grow soon, Alex*
Shea, Bob. *New socks*
Shea, Susan A. *Do you know which one will grow?*
Sheneman, Drew. *Nope!*
Sís, Peter. *Madlenka*
Slater, Dashka. *The sea serpent and me*
Sloat, Teri. *I'm a duck!*
Spinelli, Eileen. *A big boy now*
Stein, David Ezra. *Pouch!*
Stevenson, James. *Higher on the door*
　　I meant to tell you
Stewart, Amber. *I'm big enough*
Stott, Ann. *I'll be there*
Suen, Anastasia. *Baby born*
Tarpley, Todd. *Ten tiny toes*
Tavares, Matt. *Becoming Babe Ruth*
Taylor, Sean. *When a monster is born*
Teckentrup, Britta. *Little Wolf's song*
Thermes, Jennifer. *Sam Bennett's new shoes*
Thong, Roseanne. *Tummy girl*
Tildes, Phyllis Limbacher. *Billy's big-boy bed*
Torrey, Richard. *Almost*
Turner, Sandy. *Grow up*
Urban, Linda. *Little Red Henry*
Vande Griek, Susan. *Loon*
Van Leeuwen, Jean. *"Wait for me!" said Maggie McGee*
Waite, Judy. *The stray kitten*
Wells, Rosemary. *Timothy goes to school*
Weninger, Brigitte. *Bye-bye, Binky*
　　Davy in the middle
Wild, Margaret. *Puffling*
Willis, Jeanne. *Cottonball Colin*
　　Fly, chick, fly!
　　What did I look like when I was a baby?
Wilson, Gina. *Ignis*
Winter, Jeanette. *My baby*
Winters, Kay. *Tiger trail*
　　Wolf watch
Wood, Audrey. *Oh my baby bear!*
Yolen, Jane. *Baby Bear's big dreams*
Zagwÿn, Deborah Turney. *The pumpkin blanket*
Zolotow, Charlotte. *Do you know what I'll do?*
　　I like to be little

Behavior – hiding

Adler, David A. *Hiding from the Nazis*
Alter, Anna. *Disappearing Desmond*
Arnosky, Jim. *I see animals hiding*
Aruego, José. *We hide, you seek*
Asch, Frank. *Moongame*
Ashdown, Rebecca. *Bob and Flo play hide-and-seek*
Barrow, David. *Have you seen Elephant?*
Braun, Sebastien. *Who's hiding?*
Butler, John. *Ten in the meadow*
Curato, Mike. *Little Elliot, fall friends*
Dodd, Lynley. *Find me a tiger*
Dunbar, Polly. *Where's Tumpty?*
Egan, Tim. *Dodsworth in New York*
Fleming, Candace. *Tippy-tippy-tippy, hide!*
Gottesfeld, Jeff. *The tree in the courtyard*
Gravett, Emily. *Bear and Hare—where's Bear?*
Greene, Carol. *Where is that cat?*
Grifalconi, Ann. *The village that vanished*

Hutchins, Pat. *Titch and Daisy*
Jahn-Clough, Lisa. *Missing Molly*
Jennings, Linda. *Hide and seek birthday treat*
Joosse, Barbara. *Evermore Dragon*
Lewis, Kim. *Seymour and Henry*
Mayr, Diane. *Run, Turkey, run*
Mazer, Norma Fox. *Has anyone seen my Emily Greene?*
Na, Il Sung. *Hide and seek*
Oliver, Narelle. *Twilight hunt*
Panzieri, Lucia. *The kindhearted crocodile*
Paquette, Ammi-Joan. *The tiptoe guide to tracking fairies*
Pfister, Marcus. *You can't win them all, rainbow fish*
Philpot, Graham. *Where is Little Harry?*
Polacco, Patricia. *The butterfly*
Raschka, Chris. *Whaley Whale*
Santore, Charles. *A stowaway on Noah's Ark*
Schertle, Alice. *Jeremy Bean's St. Patrick's Day*
Steffensmeier, Alexander. *Millie and the big rescue*
Steig, William. *Toby, where are you?*
Stoeke, Janet Morgan. *Hide and seek*
Surplice, Holly. *Peek-a-boo Bunny*
Tafuri, Nancy. *Where did Bunny go?*
Van Leeuwen, Jean. *Chicken soup*
Walsh, Ellen Stoll. *Mouse paint*
　　Where is Jumper?
Walsh, Melanie. *Hide and sleep*
Williamson, Sarah. *Where are you?*
Wilson, Steve. *Hedgehugs: autumn hide-and-squeak*
Wong, Janet S. *Hide and seek*
Woodcock, Fiona. *Hiding Heidi*

Behavior – hiding things

Barclay, Eric. *Hiding Phil*
Beck, Andrea. *Elliot digs for treasure*
Dunrea, Olivier. *Ollie's Easter eggs*
Hines, Anna Grossnickle. *No, no Jack!*
Jackson, Richard. *In plain sight*
Modesitt, Jeanne. *Little Bunny's Easter surprise*
Ross, Tony. *Rita's rhino*
Stephens, Helen. *How to hide a lion*
Vainio, Pirkko. *Who hid the Easter eggs?*

Behavior – hurrying

Alda, Arlene. *Hurry Granny Annie*
Bogan, Paulette. *Virgil and Owen stick together*
Egan, Kate. *Kate and Nate are running late!*
McCully, Emily Arnold. *Hurry!*
Marlow, Layn. *Hurry up and slow down*
Pfister, Marcus. *Wake up, Santa Claus!*
Portis, Antoinette. *Wait*

Behavior – imitation

Allen, Jonathan. *Don't copy me!*
Asch, Frank. *Just like daddy*
Barrett, Judi. *Animals should definitely not act like people*
　　Animals should definitely not wear clothing
Bonwill, Ann. *I am not a copycat!*
Brown, Lisa. *How to be*
Chou, Yih-Fen. *Mimi loves to mimic*
Clanton, Ben. *Mo's mustache*
Cordell, Matthew. *Another brother*
Cort, Ben. *Pigs can't fly!*
Dicmas, Courtney. *Harold finds a voice*
Elliott, George. *The boy who loved bananas*

Gauch, Patricia Lee. *Dance, Tanya*
Gill-Brown, Vanessa. *Rufferella*
Harper, Jamie. *Me too!*
Harrison, David L. *Dylan, the eagle-hearted chicken*
Inkpen, Mick. *Kipper*
Kellogg, Steven. *A rose for Pinkerton*
Kvasnosky, Laura McGee. *Little Wolf's first howling*
Lavis, Steve. *Jump!*
Lawrence, Michael. *The caterpillar that roared*
Marzollo, Jean. *Pretend you're a cat*
Merz, Jennifer J. *Playground day*
Meyers, Susan. *This is the way a baby rides*
Munsch, Robert N. *Stephanie's ponytail*
Numeroff, Laura Joffe. *If you give a mouse a cookie*
Pfister, Marcus. *Bertie*
Rathmann, Peggy. *Ruby the copycat*
Schwartz, Amy. *Bea and Mr. Jones*
Shields, Carol Diggory. *I am really a princess*
Siminovich, Lorena. *Monkey see, look at me!*
Slobodkina, Esphyr. *Caps for sale*
    Caps for sale and the mindful monkeys
    More caps for sale
Steig, William. *Toby, what are you?*

Behavior – indecision

Barton, Chris. *88 instruments*
Boelts, Maribeth. *A bike like Sergio's*
Cooper, Elisha. *Magic thinks big*
Reidy, Jean. *Too purpley!*
Seuss, Dr. *What pet should I get?*

Behavior – indifference

Bee, William. *Whatever*
Donnelly, Liza. *A hippo in our yard*
Könnecke, Ole. *Anthony and the girls*
Kroll, Steven. *Will you be my valentine?*
Sendak, Maurice. *Pierre*

Behavior – lost

Alborough, Jez. *Hug*
Anderson, Lena. *The hedgehog, the pig, and their little friend*
Anholt, Catherine. *Chimp and Zee and the big storm*
Arnosky, Jim. *Armadillo's orange*
Baeten, Lieve. *Happy birthday, Little Witch!*
Bauer, Marion Dane. *A mama for Owen*
Beck, Ian. *Home before dark*
    Teddy's snowy day
Bedford, David. *Little Otter's big journey*
Bemelmans, Ludwig. *Madeline and the gypsies*
Billingsley, Franny. *Big bad bunny*
Blake, Robert J. *Little devils*
Brennan-Nelson, Denise. *Grady the goose*
Brett, Jan. *Daisy comes home*
Brill, Calista. *Little Wing learns to fly*
Brown, Marc. *Arthur lost and found*
Brown, Ruth. *Gracie the lighthouse cat*
Browne, Anthony. *Me and you*
Brunhoff, Laurent de. *Babar's little girl*
Buckingham, Matt. *Bright Stanley*
Bush, Timothy. *Teddy bear, teddy bear*
Buzzeo, Toni. *Adventure Annie goes to work*
Byrne, Richard. *We're in the wrong book!*
Carle, Eric. *Have you seen my cat?*
Chaud, Benjamin. *The bear's song*
Cohen, Miriam. *Lost in the museum*
Cooper, Elisha. *Beaver is lost*

Cordell, Matthew. *Wolf in the snow*
Côté, Geneviève. *With you always, Little Monday*
D'Amico, Carmela. *Suki the very loud bunny*
Davis, Jerry. *Little Chicken's big day*
Donovan, Gail. *Lost at sea*
Dormer, Frank W. *The sword in the stove*
Doyle, Malachy. *Too noisy!*
Dunbar, Joyce. *The very small*
Du Quette, Keith. *Little Monkey lost*
Edwards, Richard. *Always Copycub*
Emmett, Jonathan. *This way, Ruby!*
Empson, Jo. *Rabbityness*
Fitzpatrick, Marie-Louise. *Lizzy and Skunk*
Fleischman, Paul. *Lost!*
Fletcher, Ralph. *The circus surprise*
Foreman, Michael. *Tufty*
Frazee, Marla. *The farmer and the clown*
Freschet, Gina. *Naty's parade*
Gomi, Taro. *I lost my dad*
Goodings, Christina. *Lost sheep story*
Goodrich, Carter. *We forgot Brock!*
Gorbachev, Valeri. *The missing chick*
Grimm, Jacob and Wilhelm. *Hansel and Gretel*, ill. by Jen Corace
    Hansel and Gretel, ill. by Holly Hobbie
    Hansel and Gretel, ill. by Rachel Isadora
    Hansel and Gretel, ill. by Susan Jeffers
    Hansel and Gretel, ill. by James Marshall
    Hansel and Gretel, ill. by Jane Ray
    Hansel and Gretel, ill. by Claudia Wolf
    Hansel and Gretel, ill. by Paul O. Zelinsky
    Hansel and Gretel, ill. by Lisbeth Zwerger
    Hansel and Gretel / Hansel y Gretel
    Hansel and Gretel: a retelling from the original tale by the Brothers Grimm
Grindley, Sally. *Where are my chicks?*
Gutman, Anne. *Lisa in New York*
Hakte, Ben. *Julia's house for lost creatures*
Hänel, Wolfram. *Little elephant runs away*
Hatkoff, Craig, et al. *Looking for Miza*
Haughton, Chris. *Little Owl lost*
Hawkes, Kevin. *The wicked big toddlah goes to New York*
Heck, Ed. *Monkey lost*
Heiligman, Deborah. *Snow dog, go dog*
Henkes, Kevin. *Sheila Rae, the brave*
Hest, Amy. *When you meet a bear on Broadway*
Hill, Eric. *Where's Spot?*
Hodgkins, Fran. *The cat of Strawberry Hill*
Holabird, Katharine. *Angelina and Henry*
Holt, Kimberly Willis. *The adventures of Granny Clearwater and Little Critter*
Horácek, Petr. *Puffin Peter*
    Suzy Goose and the Christmas star
Horse, Harry. *Little Rabbit lost*
Huneck, Stephen. *Sally's snow adventure*
Hutchins, Pat. *Where, oh where, is Rosie's chick?*
    Where's the baby?
Ichikawa, Satomi. *La La Rose*
Inches, Alison. *Corduroy's hike*
Itaya, Satoshi. *Buttons and Bo*
Jeffers, Oliver. *Lost and found*
Jennings, Linda. *Little puppy lost*
Johnson, Paul Brett. *Lost*
Johnston, Lynn. *Farley follows his nose*
Jonas, Ann. *Two bear cubs*
Jonathan, Langley. *Missing*
Kato, Yukiko. *In the meadow*
Keane, Michael. *The night Santa got lost*

Keats, Ezra Jack. *My dog is lost!*
Kelly, L. J. R. *Sometimes it's storks*
Kelly, Mij. *Where's my darling daughter?*
Kim, Julie. *Where's Halmoni?*
Kimmel, Eric A. *Rip Van Winkle's return*
Kinsey-Warnock, Natalie. *The bear that heard crying*
Kleven, Elisa. *Glasswings*
Kroll, Steven. *Pooch on the loose*
LaMarche, Jim. *Lost and found: three dog stories*
Lambert, Martha Lewis. *I won't get lost*
Lears, Laurie. *Ian's walk*
Lee . *The lost kitten*
Levine, Ellen. *Seababy*
Lindbergh, Reeve. *Bridget and the gray wolves*
Litten, Kristyna. *Blue and Bertie*
Lobel, Gillian. *Little Honey Bear and the smiley moon*
Lomp, Stephan. *Mamasaurus*
London, Jonathan. *Ali, child of the desert*
    Duck and Hippo lost and found
    Little lost tiger
Long, Loren. *Drummer boy*
Loupy, Christophe. *Don't worry, Wags*
McAllister, Angela. *Found you, Little Wombat!*
    Mama and Little Joe
McCleery, Peter. *Bob and Joss get lost!*
McCloskey, Robert. *Blueberries for Sal*
McCully, Emily Arnold. *Picnic*
MacDonald, Alan. *Wilfred to the rescue*
McDonald, Megan. *When the library lights go out*
McFarland, Lyn Rossiter. *Widget and the puppy*
McGraw, Sheila. *Pussycats everywhere*
McHenry, E. B. *Has anyone seen Winnie and Jean?*
McKee, David. *Elmer and Wilbur*
McMullan, Kate. *I'm big!*
McPhail, David. *Lost*
Mader, C. Roger. *Lost cat*
Marzollo, Jean. *Snow angel*
Mauner, Claudia. *Zoe Sophia's scrapbook*
May, Robert L. *Rudolph shines again*
Meadows, Michelle. *Itsy-bitsy baby mouse*
Melmed, Laura Krauss. *Little Oh*
Minarik, Else Holmelund. *Little Bear's new friend*
Mitton, Tony. *Playful little penguins*
Moerbeek, Kees. *The diary of Hansel and Gretel*
Morpurgo, Michael. *Wombat goes walkabout*
Moss, Miriam. *The snow bear*
Murphy, Stuart J. *Freda is found*
Nelson, Kadir. *Baby Bear*
Nishimura, Kae. *Dinah*
Norman, Kim. *Puddle pug*
Peet, Bill. *Ella*
Pfister, Marcus. *Snow puppy*
Pham, LeUyen. *The bear who wasn't there*
Pinkwater, Daniel. *Beautiful Yetta*
Preston-Gannon, Frann. *How to lose a lemur*
Puttock, Simon. *Little lost cowboy*
Ramsden, Ashley. *Seven fathers*
Raschka, Chris. *Daisy gets lost*
Rey, Margret. *Curious George goes to the hospital*
Root, Phyllis. *Oliver finds his way*
    Scrawny cat
Rosenberry, Vera. *Vera's Halloween*
Salat, Cristina. *Peanut's emergency*
Scheffler, Ursel. *Taking care of Sister Bear*
Schertle, Alice. *Little Frog's song*
Schiller, Abbie. *When Lyla got lost (and found)*
Simmons, Jane. *Come along, Daisy!*
    Quack, Daisy, quack!

Skalak, Barbara Anne. *Waddle, waddle, quack, quack, quack*
Sloat, Teri. *Pablo in the snow*
Smath, Jerry. *Sammy Salami*
Smee, Nicola. *What's the matter, Bunny Blue?*
Snitselaar, Nicole. *Little Fox, lost*
Sockabasin, Allen. *Thanks to the animals*
Stead, Philip C. *Jonathan and the big blue boat*
Stevenson, James. *Howard*
Stoop, Naoko. *Red Knit Cap Girl to the rescue*
Sykes, Julie. *Dora's chicks*
Tafuri, Nancy. *Goodnight, my duckling*
Titherington, Jeanne. *Where are you going, Emma?*
Tokuda, Wendy. *Humphrey the lost whale*
Uhlberg, Myron. *A storm called Katrina*
Vischer, Frans. *Fuddles*
Waddell, Martin. *A kitten called Moonlight*
    Sailor Bear
    Small Bear lost
    Webster J. Duck
Waite, Judy. *The stray kitten*
Waring, Richard. *Alberto the dancing alligator*
Watanabe, Shigeo. *Where's my daddy?*
Webb, Holly. *Little puppy lost*
Wells, Rosemary. *McDuff comes home*
    Max's dragon shirt
Wheeler, Lisa. *Castaway cats*
Whybrow, Ian. *Harry and the dinosaurs at the museum*
Wild, Margaret. *The pocket dogs*
Wilson, Karma. *Bear feels scared*
    Where is home, Little Pip?

Behavior – lost & found possessions

Alborough, Jez. *Duck's key where can it be?*
Andrews, Julie. *Dumpy to the rescue!*
Antony, Steve. *The queen's handbag*
    The Queen's hat
Arnold, Marsha Diane. *Lost. found*
Aylesworth, Jim. *The mitten*
Beaumont, Karen. *Where's my t-r-u-c-k?*
    Who ate all the cookie dough?
Berger, Joe. *My special one and only*
Birchall, Mark. *Rabbit's birthday surprise*
Blackaby, Susan. *Rembrandt's hat*
Blankenship, Lee Ann. *Mr. Tuggle's troubles*
Bogan, Paulette. *Spike in the city*
Bottner, Barbara. *Pish and Posh*
Brandle, Bine. *Flusi, the sock monster*
Brett, Jan. *The mitten*
Briere-Haquet, Alice. *Zebedee's balloon*
Brown, Alan James. *Love-a-Duck*
Brown, Marc. *D. W.'s lost blankie*
Bunting, Eve. *Have you seen my new blue socks?*
    Whose shoe?
Burks, James. *Beep and Bah*
Busch, Miriam. *Lion, lion*
Butler, Kristi T. *Rip's secret spot*
Butler, M. Christina. *The special blankie*
Bynum, Janie. *Kiki's blankie*
Calmenson, Stephanie. *Oopsy, teacher!*
Carmichael, Clay. *Lonesome bear*
Castillo, Lauren. *The troublemaker*
Cate, Annette LeBlanc. *The magic rabbit*
Chessa, Francesca. *Holly's red boots*
Child, Lauren. *I completely know about guinea pigs*
Choldenko, Gennifer. *Dad and the dinosaur*
Cole, Henry. *Spot, the cat*

Cooper, Helen. *Tatty-Ratty*
Crimi, Carolyn. *Principal Fred won't go to bed*
Cronin, B. B. *The lost house*
    The lost picnic
Davies, Matt. *Ben draws trouble*
Davis, Aubrey. *A hen for Izzy Pippik*
Daywalt, Drew. *The day the crayons came home*
Derby, Sally. *Two fools and a horse*
De Sève, Randall. *Mi barco / Toy boat*
    Toy boat
Desrosiers, Sylvie. *Hocus Pocus takes the train*
De Vries, Anke. *Raf*
Diesen, Deborah. *The pout-pout fish in the big-big dark*
DiFiori, Lawrence. *Jackie and the Shadow Snatcher*
Donaldson, Julia. *Room on the broom*
Dornbusch, Erica. *Finding Kate's shoes*
Dunbar, Joyce. *Where's my sock?*
Dunrea, Olivier. *Gideon and Otto*
Edgemon, Darcie. *Seamore, the very forgetful porpoise*
Ellwand, David. *Alfred's camera*
    Alfred's party
Ernst, Lisa Campbell. *Stella Louella's runaway book*
Falconer, Ian. *Olivia — and the missing toy*
Feeney, Tatyana. *Little Owl's orange scarf*
Feiffer, Jules. *I lost my bear*
Findlay, Lisa. *What's in Oscar's trashcan?*
Fisman, Karen. *Nonna's Hanukkah surprise*
Fitzgerald, Ella. *A-tisket, a-tasket*
Flynn, Kitson. *Carrot in my pocket*
Freedman, Claire. *Night-night, Emily*
Garton, Sam. *I am Otter*
Geisert, Arthur. *The giant ball of string*
George, Lindsay Barrett. *Maggie's ball*
George, Margaret. *Lucille lost*
Geser, Gretchen. *One bright ring*
Gliori, Debi. *Flora's blanket*
Gorbachev, Valeri. *Whose hat is it?*
Grey, Mini. *Hermelin the detective mouse*
    Traction Man meets Turbodog
Gulbis, Stephen. *Cowgirl Rosie and her five baby bison*
Hall, Michael. *Little i*
Handford, Martin. *Where's Waldo?*
    Where's Waldo? The wonder book
Harley, Bill. *Lost and found*
Harvey, Matthea. *Cecil the pet glacier*
Havill, Juanita. *Jamaica's find*
Hayes, Sarah. *Lucy Anna and the Finders*
Hernandez, Leeza. *Cat napped*
    Dog gone!
Hoberman, Mary Ann. *The looking book*
Hodgkinson, Leigh. *Smile!*
Holmes, Janet A. *Have you seen Duck?*
Hoppe, Paul. *Hat*
    The woods
Hughes, Shirley. *Bobbo goes to school*
Ichikawa, Satomi. *The first bear in Africa!*
Jackson, Alison. *When the wind blew*
Jesset, Aurore. *Loopy*
Johnson, G. Francis. *Has anybody lost a glove?*
Jonas, Ann. *Where can it be?*
Jonovitz, Marilyn. *Three little kittens*
Kako, Satoshi. *Little Daruma and little Kaminari*
Kasza, Keiko. *Finders keepers*
Kellogg, Steven. *The mystery of the magic green ball*
    The mystery of the missing red mitten
Kelly, Luke. *Blanket and bear, a remarkable pair*
Klassen, Jon. *I want my hat back*

    We found a hat
Ko, Sangmi. *A dog wearing shoes*
Kovacs, Deborah. *Katie Copley*
Kroll, Steven. *Patches*
    Patches lost and found
Kruusval, Catarina. *Franny's friends*
LaMarche, Jim. *Lost and found: three dog stories*
Lamb, Albert. *Sam's winter hat*
Landström, Lena. *Where is Pim?*
Lewis, Kim. *First snow*
    Hooray for Harry
Light, Steve. *Have you seen my lunch box?*
    Have you seen my monster?
Lobel, Anita. *Nini lost and found*
London, Jonathan. *Let's go, Froggy!*
Long, Loren. *Otis and the puppy*
Long, Matty. *Super Happy Magic Forest*
Low, Alice. *Aunt Lucy went to buy a hat*
Luciani, Brigitte. *Those messy Hempels*
McClintock, Barbara. *Adele and Simon*
    Adele and Simon in America
    Lost and found: Adele and Simon in China
McCourt, Lisa. *Chicken soup for little souls: The never-forgotten doll*
MacDonald, Amy. *Cousin Ruth's tooth*
McDonnell, Christine. *Goyangi means cat*
McElmurry, Jill. *Mad about plaid*
McGinty, Alice B. *Eliza's kindergarten pet*
McKee, David. *Elmer and the lost teddy*
McPhail, David. *The teddy bear*
Mahy, Margaret. *Down the back of the chair*
    Mister Whistler
Maidment, Stella. *Cowboy puzzles*
Mann, Jennifer K. *Sam and Jump*
Manning, Maurie J. *Laundry day*
Meserve, Jessica. *Bedtime without Arthur*
Meyers, Susan. *Bear in the air*
Miyares, Daniel. *Float*
Montes, Marisa. *Egg-napped!*
Moss, Miriam. *Bare bear*
    Matty takes off!
    Wibble wobble
Mother Goose. *The three little kittens*
Myers, Tim. *Looking for Luna*
Norris, Leslie. *Albert and the angels*
Ohi, Debbie Ridpath. *Where are my books?*
Ohi, Ruth. *Kenta and the big wave*
Olien, Jessica. *Shark Detective!*
Pericoli, Matteo. *Tommaso and the missing line*
Perkins, Lynne Rae. *Snow music*
Pett, Mark. *The boy and the airplane*
Pinkney, Jerry. *Three little kittens*
Plourde, Lynn. *A mountain of mittens*
Polacco, Patricia. *Bun Bun Button*
Poydar, Nancy. *Busy Bea*
Priest, Robert H. *The pirate's eye*
Quattlebaum, Mary. *Winter friends*
Randall, Alison L. *The wheat doll*
Rickert, Janet Elizabeth. *Russ and the almost perfect day*
Robinson, Michelle. *Odd socks*
Rosen, Michael. *Red Ted and the lost things*
Rosenthal, Eileen. *Bobo the sailor man!*
    I must have Bobo!
Schachner, Judith Byron. *Bits and pieces*
Scotton, Rob. *Secret Agent Splat!*
Siegel, Randy. *Grandma's smile*
Simhaee, Rebeka. *Sara finds a mitzva*
Simon, Charnan. *Messy Molly*

Singer, Isaac Bashevis. *The parakeet named Dreidel*
Siomades, Lorianne. *Cuckoo can't find you*
　Three little kittens
Slonim, David. *Oh, Ducky*
Smee, Nicola. *No bed without Ted*
Soman, David. *Ladybug Girl and Bingo*
Springstubb, Tricia. *Phoebe and Digger*
Stadler, John. *Catilda*
Stainton, Sue. *Santa's snow cat*
Stephens, Helen. *The big adventure of the Smalls*
Sturm, James. *Sleepless knight*
Teague, Mark. *The lost and found*
Trasler, Janee. *Mimi and Bear in the snow*
Trewin, Trudie. *I lost my kisses*
Tupera, Tupera. *Polar Bear's underwear*
Velasquez, Eric. *Looking for Bongo*
Villeneuve, Anne. *The red scarf*
Vogel, Vin. *Bedtime for Yeti*
Walsh, Ellen Stoll. *Hamsters to the rescue*
Wells, Rosemary. *Max and Ruby at the Warthogs'*
　wedding
Weninger, Brigitte. *What's the matter, Davy?*
West, Judy. *Have you got my purr?*
White, Marsha. *Hooper has lost his owner*
Willems, Mo. *Knuffle Bunny*
　Knuffle Bunny free
Wood, Audrey. *Alphabet adventure*
Yoon, Salina. *Found*
　Penguin in love
Yorinks, Arthur. *Christmas in July*
Young, Cybèle. *Some things I've lost*
Zagarenski, Pamela. *Henry and Leo*

Behavior – lying

Abercrombie, Barbara. *The show-and-tell lion*
Aesop. *The boy who cried wolf*
Arsenault, Isabelle. *Colette's lost pet*
Ashdown, Rebecca. *The Whopper*
Berenstain, Stan and Jan. *The Berenstain bears and*
　the truth
Brown, Marc. *Arthur and the true Francine*
Buehner, Caralyn. *Would I ever lie to you?*
Cocca-Leffler, Maryann. *Princess K.I.M. and the lie*
　that grew
Cuyler, Margery. *I repeat, don't cheat!*
deGroat, Diane. *Liar, liar, pants on fire*
Diakité, Baba Wagué. *The hunterman and the*
　crocodiles
Duddle, Johnny. *Gigantosaurus*
Hale, Dean. *Scapegoat*
Hayes, Joe. *Juan Verdades, the man who could not tell*
　a lie
Hennessy, B. G. *The boy who cried wolf*
Kaplan, Michael B. *Betty Bunny didn't do it*
Latimer, Alex. *The boy who cried ninja*
McKissack, Patricia C. *The honest-to-goodness truth*
Magoon, Scott. *The boy who cried bigfoot!*
Miller, John. *Winston and George*
Poydar, Nancy. *Zip, zip . . . homework*
Rankin, Laura. *Ruthie and the (not so) teeny tiny lie*
Robberecht, Thierry. *Sam tells stories*
　Sarah's little ghosts
Rocco, John. *Wolf! wolf!*
Ross, Tony. *The boy who cried wolf*
Singer, Marilyn. *The boy who cried alien*
Wells, Rosemary. *Fiona's little lie*

Behavior – messy

Amant, Kathleen. *Little Rabbit gets messy*
Blankenship, Lee Ann. *Mr. Tuggle's troubles*
Booth, Anne. *The fairiest fairy*
Bowles, Paula. *Messy Jesse*
Breen, Steve. *A perfect mess*
Brennan, Eileen. *Dirtball Pete*
Coats, Lucy. *Captain Beastlie's pirate party*
Cronin, B. B. *The lost house*
Cronin, Doreen. *Bloom*
Cuyler, Margery. *Monster mess!*
Diesen, Deborah. *Picture day perfection*
Dunrea, Olivier. *Jasper and Joop*
Eaton, Jason Carter. *Great, now we've got barbarians!*
Elschner, Geraldine. *Mark's messy room*
Ericsson, Jennifer A. *She did it!*
Garton, Sam. *I am Otter*
Gay, Marie-Louise. *What are you doing, Sam?*
Gershator, Phillis. *Time for a bath*
Harris, Robie H. *I love messes!*
Helakoski, Leslie. *Big pigs*
Hodgkinson, Leigh. *Troll swap*
Jones, Stella J. *Glitter*
Keane, Dave. *Sloppy Joe*
Killen, Nicola. *Not me!*
Klise, Kate. *Little Rabbit and the Meanest Mother on*
　Earth
Lester, Helen. *The loch mess monster*
Lichtenheld, Tom. *What's with this room?*
McDonnell, Patrick. *A perfectly messed-up story*
McKissack, Patricia C. *Messy Bessey*
　Messy Bessey / Ada, la desordenada
　Messy Bessey's closet
Malbrough, Mike. *Marigold bakes a cake*
Meschenmoser, Sebastian. *Gordon and Tapir*
Modan, Rutu. *Maya makes a mess*
Moss, Miriam. *Matty in a mess!*
Powell-Tuck, Maudie. *The messy book*
Provencher, Rose-Marie. *Mouse cleaning*
Reynolds, Aaron. *Here comes Destructosaurus!*
Riley, Linnea Asplind. *Mouse mess*
Robinson, Michelle. *Ding dong! Gorilla!*
Simon, Charnan. *Messy Molly*
Stein, Janet. *This little bunny can bake*
Telchin, Eric. *The Black and White Factory*
Tuma, Refe. *What the dinosaurs did at school*
Waldman, Debby. *Room enough for Daisy*
Winstead, Rosie. *Sprout helps out*
Ziefert, Harriet. *Messy Bessie*

Behavior – misbehavior

Abramson, Jill. *Ready or not, here comes Scout*
Alexander, Lloyd. *How the cat swallowed thunder*
Alexander, Martha G. *We're in big trouble,*
　Blackboard Bear
Allard, Harry. *Miss Nelson is back*
　Miss Nelson is missing!
Anderson, Laurie Halse. *The hair of Zoe*
　Fleefenbacher goes to school
Anderson, Peggy Perry. *Out to lunch*
Aralan, Haydé. *Milton's Christmas*
Arnold, Tedd. *Huggly takes a bath*
　No jumping on the bed!
Asch, Frank. *Moonbear's dream*
Ashman, Linda. *Desmond and the naughtybugs*
　M is for mischief
Baek, Matthew J. *Be gentle with the dog, dear*
Baker, Leslie A. *You bad dog!*

Barba, Ale. *Time out!*
Bardhan-Quallen, Sudipta. *Chicks run wild*
   Tyrannosaurus wrecks!
Barnett, Mac. *Billy Twitters and his big blue whale*
   problem
   Rules of the house
   Triangle
Bemelmans, Ludwig. *Madeline and the bad hat*
Berenstain, Stan and Jan. *The Berenstain bears and*
   the truth
Bingham, Kelly. *Circle, square, Moose*
Blabey, Aaron. *Pig the winner*
Blake, Quentin. *Three little monkeys*
Bottner, Barbara. *An annoying ABC*
Brennan-Nelson, Denise. *He's been a monster all*
   day!
Bright, Paul. *There's a bison bouncing on the bed!*
Brown, Marc. *Arthur's computer disaster*
   Arthur's first sleepover
Brown, Margaret Wise. *Sneakers, the seaside cat*
Bruel, Nick. *Bad Kitty*
   A Bad Kitty Christmas
Burningham, John. *Edwardo*
Buzzeo, Toni. *No T. Rex in the library*
Carlson, Nancy. *Loudmouth George earns his*
   allowance
Castillo, Lauren. *The troublemaker*
Catalanotto, Peter. *Ivan the terrier*
Cecka, Melanie. *Violet comes to stay*
Chamberlain, Margaret. *Please don't tease Tootsie*
Chorao, Kay. *Bad boy, good boy*
Christelow, Eileen. *Five little monkeys jumping on*
   the bed
   Five little monkeys sitting in a tree
   Letters from a desperate dog
Chung, Arree. *Out!*
Church, Caroline Jayne. *Digby takes charge*
Clanton, Ben. *Rex wrecks it!*
Cohen, Miriam. *Starring first grade*
Collins, Ross. *Doodleday*
Cordell, Matthew. *Trouble gum*
Cullen, Lynn. *Dear Mr. Washington*
Curious George and the puppies
Curious George goes to a chocolate factory
Curious George goes to a movie
Curious George in the snow
Davies, Gill. *Can't, don't, won't*
Day, Alexandra. *Carl's birthday*
Debecker, Benoît. *The naughty prince*
deGroat, Diane. *Roses are pink, your feet really stink*
Delacroix, Sibylle. *Blanche hates the night*
Demas, Corinne. *Always in trouble*
DePalma, Mary Newell. *Uh-oh!*
Devlin, Jane. *Hattie the bad*
Dewdney, Anna. *Nobunny's perfect*
Dieterlé, Nathalie. *I am the king!*
DiPucchio, Kelly. *Dragon was terrible*
Dodds, Dayle Ann. *The prince won't go to bed*
Dunn, Jancee. *I'm afraid your teddy is in trouble today*
Durant, Alan. *Big Bad Bunny*
Dyckman, Ame. *Horrible Bear!*
Elliott, David. *Finn throws a fit!*
Emmett, Jonathan. *The Santa trap*
Enersen, Adele. *Vincent and the night*
Esbaum, Jill. *Stanza*
Feeney, Tatyana. *Small Elephant's bathtime*
Fergus, Maureen. *The day my mom came to*
   kindergarten
Ferrell, Sean. *The Snurtch*

Flack, Marjorie. *The story about Ping*
Ford, Bernette. *No more biting for Billy Goat!*
Fredrickson, Lane. *Watch your tongue, Cecily Beasley*
Funke, Cornelia. *Princess Pigsty*
Gall, Chris. *Revenge of the Dinotrux*
Gantos, Jack. *Happy birthday, Rotten Ralph*
   The nine lives of Rotten Ralph
   Not so Rotten Ralph
   Rotten Ralph
   Rotten Ralph's rotten romance
   Wedding bells for Rotten Ralph
   Worse than Rotten Ralph
Gassman, Julie. *Crabby pants*
Gerstein, Mordicai. *Minifred goes to school*
Going, K. L. *Dog in charge*
Goodrich, Carter. *Mister Bud wears the cone*
Grant, Jacob. *Little Bird's bad word*
Grogan, John. *Bad dog, Marley!*
Gutman, Anne. *Gaspard and Lisa's rainy day*
Hale, Bruce. *Big Bad Baby*
   Clark the Shark
Haughton, Chris. *Oh no, George!*
Havill, Juanita. *Jamaica and the substitute teacher*
Heide, Florence Parry. *Always listen to your mother*
Hemingway, Edward. *Field guide to the*
   Grumpasaurus
Henkes, Kevin. *A weekend with Wendell*
Henry, Jed. *I speak dinosaur*
Heo, Yumi. *The green frogs*
Hodgkinson, Jo. *A big day for Migs*
Hodgkinson, Leigh. *Goldilocks and just one bear*
Holabird, Katharine. *Angelina, star of the show*
Hood, Susan. *Meet Trouble*
Horáček, Petr. *My elephant*
Houran, Lori Haskins. *A dozen cousins*
Hurd, Thacher. *Bad frogs*
Hutchins, Pat. *Three-star Billy*
   Where's the baby?
Inkpen, Mick. *I will love you anyway*
Isadora, Rachel. *Uh-oh!*
Ismail, Yasmeen. *Time for bed, Fred!*
Isol. *Petit, the monster*
Jenkins, Emily. *Love you when you whine*
Jennings, Patrick. *Naughty Claudine's Christmas*
John, Jory. *The bad seed*
Johnson, Paul Brett. *Little Bunny Foo Foo*
Joosse, Barbara. *Please is a good word to say*
Juster, Norton. *Sourpuss and sweetie pie*
Kaplan, Bruce Eric. *Monsters eat whiny children*
Kellogg, Steven. *Pinkerton, behave!*
   Prehistoric Pinkerton
Kerley, Barbara. *What to do about Alice?*
Kipling, Rudyard. *How the camel got his hump*
Kirk, Katie. *Eli, no!*
Kirwan, Wednesday. *Nobody notices Minerva*
Knapman, Timothy. *Dinosaurs don't have bedtimes!*
Koehler, Fred. *How to cheer up Dad*
Kumin, Maxine. *Oh, Harry!*
Laden, Nina. *Bad dog*
Lane, Nathan. *Naughty Mabel*
Langreuter, Jutta. *Little Bear and the big fight*
LaReau, Kara. *No slurping, no burping!*
LaRochelle, David. *Moo!*
Lindbergh, Reeve. *The awful aardvarks go to school*
   The awful aardvarks shop for school
   The day the goose got loose
Lindgren, Barbro. *Oink, oink, Benny*
London, Jonathan. *Froggy eats out*
   Froggy goes to the library

McAnulty, Stacy. *Dear Santasaurus*
McBratney, Sam. *The caterpillow fight*
McClements, George. *Baron von Baddie and the ice ray incident*
  Night of the Veggie Monster
MacDonald, Amy. *Quentin Fenton Herter three*
McDonnell, Patrick. *The monsters' monster*
McElligott, Matthew. *The lion's share*
Mack, Jeff. *Duck in the fridge*
McNaughton, Colin. *Captain Abdul's pirate school*
McPhail, David. *Bad dog*
Manning, Jane. *Millie Fierce*
Mansfield, Howard. *Hogwood steps out*
Marshall, James. *The Cut-Ups*
  The Cut-Ups at Camp Custer
  The Cut-Ups crack up
  The Cut-Ups cut loose
  George and Martha back in town
Martin, David. *Monkey trouble*
Milgrim, David. *Dog brain*
Monroe, Chris. *Sneaky sheep*
Moss, Miriam. *Bad hare day*
Mozelle, Shirley. *The pig is in the pantry, the cat is on the shelf*
Munsch, Robert N. *Angela's airplane*
  Moira's birthday
Murphy, Patti Beling. *Elinor and Violet*
O'Connor, Jane. *Fancy Nancy: fanciest doll in the universe*
Offill, Jenny. *17 things I'm not allowed to do anymore*
Palatini, Margie. *Goldie and the three hares*
  No nap! yes nap!
Pallotta, Jerry. *A giraffe did one*
Parsley, Elise. *If you ever want to bring an alligator to school, don't!*
Partis, Joanne. *Stripe*
Patterson, Rebecca. *My no, no, no day!*
Paul, Ruth. *Bad dog, Flash*
  Go home Flash
Pearce, Clemency. *Frangoline and the midnight dream*
Phillips, Betty Lou. *Emily goes wild*
Pichon, Liz. *The three horrid little pigs*
Pinfold, Levi. *The Django*
Pinkwater, Daniel. *Bad bears in the big city*
  Ice-cream Larry
  Irving and Muktuk
  The picture of Morty and Ray
Potter, Beatrix. *The complete adventures of Peter Rabbit*
  The tale of Benjamin Bunny
  The tale of Peter Rabbit, ill. by Margot Apple
  The tale of Peter Rabbit, ill. by Beatrix Potter
  The tale of two bad mice
  The two bad mice
  Where's Peter Rabbit?
Redmond, E. S. *The Unruly Queen*
Reidy, Jean. *Time out for monsters!*
Rice, Eve. *Benny bakes a cake*
Richards, Dan. *The problem with not being scared of monsters*
Robberecht, Thierry. *I can't do anything!*
Robinson, Michelle. *Ding dong! Gorilla!*
Rockwell, Anne. *The boy who wouldn't obey*
Rosoff, Meg. *Wild boars cook*
Ross, Tony. *I didn't do it!*
Russo, Marisabina. *The bunnies are not in their beds*
  Under the table
Sanders, Rob. *Rodzilla*

Sattler, Jennifer. *Uh-oh, Dodo!*
Say, Allen. *Allison*
Schmid, Paul. *Petunia goes wild*
Schneider, Josh. *Everybody sleeps (but not Fred)*
  You'll be sorry
Schotter, Roni. *When the Wizzy Foot goes walking*
Scotton, Rob. *Merry Christmas, Splat*
Sendak, Maurice. *Where the wild things are*
Shannon, David. *David gets in trouble*
  David goes to school
  Good boy, Fergus!
  No, David!
  Oh, David!
Shannon, Molly. *Tilly the trickster*
Shaw, Hannah. *School for bandits*
Shea, Bob. *Big plans*
  Dinosaur vs. Mommy
Shields, Gillian. *Elephantantrum!*
Simmons, Steven J. *Alice and Greta's color magic*
  Greta's revenge
Smith, Ben Bailey. *I am Bear*
Smith, Shoham. *An after bedtime story*
Snicket, Lemony. *The bad mood and the stick*
Soman, David. *Three bears in a boat*
Stephens, Helen. *Poochie-poo*
Sternberg, Julie. *Bedtime at Bessie and Lil's*
Stevenson, James. *Worse than the worst*
The three bears. *The 3 bears and Goldilocks*
Tillman, Nancy. *Tumford the terrible*
  Tumford's rude noises
Tobin, Jim. *The very inappropriate word*
Tougas, Chris. *Dojo Daycare*
Trivizas, Eugenios. *The three little wolves and the big bad pig*
Underwood, Deborah. *Here comes Santa Cat*
Urdahl, Catherine. *Polka-dot fixes kindergarten*
Van Allsburg, Chris. *The garden of Abdul Gasazi*
Vidal, Beatriz A. *Federico and the Magi's gift*
Viorst, Judith. *Alexander, who's trying his best to be the best boy ever*
  Nobody here but me
Walton, Rick. *I need my own country!*
Warburton, Tom. *1000 times no*
Ward, Cindy. *Cookie's week*
Watson, Richard Jesse. *The boy who went ape*
Watt, Mélanie. *You're finally here!*
We wish you a merry Christmas
Weaver, Tess. *Cat jumped in!*
Weis, Carol. *When the cows got loose*
Weiss, Ellen. *The taming of Lola*
Wells, Rosemary. *Fritz and the mess fairy*
  Hands off, Harry!
  Hazel's amazing mother
  Sophie's terrible twos
  Time-out for Sophie
  Yoko's show-and-tell
Weston, Carrie. *If a chicken stayed for supper*
Whybrow, Ian. *Badness for beginners*
Willems, Mo. *Goldilocks and the three dinosaurs*
Wood, Audrey. *Elbert's bad word*
Yee, Wong Herbert. *Big black bear*
Yokococo. *Matilda and Hans*
Ziefert, Harriet. *The princess and the peas and carrots*
  There was a little girl who had a little curl

Behavior – mistakes

Aliki. *Jack and Jake*
Becker, Bonny. *The Christmas crocodile*

Bedford, David. *Mole's in love*
Brett, Jan. *Armadillo rodeo*
Bridwell, Norman. *Clifford's good deeds*
Burdett, Lois. *Twelfth night for kids*
Dodd, Emma. *Foxy*
Dubosarsky, Ursula. *The terrible plop*
Inkpen, Mick. *Kipper's birthday*
Luyken, Corinna. *The book of mistakes*
McFarland, Lyn Rossiter. *The pirate's parrot*
Medearis, Angela Shelf. *Poppa's new pants*
Parr, Todd. *It's okay to make mistakes*
Root, Phyllis. *Contrary bear*
Rylant, Cynthia. *Brownie and Pearl make good*
Saltzberg, Barney. *Crazy hair day*
Sauer, Tammi. *I love cake!*
Savage, Stephen. *The mixed-up truck*
Scheffler, Axel. *Pip and Posy: the little puddle*
Schwartz, Amy. *Starring Miss Darlene*
Singer, Marilyn. *Tallulah's Nutcracker*
Spinelli, Eileen. *Somebody loves you, Mr. Hatch*
Stoeke, Janet Morgan. *A friend for Minerva Louise*
    Minerva Louise at the fair
Tsurumi, Andrea. *Accident!*
Weigelt, Udo. *The Easter Bunny's baby*
Willard, Nancy. *Gum*
Willems, Mo. *Nanette's baguette*

Behavior – misunderstanding

Allard, Harry. *The Stupids die*
Ashman, Linda. *Ella who?*
Bently, Peter. *The prince and the porker*
Breen, Steve. *Pug and Doug*
Brown, Don. *Odd boy out*
Brown, Peter. *My teacher is a monster! (no, I am not)*
Cottle, Joan. *Miles away from home*
Cuyler, Margery. *Skeleton for dinner*
Falconer, Ian. *Olivia the spy*
Henkes, Kevin. *Kitten's first full moon*
Horowitz, Ruth. *Are we still friends?*
Light, Kelly. *Louise and Andie*
Lionni, Leo. *Fish is fish*
Mayer, Marianna. *The prince and the pauper*
Mayer, Mercer. *Bun Bun's birthday*
Meisel, Paul. *Good night, bat! good morning, squirrel!*
Rosenberg, Liz. *What James said*
Ross, Tony. *I didn't do it!*
Salley, Coleen. *Epossumondas*
Shannon, David. *The rain came down*
Sharmat, Marjorie Weinman. *Gila monsters meet you at the airport*
Simmons, Jane. *Ebb and Flo and the greedy gulls*
Stoeke, Janet Morgan. *A hat for Minerva Louise*
    Minerva Louise
    Minerva Louise at school
Thornhill, Jan. *The rumor*
Waber, Bernard. *Funny, funny Lyle*
Waldron, Kevin. *Mr. Peek and the misunderstanding at the zoo*
Willis, Jeanne. *Gorilla! Gorilla!*
Yorinks, Arthur. *Company's coming*
Young, Ed. *Donkey trouble*

Behavior – name calling

Clanton, Ben. *Vote for me!*
Eaton, Maxwell. *Two dumb ducks*
Luthardt, Kevin. *You're weird!*

Behavior – naughty *see* Behavior – misbehavior

Behavior – needing someone

Aardema, Verna. *The lonely lioness and the ostrich chicks*
Alborough, Jez. *Hug*
Aruego, José. *Weird friends*
Austin, Margot. *A friend for Growl Bear*
Birtha, Becky. *Far apart, close in heart*
Boase, Susan. *Lucky boy*
Cabrera, Jane. *The lonesome polar bear*
Casanova, Mary. *Utterly otterly day*
Chichester Clark, Emma. *I love you, Blue Kangaroo!*
Crimi, Carolyn. *Don't need friends*
Folgueira, Rodrigo. *Ribbit!*
Godard, Alex. *Mama, across the sea*
Goodhart, Pippa. *Pudgy, a puppy to love*
Jonell, Lynne. *Bravemole*
    Mom pie
Keats, Ezra Jack. *Louie's search*
Lewis, Kim. *Emma's lamb*
Lottridge, Celia Barker. *Berta, a remarkable dog*
McAllister, Angela. *The little blue rabbit*
McBratney, Sam. *Once there was a Hoodie*
McCormick, Wendy. *Daddy, will you miss me?*
McGuirk, Leslie. *Snail boy*
McPhail, David. *Emma's pet*
Meggs, Libby Phillips. *Go home!*
Pearson, Julie. *Elliot*
Peet, Bill. *Zella, Zack, and Zodiac*
Pelton, Mindy L. *When Dad's at sea*
Robertson, M. P. *The egg*
Rudge, Leila. *A perfect place for Ted*
Schneider, Christine M. *Horace P. Tuttle, magician extraordinaire*
Scott, Ann Herbert. *On mother's lap*
Seeber, Dorothea P. *A pup just for me . . . A boy just for me*
Sendak, Maurice. *Very far away*
Smith, Maggie. *Paisley*
Sperring, Mark. *I'll catch you if you fall*
Sterling, Cheryl. *Some bunny to talk to*
Thompson, Colin. *Unknown*
Tibo, Gilles. *The grand journey of Mr. Man*
Tokuda, Wendy. *Humphrey the lost whale*
Turnbull, Victoria. *Pandora*
Viorst, Judith. *Nobody here but me*
Wells, Rosemary. *McDuff moves in*
    Noisy Nora
Wenxuan, Cao. *Feather*
Wheeler, Lisa. *Porcupining*
Wilhelm, Hans. *Schnitzel's first Christmas*
Williams, Vera B. *Home at last*
Wyeth, Sharon Dennis. *Always my dad*

Behavior – potty training *see* Toilet training

Behavior – promptness, tardiness

Axelrod, Amy. *Pigs on a blanket*
Burningham, John. *John Patrick Norman McHennessy — the boy who was always late*
Cali, Davide. *A funny thing happened on the way to school . . .*
Calmenson, Stephanie. *Late for school!*
Edwards, Pamela Duncan. *The grumpy morning*
Egan, Kate. *Kate and Nate are running late!*

Gregory, Nan. *Amber waiting*
Hines, Anna Grossnickle. *What Joe saw*
Hutchins, Pat. *Little pink pig*
Lachtman, Ofelia Dumas. *Pepita takes time / Pepita, siempre tarde*
Perl, Erica S. *Totally tardy Marty*
Reiss, Mike. *Late for school*
Ross, Tony. *Our Kid*
Sykes, Julie. *Hurry, Santa!*
Teague, Mark. *The secret shortcut*

Behavior – resourcefulness

Boelts, Maribeth. *Happy like soccer*
Bouler, Olivia. *Olivia's birds*
Breen, Steve. *Violet the pilot*
Brown, Monica. *Maya's blanket*
Cabrera, Jane. *There was an old woman who lived in a shoe*
Cali, Davide. *I didn't do my homework because . . .*
Chapman, Jared. *Pirate, Viking, and Scientist*
Chase, Kit. *Oliver's tree*
Divakaruni, Chitra Banerjee. *Grandma and the great gourd*
Drummond, Allan. *Green city*
Engle, Margarita. *All the way to Havana*
Foreman, Michael. *Fortunately, unfortunately*
Geisert, Arthur. *The giant seed*
Hakte, Ben. *Julia's house for lost creatures*
Hayes, Sarah. *Lucy Anna and the Finders*
Heine, Theresa. *Chandra's magic light*
Hood, Susan. *The fix-it man*
Hopkinson, Deborah. *Steamboat school*
Imai, Ayano. *Puss and boots*
Juster, Norton. *Neville*
Kamkwamba, William. *The boy who harnessed the wind*
Keller, Holly. *Help!*
Latimer, Alex. *Penguin's hidden talent*
Layton, Neal. *Hot, hot, hot*
McAllister, Angela. *Trust me, Mom!*
Macaulay, David. *How machines work: zoo break!*
McBrier, Page. *Beatrice's goat*
McKee, David. *Elmer and the flood*
McMillan, Bruce. *How the ladies stopped the wind*
The problem with chickens
Marshall, Linda Elovitz. *Rainbow weaver / Tejedora del arcoíris*
Medina, Meg. *Tía Isa wants a car*
Meisel, Paul. *Zara's hats*
Ørdal, Stina Langlo. *Princess Aasta*
Paul, Alison. *The plan*
Perrow, Angeli. *Sirius, the dog star*
Phi, Bao. *A different pond*
Phillipps, J. C. *Monkey Ono*
Pryor, Katherine. *Zora's zucchini*
Rayner, Catherine. *Ernest, the moose who doesn't fit*
Rees, Douglas. *Jeannette Claus saves Christmas*
Reynolds, Peter H. *Going places*
Robinson, Michelle. *A beginner's guide to bear spotting*
Rosenthal, Amy Krouse. *Yes Day!*
Rudge, Leila. *Gary*
Sauer, Tammi. *Nugget and Fang*
Singleton, Linda Joy. *Snow dog, sand dog*
Spires, Ashley. *The most magnificent thing*
Stohner, Anu. *Brave Charlotte*
Stuve-Bodeen, Stephanie. *A small brown dog with a wet pink nose*

Van Dusen, Chris. *Randy Riley's really big hit*
Wilson, Troy. *Liam takes a stand*
Woollvin, Bethan. *Little Red*
Yoon, Salina. *Penguin's Christmas wish*
Young, Cybèle. *A few blocks*
Some things I've lost
Zapf, Marlena. *Underpants dance*

Behavior – rumors *see* Behavior – gossip, rumors

Behavior – running away

Ahlberg, Allan. *The runaway dinner*
Alexander, Martha G. *And my mean old mother will be sorry, Blackboard Bear*
Allen, Elanna. *Itsy Mitsy runs away*
Apple, Sam. *The saddest toilet in the world*
Bailey, Linda. *Stanley's wild ride*
Barton, Byron. *The wee little woman*
Bogan, Paulette. *Lulu the big little chick*
Brett, Jan. *Home for Christmas*
Brown, Margaret Wise. *The runaway bunny*
Brunhoff, Jean de. *The story of Babar, the little elephant*
Bunting, Eve. *Emma's turtle*
Cadow, Kenneth M. *Alfie runs away*
Chichester Clark, Emma. *Piper*
Christelow, Eileen. *The great pig escape*
The great pig search
Coh, Smiljana. *Princesses on the run*
Cotterill, Samantha. *No more bows*
Davies, Gill. *Can't, don't, won't*
Durand, Hallie. *Catch that cookie!*
Dyer, Heather. *Tina and the penguin*
Eaton, Jason Carter. *The day my runny nose ran away*
Edwards, Pamela Duncan. *Barefoot: escape on the Underground Railroad*
Ernst, Lisa Campbell. *The Gingerbread Girl goes animal crackers*
Fearnley, Jan. *Martha in the middle*
Fleming, Denise. *Buster*
Freeman, Don. *Beady Bear*
Garland, Michael. *Last night at the zoo*
The gingerbread boy. *Can't catch me*
Gingerbread baby
The gingerbread boy, ill. by Emily Bolam
The gingerbread boy, ill. by Richard Egielski
The gingerbread boy, ill. by Paul Galdone
The Gingerbread Cowboy
The gingerbread girl
The gingerbread man, ill. by Carol Jones
The gingerbread man, ill. by Megan Lloyd
The gingerbread man, ill. by Barbara McClintock
The gingerbread man, ill. by Béatrice Rodriguez
The Gingerbread Man loose in the school
The Gingerbread Man loose on the fire truck
The Library Gingerbread Man
The pancake boy
Señorita Gordita
Whiff, sniff, nibble and chew
Goodhart, Pippa. *Pudgy, a puppy to love*
Grant, Jacob. *Through with the zoo*
Hänel, Wolfram. *Little elephant runs away*
Harrison, David L. *Piggy Wiglet*
Hernandez, Leeza. *Dog gone!*
Hoban, Russell. *A baby sister for Frances*

Horse, Harry. *Little Rabbit runaway*
Howland, Naomi. *The matzah man*
Huget, Jennifer LaRue. *The beginner's guide to running away from home*
Ichikawa, Satomi. *I am Pangoo the penguin*
Imai, Ayano. *Chester*
Jagtenberg, Yvonne. *Jack's rabbit*
Johnson, Angela. *The day Ray got away*
Johnston, Lynn. *Farley follows his nose*
Kenah, Katharine. *Ferry tail*
Kimmel, Eric A. *The runaway tortilla*
   The three little tamales
Kimmelman, Leslie. *The runaway latkes*
Kraus, Robert. *Where are you going, little mouse?*
Lindgren, Barbro. *Benny's had enough*
Lloyd, Sam. *Mr. Pusskins*
Lobel, Gillian. *Does anybody love me?*
Long, Kathy. *The runaway shopping cart*
McCully, Emily Arnold. *My real family*
McDonnell, Patrick. *The little red cat who ran away and learned his ABC's (the hard way)*
McHenry, E. B. *Has anyone seen Winnie and Jean?*
Macomber, Debbie. *The yippy, yappy Yorkie in the green doggy sweater*
Martín Larrañaga, Ana. *Woo! the not-so-scary Ghost*
Massini, Sarah. *Trixie ten*
Meade, Holly. *John Willy and Freddy McGee*
Moss, Miriam. *Smudge's grumpy day*
Munsch, Robert N. *Aaron's hair*
Murray, Andrew. *Have you seen Chester?*
Ohi, Ruth. *And you can come too*
O'Malley, Kevin. *Little Buggy runs away*
Peet, Bill. *Pamela Camel*
Rand, Betseygail. *Big Bunny*
Rex, Michael. *Runaway mummy*
Rosen, Michael. *Crow and Hawk*
Rosenberry, Vera. *Vera runs away*
Rostoker-Gruber, Karen. *Bandit*
Roth, Susan L. *Cinnamon's day out*
Savage, Stephen. *Where's Walrus?*
   Where's Walrus? and Penguin?
Scieszka, Jon. *Walt Disney's Alice in Wonderland*
Segal, John. *Far far away!*
Sendak, Maurice. *Very far away*
Shulman, Goldie. *Way too much challah dough*
Slangerup, Erik Jon. *Dirt Boy*
Steig, William. *Zeke Pippin*
Stevens, Janet. *And the dish ran away with the spoon*
   My big dog
Sykes, Julie. *I don't want to take a bath!*
Tsurumi, Andrea. *Accident!*
Urbanovic, Jackie. *Duck and cover*
Van Laan, Nancy. *Little baby Bobby*
Villeneuve, Anne. *Loula is leaving for Africa*
Voake, Charlotte. *Ginger*
Waber, Bernard. *A lion named Shirley Williamson*
Waddell, Martin. *Bee frog*
Wahl, Jan. *Mabel ran away with the toys*
Weeks, Sarah. *Oh my gosh, Mrs. McNosh!*
Wojtowycz, David. *A cuddle for Claude*
Yorinks, Arthur. *Hey, Al*
Zion, Gene. *Harry, the dirty dog*

Behavior – saving things

Carlson, Nancy. *Start saving, Henry!*
Child, Lauren. *But I've used all my pocket change*
Perez, Monica. *Curious George saves his pennies*

Behavior – secrets

Aardema, Verna. *What's so funny, Ketu?*
Allard, Harry. *Miss Nelson has a field day*
Asch, Frank. *Mrs. Marlowe's mice*
Bang, Molly. *Dawn*
Battut, Éric. *Little Mouse's big secret*
Brandt, Lois. *Maddi's fridge*
Coombs, Kate. *The secret-keeper*
Falconer, Ian. *Olivia the spy*
Farley, Carol J. *The king's secret*
Freeman, Tor. *Olive and the big secret*
George, Kallie. *Secrets I know*
George, Lindsay Barrett. *The secret*
Gray, Kes. *006 and a half*
Griffin, Kitty. *Cowboy Sam and those confounded secrets*
Heide, Florence Parry. *The day of Ahmed's secret*
Hines, Anna Grossnickle. *The secret keeper*
Jarvis , Peter. *Alan's big, scary teeth*
Kang, Anna. *Can I tell you a secret?*
Kelley, True. *Blabber Mouse*
Lehman, Barbara. *The secret box*
Naylor, Phyllis Reynolds. *Keeping a Christmas secret*
Polacco, Patricia. *The butterfly*
Rappaport, Doreen. *The long-haired girl*
Riggio, Anita. *Secret signs*
San Souci, Robert D. *The snow wife*
Schoenherr, Ian. *Don't spill the beans!*
Winter, Jeanette. *Nasreen's secret school*

Behavior – seeking better things

Adler, David A. *A picture book of Cesar Chavez*
Alter, Anna. *What can you do with an old red shoe?*
Altman, Linda Jacobs. *Amelia's road*
Asim, Jabari. *Fifty cents and a dream*
Bradby, Marie. *More than anything else*
Buckley, Richard. *The foolish tortoise*
Buitrago, Jairo. *Two white rabbits*
DiPucchio, Kelly. *Grace for president*
Drummond, Allan. *Green city*
Feiffer, Kate. *President Pennybaker*
Hamilton, Virginia. *Jaguarundi*
Hopkinson, Deborah. *Sweet Clara and the freedom quilt*
Kimmel, Elizabeth Cody. *A taste of freedom*
Kraus, Robert. *Where are you going, little mouse?*
Lionni, Leo. *Tillie and the wall*
McBrier, Page. *Beatrice's goat*
McGinty, Alice B. *Gandhi*
McPhail, David. *Weezer changes the world*
Markel, Michelle. *Brave girl*
Martin, Jacqueline Briggs. *Farmer Will Allen and the growing table*
Milway, Katie Smith. *One hen*
Mortenson, Greg. *Listen to the wind*
Myers, Walter Dean. *Looking for the easy life*
Odone, Jamison. *Mole had everything*
Parish, Herman. *Amelia Bedelia's first vote*
Paul, Miranda. *One plastic bag*
Proimos, James. *Paulie Pastrami achieves world peace*
Richards, Doyin. *What's the difference? being different is amazing*
Sanna, Francesca. *The journey*
Schrock, Jan West. *Give a goat*
Shulevitz, Uri. *How I learned geography*
Slade, Suzanne. *Dangerous Jane*
Smith, Lane. *Madam President*
Spinelli, Eileen. *Peace Week in Miss Fox's class*

Stone, Tanya Lee. *Elizabeth leads the way*
  The house that Jane built
Warren, Sarah. *Dolores Huerta*
Weatherford, Carole Boston. *Be a King: Dr. Martin Luther King Jr.'s dream and you*
Wells, Rosemary. *Otto runs for President*
  Otto se presenta para presidente / Otto runs for President
Williams, Vera B. *A chair for my mother*
Winter, Jeanette. *Malala, a brave girl from Pakistan / Iqbal, a brave boy from Pakistan*
Yolen, Jane. *Naming Liberty*
Yousafzai, Malala. *Malala's magic pencil*

Behavior – sharing

Aesop. *Smog, the city dog*
Alexander, Martha G. *I'll never share you, Blackboard Bear*
Antony, Steve. *Please, Mr. Panda*
Arnold, Katya. *That apple is mine!*
Ashman, Linda. *William's winter nap*
Backx, Patsy. *Josie and Mr. Fernandez*
Bardhan-Quallen, Sudipta. *The Mine-o-saur*
Battut, Éric. *Little Mouse's big secret*
Beaumont, Karen. *Move over, Rover*
Benjamin, A. H. *Mouse, mole and the falling star*
Berger, Samantha. *Martha doesn't share!*
Bergmann, Andy. *The starry giraffe*
Bernstein, Ariel. *I have a balloon*
Blabey, Aaron. *Pig the pug*
Blegvad, Lenore. *First friends*
Boldt, Claudia. *Odd dog*
Bosca, Francesca. *The apple king*
Brett, Jan. *Christmas trolls*
Bright, Rachel. *Love Monster and the last chocolate*
Bryant, Jen. *Abe's fish*
Burks, James. *Pigs and a blanket*
Cameron, C. C. *One for me, one for you*
Caudill, Rebecca. *A pocketful of cricket*
Chaconas, Dori. *Looking for Easter*
Claire, Céline. *Shelter*
Cohen, Caron Lee. *Digger Pig and the turnip*
Cohen, Miriam. *Don't eat too much turkey!*
Cole, Joanna. *Sharing is fun*
Costa, Nicoletta. *The little tree that would not share*
Cote, Nancy. *It feels like snow*
Cousins, Lucy. *Maisy makes lemonade*
Crum, Shutta. *Mine!*
Deacon, Alexis. *Cheese belongs to you!*
Deedman, Heidi. *Too many toys!*
deGroat, Diane. *Last one in is a rotten egg!*
Demi. *The shady tree*
dePaola, Tomie. *Look and be grateful*
Devlin, Wende. *Cranberry Christmas*
Dewdney, Anna. *Llama Llama time to share*
Dickson, Irene. *Blocks*
Dunbar, Joyce. *The very small*
Dunbar, Polly. *Happy Hector*
Ehlert, Lois. *Top cat*
Emberley, Ed. *The red hen*
Farrell, Darren. *Stop following me, Moon!*
Forest, Heather. *Stone soup*
Forward, Toby. *Ben's Christmas carol*
Freeman, Tor. *Olive and the bad mood*
Galdone, Paul. *The magic porridge pot*
Garland, Sally Anne. *Share*
Garton, Sam. *Otter loves Easter!*
Gehl, Laura. *One big pair of underwear*

The gingerbread boy. *The Gingerbread Man loose at Christmas*
Goodhart, Pippa. *My very own space*
Graegin, Stephanie. *Little fox in the forest*
Gravett, Emily. *Bear and Hare: share!*
Grimm, Jacob and Wilhelm. *The star child*
Grindley, Sally. *Can we play too, Piglittle?*
Hamilton, Richard. *Polly's picnic*
Hawcock, Claire. *Mine, all mine!*
Heap, Sue. *Mine!*
Henkes, Kevin. *Sheila Rae's peppermint stick*
Henn, Sophy. *Pass it on*
Himmelman, John. *Katie and the puppy next door*
Hoberman, Mary Ann. *One of each*
Horáček, Petr. *Jonathan and Martha*
Hutchins, Pat. *The doorbell rang*
  It's my birthday!
Jin, Susie Lee. *Mine!*
Kang, Anna. *That's not mine*
Keats, Ezra Jack. *Peter's chair*
Ketteman, Helen. *Armadilly chili*
Kirk, Daniel. *You are not my friend, but I miss you*
Kirsch, Vincent X. *Forsythia and me*
Kortepeter, Paul. *Oliver's red toboggan*
Kroll, Steven. *Jungle bullies*
Landa, Norbert. *Little Bear and the wishing tree*
LaReau, Kara. *Ugly fish*
Lester, Helen. *All for me and none for all*
Lindgren, Barbro. *Sam's car*
  Sam's cookie
Lister, Mary. *The Winter King and the Summer Queen*
The little red hen. *The little red hen*, ill. by Byron Barton
  The little red hen, ill. by Emily Bolam
  The little red hen, ill. by Paul Galdone
  Little red hen
  The little red hen, ill. by Jerry Pinkney
  The little red hen, ill. by Kate Slater
  The little red hen, ill. by Annie West
  The little red hen, ill. by Margot Zemach
  The little red hen: an old fable
  The Little Red Hen and the Passover matzah
  The Little Red Hen makes a pizza
Litwin, Eric. *Groovy Joe: ice cream and dinosaurs*
Luthardt, Kevin. *Mine*
McDaniels, Preston. *A perfect snowman*
McKissack, Patricia C. *The all-I'll-ever-want Christmas doll*
Martin, David. *All for pie, pie for all*
Martins, Isabel Minhós. *Little lamb, have you any wool?*
Masurel, Claire. *Christmas is coming*
Medina, Tony. *Christmas makes me think*
Meserve, Adria. *No room for Napoleon*
Messner, Kate. *How to read a story*
Miller, Pat Zietlow. *Sharing the bread*
Mills, Lauren A. *The rag coat*
Miyares, Daniel. *Pardon me!*
Moss, Miriam. *It's my turn, Smudge*
Munsch, Robert N. *We share everything!*
Murphy, Stuart J. *Give me half!*
  Let's fly a kite
  Seaweed soup
Muth, Jon J. *Zen socks*
Nakagawa, Rieko. *Guri and Gura*
  Guri and Gura's special gift
Nanji, Shenaaz. *Treasure for lunch*
Oram, Hiawyn. *My friend Fred*
Orloff, Karen Kaufman. *I wanna new room*

Pacilio, V. J. *Ling Cho and his three friends*
Parenteau, Shirley. *Bears in the snow*
  Bears on chairs
Parkinson, Kathy. *The enormous turnip*
Paschkis, Julie. *Mooshka*
Patten, Brian. *The big snuggle-up*
Peck, Jan. *The giant carrot*
Perlman, Janet. *The delicious bug*
Pfister, Marcus. *The rainbow fish*
Pienkowski, Jan. *Bel and Bub and the big brown box*
Pinder, Eric. *How to share with a bear*
Pinkwater, Daniel. *Bear in love*
Proimos, James. *Paulie Pastrami achieves world peace*
Ransome, James. *New red bike!*
Rathmann, Peggy. *Officer Buckle and Gloria*
Rayner, Catherine. *The bear who shared*
Rockliff, Mara. *Chik chak Shabbat*
  My heart will not sit down
Rosen, Michael. *This is our house*
Rosenthal, Amy Krouse. *Plant a kiss*
Rostoker-Gruber, Karen. *Bandit's surprise*
Russo, Marisabina. *The big brown box*
Ruzzier, Sergio. *Bear and Bee*
Rylant, Cynthia. *Birthday presents*
Sasso, Sandy Eisenberg. *God said amen*
Savadier, Elivia. *Will Sheila share?*
Sawyer, Ruth. *The remarkable Christmas of the cobbler's sons*
Schmid, Paul. *Peanut and Fifi have a ball*
Seeger, Laura Vaccaro. *What if?*
Shannon, George. *Rabbit's gift*
Simmons, Jane. *Ebb and Flo and the new friend*
Siomades, Lorianne. *A place to bloom*
Smallman, Steve. *The very greedy bee*
Smalls-Hector, Irene. *Because you're lucky*
Smith, Monique Gray. *You hold me up*
Spelman, Cornelia Maude. *When I care about others*
Spinelli, Eileen. *Thanksgiving at the Tappletons'*
Stein, Mathilde. *Mine!*
Stewart, Paul. *The birthday presents*
Stoop, Naoko. *Red Knit Cap Girl and the reading tree*
Sullivan, Mary. *Frankie*
Tankard, Jeremy. *Hungry Bird*
Taylor, Thomas. *Little Mouse and the big cupcake*
Thayer, Jane. *Part-time dog*
Toscano, Charles. *Papa's pastries*
Trimmer, Christian. *Simon's new bed*
Valentine, Madeline. *I want that nut!*
van Lieshout, Maria. *Tumble!*
Vere, Ed. *Banana!*
Waldman, Debby. *Room enough for Daisy*
Weninger, Brigitte. *Merry Christmas, Davy!*
Willems, Mo. *The duckling gets a cookie!?*
Williams, Karen Lynn. *Four feet, two sandals*
Wilson, Karma. *Bear says thanks*
Wolff, Ferida. *The story blanket*
Wood, Don. *Merry Christmas, big hungry bear*
Yaccarino, Dan. *Happyland: birthday cake*
Yim, Natasha. *Goldy Luck and the three pandas*
Young, Ed. *The cat from Hunger Mountain*
Yum, Hyewon. *The twins' blanket*
Ziefert, Harriet. *Be fair, share!*

Behavior – showing off *see* Behavior – boasting, showing off

Behavior – solitude

Asher, Sandy. *Too many frogs!*
Bloom, Suzanne. *Alone together*
Brosgol, Vera. *Leave me alone!*
Davies, Benji. *The storm whale*
  The storm whale in winter
Doyle, Malachy. *Too noisy!*
Frith, Nicholas John. *Hector and Hummingbird*
Goodhart, Pippa. *My very own space*
Guion, Melissa. *Baby penguins everywhere!*
Horáček, Petr. *Look out, Suzy Goose*
Lemniscates. *Silence*
McKee, David. *Elmer and the flood*
Sif, Birgitta. *Oliver*
Underwood, Deborah. *The quiet book*
van Lieshout, Elle. *The wish*

Behavior – stealing

Ada, Alma Flor. *The gold coin*
Ahlberg, Janet. *Jeremiah in the dark wood*
Alborough, Jez. *It's the bear*
Amado, Elisa. *Tricycle*
Arabian Nights *The tale of Ali Baba and the forty thieves*
Barton, Byron. *The wee little woman*
Beaver steals fire
Biddulph, Rob. *The grizzly bear who lost his grrrrr!*
Brett, Jan. *Christmas trolls*
Bromley, Anne C. *The lunch thief*
Carlson, Nancy. *Loudmouth George and the sixth-grade bully*
Davies, Nicola. *The promise*
dePaola, Tomie. *Bill and Pete go down the Nile*
Devlin, Wende. *Cranberry Halloween*
The firebird. *The firebird*, ill. by Demi
  The firebird, ill. by Rachel Isadora
  The tale of the firebird
Hancocks, Helen. *Penguin in peril*
Hennessy, B. G. *The missing tarts*
Khing, T. T. *Where is the cake?*
  Where is the cake now?
MacDonald, Margaret Read. *Tunjur! Tunjur! Tunjur!*
Pinkwater, Daniel. *Bad bear detectives*
Vere, Ed. *The getaway*
Watts, Bernadette. *The golden plate*
Weigelt, Udo. *It wasn't me*
  Who stole the gold?
Yolen, Jane. *Piggins*

Behavior – talking to strangers

Berenstain, Stan and Jan. *The Berenstain bears learn about strangers*
Ernst, Lisa Campbell. *Little Red Riding Hood: a newfangled prairie tale*
Grimm, Jacob and Wilhelm. *Little red cap*
  Little Red Riding Hood, ill. by Célia Chauffrey
  Little Red Riding Hood, ill. by Gwen Connelly
  Little Red Riding Hood, ill. by Trina Schart Hyman
  Little Red Riding Hood, ill. by Jerry Pinkney
  Little Red Riding Hood, ill. by Gennady Spirin
  Little Red Riding Hood, ill. by Bernadette Watts
  Little Red Riding Hood, ill. by Andrea Wisnewski
  The story of Little Red Riding Hood
Heapy, Teresa. *Very little Red Riding Hood*
Kaczman, James. *A bird and his worm*

Kevi. *Don't talk to strangers*
Marshall, James. *Red Riding Hood*
Potter, Beatrix. *The tale of Little Pig Robinson*
Schwartz, Corey Rosen. *Ninja Red Riding Hood*
Wood, Audrey. *Heckedy Peg*
Woollvin, Bethan. *Little Red*

Behavior – tardiness *see* Behavior – promptness, tardiness

Behavior – teasing *see* Behavior – bullying, teasing

Behavior – toilet training *see* Toilet training

Behavior – trickery

Aardema, Verna. *Anansi finds a fool*
 Borreguita and the coyote
 Jackal's flying lesson
 Rabbit makes a monkey of lion
Aesop. *The boy who cried wolf*
 The donkey in the lion's skin
 Fox tails
 Three Aesop fox fables
 The wolf in sheep's clothing
Alexander, Lloyd. *The house Gobbaleen*
Barton, Chris. *That's not Bunny!*
Bateman, Teresa. *Keeper of soles*
Beaver steals fire
Bently, Peter. *The great sheep shenanigans*
Bernstrom, Daniel. *One day in the eucalyptus, eucalyptus tree*
Blackaby, Susan. *Brownie Groundhog and the February Fox*
Brown, Marc. *Arthur tricks the tooth fairy*
Browning, Robert. *The pied piper of Hamelin*, ill. by Mercer Mayer
 The pied piper of Hamelin, ill. by Drahos Zak
Burdett, Lois. *Twelfth night for kids*
Burningham, John. *Tug-of-war*
Campoy, F. Isabel. *Rosa Raposa*
Chicken Little. *Brave Chicken Little*
 Chicken Little
 Henny Penny, ill. by Emily Bolam
 Henny Penny, ill. by Paul Galdone
 Henny-Penny, ill. by Jane Wattenberg
 Henny Penny, ill. by Sophie Windham
 The sky is falling
Christelow, Eileen. *Five little monkeys trick-or-treat*
Crummel, Susan Stevens. *Tumbleweed stew*
Daly, Niki. *Pretty Salma*
Davis, David. *Fandango stew*
DeFelice, Cynthia C. *Cold feet*
DeSpain, Pleasant. *The dancing turtle*
Divakaruni, Chitra Banerjee. *Grandma and the great gourd*
Emberley, Rebecca. *Chicken Little*
 The crocodile and the scorpion
Friend, Catherine. *The perfect nest*
Goble, Paul. *Iktomi and the buffalo skull*
 Iktomi and the buzzard
 Iktomi and the coyote
 Iktomi and the ducks
Greene, Rhonda Gowler. *Eek! creak! snicker, sneak*
Hausman, Gerald. *Coyote walks on two legs*

Helmer, Marilyn. *Three tales of trickery*
Hennessy, B. G. *The boy who cried wolf*
Janisch, Heinz. *The merry pranks of Till Eulenspiegel*
Johnson, Paul Brett. *Jack outwits the giants*
Johnston, Tony. *The badger and the magic fan*
Kasbarian, Lucine. *The greedy sparrow*
Kasza, Keiko. *My lucky birthday*
Kellogg, Steven. *Chicken Little*
Kelly, Mij. *One more sheep*
Kimmel, Eric A. *Anansi and the moss-covered rock*
 Anansi and the talking melon
 Anansi goes fishing
 Anansi's party time
Knapman, Timothy. *Can't catch me!*
Knutson, Barbara. *Love and roast chicken*
Kraus, Robert. *Come out and play, little mouse*
Krause, Ute. *Oscar and the very hungry dragon*
Latimer, Alex. *Lion vs Rabbit*
Leroy, Jean. *A well-mannered young wolf*
McCaughrean, Geraldine. *One bright Penny*
McDermott, Gerald. *Jabutí the tortoise*
 Monkey
 Pig-Boy
 Raven
 Tim O'Toole and the wee folk
 Zomo the rabbit
MacDonald, Amy. *Please, Malese!*
MacDonald, Margaret Read. *Conejito*
 Pickin' peas
McGuinness-Kelly, Tracy-Lee. *Bad Cat puts on his top hat*
McKee, David. *Elmer and Snake*
Mahy, Margaret. *The great white man-eating shark*
Martin, Bill, Jr.. *Trick or treat?*
Miller, John. *Winston and George*
Mollel, Tololwa M. *Ananse's feast*
 The flying tortoise
Mora, Pat. *The race of toad and deer*
Morales, Yuyi. *Just a minute: a trickster tale and counting book*
 Just in case: a trickster tale and Spanish alphabet book
Munsch, Robert N. *Mmm, cookies!*
Nadimi, Suzan. *The rich man and the parrot*
Niemann, Christoph. *The potato king*
Oram, Hiawyn. *Baba Yaga and the wise doll*
Pauli, Lorenz. *The fox in the library*
Potter, Beatrix. *The pie and the patty-pan*
 The story of Miss Moppet
Rocco, John. *Wolf! wolf!*
Root, Phyllis. *Aunt Nancy and Old Man Trouble*
Ross, Tony. *The boy who cried wolf*
San Souci, Robert D. *Feathertop*
Scott, Nathan Kumar. *Mangoes and bananas*
 The sacred banana leaf
Shannon, Margaret. *Gullible's troubles*
Shea, Bob. *Cheetah can't lose*
Singleton, Debbie. *The king who wouldn't sleep*
Smith, Alex T. *Foxy and Egg*
Snyder, Dianne. *The boy of the three-year nap*
Souhami, Jessica. *Foxy!*
 No dinner!
Steig, William. *Solomon the rusty nail*
Stevens, Janet. *Tops and bottoms*
Stevenson, James. *Emma*
 Fried feathers for Thanksgiving
Strete, Craig Kee. *How the Indians bought the farm*
Subramaniam, Manasi. *The fox and the crow*
Sunami, Kitoba. *How the fisherman tricked the genie*

Taylor, Sean. *The grizzly bear with the frizzly hair*
Teague, Mark. *The sky is falling!*
Temple, Frances. *Tiger soup*
Tingle, Tim. *When Turtle grew feathers*
Turkle, Brinton. *Do not open*
Twohy, Mike. *Outfoxed*
Willems, Mo. *That is not a good idea!*
Yep, Laurence. *The man who tricked a ghost*
Young, Ed. *Monkey King*

Behavior – unnoticed, unseen

Bridges, Shirin Yim. *Mary Wrightly, so politely*
Ludwig, Trudy. *The invisible boy*
Rudge, Leila. *A perfect place for Ted*
Scott, Ann Herbert. *Hi!*

Behavior – wishing

Addy, Sharon Hart. *When wishes were horses*
Allard, Harry. *Starlight goes to town*
Aman, Kimiko. *The fox wish*
Barnett, Mac. *The magic word*
Base, Graeme. *Jungle drums*
Baumgart, Klaus. *Laura's secret*
Brett, Jan. *Fritz and the beautiful horses*
Brown, Margaret Wise. *The fierce yellow pumpkin*
Callahan, Sean. *Shannon and the world's tallest leprechaun*
Cleminson, Katie. *Magic box*
Clifton, Lucille. *Three wishes*
Conahan, Carolyn. *The big wish*
Cordell, Matthew. *Wish*
Davis, Aubrey. *Kishka for Koppel*
DiPucchio, Kelly. *Dog days of school*
Dyckman, Ame. *You don't want a unicorn!*
Ellwand, David. *Midas Mouse*
Fagan, Cary. *Ella May and the wishing stone*
Foley, Greg. *Make a wish Bear*
  Willoughby and the lion
Fox, Mem. *Possum magic*
Geras, Adèle. *My wishes for you*
Hächler, Bruno. *Anna's wish*
Heidbreder, Robert. *I wished for a unicorn*
Holub, Joan. *Twinkle, star of the week*
Horn, Sandra Ann. *The dandelion wish*
Howe, James. *I wish I were a butterfly*
Hru, Dakari. *Joshua's Masai mask*
Jackson, Shirley. *9 magic wishes*
Kimmel, Eric A. *Joha makes a wish*
Kirk, Daniel. *Jack and Jill*
Kleven, Elisa. *The wishing ball*
Klinting, Lars. *What do you want?*
Krensky, Stephen. *The youngest fairy godmother ever*
Landa, Norbert. *Little Bear and the wishing tree*
Lesynski, Loris. *Rocksy*
Lipp, Frederick. *The caged birds of Phnom Penh*
McClintock, Barbara. *Molly and the magic wishbone*
McGrory, Anik. *Mouton's impossible dream*
Maclear, Kyo. *The wish tree*
Magerl, Caroline. *Rose and the wish thing*
Meddaugh, Susan. *The witch's walking stick*
Meschenmoser, Sebastian. *Pug Man's 3 wishes*
Michelin, Linda. *Zuzu's wishing cake*
Morgan, Michaela. *Bunny wishes*
Moser, Lisa. *Watermelon wishes*
Munsch, Robert N. *Wait and see*
Murphy, Mary. *Caterpillar's wish*
Napoli, Donna Jo. *The wishing club*

Newman, Marlene. *Myron's magic cow*
Nolen, Jerdine. *Irene's wish*
Petty, Dini. *The queen, the bear and the bumblebee*
Pfister, Marcus. *Make a wish, Honey Bear!*
Pizzoli, Greg. *Templeton gets his wish*
Polacco, Patricia. *Luba and the wren*
Primavera, Elise. *The house at the end of Ladybug Lane*
Proimos, James. *Joe's wish*
Pulver, Robin. *Alicia's tutu*
Puttock, Simon. *A ladder to the stars*
Reynolds, Peter H. *The smallest gift of Christmas*
Robertson, M. P. *The sandcastle*
Rock, Lois. *I wish tonight*
Rose, Marion. *The Christmas tree fairy*
Rosenthal, Amy Krouse. *I wish you more*
  Yes Day!
Roth, Susan L. *Happy birthday Mr. Kang*
Shepard, Aaron. *The gifts of Wali Dad*
Shields, Carol Diggory. *I wish my brother was a dog*
Souhami, Jessica. *Sausages*
Stanley, Diane. *The trouble with wishes*
Stevenson, James. *The wish card ran out!*
Tan, Amy. *The moon lady*
Thong, Roseanne. *Wish: wishing traditions around the world*
Tobias, Tobi. *Wishes for you*
Turkle, Brinton. *Do not open*
van Lieshout, Elle. *The wish*
Vigna, Judith. *I wish my daddy didn't drink so much*
Wallace, Ivy. *Pookie puts the world right*
Washington, Ned. *When you wish upon a star*
Wheeler, Lisa. *The Christmas boot*
Whybrow, Ian. *Wish, change, friend*
Williams, Suzanne. *My dog never says please*
Wishinsky, Frieda. *Please, Louise!*
Wood, Audrey. *Jubal's wish*
Wooldridge, Connie Nordhielm. *Wicked Jack*
Zemach, Margot. *The three wishes*
Zoboli, Giovanna. *I wish I had . . .*

Behavior – worrying

Andrews, Julie. *The very fairy princess: graduation girl!*
Arnaldo, Monica. *Margo thinks twice*
Berger, Samantha. *Back to school with Bigfoot*
Birtha, Becky. *Far apart, close in heart*
Borden, Louise. *Off to first grade*
Bourgeois, Paulette. *Franklin says "I love you"*
Brown, Marc. *Arthur's underwear*
  Monkey: not ready for kindergarten
  Monkey: not ready for the baby
Browne, Anthony. *Silly Billy*
  What if . . . ?
Brun-Cosme, Nadine. *Big Wolf and Little Wolf, such a beautiful orange!*
  Daddy long legs
Bunting, Eve. *Yard sale*
Burg, Sarah Emmanuelle. *Do you still love me?*
Cannon, A. E. *Sophie's fish*
Carlstrom, Nancy White. *It's your first day of school, Annie Claire*
Clarke, Jane. *The best of both nests*
Cocca-Leffler, Maryann. *Jack's talent*
Collet, Géraldine. *All by myself!*
Cooper, Helen. *Dog biscuit*
Corey, Dorothy. *You go away*
Cuyler, Margery. *Bullies never win*

Hooray for Reading Day!
Stop drop and roll
Devlin, Wende. *Cranberry Easter*
Diesen, Deborah. *The pout-pout fish goes to school*
Dodd, Emma. *Foxy*
Edwards, Pamela Duncan. *Dinosaur starts school*
The worrywarts
Ehrlich, Nikki. *Twindergarten*
Falconer, Ian. *Olivia the spy*
Foley, Greg. *Don't worry Bear*
Gaiman, Neil. *Chu's first day of school*
Gavril, David. *Penelope Nuthatch and the big surprise*
Gehl, Laura. *Peep and Egg: I'm not hatching*
George, Lucy M. *Back to school Tortoise*
Gordon, Domenica More. *Archie's vacation*
Graves, Keith. *The unexpectedly bad hair of Barcelona Smith*
Griffin, Molly Beth. *Loon baby*
Hartt-Sussman, Heather. *Noni is nervous*
Henkes, Kevin. *Wemberly worried*
Horton, Joan. *Math attack!*
Jackson, Kathryn. *The saggy baggy elephant*
Jacobs, Julie. *My heart is a magic house*
Jadoul, Émile. *Good night, Chickie*
Johnson, Neil. *The falling raindrop*
Kasza, Keiko. *Ready for anything*
Kelley, Marty. *Winter woes*
Kempter, Christa. *When Mama can't sleep*
Klise, Kate. *Little Rabbit and the Night Mare*
Lasky, Kathryn. *Lunch bunnies*
Latimer, Miriam. *Dear Panda*
Leijten, Aileen. *Hugging hour!*
Lester, Helen. *Something might happen*
Lewis, Paeony. *I'll always love you*
Loupy, Christophe. *Don't worry, Wags*
Lyon, Tammie. *Olive and Snowflake*
McCarney, Rosemary. *Where will I live?*
McCarthy, Jenna. *Lola knows a lot*
McCleery, Peter. *Bob and Joss get lost!*
McGinty, Alice B. *Eliza's kindergarten pet*
McPhail, David. *Pig Pig returns*
Mahoney, Daniel J. *Monstergarten*
Mann, Jennifer K. *Sam and Jump*
Marino, Gianna. *Following Papa's song*
Marshall, James. *Portly McSwine*
Millner, Denene. *Early Sunday morning*
Milord, Susan. *Happy school year!*
Montanari, Eva. *A very full morning*
Moss, Miriam. *A babysitter for Billy Bear*
Ohi, Ruth. *A trip with Grandma*
Pennypacker, Sara. *Stuart's cape*
Pett, Mark. *The girl who never made mistakes*
Pizzoli, Greg. *The watermelon seed*
Poydar, Nancy. *The bad-news report card*
The biggest test in the universe
Quackenbush, Robert M. *First grade jitters*
Raschka, Chris. *Waffle*
Ray, Jane. *The dollhouse fairy*
Rex, Adam. *School's first day of school*
Roche, Denis. *Little Pig is capable*
Rylant, Cynthia. *Herbert's first Halloween*
Schiller, Abbie. *When Lyla got lost (and found)*
Scieszka, Jon. *Melvin might?*
Seeger, Laura Vaccaro. *I used to be afraid*
Sher, Emil. *Away*
Spelman, Cornelia Maude. *When I feel worried*
Stadler, Alexander. *Beverly Billingsly borrows a book*
Stead, Philip C. *Samson in the snow*
Stein, Garth. *Enzo's very scary Halloween*

Sterling, Cheryl. *Some bunny to talk to*
Urdahl, Catherine. *Emma's question*
Vernick, Audrey. *Second grade holdout*
Viorst, Judith. *Just in case*
Waddell, Martin. *Mimi's Christmas*
Wagner, Anke. *Tim's big move!*
Waldron, Kevin. *Mr. Peek and the misunderstanding at the zoo*
Weatherford, Carole Boston. *In your hands*
Wells, Rosemary. *Ten kisses for Sophie!*
Whybrow, Ian. *Bella gets her skates on*
Williams, Vera B. *Home at last*
Yaccarino, Dan. *Happyland: rainy day*
Yamada, Kobi. *What do you do with a problem?*
Yin. *Dear Santa, please come to the 19th floor*
Yum, Hyewon. *Mom, it's my first day of kindergarten!*
Zuppardi, Sam. *Jack's worry*

Being different *see* Character traits – being different

Bereavement *see* Death; Emotions – grief

Bible *see* Religion

Bicycling *see* Sports – bicycling

Bigotry *see* Prejudice

Bilingual *see* Foreign languages

Birds

Aardema, Verna. *Jackal's flying lesson*
Adams, Sarah. *Gary and Ray*
Aesop. *Bat's big game*
Feed me!
Aliki. *My visit to the zoo*
Amann, Jürg. *Ten birds*
Anholt, Laurence. *Billy and the big new school*
Two nests
Apperley, Dawn. *Good night, sleep tight, little bunnies*
Arnosky, Jim. *Crinkleroot's 25 birds every child should know*
Mouse writing
Asch, Frank. *Baby Bird's first nest*
Bear's bargain
Moonbear
Moonbear's dream
Moonbear's pet
Mooncake
Aston, Dianna Hutts. *Mama Outside, Mama Inside*
A nest is noisy
Baker, Jeannie. *Circle*
Baker, Keith. *Just how long can a long string be?!*
No two alike
Barnes, Laura T. *Ernest and the big itch*
Barnett, Mac. *Telephone*
Barton, Suzanne. *The sleepy songbird*
Bash, Barbara. *Urban roosts*
Bauer, Marion Dane. *The longest night*
Beck, Scott. *Pepito the brave*
Bender, Rebecca. *Giraffe meets Bird*
Not friends

Berger, Carin. *Forever friends*
Berkes, Marianne. *Marsh music*
Berne, Jennifer. *Calvin can't fly*
    Calvin, look out!
Bonwill, Ann. *I am not a copycat!*
Bouler, Olivia. *Olivia's birds*
Boyer, Cécile. *Woof meow tweet-tweet*
Brett, Jan. *Honey, honey — lion!*
Brian, Janeen. *Where does Thursday go?*
Brown, Margaret Wise. *The dead bird*
    North, south, east, west
Bruchac, Joseph. *The great ball game*
Brunhoff, Laurent de. *Babar and the succotash bird*
Buchanan, Jane. *Seed magic*
Cannon, Janell. *Stellaluna*
Carney, Margaret. *Where does a tiger-heron spend the
    night?*
Charles, Veronika Martenova. *The birdman*
Chast, Roz. *Marco goes to school*
Chivers, Natalie. *Rhino's great big itch!*
Climo, Shirley. *Tuko and the birds*
Collard, Sneed B. *Beaks!*
Cousins, Lucy. *Doctor Maisy*
    Hooray for birds!
Cronin, Doreen. *Click, clack, moo*
Crow, Kristyn. *Hello, Hippo! Goodbye, Bird!*
Crowther, Kitty. *Jack and Jim*
Cruickshank, Margrit. *We're going to feed the ducks*
Davies, Jacqueline. *The boy who drew birds*
Del Rizzo, Suzanne. *My beautiful birds*
DePalma, Mary Newell. *The strange egg*
    Two little birds
dePaola, Tomie. *The birds of Bethlehem*
    The song of Francis
DiPucchio, Kelly. *What's the magic word?*
Dominguez, Angela. *Let's go, Hugo!*
Doolittle, Bev. *Reading the wild*
Dubuc, Marianne. *The lion and the bird*
Dunning, Joan. *Seabird in the forest*
Ehlert, Lois. *Cuckoo, a Mexican folktale / Cucú: un
    cuento folklórico mexicano*
    Feathers for lunch
Elliott, David. *And here's to you!*
    On the wing
Empson, Jo. *Little home bird*
Engle, Margarita. *The sky painter*
Esbaum, Jill. *I hatched!*
    Tom's tweet
Eure, Wesley. *A fish out of water*
Fleming, Candace. *Seven hungry babies*
    When Agnes caws
Foley, Greg. *Purple Little Bird*
Franco, Betsy. *Birdsongs*
Frazier, Craig. *Bee and Bird*
Fredrickson, Lane. *Watch your tongue, Cecily Beasley*
Freedman, Deborah. *Shy*
Friend, Catherine. *The perfect nest*
Frost, Helen. *Sweep up the sun*
Gallo, Frank. *Bird calls*
Garcia, Emma. *Chugga chugga choo choo*
Garland, Michael. *Birds make nests*
Gavril, David. *Penelope Nuthatch and the big surprise*
Genechten, Guido van. *The big woods orchestra*
Goble, Paul. *The great race of the birds and animals*
Goodall, Jane. *The eagle and the wren*
Gordon, Gus. *Somewhere else*
Graham, Bob. *How to heal a broken wing*
Grant, Jacob. *Little Bird's bad word*
Gray, Rita. *Have you heard the nesting bird?*

Gray, Samantha. *Birds*
Green, Jen. *Birds*
Grimm, Jacob and Wilhelm. *Battle of the beasts*
Haas, Irene. *Bess and Bella*
Han, Eun-sun. *The flying birds*
Harper, Charise Mericle. *Amy and Ivan*
Haughton, Chris. *Shh! we have a plan*
Hayles, Marsha. *The feathered crown*
Helmer, Marilyn. *Three barnyard tales*
Henkes, Kevin. *Birds*
    Egg
Herkert, Barbara. *Birds in your backyard*
Hills, Tad. *How Rocket learned to read*
    Rocket writes a story
    Rocket's mighty words
Himmelman, John. *Noisy bird sing-along*
Hines, Anna Grossnickle. *Miss Emma's wild garden*
Hirschi, Ron. *When morning comes*
    When night comes
Hoban, Tana. *A children's zoo*
Hunter, Anne. *What's in the meadow?*
Imai, Ayano. *Mr. Brown's fantastic hat*
Iwamura, Kazuo. *Hooray for snow!*
James, Ann. *Bird and Bear*
James, Simon. *The birdwatchers*
    George flies south
Jenkins, Steve. *Animals in flight*
Jonas, Ann. *Bird talk*
Jules, Jacqueline. *Feathers for peacock*
Kaczman, James. *A bird and his worm*
Kasza, Keiko. *A mother for Choco*
Katschke, Judy. *Take a hike, Snoopy*
Kellogg, Steven. *Aster Aardvark's alphabet adventures*
Kelly, Irene. *Even an ostrich needs a nest*
Kimmel, Eric A. *The birds' gift*
King, Stephen Michael. *You*
Kirk, David. *Little bird, Biddle bird*
Kleven, Elisa. *The dancing deer and the foolish hunter*
Könnecke, Ole. *You can do it, Bert!*
Kono, Erin Eitter. *Caterina and the perfect party*
Krilanovich, Nadia. *Chicken, chicken, duck!*
Lachenmeyer, Nathaniel. *The origami master*
Lavis, Steve. *Jump!*
Lent, Blair. *Ruby and Fred*
Lerner, Harriet Goldhor. *Franny B. Kranny, there's
    a bird in your hair*
Lionni, Leo. *Inch by inch*
    Tico and the golden wings
Lipp, Frederick. *The caged birds of Phnom Penh*
Long, Ethan. *Bird and Birdie in a fine day*
    Up, tall and high
Louie, Therese On. *Raymond's perfect present*
McDonnell, Patrick. *South*
McGrory, Anik. *Mouton's impossible dream*
McKee, David. *Elmer and the big bird*
MacLear, Kyo. *The fog*
McPhail, David. *Farm morning*
Malbrough, Mike. *Marigold bakes a cake*
Malnor, Carol L. *The Blues go birding across America*
Marley, Cedella. *Every little thing*
Mathers, Petra. *Herbie's secret Santa*
    Lottie's new friend
Mazzola, Frank. *Counting is for the birds*
Mead, Alice. *Billy and Emma*
Meade, Holly. *If I never forever endeavor*
Meddaugh, Susan. *Tree of birds*
Melvin, Alice. *Counting birds*
Meres, Jonathan. *The big bad rumor*
Merino, Gemma. *The sheep who hatched an egg*

Miyares, Daniel. *Pardon me!*
Mollel, Tololwa M. *Song bird*
Mortimer, Rachael. *Song for a princess*
Munari, Bruno. *Bruno Munari's zoo*
Munro, Roxie. *Hatch!*
Murguia, Bethanie Deeney. *Cockatoo, too*
Myers, Christopher. *Sparrows*
Na, Il Sung. *Bird, balloon, Bear*
Napoli, Donna Jo. *Albert*
Nathan, Emma. *What do you call a group of turkeys?*
Neitzel, Shirley. *The house I'll build for the wrens*
Newman, Marjorie. *Mole and the baby bird*
Norling, Beth. *The stone baby*
Oberman, Sheldon. *The wisdom bird*
O'Connor, Jane. *Fancy Nancy: explorer extraordinaire!*
Palatini, Margie. *Gorgonzola*
Paulsen, Gary. *Canoe days*
Pearson, Tracey Campbell. *The purple hat*
Peet, Bill. *The kweeks of Kookatumdee*
    The pinkish, purplish, bluish egg
Perry, Andrea. *The Bicklebys' birdbath*
Pienkowski, Jan. *Bel and Bub and the baby bird*
Pierce, Christa. *Did you know that I love you?*
Pierce, Terry. *My busy green garden*
Polacco, Patricia. *Mr. Lincoln's way*
Pomerantz, Charlotte. *Flap your wings and try*
Portis, Antoinette. *Froodle*
Prosek, James. *Bird, butterfly, eel*
Reed, Lynn Rowe. *Basil's birds*
Reynolds, Aaron. *Nerdy birdy*
Robey, Katharine Crawford. *Where's the party?*
Robinson, Tim. *Tobias, the quig, and the rumplenut tree*
Rockwell, Anne. *Our yard is full of birds*
Rohmann, Eric. *Time flies*
Rose, Caroline Starr. *Over in the wetlands*
Roth, Susan L. *Happy birthday Mr. Kang*
Roussen, Jean. *Beautiful birds*
Rubin, Adam. *Those darn squirrels!*
    Those darn squirrels and the cat next door
    Those darn squirrels fly south
Ruddell, Deborah. *Today at the Bluebird Cafe*
Runton, Andy. *Owly and Wormy: friends all aflutter!*
Russo, Marisabina. *Little Bird takes a bath*
Ruzzier, Sergio. *A letter for Leo*
Ryder, Joanne. *Wild birds*
Rylant, Cynthia. *The bird house*
San Souci, Robert D. *The birds of Killingworth*
Sayre, April Pulley. *If you should hear a honey guide*
Sazaklis, John. *Fowl play*
Scanlon, Elizabeth Garton. *Noodle and Lou*
Schaefer, Carole Lexa. *Two scarlet songbirds*
Segal, John. *The lonely moose*
Seuss, Dr. *Horton hatches the egg*
    Thidwick, the big-hearted moose
Sharratt, Nick. *Shark in the park*
Sheneman, Drew. *Nope!*
Shulevitz, Uri. *What is a wise bird like you doing in a silly tale like this?*
Simler, Isabelle. *Plume*
Simple gifts
Skofield, James. *Bear and Bird*
Slack, Michael. *Shorty and Clem*
Snicket, Lemony. *Thirteen words*
Spink, Matt. *Some birds*
Stead, Philip C. *Hello, my name is Ruby*
    A home for Bird
    Samson in the snow

Stevens, Janet. *Find a cow now!*
Stewart, Melissa. *Feathers*
    A place for birds
Stileman, Kali. *Roly-poly egg*
    Snack time for Confetti
Stockdale, Susan. *Bring on the birds*
Tafuri, Nancy. *Where did Bunny go?*
    Whose chick are you?
    Will you be my friend?
Tankard, Jeremy. *Boo hoo Bird*
    Grumpy Bird
    Hungry Bird
Teevin, Toni. *What to do? What to do?*
Thong, Roseanne. *Fly free!*
Thornhill, Jan. *Is this Panama?*
    Wild in the city
Tildes, Phyllis Limbacher. *Baby's first book of birds and colors*
Timmers, Leo. *Crow*
Turnbull, Victoria. *Pandora*
Valckx, Catharina. *Lizette's green sock*
Vanderwater, Amy Ludwig. *Every day birds*
Van Fleet, Matthew. *Fuzzy yellow ducklings*
Vere, Ed. *Max and Bird*
Ward, Helen. *The king of the birds*
Ward, Jennifer. *Mama built a little nest*
Ward, Lindsay. *When Blue met Egg*
Wellington, Monica. *Riki's birdhouse*
Wenxuan, Cao. *Feather*
Winer, Yvonne. *Birds build nests*
Winstead, Rosie. *Ruby and Bubbles*
Wood, Audrey. *Birdsong*
    Little Penguin's tale
Yerkes, Jennifer. *A funny little bird*
Yolen, Jane. *On Bird Hill*
    Welcome to the river of grass
    You nest here with me
Young, Cybèle. *Ten birds*
    Ten birds meet a monster
Yuly, Toni. *Early bird*
    The Jelly Bean tree
Ziefert, Harriet. *Robin, where are you?*
Zoehfeld, Kathleen Weidner. *Did dinosaurs have feathers?*
Zullo, Germano. *Little bird*

Birds – blackbirds

Bryan, Ashley. *Beautiful blackbird*

Birds – bluebirds

Ketteman, Helen. *Armadilly chili*
Kirby, Pamela F. *What bluebirds do*
Lucas, David. *The robot and the bluebird*
Martin, David. *Peep and Ducky*
    Peep and Ducky: rainy day
Staake, Bob. *Bluebird*
Yankey, Lindsey. *Bluebird*

Birds – bluejays

Rockwell, Anne. *Two blue jays*

Birds – buzzards

Goble, Paul. *Iktomi and the buzzard*

Birds – canaries

Freeman, Don. *Quiet! There's a canary in the library*
Yolen, Jane. *Elsie's bird*

Birds – cardinals

Preller, James. *Cardinal and sunflower*
Tavares, Matt. *Red and Lulu*

Birds – chickadees

Ziefert, Harriet. *Birdhouse for rent*

Birds – chickens, roosters

Ada, Alma Flor. *The rooster who went to his uncle's wedding*
Alakija, Polly. *Counting chickens*
Alborough, Jez. *Six little chicks*
Alexander, Kwame. *Acoustic Rooster and his barnyard band*
Allard, Harry. *Starlight goes to town*
Allen, Jonathan. *I'm not reading!*
Alter, Anna. *Abigail spells*
Amato, Mary. *The chicken of the family*
Arnold, Caroline. *Hatching chicks in Room 6*
Arnold, Tedd. *The twin princes*
Asher, Sandy. *Chicken story time*
Asim, Jabari. *Preaching to the chickens*
Auch, Mary Jane. *Bantam of the opera*
  Beauty and the beaks
  The buk buk buk festival
  Chickerella
  The Easter egg farm
  Eggs mark the spot
  Hen lake
  Peeping Beauty
  The plot chickens
  Poultrygeist
  Souperchicken
Baddiel, Ivor. *Cock-a-doodle quack! quack!*
Baehr, Patricia. *Boo Cow*
Bardhan-Quallen, Sudipta. *Chicks run wild*
Battut, Eric. *The fox and the hen*
Berry, Lynne. *What floats in a moat?*
Birchall, Mark. *Hen goes shopping*
Black, Michael Ian. *Cock-a-doodle-doo-bop!*
Bogan, Paulette. *Goodnight Lulu*
  Lulu the big little chick
Bogart, Jo Ellen. *Count your chickens*
Bowles, Paula. *Scary Mary*
Boynton, Sandra. *Eek! Halloween!*
Brett, Jan. *Cinders*
  Daisy comes home
  Hedgie's surprise
Brown, Jo. *Hoppity skip Little Chick*
  Where's my mommy?
Brown, Ken. *The scarecrow's hat*
Browne, Eileen. *Handa's hen*
Bunting, Eve. *Hurry! hurry!*
Burg, Sarah Emmanuelle. *One more egg*
Carle, Eric. *The rooster who set out to see the world*
  Rooster's off to see the world
Cazet, Denys. *Elvis the rooster almost goes to heaven*
Chaconas, Dori. *Dori the contrary hen*
Chambers, Angela. *Follow that chicken!*
Chaucer, Geoffrey. *Chanticleer and the fox*
Chen, Chih-Yuan. *The featherless chicken*
Chicken Little. *Brave Chicken Little*

Chicken Little
Henny Penny, ill. by Emily Bolam
Henny Penny, ill. by Paul Galdone
Henny-Penny, ill. by Jane Wattenberg
Henny Penny, ill. by Sophie Windham
  The sky is falling
Chukovskii, Kornei Ivanovich. *Good morning, chick*
Clark, Leslie Ann. *Peepsqueak!*
Clarke, Jane. *Stuck in the mud*
Cole, Henry. *Eddie the bully*
Collet, Géraldine. *All by myself!*
Cousins, Lucy. *Count with Maisy, cheep, cheep, cheep!*
Crimi, Carolyn. *Henry and the Crazed Chicken Pirates*
Cronin, Doreen. *Smick!*
Crum, Shutta. *Fox and Fluff*
Czernecki, Stefan. *Huevos rancheros*
Dallas-Conte, Juliet. *Cock-a-moo-moo*
Daly, Niki. *Welcome to Zanzibar Road*
  What's cooking, Jamela?
Darbyshire, Kristen. *Put it on the list!*
Davis, Aubrey. *A hen for Izzy Pippik*
Davis, Jerry. *Little Chicken's big day*
Deedy, Carmen Agra. *The rooster who would not be quiet!*
de Las Casas, Dianne. *The Little "Read" Hen*
Dempsey, Kristy. *Surfer chick*
Denchfield, Nick. *Charlie Chick*
Desmoinaux, Christel. *Mrs. Hen's big surprise*
Diakité, Penda. *I lost my tooth in Africa*
DiCamillo, Kate. *Louise*
Dorros, Arthur. *City chicken*
Dumont, Jean-François. *The chickens build a wall*
Edwards, Pamela Duncan. *The mixed-up rooster*
Elliott, David. *One little chicken*
Emberley, Ed. *The red hen*
Emberley, Rebecca. *Chicken Little*
Falatko, Julie. *Snappsy the alligator and his best friend forever (probably)*
Fox, Mem. *Hattie and the fox*
Franceschelli, Christopher. *(Oliver)*
Freedman, Deborah. *Blue chicken*
Gehl, Laura. *Peep and Egg: I'm not hatching*
  Peep and Egg: I'm not taking a bath
  Peep and Egg: I'm not trick-or-treating
Ginsburg, Mirra. *Across the stream*
  The chick and the duckling
Golan, Avirama. *Little Naomi, Little Chick*
Golson, Terry. *Tillie lays an egg*
Gorbachev, Valeri. *Chicken chickens*
  Chicken chickens go to school
  The missing chick
Graves, Keith. *Chicken Big*
Grindley, Sally. *Where are my chicks?*
Hader, Berta Hoerner. *Cock-a-doodle doo*
Halls, Kelly Milner. *I bought a baby chicken*
Harrington, Janice N. *Busy-busy Little Chick*
  The chicken-chasing queen of Lamar County
Harrison, David L. *Dylan, the eagle-hearted chicken*
Hayward, Linda. *The King's chorus*
Helakoski, Leslie. *Big chickens*
  Big chickens fly the coop
  Big chickens go to town
Hest, Amy. *Little chick*
Himmelman, John. *Chickens to the rescue*
Ho, Jannie. *Bear and Chicken*
Hopkins, Jackie Mims. *Prairie chicken little*
Horowitz, Dave. *Chico the brave*
Hutchins, Pat. *Bumpety bump*

Rosie's walk
Where, oh where, is Rosie's chick?
Idle, Molly. *Flora and the chicks*
Jadoul, Émile. *Good night, Chickie*
Jennewein, Lenore. *Chick-o-Saurus Rex*
Johnston, Tony. *Chicken in the kitchen*
Joosse, Barbara. *Higgledy-piggledy chicks*
Kasza, Keiko. *The wolf's chicken stew*
Kelley, Ellen A. *My life as a chicken*
Kellogg, Steven. *Chicken Little*
Kimmel, Eric A. *Medio Pollito*
Kishira, Mayuko. *Who's next door?*
Knudsen, Michelle. *Argus*
Kromhout, Rindert. *Little Donkey and the baby-sitter*
Laminack, Lester L. *Three hens and a peacock*
Latter, Jill. *Mama Hen's big day*
Lawrence, John. *This little chick*
Lehrhaupt, Adam. *Chicken in school*
    Chicken in space
Leslie, Amanda. *Are chickens stripy?*
Lester, Helen. *The revenge of the magic chicken*
Lin, Grace. *Olvina flies*
    Olvina swims
The little red hen. *The little red hen*, ill. by Byron
    Barton
    The little red hen, ill. by Emily Bolam
    The little red hen, ill. by Paul Galdone
    Little red hen
    The little red hen, ill. by Jerry Pinkney
    The little red hen, ill. by Kate Slater
    The little red hen, ill. by Annie West
    The little red hen, ill. by Margot Zemach
    The little red hen: an old fable
    The Little Red Hen and the Passover matzah
    The Little Red Hen makes a pizza
Lottridge, Celia Barker. *The little rooster and the
    diamond button*
MacDonald, Margaret Read. *Little Rooster's
    diamond button*
McDonald, Megan. *Hen hears gossip*
MacLachlan, Patricia. *Nora's chicks*
McLellan, Stephanie Simpson. *The chicken cat*
McMillan, Bruce. *The problem with chickens*
Maguire, Gregory. *Crabby Cratchitt*
Manning, Mick. *Cock-a-doodle hoooooo!*
Marshall, James. *Wings: a tale of two chickens*
Martin, Bill, Jr.. *Chicken Chuck*
Martin, Jacqueline Briggs. *Chicken joy on Redbean
    Road*
Martín Larrañaga, Ana. *Pepo and Lolo and the red
    apple*
    Pepo and Lolo are friends
Mathers, Petra. *Lottie's new beach towel*
    When Aunt Mattie got her wings
Matthews, Tina. *Out of the egg*
Meng, Cece. *Tough chicks*
Milway, Katie Smith. *One hen*
Mollel, Tololwa M. *Kele's secret*
Montanari, Susan McElroy. *My dog's a chicken*
Mortensen, Lori. *Chicken Lily*
Most, Bernard. *Cock-a-doodle-moo!*
Murphy, Patti Beling. *Elinor and Violet*
Nimmo, Jenny. *Something wonderful*
Numeroff, Laura Joffe. *The Chicken sisters*
Ohi, Ruth. *Chicken, Pig, Cow and the class pet*
    Chicken, Pig, Cow horse around
    Chicken, Pig, Cow's first fight
O'Malley, Kevin. *Gimme cracked corn and I will share*
Oxley, Jennifer. *The chicken problem*

Palatini, Margie. *Bad boys get henpecked!*
    Shelly
    Three French hens
Partridge, Elizabeth. *Pig's eggs*
Paschkis, Julie. *P. Zonka lays an egg*
Pauli, Lorenz. *The fox in the library*
Paye, Won-Ldy. *Mrs. Chicken and the hungry crocodile*
Pearson, Tracey Campbell. *Bob*
Peet, Bill. *Cock-a-doodle Dudley*
Perl, Erica S. *Chicken Butt's back!*
Pinkwater, Daniel. *Beautiful Yetta*
    Beautiful Yetta's Hanukkah kitten
Pomerantz, Charlotte. *Here comes Henny*
Poole, Amy Lowry. *How the rooster got his crown*
Purcell, Rebecca. *Super Chicken*
Rankin, Joan. *You're somebody special, Walliwigs!*
Rave, Friederike. *Outfoxing the fox*
Rees, Douglas. *Tyrannosaurus Rex vs. Edna the very
    first chicken*
Reiser, Lynn. *The surprise family*
Reynolds, Aaron. *Buffalo wings*
    Chicks and salsa
Rodriguez, Béatrice. *The chicken thief*
    Fox and hen together
Ruurs, Margriet. *Wake up, Henry Rooster!*
Sattler, Jennifer. *Chick 'n' Pug*
    Chick 'n' Pug: the love pug
    A Chick 'n' Pug Christmas
    Chick 'n' Pug meet the Dude
Sauer, Tammi. *Bawk and roll*
    Chicken dance
Schuh, Mari C. *Chickens on the farm*
Schwartz, Corey Rosen. *Hensel and Gretel*
Scillian, Devin. *Brewster the rooster*
Shah, Idries. *The silly chicken*
Shannon, George. *The Secret Chicken Club*
    Tippy-toe chick, go
Sharmat, Marjorie Weinman. *Hooray for Mother's
    Day!*
Shea, Bob. *New socks*
Sidjanski, Brigitte. *Little Chicken and Little Duck*
Sklansky, Amy E. *Where do chicks come from?*
Stampler, Ann Redisch. *The rooster prince of Breslov*
Stanton, Elizabeth Rose. *Henny*
Stein, David Ezra. *Interrupting chicken*
Stevens, Janet. *Cook-a-doodle-doo!*
Stoeke, Janet Morgan. *A friend for Minerva Louise*
    A hat for Minerva Louise
    Hide and seek
    The Loopy Coop hens
    The Loopy Coop hens: letting go
    Minerva Louise
    Minerva Louise and the colorful eggs
    Minerva Louise and the red truck
    Minerva Louise at school
    Minerva Louise at the fair
    Minerva Louise on Christmas Eve
    Minerva Louise on Halloween
    Oh no! a fox!
    Pip's trip
Stuchner, Joan Betty. *Can hens give milk?*
Sykes, Julie. *Dora's chicks*
    Dora's eggs
Tafuri, Nancy. *Five little chicks*
Teague, Mark. *The sky is falling!*
Thomas, Jan. *Is everyone ready for fun?*
Thompson, Lauren. *Wee little chick*
The three little pigs *The three little pigs and the fox*
Twohy, Mike. *Wake up, Rupert!*

Valentina, Marina. *Lost in the roses*
Van Leeuwen, Jean. *Chicken soup*
van Lieshout, Maria. *Peep!*
Varon, Sara. *Chicken and Cat*
    Chicken and Cat clean up
Vere, Ed. *Chick*
Wahl, Phoebe. *Sonya's chickens*
Walker, Anna. *Peggy*
Ward, Helen. *The rooster and the fox*
Waring, Richard. *Hungry hen*
Weston, Carrie. *If a chicken stayed for supper*
    Why did the chicken cross the road?
Willis, Jeanne. *Mommy do you love me?*
Wisnewski, Andrea. *Trio*
Wormell, Christopher. *Henry and the fox*
Wormell, Mary. *Bernard the angry rooster*
    Hilda Hen's happy birthday
    Hilda Hen's search
Young, Ed. *Hook*

Birds – cockatoos

Murguia, Bethanie Deeney. *Cockatoo, too*
    Toucans, too

Birds – cranes

Bang, Molly. *Dawn*
    The paper crane
Bodkin, Odds. *The crane wife*
Chen, Kerstin. *Lord of the cranes*
Coerr, Eleanor. *Sadako*
George, Jean Craighead. *Luck*
Jiang, Ji-li. *Lotus and Feather*
Say, Allen. *The boy in the garden*
Wells, Rosemary. *Yoko's paper cranes*
Yagawa, Sumiko. *The crane wife*

Birds – crows

Aesop. *The crow and the pitcher*
Appelt, Kathi. *Counting crows*
    Merry Christmas, merry crow
Chorao, Kay. *Pig and Crow*
Goble, Paul. *Crow chief*
Grant, Rose Marie. *Andiamo, Weasel*
Johnson, Paul Brett. *Bearhide and crow*
Kleven, Elisa. *The wishing ball*
Lionni, Leo. *Six crows*
Loux, Lynn C. *The day I could fly*
Lowry, Lois. *Crow call*
McDermott, Gerald. *Coyote*
Paul, Alison. *The crow (a not so scary story)*
Pringle, Laurence P. *Crows*
Raschka, Chris. *Little black crow*
Rosen, Michael. *Crow and Hawk*
Sillifant, Alec. *Farmer Ham*
Singer, Marilyn. *The company of crows*
Spirin, Gennady. *Martha*
Subramaniam, Manasi. *The fox and the crow*
Timmers, Leo. *Crow*
Van Laan, Nancy. *Rainbow crow*
Wheeler, Lisa. *Old Cricket*

Birds – cuckoos

Ehlert, Lois. *Cuckoo, a Mexican folktale / Cucú: un cuento folklórico mexicano*
Roberton, Fiona. *Cuckoo!*

Birds – dodos

Mathers, Petra. *Dodo gets married*
Sattler, Jennifer. *Uh-oh, Dodo!*

Birds – doves

Ford, Gilbert. *Flying lessons*
Peet, Bill. *The pinkish, purplish, bluish egg*
Potter, Beatrix. *The tale of the faithful dove*
Singer, Isaac Bashevis. *Why Noah chose the dove*
Wells, Rosemary. *The language of doves*
Yang, Belle. *Always come home to me*

Birds – ducks

Abrahams, Peter. *Quacky baseball*
Alborough, Jez. *Captain Duck*
    Duck in the truck
    Duck's key where can it be?
    Fix-it Duck
    Hit the ball Duck
    Super Duck
Anastas, Margaret. *A hug for you*
Andersen, Hans Christian. *The ugly duckling*, ill. by Adrienne Adams
    The ugly duckling, ill. by Sebastien Braun
    The ugly duckling, ill. by Lorinda Bryan Cauley
    The ugly duckling, ill. by Charlene DeLage
    The ugly duckling, ill. by Robert Ingpen
    The ugly duckling, ill. by Rachel Isadora
    The ugly duckling, ill. by Steve Johnson
    The ugly duckling, ill. by Jerry Pinkney
    The ugly duckling, ill. by Meilo So
    The ugly duckling, ill. by Pirkko Vainio
    The ugly duckling, ill. by Bernadette Watts
    The ugly duckling, ill. by Roberta Wilson
Arnosky, Jim. *All night near the water*
Aruego, José. *The last laugh*
Asch, Frank. *Baby Duck's new friend*
Auch, Mary Jane. *The nutquacker*
Bardhan-Quallen, Sudipta. *Hampire!*
Barnett, Mac. *The wolf, the duck, and the mouse*
Barry, Frances. *Duckie's ducklings*
    Duckie's rainbow
Bates, Ivan. *Five little ducks*
Bechtold, Lisze. *Sally and the purple socks*
Berry, Lynne. *Duck dunks*
    Duck skates
    Duck tents
    Ducking for apples
Bramsen, Carin. *Hey, duck!*
    Just a duck?
Bromley, Nick. *Open very carefully*
Brown, Alan James. *Love-a-Duck*
Brown, Margaret Wise. *The golden egg book*
Bryant, Megan E. *Dump Truck Duck*
Bunting, Eve. *Happy birthday, dear duck*
    Have you seen my new blue socks?
Capucilli, Alyssa Satin. *Biscuit finds a friend*
    Katy Duck
    Katy Duck, big sister
    Katy Duck is a caterpillar
Carle, Eric. *10 little rubber ducks*
Chae, In Seon. *How do you count a dozen ducklings?*
Chen, Chih-Yuan. *Guji Guji*
Church, Caroline Jayne. *Ruff!*
Claflin, Willy. *The uglified ducky*
Cooper, Helen. *Delicious!*
    A pipkin of pepper

Costello, David Hyde. *I can help*
Cronin, Doreen. *Click, clack, ho! ho! ho!*
  Click, clack, moo I love you!
  Click, clack, peep!
  Click, clack, quackity-quack
  Click, clack, surprise!
  Duck for President
  Giggle, giggle, quack
  Thump, quack, moo
Cruickshank, Margrit. *We're going to feed the ducks*
Curious George and the dump truck (1999)
Davies, Nicola. *Just ducks!*
Deschamps, Nicola. *Duckling*
Dormer, Frank W. *Firefighter Duckies!*
Eaton, Maxwell. *Two dumb ducks*
Egan, Tim. *Dodsworth in London*
  Dodsworth in New York
  Dodsworth in Paris
  Dodsworth in Rome
Emmett, Jonathan. *Ruby in her own time*
  This way, Ruby!
Ering, Timothy Basil. *The unexpected love story of*
  Alfred Fiddleduckling
Escoffier, Michaël. *Me first!*
Faulkner, Keith. *Do you have my quack?*
Fierstein, Harvey. *The sissy duckling*
Flack, Marjorie. *The story about Ping*
Flake, Sharon G. *You are not a cat!*
Fleming, Denise. *5 little ducks*
Ford, Bernette. *No more blanket for Lambkin!*
  No more diapers for Ducky!
Foreman, Michael. *Tufty*
Gavin, Ciara. *Bear is not tired*
  Bear likes jam
  Room for Bear
Gerstein, Mordicai. *You can't have too many friends!*
Gibbons, Gail. *Ducks*
Ginsburg, Mirra. *Across the stream*
  The chick and the duckling
Goble, Paul. *Iktomi and the ducks*
Goldin, Augusta. *Ducks don't get wet*
Goldsboro, Bobby. *Noah and the ark; and, David*
  and Goliath
Gravett, Emily. *The odd egg*
Grimm, Jacob and Wilhelm. *The twelve princesses*
Grindley, Sally. *Mucky Duck*
  Silly Goose and Dizzy Duck play hide-and-seek
Hader, Berta Hoerner. *Cock-a-doodle doo*
Hamburg, Jennifer. *Monkey and Duck quack up!*
Hest, Amy. *Baby Duck and the bad eyeglasses*
  Baby Duck and the cozy blanket
  Guess who, Baby Duck
  Make the team, Baby Duck
  Off to school, Baby Duck
  You're the boss, Baby Duck
Hills, Tad. *Duck and Goose*
  Duck and Goose find a pumpkin
  Duck and Goose go to the beach
  Duck and Goose, honk! quack! boo!
  Duck and Goose, how are you feeling?
  Duck and Goose, 1, 2, 3
  Duck, Duck, Goose
  What's up, Duck?
Himmelman, John. *Duck to the rescue*
Hindley, Judy. *Do like a duck does*
Holmes, Janet A. *Have you seen Duck?*
Horowitz, Dave. *Duck, duck, moose*
Hudson, Katy. *Bear and Duck*
Ives, Penny. *Celestine, drama queen*

James, Simon. *Little One Step*
Johansen, Hanna. *The duck and the owl*
John, Jory. *Come home already!*
  Goodnight already!
  I love you already!
Jonas, Ann. *Watch William walk*
Joyce, William. *Bently and egg*
Kasza, Keiko. *Ready for anything*
Keller, John G. *The rubber-legged ducky*
Kohuth, Jane. *Duck sock hop*
Lewis, Kim. *Seymour and Henry*
Linch, Tanya. *My duck*
Llewellyn, Claire. *Duck*
London, Jonathan. *Duck and Hippo in the rainstorm*
  Duck and Hippo lost and found
Long, Ethan. *The Wing Wing brothers carnival de*
  math
  The Wing Wing brothers geometry palooza!
  The Wing Wing brothers math spectacular!
Lurie, Susan. *Swim, duck, swim!*
McCloskey, Robert. *Make way for ducklings*
Mack, Jeff. *Duck in the fridge*
McMillan, Bruce. *Days of the ducklings*
McPhail, David. *Waddles*
Magloff, Lisa. *Duckling*
Mallat, Kathy. *Just ducky*
Marshall, Natalie. *Five little ducks: a fingers and toes*
  nursery rhyme book
Martin, David. *Peep and Ducky*
  Peep and Ducky: rainy day
Mathers, Petra. *A cake for Herbie*
  When Aunt Mattie got her wings
Milgrim, David. *Santa Duck*
  Santa Duck and his merry helpers
Miller, Tim. *Moo Moo in a tutu*
Moore, Eva. *Lucky ducklings*
Mulryan, Doreen. *Lucky Ducky*
Murphy, Mary. *Quick Duck!*
Nedwidek, John. *Ducks don't wear socks*
Nolan, Lucy A. *Jack Quack*
Palatini, Margie. *Earthquack*
Parker, Marjorie Blain. *Mama's little duckling*
Paterson, Katherine. *The tale of the Mandarin ducks*
Peters, Lisa Westberg. *Cold little duck, duck, duck*
Pfeffer, Wendy. *Mallard duck at Meadow View Pond*
Pfister, Marcus. *Charlie at the zoo*
Pham, LeUyen. *The bear who wasn't there*
Pomerantz, Charlotte. *One duck, another duck*
Potter, Beatrix. *The tale of Jemima Puddle-Duck*
Rankin, Joan. *Wow! It's great being a duck*
Rankin, Laura. *Fluffy and Baron*
Reiser, Lynn. *The surprise family*
Reynolds, Adrian. *Pete and Polo's farmyard adventure*
Ritchie, Alison. *Duck says don't!*
Roberton, Fiona. *The perfect present*
  Wanted: the perfect pet
Rock, Brian. *The deductive detective*
Roddie, Shen. *Not now, Mrs. Wolf*
Root, Phyllis. *One duck stuck*
Rosenthal, Amy Krouse. *Duck! Rabbit!*
Ruzzier, Sergio. *This is not a picture book*
Salzano, Tammi. *One rainy day*
Sauer, Tammi. *Mr. Duck means business*
Shannon, David. *Duck on a bike*
  Duck on a tractor
Sidjanski, Brigitte. *Little Chicken and Little Duck*
Simmons, Jane. *Bouncy bouncy Daisy*
  Come along, Daisy!
  Daisy and the Beastie

Daisy and the egg
Daisy says coo!
Daisy says, "Here we go round the mulberry bush"
Daisy says, "If you're happy and you know it"
Daisy, the little duck with big feet
Daisy's day out
Daisy's favorite things
Daisy's hide-and-seek
Go to sleep, Daisy
Quack, Daisy, quack!
Splish splash Daisy
Skalak, Barbara Anne. *Waddle, waddle, quack, quack, quack*
Sklansky, Amy E. *The duck who played the kazoo*
Slade-Robinson, Nikki. *Muddle and Mo's worm surprise*
Muddle and Mo
Sloat, Teri. *I'm a duck!*
Soffer, Gilad. *Duck's vacation*
Sones, Sonya. *Violet and Winston*
Stevenson, James. *Howard*
Monty
Stewart, Amber. *Puddle's new school*
Straaten, Harmen van. *Duck's tale*
For me?
Sweeney, Jacqueline. *What about Bettie?*
Tafuri, Nancy. *Goodnight, my duckling*
Have you seen my duckling?
Thomas, Jan. *Pumpkin trouble*
Thompson, Lauren. *Little Quack*
Little Quack: dial-a-duck
Little Quack's bedtime
Little Quack's hide and seek
Little Quack's new friend
Tryon, Leslie. *Albert's alphabet*
Albert's birthday
Albert's Christmas
Albert's Halloween
Twohy, Mike. *Outfoxed*
Urbanovic, Jackie. *Duck and cover*
Duck at the door
Duck soup
Sitting duck
Van Laan, Nancy. *Shingebiss*
Verboven, Agnes. *Ducks like to swim*
Verdick, Elizabeth. *Peep leap*
Waddell, Martin. *Farmer Duck*
It's quacking time
Webster J. Duck
Ward, Nick. *Come on Baby Duck*
Wells, Rosemary. *The itsy-bitsy spider*
A visit to Dr. Duck
Whippo, Walt. *Little white duck*
Wildsmith, Brian. *The little wood duck*
Wilhelm, Hans. *Quacky Ducky's Easter egg*
Quacky Ducky's Easter fun
Willems, Mo. *The duckling gets a cookie!?*
The pigeon finds a hot dog!
Wilson, Karma. *Duddle Puck*
Winthrop, Elizabeth. *Bear and Mrs. Duck*
Bear's Christmas surprise
Wong, Liz. *Quackers*
Yaccarino, Dan. *Five little ducks*
Yolen, Jane. *Dimity Duck*
Yorinks, Arthur. *Quack!*
Ziefert, Harriet. *A dozen ducklings lost and found*

Birds – eagles

Bardhan-Quallen, Sudipta. *Flying eagle*
The bear
Brett, Jan. *The three little dassies*
George, Jean Craighead. *The eagles are back*
Gibbons, Gail. *Soaring with the wind*
Goble, Paul. *Adopted by the eagles*
Gregorowski, Christopher. *Fly, eagle, fly!*
Harrison, David L. *Dylan, the eagle-hearted chicken*
Hausman, Gerald. *Eagle boy*
Hodge, Deborah. *Eagles*
Martin-James, Kathleen. *Soaring bald eagles*
Minshull, Evelyn White. *Eaglet's world*
Vaughan, Richard Lee. *Eagle boy*
Young, Ed. *Hook*

Birds – falcons

George, Jean Craighead. *Frightful's daughter*
Frightful's daughter meets the Baron Weasel
Jenkins, Priscilla Belz. *Falcons nest on skyscrapers*
Jessell, Tim. *Falcon*

Birds – finches

Pericoli, Matteo. *The true story of Stellina*

Birds – flamingos

Grambling, Lois G. *Miss Hildy's missing cape caper*
Guiberson, Brenda Z. *Mud city*
Harper, Jamie. *Miss Mingo and the fire drill*
Miss Mingo and the first day of school
Hewett, Joan. *A flamingo chick grows up*
Idle, Molly. *Flora and the flamingo*
London, Jonathan. *Flamingo sunset*
Oswald, Pete. *Mingo the flamingo*
Sattler, Jennifer. *Sylvie*
Walsh, Ellen Stoll. *For Pete's sake*

Birds – geese

Aesop. *The goose that laid the golden egg*
Asher, Sandy. *Here comes Gosling!*
Bang, Molly. *Goose*
Bloom, Suzanne. *Alone together*
Bear can dance!
Fox forgets
Oh! what a surprise!
A splendid friend, indeed
What about Bear?
Bonnet, Rosalinde. *Daddy Honk Honk!*
Brennan-Nelson, Denise. *Grady the goose*
Church, Caroline Jayne. *One smart goose*
Cox, Phil Roxbee. *Goose on the loose*
Cyrus, Kurt. *Shake a leg, egg!*
Dumont, Jean-François. *The geese march in step*
Dunrea, Olivier. *Gemma and Gus*
Gideon
Gideon and Otto
Gossie's busy day
Jasper and Joop
Merry Christmas, Ollie!
Ollie
Ollie the stomper
Ollie's Easter eggs
Ollie's Halloween
Peedie
Duvoisin, Roger Antoine. *Petunia*

Fox, Mem. *Boo to a goose*
Fredericks, Anthony D. *In one tidepool*
Gehrmann, Katja. *Goose the bear*
Greenstein, Elaine. *The goose man*
Grimm, Jacob and Wilhelm. *The golden goose*
Grindley, Sally. *Silly Goose and Dizzy Duck play hide-and-seek*
Harper, Charise Mericle. *When Randolph turned rotten*
Hawkins, Emily. *Little snow goose*
Higgins, Ryan T. *Hotel Bruce*
    Mother Bruce
Hills, Tad. *Duck and Goose*
    Duck and Goose find a pumpkin
    Duck and Goose go to the beach
    Duck and Goose, honk! quack! boo!
    Duck and Goose, how are you feeling?
    Duck and Goose, 1, 2, 3
    Duck, Duck, Goose
    What's up, Duck?
Horácek, Petr. *Look out, Suzy Goose*
    Silly Suzy Goose
    Suzy Goose and the Christmas star
Inkpen, Mick. *Honk!*
Jackson, Chris. *The Gaggle sisters river tour*
Johnson, Paul Brett. *The goose who went off in a huff*
Kasza, Keiko. *Silly Goose's big story*
Kindermans, Martine. *You and me*
Lears, Laurie. *Waiting for Mr. Goose*
Lindbergh, Reeve. *The day the goose got loose*
Loth, Sebastian. *Remembering Crystal*
    Zelda the Varigoose
McBratney, Sam. *Just you and me*
Mahy, Margaret. *A summery Saturday morning*
Montes, Marisa. *Egg-napped!*
Mraz, David. *Little Goose*
Oram, Hiawyn. *Gerda the goose*
Pilkey, Dav. *The Silly Gooses*
Polacco, Patricia. *I can hear the sun*
    Rechenka's eggs
Ritchie, Alison. *Duck says don't!*
Rong, Yu. *A lovely day for Amelia Goose*
Root, Phyllis. *Grandmother Winter*
Sansone, Adele. *The little green goose*
Sayre, April Pulley. *Honk, honk, goose!*
Schoenherr, John. *Rebel*
Schubert, Ingrid. *Bear's eggs*
Simmons, Jane. *Ebb and Flo and the new friend*
Simont, Marc. *The goose that almost got cooked*
Spinelli, Eileen. *Silly Tilly*
Strand, Keith. *Grandfather's Christmas tree*
Tafuri, Nancy. *Silly little goose!*
Wall, Laura. *Goose*
    Goose goes to school
    Goose goes to the zoo
    Goose on the farm
Walsh, Ellen Stoll. *You silly goose*
Wild, Margaret. *Lucy Goosey*
Willems, Mo. *That is not a good idea!*
Wood, Jakki. *Never say boo to a goose!*

Birds – guinea fowl

Paterson, Brian. *Zigby camps out*
Ward, Helen. *Spots in a box*

Birds – hawks

Barton, Chris. *That's not Bunny!*

Baylor, Byrd. *Hawk, I'm your brother*
Hayes, Joe. *Little Gold Star / Estrellita de oro*
Kimura, Ken. *999 tadpoles*
McCarthy, Meghan. *City hawk*
Pia Toya
Rosen, Michael. *Crow and Hawk*
Schulman, Janet. *Pale Male*
Winter, Jeanette. *The tale of Pale Male*

Birds – herons

Gorbachev, Valeri. *Heron and Turtle*
McGaw, Wayne T. *T-boy of the bayou*
Quigley, Mary. *Granddad's fishing buddy*
Yolen, Jane. *An egret's day*

Birds – hummingbirds

Dudley, Rebecca. *Hank finds an egg*
Frith, Nicholas John. *Hector and Hummingbird*
Sayre, April Pulley. *The hungry hummingbird*
Yahgulanaas, Michael Nicoll. *The little hummingbird*

Birds – kestrels

Blake, Robert J. *Fledgling*

Birds – larks

Nelson, Marilyn. *Ostrich and Lark*

Birds – loons

Aston, Dianna Hutts. *Loony Little*
Griffin, Molly Beth. *Loon baby*
London, Jonathan. *Loon Lake*
Santucci, Barbara. *Loon summer*
Vande Griek, Susan. *Loon*

Birds – macaws

Mead, Alice. *Billy and Emma*

Birds – magpies

Springman, I. C. *More*
Wild, Margaret. *Fox*
Wilson, April. *April Wilson's magpie magic*

Birds – nightingales

Andersen, Hans Christian. *The nightingale*, ill. by Nancy Ekholm Burkert
    The nightingale, ill. by Pirkko Vainio
    The nightingale, ill. by Lisbeth Zwerger

Birds – ostriches

Aardema, Verna. *The lonely lioness and the ostrich chicks*
Idle, Molly. *Flora and the ostrich*
Nelson, Marilyn. *Ostrich and Lark*
Peet, Bill. *Zella, Zack, and Zodiac*
Weigelt, Udo. *The Easter Bunny's baby*

Birds – owls

Aesop. *Town mouse, country mouse*
Ainsworth, Kimberly. *Hootenanny!*
Allen, Jonathan. *"I'm not cute!"*

I'm not reading!
"I'm not Santa!"
"I'm not scared!"
Bernstein, Ariel. *I have a balloon*
Blaich, Ute. *The star*
Boiger, Alexandra. *Max and Marla*
Brown, Alan James. *Hoot and Holler*
Brunelle, Nicholas. *Snow moon*
Chapman, Jane. *I'm not sleepy!*
Chase, Kit. *Charlie's boat*
    Oliver's tree
Clifton-Brown, Holly. *Annie Hoot and the knitting extravaganza*
Corderoy, Tracey. *The little white owl*
Davies, Nicola. *White owl, barn owl*
Desbordes, Astrid. *Edmond, the moonlit party*
Dodd, Emma. *Happy*
Edwards, Pamela Duncan. *While the world is sleeping*
Ericsson, Jennifer A. *Whoo goes there?*
Feeney, Tatyana. *Little Owl's orange scarf*
Gallaher, Jason. *Whobert Whover, owl detective*
Gibbons, Gail. *Owls*
Gliori, Debi. *Little Owl's egg*
Godwin, Laura. *Owl sees owl*
Haughton, Chris. *Little Owl lost*
Hills, Tad. *Rocket writes a story*
Hiscock, Bruce. *Ookpik*
Hissey, Jane. *Hoot*
Holland, Mary. *Otis the owl*
Hopgood, Tim. *Wow! said the owl*
Hutchins, Pat. *Good-night Owl*
Iwamura, Kazuo. *Bedtime in the forest*
Johansen, Hanna. *The duck and the owl*
Johnston, Tony. *The barn owls*
Jones, Christianne C. *Lacey Walker, nonstop talker*
Judge, Lita. *Hoot and Peep*
    Hoot and Peep: a song for snow
Kishira, Mayuko. *Who's next door?*
Lear, Edward. *The owl and the pussycat*, ill. by Jan Brett
    The owl and the pussycat, ill. by Paul Galdone
    The owl and the pussycat, ill. by Anne Mortimer
Lears, Laurie. *Nathan's wish*
Lionni, Leo. *Six crows*
Lobel, Arnold. *Odd owls and stout pigs*
London, Jonathan. *The owl who became the moon*
Luzzati, Emanuele. *Three little owls*
McClure, Nikki. *In*
McDonald, Megan. *Whoo-oo is it?*
McPhail, David. *Olivia loves Owl*
Manning, Mick. *Cock-a-doodle hooooooo!*
Marino, Gianna. *Too tall houses*
Modarressi, Mitra. *Owlet's first flight*
Most, Bernard. *Z-Z-Zoink!*
Na, Il Sung. *A book of sleep*
Nicholls, Judith. *Billywise*
Oliver, Narelle. *Twilight hunt*
Pizzoli, Greg. *Good night Owl*
Potter, Beatrix. *The tale of Squirrel Nutkin*
Preston-Gannon, Frann. *What a hoot!*
Rosenthal, Amy Krouse. *Little Hoot*
Ruddell, Deborah. *Who said coo?*
Runton, Andy. *Owly and Wormy: bright lights and starry nights!*
Schatell, Brian. *Owl boy*
Serfozo, Mary. *Whooo's there?*
Smallman, Steve. *Scowl*
Srinivasan, Divya. *Little Owl's day*

    Little Owl's night
Taylor, Sean. *Hoot owl, master of disguise*
Tomlinson, Jill. *The owl who was afraid of the dark*
Townsend, Emily Rose. *Owls*
Waddell, Martin. *Owl babies*
Willis, Jeanne. *Fly, chick, fly!*
Won, Brian. *Hooray for today!*
Yolen, Jane. *Owl moon*
Yuly, Toni. *Night owl*

Birds – parakeets, parrots

Agee, Jon. *Terrific*
Bee, William. *And the train goes . . .*
Best, Cari. *Ava and the real Lucille*
Davis, Patricia Anne. *Brian's bird*
DePalma, Mary Newell. *The perfect gift*
Dicmas, Courtney. *Harold finds a voice*
Ferry, Beth. *Pirate's perfect pet*
Fox, Mem. *Tough Boris*
Friedman, Laurie. *Ruby Valentine and the sweet surprise*
Harris, Trudy. *Say something, Perico*
Javaherbin, Mina. *The secret message*
Judge, Lita. *Good morning to me!*
Kennedy, Kim. *Pirate Pete's giant adventure*
Lester, Helen. *Princess Penelope's parrot*
Ljungkvist, Laura. *Pepi sings a new song*
McFarland, Lyn Rossiter. *The pirate's parrot*
Meddaugh, Susan. *Martha walks the dog*
Medina, Meg. *Mango, Abuela, and me*
Nadimi, Suzan. *The rich man and the parrot*
Pinkwater, Daniel. *Beautiful Yetta*
Rankin, Joan. *You're somebody special, Walliwigs!*
Rawson, Katherine. *If you were a parrot*
Roth, Susan L. *Parrots over Puerto Rico*
Singer, Isaac Bashevis. *The parakeet named Dreidel*
Steig, William. *Wizzil*
Witte, Anna. *The parrot Tico Tango*

Birds – peacocks, peahens

Auch, Mary Jane. *Hen lake*
Hodgkinson, Leigh. *Limelight Larry*
Idle, Molly. *Flora and the peacocks*
Jules, Jacqueline. *Feathers for peacock*
Laminack, Lester L. *Three hens and a peacock*
Peet, Bill. *The spooky tail of Prewitt Peacock*
Polacco, Patricia. *Just plain Fancy*
Sehgal, Kabir. *A bucket of blessings*

Birds – pelicans

Johnson, Rebecca. *The proud pelican's secret*
Reed, Lynn Rowe. *Roscoe and the pelican rescue*

Birds – penguins

Anderson, Derek. *Romeo and Lou blast off*
Andreae, Giles. *Be brave, little penguin*
Antony, Steve. *I'll wait, Mr. Panda*
Apperley, Dawn. *Flip and Flop*
Arnold, Caroline. *A penguin's world*
Ashdown, Rebecca. *Bob and Flo*
    Bob and Flo play hide-and-seek
Aspinall, Sarah. *Penguins love colors*
Barner, Bob. *Penguins, penguins, everywhere!*
Bentley, Tadgh. *Little Penguin gets the hiccups*
Biddulph, Rob. *Blown away*
Bishop, Nic. *Penguin day*

Bogan, Paulette. *Virgil and Owen*
  Virgil and Owen stick together
Brooks, Erik. *Polar opposites*
Buzzeo, Toni. *One cool friend*
Clayton, Dallas. *Lily the unicorn*
Corderoy, Tracey. *The magical snow garden*
Coudray, Jean-Luc. *A goofy guide to penguins*
Cuyler, Margery. *Please play safe!*
Davies, Gill. *Can't, don't, won't*
Dodd, Emma. *I am small*
Dunbar, Polly. *Penguin*
  Pingüino / penguin
Duquennoy, Jacques. *North Pole, South Pole*
Dyer, Heather. *Tina and the penguin*
Ferry, Beth. *A small blue whale*
Fromental, Jean-Luc. *365 penguins*
Genechten, Guido van. *No ghost under my bed*
Gibbons, Gail. *Penguins!*
Gliori, Debi. *Dragon's extraordinary egg*
  Penguin post
Gorbachev, Valeri. *Turtle's penguin day*
Gourounas, Jean. *Something's fishy*
Guiberson, Brenda Z. *The emperor lays an egg*
Guion, Melissa. *Baby penguins everywhere!*
  Baby penguins love their Mama
Hancocks, Helen. *Penguin in peril*
Harper, Lee. *The Emperor's cool clothes*
Hewett, Joan. *A penguin chick grows up*
Horáček, Petr. *Flip's day*
  Blue Penguin
Ichikawa, Satomi. *I am Pangoo the penguin*
Idle, Molly. *Flora and the penguin*
Jadoul, Emile. *All by myself!*
  No room for baby!
Jeffers, Oliver. *Lost and found*
  Up and down
John, Jory. *Penguin problems*
Judge, Lita. *Flight school*
Karas, G. Brian. *Skidamarink*
Kellogg, Steven. *A penguin pup for Pinkerton*
Kimmel, Elizabeth Cody. *My penguin Osbert*
  My penguin Osbert in love
Latimer, Alex. *Penguin's hidden talent*
Lester, Helen. *Happy birdday, Tacky!*
  Tacky and the Emperor
  Tacky and the haunted igloo
  Tacky and the Winter Games
  Tacky goes to camp
  Tacky in trouble
  Tacky the penguin
  Tackylocks and the three bears
  Tacky's Christmas
  Three cheers for Tacky
Lin, Grace. *Olvina swims*
London, Jonathan. *Little penguin*
McDonald, Megan. *Penguin and Little Blue*
McMillan, Bruce. *Puffins climb, penguins rhyme*
McPhail, David. *Peter loves Penguin*
Magloff, Lisa. *Penguin*
Markle, Sandra. *A mother's journey*
Marzollo, Jean. *Pierre the penguin*
Maynor, Megan. *Ella and Penguin: stick together*
Meschenmoser, Sebastian. *Gordon and Tapir*
Messer, Claire. *Grumpy pants*
Minor, Florence. *If you were a penguin*
Mitton, Tony. *Playful little penguins*
Morison, Toby. *Little Louie takes off*
Murphy, Mary. *I like it when . . .*
  Please be quiet!

Some things change
Perlman, Janet. *The Emperor Penguin's new clothes*
  The penguin and the pea
Pfister, Marcus. *Penguin Pete and Little Tim*
Pichon, Liz. *Penguins*
Portis, Antoinette. *A penguin story*
Proimos, James. *Waddle! waddle!*
Radcliffe, Theresa. *Nanu, penguin chick*
Rash, Andy. *Archie the daredevil penguin*
Richardson, Justin. *And Tango makes three*
Rickards, Lynne. *Pink!*
Rodriguez, Edel. *Sergio makes a splash*
  Sergio saves the game!
Ryan, Pam Muñoz. *Tony Baloney*
  Tony Baloney: buddy trouble
Rylant, Cynthia. *Little penguins*
Savage, Stephen. *Where's Walrus? and Penguin?*
Schafer, Kevin. *Penguins A B C*
  Penguins 1 2 3
Schindel, John. *Busy penguins*
Schrey, Sophie. *Where's the penguin?*
Seibold, J. Otto. *Penguin dreams*
Shields, Carol Diggory. *Martian rock*
Tatham, Betty. *Penguin chick*
Telchin, Eric. *The Black and White Factory*
Townsend, Emily Rose. *Penguins*
Weeks, Sarah. *Without you*
Whybrow, Ian. *Wish, change, friend*
Wiesmüller, Dieter. *The adventures of Marco and Polo*
Willis, Jeanne. *Poles apart*
Wilson, Karma. *Don't be afraid, Little Pip*
  What's in the egg, Little Pip?
  Where is home, Little Pip?
Wood, Audrey. *Little Penguin's tale*
Yoon, Salina. *Penguin and Pinecone*
  Penguin and Pumpkin
  Penguin in love
  Penguin on vacation
  Penguin's big adventure
  Penguin's Christmas wish

Birds – pigeons

Eitzen, Ruth. *Tara's flight*
Farmer, Nancy. *Clever Ali*
Keller, Holly. *Sophie's window*
Macaulay, David. *Angelo*
McCloskey, Kevin. *The real poop on pigeons!*
McLaren, Meg. *Pigeon P.I.*
Murray, Diana. *City shapes*
Peet, Bill. *Fly, Homer, fly*
Richmond, Lori. *Pax and Blue*
Ruddell, Deborah. *Who said coo?*
Rudge, Leila. *Gary*
San Souci, Daniel. *The Mighty Pigeon Club*
Wells, Rosemary. *The language of doves*
Willems, Mo. *Don't let the pigeon drive the bus*
  Don't let the pigeon stay up late!
  The duckling gets a cookie!?
  The pigeon finds a hot dog!
  The pigeon has feelings, too!
  The pigeon loves things that go!
  The pigeon needs a bath
  The pigeon wants a puppy!

Birds – plovers

dePaola, Tomie. *Bill and Pete*

Bill and Pete go down the Nile
Bill and Pete to the rescue
Miller, John. *Winston and George*

Birds – ptarmigans

Guenther, James. *Turnagain, Ptarmigan, where did you go?*
London, Jonathan. *Gone again ptarmigan*

Birds – puffins

Allen, Jonathan. *Don't copy me!*
Bentley, Dawn. *Welcome back, Puffin*
De Beer, Hans. *Little Polar Bear and the big balloon*
Horácek, Petr. *Puffin Peter*
London, Jonathan. *Little Puffin's first flight*
McMillan, Bruce. *Nights of the pufflings*
  Puffins climb, penguins rhyme
Soltis, Sue. *Nothing like a puffin*
Wild, Margaret. *Puffling*
Zecca, Katherine. *A puffin's year*

Birds – ravens

Bansch, Helga. *Odd bird out*
  Rosie the raven
Battle-Lavert, Gwendolyn. *The shaking bag*
Dupre, Kelly. *The raven's gift*
Johnson, Amy Crane. *Cinnamon and the April shower / Canela y el aguacero de abril*
  Mason moves away / Mason se muda
McDermott, Gerald. *Raven*
Pfister, Marcus. *The little moon raven*
Weigelt, Udo. *It wasn't me*

Birds – roadrunners

Anaya, Rudolfo A. *Roadrunner's dance*

Birds – robins

Atkins, Jeannine. *Robin's home*
Fisher, Aileen Lucia. *You don't look like your mother*
Holmes, Anita. *Where robins fly*
Hurley, Jorey. *Nest*
Jenkins, Priscilla Belz. *A nest full of eggs*
Ketcham, Sallie. *The Christmas bird*
Mackall, Dandi Daley. *The story of the Easter robin*
Posada, Mia. *Robins*
Rockwell, Anne. *My spring robin*
Schwartz, Amy. *A beautiful girl*

Birds – sandpipers

Willis, Nancy Carol. *Red knot*

Birds – seagulls

Allen, Jonathan. *Don't copy me!*
Clark, Katie. *Seagull Sam*
Eaton, Maxwell. *Two dumb ducks*
Engels-Fietzek, Petra. *Sophie and the seagull*
Gibbons, Gail. *Gulls — gulls — gulls*
Simmons, Jane. *Ebb and Flo and the greedy gulls*
Turkle, Brinton. *Thy friend, Obadiah*
Walsh, Ellen Stoll. *Hamsters to the rescue*
Waugh, Peter. *The great cannon beach mouse caper*

Birds – sparrows

Evans, Lezlie. *Finding Christmas*
Kasbarian, Lucine. *The greedy sparrow*
Lee, Y. J. *The little moon princess*
Myers, Christopher. *Sparrows*
Sheehan, Kevin. *The dandelion's tale*

Birds – storks

Brown, Margaret Wise. *Wheel on the chimney*
Clarke, Jane. *The best of both nests*
Kelly, L. J. R. *Sometimes it's storks*
Olson, David J. *The thunderstruck stork*

Birds – swallows

Politi, Leo. *Song of the swallows*
Ryan, Pam Muñoz. *Nacho and Lolita*
Swinburne, Stephen R. *Swallows in the birdhouse*

Birds – swans

Andersen, Hans Christian. *The ugly duckling*, ill. by Adrienne Adams
  The ugly duckling, ill. by Sebastien Braun
  The ugly duckling, ill. by Lorinda Bryan Cauley
  The ugly duckling, ill. by Charlene DeLage
  The ugly duckling, ill. by Robert Ingpen
  The ugly duckling, ill. by Rachel Isadora
  The ugly duckling, ill. by Steve Johnson
  The ugly duckling, ill. by Jerry Pinkney
  The ugly duckling, ill. by Meilo So
  The ugly duckling, ill. by Pirkko Vainio
  The ugly duckling, ill. by Bernadette Watts
  The ugly duckling, ill. by Roberta Wilson
  The wild swans, ill. by Anne Yvonne Gilbert
  The wild swans, ill. by Susan Jeffers
Antony, Steve. *The queen's handbag*
Bunting, Eve. *Swan in love*
Edwards, Pamela Duncan. *Honk!*
Geras, Adèle. *Swan Lake*
Grimm, Jacob and Wilhelm. *Princess Sophie and the six swans*
  The six swans
Kent, Allegra. *Ballerina swan*
London, Jonathan. *Little swan*
Morpurgo, Michael. *The silver swan*
Shulman, Lisa. *Over in the meadow at the big ballet*
Sones, Sonya. *Violet and Winston*
Tafuri, Nancy. *Whose chick are you?*

Birds – toucans

Antony, Steve. *Betty goes bananas*
Lehrhaupt, Adam. *Warning: do not open this book!*
Murguia, Bethanie Deeney. *Toucans, too*

Birds – turkeys

Anderson, Derek. *Over the river*
Archer, Peggy. *Turkey surprise*
Arnosky, Jim. *All about turkeys*
  I'm a turkey!
Auch, Mary Jane. *Beauty and the beaks*
Balian, Lorna. *Sometimes it's turkey*
Bateman, Teresa. *Gus, the pilgrim turkey*
  A plump and perky turkey
Bunting, Eve. *A turkey for Thanksgiving*
Cazet, Denys. *Bob and Tom*

Cole, Brock. *The money we'll save*
Cowley, Joy. *Gracias, the Thanksgiving turkey*
Falwell, Cathryn. *Gobble gobble*
Kenah, Katharine. *The very stuffed turkey*
Kroll, Steven. *One tough turkey*
Mayr, Diane. *Run, Turkey, run*
Nathan, Emma. *What do you call a group of turkeys?*
Pilkey, Dav. *'Twas the night before Thanksgiving*
Pollock, Penny. *The turkey girl*
Reed, Lynn Rowe. *Thelonius Turkey lives!*
Shannon, George. *Turkey Tot*
Silvano, Wendi. *Turkey Claus*
    Turkey trouble
Stiegemeyer, Julie. *Gobble gobble crash!*
Sturgis, Brenda Reeves. *Ten turkeys in the road*
Waddell, Martin. *Captain Small Pig*
Wheeler, Lisa. *Turk and Runt*
White, Linda. *Too many turkeys*

Birds – vultures

Grindley, Sally. *The sulky vulture*
Peet, Bill. *Eli*
Sayre, April Pulley. *Vulture view*

Birds – woodpeckers

Breen, Steve. *Woodpecker wants a waffle*
Cousins, Lucy. *Peck, peck, peck*
Sayre, April Pulley. *Woodpecker wham!*
Townsend, Emily Rose. *Woodpeckers*

Birds – wrens

Polacco, Patricia. *Luba and the wren*

Birth

Alexander, Sue. *One more time, Mama*
Andreae, Giles. *There's a house inside my mommy*
Anholt, Laurence. *Sophie and the new baby*
Aston, Dianna Hutts. *Mama Outside, Mama Inside*
Batten, Mary. *Who has a belly button?*
Bauer, Marion Dane. *Grandmother's song*
Carlstrom, Nancy White. *Before you were born*
Cocovini, Abby. *What's inside your tummy, Mommy?*
Cole, Joanna. *How you were born*
    My puppy is born
    When you were inside mommy
Dixon, Ann. *Waiting for Noël*
Douglas, Ann. *Before you were born*
Fearnley, Jan. *A special something*
Fox, Mem. *Sophie*
Frasier, Debra. *On the day you were born*
Grambling, Lois G. *Grandma tells a story*
Harris, Robie H. *What's in there?*
Holt, Kimberly Willis. *Waiting for Gregory*
Holt, Sharon. *Did my mother do that?*
Kallok, Emma. *Gem*
Lohans, Alison. *Waiting for the sun*
Lund, Deb. *Tell me my story, Mama*
Mackall, Dandi Daley. *There's a baby in there!*
MacLachlan, Patricia. *All the places to love*
Overend, Jenni. *Welcome with love*
Pringle, Laurence P. *Everybody has a bellybutton*
Radunsky, Vladimir. *Ten*
Roberts, Jillian. *Where do babies come from? our first talk about birth*
Rockwell, Lizzy. *Hello baby!*

Rosenberg, Maxine B. *Mommy's in the hospital having a baby*
Saltz, Gail. *Amazing you*
Sears, William, M.D.. *Baby on the way*
Simpson-Enock, Sarah. *Mommy, Mommy, what's in your tummy?*
Sykes, Julie. *Dora's eggs*
    This and that
Tillman, Nancy. *On the night you were born*
Van Steenwyk, Elizabeth. *Prairie Christmas*
Waiting for baby
Yolen, Jane. *Grandma's hurrying child*

Birthdays

Aliki. *Use your head, dear*
Allen, Nancy Kelly. *"Happy birthday"*
Anholt, Catherine. *Happy birthday, Chimp and Zee*
Asch, Frank. *Happy birthday, Big Bad Wolf*
    Happy birthday, moon!
Asher, Sandy. *What a party!*
Ashman, Linda. *Maxwell's magic mix-up*
Averbeck, Jim. *One word from Sophia*
Avraham, Kate Aver. *What will you be, Sara Mee?*
Awdry, W. *Happy birthday, Thomas!*
Bach, Annie. *Monster party!*
Badescu, Ramona. *Big Rabbit's bad mood*
Baeten, Lieve. *Happy birthday, Little Witch!*
Baker, Roberta. *Olive's pirate party*
Bastianich, Lidia. *Nonna's birthday surprise*
Beck, Andrea. *Elliot bakes a cake*
Beck, Scott. *Happy birthday, Monster!*
    A mud pie for mother
Becker, Bonny. *A birthday for Bear*
Bemelmans, Ludwig. *Madeline in London*
Berenstain, Stan and Jan. *The Berenstain bears and too much birthday*
Bergel, Colin. *Mail by the pail*
Bertrand, Diane Gonzales. *The last doll / La última muñeca*
    The party for Papá Luis / La fiesta para Papá Luis
Best, Cari. *Three cheers for Catherine the Great!*
Blackstone, Stella. *Bear's birthday*
Borden, Louise. *A. Lincoln and me*
Bourgeois, Paulette. *Franklin says "I love you"*
    Postal workers
Boynton, Sandra. *Happy birthday, Little Pookie*
Breen, Steve. *Pug and Doug*
Brown, Marc. *Arthur's birthday*
Browne, Anthony. *Gorilla*
Brunhoff, Laurent de. *Babar's birthday surprise*
Bunting, Eve. *Flower garden*
    Happy birthday, dear duck
    Little Badger's just-about birthday
    A picnic in October
    The Wednesday surprise
Cabrera, Jane. *One, two, buckle my shoe*
Calmenson, Stephanie. *Birthday at the Panda Palace*
Capucilli, Alyssa Satin. *Happy birthday, Biscuit!*
    This bear's birthday
Carle, Eric. *Hello, red fox*
    The secret birthday message
Carlstrom, Nancy White. *Happy birthday, Jesse Bear!*
Cazet, Denys. *December 24th*
    A fish in his pocket
Chapin, Tom. *The backwards birthday party*
Charlip, Remy. *Handtalk birthday*
Chavarría-Cháirez, Becky. *Magda's piñata magic / Magda y la piñata mágica*

Magda's tortillas / Las tortillas de Magada
Cheng, Andrea. *The lemon sisters*
Chodos-Irvine, Margaret. *Best best friends*
Christelow, Eileen. *Don't wake up Mama!*
Clarke, Jane. *Trumpet*
Cleminson, Katie. *Magic box*
Coats, Lucy. *Captain Beastlie's pirate party*
   Neil's numberless world
Cooke, Trish. *So much*
Cousins, Lucy. *Happy birthday, Maisy*
Cox, Judy. *Happy birthday, Mrs. Millie!*
Cronin, Doreen. *Click, clack, surprise!*
Cummins, Lucy Ruth. *A hungry lion; or, a dwindling
   assortment of animals*
Dale, Penny. *Dinosaur zoom!*
Daly, Niki. *Happy birthday, Jamela!*
Day, Alexandra. *Carl's birthday*
deGroat, Diane. *Happy birthday to you, you belong
   in a zoo*
Demas, Corinne. *The boy who was generous with salt*
   The disappearing island
Díaz, Katacha. *Carolina's gift*
DiPucchio, Kelly. *Crafty Chloe*
Dixon, Ann. *Waiting for Noël*
Dodd, Emma. *The entertainer*
Edwards, Pamela Duncan. *Rosie's roses*
Ellwand, David. *Alfred's party*
Elya, Susan Middleton. *F is for fiesta*
Evans, Cambria. *Martha Moth makes socks*
Faglia, Matteo. *Happy birthday, I'm 1*
   Happy birthday, I'm 2
   Happy birthday, I'm 3
   Happy birthday, I'm 4
Fearnley, Jan. *Mr. Wolf and the three bears*
Fernandes, Eugenie. *Big week for little mouse*
Ferry, Beth. *Land shark*
Flack, Marjorie. *Ask Mr. Bear*
Fleming, Candace. *Bulldozer's big day*
   Clever Jack takes the cake
Fliess, Sue. *A gluten-free birthday for me!*
Fogliano, Julie. *When's my birthday?*
Foreman, George. *Let George do it!*
Fox, Mem. *Night noises*
Frasier, Debra. *A birthday cake is no ordinary cake*
Freeman, Tor. *Hooray! I'm five today!*
Gantos, Jack. *Happy birthday, Rotten Ralph*
Gibbons, Gail. *Happy birthday!*
Gillmor, Don. *Yuck, a love story*
Glass, Julie. *A dollar for Penny*
Gliori, Debi. *What's the time, Mr. Wolf?*
Goble, Paul. *Iktomi and the boulder*
Godin, Thelma Lynne. *The hula-hoopin' queen*
Goodall, John S. *Shrewbettina's birthday*
Goode, Diane. *Mama's perfect present*
Gorbachev, Valeri. *Nicky and the fantastic birthday
   gift*
   What's the big idea, Molly?
Graham, Bob. *Oscar's half birthday*
Hardy, Sarah Frances. *Puzzled by pink*
Harper, Charise Mericle. *The best birthday ever!*
   When Randolph turned rotten
Harrison, Hannah E. *Bernice gets carried away*
Heder, Thyra. *Alfie: (the turtle that disappeared)*
Hennessy, B. G. *Corduroy's birthday*
Hest, Amy. *Nana's birthday party*
Hill, Eric. *Spot bakes a cake*
   Spot's birthday party
Hoban, Russell. *A birthday for Frances*
Hobbie, Holly. *Everything but the horse*

Toot and Puddle, a present for Toot
Hoberman, Mary Ann. *The seven silly eaters*
Hosford, Kate. *Big birthday*
Howe, James. *Houndsley and Catina and the birthday
   surprise*
Huget, Jennifer LaRue. *The best birthday party ever*
Hughes, Shirley. *Alfie and the birthday surprise*
Hunter, Sally. *Humphrey's birthday*
Hutchins, Pat. *Happy birthday, Sam*
   It's my birthday!
Inkpen, Mick. *Kipper and Roly*
   Kipper's birthday
Janni, Rebecca. *Every cowgirl needs a horse*
Jennings, Linda. *Hide and seek birthday treat*
Jocelyn, Marthe. *Hannah and the seven dresses*
Jonas, Ann. *The thirteenth clue*
Jonell, Lynne. *It's my birthday, too!*
Jorgensen, Gail. *Gotcha!*
Kasza, Keiko. *My lucky birthday*
Keane, Dave. *Who wants a tortoise?*
Keller, Holly. *Henry's happy birthday*
Khan, Rukhsana. *Big red lollipop*
Kirk, David. *Miss Spider's ABC*
Kleven, Elisa. *Ernst*
Kroll, Virginia L. *Jason takes responsibility*
Kromhout, Rindert. *Little Donkey and the birthday
   present*
Kulka, Joe. *Wolf's coming*
Larsen, Andrew. *The not-so-faraway adventure*
Lasky, Kathryn. *Starring Lucille*
Lears, Laurie. *Megan's birthday tree*
Leedy, Loreen. *Crazy like a fox*
Lester, Helen. *Happy birdday, Tacky!*
Levine, Gail Carson. *Betsy Red Hoodie*
Lewin, Ted. *Amazon boy*
Lewis, Rose A. *Every year on your birthday*
Linders, Clara. *The very best door of all*
Lodge, Jo. *Happy birthday, Moo Moo*
London, Jonathan. *Froggy's birthday wish*
Long, Ethan. *Snickerdoodle takes the cake*
Look, Lenore. *Henry's first-moon birthday*
Lord, Cynthia. *Happy birthday, Hamster*
Lucas, David. *Cake girl*
McClatchy, Lisa. *Dear Tyrannosaurus Rex*
McClure, Wendy. *The princess and the peanut allergy*
McCormack, Caren McNelly. *The fiesta dress*
McCourt, Lisa. *Chicken soup for little souls: Della
   Splatnuk birthday girl*
   Chicken soup for little souls: The never-forgotten doll
McElligott, Matthew. *Backbeard and the birthday suit*
Machado, Ana Maria. *What a party!*
Mackintosh, David. *Marshall Armstrong is new to our
   school*
McKissack, Patricia C. *Messy Bessey and the birthday
   overnight*
McLaughlin, Lauren. *Mitzi Tulane, preschool
   detective, in What's that smell*
McNamara, Margaret. *George Washington's birthday*
McNaughton, Colin. *Not last night but the night
   before*
McPhail, David. *Big Brown Bear's birthday surprise*
Madrigal, Antonio Hernandez. *Erandi's braids*
Mann, Jennifer K. *Two speckled eggs*
Martin, Bill, Jr.. *Fire! Fire! said Mrs. McGuire*
   "Fire! Fire!" said Mrs. McGuire
Martin, David. *Monkey business*
Mayer, Mercer. *Bun Bun's birthday*
Meddaugh, Susan. *Martha says it with flowers*
Milord, Susan. *Happy one hundredth day!*

Miranda, Anne. *Alphabet fiesta*
  Monster math
Modell, Frank. *Ice cream soup*
Modesitt, Jeanne. *Little Mouse's happy birthday*
Monroe, Chris. *Bug on a bike*
Mora, Pat. *A birthday basket for Tía*
  One, two, three / Uno, dos, tres
  Pablo's tree
Morales, Yuyi. *Just in case: a trickster tale and Spanish alphabet book*
Moss, Miriam. *I'll be your friend, Smudge*
Muir, Leslie. *The little bitty bakery*
Munsch, Robert N. *Moira's birthday*
  Wait and see
Murguia, Bethanie Deeney. *I feel five!*
Murphy, Stuart J. *Too many kangaroo things to do!*
Myller, Rolf. *How big is a foot?*
Neuschwander, Cindy. *Sir Cumference and all the king's tens*
Noble, Trinka Hakes. *Jimmy's boa and the big splash birthday bash*
Numeroff, Laura Joffe. *Otis and Sydney and the best birthday ever*
O'Connor, Jane. *Bonjour, butterfly*
  Fancy Nancy: ooh la la! it's beauty day
Oxenbury, Helen. *It's my birthday*
Parenteau, Shirley. *Bears and a birthday*
Patricelli, Leslie. *The birthday box*
Paul, Ann Whitford. *Fiesta fiasco*
Peek, Merle. *Mary wore her red dress and Henry wore his green sneakers*
Pfister, Marcus. *Happy birthday, Bertie!*
  Make a wish, Honey Bear!
Pham, LeUyen. *A piece of cake*
Pilgrim, Elza. *The china doll*
Polacco, Patricia. *Some birthday!*
Pomerantz, Charlotte. *You're not my best friend anymore*
Reed, Lynn Rowe. *Pedro, his perro, and the alphabet sombrero*
Rempt, Fiona. *Snail's birthday wish*
Reynolds, Marilynn. *A present for Mrs. Kazinski*
Rice, Eve. *Benny bakes a cake*
Rim, Sujean. *Birdie's big-girl dress*
Roberton, Fiona. *The perfect present*
Roberts, Bethany. *Birthday mice*
Robinson, Sharon. *Under the same sun*
Rodman, Mary Ann. *A tree for Emmy*
Rollings, Susan. *New shoes, red shoes*
Rose, Deborah Lee. *Birthday zoo*
Ross, Tony. *I want two birthdays!*
Rossell, Judith. *Ruby and Leonard and the great big surprise*
Ryan, Pam Muñoz. *Mice and beans*
Rylant, Cynthia. *Birthday presents*
Sáenz, Benjamin Alire. *A gift from papá Diego / Un regalo de papá Diego*
  Grandma Fina and her wonderful umbrellas / La abuelita Fina y sus sombrillas maravillosas
Sage, Angie. *Molly and the birthday party*
Saltzberg, Barney. *Hi, Blueberry!*
  Hip, hip, hooray day!
Samuels, Barbara. *Fred's beds*
  Happy birthday, Dolores
Sauer, Tammi. *I love cake!*
Sayre, April Pulley. *It's my city*
Scanlon, Elizabeth Garton. *Happy birthday, Bunny!*
Schachner, Judith Byron. *Yo, Vikings*
Schoenherr, Ian. *Don't spill the beans!*

  Pip and Squeak
Schotter, Roni. *Mama, I'll give you the world*
Schubert, Leda. *Winnie plays ball*
Scieszka, Jon. *Battle Bunny*
Segal, Lore Groszmann. *Morris the artist*
Selkowe, Valrie M. *Happy birthday to me!*
Sendak, Maurice. *Bumble-ardy*
Seuss, Dr. *Happy birthday to you!*
Shannon, George. *The surprise*
Silbaugh, Elizabeth. *Raggedy Ann's birthday party book*
Simpson, Lesley. *The Purim surprise*
Sirett, Dawn. *Happy birthday Sophie!*
Slingsby, Janet. *Hetty's 100 hats*
Soto, Gary. *Chato and the party animals*
Sperring, Mark. *The fairytale cake*
  How many sleeps 'til my birthday?
Spinelli, Eileen. *In my new yellow shirt*
Stanton, Karen. *Papi's gift*
Starr, Meg. *Alicia's happy day*
Stevens, April. *Edwin speaks up*
Stewart, Paul. *The birthday presents*
Stewart, Sarah. *The journey*
Stock, Catherine. *The birthday present*
Stolz, Mary. *Emmett's pig*
Swanson, Susan Marie. *The first thing my mama told me*
Sykes, Julie. *Little Rocket's special star*
Tafuri, Nancy. *The barn party*
Tatcheva, Eva. *Witch Zelda's birthday cake*
Thomas, Jan. *A birthday for Cow!*
Thomas, Naturi. *Uh-oh! It's Mama's birthday!*
Tougas, Chris. *Dojo surprise*
Tryon, Leslie. *Albert's birthday*
Uff, Caroline. *Happy birthday, Lulu*
Vigna, Judith. *My two uncles*
Viva, Frank. *Outstanding in the rain*
Waber, Bernard. *Lyle and the birthday party*
Walker, Anna. *I love birthdays*
Wallace, John. *Tiny Rabbit goes to a birthday party*
Wallace, Nancy Elizabeth. *Tell-a-bunny*
Watt, Mélanie. *Scaredy Squirrel has a birthday party*
Wells, Rosemary. *Bunny party*
  Fiona's little lie
  Max's birthday
  Sophie's terrible twos
  Yoko's paper cranes
Weninger, Brigitte. *Double birthday*
  Happy birthday, Davy
White, Linda Arms. *Comes a wind*
Wilcox, Brian. *Full moon*
Willard, Nancy. *The mouse, the cat and Grandmother's hat*
Williams, Barbara. *Albert's gift for grandmother*
Williams, Vera B. *Something special for me*
Willis, Jeanne. *Boa's bad birthday*
Wilson, Karma. *Whopper cake*
Witte, Anna. *Lola's fandango*
Wood, Audrey. *The Birthday Queen*
Wormell, Mary. *Hilda Hen's happy birthday*
Wright, Betty Ren. *The blizzard*
Wright, Maureen. *Earth Day, birthday!*
Yaccarino, Dan. *The birthday fish*
  Happyland: birthday cake
Yashima, Taro. *Umbrella*
Yezerski, Thomas. *Queen of the world*
Yolen, Jane. *Picnic with Piggins*
Zolotow, Charlotte. *Mr. Rabbit and the lovely present*

Blackouts *see* Power failures

Blindness *see* Disabilities – blindness; Senses – sight

Board books *see* Format, unusual – board books

Boasting *see* Behavior – boasting, showing off

Boats, ships

Alborough, Jez. *Captain Duck*
Allen, Pamela. *Who sank the boat?*
Arnosky, Jim. *Parrotfish and sunken ships*
Arro, Lena. *By geezers and galoshes!*
Auld, Mary. *Noah's ark*
Austin, Mike. *Rescue Squad No. 9*
Bagley, Jessixa. *Boats for Papa*
Bartoletti, Susan Campbell. *Naamah and the ark at night*
Barton, Byron. *Boats*
Base, Graeme. *The legend of the Golden Snail*
Beck, Andrea. *Elliot's shipwreck*
Bergel, Colin. *Mail by the pail*
Berger, Melvin. *Dive! a book of deep sea creatures*
Blackstone, Stella. *Ship shapes*
Braun, Sebastien. *Toot and Pop!*
Brill, Calista. *Tugboat Bill and the river rescue*
Brunhoff, Laurent de. *Babar on Paradise Island*
Bunting, Eve. *Big Bear's big boat*
    Swan in love
Burdett, Lois. *Twelfth night for kids*
Burningham, John. *Mr. Gumpy's outing*
Cabrera, Jane. *Row, row, row your boat*
Calhoun, Mary. *Henry the sailor cat*
Carbone, Elisa. *Heroes of the surf*
Chan, Arlene. *Awakening the dragon*
Christian, Mary Blount. *If not for the calico cat*
Clark, Mary Higgins. *Ghost ship*
Corey, Shana. *Boats!*
Costello, David Hyde. *Little Pig saves the ship*
Cotten, Cynthia. *The book boat's in*
Cousins, Lucy. *Noah's ark*
Crampton, Gertrude. *Scuffy the tugboat*
Crews, Donald. *Harbor*
    Sail away
Cullen, Lynn. *Little Scraggly Hair*
Cumming, Hannah. *The red boat*
De Beer, Hans. *Little Polar Bear and the submarine*
Demas, Corinne. *The disappearing island*
Dickson, Louise. *The vanishing cat*
Dubuc, Marianne. *The animals' ark*
Duke, Kate. *Twenty is too many*
Dunbar, Polly. *Arthur's dream boat*
Ering, Timothy Basil. *The unexpected love story of Alfred Fiddleduckling*
Fitzpatrick, Marie-Louise. *You, me and the big blue sea*
Flanagan, Alice K. *Riding the ferry with Captain Cruz*
Fleming, Candace. *Papa's mechanical fish*
Floca, Brian. *Lightship*
Garland, Michael. *Tugboat*
Garland, Sherry. *My father's boat*
Gibbons, Gail. *Boat book*
    Exploring the deep, dark sea

Goldsboro, Bobby. *Noah and the ark; and, David and Goliath*
Goodhart, Pippa. *Noah makes a boat*
Gorbachev, Valeri. *The fool of the world and the flying ship: a Ukrainian folk tale*
Gramatky, Hardie. *Little Toot*
Greene, Rhonda Gowler. *Noah and the mighty ark*
Greenwood, Mark. *The Mayflower*
Gutman, Anne. *Gaspard on vacation*
Haas, Rick de. *Peter and the seal*
Harker, Lesley. *Annie's ark*
Harrison, Troon. *The floating orchard*
Holabird, Katharine. *Angelina, star of the show*
Hubbell, Patricia. *Boats: speeding! sailing! cruising!*
Hutchins, Hazel. *Beneath the bridge*
Hyde, Heidi Smith. *Emanuel and the Hanukkah rescue*
Jonas, Ann. *Aardvarks, disembark!*
Kellogg, Steven. *The island of the skog*
    Mike Fink
Kenah, Katharine. *Ferry tail*
Kimmel, Eric A. *The Erie Canal pirates*
Krensky, Stephen. *Noah's bark*
LaMarche, Jim. *The raft*
Lamb, Albert. *The abandoned lighthouse*
Lenski, Lois. *The little sailboat*
Lewin, Ted. *Amazon boy*
Light, Steve. *Swap!*
Lloyd-Jones, Sally. *Old MacNoah had an ark*
London, Jonathan. *Where the big fish are*
Lyon, George Ella. *Boats float!*
Maass, Robert. *Tugboats*
McCarthy, Michael. *The story of Noah and the ark*
McCleery, Peter. *Bob and Joss get lost!*
McCully, Emily Arnold. *The pirate queen*
McDonnell, Flora. *I love boats*
McNeil, Florence. *Sail away*
McPhail, David. *Pigs ahoy*
Martin, Jacqueline Briggs. *On Sand Island*
Matteson, George. *The Christmas tugboat*
Meddaugh, Susan. *Harry on the rocks*
Mitton, Tony. *All afloat on Noah's boat!*
Miyares, Daniel. *Float*
Morrissey, Dean. *The Christmas ship*
O'Neill, Alexis. *Loud Emily*
Oppel, Kenneth. *Peg and the whale*
Paley, Joan. *One more river*
Pallotta, Jerry. *Dory story*
Peacock, Carol Antoinette. *Pilgrim cat*
Pelton, Mindy L. *When Dad's at sea*
Perrow, Angeli. *Sirius, the dog star*
Philip, Neil. *Noah and the devil*
Pinkney, Jerry. *Noah's ark*
Potter, Beatrix. *The tale of Little Pig Robinson*
Priest, Robert H. *The old pirate of Central Park*
Prince, April Jones. *Goldenlocks and the three pirates*
Rand, Gloria. *Sailing home*
Ransome, Arthur. *The fool of the world and the flying ship*
Rappaport, Doreen. *Freedom ship*
Reynolds, Peter H. *Sydney's star*
Rockwell, Anne. *Boats*
    Ferryboat ride!
Rohmann, Eric. *The cinder-eyed cats*
Rotner, Shelley. *Boats afloat*
Rumford, James. *The Island-below-the-star*
Ruzzier, Sergio. *Two mice*
San Souci, Robert D. *Brave Margaret*
Santore, Charles. *A stowaway on Noah's Ark*

Savage, Stephen. *Little Tug*
Schachner, Judith Byron. *Yo, Vikings*
Schaefer, Lola M. *Tugboats*
Segal, John. *Alistair and Kip's great adventure*
Shapiro, Zachary. *We're all in the same boat*
Shaw, Nancy. *Sheep on a ship*
Singer, Isaac Bashevis. *Why Noah chose the dove*
Sís, Peter. *Ship ahoy!*
Slack, Michael. *Turtle Tug to the rescue*
Slater, Dashka. *The antlered ship*
Soman, David. *Three bears in a boat*
Soto, Gary. *Chato goes cruisin'*
Spier, Peter. *Noah's ark*
Stafford, Liliana. *Just dragon*
Starkoff, Vanina. *Along the river*
Stead, Philip C. *Jonathan and the big blue boat*
Steggall, Susan. *Busy boats*
Stephens, Helen. *Ahoyty-toyty*
Stevenson, James. *The stowaway*
Stewig, John Warren. *The animals watched*
Sting [Musician]. *Rock steady*
Swift, Hildegarde Hoyt. *The little red lighthouse and the great gray bridge*
Tebbs, Victoria. *Noah's Ark story*
Titherington, Jeanne. *Baby's boat*
Todd, Traci. *T is for tugboat*
Trapani, Iza. *Row, row, row your boat*
Van Allsburg, Chris. *The wreck of the Zephyr*
Van Dusen, Chris. *The circus ship*
  Down to the sea with Mr. Magee
Van Leeuwen, Jean. *Across the wide dark sea*
Virján, Emma J. *What this story needs is a pig in a wig*
Waddell, Martin. *Captain Small Pig*
  Sailor Bear
Walton, Rick. *Noah's square dance*
Wick, Walter. *Can you see what I see? Seymour and the juice box boat*
  Can you see what I see? treasure ship
Williams, Vera B. *Three days on a river in a red canoe*
Wilson, Anne. *Noah's ark*
Winter, Jeanette. *The Christmas tree ship*
Winter, Jonah. *Here comes the garbage barge!*
Winters, Kari-Lynn. *Good pirate*
Wynne-Jones, Tim. *The boat in the tree*
Yeh, Kat. *The friend ship*
Zagwỹn, Deborah Turney. *The sea house*

Bombs *see* Weapons

Boogy man *see* Monsters

Books, reading *see also* Libraries

Alexander, Kwame. *Surf's up*
Aliki. *How a book is made*
Allen, Jonathan. *I'm not reading!*
Allen, Susan. *Read anything good lately?*
Amado, Elisa. *What are you doing?*
Anholt, Catherine. *Come back, Jack!*
Asch, Frank. *Moonbear's books*
Asher, Sandy. *Chicken story time*
Asim, Jabari. *Fifty cents and a dream*
Auch, Mary Jane. *The buk buk buk festival*
  The plot chickens
  Souperchicken
Banks, Kate. *The bear in the book*
Barnett, Mac. *Chloe and the lion*

  How this book was made
Barton, Chris. *Book or bell?*
Battle-Lavert, Gwendolyn. *Papa's mark*
Becker, Bonny. *A library book for Bear*
Becker, Helaine. *You can read*
Beebe, Katy. *Brother Hugo and the bear*
Bendall-Brunello, Tiziana. *I wish I could read!*
Benton, Jim. *The end (almost)*
Berne, Jennifer. *Calvin can't fly*
  Calvin, look out!
Bernheimer, Kate. *The lonely book*
Bertram, Debbie. *The best book to read*
  The best place to read
  The best time to read
Bishop, Poppy. *Bear's house of books*
Blatt, Jane. *Books always everywhere*
Boatfield, Jonny. *The twilight book*
Bonilla, Rocio. *The highest mountain of books in the world*
Borden, Louise. *The day Eddie met the author*
Bottner, Barbara. *Miss Brooks loves books! (and I don't)*
Bradby, Marie. *More than anything else*
Briant, Ed. *Seven stories*
Bromley, Nick. *Open very carefully*
Brown, Ken. *The scarecrow's hat*
Brown, Marc. *Arthur's really helpful word book*
  D. W.'s library card
Brown, Monica. *Maya's blanket*
  Waiting for the Biblioburro
Browne, Anthony. *I like books*
  Willy's stories
Bruss, Deborah. *Book! book! book!*
Bryant, Jen. *The right word*
Buitrago, Jairo. *Jimmy the greatest*
Bunting, Eve. *Our library*
  The Wednesday surprise
Burfoot, Ella. *How to bake a book*
Burgess, Mark. *Where teddy bears come from*
Burleigh, Robert. *I love going through this book*
Bush, Laura. *Read all about it!*
Buzzeo, Toni. *Inside the books*
  Penelope Popper book doctor
Byrne, Richard. *This book is out of control!*
  This book just ate my dog!
  We're in the wrong book!
Cabrera, Jane. *Baa, baa, black sheep*
Carlson, Nancy. *I don't like to read!*
Carnavas, Peter. *The children who loved books*
Casanova, Mary. *The day Dirk Yeller came to town*
Caseley, Judith. *Sophie and Sammy's library sleepover*
Cazet, Denys. *Will you read to me?*
Chapin, Tom. *The library book*
Charlip, Remy. *Why I will never ever ever ever have enough time to read this book*
Cheng, Andrea. *Anna the bookbinder*
Child, Lauren. *But, excuse me, that is my book*
  Who's afraid of the big bad book?
Chin, Jason. *Coral reefs*
Christelow, Eileen. *Five little monkeys reading in bed*
Cleminson, Katie. *Otto the book bear*
Cline-Ransome, Lesa. *Light in the darkness*
  Words set me free
Coelho, Joseph. *Luna loves library day*
Cohen, Miriam. *When will I read?*
Colandro, Lucille. *There was an old lady who swallowed some books!*
Conover, Chris. *The lion's share*
Cotten, Cynthia. *The book boat's in*

Cousins, Lucy. *Maisy goes to the library*
Cowley, Joy. *Mrs. Goodstory*
Crimi, Carolyn. *Henry and the Buccaneer Bunnies*
  Henry and the Crazed Chicken Pirates
Crossley-Holland, Kevin. *The Riddlemaster*
Crum, Shutta. *Mouseling's words*
Cuyler, Margery. *Hooray for Reading Day!*
Dakos, Kalli. *Our principal promised to kiss a pig*
Daly, Niki. *Once upon a time*
Deedy, Carmen Agra. *Return of the library dragon*
DeFelice, Cynthia C. *The real, true Dulcie Campbell*
de Las Casas, Dianne. *There's a dragon in the library*
DePalma, Mary Newell. *The perfect gift*
DiPucchio, Kelly. *Alfred Zector, book collector*
  Dragon was terrible
Docherty, Helen. *The Snatchabook*
  The storybook knight
Donaldson, Julia. *Charlie Cook's favorite book*
Donovan, Sandy. *Bob the Alien discovers the Dewey Decimal System*
  Bored Bella learns about fiction and nonfiction
  Karl and Carolina uncover the parts of a book
  Pingpong Perry experiences how a book is made
Dotlich, Rebecca Kai. *One day, the end*
Driscoll, Amanda. *Duncan the story dragon*
Dunlap, Cirocco. *This book will not be fun*
Duvoisin, Roger Antoine. *Petunia*
Dyckman, Ame. *Read the book, lemmings!*
Edwards, Pamela Duncan. *The neat line*
Ehlert, Lois. *The scraps book*
Elliott, David. *Baabwaa and Wooliam*
Elya, Susan Middleton. *Fairy trails*
Falatko, Julie. *Snappsy the alligator (did not ask to be in this book)*
Faulkner, Keith. *The monster who loved books*
Finchler, Judy. *Miss Malarkey leaves no reader behind*
Flanagan, Alice K. *Ms. Davison, our librarian*
Fletcher, Tom. *There's a monster in your book*
Fliess, Sue. *Books for me!*
Fore, S. J. *Read to Tiger*
Fosberry, Jennifer. *Isabella star of the story*
Foster, Travis. *Give me back my book!*
Fox, Diane. *The cat, the dog, Little Red, the exploding eggs, the wolf, and Grandma*
Fox, Kathleen. *The pirates of plagiarism*
Freedman, Deborah. *Shy*
  The Story of Fish and Snail
Funke, Cornelia. *The book no one ever read*
Gall, Chris. *Revenge of the Dinotrux*
Garland, Michael. *King Puck*
  Miss Smith and the haunted library
  Miss Smith reads again!
  Miss Smith's incredible storybook
Gay, Marie-Louise. *Any questions?*
  Read me a story, Stella
Gerstein, Mordicai. *A book*
Goodhart, Pippa. *Little Nelly's big book*
Gore, Leonid. *The wonderful book*
Gravett, Emily. *Again!*
  Spells
Greene, Rhonda Gowler. *No pirates allowed! said Library Lou*
Griswell, Kim T. *Rufus blasts off!*
  Rufus goes to school
  Rufus goes to sea
Hall, Kirsten. *The jacket*
Hall, Michael. *Frankencrayon*
Hall, Patricia. *Hooray for reading!*

Harper, Charise Mericle. *A big surprise for Little Card*
Harris, Robie H. *Maybe a bear ate it!*
Haseley, Dennis. *A story for Bear*
Hayward, Linda. *I am a book*
Hector, Julian. *The gentleman bug*
Hest, Amy. *The reader*
Higgins, Ryan T. *Be quiet!*
Hillenbrand, Will. *My book box*
Hills, Tad. *How Rocket learned to read*
  Rocket writes a story
Hoban, Tana. *I read signs*
  I read symbols
  I walk and read
Hodge, Deborah. *Lily and the mixed-up letters*
Hodgkinson, Leigh. *A place to read*
Hood, Susan. *Look! I can read!*
Hopkins, Lee Bennett. *Good books, good times*
  Jumping off library shelves
Houston, Gloria. *Miss Dorothy and her bookmobile*
Hubbell, Patricia. *Check it out! reading, finding, helping*
Ivey, Randall. *Jay and the bounty of books*
Jackson, Richard. *Have a look, says Book*
Jeffers, Oliver. *A child of books*
  The incredible book eating boy
Jeram, Anita. *I love my little storybook*
John, Jory. *I will chomp you!*
Johnson, Angela. *Lottie Paris and the best place*
Jorgensen, Richard. *Reading with Dad*
Joyce, William. *Billy's booger*
  The fantastic flying books of Mr. Morris Lessmore
Kanninen, Barbara. *A story with pictures*
Kerley, Barbara. *A home for Mr. Emerson*
Kirk, Daniel. *Library mouse*
  Library mouse: a friend's tale
  Library mouse: home sweet home
Klausmeier, Jesse. *Open this little book*
Kloske, Geoffrey. *Once upon a time, the end (asleep in 60 seconds)*
Kohara, Kazuno. *The Midnight Library*
Krull, Kathleen. *The boy on Fairfield Street*
Lakin, Patricia. *Fat chance Thanksgiving*
  Rainy day
Lamm, C. Drew. *Pirates*
Lammle, Leslie. *Princess wannabe*
Larsen, Andrew. *The man who loved libraries*
Lê, Minh. *Let me finish!*
Lehman, Barbara. *Red again*
  The red book
Lehrhaupt, Adam. *Please, open this book!*
  This is a good story
  Warning: do not open this book!
Léonard, Marie. *Tibili, the little boy who didn't want to go to school*
Lies, Brian. *Bats at the library*
London, Jonathan. *Froggy goes to the library*
Long, Ethan. *The book that Zack wrote*
Lyon, George Ella. *Book*
McDonnell, Patrick. *A perfectly messed-up story*
McGee, Marni. *Winston the book wolf*
McGill, Alice. *Molly Bannaky*
Mack, Jeff. *Duck in the fridge*
  Look!
  The things I can do
McNaughton, Colin. *Not last night but the night before*
McPhail, David. *Edward and the pirates*
  Fix-it

Santa's book of names
McQuinn, Anna. *Lola at the library*
 Lola loves stories
 Lola reads to Leo
Mahoney, Daniel J. *The Saturday escape*
Manley, Curtis. *The summer Nick taught his cats to read*
Marcotte, Danielle. *Mom, dad, our books, and me*
Markel, Michelle. *Balderdash!*
Marshall, James. *Wings: a tale of two chickens*
Mattick, Lindsay. *Finding Winnie*
Meddaugh, Susan. *Hog-eye*
Meng, Cece. *I will not read this book*
Messner, Kate. *How to read a story*
Miller, Pat. *We're going on a book hunt*
Miller, William. *Richard Wright and the library card*
Milord, Susan. *Happy one hundredth day!*
Montanari, Eva. *My first . . .*
Mora, Pat. *Book fiesta! celebrate Children's Day/Book Day / Celebremos El día de los niños/El día de los libros*
 A library for Juana
 Tomás and the library lady
Morris, Carla. *The boy who was raised by librarians*
Morrison, Toni. *Please, Louise*
Muntean, Michaela. *Do not open this book!*
Nelson, Vaunda Micheaux. *The book itch*
Nez, John. *One smart Cookie*
Nikola-Lisa, W. *Magic in the margins*
Novak, B. J. *The book with no pictures*
Numeroff, Laura Joffe. *The Jellybeans and the big book bonanza*
Ohi, Debbie Ridpath. *Where are my books?*
OHora, Zachariah. *The not so quiet library*
O'Leary, Sara. *This is Sadie*
Olofsson, Helena. *The little jester*
Orozco, Jose-Luis. *Rin, rin, rin / do, re, mi*
Palatini, Margie. *The three silly billies*
 Under a pig tree
Panzieri, Lucia. *The kindhearted crocodile*
Papp, Lisa. *Madeline Finn and the library dog*
Parachini, Jodie. *This is a serious book*
Parish, Herman. *Amelia Bedelia's first library card*
Parlato, Stephen. *The world that loved books*
Parr, Todd. *Reading makes you feel good*
Paschkis, Julie. *Apple cake*
Patschke, Steve. *The spooky book*
Pauli, Lorenz. *The fox in the library*
Pearson, Susan. *How to teach a slug to read*
Pearson, Tracey Campbell. *Elephant's story*
Perry, John. *The book that eats people*
Pham, LeUyen. *The bear who wasn't there*
Pinczes, Elinor J. *My full moon is square*
Pinkney, Sandra L. *Read and rise*
Plourde, Lynn. *Book Fair Day*
Polacco, Patricia. *Aunt Chip and the great Triple Creek dam affair*
 The mermaid's purse
 Thank you, Mr. Falker
Radabaugh, Melinda Beth. *Going to the library*
Rahaman, Vashanti. *Read for me, Mama*
Ramadier, Cédric. *Shh! this book is sleeping*
Rau, Dana Meachen. *The secret code*
Robb, Diane Burton. *The alphabet war*
Robberecht, Thierry. *The wolf who fell out of a book*
Rockwell, Anne. *Father's Day*
 Library day
Rogers, Jacqueline. *Kindergarten ABC*
Rosen, Michael. *Send for a superhero!*

Rosenstock, Barb. *Thomas Jefferson builds a library*
Roth, Susan L. *Hands around the library*
Ruzzier, Sergio. *This is not a picture book*
Saltzberg, Barney. *Hug this book!*
 Inside this book (are three books)
Schoenherr, Ian. *Read it, don't eat it!*
Schubert, Leda. *Reading to Peanut*
Scieszka, Jon. *Battle Bunny*
Sheth, Kashmira. *Tiger in my soup*
Shields, Gillian. *Library Lily*
Shoulders, Michael. *Goodnight Baby Bear*
 Say Daddy!
Sierra, Judy. *Born to read*
 Imagine that! how Dr. Seuss wrote The Cat in the Hat
 Make way for readers
 Wild about books
Silvestro, Annie. *Bunny's book club*
Slade, Suzanne. *With books and bricks*
Smalls, Irene. *Don't say ain't*
Smith, Lane. *It's a book*
Sperring, Mark. *The fairytale cake*
Staake, Bob. *The Book of Gold*
 Look! a book!
 Look! another book!
 My pet book
Stadler, Alexander. *Beverly Billingsly borrows a book*
Stadler, John. *What's so scary?*
Stanley, Diane. *Raising Sweetness*
Stewart, Sarah. *The library*
Stoop, Naoko. *Red Knit Cap Girl and the reading tree*
Straaten, Harmen van. *Duck's tale*
Thomas, Shelley Moore. *Take care, Good Knight*
Tirabosco, Tom. *At the same time*
Tobin, Jim. *Sue MacDonald had a book*
Tokuda-Hall, Maggie. *Also an octopus*
Tullet, Hervé. *Help! we need a title!*
Twohy, Mike. *Poindexter makes a friend*
Van Biesen, Koen. *Roger is reading a book*
Viorst, Judith. *The good-bye book*
Walker, Sally M. *Winnie*
Waller, Curt. *Baby's first signs*
 More baby's first signs
Wallner, Alexandra. *Lucy Maud Montgomery*
Watt, Mélanie. *Have I got a book for you!*
 You're finally here!
Wayne-von Königslöw, Andrea. *How do you read to a rabbit?*
Weeks, Sarah. *Bite me, I'm a book*
 Catfish Kate and the sweet swamp band
Wells, Rosemary. *Read to your bunny*
 Yoko learns to read
Whybrow, Ian. *Wish, change, friend*
Wiesner, David. *Free fall*
 The three pigs
Wild, Margaret. *The treasure box*
Williams, Suzanne. *Library Lil*
Winter, Jeanette. *Biblioburro*
Winters, Kay. *Abe Lincoln, the boy who loved books*
Yaccarino, Dan. *I am a story*
Yates, Louise. *Dog loves books*
 Dog loves counting
Yolen, Jane. *Baby Bear's books*
Zagarenski, Pamela. *The whisper*

Boredom *see* Behavior – boredom

Bossy *see* Behavior – bossy

Bragging *see* Behavior – boasting, showing off

Bravery *see* Character traits – bravery

Bridges

Bell, Babs. *The bridge is up!*
Biggs, Brian. *Tinyville town gets to work*
Keely, Cheryl. *Here to there and me to you*
Kooser, Ted. *The bell in the bridge*
Prince, April Jones. *Twenty-one elephants and still standing*
Swift, Hildegarde Hoyt. *The little red lighthouse and the great gray bridge*

Brothers *see* Family life – brothers; Family life – brothers & sisters; Sibling rivalry

Brownies *see* Mythical creatures – elves

Bubbles

Bradley, Kimberly Brubaker. *Pop!*
Bridwell, Norman. *Clifford counts bubbles*
dePaola, Tomie. *Strega Nona takes a vacation*
Inkpen, Mick. *Thing*
Mahy, Margaret. *Bubble trouble*
Rubin, Adam. *Big bad bubble*
Van Camp, Katie. *Harry and Horsie*

Bugs *see* Insects

Buildings

Beaty, Andrea. *Iggy Peck, architect*
Cooper, Elisha. *Building*
Curlee, Lynn. *Skyscraper*
Cyrus, Kurt. *Billions of bricks*
Drummond, Allan. *Green city*
Edwards, Pamela Duncan. *Jack and Jill's treehouse*
Gibbons, Gail. *Up goes the skyscraper!*
Hale, Christy. *Dreaming up*
Hill, Isabel. *Building stories*
Hudson, Cheryl Willis. *Construction zone*
Johnson, D. B. *Palazzo inverso*
Kirk, Daniel. *Library mouse: home sweet home*
Lewis, Kevin. *The lot at the end of my block*
Merriam, Eve. *Bam, bam, bam*
Newhouse, Maxwell. *The house that Max built*
Numeroff, Laura Joffe. *What daddies do best*
Rex, Adam. *School's first day of school*
Rockliff, Mara. *Me and Momma and Big John*
Slade, Suzanne. *The house that George built*
Smith, Charles R. *Brick by brick*
Suen, Anastasia. *Raise the roof
Up! up! up! skyscraper*
Tarsky, Sue. *The busy building book*
Vila, Laura. *Building Manhattan*

Bulldozers *see* Machines

Bullying *see* Behavior – bullying, teasing

Burros *see* Animals – donkeys

Buses

Barton, Byron. *My bus*
Brillhart, Julie. *Molly rides the school bus*
Brown, Marc. *Arthur lost and found*
Bus-a-saurus bop
Cabrera, Jane. *The wheels on the bus*
Cocca-Leffler, Maryann. *Bus route to Boston*
Cole, Joanna. *The magic school bus and the science fair expedition*
The magic school bus in the time of the dinosaurs
The magic school bus inside a beehive
The magic school bus lost in the solar system
The magic school bus on the ocean floor
Crews, Donald. *School bus*
Cuyler, Margery. *The little school bus*
Dale, Penny. *The boy on the bus*
Davies, Stephen. *All aboard for the Bobo Road*
Dean, James. *Pete the Cat: the wheels on the bus*
de la Peña, Matt. *Last stop on Market Street*
Deneux, Xavier. *Vehicles*
Graham, Bob. *A bus called Heaven*
Grandits, John. *Ten rules you absolutely must not break if you want to survive the school bus*
Helakoski, Leslie. *The smushy bus*
Hirst, Robin. *My place in space*
Katz, Karen. *The babies on the bus*
Kirk, Daniel. *Bus stop, bus go*
Kovalski, Maryann. *The wheels on the bus*
Liu, Julia. *Gus, the dinosaur bus*
McCarthy, Meghan. *The adventures of Patty and the big red bus*
McMullan, Kate. *I'm smart!*
Moore, Mary-Alice. *The wheels on the school bus*
Owen, Ann. *Taking your places*
Paquette, Ammi-Joan. *Bunny Bus*
Redeker, Kent. *Don't squish the sasquatch!*
Rosen, Michael. *The bus is for us!*
Roth, Carol. *The little school bus*
Silvano, Wendi. *Just one more*
Singer, Marilyn. *I'm your bus*
Stoeke, Janet Morgan. *The bus stop*
Walters, Eric. *The matatu*
Willis, Jeanne. *The wheels on the bus: a read-along sing-along trip to the zoo*
Zelinsky, Paul O. *The wheels on the bus*

Cabs *see* Taxis

Cafés *see* Restaurants

Caldecott award books

Aardema, Verna. *Why mosquitoes buzz in people's ears*

Ackerman, Karen. *Song and dance man*
Alger, Leclaire Gowans. *Always room for one more*
Aulaire, Ingri Mortenson d'. *Abraham Lincoln*
Bemelmans, Ludwig. *Madeline's rescue*
Brown, Marcia. *Once a mouse . . .*
Brown, Margaret Wise. *The little island*
Bunting, Eve. *Smoky night*
Burton, Virginia Lee. *The little house*
Cendrars, Blaise. *Shadow*
Chaucer, Geoffrey. *Chanticleer and the fox*
Cordell, Matthew. *Wolf in the snow*
De Regniers, Beatrice Schenk. *May I bring a friend?*
Emberley, Barbara. *Drummer Hoff*
Ets, Marie Hall. *Nine days to Christmas*
Field, Rachel Lyman. *Prayer for a child*
Floca, Brian. *Locomotive*
A frog he would a-wooing go [folk-song] *Frog went a-courtin'*
Gerstein, Mordicai. *The man who walked between the towers*
Goble, Paul. *The girl who loved wild horses*
Grimm, Jacob and Wilhelm *Rapunzel*
Hader, Berta Hoerner. *The big snow*
Haley, Gail E. *A story, a story*
Hall, Donald. *Ox-cart man*
Handforth, Thomas. *Mei Li*
Henkes, Kevin. *Kitten's first full moon*
Hodges, Margaret. *Saint George and the dragon*
Hogrogian, Nonny. *One fine day*
Juster, Norton. *The hello, goodbye window*
Keats, Ezra Jack. *The snowy day*
Klassen, Jon. *This is not my hat*
Lawson, Robert. *They were strong and good*
Lipkind, William. *Finders keepers*
Lobel, Arnold. *Fables*
Macaulay, David. *Black and white*
McCloskey, Robert. *Make way for ducklings*
  Time of wonder
McCully, Emily Arnold. *Mirette on the high wire*
McDermott, Gerald. *Arrow to the sun*
Martin, Jacqueline Briggs. *Snowflake Bentley*
Mattick, Lindsay. *Finding Winnie*
Milhous, Katherine. *The egg tree*
Mosel, Arlene. *The funny little woman*
Musgrove, Margaret. *Ashanti to Zulu*
Ness, Evaline. *Sam, Bangs, and moonshine*
Perrault, Charles. *Cinderella: or, the little glass slipper*
Petersham, Maud. *The rooster crows*
Pinkney, Jerry. *The lion and the mouse*
Politi, Leo. *Song of the swallows*
Provensen, Alice. *The glorious flight*
Ransome, Arthur. *The fool of the world and the flying ship*
Raschka, Chris. *A ball for Daisy*
Rathmann, Peggy. *Officer Buckle and Gloria*
Robbins, Ruth. *Baboushka and the three kings*
Rohmann, Eric. *My friend Rabbit*
St. George, Judith. *So you want to be president?*
Santat, Dan. *The adventures of Beekle*
Say, Allen. *Grandfather's journey*
Selznick, Brian. *The invention of Hugo Cabret*
Sendak, Maurice. *Where the wild things are*
Spier, Peter. *Noah's ark*
Stead, Philip C. *A sick day for Amos McGee*
Steig, William. *Sylvester and the magic pebble*
Steptoe, Javaka. *Radiant child*
Swanson, Susan Marie. *The house in the night*
Taback, Simms. *Joseph had a little overcoat*
Thurber, James. *Many moons*

Tresselt, Alvin R. *White snow, bright snow*
Udry, Janice May. *A tree is nice*
Van Allsburg, Chris. *Jumanji*
  The polar express
Ward, Lynd. *The biggest bear*
Wiesner, David. *Flotsam*
  The three pigs
  Tuesday
Wisniewski, David. *Golem*
Yolen, Jane. *Owl moon*
Yorinks, Arthur. *Hey, Al*
Young, Ed. *Lon Po Po*
Zemach, Harve. *Duffy and the devil*

Caldecott award honor books

Alger, Leclaire Gowans. *All in the morning early*
Andersen, Hans Christian. *The ugly duckling*
Andrews, Troy. *Trombone Shorty*
Artzybasheff, Boris. *Seven Simeons*
Baker, Olaf. *Where the buffaloes begin*
Bang, Molly. *The grey lady and the strawberry snatcher*
  Ten, nine, eight
  When Sophie gets angry — really, really angry . . .
Barnes, Derrick. *Crown*
Barnett, Mac. *Extra yarn*
  Sam and Dave dig a hole
Bartone, Elisa. *Peppe the lamplighter*
Baskin, Leonard. *Hosie's alphabet*
Baylor, Byrd. *The desert is theirs*
  Hawk, I'm your brother
  The way to start a day
  When clay sings
Becker, Aaron. *Journey*
Belting, Natalia Maree. *The sun is a golden earring*
Bemelmans, Ludwig. *Madeline*
Birnbaum, Abe. *Green eyes*
Brosgol, Vera. *Leave me alone!*
Brown, Marcia. *Stone soup*
Brown, Margaret Wise. *Wheel on the chimney*
Bryant, Jen. *The right word*
  A river of words
Buzzeo, Toni. *One cool friend*
Castillo, Lauren. *Nana in the city*
Caudill, Rebecca. *A pocketful of cricket*
Chan, Chin-Yi. *Good luck horse*
A child's calendar
Chin, Jason. *Grand Canyon*
Chodos-Irvine, Margaret. *Ella Sarah gets dressed*
Clark, Ann Nolan. *In my mother's house*
Cooper, Elisha. *Big cat, little cat*
Crews, Donald. *Freight train*
  Truck
Cronin, Doreen. *Click, clack, moo*
Dalgliesh, Alice. *The Thanksgiving story*
Daugherty, James Henry. *Andy and the lion*
Dayrell, Elphinstone. *Why the sun and the moon live in the sky*
de la Peña, Matt. *Last stop on Market Street*
dePaola, Tomie. *Strega Nona*
Dick Whittington and his cat. *Dick Whittington and his cat*
Domanska, Janina. *If all the seas were one sea*
Du Bois, William Pène. *Bear party*
  Lion
Ehlert, Lois. *Color zoo*
Eichenberg, Fritz. *Ape in cape*
Ellis, Carson. *Du iz tak?*
Emberley, Barbara. *One wide river to cross*

Ets, Marie Hall. *In the forest*
  Just me
  Mister Penny
  Mr. Penny's race horse
  Mr. T. W. Anthony Woo
  Play with me
Falconer, Ian. *Olivia*
Feelings, Muriel. *Jambo means hello*
  Moja means one
Fleming, Denise. *In the small, small pond*
Ford, Lauren. *The ageless story*
The fox went out on a chilly night
Frazee, Marla. *A couple of boys have the best week ever*
Giovanni, Nikki. *Rosa*
Goudey, Alice E. *The day we saw the sun come up*
  Houses from the sea
Grifalconi, Ann. *The village of round and square houses*
Grimm, Jacob and Wilhelm. *Hansel and Gretel*
  Little Red Riding Hood
  Snow White and the seven dwarfs
Hader, Berta Hoerner. *Cock-a-doodle doo*
  The mighty hunter
Henkes, Kevin. *Owen*
  Waiting
Hill, Laban Carrick. *Dave the potter*
Ho, Minfong. *Hush!*
Hodges, Margaret. *The wave*
Hogrogian, Nonny. *The contest*
Holbrook, Stewart. *America's Ethan Allen*
Holling, Holling C. *Paddle-to-the-sea*
Howitt, Mary Botham. *Mary Howitt's The spider and the fly*
Idle, Molly. *Flora and the flamingo*
Isaacs, Anne. *Swamp Angel*
Isadora, Rachel. *Ben's trumpet*
Jenkins, Steve. *What do you do with a tail like this?*
Johnson, Stephen T. *Alphabet city*
Keats, Ezra Jack. *Goggles*
Kepes, Juliet. *Five little monkeys*
Kimmel, Eric A. *Hershel and the Hanukkah goblins*
Krauss, Ruth. *The happy day*
  A very special house
Leaf, Munro. *Wee Gillis*
Lehman, Barbara. *The red book*
Lester, Julius. *John Henry*
Levine, Ellen. *Henry's freedom box*
Lionni, Leo. *Alexander and the wind-up mouse*
  Frederick
  Inch by inch
  Swimmy
Little old lady who swallowed a fly. *There was an old lady who swallowed a fly*
Lobel, Arnold. *Frog and Toad are friends*
  On Market Street
Logue, Mary. *Sleep like a tiger*
Low, Joseph. *Mice twice*
Macaulay, David. *Castle*
  Cathedral
McCarty, Peter. *Hondo and Fabian*
McCloskey, Robert. *Blueberries for Sal*
  One morning in Maine
McDermott, Gerald. *Anansi the spider*
  Raven
MacDonald, Suse. *Alphabatics*
McDonnell, Patrick. *Me . . . Jane*
McKissack, Patricia C. *Mirandy and Brother Wind*
McLimans, David. *Gone wild*
Morales, Yuyi. *Viva Frida*

Moss, Lloyd. *Zin! zin! zin! A violin*
Mother Goose. *Mother Goose*
  The three jovial huntsmen
Muth, Jon J. *Zen shorts*
Myers, Walter Dean. *Harlem*
Newberry, Clare Turlay. *April's kittens*
  Barkis
  Marshmallow
Peet, Bill. *Bill Peet*
Pelletier, David. *The graphic alphabet*
Perrault, Charles. *Puss in boots*, ill. by Marcia Brown
  Puss in boots, ill. by Fred Marcellino
Petersham, Maud. *An American ABC*
Phi, Bao. *A different pond*
Pilkey, Dav. *The paperboy*
Pinkney, Andrea Davis. *Duke Ellington*
Pinkney, Jerry. *Noah's ark*
Politi, Leo. *Juanita*
  Pedro, the angel of Olvera Street
Priceman, Marjorie. *Hot air*
Rappaport, Doreen. *Martin's big words*
Raschka, Chris. *Yo! Yes?*
Reyher, Rebecca. *My mother is the most beautiful woman in the world*
Reynolds, Aaron. *Creepy carrots!*
Ringgold, Faith. *Tar Beach*
Rocco, John. *Blackout*
Rohmann, Eric. *Time flies*
Rosenstock, Barb. *The noisy paint box*
Ryan, Cheli Durán. *Hildilid's night*
Rylant, Cynthia. *The relatives came*
  When I was young in the mountains
San Souci, Robert D. *The faithful friend*
  The talking eggs
Sawyer, Ruth. *Journey cake, ho!*
Scanlon, Elizabeth Garton. *All the world*
Scheer, Julian. *Rain makes applesauce*
Schreiber, Georges. *Bambino the clown*
Scieszka, Jon. *The Stinky Cheese Man and other fairly stupid tales*
Seeger, Laura Vaccaro. *First the egg*
  Green
Sendak, Maurice. *In the night kitchen*
  Outside over there
Seuss, Dr. *Bartholomew and the Oobleck*
  If I ran the zoo
  McElligot's pool
Shannon, David. *No, David!*
Shulevitz, Uri. *How I learned geography*
  Snow
  The treasure
Sidman, Joyce. *Red sings from treetops*
  Song of the water boatman
Simont, Marc. *The stray dog*
Sís, Peter. *Starry messenger*
  Tibet through the red box
  The wall: growing up behind the Iron Curtain
Sleator, William. *The angry moon*
Smith, Lane. *Grandpa Green*
Snyder, Dianne. *The boy of the three-year nap*
Steig, William. *The amazing bone*
Stein, David Ezra. *Interrupting chicken*
Steptoe, John. *Mufaro's beautiful daughters*
  The story of jumping mouse
Stevens, Janet. *Tops and bottoms*
Stewart, Sarah. *The gardener*
Tafuri, Nancy. *Have you seen my duckling?*
Tamaki, Mariko. *This one summer*

Thayer, Ernest Lawrence. *Casey at the bat: a ballad of the Republic, sung in the year 1888*
The three bears. *Goldilocks and the three bears*
Titus, Eve. *Anatole*
　Anatole and the cat
Tom Tit Tot. *Tom Tit Tot*
Tresselt, Alvin R. *Hide and seek fog*
　Rain drop splash
Tudor, Tasha. *1 is one*
Turkle, Brinton. *Thy friend, Obadiah*
Udry, Janice May. *The moon jumpers*
Van Allsburg, Chris. *The garden of Abdul Gasazi*
Weatherford, Carole Boston. *Freedom in Congo Square*
　Moses: when Harriet Tubman led her people to freedom
　Voice of freedom
Wenzel, Brendan. *They all saw a cat*
Wheeler, Opal. *Sing in praise*
　Sing Mother Goose
Wiese, Kurt. *Fish in the air*
　You can write Chinese
Wiesner, David. *Free fall*
　Mr. Wuffles!
　Sector 7
Willard, Nancy. *A visit to William Blake's inn*
Willems, Mo. *Don't let the pigeon drive the bus*
　Knuffle Bunny
　Knuffle Bunny too
Williams, Sherley Anne. *Working cotton*
Williams, Vera B. *A chair for my mother*
　"More more more," said the baby
Wood, Audrey. *King Bidgood's in the bathtub*
Woodson, Jacqueline. *Coming on home soon*
Yashima, Taro. *Crow boy*
　Umbrella
Yolen, Jane. *The emperor and the kite*
Young, Ed. *Seven blind mice*
Zemach, Harve. *The judge*
Zemach, Margot. *It could always be worse*
Zolotow, Charlotte. *Mr. Rabbit and the lovely present*
　The storm book

Calendars

A child's calendar
Frasier, Debra. *A birthday cake is no ordinary cake*
Hague, Kathleen. *Calendarbears*
Livingston, Myra Cohn. *Calendar*
Murphy, Stuart J. *Pepper's journal*

Camouflages *see* Disguises

Camps, camping

Bateman, Teresa. *Hamster Camp*
The bear
Berenstain, Stan and Jan. *The Berenstain bears go to camp*
Berry, Lynne. *Duck tents*
Birdseye, Tom. *Oh yeah!*
Brown, Marc. *Arthur goes to camp*
　Arthur's first sleepover
Carlin, Patricia. *Alfie is not afraid*
Christelow, Eileen. *Jerome camps out*
Clements, Andrew. *Because your mommy loves you*
Côté, Geneviève. *Goodnight, you*
Coyle, Carmela LaVigna. *Do princesses make happy campers?*

Cummins, Julie. *Country kid, city kid*
Curious George goes camping
deGroat, Diane. *Good night, sleep tight, don't let the bedbugs bite*
Fleming, Denise. *Buster goes to Cowboy Camp*
Genechten, Guido van. *Ricky is brave*
Gifaldi, David. *Ben, king of the river*
Gutman, Anne. *Gaspard at the seashore*
Hafner, Marylin. *Molly and Emmett's camping adventure*
Henkes, Kevin. *Bailey goes camping*
Holabird, Katharine. *Angelina and Henry*
Hume, Stephen Eaton. *Red moon follows truck*
Hundal, Nancy. *Camping*
Huneck, Stephen. *Sally goes to the mountains*
Idle, Molly. *Camp Rex*
Inkpen, Mick. *Kipper's monster*
　Wibbly Pig can make a tent
Jagtenberg, Yvonne. *Jack's kite*
John, Jory. *Come home already!*
Johnson, Paul Brett. *Lost*
Jules, Jacqueline. *Picnic at Camp Shalom*
Katschke, Judy. *Take a hike, Snoopy*
Korda, Lerryn. *Into the wild*
Lakin, Patricia. *Camping day*
Lasky, Kathryn. *Lucille camps in*
Lester, Helen. *Tacky goes to camp*
London, Jonathan. *Froggy goes to camp*
McCully, Emily Arnold. *Monk camps out*
McPhail, David. *Pig Pig goes to camp*
Manning, Jane. *Millie Fierce sleeps out*
Marshall, James. *The Cut-Ups at Camp Custer*
Mayer, Mercer. *Just me and my dad*
　You're the scaredy cat
Nolen, Jerdine. *Plantzilla goes to camp*
Numeroff, Laura Joffe. *The Jellybeans and the big camp kickoff*
Orr, Wendy. *The princess and her panther*
Paterson, Brian. *Zigby camps out*
Powell-Tuck, Maudie. *Pirates aren't afraid of the dark!*
Pringle, Laurence P. *Bear hug*
Rosenstock, Barb. *The camping trip that changed America*
Ross, Tony. *I want to do it myself!*
Ruurs, Margriet. *When we go camping*
Sauer, Tammi. *Cowboy camp*
　Princess in training
Schatell, Brian. *Owl boy*
Schwartz, Henry. *How I captured a dinosaur*
Sher, Emil. *Away*
Shulevitz, Uri. *Dawn*
Singer, Marilyn. *I'm gonna climb a mountain in my patent leather shoes*
　Quiet night
Snyder, Laurel. *Good night, laila tov*
Soman, David. *Ladybug Girl and Bingo*
Sturm, James. *Sleepless knight*
Taback, Simms. *Postcards from camp*
Tafuri, Nancy. *Do not disturb*
Watt, Mélanie. *Scaredy Squirrel goes camping*
Wegman, William. *Flo and Wendell explore*
Williams, Brenda. *Outdoor opposites*
Williams, Vera B. *Three days on a river in a red canoe*
Wilson, Karma. *Sweet Briar goes to camp*
Wolff, Ashley. *Stella and Roy go camping*
Zuill, Andrea. *Wolf camp*

Canoes & canoeing

Asch, Frank. *Moonbear's canoe*
Casanova, Mary. *One-dog canoe*
Davidson, Leslie A. *In the red canoe*
Drawson, Blair. *All along the river*
Ford, Christine. *Ocean's child*
London, Jonathan. *Loon Lake*
Maggi, María Elena. *The great canoe*
Oldland, Nicholas. *Up the creek*
Paterson, Brian. *Zigby hunts for treasure*
Paulsen, Gary. *Canoe days*
Pendziwol, Jean E. *Me and you and the red canoe*

Canyons

Cameron, Eileen. *Canyon*
Chin, Jason. *Grand Canyon*
London, Jonathan. *Mustang canyon*

Cards *see* Letters, cards

Careers

Baker, Keith. *LMNO pea-quel*
    LMNO peas
Berenstain, Stan and Jan. *The Berenstain bears and mama's new job*
Berne, Jennifer. *Manfish*
Blackstone, Stella. *Bear at work*
Blumenthal, Deborah. *Fancy party gowns*
Bond, Michael. *Paddington Bear and the Christmas surprise*
Bond, Rebecca. *Bravo, Maurice!*
Bunting, Eve. *Girls A to Z*
Buzzeo, Toni. *Adventure Annie goes to work*
Catalanotto, Peter. *Kitten red, yellow, blue*
Cordsen, Carol Foskett. *The milkman*
DiPucchio, Kelly. *Grace for president*
Ericsson, Jennifer A. *Home to me, home to you*
Gardiner, Lindsey. *When Poppy and Max grow up*
Gibbons, Gail. *Emergency!*
    Farming
    Fill it up!
    The pottery place
Gibson, Karen Bush. *Child care workers*
    Emergency medical technicians
Glassman, Peter. *My dad's job*
Goodings, Lennie. *When you grow up*
Green, John Patrick. *Hippopotamister*
Hartland, Jessie. *Night shift*
Hatanaka, Kellen. *Work: an occupational ABC*
Havill, Juanita. *Just like a baby*
Heling, Kathryn. *Clothesline clues to jobs people do*
High, Linda Oatman. *The last chimney of Christmas eve*
Horton, Joan. *Working mummies*
Jordan, Deloris. *Salt in his shoes*
Judes, Marie-Odile. *Max, the stubborn little wolf*
Karas, G. Brian. *The village garage*
Kerley, Barbara. *The world is waiting for you*
Krensky, Stephen. *How Santa got his job*
    How Santa lost his job
Larsen, Andrew. *The man who loved libraries*
Liebman, Daniel. *I want to be a cowboy*
Lloyd-Jones, Sally. *How to get a job — by me, the boss*
McMullan, Kate. *Bulldog's big day*
McNaughton, Colin. *When I grow up*
McPhail, David. *Pig Pig gets a job*

Mellage, Nanette. *Coming home*
Miller, Margaret. *Who uses this?*
    Whose hat?
Morris, Ann. *Work*
Nettleton, Pamela Hill. *George Washington*
Nolen, Jerdine. *Raising dragons*
Paul, Miranda. *Whose hands are these?*
Paulsen, Gary. *Worksong*
Ray, Mary Lyn. *Basket moon*
Reed, Lynn Rowe. *Please don't upset P.U. Zorilla!*
Reichert, Amy. *Take your mama to work today*
Reiser, Lynn. *Hardworking puppies*
Rockliff, Mara. *Me and Momma and Big John*
Rockwell, Anne. *Career day*
Roth, Carol. *All aboard to work — choo-choo!*
Rotner, Shelley. *Everybody works*
Sava, Donna Lynn. *Teddy bear dreams*
Schaefer, Lola M. *Airport*
Spinelli, Jerry. *I can be anything!*
Stevenson, James. *Sam the Zamboni man*
Swinburne, Stephen R. *Whose shoes? a shoe for every job*
Turner, Sandy. *Grow up*
Wax, Wendy. *Even firefighters go to the potty*
Yankovic, Al. *When I grow up*
Ziefert, Harriet. *The biggest job of all*

Careers – acrobats

Filleul, Liz. *Tumbler*
Schachner, Judith Byron. *Skippyjon Jones Cirque de Olé*

Careers – actors

Ackerman, Karen. *Bean's big day*
Bell, Cece. *Sock Monkey boogie-woogie*
    Sock Monkey goes to Hollywood
    Sock Monkey rides again
Blumenthal, Deborah. *Charlie hits it big*
Dunrea, Olivier. *Appearing tonight! Mary Heather Elizabeth Livingstone*
Francis, Pauline. *Sam stars at Shakespeare's Globe*
Herzog, Kenny. *Phil Pickle*
LaChanze. *Little diva*
Littlesugar, Amy. *Tree of hope*
McCully, Emily Arnold. *Strongheart*
McLean, Dirk. *Curtain up!*
Milgrim, David. *Amelia makes a movie*
Schwartz, Amy. *Starring Miss Darlene*
Waber, Bernard. *Evie and Margie*
Wallis, Quvenzhané. *A night out with Mama*

Careers – aerialists

Gerstein, Mordicai. *The man who walked between the towers*
McCully, Emily Arnold. *Mirette and Bellini cross Niagara Falls*
    Mirette on the high wire

Careers – airplane pilots

Adler, David A. *A picture book of Amelia Earhart*
Barton, Byron. *Airport*
Bildner, Phil. *The hallelujah flight*
Breen, Steve. *Violet the pilot*
Brown, Don. *Ruth Law thrills a nation*
Brown, Tami Lewis. *Soar, Elinor!*
Duble, Kathleen Benner. *Pilot mom*

Edwards, Pamela Duncan. *The Wright brothers*
Flanagan, Alice K. *Flying an agricultural plane with Mr. Miller*
Johnson, Angela. *Wind flyers*
Joseph, Lynn. *Fly, Bessie, fly*
Lang, Heather. *Fearless flyer*
Lenski, Lois. *The little airplane*
Meadows, Michelle. *Pilot pups*
Moss, Marissa. *Sky high*
Pelton, Mindy L. *When Dad's at sea*
Poletti, Frances. *Miss Todd and her wonderful flying machine*
Raven, Margot Theis. *Mercedes and the chocolate pilot*
Sidman, Joyce. *Before morning*
Sís, Peter. *The pilot and the Little Prince*
Tarpley, Natasha Anastasia. *Joe-Joe's first flight*
Whitaker, Suzanne George. *The daring Miss Quimby*
Yolen, Jane. *My brothers' flying machine*

Careers – architects

Beaty, Andrea. *Iggy Peck, architect*
Cooper, Elisha. *Building*
Eldarova, Sofia. *Builder mouse*
Guarnaccia, Steven. *The three little pigs: an architectural tale*
Harvey, Jeanne Walker. *Maya Lin: artist-architect of light and lines*
Laden, Nina. *Roberto, the insect architect*
Winter, Jeanette. *The world is not a rectangle*

Careers – artists *see also* Activities – painting; Art

Adams, Adrienne. *The great Valentine's Day balloon race*
Arnold, Tedd. *Vincent paints his house*
Arrigan, Mary. *Mario's angels*
Beaty, Andrea. *Artist Ted*
Belton, Sandra. *Pictures for Miss Josie*
Browne, Anthony. *Willy's pictures*
Browning, Diane. *Signed, Abiah Rose*
Bryant, Jen. *A splash of red*
Burleigh, Robert. *Edward Hopper paints his world*
Carle, Eric. *What's your favorite color?*
Carle, Eric. *The artist who painted a blue horse*
Catalanotto, Peter. *Emily's art*
Christelow, Eileen. *Letters from a desperate dog*
What do authors do?
Davies, Jacqueline. *The boy who drew birds*
Demi. *The boy who painted dragons*
DeNoble, Augustine. *Brother Joseph*
Domney, Alexis. *Splish, splat!*
Ehlert, Lois. *The scraps book*
Engle, Margarita. *The sky painter*
Flanagan, Alice K. *Mrs. Scott's beautiful art*
The Wilsons, a house-painting team
Freedman, Deborah. *Blue chicken*
Frith, Margaret. *Frida Kahlo*
Gibbons, Gail. *The art box*
Hanson, Faye. *The wonder*
Haring, Kay A. *Keith Haring*
Harvey, Jeanne Walker. *Maya Lin: artist-architect of light and lines*
My hands sing the blues
Haseley, Dennis. *Twenty heartbeats*
Hawkes, Kevin. *Remy and Lulu*

Hershenhorn, Esther. *Fancy that*
Hest, Amy. *Nana's birthday party*
Holub, Joan. *Vincent van Gogh*
Hong, Chen Jiang. *The magic horse of Han Gan*
Hyde, Margaret E. *Matisse for kids*
Van Gogh for kids
Jahn-Clough, Lisa. *Little dog*
Johnson, Angela. *Daddy calls me man*
Johnson, D. B. *Magritte's marvelous hat*
Palazzo inverso
Kelley, True. *Claude Monet*
Kirk, Daniel. *Library mouse: a museum adventure*
Kitamura, Satoshi. *Pablo the artist*
Kulling, Monica. *Grant and Tillie go walking*
Lakin, Patricia. *Subway sonata*
Lichtenheld, Tom. *Bridget's beret*
Lionni, Leo. *Matthew's dream*
Lithgow, John. *Micawber*
Lodding, Linda Ravin. *Painting Pepette*
Look, Lenore. *Brush of the gods*
MacLachlan, Patricia. *The iridescence of birds*
Painting the wind
MacLean, Kerry Lee. *Peaceful piggy meditation*
McPhail, David. *Beatrix Potter and her paint box*
Drawing lessons from a bear
Magnier, Thierry. *Isabelle and the angel*
Maltbie, P. I. *Claude Monet: the painter who stopped the trains*
Markel, Michelle. *The fantastic jungles of Henri Rousseau*
Mayhew, James. *Katie and the Mona Lisa*
Katie meets the Impressionists
Merberg, Julie. *In the garden with Van Gogh*
A magical day with Matisse
Morales, Yuyi. *Viva Frida*
Moss, Marissa. *Regina's big mistake*
Napoli, Donna Jo. *Ready to dream*
Nikola-Lisa, W. *The year with Grandma Moses*
Novesky, Amy. *Georgia in Hawaii*
Parker, Marjorie Blain. *Colorful dreamer*
Pinkwater, Daniel. *Bear's Picture*
Raczka, Bob. *No one saw*
Reynolds, Peter H. *Sky color*
Rhodes-Pitts, Sharifa. *Jake makes a world*
Ringgold, Faith. *Henry Ossawa Tanner*
Robinson, Fiona. *Whale shines*
Rodríguez, Rachel Victoria. *Through Georgia's eyes*
Rosenstock, Barb. *The noisy paint box*
Vincent can't sleep
Ross, Tom. *Eggbert, the slightly cracked egg*
Rubin, Susan Goldman. *The yellow house*
Rusch, Elizabeth. *A day with no crayons*
Segal, Lore Groszmann. *Morris the artist*
Shapiro, J. H. *Magic trash*
Sherry, Kevin. *I'm the best artist in the ocean*
Sierra, Judy. *Ballyhoo Bay*
Sís, Peter. *The wall: growing up behind the Iron Curtain*
Spohn, Kate. *By word of mouse*
Stadler, John. *What's so scary?*
Stein, Joel Edward. *A Hanukkah with Mazel*
Steptoe, Javaka. *Radiant child*
Stevenson, James. *Fun, no fun*
I meant to tell you
Stock, Catherine. *Gugu's house*
Stone, Tanya Lee. *Sandy's circus*
Sweeney, Joan. *Suzette and the puppy*
Tonatiuh, Duncan. *Diego Rivera: his world and ours*
Tunnell, Michael O. *The joke's on George*

Vande Griek, Susan. *The art room*
Waldman, Neil. *The starry night*
Warhola, James. *Uncle Andy's*
   Uncle Andy's cats
Wheatley, Nadia. *Luke's way of looking*
Wiesner, David. *Art and Max*
Willard, Nancy. *Pish posh, said Hieronymous Bosch*
Winter, Jeanette. *Cowboy Charlie*
   Henri's scissors
   Mr. Cornell's dream boxes
Winter, Jonah. *Diego*
   Just behave, Pablo Picasso!
Wolkstein, Diane. *Little Mouse's painting*
Wood, Michele. *Going back home*
Zalben, Jane Breskin. *Mousterpiece*
Ziefert, Harriet. *Lunchtime for a purple snake*

Careers – astronauts

Agee, Jon. *Dmitri the astronaut*
   Life on Mars
Aldrin, Buzz. *Look to the stars*
   Reaching for the moon
Barrett, Judi. *Cloudy with a chance of meatballs 3*
Barton, Byron. *I want to be an astronaut*
Bartram, Simon. *Bob's best-ever friend*
   Man on the moon: a day in the life of Bob
Branley, Franklyn M. *Floating in space*
Brett, Jan. *Hedgie blasts off!*
Brown, Don. *One giant leap: the story of Neil*
   Armstrong
Burleigh, Robert. *One giant leap*
Floca, Brian. *Moonshot*
Fox, Christyan. *Astronaut PiggyWiggy*
Grey, Mini. *Space Dog*
Hadfield, Chris. *The darkest dark*
Hilliard, Richard. *Godspeed, John Glenn*
Houran, Lori Haskins. *A trip into space*
Kelly, Mark. *Mousetronaut*
   Mousetronaut goes to Mars
Kelly, Scott. *My journey to the stars*
McCarthy, Meghan. *Astronaut handbook*
McReynolds, Linda. *Eight days gone*
Mayo, Margaret. *Zoom, rocket, zoom!*
Naden, Corinne J. *Ron's big mission*
Nettleton, Pamela Hill. *Sally Ride*
Price, Ben Joel. *Earth space moon base*
Rau, Dana Meachen. *Neil Armstrong*
Van Vleet, Carmella. *To the stars!*

Careers – astronomers

Gerber, Carole. *Annie Jump Cannon, astronomer*
Hopkinson, Deborah. *Maria's comet*
Pettenati, Jeanne K. *Galileo's journal, 1609–1610*
Pinkney, Andrea Davis. *Dear Benjamin Banneker*
Sís, Peter. *Starry messenger*
Sisson, Stephanie Roth. *Star stuff*

Careers – authors *see* Careers – writers

Careers – bakers

Carle, Eric. *Walter the baker*
dePaola, Tomie. *Tony's bread*
Ericsson, Jennifer A. *Out and about at the bakery*
Flanagan, Alice K. *Mr. Santizo's tasty treats!*
Heath, Amy. *Sofie's role*
Holt, Kimberly Willis. *Skinny brown dog*

Jackson, Kathryn. *Pantaloon*
Kleven, Elisa. *Sun bread*
Kneen, Maggie. *Chocolate moose*
Levitin, Sonia. *Boom town*
McMullan, Kate. *Bulldog's big day*
Mathers, Petra. *Herbie's secret Santa*
O'Callahan, Jay. *Raspberries!*
Ogburn, Jacqueline K. *The bake shop ghost*
Rylant, Cynthia. *The cookie-store cat*
Shepard, Aaron. *The baker's dozen*
Simmonds, Posy. *Baker cat*
Stewart, Sarah. *The gardener*
Wellington, Monica. *Mr. Cookie Baker*
Westcott, Nadine Bernard. *Peanut butter and jelly*
Willard, Nancy. *The flying bed*
Willey, Margaret. *Clever Beatrice and the best little*
   pony

Careers – barbers

Barnes, Derrick. *Crown*
Burnard, Damon. *Dave's haircut*
Cole, Kenneth, Dr. *No bad news*
Hamilton, Martha. *The ghost catcher*
Koren, Edward. *Very hairy Harry*
McElligott, Matthew. *Even monsters need haircuts*
Mayer, Kirsten. *Go big or go gnome!*
Mitchell, Margaree King. *Uncle Jed's barbershop*
Peet, Bill. *Hubert's hair-raising adventures*
Radabaugh, Melinda Beth. *Getting a haircut*
Robbins, Beth. *Tom's new haircut*
Rocco, John. *Super Hair-o and the barber of doom*
Tarpley, Natasha Anastasia. *Bippity Bop barbershop*

Careers – beekeepers

Flanagan, Alice K. *Learning about bees from Mr.*
   Krebs
Kessler, Cristina. *The best beekeeper of Lalibela*
Krebs, Laurie. *The beeman*, ill. by Valeria Cis
   The beeman, ill. by Melissa Iwai
Nargi, Lela. *The honeybee man*

Careers – beggars

Oppenheim, Shulamith Levey. *Ali and the magic*
   stew

Careers – blacksmiths

High, Linda Oatman. *Winter shoes for Shadow Horse*

Careers – bookbinders

Cheng, Andrea. *Anna the bookbinder*

Careers – bus drivers

Anstee, Ashlyn. *Are we there, Yeti?*
Brown, Marc. *Arthur lost and found*
Flanagan, Alice K. *Riding the school bus with Mrs.*
   Kramer
Helakoski, Leslie. *The smushy bus*
Marin, Cheech. *Cheech and the spooky ghost bus*
Owen, Ann. *Taking your places*
Poydar, Nancy. *First day, hooray!*
Pulver, Robin. *Axle Annie*
   Axle Annie and the speed grump
Willems, Mo. *Don't let the pigeon drive the bus*

Careers – butchers

Yorinks, Arthur. *Louis the fish*

Careers – carpenters

Barros, Bruna. *The carpenter*
Lucado, Max. *Jacob's gift*
Pickthall, Marjorie L. C. *The worker in sandalwood*

Careers – cartographers

Burleigh, Robert. *Solving the puzzle under the sea*
Chancellor, Deborah. *Maps and mapping*

Careers – chauffeurs

Villeneuve, Anne. *Loula is leaving for Africa*

Careers – chefs, cooks

Anderson, Brian. *Monster chefs*
Barasch, Lynne. *Hiromi's hands*
Demas, Corinne. *The boy who was generous with salt*
Egan, Tim. *The experiments of Doctor Vermin*
Hartland, Jessie. *Bon appetit!*
Martin, Jacqueline Briggs. *Alice Waters and the trip
    to delicious*
Medearis, Angela Shelf. *The ghost of Sifty-Sifty Sam*
Miller, Pat. *The hole story of the doughnut*
Ochiltree, Dianne. *Molly, by golly!*
Radabaugh, Melinda Beth. *Going to a restaurant*
Reich, Susanna. *Minette's feast*
Slegers, Liesbet. *Chefs and what they do*
Staake, Bob. *The donut chef*
Stein, Janet. *This little bunny can bake*
Stimpson, Colin. *Jack and the baked beanstalk*
Stowell, Penelope. *The greatest potatoes*
Wellington, Monica. *Pizza at Sally's*
Whelan, Gloria. *The boy who wanted to cook*

Careers – clergy

Asim, Jabari. *Preaching to the chickens*
Beebe, Katy. *Brother Hugo and the bear*
DeNoble, Augustine. *Brother Joseph*
Dollinger, Renate. *The rabbi who flew*
I've seen the promised land
Johnson, Paul Brett. *Old Dry Fry*
Kelley, Kitty. *Martin's dream day*
Kimmel, Eric A. *Zigazak!*
Muth, Jon J. *Stone soup*
Nettleton, Pamela Hill. *Martin Luther King, Jr*
Norris, Kathleen. *The holy twins*
Olofsson, Helena. *The little jester*
Rappaport, Doreen. *Martin's big words*
Sexton, Colleen A. *Let's meet Martin Luther King, Jr*
Swain, Gwenyth. *I wonder as I wander*

Careers – coaches

Finchler, Judy. *You're a good sport, Miss Malarkey*
Flanagan, Alice K. *Coach John and his soccer team*

Careers – composers

Anderson, M. T. *Strange Mr. Satie*
Celenza, Anna Harwell. *The farewell symphony*
Costanza, Stephen. *Vivaldi and the invisible orchestra*
Newman, Lesléa. *Ketzel, the cat who composed*

Robinson, Fiona. *What animals really like*
Schaefer, Carole Lexa. *Two scarlet songbirds*
Swain, Gwenyth. *I wonder as I wander*

Careers – conductors (music)

Costello, David Hyde. *Little Pig joins the band*
Devernay, Laetitia. *The conductor*
Lithgow, John. *The remarkable Farkle McBride*
Robinson, Fiona. *What animals really like*

Careers – construction workers

Ashburn, Boni. *Builder Goose*
Banks, Kate. *The night worker*
Bean, Jonathan. *Building our house*
Bee, William. *Stanley the builder*
Beil, Karen Magnuson. *Jack's house*
Big noisy trucks and diggers
Biggs, Brian. *Tinyville town gets to work*
Bryant, Megan E. *Dump Truck Duck*
Buzzeo, Toni. *Whose tools?*
Clement, Nathan. *Job site*
Copeland, Cynthia L. *What are you waiting for?*
Cyrus, Kurt. *Billions of bricks*
Dale, Penny. *Dinosaur dig!*
Elliott, Rebecca. *Dalmatian in a digger*
Evans, Nate. *Bang! Boom! Roar!*
Flanagan, Alice K. *Mr. Paul and Mr. Luecke build
    communities*
Fleming, Meg. *Ready, set, build!*
Freedman, Claire. *Beep beep beep: time for sleep!*
Goodwin-Sturges, Judy Sue. *Construction Kitties*
Greene, Rhonda Growler. *Push! dig! scoop!*
Hayward, Linda. *A day in the life of a builder*
Hennessy, B. G. *Road builders*
Hill, Lee Sullivan. *Earthmovers*
Horvath, James. *Dig, dogs, dig
    Work, dogs, work*
Hudson, Cheryl Willis. *Construction zone*
Johnson, Angela. *Those building men*
Keller, Joy. *Monster trucks*
Kilby, Don. *At a construction site*
Lewis, Kevin. *The lot at the end of my block*
Liebman, Daniel. *I want to be a builder*
Lund, Deb. *Monsters on machines*
McMullan, Kate. *I'm dirty!*
Mandel, Peter. *Jackhammer Sam*
Meltzer, Lynn. *The construction crew*
Nevius, Carol. *Building with Dad*
Newhouse, Maxwell. *The house that Max built*
Paul, Ann Whitford. *Word builder*
Reidy, Jean. *Busy builders, busy week!*
Rinker, Sherri Duskey. *Goodnight, goodnight,
    construction site
    Mighty, mighty construction site*
Schaefer, Lola M. *Construction site*
Shoulders, Michael. *D is for dump truck*
Skultety, Nancy. *From here to there*
Steggall, Susan. *The diggers are coming!*
Stoeke, Janet Morgan. *Minerva Louise and the red
    truck*
Suen, Anastasia. *Raise the roof
    Up! up! up! skyscraper*
Sutton, Sally. *Construction
    Demolition
    Roadwork*
Wood, Jakki. *A hole in the road*

Careers – cooks *see* Careers – chefs, cooks

Careers – custodians, janitors

Brett, Jan. *Hedgie blasts off!*
Flanagan, Alice K. *Call Mr. Vasquez, he'll fix it!*
Harley, Bill. *Lost and found*
Reed, Lynn Rowe. *Basil's birds*
Schotter, Roni. *Doo-Wop Pop*

Careers – dancers

Copeland, Misty. *Firebird*
Crow, Kristyn. *Zombelina*
Dempsey, Kristy. *A dance like starlight*
Ferguson, Sarah. *Ballerina Rosie*
Gravel, Elise. *The cranky ballerina*
Hayward, Linda. *A day in the life of a dancer*
Isadora, Rachel. *Lili on stage*
Kent, Allegra. *Ballerina gets ready*
Membrino, Anna. *I want to be a ballerina*
Pace, Anne Marie. *Vampirina ballerina*
    Vampirina ballerina hosts a sleepover
Pavlova, Anna. *I dreamed I was a ballerina*
Pinkney, Andrea Davis. *Alvin Ailey*
Sís, Peter. *Ballerina*
Snyder, Laurel. *Swan*

Careers – dentists

Berenstain, Stan and Jan. *The Berenstain bears visit the dentist*
Cousins, Lucy. *Maisy, Charley, and the wobbly tooth*
Davis, Katie. *Mabel the Tooth Fairy and how she got her job*
Dungy, Tony. *You can do it!*
Flanagan, Alice K. *Dr. Kanner, dentist with a smile*
Gomi, Taro. *The crocodile and the dentist*
Keller, Laurie. *Open wide*
Murkoff, Heidi Eisenberg. *What to expect when you go to the dentist*
Rey, Margret. *Curious George goes to the dentist*
Rockwell, Harlow. *My dentist*
Rosenberry, Vera. *Vera goes to the dentist*
Schaefer, Lola M. *Dental office*
Steig, William. *Doctor De Soto goes to Africa*
Swanson, Diane. *The dentist and you*
Whybrow, Ian. *Harry and the dinosaurs say "Raahh"*
Ziefert, Harriet. *ABC dentist*

Careers – detectives

Berenstain, Stan and Jan. *The bear detectives*
Biedrzycki, David. *Ace Lacewing, Bug Detective*
Christelow, Eileen. *Where's the big bad wolf?*
Crummel, Susan Stevens. *Sherlock Bones and the missing cheese*
Dickson, Louise. *The vanishing cat*
Gallaher, Jason. *Whobert Whover, owl detective*
Geisert, Arthur. *Mystery*
Grey, Mini. *Hermelin the detective mouse*
Lazar, Tara. *7 ate 9*
Levinthal, David. *Who pushed Humpty Dumpty?*
McLaren, Meg. *Pigeon P.I.*
McLaughlin, Lauren. *Mitzi Tulane, preschool detective, in The secret ingredient*
    Mitzi Tulane, preschool detective, in What's that smell
Mason, Adrienne. *Lu and Clancy sound off*
    Lu and Clancy's spy stuff
Meddaugh, Susan. *Perfectly Martha*
Metzger, Steve. *Detective Blue*
Nash, Scott. *Tuff Fluff*
Olien, Jessica. *Shark Detective!*
Palatini, Margie. *The web files*
Pinkwater, Daniel. *Bad bear detectives*
Rash, Andy. *Agent A to Agent Z*
Schaefer, Lola M. *Police station*
Scotton, Rob. *Secret Agent Splat!*
Teague, Mark. *Detective LaRue*
Tryon, Leslie. *Albert's Halloween*
Yee, Wong Herbert. *Detective Small in the amazing banana caper*
Young, Jessica. *Spy Guy*

Careers – doctors

Beaty, Andrea. *Doctor Ted*
Berenstain, Stan and Jan. *The Berenstain bears go to the doctor*
Charlip, Remy. *"Mother, mother I feel sick"*
Cole, Joanna. *My friend the doctor*
Donaldson, Julia. *Zog and the flying doctors*
Freeman, Don. *Corduroy's busy street and Corduroy goes to the doctor*
Grimm, Jacob and Wilhelm. *Doctor All-Knowing*
Harness, Cheryl. *Mary Walker wears the pants*
Ketteman, Helen. *If Beaver had a fever*
Liebman, Daniel. *I want to be a doctor*
Lloyd, Sam. *Doctor Meow's big emergency*
London, Jonathan. *Froggy goes to the doctor*
    Here comes Doctor Hippo
Murkoff, Heidi Eisenberg. *What to expect when you go to the doctor*
Murphy, Liz. *ABC doctor*
Oelschlager, Vanita. *Bonyo Bonyo*
Owen, Ann. *Keeping you healthy*
Piumini, Roberto. *Doctor Me Di Cin*
Robbins, Beth. *Tom and Ally visit the doctor*
Rockwell, Harlow. *My doctor*
Rogers, Fred. *Going to the doctor*
Rylant, Cynthia. *Silver packages*
Schaefer, Lola M. *Hospital*
Singer, Marilyn. *I'm getting a checkup*
Slegers, Liesbet. *Katie goes to the doctor*
Stone, Tanya Lee. *Who says women can't be doctors?*
Swanson, Diane. *The doctor and you*
Viorst, Judith. *The tenth good thing about Barney*
Wells, Rosemary. *A visit to Dr. Duck*

Careers – doormen

Grimm, Edward. *The doorman*

Careers – electricians

Cole, Joanna. *The magic school bus and the electric field trip*

Careers – emergency medical technicians

Levine, Michelle. *Ambulances*
Mayo, Margaret. *Emergency!*

Careers – engineers

Beaty, Andrea. *Rosie Revere, engineer*
Biggs, Brian. *Tinyville town gets to work*
Davis, Kathryn Gibbs. *Mr. Ferris and his wheel*

Drummond, Allan. *Casey Jones*
Highet, Alistair. *The yellow train*
Kraft, Betsy Harvey. *The fantastic Ferris wheel*
Moss, Marissa. *True heart*
Underwood, Deborah. *Interstellar Cinderella*

Careers – entertainers

Newman, Lesléa. *Pigs, pigs, pigs*

Careers – explorers

Atkinson, Cale. *Explorers of the wild*
Brown, Don. *Uncommon traveler*
Hopkinson, Deborah. *Keep on!*
Kirk, Daniel. *Library mouse: a museum adventure*
　Library mouse: a world to explore
Kroll, Steven. *Lewis and Clark*
St. George, Judith. *So you want to be an explorer?*
Schachner, Judith Byron. *Yo, Vikings*
Sís, Peter. *Follow the dream*
Thomas, Frances. *One day, Daddy*
Weatherford, Carole Boston. *I, Matthew Henson*
Yorinks, Arthur. *The Miami giant*

Careers – farmers

Aesop. *The goose that laid the golden egg*
Aliki. *Milk from cow to carton*
Asch, Frank. *Barnyard lullaby*
Baker, Ken. *Old MacDonald had a dragon*
Barbour, Karen. *Mr. Williams*
Bee, William. *Stanley the farmer*
Bock, Lee. *Oh, crumps! / Ay, caramba!*
Carlson, Melody. *Farmer Brown's field trip*
Carney, Margaret. *At Grandpa's sugar bush*
Carter, David A. *Old MacDonald had a farm: a pop-up book*
Carter, Don. *Old MacDonald drives a tractor*
Christelow, Eileen. *The great pig escape*
Cordsen, Carol Foskett. *Market day*
Cronin, Doreen. *Click, clack, moo*
　Dooby dooby moo
　Thump, quack, moo
Crunk, Tony. *Grandpa's overalls*
Douglas, Erin. *Get that pest!*
Duffield, Katy. *Farmer McPeepers and his missing milk cows*
Egan, Tim. *Serious farm*
The farmer in the dell. *The farmer in the dell*, ill. by John O'Brien
　The farmer in the dell, ill. by Alexandra Wallner
Fitz-Gibbon, Sally. *On Uncle John's farm*
Flanagan, Alice K. *Raising cows on the Koebels' farm*
　A visit to the Gravesens' farm
　The Zieglers and their apple orchard
Florian, Douglas. *I love my hat*
Frazee, Marla. *The farmer and the clown*
Goodhart, Pippa. *Arthur's tractor*
Haas, Jessie. *Hurry!*
Karas, G. Brian. *On the farm, at the market*
Lasky, Kathryn. *The emperor's old clothes*
Maccarone, Grace. *Oink! moo! how do you do?*
Maguire, Gregory. *Crabby Cratchitt*
Marciano, John Bemelmans. *Delilah*
Most, Bernard. *Cock-a-doodle-moo!*
Nettleton, Pamela Hill. *George Washington*
Old MacDonald had a farm. *Grandma's nursery rhymes: Old MacDonald*
　Old MacDonald

Old MacDonald had a farm, ill. by Holly Berry
Old MacDonald had a farm, ill. by Jane Cabrera
Old MacDonald had a farm, ill. by Carol Jones
Old MacDonald had a farm, ill. by Tracey Campbell Pearson
Old MacDonald had a farm, ill. by Glen Rounds
Old MacDonald had a farm, ill. by Jessica Souhami
Old MacDonald had a farm, ill. by Prue Theobalds
Old MacDonald had a truck
Pete the Cat: Old MacDonald had a farm
Palatini, Margie. *The cheese*
Parks, Carmen. *Farmers market*
Pelletier, Andrew T. *The toy farmer*
Peterson, Cris. *Extra cheese, please!*
Plourde, Lynn. *Grandpappy snippy snappies*
Powell, Consie. *Amazing apples*
Preston-Gannon, Frann. *Dinosaur farm*
Purmell, Ann. *Apple cider making days*
　Christmas tree farm
Raschka, Chris. *Give and take*
Rotner, Shelley. *Grow! raise! catch!*
Sandburg, Carl. *The Huckabuck family and how they raised popcorn in Nebraska and quit and came back*
Schaub, Michelle. *Fresh-picked poetry*
Schotter, Roni. *Go, Little Green Truck!*
Sillifant, Alec. *Farmer Ham*
Skrypuch, Marsha Forchuk. *Enough*
Slate, Joseph. *The great big wagon that rang*
Sloat, Teri. *The thing that bothered Farmer Brown*
Steig, William. *Wizzil*
Stock, Catherine. *A porc in New York*
Sturgis, Brenda Reeves. *Ten turkeys in the road*
Tafuri, Nancy. *This is the farmer*
Taylor, Joanne. *Full moon rising*
Trent, Shanda. *Farmers' market day*
Van Leeuwen, Jean. *Nothing here but trees*
　Sorry
Waddell, Martin. *Farmer Duck*
　The pig in the pond
Wellington, Monica. *Apple farmer Annie*
Wilson, Karma. *Horseplay*
Yee, Wong Herbert. *Fireman Small to the rescue*
Yolen, Jane. *The flying witch*
　Harvest home

Careers – firefighters

Armstrong, Jennifer. *Magnus at the fire*
Austin, Mike. *Fire Engine No. 9*
Beaty, Andrea. *Firefighter Ted*
Bingham, Caroline. *Big book of rescue vehicles*
Bourgeois, Paulette. *Fire fighters*
Bridwell, Norman. *Clifford's good deeds*
Butler, Dori Hillestad. *F is for firefighting*
Carabine, Sue. *A firefighter's night before Christmas*
Child, Lauren. *Clarice Bean, guess who's babysitting?*
Curious George at the fire station
Cutlip, Kimbra L. *Firefighter's night before Christmas*
Cuyler, Margery. *The little fire truck*
Demarest, Chris L. *Firefighters A to Z*
　Hotshots!
　Smokejumpers one to ten
Deschamps, Nicola. *Emergency!*
Desimini, Lisa. *Dot the Firedog*
Dormer, Frank W. *Firefighter Duckies!*
Dubois, Muriel L. *Out and about at the fire station*

Elya, Susan Middleton. *Fire! ¡Fuego! Brave bomberos*
Flanagan, Alice K. *Ms. Murphy fights fires*
Fox, Christyan. *Fire fighter PiggyWiggy*
Frampton, David. *Mr. Ferlinghetti's poem*
Gergely, Tibor. *The great big fire engine book*
Gibbons, Gail. *Fire! Fire!*
Godwin, Laura. *This is the firefighter*
Gorbachev, Valeri. *The missing chick*
Graham, Tom. *Five little firefighters*
Grambling, Lois G. *My mom is a firefighter*
Greene, Rhonda Gowler. *Firebears*
Hamilton, Kersten. *Firefighters to the rescue!*
Harper, Jamie. *Miss Mingo and the fire drill*
Hayward, Linda. *A day in the life of a firefighter*
Hubbell, Patricia. *Firefighters!*
Jane, Pamela. *Milo and the fire engine parade*
Krensky, Stephen. *Spark the firefighter*
Lenski, Lois. *The little fire engine*
Liebman, Daniel. *I want to be a firefighter*
Lloyd, Sam. *Chief Rhino to the rescue!*
London, Jonathan. *Here comes firefighter Hippo*
Long, Loren. *Otis and the kittens*
Lukasewich, Lori. *The night fire*
McMullan, Kate. *I'm brave!*
Mammano, Julie. *Rhinos who rescue*
Martin, Bill, Jr.. *Fire! Fire! said Mrs. McGuire*
　　"Fire! Fire!" said Mrs. McGuire
Mayo, Margaret. *Emergency!*
Miller, Edward. *Fireboy to the rescue!*
Mitton, Tony. *Flashing fire engines*
Munsch, Robert N. *The fire station*
Nolan, Janet. *The firehouse light*
Ochiltree, Dianne. *Molly, by golly!*
Osborne, Mary Pope. *New York's bravest*
Owen, Ann. *Protecting your home*
Penn, Audrey. *Kai to the rescue!*
Rex, Michael. *My fire engine*
Rey, H. A. *Curious George*
　　The original Curious George
Rockwell, Anne. *At the firehouse*
　　Fire engines
Root, Andrew. *Hamsters don't fight fires!*
Santoro, Scott. *Isaac the Ice Cream Truck*
Sís, Peter. *Fire truck*
Slater, Dashka. *Firefighters in the dark*
Teague, Mark. *Firehouse!*
Whiting, Sue. *The firefighters*
Wood, Audrey. *Alphabet rescue*
Yee, Wong Herbert. *Fireman Small*
　　Fireman Small, fire down below
　　Fireman Small to the rescue
　　A small Christmas
Zimmerman, Andrea Griffing. *Fire engine man*

Careers – fishermen

Bateman, Teresa. *The merbaby*
Demas, Corinne. *The boy who was generous with salt*
Demers, Dominique. *Old Thomas and the little fairy*
Garland, Sherry. *My father's boat*
Gerstein, Mordicai. *The boy and the whale*
Gibbons, Gail. *Surrounded by sea*
LaMarche, Jim. *Up*
McGaw, Wayne T. *T-boy of the bayou*
Pennypacker, Sara. *Pierre in love*
Rotner, Shelley. *Grow! raise! catch!*
San Souci, Robert D. *Nicholas Pipe*
Sunami, Kitoba. *How the fisherman tricked the genie*
Van, Muon. *In a village by the sea*

Careers – forest rangers *see* Careers – park rangers

Careers – fortune tellers

Alexander, Lloyd. *Fortune tellers*
Shepard, Aaron. *Forty fortunes*

Careers – fur traders

Pendziwol, Jean E. *The red sash*

Careers – garbage collectors *see* Careers – sanitation workers

Careers – geologists

Burleigh, Robert. *Solving the puzzle under the sea*
Chin, Jason. *Grand Canyon*
Cole, Joanna. *The magic school bus inside the earth*

Careers – handymen

Flanagan, Alice K. *Call Mr. Vasquez, he'll fix it!*
Rockwell, Anne. *Let's go to the hardware store*

Careers – harpists

Edwards, Pamela Duncan. *The leprechaun's gold*

Careers – housekeepers

Hanson, Warren. *It's Monday, Mrs. Jolly Bones!*
McKissack, Patricia C. *Ma Dear's aprons*
Polacco, Patricia. *Gifts of the heart*

Careers – illustrators

Barnett, Mac. *How this book was made*
Browne, Anthony. *The shape game*
Carle, Eric. *What's your favorite color?*
Kanninen, Barbara. *A story with pictures*
Krull, Kathleen. *The boy on Fairfield Street*
Lehrhaupt, Adam. *This is a good story*
Luyken, Corinna. *The book of mistakes*
Myers, Walter Dean. *Harlem*
Peet, Bill. *Bill Peet*
Rau, Dana Meachen. *Dr. Seuss*
Rinker, Sherri Duskey. *Big machines*
Sierra, Judy. *Imagine that! how Dr. Seuss wrote The Cat in the Hat*
Steig, William. *When everybody wore a hat*
Whatley, Bruce. *Wait! no paint!*

Careers – inventors

Barretta, Gene. *Neo Leo*
　　Now and Ben
　　Timeless Thomas
Brill, Marlene Targ. *Margaret Knight, girl inventor*
Brown, Don. *A wizard from the start*
Davis, Kathryn Gibbs. *Mr. Ferris and his wheel*
Fleming, Candace. *Papa's mechanical fish*
Ford, Gilbert. *The marvelous thing that came from a spring*
Gall, Chris. *Awesome Dawson*
　　NanoBots
Glass, Andrew. *The wondrous whirligig*

GrandPre, Mary. *Cleonardo, the little inventor*
Hood, Susan. *The fix-it man*
Keller, Shana. *Ticktock Banneker's clock*
Kelly, David A. *Miracle mud*
Kraft, Betsy Harvey. *The fantastic Ferris wheel*
Krensky, Stephen. *Ben Franklin and his first kite*
Kulling, Monica. *All aboard! Elijah McCoy's steam engine*
McCall, Bruce. *Marveltown*
McCarthy, Meghan. *Earmuffs for everyone!*
Milgrim, David. *Young MacDonald*
Nettleton, Pamela Hill. *Benjamin Franklin*
Pelley, Kathleen T. *Inventor McGregor*
Priceman, Marjorie. *Hot air*
It's me, Marva!
Reynolds, Peter H. *Sydney's star*
Schaefer, Lola M. *The Wright brothers*
Schanzer, Rosalyn. *How Ben Franklin stole the lightning*
Taylor, Barbara. *I wonder why zippers have teeth and other questions about inventions*
Weston, Mark. *Honda*
Yolen, Jane. *My brothers' flying machine*

Careers – janitors *see* Careers – custodians, janitors

Careers – jockeys

Trollinger, Patsi B. *Perfect timing*

Careers – journalists

Dray, Philip. *Yours for justice, Ida B. Wells*
Hawkins, Colin. *Fairytale news*
Leedy, Loreen. *The Furry News*
Shea, Kitty. *Out and about at the newspaper*

Careers – judges

Winter, Jonah. *Sonia Sotomayor*
Zemach, Harve. *The judge*

Careers – lawyers

Flanagan, Alice K. *A day in court with Mrs. Trinh*
McKissack, Patricia C. *Ol' Clip-Clop*

Careers – librarians

Asch, Frank. *The Lending Zoo*
Asher, Sandy. *Chicken story time*
Bottner, Barbara. *Miss Brooks' Story Nook (where tales are told and ogres are welcome)*
Deedy, Carmen Agra. *Return of the library dragon*
Ernst, Lisa Campbell. *Stella Louella's runaway book*
Flanagan, Alice K. *Ms. Davison, our librarian*
Gonzalez, Lucia. *The storyteller's candle / La velita de los cuentos*
Grambling, Lois G. *Can I bring Woolly to the library, Ms. Reeder?*
Greene, Rhonda Gowler. *No pirates allowed! said Library Lou*
King, M. G. *Librarian on the roof!*
Liebman, Daniel. *I want to be a librarian*
Mora, Pat. *Tomás and the library lady*
Morris, Carla. *The boy who was raised by librarians*
OHora, Zachariah. *The not so quiet library*
Radabaugh, Melinda Beth. *Going to the library*

Ruurs, Margriet. *My librarian is a camel*
Shea, Kitty. *Out and about at the public library*
Sierra, Judy. *Wild about books*
Silvestro, Annie. *Bunny's book club*
Stadler, Alexander. *Beverly Billingsly borrows a book*
Williams, Suzanne. *Library Lil*
Winter, Jeanette. *The librarian of Basra*

Careers – lifeguards

Bingham, Caroline. *Big book of rescue vehicles*
Pinkwater, Daniel. *At the Hotel Larry*
Young Larry

Careers – lumberjacks

Balcziak, Bill. *Paul Bunyan*
Bateman, Teresa. *Paul Bunyan vs. Hals Halson*
Beedie, Duncan. *The lumberjack's beard*
Kellogg, Steven. *Paul Bunyan: a tall tale*
Lange, Willem. *John and Tom*
Luckhurst, Matt. *Paul Bunyan and Babe the Blue Ox*

Careers – magicians

Adler, David A. *A picture book of Harry Houdini*
Agee, Jon. *Milo's hat trick*
Ashman, Linda. *Maxwell's magic mix-up*
Bardill, Linard. *The great golden thing*
Baynton, Martin. *Jane and the magician*
Cate, Annette LeBlanc. *The magic rabbit*
Desrosiers, Sylvie. *Hocus Pocus takes the train*
Faller, Regis. *Polo and the magician!*
Geras, Adèle. *Swan Lake*
Kennedy, Kim. *Hee-Haw-Dini and the Great Zambini*
McGill, Erin. *I do not like Al's hat*
McLaren, Meg. *Rabbit magic*
Many, Paul. *The great pancake escape*
Paschkis, Julie. *Magic spell*
Paul, Ruth. *Hedgehog's magic tricks*
Schneider, Christine M. *Horace P. Tuttle, magician extraordinaire*
Seeger, Pete. *Abiyoyo returns*
Villeneuve, Anne. *The red scarf*

Careers – mail carriers *see* Careers – postal workers

Careers – mathematicians

Heiligman, Deborah. *The boy who loved math*

Careers – mechanics

Bee, William. *Stanley's garage*
Flanagan, Alice K. *Mr. Yee fixes cars*
Liebman, Daniel. *I want to be a mechanic*
Merlin, Christophe. *Under the hood*
Shulman, Mark. *Gorilla Garage*
Timmers, Leo. *Gus's garage*

Careers – messengers

Burleigh, Robert. *Messenger, messenger*

Careers – meteorologists

Bahr, Mary. *My brother loved snowflakes*
Kespert, Deborah. *Rain and shine*

Kudlinski, Kathleen V. *Boy, were we wrong about the weather!*
Schmidt, Karen Lee. *Carl's nose*

Careers – migrant workers

Adler, David A. *A picture book of Cesar Chavez*
Altman, Linda Jacobs. *Amelia's road*
Dorros, Arthur. *Radio Man / Don Radio*
Malone, Cheryl Lawton. *Dario and the whale*
Mora, Pat. *Tomás and the library lady*
Pérez, L. King. *First day in grapes*
Stanton, Karen. *Papi's gift*
Thomas, Jane Resh. *Lights on the river*
Tonatiuh, Duncan. *Pancho Rabbit and the coyote*
Warren, Sarah. *Dolores Huerta*
Williams, Sherley Anne. *Working cotton*

Careers – military

Andersen, Hans Christian. *The tinderbox*
Biden, Jill. *Don't forget, God bless our troops*
Brisson, Pat. *Sometimes we were brave*
Brown, Marcia. *Stone soup*
Bunting, Eve. *My red balloon*
    The wall
Carroll, James Christopher. *Papa's backpack*
Collins, Suzanne. *Year of the jungle*
Demarest, Chris L. *Alpha Bravo Charlie*
Dennis, Major Brian. *Nubs*
Dewan, Ted. *One true bear*
Duble, Kathleen Benner. *Pilot mom*
Emberley, Barbara. *Drummer Hoff*
Farish, Terry. *Luis paints the world*
Hardin, Melinda. *Hero dad*
Keane, Michael. *The night Santa got lost*
Kerley, Barbara. *Brave like me*
Lee, Jeanne M. *The song of Mu Lan*
Littlesugar, Amy. *Lisette's angel*
McElroy, Lisa Tucker. *Love, Lizzie*
Mackintosh, David. *The Frank show*
Messner, Kate. *Rolling Thunder*
Montalván, Luis Carlos. *Tuesday tucks me in*
Nadel, Carolina. *Daddy's home*
Nelson, S. D. *Quiet hero*
Nettleton, Pamela Hill. *George Washington*
Norman, Geoffrey. *Stars above us*
Pelton, Mindy L. *When Dad's at sea*
Polacco, Patricia. *Remembering Vera*
Ruth, Greg. *Coming home*
Seeger, Pete. *Some friends to feed*
Tomp, Sarah Wones. *Red, white, and blue goodbye*
Walker, Sally M. *Winnie*

Careers – miners

Addy, Sharon Hart. *Lucky Jake*
Amsden, Janet. *Grizzly Pete and the ghosts*
Kay, Verla. *Gold fever*
Levitin, Sonia. *Boom town*
Lyon, George Ella. *Mama is a miner*
Provensen, Alice. *Klondike gold*
Schwartz, Joanne. *Town is by the sea*

Careers – motion picture producers

Brown, Don. *Mack made movies*
Milgrim, David. *Amelia makes a movie*

Careers – musicians

Alexander, Kwame. *Acoustic Rooster and his barnyard band*
Andrews, Julie. *Simeon's gift*
Andrews, Troy. *Trombone Shorty*
Battle-Lavert, Gwendolyn. *The music in Derrick's heart*
Burleigh, Robert. *Lookin' for Bird in the big city*
Carter, Don. *Heaven's all-star jazz band*
Celenza, Anna Harwell. *Duke Ellington's Nutcracker Suite*
Christensen, Bonnie. *Woody Guthrie, poet of the people*
Cline-Ransome, Lesa. *Just a lucky so and so*
Cox, Judy. *My family plays music*
DeFelice, Cynthia C. *Cold feet*
de la Peña, Matt. *Miguel and the grand harmony*
Dillon, Leo. *Jazz on a Saturday night*
Dominguez, Angela. *Sing, don't cry*
Francis, Panama. *David gets his drum*
Golio, Gary. *Bird and Diz*
Grimm, Jacob and Wilhelm. *The Bremen town band*
    The Bremen town musicians, ill. by Bill Dickson
    The Bremen town musicians, ill. by Ilse Plume
    The Bremen town musicians, ill. by Bernadette Watts
    The Bremen town musicians, ill. by Lisbeth Zwerger
    Musicians of Bremen
    Musicians of Bremen / Los musicos de Bremner
Huling, Jan. *Ol' Bloo's boogie-woogie band and blues ensemble*
Ingalls, Ann. *The little piano girl*
Johnson, Angela. *Violet's music*
Liebman, Daniel. *I want to be a musician*
Lithgow, John. *The remarkable Farkle McBride*
Long, Loren. *Drummer boy*
Manders, John. *The really awful musicians*
Marsalis, Wynton. *Squeak, rumble, whomp! Whomp! Whomp!*
Martin, Bill, Jr.. *Maestro plays*
Orgill, Roxane. *If I only had a horn*
Parker, Robert Andrew. *Piano starts here*
Pinkney, Andrea Davis. *Duke Ellington*
Pinkwater, Daniel. *Bongo Larry*
Price, Kathy. *The Bourbon Street musicians*
Raschka, Chris. *Charlie Parker played be bop*
    Mysterious Thelonious
Richards, Keith. *Gus and me*
Ringgold, Faith. *Harlem Renaissance party*
Seeger, Pete. *The deaf musicians*
Shepard, Aaron. *The sea king's daughter*
Sís, Peter. *Play, Mozart, play*
Stinson, Kathy. *The dance of the violin*
    The man with the violin
Troupe, Quincy. *Little Stevie Wonder*
Turner, Barbara J. *Out and about at the orchestra*
Weatherford, Carole Boston. *Before John was a jazz giant*
Weller, Frances Ward. *The angel of Mill Street*
Winter, Jeanette. *Once upon a time in Chicago*
Winter, Jonah. *Dizzy*
    How Jelly Roll Morton invented jazz

Careers – naturalists

Armentrout, David. *John Muir*
Davies, Jacqueline. *The boy who drew birds*

Rosenstock, Barb. *The camping trip that changed America*
Smith, Matthew Clark. *Small wonders: Jean-Henri Fabre and his world of insects*

Careers – nuns

Mora, Pat. *A library for Juana*
Norris, Kathleen. *The holy twins*
Ransom, Candice F. *Mother Teresa*

Careers – nurses

Demi. *Florence Nightingale*
Flanagan, Alice K. *Ask Nurse Pfaff, she'll help you!*
James, Simon. *Nurse Clementine*
Liebman, Daniel. *I want to be a nurse*
Polacco, Patricia. *Clara and Davie*
Schaefer, Lola M. *Hospital*
Wohlrabe, Sarah C. *Helping you heal, a book about nurses*

Careers – oceanographers

Nivola, Claire A. *Life in the ocean*
Yaccarino, Dan. *The fantastic undersea life of Jacques Cousteau*

Careers – opera singers *see* Careers – singers

Careers – opticians, optometrists

Barclay, Eric. *I can see just fine*
Flanagan, Alice K. *Choosing eyeglasses with Mrs. Koutris*

Careers – ornithologists

Davies, Jacqueline. *The boy who drew birds*

Careers – painters *see* Careers – artists

Careers – paleontologists

Atkins, Jeannine. *Mary Anning and the sea dragon*
Barner, Bob. *Dinosaur bones*
Brown, Don. *Rare treasure*
Hartland, Jessie. *How the dinosaur got to the museum*
Houran, Lori Haskins. *Dig those dinosaurs*

Careers – park rangers

Flanagan, Alice K. *Exploring parks with Ranger Dockett*

Careers – peddlers

Derby, Sally. *Two fools and a horse*
Diakité, Baba Wagué. *The hatseller and the monkeys*
Johnson, Angela. *The Rolling Store*
Miller, William. *Jenny and the peddler*
Slobodkina, Esphyr. *Caps for sale*
    Caps for sale and the mindful monkeys
    Circus caps for sale
    More caps for sale

Careers – pharmacists

Gibson, Karen Bush. *Pharmacists*

Careers – photographers

Alter, Anna. *A photo for Greta*
Bahr, Mary. *My brother loved snowflakes*
Bibbons, Faye. *The day the picture man came*
Davis, Jill. *Orangutans are ticklish*
High, Linda Oatman. *The girl on the high-diving horse*
Jenson-Elliott, Cindy. *Antsy Ansel*
Martin, Jacqueline Briggs. *Snowflake Bentley*
Rosenstock, Barb. *Dorothea's eyes*
Weatherford, Carole Boston. *Gordon Parks*

Careers – physicians *see* Careers – doctors

Careers – plasterers

Carle, Eric. *My apron*

Careers – poets

Burleigh, Robert. *Langston's train ride*
Gollub, Matthew. *Cool melons — turn to frogs*
Malaspina, Ann. *Phillis sings out freedom*
Perdorno, Willie. *Visiting Langston*
Yolen, Jane. *My Uncle Emily*

Careers – police officers

Biggs, Brian. *Tinyville town: I'm a police officer*
Bourgeois, Paulette. *Police officers*
Braithwaite, Jill. *Police cars*
Carter, Anne Laurel. *Under a prairie sky*
Dunn, Jancee. *I'm afraid your teddy is in trouble today*
Flanagan, Alice K. *Officer Brown keeps neighborhoods safe*
Gorbachev, Valeri. *The missing chick*
Hamilton, Kersten. *Police officers on patrol*
Hubbell, Patricia. *Police*
Keats, Ezra Jack. *My dog is lost!*
Lenski, Lois. *Policeman Small*
Liebman, Daniel. *I want to be a police officer*
McCloskey, Robert. *Make way for ducklings*
Meadows, Michelle. *Traffic pups*
Mortensen, Denise Dowling. *Bug Patrol*
Niemann, Christoph. *The police cloud*
Numeroff, Laura Joffe. *Sherman Crunchley*
Owen, Ann. *Keeping you safe*
Rathmann, Peggy. *Officer Buckle and Gloria*
Russell, Joan Plummer. *Aero and Officer Mike*
Schaefer, Lola M. *Police station*
Smith, Janice Lee. *Jess and the stinky cowboys*
Whitehead, Kathy. *Looking for Uncle Louie on the Fourth of July*
Yee, Wong Herbert. *The Officers' Ball*

Careers – postal workers

Ahlberg, Janet. *The jolly Christmas postman*
    The jolly pocket postman
    The jolly postman
Bee, William. *Stanley the mailman*
Blackstone, Stella. *Bear at work*
Bottner, Barbara. *Raymond and Nelda*
Bourgeois, Paulette. *Postal workers*

Bradby, Marie. *The longest wait*
Brill, Marlene Targ. *Bronco Charlie and the Pony
    Express*
Carter, Don. *Send it!*
Clanton, Ben. *It came in the mail*
Day, Alexandra. *Special deliveries*
Dubuc, Marianne. *Mr. Postmouse takes a trip
    Mr. Postmouse's rounds*
Flanagan, Alice K. *Here comes Mr. Eventoff with the
    mail!*
Gibbons, Gail. *The post office book*
Grindley, Sally. *The giant postman*
Henkes, Kevin. *Good-bye, Curtis*
Holabird, Katharine. *Angelina's Christmas*
Horning, Sandra. *The giant hug*
Isern, Susanna. *The lonely mailman*
Kay, Verla. *Whatever happened to the Pony Express?*
Kerby, Mona. *Owney, the mail-pouch pooch*
Lendroth, Susan. *Calico Dorsey*
Lillegard, Dee. *Tortoise brings the mail*
Olshan, Matthew. *The mighty Lalouche*
Owen, Ann. *Delivering your mail*
Ruzzier, Sergio. *A letter for Leo*
Rylant, Cynthia. *Mr. Griggs' work*
Salzano, Tammi. *One windy day*
Schneider, Howie. *Fast 'n Snappy*
Shea, Kitty. *Out and about at the post office*
Spinelli, Eileen. *Somebody loves you, Mr. Hatch*
Spradlin, Michael P. *Off like the wind!*
Steffensmeier, Alexander. *Millie waits for the mail*
Tunnell, Michael O. *Mailing May*

Careers – potters

Andrews-Goebel, Nancy. *The pot that Juan built*
Hill, Laban Carrick. *Dave the potter*

Careers – preachers *see* Careers – clergy

Careers – principals *see* Careers – school
    principals

Careers – printers

Fisher, Leonard Everett. *Gutenberg*
Markel, Michelle. *Balderdash!*
Nettleton, Pamela Hill. *Benjamin Franklin*

Careers – publishers

Markel, Michelle. *Balderdash!*

Careers – race car drivers

Clement, Nathan. *Speed*
Rex, Michael. *My race car*

Careers – railroad engineers

Kimmel, Eric A. *Stormy's hat*
Lenski, Lois. *The little train*
Moser, Lisa. *Railroad Hank*
Rex, Michael. *My freight train*

Careers – ranchers

Drummond, Ree. *Charlie and the new baby
    Charlie the ranch dog*

Hoefler, Kate. *Real cowboys*
Lawson, Dorie McCullough. *Tex*
Moser, Lisa. *Cowboy Boyd and Mighty Calliope*
Parish, Herman. *Go west, Amelia Bedelia!*
Peterson, Cris. *Amazing grazing*
Urbigkit, Cat. *A young shepherd*

Careers – rangers *see* Careers – park rangers

Careers – sailors *see* Careers – military; Sailors

Careers – salespeople

Horowitz, Dave. *Buy my hats!*
Palatini, Margie. *Ding dong ding dong*
Rozen, Anna. *The merchant of noises*
Watt, Mélanie. *Have I got a book for you!*

Careers – sanitation workers

Bourgeois, Paulette. *Garbage collectors*
Kirk, Daniel. *Trash trucks!*
Maass, Robert. *Garbage*
McMullan, Kate. *I stink!*
Odanaka, Barbara. *Smash! mash! crash! there goes
    the trash!*
Savage, Stephen. *Supertruck*
Showers, Paul. *Where does the garbage go?*
Steig, William. *Tiffky Doofky*
Ward, D. J. *What happens to our trash?*
Winter, Jonah. *Here comes the garbage barge!*
Zimmerman, Andrea Griffing. *Trashy town*

Careers – school principals

Calmenson, Stephanie. *The frog principal
    The principal's new clothes*
Cocca-Leffler, Maryann. *Mr. Tanen's ties rule!*
Creech, Sharon. *A fine, fine school*
Crimi, Carolyn. *Principal Fred won't go to bed*
Dakos, Kalli. *Our principal promised to kiss a pig*
Griswell, Kim T. *Rufus goes to school*
Polacco, Patricia. *Mr. Lincoln's way*
Poydar, Nancy. *First day, hooray!*

Careers – scientists

Andros, Camille. *Charlotte the scientist is squished*
Beaty, Andrea. *Ada Twist, scientist*
Berne, Jennifer. *On a beam of light*
Brown, Don. *Odd boy out*
Buzzeo, Toni. *A passion for elephants*
Chambers, Roland. *Rooftop rocket party*
Chapman, Jared. *Pirate, Viking, and Scientist*
Elliott, David. *Hazel Nutt, mad scientist*
Greenstein, Elaine. *The goose man*
Houran, Lori Haskins. *How to spy on a shark*
James, Brian. *Supertwins meet the dangerous dino-
    robots*
Keating, Jess. *Shark lady*
Krensky, Stephen. *Ben Franklin and his first kite
    A man for all seasons*
Kudlinski, Kathleen V. *Boy, were we wrong about the
    weather!*
Lang, Heather. *Swimming with sharks*
Lawlor, Laurie. *Rachel Carson and her book that
    changed the world*
Lazar, Tara. *Normal Norman*

Lehn, Barbara. *What is a scientist?*
McCully, Emily Arnold. *Marvelous Mattie*
McDonnell, Patrick. *Me . . . Jane*
Martin, Jacqueline Briggs. *Snowflake Bentley*
Marzollo, Jean. *The little plant doctor*
Meltzer, Brad. *I am Albert Einstein*
Mosca, Julia Finley. *The girl who thought in pictures*
Nettleton, Pamela Hill. *Benjamin Franklin*
O'Connor, Teddy. *A new brain for Igor*
Offill, Jenny. *11 experiments that failed*
Pettenati, Jeanne K. *Galileo's journal, 1609–1610*
Rabinowitz, Alan. *A boy and a jaguar*
Robbins, Dean. *Margaret and the moon*
Schanzer, Rosalyn. *How Ben Franklin stole the lightning*
Shaffer, Jody Jensen. *Prudence the part-time cow*
Verstraete, Larry. *S is for scientists*
Winter, Jeanette. *The watcher*

Careers – sculptors

Rappaport, Doreen. *Lady Liberty*
Stanley, Diane. *The trouble with wishes*
Stevenson, Harvey. *Looking at liberty*
Ziarnik, Natalie. *Madeleine's light*

Careers – seamstresses

Brown, Margaret Wise. *Bunny's noisy book*
Heo, Yumi. *Lady Hahn and her seven friends*

Careers – shepherds

Calhoun, Mary. *A shepherd's gift*
Daly, Niki. *The herd boy*
Levine, Gail Carson. *Betsy Red Hoodie*
  Betsy who cried wolf
Lewis, Kim. *The shepherd boy*
Moser, Barry. *Psalm 23*
Urbigkit, Cat. *A young shepherd*

Careers – sheriffs

Crummel, Susan Stevens. *Ten-Gallon Bart*
Rumford, James. *Don't touch my hat!*
Shea, Bob. *Kid Sheriff and the terrible Toads*
Sneed, Brad. *Deputy Harvey and the ant cow caper*
Yorinks, Arthur. *Whitefish Will rides again*

Careers – shoe shiners

Quattlebaum, Mary. *The shine man*

Careers – shoemakers

Barrett, Mary Brigid. *Shoebox Sam*
Bateman, Teresa. *Keeper of soles*
Dollinger, Renate. *The rabbi who flew*
Grimm, Jacob and Wilhelm. *The elves and the shoemaker*, ill. by Kirill Chelushkin
  The elves and the shoemaker, ill. by Paul Galdone
  The elves and the shoemaker, ill. by Margaret Walty
  The shoemaker and his elves
  The shoemaker and the elves, ill. by Adrienne Adams
  The shoemaker and the elves, ill. by Ilse Plume
Imai, Ayano. *Puss and boots*
Johnson, Grace. *The candle in the window*
Light, Steve. *The shoemaker extraordinaire*
Lowell, Susan. *The bootmaker and the elves*

Madonna. *Yakov and the seven thieves*
San Souci, Robert D. *The red heels*
Stampler, Ann Redisch. *The wooden sword*
Tegen, Katherine Brown. *The story of the leprechaun*

Careers – singers

Fisher, Mary M. *Rosita's bridge*
Nolan, Nina. *Mahalia Jackson*
Orgill, Roxane. *Skit-scat raggedy cat*
Pinkney, Andrea Davis. *Martin and Mahalia*
Ryan, Pam Muñoz. *When Marian sang*
Schroeder, Alan. *Baby Flo*
Sciurba, Katie. *Oye, Celia!*
Watson, Renée. *Harlem's little blackbird*
Weatherford, Carole Boston. *Leontyne Price*
Weaver, Tess. *Opera cat*

Careers – soldiers *see* Careers – military

Careers – storekeepers

Flanagan, Alice K. *A busy day at Mr. Kang's grocery store*
  Buying a pet from Ms. Chavez
  Choosing eyeglasses with Mrs. Koutris
Heo, Yumi. *Father's rubber shoes*
Schaefer, Lola M. *Supermarket*
Shea, Kitty. *Out and about at the supermarket*
Wisniewski, David. *Sumo Mouse*
Yorinks, Arthur. *The invisible man*

Careers – tailors

Aylesworth, Jim. *My grandfather's coat*
Calmenson, Stephanie. *The principal's new clothes*
Charles, Veronika Martenova. *The birdman*
Green, Stephanie. *Betsy Ross and the silver thimble*
Grimm, Jacob and Wilhelm. *The brave little tailor*, ill. by Olga Dugina
  The brave little tailor, ill. by David Shaw
  Seven at one blow
Hest, Amy. *The purple coat*
Luxbacher, Irene. *Mr. Frank*
Oddino, Licia. *Finn and the fairies*
Osborne, Mary Pope. *The brave little seamstress*
Potter, Beatrix. *The tailor of Gloucester*

Careers – teachers

Allard, Harry. *Miss Nelson is back*
  Miss Nelson is missing!
Anderson, Laurie Halse. *The hair of Zoe Fleefenbacher goes to school*
Bowen, Anne. *I know an old teacher*
Brandt, Amy. *When Katie was our teacher / Cuando Katie era nuestra maestra*
Brennan-Nelson, Denise. *Willow*
Brenner, Emily. *On the first day of grade school*
Brisson, Pat. *I remember Miss Perry*
Brown, Marc. *Arthur's teacher moves in*
Brown, Peter. *My teacher is a monster! (no, I am not)*
Calmenson, Stephanie. *Late for school!*
  Oopsy, teacher!
  The teeny tiny teacher
Carlson, Nancy. *Henry and the Valentine surprise*
Cole, Joanna. *The magic school bus and the science fair expedition*
  The magic school bus in the time of the dinosaurs

The magic school bus inside a beehive
The magic school bus lost in the solar system
The magic school bus on the ocean floor
Cook, Lisa Broadie. *Peanut butter and homework
  sandwiches*
Cox, Judy. *Happy birthday, Mrs. Millie!*
  Pick a pumpkin, Mrs. Millie!
Cusimano, Maryann K. *You are my wonders*
Cuyler, Margery. *Kindness is cooler, Mrs. Ruler*
Danneberg, Julie. *First day jitters*
  First year letters
  Last day blues
deGroat, Diane. *No more pencils, no more books, no
  more teacher's dirty looks!*
Dodds, Dayle Ann. *Teacher's pets*
Edwards, Pamela Duncan. *Ms. Bitsy Bat's
  kindergarten*
Fern, Tracey. *W is for Webster*
Ferris, Jeri Chase. *Noah Webster and his words*
Figley, Marty Rhodes. *The schoolchildren's blizzard*
Finchler, Judy. *Congratulations, Miss Malarkey!*
  Miss Malarkey leaves no reader behind
  Miss Malarkey won't be in today
  Testing Miss Malarkey
  You're a good sport, Miss Malarkey
Flanagan, Alice K. *Learning is fun with Mrs. Perez*
Gall, Chris. *Substitute creacher*
Garland, Michael. *Miss Smith and the haunted
  library*
  Miss Smith reads again!
  Miss Smith's incredible storybook
Garton, Sam. *Otter goes to school*
George, Lucy M. *Back to school Tortoise*
Harper, Jamie. *Miss Mingo and the first day of school*
Havill, Juanita. *Jamaica and the substitute teacher*
Hayes, Sarah. *Dog day*
Hayward, Linda. *A day in the life of a teacher*
Henkes, Kevin. *El gran día de Lily / Lilly's big day*
  Lilly's big day
  Lilly's purple plastic purse
Hennessy, B. G. *Mr. Ouchy's first day*
Hopkinson, Deborah. *Annie and Helen*
  A letter to my teacher
  Steamboat school
Houston, Gloria. *My Great-Aunt Arizona*
Hubbell, Patricia. *Teacher!*
James, Simon. *Dear Mr. Blueberry*
Janousky, Peggy Robbins. *Move it, Miss Macintosh!*
Johnson, Doug. *Substitute teacher plans*
Krensky, Stephen. *My teacher's secret life*
Laminack, Lester L. *Snow day!*
Layne, Steven L. *T is for teachers*
Lehn, Barbara. *What is a teacher?*
Liebman, Daniel. *I want to be a teacher*
Linch, Tanya. *My duck*
McKissack, Robert L. *Try your best*
McLellan, Gretchen Brandenburg. *Mrs. McBee
  leaves Room 3*
McNaughton, Colin. *Once upon an ordinary school
  day*
Mann, Jennifer K. *I will never get a star on Mrs.
  Benson's blackboard*
Marshall, James. *Eugene*
Montanari, Eva. *A very full morning*
Munsch, Robert N. *Thomas' snowsuit*
Parr, Todd. *Teachers rock!*
Passen, Lisa. *Attack of the 50-foot teacher*
  The incredible shrinking teacher
Pattou, Edith. *Mrs. Spitzer's garden*

Polacco, Patricia. *An A from Miss Keller*
  The art of Miss Chew
  The junkyard wonders
  The lemonade club
  Mr. Wayne's masterpiece
  Thank you, Mr. Falker
Poydar, Nancy. *First day, hooray!*
Priceman, Marjorie. *Emeline at the circus*
Primavera, Elise. *Louise the big cheese and the back-to-
  school smarty-pants*
Pulver, Robin. *The case of the incapacitated capitals*
  Mrs. Toggle and the dinosaur
  Mrs. Toggle's beautiful blue shoe
  Mrs. Toggle's zipper
Puttock, Simon. *Miss Fox*
Radabaugh, Melinda Beth. *Going to school*
Ransome, James. *My teacher*
Rappaport, Doreen. *Helen's big world*
Reagan, Jean. *How to get your teacher ready*
Reynolds, Marilynn. *The magnificent piano recital*
Rissi, Anica Mrose. *The teacher's pet*
Roche, Denis. *The best class picture ever*
Rosen, Michael. *Totally wonderful Miss Plumberry*
Slate, Joseph. *Miss Bindergarten celebrates the last day
  of kindergarten*
  *Miss Bindergarten celebrates the 100th day of
  kindergarten*
  Miss Bindergarten gets ready for kindergarten
  Miss Bindergarten has a wild day in kindergarten
  Miss Bindergarten stays home from kindergarten
  *Miss Bindergarten takes a field trip with
  kindergarten*
Spinelli, Eileen. *Miss Fox's class gets it wrong*
  Miss Fox's class shapes up
Stadler, John. *Wilson and Miss Lovely*
Teyssèdre, Fabienne. *Joseph wants to read*
Trent, Tereai. *The girl who buried her dreams in a can*
Underwood, Deborah. *Here comes teacher cat*
Wheatley, Nadia. *Luke's way of looking*
Wohlrabe, Sarah C. *Helping you learn, a book about
  teachers*
Wood, Douglas. *What teachers can't do*
Woodson, Jacqueline. *Each kindness*
Yankovic, Al. *My new teacher and me!*
Zemach, Kaethe. *Ms. McCaw learns to draw*

Careers – toy makers

Geras, Adèle. *The nutcracker*
Hague, Michael. *The nutcracker*
Hoffmann, E. T. A. *The nutcracker*, ill. by Renée
  Graef
  The nutcracker, ill. by Peter Malone
  The nutcracker, ill. by Niroot Puttapipat
  The nutcracker, ill. by Maurice Sendak
  The nutcracker, ill. by Lisbeth Zwerger
  The Nutcracker and the Mouse King
  The nutcracker ballet
Thurber, James. *The great Quillow*

Careers – train engineers *see* Careers –
  railroad engineers

Careers – truck drivers

Clement, Nathan. *Drive*
Coffelt, Nancy. *Pug in a truck*
Cowley, Joy. *Gracias, the Thanksgiving turkey*

Day, Alexandra. *Frank and Ernest on the road*
Gibson, Karen Bush. *Truck drivers*
Liebman, Daniel. *I want to be a truck driver*
London, Jonathan. *I'm a truck driver*
Mitchell, Joyce Slayton. *Tractor-trailer trucker*
Sturges, Philemon. *I love trucks!*
Wellington, Monica. *Truck driver Tom*

Careers – veterinarians

Biggs, Brian. *Tinyville town: I'm a veterinarian*
Flanagan, Alice K. *Dr. Friedman helps animals*
Gibbons, Gail. *Say woof!*
Hull, Rod. *Mr. Betts and Mr. Potts*
Kang, A. N. *Papillon goes to the vet*
Lee, Chinlun. *Good dog, Paw*
Liebman, Daniel. *I want to be a vet*
McCully, Emily Arnold. *Wonder horse*
Owen, Ann. *Caring for your pet*
Perkins, Lynne Rae. *The broken cat*
Shea, Kitty. *Out and about at the vet clinic*

Careers – waiters, waitresses

Downey, Lynn. *Matilda's humdinger*
Radabaugh, Melinda Beth. *Going to a restaurant*

Careers – weather reporters *see* Careers –
meteorologists

Careers – weavers

Musgrove, Margaret. *The spider weaver*

Careers – window cleaners

Dahl, Roald. *The giraffe and the pelly and me*
Rey, H. A. *Curious George takes a job*

Careers – woodcarvers

Cohn, Diana. *Dream carver*
Dorros, Arthur. *Julio's magic*
Rosen, Michael J. *Elijah's angel*
Wojciechowski, Susan. *The Christmas miracle of Jonathan Toomey*

Careers – writers

Barnett, Mac. *How this book was made*
Borden, Louise. *The day Eddie met the author*
Bram, Elizabeth. *Rufus the writer*
Brown, Monica. *My name is Gabito / Me llamo Gabito*
Browne, Anthony. *The shape game*
Bunting, Eve. *My special day at third street school*
Christelow, Eileen. *What do authors do?*
Clinton, Catherine. *Phillis's big test*
Corpi, Lucha. *Where fireflies dance / Ahí, donde bailan las luciérnagas*
Davidson, Rebecca Piatt. *All the world's a stage*
Dunlap, Julie. *Louisa May and Mr. Thoreau's flute*
Fagan, Cary. *Mr. Zinger's hat*
Freedman, Deborah. *By Mouse and Frog*
Gay, Marie-Louise. *Any questions?*
Joyce, William. *Billy's booger*, ill. by William Joyce
    Billy's booger, ill. by William Joyce
Kanninen, Barbara. *A story with pictures*
Kerley, Barbara. *A home for Mr. Emerson*

Kirk, Daniel. *Library mouse*
    Library mouse: a friend's tale
Krull, Kathleen. *The boy on Fairfield Street*
Lehrhaupt, Adam. *This is a good story*
Lester, Helen. *Author*
McElroy, Lisa Tucker. *Meet my grandmother. She's a children's book author*
MacLachlan, Patricia. *Someone like me*
MacLean, Kerry Lee. *Peaceful piggy meditation*
McNamara, Margaret. *A poem in your pocket*
McPhail, David. *Beatrix Potter and her paint box*
Macy, Sue. *Miss Mary reporting*
Mora, Pat. *A library for Juana*
Myers, Walter Dean. *Harlem*
Nesbitt, Kenn. *More bears!*
Palatini, Margie. *Under a pig tree*
Peet, Bill. *Bill Peet*
Pulver, Robin. *Author day for room 3T*
Rau, Dana Meachen. *Dr. Seuss*
Ray, Mary Lyn. *A lucky author has a dog*
Ringgold, Faith. *Harlem Renaissance party*
Rinker, Sherri Duskey. *Big machines*
Rylant, Cynthia. *Best wishes*
Sierra, Judy. *Imagine that! how Dr. Seuss wrote The Cat in the Hat*
Sís, Peter. *The pilot and the Little Prince*
Stead, Philip C. *Ideas are all around*
Steig, William. *When everybody wore a hat*
Stevenson, James. *Fun, no fun*
    I meant to tell you
Tullet, Hervé. *Help! we need a title!*
Wallner, Alexandra. *Beatrix Potter*
Yaccarino, Dan. *All the way to America*

Careers – zookeepers

Goodman, Susan E. *What do you do — at the zoo?*
Liebman, Daniel. *I want to be a zookeeper*
Lyon, George Ella. *Mother to tigers*
Rathmann, Peggy. *Good night, Gorilla*
Savage, Stephen. *Where's Walrus?*
    Where's Walrus? and Penguin?
Waldron, Kevin. *Panda-monium at Peek Zoo*

Carelessness *see* Behavior – carelessness

Caribou *see* Animals – reindeer

Carnivals *see* Fairs, festivals

Carousels *see* Merry-go-rounds

Cars *see* Automobiles

Castles

Ashburn, Boni. *Over at the castle*
Bernheimer, Kate. *The girl in the castle inside the museum*
Berry, Lynne. *What floats in a moat?*
Brunhoff, Laurent de. *Babar and the ghost*
Clavel, Bernard. *Castle of books*
Hawkins, Colin. *Creepy castle*
Kenney, Sean. *Cool castles*
Walton, Rick. *Pig, pigger, piggest*

Yee, Brenda Shannon. *Sand castle*

Caterpillars *see* Insects – butterflies, caterpillars

Cave drawings *see* Petroglyphs

Cave dwellers

Elliott, David. *This Orq. (He #1!)*
　　This Orq. (He cave boy.)
　　This Orq. (He say "ugh!")
McDonnell, Patrick. *Tek*
Sauer, Tammi. *Me want pet!*
Winter, Jeanette. *Kali's song*
Wood, Audrey. *The Tickleoctopus*

Caves

Brett, Jan. *The first dog*
Galko, Francine. *Cave animals*
Galloway, Ruth. *Fidgety fish*
Harrison, David L. *Caves*
McCully, Emily Arnold. *The secret cave*
Pfister, Marcus. *Rainbow fish and the sea monsters' cave*
Rau, Dana Meachen. *Explore in a cave*
Siebert, Diane. *Cave*
Taylor, Harriet Peck. *Secrets of the stone*

Cell phone *see* Telephone, cell phone

Centipedes *see* Crustaceans – centipedes, millipedes

Chanukah *see* Holidays – Hanukkah

Character traits

Burdett, Lois. *Twelfth night for kids*
Javernick, Ellen. *What if everybody did that?*
Kirk, Daniel. *Ten thank-you letters*
Lee, Spike. *Giant steps to change the world*
Lucas, David. *The robot and the bluebird*
McPhail, David. *No!*
Martin, Emily Winfield. *The wonderful things you will be*
Mora, Pat. *Gracias / Thanks*
Morstad, Julie. *How to*
Obama, Barack. *Of thee I sing*
Parr, Todd. *The thankful book*
Rosenthal, Amy Krouse. *Christmas cookies*
　　Cookies
　　One smart cookie: bite-size lessons for the school years and beyond
Thomas, Joan G. *If Jesus came to my house*
Walker, Alice. *Finding the green stone*
Yahgulanaas, Michael Nicoll. *The little hummingbird*

Character traits – ambition

Aska, Warabe. *Tapicero tap tap*
Barton, Byron. *I want to be an astronaut*
Clanton, Ben. *Vote for me!*
Cronin, Doreen. *Duck for President*
Czajak, Paul. *Monster needs your vote*

Daly, Niki. *The herd boy*
DiPucchio, Kelly. *Grace for president*
Dungy, Tony. *You can do it!*
Evans, Richard Paul. *The spyglass*
Feiffer, Kate. *President Pennybaker*
Gramatky, Hardie. *Little Toot*
Heide, Florence Parry. *How to be a hero*
Herzog, Kenny. *Phil Pickle*
Lester, Helen. *Score one for the sloths*
Miller, Tim. *Moo Moo in a tutu*
Palatini, Margie. *Hogg, Hogg, and Hog*
Pavlova, Anna. *I dreamed I was a ballerina*
Primavera, Elise. *Louise the big cheese and the back-to-school smarty-pants*
　　Louise the big cheese and the Ooh-la-la Charm School
Rappaport, Doreen. *To dare mighty things*
Shannon, David. *Bizzy Mizz Lizzie*
Smith, Lane. *Madam President*
Spires, Ashley. *The most magnificent thing*
Spirin, Gennady. *Philipok*
Teague, Mark. *LaRue for mayor*
Tucker, Lindy. *Porkelia*
Wells, Rosemary. *Otto runs for President*
　　Otto se presenta para presidente / Otto runs for President
Yamaguchi, Kristi. *Dream big, little pig!*

Character traits – appearance

Allen, Jonathan. *"I'm not cute!"*
Andersen, Hans Christian. *The ugly duckling*, ill. by Adrienne Adams
　　The ugly duckling, ill. by Sebastien Braun
　　The ugly duckling, ill. by Lorinda Bryan Cauley
　　The ugly duckling, ill. by Charlene DeLage
　　The ugly duckling, ill. by Robert Ingpen
　　The ugly duckling, ill. by Rachel Isadora
　　The ugly duckling, ill. by Steve Johnson
　　The ugly duckling, ill. by Jerry Pinkney
　　The ugly duckling, ill. by Meilo So
　　The ugly duckling, ill. by Pirkko Vainio
　　The ugly duckling, ill. by Bernadette Watts
　　The ugly duckling, ill. by Roberta Wilson
Barnett, Mac. *Mustache!*
Beaumont, Karen. *Hats off to you!*
　　Shoe-la-la!
　　Wild about us!
Bell, Cece. *Bee-Wigged*
Bently, Peter. *The prince and the porker*
Billstrom, Dianne. *You can't go to school naked!*
Boelts, Maribeth. *Those shoes*
Brisson, Pat. *Melissa Parkington's beautiful, beautiful hair*
Britt, Chris. *The most perfect snowman*
Brown, Jeff. *Flat Stanley*, ill. by Scott Nash
　　Flat Stanley, ill. by Tomi Ungerer
Campisi, Stephanie. *The ugly dumpling*
Carlson, Nancy. *Think big!*
Chen, Chih-Yuan. *The featherless chicken*
Choldenko, Gennifer. *How to make friends with a giant*
Claflin, Willy. *The uglified ducky*
Clanton, Ben. *Rot, the cutest in the world!*
Cohen, Jeff. *Eva and Sadie and the worst haircut ever!*
Cotterill, Samantha. *No more bows*
Craft, Mahlon F. *Beauty and the beast*
Crocker, Nancy. *Betty Lou Blue*
dePaola, Tomie. *Big Anthony and the magic ring*
DiPucchio, Kelly. *Everyone loves Cupcake*

Ditchfield, Christin. *Cowlick!*
Duke, Shirley Smith. *No bows!*
Dunbar, Polly. *Arthur's dream boat*
  Pretty Pru
Fox, Mem. *The goblin and the empty chair*
Freeman, Don. *Dandelion*
Gaiman, Neil. *Crazy hair*
Glass, Eleri. *The red shoes*
Goble, Paul. *Star boy*
Greenfield, Eloise. *Grandpa's face*
Hall, Michael. *Red: a crayon's story*
Harper, Charise Mericle. *Cupcake*
Harper, Lee. *The Emperor's cool clothes*
Heos, Bridget. *Mustache Baby*
  Mustache Baby meets his match
Hogg, Gary. *Beautiful Buehla and the zany zoo*
  makeover
Hosford, Kate. *Big bouffant*
Hovland, Henrik. *John Jensen feels different*
Hume, Lachie. *Clancy the courageous cow*
Jenkins, Steve. *Creature features*
Johnson, Rebecca. *The proud pelican's secret*
Jones, Ursula. *Beauty and the beast*
King-Chai, Sharon. *Lucy Ladybug*
Kochan, Vera. *What if your best friend were blue?*
Krensky, Stephen. *Milo and the really big bunny*
Landau, Orna. *Leopardpox!*
Langen, Annette. *I won't comb my hair!*
LaReau, Kara. *Ugly fish*
Lee, H. Chuku. *Beauty and the beast: a retelling*
Long, Ethan. *Chamelia*
McAnulty, Stacy. *Beautiful*
MacDonald, Margaret Read. *The great smelly,*
  slobbery small-toothed dog
Mayer, Kirsten. *Game of gnomes*
  Go big or go gnome!
Mayer, Marianna. *Beauty and the beast*
Meddaugh, Susan. *Just Teenie*
Merino, Gemma. *The sheep who hatched an egg*
Montserrat, Pep. *Ms. Rubinstein's beauty*
Munsch, Robert N. *Makeup mess*
  The paper bag princess
  Stephanie's ponytail
Murguia, Bethanie Deeney. *Zoe gets ready*
Napoli, Donna Jo. *Bobby the bold*
Newman, Barbara Johansen. *Glamorous glasses*
Numeroff, Laura Joffe. *Why a disguise?*
O'Connor, Jane. *Fancy Nancy and the posh puppy*
Olien, Jessica. *The blobfish book*
O'Neill, Gemma. *Monty's magnificent mane*
Ormondroyd, Edward. *Theodore*
Otto, Carolyn. *What color is camouflage?*
Palacio, R. J. *We're all wonders*
Palatini, Margie. *Piggie pie*
Pfister, Marcus. *The rainbow fish*
  Rainbow fish to the rescue!
Pichon, Liz. *The very ugly bug*
Primavera, Elise. *Louise the big cheese and the la-di-*
  da shoes
Raschka, Chris. *Crabby crab*
Reidy, Jean. *Too purpley!*
Reinhardt, Jennifer Black. *Blue Ethel*
Rickards, Lynne. *Pink!*
Rylant, Cynthia. *Brownie and Pearl get dolled up*
Sabuda, Robert. *Beauty and the beast: a pop-up book*
  of the classic fairy tale
Sauer, Tammi. *Mary had a little glam*
Schwartz, Amy. *A beautiful girl*
  Polka dots for Poppy

Skeers, Linda. *Tutus aren't my style*
Small, David. *Imogene's antlers*
Stern, Ellen. *I saw a bullfrog*
Willis, Jeanne. *Slug needs a hug!*
  What did I look like when I was a baby?
Winters, Kari-Lynn. *Good pirate*
Yerkes, Jennifer. *A funny little bird*
Ziefert, Harriet. *There was a little girl who had a little*
  curl

Character traits – assertiveness

Bridges, Shirin Yim. *Mary Wrightly, so politely*
Burach, Ross. *I am not a chair!*
Chou, Yih-Fen. *Mimi says no*
Czajak, Paul. *Monster needs your vote*
Dodd, Emma. *I don't want a posh dog*
Dunklee, Annika. *My name is Elizabeth!*
Fleming, Candace. *Imogene's last stand*
Fradin, Dennis. *The price of freedom*
Garza, Cynthia Leonor. *Lucía the luchadora*
Greenawalt, Kelly. *Princess Truly in I am Truly*
Harness, Cheryl. *Mary Walker wears the pants*
Harvey, Jeanne Walker. *Maya Lin: artist-architect of*
  light and lines
Henkes, Kevin. *Lilly's big day*
Joyner, Andrew. *The pink hat*
Latimer, Alex. *Penguin's hidden talent*
Lindgren, Astrid. *Pippi Longstocking's after-*
  Christmas party
McAnulty, Stacy. *Beautiful*
Manning, Jane. *Millie Fierce sleeps out*
Meade, Holly. *If I never forever endeavor*
Milgrim, David. *Eddie gets ready for school*
Novesky, Amy. *Georgia in Hawaii*
Stein, David Ezra. *Ol' Mama Squirrel*
Stone, Tanya Lee. *Elizabeth leads the way*
  Who says women can't be doctors?
Urdahl, Catherine. *Polka-dot fixes kindergarten*
Wells, Rosemary. *Felix stands tall*
Winthrop, Elizabeth. *I'm the Boss!*
Woollvin, Bethan. *Little Red*

Character traits – being different

Andersen, Hans Christian. *The ugly duckling*, ill. by
  Adrienne Adams
  The ugly duckling, ill. by Sebastien Braun
  The ugly duckling, ill. by Lorinda Bryan Cauley
  The ugly duckling, ill. by Charlene DeLage
  The ugly duckling, ill. by Robert Ingpen
  The ugly duckling, ill. by Rachel Isadora
  The ugly duckling, ill. by Steve Johnson
  The ugly duckling, ill. by Jerry Pinkney
  The ugly duckling, ill. by Meilo So
  The ugly duckling, ill. by Pirkko Vainio
  The ugly duckling, ill. by Bernadette Watts
  The ugly duckling, ill. by Roberta Wilson
Arnold, Tedd. *Green Wilma*
Baek, Matthew J. *Panda and polar bear*
Bansch, Helga. *Odd bird out*
  Rosie the raven
Bar-el, Dan. *Not your typical dragon*
Baryshnikov, Mikhail. *Because . . .*
Bradley, Kimberly Brubaker. *Ballerino Nate*
Briggs, John. *Leaping lemmings!*
Brown, Margaret Wise. *Robin's room*
Brown, Peter. *Chowder*
Campisi, Stephanie. *The ugly dumpling*

Wilson, Karma. *Duddle Puck*
Wong, Liz. *Quackers*
Wood, Audrey. *Weird parents*
Woodson, Jacqueline. *Each kindness*
Yoon, Salina. *Be a friend*
Yorinks, Arthur. *The invisible man*
Young, Amy. *The mud fairy*
Young, Ed. *Hook*

Character traits – bravery

Andersen, Hans Christian. *The snow queen*, ill. by
    Angela Barrett
    The snow queen, ill. by Sally Holmes
    The snow queen, ill. by Susan Jeffers
    The snow queen: a retelling of the fairy tale
Anglund, Joan Walsh. *The brave cowboy*
Arnold, Marsha Diane. *The bravest of us all*
Asare, Meshack. *Sosu's call*
Bailey, Linda. *The farm team*
Barbero, Maria. *The bravest mouse*
Battersby, Katherine. *Brave Squish Rabbit*
Beck, Scott. *Pepito the brave*
Biden, Jill. *Don't forget, God bless our troops*
Birdseye, Tom. *Oh yeah!*
Brill, Calista. *Tugboat Bill and the river rescue*
Buckley, Michael. *Kel Gilligan's daredevil stunt show*
Bynum, Janie. *Kiki's blankie*
Carlson, Nancy. *Arnie and the skateboard gang*
    Harriet and the roller coaster
Carr, Matt. *Superbat*
Coles, Robert. *The story of Ruby Bridges*
Cornwall, Gaia. *Jabari jumps*
Cowell, Cressida. *Hiccup the seasick Viking*
Crum, Shutta. *The bravest of the brave*
Curtis, Jamie Lee. *My brave year of firsts*
Danticat, Edwidge. *Eight days*
Deedy, Carmen Agra. *The yellow star*
Demi. *The boy who painted dragons*
Dierssen, Andreas. *Timid Timmy*
Doyen, Denise. *Once upon a twice*
Duncan, Lois. *Song of the circus*
Ehlert, Lois. *Cuckoo, a Mexican folktale / Cucú: un
    cuento folklórico mexicano*
Elvgren, Jennifer. *The whispering town*
Esbaum, Jill. *Frankenbunny*
    I am cow, hear me moo!
Foreman, Michael. *The littlest dinosaur*
Fradin, Dennis. *The price of freedom*
Frasier, Debra. *Spike*
Genechten, Guido van. *Ricky is brave*
Giovanni, Nikki. *Rosa*
Gliori, Debi. *The scariest thing of all*
Golenbock, Peter. *Hank Aaron*
Griffin, Kitty. *The ride*
Grimm, Jacob and Wilhelm. *The brave little tailor*,
    ill. by Olga Dugina
    The brave little tailor, ill. by David Shaw
    Seven at one blow
Harrison, Troon. *Courage to fly*
Hearne, Betsy Gould. *Seven brave women*
Henkes, Kevin. *Sheila Rae, the brave*
Hood, Susan. *The Tooth Mouse*
Hopkinson, Deborah. *Abe Lincoln crosses a creek*
    Steamboat school
Hoppe, Paul. *The woods*
Horowitz, Dave. *Chico the brave*
    Humpty Dumpty climbs again
Jakes, John. *Susanna of the Alamo*

Jennewein, Lenore. *Chick-o-Saurus Rex*
Jordan, Sandra. *Mr. and Mrs. Portly and their little
    dog Snack*
Joyce, William. *Jack Frost*
Julian, Alison. *Brave as a bunny can be*
Keller, Holly. *Brave Horace*
Kelly, Mark. *Mousetronaut*
Kerley, Barbara. *Brave like me*
Kipling, Rudyard. *Rikki-tikki-tavi*, ill. by Lambert
    Davis
    Rikki-tikki-tavi, ill. by Jerry Pinkney
Kirk, Daniel. *Library mouse: a world to explore*
Kirk, David. *Oh so brave dragon*
Krensky, Stephen. *Sisters of Scituate Light*
Lears, Laurie. *Becky the brave*
Lee, Jeanne M. *The song of Mu Lan*
Lester, Alison. *Running with the horses*
Lloyd, Sam. *Chief Rhino to the rescue!*
Long, Loren. *Otis and the kittens*
    An Otis Christmas
McAnulty, Stacy. *Brave*
McDonald, Megan. *Beetle McGrady eats bugs!*
McGhee, Alison. *The sweetest witch around*
    A very brave witch
McKissack, Patricia C. *Precious and the Boo Hag*
McMullan, Kate. *I'm brave!*
Mader, C. Roger. *Tiptop cat*
Markel, Michelle. *Brave girl*
Martin, Bill, Jr.. *Knots on a counting rope*
Masini, Beatrice. *A brave little princess*
Mayer, Marianna. *The unicorn and the lake*
Mayer, Mercer. *Liza Lou and the Yeller Belly Swamp*
Meade, Holly. *If I never forever endeavor*
Minor, Florence. *How to be a bigger bunny*
Mitchell, Margaree King. *Granddaddy's gift*
Morgan, Michaela. *Brave, brave mouse*
Nash, Ogden. *The adventures of Isabel*, ill. by James
    Marshall
    The adventures of Isabel, ill. by Bridget Starr
    Taylor
    Custard the dragon and the wicked knight
Newgarden, Mark. *Bow-Wow's nightmare neighbors*
Nobisso, Josephine. *John Blair and the great Hinckley
    fire*
Osborne, Mary Pope. *The brave little seamstress*
    New York's bravest
Otoshi, Kathryn. *One*
Peet, Bill. *Cowardly Clyde*
Pfister, Marcus. *The little moon raven*
Pienkowski, Jan. *Bel and Bub and the black hole*
Polacco, Patricia. *Remembering Vera*
Pryor, Bonnie. *The porcupine mouse*
Puckett, Kelley. *Batman's dark secret*
Rappaport, Doreen. *Freedom river*
    Jack's path of courage
    The long-haired girl
    The secret seder
Raschka, Chris. *Waffle*
Ray, Mary Lyn. *Boom!*
Reynolds, Aaron. *Back of the bus*
Reynolds, Marilynn. *The name of the child*
Robertson, David A. *When we were alone*
Robinson, Sharon. *Testing the ice*
Rockwell, Anne. *Big George*
Roscoe, Charlie. *The red prince*
Sanna, Francesca. *The journey*
San Souci, Robert D. *The enchanted tapestry*
    The samurai's daughter
Sazaklis, John. *Fowl play*

Schmid, Eleonore. *Hare's Christmas gift*
Schwarz, Viviane. *Timothy and the strong pajamas*
Scieszka, Jon. *Melvin might?*
Shannon, George. *Tippy-toe chick, go*
Simon, Charnan. *Big bad Buzz*
Slack, Michael. *Turtle Tug to the rescue*
Sliwerski, Jessica Reid. *Cancer hates kisses*
Spinelli, Eileen. *Hero cat*
Steig, William. *Brave Irene*
Stein, Mathilde. *Brave Ben*
Stein, Peter. *Little Red's riding 'hood*
Stephens, Ann Marie. *Cy makes a friend*
Stoeke, Janet Morgan. *Pip's trip*
Stohner, Anu. *Brave Charlotte*
    Brave Charlotte and the wolves
Stone, Tanya Lee. *Elizabeth leads the way*
Stryer, Andrea Stenn. *Kami and the yaks*
Sullivan, Deirdre. *Ming goes to school*
Sweet, Melissa. *Tupelo rides the rails*
Tessler, Manya. *Yuki's ride home*
Thompson, Lauren. *Little Quack*
Titus, Eve. *Anatole and the cat*
Tonatiuh, Duncan. *Separate is never equal*
Uchida, Yoshiko. *The magic purse*
Van Allsburg, Chris. *Queen of the falls*
Van Woerkom, Dorothy. *Becky and the bear*
Vere, Ed. *Max the brave*
Waber, Bernard. *Courage*
Watt, Mélanie. *Scaredy Squirrel*
Weitzman, Jacqueline Preiss. *Superhero Joe*
Willems, Mo. *Knuffle Bunny free*
Winter, Jeanette. *Malala, a brave girl from Pakistan / Iqbal, a brave boy from Pakistan*
Wolkstein, Diane. *The banza*
Yolen, Jane. *Beneath the ghost moon*
Yousafzai, Malala. *Malala's magic pencil*

Character traits – cleanliness

Allen, Jonathan. *Mucky moose*
Bell, Cece. *Sock Monkey goes to Hollywood*
Bernheimer, Kate. *The girl who wouldn't brush her hair*
Best, Cari. *A perfect day for digging*
Bradford, Wade. *Why do I have to make my bed?*
Braeuner, Shellie. *The great dog wash*
Breen, Steve. *A perfect mess*
Brennan, Eileen. *Dirtball Pete*
Brown, Margaret Wise. *The dirty little boy*
Bunting, Eve. *Washday*
Bynum, Janie. *Otis*
Child, Lauren. *Say cheese!*
Church, Caroline Jayne. *One smart goose*
Cohen, Caron Lee. *Broom, zoom!*
Cummings, Pat. *Clean your room, Harvey Moon!*
Cuyler, Margery. *Monster mess!*
Dunrea, Olivier. *Jasper and Joop*
Eaton, Jason Carter. *Great, now we've got barbarians!*
Ehrlich, Fred. *Does an elephant take a bath?*
Elschner, Geraldine. *Mark's messy room*
Ernst, Lisa Campbell. *This is the van that Dad cleaned*
Funke, Cornelia. *Princess Pigsty*
Garelli, Cristina. *Farm friends clean up*
Geisert, Arthur. *Hogwash*
Gravett, Emily. *Tidy*
Grindley, Sally. *Mucky Duck*
Hanson, Warren. *It's Monday, Mrs. Jolly Bones!*
Harris, Robie H. *I love messes!*

Howie, Betsy. *The Block Mess Monster*
Huget, Jennifer LaRue. *How to clean your room in ten easy steps*
Hutchins, Pat. *Where's the baby?*
Kamish, Daniel. *Diggy Dan*
Keane, Dave. *Sloppy Joe*
Kempter, Christa. *Wally and Mae*
Kirk, David. *Little pig, Biddle pig*
Krall, Dan. *Sick Simon*
Krensky, Stephen. *What a mess!*
Kroll, Virginia L. *Really rabbits*
Lattimore, Deborah Nourse. *Cinderhazel*
Lauber, Patricia. *What you never knew about tubs, toilets and showers*
Lichtenheld, Tom. *What's with this room?*
Luciani, Brigitte. *Those messy Hempels*
McElligott, Matthew. *Backbeard and the birthday suit*
McElmurry, Jill. *Mess pets*
McHenry, E. B. *Poodlena*
McKissack, Patricia C. *Messy Bessey*
    Messy Bessey / Ada, la desordenada
    Messy Bessey and the birthday overnight
    Messy Bessey's family reunion
    Messy Bessey's holidays
McNaulty, Stacy. *101 reasons why I'm not taking a bath*
Maloney, Peter. *Belly button boy*
Meade, Rita. *Edward gets messy*
Meschenmoser, Sebastian. *Gordon and Tapir*
Milway, Katie Smith. *Mimi's village and how basic health care transformed it*
Moss, Miriam. *Matty in a mess!*
Munsch, Robert N. *Mud puddle*
Myers, Tim. *Down at the Dino Wash Deluxe*
Noonan, Julia. *Hare and Rabbit, friends forever*
Novak, Matt. *The everything machine*
Papineau, Lucie. *Lulu's pajamas*
Potter, Beatrix. *The tale of Mrs. Tittlemouse*
Powell-Tuck, Maudie. *The messy book*
Primavera, Elise. *The house at the end of Ladybug Lane*
Provencher, Rose-Marie. *Mouse cleaning*
Puttock, Simon. *Yours truly, Louisa*
Riddell, Chris. *Wendel's workshop*
Roberts, David. *Dirty Bertie*
Root, Phyllis. *Mrs. Potter's pig*
Rosenthal, Amy Krouse. *Little Oink*
Sayre, April Pulley. *Stars beneath your bed*
Schertle, Alice. *The adventures of old Bo Bear*
Sloat, Teri. *This is the house that was tidy and neat*
Smith, Janice Lee. *Jess and the stinky cowboys*
Stephens, Helen. *Ruby and the muddy dog*
Stewart, Amber. *Rabbit ears*
Taylor, Sean. *Robomop*
Teague, Mark. *Pigsty*
Teckentrup, Britta. *Big smelly bear*
Upton, Elizabeth. *Maxi the little taxi*
Varon, Sara. *Chicken and Cat clean up*
Viorst, Judith. *Super-completely and totally the messiest*
Wallace, Nancy Elizabeth. *Count down to clean up*
Watt, Mélanie. *Bug in a vacuum*
Weinert, Matthias. *No bath, no cake!*
Wells, Rosemary. *Clean-up time*
    Fritz and the mess fairy
    Max cleans up
Westaway, Kylie. *A whale in the bathtub*
Wilson, Karma. *Hogwash!*

Character traits – cleverness

Aesop. *The crow and the pitcher*
Ahlberg, Janet. *It was a dark and stormy night*
Andersen, Hans Christian. *The swineherd*
Asbjørnsen, P. C. *The three billy goats Gruff*, ill. by Stephen Carpenter
The three billy goats Gruff, ill. by Paul Galdone
The three billy goats gruff, ill. by Jerry Pinkney
The three billy goats Gruff, ill. by Glen Rounds
The three billy goats Gruff, ill. by Janet Stevens
The three Billygoats Gruff and Mean Calypso Joe
Who's that tripping over my bridge?
Asch, Frank. *Ziggy Piggy and the three little pigs*
Bang, Molly. *Wiley and the hairy man*
Bannerman, Helen. *The story of Little Babaji*
The story of Little Black Sambo (1996)
The story of Little Black Sambo (1990)
The story of Little Black Sambo (2003)
Barnett, Mac. *Rules of the house*
Bernstrom, Daniel. *One day in the eucalyptus, eucalyptus tree*
Birdsall, Jeanne. *Lucky and Squash*
Birtha, Becky. *Lucky beans*
Bishop, Claire Huchet. *The five Chinese brothers*
Bonning, Tony. *Fox tale soup*
Breen, Steve. *Woodpecker wants a waffle*
Brett, Jan. *Fritz and the beautiful horses*
Hedgie's surprise
The trouble with trolls
Brown, Marcia. *Stone soup*
Buchanan, Sue. *Mud Pie Annie*
Burningham, John. *The shopping basket*
Calhoun, Mary. *Cross-country cat*
Cole, Brock. *Good enough to eat*
Collington, Peter. *Clever cat*
Compestine, Ying Chang. *The real story of stone soup*
Czernecki, Stefan. *Huevos rancheros*
Davis, David. *Fandango stew*
Dee, Ruby. *Two ways to count to ten*
Demi. *One grain of rice*
Desrosiers, Sylvie. *Hocus Pocus*
Esbaum, Jill. *Frankenbunny*
Forest, Heather. *Stone soup*
Galdone, Paul. *What's in fox's sack?*
Garza, Cynthia Leonor. *Lucía the luchadora*
Geisert, Arthur. *Ice*
Lights out
Glaser, Linda. *Stone soup with matzoh balls*
Gorbachev, Valeri. *The fool of the world and the flying ship: a Ukrainian folk tale*
Gravett, Emily. *Little Mouse's big book of beasts*
Greenawalt, Kelly. *Princess Truly in I am Truly*
Grimm, Jacob and Wilhelm. *The rabbit's bride*
Guarnaccia, Steven. *The three little pigs: an architectural tale*
Hodgkinson, Leigh. *The big monster snorey book*
Hood, Susan. *The Tooth Mouse*
Huck, Charlotte S. *Princess Furball*
Huling, Jan. *Puss in cowboy boots*
Imai, Ayano. *Puss and boots*
Isaacs, Anne. *Pancakes for supper!*
Johnson, Rebecca. *Sea turtle's clever plan*
Johnson-Davies, Denys. *Goha, the wise fool*
Kimmel, Eric A. *The three cabritos*
Kipling, Rudyard. *Rikki-tikki-tavi*, ill. by Lambert Davis
Rikki-tikki-tavi, ill. by Jerry Pinkney
Krause, Ute. *Oscar and the very hungry dragon*

Larsen, Andrew. *A squiggly story*
Lester, Julius. *Sam and the tigers*
Lowell, Susan. *The three little javelinas*
McDermott, Gerald. *Monkey*
McMillan, Bruce. *The problem with chickens*
McNaughton, Colin. *Oops!*
Maddern, Eric. *Nail soup*
Mahy, Margaret. *The seven Chinese brothers*
Mandell, Muriel. *A donkey reads*
Mathers, Petra. *Lottie's new beach towel*
Muth, Jon J. *Stone soup*
Nichols, Lori. *Maple and Willow's Christmas tree*
Olaleye, Isaac. *Bitter bananas*
Perrault, Charles. *Puss in boots*, ill. by Marcia Brown
Puss in boots, ill. by Lorinda Bryan Cauley
Puss in boots, ill. by Paul Galdone
Puss in boots, ill. by Steve Light
Puss in boots, ill. by Giuliano Lunelli
Puss in boots, ill. by Fred Marcellino
Puss in boots, ill. by Bernhard Oberdieck
Puss in boots, ill. by Jerry Pinkney
Puss in boots, ill. by Alain Vaës
Potter, Beatrix. *The sly old cat*
The tale of the Flopsy Bunnies, ill. by Beatrix Potter
The tale of the Flopsy Bunnies, ill. by Wendy Rasmussen
Prokofiev, Sergei Sergeievitch. *Peter and the wolf*, ill. by Charles Mikolaycak
Peter and the wolf, ill. by Josef Palecek
Peter and the wolf, ill. by Chris Raschka
Peter and the wolf, ill. by Vladimir Vagin
Pullman, Philip. *Puss in boots: the adventures of that most enterprising feline*
Ransome, Arthur. *The fool of the world and the flying ship*
Reynolds, Peter H. *Going places*
Rozen, Anna. *The merchant of noises*
Rueda, Claudia. *Huff and puff*
San Souci, Robert D. *Callie Ann and Mistah Bear*
Little Pierre
Seeger, Pete. *Some friends to feed*
Shannon, George. *Lizard's home*
Shea, Bob. *Cheetah can't lose*
Sierra, Judy. *Wiley and the Hairy Man*
Singleton, Debbie. *The king who wouldn't sleep*
Singleton, Linda Joy. *Snow dog, sand dog*
Souhami, Jessica. *Mrs. McCool and the giant Cuhullin*
Steig, William. *Doctor De Soto*
Stevens, Janet. *Tops and bottoms*
Stewart, Joel. *Dexter Bexley and the big blue beastie*
Stewig, John Warren. *Clever Gretchen*
Stone soup
Stine, R.L. *Mary McScary*
Taylor, Sean. *The grizzly bear with the frizzly hair*
Tchana, Katrin. *Sense Pass King*
The three little pigs. *The three little pigs*, ill. by Gavin Bishop
The three little pigs, ill. by Paul Galdone
The three little pigs, ill. by Rob Hefferan
The three little pigs, ill. by Steven Kellogg
The three little pigs, ill. by David McPhail
The three little pigs, ill. by James Marshall
The three little pigs, ill. by Bernadette Watts
The three little pigs, ill. by Margot Zemach
The three little pigs / Los tres cerditos
The three little pigs and the big bad wolf

The three little pigs and the fox
Thurber, James. *The great Quillow*
Twohy, Mike. *Outfoxed*
Van Dusen, Chris. *Randy Riley's really big hit*
Van Woerkom, Dorothy. *The rat, the ox and the zodiac*
Wahl, Jan. *Little Johnny Buttermilk*
Ward, Helen. *The king of the birds*
The rooster and the fox
Wheeler, Lisa. *Turk and Runt*
Wiesner, David. *The three pigs*
Willey, Margaret. *Clever Beatrice, an Upper Peninsula conte*
Clever Beatrice and the best little pony
Clever Beatrice Christmas
Wood, Audrey. *Heckedy Peg*
Yamashita, Haruo. *Seven little mice go to school*
Yolen, Jane. *The flying witch*
Young, Ed. *Little Plum*

Character traits – clumsiness

Aruego, José. *Splash!*
Edwards, Pamela Duncan. *Slop goes the soup*
Fox, Mem. *Harriet, you'll drive me wild*
Kleven, Elisa. *Welcome home, Mouse*
Kroll, Steven. *Oh, Tucker!*
McNaughton, Colin. *Preston's goal!*
McPhail, David. *Crash! the cat*
O'Neill, Gemma. *Oh dear, Geoffrey!*
Rodriguez, Edel. *Sergio saves the game!*
Simon, Charnan. *Jeremy Jones, clumsy guy*
Stower, Adam. *Two left feet*
Wardlaw, Lee. *The chair where bear sits*

Character traits – completing things

Alda, Arlene. *Lulu's piano lesson*
Gorbachev, Valeri. *Pizza-pie snowman*
Mortenson, Greg. *Listen to the wind*

Character traits – compromising

Bender, Rebecca. *Giraffe meets Bird*
Côté, Geneviève. *Starring me and you*
Covell, David. *Rat and Roach rock on!*
Dumont, Jean-François. *The sheep go on strike*
Eure, Wesley. *A fish out of water*
Freedman, Deborah. *By Mouse and Frog*
Gude, Paul. *When Elephant met Giraffe*
Janni, Rebecca. *Every cowgirl needs dancing boots*
Lee, Michelle. *Play with me!*
O'Connor, Jane. *Fancy Nancy and the wedding of the century*
Rudy, Maggie. *City mouse, country mouse*
Sauer, Tammi. *Mr. Duck means business*
Torrey, Richard. *The almost terrible playdate*
Trimmer, Christian. *Simon's new bed*
Weeks, Sarah. *Catfish Kate and the sweet swamp band*

Character traits – conceit

Goble, Paul. *Iktomi and the boulder*
Iktomi and the buffalo skull
Marino, Gianna. *I am the Mountain Mouse*
Martin, Ann M. *Rachel Parker, kindergarten show-off*
Peet, Bill. *Ella*
Reynolds, Aaron. *President Squid*
Sauer, Tammi. *Oh, nuts!*
Sharmat, Marjorie Weinman. *I'm terrific*

Character traits – confidence

Alexander, Claire. *Small Florence*
Aliki. *All by myself!*
Asch, Frank. *Baby Duck's new friend*
Boyce, Katie. *Hector the hermit crab*
Corey, Shana. *Ballerina bear*
Cumming, Hannah. *The red boat*
Curtis, Jamie Lee. *My brave year of firsts*
Dempsey, Kristy. *Surfer chick*
Diesen, Deborah. *The pout-pout fish goes to school*
Esham, Barbara. *Last to finish*
Furrow, Eva. *Take your time*
Gorbachev, Valeri. *Chicken chickens*
Grant, Rose Marie. *Andiamo, Weasel*
Greenawalt, Kelly. *Princess Truly in I am Truly*
Hest, Amy. *Make the team, Baby Duck*
You can do it, Sam
Hillenbrand, Jane. *What a treasure!*
Kerley, Barbara. *What to do about Alice?*
Könnecke, Ole. *You can do it, Bert!*
Krensky, Stephen. *I know a lot!*
Krumwiede, Lana. *Just Itzy*
Latifah, Queen. *Queen of the scene*
Lehrhaupt, Adam. *Chicken in space*
Lewis, Wendy A. *In Abby's hands*
McAnulty, Stacy. *Beautiful*
McCarthy, Jenna. *Lola knows a lot*
Mack, Jeff. *The things I can do*
Milgrim, David. *Eddie gets ready for school*
Papp, Lisa. *Madeline Finn and the library dog*
Pérez, L. King. *First day in grapes*
Reynolds, Peter H. *The dot*
Robinson, Fiona. *Whale shines*
Rosenthal, Amy Krouse. *Dear Girl,*
Rylant, Cynthia. *Herbert's first Halloween*
Sauer, Tammi. *Mary had a little glam*
Schotter, Roni. *Doo-Wop Pop*
Shea, Bob. *New socks*
Sif, Birgitta. *Frances Dean who loved to dance and dance*
Stinson, Kathy. *The dance of the violin*
Thompson, Lauren. *Wee little chick*
Viorst, Judith. *And two boys booed*
Waddell, Martin. *Good job, Little Bear!*
Wagner, Karen. *Bravo, Mildred and Ed!*
Weatherford, Carole Boston. *Be a King: Dr. Martin Luther King Jr.'s dream and you*
Wormell, Christopher. *Henry and the fox*
Wright, Joanna. *Bunnies on ice*
Yankey, Lindsey. *Bluebird*
Yoshitake, Shinsuke. *Still stuck*

Character traits – cooperation

Aliki. *A play's the thing*
Armo, Nancy. *A friend for Mole*
Barasch, Lynne. *First come the zebra*
Belloni, Giulia. *Anything is possible*
Bender, Rebecca. *Giraffe meets Bird*
Bertier, Anne. *Wednesday*
Biddulph, Rob. *The grizzly bear who lost his grrrrr!*
Braun, Sebastien. *Digger and Tom!*
Brett, Jan. *The turnip*
Brimner, Larry Dane. *The big, beautiful, brown box*
Brooks, Jeremy. *Let there be peace*
Bunting, Eve. *Our library*
Cecil, Randy. *Horsefly and Honeybee*
Chin, Oliver. *The year of the sheep*
Clanton, Ben. *Rex wrecks it!*

Cohen, Caron Lee. *Broom, zoom!*
Conahan, Carolyn. *The big wish*
Cordell, Matthew. *Wolf in the snow*
Corr, Christopher. *Deep in the woods*
Côté, Geneviève. *Mr. King's machine*
Cowcher, Helen. *Desert elephants*
Dominguez, Angela. *Knit together*
Dorros, Alex. *Número uno*
Dubuc, Marianne. *The animals' ark*
Flory, Neil. *The short giraffe*
Fraser, Mary Ann. *Pet shop follies*
Freedman, Deborah. *By Mouse and Frog*
Gainer, Cindy. *I'm like you, you're like me*
Geisert, Arthur. *The giant ball of string*
  Ice
Goodall, Jane. *The eagle and the wren*
Graham, Bob. *A bus called Heaven*
Grey, Mini. *Three by the sea*
Heide, Florence Parry. *Always listen to your mother*
Hester, Denia Lewis. *Grandma Lena's big ol' turnip*
Hiscock, Bruce. *Coyote and badger*
Holub, Joan. *Tool school*
Hopkins, Lee Bennett. *Full moon and star*
Horáček, Petr. *The mouse who reached the sky*
Hudelhoff, Allen H. *Cats and kids*
Hutchins, Hazel. *Mattland*
Ishida, Sanae. *Little Kunoichi, the ninja girl*
Jackson, Jill. *Let there be peace on earth*
Jennings, Sharon. *Priscilla's paw de deux*
Kako, Satoshi. *Little Daruma and little Daikoku*
Klausmeier, Jesse. *Open this little book*
Kuiper, Nannie. *Bravo, brave beavers*
LaMarche, Jim. *Pond*
Light, Kelly. *Louise and Andie*
Lobe, Mira. *Hoppelpopp and the best bunny*
McKee, David. *Elmer and the big bird*
  Elmer and the hippos
Mahoney, Daniel J. *The perfect clubhouse*
Manzano, Sonia. *Miracle on 133rd Street*
Marino, Gianna. *Too tall houses*
Martín Larrañaga, Ana. *Pepo and Lolo and the red apple*
Martins, Isabel Minhós. *Little lamb, have you any wool?*
Meshon, Aaron. *Tools rule!*
Messier, Mireille. *The branch*
Miller, Pat Zietlow. *The quickest kid in Clarksville*
Miyares, Daniel. *That neighbor kid*
Nelson, Kadir. *If you plant a seed*
Numeroff, Laura Joffe. *The Jellybeans and the big art adventure*
  The Jellybeans and the big camp kickoff
  The Jellybeans and the big dance
Ohi, Debbie Ridpath. *Sam and Eva*
Otoshi, Kathryn. *Zero*
Parkinson, Kathy. *The enormous turnip*
Paschkis, Julie. *Magic spell*
Paye, Won-Ldy. *Head, body, legs*
Peck, Jan. *Giant peach yodel!*
Pham, LeUyen. *A piece of cake*
Rankin, Laura. *My turn!*
Reed, Liz. *Sweet competition*
Reid, Barbara. *Perfect snow*
Reynolds, Peter H. *Going places*
Rinker, Sherri Duskey. *Mighty, mighty construction site*
Roberts, Bethany. *Double trouble Groundhog Day*
Roscoe, Charlie. *The red prince*
Rouss, Sylvia A. *The littlest pair*

Ruddell, Deborah. *Who said coo?*
Ryan, Candace. *Ewe and Aye*
Scheffler, Axel. *Pip and Posy: the snowy day*
Singer, Marilyn. *Let's build a clubhouse*
  Tallulah's tap shoes
Soman, David. *Ladybug Girl and the Bug Squad*
Starin, Liz. *Splashdance*
Stevens, Janet. *The little red pen*
Stihler, Chérie B. *The giant cabbage turnip*
Swann, Rick. *Our school garden!*
Tolstoy, Aleksey Nikolayevich. *The enormous turnip*
  The gigantic turnip
Vail, Rachel. *Righty and Lefty*
Wallace, Nancy Elizabeth. *Ready, set, 100th day!*
Zommer, Yuval. *The big blue thing on the hill*

Character traits – courage *see* Character traits – bravery

Character traits – cruelty to animals *see* Character traits – kindness to animals

Character traits – curiosity

Adler, David A. *Magnets push, magnets pull*
  Things that float and things that don't
Arnosky, Jim. *Raccoon on his own*
Bang, Molly. *Dawn*
Banks, Kate. *How to find an elephant*
Beaty, Andrea. *Ada Twist, scientist*
Bogan, Carmen. *Where's Rodney?*
Bonnett-Rampersaud, Louise. *Polly Hopper's pouch*
Bryan, Ashley. *Can't scare me!*
Bunting, Eve. *Tweak tweak*
Buzzeo, Toni. *My Bibi always remembers*
Campbell, K. G. *The mermaid and the shoe*
Catalanotto, Peter. *Question Boy meets Little Miss Know-It-All*
Cecka, Melanie. *Violet goes to the country*
Chou, Yih-Fen. *Mimi loves to mimic*
Curious George and the dump truck (1984)
Curious George and the pizza
Curious George at the fire station
Curious George goes hiking
Curious George goes sledding
Curious George goes to the aquarium
Curious George goes to the circus
Curious George in the big city
Curious George takes a train
Curious George visits a toy store
Curious George visits the zoo
Curtis, Jamie Lee. *Is there really a human race?*
De Beer, Hans. *Oh no, Ono!*
Denos, Julia. *Windows*
Dotlich, Rebecca Kai. *The knowing book*
Gorbachev, Valeri. *Red red red*
Gravdahl, John. *Curious catwalk*
Hapka, Cathy. *Margret and H. A. Rey's Merry Christmas, Curious George*
Henkes, Kevin. *Little white rabbit*
Hopgood, Tim. *Wow! said the owl*
Kipling, Rudyard. *The elephant's child*
  How the elephant got his trunk
Lamb, Rosy. *Paul meets Bernadette*
Lewis, Kevin. *Not inside this house!*
Loupy, Christophe. *Wiggles*
McBratney, Sam. *The dark at the top of the stairs*

McGhee, Alison. *The sweetest witch around*
Meltzer, Brad. *I am Albert Einstein*
Merino, Gemma. *The cow who climbed a tree*
Mitton, Tony. *A very curious bear*
Morgan-Vanroyen, Mary. *Curious Rosie*
Murphy, Mary. *Koala and the flower*
Perkins, Lynne Rae. *Frank and Lucky get schooled*
Rey, H. A. *Curious George*
　Curious George gets a medal
　Curious George learns the alphabet
　Curious George rides a bike
　Curious George takes a job
　The original Curious George
Rey, Margret. *Curious George flies a kite*
　Curious George goes to the hospital
Richards, Dan. *Can one balloon make an elephant fly?*
Rylant, Cynthia. *Miss Maggie*
Schoenherr, John. *Rebel*
Slack, Michael. *Shorty and Clem*
Slater, Dashka. *The antlered ship*
Swanson, Matthew. *Everywhere, wonder*
Torrey, Richard. *Why?*
Waber, Bernard. *Lorenzo*

Character traits – flattery

Aesop. *Three Aesop fox fables*
Chaucer, Geoffrey. *Chanticleer and the fox*

Character traits – foolishness

Aardema, Verna. *Sebgugugu the glutton*
Alexander, Lloyd. *The house Gobbaleen*
Carlson, Nancy. *Arnie and the skateboard gang*
Davis, Aubrey. *Kishka for Koppel*
Hurston, Zora Neale. *The six fools*
Jacobs, Joseph. *The three sillies*
Johnson-Davies, Denys. *Goha, the wise fool*
Pilkey, Dav. *The Dumb Bunnies*
　The Dumb Bunnies' Easter
　The Dumb Bunnies go to the zoo
　Make way for Dumb Bunnies
San Souci, Robert D. *Six foolish fishermen*
Souhami, Jessica. *Sausages*
Spinelli, Eileen. *Silly Tilly*
Uhlberg, Myron. *Lemuel, the fool*
Van Nutt, Julia. *Pignapped!*
Zemach, Margot. *The three wishes*

Character traits – fortune *see* Character traits – luck

Character traits – freedom

Aesop. *The dog and the wolf*
Amnesty International. *We are all born free*
Andersen, Hans Christian. *The nightingale*, ill. by Nancy Ekholm Burkert
　The nightingale, ill. by Pirkko Vainio
　The nightingale, ill. by Lisbeth Zwerger
Baylor, Byrd. *Hawk, I'm your brother*
Bryant, Jen. *Abe's fish*
Bunting, Eve. *How many days to America?*
Cooper, Floyd. *Juneteenth for Mazie*
Drummond, Allan. *Liberty*
Elvgren, Jennifer. *The whispering town*
Evans, Shane W. *Underground: finding the light to freedom*
Grady, Cynthia. *I lay my stitches down*

Grifalconi, Ann. *Ain't nobody a stranger to me*
Levine, Ellen. *Henry's freedom box*
Lyons, Kelly Starling. *Hope's gift*
Meade, Holly. *John Willy and Freddy McGee*
Murphy, Mary. *The Alphabet Keeper*
Nadimi, Suzan. *The rich man and the parrot*
Nelson, Vaunda Micheaux. *Almost to freedom*
Park, Frances. *My freedom trip*
Pinkney, Andrea Davis. *Sojourner Truth's step-stomp stride*
Polacco, Patricia. *The butterfly*
Rappaport, Doreen. *Freedom river*
　Freedom ship
Roth, Susan L. *Happy birthday Mr. Kang*
Sanders, Scott R. *A place called Freedom*
Shange, Ntozake. *Freedom's a-callin me*
Shulevitz, Uri. *What is a wise bird like you doing in a silly tale like this?*
Siegelson, Kim L. *In the time of the drums*
Stroud, Bettye. *The patchwork path*
Sundgaard, Arnold. *The lamb and the butterfly*
Walker, Sally M. *Freedom song*
Winter, Jeanette. *Malala, a brave girl from Pakistan / Iqbal, a brave boy from Pakistan*
Woelfle, Gretchen. *Mumbet's Declaration of Independence*
Wright, Courtni Crump. *Journey to freedom*
Yousafzai, Malala. *Malala's magic pencil*

Character traits – generosity

Aliki. *The story of Johnny Appleseed*
Anglund, Joan Walsh. *Christmas is a time of giving*
Barrett, Mary Brigid. *Shoebox Sam*
Battle-Lavert, Gwendolyn. *The shaking bag*
Beck, Scott. *A mud pie for mother*
Bergmann, Andy. *The starry giraffe*
Biedrzycki, David. *Me and my dragon: Christmas spirit*
Blackwood, Freya. *Ivy loves to give*
Bouler, Olivia. *Olivia's birds*
Brisson, Pat. *Melissa Parkington's beautiful, beautiful hair*
Butler, M. Christina. *One snowy night*
Chamberlin, Mary. *Mama Panya's pancakes*
Child, Lauren. *But I've used all my pocket change*
Chinn, Karen. *Sam and the lucky money*
Compestine, Ying Chang. *The runaway rice cake*
Danowski, Sonja. *Little night cat*
Demas, Corinne. *The magic apple*
DiSalvo, DyAnne. *A castle on Viola Street*
Edwards, Michelle. *A hat for Mrs. Goldman*
Elliott, Zetta. *Melena's jubilee*
Fleming, Candace. *Boxes for Katje*
Frazee, Marla. *Hush, little baby: a folk song with pictures*
Gibfried, Diane. *Brother Juniper*
Graegin, Stephanie. *Little fox in the forest*
Grimm, Jacob and Wilhelm. *The star child*
Hamilton, Martha. *The ghost catcher*
Hayes, Joe. *Don't say a word, Mamá/No digas nada, Mamá*
Heller, Linda. *How Dalia put a big yellow comforter inside a tiny blue box*
Hughes, Shirley. *Giving*
Hush, little baby
Janice. *Little Bear's Christmas*
Jules, Jacqueline. *Feathers for peacock*
Kasza, Keiko. *The wolf's chicken stew*

King-Chai, Sharon. *Lucy Ladybug*
Kromhout, Rindert. *Little Donkey and the birthday present*
Larsen, Andrew. *The man who loved libraries*
Lionni, Leo. *Tico and the golden wings*
Lucado, Max. *All you ever need*
McCourt, Lisa. *Chicken soup for little souls: The best night out with Dad*
McGinley, Phyllis. *The year without a Santa Claus*
Marshall, Linda Elovitz. *Grandma Rose's magic*
Mitchell, Marianne. *Gullywasher gulch*
Munsch, Robert N. *Ribbon rescue*
O'Connor, Jane. *Fancy Nancy and the fabulous fashion boutique*
Patten, Brian. *The big snuggle-up*
Pilkey, Dav. *Dragon's merry Christmas*
Pinkney, Brian. *Hush, little baby*
Pomerantz, Charlotte. *The mousery*
Priest, Robert H. *The pirate's eye*
Quattlebaum, Mary. *The shine man*
Rockliff, Mara. *My heart will not sit down*
Rylant, Cynthia. *Silver packages*
Sacre, Antonio. *A mango in the hand*
Sandman, Rochel. *Perfect porridge*
Schotter, Roni. *Captain Snap and the children of Vinegar Lane*
Schrock, Jan West. *Give a goat*
Shepard, Aaron. *The baker's dozen*
Shollar, Leah. *A thread of kindness*
Silverstein, Shel. *The giving tree*
Smith, Monique Gray. *You hold me up*
Spinelli, Eileen. *Thankful*
Tada, Joni Eareckson. *The incredible discovery of Lindsey Renee*
Toscano, Charles. *Papa's pastries*
Tutu, Archbishop Desmond. *God's dream*
Underwood, Deborah. *Here comes Santa Cat*
Villnave, Erica Pelton. *Sophie's lovely locks*
Weatherford, Carole Boston. *Be a King: Dr. Martin Luther King Jr.'s dream and you*
Williams, Laura E. *The can man*
Winget, Susan. *Sam the Snowman*
Yaccarino, Dan. *Happyland: big berry*
Young, Ed. *The cat from Hunger Mountain*
Young, Ned. *Zoomer's out-of-this-world Christmas*
Ziefert, Harriet. *Surprise!*

Character traits – helpfulness

Adams, Diane. *I want to help!*
Aesop. *Androcles and the lion*, ill. by Dennis Nolan
Androcles and the lion, ill. by Janet Stevens
Androcles and the lion: and other Aesop fables
The lion and the mouse, ill. by Lisa McCue
The lion and the mouse, ill. by Sara Rojo
The lion and the mouse, ill. by Bernadette Watts
Mouse and lion
Aliki. *The two of them*
Ancona, George. *Mis quehaceres / My chores*
Anderson, Derek. *How the Easter Bunny saved Christmas*
Asch, Frank. *Baby Bird's first nest*
Monsieur Saguette and his baguette
Bagley, Jessixa. *Laundry day*
Barnes, Laura T. *Ernest's special Christmas*
Barton, Chris. *Mighty truck*
Mighty truck: muddymania!
Bloom, Suzanne. *Bear can dance!*
Bogacki, Tomasz. *Circus girl*

Booth, Anne. *The fairiest fairy*
Bouler, Olivia. *Olivia's birds*
Bourgeois, Paulette. *Franklin and Harriet*
Brandt, Lois. *Maddi's fridge*
Brett, Jan. *Home for Christmas*
Bridwell, Norman. *Clifford's good deeds*
Brisson, Pat. *Before we eat*
Bunting, Eve. *December*
Burningham, John. *Harvey Slumfenburger's Christmas present*
Bushey, Jeanne. *The polar bear's gift*
Calhoun, Mary. *Blue-ribbon Henry*
Cannon, Janell. *Crickwing*
Chiew, Suzanne. *When you need a friend*
Clarke, Jane. *Stuck in the mud*
Clinton, Hillary Rodham. *It takes a village*
Coffelt, Nancy. *Aunt Ant leaves through the leaves*
Costello, David Hyde. *I can help*
Cousins, Lucy. *Maisy makes lemonade*
Cunnane, Kelly. *Chirchir is singing*
Curato, Mike. *Little Elliot, big city*
D'Amico, Carmela. *Ella takes the cake*
Day, Alexandra. *Frank and Ernest*
Daywalt, Drew. *BB-8 on the run*
deGroat, Diane. *Lola the elf*
Mother, you're the best! (but Sister, you're a pest!)
de la Peña, Matt. *Last stop on Market Street*
Devlin, Wende. *Cranberry autumn*
Cranberry Christmas
DiCamillo, Kate. *Great joy*
Dillon, Leo. *If kids ran the world*
Donaldson, Julia. *Superworm*
Dormer, Frank W. *Firefighter Duckies!*
Durango, Julia. *The one day house*
Elliott, David. *This Orq. (He #1!)*
Emberley, Ed. *The red hen*
Ernst, Lisa Campbell. *Sylvia Jean, scout supreme*
Esbaum, Jill. *To the big top*
Ethan, Eric. *Helicopters*
Fackelmayer, Regina. *The gifts*
Freedman, Deborah. *Blue chicken*
Gall, Chris. *NanoBots*
Garland, Sarah. *Eddie's toolbox and how to make and mend things*
Gianferrari, Maria. *Hello goodbye dog*
Gibbons, Gail. *Emergency!*
Gill, Timothy. *Flip and Fin: super sharks to the rescue!*
Graham, Tom. *Five little firefighters*
Grambling, Lois G. *Here comes T. Rex Cottontail*
Granowsky, Alvin. *Can I help?*
Grimm, Jacob and Wilhelm. *The elves and the shoemaker*, ill. by Kirill Chelushkin
The elves and the shoemaker, ill. by Paul Galdone
The elves and the shoemaker, ill. by Margaret Walty
The shoemaker and his elves
The shoemaker and the elves, ill. by Adrienne Adams
The shoemaker and the elves, ill. by Ilse Plume
Hamilton, Kersten. *Red truck*
Heide, Iris van der. *A strange day*
Hill, Elizabeth Starr. *Evan's corner*
Himmelman, John. *Chickens to the rescue*
Pigs to the rescue
Ho, Jannie. *Bear and Chicken*
Horácek, Petr. *The mouse who reached the sky*
Isabella, Jude. *The red bicycle*
Jackson, Ellen. *Sometimes bad things happen*
Jackson, Kathryn. *Pantaloon*
Jeffers, Oliver. *The way back home*

Jenkins, Emily. *Up, up, up!*
Joyce, William. *Bently and egg*
 The Leaf Men and the brave good bugs
Keller, Holly. *Nosy Rosie*
Kinch, Devon. *Pretty Penny makes ends meet*
Kinerk, Robert. *Clorinda plays baseball!*
Kirsch, Vincent X. *Forsythia and me*
 Natalie and Naughtily
Klise, Kate. *Grammy Lamby and the secret handshake*
Knudsen, Michelle. *Library lion*
Koehler, Fred. *Super Jumbo*
Kroll, Virginia L. *Good citizen Sarah*
 Makayla cares about others
Krosoczka, Jarrett J. *Giddy up, Cowgirl*
Kwan, James. *Dear Yeti*
Laminack, Lester L. *Saturdays and teacakes*
Lehman, Barbara. *Trainstop*
Loki. *Jake Greenthumb*
Lord, Janet. *Albert the fix-it man*
Lowell, Susan. *The bootmaker and the elves*
Lum, Kate. *Princesses are not just pretty*
McKee, David. *Elmer and Butterfly*
McKissack, Patricia C. *Messy Bessey and the birthday overnight*
Maclear, Kyo. *The wish tree*
McLellan, Stephanie Simpson. *Tweezle into everything*
McPhail, David. *Santa's book of names*
Mahoney, Daniel J. *A really good snowman*
Manning, Mick. *Cock-a-doodle hooooooo!*
Manzano, Sonia. *A box full of kittens*
May, Robert L. *Rudolph shines again*
Mayer, Mercer. *Just for you*
Meadows, Michelle. *Super bugs*
Melling, David. *Don't worry, Douglas!*
Miller, Pat. *Squirrel's New Year's resolution*
Muth, Jon J. *Mama Lion wins the race*
 Zen ties
Nolen, Jerdine. *Pitching in for Eubie*
Numeroff, Laura Joffe. *What brothers do best; What sisters do best*
Oswald, Pete. *Mingo the flamingo*
Otoshi, Kathryn. *Beautiful hands*
Oyibo, Papa. *Big brother, little sister*
Panzieri, Lucia. *The kindhearted crocodile*
Paraskevas, Betty. *Maggie and the Ferocious Beast, the big carrot*
Paul, Miranda. *Whose hands are these?*
Peet, Bill. *The ant and the elephant*
 Cyrus the unsinkable sea serpent
Petrillo, Genevieve. *Keep your ear on the ball*
Pinkney, Jerry. *The lion and the mouse*
Potter, Beatrix. *The tailor of Gloucester*
Prince, April Jones. *Goldenlocks and the three pirates*
Randall, Angel. *Snow angels*
Rau, Dana Meachen. *In the yard*
Reider, Katja. *The big little sneeze*
Reynolds, Aaron. *President Squid*
Ries, Lori. *Fix it, Sam*
Rocco, John. *Blizzard*
Sauer, Tammi. *Nugget and Fang*
Savage, Stephen. *Little Tug*
Schneider, Josh. *Kid Amazing vs. the Blob*
Schubert, Leda. *Here comes Darrell*
Schuch, Steve. *A symphony of whales*
Schwartz, Roslyn. *The mole sisters and the piece of moss*
Scieszka, Jon. *Melvin might?*
Scotton, Rob. *Russell's Christmas magic*

Seuss, Dr. *Horton hatches the egg*
Shah, Idries. *The clever boy and the terrible, dangerous animal*
Shaw, Hannah. *School for bandits*
Sierra, Judy. *Preschool to the rescue*
Slack, Michael. *Monkey Truck*
Slade, Suzanne. *Dangerous Jane*
Slobodkina, Esphyr. *Caps for sale and the mindful monkeys*
Snyder, Laurel. *The forever garden*
Soto, Gary. *The old man and his door*
Staniszewski, Anna. *Dogosaurus Rex*
Stead, Philip C. *Bear has a story to tell*
Steffensmeier, Alexander. *Millie in the snow*
Stevenson, James. *Will you please feed our cat?*
Stone, Tanya Lee. *The house that Jane built*
Stoop, Naoko. *Red Knit Cap Girl to the rescue*
Strauss, Anna. *Hush, Mama loves you*
Thomas, Shelley Moore. *Take care, Good Knight*
Thorpe, Kiki. *A comfy, cozy Thanksgiving*
Toten, Teresa. *Bright red kisses*
Tutu, Archbishop Desmond. *God's dream*
Verdick, Elizabeth. *On-the-go time*
Vernick, Audrey. *I won a what?*
Waber, Bernard. *Lyle, Lyle Crocodile*
Waddell, Martin. *Farmer Duck*
 Good job, Little Bear!
Watson, Wendy. *Holly's Christmas eve*
Weatherford, Carole Boston. *Be a King: Dr. Martin Luther King Jr.'s dream and you*
Weninger, Brigitte. *Davy in the middle*
Wheeler, Lisa. *Old Cricket*
White, Ellen Emerson. *Santa paws*
Winstead, Rosie. *Sprout helps out*
Winters, Kari-Lynn. *Bad pirate*
Woollard, Elli. *The giant of Jum*
Ziefert, Harriet. *Ode to Humpty Dumpty*

Character traits – honesty

Aardema, Verna. *Pedro and the padre*
Abercrombie, Barbara. *The show-and-tell lion*
Ashdown, Rebecca. *The Whopper*
Boelts, Maribeth. *A bike like Sergio's*
Breathed, Berkeley. *Edwurd Fudwupper fibbed big*
Bunting, Eve. *A day's work*
Cocca-Leffler, Maryann. *Princess K.I.M. and the lie that grew*
 Princess Kim and too much truth
Cuyler, Margery. *I repeat, don't cheat!*
deGroat, Diane. *Liar, liar, pants on fire*
Demi. *The empty pot*
Dierssen, Andreas. *Timid Timmy*
Donovan, Gail. *A fishy story*
Earnhardt, Donna W. *Being Frank*
Finlay, Lizzie. *Little Croc's purse*
Geser, Gretchen. *One bright ring*
Grambling, Lois G. *The witch who wanted to be a princess*
Gutman, Anne. *Lisa in the jungle*
Havill, Juanita. *Jamaica's find*
Hesse, Karen. *Spuds*
Hobbie, Holly. *Fanny and Annabelle*
Hood, Susan. *The Tooth Mouse*
Kaplan, Michael B. *Betty Bunny didn't do it*
Keller, Holly. *That's mine, Horace*
Kroll, Virginia L. *Honest Ashley*
Latimer, Alex. *The boy who cried ninja*
McKissack, Patricia C. *The honest-to-goodness truth*

Madonna. *Mr. Peabody's apples*
Mathers, Petra. *Herbie's secret Santa*
Poydar, Nancy. *Zip, zip . . . homework*
Rahaman, Vashanti. *Divali rose*
Rankin, Laura. *Ruthie and the (not so) teeny tiny lie*
Robberecht, Thierry. *Sam tells stories*
Schroeder, Alan. *The stone lion*
Sierra, Judy. *Tell the truth, B. B. Wolf*
Singer, Marilyn. *The boy who cried alien*
Stephens, Helen. *Ruby and the muddy dog*

Character traits – hopefulness

Clinton, Hillary Rodham. *It takes a village*
Cocca-Leffler, Maryann. *Rain brings frogs*
Cordell, Matthew. *Dream*
    Wish
Daly, Niki. *The herd boy*
Davies, Nicola. *The promise*
de la Peña, Matt. *Miguel and the grand harmony*
Kittinger, Jo S. *The house on Dirty-Third Street*
Krensky, Stephen. *The last Christmas tree*
Lennon, John. *Imagine*
MacLachlan, Patricia. *Snowflakes fall*
Our children can soar
Sasso, Sandy Eisenberg. *Butterflies under our hats*
Watson, Jesse Joshua. *Hope for Haiti*
Weatherford, Carole Boston. *In your hands*
Young, Rebecca. *Teacup*

Character traits – incentive *see* Character
    traits – ambition

Character traits – individuality

Alexander, Martha G. *Max and the dumb flower*
    picture
Aliki. *All by myself!*
    Jack and Jake
Andreae, Giles. *Giraffes can't dance*
Appelt, Kathi. *Incredible me!*
Auerbach, Adam. *Edda*
Azore, Barbara. *Wanda and the wild hair*
Baicker, Karen. *Pea pod babies*
Baker, Keith. *No two alike*
Baker, Roberta. *No ordinary Olive*
Banks, Kate. *That's Papa's way*
Bansch, Helga. *Rosie the raven*
Bar-el, Dan. *Not your typical dragon*
Barton, Suzanne. *The sleepy songbird*
Bates, Ivan. *All by myself*
Battut, Éric. *The little pea*
Beaumont, Karen. *Wild about us!*
Berne, Jennifer. *On a beam of light*
Blabey, Aaron. *Pearl Barley and Charlie Parsley*
Bloom, Suzanne. *Alone together*
Boutignon, Beatrice. *Not all animals are blue*
Boynton, Sandra. *Yay, you!*
Bradley, Sandra. *Henry Holton takes the ice*
Breen, Steve. *Violet the pilot*
Bridges, Shirin Yim. *The Umbrella Queen*
Briggs, John. *Leaping lemmings!*
Britt, Paige. *Why am I me?*
Brooks, Erik. *Polar opposites*
Brown, Don. *Odd boy out*
Brown, Peter. *Mr. Tiger goes wild*
Brumbeau, Jeff. *Miss Hunnicutt's hat*
Bynum, Janie. *Otis*

Carlson, Nancy. *I like me*
Carrer, Chiara. *Otto Carrotto*
Cartaya, Pablo. *Tina Cocolina*
Cave, Kathryn. *Henry's song*
Chapman, Jared. *Steve, raised by wolves*
Child, Lauren. *Who wants to be a poodle*
Chodos-Irvine, Margaret. *Ella Sarah gets dressed*
Clanton, Ben. *Mo's mustache*
Cocca-Leffler, Maryann. *Janine*
    Janine and the field day finish
Cochran, Bill. *My parents are divorced, my elbows*
    have nicknames, and other facts about me
Collington, Peter. *Clever cat*
Corderoy, Tracey. *Hubble bubble, Granny trouble*
Corey, Shana. *First graders from Mars: The problem*
    with Pelly
Côté, Geneviève. *Me and you*
deGennaro, Sue. *The pros and cons of being a frog*
dePaola, Tomie. *Oliver Button is a sissy*
Desbordes, Astrid. *Edmond, the moonlit party*
Dicmas, Courtney. *Harold finds a voice*
Diggs, Taye. *Chocolate me!*
Diller, Kevin. *Hello, my name is Octicorn*
DiPucchio, Kelly. *Antoinette*
    Gaston
Dolenz, Micky. *Gakky Two-Feet*
Duke, Shirley Smith. *No bows!*
Dumont, Jean-François. *The geese march in step*
Eaton, Jason Carter. *The catawampus cat*
Ehlert, Lois. *Oodles of animals*
Evans, Kristina. *What's special about me, Mama?*
Falconer, Ian. *Olivia and the fairy princesses*
Frankel, Erin. *Weird!*
Friedman, Laurie. *A style all her own*
Gainer, Cindy. *I'm like you, you're like me*
Genechten, Guido van. *Flop-Ear*
Gilbert, Jane. *Indescribably Arabella*
Goldstyn, Jacques. *Bertolt*
Goodhart, Pippa. *You choose*
Gore, Emily. *And Nick*
Gutman, Dan. *Rappy the raptor*
Hall, Michael. *Perfect square*
Hardy, Sarah Frances. *Puzzled by pink*
Harris, Robie H. *I'm all dressed!*
    Who we are!
Heide, Florence Parry. *The one and only Marigold*
Heiligman, Deborah. *The boy who loved math*
Helakoski, Leslie. *Fair cow*
    Woolbur
Henderson, Alicia Terry. *Call me black, call me*
    beautiful
Himmelman, John. *Tudley didn't know*
Hines, Anna Grossnickle. *What Joe saw*
Hobbie, Holly. *Fanny*
Hodgkinson, Leigh. *Troll swap*
Hofmann-Maniyar, Ariane. *That's NOT how you*
    do it!
Hogrogian, Nonny. *The tiger of Turkestan*
Hong, Jess. *Lovely*
Hood, Morag. *Carrot and pea*
Horácek, Petr. *Look out, Suzy Goose*
    Silly Suzy Goose
Hosford, Kate. *Big birthday*
    Big bouffant
Hovland, Henrik. *John Jensen feels different*
Howe, James. *Big Bob, Little Bob*
Hughes, Susan. *Earth to Audrey*
Hume, Lachie. *Clancy the courageous cow*
Ismail, Yasmeen. *I'm a girl!*

Wheatley, Nadia. *Luke's way of looking*
Willems, Mo. *Naked mole rat gets dressed*
Winans, CeCe, et al. *Colorful world*
Winter, Jeanette. *Kali's song*
Woo, Alan. *Maggie's chopsticks*
Yolen, Jane. *Not all princesses dress in pink*
Yoon, Salina. *Be a friend*
Yum, Hyewon. *The twins' blanket*

Character traits – kindness

Aesop. *The lion and the mouse*
   Mouse and lion
Aliki. *The story of William Penn*
Andreasen, Dan. *The giant of Seville*
Aston, Dianna Hutts. *Not so tall for six*
Bang, Molly. *The paper crane*
Barrett, Mary Brigid. *Shoebox Sam*
Blaich, Ute. *The star*
Bloom, Becky. *Crackers*
Booth, Anne. *The fairiest fairy*
Brandt, Lois. *Maddi's fridge*
Bromley, Anne C. *The lunch thief*
Butler, M. Christina. *One winter's day*
Caraballo, Samuel. *My big sister / Mi hermana mayor*
Cazet, Denys. *A fish in his pocket*
Church, Caroline Jayne. *Ruff!*
Cocca-Leffler, Maryann. *Janine*
   Janine and the field day finish
Cole, Henry. *Eddie the bully*
Compton, Joanne. *Ashpet*
Cuyler, Margery. *Kindness is cooler, Mrs. Ruler*
de la Peña, Matt. *Last stop on Market Street*
dePaola, Tomie. *Look and be grateful*
Dewan, Ted. *One true bear*
Dudley, Rebecca. *Hank finds an egg*
Earnhardt, Donna W. *Being Frank*
Edwards, Nancy. *Glenna's seeds*
Ehrlich, Nikki. *Twindergarten*
Elliott, Zetta. *Melena's jubilee*
Evans, Richard Paul. *The light of Christmas*
Fackelmayer, Regina. *The gifts*
Fields, Terri. *One good deed*
Gainer, Cindy. *I'm like you, you're like me*
Grimm, Jacob and Wilhelm. *The golden goose*
Harry, Rebecca. *Snow Bunny's Christmas wish*
Hasler, Eveline. *A tale of two brothers*
Henn, Sophy. *Pass it on*
Hennessy, B. G. *Because of you*
Heyward, Du Bose. *The country bunny and the little gold shoes*
Holmquist, Delano. *SantaSaurus*
Idle, Molly. *Flora and the penguin*
Isern, Susanna. *The lonely mailman*
Jantzen, Doug. *Henry Hyena, why won't you laugh?*
Jiménez, Francisco. *The Christmas gift / El regalo de Navidad*
Johnson, Grace. *The candle in the window*
Jules, Jacqueline. *No English*
Juster, Norton. *The odious ogre*
Kasza, Keiko. *Ready for anything*
Kelly, Mij. *Friendly Day*
Kirk, Daniel. *Ten thank-you letters*
Kroll, Virginia L. *Good neighbor Nicholas*
Lamstein, Sarah Marwil. *I like your buttons!*
McCourt, Lisa. *Chicken soup for little souls: The Goodness Gorillas*
   Chicken soup for little souls: The never-forgotten doll
MacDonald, Margaret Read. *Slop!*

McDonnell, Patrick. *Thank you and good night*
McKinley, Cindy. *One smile*
McNaughton, Janet. *Brave Jack and the unicorn*
Millner, Denene. *Early Sunday morning*
Munsch, Robert N. *David's father*
Murphy, Mary. *How kind*
Muth, Jon J. *Zen socks*
Neal, Kate Jane. *Words and your heart*
Nelson, Kadir. *If you plant a seed*
O'Callahan, Jay. *Raspberries!*
Orloff, Karen Kaufman. *Miles of smiles*
Ormondroyd, Edward. *Theodore*
Proimos, James. *Paulie Pastrami achieves world peace*
Reynolds, Aaron. *Nerdy birdy*
Robberecht, Thierry. *Sam's new friend*
Roberts, Justin. *The smallest girl in the smallest grade*
Rohmer, Harriet. *Atariba and Niguayona*
Rylant, Cynthia. *If you'll be my Valentine*
San Souci, Robert D. *The talking eggs*
Sauer, Tammi. *Ginny Louise and the school showdown*
Say, Allen. *The boy in the garden*
Schnur, Steven. *The tie man's miracle*
Schotter, Roni. *Captain Snap and the children of Vinegar Lane*
Schroeder, Alan. *The stone lion*
Schwartz, Howard. *Gathering sparks*
Scotton, Rob. *Splat says thank you!*
Seuss, Dr. *Horton hears a Who!*
Silverman, Erica. *Gittel's hands*
Simmons, Steven J. *Alice and Greta*
Simon, Richard. *Oskar and the eight blessings*
Smith, Monique Gray. *You hold me up*
Spelman, Cornelia Maude. *When I care about others*
Spinelli, Eileen. *Thankful*
Steig, William. *Wizzil*
Stein, David Ezra. *Because Amelia smiled*
Steptoe, John. *Mufaro's beautiful daughters*
Stock, Catherine. *Secret Valentine*
Stroud, Bettye. *Down home at Miss Dessa's*
Thong, Roseanne. *Fly free!*
Toscano, Charles. *Papa's pastries*
Ungar, Richard. *Rachel's gift*
Van Dusen, Chris. *Hattie and Hudson*
Wallace, Nancy Elizabeth. *The kindness quilt*
Watkins, Rowboat. *Rude cakes*
Weatherford, Carole Boston. *Be a King: Dr. Martin Luther King Jr.'s dream and you*
Wheeler, Eliza. *Miss Maple's seeds*
Wilde, Oscar. *The selfish giant*, ill. by S. Saelig Gallagher
   The selfish giant, ill. by Fabian Negrin
   The selfish giant, ill. by Lisbeth Zwerger
Wojciechowski, Susan. *A fine St. Patrick's Day*
Zolotow, Charlotte. *I know a lady*

Character traits – kindness to animals

Aardema, Verna. *Koi and the kola nuts*
Adderson, Caroline. *Norman, speak!*
Aesop. *Androcles and the lion*, ill. by Dennis Nolan
   Androcles and the lion, ill. by Janet Stevens
   Androcles and the lion: and other Aesop fables
Applegate, Katherine. *Ivan*
Arnosky, Jim. *Slow down for manatees*
Baek, Matthew J. *Be gentle with the dog, dear*
Banks, Kate. *Pup and bear*
Bodkin, Odds. *The crane wife*
Bonnet, Rosalinde. *Daddy Honk Honk!*
Brett, Jan. *Mossy*

Britt, Chris. *The most perfect snowman*
Brunhoff, Laurent de. *Babar's little girl*
Bunting, Eve. *Night tree*
Burleigh, Robert. *Trapped! a whale's rescue*
Butterworth, Nick. *One snowy night*
Camcam, Princesse. *Fox's garden*
Capucilli, Alyssa Satin. *Tulip loves Rex*
Chall, Marsha Wilson. *Pick a pup*
Chamberlain, Margaret. *Please don't tease Tootsie*
Chichester Clark, Emma. *Piper*
Church, Caroline Jayne. *Digby takes charge*
Claire, Céline. *Shelter*
Collicott, Sharleen. *Toestomper and the caterpillars*
Cordell, Matthew. *Wolf in the snow*
Cousteau, Philippe. *Follow the moon home*
Cowcher, Helen. *Desert elephants*
Cox, Lynne. *Elizabeth, queen of the seas*
Daly, Niki. *Thank you, Jackson*
Daugherty, James Henry. *Andy and the lion*
Davis, Anne. *No dogs allowed!*
Dennis, Major Brian. *Nubs*
Dockray, Tracy. *The lost and found pony*
Dubuc, Marianne. *The lion and the bird*
Elschner, Geraldine. *Like a wolf*
Evans, Lezlie. *Finding Christmas*
Faulconer, Maria. *A mom for Umande*
Federspiel, Jurg. *Alligator Mike*
Ferry, Beth. *A small blue whale*
Fischer, Ellen. *Latke, the lucky dog*
Foreman, Michael. *Tufty*
Furstinger, Nancy. *Maggie's second chance*
Galing, Ed. *Tony*
Gerstein, Mordicai. *The boy and the whale*
Gianferrari, Maria. *Hello goodbye dog*
Gottfried, Maya. *Our farm*
Graham, Bob. *How to heal a broken wing*
Grover, Jan Zitz. *A home for Dakota*
Hatkoff, Craig, et al. *Winter's tail*
Havill, Juanita. *Call the horse lucky*
Henrichs, Wendy. *When Anju loved being an elephant*
Hernandez, Leeza. *Cat napped*
Hest, Amy. *Charley's first night*
Hill, Meggan. *Nico and Lola*
Ho, Jannie. *Bear and Chicken*
Hobbie, Holly. *A cat named Swan*
Hoose, Philip M. *Hey little ant*
Jackson, Ellen. *Abe Lincoln loved animals*
Jackson, Emma. *A home for Dixie*
Jay, Alison. *Out of the blue*
Jiang, Ji-li. *Lotus and Feather*
Johnson, Mariana Ruiz. *I know a bear*
Joosse, Barbara. *Nugget and Darling*
Juan, Ana. *The pet shop revolution*
Keats, Ezra Jack. *Jennie's hat*
Kim, Aram. *Cat on the bus*
Kimmel, Eric A. *The birds' gift*
Kirk, Daniel. *Rhino in the house*
Klise, Kate. *Stay: a girl, a dog, a bucket list*
Knudsen, Michelle. *Big Mean Mike*
Ko, Sangmi. *A dog wearing shoes*
Lamstein, Sarah Marwil. *Big night for salamanders*
Lears, Laurie. *Waiting for Mr. Goose*
London, Jonathan. *Jackrabbit*
Luján, Jorge. *Stephen and the beetle*
Macaulay, David. *Angelo*
McCardie, Amanda. *Our very own dog*
McCully, Emily Arnold. *Clara*
McDonald, Megan. *Shoe dog*
McDonnell, Flora. *I love animals*

McMillan, Bruce. *Nights of the pufflings*
McPhail, David. *The bear's toothache*
McQuinn, Anna. *Lola gets a cat*
Mantchev, Lisa. *Someday, narwhal*
Martin, Rafe. *The language of birds*
  The Shark God
Marzollo, Jean. *Pierre the penguin*
Meddaugh, Susan. *Tree of birds*
Miller, Edna. *Mousekin's frosty friend*
Mitchell, Hazel. *Toby*
Moore, Eva. *Lucky ducklings*
Mora, Pat. *The song of Francis and the animals*
Newman, Lesléa. *Ketzel, the cat who composed*
Nogales, Jill. *Zebra on the go*
Numeroff, Laura Joffe. *If you give a cat a cupcake*
  If you give a dog a donut
  If you give a moose a muffin
  If you give a mouse a cookie
  If you give a pig a pancake
Parker, Danny. *Parachute*
Peet, Bill. *Huge Harold*
Peet, Mal. *Cloud tea monkeys*
Perepeczko, Jenny. *Moses: the true story of an elephant baby*
Pericoli, Matteo. *The true story of Stellina*
Perkins, Lynne Rae. *Frank and Lucky get schooled*
Pinkwater, Daniel. *Rainy morning*
Polacco, Patricia. *Remembering Vera*
Reed, Lynn Rowe. *Roscoe and the pelican rescue*
Root, Barry. *Gumbrella*
Roth, Ruby. *V is for vegan*
Rumford, James. *Dog-of-the-Sea-Waves*
Ryder, Joanne. *Each living thing*
Rylant, Cynthia. *The bookshop dog*
Sampson, Michael R. *Caddie, the golf dog*
Sayre, April Pulley. *Turtle, turtle, watch out!*, ill. by Lee Christiansen
  Turtle, turtle, watch out!, ill. by Annie Patterson
Simont, Marc. *The stray dog*
Sirotich, Erica. *Found dogs*
Soros, Barbara. *Tenzin's deer*
Soule, Jean Conder. *Never tease a weasel*
Staake, Bob. *Beachy and me*
Stead, Philip C. *The only fish in the sea*
Strand, Keith. *Grandfather's Christmas tree*
Tada, Satoshi. *Mr. Beetle*
Thayer, Jane. *Part-time dog*
Thomas, Jane Resh. *Scaredy dog*
Tompert, Ann. *The pied piper of Peru*
Ts'o, Pauline. *Whispers of the wolf*
Turkle, Brinton. *Thy friend, Obadiah*
Van Allsburg, Chris. *The misadventures of Sweetie Pie*
Ward, Lynd. *The biggest bear*
Wardlaw, Lee. *Won Ton*
Yagawa, Sumiko. *The crane wife*
Yuly, Toni. *The Jelly Bean tree*

Character traits – laziness

Cohen, Caron Lee. *Digger Pig and the turnip*
Davies, Gill. *Can't, don't, won't*
dePaola, Tomie. *Jamie O'Rourke and the big potato*
  Jamie O'Rourke and the pooka
Egan, Tim. *The pink refrigerator*
Finn, Isobel. *The very lazy ladybug*
Grimm, Jacob and Wilhelm. *The three spinning fairies*
Hogg, Gary. *Look what the cat dragged in!*
Johnson, D. B. *Four legs bad, two legs good!*

Jordan, Mary Ellen. *Lazy Daisy, cranky Frankie*
Ketteman, Helen. *Armadilly chili*
Lester, Helen. *Score one for the sloths*
The little red hen. *The little red hen*, ill. by Byron Barton
　The little red hen, ill. by Emily Bolam
　The little red hen, ill. by Paul Galdone
　Little red hen
　The little red hen, ill. by Jerry Pinkney
　The little red hen, ill. by Kate Slater
　The little red hen, ill. by Annie West
　The little red hen, ill. by Margot Zemach
　The little red hen: an old fable
　The Little Red Hen and the Passover matzah
　The Little Red Hen makes a pizza
McGrath, Barbara Barbieri. *The little gray bunny*
　The little green witch
Murphy, Jim. *Fergus and the Night-Demon*
Paul, Ann Whitford. *Mañana Iguana*
Root, Phyllis. *Aunt Nancy and Cousin Lazybones*
San Souci, Robert D. *The hired hand*
Snyder, Dianne. *The boy of the three-year nap*
Stampler, Ann Redisch. *Shlemazel and the remarkable spoon of Pohost*

Character traits – loyalty

Aliki. *The two of them*
Bridwell, Norman. *Clifford goes to Hollywood*
Craft, Mahlon F. *Beauty and the beast*
Cullen, Lynn. *The mightiest heart*
Gregory, Nan. *How Smudge came*
Hautzig, Deborah. *Beauty and the beast*
Jennings, Sharon. *Priscilla and Rosy*
Jones, Ursula. *Beauty and the beast*
Lee, H. Chuku. *Beauty and the beast: a retelling*
Lester, Alison. *Running with the horses*
McGhee, Alison. *Always*
Mayer, Marianna. *Beauty and the beast*
Nelson, Marilyn. *Snook alone*
Pollock, Penny. *The turkey girl*
Potter, Beatrix. *The tale of the faithful dove*
Sabuda, Robert. *Beauty and the beast: a pop-up book of the classic fairy tale*
Tonatiuh, Duncan. *The princess and the warrior*
Waite, Michael P. *Jojofu*

Character traits – luck

Addy, Sharon Hart. *Lucky Jake*
Alexander, Lloyd. *The house Gobbaleen*
Aliki. *Three gold pieces*
Bateman, Teresa. *Fiona's luck*
Borden, Louise. *Kindergarten luck*
Brown, Margaret Wise. *Wheel on the chimney*
Christian, Mary Blount. *If not for the calico cat*
D'Amico, Carmela. *Ella sets sail*
Foley, Greg. *Good luck Bear*
Friday, Mary Ellen. *It's a bad day*
Harjo, Joy. *The good luck cat*
Landström, Lena. *Pom and Pim*
Lin, Grace. *Fortune cookie fortunes*
McGuirk, Leslie. *Lucky Tucker*
Mulryan, Doreen. *Lucky Ducky*
Nishizuka, Koko. *The beckoning cat*
Polacco, Patricia. *Bun Bun Button*
Riddell, Chris. *Platypus and the lucky day*
Sasso, Sandy Eisenberg. *Butterflies under our hats*
Seibold, J. Otto. *Lost sloth*

Seki, Sunny. *The tale of the lucky cat*
Seuss, Dr. *Did I ever tell you how lucky you are?*
Soto, Gary. *Lucky Luis*
Stampler, Ann Redisch. *Shlemazel and the remarkable spoon of Pohost*
Sutton, Jane. *The trouble with cauliflower*

Character traits – meanness

Brown, Marc. *D. W., go to your room!*
Debecker, Benoît. *The naughty prince*
Gantos, Jack. *Rotten Ralph's rotten Christmas*
　Rotten Ralph's show and tell
　Rotten Ralph's trick or treat
　Worse than Rotten Ralph
Goble, Paul. *The lost children*
Hasler, Eveline. *A tale of two brothers*
McKissack, Patricia C. *Ol' Clip-Clop*
Morrison, Toni. *The book of mean people*
O'Malley, Kevin. *Humpty Dumpty egg-splodes*
Prelutsky, Jack. *The mean old mean hyena*
Roberts, Lynn. *Rapunzel, a groovy fairy tale*
San Souci, Robert D. *Sootface*
Sauer, Tammi. *Ginny Louise and the school showdown*
Seuss, Dr. *How the Grinch stole Christmas*
Silverman, Erica. *Gittel's hands*
Simmons, Steven J. *Alice and Greta*
Somers, Kevin. *Meaner than meanest*
Steptoe, John. *Mufaro's beautiful daughters*
Stevenson, James. *Fried feathers for Thanksgiving*
　Happy Valentine's Day, Emma!
　The worst person's Christmas
Sturm, James. *Birdsong: a story in pictures*
Wooldridge, Connie Nordhielm. *Wicked Jack*

Character traits – optimism

Aliki. *The twelve months*
Carlson, Nancy. *Smile a lot!*
Cocca-Leffler, Maryann. *Rain brings frogs*
Dominguez, Angela. *Sing, don't cry*
Elliott, Zetta. *Melena's jubilee*
Hubbard, Woodleigh Marx. *All that you are*
Krauss, Ruth. *The carrot seed*
Krosoczka, Jarrett J. *It's tough to lose your balloon*
Lionni, Leo. *Theodore and the talking mushroom*
Lloyd-Jones, Sally. *Poor Doreen*
Mack, Jeff. *Good news, bad news*
Martin, Stephen W. *Charlotte and the rock*
Otoshi, Kathryn. *Beautiful hands*
Peet, Bill. *The Whingdingdilly*
Sauer, Tammi. *Ginny Louise and the school showdown*
Schwartz, Roslyn. *The mole sisters and the piece of moss*

Character traits – orderliness

Blankenship, Lee Ann. *Mr. Tuggle's troubles*
Bottner, Barbara. *Wallace's lists*
Braybrooks, Ann. *Plenty of pockets*
Eaton, Jason Carter. *Great, now we've got barbarians!*
Elliot, David. *Henry's map*
Glaser, Linda. *Mrs. Greenberg's messy Hanukkah*
Gravett, Emily. *Tidy*
Guest, Elissa Haden. *Harriet's had enough!*
Harris, Robie H. *I love messes!*
Hassett, John. *Mouse in the house*
Hodgkinson, Leigh. *Troll swap*
Kamish, Daniel. *Diggy Dan*
MacDonald, Alan. *Beware of the bears!*

McDonnell, Patrick. *A perfectly messed-up story*
McElmurry, Jill. *Mess pets*
McKissack, Patricia C. *Messy Bessey*
Malbrough, Mike. *Marigold bakes a cake*
Mariconda, Barbara. *Sort it out!*
Meade, Rita. *Edward gets messy*
Odone, Jamison. *Mole had everything*
O'Malley, Kevin. *Bud*
Piers, Helen. *Who's in my bed?*
Prigger, Mary Skillings. *Aunt Minnie McGranahan*
Root, Phyllis. *Mrs. Potter's pig*
Schotter, Roni. *Captain Bob takes flight*
Schwab, Eva. *Robert and the Robot*
Simon, Charnan. *Messy Molly*
Teague, Mark. *Pigsty*
Viorst, Judith. *Super-completely and totally the messiest*
Yolen, Jane. *How do dinosaurs clean their rooms?*

Character traits – ostracism *see* Character
traits – being different

Character traits – patience, impatience

Alakija, Polly. *Counting chickens*
Antony, Steve. *I'll wait, Mr. Panda*
Arnold, Marsha Diane. *Waiting for snow*
Asim, Jabari. *Preaching to the chickens*
Barton, Bethany. *This monster cannot wait!*
Bogan, Paulette. *Virgil and Owen stick together*
Corderoy, Tracey. *Now!*
Dunrea, Olivier. *Ollie*
Ehrlich, Amy. *Baby Dragon*
Elliott, David. *Nobody's perfect*
Fogliano, Julie. *If you want to see a whale*
Hannigan, Katherine. *Gwendolyn Grace*
Henkes, Kevin. *Waiting*
Higgins, Ryan T. *Be quiet!*
Himmelman, John. *Katie loves the kittens*
Horowitz, Dave. *Soon, Baboon, soon*
Jordan, Laurie. *Yawning yoga*
Kaplan, Michael B. *Betty Bunny loves chocolate cake*
Kleber, Dori. *More-igami*
Lemniscates. *Silence*
Leonetti, Mike. *Swinging for the fences*
MacKay, Elly. *If you hold a seed*
Magruder, Nilah. *How to find a fox*
Marlowe, Sara. *No ordinary apple*
May, Eleanor. *Albert's amazing snail*
Menchin, Scott. *What are you waiting for?*
Mollel, Tololwa M. *Subira subira*
Morgan-Vanroyen, Mary. *Patient Rosie*
Muth, Jon J. *Zen socks*
Papp, Lisa. *Madeline Finn and the library dog*
Paschkis, Julie. *Magic spell*
Paul, Miranda. *Are we pears yet?*
Portis, Antoinette. *Now*
    Wait
Poydar, Nancy. *Mailbox magic*
Reynolds, Peter H. *Happy dreamer*
Rockwell, Anne. *Chip and the karate kick*
Ross, Tony. *I want snow!*
Russo, Brian. *Yoga Bunny*
Schachner, Judith Byron. *Sarabella's thinking cap*
Schwartz, Amy. *I can't wait!*
Slack, Michael. *Shorty and Clem*
Sperring, Mark. *How many sleeps 'til my birthday?*
Stewart, Whitney. *Meditation is an open sky*
Train, Mary. *Time for the fair*

Usher, Sam. *Rain*
    Snow
Verde, Susan. *I am yoga*
Walters, Catherine. *When will it be spring?*
Wells, Rosemary. *Max's breakfast*
Whitford, Rebecca. *Little yoga*
    Sleepy little yoga
Yuly, Toni. *The Jelly Bean tree*
Ziefert, Harriet. *Robin, where are you?*

Character traits – perfectionism

Elliott, David. *Nobody's perfect*
Fearnley, Jan. *The search for the perfect child*
Harris, Peter. *Perfect Prudence*
Kono, Erin Eitter. *Caterina and the perfect party*
Malbrough, Mike. *Marigold bakes a cake*
Pett, Mark. *The girl who never made mistakes*
Ziefert, Harriet. *The princess and the peas and carrots*

Character traits – perseverance

Aliki. *A weed is a flower*
Asim, Jabari. *Fifty cents and a dream*
Balcziak, Bill. *John Henry*
Barber, Tiki. *Teammates*
Beaty, Andrea. *Ada Twist, scientist*
    Rosie Revere, engineer
Beck, Robert. *A bunny in the ballet*
Belloni, Giulia. *Anything is possible*
Best, Cari. *Sally Jean, the Bicycle Queen*
Bildner, Phil. *Marvelous Cornelius*
Blades, Ann. *Mary of mile 18*
Braun, Sebastien. *Whoosh and Chug!*
Braver, Vanita. *Madison and the two wheeler*
Brown, Don. *Teedie*
Bryant, Jen. *A splash of red*
Carle, Eric. *The very clumsy click beetle*
Carter, Anne Laurel. *The F team*
Corderoy, Tracey. *The magical snow garden*
Curtis, Jamie Lee. *My brave year of firsts*
Cutler, Jane. *Guttersnipe*
Davis, Aubrey. *A hen for Izzy Pippik*
Dempsey, Kristy. *Surfer chick*
DiCamillo, Kate. *La la la*
Drummond, Allan. *Green city*
Engle, Margarita. *All the way to Havana*
Francis, Lee DeCora. *Kunu's basket*
Garland, Michael. *Hooray José!*
Hodge, Deborah. *Lily and the mixed-up letters*
Hubbard, Crystal. *Catching the moon: the story of a
    young girl's baseball dream*
Isadora, Rachel. *Luke goes to bat*
Isern, Susanna. *Middle bear*
Jordan, Deloris. *Dream big*
Judge, Lita. *Flight school*
Kaplan, Michael B. *Betty Bunny wants a goal*
Keats, Ezra Jack. *John Henry*
Keller, Shana. *Ticktock Banneker's clock*
Kerley, Barbara. *Brave like me*
Kessler, Cristina. *The best beekeeper of Lalibela*
Kimmel, Elizabeth Cody. *A taste of freedom*
Kinerk, Robert. *Clorinda*
    Clorinda takes flight
    Timothy Cox will not change his socks
Kleber, Dori. *More-igami*
Krumwiede, Lana. *Just Itzy*
Kurtz, Jane. *In the small, small night*
Lee, Spike. *Giant steps to change the world*

Lester, Julius. *John Henry*
London, Jonathan. *Where the big fish are*
MacDonald, Margaret Read. *Give up, Gecko!*
McGinty, Alice B. *Gandhi*
Malaspina, Ann. *Touch the sky*
Marcero, Deborah. *Ursa's light*
Markel, Michelle. *The fantastic jungles of Henri Rousseau*
Marshall, Linda Elovitz. *Rainbow weaver / Tejedora del arcoíris*
Mitchell, Margaree King. *Uncle Jed's barbershop*
Mortenson, Greg. *Listen to the wind*
O'Brien, Anne Sibley. *A path of stars*
O'Callahan, Jay. *Raspberries!*
Pace, Anne Marie. *Vampirina ballerina*
Pinkney, Brian. *Jojo's flying side kick*
Piper, Watty. *The little engine that could*, ill. by George Hauman
   The little engine that could, ill. by Loren Long
Polacco, Patricia. *Fiona's lace*
Potter, Alicia. *Mrs. Harkness and the panda*
Rappaport, Doreen. *Eleanor, quiet no more*
   To dare mighty things
Robertson, David A. *When we were alone*
Root, Andrew. *Hamsters don't fight fires!*
Ruzzier, Sergio. *Amandina*
Santat, Dan. *After the fall (how Humpty Dumpty got back up again)*
Saunders, Dave. *So slow!*
Savage, Stephen. *The mixed-up truck*
Schubert, Leda. *Reading to Peanut*
Seim, Donna Marie. *Where is Simon, Sandy?*
Singer, Marilyn. *Tallulah's tap shoes*
   Tallulah's toe shoes
   Tallulah's tutu
Slade, Suzanne. *With books and bricks*
Sliwerski, Jessica Reid. *Cancer hates kisses*
Spinelli, Eileen. *Sophie's masterpiece*
Steig, William. *Brave Irene*
Stewart, Amber. *Little by little*
Stone, Tanya Lee. *Who says women can't be doctors?*
Thomas, Jane Resh. *Scaredy dog*
Verde, Susan. *The water princess*
Warwick, Dionne. *Little Man*
Watanabe, Shigeo. *Where's my daddy?*
Weatherford, Carole Boston. *Be a King: Dr. Martin Luther King Jr.'s dream and you*
Wild, Margaret. *Bobbie Dazzler*
Winters, Kari-Lynn. *Gift days*
Wisnewski, Andrea. *Trio*
Young, Jessica. *Spy Guy*
Ziefert, Harriet. *Murphy jumps a hurdle*

Character traits – persistence

Adler, David A. *Helen Keller*
Agee, Jon. *Lion lessons*
Anderson, Laurie Halse. *The big cheese of Third Street*
Asim, Jabari. *Preaching to the chickens*
Bandy, Michael S. *Granddaddy's turn*
Bloom, C. P. *The Monkey goes bananas*
Blumenthal, Deborah. *Fancy party gowns*
Boiger, Alexandra. *Max and Marla*
Braun, Sebastien. *Digger and Tom!*
Breen, Steve. *Woodpecker wants a waffle*
Brown-Wood, JaNay. *Imani's moon*
Clinton, Chelsea. *She persisted*
Crow, Kristyn. *Hello, Hippo! Goodbye, Bird!*

Czernecki, Stefan. *Paper lanterns*
Daly, Cathleen. *Prudence wants a pet*
Dudley, Rebecca. *Hank finds an egg*
Edwards, Michelle. *A hat for Mrs. Goldman*
Egielski, Richard. *Itsy bitsy spider*
Gray, Karlin. *Nadia*
Gray, Kes. *Eat your peas*
Hopkins, H. Joseph. *The tree lady*
Howe, James. *Horace and Morris join the chorus (but what about Dolores?)*
Ishida, Sanae. *Little Kunoichi, the ninja girl*
Jordan, Deloris. *Michael's golden rules*
Keating, Jess. *Shark lady*
Keller, Holly. *Pearl's new skates*
Kennedy, Kim. *Hee-Haw-Dini and the Great Zambini*
Koehler, Lora. *The little snowplow*
Krull, Kathleen. *Hillary Rodham Clinton: dreams taking flight*
Lang, Heather. *Fearless flyer*
   Swimming with sharks
Liu, Cynthea. *Bike on, Bear!*
McCully, Emily Arnold. *Mouse practice*
McGhee, Alison. *Only a witch can fly*
Mortensen, Lori. *Cindy Moo*
Murphy, Stuart J. *Same old horse*
O'Connor, Jane. *Ready, set, skip!*
Palatini, Margie. *The perfect pet*
Paul, Chris. *Long shot*
Penner, Fred. *The cat came back*
Poydar, Nancy. *No fair science fair*
Ramsden, Ashley. *Seven fathers*
Raschka, Chris. *Everyone can learn to ride a bicycle*
Ray, Mary Lyn. *A violin for Elva*
Rex, Adam. *XO, Ox*
Rockliff, Mara. *Me and Momma and Big John*
Rodriguez, Alex. *Out of the ballpark*
Savage, Stephen. *Little Plane learns to write*
Schachner, Judith Byron. *Yo, Vikings*
Shannon, George. *Turkey Tot*
Siomades, Lorianne. *The itsy bitsy spider*
Spires, Ashley. *The most magnificent thing*
   The thing Lou couldn't do
Stanton, Elizabeth Rose. *Peddles*
Teague, David. *The red hat*
Trapani, Iza. *The itsy bitsy spider*
Tryon, Leslie. *The thumbtack dancer*
Uegaki, Chieri. *Hana Hashimoto, sixth violin*
Van Allsburg, Chris. *Queen of the falls*
Van Leeuwen, Jean. *Sorry*
Verdick, Elizabeth. *Small Walt*
Willard, Nancy. *Gum*
Woo, Alan. *Maggie's chopsticks*
Yamaguchi, Kristi. *Dream big, little pig!*
Young, Ed. *Hook*
Zagwÿn, Deborah Turney. *Apple batter*

Character traits – practicality

Aylesworth, Jim. *Mother Halverson's new cat*
Gág, Wanda. *Millions of cats*
Modell, Frank. *One zillion valentines*
Wells, Rosemary. *Otto runs for President*
   Otto se presenta para presidente / Otto runs for President

Character traits – pride

Andersen, Hans Christian. *The dinosaur's new clothes*

The emperor's new clothes, ill. by Angela Barrett
The emperor's new clothes, ill. by Virginia Lee
   Burton
The emperor's new clothes, ill. by Robert Byrd
The emperor's new clothes, ill. by Serena Curmi
The emperor's new clothes, ill. by Charlene DeLage
The emperor's new clothes, ill. by Jack Delano
The emperor's new clothes, ill. by Anne Rockwell
The emperor's new clothes, ill. by Janet Stevens
The emperor's new clothes, ill. by Eve Tharlet
The emperor's new clothes: a tale set in China
Balcziak, Bill. *John Henry*
Calmenson, Stephanie. *The principal's new clothes*
Cousins, Lucy. *I'm the best*
Duvoisin, Roger Antoine. *Petunia*
Evans, Richard Paul. *The tower*
Grimm, Jacob and Wilhelm. *The water of life*
Hillenbrand, Jane. *What a treasure!*
Hughes, Langston. *My people*
Jackson, Chris. *The Gaggle sisters river tour*
Johnson, Rebecca. *The proud pelican's secret*
Keats, Ezra Jack. *John Henry*
Kirk, Daniel. *Keisha Ann can!*
Lester, Julius. *John Henry*
McCaughrean, Geraldine. *How the reindeer got their
   antlers*
Naberhaus, Sarvinder. *Blue sky white stars*
Perlman, Janet. *The Emperor Penguin's new clothes*
Quattlebaum, Mary. *Sparks fly high*
Radunsky, Vladimir. *One: a nice story about an awful
   braggart*
Ramos, Mario. *I am so handsome*
Rumford, James. *Nine animals and the well*
Rylant, Cynthia. *Mr. Griggs' work*
Sasso, Sandy Eisenberg. *God said amen*
Schwartz, Amy. *Annabelle Swift, kindergartner*
Sharmat, Marjorie Weinman. *I'm terrific*
Ward, Helen. *The rooster and the fox*
Yolen, Jane. *King Long Shanks*

Character traits – questioning

Adler, David A. *A little at a time*
Beaty, Andrea. *Ada Twist, scientist*
Blackall, Sophie. *Are you awake?*
   The baby tree
Britt, Paige. *Why am I me?*
Brown, Calef. *Boy wonders*
Calmenson, Stephanie. *Ollie's class trip*
   Ollie's school day
Campbell, K. G. *The mermaid and the shoe*
Carter, David A. *Whoo? Whoo?*
Catalanotto, Peter. *Question Boy meets Little Miss
   Know-It-All*
Chang, Victoria. *Is Mommy?*
Cole, Rachael. *City moon*
Coyle, Carmela LaVigna. *Do princesses make happy
   campers?*
   Do princesses really kiss frogs?
   Do super heroes have teddy bears?
Crumpacker, Bunny. *Alexander's pretending day*
Erlbruch, Wolf. *The big question*
Gay, Marie-Louise. *Any questions?*
Gonyea, Mark. *The spooky box*
Goodhart, Pippa. *You choose*
Gorbachev, Valeri. *Where is the apple pie?*
Hines, Anna Grossnickle. *Even if I spill my milk?*
Holub, Joan. *Why do cats meow?*
   Why do dogs bark?

Hornsey, Chris. *Why do I have to eat off the floor?*
Jackson, Richard. *Snow scene*
Jenkins, Steve. *How to swallow a pig*
   Who am I? an animal guessing game
Kuskin, Karla. *Green as a bean*
Laden, Nina. *Once upon a memory*
Lionni, Leo. *Tico and the golden wings*
Luthardt, Kevin. *Flying*
McClure, Nikki. *Mama, is it summer yet?*
Mamada, Mineko. *Which is round? which is bigger?*
Marshall, Linda Elovitz. *The passover lamb*
Menchin, Scott. *Taking a bath with the dog and other
   things that make me happy*
   What are you waiting for?
   What if everything had legs?
Miller, Margaret. *Can you guess?*
Mitton, Tony. *A very curious bear*
Munro, Roxie. *Hatch!*
Murphy, Mary. *Koala and the flower*
Offill, Jenny. *11 experiments that failed*
Pfister, Marcus. *Questions, questions*
Phillips, Christopher. *Ceci Ann's day of why*
Raab, Brigitte. *Where does pepper come from?*
Raschka, Chris. *Little black crow*
Reibstein, Mark. *Wabi Sabi*
Roderick, Stacey. *Ocean animals from head to tail*
Rosenthal, Amy Krouse. *It's not fair!*
   Yes Day!
Rossell, Judith. *Oliver*
Simpson-Enock, Sarah. *Mommy, Mommy, what's in
   your tummy?*
Slater, Dashka. *The antlered ship*
Sperring, Mark. *I'll catch you if you fall*
Staake, Bob. *The Book of Gold*
Steven, Kenneth. *The biggest thing in the world*
Stewart, Melissa. *Can an aardvark bark?*
Stott, Ann. *Always*
Tallec, Olivier. *Who what where?*
Taylor, Barbara. *I wonder why zippers have teeth and
   other questions about inventions*
Torrey, Richard. *Why?*
Tucker, Kathy. *Do cowboys ride bikes?*
Vega, Denise. *Grandmother, have the angels come?*
Waber, Bernard. *Ask me*
Walsh, Melanie. *Do lions live on lily pads?*
Weeks, Sarah. *My somebody special*
Wheeler, Valerie. *Yes, please! no, thank you!*
Wilson, Karma. *Mama, why?*
Wormell, Mary. *Why not?*
Young, Ruth. *Who says moo?*

Character traits – responsibility

Bowen, Anne. *Scooter in the outside*
Cutler, Jane. *Guttersnipe*
Davies, Stephen. *Don't spill the milk!*
Godin, Thelma Lynne. *The hula-hoopin' queen*
Gorbachev, Valeri. *Pizza-pie snowman*
Graves, Keith. *Pet boy*
Hakte, Ben. *Julia's house for lost creatures*
Hawkins, Emily. *Little snow goose*
Johnson, Jen Cullerton. *Seeds of change*
Killen, Nicola. *Not me!*
Kroll, Virginia L. *Cristina keeps a promise*
   Jason takes responsibility
Liersch, Anne. *Nell and Fluffy*
Long, Ethan. *Snickerdoodle takes the cake*
Mahoney, Daniel J. *The Saturday escape*
Napoli, Donna Jo. *Mama Miti*

Park, Linda Sue. *The firekeeper's son*
Rudy, Maggie. *I wish I had a pet*
Ryan, Pam Muñoz. *Tony Baloney: buddy trouble*
Schachner, Judith Byron. *The Grannyman*
Schwartz, Howard. *Gathering sparks*
Stephens, Helen. *Ruby and the muddy dog*
Twohy, Mike. *Wake up, Rupert!*
Watts, Bernadette. *The golden plate*
Winter, Jeanette. *Wangari's trees of peace*
Yoon, Salina. *Found*
Zuppardi, Sam. *Things to do with Dad*

Character traits – selfishness

Andersen, Hans Christian. *The swineherd*
Barnett, Mac. *The magic word*
Blabey, Aaron. *Pig the elf*
   Pig the pug
Davidson, Ellen Dee. *Princess Justina Albertina*
Deacon, Alexis. *Cheese belongs to you!*
Demi. *One grain of rice*
Gantos, Jack. *Back to school for Rotten Ralph*
Gravett, Emily. *Bear and Hare: share!*
Grindley, Sally. *Can we play too, Piglittle?*
Henkes, Kevin. *A weekend with Wendell*
Jin, Susie Lee. *Mine!*
Kimmel, Eric A. *The mysterious guests*
Lester, Helen. *Me first*
   Princess Penelope's parrot
Lipkind, William. *Finders keepers*
Long, Ethan. *Snickerdoodle takes the cake*
Meserve, Adria. *No room for Napoleon*
Peet, Bill. *The ant and the elephant*
Rolli, Jennifer Hansen. *Just one more*
Rosen, Michael. *This is our house*
Schroeder, Alan. *The stone lion*
Stein, Mathilde. *Mine!*
Watkins, Rowboat. *Rude cakes*
Wilde, Oscar. *The selfish giant*, ill. by S. Saelig
   Gallagher
   The selfish giant, ill. by Fabian Negrin
   The selfish giant, ill. by Lisbeth Zwerger
Winters, Kari-Lynn. *Bad pirate*
Wisdom, Jude. *Whatever Wanda wanted*
Yaccarino, Dan. *Happyland: big berry*

Character traits – shyness

Adams, Sarah. *Dave and Violet*
Alter, Anna. *Disappearing Desmond*
Bell, Cece. *Chuck and Woodchuck*
Bracken, Beth. *Too shy for show-and-tell*
Bunge, Daniela. *Cherry time*
Child, Lauren. *Maude*
Choldenko, Gennifer. *A giant crush*
   Louder, Lili
D'Amico, Carmela. *Ella sets the stage*
Desbordes, Astrid. *Edmond, the moonlit party*
Devlin, Wende. *Cranberry Valentine*
Freedman, Deborah. *Shy*
Goble, Paul. *Love flute*
Goldfinger, Jennifer P. *Hello, my name is Tiger*
Gorbachev, Valeri. *Chicken chickens go to school*
Graham, Bob. *Dimity Dumpty*
Haseley, Dennis. *The invisible moose*
Hodgkinson, Jo. *A big day for Migs*
Hurwitz, Johanna. *Mighty Monty*
Hutchins, Pat. *Titch and Daisy*
Jarman, Julia. *Two shy pandas*

Keats, Ezra Jack. *Louie*
Kirk, Daniel. *Library mouse*
   Library mouse: a friend's tale
Lin, Grace. *Lissy's friends*
Lucas, David. *Halibut Jackson*
Lurie, Susan. *Will you be my friend?*
Maccarone, Grace. *Miss Lina's ballerinas and the
   prince*
McCourt, Lisa. *Chicken soup for little souls: The new
   kid and the cookie thief*
Miller, Pat Zietlow. *Sophie's squash go to school*
Montenegro, Laura Nyman. *A bird about to sing*
Morgan, Michaela. *Dear bunny*
Mortensen, Lori. *Chicken Lily*
Na, Il Sung. *Bird, balloon, Bear*
Newman, Jeff. *The boys*
Paraskevas, Betty. *Chocolate at the Four Seasons*
Pearson, Susan. *Slugs in love*
Polacco, Patricia. *Mr. Wayne's masterpiece*
Pomranz, Craig. *Made by Raffi*
Potter, Alicia. *Miss Hazeltine's Home for Shy and
   Fearful Cats*
Puttock, Simon. *Mouse's first night at Moonlight
   School*
Rappaport, Doreen. *Eleanor, quiet no more*
Rockwell, Anne. *Big George*
Rosenberry, Vera. *Vera's first day of school*
Ruzzier, Sergio. *Amandina*
Sattler, Jennifer. *Pig kahuna: who's that pig?*
Schmid, Paul. *Oliver and his alligator*
Song, Mika. *Tea with Oliver*
Spinelli, Eileen. *When no one is watching*
Srinivasan, Divya. *Octopus alone*
Stephens, Ann Marie. *Cy makes a friend*
Thompson, Lauren. *Wee little lamb*
Turnbull, Victoria. *The sea tiger*
Twohy, Mike. *Poindexter makes a friend*
Udry, Janice May. *What Mary Jo shared*
Weinstone, David. *Music class today!*
Wells, Rosemary. *Say hello, Sophie!*
Winter, Jeanette. *Mr. Cornell's dream boxes*
Yashima, Taro. *Crow boy*
Zolotow, Charlotte. *A tiger called Thomas*, ill. by
   Diana Cain Bluthenthal
   A tiger called Thomas, ill. by Catherine Stock

Character traits – smallness

Adoff, Jaime. *Small fry*
Alborough, Jez. *Tall*
Andersen, Hans Christian. *Sylvia Long's
   Thumbelina*
   Thumbelina, ill. by Charlene DeLage
   Thumbelina, ill. by Demi
   Thumbelina, ill. by Arlene Graston
   Thumbelina, ill. by Bagram Ibatoulline
   Thumbelina, ill. by Susan Jeffers
   Thumbelina, ill. by Lauren A. Mills
   Thumbeline
Aston, Dianna Hutts. *Not so tall for six*
Baguley, Elizabeth. *Ready, steady, ghost!*
Balouch, Kristen. *The little little girl with the big big
   voice*
Base, Graeme. *Little elephants*
Battersby, Katherine. *Brave Squish Rabbit*
   Squish Rabbit
Bell, Cece. *Itty Bitty*
Bentley, Jonathan. *Little big*
Bogan, Paulette. *Lulu the big little chick*

Braun, Sebastien. *Toot and Pop!*
Bright, Rachel. *The lion inside*
Brown-Wood, JaNay. *Imani's moon*
Cali, Davide. *The tiny tale of Little Pea*
Cantrell, Charlie. *A friend for Einstein*
Carlson, Nancy. *Think big!*
Clark, Katie. *Seagull Sam*
Cohen, Laurie. *The flea*
Costello, David Hyde. *Little Pig joins the band*
    Little Pig saves the ship
Curato, Mike. *Little Elliot, big city*
Dewdney, Anna. *Little Excavator*
Dodd, Emma. *I am small*
Durant, Alan. *A dinosaur called Tiny*
Emmett, Jonathan. *Ruby in her own time*
    This way, Ruby!
Engle, Margarita. *Tiny rabbit's big wish*
Flory, Neil. *The short giraffe*
Foreman, Michael. *The littlest dinosaur*
Gall, Chris. *NanoBots*
Gay, Marie-Louise. *When Stella was very, very small*
Gorbachev, Valeri. *Big Little Hippo*
Gore, Emily. *And Nick*
Grant, Holly. *Wee Sister Strange*
Hartt-Sussman, Heather. *Seamus's short story*
Heapy, Teresa. *Very little Red Riding Hood*
Hosford, Kate. *Infinity and me*
Inches, Alison. *I'm not little!*
Kang, Anna. *You are (not) small*
Keane, Claire. *Little big girl*
Kimura, Ken. *999 frogs and a little brother*
Kirk, David. *Oh So Tiny bunny*
Koehler, Lora. *The little snowplow*
Kuhlman, Evan. *Hank's big day*
LaMarche, Jim. *Up*
Latimer, Alex. *Pig and small*
Lepp, Bil. *The King of Little Things*
Lichtenheld, Tom. *Cloudette*
Litwin, Eric. *The Nuts: keep rolling!*
McGrory, Anik. *Kidogo*
Martin, David. *Little Bunny and the magic Christmas tree*
Martin, Emily Winfield. *The littlest family's big day*
Marx, Patricia. *Dot in Larryland*
Masurel, Claire. *Domino*
Meserve, Jessica. *Small sister*
Miura, Taro. *The tiny king*
Miyares, Daniel. *Bring me a rock!*
Nakagawa, Chihiro. *Who made this cake?*
Nolen, Jerdine. *Hewitt Anderson's great big life*
O'Leary, Sara. *When you were small*
Palatini, Margie. *Shelly*
Paul, Chris. *Long shot*
Penn, Audrey. *Kai to the rescue!*
Pham, LeUyen. *There's no such thing as little*
Roberts, Justin. *The smallest girl in the smallest grade*
Root, Andrew. *Hamsters don't fight fires!*
Schwarz, Viviane. *Timothy and the strong pajamas*
Shulevitz, Uri. *Troto and the trucks*
Silverman, Erica. *There was a wee woman . . .*
Spires, Ashley. *Small Saul*
Stead, Philip C. *Hello, my name is Ruby*
Stewart, Amber. *Too small for my big bed*
Symes, Ruth. *Little Rex, big brother*
Thompson, Lauren. *Wee little chick*
Verdick, Elizabeth. *Small Walt*
Watts, Bernadette. *The smallest snowflake*
Wohl, Lauren L. *A teeny tiny Halloween*
Yolen, Jane. *The emperor and the kite*

Young, Ed. *Little Plum*

Character traits – stubbornness

Berger, Samantha. *Martha doesn't say sorry*
Chaconas, Dori. *Dori the contrary hen*
Chou, Yih-Fen. *Mimi says no*
Dormer, Frank W. *The obstinate pen*
Keller, Holly. *Merry Christmas, Geraldine*
Langen, Annette. *I won't comb my hair!*
Letourneau, Marie. *Argyle Fox*
Miller, Pat Zietlow. *Sophie's squash go to school*
Plourde, Lynn. *Pigs in the mud in the middle of the rud*
Priceman, Marjorie. *Princess Picky*
Sheneman, Drew. *Nope!*
Steig, William. *Spinky sulks*
Tarbescu, Edith. *The boy who stuck out his tongue*
Tyler, Anne. *Timothy Tugbottom says no!*
Viorst, Judith. *Alexander, who's not (do you hear me? I mean it!) going to move*

Character traits – vanity

Andersen, Hans Christian. *The dinosaur's new clothes*
    The emperor's new clothes, ill. by Angela Barrett
    The emperor's new clothes, ill. by Virginia Lee Burton
    The emperor's new clothes, ill. by Robert Byrd
    The emperor's new clothes, ill. by Serena Curmi
    The emperor's new clothes, ill. by Charlene DeLage
    The emperor's new clothes, ill. by Jack Delano
    The emperor's new clothes, ill. by Anne Rockwell
    The emperor's new clothes, ill. by Janet Stevens
    The emperor's new clothes, ill. by Eve Tharlet
    The emperor's new clothes: a tale set in China
    It's perfectly true!
Barnett, Mac. *Mustache!*
Braun, Sebastien. *Toot and Pop!*
Brown, Marcia. *Once a mouse . . .*
Calmenson, Stephanie. *The principal's new clothes*
Costa, Nicoletta. *The little tree that would not share*
Cousins, Lucy. *I'm the best*
DeLaporte, Bérengère. *Superfab saves the day*
dePaola, Tomie. *Strega Nona does it again*
DiPucchio, Kelly. *Everyone loves Bacon*
    Everyone loves Cupcake
Evans, Richard Paul. *The tower*
Harper, Lee. *The Emperor's cool clothes*
Hausman, Gerald. *Coyote walks on two legs*
Heo, Yumi. *Lady Hahn and her seven friends*
Lum, Kate. *Princesses are not just pretty*
MacDonald, Margaret Read. *The girl who wore too much*
Marshall, James. *George and Martha, tons of fun*
Perlman, Janet. *The Emperor Penguin's new clothes*
Primavera, Elise. *Louise the big cheese and the la-di-da shoes*
Radunsky, Vladimir. *One: a nice story about an awful braggart*
Ramos, Mario. *I am so handsome*
Rumford, James. *Nine animals and the well*
Sasso, Sandy Eisenberg. *God said amen*
Shields, Carol Diggory. *I am really a princess*
Ward, Helen. *The rooster and the fox*
Weeks, Sarah. *Glamourpuss*
Yolen, Jane. *King Long Shanks*
    Pegasus, the flying horse

Character traits – willfulness

Barnett, Mac. *The magic word*
Bottner, Barbara. *Priscilla gorilla*
Carlson, Nancy. *Loudmouth George earns his allowance*
Davidson, Ellen Dee. *Princess Justina Albertina*
Fox, Mem. *Nellie Belle*
Garton, Sam. *Otter loves Easter!*
Maloney, Brenna. *Ready Rabbit gets ready!*
Torrey, Richard. *Ally-Saurus and the first day of school*

Character traits – wisdom

dePaola, Tomie. *Look and be grateful*
French, Vivian. *The most wonderful thing in the world*
Hoffman, Mary. *Three wise women*
Kajikawa, Kimiko. *Tsunami!*
Marlowe, Sara. *No ordinary apple*
Oberman, Sheldon. *The wisdom bird*
Portis, Antoinette. *Now*
Uchida, Yoshiko. *The wise old woman*
Wisniewski, David. *The warrior and the wise man*

Cheating *see* Behavior – cheating

Cheerleading

Lester, Helen. *Three cheers for Tacky*

Cherubs *see* Angels

Child abuse

Clifton, Lucille. *One of the problems of Everett Anderson*
International Center for Assault Prevention. *My body belongs to me from my head to my toes*
Kleven, Sandy. *The right touch*
Riggs, Shannon. *Not in Room 204*
Sherman, Joanne. *Because it's my body*
Spelman, Cornelia Maude. *Your body belongs to you*
Starishevsky, Jill. *My body belongs to me*
Trottier, Maxine. *A safe place*

Children as authors

Adedjouma, Davida. *The palm of my heart*
Baskin, Leonard. *Hosie's alphabet*
The best part of me
Burdett, Lois. *Hamlet for kids*
　Macbeth for kids
　A midsummer night's dream for kids
　Romeo and Juliet for kids
　The tempest for kids
　Twelfth night for kids
Kallok, Emma. *Gem*
Kroll, Steven. *Patches*
Kunkel, Jeff. *Noah, build your boat*
Lehrhaupt, Adam. *This is a good story*
Michels-Gualtieri, Akaela S. *I was born to be a sister*
Pia Toya
Rosen, Michael. *Poems for the very young*
Saltzberg, Barney. *Inside this book (are three books)*
Wiener, Lori S., et al *Be a friend: children who live with HIV speak*

Children as illustrators

Burdett, Lois. *Hamlet for kids*
　Macbeth for kids
　A midsummer night's dream for kids
　Romeo and Juliet for kids
　The tempest for kids
　Twelfth night for kids
Hughes, Langston. *The sweet and sour animal book*
Kamish, Daniel. *Diggy Dan*
Kroll, Steven. *Patches*
Kunkel, Jeff. *Noah, build your boat*
Lehrhaupt, Adam. *This is a good story*
Miranda, Anne. *Alphabet fiesta*
Pia Toya
Tusa, Tricia. *Bunnies in my head*
Wiener, Lori S., et al *Be a friend: children who live with HIV speak*

Children as inventors

Brill, Marlene Targ. *Margaret Knight, girl inventor*
GrandPre, Mary. *Cleonardo, the little inventor*

Church

Bolden, Tonya. *Rock of ages*
Howard, Ellen. *The log cabin church*
McGowan, Michael. *Sunday is for God*
Millner, Denene. *Early Sunday morning*

Circular tales

Ada, Alma Flor. *The gold coin*
Carle, Eric. *Draw me a star*
Czekaj, Jef. *Oink-a-doodle-moo*
Fagan, Cary. *Mr. Zinger's hat*
Gorbachev, Valeri. *Where is the apple pie?*
Johnston, Tony. *Big red apple*
Lawson, JonArno. *Leap!*
Lodding, Linda Ravin. *A gift for Mama*
McKinley, Cindy. *One smile*
Murphy, Mary. *How kind*
Numeroff, Laura Joffe. *If you give a cat a cupcake*
　If you give a dog a donut
　If you give a moose a muffin
　If you give a mouse a cookie
　If you give a pig a pancake
　If you give a pig a party
Shaskan, Stephen. *A dog is a dog*
Van Laan, Nancy. *This is the hat*
Virján, Emma J. *What this story needs is a pig in a wig*
Ziefert, Harriet. *A polar bear can swim*

Circus

Alsenas, Linas. *Peanut*
Andreasen, Dan. *The giant of Seville*
Barton, Byron. *My bike*
Bogacki, Tomasz. *Circus girl*
Bronson, Linda. *The circus alphabet*
Brown, Marc. *Arthur's chicken pox*
Campbell, K. G. *Lester's dreadful sweaters*
Carlson, Melody. *The day the circus came to town*
Carter, Anne Laurel. *Circus play*
Chaud, Benjamin. *The bear's surprise*
Clements, Andrew. *Circus family dog*
Cneut, Carll. *The amazing love story of Mr. Morf*
Coerr, Eleanor. *Circus day in Japan*

Curious George goes to the circus
dePaola, Tomie. *Jingle, the Christmas clown*
Dockray, Tracy. *The lost and found pony*
Dodds, Dayle Ann. *Where's Pup?*
Downs, Mike. *You see a circus, I see —*
Duncan, Lois. *Song of the circus*
Ehlert, Lois. *Circus*
Emberley, Ed. *Thanks, Mom!*
Esbaum, Jill. *To the big top*
Falconer, Ian. *Olivia saves the circus*
Faller, Regis. *Polo and the magician!*
Fleischman, Paul. *Sidewalk circus*
Fleming, Candace. *Emma's circus*
Fletcher, Ralph. *The circus surprise*
Frazee, Marla. *The farmer and the clown*
Freeman, Don. *Bearymore*
Gottfried, Maya. *Last night I dreamed a circus*
Graham, Bob. *Dimity Dumpty*
Graves, Keith. *Second banana*
Gravett, Emily. *Wolf won't bite!*
Harrison, Hannah E. *Extraordinary Jane*
Hayes, Geoffrey. *Patrick at the circus*
Henrichs, Wendy. *When Anju loved being an elephant*
Hill, Eric. *Spot goes to the circus*
Jackson, Kathryn. *The golden circus book*
Klise, Kate. *Little Rabbit and the Meanest Mother on Earth*
Krosoczka, Jarrett J. *Ollie the purple elephant*
Landry, Leo. *Eat your peas, Ivy Louise!*
Littlesugar, Amy. *Clown child*
Lobel, Anita. *Animal antics: A to Z*
McCourt, Lisa. *Chicken soup for little souls: The best night out with Dad*
MacDonald, Suse. *Circus opposites*
  Elephants on board
McGuirk, Leslie. *Tucker over the top*
Martin, Bill, Jr.. *Chicken Chuck*
Millman, Isaac. *Moses goes to the circus*
Montserrat, Pep. *Ms. Rubinstein's beauty*
Munro, Roxie. *Circus*
Murphy, Stuart J. *Circus shapes*
Nimmo, Jenny. *Esmeralda and the children next door*
Nogales, Jill. *Zebra on the go*
Noonan, Julia. *Hare and Rabbit, friends forever*
Parsley, Elise. *If you ever want to bring a circus to the library, don't!*
Peet, Bill. *Chester the worldly pig*
  Ella
  Randy's dandy lions
Pinkwater, Daniel. *Rainy morning*
Prelutsky, Jack. *Circus*
Priceman, Marjorie. *Emeline at the circus*
Rau, Dana Meachen. *Clown around*
Rey, H. A. *Curious George rides a bike*
Robertson, Patrisha Grainger. *Cirque du Soleil*
Schachner, Judith Byron. *Skippyjon Jones Cirque de Olé*
Seuss, Dr. *If I ran the circus*
Slobodkina, Esphyr. *Circus caps for sale*
Smith, Joseph A. *Circus train*
Spier, Peter. *Peter Spier's circus!*
Stills, Caroline. *Mice mischief*
Stone, Tanya Lee. *Sandy's circus*
Sturgis, Brenda Reeves. *Ten turkeys in the road*
Teague, Mark. *Baby tamer*
Van Dusen, Chris. *The circus ship*
Villeneuve, Anne. *The red scarf*
Vincent, Gabrielle. *Ernest and Celestine at the circus*
Weis, Carol. *When the cows got loose*

Yaccarino, Dan. *Deep in the jungle*
Ziefert, Harriet. *Circus parade*

Cities, towns

Ackerman, Karen. *Bean's big day*
Adoff, Arnold. *Street music*
Aesop. *The country mouse and the city mouse*
  Milly and Tilly
  The town mouse and the country mouse, ill. by Lorinda Bryan Cauley
  The town mouse and the country mouse, ill. by Janet Stevens
  The town mouse and the country mouse: an Aesop fable, ill. by Helen Ward
  The town mouse and the country mouse: an Aesop fable, ill. by Bernadette Watts
  Town mouse, country mouse, ill. by Jan Brett
  Town mouse, country mouse, ill. by Carol Jones
Alko, Selina. *B is for Brooklyn*
Barracca, Debra. *Maxi, the hero*
  A taxi dog Christmas
Barracca, Sal. *The adventures of taxi dog*
Bartone, Elisa. *Peppe the lamplighter*
Bash, Barbara. *Urban roosts*
Berger, Barbara. *Angels on a pin*
Berner, Rotraut Susanne. *In the town all year 'round*
Bernhard, Durga. *To and fro, fast and slow*
Biggs, Brian. *Tinyville town gets to work*
Blake, Robert J. *Fledgling*
Bloom, Suzanne. *No place for a pig*
Bluemle, Elizabeth. *Tap tap boom boom*
Bogan, Paulette. *Spike in the city*
Bradby, Marie. *Momma, where are you from?*
Brooks, Nigel. *Town mouse house*
Brown, Marc. *In New York*
Brown, Peter. *The curious garden*
Brown, Tameka Fryer. *Around our way on Neighbors' Day*
Browne, Anthony. *Me and you*
Buchanan, Jane. *Seed magic*
Buitrago, Jairo. *Jimmy the greatest*
Bunting, Eve. *Riding the tiger*
  Smoky night
Burleigh, Robert. *Clang-clang! beep-beep!*
  Lookin' for Bird in the big city
  Messenger, messenger
  Zoom! zoom!
Burton, Virginia Lee. *Katy and the big snow*
  The little house
Castillo, Lauren. *Nana in the city*
Chall, Marsha Wilson. *Prairie train*
Chaud, Benjamin. *The bear's song*
Chocolate, Deborah. *El barrio*
Christie, R. Gregory. *Mousetropolis*
Cocca-Leffler, Maryann. *Bus route to Boston*
Cole, Henry. *On Meadowview Street*
  Spot, the cat
Cole, Kenneth, Dr. *No bad news*
Cole, Rachael. *City moon*
Collier, Bryan. *Uptown*
Corey, Shana. *Milly and the Macy's Parade*
  The secret subway
Crews, Donald. *Parade*
Crews, Nina. *One hot summer day*
Cummins, Julie. *Country kid, city kid*
Curato, Mike. *Little Elliot, big city*
Curious George in the big city
Curlee, Lynn. *Skyscraper*

Dahlie, Elizabeth. *Bernelly and Harriet*
Daly, Niki. *Not so fast Songololo*
de la Peña, Matt. *Last stop on Market Street*
Donnelly, Liza. *Dinosaurs' Halloween*
Dorros, Arthur. *Abuela*
    City chicken
Dugan, Joanne. *ABC NYC*
Eaton, Jason Carter. *The catawampus cat*
Emberley, Rebecca. *My city / Mi cuidad*
    Three cool kids
Fitzgerald, Joanne. *This is me and where I am*
Fleischman, Paul. *Sidewalk circus*
Franceschelli, Christopher. *Cityblock*
Garhan Attebury, Nancy. *Out and about at city hall*
Geisert, Bonnie. *Desert town*
    Mountain town
Gertsberg, Inna. *The way downtown*
Geser, Gretchen. *One bright ring*
Gianferrari, Maria. *Coyote moon*
Gibbons, Gail. *Up goes the skyscraper!*
Godwin, Laura. *Central Park serenade*
    One moon, two cats
Goode, Diane. *Tiger trouble*
Gordon, Gus. *Herman and Rosie*
Graham, Bob. *The silver button*
Greenfield, Eloise. *Night on Neighborhood Street*
Grimes, Nikki. *A pocketful of poems*
Harrison, Troon. *Courage to fly*
Helakoski, Leslie. *Big chickens go to town*
Henry, Steve. *Here is Big Bunny*
Heo, Yumi. *One afternoon*
    One Sunday morning
Hest, Amy. *Nana's birthday party*
    When you meet a bear on Broadway
High, Linda Oatman. *Tenth Avenue cowboy*
    Under New York
Hoban, Tana. *Is it red? Is it yellow? Is it blue?*
Hodge, Deborah. *Watch me grow!*
Hodgkinson, Leigh. *Goldilocks and just one bear*
Hopkins, H. Joseph. *The tree lady*
Hopkins, Lee Bennett. *City I love*
Hubbell, Patricia. *City kids*
    Sidewalk trip
Hurd, Thacher. *Zoom City*
Isadora, Rachel. *Listen to the city*
    Say hello!
Jack and the beanstalk. *Jack and the beanstalk*
Jay, Alison. *Bee and me*
Jenkins, Priscilla Belz. *Falcons nest on skyscrapers*
Jocelyn, Marthe. *Mayfly*
Joel, Billy. *New York state of mind*
Johnson, Stephen T. *Alphabet city*
Jonas, Ann. *Round trip*
Karas, G. Brian. *The village garage*
Keats, Ezra Jack. *Apt. 3*
    Goggles
    Hi, cat!
    Pet show!
Kenney, Sean. *Cool city*
Kiernan, Pat. *Good morning, city*
Kilby, Don. *In the city*
Kleven, Elisa. *Glasswings*
Kroll, Steven. *Mary McLean and the St. Patrick's Day
    parade*
Kroll, Virginia L. *Faraway drums*
Krupinski, Loretta. *Christmas in the city*
Kuhlmann, Torben. *Moletown*
Lakin, Patricia. *Subway sonata*
Lamba, Marie. *Green green*

Lendroth, Susan. *Old Manhattan has some farms*
Lenski, Lois. *Policeman Small*
Levitin, Sonia. *Boom town*
Lewin, Ted. *Amazon boy*
Light, Steve. *Have you seen my dragon?*
Lodge, Jo. *Moo Moo goes to the city*
Low, William. *Machines go to work in the city*
McCarthy, Meghan. *City hawk*
McCloskey, Robert. *Make way for ducklings*
McDermott, Gerald. *Tim O'Toole and the wee folk*
McFarland, Clive. *The fox and the wild*
McFarlane, Sheryl. *In the city*
Maitland, Barbara. *Moo in the morning*
Mak, Kam. *My Chinatown*
Martin, Jacqueline Briggs. *Farmer Will Allen and the
    growing table*
Medina, Tony. *DeShawn days*
Meister, Cari. *Busy, busy city street*
Melmed, Laura Krauss. *Capital! Washington D.C.
    from A to Z*
    New York, New York!
Merriam, Eve. *Bam, bam, bam*
Milich, Zoran. *The city ABC book*
    City colors
    City 1 2 3
    City signs
Milway, Katie Smith. *Cappuccina goes to town*
Miyakoshi, Akiko. *The way home in the night*
Moreton, Daniel. *La Cucaracha Martina*
Munro, Roxie. *The inside-outside book of London*
    The inside-outside book of New York City
    The inside-outside book of Paris
    The inside-outside book of Texas
    The inside-outside book of Washington, D.C.
    Mazescapes
Murray, Diana. *City shapes*
Myers, Christopher. *Sparrows*
Myers, Walter Dean. *Harlem*
Nastro, Caroline. *The bear who couldn't sleep*
Neubecker, Robert. *Wow! city!*
Niemann, Christoph. *Subway*
Numeroff, Laura Joffe. *What daddies do best*
Osborne, Mary Pope. *New York's bravest*
Palatini, Margie. *Hogg, Hogg, and Hog*
Patton, Julia. *The very very very long dog*
Pearson, Debora. *Big city song*
Peet, Bill. *Fly, Homer, fly*
Pericoli, Matteo. *See the city*
Pinkwater, Daniel. *Bad bears in the big city*
    Beautiful Yetta
Poffenberger, Nancy M. *September 11, 2001*
Poydar, Nancy. *Cool Ali*
Proimos, James. *The loudness of Sam*
Provensen, Alice. *Murphy in the city*
    Town and country
Pryor, Bonnie. *The dream jar*
Raschka, Chris. *New York is English, Chattanooga is
    Creek*
Reidy, Jean. *All through my town*
Reiss, Mike. *Late for school*
Reynolds, Peter H. *Rose's garden*
Richmond, Lori. *Pax and Blue*
Ringgold, Faith. *Tar Beach*
Root, Phyllis. *Anywhere farm*
Roth, Susan L. *Happy birthday Mr. Kang*
Rotner, Shelley. *Citybook*
    Senses in the city
Rudge, Leila. *Gary*
Rudy, Maggie. *City mouse, country mouse*

Russell, Natalie. *Brown Rabbit in the city*
   Moon rabbit
Russo, Marisabina. *Little Bird takes a bath*
   Mama talks too much
Santangelo, Colony Elliott. *Brother Wolf of Gubbio*
Sarcone-Roach, Julia. *The bear ate your sandwich*
Sayre, April Pulley. *It's my city*
Schaefer, Carole Lexa. *The children's garden*
Schertle, Alice. *Little Blue Truck leads the way*
Schulman, Janet. *Pale Male*
Schwartz, Joanne. *Town is by the sea*
Shapiro, J. H. *Magic trash*
Shewchuk, Pat. *In Lucia's neighborhood*
Shulevitz, Uri. *Dusk*
   One Monday morning
   Snow
Shuttlewood, Craig. *Through the town*
Silverman, Erica. *Wake up, city!*
Singer, Marilyn. *City lullaby*
Smalls-Hector, Irene. *Jonathan and his mommy*
Smith, Marie. *N is for our nation's capital*
Soto, Gary. *Chato's kitchen*
Spinelli, Eileen. *City angel*
Stadler, John. *The cats of Mrs. Calamari*
Stainton, Sue. *Santa's snow cat*
Stevenson, James. *Grandpa's great city tour*
Stewart, Joel. *Addis Berner Bear forgets*
Stewart, Sarah. *The journey*
Stolz, Mary. *Emmett's pig*
Stutson, Caroline. *Cats' night out*
Sweeney, Linda Booth. *When the snow falls*
Taback, Simms. *Simms Taback's city animals*
Tafolla, Carmen. *What can you do with a paleta?*
Takabayashi, Mari. *I live in Brooklyn*
   I live in Tokyo
Tamar, Erika. *The garden of happiness*
Tauss, Marc. *Superhero*
Teckentrup, Britta. *Busy bunny days*
Thornhill, Jan. *Wild in the city*
Uhlberg, Myron. *Lemuel, the fool*
Ungar, Richard. *Rachel's library*
Van Nutt, Julia. *Skyrockets and snickerdoodles*
Vila, Laura. *Building Manhattan*
Walker, Anna. *Peggy*
Watson, Renée. *A place where hurricanes happen*
Watts, Leslie Elizabeth. *The Baabaasheep Quartet*
Weitzman, Jacqueline Preiss. *You can't take a balloon into the Metropolitan Museum*
   You can't take a balloon into the National Gallery
Wilcox, Brian. *Full moon*
Wilde, Oscar. *The happy prince*
Wilder, Laura Ingalls. *Going to town*
Williams, Karen Lynn. *Beatrice's dream*
Williams, Sherley Anne. *Girls together*
Williams, Suzanne. *Old MacDonald in the city*
Woodson, Jacqueline. *The other side*
Wyeth, Sharon Dennis. *Something beautiful*
Yaccarino, Dan. *Doug unplugged*
Yashima, Taro. *Umbrella*
Zimmerman, Andrea Griffing. *Trashy town*
Zullo, Germano. *Line 135*

Cleanliness *see* Character traits – cleanliness

Cleverness *see* Character traits – cleverness

Climate change *see* Ecology

Cloaks *see* Clothing – coats

Clocks, watches

Appelt, Kathi. *Bats around the clock*
Axelrod, Amy. *Pigs on a blanket*
Aylesworth, Jim. *The completed hickory dickory dock*
Baker, Keith. *Hickory dickory dock*
Blackstone, Stella. *Bear takes a trip*
Chast, Roz. *Around the clock!*
Coats, Lucy. *Neil's numberless world*
Fraser, Mary Ann. *I.Q., it's time*
Gibbons, Gail. *Clocks and how they go*
Harper, Dan. *Telling time with Big Mama Cat*
Hutchins, Pat. *Clocks and more clocks*
Jaramillo, Susie. *Little skeletons / Esqueletitos*
Keller, Shana. *Ticktock Banneker's clock*
McCaughrean, Geraldine. *My grandmother's clock*
McMillan, Bruce. *Time to . . .*
Metzger, Steve. *The dancing clock*
Mother Goose. *Hickory, dickory, dock*
Murphy, Stuart J. *Game time*
   It's about time!
Older, Jules. *Telling time*
Pilegard, Virginia Walton. *The warlord's alarm*
Richards, Kitty. *It's about time, Max!*
Stead, Philip C. *A home for Bird*
Verdet, Andre. *All about time*
Wood, Audrey. *It's Duffy time!*

Clothing

Aesop. *The donkey in the lion's skin*
   The wolf in sheep's clothing
Ajmera, Maya, et al. *What we wear*
Alko, Selina. *Every-day dress-up*
Andersen, Hans Christian. *The dinosaur's new clothes*
   The emperor's new clothes, ill. by Angela Barrett
   The emperor's new clothes, ill. by Virginia Lee Burton
   The emperor's new clothes, ill. by Robert Byrd
   The emperor's new clothes, ill. by Serena Curmi
   The emperor's new clothes, ill. by Charlene DeLage
   The emperor's new clothes, ill. by Jack Delano
   The emperor's new clothes, ill. by Anne Rockwell
   The emperor's new clothes, ill. by Janet Stevens
   The emperor's new clothes, ill. by Eve Tharlet
   The emperor's new clothes: a tale set in China
Aponte, Carlos. *A season to bee*
Arnold, Tedd. *Huggly gets dressed*
Bae, Hyun-Joo. *New clothes for New Year's day*
Barrett, Judi. *Animals should definitely not wear clothing*
Beaton, Clare. *Daisy gets dressed*
Beaumont, Karen. *Dini Dinosaur*
Bentley, Dawn. *Fuzzy bear*
Billstrom, Dianne. *You can't go to school naked!*
Black, Michael Ian. *Naked!*
Blankenship, Lee Ann. *Mr. Tuggle's troubles*
Blumenthal, Deborah. *Fancy party gowns*
Brett, Jan. *The hat*
   The trouble with trolls
Brown, Marc. *Arthur's underwear*
Calmenson, Stephanie. *The principal's new clothes*
Carlstrom, Nancy White. *Jesse Bear, what will you wear?*
Carluccio, Maria. *D is for dress up*
Carter, David A. *Who's under that hat?*

Catchpool, Michael. *The cloud spinner*
Chocolate, Deborah. *Kente colors*
Chodos-Irvine, Margaret. *Ella Sarah gets dressed*
Chwast, Seymour. *Get dressed!*
Cole, Brock. *Buttons*
Corey, Shana. *You forgot your skirt, Amelia Bloomer*
Cullen, Catherine Ann. *The magical, mystical, marvelous coat*
Cunnane, Kelly. *Deep in the Sahara*
Cuyler, Margery. *Princess Bess gets dressed*
De Regniers, Beatrice Schenk. *What did you put in your pocket?*
Dodds, Dayle Ann. *Hello, sun!*
   The Kettles get new clothes
Ehrlich, Fred. *Does a chimp wear clothes?*
Emberley, Rebecca. *My clothes / Mi ropa*
Fleming, Denise. *Maggie and Michael get dressed*
Florian, Douglas. *I love my hat*
Fox, Mem. *Shoes from grandpa*
Freeman, Don. *Corduroy*
   A pocket for Corduroy
Gay, Marie-Louise. *Good morning Sam*
Gibert, Bruno. *The king is naked!*
Gordon, Domenica More. *Archie*
Harley, Bill. *Dirty Joe, the pirate*
Harper, Lee. *The Emperor's cool clothes*
Harris, Robie H. *I'm all dressed!*
Heling, Kathryn. *Clothesline clues to jobs people do*
Hennessy, B. G. *A Christmas wish for Corduroy*
Hickox, Rebecca. *The golden sandal*
Hoberman, Mary Ann. *I like old clothes*
Hopkinson, Deborah. *Knit your bit*
Hutchins, Pat. *You'll soon grow into them, Titch*
Jocelyn, Marthe. *Ready for autumn*
   Ready for spring
   Ready for summer
   Ready for winter
Kuskin, Karla. *The Philharmonic gets dressed*
   Under my hood I have a hat
Larson, Kirby. *The magic kerchief*
Lasky, Kathryn. *The emperor's old clothes*
   Lucille's snowsuit
Lester, Helen. *The sheep in wolf's clothing*
   Tacky and the Emperor
Lester, Julius. *Sam and the tigers*
Lewis, Rose A. *Orange Peel's pocket*
Lindaman, Jane. *Zip it!*
Litwin, Eric. *Pete the Cat and his four groovy buttons*
London, Jonathan. *Froggy gets dressed*
   Froggy goes to school
Long, Ethan. *Chamelia*
Lottridge, Celia Barker. *The little rooster and the diamond button*
Lucas, David. *Halibut Jackson*
Lunge-Larsen, Lise. *Noah's mittens*
Luxbacher, Irene. *Mr. Frank*
McAnulty, Stacy. *Beautiful*
MacDonald, Margaret Read. *The girl who wore too much*
   Little Rooster's diamond button
McElligott, Matthew. *Backbeard and the birthday suit*
McKee, David. *Elmer and Super El*
McKissack, Patricia C. *Nettie Jo's friends*
Makhijani, Pooja. *Mama's saris*
Markel, Michelle. *Brave girl*
Martins, Isabel Minhós. *Little lamb, have you any wool?*
Medearis, Angela Shelf. *Poppa's itchy Christmas*
   Poppa's new pants

Mills, Lauren A. *The rag coat*
Morris, Ann. *Weddings*
Moss, Miriam. *Bare bear*
Mould, Wendy. *Ants in my pants*
Müller, Birte. *I can dress myself!*
Munsch, Robert N. *Thomas' snowsuit*
Murguia, Bethanie Deeney. *Zoe gets ready*
Nedwidek, John. *Ducks don't wear socks*
Neitzel, Shirley. *The dress I'll wear to the party*
   The jacket I wear in the snow
Oberman, Sheldon. *The always prayer shawl*
O'Connor, Jane. *Fancy Nancy*
   Nancy la elegante / Fancy Nancy
Ohi, Ruth. *Pants off first*
Parr, Todd. *Underwear do's and don'ts*
Perlman, Janet. *The Emperor Penguin's new clothes*
Plourde, Lynn. *Grandpappy snippy snappies*
   You're wearing that to school?!
Potter, Beatrix. *The tale of Mrs. Tiggy-Winkle*
Rao, Sandhya. *My mother's sari*
Reidy, Hannah. *All sorts of clothes*
Reidy, Jean. *Too purpley!*
Rothenberg, Joan Keller. *Inside-out grandma*
Sanders, Scott R. *Warm as wool*
Sauer, Tammi. *Mary had a little glam*
Savadier, Elivia. *Time to get dressed!*
Schertle, Alice. *Button up!*
   The skeleton in the closet
Schnur, Steven. *The tie man's miracle*
Schwartz, Amy. *Polka dots for Poppy*
Senior, Olive. *Birthday suit*
Sheth, Kashmira. *My Dadima wears a sari*
Stoeke, Janet Morgan. *A hat for Minerva Louise*
Szekeres, Cyndy. *The mouse that Jack built*
Tafolla, Carmen. *What can you do with a rebozo?*
Vigil-Piñón, Evangelina. *Marina's muumuu / El muumuu de Marina*
Weiss, Nicki. *The world turns round and round*
Wells, Rosemary. *Max's dragon shirt*
   Max's new suit
Wild, Margaret. *The pocket dogs*
Willems, Mo. *Naked mole rat gets dressed*
Winter, Jeanette. *My baby*
Wright, Maureen. *Sneezy the snowman*
Yolen, Jane. *King Long Shanks*
Yorinks, Arthur. *Christmas in July*
Ziefert, Harriet. *Clara Ann Cookie*
Zion, Gene. *No roses for Harry*

Clothing – aprons

Carle, Eric. *My apron*
McKissack, Patricia C. *Ma Dear's aprons*
Payne, Emmy. *Katy no-pocket*

Clothing – boots

Chessa, Francesca. *Holly's red boots*
DeFelice, Cynthia C. *Cold feet*
Dunrea, Olivier. *Ollie the stomper*
Havill, Juanita. *Jamaica and Brianna*
Huling, Jan. *Puss in cowboy boots*
Lewison, Wendy Cheyette. *So many boots*
London, Jonathan. *Puddles*
Lowell, Susan. *The bootmaker and the elves*
Millard, Glenda. *And red galoshes*
Mitchell, Marianne. *Joe Cinders*
Moran, Alex. *Boots for Beth*
Olson-Brown, Ellen. *Ooh la la polka-dot boots*

Perrault, Charles. *Puss in boots*, ill. by Steve Light
    Puss in boots, ill. by Jerry Pinkney
Ray, Mary Lyn. *Red rubber boot day*
Wells, Rosemary. *Red boots*
Wheeler, Lisa. *The Christmas boot*

Clothing – coats

Aylesworth, Jim. *My grandfather's coat*
David, Ryan. *The magic raincoat*
dePaola, Tomie. *Charlie needs a cloak*
Hest, Amy. *The purple coat*
Kassirer, Sue. *Joseph and his coat of many colors*
Lacome, Julie. *Ruthie's big old coat*
Milligan, Bryce. *Brigid's cloak*
Oram, Hiawyn. *The wrong overcoat*
Plourde, Lynn. *Bella's fall coat*
Pulver, Robin. *Mrs. Toggle's zipper*
Taback, Simms. *Joseph had a little overcoat*
Wheeler, Lisa. *Jam and jelly by Holly and Nellie*
Woodruff, Elvira. *The memory coat*
Ziefert, Harriet. *A new coat for Anna*

Clothing – costumes

Andrews, Julie. *The very fairy princess: a spooky, sparkly Halloween*
Biedrzycki, David. *Me and my dragon: scared of Halloween*
Billingsley, Franny. *Big bad bunny*
Bollinger, Peter. *Algernon Graeves is scary enough*
Boynton, Sandra. *Spooky Pookie*
Chess, Victoria. *The costume party*
Christelow, Eileen. *Five little monkeys trick-or-treat*
Cousins, Lucy. *Maisy dresses up*
David, Lawrence. *Superhero Max*
Day, Alexandra. *Carl's Halloween*
deGennaro, Sue. *The pros and cons of being a frog*
deGroat, Diane. *Trick or treat, smell my feet*
DeLaporte, Bérengère. *Superfab saves the day*
Demas, Corinne. *Halloween surprise*
DiPucchio, Kelly. *Crafty Chloe: dress-up mess-up*
Ernst, Lisa Campbell. *Sylvia Jean, drama queen*
Flesher, Vivienne. *Alfred's nose*
Gallion, Sue Lowell. *Pug and Pig trick-or-treat*
Goldfinger, Jennifer P. *Hello, my name is Tiger*
Goodrich, Carter. *Zorro gets an outfit*
Grey, Mini. *Traction Man is here*
Hennessy, B. G. *Corduroy's Halloween*
Hills, Tad. *Duck and Goose, honk! quack! boo!*
Hohn, Nadia L. *Malaika's costume*
Hort, Lenny. *We're going on a treasure hunt*
    We're going on safari
Joosse, Barbara. *Dog parade*
Kovalski, Maryann. *Omar's Halloween*
Landry, Leo. *Trick or treat*
Lester, Helen. *Tacky and the haunted igloo*
Lobel, Anita. *Lena's sleep sheep*
London, Jonathan. *Froggy's Halloween*
McCue, Lisa. *Corduroy's best Halloween ever!*
McDonald, Megan. *Ant and Honey Bee, what a pair!*
McGuirk, Leslie. *Tucker's spooky Halloween*
Mayer, Pamela. *The scariest monster in the whole wide world*
Milgrim, David. *Wild feelings*
Neitzel, Shirley. *Who will I be?*
O'Connell, Jennifer. *It's Halloween night!*
Patricelli, Leslie. *Boo!*
Pinder, Eric. *How to share with a bear*

Poydar, Nancy. *The perfectly horrible Halloween*
Rim, Sujean. *Birdie's happiest Halloween*
Rockwell, Anne. *Halloween Day*
Saltzberg, Barney. *The problem with pumpkins*
    Soccer mom from outer space
Scheffler, Axel. *Pip and Posy: the scary monster*
Scotton, Rob. *Scaredy-cat, Splat!*
Silvano, Wendi. *Turkey Claus*
    Turkey trouble
Sís, Peter. *Robinson*
Soman, David. *Ladybug Girl and the dress-up dilemma*
Todd, Mark. *What will you be for Halloween?*
Winter, Jeanette. *Niño's mask*
Wojciechowski, Susan. *The best Halloween of all*
Wolff, Ferida. *On Halloween night*

Clothing – dresses

Ashburn, Boni. *I had a favorite dress*
Baldacchino, Christine. *Morris Micklewhite and the tangerine dress*
Bertrand, Diane Gonzales. *Sofía and the purple dress / Sofía y el vestido morado*
Daly, Niki. *Jamela's dress*
Friedman, Laurie. *A style all her own*
Hoffman, Sarah. *Jacob's new dress*
Jenkins, Emily. *Daffodil*
Jocelyn, Marthe. *Hannah and the seven dresses*
McCormack, Caren McNelly. *The fiesta dress*
McDonald, Megan. *The Hinky Pink*
Masini, Beatrice. *Here comes the bride*
Munsch, Robert N. *Ribbon rescue*
Norwich, William D. *Molly and the magic dress*
Rim, Sujean. *Birdie's big-girl dress*
Schaefer, Carole Lexa. *The Bora-Bora dress*
Seymour, Dorothy Z. *Ann likes red*
Strauss, Linda Leopold. *The princess gown*
Yolen, Jane. *Come to the fairies' ball*
Ziefert, Harriet. *My forever dress*

Clothing – gloves, mittens

Johnson, G. Francis. *Has anybody lost a glove?*
Jonovitz, Marilyn. *Three little kittens*
Kellogg, Steven. *The mystery of the missing red mitten*
Mother Goose. *The three little kittens*
Pinkney, Jerry. *Three little kittens*
Plourde, Lynn. *A mountain of mittens*
Quattlebaum, Mary. *Winter friends*
Siomades, Lorianne. *Three little kittens*
Yoon, Salina. *Penguin in love*

Clothing – handbags, purses

Antony, Steve. *The queen's handbag*
Bogan, Paulette. *Momma's magical purse*
Dunbar, Polly. *Pretty Pru*
Finlay, Lizzie. *Little Croc's purse*
Hansen, P. *My granny's purse*
Henkes, Kevin. *Lilly's purple plastic purse*
McElmurry, Jill. *Mad about plaid*
Uchida, Yoshiko. *The magic purse*
Westcott, Nadine Bernard. *The lady with the alligator purse*

Clothing – hats

Antony, Steve. *The Queen's hat*
Beaumont, Karen. *Hats off to you!*

Bijsterbosch, Anita. *Whose hat is that?*
Blackaby, Susan. *Rembrandt's hat*
Brown, Ken. *The scarecrow's hat*
Brumbeau, Jeff. *Miss Hunnicutt's hat*
Butler, M. Christina. *One snowy night*
Chaconas, Dori. *Virginnie's hat*
D'Amico, Carmela. *Ella, the elegant elephant*
DeRubertis, Barbara. *Corky Cub's crazy caps*
Diakité, Baba Wagué. *The hatseller and the monkeys*
Dunrea, Olivier. *Peedie*
Edwards, Michelle. *A hat for Mrs. Goldman*
Fagan, Cary. *Mr. Zinger's hat*
Freeman, Tor. *Olive and the embarrassing gift*
Gorbachev, Valeri. *Whose hat is it?*
Grifalconi, Ann. *Tiny's hat*
Harley, Bill. *Lost and found*
Hillenbrand, Will. *Snowman's story*
Holm, Sharon Lane. *Zoe's hats*
Hoppe, Paul. *Hat*
Horowitz, Dave. *Buy my hats!*
Howard, Elizabeth Fitzgerald. *Aunt Flossie's hats
    (and crab cakes later)*
Imai, Ayano. *Mr. Brown's fantastic hat*
Johnson, D. B. *Magritte's marvelous hat*
Joyner, Andrew. *The pink hat*
Judge, Lita. *Red hat*
Kasza, Keiko. *Finders keepers*
Katz, Karen. *Twelve hats for Lena*
Keats, Ezra Jack. *Jennie's hat*
Kimmel, Eric A. *Stormy's hat*
Klassen, Jon. *I want my hat back
    This is not my hat
    We found a hat*
Könnecke, Ole. *Anton can do magic*
Lamb, Albert. *Sam's winter hat*
Langdo, Bryan. *Tornado Slim and the magic cowboy
    hat*
Lear, Edward. *The Quangle Wangle's hat*
Lichtenheld, Tom. *Bridget's beret*
Low, Alice. *Aunt Lucy went to buy a hat*
Lowell, Susan. *Little Red Cowboy Hat*
Luthardt, Kevin. *Hats*
Meisel, Paul. *Zara's hats*
Melling, David. *Don't worry, Douglas!*
Miller, Margaret. *What's on my head?
    Whose hat?*
Moore, Lilian. *While you were chasing a hat*
Morris, Ann. *Hats, hats, hats*
Numeroff, Laura Joffe. *Sherman Crunchley*
Pearson, Tracey Campbell. *The purple hat*
Philip, Simon. *You must bring a hat!*
Reed, Lynn Rowe. *Pedro, his perro, and the alphabet
    sombrero*
Rumford, James. *Don't touch my hat!*
Sadler, Judy Ann. *Sandwiches for Duke*
Savage, Stephen. *Where's Walrus?*
Slingsby, Janet. *Hetty's 100 hats*
Slobodkina, Esphyr. *Caps for sale
    Caps for sale and the mindful monkeys
    Circus caps for sale
    More caps for sale*
Steig, William. *When everybody wore a hat
    Which would you rather be?*
Stephens, Helen. *How to hide a lion*
Stoop, Naoko. *Red Knit Cap Girl*
Tafuri, Nancy. *Silly little goose!*
Turner-Denstaedt, Melanie. *The hat that wore Clara
    B.*
Van Laan, Nancy. *This is the hat*

Weninger, Brigitte. *The elf's hat*
Williams, Karen Lynn. *Tap-tap*
Winthrop, Elizabeth. *Halloween hats*
Won, Brian. *Hooray for hat!*
Ziefert, Harriet. *Grandma, it's for you!
    Hats off for the Fourth of July!*

Clothing – kimonos

Uegaki, Chieri. *Suki's kimono*

Clothing – neckties

Cocca-Leffler, Maryann. *Mr. Tanen's ties rule!*
Cotterill, Samantha. *No more bows*

Clothing – pajamas

Brooks, Erik. *The practically perfect pajamas*
Graber, Janet. *Jacob and the polar bears*
Hayles, Marsha. *Pajamas anytime*
Jackson, Isaac. *Somebody's new pajamas*
Papineau, Lucie. *Lulu's pajamas*
Plourde, Lynn. *Pajama day*
Schwarz, Viviane. *Timothy and the strong pajamas*

Clothing – pants

Andreae, Giles. *Pants*
Crunk, Tony. *Grandpa's overalls*
Davies, Jacqueline. *Panda pants*
Gassman, Julie. *Crabby pants*
Gilani-Williams, Fawzia. *Nabeel's new pants*
Good, Merle, et al. *Dan's pants*
Johnston, Tony. *Levi Strauss gets a bright idea*
Kraegel, Kenneth. *Green pants*
Medearis, Angela Shelf. *Poppa's new pants*
Raschka, Chris. *Moosey Moose*
Rice, Eve. *Peter's pockets*
Watkins, Rowboat. *Pete with no pants*

Clothing – pockets

Braybrooks, Ann. *Plenty of pockets*
Payne, Emmy. *Katy no-pocket*
Rice, Eve. *Peter's pockets*
Scanlon, Elizabeth Garton. *A sock is a pocket for
    your toes*

Clothing – scarves

Arnold, Marsha Diane. *Lost. found*
Bunge, Daniela. *The scarves*
Feeney, Tatyana. *Little Owl's orange scarf*
Villeneuve, Anne. *The red scarf*
Wright, Dare. *A gift from the lonely doll*

Clothing – shirts

Spinelli, Eileen. *In my new yellow shirt*

Clothing – shoes

Barrett, Mary Brigid. *Shoebox Sam*
Bateman, Teresa. *Keeper of soles*
Beaumont, Karen. *Shoe-la-la!*
Blessing, Charlotte. *New old shoes*
Boelts, Maribeth. *Those shoes*
Browne, Anthony. *Willy the wizard*
Bunting, Eve. *Whose shoe?*

Cabrera, Jane. *There was an old woman who lived in a shoe*
Campbell, K. G. *The mermaid and the shoe*
Colato Laínez, René. *My shoes and I*
Daly, Niki. *Happy birthday, Jamela!*
Dornbusch, Erica. *Finding Kate's shoes*
Dunbar, Joyce. *Shoe baby*
Fitz-Gibbon, Sally. *Two shoes, blue shoes, new shoes!*
Fliess, Sue. *Shoes for me!*
Fullerton, Alma. *A good trade*
Glass, Eleri. *The red shoes*
Gormley, Greg. *Dog in boots*
Grimes, Nikki. *Shoe magic*
Hartt-Sussman, Heather. *Seamus's short story*
Hayles, Marsha. *Bunion Burt*
Heo, Yumi. *Father's rubber shoes*
Hines, Anna Grossnickle. *Whose shoes?*
Hoe, Susan. *Which shoes would you choose?*
Johnson, Angela. *Shoes like Miss Alice's*
Johnson, Marion. *Caillou, new shoes*
Ko, Sangmi. *A dog wearing shoes*
Light, Steve. *The shoemaker extraordinaire*
Lipp, Frederick. *Running shoes*
Litwin, Eric. *Pete the Cat: I love my white shoes*
    Pete the Cat: rocking in my school shoes
Lodge, Bernard. *Shoe Shoe Baby*
McDonald, Megan. *Shoe dog*
Mader, C. Roger. *Lost cat*
Meunier, Brian. *Bravo, Tavo!*
Meyer, Susan Lynn. *New shoes*
Miller, Margaret. *Whose shoe?*
Morris, Ann. *Shoes, shoes, shoes*
Novak, Matt. *Flip flop bop*
Paul, Ann Whitford. *Hello toes! Hello feet!*
Primavera, Elise. *Louise the big cheese and the la-di-da shoes*
Pulver, Robin. *Mrs. Toggle's beautiful blue shoe*
Rim, Sujean. *Birdie's big-girl shoes*
Rollings, Susan. *New shoes, red shoes*
Rosenthal, Betsy R. *Which shoes would you choose?*
Ross, Tony. *Centipede's 100 shoes*
Silverman, Erica. *There was a wee woman . . .*
Singer, Marilyn. *Shoe bop!*
    Tallulah's toe shoes
Slater, Dashka. *Baby shoes*
Swinburne, Stephen R. *Whose shoes? a shoe for every job*
Thermes, Jennifer. *Sam Bennett's new shoes*
Tucker, Kathy. *The leprechaun in the basement*
Uff, Caroline. *Hello, Lulu*
Vigna, Judith. *Boot weather*
Williams, Karen Lynn. *Four feet, two sandals*
Winthrop, Elizabeth. *Shoes*
Wynne-Jones, Tim. *Secret Agent Man goes shopping for shoes*
Young, Amy. *Belinda in Paris*

Clothing – socks

Bechtold, Lisze. *Sally and the purple socks*
Brandle, Bine. *Flusi, the sock monster*
Bunting, Eve. *Have you seen my new blue socks?*
Burks, James. *Beep and Bah*
Dormer, Frank W. *Socksquatch*
Dunbar, Joyce. *Where's my sock?*
Evans, Cambria. *Martha Moth makes socks*
Kinerk, Robert. *Timothy Cox will not change his socks*
Kohuth, Jane. *Duck sock hop*
Murphy, Stuart J. *A pair of socks*

Robinson, Michelle. *Odd socks*
Shea, Bob. *New socks*
Sohn, Tania. *Socks!*
Valckx, Catharina. *Lizette's green sock*

Clothing – suits

Chapman, Jared. *Fruits in suits*
Rader, Laura. *Santa's new suit*

Clothing – sweaters

Birchall, Mark. *Rabbit's wooly sweater*
Campbell, K. G. *Lester's dreadful sweaters*
Jeffers, Oliver. *The Hueys in The new sweater*
Larsen, Andrew. *Bella and the bunny*
Olsen, Sylvia. *Yetsa's sweater*
Waterton, Betty. *A bumblebee sweater*

Clothing – underwear

Berger, Samantha. *Monster's new undies*
Chapman, Jared. *Vegetables in underwear*
Doodler, Todd H. *Veggies with wedgies*
Escoffier, Michaël. *Brief thief*
Freedman, Claire. *Dinosaurs love underpants*
    Pirates love underpants
Piggy and Bear in their underwear
Reynolds, Aaron. *Creepy pair of underwear!*
Sendelbach, Brian. *The underpants zoo*
Swain, Ruth Freeman. *Underwear*
Tupera, Tupera. *Polar Bear's underwear*
Zapf, Marlena. *Underpants dance*

Clowns, jesters

Barton, Byron. *My bike*
Baynton, Martin. *Jane and the dragon*
Campbell, K. G. *Lester's dreadful sweaters*
dePaola, Tomie. *Jingle, the Christmas clown*
Dodds, Dayle Ann. *Where's Pup?*
Fletcher, Ralph. *The circus surprise*
Fox, Christyan. *What color is that, PiggyWiggy?*
Frazee, Marla. *The farmer and the clown*
Harper, Jo. *Ollie Jolly, rodeo clown*
Hayes, Geoffrey. *Patrick at the circus*
Jones, Ursula. *The princess who had no kingdom*
Kotzwinkle, William. *Walter, the farting dog: trouble at the yard sale*
Laden, Nina. *Clowns on vacation*
Littlesugar, Amy. *Clown child*
Olofsson, Helena. *The little jester*
Rau, Dana Meachen. *Clown around*
Salley, Coleen. *Epossumondas*
Schreiber, Georges. *Bambino the clown*
Schubert, Leda. *Monsieur Marceau*
Thurber, James. *Many moons*, ill. by Marc Simont
    Many moons, ill. by Louis Slobodkin

Clubs, gangs

Bateman, Teresa. *The Bully Blockers Club*
Berenstain, Stan and Jan. *The Berenstain bears no girls allowed*
Bourgeois, Paulette. *Franklin's secret club*
Bunting, Eve. *Riding the tiger*
Collicott, Sharleen. *Toestomper and the caterpillars*
Corey, Shana. *Here come the Girl Scouts!*
Ernst, Lisa Campbell. *Sylvia Jean, scout supreme*
Howe, James. *Horace and Morris but mostly Dolores*

Long, Ethan. *Fright club*
 Valensteins: (a love story)
McCourt, Lisa. *Chicken soup for little souls: The Goodness Gorillas*
Mahoney, Daniel J. *The perfect clubhouse*
Murphy, Stuart J. *Treasure map*
O'Connor, Jane. *Fancy Nancy: explorer extraordinaire!*
Powell, Alma. *America's promise*
San Souci, Daniel. *The Mighty Pigeon Club*
Shannon, George. *The Secret Chicken Club*
Singer, Marilyn. *Let's build a clubhouse*
Stohner, Anu. *Brave Charlotte and the wolves*

Clumsiness *see* Character traits – clumsiness

Cold *see* Concepts – cold & heat; Weather – cold

Collecting things *see* Behavior – collecting things

Communication

Acredolo, Linda P. *My first baby signs*
Allen, Kathryn Madeline. *A kiss means I love you*
 Show me happy
Barnett, Mac. *Telephone*
Beeke, Tiphanie. *Roar like a lion!*
Charlip, Remy, et al. *Handtalk*
Cheng, Andrea. *Grandfather counts*
Chrustowski, Rick. *Bee dance*
Cruise, Robin. *Bartleby speaks!*
de Lestrade, Agnès. *Phileas's fortune*
Dorros, Arthur. *Radio Man / Don Radio*
Ehrlich, Fred. *Does a seal smile?*
Felix, Monique. *The rumor*
Fisher, Leonard Everett. *Gutenberg*
Gibbons, Gail. *The post office book*
 Puff — flash — bang!
Heelan, Jamee Riggio. *Can you hear a rainbow?*
Hoban, Tana. *I read signs*
 I read symbols
Jenkins, Steve. *Slap, squeak, and scatter*
Leedy, Loreen. *The Furry News*
Meres, Jonathan. *The big bad rumor*
Milich, Zoran. *City signs*
Miller, Mary Beth. *Handtalk zoo*
Millman, Isaac. *Moses goes to a concert*
 Moses goes to the circus
Mortimer, Rachael. *Song for a princess*
Pfeffer, Wendy. *Dolphin talk*
Potter, Beatrix. *Yours affectionately, Peter Rabbit*
Reynolds, Aaron. *Pirates vs. cowboys*
Roberton, Fiona. *Cuckoo!*
Seuss, Dr. *Gerald McBoing Boing*
 Gerald McBoing Boing sound book
Sherman, Joanne. *Because it's my body*
Showers, Paul. *How you talk*
Stewart, Melissa. *Can an aardvark bark?*
Van Woerkom, Dorothy. *Hidden messages*
Walton, Rick. *My two hands, my two feet*
Wells, Rosemary. *Letters and sounds*
 Say hello, Sophie!
 Use your words, Sophie!
Williams, Karen Lynn. *My name is Sangoel*
Yaccarino, Dan. *I am a story*

Communities, neighborhoods

Alda, Arlene. *Morning glory Monday*
Alko, Selina. *B is for Brooklyn*
Ancona, George. *Barrio*
Best, Cari. *When Catherine the Great and I were eight!*
Block party today
Bluemle, Elizabeth. *How do you wokka-wokka?*
Boelts, Maribeth. *Happy like soccer*
Bourgeois, Paulette. *Fire fighters*
 Garbage collectors
 Police officers
 Postal workers
Brown, Marc. *Arthur's neighborhood*
Brown, Tameka Fryer. *Around our way on Neighbors' Day*
Bunting, Eve. *Smoky night*
Campoy, F. Isabel. *Maybe something beautiful*
Caseley, Judith. *On the town*
Chocolate, Deborah. *El barrio*
Christensen, Bonnie. *Plant a little seed*
Clinton, Hillary Rodham. *It takes a village*
Cole, Kenneth, Dr. *No bad news*
Cooper, Elisha. *A good night walk*
Cumpiano, Ina. *Quinito's neighborhood / El vecindario de Quinito*
De Anda, Diane. *The patchwork garden / pedacitos de huerto*
Denos, Julia. *Windows*
DiSalvo, DyAnne. *Grandpa's corner store*
Dooley, Norah. *Everybody brings noodles*
Durango, Julia. *The one day house*
Eclare, Melanie. *A harvest of color*
Edwards, Nancy. *Glenna's seeds*
Flanagan, Alice K. *A busy day at Mr. Kang's grocery store*
 Buying a pet from Ms. Chavez
 Coach John and his soccer team
 Here comes Mr. Eventoff with the mail!
 Ms. Davison, our librarian
 Ms. Murphy fights fires
 Officer Brown keeps neighborhoods safe
 Riding the school bus with Mrs. Kramer
 A visit to the Gravesens' farm
Forman, Ruth. *Young Cornrows callin out the moon*
Freeman, Don. *Corduroy's busy street and Corduroy goes to the doctor*
Fries, Claudia. *A pig is moving in*
Gal, Susan. *Day by day*
Garland, Sarah. *Eddie's toolbox and how to make and mend things*
Geras, Adèle. *The Cats of Cuckoo Square, Geejay the Hero*
Gibson, Karen Bush. *Child care workers*
 Emergency medical technicians
 Pharmacists
 Truck drivers
Graham, Bob. *A bus called Heaven*
Greenfield, Eloise. *Night on Neighborhood Street*
Grey, Mini. *Hermelin the detective mouse*
Harshman, Marc. *Only one neighborhood*
Henkes, Kevin. *Good-bye, Curtis*
Heo, Yumi. *One afternoon*
Herrera, Juan Felipe. *Grandma and Me at the flea / Los meros meros remateros*
Hubbell, Patricia. *Sidewalk trip*
Hudes, Quiara Alegría. *Welcome to my neighborhood!*
Isadora, Rachel. *Over the green hills*
 Say hello!

Yo, Jo!
Johnson, D. B. *Eddie's kingdom*
Johnson, G. Francis. *Has anybody lost a glove?*
Johnson, Paul Brett. *Mr. Persnickety and Cat Lady*
Johnston, Tony. *The cat with seven names*
Keats, Ezra Jack. *Pet show!*
Kittinger, Jo S. *The house on Dirty-Third Street*
Kraus, Robert. *Mouse in love*
Krensky, Stephen. *My teacher's secret life*
Lakin, Patricia. *Fat chance Thanksgiving*
Lamba, Marie. *Green green*
Leedahl, Shelley A. *The bone talker*
Leedy, Loreen. *The Furry News*
Lewis, Rob. *Friends*
Liebman, Daniel. *I want to be a firefighter*
   I want to be a police officer
Lord, Janet. *Albert the fix-it man*
Louie, Therese On. *Raymond's perfect present*
Lyon, George Ella. *You and me and home sweet home*
Machado, Ana Maria. *What a party!*
Manning, Maurie J. *Laundry day*
Manzano, Sonia. *Miracle on 133rd Street*
Marsalis, Wynton. *Squeak, rumble, whomp! Whomp!*
   Whomp!
Martin, Jacqueline Briggs. *Farmer Will Allen and the*
   growing table
Medearis, Angela Shelf. *Rum-a-tum-tum*
Modarressi, Mitra. *Yard sale*
Nielsen, Laura. *Mrs. Muddle's holidays*
Novak, Matt. *The Robobots*
Owen, Ann. *Taking your places*
Pedersen, Judy. *When night time comes near*
Pinkney, Brian. *The adventures of sparrowboy*
Pittman, Helena Clare. *The angel tree*
Powell, Alma. *America's promise*
Reidy, Jean. *Busy builders, busy week!*
Ritchie, Scot. *Look where we live!*
Rockliff, Mara. *Chik chak Shabbat*
Rockwell, Anne. *Backyard bear*
Rogers, Fred. *Moving*
Rose, Naomi C. *Tashi and the Tibetan flower cure*
Rosen, Michael. *A Thanksgiving wish*
Russo, Marisabina. *Mama talks too much*
SanAngelo, Ryan. *Eddie spaghetti*
Schubert, Leda. *Here comes Darrell*
Shewchuk, Pat. *In Lucia's neighborhood*
Sís, Peter. *Madlenka, soccer star*
Smalls-Hector, Irene. *Jonathan and his mommy*
Spinelli, Eileen. *Cold snap*
   Somebody loves you, Mr. Hatch
Stead, Philip C. *Ideas are all around*
Stevens, April. *Waking up Wendell*
Sutherland, Marc. *MacMurtrey's wall*
Tamar, Erika. *The garden of happiness*
Taulbert, Clifton L. *Little Cliff and the porch people*
Thayer, Jane. *Part-time dog*
Thomson, Sarah L. *Around the neighborhood*
Watson, Renée. *A place where hurricanes happen*
Wells, Rosemary. *McDuff goes to school*
Wong, Janet S. *The dumpster diver*
Wyeth, Sharon Dennis. *Something beautiful*
Yolen, Jane. *Raising Yoder's barn*

Competition *see* Contests; Sibling rivalry;
   Sports; Sportsmanship

Completing things *see* Character traits –
   completing things

Compromising *see* Character traits –
   compromising

Computers *see also* Technology

Alemagna, Beatrice. *On a magical do-nothing day*
Brown, Marc. *Arthur's computer disaster*
Carrick, Carol. *Patrick's dinosaurs on the Internet*
Collins, Suzanne. *When Charlie McButton lost power*
Dormer, Frank W. *Click!*
Gutch, Michael. *Sticky, sticky, stuck!*
Robbins, Dean. *Margaret and the moon*
Saltzberg, Barney. *Tea with Grandpa*
Wallmark, Laurie. *Ada Byron Lovelace and the*
   thinking machine
Zuckerberg, Randi. *Dot*

Conceit *see* Character traits – conceit

Concepts

Adler, David A. *Perimeter, area, and volume*
   Things that float and things that don't
Anno, Mitsumasa. *Anno's math games*
   Anno's math games II
   Anno's math games III
Berenstain, Stan and Jan. *Inside outside upside down*
Berry, Lynne. *What floats in a moat?*
Boutignon, Beatrice. *Not all animals are blue*
Boyd, Lizi. *Inside outside*
Brown, Margaret Wise. *Sailor boy jig*
Burningham, John. *First steps*
Carle, Eric. *My very first book of motion*
Cousins, Lucy. *Maisy's amazing big book of learning*
Crews, Donald. *Light*
   We read
Dunn, Todd. *We go together*
Ehlert, Lois. *In my world*
Einhorn, Edward. *A very improbable story*
Fisher, Valorie. *Everything I need to know before I'm*
   five
   I can do it myself
Fleming, Denise. *The everything book*
Goldstone, Bruce. *Great estimations*
   That's a possibility!
Hammersmith, Craig. *Patterns*
Hays, Anna Jane. *Ready, set, preschool!*
Hoban, Tana. *All about where*
   Black on white
   Dots, spots, speckles, and stripes
   Is it rough? Is it smooth? Is it shiny?
   Look! look! look!
   More, fewer, less
   Over, under and through
   White on black
Jenkins, Steve. *Biggest, strongest, fastest*
Jocelyn, Marthe. *Same same*
Johnson, Stephen T. *Alphabet city*
Jonas, Ann. *Reflections*
Jullien, Jean. *Before and after*
Killion, Bette. *Just think!*
Leedy, Loreen. *Seeing symmetry*
McCarthy, Mary. *A closer look*
McMillan, Bruce. *Dry or wet?*
   One, two, one pair!
   Sense suspense
Maloney, Peter. *One foot two feet*
Mamada, Mineko. *Which is round? which is bigger?*

Marzollo, Jean. *I love you*
May, Eleanor. *Albert's amazing snail*
Montanari, Eva. *The crocodile's true colors*
Murphy, Mary. *Quick Duck!*
    Slow snail
Murphy, Stuart J. *The greatest gymnast of all*
    Let's fly a kite
    Missing mittens
    Probably pistachio
Neuschwander, Cindy. *Pastry school in Paris*
Pelletier, David. *The graphic alphabet*
Pham, LeUyen. *There's no such thing as little*
Pinto, Sara. *Apples and oranges*
Rockwell, Anne. *What we like*
Rosenthal, Amy Krouse. *This plus that*
Ross, Michael Elsohn. *Earth cycles*
Rotner, Shelley. *Parts*
Scarry, Richard. *Richard Scarry's best first book ever!*
Schwartz, David M. *If you hopped like a frog*
Seuss, Dr. *Gerald McBoing Boing*
    Gerald McBoing Boing sound book
Shannon, George. *Tomorrow's alphabet*
Sís, Peter. *Beach ball*
Spohn, Kate. *The wet dry book*
Swinburne, Stephen R. *What's a pair? What's a dozen?*
Tompert, Ann. *Just a little bit*
Walsh, Ellen Stoll. *Balancing act*
Ward, Helen. *Spots in a box*
Wells, Rosemary. *How many? How much?*
Yektai, Niki. *Bears in pairs*

Concepts – change

Aregui, Matthias. *Before after*
Clinton, Hillary Rodham. *It takes a village*
Jullien, Jean. *Before and after*
Kirk, Daniel. *The thing about spring*
Long, Loren. *Little tree*
McPhail, David. *Weezer changes the world*
Murphy, Mary. *Some things change*
Reinhardt, Jennifer Black. *Blue Ethel*
Seeger, Laura Vaccaro. *First the egg*
Shea, Susan A. *Do you know which one will grow?*
Wagner, Anke. *Tim's big move!*
Young, Cybèle. *Some things I've lost*

Concepts – cold & heat

Arnold, Caroline. *Too hot? too cold?*
Best, Cari. *When Catherine the Great and I were eight!*
Bynum, Janie. *Altoona up north*
Chambers, Catherine. *Heat wave*
Floyd, Madeleine. *Cold paws, warm heart*
Rau, Dana Meachen. *Chilly Charlie*
Schwartz, Roslyn. *The mole sisters and the cool breeze*
Stewart, Melissa. *Beneath the sun*
Taulbert, Clifton L. *Little Cliff and the cold place*

Concepts – color

Alda, Arlene. *Except the color grey*
Anderson, Airlie. *Cat's colors*
Anderson, Brian. *The prince's new pet*
Aponte, Carlos. *A season to bee*
Arnold, Tedd. *Vincent paints his house*
Aspinall, Sarah. *Penguins love colors*
Austin, Mike. *Monsters love colors*
Averbeck, Jim. *In a blue room*
Baker, Alan. *White Rabbit's color book*

Baker, Keith. *Little green peas*
Barnes, Brynne. *Colors of me*
Barnett, Mac. *Extra yarn*
Barry, Frances. *Duckie's rainbow*
Bass, Jennifer Vogel. *Edible colors*
Bauer, Marion Dane. *One brown bunny*
Beautiful moments in the wild
Beck, Andrea. *Elliot's great big lift-the-flap book*
Bee, William. *Stanley's colors*
Benevelli, Alberto. *The colors of the chameleon*
Bilgrami, Shaheen. *Farmyard painting party*
    Jungle art show
Black, Harley. *Amazing magic school*
    Magic art class
Blackstone, Stella. *Bear's busy family*
    Cleo's color book
Boldt, Mike. *Colors versus shapes*
Borando, Silvia. *Now you see me, now you don't*
Brocket, Jane. *Ruby, violet, lime*
Brown, Margaret Wise. *My world of color*
Brown, Tameka Fryer. *My cold plum lemon pie bluesy mood*
Bryant, Megan E. *Colorasaurus*
Burningham, John. *First steps*
Carle, Eric. *What's your favorite color?*
Carle, Eric. *The artist who painted a blue horse*
    Hello, red fox
    The mixed-up chameleon
    My very first book of colors
Catalanotto, Peter. *Kitten red, yellow, blue*
Chernesky, Felicia Sanzari. *Sugar white snow and evergreens*
Chichester Clark, Emma. *Eliza and the moonchild*
Chocolate, Deborah. *Kente colors*
Cottin, Menena. *The black book of colors*
Court, Rob. *Color*
Cousins, Lucy. *Maisy's colors*
    Maisy's rainbow dream
Cronin, B. B. *The lost house*
Crowther, Robert. *Colors*
Daywalt, Drew. *The day the crayons came home*
    The day the crayons quit
Delessert, Etienne. *Full color*
dePaola, Tomie. *Marcos*
Dodd, Emma. *Dog's colorful day*
Doerrfeld, Cori. *Penny loves pink*
Dunbar, Polly. *Dog Blue*
    Flyaway Katie
Edwards, Pamela Duncan. *Warthogs paint*
Ehlert, Lois. *Color farm*
    Color zoo
    Fish eyes
Emberley, Rebecca. *My colors / Mis colores*
Ericsson, Jennifer A. *A piece of chalk*
Feiffer, Kate. *Double pink*
Félix, Lucie. *Apples and robins*
Ficocelli, Elizabeth. *Kid tea*
Fleming, Denise. *Lunch*
    Maggie and Michael get dressed
Foley, Greg. *Purple Little Bird*
Fontes, Justine Korman. *Black meets White*
Fox, Christyan. *What color is that, PiggyWiggy?*
Freedman, Deborah. *Blue chicken*
Freymann, Saxton. *Food for thought*
Gibbs, Edward. *I spy on the farm*
    I spy with my little eye
Godwin, Laura. *Little white dog*
Gold-Vukson, Marji E. *The colors of my Jewish Year*
Gonyea, Mark. *A book about color*

Gorbachev, Valeri. *Red red red*
Gravett, Emily. *Blue chameleon*
   Orange pear apple bear
Gregory, Nan. *Pink*
Gunzi, Christiane. *Colors*
Hall, Michael. *It's an orange aardvark!*
   Red: a crayon's story
Harper, Charise Mericle. *Pink me up*
Harshman, Marc. *Red are the apples*
Hassett, John. *Father Sun, Mother Moon*
Heller, Ruth. *Color, color, color, color*
Henkes, Kevin. *Birds*
Hest, Amy. *The purple coat*
Hicks, Barbara Jean. *I like black and white*
Hill, Eric. *Spot looks at colors*
Hoban, Tana. *Colors everywhere*
   Dots, spots, speckles, and stripes
   Is it red? Is it yellow? Is it blue?
   Of colors and things
Holm, Sharon Lane. *Zoe's hats*
Hopgood, Tim. *Wow! said the owl*
Horacek, Judy. *Yellow is my color star*
Horácek, Petr. *Butterfly butterfly*
   Strawberries are red
   What is black and white?
Horwood, Annie. *Butterfly, butterfly what colors do you see?*
Houblon, Marie. *A world of colors*
Hubbard, Patricia. *My crayons talk*
Hutchins, Hazel. *Snap!*
Inkpen, Mick. *Kipper's book of colors*
Iyengar, Malathi Michelle. *Tan to tamarind*
Jackson, Ellen. *The seven seas*
Jay, Alison. *Red green blue*
Jenkins, Steve. *Living color*
Jonas, Ann. *Color dance*
Kaiser, Ruth. *The smiley book of colors*
Kann, Victoria. *Pinkalicious*
   Purplicious
Katz, Karen. *The colors of us*
Klausmeier, Jesse. *Open this little book*
Kono, Erin Eitter. *Every color*
Kumin, Maxine. *What color is Caesar?*
Lallemand, Orianne. *The wolf who wanted to change his color*
Larios, Julie. *Yellow elephant*
Leslie, Amanda. *Do crocodiles moo?*
Lionni, Leo. *A color of his own*
   A color of his own [Spanish-English bilingual edition]
   Little blue and little yellow
Litwin, Eric. *Pete the Cat: I love my white shoes*
Liu, Jae Soo. *Yellow umbrella*
Lobel, Anita. *Ten hungry rabbits*
Lottridge, Celia Barker. *One watermelon seed*
Luján, Jorge. *Colors! / ¡Colores!*
Macdonald, Maryann. *The pink party*
McGrath, Barbara Barbieri. *Kellogg's froot loops color fun book*
   Teddy bear counting
McMillan, Bruce. *Growing colors*
Martin, Bill, Jr.. *Brown bear, brown bear, what do you see?*
Milich, Zoran. *City colors*
Miller, Margaret. *I love colors*
Munsch, Robert N. *Purple, green and yellow*
Neubecker, Robert. *Courage of the blue boy*
Norman, Kim. *I know a wee piggy*
Otoshi, Kathryn. *One*

   Pantone
Park, Linda Sue. *What does Bunny see?*
Parr, Todd. *Black and white*
Paschkis, Julie. *P. Zonka lays an egg*
Patent, Dorothy Hinshaw. *Bold and bright, black-and-white animals*
Patricelli, Leslie. *Hop! hop!*
Peek, Merle. *Mary wore her red dress and Henry wore his green sneakers*
Penn, Audrey. *A color game for Chester Raccoon*
Pinkney, Sandra L. *A rainbow all around me*
Pinkwater, Daniel. *Bear's Picture*
Portis, Antoinette. *A penguin story*
Porto, Tony. *Blue aliens*
   Get red
Priceman, Marjorie. *It's me, Marva!*
Raschka, Chris. *Mysterious Thelonious*
Rau, Dana Meachen. *Lots of balloons*
Reasoner, Charles. *One blue fish*
Reed, Lynn Rowe. *Color chaos!*
Reynolds, Peter H. *Sky color*
Rickards, Lynne. *Pink!*
Robertson, Patrisha Grainger. *Cirque du Soleil*
Rosen, Michael. *How the animals got their colors*
Rotner, Shelley. *Shades of people*
Rubinger, Ami. *I dream of an elephant*
Rusch, Elizabeth. *A day with no crayons*
Ryan, Pam Muñoz. *The crayon counting book*
Salzano, Tammi. *One rainy day*
Seeger, Laura Vaccaro. *Green*
   Lemons are not red
Selig, Josh. *Red and Yellow's noisy night*
Serfozo, Mary. *Who said red?*
Seymour, Dorothy Z. *Ann likes red*
Shannon, George. *White is for blueberry*
Shirotani, Hideo. *What color? / Qué color?*
Siddals, Mary McKenna. *Shivery shades of Halloween*
   Tell me a season
Sidman, Joyce. *Red sings from treetops*
Simler, Isabelle. *The blue hour*
Simmons, Steven J. *Alice and Greta's color magic*
Siomades, Lorianne. *My box of color*
Slater, Dashka. *Baby shoes*
Smith, Danna. *Arctic white*
   Pirate nap
Smythe, Theresa. *Chester's colorful Easter eggs*
Snyder, Carol. *We're painting*
Spafford, Suzy. *Witzy's colors*
Spier, Peter. *Oh, were they ever happy!*
Spinelli, Eileen. *In my new yellow shirt*
Staake, Bob. *My little color book*
Steggall, Susan. *Colors*
   Red car, red bus
Strete, Craig Kee. *They thought they saw him*
Stringer, Lauren. *Yellow time*
Sullivan, Tom. *Blue vs. Yellow*
Sweet, Melissa. *Carmine*
Swinburne, Stephen R. *Lots and lots of zebra stripes*
   What color is nature?
Tafuri, Nancy. *Blue goose*
Telchin, Eric. *The Black and White Factory*
Thomas, Valerie. *Winnie the witch*
Thong, Roseanne. *Green is a chile pepper*
Tildes, Phyllis Limbacher. *Baby's first book of birds and colors*
Trimble, Marcia. *Flower Green*
Tullet, Herve. *Let's play*
   Mix it up!
Tusa, Tricia. *Follow me*

Van Fleet, Matthew. *Fuzzy yellow ducklings*
    One yellow lion
    Spotted yellow frogs
Van Laan, Nancy. *Rainbow crow*
Walsh, Ellen Stoll. *Mouse magic*
    Mouse paint
Watt, Mélanie. *Leon the chameleon*
Weeks, Sarah. *Counting Ovejas*
Wellington, Monica. *Colors for Zena*
Wiley, Thom. *One sheep, blue sheep*
Williams, Sue. *I went walking*
Wilson, April. *April Wilson's magpie magic*
Wilson, Karma. *Bear sees colors*
Winne, Joanne. *Blue in my world*
    Green in my world
    Red in my world
Wolff, Ashley. *Baby Bear sees blue*
Wood, Audrey. *The deep blue sea*
Wood, Jakki. *Moo moo, brown cow*
Ying, Jonathan. *Not quite black and white*
Yolen, Jane. *How do dinosaurs learn their colors?*
Young, Jessica. *My blue is happy*
Ziefert, Harriet. *Lunchtime for a purple snake*
Zolotow, Charlotte. *Mr. Rabbit and the lovely present*

Concepts – counting *see* Counting, numbers

Concepts – distance

Axelrod, Amy. *Pigs on the move*

Concepts – left & right

Barrett, Judi. *The marshmallow incident*
May, Eleanor. *Albert is not scared*
Murphy, Stuart J. *Left, right, Emma!*

Concepts – measurement

Aber, Linda Williams. *Carrie measures up!*
Adler, David A. *Perimeter, area, and volume*
Axelrod, Amy. *Pigs on the move*
Barner, Bob. *Ants rule*
Limentani, Alison. *How long is a whale?*
Lionni, Leo. *Inch by inch*
Murphy, Stuart J. *Bigger, better, best*
    Polly's pen pal
Myller, Rolf. *How big is a foot?*
Pelley, Kathleen T. *Magnus Maximus, a marvelous measurer*
Pinczes, Elinor J. *Inchworm and a half*
Schwartz, David M. *Ready! set! measure!*
Sweeney, Joan. *Me and the measure of things*
    Me counting time

Concepts – motion

Dotlich, Rebecca Kai. *In the spin of things*
Ehrlich, Fred. *Does a giraffe drive?*
Jenkins, Steve. *Move!*
Lillegard, Dee. *Go! poetry in motion: poems*
Rau, Dana Meachen. *Rolling*
Seder, Rufus Butler. *Waddle!*
Waring, Geoff. *Oscar and the cricket*
Ziefert, Harriet. *Beach party!*

Concepts – opposites

Alda, Arlene. *Hello, good-bye*

Arena, Jen. *Marta! big and small*
Austin, Richard. *Pocket piggies opposites!*
Badescu, Ramona. *Pomelo's opposites*
Baruzzi, Agnese. *Opposite surprise*
Bee, William. *Stanley's opposites*
Bernhard, Durga. *Earth, sky, wet, dry*
    To and fro, fast and slow
Biggs, Brian. *Stop! go!*
Blackstone, Stella. *Octopus opposites*
    You and me
Boyd, Lizi. *Big bear little chair*
Brooks, Erik. *Polar opposites*
Burningham, John. *First steps*
Chambers, Angela. *Follow that chicken!*
Chernesky, Felicia Sanzari. *Sun above and blooms below*
Child, Lauren. *Charlie and Lola's opposites*
Coat, Janik. *Hippopposites*
Cousins, Lucy. *Maisy big, Maisy small*
Crews, Nina. *A high, low, near, far, loud, quiet story*
Crowther, Robert. *Opposites*
Cumpiano, Ina. *Quinito, day and night / Quinito, dia y noche*
Davis, Nancy. *A garden of opposites*
Deegan, Kim. *My first book of opposites*
Emberley, Rebecca. *My opposites / Mis opuestos*
Falconer, Ian. *Olivia's opposites*
Fernandes, Eugenie. *Big week for little mouse*
Freymann, Saxton. *Food for thought*
Friedland, Katy. *Art museum opposites*
Guy, Ginger Foglesong. *Perros! perros! dogs! dogs!*
Hatanaka, Kellen. *Drive: a look at roadside opposites*
High, Linda Oatman. *Under New York*
Hill, Eric. *Spot looks at opposites*
Hills, Tad. *What's up, Duck?*
Hoban, Tana. *Exactly the opposite*
Hood, Susan. *Double take!*
Horácek, Petr. *Animal opposites*
Hunter, Tom. *Build it up and knock it down*
Idle, Molly. *Flora and the ostrich*
Inkpen, Mick. *Kipper's book of opposites*
Intriago, Patricia. *Dot*
Jeffers, Oliver. *The Hueys in What's the opposite?*
Krensky, Stephen. *I know a lot!*
L'Arronge, Lilli. *Me tall, you small*
Lewis, J. Patrick. *Big is big and little little*
Litton, Jonathan. *Big fish little fish*
MacDonald, Suse. *Circus opposites*
Milgrim, David. *My friend Lucky*
Miller, Margaret. *Big and little*
Minters, Frances. *Too big, too small, just right*
Na, Il Sung. *The opposite zoo*
National Wildlife Federation. *My first book of animal opposites*
Preston-Gannon, Frann. *What a hoot!*
Reich, Kass. *Up hamster, down hamster*
Reinhart, Matthew. *Animal popposites*
Rosenthal, Marc. *Big bot, small bot*
Rueda, Claudia. *Is it big or is it little?*
Rylant, Cynthia. *We love you, Rosie!*
Salzano, Tammi. *One windy day*
Seeger, Laura Vaccaro. *Black? white! day? night! a book of opposites*
Serfozo, Mary. *What's what?*
Siminovich, Lorena. *I like vegetables*
Staake, Bob. *My little opposites book*
Stevenson, James. *Fun, no fun*
Stickland, Paul. *Dinosaur roar!*
Swinburne, Stephen R. *What's opposite?*

Sperring, Mark. *The shape of my heart*
Tafuri, Nancy. *The brass ring*
Thong, Roseanne. *Round is a mooncake*
 Round is a tortilla
Van Fleet, Matthew. *Fuzzy yellow ducklings*
 Spotted yellow frogs
Walsh, Ellen Stoll. *Mouse shapes*
Weeks, Sarah. *Bite me, I'm a shape*
Wildsmith, Brian. *Brian Wildsmith 1 2 3*
Wilson, April. *April Wilson's magpie magic*
Ziefert, Harriet. *Squarehead*

Concepts – size

Ahlberg, Allan. *The snail house*
Alborough, Jez. *Tall*
 Watch out! Big Bro's coming!
Alexander, Martha G. *Blackboard Bear*
Alter, Anna. *Estelle and Lucy*
Anderson, Laurie Halse. *The big cheese of Third*
 Street
Barner, Bob. *Ants rule*
Barnes, Laura T. *Teeny tiny Ernest*
Bechtold, Lisze. *Sally and the purple socks*
Bedford, David. *Big bears can!*
Bentley, Jonathan. *Little big*
Berenstain, Stan and Jan. *Old hat, new hat*
Berger, Barbara. *Angels on a pin*
Blackstone, Stella. *Bear in a square*
Blades, Ann. *Too small*
Bogan, Paulette. *Lulu the big little chick*
Bogart, Jo Ellen. *Big and small, room for all*
Boyd, Lizi. *Big bear little chair*
Bridges, Margaret Park. *Am I big or little?*
Brière-Haquet, Alice. *One very big bear*
Brown, Marcia. *Once a mouse . . .*
Brownlow, Mike. *Mickey Moonbeam*
Buehner, Caralyn. *Superdog, the heart of a hero*
Cali, Davide. *The tiny tale of Little Pea*
Callahan, Sean. *Shannon and the world's tallest*
 leprechaun
Carlson, Nancy. *Think big!*
Choldenko, Gennifer. *How to make friends with a*
 giant
Clements, Andrew. *Big Al and Shrimpy*
Cohen, Laurie. *The flea*
Cole, Henry. *Big bug*
Cuyler, Margery. *The biggest, best snowman*
Docherty, Thomas. *Big scary monster*
Dunbar, Joyce. *The very small*
Durant, Alan. *A dinosaur called Tiny*
Emmett, Jonathan. *Someone bigger*
Engle, Margarita. *Tiny rabbit's big wish*
Florian, Douglas. *A pig is big*
Gall, Chris. *NanoBots*
Garland, Michael. *Hooray José!*
Gavin, Ciara. *Room for Bear*
Goodhart, Pippa. *Little Nelly's big book*
Gorbachev, Valeri. *Big Little Elephant*
 Big Little Hippo
Graves, Keith. *Chicken Big*
Grindley, Sally. *The giant postman*
Gunzi, Christiane. *Sizes*
Hall, Algy Craig. *Dino bites!*
Hartt-Sussman, Heather. *Seamus's short story*
Helakoski, Leslie. *Big pigs*
Helmer, Marilyn. *Three teeny tiny tales*
Henkes, Kevin. *The biggest boy*
 Birds

Henry, Steve. *Here is Big Bunny*
Hoban, Tana. *Is it larger? Is it smaller?*
 Is it red? Is it yellow? Is it blue?
 Spirals, curves, fanshapes and lines
Hosford, Kate. *Infinity and me*
Howe, James. *Brontorina*
Hutchins, Hazel. *Two so small*
Hutchins, Pat. *Shrinking mouse*
 Titch
Jenkins, Emily. *Small medium large*
Jenkins, Steve. *Actual size*
 Big and little
 Prehistoric actual size
Jordan, Deloris. *Salt in his shoes*
Joyce, William. *Big time Olie*
 George shrinks
Judge, Lita. *How big were dinosaurs?*
Kalan, Robert. *Blue sea*
Kang, Anna. *You are (not) small*
Keller, Holly. *Jacob's tree*
Kimura, Ken. *999 frogs and a little brother*
Kirk, Daniel. *Bigger*
Kliphuis, Christine. *Robbie and Ronnie*
Klise, Kate. *Stand straight, Ella Kate*
Latimer, Alex. *Pig and small*
Lepp, Bil. *The King of Little Things*
Lichtenheld, Tom. *Cloudette*
Litwin, Eric. *The Nuts: keep rolling!*
Long, Ethan. *Me and my big mouse*
 Up, tall and high
MacDonald, Ross. *Bad baby*
McEvoy, Anne. *Betsy B. Little*
McGrory, Anik. *Kidogo*
McGuirk, Leslie. *Snail boy*
Markle, Sandra. *Bats: biggest! littlest!*
 Sharks: biggest! littlest!
Marks, Jennifer L. *Sorting by size*
Martin, Emily Winfield. *The littlest family's big day*
Marx, Patricia. *Dot in Larryland*
Masurel, Claire. *Too big!*
Mayer, Mercer. *Just big enough*
Meddaugh, Susan. *Just Teenie*
Miller, Margaret. *Big and little*
 Now I'm big
Miura, Taro. *The big princess*
Most, Bernard. *How big were the dinosaurs?*
Mueller, Doris L. *Small One's adventure*
Murphy, Kelly. *The boll weevil ball*
Murphy, Stuart J. *Bigger, better, best*
Nickle, John. *The ant bully*
Nimmo, Jenny. *Esmeralda and the children next door*
Nolen, Jerdine. *Hewitt Anderson's great big life*
Norac, Carl. *My daddy is a giant*
O'Brien, Patrick. *Gigantic!*
Ohmura, Tomoko. *The long, long line*
O'Leary, Sara. *When you were small*
Packard, Edward. *Big numbers*
Parr, Todd. *Big and little*
Passen, Lisa. *Attack of the 50-foot teacher*
 The incredible shrinking teacher
Peet, Bill. *Huge Harold*
Pinfold, Levi. *Black dog*
Poydar, Nancy. *Cool Ali*
Rand, Betseygail. *Big Bunny*
Rayner, Catherine. *Ernest, the moose who doesn't fit*
Roberts, Justin. *The smallest girl in the smallest grade*
Rueda, Claudia. *Is it big or is it little?*
Russo, Marisabina. *A very big bunny*
Ruzzier, Sergio. *The little giant*

San Souci, Robert D. *Little Pierre*
Schotter, Roni. *When the Wizzy Foot goes walking*
Schwartz, David M. *How much is a million?*
Sherry, Kevin. *I'm the biggest thing in the ocean*
Tafuri, Nancy. *The brass ring*
Turner, Sandy. *Otto's trunk*
Van Leeuwen, Jean. *"Wait for me!" said Maggie McGee*
Verdick, Elizabeth. *Small Walt*
Vere, Ed. *Everyone's little*
Walton, Rick. *Bertie was a watchdog*
Wheeler, Lisa. *Turk and Runt*
Willems, Mo. *Big Frog can't fit in*
Wilson, April. *April Wilson's magpie magic*
Yaccarino, Dan. *So big*
Ziefert, Harriet. *Bigger than Daddy*
Zoehfeld, Kathleen Weidner. *Dinosaurs big and small*

Concepts – speed

Braun, Sebastien. *Whoosh and Chug!*
Cartier, Wesley. *Marco's run*
Furrow, Eva. *Take your time*
Munro, Roxie. *Go! go! go!*
Munsch, Robert N. *Zoom*
Patricelli, Leslie. *Faster! faster!*
Rozier, Lucy Margaret. *Jackrabbit McCabe and the electric telegraph*
Saunders, Dave. *So slow!*
Smee, Nicola. *Clip-clop*

Concepts – up & down

George, Kristine O'Connell. *Up!*
Harris, Trudy. *Up bear, down bear*
Hoban, Tana. *Look up, look down*
May, Eleanor. *Albert is not scared*
Redding, Sue. *Up above and down below*

Concepts – weight

Cobb, Vicki. *I fall down*
Limentani, Alison. *How much does a ladybug weigh?*
Schwartz, David M. *Ready! set! measure!*
Sweeney, Joan. *Me and the measure of things*

Confidence *see* Character traits – confidence

Conservation *see* Ecology

Contests

Aesop. *The contest between the Sun and the Wind*
Alexander, Kwame. *Acoustic Rooster and his barnyard band*
Alter, Anna. *Abigail spells*
Arnold, Tedd. *The twin princes*
Bailey, Linda. *Stanley's beauty contest*
Barton, Chris. *Shark vs. train*
Bateman, Teresa. *Paul Bunyan vs. Hals Halson*
Bee, William. *Worst in show*
Best, Cari. *Ava and the real Lucille*
Biddulph, Rob. *The grizzly bear who lost his grrrrr!*
Birtha, Becky. *Lucky beans*
Bond, Michael. *Paddington Bear and the Busy Bee Carnival*
Booth, Tom. *Don't blink!*

Brett, Jan. *The Easter egg*
Bridwell, Norman. *Clifford the champion*
Callahan, Sean. *Shannon and the world's tallest leprechaun*
Calvert, Pam. *Princess Peepers picks a pet*
Campbell, K. G. *Dylan the villain*
Caple, Kathy. *Worm gets a job*
Cartaya, Pablo. *Tina Cocolina*
Catalanotto, Peter. *Emily's art*
Clanton, Ben. *Rot, the cutest in the world!*
Clayton, Elaine. *A blue ribbon for Sugar*
Cocca-Leffler, Maryann. *Janine and the field day finish*
Cole, Barbara Hancock. *Anna and Natalie*
Conahan, Carolyn. *The big wish*
Cousins, Lucy. *Maisy's field day*
Czekaj, Jef. *Hip and Hop, don't stop!*
Darrow, Sharon. *Old Thunder and Miss Raney*
Demas, Corinne. *Nina's waltz*
Dorros, Alex. *Número uno*
Dorros, Arthur. *Julio's magic*
Durango, Julia. *Pest fest*
Esbaum, Jill. *Stanza*
Frasier, Debra. *Spike*
Godin, Thelma Lynne. *The hula-hoopin' queen*
GrandPre, Mary. *Cleonardo, the little inventor*
Grigsby, Susan. *First peas to the table*
Hamburg, Jennifer. *Monkey and Duck quack up!*
Heide, Iris van der. *A strange day*
Helmore, Jim. *Oh no, monster tomato!*
Heos, Bridget. *Mustache Baby meets his match*
Himes, Rachel. *Princess and the peas*
Ishida, Sanae. *Little Kunoichi, the ninja girl*
Joyce, William. *Billy's booger*
Kaner, Etta. *And the winner is . . .*
Khan, Rukhsana. *King for a day*
Kinney, Jessica. *The pig scramble*
Kroll, Steven. *Super-dragon*
Kulka, Joe. *My crocodile does not bite*
Lazar, Tara. *Little Red Gliding Hood*
Leedy, Loreen. *The great graph contest*
Lobe, Mira. *Hoppelpopp and the best bunny*
London, Jonathan. *Froggy plays in the band*
Lum, Kate. *Princesses are not just pretty*
McKee, David. *Elmer and the race*
McMullan, Kate. *I'm fast*
Mahoney, Daniel J. *A really good snowman*
Marshall, James. *The Cut-Ups carry on*
Mathers, Petra. *A cake for Herbie*
Mayer, Kirsten. *Game of gnomes*
Munsch, Robert N. *More pies*
Neugebauer, Charise. *The real winner*
Olaleye, Isaac. *In the Rainfield*
Oldland, Nicholas. *Walk on the wild side*
Park, Frances. *The royal bee*
Paul, Ellis. *The night the lights went out on Christmas*
Pizzoli, Greg. *Number one Sam*
Polacco, Patricia. *Rotten Richie and the ultimate dare*
Quattlebaum, Mary. *Pirate vs. pirate*
Sparks fly high
Reed, Liz. *Sweet competition*
Reynolds, Peter H. *Going places*
Sydney's star
Root, Phyllis. *Rosie's fiddle*
Rose, Deborah Lee. *The spelling bee before recess*
Rosen, Michael J. *Night of the pumpkinheads*
Ross, Tony. *I want to win!*
Rozier, Lucy Margaret. *Jackrabbit McCabe and the electric telegraph*

Sage, James. *Farmer Smart's fat cat*
Samuels, Barbara. *Aloha, Dolores*
Sauer, Tammi. *Chicken dance*
Sayres, Brianna Caplan. *Tiara Saurus Rex*
Shannon, David. *Bizzy Mizz Lizzie*
Shannon, George. *A very witchy spelling bee*
Shea, Bob. *Cheetah can't lose*
Shields, Carol Diggory. *The bugliest bug*
Shulevitz, Uri. *Troto and the trucks*
Spinelli, Eileen. *The best story*
  Callie Cat, ice skater
Stinson, Kathy. *The dance of the violin*
Stower, Adam. *Two left feet*
Sullivan, Tom. *Blue vs. Yellow*
Tabor, Corey R. *Fox and the jumping contest*
Wallace, Nancy Elizabeth. *Recycle every day!*
Weaver, Tess. *Frederick Finch, loudmouth*
Weninger, Brigitte. *Davy, soccer star!*
White, Linda Arms. *Comes a wind*
Winters, Kay. *The teeny tiny ghost and the monster*
Wojciechowski, Susan. *A fine St. Patrick's Day*
Yamada, Utako. *The story of Cherry the pig*
Yamaguchi, Kristi. *It's a big world, little pig!*

Cooking *see* Activities – baking, cooking

Cooks *see* Careers – bakers; Careers – chefs, cooks

Cooperation *see* Character traits – cooperation

Counting, numbers

Adler, David A. *Fun with Roman numerals*
  Millions, billions, and trillions
  Money madness
  Place value
  Triangles
Ainsworth, Kimberly. *Hootenanny!*
Alakija, Polly. *Catch that goat!*
  Counting chickens
Alda, Arlene. *Arlene Alda's 1 2 3*
Allen, Susan. *Used any numbers lately?*
Amann, Jürg. *Ten birds*
Anderson, Derek. *Ten hungry pigs*
  Ten pigs
  Animal 123
Anno, Mitsumasa. *Anno's counting book*
  Anno's counting house
  Anno's hat tricks
  Anno's magic seeds
  Anno's math games
  Anno's math games II
  Anno's math games III
Appelt, Kathi. *Bats on parade*
  Counting crows
  Rain dance
Arena, Jen. *One hundred snowmen*
Armstrong-Ellis, Carey. *Ten creepy monsters*
Arnold, Tedd. *Five ugly monsters*
Arnosky, Jim. *Mouse numbers and letters*
Ashburn, Boni. *Over at the castle*
Austin, Mike. *Countdown with Milo*
Axelrod, Amy. *Pigs in the pantry*
  Pigs on the ball
Aylesworth, Jim. *The completed hickory dickory dock*
  One crow

Bailey, Linda. *Goodnight, sweet pig*
Bair, Sheila. *Isabel's car wash*
Baker, Alan. *Gray Rabbit's one, two, three*
  Little Rabbit's first number book
Baker, Keith. *1-2-3 peas*
  Potato Joe
Bang, Molly. *Ten, nine, eight*
Banks, Kate. *Max's math*
Barber, Patti. *First number book*
Barclay, Eric. *Counting dogs*
Barnett, Mac. *Count the monkeys*
Barry, Frances. *Duckie's ducklings*
Barton, Byron. *My bus*
Baruzzi, Agnese. *Look, look again*
Base, Graeme. *The water hole*
Bass, Jennifer Vogel. *Edible numbers*
Bateman, Donna M. *Deep in the swamp*
Bates, Ivan. *Five little ducks*
Bauer, Marion Dane. *One brown bunny*
Beaton, Clare. *One moose, twenty mice*
Beaty, Andrea. *Hide and sheep*
Beaumont, Karen. *Doggone dogs!*
Beck, Andrea. *Elliot's great big lift-the-flap book*
Becker, John Leonard. *Seven little rabbits*
Bee, William. *Stanley's numbers*
Beeler, Selby B. *How many Elephants?*
Benzwie, Teresa. *Numbers on the move*
Berenstain, Stan and Jan. *Bears on wheels*
  The Berenstain bears' counting book
Berkes, Marianne. *Over in a river*
  Over in Australia
  Over in the Arctic
  Over in the forest
  Over in the jungle
  Over on a mountain
  Seashells by the seashore
Berry, Lynne. *Duck dunks*
Biggs, Brian. *123 beep beep beep!*
Billin-Frye, Paige. *One, two, buckle my shoe*
Birtha, Becky. *Lucky beans*
Blackstone, Stella. *Bear in a square*
  Bear's birthday
  Cleo's counting book
Blechman, Nicholas. *Night light*
Bleiman, Andrew. *1-2-3 zooborns!*
Bloom, Suzanne. *A number slumber*
Bogart, Jo Ellen. *Count your chickens*
Boldt, Mike. *123 versus ABC*
Bowen, Anne. *The great math tattle battle*
Bozik, Chrissy. *The ghosts go scaring*
Bridwell, Norman. *Clifford counts bubbles*
Brière-Haquet, Alice. *One very big bear*
Brooks, Alan. *Frogs jump*
Brown, Margaret Wise. *Goodnight moon 123: a counting book*
Brown-Wood, JaNay. *Grandma's tiny house*
Browne, Anthony. *One gorilla: a counting book*
Browne, Eileen. *Handa's hen*
Bruce, Lisa. *Engines, engines*
Bruel, Nick. *Poor puppy*
Bryant, Megan E. *Countasaurus*
Buitrago, Jairo. *Two white rabbits*
Burningham, John. *First steps*
Butler, John. *Bedtime in the jungle*
  Ten in the den
  While you were sleeping
Cabatingan, Erin. *Musk Ox counts*
Cabrera, Jane. *One, two, buckle my shoe*
  Ten in the bed

Cameron, C. C. *One for me, one for you*
Capucilli, Alyssa Satin. *Mrs. McTats and her houseful of cats*
Carle, Eric. *My very first book of numbers*
    1, 2, 3 to the zoo
    The rooster who set out to see the world
    Rooster's off to see the world
    10 little rubber ducks
Carlson, Nancy. *Henry's 100 days of kindergarten*
Carlstrom, Nancy White. *Let's count it out, Jesse Bear*
Carter, David A. *One red dot*
Cave, Kathryn. *One child, one seed*
Chae, In Seon. *How do you count a dozen ducklings?*
Chall, Marsha Wilson. *One pup's up*
Chamberlin-Calamar, Pat. *Alaska's twelve days of summer*
Chernesky, Felicia Sanzari. *Cheers for a dozen ears*
Chichester Clark, Emma. *Little Miss Muffet counts to ten*
Child, Lauren. *Absolutely one thing*
    Charlie and Lola's numbers
Christelow, Eileen. *Five little monkeys go shopping*
    Five little monkeys jumping on the bed
    Five little monkeys sitting in a tree
Clements, Andrew. *A million dots*
Cline-Ransome, Lesa. *Quilt counting*
Coats, Lucy. *Neil's numberless world*
Cobb, Annie. *The long wait*
Cohn, Scotti. *One wolf howls*
Cook, Grace. *Two little eyes and other action rhymes*
Cooper, Elisha. *Eight, an animal alphabet*
Cotten, Cynthia. *At the edge of the woods*
Cotton, Katie. *Counting lions*
Cousins, Lucy. *Count with Maisy*
    Count with Maisy, cheep, cheep, cheep!
    Maisy's twinkly, crinkly counting book
Cox, Judy. *Sheep won't sleep*
Crews, Donald. *Bicycle race*
    Ten black dots
Crimi, Carolyn. *Pugs in a Bug*
Cronin, Doreen. *Click, clack, splish, splash*
Crum, Shutta. *The bravest of the brave*
Curious George's 1 to 10 and back again
Cuyler, Margery. *Guinea pigs add up*
    100th day worries
Cyrus, Kurt. *Billions of bricks*
Dahl, Michael. *Downhill fun*
    Eggs and legs
    Footprints in the snow
    From the garden
    Hands down
    Lots of ladybugs!
    On the launch pad
    One big building
    One checkered flag
    One giant splash
    Pie for piglets
    Starry arms
Dale, Penny. *Dinosaur dig!*
Daniels, Teri. *Math man*
Davies, Jacqueline. *Tricking the Tallyman*
Davies, Stephen. *All aboard for the Bobo Road*
Day, Nancy Raines. *What in the world?*
Dean, Kim. *Pete the Cat and the missing cupcakes*
Deegan, Kim. *My first book of numbers*
Degman, Lori. *One zany zoo*
Delessert, Etienne. *Hungry for numbers*
Demarest, Chris L. *Smokejumpers one to ten*
Demi. *One grain of rice*

Dempsey, Kristy. *Ten little fingers, two small hands*
    Ten little toes, two small feet
Denega, Danielle. *Numbers*
Denise, Anika. *Pigs love potatoes*
Dernavich, Drew. *It's not easy being Number Three*
DeRubertis, Barbara. *Bobby Baboon's banana be-bop*
Deschamps, Nicola. *Duckling*
Dickinson, Rebecca. *Over in the Hollow*
DiTerlizzi, Tony. *G is for one gzonk!*
Dobbins, Jan. *Driving my tractor*
Dodd, Emma. *Dog's colorful day*
Donaldson, Julia. *One mole digging a hole*
    One Ted falls out of bed
Dotlich, Rebecca Kai. *Race car count*
Downing, Johnette. *Down in Louisiana*
Duke, Kate. *One guinea pig is not enough*
    Twenty is too many
Dunrea, Olivier. *Me and Annie McPhee*
Dupasquier, Philippe. *1 2 3, follow me!*
Durango, Julia. *Cha-cha chimps*
Edwards, Pamela Duncan. *Roar*
    Warthogs in the kitchen
Ehlert, Lois. *Fish eyes*
Einhorn, Edward. *Fractions in disguise*
Elliott, David. *One little chicken*
Ellwand, David. *Ten in the bed*
Elya, Susan Middleton. *Eight animals on the town*
Emberley, Rebecca. *My numbers / Mis números*
    Ten little beasties
Esham, Barbara. *Last to finish*
Evans, Lezlie. *Can you count ten toes?*
Falconer, Ian. *Olivia counts*
Falwell, Cathryn. *Christmas for 10*
    Feast for ten
    Turtle splash!
Faulkner, Keith. *Pop! went another balloon!*
Fearrington, Ann. *Who sees the lighthouse?*
Feelings, Muriel. *Moja means one*
Fisher, Aileen Lucia. *Know what I saw?*
Fisher, Doris. *My even day*
    One odd day
Fisher, Valorie. *Everything I need to know before I'm five*
    How high can a dinosaur count?
    I can do it myself
Five little pumpkins, ill. by Ben Mantle
    Five little pumpkins, ill. by Iris Van Rynbach
    Five little pumpkins, ill. by Dan Yaccarino
Fleming, Candace. *Seven hungry babies*
    Who invited you?
Fleming, Denise. *Count!*
    The first day of winter
    5 little ducks
    Shout! shout it out!
Formento, Alison. *These bees count!*
    These rocks count!
    These seas count!
    This tree counts!
    This tree, 1, 2, 3
Fox, Christyan. *Count to ten, PiggyWiggy!*
Fox, Mem. *Let's count goats!*
Franceschelli, Christopher. *Countablock*
Franco, Betsy. *Birdsongs*
    Double play!
Freymann, Saxton. *Food for thought*
    One lonely seahorse
Fromental, Jean-Luc. *365 penguins*
Fry, Jenny. *Building numbers*
Garcia, Emma. *Chugga chugga choo choo*

Gardiner, Lindsey. *Good night, Poppy and Max*
Garland, Michael. *How many mice?*
Gehl, Laura. *One big pair of underwear*
George, Bobby. *Montessori number work*
George, Kristine O'Connell. *The great frog race and other poems*
Gerber, Carole. *Ten busy brooms*
Gershator, Phillis. *Zoo day, olé!*
Geser, Gretchen. *One bright ring*
Ghahremani, Susie. *Stack the cats*
Gibbs, Edward. *I spy under the sea*
Giganti, Paul. *Each orange had eight slices*
  How many blue birds flew away?
  How many snails?
Gill, Shelley. *The big buck adventure*
Gillham, Bill. *How many sharks in the bath?*
Ginkel, Anne. *I've got an elephant*
Giogas, Valarie. *In my backyard*
Girnis, Margaret. *1, 2, 3 for you and me*
Glicksman, Caroline. *Eric the math bear*
Goldstone, Bruce. *Great estimations*
  That's a possibility!
Gollub, Matthew. *Ten oni drummers*
Gomi, Taro. *I know numbers!*
Gorbachev, Valeri. *Christopher counting*
  One rainy day
Grabill, Rebecca. *Halloween good night*
Gravett, Emily. *Bear and Hare—where's Bear?*
  The rabbit problem
Greene, Rhonda Growler. *Push! dig! scoop!*
Greenstein, Elaine. *Dreaming*
Grindley, Sally. *Where are my chicks?*
Grossman, Bill. *My little sister ate one hare*
Grossman, Virginia. *Ten little rabbits*
Gunzi, Christiane. *Numbers*
Guy, Ginger Foglesong. *Fiesta*
Hague, Kathleen. *Numbears*
  Ten little bears
Halfmann, Janet. *Eggs 1, 2, 3*
Halls, Kelly Milner. *I bought a baby chicken*
Han, Eun-sun. *The flying birds*
Harper, Charise Mericle. *Amy and Ivan*
Harrington, Tim. *This little piggy*
Harris, Trudy. *Jenny found a penny*
  100 days of school
  Tally cat keeps track
  Twenty hungry piggies
Harshman, Marc. *Only one neighborhood*
Harvey, Jayne. *Busy bugs*
Haskins, Jim. *Count your way through Afghanistan*
  Count your way through Africa
  Count your way through Brazil
  Count your way through Canada
  Count your way through China
  Count your way through France
  Count your way through Germany
  Count your way through Greece
  Count your way through India
  Count your way through Iran
  Count your way through Ireland
  Count your way through Israel
  Count your way through Italy
  Count your way through Japan
  Count your way through Korea
  Count your way through Mexico
  Count your way through Russia
  Count your way through the Arab world
Hawk, Fran. *Count down to fall*
Hawkins, Colin. *One, two, guess who?*

Hays, Anna Jane. *Kindergarten countdown*
Heiligman, Deborah. *The boy who loved math*
Helakoski, Leslie. *The smushy bus*
Hennessy, B. G. *Mr. Ouchy's first day*
  One little, two little, three little pilgrims
Hill, Eric. *Spot counts from 1 to 10*
Hill, Susanna Leonard. *Can't sleep without sheep*
Hills, Tad. *Duck and Goose, 1, 2, 3*
Himmelman, John. *Ten little hot dogs*
Hoban, Tana. *Count and see*
  Let's count
  More, fewer, less
  26 letters and 99 cents
Hoberman, Mary Ann. *The looking book*
Hoffman, Don. *A counting book with Billy and Abigail*
Holub, Joan. *Apple countdown*
  Pumpkin countdown
  Zero the hero
Hooks, William H. *A dozen dizzy dogs*
Horácek, Petr. *One spotted giraffe*
  When the moon smiled
Horton, Joan. *Math attack!*
Hosford, Kate. *Infinity and me*
Hruby, Emily. *Counting in the garden*
Hubbard, Patricia. *Trick or treat countdown*
Huck, Charlotte S. *A creepy countdown*
Hughes, Shirley. *Olly and me 1-2-3*
Hulme, Joy N. *Easter babies*
Hutchins, Pat. *One hunter*
  Ten red apples
Idle, Molly. *Flora and the chicks*
Imai, Ayano. *The 108th sheep*
Inkpen, Mick. *Kipper's book of numbers*
  Kipper's toybox
Isadora, Rachel. *123 pop!*
Jackson, Ellen. *Octopuses one to ten*
Jacobs, Paul DuBois. *Count on the subway*
Jane, Pamela. *Little elfie one*
  Little goblins ten
  Monster countdown
Jay, Alison. *1 2 3*
Jeffers, Oliver. *The Hueys in None the number*
Jenkins, Emily. *Lemonade in winter*
Jocelyn, Marthe. *Ones and twos*
Johnson, Stephen T. *City by numbers*
Jonas, Ann. *Splash!*
Joyce, William. *The Numberlys*
Kassirer, Sue. *Math fair blues*
Katz, Karen. *Counting kisses*
  Daddy hugs 1 2 3
  Ten tiny babies
  Ten tiny tickles
Keats, Ezra Jack. *One red sun*
Keller, Laurie. *Grandpa Gazillion's number yard*
Kellogg, Steven. *Give the dog a bone*
Kerr, Judith. *One night in the zoo*
Ketteman, Helen. *At the old haunted house*
Kimmelman, Leslie. *How do I love you?*
Kinch, Devon. *Pretty Penny makes ends meet*
  Knick knack paddy whack
Koller, Jackie French. *One monkey too many*
Krans, Kim. *1, 2, 3 dream*
Krebs, Laurie. *We all went on safari*
Kroll, Virginia L. *Equal shmequal*
  Uno, dos, tres, posada!
Kunhardt, Katharine. *Let's count the puppies*
Laminack, Lester L. *Jake's 100th day of school*
Langstaff, John M. *Over in the meadow*

Larochelle, David. *1+1=5*
Lavis, Steve. *Cock-a-doodle-doo*
Law, Diane. *Come out and play: count around the world in five languages*
Lawler, Janet. *Ocean counting*
Lazar, Tara. *7 ate 9*
Ledwon, Peter. *Midnight math twelve terrific math games*
Lee, Huy Voun. *1, 2, 3 go!*
Lee, Mark. *20 big trucks in the middle of the street*
Leedy, Loreen. *Fraction action*
  The great graph contest
  Missing math
  Mission — addition
  2 x 2 = boo!
Lessac, Frané. *Island Counting 123*
Leuck, Laura. *One witch*
Levine, Arthur A. *Monday is one day*
Lewis, J. Patrick. *Arithme-tickle*
Lewison, Wendy Cheyette. *Two is for twins*
Light, Steve. *Have you seen my dragon?*
Limentani, Alison. *How long is a whale?*
  How much does a ladybug weigh?
Lindbergh, Reeve. *Midnight farm*
Litwin, Eric. *Groovy Joe: dance party countdown*
  Pete the Cat and his four groovy buttons
Ljungkvist, Laura. *Follow the line*
Lobel, Anita. *One lighthouse, one moon*
  Ten hungry rabbits
Lodge, Bernard. *How scary*
London, Jonathan. *Count the ways, Little Brown Bear*
Long, Ethan. *One drowsy dragon*
  Soup for one
  The Wing Wing brothers carnival de math
  The Wing Wing brothers geometry palooza!
  The Wing Wing brothers math spectacular!
Lottridge, Celia Barker. *One watermelon seed*
Lynn, Sarah. *1-2-3 va-va-vroom!*
Lyon, George Ella. *Counting on the woods*
Lyons, Kelly Starling. *One more dino on the floor*
Maccarone, Grace. *Miss Lina's ballerinas*
  The three little pigs count to 100
MacDonald, Margaret Read. *A hen, a chick, and a string guitar*
  How many donkeys?
MacDonald, Suse. *Fish, swish! splash, dash!*
  Look whooo's counting
McElligott, Matthew. *Bean thirteen*
  The lion's share
McFarland, Lyn Rossiter. *Mouse went out to get a snack*
McGinty, Alice B. *Ten little lambs*
McGrath, Barbara Barbieri. *Kellogg's froot loops counting fun book*
  Teddy bear addition
  Teddy bear counting
McKellar, Danica. *Goodnight, numbers*
McMillan, Bruce. *Counting wildflowers*
  Eating fractions
  Jelly beans for sale
  One, two, one pair!
McMullan, Kate. *I'm dirty!*
McNamara, Margaret. *How many seeds in a pumpkin?*
McQuinn, Anna. *The sleep sheep*
Maestro, Betsy. *Dollars and cents for Harriet*
Maloney, Peter. *One foot two feet*
Manning, Maurie J. *The aunts go marching*

Mannis, Celeste Davidson. *One leaf rides the wind*
Mansfield, Andy. *One lonely fish*
Mariconda, Barbara. *Sort it out!*
Marino, Gianna. *One too many*
Markel, Michelle. *Tyrannosaurus math*
Markes, Julie. *Sidewalk 1 2 3*
Markle, Sandra. *How many baby pandas?*
Marshall, Natalie. *Five little ducks: a fingers and toes nursery rhyme book*
Martin, Bill, Jr.. *Rock it, sock it, number line*
  Ten little caterpillars
Marzollo, Jean. *Help me learn addition*
  Help me learn numbers 0–20
  Help me learn subtraction
  I spy little numbers
  Ten cats have hats
  Ten little Christmas presents
Massie, Felix. *Dogs in cars*
May, Eleanor. *Albert the muffin-maker*
  The mousier the merrier
Mazzola, Frank. *Counting is for the birds*
Medina, Juana. *One big salad*
Melmed, Laura Krauss. *This first Thanksgiving*
Melvin, Alice. *Counting birds*
Menotti, Andrea. *How many jelly beans?*
Merriam, Eve. *12 ways to get to 11*
Michelson, Richard. *Ten times better*
Micklos, John. *One leaf, two leaves, count with me!*
Milich, Zoran. *City 1 2 3*
Miller, Virginia. *Ten red apples*
Milord, Susan. *Happy one hundredth day!*
Miranda, Anne. *Monster math*
  Vroom, chugga, vroom-vroom
Mitter, Matt. *1, 2, 3, counting rhymes*
Modesitt, Jeanne. *Oh, what a beautiful day!*
Moore, Elaine. *Roly-poly puppies*
Mora, Pat. *One, two, three / Uno, dos, tres*
Morales, Yuyi. *Just a minute: a trickster tale and counting book*
Morozumi, Atsuko. *One gorilla*
Mortensen, Lori. *Mousequerade ball*
Moseley, Keith. *Where's the dinosaur?*
Moss, Lloyd. *Zin! zin! zin! A violin*
Moss, Marissa. *Knick knack paddywack*
Mother Goose. *Mother Goose numbers on the loose*
  1, 2, buckle my shoe
Mullins, Patricia. *One horse waiting for me*
Murphy, Stuart J. *Animals on board*
  Beep beep, vroom vroom!
  The best bug parade
  Betcha!
  Bug dance
  Captain Invincible and the space shapes
  Dave's down-to-earth rock shop
  Dinosaur deals
  Earth Day — hooray!
  Elevator magic
  Every buddy counts
  A fair bear share
  Give me half!
  The greatest gymnast of all
  Henry the fourth
  Jack the builder
  Just enough carrots
  Leaping lizards
  Mall mania
  Missing mittens
  Monster musical chairs
  More or less

The right place for Albert
Tightwad Tod
Slade, Suzanne. *What's new at the zoo?: an animal adding adventure*
What's the difference?
Slate, Joseph. *Miss Bindergarten celebrates the 100th day of kindergarten*
Slingsby, Janet. *Hetty's 100 hats*
Sloat, Teri. *Zip! zoom! on a broom*
Smith, Danna. *Swallow the leader*
Smith, David J. *If America were a village*
Smith, Maggie. *Counting our way to Maine*
Dear Daisy, get well soon
One naked baby
Sorenson, Ashley. *The very cold, freezing, no-numbers day*
Souders, Taryn. *Whole-y cow!*
Spanyol, Jessica. *Carlo likes counting*
Sper, Emily. *Hanukkah: a counting book in English, Hebrew, and Yiddish*
Spinelli, Eileen. *Miss Fox's class earns a field trip*
Together at Christmas
Spurr, Elizabeth. *Two bears beneath the stairs*
Staake, Bob. *My little 1 2 3 book*
Stevens, April. *Waking up Wendell*
Stickland, Paul. *A number of dinosaurs*
Ten terrible dinosaurs
Stiegemeyer, Julie. *Gobble gobble crash!*
Seven little bunnies
Stills, Caroline. *The house of twelve bunnies*
Mice mischief
Sturges, Philemon. *Ten flashing fireflies*
Sturgis, Brenda Reeves. *Ten turkeys in the road*
Surplice, Holly. *Guinea pig party*
Swinburne, Stephen R. *Water for one, water for everyone*
What's a pair? What's a dozen?
Sykes, Julie. *Dora's chicks*
Szekeres, Cyndy. *I can count 100 bunnies, and so can you!*
Tafuri, Nancy. *The big storm*
Counting to Christmas
Who's counting?
Tang, Greg. *Math appeal*
Math fables
Math fables too
Thomas, Jan. *Is that wise, Pig?*
Thompson, Lauren. *How many cats?*
Little Quack
Little Quack: dial-a-duck
Little Quack's hide and seek
One riddle, one answer
Thomson, Sarah L. *Around the neighborhood*
Todd, Mark. *Start your engines*
Toft, Kim Michelle. *One less fish*
Trapani, Iza. *Haunted party*
Tudor, Tasha. *1 is one*
Van Fleet, Matthew. *One yellow lion*
Van Laan, Nancy. *Mama rocks, Papa sings*
A tree for me
Van Lieshout, Maria. *Flight 1-2-3*
Van Woerkom, Dorothy. *Abu Ali counts his donkeys*
Vega, Denise. *Build a burrito*
Verdick, Elizabeth. *Peep leap*
Voce, Louise. *Over in the meadow*
Waber, Bernard. *Lyle walks the dogs*
Wadsworth, Ginger. *One tiger growls*
Wahman, Joe. *Snowboy 1, 2, 3*
Wallace, Nancy Elizabeth. *Count down to clean up*

Planting seeds
Ready, set, 100th day!
Wallmark, Laurie. *Ada Byron Lovelace and the thinking machine*
Walsh, Ellen Stoll. *Mouse count*
Walton, Rick. *One more bunny*
So many bunnies
Ward, Jennifer. *Over in the garden*
Somewhere in the ocean
Way up in the Arctic
Weeks, Sarah. *Counting Ovejas*
Wells, Rosemary. *Emily's first 100 days of school*
How many? How much?
Max counts his chickens
Max's toys
Weston, Carrie. *If a chicken stayed for supper*
Wildsmith, Brian. *Brian Wildsmith 1 2 3*
Wiley, Thom. *One sheep, blue sheep*
Williams, Brenda. *The real princess*
Williams, Rozanne Lanczak. *The coin counting book*
Williams, Sue. *Dinnertime*
Let's go visiting
Williams, Suzanne. *Old MacDonald in the city*
Ten naughty little monkeys
Wilson, Anna. *Over in the grasslands*
Wilson, Karma. *Bear counts*
Wojtowycz, David. *Animal antics from 1 to 10*
Wolff, Ashley. *Baby Bear counts one*
Wolff, Ferida. *On Halloween night*
Wong, Janet S. *Hide and seek*
Wood, Audrey. *Ten little fish*
Wood, Jakki. *Moo moo, brown cow*
Yates, Louise. *Dog loves counting*
Yates, Philip. *Ten little mummies*
Yektai, Niki. *Bears at the beach*
Yolen, Jane. *How do dinosaurs count to ten?*
Young, Cybèle. *Ten birds*
Ten birds meet a monster
Ziefert, Harriet. *Counting chickens*
A dozen ducklings lost and found
Knick-knack paddywhack
Rockheads
Two little witches
You can't buy a dinosaur with a dime
Zuffi, Stefano. *Art 123*

Countries, foreign *see* Foreign lands

Country

Aesop. *The country mouse and the city mouse*
Milly and Tilly
The town mouse and the country mouse, ill. by Lorinda Bryan Cauley
The town mouse and the country mouse, ill. by Janet Stevens
The town mouse and the country mouse: an Aesop fable, ill. by Helen Ward
The town mouse and the country mouse: an Aesop fable, ill. by Bernadette Watts
Town mouse, country mouse, ill. by Jan Brett
Town mouse, country mouse, ill. by Carol Jones
Bernhard, Durga. *To and fro, fast and slow*
Brooks, Nigel. *Country mouse cottage*
Burton, Virginia Lee. *The little house*
Carlstrom, Nancy White. *The snow speaks*
Cecka, Melanie. *Violet goes to the country*
Chall, Marsha Wilson. *Prairie train*

Christie, R. Gregory. *Mousetropolis*
Cline-Ransome, Lesa. *Quilt alphabet*
  Quilt counting
Cummins, Julie. *Country kid, city kid*
Curato, Mike. *Little Elliot, fall friends*
Dahlie, Elizabeth. *Bernelly and Harriet*
Davies, Jacqueline. *The night is singing*
Dennard, Deborah. *Hedgehog haven*
Dorros, Arthur. *City chicken*
Gibbons, Gail. *County fair*
Gray, Rita. *Nonna's porch*
Hesse, Karen. *Spuds*
Hoffman, Elizabeth Stokes. *Miss Renée's mice go to*
  an exhibition
Jocelyn, Marthe. *Mayfly*
Johnson, Angela. *Down the winding road*
Kilby, Don. *In the country*
Lawrence, Mary. *What's that sound?*
Lewin, Ted. *Fair!*
Lewis, Kim. *One summer day*
Loomis, Christine. *Cowboy bunnies*
MacLachlan, Patricia. *All the places to love*
Martin, Bill, Jr.. *Barn dance!*
Miller, William. *Jenny and the peddler*
Mollel, Tololwa M. *Ananse's feast*
Munro, Roxie. *The inside-outside book of Texas*
  Mazescapes
Parks, Carmen. *Farmers market*
Polacco, Patricia. *Meteor!*
Provensen, Alice. *Town and country*
Rockwell, Anne. *Willy can count*
Rudy, Maggie. *City mouse, country mouse*
Rylant, Cynthia. *Appalachia*
  Christmas in the country
  Night in the country
  Scarecrow
Schertle, Alice. *Down the road*
Southwell, Jandelyn. *The little country town*
Sweeney, Linda Booth. *When the snow falls*
Tucker, Kathy. *Do cowboys ride bikes?*
Van Allsburg, Chris. *The stranger*
Wyeth, Sharon Dennis. *Always my dad*
Yolen, Jane. *Letting Swift River go*
Zullo, Germano. *Line 135*

Courage *see* Character traits – bravery

Cowboys, cowgirls

Anglund, Joan Walsh. *The brave cowboy*
  The cowboy's Christmas
Appelt, Kathi. *Cowboy dreams*
Balcziak, Bill. *Pecos Bill*
Bell, Cece. *Sock Monkey rides again*
Brownlow, Mike. *Way out West — with a baby!*
Bruins, David. *The call of the cowboy*
Cowley, Joy. *Where horses run free*
Danneberg, Julie. *Cowboy Slim*
Diterlizzi, Angela. *I wanna be a cowgirl*
Elya, Susan Middleton. *Cowboy José*
Fleming, Denise. *Buster goes to Cowboy Camp*
Frank, John. *The toughest cowboy, Or, How the Wild*
  West was tamed
Gibbons, Gail. *Yippee-yay!*
The gingerbread boy. *The Gingerbread Cowboy*
Greathouse, Carol. *The dinosaur tamer*
Gulbis, Stephen. *Cowgirl Rosie and her five baby*
  bison

Harper, Jo. *Ollie Jolly, rodeo clown*
High, Linda Oatman. *Tenth Avenue cowboy*
Hill, Eric. *Spot goes to a party*
Hoefler, Kate. *Real cowboys*
Holub, Joan. *Cinderdog and the wicked stepcat*
Janni, Rebecca. *Every cowgirl goes to school*
  Every cowgirl loves a rodeo
  Every cowgirl needs a horse
  Every cowgirl needs dancing boots
Johnston, Tony. *The cowboy and the black-eyed pea*
Kellogg, Steven. *Pecos Bill*
Ketteman, Helen. *Bubba the cowboy prince*
Kimmel, Eric A. *Little Britches and the rattlers*
Knowlton, Laurie Lazzaro. *Why cowgirls are such*
  sweet talkers
Langdo, Bryan. *Tornado Slim and the magic cowboy*
  hat
Lawson, Dorie McCullough. *Tex*
Lawson, Julie. *Arizona Charlie and the Klondike Kid*
Lester, Julius. *Black cowboy, wild horses*
Liebman, Daniel. *I want to be a cowboy*
Little old lady who swallowed a fly. *There once was a*
  cowpoke who swallowed an ant
Loomis, Christine. *Cowboy bunnies*
Lowell, Susan. *The bootmaker and the elves*
McClements, George. *Ridin' dinos with Buck Bronco*
Maidment, Stella. *Cowboy puzzles*
Mitchell, Marianne. *Joe Cinders*
Montijo, Rhode. *The Halloween Kid*
Mortensen, Lori. *Cowpoke Clyde and Dirty Dawg*
  Cowpoke Clyde rides the range
Moser, Lisa. *Cowboy Boyd and Mighty Calliope*
Munro, Roxie. *The inside-outside book of Texas*
Perkins, Maripat. *Rodeo Red*
Pinkney, Andrea Davis. *Bill Pickett, rodeo ridin'*
  cowboy
Rash, Andy. *Are you a horse?*
Reynolds, Aaron. *Pirates vs. cowboys*
Roberts, Bethany. *Birthday mice*
Rounds, Glen. *Cowboys*
Rubel, Nicole. *A cowboy named Ernestine*
Sadler, Marilyn. *Alice from Dallas*
Sanders, Rob. *Cowboy Christmas*
Sauer, Tammi. *Cowboy camp*
Schanzer, Rosalyn. *The Old Chisholm Trail*
Schnitzler, Pattie L. *Widdermaker*
Scieszka, Jon. *Cowboy and Octopus*
Smith, Janice Lee. *Jess and the stinky cowboys*
Stein, David Ezra. *Cowboy Ned and Andy*
  Ned's new friend
Stutson, Caroline. *Cowpokes*
Thomas, Jan. *Let's sing a lullaby with the Brave*
  Cowboy
Tibo, Gilles. *The cowboy kid*
Tucker, Kathy. *Do cowboys ride bikes?*
Van Slyke, Rebecca. *Lexie the word wrangler*
Wheeler, Lisa. *Sixteen cows*
Winter, Jeanette. *Cowboy Charlie*
Wood, Audrey. *A cowboy Christmas*

Cows *see* Animals – bulls, cows

Crafts *see* Activities – making things

Creation

Alexander, Cecil Frances. *All creatures great and*
  small

All things bright and beautiful, ill. by Ashley Bryan
All things bright and beautiful, ill. by Anna Vojtech
All things bright and beautiful, ill. by Bruce Whatley
Anaya, Rudolfo A. *Roadrunner's dance*
Bible. Old Testament. Genesis. *Genesis*
　The Genesis of it all
　Let there be light
Boroson, Martin. *Becoming me*
Brown, Kerry. *Tupag the dreamer*
Cohen, Deborah Bodin. *The seventh day*
dePaola, Tomie. *Let the whole earth sing praise*
Downey, Lynn. *This is the earth that God made*
Fisher, Leonard Everett. *The seven days of creation*
Fleischman, Paul. *First light, first life*
Goble, Paul. *The great race of the birds and animals*
　Remaking the earth
Goodings, Christina. *Creation story*
Greene, Rhonda Gowler. *The beautiful world that God made*
Grimes, Nikki. *At break of day*
Haley, Gail E. *Two bad boys*
Hansen, Felicity. *The first bear*
Hofmeyr, Dianne. *The star-bearer*
Jaffe, Nina. *The golden flower*
Johnson, James Weldon. *The Creation*
King, Thomas. *Coyote sings to the moon*
Lester, Julius. *What a truly cool world*
Lewis, Jacqueline Janette. *You are so wonderful*
Lindbergh, Reeve. *The circle of days*
Pia Toya
Poole, Amy Lowry. *How the rooster got his crown*
Rodanas, Kristina. *Follow the stars*
Rohmer, Harriet. *How we came to the fifth world*
Root, Phyllis. *Big Momma makes the world*
Rosen, Michael J. *The dog who walked with God*
Rylant, Cynthia. *Creation*
Slate, Joseph. *Story time for Little Porcupine*
Strauss, Susan. *When woman became the sea*
Van Kampen, Vlasta. *Bear tales*
Van Laan, Nancy. *Rainbow crow*
Wolkstein, Diane. *Sun Mother wakes the world*
Wood, Audrey. *The rainbow bridge*
Wood, Nancy C. *Mr. and Mrs. God in the creation kitchen*
Ziefert, Harriet. *First He made the sun*

Creatures *see* Monsters; Mythical creatures

Creeks *see* Rivers

Crime

Ada, Alma Flor. *The gold coin*
Agee, Jon. *My rhinoceros*
Ahlberg, Janet. *It was a dark and stormy night*
Auch, Mary Jane. *Eggs mark the spot*
Balouch, Kristen. *The king and the three thieves*
Barracca, Debra. *Maxi, the hero*
Base, Graeme. *The Jewel Fish of Karnak*
Biedrzycki, David. *Ace Lacewing, Bug Detective*
　Breaking news: bears to the rescue
Birtha, Becky. *Far apart, close in heart*
Burdett, Lois. *Hamlet for kids*
　Macbeth for kids
Casanova, Mary. *The day Dirk Yeller came to town*

Crummel, Susan Stevens. *Sherlock Bones and the missing cheese*
Dahl, Roald. *The giraffe and the pelly and me*
Davies, Matt. *Ben rides on*
Delessert, Etienne. *Alert!*
Derby, Sally. *Two fools and a horse*
DiFiori, Lawrence. *Jackie and the Shadow Snatcher*
Docherty, Helen. *The Snatchabook*
Donaldson, Julia. *The Highway Rat*
Douglas, Erin. *Get that pest!*
Durant, Alan. *Big Bad Bunny*
Egan, Tim. *The trial of Cardigan Jones*
Escoffier, Michaël. *Brief thief*
Flanagan, Alice K. *A day in court with Mrs. Trinh*
　Officer Brown keeps neighborhoods safe
Geisert, Arthur. *Mystery*
　Nursery crimes
　Pigaroons
Glicksman, Caroline. *Eric the math bear*
Goode, Diane. *Tiger trouble*
Grey, Mini. *The adventures of the dish and the spoon*
Grimm, Jacob and Wilhelm. *The Bremen town band*
　The Bremen town musicians, ill. by Bill Dickson
　The Bremen town musicians, ill. by Ilse Plume
　The Bremen town musicians, ill. by Bernadette Watts
　The Bremen town musicians, ill. by Lisbeth Zwerger
　Musicians of Bremen
　Musicians of Bremen / Los musicos de Bremner
Hancocks, Helen. *Penguin in peril*
Hoffman, Eric. *Play Lady / La Señora Juguetona*
Hogrogian, Nonny. *The contest*
Huling, Jan. *Ol' Bloo's boogie-woogie band and blues ensemble*
James, Brian. *The Supertwins and tooth trouble*
Jordan, Sandra. *Mr. and Mrs. Portly and their little dog Snack*
Klassen, Jon. *This is not my hat*
Knapp, Ruthie. *Who stole Mona Lisa?*
Kotzwinkle, William. *Walter, the farting dog: trouble at the yard sale*
Krall, Dan. *The great lollipop caper*
Lane, Adam J. B. *Stop thief!*
Lawson, Julie. *Arizona Charlie and the Klondike Kid*
McCully, Emily Arnold. *An outlaw Thanksgiving*
McLaren, Meg. *Pigeon P.I.*
McPhail, David. *Moony B. Finch, fastest draw in the West*
Madonna. *Yakov and the seven thieves*
Magoon, Scott. *The boy who cried bigfoot!*
Marciano, John Bemelmans. *Madeline and the cats of Rome*
Mead, Alice. *Billy and Emma*
Moss, P. Buckley. *Reuben and the quilt*
Poffenberger, Nancy M. *September 11, 2001*
Price, Kathy. *The Bourbon Street musicians*
Richardson, Bill. *The alphabet thief*
Rock, Brian. *The deductive detective*
Rubin, Adam. *Secret pizza party*
SanAngelo, Ryan. *Eddie spaghetti*
Sazaklis, John. *Fowl play*
Schneider, Howie. *Fast 'n Snappy*
Shea, Bob. *Kid Sheriff and the terrible Toads*
Skolsky, Mindy Warshaw. *Hannah and the whistling tea kettle*
Slobodkina, Esphyr. *Circus caps for sale*
Sneed, Brad. *Deputy Harvey and the ant cow caper*
Stephens, Helen. *How to hide a lion*

Ungerer, Tomi. *The three robbers*
Van Nutt, Julia. *The monster in the shadows*
Walton, Rick. *Bertie was a watchdog*
Warnes, Tim. *The great cheese robbery*
Weigelt, Udo. *It wasn't me*
Wisniewski, David. *Sumo Mouse*
Yee, Wong Herbert. *Detective Small in the amazing banana caper*
   The Officers' Ball
Young, Jessica. *Spy Guy*
Zommer, Yuval. *One hundred sausages*

Crocodiles *see* Reptiles – alligators, crocodiles

Cruelty to animals *see* Character traits – kindness to animals

Crustaceans

Fenske, Jonathan. *Barnacle is bored*
Himmelman, John. *A pill bug's life*
Tokuda, Yukihisa. *I'm a pill bug*

Crustaceans – centipedes, millipedes

Greenaway, Theresa. *Centipedes and millipedes*
Ross, Tony. *Centipede's 100 shoes*

Crustaceans – crabs

Boyce, Katie. *Hector the hermit crab*
Carle, Eric. *A house for Hermit Crab*
Galloway, Ruth. *Clumsy crab*
Horowitz, Ruth. *Crab moon*
Kalan, Robert. *Moving day*
McDonald, Megan. *Is this a house for Hermit Crab?*
Mason, Janeen I. *Ocean commotion*
Peet, Bill. *Kermit the hermit*
Raschka, Chris. *Crabby crab*
Riddell, Chris. *Platypus*
Tafuri, Nancy. *Follow me!*
Walsh, Ellen Stoll. *Hamsters to the rescue*
Ward, Helen. *Old shell, new shell*

Crustaceans – lobsters

Schwarz, Viviane. *Shark and Lobster's amazing undersea adventure*

Crustaceans – shrimp

McGaw, Wayne T. *T-boy of the bayou*
Reynolds, Aaron. *Sea Monkey and Bob*

Crying *see* Emotions

Cumulative tales

Aardema, Verna. *Bringing the rain to Kapiti Plain*
   The riddle of the drum
Ada, Alma Flor. *The Christmas tree / El arbol de Navidad*
   The gold coin
   The rooster who went to his uncle's wedding
Alexander, Lloyd. *Fortune tellers*
Alger, Leclaire Gowans. *Always room for one more*
Arnold, Tedd. *No more water in the tub!*

Asbjørnsen, P. C. *The three billy goats Gruff*, ill. by Stephen Carpenter
   The three billy goats Gruff, ill. by Paul Galdone
   The three billy goats gruff, ill. by Jerry Pinkney
   The three billy goats Gruff, ill. by Glen Rounds
   The three billy goats Gruff, ill. by Janet Stevens
Aston, Dianna Hutts. *Loony Little*
Azore, Barbara. *Wanda and the wild hair*
Baker, Alan. *Black and White Rabbit's ABC*
Baker, Ken. *Old MacDonald had a dragon*
Barton, Byron. *Buzz, buzz, buzz*
Beil, Karen Magnuson. *Jack's house*
Bell, Babs. *The bridge is up!*
Bertrand, Diane Gonzales. *The party for Papa Luis / La fiesta para Papa Luis*
Birdseye, Tom. *Soap! soap! don't forget the soap!*
Blackstone, Stella. *An island in the sun*
Bond, Rebecca. *The great doughnut parade*
Bowen, Anne. *I know an old teacher*
Brendler, Carol. *Not very scary*
Brenner, Emily. *On the first day of grade school*
Brett, Jan. *Berlioz the bear*
   The mitten
   The turnip
Brisson, Pat. *Hobbledy-clop*
Brown, Ruth. *A dark, dark tale*
Bryan, Ashley. *Beat the story-drum, pum-pum*
Burningham, John. *Mr. Gumpy's outing*
Burton, Virginia Lee. *Katy and the big snow*
Capucilli, Alyssa Satin. *Inside a zoo in the city*
Carle, Eric. *Pancakes, pancakes*
Carter, David A. *Old MacDonald had a farm: a pop-up book*
Cazet, Denys. *Nothing at all*
Chaconas, Dori. *Don't slam the door!*
Chicken Little. *Brave Chicken Little*
   Chicken Little
   Henny Penny, ill. by Emily Bolam
   Henny Penny, ill. by Paul Galdone
   Henny-Penny, ill. by Jane Wattenberg
   Henny Penny, ill. by Sophie Windham
   The sky is falling
Clarke, Jane. *Stuck in the mud*
   Who woke the baby?
Cohen, Caron Lee. *Digger Pig and the turnip*
Colandro, Lucille. *There was a cold lady who swallowed some snow!*
   There was an old lady who swallowed a clover!
   There was an old lady who swallowed a frog!
   There was an old lady who swallowed some books!
Cooke, Trish. *So much*
Corr, Christopher. *Deep in the woods*
Davidson, Rebecca Piatt. *All the world's a stage*
Deacon, Alexis. *Cheese belongs to you!*
de Las Casas, Dianne. *The house that Witchy built*
dePaola, Tomie. *Jack*
De Regniers, Beatrice Schenk. *What did you put in your pocket?*
Donaldson, Julia. *The Giant Jumperee*
Downey, Lynn. *This is the earth that God made*
Downing, Johnette. *There was an old lady who swallowed some bugs*
Dunrea, Olivier. *Bear Noel*
   Me and Annie McPhee
Edwards, David. *The pen that Pa built*
Edwards, Pamela Duncan. *Jack and Jill's treehouse*
   The Wright brothers
Egielski, Richard. *The sleepless little vampire*
Emberley, Barbara. *Drummer Hoff*

Emberley, Ed. *The red hen*
Emberley, Rebecca. *Chicken Little*
Emberley, Rebecca, et al. *There was an old monster*
Ernst, Lisa Campbell. *The Gingerbread Girl goes animal crackers*
   Stella Louella's runaway book
Fleming, Candace. *Oh, no!*
Fox, Mem. *Hattie and the fox*
   Shoes from grandpa
Frazee, Marla. *Hush, little baby: a folk song with pictures*
Gág, Wanda. *Millions of cats*
Galdone, Paul. *Cat goes fiddle-i-fee*
Garriel, Barbara S. *I know a shy fellow who swallowed a cello*
Gershator, Phillis. *Who's awake in springtime?*
The gingerbread boy. *Can't catch me*
   Gingerbread baby
   The gingerbread boy, ill. by Emily Bolam
   The gingerbread boy, ill. by Richard Egielski
   The gingerbread boy, ill. by Paul Galdone
   The Gingerbread Cowboy
   The gingerbread girl
   The gingerbread man, ill. by Carol Jones
   The gingerbread man, ill. by Megan Lloyd
   The gingerbread man, ill. by Barbara McClintock
   The gingerbread man, ill. by Béatrice Rodriguez
   The Gingerbread Man loose in the school
   The Library Gingerbread Man
   The Ninjabread Man
   The pancake boy
   Señorita Gordita
   Whiff, sniff, nibble and chew
Gold-Vukson, Marji E. *Grandpa and me on Tu B'Shevat*
Gorbachev, Valeri. *Dragon is coming!*
Gutch, Michael. *Sticky, sticky, stuck!*
Hall, Algy Craig. *Dino bites!*
Harper, Charise Mericle. *There was a bold lady who wanted a star*
Hatch, Elizabeth. *Halloween night*
Hester, Denia Lewis. *Grandma Lena's big ol' turnip*
Hill, Susanna Leonard. *The house that Mack built*
Hillenbrand, Will. *Fiddle-i-fee*
Hogrogian, Nonny. *One fine day*
Hopkins, Jackie Mims. *Prairie chicken little*
Horning, Sandra. *The giant hug*
Horsbrugh, Wilma. *The train to Glasgow*
House, Catherine. *A stork in a baobab tree*
The house that Jack built. *The house that Jack built*, ill. by Diana Mayo
   The house that Jack built, ill. by Jeanette Winter
   This is the house that Jack built
Howland, Naomi. *The matzah man*
Hughes, Shirley. *Alfie gets in first*
Hush, little baby
Hutchins, Pat. *Don't forget the bacon!*
   Good-night Owl
   Titch
Isadora, Rachel. *Old Mikamba had a farm*
   There was a tree
Jackson, Alison. *I know an old lady who swallowed a pie*
Jones, Stella J. *The very grumpy day*
Kalan, Robert. *Jump, frog, jump!*
   Moving day
Kimmel, Eric A. *The runaway tortilla*
Klostermann, Penny Parker. *There was an old dragon who swallowed a knight*

Knick knack paddy whack
Lendroth, Susan. *Old Manhattan has some farms*
Lester, Helen. *It wasn't my fault*
Levine, Abby. *This is the pumpkin*
Lewis, Kevin. *The lot at the end of my block*
Lewison, Wendy Cheyette. *"Buzz," said the bee*
   Going to sleep on the farm
Little old lady who swallowed a fly. *I know an old lady*
   I know an old lady who swallowed a fly, ill. by Stephen Gulbis
   I know an old lady who swallowed a fly, ill. by Glen Rounds
   I know an old lady who swallowed a fly, ill. by Nadine Bernard Westcott
   There once was a cowpoke who swallowed an ant
   There was an old lady who swallowed a fly, ill. by Pam Adams
   There was an old lady who swallowed a fly, ill. by Rashin Kheiriyeh
   There was an old lady who swallowed a fly, ill. by Simms Taback
   There was an old monkey who swallowed a frog
   There was an old mummy who swallowed a spider
   There was an old pirate who swallowed a fish
The little red hen. *The little red hen*, ill. by Byron Barton
   The little red hen, ill. by Emily Bolam
   The little red hen, ill. by Paul Galdone
   Little red hen
   The little red hen, ill. by Jerry Pinkney
   The little red hen, ill. by Kate Slater
   The little red hen, ill. by Annie West
   The little red hen, ill. by Margot Zemach
   The little red hen: an old fable
   The Little Red Hen makes a pizza
Lloyd-Jones, Sally. *Old MacNoah had an ark*
Long, Ethan. *The book that Zack wrote*
Long, Kathy. *The runaway shopping cart*
Lupton, Hugh. *Pirican Pic and Pirican Mor*
MacDonald, Elizabeth. *The wolf is coming!*
MacDonald, Margaret Read. *A hen, a chick, and a string guitar*
   The squeaky door
   Teeny Weeny Bop
Mack, Jeff. *Ah ha!*
Mahy, Margaret. *The Christmas tree tangle*
Manning, Maurie J. *The aunts go marching*
Margolin, H. Ellen. *Goin' to Boston*
Martin, Bill, Jr.. *Baby bear, baby bear, what do you see?*
   Brown bear, brown bear, what do you see?
   Old devil wind
Mayhew, James. *Where's my hug?*
Medearis, Angela Shelf. *Too much talk*
Melvin, Alice. *The high street*
Metzger, Steve. *This is the house that monsters built*
Millard, Glenda. *Isabella's garden*
Mollel, Tololwa M. *Rhinos for lunch and elephants for supper*
Monroe, Chris. *Bug on a bike*
Mora, Pat. *A piñata in a pine tree*
Moser, Lisa. *Perfect soup*
Moss, Marissa. *Knick knack paddywack*
Munsch, Robert N. *Stephanie's ponytail*
Murray, Alison. *The house that Zack built*
Neitzel, Shirley. *The bag I'm taking to Grandma's*
   The dress I'll wear to the party
   The house I'll build for the wrens
   I'm not feeling well today

Curiosity *see* Character traits – curiosity

Currency *see* Money

Cycles *see* Activities – bicycling; Motorcycles

Dark *see* Night; Power failures

Darkness – fear *see* Emotions – fear

Dawn *see* Morning

Day

Andreasen, Dan. *Saturday with Daddy*
Ashman, Linda. *Just another morning*
Ballard, Robin. *My day, your day*
Berger, Carin. *A perfect day*
Bernhard, Durga. *While you are sleeping: a lift-the-flap book of time around the world*
Borando, Silvia. *Black cat, white cat*
Bradley, Kimberly Brubaker. *Favorite things*
Braun, Sebastien. *I love my daddy*
Brown, Margaret Wise. *Good day, good night*
Calmenson, Stephanie. *Ollie's school day*
Carluccio, Maria. *The sounds around town*
Charlip, Remy. *A perfect day*
    Why I will never ever ever ever have enough time to read this book
Chast, Roz. *Around the clock!*
Cocca-Leffler, Maryann. *Time to say bye-bye*
Freedman, Claire. *One magical day*
George, Jean Craighead. *Morning, noon, and night*
Geras, Adèle. *My wishes for you*
Gomi, Taro. *The great day*
Graham, Bob. *How the sun got to Coco's house*
Haley, Amanda. *It's a baby's world*
Heidbreder, Robert. *Noisy poems for a busy day*
Hopgood, Tim. *Wow! said the owl*
Jenkins, Emily. *Water in the park*
    What happens on Wednesdays
Johnson, Angela. *Lottie Paris lives here*
Kavanagh, Peter. *I love my mama*
Kerley, Barbara. *One world, one day*
Lamb, Albert. *Tell me the day backwards*
Lobel, Anita. *Hello, day!*
Low, William. *Daytime nighttime*
McGee, Marni. *The noisy farm*
Marley, Cedella. *Every little thing*
Martin, Ruth. *Moon dreams*
Melmed, Laura Krauss. *A hug goes around*
Minor, Wendell. *Daylight starlight wildlife*
Modesitt, Jeanne. *Oh, what a beautiful day!*
Munro, Roxie. *Desert days, desert nights*
Murphy, Stuart J. *It's about time!*
Rong, Yu. *A lovely day for Amelia Goose*
Rosenthal, Amy Krouse. *Awake beautiful child*
Ross, Michael Elsohn. *Earth cycles*
Rylant, Cynthia. *All in a day*
Schaefer, Carole Lexa. *Someone says*
Seven spunky monkeys
Srinivasan, Divya. *Little Owl's day*
Turner, Ann Warren. *In the heart*
Underwood, Deborah. *The loud book!*
Waring, Geoff. *Oscar and the moth*
Yee, Wong Herbert. *Summer days and nights*

Day care *see* School – nursery

Daydreams *see* Dreams

Days of the week, months of the year

Alakija, Polly. *Counting chickens*
Archer, Micha. *Daniel finds a poem*
Baker, Keith. *Hap-pea all year*
Boling, Katherine. *New year be coming!*
Boling, Ruth L. *Come worship with me*
Brian, Janeen. *Where does Thursday go?*
Bunting, Eve. *Sing a song of piglets*

Butterworth, Nick. *Jasper's beanstalk*
Carle, Eric. *Today is Monday*
    The very hungry caterpillar
Carlstrom, Nancy White. *How do you say it today, Jesse Bear?*
A child's calendar
Cohn, Scotti. *One wolf howls*
Day, Nancy Raines. *A kitten's year*
Demas, Corinne. *Valentine surprise*
De Regniers, Beatrice Schenk. *What did you put in your pocket?*
Downing, Johnette. *Today is Monday in Louisiana*
Downing, Julie. *No hugs till Saturday*
Elya, Susan Middleton. *A year full of holidays*
Fernandes, Eugenie. *Big week for little mouse*
Ficocelli, Elizabeth. *Kid tea*
Firmin, Josie. *My week*
Fleming, Denise. *5 little ducks*
Gershator, Phillis. *This is the day!*
Glenn, Sharlee. *Just what Mama needs*
Gravett, Emily. *The rabbit problem*
Guion, Melissa. *Baby penguins love their Mama*
Hague, Kathleen. *Calendarbears*
Hanson, Warren. *It's Monday, Mrs. Jolly Bones!*
Harness, Cheryl. *Our colonial year*
Hayles, Marsha. *Pajamas anytime*
Hewitt, Kathryn. *No dogs here!*
Hubbell, Patricia. *Rabbit moon*
Jackson, Ellen. *April*
    August
    December
    February
    January
    July
    June
    March
    May
    November
    October
    September
Katz, Bobbi. *Once around the sun*
Katz, Karen. *Twelve hats for Lena*
Katz, Susan B. *All year round*
Leduc, Emilie. *All year round*
Lesser, Carolyn. *What a wonderful day to be a cow*
Levine, Arthur A. *Monday is one day*
Livingston, Myra Cohn. *Calendar*
Lobel, Anita. *One lighthouse, one moon*
McCurdy, Michael. *An Algonquian year*
McGowan, Michael. *Sunday is for God*
Martin, Bill, Jr.. *The turning of the year*
Marzollo, Jean. *I spy, year-round challenger!*
Newman, Jeff. *The boys*
Obed, Ellen Bryan. *Who would like a Christmas tree?*
Otten, Charlotte F. *January rides the wind*
Peters, Lisa Westberg. *October smiled back*
Polacco, Patricia. *Because of Thursday*
Preston-Gannon, Frann. *Pepper and Poe*
Provensen, Alice. *The year at Maple Hill Farm*
Rau, Dana Meachen. *I'll make you a card*
Reidy, Jean. *Busy builders, busy week!*
Rosenberg, Madelyn. *The Schmutzy Family*
Rylant, Cynthia. *Bless us all*
    Give me grace
Santos, Rosa. *Play date*
Sayre, April Pulley. *Eat like a bear*
Scarry, Richard. *Richard Scarry's best first book ever!*
Sendak, Maurice. *Chicken soup with rice*
Seven, John. *A year with friends*

Shahan, Sherry. *Fiesta!*
Shields, Carol Diggory. *Day by day a week goes round*
  Month by month a year goes round
Shulevitz, Uri. *One Monday morning*
Singer, Marilyn. *Turtle in July*
Smith, Maggie. *Dear Daisy, get well soon*
Spinelli, Eileen. *Heat wave*
  Here comes the year
Tafuri, Nancy. *Snowy flowy blowy*
Taylor, Joanne. *Full moon rising*
Thomas, Joyce Carol. *Gingerbread days*
Thompson, Richard. *The follower*
Van der Meer, Mara. *Can we play?*
Verdet, Andre. *All about time*
Wang, Xiaohong. *One year in Beijing*
Ward, Cindy. *Cookie's week*
Wells, Rosemary. *My kindergarten*
Winnick, Karen B. *A year goes round*
Wolff, Ashley. *When Lucy goes out walking*
Wood, Audrey. *Heckedy Peg*
Young, Ed. *Seven blind mice*

Deafness *see* Anatomy – ears; Disabilities –
  deafness; Senses – hearing

Death

Abley, Mark. *Ghost cat*
Aliki. *Mummies made in Egypt*
Alvarez, Julia. *Where do they go?*
Anaya, Rudolfo A. *Farolitos for Abuelo*
Andersen, Hans Christian. *It's perfectly true!*
  The little match girl, ill. by Rachel Isadora
  The little match girl, ill. by Blair Lent
  The little match girl, ill. by Jerry Pinkney
  The little matchstick girl
Anholt, Laurence. *Seven for a secret*
Bagley, Jessixa. *Boats for Papa*
Barron, T. A. *Where is Grandpa?*
Bateman, Teresa. *Keeper of soles*
The best cat in the world
Bley, Anette. *And what comes after a thousand?*
Blumenthal, Deborah. *The blue house dog*
Boyden, Linda. *The blue roses*
Brisson, Pat. *I remember Miss Perry*
Brown, Laurie Krasny. *When dinosaurs die*
Brown, Margaret Wise. *The dead bird*
Bunting, Eve. *Rudi's pond*
Burleigh, Robert. *Good-bye, Sheepie*
Burrowes, Adjoa J. *Grandma's purple flowers*
Castellucci, Cecil. *Grandma's gloves*
Cazet, Denys. *A fish in his pocket*
Clifton, Lucille. *Everett Anderson's goodbye*
Cobb, Rebecca. *Missing Mommy*
Cochran, Bill. *The forever dog*
Coerr, Eleanor. *Sadako*
Cohen, Miriam. *Jim's dog Muffins*, ill. by Ronald
  Himler
  Jim's dog Muffins, ill. by Lillian Hoban
Cooke, Trish. *The grandad tree*
Cooper, Elisha. *Big cat, little cat*
Crowe, Carole. *Turtle girl*
Davies, Nicola. *The pond*
dePaola, Tomie. *Nana Upstairs and Nana
  Downstairs*
Doray, Malika. *One more Wednesday*
Fletcher, Ralph. *Grandpa never lies*
Fox, Mem. *Sophie*

Fraustino, Lisa Rowe. *The hickory chair*
Fritts, Mary Bahr. *If Nathan were here*
Genechten, Guido van. *Ricky and the squirrel*
Goble, Paul. *Beyond the ridge*
Goldman, Judy. *Uncle Monarch and the Day of the
  Dead*
Goldstyn, Jacques. *Bertolt*
Gregory, Nan. *Wild Girl and Gran*
Grimm, Edward. *The doorman*
Hanson, Regina. *A season for mangoes*
Harris, Robie H. *Goodbye, Mousie*
Haynes, Max. *Grandma's gone to live in the stars*
Hest, Amy. *My old pal, Oscar*
Hill, Frances. *The bug cemetery*
Hole, Stian. *Anna's heaven*
Hopkinson, Deborah. *Bluebird summer*
Huneck, Stephen. *Sally goes to heaven*
Jeffers, Oliver. *The heart and the bottle*
Jeffs, Stephanie. *Jenny*
  Josh
Johnston, Tony. *That summer*
Joosse, Barbara. *Ghost wings*
Keats, Ezra Jack. *Maggie and the pirate*
Kerner, Susan. *Always by my side*
Krishnaswami, Uma. *Remembering Grandpa*
Levis, Caron. *Ida, always*
Londner, Renee. *Stones for Grandpa*
Loth, Sebastian. *Remembering Crystal*
Luenn, Nancy. *A gift for Abuelita*
Lunde, Stein Erik. *My father's arms are a boat*
Lupton, David. *Goodbye, Brecken*
Maier, Inger. *Ben's flying flowers*
Mathers, Petra. *When Aunt Mattie got her wings*
Meng, Cece. *Always remember*
Monk, Isabell. *Blackberry stew*
Mora, Pat. *The remembering day / El día de los
  muertos*
Moundlic, Charlotte. *The scar*
Murphy, Sally. *Pearl verses the world*
Napoli, Donna Jo. *Flamingo dream*
Nobisso, Josephine. *Grandpa loved*
O'Brien, Anne Sibley. *A path of stars*
Onyefulu, Ifeoma. *Saying goodbye*
Oskarsson, Bardur. *The flat rabbit*
Parker, Marjorie Blain. *Jasper's day*
Partridge, Elizabeth. *Big Cat Pepper*
Pitcher, Caroline. *Nico's octopus*
Polacco, Patricia. *An A from Miss Keller*
Portnoy, Mindy Avra. *Where do people go when they
  die?*
Puttock, Simon. *A story for Hippo*
Rappaport, Doreen. *The new king*
Raschka, Chris. *The purple balloon*
Ringtved, Glenn. *Cry, heart, but never break*
Roberts, Jillian. *What happens when a loved one dies?*
Rogers, Fred. *When a pet dies*
Rohmann, Eric. *Bone dog*
Roper, Janice M. *Dancing on the moon*
Rosen, Michael. *A Thanksgiving wish*
Rosenberg, Liz. *The carousel*
Russo, Marisabina. *Grandpa Abe*
Rylant, Cynthia. *Dog Heaven*
Sanna, Francesca. *The journey*
Santucci, Barbara. *Anna's corn*
Schick, Eleanor. *Mama*
Schotter, Roni. *In the piney woods*
Simon, Norma. *The saddest time*
Sinykin, Sheri. *Zayde comes to live*
Skofield, James. *Bear and Bird*

Smith, Maggie. *Desser, the best ever cat*
Staake, Bob. *Bluebird*
Stafford, Liliana. *Just dragon*
Thomas, Jane Resh. *Saying good-bye to grandma*
Tibo, Gilles. *The grand journey of Mr. Man*
Turner, Pamela S. *Hachiko*
Varley, Susan. *Badger's parting gifts*
Vigna, Judith. *Saying goodbye to daddy*
Viorst, Judith. *The tenth good thing about Barney*
Wahl, Phoebe. *Sonya's chickens*
Walker, Alice. *To hell with dying*
Warner, Sunny. *The moon quilt*
Weigelt, Udo. *Bear's last journey*
Weitzman, Elizabeth. *Let's talk about when a parent dies*
Wells, Rosemary. *The language of doves*
Wild, Margaret. *Harry and Hopper*
    Old Pig
Wilhelm, Hans. *I'll always love you*
Wood, Douglas. *Aunt Mary's rose*
    Grandad's prayers of the earth
Woodson, Jacqueline. *Sweet, sweet memory*
Yeh, Kat. *The magic brush*
Yolen, Jane. *The day Tiger Rose said goodbye*
    The stranded whale
Zalben, Jane Breskin. *Pearl's marigolds for grandpa*
Zolotow, Charlotte. *My grandson Lew*
    The old dog
Zucker, Bonnie. *Something very sad happened*

Demons *see* Devil; Monsters

Department stores *see* Shopping; Stores

Desert

Anaya, Rudolfo A. *Roadrunner's dance*
Arnosky, Jim. *Coyote raid in Cactus Canyon*
Bash, Barbara. *Desert giant*
Baylor, Byrd. *The desert is theirs*
Brett, Jan. *The three little dassies*
Geisert, Bonnie. *Desert town*
Guiberson, Brenda Z. *Cactus hotel*
Hiscock, Bruce. *Coyote and badger*
Johnson, Paul Brett. *Lost*
Johnston, Tony. *Desert dog*
    Desert song
Keats, Ezra Jack. *Clementina's cactus*
Lawlor, Laurie. *Old Crump*
Levinson, Nancy Smiler. *Death Valley*
London, Jonathan. *Ali, child of the desert*
Lowell, Susan. *The tortoise and the jackrabbit*
McLerran, Alice. *Roxaboxen*
Mora, Pat. *Delicious hullabaloo / Pachanga deliciosa*
    The desert is my mother / El desierto es mi madre
    Listen to the desert / Oye al desierto
    This big sky
Moss, Miriam. *This is the oasis*
Munro, Roxie. *Desert days, desert nights*
Pattison, Darcy. *Desert baths*
Paul, Ann Whitford. *Count on Culebra*
    Fiesta fiasco
    Mañana Iguana
    Tortuga in trouble
Reynolds, Jan. *Sahara*
Sayre, April Pulley. *Dig, wait, listen*
Serafini, Frank. *Looking closely across the desert*
Siebert, Diane. *Mojave*

Spurling, Margaret. *Bilby moon*
Yolen, Jane. *Welcome to the sea of sand*
Young, Ed. *Donkey trouble*

Detective stories *see* Careers – detectives; Mystery stories; Problem solving

Devil

Philip, Neil. *Noah and the devil*
Quattlebaum, Mary. *Sparks fly high*
Root, Phyllis. *Rosie's fiddle*
Stewig, John Warren. *Clever Gretchen*
Wooldridge, Connie Nordhielm. *The legend of Strap Buckner*
    Wicked Jack
Zemach, Harve. *Duffy and the devil*

Dictionaries

Bergen, Lara Rice. *Blue's world of words*
Day, Alexandra. *Frank and Ernest play ball*
Fern, Tracey. *W is for Webster*
Ferris, Jeri Chase. *Noah Webster and his words*
Got, Yves. *Sam's big book of words*
Stanley, Mandy. *First word book*

Diet *see* Food; Health & fitness

Diggers *see* Careers – construction workers; Machines

Diners *see* Restaurants

Dinosaurs

Aliki. *Digging up dinosaurs*
    Dinosaur bones
    Dinosaurs are different
    Fossils tell of long ago
    My visit to the dinosaurs
Alphin, Elaine Marie. *Dinosaur hunter*
Andersen, Hans Christian. *The dinosaur's new clothes*
Andreae, Giles. *Captain Flinn and the pirate dinosaurs*
    Captain Flinn and the pirate dinosaurs: missing treasure!
    Dinosaurs galore!
Atkins, Jeannine. *Mary Anning and the sea dragon*
Bailey, Linda. *If you happen to have a dinosaur*
Baker, Liza. *Dinosaur days*
Bardhan-Quallen, Sudipta. *The Mine-o-saur*
    Tyrannosaurus wrecks!
Barner, Bob. *Dinosaur bones*
    Dinosaurs roar, butterflies soar!
Barry, Frances. *Let's look at dinosaurs*
Barton, Byron. *Bones, bones, dinosaur bones*
    Dinosaurs, dinosaurs
Bateman, Teresa. *Hunting the daddyosaurus*
Bauer, Marion Dane. *Dinosaur thunder*
Beaumont, Karen. *Dini Dinosaur*
Benton, Jim. *Where did all the dinos go?*
Berger, Melvin. *Why did the dinosaurs disappear?*
Berkner, Laurie. *We are the dinosaurs*
Bilgrami, Shaheen. *Amazing dinosaur discovery*

Blackstone, Stella. *I dreamt I was a dinosaur*
Bourgeois, Paulette. *Franklin's class trip*
Boynton, Sandra. *Dinosaur dance!*
Broach, Elise. *When dinosaurs came with everything*
Brockenbrough, Martha. *The Dinosaur Tooth Fairy*
Brown, Laurie Krasny. *Dinosaurs alive and well*
   Dinosaurs divorce
   Dinosaurs to the rescue
   Dinosaurs travel
   How to be a friend
   When dinosaurs die
Brown, Marc. *Dinosaurs, beware!*
Bryant, Megan E. *Alphasaurus*
   Colorasaurus
   Countasaurus
   Shapeasaurus
Buzzeo, Toni. *No T. Rex in the library*
Calmenson, Stephanie. *No honking allowed*
Carrick, Carol. *Big old bones*
   Patrick's dinosaurs
   Patrick's dinosaurs on the Internet
   What happened to Patrick's dinosaurs?
Carter, David A. *Flapdoodle dinosaurs*
Choldenko, Gennifer. *Dad and the dinosaur*
Clanton, Ben. *Rex wrecks it!*
Clarke, Jane. *Dancing with the Dinosaurs*
   Dippy's sleepover
Climo, Liz. *Rory the dinosaur: me and my dad*
   Rory the dinosaur needs a Christmas tree
   Rory the dinosaur wants a pet
Cohen, Daniel. *Apatosaurus*
   Pteranodon
   Stegosaurus
   Triceratops
   Tyrannosaurus rex
   Velociraptor
Cole, Joanna. *The magic school bus in the time of the dinosaurs*
Crowther, Robert. *Robert Crowther's pop-up dinosaur ABC*
Cyrus, Kurt. *Tadpole Rex*
   The voyage of turtle Rex
Dale, Penny. *Dinosaur dig!*
   Dinosaur rescue!
   Dinosaur rocket!
   Dinosaur zoom!
Daniels, Teri. *G-Rex*
DePalma, Mary Newell. *Uh-oh!*
dePaola, Tomie. *Little Grunt and the big egg*
Desmoinaux, Christel. *Mrs. Hen's big surprise*
DiPucchio, Kelly. *Dinosnores*
DiSiena, Laura Lyn. *Dinosaurs live on!*
Donaldson, Julia. *Tyrannosaurus Drip*
Donnelly, Liza. *Dinosaurs' Halloween*
Drehsen, Britta. *Flip-o-storic*
Duddle, Johnny. *Gigantosaurus*
Durant, Alan. *A dinosaur called Tiny*
Edwards, Pamela Duncan. *Dinosaur starts school*
Edwards, Wallace. *The extinct files*
Evans, Nate. *Bang! Boom! Roar!*
Faulkner, Keith. *Rexerella*
Fletcher, Tom. *The dinosaur that pooped a planet!*
Florian, Douglas. *Dinothesaurus*
Foreman, Michael. *The littlest dinosaur*
Fox, Diane. *Tyson the terrible*
Franceschelli, Christopher. *Dinoblock*
Freedman, Claire. *Dinosaurs love underpants*
Fuge, Charles. *Three little dinosaurs*
Funk, Josh. *Pirasaurs!*

Gall, Chris. *Dinotrux*
   Dinotrux dig the beach
   Revenge of the Dinotrux
Garland, Michael. *Miss Smith reads again!*
Gibbons, Gail. *Dinosaur discoveries*
   Dinosaurs!
Granowsky, Alvin. *Dinosaurs*
Greathouse, Carol. *The dinosaur tamer*
Greenfield, Eloise. *I can draw a weeposaur and other dinosaurs*
Gurney, John Steven. *Dinosaur train*
Gutman, Dan. *Rappy the raptor*
Hall, Algy Craig. *Dino bites!*
Halls, Kelly Milner. *Dinosaur parade: a spectacle of prehistoric proportions*
Halpern, Shari. *Dinosaur parade*
Harrison, Carol. *Dinosaurs everywhere!*
Hartland, Jessie. *How the dinosaur got to the museum*
Hartmann, Wendy. *The dinosaurs are back and it's all your fault, Edward!*
Heidbreder, Robert. *Drumheller dinosaur dance*
Hennessy, B. G. *Busy Dinah Dinosaur*
   The dinosaur who lived in my backyard
   Meet Dinah Dinosaur
Henry, Jed. *I speak dinosaur*
Hines, Anna Grossnickle. *I am a Tyrannosaurus*
Holmquist, Delano. *SantaSaurus*
Hort, Lenny. *Did dinosaurs eat pizza?*
Houran, Lori Haskins. *Dig those dinosaurs*
Howe, James. *Brontorina*
Idle, Molly. *Camp Rex*
   Santa Rex
   Sea Rex
   Tea Rex
James, Brian. *Supertwins meet the dangerous dino-robots*
James, Simon. *Rex*
Jenkins, Steve. *Animals in flight*
Jennewein, Lenore. *Chick-o-Saurus Rex*
Joyce, William. *Dinosaur Bob*
Judge, Lita. *How big were dinosaurs?*
Kastner, Jill. *Merry Christmas, Princess Dinosaur*
   Princess Dinosaur
Kellogg, Steven. *Prehistoric Pinkerton*
Kirsch, Vincent X. *Freddie and Gingersnap*
Knapman, Timothy. *Dinosaurs don't have bedtimes!*
Krensky, Stephen. *Dinosaurs in disguise*
Kroll, Steven. *The Tyrannosaurus game*
Kudlinski, Kathleen V. *Boy, were we wrong about dinosaurs!*
Lach, Will. *I am not a dinosaur!*
Lawler, Janet. *Tyrannoclaus*
Lewis, Kevin. *Dinosaur dinosaur*
Litwin, Eric. *Groovy Joe: ice cream and dinosaurs*
Liu, Julia. *Gus, the dinosaur bus*
Lomp, Stephan. *Mamasaurus*
Lund, Deb. *All aboard the dinotrain*
   Dinosailors
   Dinosoaring
Lyons, Kelly Starling. *One more dino on the floor*
McAnulty, Stacy. *Dear Santasaurus*
McClatchy, Lisa. *Dear Tyrannosaurus Rex*
McClements, George. *Dinosaur Woods*
   Ridin' dinos with Buck Bronco
MacDonald, Suse. *Shape by shape*

MacLeod, Elizabeth. *What did dinosaurs eat?*
McMullan, Kate. *I'm bad!*
    I'm big!
Mandell, B. B. *Samanthasaurus Rex*
Manning, Mick. *Dino-dinners*
Markel, Michelle. *Tyrannosaurus math*
Martin, Stephen W. *Charlotte and the rock*
Masurel, Claire. *Too big!*
Mayer, Mercer. *Too many dinosaurs*
Mayo, Margaret. *Stomp, dinosaur, stomp!*
Middleton, Julie. *Are the dinosaurs dead, Dad?*
Mitton, Tony. *Dinosaurumpus*
    Rumble, roar, dinosaur!
Montanari, Eva. *Dino bikes*
Moseley, Keith. *Where's the dinosaur?*
Most, Bernard. *ABC T-Rex*
    A dinosaur named after me
    Dinosaur questions
    How big were the dinosaurs?
    If the dinosaurs came back
    A pair of protoceratops
    A trio of triceratops
    Whatever happened to the dinosaurs?
Muecke, Anne. *The dinosaurs' night before Christmas*
Munro, Roxie. *Inside-outside dinosaurs*
Murphy, Stuart J. *Dinosaur deals*
Myers, Tim. *Down at the Dino Wash Deluxe*
Neubecker, Robert. *Linus the vegetarian T. rex*
O'Brien, Patrick. *Gigantic!*
    Sabertooth
O'Connor, George. *If I had a raptor*
    If I had a triceratops
Oldland, Nicholas. *Dinosaur countdown*
O'Malley, Kevin. *Captain Raptor and the moon mystery*
    Captain Raptor and the space pirates
Otto, Carolyn. *Dinosaur chase*
Palatini, Margie. *Gorgonzola*
Pett, Mark. *Lizard from the park*
Pfister, Marcus. *Dazzle the dinosaur*
Plourde, Lynn. *Dino pets*
    Dino pets go to school
Prap, Lila. *Dinosaurs?!*
Prasadam-Halls, Smriti. *T. Veg*
Prelutsky, Jack. *Tyrannosaurus was a beast*
Preston-Gannon, Frann. *Dinosaur farm*
Pulver, Robin. *Mrs. Toggle and the dinosaur*
Rees, Douglas. *Tyrannosaurus Rex vs. Edna the very first chicken*
Rennert, Laura Joy. *Buying, training and caring for your dinosaur*
Rey, Margret. *Curious George and the dinosaur*
Roderick, Stacey. *Dinosaurs from head to tail*
Rohmann, Eric. *Time flies*
Rosenberg, Liz. *Tyrannosaurus dad*
Ryder, Joanne. *Tyrannosaurus time*
Sabuda, Robert. *Encyclopedia prehistorica: dinosaurs*
Sansone, Adele. *The little green goose*
Sayres, Brianna Caplan. *Tiara Saurus Rex*
Schachner, Judith Byron. *Skippyjon Jones and the big bones*
Schwartz, Henry. *How I captured a dinosaur*
Sedaka, Marc. *Dinosaur pet*
Sharkey, Niamh. *Santasaurus*
Shea, Bob. *Dinosaur vs. bedtime*
    Dinosaur vs. Mommy
    Dinosaur vs. Santa
    Dinosaur vs. school
    Dinosaur vs. the library

    Dinosaur vs. the potty
    Kid Sheriff and the terrible Toads
Shields, Carol Diggory. *Saturday night at the dinosaur stomp*
Sierra, Judy. *Suppose you meet a dinosaur*
Sís, Peter. *Dinosaur!*
Slack, Michael. *Shorty and Clem*
Staniszewski, Anna. *Dogosaurus Rex*
Stein, David Ezra. *Dinosaur kisses*
Stevenson, James. *The most amazing dinosaur*
Stickland, Paul. *Dinosaur roar!*
    Dinosaur stomp!
    A number of dinosaurs
    Ten terrible dinosaurs
Symes, Ruth. *Little Rex, big brother*
Tuma, Refe. *What the dinosaurs did at school*
Underwood, Deborah. *Super Saurus saves kindergarten*
Waddell, Martin. *The Super Hungry Dinosaur*
Wahl, Jan. *The field mouse and the dinosaur named Sue*
    I met a dinosaur
Wallace, Karen. *I am an ankylosaurus*
Weinberg, Steven. *Rex finds an egg! egg! egg!*
Werner, Sharon. *Alphasaurs and other prehistoric types*
Wheeler, Lisa. *Dino-baseball*
    Dino-basketball
    Dino-boarding
    Dino-football
    Dino-hockey
    Dino-racing
    Dino-soccer
    Dino-swimming
    Dino-wrestling
Whybrow, Ian. *Harry and the bucketful of dinosaurs*
    Harry and the dinosaurs at the museum
    Harry and the dinosaurs go to school
    Harry and the dinosaurs say "Raahh"
Wick, Walter. *Can you see what I see? cool collections*
Willems, Mo. *Edwina, the dinosaur who didn't know she was extinct*
    Goldilocks and the three dinosaurs
Willis, Jeanne. *I'm sure I saw a dinosaur*
Wilson, Karma. *Dinos in the snow!*
Wing, Natasha. *How to raise a dinosaur*
Wise, William. *Dinosaurs forever*
Wood, Douglas. *What teachers can't do*
Yolen, Jane. *How do dinosaurs clean their rooms?*
    How do dinosaurs count to ten?
    How do dinosaurs eat their food?
    How do dinosaurs get well soon?
    How do dinosaurs go to school?
    How do dinosaurs go to sleep?
    How do dinosaurs learn their colors?
    How do dinosaurs play with their friends?
    How do dinosaurs say good night?
    How do dinosaurs say Happy Chanukah?
    How do dinosaurs say I love you?
    How do dinosaurs say I'm mad?
    How do dinosaurs say Merry Christmas?
    How do dinosaurs stay friends?
    How do dinosaurs stay safe?
Zoehfeld, Kathleen Weidner. *Did dinosaurs have feathers?*
    Dinosaur tracks
    Dinosaurs big and small
    Where did dinosaurs come from?
Zommer, Yuval. *One hundred bones*

Disabilities – mental disabilities

Gifaldi, David. *Ben, king of the river*
Rickert, Janet Elizabeth. *Russ and the almost perfect day*
Shriver, Maria. *What's wrong with Timmy?*

Disabilities – physical disabilities

Adler, David A. *Campy*
Buchanan, Jane. *Seed magic*
Burnett, Frances Hodgson. *The secret garden*
Cowen-Fletcher, Jane. *Mama zooms*
De Anda, Diane. *Dancing Miranda / Baila, Miranda, baila*
Elliott, Rebecca. *Just because*
Emmons, Chip. *Sammy wakes his dad*
Garoche, Camille. *The snow rabbit*
Gianferrari, Maria. *Hello goodbye dog*
Heelan, Jamee Riggio. *The making of my special hand, Madison's story*
Rolling along, the story of Taylor and his wheelchair
Hines, Anna Grossnickle. *Gramma's walk*
Hoffman, Eric. *No fair to tigers / No es justo para los tigres*
Hong, Nari. *Days with Dad*
Hudson, Cheryl Willis. *My friend Maya loves to dance*
Jurmain, Suzanne Tripp. *Nice work, Franklin!*
Khan, Rukhsana. *King for a day*
Lee, Jeanne M. *Silent lotus*
Moore, Genevieve. *Catherine's story*
Moore-Mallinos, Jennifer. *It's ok to be me!*
Munsch, Robert N. *Zoom*
Palacio, R. J. *We're all wonders*
Razi, Michaele. *Frank the seven-legged spider*
Senisi, Ellen B. *All kinds of friends, even green*
Stewart, Shannon. *Sea crow*
Thompson, Laurie Ann. *Emmanuel's dream*
Wells, Rosemary. *The little lame prince*
Willis, Jeanne. *Susan laughs*
Wisnewski, Andrea. *Trio*
Yin. *Dear Santa, please come to the 19th floor*

Disabilities – stuttering

Lears, Laurie. *Ben has something to say*
Rabinowitz, Alan. *A boy and a jaguar*

Disbelief *see* Behavior – disbelief

Discrimination *see* Prejudice

Diseases *see* Illness

Disguises

Aesop. *The donkey in the lion's skin*
The wolf in sheep's clothing
Anderson, Derek. *Ten hungry pigs*
Bell, Cece. *Bee-Wigged*
Bestor, Sheri Mabry. *Good trick, walking stick!*
Borando, Silvia. *Now you see me, now you don't*
Cannon, Janell. *Little Yau*
Ehlert, Lois. *Lots of spots*
Ernst, Lisa Campbell. *Sylvia Jean, scout supreme*
Fairgray, Richard. *Gorillas in our midst*

Fenton, Joe. *Boo!*
Gentle, Victor. *Shark camouflage and armor*
Holmes, Anita. *Can you find us?*
Hutchins, Hazel. *I'd know you anywhere*
Krensky, Stephen. *Dinosaurs in disguise*
Lester, Helen. *The sheep in wolf's clothing*
McNaughton, Colin. *Boo!*
Mason, Adrienne. *Lu and Clancy's spy stuff*
Oliver, Narelle. *Twilight hunt*
Onishi, Satoru. *Who's hiding*
Peters, Bernadette. *Stella is a star!*
Roberton, Fiona. *Wanted: the perfect pet*
Savage, Stephen. *Where's Walrus?*
Schwartz, David M. *Where else in the wild?*
Where in the wild
Shaskan, Stephen. *A dog is a dog*
Stevenson, Emma. *Hide-and-seek science*
Stockdale, Susan. *Spectacular spots*
Swinburne, Stephen R. *Lots and lots of zebra stripes*
Taylor, Sean. *Hoot owl, master of disguise*
Tildes, Phyllis Limbacher. *Animals in camouflage*
Weigelt, Udo. *Super Guinea Pig to the rescue*
Yep, Laurence. *Auntie Tiger*

Dissatisfaction *see* Behavior – dissatisfaction

Diversity *see* Ethnic groups in the U.S.

Diving *see* Sports – skin diving

Divorce

Adams, Eric J. *On the day his daddy left*
Appelt, Kathi. *When Otis courted Mama*
Bernhard, Durga. *To and fro, fast and slow*
Brown, Laurie Krasny. *Dinosaurs divorce*
Bunting, Eve. *The days of summer*
My mom's wedding
Clarke, Jane. *The best of both nests*
Cochran, Bill. *My parents are divorced, my elbows have nicknames, and other facts about me*
Coelho, Joseph. *Luna loves library day*
Coffelt, Nancy. *Fred stays with me!*
Cook, Julia. *The "D" word*
Coy, John. *Two old potatoes and me*
Daly, Cathleen. *Emily's blue period*
Grindley, Sally. *A new room for William*
Haughton, Emma. *Rainy day*
Holmberg, Bo R. *A day with Dad*
Lansky, Vicki. *It's not your fault, KoKo Bear*
Levins, Sandra. *Do you sing Twinkle?*
Masurel, Claire. *Two homes*
Moore-Mallinos, Jennifer. *When my parents forgot how to be friends*
Portnoy, Mindy Avra. *A tale of two seders*
Ransom, Jeanie Franz. *I don't want to talk about it*
Rogers, Fred. *Divorce*
Santucci, Barbara. *Loon summer*
Schotter, Roni. *Room for Rabbit*
Shreeve, Elizabeth. *Oliver at the window*
Smet, Marian De. *I have two homes*
Spelman, Cornelia Maude. *Mama and Daddy Bear's divorce*
Stanton, Karen. *Monday, Wednesday, and every other weekend*
Thomas, Pat. *My family's changing*

Walsh, Melanie. *Living with Mom and living with Dad*
Weninger, Brigitte. *Good-bye, Daddy!*
Willhoite, Michael. *Daddy's roommate*
Winthrop, Elizabeth. *As the crow flies*

Down & up *see* Concepts – up & down

Dragons

Adams, Sarah. *Dave and Violet*
Ashburn, Boni. *Over at the castle*
Atkins, Jeannine. *Mary Anning and the sea dragon*
Averbeck, Jim. *Oh no, Little Dragon!*
Baillie, Allan. *Dragonquest*
Baker, Ken. *Old MacDonald had a dragon*
Banks, Kate. *Max's dragon*
Bar-el, Dan. *Not your typical dragon*
Baynton, Martin. *Jane and the dragon*
    Jane and the magician
Beck, Scott. *Happy birthday, Monster!*
Berkeley, Jon. *Chopsticks*
Biedrzycki, David. *Me and my dragon*
    Me and my dragon: Christmas spirit
    Me and my dragon: scared of Halloween
Brill, Calista. *Little Wing learns to fly*
Brunhoff, Laurent de. *Babar on Paradise Island*
Calvert, Pam. *Princess Peepers picks a pet*
Cave, Kathryn. *You've got dragons*
Clanton, Ben. *It came in the mail*
Deedy, Carmen Agra. *Return of the library dragon*
de Las Casas, Dianne. *There's a dragon in the library*
Demi. *The boy who painted dragons*
    The dragon's tale and other animal fables of the Chinese zodiac
dePaola, Tomie. *The knight and the dragon*
DiPucchio, Kelly. *Dragon was terrible*
Docherty, Helen. *The storybook knight*
Donaldson, Julia. *A gold star for Zog*
    Room on the broom
    Zog and the flying doctors
Downing, Julie. *No hugs till Saturday*
Driscoll, Amanda. *Duncan the story dragon*
Ehrlich, Amy. *Baby Dragon*
Ellery, Amanda. *If I had a dragon*
Eversole, Robyn. *East Dragon, West Dragon*
Falkenstern, Lisa. *A dragon moves in*
Faller, Regis. *Polo and the dragon*
Fletcher, Ralph. *The Sandman*
Florian, Douglas. *How to draw a dragon*
Funk, Josh. *Dear dragon*
Gliori, Debi. *Dragon's extraordinary egg*
    The trouble with dragons
Goodhart, Pippa. *Arthur's tractor*
Gorbachev, Valeri. *How to be friends with a dragon*
Grahame, Kenneth. *The reluctant dragon*
Gravett, Emily. *Again!*
Hale, Bruce. *Snoring Beauty*
Hoban, Russell. *Ace Dragon Ltd*
Hodges, Margaret. *Saint George and the dragon*
Howe, James. *There's a dragon in my sleeping bag*
Hunter, Jana Novotny. *Little ones do*
Joosse, Barbara. *Evermore Dragon*
    Lovabye Dragon
    Sail away Dragon
Julian, Sean. *Sloppy wants a hug*
Kaufman, Jeanne. *Young Henry and the dragon*
Kirk, David. *Oh so brave dragon*

Kirsch, Vincent X. *Freddie and Gingersnap*
Klostermann, Penny Parker. *There was an old dragon who swallowed a knight*
Knudsen, Michelle. *Argus*
Kraegel, Kenneth. *King Arthur's very great grandson*
Krause, Ute. *Oscar and the very hungry dragon*
Krensky, Stephen. *Spark the firefighter*
Kroll, Steven. *Super-dragon*
Lambert, Martha Lewis. *I won't get lost*
Leedy, Loreen. *The dragon Halloween party*
    The dragon Thanksgiving feast
Lehrhaupt, Adam. *I will not eat you*
Light, Steve. *Have you seen my dragon?*
Long, Ethan. *One drowsy dragon*
Mayhew, James. *The knight who took all day*
Meddaugh, Susan. *Harry on the rocks*
Merino, Gemma. *The crocodile who didn't like water*
Moore, Jodi. *When a dragon moves in*
Moore, Lilian. *Beware, take care*
Morgan, Mary. *Dragon pizzeria*
Munsch, Robert N. *The paper bag princess*
Nash, Ogden. *Custard the dragon and the wicked knight*
Niemann, Christoph. *The pet dragon*
Nolen, Jerdine. *Raising dragons*
Nunes, Susan Miho. *The last dragon*
Peet, Bill. *How Droofus the dragon lost his head*
Pendziwol, Jean E. *No dragons for tea*
    The tale of Sir Dragon
    A treasure at sea for dragon and me
Pienkowski, Jan. *Bel and Bub and the black hole*
Pilkey, Dav. *Dragon's fat cat*
    Dragon's merry Christmas
    A friend for Dragon
Ramos, Mario. *I am so strong*
Robertson, M. P. *The dragon snatcher*
    The egg
Robinson, Michelle. *The forgetful knight*
Roth, Judith L. *Goodnight, dragons*
Rubin, Adam. *Dragons love tacos*
    Dragons love tacos 2
Sabuda, Robert. *The dragon and the knight*
San Souci, Daniel. *The rabbit and the dragon king*
Schaefer, Carole Lexa. *Dragon dancing*
Sierra, Judy. *'Twas the fright before Christmas*
Smallman, Steve. *Dragon stew*
Sperring, Mark. *The sunflower sword*
Thayer, Jane. *The popcorn dragon*
Thomas, Shelley Moore. *A cold winter's Good Knight*
    A Good Knight's rest
    Good night, Good Knight
    Take care, Good Knight
Thomas, Valerie. *Winnie's midnight dragon*
Tucker, Kathy. *The seven Chinese sisters*
Ward, Helen. *The dragon machine*
Wiesner, David. *Free fall*
    The loathsome dragon
Wilson, Gina. *Ignis*
Wojtowycz, David. *Elephant Joe, Brave Knight!*
Wong, Benedict Norbert. *Lo and behold*
    Lo and behold, good enough to eat
Yarrow, Peter. *Puff, the magic dragon*
Yep, Laurence. *Dragon prince*
Yolen, Jane. *Waking dragons*
Ziefert, Harriet. *William and the dragon*

Dreams *see also* Nightmares

Adlerman, Daniel. *Africa calling*

Alborough, Jez. *Ice cream bear*

Alexander, Martha G. *You're a genius, Blackboard Bear*

Anholt, Laurence. *Jack and the dreamsack*

Appelt, Kathi. *Cowboy dreams*

Argueta, Jorge. *Trees are hanging from the sky*

Arnold, Tedd. *Green Wilma*
  No jumping on the bed!

Asch, Frank. *Moonbear's dream*

Banks, Kate. *Close your eyes*

Bar-el, Dan. *A fish named Glub*

Berenstain, Stan and Jan. *The Berenstain bears and the bad dream*

Blackstone, Stella. *I dreamt I was a dinosaur*

Browne, Anthony. *Willy the dreamer*

Burdett, Lois. *A midsummer night's dream for kids*

Burningham, John. *The magic bed*

Byun, You. *Dream friends*

Carlson, Nancy. *It's going to be perfect*

Chapman, Nancy Kapp. *Doggie dreams*

Chriscoe, Sharon. *Race car dreams*

Cohen, Caron Lee. *Martin and the giant lions*

Cousins, Lucy. *Maisy's bedtime*
  Maisy's rainbow dream

deGroat, Diane. *Homer*

Demi. *The magic pillow*

Dudley, Rebecca. *Hank has a dream*

Dunbar, Polly. *Arthur's dream boat*

Dunnick, Regan. *Sweet dreams, Douglas*

Durango, Julia. *Dream hop*

Enersen, Adele. *When my baby dreams*

Farmer, Bonnie. *Isaac's dreamcatcher*

Ginsburg, Mirra. *Across the stream*

Gorbachev, Valeri. *Nicky and the big, bad wolves*
  When someone is afraid

Gottfried, Maya. *Last night I dreamed a circus*

Hanson, Faye. *The wonder*

Henkes, Kevin. *Old Bear*

Hoban, Russell. *Rosie's magic horse*

Hoffmann, E. T. A *The Nutcracker in Harlem*

Howard, Arthur. *My dream dog*

Hurd, Thacher. *The weaver*

Hutchins, Hazel. *Beneath the bridge*

Isadora, Rachel. *Caribbean dream*

Jay, Alison. *1 2 3*

Johnson, Angela. *I dream of trains*

Johnson, Lindan Lee. *The dream jar*

Jonas, Ann. *The quilt*

Joyce, William. *The Sandman: the story of Sanderson Mansnoozie*

Keats, Ezra Jack. *Dreams*

Kenah, Katharine. *The dream shop*

King, Martin Luther, Jr.. *I have a dream*

Kirk, David. *Oh So Tiny bunny*

Lawson, Dorie McCullough. *Tex*

Le Guin, Ursula K. *Cat dreams*

Lester, Julius. *Albidaro and the mischievous dream*

Lithgow, John. *Never play music right next to the zoo*

London, Jonathan. *Froggy goes to school*

McCain, Becky R. *Grandmother's dreamcatcher*

McCarty, Peter. *Bunny dreams*

McDermott, Gerald. *Daniel O'Rourke*

MacDonald, Ross. *Another perfect day*

Mack, Jeff. *Hush little polar bear*

Maconie, Robin. *Alice and her fabulous teeth*

McPhail, David. *Boy on the brink*

Marcero, Deborah. *Ursa's light*

Martin, Bill, Jr.. *Barn dance!*
  Little granny quarterback

Martin, Emily Winfield. *Day dreamers*
  Dream animals

Martin, Ruth. *Moon dreams*

Melmed, Laura Krauss. *Jumbo's lullaby*

Mendes, Valerie. *Look at me, Grandma!*

Milgrim, David. *Another day in the Milky Way*

Nahas, Sylvaine. *Nicolo's unicorn*

Napoli, Donna Jo. *Ready to dream*

Neuschwander, Cindy. *Amanda Bean's amazing dream*

Osofsky, Audrey. *Dreamcatcher*

Owens, Mary Beth. *Panda whispers*

Pfister, Marcus. *Wake up, Santa Claus!*

Pilkey, Dav. *When cats dream*

Polacco, Patricia. *Appelemando's dreams*

Potter, Giselle. *Tell me what to dream about*

Ringgold, Faith. *My dream of Martin Luther King*
  Tar Beach

Rock, Lois. *I wish tonight*

Rockhill, Dennis. *Polar slumber / Sueño polar*

Rohmann, Eric. *The cinder-eyed cats*

Roper, Janice M. *Dancing on the moon*

Sava, Donna Lynn. *Teddy bear dreams*

Say, Allen. *A river dream*

Sayles, Elizabeth. *The goldfish yawned*

Schaefer, Carole Lexa. *Down in the woods at sleepytime*

Schuch, Steve. *A symphony of whales*

Seibold, J. Otto. *Penguin dreams*

Sendak, Maurice. *In the night kitchen*

Senshu, Noriko. *Sonny's dream*

Shah, Idries. *The boy without a name*

Sheldon, Dyan. *Under the moon*

Showers, Paul. *Sleep is for everyone*

Shulevitz, Uri. *The treasure*

Simmons, Jane. *Go to sleep, Daisy*

Sís, Peter. *Robinson*

Slater, Dashka. *Firefighters in the dark*

Steig, William. *The Zabajaba Jungle*

Stewart, Amber. *Bedtime for Button*

Tafuri, Nancy. *Junglewalk*
  What the sun sees / What the moon sees

Teague, David. *Franklin's big dreams*

Tudor, Tasha. *A tale for Easter*

Wahl, Jan. *Elf night*

Ward, Helen. *The tin forest*

Washington, Ned. *When you wish upon a star*

Watt, Mélanie. *Scaredy Squirrel at night*

Weber, Linda Kay. *Louie Larkey and the bad dream patrol*

Wick, Walter. *Can you see what I see? dream machine*

Wiebe, Rudy. *Hidden buffalo*

Wiesner, David. *Free fall*

Wild, Margaret. *Going home*

Winter, Jeanette. *Mr. Cornell's dream boxes*

Wood, Audrey. *Sweet dream pie*

Yaccarino, Dan. *Good night, Mr. Night*

Yolen, Jane. *Moon ball*

Yorinks, Arthur. *Hey, Al*

Young, Ed. *Night visitors*

Yum, Hyewon. *Last night*

Zalben, Jane Breskin. *Baby shower*

Ziefert, Harriet. *Squarehead*
  What do ducks dream?

Dwarfs, midgets

Delessert, Etienne. *The seven dwarfs*

Grimm, Jacob and Wilhelm. *Rose Red and the bear prince*
  Snow White, ill. by Melinda Copper
  Snow White, ill. by Quentin Gréban
  Snow White, ill. by Trina Schart Hyman
  Snow White, ill. by Charles Santore
  Snow White and the seven dwarfs, ill. by Wanda Gág
  Snow White and the seven dwarfs, ill. by Laura Ljungkvist
Ruzzier, Sergio. *The little giant*

Dwellings *see* Buildings; Homes, houses

Dying *see* Death

Ears *see* Anatomy – ears; Disabilities – deafness; Senses – hearing

Earth

Asch, Frank. *The earth and I*
Bang, Molly. *Buried sunlight*
Branley, Franklyn M. *Earthquakes*
  The sun, our nearest star
  What makes day and night
Cameron, Eileen. *Canyon*
Cole, Joanna. *The magic school bus inside the earth*
Elschner, Geraldine. *Moonchild, star of the sea*
Ernst, Lisa Campbell. *Round like a ball!*
Gifford, Peggy. *The great big green*
Glaser, Linda. *Our big home*
Greene, Rhonda Gowler. *The beautiful world that God made*
Guiberson, Brenda Z. *Earth*
Jeffers, Oliver. *Here we are*
Jenkins, Steve. *Hottest, coldest, highest, deepest*
Karas, G. Brian. *On Earth*
Lauber, Patricia. *You're aboard spaceship Earth*
Lewis, J. Patrick. *Earth and me, our family tree*
  Earth and you, a closer view
Luenn, Nancy. *Mother earth*
Martin, Bill, Jr.. *I love our Earth*
Milgrim, David. *Here in space*
Munro, Roxie. *Ecomazes*
Parr, Todd. *The earth book*
Reiser, Lynn. *Earthdance*
Rockwell, Anne. *What's so bad about gasoline?*
Ross, Michael Elsohn. *Earth cycles*
Shore, Diane Z. *This is the Earth*
Siomades, Lorianne. *A place to bloom*
Staub, Leslie. *Bless this house*
Wells, Robert E. *What's so special about planet Earth?*
Zoehfeld, Kathleen Weidner. *How mountains are made*

Earthquakes

Danticat, Edwidge. *Eight days*
Harrison, David L. *Earthquakes*
Lee, Milly. *Earthquake*
Oelschlager, Vanita. *I came from the water*
Palatini, Margie. *Earthquack*
Perry, Phyllis J. *Pandas' earthquake escape*
Watson, Jesse Joshua. *Hope for Haiti*

Eating *see* Food

Ecology

Alexander, Sue. *Behold the trees*
Aliki. *My visit to the zoo*
Alter, Anna. *What can you do with an old red shoe?*
Ambrose, Sophie. *The lonely giant*
Appelt, Kathi. *Miss Lady Bird's wildflowers*
Armentrout, David. *John Muir*
Arnold, Caroline. *A warmer world*
Arnosky, Jim. *Crinkleroot's guide to giving back to nature*
  Crinkleroot's visit to Crinkle Cove
Atwell, Debby. *River*
Austin, Mike. *Junkyard*
Baker, Jeannie. *The story of rosy dock*
  Where the forest meets the sea
  Window
Bang, Molly. *Rivers of sunlight*
Barroux. *Where's the elephant?*
Bateman, Donna M. *Deep in the swamp*
  Out on the prairie
Baylor, Byrd. *The desert is theirs*
Beard, Alex. *Crocodile's tears*
Berenstain, Stan and Jan. *The Berenstain bears don't pollute anymore*
Berger, Carin. *OK go*
Berger, Melvin. *Oil spill!*
Bonfield, Chloe. *The perfect tree*
Brenner, Barbara A. *One small place by the sea*
Brett, Jan. *Mossy*
Brown, Laurie Krasny. *Dinosaurs to the rescue*
Brown, Marc. *Arthur turns green*
Brown, Peter. *The curious garden*
Brown, Ruth. *The old tree*
Burton, Virginia Lee. *The little house*
Catchpool, Michael. *The cloud spinner*
Cherry, Lynne. *The great kapok tree*
  A river ran wild
Child, Lauren. *What planet are you from Clarice Bean?*
Chin, Jason. *Coral reefs*
Cole, Henry. *The littlest evergreen*
  On Meadowview Street
Cole, Joanna. *The magic school bus and the climate challenge*
Corr, Christopher. *Whole world*
Côté, Geneviève. *Mr. King's machine*
  Mr. King's things
Cousteau, Philippe. *Follow the moon home*
Crowe, Carole. *Turtle girl*
Davies, Nicola. *Many*
  Oceans and seas
deGroat, Diane. *Ants in your pants, worms in your plants!*
Delacre, Lulu. *¡Olinguito, de la A a la Z! / Olinguito, from A to Z!*
Dennard, Deborah. *Hedgehog haven*

DePalma, Mary Newell. *A grand old tree*
Drummond, Allan. *Green city*
Duvall, John. *The great spruce*
Formento, Alison. *These seas count!*
Franco, Betsy. *Pond circle*
Galko, Francine. *Cave animals*
Gall, Chris. *Awesome Dawson*
George, Jean Craighead. *The buffalo are back*
    The eagles are back
    Everglades
    The last polar bear
    The wolves are back
Gerardi, Jan. *The little recycler*
Gibbons, Gail. *Coral reefs*
    Exploring the deep, dark sea
    Nature's green umbrella
    Recycle!
Glaser, Linda. *Garbage helps our garden grow*
Gliori, Debi. *The trouble with dragons*
Grupper, Jonathan. *Destination — Rocky Mountains*
    Destination, rain forest
Guiberson, Brenda Z. *Cactus hotel*
    Earth
Hader, Berta Hoerner. *The mighty hunter*
Hamilton, Virginia. *Drylongso*
    Jaguarundi
Heinz, Brian J. *Butternut Hollow Pond*
Hewitt, Sally. *All year round*
    Woods and meadows
Himmelman, John. *Mouse in a meadow*
Hines, Gary. *A Christmas tree in the White House*
Hobbie, Holly. *Gem*
Isabella, Jude. *The red bicycle*
Jackson, Ellen. *Earth Mother*
Jeffers, Oliver. *The great paper caper*
    Here we are
Jenkins, Steve. *I see a kookaburra*
Johanasen, Heather. *About the rain forest*
Johnson, Amy Crane. *Mason moves away / Mason se muda*
Johnson, Jen Cullerton. *Seeds of change*
Johnston, Tony. *The whole green world*
Kann, Victoria. *Emeraldalicious*
Karas, G. Brian. *As an oak tree grows*
Keister, Douglas. *Fernando's gift / El regalo de Fernando*
Kleven, Elisa. *The dancing deer and the foolish hunter*
    Glasswings
Kroll, Steven. *Stuff!*
Kudlinski, Kathleen V. *The seaside switch*
Kuhlmann, Torben. *Moletown*
Kurtz, Kevin. *A day in the salt marsh*
LaMarche, Jim. *Pond*
Lamstein, Sarah Marwil. *Big night for salamanders*
Lauber, Patricia. *Be a friend to trees*
    Who eats what?
Lawlor, Laurie. *Rachel Carson and her book that changed the world*
Layton, Neal. *The tree*
Leedy, Loreen. *The great trash bash*
Lennon, Julian. *Touch the earth*
Levinson, Nancy Smiler. *Death Valley*
    Rain forests
Lewin, Ted. *Amazon boy*
Lewis, J. Patrick. *Earth and you, a closer view*
London, Jonathan. *Gone again ptarmigan*
Luenn, Nancy. *Mother earth*
    Squish!
Lumry, Amanda. *Polar bear puzzle*

    Safari in South Africa
Maass, Robert. *Garbage*
McClements, George. *Dinosaur Woods*
MacDonald, Margaret Read. *Surf war!*
MacLear, Kyo. *The fog*
McMillan, Bruce. *Days of the ducklings*
McPhail, David. *The family tree*
Markle, Sandra. *Waiting for ice*
Martin, Jacqueline Briggs. *Creekfinding*
Mazer, Anne. *The salamander room*
Messner, Kate. *Tree of wonder*
Middleton, Charlotte. *Nibbles*
Miller, Debbie S. *Are trees alive?*
    River of life
Moss, Miriam. *This is the tree*
Muldrow, Diane. *We planted a tree*
Munro, Roxie. *Desert days, desert nights*
    Ecomazes
Murphy, Stuart J. *Earth Day — hooray!*
Napoli, Donna Jo. *Mama Miti*
Nivola, Claire A. *Life in the ocean*
    Planting the trees of Kenya
Oldland, Nicholas. *Big bear hug*
Pandell, Karen. *I love you sun, I love you moon*
Parr, Todd. *The earth book*
Paul, Miranda. *One plastic bag*
Peet, Bill. *The caboose who got loose*
    Farewell to Shady Glade
    Fly, Homer, fly
    The gnats of knotty pine
    The wump world
Perez, Monica. *Curious George plants a tree*
Peterson, Cris. *Amazing grazing*
Prevot, Franck. *Wangari Maathai*
Quattlebaum, Mary. *Jo MacDonald had a garden*
Rabinowitz, Alan. *A boy and a jaguar*
Rand, Gloria. *Prince William*
Reed, Lynn Rowe. *Roscoe and the pelican rescue*
Reed-Jones, Carol. *The tree in the ancient forest*
Reynolds, Aaron. *Carnivores*
Robinson, Tim. *Tobias, the quig, and the rumplenut tree*
Rockwell, Anne. *What's so bad about gasoline?*
Roop, Connie. *Let's celebrate Earth Day*
Root, Phyllis. *Big belching bog*
Rosenberg, Madelyn. *Happy birthday, tree!*
Rosenstock, Barb. *The camping trip that changed America*
Roth, Susan L. *Parrots over Puerto Rico*
Rotner, Shelley. *The buzz on bees*
Rowe, John A. *Moondog*
Ryder, Joanne. *The waterfall's gift*
St. Pierre, Stephanie. *What the sea saw*
Sanders, Scott R. *Crawdad Creek*
San Souci, Robert D. *The birds of Killingworth*
Sayre, April Pulley. *The shape of Betts Meadow*
    Trout are made of trees
Sazaklis, John. *Fowl play*
Seattle, Chief. *Brother eagle, sister sky*
Sensel, Joni. *Bears barge in*
Seuss, Dr. *The Lorax*
Seven, John. *The ocean story*
Shore, Diane Z. *This is the Earth*
Showers, Paul. *Where does the garbage go?*
Siddals, Mary McKenna. *Compost stew*
Sierra, Judy. *Ballyhoo Bay*
Siomades, Lorianne. *A place to bloom*
Sirett, Dawn. *Love your world*
Spinelli, Eileen. *Miss Fox's class goes green*

Staub, Leslie. *Bless this house*
Stewart, Melissa. *A place for birds*
 A place for frogs
Strauss, Rochelle. *One well*
Suzuki, David. *Salmon forest*
Swamp, Jake. *Giving thanks*
Tafolla, Carmen. *Baby Coyote and the old woman / El coyotito y la viejita*
Thompson, Jolene. *Faraway fox*
Thornhill, Jan. *Wild in the city*
Toft, Kim Michelle. *The world that we want*
Tresselt, Alvin R. *The gift of the tree*
Trice, Linda. *Kenya's art*
Waldman, Neil. *They came from the Bronx*
Wallace, Nancy Elizabeth. *Recycle every day!*
 Water! water! water!
Walsh, Melanie. *10 things I can do to help my world*
Ward, D. J. *What happens to our trash?*
Ward, Helen. *The tin forest*
Weninger, Brigitte. *Precious water*
Winer, Yvonne. *Frogs sing songs*
Winkelman, Barbara Gaines. *Sockeye's journey home*
Winter, Jeanette. *Nanuk the ice bear*
 Wangari's trees of peace
Wong, Janet S. *The dumpster diver*
Wood, Douglas. *Old Turtle*
Wright, Maureen. *Earth Day, birthday!*
Yahgulanaas, Michael Nicoll. *The little hummingbird*
Yezerski, Thomas. *Meadowlands*
Yolen, Jane. *Welcome to the river of grass*
 Welcome to the sea of sand
 Where have the unicorns gone?
Yuly, Toni. *Thank you, bees*
Ziefert, Harriet. *My forever dress*
Zoehfeld, Kathleen Weidner. *Secrets of the garden*

Education *see* School

Eggs

Aesop. *The goose that laid the golden egg*
Andersen, Hans Christian. *The woman with the eggs*
Arnold, Caroline. *Hatching chicks in Room 6*
Aston, Dianna Hutts. *An egg is quiet*
Auch, Mary Jane. *The Easter egg farm*
 Eggs mark the spot
Averbeck, Jim. *Except if*
Balian, Lorna. *Humbug rabbit*
Bateson-Hill, Margaret. *Masha and the firebird*
Battut, Eric. *The fox and the hen*
Berenstain, Stan and Jan. *The Berenstain bears and the real Easter eggs*
Brett, Jan. *The Easter egg*
 Hedgie's surprise
Brown, Margaret Wise. *The golden egg book*
Burg, Sarah Emmanuelle. *One more egg*
Carter, David A. *Easter bugs*
Cutbill, Andy. *The cow that laid an egg*
Cyrus, Kurt. *Shake a leg, egg!*
Dahl, Michael. *Eggs and legs*
DePalma, Mary Newell. *The strange egg*
Desmoinaux, Christel. *Mrs. Hen's big surprise*
Douglas, Erin. *Get that pest!*
Dudley, Rebecca. *Hank finds an egg*
Dunrea, Olivier. *Ollie*
 Ollie's Easter eggs
Fox, Mem. *Hunwick's egg*
Franceschelli, Christopher. *(Oliver)*

Friend, Catherine. *The perfect nest*
Gehl, Laura. *Peep and Egg: I'm not hatching*
Gill, Shelley. *The egg*
Gliori, Debi. *Little Owl's egg*
Golson, Terry. *Tillie lays an egg*
Graham, Bob. *Dimity Dumpty*
Grambling, Lois G. *Here comes T. Rex Cottontail*
Gravett, Emily. *The odd egg*
Halfmann, Janet. *Eggs 1, 2, 3*
Hartmann, Wendy. *The dinosaurs are back and it's all your fault, Edward!*
Heller, Ruth. *Chickens aren't the only ones*
Henkes, Kevin. *Egg*
Higgins, Ryan T. *Mother Bruce*
Hill, Eric. *Spot's first Easter*
Horowitz, Dave. *Humpty Dumpty climbs again*
Howard, Reginald. *The big, big wall*
Hughes, Laura. *We're going on an egg hunt*
Jenkins, Priscilla Belz. *A nest full of eggs*
Joyce, William. *Bently and egg*
Kangas, Juli. *The surprise visitor*
Kaplan, Michael B. *Betty Bunny loves Easter*
Kellogg, Steven. *A penguin pup for Pinkerton*
Kimmel, Eric A. *The birds' gift*
Latter, Jill. *Mama Hen's big day*
Lionni, Leo. *An extraordinary egg*
Meddaugh, Susan. *Harry on the rocks*
Milhous, Katherine. *The egg tree*
Montes, Marisa. *Egg-napped!*
Mortimer, Anne. *Bunny's Easter egg*
Mother Goose. *Humpty Dumpty*
Munro, Roxie. *Hatch!*
Nakagawa, Rieko. *Guri and Gura*
Nolen, Jerdine. *Raising dragons*
Partridge, Elizabeth. *Pig's eggs*
Paschkis, Julie. *P. Zonka lays an egg*
Patricelli, Leslie. *Hop! hop!*
Peet, Bill. *The pinkish, purplish, bluish egg*
Polacco, Patricia. *Chicken Sunday*
 Just plain Fancy
 Rechenka's eggs
Polhemus, Coleman. *The crocodile blues*
Posada, Mia. *Guess what is growing inside this egg*
Potter, Beatrix. *The tale of Jemima Puddle-Duck*
Rand, Betseygail. *Big Bunny*
Roberts, Bethany. *Easter mice*
Robertson, M. P. *The dragon snatcher*
 The egg
Ross, Tom. *Eggbert, the slightly cracked egg*
Rouillard, Wendy. *Barnaby's bunny*
San Souci, Robert D. *The talking eggs*
Santat, Dan. *After the fall (how Humpty Dumpty got back up again)*
Schertle, Alice. *Down the road*
Schmid, Paul. *Oliver and his egg*
Schubert, Ingrid. *Bear's eggs*
Schulman, Janet. *Ten Easter egg hunters*
Seuss, Dr. *Horton hatches the egg*
Simmons, Jane. *Daisy and the egg*
Singer, Marilyn. *Eggs*
Sklansky, Amy E. *Where do chicks come from?*
Slegers, Liesbet. *Happy Easter!*
Smith, Alex T. *Foxy and Egg*
Smythe, Theresa. *Chester's colorful Easter eggs*
Stalder, Päivi. *Ernest's first Easter*
Stevenson, James. *The great big especially beautiful Easter egg*
Stileman, Kali. *Roly-poly egg*

Stoeke, Janet Morgan. *Minerva Louise and the colorful eggs*
Sykes, Julie. *Dora's eggs*
Tafuri, Nancy. *Whose chick are you?*
Taylor, Shirley. *The cross in the egg*
Thomas, Jan. *The Easter Bunny's assistant*
Tudor, Tasha. *A tale for Easter*
Vainio, Pirkko. *Who hid the Easter eggs?*
Waddell, Martin. *It's quacking time*
Ward, Jennifer. *What will hatch?*
Ward, Lindsay. *When Blue met Egg*
Weigelt, Udo. *The Easter Bunny's baby*
Weinberg, Steven. *Rex finds an egg! egg! egg!*
Wilhelm, Hans. *More bunny trouble*
    Quacky Ducky's Easter egg
Wilson, Karma. *What's in the egg, Little Pip?*
Wormell, Mary. *Hilda Hen's search*
Zuniga, Elisabeth. *A friend for Bo*

Egyptian language *see* Hieroglyphics

Elderly *see* Old age

Elevators, escalators

Murphy, Stuart J. *Elevator magic*

Emotions

Aliki. *Feelings*
Allen, Kathryn Madeline. *A kiss means I love you*
    Show me happy
Alrawi, Karim. *The girl who lost her smile*
Anderson, Stephen Axel. *I know the moon*
Anholt, Catherine. *What makes me happy?*
Bang, Molly. *When Sophie's feelings are really, really hurt*
Barnett, Mac. *I love you like a pig*
    Places to be
Beaumont, Karen. *Crybaby*
Berger, Samantha. *Crankenstein*
Berkner, Laurie. *The story of my feelings*
Bluthenthal, Diana Cain. *I'm not invited?*
Boyden, Linda. *The blue roses*
Brisson, Pat. *Sometimes we were brave*
Brown, Alan James. *Hoot and Holler*
Brown, Laurie Krasny. *When dinosaurs die*
Brown, Tameka Fryer. *My cold plum lemon pie bluesy mood*
Browne, Anthony. *How do you feel?*
Burdett, Lois. *The tempest for kids*
Burrowes, Adjoa J. *Grandma's purple flowers*
Cain, Janan. *The way I feel*
Carter, David A. *If you're happy and you know it, clap your hands*
Cocca-Leffler, Maryann. *Theo's mood*
Côté, Geneviève. *Starring me and you*
Cowell, Cressida. *What shall we do with the Boo-Hoo Baby?*
Curtis, Jamie Lee. *Today I feel silly and other moods that make my day*
Daly, Cathleen. *Emily's blue period*
Daly, Niki. *What's cooking, Jamela?*
Dewdney, Anna. *Grumpy Gloria*
    Llama Llama misses Mama
DiCamillo, Kate. *Great joy*
Doughty, Rebecca. *Oh no! Time to go!*
Dunbar, Polly. *Flyaway Katie*

Edvall, Lilian. *The rabbit who longed for home*
Edwards, Becky. *My first day at nursery school*
Emberley, Ed. *Glad monster, sad monster*
Fernandes, Eugenie. *Sleepy little mouse*
Frame, Jeron Ashford. *Yesterday I had the blues*
Freedman, Claire. *Where's your smile, crocodile?*
Freymann, Saxton. *How are you peeling?*
Galdone, Paul. *The teeny-tiny woman*
Got, Yves. *Sam loves kisses*
Grossman, Bill. *My little sister hugged an ape*
Hall, Michael. *My heart is like a zoo*
Harper, Charise Mericle. *Henry's heart*
Harper, Jessica. *Lizzy's ups and downs*
Hills, Tad. *Duck and Goose, how are you feeling?*
Hines, Anna Grossnickle. *Even if I spill my milk?*
Hobbie, Holly. *Toot and Puddle, you are my sunshine*
Hodgkinson, Leigh. *Smile!*
Hopkinson, Deborah. *Bluebird summer*
Hout, Mies van. *Happy*
Inkpen, Mick. *Wibbly Pig is upset*
Isadora, Rachel. *At the crossroads*
Jackson, Ellen. *Sometimes bad things happen*
Johnson, Angela. *The leaving morning*
Kimmel, Haven. *Orville, a dog story*
Klise, Kate. *Why do you cry?*
Könnecke, Ole. *Anthony and the girls*
Krauss, Ruth. *You're just what I need*
Krosoczka, Jarrett J. *It's tough to lose your balloon*
    My buddy, Slug
Lairla, Sergio. *Abel and the wolf*
Lester, Helen. *Hurty feelings*
Lewin, Hugh. *Jafta*
    Jafta — the homecoming
Lodge, Jo. *Happy Snappy!*
McAllister, Angela. *The little blue rabbit*
Maclear, Kyo. *Virginia Wolf*
Making faces: a first book of emotions
Melmed, Laura Krauss. *A hug goes around*
Milgrim, David. *Wild feelings*
Munsch, Robert N. *Aaron's hair*
Murphy, Mary. *I feel happy, and sad, and angry, and glad*
Napoli, Donna Jo. *Flamingo dream*
Neal, Christopher Silas. *Everyone*
Nemiroff, Marc A. *Shy spaghetti and excited eggs*
Nicholls, Judith. *Someone I like*
Norling, Beth. *The stone baby*
Numeroff, Laura Joffe. *The hope tree*
Otoshi, Kathryn. *One*
Parr, Todd. *The feelings book*
    Things that make you feel good, things that make you feel bad
Patricelli, Leslie. *Baby happy, baby sad*
Patterson, Rebecca. *My no, no, no day!*
Peacock, Carol Antoinette. *Mommy far, Mommy near*
Proimos, James. *The loudness of Sam*
Raczka, Bob. *Niko draws a feeling*
Raschka, Chris. *Ring! Yo?*
    Yo! Yes?
Robberecht, Thierry. *Stolen smile*
Rockliff, Mara. *The Grudge Keeper*
Rogers, Fred. *Adoption*
    Making friends
    Moving
Ross, Dave. *A book of hugs*
    A book of kisses
Rotner, Shelley. *Feeling thankful*
Say, Allen. *Allison*

Seeger, Laura Vaccaro. *Walter was worried*
Senisi, Ellen B. *Hurray for pre-K!*
Simon, Norma. *How do I feel?*
Smith, A. J. *Even monsters*
Smith, Linda. *Mrs. Biddlebox*
Smith, Maggie. *Desser, the best ever cat*
Spelman, Cornelia Maude. *Mama and Daddy Bear's divorce*
    When I care about others
Sperring, Mark. *I'll catch you if you fall*
Spinelli, Eileen. *When you are happy*
Stanley, Malaika Rose. *Baby Ruby bawled*
Sterling, Cheryl. *Some bunny to talk to*
Stevenson, James. *Fun, no fun*
Stewart, Whitney. *Meditation is an open sky*
Strauss, Anna. *Hush, Mama loves you*
Tabby, Abigail. *Baby face*
Tankard, Jeremy. *Grumpy Bird*
Thomas, Jane Resh. *Lights on the river*
Vigna, Judith. *Saying goodbye to daddy*
Waber, Bernard. *Ira says goodbye*
Walter, Mildred Pitts. *Two too much*
Watts, Bernadette. *The golden plate*
Weeks, Sarah. *My somebody special*
Weninger, Brigitte. *Good-bye, Daddy!*
Wight, Tamra. *The three grumpies*
Willems, Mo. *The pigeon has feelings, too!*
Willis, Jeanne. *Susan laughs*
Winthrop, Elizabeth. *Promises*
Yoon, Salina. *Found*
Young, Jessica. *My blue is happy*
Yum, Hyewon. *Last night*
Ziefert, Harriet. *Bunny's lessons*

Emotions – anger

Alexander, Martha G. *And my mean old mother will be sorry, Blackboard Bear*
Aliki. *We are best friends*
Antony, Steve. *Betty goes bananas*
Bang, Molly. *When Sophie gets angry — really, really angry . . .*
Birtha, Becky. *Far apart, close in heart*
Blabey, Aaron. *Pig the winner*
Bunting, Eve. *Smoky night*
Burnell, Heather Ayris. *Bedtime monster / ¡A dormir, pequeño monstruo!*
Clarke, Jane. *Trumpet*
Coh, Smiljana. *The seven princesses*
Demers, Dominique. *Old Thomas and the little fairy*
Dewdney, Anna. *Llama Llama mad at Mama*
DiPucchio, Kelly. *Dragon was terrible*
Du Bois, William Pène. *Bear party*
Elliott, David. *Finn throws a fit!*
Everitt, Betsy. *Mean soup*
Fox, Mem. *Harriet, you'll drive me wild*
Gassman, Julie. *Crabby pants*
Gilmore, Rachna. *Making grizzle grow*
Harrington, Janice N. *Roberto walks home*
Harris, Robie H. *The day Leo said I hate you!*
Hemingway, Edward. *Field guide to the Grumpasaurus*
Henkes, Kevin. *Lilly's big day*
    Lilly's purple plastic purse
Henn, Sophy. *Pom Pom Panda gets the grumps*
Hooks, Bell. *Grump groan growl*
Howe, James. *Horace and Morris join the chorus (but what about Dolores?)*
Hughes, Shirley. *Don't want to go!*

Inches, Alison. *I'm not little!*
John, Jory. *The bad seed*
Jonell, Lynne. *When Mommy was mad*
Jones, Elizabeth. *Sunshine and Storm*
Kaplan, Michael B. *Betty Bunny wants everything*
Kroll, Steven. *That makes me mad*
Krosoczka, Jarrett J. *Naptastrophe!*
Landa, Norbert. *Little Bear and the wishing tree*
Langreuter, Jutta. *Little Bear and the big fight*
Lester, Helen. *Princess Penelope's parrot*
Lewis, Kim. *Friends*
Lyon, George Ella. *No dessert forever!*
McBratney, Sam. *I'll always be your friend*
    I'm sorry
McDonnell, Patrick. *A perfectly messed-up story*
Moroney, Trace. *When I'm feeling angry*
Morrison, Toni. *The book of mean people*
Moss, Miriam. *Smudge's grumpy day*
Murphy, Jill. *Meltdown!*
Nadel, Carolina. *Daddy's home*
OHora, Zachariah. *No fits, Nilson!*
O'Malley, Kevin. *Humpty Dumpty egg-splodes*
Palatini, Margie. *Goldie is mad*
Perl, Erica S. *Dotty*
Pfister, Marcus. *You can't win them all, rainbow fish*
Pienkowski, Jan. *Bel and Bub and the bad snowball*
Rankin, Laura. *Ruthie and the (not so) very busy day*
Reynolds, Aaron. *Here comes Destructosaurus!*
Sakai, Komako. *Mad at Mommy*
Sasso, Sandy Eisenberg. *Cain and Abel*
Seeger, Laura Vaccaro. *Bully*
Shannon, David. *The amazing Christmas extravaganza*
Shea, Pegi Deitz. *The boy and the spell*
Shields, Carol Diggory. *I wish my brother was a dog*
Shields, Gillian. *Elephantantrum!*
Spelman, Cornelia Maude. *When I feel angry*
Spires, Ashley. *The most magnificent thing*
Sunami, Kitoba. *How the fisherman tricked the genie*
Sykes, Julie. *Little Tiger's big surprise*
Tutu, Archbishop Desmond. *Desmond and the very mean word*
Urban, Linda. *Mouse was mad*
Vail, Rachel. *Flabbersmashed about you*
    Sometimes I'm Bombaloo
Waddell, Martin. *The Super Hungry Dinosaur*
Weiss, Ellen. *The taming of Lola*
Wells, Rosemary. *Miracle melts down*
Wormell, Mary. *Bernard the angry rooster*
Yolen, Jane. *How do dinosaurs say I'm mad?*
Yorinks, Arthur. *Harry and Lulu*
Zolotow, Charlotte. *The quarreling book*

Emotions – embarrassment

Altman, Alexandra Jessup. *Waiting for Benjamin*
Baryshnikov, Mikhail. *Because . . .*
Birtha, Becky. *Far apart, close in heart*
Brown, Marc. *Arthur's underwear*
Bunting, Eve. *A picnic in October*
Carlson, Nancy. *Sometimes you barf*
Cotterill, Samantha. *No more bows*
Feiffer, Kate. *My mom is trying to ruin my life*
Foreman, Michael. *Oh! if only . . .*
Freeman, Don. *Quiet! There's a canary in the library*
Freeman, Tor. *Olive and the embarrassing gift*
Goodrich, Carter. *Zorro gets an outfit*
Merino, Gemma. *The sheep who hatched an egg*
Moore-Mallinos, Jennifer. *My brother is autistic*

Raschka, Chris. *The blushful hippopotamus*
Singer, Marilyn. *Tallulah's Nutcracker*
Vernick, Audrey. *First grade dropout*
Wood, Audrey. *Weird parents*

Emotions – envy, jealousy

Alexander, Martha G. *Nobody asked me if I wanted a baby sister*
　When the new baby comes, I'm moving out
Asch, Frank. *Bear's bargain*
Britt, Chris. *The most perfect snowman*
Busch, Miriam. *Raisin, the littlest cow*
Calhoun, Mary. *High-wire Henry*
Chichester Clark, Emma. *Plenty of love to go around*
Child, Lauren. *The new small person*
Cole, Joanna. *The new baby at your house*
Colleen, Marcie. *Love, triangle*
Desmond, Jenni. *Red cat blue cat*
Dierssen, Andreas. *The old red tractor*
Drummond, Ree. *Charlie and the new baby*
Egan, Tim. *A mile from Ellington Station*
Enderle, Judith Ross. *Smile, Principessa!*
Fenske, Jonathan. *Barnacle is bored*
Fleming, Denise. *Buster*
Frazee, Marla. *The bossier baby*
Gantos, Jack. *Back to school for Rotten Ralph*
　Rotten Ralph's rotten Christmas
Grant, Jacob. *Cat knit*
Grimm, Jacob and Wilhelm. *Snow White*, ill. by Melinda Copper
　Snow White, ill. by Quentin Gréban
　Snow White, ill. by Trina Schart Hyman
　Snow White, ill. by Charles Santore
　Snow White and the seven dwarfs, ill. by Wanda Gág
　Snow White and the seven dwarfs, ill. by Laura Ljungkvist
Hamilton, Arlene. *Only a cow*
Harper, Anita. *It's not fair!*
Hartt-Sussman, Heather. *Here comes Hortense!*
Havill, Juanita. *Jamaica and Brianna*
Hest, Amy. *You're the boss, Baby Duck*
Hoban, Russell. *A baby sister for Frances*
　A birthday for Frances
Howe, James. *I wish I were a butterfly*
Hubbard, Woodleigh Marx. *Whoa, jealousy*
Idle, Molly. *Flora and the peacocks*
Joosse, Barbara. *Nugget and Darling*
Keller, Holly. *Geraldine's baby brother*
Kellogg, Steven. *Best friends*
Layne, Steven L. *Love the baby*
Lindenbaum, Pija. *Mini Mia and her darling uncle*
Lionni, Leo. *Alexander and the wind-up mouse*
Lloyd-Jones, Sally. *His Royal Highness, King Baby*
Macdonald, Maryann. *The pink party*
Martin, Ann M. *Rachel Parker, kindergarten show-off*
Mathers, Petra. *Lottie's new friend*
Mayer, Mercer. *One frog too many*
Milligan, Bryce. *The prince of Ireland and the three magic stallions*
Moore, Liz. *Zizi and Tish*
Ormerod, Jan. *The baby swap*
Peet, Bill. *The luckiest one of all*
Reynolds, Peter H. *The best kid in the world*
Robberecht, Thierry. *Back into Mommy's tummy*
Roper, Janice M. *Dancing on the moon*
Rosen, Michael. *Howler*
Russo, Marisabina. *The trouble with baby*

San Souci, Robert D. *Peter and the blue witch baby*
Satoshi, Kako. *Little Daruma and little Tengu*
Schneider, Josh. *Princess Sparkle-Heart gets a makeover*
Shea, Bob. *Unicorn thinks he's pretty great*
Smalls-Hector, Irene. *Because you're lucky*
Stein, David Ezra. *Ned's new friend*
Stephens, Helen. *What about me?*
Sykes, Julie. *Little Tiger's big surprise*
Townsend, Michael. *Cute and cuter*
Umansky, Kaye. *I don't like Gloria!*
Voake, Charlotte. *Ginger*
Waber, Bernard. *Evie and Margie*
　Lyle and the birthday party
Wahl, Jan. *Mabel ran away with the toys*
Weeks, Sarah. *Glamourpuss*
Wewer, Iris. *My wild sister and me*
Wild, Margaret. *Fox*
Wortche, Allison. *Rosie Sprout's time to shine*
Yankey, Lindsey. *Sun and Moon*
Yep, Laurence. *Dragon prince*
Young, Amy. *A new friend for Sparkle*

Emotions – fear

Alborough, Jez. *It's the bear*
　Watch out! Big Bro's coming!
Alexander, Martha G. *I'll protect you from the jungle beasts*
Allen, Jonathan. *"I'm not scared!"*
Andreae, Giles. *Be brave, little penguin*
Apple, Margot. *Brave Martha*
Armo, Nancy. *A friend for Mole*
Arnaldo, Monica. *Margo thinks twice*
Arnold, Marsha Diane. *The bravest of us all*
Aylesworth, Jim. *Teddy bear tears*
　Two terrible frights
Baguley, Elizabeth. *Ready, steady, ghost!*
Baker, Ken. *Brave little monster*
Baker, Roberta. *Olive's first sleepover*
Balmes, Santi. *I will fight monsters for you*
Barton, Bethany. *Give bees a chance*
Battersby, Katherine. *Brave Squish Rabbit*
Bauer, Marion Dane. *Dinosaur thunder*
　Halloween forest
　Jason's bears
Baum, Louis. *The mouse who braved bedtime*
Beaty, Andrea. *Hush, Baby Ghostling*
Beck, Scott. *Pepito the brave*
Bently, Peter. *King Jack and the dragon*
Berenstain, Stan and Jan. *The Berenstain bears get stage fright*
　The Berenstain bears learn about strangers
Bergman, Mara. *Snip snap!*
Bertram, Debbie. *My new big-kid bed*
Bird, Betsy. *Giant dance party*
Blake, Stephanie. *I don't want to go to school!*
Bonnett-Rampersaud, Louise. *Bubble and Squeak*
Bourgeois, Paulette. *Franklin and the thunderstorm*
　Franklin in the dark
Boxall, Ed. *Francis the scaredy cat*
Bradbury, Ray. *Switch on the night*
Brendler, Carol. *Not very scary*
Bright, Paul. *The bears in the bed and the great big storm*
Bright, Rachel. *The koala who could*
　Love Monster and the scary something
Bruel, Nick. *Bad Kitty, scaredy-cat*
Bunting, Eve. *Ghost's hour, spook's hour*

London, Jonathan. *Froggy learns to swim*
Lucke, Deb. *The boy who wouldn't swim*
Lyon, George Ella. *Cecil's story*
McAllister, Angela. *Trust me, Mom!*
McBratney, Sam. *The dark at the top of the stairs*
McCarthy, Jenna. *Poppy Louise is not afraid of anything*
McCully, Emily Arnold. *Mirette on the high wire*
MacDonald, Margaret Read. *The squeaky door*
McGhee, Alison. *Countdown to kindergarten*
　　Song of middle C
McKee, David. *Elmer and the monster*
McPhail, David. *Water boy*
Mader, C. Roger. *Tiptop cat*
Manceau, Edouard. *Tickle monster*
Marino, Gianna. *Night animals*
Martín Larrañaga, Ana. *Woo! the not-so-scary Ghost*
Mathews, Judith. *Nathaniel Willy, scared silly*
May, Eleanor. *Albert is not scared*
Mayer, Mercer. *There are monsters everywhere*
　　There's a nightmare in my closet
　　There's an alligator under my bed
　　You're the scaredy cat
Maynor, Megan. *Ella and Penguin: stick together*
Meserve, Jessica. *Bedtime without Arthur*
Michelson, Richard. *Oh no, not ghosts!*
Miller, William. *A house by the river*
Milord, Susan. *Happy school year!*
Modarressi, Mitra. *Owlet's first flight*
Mollel, Tololwa M. *Rhinos for lunch and elephants for supper*
Monfreid, Dorothée de. *Dark night*
Moodie, Fiona. *Noko and the night monster*
Moore, Lilian. *Beware, take care*
Morgan, Michaela. *Brave, brave mouse*
Moroney, Trace. *When I'm feeling scared*
Morrison, Toni. *Please, Louise*
Mortensen, Lori. *Chicken Lily*
Murphy, Jim. *Fergus and the Night-Demon*
Nash, Ogden. *The adventures of Isabel*, ill. by James Marshall
　　The adventures of Isabel, ill. by Bridget Starr Taylor
Newman, Lesléa. *Miss Tutu's star*
Nivola, Claire A. *The forest*
Norman, Geoffrey. *Stars above us*
Paraskevas, Betty. *Maggie and the Ferocious Beast, the big scare*
Parker, Danny. *Parachute*
Patricelli, Leslie. *The Patterson puppies and the midnight monster party*
Patschke, Steve. *The spooky book*
Paul, Alison. *The crow (a not so scary story)*
Peck, Richard. *Monster night at Grandma's house*
Penn, Audrey. *A bedtime kiss for Chester Raccoon*
Pfister, Marcus. *Rainbow fish to the rescue!*
Pinfold, Levi. *Black dog*
Pitzer, Susanna. *Not afraid of dogs*
Polacco, Patricia. *Mr. Wayne's masterpiece*
　　Thunder cake
Potter, Alicia. *Miss Hazeltine's Home for Shy and Fearful Cats*
Powell, Polly. *Just dessert*
Powell-Tuck, Maudie. *Pirates aren't afraid of the dark!*
Pryor, Bonnie. *The porcupine mouse*
Puckett, Kelley. *Batman's dark secret*
Pumphrey, Jerome. *Creepy things are scaring me*
Raschka, Chris. *Can't sleep*
　　Daisy gets lost

　　Waffle
Rash, Andy. *Archie the daredevil penguin*
Ray, Mary Lyn. *Boom!*
Reynolds, Aaron. *Creepy carrots!*
　　Creepy pair of underwear!
　　Sea Monkey and Bob
Reynolds, Marilynn. *The name of the child*
Riggs, Shannon. *Not in Room 204*
Rim, Sujean. *Birdie's first day of school*
Robberecht, Thierry. *Sam is never scared*
Robbins, Beth. *Tom, Ally, and the baby-sitter*
　　Tom and Ally visit the doctor
　　Tom's afraid of the dark
　　Tom's new haircut
Rockwell, Anne. *Katie Catz makes a splash*
　　Welcome to kindergarten
Rodriguez, Edel. *Sergio makes a splash*
Rosenberry, Vera. *Vera's first day of school*
Rosoff, Meg. *Jumpy Jack and Googily*
Ross, Tony. *I want my light on!*
Rubin, Adam. *Big bad bubble*
Runton, Andy. *Owly and Wormy: bright lights and starry nights!*
Salley, Coleen. *Epossumondas plays possum*
Sanna, Francesca. *The journey*
Sanromán, Susana. *Señora Reganona*
Santat, Dan. *After the fall (how Humpty Dumpty got back up again)*
Sattler, Jennifer. *Pig kahuna*
Saunders, Karen. *Baby Badger's wonderful night*
Savadier, Elivia. *No haircut today!*
Schaefer, Carole Lexa. *Who's there?*
Schmid, Paul. *Oliver and his alligator*
Schneider, Josh. *Bedtime monsters*
Schuurmans, Hilde. *Sydney won't swim*
Schwarz, Viviane. *Shark and Lobster's amazing undersea adventure*
Scotton, Rob. *Splish, splash, splat!*
Seeger, Laura Vaccaro. *I used to be afraid*
Senshu, Noriko. *Sonny's dream*
Seuss, Dr. *The Sneetches, and other stories*
Shah, Idries. *The clever boy and the terrible, dangerous animal*
Shea, Bob. *I'm a shark*
　　The scariest book ever
Shum, Benson. *Holly's day at the pool*
Simon, Charnan. *Big bad Buzz*
Snicket, Lemony. *The dark*
Soman, David. *Ladybug Girl at the beach*
Spelman, Cornelia Maude. *When I feel scared*
Spinelli, Eileen. *A safe place called home*
　　Wanda's monster
Staub, Leslie. *Time for (Earth) school, Dewey Dew*
Stein, Mathilde. *Brave Ben*
Stevenson, Harvey. *Big scary wolf*
Stevenson, James. *What's under my bed?*
Stewart, Amber. *No babysitters allowed*
Stewart, Shannon. *Sea crow*
Stine, R.L. *Mary McScary*
Stock, Catherine. *Halloween monster*
Stroud, Bettye. *Dance y'all*
Taulbert, Clifton L. *Little Cliff's first day of school*
Taylor, Sean. *I want to be in a scary story*
Tessler, Manya. *Yuki's ride home*
Thach, James Otis. *A child's guide to common household monsters*
Thomas, Jan. *The doghouse*
　　Let's sing a lullaby with the Brave Cowboy
Thompson, Richard. *The night walker*

Thornhill, Jan. *The rumor*
Tomlinson, Jill. *The owl who was afraid of the dark*
Tsurumi, Andrea. *Accident!*
Tyger, Rory. *Newton*
Vail, Rachel. *Jibberwillies at night*
van Lieshout, Maria. *Peep!*
Viorst, Judith. *And two boys booed*
  My mama says there aren't any zombies, ghosts, vampires, creatures, demons, monsters, fiends, goblins, or things
Vogel, Vin. *Bedtime for Yeti*
Waddell, Martin. *Can't you sleep, Little Bear?*
  Let's go home, Little Bear
  Owl babies
  Tom Rabbit
Waechter, Phillip. *Rosie and the nightmares*
Waldron, Jan L. *John Pig's Halloween*
Wallace, Ian. *Chin Chiang and the dragon's dance*
Wallen, Ila. *The moon in my room*
Walsh, Ellen Stoll. *Pip's magic*
Ward, Nick. *Come on Baby Duck*
Warnes, Tim. *The great cheese robbery*
Watt, Mélanie. *Scaredy Squirrel*
  Scaredy Squirrel at night
  Scaredy Squirrel at the beach
  Scaredy Squirrel goes camping
  Scaredy Squirrel has a birthday party
  Scaredy Squirrel makes a friend
  Scaredy Squirrel prepares for Christmas
  Scaredy Squirrel prepares for Halloween
Weitzman, Jacqueline Preiss. *Superhero Joe*
  Superhero Joe and the creature next door
Wells, Rosemary. *A visit to Dr. Duck*
Weston, Martha. *Tuck in the pool*
Whybrow, Ian. *Harry and the dinosaurs say "Raahh"*
Willems, Mo. *Sam the most scaredy-cat kid in the whole world*
Williams, Linda. *The little old lady who was not afraid of anything*
Willis, Jeanne. *Fly, chick, fly!*
Wilson, Karma. *Bear feels scared*
  Don't be afraid, Little Pip
  Who goes there?
Wilson-Max, Ken. *Max's starry night*
Winters, Kay. *The teeny tiny ghost*
  Whooo's haunting the teeny tiny ghost?
Winton, Tim. *The deep*
Wormell, Christopher. *Henry and the fox*
Wright, Michael. *Jake starts school*
Yarlett, Emma. *Orion and the Dark*
Yoon, Salina. *Stormy night*
Yum, Hyewon. *There are no scary wolves*
Zolotow, Charlotte. *The storm book*

Emotions – grief

Alvarez, Julia. *Where do they go?*
Bagley, Jessixa. *Boats for Papa*
Barron, T. A. *Where is Grandpa?*
The best cat in the world
Bley, Anette. *And what comes after a thousand?*
Blumenthal, Deborah. *The blue house dog*
Boase, Susan. *Lucky boy*
Brisson, Pat. *I remember Miss Perry*
Brown, Margaret Wise. *The dead bird*
Bunting, Eve. *The memory string*
  Rudi's pond
Charles, Veronika Martenova. *The birdman*
Clifton, Lucille. *Everett Anderson's goodbye*

Cobb, Rebecca. *Missing Mommy*
Cochran, Bill. *The forever dog*
Cohen, Miriam. *Jim's dog Muffins*, ill. by Ronald Himler
  Jim's dog Muffins, ill. by Lillian Hoban
Cooke, Trish. *The grandad tree*
Davies, Nicola. *The pond*
dePaola, Tomie. *Nana Upstairs and Nana Downstairs*
Doray, Malika. *One more Wednesday*
Edwards, Michelle. *Papa's latkes*
Ewart, Claire. *The giant*
Fletcher, Ralph. *Grandpa never lies*
Fritts, Mary Bahr. *If Nathan were here*
Gregory, Nan. *Wild Girl and Gran*
Grifalconi, Ann. *Tiny's hat*
Grimm, Edward. *The doorman*
Hanson, Regina. *A season for mangoes*
Harris, Robie H. *Goodbye, Mousie*
Haynes, Max. *Grandma's gone to live in the stars*
Heard, Georgia. *This place I know*
Hest, Amy. *My old pal, Oscar*
Hill, Frances. *The bug cemetery*
Hole, Stian. *Anna's heaven*
Jeffers, Oliver. *The heart and the bottle*
Jeffs, Stephanie. *Jenny*
  Josh
Johnston, Tony. *That summer*
Kerner, Susan. *Always by my side*
Krishnaswami, Uma. *Remembering Grandpa*
Leiner, Katherine. *Mama does the mambo*
Levis, Caron. *Ida, always*
Lunde, Stein Erik. *My father's arms are a boat*
Maier, Inger. *Ben's flying flowers*
Monk, Isabell. *Blackberry stew*
Moundlic, Charlotte. *The scar*
Murphy, Sally. *Pearl verses the world*
Napoli, Donna Jo. *Flamingo dream*
Nickle, John. *TV Rex*
Nobisso, Josephine. *Grandpa loved*
O'Brien, Anne Sibley. *A path of stars*
Onyefulu, Ifeoma. *Saying goodbye*
Parker, Marjorie Blain. *Jasper's day*
Parr, Todd. *The goodbye book*
Polacco, Patricia. *An A from Miss Keller*
Puttock, Simon. *A story for Hippo*
Rappaport, Doreen. *The new king*
Raschka, Chris. *The purple balloon*
Ringtved, Glenn. *Cry, heart, but never break*
Roberts, Jillian. *What happens when a loved one dies?*
Rogers, Fred. *When a pet dies*
Roper, Janice M. *Dancing on the moon*
Rosenberg, Liz. *The carousel*
Russo, Marisabina. *Grandpa Abe*
Santucci, Barbara. *Anna's corn*
Schick, Eleanor. *Mama*
Simon, Norma. *The saddest time*
Skofield, James. *Bear and Bird*
Stafford, Liliana. *Just dragon*
Thomas, Jane Resh. *Saying good-bye to grandma*
Tibo, Gilles. *The grand journey of Mr. Man*
Vigna, Judith. *Saying goodbye to daddy*
Viorst, Judith. *The tenth good thing about Barney*
Weigelt, Udo. *Bear's last journey*
Weitzman, Elizabeth. *Let's talk about when a parent dies*
Wild, Margaret. *Harry and Hopper*
Wilhelm, Hans. *I'll always love you*
Wood, Douglas. *Grandad's prayers of the earth*

Woodson, Jacqueline. *Sweet, sweet memory*
Zalben, Jane Breskin. *Pearl's marigolds for grandpa*
Ziefert, Harriet. *Ode to Humpty Dumpty*
Zolotow, Charlotte. *My grandson Lew*
    The old dog
Zucker, Bonnie. *Something very sad happened*

Emotions – happiness

Cabrera, Jane. *If you're happy and you know it*
Carlson, Nancy. *Think happy!*
Cohen, Caron Lee. *Happy to you!*
Doyle, Malachy. *Get happy*
Emberley, Rebecca. *If you're a monster and you know it*
Gray Smith, Monique. *My heart fills with happiness*
Hall, Michael. *Perfect square*
Henn, Sophy. *Pass it on*
Jackson, Ellen. *Sometimes bad things happen*
Kaiser, Ruth. *The smiley book of colors*
Lloyd, David. *Polly Molly Woof Woof*
McBratney, Sam. *Once there was a Hoodie*
Menchin, Scott. *Taking a bath with the dog and other things that make me happy*
Miura, Taro. *The tiny king*
Moroney, Trace. *When I'm feeling happy*
Ormerod, Jan. *If you're happy and you know it!*
Parr, Todd. *The feel good book*
Portis, Antoinette. *Now*
Rayner, Catherine. *Augustus and his smile*
Rylant, Cynthia. *The wonderful happens*
Schwartz, Amy. *One hundred things that make me happy*
Schwarz, Viviane. *The adventures of a nose*
Shea, Bob. *The happiest book ever*
Starr, Meg. *Alicia's happy day*
Steig, William. *Spinky sulks*
Stein, David Ezra. *Because Amelia smiled*
Thomas, Joyce Carol. *Joy*
Warhola, James. *If you're happy and you know it: jungle edition*
Wilcox, Brad. *Hip, hip, hooray for Annie McRae!*
Williams, Pharrell. *Happy!*
Willis, Jeanne. *Misery Moo*
Wood, Douglas. *The secret of saying thanks*

Emotions – hate

Harris, Robie H. *The day Leo said I hate you!*
Thompson, Lauren. *The forgiveness garden*
Udry, Janice May. *Let's be enemies*
Zolotow, Charlotte. *The hating book*

Emotions – jealousy *see* Emotions – envy, jealousy

Emotions – loneliness

Aardema, Verna. *The lonely lioness and the ostrich chicks*
Abley, Mark. *Ghost cat*
Ahlberg, Allan. *The pencil*
Alborough, Jez. *My friend bear*
Aliki. *We are best friends*
Andros, Camille. *Charlotte the scientist is squished*
Barnett, Mac. *Leo: a ghost story*
Battersby, Katherine. *Squish Rabbit*
Bernheimer, Kate. *The girl in the castle inside the museum*

    The lonely book
Bowles, Paula. *Scary Mary*
Brett, Jan. *Annie and the wild animals*
Brun-Cosme, Nadine. *Big Wolf and Little Wolf*
Byun, You. *Dream friends*
Cecil, Randy. *Lucy*
Chichester Clark, Emma. *Melrose and Croc*
Colfer, Eoin. *Imaginary Fred*
Corderoy, Tracey. *Just right for two*
Cort, Ben. *Pigs can't fly!*
Cuevas, Michelle. *The uncorker of ocean bottles*
Cumming, Hannah. *The red boat*
Curato, Mike. *Little Elliot, big family*
Daly, Niki. *Welcome to Zanzibar Road*
Davies, Benji. *The storm whale*
    The storm whale in winter
DiCamillo, Kate. *La la la*
DiPucchio, Kelly. *Zombie in love*
Dunrea, Olivier. *Little cub*
Ellis, Sarah. *Ben says goodbye*
Emberley, Rebecca. *Spare parts*
Esbaum, Jill. *Tom's tweet*
Ferry, Beth. *A small blue whale*
    Stick and Stone
Floyd, Madeleine. *Cold paws, warm heart*
Foggo, Cheryl. *Dear baobab*
Foreman, Jack. *Say hello*
Fox, Mem. *The goblin and the empty chair*
Ginkel, Anne. *I've got an elephant*
Goldstyn, Jacques. *Bertolt*
Gorbachev, Valeri. *Big Little Elephant*
Gordon, Gus. *Herman and Rosie*
Grey, Mini. *Ginger bear*
Haas, Irene. *Bess and Bella*
Halpern, Julie. *Toby and the snowflakes*
Hest, Amy. *The dog who belonged to no one*
Horácek, Petr. *Blue Penguin*
Ikegami, Aiko. *Friends*
Imai, Ayano. *Mr. Brown's fantastic hat*
Isern, Susanna. *The lonely mailman*
Jahn-Clough, Lisa. *On the hill*
James, J. Alison. *The bears' Christmas surprise*
Janni, Rebecca. *Every cowgirl needs dancing boots*
Jeffers, Oliver. *The heart and the bottle*
    Lost and found
Jiang, Ji-li. *Lotus and Feather*
Johnston, Tony. *The cat with seven names*
Joosse, Barbara. *Lovabye Dragon*
Jules, Jacqueline. *No English*
Juster, Norton. *Neville*
Keats, Ezra Jack. *The trip*
King-Chai, Sharon. *Lucy Ladybug*
Kleven, Elisa. *The friendship wish*
Kohara, Kazuno. *Here comes Jack Frost*
Kolanovic, Dubravka. *Everyone needs a friend*
Kooser, Ted. *The bell in the bridge*
Kroll, Steven. *The hand-me-down doll*
Lacombe, Benjamin. *Cherry and Olive*
Lambert, Jonny. *The only lonely panda*
LaReau, Kara. *Mr. Prickles*
    Snowbaby could not sleep
    Ugly fish
Le Neouanic, Lionel. *Little smudge*
Lerch. *Swim! swim!*
Litchfield, David. *The bear and the piano*
Lucas, David. *Cake girl*
Ludwig, Trudy. *The invisible boy*
McCarty, Peter. *Jeremy draws a monster*
McCormick, Wendy. *Daddy, will you miss me?*

McDonnell, Christine. *Goyangi means cat*
McDonnell, Patrick. *South*
McElroy, Lisa Tucker. *Love, Lizzie*
MacLachlan, Patricia. *Nora's chicks*
Magerl, Caroline. *Rose and the wish thing*
Marx, Patricia. *Dot in Larryland*
Maturana, Andrea. *Life without Nico*
Mitchell, Hazel. *Toby*
Morison, Toby. *Little Louie takes off*
Mortimer, Rachael. *Song for a princess*
Murphy, Sally. *Pearl verses the world*
Na, Il Sung. *Bird, balloon, Bear*
Nichols, Lori. *Maple and Willow apart*
Norac, Carl. *I love to cuddle*
Norwich, William D. *Molly and the magic dress*
Pfister, Marcus. *The rainbow fish*
Pilcher, Steve. *Over there*
Pilkey, Dav. *A friend for Dragon*
Pizzoli, Greg. *Templeton gets his wish*
Radunsky, Vladimir. *You?*
Rex, Adam. *Nothing rhymes with orange*
Root, Phyllis. *Scrawny cat*
Rowe, John A. *I want a hug*
Ruzzier, Sergio. *A letter for Leo*
Segal, John. *The lonely moose*
Shapiro, Esmé. *Ooko*
Sherry, Kevin. *Turtle Island*
Snicket, Lemony. *Goldfish Ghost*
Song, Mika. *Tea with Oliver*
Spelman, Cornelia Maude. *When I miss you*
Spinelli, Eileen. *Somebody loves you, Mr. Hatch*
Staake, Bob. *Bluebird*
Stevenson, James. *Mr. Hacker*
Swaim, Jessica. *The hound from the pound*
Swann, Rick. *Our school garden!*
Taback, Simms. *I miss you every day*
Teckentrup, Britta. *Grumpy cat*
Teevin, Toni. *What to do? What to do?*
Titherington, Jeanne. *A place for Ben*
Turnbull, Victoria. *Pandora*
Vail, Rachel. *Flabbersmashed about you*
Viorst, Judith. *Nobody here but me*
Waber, Bernard. *Gina*
Waddell, Martin. *Sam Vole and his brothers*
　　Sleep tight, Little Bear
Wall, Laura. *Goose*
Wallner, Alexandra. *Beatrix Potter*
Walter, Mildred Pitts. *My mama needs me*
Ward, Helen. *The dragon machine*
Watt, Mélanie. *Scaredy Squirrel makes a friend*
Wells, Rosemary. *Small world of Binky Braverman*
Wheeler, Lisa. *The Christmas boot*
　　Porcupining
Wild, Margaret. *Fox*
Wilson, Karma. *Sweet Briar goes to camp*
Winter, Jeanette. *Angelina's island*
Wright, Dare. *A gift from the lonely doll*
　　The lonely doll
Yashima, Taro. *Crow boy*
Yeh, Kat. *The friend ship*
Yerkes, Jennifer. *A funny little bird*
Yolen, Jane. *Elsie's bird*
Yoon, Salina. *Be a friend*
Young, Rebecca. *Teacup*
Zolotow, Charlotte. *The bunny who found Easter*
　　A tiger called Thomas, ill. by Diana Cain
　　　　Bluthenthal
　　A tiger called Thomas, ill. by Catherine Stock
Zuniga, Elisabeth. *A friend for Bo*

Emotions – love

Adoff, Arnold. *Love letters*
Aigner-Clark, Julie. *You are the best medicine*
Anastas, Margaret. *A hug for you*
　　Mommy's best kisses
Andersen, Hans Christian. *The snow queen*, ill. by
　　Angela Barrett
　　The snow queen, ill. by Sally Holmes
　　The snow queen, ill. by Susan Jeffers
　　The snow queen: a retelling of the fairy tale
Anholt, Laurence. *Seven for a secret*
Appelt, Kathi. *Oh my baby, little one*
Ashman, Linda. *What could be better than this*
Austrian, J. J. *Worm loves Worm*
Baker, Liza. *I love you because you're you*
Bang, Molly. *In my heart*
Bedford, David. *Mole's in love*
　　The way I love you
Bianco, Margery Williams. *The velveteen rabbit*, ill.
　　by David Jorgensen
　　The velveteen rabbit, ill. by Thea Kliros
　　The velveteen rabbit, ill. by Komako Sakai
　　The velveteen rabbit, ill. by Gennady Spirin
　　The velveteen rabbit: or, How toys became real, ill. by
　　　　Allen Atkinson
　　The velveteen rabbit: or, How toys became real, ill. by
　　　　Steve Johnson
Bible. New Testament. Corinthians 1st, XIII. *Love
　　is*
Bright, Rachel. *Love Monster*
Bunting, Eve. *Baby can*
　　Swan in love
　　You were loved before you were born
Burdett, Lois. *Romeo and Juliet for kids*
Calmenson, Stephanie. *Perfect puppy*
Capucilli, Alyssa Satin. *Bear hugs*
　　I will love you
Cheshire, Marc. *Love and kisses, Eloise*
Chichester Clark, Emma. *Love is my favorite thing*
Clayton, Dallas. *An awesome book of love!*
Clements, Andrew. *Because your daddy loves you*
　　Because your mommy loves you
Clifton, Lucille. *Everett Anderson's goodbye*
Cole, Babette. *Truelove*
Conway, David. *The most important gift of all*
Craft, Mahlon F. *Beauty and the beast*
Cruise, Robin. *Only you*
Davies, Stephen. *Don't spill the milk!*
Delacre, Lulu. *How far do you love me?*
Denise, Anika. *Baking day at Grandma's*
DiTerlizzi, Angela. *Baby love*
Dodd, Emma. *Always*
　　Everything
　　Forever
　　Foxy in love
　　Happy
　　Love
　　More and more
　　No matter what
Duncan, Alice Faye. *Honey baby sugar child*
Dunrea, Olivier. *Old Bear and his cub*
Durant, Alan. *I love you, little monkey*
Dylan, Bob. *If not for you*
Edwards, Nicola. *Goodnight Baxter*
Elffers, Joost. *Do you love me?*
Emmett, Jonathan. *I love you always and forever*
Eure, Wesley. *A fish out of water*
Evans, Kristina. *What's special about me, Mama?*

Evans, Lezlie. *Who loves the little lamb?*
Farrington, Susan. *What I love about you*
Ferber, Brenda A. *The yuckiest, stinkiest, best Valentine ever*
Flack, Marjorie. *Ask Mr. Bear*
Fleming, Meg. *I heart you*
Foreman, Michael. *I love you, too!*
Fox, Mem. *Koala Lou*
    Sophie
Freeman, Don. *Corduroy*
George, Lindsay Barrett. *The secret*
Gliori, Debi. *No matter what*
Goble, Paul. *Love flute*
Hample, Stoo. *I will kiss you (lots and lots and lots!)*
Hautzig, Deborah. *Beauty and the beast*
Hesse, Karen. *Spuds*
Hines, Anna Grossnickle. *When we married Gary*
Howe, James. *Otter and odder*
Jacobs, Julie. *My heart is a magic house*
Jaffe, Nina. *The way meat loves salt*
Jenkins, Emily. *Love you when you whine*
Jones, Ursula. *Beauty and the beast*
Joosse, Barbara. *Grandma calls me Beautiful*
    Love is a good thing to feel
    Mama, do you love me?
    Papa do you love me?
Jordan, Deloris. *Baby blessings*
Juster, Norton. *Sourpuss and sweetie pie*
Karas, G. Brian. *Skidamarink*
Kasza, Keiko. *A mother for Choco*
Katz, Karen. *Daddy hugs 1 2 3*
    Mommy hugs
Kern, Noris. *I love you with all my heart*
Kimmel, Elizabeth Cody. *My penguin Osbert in love*
Kimmelman, Leslie. *How do I love you?*
Kindermans, Martine. *You and me*
Kirk, David. *Little Miss Spider*
Kraus, Robert. *Mouse in love*
Krauss, Ruth. *And I love you*
Kuklin, Susan. *Families*
Laird, Elizabeth. *A book of promises*
Lawler, Janet. *A father's song*
    Love is real
Lawrence, Michael. *Baby loves*
Lee, Chinlun. *Good dog, Paw*
Lee, H. Chuku. *Beauty and the beast: a retelling*
Lloyd-Jones, Sally. *Just because you're mine*
London, Jonathan. *Count the ways, Little Brown Bear*
    Froggy's first kiss
    What do you love?
Long, Ethan. *Valensteins: (a love story)*
McAllister, Angela. *Mama and Little Joe*
McBratney, Sam. *Guess how much I love you*
    There, there
McCarty, Peter. *Henry in love*
McCaughrean, Geraldine. *Beauty and the beast*
McCourt, Lisa. *I love you, Stinky Face*
MacDonald, Margaret Read. *The great smelly, slobbery small-toothed dog*
MacLachlan, Patricia. *Who loves me?*
McNaughton, Colin. *Oomph!*
McPhail, David. *Brothers*
    I promise
    The teddy bear
Marley, Cedella. *One love*
Martin, Bill, Jr.. *Knots on a counting rope*
Marzollo, Jean. *I love you*
Massini, Sarah. *Love always everywhere*

Masurel, Claire. *Two homes*
Mayer, Marianna. *Beauty and the beast*
Mayer, Mercer. *Just for you*
Milord, Susan. *If I could*
    Love that baby
Morgan, Michaela. *Dear bunny*
Morris, Ann. *Loving*
Morrow, Tara Jaye. *Mommy loves her baby; Daddy loves his baby*
Munsch, Robert N. *Love you forever*
Newman, Lesléa. *Daddy's song*
Newman, Marjorie. *Mole and the baby bird*
Nobisso, Josephine. *Grandpa loved*
Norac, Carl. *I love you so much*
North, Sherry. *Because you are my baby*
O'Keefe, Susan Heyboer. *Love me, love you*
Oppenheim, Shulamith Levey. *I love you, Bunny Rabbit*
Oram, Hiawyn. *Kiss it better*
Otsuka, Yuzo. *Suho's white horse*
Paradis, Susan. *My mommy*
Parr, Todd. *The I love you book*
Paschkis, Julie. *Apple cake*
Paul, Ann Whitford. *If animals said I love you*
Pearce, Clemency. *Three little words*
Pearson, Susan. *Slugs in love*
Pennypacker, Sara. *Pierre in love*
Pham, LeUyen. *All the things I love about you*
Pierce, Christa. *Did you know that I love you?*
Pignataro, Anna. *Our love grows*
Pow, Tom. *Tell me one thing, Dad*
Prasadam-Halls, Smriti. *I love you night and day*
Price, Leontyne. *Aïda*
Quattlebaum, Mary. *Pirate vs. pirate*
Rankin, Joan. *You're somebody special, Walliwigs!*
Ransom, Jeanie Franz. *I don't want to talk about it*
Reiser, Lynn. *The surprise family*
Reynolds, Luke. *If my love were a fire truck*
Ritchie, Alison. *Me and my dad!*
    Me and my mom!
Robinson, Michelle. *Odd socks*
Rock, Brian. *With all my heart*
Rock, Lois. *Now we have a baby*
Rohmer, Harriet. *Mother scorpion country*
Rose, Deborah Lee. *All the seasons of the year*
Rosenthal, Amy Krouse. *Plant a kiss*
Rossetti-Shustak, Bernadette. *I love you through and through*
Roth, Carol. *Will you still love me?*
Rotner, Shelley. *Lots of grandparents*
    What's love?
Rueda, Claudia. *My little polar bear*
Rusackas, Francesca. *Daddy all day long*
Ryder, Joanne. *Bear of my heart*
Rylant, Cynthia. *Baby face: a book of love for baby*
    If you'll be my Valentine
    Puppies and piggies
Sabuda, Robert. *Beauty and the beast: a pop-up book of the classic fairy tale*
Saltzberg, Barney. *Kisses*
Salzano, Tammi. *I love you just the way you are*
Samuels, Barbara. *Faye and Dolores*
San Souci, Robert D. *Nicholas Pipe*
Schlessinger, Laura. *Why do you love me?*
Scott, Ann Herbert. *On mother's lap*
Shannon, George. *Hands say love*
Shapiro, Jody Fickes. *Family lullaby*
Sheehan, Monica. *Love is you and me*
Slonim, David. *I loathe you*

Snyder, Betsy E. *I haiku you*
Spelman, Cornelia Maude. *Mama and Daddy Bear's divorce*
Steig, William. *Potch and Polly*
   Tiffky Doofky
Steven, Kenneth. *The biggest thing in the world*
Stott, Ann. *Always*
   I'll be there
Stuve-Bodeen, Stephanie. *Elizabeti's doll*
Summers, Kate. *Milly's wedding*
Taback, Simms. *I miss you every day*
Tafuri, Nancy. *I love you, little one*
Thomas, Eliza. *The red blanket*
Thompson, Kay. *Kay Thompson's Eloise's what I absolutely love love love*
Tillman, Nancy. *Wherever you are*
Tinkham, Kelly A. *Hair for Mama*
Tonatiuh, Duncan. *The princess and the warrior*
Trotter, Deborah W. *How do you know?*
Tupper Ling, Nancy. *The story I'll tell*
Van Buren, David. *I love you as big as the world*
van Lieshout, Elle. *The wish*
Verburg, Bonnie. *The kiss box*
Vischer, Phil. *Sidney and Norman*
Waddell, Martin. *Who do you love?*
Walton, Rick. *What do we do with the baby?*
Wan, Joyce. *Hug you, kiss you, love you*
Watson, Wendy. *A Valentine for you*
Weeks, Sarah. *Woof*
Weiss, Ellen. *I love you, Little Monster*
Wells, Rosemary. *Carry me!*
   Love waves
Wild, Margaret. *Piglet and Mama*
   Piglet and Papa
Williams, Sam. *That's love*
Willis, Jeanne. *Mommy do you love me?*
Wilson, Sarah. *Love and kisses*
Wood, Douglas. *When a dad says "I love you"*
   When a grandpa says "I love you"
Xinran, Xue. *Motherbridge of love*
Yolen, Jane. *How do dinosaurs say I love you?*
Yoon, Salina. *Penguin in love*
Yorinks, Arthur. *Harry and Lulu*
Young, Ed. *My Mei Mei*
Zolotow, Charlotte. *Do you know what I'll do?*
   Say it!
   Some things go together
Zuckerman, Linda. *I will hold you 'til you sleep*

Emotions – sadness

Abley, Mark. *Ghost cat*
Bang, Molly. *When Sophie's feelings are really, really hurt*
Beaty, Daniel. *Knock knock*
Birtha, Becky. *Far apart, close in heart*
Brown, Margaret Wise. *The dead bird*
Carroll, James Christopher. *Papa's backpack*
Cobb, Rebecca. *Missing Mommy*
Cora, Cat. *A suitcase surprise for Mommy*
Diesen, Deborah. *The pout-pout fish*
Havill, Juanita. *Jamaica's blue marker*
Henry, Jed. *Cheer up, Mouse!*
Kerner, Susan. *Always by my side*
Kobald, Irena. *My two blankets*
Lawrence, Jennifer B. *Sad doggy*
Levis, Caron. *Stuck with the Blooz*
Maier, Inger. *Ben's flying flowers*
Medina, Sarah. *Sad*

Monk, Isabell. *Blackberry stew*
Moroney, Trace. *When I'm feeling sad*
Parr, Todd. *The goodbye book*
Paul, Alison. *The plan*
Plecas, Jennifer. *Olive's perfect world*
Pulver, Robin. *Saturday is Dadurday*
Santat, Dan. *After the fall (how Humpty Dumpty got back up again)*
Spelman, Cornelia Maude. *When I feel sad*
Willis, Jeanne. *Misery Moo*
Yolen, Jane. *The stranded whale*
Zucker, Bonnie. *Something very sad happened*

Emotions – unhappiness *see* Emotions – happiness; Emotions – sadness

Engineered books *see* Format, unusual – toy & movable books

Entertainment *see* Theater

Entrepreneur *see* Money

Environment *see* Ecology

Eskimos, *see also* Indians of North America – Inuit

Brown, Kerry. *Tupag the dreamer*
Edwardson, Debby Dahl. *Whale snow*
George, Jean Craighead. *Nutik and Amaroq play ball*
   Nutik, the wolf pup
   Snow bear
Joosse, Barbara. *Mama, do you love me?*
Luenn, Nancy. *Nessa's fish*
   Nessa's story
Munsch, Robert N. *A promise is a promise*
San Souci, Robert D. *Song of Sedna*
Scott, Ann Herbert. *On mother's lap*
Sís, Peter. *A small tall tale from the far Far North*

Ethnic groups in the U.S.

Alko, Selina. *I'm your peanut butter big brother*
Averbeck, Jim. *One word from Sophia*
Bunting, Eve. *Smoky night*
Cohen, Miriam. *Will I have a friend?*, ill. by Ronald Himler
   Will I have a friend?, ill. by Lillian Hoban
de la Peña, Matt. *Last stop on Market Street*
Diggs, Taye. *Mixed me!*
Dooley, Norah. *Everybody brings noodles*
   Everybody cooks rice
   Everybody serves soup
Dorros, Arthur. *Abuela*
Edwards, Nancy. *Glenna's seeds*
Faruqi, Reem. *Lailah's lunchbox*
Fergus, Maureen. *The day Santa stopped believing in Harold*
Golding, Theresa Martin. *Memorial Day surprise*
Graham, Bob. *Oscar's half birthday*
Harris, Robie H. *Who we are!*
   Who's in my family?
Kallok, Emma. *Gem*

Katz, Karen. *The colors of us*
Keats, Ezra Jack. *My dog is lost!*
Lester, Julius. *Let's talk about race*
Maestro, Betsy. *Coming to America*
Manushkin, Fran. *Happy in our skin*
Miller, J. Philip. *We all sing with the same voice*
Moss, Jenny Jackson. *Cajun night after Christmas*
Nikola-Lisa, W. *Bein' with you this way*
Petricic, Dusan. *My family tree and me*
Pinkney, Sandra L. *A rainbow all around me*
Polacco, Patricia. *In our mothers' house*
Richards, Doyin. *What's the difference? being different is amazing*
Rotner, Shelley. *Lots of moms*
   Shades of people
Schaefer, Carole Lexa. *Snow pumpkin*
Shannon, George. *One family*
Shelby, Anne. *Potluck*
Smith, Charles R. *I am the world*
Stowell, Penelope. *The greatest potatoes*
Udry, Janice May. *What Mary Jo shared*
Vigil-Piñón, Evangelina. *Marina's muumuu / El muumuu de Marina*
Washington, Kathy Gates. *Three colors of Katie*
Weiss, Nicki. *The world turns round and round*
Williams, Vera B. *"More more more," said the baby*
Wing, Natasha. *Jalapeño bagels*
Wong, Janet S. *This next New Year*

Ethnic groups in the U.S. – African Americans

Ackerman, Karen. *By the dawn's early light*
Adedjouma, Davida. *The palm of my heart*
Adler, David A. *Campy*
   Heroes for civil rights
   Joe Louis
   A picture book of Martin Luther King, Jr
   Satchel Paige
Adoff, Arnold. *In for winter, out for spring*
Alexander, Elizabeth. *Praise song for the day*
Aliki. *A weed is a flower*
Allen, Debbie. *Dancing in the wings*
Altman, Linda Jacobs. *The legend of Freedom Hill*
   Singing with Momma Lou
Altman, Susan. *Followers of the north star*
Andrews, Troy. *Trombone Shorty*
Armand, Glenda. *Love twelve miles long*
Ashley Bryan's ABC of African American poetry
Asim, Jabari. *Daddy goes to work*
   Fifty cents and a dream
   Preaching to the chickens
Aston, Dianna Hutts. *The moon over Star*
Baicker, Karen. *You can do it too!*
Balcziak, Bill. *John Henry*
Bandy, Michael S. *Granddaddy's turn*
   White water
Bang, Molly. *Ten, nine, eight*
   Wiley and the hairy man
Barber, Tiki. *By my brother's side*
   Game day
   Teammates
Barbour, Karen. *Mr. Williams*
Barnes, Derrick. *Crown*
Barnwell, Ysaye M. *No mirrors in my Nana's house*
Barrett, Mary Brigid. *Shoebox Sam*
Bass, Hester. *Seeds of freedom*
Battle-Lavert, Gwendolyn. *The music in Derrick's heart*

   Papa's mark
   The shaking bag
Bauer, Marion Dane. *Harriet Tubman*
Beaty, Andrea. *Ada Twist, scientist*
Beaty, Daniel. *Knock knock*
Belton, Sandra. *Pictures for Miss Josie*
Bennett, Kelly. *Not Norman*
Best, Cari. *My three best friends and me, Zulay*
Bible. New Testament. *The Lord's prayer*
Bildner, Phil. *The hallelujah flight*
   Marvelous Cornelius
Birtha, Becky. *Grandmama's pride*
   Lucky beans
Blackstone, Stella. *Bear on a bike*
Blumenthal, Deborah. *Fancy party gowns*
Boelts, Maribeth. *Happy like soccer*
   Those shoes
Bolden, Tonya. *Beautiful moon*
   Rock of ages
Bonnice, Lindsey. *Libby and Pearl: the best of friends*
Boswell, Addie. *The rain stomper*
Bradby, Marie. *Momma, where are you from?*
   More than anything else
   Once upon a farm
Brantley-Newton, Vanessa. *Let freedom sing*
Brooks, Gwendolyn. *Bronzeville boys and girls*
Brown, Tameka Fryer. *My cold plum lemon pie bluesy mood*
Brown-Wood, JaNay. *Grandma's tiny house*
Broyles, Anne. *Priscilla and the hollyhocks*
Bryan, Ashley. *All night, all day*
Bryant, Jen. *A splash of red*
Buchanan, Jane. *Seed magic*
Bunting, Eve. *The blue and the gray*
   The cart that carried Martin
Burleigh, Robert. *Langston's train ride*
   Lookin' for Bird in the big city
   Stealing home
Busch, Miriam. *Lion, lion*
Campbell, Bebe Moore. *I get so hungry*
Carbone, Elisa. *Night running*
Carter, Don. *Heaven's all-star jazz band*
Cash, Megan Montague. *What makes the seasons?*
Celenza, Anna Harwell. *Duke Ellington's Nutcracker Suite*
Chapin, Tom. *The library book*
Child, Lauren. *The new small person*
Chocolate, Deborah. *Kwanzaa*
Clifton, Lucille. *Everett Anderson's goodbye*
   One of the problems of Everett Anderson
   Three wishes
Cline-Ransome, Lesa. *Before she was Harriet*
   Freedom's school
   Just a lucky so and so
   Light in the darkness
   Words set me free
Clinton, Catherine. *Phillis's big test*
   When Harriet met Sojourner
Cole, Henry. *Unspoken*
Cole, Kenneth, Dr. *No bad news*
Coles, Robert. *The story of Ruby Bridges*
Collier, Bryan. *Uptown*
Cooper, Floyd. *Coming home: from the life of Langston Hughes*
   Juneteenth for Mazie
   Max and the tag-along moon
   The ring bearer
   Willie and the All-Stars
Copeland, Misty. *Firebird*

Cornwall, Gaia. *Jabari jumps*
Crews, Donald. *Cloudy day/sunny day*
  Shortcut
Crews, Nina. *A ghost story*
  One hot summer day
  You are here
Crowe, Chris. *Just as good*
Cummings, Pat. *Angel baby*
  Clean your room, Harvey Moon!
  My aunt came back
Curtis, Gavin. *The bat boy and his violin*
Dawes, Kwame Senu Neville. *I saw your face*
Deans, Karen. *Playing to win*
de la Peña, Matt. *A nation's hope*
Dempsey, Kristy. *A dance like starlight*
Derby, Sally. *No mush today*
Diggs, Taye. *Chocolate me!*
Dray, Philip. *Yours for justice, Ida B. Wells*
DuBurke, Randy. *The moon ring*
Duncan, Alice Faye. *Honey baby sugar child*
Dungy, Tony. *You can do it!*
Edwards, Pamela Duncan. *Barefoot: escape on the
  Underground Railroad*
  The bus ride that changed history
Ehrhardt, Karen. *This jazz man*
Elliott, Zetta. *Melena's jubilee*
Elster, Jean Alicia. *Just call me Joe Joe*
English, Karen. *The baby on the way*
  Hot day on Abbott Avenue
Evans, Kristina. *What's special about me, Mama?*
Evans, Shane W. *Underground: finding the light to
  freedom*
  We march
Falwell, Cathryn. *Christmas for 10*
  David's drawing
  Feast for ten
Farris, Christine King. *March on!*
  My brother Martin
Feiffer, Kate. *Which puppy?*
Fishman, Cathy Goldberg. *When Jackie and Hank
  met*
Flournoy, Valerie. *The patchwork quilt*
Ford, Juwanda G. *K is for Kwanzaa*
  Together for Kwanzaa
Forman, Ruth. *Young Cornrows callin out the moon*
Fradin, Dennis. *The price of freedom*
Frame, Jeron Ashford. *Yesterday I had the blues*
Fredrickson, Lane. *Monster trouble!*
Freeman, Don. *Corduroy*
  A pocket for Corduroy
Giovanni, Nikki. *Lincoln and Douglass*
  Rosa
  The sun is so quiet
Godin, Thelma Lynne. *The hula-hoopin' queen*
Golenbock, Peter. *Hank Aaron*
Golio, Gary. *Bird and Diz*
Goodman, Susan E. *The first step*
Gourley, Robbin. *Bring me some apples and I'll make
  you a pie*
Grady, Cynthia. *I lay my stitches down*
Greenawalt, Kelly. *Princess Truly in I am Truly*
Greenfield, Eloise. *Angels*
  Big friend, little friend
  Brothers and sisters
  Daydreamers
  Easter parade
  First pink light
  I make music
  Me and Neesie

My doll, Keshia
Nathaniel talking
Night on Neighborhood Street
Water, water
Greenfield, Monica. *Waiting for Christmas*
Grifalconi, Ann. *Ain't nobody a stranger to me*
  Tiny's hat
  The village that vanished
Grigsby, Susan. *In the garden with Dr. Carver*
Grimes, Nikki. *Barack Obama*
  Danitra Brown, class clown
  Welcome, Precious
  When Daddy prays
  When Gorilla goes walking
Hamilton, Virginia. *Drylongso*
Harrington, Janice N. *The chicken-chasing queen of
  Lamar County*
Harris, Teresa E. *Summer Jackson*
Harrison, Troon. *Courage to fly*
Harvey, Jeanne Walker. *My hands sing the blues*
Haskins, Jim. *Delivering justice*
Havill, Juanita. *Jamaica and Brianna*
  Jamaica and the substitute teacher
  Jamaica is thankful
  Jamaica Tag-Along
  Jamaica's blue marker
  Jamaica's find
Heath, Amy. *Sofie's role*
Heder, Thyra. *Alfie: (the turtle that disappeared)*
Henderson, Alicia Terry. *Call me black, call me
  beautiful*
Herkert, Barbara. *Sewing stories*
Hesse, Karen. *Come on, rain*
Hester, Denia Lewis. *Grandma Lena's big ol' turnip*
Hill, Elizabeth Starr. *Evan's corner*
Hill, Laban Carrick. *Dave the potter*
Himes, Rachel. *Princess and the peas*
Hoffman, Mary. *Amazing Grace*
  Grace at Christmas
  Princess Grace
Hoffmann, E. T. A *The Nutcracker in Harlem*
Hood, Susan. *Look! I can read!*
Hooks, Bell. *Be boy buzz*
  Happy to be nappy
Hopkinson, Deborah. *Keep on!*
  Steamboat school
  Sweet Clara and the freedom quilt
Howard, Elizabeth Fitzgerald. *Aunt Flossie's hats
  (and crab cakes later)*
  Chita's Christmas tree
  Virgie goes to school with us boys
Hru, Dakari. *Joshua's Masai mask*
Hubbard, Crystal. *Catching the moon: the story of a
  young girl's baseball dream*
Hudson, Cheryl Willis. *Bright eyes, brown skin*
  My friend Maya loves to dance
Hudson, Wade. *Pass it on: African-American poetry
  for children*
Hughes, Langston. *Carol of the brown king*
  I, too, am America
  Lullaby (for a Black mother)
  My people
  The Negro speaks of rivers
  That is my dream!
Hurston, Zora Neale. *The six fools*
Hush songs
Hutchins, Pat. *My best friend*
In daddy's arms I am tall
Ingalls, Ann. *The little piano girl*

San Souci, Robert D. *The boy and the ghost*
   Callie Ann and Mistah Bear
   The hired hand
   The secret of the stones
   Sukey and the mermaid
Sauer, Tammi. *Mary had a little glam*
Schaefer, Lola M. *Kwanzaa*
Schertle, Alice. *Down the road*
Schofield-Morrison, Connie. *I got the rhythm*
Schroeder, Alan. *Baby Flo*
   Minty
   Ragtime Tumpie
Scruggs, Afi. *Jump rope magic*
Serfozo, Mary. *What's what?*
Seskin, Steve. *A chance to shine*
Sexton, Colleen A. *Let's meet Martin Luther King, Jr*
Shange, Ntozake. *Coretta Scott*
   Ellington was not a street
   Freedom's a-callin me
   Whitewash
Shapiro, J. H. *Magic trash*
Shelton, Paula Young. *Child of the civil rights movement*
Shore, Diane Z. *This is the dream*
Showers, Paul. *Look at your eyes*
   Your skin and mine
Siegelson, Kim L. *In the time of the drums*
Sierra, Judy. *Wiley and the Hairy Man*
Skead, Robert. *Something to prove*
Slade, Suzanne. *Climbing Lincoln's steps*
   Friends for freedom
   With books and bricks
Slate, Joseph. *I want to be free*
Smalls, Irene. *Don't say ain't*
   My Nana and me
   My Pop Pop and me
Smalls-Hector, Irene. *Because you're lucky*
   Beginning school
   Jenny Reen and the Jack Muh Lantern
   Jonathan and his mommy
   Kevin and his dad
Smith, Charles R. *Brick by brick*
   Loki and Alex
   Twenty-eight days
Smothers, Ethel Footman. *Auntee Edna*
Stauffacher, Sue. *Nothing but trouble*
Steggall, Susan. *Rattle and rap*
Stephens, Helen. *What about me?*
Steptoe, Javaka. *The Jones family express*
Steptoe, John. *Creativity*
   Stevie
Stolz, Mary. *Storm in the night*
Stroud, Bettye. *Dance y'all*
   Down home at Miss Dessa's
   The leaving
   The patchwork path
Swain, Gwenyth. *Riding to Washington*
Tarpley, Natasha Anastasia. *Bippity Bop barbershop*
   I love my hair!
   Joe-Joe's first flight
Tate, Don. *It jes' happened*
Taulbert, Clifton L. *Little Cliff and the porch people*
   Little Cliff's first day of school
Tauss, Marc. *Superhero*
Tavares, Matt. *Henry Aaron's dream*
Taylor, Ann. *Baby dance*
Teague, Mark. *Baby tamer*
Temple, Charles A. *Train*
This little light of mine

Thomas, Jane Resh. *Celebration!*
Thomas, Joyce Carol. *The blacker the berry*
   Brown honey in broomwheat tea
   Cherish me
   Crowning glory
   Gingerbread days
   The gospel Cinderella
   In the land of milk and honey
   Joy
   You are my perfect baby
Thomas, Naturi. *Uh-oh! It's Mama's birthday!*
Tinkham, Kelly A. *Hair for Mama*
Tokunbo, Dimitrea. *The sound of Kwanzaa*
Trice, Linda. *Kenya's art*
   Kenya's word
Trollinger, Patsi B. *Perfect timing*
Troupe, Quincy. *Little Stevie Wonder*
Tryon, Leslie. *The thumbtack dancer*
Turner, Ann Warren. *Nettie's trip south*
Turner, Glennette Tilley. *An apple for Harriet Tubman*
Turner-Denstaedt, Melanie. *The hat that wore Clara B.*
Udry, Janice May. *What Mary Jo shared*
Uhlberg, Myron. *Dad, Jackie, and me*
   A storm called Katrina
Vernick, Audrey. *She loved baseball*
Walker, Alice. *Finding the green stone*
   To hell with dying
Walker, Sally M. *Freedom song*
Wallis, Quvenzhané. *A night out with Mama*
Walter, Mildred Pitts. *My mama needs me*
   Two too much
Wangerin, Walter. *Probity Jones and the Fear Not Angel*
Warwick, Dionne. *Little Man*
Washington, Donna L. *The story of Kwanzaa*
Watkins, Angela Farris. *Love will see you through*
   My Uncle Martin's big heart
   My Uncle Martin's words for America
Watson, Renée. *Harlem's little blackbird*
Weatherford, Carole Boston. *Be a King: Dr. Martin Luther King Jr.'s dream and you*
   The Beatitudes
   Before John was a jazz giant
   Champions on the bench
   Freedom in Congo Square
   Freedom on the menu
   Gordon Parks
   I, Matthew Henson
   In your hands
   Juneteenth jamboree
   Leontyne Price
   Moses: when Harriet Tubman led her people to freedom
   Sugar Hill
   Voice of freedom
Wiles, Debbie. *Freedom summer*
Williams, Karen Lynn. *A beach tail*
Williams, Sherley Anne. *Girls together*
   Working cotton
Williams, Vera B. *Cherries and cherry pits*
Williams-Garcia, Rita. *Catching the wild waiyuuzee*
Wilson-Max, Ken. *Max's starry night*
Winne, Joanne. *Let's get ready for Kwanzaa*
Winter, Jeanette. *Follow the drinking gourd*
Winter, Jonah. *Barack*
   Dizzy
   How Jelly Roll Morton invented jazz

Ethnic groups in the U.S. – Amish

Ethnic groups in the U.S. – Arab Americans

Ethnic groups in the U.S. – Asian Americans

Ethnic groups in the U.S. – Black Americans *see* Ethnic groups in the U.S. – African Americans

Ethnic groups in the U.S. – Cajuns

Ethnic groups in the U.S. – Cambodian Americans

Ethnic groups in the U.S. – Chinese Americans

Ethnic groups in the U.S. – Cuban Americans

Ada, Alma Flor. *With love, Little Red Hen*
Chapra, Mimi. *Amelia's show-and-tell fiesta / Amelia y la fiesta de "muestra y cuenta"*
Sacre, Antonio. *La Noche Buena*

Ethnic groups in the U.S. – Dominican Americans

Farish, Terry. *Luis paints the world*

Ethnic groups in the U.S. – East Indian Americans

Iyengar, Malathi Michelle. *Romina's rangoli*
Krishnaswami, Uma. *Bringing Asha home*
    Chachaji's cup
    The happiest tree
Makhijani, Pooja. *Mama's saris*
Rao, Sandhya. *My mother's sari*
Sebra, Richard. *It's Diwali!*
Sheth, Kashmira. *My Dadima wears a sari*
Zia, F. *Hot, hot roti for Dada-ji*

Ethnic groups in the U.S. – Filipino Americans

Giles, Almira Astudillo. *Willie wins*

Ethnic groups in the U.S. – French Americans

McCully, Emily Arnold. *Mirette and Bellini cross Niagara Falls*

Ethnic groups in the U.S. – German Americans

Bodkin, Odds. *The Christmas cobwebs*
Jaspersohn, William. *The two brothers*

Ethnic groups in the U.S. – Greek Americans

D'Arc, Karen Scourby. *My grandmother is a singing Yaya*

Ethnic groups in the U.S. – Guatemalan Americans

Flanagan, Alice K. *Mr. Santizo's tasty treats!*
O'Brien, Anne Sibley. *I'm new here*

Ethnic groups in the U.S. – Haitian Americans

Steptoe, Javaka. *Radiant child*

Ethnic groups in the U.S. – Hispanic Americans

Aliki. *Tabby*
Ancona, George. *Barrio*
    Mi música / My music
    Mis abuelos / My grandparents
    Mis comidas / My foods
    Mis fiestas / My celebrations
    Mis juegos / My games
    Mis quehaceres / My chores
Arena, Jen. *Marta! big and small*
Caraballo, Samuel. *My big sister / Mi hermana mayor*
Carlson, Lori Marie. *Hurray for Three Kings' Day*
Chapra, Mimi. *Sparky's bark / El ladrido de Sparky*
Chocolate, Deborah. *El barrio*
Colato Laínez, René. *Mamá the alien / Mamá la extraterrestre*
Cumpiano, Ina. *Quinito, day and night / Quinito, día y noche*
    Quinito's neighborhood / El vecindario de Quinito
De Anda, Diane. *Dancing Miranda / Baila, Miranda, baila*
    A day without sugar / Un día sin azúcar
dePaola, Tomie. *A new Barker in the house*
Dorros, Arthur. *Mama and me*
    Papa and me
Elya, Susan Middleton. *Adiós, tricycle*
    Tooth on the loose
English, Karen. *Speak English for us, Marisol*
Griessman, Annette. *The fire*
Harrington, Janice N. *Roberto walks home*
Hayes, Joe. *Don't say a word, Mamá/No digas nada, Mamá*
Hudes, Quiara Alegría. *Welcome to my neighborhood!*
Kroll, Virginia L. *Uno, dos, tres, posada!*
Kyle, Tracey. *Gazpacho for Nacho*
Lachtman, Ofelia Dumas. *Pepita takes time / Pepita, siempre tarde*
Lomas Garza, Carmen. *In my family*
McCormack, Caren McNelly. *The fiesta dress*
Manning, Maurie J. *Kitchen dance*
Medina, Meg. *Tía Isa wants a car*
Miller, Elizabeth I. *Just like home / Como en mi tierra*
Mora, Pat. *Abuelos*
    Gracias / Thanks
Morris, Ann. *Grandma Francisca remembers*
Pinkney, Sandra L. *I am Latino*
San Souci, Robert D. *Little gold star*
Shea, Pegi Deitz. *New moon*
Starr, Meg. *Alicia's happy day*
Thong, Roseanne. *Green is a chile pepper*
    Round is a tortilla
Velasquez, Eric. *Looking for Bongo*
Winter, Jonah. *Sonia Sotomayor*
Witte, Anna. *Lola's fandango*
Yin. *Dear Santa, please come to the 19th floor*
Zepeda, Gwendolyn. *Growing up with tamales / Los tamales de Ana*

Ethnic groups in the U.S. – Hmong Americans

Gerdner, Linda. *Grandfather's story cloth / Yawg daim paj ntaub dab neeg*
Shea, Pegi Deitz. *The whispering cloth*

Ethnic groups in the U.S. – Hungarian Americans

Couric, Katie. *The brand new kid*

Ethnic groups in the U.S. – Irish Americans

Connor, Leslie. *Miss Bridie chose a shovel*
Dillon, Jana. *Lucky O'Leprechaun comes to America*
Hazen, Barbara Shook. *Katie's wish*

Kroll, Steven. *Mary McLean and the St. Patrick's Day parade*
Nolan, Janet. *The St. Patrick's Day shillelagh*
Polacco, Patricia. *Fiona's lace*
Weller, Frances Ward. *The angel of Mill Street*

Ethnic groups in the U.S. – Italian Americans

Akin, Sara Laux. *Three scoops and a fig*
Alda, Arlene. *Morning glory Monday*
Bartone, Elisa. *Peppe the lamplighter*
Bastianich, Lidia. *Nonna tell me a story*
   Nonna's birthday surprise
Bunting, Eve. *A picnic in October*
Fleischman, Paul. *The matchbox diary*
Yaccarino, Dan. *All the way to America*

Ethnic groups in the U.S. – Jamaican Americans

Winter, Jeanette. *Angelina's island*

Ethnic groups in the U.S. – Japanese Americans

Barasch, Lynne. *Hiromi's hands*
Bunting, Eve. *So far from the sea*
DaCosta, Barbara. *Nighttime Ninja*
Kroll, Virginia L. *Pink paper swans*
Lang, Heather. *Swimming with sharks*
Lee-Tai, Amy. *A place where sunflowers grow / Sabaku ni saita himawari*
Meshon, Aaron. *Take me out to the Yakyu*
Mochizuki, Ken. *Baseball saved us*
Noguchi, Rick. *Flowers from Mariko*
Sanger, Amy Wilson. *First book of sushi*
Say, Allen. *Emma's rug*
   The favorite daughter
   Grandfather's journey
   Tea with milk
Terasaki, Stanley Todd. *Ghosts for breakfast*
Uchida, Yoshiko. *The bracelet*
Uegaki, Chieri. *Hana Hashimoto, sixth violin*
   Suki's kimono
Wells, Rosemary. *Yoko*
   Yoko finds her way
   Yoko learns to read
   Yoko writes her name
   Yoko's paper cranes
   Yoko's show-and-tell
Yamasaki, Katie. *Fish for Jimmy*
Yashima, Taro. *Umbrella*

Ethnic groups in the U.S. – Jewish Americans *see* Jewish culture

Ethnic groups in the U.S. – Korean Americans

Avraham, Kate Aver. *What will you be, Sara Mee?*
Bercaw, Edna Coe. *Halmoni's day*
Bunting, Eve. *Jin Woo*
Choi, Sook Nyul. *Halmoni and the picnic*
Choi, Yangsook. *Behind the mask*
   The name jar
Choung, Euh-hee. *Minji's Salon*
Czech, Jan M. *An American face*

Flanagan, Alice K. *A busy day at Mr. Kang's grocery store*
Heo, Yumi. *Father's rubber shoes*
   Ten days and nine nights
Kim, Aram. *No kimchi for me!*
McDonnell, Christine. *Goyangi means cat*
O'Brien, Anne Sibley. *I'm new here*
Pak, Soyung. *Dear Juno*
   A place to grow
   Sumi's first day of school ever
Park, Frances. *Good-bye, 382 Shin Dang Dong*
   The Have a Good Day Cafe
Patz, Nancy. *Babies can't eat kimchee!*
Recorvits, Helen. *My name is Yoon*
   Yoon and the Christmas mitten
   Yoon and the jade bracelet
Watts, Jeri. *A piece of home*
Williams, Laura E. *The best winds*
Wong, Janet S. *The trip back home*

Ethnic groups in the U.S. – Lebanese Americans

Khan, Hena. *The night of the moon*

Ethnic groups in the U.S. – Mexican Americans

Ada, Alma Flor. *I love Saturdays y domingos*
Adler, David A. *A picture book of Cesar Chavez*
Anaya, Rudolfo A. *Farolitos for Abuelo*
Bertrand, Diane Gonzales. *Family / familia*
   The last doll / La última muñeca
   The party for Papa Luis / La fiesta para Papa Luis
   Sofía and the purple dress / Sofía y el vestido morado
   Uncle Chente's picnic / El picnic de Tío Chente
Brown, Monica. *Chavela and the magic bubble*
   Side by side / Lado a lado
Bunting, Eve. *A day's work*
   Going home
Colato Laínez, René. *The Tooth Fairy meets El Ratón Pérez*
Compos, Tito. *Muffler man / El hombre mofle*
Cox, Judy. *Carmen learns English*
Cruise, Robin. *Little Mama forgets*
da Costa, Deborah. *Hanukkah moon*
Dorros, Arthur. *Radio Man / Don Radio*
   When the pigs took over
Edwards, Michelle. *A hat for Mrs. Goldman*
Ets, Marie Hall. *Gilberto and the wind*
   Nine days to Christmas
Fisher, Mary M. *Rosita's bridge*
Flanagan, Alice K. *Cinco de Mayo*
Freschet, Gina. *Beto and the bone dance*
Galindo, Mary Sue. *Icy watermelon / Sandía fría*
Head, Judith. *Mud soup*
Herrera, Juan Felipe. *Grandma and Me at the flea / Los meros meros remateros*
Iyengar, Malathi Michelle. *Romina's rangoli*
Jiménez, Francisco. *The Christmas gift / El regalo de Navidad*
Johnston, Tony. *My abuelita*
Luenn, Nancy. *A gift for Abuelita*
Mora, Pat. *The bakery lady / La señora de la panadería*
   A birthday basket for Tía
   Confetti
   I pledge allegiance
   Pablo's tree

The rainbow tulip
Tomás and the library lady
Morales, Yuyi. *Niño wrestles the world*
Rudas
O'Neill, Alexis. *Estela's swap*
Pérez, Amada Irma. *My diary from here to there / Mi diario de aquí hasta allá*
My very own room / Mi propio cuartito
Pérez, L. King. *First day in grapes*
Politi, Leo. *Juanita*
Pedro, the angel of Olvera Street
Song of the swallows
Price, Mara. *Grandma's chocolate / El chocolate de Abuelita*
Roe, Eileen. *With my brother / Con mi hermano*
Ruiz-Flores, Lupe. *Alicia's fruity drinks / Las aguas frescas de Alicia*
Sáenz, Benjamin Alire. *A gift from papá Diego / Un regalo de papá Diego*
Grandma Fina and her wonderful umbrellas / La abuelita Fina y sus sombrillas maravillosas
Schaefer, Lola M. *Cinco de Mayo*
Schreck, Karen Halvorsen. *Lucy's family tree*
Soto, Gary. *Chato goes cruisin'*
Lucky Luis
My little car / Mi carrito
The old man and his door
Snapshots from the wedding
Too many tamales
Stewart, Sarah. *The quiet place*
Tafolla, Carmen. *Fiesta babies*
What can you do with a paleta?
What can you do with a rebozo?
Thomas, Jane Resh. *Lights on the river*
Tonatiuh, Duncan. *Dear Primo*
Separate is never equal
Warren, Sarah. *Dolores Huerta*

Ethnic groups in the U.S. – Pakistani Americans

English, Karen. *Nadia's hands*
Khan, Rukhsana. *Big red lollipop*

Ethnic groups in the U.S. – Puerto Rican Americans

Cowley, Joy. *Gracias, the Thanksgiving turkey*
Gonzalez, Lucia. *The storyteller's candle / La velita de los cuentos*
Keats, Ezra Jack. *My dog is lost!*
Manzano, Sonia. *A box full of kittens*
Miracle on 133rd Street
No dogs allowed
Steptoe, Javaka. *Radiant child*
Steptoe, John. *Creativity*
Velasquez, Eric. *Grandma's gift*
Grandma's records

Ethnic groups in the U.S. – Russian Americans

Best, Cari. *When Catherine the Great and I were eight!*
Broyles, Anne. *Shy Mama's Halloween*
Polacco, Patricia. *The trees of the dancing goats*
Pryor, Bonnie. *The dream jar*
Tarbescu, Edith. *Annushka's voyage*
Woodruff, Elvira. *The memory coat*
Yolen, Jane. *Naming Liberty*

Ethnic groups in the U.S. – Shakers

Ray, Mary Lyn. *Shaker boy*

Ethnic groups in the U.S. – Somali Americans

O'Brien, Anne Sibley. *I'm new here*

Ethnic groups in the U.S. – Sudanese Americans

Williams, Karen Lynn. *My name is Sangoel*

Ethnic groups in the U.S. – Swedish Americans

Peterson, Melissa. *Hanna's Christmas*

Ethnic groups in the U.S. – Tibetan Americans

Rose, Naomi C. *Tashi and the Tibetan flower cure*

Ethnic groups in the U.S. – Vietnamese Americans

Garland, Sherry. *The lotus seed*
My father's boat
Jules, Jacqueline. *Duck for Turkey Day*
Phi, Bao. *A different pond*
Surat, Michele Maria. *Angel child, dragon child*

Etiquette

Ainslie, Tamsin. *I can say please*
I can say thank you
Aliki. *Manners*
Anderson, Peggy Perry. *Out to lunch*
Antony, Steve. *Please, Mr. Panda*
Barnett, Mac. *The magic word*
Berenstain, Stan and Jan. *The Berenstain bears forget their manners*
Best, Cari. *Are you going to be good?*
Bishop, Poppy. *Bear's house of books*
Bloom, Suzanne. *Piggy Monday*
Breznak, Irene. *Sneezy Louise*
Bridges, Shirin Yim. *Mary Wrightly, so politely*
Brown, Marc. *Perfect pigs*
Cole, Babette. *Lady Lupin's book of etiquette*
Cullen, Lynn. *Dear Mr. Washington*
Dahl, Michael. *Bear says "thank you"*
Hippo says "excuse me."
Daly, Niki. *Thank you, Jackson*
Delaunois, Angèle. *Magic little words*
Demas, Corinne. *Are pirates polite?*
Dewdney, Anna. *Nobunny's perfect*
Dutton, Sandra. *Dear Miss Perfect*
Dyckman, Ame. *Tea party rules*
Edwards, Pamela Duncan. *Rude mule*
Ferguson, Sarah. *Tea for Ruby*
Fredrickson, Lane. *Watch your tongue, Cecily Beasley*
Gibbs, Lynne. *Don't slurp your soup!*
Goldberg, Whoopi. *Whoopi's big book of manners*
Gorbachev, Valeri. *How to be friends with a dragon*
Greenberg, David. *Don't forget your etiquette!*
Hamilton, Martha. *The hidden feast*
Harper, Charise Mericle. *The best birthday ever!*
Helmer, Diana Star. *The cat who came for tacos*
Henry, Jed. *I speak dinosaur*

Holt, Kimberly Willis. *Dinner with the Highbrows*
Holub, Joan. *Turkeys never gobble*
Hood, Susan. *Just say boo!*
Huget, Jennifer LaRue. *Thanks a lot, Emily Post!*
Idle, Molly. *Tea Rex*
Jones, Christianne C. *Lacey Walker, nonstop talker*
Joosse, Barbara. *Please is a good word to say*
Katz, Alan. *Don't say that word!*
Keller, Laurie. *Do unto otters*
Kelly, Mij. *Achoo!*
Kopelke, Lisa. *Excuse me!*
Lane, Nathan. *Naughty Mabel*
LaReau, Kara. *No slurping, no burping!*
Leroy, Jean. *A well-mannered young wolf*
Levitin, Sonia. *When Elephant goes to a party*
   When Kangaroo goes to school
Lloyd-Jones, Sally. *Being a pig is nice*
McElligott, Matthew. *The lion's share*
Manners mash-up
Marciano, John Bemelmans. *Madeline says merci*
Melling, David. *The Scallywags*
Metzger, Steve. *Will Princess Isabel ever say please?*
Miller, Virginia. *On your potty!*
Modan, Rutu. *Maya makes a mess*
Monster, be good!
Montanari, Donata. *Children around the world*
Morris, Jennifer E. *May I please have a cookie?*
Parr, Todd. *Do's and don'ts*
Paxton, Tom. *Engelbert the elephant*
Pearson, Peter. *How to eat an airplane*
Post, Peggy. *Emily's everyday manners*
Potter, Beatrix. *The sly old cat*
Primavera, Elise. *Louise the big cheese and the Ooh-la-la Charm School*
Riehle, Mary Ann McCabe. *The little kids' table*
Robberecht, Thierry. *I can't do anything!*
Rosenthal, Amy Krouse. *Cookies*
Scarry, Richard. *Richard Scarry's please and thank you book*
Senning, Cindy Post. *Emily's out and about book*
Shaw, Hannah. *School for bandits*
Sierra, Judy. *Mind your manners, B. B. Wolf*
   Suppose you meet a dinosaur
Stein, David Ezra. *The nice book*
Stephens, Helen. *Ahoyty-toyty*
Sweetland, Nancy Rose. *Yelly Kelly*
Szekeres, Cyndy. *Toby's please and thank you*
Tekavec, Heather. *Manners are not for monkeys*
Thomas, Shelley Moore. *A cold winter's Good Knight*
Tillman, Nancy. *Tumford's rude noises*
Tryon, Leslie. *Patsy says*
Vestergaard, Hope. *Potty animals*
Watkins, Rowboat. *Rude cakes*
Watt, Mélanie. *You're finally here!*
Wells, Rosemary. *Say hello, Sophie!*
Weninger, Brigitte. *Davy loves his mommy*
Wheeler, Valerie. *Yes, please! no, thank you!*
Willems, Mo. *The duckling gets a cookie!?*
   Time to say "please"!
Wilson, Karma. *Bear says thanks*
Yee, Wong Herbert. *Big black bear*
Yolen, Jane. *How do dinosaurs eat their food?*
Ziefert, Harriet. *Mother Goose manners*
   Someday we'll have very good manners

Evening *see* Twilight

Evolution

Heos, Bridget. *Shell, beak, tusk*
Sullivan, Tom. *I used to be a fish*
Tweet, Jonathan. *Grandmother Fish*

Exercise *see* Health & fitness – exercise

Experiments *see* Science

Extraterrestrial beings *see* Aliens

Eye glasses *see* Glasses

Eyes *see* Anatomy – eyes; Glasses; Disabilities – blindness; Senses – sight

Fables *see* Folk & fairy tales

Fairies

Bar-el, Dan. *Such a prince*
Bate, Lucy. *Little Rabbit's loose tooth*
Batt, Tanya Robyn. *The faerie's gift*
Booth, Anne. *The fairiest fairy*
Bottner, Barbara. *Pish and Posh*
Bouchard, Dave. *Fairy*
Bowen, Anne. *Tooth Fairy's first night*
Brockenbrough, Martha. *The Dinosaur Tooth Fairy*
Brown, Marc. *Arthur tricks the tooth fairy*
Cash, Rosanne. *Penelope Jane*
Clibbon, Meg. *Imagine you're a fairy!*
Climo, Shirley. *The Persian Cinderella*
Colato Laínez, René. *The Tooth Fairy meets El Ratón Pérez*
Coombs, Kate. *The tooth fairy wars*
Cronin, Doreen. *Bloom*
Davis, Katie. *Mabel the Tooth Fairy and how she got her job*
Demers, Dominique. *Old Thomas and the little fairy*
Durant, Alan. *Dear tooth fairy*
Edwards, Pamela Duncan. *Dear Tooth Fairy*
Evans, Dilys. *Fairies, trolls and goblins galore*
Fliess, Sue. *A fairy friend*
Garland, Michael. *King Puck*
Gay, Marie-Louise. *Stella, fairy of the forest*
Graham, Bob. *April and Esme, tooth fairies*
   Jethro Byrd, fairy child
Grambling, Lois G. *This whole Tooth Fairy thing's nothing but a big rip-off!*
Grimm, Jacob and Wilhelm. *Sleeping Beauty*, ill. by Maja Dusíková
   Sleeping beauty, ill. by Sarah Gibb

The sleeping beauty
The three spinning fairies
Hague, Kathleen. *Good night, fairies*
Hundal, Nancy. *Twilight fairies*
Inkpen, Deborah. *Harriet and the little fat fairy*
James, Brian. *The Supertwins and tooth trouble*
Jay, Betsy. *Jane vs. the Tooth Fairy*
Johnson, Paul Brett. *Little Bunny Foo Foo*
Kann, Victoria. *Silverlicious*
Kaye, Marilyn. *The real tooth fairy*
Krensky, Stephen. *The youngest fairy godmother ever*
Lowell, Susan. *Cindy Ellen*
McClintock, Barbara. *Molly and the magic wishbone*
MacDonald, Margaret Read. *Slop!*
Too many fairies
Maconie, Robin. *Alice and her fabulous teeth*
Milord, Susan. *Willa the wonderful*
Munsch, Robert N. *Andrew's loose tooth*
Numeroff, Laura Joffe. *Ponyella*
Oddino, Licia. *Finn and the fairies*
Olson, Mary. *Nice try, Tooth Fairy*
Palatini, Margie. *Gone with the wand*
Paquette, Ammi-Joan. *The tiptoe guide to tracking fairies*
Paxton, Tom. *The story of the Tooth Fairy*
Perrault, Charles. *Sleeping Beauty*
Pomeranc, Marion Hess. *The American Wei*
Prelutsky, Jack. *Monday's troll*
Ray, Jane. *The dollhouse fairy*
Reinhart, Matthew. *Fairies and magical creatures*
Rose, Marion. *The Christmas tree fairy*
Sabuda, Robert. *Peter Pan*
Sierra, Judy. *The gift of the crocodile*
Simmons, Jane. *The dreamtime fairies*
Smith, Lane. *Pinocchio, the boy*
Taylor, Jane. *Twinkle, twinkle, little star*, ill. by Heather Collins
Twinkle, twinkle, little star, ill. by Michael Hague
Underwood, Deborah. *Here comes the Tooth Fairy Cat*
Wallace, Ivy. *Pookie*
Ward, Helen. *Little Moon Dog*
Wells, Rosemary. *Fritz and the mess fairy*
Weninger, Brigitte. *The elf's hat*
Yolen, Jane. *Come to the fairies' ball*
Young, Amy. *The mud fairy*

Fairs, festivals

Berger, Samantha. *Snoozefest at the Nuzzledome*
Blumenthal, Deborah. *Ice palace*
Bond, Michael. *Paddington Bear and the Busy Bee Carnival*
Browne, Anthony. *Animal fair*
Bunting, Eve. *The pumpkin fair*
Calhoun, Mary. *Blue-ribbon Henry*
Castaneda, Omar S. *Abuela's weave*
Cave, Kathryn. *The boy who became an eagle*
Chaconas, Dori. *Hurry down to Derry Fair*
Chan, Arlene. *Awakening the dragon*
Colato Laínez, René. *Playing lotería / El juego de la lotería*
Cousins, Lucy. *Maisy at the fair*
Crews, Donald. *Night at the fair*
D'Amico, Carmela. *Ella sets sail*
Darrow, Sharon. *Old Thunder and Miss Raney*
Davis, Kathryn Gibbs. *Mr. Ferris and his wheel*
Dorros, Arthur. *Tonight is carnaval*
Dubuc, Marianne. *Animal masquerade*

Ets, Marie Hall. *Mr. Penny's race horse*
Flanagan, Alice K. *Chinese New Year*
Fraser, Mary Ann. *Heebie-Jeebie Jamboree*
Frasier, Debra. *A fabulous fair alphabet*
Geisert, Arthur. *Pigaroons*
Gibbons, Gail. *County fair*
Goembel, Ponder. *Animal fair*
Gorbachev, Valeri. *Molly who flew away*
Greenwood, Mark. *Drummer boy of John John*
Guy, Ginger Foglesong. *Fiesta*
Hamilton, Arlene. *Only a cow*
Helakoski, Leslie. *Fair cow*
Hill, Eric. *Spot at the fair*
Himmelman, John. *Cows to the rescue*
Hoffman, Elizabeth Stokes. *Miss Renée's mice go to an exhibition*
Hohn, Nadia L. *Malaika's costume*
Holabird, Katharine. *Angelina at the fair*
Horn, Sandra Ann. *The dandelion wish*
Jackson, Ellen. *The autumn equinox*
Janni, Rebecca. *Every cowgirl loves a rodeo*
Kassirer, Sue. *Math fair blues*
Khan, Rukhsana. *King for a day*
Kinney, Jessica. *The pig scramble*
Kraft, Betsy Harvey. *The fantastic Ferris wheel*
Krishnaswami, Uma. *Holi*
Lasky, Kathryn. *Science fair bunnies*
Lewin, Ted. *Fair!*
Light, Steve. *Have you seen my monster?*
Lin, Grace. *Thanking the moon*
Lord, Cynthia. *Hot Rod Hamster: monster truck mania!*
McLean, Dirk. *Play mas'! a carnival ABC*
Murphy, Stuart J. *The penny pot*
Norman, Kim. *I know a wee piggy*
O'Malley, Kevin. *Roller coaster*
Paraskevas, Betty. *Marvin, the tap-dancing horse*
Polacco, Patricia. *Oh, look!*
Reynolds, Jan. *Celebrate!*
Rosen, Michael. *Bear flies high*
Seto, Loretta. *Mooncakes*
Shireen, Nadia. *Hey, Presto!*
Speed, Toby. *Brave potatoes*
Stevenson, James. *All aboard!*
Stihler, Chérie B. *The giant cabbage turnip*
Stoeke, Janet Morgan. *Minerva Louise at the fair*
Tafolla, Carmen. *Fiesta babies*
Train, Mary. *Time for the fair*
Van Nutt, Julia. *Pumpkins from the sky?*
Watson, Clyde. *Applebet*
Weaver, Tess. *Frederick Finch, loudmouth*
Winter, Jeanette. *Niño's mask*
Yaccarino, Dan. *Billy and Goat at the state fair*
Yacowitz, Caryn. *Pumpkin fiesta*
Ziefert, Harriet. *Pumpkin Pie*

Fairy tales *see* Folk & fairy tales

Family life

Adams, Eric J. *On the day his daddy left*
Adler, David A. *Hiding from the Nazis*
It's time to sleep, it's time to dream
Adoff, Arnold. *Black is brown is tan*
In for winter, out for spring
Ahlberg, Janet. *The baby's catalogue*
Peek-a-boo!
Ajmera, Maya. *To be a kid*

Collicott, Sharleen. *Mildred and Sam*
Cooke, Trish. *So much*
Cooney, Barbara. *Eleanor*
Cooper, Floyd. *Coming home: from the life of Langston Hughes*
Cordell, Matthew. *Wish*
Corderoy, Tracey. *It's Christmas! Now!*
Corey, Dorothy. *You go away*
Corpi, Lucha. *Where fireflies dance / Ahí, donde bailan las luciérnagas*
Coste, Marion. *Finding Joy*
Cox, Judy. *My family plays music*
Crews, Donald. *Sail away*
Crews, Nina. *A ghost story*
    You are here
Cruise, Robin. *Only you*
Crum, Shutta. *Dozens of cousins*
Cumpiano, Ina. *Quinito, day and night / Quinito, dia y noche*
Cunnane, Kelly. *Chirchir is singing*
Curato, Mike. *Little Elliot, big family*
Curtis, Jamie Lee. *Tell me again about the night I was born*
    Today I feel silly and other moods that make my day
da Costa, Deborah. *Hanukkah moon*
D'Antonio, Nancy. *Our baby from China*
Darbyshire, Kristen. *Put it on the list!*
DeFelice, Cynthia C. *The real, true Dulcie Campbell*
de la Peña, Matt. *Miguel and the grand harmony*
Denim, Sue. *The Dumb Bunnies*
    The Dumb Bunnies' Easter
    The Dumb Bunnies go to the zoo
    Make way for Dumb Bunnies
dePaola, Tomie. *The art lesson*
    The family Christmas tree book
Devine, Monica. *Carry me, Mama*
Dewey, Jennifer Owings. *Once I knew a spider*
Dieterlé, Nathalie. *I am the king!*
DiPucchio, Kelly. *Littles*
Dixon, Ann. *Waiting for Noël*
Dodd, Emma. *I am small*
    What pet to get?
Dooley, Norah. *Everybody cooks rice*
Dotlich, Rebecca Kai. *A family like yours*
Doughty, Rebecca. *Oh no! Time to go!*
Douglas, Ann. *Before you were born*
Downing, Julie. *No hugs till Saturday*
Downs, Mike. *You see a circus, I see —*
Doyle, Malachy. *Too noisy!*
Dungy, Tony. *You can do it!*
Ehlert, Lois. *Hands*
Elliott, David. *Knitty Kitty*
    Nobody's perfect
Elvgren, Jennifer Riesmeyer. *Josias, hold the book*
Elya, Susan Middleton. *N is for Navidad*
Emerman, Ellen. *Just right: the story of a Jewish home*
Engle, Margarita. *All the way to Havana*
English, Karen. *Nadia's hands*
Eschbacher, Roger. *Road trip*
Falwell, Cathryn. *Feast for ten*
    We have a baby
Fearing, Mark. *The great Thanksgiving escape*
Fearnley, Jan. *A special something*
Federle, Tim. *Tommy can't stop!*
Feiffer, Jules. *I lost my bear*
Feiffer, Kate. *No go sleep!*
    Which puppy?
Fishman, Cathy Goldberg. *On Purim*

On Shabbat
Flanagan, Alice K. *A visit to the Gravesens' farm*
Fleming, Candace. *Papa's mechanical fish*
Foggo, Cheryl. *Dear baobab*
Foreman, George. *Let George do it!*
Fox, Mem. *Time for bed*
Fraggalosch, Audrey. *Great grizzly wilderness*
Frame, Jeron Ashford. *Yesterday I had the blues*
Francis, Panama. *David gets his drum*
Friedman, Ina R. *How my parents learned to eat*
Friedrich, Molly. *You're not my real mother!*
Gal, Susan. *Day by day*
Galvin, Laura Gates. *River Otter at Autumn Lane*
Gavin, Ciara. *Bear is not tired*
Gerrard, K.A. *My family is a zoo*
Gilani-Williams, Fawzia. *Nabeel's new pants*
Gleeson, Libby. *Cuddle time*
Gliori, Debi. *Mr. Bear's new baby*
    No matter what
Goodman, Susan E. *Chopsticks for my noodle soup*
Goudey, Alice E. *The day we saw the sun come up*
Gourley, Robbin. *Bring me some apples and I'll make you a pie*
Graff, Lisa. *It is not time for sleeping*
Graham, Bob. *"Let's get a pup!" said Kate*
    Oscar's half birthday
Gray, Nigel. *Time to play!*
Greenfield, Eloise. *I make music*
    Me and Neesie
Greenfield, Monica. *Waiting for Christmas*
Gregory, Nan. *Pink*
Grey, Mini. *Traction Man is here*
Griessman, Annette. *The fire*
Grindley, Sally. *A new room for William*
Guest, Elissa Haden. *Harriet's had enough!*
Guiberson, Brenda Z. *The emperor lays an egg*
Gutch, Michael. *Sticky, sticky, stuck!*
Guy, Ginger Foglesong. *My grandma / Mi abuelita*
Hall, Donald. *Lucy's Christmas*
Hammersmith, Craig. *What is a family?*
Hänel, Wolfram. *Little elephant's song*
Hannigan, Katherine. *Gwendolyn Grace*
Harris, Robie H. *Don't forget to come back*
    Go! go! Maria!
    Who's in my family?
Harris, Teresa E. *Summer Jackson*
Hartman, Bob. *Granny Mae's Christmas play*
Havill, Juanita. *Just like a baby*
Hazen, Barbara Shook. *Who is your favorite monster, Mama?*
Hearne, Betsy Gould. *Seven brave women*
Heath, Amy. *Sofie's role*
Heide, Florence Parry. *Sami and the time of the troubles*
Helakoski, Leslie. *Doggone feet!*
Helmer, Marilyn. *One splendid tree*
Henkes, Kevin. *Bailey goes camping*
    Julius, the baby of the world
    Shhhh
Heo, Yumi. *Ten days and nine nights*
Herman, Charlotte. *The memory cupboard*
Hesse, Karen. *Spuds*
Hest, Amy. *The purple coat*
Hill, Elizabeth Starr. *Evan's corner*
Hill, Eric. *Spot goes to the beach*
Hindley, Judy. *What's in baby's morning*
Hines, Anna Grossnickle. *Big like me*
    Daddy makes the best spaghetti
    Even if I spill my milk?

London, Jonathan. *Hurricane!*
Long, Melinda. *Hiccup snickup*
Longstreth, Galen Goodwin. *Yes, let's*
Loomis, Christine. *Across America, I love you*
López, Susana. *The best family in the world*
Luxbacher, Irene. *Mr. Frank*
Lyon, George Ella. *Cecil's story*
　Come a tide
　No dessert forever!
　One lucky girl
McAllister, Angela. *Yuck! That's not a monster*
McAnulty, Stacy. *Excellent Ed*
Macaulay, David. *Black and white*
McCarty, Peter. *Chloe*
McCloskey, Robert. *Blueberries for Sal*
　One morning in Maine
McClure, Nikki. *Waiting for high tide*
McCully, Emily Arnold. *Monk camps out*
　My real family
McCutcheon, John. *Happy adoption day!*
MacDonald, Amy. *Cousin Ruth's tooth*
McDonald, Megan. *Insects are my life*
McGowan, Michael. *Sunday is for God*
Mackintosh, David. *Lucky*
McKissack, Patricia C. *Messy Bessey's family reunion*
　Nettie Jo's friends
　Stitchin' and pullin'
MacLachlan, Patricia. *All the places to love*
　Who loves me?
　You were the first
McLaughlin, Lauren. *Wonderful you*
McLellan, Stephanie Simpson. *Tweezle into everything*
McPhail, David. *Emma's pet*
　Emma's vacation
McQuade, Jacqueline. *Good times with Teddy Bear*
Mahy, Margaret. *The rattlebang picnic*
　The seven Chinese brothers
Maloney, Peter. *His mother's nose*
Mandell, B. B. *Samanthasaurus Rex*
Manning, Maurie J. *Kitchen dance*
Manning, Peyton. *Family huddle*
Manushkin, Fran. *Happy in our skin*
Manzano, Sonia. *No dogs allowed*
Marcotte, Danielle. *Mom, dad, our books, and me*
Markle, Sandra. *A mother's journey*
Martin, David. *Five little piggies*
Martin, Emily Winfield. *The littlest family's big day*
Martín, Hugo C. *Pablo's Christmas*
Martin, Jacqueline Briggs. *On Sand Island*
Matteson, George. *The Christmas tugboat*
Mauner, Claudia. *Zoe Sophia in New York*
May, Kathy. *Molasses man*
Mayhew, James. *Where's my hug?*
Medina, Tony. *DeShawn days*
Melmed, Laura Krauss. *A hug goes around*
　Little Oh
Meltzer, Amy. *The Shabbat Princess*
Meng, Cece. *I will not read this book*
Messinger, Carla. *When the shadbush blooms*
Miller, Margaret. *I love colors*
Miller, Pat Zietlow. *Sharing the bread*
Modesitt, Jeanne. *Little Mouse's happy birthday*
Monk, Isabell. *Family*
Montanari, Susan McElroy. *My dog's a chicken*
Moore, Raina. *How do you say good night?*
Moore-Mallinos, Jennifer. *When my parents forgot how to be friends*
Moorman, Margaret. *Light the lights!*

Mora, Pat. *I pledge allegiance*
　Let's eat! / A comer!
Morozumi, Atsuko. *Helping daddy*
Morris, Ann. *Families*
　Loving
Moses, Will. *Silent night*
Munsch, Robert N. *I have to go!*
　Mmm, cookies!
Murguia, Bethanie Deeney. *Snippet the early riser*
Murphy, Jill. *A quiet night in*
Murphy, Stuart J. *The best vacation ever*
Myers, Anna. *Tumbleweed Baby*
Nicholls, Judith. *Someone I like*
Nikola-Lisa, W. *One, two, three Thanksgiving!*
　Summer sun risin'
Nolen, Jerdine. *Hewitt Anderson's great big life*
　In my momma's kitchen
　Pitching in for Eubie
Norac, Carl. *I love you so much*
Novak, Matt. *A wish for you*
O'Connell, Rebecca. *Baby parade*
O'Connor, Jane. *Fancy Nancy*
　Fancy Nancy and the posh puppy
　Fancy Nancy splendiferous Christmas
　Nancy la elegante / Fancy Nancy
　The snow globe family
Oelschlager, Vanita. *Made in China*
Ohi, Ruth. *And you can come too*
O'Keefe, Susan Heyboer. *Baby day*
Onyefulu, Ifeoma. *Omer's favorite place*
Orloff, Karen Kaufman. *I wanna new room*
Ormerod, Jan. *Who's whose?*
Orona-Ramirez, Kristy. *Kiki's journey*
Osborne, Mary Pope. *Happy birthday, America*
Osofsky, Audrey. *Dreamcatcher*
Overend, Jenni. *Welcome with love*
Palatini, Margie. *Tub-boo-boo*
Parr, Todd. *We belong together*
Paterson, Diane. *Hurricane wolf*
Pelley, Kathleen T. *Inventor McGregor*
Pennypacker, Sara. *Meet the Dullards*
Pérez, Amada Irma. *My diary from here to there / Mi diario de aquí hasta allá*
　My very own room / Mi propio cuartito
Perkins, Lynne Rae. *The broken cat*
　Home lovely
　Pictures from our vacation
Perl, Erica S. *Ninety-three in my family*
Peterson, Jeanne Whitehouse. *Don't forget Winona*
Petricic, Dusan. *My family tree and me*
Pfeffer, Wendy. *Mallard duck at Meadow View Pond*
Phillipps, J. C. *The Simples love a picnic*
Piernas-Davenport, Gail. *Shanté Keys and the New Year's peas*
Pilkey, Dav. *The Dumb Bunnies*
　The Dumb Bunnies' Easter
　The Dumb Bunnies go to the zoo
　The Hallo-wiener
　Make way for Dumb Bunnies
Pinfold, Levi. *Black dog*
Pinkney, Andrea Davis. *Mim's Christmas jam*
Pinkney, Brian. *Jojo's flying side kick*
Pinkney, Gloria Jean. *Back home*
　The Sunday outing
Pizzoli, Greg. *Templeton gets his wish*
Polacco, Patricia. *The blessing cup*
　Gifts of the heart
Portnoy, Mindy Avra. *A tale of two seders*
　Where do people go when they die?

Family life – aunts, uncles

Family life – brothers *see also* Family life;
Family life – brothers & sisters; Sibling rivalry

Hartmann, Wendy. *The dinosaurs are back and it's all your fault, Edward!*
Henry, Steve. *Nobody asked me!*
Hiatt, Fred. *Baby talk*
Hoban, Russell. *Best friends for Frances*
Howe, James. *There's a dragon in my sleeping bag*
Isern, Susanna. *Middle bear*
Itaya, Satoshi. *Buttons and Bo*
James, Simon. *Little One Step*
Jaspersohn, William. *The two brothers*
Johnston, Tony. *The iguana brothers, a perfect day*
   That summer
Jonell, Lynne. *It's my birthday, too!*
Joosse, Barbara. *I love you the purplest*
Kirsch, Vincent X. *Two little boys from Toolittle Toys*
Kleven, Elisa. *A monster in the house*
   The puddle pail
Kling, Kevin. *Big little brother*
Kraus, Robert. *Little Louie the baby bloomer*
Kushner, Donn. *Peter's pixie*
Larsen, Andrew. *In the tree house*
Layne, Steven L. *My brother Dan's delicious*
Lehman-Wilzig, Tami. *Nathan blows out the Hanukkah candles*
Leuck, Laura. *My beastly brother*
Lindgren, Barbro. *Oink, oink, Benny*
London, Jonathan. *Moshi moshi*
Long, Ethan. *The Wing Wing brothers carnival de math*
   The Wing Wing brothers geometry palooza!
   The Wing Wing brothers math spectacular!
Long, Heather. *Max and Milo go to sleep!*
Luthardt, Kevin. *Mine*
McPhail, David. *Brothers*
Moore-Mallinos, Jennifer. *My brother is autistic*
Numeroff, Laura Joffe. *What brothers do best*
Olson, Mary. *An alligator ate my brother*
Palatini, Margie. *Tub-boo-boo*
Penfold, Alexandra. *We are brothers, we are friends*
Perry, Michael. *Daniel's ride*
Pinder, Eric. *How to share with a bear*
Pinkwater, Daniel. *Young Larry*
Rodman, Mary Ann. *Surprise soup*
Roe, Eileen. *With my brother / Con mi hermano*
Rossiter, Nan Parson. *Sugar on snow*
Rumford, James. *Dog-of-the-Sea-Waves*
   The Island-below-the-star
Russo, Marisabina. *The big brown box*
Saltzberg, Barney. *Cornelius P. Mud, are you ready for baby?*
San Souci, Robert D. *The enchanted tapestry*
   Little Pierre
Sasso, Sandy Eisenberg. *Cain and Abel*
Sattler, Jennifer. *Pig kahuna pirates!*
Schaefer, Lola M. *One special day*
Schertle, Alice. *Witch Hazel*
Schwartz, Roslyn. *The Vole brothers*
Shields, Carol Diggory. *I wish my brother was a dog*
Silverman, Erica. *Follow the leader*
Soman, David. *The amazing adventures of Bumblebee Boy*
Steig, William. *The toy brother*
Stevenson, James. *That's exactly the way it wasn't*
Stuve-Bodeen, Stephanie. *Mama Elizabeti*
Symes, Ruth. *Little Rex, big brother*
Titherington, Jeanne. *A place for Ben*
Van Allsburg, Chris. *Zathura*
Van Leeuwen, Jean. *Sorry*
Vernick, Audrey. *Brothers at bat*

Vulliamy, Clara. *Ellen and Penguin and the new baby*
Waddell, Martin. *Sam Vole and his brothers*
Ward, Lindsay. *Brobarians*
Wheeler, Lisa. *Turk and Runt*
White, Linda Arms. *Comes a wind*
Wilhelm, Hans. *More bunny trouble*
Wilson, Sarah. *Friends and pals and brothers, too*
Wilson, Troy. *Liam takes a stand*
Yaccarino, Dan. *Morris Mole*
Yin. *Coolies*
Yolen, Jane. *My brothers' flying machine*
Yoon, Salina. *Penguin and Pumpkin*
Zimmerman, Andrea Griffing. *Train man*

Family life – brothers & sisters

Alborough, Jez. *Watch out! Big Bro's coming!*
Andros, Camille. *Charlotte the scientist is squished*
Archer, Peggy. *Turkey surprise*
Baicker, Karen. *You can do it too!*
Barclay, Eric. *Hiding Phil*
Barnett, Mac. *Rules of the house*
Bartone, Elisa. *Peppe the lamplighter*
Bassède, Francine. *A day with the Bellyflops*
Baumgart, Klaus. *Laura's secret*
Bedford, David. *Ella's games*
Bennett, Kelly. *Vampire baby*
Berenstain, Stan and Jan. *The Berenstain bears no girls allowed*
Bergman, Mara. *Snip snap!*
Berry, Lynne. *Squid Kid the Magnificent*
Birdsall, Jeanne. *Flora's very windy day*
Boelts, Maribeth. *You're a brother, Little Bunny!*
Bonnett-Rampersaud, Louise. *Bubble and Squeak*
Bourgeois, Paulette. *Franklin and Harriet*
   Franklin's baby sister
Bowen, Anne. *When you visit Grandma and Grandpa*
Bower, Gary. *Ivy's icicle*
Breathed, Berkeley. *Edwurd Fudwupper fibbed big*
Broach, Elise. *What the no-good baby is good for*
Brown, Marc. *Arthur tricks the tooth fairy*
   Arthur turns green
   Arthur's first sleepover
   D. W. rides again!
   D. W. thinks big
   D. W.'s library card
   Glasses for D. W.
   Monkey: not ready for the baby
Browne, Anthony. *My brother*
Burks, James. *Pigs and a blanket*
Busch, Miriam. *Raisin, the littlest cow*
Buzzeo, Toni. *Lighthouse Christmas*
Capucilli, Alyssa Satin. *Katy Duck, big sister*
Caraballo, Samuel. *My big sister / Mi hermana mayor*
Carter, Alden R. *Big brother Dustin*
Caseley, Judith. *Sophie and Sammy's library sleepover*
Chaconas, Dori. *Dancing with Katya*
Chavarría-Cháirez, Becky. *Magda's piñata magic / Magda y la piñata mágica*
Cheng, Andrea. *The lemon sisters*
Chessa, Francesca. *The mysterious package*
Child, Lauren. *Absolutely one thing*
   But, excuse me, that is my book
   But I've used all my pocket change
   Charlie and Lola's numbers
   Charlie and Lola's opposites
   I am too absolutely small for school
   I completely know about guinea pigs
   I really, really need actual ice skates

I will never not ever eat a tomato
My best, best friend
Say cheese!
Snow is my favorite and my best
Clark, Katie. *Seagull Sam*
Collins, Suzanne. *When Charlie McButton lost power*
Corderoy, Tracey. *Monty and Milli*
Corpi, Lucha. *Where fireflies dance / Ahí, donde*
bailan las luciérnagas
Crews, Nina. *A high, low, near, far, loud, quiet story*
Crow, Kristyn. *The middle-child blues*
Cullen, Lynn. *Dear Mr. Washington*
Cummings, Pat. *Angel baby*
Cuyler, Margery. *The bumpy little pumpkin*
David, Lawrence. *The land of the hungry armadillos*
Davies, Gill. *Wilbur waited*
Dealey, Erin. *Goldie Locks has chicken pox*
deGroat, Diane. *Mother, you're the best! (but Sister,*
you're a pest!)
Trick or treat, smell my feet
dePaola, Tomie. *Boss for a day*
Marcos
Meet the Barkers
A new Barker in the house
Dewan, Ted. *Crispin and the 3 little piglets*
Dixon, Ann. *Winter is . . .*
Doerrfeld, Cori. *Maggie and Wendel*
Penny loves pink
Downey, Lynn. *The tattletale*
Duke, Kate. *The tale of Pip and Squeak*
Dunrea, Olivier. *Gemma and Gus*
Dyer, Sarah. *Clementine and Mungo*
Ellery, Amanda. *If I had a dragon*
Elliott, Laura Malone. *Hunter's big sister*
Elliott, Rebecca. *Just because*
Ellis, Sarah. *Big Ben*
Elya, Susan Middleton. *Sophie's trophy*
Escoffier, Michaël. *Me first!*
Farris, Christine King. *My brother Martin*
Fearnley, Jan. *Martha in the middle*
Feeney, Tatyana. *Little Frog's tadpole trouble*
Feiffer, Kate. *But I wanted a baby brother!*
Fleming, Denise. *Mama cat has three kittens*
Ford, Juwanda G. *Together for Kwanzaa*
Fraser, Mary Ann. *Heebie-Jeebie Jamboree*
Frazee, Marla. *The bossier baby*
Freedman, Deborah. *Scribble*
Funke, Cornelia. *The wildest brother*
Gammell, Stephen. *How about going for a ride*
Gary, Meredith. *Sometimes you get what you want*
Gay, Marie-Louise. *Good morning Sam*
Read me a story, Stella
Stella, fairy of the forest
Stella, queen of the snow
Stella, star of the sea
What are you doing, Sam?
When Stella was very, very small
George, Jean Craighead. *Nutik, the wolf pup*
Going, K. L. *Bumpety, dunkety, thumpety-thump!*
Goode, Diane. *Mama's perfect present*
Gorbachev, Valeri. *The best cat*
How to be friends with a dragon
Nicky and the rainy day
Gordon, David. *The ugly truckling*
Got, Yves. *Sam's little sister*
Graham, Bob. *Dimity Dumpty*
Green, Jen. *Our new baby*
Greenfield, Eloise. *Brothers and sisters*

Grimm, Jacob and Wilhelm. *Princess Sophie and the*
six swans
The six swans
Grindley, Sally. *It's my school*
Gutierrez, Akemi. *The mummy and other adventures*
of Sam and Alice
Guy, Ginger Foglesong. *Siesta*
Hänel, Wolfram. *Little elephant runs away*
Harley, Bill. *Dirty Joe, the pirate*
Harper, Anita. *It's not fair!*
Harper, Jamie. *Me too!*
Harris, Robie H. *Hi, new baby*
Hasler, Eveline. *A tale of two brothers*
Havill, Juanita. *Jamaica is thankful*
Jamaica Tag-Along
Heller, Linda. *How Dalia put a big yellow comforter*
inside a tiny blue box
Hershenhorn, Esther. *Fancy that*
Hest, Amy. *You're the boss, Baby Duck*
Hoberman, Mary Ann. *And to think that we thought*
that we'd never be friends
The seven silly eaters
Hood, Susan. *Mission: new baby*
Hooks, William H. *The legend of the Christmas rose*
Hughes, Shirley. *Alfie's ABC*
Annie Rose is my little sister
Olly and me
Olly and me 1-2-3
Rhymes for Annie Rose
Hunter, Sally. *Humphrey's bedtime*
Humphrey's Christmas
Hurwitz, Johanna. *Russell's secret*
Hutchins, Pat. *Silly Billy!*
Isadora, Rachel. *Yo, Jo!*
Jalali, Reza. *Moon watchers*
James, Brian. *Supertwins and the sneaky, slimy book*
worms
The Supertwins and tooth trouble
The Supertwins meet the bad dogs from space
Supertwins meet the dangerous dino-robots
Javaherbin, Mina. *Soccer star*
Jeffs, Stephanie. *Jenny*
Jenkins, Emily. *Lemonade in winter*
Johnson, Angela. *Do like Kyla*
Johnson, Gillian. *My sister Gracie*
Johnson, Lindan Lee. *The dream jar*
Joyce, William. *Santa calls*
Judge, Chris. *Tin*
Judge, Lita. *Hoot and Peep*
Hoot and Peep: a song for snow
Kann, Victoria. *Silverlicious*
Kaplan, Bruce Eric. *Meaniehead*
Monsters eat whiny children
Karas, G. Brian. *Bebe's bad dream*
Kay, Verla. *Orphan train*
Keane, Claire. *Little big girl*
Keller, Holly. *Geraldine and Mrs. Duffy*
Kim, Aram. *No kimchi for me!*
Kim, Julie. *Where's Halmoni?*
Knapman, Timothy. *Time now to dream*
Knudsen, Michelle. *A moldy mystery*
Koch, Ed. *Eddie's little sister makes a splash*
Koller, Jackie French. *Baby for sale*
Kornell, Max. *Me first*
Kortepeter, Paul. *Oliver's red toboggan*
Krensky, Stephen. *We just had a baby*
Kurtz, Jane. *In the small, small night*
Kushner, Tony. *Brundibar*
Lam, Maple. *My little sister and me*

LaMarche, Jim. *Up*
Lamm, C. Drew. *Pirates*
Landa, Norbert. *Little Bear and the wishing tree*
Landolf, Diane Wright. *What a good big brother!*
LaRochelle, David. *The haunted hamburger and other ghostly stories*
Larsen, Andrew. *A squiggly story*
Lasky, Kathryn. *Lucille's snowsuit*
  Starring Lucille
Lazar, Tara. *The Monstore*
Lears, Laurie. *Ian's walk*
Light, Kelly. *Louise loves art*
Lloyd-Jones, Sally. *His Royal Highness, King Baby*
  How to be a baby — by me, the big sister
Lobe, Mira. *Hoppelpopp and the best bunny*
Look, Lenore. *Henry's first-moon birthday*
Lucke, Deb. *The boy who wouldn't swim*
McClintock, Barbara. *Adele and Simon*
  Adele and Simon in America
  Lost and found: Adele and Simon in China
  Molly and the magic wishbone
McCormick, Wendy. *The night you were born*
McCullough, Sharon Pierce. *Bunbun, the middle one*
McDonald, Rae A. *A fishing surprise*
MacDonald, Ross. *Bad baby*
McKissack, Patricia C. *The all-I'll-ever-want Christmas doll*
McKy, Katie. *Pumpkin town!*
McQuinn, Anna. *Lola reads to Leo*
Mahoney, Daniel J. *A really good snowman*
Mair, Samia J. *The perfect gift*
Manson, Ainslie. *Ballerinas don't wear glasses*
Massini, Sarah. *Trixie ten*
Meade, Holly. *Inside, inside, inside*
Meddaugh, Susan. *Cinderella's rat*
Mendes, Valerie. *Look at me, Grandma!*
Meng, Cece. *The wonderful thing about hiccups*
Merino, Gemma. *The cow who climbed a tree*
Meserve, Jessica. *Bedtime without Arthur*
  Small sister
Michels-Gualtieri, Akaela S. *I was born to be a sister*
Michelson, Richard. *Oh no, not ghosts!*
Milgrim, David. *Amelia makes a movie*
  Santa Duck and his merry helpers
Molk, Laurel. *Eeny, Meeny, Miney, Mo and Flo!*
Moon, Nicola. *Something special*
Morales, Yuyi. *Niño wrestles the world*
  Rudas
Morrissey, Dean. *The crimson comet*
Munsch, Robert N. *Alligator baby*
Murkoff, Heidi Eisenberg. *What to expect when the new baby comes home*
Muth, Jon J. *Zen ghosts*
  Zen shorts
  Zen socks
  Zen ties
Napoli, Donna Jo. *The wishing club*
Nelson, S. D. *The Star People*
Neubecker, Robert. *Fall is for school*
  Winter is for snow
Neuschwander, Cindy. *Pastry school in Paris*
Newman, Lesléa. *Sparkle boy*
Newman, Marjorie. *Just like me*
Norris, Kathleen. *The holy twins*
Novak, Matt. *The Pillow War*
Numeroff, Laura Joffe. *What brothers do best; What sisters do best*
Offill, Jenny. *While you were napping*

Ohi, Ruth. *The couch was a castle*
  Me and my brother
  Me and my sister
  A trip with Grandma
Olson, Jennifer Gray. *Ninja Bunny: sister vs. brother*
Ormerod, Jan. *The baby swap*
Palatini, Margie. *Goldie is mad*
  Good as Goldie
Parkhurst, Carolyn. *Cooking with Henry and Elliebelly*
Partis, Joanne. *Stripe's naughty sister*
Patz, Nancy. *Babies can't eat kimchee!*
Peete, Holly Robinson. *My brother Charlie*
Pegram, Laura. *Daughter's Day blues*
Pelham, David. *Sam's pizza*
  Sam's sandwich
Pendziwol, Jean E. *Me and you and the red canoe*
Perkins, Maripat. *Rodeo Red*
Pham, LeUyen. *Big sister, little sister*
Polacco, Patricia. *My rotten redheaded older brother*
  Rotten Richie and the ultimate dare
Powell-Tuck, Maudie. *Pirates aren't afraid of the dark!*
Prigger, Mary Skillings. *Aunt Minnie McGranahan*
Pulver, Robin. *Way to go, Alex!*
Raschka, Chris. *The blushful hippopotamus*
Regan, Dian Curtis. *Space Boy and his dog*
  Space Boy and the space pirate
Reiser, Lynn. *My baby and me*
Reiss, Mike. *The boy who wouldn't share*
Reynolds, Peter H. *The best kid in the world*
  Ish
Ries, Lori. *Fix it, Sam*
Robbins, Beth. *Tom, Ally, and the new baby*
  Tom and Ally visit the doctor
Roberts, Bethany. *Double trouble Groundhog Day*
Robertson, M. P. *Hieronymous Betts and his unusual pets*
Rockwell, Anne. *Brendan and Belinda and the slam dunk!*
Rockwell, Lizzy. *Hello baby!*
Roddie, Shen. *Toes are to tickle*
Rogers, Jacqueline. *Tiptoe into kindergarten*
Roper, Janice M. *Dancing on the moon*
Rossell, Judith. *Ruby and Leonard and the great big surprise*
Rubel, Nicole. *Ham and Pickles*
Rusch, Elizabeth. *Ready, set . . . baby!*
Russo, Marisabina. *Hannah's baby sister*
  Peter is just a baby
  The trouble with baby
Ryan, Pam Muñoz. *Mud is cake*
  Tony Baloney
  Tony Baloney: buddy trouble
Saltzberg, Barney. *Inside this book (are three books)*
Samuels, Barbara. *Dolores meets her match*
  Happy Valentine's Day, Dolores
Sanders, Scott R. *Crawdad Creek*
Sanders-Wells, Linda. *Maggie's monkeys*
Sayre, April Pulley. *It's my city*
Schaefer, Lola M. *One busy day*
Scheffler, Ursel. *Taking care of Sister Bear*
Schneider, Christine M. *Saxophone Sam and his snazzy jazz band*
Schneider, Josh. *Kid Amazing vs. the Blob*
  You'll be sorry
Scrimger, Richard. *Eugene's story*
  Princess Bun Bun
Shea, Pegi Deitz. *New moon*
Sheldon, Annette. *Big sister now*

Sheth, Kashmira. *Tiger in my soup*
Sif, Birgitta. *Swish and Squeak's noisy day*
Simmons, Jane. *Daisy and the Beastie*
    Daisy and the egg
    Little Fern's first winter
Singer, Marilyn. *I'm gonna climb a mountain in my patent leather shoes*
    Tallulah's solo
Skinner, Daphne. *Henry keeps score*
Smallcomb, Pam. *Earth to Clunk*
Smith, Linda. *Sir Cassie to the rescue*
Snicket, Lemony. *Twenty-nine myths on the Swinster Pharmacy*
Stanton, Andy. *Danny McGee drinks the sea*
Stewart, Amber. *Little by little*
Stewart, Shannon. *Sea crow*
Stiegemeyer, Julie. *Under the baobab tree*
Stoeke, Janet Morgan. *Waiting for May*
Sturges, Philemon. *I love school*
Stuve-Bodeen, Stephanie. *We'll paint the octopus red*
Sullivan, Sarah. *Dear Baby*
Sweeney, Jacqueline. *What about Bettie?*
Sykes, Julie. *Wait for me, Little Tiger*
Taylor, Sean. *The snowbear*
Thomas, Louis. *Hug it out!*
Vail, Rachel. *Sometimes I'm Bombaloo*
Van Leeuwen, Jean. *Five funny bunnies*
    "Wait for me!" said Maggie McGee
Voake, Charlotte. *Hello twins*
Waddell, Martin. *When the teddy bears came*
Walter, Mildred Pitts. *Two too much*
Walters, Catherine. *Play gently, Alfie Bear*
Ward, Nick. *Don't eat the babysitter!*
Wegman, William. *Flo and Wendell explore*
Wells, Rosemary. *Bunny cakes*
    Bunny mail
    Bunny money
    Bunny party
    Clean-up time
    Goodnight Max
    Max and Ruby's bedtime book
    Max and Ruby's Midas
    Max and Ruby's treasure hunt
    Max cleans up
    Max's apples
    Max's bunny business
    Max's dragon shirt
    Max's Easter surprise
    Max's worm cake
    Peek-a-boo
    Red boots
    Ruby's beauty shop
    Shopping
Weninger, Brigitte. *Davy in the middle*
Weston, Martha. *Tuck's haunted house*
Wewer, Iris. *My wild sister and me*
Whybrow, Ian. *Badness for beginners*
Wiesner, David. *Hurricane*
Winters, Kari-Lynn. *Gift days*
Winthrop, Elizabeth. *Lucy and Henry are twins*
Wishinsky, Frieda. *Please, Louise!*
Wynne-Jones, Tim. *The boat in the tree*
Yin. *Brothers*
Yolen, Jane. *Soft house*
Young, Cybèle. *A few bites*
    A few blocks
Young, Ed. *My Mei Mei*
Zalben, Jane Breskin. *Baby Babka*
Zemach, Margot. *Eating up Gladys*

Zimmerman, Andrea Griffing. *Fire engine man*

Family life – cousins

Brownlee, Sophia Grace. *Show time with Sophia Grace and Rosie*
    Tea time with Sophia Grace and Rosie
Buehner, Caralyn. *Would I ever lie to you?*
Campbell, K. G. *Lester's dreadful sweaters*
Carlstrom, Nancy White. *Guess who's coming, Jesse Bear*
Crum, Shutta. *Dozens of cousins*
    My mountain song
Dahlie, Elizabeth. *Bernelly and Harriet*
D'Amico, Carmela. *Suki and Mirabella*
deGroat, Diane. *Last one in is a rotten egg!*
Garland, Sally Anne. *Share*
Greenfield, Eloise. *Easter parade*
Hest, Amy. *Nana's birthday party*
Holabird, Katharine. *Angelina's big city ballet*
    Angelina's Christmas
Holt, Kimberly Willis. *Waiting for Gregory*
Houran, Lori Haskins. *A dozen cousins*
Kinsey-Warnock, Natalie. *A farm of her own*
McCarty, Peter. *First snow*
McKay, Hilary. *Pirates ahoy!*
McKee, David. *Elmer and the whales*
Newman, Barbara Johansen. *Glamorous glasses*
OHora, Zachariah. *My cousin Momo*
Perret, Delphine. *Pedro and George*
Rodriguez, Bobbie. *Sarah's sleepover*
Root, Phyllis. *Aunt Nancy and Cousin Lazybones*
Rose, Nancy. *Merry Christmas, squirrels!*
    The secret life of squirrels
Schaefer, Carole Lexa. *The little French whistle*
Smalls-Hector, Irene. *Because you're lucky*
Stine, R.L. *Mary McScary*
Thomassie, Tynia. *Cajun through and through*
Tonatiuh, Duncan. *Dear Primo*
Weiss, Ellen. *The taming of Lola*

Family life – daughters

Baker, Roberta. *No ordinary Olive*
Bartoletti, Susan Campbell. *The Christmas promise*
Buitrago, Jairo. *Two white rabbits*
Burke, Bobby. *Daddy's little girl*
Campbell, Ann-Jeanette. *Queenie Farmer had fifteen daughters*
Cole, Brock. *Buttons*
Coy, John. *Two old potatoes and me*
Day, Jan. *The pirate, Pink*
    Pirate Pink and treasures of the reef
De Anda, Diane. *Dancing Miranda / Baila, Miranda, baila*
Dominguez, Angela. *Knit together*
Duble, Kathleen Benner. *Pilot mom*
Feiffer, Jules. *The daddy mountain*
Fruisen, Catherine Myler. *My mother's pearls*
Gilmore, Rachna. *Making grizzle grow*
Gray, Kes. *Eat your peas*
    006 and a half
Hesse, Karen. *Come on, rain*
Krosoczka, Jarrett J. *Giddy up, Cowgirl*
McCourt, Lisa. *Good night, Princess Pruney Toes*
Makhijani, Pooja. *Mama's saris*
Newman, Lesléa. *Heather has two mommies*
Paul, Alison. *The plan*
Pow, Tom. *Tell me one thing, Dad*

Rao, Sandhya. *My mother's sari*
Santucci, Barbara. *Loon summer*
Say, Allen. *The favorite daughter*
Simpson, Lesley. *The Purim surprise*
Singer, Marilyn. *Didi and Daddy on the Promenade*
Slawson, Michele Benoit. *Signs for sale*
Stephens, J. Moria. *Persephone, the ladybug*
Stevenson, James. *I meant to tell you*
Thiesing, Lisa. *Me and you: a mother-daughter album*
Waber, Bernard. *Ask me*
Winters, Kari-Lynn. *Bad pirate*
Winthrop, Elizabeth. *Promises*

Family life – fathers

Alexie, Sherman. *Thunder Boy Jr.*
Allen, Elanna. *Itsy Mitsy runs away*
Alter, Anna. *A photo for Greta*
Anderson, Peggy Perry. *To the tub*
Andreae, Giles. *I love my daddy*
Andreasen, Dan. *Saturday with Daddy*
Asch, Frank. *Just like daddy*
Asim, Jabari. *Daddy goes to work*
Auld, Mary. *My dad*
Banks, Kate. *The night worker*
    That's Papa's way
Bartoletti, Susan Campbell. *The Christmas promise*
Bartone, Elisa. *Peppe the lamplighter*
Bateman, Teresa. *Hunting the daddyosaurus*
Battle-Lavert, Gwendolyn. *Papa's mark*
Bauer, Marion Dane. *Sleep, little one, sleep*
Beaty, Daniel. *Knock knock*
Becker, Aaron. *Return*
Bee, William. *Whatever*
Bennett, Kelly. *Dad and Pop*
    Your daddy was just like you
Bergel, Colin. *Mail by the pail*
Berger, Lou. *Dream dog*
Berry, Matt. *Up on Daddy's shoulders*
Bildner, Phil. *The greatest game ever played*
Black, Birdie. *Just right for Christmas*
Bluemle, Elizabeth. *My father the dog*
Boelts, Maribeth. *Big Daddy, frog wrestler*
    Looking for Sleepy
Boyd, Lizi. *I love Daddy*
Bradman, Tony. *Daddy's lullaby*
Braun, Sebastien. *I love my daddy*
Briant, Ed. *A day at the beach*
Brisson, Pat. *Star blanket*
Brown, Margaret Wise. *The fathers are coming home*
Browne, Anthony. *Gorilla*
    My dad
Bruchac, Joseph. *My father is taller than a tree*
Brun-Cosme, Nadine. *Daddy long legs*
    With Dad, it's like that
Brutschy, Jennifer. *Just one more story*
Buitrago, Jairo. *Two white rabbits*
Bunting, Eve. *Fly away home*
    My red balloon
    A perfect Father's Day
Burke, Bobby. *Daddy's little girl*
Burleigh, Robert. *Good-bye, Sheepie*
Butterworth, Nick. *My dad is awesome*
Buzzeo, Toni. *Just like my Papa*
Capucilli, Alyssa Satin. *Hush a bye, baby*
    Only my dad and me
Carroll, James Christopher. *Papa's backpack*
Chaconas, Dori. *On a wintry morning*
Chaud, Benjamin. *The bear's sea escape*

    The bear's song
Cheng, Andrea. *Anna the bookbinder*
Choldenko, Gennifer. *Dad and the dinosaur*
Clements, Andrew. *Because your daddy loves you*
Climo, Liz. *Rory the dinosaur: me and my dad*
    Rory the dinosaur needs a Christmas tree
Colato Laínez, René. *My shoes and I*
Cole, Brock. *Buttons*
Collins, Billy. *Daddy's little boy*
Collins, Pat Lowery. *The deer watch*
Collins, Suzanne. *Year of the jungle*
Compos, Tito. *Muffler man / El hombre mofle*
Corderoy, Tracey. *I want my daddy*
Costain, Meredith. *Daddies are awesome*
Cotter, Bill. *Beard in a box*
Cousins, Lucy. *Peck, peck, peck*
Cowley, Joy. *Gracias, the Thanksgiving turkey*
Coy, John. *Two old potatoes and me*
Coyle, Carmela LaVigna. *Do princesses really kiss frogs?*
Creech, Sharon. *Fishing in the air*
Crowther, Kitty. *Scritch scratch scraww plop*
Crum, Shutta. *Fox and Fluff*
Dahl, Michael. *Goodnight baseball*
Davies, Benji. *The storm whale*
    The storm whale in winter
Day, Jan. *The pirate, Pink*
    Pirate Pink and treasures of the reef
Demas, Corinne. *Nina's waltz*
Demers, Dominique. *Every single night*
Dewdney, Anna. *Nelly Gnu and Daddy too*
DiTerlizzi, Tony. *Ted*
Dodd, Emma. *Just like you*
Dorros, Arthur. *Papa and me*
Dotlich, Rebecca Kai. *Papa loves*
Dunrea, Olivier. *A Christmas tree for Pyn*
    Old Bear and his cub
Durand, Hallie. *Mitchell goes bowling*
    Mitchell's license
Dyer, Sarah. *Monster day at work*
Dylan, Bob. *If not for you*
Eaton, Maxwell. *I'm awake!*
Edwards, Michelle. *Papa's latkes*
Ehrlich, Fred. *Does a duck have a daddy?*
Eilenberg, Max. *Cowboy Kid*
Emmons, Chip. *Sammy wakes his dad*
Ernst, Lisa Campbell. *This is the van that Dad cleaned*
Ewart, Claire. *The giant*
Farmer, Nancy. *Clever Ali*
Feiffer, Jules. *The daddy mountain*
Feiffer, Kate. *My side of the car*
Foreman, Michael. *I love you, too!*
Fortenberry, Julie. *Lily's cat mask*
Frederick, Heather Vogel. *Hide and squeak*
Galbraith, Kathryn O. *Arbor Day square*
Gay, Marie-Louise. *Roslyn Rutabaga and the biggest hole on earth!*
George, Jean Craighead. *Cliff hanger*
George, Kristine O'Connell. *Up!*
George, William T. *Christmas at Long Pond*
Germein, Katrina. *My dad thinks he's funny*
Gerstein, Mordicai. *The boy and the whale*
Gibala-Broxholm, Scott. *Maddie's monster dad*
Giles, Almira Astudillo. *Willie wins*
Gilmore, Rachna. *Making grizzle grow*
Glass, Beth Raisner. *Blue-ribbon dad*
Glassman, Peter. *My dad's job*
Gomi, Taro. *I lost my dad*

Napoli, Donna Jo. *Flamingo dream*
Newman, Lesléa. *Daddy, Papa, and me*
    Daddy's song
Niemann, Christoph. *Subway*
Nolan, Janet. *A Father's Day thank you*
Nolen, Jerdine. *Irene's wish*
Norac, Carl. *My daddy is a giant*
Norman, Geoffrey. *Stars above us*
North, Sherry. *Because I am your daddy*
Numeroff, Laura Joffe. *What daddies do best*
Ochiltree, Dianne. *It's a firefly night*
Oelschlager, Vanita. *A tale of two daddies*
O'Leary, Sara. *When you were small*
O'Malley, Kevin. *Little Buggy*
    Little Buggy runs away
O'Neill, Alexis. *Estela's swap*
Oppenheim, Shulamith Levey. *Ali and the magic*
    stew
Ormerod, Jan. *Molly and her dad*
Pak, Soyung. *A place to grow*
Paradis, Susan. *My Daddy*
    Snow princess
Park, Linda Sue. *The firekeeper's son*
    The third gift
Parker, Marjorie Blain. *When dads don't grow up*
Parr, Todd. *The daddy book*
Patricelli, Leslie. *Faster! faster!*
Paul, Alison. *The plan*
Pelton, Mindy L. *When Dad's at sea*
Pfister, Marcus. *Bertie*
    Penguin Pete and Little Tim
Phelan, Matt. *Druthers*
Phi, Bao. *A different pond*
Plecas, Jennifer. *Pretend*
Plourde, Lynn. *Dad, aren't you glad?*
Polacco, Patricia. *My ol' man*
    Some birthday!
Posey, Lee. *Night rabbits*
Pow, Tom. *Tell me one thing, Dad*
Prap, Lila. *Daddies*
Pringle, Laurence P. *Bear hug*
Pullen, Zachary. *Friday my Radio Flyer flew*
Pulver, Robin. *Saturday is Dadurday*
Rappaport, Doreen. *The new king*
Raschka, Chris. *Everyone can learn to ride a bicycle*
Ray, Jane. *The dollhouse fairy*
Ray, Mary Lyn. *Basket moon*
Reagan, Jean. *How to surprise a dad*
Rex, Michael. *You can do anything, Daddy!*
Reynolds, Luke. *Bedtime blastoff!*
    If my love were a fire truck
Rice, Eve. *Swim!*
Richards, Doyin. *I wonder*
Ritchie, Alison. *Me and my dad!*
Robinson, Sharon. *Testing the ice*
Rockwell, Anne. *Ducklings and pollywogs*
    Father's Day
Root, Phyllis. *Contrary bear*
Rosenberg, Liz. *Tyrannosaurus dad*
Rusackas, Francesca. *Daddy all day long*
Ryder, Joanne. *My father's hands*
Rylant, Cynthia. *Herbert's first Halloween*
San Souci, Robert D. *The samurai's daughter*
Santucci, Barbara. *Loon summer*
Saudo, Coralie. *My dad at the zoo*
    My dad is big and strong, but . . .
Saunders, Karen. *Baby Badger's wonderful night*
Savadier, Elivia. *Time to get dressed!*
Schaefer, Lola M. *Toolbox twins*

Schlessinger, Laura. *Dr. Laura Schlessinger's*
    Growing up is hard
Schotter, Roni. *Room for Rabbit*
Schwartz, Amy. *Bea and Mr. Jones*
Schwartz, Joanne. *Town is by the sea*
The scrubbly-bubbly car wash
Shahan, Sherry. *That's not how you play soccer,*
    Daddy
Shannon, David. *Jangles*
Shea, Bob. *Oh, Daddy!*
Shipton, Jonathan. *How to be a happy hippo*
Sidman, Joyce. *Just us two*
Silverman, Erica. *Wake up, city!*
Singer, Marilyn. *Didi and Daddy on the Promenade*
Sitomer, Alan Lawrence. *Daddies do it different*
Slate, Joseph. *Story time for Little Porcupine*
Slawson, Michele Benoit. *Signs for sale*
Smallman, Steve. *My dad!*
Smalls-Hector, Irene. *Kevin and his dad*
Smith, Hope Anita. *My daddy rules the world*
Smith, Will. *Just the two of us*
Sockabasin, Allen. *Thanks to the animals*
Sperring, Mark. *How many sleeps 'til my birthday?*
Spinelli, Eileen. *A big boy now*
    Night shift daddy
    When Papa comes home tonight
Spinelli, Jerry. *My daddy and me*
Stanton, Karen. *Papi's gift*
Steen, Sandra. *Car wash*
Steig, William. *Pete's a pizza*
Stein, David Ezra. *Tad and Dad*
Stevenson, James. *I meant to tell you*
    Sam the Zamboni man
Stewart, Amber. *Bedtime for Button*
Stock, Catherine. *Christmas time*
Tafuri, Nancy. *Daddy hugs*
Tarbescu, Edith. *Annushka's voyage*
Tarpley, Natasha Anastasia. *Bippity Bop barbershop*
Taylor, Ann. *Baby dance*
Taylor, Sean. *A brave bear*
Tellis, Annabel. *If my dad were a dog*
Thompson, Lauren. *Mouse's first snow*
Thomson, Sarah L. *Quick, Little Monkey!*
Tomp, Sarah Wones. *Red, white, and blue goodbye*
Tonatiuh, Duncan. *Pancho Rabbit and the coyote*
Trottier, Maxine. *A safe place*
Udry, Janice May. *What Mary Jo shared*
Uhlberg, Myron. *Dad, Jackie, and me*
    The printer
Van Slyke, Rebecca. *Dad school*
Vigna, Judith. *I wish my daddy didn't drink so much*
    Saying goodbye to daddy
Waber, Bernard. *Ask me*
Waboose, Jan Bourdeau. *Morning on the lake*
Waddell, Martin. *Can't you sleep, Little Bear?*
    Let's go home, Little Bear
Walker, Anna. *I love my dad*
Walters, Virginia. *Are we there yet, Daddy?*
Warnes, Tim. *Daddy hug*
Watanabe, Shigeo. *Let's go swimming*
    Where's my daddy?
Watts, Frances. *Kisses for Daddy*
Wechterowicz, Przemyslaw. *Hug me, please!*
Weigel, Jeff. *Atomic Ace (he's just my dad)*
Welch, Willy. *Dancing with Daddy*
Wells, Rosemary. *The island light*
Weninger, Brigitte. *Good-bye, Daddy!*
Weulersse, Odile. *Nasreddine*
Wild, Margaret. *Piglet and Papa*

Willhoite, Michael. *Daddy's roommate*
Winters, Kari-Lynn. *Bad pirate*
Winthrop, Elizabeth. *As the crow flies*
Wohnoutka, Mike. *Dad's first day*
Wolf, Jake. *Daddy, could I have an elephant?*
Wood, Douglas. *What dads can't do*
    When a dad says "I love you"
Wyeth, Sharon Dennis. *Always my dad*
Yaccarino, Dan. *Every Friday*
Yolen, Jane. *All those secrets of the world*
    Baby Bear's chairs
    The emperor and the kite
    My father knows the names of things
    Owl moon
Young, Ed. *Mouse match*
Young, Jessica. *Spy Guy*
Yu, Li-Qiong. *A New Year's reunion*
Zappa, Ahmet. *Because I'm your dad*
Ziefert, Harriet. *Bigger than Daddy*
Zolotow, Charlotte. *A father like that*
Zuppardi, Sam. *Things to do with Dad*

Family life – grandfathers

Acheson, Alison. *Grandpa's music*
Ackerman, Karen. *Song and dance man*
Adler, David A. *A little at a time*
Aliki. *The two of them*
Altes, Marta. *My grandpa*
Anaya, Rudolfo A. *Farolitos for Abuelo*
Andrews, Julie. *Dumpy the dump truck*
Anholt, Laurence. *Seven for a secret*
Appelt, Kathi. *Where, where is Swamp Bear?*
Asher, Sandy. *What a party!*
Aska, Warabe. *Tapicero tap tap*
Aylesworth, Jim. *My grandfather's coat*
Balouch, Kristen. *Mystery bottle*
Bandy, Michael S. *Granddaddy's turn*
Barrett, Judi. *Cloudy with a chance of meatballs*
    Cloudy with a chance of meatballs 3
Barron, T. A. *Where is Grandpa?*
Beardshaw, Rosalind. *Grandpa's surprise*
Boyden, Linda. *The blue roses*
Bradford, Karleen. *You can't rush a cat*
Briggs, Raymond. *The puddleman*
Bunting, Eve. *Butterfly house*
    A day's work
    So far from the sea
Butler, Dori Hillestad. *My grandpa had a stroke*
Callahan, Sean. *The leprechaun who lost his rainbow*
Carney, Margaret. *The biggest fish in the lake*
Carter, Don. *Heaven's all-star jazz band*
Cazet, Denys. *December 24th*
Cheng, Andrea. *Grandfather counts*
Choi, Yangsook. *Behind the mask*
Cocca-Leffler, Maryann. *A vacation for Pooch*
Cohen, Deborah Bodin. *Papa Jethro*
Compestine, Ying Chang. *Crouching tiger*
Cooke, Trish. *The grandad tree*
Cooper, Floyd. *Max and the tag-along moon*
Costello, David Hyde. *Little Pig saves the ship*
Cronin, B. B. *The lost house*
    The lost picnic
Crunk, Tony. *Grandpa's overalls*
Cumberbatch, Judy. *Can you hear the sea?*
Cummings, Phil. *Newspaper hats*
Daly, Niki. *Old Bob's brown bear*
Davidson, Leslie A. *In the red canoe*
Davies, Nicola. *White owl, barn owl*

Davis, Aubrey. *Bagels from Benny*
dePaola, Tomie. *Now one foot, now the other*
    Tom
De Sève, Randall. *A fire truck named Red*
DiSalvo, DyAnne. *Grandpa's corner store*
Dominguez, Angela. *Sing, don't cry*
Dorros, Arthur. *Abuelo*
Drawson, Blair. *All along the river*
Drummond, Allan. *Tin Lizzie*
Duvall, John. *The great spruce*
Earnhardt, Donna W. *Being Frank*
Falwell, Cathryn. *Rainbow Stew*
Fletcher, Ralph. *Grandpa never lies*
Fox, Mem. *Shoes from grandpa*
    Sophie
Francis, Lee DeCora. *Kunu's basket*
Fry, Stella. *Grandpa's garden*
Garland, Michael. *Grandpa's tractor*
Geisert, Arthur. *Mystery*
George, William T. *Fishing at Long Pond*
Gerdner, Linda. *Grandfather's story cloth / Yawg*
    daim paj ntaub dab neeg
Gillard, Denise. *Music from the sky*
Gold-Vukson, Marji E. *Grandpa and me on Tu*
    B'Shevat
Golding, Theresa Martin. *Memorial Day surprise*
Gower, Catherine. *Long-Long's new year*
Greenfield, Eloise. *Grandpa's face*
Grifalconi, Ann. *Ain't nobody a stranger to me*
Grist, Julie. *Flying, just plane fun*
Henkes, Kevin. *Grandpa and Bo*
Henson, Heather. *Grumpy Grandpa*
Hest, Amy. *Baby Duck and the bad eyeglasses*
    Guess who, Baby Duck
    Make the team, Baby Duck
    Off to school, Baby Duck
    The purple coat
    When Charley met Grampa
    You're the boss, Baby Duck
Highet, Alistair. *The yellow train*
Hopkinson, Deborah. *Bluebird summer*
Hurst, Carol Otis. *Terrible storm*
Hutchins, Pat. *Bumpety bump*
    Happy birthday, Sam
Isadora, Rachel. *Happy belly, happy smile*
    Yo, Jo!
Ismail, Yasmeen. *Imagine that!*
Jackson, Richard. *In plain sight*
James, Simon. *The birdwatchers*
Jiang, Ji-li. *Lotus and Feather*
Johnson, Angela. *Julius*
    The Rolling Store
    When I am old with you
Johnston, Tony. *Little Rabbit goes to sleep*
Kasza, Keiko. *Grandpa Toad's last secret*
Kimmelman, Leslie. *The Shabbat puppy*
Krebs, Laurie. *The beeman*, ill. by Valeria Cis
    The beeman, ill. by Melissa Iwai
Larsen, Andrew. *The imaginary garden*
    The not-so-faraway adventure
Latimer, Alex. *Stay! a top dog story*
LeBox, Annette. *Wild bog tea*
Levine, Arthur A. *What a beautiful morning*
Liu, Sylvia. *A morning with grandpa*
Liwska, Renata. *Little panda*
Lobel, Gillian. *Does anybody love me?*
Locker, Thomas. *Where the river begins*
Londner, Renee. *Stones for Grandpa*
Lynn, Sarah. *Tip-tap pop*

McCully, Emily Arnold. *The Christmas gift*
McDonald, Megan. *The great pumpkin switch*
McKee, David. *Elmer and Grandpa Eldo*
McKenna, Sharon. *Good morning, sunshine*
Mackintosh, David. *The Frank show*
Martin, Bill, Jr.. *Knots on a counting rope*
Martin, Jacqueline Briggs. *The water gift and the pig of the pig*
Mason, Margaret H. *These hands*
May, Kathy. *Molasses man*
Mayer, Mercer. *Just big enough*
Meshon, Aaron. *Take me out to the Yakyu*
Messner, Kate. *Rolling Thunder*
Michelson, Richard. *Too young for Yiddish*
Mitchell, Margaree King. *Granddaddy's gift*
Monk, Isabell. *Blackberry stew*
Moon, Nicola. *Lucy's picture*
Moore, Lilian. *While you were chasing a hat*
Mora, Pat. *Pablo's tree*
Moseley, Keith. *Where's the dinosaur?*
Moser, Lisa. *Watermelon wishes*
Muller, Gerda. *How does my garden grow?*
Murphy, Yannick. *Ahwooooooooo!*
Nanji, Shenaaz. *An alien in my house*
Newman, Lesléa. *A sweet Passover*
Nickle, John. *TV Rex*
Nobisso, Josephine. *Grandpa loved*
Numeroff, Laura Joffe. *What grandmas do best; What grandpas do best*
Oberman, Sheldon. *The always prayer shawl*
   By the Hanukkah light
O'Malley, Kevin. *Bud*
Oram, Hiawyn. *Going to Grandpa's*
Otto, Carolyn. *That sky, that rain*
Parr, Todd. *The grandpa book*
Paul, Ann Whitford. *Everything to spend the night . . . from A to Z*
Perret, Delphine. *The Big Bad Wolf goes on vacation*
Pfister, Marcus. *The happy hedgehog*
Proimos, James. *Joe's wish*
Purmell, Ann. *Apple cider making days*
Quigley, Mary. *Granddad's fishing buddy*
Rahaman, Vashanti. *Divali rose*
Reagan, Jean. *How to babysit a grandpa*
Reynolds, Adrian. *Pete and Polo's farmyard adventure*
Richards, Keith. *Gus and me*
Roberts, Bethany. *Gramps and the fire dragon*
Rose, Naomi C. *Tashi and the Tibetan flower cure*
Rosenberry, Vera. *Vera's baby sister*
Roth, Susan L. *Happy birthday Mr. Kang*
Russo, Marisabina. *Grandpa Abe*
Sáenz, Benjamin Alire. *A gift from papá Diego / Un regalo de papá Diego*
Saltzberg, Barney. *Tea with Grandpa*
Santucci, Barbara. *Anna's corn*
Say, Allen. *Grandfather's journey*
Schaefer, Carole Lexa. *The little French whistle*
Schlessinger, Laura. *Dr. Laura Schlessinger's Where's God?*
Schotter, Roni. *In the piney woods*
Schwartz, Howard. *Gathering sparks*
Sheth, Kashmira. *Monsoon afternoon*
Shields, Carol Diggory. *Lucky pennies and hot chocolate*
Shulevitz, Uri. *Dawn*
   Dusk
Sinykin, Sheri. *Zayde comes to live*
Sís, Peter. *Ice cream summer*
Smalls, Irene. *My Pop Pop and me*

Smith, Danna. *Arctic white*
Soman, David. *Ladybug Girl's day out with Grandpa*
Soto, Gary. *My little car / Mi carrito*
Stafford, Liliana. *Just dragon*
Sterer, Gideon. *Skyfishing*
Stevenson, James. *Brr!*
   "Could be worse!"
   Grandpa's great city tour
   Grandpa's too-good garden
   The great big especially beautiful Easter egg
   No friends
   That dreadful day
   That terrible Halloween night
   That's exactly the way it wasn't
   There's nothing to do!
   We can't sleep
   What's under my bed?
   Will you please feed our cat?
   Worse than Willy!
Stiles, Martha Bennett. *Island magic*
Stock, Catherine. *Thanksgiving treat*
Stolz, Mary. *Storm in the night*
Tavares, Matt. *Oliver's game*
Titherington, Jeanne. *Where are you going, Emma?*
Tompert, Ann. *Grandfather Tang's story*
Uegaki, Chieri. *Hana Hashimoto, sixth violin*
Usher, Sam. *Rain*
   Snow
Van Leeuwen, Jean. *The tickle stories*
Vigna, Judith. *My two uncles*
Wallace, Ian. *Chin Chiang and the dragon's dance*
Wallace, Nancy Elizabeth. *Seeds! seeds! seeds!*
   Snow
Walters, Eric. *The matatu*
Wells, Rosemary. *The language of doves*
Williams, Laura E. *The best winds*
Winch, John. *Keeping up with Grandma*
Wolff, Ashley. *I call my grandpa Papa*
Wood, Douglas. *Grandad's prayers of the earth*
   When a grandpa says "I love you"
Woodruff, Elvira. *Can you guess where we're going?*
Yeh, Kat. *The magic brush*
Zalben, Jane Breskin. *Pearl's marigolds for grandpa*
Zia, F. *Hot, hot roti for Dada-ji*
Ziefert, Harriet. *Lunchtime for a purple snake*
   No kiss for Grandpa!
   Robin, where are you?
   That's what grandpas are for
Zolotow, Charlotte. *My grandson Lew*

Family life – grandmothers

Abeele, Veronique van den. *Still my Grandma*
Aber, Linda Williams. *Carrie measures up!*
Ackerman, Karen. *By the dawn's early light*
Addasi, Maha. *Time to pray*
Ahlberg, Allan. *The snail house*
Alcott, Louisa May. *An old-fashioned Thanksgiving*
Alda, Arlene. *Hurry Granny Annie*
Altman, Linda Jacobs. *Singing with Momma Lou*
Anderson, Laurie Halse. *Turkey pox*
Anderson, Peggy Perry. *Joe on the go*
Balian, Lorna. *Humbug rabbit*
Barnwell, Ysaye M. *No mirrors in my Nana's house*
Baryshnikov, Mikhail. *Because . . .*
Bastianich, Lidia. *Nonna tell me a story*
   Nonna's birthday surprise
Bauer, Marion Dane. *Grandmother's song*
Beardshaw, Rosalind. *Grandma's beach*

Vigil-Piñón, Evangelina. *Marina's muumuu / El muumuu de Marina*
Vulliamy, Clara. *Small*
Waboose, Jan Bourdeau. *Firedancers*
Waldman, Neil. *They came from the Bronx*
Watts, Jeri. *A piece of home*
Weiss, Ellen. *The taming of Lola*
Weitzman, Jacqueline Preiss. *You can't take a balloon into the Metropolitan Museum*
You can't take a balloon into the National Gallery
Wells, Rosemary. *Bunny cakes*
Bunny mail
Bunny money
Bunny party
Max and Ruby's bedtime book
Max and Ruby's treasure hunt
Ruby's beauty shop
Yoko's paper cranes
Whybrow, Ian. *Sammy and the robots*
Wigersma, Tanneke. *Baby brother*
Wilcox, Brian. *Full moon*
Wild, Margaret. *Old Pig*
Our granny
Piglet and Granny
Willard, Nancy. *The mouse, the cat and Grandmother's hat*
Williams, Barbara. *Albert's gift for grandmother*
Williams, Vera B. *Music, music for everyone*
Winch, John. *Keeping up with Grandma*
Wojtowycz, David. *A cuddle for Claude*
Wolff, Ashley. *I call my grandma Nana*
Wood, Audrey. *The full moon at the napping house*
The napping house
The napping house wakes up
Wood, Douglas. *What grandmas can't do*
Woodson, Jacqueline. *Coming on home soon*
Yolen, Jane. *Grandma's hurrying child*
Zagwÿn, Deborah Turney. *The winter gift*
Zelinsky, Paul O. *The wheels on the bus*
Ziefert, Harriet. *Grandma, it's for you!*
My forever dress
That's what grandmas are for
Zolotow, Charlotte. *William's doll*

Family life – grandparents

Ada, Alma Flor. *I love Saturdays y domingos*
Ajmera, Maya, et al. *Our grandparents*
Ancona, George. *Mis abuelos / My grandparents*
Auld, Mary. *My grandparents*
Barrett, Judi. *Pickles to Pittsburgh*
Bateman, Teresa. *April foolishness*
Bergman, Tamar. *Where is?*
Bowen, Anne. *When you visit Grandma and Grandpa*
Bryne, Gayle. *Sometimes it's grandmas and grandpas, not mommies and daddies*
Bunge, Daniela. *The scarves*
Bunting, Eve. *The days of summer*
Carlson, Nancy. *Hooray for Grandparent's Day!*
Cazet, Denys. *The octopus*
Child, Lydia Maria. *Over the river and through the wood*
Over the river and through the wood: the New England boy's song about Thanksgiving Day
Crum, Shutta. *All on a sleepy night*
My mountain song
Cusimano, Maryann K. *You are my wish*
Dewdney, Anna. *Llama Llama Gram and Grandpa*
Frazee, Marla. *A couple of boys have the best week ever*

Galindo, Mary Sue. *Icy watermelon / Sandía fría*
Grambling, Lois G. *Grandma tells a story*
Haas, Jessie. *Hurry!*
Hazen, Barbara Shook. *Katie's wish*
Hill, Eric. *Spot visits his grandparents*
Hittleman, Carol G. *A grand celebration*
Hoberman, Mary Ann. *I'm going to Grandma's*
Holabird, Katharine. *Angelina, star of the show*
Horácek, Petr. *My elephant*
Horrocks, Anita. *Silas' seven grandparents*
Hunter, Dette. *38 ways to entertain your grandparents*
Hutchins, Hazel. *One dark night*
Jennings, Sharon. *Franklin's Thanksgiving*
Juster, Norton. *The hello, goodbye window*
Sourpuss and sweetie pie
Kinsey-Warnock, Natalie. *Nora's ark*
Kooser, Ted. *The bell in the bridge*
Krishnaswami, Uma. *Remembering Grandpa*
Kropf, Latifa Berry. *It's Hanukkah time!*
Lloyd-Jones, Sally. *The ultimate guide to grandmas and grandpas!*
Long, Kathy. *Christopher sat straight up in bed*
Long, Melinda. *When Papa snores*
Look, Lenore. *Polka Dot Penguin Pottery*
Mollel, Tololwa M. *Kele's secret*
Oppenheim, Shulamith Levey. *Fireflies for Nathan*
Orloff, Karen Kaufman. *I wanna go home*
Palacios, Argentina. *A Christmas surprise for Chabelita*
Parish, Herman. *Amelia Bedelia's first apple pie*
Polacco, Patricia. *My rotten redheaded older brother*
The trees of the dancing goats
Rice, Eve. *At Grammy's house*
Rosen, Michael. *A Thanksgiving wish*
Rotner, Shelley. *Lots of grandparents*
Rylant, Cynthia. *Christmas in the country*
Schwartz, Joanne. *Our corner grocery store*
Shapiro, Jody Fickes. *Up, up, up! It's apple-picking time*
Shulimson, Sarene. *Lights out Shabbat*
Skolsky, Mindy Warshaw. *Hannah and the whistling tea kettle*
Stevenson, James. *Higher on the door*
July
Stojic, Manya. *Wet pebbles under our feet*
Thomson, Pat. *The squeaky, creaky bed*
Tsubakiyama, Margaret. *Mei-Mei loves the morning*
Tunnell, Michael O. *Mailing May*
Uslander, Arlene. *That's what grandparents are for*
Van Leeuwen, Jean. *Touch the sky summer*
Woodson, Jacqueline. *Sweet, sweet memory*
Wyeth, Sharon Dennis. *Always my dad*
Yolen, Jane. *Off we go!*
Ziefert, Harriet. *Grandma's wedding album*

Family life – great-grandparents

dePaola, Tomie. *Nana Upstairs and Nana Downstairs*
Fleischman, Paul. *The matchbox diary*
Judd, Naomi. *Naomi Judd's guardian angels*
MacLachlan, Patricia. *Three names*
Nelson, Vaunda Micheaux. *Don't call me Grandma*
Rochelle, Belinda. *Jewels*
Smith, Lane. *Grandpa Green*
Taulbert, Clifton L. *Little Cliff's first day of school*

Family life – mothers

Ackerman, Karen. *By the dawn's early light*
Aigner-Clark, Julie. *You are the best medicine*
Alborough, Jez. *Hug*
    It's the bear
Alda, Arlene. *Morning glory Monday*
Alexander, Sue. *One more time, Mama*
Anastas, Margaret. *Mommy's best kisses*
Anderson, Laurie Halse. *No time for Mother's Day*
Andreae, Giles. *I love my mommy*
    There's a house inside my mommy
Appelt, Kathi. *Oh my baby, little one*
    When Otis courted Mama
Armand, Glenda. *Love twelve miles long*
Ashman, Linda. *All we know*
    Mama's day
Aston, Dianna Hutts. *Mama Outside, Mama Inside*
Auld, Mary. *My mom*
Averbeck, Jim. *Oh no, Little Dragon!*
Bagley, Jessixa. *Boats for Papa*
Baker, Liza. *I love you because you're you*
Balian, Lorna. *Mother's Mother's Day*
Banks, Kate. *The bear in the book*
    Close your eyes
    Mama's coming home
    Pup and bear
Bardhan-Quallen, Sudipta. *Chicks run wild*
Bassède, Francine. *A day with the Bellyflops*
Bauer, Marion Dane. *Grandmother's song*
    A mama for Owen
    My mother is mine
Beaty, Andrea. *Hush, Baby Ghostling*
Beck, Scott. *A mud pie for mother*
Bedford, David. *Little Otter's big journey*
    Touch the sky, my little bear
Berger, Carin. *Good night! Good night!*
Bergman, Tamar. *Where is?*
Bertram, Debbie. *The best place to read*
Best, Cari. *If I could drive, Mama*
Black, Sonia. *Hanging out with Mom*
Blackall, Sophie. *Are you awake?*
Blake, Robert J. *Little devils*
Bogan, Paulette. *Goodnight Lulu*
    Lulu the big little chick
    Momma's magical purse
Bottner, Barbara. *Rosa's room*
Bourgeois, Paulette. *Franklin says "I love you"*
Bourguignon, Laurence. *Heart in the pocket*
Boyd, Lizi. *I love Mommy*
Boynton, Sandra. *Happy birthday, Little Pookie*
    Little Pookie
Bradby, Marie. *Momma, where are you from?*
Bradford, Wade. *Why do I have to make my bed?*
Bradley, Kimberly Brubaker. *Favorite things*
Brami, Elisbeth. *Mommy time*
Brandt, Amy. *Benjamin comes back / Benjamin regresa*
Braun, Sebastien. *I love my mommy*
Breathed, Berkeley. *Mars needs moms!*
Bridges, Margaret Park. *Am I big or little?*
Brill, Calista. *Little Wing learns to fly*
Brisson, Pat. *Sometimes we were brave*
Brown, Jo. *Where's my mommy?*
Brown, Margaret Wise. *The runaway bunny*
Brown, Susan Taylor. *Oliver's must-do list*
Browne, Anthony. *My mom*
Bulion, Leslie. *Fatuma's new cloth*
Bunting, Eve. *Flower garden*

My mom's wedding
Pirate boy
Tweak tweak
Buzzeo, Toni. *Adventure Annie goes to work*
    Stay close to Mama
Cabrera, Jane. *Mommy, carry me please!*
    There was an old woman who lived in a shoe
Cadow, Kenneth M. *Alfie runs away*
Campbell, Ann-Jeanette. *Queenie Farmer had fifteen daughters*
Cannon, Janell. *Stellaluna*
Capucilli, Alyssa Satin. *I will love you*
    Only my mom and me
    What kind of kiss?
Carle, Eric. *Does a kangaroo have a mother, too?*
Carlstrom, Nancy White. *It's your first day of school, Annie Claire*
    Mama, will it snow tonight?
Carrick, Carol. *Valentine*
Chaconas, Dori. *Christmas mouseling*
Chang, Victoria. *Is Mommy?*
Charlip, Remy. *Sleepytime rhyme*
Christelow, Eileen. *Don't wake up Mama!*
Church, Caroline Jayne. *One more hug for Madison*
Clements, Andrew. *Because your mommy loves you*
Cobb, Rebecca. *Missing Mommy*
Cocovini, Abby. *What's inside your tummy, Mommy?*
Cohen, Caron Lee. *Happy to you!*
Colato Laínez, René. *Mamá the alien / Mamá la extraterrestre*
Cole, Joanna. *When you were inside mommy*
Collet, Géraldine. *All by myself!*
Collins, Ross. *Doodleday*
Cora, Cat. *A suitcase surprise for Mommy*
Côté, Geneviève. *With you always, Little Monday*
Cotton, Katie. *The road home*
Cousins, Lucy. *Hooray for fish!*
Cowen-Fletcher, Jane. *Mama zooms*
Crimi, Carolyn. *Where's my mummy?*
Cronin, Doreen. *M.O.M. (Mom Operating Manual)*
Crumpacker, Bunny. *Alexander's pretending day*
Curtis, Jamie Lee. *My mommy hung the moon*
DaCosta, Barbara. *Nighttime Ninja*
Dahl, Michael. *Bear says "thank you"*
Danowski, Sonja. *Little night cat*
Davis, Jerry. *Little Chicken's big day*
De Anda, Diane. *Dancing Miranda / Baila, Miranda, baila*
de Las Casas, Dianne. *Mama's bayou*
dePaola, Tomie. *My mother is so smart*
Dewdney, Anna. *Llama Llama home with Mama*
    Llama Llama mad at Mama
    Llama Llama misses Mama
    Llama, Llama red pajama
Diesen, Deborah. *Bloom*
Diggs, Taye. *Chocolate me!*
Dijs, Carla. *Mommy, what if —?*
Dodd, Emma. *Everything*
    Forever
    Happy
    No matter what
Dominguez, Angela. *Knit together*
Donaldson, Julia. *Where's my mom?*
Dornbusch, Erica. *Finding Kate's shoes*
Dorros, Arthur. *Mama and me*
Dotlich, Rebecca Kai. *Mama loves*
Douglas, Ann. *Before you were born*
Dowson, Nick. *Tigress*
Duble, Kathleen Benner. *Pilot mom*

Duncan, Alice Faye. *Honey baby sugar child*
Dunrea, Olivier. *It's snowing*
Dwyer, Mindy. *Quilt of dreams*
Eaton, Jason Carter. *Great, now we've got barbarians!*
Edwards, Richard. *Copy me, Copycub*
Ehrlich, Amy. *Baby Dragon*
Ehrlich, Fred. *Does a mouse have a mommy?*
Ehrlich, H. M. *Gotcha, Louie!*
Emberley, Ed. *Thanks, Mom!*
Ericsson, Jennifer A. *Home to me, home to you*
Evans, Kristina. *What's special about me, Mama?*
Evans, Lezlie. *Who loves the little lamb?*
Falwell, Cathryn. *P.J. and Puppy*
Fearnley, Jan. *Watch out!*
Feeney, Tatyana. *Little Owl's orange scarf*
Fergus, Maureen. *The day my mom came to kindergarten*
Fitzpatrick, Marie-Louise. *You, me and the big blue sea*
Flack, Marjorie. *Ask Mr. Bear*
Flattinger, Hubert. *Stormy night*
Fleming, Denise. *Sleepy, oh so sleepy*
Ford, Christine. *Ocean's child*
Ford, Miela. *Mom and me*
Fox, Mem. *Harriet, you'll drive me wild*
  Koala Lou
  This and that
Fraggalosch, Audrey. *Grizzly bear family*
  Trails above the tree line
Frasier, Debra. *Out of the ocean*
Freedman, Claire. *One magical morning*
Fruisen, Catherine Myler. *My mother's pearls*
Gal, Susan. *Night lights*
Galindo, Renata. *My new mom and me*
Garden, Nancy. *Molly's family*
Gardner, Sally. *Mama, don't go out tonight*
Genechten, Guido van. *Because you are my friend*
Gershator, Phillis. *This is the day!*
  Time for a hug
Gerstein, Mordicai. *Leaving the nest*
Glenn, Sharlee. *Just what Mama needs*
Gliori, Debi. *Little Owl's egg*
  Stormy weather
Godard, Alex. *Mama, across the sea*
Goode, Diane. *Mama's perfect present*
  The most perfect spot
Goodings, Lennie. *When you grow up*
Gorbachev, Valeri. *Nicky and the fantastic birthday gift*
Gore, Leonid. *Mommy, where are you?*
Grambling, Lois G. *My mom is a firefighter*
Gray, Kes. *Eat your peas*
  006 and a half
Greene, Rhonda Gowler. *Mommy is a soft, warm kiss*
Greenstein, Elaine. *As big as you*
Guion, Melissa. *Baby penguins love their Mama*
Hague, Kathleen. *Good night, fairies*
Hall, Pamela. *Miss you like crazy*
Hample, Stoo. *I will kiss you (lots and lots and lots!)*
Harper, Jessica. *Lizzy's do's and don'ts*
  Lizzy's ups and downs
Harris, Robie H. *The day Leo said I hate you!*
Heo, Yumi. *One afternoon*
Hesse, Karen. *Come on, rain*
Hest, Amy. *Are you sure, Mother Bear?*
  Kiss good night
  When you meet a bear on Broadway
  You can do it, Sam
Ho, Minfong. *Hush!*

Hoberman, Mary Ann. *The seven silly eaters*
Horton, Joan. *Working mummies*
Howie, Betsy. *The Block Mess Monster*
Hubbell, Patricia. *Sea, sand, me!*
  Sidewalk trip
Huget, Jennifer LaRue. *Thanks a lot, Emily Post!*
Hughes, Langston. *Lullaby (for a Black mother)*
Hunter, Sally. *Humphrey's corner*
Hutchins, Pat. *Where, oh where, is Rosie's chick?*
Iwai, Melissa. *Soup day*
Jadoul, Émile. *Good night, Chickie*
Janowitz, Tama. *Hear that?*
Jenkins, Emily. *Love you when you whine*
Jennings, Sharon. *Bearcub and Mama*
Jewel. *That's what I'd do*
Johnson, Angela. *Tell me a story, Mama*
Johnson, Marion. *Caillou, new shoes*
Johnson, Paul Brett. *The goose who went off in a huff*
Johnston, Tony. *My best friend Bear*
Jonas, Ann. *Two bear cubs*
Jonell, Lynne. *Bravemole*
  I need a snake
  Mom pie
  When Mommy was mad
Joosse, Barbara. *I love you the purplest*
  Mama, do you love me?
Kaplanoglou, Mania. *Mama Bear, Little Bear*
Kasza, Keiko. *A mother for Choco*
Katz, Karen. *Mommy hugs*
  Where is baby's mommy?
Kavanagh, Peter. *I love my mama*
Keller, Holly. *Miranda's beach day*
Kempter, Christa. *When Mama can't sleep*
Kern, Noris. *I love you with all my heart*
Ketteman, Helen. *If Beaver had a fever*
Killion, Bette. *Just think!*
Kindermans, Martine. *You and me*
Kirk, David. *Little Miss Spider*
Klise, Kate. *Little Rabbit and the Meanest Mother on Earth*
Knapman, Timothy. *Soon*
  Time now to dream
Koller, Jackie French. *No such thing*
Kono, Erin Eitter. *Hula lullaby*
Krauss, Ruth. *You're just what I need*
Kroll, Steven. *That makes me mad*
Krosoczka, Jarrett J. *Bubble bath pirates*
  Giddy up, Cowgirl
  Good night, Monkey Boy
Kuiper, Nannie. *Bailey the bear cub*
Kuskin, Karla. *A boy had a mother who bought him a hat*
LaChanze. *Little diva*
Lamb, Albert. *Tell me the day backwards*
Landau, Orna. *Leopardpox!*
Lasky, Kathryn. *Mommy's hands*
Lawler, Janet. *A mother's song*
Lee, Tae-Jun. *Waiting for Mama*
Leuck, Laura. *My monster mama loves me so*
Lewin, Hugh. *Jafta's mother*
Lewis, Anne Margaret. *Puddle jumpers*
Lewis, Kim. *Seymour and Henry*
Lewis, Paeony. *I'll always love you*
Lindgren, Barbro. *Benny's had enough*
Lindsay, Jeanne Warren. *Do I have a daddy?*
Lipan, Sabine. *Mom, there's a bear at the door*
Lish, Ted. *The three little puppies and the big bad flea*
Little Bear's Valentine
Lobel, Anita. *Taking care of Mama Rabbit*

Lobel, Gillian. *Little Honey Bear and the smiley moon*
Lomp, Stephan. *Mamasaurus*
London, Jonathan. *Count the ways, Little Brown Bear*
 Here comes Doctor Hippo
 What do you love?
Lyon, George Ella. *Mama is a miner*
McAllister, Angela. *My mom has x-ray vision*
 Night-night, little one
 Trust me, Mom!
McBratney, Sam. *I'll always be your friend*
McCourt, Lisa. *Happy Halloween, Stinky Face*
 I love you, Stinky Face
 I miss you, Stinky Face
 It's time for school, Stinky Face
 Merry Christmas, Stinky Face
McElroy, Lisa Tucker. *Love, Lizzie*
McGhee, Alison. *Someday*
McGinty, Alice B. *Eliza's kindergarten surprise*
Macken, JoAnn Early. *Waiting out the storm*
MacLachlan, Patricia. *Before you came*
 Lala salama
McMullan, Kate. *If you were my bunny*
 Mama's kisses
McNiff, Dawn. *Mommy's little monster*
McPhail, David. *I promise*
Madrigal, Antonio Hernandez. *Erandi's braids*
Mahy, Margaret. *Boom Baby boom, boom*
Makhijani, Pooja. *Mama's saris*
Manning, Mick. *Supermom*
Marino, Gianna. *Meet me at the moon*
Martin, David. *Monkey business*
Marzollo, Jean. *Mama, Mama*
Matthies, Janna. *The goodbye cancer garden*
Mayer, Mercer. *Just for you*
Melmed, Laura Krauss. *I love you as much . . .*
Micklos, John. *Mommy poems*
Miller, William. *A house by the river*
Milord, Susan. *If I could*
Minarik, Else Holmelund. *Am I beautiful?*
Mitchard, Jacquelyn. *Baby bat's lullaby*
Miyakoshi, Akiko. *The way home in the night*
Modarressi, Mitra. *Taking care of Mama*
Monnier, Miriam. *Just right*
Moore, Eva. *Lucky ducklings*
Moore-Mallinos, Jennifer. *Mom has cancer!*
Mora, Pat. *Love to mamá*
Morgan-Vanroyen, Mary. *Sleep tight, little mouse*
Morris, Ann. *The mommy book*
Morrow, Tara Jaye. *Panda goes to school*
Moss, Miriam. *The snow bear*
Moundlic, Charlotte. *The scar*
Mraz, David. *Little Goose*
Müller, Birte. *Finn cooks*
Munsch, Robert N. *Love you forever*
Murphy, Jill. *Meltdown!*
Murphy, Mary. *Please be quiet!*
Murphy, Patricia J. *Mama, look!*
Murphy, Stuart J. *Rabbit's pajama party*
Murphy, Yannick. *Baby Polar*
Murray, Alison. *Little Mouse*
Napoli, Donna Jo. *Hands and hearts*
Neitzel, Shirley. *We're making breakfast for mother*
Newman, Lesléa. *Donovan's big day*
 Heather has two mommies
 Just like Mama
 Mommy, Mama, and Me
Nicholls, Judith. *Billywise*
Noble, Sheilagh. *More*

Norac, Carl. *My mommy is magic*
North, Sherry. *Because you are my baby*
Numeroff, Laura Joffe. *The hope tree*
 Nighty-night, Cooper
Oelschlager, Vanita. *A tale of two mommies*
Ohi, Ruth. *Pants off first*
O'Keefe, Susan Heyboer. *Love me, love you*
Palacios, Argentina. *A Christmas surprise for Chabelita*
Palatini, Margie. *Zak's lunch*
Paradis, Susan. *My mommy*
Parker, Marjorie Blain. *Mama's little duckling*
 Your kind of mommy
Parr, Todd. *The mommy book*
Patrick, Jean L. S. *If I had a snowplow*
Peacock, Carol Antoinette. *Mommy far, Mommy near*
Peet, Mal. *Cloud tea monkeys*
Peterson, Jeanne Whitehouse. *My mama sings*
Pham, LeUyen. *All the things I love about you*
Pignataro, Anna. *Our love grows*
Pinkwater, Daniel. *Young Larry*
Platt, Cynthia. *A little bit of love*
Poh, Jennifer. *Herbie's big adventure*
Polacco, Patricia. *Betty Doll*
 In our mothers' house
 Mommies say shhh!
Portis, Antoinette. *Wait*
Posthuma, Sieb. *Benny*
Price, Hope Lynne. *These hands*
Pulver, Robin. *Nobody's mother is in second grade*
Radcliffe, Theresa. *Bashi, elephant baby*
Raff, Courtney Granet. *Giant of the sea*
Rahaman, Vashanti. *Read for me, Mama*
Ransom, Candice F. *The Christmas dolls*
Rao, Sandhya. *My mother's sari*
Reagan, Jean. *How to raise a mom*
Reichert, Amy. *Take your mama to work today*
Reiser, Lynn. *Any kind of dog*
Rex, Michael. *Runaway mummy*
Reyher, Rebecca. *My mother is the most beautiful woman in the world*
Reynolds, Marilynn. *The magnificent piano recital*
Richards, Dan. *Can one balloon make an elephant fly?*
Richmond, Marianne. *I'm not tired yet!*
 Oh, the things my mom will do . . .
Rim, Sujean. *Birdie's big-girl hair*
Rinker, Sherri Duskey. *Silly wonderful you*
Ritchie, Alison. *Me and my mom!*
Robberecht, Thierry. *Back into Mommy's tummy*
Robbins, Maria Polushkin. *Mother, Mother, I want another*
Robinson, Sue. *I want to play*
Rock, Brian. *With all my heart*
Rockliff, Mara. *Me and Momma and Big John*
Rockwell, Anne. *Willy can count*
Roddie, Shen. *Not now, Mrs. Wolf*
Rose, Deborah Lee. *All the seasons of the year*
 Someone's sleepy
Rosenberg, Liz. *The carousel*
Rosenthal, Amy Krouse. *Bedtime for Mommy*
Ross, Michael Elsohn. *Mama's milk*
Roth, Carol. *Where's my mommy?*
 Will you still love me?
Rotner, Shelley. *Lots of moms*
Rubel, Nicole. *No more vegetables!*
Rudolph, Shaina. *All my stripes*
Rueda, Claudia. *My little polar bear*

Surprise!
Zolotow, Charlotte. *I like to be little*
Mr. Rabbit and the lovely present
Say it!
This quiet lady

Family life – new sibling

Alexander, Martha G. *Nobody asked me if I wanted a baby sister*
    When the new baby comes, I'm moving out
Anholt, Laurence. *Sophie and the new baby*
Appelt, Kathi. *Brand-new baby blues*
Apperley, Dawn. *Don't wake the baby*
Ashman, Linda. *When I was king*
Banks, Kate. *This baby*
Beaton, Kate. *King Baby*
Boelts, Maribeth. *You're a brother, Little Bunny!*
Borden, Louise. *Big brothers don't take naps*
Bradman, Tony. *The perfect baby*
Broach, Elise. *What the no-good baby is good for*
Brown, Marc. *Arthur's baby*
    Monkey: not ready for the baby
Bunting, Eve. *Baby can*
    Will it be a baby brother?
Burningham, John. *There's going to be a baby*
Busch, Miriam. *Raisin, the littlest cow*
Chaud, Benjamin. *The bear's surprise*
Cocca-Leffler, Maryann. *Theo's mood*
Cole, Joanna. *I'm a big sister*
    The new baby at your house
Conway, David. *The most important gift of all*
Cote, Nancy. *It's all about me!*
Davies, Gill. *Wilbur waited*
Dempsey, Sheena. *Bye-bye baby brother!*
dePaola, Tomie. *The baby sister*
Derby, Sally. *No mush today*
Dewan, Ted. *Crispin and the 3 little piglets*
Doerrfeld, Cori. *Penny loves pink*
Dunrea, Olivier. *Ollie*
Dyer, Jane. *Little Brown Bear and the bundle of joy*
Elkin, Mark. *Samuel's baby*
Enderle, Judith Ross. *Smile, Principessa!*
Fearnley, Jan. *A special something*
Feeney, Tatyana. *Little Frog's tadpole trouble*
Frazee, Marla. *The bossier baby*
Fucile, Tony. *Poor Louie*
Gliori, Debi. *Little Owl's egg*
    Where did that baby come from?
Gutman, Anne. *Lisa's baby sister*
Hall, Algy Craig. *Fine as we are*
Hanson, Mary Elizabeth. *The difference between babies and cookies*
Harper, Anita. *It's not fair!*
Harris, Robie H. *Hi, new baby*
    Mail Harry to the moon!
    What's in there?
Henry, Steve. *Nobody asked me!*
Heos, Bridget. *Queen Dog*
Hill, Susanna Leonard. *Not yet, Rose*
Holabird, Katharine. *Angelina's baby sister*
Horse, Harry. *Little Rabbit's new baby*
Huget, Jennifer LaRue. *The beginner's guide to running away from home*
Jacobs, Julie. *My heart is a magic house*
Jadoul, Émile. *No room for baby!*
Kallok, Emma. *Gem*
Keane, Claire. *Little big girl*
Keats, Ezra Jack. *Peter's chair*

Keller, Holly. *Geraldine's baby brother*
Krensky, Stephen. *We just had a baby*
Kushner, Donn. *Peter's pixie*
Layne, Steven L. *Love the baby*
Lloyd-Jones, Sally. *His Royal Highness, King Baby*
Lohans, Alison. *Waiting for the sun*
McCormick, Wendy. *The night you were born*
MacDonald, Ross. *Bad baby*
Mackall, Dandi Daley. *There's a baby in there!*
McQuinn, Anna. *Lola reads to Leo*
Mendes, Valerie. *Look at me, Grandma!*
Morris, Richard T. *Bye-bye, baby!*
Munsch, Robert N. *Alligator baby*
Murkoff, Heidi Eisenberg. *What to expect when the new baby comes home*
My new baby
Newman, Marjorie. *Just like me*
Nichols, Lori. *Maple*
Ormerod, Jan. *The baby swap*
Paschkis, Julie. *Mooshka*
Patz, Nancy. *Babies can't eat kimchee!*
Penfold, Alexandra. *We are brothers, we are friends*
Perkins, Maripat. *Rodeo Red*
Rheingrover, Jean Sasso. *Veronica's first year*
Robberecht, Thierry. *Back into Mommy's tummy*
Robbins, Beth. *Tom, Ally, and the new baby*
Rock, Lois. *Now we have a baby*
Rockwell, Lizzy. *Hello baby!*
Rodman, Mary Ann. *Surprise soup*
Rogers, Fred. *The new baby*
Rosenberg, Maxine B. *Mommy's in the hospital having a baby*
Rosenberry, Vera. *Vera's baby sister*
Rosenthal, Amy Krouse. *Little Miss, big sis*
Roth, Carol. *Will you still love me?*
Rusch, Elizabeth. *Ready, set . . . baby!*
Russo, Marisabina. *Hannah's baby sister*
Schaefer, Lola M. *One special day*
Schindel, John. *Frog face, my little sister and me*
Sears, William, M.D., et al.. *What baby needs*
Sheldon, Annette. *Big sister now*
Shields, Carol Diggory. *I wish my brother was a dog*
Shields, Gillian. *When the world was waiting for you*
Shipton, Jonathan. *Baby baby blah blah blah!*
Simmons, Jane. *Daisy and the egg*
Springstubb, Tricia. *Phoebe and Digger*
Stevenson, James. *Worse than Willy!*
Stinson, Kathy. *A pocket can have a treasure in it*
Stuve-Bodeen, Stephanie. *Mama Elizabeti*
Sullivan, Sarah. *Once upon a baby brother*
Swanson, Matthew. *Babies ruin everything*
Sykes, Julie. *Little Tiger's big surprise*
Thomas, Joyce Carol. *You are my perfect baby*
Thomas, Shelley Moore. *A baby's coming to your house*
Titherington, Jeanne. *A place for Ben*
Van Leeuwen, Jean. *Benny and beautiful baby Delilah*
Vulliamy, Clara. *Ellen and Penguin and the new baby*
Waddell, Martin. *Rosie's babies*
    When the teddy bears came
Wahl, Jan. *Mabel ran away with the toys*
Walters, Catherine. *Are you there, Baby Bear?*
Weeks, Sarah. *Sophie Peterman tells the truth!*
Wells, Rosemary. *Use your words, Sophie!*
Weninger, Brigitte. *Will you mind the baby, Davy?*
Whybrow, Ian. *A baby for Grace*
Wigersma, Tanneke. *Baby brother*
Wild, Margaret. *Rosie and Tortoise*
Wilson, Karma. *What's in the egg, Little Pip?*

Woodson, Jacqueline. *Pecan pie baby*
You and me
Young, Amy. *Don't eat the baby!*
Zagwÿn, Deborah Turney. *Turtle spring*
Zeltser, David. *Ninja baby*
Ziefert, Harriet. *Talk, baby!*
   Waiting for baby

Family life – only child

Best, Cari. *What's so bad about being an only child?*

Family life – parents

Alko, Selina. *Daddy Christmas and Hanukkah Mama*
Anastas, Margaret. *A hug for you*
Ashman, Linda. *What could be better than this*
Baker, Roberta. *No ordinary Olive*
Ballard, Robin. *My day, your day*
Bently, Peter. *Meet the parents*
Burg, Sarah Emmanuelle. *Do you still love me?*
Carlstrom, Nancy White. *Before you were born*
Cole, Joanna. *When Mommy and Daddy go to work*
Cusimano, Maryann K. *You are my I love you*
DiTerlizzi, Angela. *Baby love*
Elya, Susan Middleton. *No more, por favor*
Farrington, Susan. *What I love about you*
Fearnley, Jan. *Just like you*
Feiffer, Kate. *My mom is trying to ruin my life*
Fleming, Meg. *I heart you*
Fraser, Mary Ann. *How animal babies stay safe*
Gay, Michel. *Zee is not scared*
Geras, Adèle. *My wishes for you*
Gerber, Carole. *Tuck-in time*
Godwin, Laura. *What the baby hears*
Harper, Jamie. *Don't grown-ups ever have fun?*
Harper, Jo. *I could eat you up!*
Hest, Amy. *Mabel dancing*
Houran, Lori Haskins. *I will keep you safe and sound*
Hunter, Jana Novotny. *Little ones do*
Iijima, Geneva Cobb. *The way we do it in Japan*
Johnston, Tony. *Go track a yak*
Jonovitz, Marilyn. *Maybe, my baby*
Jordan, Deloris. *Baby blessings*
Kerley, Barbara. *You and me together*
Kirk, Daniel. *Snow family*
Kurtz, Jane. *Rain romp*
L'Arronge, Lilli. *Me tall, you small*
Larsen, Mylisa. *How to put your parents to bed*
Lerman, Josh. *How to raise Mom and Dad*
Lobel, Gillian. *Does anybody love me?*
London, Jonathan. *Froggy eats out*
Lund, Deb. *Tell me my story, Mama*
McGee, Marni. *Wake up, me!*
Mack, Todd. *Princess Penelope*
Martin, Emily Winfield. *The wonderful things you will be*
Masurel, Claire. *Two homes*
Milgrim, David. *Best baby ever*
Mitchard, Jacquelyn. *Ready, set, school!*
Modarressi, Mitra. *Stay awake, Sally*
Morrow, Tara Jaye. *Mommy loves her baby; Daddy loves his baby*
Murphy, Mary. *I like it when . . .*
Numeroff, Laura Joffe. *Would I trade my parents?*
Okimoto, Jean Davies. *The White Swan express*
O'Mara, Carmel. *Good morning*
   Good night
Parks, Carmen. *Farmers market*

Pedersen, Marika. *Mommy works, Daddy works*
Pow, Tom. *Who is the world for?*
Proimos, James. *Todd's TV*
Ramos, Jorge. *I'm just like my mom / Me parezco tanto a mi mamá; I'm just like my dad / Me parezco tanto a mi papá*
Ransom, Jeanie Franz. *I don't want to talk about it*
   What do parents do? (. . . When you're not home)
Rau, Dana Meachen. *In the yard*
Roberts, Bethany. *Rosie to the rescue*
Robledo, Honorio. *Nico visits the moon*
Rockwell, Anne. *Two blue jays*
Root, Phyllis. *Oliver finds his way*
Rosenberg, Liz. *Nobody*
   We wanted you
Ross, Michael Elsohn. *Play with me*
Schmid, Paul. *Petunia goes wild*
Spelman, Cornelia Maude. *When I miss you*
Steig, William. *Toby, who are you?*
Swinburne, Stephen R. *Safe, warm, and snug*
Thomas, Frances. *One day, Daddy*
Tobias, Tobi. *Wishes for you*
Wadham, Tim. *The queen of France*
Walsh, Melanie. *Living with Mom and living with Dad*
Weeks, Sarah. *My somebody special*
   Without you
Weigelt, Udo. *The Easter Bunny's baby*
Wells, Rosemary. *Love waves*
Wild, Margaret. *Puffling*
Willems, Mo. *Welcome: a Mo Willems guide for new arrivals*

Family life – same-sex parents

Newman, Lesléa. *Daddy, Papa, and me*
   Heather has two mommies
   Mommy, Mama, and Me
Polacco, Patricia. *In our mothers' house*
Richardson, Justin. *And Tango makes three*
Rotner, Shelley. *Families*
Schiffer, Miriam B. *Stella brings the family*
Willhoite, Michael. *Daddy's roommate*
Williams, Vera B. *Home at last*

Family life – single-parent families

Beaty, Daniel. *Knock knock*
Edwards, Michelle. *Papa's latkes*
Egan, Kate. *Kate and Nate are running late!*
Moore, Genevieve. *Catherine's story*
Polacco, Patricia. *Something about Hensley's*
Rotner, Shelley. *Families*
Schotter, Roni. *Mama, I'll give you the world*
Thomas, Eliza. *The red blanket*
Woodson, Jacqueline. *Pecan pie baby*
Zolotow, Charlotte. *A father like that*

Family life – sisters see also Family life; Family life – brothers & sisters; Sibling rivalry

Alcott, Louisa May. *Little women*
Alexander, Claire. *Small Florence*
Alexander, Martha G. *Nobody asked me if I wanted a baby sister*
Alter, Anna. *Estelle and Lucy*
Amato, Mary. *The chicken of the family*
Arnold, Marsha Diane. *The bravest of us all*
Auld, Mary. *My sister*

Bang, Molly. *When Sophie gets angry — really, really angry . . .*
Barasch, Lynne. *The reluctant flower girl*
Best, Cari. *Ava and the real Lucille*
Blumenthal, Deborah. *Don't let the peas touch!*
Bonwill, Ann. *Naughty toes*
Brown, Marc. *Arthur meets the president*
    D. W., go to your room!
Bunting, Eve. *The days of summer*
Coh, Smiljana. *The seven princesses*
Cohen, Jeff. *Eva and Sadie and the best classroom ever!*
    Eva and Sadie and the worst haircut ever!
Cole, Joanna. *I'm a big sister*, ill. by Maxie Chambliss
    I'm a big sister, ill. by Rosalinda Kightley
Cox, Judy. *Carmen learns English*
Demas, Corinne. *The magic apple*
dePaola, Tomie. *The baby sister*
Ericsson, Jennifer A. *She did it!*
Figley, Marty Rhodes. *The schoolchildren's blizzard*
Fraser, Mary Ann. *Mermaid sister*
Garoche, Camille. *The snow rabbit*
George, Kristine O'Connell. *Emma dilemma*
Graham, Bob. *April and Esme, tooth fairies*
Gritton, Steve. *The trouble with sisters and robots*
Grossman, Bill. *My little sister hugged an ape*
Gutman, Anne. *Lisa's baby sister*
Hanson, Mary Elizabeth. *The difference between babies and cookies*
Hardy, Sarah Frances. *Puzzled by pink*
Hayes, Joe. *Don't say a word, Mamá/No digas nada, Mamá*
Heine, Theresa. *Chandra's magic light*
Henkes, Kevin. *Sheila Rae, the brave*
    Sheila Rae's peppermint stick
Hoban, Russell. *Best friends for Frances*
Holabird, Katharine. *Angelina's baby sister*
Jackson, Chris. *The Gaggle sisters river tour*
Jenkins, Emily. *Daffodil*
    Daffodil, crocodile
Johnson, Angela. *One of three*
    A sweet smell of roses
    The wedding
Kassirer, Sue. *What's next, Nina?*
Keefer, Janice Kulyk. *Anna's goat*
Khan, Rukhsana. *Big red lollipop*
Kirsch, Vincent X. *Natalie and Naughtily*
Krensky, Stephen. *Sisters of Scituate Light*
Kroll, Virginia L. *Faraway drums*
Lears, Laurie. *Becky the brave*
McCarthy, Jenna. *Lola knows a lot*
    Poppy Louise is not afraid of anything
McCarthy, Meghan. *The adventures of Patty and the big red bus*
McCormack, Caren McNelly. *The fiesta dress*
McElmurry, Jill. *Mess pets*
McGhee, Alison. *The sweetest witch around*
Maclear, Kyo. *Virginia Wolf*
McPhail, David. *Crash! the cat*
Mantchev, Lisa. *Sister day!*
Martin, Rafe. *The rough-face girl*
Membrino, Anna. *I want to be a ballerina*
Montanari, Eva. *Tiff, Taff, and Lulu*
Moore, Liz. *Zizi and Tish*
Murguia, Bethanie Deeney. *Zoe's jungle*
    Zoe's room (no sisters allowed)
Nichols, Lori. *Maple and Willow apart*
    Maple and Willow together

Maple and Willow's Christmas tree
Norling, Beth. *Sister night and sister day*
Numeroff, Laura Joffe. *The Chicken sisters*
O'Connor, Jane. *Fancy Nancy: fanciest doll in the universe*
    Fancy Nancy and the fabulous fashion boutique
Orr, Wendy. *The princess and her panther*
Peterson, Jeanne Whitehouse. *Don't forget Winona*
Player, Micah. *Chloe, instead*
Plourde, Lynn. *Spring's sprung*
Potter, Giselle. *Tell me what to dream about*
Pryor, Bonnie. *Amanda and April*
    Merry Christmas, Amanda and April
Rheingrover, Jean Sasso. *Veronica's first year*
Rosenberg, Liz. *The carousel*
Rosenthal, Amy Krouse. *Little Miss, big sis*
Rothenberg, Joan Keller. *Matzah ball soup*
Samuels, Barbara. *Aloha, Dolores*
    Duncan and Dolores
    What's so great about Cindy Snappleby?
San Souci, Robert D. *Sootface*
Schindel, John. *Frog face, my little sister and me*
Schmid, Paul. *Peanut and Fifi have a ball*
Schwartz, Amy. *Dee Dee and me*
    Polka dots for Poppy
Schwartz, Roslyn. *The mole sisters and the cool breeze*
    The mole sisters and the fairy ring
    The mole sisters and the piece of moss
    The mole sisters and the question
    The mole sisters and the rainy day
Spohn, Kate. *By word of mouse*
Stewig, John Warren. *Mother Holly*
Stroud, Bettye. *Down home at Miss Dessa's*
Tarbescu, Edith. *Annushka's voyage*
Tuck, Justin. *Home-field advantage*
Tucker, Kathy. *The seven Chinese sisters*
Tupper Ling, Nancy. *My sister, Alicia May*
Viorst, Judith. *Super-completely and totally the messiest*
Waboose, Jan Bourdeau. *SkySisters*
Wells, Rosemary. *Use your words, Sophie!*
Whybrow, Ian. *A baby for Grace*
Wilder, Laura Ingalls. *Going to town*
Wilhelm, Hans. *More bunny trouble*
Wishinsky, Frieda. *You're mean, Lily Jean!*
Yep, Laurence. *Auntie Tiger*
    Dragon prince
Yezerski, Thomas. *Queen of the world*
Yum, Hyewon. *The twins' blanket*
    The twins' little sister
Zapf, Marlena. *Underpants dance*
Zehler, Antonia. *Two fine ladies*
    Two fine ladies have a tiff

Family life – sons

Boelts, Maribeth. *Looking for Sleepy*
Boyd, Lizi. *I love Daddy*
    I love Mommy
Braun, Sebastien. *I love my daddy*
Collins, Billy. *Daddy's little boy*
Compos, Tito. *Muffler man / El hombre mofle*
Creech, Sharon. *Fishing in the air*
Dorros, Arthur. *Papa and me*
Granowsky, Alvin. *At the park*
Jennings, Sharon. *Bearcub and Mama*
Jonovitz, Marilyn. *Good morning, Little Fox*
Krosoczka, Jarrett J. *Good night, Monkey Boy*
Lewin, Ted. *Big Jimmy's Kum Kau Chinese take out*
London, Jonathan. *Loon Lake*

Rusackas, Francesca. *Daddy all day long*
Schlessinger, Laura. *Dr. Laura Schlessinger's Growing up is hard*
Why do you love me?
Smith, Will. *Just the two of us*
Spinelli, Jerry. *My daddy and me*
Sullivan, Paula. *Todd's box*
Tarpley, Natasha Anastasia. *Bippity Bop barbershop*
Thomas, Joyce Carol. *Joy*
Weatherford, Carole Boston. *In your hands*

Family life – stepchildren *see* Divorce; Family life – stepfamilies

Family life – stepfamilies

Appelt, Kathi. *When Otis courted Mama*
Bell, Anthea. *Vasilisa the beautiful*
Bennett, Kelly. *Dad and Pop*
Bullard, Lisa. *Trick-or-treat on Milton Street*
Bunting, Eve. *The memory string*
Carey, Lorraine. *Cinderella's stepsister and the big bad wolf*
Cinderella
Climo, Shirley. *The Egyptian Cinderella*
The Korean Cinderella
The Persian Cinderella
Coburn, Jewell Reinhart. *Angkat*
Jouanah
Cooper, Floyd. *The ring bearer*
Daly, Jude. *Fair, brown and trembling*
Day, Nancy Raines. *The lion's whiskers*
Geras, Adèle. *Sleeping beauty*
Hickox, Rebecca. *The golden sandal*
Hines, Anna Grossnickle. *When we married Gary*
Horrocks, Anita. *Silas' seven grandparents*
Levins, Sandra. *Do you sing Twinkle?*
Lowell, Susan. *Cindy Ellen*
McCaughrean, Geraldine. *Grandma Chickenlegs*
Manna, Anthony L. *The orphan*
Perkins, Chloe. *Cinderella*
Perrault, Charles *Cinderella*, ill. by Nicoletta Ceccoli
Cinderella, ill. by Susan Jeffers
Cinderella, ill. by Loek Koopmans
Cinderella, ill. by Barbara McClintock
Cinderella, ill. by James Marshall
Cinderella / Cenicienta
Cinderella: a pop-up fairy tale
Cinderella: or, the little glass slipper
Roberts, Lynn. *Cinderella, an Art Deco love story*
Rotner, Shelley. *Families*
Sanderson, Ruth. *Cinderella*
San Souci, Robert D. *Cinderella Skeleton*
Little gold star
Schotter, Roni. *Room for Rabbit*
Schroeder, Alan. *Smoky Mountain Rose*
Shaskan, Trisha Speed. *Seriously, Cinderella is so annoying!*
Sierra, Judy. *The gift of the crocodile*
Stewig, John Warren. *Mother Holly*
Thomas, Joyce Carol. *The gospel Cinderella*
Underwood, Deborah. *Interstellar Cinderella*
Winthrop, Elizabeth. *Vasilissa the beautiful*

Family life – stepparents *see* Divorce; Family life – stepfamilies

Farms

Adler, David A. *A picture book of Cesar Chavez*
Alborough, Jez. *The gobble gobble moooooo tractor book*
Alsdurf, Phyllis. *It's milking time*
Amato, Mary. *The chicken of the family*
Ammon, Richard. *Amish horses*
Anderson, Derek. *Story county*
Anderson, Peggy Perry. *Chuck's band*
Andrews, Julie. *Dumpy the dump truck*
Arnosky, Jim. *Raccoons and ripe corn*
Ashforth, Camilla. *Willow at Christmas*
Asim, Jabari. *Preaching to the chickens*
Auch, Mary Jane. *The nutquacker*
Aylesworth, Jim. *Cock-a-doodle-doo, creak, pop-pop, moo*
One crow
Baddiel, Ivor. *Cock-a-doodle quack! quack!*
Bailey, Linda. *The farm team*
Baker, Ken. *Old MacDonald had a dragon*
Banks, Kate. *What's coming for Christmas?*
Barbour, Karen. *Mr. Williams*
Base, Graeme. *Little elephants*
Bateman, Teresa. *April foolishness*
Farm flu
Job wanted
Battut, Eric. *The fox and the hen*
Beaton, Clare. *Clare Beaton's farmyard rhymes*
Beaumont, Karen. *Duck, duck, goose!*
No sleep for the sheep!
Bee, William. *Stanley the farmer*
Beeke, Jemma. *The Rickety Barn show*
Bibbons, Faye. *The day the picture man came*
Bilgrami, Shaheen. *Farmyard painting party*
Black, Michael Ian. *Cock-a-doodle-doo-bop!*
Blackstone, Stella. *How big is a pig?*
Blades, Ann. *Mary of mile 18*
Bock, Lee. *Oh, crumps! / Ay, caramba!*
Bonning, Tony. *Fox tale soup*
Bradby, Marie. *Once upon a farm*
Brett, Jan. *The turnip*
Bright, Robert. *Georgie*
Brown, James. *Farm*
Brown, Margaret Wise. *Christmas in the barn*
Bunting, Eve. *Hurry! hurry!*
Burg, Sarah Emmanuelle. *One more egg*
Campbell, Rod. *Farm animals*
Carle, Eric. *Dream snow*
Carlstrom, Nancy White. *The way to Wyatt's house*
Carr, Jan. *Big Truck and Little Truck*
Carter, David A. *Old MacDonald had a farm: a pop-up book*
Carter, Don. *Old MacDonald drives a tractor*
Caudill, Rebecca. *A pocketful of cricket*
Cazet, Denys. *Nothing at all*
Chaconas, Dori. *Dori the contrary hen*
Chaucer, Geoffrey. *Chanticleer and the fox*
Chernesky, Felicia Sanzari. *Cheers for a dozen ears*
From apple trees to cider, please!
Pick a circle, gather squares
Sun above and blooms below
Child, Lydia Maria. *Over the river and through the wood*
Over the river and through the wood: the New England boy's song about Thanksgiving Day
Chitwood, Suzanne Tanner. *Wake up, big barn!*
Church, Caroline Jayne. *Digby takes charge*
One smart goose

The web files
Parish, Herman. *Amelia Bedelia's first field trip*
Peet, Bill. *Cock-a-doodle Dudley*
Pelletier, Andrew T. *The toy farmer*
Perrin, Martine. *Cock-a-doodle who?*
Peterson, Cris. *Extra cheese, please!*
    Fantastic farm machines
Peterson, Mary. *Piggies in the pumpkin patch*
Pfeffer, Wendy. *The big flood*
Phillips, Mildred. *And the cow said, "moo"!*
Piers, Helen. *Who's in my bed?*
Pinkney, Gloria Jean. *Back home*
    The Sunday outing
Plourde, Lynn. *Field trip day*
    Only cows allowed!
Polacco, Patricia. *Just plain Fancy*
Potter, Beatrix. *The tale of Peter Rabbit*
Preston-Gannon, Frann. *Dinosaur farm*
Prigger, Mary Skillings. *Aunt Minnie and the twister*
Provensen, Alice. *The year at Maple Hill Farm*
Purmell, Ann. *Apple cider making days*
    Christmas tree farm
Puttock, Simon. *Yours truly, Louisa*
Ransom, Candice F. *Tractor day*
Raschka, Chris. *Give and take*
Ray, Mary Lyn. *Go to sleep, little farm*
Reed, Lynn Rowe. *Thelonius Turkey lives!*
Regan, Dian Curtis. *Barnyard slam*
Reynolds, Aaron. *Chicks and salsa*
Reynolds, Adrian. *Pete and Polo's farmyard adventure*
Reynolds, Marilynn. *The new land*
    The prairie fire
Robart, Rose. *The cake that Mack ate*
Robbins, Ken. *Apples*
Root, Phyllis. *Anywhere farm*
    What Baby wants
Rossiter, Nan Parson. *Sugar on snow*
Roth, Carol. *Where's my mommy?*
Ryder, Joanne. *Dance by the light of the moon*
Rylant, Cynthia. *Scarecrow*
Sadler, Judy Ann. *Sandwiches for Duke*
Sage, James. *Farmer Smart's fat cat*
Sandburg, Carl. *From daybreak to good night*
    The Huckabuck family and how they raised popcorn
      in Nebraska and quit and came back
Santoro, Scott. *Farm-fresh cats*
Schnur, Steven. *Spring thaw*
Schotter, Roni. *Go, Little Green Truck!*
Schubert, Leda. *Feeding the sheep*
Schuh, Mari C. *Chickens on the farm*
    Cows on the farm
    Pigs on the farm
    Sheep on the farm
Selsam, Millicent E. *Keep looking!*
Shannon, George. *Turkey Tot*
Shapiro, Jody Fickes. *Up, up, up! It's apple-picking time*
    time
Sierra, Judy. *E-I-E-I-O*
Sillifant, Alec. *Farmer Ham*
Silvano, Wendi. *Turkey trouble*
Simmons, Jane. *Daisy and the Beastie*
Simont, Marc. *The goose that almost got cooked*
Sims, Nat. *Peekaboo barn*
Slack, Michael. *Wazdot?*
Sloat, Teri. *Farmer Brown goes round and round*
    Farmer Brown shears his sheep
Spinelli, Eileen. *Princess Pig*
    Silly Tilly
Staines, Bill. *All God's critters*

Steffensmeier, Alexander. *Millie and the big rescue*
    Millie waits for the mail
Stevens, Jan Romero. *Carlos and the skunk / Carlos*
    y el zorrillo
Stevens, Janet. *Find a cow now!*
Stevenson, James. *"Could be worse!"*
Stewig, John Warren. *Making plum jam*
Stiegemeyer, Julie. *Gobble gobble crash!*
Stinson, Kathy. *A pocket can have a treasure in it*
Stockland, Patricia M. *In the horse stall*
    In the pig pen
    In the sheep pasture
Stoeke, Janet Morgan. *Hide and seek*
    The Loopy Coop hens
    Pip's trip
Strete, Craig Kee. *How the Indians bought the farm*
Stroud, Bettye. *Dance y'all*
Stuchner, Joan Betty. *Can hens give milk?*
Stutson, Caroline. *Prairie primer A to Z*
Sweet, Melissa. *Fiddle-i-fee*
Sykes, Julie. *Dora's eggs*
    This and that
Taback, Simms. *Simms Taback's farm animals*
Tafuri, Nancy. *Blue goose*
    Early morning in the barn
    This is the farmer
    Who's counting?
Teague, Mark. *Funny farm*
Teckentrup, Britta. *Busy bunny days*
Terasaki, Stanley Todd. *Ghosts for breakfast*
Thermes, Jennifer. *Sam Bennett's new shoes*
Thomas, Jane Resh. *Lights on the river*
Thompson, Lauren. *Wee little chick*
Tolstoy, Aleksey Nikolayevich. *The enormous turnip*
    The gigantic turnip
Tougas, Chris. *Dojo daytrip*
Tresselt, Alvin R. *Sun up*
    Wake up, farm!
Tricarico, Christine. *Cock-a-doodle dance!*
Tudor, Tasha. *Pumpkin moonshine*
Turner, Ann Warren. *Dakota dugout*
Twohy, Mike. *Wake up, Rupert!*
Vagin, Vladimir. *The enormous carrot*
Vamos, Samantha R. *The cazuela that the farm*
    maiden stirred
Van Fleet, Matthew. *Moo*
Van Leeuwen, Jean. *Chicken soup*
    The strange adventures of Blue Dog
Verboven, Agnes. *Ducks like to swim*
Waddell, Martin. *Farmer Duck*
    Tom Rabbit
Wahl, Phoebe. *Sonya's chickens*
Wall, Laura. *Goose on the farm*
Wallace, Nancy Elizabeth. *Apples, apples, apples*
    Pumpkin day
Ward, Helen. *The rooster and the fox*
Watterson, Carol. *An edible alphabet*
Wellington, Monica. *Apple farmer Annie*
Westcott, Nadine Bernard. *Skip to my Lou*
    There's a hole in the bucket
White, Linda. *Too many turkeys*
Whybrow, Ian. *Faraway farm*
Wild, Margaret. *Piglet and Granny*
    Piglet and Mama
    Piglet and Papa
Wiley, Thom. *One sheep, blue sheep*
Williams, Linda. *Horse in the pigpen*
Wilson, Karma. *The cow loves cookies*
    Duddle Puck

Hogwash!
Horseplay
Wood, Jakki. *Moo moo, brown cow*
   Never say boo to a goose!
Wormell, Mary. *Hilda Hen's happy birthday*
   Hilda Hen's search
   Why not?
Wright, Maureen. *Barnyard fun*
Yaccarino, Dan. *Doug unplugs on the farm*
Yolen, Jane. *Harvest home*
   Jane Yolen's Old MacDonald songbook
   Raising Yoder's barn
Yoon, Salina. *Do cows meow?*
   Penguin and Pumpkin
Zarins, Kim. *The helpful puppy*
Ziefert, Harriet. *I swapped my dog*
   Pumpkin Pie
   What do ducks dream?

Feathers

Piven, Hanoch. *The perfect purple feather*
Simler, Isabelle. *Plume*
Stewart, Melissa. *Feathers*
Ward, Jennifer. *Feathers and hair, what animals wear*
Wenxuan, Cao. *Feather*

Feeling *see* Senses – touch

Feelings *see* Emotions

Fidgeting *see* Behavior – fidgeting

Fighting *see* Behavior – fighting, arguing

Fingers *see* Anatomy – hands

Finishing things *see* Character traits –
   completing things

Fire

Beaver steals fire
Bourgeois, Paulette. *Fire fighters*
Cash, Rosanne. *Penelope Jane*
Cuyler, Margery. *Stop drop and roll*
Demarest, Chris L. *Firefighters A to Z*
   Hotshots!
Deschamps, Nicola. *Emergency!*
Dubois, Muriel L. *Out and about at the fire station*
Ehlert, Lois. *Cuckoo, a Mexican folktale / Cucú: un
   cuento folklórico mexicano*
Elya, Susan Middleton. *Fire! ¡Fuego! Brave bomberos*
Flanagan, Alice K. *Ms. Murphy fights fires*
Griessman, Annette. *The fire*
Hayward, Linda. *A day in the life of a firefighter*
Heos, Bridget. *Be safe around fire*
Hoberman, Mary Ann. *Mrs. O'Leary's cow*
Jacobs, Paul DuBois. *Fire drill*
Kaufman, Jeanne. *Young Henry and the dragon*
Liebman, Daniel. *I want to be a firefighter*
London, Jonathan. *Little lost tiger*
Long, Loren. *Otis and the kittens*
Markle, Sandra. *Finding home*

Martin, Bill, Jr.. *Fire! Fire! said Mrs. McGuire*
   "Fire! Fire!" said Mrs. McGuire
Nelson, S. D. *The Star People*
Nez, John. *One smart Cookie*
Nobisso, Josephine. *John Blair and the great Hinckley
   fire*
Nolan, Janet. *The firehouse light*
Owen, Ann. *Protecting your home*
Pendziwol, Jean E. *No dragons for tea*
Penn, Audrey. *Kai to the rescue!*
Polacco, Patricia. *Tikvah means hope*
Rex, Michael. *My fire engine*
Reynolds, Marilynn. *The prairie fire*
Roberts, Bethany. *Gramps and the fire dragon*
Sandburg, Carl. *The Huckabuck family and how they
   raised popcorn in Nebraska and quit and came
   back*
Spinelli, Eileen. *Hero cat*
Thompson, Colin. *Unknown*
Uhlberg, Myron. *The printer*
Van Laan, Nancy. *Rainbow crow*
Wilson, Gina. *Ignis*
Yee, Wong Herbert. *Fireman Small*
   Fireman Small, fire down below
   Fireman Small to the rescue

Fire engines *see* Careers – firefighters; Trucks

Fish

Aliki. *The long lost coelacanth and other living fossils*
   My visit to the aquarium
Allen, Elanna. *Poor little guy*
Arenson, Roberta. *Manu and the talking fish*
Arnosky, Jim. *Crinkleroot's 25 fish every child should
   know*
Aruego, José. *Weird friends*
Asch, Frank. *Moonbear's pet*
Bar-el, Dan. *A fish named Glub*
Bennett, Kelly. *Not Norman*
Berger, Melvin. *Dive! a book of deep sea creatures*
Blackstone, Stella. *Secret seahorse*
Buckingham, Matt. *Bright Stanley*
Bunting, Eve. *Finn McCool and the great fish*
   Gleam and Glow
Cannon, A. E. *Sophie's fish*
Clements, Andrew. *Big Al and Shrimpy*
Cook, Bernadine. *The little fish that got away*
Cousins, Lucy. *Hooray for fish!*
Curious George goes to the aquarium
Dahl, Michael. *One giant splash*
Diesen, Deborah. *The not very merry pout-pout fish*
   The pout-pout fish
   The pout-pout fish, far, far from home
   The pout-pout fish goes to school
   The pout-pout fish in the big-big dark
DiPucchio, Kelly. *Gilbert goldfish wants a pet*
Donaldson, Julia. *The fish who cried wolf*
Donovan, Gail. *The copycat fish*
   A fishy story
   Hidden treasures
   Lost at sea
Ehlert, Lois. *Fish eyes*
   Rain fish
Elschner, Geraldine. *Fritz's fish*
Eure, Wesley. *A fish out of water*
Fenske, Jonathan. *Barnacle is bored*
Foreman, Michael. *Friends*

Freedman, Deborah. *The Story of Fish and Snail*
Galloway, Ruth. *Fidgety fish*
Geist, Ken. *The three little fish and the big bad shark*
Goldfinger, Jennifer P. *A fish named Spot*
Grant, Joan. *Cat and Fish*
Gunnufson, Charlotte. *Prince and Pirate*
Harris, Trudy. *Pattern fish*
Hendra, Sue. *Barry, the fish with fingers*
Hodge, Deborah. *Salmon*
Hout, Mies van. *Happy*
Howe, James. *Otter and odder*
Jonas, Ann. *Splash!*
Kalan, Robert. *Blue sea*
Klassen, Jon. *This is not my hat*
Krykorka, Ian. *Carl, the Christmas carp*
Lamb, Rosy. *Paul meets Bernadette*
LaReau, Kara. *Ugly fish*
LeBox, Annette. *Salmon Creek*
Lerch. *Swim! swim!*
Lionni, Leo. *Fish is fish*
    Swimmy
Little old lady who swallowed a fly. *There was an old pirate who swallowed a fish*
Lloyd-Jones, Sally. *Poor Doreen*
London, Jonathan. *Where the big fish are*
MacDonald, Suse. *Fish, swish! splash, dash!*
McGaw, Wayne T. *T-boy of the bayou*
Mansfield, Andy. *One lonely fish*
Martin, David. *Piggy and Dad go fishing*
Olien, Jessica. *The blobfish book*
Pallotta, Jerry. *Dory story*
Paulsen, Gary. *Canoe days*
Pfeffer, Wendy. *What's it like to be a fish?*
Pfister, Marcus. *Good night, little rainbow fish*
    The rainbow fish
    Rainbow fish ABC
    Rainbow fish and the big blue whale
    Rainbow fish and the sea monsters' cave
    Rainbow fish to the rescue!
    You can't win them all, rainbow fish
Poydar, Nancy. *Fish school*
Prosek, James. *Bird, butterfly, eel*
Raschka, Chris. *Arlene sardine*
Rechner, Amy. *Out and about at the aquarium*
Reynolds, Aaron. *Sea Monkey and Bob*
Roderick, Stacey. *Ocean animals from head to tail*
Rohmann, Eric. *Clara and Asha*
Rylant, Cynthia. *Henny, Penny, Lenny, Denny, and Mike*
Sauer, Tammi. *Nugget and Fang*
Sayre, April Pulley. *Trout are made of trees*
    Trout, trout, trout
Schwartz, Amy. *A beautiful girl*
Seuss, Dr. *McElligot's pool*
Shannon, David. *Jangles*
Shields, Gillian. *Dogfish*
Simeon, Jean-Pierre. *This is a poem that heals fish*
Sloat, Teri. *There was an old lady who swallowed a trout*
Smith, Danna. *Swallow the leader*
Snicket, Lemony. *Goldfish Ghost*
Stead, Philip C. *The only fish in the sea*
Stevenson, James. *Which one is Whitney?*
Stockdale, Susan. *Fabulous Fishes*
Suzuki, David. *Salmon forest*
Toft, Kim Michelle. *One less fish*
Van Laan, Nancy. *Little Fish lost*
Waber, Bernard. *Lorenzo*
Weeks, Sarah. *Catfish Kate and the sweet swamp band*

Winkelman, Barbara Gaines. *Puffer's surprise*
    Sockeye's journey home
Wood, Audrey. *Ten little fish*
Wright, Catherine. *Steamboat Annie and the thousand-pound catfish*
Yaccarino, Dan. *The birthday fish*
Yoo, Taeeun. *The little red fish*
Yorinks, Arthur. *Louis the fish*

Fish – seahorses

Blackstone, Stella. *Secret seahorse*
Butterworth, Chris. *Sea horse*
Curtis, Jennifer Keats. *Seahorses*
Damjan, Mischa. *The little seahorse and the Christmas pearl*
Freymann, Saxton. *One lonely seahorse*

Fish – sharks

Adamson, Ged. *Shark Dog!*
Arnold, Caroline. *Giant shark*
Barton, Chris. *Shark vs. train*
Bloom, C. P. *The Monkey goes bananas*
Clarke, Ginjer L. *Sharks!*
Clarke, Jane. *Gilbert the hero*
Cox, Phil Roxbee. *Shark in the park*
Diffily, Deborah. *Jurassic shark*
Ferry, Beth. *Land shark*
Geist, Ken. *The three little fish and the big bad shark*
Gentle, Victor. *Baby sharks*
    Killer sharks, killer people
    Shark camouflage and armor
    Very big sharks
    The world's strangest shark
Gibbons, Gail. *Sharks*
Gill, Timothy. *Flip and Fin: super sharks to the rescue!*
    Flip and Fin: we rule the school!
Griff. *Shark-mad Stanley*
Hale, Bruce. *Clark the Shark*
Houran, Lori Haskins. *How to spy on a shark*
Keating, Jess. *Shark lady*
Lang, Heather. *Swimming with sharks*
Mahy, Margaret. *The great white man-eating shark*
Manley, Curtis. *Shawn loves sharks*
Markle, Sandra. *Sharks: biggest! littlest!*
Martin, Rafe. *The Shark God*
O'Brien, Patrick. *Megatooth*
Olien, Jessica. *Shark Detective!*
Pfister, Marcus. *Rainbow fish to the rescue!*
Reed, Lynn Rowe. *Benny Shark goes to friend school*
Reynolds, Aaron. *Carnivores*
Rockwell, Anne. *Little shark*
Sabuda, Robert. *Encyclopedia prehistorica: sharks and other seamonsters*
Sauer, Tammi. *Nugget and Fang*
Schwarz, Viviane. *Shark and Lobster's amazing undersea adventure*
Sharratt, Nick. *Shark in the park*
Shea, Bob. *I'm a shark*
Troll, Ray. *Sharkabet*
Ward, Nick. *Don't eat the babysitter!*
Waters, John F. *Sharks have six senses*

Fitness *see* Health & fitness

Flags

Bartoletti, Susan Campbell. *The flag maker*

Cohan, George M. *You're a grand old flag*
Fisher, Leonard Everett. *Stars and stripes: our national flag*
Fulton, Kristen. *Long may she wave*
Gillingham, Sara. *Alpha, Bravo, Charlie: the complete book of nautical codes*
Green, Stephanie. *Betsy Ross and the silver thimble*
Key, Francis Scott. *The Star Spangled Banner*
  The Star-Spangled Banner
Kroll, Steven. *By the dawn's early light: the story of the Star Spangled Banner*
Martin, Bill, Jr.. *I pledge allegiance*
Naberhaus, Sarvinder. *Blue sky white stars*
White, Becky. *Betsy Ross*

Flattery *see* Character traits – flattery

Flowers

Alda, Arlene. *Morning glory Monday*
Appelt, Kathi. *Miss Lady Bird's wildflowers*
Bardill, Linard. *The great golden thing*
Blackstone, Stella. *What's this?*
Blossom tales
Bruce, Lisa. *Fran's flower*
Bunting, Eve. *Flower garden*
  Sunflower house
Cooney, Barbara. *Miss Rumphius*
dePaola, Tomie. *The legend of the bluebonnet*
  The legend of the Indian paintbrush
Eclare, Melanie. *A handful of sunshine*
Ehlert, Lois. *Planting a rainbow*
Elschner, Geraldine. *Max's magic seeds*
Ford, Miela. *Sunflower*
Foreman, Michael. *Mia's story*
Gerber, Carole. *Spring blossoms*
Heller, Ruth. *The reason for a flower*
Himmelman, John. *A dandelion's life*
Hines, Anna Grossnickle. *Miss Emma's wild garden*
Hoban, Julia. *Amy loves the sun*
Holmes, Anita. *Flowers and friends*
Karon, Jan. *The trellis and the seed*
Lawson, Jonarno. *Sidewalk flowers*
Lee-Tai, Amy. *A place where sunflowers grow / Sabaku ni saita himawari*
Lin, Grace. *The ugly vegetables*
Lind, Michael. *Bluebonnet girl*
Lobel, Anita. *Alison's zinnia*
Louie, Therese On. *Raymond's perfect present*
McMillan, Bruce. *Counting wildflowers*
McQuinn, Anna. *Lola plants a garden*
Marshall, Janet Perry. *A honey of a day*
Maurer, Tracy. *Growing flowers*
Milne, A. A. *The magic hill*
Murphy, Mary. *Koala and the flower*
Noda, Takayo. *Song of the flowers*
Park, Linda Sue. *What does Bunny see?*
Pfister, Marcus. *Ava's poppy*
Pomeroy, Diana. *Wildflower ABC*
Posada, Mia. *Dandelions, stars in the grass*
Preller, James. *Cardinal and sunflower*
Ramirez, Melissa Bourbon. *The flight of the sunflower*
Rawlinson, Julia. *Fletcher and the springtime blossoms*
Reynolds, Peter H. *Rose's garden*
Rockwell, Anne. *Bumblebee, bumblebee, do you know me?*

  My spring robin
Schaefer, Lola M. *This is the sunflower*
Stephens, J. Moria. *Persephone, the ladybug*
Swanson, Susan Marie. *To be like the sun*
Tamar, Erika. *The garden of happiness*
Taylor, Sean. *Huck runs amuck!*
Trimble, Marcia. *Flower Green*
Waber, Bernard. *A lion named Shirley Williamson*
Wallace, Nancy Elizabeth. *Paperwhite*
Watts, Jeri. *A piece of home*
Wellington, Monica. *Zinnia's flower garden*
Wood, Audrey. *Birdsong*
  When the root children wake up

Flowers – roses

Edwards, Pamela Duncan. *Rosie's roses*
Hooks, William H. *The legend of the Christmas rose*
Valentina, Marina. *Lost in the roses*
Wood, Douglas. *Aunt Mary's rose*

Fold-out books *see* Format, unusual – toy & movable books

Folk & fairy tales

Aardema, Verna. *Anansi does the impossible!*
  Anansi finds a fool
  Bimwili and the Zimwi
  Borreguita and the coyote
  Bringing the rain to Kapiti Plain
  Half-a-ball-of-kenki
  Jackal's flying lesson
  Ji-nongo-nongo means riddles
  Koi and the kola nuts
  The lonely lioness and the ostrich chicks
  Misoso
  Oh, Kojo! How could you!
  Pedro and the padre
  Princess Gorilla and a new kind of water
  The riddle of the drum
  Sebgugugu the glutton
  Traveling to Tondo
  The vingananee and the tree toad
  Who's in Rabbit's house?
  Why mosquitoes buzz in people's ears
Ada, Alma Flor. *Dear Peter Rabbit*
  The rooster who went to his uncle's wedding
Aesop. *Aesop's fables*, ill. by Piet Grobler
  Aesop's fables, ill. by Michael Hague
  Aesop's fables, ill. by Heidi Holder
  Aesop's fables, ill. by Martin Jarrie
  Aesop's fables, ill. by Jerry Pinkney
  Aesop's fables, ill. by Fulvio Testa
  Androcles and the lion, ill. by Dennis Nolan
  Androcles and the lion, ill. by Janet Stevens
  Androcles and the lion: and other Aesop fables
  Animal fables from Aesop
  Anno's Aesop
  The ant and the grasshopper, ill. by Amy Lowry Poole
  The ant and the grasshopper, ill. by Sara Rojo
  Bat's big game
  Belling the cat
  Belling the cat and other Aesop fables
  The best of Aesop's fables
  The boy who cried wolf
  The contest between the Sun and the Wind

The country mouse and the city mouse
The crow and the pitcher
Doctor Coyote
The dog and the wolf
Fables from Aesop
Feed me!
The fox and the grapes
Fox tails
The goose that laid the golden egg
The grasshopper and the ants
The hare and the tortoise, ill. by Paul Galdone
The hare and the tortoise, ill. by Carol Jones
The hare and the tortoise, ill. by Helen Ward
The hare and the tortoise / La liebre y la tortuga
Hare and Tortoise
The lion and the mouse, ill. by Lisa McCue
The lion and the mouse, ill. by Sara Rojo
The lion and the mouse, ill. by Bernadette Watts
The lion and the mouse and other Aesop fables
Milly and Tilly
Mouse and lion
The race
Road signs
Smog, the city dog
Three Aesop fox fables
The tortoise and the hare, ill. by Jerry Pinkney
The tortoise and the hare, ill. by Sara Rojo
The tortoise and the hare: an Aesop fable
The town mouse and the country mouse, ill. by Lorinda Bryan Cauley
The town mouse and the country mouse, ill. by Janet Stevens
The town mouse and the country mouse: an Aesop fable, ill. by Helen Ward
The town mouse and the country mouse: an Aesop fable, ill. by Bernadette Watts
Town mouse, country mouse, ill. by Jan Brett
Town mouse, country mouse, ill. by Carol Jones
The wolf in sheep's clothing
Ahlberg, Allan. *The Goldilocks variations*
Previously
Ahlberg, Jessica. *Fairy tales for Mr. Barker*
Ahmed, Said Salah. *The lion's share / Qayb Libaax*
Aleichem, Sholem. *Hanukah money*
Alger, Leclaire Gowans. *All in the morning early*
Always room for one more
Aliki. *Three gold pieces*
The twelve months
Allen, Debbie. *Brothers of the knight*
Alley, Zoe B. *There's a princess in the palace*
There's a wolf at the door
Alvarez, Julia. *The secret footprints*
Andersen, Hans Christian. *The dinosaur's new clothes*
The emperor's new clothes, ill. by Angela Barrett
The emperor's new clothes, ill. by Virginia Lee Burton
The emperor's new clothes, ill. by Robert Byrd
The emperor's new clothes, ill. by Serena Curmi
The emperor's new clothes, ill. by Charlene DeLage
The emperor's new clothes, ill. by Jack Delano
The emperor's new clothes, ill. by Anne Rockwell
The emperor's new clothes, ill. by Janet Stevens
The emperor's new clothes, ill. by Eve Tharlet
The emperor's new clothes: a tale set in China
The fir tree, ill. by Diane Goode
The fir tree, ill. by Bernadette Watts
It's perfectly true!
La princesa and the pea

The little match girl, ill. by Rachel Isadora
The little match girl, ill. by Blair Lent
The little match girl, ill. by Jerry Pinkney
The little matchstick girl
The little mermaid, ill. by Charlene DeLage
The little mermaid, ill. by Michael Hague
The little mermaid, ill. by Rachel Isadora
The nightingale, ill. by Nancy Ekholm Burkert
The nightingale, ill. by Pirkko Vainio
The nightingale, ill. by Lisbeth Zwerger
The princess and the pea, ill. by Emily Bolam
The princess and the pea, ill. by Charlene DeLage
The princess and the pea, ill. by Dorothée Duntze
The princess and the pea, ill. by Maja Dusíková
The princess and the pea, ill. by Paul Galdone
The princess and the pea, ill. by Rachel Isadora
The princess and the pea, ill. by Bernhard Oberdieck
The princess and the pea, ill. by Janet Stevens
The princess and the pea, ill. by Alain Vaës
The princess and the pea in miniature
The snow queen, ill. by Angela Barrett
The snow queen, ill. by Sally Holmes
The snow queen, ill. by Susan Jeffers
The snow queen: a retelling of the fairy tale
The steadfast tin soldier, ill. by Jen Corace
The steadfast tin soldier, ill. by Charlene DeLage
The steadfast tin soldier, ill. by Paul Galdone
The steadfast tin soldier, ill. by Rachel Isadora
The steadfast tin soldier, ill. by P. J. Lynch
The steadfast tin soldier, ill. by Fred Marcellino
The steadfast tin soldier, ill. by JooHee Yoon
The swineherd
Sylvia Long's Thumbelina
Thumbelina, ill. by Charlene DeLage
Thumbelina, ill. by Demi
Thumbelina, ill. by Arlene Graston
Thumbelina, ill. by Bagram Ibatoulline
Thumbelina, ill. by Susan Jeffers
Thumbelina, ill. by Lauren A. Mills
Thumbeline
The tinderbox, ill. by Warwick Hutton
The tinderbox, ill. by Bagram Ibatoulline
The tinderbox, ill. by Barry Moser
The ugly duckling, ill. by Adrienne Adams
The ugly duckling, ill. by Sebastien Braun
The ugly duckling, ill. by Lorinda Bryan Cauley
The ugly duckling, ill. by Charlene DeLage
The ugly duckling, ill. by Robert Ingpen
The ugly duckling, ill. by Rachel Isadora
The ugly duckling, ill. by Steve Johnson
The ugly duckling, ill. by Jerry Pinkney
The ugly duckling, ill. by Meilo So
The ugly duckling, ill. by Pirkko Vainio
The ugly duckling, ill. by Bernadette Watts
The ugly duckling, ill. by Roberta Wilson
The wild swans, ill. by Anne Yvonne Gilbert
The wild swans, ill. by Susan Jeffers
The woman with the eggs
Arabian Nights *The tale of Ali Baba and the forty thieves*
Arenson, Roberta. *Manu and the talking fish*
Arnold, Katya. *That apple is mine!*
Artell, Mike. *Petite Rouge*
Asbjørnsen, P. C. *The three billy goats Gruff*, ill. by Stephen Carpenter
The three billy goats Gruff, ill. by Paul Galdone
The three billy goats gruff, ill. by Jerry Pinkney
The three billy goats Gruff, ill. by Glen Rounds

Day, Nancy Raines. *The lion's whiskers*
Dayrell, Elphinstone. *Why the sun and the moon live in the sky*
Dee, Ruby. *Two ways to count to ten*
Deedy, Carmen Agra. *Martina the beautiful cockroach*
DeFelice, Cynthia C. *Nelly May has her say*
de Las Casas, Dianne. *Blue frog*
  The Little "Read" Hen
Delessert, Etienne. *The seven dwarfs*
Demas, Corinne. *The magic apple*
Demi. *The dragon's tale and other animal fables of the Chinese zodiac*
  The empty pot
  The greatest treasure
  One grain of rice
  The shady tree
dePaola, Tomie. *Big Anthony, his story*
  Favorite nursery tales
  Fin M'Coul
  Jamie O'Rourke and the big potato
  The legend of Old Befana
  The legend of the bluebonnet
  The legend of the Indian paintbrush
  Little Grunt and the big egg
  Strega Nona meets her match
  Tony's bread
DeSpain, Pleasant. *The dancing turtle*
Diakité, Baba Wagué. *The hatseller and the monkeys*
  The hunterman and the crocodiles
  The magic gourd
  Mee-an and the magic serpent
Dick Whittington and his cat. *Dick Whittington and his cat*, ill. by Marcia Brown
  Dick Whittington and his cat, ill. by Mélisande Potter
Divakaruni, Chitra Banerjee. *Grandma and the great gourd*
Dodd, Emma. *Cinderelephant*
Donnelly, Jennifer. *Humble pie*
Downing, Johnette. *There was an old lady who swallowed some bugs*
Durand, Hallie. *Catch that cookie!*
Duvall, Deborah L. *The opossum's tale*
Edwards, Pamela Duncan. *Princess Pigtoria and the pea*
Ehlert, Lois. *Cuckoo, a Mexican folktale / Cucú: un cuento folklórico mexicano*
  Mole's hill
  Moon rope / Un lazo a la luna
Eisner, Will. *Sundiata*
Ellwand, David. *Cinderlily*
Elya, Susan Middleton. *Little Roja Riding Hood*
  Rubia and the three osos
Emberley, Barbara. *One wide river to cross*
Emberley, Ed. *The red hen*
Emberley, Rebecca. *Chicken Little*
  The crocodile and the scorpion
  Three cool kids
Emmett, Jonathan. *Prince Ribbit*
Ernst, Lisa Campbell. *Goldilocks returns*
  Little Red Riding Hood: a newfangled prairie tale
Evans, Cambria. *Bone soup*
The firebird. *The firebird*, ill. by Demi
  The firebird, ill. by Rachel Isadora
  The tale of the firebird
Fisher, Leonard Everett. *Cyclops*
  Theseus and the Minotaur
  William Tell

Fleischman, Paul. *First light, first life*
  Glass slipper, gold sandal
Fleming, Candace. *Clever Jack takes the cake*
Forest, Heather. *Stone soup*
Fox, Diane. *The cat, the dog, Little Red, the exploding eggs, the wolf, and Grandma*
The fox went out on a chilly night
Franco, Betsy. *Why the frog has big eyes*
French, Vivian. *The most wonderful thing in the world*
Galdone, Paul. *The magic porridge pot*
  The teeny-tiny woman
  What's in fox's sack?
Geras, Adèle. *The nutcracker*
  Sleeping beauty
  Swan Lake
Gershator, Phillis. *Only one cowry*
  Zzzng! zzzng! zzzng!
Gerson, Mary-Joan. *Why the sky is far away*
The gingerbread boy. *Gingerbread baby*
  The gingerbread boy, ill. by Emily Bolam
  The gingerbread boy, ill. by Richard Egielski
  The gingerbread boy, ill. by Paul Galdone
  The Gingerbread Cowboy
  The gingerbread girl
  The gingerbread man, ill. by Carol Jones
  The gingerbread man, ill. by Megan Lloyd
  The gingerbread man, ill. by Barbara McClintock
  The gingerbread man, ill. by Béatrice Rodriguez
  The Gingerbread Man loose at Christmas
  The Gingerbread Man loose at the zoo
  The Gingerbread Man loose in the school
  The Gingerbread Man loose on the fire truck
  The Ninjabread Man
  The pancake boy
  Señorita Gordita
  Whiff, sniff, nibble and chew
Ginsburg, Mirra. *Clay boy*
Glaser, Linda. *Stone soup with matzoh balls*
Go tell Aunt Rhody
Goble, Paul. *Adopted by the eagles*
  Buffalo woman
  Crow chief
  The dream wolf
  The gift of the sacred dog
  The great race of the birds and animals
  Her seven brothers
  Iktomi and the berries
  Iktomi and the boulder
  Iktomi and the buffalo skull
  Iktomi and the buzzard
  Iktomi and the coyote
  Iktomi and the ducks
  The legend of the White Buffalo Woman
  The lost children
  Love flute
  Mystic horse
  Remaking the earth
  The return of the buffaloes
  Star boy
Goodall, Jane. *The eagle and the wren*
Goode, Diane. *Diane Goode's book of silly stories and songs*
Gorbachev, Valeri. *The fool of the world and the flying ship: a Ukrainian folk tale*
Grambling, Lois G. *The witch who wanted to be a princess*
Granfield, Linda. *The legend of the panda*
Gray, Luli. *Ant and Grasshopper*
Gregorowski, Christopher. *Fly, eagle, fly!*

The Helen Oxenbury nursery collection
Helmer, Marilyn. *Three barnyard tales*
  Three cat and mouse tales
  Three prince charming tales
  Three royal tales
  Three tales of enchantment
  Three tales of three
  Three tales of trickery
  Three teeny tiny tales
  Three tuneful tales
Hennessy, B. G. *The boy who cried wolf*
Henrichs, Wendy. *I am Tama, lucky cat*
Heo, Yumi. *The green frogs*
Heyer, Marilee. *The weaving of a dream*
Hickox, Rebecca. *The golden sandal*
Hill, Eric. *Spot's birthday party*
  Where's Spot?
Himes, Rachel. *Princess and the peas*
Ho, Minfong. *Brother Rabbit*
Hodges, Margaret. *Saint George and the dragon*
  The wave
Hodgkinson, Leigh. *Goldilocks and just one bear*
Hoffman, Mary. *Clever Katya*
Hoffmann, E. T. A. *The nutcracker*, ill. by Renée
  Graef
  The nutcracker, ill. by Alison Jay
  The nutcracker, ill. by Peter Malone
  The nutcracker, ill. by Niroot Puttapipat
  The nutcracker, ill. by Maurice Sendak
  The nutcracker, ill. by Lisbeth Zwerger
  The Nutcracker and the Mouse King
  The nutcracker ballet
Hogrogian, Nonny. *The contest*
Hong, Chen Jiang. *The magic horse of Han Gan*
Hooks, William H. *Moss gown*
Hopkins, Jackie Mims. *The gold miner's daughter*
  Prairie chicken little
Horn, Sandra Ann. *Babushka*
Howland, Naomi. *Latkes, latkes, good to eat*
Huck, Charlotte S. *Princess Furball*
Huling, Jan. *Ol' Bloo's boogie-woogie band and blues*
  ensemble
  Puss in cowboy boots
Hurst, Margaret M. *Grannie and the Jumbie*
Hurston, Zora Neale. *The six fools*
Imai, Ayano. *Puss and boots*
Irving, Washington. *The legend of Sleepy Hollow*, ill.
  by R. W. Alley
  The legend of Sleepy Hollow, ill. by Daniel San
  Souci
Jack and the beanstalk. *Jack and the beanstalk*, ill.
  by Aljoscha Blau
  Jack and the beanstalk, ill. by Steve Cox
  Jack and the beanstalk, ill. by Nina Crews
  Jack and the beanstalk, ill. by Julek Heller
  Jack and the beanstalk, ill. by John Howe
  Jack and the beanstalk, ill. by Steven Kellogg
  Jack and the beanstalk, ill. by Albert Lorenz
  Jack and the beanstalk, ill. by Niamh Sharkey
  Jack and the beanstalk, ill. by Gennady Spirin
  Jack and the beanstalk, ill. by Matt Tavares
  Jack and the beanstalk and the french fries
  Jacques and de beanstalk
Jackson, Alison. *I know an old lady who swallowed*
  a pie
  Thea's tree
Jackson, Ellen. *Cinder Edna*
Jacobs, Joseph. *King of the cats*
  The three sillies

Jaffe, Nina. *The golden flower*
  In the month of Kislev
  Tales for the seventh day
  The way meat loves salt
Janisch, Heinz. *The merry pranks of Till Eulenspiegel*
Javaherbin, Mina. *Elephant in the dark*
  The secret message
Jay, Alison. *1 2 3*
Jiang, Ji-li. *The magical Monkey King, mischief in*
  heaven
Johnson, Paul Brett. *Jack outwits the giants*
  Old Dry Fry
Johnson-Davies, Denys. *Goha, the wise fool*
Johnston, Tony. *The badger and the magic fan*
  Bigfoot Cinderrrrella
  The cowboy and the black-eyed pea
  Go track a yak
  The tale of Rabbit and Coyote
Jones, Ursula. *Beauty and the beast*
  The princess who had no kingdom
Joyce, William. *A bean, a stalk, and a boy named Jack*
Jules, Jacqueline. *Feathers for peacock*
Kajikawa, Kimiko. *Tsunami!*
  Yoshi's feast
Kasbarian, Lucine. *The greedy sparrow*
Keats, Ezra Jack. *John Henry*
Keens-Douglas, Richardo. *Anancy and the haunted*
  house
Keller, Emily Snowell. *Sleeping Bunny*
Kellogg, Steven. *Chicken Little*
  I was born about 10,000 years ago
  The Pied Piper's magic
Ketcham, Sallie. *The Christmas bird*
Ketteman, Helen. *Bubba the cowboy prince*
  The three little gators
  Waynetta and the cornstalk
Kilaka, John. *True friends*
Kim, Hanmin. *Tiptoe tapirs*
Kim, Julie. *Where's Halmoni?*
Kimmel, Eric A. *Anansi and the magic stick*
  Anansi and the moss-covered rock
  Anansi and the talking melon
  Anansi goes fishing
  Anansi's party time
  The birds' gift
  Easy work!
  The Erie Canal pirates
  The frog princess: a Tlingit legend from Alaska
  Gershon's monster
  Joseph and the Sabbath fish
  Little Red Hot
  The magic dreidels
  Medio Pollito
  Rattlestiltskin
  Rip Van Winkle's return
  The runaway tortilla
  The three cabritos
  The three little tamales
  The three princes
  The two mountains
King, Thomas. *Coyote sings to the moon*
Kloske, Geoffrey. *Once upon a time, the end (asleep in*
  60 seconds)
Klostermann, Penny Parker. *A cooked-up fairy tale*
Knutson, Barbara. *Love and roast chicken*
Kosofsky, Chaim. *Much, much better*
Koster, Gloria. *Little Red Ruthie*
Krensky, Stephen. *Too many leprechauns*
Krudop, Walter Lyon. *The man who caught fish*

Moerbeek, Kees. *The diary of Hansel and Gretel*
Mollel, Tololwa M. *Ananse's feast*
   The flying tortoise
   Kitoto the mighty
   Orphan boy
   Song bird
   Subira subira
Montes, Marisa. *Juan Bobo goes to work*
Moore, Marian. *Dear Cinderella*
Mora, Pat. *The night the moon fell*
   The race of toad and deer
Morales, Yuyi. *Just a minute: a trickster tale and counting book*
   Just in case: a trickster tale and Spanish alphabet book
Moreton, Daniel. *La Cucaracha Martina*
Morgan, Mary. *Dragon pizzeria*
Morrison, Toni. *The tortoise or the hare*
Mortimer, Rachael. *Red Riding Hood and the sweet little wolf*
Mosel, Arlene. *Tikki Tikki Tembo*
Muller, Robin. *The lucky old woman*
Munsch, Robert N. *A promise is a promise*
Musgrove, Margaret. *The spider weaver*
Muth, Jon J. *Stone soup*
   Zen shorts
Nadimi, Suzan. *The rich man and the parrot*
Newman, Marlene. *Myron's magic cow*
Nishizuka, Koko. *The beckoning cat*
Noble, Trinka Hakes. *A Christmas spider's miracle*
Norling, Beth. *Sister night and sister day*
Numeroff, Laura Joffe. *Ponyella*
Oberman, Sheldon. *The wisdom bird*
Ogburn, Jacqueline K. *The magic nesting doll*
Olaleye, Isaac. *In the Rainfield*
The old woman and her pig *The old woman and her pig*
   The old woman and her pig: an Appalachian folktale
O'Malley, Kevin. *The great race*
O'Neill, Richard. *Yokki and the Parno Gry*
Onyefulu, Obi. *Chinye*
Oppenheim, Joanne. *The Christmas witch*
Oram, Hiawyn. *Baba Yaga and the wise doll*
Orgel, Doris. *The cat's tale*
Osborne, Mary Pope. *The brave little seamstress*
   Kate and the beanstalk
   Sleeping Bobby
Osofsky, Audrey. *Dreamcatcher*
Otsuka, Yuzo. *Suho's white horse*
Oughton, Jerrie. *How the stars fell into the sky*
   The magic weaver of rugs
Over in the meadow
Palatini, Margie. *Lousy rotten stinkin' grapes*
Parkinson, Kathy. *The enormous turnip*
Paterson, Katherine. *The tale of the Mandarin ducks*
Paul, Ann Whitford. *Tortuga in trouble*
Paxton, Tom. *The story of Santa Claus*
   The story of the Tooth Fairy
Paye, Won-Ldy. *Head, body, legs*
   Mrs. Chicken and the hungry crocodile
Peck, Jan. *The giant carrot*
   Giant peach yodel!
Perkins, Chloe. *Cinderella*
Perlman, Janet. *The Emperor Penguin's new clothes*
   The penguin and the pea
Perrault, Charles *Cinderella*, ill. by Nicoletta Ceccoli
   Cinderella, ill. by Susan Jeffers
   Cinderella, ill. by Loek Koopmans

   Cinderella, ill. by Barbara McClintock
   Cinderella, ill. by James Marshall
   Cinderella / Cenicienta
   Cinderella: a pop-up fairy tale
   Cinderella: or, the little glass slipper
   Puss in boots, ill. by Marcia Brown
   Puss in boots, ill. by Lorinda Bryan Cauley
   Puss in boots, ill. by Paul Galdone
   Puss in boots, ill. by Steve Light
   Puss in boots, ill. by Giuliano Lunelli
   Puss in boots, ill. by Fred Marcellino
   Puss in boots, ill. by Bernhard Oberdieck
   Puss in boots, ill. by Jerry Pinkney
   Puss in boots, ill. by Alain Vaës
   Sleeping Beauty
Petach, Heidi. *Goldilocks and the three hares*
Philip, Neil. *Noah and the devil*
Pia Toya
Pilegard, Virginia Walton. *The warlord's puzzle*
Pinkney, Jerry. *The lion and the mouse*
Pitcher, Caroline. *Mariana and the merchild*
Polacco, Patricia. *Babushka's Mother Goose*
   Luba and the wren
   Rechenka's eggs
Pollock, Penny. *The turkey girl*
   When the moon is full
Poole, Amy Lowry. *The pea blossom*
Price, Kathy. *The Bourbon Street musicians*
Prince, April Jones. *Goldenlocks and the three pirates*
Prokofiev, Sergei Sergeievitch. *Peter and the wolf*, ill. by Charles Mikolaycak
   Peter and the wolf, ill. by Josef Palecek
   Peter and the wolf, ill. by Chris Raschka
   Peter and the wolf, ill. by Vladimir Vagin
Pullman, Philip. *Puss in boots: the adventures of that most enterprising feline*
Quattlebaum, Mary. *Sparks fly high*
Radunsky, Vladimir. *Manneken pis*
Ramos, Mario. *I am so handsome*
Ramsden, Ashley. *Seven fathers*
Ransome, Arthur. *The fool of the world and the flying ship*
Rappaport, Doreen. *The long-haired girl*
   The new king
Ray, Jane. *The apple-pip princess*
Riggio, Anita. *Beware the Brindlebeast*
Ringgold, Faith. *The invisible princesses*
Robberecht, Thierry. *The wolf who fell out of a book*
Robbins, Ruth. *Baboushka and the three kings*
Roberts, Lynn. *Cinderella, an Art Deco love story*
   Rapunzel, a groovy fairy tale
Robins, Arthur. *The teeny tiny woman*
Rocco, John. *Wolf! wolf!*
Rockwell, Anne. *The boy who wouldn't obey*
Rodanas, Kristina. *The dragonfly's tale*
   Follow the stars
Rohmer, Harriet. *How we came to the fifth world*
   Mother scorpion country
Rohmer, Harriet, et al. *The invisible hunters*
Root, Phyllis. *Aunt Nancy and Old Man Trouble*
   Grandmother Winter
Rosales, Melodye Benson. *Leola and the honeybears*
Rosen, Michael. *Crow and Hawk*
Ross, Gayle. *How Turtle's back was cracked*
   The legend of the Windigo
Ross, Tony. *The boy who cried wolf*
Roth, Susan L. *Kanahena*
Rothenberg, Joan Keller. *Inside-out grandma*
Rumford, James. *Nine animals and the well*

Zemach, Margot. *It could always be worse*
    The three wishes
Zeman, Ludmila. *Sindbad*
Ziefert, Harriet. *When I first came to this land*

Folk & fairy tales – pourquoi tales

Alexander, Lloyd. *How the cat swallowed thunder*
Bruchac, James. *Rabbit's snow dance*
Bruchac, Joseph. *How Chipmunk got his stripes*
Cummings, Pat. *Ananse and the lizard*
Kipling, Rudyard. *How the camel got his hump*
    How the elephant got his trunk
    How the leopard got his spots
Larson, Bonnie. *When animals were people / Cuando
    los animales eran personas*
Lester, Julius. *Why heaven is far away*
McDermott, Gerald. *Jabutí the tortoise*
Poole, Amy Lowry. *How the rooster got his crown*
Rosen, Michael. *How the animals got their colors*
Shepard, Aaron. *Master man*
Sherman, Pat. *The sun's daughter*
Wolkstein, Diane. *The day Ocean came to visit*

Food

Abrams, Pam. *Now I eat my ABC's*
Aesop. *The fox and the grapes*
Ahlberg, Allan. *Hooray for bread*
    The runaway dinner
Akin, Sara Laux. *Three scoops and a fig*
Alalou, Elizabeth. *The butter man*
Alborough, Jez. *Ice cream bear*
    It's the bear
Alcott, Louisa May. *An old-fashioned Thanksgiving*
Aliki. *Milk from cow to carton*
Ancona, George. *Mis comidas / My foods*
Anderson, Derek. *Gladys goes out to lunch*
    Ten hungry pigs
Andrews, Julie. *Dumpy's apple shop*
Angelou, Maya. *Angelina of Italy*
Antony, Steve. *Betty goes bananas*
Argueta, Jorge. *Arroz con leche / Rice pudding*
    Guacamole
    *Sopa de frijoles: un poema para cocinar / Bean soup:
        a cooking poem*
    Tamalitos
Armstrong, Jennifer. *Once upon a banana*
Arnosky, Jim. *Gobble it up!*
    Raccoons and ripe corn
Asch, Frank. *Monsieur Saguette and his baguette*
    Moonbear
    Pizza
    Popcorn
Aston, Dianna Hutts. *An orange in January*
Auch, Mary Jane. *The princess and the pizza*
Averbeck, Jim. *The market bowl*
Axelrod, Amy. *Pigs in the pantry*
    Pigs will be pigs
Aylesworth, Jim. *The burger and the hot dog*
Backx, Patsy. *Josie and Mr. Fernandez*
Bailey, Linda. *Toads on toast*
Baker, Keith. *Hap-pea all year*
    Little green peas
    LMNO pea-quel
    LMNO peas
    1-2-3 peas
Baranski, Joan Sullivan. *Round is a pancake*
Barasch, Lynne. *Hiromi's hands*

Barbour, Karen. *Little Nino's pizzeria*
Bardhan-Quallen, Sudipta. *Hampire!*
Barrett, Judi. *Cloudy with a chance of meatballs*
    Cloudy with a chance of meatballs 3
    The marshmallow incident
    Pickles to Pittsburgh
Barron, Rex. *Fed up!*
Bass, Jennifer Vogel. *Edible colors*
    Edible numbers
Bastianich, Lidia. *Nonna tell me a story*
    Nonna's birthday surprise
Baum, Maxie. *I have a little dreidel*
Berenstain, Stan and Jan. *The Berenstain bears and
    too much junk food*
Bergman, Mara. *Yum yum! What fun!*
Bergmann, Andy. *The starry giraffe*
Berry, Lynne. *Ducking for apples*
Bertrand, Diane Gonzales. *Sofia and the purple
    dress / Sofia y el vestido morado*
Best, Cari. *Easy as pie*
Black, Michael Ian. *I'm bored*
Blackstone, Stella. *Making minestrone*
Bloch, Serge. *You are what you eat*
Bloom, Suzanne. *Feeding friendsies*
Boldt, Claudia. *Odd dog*
Bond, Rebecca. *The great doughnut parade*
Bonning, Tony. *Fox tale soup*
Border, Terry. *Merry Christmas, Peanut!*
    Milk goes to school
    Peanut Butter and Cupcake!
Brandt, Lois. *Maddi's fridge*
Breen, Steve. *Woodpecker wants a waffle*
Brenner, Barbara A. *Beef stew*
Brett, Jan. *Hedgie's surprise*
Bright, Rachel. *Love Monster and the last chocolate*
Brisson, Pat. *Before we eat*
Brokamp, Elizabeth. *The picky little witch*
Brown, Marc. *D. W., the picky eater*
Brown, Marcia. *Stone soup*
Brown-Wood, JaNay. *Grandma's tiny house*
Bruel, Nick. *Bad Kitty*
Bunting, Eve. *One green apple*
Burach, Ross. *There's a giraffe in my soup*
Butterworth, Chris. *How did that get in my lunchbox?*
Caldicott, Chris. *World food alphabet*
Campisi, Stephanie. *The ugly dumpling*
Capucilli, Karen. *The jelly bean fun book*
Carle, Eric. *My very first book of food*
    Pancakes, pancakes
    Today is Monday
    Walter the baker
Carlson, Nancy. *Harriet and George's Christmas treat*
Carney, Margaret. *At Grandpa's sugar bush*
Carrer, Chiara. *Otto Carrotto*
Cartaya, Pablo. *Tina Cocolina*
Catalanotto, Peter. *The secret lunch special*
Cazet, Denys. *The perfect pumpkin pie*
Chall, Marsha Wilson. *Sugarbush spring*
Chamberlin, Mary. *Mama Panya's pancakes*
Chapman, Jared. *Fruits in suits*
    Vegetables in underwear
Chavarría-Cháirez, Becky. *Magda's tortillas / Las
    tortillas de Magada*
Chen, Chih-Yuan. *On my way to buy eggs*
Chernesky, Felicia Sanzari. *Cheers for a dozen ears*
    From apple trees to cider, please!
Cherry, Lynne. *How Groundhog's garden grew*
Child, Lauren. *I will never not ever eat a tomato*
Christelow, Eileen. *Don't wake up Mama!*

Church, Caroline Jayne. *Little Apple Goat*
Clanton, Ben. *Rot, the cutest in the world!*
Collins, Ross. *Alvie eats soup*
Compestine, Ying Chang. *Boy dumplings*
   The real story of stone soup
   The runaway rice cake
   The story of chopsticks
   The story of noodles
Cooper, Elisha. *Ice cream*
Cooper, Helen. *Dog biscuit*
Cordsen, Carol Foskett. *The milkman*
Cousins, Lucy. *Maisy makes gingerbread*
Coy, John. *Two old potatoes and me*
Cruickshank, Margrit. *We're going to feed the ducks*
Curious George and the pizza
Curious George goes to a chocolate factory
Curious George makes pancakes
Curtis, Andrea. *What's for lunch?*
Dahl, Michael. *From the garden*
Darrow, Sharon. *Old Thunder and Miss Raney*
Davis, Aubrey. *Bagels from Benny*
Davis, David. *Fandango stew*
Davis, Jacky. *Black Belt Bunny*
Davis, Lee. *Feeding time*
Deacon, Alexis. *Cheese belongs to you!*
Dealey, Erin. *Deck the walls!*
Dean, Kim. *Pete the Cat and the missing cupcakes*
De Anda, Diane. *A day without sugar / Un dia sin azucar*
DeFelice, Cynthia C. *One potato, two potato*
de Las Casas, Dianne. *Blue frog*
Delessert, Etienne. *Hungry for numbers*
Denise, Anika. *Pigs love potatoes*
dePaola, Tomie. *Pancakes for breakfast*
   The popcorn book
   Tony's bread
De Regniers, Beatrice Schenk. *What did you put in your pocket?*
Detlefsen, Lisl H. *Time for cranberries*
DiPucchio, Kelly. *Everyone loves Bacon*
   Everyone loves Cupcake
DiTerlizzi, Tony. *Jimmy Zangwow's out-of-this-world, moon pie adventure*
Dolan, Elys. *Nuts in space*
Donnelly, Jennifer. *Humble pie*
Donnio, Sylviane. *I'd really like to eat a child*
Donohue, Dorothy. *Veggie soup*
Doodler, Todd H. *Veggies with wedgies*
Dooley, Norah. *Everybody brings noodles*
   Everybody cooks rice
   Everybody serves soup
Downing, Johnette. *Today is Monday in Louisiana*
Doyle, Malachy. *Hungry! hungry! hungry!*
Drescher, Henrik. *Hubert the Pudge*
Durant, Alan. *Burger boy*
Duval, Kathy. *Take me to your BBQ*
Eaton, Maxwell. *Best buds*
Eclare, Melanie. *A harvest of color*
Edwards, Michelle. *Max makes a cake*
Egan, Tim. *The trial of Cardigan Jones*
Ehlert, Lois. *Eating the alphabet*
   Growing vegetable soup
Ehrlich, Fred. *Does a camel cook?*
Eldarova, Sofia. *Builder mouse*
Elliott, George. *The boy who loved bananas*
Elvgren, Jennifer Riesmeyer. *Josias, hold the book*
Elya, Susan Middleton. *No more, por favor*
Emberley, Ed. *Thanks, Mom!*
Emberley, Rebecca. *My food / Mi comida*

Ernst, Lisa Campbell. *The Gingerbread Girl goes animal crackers*
Evans, Cambria. *Bone soup*
Evans, Lezlie. *The bunnies' picnic*
Everitt, Betsy. *Mean soup*
Faglia, Matteo. *Happy birthday, I'm 1*
   Happy birthday, I'm 2
   Happy birthday, I'm 3
   Happy birthday, I'm 4
Falwell, Cathryn. *Mystery vine*
   Rainbow Stew
Farish, Terry. *The cat who liked potato soup*
Fearnley, Jan. *Mr. Wolf's pancakes*
Fitzgerald, Joanne. *Yum! yum!*
Flaherty, A. W. *The luck of the Loch Ness monster*
Flanagan, Alice K. *The Zieglers and their apple orchard*
Fleming, Candace. *Clever Jack takes the cake*
   Gator gumbo
Fleming, Denise. *Lunch*
Fliess, Sue. *A gluten-free birthday for me!*
Florence, Tyler. *Tyler makes pancakes!*
   Tyler makes spaghetti!
Foges, Clare. *Kitchen disco*
Forest, Heather. *Stone soup*
Fox, Christyan. *Count to ten, PiggyWiggy!*
Fox, Mem. *Possum magic*
Freedman, Claire. *Spider sandwiches*
Freymann, Saxton. *Baby food*
   Dog food
   Fast food
   Food for thought
   Food play
   How are you peeling?
Friedman, Caitlin. *How do you feed a hungry giant?*
Galdone, Paul. *The magic porridge pot*
Garland, Michael. *The President and Mom's apple pie*
Gavin, Ciara. *Bear likes jam*
Gibbons, Gail. *Apples*
   The berry book
   Corn
   The fruits we eat
   The honey makers
   Ice cream: the full scoop
   The milk makers
   The missing maple syrup sap mystery
   The seasons of Arnold's apple tree
   The vegetables we eat
Gilman, Rita Golden. *Rice is life*
The gingerbread boy. *Gingerbread baby*
   The gingerbread boy, ill. by Richard Egielski
   The gingerbread boy, ill. by Paul Galdone
   The Gingerbread Cowboy
   The gingerbread girl
   The gingerbread man, ill. by Carol Jones
   The gingerbread man, ill. by Barbara McClintock
   The gingerbread man, ill. by Béatrice Rodriguez
   The Gingerbread Man loose at Christmas
   The Gingerbread Man loose at the zoo
   The Gingerbread Man loose in the school
   The Gingerbread Man loose on the fire truck
   The Library Gingerbread Man
   The Ninjabread Man
   The pancake boy
   Señorita Gordita
Glaser, Linda. *Mrs. Greenberg's messy Hanukkah*
   Stone soup with matzoh balls
Goble, Paul. *The return of the buffaloes*
Goldin, Barbara Diamond. *A mountain of blintzes*

Gorbachev, Valeri. *Pizza-pie snowman*
Gore, Leonid. *Worms for lunch?*
Gourley, Robbin. *Bring me some apples and I'll make you a pie*
　First garden
Gray, Kes. *Eat your peas*
Gretz, Susanna. *Rabbit food*
Grey, Mini. *Ginger bear*
Grigsby, Susan. *First peas to the table*
Gutierrez, Elisa. *Letter lunch*
Hacohen, Dean. *Who's hungry?*
Hafner, Marylin. *Molly and Emmett's surprise garden*
Hall, Margaret. *Corn*
　Peanuts
Hall, Zoe. *The apple pie tree*
Harper, Charise Mericle. *Cupcake*
Harris, Robie H. *What's so yummy?*
Hart, Caryl. *The princess and the peas*
Hartland, Jessie. *Bon appetit!*
Hartman, Bob. *The wolf who cried boy*
Head, Judith. *Mud soup*
Heller, Nicholas. *Ogres! ogres! ogres!*
Helmer, Marilyn. *Yummy riddles*
Hemingway, Edward. *Bad apple*
Henkes, Kevin. *Sheila Rae's peppermint stick*
Heras, Theo. *Baby cakes*
Herzog, Kenny. *Phil Pickle*
Hesse, Karen. *Spuds*
Hest, Amy. *You can do it, Sam*
Hester, Denia Lewis. *Grandma Lena's big ol' turnip*
Hicks, Barbara Jean. *Monsters don't eat broccoli*
Hill, Eric. *Spot bakes a cake*
Hill, Mary. *Let's make pizza*
　Let's make tacos
Himes, Rachel. *Princess and the peas*
Hirsh, Marilyn. *Potato pancakes all around*
Hoban, Russell. *Bread and jam for Frances*
Hoberman, Mary Ann. *The seven silly eaters*
Holt, Kimberly Willis. *Dinner with the Highbrows*
Holub, Joan. *Apple countdown*
　The pizza that we made
　Pumpkin countdown
Hood, Morag. *Carrot and pea*
Hopkins, Lee Bennett. *Yummy! eating through a day*
Horácek, Petr. *Strawberries are red*
Horowitz, Dave. *The ugly pumpkin*
Howe, James. *Horace and Morris say cheese (which makes Dolores sneeze!)*
Howland, Naomi. *The matzah man*
Hurwitz, Johanna. *Ethan out and about*
Hutchins, Pat. *Don't forget the bacon!*
　Ten red apples
Inkpen, Mick. *Wibbly Pig likes bananas*
Isaacs, Anne. *Pancakes for supper!*
Isadora, Rachel. *Happy belly, happy smile*
Iwai, Melissa. *Pizza day*
　Soup day
Jack and the beanstalk. *Jack and the beanstalk and the french fries*
Jackson, Alison. *I know an old lady who swallowed a pie*
Jeffers, Oliver. *The incredible book eating boy*
Jenkins, Emily. *A fine dessert*
Jenkins, Steve. *Time to eat*
Jocelyn, Marthe. *Eats*
John, Jory. *I will chomp you!*
Johnson, Paul Brett. *On top of spaghetti*
Jonovitz, Marilyn. *Good morning, Little Fox*
Kalz, Jill. *Fruits*

Kann, Victoria. *Pinkalicious*
Kaplan, Michael B. *Betty Bunny loves chocolate cake*
Kasza, Keiko. *Badger's fancy meal*
　The wolf's chicken stew
Keller, Laurie. *Arnie the doughnut*
Kenah, Katharine. *The very stuffed turkey*
Ketteman, Helen. *Armadilly chili*
Khing, T. T. *Where is the cake?*
　Where is the cake now?
Kim, Aram. *No kimchi for me!*
Kimmel, Eric A. *Hanukkah bear*
　Jack and the giant barbecue
　Little Red Hot
　Rattlestiltskin
　The three little tamales
Kirk, David. *Little bird, Biddle bird*
Kladstrup, Kristin. *The gingerbread pirates*
Kleven, Elisa. *The apple doll*
　Sun bread
Koda-Callan, Elizabeth. *The squiggly Wigglys*
Koponen, Libby. *Mmm . . . let's eat!*
Koster, Gloria. *Little Red Ruthie*
　The peanut-free cafe
Krall, Dan. *The great lollipop caper*
Krull, Kathleen. *Supermarket*
Kyle, Tracey. *Gazpacho for Nacho*
Landry, Leo. *Eat your peas, Ivy Louise!*
LaReau, Kara. *No slurping, no burping!*
LaRochelle, David. *How Martha saved her parents from green beans*
Lass, Bonnie. *Who took the cookies from the cookie jar?*
Lauber, Patricia. *Who eats what?*
Leedy, Loreen. *The dragon Thanksgiving feast*
　The edible pyramid
　Jack and the hungry giant eat right with MyPlate
Lendler, Ian. *An undone fairy tale*
Levert, Mireille. *An island in the soup*
Lewin, Betsy. *Good night, Knight*
Lewis, Paeony. *No more cookies!*
Lin, Grace. *Dim sum for everyone*
　Fortune cookie fortunes
　Our food
　Thanking the moon
　The ugly vegetables
Lipson, Eden Ross. *Applesauce season*
Litwin, Eric. *Groovy Joe: ice cream and dinosaurs*
Livingston, A. A. B. *Bear and Lolly: catch that cookie!*
Ljungkvist, Laura. *Toni's topsy-turvy telephone day*
Llewellyn, Claire. *Tree*
Lo, Ginnie. *Auntie Yang's great soybean picnic*
Lobel, Anita. *Ten hungry rabbits*
Loehr, Patrick. *Mucumber McGee and the lunch lady's liver*
London, Jonathan. *Crunch munch*
　Froggy eats out
　The sugaring-off party
Long, Ethan. *Snickerdoodle takes the cake*
　Soup for one
Luciani, Brigitte. *Those messy Hempels*
Luckhurst, Matt. *Paul Bunyan and Babe the Blue Ox*
McAlister, Caroline. *Holy Molé!*
McClements, George. *Night of the Veggie Monster*
McCloskey, Robert. *Blueberries for Sal*
McClure, Nikki. *Apple*
McCully, Emily Arnold. *Popcorn at the palace*
McCurdy, Michael. *An Algonquian year*
McDonald, Megan. *Beetle McGrady eats bugs!*
McDonald, Rae A. *A fishing surprise*
McElligott, Matthew. *Even aliens need snacks*

Thomas, Jan. *A birthday for Cow!*
Thompson, Lauren. *The apple pie that Papa baked*
  Chew, chew, gulp!
Thurman, Kathryn K. *A garden for Pig*
Todd, Mark. *Food trucks!*
Tone, Satoe. *The very big carrot*
Torres, Leyla. *Saturday sancocho*
Toscano, Charles. *Papa's pastries*
Trukhan, Ekaterina. *Apples for little Fox*
Tudor, Tasha. *Pumpkin moonshine*
Tunnell, Michael O. *Halloween pie*
Uchida, Yoshiko. *The two foolish cats*
Vamos, Samantha R. *The cazuela that the farm
  maiden stirred*
Van Camp, Katie. *CookieBot!*
VanHecke, Susan. *An apple pie for dinner*
Van Laan, Nancy. *Tickle tum*
Van Leeuwen, Jean. *Chicken soup*
Vega, Denise. *Build a burrito*
Voake, Charlotte. *Pizza kittens*
Waber, Bernard. *Fast food! gulp! gulp!*
Waddell, Martin. *Yum, yum, yummy*
Walburg, Lori. *The legend of the candy cane*
Wallace, Karen. *Scarlette Beane*
Wallace, Nancy Elizabeth. *Pumpkin day*
Wardlaw, Lee. *The chair where bear sits*
Watkins, Rowboat. *Rude cakes*
Watson, Clyde. *Valentine foxes*
Weinstock, Robert. *Food hates you, too, and other
  poems*
Wellington, Monica. *Apple farmer Annie*
  Mr. Cookie Baker
  Pizza at Sally's
Wells, Rosemary. *McDuff saves the day*
  Max and Ruby's Midas
  Max's apples
  Yoko
Weninger, Brigitte. *Little apple*
Westcott, Nadine Bernard. *Peanut butter and jelly*
Wheeler, Lisa. *Jam and jelly by Holly and Nellie*
  Turk and Runt
  Ugly pie
White, Linda. *Too many pumpkins*
Who took the cookie?
Willard, Nancy. *The Moon and Riddles Diner and the
  Sunnyside Café*
Willems, Mo. *The duckling gets a cookie!?*
  Nanette's baguette
  The pigeon finds a hot dog!
Williams, Sam. *Angel's Christmas cookies*
Wilson, Karma. *The cow loves cookies*
  Whopper cake
Wing, Natasha. *Jalapeño bagels*
Wisniewski, David. *Tough cookie*
Wolff, Nancy. *Tallulah in the kitchen*
Wong, Benedict Norbert. *Lo and behold*
  Lo and behold, good enough to eat
Woo, Alan. *Maggie's chopsticks*
Wood, Audrey. *Heckedy Peg*
Wright, Michael. *Jake goes peanuts*
Yaccarino, Dan. *The lima bean monster*
  Morris Mole
Yee, Wong Herbert. *Hamburger Heaven*
Yolen, Jane. *How do dinosaurs eat their food?*
Young, Cybèle. *A few bites*
Zagwÿn, Deborah Turney. *Apple batter*
Zalben, Jane Breskin. *Saturday night at the Beastro*
Zamorano, Ana. *Let's eat!*

Zepeda, Gwendolyn. *Growing up with tamales / Los
  tamales de Ana*
Zia, F. *Hot, hot roti for Dada-ji*
Zoehfeld, Kathleen Weidner. *Apples, apples*
  Secrets of the garden
Zommer, Yuval. *One hundred sausages*

Foolishness *see* Character traits – foolishness

Foreign lands

Ada, Alma Flor. *The rooster who went to his uncle's
  wedding*
Ajmera, Maya. *Back to school*
  Come out and play
  To be a kid
Aleichem, Sholem. *Hanukah money*
Aliki. *Marianthe's story one: painted words;
  Marianthe's story two: spoken memories*
Baylor, Byrd. *The way to start a day*
Blossom tales
Coburn, Jewell Reinhart. *Jouanah*
Dooley, Norah. *Everybody brings noodles*
Fleischman, Paul. *First light, first life*
  Glass slipper, gold sandal
Frank, John. *How to catch a fish*
Handford, Martin. *Where's Waldo?*
Höjer, Dan. *Heart of mine*
Kinkade, Sheila. *My family*
Knight, Margy Burns. *Talking walls*
Lewin, Ted. *Market!*
MacDonald, Margaret Read. *Surf war!*
Marlowe, Pete. *One Arabian morning*
Montanari, Donata. *Children around the world*
Morris, Ann. *Houses and homes*
  Loving
  On the go
  Play
  Work
Niemann, Christoph. *The potato king*
Raffi. *Like me and you*
Reynolds, Jan. *Celebrate!*
Rogers, Gregory. *The hero of Little Street*
Seim, Donna Marie. *Where is Simon, Sandy?*
Shah, Idries. *Fatima the spinner and the tent*
Singer, Marilyn. *Nine o'clock lullaby*
Sís, Peter. *Madlenka*
Soto, Gary. *The old man and his door*
Stein, David Ezra. *Because Amelia smiled*
Trapani, Iza. *I'm a little teapot*
Tupper Ling, Nancy. *The story I'll tell*
Van Laan, Nancy. *Sleep, sleep, sleep*

Foreign lands – Afghanistan

Haskins, Jim. *Count your way through Afghanistan*
King, Dedie. *I see the sun in Afghanistan*
Stampler, Ann Redisch. *The wooden sword*
Williams, Karen Lynn. *Four feet, two sandals*
Winter, Jeanette. *Nasreen's secret school*

Foreign lands – Africa

Aardema, Verna. *Anansi does the impossible!*
  Bimwili and the Zimwi
  Bringing the rain to Kapiti Plain
  Half-a-ball-of-kenki
  Jackal's flying lesson
  Ji-nongo-nongo means riddles

O'Neill, Gemma. *Oh dear, Geoffrey!*
Onyefulu, Ifeoma. *An African Christmas*
　　A triangle for Adaora
Onyefulu, Obi. *Chinye*
Pritchett, Dylan. *The first music*
Radcliffe, Theresa. *Bashi, elephant baby*
San Souci, Robert D. *The secret of the stones*
Sayre, April Pulley. *If you should hear a honey guide*
Schaefer, Carole Lexa. *Cool time song*
Smith, Alex T. *Little Red and the very hungry lion*
Souhami, Jessica. *The leopard's drum*
Steig, William. *Doctor De Soto goes to Africa*
Steptoe, John. *Mufaro's beautiful daughters*
Stiegemeyer, Julie. *Under the baobab tree*
Stojic, Manya. *Rain*
Swann, Brian. *The house with no door*
Swinburne, Stephen R. *Water for one, water for*
　　everyone
Trimble, Marcia. *Hello sun*
Tulloch, Shirley. *Who made me?*
Unobagha, Uzoamaka Chinyelu. *Off to the sweet*
　　shores of Africa and other talking drum rhymes
Van Laan, Nancy. *Little Fish lost*
Verde, Susan. *The water princess*
Wallace, Joseph E. *Big and noisy Simon*
Walter, Mildred Pitts. *Brother to the wind*
Walters, Eric. *An African alphabet*
Williams, Karen Lynn. *Galimoto*
　　When Africa was home
Wilson, Anna. *Over in the grasslands*
Winter, Jeanette. *My baby*
Wolkstein, Diane. *The day Ocean came to visit*

Foreign lands – Antarctic

Bishop, Nic. *Penguin day*
Brooks, Erik. *Polar opposites*
Duquennoy, Jacques. *North Pole, South Pole*
Dyer, Heather. *Tina and the penguin*
Gibbons, Gail. *Penguins!*
Jeffers, Oliver. *Lost and found*
Kimmel, Elizabeth Cody. *My penguin Osbert in love*
Lester, Alison. *Sophie Scott goes south*
Livinson, Nancy Smiler. *North Pole, South Pole*
London, Jonathan. *Little penguin*
McDonald, Megan. *Penguin and Little Blue*
McQuade, Jacqueline. *Snow babies*
Radcliffe, Theresa. *Nanu, penguin chick*
Schofield, Jennifer. *Animal babies in polar lands*
Seibold, J. Otto. *Penguin dreams*
Townsend, Emily Rose. *Penguins*
Viva, Frank. *A trip to the bottom of the world with*
　　Mouse
Wilson, Karma. *Where is home, Little Pip?*
Wood, Audrey. *Little Penguin's tale*

Foreign lands – Arabia

Haskins, Jim. *Count your way through the Arab world*
Kimmel, Eric A. *The three princes*
Vallverdu, Josep. *Aladdin and the magic lamp /*
　　Aldino y la lampara maravillosa
Zeman, Ludmila. *Sindbad*

Foreign lands – Arctic

Agee, Jon. *Little Santa*
Aston, Dianna Hutts. *Loony Little*
Banks, Kate. *Pup and bear*
Berger, Melvin. *Brrr! a book about polar animals*

Berkes, Marianne. *Over in the Arctic*
Blaikie, Lynn. *Beyond the northern lights*
Brett, Jan. *The three snow bears*
Brooks, Erik. *Polar opposites*
Brown, Kerry. *Tupag the dreamer*
Crawford, Laura. *In arctic waters*
Crowley, Ned. *Nanook and Pryce*
De Beer, Hans. *Little Polar Bear and the whales*
Duquennoy, Jacques. *North Pole, South Pole*
Ford, Christine. *Ocean's child*
Ford, Miela. *Mom and me*
George, Jean Craighead. *The last polar bear*
　　Nutik and Amaroq play ball
　　Nutik, the wolf pup
　　Snow bear
Guiberson, Brenda Z. *Ice bears*
Heder, Thyra. *The bear report*
Hopkinson, Deborah. *Keep on!*
Livinson, Nancy Smiler. *North Pole, South Pole*
London, Jonathan. *Gone again ptarmigan*
　　Ice Bear and Little Fox
Luenn, Nancy. *Nessa's story*
McQuade, Jacqueline. *Snow babies*
Merski, P. K. *Roaring, boring, Alice*
Moss, Miriam. *The snow bear*
Primavera, Elise. *Auntie Claus*
　　Auntie Claus and the key to Christmas
Raffi. *Baby beluga*
Reynolds, Jan. *Far north*
Rives. *If I were a polar bear*
Rueda, Claudia. *My little polar bear*
Ryder, Joanne. *White bear, ice bear*
Sabuda, Robert. *The Blizzard's robe*
Schofield, Jennifer. *Animal babies in polar lands*
Sís, Peter. *A small tall tale from the far Far North*
Smith, Danna. *Arctic white*
Spinelli, Eileen. *Polar bear, arctic hare*
Taulbert, Clifton L. *Little Cliff and the cold place*
Taylor, Harriet Peck. *Ulaq and the northern lights*
Taylor, Theodore. *Hello, Arctic!*
Thompson, Lauren. *Polar bear morning*
Thomson, Sarah L. *Where do polar bears live?*
Townsend, Emily Rose. *Arctic foxes*
　　Polar bears
Votaw, Carol. *Good morning, little polar bear*
Wallace, Mary. *I is for Inuksuk*
Ward, Jennifer. *Way up in the Arctic*
Ward, Lindsay. *Please bring balloons*
Weatherford, Carole Boston. *I, Matthew Henson*
Wild, Margaret. *Thank you, Santa*
Winter, Jeanette. *Nanuk the ice bear*
Yolen, Jane. *Welcome to the icehouse*
Yoon, Salina. *Penguin's big adventure*

Foreign lands – Argentina

Dorros, Arthur. *Abuelo*
Lamm, C. Drew. *Gauchada*
Van Laan, Nancy. *The magic bean tree*

Foreign lands – Armenia

Hogrogian, Nonny. *The contest*
San Souci, Robert D. *A weave of words*

Foreign lands – Asia

Chin-Lee, Cynthia. *A is for Asia*
Sierra, Judy. *Counting crocodiles*

Foreign lands – Australia

Arnold, Caroline. *Australian animals*
  A platypus' world
  A wombat's world
Baker, Jeannie. *Mirror*
  The story of rosy dock
  Where the forest meets the sea
  Window
Berkes, Marianne. *Over in Australia*
Bonnett-Rampersaud, Louise. *Polly Hopper's pouch*
Brown, Marc. *Arthur's animal adventure*
Cheng, Christopher. *Python*
Dennard, Deborah. *Koala country*
Fox, Mem. *Possum magic*
French, Jackie. *Josephine wants to dance*
Lester, Alison. *Ernie dances to the didgeridoo*
Markle, Sandra. *Finding home*
  Hip-pocket papa
Morpurgo, Michael. *Wombat goes walkabout*
Napoli, Donna Jo. *Ready to dream*
Pettitt, Linda. *Yafi's family*
Reynolds, Jan. *Down under*
Roth, Susan L. *The biggest frog in Australia*
Shields, Carol Diggory. *Wombat walkabout*
Spurling, Margaret. *Bilby moon*
Votaw, Carol. *Waking up down under*
Ward, Helen. *Old shell, new shell*
Wild, Margaret. *Bobbie Dazzler*
  Thank you, Santa
Wolkstein, Diane. *Sun Mother wakes the world*

Foreign lands – Austria

Greenstein, Elaine. *The goose man*
Lester, Alison. *Running with the horses*
Lodding, Linda Ravin. *A gift for Mama*
Tompert, Ann. *A carol for Christmas*

Foreign lands – Bangladesh

Malaspina, Ann. *Yasmin's hammer*

Foreign lands – Bavaria *see* Foreign lands –
  Austria; Foreign lands – Germany

Foreign lands – Belarus

Manushkin, Fran. *How mama brought the spring*

Foreign lands – Belgium

Radunsky, Vladimir. *Manneken pis*

Foreign lands – Bosnia-Herzegovina

Bunting, Eve. *Gleam and Glow*

Foreign lands – Brazil

Brown, Monica. *Pelé, king of soccer / Pelé, el rey del
  fútbol*
Cherry, Lynne. *The great kapok tree*
Cline-Ransome, Lesa. *Young Pelé*
DeSpain, Pleasant. *The dancing turtle*
Haskins, Jim. *Count your way through Brazil*
Javaherbin, Mina. *Soccer star*
Lewin, Ted. *Amazon boy*
Malone, Cheryl Lawton. *Dario and the whale*

Van Laan, Nancy. *So say the little monkeys*

Foreign lands – British Columbia

Manuel, Lynn. *Camels always do*
Olsen, Sylvia. *Yetsa's sweater*

Foreign lands – Burkina Faso

Davies, Stephen. *All aboard for the Bobo Road*
Isabella, Jude. *The red bicycle*

Foreign lands – Cambodia

Coburn, Jewell Reinhart. *Angkat*
Ho, Minfong. *Brother Rabbit*
Lee, Jeanne M. *Silent lotus*
Lipp, Frederick. *Running shoes*
Riecherter, Daryn. *The Cambodian dancer*

Foreign lands – Cameroon

Alexander, Lloyd. *Fortune tellers*
Averbeck, Jim. *The market bowl*
Rockliff, Mara. *My heart will not sit down*
Tchana, Katrin. *Sense Pass King*

Foreign lands – Canada

Becker, Helaine. *Mama likes to mambo*
Blades, Ann. *Mary of mile 18*
  Too small
Brebeuf, Jean de. *The Huron carol*
Bushey, Jeanne. *The polar bear's gift*
Butler, Geoff. *Ode to Newfoundland*
Carney, Margaret. *At Grandpa's sugar bush*
Carter, Anne Laurel. *My home bay*
  Under a prairie sky
Clements, Andrew. *Tara and Tiree, fearless friends*
Cutler, Jane. *Guttersnipe*
Downie, Mary Alice. *A pioneer ABC*
Grassby, Donna. *A seaside alphabet*
Gregory, Nan. *Wild Girl and Gran*
Haskins, Jim. *Count your way through Canada*
Hodge, Deborah. *Emma's story*
Holling, Holling C. *Paddle-to-the-sea*
Hume, Stephen Eaton. *Red moon follows truck*
Lawson, Julie. *Arizona Charlie and the Klondike Kid*
Lee, Dennis. *Bubblegum delicious*
Lipp, Frederick. *The caged birds of Phnom Penh*
Little old lady who swallowed a fly. *There was an old
  lady who swallowed a fly*
London, Jonathan. *The sugaring-off party*
Lumry, Amanda. *Polar bear puzzle*
MacGregor, Roy. *The highest number in the world*
McNaughton, Janet. *Brave Jack and the unicorn*
Major, Kevin. *Eh to zed?*
Miles, Victoria. *Old Mother Bear*
Milord, Susan. *The ghost on the hearth*
Munsch, Robert N. *Love you forever*
  Mud puddle
  A promise is a promise
  Thomas' snowsuit
  Wait and see
  Where is Gah-Ning?
Pendziwol, Jean E. *The red sash*
Perkins, Lynne Rae. *Pictures from our vacation*
Pickthall, Marjorie L. C. *The worker in sandalwood*
Pinkwater, Daniel. *Young Larry*
Reynolds, Marilynn. *The name of the child*

Stuchner, Joan Betty. *The Kugel Valley Klezmer Band*
Thien, Madeleine. *The Chinese violin*
Walker, Sally M. *Winnie*
Ward, Lynd. *The biggest bear*
Wiebe, Rudy. *Hidden buffalo*
Wishinsky, Frieda. *Where are you, Bear?*
Zagwӳn, Deborah Turney. *The pumpkin blanket*

Foreign lands – Caribbean Islands

Asbjørnsen, P. C. *The three Billygoats Gruff and Mean Calypso Joe*
Bryan, Ashley. *Can't scare me!*
   Sing to the sun
Godard, Alex. *Mama, across the sea*
Hallworth, Grace. *Sing me a story*
Hohn, Nadia L. *Malaika's costume*
Hurst, Margaret M. *Grannie and the Jumbie*
Isadora, Rachel. *Caribbean dream*
Lessac, Frané. *Island Counting 123*
McLean, Dirk. *Play mas'! a carnival ABC*
McMillan, Bruce. *Sense suspense*
Moreton, Daniel. *La Cucaracha Martina*
Moser, Barry. *Psalm 23*
Rahaman, Vashanti. *O Christmas tree*
San Souci, Robert D. *Cendrillon*
   The faithful friend
   The house in the sky

Foreign lands – Central America

Ada, Alma Flor. *The gold coin*
Tortillas and lullabies / Tortillas y cancioncitas
Wisniewski, David. *Rain player*

Foreign lands – Chad

Rumford, James. *Rain school*

Foreign lands – Chile

Foreman, Michael. *Mia's story*
Pitcher, Caroline. *Mariana and the merchild*
Rand, Gloria. *A pen pal for Max*

Foreign lands – China

Aesop. *The ant and the grasshopper*
Andersen, Hans Christian. *The emperor's new clothes*
   The emperor's new clothes: a tale set in China
   The nightingale, ill. by Nancy Ekholm Burkert
   The nightingale, ill. by Pirkko Vainio
   The nightingale, ill. by Lisbeth Zwerger
Berkeley, Jon. *Chopsticks*
Bishop, Claire Huchet. *The five Chinese brothers*
Brett, Jan. *Daisy comes home*
Bridges, Shirin Yim. *Ruby's wish*
Casanova, Mary. *The hunter*
Chan, Arlene. *Awakening the dragon*
Chen, Kerstin. *Lord of the cranes*
Clark, Karen Henry. *Sweet moon baby*
Compestine, Ying Chang. *Boy dumplings*
   D is for dragon dance
   The real story of stone soup
   The runaway rice cake
   The runaway wok
   The story of chopsticks
   The story of noodles
   The story of paper
Coste, Marion. *Finding Joy*

Crane, Carol. *D is for dancing dragon*
Czernecki, Stefan. *Paper lanterns*
D'Antonio, Nancy. *Our baby from China*
Demi. *The dragon's tale and other animal fables of the Chinese zodiac*
   The empty pot
   The girl who drew a phoenix
   The greatest treasure
   The magic pillow
   The shady tree
Flack, Marjorie. *The story about Ping*
Gibbons, Gail. *Giant pandas*
Granfield, Linda. *The legend of the panda*
Handforth, Thomas. *Mei Li*
Haskins, Jim. *Count your way through China*
Heyer, Marilee. *The weaving of a dream*
Hodge, Deborah. *Emma's story*
Hong, Chen Jiang. *The magic horse of Han Gan*
Hyde, Heidi Smith. *Shanghai Sukkah*
Jiang, Ji-li. *The magical Monkey King, mischief in heaven*
   Red kite, blue kite
Keister, Douglas. *To grandmother's house*
Krebs, Laurie. *We're riding on a caravan*
Lee, Jeanne M. *The song of Mu Lan*
Lewis, Rose A. *I love you like crazy cakes*
Lin, Grace. *The red thread*
Lobel, Arnold. *Ming Lo moves the mountain*
Loo, Sanne te. *Ping-Li's kite*
Look, Lenore. *Brush of the gods*
Louie, Ai-Ling. *Yeh Shen*
Louis, Catherine. *Liu and the bird*
McClintock, Barbara. *Lost and found: Adele and Simon in China*
Mahy, Margaret. *The seven Chinese brothers*
Maples in the mist
Markle, Sandra. *How many baby pandas?*
Marx, Trish. *Kindergarten day USA and China*
Morris, Ann. *Grandma Lai Goon remembers*
Mosel, Arlene. *Tikki Tikki Tembo*
Muth, Jon J. *Stone soup*
Nagda, Anne Whitehead. *A home for panda*
Niemann, Christoph. *The pet dragon*
Okimoto, Jean Davies. *The White Swan express*
Orgel, Doris. *The cat's tale*
Pacilio, V. J. *Ling Cho and his three friends*
Partridge, Elizabeth. *Oranges on Golden Mountain*
Perry, Phyllis J. *Pandas' earthquake escape*
Pilegard, Virginia Walton. *The warlord's alarm*
   The warlord's beads
   The warlord's puzzle
Piumini, Roberto. *Doctor Me Di Cin*
Poole, Amy Lowry. *How the rooster got his crown*
   The pea blossom
Potter, Alicia. *Mrs. Harkness and the panda*
Rappaport, Doreen. *The long-haired girl*
Rocco, John. *Wolf! wolf!*
Rumford, James. *Chee-lin*
Ryder, Joanne. *Panda kindergarten*
San Souci, Robert D. *The enchanted tapestry*
Schaefer, Lola M. *Chinese New Year*
So, Sungwan. *Shanyi goes to China*
Stevens, Jan Romero. *Carlos digs to China / Carlos excava hasta la China*
Stoeke, Janet Morgan. *Waiting for May*
Tan, Amy. *The Chinese Siamese cat*
   The moon lady
Thisdale, François. *Nini*
Tompert, Ann. *Grandfather Tang's story*

Tseng, Grace. *White tiger, blue serpent*
Tsubakiyama, Margaret. *Mei-Mei loves the morning*
Tucker, Kathy. *The seven Chinese sisters*
Van Woerkom, Dorothy. *The rat, the ox and the zodiac*
Wade, Mary Dodson. *No year of the cat*
Wang, Andrea. *The Nian Monster*
Wang, Gabrielle. *The race for the Chinese zodiac*
Wang, Xiaohong. *One year in Beijing*
Whitfield, Susan. *The animals of the Chinese zodiac*
Wiese, Kurt. *Fish in the air*
Yang, Belle. *Always come home to me*
Yee, Paul. *Bamboo*
Yep, Laurence. *Auntie Tiger*
   Dragon prince
   The man who tricked a ghost
   The shell woman and the king
Yi, Hu Yong. *Good morning China*
Yolen, Jane. *The emperor and the kite*
Young, Ed. *Cat and Rat*
   Little Plum
   Lon Po Po
   The lost horse
   Monkey King
   Mouse match
   Night visitors
Yu, Li-Qiong. *A New Year's reunion*
Zhang, Song Nan. *The ballad of Mulan*

Foreign lands – Colombia

Brown, Monica. *My name is Gabito / Me llamo Gabito*
   Waiting for the Biblioburro
Torres, Leyla. *Saturday sancocho*
Winter, Jeanette. *Biblioburro*

Foreign lands – Congo (Democratic Republic)

Aardema, Verna. *Traveling to Tondo*
Hatkoff, Craig, et al. *Looking for Miza*

Foreign lands – Costa Rica

Burns, Loree Griffin. *Handle with care*
Keister, Douglas. *Fernando's gift / El regalo de Fernando*
Strauss, Susan. *When woman became the sea*

Foreign lands – Cuba

Deedy, Carmen Agra. *Martina the beautiful cockroach*
Engle, Margarita. *All the way to Havana*
   Drum dream girl
Leiner, Katherine. *Mama does the mambo*
Sacre, Antonio. *A mango in the hand*
Sciurba, Katie. *Oye, Celia!*

Foreign lands – Czechoslovakia

Krykorka, Ian. *Carl, the Christmas carp*
Marshak, S. *The Month-Brothers*
Sís, Peter. *The wall: growing up behind the Iron Curtain*
Van Kampen, Vlasta. *Bear tales*
Wisniewski, David. *Golem*

Foreign lands – Denmark

Burdett, Lois. *Hamlet for kids*
Deedy, Carmen Agra. *The yellow star*
Drummond, Allan. *Energy island*
Elvgren, Jennifer. *The whispering town*
MacDonald, Margaret Read. *Fat cat*

Foreign lands – Dominican Republic

Alvarez, Julia. *The secret footprints*
Tavares, Matt. *Growing up Pedro*

Foreign lands – Ecuador

Delacre, Lulu. *¡Olinguito, de la A a la Z! / Olinguito, from A to Z!*

Foreign lands – Egypt

Aliki. *Mummies made in Egypt*
Auld, Mary. *Exodus from Egypt*
Base, Graeme. *The Jewel Fish of Karnak*
Bower, Tamara. *The shipwrecked sailor*
Climo, Shirley. *The Egyptian Cinderella*
dePaola, Tomie. *Bill and Pete go down the Nile*
Ewert, Marcus. *Mummy cat*
Farmer, Nancy. *Clever Ali*
Hartland, Jessie. *How the sphinx got to the museum*
Heide, Florence Parry. *The day of Ahmed's secret*
Hofmeyr, Dianne. *The star-bearer*
Krebs, Laurie. *We're sailing down the Nile*
Marcellino, Fred. *I, crocodile*
Price, Leontyne. *Aïda*
Roth, Susan L. *Hands around the library*
Rouss, Sylvia A. *The littlest frog*
Sabuda, Robert. *Tutankhamen's gift*
St. George, Judith. *Zarafa*
Stolz, Mary. *Zekmet, the stone carver*
Yates, Philip. *Ten little mummies*

Foreign lands – El Salvador

Argueta, Jorge. *Trees are hanging from the sky*
Colato Laínez, René. *My shoes and I*

Foreign lands – England

Ahlberg, Allan. *The baby in the hat*
Anno, Mitsumasa. *Anno's Britain*
Antony, Steve. *The Queen's hat*
Atkins, Jeannine. *Mary Anning and the sea dragon*
Beardshaw, Rosalind. *Grandpa's surprise*
Bemelmans, Ludwig. *Madeline in London*
Bennett, Jill. *Teeny tiny*
Brooks, Nigel. *Country mouse cottage*
   Town mouse house
Brown, Don. *Rare treasure*
   Uncommon traveler
Brown, Ruth. *A dark, dark tale*
Burnett, Frances Hodgson. *A little princess*, ill. by Barbara McClintock
   A little princess, ill. by Graham Rust
   The secret garden
Cousins, Lucy. *Maisy goes to London*
DeFelice, Cynthia C. *Nelly May has her say*
Dennard, Deborah. *Hedgehog haven*
Dick Whittington and his cat. *Dick Whittington and his cat*, ill. by Marcia Brown

Dick Whittington and his cat, ill. by Mélisande
Potter
Egan, Tim. *Dodsworth in London*
Francis, Pauline. *Sam stars at Shakespeare's Globe*
Grahame, Kenneth. *The wind in the willows*
Hodges, Margaret. *Saint George and the dragon*
Hopkinson, Deborah. *The humblebee hunter*
Hughes, Shirley. *Alfie and the big boys*
 Out and about
Jack and the beanstalk. *Jack and the beanstalk*
Kennedy, Cindy. *The star of Christmas*
Ketcham, Sallie. *The Christmas bird*
Little old lady who swallowed a fly. *I know an old
 lady*
 I know an old lady who swallowed a fly, ill. by
 Stephen Gulbis
 I know an old lady who swallowed a fly, ill. by Glen
 Rounds
 I know an old lady who swallowed a fly, ill. by
 Nadine Bernard Westcott
Long, Sylvia. *Deck the hall*
McCully, Emily Arnold. *Popcorn at the palace*
MacDonald, Alan. *Wilfred to the rescue*
MacDonald, Margaret Read. *The old woman who
 lived in a vinegar bottle*
Munro, Roxie. *The inside-outside book of London*
Richardson, Justin. *Christian, the hugging lion*
Riggio, Anita. *Beware the Brindlebeast*
Robins, Arthur. *The teeny tiny woman*
Rogers, Gregory. *The boy, the bear, the baron, the bard*
 Midsummer knight
San Souci, Robert D. *The Hobyahs*
 Robin Hood and the golden arrow
Wahl, Jan. *Little Johnny Buttermilk*
Whelan, Gloria. *Queen Victoria's bathing machine*
Zemach, Harve. *Duffy and the devil*

Foreign lands – Ethiopia

Day, Nancy Raines. *The lion's whiskers*
Kessler, Cristina. *The best beekeeper of Lalibela*
Kurtz, Jane. *Faraway home*
Onyefulu, Ifeoma. *Omer's favorite place*
Pettitt, Linda. *Yafi's family*
Schur, Maxine Rose. *Day of delight*

Foreign lands – Europe

Banks, Kate. *City cat*
Jaffe, Nina. *The way meat loves salt*
Keefer, Janice Kulyk. *Anna's goat*

Foreign lands – Finland

Shepard, Aaron. *The princess mouse*

Foreign lands – France

Anderson, M. T. *Strange Mr. Satie*
Arnold, Marsha Diane. *Metro cat*
Bemelmans, Ludwig. *Madeline*
 Madeline and the bad hat
 Madeline and the gypsies
 Madeline's Christmas
 Madeline's rescue
Brunhoff, Jean de. *The story of Babar, the little
 elephant*
Brunhoff, Laurent de. *Babar's guide to Paris*
Chall, Marsha Wilson. *Bonaparte*
Chaud, Benjamin. *The bear's song*

Coxe, Molly. *Bunny and the beast*
Demi. *Joan of Arc*
Dicmas, Courtney. *Harold finds a voice*
Dominguez, Angela. *Let's go, Hugo!*
Egan, Tim. *Dodsworth in Paris*
Ellwand, David. *Cinderlily*
Goode, Diane. *Mama's perfect present*
Hartland, Jessie. *Bon appétit!*
Haskins, Jim. *Count your way through France*
Hawkes, Kevin. *Remy and Lulu*
Hobbie, Holly. *Toot and Puddle, top of the world*
Holmes, Mary Tavener. *A giraffe goes to Paris*
Huling, Jan. *Puss in cowboy boots*
Ichikawa, Satomi. *Come fly with me*
 La La Rose
Johnson, D. B. *Magritte's marvelous hat*
Kelley, True. *Claude Monet*
Kimmelman, Leslie. *Everybody bonjours!*
Littlesugar, Amy. *Lisette's angel*
Lodding, Linda Ravin. *Painting Pepette*
McCaughrean, Geraldine. *Beauty and the beast*
McClintock, Barbara. *Adele and Simon*
McCully, Emily Arnold. *Mirette on the high wire*
McLaren, Chesley. *Zat cat!*
Mader, C. Roger. *Tiptop cat*
Magoon, Scott. *Hugo and Miles in I've painted
 everything!*
Marcellino, Fred. *I, crocodile*
Marciano, John Bemelmans. *Madeline and the old
 house in Paris*
Markel, Michelle. *The fantastic jungles of Henri
 Rousseau*
Muller, Gerda. *How does my garden grow?*
Munro, Roxie. *The inside-outside book of Paris*
Neuschwander, Cindy. *Pastry school in Paris*
Olofsson, Helena. *The little jester*
Olshan, Matthew. *The mighty Lalouche*
Palatini, Margie. *Three French hens*
Parker, Marjorie Blain. *Colorful dreamer*
Perrault, Charles. *Cinderella / Cenicienta*
Polacco, Patricia. *The butterfly*
Poole, Josephine. *Joan of Arc*
Pullman, Philip. *Puss in boots: the adventures of that
 most enterprising feline*
Raffi. *Wheels on the bus*
Rappaport, Doreen. *The secret seder*
Reich, Susanna. *Minette's feast*
Rubin, Susan Goldman. *The yellow house*
St. George, Judith. *Zarafa*
Schubert, Leda. *Monsieur Marceau*
Selznick, Brian. *The invention of Hugo Cabret*
Sís, Peter. *The pilot and the Little Prince*
Smith, Matthew Clark. *Lighter than air*
 *Small wonders: Jean-Henri Fabre and his world of
 insects*
Stevenson, Harvey. *Looking at liberty*
Sweeney, Joan. *Suzette and the puppy*
Titus, Eve. *Anatole*
 Anatole and the cat
Wells, Rosemary. *The miraculous tale of the two
 Maries*
Whelan, Gloria. *The boy who wanted to cook*
Willems, Mo. *Nanette's baguette*
Winter, Jeanette. *Henri's scissors*
Yolleck, Joan. *Paris in the spring with Picasso*
Yorinks, Arthur. *Harry and Lulu*
Young, Amy. *Belinda in Paris*
Ziarnik, Natalie. *Madeleine's light*

Foreign lands – French Guiana

Ryder, Joanne. *Jaguar in the rain forest*

Foreign lands – Galapagos Islands

Furrow, Eva. *Take your time*
George, Jean Craighead. *Galápagos George*
Jacobs, Francine. *Lonesome George, the giant tortoise*
Krebs, Laurie. *We're sailing to Galapagos*
Winkelman, Barbara Gaines. *Puffer's surprise*

Foreign lands – Gambia

Paul, Miranda. *One plastic bag*

Foreign lands – Germany

Allen, Debbie. *Brothers of the knight*
Bauer, Sepp. *The Christmas rose*
Browning, Robert. *The pied piper of Hamelin*, ill. by
    Mercer Mayer
    The pied piper of Hamelin, ill. by Drahos Zak
Delessert, Etienne. *The seven dwarfs*
Grimm, Jacob and Wilhelm. *As luck would have it*
    The brave little tailor, ill. by Olga Dugina
    The brave little tailor, ill. by David Shaw
    The elves and the shoemaker, ill. by Kirill
        Chelushkin
    The elves and the shoemaker, ill. by Paul Galdone
    The elves and the shoemaker, ill. by Margaret Walty
    Hans my hedgehog
    Iron John, ill. by Trina Schart Hyman
    Iron John, ill. by Winslow Pels
    The rabbit's bride
    Seven at one blow
    The shoemaker and his elves
    The shoemaker and the elves, ill. by Adrienne
        Adams
    The shoemaker and the elves, ill. by Ilse Plume
    The three spinning fairies
Haskins, Jim. *Count your way through Germany*
Janisch, Heinz. *The merry pranks of Till Eulenspiegel*
Johnson, Grace. *The candle in the window*
Norling, Beth. *Sister night and sister day*
Raven, Margot Theis. *Mercedes and the chocolate
    pilot*
Root, Phyllis. *Grandmother Winter*
Seeger, Pete. *Some friends to feed*
Stewig, John Warren. *Mother Holly*
Ungerer, Tomi. *Otto: the autobiography of a teddy bear*
Wiviott, Meg. *Benno and the night of broken glass*

Foreign lands – Ghana

Angelou, Maya. *Kofi and his magic*
Cumberbatch, Judy. *Can you hear the sea?*
Cummings, Pat. *Ananse and the lizard*
Kurtz, Jane. *In the small, small night*
Medearis, Angela Shelf. *Seven spools of thread*
    Too much talk
Milway, Katie Smith. *One hen*
Mollel, Tololwa M. *Ananse's feast*
Musgrove, Margaret. *The spider weaver*
Onyefulu, Ifeoma. *Deron goes to nursery school*
    Grandma comes to stay
Thompson, Laurie Ann. *Emmanuel's dream*

Foreign lands – Gilbert Islands *see* Foreign
    lands – South Sea Islands

Foreign lands – Great Britain

Antony, Steve. *The queen's handbag*
Browne, Anthony. *The shape game*

Foreign lands – Greece

Aliki. *Three gold pieces*
    The twelve months
Haskins, Jim. *Count your way through Greece*
Manna, Anthony L. *The orphan*
Mayer, Marianna. *Pegasus*
    Perseus
Rumford, James. *There's a monster in the alphabet*
Stewig, John Warren. *King Midas*

Foreign lands – Greenland

Dupre, Kelly. *The raven's gift*

Foreign lands – Guatemala

Carling, Amelia Lau. *Mama and Papa have a store*
Castaneda, Omar S. *Abuela's weave*
Marshall, Linda Elovitz. *Rainbow weaver / Tejedora
    del arcoíris*
Mora, Pat. *The race of toad and deer*

Foreign lands – Haiti

Danticat, Edwidge. *Eight days*
Elvgren, Jennifer Riesmeyer. *Josias, hold the book*
Lauture, Denizé. *Running the road to ABC*
MacDonald, Amy. *Please, Malese!*
Oelschlager, Vanita. *I came from the water*
Van Laan, Nancy. *Mama rocks, Papa sings*
Watson, Jesse Joshua. *Hope for Haiti*
Williams, Karen Lynn. *Painted dreams*
    Tap-tap

Foreign lands – Himalayas

Fleming, Candace. *When Agnes caws*
Nagda, Anne Whitehead. *World above the clouds*
Peet, Mal. *Cloud tea monkeys*

Foreign lands – Holland

Fleming, Candace. *Boxes for Katje*
Gottesfeld, Jeff. *The tree in the courtyard*
Rosenstock, Barb. *Vincent can't sleep*
Woelfle, Gretchen. *Katje the windmill cat*

Foreign lands – Honduras

Milway, Katie Smith. *The good garden*

Foreign lands – Hungary

Brown, Margaret Wise. *Wheel on the chimney*
Heiligman, Deborah. *The boy who loved math*
Lottridge, Celia Barker. *The little rooster and the
    diamond button*
MacDonald, Margaret Read. *Little Rooster's
    diamond button*

Foreign lands – Iceland

McMillan, Bruce. *Days of the ducklings*
    How the ladies stopped the wind

Nights of the pufflings
The problem with chickens
Wisniewski, David. *Elfwyn's saga*

Foreign lands – India

Appelt, Kathi. *Elephants aloft*
Arenson, Roberta. *Manu and the talking fish*
Bannerman, Helen. *The story of Little Babaji*
    The story of Little Black Sambo (1996)
    The story of Little Black Sambo (1990)
    The story of Little Black Sambo (2003)
Brown, Marcia. *Once a mouse . . .*
Bruce, Lisa. *Engines, engines*
Charles, Veronika Martenova. *The birdman*
Divakaruni, Chitra Banerjee. *Grandma and the
    great gourd*
Gardeski, Christina Mia. *Diwali*
Hamilton, Martha. *The ghost catcher*
Haskins, Jim. *Count your way through India*
Javaherbin, Mina. *Elephant in the dark*
Jeyaveeran, Ruth. *The road to Mumbai*
Kimmel, Elizabeth Cody. *A taste of freedom*
Kipling, Rudyard. *Rikki-tikki-tavi*, ill. by Lambert
    Davis
    Rikki-tikki-tavi, ill. by Jerry Pinkney
Kostecki-Shaw, Jenny Sue. *Same, same but different*
Kroll, Virginia L. *Selvakumar knew better*
Lester, Julius. *Sam and the tigers*
McDermott, Gerald. *Monkey*
McGinty, Alice B. *Gandhi*
Noyes, Deborah. *When I met the wolf girls*
Rumford, James. *Nine animals and the well*
Sebra, Richard. *It's Diwali!*
Sehgal, Kabir. *A bucket of blessings*
    The wheels on the tuk tuk
Shepard, Aaron. *The gifts of Wali Dad*
Sheth, Kashmira. *Monsoon afternoon*
So, Meilo. *Gobble, gobble, slip, slop*
Souhami, Jessica. *No dinner!*
    Rama and the demon king
Thornhill, Jan. *The rumor*
Verma, Jatinder Nath. *The story of Divaali*
Young, Ed. *Seven blind mice*
Zacharias, Ravi. *The merchant and the thief*

Foreign lands – Indonesia

Gilman, Rita Golden. *Rice is life*
Henrichs, Wendy. *When Anju loved being an elephant*
Scott, Nathan Kumar. *Mangoes and bananas*
    The sacred banana leaf
Sierra, Judy. *The gift of the crocodile*

Foreign lands – Iran

Balouch, Kristen. *The king and the three thieves*
    Mystery bottle
Haskins, Jim. *Count your way through Iran*
Javaherbin, Mina. *The secret message*
Oppenheim, Shulamith Levey. *Ali and the magic
    stew*
Shepard, Aaron. *Forty fortunes*

Foreign lands – Iraq

Alrawi, Karim. *The girl who lost her smile*
Dennis, Major Brian. *Nubs*
Hickox, Rebecca. *The golden sandal*
Kosofsky, Chaim. *Much, much better*

Rumford, James. *Silent music*
Winter, Jeanette. *The librarian of Basra*
    The world is not a rectangle

Foreign lands – Ireland

Balian, Lorna. *Leprechauns never lie*
Bateman, Teresa. *Fiona's luck*
    Traveling Tom and the leprechaun
Bunting, Eve. *Ballywhinney Girl*
    Finn McCool and the great fish
    Walking to school
Climo, Shirley. *The Irish Cinderlad*
Daly, Jude. *Fair, brown and trembling*
dePaola, Tomie. *Fin M'Coul*
    Jamie O'Rourke and the big potato
    Jamie O'Rourke and the pooka
    Patrick
Edwards, Pamela Duncan. *The leprechaun's gold*
Esckelson, Laura. *The copper braid of Shannon
    O'Shea*
Garland, Michael. *King Puck*
Haskins, Jim. *Count your way through Ireland*
Hazen, Barbara Shook. *Katie's wish*
Krensky, Stephen. *Too many leprechauns*
McCully, Emily Arnold. *The pirate queen*
McDermott, Gerald. *Daniel O'Rourke*
Milligan, Bryce. *Brigid's cloak*
    The prince of Ireland and the three magic stallions
Murphy, Jim. *Fergus and the Night-Demon*
Nolan, Janet. *The St. Patrick's Day shillelagh*
San Souci, Robert D. *Brave Margaret*
Souhami, Jessica. *Mrs. McCool and the giant
    Cuhullin*
Taylor, Alice. *A child's treasury of Irish rhymes*
Tompert, Ann. *Saint Patrick*
Welling, Peter J. *Shawn O'Hisser, the last snake in
    Ireland*
Woodruff, Elvira. *Small beauties*

Foreign lands – Israel

Abraham, Michelle Shapiro. *My cousin Tamar lives
    in Israel*
Adler, David A. *A picture book of Israel*
Alexander, Sue. *Behold the trees*
Auld, Mary. *David and Goliath*
Biers-Ariel, Matt. *Solomon and the trees*
Cohen, Deborah Bodin. *Engineer Ari and the Rosh
    Hashana ride*
da Costa, Deborah. *Snow in Jerusalem*
Fisher, Leonard Everett. *David and Goliath*
Goldsboro, Bobby. *Noah and the ark; and, David
    and Goliath*
Haskins, Jim. *Count your way through Israel*
Herman, Charlotte. *First rain*
Oberman, Sheldon. *The wisdom bird*
Ofanansky, Allison. *Harvest of light*

Foreign lands – Italy

Aesop. *Androcles and the lion*, ill. by Dennis Nolan
    Androcles and the lion, ill. by Janet Stevens
    Androcles and the lion: and other Aesop fables
Angelou, Maya. *Angelina of Italy*
Anno, Mitsumasa. *Anno's Italy*
Barton, Bob. *Paul Gallico's The small miracle*
Costanza, Stephen. *Vivaldi and the invisible orchestra*
dePaola, Tomie. *Big Anthony, his story*
    The clown of God

Jingle, the Christmas clown
The legend of Old Befana
Merry Christmas, Strega Nona
Tony's bread
DiLorenzo, Barbara. *Renato and the lion*
Egan, Tim. *Dodsworth in Rome*
Egielski, Richard. *St. Francis and the wolf*
Falconer, Ian. *Olivia goes to Venice*
Fleming, Candace. *Gabriella's song*
Gibfried, Diane. *Brother Juniper*
Grant, Rose Marie. *Andiamo, Weasel*
Gutman, Anne. *Gaspard on vacation*
Hamilton, Martha. *Priceless gifts*
Haskins, Jim. *Count your way through Italy*
Marciano, John Bemelmans. *Madeline and the cats
    of Rome*
Mauner, Claudia. *Zoe Sophia's scrapbook*
Nivola, Claire A. *Orani*
Norris, Kathleen. *The holy twins*
Pericoli, Matteo. *Tommaso and the missing line*
Potter, Giselle. *The year I didn't go to school*
Russo, Marisabina. *I will come back for you*
Sanderson, Ruth. *Papa Gatto*
Weaver, Tess. *Opera cat*
Willard, Nancy. *The flying bed*
Yorinks, Arthur. *The Miami giant*

Foreign lands – Jamaica

Hanson, Regina. *A season for mangoes*
Temple, Frances. *Tiger soup*

Foreign lands – Japan

Bang, Molly. *Dawn*
Bauld, Jane Scoggins. *Journey of the third seed*
Bodkin, Odds. *The crane wife*
Christian, Mary Blount. *If not for the calico cat*
Coerr, Eleanor. *Circus day in Japan*
    Sadako
Gershator, Phillis. *Sky sweeper*
Goldsaito, Katrina. *The sound of silence*
Gollub, Matthew. *Cool melons — turn to frogs*
    Ten oni drummers
Haskins, Jim. *Count your way through Japan*
Henrichs, Wendy. *I am Tama, lucky cat*
Hodges, Margaret. *The wave*
Iijima, Geneva Cobb. *The way we do it in Japan*
Issa, Kobayashi. *Today and today*
Johnston, Tony. *The badger and the magic fan*
Kajikawa, Kimiko. *Tsunami!*
    Yoshi's feast
Kako, Satoshi. *Little Daruma and little Daikoku*
    Little Daruma and little Kaminari
Kimura, Yuichi. *One stormy night . . .*
    One sunny day . . .
Lachenmeyer, Nathaniel. *The origami master*
London, Jonathan. *Moshi moshi*
Mayer, Mercer. *Shibumi and the kitemaker*
Melmed, Laura Krauss. *The first song ever sung*
Meshon, Aaron. *Take me out to the Yakyu*
Mosel, Arlene. *The funny little woman*
Namioka, Lensey. *Hungriest boy in the world*
Nishizuka, Koko. *The beckoning cat*
Ohi, Ruth. *Kenta and the big wave*
Parot, Annelore. *Kimonos*
Paterson, Katherine. *The tale of the Mandarin ducks*
Preus, Margi. *The Peace Bell*
San Souci, Robert D. *The samurai's daughter*

The silver charm
The snow wife
Satoshi, Kako. *Little Daruma and little Tengu*
Say, Allen. *The bicycle man*
The boy in the garden
Erika-San
Grandfather's journey
Kamishibai man
Once under the cherry blossom tree
Tea with milk
Tree of cranes
Seki, Sunny. *The tale of the lucky cat*
Shannon, George. *Spring: a haiku story*
Sierra, Judy. *Tasty baby belly buttons*
Takabayashi, Mari. *I live in Tokyo*
Turner, Pamela S. *Hachiko*
Uchida, Yoshiko. *The magic purse*
The wise old woman
Waite, Michael P. *Jojofu*
Wells, Rosemary. *Yoko finds her way*
Yoko's paper cranes
Weston, Mark. *Honda*
Wisniewski, David. *Sumo Mouse*
The warrior and the wise man
Wright, Danielle. *Japanese nursery rhymes*
Yagawa, Sumiko. *The crane wife*
Yamada, Utako. *The story of Cherry the pig*
Yashima, Taro. *Crow boy*

Foreign lands – Kenya

Barasch, Lynne. *First come the zebra*
Browne, Eileen. *Handa's hen*
Chamberlin, Mary. *Mama Panya's pancakes*
Conway, David. *Lila and the secret of rain*
Cunnane, Kelly. *Chirchir is singing*
    For you are a Kenyan child
Doner, Kim. *On a road in Africa*
Ellis, Gerry. *Natumi takes the lead*
Johnson, Jen Cullerton. *Seeds of change*
Johnston, Tony. *A Kenya Christmas*
Kirk, Daniel. *Rhino in the house*
Milway, Katie Smith. *Mimi's village and how basic
    health care transformed it*
Mollel, Tololwa M. *Orphan boy*
    Rhinos for lunch and elephants for supper
Napoli, Donna Jo. *Mama Miti*
Nivola, Claire A. *Planting the trees of Kenya*
Oelschlager, Vanita. *Bonyo Bonyo*
Prevot, Franck. *Wangari Maathai*
Richardson, Justin. *Christian, the hugging lion*
Walters, Eric. *The matatu*
Williams, Karen Lynn. *Beatrice's dream*
Wilson-Max, Ken. *Fuhara means happy*
Winter, Jeanette. *Wangari's trees of peace*

Foreign lands – Korea

Bae, Hyun-Joo. *New clothes for New Year's day*
Chung, Hyechong. *K is for Korea*
Climo, Shirley. *The Korean Cinderella*
Farley, Carol J. *The king's secret*
Haskins, Jim. *Count your way through Korea*
Heo, Yumi. *The green frogs*
    Lady Hahn and her seven friends
Kim, Julie. *Where's Halmoni?*
Lee, Tae-Jun. *Waiting for Mama*
Park, Frances. *Good-bye, 382 Shin Dang Dong*
    The royal bee

Where on earth is my bagel?
Park, Linda Sue. *Bee-bim bop!*
  The firekeeper's son
San Souci, Daniel. *The rabbit and the dragon king*
Wong, Janet S. *The trip back home*

Foreign lands – Korea (North)

Park, Frances. *My freedom trip*

Foreign lands – Laos

Xiong, Blia. *Nine-in-one Grr! Grr!*
Youme. *Mali under the night sky*

Foreign lands – Lapland

Reynolds, Jan. *Far north*

Foreign lands – Latin America

Argueta, Jorge. *Salsa*
Mora, Pat. *A piñata in a pine tree*
Shahan, Sherry. *Fiesta!*
Stanton, Karen. *Papi's gift*
Thong, Roseanne. *Día de los muertos*
  'Twas nochebuena
Torres, Leyla. *Liliana's grandmothers*
Vidal, Beatriz A. *Federico and the Magi's gift*

Foreign lands – Lebanon

Heide, Florence Parry. *Sami and the time of the troubles*

Foreign lands – Liberia

Aardema, Verna. *Koi and the kola nuts*
  The vingananee and the tree toad
Paye, Won-Ldy. *Head, body, legs*
  Mrs. Chicken and the hungry crocodile

Foreign lands – Madagascar

Dennard, Deborah. *Lemur landing*
Rappaport, Doreen. *The new king*

Foreign lands – Malawi

Kamkwamba, William. *The boy who harnessed the wind*

Foreign lands – Malaysia

Goodman, Susan E. *Chopsticks for my noodle soup*

Foreign lands – Mali

Cowcher, Helen. *Desert elephants*
Diakité, Baba Wagué. *The magic gourd*
  Mee-an and the magic serpent
Diakité, Penda. *I lost my tooth in Africa*
Eisner, Will. *Sundiata*
Wisniewski, David. *Sundiata: lion king of Mali*

Foreign lands – Martinique

San Souci, Robert D. *The faithful friend*

Foreign lands – Mauritania

Cunnane, Kelly. *Deep in the Sahara*

Foreign lands – Mexico

Aardema, Verna. *Borreguita and the coyote*
  Pedro and the padre
  The riddle of the drum
Alarcón, Francisco X. *From the bellybutton of the moon and other summer poems / Del ombligo de la luna y otros poemas de verano*
Amado, Elisa. *What are you doing?*
Bernier-Grand, Carmen T. *Our Lady of Guadalupe*
Bullard, Lisa. *Marco's Cinco de Mayo*
Bunting, Eve. *Going home*
Cohn, Diana. *Dream carver*
Colato Laínez, René. *Playing lotería / El juego de la lotería*
Corpi, Lucha. *Where fireflies dance / Ahí, donde bailan las luciérnagas*
de la Peña, Matt. *Miguel and the grand harmony*
de Las Casas, Dianne. *Blue frog*
dePaola, Tomie. *The Lady of Guadalupe*
Dominguez, Angela. *Sing, don't cry*
Dorros, Arthur. *Julio's magic*
Ehlert, Lois. *Cuckoo, a Mexican folktale / Cucú: un cuento folklórico mexicano*
Elya, Susan Middleton. *N is for Navidad*
Ets, Marie Hall. *Nine days to Christmas*
Flanagan, Alice K. *Cinco de Mayo*
Frith, Margaret. *Frida Kahlo*
Garza, Cynthia Leonor. *Lucía the luchadora*
Goldman, Judy. *Uncle Monarch and the Day of the Dead*
Gonzales, Mark. *Yo soy Muslim*
Grimm, Jacob and Wilhelm *The fisherman and the turtle*
Grossman, Patricia. *Saturday market*
Guy, Ginger Foglesong. *Fiesta*
Haskins, Jim. *Count your way through Mexico*
Johnston, Tony. *Day of the Dead*
  The iguana brothers, a perfect day
  My Mexico / México mío
  P is for piñata
  The tale of Rabbit and Coyote
Joosse, Barbara. *Ghost wings*
Keep, Linda Lowery. *Day of the Dead*
Kimmel, Eric A. *The two mountains*
Krebs, Laurie. *Off we go to Mexico*
Larson, Bonnie. *When animals were people / Cuando los animales eran personas*
Levy, Janice. *Celebrate! It's cinco de mayo! / Celebremos! Es el cinco de mayo!*
McAlister, Caroline. *Holy Molé!*
McDermott, Gerald. *Musicians of the sun*
Madrigal, Antonio Hernandez. *Erandi's braids*
Martín, Hugo C. *Pablo's Christmas*
Meunier, Brian. *Bravo, Tavo!*
Mora, Pat. *The beautiful lady*
  The gift of the poinsettia / El regalo de la flor de nochebuena
  A library for Juana
  The night the moon fell
  The remembering day / El día de los muertos
Morales, Yuyi. *Just a minute: a trickster tale and counting book*
  Viva Frida
Perkins, Chloe. *Cinderella*
Rohmer, Harriet. *How we came to the fifth world*

Ross, Michael Elsohn. *Mexican Christmas*
Ryan, Pam Muñoz. *Mice and beans*
Sahagun, Bernardino de. *Spirit child*
Sanromán, Susana. *Señora Reganoña*
Schaefer, Lola M. *Cinco de Mayo*
Sobol, Richard. *Adelina's whales*
Swope, Sam. *Gotta go! Gotta go!*
Tafolla, Carmen. *What can you do with a rebozo?*
Tonatiuh, Duncan. *Dear Primo*
    Diego Rivera: his world and ours
Van Laan, Nancy. *La boda*
Volkmer, Jane Anne. *Song of Chirimia / La Musica de la Chirimia*
Wade, Mary Dodson. *Cinco de Mayo*
Weill, Cynthia. *Animal talk: Mexican folk art animal sounds in English and Spanish*
Winter, Jeanette. *Niño's mask*
Wisniewski, David. *Rain player*
Yacowitz, Caryn. *Pumpkin fiesta*
Ziefert, Harriet. *Home for Navidad*

Foreign lands – Middle East

Addasi, Maha. *Time to pray*
Arabian Nights *The tale of Ali Baba and the forty thieves*
Johnson-Davies, Denys. *Goha, the wise fool*
Kimmel, Eric A. *Joha makes a wish*
Shah, Idries. *The boy without a name*
    The clever boy and the terrible, dangerous animal
    The silly chicken
Weulersse, Odile. *Nasreddine*
Young, Ed. *What about me?*

Foreign lands – Mongolia

Baasansuren, Bolormaa. *My little round house*
Lewin, Ted. *Horse song*
Otsuka, Yuzo. *Suho's white horse*
Yep, Laurence. *The Khan's daughter*

Foreign lands – Morocco

Alalou, Elizabeth. *The butter man*
Baker, Jeannie. *Mirror*
Ichikawa, Satomi. *My father's shop*
London, Jonathan. *Ali, child of the desert*
Turk, Evan. *The storyteller*

Foreign lands – Namibia

Aardema, Verna. *Jackal's flying lesson*

Foreign lands – Nepal

Heine, Theresa. *Chandra's magic light*
Hobbie, Holly. *Toot and Puddle, top of the world*
Nagda, Anne Whitehead. *A tiger tale*
Reynolds, Jan. *Himalaya*
Stryer, Andrea Stenn. *Kami and the yaks*

Foreign lands – Netherlands *see* Foreign lands – Holland

Foreign lands – Nicaragua

Rohmer, Harriet. *Mother scorpion country*
Rohmer, Harriet, et al. *The invisible hunters*

Foreign lands – Nigeria

Daly, Niki. *Why the sun and moon live in the sky*
Gerson, Mary-Joan. *Why the sky is far away*
Medearis, Angela Shelf. *The singing man*
Mollel, Tololwa M. *The flying tortoise*
Olaleye, Isaac. *Bikes for rent!*
    Bitter bananas
    The distant talking drum
    In the Rainfield
Onyefulu, Ifeoma. *Ife's first haircut*
    Ogbo
    Saying goodbye
Shepard, Aaron. *Master man*

Foreign lands – Norway

Brett, Jan. *Who's that knocking on Christmas eve?*
Harvey, Matthea. *Cecil the pet glacier*
Kimmel, Eric A. *Easy work!*
Lunge-Larsen, Lise. *The race of the Birkebeiners*
Reynolds, Jan. *Far north*

Foreign lands – Pakistan

Khan, Rukhsana. *King for a day*
Mortenson, Greg. *Listen to the wind*
Shepard, Aaron. *The gifts of Wali Dad*
Williams, Karen Lynn. *Four feet, two sandals*
Winter, Jeanette. *Malala, a brave girl from Pakistan / Iqbal, a brave boy from Pakistan*
Yousafzai, Malala. *Malala's magic pencil*

Foreign lands – Palestine

MacDonald, Margaret Read. *Tunjur! Tunjur! Tunjur!*
Nye, Naomi Shihab. *Sitti's secrets*

Foreign lands – Panama

MacDonald, Margaret Read. *Conejito*
Palacios, Argentina. *A Christmas surprise for Chabelita*
Sayre, April Pulley. *Army ant parade*

Foreign lands – Persia

Climo, Shirley. *The Persian Cinderella*
Nadimi, Suzan. *The rich man and the parrot*

Foreign lands – Peru

Díaz, Katacha. *Carolina's gift*
Dominguez, Angela. *Maria had a little llama/Maria tenia una llama pequena*
Dorros, Arthur. *Tonight is carnaval*
Ehlert, Lois. *Moon rope / Un lazo a la luna*
Horowitz, Dave. *Chico the brave*
Krebs, Laurie. *Up and down the Andes*
Tompert, Ann. *The pied piper of Peru*

Foreign lands – Philippines

Climo, Shirley. *Tuko and the birds*
San Souci, Robert D. *Pedro and the monkey*

Foreign lands – Poland

Carnesi, Monica. *Little dog lost*

Sasso, Sandy Eisenberg. *Butterflies under our hats*
Ungar, Richard. *Rachel's library*

Foreign lands – Puerto Rico

Gugler, Laurel Dee. *There's a billy goat in the garden*
Jaffe, Nina. *The golden flower*
London, Jonathan. *Hurricane!*
Montes, Marisa. *Juan Bobo goes to work*
Rohmer, Harriet. *Atariba and Niguayona*
Roth, Susan L. *Parrots over Puerto Rico*
Santiago, Esmeralda. *A doll for Navidades*

Foreign lands – Romania

Gray, Karlin. *Nadia*
Philip, Neil. *Noah and the devil*

Foreign lands – Russia

Arnold, Katya. *That apple is mine!*
Bateson-Hill, Margaret. *Masha and the firebird*
Bell, Anthea. *Vasilisa the beautiful*
Brett, Jan. *The turnip*
Brown, Marcia. *Stone soup*
Cole, Joanna. *Bony-legs*
Corr, Christopher. *Deep in the woods*
Croll, Carolyn. *The little snowgirl*
The firebird. *The firebird*, ill. by Demi
    The firebird, ill. by Rachel Isadora
    The tale of the firebird
Ginsburg, Mirra. *Clay boy*
Haskins, Jim. *Count your way through Russia*
Hoffman, Mary. *Clever Katya*
Horn, Sandra Ann. *Babushka*
Howland, Naomi. *Latkes, latkes, good to eat*
Joosse, Barbara. *Nikolai, the only bear*
Kabakov, Vladimir. *R is for Russia*
King, Dedie. *I see the sun in Russia*
London, Jonathan. *Little lost tiger*
McCaughrean, Geraldine. *Grandma Chickenlegs*
Martin, Rafe. *The language of birds*
Mayer, Marianna. *Baba Yaga and Vasilisa the Brave*
Oram, Hiawyn. *Baba Yaga and the wise doll*
Parkinson, Kathy. *The enormous turnip*
Pavlova, Anna. *I dreamed I was a ballerina*
Peck, Jan. *The giant carrot*
Polacco, Patricia. *Babushka's Mother Goose*
Prokofiev, Sergei Sergeievitch. *Peter and the wolf*,
    ill. by Charles Mikolaycak
    Peter and the wolf, ill. by Josef Palecek
    Peter and the wolf, ill. by Chris Raschka
    Peter and the wolf, ill. by Vladimir Vagin
Robbins, Ruth. *Baboushka and the three kings*
Sanderson, Ruth. *The golden mare, the firebird, and
    the magic ring*
San Souci, Robert D. *Peter and the blue witch baby*
Schuch, Steve. *A symphony of whales*
Shepard, Aaron. *The sea king's daughter*
Spirin, Gennady. *Martha*
    Philipok
Thompson, Kay. *Kay Thompson's Eloise in Moscow*
Tolstoy, Aleksey Nikolayevich. *The enormous turnip*
    The gigantic turnip
Vagin, Vladimir. *The enormous carrot*
Van Kampen, Vlasta. *Bear tales*
Winthrop, Elizabeth. *Vasilissa the beautiful*
Yolen, Jane. *The firebird*
    The flying witch

Foreign lands – Rwanda

Aardema, Verna. *Sebgugugu the glutton*

Foreign lands – Sahara Desert

Reynolds, Jan. *Sahara*

Foreign lands – Saudi Arabia

MacDonald, Margaret Read. *How many donkeys?*

Foreign lands – Scandinavia

Manning, Mick. *What a Viking!*

Foreign lands – Scotland

Alger, Leclaire Gowans. *All in the morning early*
    Always room for one more
Burdett, Lois. *Macbeth for kids*
Leaf, Munro. *Wee Gillis*
Lester, Helen. *The loch mess monster*
Lupton, Hugh. *Pirican Pic and Pirican Mor*
Thompson, Emma. *The further tale of Peter Rabbit*

Foreign lands – Siam *see* Foreign lands –
    Thailand

Foreign lands – Somalia

Ahmed, Said Salah. *The lion's share / Qayb Libaax*
McQuinn, Anna. *My friend Jamal*

Foreign lands – South Africa

Angelou, Maya. *My painted house, my friendly
    chicken, and me*
Bildner, Phil. *The soccer fence*
Cave, Kathryn. *One child, one seed*
Daly, Niki. *Happy birthday, Jamela!*
    The herd boy
    Jamela's dress
    Not so fast Songololo
    Once upon a time
    A song for Jamela
    Thank you, Jackson
    What's cooking, Jamela?
Isadora, Rachel. *At the crossroads*
    Over the green hills
    A South African night
Javaherbin, Mina. *Goal!*
Lewin, Hugh. *Jafta — the homecoming*
Lumry, Amanda. *Safari in South Africa*
Nelson, Kadir. *Nelson Mandela*
Seeger, Pete. *Abiyoyo returns*
Tutu, Archbishop Desmond. *Desmond and the very
    mean word*
Wilson-Max, Ken. *Halala means welcome*

Foreign lands – South America

Bateman, Teresa. *The frog with the big mouth*
Buxton, Jane. *The littlest llama*
Campoy, F. Isabel. *Rosa Raposa*
Downing, Johnette. *Amazon alphabet*
Knutson, Barbara. *Love and roast chicken*
McDermott, Gerald. *Jabutí the tortoise*
Reynolds, Jan. *Amazon*

Silvano, Wendi. *Just one more*
Yahgulanaas, Michael Nicoll. *The little hummingbird*

Foreign lands – South Sea Islands

Blackstone, Stella. *Secret seahorse*
Wood, Audrey. *Ten little fish*

Foreign lands – Spain

Aska, Warabe. *Tapicero tap tap*
Davis, Aubrey. *Bagels from Benny*
Kimmel, Eric A. *Medio Pollito*
Leaf, Munro. *The story of Ferdinand the bull*
Sierra, Judy. *The beautiful butterfly*
Zamorano, Ana. *Let's eat!*

Foreign lands – Sudan

Aardema, Verna. *What's so funny, Ketu?*
Kessler, Cristina. *My great-grandmother's gourd*

Foreign lands – Sweden

Hooks, William H. *The legend of the Christmas rose*
Lindgren, Astrid. *Pippi Longstocking's after-
    Christmas party*
Maddern, Eric. *Nail soup*

Foreign lands – Switzerland

Fisher, Leonard Everett. *William Tell*
Hasler, Eveline. *A tale of two brothers*

Foreign lands – Syria

Del Rizzo, Suzanne. *My beautiful birds*

Foreign lands – Taiwan

Chen, Chih-Yuan. *On my way to buy eggs*

Foreign lands – Tanzania

Bardhan-Quallen, Sudipta. *Flying eagle*
Kilaka, John. *True friends*
Krebs, Laurie. *We all went on safari*
MacLachlan, Patricia. *Lala salama*
Markle, Sandra. *Thirsty, thirsty elephants*
Martin, Francesca. *Clever Tortoise*
Mollel, Tololwa M. *Kele's secret*
    My rows and piles of coins
    Song bird
    Subira subira
Robinson, Sharon. *Under the same sun*
Stuve-Bodeen, Stephanie. *Elizabeti's doll*
    Elizabeti's school
    Mama Elizabeti
Winter, Jeanette. *The watcher*

Foreign lands – Tasmania

Baker, Jeannie. *The hidden forest*

Foreign lands – Thailand

Arnold, Katya. *Elephants can paint, too!*
Bridges, Shirin Yim. *The Umbrella Queen*
Ho, Minfong. *Hush!*
Krudop, Walter Lyon. *The man who caught fish*

MacDonald, Margaret Read. *The girl who wore too
    much*
Shea, Pegi Deitz. *The whispering cloth*

Foreign lands – Tibet

Berger, Barbara. *All the way to Lhasa*
Martin, Jacqueline Briggs. *The chiru of High Tibet*
Schroeder, Alan. *The stone lion*
Sís, Peter. *Tibet through the red box*
Soros, Barbara. *Tenzin's deer*

Foreign lands – Trinidad

Bootman, Colin. *Fish for the Grand Lady*
Greenwood, Mark. *Drummer boy of John John*
Joseph, Lynn. *Coconut kind of day*
    An island Christmas
Rahaman, Vashanti. *Divali rose*

Foreign lands – Turkey

Gilani-Williams, Fawzia. *Nabeel's new pants*
Mandell, Muriel. *A donkey reads*

Foreign lands – Tyrol

Sawyer, Ruth. *The remarkable Christmas of the
    cobbler's sons*

Foreign lands – Uganda

Fullerton, Alma. *A good trade*
McBrier, Page. *Beatrice's goat*
MacDonald, Margaret Read. *Give up, Gecko!*
Schrock, Jan West. *Give a goat*
Winters, Kari-Lynn. *Gift days*

Foreign lands – Ukraine

Aylesworth, Jim. *The mitten*
Brett, Jan. *The mitten*
Gorbachev, Valeri. *The fool of the world and the flying
    ship: a Ukrainian folk tale*
Kimmel, Eric A. *The birds' gift*
Polacco, Patricia. *Luba and the wren*
Ransome, Arthur. *The fool of the world and the flying
    ship*
Skrypuch, Marsha Forchuk. *Enough*
Tresselt, Alvin R. *The mitten: an old Ukrainian
    folktale*

Foreign lands – Uzbekistan

Sandman, Rochel. *Perfect porridge*

Foreign lands – Venezuela

Nazoa, Aquiles. *A small Nativity*

Foreign lands – Vietnam

Alberti, Theresa Jarosz. *Vietnam ABCs*
Garland, Sherry. *The lotus seed*
Lee, Jeanne M. *Toad is the uncle of heaven*
Shepard, Aaron. *The crystal heart*
Sugarman, Brynn Olenberg. *Rebecca's journey home*
Thong, Roseanne. *Fly free!*
Van, Muon. *In a village by the sea*
Vander Zee, Ruth. *Always with you*

Foreign lands – Wales

Cullen, Lynn. *The mightiest heart*
MacDonald, Margaret Read. *Slop!*

Foreign lands – West Indies

Hamilton, Virginia. *The girl who spun gold*
Rahaman, Vashanti. *O Christmas tree*

Foreign lands – Yukon Territory

Provensen, Alice. *Klondike gold*

Foreign lands – Zaire

Aardema, Verna. *Traveling to Tondo*

Foreign lands – Zambia

Bryan, Ashley. *Beautiful blackbird*

Foreign lands – Zanzibar

Aardema, Verna. *Bimwili and the Zimwi*

Foreign lands – Zimbabwe

Stock, Catherine. *Gugu's house*
Trent, Tereai. *The girl who buried her dreams in a can*

Foreign languages

Ada, Alma Flor. *The Christmas tree / El arbol de
    Navidad*
    Gathering the sun
    I love Saturdays y domingos
    ¡Muu, moo!
    Pio peep!
Addasi, Maha. *Time to pray*
Adderson, Caroline. *Norman, speak!*
Aesop. *The hare and the tortoise / La liebre y la tortuga*
Ahmed, Said Salah. *The lion's share / Qayb Libaax*
Aigner-Clark, Julie. *Language nursery*
Alarcón, Francisco X. *From the bellybutton of the
    moon and other summer poems / Del ombligo de la
    luna y otros poemas de verano*
    *Iguanas in the snow and other winter poems /
    Iguanas en la nieve y otros poemas de invierno*
Ancona, George. *Mi música / My music*
    Mis abuelos / My grandparents
    Mis comidas / My foods
    Mis fiestas / My celebrations
    Mis juegos / My games
    Mis quehaceres / My chores
Andersen, Hans Christian. *La princesa and the pea*
Arena, Jen. *Marta! big and small*
Argueta, Jorge. *Arroz con leche / Rice pudding*
    Guacamole
    Moony Luna / Luna, Lunita Lunera
    Salsa
    *Sopa de frijoles: un poema para cocinar / Bean soup:
    a cooking poem*
    Tamalitos
Barner, Bob. *The Day of the Dead / El Día de los
    Muertos*
Beaton, Clare. *At home / A la maison*
Bertrand, Diane Gonzales. *Family / familia*
    The last doll / La última muñeca
    Sofía and the purple dress / Sofía y el vestido morado

Uncle Chente's picnic / El picnic de Tío Chente
Bloom, Suzanne. *Nuestro autobús / The bus for us*
Bock, Lee. *Oh, crumps! / Ay, caramba!*
Bouchard, Dave. *Nokum is my teacher*
Brandt, Amy. *Benjamin comes back / Benjamin
    regresa*
    *When Katie was our teacher / Cuando Katie era
    nuestra maestra*
Brimner, Larry Dane. *Trick or treat, Old Armadillo*
Brown, Monica. *Maya's blanket*
    My name is Gabito / Me llamo Gabito
    Pelé, king of soccer / Pelé, el rey del fútbol
    Side by side / Lado a lado
Bruzzone, Catherine. *Puppy finds a friend /
    Cachorrito encuentra un amigo*
    Puppy finds a friend / Le petit chien se trouve un ami
Burnell, Heather Ayris. *Bedtime monster / ¡A dormir,
    pequeño monstruo!*
Caraballo, Samuel. *My big sister / Mi hermana mayor*
Chapra, Mimi. *Amelia's show-and-tell fiesta / Amelia
    y la fiesta de "muestra y cuenta"*
    Sparky's bark / El ladrido de Sparky
Chavarría-Cháirez, Becky. *Magda's piñata magic /
    Magda y la piñata mágica*
    Magda's tortillas / Las tortillas de Magada
Chen, Yong. *A gift*
Chin, Oliver. *The year of the monkey*
Coerr, Eleanor. *Circus day in Japan*
Colato Laínez, René. *Mamá the alien / Mamá la
    extraterrestre*
    Playing lotería / El juego de la lotería
    Señor Pancho had a rancho
Compos, Tito. *Muffler man / El hombre mofle*
Corpi, Lucha. *Where fireflies dance / Ahí, donde
    bailan las luciérnagas*
Cox, Judy. *Carmen learns English*
Cumpiano, Ina. *Quinito, day and night / Quinito,
    dia y noche*
    Quinito's neighborhood / El vecindario de Quinito
De colores / Bright with colors
De Anda, Diane. *Dancing Miranda / Baila,
    Miranda, baila*
    A day without sugar / Un dia sin azucar
    The patchwork garden / pedacitos de huerto
Delacre, Lulu. *Arroz con leche*
    Las Navidades
    ¡Olinguito, de la A a la Z! / Olinguito, from A to Z!
dePaola, Tomie. *Brava Strega Nona!*
    Marcos
De Sève, Randall. *Mi barco / Toy boat*
Dominguez, Angela. *How do you say? / ¿Cómo se
    dice?*
    *Maria had a little llama/Maria tenia una llama
    pequena*
Dorros, Alex. *Número uno*
Dorros, Arthur. *Abuela*
    Abuelo
    Mama and me
    Papa and me
    Radio Man / Don Radio
Dunbar, Polly. *Pingüino / penguin*
Ehlert, Lois. *Cuckoo, a Mexican folktale / Cucú: un
    cuento folklórico mexicano*
    Moon rope / Un lazo a la luna
Elya, Susan Middleton. *Adiós, tricycle*
    Bebé goes shopping
    Bebé goes to the beach
    Cowboy Jose
    Eight animals bake a cake

Eight animals on the town

F is for fiesta

Fairy trails

Fire! ¡Fuego! Brave bomberos

Little Roja Riding Hood

N is for Navidad

No more, por favor

Oh no, gotta go #2

Rubia and the three osos

Say hola to Spanish

Sophie's trophy

Tooth on the loose

Emberley, Rebecca. *My animals / Mis animales*

My big book of Spanish words

My city / Mi cuidad

My clothes / Mi ropa

My colors / Mis colores

My food / Mi comida

My garden / Mi jardin

My house / Mi casa

My numbers / Mis números

My opposites / Mis opuestos

My room / Mi cuarto

My school / Mi escuela

My shapes / Mis formas

My toys / Mi juguetes

English, Karen. *Speak English for us, Marisol*

Evans, Lezlie. *Can you count ten toes?*

Can you greet the whole wide world?

Farish, Terry. *Luis paints the world*

Farley, Carol J. *The king's secret*

Feelings, Muriel. *Jambo means hello*

Moja means one

Flanagan, Alice K. *Learning is fun with Mrs. Perez*

Galindo, Mary Sue. *Icy watermelon / Sandía fría*

Gershator, Phillis. *Zoo day, olé!*

The gingerbread boy. *Señorita Gordita*

Gollub, Matthew. *Jazz Fly 2*

Ten oni drummers

Gonzalez, Lucia. *The storyteller's candle / La velita de los cuentos*

Grant, Brianna K. *We are girls who love to run / Somos chicas y a nosotras nos encanta correr*

Grimm, Jacob and Wilhelm. *Hansel and Gretel / Hansel y Gretel*

Musicians of Bremen / Los musicos de Bremner

Groner, Judyth Saypol. *My first Hebrew word book*

Guy, Ginger Foglesong. *¡Bravo!*

Fiesta

My grandma / Mi abuelita

My school / Mi escuela

Perros! perros! dogs! dogs!

Siesta

Harris, Trudy. *Say something, Perico*

Haskins, Jim. *Count your way through Afghanistan*

Count your way through Africa

Count your way through Brazil

Count your way through China

Count your way through France

Count your way through Germany

Count your way through Greece

Count your way through India

Count your way through Iran

Count your way through Israel

Count your way through Italy

Count your way through Japan

Count your way through Korea

Count your way through Mexico

Count your way through Russia

Count your way through the Arab world

Hayes, Joe. *Don't say a word, Mamá/No digas nada, Mamá*

Juan Verdades, the man who could not tell a lie

Little Gold Star / Estrellita de oro

Head, Judith. *Mud soup*

Henderson, Kathy. *Hush, baby, hush!*

Henkes, Kevin. *El gran día de Lily / Lilly's big day*

Herrera, Juan Felipe. *Grandma and Me at the flea / Los meros meros remateros*

Hill, Eric. *Spot's big book of words / El libro grande de las palabras de Spot*

Hoffman, Eric. *No fair to tigers / No es justo para los tigres*

Play Lady / La Señora Juguetona

Hood, Susan. *Spike, the mixed-up monster*

Hoshino, Felicia. *Sora and the cloud*

Hudes, Quiara Alegría. *Welcome to my neighborhood!*

Iijima, Geneva Cobb. *The way we do it in Japan*

Isadora, Rachel. *Say hello!*

Jaramillo, Susie. *Elefantitos / little elephants*

Little skeletons / Esqueletitos

Jenkins, Steve. *Perros y gatos / dogs and cats*

Jiménez, Francisco. *The Christmas gift / El regalo de Navidad*

Jocelyn, Marthe. *ABC x 3*

Johnson, Amy Crane. *Cinnamon and the April shower / Canela y el aguacero de abril*

Mason moves away / Mason se muda

Johnston, Tony. *My abuelita*

My Mexico / México mío

Katz, Karen. *Can you say peace?*

Keats, Ezra Jack. *My dog is lost!*

Keister, Douglas. *Fernando's gift / El regalo de Fernando*

Kimmel, Eric A. *Rattlestiltskin*

Kimmelman, Leslie. *Everybody bonjours!*

King, Dedie. *I see the sun in Afghanistan*

I see the sun in Russia

Krebs, Laurie. *Off we go to Mexico*

We all went on safari

Kyle, Tracey. *Gazpacho for Nacho*

Lachtman, Ofelia Dumas. *Pepita takes time / Pepita, siempre tarde*

Larson, Bonnie. *When animals were people / Cuando los animales eran personas*

Law, Diane. *Come out and play: count around the world in five languages*

Lee, Huy Voun. *In the leaves*

1, 2, 3 go!

Lee-Tai, Amy. *A place where sunflowers grow / Sabaku ni saita himawari*

Levy, Janice. *Celebrate! It's cinco de mayo! / Celebremos! Es el cinco de mayo!*

Lionni, Leo. *A color of his own [Spanish-English bilingual edition]*

Ljungkvist, Laura. *Pepi sings a new song*

Lomas Garza, Carmen. *In my family*

Luenn, Nancy. *A gift for Abuelita*

Luján, Jorge. *Colors! / ¡Colores!*

Moví la mano / I moved my hand

Sky blue accident / Accidente celeste

MacDonald, Margaret Read. *Conejito*

How many donkeys?

McKissack, Patricia C. *Messy Bessey / Ada, la desordenada*

McLean, Dirk. *Play mas'! a carnival ABC*

Marshall, Linda Elovitz. *Rainbow weaver / Tejedora del arcoíris*

Medina, Meg. *Mango, Abuela, and me*
Meshon, Aaron. *Take me out to the Yakyu*
Miller, Elizabeth I. *Just like home / Como en mi tierra*
Montes, Marisa. *Los gatos black on Halloween*
Mora, Pat. *The bakery lady / La señora de la panadería*
    Book fiesta! celebrate Children's Day/Book Day / Celebremos El día de los niños/El día de los libros
    Confetti
    Delicious hullabaloo / Pachanga deliciosa
    The desert is my mother / El desierto es mi madre
    The gift of the poinsettia / El regalo de la flor de nochebuena
    Gracias / Thanks
    Here, kitty, kitty! / ¡Ven, gatita, ven!
    I pledge allegiance
    Let's eat! / A comer!
    Listen to the desert / Oye al desierto
    Love to mamá
    Marimba!
    One, two, three / Uno, dos, tres
    A piñata in a pine tree
    The race of toad and deer
    The remembering day / El día de los muertos
    Sweet dreams / Dulces suenos
    Water rolls, water rises / el agua ruda, el agua sube
Morales, Yuyi. *Just in case: a trickster tale and Spanish alphabet book*
    Niño wrestles the world
    Rudas
    Viva Frida
Moreton, Daniel. *La Cucaracha Martina*
Morton, Lone. *Hurry up, Molly / Apúrate, Molly*
    Hurry up, Molly / Dépêche-toi, Molly
Mother Goose. *La Madre Goose*
Niemann, Christoph. *The pet dragon*
Nye, Naomi Shihab. *Sitti's secrets*
O'Connor, Jane. *Nancy la elegante / Fancy Nancy*
Ogburn, Jacqueline K. *Little treasures*
Orozco, Jose-Luis. *Pancho Claus*
    Rin, rin, rin / do, re, mi
Pak, Soyung. *Dear Juno*
Park, Linda Sue. *Yum! yuck!*
Paul, Ann Whitford. *Count on Culebra*
    Fiesta fiasco
    Mañana Iguana
    Tortuga in trouble
Pérez, Amada Irma. *My diary from here to there / Mi diario de aquí hasta allá*
    My very own room / Mi propio cuartito
Perrault, Charles. *Cinderella / Cenicienta*
Pinkwater, Daniel. *Beautiful Yetta*
    Beautiful Yetta's Hanukkah kitten
Portis, Antoinette. *No es una caja / not a box*
Prap, Lila. *Animals speak*
Price, Mara. *Grandma's chocolate / El chocolate de Abuelita*
Puck. *Babies around the world*
Reed, Lynn Rowe. *Pedro, his perro, and the alphabet sombrero*
Reiser, Lynn. *My way / A mi manera*
Roe, Eileen. *With my brother / Con mi hermano*
Rosa-Mendoza, Gladys. *What time is it? / Qué hora es?*
Ruiz-Flores, Lupe. *Alicia's fruity drinks / Las aguas frescas de Alicia*
Rumford, James. *Dog-of-the-Sea-Waves*
    Sequoyah
    There's a monster in the alphabet

Russo, Marisabina. *Peter is just a baby*
Ryan, Pam Muñoz. *Hello Ocean / Hola mar*
    Mice and beans
Sacre, Antonio. *A mango in the hand*
Sáenz, Benjamin Alire. *A gift from papá Diego / Un regalo de papá Diego*
    Grandma Fina and her wonderful umbrellas / La abuelita Fina y sus sombrillas maravillosas
San Souci, Robert D. *Little gold star*
Schotter, Roni. *All about grandmas*
Shannon, David. *Demasiados juguetes / too many toys*
Shirotani, Hideo. *Let's eat / Vamos a comer*
    Let's take a walk / Vamos a caminar
    What color? / Qué color?
Silvano, Wendi. *Counting coconuts / Contando cocos*
Singh, Rina. *My first book of Hindi words*
Soto, Gary. *Chato goes cruisin'*
    Chato's kitchen
    My little car / Mi carrito
    Too many tamales
Sper, Emily. *Hanukkah: a counting book in English, Hebrew, and Yiddish*
Stevens, Jan Romero. *Carlos and the skunk / Carlos y el zorrillo*
    Carlos digs to China / Carlos excava hasta la China
Sweetland, Nancy Rose. *If I could / Si yo pudiera*
Tafolla, Carmen. *Baby Coyote and the old woman / El coyotito y la viejita*
Thong, Roseanne. *Día de los muertos*
    'Twas nochebuena
The three little pigs *The three little pigs / Los tres cerditos*
Tortillas and lullabies / Tortillas y cancioncitas
Vagin, Vladimir. *Here comes the cat*
Vallverdu, Josep. *Aladdin and the magic lamp / Aldino y la lampara maravillosa*
Vamos, Samantha R. *Before you were here, mi amor*
    The cazuela that the farm maiden stirred
Van Laan, Nancy. *La boda*
    Sleep, sleep, sleep
Vega, Denise. *Build a burrito*
    Grandmother, have the angels come?
Velasquez, Eric. *Grandma's gift*
Vidal, Beatriz A. *Federico and the Magi's gift*
Vigil-Piñón, Evangelina. *Marina's muumuu / El muumuu de Marina*
Volkmer, Jane Anne. *Song of Chirimia / La Musica de la Chirimia*
Walker, Rob D. *Mama says*
Wallace, Mary. *I is for Inuksuk*
Warburton, Tom. *1000 times no*
Weeks, Sarah. *Counting Ovejas*
Weill, Cynthia. *Animal talk: Mexican folk art animal sounds in English and Spanish*
Weinstein, Ellen Slusky. *Everywhere the cow says "Moo!"*
Wells, Rosemary. *McDuff goes to school*
    Otto se presenta para presidente / Otto runs for President
Wiese, Kurt. *You can write Chinese*
Wilson-Max, Ken. *Fuhara means happy*
    Halala means welcome
Winter, Jonah. *Diego*
    Sonia Sotomayor
Wolff, Ashley. *I call my grandma Nana*
    I call my grandpa Papa
Wu, Faye-Lynn. *Chinese and English nursery rhymes*
Yeh, Kat. *The magic brush*

Zepeda, Gwendolyn. *Growing up with tamales / Los tamales de Ana*
Ziefert, Harriet. *Home for Navidad*

Forest, woods

Adler, David A. *Redwoods are the tallest trees in the world*
Ahlberg, Janet. *Jeremiah in the dark wood*
Alborough, Jez. *Where's my teddy?*
Ambrose, Sophie. *The lonely giant*
Arnold, Marsha Diane. *Waiting for snow*
Arnosky, Jim. *Crinkleroot's guide to knowing the trees*
Atkinson, Cale. *Explorers of the wild*
Baker, Jeannie. *Where the forest meets the sea*
Bauer, Marion Dane. *Halloween forest*
    Winter dance
Berenstain, Stan and Jan. *The Berenstain bears and the ghost of the forest*
Berkes, Marianne. *Over in the forest*
Bissonette, Aimée. *North woods girl*
Claire, Céline. *Shelter*
Collins, Pat Lowery. *The deer watch*
Cotten, Cynthia. *At the edge of the woods*
Crum, Shutta. *The bravest of the brave*
Delacre, Lulu. *¡Olinguito, de la A a la Z! / Olinguito, from A to Z!*
Delessert, Etienne. *The seven dwarfs*
Demarest, Chris L. *Hotshots!*
    Smokejumpers one to ten
Dennard, Deborah. *Koala country*
    Lemur landing
DePrisco, Dorothea. *Snowbear's winter day*
Docherty, Helen. *The Snatchabook*
Doi, Kaya. *Chirri and Chirra*
Ets, Marie Hall. *In the forest*
Fredericks, Anthony D. *In one tidepool*
Frost, Robert. *Stopping by woods on a snowy evening*
Gay, Marie-Louise. *Stella, fairy of the forest*
Genechten, Guido van. *The big woods orchestra*
George, Lindsay Barrett. *In the woods*
George, William T. *Christmas at Long Pond*
Gershator, Phillis. *Who's in the forest?*
Gliori, Debi. *Mr. Bear to the rescue*
Gore, Leonid. *The wonderful book*
Graham-Barber, Lynda. *Spy hops and belly flops*
Grant, Holly. *Wee Sister Strange*
Grimm, Jacob and Wilhelm. *Hansel and Gretel*, ill. by Jen Corace
    Hansel and Gretel, ill. by Holly Hobbie
    Hansel and Gretel, ill. by Rachel Isadora
    Hansel and Gretel, ill. by Susan Jeffers
    Hansel and Gretel, ill. by James Marshall
    Hansel and Gretel, ill. by Jane Ray
    Hansel and Gretel, ill. by Claudia Wolf
    Hansel and Gretel, ill. by Paul O. Zelinsky
    Hansel and Gretel, ill. by Lisbeth Zwerger
    Hansel and Gretel / Hansel y Gretel
    Hansel and Gretel: a retelling from the original tale by the Brothers Grimm
Hewitt, Sally. *Woods and meadows*
Himmelman, John. *A wood frog's life*
Holabird, Katharine. *Angelina and Henry*
Itaya, Satoshi. *Buttons and Bo*
Jackson, Richard. *All ears, all eyes*
Johnson, Amy Crane. *Cinnamon and the April shower / Canela y el aguacero de abril*
Johnston, Tony. *Bigfoot Cinderrrrella*
    Winter is coming

Judge, Lita. *Red hat*
Keister, Douglas. *Fernando's gift / El regalo de Fernando*
Kherdian, David. *Come back, Moon*
Kleven, Elisa. *The dancing deer and the foolish hunter*
Knapman, Timothy. *Time now to dream*
Lairla, Sergio. *Abel and the wolf*
Landström, Olof. *Boo and Baa in the woods*
Lyon, George Ella. *Counting on the woods*
    What forest knows
McClements, George. *Dinosaur Woods*
McFarland, Clive. *A bed for Bear*
    The fox and the wild
Martin, Bill, Jr.. *A beasty story*
Martin, David. *Let's have a tree party!*
Miller, Debbie S. *Are trees alive?*
Miller, Edna. *Mousekin's Thanksgiving*
Miyakoshi, Akiko. *The tea party in the woods*
Moerbeek, Kees. *The diary of Hansel and Gretel*
Nivola, Claire A. *The forest*
Olaleye, Isaac. *Lake of the Big Snake*
Pearson, Tracey Campbell. *The purple hat*
Peet, Bill. *Big bad Bruce*
Quattlebaum, Mary. *Jo MacDonald hiked in the woods*
Reed-Jones, Carol. *The tree in the ancient forest*
Ryder, Joanne. *The waterfall's gift*
Sayre, April Pulley. *Army ant parade*
Schaefer, Carole Lexa. *Down in the woods at sleepytime*
Schofield, Jennifer. *Animal babies in rain forests*
Schotter, Roni. *In the piney woods*
Serafini, Frank. *Looking closely through the forest*
Serfozo, Mary. *Whooo's there?*
Sharratt, Nick. *The foggy, foggy forest*
Simple gifts
Srinivasan, Divya. *Little Owl's day*
Stojic, Manya. *Snow*
Stoop, Naoko. *Red Knit Cap Girl*
Tresselt, Alvin R. *The gift of the tree*
Waddell, Martin. *Let's go home, Little Bear*
Wallen, Ila. *The moon in my room*
Ward, Helen. *The tin forest*
Ward, Jennifer. *Forest bright, forest night*
Wells, Rosemary. *Moss pillows*
Wilson, Karma. *Bear stays up for Christmas*
Yolen, Jane. *All in the woodland early*
    Owl moon

Forgetfulness *see* Behavior – forgetfulness

Forgiving *see* Behavior – forgiving

Format, unusual

Ahlberg, Janet. *The jolly Christmas postman*
Ahlberg, Jessica. *Fairy tales for Mr. Barker*
Aliki. *Marianthe's story one: painted words; Marianthe's story two: spoken memories*
Baeten, Lieve. *The clever little witch*
    The curious little witch
Barnett, Mac. *Guess again!*
Behrens, Janice. *Let's find rain forest animals*
Blechman, Nicholas. *Night light*
Boyd, Lizi. *Inside outside*
Bridwell, Norman. *Glow-in-the-dark Halloween*
Brown, Ruth. *The tale of two mice*
Budnitz, Paul. *The hole in the middle*

Capucilli, Alyssa Satin. *My first soccer game*
Carle, Eric. *My very first book of colors*
  My very first book of growth
  My very first book of homes
  My very first book of motion
  My very first book of numbers
  My very first book of shapes
  My very first book of touch
  My very first book of words
  10 little rubber ducks
  The very hungry caterpillar
  The very quiet cricket
Carter, David A. *If you're happy and you know it, clap your hands*
Chedru, Delphine. *Spot it again!*
Dennard, Deborah. *Hedgehog haven*
Donovan, Gail. *The copycat fish*
  A fishy story
  Lost at sea
Ehlert, Lois. *Color farm*
  Color zoo
  In my world
  Leaf man
Franceschelli, Christopher. *(Oliver)*
Goodall, John S. *Creepy castle*
  Shrewbettina's birthday
Gore, Leonid. *Worms for lunch?*
Gravett, Emily. *Spells*
Halfmann, Janet. *Eggs 1, 2, 3*
Hoban, Tana. *Look! look! look!*
  26 letters and 99 cents
Hood, Susan. *Leaps and bounce*
Horácek, Petr. *Butterfly butterfly*
  Jonathan and Martha
Jenkins, Steve. *Dogs and cats*
  Perros y gatos / dogs and cats
Johnson, D. B. *Palazzo inverso*
Jonas, Ann. *Reflections*
  The thirteenth clue
Joyce, William. *The Numberlys*
Little old lady who swallowed a fly. *There was an old lady who swallowed a fly*
Llewellyn, Claire. *Crocodile*
  Duck
  Ladybug
  Tree
Long, Ethan. *The book that Zack wrote*
Loth, Sebastian. *Clementine*
  Zelda the Varigoose
MacDonald, Suse. *Fish, swish! splash, dash!*
  Shape by shape
MacKinnon, Debbie. *Eye spy shapes*
Marx, Trish. *Kindergarten day USA and China*
Menotti, Andrea. *How many jelly beans?*
Moffatt, Judith. *Trick-or-treat faces*
Morrow, Tara Jaye. *Mommy loves her baby; Daddy loves his baby*
Mother Goose. *Hickory dickory dock and other nursery rhymes*
Nelson-Schmidt, Michelle. *Cats, cats!*
  Dogs, dogs!
Numeroff, Laura Joffe. *What grandmas do best; What grandpas do best*
Old MacDonald had a farm. *Old MacDonald had a farm*
Olson-Brown, Ellen. *Ooh la la polka-dot boots*
Pericoli, Matteo. *See the city*
Perrin, Martine. *Cock-a-doodle who?*
Pfister, Marcus. *Charlie at the zoo*

Potter, Beatrix. *Where's Peter Rabbit?*
Ramos, Jorge. *I'm just like my mom / Me parezco tanto a mi mamá; I'm just like my dad / Me parezco tanto a mi papá*
Rasmussen, Halfdan. *The ladder*
Roth, Carol. *Ten dirty pigs / Ten clean pigs*
Seeger, Laura Vaccaro. *One boy*
Seuss, Dr. *Gerald McBoing Boing sound book*
Sharratt, Nick. *The foggy, foggy forest*
Siminovich, Lorena. *I like vegetables*
Simmons, Jane. *Daisy, the little duck with big feet*
Taback, Simms. *Postcards from camp*
Tafuri, Nancy. *What the sun sees / What the moon sees*
Toft, Kim Michelle. *The world that we want*
Tullet, Hervé. *The book with a hole*
  Mix it up!
  Press here
Viva, Frank. *A long way away*
Wildsmith, Brian. *Give a dog a bone*
  Goat's trail
Young, Ed. *Mouse match*
Ziefert, Harriet. *Counting chickens*
  Hanukkah haiku
  Messy Bessie

Format, unusual – board books

Abrams, Pam. *Now I eat my ABC's*
Acredolo, Linda P. *My first baby signs*
Aigner-Clark, Julie. *Language nursery*
Ajmera, Maya. *Animal friends: a global celebration of children and their animals*
  Global baby boys
  Global baby girls
Alborough, Jez. *Tall*
Alexander, Cecil Frances. *All creatures great and small*
Alley, R. W. *There once was a witch*
American babies
American Museum of Natural History. *ABC insects*
Anholt, Catherine. *Chimp and Zee's noisy book*
  Monkey around with Chimp and Zee [board book]
Animal I spy
Animal 123
Asch, Frank. *Moonbear's books*
  Moonbear's canoe
Austin, Mike. *Countdown with Milo*
Austin, Richard. *Pocket piggies opposites!*
Baby animals at the zoo
Barack, Marcy. *Season song*
Barclay, Eric. *Counting dogs*
Barrett, Mary Brigid. *All fall down*
  Pat-a-cake
Basher, Simon. *Go! go! Bobo*
Beall, Pamela Conon. *Wee Sing if you're happy and you know it*
Beaton, Clare. *Clare Beaton's action rhymes*
  Clare Beaton's bedtime rhymes
  Clare Beaton's farmyard rhymes
  Clare Beaton's nursery rhymes
Bee, William. *Stanley's colors*
  Stanley's numbers
  Stanley's opposites
Benton, Jim. *Where did all the dinos go?*
Biggs, Brian. *123 beep beep beep!*
  Stop! go!
  Tinyville town: I'm a police officer
  Tinyville town: I'm a veterinarian
Blackstone, Stella. *Baby talk*

Boelts, Maribeth. *Sweet dreams, Little Bunny!*
Bolam, Emily. *Animals talk*
  I go potty
Boynton, Sandra. *Dinosaur dance!*
  Eek! Halloween!
  Happy birthday, Little Pookie
  Little Pookie
  Night-night, Little Pookie
  Spooky Pookie
Brantz, Loryn. *Feminist Baby*
Brown, James. *Farm*
Brown, Marc. *Arthur goes to school*
  Arthur's animal adventure
Brunhoff, Laurent de. *B is for Babar*
Bryant, Megan E. *Alphasaurus*
  Colorasaurus
  Countasaurus
  Shapeasaurus
Burg, Ann. *Autumn walk*
Burnard, Damon. *I spy in the jungle*
  I spy in the ocean
Buzzeo, Toni. *Whose truck?*
Cabrera, Jane. *Monkey's play time*
Callery, Sean. *Hide and seek in the jungle*
Campbell, Rod. *Farm animals*
Capucilli, Alyssa Satin. *Biscuit gives a gift*
  Hush a bye, baby
  Katy Duck
  Katy Duck, big sister
Carle, Eric. *From head to toe*
  My first peek-a-boo: animals
Chambers, Angela. *Follow that chicken!*
  How now, cow?
Child, Lauren. *Charlie and Lola's numbers*
  Charlie and Lola's opposites
Church, Caroline Jayne. *I love my bunny*
  I love my robot
Chwast, Seymour. *Get dressed!*
Coat, Janik. *Rhymoceros*
Cocoretto . *Toot! toot!*
Cole, Joanna. *Sharing is fun*
Cousins, Lucy. *Count with Maisy*
  Happy Easter, Maisy!
  Maisy's Christmas tree
  Maisy's Halloween
  Maisy's noisy day
Curious George's 1 to 10 and back again
Dahl, Michael. *Bear says "thank you"*
  Hippo says "excuse me."
  Nap time for Kitty
Dann, Penny. *Eensy weensy spider*
Davis, Caroline. *My little rocking horse lullabies*
  My little rowboat
Davis, Sarah. *My first trucks*
Deegan, Kim. *My first book of numbers*
  My first book of opposites
dePaola, Tomie. *Get dressed, Santa!*
  Marcos
Deschamps, Nicola. *Duckling*
  Emergency!
Diehl, David. *Goal! my soccer book*
Doepker, David. *Animal babies*
  Farm babies
Dupasquier, Philippe. *1 2 3, follow me!*
Edwards, Pamela Duncan. *Warthogs in a box*
Ellwand, David. *Ten in the bed*
Emberley, Ed. *Where's my sweetie pie?*
Emberley, Rebecca. *My animals / Mis animales*
  My city / Mi cuidad

My clothes / Mi ropa
My colors / Mis colores
My food / Mi comida
My garden / Mi jardin
My house / Mi casa
My numbers / Mis números
My opposites / Mis opuestos
My room / Mi cuarto
My school / Mi escuela
My shapes / Mis formas
My toys / Mi juguetes
Faglia, Matteo. *Happy birthday, I'm 1*
  Happy birthday, I'm 2
  Happy birthday, I'm 3
  Happy birthday, I'm 4
Falconer, Ian. *Olivia — and the missing toy*
  Olivia counts
  Olivia's opposites
Ferri, Giuliano. *Peekaboo*
Five little pumpkins, ill. by Ben Mantle
  Five little pumpkins, ill. by Dan Yaccarino
Ford, Bernette. *No more diapers for Ducky!*
Formento, Alison. *This tree, 1, 2, 3*
Fox, Christyan. *Count to ten, PiggyWiggy!*
  What color is that, PiggyWiggy?
  What shape is that, PiggyWiggy?
Franceschelli, Christopher. *Dinoblock*
Frazee, Marla. *Hush, little baby: a folk song with*
  pictures
Freeman, Don. *Corduroy's busy street and Corduroy*
  goes to the doctor
Freymann, Saxton. *Baby food*
  Dog food
  Food for thought
Fronis, Aly. *If you're spooky and you know it*
Fuge, Charles. *Where to, Little Wombat?*
Gardiner, Lindsey. *Good night, Poppy and Max*
George, Bobby. *Montessori number work*
  My first book of patterns
Gerardi, Jan. *The little recycler*
Gergely, Tibor. *The great big fire engine book*
Gillingham, Sara. *Friends*
  Trucks
Gliori, Debi. *Can I have a hug?*
Gold-Vukson, Marji E. *The colors of my Jewish Year*
Good morning
Got, Yves. *Sam loves kisses*
  Sam's little sister
Gray Smith, Monique. *My heart fills with happiness*
Greenfield, Eloise. *Big friend, little friend*
  I make music
  My doll, Keshia
Gundersheimer, Karen. *Find cat, wear hat*
Harper, Jamie. *Night night, Baby Bundt*
  Splish splash, Baby Bundt
Harris, Trudy. *Up bear, down bear*
Hegarty, Patricia. *Good night farm*
Henkes, Kevin. *Lilly's chocolate heart*
  Sheila Rae's peppermint stick
Hest, Amy. *Baby Duck and the cozy blanket*
Hill, Eric. *Spot at home*
  Spot at the fair
  Spot counts from 1 to 10
  Spot goes to the circus
  Spot goes to the farm
  Spot looks at colors
  Spot looks at opposites

Spot looks at shapes
Spot looks at weather
Spot on the farm
Spot visits his grandparents
Spot's first words
Spot's magical Christmas
Hills, Tad. *Duck and Goose find a pumpkin*
Duck and Goose, how are you feeling?
Duck and Goose, 1, 2, 3
Rocket's mighty words
What's up, Duck?
Hines, Anna Grossnickle. *What can you do in the rain?*
What can you do in the snow?
What can you do in the sun?
What can you do in the wind?
Hoban, Tana. *What is that?*
White on black
Who are they?
Hoe, Susan. *Which shoes would you choose?*
Hoffman, Don. *A counting book with Billy and Abigail*
Good morning, good night Billy and Abigail
Holabird, Katharine. *Angelina dances*
Holm, Jennifer L. *I'm Grumpy*
Holub, Joan. *Turkeys never gobble*
Hood, Susan. *Tickly toes*
Hop a little, jump a little!
Horácek, Petr. *Beep beep*
Choo choo
A surprise for Tiny Mouse
Time for bed
Hubbell, Patricia. *Pots and pans*
Wrapping paper romp
Hurd, Thacher. *Cat's pajamas*
Hutchins, Hazel. *Up dog*
Hyde, Margaret E. *Matisse for kids*
Van Gogh for kids
Imershein, Betsy. *Trucks*
Inkpen, Mick. *Wibbly Pig can make a tent*
Wibbly Pig is upset
Wibbly Pig likes bananas
Wibbly Pig opens his presents
Intrater, Roberta Grobel. *Peek-a-boo!*
Smile!
Jackson, Kathryn. *The golden circus book*
Janovitz, Marilyn. *Baby, Baby, Baby!*
Jaramillo, Susie. *Elefantitos / little elephants*
Jenkins, Emily. *Num, num, num!*
Plonk, plonk, plonk!
Up, up, up!
Jocelyn, Marthe. *Ready for autumn*
Ready for spring
Ready for summer
Ready for winter
Johnson, Angela. *Joshua by the sea*
Joshua's night whispers
Rain feet
Jones, Christianne C. *The Santa shimmy*
Jullien, Jean. *Before and after*
Just like father
Katz, Karen. *Baby loves winter!*
Katz, Susan B. *ABC, baby me!*
Keats, Ezra Jack. *One red sun*
Kim, Sue. *How does a seed grow?*
Kirwan, Wednesday. *Baby loves to boogie!*
Könnecke, Ole. *The big book of words and pictures*
Krensky, Stephen. *I am so brave!*
I know a lot!

Laden, Nina. *Peek-a-who?*
Peek-a-choo-choo!
Lawrence, Michael. *Baby loves*
Lemke, Donald. *Book-o-beards*
Lester, J. D. *Mommy calls me Monkeypants*
Libney, Varda. *What I like about Passover*
Light, Steve. *Diggers go*
Have you seen my lunch box?
Planes go
Trains go
Litton, Jonathan. *Big fish little fish*
Lodge, Jo. *Happy Snappy!*
Logan, Bob. *Rocket town*
Look at me!
Low, William. *Trucks to the rescue!*
McFarlane, Sheryl. *In the city*
On the farm
McGrath, Barbara Barbieri. *Kellogg's froot loops color fun book*
McMullan, Kate. *Supercat*
McNeil, Kelli. *Sleepy toes*
McPhail, David. *Baby Pig Pig talks*
Bella loves Bunny
Ben loves Bear
Olivia loves Owl
Peter loves Penguin
McQuade, Jacqueline. *At preschool with Teddy Bear*
At the petting zoo with Teddy Bear
Making faces: a first book of emotions
Mara, Nichole. *So many feet*
Marchon, Benoit. *Spoonful!*
Markes, Julie. *Sidewalk ABC*
Sidewalk 1 2 3
Marshall, James. *Eugene*
Marshall, Natalie. *Five little ducks: a fingers and toes nursery rhyme book*
Martin, David. *Hanukkah lights*
Marzollo, Jean. *Do you know new?*
I spy little animals
I spy little book
I spy little wheels
Mama, Mama
Papa, Papa
Mayo, Margaret. *Choo choo clickety-clack*
Melmed, Laura Krauss. *I love you as much . . .*
Merberg, Julie. *In the garden with Van Gogh*
A magical day with Matisse
Miller, Margaret. *Baby faces*
Guess who?
I love colors
What's on my head?
Monfreid, Dorothée de. *Shhh! I'm sleeping*
Morozumi, Atsuko. *Helping daddy*
In the park
Playing
Time for bed
Mother Goose. *Hey, diddle, diddle [board book]*
Hickory, dickory, dock
Humpty Dumpty
Humpty Dumpty and other rhymes
Jack and Jill [board book]
Little Boy Blue and other rhymes
Little Miss Muffet [board book]
Little Miss Muffet
My first real Mother Goose [board book]
One, two, buckle my shoe [board book]
Pat-a-cake, ill. by Olga Ivanov
Pat-a-cake, ill. by Annie Kubler
Pat-a-cake [board book]

Pussycat, pussycat and other rhymes
Rock-a-bye baby [board book]
Snuggle up with Mother Goose
This little piggy [board book]
Wee Willie Winkie [board book]
Wee Willie Winkie and other rhymes
Mühle, Jörg. *Tickle my ears*
Murphy, Mary. *Crocopotamus*
  Quick Duck!
  Slow snail
My big book of trucks and diggers
My new baby
Naberhaus, Sarvinder. *Lines*
National Wildlife Federation. *My first book of*
  animal opposites
  My first book of baby animals
Newgarden, Mark. *Bow-Wow orders lunch*
Newman, Lesléa. *Daddy, Papa, and me*
  Mommy, Mama, and Me
Neyer, Andrew. *Letters are for learning*
Nieminen, Lotta. *Pancakes! an interactive recipe book*
Norac, Carl. *I love to cuddle*
Novesky, Amy. *Love is a truck*
Numeroff, Laura Joffe. *Happy Valentine's Day,*
  Mouse!
  What brothers do best
Ohi, Ruth. *Pants off first*
Old MacDonald had a farm. *Grandma's nursery*
  rhymes: Old MacDonald
O'Mara, Carmel. *Rainy day*
  Sunny day
Pantone
Parr, Todd. *Big and little*
  Black and white
Patricelli, Leslie. *Baby happy, baby sad*
  Binky
  Blankie
  Boo!
  Fa la la
  Hair
  Hop! hop!
  Nighty-night
  No no, yes yes
Pearson, Tracey Campbell. *Diddle diddle dumpling*
  Hector Protector [board book]
Penn, Audrey. *A bedtime kiss for Chester Raccoon*
  A color game for Chester Raccoon
Perkins, Chloe. *Cinderella*
Peterson, Melissa. *Hanna's Christmas*
Pfister, Marcus. *Where is my friend?*
Prelutsky, Jack. *Halloween countdown*
Preston-Gannon, Frann. *Deep deep sea*
  What a hoot!
Puck. *Babies around the world*
Purcell, Rebecca. *Super Chicken*
Ramadier, Cédric. *Help! the wolf is coming!*
  Shh! this book is sleeping
Reasoner, Charles. *Peek-a-boo monsters*
Reich, Kass. *Up hamster, down hamster*
Riggs, Kate. *Time to build*
Rock, Lois. *Now we have a baby*
Rosa-Mendoza, Gladys. *What time is it? / Qué hora*
  es?
Rossetti-Shustak, Bernadette. *I love you through and*
  through
Rubin, Susan Goldman. *Matisse dance for joy*
Salariya, David. *All about me!*
Saltzberg, Barney. *I love dogs*
Salzano, Tammi. *One rainy day*

Sanger, Amy Wilson. *First book of sushi*
Sasso, Sandy Eisenberg. *Naamah, Noah's wife*
Savage, Stephen. *Seven orange pumpkins*
Schindel, John. *The babies and doggies book*
  Busy penguins
Shannon, David. *David smells*
  Oh, David!
  Oops! a diaper David book
Shapes
Shea, Pegi Deitz. *I see me!*
Shirotani, Hideo. *Let's eat / Vamos a comer*
  Let's play
  Let's take a walk / Vamos a caminar
  What color? / Qué color?
Shuttlewood, Craig. *Through the town*
Siminovich, Lorena. *I like bugs*
Simmons, Jane. *Daisy says coo!*
  Daisy says, "Here we go round the mulberry bush"
  Daisy says, "If you're happy and you know it"
  Daisy's day out
  Daisy's favorite things
  Splish splash Daisy
Sims, Nat. *Peekaboo barn*
Slegers, Liesbet. *Fall leaves*
  Funny ears
  Funny feet
  Funny tails
  Playing
  Winter snow
Smith, Charles R. *I'll be there*
  My gal
Spohn, Kate. *Snow play*
Spurr, Elizabeth. *In the garden*
Staake, Bob. *My little ABC book*
  My little color book
  My little 1 2 3 book
  My little opposites book
Stanley, Mandy. *At the pool*
  In the park
  On the move
  Perfect pets
Stephens, Helen. *I'm too busy*
Stoeke, Janet Morgan. *Hide and seek*
Szekeres, Cyndy. *Toby's please and thank you*
Tafolla, Carmen. *Baby Coyote and the old woman / El*
  coyotito y la viejita
Tafuri, Nancy. *Where we sleep*
Taylor, Ann. *Baby dance*
Taylor, Jane. *Twinkle, twinkle little star*
Thomas, Joyce Carol. *Joy*
Thompson, Lauren. *Little Quack: dial-a-duck*
Tildes, Phyllis Limbacher. *Baby's first book of birds*
  and colors
Trapani, Iza. *How much is that doggie in the window?*
Verdick, Elizabeth. *On-the-go time*
  Tails are not for pulling
Waiting for baby
Waller, Curt. *Baby's first signs*
  More baby's first signs
Walters, Eric. *An African alphabet*
Wan, Joyce. *Hug you, kiss you, love you*
Wax, Wendy. *A very mice Christmas*
Weeks, Sarah. *Bite me, I'm a book*
  Bite me, I'm a shape
Wegerif, Gay. *Up close*
Weiss, Ellen. *Playtime for twins*
Wellington, Monica. *Bunny's first snowflake*
Wells, Rosemary. *Bingo*
  Clean-up time

The itsy-bitsy spider
Max's bath
Max's bedtime
Max's birthday
Max's breakfast
Max's first word
Max's new suit
Max's ride
Max's toys
Peek-a-boo
Red boots
Shopping
A visit to Dr. Duck
Wheeler, Valerie. *Yes, please! no, thank you!*
Who took the cookie?
Wick, Walter. *Can you see what I see? Christmas*
Wiley, Thom. *One sheep, blue sheep*
Wilhelm, Hans. *Quacky Ducky's Easter egg*
Quacky Ducky's Easter fun
Willems, Mo. *The pigeon has feelings, too!*
The pigeon loves things that go!
Welcome: a Mo Willems guide for new arrivals
Wilson, Karma. *Hello, Calico!*
Wright, Cliff. *Bear and ball*
Bear and kite
Yaccarino, Dan. *Five little ducks*
Happyland: big berry
Happyland: birthday cake
Happyland: rainy day
Yolen, Jane. *How do dinosaurs clean their rooms?*
How do dinosaurs count to ten?
How do dinosaurs go to sleep?
Yoon, Salina. *At the beach*
You and me
Ziefert, Harriet. *Beach party!*
It's time to go to sleep
It's time to take a nap
Knick-knack paddywhack
Wiggle like an octopus
Zoehfeld, Kathleen Weidner. *Apples, apples*

Format, unusual – graphic novels

Brunetti, Ivan. *Wordplay*
Coudray, Jean-Luc. *A goofy guide to penguins*
Desrosiers, Sylvie. *Hocus Pocus takes the train*
Green, John Patrick. *Hippopotamister*
Kim, Julie. *Where's Halmoni?*
McCloskey, Kevin. *The real poop on pigeons!*
Modan, Rutu. *Maya makes a mess*
Nordling, Lee. *Belinda the unbeatable*
The bramble
Shehewe
Richards, Barnaby. *Blip!*
Sazaklis, John. *Fowl play*
Sturm, James. *Birdsong: a story in pictures*
Gryphons aren't so great
Ogres awake!
Sleepless knight
Tamaki, Mariko. *This one summer*
Viva, Frank. *A trip to the bottom of the world with Mouse*

Format, unusual – toy & movable books

Aesop. *The hare and the tortoise*
Ahlberg, Allan. *The Goldilocks variations*
Ahlberg, Janet. *The jolly pocket postman*
The jolly postman

Peek-a-boo!
Playmates
Alborough, Jez. *Duck's key where can it be?*
Allen, Judy. *Whales and dolphins*
American Museum of Natural History. *Spot the animals*
Arnosky, Jim. *Wild and swampy*
Baby animals
Baeten, Lieve. *Happy birthday, Little Witch!*
Baker, Jeannie. *Mirror*
Barry, Frances. *Duckie's rainbow*
Let's look at dinosaurs
Let's save the animals
Baruzzi, Agnese. *Look, look again*
Opposite surprise
Bataille, Marion. *ABC3D*
Bauer, Marion Dane. *Christmas lights*
I'm not afraid of Halloween!
Toes, ears, and nose!
Uh-oh! a lift-the-flap story
Beck, Andrea. *Elliot's great big lift-the-flap book*
Beeler, Selby B. *How many Elephants?*
Bentley, Dawn. *Fuzzy bear*
Fuzzy Bear's potty book
Berenstain, Jan. *The Berenstain bears trim the tree*
Berger, Melvin. *Early humans*
Bernhard, Durga. *In the fiddle is a song*
While you are sleeping: a lift-the-flap book of time around the world
Big noisy trucks and diggers
Bilgrami, Shaheen. *Amazing dinosaur discovery*
Farmyard painting party
Incredible animal discovery
Jungle art show
Birchall, Mark. *Hen goes shopping*
Black, Harley. *Amazing magic school*
Magic art class
Blum, Mark. *Big trucks and diggers in 3-D*
Braun, Sebastien. *Who's hiding?*
Bridwell, Norman. *Clifford's neighborhood*
Brown, Heather. *Chomp!*
Brown, Marc. *Arthur goes to school*
Arthur's neighborhood
Arthur's spookiest Halloween
Brown, Ruth. *Monkey's friends*
The old tree
Browne, Anthony. *Animal fair*
Brownlow, Mike. *The big white book with almost nothing in it*
Butler, M. Christina. *One snowy night*
Butterfield, Moira. *Magic world of learning*
Buzzeo, Toni. *Whose tools?*
Cabrera, Jane. *Bear's good night*
Campbell, Rod. *Dear zoo*
Capucilli, Alyssa Satin. *Biscuit loves school*
Biscuit's Valentine's Day
Happy Hanukkah, Biscuit
My first ballet class
Only my dad and me
Only my mom and me
Carle, Eric. *Dream snow*
My first peek-a-boo: animals
My very first book of food
My very first book of heads and tails
My very first book of sounds
My very first book of tools
Papa, please get the moon for me
The secret birthday message
The very lonely firefly

Watch out! A giant!
Carney, Margaret. *Where does a tiger-heron spend the
    night?*
Carter, David A. *Blue 2*
    Chanukah bugs
    Easter bugs
    Flapdoodle dinosaurs
    How many bugs in a box?
    In a dark, dark wood
    Old MacDonald had a farm: a pop-up book
    One red dot
    Peekaboo bugs
    600 black spots
    Whoo? Whoo?
    Who's under that hat?
    Yellow square
Chambers, Angela. *Follow that chicken!*
    How now, cow?
Cheshire, Marc. *Here comes Eloise!*
    Merry Christmas, Eloise!
Child, Lauren. *My dream bed*
Chwast, Seymour. *Get dressed!*
Ciboul, Adele. *The five senses*
Cocoretto . *Toot! toot!*
Comden, Betty. *What's new at the zoo?*
Cousins, Lucy. *Count with Maisy, cheep, cheep, cheep!*
    Ha ha, Maisy!
    Happy birthday, Maisy
    Maisy at the farm
    Maisy's amazing big book of learning
    Maisy's amazing big book of words
    Maisy's book of things that go
    Maisy's farm
    Maisy's first clock
    Maisy's pirate treasure hunt
    Maisy's twinkly, crinkly counting book
    Maisy's wonderful weather book
    More fun with Maisy!
    Stop and go, Maisy
    With love from Maisy
Cox, Phil Roxbee. *Fox on a box*
    Goose on the loose
    Shark in the park
Crews, Donald. *Inside freight train*
Crowther, Robert. *Amazing pop-up trucks*
    Colors
    Opposites
    Robert Crowther's pop-up dinosaur ABC
    Shapes
Curtis, Jamie Lee. *Today I feel silly and other moods
    that make my day*
Davis, Kate. *Barnyard babies*
Davis, Nancy. *A garden of opposites*
Day, Trevor. *Youch! it bites!*
deGroat, Diane. *Lola the elf*
Denchfield, Nick. *Charlie Chick*
Denega, Danielle. *Numbers*
    Rain or shine
Deneux, Xavier. *Vehicles*
dePaola, Tomie. *Brava Strega Nona!*
DePrisco, Dorothea. *Snowbear's winter day*
    What will I become?
    Who lives here?
Dijs, Carla. *Mommy, what if —?*
Dodds, Dayle Ann. *Where's Pup?*
Dowley, Tim. *The shepherds' tale*
    The wise men's tale
Doyle, Malachy. *Baby see, baby do!*
    Well, a crocodile can!

Drehsen, Britta. *Flip-o-storic*
Dunrea, Olivier. *Gossie's busy day*
Durant, Alan. *Dear tooth fairy*
Egielski, Richard. *Itsy bitsy spider*
Ehlert, Lois. *Hands*
    Waiting for wings
Emberley, Ed. *Ed Emberley's bye-bye, big bad bullybug!*
    Glad monster, sad monster
    Go away, big green monster!
    Nighty night Little Green Monster
    Where's my sweetie pie?
Faulkner, Keith. *Charlie Chimp's Christmas*
    Do you have my quack?
    The giraffe who cock-a-doodle-doo'd
    Jumbled jungle
    The monster who loved books
    Pop! went another balloon!
    Rexerella
    The scared little bear
    *The tallest shortest longest greenest brownest animal
        in the jungle!*
    A trick or a treat?
Félix, Lucie. *Apples and robins*
Ferri, Giuliano. *Peekaboo*
Findlay, Lisa. *What's in Oscar's trashcan?*
Firmin, Josie. *My week*
Fischer, Scott M. *Twinkle*
Foley, Greg. *I miss you Mouse*
Fontes, Justine Korman. *Black meets White*
Fox, Diane. *Tyson the terrible*
Franceschelli, Christopher. *Alphablock*
    Cityblock
    Countablock
Friedman, Caitlin. *How do you feed a hungry giant?*
Gabriel, Ashala. *Night night toes*
Gallo, Frank. *Bird calls*
    Night sounds
Gamble, Isobel. *Who's that?*
Genechten, Guido van. *Guess what?*
    Guess where?
Gerstein, Mordicai. *The man who walked between the
    towers*
Gibbs, Edward. *I spy on the farm*
    I spy pets
    I spy under the sea
    I spy with my little eye
Gillingham, Sara. *Friends*
    Trucks
The gingerbread boy. *Gingerbread baby*
Gonyea, Mark. *The spooky box*
Gore, Leonid. *Mommy, where are you?*
Graves, Keith. *The monsterator*
Gravett, Emily. *Little Mouse's big book of beasts*
    Little Mouse's big book of fears
    Meerkat mail
    The rabbit problem
Gray, Nigel. *Time to play!*
Green, Dan. *Wild alphabet*
Green, Rod. *Giant vehicles*
Gukova, Julia. *All mixed-up!*
Hacohen, Dean. *Tuck me in!*
    Who's hungry?
Haines, Mike. *Countdown to bedtime*
Hall, Michael. *It's an orange aardvark!*
Hamilton, Libby. *The monstrous book of monsters*
Hansen, P. *My granny's purse*
Harper, Charise Mericle. *Amy and Ivan*
Harper, Dan. *Telling time with Big Mama Cat*
Hawkins, Colin. *Creepy castle*

One, two, guess who?
Hennessy, B. G. *Corduroy at the zoo*
  Corduroy's birthday
  Corduroy's Christmas
  Corduroy's Easter
  Corduroy's Halloween
Hernandez, Keith. *First-base hero*
Hewitt, Sally. *Face to face safari*
Hill, Eric. *Spot bakes a cake*
  Spot goes to a party
  Spot goes to school
  Spot goes to the beach
  Spot goes to the park
  Spot sleeps over
  Spot's baby sister
  Spot's birthday party
  Spot's first Christmas
  Spot's first Easter
  Spot's first walk
  Where's Spot?
Hill, Susanna Leonard. *The house that Mack built*
Hines, Anna Grossnickle. *No, no Jack!*
  Whose shoes?
Hoban, Tana. *Just look*
  Look book
Hoffmann, E. T. A. *The nutcracker*
Horácek, Petr. *Animal opposites*
  Flip's day
  The mouse who reached the sky
  One spotted giraffe
  Strawberries are red
  The mouse who ate the moon
  A surprise for Tiny Mouse
Horwood, Annie. *Butterfly, butterfly what colors do you see?*
How much does God love me?
Hughes, Laura. *We're going on an egg hunt*
Hutchins, Hazel. *Two so small*
Idle, Molly. *Flora and the chicks*
  Flora and the flamingo
  Flora and the ostrich
  Flora and the peacocks
  Flora and the penguin
Inkpen, Mick. *Kipper's Christmas eve*
  Kipper's rainy day
  Kipper's sunny day
Janovitz, Marilyn. *A, B, see!*
Jaramillo, Susie. *Little skeletons / Esqueletitos*
Jenkins, Steve. *Animals upside down*
Johnson, Stephen T. *My little blue robot*
Jonas, Ann. *Where can it be?*
Jullien, Jean. *Before and after*
Kaner, Etta. *Who likes the rain?*
  Who likes the sun?
  Who likes the wind?
Karas, G. Brian. *Skidamarink*
Katz, Karen. *A potty for me!*
  Where is baby's mommy?
Klausmeier, Jesse. *Open this little book*
Koda-Callan, Elizabeth. *The squiggly Wigglys*
Koponen, Libby. *Mmm . . . let's eat!*
Lavis, Steve. *On the farm*
Lawrence, Jennifer B. *Sad doggy*
Lemke, Donald. *Book-o-beards*
Leslie, Amanda. *Alfie and Betty Bug*
  Are chickens stripy?
  Do crocodiles moo?
  Flappy, waggy, wiggly
  Who's that scratching at my door?

Lewin, Betsy. *Where is Tippy Toes?*
Lewis, Anne Margaret. *What am I? Christmas*
Lithgow, John. *The remarkable Farkle McBride*
Little old lady who swallowed a fly. *I know an old lady who swallowed a fly*
  There was an old lady who swallowed a fly
Litton, Jonthan. *Snip snap*
Lobel, Arnold. *The Frog and Toad pop-up book*
Lodge, Jo. *Happy birthday, Moo Moo*
  Happy Snappy!
  Moo Moo goes to the city
Long, Ethan. *Up, tall and high*
Low, William. *Machines go to work*
  Machines go to work in the city
Macaulay, David. *How machines work: zoo break!*
MacDonald, Suse. *Circus opposites*
McNamara, Margaret. *The whistle on the train*
Martin, Ruth. *Santa's on his way*
Merlin, Christophe. *Under the hood*
Michelson, Richard. *Ten times better*
Mitton, Tony. *Rumble, roar, dinosaur!*
Moerbeek, Kees. *The diary of Hansel and Gretel*
Moore, Clement Clarke. *The night before Christmas: a pop-up*
Morgan, Mary. *My good night book*
Morris, Dewi. *Sandy's street*
Munro, Roxie. *Circus*
  Go! go! go!
Murphy, Mary. *Crocopotamus*
  Good night like this
  A kiss like this
  Say hello like this!
Mystery manor
Nobles, Kristen M. *Drive this book*
Noonan, Julia. *Mouse by mouse*
Novak, Matt. *Too many bunnies*
O'Brien, Anne Sibley. *Abracadabra, it's spring!*
  Hocus pocus, it's fall!
Old MacDonald had a farm. *Old MacDonald had a farm*
Park, Linda Sue. *Yum! yuck!*
Parot, Annelore. *Kimonos*
Pelham, David. *A is for animals*
  Crawlies creep
  Sam's pizza
  Sam's sandwich
Perrault, Charles. *Cinderella: a pop-up fairy tale*
Perrin, Martine. *Look who's there!*
Pfister, Marcus. *Just the way you are*
  Milo and the magical stones
Pham, LeUyen. *There's no such thing as little*
Philpot, Graham. *Where is Little Harry?*
Pienkowski, Jan. *Good night, a pop-up lullaby*
  Haunted house
  Pizza!
Piers, Helen. *Who's in my bed?*
Piggy and Bear in their underwear
Pittau, Francisco. *Out of sight*
Porter, Sue. *Parsnip*
Potter, Beatrix. *The two bad mice*
Previn, Stacey. *Find spot!*
Rayner, Catherine. *Ernest, the moose who doesn't fit*
Reasoner, Charles. *One blue fish*
Regan, Dian Curtis. *How do you know it's Halloween?*
Reinhart, Matthew. *Animal popposites*
  Fairies and magical creatures
  Gods and heroes
Reiser, Lynn. *My cat Tuna*

My dog Truffle
Play ball with me!
Reitman, Andrea. *Mouse in the house*
Rives. *If I were a polar bear*
Rosen, Michael J. *Chanukah lights*
Rosenthal, Marc. *Big bot, small bot*
Rowe, Jeannette. *Whose ears?*
Whose feet?
Whose nose?
Rubin, Adam. *Robo-Sauce*
Rueda, Claudia. *Bunny slopes*
Huff and puff
Sabuda, Robert. *Beauty and the beast: a pop-up book of the classic fairy tale*
The Christmas alphabet
The dragon and the knight
Encyclopedia prehistorica: dinosaurs
Encyclopedia prehistorica: mega-beasts
Encyclopedia prehistorica: sharks and other seamonsters
The movable Mother Goose
Peter Pan
Winter in white
Winter's tale
Safran, Sheri. *All kinds of families: a lift-the-flap book*
Sage, Angie. *Molly and the birthday party*
Saltzberg, Barney. *Andrew drew and drew*
Baby animal kisses
Hi, Blueberry!
Kisses
Santa Claus is coming to town
Santoro, Lucio. *Wild oceans*
Scarry, Huck. *Looking into the Middle Ages*
Scheffler, Axel. *Axel Scheffler's Flip flap safari*
Schindel, John. *What did they see?*
Schwartz, David M. *Where else in the wild?*
Where in the wild
Schwarz, Viviane. *Is there a dog in this book?*
There are cats in this book
There are no cats in this book
Seder, Rufus Butler. *Waddle!*
The Wizard of Oz
Seeber, Dorothea P. *A pup just for me . . . A boy just for me*
Seeger, Laura Vaccaro. *Black? white! day? night! a book of opposites*
First the egg
The hidden alphabet
Lemons are not red
Sendak, Maurice. *Mommy?*
Sharratt, Nick. *Shark in the park*
What's in the witch's kitchen?
Shea, Susan A. *Do you know which one will grow?*
Sheehy, Shawn. *Welcome to the neighborwood*
Shuttlewood, Craig. *Who's in the tree?*
Simmons, Jane. *Bouncy bouncy Daisy*
Daisy's hide-and-seek
Simpson-Enock, Sarah. *Mommy, Mommy, what's in your tummy?*
Sims, Nat. *Peekaboo barn*
Sirett, Dawn. *Happy birthday Sophie!*
Sís, Peter. *Fire truck*
Trucks, trucks, trucks
Smee, Nicola. *No bed without Ted*
Smith, Kathryn. *Little Donkey's Christmas story*
Little Lamb's Christmas story
Smith, Lois T. *Carrie and Carl play*
Smith, Mavis. *'Twas the day after Thanksgiving*
Snyder, Betsy. *I can dance*, ill. by Betsy E. Snyder

I can dance, ill. by Betsy E. Snyder
I can play, ill. by Betsy E. Snyder
I can play, ill. by Betsy E. Snyder
Spafford, Suzy. *Witzy's colors*
Sper, Emily. *The Passover seder*
Spurr, Elizabeth. *Two bears beneath the stairs*
Stadler, John. *Take me out to the ball game: a pop-up book*
Stanley, Mandy. *Bloomer, the dog you can play with*
Steele, Philip. *A knight's city*
Trains: the slide-out, see-through story of world-famous trains and railroads
Stickland, Paul. *Dinosaur stomp!*
A number of dinosaurs
Truck jam
Stileman, Kali. *Roly-poly egg*
Taback, Simms. *Simms Taback's city animals*
Simms Taback's farm animals
Simms Taback's safari animals
Tabby, Abigail. *Baby face*
Tatcheva, Eva. *Witch Zelda's birthday cake*
Teckentrup, Britta. *Bee*
Get out of my bath!
Tree: a peek-through picture book
Thompson, Lauren. *Little Quack: dial-a-duck*
Tildes, Phyllis Limbacher. *Eye guess*
Torres, Melissa A. *The great Christmas tree celebration*
Tupera, Tupera. *Polar Bear's underwear*
Van der Meer, Mara. *Can we play?*
Van Fleet, Matthew. *Fuzzy yellow ducklings*
Heads
Moo
One yellow lion
Spotted yellow frogs
Verdet, Andre. *All about time*
Vere, Ed. *Everyone's little*
Viorst, Judith. *And two boys booed*
Viva, Frank. *Outstanding in the rain*
Walsh, Melanie. *Living with Mom and living with Dad*
Monster, monster
Wax, Wendy. *Even firefighters go to the potty*
Weeks, Sarah. *Be mine, be mine, sweet valentine*
Wells, Rosemary. *Goodnight Max*
McDuff's hide-and-seek
Max and Ruby at the Warthogs' wedding
Max and Ruby's treasure hunt
Weninger, Brigitte. *Special delivery*
White, Marsha. *Hooper has lost his owner*
Whybrow, Ian. *Good night, monster*
Hello! Is this grandma?
Sammy and the robots
Wick, Walter. *Hey, Seymour!*
Willems, Mo. *Big Frog can't fit in*
Time to say "please"!
Wing, Natasha. *How to raise a dinosaur*
Wood, Audrey. *The napping house wakes up*
Yaccarino, Dan. *So big*
Yoon, Salina. *Do cows meow?*
Do crocs kiss?
Opposnakes
Young, Cybèle. *Some things I've lost*
Zelinsky, Paul O. *The wheels on the bus*
Ziefert, Harriet. *Mommies are for counting stars*
Robin, where are you?
Talk, baby!

Fortune *see* Character traits – luck

Fossils

Aliki. *Fossils tell of long ago*
    The long lost coelacanth and other living fossils
Alphin, Elaine Marie. *Dinosaur hunter*
Atkins, Jeannine. *Mary Anning and the sea dragon*
Barner, Bob. *Dinosaur bones*
    Dinosaurs roar, butterflies soar!
Brown, Don. *Rare treasure*
Cohen, Daniel. *Apatosaurus*
    Pteranodon
    Stegosaurus
    Triceratops
    Tyrannosaurus rex
    Velociraptor
Diffily, Deborah. *Jurassic shark*
DiSiena, Laura Lyn. *Dinosaurs live on!*
Houran, Lori Haskins. *Dig those dinosaurs*
Johansen, K. V. *Pippin and the bones*
Lach, Will. *I am not a dinosaur!*
Pellant, Chris. *The best book of fossils, rocks, and
    minerals*
Sabuda, Robert. *Encyclopedia prehistorica: mega-
    beasts*
    *Encyclopedia prehistorica: sharks and other
    seamonsters*
Thomson, Bill. *Fossil*
Zoehfeld, Kathleen Weidner. *Dinosaur tracks*
Zommer, Yuval. *One hundred bones*

Foster children, foster homes

O'Leary, Sara. *A family is a family is a family*
Pearson, Julie. *Elliot*
Rosenthal, Amy Krouse. *That's me loving you*

Freedom *see* Character traits – freedom

Friendship

Ada, Alma Flor. *Friend frog*
Adams, Sarah. *Dave and Violet*
    Gary and Ray
Alborough, Jez. *My friend bear*
Alborozo, Gabriel. *The mouse and the moon*
Alexander, Claire. *Monkey and the little one*
Alexander, Kwame. *Surf's up*
Aliki. *Best friends together again*
    Feelings
    Overnight at Mary Bloom's
    We are best friends
Alter, Anna. *Abigail spells*
Amado, Elisa. *Tricycle*
Anastas, Margaret. *A hug for you*
Anderson, Derek. *Romeo and Lou blast off*
Anglund, Joan Walsh. *A friend is someone who likes
    you*
Apperley, Dawn. *Blossom and Boo*
Armo, Nancy. *A friend for Mole*
Armstrong, Matthew S. *Jane and Mizmow*
Arnosky, Jim. *Armadillo's orange*
Arsenault, Isabelle. *Colette's lost pet*
Asch, Frank. *Moonbear's friend*
    Moonbear's pet
Ashdown, Rebecca. *Bob and Flo*
Ashman, Linda. *Ella who?*
Askani, Tanja. *A friend like you*
Bagley, Jessixa. *Before I leave*
Bailey, Linda. *Stanley's little sister*

Baker, Roberta. *Olive's first sleepover*
Barasch, Lynne. *The reluctant flower girl*
Bardhan-Quallen, Sudipta. *The Mine-o-saur*
Barnes, Laura T. *Ernest and the big itch*
    Ernest's special Christmas
    Twist and Ernest
Barnett, Mac. *I love you like a pig*
    Leo: a ghost story
    Places to be
Barrett, Ron. *Cats got talent*
Barringer, William. *Gregory and Alexander*
Bateman, Teresa. *The leprechaun under the bed*
Battersby, Katherine. *Squish Rabbit*
Bauer, Marion Dane. *Frog's best friend*
Baumgart, Klaus. *Laura's star*
Beck, Andrea. *Elliot's Christmas surprise*
    Elliot's emergency
    Elliot's shipwreck
Becker, Bonny. *A bedtime for Bear*
    A birthday for Bear
    A Christmas for Bear
    A library book for Bear
    The sniffles for Bear
    A visitor for Bear
Bell, Cece. *Bee-Wigged*
    Chuck and Woodchuck
Belloni, Giulia. *Anything is possible*
Belton, Sandra. *Pictures for Miss Josie*
Bendall-Brunello, Tiziana. *I wish I could read!*
Bender, Rebecca. *Giraffe meets Bird*
    Not friends
Benjamin, A. H. *Mouse, mole and the falling star*
Bennett, Kelly. *Not Norman*
Berenstain, Stan and Jan. *The Berenstain bears and
    the trouble with friends*
    The Berenstain bears' moving day
Berger, Carin. *Forever friends*
Bertier, Anne. *Wednesday*
Biddulph, Rob. *The grizzly bear who lost his grrrrr!*
Biedrzycki, David. *Groundhog's runaway shadow*
Birdsall, Jeanne. *Lucky and Squash*
Blabey, Aaron. *Pearl Barley and Charlie Parsley*
Blackaby, Susan. *Brownie Groundhog and the
    February Fox*
    Brownie Groundhog and the wintry surprise
Blackstone, Stella. *Cleo and Caspar*
    Cleo in the snow
    Cleo on the move
    Cleo the cat
Blake, Quentin. *Fantastic Daisy Artichoke*
Blake, Robert J. *Painter and Ugly*
Blegvad, Lenore. *First friends*
Bley, Anette. *A friend*
Block party today
Bloom, Suzanne. *Alone together*
    A splendid friend, indeed
    What about Bear?
Bluthenthal, Diana Cain. *I'm not invited?*
Bogacki, Tomasz. *Circus girl*
Bogan, Paulette. *Virgil and Owen*
    Virgil and Owen stick together
Boldt, Claudia. *Odd dog*
Bonnice, Lindsey. *Libby and Pearl: the best of friends*
Bonwill, Ann. *Bug and Bear*
    I am not a copycat!
Borando, Silvia. *Black cat, white cat*
Border, Terry. *Peanut Butter and Cupcake!*
Bosca, Francesca. *The three grasshoppers*
Bottner, Barbara. *Raymond and Nelda*

Daly, Niki. *Once upon a time*
Davis, Anne. *No dogs allowed!*
Day, Marie. *Edward the "crazy man"*
DeBear, Kirsten. *Be quiet, Marina!*
deGennaro, Sue. *The pros and cons of being a frog*
deGroat, Diane. *Happy birthday to you, you belong in a zoo*
   No more pencils, no more books, no more teacher's dirty looks!
Demas, Corinne. *Here comes trouble!*
DePalma, Mary Newell. *The strange egg*
dePaola, Tomie. *My first Thanksgiving*
   Tom
De Regniers, Beatrice Schenk. *May I bring a friend?*
DeRubertis, Barbara. *Corky Cub's crazy caps*
de Varennes, Monique. *The jewel box ballerinas*
Dewdney, Anna. *Roly Poly pangolin*
Dierssen, Andreas. *Timmy's new friend*
Diesen, Deborah. *The pout-pout fish*
DiPucchio, Kelly. *Crafty Chloe: dress-up mess-up*
Dominguez, Angela. *How do you say? / ¿Cómo se dice?*
Donofrio, Beverly. *Mary and the mouse, the mouse and Mary*
   Where's Mommy?
Donohue, Dorothy. *Veggie soup*
Dorros, Arthur. *Julio's magic*
Doyle, Malachy. *Storm cats*
Dubuc, Marianne. *The lion and the bird*
   Lucy and company
Dunbar, Polly. *Happy Hector*
   Hello Tilly
   Pretty Pru
   Where's Tumpty?
Dunrea, Olivier. *Jasper and Joop*
Duvoisin, Roger Antoine. *Petunia*
Dyckman, Ame. *Boy + Bot*
Eaton, Maxwell. *Best buds*
   The mystery
   Superheroes
Edgemon, Darcie. *Seamore, the very forgetful porpoise*
Edwards, Karl Newsom. *I got a new friend*
Edwards, Nicola. *Goodnight Baxter*
Edwards, Pamela Duncan. *Gigi and Lulu's gigantic fight*
   The old house
   Warthogs in a box
Egan, Tim. *Roasted peanuts*
Elliott, David. *Baabwaa and Wooliam*
   Hunter's best friend at school
   The two Tims
Elliott, Laura Malone. *Hunter and Stripe and the soccer showdown*
   A string of hearts
Ellis, Sarah. *Ben says goodbye*
Emberley, Rebecca. *Spare parts*
Emmett, Jonathan. *The best gift of all*
Engels-Fietzek, Petra. *Sophie and the seagull*
Engler, Michael. *Elephantastic!*
English, Karen. *Hot day on Abbott Avenue*
Esbaum, Jill. *To the big top*
   Tom's tweet
Fagan, Cary. *Ella May and the wishing stone*
Falatko, Julie. *Snappsy the alligator and his best friend forever (probably)*
Faller, Regis. *Polo and Lily*
Falwell, Cathryn. *David's drawing*
Farish, Terry. *The cat who liked potato soup*
   Joseph's big ride

Faulkner, Keith. *The tallest shortest longest greenest brownest animal in the jungle!*
Fearnley, Jan. *Arthur and the meanies*
   A perfect day for it
Fergus, Maureen. *Buddy and Earl*
   Buddy and Earl go exploring
Ferry, Beth. *A small blue whale*
   Stick and Stone
Floyd, Madeleine. *Cold paws, warm heart*
Foley, Greg. *I miss you Mouse*
   Make a wish Bear
   Thank you, Bear
   Willoughby and the lion
Folgueira, Rodrigo. *Ribbit!*
Ford, Bernette. *No more blanket for Lambkin!*
Foreman, Michael. *Friends*
   The littlest dinosaur
Fox, Diane. *Tyson the terrible*
Fox, Mem. *Hunwick's egg*
Frankel, Erin. *Tough!*
Frazee, Marla. *Boot and Shoe*
Freedman, Deborah. *Shy*
Freeman, Tor. *Olive and the bad mood*
   Olive and the embarrassing gift
Freymann, Saxton. *One lonely seahorse*
Frith, Nicholas John. *Hector and Hummingbird*
Fritts, Mary Bahr. *If Nathan were here*
Fuge, Charles. *Swim, Little Wombat, swim!*
Galbraith, Kathryn O. *Two bunny buddies*
Gall, Chris. *Dog vs. Cat*
Gantos, Jack. *Back to school for Rotten Ralph*
Garland, Sarah. *Eddie's toolbox and how to make and mend things*
Garton, Sam. *I am Otter*
Gauch, Patricia Lee. *Tanya and Emily in a dance for two*
Genechten, Guido van. *Because you are my friend*
George, Kallie. *Secrets I know*
Geraghty, Paul. *The hoppameleon*
Gerstein, Mordicai. *You can't have too many friends!*
Gianferrari, Maria. *Penny and Jelly: the school show*
Gillingham, Sara. *Friends*
Gillmor, Don. *Yuck, a love story*
Giovanni, Nikki. *Lincoln and Douglass*
Glaser, Linda. *Hannah's way*
Gleeson, Libby. *Clancy and Millie and the very fine house*
   Half a world away
Goodhart, Pippa. *Pudgy, a puppy to love*
Goodrich, Carter. *We forgot Brock!*
Goossens, Philippe. *Knock! knock! knock! who's there?*
Gorbachev, Valeri. *Big Little Elephant*
   Catty Jane who hated the rain
   Catty Jane who loved to dance
   Chicken chickens go to school
   Heron and Turtle
   Me too!
   That's what friends are for
Gordon, Gus. *Herman and Rosie*
Grant, Jacob. *Cat knit*
Grant, Joan. *Cat and Fish*
Gravett, Emily. *Bear and Hare: share!*
   Bear and Hare: snow!
   Bear and Hare go fishing
   Bear and Hare—where's Bear?
Gray, Luli. *Ant and Grasshopper*
Greenfield, Eloise. *Big friend, little friend*
Gregory, Nan. *Wild Girl and Gran*
Gretz, Susanna. *Riley and Rose in the picture*

Katzler, Eva. *Florentine and Pig*
Keats, Ezra Jack. *A letter to Amy*
    Peter's chair
Keller, Holly. *Help!*
    Sophie's window
Kellogg, Steven. *Best friends*
Kenah, Katharine. *The very stuffed turkey*
Kerley, Barbara. *With a friend by your side*
Ketteman, Helen. *Armadilly chili*
Kilaka, John. *True friends*
Kimura, Ken. *999 frogs and a little brother*
Kimura, Yuichi. *One stormy night . . .*
    One sunny day . . .
Kinerk, Robert. *Clorinda plays baseball!*
King, Stephen Michael. *You*
Kirk, Daniel. *Library mouse: a world to explore*
    Ten things I love about you
    You are not my friend, but I miss you
Kirk, David. *Oh so brave dragon*
Kirsch, Vincent X. *Forsythia and me*
    Freddie and Gingersnap
Kitamura, Satoshi. *Pablo the artist*
Kleven, Elisa. *The friendship wish*
    Welcome home, Mouse
Kliphuis, Christine. *Robbie and Ronnie*
Knudsen, Michelle. *Marilyn's monster*
Kochan, Vera. *What if your best friend were blue?*
Kolanovic, Dubravka. *Everyone needs a friend*
Korda, Lerryn. *Into the wild*
    It's vacation time
Kostecki-Shaw, Jenny Sue. *Same, same but different*
Kraegel, Kenneth. *King Arthur's very great grandson*
Kroll, Virginia L. *Forgiving a friend*
Krosoczka, Jarrett J. *Max for president*
    My buddy, Slug
Kuhlman, Evan. *Hank's big day*
Lairla, Sergio. *Abel and the wolf*
Lakin, Patricia. *Camping day*
Lambert, Jonny. *The only lonely panda*
Landström, Lena. *Pom and Pim*
    Where is Pim?
Langreuter, Jutta. *Little Bear and the big fight*
    Little Bear goes to kindergarten
LaReau, Kara. *Mr. Prickles*
Lasky, Kathryn. *Fourth of July bear*
Latimer, Alex. *Pig and small*
Latimer, Miriam. *Dear Panda*
Leeson, Christine. *Molly and the storm*
Lehman, Barbara. *Red again*
    The red book
Le Neouanic, Lionel. *Little smudge*
Lerch. *Swim! swim!*
Lester, Helen. *Three cheers for Tacky*
Levis, Caron. *Ida, always*
Levy, Janice. *Thomas the toadilly terrible bully*
Lewis, Kim. *Friends*
    Good night, Harry
    Here we go Harry
    Hooray for Harry
Lewis, Rob. *Friends*
Light, Kelly. *Louise and Andie*
Light, Steve. *The Christmas giant*
    Swap!
Lin, Grace. *Lissy's friends*
    Okie-dokie, Artichokie
Linders, Clara. *The very best door of all*
Lionni, Leo. *Alexander and the wind-up mouse*
    An extraordinary egg
    Fish is fish

    Little blue and little yellow
    Mr. McMouse
    Nicolas, where have you been?
Litchfield, David. *The bear and the piano*
Litten, Kristyna. *Blue and Bertie*
Livingston, A. A. *B. Bear and Lolly: off to school*
Livingston, Irene. *Finklehopper Frog cheers*
Lobel, Arnold. *Days with Frog and Toad*
    Frog and Toad all year
    Frog and Toad are friends
    Frog and Toad together
London, Jonathan. *Duck and Hippo in the rainstorm*
    Duck and Hippo lost and found
Long, Ethan. *Bird and Birdie in a fine day*
Long, Loren. *Otis and the puppy*
Lovell, Patty. *Have fun, Molly Lou Melon*
Lucas, David. *Cake girl*
Ludwig, Trudy. *Better than you*
    The invisible boy
Lundquist, Mary. *Cat and Bunny*
Lundy, Charlotte. *Thank you, Ruth and Naomi*
Lurie, Susan. *Will you be my friend?*
Luthardt, Kevin. *Hats*
    You're weird!
Macaulay, David. *Angelo*
McBratney, Sam. *I'm sorry*
    Yes we can!
McCarthy, Jenna. *Lola's rules for friendship*
McCarty, Peter. *The monster returns*
McClurkan, Rob. *Playdates rule!*
McCourt, Lisa. *Chicken soup for little souls: Della Splatnuk birthday girl*
    Chicken soup for little souls: The new kid and the cookie thief
McCue, Lisa. *Quiet Bunny and Noisy Puppy*
Macdonald, Maryann. *The pink party*
McDonald, Megan. *Reptiles are my life*
McDonnell, Patrick. *The gift of nothing*
    Thank you and good night
McGhee, Alison. *Making a friend*
McKee, David. *Elmer and Wilbur*
    Elmer in the snow
McKissack, Patricia C. *Messy Bessey and the birthday overnight*
MacLachlan, Patricia. *Nora's chicks*
McLellan, Stephanie Simpson. *The chicken cat*
McPhail, David. *Bella loves Bunny*
    Ben loves Bear
    Big Brown Bear goes to town
    Big Brown Bear's birthday surprise
    Big Brown Bear's up and down day
    Budgie and Boo
    Olivia loves Owl
    Peter loves Penguin
    Pig Pig meets the lion
    Sylvie and True
    Waddles
McQuinn, Anna. *My friend Jamal*
    My friend Mei Jing
Magerl, Caroline. *Rose and the wish thing*
Mahoney, Daniel J. *The perfect clubhouse*
Mallat, Kathy. *Just ducky*
Manley, Curtis. *Shawn loves sharks*
Mann, Jennifer K. *Sam and Jump*
    Two speckled eggs
Mantchev, Lisa. *Someday, narwhal*
Marciano, John Bemelmans. *Delilah*
Marshall, James. *The Cut-Ups cut loose*
    George and Martha

Louise the big cheese and the Ooh-la-la Charm School
Proimos, James. *Waddle! waddle!*
Puttock, Simon. *Big bad wolf is good*
    Goat and Donkey in strawberry sunglasses
    Goat and Donkey in the great outdoors
    A story for Hippo
Quattlebaum, Mary. *Winter friends*
Rand, Gloria. *A pen pal for Max*
Rania, Queen, consort of Abdullah II, King of
    Jordan. *The sandwich swap*
Rankin, Laura. *Fluffy and Baron*
    My turn!
Raschka, Chris. *Ring! Yo?*
    Yo! Yes?
Rawlinson, Julia. *Fletcher and the snowflake*
    Christmas
Rayner, Catherine. *The bear who shared*
    Solomon Crocodile
Reed, Lynn Rowe. *Benny Shark goes to friend school*
Reiser, Lynn. *My way / A mi manera*
    Two mice in three fables
Reynolds, Aaron. *Nerdy birdy*
Reynolds, Peter H. *I'm here*
Richards, Barnaby. *Blip!*
Richards, Dan. *The problem with not being scared of*
    monsters
Richmond, Lori. *Pax and Blue*
Ritchie, Alison. *What Bear likes best!*
Ritz, Karen. *Windows with birds*
Robberecht, Thierry. *Sam tells stories*
    Sam's new friend
Robbins, Jacqui. *The new girl . . . and me*
    Two of a kind
Robinson, Sue. *I want to play*
Roche, Denis. *Mim, gym, and June*
Roddie, Shen. *Sandbear*
Rodman, Mary Ann. *My best friend*
Rodriguez, Béatrice. *Fox and hen together*
Rogers, Fred. *Extraordinary friends*
    Making friends
    Moving
Rohmann, Eric. *My friend Rabbit*
Root, Phyllis. *Toot toot zoom!*
Rosen, Michael. *Bear's day out*
Rosen, Michael J. *Elijah's angel*
Rosenberg, Liz. *What James said*
Rosenthal, Amy Krouse. *Chopsticks*
    Friendshape
    Uni the unicorn
Rosenthal, Marc. *Archie and the pirates*
Rosoff, Meg. *Jumpy Jack and Googily*
Ross, Tony. *I want a friend!*
Roth, Carol. *Little Bunny's sleepless night*
Roth, Roger. *Fishing for Methuselah*
Rotner, Shelley. *All kinds of friends*
Rudy, Maggie. *City mouse, country mouse*
Rumford, James. *Dog-of-the-Sea-Waves*
    Tiger and turtle
Runton, Andy. *Owly and Wormy: bright lights and*
    starry nights!
    Owly and Wormy: friends all aflutter!
Russell, Natalie. *Brown Rabbit in the city*
    Moon rabbit
Russo, Marisabina. *Sophie sleeps over*
    A very big bunny
Ruzzier, Sergio. *Hey, Rabbit!*
    A letter for Leo
    The little giant
    Too busy

Ryan, Candace. *Ribbit rabbit*
Rylant, Cynthia. *All I see*
    The bookshop dog
    Miss Maggie
Sadler, Marilyn. *Alice from Dallas*
Sakai, Komako. *Emily's balloon*
Saltzberg, Barney. *Hip, hip, hooray day!*
    The problem with pumpkins
Sandu, Anca. *Churchill's tale of tails*
Sanromán, Susana. *Señora Reganoña*
Santat, Dan. *The adventures of Beekle*
Sarah, Linda. *Big friends*
Sasso, Sandy Eisenberg. *For heaven's sake*
Satoshi, Kako. *Little Daruma and little Tengu*
Sauer, Tammi. *I love cake!*
    Your alien
    Your alien returns
Scanlon, Elizabeth Garton. *The good-pie party*
    Noodle and Lou
Schachner, Judith Byron. *Dewey Bob*
Schaefer, Lola M. *Frankie Stein starts school*
Scheer, Julian. *By the light of the captured moon*
Scheffler, Axel. *Pip and Posy: the new friend*
    Pip and Posy: the scary monster
    Pip and Posy: the snowy day
    Pip and Posy: the super scooter
Scheffler, Ursel. *Who has time for Little Bear?*
Schertle, Alice. *Little Blue Truck*
Schick, Eleanor. *My Navajo sister*
Schmid, Paul. *Oliver and his egg*
Schneider, Josh. *Princess Sparkle-Heart gets a*
    makeover
Schubert, Ingrid. *There's always room for one more*
Schulz, Heidi. *Giraffes ruin everything*
Schwartz, Amy. *I can't wait!*
    100 things I love to do with you
    Tiny and Hercules
Schwartz, Corey Rosen. *Hop! Plop!*
Schwarz, Viviane. *How to find gold*
Scieszka, Jon. *Cowboy and Octopus*
    Smash! crash!
Scott, Elaine. *Friends!*
Scotton, Rob. *Splat says thank you!*
    Splish, splash, splat!
Seeger, Laura Vaccaro. *Dog and Bear: three to get*
    ready
    Dog and Bear: tricks and treats
    Dog and Bear: two friends, three stories
    Dog and Bear: two's company
    What if?
Segal, John. *The lonely moose*
Seven, John. *A year with friends*
Shannon, George. *Heart to heart*
    Rabbit's gift
Sharmat, Marjorie Weinman. *The 329th friend*
Shaskan, Tricia Speed. *Punk skunks*
Shaw, Hannah. *Sneaky Weasel*
Shea, Bob. *Unicorn thinks he's pretty great*
Sheehan, Kevin. *The dandelion's tale*
Sherry, Kevin. *Turtle Island*
Shields, Gillian. *Library Lily*
Shireen, Nadia. *Hey, Presto!*
Shriver, Maria. *What's wrong with Timmy?*
Sidjanski, Brigitte. *Little Chicken and Little Duck*
Sif, Birgitta. *Oliver*
Silverhardt, Lauryn. *Happy Chinese New Year, Kai-*
    lan!
Siminovich, Lorena. *Alex and Lulu*
Simmons, Jane. *Together*

Wick, Walter. *Can you see what I see? Seymour makes*
 new friends
Wild, Margaret. *Fox*
 Mr. Nick's knitting
Wiles, Debbie. *Freedom summer*
Wilhelm, Hans. *Quacky Ducky's Easter egg*
Willems, Mo. *City dog, country frog*
 Leonardo the terrible monster
 Sam the most scaredy-cat kid in the whole world
Williams, Karen Lynn. *When Africa was home*
Williams, Sherley Anne. *Girls together*
Willis, Jeanne. *Misery Moo*
 Poles apart
Wilson, Karma. *Bear feels scared*
 Bear feels sick
Wilson, Sarah. *Friends and pals and brothers, too*
Wilson, Steve. *Hedgehugs*
Winget, Susan. *Tucker's four-carrot school day*
Winstead, Rosie. *Ruby and Bubbles*
Wishinsky, Frieda. *You're mean, Lily Jean!*
Wojciechowski, Susan. *The Christmas miracle of*
 Jonathan Toomey
Wolff, Ferida. *The story blanket*
Wolkstein, Diane. *Little Mouse's painting*
 Step by step
Wong, Liz. *Quackers*
Wood, Audrey. *Jubal's wish*
Woodcock, Fiona. *Hiding Heidi*
Wormell, Christopher. *Blue Rabbit and friends*
Yaccarino, Dan. *Billy and Goat at the state fair*
 Happyland: big berry
 Happyland: rainy day
 Unlovable
Yeh, Kat. *The friend ship*
Yin. *Brothers*
Yolen, Jane. *Dimity Duck*
 How do dinosaurs play with their friends?
 How do dinosaurs stay friends?
Yoon, Salina. *Be a friend*
 Penguin and Pinecone
 Penguin on vacation
 Penguin's Christmas wish
Young, Amy. *A new friend for Sparkle*
Young, Ruth. *Golden Bear*
Zalben, Jane Breskin. *Beni's first Chanukah*
Zehler, Antonia. *Two fine ladies*
 Two fine ladies have a tiff
Ziefert, Harriet. *Bunny's lessons*
 Fun Land fun!
 39 uses for a friend
Zolotow, Charlotte. *The hating book*
 My friend John
Zuniga, Elisabeth. *A friend for Bo*

Frogs & toads

Ada, Alma Flor. *Friend frog*
Alexander, Kwame. *Surf's up*
Allchin, Rosalind. *The frog princess*
Anderson, Peggy Perry. *Joe on the go*
 Out to lunch
 Time for bed, the babysitter said
 To the tub
Angleberger, Tom. *McToad mows Tiny Island*
Arnold, Tedd. *Green Wilma*
 Green Wilma, frog in space
Arnosky, Jim. *All about frogs*
Asch, Frank. *Baby Bird's first nest*
 Moonbear's pet

Asher, Sandy. *Here comes Gosling!*
 Too many frogs!
 What a party!
Azore, Barbara. *Wanda and the frogs*
Bailey, Linda. *Toads on toast*
Bartles, Veronica. *The princess and the frogs*
Bateman, Teresa. *The frog with the big mouth*
Bauer, Marion Dane. *Frog's best friend*
Berkes, Marianne. *Marsh music*
Boelts, Maribeth. *Big Daddy, frog wrestler*
Bonning, Tony. *Snog the frog*
Boyd, Lizi. *I love Daddy*
 I love Mommy
Breen, Steve. *Stick*
Brenning, Juli. *Maggi and Milo*
Bynum, Janie. *Otis*
Calmenson, Stephanie. *The frog principal*
Carle, Eric. *Hello, red fox*
Carlson, Nancy. *Smile a lot!*
 Think big!
 Think happy!
Cecil, Randy. *Horsefly and Honeybee*
Chrustowski, Rick. *Hop frog*
Cooper, Susan. *Frog*
Cowan, Charlotte. *Peeper has a fever*
Crowther, Kitty. *Scritch scratch scraww plop*
Cyrus, Kurt. *Tadpole Rex*
Debecker, Benoît. *The naughty prince*
Dennard, Deborah. *Bullfrog at Magnolia Circle*
Donaldson, Julia. *The Giant Jumperee*
Downing, Johnette. *There was an old lady who*
 swallowed some bugs
Elya, Susan Middleton. *Sophie's trophy*
Emmett, Jonathan. *Prince Ribbit*
Fearnley, Jan. *Martha in the middle*
Feeney, Tatyana. *Little Frog's tadpole trouble*
Ferri, Giuliano. *Little Tad grows up*
FitzSimmons, David. *Curious critters*
 Curious critters, vol. 2
Fleming, Denise. *In the small, small pond*
Florian, Douglas. *Lizards, frogs, and polliwogs*
Folgueira, Rodrigo. *Ribbit!*
Franco, Betsy. *Why the frog has big eyes*
Freedman, Deborah. *By Mouse and Frog*
French, Vivian. *Growing frogs*
A frog he would a-wooing go [folk-song] *Frog went*
 a-courtin'
 Frog went a-courting
 Froggie went a courting
 Froggy went a-courtin'
Gardner, Carol. *Princess Zelda and the frog*
Geraghty, Paul. *The hoppameleon*
Gibbons, Gail. *Frogs*
Grahame, Kenneth. *The wind in the willows*
Gravett, Emily. *Spells*
Gray, Kes. *Frog on a log?*
Grimm, Jacob and Wilhelm. *The frog prince*, ill. by
 Anne Yvonne Gilbert
 The frog prince, ill. by Todd Ouren
Grobler, Piet. *Hey, frog!*
Guiberson, Brenda Z. *Frog song*
Hall, Algy Craig. *Fine as we are*
Hassett, Ann. *Too many frogs!*
Heo, Yumi. *The green frogs*
Himmelman, John. *Noisy frog sing-along*
 A wood frog's life
Hobbie, Holly. *Gem*
Hood, Susan. *Leaps and bounce*
Hunter, Anne. *Possum and the peeper*

Hurd, Thacher. *Bad frogs*
Hurley, Jorey. *Ribbit*
Isherwood, Shirley. *Flora the frog*
James, Betsy. *Tadpoles*
Jenkins, Martin. *Fabulous frogs*
Johnson, Rebecca. *Tree frog hears a sound*
Johnson, Suzanne C. *Fribbity ribbit*
Jordan, Sandra. *Frog hunt*
Joyce, William. *Bently and egg*
Kalan, Robert. *Jump, frog, jump!*
Kang, Anna. *Can I tell you a secret?*
Kasza, Keiko. *Grandpa Toad's last secret*
Kellogg, Steven. *The mysterious tadpole*
Ketteman, Helen. *Armadilly chili*
Kimmel, Eric A. *The frog princess: a Tlingit legend
    from Alaska*
Kimura, Ken. *999 frogs and a little brother*
    999 frogs wake up
    999 tadpoles
Kopelke, Lisa. *Excuse me!*
Lee, Jeanne M. *Toad is the uncle of heaven*
Leedy, Loreen. *The great graph contest*
Levy, Janice. *Thomas the toadilly terrible bully*
Lionni, Leo. *An extraordinary egg*
    Fish is fish
    It's mine!
Little old lady who swallowed a fly. *There was an old
    monkey who swallowed a frog*
Livingston, Irene. *Finklehopper Frog*
    Finklehopper Frog cheers
Lobel, Arnold. *Days with Frog and Toad*
    Frog and Toad all year
    Frog and Toad are friends
    The Frog and Toad pop-up book
    Frog and Toad together
    The frogs and toads all sang
London, Jonathan. *Froggy eats out*
    Froggy gets a doggy
    Froggy gets dressed
    Froggy goes to bed
    Froggy goes to camp
    Froggy goes to Hawaii
    Froggy goes to school
    Froggy goes to the doctor
    Froggy goes to the library
    Froggy learns to swim
    Froggy plays in the band
    Froggy plays soccer
    Froggy plays T-ball
    Froggy rides a bike
    Froggy's birthday wish
    Froggy's first Christmas
    Froggy's first kiss
    Froggy's Halloween
    Let's go, Froggy!
Long, Ethan. *The croaky pokey!*
Mack, Jeff. *Ah ha!*
    Frog and Fly
McLeod, Heather. *Kiss me!*
Magloff, Lisa. *Frog*
Markle, Sandra. *Hip-pocket papa*
    Toad weather
Mayer, Mercer. *A boy, a dog, a frog and a friend*
    A boy, a dog and a frog
    Frog goes to dinner
    Frog on his own
    Frog, where are you?
    One frog too many
Mitton, Tony. *Down by the cool of the pool*

Murphy, Stuart J. *Ready, set, hop!*
Northey, Lawrence. *I'm a hop hop hoppity frog*
Parenteau, Shirley. *One frog sang*
Petty, Dev. *I don't want to be a frog*
    I don't want to be big
    There's nothing to do!
Pfeffer, Wendy. *From tadpole to frog*
Pfister, Marcus. *Hopper hunts for spring*
Pinczes, Elinor J. *My full moon is square*
Pinkwater, Daniel. *Bear and Bunny*
Potter, Beatrix. *The tale of Mr. Jeremy Fisher*, ill. by
    David Jorgensen
    The tale of Mr. Jeremy Fisher, ill. by Beatrix Potter
Rong, Yu. *A lovely day for Amelia Goose*
Roth, Susan L. *The biggest frog in Australia*
Rouss, Sylvia A. *The littlest frog*
Ryan, Candace. *Ribbit rabbit*
Ryder, Joanne. *Toad by the road*
Samuels, Barbara. *What's so great about Cindy
    Snappleby?*
Sayre, April Pulley. *Dig, wait, listen*
Schertle, Alice. *Advice for a frog and other poems*
    Little Frog's song
Schneider, Howie. *Fast 'n Snappy*
Scieszka, Jon. *The frog prince, continued*
Shannon, George. *April showers*
    Frog legs
Shaskan, Stephen. *Toad on the road*
Shea, Bob. *The happiest book ever*
    Kid Sheriff and the terrible Toads
Stead, Philip C. *A home for Bird*
Steig, William. *Gorky rises*
Stein, David Ezra. *Tad and Dad*
Steptoe, John. *The story of jumping mouse*
Stevenson, James. *Monty*
Stewart, Melissa. *A place for frogs*
Straaten, Harmen van. *Duck's tale*
    For me?
Tagholm, Sally. *The frog*
Tashiro, Chisato. *Five nice mice*
Thomas, Jan. *Can you make a scary face?*
Thompson, Lauren. *Leap back home to me*
    Little Quack's new friend
Tripp, Paul. *Tubby the tuba*
Vern, Alex. *Where do frogs come from?*
Waddell, Martin. *Bee frog*
Wiesner, David. *Tuesday*
Willems, Mo. *Big Frog can't fit in*
    City dog, country frog
    Nanette's baguette
Willis, Jeanne. *Tadpole's promise*
Winer, Yvonne. *Frogs sing songs*
Wood, Audrey. *Jubal's wish*
Yolen, Jane. *Dimity Duck*
    King Long Shanks
Young, Amy. *The mud fairy*

Frontier life *see* U.S. history – frontier &
    pioneer life

Furniture

Lillegard, Dee. *Wake up house!*
Slonim, David. *He came with the couch*

Furniture – beds

Arnold, Tedd. *No jumping on the bed!*

Bergstein, Rita M. *Your own big bed*
Bertram, Debbie. *My new big-kid bed*
Bibbel, Mark. *Oh, Harry!*
Bluemle, Elizabeth. *Dogs on the bed*
Bottner, Barbara. *Rosa's room*
Bright, Paul. *There's a bison bouncing on the bed!*
Burningham, John. *The magic bed*
Camp, Lindsay. *The biggest bed in the world*
Child, Lauren. *My dream bed*
Ferreri, Della Ross. *How will I ever sleep in this bed?*
Hines, Anna Grossnickle. *My own big bed*
Howe, James. *There's a monster under my bed*
Lum, Kate. *What! cried Granny*
McGhee, Alison. *Bye-bye, crib*
Pulver, Robin. *Alicia's tutu*
Root, Phyllis. *Creak! said the bed*
Samuels, Barbara. *Fred's beds*
Singer, Marilyn. *Fred's bed*
Stevenson, James. *What's under my bed?*
Thomson, Pat. *The squeaky, creaky bed*
Willard, Nancy. *The flying bed*

Furniture – chairs

Bertram, Debbie. *The best place to read*
Collins, Ross. *There's a bear on my chair*
Keats, Ezra Jack. *Peter's chair*
Mahy, Margaret. *Down the back of the chair*
Manuel, Lynn. *The trouble with Tilly Trumble*
Parenteau, Shirley. *Bears on chairs*
Williams, Vera B. *A chair for always*
    A chair for my mother

Games

Agee, Jon. *Mr. Putney's quacking dog*
Ahlberg, Janet. *Each peach pear plum*
    Peek-a-boo!
Alemagna, Beatrice. *On a magical do-nothing day*
Ancona, George. *Mis juegos / My games*
Anglund, Joan Walsh. *The brave cowboy*
Anno, Mitsumasa. *Anno's Britain*
    Anno's counting house
    Anno's Italy
    Anno's journey
    Anno's U.S.A.
Aruego, José. *We hide, you seek*
Ashdown, Rebecca. *Bob and Flo play hide-and-seek*
Barnett, Mac. *Guess again!*
Barrett, Mary Brigid. *All fall down*
    Pat-a-cake
Barrow, David. *Have you seen Elephant?*
Beaton, Clare. *Clare Beaton's action rhymes*
Behrens, Janice. *Let's find rain forest animals*
Boatfield, Jonny. *The twilight book*
Brown, Marc. *Finger rhymes*
    Hand rhymes
    Play rhymes
Burnard, Damon. *I spy in the jungle*

Burningham, John. *Tug-of-war*
Butler, John. *Ten in the meadow*
Butterfield, Moira. *Magic world of learning*
Carter, David A. *Peekaboo bugs*
    Whoo? Whoo?
Cauley, Lorinda Bryan. *Clap your hands*
Chichester Clark, Emma. *Follow the leader!*
Cuyler, Margery. *We're going on a lion hunt*
Dann, Penny. *Eensy weensy spider*
Davenier, Christine. *It's raining, it's pouring*
Daywalt, Drew. *The legend of rock paper scissors*
Delacre, Lulu. *Arroz con leche*
dePaola, Tomie. *Hide-and-seek all week*
Edwards, Richard. *Always Copycub*
Einhorn, Edward. *A very improbable story*
The farmer in the dell. *The farmer in the dell*, ill. by
    John O'Brien
    The farmer in the dell, ill. by Alexandra Wallner
Go tell Aunt Rhody
Grindley, Sally. *Silly Goose and Dizzy Duck play hide-
    and-seek*
Hague, Michael. *Teddy bear, teddy bear*
Handford, Martin. *Find Waldo now*
    The great Waldo search
    Where's Waldo?
    Where's Waldo? In Hollywood
    Where's Waldo? The fantastic journey
    Where's Waldo? The wonder book
    Where's Waldo now?
Hays, Anna Jane. *Ready, set, preschool!*
Hines, Anna Grossnickle. *What can you do in the
    wind?*
Hort, Lenny. *We're going on a treasure hunt*
Hru, Dakari. *Tickle, tickle*
Hughes, Sarah. *Let's play hopscotch*
    Let's play jacks
Hunter, Dette. *38 ways to entertain your babysitter*
    38 ways to entertain your grandparents
Hutchins, Pat. *What game shall we play?*
    Which witch is which?
Intrater, Roberta Grobel. *Peek-a-boo!*
Isadora, Rachel. *Peekaboo bedtime*
    Peekaboo morning
Jackson, Richard. *In plain sight*
Jahn-Clough, Lisa. *Missing Molly*
James, Simon. *Little One Step*
Jenkins, Steve. *What do you do with a tail like this?*
Jennings, Linda. *Hide and seek birthday treat*
Jonas, Ann. *The trek*
Joosse, Barbara. *Evermore Dragon*
Katz, Karen. *Where is baby's mommy?*
Kraus, Robert. *Mort the sport*
Krauss, Ruth. *You're just what I need*
Krilanovich, Nadia. *Chicken, chicken, duck!*
Kroll, Steven. *The Tyrannosaurus game*
Ledwon, Peter. *Midnight math twelve terrific math
    games*
Lewis, J. Patrick. *The bookworm's feast*
Long, Ethan. *Lion and Tiger and Bear*
McCall, Francis X. *A huge hog is a big pig*
Manning, Jane. *My first baby games*
Mayer, Kirsten. *Game of gnomes*
Meade, Holly. *Inside, inside, inside*
Miller, Margaret. *Whose shoe?*
Monson, A. M. *Wanted . . . best friend*
Moore, Julianne. *Freckleface Strawberry and the
    dodgeball bully*
Mother Goose *Pat-a-cake*
Munro, Roxie. *Mazescapes*

Murphy, Stuart J. *Monster musical chairs*
  More or less
Murray, Martine. *A moose called Mouse*
Na, Il Sung. *Hide and seek*
Newman, Lesléa. *Runaway dreidel*
Nordling, Lee. *Belinda the unbeatable*
Palatini, Margie. *The cheese*
Petrillo, Genevieve. *Keep your ear on the ball*
Pfister, Marcus. *You can't win them all, rainbow fish*
Philpot, Graham. *Where is Little Harry?*
Pow, Tom. *Tell me one thing, Dad*
Ray, Karen. *Sleep song*
Robberecht, Thierry. *Sam is not a loser*
Roddie, Shen. *Toes are to tickle*
Rodriguez, Bobbie. *Sarah's sleepover*
Root, Phyllis. *Looking for a moose*
Rosen, Michael. *We're going on a bear hunt*
Rueda, Claudia. *Let's play in the forest while the wolf
  is not around*
Russo, Marisabina. *The big brown box*
Scruggs, Afi. *Jump rope magic*
Shaw, Charles Green. *It looked like spilt milk*
Simmons, Jane. *Daisy's hide-and-seek*
  Little Fern's first winter
Steffensmeier, Alexander. *Millie and the big rescue*
Steig, William. *Pete's a pizza*
  Toby, what are you?
Stoeke, Janet Morgan. *Hide and seek*
Surplice, Holly. *Peek-a-boo Bunny*
Tafuri, Nancy. *Where did Bunny go?*
Thompson, Lauren. *Little Quack's hide and seek*
Trapani, Iza. *What am I?*
Van Allsburg, Chris. *Jumanji*
  Zathura
Van Laan, Nancy. *Tickle tum*
Viorst, Judith. *The alphabet from Z to A*
Walsh, Ellen Stoll. *Where is Jumper?*
Walsh, Melanie. *Hide and sleep*
Wells, Rosemary. *McDuff's hide-and-seek*
  Peek-a-boo
Weninger, Brigitte. *Special delivery*
Westcott, Nadine Bernard. *The lady with the
  alligator purse*
White, Kathryn. *The tickle test*
Wick, Walter. *Can you see what I see? cool collections*
Wildsmith, Brian. *Brian Wildsmith's puzzles*
Wilner, Isabel. *The baby's game book*
Wisniewski, David. *Rain player*
Wood, Don. *Piggies*
Yaccarino, Dan. *So big*
Yee, Wong Herbert. *Who likes rain?*
Yoon, Salina. *Tap to play!*

Gangs *see* Clubs, gangs

Garage sales, rummage sales

Bunting, Eve. *Yard sale*
Devlin, Wende. *Cranberry autumn*
Elya, Susan Middleton. *Adiós, tricycle*
Kotzwinkle, William. *Walter, the farting dog: trouble
  at the yard sale*
Kroll, Steven. *Stuff!*
Stevenson, James. *Yard sale*

Garbage collectors *see* Careers – sanitation
  workers

Gardens, gardening

Aliki. *Corn is maize*
  Quiet in the garden
  The story of Johnny Appleseed
Ancona, George. *It's our garden*
Anno, Mitsumasa. *Anno's magic seeds*
Anstee, Ashlyn. *No, no, Gnome!*
Ayres, Katherine. *Up, down, and around*
Azarian, Mary. *A gardener's alphabet*
Baicker, Karen. *Pea pod babies*
Bauld, Jane Scoggins. *Journey of the third seed*
Beames, Margaret. *Night cat*
Beck, Andrea. *Elliot digs for treasure*
Best, Cari. *A perfect day for digging*
Blackstone, Stella. *What's this?*
Bogacki, Tomasz. *My first garden*
Bond, Michael. *Paddington Bear in the garden*
Boyden, Linda. *The blue roses*
Braun, Sebastien. *Who's hiding?*
Brenner, Barbara A. *Good morning, garden*
Brett, Jan. *Mossy*
Brown, Peter. *The curious garden*
Bruce, Lisa. *Fran's flower*
Bunting, Eve. *A day's work*
  Flower garden
  Sunflower house
Burnett, Frances Hodgson. *The secret garden*
Carbone, Elisa. *Diana's White House garden*
Castellucci, Cecil. *Grandma's gloves*
Cherry, Lynne. *How Groundhog's garden grew*
Christensen, Bonnie. *Plant a little seed*
Codell, Esme Raji. *Seed by seed*
Colandro, Lucille. *There was an old lady who
  swallowed a frog!*
Corderoy, Tracey. *The magical snow garden*
Dahl, Michael. *From the garden*
Davis, Nancy. *A garden of opposites*
Deak, Erzsi. *Pumpkin time!*
De Anda, Diane. *The patchwork garden / pedacitos
  de huerto*
Demi. *The empty pot*
dePaola, Tomie. *Strega Nona's harvest*
Diesen, Deborah. *Bloom*
Donaldson, Julia. *One mole digging a hole*
Duke, Kate. *Ready for pumpkins*
Eclare, Melanie. *A handful of sunshine*
  A harvest of color
Ehlert, Lois. *Growing vegetable soup*
  Holey Moley
  Planting a rainbow
Ellis, Carson. *Du iz tak?*
Elvgren, Jennifer Riesmeyer. *Josias, hold the book*
Emberley, Rebecca. *My garden / Mi jardin*
Falwell, Cathryn. *Mystery vine*
Fan, Terry. *The Night Gardener*
Fine, Edith Hope. *Water, weed, and wait*
Fleischman, Paul. *Weslandia*
Fleming, Candace. *Muncha! muncha! muncha!*
Fogliano, Julie. *And then it's spring*
Ford, Miela. *Sunflower*
French, Vivian. *Yucky worms*
Fry, Stella. *Grandpa's garden*
George, Lindsay Barrett. *In the garden: who's been
  here?*
Gershator, Phillis. *Sky sweeper*
Gibbons, Gail. *Corn*
  The fruits we eat
  The pumpkin book

Glaser, Linda. *Garbage helps our garden grow*
Gliori, Debi. *Flora's surprise*
Gourley, Robbin. *First garden*
Grigsby, Susan. *First peas to the table*
   In the garden with Dr. Carver
Guest, C. Z. *Tiny green thumbs*
Hafner, Marylin. *Molly and Emmett's surprise garden*
Hall, Zoe. *The surprise garden*
Harrison, David L. *Farmer's garden*
Harshman, Marc. *Red are the apples*
Hayes, Joe. *Don't say a word, Mamá/No digas nada,*
   Mamá
Heap, Sue. *Four friends in the garden*
Helmore, Jim. *Oh no, monster tomato!*
Henderson, Kathy. *And the good brown earth*
Henkes, Kevin. *My garden*
Henterly, Jamichael. *Good night, garden gnome*
Hest, Amy. *Little chick*
Hines, Anna Grossnickle. *Miss Emma's wild garden*
Hodge, Deborah. *Watch me grow!*
Hoffman, Eric. *Play Lady / La Señora Juguetona*
Holmes, Anita. *Flowers and friends*
Honey, Elizabeth. *That's not a daffodil!*
Hopkins, H. Joseph. *The tree lady*
Hruby, Emily. *Counting in the garden*
Hubbell, Patricia. *Black earth, gold sun*
Inches, Alison. *Corduroy's garden*
Iwai, Melissa. *Pizza day*
Jack and the beanstalk. *Jack and the beanstalk and*
   the french fries
Jordan, Helene J. *How a seed grows*
Joyce, William. *The Leaf Men and the brave good bugs*
Kann, Victoria. *Emeraldalicious*
Kellogg, Steven. *Johnny Appleseed: a tall tale*
Krauss, Ruth. *The carrot seed*
Lamba, Marie. *Green green*
Larsen, Andrew. *The imaginary garden*
Lendroth, Susan. *Old Manhattan has some farms*
Levenson, George. *Pumpkin circle*
Lin, Grace. *The ugly vegetables*
Lindbergh, Reeve. *Johnny Appleseed*
Lobel, Anita. *Ten hungry rabbits*
Loki. *Jake Greenthumb*
Lottridge, Celia Barker. *One watermelon seed*
Maass, Robert. *Garden*
MacDonald, Margaret Read. *Pickin' peas*
McLeod, Elaine. *Lessons from Mother Earth*
McQuinn, Anna. *Lola plants a garden*
Mannis, Celeste Davidson. *One leaf rides the wind*
Marshall, Linda Elovitz. *Talia and the rude*
   vegetables
Martin, Jacqueline Briggs. *Farmer Will Allen and the*
   growing table
Matheson, Christie. *Plant the tiny seed*
Matthies, Janna. *The goodbye cancer garden*
Maurer, Tracy. *Growing flowers*
Messner, Kate. *Up in the garden and down in the dirt*
Middleton, Charlotte. *Nibbles*
   Nibbles' garden
Millard, Glenda. *Isabella's garden*
Miller, Pat Zietlow. *Sophie's squash*
Milway, Katie Smith. *The good garden*
Molk, Laurel. *Good job, Oliver!*
Mora, Pat. *The remembering day / El día de los*
   muertos
Mortimer, Anne. *Pumpkin cat*
Moser, Lisa. *Stories from Bug Garden*
Moulton, Mark Kimball. *The very best pumpkin*
Muller, Gerda. *How does my garden grow?*

Nelson, Kadir. *If you plant a seed*
Noguchi, Rick. *Flowers from Mariko*
Nolen, Jerdine. *Irene's wish*
O'Malley, Kevin. *Bud*
Oxenbury, Helen. *Tom and Pippo in the garden*
Pak, Soyung. *A place to grow*
Paraskevas, Betty. *Maggie and the Ferocious Beast,*
   the big carrot
Park, Linda Sue. *What does Bunny see?*
Parker, Kim. *Counting in the garden*
Pattou, Edith. *Mrs. Spitzer's garden*
Peppa Pig and the vegetable garden
Perkins, Lynne Rae. *Home lovely*
Peterson, Cris. *Seed soil sun*
Pierce, Terry. *My busy green garden*
Pinczes, Elinor J. *Inchworm and a half*
Pinfold, Levi. *Greenling*
Pryor, Katherine. *Zora's zucchini*
Quattlebaum, Mary. *Jo MacDonald had a garden*
Ray, Deborah Kogan. *Lily's garden*
Reynolds, Peter H. *Rose's garden*
Robbins, Ken. *Pumpkins*
Roberts, Bethany. *The wind's garden*
Root, Phyllis. *Anywhere farm*
Rosenberry, Vera. *Who is in the garden?*
Rotner, Shelley. *Grow! raise! catch!*
Rubel, Nicole. *No more vegetables!*
Ryder, Joanne. *My father's hands*
Rylant, Cynthia. *This year's garden*
Say, Allen. *The boy in the garden*
Schaefer, Carole Lexa. *The children's garden*
Schoonmaker, Elizabeth. *Square cat ABC*
Schulman, Janet. *A bunny for all seasons*
Schumaker, Ward. *In my garden*
Segal, John. *Carrot soup*
Selkowe, Valrie M. *Happy birthday to me!*
Serafini, Frank. *Looking closely inside the garden*
Shannon, George. *Busy in the garden*
Sierra, Judy. *E-I-E-I-O*
Siminovich, Lorena. *I like vegetables*
Smith, Lane. *Grandpa Green*
Smith, Maggie. *This is your garden*
Snyder, Laurel. *The forever garden*
Spurr, Elizabeth. *In the garden*
Stevens, Janet. *Tops and bottoms*
Stevenson, James. *Grandpa's too-good garden*
Stewart, Sarah. *The gardener*
Swain, Gwenyth. *Johnny Appleseed*
Swann, Rick. *Our school garden!*
Tamar, Erika. *The garden of happiness*
Thompson, Lauren. *The forgiveness garden*
Thurman, Kathryn K. *A garden for Pig*
Titherington, Jeanne. *Pumpkin pumpkin*
Trapani, Iza. *Here we go 'round the mulberry bush*
Voake, Steve. *Insect detective*
Waldherr, Kris. *Harvest*
Wallace, Karen. *Scarlette Beane*
Wallace, Nancy Elizabeth. *Paperwhite*
   Planting seeds
Ward, Jennifer. *Over in the garden*
   What will grow?
Weeks, Sarah. *Mrs. McNosh and the great big squash*
Wellington, Monica. *Zinnia's flower garden*
Wells, Rosemary. *First tomato*
   Max's worm cake
White, Linda. *Too many turkeys*
Wilde, Oscar. *The selfish giant*, ill. by S. Saelig
   Gallagher
   The selfish giant, ill. by Fabian Negrin

The selfish giant, ill. by Lisbeth Zwerger
Wilner, Isabel. *A garden alphabet*
Wilson, Karma. *Mortimer's first garden*
Wood, Douglas. *Aunt Mary's rose*
Wortche, Allison. *Rosie Sprout's time to shine*
Wunderli, Stephen. *Little Boo*
Yacowitz, Caryn. *Pumpkin fiesta*
Yolen, Jane. *Johnny Appleseed: the legend and the truth*
Zagwÿn, Deborah Turney. *Apple batter*
  The pumpkin blanket
Zoehfeld, Kathleen Weidner. *Secrets of the garden*

Gender identity

Baldacchino, Christine. *Morris Micklewhite and the tangerine dress*
Herthel, Jessica. *I am Jazz*
Hoffman, Sarah. *Jacob's new dress*
Howe, James. *Big Bob, Little Bob*
Newman, Lesléa. *Sparkle boy*
Walton, Jessica. *Introducing Teddy*

Gender roles

Adler, David A. *A picture book of Amelia Earhart*
  A picture book of Eleanor Roosevelt
Baguley, Elizabeth. *Meggie moon*
Banks, Kate. *Mama's coming home*
Brantz, Loryn. *Feminist Baby*
Bridges, Shirin Yim. *Ruby's wish*
Brown, Don. *Rare treasure*
  Ruth Law thrills a nation
Brown, Tami Lewis. *Soar, Elinor!*
Browning, Diane. *Signed, Abiah Rose*
Burleigh, Robert. *Solving the puzzle under the sea*
Clinton, Chelsea. *She persisted*
Codell, Esmé Raji. *The basket ball*
Corey, Shana. *You forgot your skirt, Amelia Bloomer*
Cristaldi, Kathryn. *Baseball ballerina*
Demi. *Florence Nightingale*
DiPucchio, Kelly. *Grace for president*
Donaldson, Julia. *Zog and the flying doctors*
Dray, Philip. *Yours for justice, Ida B. Wells*
Engle, Margarita. *Drum dream girl*
Fierstein, Harvey. *The sissy duckling*
Garza, Cynthia Leonor. *Lucía the luchadora*
Gerber, Carole. *Annie Jump Cannon, astronomer*
GrandPre, Mary. *Cleonardo, the little inventor*
Grant, Brianna K. *We are girls who love to run / Somos chicas y a nosotras nos encanta correr*
Harness, Cheryl. *Mary Walker wears the pants*
Hill, Susanna Leonard. *Punxsutawney Phyllis*
Hines, Anna Grossnickle. *Daddy makes the best spaghetti*
Hoffman, Sarah. *Jacob's new dress*
Hooks, Bell. *Be boy buzz*
Hopkins, H. Joseph. *The tree lady*
Hopkinson, Deborah. *Knit your bit*
Howard, Elizabeth Fitzgerald. *Virgie goes to school with us boys*
Hubbard, Crystal. *Catching the moon: the story of a young girl's baseball dream*
Ismail, Yasmeen. *I'm a girl!*
Joyner, Andrew. *The pink hat*
Keating, Jess. *Shark lady*
Kessler, Cristina. *The best beekeeper of Lalibela*
Kilodavis, Cheryl. *My princess boy*
Kroll, Virginia L. *Girl, you're amazing!*

Krull, Kathleen. *Hillary Rodham Clinton: dreams taking flight*
Landman, Tanya. *Mary's penny*
Lang, Heather. *Fearless flyer*
  Swimming with sharks
Lawlor, Laurie. *Rachel Carson and her book that changed the world*
Lyon, George Ella. *Mama is a miner*
McCully, Emily Arnold. *Queen of the diamond*
MacGregor, Roy. *The highest number in the world*
Mackall, Dandi Daley. *A girl named Dan*
Macy, Sue. *Miss Mary reporting*
Milgrim, David. *Time to get up, time to go*
Moore, Julianne. *Freckleface Strawberry: best friends forever*
Mortenson, Greg. *Listen to the wind*
Moss, Marissa. *Sky high*
  True heart
Nordling, Lee. *Shehewe*
Numeroff, Laura Joffe. *What daddies do best*
  What mommies do best
Ochiltree, Dianne. *Molly, by golly!*
Plourde, Lynn. *Margaret Chase Smith*
Poletti, Frances. *Miss Todd and her wonderful flying machine*
Pomranz, Craig. *Made by Raffi*
Raczka, Bob. *Joy in Mudville*
Robbins, Dean. *Margaret and the moon*
  Two friends
Rosenstock, Barb. *Dorothea's eyes*
Rosenthal, Amy Krouse. *Dear Girl,*
Russell-Brown, Katheryn. *Little Melba and her big trombone*
San Souci, Robert D. *Brave Margaret*
  A weave of words
Sierra, Judy. *Tasty baby belly buttons*
Slade, Suzanne. *Dangerous Jane*
  Friends for freedom
Smith, Jada Pinkett. *Girls hold up this world*
Smith, Lane. *Madam President*
Smith, Matthew Clark. *Lighter than air*
Smith, Nikkolas. *The golden girls of Rio*
Stone, Tanya Lee. *Elizabeth leads the way*
  The house that Jane built
  Who says women can't be doctors?
Trent, Tereai. *The girl who buried her dreams in a can*
U'Ren, Andrea. *Pugdog*
Van Vleet, Carmella. *To the stars!*
Vernick, Audrey. *She loved baseball*
Wallmark, Laurie. *Ada Byron Lovelace and the thinking machine*
Wallner, Alexandra. *Susan B. Anthony*
Whitaker, Suzanne George. *The daring Miss Quimby*
Winter, Jeanette. *Nasreen's secret school*
  The world is not a rectangle
Winter, Jonah. *Hillary*
Wooldridge, Connie Nordhielm. *When Esther Morris headed west*
Yolen, Jane. *Not all princesses dress in pink*
Zhang, Song Nan. *The ballad of Mulan*
Ziarnik, Natalie. *Madeleine's light*

Genealogy

Schreck, Karen Halvorsen. *Lucy's family tree*
Sweeney, Joan. *Me and my family tree*
Wyeth, Sharon Dennis. *The granddaughter necklace*

Generosity *see* Character traits – generosity

Geography

Cuyler, Margery. *That's good! that's bad! in Washington, D.C.*
Holub, Joan. *Geogra-fleas*
Jackson, Ellen. *The seven seas*
Jenkins, Steve. *Hottest, coldest, highest, deepest*
Keller, Laurie. *The scrambled states of America*
    The scrambled states of America talent show
Lewis, J. Patrick. *Earth and you, a closer view*
Ljungkvist, Laura. *Follow the line around the world*
National Geographic Society [U.S.]. *National Geographic our world*
Piepmeier, Charlotte. *Lucy's journey to the wild west*
Schuett, Stacey. *Somewhere in the world right now*
Shulevitz, Uri. *How I learned geography*
Vyner, Tim. *World team*

Ghosts

Ahlberg, Janet. *Funnybones*
Allard, Harry. *Bumps in the night*
Amsden, Janet. *Grizzly Pete and the ghosts*
Auch, Mary Jane. *Poultrygeist*
Baehr, Patricia. *Boo Cow*
Baguley, Elizabeth. *Ready, steady, ghost!*
Bailey, Ella. *No such thing*
Barnett, Mac. *Leo: a ghost story*
Beaty, Andrea. *Hush, Baby Ghostling*
Bennett, Jill. *Teeny tiny*
Berenstain, Stan and Jan. *The Berenstain bears and the ghost of the forest*
Bozik, Chrissy. *The ghosts go scaring*
Bright, Robert. *Georgie*
    Georgie's Christmas carol
    Georgie's Halloween
Brunhoff, Laurent de. *Babar and the ghost*
Bunting, Eve. *Ghost cat*
Calmenson, Stephanie. *The teeny tiny teacher*
Carter, David A. *In a dark, dark wood*
Cazet, Denys. *The perfect pumpkin pie*
Chase, Mary. *The wicked, wicked ladies in the haunted house*
Clanton, Ben. *Boo who?*
Clark, Mary Higgins. *Ghost ship*
Compestine, Ying Chang. *Boy dumplings*
Côté, Geneviève. *Bob's hungry ghost*
Crews, Nina. *A ghost story*
Cuyler, Margery. *Skeleton hiccups*
deGroat, Diane. *Good night, sleep tight, don't let the bedbugs bite*
Diviny, Sean. *Halloween Motel*
Eeckhout, Emmanuelle. *There's no such thing as ghosts!*
Evans, Cambria. *Bone soup*
Fenton, Joe. *Boo!*
Galdone, Joanna. *The tailypo*
Galdone, Paul. *The teeny-tiny woman*
Goldie, Sonia. *Ghosts*
Goodhart, Pippa. *Three little ghosties*
Hamilton, Martha. *The ghost catcher*
Hawkins, Colin. *Creepy castle*
Jacobs, Joseph. *King of the cats*
Johnston, Tony. *The ghost of Nicholas Greebe*
Ketteman, Helen. *The ghosts go haunting*
Kohara, Kazuno. *Ghosts in the house!*
Landry, Leo. *The snow ghosts*

Trick or treat
LaRochelle, David. *The haunted hamburger and other ghostly stories*
Lester, Julius. *The hungry ghosts*
Lewis, J. Patrick. *The house of Boo*
McKissack, Patricia C. *Ol' Clip-Clop*
Marciano, John Bemelmans. *Madeline and the old house in Paris*
Marin, Cheech. *Cheech and the spooky ghost bus*
Martin, Bill, Jr.. *Old devil wind*
Martín Larrañaga, Ana. *Woo! the not-so-scary Ghost*
Marzollo, Jean. *I spy spooky night*
Matheis, Mickie. *Bedtime for Boo*
Medearis, Angela Shelf. *The ghost of Sifty-Sifty Sam*
Milord, Susan. *The ghost on the hearth*
Moore, Lilian. *Beware, take care*
Murphy, Jim. *Fergus and the Night-Demon*
Muth, Jon J. *Zen ghosts*
Mystery manor
Newgarden, Mark. *Bow-Wow's nightmare neighbors*
Ogburn, Jacqueline K. *The bake shop ghost*
Paquette, Ammi-Joan. *Ghost in the house*
Pearson, Susan. *We're going on a ghost hunt*
Pienkowski, Jan. *Haunted house*
Prelutsky, Jack. *Halloween countdown*
Pulver, Robin. *Never say boo!*
Reiner, Carl. *Tell me a scary story — but not too scary!*
Richardson, Bill. *Sally Dog Little*
Robberecht, Thierry. *Sarah's little ghosts*
Robins, Arthur. *The teeny tiny woman*
Rocklin, Joanne. *This book is haunted*
Ross, Tony. *I want my light on!*
San Souci, Robert D. *The boy and the ghost*
Shea, Bob. *The scariest book ever*
Silverman, Erica. *The Halloween house*
Smith, Lane. *Abe Lincoln's dream*
Snicket, Lemony. *Goldfish Ghost*
Stein, Mathilde. *Mine!*
Terasaki, Stanley Todd. *Ghosts for breakfast*
Trapani, Iza. *Haunted party*
Vaughan, Marcia Kapok. *We're going on a ghost hunt*
Winters, Kay. *The teeny tiny ghost*
    The teeny tiny ghost and the monster
    Whooo's haunting the teeny tiny ghost?
Yep, Laurence. *The man who tricked a ghost*

Giants

Ambrose, Sophie. *The lonely giant*
Andreasen, Dan. *The giant of Seville*
Auld, Mary. *David and Goliath*
Balian, Lorna. *A sweetheart for Valentine*
Beaty, Andrea. *When giants come to play*
Bertrand, Lynne. *Granite baby*
Bird, Betsy. *Giant dance party*
Birdseye, Tom. *Look out, Jack! The giant is back*
Braun, Eric. *Trust me, Jack's beanstalk stinks*
Briggs, Raymond. *Jim and the beanstalk*
Bryan, Ashley. *Can't scare me!*
Bunting, Eve. *Finn McCool and the great fish*
Carle, Eric. *Watch out! A giant!*
Christopher, Neil. *On the shoulder of a giant*
dePaola, Tomie. *Fin M'Coul*
Fisher, Leonard Everett. *David and Goliath*
Friedman, Caitlin. *How do you feed a hungry giant?*
Goldsboro, Bobby. *Noah and the ark; and, David and Goliath*
Grimm, Jacob and Wilhelm. *The brave little tailor*, ill. by Olga Dugina

The brave little tailor, ill. by David Shaw
  Seven at one blow
Harrison, David L. *The book of giant stories*
Hawkes, Kevin. *The wicked big toddlah*
  The wicked big toddlah goes to New York
Higgins, Ryan T. *Wilfred*
Hutchins, Hazel. *Two so small*
Ivey, Randall. *Jay and the bounty of books*
Jack and the beanstalk. *Jack and the beanstalk*, ill.
  by Aljoscha Blau
  Jack and the beanstalk, ill. by Steve Cox
  Jack and the beanstalk, ill. by Nina Crews
  Jack and the beanstalk, ill. by Julek Heller
  Jack and the beanstalk, ill. by John Howe
  Jack and the beanstalk, ill. by Steven Kellogg
  Jack and the beanstalk, ill. by Albert Lorenz
  Jack and the beanstalk, ill. by Niamh Sharkey
  Jack and the beanstalk, ill. by Gennady Spirin
  Jack and the beanstalk, ill. by Matt Tavares
  Jack and the beanstalk and the french fries
  Jacques and de beanstalk
Johnson, Paul Brett. *Jack outwits the giants*
Joyce, William. *A bean, a stalk, and a boy named Jack*
Kasza, Keiko. *The mightiest*
Kennedy, Kim. *Pirate Pete's giant adventure*
Ketteman, Helen. *Waynetta and the cornstalk*
Kimmel, Eric A. *Jack and the giant barbecue*
Klausmeier, Jesse. *Open this little book*
Klise, Kate. *Stand straight, Ella Kate*
Leedy, Loreen. *Jack and the hungry giant eat right
  with MyPlate*
Light, Steve. *The Christmas giant*
  The shoemaker extraordinaire
Mora, Pat. *Doña Flor*
Munsch, Robert N. *David's father*
Nash, Ogden. *The adventures of Isabel*, ill. by James
  Marshall
  The adventures of Isabel, ill. by Bridget Starr
  Taylor
Nolen, Jerdine. *Hewitt Anderson's great big life*
O'Connor, George. *Uncle Bigfoot*
O'Malley, Kevin. *Once upon a cool motorcycle dude*
Osborne, Mary Pope. *The brave little seamstress*
  Kate and the beanstalk
Ruzzier, Sergio. *The little giant*
San Souci, Robert D. *Brave Margaret*
  Peter and the blue witch baby
Schotter, Roni. *When the Wizzy Foot goes walking*
Seeger, Pete. *Abiyoyo returns*
Souhami, Jessica. *Mrs. McCool and the giant
  Cuhullin*
Spalding, Andrea. *It's raining, it's pouring*
Stanley, Diane. *The Giant and the beanstalk*
Stimpson, Colin. *Jack and the baked beanstalk*
Thurber, James. *The great Quillow*
Tom Thumb. *The adventures of Tom Thumb*
Wilde, Oscar. *The selfish giant*, ill. by S. Saelig
  Gallagher
  The selfish giant, ill. by Fabian Negrin
  The selfish giant, ill. by Lisbeth Zwerger
Willey, Margaret. *Clever Beatrice, an Upper
  Peninsula conte*
Woollard, Elli. *The giant of Jum*
Yorinks, Arthur. *The Miami giant*

Gifts

Anderson, Laurie Halse. *No time for Mother's Day*
Beck, Andrea. *Elliot's Christmas surprise*

Beck, Scott. *A mud pie for mother*
Becker, Bonny. *A Christmas for Bear*
Best, Cari. *Three cheers for Catherine the Great!*
Black, Birdie. *Just right for Christmas*
Blackwood, Freya. *Ivy loves to give*
Bloom, Suzanne. *Oh! what a surprise!*
Bourgeois, Paulette. *Franklin says "I love you"*
  Franklin's Christmas gift
Bridges, Shirin Yim. *Mary Wrightly, so politely*
Bright, Rachel. *Love Monster and the perfect present*
Brown, Marc. *Arthur's Christmas*
Bruce, Lisa. *Fran's friend*
Buehner, Caralyn. *Snowmen at Christmas*
Bunting, Eve. *The baby shower*
  Mr. Goat's valentine
Butler, M. Christina. *One snowy night*
  One special Christmas
Calhoun, Mary. *A shepherd's gift*
Calmenson, Stephanie. *Birthday at the Panda Palace*
Capucilli, Alyssa Satin. *Happy Hanukkah, Biscuit*
Chen, Chih-Yuan. *The best Christmas ever*
Cocca-Leffler, Maryann. *A homemade together
  Christmas*
Conway, David. *The most important gift of all*
Cousins, Lucy. *With love from Maisy*
Danneberg, Julie. *Last day blues*
Deedman, Heidi. *Too many toys!*
deGroat, Diane. *Happy birthday to you, you belong
  in a zoo*
DePalma, Mary Newell. *The perfect gift*
Díaz, Katacha. *Carolina's gift*
Diesen, Deborah. *The not very merry pout-pout fish*
DiPucchio, Kelly. *Crafty Chloe*
Dooley, Norah. *Everybody serves soup*
Dunrea, Olivier. *A Christmas tree for Pyn*
Edwards, Pamela Duncan. *Rosie's roses*
Elya, Susan Middleton. *Tooth on the loose*
Emmett, Jonathan. *The best gift of all*
Engelbreit, Mary. *Queen of Christmas*
Evans, Cambria. *Martha Moth makes socks*
Foley, Greg. *Thank you, Bear*
Frazee, Marla. *Santa Claus*
Freeman, Tor. *Olive and the embarrassing gift*
French, Vivian. *A present for mom*
Friedman, Laurie. *Love, Ruby Valentine*
Gardella, Tricia. *Blackberry booties*
The gingerbread boy. *The Gingerbread Man loose at
  Christmas*
Gliori, Debi. *What can I give him?*
Goble, Paul. *The gift of the sacred dog*
Gorbachev, Valeri. *What's the big idea, Molly?*
Gutman, Anne. *Gaspard and Lisa's Christmas
  surprise*
Hamilton, Martha. *Priceless gifts*
Harper, Charise Mericle. *Amy and Ivan*
Hayles, Marsha. *The feathered crown*
Helldorfer, M. C. *Hog music*
Hobbie, Holly. *Toot and Puddle: let it snow*
  Toot and Puddle, a present for Toot
Hubbell, Patricia. *Wrapping paper romp*
Hughes, Shirley. *Alfie and the birthday surprise*
Hutchins, Pat. *It's my birthday!*
Inkpen, Mick. *Kipper and Roly*
  Wibbly Pig opens his presents
Jeffers, Susan. *The twelve days of Christmas*
Keane, Claire. *Once upon a cloud*
Keats, Ezra Jack. *The little drummer boy*
Keister, Douglas. *Fernando's gift / El regalo de
  Fernando*

Kimmel, Elizabeth Cody. *My penguin Osbert*
Krensky, Stephen. *Mother's Day surprise*
Kromhout, Rindert. *Little Donkey and the birthday present*
Linders, Clara. *The very best door of all*
Little, Jean. *Pippin the Christmas pig*
Lodding, Linda Ravin. *A gift for Mama*
Louie, Therese On. *Raymond's perfect present*
McClure, Gillian. *Tom Finger*
McCourt, Lisa. *Chicken soup for little souls: The never-forgotten doll*
McCully, Emily Arnold. *The Christmas gift*
McDonnell, Patrick. *The gift of nothing*
McGhee, Alison. *Star bright*
McGinley, Phyllis. *The year without a Santa Claus*
Mair, Samia J. *The perfect gift*
Marzollo, Jean. *Ten little Christmas presents*
Mathers, Petra. *Lottie's new beach towel*
Meddaugh, Susan. *Martha says it with flowers*
Medearis, Angela Shelf. *Annie's gifts*
Montanari, Eva. *My first . . .*
Mora, Pat. *A birthday basket for Tía*
    The gift of the poinsettia / El regalo de la flor de nochebuena
Morales, Yuyi. *Just in case: a trickster tale and Spanish alphabet book*
Morrissey, Dean. *The Christmas ship*
Naylor, Phyllis Reynolds. *Keeping a Christmas secret*
Nolan, Janet. *A Father's Day thank you*
Ommen, Sylvia van. *The surprise*
Paul, Ann Whitford. *Fiesta fiasco*
Pett, Mark. *The boy and the airplane*
Pilgrim, Elza. *The china doll*
Polacco, Patricia. *Gifts of the heart*
Pomerantz, Charlotte. *You're not my best friend anymore*
Price, Mara. *Grandma's chocolate / El chocolate de Abuelita*
Rempt, Fiona. *Snail's birthday wish*
Reynolds, Peter H. *The smallest gift of Christmas*
Roberton, Fiona. *The perfect present*
Rodanas, Kristina. *The little drummer boy*
Rumford, James. *Nine animals and the well*
Rylant, Cynthia. *Birthday presents*
Sabuda, Robert. *Tutankhamen's gift*
Sage, Angie. *Molly and the birthday party*
Saint James, Synthia. *The gifts of Kwanzaa*
Santiago, Esmeralda. *A doll for Navidades*
Segal, Lore Groszmann. *Morris the artist*
Shepard, Aaron. *The gifts of Wali Dad*
Skolsky, Mindy Warshaw. *Hannah and the whistling tea kettle*
Speirs, John. *The little boy's Christmas gift*
Spinelli, Eileen. *In my new yellow shirt*
Stanton, Karen. *Papi's gift*
Steptoe, Javaka. *The Jones family express*
Stewart, Paul. *The birthday presents*
Tazewell, Charles. *The littlest angel*, ill. by Deborah Lanino
    The littlest angel, ill. by Paul Micich
    The littlest angel, ill. by Rebecca Thornburgh
Thomas, Naturi. *Uh-oh! It's Mama's birthday!*
Thury, Frederick. *The last straw*
Uff, Caroline. *Happy birthday, Lulu*
Underwood, Deborah. *Here comes Santa Cat*
Ungar, Richard. *Yitzi and the giant menorah*
Varley, Susan. *Badger's parting gifts*
Velasquez, Eric. *Grandma's gift*
Wallace, John. *Tiny Rabbit goes to a birthday party*

Walton, Rick. *The remarkable friendship of Mr. Cat and Mr. Rat*
Weeks, Sarah. *Be mine, be mine, sweet valentine*
Wells, Rosemary. *Morris's disappearing bag*
    Yoko's show-and-tell
Weninger, Brigitte. *Double birthday*
    Happy Easter, Davy
    Happy Easter, Davy!
Williams, Barbara. *Albert's gift for grandmother*
Williams, Vera B. *Something special for me*
Willis, Jeanne. *Boa's bad birthday*
Wood, Don. *Merry Christmas, big hungry bear*
Wright, Dare. *A gift from the lonely doll*
Yoon, Salina. *Penguin's Christmas wish*
Ziefert, Harriet. *Grandma, it's for you!*

Gilbert Islands *see* Foreign lands – South Sea Islands

Glasses *see also* Careers – opticians, optometrists

Adamson, Ged. *Douglas, you need glasses!*
Barclay, Eric. *I can see just fine*
Bedford, David. *Mole's in love*
Berne, Jennifer. *Calvin, look out!*
Brown, Marc. *Arthur's eyes*
    Glasses for D. W.
Calvert, Pam. *Princess Peepers*
    Princess Peepers picks a pet
Carlson, Melody. *Farmer Brown's field trip*
Cohen, Peter Zachary. *Boris's glasses*
Dean, James. *Pete the Cat and his magic sunglasses*
Duffield, Katy. *Farmer McPeepers and his missing milk cows*
Flanagan, Alice K. *Choosing eyeglasses with Mrs. Koutris*
Headley, Justina Chen. *The patch*
Hest, Amy. *Baby Duck and the bad eyeglasses*
Ismail, Yasmeen. *Specs for Rex*
Lane, Nathan. *Naughty Mabel sees it all*
Newman, Barbara Johansen. *Glamorous glasses*
Scillian, Devin. *Brewster the rooster*
Smith, Lane. *Glasses . . . who needs 'em?*
Stadler, John. *The cats of Mrs. Calamari*

Global warming *see* Ecology

Gossip *see* Behavior – gossip, rumors

Grammar *see* Language

Graphic novels *see* Format, unusual – graphic novels

Greed *see* Behavior – greed

Grocery stores *see* Shopping; Stores

Growing up *see* Behavior – growing up

Guns *see* Weapons

Gypsies *see* Romani

Habits *see* Thumb sucking

Hair

Anderson, Laurie Halse. *The hair of Zoe Fleefenbacher goes to school*
Azore, Barbara. *Wanda and the wild hair*
Barnes, Derrick. *Crown*
Barton, Bethany. *This monster needs a haircut*
Bernheimer, Kate. *The girl who wouldn't brush her hair*
Brisson, Pat. *Melissa Parkington's beautiful, beautiful hair*
Burnard, Damon. *Dave's haircut*
Cohen, Jeff. *Eva and Sadie and the worst haircut ever!*
Daly, Catherine. *Whiskers*
Diouf, Sylviane A,. *Bintou's braids*
Ditchfield, Christin. *Cowlick!*
Driscoll, Amanda. *Wally does not want a haircut*
Esckelson, Laura. *The copper braid of Shannon O'Shea*
Fisher, Jeff. *The hair scare*
Fox, Lee. *Ella Kazoo will not brush her hair*
Gaiman, Neil. *Crazy hair*
Graves, Keith. *The unexpectedly bad hair of Barcelona Smith*
Grimm, Jacob and Wilhelm. *Rapunzel*, ill. by Sarah Gibb
    Rapunzel, ill. by Trina Schart Hyman
    Rapunzel, ill. by Rachel Isadora
    Rapunzel, ill. by Joma
    Rapunzel, ill. by Kris Waldherr
    Rapunzel, ill. by Paul O. Zelinsky
    Rapunzel: a fairy tale
Higgins, Ryan T. *Wilfred*
Hilton, Perez. *The boy with pink hair*
Hooks, Bell. *Happy to be nappy*
Hosford, Kate. *Big bouffant*
Koren, Edward. *Very hairy Harry*
Krosoczka, Jarrett J. *Baghead*
Krull, Kathleen. *Big wig*
Langen, Annette. *I won't comb my hair!*
Lemke, Donald. *Book-o-beards*
Lerner, Harriet Goldhor. *Franny B. Kranny, there's a bird in your hair*
Lubner, Susan. *Ruthie Bon Bair, do not go to bed with wringing wet hair!*
MacDonald, Alan. *The pig in a wig*
McElligott, Matthew. *Backbeard and the birthday suit*
Madrigal, Antonio Hernandez. *Erandi's braids*
Many, Paul. *Dad's bald head*
Moss, Miriam. *Bad hare day*
Munsch, Robert N. *Aaron's hair*
    Stephanie's ponytail
Napoli, Donna Jo. *Bobby the bold*

Onyefulu, Ifeoma. *Ife's first haircut*
Palatini, Margie. *Bedhead*
    Moosetache
Parr, Todd. *This is my hair*
Patricelli, Leslie. *Hair*
Radabaugh, Melinda Beth. *Getting a haircut*
Ries, Lori. *Punk wig*
Rim, Sujean. *Birdie's big-girl hair*
Robbins, Beth. *Tom's new haircut*
Roberts, Lynn. *Rapunzel, a groovy fairy tale*
Rocco, John. *Super Hair-o and the barber of doom*
Saltzberg, Barney. *Crazy hair day*
Savadier, Elivia. *No haircut today!*
Shannon, David. *Bugs in my hair!*
Tarpley, Natasha Anastasia. *Bippity Bop barbershop*
    I love my hair!
Thomas, Joyce Carol. *Crowning glory*
Tinkham, Kelly A. *Hair for Mama*
Tuck, Justin. *Home-field advantage*
Villnave, Erica Pelton. *Sophie's lovely locks*
Ward, Jennifer. *Feathers and hair, what animals wear*
Watters, Debbie, et al. *Where's Mom's hair?*
Williams-Garcia, Rita. *Catching the wild waiyuuzee*
Woollvin, Bethan. *Rapunzel*
Ziefert, Harriet. *There was a little girl who had a little curl*

Handicaps *see* Disabilities

Hares *see* Animals – rabbits

Hawaii

Guback, Georgia. *Luka's quilt*
Hayashi, Leslie Ann. *Fables from the sea*
Joosse, Barbara. *Grandma calls me Beautiful*
Kono, Erin Eitter. *Hula lullaby*
Lin, Grace. *Olvina swims*
London, Jonathan. *Froggy goes to Hawaii*
McDermott, Gerald. *Pig-Boy*
Martin, Rafe. *The Shark God*
Novesky, Amy. *Georgia in Hawaii*
Rumford, James. *Dog-of-the-Sea-Waves*
    The Island-below-the-star
Samuels, Barbara. *Aloha, Dolores*
Stanley, Fay. *The last princess*
Vigil-Piñón, Evangelina. *Marina's muumuu / El muumuu de Marina*

Health & fitness

Ajmera, Maya, et al. *Healthy kids*
Bridge, Chris. *Andrew's story*
Brown, Laurie Krasny. *Dinosaurs alive and well*
Bunting, Eve. *My dog Jack is fat*
Butterworth, Chris. *How did that get in my lunchbox?*
Campbell, Bebe Moore. *I get so hungry*
Cleland, Jo. *Getting your zzzzs*
Cole, Joanna. *My friend the doctor*
Corey, Shana. *First graders from Mars: Nergal and the Great Space Race*
Davis, Jacky. *Black Belt Bunny*
De Anda, Diane. *A day without sugar / Un dia sin azucar*
Drescher, Henrik. *Hubert the Pudge*
Fraser, Mary Ann. *I.Q. gets fit*
Gavin, Ciara. *Bear likes jam*
Glaser, Jason. *Pinkeye*

Gordon, Sharon. *Asthma*
  Bruises
  Cuts and scrapes
  Pinkeye
  Seeing
  Smelling
Harper, Charise Mericle. *Flush!*
  Henry's heart
Harris, Robie H. *What's so yummy?*
International Center for Assault Prevention. *My body belongs to me from my head to my toes*
Kalz, Jill. *Fruits*
Keller, Laurie. *Open wide*
Kelly, Mij. *Achoo!*
Kostecki-Shaw, Jenny Sue. *My travelin' eye*
Krall, Dan. *Sick Simon*
Krishnaswami, Uma. *The happiest tree*
Leedy, Loreen. *The edible pyramid*
  Jack and the hungry giant eat right with MyPlate
Lin, Grace. *Our food*
McElmurry, Jill. *Mess pets*
McLaughlin, Lauren. *Mitzi Tulane, preschool detective, in The secret ingredient*
Martin, Jacqueline Briggs. *Alice Waters and the trip to delicious*
Miller, Edward. *The tooth book*
Milway, Katie Smith. *Mimi's village and how basic health care transformed it*
Müller, Birte. *Finn cooks*
Murkoff, Heidi Eisenberg. *What to expect when you go to the dentist*
  What to expect when you go to the doctor
Murphy, Liz. *ABC doctor*
Newcome, Zita. *Pop-up toddlerobics*
Owen, Ann. *Keeping you healthy*
Rockwell, Harlow. *My doctor*
Rosenberry, Vera. *Vera goes to the dentist*
Roth, Ruby. *V is for vegan*
Ruiz-Flores, Lupe. *Alicia's fruity drinks / Las aguas frescas de Alicia*
Sears, William, M.D., et al.. *Eat healthy, feel great*
Showers, Paul. *Sleep is for everyone*
Singer, Marilyn. *I'm getting a checkup*
Slangerup, Erik Jon. *Dirt Boy*
Spelman, Cornelia Maude. *Your body belongs to you*
Starishevsky, Jill. *My body belongs to me*
Stewart, Whitney. *Meditation is an open sky*
Swanson, Diane. *The dentist and you*
  The doctor and you
Taylor, Sean. *Boing!*
Wells, Rosemary. *The gulps*
Yoo, Taeeun. *You are a lion!*
Zamorano, Ana. *Let's eat!*

Health & fitness – exercise

Bateman, Teresa. *Hamster Camp*
Beliveau, Kathy. *The yoga game by the sea*
Bertrand, Diane Gonzales. *Sofia and the purple dress / Sofia y el vestido morado*
Carlson, Nancy. *Get up and go!*
Cronin, Doreen. *Stretch*
Jordan, Laurie. *Yawning yoga*
Liu, Sylvia. *A morning with grandpa*
McKinlay, Penny. *Flabby Tabby*
Martin, Bill, Jr.. *Spunky Little Monkey*
Pajalunga, Lorena V. *Yoga for kids*
Rockwell, Lizzy. *The busy body book*
Russo, Brian. *Yoga Bunny*

Spinelli, Eileen. *Miss Fox's class shapes up*
Thompson, Lauren. *Hop, hop, jump!*
Tsubakiyama, Margaret. *Mei-Mei loves the morning*
Verde, Susan. *I am yoga*
Wells, Rosemary. *The gulps*
Whitford, Rebecca. *Little yoga*
  Sleepy little yoga
Ziefert, Harriet. *Murphy meets the treadmill*

Hearing *see* Anatomy – ears; Disabilities – deafness; Senses – hearing

Heat *see* Concepts – cold & heat

Heavy equipment *see* Machines

Helicopters

Austin, Mike. *Rescue Squad No. 9*
Ethan, Eric. *Helicopters*
Glass, Andrew. *The wondrous whirligig*
Kimmel, Elizabeth Cody. *My penguin Osbert in love*
Slack, Michael. *Elecopter*

Helpfulness *see* Character traits – helpfulness

Hens *see* Birds – chickens, roosters

Hibernation

Arnosky, Jim. *Every autumn comes the bear*
Banks, Kate. *The bear in the book*
Bauer, Marion Dane. *Winter dance*
Berger, Carin. *Finding spring*
Blecha, Aaron. *Goodnight, Grizzle Grump!*
Bright, Paul. *Grumpy Badger's Christmas*
Carnesi, Monica. *Sleepover with Beatrice and Bear*
Chaud, Benjamin. *The bear's sea escape*
Cooper, Elisha. *Bear dreams*
Cox, Judy. *Go to sleep, Groundhog*
Cuyler, Margery. *Groundhog stays up late*
Fleming, Denise. *Time to sleep*
Fraggalosch, Audrey. *Grizzly bear family*
Freeman, Don. *Bearymore*
Gammell, Stephen. *Wake up, bear . . . It's Christmas!*
Gavin, Ciara. *Bear is not tired*
Gerber, Carole. *Little red bat*
Grindley, Sally. *What will I do without you?*
Heder, Thyra. *Alfie: (the turtle that disappeared)*
Helquist, Brett. *Bedtime for Bear*
Henkes, Kevin. *Old Bear*
Hest, Amy. *Are you sure, Mother Bear?*
Jackson, Gwen. *Lump Lump and the blanket of dreams*
Janice. *Little Bear's Christmas*
Krauss, Ruth. *The happy day*
London, Jonathan. *Froggy gets dressed*
McFarland, Clive. *A bed for Bear*
Martin, David. *Shh! bears sleeping*
Meadows, Michelle. *Hibernation station*
Messner, Kate. *Over and under the snow*
Miller, Edna. *Mousekin's golden house*
Nastro, Caroline. *The bear who couldn't sleep*
Partridge, Elizabeth. *Moon glowing*
Rueda, Claudia. *No*

Sayre, April Pulley. *Eat like a bear*
Schertle, Alice. *Very hairy bear*
Senshu, Noriko. *Sonny's dream*
Stead, Philip C. *Bear has a story to tell*
Stein, David Ezra. *Leaves*
Stewart, Paul. *A little bit of winter*
Tibi, Marie. *The bear who didn't want to miss Christmas*
Walters, Catherine. *When will it be spring?*
Welling, Peter J. *Andrew McGroundhog and his shady shadow*
Wilson, Karma. *Bear stays up for Christmas*
Wolff, Ashley. *Baby Bear counts one*
Wright, Maureen. *Sleep, Big Bear, sleep!*
Yolen, Jane. *Sleep, black bear, sleep*
Zagwÿn, Deborah Turney. *Turtle spring*

Hiccups

Bentley, Tadgh. *Little Penguin gets the hiccups*
Berger, Melvin. *Why I sneeze, shiver, hiccup, and yawn*
Cuyler, Margery. *Skeleton hiccups*
Kang, A. N. *Papillon goes to the vet*
Kenyon, Tony. *Hyacinth Hop has the hic-hops*
Long, Melinda. *Hiccup snickup*
Meng, Cece. *The wonderful thing about hiccups*
Newman, Tracy. *Shabbat hiccups*
Sterling, Holly. *Hiccups!*

Hiding *see* Behavior – hiding

Hiding things *see* Behavior – hiding things

Hieroglyphics

Bower, Tamara. *The shipwrecked sailor*

Hobby horses *see* Toys – rocking horses

Hogs *see* Animals – pigs

Holidays

Adler, David A. *The children's book of Jewish holidays*
   A picture book of Jewish holidays
Ancona, George. *Mis fiestas / My celebrations*
Biers-Ariel, Matt. *Solomon and the trees*
Bullard, Lisa. *Rashad's Ramadan and Eid al-Fitr*
Capucilli, Alyssa Satin. *Biscuit gives a gift*
Carle, Eric. *Hello, red fox*
Carlson, Lori Marie. *Hurray for Three Kings' Day*
Cazet, Denys. *December 24th*
Chancellor, Deborah. *Holidays!*
Cooney, Barbara. *The story of Christmas*
dePaola, Tomie. *Strega Nona's gift*
Elya, Susan Middleton. *A year full of holidays*
Emerman, Ellen. *Is it Shabbos yet?*
Fishman, Cathy Goldberg. *On Shabbat*
Freschet, Gina. *Naty's parade*
Galbraith, Kathryn O. *Arbor Day square*
Gold-Vukson, Marji E. *Grandpa and me on Tu B'Shevat*
Hubbell, Patricia. *Rabbit moon*
Jackson, Ellen. *April*
   August

The autumn equinox
December
February
January
July
June
March
May
November
October
September
The spring equinox
The summer solstice
The winter solstice
Kimmelman, Leslie. *Dance, sing, remember*
Lewis, J. Patrick. *World Rat Day*
Lin, Grace. *Thanking the moon*
Livingston, Myra Cohn. *Celebrations*
McGee, Marni. *The colt and the king*
Mair, Samia J. *The perfect gift*
Mobin-Uddin, Asma. *The best Eid ever*
Mora, Pat. *The bakery lady / La señora de la panadería*
   Book fiesta! celebrate Children's Day/Book Day / Celebremos El día de los niños/El día de los libros
Morris, Ann. *Light the candle! bang the drum!*
Murphy, Stuart J. *Earth Day — hooray!*
Newman, Lesléa. *Here is the world*
Nielsen, Laura. *Mrs. Muddle's holidays*
Pandya, Meenal. *Here comes Diwali*
Podwal, Mark H. *A sweet year*
Rau, Dana Meachen. *I'll make you a card*
Reiss, Mike. *Santa claustrophobia*
Reynolds, Jan. *Celebrate!*
Rockwell, Anne. *President's Day*
Rosenfeld, Dina Herman. *Five alive*
Rosenthal, Amy Krouse. *Yes Day!*
Shahan, Sherry. *Fiesta!*
Shulimson, Sarene. *Lights out Shabbat*
Singer, Marilyn. *Every day's a dog's day*
Tunnell, Michael O. *Halloween pie*
Yolen, Jane. *The three bears holiday rhyme book*

Holidays – April Fools' Day

Bateman, Teresa. *April foolishness*
Brown, Marc. *Arthur's April fool*
deGroat, Diane. *April Fool! watch out at school!*
Hill, Susanna Leonard. *April Fool, Phyllis!*
Kroll, Steven. *It's April Fools' Day!*
Modell, Frank. *Look out, it's April Fools' Day*
Morton, Carlene. *The library pages*
Wright, Maureen. *Barnyard fun*

Holidays – Chanukah *see* Holidays – Hanukkah

Holidays – Chinese New Year

Chen, Yong. *A gift*
Chinn, Karen. *Sam and the lucky money*
Compestine, Ying Chang. *Crouching tiger*
   D is for dragon dance
   The runaway rice cake
   The runaway wok
Flanagan, Alice K. *Chinese New Year*
Gower, Catherine. *Long-Long's new year*
Handforth, Thomas. *Mei Li*

Schaefer, Lola M. *Chinese New Year*
Silverhardt, Lauryn. *Happy Chinese New Year, Kai-lan!*
Wallace, Ian. *Chin Chiang and the dragon's dance*
Wang, Andrea. *The Nian Monster*
Waters, Kate. *Lion dancer*
Wong, Janet S. *This next New Year*
Yim, Natasha. *Goldy Luck and the three pandas*
Yu, Li-Qiong. *A New Year's reunion*

Holidays – Christmas

Ada, Alma Flor. *The Christmas tree / El arbol de Navidad*
Adams, Adrienne. *The Christmas party*
Agee, Jon. *Little Santa*
Ahlberg, Janet. *The jolly Christmas postman*
Aliki. *Christmas tree memories*
Alko, Selina. *Daddy Christmas and Hanukkah Mama*
Allen, Jonathan. *"I'm not Santa!"*
Alsenas, Linas. *Mrs. Claus takes a vacation*
Ammon, Richard. *An Amish Christmas*
Anaya, Rudolfo A. *Farolitos for Abuelo*
Andersen, Hans Christian. *The fir tree*, ill. by Diane Goode
  The fir tree, ill. by Bernadette Watts
Anderson, Derek. *How the Easter Bunny saved Christmas*
Angelou, Maya. *Amazing peace*
Anglund, Joan Walsh. *Christmas is a time of giving*
  The cowboy's Christmas
Appelt, Kathi. *Merry Christmas, merry crow*
Apperley, Dawn. *Santa Claus will come tonight*
Aralan, Haydé. *Milton's Christmas*
Arnold, Katya. *The adventures of Snowwoman*
Ashforth, Camilla. *Willow at Christmas*
Auch, Mary Jane. *The nutquacker*
Autry, Gene. *Here comes Santa Claus*
Axelrod, Amy. *Pigs on the move*
Bailey, Mary Bryant. *Jeoffry's Christmas*
Balian, Lorna. *Bah! Humbug?*
Banks, Kate. *What's coming for Christmas?*
Barracca, Debra. *A taxi dog Christmas*
Barrett, Judi. *Santa from Cincinnati*
Bartoletti, Susan Campbell. *The Christmas promise*
Bastianich, Lidia. *Nonna tell me a story*
Bastin, Marjolein. *Christmas with Vera*
Bauer, Marion Dane. *Christmas lights*
Bauer, Sepp. *The Christmas rose*
Baumgart, Klaus. *Laura's Christmas star*
Beck, Andrea. *Elliot's Christmas surprise*
Becker, Bonny. *The Christmas crocodile*
  A Christmas for Bear
Bedford, David. *I've seen Santa!*
Bemelmans, Ludwig. *Madeline's Christmas*
Berenstain, Jan. *The Berenstain bears trim the tree*
Berenstain, Stan and Jan. *The Berenstain bears' Christmas tree*
  The Berenstain bears meet Santa Bear
Bible. New Testament. Gospels. *Bethlehem*
  The Christmas story: from the Gospel according to St. Luke from the King James Bible
  The story of Christmas
Biedrzycki, David. *Me and my dragon: Christmas spirit*
  Santa retires
Blabey, Aaron. *Pig the elf*
Black, Birdie. *Just right for Christmas*
Blaich, Ute. *The star*

Bodkin, Odds. *The Christmas cobwebs*
Bond, Michael. *Paddington Bear and the Christmas surprise*
Bond, Rebecca. *A city Christmas tree*
Border, Terry. *Merry Christmas, Peanut!*
Bourgeois, Paulette. *Franklin's Christmas gift*
Bowen, Anne. *Christmas is coming*
Boynton, Sandra. *Christmas parade*
Brebeuf, Jean de. *The Huron carol*
Breen, Steve. *The secret of Santa's island*
Brennan-Nelson, Denise. *Good night, reindeer*
Brenner, Tom. *And then comes Christmas*
Brett, Jan. *The animals' Santa*
  Christmas trolls
  Home for Christmas
  Who's that knocking on Christmas eve?
  The wild Christmas reindeer
Briggs, Raymond. *Father Christmas*
Bright, Paul. *Grumpy Badger's Christmas*
Bright, Robert. *Georgie's Christmas carol*
Bronson, Linda. *Sleigh bells and snowflakes*
Brown, Marc. *Arthur's Christmas*
  Arthur's perfect Christmas
Brown, Margaret Wise. *A child is born*
  Christmas in the barn
  The little fir tree
Brown, Ruth. *Holly, the true story of a cat*
Bruel, Nick. *A Bad Kitty Christmas*
Brunhoff, Jean de. *Babar and Father Christmas*
Buck, Nola. *A Christmas goodnight*
Buehner, Caralyn. *Merry Christmas, Mr. Mouse*
  Snowmen at Christmas
Bunting, Eve. *Christmas cricket*
  December
  Going home
  Night tree
  We were there
  Who was born this special day?
Burgess, Mark. *Where teddy bears come from*
Burningham, John. *Harvey Slumfenburger's Christmas present*
Butler, Christina. *One cozy Christmas*
Butler, M. Christina. *One snowy night*
  One special Christmas
Butterworth, Nick. *Jingle bells*
Buzzeo, Toni. *Lighthouse Christmas*
Byrd, Robert. *Saint Francis and the Christmas donkey*
Calhoun, Mary. *Henry the Christmas cat*
  A shepherd's gift
Capucilli, Alyssa Satin. *Merry Christmas, from Biscuit*
Carabine, Sue. *A firefighter's night before Christmas*
Carle, Eric. *Dream snow*
Carlson, Nancy. *Harriet and George's Christmas treat*
Carlstrom, Nancy White. *Where is Christmas, Jesse Bear?*
Catalano, Dominic. *Santa and the three bears*
Chaconas, Dori. *Christmas mouseling*
  Cork and Fuzz: merry merry holly holly
  When cows come home for Christmas
Chapman, Jane. *Is it Christmas yet?*
Chen, Chih-Yuan. *The best Christmas ever*
Cheshire, Marc. *Merry Christmas, Eloise!*
Chichester Clark, Emma. *Melrose and Croc*
Chorao, Kay. *The Christmas story*
Christelow, Eileen. *Not until Christmas, Walter!*
Chung, Arree. *Ninja Claus!*
Clements, Andrew. *Bright Christmas*
Climo, Liz. *Rory the dinosaur needs a Christmas tree*

Cocca-Leffler, Maryann. *A homemade together Christmas*
Cole, Brock. *The money we'll save*
Cole, Henry. *The littlest evergreen*
Conahan, Carolyn. *The twelve days of Christmas dogs*
Conover, Chris. *The Christmas bears*
Conrad, Pam. *The Tub People's Christmas*
Cooney, Barbara. *The story of Christmas*
Corderoy, Tracey. *It's Christmas!*
Corey, Shana. *Milly and the Macy's Parade*
Cousins, Lucy. *Maisy's Christmas tree*
Cowley, Joy. *Mrs. Wishy-Washy's Christmas*
Croll, Carolyn. *The little snowgirl*
Cronin, Doreen. *Click, clack, ho! ho! ho!*
Crossley-Holland, Kevin. *How many miles to Bethlehem?*
Currey, Anna. *Truffle's Christmas*
Cushman, Doug. *Christmas Eve good night*
Cutlip, Kimbra L. *Firefighter's night before Christmas*
Czajak, Paul. *Monster needs a Christmas tree*
Daly, Niki. *What's cooking, Jamela?*
Damjan, Mischa. *The little seahorse and the Christmas pearl*
David, Lawrence. *Peter Claus and the naughty list*
Deacon, Alexis. *While you are sleeping*
Dealey, Erin. *Deck the walls!*
deGroat, Diane. *Jingle bells, homework smells*
　Lola the elf
Delacre, Lulu. *Las Navidades*
Demas, Corinne. *Two Christmas mice*
Demi. *The legend of Saint Nicholas*
Denim, Sue. *The Dumb Bunnies' Easter*
DePalma, Mary Newell. *The Nutcracker doll*
dePaola, Tomie. *Baby's first Christmas*
　The clown of God
　An early American Christmas
　The family Christmas tree book
　Get dressed, Santa!
　Jingle, the Christmas clown
　Merry Christmas, Strega Nona
　The night of Las Posadas
　The story of the three wise kings
Devlin, Wende. *Cranberry Christmas*
Dewan, Ted. *Crispin, the pig who had it all*
DiCamillo, Kate. *Great joy*
Diesen, Deborah. *The not very merry pout-pout fish*
Dixon, Ann. *Waiting for Noël*
Donaldson, Julia. *Stick Man*
Dowley, Tim. *The shepherds' tale*
　The wise men's tale
Dudás, Gergely. *Bear's merry book of hidden things*
Dunrea, Olivier. *Bear Noel*
　A Christmas tree for Pyn
　Merry Christmas, Ollie!
Duquennoy, Jacques. *North Pole, South Pole*
Duval, Kathy. *The Three Bears' Christmas*
Duvall, John. *The great spruce*
Elschner, Geraldine. *Pashmina the little Christmas goat*
Elya, Susan Middleton. *N is for Navidad*
Emmett, Jonathan. *The Santa trap*
Engelbreit, Mary. *Mary Engelbreit's A merry little Christmas*
　A night of great joy
　Queen of Christmas
Ets, Marie Hall. *Nine days to Christmas*
Evans, Lezlie. *Finding Christmas*
Evans, Richard Paul. *The light of Christmas*
Evert, Lori. *The Christmas wish*

Fackelmayer, Regina. *The gifts*
Falwell, Cathryn. *Christmas for 10*
Farber, Norma. *How the hibernators came to Bethlehem*
Faulkner, Keith. *Charlie Chimp's Christmas*
Fergus, Maureen. *The day Santa stopped believing in Harold*
Fine, Howard. *A piggie Christmas*
Fisher, Aileen Lucia. *Do rabbits have Christmas?*
Flanagan, Alice K. *Christmas*
Foreman, Michael. *Cat in the manger*
Forward, Toby. *Ben's Christmas carol*
Fox, Mem. *Wombat divine*
Frazee, Marla. *Santa Claus*
French, Jackie. *Christmas wombat*
Gammell, Stephen. *Wake up, bear . . . It's Christmas!*
Gantos, Jack. *Rotten Ralph's rotten Christmas*
Garland, Michael. *Christmas City*
　Christmas magic
George, William T. *Christmas at Long Pond*
Geras, Adèle. *The nutcracker*
The gingerbread boy. *The Gingerbread Man loose at Christmas*
Gliori, Debi. *What can I give him?*
Godden, Rumer. *The story of Holly and Ivy*
Grahame, Kenneth. *A wind in the willows Christmas*
Greene, Rhonda Gowler. *The stable where Jesus was born*
Greenfield, Monica. *Waiting for Christmas*
Grimes, Nikki. *Voices of Christmas*
Grogan, John. *A very Marley Christmas*
Grün, Anselm. *The legend of Saint Nicholas*
Gutman, Anne. *Gaspard and Lisa's Christmas surprise*
Hächler, Bruno. *Anna's wish*
Hague, Michael. *The nutcracker*
Hale, Bruce. *Santa on the loose!*
Hall, Donald. *Lucy's Christmas*
Hapka, Cathy. *Margret and H. A. Rey's Merry Christmas, Curious George*
Harley, Bill. *Dear Santa*
Harness, Cheryl. *Papa's Christmas gift*
Harry, Rebecca. *Snow Bunny's Christmas wish*
Hart, Caryl. *The princess and the Christmas rescue*
Hartman, Bob. *Granny Mae's Christmas play*
Harvey, Brett. *My prairie Christmas*
Hassett, Ann. *The finest Christmas tree*
Hayles, Marsha. *The feathered crown*
Heath, Amy. *Sofie's role*
Helmer, Marilyn. *One splendid tree*
Hennessy, B. G. *A Christmas wish for Corduroy*
　Corduroy's Christmas
　The first night
Hickman, Martha Whitmore. *A baby born in Bethlehem*
High, Linda Oatman. *The last chimney of Christmas eve*
Hill, Eric. *Spot's first Christmas*
　Spot's magical Christmas
Hines, Anna Grossnickle. *The secret keeper*
Hines, Gary. *A Christmas tree in the White House*
Hobbie, Holly. *Toot and Puddle: let it snow*
　Toot and Puddle, I'll be home for Christmas
Hodges, Margaret. *Silent night: the song and its story*
Hoffman, Mary. *Grace at Christmas*
　Three wise women
Hoffmann, E. T. A. *The nutcracker*, ill. by Renée Graef
　The nutcracker, ill. by Alison Jay

The nutcracker, ill. by Peter Malone
The nutcracker, ill. by Niroot Puttapipat
The nutcracker, ill. by Maurice Sendak
The nutcracker, ill. by Lisbeth Zwerger
The Nutcracker and the Mouse King
The nutcracker ballet
The Nutcracker in Harlem
Hogrogian, Nonny. *The first Christmas*
Holabird, Katharine. *Angelina's Christmas*
    Christmas in Mouseland
    Christmas with Angelina
Holmquist, Delano. *SantaSaurus*
Hooks, William H. *The legend of the Christmas rose*
Hooper, Maureen Brett. *Silent night: a Christmas*
    carol is born
Hopkins, Lee Bennett. *Christmas presents*
Horácek, Petr. *Suzy Goose and the Christmas star*
Horn, Sandra Ann. *Babushka*
House, Catherine. *A stork in a baobab tree*
Houston, Gloria. *The year of the perfect Christmas tree*
Howard, Elizabeth Fitzgerald. *Chita's Christmas tree*
Howard, Ellen. *The log cabin Christmas*
Huddy, Delia. *The Christmas Eve tree*
Hughes, Langston. *Carol of the brown king*
Hughes, Shirley. *The Christmas Eve ghost*
Hunter, Sally. *Humphrey's Christmas*
Hurd, Thacher. *Santa Mouse and the ratdeer*
Ichikawa, Satomi. *What the little fir tree wore to the*
    Christmas party
Idle, Molly. *Santa Rex*
Inkpen, Deborah. *Harriet and the little fat fairy*
Inkpen, Mick. *Kipper's Christmas eve*
James, J. Alison. *The bears' Christmas surprise*
Jane, Pamela. *Little elfie one*
Janice. *Little Bear's Christmas*
Jay, Alison. *Christmastime*
Jeffers, Susan. *Jingle bells*
    The twelve days of Christmas
Jennings, Patrick. *Naughty Claudine's Christmas*
Jiménez, Francisco. *The Christmas gift / El regalo de*
    Navidad
Johnson, Crockett. *Harold at the North Pole*
Johnson, David. *Snow sounds*
Johnson, Grace. *The candle in the window*
Johnston, Tony. *A Kenya Christmas*
    Noel
Joosse, Barbara. *A houseful of Christmas*
Joseph, Lynn. *An island Christmas*
Joslin, Mary. *On that Christmas night*
Kasparavicius, Kestutis. *The bear family's world tour*
    Christmas
Kastner, Jill. *Merry Christmas, Princess Dinosaur*
Keane, Michael. *The night Santa got lost*
Keats, Ezra Jack. *The little drummer boy*
Keller, Holly. *Merry Christmas, Geraldine*
Kelley, True. *The dog who saved Santa*
Kellogg, Steven. *The Christmas witch*
    Santa Claus is comin' to town
Kennedy, Cindy. *The star of Christmas*
Ketcham, Sallie. *The Christmas bird*
Kidslabel. *Spot 7: Christmas*
Killen, Nicola. *The little reindeer*
Kimmel, Elizabeth Cody. *My penguin Osbert*
Kinsey-Warnock, Natalie. *A Christmas like Helen's*
Kladstrup, Kristin. *The gingerbread pirates*
Kneen, Maggie. *The Christmas surprise*
Knight, Hilary. *A firefly in a fir tree*
Krensky, Stephen. *How Santa got his job*
    How Santa lost his job

The last Christmas tree
Kroll, Steven. *Pooch on the loose*
    Santa's crash-bang Christmas
Kroll, Virginia L. *Uno, dos, tres, posada!*
Krupinski, Loretta. *Christmas in the city*
Krykorka, Ian. *Carl, the Christmas carp*
Langley, Karen. *Shine*
Langstaff, John M. *What a morning!*
Lawler, Janet. *Tyrannoclaus*
Lee, Quinlan B. *Crazy Christmas chaos*
Lee, Stan. *Stan Lee's superhero Christmas*
LeSourd, Nancy. *Christy, Christmastime at Cutter*
    Gap
Lester, Helen. *Tacky's Christmas*
Lewandowski, Frrich. *It's Christmas again*
Lewis, Anne Margaret. *What am I? Christmas*
Lewis, J. Patrick. *Long was the winter road they*
    traveled
Light, Steve. *The Christmas giant*
Lin, Grace. *Okie-dokie, Artichokie*
Lindgren, Astrid. *Pippi Longstocking's after-*
    Christmas party
Little, Jean. *Pippin the Christmas pig*
Litwin, Eric. *Pete the Cat saves Christmas*
Lloyd-Jones, Sally. *Song of the stars*
London, Jonathan. *Froggy's first Christmas*
Long, Loren. *Drummer boy*
    An Otis Christmas
Long, Sylvia. *Deck the hall*
Lucado, Max. *Alabaster's song*
Lucas, David. *Christmas at the toy museum*
Luzzati, Emanuele. *Three little owls*
McAnulty, Stacy. *Dear Santasaurus*
Maccarone, Grace. *A child was born*
McCaughrean, Geraldine. *Father and son*
    How the reindeer got their antlers
McCourt, Lisa. *Merry Christmas, Stinky Face*
McCully, Emily Arnold. *The Christmas gift*
McGhee, Alison. *Star bright*
McGinley, Phyllis. *The year without a Santa Claus*
McGinley-Nally, Sharon. *The friendly beasts*
McGuirk, Leslie. *Ho, ho, ho, Tucker!*
MacKay, Elly. *Waltz of the snowflakes*
McKee, David. *Elmer's Christmas*
McKissack, Patricia C. *The all-I'll-ever-want*
    Christmas doll
    Messy Bessey's holidays
McPhail, David. *Henry Bear's Christmas*
    Santa's book of names
McQuade, Jacqueline. *Christmas with Teddy Bear*
Mahy, Margaret. *The Christmas tree tangle*
Major, Kevin. *Aunt Olga's Christmas postcards*
Manzano, Sonia. *Miracle on 133rd Street*
Marshall, James. *Merry Christmas, space case*
Martin, Ann M. *The Doll People's Christmas*
Martin, David. *Little Bunny and the magic Christmas*
    tree
Martín, Hugo C. *Pablo's Christmas*
Martin, Ruth. *Santa's on his way*
Marzollo, Jean. *I see a star*
    I spy Christmas
    I spy little Christmas
    Ten little Christmas presents
Masurel, Claire. *Christmas is coming*
Mathers, Petra. *Herbie's secret Santa*
Matteson, George. *The Christmas tugboat*
May, Robert L. *Rudolph shines again*
    Rudolph the red-nosed reindeer
Mayer, Mercer. *The little drummer mouse*

Mayhew, James. *Ella Bella ballerina and The Nutcracker*
Mayper, Monica. *Come and see*
Medearis, Angela Shelf. *Poppa's itchy Christmas*
Medina, Tony. *Christmas makes me think*
Metzger, Steve. *Waiting for Santa*
Milgrim, David. *Santa Duck*
　Santa Duck and his merry helpers
Miller, Edna. *Mousekin's Christmas eve*
Minor, Wendell. *Christmas tree!*
Modugno, Maria. *Santa Claus and the three bears*
Mohr, Joseph. *Silent night*
Moore, Clement Clarke. *A creature was stirring*
　The night before Christmas, ill. by Jan Brett
　The night before Christmas, ill. by Tomie dePaola
　The night before Christmas, ill. by Mary Engelbreit
　The night before Christmas, ill. by David Ercolini
　The night before Christmas, ill. by Holly Hobbie
　The night before Christmas, ill. by Rachel Isadora
　The night before Christmas, ill. by Raquel Jaramillo
　The night before Christmas, ill. by Anita Lobel
　The night before Christmas, ill. by James Marshall
　The night before Christmas, ill. by Will Moses
　The night before Christmas, ill. by Ted Rand
　The night before Christmas, ill. by Barbara Reid
　The night before Christmas, ill. by Ruth Sanderson
　The night before Christmas, ill. by Gennady Spirin
　The night before Christmas, ill. by Tasha Tudor
　The night before Christmas, ill. by Richard Jesse Watson
　The night before Christmas, ill. by Wendy Watson
　The night before Christmas, ill. by Bruce Whatley
　The night before Christmas, ill. by Lisbeth Zwerger
　The night before Christmas
　The night before Christmas: a pop-up
　The teddy bears' night before Christmas
　'Twas the night before Christmas, ill. by Daniel Kirk
　'Twas the night before Christmas, ill. by Matt Tavares
　'Twas the night before Christmas, ill. by Christopher Wormell
Moorman, Margaret. *Light the lights!*
Mora, Pat. *The gift of the poinsettia / El regalo de la flor de nochebuena*
　A piñata in a pine tree
Morpurgo, Michael. *On angel wings*
Morrissey, Dean. *The Christmas ship*
Moses, Will. *Silent night*
Moss, Jenny Jackson. *Cajun night after Christmas*
Moulton, Mark Kimball. *Reindeer Christmas*
Muecke, Anne. *The dinosaurs' night before Christmas*
Murguia, Bethanie Deeney. *The best parts of Christmas*
Naylor, Phyllis Reynolds. *Keeping a Christmas secret*
Nazoa, Aquiles. *A small Nativity*
Nichols, Lori. *Maple and Willow's Christmas tree*
Nikola-Lisa, W. *Hallelujah!*
　To hear the angels sing
Noble, Trinka Hakes. *A Christmas spider's miracle*
Norris, Leslie. *Albert and the angels*
Novak, Matt. *The last Christmas present*
Numeroff, Laura Joffe. *If you take a mouse to the movies*
　Merry Christmas, Mouse!
Obed, Ellen Bryan. *Who would like a Christmas tree?*
O'Connor, Jane. *Fancy Nancy splendiferous Christmas*
Older, Effin. *My two grandmothers*

Onyefulu, Ifeoma. *An African Christmas*
Oppenheim, Joanne. *The Christmas witch*
Orozco, Jose-Luis. *Pancho Claus*
Park, Linda Sue. *The third gift*
Pasquali, Elena. *Ituku's Christmas journey*
Patricelli, Leslie. *Fa la la*
Paul, Ellis. *The night the lights went out on Christmas*
Paxton, Tom. *The story of Santa Claus*
Peet, Amanda. *Dear Santa, Love Rachel Rosenstein*
Peet, Bill. *Countdown to Christmas*
Petach, Heidi. *Wee three pigs*
Peterson, Melissa. *Hanna's Christmas*
Pfister, Marcus. *The Christmas star*
　Wake up, Santa Claus!
Pickthall, Marjorie L. C. *The worker in sandalwood*
Pilkey, Dav. *Dragon's merry Christmas*
　The Dumb Bunnies' Easter
Pingk, Rubin. *Samurai Santa*
Pinkney, Andrea Davis. *Mim's Christmas jam*
Pinkwater, Daniel. *Wolf Christmas*
Pittman, Helena Clare. *The angel tree*
Plourde, Lynn. *Merry Moosey Christmas*
Polacco, Patricia. *Gifts of the heart*
　The trees of the dancing goats
　Welcome Comfort
Politi, Leo. *Pedro, the angel of Olvera Street*
Powell, Consie. *Old dog Cora and the Christmas tree*
Primavera, Elise. *Auntie Claus*
　Auntie Claus and the key to Christmas
Pryor, Bonnie. *Merry Christmas, Amanda and April*
Pulver, Robin. *Christmas for a kitten*
　Christmas kitten, home at last
Purmell, Ann. *Christmas tree farm*
Quattlebaum, Mary. *The shine man*
Raczka, Bob. *Santa Clauses*
Rader, Laura. *Santa's new suit*
Rahaman, Vashanti. *O Christmas tree*
Ransom, Candice F. *The Christmas dolls*
Rawlinson, Julia. *Fletcher and the snowflake Christmas*
Ray, Mary Lyn. *Christmas farm*
Reagan, Jean. *How to catch Santa*
Recorvits, Helen. *Yoon and the Christmas mitten*
Rees, Douglas. *Jeannette Claus saves Christmas*
Reiser, Lynn. *Christmas counting*
Reiss, Mike. *How Murray saved Christmas*
　Merry un-Christmas
　Santa claustrophobia
Reynolds, Peter H. *The smallest gift of Christmas*
Rinker, Sherri Duskey. *The twelve sleighs of Christmas*
Robbins, Ruth. *Baboushka and the three kings*
Roberts, Bethany. *Christmas mice*
　Cookie angel
Rodanas, Kristina. *The little drummer boy*
Root, Phyllis. *All for the newborn baby*
Rosales, Melodye Benson. *'Twas the night b'fore Christmas*
Rose, Marion. *The Christmas tree fairy*
Rose, Nancy. *Merry Christmas, squirrels!*
Rosen, Michael J. *Elijah's angel*
Rosenberg, Liz. *On Christmas eve*
Rosenthal, Amy Krouse. *Christmas cookies*
Ross, Michael Elsohn. *Mexican Christmas*
Rox, John. *I want a hippopotamus for Christmas*
Ryan, Pam Muñoz. *There was no snow on Christmas Eve*
Rylant, Cynthia. *Christmas in the country*
　Little Whistle's Christmas

Wilson, Karma. *Bear stays up for Christmas*
  Mortimer's Christmas manger
Wing, Natasha. *The night before the night before*
  Christmas
Winter, Jeanette. *The Christmas tree ship*
Winthrop, Elizabeth. *Bear's Christmas surprise*
  A child is born: the Christmas story
Wojciechowski, Susan. *The Christmas miracle of*
  Jonathan Toomey
Wolff, Patricia Rae. *A new, improved Santa*
Wood, Audrey. *The Christmas adventure of Space Elf*
  Sam
  A cowboy Christmas
Wood, Don. *Merry Christmas, big hungry bear*
Wright, Dare. *A gift from the lonely doll*
Yee, Wong Herbert. *A small Christmas*
Yin. *Dear Santa, please come to the 19th floor*
Yolen, Jane. *How do dinosaurs say Merry Christmas?*
  Sister Bear
Yoon, Salina. *Penguin's Christmas wish*
Yorinks, Arthur. *Christmas in July*
Young, Ned. *Zoomer's out-of-this-world Christmas*
Zagwÿn, Deborah Turney. *The winter gift*
Zepeda, Gwendolyn. *Growing up with tamales / Los*
  tamales de Ana
Ziefert, Harriet. *Home for Navidad*
Zolotow, Charlotte. *The beautiful Christmas tree*

Holidays – Cinco de Mayo

Bullard, Lisa. *Marco's Cinco de Mayo*
Cox, Judy. *Cinco de Mouse-o!*
Flanagan, Alice K. *Cinco de Mayo*
Levy, Janice. *Celebrate! It's cinco de mayo! /*
  Celebremos! Es el cinco de mayo!
Schaefer, Lola M. *Cinco de Mayo*
Wade, Mary Dodson. *Cinco de Mayo*

Holidays – Day of the Dead

Barner, Bob. *The Day of the Dead / El Día de los*
  Muertos
Freschet, Gina. *Beto and the bone dance*
Goldman, Judy. *Uncle Monarch and the Day of the*
  Dead
Jaramillo, Susie. *Little skeletons / Esqueletitos*
Johnston, Tony. *Day of the Dead*
Joosse, Barbara. *Ghost wings*
Keep, Linda Lowery. *Day of the Dead*
Luenn, Nancy. *A gift for Abuelita*
Montes, Marisa. *Los gatos black on Halloween*
Mora, Pat. *The remembering day / El día de los*
  muertos
Thong, Roseanne. *Día de los muertos*

Holidays – Diwali

Gardeski, Christina Mia. *Diwali*
Pandya, Meenal. *Here comes Diwali*
Rahaman, Vashanti. *Divali rose*
Sebra, Richard. *It's Diwali!*
Verma, Jatinder Nath. *The story of Divaali*

Holidays – Earth Day

deGroat, Diane. *Ants in your pants, worms in your*
  plants!
Roop, Connie. *Let's celebrate Earth Day*
Wright, Maureen. *Earth Day, birthday!*

Holidays – Easter

Adams, Adrienne. *The Easter egg artists*
Auch, Mary Jane. *The Easter egg farm*
Balian, Lorna. *Humbug rabbit*
Berenstain, Stan and Jan. *The Berenstain bears and*
  the real Easter eggs
Bergren, Lisa Tawn. *God gave us Easter*
Berlin, Irving. *Easter parade*
Bible. New Testament. Gospels. *Easter: from the*
  King James Bible
Brett, Jan. *The Easter egg*
Brown, Margaret Wise. *The golden egg book*
  The runaway bunny
Burg, Sarah Emmanuelle. *One more egg*
Carlson, Melody. *The Easterville miracle*
Carter, David A. *Easter bugs*
Chaconas, Dori. *Looking for Easter*
Cousins, Lucy. *Happy Easter, Maisy!*
deGroat, Diane. *Last one in is a rotten egg!*
Denim, Sue. *The Dumb Bunnies' Easter*
Devlin, Wende. *Cranberry Easter*
Dunrea, Olivier. *Ollie's Easter eggs*
Friedrich, Priscilla. *The Easter bunny that overslept*
Garland, Michael. *The great Easter egg hunt*
Garton, Sam. *Otter loves Easter!*
Gibbons, Gail. *Easter*
Grambling, Lois G. *Here comes T. Rex Cottontail*
Greenfield, Eloise. *Easter parade*
Hennessy, B. G. *Corduroy's Easter*
Heyward, Du Bose. *The country bunny and the little*
  gold shoes
Hill, Eric. *Spot's first Easter*
Hughes, Laura. *We're going on an egg hunt*
Hulme, Joy N. *Easter babies*
Kaplan, Michael B. *Betty Bunny loves Easter*
Kimmel, Eric A. *The birds' gift*
Krensky, Stephen. *Milo and the really big bunny*
Kroll, Steven. *The big bunny and the Easter eggs*
  The big bunny and the magic show
Lenski, Lois. *The Easter Rabbit's parade*
McGrath, Barbara Barbieri. *The little gray bunny*
Mackall, Dandi Daley. *The story of the Easter robin*
Marciano, John Bemelmans. *Madeline at the White*
  House
Milhous, Katherine. *The egg tree*
Miller, Edna. *Mousekin's Easter basket*
Modesitt, Jeanne. *Little Bunny's Easter surprise*
Mortimer, Anne. *Bunny's Easter egg*
Murphy, Elspeth Campbell. *Happy Easter, God*
Paquette, Ammi-Joan. *Bunny Bus*
Paraskevas, Betty. *Nibbles O'Hare*
Patricelli, Leslie. *Hop! hop!*
Pienkowski, Jan. *Easter*
Pilkey, Dav. *The Dumb Bunnies' Easter*
Polacco, Patricia. *Chicken Sunday*
Rand, Betseygail. *Big Bunny*
Roberts, Bethany. *Easter mice*
Schulman, Janet. *Ten Easter egg hunters*
Slegers, Liesbet. *Happy Easter!*
Smythe, Theresa. *Chester's colorful Easter eggs*
Stalder, Päivi. *Ernest's first Easter*
Stock, Catherine. *Easter surprise*
Stoeke, Janet Morgan. *Minerva Louise and the*
  colorful eggs
Stohs, Anita. *An Easter alleluia*
Taylor, Shirley. *The cross in the egg*
Taylor-Butler, Christine. *Lamb's Easter surprise*

Tegen, Katherine Brown. *The story of the Easter Bunny*
Thomas, Jan. *The Easter Bunny's assistant*
Thompson, Lauren. *Love one another*
Tudor, Tasha. *A tale for Easter*
Underwood, Deborah. *Here comes the Easter Cat*
Vail, Rachel. *Piggy Bunny*
Vainio, Pirkko. *Who hid the Easter eggs?*
Vidrine, Beverly Barras. *Easter Day alphabet*
Watson, Wendy. *Happy Easter day!*
Wedeven, Carol. *The Easter cave*
Weigelt, Udo. *The Easter Bunny's baby*
Weil, Lisl. *The candy egg bunny*
Wells, Rosemary. *Max counts his chickens*
  Max's chocolate chicken
  Max's Easter surprise
Weninger, Brigitte. *Happy Easter, Davy*
  Happy Easter, Davy!
Wildsmith, Brian. *The Easter story*
Wilhelm, Hans. *More bunny trouble*
  Quacky Ducky's Easter egg
  Quacky Ducky's Easter fun
Winthrop, Elizabeth. *He is risen*
Wolf, Winfried. *The Easter bunny*
Zolotow, Charlotte. *The bunny who found Easter*
  Mr. Rabbit and the lovely present

Holidays – Father's Day

Bunting, Eve. *A perfect Father's Day*
Butterworth, Nick. *My dad is awesome*
Callahan, Sean. *A wild Father's Day*
Kroll, Steven. *Happy Father's Day*
Loomis, Christine. *The best Father's Day present ever*
Nolan, Janet. *A Father's Day thank you*
Rockwell, Anne. *Father's Day*
Sharmat, Marjorie Weinman. *Hooray for Father's Day!*

Holidays – Fourth of July

Arena, Jen. *Lady Liberty's holiday*
Bertrand, Diane Gonzales. *Uncle Chente's picnic / El picnic de Tío Chente*
Chall, Marsha Wilson. *Happy birthday, America!*
Keller, Holly. *Henry's Fourth of July*
Lasky, Kathryn. *Fourth of July bear*
Malnor, Carol L. *The Blues go birding across America*
Osborne, Mary Pope. *Happy birthday, America*
Roberts, Bethany. *Fourth of July mice*
Roosa, Karen. *Pippa at the parade*
Thomas, Jane Resh. *Celebration!*
Van Nutt, Julia. *Skyrockets and snickerdoodles*
Wardlaw, Lee. *Red, white, and boom!*
Watson, Wendy. *Hurray for the Fourth of July*
Wells, Rosemary. *McDuff saves the day*
Whitehead, Kathy. *Looking for Uncle Louie on the Fourth of July*
Ziefert, Harriet. *Hats off for the Fourth of July!*

Holidays – Groundhog Day

Blackaby, Susan. *Brownie Groundhog and the February Fox*
Cox, Judy. *Go to sleep, Groundhog*
Cuyler, Margery. *Groundhog stays up late*
Freeman, Don. *Gregory's Shadow*
Gibbons, Gail. *Groundhog Day*
Hill, Susanna Leonard. *Punxsutawney Phyllis*
Hiskey, Iris. *The secret of the first one up*

Holub, Joan. *Groundhog weather school*
Johnson, Crockett. *Will spring be early or will spring be late?*
Kroll, Steven. *It's Groundhog Day!*
Levine, Abby. *Gretchen Groundhog, it's your day!*
Lewin, Betsy. *Groundhog day*
Miller, Pat. *Substitute Groundhog*
Pallotta, Jerry. *Who will see their shadows this year?*
Pearlman, Robb. *Groundhog's day off*
Roberts, Bethany. *Double trouble Groundhog Day*
Swallow, Pamela Curtis. *Groundhog gets a say*
Tompert, Ann. *Nothing sticks like a shadow*
Welling, Peter J. *Andrew McGroundhog and his shady shadow*

Holidays – Halloween

Adams, Adrienne. *A Halloween happening*
  A woggle of witches
Agran, Rick. *Pumpkin shivaree*
Alexander, Sue. *Who goes out on Halloween?*
Alley, R. W. *There once was a witch*
Andrews, Julie. *The very fairy princess: a spooky, sparkly Halloween*
Asch, Frank. *Popcorn*
Auch, Mary Jane. *Poultrygeist*
Bailey, Ella. *No such thing*
Balian, Lorna. *Humbug witch*
Bauer, Marion Dane. *Halloween forest*
  I'm not afraid of Halloween!
Berenstain, Stan and Jan. *The Berenstain bears trick or treat*
Biedrzycki, David. *Me and my dragon: scared of Halloween*
Bollinger, Peter. *Algernon Graeves is scary enough*
Bond, Felicia. *The Halloween play*
Boynton, Sandra. *Eek! Halloween!*
  Spooky Pookie
Bozik, Chrissy. *The ghosts go scaring*
Brendler, Carol. *Not very scary*
Brennan-Nelson, Denise. *J is for jack-o-lantern*
Brenner, Tom. *And then comes Halloween*
Bridwell, Norman. *Clifford's Halloween*
  Glow-in-the-dark Halloween
Bright, Robert. *Georgie's Halloween*
Brimner, Larry Dane. *Trick or treat, Old Armadillo*
Brokamp, Elizabeth. *The picky little witch*
Brown, Lisa. *Vampire boy's good night*
Brown, Marc. *Arthur's Halloween*
  Arthur's spookiest Halloween
Brown, Margaret Wise. *The fierce yellow pumpkin*
Broyles, Anne. *Shy Mama's Halloween*
Bruel, Nick. *Bad Kitty, scaredy-cat*
Bullard, Lisa. *Trick-or-treat on Milton Street*
Bunting, Eve. *The bones of Fred McFee*
  Scary, scary Halloween
Carlson, Melody. *When the creepy things come out*
Carlstrom, Nancy White. *What a scare, Jesse Bear!*
  Who said boo?
Caseley, Judith. *Witch mama*
Caswell, Deanna. *Boo! haiku*
Cazet, Denys. *Never poke a squid*
  The perfect pumpkin pie
Chetkowski, Emily. *Pumpkin smile*
Choi, Yangsook. *Behind the mask*
Christelow, Eileen. *Five little monkeys trick-or-treat*
Christian, Cheryl. *Witches*
Cocca-Leffler, Maryann. *Jungle Halloween*
Cohen, Miriam. *The real-skin rubber monster mask*

Colby, Rebecca. *It's raining bats and frogs*
Cousins, Lucy. *Maisy's Halloween*
Cox, Judy. *Haunted house, haunted Mouse*
Cronin, Doreen. *Click, clack, boo!*
Crum, Shutta. *Who took my hairy toe?*
Cushman, Doug. *Halloween good night*
Cuyler, Margery. *The bumpy little pumpkin*
David, Lawrence. *Superhero Max*
Day, Alexandra. *Carl's Halloween*
Day, Nancy Raines. *On a windy night*
deGroat, Diane. *Trick or treat, smell my feet*
de Las Casas, Dianne. *The house that Witchy built*
Demas, Corinne. *Halloween surprise*
Desmoinaux, Christel. *"Hallo-what?"*
Devlin, Wende. *Cranberry Halloween*
Dickinson, Rebecca. *Over in the Hollow*
Diviny, Sean. *Halloween Motel*
Donnelly, Liza. *Dinosaurs' Halloween*
Druce, Arden. *Halloween night*
Dunrea, Olivier. *Ollie's Halloween*
Duval, Kathy. *The Three Bears' Halloween*
Egan, Tim. *The experiments of Doctor Vermin*
Engelbreit, Mary. *Queen of Halloween*
Faulkner, Keith. *A trick or a treat?*
Five little pumpkins, ill. by Ben Mantle
    Five little pumpkins, ill. by Iris Van Rynbach
    Five little pumpkins, ill. by Dan Yaccarino
Flanagan, Alice K. *Halloween*
Fraser, Mary Ann. *Heebie-Jeebie Jamboree*
Fronis, Aly. *If you're spooky and you know it*
Galbraith, Kathryn O. *Boo, bunny!*
Gallion, Sue Lowell. *Pug and Pig trick-or-treat*
Gantos, Jack. *Rotten Ralph's trick or treat*
Garton, Sam. *Otter loves Halloween*
Gehl, Laura. *Peep and Egg: I'm not trick-or-treating*
Gerber, Carole. *Ten busy brooms*
Gibbons, Gail. *Halloween*
    Halloween is . . .
Grabill, Rebecca. *Halloween good night*
Grambling, Lois G. *Miss Hildy's missing cape caper*
    T. Rex trick-or-treats
Graves, Keith. *The monsterator*
Grogan, John. *Trick or treat, Marley!*
Gunnufson, Charlotte. *Halloween hustle*
Hall, Zoe. *It's pumpkin time!*
Halloweena
Hatch, Elizabeth. *Halloween night*
Heidbreder, Robert. *Black and bittern was night*
Heinz, Brian J. *The monsters' test*
Hennessy, B. G. *Corduroy's Halloween*
Hills, Tad. *Duck and Goose, honk! quack! boo!*
Hines, Anna Grossnickle. *When the goblins came knocking*
Holabird, Katharine. *Angelina's Halloween*
Holub, Joan. *The Halloween Queen*
Hood, Susan. *Just say boo!*
Hopkins, Lee Bennett. *Ragged shadows*
Horowitz, Dave. *The ugly pumpkin*
Hubbard, Patricia. *Trick or treat countdown*
Hubbell, Patricia. *Boo! Halloween poems and limericks*
    Wrapping paper romp
Hubbell, Will. *Pumpkin Jack*
Huck, Charlotte S. *A creepy countdown*
Hutchins, Pat. *Which witch is which?*
Irving, Washington. *The legend of Sleepy Hollow*, ill. by R. W. Alley
    The legend of Sleepy Hollow, ill. by Daniel San Souci

Jane, Pamela. *Little goblins ten*
    Monster mischief
Johnston, Tony. *Soup bone*
    The vanishing pumpkin
Keats, Ezra Jack. *The trip*
Keens-Douglas, Richardo. *Anancy and the haunted house*
Kellogg, Steven. *The mystery of the flying orange pumpkin*
Ketteman, Helen. *At the old haunted house*
    The ghosts go haunting
Kimmelman, Leslie. *Trick ARRR treat*
Kontis, Alethea. *AlphaOops!*
Kovalski, Maryann. *Omar's Halloween*
Krieb, Mr. *We're off to find the witch's house*
Krosoczka, Jarrett J. *Annie was warned*
Kutner, Merrily. *Z is for zombie*
Landry, Leo. *Trick or treat*
Leedy, Loreen. *The dragon Halloween party*
    2 x 2 = boo!
Lester, Helen. *Tacky and the haunted igloo*
Leuck, Laura. *One witch*
Levine, Abby. *This is the pumpkin*
Lewis, J. Patrick. *The house of Boo*
Lewis, Kevin. *The runaway pumpkin*
Little old lady who swallowed a fly. *There was an old mummy who swallowed a spider*
London, Jonathan. *Froggy's Halloween*
Long, Ethan. *Fright club*
McCourt, Lisa. *Happy Halloween, Stinky Face*
McCue, Lisa. *Corduroy's best Halloween ever!*
McGhee, Alison. *Only a witch can fly*
    The sweetest witch around
    A very brave witch
McGuirk, Leslie. *Tucker's spooky Halloween*
Marshall, Edward. *Space case*
Martin, Bill, Jr.. *The magic pumpkin*
    Old devil wind
    Trick or treat?
Marzollo, Jean. *I spy spooky night*
Mayer, Pamela. *The scariest monster in the whole wide world*
Mayr, Diane. *Littlebat's Halloween story*
Meddaugh, Susan. *The witches' supermarket*
Melmed, Laura Krauss. *Fright night flight*
Merriam, Eve. *Halloween ABC*
Miller, Edna. *Mousekin's golden house*
Minor, Wendell. *Pumpkin heads*
Moffatt, Judith. *The pumpkin man*
    Trick-or-treat faces
Montes, Marisa. *Los gatos black on Halloween*
Montijo, Rhode. *The Halloween Kid*
Mortimer, Anne. *Pumpkin cat*
Murray, Marjorie Dennis. *Halloween night*
Muth, Jon J. *Zen ghosts*
Neitzel, Shirley. *Who will I be?*
Nikola-Lisa, W. *Shake dem Halloween bones*
Novak, Matt. *No zombies allowed*
O'Connell, Jennifer. *It's Halloween night!*
O'Malley, Kevin. *Velcome*
Palatini, Margie. *Piggie pie*
Pamintuan, Macky. *Twelve haunted rooms of Halloween*
Passen, Lisa. *Attack of the 50-foot teacher*
Patricelli, Leslie. *Boo!*
Pearson, Susan. *We're going on a ghost hunt*
Pilkey, Dav. *The Hallo-wiener*
Polacco, Patricia. *Picnic at Mudsock Meadow*
Poydar, Nancy. *The perfectly horrible Halloween*

Prelutsky, Jack. *Halloween countdown*
    Wild witches' ball
Preston, Tim. *Pumpkin moon*
Reeves, Howard W. *There was an old witch*
Regan, Dian Curtis. *How do you know it's
    Halloween?*
Rex, Michael. *Brooms are for flying*
Riggio, Anita. *Beware the Brindlebeast*
Rim, Sujean. *Birdie's happiest Halloween*
Rocklin, Joanne. *This book is haunted*
Rockwell, Anne. *Apples and pumpkins*
    Halloween Day
Rohmann, Eric. *Bone dog*
Rosen, Michael J. *Night of the pumpkinheads*
Rosenberry, Vera. *Vera's Halloween*
Ross, Eileen. *The Halloween showdown*
Rylant, Cynthia. *Herbert's first Halloween*
    Moonlight, the Halloween cat
Saltzberg, Barney. *The problem with pumpkins*
San Souci, Robert D. *Cinderella Skeleton*
Savage, Stephen. *Seven orange pumpkins*
    Ten orange pumpkins
Schulman, Janet. *10 trick-or-treaters*
Schweninger, Ann. *Halloween surprises*
Scotton, Rob. *Scaredy-cat, Splat!*
Seeger, Laura Vaccaro. *Dog and Bear: tricks and
    treats*
Seibold, J. Otto. *Vunce upon a time*
Seinfeld, Jerry. *Halloween*
Shaw, Nancy. *Sheep trick or treat*
Shea, Bob. *The scariest book ever*
Shute, Linda. *Halloween party*
Siddals, Mary McKenna. *Shivery shades of Halloween*
Sierra, Judy. *The house that Drac built*
Silverman, Erica. *The Halloween house*
Sloat, Teri. *Zip! zoom! on a broom*
Smalls-Hector, Irene. *Jenny Reen and the Jack Muh
    Lantern*
Soman, David. *Ladybug Girl and the dress-up
    dilemma*
Spurr, Elizabeth. *Pumpkin hill*
Stein, Garth. *Enzo's very scary Halloween*
Stevenson, James. *That terrible Halloween night*
Stock, Catherine. *Halloween monster*
Stoeke, Janet Morgan. *Minerva Louise on Halloween*
Stutson, Caroline. *By the light of the Halloween moon*
Tatcheva, Eva. *Witch Zelda's birthday cake*
Teague, Mark. *One Halloween night*
Tegen, Katherine Brown. *Dracula and Frankenstein
    are friends*
Thomas, Jan. *Pumpkin trouble*
Thompson, Lauren. *Mouse's first Halloween*
Titherington, Jeanne. *Pumpkin pumpkin*
Todd, Mark. *What will you be for Halloween?*
Trapani, Iza. *Haunted party*
Tryon, Leslie. *Albert's Halloween*
Tudor, Tasha. *Pumpkin moonshine*
Turner, Ann Warren. *Pumpkin cat*
Vasilovich, Guy. *The thirteen nights of Halloween*
Vaughan, Marcia Kapok. *We're going on a ghost hunt*
Waldron, Jan L. *John Pig's Halloween*
Walker, Sally M. *Druscilla's Halloween*
Watson, Wendy. *Boo! it's Halloween*
Watt, Mélanie. *Scaredy Squirrel prepares for Halloween*
Weston, Martha. *Tuck's haunted house*
Williams, Suzanne. *The witch casts a spell*
Winters, Kay. *The teeny tiny ghost*
    Whooo's haunting the teeny tiny ghost?
Winthrop, Elizabeth. *Halloween hats*

Wohl, Lauren L. *A teeny tiny Halloween*
Wojciechowski, Susan. *The best Halloween of all*
Wolff, Ferida. *On Halloween night*
Wunderli, Stephen. *Little Boo*
Yolen, Jane. *Beneath the ghost moon*
Ziefert, Harriet. *Two little witches*
Zolotow, Charlotte. *A tiger called Thomas*, ill. by
    Diana Cain Bluthenthal
    A tiger called Thomas, ill. by Catherine Stock

Holidays – Hanukkah

Adler, David A. *A picture book of Hanukkah*
    A picture book of Jewish holidays
    The story of Hanukkah
Aleichem, Sholem. *Hanukah money*
Alko, Selina. *Daddy Christmas and Hanukkah Mama*
Barash, Chris. *Is it Hanukkah yet?*
Baum, Maxie. *I have a little dreidel*
Bridwell, Norman. *Clifford celebrates Hanukkah*
Bunting, Eve. *One candle*
Capucilli, Alyssa Satin. *Happy Hanukkah, Biscuit*
Carter, David A. *Chanukah bugs*
Chwast, Seymour. *The miracle of Hanukkah*
Cleary, Brian P. *Eight wild nights*
da Costa, Deborah. *Hanukkah moon*
Edwards, Michelle. *The Hanukkah trike*
    Papa's latkes
    Room for the baby
Fischer, Ellen. *Latke, the lucky dog*
Fishman, Cathy Goldberg. *On Hanukkah*
Fisman, Karen. *Nonna's Hanukkah surprise*
Glaser, Linda. *Mrs. Greenberg's messy Hanukkah*
Hirsh, Marilyn. *Potato pancakes all around*
Hopkins, Lee Bennett. *Hanukkah lights*
Howland, Naomi. *Latkes, latkes, good to eat*
Hyde, Heidi Smith. *Emanuel and the Hanukkah
    rescue*
Jaffe, Nina. *In the month of Kislev*
Kimmel, Eric A. *The Chanukkah guest*
    Hanukkah bear
    Hershel and the Hanukkah goblins
    The magic dreidels
    Simon and the bear
    Zigazak!
Kimmelman, Leslie. *Hanukkah lights, Hanukkah
    nights*
    The runaway latkes
Koster, Gloria. *Little Red Ruthie*
Krensky, Stephen. *Hanukkah at Valley Forge*
Kroll, Steven. *The Hanukkah mice*
Kropf, Latifa Berry. *It's Hanukkah time!*
Krulik, Nancy E. *Is it Hanukkah yet?*
Kuskin, Karla. *A great miracle happened there*
Lehman-Wilzig, Tami. *Nathan blows out the
    Hanukkah candles*
McKissack, Patricia C. *Messy Bessey's holidays*
Manushkin, Fran. *Hooray for Hanukkah!*
    Latkes and applesauce
Martin, David. *Hanukkah lights*
Melmed, Laura Krauss. *Eight winter nights*
    Moishe's miracle
Moorman, Margaret. *Light the lights!*
Newman, Lesléa. *The eight nights of Chanukah*
    Runaway dreidel
Oberman, Sheldon. *By the Hanukkah light*
Ofananasky, Allison. *Harvest of light*
Older, Effin. *My two grandmothers*
Pinkwater, Daniel. *Beautiful Yetta's Hanukkah kitten*

Podwal, Mark H. *The menorah story*
Polacco, Patricia. *The trees of the dancing goats*
Randall, Ronne. *The Hanukkah mice*
Rosen, Michael J. *Chanukah lights*
　Chanukah lights everywhere
　Elijah's angel
　Our eight nights of Hanukkah
Rothenberg, Joan Keller. *Inside-out grandma*
Schaefer, Lola M. *Hanukkah*
Schnur, Steven. *The tie man's miracle*
Schotter, Roni. *Hanukkah!*
Silverman, Erica. *The Hanukkah hop!*
Simon, Norma. *The story of Hanukkah*
Simon, Richard. *Oskar and the eight blessings*
Singer, Isaac Bashevis. *The parakeet named Dreidel*
Smith, Dian G. *Hanukkah lights*
Sper, Emily. *Hanukkah: a counting book in English,*
　Hebrew, and Yiddish
Spinner, Stephanie. *It's a miracle*
Stein, Joel Edward. *A Hanukkah with Mazel*
Stone, Tanya Lee. *D is for dreidel*
Ungar, Richard. *Yitzi and the giant menorah*
Yolen, Jane. *How do dinosaurs say Happy Chanukah?*
Zalben, Jane Breskin. *Beni's first Chanukah*
　Pearl's eight days of Chanukah
Ziefert, Harriet. *Hanukkah haiku*

Holidays – Independence Day *see* Holidays –
Fourth of July

Holidays – Juneteenth

Cooper, Floyd. *Juneteenth for Mazie*
Weatherford, Carole Boston. *Juneteenth jamboree*

Holidays – Kwanzaa

Chocolate, Deborah. *Kente colors*
　Kwanzaa
Ford, Juwanda G. *K is for Kwanzaa*
　Together for Kwanzaa
McKissack, Patricia C. *Messy Bessey's holidays*
Medearis, Angela Shelf. *Seven spools of thread*
Saint James, Synthia. *The gifts of Kwanzaa*
Schaefer, Lola M. *Kwanzaa*
Tokunbo, Dimitrea. *The sound of Kwanzaa*
Washington, Donna L. *Li'l Rabbit's Kwanzaa*
　The story of Kwanzaa
Winne, Joanne. *Let's get ready for Kwanzaa*

Holidays – Mardi Gras *see* Mardi Gras

Holidays – Martin Luther King, Jr. Day

Adler, David A. *A picture book of Martin Luther King,*
　Jr
Brantley-Newton, Vanessa. *Let freedom sing*
Bunting, Eve. *The cart that carried Martin*
Evans, Shane W. *We march*
Farris, Christine King. *March on!*
　My brother Martin
Johnson, Angela. *A sweet smell of roses*
Kelley, Kitty. *Martin's dream day*
King, Martin Luther, III.. *My daddy, Dr. Martin*
　Luther King, Jr.
King, Martin Luther, Jr.. *I have a dream*
Myers, Walter Dean. *Young Martin's promise*
Nettleton, Pamela Hill. *Martin Luther King, Jr*

Pinkney, Andrea Davis. *Martin and Mahalia*
Rappaport, Doreen. *Martin's big words*
Ringgold, Faith. *My dream of Martin Luther King*
Sexton, Colleen A. *Let's meet Martin Luther King, Jr*
Watkins, Angela Farris. *Love will see you through*
　My Uncle Martin's big heart
　My Uncle Martin's words for America
Weatherford, Carole Boston. *Be a King: Dr. Martin*
　Luther King Jr.'s dream and you

Holidays – May Day

Mora, Pat. *The rainbow tulip*

Holidays – Memorial Day

Golding, Theresa Martin. *Memorial Day surprise*
Messner, Kate. *Rolling Thunder*

Holidays – Mother's Day

Alexander, Martha G. *Max and the dumb flower*
　picture
Anderson, Laurie Halse. *No time for Mother's Day*
Balian, Lorna. *Mother's Mother's Day*
Bauer, Marion Dane. *My mother is mine*
Bunting, Eve. *The Mother's Day mice*
deGroat, Diane. *Mother, you're the best! (but Sister,*
　you're a pest!)
French, Vivian. *A present for mom*
Grambling, Lois G. *T. Rex and the Mother's Day hug*
Krensky, Stephen. *Mother's Day surprise*
Kroll, Steven. *Happy Mother's Day*
Rockwell, Anne. *Mother's Day*
Sharmat, Marjorie Weinman. *Hooray for Mother's*
　Day!
Schiffer, Miriam B. *Stella brings the family*
Weninger, Brigitte. *Davy loves his mommy*

Holidays – New Year's

Andersen, Hans Christian. *The little match girl*, ill.
　by Rachel Isadora
　The little match girl, ill. by Blair Lent
　The little match girl, ill. by Jerry Pinkney
　The little matchstick girl
Bae, Hyun-Joo. *New clothes for New Year's day*
Fromental, Jean-Luc. *365 penguins*
Holabird, Katharine. *Angelina ice skates*
Miller, Pat. *Squirrel's New Year's resolution*
Modell, Frank. *Goodbye old year, hello new year*
Piernas-Davenport, Gail. *Shanté Keys and the New*
　Year's peas
Preus, Margi. *The Peace Bell*
Ziefert, Harriet. *First Night*

Holidays – Passover

Adler, David A. *A picture book of Jewish holidays*
　A picture book of Passover
　The story of Passover
Edwards, Michelle. *Max makes a cake*
Fishman, Cathy Goldberg. *On Passover*
Flanagan, Alice K. *Passover*
Geras, Adèle. *Rebecca's Passover*
Glaser, Linda. *Hoppy Passover!*
　Stone soup with matzoh balls
Hanft, Josh. *The miracles of Passover*
Howland, Naomi. *The matzah man*
Kimmelman, Leslie. *Hooray! it's Passover!*

Kropf, Latifa Berry. *It's seder time!*
Levine, Abby. *This is the matzah*
Libney, Varda. *What I like about Passover*
The little red hen. *The Little Red Hen and the Passover matzah*
Manushkin, Fran. *Miriam's cup*
Marshall, Linda Elovitz. *The passover lamb*
Newman, Lesléa. *Matzo ball moon*
    A sweet Passover
Portnoy, Mindy Avra. *A tale of two seders*
Rappaport, Doreen. *The secret seder*
Rothenberg, Joan Keller. *Matzah ball soup*
Rouss, Sylvia A. *Sammy Spider's first Passover*
Schotter, Roni. *Passover!*
    Passover magic
Shulevitz, Uri. *The magician*
Silverman, Erica. *Gittel's hands*
Simon, Norma. *The story of Passover*
Sper, Emily. *The Passover seder*
Strauss, Linda Leopold. *The Elijah door*
Ungar, Richard. *Rachel's gift*
Wayland, April Halprin. *More than enough*
Weber, Elka. *The Yankee at the seder*
Wohl, Lauren L. *Matzoh mouse*
Zalben, Jane Breskin. *Pearl's Passover*
Zolkower, Edie Stoltz. *Too many cooks*
Zucker, Jonny. *Four special questions*

Holidays – Purim

Fishman, Cathy Goldberg. *On Purim*
Goldin, Barbara Diamond. *Cakes and miracles*
Milhander, Laura Aron. *Not for all the hamantaschen in town*
Schotter, Roni. *Purim play*
Simpson, Lesley. *The Purim surprise*
Zucker, Jonny. *It's party time*

Holidays – Ramadan

Addasi, Maha. *The white nights of Ramadan*
Bullard, Lisa. *Rashad's Ramadan and Eid al-Fitr*
Faruqi, Reem. *Lailah's lunchbox*
Ghazi, Suhaib Hamid. *Ramadan*
Gilani-Williams, Fawzia. *Nabeel's new pants*
Jalali, Reza. *Moon watchers*
Katz, Karen. *My first Ramadan*
Khan, Hena. *The night of the moon*
Mobin-Uddin, Asma. *A party in Ramadan*
Robert, Na'ima B. *Ramadan Moon*
Whitman, Sylvia. *Under the Ramadan moon*

Holidays – Rosh Hashanah

Cohen, Deborah Bodin. *Engineer Ari and the Rosh Hashana ride*
Fishman, Cathy Goldberg. *On Rosh Hashanah and Yom Kippur*
Kimmel, Eric A. *Gershon's monster*
Kimmelman, Leslie. *Sound the shofar!*
Kropf, Latifa Berry. *It's Shofar time!*
Marshall, Linda Elovitz. *Talia and the rude vegetables*
Schnur, Susan. *Tashlich at Turtle Rock*
Wayland, April Halprin. *New Year at the pier*
Zucker, Jonny. *Apples and honey*

Holidays – Rosh Kodesh

da Costa, Deborah. *Hanukkah moon*

Holidays – Seder

Kropf, Latifa Berry. *It's seder time!*
Levine, Abby. *This is the matzah*
Marshall, Linda Elovitz. *The passover lamb*
Wayland, April Halprin. *More than enough*
Weber, Elka. *The Yankee at the seder*

Holidays – Shavuot

Goldin, Barbara Diamond. *A mountain of blintzes*
Korngold, Jamie S. *Sadie and the big mountain*
Rouss, Sylvia A. *Sammy Spider's first Shavuot*

Holidays – St. Patrick's Day

Bunting, Eve. *St. Patrick's Day in the morning*
Callahan, Sean. *The leprechaun who lost his rainbow Shannon and the world's tallest leprechaun*
Colandro, Lucille. *There was an old lady who swallowed a clover!*
Janice. *Little Bear marches in the St. Patrick's Day parade*
Kroll, Steven. *Mary McLean and the St. Patrick's Day parade*
McGuirk, Leslie. *Lucky Tucker*
Nolan, Janet. *The St. Patrick's Day shillelagh*
Rockwell, Anne. *St. Patrick's Day*
Schertle, Alice. *Jeremy Bean's St. Patrick's Day*
Tucker, Kathy. *The leprechaun in the basement*
Wojciechowski, Susan. *A fine St. Patrick's Day*

Holidays – Sukkot

Goldin, Barbara Diamond. *Night lights*
Hyde, Heidi Smith. *Shanghai Sukkah*
Kimmel, Eric A. *The mysterious guests*
Korngold, Jamie S. *Sadie's sukkah breakfast*
Polacco, Patricia. *Tikvah means hope*
Vorst, Rochel Groner. *The sukkah that I built*

Holidays – Thanksgiving

Alcott, Louisa May. *An old-fashioned Thanksgiving*
Allegra, Mike. *Sarah gives thanks*
Anderson, Derek. *Over the river*
Anderson, Laurie Halse. *Thank you, Sarah Turkey pox*
Archer, Peggy. *Turkey surprise*
Ashman, Linda. *Over the river and through the wood*
Atwell, Debby. *The Thanksgiving door*
Auch, Mary Jane. *Beauty and the beaks*
Balian, Lorna. *Sometimes it's turkey*
Bartlett, Robert Merrill. *The story of Thanksgiving*
Bateman, Teresa. *Gus, the pilgrim turkey A plump and perky turkey*
Behrens, June. *The feast of Thanksgiving*
Berenstain, Stan and Jan. *The Berenstain bears and the prize pumpkin*
Bildner, Phil. *Turkey Bowl*
Borden, Louise. *Thanksgiving is . . .*
Brown, Marc. *Arthur's Thanksgiving*
Bruchac, Joseph. *Squanto's journey*
Bunting, Eve. *How many days to America? A turkey for Thanksgiving*
Carlstrom, Nancy White. *Thanksgiving Day at our house*
Child, Lydia Maria. *Over the river and through the wood*

Over the river and through the wood: the New
England boy's song about Thanksgiving Day
Corey, Shana. *Milly and the Macy's Parade*
Cowley, Joy. *Gracias, the Thanksgiving turkey*
Cox, Judy. *One is a feast for Mouse*
Dalgliesh, Alice. *The Thanksgiving story*
dePaola, Tomie. *My first Thanksgiving*
Detlefsen, Lisl H. *Time for cranberries*
Devlin, Wende. *Cranberry Thanksgiving*
Elliott, Laura Malone. *Thanksgiving Day thanks*
Fearing, Mark. *The great Thanksgiving escape*
Flanagan, Alice K. *Thanksgiving*
Friedman, Laurie. *Thanksgiving rules*
Geisert, Arthur. *Nursery crimes*
George, Jean Craighead. *The first Thanksgiving*
Gibbons, Gail. *Thanksgiving Day*
Greene, Rhonda Gowler. *The very first Thanksgiving*
Day
Haugen, Brenda. *Thanksgiving*
Herman, Charlotte. *The memory cupboard*
Holub, Joan. *Turkeys never gobble*
Hopkins, Lee Bennett. *Merrily comes our harvest in*
Horowitz, Dave. *The ugly pumpkin*
Jackson, Alison. *I know an old lady who swallowed*
a pie
Janice. *Little Bear's Thanksgiving*
Jennings, Sharon. *Franklin's Thanksgiving*
Jules, Jacqueline. *Duck for Turkey Day*
Kenah, Katharine. *The very stuffed turkey*
Kimmelman, Leslie. *Round the turkey*
Koller, Jackie French. *Nickommoh!*
Kroll, Steven. *Oh, what a Thanksgiving!*
One tough turkey
The squirrels' Thanksgiving
Kroll, Virginia L. *The Thanksgiving bowl*
Lakin, Patricia. *Fat chance Thanksgiving*
Leedy, Loreen. *The dragon Thanksgiving feast*
Levine, Abby. *This is the turkey*
McCully, Emily Arnold. *An outlaw Thanksgiving*
Markes, Julie. *Thanks for Thanksgiving*
Marzollo, Jean. *Thanksgiving cats*
Mayr, Diane. *Run, Turkey, run*
Melmed, Laura Krauss. *This first Thanksgiving*
Metaxas, Eric. *Squanto and the miracle of*
Thanksgiving
Miller, Edna. *Mousekin's Thanksgiving*
Miller, Pat Zietlow. *Sharing the bread*
Myra, Harold Lawrence. *Thanksgiving: what makes*
it special?
Nikola-Lisa, W. *One, two, three Thanksgiving!*
Pilkey, Dav. *'Twas the night before Thanksgiving*
Pomeranc, Marion Hess. *The can-do Thanksgiving*
Rael, Elsa Okon. *Rivka's first Thanksgiving*
Reed, Lynn Rowe. *Thelonius Turkey lives!*
Rockwell, Anne. *Thanksgiving Day*
Rosen, Michael. *A Thanksgiving wish*
Shore, Diane Z. *This is the feast*
Silvano, Wendi. *Turkey trouble*
Smith, Mavis. *'Twas the day after Thanksgiving*
Spinelli, Eileen. *Thanksgiving at the Tappletons'*
Stanley, Diane. *Thanksgiving on Plymouth Plantation*
Stock, Catherine. *Thanksgiving treat*
Thorpe, Kiki. *A comfy, cozy Thanksgiving*
Tresselt, Alvin R. *Autumn harvest*
Watson, Wendy. *Thanksgiving at our house*
Wheeler, Lisa. *Turk and Runt*
Willey, Margaret. *Thanksgiving with me*
Williams, Barbara. *Chester Chipmunk's Thanksgiving*

Holidays – Tu B'Shevat

Gellman, Ellie B. *Netta and her plant*
Rosenberg, Madelyn. *Happy birthday, tree!*
Rouss, Sylvia A. *Sammy Spider's first Tu B'Shevat*

Holidays – Valentine's Day

Adams, Adrienne. *The great Valentine's Day balloon*
race
Andrews, Julie. *The very fairy princess follows her*
heart
Balian, Lorna. *A sweetheart for Valentine*
Brown, Marc. *Arthur's Valentine*
Bunting, Eve. *Mr. Goat's valentine*
The Valentine bears
Capucilli, Alyssa Satin. *Biscuit's Valentine's Day*
Carlson, Nancy. *Henry and the Valentine surprise*
Louanne Pig in the mysterious Valentine
Carr, Jan. *Sweet hearts*
Carrick, Carol. *Valentine*
Casey, Tina. *The runaway Valentine*
Cheshire, Marc. *Love and kisses, Eloise*
Choldenko, Gennifer. *A giant crush*
Cohen, Miriam. *Bee my Valentine!*
Cronin, Doreen. *Click, clack, moo I love you!*
Dean, James. *Pete the Cat: Valentine's Day is cool*
deGroat, Diane. *Roses are pink, your feet really stink*
Demas, Corinne. *Valentine surprise*
Devlin, Wende. *Cranberry Valentine*
Dodd, Emma. *Foxy in love*
Elliott, Laura Malone. *A string of hearts*
Ferber, Brenda A. *The yuckiest, stinkiest, best*
Valentine ever
Flanagan, Alice K. *Valentine's Day*
Friedman, Laurie. *Love, Ruby Valentine*
Ruby Valentine and the sweet surprise
Ruby Valentine saves the day
Gantos, Jack. *Rotten Ralph's rotten romance*
Gibbons, Gail. *Valentine's Day is —*
Henkes, Kevin. *Lilly's chocolate heart*
Hurd, Thacher. *Little Mouse's big Valentine*
Jackson, Alison. *The ballad of Valentine*
Kroll, Steven. *Will you be my valentine?*
Let me call you sweetheart
Little Bear's Valentine
Livingston, Myra Cohn. *Valentine poems*
London, Jonathan. *Froggy's first kiss*
Long, Ethan. *Valensteins: (a love story)*
Marzollo, Jean. *Valentine cats*
Modell, Frank. *One zillion valentines*
Numeroff, Laura Joffe. *Happy Valentine's Day,*
Mouse!
Pace, Anne Marie. *Groundhug Day*
Parish, Herman. *Amelia Bedelia's first valentine*
Petersen, David. *Snowy Valentine*
Poydar, Nancy. *Rhyme time Valentine*
Roberts, Bethany. *Valentine mice!*
Rockwell, Anne. *Valentine's Day*
Rylant, Cynthia. *If you'll be my Valentine*
Sabuda, Robert. *St. Valentine*
Samuels, Barbara. *Happy Valentine's Day, Dolores*
Schulman, Janet. *10 Valentine friends*
Schweninger, Ann. *Valentine friends*
Scotton, Rob. *Love, Splat*
Shannon, George. *Heart to heart*
Sharmat, Marjorie Weinman. *The best Valentine in*
the world
Spinelli, Eileen. *Somebody loves you, Mr. Hatch*
Stevenson, James. *Happy Valentine's Day, Emma!*

A village full of valentines
Stock, Catherine. *Secret Valentine*
Sutton, Benn. *Hedgehug*
Underwood, Deborah. *Here comes Valentine Cat*
Wallace, Nancy Elizabeth. *The Valentine Express*
Watson, Clyde. *Valentine foxes*
Watson, Wendy. *A Valentine for you*
Weeks, Sarah. *Be mine, be mine, sweet valentine*

Holidays – Yom Kippur

Fishman, Cathy Goldberg. *On Rosh Hashanah and Yom Kippur*
Kimmelman, Leslie. *Sound the shofar!*
Rouss, Sylvia A. *Sammy Spider's first Yom Kippur*

Holocaust

Adler, David A. *Hiding from the Nazis*
Lehman-Wilzig, Tami. *Keeping the promise*
Morris, Ann. *Grandma Esther remembers*
Oberman, Sheldon. *By the Hanukkah light*
Russo, Marisabina. *I will come back for you*
Schnur, Steven. *The tie man's miracle*
Simon, Richard. *Oskar and the eight blessings*
Ungerer, Tomi. *Otto: the autobiography of a teddy bear*
Wiviott, Meg. *Benno and the night of broken glass*

Homeless

Andersen, Hans Christian. *The little match girl*, ill. by Rachel Isadora
  The little match girl, ill. by Blair Lent
  The little match girl, ill. by Jerry Pinkney
  The little matchstick girl
Barrett, Mary Brigid. *Shoebox Sam*
Bartoletti, Susan Campbell. *The Christmas promise*
Bromley, Anne C. *The lunch thief*
Bunting, Eve. *December*
  Fly away home
Chinn, Karen. *Sam and the lucky money*
Cole, Brock. *Good enough to eat*
Day, Marie. *Edward the "crazy man"*
DiCamillo, Kate. *Great joy*
Huddy, Delia. *The Christmas Eve tree*
King, Stephen Michael. *Mutt dog!*
McPhail, David. *The teddy bear*
Meggs, Libby Phillips. *Go home!*
Myers, Christopher. *Sparrows*
Polacco, Patricia. *I can hear the sun*
Seskin, Steve. *A chance to shine*
Stewart, Joel. *Addis Berner Bear forgets*
Sweet, Melissa. *Tupelo rides the rails*
Tibo, Gilles. *The cowboy kid*
Vainio, Pirkko. *The Christmas angel*
Williams, Laura E. *The can man*

Homes, houses

Alger, Leclaire Gowans. *Always room for one more*
Alizadeh, Kate. *Quiet!*
Altman, Linda Jacobs. *Amelia's road*
Angelou, Maya. *My painted house, my friendly chicken, and me*
Anholt, Laurence. *Two nests*
Arnold, Tedd. *Vincent paints his house*
Arnosky, Jim. *Armadillo's orange*
Ashman, Linda. *Castles, caves, and honeycombs*
  Creaky old house
Aston, Dianna Hutts. *A nest is noisy*

Banks, Kate. *The great blue house*
Barnett, Mac. *Noisy night*
Barton, Byron. *Building a house*
  My house
Bean, Jonathan. *Building our house*
  This is my home, this is my school
Beaton, Clare. *At home / A la maison*
Bee, William. *Stanley the builder*
Beedie, Duncan. *The lumberjack's beard*
Beil, Karen Magnuson. *Jack's house*
Blackstone, Stella. *Bear at home*
Bloom, Suzanne. *No place for a pig*
Brett, Jan. *The three little dassies*
Brown, Margaret Wise. *Robin's room*
Brown, Petra. *When the wind blew*
Burton, Virginia Lee. *The little house*
Buzzeo, Toni. *Whose tools?*
Cabrera, Jane. *There was an old woman who lived in a shoe*
Carle, Eric. *A house for Hermit Crab*
  My very first book of homes
Carter, David A. *In a dark, dark wood*
Cecka, Melanie. *Violet comes to stay*
Chiew, Suzanne. *When you need a friend*
Clements, Andrew. *Slippers at home*
Collicott, Sharleen. *Mildred and Sam*
Corr, Christopher. *Deep in the woods*
Cotton, Katie. *The road home*
Crum, Shutta. *A family for Old Mill Farm*
Daly, Niki. *Welcome to Zanzibar Road*
Davies, Jacqueline. *The house takes a vacation*
Deacon, Alexis. *A place to call home*
dePaola, Tomie. *Jack*
DePrisco, Dorothea. *Who lives here?*
DiSalvo, DyAnne. *A castle on Viola Street*
Durango, Julia. *The one day house*
Edwards, Pamela Duncan. *Jack and Jill's treehouse*
  The old house
Ellis, Carson. *Home*
Emberley, Rebecca. *My house / Mi casa*
  My room / Mi cuarto
Emerman, Ellen. *Just right: the story of a Jewish home*
Emmett, Jonathan. *No place like home*
Empson, Jo. *Little home bird*
Falkenstern, Lisa. *A dragon moves in*
Fitzgerald, Joanne. *This is me and where I am*
Flanagan, Alice K. *Call Mr. Vasquez, he'll fix it!*
  Mr. Paul and Mr. Luecke build communities
  The Wilsons, a house-painting team
Foley, Greg. *Purple Little Bird*
Freedman, Deborah. *This house, once*
Fries, Claudia. *A pig is moving in*
Fuge, Charles. *Where to, Little Wombat?*
Gamble, Isobel. *Who's that?*
Garland, Michael. *Birds make nests*
Gavin, Ciara. *Room for Bear*
Gibbons, Gail. *How a house is built*
Gleeson, Libby. *Clancy and Millie and the very fine house*
Gliori, Debi. *Flora's surprise*
  Mr. Bear to the rescue
Godwin, Jane. *Bear make den*
Goode, Diane. *Tiger trouble*
Grahame, Kenneth. *A wind in the willows Christmas*
Grimm, Edward. *The doorman*
Grindley, Sally. *A new room for William*
Groundhog at Evergreen Road
Guthrie, Woody. *Bling blang*
Hakte, Ben. *Julia's house for lost creatures*

Wellington, Monica. *Riki's birdhouse*
Wells, Rosemary. *The house in the mail*
  Stella's Starliner
Weston, Martha. *Tuck's haunted house*
Williams, Brenda. *Home for a tiger, home for a bear*
Winer, Yvonne. *Birds build nests*
Wong, Janet S. *Homegrown house*
Wormell, Christopher. *Blue Rabbit and friends*
Yee, Wong Herbert. *Eek! There's a mouse in the house*
  Mrs. Brown went to town
Yin. *Dear Santa, please come to the 19th floor*
Yum, Hyewon. *This is our house*
Zalben, Jane Breskin. *Hey, Mama Goose*
Zelinsky, Paul O. *The maid and the mouse and the odd-shaped house*
Ziefert, Harriet. *Birdhouse for rent*

Homework

Cali, Davide. *I didn't do my homework because . . .*
Cook, Lisa Broadie. *Peanut butter and homework sandwiches*
deGroat, Diane. *Jingle bells, homework smells*
Heder, Thyra. *The bear report*
Kroll, Virginia L. *Honest Ashley*
Yorinks, Arthur. *Homework*

Homosexuality *see* LGBTQ

Honesty *see* Character traits – honesty

Honey bees *see* Insects – bees

Hope *see* Character traits – hopefulness

Hopefulness *see* Character traits – hopefulness

Horses, rocking *see* Toys – rocking horses

Hospitals

Bemelmans, Ludwig. *Madeline*
Bennett, Howard J. *Harry goes to the hospital*
Bond, Michael. *Paddington Bear goes to the hospital*
Cork, Barbara Taylor. *Katie goes to the hospital*
Cousins, Lucy. *Maisy goes to the hospital*
Curious George makes pancakes
Dooley, Virginia. *Tubes in my ears*
Flanagan, Alice K. *Ask Nurse Pfaff, she'll help you!*
Garhan Attebury, Nancy. *Out and about at the hospital*
Gutman, Anne. *Gaspard in the hospital*
Hapka, Cathy. *Margret and H. A. Rey's Merry Christmas, Curious George*
Hatkoff, Juliana Lee. *Good-bye tonsils*
Jennings, Sharon. *Franklin goes to the hospital*
Lloyd, Sam. *Doctor Meow's big emergency*
Pirner, Connie White. *Even little kids get diabetes*
Rey, Margret. *Curious George goes to the hospital*
Rogers, Fred. *Going to the hospital*
Rosenberg, Maxine B. *Mommy's in the hospital having a baby*
Ross, Tony. *I don't want to go to the hospital!*
Schaefer, Lola M. *Hospital*

Urdahl, Catherine. *Emma's question*
Whybrow, Ian. *Sammy and the robots*
Wild, Margaret. *Going home*
  Mr. Nick's knitting
Zonta, Pat. *Jessica's x-ray*

Hot air balloons *see* Activities – ballooning

Hotels

Cheshire, Marc. *Here comes Eloise!*
Diviny, Sean. *Halloween Motel*
Higgins, Ryan T. *Hotel Bruce*
Hucke, Johannes. *Pip in the Grand Hotel*
Kovacs, Deborah. *Katie Copley*
Paraskevas, Betty. *Chocolate at the Four Seasons*
Pinkwater, Daniel. *At the Hotel Larry*
  Bad bears and a bunny
Stem, J. David. *Kay Thompson's Eloise in Hollywood*
Stevens, Jan Romero. *Carlos digs to China / Carlos excava hasta la China*
Stevenson, James. *The Sea View Hotel*
Thompson, Kay. *Kay Thompson's Eloise*
  Kay Thompson's Eloise at Christmastime
  Kay Thompson's Eloise in Moscow
  Kay Thompson's Eloise takes a bawth
  Kay Thompson's Eloise's what I absolutely love love love
Waber, Bernard. *Do you see a mouse?*
Wojtowycz, David. *Animal antics from 1 to 10*
Yee, Wong Herbert. *Fireman Small, fire down below*

Houses *see* Homes, houses

Hugging

Barnett, Mac. *President Taft is stuck in the bath*
Bond, Felicia. *Big hugs, little hugs*
Cabrera, Jane. *Kitty's cuddles*
Campbell, Scott. *Hug machine*
Chapman, Jane. *No more cuddles!*
Church, Caroline Jayne. *One more hug for Madison*
Clements, Andrew. *Slippers loves to run*
Crandall, Court. *Hugville*
Downing, Julie. *No hugs till Saturday*
Gershator, Phillis. *Time for a hug*
Grambling, Lois G. *T. Rex and the Mother's Day hug*
Henry, Jed. *Cheer up, Mouse!*
Horning, Sandra. *The giant hug*
Isop, Laurie. *How do you hug a porcupine?*
Julian, Sean. *Sloppy wants a hug*
Katz, Karen. *Daddy hugs 1 2 3*
  Mommy hugs
McBratney, Sam. *There, there*
Macdonald, Maryann. *How to hug*
Mack, Jeff. *Who wants a hug?*
Mayhew, James. *Where's my hug?*
Melling, David. *Hugless Douglas*
Oldland, Nicholas. *Big bear hug*
Rowe, John A. *I want a hug*
Ryder, Joanne. *Won't you be my hugaroo?*
Saltzberg, Barney. *Cornelius P. Mud, are you ready for bed?*
Schmid, Paul. *Hugs from Pearl*
Spinelli, Eileen. *Hug a bug*
Stein, David Ezra. *Monster hug!*
Sutton, Benn. *Hedgehug*
Tafuri, Nancy. *Daddy hugs*

Thomas, Louis. *Hug it out!*
Walsh, Joanna. *The perfect hug*
Waring, Zoe. *No hugs for Porcupine*
Warnes, Tim. *Daddy hug*
Wechterowicz, Przemyslaw. *Hug me, please!*
Willis, Jeanne. *Slug needs a hug!*
Wilson, Steve. *Hedgehugs*

Humorous stories

Aardema, Verna. *Oh, Kojo! How could you!*
  What's so funny, Ketu?
  Who's in Rabbit's house?
Abbott, Bud. *Who's on first?*
Agee, Jon. *Nothing*
  The retired kid
Ahlberg, Allan. *The adventures of Bert*
  A bit more Bert
  The Goldilocks variations
  Half a pig
Aliki. *Digging up dinosaurs*
Allard, Harry. *Miss Nelson has a field day*
  Miss Nelson is back
  Miss Nelson is missing!
  Starlight goes to town
  The Stupids die
  The Stupids have a ball
  The Stupids step out
  The Stupids take off
Andersen, Hans Christian. *The emperor's new clothes*, ill. by Virginia Lee Burton
  The emperor's new clothes, ill. by Robert Byrd
  The emperor's new clothes, ill. by Serena Curmi
  The emperor's new clothes, ill. by Charlene DeLage
  The emperor's new clothes, ill. by Jack Delano
  The emperor's new clothes, ill. by Anne Rockwell
  The emperor's new clothes, ill. by Janet Stevens
  The emperor's new clothes, ill. by Eve Tharlet
  The emperor's new clothes: a tale set in China
  The princess and the pea
Anderson, Laurie Halse. *The hair of Zoe Fleefenbacher goes to school*
Andreae, Giles. *Pants*
Angleberger, Tom. *Crankee Doodle*
Apperley, Dawn. *Don't wake the baby*
Armstrong, Jennifer. *Once upon a banana*
Armstrong-Ellis, Carey. *Prudy's problem and how she solved it*
Arnold, Tedd. *Dirty Gert*
  A pet for Fly Guy
Arnosky, Jim. *Outdoors on foot*
Asch, Frank. *The Daily Comet*
  Sand cake
Asher, Sandy. *Chicken story time*
Ashman, Linda. *To the beach!*
Auch, Mary Jane. *Bantam of the opera*
  The buk buk buk festival
  Chickerella
  The plot chickens
  The princess and the pizza
Axelrod, Amy. *They'll believe me when I'm gone*
Azore, Barbara. *Wanda and the frogs*
Bachelet, Gilles. *My cat, the silliest cat in the world*
  When the silliest cat was small
Bakos, Lisa M. *The wrong side of the bed*
Balian, Lorna. *Leprechauns never lie*
Bardhan-Quallen, Sudipta. *Hampire!*
Barnett, Mac. *Extra yarn*
  Oh no!

Oh no! Not again!
  The skunk
  Triangle
  The wolf, the duck, and the mouse
Barrett, Judi. *The marshmallow incident*
  Never take a shark to the dentist and other things not to do
Bell, Cece. *Bee-Wigged*
Biedrzycki, David. *Breaking news: bear alert*
  Breaking news: bears to the rescue
Bingham, Kelly. *Circle, square, Moose*
  Z is for Moose
Birdsall, Jeanne. *My favorite pets*
Black, Michael Ian. *Naked!*
  A pig parade is a terrible idea
  The purple kangaroo
Bloch, Serge. *Butterflies in my stomach and other school hazards*
  You are what you eat
Boldt, Mike. *123 versus ABC*
Border, Terry. *Merry Christmas, Peanut!*
Braun, Eric. *Trust me, Jack's beanstalk stinks*
Bridwell, Norman. *The witch grows up*
Briggs, Raymond. *Jim and the beanstalk*
Broach, Elise. *When dinosaurs came with everything*
Brown, Jeff. *Flat Stanley*, ill. by Scott Nash
  Flat Stanley, ill. by Tomi Ungerer
Brown, Peter. *Children make terrible pets*
Buckley, Michael. *Kel Gilligan's daredevil stunt show*
Burach, Ross. *I am not a chair!*
  There's a giraffe in my soup
Burningham, John. *The shopping basket*
Buzzeo, Toni. *One cool friend*
Byous, Shawn. *Because I stubbed my toe*
Cali, Davide. *I didn't do my homework because . . .*
  The truth about my unbelievable summer . . .
Calmenson, Stephanie. *Oopsy, teacher!*
Campbell, K. G. *Dylan the villain*
Carle, Eric. *The nonsense show*
Carroll, Lewis. *Jabberwocky*
Castle, Caroline. *Naughty!*
Cazet, Denys. *Bob and Tom*
  Elvis the rooster almost goes to heaven
Chaconas, Dori. *Don't slam the door!*
Charlip, Remy. *"Mother, mother I feel sick"*
Child, Lauren. *What planet are you from Clarice Bean?*
Christelow, Eileen. *The desperate dog writes again*
  Letters from a desperate dog
  Where's the big bad wolf?
Coffelt, Nancy. *Catch that baby!*
Cole, Babette. *Truelove*
Cole, Brock. *Buttons*
Collington, Peter. *Clever cat*
Collins, Ross. *Dear Vampa*
Conway, David. *The great fairy tale disaster*
  The great nursery rhyme disaster
Cooper, Helen. *Dog biscuit*
Corey, Shana. *First graders from Mars: Horus's horrible day*
  First graders from Mars: Nergal and the Great Space Race
  First graders from Mars: Tera, star student
  First graders from Mars: The problem with Pelly
Cosentino, Ralph. *The marvelous misadventures of — Fun-Boy*
Coudray, Jean-Luc. *A goofy guide to penguins*
Cox, Judy. *Happy birthday, Mrs. Millie!*
  Pick a pumpkin, Mrs. Millie!

Crimi, Carolyn. *The Louds move in!*
Crisp, Marty. *Totally polar*
Cronin, Doreen. *Duck for President*
   M.O.M. (Mom Operating Manual)
Cutbill, Andy. *The cow that laid an egg*
   First week at cow school
Czekaj, Jef. *A call for a new alphabet*
   Cat secrets
Daugherty, James Henry. *Andy and the lion*
Davis, Katie. *Mabel the Tooth Fairy and how she got
   her job*
Day, Alexandra. *The fairy dogfather*
Daywalt, Drew. *The legend of rock paper scissors*
De Beer, Hans. *Oh no, Ono!*
DeFelice, Cynthia C. *Nelly May has her say*
   One potato, two potato
Demas, Corinne. *Always in trouble*
dePaola, Tomie. *Bill and Pete*
   Merry Christmas, Strega Nona
   Strega Nona
   Strega Nona meets her match
   Strega Nona's harvest
   Strega Nona's magic lessons
De Regniers, Beatrice Schenk. *May I bring a friend?*
Diesen, Deborah. *The barefooted, bad-tempered baby
   brigade*
Dillon, Jana. *Lucky O'Leprechaun comes to America*
DiPucchio, Kelly. *Dog days of school*
   Zombie in love
   Zombie in love 2 + 1
Ditchfield, Christin. *Cowlick!*
Dolan, Elys. *Nuts in space*
   Weasels
Donaldson, Julia. *Tyrannosaurus Drip*
Doodler, Todd H. *Veggies with wedgies*
Dormer, Frank W. *The sword in the stove*
Dorros, Alex. *Número uno*
Dorros, Arthur. *City chicken*
   When the pigs took over
Downard, Barry. *The Race of the Century*
Downs, Mike. *Pig giggles and rabbit rhymes*
Duffield, Katy. *Farmer McPeepers and his missing
   milk cows*
Durant, Alan. *Burger boy*
Duvoisin, Roger Antoine. *Petunia*
Edwards, Pamela Duncan. *Muldoon*
   Princess Pigtoria and the pea
Edwards, Wallace. *The extinct files*
Egan, Tim. *Dodsworth in New York*
Ehlert, Lois. *Rrralph*
Elliott, David. *Hazel Nutt, Alien Hunter*
   Hazel Nutt, mad scientist
Elliott, George. *The boy who loved bananas*
Elsdale, Bob. *Mac side up*
Ernst, Lisa Campbell. *Goldilocks returns*
Escoffier, Michael. *Where's the baboon?*
Falatko, Julie. *Snappsy the alligator (did not ask to be
   in this book)*
Feiffer, Jules. *Bark, George*
Feiffer, Kate. *My mom is trying to ruin my life*
Ferber, Brenda A. *The yuckiest, stinkiest, best
   Valentine ever*
Fergus, Maureen. *The day Santa stopped believing in
   Harold*
Fisher, Carolyn. *A twisted tale*
Flake, Sharon G. *You are not a cat!*
Fletcher, Tom. *The dinosaur that pooped a planet!*
Foreman, George. *Let George do it!*

Fox, Diane. *The cat, the dog, Little Red, the exploding
   eggs, the wolf, and Grandma*
Fox, Mem. *A particular cow*
Frank, John. *The toughest cowboy, Or, How the Wild
   West was tamed*
Frazee, Marla. *A couple of boys have the best week ever*
French, Jackie. *Pete the sheep-sheep*
Gaiman, Neil. *Crazy hair*
Garriel, Barbara S. *I know a shy fellow who swallowed
   a cello*
Gay, Marie-Louise. *Good morning Sam*
   Short stories for little monsters
Gerstein, Mordicai. *You can't have too many friends!*
Gill, Timothy. *Flip and Fin: super sharks to the rescue!*
Goode, Diane. *Diane Goode's book of silly stories and
   songs*
Goodhart, Pippa. *Arthur's tractor*
Graber, Janet. *Jacob and the polar bears*
Gravett, Emily. *Wolves*
Green, Stephanie. *Not just another moose*
Greenberg, David. *Crocs!*
Grey, Mini. *The adventures of the dish and the spoon*
Griffin, Kitty. *Cowboy Sam and those confounded
   secrets*
   The foot-stomping adventures of Clementine Sweet
Grimm, Jacob and Wilhelm. *As luck would have it*
Grossman, Bill. *Timothy Tunny swallowed a bunny*
Hale, Bruce. *Snoring Beauty*
Hall, Michael. *Frankencrayon*
Hammill, Matt. *Sir Reginald's logbook*
Hanson, Warren. *It's Monday, Mrs. Jolly Bones!*
Hapka, Cathy. *Margret and H. A. Rey's Merry
   Christmas, Curious George*
Harper, Lee. *The Emperor's cool clothes*
Hart, Christopher. *Merwin, master of disguise*
Hawkes, Kevin. *The wicked big toddlah*
   The wicked big toddlah goes to New York
Hayward, Linda. *Pepe and Papa*
Heide, Florence Parry. *Always listen to your mother*
   How to be a hero
Helakoski, Leslie. *Big chickens fly the coop*
Helmer, Marilyn. *Critter riddles*
Helquist, Brett. *Roger, the jolly pirate*
Herzog, Kenny. *Phil Pickle*
Hicks, Barbara Jean. *The secret life of Walter Kitty*
Himmelman, John. *Cows to the rescue*
   Duck to the rescue
Hoberman, Mary Ann. *"It's simple," said Simon*
Hodgkinson, Leigh. *Goldilocks and just one bear*
Holt, Kimberly Willis. *Dinner with the Highbrows*
Holub, Joan. *Little red writing*
   Zero the hero
Hornsey, Chris. *Why do I have to eat off the floor?*
Horowitz, Dave. *Humpty Dumpty climbs again*
Hort, Lenny. *Tie your socks and clap your feet*
Huget, Jennifer LaRue. *How to clean your room in
   ten easy steps*
Hutchins, Pat. *Clocks and more clocks*
   Don't forget the bacon!
   Rosie's walk
I invited a dragon to dinner
Isaacs, Anne. *Meanwhile, back at the ranch*
Jackson, Alison. *I know an old lady who swallowed
   a pie*
Jagtenberg, Yvonne. *Jack the wolf*
James, Simon. *Baby Brains and RoboMom*
Jeffers, Oliver. *Stuck*
Jennings, Sharon. *C'mere, boy!*
Jobling, Curtis. *Frankenstein's cat*

The three silly billies
Under a pig tree
The web files
Parachini, Jodie. *This is a serious book*
Parish, Herman. *Amelia Bedelia's first apple pie*
   Amelia Bedelia's first day of school
   Amelia Bedelia's first field trip
   Amelia Bedelia's first valentine
   Go west, Amelia Bedelia!
Parkinson, Curtis. *Emily's eighteen aunts*
Parr, Todd. *Underwear do's and don'ts*
Parsley, Elise. *If you ever want to bring a circus to the library, don't!*
   If you ever want to bring a piano to the beach, don't!
   If you ever want to bring an alligator to school, don't!
Passen, Lisa. *The incredible shrinking teacher*
Patton, Julia. *The very very very long dog*
Pearlman, Robb. *Groundhog's day off*
Pearson, Peter. *How to eat an airplane*
Pearson, Tracey Campbell. *Bob*
Peet, Bill. *Big bad Bruce*
   Buford the little bighorn
   Chester the worldly pig
   Countdown to Christmas
   Cowardly Clyde
   Eli
   Hubert's hair-raising adventures
   Huge Harold
   Jennifer and Josephine
   Jethro and Joel were a troll
   Kermit the hermit
   Merle the high flying squirrel
   Randy's dandy lions
Pennypacker, Sara. *Meet the Dullards*
Perl, Erica S. *Chicken Butt's back!*
Perret, Delphine. *Pedro and George*
Pichon, Liz. *The three horrid little pigs*
Pilkey, Dav. *The Dumb Bunnies*
   The Dumb Bunnies' Easter
   The Dumb Bunnies go to the zoo
   Make way for Dumb Bunnies
   The Silly Gooses
Pilutti, Deb. *Ten rules of being a superhero*
Pinkney, Brian. *The adventures of sparrowboy*
Pinkwater, Daniel. *At the Hotel Larry*
   Bad bear detectives
   Bad bears and a bunny
   Bad bears go visiting
   Bad bears in the big city
   Bongo Larry
   Dancing Larry
   I am the dog
   Ice-cream Larry
   The picture of Morty and Ray
   Sleepover Larry
   Young Larry
Plourde, Lynn. *Grandpappy snippy snappies*
   Only cows allowed!
   Pigs in the mud in the middle of the rud
Polacco, Patricia. *In Enzo's splendid gardens*
Portis, Antoinette. *Froodle*
Potter, Beatrix. *The tale of Tom Kitten*
Prelutsky, Jack. *The baby uggs are hatching*
   The queen of Eene
   The Random House book of poetry for children
   The snopp on the sidewalk and other poems
Primavera, Elise. *Thumb love*
Prince, Joshua. *I saw an ant in a parking lot*
   I saw an ant on the railroad track

Pulver, Robin. *Mrs. Toggle's zipper*
Rader, Laura. *Santa's new suit*
Ransom, Jeanie Franz. *What do parents do?*
   (. . . When you're not home)
Raschka, Chris. *Cowy cow*
   Crabby crab
Rausch, Molly. *My cold went on vacation*
Redeker, Kent. *Don't squish the sasquatch!*
Reeve, Rosie. *Training Tallulah*
Regan, Dian Curtis. *How do you know it's Halloween?*
Regan, Lara Jo. *What is Mr. Winkle?*
Reichert, Amy. *Take your mama to work today*
Reiss, Mike. *Late for school*
   Merry un-Christmas
   Santa claustrophobia
Rennert, Laura Joy. *Buying, training and caring for your dinosaur*
Rex, Michael. *Furious George goes bananas*
   Goodnight goon
   You can do anything, Daddy!
Rey, H. A. *Cecily G and the nine monkeys*
   Curious George
   Curious George gets a medal
   Curious George rides a bike
   Curious George takes a job
   Elizabite
   The original Curious George
Rey, Margret. *Billy's picture*
   Curious George flies a kite
   Curious George goes to the hospital
Richardson, Bill. *But if they do*
Robinson, Bruce. *The obvious elephant*
Robinson, Fiona. *What animals really like*
Robinson, Michelle. *A beginner's guide to bear spotting*
   The forgetful knight
   How to wash a woolly mammoth
   There's a lion in my cornflakes
   What to do if an elephant stands on your foot
Root, Phyllis. *Rattletrap car*
Rosen, Michael. *Howler*
Rosenberg, Madelyn. *The Schmutzy Family*
Rosenthal, Amy Krouse. *Chopsticks*
Rosenthal, Marc. *Phooey!*
Rosoff, Meg. *Jumpy Jack and Googily*
   Wild boars cook
Rovetch, Lissa. *Ook the book*
Rubin, Adam. *Big bad bubble*
Salley, Coleen. *Epossumondas*
   Epossumondas saves the day
Samuels, Barbara. *Dolores meets her match*
   Duncan and Dolores
   Happy Valentine's Day, Dolores
Sandburg, Carl. *The Huckabuck family and how they raised popcorn in Nebraska and quit and came back*
Sanders, Rob. *Rodzilla*
Sattler, Jennifer. *Chick 'n' Pug: the love pug*
Sauer, Tammi. *Chicken dance*
Savage, Stephen. *The mixed-up truck*
Sayre, April Pulley. *Noodle Man*
Scheer, Julian. *Rain makes applesauce*
Schneider, Christine M. *Horace P. Tuttle, magician extraordinaire*
Schneider, Howie. *Fast 'n Snappy*
Schnitzler, Pattie L. *Widdermaker*
Scieszka, Jon. *Robot Zot!*
Scotton, Rob. *Splat the cat*

Hurrying *see* Behavior – hurrying

Hygiene *see also* Character traits – cleanliness; Health & fitness

Bernheimer, Kate. *The girl who wouldn't brush her hair*

Brennan, Eileen. *Dirtball Pete*
Coats, Lucy. *Captain Beastlie's pirate party*
Fox, Lee. *Ella Kazoo will not brush her hair*
Garelli, Cristina. *Farm friends clean up*
Kelly, Mij. *Achoo!*
Langreuter, Jutta. *Little Bear brushes his teeth*
McNaulty, Stacy. *101 reasons why I'm not taking a bath*
Palatini, Margie. *Gorgonzola*
Puttock, Simon. *Squeaky clean*
Spector, Todd. *How to pee: potty training for boys*
    How to pee: potty training for girls
Vestergaard, Hope. *Potty animals*
Weinert, Matthias. *No bath, no cake!*

Identity *see* Self-concept

Illness

Alda, Arlene. *Iris has a virus*
Appelt, Kathi. *Mogie*
Bauer, Sepp. *The Christmas rose*
Bedford, David. *Shaggy Dog and the terrible itch*
Bemelmans, Ludwig. *Madeline's Christmas*
Bennett, Howard J. *Harry goes to the hospital*
Berger, Melvin. *Germs make me sick!*
Butler, Dori Hillestad. *My grandpa had a stroke*
Cannon, Janell. *Little Yau*
Carlson, Nancy. *Sometimes you barf*
Carter, Alden R. *Seeing things my way*
Charlip, Remy. *"Mother, mother I feel sick"*
Coerr, Eleanor. *Sadako*
Colón, Raúl. *Draw!*
Cork, Barbara Taylor. *Katie goes to the hospital*
Cowan, Charlotte. *Peeper has a fever*
    Sadie's sore throat
Cowell, Cressida. *Hiccup the seasick Viking*
dePaola, Tomie. *Now one foot, now the other*
Dewdney, Anna. *Llama Llama home with Mama*
Dooley, Virginia. *Tubes in my ears*
Evans, Lezlie. *Finding Christmas*
Finchler, Judy. *Miss Malarkey won't be in today*
Gaiman, Neil. *Chu's day*
    Chu's first day of school
Garhan Attebury, Nancy. *Out and about at the hospital*
Gibbons, Gail. *Say woof!*
Glaser, Jason. *Pinkeye*
Gordon, Sharon. *Pinkeye*
Gray, Kes. *The "Get well soon" book*
Greene, Rhonda Gowler. *Barnyard song*
Gretz, Susanna. *Teddy bears cure a cold*
Hobbie, Holly. *Toot and Puddle: wish you were here*
Hull, Rod. *Mr. Betts and Mr. Potts*
Inns, Christopher. *Next! please*
Jeffs, Stephanie. *Jenny*
Jennings, Sharon. *Franklin goes to the hospital*
Keane, Dave. *Sloppy Joe*

Ketteman, Helen. *If Beaver had a fever*
Kroll, Steven. *The big bunny and the Easter eggs*
Kroll, Virginia L. *Pink paper swans*
Lobel, Anita. *Taking care of Mama Rabbit*
Louie, Therese On. *Raymond's perfect present*
Lyon, George Ella. *Cecil's story*
MacDonald, Amy. *Rachel Fister's blister*
McKissack, Patricia C. *Precious and the Boo Hag*
MacLachlan, Patricia. *The sick day*
McPhail, David. *The bear's toothache*
Madonna. *Yakov and the seven thieves*
Maier, Inger. *Ben's flying flowers*
Marshall, James. *Yummers!*
Martin, Jacqueline Briggs. *Chicken joy on Redbean Road*
Miller, Pat. *Substitute Groundhog*
Milway, Katie Smith. *Mimi's village and how basic health care transformed it*
Modarressi, Mitra. *Taking care of Mama*
Murphy, Jill. *Mr. Large in charge*
Neitzel, Shirley. *I'm not feeling well today*
Newsome, Jill. *Dream dancer*
Nimmo, Jenny. *Esmeralda and the children next door*
Oelschlager, Vanita. *I came from the water*
Oppenheim, Shulamith Levey. *Ali and the magic stew*
Peet, Mal. *Cloud tea monkeys*
Perkins, Lynne Rae. *The broken cat*
Raschka, Chris. *The purple balloon*
Ray, Jane. *The dollhouse fairy*
Rees, Douglas. *Jeannette Claus saves Christmas*
Reider, Katja. *The big little sneeze*
Rockliff, Mara. *Chik chak Shabbat*
Rogers, Fred. *Going to the hospital*
Rohmer, Harriet. *Atariba and Niguayona*
Rose, Naomi C. *Tashi and the Tibetan flower cure*
Rosenfeld, Dina Herman. *Get well soon*
Ross, Tony. *I feel sick!*
Rylant, Cynthia. *Little Whistle's medicine*
    Silver packages
Say, Allen. *A river dream*
Schick, Eleanor. *Mama*
Schubert, Leda. *The Princess of Borscht*
Scotton, Rob. *Splat says thank you!*
Singer, Marilyn. *Boo hoo boo-boo*
Soros, Barbara. *Tenzin's deer*
Soto, Gary. *Chato goes cruisin'*
Spalding, Andrea. *It's raining, it's pouring*
Stead, Philip C. *A sick day for Amos McGee*
Stroud, Bettye. *Down home at Miss Dessa's*
Tankard, Jeremy. *Boo hoo Bird*
Thurber, James. *Many moons*, ill. by Marc Simont
    Many moons, ill. by Louis Slobodkin
Urdahl, Catherine. *Emma's question*
Vigna, Judith. *I wish my daddy didn't drink so much*
Wells, Rosemary. *The island light*
    A visit to Dr. Duck
Whybrow, Ian. *Sammy and the robots*
Wild, Margaret. *Mr. Nick's knitting*
Williams, Vera B. *Music, music for everyone*
Wilson, Karma. *Bear feels sick*
Winter, Jeanette. *Henri's scissors*
Yolen, Jane. *How do dinosaurs get well soon?*
Zonta, Pat. *Jessica's x-ray*

Illness – AIDS

Beake, Lesley. *Home now*
Haring, Kay A. *Keith Haring*

Wiener, Lori S., et al *Be a friend: children who live with HIV speak*

Illness – alcoholism

Langsen, Richard C. *When someone in the family drinks too much*

Illness – allergies

Berger, Lou. *Dream dog*
Berger, Melvin. *Why I sneeze, shiver, hiccup, and yawn*
Fliess, Sue. *A gluten-free birthday for me!*
Geras, Adèle. *The Cats of Cuckoo Square, Geejay the Hero*
Harrison, Troon. *Aaron's awful allergies*
Havill, Juanita. *Jamaica is thankful*
Howe, James. *Horace and Morris say cheese (which makes Dolores sneeze!)*
Koehler, Lana Wayne. *Ah-choo!*
Koster, Gloria. *The peanut-free cafe*
McClure, Wendy. *The princess and the peanut allergy*
Nichols, Lori. *Maple and Willow's Christmas tree*
Pulver, Robin. *Christmas kitten, home at last*
Singleton, Linda Joy. *Snow dog, sand dog*

Illness – Alzheimer's

Abeele, Veronique van den. *Still my Grandma*
Acheson, Alison. *Grandpa's music*
Altman, Linda Jacobs. *Singing with Momma Lou*
Gerdner, Linda. *Grandfather's story cloth / Yawg daim paj ntaub dab neeg*
Van Laan, Nancy. *Forget me not*

Illness – asthma

Berger, Melvin. *Why I sneeze, shiver, hiccup, and yawn*
Carter, Alden R. *I'm tougher than asthma!*
Golding, Theresa Martin. *Abby's asthma and the big race*
Gordon, Sharon. *Asthma*
Hurwitz, Johanna. *Mighty Monty*
Matthies, Janna. *Peter, the knight with asthma*
Thomas, Pat. *Why is it so hard to breathe?*

Illness – cancer

Aigner-Clark, Julie. *You are the best medicine*
Bridge, Chris. *Andrew's story*
Lin, Grace. *Robert's snowflakes*
Matthies, Janna. *The goodbye cancer garden*
Moore-Mallinos, Jennifer. *Mom has cancer!*
Napoli, Donna Jo. *Flamingo dream*
North, Sherry. *Champ's story*
Numeroff, Laura Joffe. *The hope tree*
Polacco, Patricia. *Betty Doll*
  The lemonade club
Ries, Lori. *Punk wig*
Sliwerski, Jessica Reid. *Cancer hates kisses*
Tinkham, Kelly A. *Hair for Mama*
Tusa, Tricia. *Bunnies in my head*
Watters, Debbie, et al. *Where's Mom's hair?*
Winthrop, Elizabeth. *Promises*

Illness – chicken pox

Anderson, Laurie Halse. *Turkey pox*

Brown, Marc. *Arthur's chicken pox*
Cazet, Denys. *The octopus*
Dealey, Erin. *Goldie Locks has chicken pox*
Kelley, True. *I've got chicken pox*
Rosenberry, Vera. *When Vera was sick*
Smith, Maggie. *Dear Daisy, get well soon*

Illness – cold (disease)

Becker, Bonny. *The sniffles for Bear*
Breznak, Irene. *Sneezy Louise*
Cowan, Charlotte. *Katie caught a cold*
Duffield, Katy S. *Aliens get the sniffles too! ahhh-choo!*
Emmett, Jonathan. *The best gift of all*
Hest, Amy. *Guess who, Baby Duck*
Krall, Dan. *Sick Simon*
Mandel, Peter. *Zoo ah-choooo*
Mayer, Pamela. *The Grandma cure*
Posthuma, Sieb. *Benny*
Rausch, Molly. *My cold went on vacation*
Scanlon, Elizabeth Garton. *Bob, not Bob!*
Slate, Joseph. *Miss Bindergarten stays home from kindergarten*
Van Leeuwen, Jean. *Chicken soup*

Illness – dementia

Cummings, Phil. *Newspaper hats*
Levine, Arthur A. *What a beautiful morning*

Illness – diabetes

Carter, Alden R. *I'm tougher than diabetes!*
De Anda, Diane. *A day without sugar / Un dia sin azucar*
Pirner, Connie White. *Even little kids get diabetes*
Ruiz-Flores, Lupe. *Alicia's fruity drinks / Las aguas frescas de Alicia*

Illness – epilepsy

Lears, Laurie. *Becky the brave*

Illness – influenza

Bateman, Teresa. *Farm flu*
Reynolds, Marilynn. *The name of the child*

Illness – mental illness

Day, Marie. *Edward the "crazy man"*
Niner, Holly L. *Mr. Worry*
Sterling, Cheryl. *Some bunny to talk to*

Illness – poliomyelitis

Chaconas, Dori. *Dancing with Katya*
De Anda, Diane. *Dancing Miranda / Baila, Miranda, baila*

Illness – tonsillectomy

Hatkoff, Juliana Lee. *Good-bye tonsils*

Imagination

Abercrombie, Barbara. *The show-and-tell lion*
Adlerman, Daniel. *Africa calling*
Agee, Jon. *The incredible painting of Felix Clousseau*
Ahlberg, Allan. *The pencil*

I'll catch the moon
You are here
Crisp, Marty. *Totally polar*
Crumpacker, Bunny. *Alexander's pretending day*
Cumming, Hannah. *The red boat*
DaCosta, Barbara. *Mighty Moby*
Nighttime Ninja
Dahl, Michael. *Bedtime for Batman*
Good morning, Superman
Daly, Cathleen. *Prudence wants a pet*
Davey, Owen. *Night Knight*
Dematons, Charlotte. *Let's go*
Devernay, Laetitia. *The conductor*
De Vries, Maggie. *How sleep found Tabitha*
Dewan, Ted. *Baby gets the zapper*
DiPucchio, Kelly. *Super Manny stands up!*
Diterlizzi, Angela. *I wanna be a cowgirl*
DiTerlizzi, Tony. *Jimmy Zangwow's out-of-this-world,*
moon pie adventure
Docherty, Thomas. *To the beach*
Dodd, Emma. *What pet to get?*
Dodd, Lynley. *A dragon in a wagon*
Doerrfeld, Cori. *Maggie and Wendel*
Donahue, Shari Faden. *The zebra-striped whale with*
the polka-dot tail
Donaldson, Julia. *The fish who cried wolf*
Dornbusch, Erica. *Finding Kate's shoes*
Drawson, Blair. *All along the river*
Dubosarsky, Ursula. *Rex*
Dunbar, Polly. *Dog Blue*
Flyaway Katie
Dunnick, Regan. *Sweet dreams, Douglas*
Ehlert, Lois. *Rain fish*
Ellery, Amanda. *If I had a dragon*
If I were a jungle animal
Enersen, Adele. *Vincent and the night*
Engler, Michael. *Elephantastic!*
Escoffier, Michael. *The day I lost my superpowers*
Esenwine, Matt Forrest. *Flashlight night*
Ets, Marie Hall. *In the forest*
Fagan, Cary. *Mr. Zinger's hat*
Faller, Regis. *The adventures of Polo*
Polo
Polo and the dragon
Falwell, Cathryn. *Word wizard*
Fancher, Lou. *Star climbing*
Fearnley, Jan. *A special something*
Fergus, Maureen. *Buddy and Earl*
Buddy and Earl go exploring
Fitzpatrick, Marie-Louise. *I'm a tiger, too!*
Fogliano, Julie. *If you want to see a whale*
Fosberry, Jennifer. *Isabella*
Isabella star of the story
Fox, Christyan. *Astronaut PiggyWiggy*
Fire fighter PiggyWiggy
Fox, Mem. *Tell me about your day today*
Freedman, Deborah. *Scribble*
Freeman, Don. *Quiet! There's a canary in the library*
Fuge, Charles. *I know a rhino*
Gammell, Stephen. *Mudkin*
Gardiner, Lindsey. *Here come Poppy and Max*
When Poppy and Max grow up
Gardner, Sally. *Mama, don't go out tonight*
Garton, Sam. *Otter in space*
Gay, Marie-Louise. *Any questions?*
Caramba
Short stories for little monsters
When Stella was very, very small
George, Lindsay Barrett. *My bunny and me*

Geras, Adèle. *The nutcracker*
Gerstein, Mordicai. *A book*
The first drawing
How to bicycle to the moon to plant sunflowers
Gibala-Broxholm, Scott. *Maddie's monster dad*
Gigot, Jami. *Mae and the moon*
Gill, Deirdre. *Outside*
Gilmore, Rachna. *Making grizzle grow*
Glassman, Peter. *My dad's job*
Gleeson, Libby. *Clancy and Millie and the very fine*
house
Glenn, Sharlee. *Just what Mama needs*
Godwin, Laura. *Little white dog*
Gomi, Taro. *Over the ocean*
Gorbachev, Valeri. *Turtle's penguin day*
Graham, Bob. *Max*
Gravett, Emily. *Spells*
Gray, Nigel. *Time to play!*
Greenfield, Eloise. *The friendly four*
I can draw a weeposaur and other dinosaurs
Gregory, Nan. *Wild Girl and Gran*
Grey, Mini. *Traction Man meets Turbodog*
Griff. *Shark-mad Stanley*
Gwynne, Fred. *A chocolate moose for dinner*
A little pigeon toad
Hague, Michael. *The nutcracker*
Hall, Michael. *It's an orange aardvark!*
Hamburg, Jennifer. *A moose that says mooooooooooo*
Hammill, Matt. *Sir Reginald's logbook*
Handford, Martin. *Where's Waldo? The fantastic*
journey
Hanson, Faye. *The wonder*
Harper, Charise Mericle. *The best birthday ever!*
Superlove
Harper, Jamie. *Miles to go*
Harper, Jessica. *Nora's room*
Harris, Robie H. *Mail Harry to the moon!*
Maybe a bear ate it!
Hayles, Marsha. *He saves the day*
Heap, Sue. *Danny's drawing book*
What shall we play?
Heidbreder, Robert. *I wished for a unicorn*
Heide, Florence Parry. *How to be a hero*
Henkes, Kevin. *Little white rabbit*
My garden
Hennessy, B. G. *The dinosaur who lived in my*
backyard
Hesselberth, Joyce. *Shape shift*
Hicks, Barbara Jean. *Monsters don't eat broccoli*
Hindley, Judy. *Rosy's visitors*
Hines, Anna Grossnickle. *Gramma's walk*
I am a backhoe
I am a Tyrannosaurus
Hoffman, Eric. *A dark, dark cave*
Hoffmann, E. T. A. *The nutcracker,* ill. by Renée
Graef
The nutcracker, ill. by Alison Jay
The nutcracker, ill. by Peter Malone
The nutcracker, ill. by Niroot Puttapipat
The nutcracker, ill. by Maurice Sendak
The nutcracker, ill. by Lisbeth Zwerger
The Nutcracker and the Mouse King
The nutcracker ballet
Hole, Stian. *Anna's heaven*
Honey, Elizabeth. *That's not a daffodil!*
Hoppe, Paul. *Hat*
Horácek, Petr. *My elephant*
Hoshino, Felicia. *Sora and the cloud*
Hughes, Susan. *Earth to Audrey*

Huneck, Stephen. *Sally gets a job*
Husband, Amy. *Dear Teacher*
Hutchins, Hazel. *Snap!*
Ichikawa, Satomi. *Come fly with me*
    My little train
Irwin, Michael. *Bears in my bed*
Ismail, Yasmeen. *Imagine that!*
Jackson, Ellen. *The seven seas*
James, Simon. *Dear Mr. Blueberry*
Janni, Rebecca. *Every cowgirl needs a horse*
Jarka, Jeff. *Love that kitty!*
    Love that puppy!
Jeffers, Oliver. *A child of books*
Jenkins, Emily. *Daffodil, crocodile*
    Princessland
Jennings, Sharon. *The happily ever afternoon*
Jeram, Anita. *I love my little storybook*
Jessell, Tim. *Falcon*
Jeyaveeran, Ruth. *The road to Mumbai*
Johnson, Angela. *Lily Brown's paintings*
    Lottie Paris lives here
Johnson, Crockett. *Harold and the purple crayon*
    Harold at the North Pole
    Magic beach
    A picture for Harold's room
Johnson, D. B. *Henry climbs a mountain*
Jonas, Ann. *The trek*
Jones, Sylvie. *Who's in the tub?*
Joosse, Barbara. *Roawr!*
Joyce, William. *Billy's booger*
    Jack Frost
    The Man in the Moon
Jukes, Mavis. *You're a bear*
Kamish, Daniel. *Diggy Dan*
Kanninen, Barbara. *A story with pictures*
Kay, Julia. *Gulliver Snip*
Keane, Claire. *Once upon a cloud*
Keats, Ezra Jack. *Dreams*
    The trip
Kellogg, Steven. *Ralph's secret weapon*
Kenney, Sean. *Cool cars and trucks*
    Cool castles
    Cool city
    Cool creations in 101 pieces
    Cool creations in 35 pieces
Kirk, Daniel. *Honk honk! Beep beep!*
Knapman, Timothy. *Dinosaurs don't have bedtimes!*
    A monster moved in!
Knight, Hilary. *Hilary Knight's the owl and the pussy-cat*
Kramer, Jackie Azúa. *The green umbrella*
Krauss, Ruth. *A very special house*
Kroll, Steven. *Oh, what a Thanksgiving!*
    The Tyrannosaurus game
Kroll, Virginia L. *Faraway drums*
Kruusval, Catarina. *Franny's friends*
Kuefler, Joseph. *Beyond the pond*
Kwon, Yoon-duck. *My cat copies me*
Laden, Nina. *Are we there yet?*
Lamb, Rosy. *Paul meets Bernadette*
Lammle, Leslie. *Princess wannabe*
Landa, Norbert. *The great monster hunt*
Landry, Leo. *Eat your peas, Ivy Louise!*
Landström, Lena. *Pom and Pim*
LaRochelle, David. *It's a tiger*
    1+1=5
Larsen, Andrew. *The imaginary garden*
Lawson, Dorie McCullough. *Tex*
Lawson, Janet. *Audrey and Barbara*

Lazo, Caroline. *Someday when my cat can talk*
Lee, Suzy. *Shadow*
Lehman, Barbara. *Museum trip*
    Rainstorm
    The secret box
    Trainstop
Lehrhaupt, Adam. *Chicken in school*
    Chicken in space
Leiter, Richard. *The flying hand of Marco B.*
Leroy, Jean. *Stripes the tiger*
Levert, Mireille. *An island in the soup*
    The princess who had almost everything
Lewis, Anne Margaret. *Fly blanky fly*
    Puddle jumpers
Liao, Jimmy. *The sound of colors*
Light, Steve. *Zephyr takes flight*
Lionni, Leo. *Let's make rabbits*
Lithgow, John. *Carnival of the animals*
    I'm a manatee
Liwska, Renata. *Red wagon*
Ljungkvist, Laura. *Follow the line*
    Follow the line through the house
London, Jonathan. *Here comes Doctor Hippo*
    Here comes firefighter Hippo
    My big rig
Long, Melinda. *How I became a pirate*
Loth, Sebastian. *Zelda the Varigoose*
Loux, Lynn C. *The day I could fly*
Lovell, Patty. *Have fun, Molly Lou Melon*
Lucas, David. *Nutmeg*
    Something to do
Luenn, Nancy. *Nessa's story*
Luján, Jorge. *Moví la mano / I moved my hand*
Luyken, Corinna. *The book of mistakes*
Lynn, Sarah. *1-2-3 va-va-vroom!*
Lyon, George Ella. *Who came down that road?*
McAllister, Angela. *Harry's box*
McCarthy, Meghan. *The adventures of Patty and the big red bus*
McCarty, Peter. *Chloe*
    Moon plane
McClure, Nikki. *In*
McCourt, Lisa. *Good night, Princess Pruney Toes*
    Happy Halloween, Stinky Face
    I love you, Stinky Face
    It's time for school, Stinky Face
    Merry Christmas, Stinky Face
McGhee, Alison. *Song of middle C*
McKay, Hilary. *Pirates ahoy!*
Mackintosh, David. *Lucky*
McLerran, Alice. *Roxaboxen*
McNaughton, Colin. *Not last night but the night before*
McNeil, Florence. *Sail away*
McPhail, David. *Andrew draws*
    Boy on the brink
    Edward and the pirates
    Edward in the jungle
    Emma in charge
    Moony B. Finch, fastest draw in the West
    Pig Pig and the magic photo album
    Pig Pig rides
    Tinker and Tom and the Star Baby
McQuinn, Anna. *Lola loves stories*
Mahy, Margaret. *The green bath*
    The man from the land of Fandango
Maizes, Sarah. *On my way to bed*
    On my way to the bath
Maloney, Brenna. *Ready Rabbit gets ready!*

Manceau, Edouard. *Windblown*
Manushkin, Fran. *The shivers in the fridge*
Marlowe, Pete. *One Arabian morning*
Marshall, James. *George and Martha 'round and 'round*
Martin, Emily Winfield. *Day dreamers*
Martin, Rafe. *Will's mammoth*
Marzollo, Jean. *I spy fantasy*
 Pretend you're a cat
Mayer, Mercer. *The bravest knight*
Mayhew, James. *Ella Bella ballerina and The Nutcracker*
 Katie and the sunflowers
Mazer, Anne. *The salamander room*
Melanson, Luc. *Topsy-Turvy Town*
Menchin, Scott. *Harry goes to dog school*
 What if everything had legs?
Merz, Jennifer J. *Playground day*
Milgrim, David. *Cows can't fly*
Minor, Wendell. *How big could your pumpkin grow?*
Miranda, Anne. *Beep! beep!*
Miyakoshi, Akiko. *The storm*
Moers, Hermann. *Rufus and Max*
Moore, Jodi. *When a dragon moves in*
Morris, Ann. *Play*
Morris, Bob. *Crispin the Terrible*
Morstad, Julie. *How to*
Most, Bernard. *If the dinosaurs came back*
Mould, Wendy. *Ants in my pants*
Murguia, Bethanie Deeney. *Princess! Fairy!*
 Ballerina!
 The too-scary story
 Zoe's jungle
Murphy, Stuart J. *Jack the builder*
Myers, Christopher. *My pen*
Na, Il Sung. *The thingamabob*
Neitzel, Shirley. *I'm taking a trip on my train*
Ness, Evaline. *Sam, Bangs, and moonshine*
Neubecker, Robert. *Beasty bath*
 What little boys are made of
Newman, Nanette. *What will you be, Grandma?*
Nickle, John. *TV Rex*
Niemann, Christoph. *That's how!*
Norwich, William D. *Molly and the magic dress*
Numeroff, Laura Joffe. *Chimps don't wear glasses*
O'Connor, George. *Ker-splash!*
Offill, Jenny. *While you were napping*
O'Hara, Natalia. *Hortense and the shadow*
Ohi, Debbie Ridpath. *Sam and Eva*
Ohi, Ruth. *The couch was a castle*
O'Leary, Sara. *This is Sadie*
 When you were small
O'Malley, Kevin. *Straight to the pole*
Orr, Wendy. *The princess and her panther*
Palacio, R. J. *We're all wonders*
Palatini, Margie. *Zak's lunch*
Pallotta, Jerry. *Dory story*
Paolilli, Paul. *Silver seeds*
Paradis, Susan. *Snow princess*
Park, Frances. *Where on earth is my bagel?*
Parkhurst, Carolyn. *Cooking with Henry and Elliebelly*
Parlato, Stephen. *The world that loved books*
Patricelli, Leslie. *The birthday box*
 Faster! faster!
 Higher! higher!
Paul, Miranda. *10 little ninjas*
Pearce, Philippa. *Amy's three best things*
Pearson, Susan. *We're going on a ghost hunt*

Peck, Jan. *Pirate treasure hunt!*
 Way up high in a tall green tree
Pennypacker, Sara. *Stuart's cape*
Pericoli, Matteo. *Tommaso and the missing line*
Perlman, Janet. *The Emperor Penguin's new clothes*
Peters, Lisa Westberg. *Cold little duck, duck, duck*
Phelan, Matt. *Druthers*
Pilutti, Deb. *Ten rules of being a superhero*
Pinder, Eric. *If all the animals came inside*
Pinkney, Brian. *On the ball*
Pinto, Sara. *Apples and oranges*
Piven, Hanoch. *Let's make faces*
Pizzoli, Greg. *The watermelon seed*
Plecas, Jennifer. *Pretend*
Polacco, Patricia. *Appelemando's dreams*
 Emma Kate
 My ol' man
Portis, Antoinette. *No es una caja / not a box*
 Not a box
 Not a stick
 Princess Super Kitty
Postgate, Daniel. *The snagglegrollop*
Potter, Giselle. *Tell me what to dream about*
 This is my dollhouse
Powell, Polly. *Just dessert*
Prelutsky, Jack. *The baby uggs are hatching*
 Behold the bold umbrellaphant and other poems
 Imagine that! poems of never-was
 Ride a purple pelican
 The snopp on the sidewalk and other poems
 Stardines swim high across the sky
Pringle, Laurence P. *Jesse builds a road*
Proimos, James. *The best bike ride ever*
Purcell, Rebecca. *Super Chicken*
Pym, Tasha. *Have you ever seen a sneep?*
Raschka, Chris. *Cowy cow*
 Little black crow
Rasmussen, Halfdan. *The ladder*
Redeker, Kent. *Don't splash the sasquatch!*
Reed, Neil. *The midnight unicorn*
Regan, Dian Curtis. *Space Boy and his dog*
 Space Boy and the space pirate
Reidy, Jean. *Light up the night*
 Time out for monsters!
Reiser, Lynn. *Any kind of dog*
Rex, Michael. *My fire engine*
Reynolds, Luke. *Bedtime blastoff!*
Rinck, Maranke. *I feel a foot!*
Robbins, Beth. *Tom's afraid of the dark*
Roberts, Bethany. *Gramps and the fire dragon*
 Rosie to the rescue
Roberts, Victoria. *The best pet ever*
Rogers, Gregory. *The hero of Little Street*
Rosen, Michael. *Send for a superhero!*
Rosen, Michael J. *With a dog like that, a kid like me . . .*
Rosenberg, Liz. *The carousel*
Rossell, Judith. *Oliver*
Russo, Marisabina. *The big brown box*
Ruzzier, Sergio. *Hey, Rabbit!*
Ryan, Pam Muñoz. *Mud is cake*
Ryder, Joanne. *Tyrannosaurus time*
Rymond, Lynda Gene. *Oscar and the mooncats*
Sabuda, Robert. *Peter Pan*
Salas, Laura Purdie. *A leaf can be . . .*
Saltzberg, Barney. *Andrew drew and drew*
SanAngelo, Ryan. *Eddie spaghetti*
Sanders, Rob. *Rodzilla*
Sanders-Wells, Linda. *Maggie's monkeys*

Santat, Dan. *Are we there yet?*
Sarah, Linda. *Big friends*
Sava, Donna Lynn. *Teddy bear dreams*
Say, Allen. *Emma's rug*
Scanlon, Elizabeth Garton. *Another way to climb a tree*
Schaefer, Carole Lexa. *Dragon dancing*
   Kids like us
   Someone says
Schaefer, Lola M. *One busy day*
Schmid, Paul. *Oliver and his egg*
   Petunia goes wild
Schneider, Josh. *Kid Amazing vs. the Blob*
Schotter, Roni. *Captain Bob sets sail*
   Captain Bob takes flight
Schwarz, Viviane. *How to find gold*
Scieszka, Jon. *Walt Disney's Alice in Wonderland*
Segal, John. *Pirates don't take baths*
Sendak, Maurice. *In the night kitchen*
   The sign on Rosie's door
   Where the wild things are
Seuss, Dr. *And to think that I saw it on Mulberry Street*
   McElligot's pool
Shaw, Charles Green. *It looked like spilt milk*
Shea, Bob. *Big plans*
Sheldon, Dyan. *Unicorn dreams*
Sheridan, Sara. *I'm me!*
Sheth, Kashmira. *Tiger in my soup*
Shields, Carol Diggory. *I am really a princess*
Shipton, Jonathan. *What if?*
Shulevitz, Uri. *How I learned geography*
   One Monday morning
   So sleepy story
   When I wore my sailor suit
Sif, Birgitta. *Oliver*
   Swish and Squeak's noisy day
   Where my feet go
Sís, Peter. *Ballerina*
   Dinosaur!
   Madlenka
   Madlenka, soccer star
   Robinson
   Ship ahoy!
Slate, Jenny. *Marcel the shell with shoes on*
Smith, Dana Kessimakis. *A brave spaceboy*
Smith, Linda. *Sir Cassie to the rescue*
Sohn, Tania. *Socks!*
Soman, David. *The amazing adventures of Bumblebee Boy*
   Ladybug Girl
   Ladybug Girl and Bingo
   Ladybug Girl and Bumblebee Boy
   Ladybug Girl and the best ever playdate
   Ladybug Girl and the big snow
   Ladybug Girl and the Bug Squad
Spalding, Andrea. *It's raining, it's pouring*
Spinelli, Eileen. *In my new yellow shirt*
   Someday
Stadler, Alexander. *Beverly Billingsly takes the cake*
Stanton, Elizabeth Rose. *Peddles*
Stead, Philip C. *Ideas are all around*
Steig, William. *Pete's a pizza*
   Toby, who are you?
Stein, Mathilde. *The child cruncher*
Sterer, Gideon. *Skyfishing*
Stern, Ellen. *I saw a bullfrog*
Stevenson, James. *Worse than Willy!*
Stevenson, Robert Louis. *Block city*, ill. by Daniel Kirk

Block city, ill. by Ashley Wolff
   The little land
Stubbs, Lisa. *Lily and Bear*
   Lily and Bear: grumpy feet
Stuve-Bodeen, Stephanie. *Elizabeti's doll*
Surovec, Yasmine. *I see Kitty*
Swanson, Matthew. *Everywhere, wonder*
Sweetland, Nancy Rose. *If I could / Si yo pudiera*
Swenson, Jamie A. *If you were a dog*
Tafuri, Nancy. *Junglewalk*
Tanaka, Shinsuke. *Wings*
Tarpley, Natasha Anastasia. *Joe-Joe's first flight*
Taylor, Sean. *The snowbear*
Teague, Mark. *The lost and found*
   The pirate jamboree
Thomas, Jan. *Can you make a scary face?*
Thompson, Colin. *Falling angels*
Thompson, Richard. *The night walker*
Thomson, Bill. *The typewriter*
Tibo, Gilles. *The cowboy kid*
Timmers, Leo. *Franky*
Tokuda-Hall, Maggie. *Also an octopus*
Tompert, Ann. *Little Fox goes to the end of the world*
Tone, Satoe. *The very big carrot*
Torrey, Richard. *The almost terrible playdate*
Tougas, Chris. *Art's supplies*
Trapani, Iza. *I'm a little teapot*
Tullet, Herve. *Let's play*
   The book with a hole
   Mix it up!
   Press here
   Say zoop!
Tupper Ling, Nancy. *The story I'll tell*
Turner, Sandy. *Grow up*
Tusa, Tricia. *Bunnies in my head*
   Follow me
Underwood, Deborah. *Part-time princess*
   Super Saurus saves kindergarten
Usher, Sam. *Rain*
   Snow
Valério, Geraldo. *Turn on the night*
Van Allsburg, Chris. *Bad day at Riverbend*
   The garden of Abdul Gasazi
   Jumanji
   The mysteries of Harris Burdick
   The polar express
   Probuditi!
Van Camp, Katie. *CookieBot!*
   Harry and Horsie
Van Wright, Cornelius. *When an alien meets a swamp monster*
Vaughan, Marcia Kapok. *We're going on a ghost hunt*
Verde, Susan. *I am yoga*
Vigna, Judith. *Boot weather*
Villeneuve, Anne. *Loula is leaving for Africa*
Viorst, Judith. *The good-bye book*
   My mama says there aren't any zombies, ghosts, vampires, creatures, demons, monsters, fiends, goblins, or things
Waddell, Martin. *Bee frog*
Wadham, Tim. *The queen of France*
Wahl, Jan. *I met a dinosaur*
Waldman, Neil. *The starry night*
Wallner, Alexandra. *Beatrix Potter*
Walton, Rick. *I need my own country!*
Ward, Helen. *The dragon machine*
Watkins, Rowboat. *Pete with no pants*
Weitzman, Jacqueline Preiss. *Superhero Joe*
   Superhero Joe and the creature next door

Wells, Rosemary. *A lion for Lewis*
  Small world of Binky Braverman
Whatley, Bruce. *Captain Pajamas*
  Clinton Gregory's secret
Wheatley, Nadia. *Luke's way of looking*
White, Kathryn. *Ruby's school walk*
Whiting, Sue. *The firefighters*
Whybrow, Ian. *Harry and the bucketful of dinosaurs*
Wiesner, David. *Flotsam*
  Hurricane
Willard, Nancy. *A visit to William Blake's inn*
Willems, Mo. *Leonardo the terrible monster*
Williams, Vera B. *Cherries and cherry pits*
Williams-Garcia, Rita. *Catching the wild waiyuuzee*
Willis, Jeanne. *Delilah D. at the library*
Wilson, Karma. *Princess me*
Wilson, N. D. *Ninja boy goes to school*
Wing, Natasha. *Go to bed, monster!*
Wood, Audrey. *The flying dragon room*
Wynne-Jones, Tim. *Secret Agent Man goes shopping for shoes*
Yelchin, Eugene. *Spring hare*
Yolen, Jane. *King Long Shanks*
  What to do with a box
Yoo, Taeeun. *You are a lion!*
Yoon, Salina. *Tap to play!*
Yorinks, Arthur. *Harry and Lulu*
  Hey, Al
  Louis the fish
  What a trip!
Young, Cybèle. *A few blocks*
  Some things I've lost
Young, Ned. *Zoomer*
  Zoomer's summer snowstorm
Young, Ruth. *Golden Bear*
Yum, Hyewon. *There are no scary wolves*
Zagarenski, Pamela. *The whisper*
Zalben, Jane Breskin. *Mousterpiece*
Ziefert, Harriet. *Mighty Max*
Zimmerman, Andrea Griffing. *Train man*
Zoboli, Giovanna. *I wish I had . . .*
Zuppardi, Sam. *Things to do with Dad*

Imagination – imaginary friends

Alexander, Martha G. *And my mean old mother will be sorry, Blackboard Bear*
  Blackboard Bear
  I sure am glad to see you, Blackboard Bear
  I'll protect you from the jungle beasts
  We're in big trouble, Blackboard Bear
  You're a genius, Blackboard Bear
Anglund, Joan Walsh. *The cowboy's Christmas*
Byun, You. *Dream friends*
Colfer, Eoin. *Imaginary Fred*
DiTerlizzi, Tony. *Ted*
Ferrell, Sean. *The Snurtch*
Goodrich, Carter. *We forgot Brock!*
Greenfield, Eloise. *Me and Neesie*
Henkes, Kevin. *Jessica*
Howe, James. *There's a dragon in my sleeping bag*
Klise, Kate. *Imagine Harry*
Kvasnosky, Laura McGee. *Really truly Bingo*
Magerl, Caroline. *Rose and the wish thing*
Perl, Erica S. *Dotty*
Pinfold, Levi. *The Django*
Rohmann, Eric. *Clara and Asha*
Rosenberg, Liz. *Nobody*
Santat, Dan. *The adventures of Beekle*

Imitation *see* Behavior – imitation

Immigrants, immigration *see also* Refugees

Atwell, Debby. *The Thanksgiving door*
Avi. *Silent movie*
Aylesworth, Jim. *My grandfather's coat*
Barroux. *Welcome*
Broyles, Anne. *Shy Mama's Halloween*
Buitrago, Jairo. *Two white rabbits*
Bunting, Eve. *One green apple*
  A picnic in October
Carling, Amelia Lau. *Mama and Papa have a store*
Colato Laínez, René. *Mamá the alien / Mamá la extraterrestre*
  My shoes and I
Connor, Leslie. *Miss Bridie chose a shovel*
Corey, Shana. *Milly and the Macy's Parade*
Coy, John. *Their great gift*
Curtis, Jamie Lee. *This is me*
Cutler, Jane. *Guttersnipe*
Farish, Terry. *Joseph's big ride*
Fleischman, Paul. *The matchbox diary*
Hearne, Betsy Gould. *Seven brave women*
Hyde, Heidi Smith. *Mendel's accordion*
  Shanghai Sukkah
Jaspersohn, William. *The two brothers*
Jiménez, Francisco. *The Christmas gift / El regalo de Navidad*
Jules, Jacqueline. *No English*
Kobald, Irena. *My two blankets*
Kurtz, Jane. *In the small, small night*
Larsen, Andrew. *The man who loved libraries*
Lee, Milly. *Landed*
McCully, Emily Arnold. *Mirette and Bellini cross Niagara Falls*
McGill, Alice. *Molly Bannaky*
MacLachlan, Patricia. *Nora's chicks*
McQuinn, Anna. *My friend Jamal*
Mak, Kam. *My Chinatown*
Malone, Cheryl Lawton. *Dario and the whale*
Miller, Elizabeth I. *Just like home / Como en mi tierra*
Mora, Pat. *I pledge allegiance*
Nolan, Janet. *The St. Patrick's Day shillelagh*
Oberman, Sheldon. *The always prayer shawl*
O'Brien, Anne Sibley. *I'm new here*
Pak, Soyung. *A place to grow*
Park, Frances. *The Have a Good Day Cafe*
  My freedom trip
Partridge, Elizabeth. *Oranges on Golden Mountain*
Pérez, Amada Irma. *My diary from here to there / Mi diario de aquí hasta allá*
Phi, Bao. *A different pond*
Polacco, Patricia. *The blessing cup*
  Fiona's lace
  The keeping quilt
Pomeranc, Marion Hess. *The American Wei*
Pryor, Bonnie. *The dream jar*
Rael, Elsa Okon. *Rivka's first Thanksgiving*
Recorvits, Helen. *My name is Yoon*
  Yoon and the Christmas mitten
Reynolds, Marilynn. *The new land*
Ringgold, Faith. *We came to America*
Sandman, Rochel. *Perfect porridge*
Sanna, Francesca. *The journey*
Steig, William. *When everybody wore a hat*
Stevenson, Harvey. *Looking at liberty*
Stewart, Sarah. *The quiet place*
Tarbescu, Edith. *Annushka's voyage*

Watts, Jeri. *A piece of home*
Williams, Karen Lynn. *My name is Sangoel*
Winter, Jeanette. *Angelina's island*
Woodruff, Elvira. *The memory coat*
    Small beauties
Yaccarino, Dan. *All the way to America*
Yin. *Brothers*
    Coolies
Yolen, Jane. *Naming Liberty*
Young, Rebecca. *Teacup*
Ziefert, Harriet. *When I first came to this land*

Impatience *see* Character traits – patience, impatience

Incentive *see* Character traits – ambition

Indecision *see* Behavior – indecision

Independence Day *see* Holidays – Fourth of July

Indians of Central America – Maya

Ehlert, Lois. *Cuckoo, a Mexican folktale / Cucú: un cuento folklórico mexicano*
Marshall, Linda Elovitz. *Rainbow weaver / Tejedora del arcoíris*
Mora, Pat. *The night the moon fell*
Price, Mara. *Grandma's chocolate / El chocolate de Abuelita*
Rockwell, Anne. *The boy who wouldn't obey*
Volkmer, Jane Anne. *Song of Chirimia / La Musica de la Chirimia*
Wisniewski, David. *Rain player*

Indians of Central America – Taino

Alvarez, Julia. *The secret footprints*

Indians of North America

Alexie, Sherman. *Thunder Boy Jr.*
Aliki. *Corn is maize*
Baker, Olaf. *Where the buffaloes begin*
Baylor, Byrd. *Hawk, I'm your brother*
    When clay sings
Beaver steals fire
Bouchard, Dave. *The song within my heart*
Boyden, Linda. *The blue roses*
Brown, Don. *Bright path*
Bruchac, Joseph. *Buffalo song*
    The circle of thanks
    How Chipmunk got his stripes
    Many nations
    Thirteen moons on turtle's back
Clement-Davies, David. *Spirit*
Farmer, Bonnie. *Isaac's dreamcatcher*
Francis, Lee DeCora. *Kunu's basket*
Goble, Paul. *Buffalo woman*
    The girl who loved wild horses
Grossman, Virginia. *Ten little rabbits*
Hader, Berta Hoerner. *The mighty hunter*
Harjo, Joy. *The good luck cat*
London, Jonathan. *Fireflies, fireflies, light my way*
Luenn, Nancy. *Nessa's fish*

McDermott, Gerald. *Raven*
McLeod, Elaine. *Lessons from Mother Earth*
Martin, Bill, Jr.. *Knots on a counting rope*
Olsen, Sylvia. *Yetsa's sweater*
Perrow, Angeli. *Many hands*
Pollock, Penny. *When the moon is full*
Rappaport, Doreen. *We are the many*
Shoulders, Michael. *D is for drum*
Siberell, Anne. *Whale in the sky*
Smith, Cynthia Leitich. *Jingle dancer*
Strete, Craig Kee. *How the Indians bought the farm*
Taylor, Harriet Peck. *Coyote and the laughing butterflies*
Vaughan, Richard Lee. *Eagle boy*

Indians of North America – Algonquin

McCurdy, Michael. *An Algonquian year*
Martin, Rafe. *The rough-face girl*
Ross, Gayle. *The legend of the Windigo*

Indians of North America – Aztec

Aesop. *Doctor Coyote*
de Las Casas, Dianne. *Blue frog*
Kimmel, Eric A. *The two mountains*
McDermott, Gerald. *Musicians of the sun*
Mora, Pat. *The beautiful lady*
Tonatiuh, Duncan. *The princess and the warrior*

Indians of North America – Blackfoot

Goble, Paul. *The lost children*
San Souci, Robert D. *The legend of Scarface*
Yolen, Jane. *Sky dogs*

Indians of North America – Cherokee

Duvall, Deborah L. *The opossum's tale*
Flanagan, Alice K. *Mrs. Scott's beautiful art*
Haley, Gail E. *Two bad boys*
Ross, Gayle. *How Turtle's back was cracked*
Roth, Susan L. *Kanahena*
Rumford, James. *Sequoyah*

Indians of North America – Cheyenne (Sioux)

Goble, Paul. *Death of the iron horse*
    The great race of the birds and animals
    Her seven brothers

Indians of North America – Chippewa

McCain, Becky R. *Grandmother's dreamcatcher*

Indians of North America – Choctaw

Tingle, Tim. *When Turtle grew feathers*

Indians of North America – Chumash

Wood, Audrey. *The rainbow bridge*

Indians of North America – Comanche

dePaola, Tomie. *The legend of the bluebonnet*
Lind, Michael. *Bluebonnet girl*
Waldman, Neil. *They came from the Bronx*

Indians of North America – Cree

Bouchard, Dave. *Nokum is my teacher*
Robertson, David A. *When we were alone*
Wiebe, Rudy. *Hidden buffalo*

Indians of North America – Creek

Bruchac, Joseph. *The great ball game*

Indians of North America – Crow

Goble, Paul. *Crow chief*

Indians of North America – Dakota (Sioux)

Goble, Paul. *Iktomi and the boulder*
  Iktomi and the buzzard
  Love flute
Nelson, S. D. *Gift horse*

Indians of North America – Goshute

Pia Toya

Indians of North America – Great Basin

Pia Toya

Indians of North America – Great Plains

dePaola, Tomie. *The legend of the Indian paintbrush*
Erdrich, Liselotte. *Bears make rock soup and other stories*
Goble, Paul. *Beyond the ridge*
  The dream wolf
  The gift of the sacred dog
  Iktomi and the berries
  Iktomi and the boulder
  Iktomi and the buffalo skull
  Iktomi and the buzzard
  Iktomi and the coyote
  Iktomi and the ducks
  Mystic horse
  Remaking the earth
  The return of the buffaloes

Indians of North America – Haida

Frantz, Jennifer. *Totem poles*

Indians of North America – Hopi

Dawavendewa, Gerald. *The butterfly dance*

Indians of North America – Huichol

Larson, Bonnie. *When animals were people / Cuando los animales eran personas*

Indians of North America – Inuit

Bushey, Jeanne. *The polar bear's gift*
Christopher, Neil. *On the shoulder of a giant*
Edwardson, Debby Dahl. *Whale snow*
Ford, Christine. *Ocean's child*
London, Jonathan. *Ice Bear and Little Fox*
Pasquali, Elena. *Ituku's Christmas journey*
Sís, Peter. *A small tall tale from the far Far North*

Stafford, Liliana. *The snow bear*

Indians of North America – Iroquois

Bruchac, James. *Rabbit's snow dance*
Longfellow, Henry Wadsworth. *Hiawatha*
Sherman, Pat. *The sun's daughter*

Indians of North America – Kato

Rosen, Michael J. *The dog who walked with God*

Indians of North America – Lakota

Nelson, S. D. *The Star People*

Indians of North America – Lakota (Sioux)

Bateson-Hill, Margaret. *Shota and the star quilt*
Bruchac, Joseph. *Crazy horse's vision*
Goble, Paul. *Adopted by the eagles*
  The legend of the White Buffalo Woman
  The return of the buffaloes

Indians of North America – Lenape

Messinger, Carla. *When the shadbush blooms*
Van Laan, Nancy. *Rainbow crow*

Indians of North America – Metis

Pendziwol, Jean E. *The red sash*

Indians of North America – Miwok

San Souci, Robert D. *Two bear cubs: a Miwok legend from California's Yosemite Valley*

Indians of North America – Mohawk

Swamp, Jake. *Giving thanks*

Indians of North America – Muskogee

Bruchac, Joseph. *The great ball game*

Indians of North America – Narragansett

Koller, Jackie French. *Nickommoh!*

Indians of North America – Navajo

Blood, Charles L. *The goat in the rug*
Hausman, Gerald. *Coyote walks on two legs*
  Eagle boy
Jackson, Gwen. *Lump Lump and the blanket of dreams*
Oughton, Jerrie. *How the stars fell into the sky*
  The magic weaver of rugs
Schick, Eleanor. *My Navajo sister*
Tapahonso, Luci. *Navajo ABC*

Indians of North America – Nez Perce

Kay, Verla. *Broken Feather*

Indians of North America – Ojibwa

Osofsky, Audrey. *Dreamcatcher*
Rodanas, Kristina. *Follow the stars*

San Souci, Robert D. *Sootface*
Van Laan, Nancy. *Shingebiss*
Waboose, Jan Bourdeau. *Firedancers*
  Morning on the lake
  SkySisters

Indians of North America – Papago

Baylor, Byrd. *The desert is theirs*

Indians of North America – Passamaquoddy

Sockabasin, Allen. *Thanks to the animals*

Indians of North America – Pawnee

Cohen, Caron Lee. *The mud pony*
Goble, Paul. *Mystic horse*

Indians of North America – Pima

Nelson, S. D. *Quiet hero*

Indians of North America – Powhatan

Krull, Kathleen. *Pocahontas: princess of the New World*
Nettleton, Pamela Hill. *Pocahontas*

Indians of North America – Pueblo

McDermott, Gerald. *Arrow to the sun*
Rosen, Michael. *Crow and Hawk*
Ts'o, Pauline. *Whispers of the wolf*

Indians of North America – Seminole

Medearis, Angela Shelf. *Dancing with the Indians*

Indians of North America – Seneca

Charles, Veronika Martenova. *The maiden of the mist*
Ehlert, Lois. *Mole's hill*

Indians of North America – Shoshone

Morris, Ann. *Grandma Maxine remembers*
Napoli, Donna Jo. *The crossing*
Stevens, Janet. *Old bag of bones*

Indians of North America – Siksika

Goble, Paul. *The lost children*
  Star boy
San Souci, Robert D. *The legend of Scarface*
Yolen, Jane. *Sky dogs*

Indians of North America – Sioux

Sheldon, Dyan. *Under the moon*

Indians of North America – Southwest

McDermott, Gerald. *Coyote*
Taylor, Harriet Peck. *Secrets of the stone*

Indians of North America – Suquamish

Seattle, Chief. *Brother eagle, sister sky*

Indians of North America – Taino

Jaffe, Nina. *The golden flower*

Indians of North America – Tewa

Clark, Ann Nolan. *In my mother's house*
Orona-Ramirez, Kristy. *Kiki's journey*

Indians of North America – Tlingit

Kimmel, Eric A. *The frog princess: a Tlingit legend from Alaska*
Sleator, William. *The angry moon*

Indians of North America – Tsimshian

Spalding, Andrea. *Solomon's tree*

Indians of North America – Wampanoag

Bartlett, Robert Merrill. *The story of Thanksgiving*
Bruchac, Joseph. *Squanto's journey*
Hennessy, B. G. *One little, two little, three little pilgrims*
Metaxas, Eric. *Squanto and the miracle of Thanksgiving*
Shore, Diane Z. *This is the feast*

Indians of North America – Windigos

Ross, Gayle. *The legend of the Windigo*

Indians of North America – Zapotec

Grossman, Patricia. *Saturday market*
Johnston, Tony. *The tale of Rabbit and Coyote*
Van Laan, Nancy. *La boda*

Indians of North America – Zuni

Pollock, Penny. *The turkey girl*
Rodanas, Kristina. *The dragonfly's tale*

Indians of South America

Knutson, Barbara. *Love and roast chicken*
Krebs, Laurie. *Up and down the Andes*
Reynolds, Jan. *Amazon*

Indians of South America – Karina

Maggi, María Elena. *The great canoe*

Indians of South America – Quechua

Van Laan, Nancy. *The magic bean tree*

Indians, American *see* Indians of Central America; Indians of North America; Indians of South America

Indifference *see* Behavior – indifference

Individuality *see* Character traits – individuality

Indonesian Archipelago see Foreign lands –
South Sea Islands

Insects

American Museum of Natural History. *ABC insects*
Anastas, Margaret. *A hug for you*
Andreae, Giles. *Bustle in the bushes*
Austrian, J. J. *Worm loves Worm*
Beall, Pamela Conon. *Wee Sing if you're happy and you know it*
Berger, Melvin. *Buzz! a book about insects*
Bestor, Sheri Mabry. *Good trick, walking stick!*
Biedrzycki, David. *Ace Lacewing, Bug Detective*
Bonwill, Ann. *Bug and Bear*
Carter, David A. *Chanukah bugs*
   Easter bugs
   How many bugs in a box?
   Peekaboo bugs
Cyrus, Kurt. *Big rig bugs*
Dennard, Deborah. *Bullfrog at Magnolia Circle*
DiTerlizzi, Angela. *Some bugs*
Dodd, Emma. *I love bugs!*
Donaldson, Julia. *Superworm*
Downing, Johnette. *There was an old lady who swallowed some bugs*
Durango, Julia. *Pest fest*
Edwards, Pamela Duncan. *Bravo, Livingstone Mouse!*
Ellis, Carson. *Du iz tak?*
Florian, Douglas. *Insectlopedia*
Frost, Helen. *Step gently out*
Gerber, Carole. *Seeds, bees, butterflies, and more!*
Glaser, Linda. *Not a buzz to be found*
Gran, Julia. *Big bug surprise*
Grandits, John. *Seven rules you absolutely must not break if you want to survive the cafeteria*
Green, Emily K. *Walkingsticks*
Hanson, Warren. *Bugtown Boogie*
Harris, Trudy. *Pattern bugs*
Harvey, Jayne. *Busy bugs*
Hector, Julian. *The gentleman bug*
Hegarty, Patricia. *Bug Bear*
Himmelman, John. *Noisy bug sing-along*
   There's a bug on my book!
Hines, Anna Grossnickle. *Miss Emma's wild garden*
Holmes, Anita. *Insect detector*
Hopkins, Lee Bennett. *Nasty bugs*
Hunter, Anne. *What's in the meadow?*
Jenkins, Steve. *Animals in flight*
Joyce, William. *The Leaf Men and the brave good bugs*
Kirk, David. *Little Miss Spider at Sunny Patch School*
   Miss Spider's ABC
   Miss Spider's new car
Kuhlman, Evan. *Hank's big day*
Latimer, Alex. *Pig and small*
Lawson, JonArno. *Leap!*
Leslie, Amanda. *Alfie and Betty Bug*
Lewis, J. Patrick. *Face bug*
   The little buggers
Lewison, Wendy Cheyette. *So many boots*
Limentani, Alison. *How much does a ladybug weigh?*
Lionni, Leo. *Inch by inch*
McDonald, Megan. *Beetle McGrady eats bugs!*
   Insects are my life
   Reptiles are my life
McElligott, Matthew. *Bean thirteen*
McKelvey, Douglas Kaine. *Locust pocus*

Markle, Sandra. *Creepy, crawly baby bugs*
   Insects
Martin, Bill, Jr.. *The little squeegy bug*
Meadows, Michelle. *Super bugs*
Meisel, Paul. *My awesome summer, by P. Mantis*
Miyares, Daniel. *Bring me a rock!*
Monroe, Chris. *Bug on a bike*
Morrow, Barbara Olenyik. *Mr. Mosquito put on his tuxedo*
Mortensen, Denise Dowling. *Bug Patrol*
Moser, Lisa. *Stories from Bug Garden*
Munro, Roxie. *Busy builders*
Murawski, Darlyne A. *Bug faces*
Murphy, Stuart J. *The best bug parade*
   Bug dance
Newgarden, Mark. *Bow-Wow bugs a bug*
O'Connor, Jane. *Fancy Nancy: explorer extraordinaire!*
Oppenheim, Joanne. *Have you seen bugs?*
Palatini, Margie. *The perfect pet*
Parker, Nancy Winslow. *Bugs*
Paulsen, Gary. *Canoe days*
Perlman, Janet. *The delicious bug*
Peters, Lisa Westberg. *Sleepyhead bear*
Pichon, Liz. *The very ugly bug*
Pienkowski, Jan. *Pizza!*
Pierce, Terry. *My busy green garden*
Pin, Isabel. *The seed*
Pinczes, Elinor J. *A remainder of one*
Rockwell, Anne. *Bugs are insects*
   Bumblebee, bumblebee, do you know me?
Ryder, Joanne. *My father's hands*
Sabuda, Robert. *The movable Mother Goose*
Salzano, Tammi. *One little blueberry*
Shields, Carol Diggory. *The bugliest bug*
Siminovich, Lorena. *I like bugs*
Siomades, Lorianne. *Katy did it!*
Smith, Matthew Clark. *Small wonders: Jean-Henri Fabre and his world of insects*
Stein, Peter. *Bugs galore*
Sturges, Philemon. *I love bugs*
   What's that sound, Woolly Bear?
Van Woerkom, Dorothy. *Hidden messages*
Voake, Steve. *Insect detective*
Ward, Jennifer. *Over in the garden*
Watt, Mélanie. *Bug in a vacuum*
Williams, Suzanne. *Old MacDonald in the city*
Wood, Audrey. *When the root children wake up*

Insects – ants

Aesop. *The ant and the grasshopper*, ill. by Amy Lowry Poole
   The ant and the grasshopper, ill. by Sara Rojo
   The grasshopper and the ants
Allen, Judy. *Are you an ant?*
Andreae, Giles. *Rumble in the jungle*
Baker, Keith. *Just how long can a long string be?!*
Barner, Bob. *Ants rule*
Becker, Bonny. *An ant's day off*
Cannon, Janell. *Crickwing*
Dorros, Arthur. *Ant cities*
Emberley, Rebecca. *The ant and the grasshopper*
Gray, Luli. *Ant and Grasshopper*
Hall, Michael. *It's an orange aardvark!*
Hepworth, Catherine. *ANTics! an alphabetical anthology*
Hodge, Deborah. *Ants*
Hoose, Philip M. *Hey little ant*

Landström, Olof. *Boo and Baa in the woods*
Lass, Bonnie. *Who took the cookies from the cookie jar?*
Little old lady who swallowed a fly. *There once was a cowpoke who swallowed an ant*
Loewen, Nancy. *Tiny workers*
McDonald, Megan. *Ant and Honey Bee, what a pair!*
McElligott, Matthew. *The lion's share*
Martin, David. *All for pie, pie for all*
Nickle, John. *The ant bully*
O'Malley, Kevin. *Little Buggy runs away*
Peet, Bill. *The ant and the elephant*
Philpot, Lorna. *Find Anthony Ant*
Pichard, Alexandra. *Pen pals*
Prince, Joshua. *I saw an ant in a parking lot*
    I saw an ant on the railroad track
Sayre, April Pulley. *Army ant parade*
Sneed, Brad. *Deputy Harvey and the ant cow caper*
Van Allsburg, Chris. *Two bad ants*
Wells, Rosemary. *McDuff saves the day*
Wolkstein, Diane. *Step by step*
Young, Ed. *Night visitors*

Insects – bees

Aponte, Carlos. *A season to bee*
Barton, Bethany. *Give bees a chance*
Barton, Byron. *Buzz, buzz, buzz*
Bell, Cece. *Bee-Wigged*
Cecil, Randy. *Horsefly and Honeybee*
Chrustowski, Rick. *Bee dance*
Cole, Joanna. *The magic school bus inside a beehive*
Flanagan, Alice K. *Learning about bees from Mr. Krebs*
Florian, Douglas. *Unbeelievables*
Formento, Alison. *These bees count!*
Frazier, Craig. *Bee and Bird*
Galvin, Laura Gates. *Bumblebee at Apple Tree Lane*
Gibbons, Gail. *The honey makers*
Gran, Julia. *Big bug surprise*
Green, Emily K. *Bumblebees*
Gugler, Laurel Dee. *There's a billy goat in the garden*
Heiligman, Deborah. *Honeybees*
Hodge, Deborah. *Bees*
Hopkinson, Deborah. *The humblebee hunter*
Horowitz, Ruth. *Are we still friends?*
Huber, Raymond. *Flight of the honey bee*
Jay, Alison. *Bee and me*
Kessler, Cristina. *The best beekeeper of Lalibela*
Krebs, Laurie. *The beeman*, ill. by Valeria Cis
    The beeman, ill. by Melissa Iwai
Loewen, Nancy. *Busy buzzers*
McDonald, Megan. *Ant and Honey Bee, what a pair!*
Morales, Melita. *Jam and honey*
Nargi, Lela. *The honeybee man*
Petty, Dini. *The queen, the bear and the bumblebee*
Polacco, Patricia. *In Enzo's splendid gardens*
Rockwell, Anne. *Bumblebee, bumblebee, do you know me?*
    Honey in a hive
Roode, Daniel. *Little Bea and the snowy day*
Rotner, Shelley. *The buzz on bees*
Ruzzier, Sergio. *Bear and Bee*
    Too busy
Sayre, April Pulley. *The bumblebee queen*
    If you should hear a honey guide
Shannon, David. *Bizzy Mizz Lizzie*
Smallman, Steve. *The very greedy bee*
Spinelli, Eileen. *Buzz*
Teckentrup, Britta. *Bee*

Wong, Janet S. *Buzz*

Insects – beetles

Aston, Dianna Hutts. *A beetle is shy*
Carle, Eric. *The very clumsy click beetle*
Fleming, Denise. *Beetle bop*
Gorbachev, Valeri. *Big Little Hippo*
Luján, Jorge. *Stephen and the beetle*
Murphy, Kelly. *The boll weevil ball*
Tada, Satoshi. *Mr. Beetle*

Insects – butterflies, caterpillars

Aardema, Verna. *Who's in Rabbit's house?*
Allen, Judy. *Are you a butterfly?*
Arnosky, Jim. *Crinkleroot's guide to knowing butterflies and moths*
Aston, Dianna Hutts. *A butterfly is patient*
Barner, Bob. *Dinosaurs roar, butterflies soar!*
Barringer, William. *Gregory and Alexander*
Bruel, Robert O. *Bob and Otto*
Bunting, Eve. *Butterfly house*
Burns, Loree Griffin. *Handle with care*
Carle, Eric. *The very hungry caterpillar*
Clarke, Jane. *Who woke the baby?*
Collicott, Sharleen. *Toestomper and the bad butterflies*
    Toestomper and the caterpillars
Côté, Geneviève. *Mr. King's machine*
Coville, Bruce. *The prince of butterflies*
Davol, Marguerite W. *Why butterflies go by on silent wings*
Donaldson, Julia. *Where's my mom?*
Edwards, Pamela Duncan. *Clara Caterpillar*
Ehlert, Lois. *Waiting for wings*
Elwell, Peter. *Adios Oscar!*
Engle, Margarita. *Summer birds*
Fleming, Denise. *In the tall, tall grass*
Foley, Greg. *Don't worry Bear*
Frost, Helen. *Monarch and milkweed*
Gibbons, Gail. *Monarch butterfly*
Glaser, Linda. *Magnificent monarchs*
Goldman, Judy. *Uncle Monarch and the Day of the Dead*
Heap, Sue. *Four friends in the garden*
Himmelman, John. *A monarch butterfly's life*
Horwood, Annie. *Butterfly, butterfly what colors do you see?*
Jarrett, Clare. *Arabella Miller's tiny caterpillar*
Joosse, Barbara. *Ghost wings*
Kelly, Irene. *It's a butterfly's life*
Kleven, Elisa. *Glasswings*
Kotzwinkle, William. *Walter, the farting dog: rough weather ahead*
Lawrence, Michael. *The caterpillar that roared*
Lionni, Leo. *The alphabet tree*
McBratney, Sam. *The caterpillow fight*
McFarland, Clive. *Caterpillar dreams*
McKee, David. *Elmer and Butterfly*
Madison, Alan. *Velma Gratch and the way cool butterfly*
Magloff, Lisa. *Butterfly*
Maier, Inger. *Ben's flying flowers*
Markle, Sandra. *Butterfly tree*
Martin, Bill, Jr.. *Ten little caterpillars*
Middleton, Charlotte. *Nibbles' garden*
Murphy, Mary. *Caterpillar's wish*
Ó Flatharta, Antoine. *Hurry and the monarch*
O'Connor, Jane. *Bonjour, butterfly*

Pallotta, Jerry. *Butterfly counting*
Patent, Dorothy Hinshaw. *Fabulous fluttering tropical butterflies*
Pedersen, Janet. *Houdini the amazing caterpillar*
Polacco, Patricia. *The butterfly*
Pringle, Laurence. *The secret life of the woolly bear caterpillar*
Prosek, James. *Bird, butterfly, eel*
Rockwell, Anne. *Becoming butterflies*
Rolli, Jennifer Hansen. *Claudia and Moth*
Runton, Andy. *Owly and Wormy: friends all aflutter!*
Ryder, Joanne. *Where butterflies grow*
Sandved, Kjell Bloch. *The butterfly alphabet*
Schubert, Ingrid. *There's always room for one more*
Shingu, Susumu. *Traveling butterflies*
Sierra, Judy. *The beautiful butterfly*
Singer, Marilyn. *Caterpillars*
Sturges, Philemon. *What's that sound, Woolly Bear?*
Sundgaard, Arnold. *The lamb and the butterfly*
Swope, Sam. *Gotta go! Gotta go!*
Symes, Ruth. *Harriet dancing*
Taylor, Harriet Peck. *Coyote and the laughing butterflies*
Wallace, Nancy Elizabeth. *Fly, monarch! fly!*
Willis, Jeanne. *Tadpole's promise*
Wilson, Steve. *Hedgehugs and the Hattiepillar*
Winer, Yvonne. *Butterflies fly*

Insects – cockroaches

Cannon, Janell. *Crickwing*
Covell, David. *Rat and Roach*
  Rat and Roach rock on!
Deedy, Carmen Agra. *Martina the beautiful cockroach*
Moreton, Daniel. *La Cucaracha Martina*
O'Malley, Kevin. *Leo Cockroach . . . toy tester*
Schneider, Howie. *Wilky the White House cockroach*

Insects – crickets

Bunting, Eve. *Christmas cricket*
Carle, Eric. *The very quiet cricket*
Caudill, Rebecca. *A pocketful of cricket*
Green, Emily K. *Crickets*
Waring, Geoff. *Oscar and the cricket*
Wheeler, Lisa. *Old Cricket*

Insects – dragonflies

Breen, Steve. *Stick*
Miller, Heather Lynn. *This is your life cycle*
Rodanas, Kristina. *The dragonfly's tale*

Insects – fireflies

Carle, Eric. *The very lonely firefly*
Drachman, Eric. *Leo the lightning bug*
Frost, Helen. *Among a thousand fireflies*
Loewen, Nancy. *Living lights*
Ochiltree, Dianne. *It's a firefly night*
Oppenheim, Shulamith Levey. *Fireflies for Nathan*
Pinczes, Elinor J. *My full moon is square*
Sturges, Philemon. *Ten flashing fireflies*
Thomas, Patricia. *Firefly mountain*

Insects – fleas

Cneut, Carll. *The amazing love story of Mr. Morf*
Cohen, Laurie. *The flea*

Downey, Lynn. *The flea's sneeze*
Hanson, Mary Elizabeth. *The old man and the flea*
Lish, Ted. *The three little puppies and the big bad flea*
Marcus, Kimberly. *Scritch-scratch a perfect match*
Rogers, Paul. *Tiny*
Steig, Jeanne. *Fleas!*
Weninger, Brigitte. *The elf's hat*
Wood, Audrey. *The napping house wakes up*

Insects – flies

Aardema, Verna. *Half-a-ball-of-kenki*
Arnold, Tedd. *A pet for Fly Guy*
Aylesworth, Jim. *Old Black Fly*
Cecil, Randy. *Horsefly and Honeybee*
Cronin, Doreen. *Diary of a fly*
Edwards, Karl Newsom. *Fly!*
Gollub, Matthew. *The Jazz Fly*
  Jazz Fly 2
Horácek, Petr. *The fly*
Howitt, Mary Botham. *Mary Howitt's The spider and the fly*
Jorgensen, Gail. *Gotcha!*
Little old lady who swallowed a fly. *I know an old lady*
  I know an old lady who swallowed a fly, ill. by Stephen Gulbis
  I know an old lady who swallowed a fly, ill. by Glen Rounds
  I know an old lady who swallowed a fly, ill. by Nadine Bernard Westcott
  There was an old lady who swallowed a fly, ill. by Pam Adams
  There was an old lady who swallowed a fly, ill. by Rashin Kheiriyeh
  There was an old lady who swallowed a fly, ill. by Simms Taback
Long, Ethan. *Soup for one*
Lozoff, Bo. *The wonderful life of a fly who couldn't fly*
Mack, Jeff. *Frog and Fly*
Murray, Alison. *The house that Zack built*
Rosen, Michael. *Tiny little fly*
Schwartz, Amy. *A beautiful girl*
Sierra, Judy. *Thelonius Monster's sky-high fly pie*
Trapani, Iza. *Shoo fly!*

Insects – gnats

Peet, Bill. *The gnats of knotty pine*

Insects – grasshoppers

Aesop. *The ant and the grasshopper*, ill. by Amy Lowry Poole
  The ant and the grasshopper, ill. by Sara Rojo
  The grasshopper and the ants
Allen, Judy. *Are you a grasshopper?*
Bosca, Francesca. *The three grasshoppers*
Emberley, Rebecca. *The ant and the grasshopper*
Gray, Luli. *Ant and Grasshopper*
Green, Emily K. *Grasshoppers*
Loewen, Nancy. *Hungry hoppers*
Wolkstein, Diane. *Step by step*

Insects – ladybugs

Allen, Judy. *Are you a ladybug?*
Berger, Joe. *Bridget Fidget and the most perfect pet!*
Bono, Mary. *Ugh! a bug*
Carle, Eric. *The grouchy ladybug*

Chrustowski, Rick. *Bright beetle*
Dahl, Michael. *Lots of ladybugs!*
Donaldson, Julia. *What the ladybug heard*
Finn, Isobel. *The very lazy ladybug*
Fox, Mem. *Yoo-hoo, Ladybug!*
Gibbons, Gail. *Ladybugs*
King-Chai, Sharon. *Lucy Ladybug*
Llewellyn, Claire. *Ladybug*
Loewen, Nancy. *Spotted beetles*
O'Malley, Kevin. *Little Buggy*
    Little Buggy runs away
Posada, Mia. *Ladybugs*
Primavera, Elise. *The house at the end of Ladybug Lane*
Stephens, J. Moria. *Persephone, the ladybug*
Thomas, Jan. *Can you make a scary face?*

Insects – lice

Caffey, Donna. *Yikes-lice!*
Shannon, David. *Bugs in my hair!*
Stier, Catherine. *Bugs in my hair?!*
Van Laan, Nancy. *Nit-pickin'*

Insects – lightning bugs *see* Insects – fireflies

Insects – mosquitoes

Aardema, Verna. *Why mosquitoes buzz in people's ears*
Gershator, Phillis. *Zzzng! zzzng! zzzng!*
Knudsen, Michelle. *Bugged!*
Morrow, Barbara Olenyik. *Mr. Mosquito put on his tuxedo*
Novak, Jordan P. *Mosquitoes can't bite ninjas*
Ross, Gayle. *The legend of the Windigo*
Sloat, Teri. *The thing that bothered Farmer Brown*
Uribe, Verónica. *Buzz buzz buzz*

Insects – moths

Arnosky, Jim. *Crinkleroot's guide to knowing butterflies and moths*
Evans, Cambria. *Martha Moth makes socks*
Himmelman, John. *A luna moth's life*
Loewen, Nancy. *Night fliers*
Pringle, Laurence. *The secret life of the woolly bear caterpillar*
Rolli, Jennifer Hansen. *Claudia and Moth*
Sandved, Kjell Bloch. *The butterfly alphabet*
Sturges, Philemon. *What's that sound, Woolly Bear?*

Insects – termites

Laden, Nina. *Roberto, the insect architect*
Rouss, Sylvia A. *The littlest pair*

Internet *see* Technology

Interracial marriage *see* Marriage, interracial

Inventions

Barretta, Gene. *Neo Leo*
    Now and Ben
    Timeless Thomas
Beaty, Andrea. *Rosie Revere, engineer*
Davis, Kathryn Gibbs. *Mr. Ferris and his wheel*

Elliott, David. *This Orq. (He #1!)*
Falkenstern, Lisa. *Professor Whiskerton presents Steampunk ABC*
Fisher, Leonard Everett. *Gutenberg*
Fleming, Candace. *Papa's mechanical fish*
Ford, Gilbert. *The marvelous thing that came from a spring*
Geisert, Arthur. *Lights out*
GrandPre, Mary. *Cleonardo, the little inventor*
Harper, Charise Mericle. *Imaginative inventions*
Hart, Caryl. *The princess and the Christmas rescue*
Hood, Susan. *The fix-it man*
Hopkins, Lee Bennett. *Incredible inventions*
James, Simon. *Baby Brains and RoboMom*
Joyce, William. *Sleepy time Olie*
Kelly, David A. *Miracle mud*
Kraft, Betsy Harvey. *The fantastic Ferris wheel*
Kulling, Monica. *All aboard! Elijah McCoy's steam engine*
McCarthy, Meghan. *Earmuffs for everyone!*
McCully, Emily Arnold. *Marvelous Mattie*
Milgrim, David. *Young MacDonald*
Perry, Andrea. *Here's what you do when you can't find your shoe*
Polacco, Patricia. *The junkyard wonders*
Priceman, Marjorie. *Hot air*
Rash, Andy. *Archie the daredevil penguin*
Reynolds, Peter H. *Going places*
Riddell, Chris. *Wendel's workshop*
Taylor, Barbara. *I wonder why zippers have teeth and other questions about inventions*
Varela, Barry. *Gizmo*

Islands

Blackstone, Stella. *An island in the sun*
Breen, Steve. *The secret of Santa's island*
Brown, Margaret Wise. *The little island*
Brunhoff, Laurent de. *Babar on Paradise Island*
Bunting, Eve. *Mouse island*
Burdett, Lois. *The tempest for kids*
Buzzeo, Toni. *The sea chest*
Demas, Corinne. *The disappearing island*
Field, Rachel Lyman. *Grace for an island meal*
Gay, Marie-Louise. *On my island*
Gibbons, Gail. *Surrounded by sea*
Godkin, Celia. *Wolf island*
Isadora, Rachel. *Caribbean dream*
Joseph, Lynn. *Coconut kind of day*
Kellogg, Steven. *The island of the skog*
McCloskey, Robert. *Time of wonder*
MacLachlan, Patricia. *Painting the wind*
MacLear, Kyo. *The fog*
McMillan, Bruce. *Days of the ducklings*
Martin, Jacqueline Briggs. *On Sand Island*
Meddaugh, Susan. *Harry on the rocks*
Moore, Inga. *Captain Cat*
Pfister, Marcus. *Milo and the mysterious island*
Rahaman, Vashanti. *O Christmas tree*
Rockwell, Anne. *Ferryboat ride!*
Rohmann, Eric. *The cinder-eyed cats*
Rumford, James. *The Island-below-the-star*
Schaefer, Lola M. *An island grows*
Sherry, Kevin. *Turtle Island*
Stevenson, James. *The castaway*
Stiles, Martha Bennett. *Island magic*
Stojic, Manya. *Wet pebbles under our feet*
Williams, Garth. *Benjamin's treasure*
Wisdom, Jude. *Whatever Wanda wanted*

Jackets *see* Clothing – coats

Janitors *see* Careers – custodians, janitors

Jealousy *see* Emotions – envy, jealousy

Jesters *see* Clowns, jesters

Jewelry

Andersen, Hans Christian. *The princess and the pea*
Fruisen, Catherine Myler. *My mother's pearls*
Kassirer, Sue. *What's next, Nina?*
Kinch, Devon. *Pretty Penny makes ends meet*
Lamm, C. Drew. *Gauchada*
Recorvits, Helen. *Yoon and the jade bracelet*
Wyeth, Sharon Dennis. *The granddaughter necklace*

Jewish culture

Abraham, Michelle Shapiro. *My cousin Tamar lives in Israel*
Adler, David A. *The children's book of Jewish holidays*
  Hiding from the Nazis
  A picture book of Hanukkah
  A picture book of Israel
  A picture book of Jewish holidays
  A picture book of Passover
  The story of Hanukkah
  The story of Passover
Aleichem, Sholem. *Hanukah money*
Aylesworth, Jim. *My grandfather's coat*
Baum, Maxie. *I have a little dreidel*
Biers-Ariel, Matt. *Solomon and the trees*
Capucilli, Alyssa Satin. *Happy Hanukkah, Biscuit*
Chwast, Seymour. *The miracle of Hanukkah*
Cohen, Deborah Bodin. *Papa Jethro*
Cutler, Jane. *Guttersnipe*
Davis, Aubrey. *Bagels from Benny*
  Kishka for Koppel
Dollinger, Renate. *The rabbi who flew*
Edwards, Michelle. *The Hanukkah trike*
  A hat for Mrs. Goldman
  Max makes a cake
  Papa's latkes
  Room for the baby
Elissa, Barbara. *The remarkable journey of Josh's kippah*
Elvgren, Jennifer. *The whispering town*
Emerman, Ellen. *Is it Shabbos yet?*
  Just right: the story of a Jewish home
Fagan, Cary. *Oy, feh, so?*
Fields, Terri. *One good deed*
Fishman, Cathy Goldberg. *On Hanukkah*
  On Passover
  On Purim
  On Rosh Hashanah and Yom Kippur
  On Shabbat
  When Jackie and Hank met
Flanagan, Alice K. *Passover*
Gadot, A. S. *The first gift*
Gellman, Ellie B. *Netta and her plant*
Geras, Adèle. *Rebecca's Passover*
Glaser, Linda. *Hannah's way*
  Hoppy Passover!
  Mrs. Greenberg's messy Hanukkah
  Stone soup with matzoh balls
Gold-Vukson, Marji E. *The colors of my Jewish Year*
  Grandpa and me on Tu B'Shevat
Goldin, Barbara Diamond. *Cakes and miracles*
  A mountain of blintzes
  Night lights
Gottesfeld, Jeff. *The tree in the courtyard*
Groner, Judyth Saypol. *My first Hebrew word book*
Hanft, Josh. *The miracles of Passover*
Heller, Linda. *How Dalia put a big yellow comforter inside a tiny blue box*
Herman, Charlotte. *First rain*
Hest, Amy. *The Friday nights of Nana*
Hirsh, Marilyn. *Potato pancakes all around*
Hopkins, Lee Bennett. *Hanukkah lights*
Howland, Naomi. *Latkes, latkes, good to eat*
  The matzah man
Hyde, Heidi Smith. *Emanuel and the Hanukkah rescue*
  Mendel's accordion
  Shanghai Sukkah
Jaffe, Nina. *In the month of Kislev*
  Tales for the seventh day
  The way meat loves salt
Jules, Jacqueline. *Picnic at Camp Shalom*
Kimmel, Eric A. *The Chanukkah guest*
  Gershon's monster
  Hanukkah bear
  Hershel and the Hanukkah goblins
  Joseph and the Sabbath fish
  The magic dreidels
  Simon and the bear
  Zigazak!
Kimmelman, Leslie. *Dance, sing, remember*
  Hanukkah lights, Hanukkah nights
  Hooray! it's Passover!
  The runaway latkes
  The Shabbat puppy
  Sound the shofar!
Korngold, Jamie S. *Sadie and the big mountain*
  Sadie's sukkah breakfast
Kosofsky, Chaim. *Much, much better*
Kropf, Latifa Berry. *It's Hanukkah time!*
  It's seder time!
  It's Shofar time!
Krulik, Nancy E. *Is it Hanukkah yet?*
Kuskin, Karla. *A great miracle happened there*
Lehman-Wilzig, Tami. *Keeping the promise*
  Nathan blows out the Hanukkah candles
Levine, Abby. *This is the matzah*
Libney, Varda. *What I like about Passover*
The little red hen. *The Little Red Hen and the Passover matzah*
Londner, Renee. *Stones for Grandpa*
McDonough, Yona Zeldis. *Hammerin' Hank*
Manushkin, Fran. *Hooray for Hanukkah!*
  Latkes and applesauce
  Miriam's cup

Marshall, Linda Elovitz. *Grandma Rose's magic*
  The passover lamb
Medoff, Francine. *The mouse in the matzah factory*
Melmed, Laura Krauss. *Eight winter nights*
  Moishe's miracle
Meltzer, Amy. *A mezuzah on the door*
  The Shabbat Princess
Michelson, Richard. *Across the alley*
  Too young for Yiddish
Milhander, Laura Aron. *Not for all the
    hamantaschen in town*
Miller, William. *Jenny and the peddler*
Morris, Ann. *Grandma Esther remembers*
Newman, Lesléa. *The eight nights of Chanukah*
  Here is the world
  Matzo ball moon
  Runaway dreidel
  A sweet Passover
Newman, Tracy. *Shabbat hiccups*
Oberman, Sheldon. *The always prayer shawl*
Peet, Amanda. *Dear Santa, Love Rachel Rosenstein*
Perlov, Betty Rosenberg. *Rifka takes a bow*
Podwal, Mark H. *The menorah story*
  A sweet year
Polacco, Patricia. *The blessing cup*
  The keeping quilt
  Mrs. Katz and Tush
  Someone for Mr. Sussman
  Tikvah means hope
  The trees of the dancing goats
Rael, Elsa Okon. *Rivka's first Thanksgiving*
Randall, Ronne. *The Hanukkah mice*
Rappaport, Doreen. *The secret seder*
Rockliff, Mara. *Chik chak Shabbat*
Rosen, Michael J. *Chanukah lights everywhere*
  Elijah's angel
  Our eight nights of Hanukkah
Rosenberg, Madelyn. *Happy birthday, tree!*
  The Schmutzy Family
Rosenfeld, Dina Herman. *Five alive*
  Get well soon
Rothenberg, Joan Keller. *Inside-out grandma*
  Matzah ball soup
Rouss, Sylvia A. *The littlest frog*
  Sammy Spider's first day of school
  Sammy Spider's first Passover
  Sammy Spider's first Shabbat
  Sammy Spider's first Shavuot
  Sammy Spider's first Tu B'Shevat
  Sammy Spider's first Yom Kippur
Russo, Marisabina. *I will come back for you*
Sasso, Sandy Eisenberg. *Butterflies under our hats*
Schaefer, Lola M. *Hanukkah*
Schnur, Steven. *The tie man's miracle*
Schnur, Susan. *Tashlich at Turtle Rock*
Schotter, Roni. *Hanukkah!*
  Passover!
  Passover magic
  Purim play
Schubert, Leda. *The Princess of Borscht*
Schur, Maxine Rose. *Day of delight*
Schwartz, Howard. *Gathering sparks*
Shollar, Leah. *A thread of kindness*
Shulevitz, Uri. *The magician*
Shulimson, Sarene. *Lights out Shabbat*
Shulman, Goldie. *Way too much challah dough*
Silverman, Erica. *Gittel's hands*
  The Hanukkah hop!
Simhaee, Rebeka. *Sara finds a mitzva*

Simon, Norma. *The story of Hanukkah*
  The story of Passover
Simon, Richard. *Oskar and the eight blessings*
Simpson, Lesley. *The Purim surprise*
Singer, Isaac Bashevis. *The parakeet named Dreidel*
Sinykin, Sheri. *Zayde comes to live*
Smith, Dian G. *Hanukkah lights*
Snyder, Laurel. *Baxter, the pig who wanted to be
    kosher*
  Good night, laila tov
Sper, Emily. *Hanukkah: a counting book in English,
    Hebrew, and Yiddish*
  The Passover seder
Spinner, Stephanie. *It's a miracle*
Stampler, Ann Redisch. *The rooster prince of Breslov*
  Shlemazel and the remarkable spoon of Pohost
  The wooden sword
Stone, Tanya Lee. *D is for dreidel*
Strauss, Linda Leopold. *The Elijah door*
Stuchner, Joan Betty. *Can hens give milk?*
  The Kugel Valley Klezmer Band
Sugarman, Brynn Olenberg. *Rebecca's journey home*
Sussman, Joni Kibort. *My first Yiddish word book*
Taback, Simms. *Kibitzers and fools*
Tarbescu, Edith. *Annushka's voyage*
  The boy who stuck out his tongue
Ungar, Richard. *Rachel captures the moon*
  Rachel's gift
  Rachel's library
Ungerer, Tomi. *Otto: the autobiography of a teddy bear*
Vorst, Rochel Groner. *The sukkah that I built*
Waldman, Debby. *Room enough for Daisy*
  A sack full of feathers
Wayland, April Halprin. *More than enough*
Wisniewski, David. *Golem*
Wiviott, Meg. *Benno and the night of broken glass*
Wohl, Lauren L. *Matzoh mouse*
Woodruff, Elvira. *The memory coat*
Yolen, Jane. *Naming Liberty*
Yorinks, Arthur. *The Miami giant*
Zalben, Jane Breskin. *Beni's first Chanukah*
  Beni's first wedding
  Pearl's eight days of Chanukah
  Pearl's Passover
Zemach, Margot. *It could always be worse*
Zolkower, Edie Stoltz. *Too many cooks*
Zucker, Jonny. *Apples and honey*
  Four special questions
  It's party time

Jobs *see* Careers

Jokes *see* Riddles & jokes

Jumping rope *see* Activities – jumping

Jungle

Aardema, Verna. *Rabbit makes a monkey of lion*
Alborough, Jez. *Tall*
Andreae, Giles. *Rumble in the jungle*
Ashman, Linda. *Starry safari*
Baker, Liza. *Dinosaur days*
Balouch, Kristen. *The little little girl with the big big
    voice*
Barroux. *Where's the elephant?*
Base, Graeme. *Jungle drums*

Bateman, Teresa. *The frog with the big mouth*
Beaton, Clare. *How loud is a lion?*
Behrens, Janice. *Let's find rain forest animals*
Berkes, Marianne. *Over in the jungle*
Bilgrami, Shaheen. *Jungle art show*
Bright, Paul. *Quiet!*
Broach, Elise. *Gumption!*
Burnard, Damon. *I spy in the jungle*
Butler, John. *Bedtime in the jungle*
Callery, Sean. *Hide and seek in the jungle*
Campoy, F. Isabel. *Rosa Raposa*
Cannon, Janell. *Verdi*
Carle, Eric. *"Slowly, slowly, slowly," said the sloth*
Cherry, Lynne. *The great kapok tree*
Costello, Emily. *Realm of the panther*
Cyrus, Kurt. *Invisible lizard*
Derrick, Patricia. *Riley the rhinoceros*
Downing, Johnette. *Amazon alphabet*
Duke, Kate. *In the rainforest*
Du Quette, Keith. *Little Monkey lost*
Edwards, Pamela Duncan. *Roar*
Ellery, Amanda. *If I were a jungle animal*
Elya, Susan Middleton. *No more, por favor*
Faulkner, Keith. *The giraffe who cock-a-doodle-doo'd*
   Jumbled jungle
   The tallest shortest longest greenest brownest animal
    in the jungle!
Frampton, David. *The whole night through*
Freeman, Mylo. *Potty*
Geoghegan, Adrienne. *All your own teeth*
Gibbons, Gail. *Nature's green umbrella*
Gibert, Bruno. *The king is naked!*
Gollub, Matthew. *Jazz Fly 2*
Greene, Rhonda Gowler. *Jamboree day*
Grupper, Jonathan. *Destination, rain forest*
Gutman, Anne. *Lisa in the jungle*
Hewitt, Sally. *Face to face safari*
Isadora, Rachel. *A South African night*
Jennings, Linda. *Hide and seek birthday treat*
Johanasen, Heather. *About the rain forest*
Johnson, Rebecca. *Tree frog hears a sound*
Kim, Hanmin. *Tiptoe tapirs*
Kipling, Rudyard. *The jungle book*
Krebs, Laurie. *We're roaming in the rainforest*
Kroll, Steven. *Jungle bullies*
Levinson, Nancy Smiler. *Rain forests*
McMullan, Kate. *Mama's kisses*
McPhail, David. *Edward in the jungle*
Mahy, Margaret. *17 kings and 42 elephants*
   Simply delicious!
Mangan, Anne. *The monkey who wanted the moon*
Mena, Pato. *The perfect siesta*
Messner, Kate. *Tree of wonder*
Mitchell, Susan K. *The rainforest grew all around*
Mitton, Tony. *The Jungle Run*
Newman, Jeff. *Reginald*
Parker, Victoria. *Bearum scarum*
Paterson, Brian. *Zigby camps out*
   Zigby hunts for treasure
Peck, Jan. *Way up high in a tall green tree*
Pritchett, Dylan. *The first music*
Robinson, Michelle. *What to do if an elephant stands*
   on your foot
Rosen, Michael. *Tiny little fly*
Ryder, Joanne. *Jaguar in the rain forest*
Sage, Angie. *Monkeys in the jungle*
Salerno, Steven. *Wild child*
Schaefer, Carole Lexa. *Big Little Monkey*
Slack, Michael. *Monkey Truck*

Smallman, Steve. *Hiccupotamus*
Steig, William. *The Zabajaba Jungle*
Sykes, Julie. *Wait for me, Little Tiger*
Tafuri, Nancy. *Junglewalk*
Teyssèdre, Fabienne. *Joseph wants to read*
Thomson, Sarah L. *Quick, Little Monkey!*
Tierney, Fiona. *Lion's lunch?*
Van Allsburg, Chris. *Jumanji*
Ward, Helen. *The tin forest*
Warhola, James. *If you're happy and you know it:*
   jungle edition
West, Colin. *One day in the jungle*
Wildsmith, Brian. *Jungle party*
Willis, Jeanne. *The boy who lost his bellybutton*
Witte, Anna. *The parrot Tico Tango*

Kindness *see* Character traits – kindness

Kindness to animals *see* Character traits –
   kindness to animals

Kissing

Capucilli, Alyssa Satin. *What kind of kiss?*
Daly, Niki. *No more kisses for Bernard!*
Fredrickson, Lane. *Monster trouble!*
Gibson, Amy. *Catching kisses*
Got, Yves. *Sam loves kisses*
Grimm, Jacob and Wilhelm. *The frog prince*
Hample, Stoo. *I will kiss you (lots and lots and lots!)*
Hest, Amy. *Kiss good night*
Katz, Karen. *Counting kisses*
McAllister, Angela. *Take a kiss to school*
McLeod, Heather. *Kiss me!*
Monari, Manuela. *Zero kisses for me!*
Murphy, Mary. *A kiss like this*
Oram, Hiawyn. *Kiss it better*
Plourde, Lynn. *Dad, aren't you glad?*
Robbins, Maria Polushkin. *Mother, Mother, I want*
   another
Root, Phyllis. *Kiss the cow*
Rosenthal, Amy Krouse. *Plant a kiss*
Saltzberg, Barney. *Baby animal kisses*
   Cornelius P. Mud, are you ready for school?
   Kisses
Stein, David Ezra. *Dinosaur kisses*
Tafuri, Nancy. *All kinds of kisses*
Tarpley, Todd. *How about a kiss for me?*
Trewin, Trudie. *I lost my kisses*
Verburg, Bonnie. *The kiss box*
Walsh, Joanna. *The biggest kiss*
Waring, Zoe. *No hugs for Porcupine*
Watts, Frances. *Kisses for Daddy*
Yolen, Jane. *Mama's kiss*

Kites

Alborough, Jez. *Super Duck*
Baumgart, Klaus. *Laura's secret*
Biddulph, Rob. *Blown away*
Clark, Katie. *Seagull Sam*
Dyckman, Ame. *Horrible Bear!*
Emmett, Jonathan. *Someone bigger*
Heide, Florence Parry. *Princess Hyacinth*
Hest, Amy. *Little chick*
Hillenbrand, Will. *Kite day*
Jagtenberg, Yvonne. *Jack's kite*
Jeffers, Oliver. *Stuck*
Jiang, Ji-li. *Red kite, blue kite*
Khan, Rukhsana. *King for a day*
Krensky, Stephen. *Ben Franklin and his first kite*
Lin, Grace. *Kite flying*
Mayer, Mercer. *Shibumi and the kitemaker*
Mitchell, Robin. *Windy*
Murphy, Stuart J. *Let's fly a kite*
Oskarsson, Bardur. *The flat rabbit*
Peet, Bill. *Merle the high flying squirrel*
Rey, Margret. *Curious George flies a kite*
Stafford, Liliana. *Just dragon*
Wiese, Kurt. *Fish in the air*
Williams, Laura E. *The best winds*
Wisdom, Jude. *Whatever Wanda wanted*
Wright, Cliff. *Bear and kite*
Yolen, Jane. *The emperor and the kite*

Knights

Adkins, Jan. *What if you met a knight?*
Baillie, Allan. *Dragonquest*
Banks, Kate. *Max's castle*
Baynton, Martin. *Jane and the dragon*
Davey, Owen. *Night Knight*
dePaola, Tomie. *The knight and the dragon*
Docherty, Helen. *The storybook knight*
Donaldson, Julia. *A gold star for Zog*
Dormer, Frank W. *The sword in the stove*
Gibbons, Gail. *Knights in shining armor*
Goodall, John S. *Creepy castle*
Grahame, Kenneth. *The reluctant dragon*
Klostermann, Penny Parker. *There was an old dragon who swallowed a knight*
Kraegel, Kenneth. *King Arthur's very great grandson*
Lewin, Betsy. *Good night, Knight*
Matthies, Janna. *Peter, the knight with asthma*
Mayer, Mercer. *The bravest knight*
Mayhew, James. *The knight who took all day*
Melling, David. *Good knight sleep tight*
Nash, Ogden. *Custard the dragon and the wicked knight*
Neuschwander, Cindy. *Sir Cumference and all the king's tens*
Peet, Bill. *Cowardly Clyde*
    How Droofus the dragon lost his head
Robinson, Michelle. *The forgetful knight*
Rogers, Gregory. *The boy, the bear, the baron, the bard*
    Midsummer knight
Sabuda, Robert. *The dragon and the knight*
Scarry, Huck. *Looking into the Middle Ages*
Smith, Linda. *Sir Cassie to the rescue*
Sperring, Mark. *The sunflower sword*
Steele, Philip. *A knight's city*
Sturm, James. *Gryphons aren't so great*
    Ogres awake!
    Sleepless knight
Thomas, Shelley Moore. *A cold winter's Good Knight*
    A Good Knight's rest
    Good night, Good Knight
    Take care, Good Knight
Tucker, Kathy. *Do knights take naps?*
Wheeler, Lisa. *Boogie knights*
Wojtowycz, David. *Elephant Joe, Brave Knight!*

Lady birds *see* Insects – ladybugs

Lakes, ponds

Arnosky, Jim. *Beaver pond, moose pond*
Davies, Nicola. *The pond*
Day, Alexandra. *Carl's summer vacation*
Falwell, Cathryn. *Pond babies*
    Scoot!
Fleming, Denise. *In the small, small pond*
Folgueira, Rodrigo. *Ribbit!*
Franco, Betsy. *Pond circle*
George, Lindsay Barrett. *Around the pond*
Heinz, Brian J. *Butternut Hollow Pond*
Jordan, Sandra. *Frog hunt*
Kuefler, Joseph. *Beyond the pond*
LaMarche, Jim. *Pond*
London, Jonathan. *Loon Lake*
Martin, Jacqueline Briggs. *On Sand Island*
Mitton, Tony. *Down by the cool of the pool*
Pfeffer, Wendy. *Mallard duck at Meadow View Pond*
Quattlebaum, Mary. *Jo MacDonald saw a pond*
Ritchie, Alison. *Duck says don't!*
Rockwell, Anne. *Ducklings and pollywogs*
Root, Phyllis. *Rattletrap car*
Schoenherr, John. *Rebel*
Schofield, Jennifer. *Animal babies in ponds and rivers*
Serafini, Frank. *Looking closely around the pond*
Sidman, Joyce. *Song of the water boatman*
Taylor, Harriet Peck. *Coyote and the laughing butterflies*
Thompson, Lauren. *Little Quack's new friend*
Van Dusen, Chris. *Hattie and Hudson*
Van Leeuwen, Jean. *Touch the sky summer*
Waddell, Martin. *The pig in the pond*
Wallace, Nancy Elizabeth. *Pond walk*
Yolen, Jane. *On Duck Pond*

Lambs *see* Animals – babies; Animals – sheep

Language

Alda, Arlene. *Did you say pears?*
Aliki. *Communication*
    Hello! Good-bye!
Allen, Susan. *Read anything good lately?*
Arnold, Tedd. *More parts*
Ayres, Katherine. *Up, down, and around*
Azarian, Mary. *A gardener's alphabet*

Baker, Alan. *Little Rabbit's first word book*
Banks, Kate. *Max's castle*
   Max's dragon
   Max's words
Barnett, Mac. *The magic word*
   Telephone
Barretta, Gene. *Dear deer*
Barton, Byron. *Tools*
Basher, Simon. *ABC kids*
Beaton, Clare. *Zoë and her zebra*
Bell, Cece. *I yam a donkey!*
Bergen, Lara Rice. *Blue's world of words*
Berkes, Marianne. *Animalogy*
Bertrand, Diane Gonzales. *The party for Papa Luis / La fiesta para Papa Luis*
Best, Cari. *Beatrice spells some lulus and learns to write a letter*
Bloch, Serge. *Butterflies in my stomach and other school hazards*
   You are what you eat
Brennan-Nelson, Denise. *My grandma likes to say*
Brocket, Jane. *Ruby, violet, lime*
Brown, Marc. *Arthur's really helpful word book*
Brunetti, Ivan. *Wordplay*
Bruno, Elsa Knight. *Punctuation celebration*
Bryant, Jen. *The right word*
Carle, Eric. *My very first book of words*
Carlson, Nancy. *ABC, I like me!*
Carr, Jan. *Greedy apostrophe*
Cassie, Brian. *Say it again*
Chambers, Angela. *Follow that chicken!*
Charlip, Remy. *Handtalk birthday*
Charlip, Remy, et al. *Handtalk*
Cheng, Andrea. *Grandfather counts*
Cleary, Brian P. *A lime, a mime, a pool of slime*
   Peanut butter and jellyfishes
Coffelt, Nancy. *Aunt Ant leaves through the leaves*
   Big, bigger, biggest!
Cousins, Lucy. *Maisy's amazing big book of words*
Cox, Phil Roxbee. *Fox on a box*
   Goose on the loose
   Shark in the park
Curtis, Jamie Lee. *Big words for little people*
Dahl, Michael. *If you were an adjective*
Danylyshyn, Greg. *A crash of rhinos*
Day, Alexandra. *Frank and Ernest*
   Frank and Ernest on the road
   Frank and Ernest play ball
DeFelice, Cynthia C. *Nelly May has her say*
de Las Casas, Dianne. *The Little "Read" Hen*
Delaunois, Angèle. *Magic little words*
de Lestrade, Agnès. *Phileas's fortune*
Donohue, Moira Rose. *Alfie the apostrophe*
Du Quette, Keith. *They call me Woolly*
Ellis, Carson. *Du iz tak?*
Escoffier, Michael. *Take away the A*
   Where's the baboon?
   Have you seen my trumpet?
Falwell, Cathryn. *Word wizard*
Feiffer, Kate. *Henry, the dog with no tail*
Feldman, Eve B. *Billy and Milly, short and silly*
Fern, Tracey. *W is for Webster*
Ferris, Jeri Chase. *Noah Webster and his words*
Fleming, Denise. *Shout! shout it out!*
Gibbons, Gail. *Weather words and what they mean*
Got, Yves. *Sam's big book of words*
Grant, Jacob. *Little Bird's bad word*
Groner, Judyth Saypol. *My first Hebrew word book*
Guy, Ginger Foglesong. *¡Bravo!*

Gwynne, Fred. *A chocolate moose for dinner*
   A little pigeon toad
Hall, Michael. *Cat tale*
   Little i
Hambleton, Laura. *Monkey business: fun with idioms*
Harper, Jo. *I could eat you up!*
Harris, Trudy. *Pattern bugs*
Harshman, Terry Webb. *Does a sea cow say moo?*
Heelan, Jamee Riggio. *Can you hear a rainbow?*
Heidbreder, Robert. *Lickety-split*
Heling, Kathryn. *Mouse makes magic*
   Mouse's hide-and-seek words
Heller, Ruth. *A cache of jewels and other collective nouns*
   Fantastic! wow! and unreal!
   Kites sail high
   Many luscious lollipops
   Merry-go-round
   Mine, all mine
Henry, Jed. *I speak dinosaur*
Hiatt, Fred. *Baby talk*
Hill, Eric. *Spot's big book of words / El libro grande de las palabras de Spot*
   Spot's first words
Hills, Tad. *Rocket's mighty words*
Hoban, Tana. *All about where*
Holland, Loretta. *Fall leaves*
Holub, Joan. *Little red writing*
Hunter, Tom. *Build it up and knock it down*
Hurd, Thacher. *Cat's pajamas*
Hyman, Trina Schart. *A little alphabet*
Inkpen, Mick. *Kipper's book of opposites*
Isadora, Rachel. *Yo, Jo!*
Jay, Alison. *Christmastime*
Jenkins, Emily. *Small medium large*
Jenkins, Steve. *Move!*
Jocelyn, Marthe. *Where do you look?*
Jonas, Ann. *Watch William walk*
Joyce, Susan. *ABC nature riddles*
Katz, Alan. *That stinks!*
Keller, Laurie. *Do unto otters*
Könnecke, Ole. *The big book of words and pictures*
Krauss, Ruth. *A hole is to dig*
Kubler, Annie. *My first signs*
Lawlor, Laurie. *Muddy as a duck puddle and other American similes*
Lee, Tae-Jun. *Waiting for Mama*
Leedy, Loreen. *Crazy like a fox*
   There's a frog in my throat
Lehrhaupt, Adam. *Wordplay*
Levis, Caron. *May I have a word?*
Lewis, J. Patrick. *Big is big and little little*
Long, Ethan. *In, over, and on (the farm)*
   Ms. Spell
   Up, tall and high
MacDonald, Ross. *Achoo! Bang! Crash!*
McKay, Jodi. *Where are the words?*
McLean, Dirk. *Play mas'! a carnival ABC*
McPhail, David. *Pig Pig meets the lion*
May, Eleanor. *Albert's amazing snail*
Michelson, Richard. *Too young for Yiddish*
Milgrim, David. *My friend Lucky*
Miller, Mary Beth. *Handtalk zoo*
Millman, Isaac. *Moses goes to a concert*
   Moses goes to school
   Moses goes to the circus
Mora, Pat. *Yum! mmmm! que rico!*
Mortimer, Rachael. *Song for a princess*
Moses, Will. *Raining cats and dogs*

Murguia, Bethanie Deeney. *Cockatoo, too*
  Toucans, too
Nathan, Emma. *What do you call a group of turkeys?*
O'Connor, Jane. *Fancy Nancy: aspiring artist*
  Fancy Nancy: explorer extraordinaire!
  Fancy Nancy: ooh la la! it's beauty day
  Fancy Nancy and the fabulous fashion boutique
  Fancy Nancy splendiferous Christmas
  Fancy Nancy's collection of fancy words
Ogburn, Jacqueline K. *Little treasures*
O'Malley, Kevin. *Animal crackers fly the coop*
Parish, Herman. *Amelia Bedelia's first library card*
  Amelia Bedelia's first vote
Park, Linda Sue. *Yaks yak*
Parker, Marjorie Blain. *A paddling of ducks*
Parr, Todd. *Big and little*
  Black and white
Paschkis, Julie. *Magic spell*
Paul, Alison. *The crow (a not so scary story)*
Paul, Ann Whitford. *Word builder*
Pearson, Tracey Campbell. *Elephant's story*
Perl, Erica S. *Chicken Butt's back!*
Pulver, Robin. *The case of the incapacitated capitals*
  Happy endings
  Nouns and verbs have a field day
  Punctuation takes a vacation
  Silent letters loud and clear
Rankin, Laura. *The handmade counting book*
Rappaport, Doreen. *Abe's honest words*
  Martin's big words
Reinhart, Matthew. *Animal popposites*
Richardson, Bill. *The alphabet thief*
Ringgold, Faith. *Cassie's word quilt*
Roberton, Fiona. *Cuckoo!*
Rockwell, Anne. *What we like*
Rosenthal, Amy Krouse. *Al Pha's bet*
  Exclamation mark
  I scream, ice cream!
  Wumbers
Rosenthal, Betsy R. *An ambush of tigers*
Rovetch, Lissa. *Ook the book*
Rumford, James. *There's a monster in the alphabet*
Schaefer, Carole Lexa. *ABCers*
Schotter, Roni. *The boy who loved words*
Schwartz, Amy. *One hundred things that make me happy*
Seeger, Laura Vaccaro. *One boy*
  Walter was worried
Serfozo, Mary. *What's what?*
Shannon, David. *Oops! a diaper David book*
Showers, Paul. *How you talk*
Smith, Lane. *There is a tribe of kids*
Snicket, Lemony. *Thirteen words*
Sper, Emily. *The Passover seder*
Stangl, Katrin. *Strong as a bear*
Stanley, Mandy. *At the pool*
  First word book
  In the park
Sussman, Joni Kibort. *My first Yiddish word book*
Tapahonso, Luci. *Navajo ABC*
Thomson, Bill. *The typewriter*
Tobin, Jim. *Sue MacDonald had a book*
  The very inappropriate word
Trice, Linda. *Kenya's word*
Truss, Lynne. *Eats, shoots and leaves*
Van Slyke, Rebecca. *Lexie the word wrangler*
Viorst, Judith. *The alphabet from Z to A*
Viva, Frank. *Outstanding in the rain*
Walker, Sally M. *The Vowel family*

Walsh, Liam Francis. *Fish*
Walton, Rick. *Just me and 6,000 rats*
Ward, Lindsay. *Henry finds his word*
Wells, Rosemary. *Letters and sounds*
  Max's first word
  Max's ride
  Use your words, Sophie!
Williamson, Sarah. *Where are you?*
Wimmer, Sonja. *The word collector*
Winnie-the-Pooh's A B C
Wise, William. *Zany zoo*
Wishinsky, Frieda. *What's up, bear?*
Wood, Audrey. *Elbert's bad word*

Language – sign language *see* Sign language

Languages, foreign *see* Foreign languages

Laundry

Bagley, Jessixa. *Laundry day*
Docherty, Thomas. *Wash-a-bye Bear*
Feeney, Tatyana. *Small Bunny's blue blanket*
Ford, Bernette. *No more blanket for Lambkin!*
Freeman, Don. *A pocket for Corduroy*
Ormondroyd, Edward. *Theodore*
Weeks, Sarah. *Mrs. McNosh hangs up her wash*
Willems, Mo. *Knuffle Bunny*

Law *see* Careers – judges; Careers – lawyers; Careers – police officers; Crime

Laziness *see* Character traits – laziness

Legends *see* Folk & fairy tales

Letters, cards

Ada, Alma Flor. *Dear Peter Rabbit*
  With love, Little Red Hen
Adoff, Arnold. *Love letters*
Alexander, Claire. *Back to front and upside down*
Anholt, Laurence. *Seven for a secret*
Augustin, Barbara. *Antonella and her Santa Claus*
Bauer, Marion Dane. *My mother is mine*
Chen, Yong. *A gift*
Christelow, Eileen. *The desperate dog writes again*
  Letters from a desperate dog
Clanton, Ben. *It came in the mail*
Cole, Barbara Hancock. *Anna and Natalie*
Collins, Ross. *Dear Vampa*
Crimi, Carolyn. *Dear Tabby*
Cullen, Lynn. *Dear Mr. Washington*
Danneberg, Julie. *First year letters*
Daywalt, Drew. *The day the crayons came home*
  The day the crayons quit
De Vries, Anke. *Raf*
Durant, Alan. *Dear tooth fairy*
Edwards, Pamela Duncan. *Dear Tooth Fairy*
Flanagan, Alice K. *Here comes Mr. Eventoff with the mail!*
Funk, Josh. *Dear dragon*
Gravett, Emily. *Meerkat mail*
Harley, Bill. *Dear Santa*
Heide, Iris van der. *A strange day*

LGBTQ *see also* Gender identity

Libraries *see also* Books, reading

The gingerbread boy. *The Library Gingerbread Man*
Gonzalez, Lucia. *The storyteller's candle / La velita de los cuentos*
Grambling, Lois G. *Can I bring Woolly to the library, Ms. Reeder?*
Greene, Rhonda Gowler. *No pirates allowed! said Library Lou*
Harper, Charise Mericle. *A big surprise for Little Card*
Hest, Amy. *The babies are coming!*
Hopkins, Lee Bennett. *Jumping off library shelves*
Horn, Emily. *Excuse me — are you a witch?*
Houston, Gloria. *Miss Dorothy and her bookmobile*
Hubbell, Patricia. *Check it out! reading, finding, helping*
Ivey, Randall. *Jay and the bounty of books*
Johnson, Angela. *Lottie Paris and the best place*
Joyce, William. *The fantastic flying books of Mr. Morris Lessmore*
Kimmel, Eric A. *I took my frog to the library*
King, M. G. *Librarian on the roof!*
Kirk, Daniel. *Library mouse*
   Library mouse: a friend's tale
   Library mouse: a world to explore
   Library mouse: home sweet home
Knudsen, Michelle. *Library lion*
Kohara, Kazuno. *The Midnight Library*
Lakin, Patricia. *Clarence the copy cat*
   Rainy day
Larsen, Andrew. *The man who loved libraries*
Lies, Brian. *Bats at the library*
Lindbergh, Reeve. *Homer the library cat*
London, Jonathan. *Froggy goes to the library*
McDonald, Megan. *When the library lights go out*
McGee, Marni. *Winston the book wolf*
McQuinn, Anna. *Leo loves baby time*
   Lola at the library
Mahoney, Daniel J. *The Saturday escape*
Malaspina, Ann. *Finding Lincoln*
Mayr, Diane. *Littlebat's Halloween story*
Meng, Cece. *The wonderful thing about hiccups*
Middleton, Charlotte. *Nibbles*
Miller, Pat. *We're going on a book hunt*
Miller, William. *Richard Wright and the library card*
Mora, Pat. *A library for Juana*
   Tomás and the library lady
Morris, Carla. *The boy who was raised by librarians*
Morrison, Toni. *Please, Louise*
Morton, Carlene. *The library pages*
Munro, Roxie. *The inside-outside book of libraries*
Murphy, Mary. *Koala and the flower*
Myron, Vicki. *Dewey*
Naden, Corinne J. *Ron's big mission*
Numeroff, Laura Joffe. *The Jellybeans and the big book bonanza*
OHora, Zachariah. *The not so quiet library*
Papp, Lisa. *Madeline Finn and the library dog*
Parish, Herman. *Amelia Bedelia's first library card*
Parsley, Elise. *If you ever want to bring a circus to the library, don't!*
Pauli, Lorenz. *The fox in the library*
Polacco, Patricia. *Aunt Chip and the great Triple Creek dam affair*
   The mermaid's purse
Radabaugh, Melinda Beth. *Going to the library*
Rahaman, Vashanti. *Read for me, Mama*
Rockwell, Anne. *Library day*
Rosenstock, Barb. *Thomas Jefferson builds a library*
Roth, Susan L. *Hands around the library*

Ruurs, Margriet. *My librarian is a camel*
Sadler, Marilyn. *Alistair in outer space*
Schoenherr, Ian. *Read it, don't eat it!*
Shea, Bob. *Dinosaur vs. the library*
Shea, Kitty. *Out and about at the public library*
Shields, Gillian. *Library Lily*
Sierra, Judy. *Mind your manners, B. B. Wolf*
   Wild about books
Silvestro, Annie. *Bunny's book club*
Slegers, Liesbet. *Kevin goes to the library*
Spinelli, Eileen. *The best story*
Staake, Bob. *The Book of Gold*
Stadler, Alexander. *Beverly Billingsly borrows a book*
Stewart, Sarah. *The library*
Stoeke, Janet Morgan. *It's library day*
Stoop, Naoko. *Red Knit Cap Girl and the reading tree*
Sutton, Sally. *Construction*
Turner, Ann Warren. *Pumpkin cat*
Twohy, Mike. *Poindexter makes a friend*
Ungar, Richard. *Rachel's library*
Willis, Jeanne. *Delilah D. at the library*
Winter, Jeanette. *Biblioburro*
   The librarian of Basra
Woodruff, Elvira. *Can you guess where we're going?*
Yoo, Taeeun. *The little red fish*

Light, lights

Bang, Molly. *My light*
Berger, Melvin. *Switch on, switch off*
Blechman, Nicholas. *Night light*
Boyd, Lizi. *Flashlight*
Crews, Donald. *Light*
Gal, Susan. *Night lights*
Graham, Joan Bransfield. *Flicker flash*
Hayes, Geoffrey. *The bunny's night-light*
Heine, Theresa. *Chandra's magic light*
Holderness, Jackie. *What is a shadow?*
McDonald, Megan. *When the library lights go out*
Paul, Ellis. *The night the lights went out on Christmas*
Pfeffer, Wendy. *Light is all around us*
Rocco, John. *Blackout*
Rosenberg, Liz. *Eli's night-light*
Schnur, Steven. *Night lights*
Shulevitz, Uri. *Dusk*
Snicket, Lemony. *The dark*
Swanson, Susan Marie. *The house in the night*
Swinburne, Stephen R. *Guess whose shadow?*
Waring, Geoff. *Oscar and the moth*

Lighthouses

Brett, Jan. *Comet's nine lives*
Briggs, Kelly Paul. *Lighthouse lullaby*
Brown, Ruth. *Gracie the lighthouse cat*
Bunting, Eve. *Ghost cat*
Buzzeo, Toni. *Lighthouse Christmas*
   The sea chest
Fearrington, Ann. *Who sees the lighthouse?*
Haas, Rick de. *Peter and the winter sleepers*
Krensky, Stephen. *Sisters of Scituate Light*
Lamb, Albert. *The abandoned lighthouse*
Lobel, Anita. *One lighthouse, one moon*
Perrow, Angeli. *Lighthouse dog to the rescue*
Stainton, Sue. *The lighthouse cat*
Swift, Hildegarde Hoyt. *The little red lighthouse and the great gray bridge*
Wells, Rosemary. *The island light*

Lightning bugs *see* Insects – fireflies

Little people

San Souci, Robert D. *Little Pierre*
Tom Thumb. *The adventures of Tom Thumb*
   Tom Thumb

Littleness *see* Character traits – smallness

Lost *see* Behavior – lost

Lost & found possessions *see* Behavior – lost
   & found possessions

Loyalty *see* Character traits – loyalty

Luck *see* Character traits – luck

Lullabies

Asch, Frank. *Barnyard lullaby*
Ashman, Linda. *Rock-a-bye romp*
Bang, Molly. *Ten, nine, eight*
Blomgren, Jennifer. *Where do I sleep?*
Bradman, Tony. *Daddy's lullaby*
Brown, Margaret Wise. *Goodnight songs*
Cabrera, Jane. *Twinkle, twinkle, little star*
Canyon, Christopher. *John Denver's Ancient rhymes*
Davies, Jacqueline. *The night is singing*
Davis, Caroline. *My little rocking horse lullabies*
de Las Casas, Dianne. *Mama's bayou*
Fox, Mem. *Sleepy bears*
Frampton, David. *The whole night through*
Frazee, Marla. *Hush, little baby: a folk song with
   pictures*
Ginsburg, Mirra. *Asleep, asleep*
Guthrie, James. *Last song*
Heidbreder, Robert. *Song for a summer night*
Henderson, Kathy. *Hush, baby, hush!*
Ho, Minfong. *Hush!*
Hughes, Langston. *Lullaby (for a Black mother)*
Hush, little baby
Hush songs
Jewel. *Sweet dreams*
   That's what I'd do
Kirk, Daniel. *Hush, little alien*
Kono, Erin Eitter. *Hula lullaby*
Lewis, Rose A. *Sweet dreams*
London, Jonathan. *Fireflies, fireflies, light my way*
Lullaby moons and a silver spoon
McGhee, Alison. *In the hollow of your hand*
MacLachlan, Patricia. *Lala salama*
McMullan, Kate. *If you were my bunny*
Markell, Denis. *Hush, Little Monster*
Melmed, Laura Krauss. *Jumbo's lullaby*
Metaxas, Eric. *It's time to sleep, my love*
Millen, C. M. *Blue bowl down*
Mitchard, Jacquelyn. *Baby bat's lullaby*
Newman, Lesléa. *Daddy's song*
Noda, Takayo. *Song of the flowers*
Numeroff, Laura Joffe. *Nighty-night, Cooper*
Pearson, Susan. *The drowsy hours*
Pienkowski, Jan. *Good night, a pop-up lullaby*

Pinkney, Brian. *Hush, little baby*
Pomerantz, Charlotte. *All asleep*
Prap, Lila. *Animal lullabies*
Root, Phyllis. *All for the newborn baby*
   What Baby wants
Selig, Josh. *Red and Yellow's noisy night*
Snyder, Betsy E. *Sweet dreams lullaby*
Staub, Leslie. *Bless this house*
Thomas, Jan. *Let's sing a lullaby with the Brave
   Cowboy*
Thomson, Sarah L. *Around the neighborhood*
Titherington, Jeanne. *Baby's boat*
Van Laan, Nancy. *Sleep, sleep, sleep*
   When winter comes: a lullaby
Walty, Margaret. *Rock-a-bye baby: lullabies for bedtime*
Withrow, Sarah. *Be a baby*
Yolen, Jane. *Sleep, black bear, sleep*
Zoboli, Giovanna. *The big book of slumber*

Lying *see* Behavior – lying

Machines

Angleberger, Tom. *McToad mows Tiny Island*
Ashburn, Boni. *Builder Goose*
Barton, Byron. *Machines at work*
Bee, William. *Digger Dog*
   Stanley the builder
Big noisy trucks and diggers
Biggs, Brian. *Tinyville town gets to work*
Blum, Mark. *Big trucks and diggers in 3-D*
Braun, Sebastien. *Digger and Tom!*
Burleigh, Robert. *Zoom! zoom!*
Burton, Virginia Lee. *Katy and the big snow*
   Mike Mulligan and his steam shovel
Buzzeo, Toni. *Whose truck?*
Carter, Don. *Get to work, trucks!*
Clement, Nathan. *Job site*
Copeland, Cynthia L. *What are you waiting for?*
Côté, Geneviève. *Mr. King's machine*
Dahl, Michael. *One big building*
Davis, Kathryn Gibbs. *Mr. Ferris and his wheel*
Dewdney, Anna. *Little Excavator*
Dotlich, Rebecca Kai. *What can a crane pick up?*
Elliott, Rebecca. *Dalmatian in a digger*
Fleming, Candace. *Bulldozer helps out*
   Bulldozer's big day
Freedman, Claire. *Beep beep beep: time for sleep!*
Fry, Jenny. *Building numbers*
Geisert, Arthur. *Hogwash*
Gordon, David. *Extremely cute animals operating
   heavy machinery*
   The three little rigs
Granowsky, Alvin. *Diggers and cranes*
Green, Rod. *Giant vehicles*
Harper, Charise Mericle. *Go! go! go! stop!*
Hennessy, B. G. *Road builders*
Hill, Eric. *Spot goes to the farm*

Hill, Lee Sullivan. *Earthmovers*
Hines, Anna Grossnickle. *I am a backhoe*
Hoban, Tana. *Construction zone*
    Dig, drill, dump, fill
Holub, Joan. *Mighty dads*
Horvath, James. *Dig, dogs, dig*
Hudson, Cheryl Willis. *Construction zone*
Kilby, Don. *At a construction site*
    In the city
    In the country
Koehler, Lora. *The little snowplow*
Kraft, Betsy Harvey. *The fantastic Ferris wheel*
Light, Steve. *Diggers go*
Low, William. *Machines go to work*
    Machines go to work in the city
Lund, Deb. *Monsters on machines*
Macaulay, David. *How machines work: zoo break!*
MacDonald, Suse. *Elephants on board*
McMullan, Kate. *I'm cool!*
Meltzer, Lynn. *The construction crew*
Merriam, Eve. *Bam, bam, bam*
Murphy, Andy. *Out and about at the dairy farm*
My big book of trucks and diggers
Nakagawa, Chihiro. *Who made this cake?*
Niemann, Christoph. *That's how!*
Nikola-Lisa, W. *One hole in the road*
Novak, Matt. *The everything machine*
Odgers, Sally. *Good night, Truck*
Old MacDonald had a farm. Old MacDonald had a truck
Olson-Brown, Ellen. *Hush little digger*
Pallotta, Jerry. *The construction alphabet book*
Patrick, Jean L. S. *If I had a snowplow*
Peterson, Cris. *Fantastic farm machines*
Pringle, Laurence P. *Jesse builds a road*
Rinker, Sherri Duskey. *Goodnight, goodnight, construction site*
    Mighty, mighty construction site
Rockwell, Anne. *Good morning, Digger*
Sadler, Marilyn. *Alistair's time machine*
Savage, Stephen. *Supertruck*
Sayres, Brianna Caplan. *Where do diggers sleep at night?*
Schubert, Leda. *Here comes Darrell*
Steggall, Susan. *Colors*
    The diggers are coming!
Stein, Peter. *Little Red's riding 'hood*
Stevenson, James. *Sam the Zamboni man*
Suen, Anastasia. *Up! up! up! skyscraper*
Sutton, Sally. *Construction*
    Demolition
Varela, Barry. *Gizmo*
Verdick, Elizabeth. *Small Walt*
Vestergaard, Hope. *Digger, dozer, dumper*
Watson, Wendy. *Holly's Christmas eve*
Wood, Jakki. *A hole in the road*

Magic

Adler, David A. *A picture book of Harry Houdini*
Agee, Jon. *Milo's hat trick*
Andersen, Hans Christian. *The tinderbox*, ill. by Warwick Hutton
    The tinderbox, ill. by Bagram Ibatoulline
    The tinderbox, ill. by Barry Moser
    The wild swans, ill. by Anne Yvonne Gilbert
    The wild swans, ill. by Susan Jeffers
Anno, Mitsumasa. *Anno's hat tricks*
Araki, Mie. *The magic toolbox*

Aylesworth, Jim. *The full belly bowl*
Baeten, Lieve. *The clever little witch*
Barnett, Mac. *The magic word*
Base, Graeme. *The Jewel Fish of Karnak*
    Jungle drums
    Little elephants
Bateman, Teresa. *Hamster Camp*
Baumgart, Klaus. *Laura's Christmas star*
    Laura's secret
Baynton, Martin. *Jane and the magician*
Becker, Aaron. *Journey*
    Quest
    Return
Begin, Mary Jane. *The sorcerer's apprentice*
Bemelmans, Ludwig. *Madeline's Christmas*
Berenstain, Stan and Jan. *The Berenstain bears and the sitter*
Berry, Lynne. *Squid Kid the Magnificent*
Bianco, Margery Williams. *The velveteen rabbit*, ill. by David Jorgensen
    The velveteen rabbit, ill. by Thea Kliros
    The velveteen rabbit, ill. by Komako Sakai
    The velveteen rabbit, ill. by Gennady Spirin
    The velveteen rabbit: or, How toys became real, ill. by Allen Atkinson
    The velveteen rabbit: or, How toys became real, ill. by Steve Johnson
Black, Harley. *Amazing magic school*
Bloom, Becky. *Mice make trouble*
Bogan, Paulette. *Momma's magical purse*
Booth, Anne. *The fairiest fairy*
Bottner, Barbara. *Pish and Posh*
Bower, Tamara. *The shipwrecked sailor*
Bridwell, Norman. *The witch grows up*
Briggs, Raymond. *The puddleman*
Brown, Marcia. *Once a mouse . . .*
Brown, Monica. *Chavela and the magic bubble*
Buehner, Caralyn. *Snowmen all year*
Bunting, Eve. *Thunder horse*
Burdett, Lois. *The tempest for kids*
Burningham, John. *The magic bed*
Calmenson, Stephanie. *The frog principal*
Carmody, Isobelle. *Magic night*
Cate, Annette LeBlanc. *The magic rabbit*
Chase, Mary. *The wicked, wicked ladies in the haunted house*
Cleminson, Katie. *Magic box*
Coats, Lucy. *Neil's numberless world*
Cole, Babette. *Prince Cinders*
Cole, Joanna. *Bony-legs*
    The magic school bus and the science fair expedition
    The magic school bus in the time of the dinosaurs
    The magic school bus inside a beehive
    The magic school bus lost in the solar system
    The magic school bus on the ocean floor
Compestine, Ying Chang. *The runaway wok*
Corderoy, Tracey. *Monty and Milli*
Craft, Mahlon F. *Beauty and the beast*
Cronin, Doreen. *Bloom*
Cullen, Catherine Ann. *The magical, mystical, marvelous coat*
David, Ryan. *The magic raincoat*
DeFelice, Cynthia C. *One potato, two potato*
Demi. *The magic pillow*
dePaola, Tomie. *Big Anthony and the magic ring*
    Brava Strega Nona!
    Merry Christmas, Strega Nona
    Strega Nona
    Strega Nona meets her match

Shah, Idries. *The boy without a name*
Shepard, Aaron. *One-eye! Two-eyes! Three-eyes!*
Shireen, Nadia. *Hey, Presto!*
Shulevitz, Uri. *The magician*
Simmons, Steven J. *Alice and Greta*
    Alice and Greta's color magic
    Greta's revenge
Sokol, Edward. *Meet Stinky Magee*
Somers, Kevin. *Meaner than meanest*
Sperring, Mark. *Max and the won't go to bed show*
Stainton, Sue. *The chocolate cat*
Steig, William. *The amazing bone*
    Caleb and Kate
    Gorky rises
    Solomon the rusty nail
    Sylvester and the magic pebble
    Tiffky Doofky
    Zeke Pippin
Steptoe, John. *The story of jumping mouse*
Stevenson, James. *Yuck!*
Stewig, John Warren. *Clever Gretchen*
Stimpson, Colin. *Jack and the baked beanstalk*
Taulbert, Clifton L. *Little Cliff and the porch people*
Teague, Mark. *One Halloween night*
Tegen, Katherine. *Pink cupcake magic*
Tegen, Katherine Brown. *Snowman magic*
Thomas, Shelley Moore. *Good night, Good Knight*
Thomas, Valerie. *Winnie's midnight dragon*
Thompson, Lauren. *The Christmas magic*
Thomson, Bill. *Chalk*
    The typewriter
Tibo, Gilles. *The cowboy kid*
Tom Tit Tot. *Tom Tit Tot*
Tseng, Grace. *White tiger, blue serpent*
Tunnell, Michael O. *Halloween pie*
Vallverdu, Josep. *Aladdin and the magic lamp /*
    Aldino y la lampara maravillosa
Van Allsburg, Chris. *The garden of Abdul Gasazi*
    Probuditi!
    The widow's broom
Van Dusen, Chris. *King Hugo's huge ego*
Wallace, Karen. *Scarlette Beane*
Walsh, Ellen Stoll. *Mouse magic*
    Pip's magic
Walters, Catherine. *The magical snowman*
Wiesner, David. *The loathsome dragon*
    Tuesday
Willard, Nancy. *The flying bed*
Williams, Sam. *Snowy magic*
Wisniewski, David. *Elfwyn's saga*
Wood, Audrey. *The flying dragon room*
Yep, Laurence. *The shell woman and the king*
Yolen, Jane. *The firebird*
Yoo, Taeeun. *The little red fish*
Zagarenski, Pamela. *Henry and Leo*
    The whisper

Mail *see* Careers – postal workers; Letters, cards;
    Post office

Mail carriers *see* Careers – postal workers;
    Letters, cards

Manners *see* Etiquette

Maps

Beck, Andrea. *Elliot digs for treasure*
Becker, Aaron. *Quest*
Burleigh, Robert. *Solving the puzzle under the sea*
Chancellor, Deborah. *Maps and mapping*
Elliot, David. *Henry's map*
Gertsberg, Inna. *The way downtown*
Hartman, Gail. *As the crow flies*
Keller, Laurie. *The scrambled states of America*
    The scrambled states of America talent show
Leedy, Loreen. *Mapping Penny's world*
Murphy, Stuart J. *Treasure map*
National Geographic Society [U.S.]. *National*
    Geographic our world
Paterson, Brian. *Zigby hunts for treasure*
Piepmeier, Charlotte. *Lucy's journey to the wild west*
Shulevitz, Uri. *How I learned geography*
Singer, Marilyn. *On the same day in March*
Stroud, Bettye. *The patchwork path*
Tyler, Jenny. *Big Pig on a dig*
Walters, Virginia. *Are we there yet, Daddy?*

Mardi Gras

Lionni, Leo. *The greentail mouse*

Marionettes *see* Puppets

Markets *see* Stores

Marriage, interracial

Adoff, Arnold. *Black is brown is tan*
McGill, Alice. *Molly Bannaky*
Senisi, Ellen B. *For my family, love, Allie*

Marriages *see* Weddings

Masks

Choi, Yangsook. *Behind the mask*
Cohen, Miriam. *The real-skin rubber monster mask*
Emberley, Ed. *Glad monster, sad monster*
Fortenberry, Julie. *Lily's cat mask*
Garza, Cynthia Leonor. *Lucía the luchadora*
Hru, Dakari. *Joshua's Masai mask*
Lemke, Donald. *Book-o-beards*
Spalding, Andrea. *Solomon's tree*

Math *see* Counting, numbers

Mazes

Kalz, Jill. *An a-maze-ing amusement park adventure*
    An a-maze-ing farm adventure
    An a-maze-ing school adventure
    An a-maze-ing zoo adventure
Munro, Roxie. *Ecomazes*
    Market maze
    Mazescapes
    Mazeways
Philpot, Lorna. *Find Anthony Ant*

Meanness *see* Character traits – meanness

Mechanical men *see* Robots

Medical technicians *see* Careers – emergency medical technicians

Memories, memory

Aliki. *Christmas tree memories*
Bar-el, Dan. *A fish named Glub*
Bloom, Suzanne. *Fox forgets*
Blumenthal, Deborah. *Aunt Claire's yellow beehive hair*
Bonwill, Ann. *The Frazzle family finds a way*
Bowen, Anne. *I loved you before you were born*
Brisson, Pat. *Star blanket*
Bunting, Eve. *The memory string*
Cheng, Andrea. *The lemon sisters*
Ciraolo, Simona. *The lines on Nana's face*
Cooke, Trish. *The grandad tree*
Cruise, Robin. *Little Mama forgets*
Cummings, Phil. *Newspaper hats*
Doray, Malika. *One more Wednesday*
Dunrea, Olivier. *Peedie*
Empson, Jo. *Chimpanzees for tea!*
Fitzpatrick, Marie-Louise. *You, me and the big blue sea*
Fleischman, Paul. *The matchbox diary*
Foreman, Michael. *Cat in the manger*
Garland, Michael. *Grandpa's tractor*
Gerdner, Linda. *Grandfather's story cloth / Yawg daim paj ntaub dab neeg*
Hanson, Regina. *A season for mangoes*
Hines, Anna Grossnickle. *When the goblins came knocking*
Hopkinson, Deborah. *Bluebird summer*
Johnson, Angela. *The Rolling Store*
Joosse, Barbara. *Ghost wings*
Krishnaswami, Uma. *Chachaji's cup*
Kurtz, Jane. *Faraway home*
Laden, Nina. *Once upon a memory*
Leedahl, Shelley A. *The bone talker*
Levine, Arthur A. *What a beautiful morning*
Lindbergh, Reeve. *My little grandmother often forgets*
Lloyd, Jennifer. *The best thing about kindergarten*
Lucke, Deb. *Sneezenesia*
Luxbacher, Irene. *Mr. Frank*
Lynn, Sarah. *Tip-tap pop*
Lyons, Kelly Starling. *Tea cakes for Tosh*
McKee, David. *Elmer and Grandpa Eldo*
MacLachlan, Patricia. *Snowflakes fall*
  Someone like me
Mathers, Petra. *When Aunt Mattie got her wings*
Meng, Cece. *Always remember*
Monk, Isabell. *Blackberry stew*
Mora, Pat. *The remembering day / El día de los muertos*
Morris, Ann. *Grandma Esther remembers*
  Grandma Francisca remembers
  Grandma Lai Goon remembers
  Grandma Lois remembers
  Grandma Maxine remembers
Nivola, Claire A. *Orani*
O'Brien, Anne Sibley. *A path of stars*
Parker, Marjorie Blain. *Jasper's day*
Perkins, Lynne Rae. *The broken cat*
Polacco, Patricia. *Betty Doll*
  Mrs. Mack
Priceman, Marjorie. *My nine lives / by Clio*

Robinson, Michelle. *The forgetful knight*
Rochelle, Belinda. *Jewels*
Santucci, Barbara. *Anna's corn*
Schick, Eleanor. *Mama*
Seinfeld, Jerry. *Halloween*
Sheehan, Kevin. *The dandelion's tale*
Smith, Lane. *Grandpa Green*
Steig, William. *When everybody wore a hat*
Stewart, Joel. *Addis Berner Bear forgets*
Turner, Ann Warren. *Abe Lincoln remembers*
Van Laan, Nancy. *Forget me not*
Warner, Sunny. *The moon quilt*
Winter, Jeanette. *Mr. Cornell's dream boxes*
Woodruff, Elvira. *The memory coat*
Woodson, Jacqueline. *Sweet, sweet memory*
Wyeth, Sharon Dennis. *The granddaughter necklace*
Young, Cybèle. *Nancy knows*
Young, Rebecca. *Teacup*
Zagwÿn, Deborah Turney. *The winter gift*
Zalben, Jane Breskin. *Pearl's marigolds for grandpa*

Merry-go-rounds

Cecil, Randy. *Gator*
Clements, Andrew. *Workshop*
Crews, Donald. *Carousel*
Kleven, Elisa. *A carousel tale*
Murphy, Stuart J. *Animals on board*
Rosenberg, Liz. *The carousel*
Selick, Henry. *Moongirl*
Ward, Lindsay. *Please bring balloons*

Messy *see* Behavior – messy

Metamorphosis

Aston, Dianna Hutts. *A butterfly is patient*
Barringer, William. *Gregory and Alexander*
Bunting, Eve. *Butterfly house*
Carle, Eric. *The very hungry caterpillar*
Collicott, Sharleen. *Toestomper and the bad butterflies*
Edwards, Pamela Duncan. *Clara Caterpillar*
Foley, Greg. *Don't worry Bear*
Frost, Helen. *Monarch and milkweed*
Geras, Adèle. *Swan Lake*
Gibbons, Gail. *Monarch butterfly*
Jarrett, Clare. *Arabella Miller's tiny caterpillar*
Martin, Bill, Jr.. *Ten little caterpillars*
Middleton, Charlotte. *Nibbles' garden*
Murphy, Mary. *Caterpillar's wish*
Pedersen, Janet. *Houdini the amazing caterpillar*
Rockwell, Anne. *Becoming butterflies*
Runton, Andy. *Owly and Wormy: friends all aflutter!*
Ryder, Joanne. *Where butterflies grow*
Shingu, Susumu. *Traveling butterflies*
Sturges, Philemon. *What's that sound, Woolly Bear?*
Willis, Jeanne. *Tadpole's promise*
Wilson, Steve. *Hedgehugs and the Hattiepillar*

Middle Ages

Adkins, Jan. *What if you met a knight?*
Ashburn, Boni. *Over at the castle*
Dick Whittington and his cat. *Dick Whittington and his cat*, ill. by Marcia Brown
  Dick Whittington and his cat, ill. by Mélisande Potter
Gibbons, Gail. *Knights in shining armor*
Hindley, Judy. *Princess Rosa's winter*

Hodges, Margaret. *Saint George and the dragon*
Kaufman, Jeanne. *Young Henry and the dragon*
Klostermann, Penny Parker. *There was an old dragon who swallowed a knight*
Nikola-Lisa, W. *Magic in the margins*
Olofsson, Helena. *The little jester*
Scarry, Huck. *Looking into the Middle Ages*
Steig, William. *The toy brother*
Tucker, Kathy. *Do knights take naps?*
Yep, Laurence. *The man who tricked a ghost*

Migration

Baker, Jeannie. *Circle*
Berkes, Marianne. *Going home: the mystery of animal migration*
Berne, Jennifer. *Calvin can't fly*
Cowcher, Helen. *Desert elephants*
DePalma, Mary Newell. *Two little birds*
Elwell, Peter. *Adios Oscar!*
Empson, Jo. *Little home bird*
Frost, Helen. *Monarch and milkweed*
George, Jean Craighead. *Luck*
Gerber, Carole. *Little red bat*
Lamstein, Sarah Marwil. *Big night for salamanders*
Madison, Alan. *Velma Gratch and the way cool butterfly*
Marino, Gianna. *Following Papa's song*
Markle, Sandra. *Butterfly tree*
   Toad weather
Ó Flatharta, Antoine. *Hurry and the monarch*
Oswald, Pete. *Mingo the flamingo*
Prosek, James. *Bird, butterfly, eel*
Sayre, April Pulley. *Here come the humpbacks!*
   Home at last: a song of migration
   Turtle, turtle, watch out!, ill. by Lee Christiansen
   Turtle, turtle, watch out!, ill. by Annie Patterson
Shingu, Susumu. *Traveling butterflies*
Swope, Sam. *Gotta go! Gotta go!*
Thornhill, Jan. *Is this Panama?*
Wild, Margaret. *Lucy Goosey*
Willis, Nancy Carol. *Red knot*
Winkelman, Barbara Gaines. *Sockeye's journey home*
Woodson, Jacqueline. *This is the rope*

Mimes *see* Clowns, jesters

Ministers *see* Careers – clergy

Minorities *see* Ethnic groups in the U.S.

Mirages *see* Optical illusions

Mirrors

Baker, Jeannie. *Mirror*
Cobb, Vicki. *I see myself*
Lee, Suzy. *Mirror*
Schindel, John. *What did they see?*
Wilhelm, Hans. *A hole in the wall*

Misbehavior *see* Behavior – misbehavior

Missing *see* Behavior – lost

Missions

Politi, Leo. *Song of the swallows*
Ryan, Pam Muñoz. *Nacho and Lolita*

Mist *see* Weather – fog

Mistakes *see* Behavior – mistakes

Misunderstanding *see* Behavior – misunderstanding

Mittens *see* Clothing – gloves, mittens

Money

Adler, David A. *Money madness*
Axelrod, Amy. *Pigs will be pigs*
Bair, Sheila. *Isabel's car wash*
Berenstain, Stan and Jan. *The Berenstain bears' trouble with money*
Borden, Louise. *Kindergarten luck*
Brown, Marc. *Arthur's TV trouble*
Caple, Kathy. *Worm gets a job*
Carlson, Nancy. *Start saving, Henry!*
Child, Lauren. *But I've used all my pocket change I really, really need actual ice skates*
Curious George and the puppies
Finlay, Lizzie. *Little Croc's purse*
Garhan Attebury, Nancy. *Out and about at the bank*
   Out and about at the United States Mint
Gill, Shelley. *The big buck adventure*
Glass, Julie. *A dollar for Penny*
Harris, Trudy. *Jenny found a penny*
Heine, Theresa. *Chandra's magic light*
Inkpen, Mick. *The great pet sale*
Isabella, Jude. *The red bicycle*
Jenkins, Emily. *Lemonade in winter*
Kinch, Devon. *Pretty Penny cleans up*
   Pretty Penny makes ends meet
Leedy, Loreen. *Follow the money*
McCaughrean, Geraldine. *One bright Penny*
McMillan, Bruce. *Jelly beans for sale*
Maestro, Betsy. *Dollars and cents for Harriet*
Marks, Jennifer L. *Sorting money*
Medina, Meg. *Tía Isa wants a car*
Milway, Katie Smith. *One hen*
Mollel, Tololwa M. *My rows and piles of coins*
Murphy, Stuart J. *The penny pot*
   Sluggers' car wash
O'Connor, Jane. *Fancy Nancy and the fabulous fashion boutique*
O'Neill, Alexis. *Estela's swap*
Paul, Miranda. *One plastic bag*
Perez, Monica. *Curious George saves his pennies*
Reid, Margarette S. *Lots and lots of coins*
Siegel, Randy. *One proud penny*
Skinner, Daphne. *Tightwad Tod*
Stewart, Sarah. *The money tree*
Tada, Joni Eareckson. *The incredible discovery of Lindsey Renee*
Viorst, Judith. *Alexander, who used to be rich last Sunday*
Warwick, Dionne. *Little Man*
Wells, Rosemary. *Bunny money*
   Max's bunny business

Williams, Rozanne Lanczak. *The coin counting book*
Wilson, Troy. *Liam takes a stand*
Ziefert, Harriet. *You can't buy a dinosaur with a dime*

Monsters

Adler, David A. *Perimeter, area, and volume*
Alexander, Lloyd. *The house Gobbaleen*
Alexander, Sue. *Who goes out on Halloween?*
Anderson, Brian. *Monster chefs*
Anstee, Ashlyn. *Are we there, Yeti?*
Apple, Margot. *Brave Martha*
Armstrong, Matthew S. *Jane and Mizmow*
Armstrong-Ellis, Carey. *Ten creepy monsters*
Arnold, Tedd. *Five ugly monsters*
  Huggly gets dressed
  Huggly takes a bath
Ashdown, Rebecca. *The Whopper*
Ashman, Linda. *The essential worldwide monster
  guide*
Atteberry, Kevan. *Bunnies!!!*
  Puddles!!!
Austin, Mike. *Monsters love colors*
Bach, Annie. *Monster party!*
Baker, Ken. *Brave little monster*
Balmes, Santi. *I will fight monsters for you*
Bang, Molly. *Wiley and the hairy man*
Bardhan-Quallen, Sudipta. *Hampire!*
Barnett, Mac. *Rules of the house*
Barton, Bethany. *This monster cannot wait!*
  This monster needs a haircut
Bauer, Marion Dane. *I'm not afraid of Halloween!*
Baum, Louis. *The mouse who braved bedtime*
Beaty, Andrea. *Hush, Baby Ghostling*
Beck, Scott. *Happy birthday, Monster!*
  Monster sleepover!
Bee, William. *Worst in show*
Bennett, Kelly. *Vampire baby*
Berger, Samantha. *Back to school with Bigfoot*
  Monster's new undies
Boxall, Ed. *Francis the scaredy cat*
Boyd, Colin. *The bath monster*
Brandle, Bine. *Flusi, the sock monster*
Brendler, Carol. *Not very scary*
Brennan, Herbie. *Frankenstella and the video store
  monster*
Brennan-Nelson, Denise. *He's been a monster all
  day!*
Bright, Rachel. *Love Monster*
  Love Monster and the last chocolate
  Love Monster and the perfect present
  Love Monster and the scary something
The brothers gruesome
Brown, Lisa. *Vampire boy's good night*
Brown, Marc. *Arthur's first sleepover*
Brown, Peter. *My teacher is a monster! (no, I am not)*
Bunting, Eve. *Scary, scary Halloween*
Burnell, Heather Ayris. *Bedtime monster / ¡A dormir,
  pequeño monstruo!*
Case, Chris. *Sophie and the next-door monsters*
Catrow, David. *Monster mash*
Chapman, Jane. *No more cuddles!*
Clanton, Ben. *Mo's mustache*
Cohen, Caron Lee. *Broom, zoom!*
Cohen, Miriam. *Jim meets the thing*
Collins, Ross. *Dear Vampa*
Cornell, Kevin. *Go to sleep, monster!*
Côté, Geneviève. *Mr. King's things*
Crow, Kristyn. *Bedtime at the swamp*

Zombelina
Zombelina: school days
Crum, Shutta. *Who took my hairy toe?*
Cushman, Doug. *Halloween good night*
Cuyler, Margery. *Bonaparte falls apart*
  Monster mess!
Czajak, Paul. *Monster needs a Christmas tree*
  Monster needs your vote
David, Lawrence. *The land of the hungry armadillos*
Day, Trevor. *Youch! it bites!*
Denise, Anika. *Monster trucks*
Dickinson, Rebecca. *Over in the Hollow*
DiPucchio, Kelly. *Zombie in love*
  Zombie in love 2 + 1
Diviny, Sean. *Halloween Motel*
Docherty, Thomas. *Big scary monster*
Dolan, Elys. *The mystery of the haunted farm*
Dormer, Frank W. *Socksquatch*
Doyle, Malachy. *Hungry! hungry! hungry!*
Dunbar, Joyce. *The monster who ate darkness*
Dyer, Sarah. *Clementine and Mungo*
  Monster day at work
Egielski, Richard. *The sleepless little vampire*
Elliott, David. *Hazel Nutt, mad scientist*
Emberley, Ed. *Ed Emberley's bye-bye, big bad bullybug!*
  Glad monster, sad monster
  Go away, big green monster!
  Nighty night Little Green Monster
Emberley, Rebecca. *If you're a monster and you know
  it*
  Ten little beasties
Emberley, Rebecca, et al. *There was an old monster*
Esbaum, Jill. *Frankenbunny*
Evans, Cambria. *Bone soup*
Faulkner, Keith. *The monster who loved books*
Flaherty, A. W. *The luck of the Loch Ness monster*
Fletcher, Tom. *There's a monster in your book*
Fraser, Mary Ann. *No Yeti yet*
Fredrickson, Lane. *Monster trouble!*
Freedman, Claire. *Spider sandwiches*
Fronis, Aly. *If you're spooky and you know it*
Funke, Cornelia. *The wildest brother*
Gaiman, Neil. *The dangerous alphabet*
Gall, Chris. *Substitute creacher*
Gerstein, Mordicai. *The absolutely awful alphabet*
Gibala-Broxholm, Scott. *Maddie's monster dad*
Goodall, John S. *Creepy castle*
Grabill, Rebecca. *Halloween good night*
Gravel, Elise. *I want a monster!*
Graves, Keith. *The monsterator*
Greene, Rhonda Gowler. *Eek! creak! snicker, sneak*
Gunnufson, Charlotte. *Halloween hustle*
Haber, Tiffany Strelitz. *The monster who lost his
  mean*
Hall, Michael. *Frankencrayon*
Hamilton, Libby. *The monstrous book of monsters*
Harper, Charise Mericle. *The Monster Show*
Hawkins, Colin. *Creepy castle*
Hazen, Barbara Shook. *Who is your favorite monster,
  Mama?*
Heinz, Brian J. *The monsters' test*
Heller, Nicholas. *Ogres! ogres! ogres!*
Helmer, Marilyn. *Spooky riddles*
Hemingway, Edward. *Bump in the night*
Hicks, Barbara Jean. *Jitterbug jam*
  Monsters don't eat broccoli
Hodgkinson, Leigh. *The big monster snorey book*
Horton, Joan. *Working mummies*
Hout, Mies van. *Friends*

Howe, James. *There's a monster under my bed*
Howie, Betsy. *The Block Mess Monster*
Hunter, Jana Novotny. *My tail's not tired*
Hutchins, Pat. *It's my birthday!*
   Silly Billy!
   Three-star Billy
   The very worst monster
   Where's the baby?
Imai, Ayano. *Puss and boots*
Inches, Alison. *I'm not little!*
Inkpen, Mick. *Kipper's monster*
Irving, John. *A sound like someone trying not to make a sound*
Jamison, Jocelyn. *Drac's night out*
Jane, Pamela. *Little goblins ten*
   Monster countdown
   Monster mischief
John, Jory. *I will chomp you!*
   Quit calling me a monster!
Kaplan, Bruce Eric. *Monsters eat whiny children*
Kasza, Keiko. *Grandpa Toad's last secret*
Keller, Joy. *Monster trucks*
Kellogg, Steven. *The island of the skog*
   The mysterious tadpole
Ketteman, Helen. *The ghosts go haunting*
   Goodnight, Little Monster
Kimmel, Eric A. *The three cabritos*
Kirk, David. *Truckeroo school*
Kleven, Elisa. *A monster in the house*
Knapman, Timothy. *A monster moved in!*
Knudsen, Michelle. *Marilyn's monster*
Koller, Jackie French. *No such thing*
Kraegel, Kenneth. *King Arthur's very great grandson*
Kutner, Merrily. *The Zombie Nite Cafe*
Kwan, James. *Dear Yeti*
LaRochelle, David. *Monster and son*
Layne, Steven L. *My brother Dan's delicious*
Lazar, Tara. *The Monstore*
Lester, Helen. *The loch mess monster*
Lesynski, Loris. *Night school*
Leuck, Laura. *Goodnight, baby monster*
   My beastly brother
   My monster mama loves me so
Levis, Caron. *Stuck with the Blooz*
Lewis, J. Patrick. *M is for monster*
Lia, Simone. *Red's great chase*
Lichtenheld, Tom. *Everything I know about monsters*
Light, Steve. *Have you seen my monster?*
Lodge, Bernard. *How scary*
Long, Ethan. *Fright club*
   Valensteins: (a love story)
Lund, Deb. *Monsters on machines*
Lundgren, Mary Beth. *Seven scary monsters*
McAllister, Angela. *Trust me, Mom!*
   Yuck! That's not a monster
McCarty, Peter. *Jeremy draws a monster*
   The monster returns
McDonnell, Patrick. *The monsters' monster*
McElligott, Matthew. *Even monsters need haircuts*
McGee, Joe. *Peanut butter and brains*
MacHale, D. J. *The monster princess*
McKee, David. *Elmer and the monster*
McKissack, Patricia C. *Precious and the Boo Hag*
Mahoney, Daniel J. *Monstergarten*
Manceau, Edouard. *Tickle monster*
Markell, Denis. *Hush, Little Monster*
Martin, Bill, Jr.. *A beasty story*
Mayer, Marianna. *Pegasus*
Mayer, Mercer. *The bravest knight*

   Liza Lou and the Yeller Belly Swamp
   There are monsters everywhere
   There's a nightmare in my closet
Mayer, Pamela. *The scariest monster in the whole wide world*
Medearis, Angela Shelf. *Tailypo*
Metz, Lorijo. *Floridius Bloom and the planet of Gloom*
Metzger, Steve. *This is the house that monsters built*
Milgrim, David. *Some monsters are different*
Miranda, Anne. *Monster math*
Moffatt, Judith. *Trick-or-treat faces*
Mollel, Tololwa M. *Song bird*
Monster, be good!
Montes, Marisa. *Los gatos black on Halloween*
Moodie, Fiona. *Noko and the night monster*
Moore, Lilian. *Beware, take care*
Mosel, Arlene. *The funny little woman*
Murphy, Jill. *All for one*
Murray, Diana. *Ned the knitting pirate*
Mystery manor
Namioka, Lensey. *Hungriest boy in the world*
Neubecker, Robert. *Beasty bath*
Noll, Amanda. *I need my monster*
Norac, Carl. *Monster, don't eat me!*
Nordling, Lee. *The bramble*
Numberman, Neil. *Do not build a Frankenstein!*
Numeroff, Laura Joffe. *Laura Numeroff's 10-step guide to living with your monster*
O'Connor, George. *Sally and the Some-Thing*
OHora, Zachariah. *The not so quiet library*
O'Keefe, Susan Heyboer. *Hungry monster ABC*
   One hungry monster
O'Malley, Kevin. *Velcome*
Pace, Anne Marie. *Vampirina ballerina*
   Vampirina ballerina hosts a sleepover
Paraskevas, Betty. *Maggie and the Ferocious Beast, the big carrot*
   Maggie and the Ferocious Beast, the big scare
Patricelli, Leslie. *The Patterson puppies and the midnight monster party*
Peck, Richard. *Monster night at Grandma's house*
Peet, Bill. *Cyrus the unsinkable sea serpent*
Pfister, Marcus. *Rainbow fish and the sea monsters' cave*
Pickering, Jimmy. *Skelly the skeleton girl*
Pienkowski, Jan. *Haunted house*
Pinkney, Brian. *Cosmo and the robot*
Polacco, Patricia. *Some birthday!*
Prelutsky, Jack. *The baby uggs are hatching*
Puttock, Simon. *The baby that roared*
Reasoner, Charles. *Peek-a-boo monsters*
Redeker, Kent. *Don't splash the sasquatch!*
   Don't squish the sasquatch!
Reiner, Carl. *Tell me a scary story — but not too scary!*
Rex, Michael. *Goodnight goon*
Reynolds, Aaron. *Here comes Destructosaurus!*
Richards, Dan. *The problem with not being scared of monsters*
Riggio, Anita. *Beware the Brindlebeast*
Rosoff, Meg. *Jumpy Jack and Googily*
Ross, Gayle. *The legend of the Windigo*
Rubin, Adam. *Big bad bubble*
Sage, James. *Mr. Beast*
San Souci, Robert D. *The Hobyahs*
   Pedro and the monkey
Sauer, Tammi. *Mostly monsterly*
Schaefer, Lola M. *Frankie Stein*
   Frankie Stein starts school
Scheffler, Axel. *Pip and Posy: the scary monster*

Schneider, Josh. *Bedtime monsters*
Schnitzlein, Danny. *The monster who ate my peas*
Schultz, Sam. *Monster mayhem*
Scrimger, Richard. *Princess Bun Bun*
Seeger, Pete. *Abiyoyo*
Seibold, J. Otto. *Vunce upon a time*
Selick, Henry. *Moongirl*
Sendak, Maurice. *Mommy?*
  Seven little monsters
  Where the wild things are
Shannon, Margaret. *Gullible's troubles*
Sierra, Judy. *The house that Drac built*
  Monster Goose
  Thelonius Monster's sky-high fly pie
  'Twas the fright before Christmas
  Wiley and the Hairy Man
Silverman, Erica. *The Halloween house*
Simon, Annette. *Robot zombie Frankenstein!*
Sís, Peter. *Ship ahoy!*
Slonim, David. *I loathe you*
Smith, A. J. *Even monsters*
Soman, David. *The monster next door*
Spinelli, Eileen. *Wanda's monster*
Stadler, John. *Wilson and Miss Lovely*
Stein, David Ezra. *Monster hug!*
Stein, Mathilde. *The child cruncher*
  Monstersong
Stephens, Ann Marie. *Cy makes a friend*
Stephens, Helen. *Ruby and the noisy hippo*
Stevenson, James. *"Could be worse!"*
Stewart, Joel. *Dexter Bexley and the big blue beastie*
Stine, R. L. *The Little Shop of Monsters*
Stower, Adam. *Two left feet*
Taylor, Sean. *I want to be in a scary story*
  When a monster is born
Tegen, Katherine Brown. *Dracula and Frankenstein are friends*
Thach, James Otis. *A child's guide to common household monsters*
Thomas, Frances. *One day, Daddy*
Todd, Mark. *What will you be for Halloween?*
Tunnell, Michael O. *Halloween pie*
Turkle, Brinton. *Do not open*
Turnbull, Victoria. *Kings of the castle*
Van Dusen, Chris. *Hattie and Hudson*
Van Nutt, Julia. *The monster in the shadows*
Vega, Denise. *If your monster won't go to bed*
Vere, Ed. *Bedtime for monsters*
Vestergaard, Hope. *What do you do when a monster says boo?*
Viorst, Judith. *My mama says there aren't any zombies, ghosts, vampires, creatures, demons, monsters, fiends, goblins, or things*
Vogel, Vin. *Bedtime for Yeti*
  The thing about yetis
Waechter, Phillip. *Rosie and the nightmares*
Waldron, Jan L. *John Pig's Halloween*
Walsh, Melanie. *Monster, monster*
Walton, Rick. *Frankenstein*
  Frankenstein's fright before Christmas
Wang, Andrea. *The Nian Monster*
Weston, Martha. *Tuck's haunted house*
Wheeler, Lisa. *Boogie knights*
  Even monsters need to sleep
Whitman, Candace. *Lines that wiggle*
Whybrow, Ian. *Good night, monster*
Willems, Mo. *Leonardo the terrible monster*
  Sam the most scaredy-cat kid in the whole world
Wing, Natasha. *Go to bed, monster!*

Winters, Kay. *The teeny tiny ghost and the monster*
Wohnoutka, Mike. *Little puppy and the big green monster*
Yaccarino, Dan. *The lima bean monster*
Yep, Laurence. *The Khan's daughter*
Yolen, Jane. *Creepy monsters, sleepy monsters*
  Romping monsters, stomping monsters
Zalben, Jane Breskin. *Saturday night at the Beastro*
Zemach, Harve. *The judge*
Zenz, Aaron. *Monsters go night-night*

Months of the year *see* Days of the week, months of the year

Moon

Agee, Jon. *Dmitri the astronaut*
  It's only Stanley
Alborozo, Gabriel. *The mouse and the moon*
Aldrin, Buzz. *Reaching for the moon*
Anderson, Stephen Axel. *I know the moon*
Arden, Carolyn. *Goose moon*
Asch, Frank. *Happy birthday, moon!*
  Moonbear
  Mooncake
  Moondance
  Moongame
Bartram, Simon. *Man on the moon: a day in the life of Bob*
Berenstain, Stan and Jan. *The Berenstain bears on the moon*
Berger, Barbara. *Grandfather Twilight*
Bolden, Tonya. *Beautiful moon*
Branley, Franklyn M. *What the moon is like*
Brown, Margaret Wise. *Goodnight moon*
  Goodnight moon ABC
  Goodnight moon 123: a counting book
Brown-Wood, JaNay. *Imani's moon*
Burleigh, Robert. *One giant leap*
Butler, M. Christina. *Mouse and the moon*
Cain, Sheridan. *By the light of the moon*
Carle, Eric. *Papa, please get the moon for me*
Carroll, James Christopher. *The boy and the moon*
Chambers, Roland. *Rooftop rocket party*
Chichester Clark, Emma. *Eliza and the moonchild*
Clark, Karen Henry. *Sweet moon baby*
Cole, Rachael. *City moon*
Conrad, Donna. *See you soon, Moon*
Cooper, Floyd. *Max and the tag-along moon*
Côté, Geneviève. *With you always, Little Monday*
Crews, Nina. *I'll catch the moon*
Dale, Penny. *Dinosaur rocket!*
Daly, Niki. *Why the sun and moon live in the sky*
Dayrell, Elphinstone. *Why the sun and the moon live in the sky*
DiCamillo, Kate. *La la la*
Dillon, Jana. *Lucky O'Leprechaun in school*
DiTerlizzi, Tony. *Jimmy Zangwow's out-of-this-world, moon pie adventure*
DuBurke, Randy. *The moon ring*
Ehlert, Lois. *Moon rope / Un lazo a la luna*
Elschner, Geraldine. *Moonchild, star of the sea*
Emmett, Jonathan. *Bringing down the moon*
Farrell, Darren. *Stop following me, Moon!*
Feder, Sandra. *The moon inside*
Fletcher, Ralph. *Hello, harvest moon*
Floca, Brian. *Moonshot*
Florian, Douglas. *Comets, stars, the moon, and Mars*

Foley, Greg. *Willoughby and the moon*
Gerstein, Mordicai. *How to bicycle to the moon to plant sunflowers*
Gigot, Jami. *Mae and the moon*
Gillmor, Don. *Yuck, a love story*
Goldberg, Myla. *Catching the moon*
Gollub, Matthew. *Gobble, quack, moon*
Griffith, Helen V. *Moonlight*
Hargrove, Linda. *Wings across the moon*
Harley, Bill. *Bear's all-night party*
Heller, Nicholas. *Elwood and the witch*
Henkes, Kevin. *Kitten's first full moon*
Horácek, Petr. *When the moon smiled*
    The mouse who ate the moon
Hunter, Anne. *Possum's harvest moon*
Jeffers, Oliver. *The way back home*
Joyce, William. *The Man in the Moon*
    The Sandman: the story of Sanderson Mansnoozie
Kherdian, David. *Come back, Moon*
King, Thomas. *Coyote sings to the moon*
Kirk, Daniel. *Moondogs*
Krilanovich, Nadia. *Moon child*
Lin, Grace. *Thanking the moon*
Lobel, Anita. *Lena's sleep sheep*
Lobel, Gillian. *Little Honey Bear and the smiley moon*
Loth, Sebastian. *Clementine*
McCarthy, Meghan. *The adventures of Patty and the big red bus*
McCarty, Peter. *Moon plane*
McDermott, Gerald. *Anansi the spider*
McNulty, Faith. *If you decide to go to the moon*
McReynolds, Linda. *Eight days gone*
Mangan, Anne. *The monkey who wanted the moon*
Martin, Ruth. *Moon dreams*
Mora, Pat. *The night the moon fell*
Morrissey, Dean. *The crimson comet*
Mortensen, Lori. *Cindy Moo*
Mother Goose. *Hey, diddle, diddle*
    Hey, diddle, diddle [board book]
Murray, Marjorie Dennis. *Little Wolf and the moon*
Nishimura, Kae. *Bunny Lune*
Oxenbury, Helen. *Tom and Pippo see the moon*
Pearce, Clemency. *Frangoline and the midnight dream*
Pearle, Ida. *The moon is going to Addy's house*
Pfister, Marcus. *The little moon raven*
Pollock, Penny. *When the moon is full*
Porter, Pamela. *Yellow moon, apple moon*
Preston, Tim. *Pumpkin moon*
Raschka, Chris. *Can't sleep*
Rex, Adam. *Moonday*
Robbins, Dean. *Margaret and the moon*
Robert, Na'ima B. *Ramadan Moon*
Robledo, Honorio. *Nico visits the moon*
Roper, Janice M. *Dancing on the moon*
Rowe, John A. *Moondog*
Rymond, Lynda Gene. *Oscar and the mooncats*
Scheer, Julian. *By the light of the captured moon*
Schertle, Alice. *Witch Hazel*
Selick, Henry. *Moongirl*
Shea, Pegi Deitz. *New moon*
Shulman, Lisa. *The moon might be milk*
Simon, Francesca. *Hello, Moon!*
Sleator, William. *The angry moon*
Smith, Linda. *When Moon fell down*
Speed, Toby. *Two cool cows*
Spinelli, Eileen. *Rise the moon*
Spurling, Margaret. *Bilby moon*

Stevenson, Robert Louis. *The moon*, ill. by Tracey Campbell Pearson
    The moon, ill. by Denise Saldutti
Stoop, Naoko. *Red Knit Cap Girl*
Suen, Anastasia. *Man on the moon*
The sun, the moon, and the stars
Tafuri, Nancy. *What the sun sees / What the moon sees*
Tan, Amy. *The moon lady*
Tarpley, Natasha Anastasia. *Joe-Joe's first flight*
Taylor, Joanne. *Full moon rising*
Thurber, James. *Many moons*, ill. by Marc Simont
    Many moons, ill. by Louis Slobodkin
Trimble, Marcia. *Moonbeams for Santa*
Udry, Janice May. *The moon jumpers*
Ungar, Richard. *Rachel captures the moon*
Ungerer, Tomi. *Moon man*
Vail, Rachel. *Over the moon*
Ward, Helen. *Little Moon Dog*
Wilcox, Brian. *Full moon*
Wolkstein, Diane. *The day Ocean came to visit*
Wood, Audrey. *Moonflute*
Yaccarino, Dan. *Zoom! zoom! zoom! I'm off to the moon!*
Yankey, Lindsey. *Sun and Moon*
Zolotow, Charlotte. *The moon was the best*

Mopeds *see* Motorcycles

Morning

Brenner, Barbara A. *Good morning, garden*
Brown, Margaret Wise. *A child's good morning book*
Dahl, Michael. *Good morning, Superman*
Eaton, Maxwell. *I'm awake!*
Freedman, Claire. *One magical morning*
Gay, Marie-Louise. *Good morning Sam*
Gerstein, Mordicai. *The night world*
Gleeson, Libby. *Cuddle time*
Good morning
Hannert, Todd. *Morning dance*
Hayward, Linda. *The King's chorus*
Henkes, Kevin. *Shhhh*
Hirschi, Ron. *When morning comes*
Hoffman, Don. *Good morning, good night Billy and Abigail*
Judge, Lita. *Good morning to me!*
Kiernan, Pat. *Good morning, city*
McGee, Marni. *Wake up, me!*
Mortensen, Denise Dowling. *Wake up engines*
Most, Bernard. *Cock-a-doodle-moo!*
Murguia, Bethanie Deeney. *Snippet the early riser*
Murphy, Stuart J. *Get up and go!*
O'Mara, Carmel. *Good morning*
Pedersen, Janet. *Millie wants to play*
Pilkey, Dav. *The paperboy*
Raffi. *Rise and shine*
Rosenberg, Liz. *Nobody*
Sedaka, Neil. *Waking up is hard to do*
Shulevitz, Uri. *Dawn*
Siddals, Mary McKenna. *Morning song*
Silverman, Erica. *Wake up, city!*
Stevens, April. *Waking up Wendell*
Tafuri, Nancy. *Early morning in the barn*
Tresselt, Alvin R. *Wake up, farm!*
Votaw, Carol. *Good morning, little polar bear*
Weninger, Brigitte. *"Mom, wake up and play!"*
Wick, Walter. *Can you see what I see? dream machine*
Yi, Hu Yong. *Good morning China*

Zolotow, Charlotte. *Something is going to happen*

Mother Goose *see* Nursery rhymes

Motion picture producers *see* Careers – motion picture producers

Motion pictures *see* Theater

Motorcycles

Blake, Quentin. *Mrs. Armitage*
Hill, Lee Sullivan. *Motorcycles*
Meadows, Michelle. *Traffic pups*
Messner, Kate. *Rolling Thunder*
O'Malley, Kevin. *Once upon a cool motorcycle dude*
Whitehead, Kathy. *Looking for Uncle Louie on the Fourth of July*

Mountain climbing *see* Sports – mountain climbing

Mountain lions *see* Animals – cougars

Mountains

Berkes, Marianne. *Over on a mountain*
Geisert, Bonnie. *Mountain town*
George, Jean Craighead. *Cliff hanger*
Gill, Shelley. *Up on Denali*
Grupper, Jonathan. *Destination — Rocky Mountains*
Huneck, Stephen. *Sally goes to the mountains*
Johnson, D. B. *Henry climbs a mountain*
Kimmel, Eric A. *The two mountains*
Locker, Thomas. *Mountain dance*
McCarthy, Meghan. *The adventures of Patty and the big red bus*
Moss, Miriam. *This is the mountain*
Nagda, Anne Whitehead. *World above the clouds*
Ray, Mary Lyn. *Basket moon*
Schmidt, Karen Lee. *Carl's nose*
Silvano, Wendi. *Just one more*
Wells, Rosemary. *The bear went over the mountain*
Zoehfeld, Kathleen Weidner. *How mountains are made*

Moving

Aliki. *Best friends together again*
   We are best friends
Arsenault, Isabelle. *Colette's lost pet*
Asch, Frank. *Goodbye house*
Ashman, Linda. *Ella who?*
Bagley, Jessixa. *Before I leave*
Beake, Lesley. *Home now*
Berenstain, Stan and Jan. *The Berenstain bears' moving day*
Blackstone, Stella. *Cleo on the move*
Blades, Ann. *Too small*
Bond, Felicia. *Poinsettia and her family*
Border, Terry. *Peanut Butter and Cupcake!*
Bottner, Barbara. *Rosa's room*
Bowers, Tim. *A new home*
Brown, Petra. *When the wind blew*
Bullard, Lisa. *Trick-or-treat on Milton Street*

Bunting, Eve. *Yard sale*
Byun, You. *Dream friends*
Carle, Eric. *Friends*
Carlson, Nancy. *My best friend moved away*
Carlstrom, Nancy White. *I'm not moving, Mama!*
Crum, Shutta. *A family for Old Mill Farm*
Cumming, Hannah. *The red boat*
D'Amico, Carmela. *Ella, the elegant elephant*
Denise, Anika. *Bella and Stella come home*
Ellis, Sarah. *Ben says goodbye*
Faruqi, Reem. *Lailah's lunchbox*
Glaser, Linda. *Hannah's way*
Gleeson, Libby. *Clancy and Millie and the very fine house*
   Half a world away
Grindley, Sally. *A new room for William*
Hallowell, George. *Wagons ho!*
Harrison, Troon. *Courage to fly*
Havill, Juanita. *Jamaica's blue marker*
Hobbie, Holly. *Everything but the horse*
Hume, Stephen Eaton. *Red moon follows truck*
Johnson, Amy Crane. *Mason moves away / Mason se muda*
Johnson, Angela. *The leaving morning*
Johnston, Tony. *The quilt story*
   Sunsets of the West
Juster, Norton. *Neville*
Kalan, Robert. *Moving day*
Keats, Ezra Jack. *The trip*
Kleven, Elisa. *The friendship wish*
Lawlor, Laurie. *Old Crump*
Lears, Laurie. *Megan's birthday tree*
Light, Steve. *The bunny burrow buyer's book*
Lobel, Anita. *Nini here and there*
Lobel, Arnold. *Ming Lo moves the mountain*
Lorenz, Albert. *The exceptionally, extraordinarily ordinary first day of school*
McCarthy, Jenna. *Lola's rules for friendship*
Macomber, Debbie. *The yippy, yappy Yorkie in the green doggy sweater*
Magerl, Caroline. *Rose and the wish thing*
Maturana, Andrea. *Life without Nico*
Meltzer, Amy. *A mezuzah on the door*
Michelin, Linda. *Zuzu's wishing cake*
Moss, Miriam. *I'll be your friend, Smudge*
   A new house for Smudge
Moss, Peggy. *One of us*
Numberman, Neil. *Do not build a Frankenstein!*
Park, Frances. *Good-bye, 382 Shin Dang Dong*
Pennypacker, Sara. *Meet the Dullards*
   Stuart's cape
Percival, Tom. *Herman's letter*, ill. by Tom Percival
   Herman's letter, ill. by Tom Percival
Pérez, Amada Irma. *My diary from here to there / Mi diario de aquí hasta allá*
Piepmeier, Charlotte. *Lucy's journey to the wild west*
Rim, Sujean. *Chee-Kee*
Ritz, Karen. *Windows with birds*
Rogers, Fred. *Moving*
Rostoker-Gruber, Karen. *Bandit*
Scanlon, Elizabeth Garton. *The good-pie party*
Sharmat, Marjorie Weinman. *Gila monsters meet you at the airport*
Shreeve, Elizabeth. *Oliver at the window*
Siegel, Mark. *Moving house*
Simpson, Lesley. *The Purim surprise*
Smith, Dana Kessimakis. *A brave spaceboy*
Smith, Joseph A. *Circus train*
Snyder, Laurel. *The forever garden*

Stead, Philip C. *Lenny and Lucy*
Stephens, Helen. *Fleabag*
Stevenson, James. *No friends*
Stewart, Shannon. *Sea crow*
Underwood, Deborah. *Bad bye, good bye*
Van Leeuwen, Jean. *Going west*
Viorst, Judith. *Alexander, who's not (do you hear me? I mean it!) going to move*
Waber, Bernard. *Gina*
    Ira says goodbye
Wagner, Anke. *Tim's big move!*
Watts, Jeri. *A piece of home*
Wong, Janet S. *Homegrown house*
Yaccarino, Dan. *Lawn to lawn*
    Oswald
Yolen, Jane. *Elsie's bird*
Zagwÿn, Deborah Turney. *The winter gift*

Multi-ethnic *see* Ethnic groups in the U.S.

Multiple births – triplets

Brunhoff, Jean de. *Babar and his children*
Horse, Harry. *Little Rabbit's new baby*
Jenkins, Emily. *Daffodil*
    Daffodil, crocodile

Multiple births – twins

Aliki. *Jack and Jake*
Arnold, Tedd. *The twin princes*
Atinuke. *Double trouble for Anna Hibiscus!*
Barber, Tiki. *By my brother's side*
    Game day
    Teammates
Brown, Marc. *Arthur babysits*
dePaola, Tomie. *Boss for a day*
    Hide-and-seek all week
    Marcos
    Meet the Barkers
    A new Barker in the house
Ehrlich, Nikki. *Twindergarten*
Geist, Ken. *Who's who?*
Gill, Timothy. *Flip and Fin: super sharks to the rescue!*
    Flip and Fin: we rule the school!
Hutchins, Pat. *Which witch is which?*
James, Brian. *Supertwins and the sneaky, slimy book worms*
    The Supertwins and tooth trouble
    The Supertwins meet the bad dogs from space
    Supertwins meet the dangerous dino-robots
Kirsch, Vincent X. *Natalie and Naughtily*
LaReau, Kara. *Rocko and Spanky have company*
Lewison, Wendy Cheyette. *Two is for twins*
McElmurry, Jill. *Mess pets*
Mahy, Margaret. *Down the dragon's tongue*
Neuschwander, Cindy. *Pastry school in Paris*
Norling, Beth. *Sister night and sister day*
Norris, Kathleen. *The holy twins*
Peete, Holly Robinson. *My brother Charlie*
Reed, Liz. *Sweet competition*
Roberts, Bethany. *Double trouble Groundhog Day*
Rockwell, Anne. *Brendan and Belinda and the slam dunk!*
Ryder, Joanne. *A pair of polar bears*
Simon, Norma. *How do I feel?*
Stanley, Diane. *Thanksgiving on Plymouth Plantation*
Tuck, Justin. *Home-field advantage*
Voake, Charlotte. *Hello twins*

Walters, Catherine. *Are you there, Baby Bear?*
Weiss, Ellen. *Playtime for twins*
Wilson, Troy. *Liam takes a stand*
Winthrop, Elizabeth. *Lucy and Henry are twins*
Wisniewski, David. *The warrior and the wise man*
Yang, Belle. *Always come home to me*
Yum, Hyewon. *The twins' blanket*
    The twins' little sister
Zehler, Antonia. *Two fine ladies*
    Two fine ladies have a tiff

Mummies

Bunting, Eve. *Ballywhinney Girl*
Crimi, Carolyn. *Where's my mummy?*
Ewert, Marcus. *Mummy cat*
Horton, Joan. *Working mummies*
Little old lady who swallowed a fly. *There was an old mummy who swallowed a spider*
Rex, Michael. *Runaway mummy*
Schachner, Judith Byron. *Skippyjon Jones in mummy trouble*
Yates, Philip. *Ten little mummies*

Muppets *see* Puppets

Museums

Aliki. *My visit to the dinosaurs*
Armstrong-Ellis, Carey. *Prudy's problem and how she solved it*
Beeny, Emily. *Hector the collector*
Berenstain, Stan and Jan. *The Berenstain bears and the missing dinosaur bone*
Bernheimer, Kate. *The girl in the castle inside the museum*
Bilgrami, Shaheen. *Amazing dinosaur discovery*
Bliss, Harry. *Bailey at the museum*
Bourgeois, Paulette. *Franklin's class trip*
Brett, Jan. *Mossy*
Brown, Laurie Krasny. *Visiting the art museum*
Browne, Anthony. *The shape game*
Brunhoff, Laurent de. *Babar's Museum of Art*
Cohen, Miriam. *Lost in the museum*
Cousins, Lucy. *Maisy goes to the museum*
Cressy, Judith. *Can you find it?*
    Can you find it, too?
dePaola, Tomie. *Bill and Pete go down the Nile*
DiLorenzo, Barbara. *Renato and the lion*
Friedland, Katy. *Art museum opposites*
Gall, Chris. *Revenge of the Dinotrux*
Garton, Sam. *Otter in space*
Geisert, Arthur. *Mystery*
Hartland, Jessie. *How the dinosaur got to the museum*
    How the meteorite got to the museum
    How the sphinx got to the museum
Hooper, Meredith. *Celebrity cat*
    Dogs' Night
Hopkins, Lee Bennett. *Behind the museum door*
Hurd, Thacher. *Art dog*
Johansen, K. V. *Pippin and the bones*
Katz, Susan. *Mrs. Brown on exhibit*
Kellogg, Steven. *Prehistoric Pinkerton*
Kirk, Daniel. *Library mouse: a museum adventure*
Lehman, Barbara. *Museum trip*
Lionni, Leo. *Matthew's dream*
Lithgow, John. *Carnival of the animals*
    Micawber
Lucas, David. *Christmas at the toy museum*

Magnier, Thierry. *Isabelle and the angel*
Mauner, Claudia. *Zoe Sophia in New York*
Mayhew, James. *Katie and the Mona Lisa*
   Katie and the sunflowers
   Katie meets the Impressionists
Menchin, Scott. *Grandma in blue with red hat*
Metropolitan Museum of Art, NY. *Museum shapes*
Middleton, Julie. *Are the dinosaurs dead, Dad?*
Munro, Roxie. *The inside-outside book of Texas*
   The inside-outside book of Washington, D.C.
Neubecker, Robert. *Linus the vegetarian T. rex*
Rim, Sujean. *Birdie's happiest Halloween*
Rogers, Gregory. *The hero of Little Street*
Rohmann, Eric. *Time flies*
Ruzzier, Sergio. *The room of wonders*
Shea, Kitty. *Out and about at the science center*
Smith, Marie. *S is for Smithsonian*
Soman, David. *Ladybug Girl's day out with Grandpa*
Stevenson, James. *The most amazing dinosaur*
Trenc, Milan. *Another night at the museum*
Tunnell, Michael O. *The joke's on George*
Van Nutt, Julia. *Pignapped!*
Verde, Susan. *The museum*
Wahl, Jan. *The field mouse and the dinosaur named Sue*
   I met a dinosaur
Weitzman, Jacqueline Preiss. *You can't take a balloon into the Metropolitan Museum*
   You can't take a balloon into the National Gallery
Wellington, Monica. *Squeaking of art, the mice go to the museum*
Wheatley, Nadia. *Luke's way of looking*
Whybrow, Ian. *Harry and the dinosaurs at the museum*
Zalben, Jane Breskin. *Mousterpiece*

Music

Acheson, Alison. *Grandpa's music*
Ajmera, Maya. *Music everywhere!*
Alexander, Cecil Frances. *All creatures great and small*
Alger, Leclaire Gowans. *Always room for one more*
Aliki. *Ah, music!*
Alley, R. W. *There once was a witch*
Ancona, George. *Mi música / My music*
Anderson, Peggy Perry. *Chuck's band*
Appelt, Kathi. *Bats around the clock*
   Bats on parade
Asch, Frank. *Barnyard lullaby*
Austin, Patricia. *The cat who loved Mozart*
Autry, Gene. *Here comes Santa Claus*
Baer, Gene. *Thump thump rat-a-tat-tat*
Barnwell, Ysaye M. *We are one*
Barton, Suzanne. *The sleepy songbird*
Bateman, Teresa. *Harp o' gold*
   Traveling Tom and the leprechaun
Bates, Katharine Lee. *America the beautiful*, ill. by Chris Gall
   America the beautiful, ill. by Wendell Minor
   America the beautiful: together we stand
The bear
Berkner, Laurie. *The story of my feelings*
   We are the dinosaurs
Berlin, Irving. *Easter parade*
   God bless America
Bosca, Francesca. *The three grasshoppers*
Brett, Jan. *Berlioz the bear*
Brokering, Herbert F. *Earth and all stars*

Brown, Marc. *Play rhymes*
Bryan, Ashley. *All night, all day*
Burke, Bobby. *Daddy's little girl*
Burleigh, Robert. *Lookin' for Bird in the big city*
Butler, Geoff. *Ode to Newfoundland*
Cabrera, Jane. *If you're happy and you know it*
   The wheels on the bus
Calmenson, Stephanie. *Jazzmatazz!*
Canyon, Christopher. *John Denver's Ancient rhymes*
   John Denver's Sunshine on my shoulders
Carle, Eric. *I see a song*
Carter, David A. *If you're happy and you know it, clap your hands*
   Old MacDonald had a farm: a pop-up book
Carter, Don. *Heaven's all-star jazz band*
Casterline, L. C. *The sounds of music*
Celenza, Anna Harwell. *Duke Ellington's Nutcracker Suite*
   The farewell symphony
Chapin, Tom. *The library book*
Chernaik, Judith. *Carnival of the animals: poems inspired by Saint-Saëns' music*
Christensen, Bonnie. *Woody Guthrie, poet of the people*
Collins, Billy. *Daddy's little boy*
Comden, Betty, et al. *Flying to Neverland with Peter Pan*
Costanza, Stephen. *Vivaldi and the invisible orchestra*
Crimi, Carolyn. *Rock 'n' roll Mole*
Crow, Kristyn. *Cool Daddy Rat*
Cummings, Phil. *Boom bah!*
Curtis, Gavin. *The bat boy and his violin*
Czekaj, Jef. *Hip and Hop, don't stop!*
   Yes, yes, Yaul!
Daly, Niki. *Ruby sings the blues*
Davis, David. *Jazz cats*
Dean, James. *Pete the Cat: the wheels on the bus*
de la Peña, Matt. *Miguel and the grand harmony*
Delacre, Lulu. *Arroz con leche*
   Las Navidades
Demas, Corinne. *Nina's waltz*
Dillon, Leo. *Jazz on a Saturday night*
Dominguez, Angela. *Sing, don't cry*
Donaldson, Julia. *Tabby McTat, the musical cat*
Dylan, Bob. *Blowin' in the wind*
Ehrhardt, Karen. *This jazz man*
Elliott, David. *Hazel Nutt, mad scientist*
Ellwand, David. *Ten in the bed*
Emberley, Rebecca. *The ant and the grasshopper*
Engle, Margarita. *Drum dream girl*
Falconer, Ian. *Olivia forms a band*
The farmer in the dell. *The farmer in the dell*, ill. by John O'Brien
   The farmer in the dell, ill. by Alexandra Wallner
Fine, Howard. *A piggie Christmas*
Fitzgerald, Ella. *A-tisket, a-tasket*
Fleming, Candace. *Gabriella's song*
Foges, Clare. *Kitchen disco*
Frazee, Marla. *Hush, little baby: a folk song with pictures*
A frog he would a-wooing go [folk-song]. *Frog went a-courting*
Genechten, Guido van. *The big woods orchestra*
Golio, Gary. *Bird and Diz*
Gollub, Matthew. *Gobble, quack, moon*
   The Jazz Fly
   Jazz Fly 2
Goode, Diane. *Diane Goode's book of silly stories and songs*

Gordon, Gus. *Herman and Rosie*
Greenberg, Jan. *Ballet for Martha*
Greenfield, Eloise. *I make music*
Grimm, Jacob and Wilhelm. *Hans my hedgehog*
Guthrie, Woody. *Bling blang*
　My dolly
　This land is your land
Hale, Sarah Josepha Buell. *Mary had a little lamb,*
　ill. by Tomie dePaola
　Mary had a little lamb, ill. by Laura Huliska-Beith
　Mary had a little lamb, photos by Bruce McMillan
Hallworth, Grace. *Sing me a story*
Harris, John. *Jingle bells: how the holiday classic came*
　to be
Helmer, Marilyn. *Three tuneful tales*
Here we go round the mulberry bush
High, Linda Oatman. *Cool Bopper's choppers*
Hoberman, Mary Ann. *Bill Grogan's goat*
Hodges, Margaret. *Silent night: the song and its story*
Hooper, Maureen Brett. *Silent night: a Christmas*
　carol is born
Hoose, Philip M. *Hey little ant*
Horowitz, Dave. *Soon, Baboon, soon*
House, Catherine. *A stork in a baobab tree*
Hurd, Thacher. *Mama don't allow*
Hush, little baby
Hush songs
Hyde, Heidi Smith. *Mendel's accordion*
Ingalls, Ann. *The little piano girl*
Isadora, Rachel. *Ben's trumpet*
　Bring on that beat
Ivimey, John William. *The complete story of the three*
　blind mice
　Three blind mice
Jeffers, Susan. *Jingle bells*
Jenkins, Emily. *Plonk, plonk, plonk!*
Jennings, Patrick. *Bat and Rat*
Johnson, Angela. *Violet's music*
Johnson, James Weldon. *Lift every voice and sing*
　Lift ev'ry voice and sing
Johnson, Paul Brett. *Little Bunny Foo Foo*
Judd, Naomi. *Naomi Judd's guardian angels*
Katz, Karen. *The babies on the bus*
Keats, Ezra Jack. *Apt. 3*
　The little drummer boy
Kellogg, Steven. *Yankee Doodle*
Kimmel, Eric A. *The Erie Canal pirates*
　The three cabritos
Kirk, Daniel. *Go!*
Knight, Hilary. *A firefly in a fir tree*
Kovalski, Maryann. *Take me out to the ball game*
　The wheels on the bus
Kroll, Steven. *By the dawn's early light: the story of the*
　Star Spangled Banner
Krosoczka, Jarrett J. *Punk Farm*
Krull, Kathleen. *M is for music*
Langstaff, John M. *Oh, a-hunting we will go*
　What a morning!
Lenski, Lois. *I like winter*
Lies, Brian. *Bats in the band*
Lionni, Leo. *Frederick*
　Geraldine, the music mouse
Litchfield, David. *The bear and the piano*
Lithgow, John. *Never play music right next to the zoo*
Litwin, Eric. *Groovy Joe: dance party countdown*
　Groovy Joe: ice cream and dinosaurs
Liu, Jae Soo. *Yellow umbrella*
Lloyd-Jones, Sally. *Old MacNoah had an ark*
Long, Sylvia. *Deck the hall*

McCloskey, Robert. *Lentil*
McDermott, Gerald. *Musicians of the sun*
McGhee, Alison. *Song of middle C*
McGinley-Nally, Sharon. *The friendly beasts*
McGowan, Jayme. *One bear extraordinaire*
McMullan, Kate. *Rock-a-baby band*
McPhail, David. *Mole music*
Madison, Alan. *Pecorino's first concert*
Manders, John. *The really awful musicians*
Margolin, H. Ellen. *Goin' to Boston*
Marsalis, Wynton. *Squeak, rumble, whomp! Whomp!*
　Whomp!
Martin, Jacqueline Briggs. *Chicken joy on Redbean*
　Road
Mayer, Mercer. *The little drummer mouse*
Mayhew, James. *Ella Bella ballerina and A*
　Midsummer Night's Dream
　Ella Bella ballerina and Swan Lake
　Ella Bella ballerina and The Nutcracker
　Ella Bella ballerina and The sleeping beauty
Medearis, Angela Shelf. *The singing man*
Michelson, Richard. *Across the alley*
Milgrim, David. *Young MacDonald*
Miller, J. Philip. *We all sing with the same voice*
Miller, William. *The piano*
　Rent party jazz
Millman, Isaac. *Moses goes to a concert*
Mills, Judith Christine. *The painted chest*
Mitton, Tony. *Farmer Joe and the music show*
Moore, Mary-Alice. *The wheels on the school bus*
Mora, Pat. *A piñata in a pine tree*
Moss, Lloyd. *Our marching band*
　Zin! zin! zin! A violin
Myers, Walter Dean. *The blues of Flats Brown*
Nelson, Steve. *Frosty the snowman*
Newman, Lesléa. *Ketzel, the cat who composed*
Nolan, Nina. *Mahalia Jackson*
Nygaard, Elizabeth. *Snake alley band*
Old MacDonald had a farm. *Grandma's nursery*
　rhymes: Old MacDonald
　Old MacDonald had a farm, ill. by Holly Berry
　Old MacDonald had a farm, ill. by Jane Cabrera
　Old MacDonald had a farm, ill. by Carol Jones
　Old MacDonald had a farm, ill. by Tracey
　　Campbell Pearson
　Old MacDonald had a farm, ill. by Glen Rounds
　Old MacDonald had a farm, ill. by Prue
　　Theobalds
　Pete the Cat: Old MacDonald had a farm
Olson-Brown, Ellen. *Hush little digger*
Orgill, Roxane. *Skit-scat raggedy cat*
Palatini, Margie. *The cheese*
Parenteau, Shirley. *Bears in a band*
Paxton, Tom. *Going to the zoo*
Peterson, Jeanne Whitehouse. *My mama sings*
Pinkney, Andrea Davis. *Duke Ellington*
Pinkney, Brian. *Hush, little baby*
Pinkney, Gloria Jean. *Music from our Lord's holy*
　heaven
Price, Leontyne. *Aïda*
Pritchett, Dylan. *The first music*
Prokofiev, Sergei Sergeievitch. *Peter and the wolf,*
　ill. by Charles Mikolaycak
　Peter and the wolf, ill. by Josef Palecek
　Peter and the wolf, ill. by Chris Raschka
　Peter and the wolf, ill. by Vladimir Vagin
Protopopescu, Orel. *Thelonious Mouse*
Raffi. *Baby beluga*
　Down by the bay

Everything grows
Like me and you
One light, one sun
Rise and shine
Shake my sillies out
Wheels on the bus
Raposo, Joe. *Sing!*
Raschka, Chris. *Charlie Parker played be bop*
The cosmobiography of Sun Ra
Hip Hop Dog
John Coltrane's giant steps
Ray, Mary Lyn. *Shaker boy*
Robbins, Ruth. *Baboushka and the three kings*
Rodanas, Kristina. *The little drummer boy*
Root, Phyllis. *Rosie's fiddle*
Roth, Susan L. *Do re mi*
Russell-Brown, Katheryn. *Little Melba and her big trombone*
Santa Claus is coming to town
Sauer, Tammi. *Bawk and roll*
Schaefer, Carole Lexa. *Two scarlet songbirds*
Schanzer, Rosalyn. *The Old Chisholm Trail*
Schneider, Christine M. *Saxophone Sam and his snazzy jazz band*
Schuch, Steve. *A symphony of whales*
Sciurba, Katie. *Oye, Celia!*
Sedaka, Marc. *Dinosaur pet*
Seeger, Pete. *The deaf musicians*
Seskin, Steve. *Don't laugh at me*
Shaskan, Tricia Speed. *Punk skunks*
Shea, Pegi Deitz. *The boy and the spell*
Shields, Carol Diggory. *Baby's got the blues*
Shulevitz, Uri. *So sleepy story*
Simple gifts
Sís, Peter. *Play, Mozart, play*
Sloat, Teri. *Hark! The aardvark angels sing*
Smallman, Steve. *Hiccupotamus*
Smith, Charles R. *I'll be there*
My gal
Smith, Will. *Just the two of us*
Snell, Gordon. *Twelve days, a Christmas countdown*
Sorel, Edward. *The Saturday kid*
Stadler, Alexander. *Beverly Billingsly takes a bow*
Staines, Bill. *All God's critters*
Steig, William. *Roland, the minstrel pig*
Zeke Pippin
Stevens, Jan Romero. *Twelve lizards leaping*
Stewart, Joel. *Addis Berner Bear forgets*
Stinson, Kathy. *The dance of the violin*
The man with the violin
Stohs, Anita. *An Easter alleluia*
Sweet, Melissa. *Fiddle-i-fee*
Tashiro, Chisato. *Five nice mice*
Thien, Madeleine. *The Chinese violin*
Thomas, Joyce Carol. *The gospel Cinderella*
Titcomb, Gordon. *The last train*
Trapani, Iza. *I'm a little teapot*
The itsy bitsy spider
Jingle bells
Shoo fly!
Turner, Barbara J. *Out and about at the orchestra*
The twelve days of Christmas. English folk song.
The twelve days of Christmas, ill. by Jan Brett
The twelve days of Christmas, ill. by Jane Cabrera
The twelve days of Christmas, ill. by Rachel Griffin
Twelve days of Christmas
The twelve days of Christmas, ill. by Laurel Long
The 12 days of Christmas

The twelve days of Christmas, ill. by Emma Randall
The twelve days of Christmas, ill. by Jane Ray
The twelve days of Christmas, ill. by Gennady Spirin
Vainio, Pirkko. *The Christmas angel*
Velasquez, Eric. *Grandma's records*
Voake, Charlotte. *Tweedle - dee - dee*
Wallace, Nancy Elizabeth. *Apples, apples, apples*
Walter, Mildred Pitts. *Ty's one-man band*
Walty, Margaret. *Rock-a-bye baby: lullabies for bedtime*
Wangerin, Walter. *Angels and all children*
Ward, B. J. *Farty Marty*
Ward, Jennifer. *Over in the garden*
Watts, Leslie Elizabeth. *The Baabaasheep Quartet*
Weatherford, Carole Boston. *Before John was a jazz giant*
Jazz baby
Leontyne Price
Weeks, Sarah. *Catfish Kate and the sweet swamp band*
Crocodile smile
Woof
Weinstone, David. *Music class today!*
Wells, Rosemary. *Bingo*
Westcott, Nadine Bernard. *Skip to my Lou*
There's a hole in the bucket
Wheeler, Lisa. *Jazz baby*
Wheeler, Opal. *Sing in praise*
Sing Mother Goose
Whippo, Walt. *Little white duck*
Wilder, Laura Ingalls. *My little house songbook*
Williams, Suzanne. *The witch casts a spell*
Williams, Vera B. *Music, music for everyone*
Willis, Jeanne. *The wheels on the bus: a read-along sing-along trip to the zoo*
Winter, Jeanette. *Kali's song*
Once upon a time in Chicago
Winter, Jonah. *Dizzy*
How Jelly Roll Morton invented jazz
Wolkstein, Diane. *The banza*
Yarrow, Peter. *Puff, the magic dragon*
Yolen, Jane. *Jane Yolen's Old MacDonald songbook*
Zelinsky, Paul O. *The wheels on the bus*
Ziefert, Harriet. *Animal music*

Musical instruments

Ajmera, Maya. *Music everywhere!*
Barton, Chris. *88 instruments*
Bunting, Eve. *Hey diddle diddle*
Casterline, L. C. *The sounds of music*
Cocoretto . *Toot! toot!*
Cox, Judy. *My family plays music*
Cummings, Phil. *Boom bah!*
Day, Nancy Raines. *A is for alliguitar*
Geringer, Laura. *Boom boom go away!*
Horowitz, Dave. *Soon, Baboon, soon*
Lithgow, John. *Never play music right next to the zoo*
The remarkable Farkle McBride
Madison, Alan. *Pecorino's first concert*
Marsalis, Wynton. *Squeak, rumble, whomp! Whomp! Whomp!*
Newton, Jill. *Crash bang donkey!*
Prokofiev, Sergei Sergeievitch. *Peter and the wolf,* ill. by Charles Mikolaycak
Peter and the wolf, ill. by Josef Palecek
Peter and the wolf, ill. by Chris Raschka
Peter and the wolf, ill. by Vladimir Vagin
Saaf, Donald. *The ABC animal orchestra*

Shahan, Sherry. *The jazzy alphabet*
Sklansky, Amy E. *The duck who played the kazoo*
Thorpe, Kiki. *Time to cha-cha-cha!*
Uhlberg, Myron. *A storm called Katrina*
Weinstone, David. *Music class today!*

Musical instruments – accordions

Hyde, Heidi Smith. *Mendel's accordion*
Williams, Vera B. *Music, music for everyone*

Musical instruments – bagpipes

DeFelice, Cynthia C. *Cold feet*

Musical instruments – bands

Alexander, Kwame. *Acoustic Rooster and his barnyard band*
Anderson, Peggy Perry. *Chuck's band*
Appelt, Kathi. *Bats on parade*
Baer, Gene. *Thump thump rat-a-tat-tat*
Boynton, Sandra. *Christmas parade*
Brett, Jan. *Berlioz the bear*
Carter, Don. *Heaven's all-star jazz band*
Costello, David Hyde. *Little Pig joins the band*
Covell, David. *Rat and Roach rock on!*
Emberley, Rebecca. *The ant and the grasshopper*
Gerber, Carole. *A band of babies*
Hurd, Thacher. *Mama don't allow*
Johnson, Angela. *Violet's music*
Kassirer, Sue. *Math fair blues*
London, Jonathan. *Froggy plays in the band*
McGowan, Jayme. *One bear extraordinaire*
McMullan, Kate. *Rock-a-baby band*
Moss, Lloyd. *Our marching band*
Nygaard, Elizabeth. *Snake alley band*
Orgill, Roxane. *If I only had a horn*
Parenteau, Shirley. *Bears in a band*
Raschka, Chris. *John Coltrane's giant steps*
Stuchner, Joan Betty. *The Kugel Valley Klezmer Band*
Walter, Mildred Pitts. *Ty's one-man band*
Weeks, Sarah. *Catfish Kate and the sweet swamp band*
Winter, Jeanette. *Once upon a time in Chicago*
Ziefert, Harriet. *Animal music*

Musical instruments – banjos

Busse, Sarah Martin. *Banjo granny*
Pinfold, Levi. *The Django*
Wolkstein, Diane. *The banza*

Musical instruments – cellos

Garriel, Barbara S. *I know a shy fellow who swallowed a cello*

Musical instruments – drums

Base, Graeme. *Jungle drums*
Crow, Kristyn. *Skeleton cat*
Davol, Marguerite W. *The loudest, fastest, best drummer in Kansas*
Engle, Margarita. *Drum dream girl*
Francis, Panama. *David gets his drum*
Gollub, Matthew. *The Jazz Fly*
Greenwood, Mark. *Drummer boy of John John*
Guidone, Thea. *Drum city*
Kay, Verla. *Civil War drummer boy*
Keats, Ezra Jack. *The little drummer boy*

Long, Loren. *Drummer boy*
Mayer, Mercer. *The little drummer mouse*
Patricelli, Leslie. *Be quiet, Mike!*
Pinkwater, Daniel. *Bongo Larry*
Protopopescu, Orel. *Two sticks*
Rodanas, Kristina. *The little drummer boy*
Vernick, Audrey. *Teach your buffalo to play drums*
Warwick, Dionne. *Little Man*

Musical instruments – fiddles *see* Musical instruments – violins

Musical instruments – flutes

Gillard, Denise. *Music from the sky*
Lionni, Leo. *Geraldine, the music mouse*

Musical instruments – guitars

Bryan, Ashley. *All night, all day*
Kovalski, Maryann. *The wheels on the bus*
Litwin, Eric. *Groovy Joe: dance party countdown*
Myers, Walter Dean. *The blues of Flats Brown*
Richards, Keith. *Gus and me*

Musical instruments – harmonicas

Battle-Lavert, Gwendolyn. *The music in Derrick's heart*
Keats, Ezra Jack. *Apt. 3*
McCloskey, Robert. *Lentil*
Steig, William. *Zeke Pippin*

Musical instruments – harps

Edwards, Pamela Duncan. *The leprechaun's gold*

Musical instruments – lutes

Steig, William. *Roland, the minstrel pig*

Musical instruments – orchestras

Costanza, Stephen. *Vivaldi and the invisible orchestra*
Kuskin, Karla. *The Philharmonic gets dressed*
Millman, Isaac. *Moses goes to a concert*
Saaf, Donald. *The ABC animal orchestra*
Snicket, Lemony. *The composer is dead*
Tripp, Paul. *Tubby the tuba*
Turner, Barbara J. *Out and about at the orchestra*
Wright, Johanna. *The orchestra pit*

Musical instruments – pianos

Alda, Arlene. *Lulu's piano lesson*
Austin, Patricia. *The cat who loved Mozart*
Bryan, Ashley. *All night, all day*
Ingalls, Ann. *The little piano girl*
Litchfield, David. *The bear and the piano*
McGhee, Alison. *Song of middle C*
Miller, William. *The piano*
Newman, Lesléa. *Ketzel, the cat who composed*
Parsley, Elise. *If you ever want to bring a piano to the beach, don't!*
Perkins, Lynne Rae. *The cardboard piano*
Pinkney, Andrea Davis. *Duke Ellington*
Reynolds, Marilynn. *The magnificent piano recital*
Winter, Jonah. *How Jelly Roll Morton invented jazz*

Musical instruments – saxophones

High, Linda Oatman. *Cool Bopper's choppers*
Kallok, Emma. *Gem*
Raschka, Chris. *Charlie Parker played be bop*

Musical instruments – trombones

Andrews, Troy. *Trombone Shorty*
Russell-Brown, Katheryn. *Little Melba and her big trombone*
Weeks, Sarah. *Woof*

Musical instruments – trumpets

Burleigh, Robert. *Lookin' for Bird in the big city*
Cline-Ransome, Lesa. *Just a lucky so and so*
Isadora, Rachel. *Ben's trumpet*
Orgill, Roxane. *If I only had a horn*
Stewart, Joel. *Addis Berner Bear forgets*
Zuppardi, Sam. *Jack's worry*

Musical instruments – tubas

Tripp, Paul. *Tubby the tuba*

Musical instruments – violins

Carle, Eric. *I see a song*
Curtis, Gavin. *The bat boy and his violin*
Ering, Timothy Basil. *The unexpected love story of Alfred Fiddleduckling*
Kraus, Robert. *Mort the sport*
McPhail, David. *Mole music*
Moss, Lloyd. *Zin! zin! zin! A violin*
Otsuka, Yuzo. *Suho's white horse*
Ray, Mary Lyn. *A violin for Elva*
Root, Phyllis. *Rosie's fiddle*
Sorel, Edward. *The Saturday kid*
Stinson, Kathy. *The dance of the violin*
The man with the violin
Thien, Madeleine. *The Chinese violin*
Uegaki, Chieri. *Hana Hashimoto, sixth violin*

Mystery stories

Berenstain, Stan and Jan. *The bear detectives*
The Berenstain bears and the messy room
The Berenstain bears and the missing dinosaur bone
The Berenstain bears and the missing honey
Boatfield, Jonny. *The twilight book*
Catusanu, Mircea. *The strange case of the missing sheep*
Christelow, Eileen. *Where's the big bad wolf?*
Dean, Kim. *Pete the Cat and the missing cupcakes*
Dolan, Elys. *The mystery of the haunted farm*
Fromental, Jean-Luc. *Bonesville*
Gallaher, Jason. *Whobert Whover, owl detective*
Geisert, Arthur. *Mystery*
Nursery crimes
Gibbons, Gail. *The missing maple syrup sap mystery*
Grambling, Lois G. *Miss Hildy's missing cape caper*
Hurd, Thacher. *Art dog*
Jonas, Ann. *The thirteenth clue*
Kellogg, Steven. *The mystery of the flying orange pumpkin*
The mystery of the magic green ball
The mystery of the missing red mitten
The mystery of the stolen blue paint
Lass, Bonnie. *Who took the cookies from the cookie jar?*

Lazar, Tara. *7 ate 9*
Leedy, Loreen. *Missing math*
Levinthal, David. *Who pushed Humpty Dumpty?*
McDonald, Megan. *The great pumpkin switch*
McLaren, Meg. *Pigeon P.I.*
McLaughlin, Lauren. *Mitzi Tulane, preschool detective, in The secret ingredient*
Mitzi Tulane, preschool detective, in What's that smell
Marzollo, Jean. *I spy treasure hunt*
Mauner, Claudia. *Zoe Sophia in New York*
Nash, Scott. *Tuff Fluff*
Olien, Jessica. *Shark Detective!*
Selznick, Brian. *The invention of Hugo Cabret*
Sneed, Brad. *Deputy Harvey and the ant cow caper*
Snicket, Lemony. *The composer is dead*
Twenty-nine myths on the Swinster Pharmacy
Thompson, Richard. *The follower*
Trukhan, Ekaterina. *Apples for little Fox*
Tryon, Leslie. *Albert's Halloween*
Van Nutt, Julia. *The mystery of Mineral Gorge*

Mythical creatures

Aardema, Verna. *Anansi finds a fool*
Ahlberg, Janet. *Jeremiah in the dark wood*
Ashman, Linda. *The essential worldwide monster guide*
Bartram, Simon. *Man on the moon: a day in the life of Bob*
Carmody, Isobelle. *Magic night*
Carroll, Lewis. *Jabberwocky*
Child, Lauren. *Beware of the storybook wolves*
Conover, Chris. *The lion's share*
Duddle, Jonny. *The pirate cruncher*
Esckelson, Laura. *The copper braid of Shannon O'Shea*
Evans, Dilys. *Fairies, trolls and goblins galore*
The firebird. *The firebird*, ill. by Demi
The firebird, ill. by Rachel Isadora
The tale of the firebird
Fisher, Leonard Everett. *Cyclops*
Theseus and the Minotaur
Goble, Paul. *Iktomi and the coyote*
Graham, Bob. *Max*
Greenfield, Eloise. *I can draw a weeposaur and other dinosaurs*
Hakte, Ben. *Julia's house for lost creatures*
Hayes, Sarah. *Lucy Anna and the Finders*
James, Brian. *The Supertwins meet the bad dogs from space*
Jane, Pamela. *Little goblins ten*
Johnston, Tony. *Bigfoot Cinderrrrella*
Kohara, Kazuno. *Here comes Jack Frost*
Kraegel, Kenneth. *King Arthur's very great grandson*
Larios, Julie. *Imaginary menagerie*
Long, Matty. *Super Happy Magic Forest*
McBratney, Sam. *Once there was a Hoodie*
Magoon, Scott. *The boy who cried bigfoot!*
Martin, Emily Winfield. *Day dreamers*
Mayer, Mercer. *The bravest knight*
Mora, Pat. *Abuelos*
Nobleman, Marc Tyler. *The chupacabra ate the candelabra*
Peet, Bill. *Cyrus the unsinkable sea serpent*
No such things
The pinkish, purplish, bluish egg
Plourde, Lynn. *Wild child*
Winter waits

Reinhart, Matthew. *Fairies and magical creatures*
    Gods and heroes
Richards, Jean. *The first Olympic games*
Sabuda, Robert. *The Blizzard's robe*
Shepard, Aaron. *The sea king's daughter*
Sierra, Judy. *'Twas the fright before Christmas*
Singer, Marilyn. *Creature carnival*
Slater, Dashka. *The sea serpent and me*
Spires, Ashley. *Larf*
Todd, Barbara. *The rainmaker*
Washington, Donna L. *A big, spooky house*
Wilbur, Helen L. *Z is for Zeus*
Williams, Suzanne. *The witch casts a spell*
Wisniewski, David. *Golem*
Wood, Audrey. *The Bunyans*
    The Tickleoctopus
Yolen, Jane. *The firebird*
    Pegasus, the flying horse
    Wings

Mythical creatures – aliens *see* Aliens

Mythical creatures – elves

deGroat, Diane. *Lola the elf*
Grimm, Jacob and Wilhelm. *The elves and the*
    shoemaker, ill. by Kirill Chelushkin
    The elves and the shoemaker, ill. by Paul Galdone
    The elves and the shoemaker, ill. by Margaret Walty
    The shoemaker and his elves
    The shoemaker and the elves, ill. by Adrienne
      Adams
    The shoemaker and the elves, ill. by Ilse Plume
Joyce, William. *The Leaf Men and the brave good bugs*
Kimmel, Eric A. *Rip Van Winkle's return*
Krensky, Stephen. *How Santa lost his job*
Light, Steve. *The Christmas giant*
Lowell, Susan. *The bootmaker and the elves*
Maconie, Robin. *Alice and her fabulous teeth*
May, Robert L. *Rudolph the red-nosed reindeer*
Novak, Matt. *The last Christmas present*
Rinker, Sherri Duskey. *The twelve sleighs of*
    Christmas
Wahl, Jan. *Elf night*
Williams, Sam. *Angel's Christmas cookies*
    Snowy magic

Mythical creatures – genies

Lucas, David. *Nutmeg*
Sunami, Kitoba. *How the fisherman tricked the genie*
Turk, Evan. *The storyteller*

Mythical creatures – gnomes

Anstee, Ashlyn. *No, no, Gnome!*
Henterly, Jamichael. *Good night, garden gnome*
Mayer, Kirsten. *Game of gnomes*
    Go big or go gnome!

Mythical creatures – goblins

Alexander, Lloyd. *The house Gobbaleen*
Alexander, Sue. *Who goes out on Halloween?*
Bunting, Eve. *Scary, scary Halloween*
dePaola, Tomie. *Jamie O'Rourke and the pooka*
Doyle, Malachy. *Hungry! hungry! hungry!*
Fox, Mem. *The goblin and the empty chair*
Hatke, Ben. *Nobody likes a goblin*

Kimmel, Eric A. *Hershel and the Hanukkah goblins*
McDonald, Megan. *The Hinky Pink*
Sendak, Maurice. *Outside over there*

Mythical creatures – griffins, gryphons

Sturm, James. *Gryphons aren't so great*

Mythical creatures – leprechauns

Balian, Lorna. *Leprechauns never lie*
Bateman, Teresa. *Fiona's luck*
    Leprechaun gold
    The leprechaun under the bed
    Traveling Tom and the leprechaun
Bunting, Eve. *That's what leprechauns do*
Callahan, Sean. *The leprechaun who lost his rainbow*
    Shannon and the world's tallest leprechaun
Chase, Mary. *The wicked, wicked ladies in the haunted*
    house
Colandro, Lucille. *There was an old lady who*
    swallowed a clover!
dePaola, Tomie. *Jamie O'Rourke and the big potato*
Dillon, Jana. *Lucky O'Leprechaun comes to America*
    Lucky O'Leprechaun in school
Edwards, Pamela Duncan. *The leprechaun's gold*
Krensky, Stephen. *Too many leprechauns*
Shute, Linda. *Clever Tom and the leprechaun*
Tegen, Katherine Brown. *The story of the leprechaun*
Tucker, Kathy. *The leprechaun in the basement*
Welling, Peter J. *Shawn O'Hisser, the last snake in*
    Ireland

Mythical creatures – lutins

Willey, Margaret. *Clever Beatrice and the best little*
    pony

Mythical creatures – mermaids, mermen

Andersen, Hans Christian. *The little mermaid*, ill.
    by Charlene DeLage
    The little mermaid, ill. by Michael Hague
    The little mermaid, ill. by Rachel Isadora
Bateman, Teresa. *The merbaby*
Brett, Jan. *The mermaid*
Campbell, K. G. *The mermaid and the shoe*
Clibbon, Meg. *Imagine you're a mermaid!*
Fraser, Mary Ann. *Mermaid sister*
Hakala, Marjorie Rose. *Mermaid dance*
Lucas, David. *The skeleton pirate*
Minters, Frances. *Princess Fishtail*
Pitcher, Caroline. *Mariana and the merchild*
San Souci, Robert D. *Nicholas Pipe*
    Sukey and the mermaid
Sperring, Mark. *Mermaid dreams*
Turnbull, Victoria. *The sea tiger*
Willis, Jeanne. *Do little mermaids wet their beds*

Mythical creatures – ogres

Cole, Brock. *Good enough to eat*
Heller, Nicholas. *Ogres! ogres! ogres!*
Juster, Norton. *The odious ogre*
Kimmelman, Leslie. *The three bully goats*
Prelutsky, Jack. *Awful Ogre running wild*
    Awful Ogre's awful day
San Souci, Robert D. *Little Pierre*
    The silver charm
Sierra, Judy. *Tasty baby belly buttons*

Sturm, James. *Ogres awake!*
Willard, Nancy. *Shadow story*

Mythical creatures – Pegasus

Mayer, Marianna. *Pegasus*
Yolen, Jane. *Pegasus, the flying horse*

Mythical creatures – phoenix

Demi. *The girl who drew a phoenix*

Mythical creatures – pixies

Kushner, Donn. *Peter's pixie*

Mythical creatures – pooka spirit

dePaola, Tomie. *Jamie O'Rourke and the pooka*
McDermott, Gerald. *Daniel O'Rourke*

Mythical creatures – trolls

Aardema, Verna. *Bimwili and the Zimwi*
Asbjørnsen, P. C. *The three billy goats Gruff,* ill. by
    Stephen Carpenter
    The three billy goats Gruff, ill. by Paul Galdone
    The three billy goats gruff, ill. by Jerry Pinkney
    The three billy goats Gruff, ill. by Glen Rounds
    The three billy goats Gruff, ill. by Janet Stevens
    The three Billygoats Gruff and Mean Calypso Joe
    Who's that tripping over my bridge?
Bolliger, Max. *The happy troll*
Brett, Jan. *Christmas trolls*
    Hedgie's surprise
    Home for Christmas
    The trouble with trolls
    Who's that knocking on Christmas eve?
Grimm, Jacob and Wilhelm. *The glass mountain*
Hodgkinson, Leigh. *Troll swap*
McNiff, Dawn. *Mommy's little monster*
Mayer, Mercer. *The bravest knight*
Minters, Frances. *Princess Fishtail*
Mortimer, Rachael. *The three Billy Goats Fluff*
Palatini, Margie. *The three silly billies*
Peet, Bill. *Jethro and Joel were a troll*
Polacco, Patricia. *Oh, look!*
Prelutsky, Jack. *Monday's troll*
Root, Phyllis. *Lucia and the light*
Willis, Jeanne. *Troll stinks*
Wolff, Patricia Rae. *The toll-bridge troll*
Yolen, Jane. *Sister Bear*

Mythical creatures – unicorns

Clayton, Dallas. *Lily the unicorn*
Diller, Kevin. *Hello, my name is Octicorn*
Dyckman, Ame. *You don't want a unicorn!*
Heidbreder, Robert. *I wished for a unicorn*
McNaughton, Janet. *Brave Jack and the unicorn*
Mayer, Marianna. *The unicorn and the lake*
Mitchell, Adrian. *Nobody rides the unicorn*
Nahas, Sylvaine. *Nicolo's unicorn*
Reed, Neil. *The midnight unicorn*
Rosenthal, Amy Krouse. *Uni the unicorn*
    Uni the unicorn and the dream come true
Shea, Bob. *Unicorn thinks he's pretty great*
Sheldon, Dyan. *Unicorn dreams*
Sima, Jessie. *Not quite narwhal*
Yolen, Jane. *Where have the unicorns gone?*

Young, Amy. *A new friend for Sparkle*
    A unicorn named Sparkle

Mythical creatures – werewolves

Collins, Ross. *Dear Vampa*
Salley, Coleen. *Epossumondas plays possum*

Mythology *see* Folk & fairy tales

Name calling *see* Behavior – name calling

Names

Alexie, Sherman. *Thunder Boy Jr.*
Bayer, Jane. *A my name is Alice*
Bryan, Ashley. *Turtle knows your name*
Bunting, Eve. *Girls A to Z*
Capucilli, Alyssa Satin. *Hello, Biscuit!*
Carter, Alden R. *Big brother Dustin*
Catalanotto, Peter. *Matthew A.B.C.*
Child, Lauren. *That pesky rat*
Choi, Yangsook. *The name jar*
dePaola, Tomie. *Tom*
Dunklee, Annika. *My name is Elizabeth!*
Du Quette, Keith. *They call me Woolly*
Foreman, George. *Let George do it!*
Gadot, A. S. *The first gift*
Henkes, Kevin. *Chrysanthemum*
Inkpen, Mick. *Nothing*
Katz, Karen. *Princess Baby*
Kimmel, Eric A. *Rattlestiltskin*
Lester, Helen. *A porcupine named Fluffy*
Lester, J. D. *Mommy calls me Monkeypants*
MacLachlan, Patricia. *Three names*
McQuade, Jacqueline. *Big babies*
Monk, Isabell. *Hope*
Mosel, Arlene. *Tikki Tikki Tembo*
Most, Bernard. *A dinosaur named after me*
Murphy, Stuart J. *Write on, Carlos!*
Murray, Alison. *Little Mouse*
Norac, Carl. *Hello, sweetie pie*
Philip, Simon. *I don't know what to call my cat*
Pringle, Laurence P. *Naming the cat*
Raschka, Chris. *New York is English, Chattanooga is
    Creek*
Recorvits, Helen. *My name is Yoon*
Reynolds, Marilynn. *The name of the child*
Root, Phyllis. *The name quilt*
Rubin, C. M. *Eleanor, Ellatony, Ellencake, and me*
Sadu, Itah. *Christopher changes his name*
Sasso, Sandy Eisenberg. *In God's name*
Shah, Idries. *The boy without a name*
Sutton, Jane. *Don't call me Sidney*
Swanson, Susan Marie. *The first thing my mama told
    me*
Tom Tit Tot. *Tom Tit Tot*

Waber, Bernard. *A lion named Shirley Williamson*
Whybrow, Ian. *Harry and the bucketful of dinosaurs*
Williams, Karen Lynn. *My name is Sangoel*
Wolff, Ashley. *I call my grandma Nana*
    I call my grandpa Papa
Zwillich, Julie. *Phoebe sounds it out*

Napping *see* Sleep

Native Americans *see* Eskimos; Indians of Central America; Indians of North America; Indians of South America

Nature

Alarcón, Francisco X. *From the bellybutton of the moon and other summer poems / Del ombligo de la luna y otros poemas de verano*
Alemagna, Beatrice. *On a magical do-nothing day*
Alexander, Cecil Frances. *All creatures great and small*
    All things bright and beautiful, ill. by Ashley Bryan
    All things bright and beautiful, ill. by Anna Vojtech
    All things bright and beautiful, ill. by Bruce Whatley
Alexander, Sue. *One more time, Mama*
Aliki. *Quiet in the garden*
Appelt, Kathi. *My father's house*
Archer, Micha. *Daniel finds a poem*
Aregui, Matthias. *Before after*
Arnold, Katya. *Let's find it!*
Arnosky, Jim. *At this very moment*
    Babies in the bayou
    Come out, muskrats
    Crinkleroot's guide to giving back to nature
    Crinkleroot's guide to knowing animal habitats
    Crinkleroot's guide to knowing the trees
    Crinkleroot's guide to walking in wild places
    Crinkleroot's 25 birds every child should know
    Crinkleroot's 25 fish every child should know
    Crinkleroot's 25 mammals every child should know
    Crinkleroot's visit to Crinkle Cove
    Dolphins on the sand
    I see animals hiding
    Little Burro
    Parrotfish and sunken ships
    Wild tracks!
Asch, Frank. *The earth and I*
Ashman, Linda. *All we know*
Atteberry, Kevan. *Bunnies!!!*
Bash, Barbara. *Urban roosts*
Berenstain, Stan and Jan. *The Berenstain bears and the wild, wild honey*
Berger, Melvin. *Look out for turtles!*
Berk, Ari. *Nightsong*
Berne, Jennifer. *Manfish*
Bernhard, Durga. *Earth, sky, wet, dry*
Bevis, Mary. *Wolf song*
Biro, Maureen Boyd. *Walking with Maga*
Bishop, Nic. *Penguin day*
Bissonette, Aimée. *North woods girl*
Blaikie, Lynn. *Beyond the northern lights*
Bloxam, Frances. *Antlers forever!*
Bogan, Carmen. *Where's Rodney?*
Bogart, Jo Ellen. *Big and small, room for all*
Brett, Jan. *Mossy*

Brown, Margaret Wise. *Nibble, nibble*
Bruchac, Joseph. *The circle of thanks*
Bryan, Ashley. *Sing to the sun*
Bunting, Eve. *Anna's table*
    Peepers
Burleigh, Robert. *If you spent a day with Thoreau at Walden pond*
Carlstrom, Nancy White. *What does the sky say?*
Chaikin, Miriam. *Don't step on the sky*
Cherry, Lynne. *A river ran wild*
Chin, Jason. *Grand Canyon*
Chrustowski, Rick. *Turtle crossing*
Cole, Henry. *On Meadowview Street*
Collins, Pat Lowery. *The deer watch*
Cooke, Trish. *The grandad tree*
Corr, Christopher. *Whole world*
Cousteau, Philippe. *Follow the moon home*
Davidson, Leslie A. *In the red canoe*
Davies, Nicola. *Just ducks!*
    The pond
Day, Nancy Raines. *What in the world?*
Delacre, Lulu. *How far do you love me?*
DePalma, Mary Newell. *A grand old tree*
dePaola, Tomie. *Look and be grateful*
Doi, Kaya. *Chirri and Chirra*
Doolittle, Bev. *Reading the wild*
Ellis, Gerry. *Natumi takes the lead*
Engle, Margarita. *The sky painter*
Ericsson, Jennifer A. *Whoo goes there?*
Ernst, Lisa Campbell. *Wake up, it's Spring!*
Farrar, Sid. *The year comes round*
Ferri, Giuliano. *Little Tad grows up*
Fisher, Aileen Lucia. *Do rabbits have Christmas?*
    The story goes on
FitzSimmons, David. *Curious critters*
    Curious critters, vol. 2
    Salamander dance
Fleming, Denise. *In the tall, tall grass*
    Underground
    Where once there was a wood
Fletcher, Ralph. *Hello, harvest moon*
Ford, Miela. *Sunflower*
Formento, Alison. *This tree counts!*
    This tree, 1, 2, 3
Fox, Paula. *Traces*
Franco, Betsy. *Bees, snails, and peacock tails*
Freedman, Deborah. *This house, once*
Frisch, Aaron. *The lonely pine*
Frost, Helen. *Step gently out*
    Sweep up the sun
Galbraith, Kathryn O. *Planting the wild garden*
Genechten, Guido van. *The big woods orchestra*
George, Jean Craighead. *Dear Rebecca, winter is here*
    Everglades
George, Kristine O'Connell. *The great frog race and other poems*
George, Lindsay Barrett. *Around the pond*
    In the garden: who's been here?
    In the woods
George, William T. *Beaver at Long Pond*
    Box turtle at Long Pond
    Christmas at Long Pond
Geraghty, Paul. *Help me!*
Gerber, Carole. *Seeds, bees, butterflies, and more!*
Gershator, Phillis. *Listen, listen*
Gibbons, Gail. *Beavers*
Gifford, Peggy. *The great big green*
Gill, Shelley. *The egg*
Giogas, Valarie. *In my backyard*

Pollard, Nik. *The tide*
Posada, Mia. *Who was here?*
Powell, Consie. *The first day of winter*
Poydar, Nancy. *Snip, snip . . . snow!*
Preller, James. *Cardinal and sunflower*
Raczka, Bob. *Spring things*
Rau, Dana Meachen. *Stroll by the sea*
Reynolds, Aaron. *Carnivores*
Robert, Nadine. *Toshi's little treasures*
Robey, Katharine Crawford. *Where's the party?*
Root, Phyllis. *If you want to see a caribou*
   Plant a pocket of prairie
Rotner, Shelley. *Every season*
Ruddell, Deborah. *A whiff of pine, a hint of skunk*
Ruurs, Margriet. *In my backyard*
   When we go camping
Ryder, Joanne. *Chipmunk song*
   Step into the night
   The waterfall's gift
   Where butterflies grow
   White bear, ice bear
Rylant, Cynthia. *Life*
   Snow
   The stars will still shine
San Souci, Robert D. *The birds of Killingworth*
Sayre, April Pulley. *Best in snow*
   Eat like a bear
   Honk, honk, goose!
   The shape of Betts Meadow
   Squirrels leap, squirrels sleep
   Woodpecker wham!
Schaefer, Lola M. *This is the sunflower*
Schnur, Steven. *Spring thaw*
Schoenherr, John. *Bear*
Schwartz, Roslyn. *Tales from Parc la Fontaine*
Seeger, Laura Vaccaro. *Green*
Selsam, Millicent E. *How to be a nature detective*
Shannon, George. *White is for blueberry*
Shore, Diane Z. *This is the Earth*
Shulevitz, Uri. *Snow*
Siddals, Mary McKenna. *Bringing the outside in*
   I'll play with you
Sidman, Joyce. *Butterfly eyes and other secrets of the meadow*
   Round
   Song of the water boatman
   Swirl by swirl
   Ubiquitous
   Winter bees and other poems of the cold
Siebert, Diane. *Sierra*
Sill, Cathryn. *Wetlands*
Simler, Isabelle. *The blue hour*
Simmons, Jane. *Come along, Daisy!*
Singer, Marilyn. *Turtle in July*
Smith, Matthew Clark. *Small wonders: Jean-Henri Fabre and his world of insects*
Snyder, Betsy E. *Sweet dreams lullaby*
Stiles, Martha Bennett. *Island magic*
Suzuki, David. *Salmon forest*
Swamp, Jake. *Giving thanks*
Swanson, Susan Marie. *To be like the sun*
Swinburne, Stephen R. *Lots and lots of zebra stripes*
   What color is nature?
Tafuri, Nancy. *What the sun sees / What the moon sees*
Thornhill, Jan. *Is this Panama?*
Tomecek, Steve. *Dirt*
Vanderwater, Amy Ludwig. *Every day birds*
Viano, Hannah. *B is for bear*
von Olfers, Sibylle. *Mother Earth and her children*

Waboose, Jan Bourdeau. *Morning on the lake*
Wahl, Phoebe. *Sonya's chickens*
Wallace, Karen. *Scarlette Beane*
Walsh, Melanie. *Do donkeys dance?*
   Do lions live on lily pads?
Walters, Catherine. *When will it be spring?*
Ward, Jennifer. *Mama built a little nest*
   What will hatch?
Weiss, George. *What a wonderful world*, ill. by Ashley Bryan
   What a wonderful world, ill. by Tim Hopgood
Wells, Rosemary. *Forest of dreams*
Weninger, Brigitte. *Precious water*
Wigger, J. Bradley. *Thank you, God*
Winter, Jeanette. *The watcher*
Winters, Kay. *Tiger trail*
   Wolf watch
Winton, Tim. *The deep*
Wolff, Ashley. *Baby Bear sees blue*
Wood, Audrey. *Blue sky*
   The Bunyans
   When the root children wake up
Wood, Douglas. *Grandad's prayers of the earth*
   No one but you
   The secret of saying thanks
   Where the sunrise begins
Yee, Wong Herbert. *My autumn book*
   Tracks in the snow
Yezerski, Thomas. *Meadowlands*
Yolen, Jane. *A mirror to nature*
   On Bird Hill
   On Duck Pond
   Thunder underground
   Welcome to the icehouse
Yuly, Toni. *Thank you, bees*
Ziefert, Harriet. *One red apple*
Zolotow, Charlotte. *Say it!*
   When the wind stops

Naughty *see* Behavior – misbehavior

Neatness *see* Character traits – cleanliness

Needing someone *see* Behavior – needing someone

Negotiation *see* Activities – trading

Neighborhoods *see* Communities, neighborhoods

Netherlands *see* Foreign lands – Holland

Night

Adlerman, Daniel. *Africa calling*
Adoff, Arnold. *Daring Dog and Captain Cat*
Ahlberg, Janet. *Funnybones*
Alexander, Martha G. *We're in big trouble, Blackboard Bear*
   You're a genius, Blackboard Bear
Aliki. *Overnight at Mary Bloom's*
Almond, David. *Kate, the cat and the moon*
Anholt, Laurence. *Jack and the dreamsack*

Appelt, Kathi. *Cowboy dreams*
Apperley, Dawn. *Blossom and Boo stay up late*
  Good night, sleep tight, little bunnies
Apple, Margot. *Brave Martha*
Arnold, Tedd. *Huggly gets dressed*
  Huggly takes a bath
Arnosky, Jim. *All night near the water*
  Raccoons and ripe corn
Asch, Frank. *Moonbear*
Ashman, Linda. *How to make a night*
Aylesworth, Jim. *Two terrible frights*
Baker, Ken. *Brave little monster*
Ballard, Robin. *Tonight and tomorrow*
Barnett, Mac. *Noisy night*
Bartoletti, Susan Campbell. *Naamah and the ark at night*
Bauer, Marion Dane. *The longest night*
Beames, Margaret. *Night cat*
Bean, Jonathan. *At night*
Beck, Andrea. *Elliot's noisy night*
Berenstain, Stan and Jan. *Bears in the night*
  The Berenstain bears in the dark
Berk, Ari. *Nightsong*
Bernhard, Durga. *While you are sleeping: a lift-the-flap book of time around the world*
Birdseye, Tom. *Oh yeah!*
Blackall, Sophie. *Are you awake?*
Bond, Felicia. *Poinsettia and the firefighters*
Borando, Silvia. *Black cat, white cat*
Bourgeois, Paulette. *Franklin in the dark*
Boyd, Lizi. *Flashlight*
Bradbury, Ray. *Switch on the night*
Brown, Margaret Wise. *The fathers are coming home*
Brunelle, Nicholas. *Snow moon*
Buehner, Caralyn. *Snowmen at night*
Bunting, Eve. *Ghost's hour, spook's hour*
Burningham, John. *It's a secret!*
Butler, John. *Hush, little ones*
  While you were sleeping
Butterworth, Nick. *One snowy night*
Carlson, Melody. *When the creepy things come out*
Carman, William. *What's that noise?*
Carroll, James Christopher. *The boy and the moon*
Casanova, Mary. *Utterly otterly night*
Cohen, Caron Lee. *Martin and the giant lions*
Cole, Rachael. *City moon*
Conrad, Donna. *See you soon, Moon*
Crews, Donald. *Night at the fair*
Crews, Nina. *I'll catch the moon*
DaCosta, Barbara. *Nighttime Ninja*
Davies, Jacqueline. *The night is singing*
Davies, Nicola. *Bat loves the night*
  White owl, barn owl
Deacon, Alexis. *While you are sleeping*
Delacroix, Sibylle. *Blanche hates the night*
De Roo, Elena. *The rain train*
Doyen, Denise. *Once upon a twice*
Dunbar, Joyce. *The monster who ate darkness*
Duncan, Lois. *I walk at night*
Edwards, Michelle. *What's that noise?*
Edwards, Pamela Duncan. *Wake-up kisses*
  While the world is sleeping
Emberley, Barbara. *Night's nice*
Enersen, Adele. *Vincent and the night*
Esenwine, Matt Forrest. *Flashlight night*
Fan, Terry. *The Night Gardener*
Faulkner, Keith. *A trick or a treat?*
Feder, Sandra. *The moon inside*
Feiffer, Kate. *No go sleep!*

Fletcher, Ralph. *Hello, harvest moon*
Ford, Bernette. *First snow*
Fox, Mem. *Night noises*
Fraser, Mary Ann. *Where are the night animals?*
Gabriel, Ashala. *Night night toes*
Gal, Susan. *Night lights*
Gallo, Frank. *Night sounds*
George, William T. *Beaver at Long Pond*
Gerstein, Mordicai. *The night world*
Gibbons, Gail. *Bats*
Ginsburg, Mirra. *Asleep, asleep*
Godwin, Laura. *Owl sees owl*
Goossens, Philippe. *Knock! knock! knock! who's there?*
Graber, Janet. *Jacob and the polar bears*
Grant, Holly. *Wee Sister Strange*
Greenfield, Eloise. *Night on Neighborhood Street*
Grey, Mini. *Toys in space*
Hargrove, Linda. *Wings across the moon*
Harris, Peter. *The night pirates*
Harshman, Marc. *All the way to morning*
Hartland, Jessie. *Night shift*
Heidbreder, Robert. *Song for a summer night*
Hertz, Grete Janus. *Olie's bedtime walk*
Hirschi, Ron. *When night comes*
Hissey, Jane. *Hoot*
Hoberman, Mary Ann. *I'm going to Grandma's*
Hoffman, Don. *Good morning, good night Billy and Abigail*
Hopgood, Tim. *Wow! said the owl*
Horácek, Petr. *When the moon smiled*
Hosta, Dar. *I love the night*
Howe, James. *There's a monster under my bed*
Isadora, Rachel. *A South African night*
Jackson, Richard. *All ears, all eyes*
Johnson, Angela. *Joshua's night whispers*
Johnson, D. B. *Henry's night*
Johnston, Tony. *Desert song*
  Little Rabbit goes to sleep
Jukes, Mavis. *You're a bear*
Keats, Ezra Jack. *Dreams*
Kenah, Katharine. *The dream shop*
Kudlinski, Kathleen V. *The sunset switch*
Lesynski, Loris. *Night school*
Lindbergh, Reeve. *Midnight farm*
London, Jonathan. *Fireflies, fireflies, light my way*
  The owl who became the moon
Low, William. *Daytime nighttime*
Lullaby moons and a silver spoon
McDonald, Megan. *Whoo-oo is it?*
McGinty, Alice B. *Ten little lambs*
MacLachlan, Patricia. *Fiona loves the night*
Marino, Gianna. *Night animals*
Martin, Bill, Jr.. *Barn dance!*
Martin, Ruth. *Moon dreams*
Matheson, Christie. *Touch the brightest star*
Mayer, Mercer. *You're the scaredy cat*
Milusich, Janice. *Off go their engines, off go their lights*
Minor, Wendell. *Daylight starlight wildlife*
Monfreid, Dorothée de. *Dark night*
Moodie, Fiona. *Noko and the night monster*
Mora, Pat. *Delicious hullabaloo / Pachanga deliciosa*
Morales, Yuyi. *Little night*
Morgan, Mary. *My good night book*
Munro, Roxie. *Desert days, desert nights*
Murphy, Stuart J. *It's about time!*
Murray, Martine. *A moose called Mouse*
Na, Il Sung. *A book of sleep*
Newman, Lesléa. *Cats, cats, cats*

Nobisso, Josephine. *The moon's lullaby*
Ochiltree, Dianne. *It's a firefly night*
Pearce, Clemency. *Frangoline and the midnight dream*
Pearson, Susan. *The drowsy hours*
Peck, Richard. *Monster night at Grandma's house*
Pedersen, Judy. *When night time comes near*
Pendziwol, Jean E. *Once upon a northern night*
Peters, Lisa Westberg. *Frankie works the night shift*
Pilkey, Dav. *The Moonglow Roll-O-Rama*
A pocketful of stars
Posey, Lee. *Night rabbits*
Powell, Polly. *Just dessert*
Purmell, Ann. *Where wild babies sleep*
Raschka, Chris. *Can't sleep*
Rathmann, Peggy. *Good night, Gorilla*
Ray, Mary Lyn. *Stars*
Rice, Eve. *Goodnight, goodnight*
Riley, Linnea Asplind. *Mouse mess*
Rinker, Sherri Duskey. *Steam train, dream train*
Ritchie, Scot. *My house is alive!*
Robbins, Beth. *Tom's afraid of the dark*
Rocco, John. *Blackout*
Rockwell, Anne. *Here comes the night*
Rodriguez, Bobbie. *Sarah's sleepover*
Rohmann, Eric. *The cinder-eyed cats*
Roscoe, Lily. *The night parade*
Rosenberg, Liz. *Eli's night-light*
Ross, Michael Elsohn. *Earth cycles*
Roth, Susan L. *Night-time numbers*
Runton, Andy. *Owly and Wormy: bright lights and starry nights!*
Ryan, Cheli Durán. *Hildilid's night*
Ryder, Joanne. *Step into the night*
Rylant, Cynthia. *Night in the country*
Sanromán, Susana. *Señora Reganoña*
Saunders, Karen. *Baby Badger's wonderful night*
Schnur, Steven. *Night lights*
Serfozo, Mary. *Whooo's there?*
Shulevitz, Uri. *Dusk*
So sleepy story
Simmons, Jane. *Daisy's favorite things*
Singer, Marilyn. *Quiet night*
Sloat, Teri. *The thing that bothered Farmer Brown*
Snicket, Lemony. *The dark*
Somary, Wolfgang. *Night and the candlemaker*
Southwell, Jandelyn. *The little country town*
Spinelli, Eileen. *Night shift daddy*
Rise the moon
Sproule, Gail. *Singing the dark*
Srinivasan, Divya. *Little Owl's night*
Stevenson, Robert Louis. *The moon*
Stolz, Mary. *Storm in the night*
Sturges, Philemon. *Ten flashing fireflies*
Stutson, Caroline. *Cats' night out*
Swanson, Susan Marie. *The house in the night*
Tafuri, Nancy. *Do not disturb*
What the sun sees / What the moon sees
Teague, David. *Franklin's big dreams*
Thomas, Patricia. *Firefly mountain*
Red sled
Thomas, Shelley Moore. *Putting the world to sleep*
Thompson, Lauren. *Little Quack's bedtime*
Thompson, Richard. *The night walker*
Thornhill, Jan. *Wild in the city*
Tillman, Nancy. *On the night you were born*
Tomlinson, Jill. *The owl who was afraid of the dark*
Valério, Geraldo. *Turn on the night*
Van Allsburg, Chris. *The polar express*

Waboose, Jan Bourdeau. *Firedancers*
SkySisters
Waddell, Martin. *The big big sea*
Can't you sleep, Little Bear?
Owl babies
Sleep tight, Little Bear
Walsh, Ellen Stoll. *Pip's magic*
Walter, Mildred Pitts. *Darkness*
Waring, Geoff. *Oscar and the moth*
Watt, Mélanie. *Scaredy Squirrel at night*
Weiss, Nicki. *Where does the brown bear go?*
Wellington, Monica. *Night rabbits*
Weston, Carrie. *If a chicken stayed for supper*
Whatley, Bruce. *Captain Pajamas*
Wiesner, David. *Tuesday*
Wild, Margaret. *Midnight babies*
Winnick, Karen B. *Sybil's night ride*
Wolf, Karina. *The Insomniacs*
Won, Brian. *Hooray for today!*
Wood, Audrey. *Moonflute*
Yaccarino, Dan. *Good night, Mr. Night*
Yee, Wong Herbert. *Summer days and nights*
Yolen, Jane. *Owl moon*
Zolotow, Charlotte. *When the wind stops*

Nightmares *see also* Bedtime; Monsters; Mythical creatures – goblins; Night; Sleep

Durango, Julia. *Dream hop*
Johnson, Lindan Lee. *The dream jar*
Karas, G. Brian. *Bebe's bad dream*
Klise, Kate. *Little Rabbit and the Night Mare*
Stadler, Alexander. *Beverly Billingsly borrows a book*
Waechter, Phillip. *Rosie and the nightmares*

Ninjas *see* Sports – martial arts

No text *see* Wordless

Noise, sounds

Agee, Jon. *It's only Stanley*
Alizadeh, Kate. *Quiet!*
Allard, Harry. *Bumps in the night*
Allen, Jonathan. *The little rabbit who liked to say moo*
Anholt, Catherine. *Chimp and Zee's noisy book*
Arndt, Michael. *Cat says meow and other animalopoeia*
Arnold, Katya. *Meow!*
Arnold, Marsha Diane. *Roar of a snore*
Asch, Frank. *Barnyard lullaby*
Aylesworth, Jim. *Cock-a-doodle-doo, creak, pop-pop, moo*
Country crossing
Baddiel, Ivor. *Cock-a-doodle quack! quack!*
Balouch, Kristen. *The little little girl with the big big voice*
Barnett, Mac. *Noisy night*
Beaton, Clare. *How loud is a lion?*
Beaumont, Karen. *No sleep for the sheep!*
Beck, Andrea. *Elliot's noisy night*
Bee, William. *And the cars go . . .*
And the train goes . . .
Beeke, Tiphanie. *Roar like a lion!*
Berenstain, Stan and Jan. *Bears in the night*
Berkes, Marianne. *Marsh music*
Big noisy trucks and diggers
Black, Michael Ian. *Cock-a-doodle-doo-bop!*

McCue, Lisa. *Quiet Bunny*
MacDonald, Margaret Read. *The squeaky door*
McDonald, Megan. *Whoo-oo is it?*
MacDonald, Ross. *Achoo! Bang! Crash!*
McFarlane, Sheryl. *In the city*
    On the farm
McGee, Marni. *The noisy farm*
McGovern, Ann. *Too much noise*
Macken, JoAnn Early. *Baby says "moo!"*
Mahy, Margaret. *Boom Baby boom, boom*
Maitland, Barbara. *Moo in the morning*
Mandel, Peter. *Zoo ah-choooo*
Marsalis, Wynton. *Squeak, rumble, whomp! Whomp! Whomp!*
Martin, Bill, Jr.. *Listen to our world*
    Polar bear, polar bear, what do you hear?
Mason, Adrienne. *Lu and Clancy sound off*
Massini, Sarah. *Trixie ten*
Matheis, Mickie. *Bedtime for Boo*
Mayo, Margaret. *Choo choo clickety-clack*
Medearis, Angela Shelf. *Rum-a-tum-tum*
Meister, Cari. *Busy, busy city street*
Milgrim, David. *Why Benny barks*
Miranda, Anne. *Beep! beep!*
Mitton, Tony. *Flashing fire engines*
Moon, Nicola. *Tick-tock, drip-drop*
Moore, Suzi. *Whoops!*
Mora, Pat. *Listen to the desert / Oye al desierto*
Moreton, Daniel. *La Cucaracha Martina*
Most, Bernard. *The cow that went oink*
    Z-Z-Zoink!
Mozelle, Shirley. *The bear upstairs*
Munsch, Robert N. *Mortimer*
Murphy, Jill. *Peace at last*
Murphy, Mary. *Please be quiet!*
    Say hello like this!
Murphy, Stuart J. *Percy listens up*
Murphy, Yannick. *Ahwooooooooo!*
Naberhaus, Sarvinder. *Boom boom*
Newton, Jill. *Crash bang donkey!*
Nobles, Kristen M. *Drive this book*
Nygaard, Elizabeth. *Snake alley band*
O'Neill, Alexis. *Loud Emily*
Palatini, Margie. *Boo-hoo moo*
    Moo who?
Parenteau, Shirley. *Bears in a band*
Park, Linda Sue. *Yum! yuck!*
Patricelli, Leslie. *Be quiet, Mike!*
Pearson, Debora. *Big city song*
Pearson, Tracey Campbell. *Bob*
Pedersen, Janet. *Millie wants to play*
Perkins, Lynne Rae. *Snow music*
Pfeffer, Wendy. *Dolphin talk*
Phillips, Mildred. *And the cow said, "moo"!*
Pizzoli, Greg. *Good night Owl*
Polacco, Patricia. *Mommies say shhh!*
Portis, Antoinette. *Froodle*
Raschka, Chris. *Talk to me about the alphabet*
Rauss, Ron. *Can I just take a nap?*
Ritchie, Scot. *My house is alive!*
Roques, Dominique. *Sleep tight, Anna Banana!*
Rozen, Anna. *The merchant of noises*
Schofield-Morrison, Connie. *I got the rhythm*
Schwartz, Corey Rosen. *Hop! Plop!*
Scruggs, Afi. *Jump rope magic*
Seeger, Laura Vaccaro. *I had a rooster*
Selig, Josh. *Red and Yellow's noisy night*
Serfozo, Mary. *Rain talk*
Seuss, Dr. *Gerald McBoing Boing*

    Gerald McBoing Boing sound book
Shaw, Nancy. *Raccoon tune*
Showers, Paul. *Hear your heart*
    The listening walk
Sif, Birgitta. *Swish and Squeak's noisy day*
Simmons, Jane. *Daisy says coo!*
    Daisy says, "If you're happy and you know it"
    Daisy, the little duck with big feet
    Daisy's day out
    Daisy's hide-and-seek
    Go to sleep, Daisy
    Quack, Daisy, quack!
Sims, Nat. *Peekaboo barn*
Singer, Marilyn. *City lullaby*
    Quiet night
Skolsky, Mindy Warshaw. *Hannah and the whistling tea kettle*
Slingsby, Janet. *Hush-a-bye babies*
Sloat, Teri. *Farmer Brown goes round and round*
    The thing that bothered Farmer Brown
Smallman, Steve. *Hiccupotamus*
Southwell, Jandelyn. *The little country town*
Spence, Robert, III.. *Clickety clack*
Spier, Peter. *Gobble, growl, grunt*
Spires, Elizabeth. *The big meow*
Stephens, Helen. *Ruby and the noisy hippo*
Stevens, April. *Waking up Wendell*
Stevenson, Harvey. *Big scary wolf*
Stewart, Melissa. *Can an aardvark bark?*
Sturges, Philemon. *What's that sound, Woolly Bear?*
Tafuri, Nancy. *Do not disturb*
    The donkey's Christmas song
Teckentrup, Britta. *Little Wolf's song*
Thompson, Richard. *The night walker*
Thomson, Pat. *The squeaky, creaky bed*
Tillman, Nancy. *Tumford's rude noises*
Tresselt, Alvin R. *Wake up, farm!*
Tullet, Hervé. *Say zoop!*
Turner, Sandy. *Silent night*
Tyger, Rory. *Newton*
Uhlberg, Myron. *The sound of all things*
Underwood, Deborah. *The Christmas quiet book*
    The loud book!
    The quiet book
Van Biesen, Koen. *Roger is reading a book*
Verboven, Agnes. *Ducks like to swim*
Vernick, Audrey. *Teach your buffalo to play drums*
Waber, Bernard. *The mouse that snored*
Waddell, Martin. *Let's go home, Little Bear*
    Squeak-a-lot
Wadsworth, Ginger. *One tiger growls*
Wallace, Joseph E. *Big and noisy Simon*
Walsh, Melanie. *Do monkeys tweet?*
Walter, Virginia. *"Hi, pizza man!"*
Walton, Rick. *Little dogs say "Rough!"*
Waring, Geoff. *Oscar and the bat*
Weaver, Tess. *Frederick Finch, loudmouth*
Weill, Cynthia. *Animal talk: Mexican folk art animal sounds in English and Spanish*
Weinstein, Ellen Slusky. *Everywhere the cow says "Moo!"*
West, Colin. *One day in the jungle*
West, Judy. *Have you got my purr?*
Wildsmith, Brian. *Goat's trail*
Williams, Carol Ann. *Booming Bella*
Wilson, Karma. *Duddle Puck*
    Who goes there?
Winer, Yvonne. *Frogs sing songs*
Winnick, Karen B. *Barn sneeze*

Wolff, Ferida. *It is the wind*
Wong, Janet S. *Buzz*
Woodruff, Liza. *Emerson barks*
Yolen, Jane. *On Duck Pond*
Yoon, Salina. *Do cows meow?*
    Do crocs kiss?
Young, Ruth. *Who says moo?*
Yuly, Toni. *Night owl*
Zolotow, Charlotte. *The poodle who barked at the wind*

Noise, sounds – snoring *see* Sleep – snoring

Nomads

Baasansuren, Bolormaa. *My little round house*

North Pole *see* Foreign lands – Arctic

Northern lights

Kalz, Jill. *Northern lights*
Merski, P. K. *Roaring, boring, Alice*
Sabuda, Robert. *The Blizzard's robe*
Smith, Danna. *Arctic white*
Taylor, Harriet Peck. *Ulaq and the northern lights*
Waboose, Jan Bourdeau. *SkySisters*

Noses *see* Anatomy – noses; Senses – smell

Numbers *see* Counting, numbers

Nursery rhymes

Ada, Alma Flor. *¡Muu, moo!*
    Pio peep!
Ahlberg, Janet. *The jolly Christmas postman*
Anholt, Catherine. *Come back, Jack!*
Ashburn, Boni. *Builder Goose*
Aylesworth, Jim. *The completed hickory dickory dock*
Baker, Keith. *Potato Joe*
Beaton, Clare. *Clare Beaton's bedtime rhymes*
    Clare Beaton's farmyard rhymes
    Clare Beaton's nursery rhymes
Billin-Frye, Paige. *One, two, buckle my shoe*
Brown, Marc. *Finger rhymes*
    Hand rhymes
    Play rhymes
Brown, Margaret Wise. *The find it book*
Bush, Timothy. *Teddy bear, teddy bear*
Butler, John. *Ten in the den*
Cabrera, Jane. *Baa, baa, black sheep*
    One, two, buckle my shoe
    Rock-a-bye baby
    There was an old woman who lived in a shoe
    Twinkle, twinkle, little star
Cauley, Lorinda Bryan. *Clap your hands*
Charlip, Remy. *Sleepytime rhyme*
Chichester Clark, Emma. *Little Miss Muffet counts to ten*
Chorao, Kay. *The baby's bedtime book*
    Knock at the door and other baby action rhymes
Christelow, Eileen. *Five little monkeys jumping on the bed*
Colby, Rebecca. *Motor Goose: rhymes that go!*
Conway, David. *The great nursery rhyme disaster*

Cummings, Troy. *The Eensy Weensy Spider freaks out! (big-time!)*
Dann, Penny. *Eensy weensy spider*
Davis, Caroline. *My little rowboat*
Dean, James. *Pete the Cat: twinkle, twinkle, little star*
Delessert, Etienne. *A was an apple pie*
dePaola, Tomie. *Favorite nursery tales*
    Tomie de Paola's Mother Goose
Domanska, Janina. *If all the seas were one sea*
Edwards, Pamela Duncan. *The neat line*
Egielski, Richard. *Itsy bitsy spider*
Fitzgerald, Joanne. *Yum! yum!*
Fleming, Denise. *The everything book*
Fox, Mem. *Good night, sleep tight*
Galdone, Paul. *Cat goes fiddle-i-fee*
Gliori, Debi. *What's the time, Mr. Wolf?*
Grey, Mini. *The adventures of the dish and the spoon*
Hague, Michael. *Teddy bear, teddy bear*
Hale, Sarah Josepha Buell. *Mary had a little lamb,* ill. by Tomie dePaola
    Mary had a little lamb, ill. by Laura Huliska-Beith
    Mary had a little lamb, photos by Bruce McMillan
    Mary had a little lamb, ill. by Salley Mavor
Harrington, Tim. *This little piggy*
Harris, Trudy. *The clock struck one*
    Twenty hungry piggies
The Helen Oxenbury nursery collection
Heller, Nicholas. *This little piggy*
Hennessy, B. G. *The missing tarts*
Hill, Susanna Leonard. *The house that Mack built*
Hillenbrand, Will. *Fiddle-i-fee*
    Mother Goose picture puzzles
Hoberman, Mary Ann. *Mary had a little lamb*
    Miss Mary Mack
Honey, Elizabeth. *The moon in the man*
Horowitz, Dave. *Humpty Dumpty climbs again*
The house that Jack built. The house that Jack built, ill. by Diana Mayo
    The house that Jack built, ill. by Jeanette Winter
    This is the house that Jack built
Ivimey, John William. *The complete story of the three blind mice*
    Three blind mice
Jackson, Alison. *If the shoe fits*
    When the wind blew
Jaramillo, Susie. *Elefantitos / little elephants*
Jay, Alison. *Red green blue*
Jonovitz, Marilyn. *Three little kittens*
Kirk, Daniel. *Jack and Jill*
Kroll, Virginia L. *Jaha and Jamil went down the hill*
Krumwiede, Lana. *Just Itzy*
Levinthal, David. *Who pushed Humpty Dumpty?*
McMullan, Kate. *Baby Goose*
Martin, Bill, Jr.. *Fire! Fire! said Mrs. McGuire*
    "Fire! Fire!" said Mrs. McGuire
Martin, Sarah Catherine. *Old Mother Hubbard*
    Old Mother Hubbard and her wonderful dog
Metzger, Steve. *Detective Blue*
Miranda, Anne. *To market, to market*
Mitton, Tony. *Riddledy piggledy*
Montgomery, Michael G. *Over the candlestick*
Morgan, Mary. *Dragon pizzeria*
Mortensen, Lori. *Cindy Moo*
Moses, Will. *Mary and her little lamb*
Mother Goose. *Arnold Lobel book of Mother Goose*
    The baby's lap book
    The cat and the fiddle
    The Chinese Mother Goose rhymes
    Hey, diddle, diddle

Hey, diddle, diddle [board book]
Hickory, dickory, dock
Hickory dickory dock and other nursery rhymes
Humpty Dumpty
Humpty Dumpty and other rhymes
Ian Penney's book of nursery rhymes
Jack and Jill [board book]
James Marshall's Mother Goose
La Madre Goose
Little Boy Blue and other rhymes
Little Miss Muffet [board book]
Little Miss Muffet
Mother Goose, ill. by Scott Cook
Mother Goose, ill. by Michael Hague
Mother Goose, ill. by Tasha Tudor
Mother Goose numbers on the loose
Mother Goose remembers
My first real Mother Goose [board book]
1, 2, buckle my shoe
One, two, buckle my shoe [board book]
Pat-a-cake, ill. by Olga Ivanov
Pat-a-cake, ill. by Annie Kubler
Pat-a-cake [board book]
Pussycat, pussycat and other rhymes
Richard Scarry's best Mother Goose ever
Rock-a-bye baby [board book]
Snuggle up with Mother Goose
This little piggy [board book]
The three jovial huntsmen
The three little kittens
Wee Willie Winkie [board book]
Wee Willie Winkie and other rhymes
Wendy Watson's Mother Goose
Will Moses Mother Goose
O'Malley, Kevin. *Humpty Dumpty egg-splodes*
One, two, skip a few!
Palatini, Margie. *The web files*
Pearson, Tracey Campbell. *Diddle diddle dumpling*
　　Hector Protector [board book]
Petersham, Maud. *The rooster crows*
Pierce, Terry. *Counting your way*
Pinkney, Jerry. *Three little kittens*
Polacco, Patricia. *Babushka's Mother Goose*
Potter, Beatrix. *Appley Dapply's nursery rhymes*
　　Cecily Parsley's nursery rhymes
Sabuda, Robert. *The movable Mother Goose*
Santat, Dan. *After the fall (how Humpty Dumpty got back up again)*
Schoenherr, Ian. *Cat and mouse*
Scieszka, Jon. *The book that Jack wrote*
　　Truckery rhymes
Sendak, Maurice. *Hector Protector, and As I went over the water*
Sierra, Judy. *Monster Goose*
Simple Simon. *The adventures of Simple Simon*
Siomades, Lorianne. *The itsy bitsy spider*
　　Three little kittens
Smith, Danna. *Mother Goose's pajama party*
Spirin, Gennady. *A apple pie*
Stanley, Diane. *The Giant and the beanstalk*
Stevens, Janet. *And the dish ran away with the spoon*
Stoop, Naoko. *Sing with me!*
Taylor, Alice. *A child's treasury of Irish rhymes*
Taylor, Jane. *Twinkle, twinkle, little star*, ill. by Heather Collins
　　Twinkle, twinkle, little star, ill. by Michael Hague
　　Twinkle, twinkle, little star, ill. by Julia Noonan
　　Twinkle, twinkle, little star, ill. by Jerry Pinkney
Thomson, Sarah L. *Around the neighborhood*

Trapani, Iza. *Baa baa black sheep*
　　The itsy bitsy spider
　　Old King Cole
　　Rufus and friends
Vail, Rachel. *Over the moon*
Verburg, Bonnie. *The tree house that Jack built*
Voce, Louise. *Over in the meadow*
Watson, Wendy. *Thanksgiving at our house*
Wells, Rosemary. *Max and Ruby's treasure hunt*
Wheeler, Opal. *Sing Mother Goose*
Wright, Danielle. *Japanese nursery rhymes*
Wu, Faye-Lynn. *Chinese and English nursery rhymes*
Zalben, Jane Breskin. *Hey, Mama Goose*
Zemach, Margot. *Some from the moon, some from the sun*
Ziefert, Harriet. *Mother Goose manners*
　　Ode to Humpty Dumpty

Nursery school *see* School – nursery

Nutrition *see* Food; Health & fitness

Occupations *see* Careers

Oceans *see* Sea & seashore

Octopuses

Allen, Elanna. *Poor little guy*
Baker, Keith. *My octopus arms*
Brett, Jan. *The mermaid*
Cazet, Denys. *The octopus*
Diller, Kevin. *Hello, my name is Octicorn*
Estes, Allison. *Izzy and Oscar*
Farrell, Darren. *Thank you, Octopus*
Jackson, Ellen. *Octopuses one to ten*
Lauber, Patricia. *An octopus is amazing*
McKenna, Martin. *The octopuppy*
Mayer, Mercer. *Octopus soup*
Nyeu, Tao. *Squid and Octopus*
Paterson, Brian. *Zigby dives in*
Pichard, Alexandra. *Pen pals*
Pitcher, Caroline. *Nico's octopus*
Scieszka, Jon. *Cowboy and Octopus*
Srinivasan, Divya. *Octopus alone*
Tokuda-Hall, Maggie. *Also an octopus*
Yaccarino, Dan. *An octopus followed me home*
　　Oswald

Odors *see* Senses – smell

Oil

Berger, Melvin. *Oil spill!*

Rand, Gloria. *Prince William*

Old age

Agee, Jon. *The retired kid*
Alsenas, Linas. *Peanut*
Altes, Marta. *My grandpa*
Altman, Linda Jacobs. *Singing with Momma Lou*
Arnosky, Jim. *Grandfather Buffalo*
Arro, Lena. *By geezers and galoshes!*
Barbour, Karen. *Mr. Williams*
Best, Cari. *Are you going to be good?*
Biro, Maureen Boyd. *Walking with Maga*
Bley, Anette. *And what comes after a thousand?*
Briggs, Raymond. *Jim and the beanstalk*
Bunting, Eve. *Can you do this, Old Badger?*
Cheng, Andrea. *The lemon sisters*
Ciraolo, Simona. *The lines on Nana's face*
Cruise, Robin. *Little Mama forgets*
Cummings, Phil. *Newspaper hats*
dePaola, Tomie. *Nana Upstairs and Nana Downstairs*
Edwards, Michelle. *A hat for Mrs. Goldman*
Fox, Mem. *Wilfrid Gordon McDonald Partridge*
Grimm, Jacob and Wilhelm. *The Bremen town band*
  The Bremen town musicians, ill. by Bill Dickson
  The Bremen town musicians, ill. by Ilse Plume
  The Bremen town musicians, ill. by Bernadette Watts
  The Bremen town musicians, ill. by Lisbeth Zwerger
  Musicians of Bremen
  Musicians of Bremen / Los musicos de Bremner
Henson, Heather. *Grumpy Grandpa*
Huling, Jan. *Ol' Bloo's boogie-woogie band and blues ensemble*
Johnson, Angela. *When I am old with you*
Johnston, Tony. *A small thing . . . but big*
Joyce, William. *The Leaf Men and the brave good bugs*
Klise, Kate. *Stay: a girl, a dog, a bucket list*
Leedahl, Shelley A. *The bone talker*
Levine, Arthur A. *What a beautiful morning*
Lindbergh, Reeve. *My little grandmother often forgets*
Lyons, Kelly Starling. *Tea cakes for Tosh*
Martin, Bill, Jr.. *Little granny quarterback*
Miller, William. *The piano*
Muth, Jon J. *Zen ties*
Nanji, Shenaaz. *An alien in my house*
Nelson, Vaunda Micheaux. *Don't call me Grandma*
Newman, Jeff. *The boys*
Orloff, Karen Kaufman. *I wanna go home*
Peet, Bill. *Smokey*
Powell, Consie. *Old dog Cora and the Christmas tree*
Price, Kathy. *The Bourbon Street musicians*
Proimos, James. *Joe's wish*
Puttock, Simon. *A ladder to the stars*
Ramsden, Ashley. *Seven fathers*
Ray, Mary Lyn. *A violin for Elva*
Reynolds, Marilynn. *A present for Mrs. Kazinski*
Rubin, Adam. *Those darn squirrels!*
  Those darn squirrels and the cat next door
  Those darn squirrels fly south
Schachner, Judith Byron. *The Grannyman*
Shelby, Anne. *The man who lived in a hollow tree*
Shepherd, Jessica. *Grandma*
Smith, Lane. *Grandpa Green*
Stead, Philip C. *A sick day for Amos McGee*
Stevens, Janet. *Old bag of bones*
Stroud, Bettye. *Down home at Miss Dessa's*

Tafolla, Carmen. *Baby Coyote and the old woman / El coyotito y la viejita*
Uchida, Yoshiko. *The wise old woman*
Urdahl, Catherine. *Emma's question*
Van Laan, Nancy. *Forget me not*
Vega, Denise. *Grandmother, have the angels come?*
Walker, Sally M. *Druscilla's Halloween*
Weigelt, Udo. *Old Beaver*
Wild, Margaret. *Old Pig*
Winter, Jeanette. *Henri's scissors*
Yolen, Jane. *Miz Berlin walks*
Zolotow, Charlotte. *I know a lady*

Olympics *see* Sports – Olympics

Opossums *see* Animals – possums

Optical illusions

Anno, Mitsumasa. *Anno's alphabet*
  Anno's counting book
  Anno's counting house
  Anno's Italy
  Anno's journey
Mallat, Kathy. *Just ducky*
Priceman, Marjorie. *It's me, Marva!*
Rosenthal, Amy Krouse. *Duck! Rabbit!*

Optimism *see* Character traits – optimism

Orderliness *see* Character traits – orderliness

Orphans

Beake, Lesley. *Home now*
Bemelmans, Ludwig. *Madeline*
  Madeline and the bad hat
  Madeline and the gypsies
  Madeline in London
  Madeline's Christmas
  Madeline's rescue
Burnett, Frances Hodgson. *A little princess*, ill. by Barbara McClintock
  A little princess, ill. by Graham Rust
Calhoun, Mary. *A shepherd's gift*
Crunk, Tony. *Big Mama*
Ellis, Gerry. *Natumi takes the lead*
Fan, Terry. *The Night Gardener*
Goble, Paul. *The lost children*
Godden, Rumer. *The story of Holly and Ivy*
Hershenhorn, Esther. *Fancy that*
Joosse, Barbara. *Nikolai, the only bear*
Kay, Verla. *Orphan train*
Kessler, Cristina. *Jubela*
Manna, Anthony L. *The orphan*
Marciano, John Bemelmans. *Madeline and the cats of Rome*
  Madeline and the old house in Paris
  Madeline at the White House
Martin, Jacqueline Briggs. *The water gift and the pig of the pig*
Mollel, Tololwa M. *Orphan boy*
Noyes, Deborah. *When I met the wolf girls*
Odone, Jamison. *Honey badgers*
Oelschlager, Vanita. *I came from the water*
Polacco, Patricia. *Welcome Comfort*

Pomerantz, Charlotte. *The mousery*
Prigger, Mary Skillings. *Aunt Minnie McGranahan*
Puckett, Kelley. *Batman's dark secret*
Rylant, Cynthia. *The bird house*
San Souci, Robert D. *The secret of the stones*
Selznick, Brian. *The invention of Hugo Cabret*
Stanley, Diane. *Raising Sweetness*
Ungerer, Tomi. *The three robbers*
Vander Zee, Ruth. *Always with you*
Willard, Nancy. *Shadow story*
Yolen, Jane. *The girl in the golden bower*

Outer space *see* Space & space ships

Pageants *see* Theater

Painters *see* Activities – painting; Careers – artists

Panthers *see* Animals – leopards

Paper

Compestine, Ying Chang. *The story of paper*
Czernecki, Stefan. *Paper lanterns*
Gibbons, Gail. *Deadline!*
  Paper, paper everywhere
Howell, Will C. *Zoo flakes ABC*
Jeffers, Oliver. *The great paper caper*
Kleber, Dori. *More-igami*
Kleven, Elisa. *The paper princess*
Kroll, Virginia L. *Pink paper swans*
Melmed, Laura Krauss. *Little Oh*
Moffatt, Judith. *Snow shapes*
Reynolds, Peter H. *I'm here*

Parades

Appelt, Kathi. *Bats on parade*
Baer, Gene. *Thump thump rat-a-tat-tat*
Black, Michael Ian. *A pig parade is a terrible idea*
Bond, Rebecca. *The great doughnut parade*
Boswell, Addie. *The rain stomper*
Boynton, Sandra. *Christmas parade*
Colby, Rebecca. *It's raining bats and frogs*
Corey, Shana. *Milly and the Macy's Parade*
Crews, Donald. *Parade*
Crimi, Carolyn. *Pugs in a Bug*
DiPucchio, Kelly. *Crafty Chloe: dress-up mess-up*
Ets, Marie Hall. *In the forest*
Freschet, Gina. *Naty's parade*
Greenberg, Melanie Hope. *Mermaids on parade*
Greenfield, Eloise. *Easter parade*
Guidone, Thea. *Drum city*
Hoffman, Mary. *Princess Grace*

Jane, Pamela. *Milo and the fire engine parade*
Janice. *Little Bear marches in the St. Patrick's Day parade*
Johnson, Angela. *The day Ray got away*
Joosse, Barbara. *Dog parade*
  Hooray Parade
Kroll, Steven. *Mary McLean and the St. Patrick's Day parade*
Lasky, Kathryn. *Fourth of July bear*
Lenski, Lois. *The Easter Rabbit's parade*
London, Jonathan. *Froggy plays in the band*
McKee, David. *Elmer's special day*
Mora, Pat. *The rainbow tulip*
Paquette, Ammi-Joan. *Bunny Bus*
Pitman, Gayle E. *This day in June*
Roosa, Karen. *Pippa at the parade*
Roscoe, Lily. *The night parade*
Sebe, Masayuki. *One hundred animals on parade!*
Sweet, Melissa. *Balloons over Broadway*
Waldron, Kevin. *Panda-monium at Peek Zoo*
Wardlaw, Lee. *Red, white, and boom!*
Whitehead, Kathy. *Looking for Uncle Louie on the Fourth of July*
Winthrop, Elizabeth. *Halloween hats*
Ziefert, Harriet. *Circus parade*
  First Night

Parks

Becker, Shari. *Maxwell's mountain*
Black, Sonia. *Hanging out with Mom*
Bogan, Carmen. *Where's Rodney?*
Browne, Anthony. *Voices in the park*
Cohen, Caron Lee. *Martin and the giant lions*
Cotten, Cynthia. *Rain play*
Curious George and the dump truck (1999)
Flanagan, Alice K. *Exploring parks with Ranger Dockett*
Godwin, Laura. *Central Park serenade*
Gorbachev, Valeri. *Chicken chickens*
Granowsky, Alvin. *At the park*
Heo, Yumi. *One Sunday morning*
High, Linda Oatman. *The girl on the high-diving horse*
Hill, Eric. *Spot goes to the park*
Ichikawa, Satomi. *La La Rose*
Jenkins, Emily. *Water in the park*
Jones, Ursula. *The witch's children*
Kann, Victoria. *Emeraldalicious*
McGhee, Alison. *Percy, dog of destiny*
McKissack, Patricia C. *Messy Bessey's family reunion*
McPhail, David. *Henry Bear's park*
Mahy, Margaret. *Down the dragon's tongue*
Merriam, Eve. *Where's that cat?*
Morozumi, Atsuko. *In the park*
Noble, Sheilagh. *More*
Nordling, Lee. *Shehewe*
Rosenstock, Barb. *The camping trip that changed America*
Ruelle, Karen Gray. *Bark park*
Schaefer, Carole Lexa. *ABCers*
Schwartz, Roslyn. *Tales from Parc la Fontaine*
Sharratt, Nick. *Shark in the park*
Singer, Marilyn. *Didi and Daddy on the Promenade*
Springstubb, Tricia. *Phoebe and Digger*
Sweeney, Joan. *Suzette and the puppy*
Walton, Rick. *Girl and Gorilla: out and about*
Weeks, Sarah. *Oh my gosh, Mrs. McNosh!*

Parks – amusement

Cecil, Randy. *Gator*
Cobb, Annie. *The long wait*
Curato, Mike. *Little Elliot, big fun*
Davis, Kathryn Gibbs. *Mr. Ferris and his wheel*
Frazee, Marla. *Roller coaster*
Gavril, David. *Penelope Nuthatch and the big surprise*
Hartt-Sussman, Heather. *Here comes Hortense!*
Horse, Harry. *Little Rabbit lost*
Kalz, Jill. *An a-maze-ing amusement park adventure*
Kang, Anna. *I am (not) scared*
Kraft, Betsy Harvey. *The fantastic Ferris wheel*
May, Eleanor. *Albert is not scared*
Rogalski, Mark. *Tickets to ride*
Viva, Frank. *Outstanding in the rain*
Ziefert, Harriet. *Fun Land fun!*

Parrots *see* Birds – parakeets, parrots

Participation

Borando, Silvia. *The cat book*
Brown, Marc. *Finger rhymes*
Cook, Grace. *Two little eyes and other action rhymes*
Cronin, Doreen. *Wiggle*
Cuyler, Margery. *We're going on a lion hunt*
Dempsey, Kristy. *A hop is up*
Diakité, Baba Wagué. *The hatseller and the monkeys*
Ets, Marie Hall. *Just me*
Fletcher, Tom. *There's a monster in your book*
Harrington, Tim. *Nose to toes, you are yummy!*
Hoban, Tana. *Where is it?*
Hutchins, Pat. *Good-night Owl*
Jones, Christianne C. *The Santa shimmy*
McLean, Janet. *Let's go, baby-o!*
Martin, Bill, Jr.. *Spunky Little Monkey*
Matheson, Christie. *Touch the brightest star*
Mühle, Jörg. *Tickle my ears*
Nieminen, Lotta. *Pancakes! an interactive recipe book*
Ramadier, Cédric. *Help! the wolf is coming!*
Rosen, Michael. *We're going on a bear hunt*
Rueda, Claudia. *Huff and puff*
Serafini, Frank. *Looking closely along the shore*
Seuss, Dr. *Gerald McBoing Boing sound book*
Shaw, Charles Green. *It looked like spilt milk*
Simmons, Jane. *Daisy says, "Here we go round the mulberry bush"*
   Daisy says, "If you're happy and you know it"
Slobodkina, Esphyr. *Caps for sale*
   Circus caps for sale
   More caps for sale
Smith, Kathryn. *Little Donkey's Christmas story*
   Little Lamb's Christmas story
Sorenson, Ashley. *The very cold, freezing, no-numbers day*
Spier, Peter. *Gobble, growl, grunt*
Trapani, Iza. *I'm a little teapot*
Tullet, Herve. *Let's play*
   The book with a hole
   Mix it up!
   Press here
   Say zoop!
Wells, Rosemary. *Max and Ruby's treasure hunt*
Yoon, Salina. *Tap to play!*
Ziefert, Harriet. *Wiggle like an octopus*

Parties

Adams, Adrienne. *The Christmas party*
   A Halloween happening
Allard, Harry. *The Stupids have a ball*
Allen, Joy. *Princess Palooza*
   Princess party
Anholt, Catherine. *Happy birthday, Chimp and Zee*
Asch, Frank. *Popcorn*
Asher, Sandy. *What a party!*
Ashman, Linda. *Maxwell's magic mix-up*
Avraham, Kate Aver. *What will you be, Sara Mee?*
Awdry, W. *Happy birthday, Thomas!*
Bach, Annie. *Monster party!*
Bailey, Linda. *Stanley's party*
Baker, Roberta. *Olive's pirate party*
Beck, Scott. *Happy birthday, Monster!*
Berenstain, Stan and Jan. *The Berenstain bears and the slumber party*
Berry, Lynne. *The curious demise of a contrary cat*
Bertrand, Diane Gonzales. *The party for Papa Luis / La fiesta para Papa Luis*
Best, Cari. *Are you going to be good?*
Birchall, Mark. *Rabbit's birthday surprise*
Blackstone, Stella. *Bear's birthday*
Block party today
Bluemle, Elizabeth. *How do you wokka-wokka?*
Bluthenthal, Diana Cain. *I'm not invited?*
Brendler, Carol. *Not very scary*
Brown, Marc. *Arthur's birthday*
Brown, Tameka Fryer. *Around our way on Neighbors' Day*
Browne, Anthony. *What if . . . ?*
Brownlee, Sophia Grace. *Tea time with Sophia Grace and Rosie*
Buehner, Caralyn. *Snowmen at Christmas*
Bunting, Eve. *Little Badger's just-about birthday*
Cabrera, Jane. *One, two, buckle my shoe*
Carlson, Nancy. *Armond goes to a party*
Carlstrom, Nancy White. *Happy birthday, Jesse Bear!*
Chambers, Roland. *Rooftop rocket party*
Chan, Ruth. *Where's the party?*
Chapin, Tom. *The backwards birthday party*
Chavarría-Cháirez, Becky. *Magda's piñata magic / Magda y la piñata mágica*
Chess, Victoria. *The costume party*
Chodos-Irvine, Margaret. *Ella Sarah gets dressed*
Clarke, Jane. *Trumpet*
Cohen, Miriam. *Tough Jim*
Cousins, Lucy. *Maisy dresses up*
Cox, Judy. *Happy birthday, Mrs. Millie!*
Cronin, Doreen. *Click, clack, boo!*
Dale, Penny. *Dinosaur zoom!*
Day, Alexandra. *Follow Carl!*
deGroat, Diane. *Happy birthday to you, you belong in a zoo*
Desbordes, Astrid. *Edmond, the moonlit party*
Dodd, Emma. *The entertainer*
Dooley, Norah. *Everybody brings noodles*
Du Bois, William Pène. *Bear party*
Dunn, Jancee. *I'm afraid your teddy is in trouble today*
Dyckman, Ame. *Tea party rules*
Ehlert, Lois. *Boo to you!*
Elya, Susan Middleton. *F is for fiesta*
Ets, Marie Hall. *Nine days to Christmas*
Evans, Cambria. *Martha Moth makes socks*
Fleming, Candace. *Bulldozer's big day*
Fliess, Sue. *A gluten-free birthday for me!*
Ford, Bernette. *No more bottles for Bunny!*

Patience *see* Character traits – patience, impatience

Peace *see* Violence, nonviolence

Peahens *see* Birds – peacocks, peahens

Pen pals

Perfectionism *see* Character traits – perfectionism

Perseverance *see* Character traits – perseverance

Persistence *see* Character traits – persistence

Petroglyphs

Petroleum *see* Oil

Pets

Clements, Andrew. *Dogku*
  Dolores and the big fire
  Slippers loves to run
  Tara and Tiree, fearless friends
Climo, Liz. *Rory the dinosaur wants a pet*
Cochran, Bill. *The forever dog*
Cohen, Miriam. *Jim's dog Muffins*, ill. by Ronald
    Himler
  Jim's dog Muffins, ill. by Lillian Hoban
Cole, Babette. *Princess Smartypants*
Cole, Henry. *Trudy*
Collicott, Sharleen. *Toestomper and the bad butterflies*
Cooper, Elisha. *Big cat, little cat*
Côté, Geneviève. *Bob's hungry ghost*
Cowen-Fletcher, Jane. *Hello, puppy!*
Crisp, Marty. *Black and white*
Cuyler, Margery. *Guinea pigs add up*
Daly, Cathleen. *Prudence wants a pet*
Daly, Niki. *What's cooking, Jamela?*
Davidson, Ellen Dee. *Princess Justina Albertina*
Davis, Patricia Anne. *Brian's bird*
Day, Alexandra. *Special deliveries*
dePaola, Tomie. *Little Grunt and the big egg*
DiPucchio, Kelly. *Gilbert goldfish wants a pet*
DiTerlizzi, Angela. *Some pets*
Dodd, Emma. *I don't want a posh dog*
  What pet to get?
Dodds, Dayle Ann. *Pet wash*
  Teacher's pets
Doyle, Malachy. *Sleepy Pendoodle*
Dubosarsky, Ursula. *Rex*
Duke, Kate. *Ready for pumpkins*
Dyckman, Ame. *You don't want a unicorn!*
Eaton, Jason Carter. *How to track a truck*
  How to train a train
Edwards, Karl Newsom. *I got a new friend*
Elliott, David. *This Orq. (He #1!)*
  This Orq. (He cave boy.)
  This Orq. (He say "ugh!")
Elschner, Geraldine. *Fritz's fish*
Elsdale, Bob. *Mac side up*
Estes, Allison. *Izzy and Oscar*
Falwell, Cathryn. *P.J. and Puppy*
Farish, Terry. *The cat who liked potato soup*
Feiffer, Kate. *Which puppy?*
Ferry, Beth. *Land shark*
  Pirate's perfect pet
Flanagan, Alice K. *Buying a pet from Ms. Chavez*
Fleming, Denise. *Buster*
Foster, John. *Pet poems*
Fraser, Mary Ann. *I.Q. gets fit*
  I.Q. goes to school
  I.Q. goes to the library
  I.Q., it's time
  Pet shop follies
  Pet shop lullaby
Friedman, Laurie. *Ruby Valentine and the sweet
    surprise*
Gay, Marie-Louise. *What are you doing, Sam?*
Gibbs, Edward. *I spy pets*
Giff, Patricia Reilly. *Good luck, Ronald Morgan*
Goldfinger, Jennifer P. *A fish named Spot*
  My dog Lyle
Gorbachev, Valeri. *The best cat*
  Cats are cats
Gottfried, Maya. *Good dog*
Graham, Bob. *"Let's get a pup!" said Kate*
  "The trouble with dogs," said Dad
Grambling, Lois G. *Big Dog*

Granowsky, Alvin. *At the park*
Gravel, Elise. *I want a monster!*
Graves, Keith. *Pet boy*
Gravett, Emily. *Matilda's cat*
Greenaway, Theresa. *Centipedes and millipedes*
Gregory, Nan. *How Smudge came*
Griff. *Shark-mad Stanley*
Grimes, Nikki. *When Gorilla goes walking*
Hanson, Mary Elizabeth. *The old man and the flea*
Harper, Charise Mericle. *Henry's heart*
Harris, Robie H. *Goodbye, Mousie*
Harrison, Troon. *Aaron's awful allergies*
Harvey, Amanda. *Dog days*
  Dog-eared
  Dog gone
Harvey, Matthea. *Cecil the pet glacier*
Haughton, Chris. *Oh no, George!*
Hayles, Marsha. *A pet of a pet*
Hays, Anna Jane. *The pup speaks up*
Heder, Thyra. *Alfie: (the turtle that disappeared)*
Heide, Florence Parry. *A promise is a promise*
Heiligman, Deborah. *Fun dog, sun dog*
Helakoski, Leslie. *Doggone feet!*
Hest, Amy. *Charley's first night*
  My old pal, Oscar
  When Charley met Grampa
Hill, Frances. *The bug cemetery*
Hindley, Judy. *The best thing about a puppy*
Hobbie, Holly. *A cat named Swan*
Hogg, Gary. *Look what the cat dragged in!*
Howard, Arthur. *Hoodwinked*
Hughes, Ted. *My brother Bert*
Hull, Rod. *Mr. Betts and Mr. Potts*
Huneck, Stephen. *Sally goes to heaven*
Imai, Ayano. *Chester*
Inkpen, Deborah. *Harriet and the little fat fairy*
Inkpen, Mick. *The great pet sale*
  Kipper and Roly
Jackson, Ellen. *Abe Lincoln loved animals*
Jagtenberg, Yvonne. *Jack's rabbit*
Jarka, Jeff. *Love that kitty!*
  Love that puppy!
Javernick, Ellen. *The birthday pet*
Jeffers, Oliver. *This moose belongs to me*
Johnson, Angela. *The girl who wore snakes*
  Julius
Johnson, Paul Brett. *Lost*
Jonell, Lynne. *I need a snake*
Joosse, Barbara. *Bad dog school*
Jordan, Sandra. *Mr. and Mrs. Portly and their little
    dog Snack*
Joyce, William. *Dinosaur Bob*
Juan, Ana. *The pet shop revolution*
Katz, Bobbi. *Nothing but a dog*
Katz, Susan. *Oh, Theodore!*
Keane, Dave. *Who wants a tortoise?*
Keats, Ezra Jack. *Maggie and the pirate*
  Pet show!
Kellogg, Steven. *Can I keep him?*
  The mysterious tadpole
Kerby, Johanna. *Little pink pup*
Kimmel, Eric A. *I took my frog to the library*
Klise, Kate. *Stay: a girl, a dog, a bucket list*
Koehler, Lana Wayne. *Ah-choo!*
Kroll, Steven. *Patches lost and found*
Kroll, Virginia L. *Really rabbits*
Kulka, Joe. *My crocodile does not bite*
Kwon, Yoon-duck. *My cat copies me*

LaRue for mayor
Thomas, Jane Resh. *Scaredy dog*
Thoms, Susan Collins. *Cesar takes a break*
Torrey, Richard. *My dog, Bob*
Townsend, Michael. *Cute and cuter*
Trapani, Iza. *How much is that doggie in the window?*
  Row, row, row your boat
Trukhan, Ekaterina. *Patrick wants a dog!*
Turner, Pamela S. *Hachiko*
Uff, Caroline. *Hello, Lulu*
Umansky, Kaye. *I don't like Gloria!*
Urbanovic, Jackie. *Duck and cover*
  Duck at the door
Van Allsburg, Chris. *The misadventures of Sweetie Pie*
VanSickle, Vikki. *If I had a gryphon*
Vaughan, Marcia Kapok. *Whistling Dixie*
Verdick, Elizabeth. *Tails are not for pulling*
Vernick, Audrey. *I won a what?*
Viorst, Judith. *The tenth good thing about Barney*
Voake, Charlotte. *Melissa's octopus and other unsuitable pets*
Wahman, Wendy. *Don't lick the dog*
Ward, Lynd. *The biggest bear*
Waring, Richard. *Alberto the dancing alligator*
Weigelt, Udo. *Super Guinea Pig to the rescue*
Wells, Rosemary. *Lucy comes to stay*
Weninger, Brigitte. *Miko wants a dog*
Wheeler, Lisa. *The pet project*
Wilhelm, Hans. *I'll always love you*
Willems, Mo. *The pigeon wants a puppy!*
Williams, Sue. *Let's go visiting*
Wing, Natasha. *How to raise a dinosaur*
Winstead, Rosie. *Ruby and Bubbles*
Wolf, Jake. *Daddy, could I have an elephant?*
Yaccarino, Dan. *The birthday fish*
  New pet
  An octopus followed me home
  Oswald
Young, Amy. *A unicorn named Sparkle*
Zalben, Jane Breskin. *Baby shower*
Ziefert, Harriet. *Murphy meets the treadmill*
Zimmerman, Andrea Griffing. *My dog Toby*
Zolotow, Charlotte. *The old dog*
  The poodle who barked at the wind
Zommer, Yuval. *One hundred bones*

Physicians *see* Careers – doctors

Picture puzzles

Alarcón, Francisco X. *Iguanas in the snow and other winter poems / Iguanas en la nieve y otros poemas de invierno*
Animal I spy
Animal 123
Anno, Mitsumasa. *Anno's alphabet*
  Anno's counting book
  Anno's counting house
  Anno's Italy
  Anno's journey
Barber, Patti. *First number book*
Barrett, Judi. *An excessive alphabet*
Behrens, Janice. *Let's find rain forest animals*
Berner, Rotraut Susanne. *In the town all year 'round*
Brown, Margaret Wise. *The find it book*
Bùi, Tak. *Spot the difference*
Carter, David A. *Blue 2*
  One red dot

600 black spots
Whoo? Whoo?
Who's under that hat?
Yellow square
Cauley, Lorinda Bryan. *What do you know!*
Chedru, Delphine. *Spot it!*
  Spot it again!
Cleary, Brian P. *Peanut butter and jellyfishes*
Cole, Henry. *Spot, the cat*
Cressy, Judith. *Can you find it?*
  Can you find it, too?
Cronin, B. B. *The lost house*
  The lost picnic
Dahl, Michael. *Downhill fun*
  Eggs and legs
  Footprints in the snow
  From the garden
  Hands down
  One big building
Davis, Kate. *Barnyard babies*
Dudás, Gergely. *Bear's merry book of hidden things*
Ehlert, Lois. *In my world*
Ellwand, David. *Alfred's camera*
  Alfred's party
Fairgray, Richard. *Gorillas in our midst*
Falken, Linda. *Can you find it?*
Faulkner, Keith. *A trick or a treat?*
Fox, Mem. *Yoo-hoo, Ladybug!*
Gannij, Joan. *Elusive moose*
Garland, Michael. *Americana adventure*
  Christmas City
  The great Easter egg hunt
  Super snow day seek and find
Geisert, Arthur. *Mystery*
Gross, Benedikt. *ABC: the alphabet from the sky*
Gukova, Julia. *All mixed-up!*
Hale, Bruce. *Santa on the loose!*
Handford, Martin. *Find Waldo now*
  The great Waldo search
  Where's Waldo?
Herzog, Brad. *I spy with my little eye: baseball*
Hillenbrand, Will. *Mother Goose picture puzzles*
Jackson, Richard. *In plain sight*
Jay, Alison. *Christmastime*
  Red green blue
Jenkins, Steve. *I see a kookaburra*
Kamm, Katja. *Invisible*
Khing, T. T. *Where is the cake?*
  Where is the cake now?
Kidslabel. *Spot 7: school*
  Spot 7: Christmas
Krans, Kim. *ABC dream*
Light, Steve. *Have you seen my lunch box?*
Ljungkvist, Laura. *Follow the line*
  Follow the line through the house
  Follow the line to school
  Search and spot: animals!
  Search and spot go!
MacDonald, Suse. *Look whooo's counting*
McGrath, Barbara Barbieri. *Kellogg's froot loops color fun book*
McMillan, Bruce. *Mouse views*
Marino, Gianna. *One too many*
Marzollo, Jean. *I spy*
  I spy A to Z
  I spy Christmas
  I spy extreme challenger!
  I spy fantasy
  I spy gold challenger!

I spy little animals
I spy little book
I spy little bunnies
I spy little Christmas
I spy little letters
I spy little numbers
I spy little wheels
I spy, mystery
I spy school days
I spy spooky night
I spy super challenger!
I spy treasure hunt
I spy ultimate challenger!
I spy, year-round challenger!
Micklethwait, Lucy. *In the picture*
Moseley, Keith. *Where's the dinosaur?*
Munro, Roxie. *Amazement Park*
    Circus
    Ecomazes
    Market maze
    Mazescapes
    Mazeways
Nickle, John. *Alphabet explosion!*
Oliver, Narelle. *Twilight hunt*
Onishi, Satoru. *Who's hiding*
Pamintuan, Macky. *Twelve haunted rooms of*
    Halloween
Philpot, Lorna. *Find Anthony Ant*
Raczka, Bob. *Fall mixed up*
Ringgold, Faith. *Cassie's word quilt*
Roderick, Stacey. *Dinosaurs from head to tail*
Rotner, Shelley. *Parts*
Schrey, Sophie. *Where's the penguin?*
Schwartz, David M. *If you hopped like a frog*
Seeger, Laura Vaccaro. *The hidden alphabet*
Serafini, Frank. *Looking closely along the shore*
Staake, Bob. *Look! a book!*
    Look! another book!
Stevenson, Emma. *Hide-and-seek science*
Tallec, Olivier. *Who done it?*
    Who what where?
Teckentrup, Britta. *The odd one out*
    One is not a pair
    Where's the pair?
Tildes, Phyllis Limbacher. *Animals in camouflage*
Toft, Kim Michelle. *Neptune's nursery*
    One less fish
Trapani, Iza. *Rufus and friends*
Turner, Ann Warren. *Angel hide and seek*
Wegerif, Gay. *Up close*
Weitzman, Jacqueline Preiss. *You can't take a*
    balloon into the National Gallery
Whybrow, Ian. *Faraway farm*
Wick, Walter. *Can you see what I see? Christmas*
    Can you see what I see? cool collections
    Can you see what I see? dream machine
    Can you see what I see? once upon a time
    Can you see what I see? out of this world
    Can you see what I see? picture puzzles to search and
        solve
    Can you see what I see? Seymour and the juice box
        boat
    Can you see what I see? Seymour makes new friends
    Can you see what I see? the night before Christmas
    Can you see what I see? toyland express
    Can you see what I see? treasure ship
    Hey, Seymour!
Wiesmüller, Dieter. *In the blink of an eye*
Ziefert, Harriet. *Messy Bessie*

Pilgrims

Behrens, June. *The feast of Thanksgiving*
Bruchac, Joseph. *Squanto's journey*
Bunting, Eve. *How many days to America?*
Dalgliesh, Alice. *The Thanksgiving story*
George, Jean Craighead. *The first Thanksgiving*
Gibbons, Gail. *Thanksgiving Day*
Greene, Rhonda Gowler. *The very first Thanksgiving*
    Day
Greenwood, Mark. *The Mayflower*
Hennessy, B. G. *One little, two little, three little*
    pilgrims
Kroll, Steven. *One tough turkey*
Metaxas, Eric. *Squanto and the miracle of*
    Thanksgiving
Peacock, Carol Antoinette. *Pilgrim cat*
Van Leeuwen, Jean. *Across the wide dark sea*

Pioneer life *see* U.S. history – frontier & pioneer
    life

Pirates

Ahlberg, Janet. *It was a dark and stormy night*
Andreae, Giles. *Captain Flinn and the pirate*
    dinosaurs
    Captain Flinn and the pirate dinosaurs: missing
        treasure!
Arro, Lena. *By geezers and galoshes!*
Baker, Roberta. *Olive's pirate party*
Bardhan-Quallen, Sudipta. *Pirate princess*
Bently, Peter. *Captain Jack and the pirates*
Brown, Calef. *Pirateria*
Bunting, Eve. *Little Badger, terror of the seven seas*
    P is for pirate
    Pirate boy
Burningham, John. *Come away from the water,*
    Shirley
Chapman, Jared. *Pirate, Viking, and Scientist*
Clibbon, Meg. *Imagine you're a pirate!*
Coats, Lucy. *Captain Beastlie's pirate party*
Crimi, Carolyn. *Henry and the Buccaneer Bunnies*
    Henry and the Crazed Chicken Pirates
Crowe, Caroline. *Pirates in pajamas*
Day, Jan. *The pirate, Pink*
    Pirate Pink and treasures of the reef
Demas, Corinne. *Are pirates polite?*
    Pirates go to school
DiCamillo, Kate. *Louise*
Duddle, Jonny. *The pirate cruncher*
    The pirates next door
Estes, Allison. *Izzy and Oscar*
Ferry, Beth. *Pirate's perfect pet*
Florian, Douglas. *Shiver me timbers!*
Fox, Kathleen. *The pirates of plagiarism*
Fox, Mem. *Tough Boris*
Freedman, Claire. *Pirates love underpants*
Funk, Josh. *Pirasaurs!*
Funke, Cornelia. *Pirate girl*
Gaiman, Neil. *The dangerous alphabet*
Greene, Rhonda Gowler. *No pirates allowed! said*
    Library Lou
Griswell, Kim T. *Rufus goes to sea*
Grossmann-Hensel, Katharina. *Papa is a pirate*
Gunnufson, Charlotte. *Prince and Pirate*
Harley, Bill. *Dirty Joe, the pirate*
Harris, Peter. *The night pirates*
Helquist, Brett. *Roger, the jolly pirate*

Horowitz, Dave. *Twenty-six pirates*
Kay, Julia. *Gulliver Snip*
Keats, Ezra Jack. *Maggie and the pirate*
Kennedy, Kim. *Pirate Pete's giant adventure*
Kimmel, Eric A. *The Erie Canal pirates*
    Robin Hook, pirate hunter!
Kimmelman, Leslie. *Trick ARRR treat*
Kladstrup, Kristin. *The gingerbread pirates*
Kramer, Andrew. *Pajama pirates*
Krosoczka, Jarrett J. *Bubble bath pirates*
Krupinski, Loretta. *Pirate treasure*
Lamm, C. Drew. *Pirates*
Lasky, Kathryn. *Pirate Bob*
Leuck, Laura. *I love my pirate papa*
Lichtenheld, Tom. *Everything I know about pirates*
Light, Steve. *Swap!*
Little old lady who swallowed a fly. *There was an old*
    pirate who swallowed a fish
Long, Melinda. *How I became a pirate*
    Pirates don't change diapers
Lucas, David. *The skeleton pirate*
McCully, Emily Arnold. *The pirate queen*
McElligott, Matthew. *Backbeard and the birthday suit*
McFarland, Lyn Rossiter. *The pirate's parrot*
McNaughton, Colin. *Captain Abdul's little treasure*
    Captain Abdul's pirate school
McNeil, Florence. *Sail away*
McPhail, David. *Edward and the pirates*
Marzollo, Jean. *I spy treasure hunt*
Murray, Diana. *Ned the knitting pirate*
O'Malley, Kevin. *Captain Raptor and the space*
    pirates
Peck, Jan. *Pirate treasure hunt!*
Powell-Tuck, Maudie. *Pirates aren't afraid of the dark!*
Preller, James. *A pirate's guide to first grade*
    A pirate's guide to recess
Priest, Robert H. *The pirate's eye*
Prince, April Jones. *Goldenlocks and the three pirates*
Quattlebaum, Mary. *Pirate vs. pirate*
Regan, Dian Curtis. *Space Boy and the space pirate*
Reynolds, Aaron. *Pirates vs. cowboys*
Richardson, Bill. *Sally Dog Little*
Rosenthal, Marc. *Archie and the pirates*
Rubin, Susan Goldman. *Jean Laffite*
Sattler, Jennifer. *Pig kahuna pirates!*
Schotter, Roni. *Captain Bob sets sail*
Sís, Peter. *Robinson*
Siy, Alexandra. *One tractor*
Smith, Danna. *Pirate nap*
Sobel, June. *Shiver me letters*
Spires, Ashley. *Small Saul*
Sturges, Philemon. *This little pirate*
Teague, Mark. *The pirate jamboree*
Thomson, Sarah L. *Pirates, ho!*
Tucker, Kathy. *Do pirates take baths?*
Weinert, Matthias. *No bath, no cake!*
Winters, Kari-Lynn. *Bad pirate*
    Good pirate
Wolfe, Myra. *Charlotte Jane battles bedtime*

Planes *see* Airplanes, airports

Planets

Barner, Bob. *Stars, stars, stars*
Barrett, Judi. *Cloudy with a chance of meatballs 3*
Branley, Franklyn M. *The planets in our solar system*
Florian, Douglas. *Comets, stars, the moon, and Mars*

Gibbons, Gail. *The planets*
McNamara, Margaret. *The three little aliens and the*
    big bad robot
Metzger, Steve. *Pluto visits Earth!*
O'Brien, Patrick. *You are the first kid on Mars*
Pinkney, Brian. *Cosmo and the robot*
Rau, Dana Meachen. *Mars*
Sanders, Rob. *Outer space bedtime race*
Weitekamp, Margaret A. *Pluto's secret*
Wethered, Peggy. *Touchdown Mars!*
Yaccarino, Dan. *First day on a strange new planet*
    New pet
Yorinks, Arthur. *Company's going*

Plants

Agran, Rick. *Pumpkin shivaree*
Aliki. *Corn is maize*
    My visit to the aquarium
Arnold, Katya. *Let's find it!*
Azarian, Mary. *A gardener's alphabet*
Baker, Jeannie. *The hidden forest*
    The story of rosy dock
Bang, Molly. *Living sunlight*
    Ocean sunlight
Bardill, Linard. *The great golden thing*
Bash, Barbara. *Desert giant*
Berenstain, Stan and Jan. *The Berenstain bears and*
    the prize pumpkin
    The Berenstain bears' that stump must go!
Bernhard, Durga. *Earth, sky, wet, dry*
Braun, Eric. *Trust me, Jack's beanstalk stinks*
Brett, Jan. *The turnip*
Bruce, Lisa. *Fran's flower*
Butterworth, Nick. *Jasper's beanstalk*
Cannon, Janell. *Little Yau*
Carle, Eric. *The tiny seed*
Cash, Megan Montague. *What makes the seasons?*
Cave, Kathryn. *One child, one seed*
Chapman, Jared. *Vegetables in underwear*
Cotten, Cynthia. *At the edge of the woods*
Day, Trevor. *Youch! it bites!*
Duke, Kate. *In the rainforest*
    Ready for pumpkins
Ehlert, Lois. *Leaf man*
Five little pumpkins, ill. by Ben Mantle
    Five little pumpkins, ill. by Iris Van Rynbach
    Five little pumpkins, ill. by Dan Yaccarino
Fleischman, Paul. *Weslandia*
Fleming, Denise. *Where once there was a wood*
Ford, Miela. *Sunflower*
Gellman, Ellie B. *Netta and her plant*
Gerber, Carole. *Seeds, bees, butterflies, and more!*
Gibbons, Gail. *The berry book*
    From seed to plant
    Nature's green umbrella
    The vegetables we eat
Ginsburg, Mirra. *Mushroom in the rain*
Goodman, Emily. *Plant secrets*
Gourley, Robbin. *First garden*
Grey, Mini. *The very smart pea and the princess-to-be*
Grigsby, Susan. *In the garden with Dr. Carver*
Guiberson, Brenda Z. *Cactus hotel*
Hall, Zoe. *It's pumpkin time!*
Hammersmith, Craig. *Watch it grow*
Hayward, Linda. *What homework?*
Helmore, Jim. *Oh no, monster tomato!*
Henkes, Kevin. *So happy!*
Himmelman, John. *A dandelion's life*

Plays *see* Theater

Pockets *see* Clothing

Poetry

Bates, Katharine Lee. *America the beautiful*, ill. by Chris Gall
    America the beautiful, ill. by Wendell Minor
    America the beautiful: together we stand
Becker, Helaine. *Mama likes to mambo*
Belle, Jennifer. *Animal stackers*
The best part of me
Blanco, Richard. *One today*
Bless the beasts
Bolden, Tonya. *Rock of ages*
Boling, Katherine. *New year be coming!*
Booth, Philip E. *Crossing*
Borden, Louise. *America is . . .*
Bronson, Linda. *Sleigh bells and snowflakes*
Brooks, Gwendolyn. *Bronzeville boys and girls*
Brown, Margaret Wise. *The friendly book*
    Give yourself to the rain
    The Golden sleepy book
    Love songs of the little bear
    Nibble, nibble
Browning, Robert. *The pied piper of Hamelin*
Bruchac, Joseph. *The circle of thanks*
    Thirteen moons on turtle's back
Bruno, Elsa Knight. *Punctuation celebration*
Bryan, Ashley. *Sing to the sun*
Bryant, Jen. *A river of words*
Bunting, Eve. *Anna's table*
    Sing a song of piglets
    Who was born this special day?
Burleigh, Robert. *Goal*
Bush, Timothy. *Ferocious girls, steamroller boys, and other poems in between*
Calmenson, Stephanie. *Good for you!*
    Welcome, baby!
Cameron, Eileen. *Canyon*
Carabine, Sue. *A firefighter's night before Christmas*
Carlstrom, Nancy White. *Before you were born*
    Thanksgiving Day at our house
    What does the sky say?
    Who said boo?
Carroll, Lewis. *Jabberwocky*
Carryl, Charles E. *The camel's lament*
Caswell, Deanna. *Boo! haiku*
Cendrars, Blaise. *Shadow*
Chaikin, Miriam. *Don't step on the sky*
Chernaik, Judith. *Carnival of the animals: poems inspired by Saint-Saëns' music*
A child's calendar
Chorao, Kay. *The baby's bedtime book*
Christelow, Eileen. *Five little monkeys jumping on the bed*
Clavel, Bernard. *Castle of books*
Cleary, Brian P. *If it rains pancakes*
Clements, Andrew. *Dogku*
Cline-Ransome, Lesa. *Quilt alphabet*
Clinton, Catherine. *Phillis's big test*
Come and play
Coombs, Kate. *Water sings blue*
Cooper, Floyd. *Coming home: from the life of Langston Hughes*
Cotner, June. *Amazing graces*
Crawley, Dave. *Cat poems*
Creech, Sharon. *Who's that baby?*
Cuetara, Mittie. *Baby business*
Cutlip, Kimbra L. *Firefighter's night before Christmas*
Danneberg, Julie. *Cowboy Slim*
Dawes, Kwame Senu Neville. *I saw your face*
Delacre, Lulu. *Arroz con leche*
    Las Navidades

Derby, Sally. *A new school year*
Dotlich, Rebecca Kai. *A family like yours*
    In the spin of things
    What is science?
Downes, Belinda. *Baby days*
Eastwick, Ivy O. *Some folks like cats, and other poems*
Elliott, David. *In the sea*
    In the wild
    On the wing
Emberley, Barbara. *Drummer Hoff*
    Night's nice
    One wide river to cross
Engle, Margarita. *Orangutanka*
    The sky painter
Esbaum, Jill. *Stanza*
Evans, Dilys. *Fairies, trolls and goblins galore*
Farber, Norma. *How the hibernators came to Bethlehem*
Farrar, Sid. *The year comes round*
Field, Eugene. *Wynken, Blynken and Nod*
    Wynken, Blynken, and Nod: a Dutch lullaby
Field, Rachel Lyman. *Grace for an island meal*
Figley, Marty Rhodes. *Emily and Carlo*
Fischer, Scott M. *Twinkle*
Fisher, Aileen Lucia. *Do rabbits have Christmas?*
    The story goes on
Fitch, Sheree. *No two snowflakes*
Fletcher, Ralph. *Grandpa never lies*
Florian, Douglas. *Bow wow meow meow, it's rhyming cats and dogs*
    Comets, stars, the moon, and Mars
    Dinothesaurus
    Handsprings
    Insectlopedia
    Lizards, frogs, and polliwogs
    Poem runs
    Poetrees
    Shiver me timbers!
    Summersaults
    Unbeelievables
    The wonderful habits of rabbits
    Zoo's who
Fogliano, Julie. *When green becomes tomatoes*
Forman, Ruth. *Young Cornrows callin out the moon*
Foster, John. *Pet poems*
Fox, Paula. *Traces*
Frampton, David. *Mr. Ferlinghetti's poem*
    My beastie book of ABC
Franco, Betsy. *Bees, snails, and peacock tails*
    A curious collection of cats
    A dazzling display of dogs
    A spectacular selection of sea critters
Frank, John. *A chill in the air*
    How to catch a fish
Frasier, Debra. *On the day you were born*
Frost, Helen. *Among a thousand fireflies*
    Step gently out
    Sweep up the sun
    Wake up!
Frost, Robert. *Stopping by woods on a snowy evening*
George, Kristine O'Connell. *Emma dilemma*
    The great frog race and other poems
    Little Dog and Duncan
    Old Elm speaks
Gerber, Carole. *Seeds, bees, butterflies, and more!*
Gilchrist, Jan Spivey. *My America*
Gilman, Rita Golden. *Rice is life*
Giovanni, Nikki. *The sun is so quiet*
Glaser, Linda. *Emma's poem*

Godwin, Laura. *Barnyard prayers*
Gollub, Matthew. *Cool melons — turn to frogs*
Gottfried, Maya. *Good dog*
   Our farm
Grady, Cynthia. *I lay my stitches down*
Graham, Joan Bransfield. *Flicker flash*
   The poem that will not end
   Splish splash
Grahame, Kenneth. *The reluctant dragon*
Greenberg, David. *Don't forget your etiquette!*
Greenfield, Eloise. *Angels*
   Big friend, little friend
   Brothers and sisters
   Daydreamers
   The friendly four
   I can draw a weeposaur and other dinosaurs
   I make music
   In the land of words
   My doll, Keshia
   Nathaniel talking
   Night on Neighborhood Street
Grimes, Nikki. *Danitra Brown, class clown*
   A pocketful of poems
   Shoe magic
   Voices of Christmas
   When Daddy prays
   When Gorilla goes walking
Grossman, Bill. *Timothy Tunny swallowed a bunny*
Guthrie, James. *Last song*
Gutman, Dan. *Casey back at bat*
Hague, Michael. *Animal friends: a collection of poems for children*
Harness, Cheryl. *Papa's Christmas gift*
Harrison, David L. *The alligator in the closet and other poems around the house*
   Farmer's garden
Heard, Georgia. *This place I know*
Heidbreder, Robert. *Noisy poems for a busy day*
The Helen Oxenbury nursery collection
Hines, Anna Grossnickle. *Pieces, a year in poems and quilts*
Hittleman, Carol G. *A grand celebration*
Honey, Elizabeth. *The moon in the man*
Hooper, Patricia. *Where do you sleep, little one?*
Hopkins, Lee Bennett. *All God's children*
   Alphathoughts
   April, bubbles, chocolate
   Behind the museum door
   Christmas presents
   City I love
   Good books, good times
   Good rhymes, good times
   Hanukkah lights
   Incredible inventions
   Jumping off library shelves
   Manger
   Merrily comes our harvest in
   Nasty bugs
   Ragged shadows
   School supplies
   Yummy! eating through a day
Hort, Lenny. *Tie your socks and clap your feet*
Horton, Joan. *Hippopotamus stew*
Howitt, Mary Botham. *Mary Howitt's The spider and the fly*
Hubbell, Patricia. *Black earth, gold sun*
   Boo! Halloween poems and limericks
   Bouncing time
   City kids

   Earthmates
Hudson, Cheryl Willis. *Bright eyes, brown skin*
Hudson, Wade. *Pass it on: African-American poetry for children*
Hughes, Langston. *Carol of the brown king*
   I, too, am America
   Lullaby (for a Black mother)
   My people
   The Negro speaks of rivers
   Sail away
   The sweet and sour animal book
   That is my dream!
Hughes, Shirley. *Olly and me*
Hundal, Nancy. *Camping*
I invited a dragon to dinner
In daddy's arms I am tall
Issa, Kobayashi. *Today and today*
Iyengar, Malathi Michelle. *Tan to tamarind*
Janeczko, Paul B. *Firefly July*
Jensen, Dana. *A meal of the stars*
Johnson, Angela. *Daddy calls me man*
Johnson, James Weldon. *The Creation*
Johnston, Tony. *The barn owls*
   My Mexico / México mío
   Sequoia
Joseph, Lynn. *Coconut kind of day*
Katz, Bobbi. *Once around the sun*
Katz, Susan. *Mrs. Brown on exhibit*
   Oh, Theodore!
Kay, Verla. *Broken Feather*
Kennedy, Jimmy. *The teddy bears' picnic*, ill. by Michael Hague
   The teddy bears' picnic, ill. by Prue Theobalds
Knight, Hilary. *Hilary Knight's the owl and the pussy-cat*
Krauss, Ruth. *Bears*
Kumin, Maxine. *Mites to astodons*
Kuskin, Karla. *Toots the cat*
Larios, Julie. *Imaginary menagerie*
   Yellow elephant
Latham, Irene. *Dear Wandering Wildebeest*
Lear, Edward. *The owl and the pussycat*, ill. by Jan Brett
   The owl and the pussycat, ill. by Paul Galdone
   The owl and the pussycat, ill. by Anne Mortimer
   The Quangle Wangle's hat
LeBox, Annette. *Salmon Creek*
Lee, Dennis. *Bubblegum delicious*
Lenski, Lois. *I like winter*
   Now it's fall
Lesser, Carolyn. *What a wonderful day to be a cow*
Let there be light: poems and prayers for repairing the world
Let's count the raindrops
Levine, Gail Carson. *Forgive me, I meant to do it*
Lewis, J. Patrick. *The bookworm's feast*
   Doodle dandies
   Face bug
   Good mousekeeping
   A hippopotamusn't
   The little buggers
   Long was the winter road they traveled
   Riddle-icious
   World Rat Day
Lillegard, Dee. *Go! poetry in motion: poems*
   Hello school!
   Wake up house!
Lin, Grace. *Our food*
   Robert's snowflakes

Livingston, Myra Cohn. *Abraham Lincoln: a man for all the people*
  Calendar
  Celebrations
  Keep on singing
Locker, Thomas. *Mountain dance*
  Water dance
London, Jonathan. *Sun dance, water dance*
Longfellow, Henry Wadsworth. *Hiawatha*
  Paul Revere's ride
  Paul Revere's ride: the landlord's tale
Luján, Jorge. *Beyond my hand*
  Colors! / ¡Colores!
  Moví la mano / I moved my hand
  Lullaby moons and a silver spoon
Lyon, George Ella. *Book*
  Counting on the woods
MacDonald, Suse. *Edward Lear's A was once an apple pie*
McGhee, Alison. *Only a witch can fly*
McGough, Roger. *What on earth can it be?*
MacLachlan, Patricia. *Cat talk*
  Snowflakes fall
McNamara, Margaret. *A poem in your pocket*
Maguire, John. *People*
Mak, Kam. *My Chinatown*
Mannis, Celeste Davidson. *One leaf rides the wind*
  Maples in the mist
Marshall, James. *Pocketful of nonsense*
Marzollo, Jean. *I love you*
Mathers, Petra. *A cake for Herbie*
Mayo, Margaret. *Wiggle waggle fun*
Medina, Tony. *DeShawn days*
Melmed, Laura Krauss. *The first song ever sung*
  This first Thanksgiving
Merriam, Eve. *Bam, bam, bam*
  Blackberry ink
  Halloween ABC
Micklos, John. *Daddy poems*
  Mommy poems
Montenegro, Laura Nyman. *A bird about to sing*
Moore, Clement Clarke. *A creature was stirring*
  The night before Christmas, ill. by Jan Brett
  The night before Christmas, ill. by Tomie dePaola
  The night before Christmas, ill. by Mary Engelbreit
  The night before Christmas, ill. by David Ercolini
  The night before Christmas, ill. by Holly Hobbie
  The night before Christmas, ill. by Rachel Isadora
  The night before Christmas, ill. by Raquel Jaramillo
  The night before Christmas, ill. by Anita Lobel
  The night before Christmas, ill. by James Marshall
  The night before Christmas, ill. by Will Moses
  The night before Christmas, ill. by Ted Rand
  The night before Christmas, ill. by Barbara Reid
  The night before Christmas, ill. by Ruth Sanderson
  The night before Christmas, ill. by Gennady Spirin
  The night before Christmas, ill. by Tasha Tudor
  The night before Christmas, ill. by Richard Jesse Watson
  The night before Christmas, ill. by Wendy Watson
  The night before Christmas, ill. by Bruce Whatley
  The night before Christmas, ill. by Lisbeth Zwerger
  The night before Christmas
  The night before Christmas: a pop-up
  The teddy bears' night before Christmas
  'Twas the night before Christmas, ill. by Daniel Kirk
  'Twas the night before Christmas, ill. by Matt Tavares
  'Twas the night before Christmas, ill. by Christopher Wormell
Moore, Lilian. *Beware, take care*
Mora, Pat. *Confetti*
  Delicious hullabaloo / Pachanga deliciosa
  The desert is my mother / El desierto es mi madre
  Listen to the desert / Oye al desierto
  Love to mamá
  This big sky
  Water rolls, water rises / el agua ruda, el agua sube
  Yum! mmmm! que rico!
Mortensen, Lori. *Chicken Lily*
Moser, Lisa. *Stories from Bug Garden*
Moss, Jenny Jackson. *Cajun night after Christmas*
Mother Goose. *Arnold Lobel book of Mother Goose*
Mozelle, Shirley. *The kitchen talks*
Murphy, Elspeth Campbell. *Happy Easter, God*
Murphy, Sally. *Pearl verses the world*
Muth, Jon J. *Hi, Koo!*
Myers, Tim. *Basho and the fox*
Myers, Walter Dean. *Brown angels*
  Harlem
Nash, Ogden. *The adventures of Isabel*, ill. by James Marshall
  The adventures of Isabel, ill. by Bridget Starr Taylor
  Custard the dragon and the wicked knight
Nicholls, Judith. *Someone I like*
Nidey, Kelli. *When autumn falls*
Nikola-Lisa, W. *Bein' with you this way*
Noda, Takayo. *Dear world*
Northey, Lawrence. *I'm a hop hop hoppity frog*
Numeroff, Laura Joffe. *Sometimes I wonder if poodles like noodles*
Nye, Naomi Shihab. *Come with me*
O'Connor, Jane. *Fancy Nancy: poet extraordinaire!*
O'Keefe, Susan Heyboer. *One hungry monster*
Olaleye, Isaac. *The distant talking drum*
Oliver, Lin. *Little poems for tiny ears*
Oppenheim, Joanne. *Have you seen trees?*
Otten, Charlotte F. *January rides the wind*
Otto, Carolyn. *Dinosaur chase*
Paolilli, Paul. *Silver seeds*
Pearson, Debora. *Leo's tree*
Pearson, Susan. *The drowsy hours*
  Slugs in love
Perdorno, Willie. *Visiting Langston*
Perkins, Useni Eugene. *Hey Black Child*
Perry, Andrea. *Here's what you do when you can't find your shoe*
Peters, Lisa Westberg. *Volcano wakes up!*
Philip, Neil. *The fish is me*
  Hot potato
Pickering, Jimmy. *It's fall*
  It's winter
Plourde, Lynn. *Pigs in the mud in the middle of the rud*
  A pocketful of stars
Pollock, Penny. *When the moon is full*
Pomerantz, Charlotte. *All asleep*
Powell, Consie. *Amazing apples*
Prelutsky, Jack. *Awful Ogre running wild*
  Awful Ogre's awful day
  The baby uggs are hatching
  Behold the bold umbrellaphant and other poems
  Beneath a blue umbrella
  Circus
  For laughing out louder
  The frogs wore red suspenders

Wharnsby-Ali, Dawud. *A picnic of poems in Allah's green garden*
Wheeler, Lisa. *Wool gathering*
Whitehead, Jenny. *Lunch box mail and other poems*
Whiteley, Opal Stanley. *Only Opal*
Wick, Walter. *Can you see what I see? the night before Christmas*
Wilbur, Richard. *The disappearing alphabet*
Willard, Nancy. *The Moon and Riddles Diner and the Sunnyside Café*
   Pish posh, said Hieronymous Bosch
   A visit to William Blake's inn
Wilson, Anna. *Over in the grasslands*
Winnick, Karen B. *A year goes round*
Wise, William. *Dinosaurs forever*
Wong, Janet S. *Homegrown house*
Worth, Valerie. *Pug and other animal poems*
Xinran, Xue. *Motherbridge of love*
Yolen, Jane. *An egret's day*
   A mirror to nature
   The three bears holiday rhyme book
   Thunder underground
   Welcome to the sea of sand
Zahares, Wade. *Big, bad, and a little bit scary*
Ziefert, Harriet. *A bunny is funny*
   Hanukkah haiku
Zolotow, Charlotte. *Some things go together*

Pollution *see* Ecology

Poltergeists *see* Ghosts

Ponds *see* Lakes, ponds

Ponies *see* Animals – horses, ponies

Poor *see* Homeless; Poverty

Pop-up books *see* Format, unusual – toy & movable books

Porpoises *see* Animals – dolphins

Post office

Ahlberg, Janet. *The jolly Christmas postman*
   The jolly pocket postman
   The jolly postman
Bergel, Colin. *Mail by the pail*
Carter, Don. *Send it!*
Gibbons, Gail. *The post office book*
Gliori, Debi. *Penguin post*
Horning, Sandra. *The giant hug*
Lendroth, Susan. *Calico Dorsey*
Rylant, Cynthia. *Mr. Griggs' work*
Schneider, Howie. *Fast 'n Snappy*
Scott, Ann Herbert. *Hi!*
Shea, Kitty. *Out and about at the post office*

Potty training *see* Toilet training

Pourquoi tales *see* Folk & fairy tales – pourquoi tales

Poverty

Andersen, Hans Christian. *The little match girl*, ill. by Rachel Isadora
   The little match girl, ill. by Blair Lent
   The little match girl, ill. by Jerry Pinkney
   The little matchstick girl
Bartoletti, Susan Campbell. *The Christmas promise*
Boelts, Maribeth. *Happy like soccer*
Brandt, Lois. *Maddi's fridge*
Buitrago, Jairo. *Jimmy the greatest*
Burnett, Frances Hodgson. *A little princess*
Cutler, Jane. *Guttersnipe*
Fullerton, Alma. *A good trade*
Grimm, Jacob and Wilhelm. *Doctor All-Knowing*
Javaherbin, Mina. *Soccer star*
Lipp, Frederick. *Running shoes*
Littlesugar, Amy. *Tree of hope*
Mahy, Margaret. *Down the back of the chair*
Mills, Lauren A. *The rag coat*
Milway, Katie Smith. *One hen*
Park, Frances. *The royal bee*
Poulin, Andrée. *Pablo finds a treasure*
Quattlebaum, Mary. *The shine man*
Sawyer, Ruth. *Journey cake, ho!*
Shulevitz, Uri. *How I learned geography*
Slade, Suzanne. *Dangerous Jane*
Stein, Joel Edward. *A Hanukkah with Mazel*
Stone, Tanya Lee. *The house that Jane built*
Thomas, Jane Resh. *Lights on the river*
Toscano, Charles. *Papa's pastries*
Vainio, Pirkko. *The Christmas angel*
Wilde, Oscar. *The happy prince*
Williams, Karen Lynn. *Beatrice's dream*
Woodson, Jacqueline. *Each kindness*
Ziefert, Harriet. *When I first came to this land*

Pow-wows

Bouchard, Dave. *The song within my heart*

Power failures

Rodriguez, Bobbie. *Sarah's sleepover*

Practicality *see* Character traits – practicality

Prairie wolves *see* Animals – coyotes

Prayers *see* Religion

Preachers *see* Careers – clergy

Pregnancy *see* Birth

Prehistoric man *see* Cave dwellers

Prehistory

Aliki. *Digging up dinosaurs*

Prejudice

Miller, Pat Zietlow. *The quickest kid in Clarksville*
Miller, William. *The bus ride*
Mitchell, Margaree King. *Susie Mae*
    When Grandmama sings
Morris, Ann. *Grandma Lois remembers*
Myers, Walter Dean. *Muhammad Ali: the people's champion*
Naden, Corinne J. *Ron's big mission*
Nelson, Kadir. *Nelson Mandela*
Pfister, Marcus. *Milo and the mysterious island*
Pinkney, Andrea Davis. *Boycott blues*
    Sit-in
Polacco, Patricia. *Mr. Lincoln's way*
Rahaman, Vashanti. *Divali rose*
Ramsey, Calvin Alexander. *Ruth and the Green Book*
Rappaport, Doreen. *Martin's big words*
    The school is not white!
Reynolds, Aaron. *Back of the bus*
Ringgold, Faith. *If a bus could talk*
Robertson, David A. *When we were alone*
Rosen, Michael. *This is our house*
Ruzzier, Sergio. *Bear and Bee*
Ryan, Pam Muñoz. *When Marian sang*
Sauer, Tammi. *Nugget and Fang*
Say, Allen. *The favorite daughter*
Schroeder, Alan. *Minty*
Shange, Ntozake. *Coretta Scott*
    Whitewash
Shelton, Paula Young. *Child of the civil rights movement*
Shore, Diane Z. *This is the dream*
Sidjanski, Brigitte. *Little Chicken and Little Duck*
Skead, Robert. *Something to prove*
Slade, Suzanne. *Climbing Lincoln's steps*
    With books and bricks
Smalls, Irene. *Don't say ain't*
Tarpley, Natasha Anastasia. *Joe-Joe's first flight*
Tavares, Matt. *Henry Aaron's dream*
Thompson, Laurie Ann. *Emmanuel's dream*
Tonatiuh, Duncan. *Separate is never equal*
Tutu, Archbishop Desmond. *Desmond and the very mean word*
Ungerer, Tomi. *Flix*
Van Allsburg, Chris. *The widow's broom*
Van Dusen, Chris. *Hattie and Hudson*
Vernick, Audrey. *She loved baseball*
Watkins, Angela Farris. *Love will see you through*
    My Uncle Martin's words for America
Weatherford, Carole Boston. *The Beatitudes*
    Champions on the bench
    Freedom on the menu
    Gordon Parks
    Voice of freedom
Wells, Rosemary. *Yoko*
Wiles, Debbie. *Freedom summer*
Winter, Jonah. *Lillian's right to vote*
Wittenstein, Barry. *Waiting for Pumpsie*
Woodson, Jacqueline. *The other side*
Yin. *Coolies*

Preschool *see* School – nursery

Pretending *see* Imagination

Pride *see* Character traits – pride

Priests *see* Careers – clergy

Problem solving

Aesop. *The crow and the pitcher*
Alexander, Martha G. *I'll protect you from the jungle beasts*
    We're in big trouble, Blackboard Bear
Amann, Jürg. *Ten birds*
Andros, Camille. *Charlotte the scientist is squished*
Armstrong-Ellis, Carey. *Prudy's problem and how she solved it*
Arnosky, Jim. *Mud time and more*
Asch, Frank. *Mr. Maxwell's mouse*
Berry, Lynne. *What floats in a moat?*
Brett, Jan. *The turnip*
Brown, Jeff. *Flat Stanley*, ill. by Scott Nash
    Flat Stanley, ill. by Tomi Ungerer
Butterworth, Nick. *Jingle bells*
Cabrera, Jane. *There was an old woman who lived in a shoe*
Carlson, Nancy. *Harriet and the garden*
Caston, Jane. *Will you help Doug find his dog?*
Chase, Kit. *Oliver's tree*
Chivers, Natalie. *Rhino's great big itch!*
Climo, Liz. *Rory the dinosaur needs a Christmas tree*
Cole, Babette. *Princess Smartypants*
Cousteau, Philippe. *Follow the moon home*
Deedman, Heidi. *Too many toys!*
dePaola, Tomie. *Charlie needs a cloak*
Dierssen, Andreas. *The old red tractor*
Driscoll, Amanda. *Duncan the story dragon*
Einhorn, Edward. *A very improbable story*
Flory, Neil. *The short giraffe*
Gardella, Tricia. *Blackberry booties*
George, Lindsay Barrett. *In the garden: who's been here?*
    In the woods
Gianferrari, Maria. *Penny and Jelly: slumber under the stars*
Gordon, Gus. *Somewhere else*
Grambling, Lois G. *Can I bring Woolly to the library, Ms. Reeder?*
Grindley, Sally. *Who is it?*
Harvey, Damian. *Just the thing!*
Hester, Denia Lewis. *Grandma Lena's big ol' turnip*
Hood, Susan. *The fix-it man*
Johnson, Paul Brett. *Mr. Persnickety and Cat Lady*
Jonas, Ann. *Holes and peeks*
Joyce, William. *Big time Olie*
Keats, Ezra Jack. *Goggles*
    Whistle for Willie
Kishira, Mayuko. *Who's next door?*
Knudsen, Michelle. *Bugged!*
Krosoczka, Jarrett J. *It's tough to lose your balloon*
Maccarone, Grace. *Miss Lina's ballerinas*
McCloskey, Robert. *Lentil*
McCully, Emily Arnold. *Marvelous Mattie*
McKee, David. *Elmer and the hippos*
Mamada, Mineko. *Which is round? which is bigger?*
Marino, Gianna. *Too tall houses*
Masini, Beatrice. *A brave little princess*
Mayer, Mercer. *Just big enough*
    What do you do with a kangaroo?
Murguia, Bethanie Deeney. *Snippet the early riser*
Murphy, Stuart J. *The best vacation ever*
    Treasure map
Nakagawa, Rieko. *Guri and Gura*
Olaleye, Isaac. *Bitter bananas*

Progress

Promptness *see* Behavior – promptness, tardiness

Pumas *see* Animals – cougars

Punctuality *see* Behavior – promptness, tardiness

Puppets

Purses *see* Clothing – handbags, purses

Puzzles *see also* Picture puzzles; Rebuses; Riddles & jokes

Questioning *see* Character traits – questioning

Quicksand *see* Sand

Quilts

Ransom, Candice F. *The promise quilt*
Ringgold, Faith. *Cassie's word quilt*
  Tar Beach
Root, Phyllis. *The name quilt*
Stroud, Bettye. *The patchwork path*
Torres, Leyla. *Liliana's grandmothers*
Van Leeuwen, Jean. *Papa and the pioneer quilt*
von Olfers, Sibylle. *Mother Earth and her children*
Wallace, Nancy Elizabeth. *The kindness quilt*
Warner, Sunny. *The moon quilt*
Woodson, Jacqueline. *Show way*
Yorinks, Arthur. *Quack!*
Zagwÿn, Deborah Turney. *The pumpkin blanket*

Rabbis *see* Careers – clergy

Race relations *see* Prejudice

Racially mixed *see* Ethnic groups in the U.S.

Radios

Barasch, Lynne. *Radio rescue*
Dorros, Arthur. *Radio Man / Don Radio*
Schneider, Christine M. *Saxophone Sam and his snazzy jazz band*

Railroads *see* Trains

Rain *see* Weather – rain

Rain forest *see* Jungle

Rangers *see* Careers – park rangers

Reading *see* Books, reading

Rebuses

Capucilli, Alyssa Satin. *Inside a zoo in the city*
Edwards, Pamela Duncan. *Jack and Jill's treehouse*
Gilman, Rita Golden. *Mole in a hole*
The house that Jack built. *The house that Jack built*
Lewis, J. Patrick. *The fantastic 5 and 10¢ store*
Marzollo, Jean. *I love you*
  I see a star
Mitter, Matt. *Once upon a rhyme*
Neitzel, Shirley. *The bag I'm taking to Grandma's*
  The dress I'll wear to the party
  The house I'll build for the wrens
  I'm not feeling well today
  I'm taking a trip on my train

We're making breakfast for mother
Who will I be?
Rau, Dana Meachen. *Flying*
  Riding
  Rolling
Sierra, Judy. *We love our school!*

Recycling *see* Behavior – resourcefulness;
  Ecology

Refugees *see also* Immigrants, immigration

Barroux. *Welcome*
Buitrago, Jairo. *Two white rabbits*
Del Rizzo, Suzanne. *My beautiful birds*
Farish, Terry. *Joseph's big ride*
Hyde, Heidi Smith. *Shanghai Sukkah*
McCarney, Rosemary. *Where will I live?*
Sanna, Francesca. *The journey*
Wild, Margaret. *The treasure box*
Williams, Karen Lynn. *Four feet, two sandals*
  My name is Sangoel

Religion

Addasi, Maha. *Time to pray*
Adler, David A. *A picture book of Hanukkah*
  A picture book of Israel
  The story of Hanukkah
Aesop. *Androcles and the lion*
Ajmera, Maya. *Faith*
Aleichem, Sholem. *Hanukah money*
Alexander, Cecil Frances. *All creatures great and small*
  All things bright and beautiful, ill. by Ashley Bryan
  All things bright and beautiful, ill. by Anna Vojtech
  All things bright and beautiful, ill. by Bruce Whatley
Aliki. *Mummies made in Egypt*
Ammon, Richard. *An Amish Christmas*
Appelt, Kathi. *My father's house*
Baring-Gould, S. *Now the day is over*
Bartoletti, Susan Campbell. *Naamah and the ark at night*
Barton, Bob. *Paul Gallico's The small miracle*
Baylor, Byrd. *The way to start a day*
Bea, Holly. *Bless your heart*
  My spiritual alphabet book
Bedard, Michael. *The wolf of Gubbio*
Bergren, Lisa Tawn. *God gave us Easter*
  How big is God?
Bernier-Grand, Carmen T. *Our Lady of Guadalupe*
Bible. New Testament. *The Lord's prayer*
Bible. New Testament. Corinthians 1st, XIII. *Love is*
Bible. New Testament. Gospels. *Easter: from the King James Bible*
Bible. Old Testament. Ecclesiastes. *To every thing there is a season*
  To everything there is a season
Bible. Old Testament. Genesis. *Genesis*
  The Genesis of it all
  Let there be light
Bible. Old Testament. Psalms. *I will rejoice*
  The Lord is my shepherd
  Psalms for young children
  The twenty-third Psalm

Bible. Old Testament. Ruth. *Ruth and Naomi*
Bless the beasts
Bolden, Tonya. *Beautiful moon*
  Rock of ages
Boling, Ruth L. *Come worship with me*
Borchard, Therese Johnson. *Taste and see the goodness of the Lord*
Boroson, Martin. *Becoming me*
Brokering, Herbert F. *Earth and all stars*
Brooks, Jeremy. *Let there be peace*
Bryan, Ashley. *All night, all day*
Buck, Nola. *A Christmas goodnight*
Bullard, Lisa. *Rashad's Ramadan and Eid al-Fitr*
Carlson, Lori Marie. *Hurray for Three Kings' Day*
Carlson, Melody. *The Easterville miracle*
Carlstrom, Nancy White. *Does God know how to tie shoes?*
  What does the sky say?
A children's treasury of prayers
Cohen, Deborah Bodin. *Papa Jethro*
  The seventh day
Cotner, June. *Amazing graces*
Davis, Aubrey. *Bagels from Benny*
Demi. *Joan of Arc*
dePaola, Tomie. *The clown of God*
  The Lady of Guadalupe
  The legend of Old Befana
  Let the whole earth sing praise
  Look and be grateful
  The night of Las Posadas
  Patrick
  The song of Francis
Downey, Lynn. *This is the earth that God made*
Dungy, Tony. *You can do it!*
Egielski, Richard. *St. Francis and the wolf*
Emerman, Ellen. *Is it Shabbos yet?*
Farber, Norma. *How the hibernators came to Bethlehem*
Field, Rachel Lyman. *Grace for an island meal*
  Prayer for a child
Filleul, Liz. *Tumbler*
Fisher, Leonard Everett. *The seven days of creation*
Fishman, Cathy Goldberg. *On Hanukkah*
  On Passover
  On Rosh Hashanah and Yom Kippur
  On Shabbat
Fitch, Florence Mary. *A book about God*
Foreman, Michael. *Cat in the manger*
Gadot, A. S. *The first gift*
  Tower of Babel
Ghazi, Suhaib Hamid. *Ramadan*
Gibfried, Diane. *Brother Juniper*
Gilani-Williams, Fawzia. *Nabeel's new pants*
Godwin, Laura. *Barnyard prayers*
Gold, August. *Does God hear my prayer?*
Gold-Vukson, Marji E. *The colors of my Jewish Year*
  Grandpa and me on Tu B'Shevat
Goldin, Barbara Diamond. *A mountain of blintzes*
Goodings, Christina. *Creation story*
  Lost sheep story
Grimes, Nikki. *At break of day*
  When Daddy prays
Grün, Anselm. *Jesus*
  The legend of Saint Nicholas
Hennessy, B. G. *The first night*
Hest, Amy. *The Friday nights of Nana*
Hirsh, Marilyn. *Potato pancakes all around*
Hoffman, Mary. *Miracles*
  Parables, stories Jesus told

Hole, Stian. *Anna's heaven*
Hopkins, Lee Bennett. *All God's children*
  Hanukkah lights
How much does God love me?
Howard, Ellen. *The log cabin church*
Hughes, Shirley. *The Christmas Eve ghost*
I've seen the promised land
Jaffe, Nina. *Tales for the seventh day*
Jalali, Reza. *Moon watchers*
Jeffs, Stephanie. *Jenny*
  Josh
Johnson, Grace. *The candle in the window*
Johnson, James Weldon. *The Creation*
Jordan, Deloris. *Baby blessings*
Jules, Jacqueline. *Abraham's search for God*
  Benjamin and the silver goblet
Kassirer, Sue. *Joseph and his coat of many colors*
Katz, Karen. *My first Ramadan*
Kimmel, Eric A. *The Chanukkah guest*
  Gershon's monster
  Hershel and the Hanukkah goblins
  Joseph and the Sabbath fish
  The lady in the blue cloak
Kimmelman, Leslie. *Dance, sing, remember*
  Hanukkah lights, Hanukkah nights
  Hooray! it's Passover!
  The runaway latkes
  The Shabbat puppy
  Sound the shofar!
Kittinger, Jo S. *The house on Dirty-Third Street*
Krishnaswami, Uma. *Holi*
Kropf, Latifa Berry. *It's Hanukkah time!*
  It's seder time!
  It's Shofar time!
Krulik, Nancy E. *Is it Hanukkah yet?*
Kunkel, Jeff. *Noah, build your boat*
Kushner, Lawrence. *Because Nothing Looks Like God*
Kuskin, Karla. *A great miracle happened there*
Lach, William. *I imagine angels*
Langstaff, John M. *What a morning!*
Langton, Jane. *Saint Francis and the wolf*
Lehman-Wilzig, Tami. *Keeping the promise*
LeSourd, Nancy. *Christy, Christmastime at Cutter Gap*
Lester, Julius. *What a truly cool world*
  Why heaven is far away
Let it shine
Let there be light: poems and prayers for repairing the world
Lewis, Jacqueline Janette. *You are so wonderful*
Libney, Varda. *What I like about Passover*
Lindbergh, Reeve. *The circle of days*
  On morning wings
Lumbard, Alexis York. *Everyone prays*
Lundy, Charlotte. *Thank you, Esther*
  Thank you, Ruth and Naomi
Maccarone, Grace. *A child's good night prayer*
McGee, Marni. *The colt and the king*
McGowan, Michael. *Sunday is for God*
Mackall, Dandi Daley. *The story of the Easter robin*
Madonna. *Yakov and the seven thieves*
Manushkin, Fran. *Hooray for Hanukkah!*
  Latkes and applesauce
  Miriam's cup
Martin, Bill, Jr.. *Adam, Adam, what do you see?*
Marzollo, Jean. *Miriam and her brother Moses*
Mayer, Marianna. *Perseus*
Medina, Tony. *Christmas makes me think*
Moorman, Margaret. *Light the lights!*

Religion – Daniel

Religion – David

Auld, Mary. *David and Goliath*
Fisher, Leonard Everett. *David and Goliath*
Goldsboro, Bobby. *Noah and the ark; and, David and Goliath*

Religion – Hinduism

Gardeski, Christina Mia. *Diwali*
Pandya, Meenal. *Here comes Diwali*
Rahaman, Vashanti. *Divali rose*
Sebra, Richard. *It's Diwali!*
Verma, Jatinder Nath. *The story of Divaali*

Religion – Islam

Addasi, Maha. *The white nights of Ramadan*
Cunnane, Kelly. *Deep in the Sahara*
Faruqi, Reem. *Lailah's lunchbox*
Ghazi, Suhaib Hamid. *Ramadan*
Gonzales, Mark. *Yo soy Muslim*
Katz, Karen. *My first Ramadan*
Khan, Hena. *The night of the moon*
Mair, Samia J. *The perfect gift*
Mobin-Uddin, Asma. *The best Eid ever*
  A party in Ramadan
Robert, Na'ima B. *Ramadan Moon*
Wharnsby-Ali, Dawud. *A picnic of poems in Allah's green garden*
Whitman, Sylvia. *Under the Ramadan moon*

Religion – Jonah

Auld, Mary. *The story of Jonah*
Bible. Old Testament. Jonah. *The Book of Jonah*
Goldsboro, Bobby. *Jonah and the whale; and, Daniel in the lion's den*
Spinelli, Eileen. *Jonah's whale*

Religion – Moses

Auld, Mary. *Exodus from Egypt*
Hodges, Margaret. *Moses*
Marzollo, Jean. *Miriam and her brother Moses*
Topek, Susan Remick. *Ten good rules*

Religion – Nativity

Bible. New Testament. Gospels. *Bethlehem*
  The Christmas story: from the Gospel according to St. Luke from the King James Bible
  The story of Christmas
Blaich, Ute. *The star*
Brebeuf, Jean de. *The Huron carol*
Brown, Margaret Wise. *A child is born*
  Christmas in the barn
Bryan, Ashley. *Who built the stable?*
Bunting, Eve. *We were there*
  Who was born this special day?
Byrd, Robert. *Saint Francis and the Christmas donkey*
Calhoun, Mary. *A shepherd's gift*
Chaconas, Dori. *Christmas mouseling*
Chorao, Kay. *The Christmas story*
Clements, Andrew. *Bright Christmas*
Cooney, Barbara. *The story of Christmas*
Cotten, Cynthia. *This is the stable*
Crawford, Sheryl Ann. *The baby who changed the world*
Crisp, Marty. *The most precious gift*

Crossley-Holland, Kevin. *How many miles to Bethlehem?*
Damjan, Mischa. *The little seahorse and the Christmas pearl*
dePaola, Tomie. *The birds of Bethlehem*
  The story of the three wise kings
Dowley, Tim. *The shepherds' tale*
  The wise men's tale
Engelbreit, Mary. *A night of great joy*
Gliori, Debi. *What can I give him?*
Greene, Rhonda Gowler. *The stable where Jesus was born*
Grimes, Nikki. *Voices of Christmas*
Hartman, Bob. *Granny Mae's Christmas play*
Hayles, Marsha. *The feathered crown*
Hickman, Martha Whitmore. *A baby born in Bethlehem*
Hoffman, Mary. *Three wise women*
Hogrogian, Nonny. *The first Christmas*
Hooks, William H. *The legend of the Christmas rose*
Hopkins, Lee Bennett. *Manger*
Horn, Sandra Ann. *Babushka*
Hughes, Langston. *Carol of the brown king*
Joslin, Mary. *On that Christmas night*
Keats, Ezra Jack. *The little drummer boy*
Ketcham, Sallie. *The Christmas bird*
Lewandowski, Frrich. *It's Christmas again*
Lewis, J. Patrick. *Long was the winter road they traveled*
Lloyd-Jones, Sally. *Song of the stars*
Lucado, Max. *Jacob's gift*
Maccarone, Grace. *A child was born*
McCaughrean, Geraldine. *Father and son*
MacDonald, Maryann. *The Christmas cat*
McGhee, Alison. *Star bright*
McGinley-Nally, Sharon. *The friendly beasts*
Mackall, Dandi Daley. *Off to Bethlehem!*
Mayer, Mercer. *The little drummer mouse*
Mayper, Monica. *Come and see*
Milligan, Bryce. *Brigid's cloak*
Morpurgo, Michael. *On angel wings*
Nazoa, Aquiles. *A small Nativity*
Nikola-Lisa, W. *Hallelujah!*
  To hear the angels sing
Oppenheim, Joanne. *The Christmas witch*
Pasquali, Elena. *Ituku's Christmas journey*
Pfister, Marcus. *The Christmas star*
Rodanas, Kristina. *The little drummer boy*
Root, Phyllis. *All for the newborn baby*
Ryan, Pam Muñoz. *There was no snow on Christmas Eve*
Rylant, Cynthia. *Nativity*
Sahagun, Bernardino de. *Spirit child*
Schmid, Eleonore. *Hare's Christmas gift*
Slate, Joseph. *What star is this?*
Smith, Kathryn. *Little Donkey's Christmas story*
  Little Lamb's Christmas story
Spang, Günter. *The ox and the Donkey*
Speirs, John. *The little boy's Christmas gift*
Spirin, Gennady. *We three kings*
Summers, Susan. *The fourth wise man*
Tafuri, Nancy. *The donkey's Christmas song*
Tazewell, Charles. *The littlest angel*, ill. by Deborah Lanino
  The littlest angel, ill. by Paul Micich
  The littlest angel, ill. by Rebecca Thornburgh
Thompson, Lauren. *One starry night*
Thury, Frederick. *The last straw*
Tolan, Stephanie S. *Bartholomew's blessing*

Walburg, Lori. *The legend of the candy cane*
Wangerin, Walter. *Probity Jones and the Fear Not Angel*
Wildsmith, Brian. *A Christmas story*
Wilson, Karma. *Mortimer's Christmas manger*
Winthrop, Elizabeth. *A child is born: the Christmas story*

Religion – Noah

Auld, Mary. *Noah's ark*
Cousins, Lucy. *Noah's ark*
Cullen, Lynn. *Little Scraggly Hair*
Dubuc, Marianne. *The animals' ark*
Eitzen, Ruth. *Tara's flight*
Emberley, Barbara. *One wide river to cross*
Goldsboro, Bobby. *Noah and the ark; and, David and Goliath*
Goodhart, Pippa. *Noah makes a boat*
Greene, Rhonda Gowler. *Noah and the mighty ark*
Harker, Lesley. *Annie's ark*
Jonas, Ann. *Aardvarks, disembark!*
Krensky, Stephen. *Noah's bark*
Lloyd-Jones, Sally. *Old MacNoah had an ark*
Lunge-Larsen, Lise. *Noah's mittens*
McCarthy, Michael. *The story of Noah and the ark*
Mitton, Tony. *All afloat on Noah's boat!*
Molchadsky, Yael. *The chameleon that saved Noah's ark*
Paley, Joan. *One more river*
Philip, Neil. *Noah and the devil*
Pinkney, Jerry. *Noah's ark*
Rouss, Sylvia A. *The littlest pair*
Santore, Charles. *A stowaway on Noah's Ark*
Sassi, Laura. *Goodnight, Ark*
Sasso, Sandy Eisenberg. *Naamah, Noah's wife*
Shapiro, Zachary. *We're all in the same boat*
Singer, Isaac Bashevis. *Why Noah chose the dove*
Spier, Peter. *Noah's ark*
Stewig, John Warren. *The animals watched*
Sting [Musician]. *Rock steady*
Tebbs, Victoria. *Noah's Ark story*
Walton, Rick. *Noah's square dance*
Wilson, Anne. *Noah's ark*

Remembering *see* Memories, memory

Repetitive stories *see* Cumulative tales

Reptiles

Arnosky, Jim. *Slither and crawl*
FitzSimmons, David. *Curious critters*
Curious critters, vol. 2
Florian, Douglas. *Lizards, frogs, and polliwogs*
Green, Jen. *Reptiles*
Hood, Susan. *Spike, the mixed-up monster*
MacDonald, Margaret Read. *Give up, Gecko!*
McDonald, Megan. *Reptiles are my life*

Reptiles – alligators, crocodiles

Aliki. *Use your head, dear*
Beard, Alex. *Crocodile's tears*
Becker, Bonny. *The Christmas crocodile*
Bedford, David. *Two tough crocs*
Bergman, Mara. *Snip snap!*
Bromley, Nick. *Open very carefully*

Brown, Jo. *Where's my mommy?*
Bynum, Janie. *Kiki's blankie*
Cecil, Randy. *Gator*
Chen, Chih-Yuan. *Guji Guji*
Chichester Clark, Emma. *Melrose and Croc*
Christelow, Eileen. *Five little monkeys sitting in a tree*
Five little monkeys wash the car
Jerome camps out
Cousins, Lucy. *Maisy, Charley, and the wobbly tooth*
Maisy cleans up
Maisy goes shopping
Dahl, Roald. *The enormous crocodile*
dePaola, Tomie. *Bill and Pete*
Bill and Pete go down the Nile
Bill and Pete to the rescue
Derrick, David G., Jr. *I'm the scariest thing in the jungle!*
Dillard, Sarah. *First day at Zoo School*
Donnio, Sylviane. *I'd really like to eat a child*
Emberley, Rebecca. *The crocodile and the scorpion*
Falatko, Julie. *Snappsy the alligator (did not ask to be in this book)*
Snappsy the alligator and his best friend forever (probably)
Federspiel, Jurg. *Alligator Mike*
Finlay, Lizzie. *Little Croc's purse*
Fleming, Candace. *Gator gumbo*
Freedman, Claire. *Where's your smile, crocodile?*
Gibbons, Gail. *Alligators and crocodiles*
Gomi, Taro. *The crocodile and the dentist*
Gordon, Gus. *Herman and Rosie*
Gralley, Jean. *Very boring alligator*
Gravett, Emily. *The odd egg*
Greenberg, David. *Crocs!*
Hannigan, Katherine. *Gwendolyn Grace*
Henkes, Kevin. *Egg*
Heos, Bridget. *What to expect when you're expecting hatchlings*
Hill, Eric. *Spot's baby sister*
Hovland, Henrik. *John Jensen feels different*
Huggins, Peter. *Trosclair and the alligator*
Hurd, Thacher. *Mama don't allow*
Jarvis , Peter. *Alan's big, scary teeth*
Jewell, Nancy. *Alligator wedding*
Kasza, Keiko. *My lucky birthday*
Ketteman, Helen. *The three little gators*
Kimmelman, Leslie. *How do I love you?*
Kipling, Rudyard. *How the elephant got his trunk*
Kleven, Elisa. *A carousel tale*
Ernst
The puddle pail
The wishing ball
Kulka, Joe. *My crocodile does not bite*
Lakin, Patricia. *Camping day*
Rainy day
Lehrhaupt, Adam. *Warning: do not open this book!*
Lies, Brian. *Gator dad*
Lionni, Leo. *Cornelius*
An extraordinary egg
Llewellyn, Claire. *Crocodile*
Lodge, Jo. *Happy Snappy!*
Malkin, Michele. *Pinky's sweet tooth*
Marcellino, Fred. *I, crocodile*
Mayer, Mercer. *There's an alligator under my bed*
Merino, Gemma. *The crocodile who didn't like water*
Miller, John. *Winston and George*
Miyares, Daniel. *Pardon me!*
Montanari, Eva. *The crocodile's true colors*
Morris, Jennifer E. *May I please have a cookie?*

Moss, Jenny Jackson. *Cajun night after Christmas*
Noonan, Diana. *The crocodile*
Olson, Mary. *An alligator ate my brother*
O'Neill, Gemma. *Monty's magnificent mane*
Ormerod, Jan. *The baby swap*
Palatini, Margie. *No biting, Louise*
Panzieri, Lucia. *The kindhearted crocodile*
Parsley, Elise. *If you ever want to bring an alligator to school, don't!*
Paye, Won-Ldy. *Mrs. Chicken and the hungry crocodile*
Perret, Delphine. *Pedro and George*
Pizzoli, Greg. *The watermelon seed*
Polhemus, Coleman. *The crocodile blues*
Postgate, Daniel. *The richest crocodile in the world*
Protopopescu, Orel. *Two sticks*
Rayner, Catherine. *Solomon Crocodile*
Rowe, John A. *I want a hug*
Rylant, Cynthia. *Alligator boy*
Sandall, Ellie. *Follow me!*
Schmid, Paul. *Oliver and his alligator*
Schneider, Howie. *Fast 'n Snappy*
Schubert, Ingrid. *There is a crocodile under my bed*
Schwarz, Viviane. *How to find gold*
Sedaka, Neil. *Waking up is hard to do*
Sendak, Maurice. *Alligators all around*
Shipton, Jonathan. *No biting, horrible crocodile!*
Sierra, Judy. *Counting crocodiles*
　　The gift of the crocodile
Stevenson, James. *Monty*
　　No need for Monty
Taylor, Sean. *Crocodiles are the best animals of all*
Tourville, Amanda Doering. *A crocodile grows up*
Urbanovic, Jackie. *Duck and cover*
Van Wright, Cornelius. *When an alien meets a swamp monster*
Vaughan, Marcia Kapok. *Snap!*
Vrombaut, An. *Clarabella's teeth*
Waber, Bernard. *Funny, funny Lyle*
　　Lovable Lyle
　　Lyle and the birthday party
　　Lyle at Christmas
　　Lyle at the office
　　Lyle finds his mother
　　Lyle, Lyle Crocodile
　　Lyle walks the dogs
Walsh, Ellen Stoll. *For Pete's sake*
Waring, Richard. *Alberto the dancing alligator*
Wells, Rosemary. *Hands off, Harry!*
Whybrow, Ian. *Hello! Is this grandma?*
Willis, Jeanne. *The boy who lost his bellybutton*
Zuill, Andrea. *Dance is for everyone*

Reptiles – chameleons

Benevelli, Alberto. *The colors of the chameleon*
Carle, Eric. *The mixed-up chameleon*
Cowley, Joy. *Chameleon, chameleon*
Cyrus, Kurt. *Invisible lizard*
Dubosarsky, Ursula. *Rex*
Gravett, Emily. *Blue chameleon*
Long, Ethan. *Chamelia*
Molchadsky, Yael. *The chameleon that saved Noah's ark*
Na, Il Sung. *Hide and seek*
Perlman, Janet. *The delicious bug*
Phinn, Gervase. *Who am I?*
Watt, Mélanie. *Leon the chameleon*

Reptiles – iguanas

Alarcón, Francisco X. *Iguanas in the snow and other winter poems / Iguanas en la nieve y otros poemas de invierno*
Escoffier, Michaël. *Brief thief*
Johnston, Tony. *The iguana brothers, a perfect day*
Paul, Ann Whitford. *Count on Culebra*
　　Mañana Iguana
Robbins, Jacqui. *The new girl . . . and me*
Senisi, Ellen B. *All kinds of friends, even green*
Thoms, Susan Collins. *Cesar takes a break*

Reptiles – lizards

Antony, Steve. *Green lizards vs. red rectangles*
Carle, Eric. *The mixed-up chameleon*
Cummings, Pat. *Ananse and the lizard*
Leedy, Loreen. *The great graph contest*
Lionni, Leo. *A color of his own*
　　A color of his own [Spanish-English bilingual edition]
Mora, Pat. *Delicious hullabaloo / Pachanga deliciosa*
Murphy, Stuart J. *Leaping lizards*
Shannon, George. *Lizard's home*
　　Lizard's song
Strete, Craig Kee. *They thought they saw him*
Wiesner, David. *Art and Max*
Wood, Audrey. *Jubal's wish*

Reptiles – salamanders

FitzSimmons, David. *Salamander dance*
Hood, Susan. *Spike, the mixed-up monster*
Lamstein, Sarah Marwil. *Big night for salamanders*
Mazer, Anne. *The salamander room*
Walsh, Ellen Stoll. *Pip's magic*

Reptiles – snakes

Aardema, Verna. *What's so funny, Ketu?*
Anaya, Rudolfo A. *Roadrunner's dance*
Arnosky, Jim. *Coyote raid in Cactus Canyon*
　　Crinkleroot's visit to Crinkle Cove
　　Rattlesnake dance
Aruego, José. *The last laugh*
Bernstrom, Daniel. *One day in the eucalyptus, eucalyptus tree*
Bower, Tamara. *The shipwrecked sailor*
Buckley, Richard. *The greedy python*
Burell, Sarah. *Diamond Jim Dandy and the sheriff*
Cannon, Janell. *Verdi*
Cheng, Christopher. *Python*
Davies, Nicola. *I (don't) like snakes*
Davol, Marguerite W. *The snake's tales*
Diakité, Baba Wagué. *Mee-an and the magic serpent*
Gibbons, Gail. *Snakes*
Hayes, Joe. *The gum-chewing rattler*
Jarman, Julia. *Class Two at the zoo*
Johnson, Angela. *The girl who wore snakes*
Jonell, Lynne. *I need a snake*
Keller, Holly. *Help!*
Kimmel, Eric A. *Little Britches and the rattlers*
Kimura, Ken. *999 frogs wake up*
Kipling, Rudyard. *Rikki-tikki-tavi*, ill. by Lambert Davis
　　Rikki-tikki-tavi, ill. by Jerry Pinkney
Krensky, Stephen. *Mother's Day surprise*
Lauber, Patricia. *Snakes are hunters*
Lester, Julius. *Why heaven is far away*

McKee, David. *Elmer and Snake*
McPhail, David. *Sylvie and True*
Mason, Adrienne. *Snakes*
Noble, Trinka Hakes. *The day Jimmy's boa ate the wash*
    Jimmy's boa and the big splash birthday bash
    Jimmy's boa bounces back
Nygaard, Elizabeth. *Snake alley band*
Olaleye, Isaac. *Lake of the Big Snake*
Patent, Dorothy Hinshaw. *Slinky, scaly, slithery snakes*
Paul, Ann Whitford. *Count on Culebra*
Pilkey, Dav. *A friend for Dragon*
Pringle, Laurence P. *Snakes*
Shannon, George. *Lizard's home*
Shuttlewood, Craig. *Through the town*
Siegel, Randy. *My snake Blake*
Stroud, Bettye. *Dance y'all*
Tseng, Grace. *White tiger, blue serpent*
Ungerer, Tomi. *Crictor*
Walsh, Ellen Stoll. *Mouse count*
Welling, Peter J. *Shawn O'Hisser, the last snake in Ireland*
Wildsmith, Brian. *Jungle party*
Williamson, Sarah. *Where are you?*
Willis, Jeanne. *Boa's bad birthday*
Wright, Johanna. *The orchestra pit*
Yoon, Salina. *Opposnakes*

Reptiles – turtles, tortoises

Aesop. *The hare and the tortoise*, ill. by Paul Galdone
    The hare and the tortoise, ill. by Carol Jones
    The hare and the tortoise, ill. by Helen Ward
    The hare and the tortoise / La liebre y la tortuga
    Hare and Tortoise
    The race
    Road signs
    The tortoise and the hare, ill. by Jerry Pinkney
    The tortoise and the hare, ill. by Sara Rojo
    The tortoise and the hare: an Aesop fable
Arnosky, Jim. *Turtle in the sea*
Bauer, Marion Dane. *Frog's best friend*
    A mama for Owen
Berger, Melvin. *Look out for turtles!*
Bourgeois, Paulette. *Franklin and Harriet*
    Franklin and the thunderstorm
    Franklin in the dark
    Franklin rides a bike
    Franklin says "I love you"
    Franklin's baby sister
    Franklin's Christmas gift
    Franklin's class trip
    Franklin's new friend
    Franklin's secret club
Brett, Jan. *Mossy*
Bryan, Ashley. *Turtle knows your name*
Buckley, Richard. *The foolish tortoise*
Bunting, Eve. *Emma's turtle*
Casin, Sheridan. *Little Turtle and the song of the sea*
Castillo, Lauren. *Melvin and the boy*
Chrustowski, Rick. *Turtle crossing*
Cousteau, Philippe. *Follow the moon home*
Crowe, Carole. *Turtle girl*
Cyrus, Kurt. *The voyage of turtle Rex*
Czekaj, Jef. *Hip and Hop, don't stop!*
    Yes, yes, Yaul!
Davies, Nicola. *One tiny turtle*
DeSpain, Pleasant. *The dancing turtle*

Downard, Barry. *The Race of the Century*
Falwell, Cathryn. *Scoot!*
    Turtle splash!
Fleming, Candace. *Sunny Boy!*
Furrow, Eva. *Take your time*
George, Jean Craighead. *Galápagos George*
George, Lucy M. *Back to school Tortoise*
George, Margaret. *Lucille lost*
George, William T. *Box turtle at Long Pond*
Gorbachev, Valeri. *Heron and Turtle*
    Red red red
    Turtle's penguin day
    Whose hat is it?
Guiberson, Brenda Z. *Into the sea*
Harris, Robie H. *Turtle and me*
Heder, Thyra. *Alfie: (the turtle that disappeared)*
Himmelman, John. *Tudley didn't know*
Horn, Peter. *The best father of all*
    When I grow up . . .
Horvath, David. *Just like Bossy Bear*
Jacobs, Francine. *Lonesome George, the giant tortoise*
Javernick, Ellen. *The birthday pet*
Jennings, Sharon. *Franklin forgives*
    Franklin goes to the hospital
    Franklin makes a deal
    Franklin wants a badge
    Franklin's Thanksgiving
Johnson, Rebecca. *Sea turtle's clever plan*
Joyce, William. *Bently and egg*
Keane, Dave. *Who wants a tortoise?*
Kimmel, Eric A. *Anansi goes fishing*
    Anansi's party time
Klassen, Jon. *We found a hat*
Korman, Susan. *Box turtle at Silver Pond Lane*
Lillegard, Dee. *Tortoise brings the mail*
Loth, Sebastian. *Remembering Crystal*
Lowell, Susan. *The tortoise and the jackrabbit*
Luthardt, Kevin. *You're weird!*
McDermott, Gerald. *Jabutí the tortoise*
Marlow, Layn. *Hurry up and slow down*
Marshall, James. *Eugene*
    Yummers too
Martin, Francesca. *Clever Tortoise*
Meng, Cece. *Always remember*
Mollel, Tololwa M. *Ananse's feast*
    The flying tortoise
Morrison, Toni. *The tortoise or the hare*
Ó Flatharta, Antoine. *Hurry and the monarch*
Oldland, Nicholas. *Making the moose out of life*
O'Malley, Kevin. *The great race*
Paul, Ann Whitford. *Tortuga in trouble*
Ross, Gayle. *How Turtle's back was cracked*
Rumford, James. *Tiger and turtle*
San Souci, Daniel. *The rabbit and the dragon king*
Sayre, April Pulley. *Turtle, turtle, watch out!*, ill. by Lee Christiansen
    Turtle, turtle, watch out!, ill. by Annie Patterson
Sherry, Kevin. *Turtle Island*
Slack, Michael. *Turtle Tug to the rescue*
Swinburne, Stephen R. *Turtle tide*
Tingle, Tim. *When Turtle grew feathers*
Van Woerkom, Dorothy. *Harry and Shelburt*
Williams, Barbara. *Albert's gift for grandmother*
Winter, Jeanette. *Mama: a true story, in which a baby hippo loses his mama during a tsunami, but finds a new home*
Zagwÿn, Deborah Turney. *Turtle spring*

Resourcefulness *see* Behavior –
resourcefulness

Responsibility *see* Character traits –
responsibility

Rest *see* Sleep

Restaurants

Anderson, Peggy Perry. *Out to lunch*
Ashman, Linda. *No dogs allowed*
Bee, William. *Stanley's diner*
Burach, Ross. *There's a giraffe in my soup*
Campisi, Stephanie. *The ugly dumpling*
Dorros, Arthur. *When the pigs took over*
Downey, Lynn. *Matilda's humdinger*
Florence, Tyler. *Tyler makes spaghetti!*
Isadora, Rachel. *Happy belly, happy smile*
Krause, Ute. *Oscar and the very hungry dragon*
Kutner, Merrily. *The Zombie Nite Cafe*
Lewin, Ted. *Big Jimmy's Kum Kau Chinese take out*
Lin, Grace. *Dim sum for everyone*
London, Jonathan. *Froggy eats out*
Odanaka, Barbara. *A crazy day at the Critter Café*
Park, Frances. *The Have a Good Day Cafe*
Pearson, Tracey Campbell. *Where does Joe go?*
Perry, Robert. *Down at the Seaweed Café*
Polacco, Patricia. *Because of Thursday*
In Enzo's splendid gardens
Radabaugh, Melinda Beth. *Going to a restaurant*
Rockwell, Anne. *Truck stop*
Slegers, Liesbet. *Chefs and what they do*
Stowell, Penelope. *The greatest potatoes*
Waber, Bernard. *Fast food! gulp! gulp!*
Weatherford, Carole Boston. *Freedom on the menu*
Wellington, Monica. *Pizza at Sally's*
Whelan, Gloria. *The boy who wanted to cook*
Willard, Nancy. *The Moon and Riddles Diner and the
Sunnyside Café*
Yee, Wong Herbert. *Hamburger Heaven*

Rhyming text

Aardema, Verna. *Bringing the rain to Kapiti Plain*
The riddle of the drum
Ada, Alma Flor. *The Christmas tree / El arbol de
Navidad*
Adams, Diane. *I can do it myself!*
I want to help!
Adler, Victoria. *All of baby nose to toes*
Adlerman, Daniel. *Africa calling*
Adoff, Arnold. *Black is brown is tan*
Aesop. *Androcles and the lion: and other Aesop fables*
The race
Agee, Jon. *It's only Stanley*
Ahlberg, Allan. *Hooray for bread*
Ahlberg, Janet. *Each peach pear plum*
The jolly Christmas postman
The jolly pocket postman
The jolly postman
Peek-a-boo!
Alborough, Jez. *Captain Duck*
Duck in the truck
Duck's key where can it be?
Fix-it Duck
Hit the ball Duck

Ice cream bear
It's the bear
Six little chicks
Tall
Where's my teddy?
Alda, Arlene. *Here a face, there a face*
Sheep, sheep, sheep, help me fall asleep
Alexander, Kwame. *Acoustic Rooster and his
barnyard band*
Alexander, Sue. *Who goes out on Halloween?*
Aliki. *Push button*
Allen, Joy. *Princess Palooza*
Princess party
Allen, Kathryn Madeline. *I am a baby*
A kiss means I love you
Show me happy
Allen, Pamela. *Who sank the boat?*
Allenby, Victoria. *Nat the cat can sleep like that*
Alvarez, Julia. *Where do they go?*
Anastas, Margaret. *A hug for you*
Mommy's best kisses
Andersen, Hans Christian. *La princesa and the pea*
Anderson, Derek. *Ten hungry pigs*
Ten pigs
Anderson, Lena. *The hedgehog, the pig, and their
little friend*
Anderson, Peggy Perry. *Chuck's band*
Chuck's truck
Out to lunch
Anderson, Stephen Axel. *I know the moon*
Andreae, Giles. *Be brave, little penguin*
Giraffes can't dance
I love my daddy
I love my mommy
Pants
Rumble in the jungle
There's a house inside my mommy
Andrews, Sylvia. *Dancing in my bones*
Andrews-Goebel, Nancy. *The pot that Juan built*
Anholt, Catherine. *Happy birthday, Chimp and Zee*
What makes me happy?
Anholt, Laurence. *Two nests*
Aponte, Carlos. *A season to bee*
Appelt, Kathi. *The Alley Cat's Meow*
Bats around the clock
Bats on parade
Brand-new baby blues
Counting crows
Cowboy dreams
Incredible me!
Merry Christmas, merry crow
Oh my baby, little one
Rain dance
Apperley, Dawn. *Good night, sleep tight, little bunnies*
Santa Claus will come tonight
Arena, Jen. *One hundred snowmen*
Armstrong-Ellis, Carey. *Ten creepy monsters*
Arnold, Marsha Diane. *Roar of a snore*
Arnold, Tedd. *Dirty Gert*
Five ugly monsters
Green Wilma
Green Wilma, frog in space
More parts
Parts
Arnosky, Jim. *Gobble it up!*
I'm a turkey!
A manatee morning
Arquette, Kerry. *What did you do today?*
Artell, Mike. *Petite Rouge*

Ashburn, Boni. *The class*
   The fort that Jack built
   Over at the castle
Ashman, Linda. *All we know*
   Babies on the go
   Castles, caves, and honeycombs
   Creaky old house
   Henry wants more!
   How to make a night
   Just another morning
   M is for mischief
   Mama's day
   Maxwell's magic mix-up
   Samantha on a roll
   Starry safari
   Stella, unleashed
   To the beach!
   When I was king
   William's winter nap
Asim, Jabari. *Daddy goes to work*
Aylesworth, Jim. *Cock-a-doodle-doo, creak, pop-pop, moo*
   The folks in the valley
   Little Bitty Mousie
   My sister's rusty bike
   Old Black Fly
   One crow
Ayres, Katherine. *Up, down, and around*
Bach, Annie. *Monster party!*
Backx, Patsy. *Skippy and Jack*
Baer, Edith. *This is the way we go to school*
Baicker, Karen. *Pea pod babies*
   You can do it too!
Bailey, Ella. *No such thing*
Bailey, Linda. *Goodnight, sweet pig*
Bailey, Mary Bryant. *Jeoffry's Christmas*
Baillie, Marilyn. *Nose to toes*
Baker, Keith. *Hap-pea all year*
   Just how long can a long string be?!
   Little green peas
   LMNO pea-quel
   LMNO peas
   My octopus arms
   No two alike
   1-2-3 peas
Baker, Liza. *I love you because you're you*
Bakos, Lisa. *Too many moose!*
Bang, Molly. *Ten, nine, eight*
Banks, Kate. *City cat*
Bar-el, Dan. *A fish named Glub*
Barack, Marcy. *Season song*
Baranski, Joan Sullivan. *Round is a pancake*
Barash, Chris. *Is it Hanukkah yet?*
Bardhan-Quallen, Sudipta. *Chicks run wild*
   Pirate princess
   Snoring Beauty
   Tyrannosaurus wrecks!
Barner, Bob. *Bears! bears! bears!*
   Dinosaur bones
   Penguins, penguins, everywhere!
   Stars, stars, stars
Barnes, Brynne. *Colors of me*
Barnett, Mac. *Guess again!*
Barracca, Debra. *Maxi, the hero*
   Maxi, the star
   A taxi dog Christmas
Barracca, Sal. *The adventures of taxi dog*
Barrett, Judi. *Which witch is which?*

Bartoletti, Susan Campbell. *Nobody's nosier than a cat*
Bateman, Donna M. *Deep in the swamp*
Bateman, Teresa. *April foolishness*
   Farm flu
   Hamster Camp
   Hunting the daddyosaurus
   A plump and perky turkey
   The princesses have a ball
Bauer, Marion Dane. *Halloween forest*
   In like a lion out like a lamb
   My mother is mine
   One brown bunny
   Thank you for me!
Baylor, Byrd. *The desert is theirs*
   Everybody needs a rock
Bea, Holly. *Bless your heart*
   My spiritual alphabet book
Beaton, Clare. *Daisy gets dressed*
Beaty, Andrea. *Ada Twist, scientist*
   Hide and sheep
   Iggy Peck, architect
   Rosie Revere, engineer
Beaumont, Karen. *Crybaby*
   Dini Dinosaur
   Doggone dogs!
   Duck, duck, goose!
   Hats off to you!
   I ain't gonna paint no more!
   Move over, Rover
   No sleep for the sheep!
   Shoe-la-la!
   Who ate all the cookie dough?
   Wild about us!
Becker, Bonny. *Tickly prickly*
Becker, Shelly. *Even superheroes have bad days*
Bell, Babs. *Sputter, sputter, sput!*
Bemelmans, Ludwig. *Madeline*
   Madeline and the bad hat
   Madeline and the gypsies
   Madeline in London
   Madeline's Christmas
   Madeline's rescue
Bennett, Artie. *The butt book*
Bentley, Dawn. *Fuzzy bear*
   Fuzzy Bear's potty book
Bently, Peter. *Captain Jack and the pirates*
   The great sheep shenanigans
   King Jack and the dragon
   Meet the parents
   The prince and the porker
   A recipe for bedtime
   Those magnificent sheep in their flying machine
Benton, Jim. *Where did all the dinos go?*
Berenstain, Stan and Jan. *The bear detectives*
   The Berenstain bears and the missing dinosaur bone
   The Berenstain bears and the spooky old tree
   The Berenstain bears' Christmas tree
   The Berenstain bears' that stump must go!
   He bear, she bear
Berger, Samantha. *Monster's new undies*
   Snoozefest at the Nuzzledome
Bergman, Mara. *Yum yum! What fun!*
Berkes, Marianne. *Marsh music*
   Over in a river
   Over in Australia
   Over in the Arctic
   Over in the forest
   Over in the jungle

Over on a mountain
Bernhard, Durga. *In the fiddle is a song*
Berry, Lynne. *Duck dunks*
  Duck skates
  Duck tents
  Ducking for apples
Bertram, Debbie. *The best book to read*
  The best place to read
  The best time to read
  My new big-kid bed
Bible. Old Testament. Psalms. *I will rejoice*
Biddulph, Rob. *Blown away*
  The grizzly bear who lost his grrrrr!
Billin-Frye, Paige. *One, two, buckle my shoe*
Billstrom, Dianne. *You can't go to school naked!*
Blabey, Aaron. *Pig the elf*
  Pig the pug
  Pig the winner
Black, Sonia. *Hanging out with Mom*
Blackstone, Stella. *Alligator alphabet*
  Bear at home
  Bear at work
  Bear in sunshine
  Bear's birthday
  Bear's busy family
  Bear's school day
  Cleo and Caspar
  Cleo in the snow
  Cleo on the move
  Cleo the cat
  Cleo's alphabet book
  Cleo's color book
  Cleo's counting book
  Come here, Cleo
  How big is a pig?
  I dreamt I was a dinosaur
  An island in the sun
  Octopus opposites
  Secret seahorse
  Ship shapes
Blaikie, Lynn. *Beyond the northern lights*
Blake, Quentin. *Fantastic Daisy Artichoke*
Blatt, Jane. *Books always everywhere*
Blechman, Nicholas. *Night light*
Blegvad, Lenore. *First friends*
Blomgren, Jennifer. *Where do I sleep?*
Bloom, Suzanne. *A number slumber*
Bluemle, Elizabeth. *Dogs on the bed*
  Tap tap boom boom
Boedoe, Geefwee. *Arrowville*
Bogart, Jo Ellen. *Count your chickens*
Bolam, Emily. *I go potty*
Bonnett-Rampersaud, Louise. *How do you sleep?*
  Never ask a bear
Bono, Mary. *Ugh! a bug*
Booth, Anne. *The fairiest fairy*
Bowen, Anne. *I know an old teacher*
Bowie, C. W. *Busy fingers*
  Busy toes
Boynton, Sandra. *Christmas parade*
  Dinosaur dance!
  Eek! Halloween!
  Happy birthday, Little Pookie
  Little Pookie
  Night-night, Little Pookie
  Spooky Pookie
  Yay, you!
Bozik, Chrissy. *The ghosts go scaring*
Bradby, Marie. *Once upon a farm*

Braeuner, Shellie. *The great dog wash*
Bramsen, Carin. *Hey, duck!*
  Just a duck?
Brantz, Loryn. *Feminist Baby*
Brennan, Eileen. *Bad Astrid*
Brennan, Linda Crotta. *Marshmallow kisses*
Brennan-Nelson, Denise. *Good night, reindeer*
  He's been a monster all day!
  My grandma likes to say
Brenner, Barbara A. *Good morning, garden*
Brenner, Emily. *On the first day of grade school*
Bridwell, Norman. *Clifford's neighborhood*
Briere-Haquet, Alice. *Zebedee's balloon*
Briggs, Kelly Paul. *Lighthouse lullaby*
Bright, Rachel. *The koala who could*
  The lion inside
  Side by side
Brisson, Pat. *Before we eat*
Bronson, Linda. *The circus alphabet*
The brothers gruesome
Brown, Calef. *Boy wonders*
  Pirateria
  Tippintown
Brown, Ken. *What's the time, Grandma Wolf?*
Brown, Margaret Wise. *Another important book*
  A child is born
  Christmas in the barn
  Good day, good night
  My world of color
  Sailor boy jig
  Sleepy ABC, ill. by Karen Katz
  Sleepy ABC, ill. by Esphyr Slobodkina
  Where have you been?
Brown, Tameka Fryer. *Around our way on Neighbors'
    Day*
  My cold plum lemon pie bluesy mood
Brown-Wood, JaNay. *Grandma's tiny house*
Brownlow, Mike. *The big white book with almost
    nothing in it*
  Way out West — with a baby!
Bruce, Lisa. *Engines, engines*
Bruchac, Joseph. *My father is taller than a tree*
Bruel, Nick. *A Bad Kitty Christmas*
Bryan, Ashley. *Beat the story-drum, pum-pum*
  Can't scare me!
  The cat's purr
  Who built the stable?
Bryan, Sean. *A bear and his boy*
Bryant, Megan E. *Dump Truck Duck*
Buchanan, Sue. *Mud Pie Annie*
Buck, Nola. *A Christmas goodnight*
Buckley, Richard. *The foolish tortoise*
  The greedy python
Buehner, Caralyn. *Merry Christmas, Mr. Mouse*
  Snowmen all year
  Snowmen at Christmas
  Snowmen at night
  Would I ever lie to you?
Bunting, Eve. *The baby shower*
  The bones of Fred McFee
  Butterfly house
  Flower garden
  Happy birthday, dear duck
  Have you seen my new blue socks?
  Hey diddle diddle
  The pumpkin fair
  Scary, scary Halloween
  Sunflower house
  Whose shoe?

Burdett, Lois. *Hamlet for kids*
   A midsummer night's dream for kids
   Romeo and Juliet for kids
   The tempest for kids
Burfoot, Ella. *How to bake a book*
Burleigh, Robert. *Clang-clang! beep-beep!*
   Hit the road, Jack
   I love going through this book
   Messenger, messenger
   Zoom! zoom!
Bus-a-saurus bop
Butler, John. *Can you growl like a bear?*
   Hush, little ones
Buxton, Jane. *The littlest llama*
Buzzeo, Toni. *Inside the books*
Byous, Shawn. *Because I stubbed my toe*
Cabrera, Jane. *Baa, baa, black sheep*
   Row, row, row your boat
   There was an old woman who lived in a shoe
Caffey, Donna. *Yikes-lice!*
Cain, Janan. *The way I feel*
Calmenson, Stephanie. *Birthday at the Panda Palace*
   Jazzmatazz!
   Late for school!
   No honking allowed
   Oopsy, teacher!
Cameron, C. C. *One for me, one for you*
Capucilli, Alyssa Satin. *Bear hugs*
   I will love you
   Inside a zoo in the city
   Mrs. McTats and her houseful of cats
   What kind of kiss?
Carle, Eric. *The nonsense show*
Carlson, Melody. *The Easterville miracle*
   Farmer Brown's field trip
   When the creepy things come out
Carlstrom, Nancy White. *Better not get wet, Jesse Bear*
   Guess who's coming, Jesse Bear
   Happy birthday, Jesse Bear!
   How do you say it today, Jesse Bear?
   It's about time, Jesse Bear
   It's your first day of school, Annie Claire
   Let's count it out, Jesse Bear
   What a scare, Jesse Bear!
   Where is Christmas, Jesse Bear?
Carney, Margaret. *Where does a tiger-heron spend the night?*
Carr, Jan. *Dappled apples*
   Splish, splash, spring
Carter, David A. *Flapdoodle dinosaurs*
Carter, Don. *Old MacDonald drives a tractor*
Cartwright, Reg. *What we do*
Casanova, Mary. *One-dog canoe*
   One-dog sleigh
Cash, Megan Montague. *I saw the sea and the sea saw me*
Casteel, Seth. *Puppy pool party!*
   Underwater dogs
Caswell, Deanna. *Beach house*
   Train trip
Cazet, Denys. *Nothing at all*
Chaconas, Dori. *Don't slam the door!*
   Hurry down to Derry Fair
   On a wintry morning
   Virginnie's hat
   When cows come home for Christmas
Chall, Marsha Wilson. *One pup's up*
Chamberlain, Margaret. *Please don't tease Tootsie*

Chapman, Nancy Kapp. *Doggie dreams*
Charlip, Remy. *Baby hearts and baby flowers*
   "Mother, mother I feel sick"
   Sleepytime rhyme
Chast, Roz. *Around the clock!*
Chernesky, Felicia Sanzari. *Cheers for a dozen ears*
   From apple trees to cider, please!
   Pick a circle, gather squares
   Sugar white snow and evergreens
   Sun above and blooms below
Chetkowski, Emily. *Pumpkin smile*
Chichester Clark, Emma. *Little Miss Muffet counts to ten*
Chitwood, Suzanne Tanner. *Wake up, big barn!*
Chorao, Kay. *Knock at the door and other baby action rhymes*
Chriscoe, Sharon. *Race car dreams*
Christelow, Eileen. *Five little monkeys reading in bed*
   Five little monkeys sitting in a tree
   Five little monkeys wash the car
Christian, Cheryl. *Witches*
Chrustowski, Rick. *My Little Fox*
Church, Caroline Jayne. *I love my bunny*
   I love my robot
Churchill, Vicki. *Sometimes I like to curl up in a ball*
Clarke, Jane. *Dancing with the Dinosaurs*
   Stuck in the mud
Clarkson, Stephanie. *Sleeping Cinderella and other princess mix-ups*
Clayton, Dallas. *An awesome book!*
   An awesome book of love!
Cleary, Beverly. *The hullabaloo ABC*
Cleary, Brian P. *Eight wild nights*
   A lime, a mime, a pool of slime
   Peanut butter and jellyfishes
Clements, Andrew. *The handiest things in the world*
Clifton, Lucille. *Everett Anderson's goodbye*
   One of the problems of Everett Anderson
Cline-Ransome, Lesa. *Quilt alphabet*
   Quilt counting
Coat, Janik. *Rhymoceros*
Cocca-Leffler, Maryann. *Jungle Halloween*
   Let it rain
Colandro, Lucille. *There was a cold lady who swallowed some snow!*
   There was an old lady who swallowed a clover!
   There was an old lady who swallowed a frog!
   There was an old lady who swallowed some books!
Colborn, Mary Palenick. *Rainy day slug*
Collins, Ross. *There's a bear on my chair*
Collins, Suzanne. *When Charlie McButton lost power*
Conover, Chris. *The Christmas bears*
Cook, Grace. *Two little eyes and other action rhymes*
Corderoy, Tracey. *Hubble bubble, Granny trouble*
Cordsen, Carol Foskett. *Market day*
   The milkman
Corey, Shana. *Boats!*
Costain, Meredith. *Daddies are awesome*
Cote, Nancy. *Jackson's blanket*
Cotten, Cynthia. *At the edge of the woods*
   Rain play
Cotton, Katie. *The road home*
Couric, Katie. *The brand new kid*
Cousins, Lucy. *Hooray for birds!*
   Hooray for fish!
   Peck, peck, peck
Cowley, Joy. *Mrs. Wishy-Washy's Christmas*
Cox, Judy. *Snow day for Mouse*
Cox, Phil Roxbee. *Fox on a box*

    Goose on the loose
    Shark in the park
Coyle, Carmela LaVigna. *Do princesses have best*
    friends forever?
    Do princesses make happy campers?
    Do super heroes have teddy bears?
Craig, Lindsey. *Dancing feet!*
    Farmyard beat
Crandall, Court. *Hugville*
Crawford, Laura. *In arctic waters*
Crimi, Carolyn. *Principal Fred won't go to bed*
    Pugs in a Bug
Crisp, Marty. *Totally polar*
Crocker, Nancy. *Betty Lou Blue*
Cronin, Doreen. *Bounce*
    Click, clack, splish, splash
    Stretch
    Wiggle
Crouse, Livingstone. *Kisses for kindergarten*
Crow, Kristyn. *Bedtime at the swamp*
    Cool Daddy Rat
    The middle-child blues
    Skeleton cat
    Zombelina
    Zombelina: school days
Crowe, Caroline. *Pirates in pajamas*
Crowley, Ned. *Nanook and Pryce*
Cruise, Robin. *Only you*
Crum, Shutta. *All on a sleepy night*
    The bravest of the brave
    A family for Old Mill Farm
Cullen, Catherine Ann. *The magical, mystical,*
    marvelous coat
    Thirsty baby
Cummings, Pat. *Angel baby*
    Clean your room, Harvey Moon!
    My aunt came back
Curtis, Jamie Lee. *Big words for little people*
    I'm gonna like me
    Is there really a human race?
    It's hard to be five
    My brave year of firsts
    My mommy hung the moon
    This is me
    Today I feel silly and other moods that make my day
    Where do balloons go?
Cushman, Doug. *Christmas Eve good night*
    Halloween good night
Cusimano, Maryann K. *You are my I love you*
    You are my wish
    You are my wonders
Cuyler, Margery. *Guinea pigs add up*
    The little dump truck
    The little fire truck
    The little school bus
    Monster mess!
    Princess Bess gets dressed
    Skeleton for dinner
Cyrus, Kurt. *Big rig bugs*
    Billions of bricks
    Motor Dog
    Shake a leg, egg!
    Tadpole Rex
    The voyage of turtle Rex
Czajak, Paul. *Monster needs a Christmas tree*
    Monster needs your vote
Dahl, Michael. *Goodnight baseball*
    Goodnight football
Daniels, Teri. *Just enough*

Danylyshyn, Greg. *A crash of rhinos*
Davenier, Christine. *It's raining, it's pouring*
Davick, Linda. *I love you, nose! I love you, toes!*
Davidson, Leslie A. *In the red canoe*
Davidson, Rebecca Piatt. *All the world's a stage*
Davies, Jacqueline. *The night is singing*
Davies, Sarah. *Happy to be girls*
Davis, David. *Jazz cats*
Day, Nancy Raines. *A is for alliguitar*
    What in the world?
Deady, Kathleen W. *All year long*
    It's time!
Dealey, Erin. *Goldie Locks has chicken pox*
Dean, James. *Pete the Cat and the new guy*
Dean, Kim. *Pete the Cat and the missing cupcakes*
Degman, Lori. *One zany zoo*
de Las Casas, Dianne. *Mama's bayou*
Demarest, Chris L. *Firefighters A to Z*
    Hotshots!
Demas, Corinne. *Are pirates polite?*
    Pirates go to school
Dempsey, Kristy. *A hop is up*
    Mini racer
    Ten little fingers, two small hands
    Ten little toes, two small feet
Denise, Anika. *Baking day at Grandma's*
    Pigs love potatoes
DePalma, Mary Newell. *Bow-wow wiggle-waggle*
dePaola, Tomie. *Get dressed, Santa!*
De Regniers, Beatrice Schenk. *May I bring a friend?*
Dewdney, Anna. *Grumpy Gloria*
    Little Excavator
    Llama Llama and the bully goat
    Llama Llama home with Mama
    Llama Llama mad at Mama
    Llama Llama misses Mama
    Llama, Llama red pajama
    Llama Llama time to share
    Nelly Gnu and Daddy too
    Nobunny's perfect
    Roly Poly pangolin
Dickinson, Rebecca. *Over in the Hollow*
Diesen, Deborah. *The barefooted, bad-tempered baby*
    brigade
    The not very merry pout-pout fish
    The pout-pout fish
    The pout-pout fish, far, far from home
    The pout-pout fish goes to school
    The pout-pout fish in the big-big dark
Diggs, Taye. *Mixed me!*
Dionne, Wanda. *Little Thumb*
DiPucchio, Kelly. *Alfred Zector, book collector*
    Dinosnores
    Littles
DiTerlizzi, Angela. *Baby love*
    I wanna be a cowgirl
    Say what?
    Some bugs
    Some pets
DiTerlizzi, Tony. *G is for one gzonk!*
Diviny, Sean. *Halloween Motel*
Dixon, Ann. *Winter is . . .*
Dobbins, Jan. *Driving my tractor*
Docherty, Helen. *The Snatchabook*
    The storybook knight
Docherty, Thomas. *Wash-a-bye Bear*
Dodd, Emma. *Always*
    Best bear
    The entertainer

Everything
Happy
I don't want a cool cat!
I don't want a posh dog
I love bugs!
Just like you
Love
More and more
No matter what
When I grow up
Dodd, Lynley. *A dragon in a wagon*
 Find me a tiger
Dodds, Dayle Ann. *Hello, sun!*
 Pet wash
 The prince won't go to bed
 Where's Pup?
Dominguez, Angela. *Maria had a little llama/Maria tenia una llama pequena*
Donahue, Shari Faden. *The zebra-striped whale with the polka-dot tail*
Donaldson, Julia. *Charlie Cook's favorite book*
 The fish who cried wolf
 The Giant Jumperee
 A gold star for Zog
 The Highway Rat
 One mole digging a hole
 Room on the broom
 Stick Man
 Superworm
 Tabby McTat, the musical cat
 Tyrannosaurus Drip
 What the ladybug heard
 Where's my mom?
 Zog and the flying doctors
Doner, Kim. *On a road in Africa*
Doodler, Todd H. *The zoo I drew*
Dorfman, Craig. *I knew you could!*
Dotlich, Rebecca Kai. *All aboard!*
 Race car count
 What can a crane pick up?
 What is round?
 What is square?
Doughty, Rebecca. *Oh no! Time to go!*
Downey, Lynn. *The flea's sneeze*
 This is the earth that God made
Downs, Mike. *You see a circus, I see —*
Doyle, Charlotte Lackner. *The bouncing, dancing, galloping ABC*
Doyle, Malachy. *Get happy*
 Storm cats
Dragonwagon, Crescent. *All the awake animals are almost asleep*
Druce, Arden. *Halloween night*
Drummond, Allan. *Casey Jones*
Dubosarsky, Ursula. *The terrible plop*
Duddle, Johnny. *Gigantosaurus*
Duddle, Jonny. *The pirate cruncher*
 The pirates next door
Dunbar, Joyce. *Pat-a-cake baby*
 Shoe baby
Duncan, Lois. *I walk at night*
 Song of the circus
Dunn, Todd. *We go together*
Dunrea, Olivier. *Me and Annie McPhee*
Durango, Julia. *Cha-cha chimps*
 Go-go gorillas
Duval, Kathy. *A bear's year*
 Take me to your BBQ
Edens, Cooper. *The Animal Mall*

Edwards, David. *The pen that Pa built*
Edwards, Pamela Duncan. *The grumpy morning*
 Roar
 Wake-up kisses
 Warthogs in the kitchen
 Warthogs paint
 While the world is sleeping
Ehlert, Lois. *Boo to you!*
 Feathers for lunch
 Fish eyes
 Holey Moley
 Lots of spots
 Market day
 Nuts to you!
 Oodles of animals
 Top cat
 Waiting for wings
Ehrhardt, Karen. *This jazz man*
Elffers, Joost. *Do you love me?*
Elliott, David. *And here's to you!*
 One little chicken
Ellwand, David. *Cinderlily*
Elya, Susan Middleton. *Adiós, tricycle*
 Bebé goes shopping
 Bebé goes to the beach
 Cowboy Jose
 Eight animals bake a cake
 Eight animals on the town
 F is for fiesta
 Fire! ¡Fuego! Brave bomberos
 Little Roja Riding Hood
 No more, por favor
 Oh no, gotta go #2
 Rubia and the three osos
 Tooth on the loose
 A year full of holidays
Emberley, Ed. *The wing on a flea*
Emberley, Rebecca. *Mice on ice*
 Spare parts
Emmett, Jonathan. *Someone bigger*
Engelbreit, Mary. *Mary Engelbreit's A merry little Christmas*
Ericsson, Jennifer A. *She did it!*
Ernst, Lisa Campbell. *Round like a ball!*
 This is the van that Dad cleaned
Esbaum, Jill. *Estelle takes a bath*
 I am cow, hear me moo!
 I hatched!
 Stanza
Eschbacher, Roger. *Nonsense! He yelled*
 Road trip
Esenwine, Matt Forrest. *Flashlight night*
Estefan, Gloria. *Noelle's treasure tale*
Evans, Lezlie. *The bunnies' picnic*
 The bunnies' trip
 Can you count ten toes?
 Who loves the little lamb?
Evans, Nate. *Bang! Boom! Roar!*
Ewert, Marcus. *Mummy cat*
Fallon, Jimmy. *Snowball fight!*
Falwell, Cathryn. *Christmas for 10*
 Feast for ten
 Gobble gobble
 Mystery vine
 Rainbow Stew
 Scoot!
 Shape capers
 Turtle splash!
Fearrington, Ann. *Who sees the lighthouse?*

Feldman, Eve B. *Billy and Milly, short and silly*
Fernandes, Eugenie. *Big week for little mouse*
  Busy little mouse
  Kitten's spring
  Kitten's winter
Ferreri, Della Ross. *How will I ever sleep in this bed?*
Ferry, Beth. *Stick and Stone*
Ficocelli, Elizabeth. *Kid tea*
Fischer, Scott M. *Jump!*
Fisher, Aileen Lucia. *Know what I saw?*
  You don't look like your mother
Fisher, Doris. *My even day*
  One odd day
Fitzpatrick, Marie-Louise. *I'm a tiger, too!*
Five little pumpkins, ill. by Ben Mantle
  Five little pumpkins, ill. by Iris Van Rynbach
  Five little pumpkins, ill. by Dan Yaccarino
Fleming, Candace. *Seven hungry babies*
  Who invited you?
Fleming, Denise. *Barnyard banter*
  Beetle bop
  The first day of winter
  In the small, small pond
  Underground
Fleming, Meg. *I heart you*
  Ready, set, build!
Fliess, Sue. *Books for me!*
  Calling all cars
  A fairy friend
  A gluten-free birthday for me!
  Race!
  Shoes for me!
Florian, Douglas. *The curious cares of bears*
  How to draw a dragon
  I love my hat
  A pig is big
Flynn, Kitson. *Carrot in my pocket*
Foges, Clare. *Kitchen disco*
Fogliano, Julie. *Old dog baby baby*
Foreman, Jack. *Say hello*
Fox, Lee. *Ella Kazoo will not brush her hair*
Fox, Mem. *Boo to a goose*
  Good night, sleep tight
  Hello, baby!
  Let's count goats!
  The magic hat
  Nellie Belle
  Shoes from grandpa
  Sleepy bears
  Ten little fingers and ten little toes
  This and that
  Time for bed
  Two little monkeys
  Where is the green sheep?
  Where the giant sleeps
  Yoo-hoo, Ladybug!
  Zoo-looking
Frampton, David. *The whole night through*
Franco, Betsy. *Double play!*
Frazier, Craig. *Lots of dots*
Frederick, Heather Vogel. *Babyberry pie*
  Hide and squeak
Fredrickson, Lane. *Watch your tongue, Cecily Beasley*
Freedman, Claire. *Dinosaurs love underpants*
  One magical day
  One magical morning
  Pirates love underpants
  Snuggle up, sleepy ones
  Spider sandwiches

Freymann, Saxton. *Dr. Pompo's nose*
  One lonely seahorse
Friedman, Laurie. *Ruby Valentine and the sweet surprise*
  Ruby Valentine saves the day
  Thanksgiving rules
Friend, David. *With any luck, I'll drive a truck*
Fronis, Aly. *If you're spooky and you know it*
Fuge, Charles. *Astonishing animal ABC*
  I know a rhino
Funk, Josh. *Dear dragon*
  Pirasaurs!
Fyleman, Rose. *Mice*
Gaiman, Neil. *Crazy hair*
  The dangerous alphabet
Galbraith, Kathryn O. *Boo, bunny!*
Gall, Chris. *Substitute creacher*
Gannij, Joan. *Hidden hippo*
Garland, Michael. *Christmas City*
  The great Easter egg hunt
  Hooray José!
  Last night at the zoo
Garland, Sally Anne. *Share*
Garriel, Barbara S. *I know a shy fellow who swallowed a cello*
Gehl, Laura. *One big pair of underwear*
Geist, Ken. *Who's who?*
George, Kristine O'Connell. *Up!*
Geras, Adèle. *Sleep tight, Ginger Kitten*
Gerber, Carole. *A band of babies*
  Spring blossoms
  Ten busy brooms
Geringer, Laura. *Boom boom go away!*
Gerrard, K.A. *My family is a zoo*
Gershator, Phillis. *Listen, listen*
  Moo, moo, brown cow! Have you any milk?
  Summer is summer
  Time for a bath
  Time for a hug
  When it starts to snow
  Who's awake in springtime?
  Who's in the farmyard?
  Who's in the forest?
Ghigna, Charles. *I see winter*
Gibson, Amy. *By day, by night*
  Split! splat!
Gilman, Rita Golden. *Mole in a hole*
The gingerbread boy. *The gingerbread boy*
  The Gingerbread Man loose at Christmas
  The Gingerbread Man loose at the zoo
  The Gingerbread Man loose in the school
  The Gingerbread Man loose on the fire truck
  Whiff, sniff, nibble and chew
Ginkel, Anne. *I've got an elephant*
Giogas, Valarie. *In my backyard*
Glass, Beth Raisner. *Blue-ribbon dad*
  Noises at night
Glass, Julie. *A dollar for Penny*
Gliori, Debi. *Goodnight world*
  No matter what
  Polar Bolero
  Stormy weather
  What can I give him?
  Where did that baby come from?
Godwin, Laura. *Central Park serenade*
  Little white dog
  One moon, two cats
  This is the firefighter
  What the baby hears

Goembel, Ponder. *Animal fair*
Going, K. L. *Bumpety, dunkety, thumpety-thump!*
Gold-Vukson, Marji E. *Grandpa and me on Tu B'Shevat*
Gollub, Matthew. *The Jazz Fly*
   Jazz Fly 2
   Ten oni drummers
Good, Merle, et al. *Dan's pants*
Goodhart, Pippa. *My very own space*
Gow, Nancy. *Ten big toes and a prince's nose*
Grabill, Rebecca. *Halloween good night*
Graham, Joan Bransfield. *The poem that will not end*
Graham-Barber, Lynda. *Spy hops and belly flops*
Graham-Yooll, Liz. *Timothy Tib*
Gralley, Jean. *Very boring alligator*
Grant, Holly. *Wee Sister Strange*
Gravdahl, John. *Curious catwalk*
Graves, Keith. *The monsterator*
   Pet boy
Gravett, Emily. *Monkey and me*
   Tidy
Gray, Kes. *Frog on a log?*
Gray, Rita. *Have you heard the nesting bird?*
   The wild little horse
Greenawalt, Kelly. *Princess Truly in I am Truly*
Greenberg, David. *Crocs!*
   Skunks
Greene, Rhonda Gowler. *At grandma's*
   Barnyard song
   Daddy is a cozy hug
   Eek! creak! snicker, sneak
   Jamboree day
   Mommy is a soft, warm kiss
   No pirates allowed! said Library Lou
   The stable where Jesus was born
   The very first Thanksgiving Day
Greene, Rhonda Growler. *Push! dig! scoop!*
Greenfield, Eloise. *Water, water*
Griffith, Helen V. *Moonlight*
Grossman, Bill. *My little sister ate one hare*
   My little sister hugged an ape
Grossman, Virginia. *Ten little rabbits*
Guarino, Deborah. *Is your mama a llama?*
Guenther, James. *Turnagain, Ptarmigan, where did you go?*
Guidone, Thea. *Drum city*
Gulbis, Stephen. *Cowgirl Rosie and her five baby bison*
Gundersheimer, Karen. *Find cat, wear hat*
Gunnufson, Charlotte. *Halloween hustle*
Gutman, Dan. *Rappy the raptor*
Haber, Tiffany Strelitz. *The monster who lost his mean*
   Ollie and Claire
Hächler, Bruno. *What does my teddy bear do all night?*
Hager, Sarah. *Dancing Matilda*
Hague, Kathleen. *Alphabears*
   Calendarbears
   Ten little bears
Hall, Algy Craig. *Dino bites!*
Hall, Marcellus. *Everyone sleeps*
Hall, Michael. *Cat tale*
   Little i
   My heart is like a zoo
Halls, Kelly Milner. *Dinosaur parade: a spectacle of prehistoric proportions*
Halpern, Shari. *Dinosaur parade*
Hamburg, Jennifer. *Monkey and Duck quack up!*

   A moose that says mooooooooooo
Hamilton, K. R. *This is the ocean*
Hamilton, Kersten. *Police officers on patrol*
   Red truck
Hamilton, Richard. *Let's take over the kindergarten*
   Polly's picnic
Hample, Stoo. *I will kiss you (lots and lots and lots!)*
Hamsa, Bobbie. *Fast-draw Freddie*
Hanson, Warren. *Bugtown Boogie*
Harby, Melanie. *All aboard for Dreamland!*
Hargrove, Linda. *Wings across the moon*
Harley, Bill. *Dirty Joe, the pirate*
Harper, Charise Mericle. *There was a bold lady who wanted a star*
Harper, Jessica. *I'm not going to chase the cat today*
   Lizzy's do's and don'ts
   Lizzy's ups and downs
   Nora's room
Harrington, Tim. *Nose to toes, you are yummy!*
Harris, Trudy. *Jenny found a penny*
   100 days of school
   Pattern bugs
   Pattern fish
   Twenty hungry piggies
Harrison, David L. *Piggy Wiglet*
Harshman, Marc. *Red are the apples*
Harshman, Terry Webb. *Does a sea cow say moo?*
Hart, Caryl. *The princess and the Christmas rescue*
   The princess and the peas
Harvey, Jayne. *Busy bugs*
Hatch, Elizabeth. *Halloween night*
Hawkins, Colin. *One, two, guess who?*
Hayles, Marsha. *Bunion Burt*
   The feathered crown
   He saves the day
   Pajamas anytime
Hays, Anna Jane. *Kindergarten countdown*
Hegarty, Patricia. *Bug Bear*
   Good night farm
Hegg, Tom. *Peef and his best friend*
Heidbreder, Robert. *Black and bittern was night*
   I wished for a unicorn
   A sea-wishing day
   Song for a summer night
Heiligman, Deborah. *Cool dog, school dog*
   Snow dog, go dog
Heim, Alastair. *Love you too*
Heinz, Brian J. *The monsters' test*
   Red Fox at McCloskey's farm
Helakoski, Leslie. *Doggone feet!*
Heling, Kathryn. *Mouse's hide-and-seek words*
Heller, Ruth. *A cache of jewels and other collective nouns*
   Color, color, color, color
   Fantastic! wow! and unreal!
   Kites sail high
   Many luscious lollipops
   Merry-go-round
   Mine, all mine
   The reason for a flower
Henderson, Kathy. *Baby knows best*
Henkes, Kevin. *Oh!*
Hennessy, B. G. *The missing tarts*
Heras, Theo. *What will we do with the baby-o?*
Hesse, Karen. *My thumb*
Hicks, Barbara Jean. *I like black and white*
   Monsters don't eat broccoli
Hill, Isabel. *Building stories*
Hill, Susanna Leonard. *The house that Mack built*

Johnston, Tony. *Chicken in the kitchen*
  Desert dog
  Off to kindergarten
  The whole green world
Jones, Christianne C. *The Santa shimmy*
Jones, Sylvie. *Who's in the tub?*
Joosse, Barbara. *Hooray Parade*
Jordan, Mary Ellen. *Lazy Daisy, cranky Frankie*
Jorgensen, Gail. *Crocodile beat*
Jorgensen, Richard. *Reading with Dad*
Joyce, Susan. *ABC nature riddles*
  ABC school riddles
Joyce, William. *Rolie Polie Olie*
  Sleepy time Olie
Jukes, Mavis. *You're a bear*
Kalan, Robert. *Moving day*
Karas, G. Brian. *Skidamarink*
Katz, Alan. *Don't say that word!*
Katz, Karen. *Ten tiny babies*
  Twelve hats for Lena
Katz, Susan B. *ABC school's for me!*
  All year round
Kaufman, Jeanne. *Young Henry and the dragon*
Kavanagh, Peter. *I love my mama*
Kay, Julia. *Gulliver Snip*
Kay, Verla. *Civil War drummer boy*
  Covered wagons, bumpy trails
  Gold fever
  Hornbooks and inkwells
  Iron horses
  Orphan train
  Whatever happened to the Pony Express?
Keillor, Garrison. *Daddy's girl*
Keller, Joy. *Monster trucks*
Keller, Laurie. *Grandpa Gazillion's number yard*
Kelley, Marty. *The rules*
  Summer stinks
  Winter woes
Kelly, L. J. R. *Sometimes it's storks*
Kelly, Luke. *Blanket and bear, a remarkable pair*
Kelly, Mij. *Achoo!*
  A bed of your own!
  Friendly Day
  One more sheep
  Where's my darling daughter?
Kennedy, Anne Vittur. *The farmer's away! baa! neigh!*
Kerner, Susan. *Always by my side*
Kerr, Judith. *One night in the zoo*
Ketteman, Helen. *At the old haunted house*
  Goodnight, Little Monster
  If Beaver had a fever
Khalsa, Dayal Kaur. *Green cat*
Killion, Bette. *Just think!*
Kimmel, Eric A. *The Erie Canal pirates*
Kimmelman, Leslie. *Everybody bonjours!*
  How do I love you?
  Round the turkey
  Trick ARRR treat
Kindermans, Martine. *You and me*
Kinerk, Robert. *Clorinda*
  Clorinda plays baseball!
  Clorinda takes flight
  Timothy Cox will not change his socks
King, Stephen Michael. *Emily loves to bounce*
Kirk, Daniel. *Bus stop, bus go*
  Honk honk! Beep beep!
  Keisha Ann can!
  Moondogs

Snow family
Trash trucks!
Kirk, David. *Little bird, Biddle bird*
  Little bunny, Biddle bunny
  Little Miss Spider
  Little Miss Spider at Sunny Patch School
  Little pig, Biddle pig
  Miss Spider's ABC
  Miss Spider's new car
  Miss Spider's tea party
  Truckeroo school
Kleven, Elisa. *Cozy light, cozy night*
  Sun bread
Kneen, Maggie. *The Christmas surprise*
Koda-Callan, Elizabeth. *The squiggly Wigglys*
Koehler, Lana Wayne. *Ah-choo!*
Kohuth, Jane. *Duck sock hop*
Koller, Jackie French. *Bouncing on the bed*
  One monkey too many
Kono, Erin Eitter. *Hula lullaby*
Kramer, Andrew. *Pajama pirates*
Kranking, Kathy. *The ocean is . . .*
Krasnesky, Thad. *That cat can't stay*
Kraus, Robert. *Mouse in love*
  Whose mouse are you?
Krauss, Ruth. *Goodnight, goodnight, sleepyhead*
Krebs, Laurie. *The beeman*, ill. by Valeria Cis
  The beeman, ill. by Melissa Iwai
  Off we go to Mexico
  Up and down the Andes
  We're roaming in the rainforest
  We're sailing down the Nile
  We're sailing to Galapagos
Krensky, Stephen. *I am so brave!*
  I know a lot!
Krieb, Mr. *We're off to find the witch's house*
Kroll, Virginia L. *Boy, you're amazing!*
  Everybody has a teddy
  Girl, you're amazing!
  On the way to kindergarten
  Uno, dos, tres, posada!
Kumin, Maxine. *Oh, Harry!*
Kurtz, Jane. *Rain romp*
Kurtz, Kevin. *A day in the salt marsh*
Kuskin, Karla. *A boy had a mother who bought him a hat*
  Green as a bean
  So, what's it like to be a cat?
  Under my hood I have a hat
Kutner, Merrily. *Z is for zombie*
  The Zombie Nite Cafe
Kyle, Tracey. *Gazpacho for Nacho*
Laden, Nina. *Clowns on vacation*
  Peek-a-who?
  Peek-a-choo-choo!
Lamba, Marie. *Green green*
Lang, Suzanne. *Families, families, families!*
LaRochelle, David. *Monster and son*
Larsen, Mylisa. *If I were a kangaroo*
Lass, Bonnie. *Who took the cookies from the cookie jar?*
Latifah, Queen. *Queen of the scene*
Lawler, Janet. *A father's song*
  Love is real
  A mother's song
  Snowzilla
  Tyrannoclaus
Lawrence, Jennifer B. *Sad doggy*
Lawrence, John. *This little chick*
Lawson, JonArno. *Leap!*

Quentin Fenton Herter three
Rachel Fister's blister
McDonald, Megan. *It's picture day today!*
McDonald, Rae A. *A fishing surprise*
MacDonald, Suse. *Elephants on board*
McDonnell, Patrick. *Art*
McEvoy, Anne. *Betsy B. Little*
McGee, Marni. *Sleepy me*
    Wake up, me!
McGinley, Phyllis. *The year without a Santa Claus*
McGinty, Alice B. *Ten little lambs*
    Thank you, world
McGough, Roger. *What on earth can it be?*
McGrath, Barbara Barbieri. *Kellogg's froot loops*
    color fun book
    Kellogg's froot loops counting fun book
    Teddy bear addition
    Teddy bear counting
McHenry, E. B. *Poodlena*
Mack, Jeff. *Hush little polar bear*
    The things I can do
Mackall, Dandi Daley. *Off to Bethlehem!*
McKelvey, Douglas Kaine. *Locust pocus*
Macken, JoAnn Early. *Baby says "moo!"*
    Waiting out the storm
McKissack, Patricia C. *Messy Bessey and the birthday*
    overnight
    Messy Bessey's closet
    Messy Bessey's holidays
MacLachlan, Patricia. *The moon's almost here*
McLaren, Chesley. *Zat cat!*
McLaughlin, Lauren. *Wonderful you*
McLean, Janet. *Let's go, baby-o!*
MacLennan, Cathy. *Chicky Chicky Chook Chook*
McMillan, Bruce. *Puffins climb, penguins rhyme*
McMullan, Kate. *Mama's kisses*
    Rock-a-baby band
McNaughton, Colin. *Not last night but the night*
    before
    We're off to look for aliens
    When I grow up
Maconie, Robin. *Alice and her fabulous teeth*
McPhail, David. *Pigs ahoy*
    Pigs aplenty, pigs galore!
    Those can-do pigs
McPike, Elizabeth. *Little bitty friends*
    Little sleepyhead
McReynolds, Linda. *Eight days gone*
Magliaro, Elaine. *Things to do*
Maguire, Gregory. *Crabby Cratchitt*
Mahy, Margaret. *Bubble trouble*
    The Christmas tree tangle
    Down the back of the chair
    The man from the land of Fandango
    17 kings and 42 elephants
    A summery Saturday morning
Mallat, Kathy. *Papa pride*
Maloney, Peter. *Belly button boy*
Mandel, Peter. *Jackhammer Sam*
    Say hey
Manning, Maurie J. *The aunts go marching*
Manushkin, Fran. *Bamboo for me, bamboo for you!*
    Happy in our skin
Many, Paul. *The great pancake escape*
Marciano, John Bemelmans. *Madeline and the cats*
    of Rome
    Madeline and the old house in Paris
    Madeline says merci
Marcus, Kimberly. *Scritch-scratch a perfect match*

Margalith, Joan. *The babies are landing*
Mariconda, Barbara. *Sort it out!*
Markell, Denis. *Hush, Little Monster*
Markes, Julie. *Shhhhh! Everybody's sleeping*
    Thanks for Thanksgiving
Marshak, S. *The Month-Brothers*
Marshall, Linda Elovitz. *Kindergarten is cool!*
Marshall, Natalie. *Five little ducks: a fingers and toes*
    nursery rhyme book
Martin, Bill, Jr.. *Adam, Adam, what do you see?*
    Baby bear, baby bear, what do you see?
    Barn dance!
    Brown bear, brown bear, what do you see?
    Chicka chicka boom boom
    Here are my hands
    Kitty Cat, Kitty Cat, are you going to school?
    Kitty Cat, Kitty Cat, are you going to sleep?
    Kitty Cat, Kitty Cat, are you waking up?
    Listen to the rain
    Little granny quarterback
    Maestro plays
    The magic pumpkin
    Polar bear, polar bear, what do you hear?
    Spunky Little Monkey
    Ten little caterpillars
    The turning of the year
Martin, David. *Hanukkah lights*
    Let's have a tree party!
    Peep and Ducky
    Peep and Ducky: rainy day
    Shh! bears sleeping
    We've all got bellybuttons
Martin, Emily Winfield. *Day dreamers*
    Dream animals
    The wonderful things you will be
Marzollo, Jean. *Do you know new?*
    I spy
    I spy Christmas
    I spy extreme challenger!
    I spy fantasy
    I spy gold challenger!
    I spy little animals
    I spy little book
    I spy little bunnies
    I spy little Christmas
    I spy little letters
    I spy little numbers
    I spy little wheels
    I spy, mystery
    I spy school days
    I spy spooky night
    I spy super challenger!
    I spy treasure hunt
    I spy ultimate challenger!
    I spy, year-round challenger!
    Mama, Mama
    Papa, Papa
    Pierre the penguin
    Pretend you're a cat
    Sun song
    Ten cats have hats
    Thanksgiving cats
    Valentine cats
Massini, Sarah. *Love always everywhere*
Matheson, Christie. *Plant the tiny seed*
    Tap the magic tree
Mathews, Judith. *Nathaniel Willy, scared silly*
May, Robert L. *Rudolph shines again*
    Rudolph the red-nosed reindeer

Mayer, Lynne. *Newton and me*
Maynard, Bill. *Santa's time off*
Mayo, Margaret. *Dig dig digging*
 Emergency!
 Stomp, dinosaur, stomp!
 Wiggle waggle fun
Mazer, Norma Fox. *Has anyone seen my Emily Greene?*
Mazzola, Frank. *Counting is for the birds*
Meade, Holly. *If I never forever endeavor*
 A place to sleep
Meadows, Michelle. *Hibernation station*
 Itsy-bitsy baby mouse
 Piggies in pajamas
 Piggies in the kitchen
 Pilot pups
 Super bugs
Medearis, Angela Shelf. *Dancing with the Indians*
 The ghost of Sifty-Sifty Sam
 Rum-a-tum-tum
Meister, Cari. *Busy, busy city street*
Melmed, Laura Krauss. *Capital! Washington D.C. from A to Z*
 Eight winter nights
 Fright night flight
 A hug goes around
 I love you as much . . .
 Jumbo's lullaby
Meltzer, Lynn. *The construction crew*
Melvin, Alice. *Counting birds*
Merberg, Julie. *In the garden with Van Gogh*
 A magical day with Matisse
Merriam, Eve. *Low song*
 Where's that cat?
Merski, P. K. *Roaring, boring, Alice*
Merz, Jennifer J. *Playground day*
Messner, Kate. *Rolling Thunder*
Metzger, Steve. *This is the house that monsters built*
Meyers, Susan. *Bear in the air*
 Everywhere babies
 Kittens! kittens! kittens!
 Puppies! puppies! puppies!
 Rock-a-bye room
 This is the way a baby rides
Michelson, Richard. *Oh no, not ghosts!*
 Ten times better
Micklos, John. *One leaf, two leaves, count with me!*
Milgrim, David. *Cows can't fly*
 Here in space
 How you got so smart
 Why Benny barks
Millard, Glenda. *And red galoshes*
 Isabella's garden
Millen, C. M. *Blue bowl down*
Miller, J. Philip. *We all sing with the same voice*
Miller, Pat. *We're going on a book hunt*
Miller, Pat Zietlow. *Sharing the bread*
 Wherever you go
Miller, Ruth. *The bear on the bed*
 I went to the farm
Milord, Susan. *If I could*
Milusich, Janice. *Off go their engines, off go their lights*
Minor, Florence. *If you were a penguin*
Minor, Wendell. *Christmas tree!*
 My farm friends
Minters, Frances. *Cinder-Elly*
 Princess Fishtail
 Sleepless Beauty

 Too big, too small, just right
Miranda, Anne. *Beep! beep!*
 Monster math
Mitter, Matt. *ABC: alphabet rhymes*
 Once upon a rhyme
 1, 2, 3, counting rhymes
Mitton, Tony. *All afloat on Noah's boat!*
 Cool cars
 Dinosaurumpus
 Down by the cool of the pool
 Farmer Joe and the music show
 Flashing fire engines
 The Jungle Run
 Playful little penguins
 Snowy Bear
 A very curious bear
Mizzoni, Chris. *Clancy with the puck*
Modarressi, Mitra. *Owlet's first flight*
 Stay awake, Sally
Modesitt, Jeanne. *Oh, what a beautiful day!*
Moffatt, Judith. *The pumpkin man*
 Trick-or-treat faces
Molk, Laurel. *Eeny, Meeny, Miney, Mo and Flo!*
Monks, Lydia. *The cat barked?*
Monroe, Chris. *Bug on a bike*
Montes, Marisa. *Egg-napped!*
 Los gatos black on Halloween
Moore, Elaine. *Roly-poly puppies*
Moore, Raina. *How do you say good night?*
Moore, Suzi. *Whoops!*
Mora, Pat. *Marimba!*
 One, two, three / Uno, dos, tres
Morales, Melita. *Jam and honey*
Moreillon, Judi. *Ready and waiting for you*
Morgan, Mary. *My good night book*
Morgan, Michaela. *Brave, brave mouse*
Morris, Ann. *Shoes, shoes, shoes*
Morrison, Cathy. *I want a pet!*
Morrison, Toni. *Peeny butter fudge*
 Please, Louise
Morrow, Barbara Olenyik. *Mr. Mosquito put on his tuxedo*
Morrow, Tara Jaye. *Mommy loves her baby; Daddy loves his baby*
Mortensen, Denise Dowling. *Bug Patrol*
 Wake up engines
Mortensen, Lori. *Cindy Moo*
 Cowpoke Clyde rides the range
 Mousequerade ball
Morton-Shaw, Christine. *Wake up, sleepy bear!*
Mosca, Julia Finley. *The girl who thought in pictures*
Moss, Lloyd. *Our marching band*
 Zin! zin! zin! A violin
Moss, Miriam. *Bare bear*
Mother Goose. *Hickory, dickory, dock*
 Humpty Dumpty
 1, 2, buckle my shoe
 Pat-a-cake
Moulton, Mark Kimball. *Reindeer Christmas*
Muecke, Anne. *The dinosaurs' night before Christmas*
Muir, Leslie. *The little bitty bakery*
Munro, Roxie. *Circus*
Murguia, Bethanie Deeney. *Toucans, too*
Murphy, Mary. *Good night like this*
Murphy, Stuart J. *Animals on board*
 The best vacation ever
 Circus shapes
 Elevator magic
 Every buddy counts

Get up and go!
Rabbit's pajama party
Same old horse
Murray, Alison. *Hickory dickory dog*
The house that Zack built
One two that's my shoe!
Murray, Diana. *City shapes*
Ned the knitting pirate
Murray, Marjorie Dennis. *Halloween night*
Myers, Tim. *Looking for Luna*
Naberhaus, Sarvinder. *Boom boom*
Neitzel, Shirley. *The bag I'm taking to Grandma's*
The dress I'll wear to the party
The house I'll build for the wrens
I'm not feeling well today
I'm taking a trip on my train
The jacket I wear in the snow
We're making breakfast for mother
Who will I be?
Neubecker, Robert. *Beasty bath*
Fall is for school
What little boys are made of
Winter is for snow
Nevius, Carol. *Baseball hour*
Building with Dad
Karate hour
Soccer hour
Newbery, Linda. *Posy*
Newcome, Zita. *Pop-up toddlerobics*
Newman, Lesléa. *Cats, cats, cats*
Daddy's song
Dogs, dogs, dogs
Just like Mama
Pigs, pigs, pigs
Runaway dreidel
Skunk's spring surprise
Nichol, Barbara. *Trunks all aboard*
Niemann, Christoph. *Subway*
Nikola-Lisa, W. *Shake dem Halloween bones*
Summer sun risin'
To hear the angels sing
Nogales, Jill. *Zebra on the go*
Noonan, Julia. *Bath day*
Breakfast time
Mouse by mouse
Norman, Kim. *I know a wee piggy*
If it's snowy and you know it, clap your paws!
Still a gorilla!
Ten on the sled
North, Sherry. *Because I am your daddy*
Because you are my baby
Northey, Lawrence. *I'm a hop hop hoppity frog*
Novak, Matt. *Flip flop bop*
The Pillow War
A wish for you
Numeroff, Laura Joffe. *Chimps don't wear glasses*
When sheep sleep
O'Brien, Anne Sibley. *Abracadabra, it's spring!*
Hocus pocus, it's fall!
Ochiltree, Dianne. *It's a firefly night*
Pillow pup
O'Connor, Jane. *Ready, set, skip!*
Odanaka, Barbara. *A crazy day at the Critter Café*
Smash! mash! crash! there goes the trash!
Odgers, Sally. *Good night, Truck*
Oelschlager, Vanita. *Made in China*
O'Hair, Margaret. *My kitten*
My pup
Star baby

Sweet baby feet
Ohi, Ruth. *Me and my brother*
Me and my sister
O'Keefe, Susan Heyboer. *Baby day*
Good night, God bless
Hungry monster ABC
Love me, love you
Old MacDonald had a farm. *Old MacDonald's things that go*
Olson, David J. *The thunderstruck stork*
Olson-Brown, Ellen. *Ooh la la polka-dot boots*
One, two, skip a few!
Oppenheim, Joanne. *Have you seen bugs?*
Ormerod, Jan. *If you're happy and you know it!*
Ms. MacDonald has a class
Orozco, Jose-Luis. *Pancho Claus*
Over in the meadow
Owen, Karen. *I could be, you could be*
Owens, Mary Beth. *Panda whispers*
Oxenbury, Helen. *Pig tale*
Pacilio, V. J. *Ling Cho and his three friends*
Palatini, Margie. *No nap! yes nap!*
Pallotta, Jerry. *A giraffe did one*
Pamintuan, Macky. *Twelve haunted rooms of Halloween*
Paquette, Ammi-Joan. *Bunny Bus*
Ghost in the house
Parenteau, Shirley. *Bears and a birthday*
Bears in beds
Bears in the bath
Bears in the snow
Bears on chairs
Park, Linda Sue. *Bee-bim bop!*
What does Bunny see?
Xander's panda party
Parker, Marjorie Blain. *Your kind of mommy*
Parker, Victoria. *Bearum scarum*
Partridge, Elizabeth. *Big Cat Pepper*
Moon glowing
Patrick, Jean L. S. *If I had a snowplow*
Patten, Brian. *The big snuggle-up*
Paul, Ann Whitford. *Everything to spend the night . . . from A to Z*
If animals kissed goodnight
If animals said I love you
Paul, Ellis. *The night the lights went out on Christmas*
Paul, Miranda. *10 little ninjas*
Whose hands are these?
Paulsen, Gary. *Worksong*
Pearce, Clemency. *Frangoline and the midnight dream*
Three little words
Pearson, Debora. *Big city song*
Pearson, Susan. *Hooray for feet!*
Pearson, Tracey Campbell. *Where does Joe go?*
Peck, Jan. *Way up high in a tall green tree*
Peddicord, Jane Ann. *That special little baby*
Peet, Bill. *Ella*
Hubert's hair-raising adventures
Huge Harold
Kermit the hermit
The kweeks of Kookatumdee
The luckiest one of all
No such things
The pinkish, purplish, bluish egg
Randy's dandy lions
Smokey
Zella, Zack, and Zodiac
Pelham, David. *Sam's pizza*

Sam's sandwich
Pendziwol, Jean E. *No dragons for tea*
  The tale of Sir Dragon
  A treasure at sea for dragon and me
Penn, Audrey. *A bedtime kiss for Chester Raccoon*
Perl, Erica S. *Ferocious Fluffity*
  Ninety-three in my family
Perlman, Willa. *Good night, world*
Perrin, Martine. *Cock-a-doodle who?*
Perry, Andrea. *The Bicklebys' birdbath*
Perry, Robert. *Down at the Seaweed Café*
Peters, Lisa Westberg. *October smiled back*
  Sleepyhead bear
Pfister, Marcus. *Questions, questions*
Phillips, Christopher. *Ceci Ann's day of why*
Pickering, Jimmy. *It's fall*
Pierce, Christa. *Did you know that I love you?*
Pilkey, Dav. *The Moonglow Roll-O-Rama*
  'Twas the night before Thanksgiving
Pinczes, Elinor J. *Inchworm and a half*
  My full moon is square
  A remainder of one
Pinder, Eric. *If all the animals came inside*
Pinfold, Levi. *Greenling*
Pitman, Gayle E. *This day in June*
Piven, Hanoch. *The perfect purple feather*
Plourde, Lynn. *Dino pets*
  Dino pets go to school
  Grandpappy snippy snappies
  Spring's sprung
  Wild child
  Winter waits
Pollard, Nik. *The river*
Pomerantz, Charlotte. *Flap your wings and try*
  Here comes Henny
  The mousery
  The piggy in the puddle
Porter, Pamela. *Yellow moon, apple moon*
Posada, Mia. *Ladybugs*
  Robins
  Who was here?
Postgate, Daniel. *Smelly Bill*
  Smelly Bill: love stinks
Poydar, Nancy. *Rhyme time Valentine*
Prap, Lila. *Animal lullabies*
  Daddies
Prasadam-Halls, Smriti. *I love you night and day*
  T. Veg
Prelutsky, Jack. *The mean old mean hyena*
  The terrible tiger
  Wild witches' ball
  The wizard
Preston-Gannon, Frann. *What a hoot!*
Previn, Stacey. *Find spot!*
Price, Ben Joel. *Earth space moon base*
Price, Hope Lynne. *These hands*
Prince, April Jones. *What do wheels do all day?*
Prince, Joshua. *I saw an ant in a parking lot*
  I saw an ant on the railroad track
Prochovnic, Dawn Babb. *The big blue bowl*
  Hip hip hooray! It's Family Day!
Protopopescu, Orel. *Two sticks*
Pumphrey, Jerome. *Creepy things are scaring me*
Pym, Tasha. *Have you ever seen a sneep?*
Quattlebaum, Mary. *Jo MacDonald hiked in the woods*
Raczka, Bob. *Art is . . .*
  Fall mixed up
  Joy in Mudville

Snowy, blowy winter
Spring things
Summer wonders
Who loves the fall?
Rader, Laura. *Tea for me, tea for you*
Radzinski, Kandy. *Where to sleep*
Randall, Ronne. *The Hanukkah mice*
Ransom, Candice F. *Tractor day*
Rau, Dana Meachen. *Chilly Charlie*
  Clown around
  I'll make you a card
  Rubber duck
  Shoo crow, shoo!
Rauss, Ron. *Can I just take a nap?*
Ray, Karen. *Sleep song*
Ray, Mary Lyn. *Go to sleep, little farm*
Reasoner, Charles. *Peek-a-boo monsters*
Redding, Sue. *Up above and down below*
Redmond, E. S. *The Unruly Queen*
Reeves, Howard W. *There was an old witch*
Regan, Dana. *Monkey see, monkey do*
Reid, Barbara. *The party*
Reidy, Jean. *All through my town*
  Busy builders, busy week!
  Light up the night
  Too pickley!
  Too purpley!
Reiser, Lynn. *My baby and me*
Reiss, Mike. *The boy who wouldn't share*
  How Murray saved Christmas
  Late for school
  Santa claustrophobia
Reitman, Andrea. *Mouse in the house*
Rex, Adam. *Nothing rhymes with orange*
Rex, Michael. *Dunk skunk*
  Goodnight goon
Rey, H. A. *Elizabite*
Reynolds, Aaron. *Snowbots*
Reynolds, Luke. *If my love were a fire truck*
Richardson, Bill. *The alphabet thief*
  But if they do
Rickards, Lynne. *Jacob O'Reilly wants a pet*
Riehle, Mary Ann McCabe. *The little kids' table*
Rinker, Sherri Duskey. *Goodnight, goodnight, construction site*
  Mighty, mighty construction site
  Steam train, dream train
  The twelve sleighs of Christmas
Ritchie, Alison. *Me and my dad!*
  Me and my mom!
Rives. *If I were a polar bear*
Robbins, Ruth. *Baboushka and the three kings*
Roberts, Bethany. *Birthday mice*
  Christmas mice
  Easter mice
  Fourth of July mice
  Valentine mice!
Roberts, Justin. *The smallest girl in the smallest grade*
Robertson, Patrisha Grainger. *Cirque du Soleil*
Robinson, Michelle. *And the robot went . . .*
  The forgetful knight
Robinson, Tim. *Tobias, the quig, and the rumplenut tree*
Rock, Lois. *God bless me, God bless you*
  I wish tonight

I wonder why?
Roemer, Heidi Bee. *What kind of seeds are these?*
Rogers, Paul. *Ruby's dinnertime*
    Ruby's potty
    What will the weather be like today?
Rollings, Susan. *New shoes, red shoes*
Roode, Daniel. *Little Bea and the snowy day*
Roosa, Karen. *Beach day*
    Pippa at the parade
Root, Phyllis. *Anywhere farm*
    Creak! said the bed
    Flip, flap, fly!
    One duck stuck
    Rattletrap car
    Ten sleepy sheep
Roscoe, Lily. *The night parade*
Rose, Deborah Lee. *All the seasons of the year*
    Birthday zoo
    Someone's sleepy
    The spelling bee before recess
Rosen, Michael. *The bus is for us!*
Rosen, Michael J. *Avalanche*
Rosenbaum, Andria Warmflash. *Trains don't sleep*
Rosenberg, Liz. *Eli's night-light*
Rosenfeld, Dina Herman. *How in the world does*
    bread come from the earth?
Rosenthal, Amy Krouse. *It's not fair!*
    Little Miss, big sis
Rosenthal, Betsy R. *An ambush of tigers*
    Which shoes would you choose?
Ross, Michael Elsohn. *Mama's milk*
    Play with me
Rossetti-Shustak, Bernadette. *I love you through and*
    through
Roth, Carol. *All aboard to work — choo-choo!*
    The little school bus
    Will you still love me?
Roth, Ruby. *V is for vegan*
Roth, Susan L. *Night-time numbers*
Rothstein, Gloria. *Sheep asleep*
Rotner, Shelley. *Citybook*
    Parts
Rubin, C. M. *Eleanor, Ellatony, Ellencake, and me*
Rubinger, Ami. *Dog number 1 dog number 10*
    I dream of an elephant
Ryan, Candace. *Zoo zoom!*
Ryan, Pam Muñoz. *Armadillos sleep in dugouts*
    The crayon counting book
    Hello, Ocean!
    Hello Ocean / Hola mar
    Mud is cake
    There was no snow on Christmas Eve
Ryder, Joanne. *Bear of my heart*
    Big bear ball
    Chipmunk song
    Dance by the light of the moon
    Each living thing
    A fawn in the grass
    Won't you be my hugaroo?
Rylant, Cynthia. *All in a day*
    Alligator boy
    Bear day
    Bless us all
    Bunny bungalow
    Give me grace
    If you'll be my Valentine
    Puppies and piggies
    The stars will still shine
Sabuda, Robert. *Winter in white*

Sadler, Marilyn. *Tony Baroni loves macaroni*
Sage, Angie. *Monkeys in the jungle*
Salas, Laura Purdie. *A leaf can be . . .*
    Water can be . . .
Saltzberg, Barney. *All around the seasons*
    Hug this book!
    I love cats
    I love dogs
    Kisses
    Tea with Grandpa
Salzano, Tammi. *I love you just the way you are*
Sandall, Ellie. *Everybunny dance!*
    Follow me!
Sanders, Rob. *Outer space bedtime race*
Sanderson, Ruth. *A castle full of cats*
Sanfield, Steve. *Snow*
Sanger, Amy Wilson. *First book of sushi*
San Souci, Robert D. *Cinderella Skeleton*
    The Hobyahs
Santoro, Scott. *Which way to witch school?*
Sartell, Debra. *Time for bed, Baby Ted*
Sassi, Laura. *Goodnight, Ark*
Saul, Carol P. *Barn cat*
Sava, Donna Lynn. *Teddy bear dreams*
Savage, Stephen. *Ten orange pumpkins*
Sayles, Elizabeth. *The goldfish yawned*
Sayre, April Pulley. *Full of fall*
    Go, go, grapes!
    Hush, little puppy
    If you're hoppy
    It's my city
    Let's go nuts! seeds we eat
    Rah, rah, radishes!
    Squirrels leap, squirrels sleep
    Trout, trout, trout
    Vulture view
    Woodpecker wham!
Sayres, Brianna Caplan. *Tiara Saurus Rex*
    Where do diggers sleep at night?
Scanlon, Elizabeth Garton. *Happy birthday, Bunny!*
    A sock is a pocket for your toes
    Think big!
Schaefer, Lola M. *An island grows*
    Loose tooth
    This is the sunflower
    Toolbox twins
Schafer, Milton. *That crazy Barb'ra*
Scheffler, Axel. *Axel Scheffler's Flip flap safari*
Schertle, Alice. *Little Blue Truck*
    Little Blue Truck leads the way
    The skeleton in the closet
Schindel, John. *Busy penguins*
Schneider, Christine M. *Picky Mrs. Pickle*
    Saxophone Sam and his snazzy jazz band
Schneider, Josh. *Everybody sleeps (but not Fred)*
Schnitzlein, Danny. *The monster who ate my peas*
Schnur, Steven. *Night lights*
Schoenherr, Ian. *Cat and mouse*
    Don't spill the beans!
    Read it, don't eat it!
Schotter, Roni. *All about grandmas*
    Doo-Wop Pop
    When the Wizzy Foot goes walking
Schroeder, Lisa. *Baby can't sleep*
Schubert, Leda. *Feeding the sheep*
Schulman, Janet. *Ten Easter egg hunters*
    10 trick-or-treaters
    10 Valentine friends
Schumaker, Ward. *Dance!*

Schwartz, Amy. *Lucy can't sleep*
  100 things I love to do with you
  One hundred things that make me happy
Schwartz, Corey Rosen. *Hensel and Gretel*
  Ninja Red Riding Hood
  The three ninja pigs
Scillian, Devin. *Brewster the rooster*
The scrubbly-bubbly car wash
Scruggs, Afi. *Jump rope magic*
Seeber, Dorothea P. *A pup just for me . . . A boy just*
  for me
Seibold, J. Otto. *Penguin dreams*
Sendak, Maurice. *Bumble-ardy*
  Pierre
  Seven little monsters
Sendelbach, Brian. *The underpants zoo*
Sensel, Joni. *Bears barge in*
Serfozo, Mary. *There's a square*
  Who wants one?
  Whooo's there?
Seuling, Barbara. *Spring song*
Seuss, Dr. *And to think that I saw it on Mulberry Street*
  The butter battle book
  Did I ever tell you how lucky you are?
  Gerald McBoing Boing
  Gerald McBoing Boing sound book
  Happy birthday to you!
  Horton and the Kwuggerbug and more lost stories
  Horton hatches the egg
  Horton hears a Who!
  How the Grinch stole Christmas
  Hunches in bunches
  I can lick 30 tigers today and other stories
  I had trouble getting to Solla Sollew
  If I ran the circus
  If I ran the zoo
  The king's stilts
  McElligot's pool
  On beyond zebra
  Scrambled eggs super!
  The Sneetches, and other stories
  Thidwick, the big-hearted moose
  What pet should I get?
Seven spunky monkeys
Shahan, Sherry. *The jazzy alphabet*
Shannon, George. *Hands say love*
  Who put the cookies in the cookie jar?
Shannon, Terry Miller. *Tub toys*
Sharratt, Nick. *The foggy, foggy forest*
  Shark in the park
  What's in the witch's kitchen?
Shaskan, Stephen. *A dog is a dog*
Shaw, Nancy. *Raccoon tune*
  Sheep blast off!
  Sheep in a jeep
  Sheep in a shop
  Sheep on a ship
  Sheep out to eat
  Sheep take a hike
  Sheep trick or treat
Shaw, Stephanie. *A cookie for Santa*
Shea, Bob. *Race you to bed*
Shea, Pegi Deitz. *I see me!*
Shea, Susan A. *Do you know which one will grow?*
Sheehan, Monica. *Love is you and me*
Shields, Carol Diggory. *Baby's got the blues*
  Day by day a week goes round
  Martian rock
  Month by month a year goes round

Saturday night at the dinosaur stomp
Wombat walkabout
Shields, Gillian. *When the world was waiting for you*
Shindler, Ramon. *Found alphabet*
Shore, Diane Z. *Look both ways*
  This is the dream
Shoulders, Michael. *D is for dump truck*
Shulevitz, Uri. *Rain rain rivers*
Shulman, Lisa. *Over in the meadow at the big ballet*
Shulman, Mark. *Gorilla Garage*
Shute, Linda. *Halloween party*
Shuttlewood, Craig. *Who's in the tree?*
Siddals, Mary McKenna. *Bringing the outside in*
  Compost stew
  Millions of snowflakes
  Shivery shades of Halloween
  Tell me a season
Sidman, Joyce. *Before morning*
Siebert, Diane. *Cave*
  Plane song
  Train song
  Truck song
Sierra, Judy. *Ballyhoo Bay*
  Born to read
  E-I-E-I-O
  The house that Drac built
  Make way for readers
  The secret science project that almost ate school
  Sleepy little alphabet
  Suppose you meet a dinosaur
  Thelonius Monster's sky-high fly pie
  There's a zoo in room 22
  'Twas the fright before Christmas
  We love our school!
  Wild about books
  Wild about you!
  Zoozical
Silvano, Wendi. *What does the wind say?*
Silverman, Erica. *Follow the leader*
  The Halloween house
  The Hanukkah hop!
  There was a wee woman . . .
  Wake up, city!
Silverstein, Shel. *A giraffe and a half*
  The giving tree
Simmons, Jane. *Daisy's favorite things*
Simon, Francesca. *Calling all toddlers*
Singer, Marilyn. *Boo hoo boo-boo*
  The boy who cried alien
  City lullaby
  Fred's bed
  I'm gonna climb a mountain in my patent leather
    shoes
  I'm your bus
  Let's build a clubhouse
  Shoe bop!
  Solomon sneezes
  What is your dog doing?
Singh, Rina. *My first book of Hindi words*
Siomades, Lorianne. *Cuckoo can't find you*
  Kangaroo and cricket
  A place to bloom
Sirotich, Erica. *Found dogs*
Siy, Alexandra. *One tractor*
Skalak, Barbara Anne. *Waddle, waddle, quack,*
  quack, quack
Slack, Michael. *Elecopter*
  Monkey Truck
  Turtle Tug to the rescue

Slate, Joseph. *The great big wagon that rang*
  I want to be free
  Miss Bindergarten celebrates the last day of
    kindergarten
  Miss Bindergarten celebrates the 100th day of
    kindergarten
  Miss Bindergarten has a wild day in kindergarten
  Miss Bindergarten stays home from kindergarten
  Miss Bindergarten takes a field trip with
    kindergarten
  What star is this?
  Who is coming to our house?
Slater, Dashka. *Baby shoes*
Slater, Teddy. *Smooch your pooch*
Slayton, Fran Cannon. *Snowball moon*
Sloat, Teri. *Farmer Brown goes round and round*
  Farmer Brown shears his sheep
  Patty's pumpkin patch
  Pieces of Christmas
  There was an old lady who swallowed a trout
  The thing that bothered Farmer Brown
  This is the house that was tidy and neat
  Zip! zoom! on a broom
Slonim, David. *I loathe you*
Small, David. *George Washington's cows*
Smallman, Steve. *Dragon stew*
  Hiccupotamus
  My dad!
Smalls, Irene. *My Pop Pop and me*
Smalls-Hector, Irene. *Kevin and his dad*
Smee, Nicola. *What's the matter, Bunny Blue?*
Smith, Charles R. *Dance with me*
  I am the world
Smith, Danna. *Pirate nap*
  Swallow the leader
Smith, Jada Pinkett. *Girls hold up this world*
Smith, Linda. *Mrs. Biddlebox*
  When Moon fell down
Smith, Maggie. *One naked baby*
  Pigs in pajamas
Smith, Mavis. *'Twas the day after Thanksgiving*
Smith, Shoham. *An after bedtime story*
Smith, Stu. *The bubble gum kid*
Snell, Gordon. *'Twas the day after Christmas*
Snyder, Betsy E. *Sweet dreams lullaby*
Snyder, Laurel. *Good night, laila tov*
Sobel, June. *The goodnight train*
  Shiver me letters
Souders, Taryn. *Whole-y cow!*
Soule, Jean Conder. *Never tease a weasel*
Southwell, Jandelyn. *The little country town*
Speed, Toby. *Two cool cows*
Spence, Robert, III.. *Clickety clack*
Sperring, Mark. *The fairytale cake*
  The shape of my heart
Spier, Peter. *Noah's ark*
Spinelli, Eileen. *City angel*
  Do you have a cat?
  Do you have a dog?
  Here comes the year
  Hug a bug
  I know it's autumn
  The perfect Christmas
  Rise the moon
  A safe place called home
  Silly Tilly
  Thankful
  Together at Christmas
  What do angels wear?

  When Mama comes home tonight
  When no one is watching
  When Papa comes home tonight
Spinelli, Jerry. *I can be anything!*
Spink, Matt. *Some birds*
Spohn, Kate. *Snow play*
  The wet dry book
Spurr, Elizabeth. *In the garden*
  Two bears beneath the stairs
Staake, Bob. *Beachy and me*
  The donut chef
  Look! a book!
  Look! another book!
  My pet book
Stainton, Sue. *I love dogs!*
Stanton, Andy. *Danny McGee drinks the sea*
Steggall, Susan. *The diggers are coming!*
Stein, Mathilde. *Monstersong*
Stein, Peter. *Bugs galore*
  Cars galore
  Trucks galore
Stern, Ellen. *I saw a bullfrog*
Stewart, Sarah. *The library*
Stickland, Paul. *Bears*
  Dinosaur roar!
  Dinosaur stomp!
  Ten terrible dinosaurs
Stiegemeyer, Julie. *Gobble gobble crash!*
  Seven little bunnies
Sting [Musician]. *Rock steady*
Stockdale, Susan. *Bring on the birds*
  Fabulous Fishes
  Spectacular spots
Stoeke, Janet Morgan. *The bus stop*
  It's library day
Stohs, Anita. *An Easter alleluia*
Stone, Tanya Lee. *D is for dreidel*
Sturges, Philemon. *How do you make a baby smile?*
  I love bugs
  I love school
  I love tools!
  I love trains
  I love trucks!
  Ten flashing fireflies
  This little pirate
  Waggers
Sturgis, Brenda Reeves. *Ten turkeys in the road*
Stutson, Caroline. *By the light of the Halloween moon*
  Cats' night out
  Cowpokes
  Night train
  Prairie primer A to Z
Suen, Anastasia. *Baby born*
  Delivery
  Raise the roof
  Red light, green light
  Road work ahead
  Subway
  Window music
Surplice, Holly. *Guinea pig party*
  Peek-a-boo Bunny
Swaim, Jessica. *The hound from the pound*
Sweeney, Linda Booth. *When the snow falls*
  When the wind blows
Swenson, Jamie A. *Boom! boom! boom!*
Szekeres, Cyndy. *Toby's please and thank you*
Taback, Simms. *I miss you every day*
Tafolla, Carmen. *Fiesta babies*
Tafuri, Nancy. *Snowy flowy blowy*

Somewhere in the ocean
Way up in the Arctic
Ward, Lindsay. *The importance of being 3*
Wardlaw, Lee. *The chair where bear sits*
Red, white, and boom!
Wargin, Kathy-jo. *Scare a bear*
Warnes, Tim. *Daddy hug*
Watson, Clyde. *Applebet*
Wax, Wendy. *A very mice Christmas*
Weatherford, Carole Boston. *Jazz baby*
Sugar Hill
Weeks, Sarah. *Be mine, be mine, sweet valentine*
Bite me, I'm a book
Bite me, I'm a shape
Bunny fun
I'm a pig
Mrs. McNosh and the great big squash
My somebody special
Oh my gosh, Mrs. McNosh!
Overboard!
Woof
Weigel, Jeff. *Atomic Ace (he's just my dad)*
Weingarten, Gene. *Me and dog*
Weinstone, David. *Music class today!*
Weiss, Nicki. *The world turns round and round*
Welch, Willy. *Dancing with Daddy*
Grumpy Bunnies
Wells, Rosemary. *Clean-up time*
First tomato
Hand in hand
Love waves
Moss pillows
My kindergarten
Noisy Nora
Read to your bunny
Red boots
Shy Charles
Weninger, Brigitte. *The elf's hat*
Wensink, Patrick. *Go go gorillas*
Westcott, Nadine Bernard. *Peanut butter and jelly*
Wheeler, Lisa. *Babies can sleep anywhere*
Boogie knights
Castaway cats
Dino-baseball
Dino-basketball
Dino-boarding
Dino-football
Dino-hockey
Dino-racing
Dino-soccer
Dino-swimming
Dino-wrestling
Even monsters need to sleep
Jazz baby
Mammoths on the move
The pet project
Sixteen cows
Whelan, Gloria. *Queen Victoria's bathing machine*
White, Alexina B. *Frisky brisky hippity hop*
White, Becky. *Betsy Ross*
White, Dianne. *Blue on blue*
White, Kathryn. *Ruby's school walk*
Whitman, Candace. *Lines that wiggle*
Whybrow, Ian. *Faraway farm*
Wick, Walter. *Can you see what I see? Christmas*
Can you see what I see? cool collections
Can you see what I see? dream machine
Can you see what I see? once upon a time
Can you see what I see? out of this world

Can you see what I see? picture puzzles to search and
solve
Can you see what I see? Seymour and the juice box
boat
Can you see what I see? Seymour makes new friends
Can you see what I see? treasure ship
Hey, Seymour!
Wickberg, Susan. *Hey Mr. Choo-Choo, where are you
going?*
Wilcox, Leah. *Waking Beauty*
Wild, Margaret. *Itsy-bitsy babies*
Willard, Nancy. *The mouse, the cat and
Grandmother's hat*
Willems, Mo. *Nanette's baguette*
Willey, Margaret. *Thanksgiving with me*
Williams, Brenda. *Home for a tiger, home for a bear*
Williams, Linda. *Horse in the pigpen*
Williams, Rozanne Lanczak. *The coin counting book*
Williams, Sam. *That's love*
Williams, Sue. *Dinnertime*
I went walking
Let's go visiting
Williams, Suzanne. *Old MacDonald in the city*
Ten naughty little monkeys
Willis, Jeanne. *Do little mermaids wet their beds*
Hippospotamus
I'm sure I saw a dinosaur
Slug needs a hug!
Susan laughs
Troll stinks
Wilner, Isabel. *A garden alphabet*
Wilson, Karma. *Animal strike at the zoo, it's true!*
Bear counts
Bear says thanks
Bear sees colors
Bear stays up for Christmas
Bear's loose tooth
Big bear, small mouse
The cow loves cookies
Dinos in the snow!
Duddle Puck
Hogwash!
Horseplay
How to bake an American pie
Mama always comes home
Mama, why?
Moose tracks!
Princess me
Sakes alive!
Sleepyhead
Whopper cake
Wilson, Sarah. *Friends and pals and brothers, too*
Love and kisses
Wing, Natasha. *The night before the night before
Christmas*
Winters, Kay. *Wolf watch*
Winthrop, Elizabeth. *Halloween hats*
Lucy and Henry are twins
Shoes
Sledding
Witte, Anna. *The parrot Tico Tango*
Wojtusik, Elizabeth. *Kitty up!*
Wolf, Sallie. *Truck stuck*
Wolff, Ashley. *I call my grandma Nana*
I call my grandpa Papa
When Lucy goes out walking
Wolff, Ferida. *On Halloween night*
Wong, Janet S. *Grump*
Hide and seek

Riddles & jokes

I spy, mystery
I spy school days
I spy spooky night
I spy super challenger!
I spy treasure hunt
I spy ultimate challenger!
I spy, year-round challenger!
Medearis, Angela Shelf. *The freedom riddle*
Mitton, Tony. *Riddledy piggledy*
Modell, Frank. *Look out, it's April Fools' Day*
Potter, Beatrix. *The tale of Squirrel Nutkin*
Regan, Dian Curtis. *How do you know it's Halloween?*
Schultz, Sam. *Animal antics: the beast jokes ever*
    Monster mayhem
Sidman, Joyce. *Butterfly eyes and other secrets of the meadow*
Sloat, Teri. *Rib-ticklers*
Swann, Brian. *The house with no door*
Thompson, Lauren. *One riddle, one answer*
Warrick, Karen Clemens. *If I had a tail*
    Who needs that nose?
Wick, Walter. *Can you see what I see? treasure ship*
Wolff, Patricia Rae. *The toll-bridge troll*
Wright, Maureen. *Barnyard fun*
Young, Ruth. *Who says moo?*
Ziefert, Harriet. *What is part this, part that?*

Right & left *see* Concepts – left & right

Riots *see* Violence, nonviolence

Rivers

Ashforth, Camilla. *Willow on the river*
Atwell, Debby. *River*
Berkes, Marianne. *Over in a river*
Cameron, Eileen. *Canyon*
Cherry, Lynne. *A river ran wild*
Crampton, Gertrude. *Scuffy the tugboat*
Downing, Johnette. *Amazon alphabet*
Drawson, Blair. *All along the river*
George, Jean Craighead. *Everglades*
Harrison, David L. *Rivers*
Holling, Holling C. *Paddle-to-the-sea*
Hooper, Meredith. *River story*
Kellogg, Steven. *Mike Fink*
Kurtz, Jane. *River friendly, river wild*
LaMarche, Jim. *The raft*
Lewin, Ted. *Amazon boy*
Locker, Thomas. *Where the river begins*
London, Jonathan. *White water*
Martin, Jacqueline Briggs. *Creekfinding*
Miller, Debbie S. *River of life*
Pfeffer, Wendy. *The big flood*
Pollard, Nik. *The river*
Reynolds, Jan. *Amazon*
Sanders, Scott R. *Crawdad Creek*
Schofield, Jennifer. *Animal babies in ponds and rivers*
Starkoff, Vanina. *Along the river*
Walsh, Ellen Stoll. *Dot and Jabber and the mystery of the missing stream*

Roads

Hennessy, B. G. *Road builders*
Horvath, James. *Work, dogs, work*

Kilby, Don. *On the road*
Krishnaswami, Uma. *Out of the way! Out of the way!*
Lyon, George Ella. *Who came down that road?*
Morris, Dewi. *Sandy's street*
Nikola-Lisa, W. *One hole in the road*
Plourde, Lynn. *Pigs in the mud in the middle of the rud*
Pringle, Laurence P. *Jesse builds a road*
Skultety, Nancy. *From here to there*
Suen, Anastasia. *Road work ahead*
Sutton, Sally. *Roadwork*

Robbers *see* Crime

Robots

Austin, Mike. *Junkyard*
Barnett, Mac. *Oh no!*
Burks, James. *Beep and Bah*
Church, Caroline Jayne. *I love my robot*
Cushman, Doug. *Space cat*
Cyrus, Kurt. *Motor Dog*
Daywalt, Drew. *BB-8 on the run*
Duddle, Jonny. *The king of space*
Dyckman, Ame. *Boy + Bot*
Emberley, Rebecca. *Spare parts*
Gall, Chris. *Awesome Dawson*
    NanoBots
Gritton, Steve. *The trouble with sisters and robots*
Houran, Lori Haskins. *How to spy on a shark*
James, Brian. *Supertwins meet the dangerous dino-robots*
James, Simon. *Baby Brains and RoboMom*
Johnson, Stephen T. *My little blue robot*
Joyce, William. *Rolie Polie Olie*
    Sleepy time Olie
    Snowie Rolie
Judge, Chris. *Tin*
Kuszyk, R. Nicholas. *R Robot saves lunch*
Lester, Helen. *Wodney Wat's wobot*
Lucas, David. *The robot and the bluebird*
McCall, Bruce. *Marveltown*
McCanna, Tim. *Bitty Bot*
McNamara, Margaret. *The three little aliens and the big bad robot*
Marshall, Edward. *Space case*
Novak, Matt. *The Robobots*
Paul, Miranda. *Trainbots*
Pinkney, Brian. *Cosmo and the robot*
Price, Ben Joel. *Earth space moon base*
Reynolds, Aaron. *Snowbots*
Richards, Barnaby. *Blip!*
Riddell, Chris. *Wendel's workshop*
Robinson, Michelle. *And the robot went . . .*
Rosenthal, Marc. *Big bot, small bot*
Rubin, Adam. *Robo-Sauce*
Schwab, Eva. *Robert and the Robot*
Scieszka, Jon. *Robot Zot!*
Selznick, Brian. *The invention of Hugo Cabret*
Simon, Annette. *Robot zombie Frankenstein!*
Staniszewski, Anna. *Power down, Little Robot*
Tarpley, Todd. *Beep! beep! go to sleep!*
Tauss, Marc. *Superhero*
Taylor, Sean. *Robomop*
Thorpe, Kiki. *Lots of bots*
Timmers, Leo. *Franky*
Van Camp, Katie. *CookieBot!*
Van Dusen, Chris. *Randy Riley's really big hit*

Watkins, Adam F. *R is for robot*
Whybrow, Ian. *Sammy and the robots*
Yaccarino, Dan. *Doug unplugged*
 Doug unplugs on the farm
 If I had a robot

Rockets *see* Space & space ships

Rocks

Aston, Dianna Hutts. *A rock is lively*
Baylor, Byrd. *Everybody needs a rock*
Bertrand, Lynne. *Granite baby*
Christian, Peggy. *If you find a rock*
Cole, Joanna. *The magic school bus inside the earth*
Ferry, Beth. *Stick and Stone*
Formento, Alison. *These rocks count!*
Goble, Paul. *Iktomi and the boulder*
Hurst, Carol Otis. *Rocks in his head*
Lesynski, Loris. *Rocksy*
McGuirk, Leslie. *If rocks could sing*
Martin, Stephen W. *Charlotte and the rock*
Pellant, Chris. *The best book of fossils, rocks, and minerals*
Polacco, Patricia. *My ol' man*
Stuve-Bodeen, Stephanie. *Elizabeti's doll*
Walker, Alice. *Finding the green stone*
Wallace, Nancy Elizabeth. *Rocks! rocks! rocks!*

Rodeos

Elya, Susan Middleton. *Cowboy Jose*
Gibbons, Gail. *Yippee-yay!*
Harper, Jo. *Ollie Jolly, rodeo clown*
Janni, Rebecca. *Every cowgirl loves a rodeo*
Munro, Roxie. *Rodeo*
Murphy, Stuart J. *Rodeo time*

Romani

Bemelmans, Ludwig. *Madeline and the gypsies*
Kellogg, Steven. *The mystery of the magic green ball*
O'Neill, Richard. *Yokki and the Parno Gry*
Pinfold, Levi. *The Django*

Roosters *see* Birds – chickens, roosters

Royalty

Aardema, Verna. *The riddle of the drum*
Brunhoff, Laurent de. *Babar's USA*
Carle, Eric. *Walter the baker*
Climo, Shirley. *The Egyptian Cinderella*
 The Korean Cinderella
Cronin, Doreen. *Bloom*
Delessert, Etienne. *The seven dwarfs*
De Regniers, Beatrice Schenk. *May I bring a friend?*
Fisher, Leonard Everett. *Theseus and the Minotaur*
Fleischman, Paul. *Glass slipper, gold sandal*
Geras, Adèle. *The nutcracker*
Grimm, Jacob and Wilhelm *The goose girl*
 Hans my hedgehog
 Rumpelstiltskin, ill. by Paul Galdone
 Rumpelstiltskin, ill. by David Shaw
 Rumpelstiltskin, ill. by Paul O. Zelinsky
 The water of life
Hague, Michael. *The nutcracker*
Helmer, Marilyn. *Three royal tales*

Hoffmann, E. T. A. *The nutcracker*, ill. by Renée Graef
 The nutcracker, ill. by Alison Jay
 The nutcracker, ill. by Peter Malone
 The nutcracker, ill. by Niroot Puttapipat
 The nutcracker, ill. by Maurice Sendak
 The nutcracker, ill. by Lisbeth Zwerger
 The Nutcracker and the Mouse King
 The nutcracker ballet
Lee, Jeanne M. *Toad is the uncle of heaven*
Lin, Grace. *The red thread*
Marlowe, Pete. *One Arabian morning*
Martin, Bill, Jr.. *Rock it, sock it, number line*
Mayer, Marianna. *Baba Yaga and Vasilisa the Brave*
Neuschwander, Cindy. *Sir Cumference and all the king's tens*
O'Malley, Kevin. *Once upon a royal superbaby*
Oppel, Kenneth. *The king's taster*
Price, Leontyne. *Aïda*
Rappaport, Doreen. *The new king*
Sanderson, Ruth. *A castle full of cats*
San Souci, Robert D. *The white cat*
Seuss, Dr. *Bartholomew and the Oobleck*
Shulevitz, Uri. *One Monday morning*
Steig, William. *Roland, the minstrel pig*
Thomas, Shelley Moore. *Good night, Good Knight*
Wiesner, David. *The loathsome dragon*
Williams, Brenda. *The real princess*
Wisniewski, David. *The warrior and the wise man*

Royalty – emperors

Aesop. *The ant and the grasshopper*
Andersen, Hans Christian. *The dinosaur's new clothes*
 The emperor's new clothes, ill. by Angela Barrett
 The emperor's new clothes, ill. by Virginia Lee Burton
 The emperor's new clothes, ill. by Robert Byrd
 The emperor's new clothes, ill. by Serena Curmi
 The emperor's new clothes, ill. by Charlene DeLage
 The emperor's new clothes, ill. by Jack Delano
 The emperor's new clothes, ill. by Anne Rockwell
 The emperor's new clothes, ill. by Janet Stevens
 The emperor's new clothes, ill. by Eve Tharlet
 The emperor's new clothes: a tale set in China
 The nightingale, ill. by Nancy Ekholm Burkert
 The nightingale, ill. by Pirkko Vainio
 The nightingale, ill. by Lisbeth Zwerger
Bauld, Jane Scoggins. *Journey of the third seed*
Demi. *The empty pot*
Lasky, Kathryn. *The emperor's old clothes*
Marcellino, Fred. *I, crocodile*
Mayer, Mercer. *Shibumi and the kitemaker*
Perlman, Janet. *The Emperor Penguin's new clothes*
Shulevitz, Uri. *What is a wise bird like you doing in a silly tale like this?*
Wade, Mary Dodson. *No year of the cat*
Wang, Gabrielle. *The race for the Chinese zodiac*
Yolen, Jane. *The emperor and the kite*
Young, Ed. *Cat and Rat*

Royalty – khans

Yep, Laurence. *The Khan's daughter*

Royalty – kings

Anderson, Brian. *Monster chefs*
Balouch, Kristen. *The king and the three thieves*

Baranski, Joan Sullivan. *Round is a pancake*
Barnett, Mac. *Mustache!*
Biers-Ariel, Matt. *Solomon and the trees*
Black, Birdie. *Just right for Christmas*
Bosca, Francesca. *The apple king*
Brunhoff, Jean de. *Babar the king*
    Babar the king [facsimile ed.]
Burdett, Lois. *Macbeth for kids*
Catchpool, Michael. *The cloud spinner*
Deedy, Carmen Agra. *The yellow star*
Diakité, Baba Wagué. *The magic gourd*
Dieterlé, Nathalie. *I am the king!*
Eisner, Will. *Sundiata*
Evans, Richard Paul. *The spyglass*
Farley, Carol J. *The king's secret*
Fisher, Jeff. *The hair scare*
Gershator, Phillis. *Only one cowry*
Gerstein, Mordicai. *You can't have too many friends!*
Gibert, Bruno. *The king is naked!*
Grimm, Jacob and Wilhelm *Iron John*, ill. by Trina
    Schart Hyman
    Iron John, ill. by Winslow Pels
Hawthorne, Nathaniel. *King Midas and the golden
    touch*
Huling, Jan. *Puss in cowboy boots*
Krudop, Walter Lyon. *The man who caught fish*
Lepp, Bil. *The King of Little Things*
Lewis, Jill. *Don't read this book!*
Lloyd-Jones, Sally. *His Royal Highness, King Baby*
MacDonald, Margaret Read. *Little Rooster's
    diamond button*
Mahy, Margaret. *17 kings and 42 elephants*
Manders, John. *The really awful musicians*
Martin, Rafe. *The Shark God*
Mayer, Marianna. *The prince and the pauper*
Medearis, Angela Shelf. *Too much talk*
Mitchell, Adrian. *Nobody rides the unicorn*
Miura, Taro. *The tiny king*
Miyares, Daniel. *Bring me a rock!*
Myller, Rolf. *How big is a foot?*
Niemann, Christoph. *The potato king*
Nobisso, Josephine. *The weight of a Mass*
Oberman, Sheldon. *The wisdom bird*
Ørdal, Stina Langlo. *Princess Aasta*
Osborne, Mary Pope. *The brave little seamstress*
Peet, Bill. *How Droofus the dragon lost his head*
Perrault, Charles. *Puss in boots*, ill. by Marcia
    Brown
    Puss in boots, ill. by Lorinda Bryan Cauley
    Puss in boots, ill. by Paul Galdone
    Puss in boots, ill. by Steve Light
    Puss in boots, ill. by Giuliano Lunelli
    Puss in boots, ill. by Fred Marcellino
    Puss in boots, ill. by Bernhard Oberdieck
    Puss in boots, ill. by Jerry Pinkney
    Puss in boots, ill. by Alain Vaës
Pfister, Marcus. *How Leo learned to be king*
Pienkowski, Jan. *Pizza!*
Pullman, Philip. *Puss in boots: the adventures of that
    most enterprising feline*
Rosenthal, Amy Krouse. *Al Pha's bet*
St. George, Judith. *Zarafa*
San Souci, Robert D. *A weave of words*
Sawyer, Ruth. *The remarkable Christmas of the
    cobbler's sons*
Seuss, Dr. *The king's stilts*
Sierra, Judy. *The beautiful butterfly*
Singleton, Debbie. *The king who wouldn't sleep*
Souhami, Jessica. *Rama and the demon king*

Steptoe, John. *Mufaro's beautiful daughters*
Stewig, John Warren. *King Midas*
Sturm, James. *Ogres awake!*
Tchana, Katrin. *Sense Pass King*
Tom Thumb. *The adventures of Tom Thumb*
Van Dusen, Chris. *King Hugo's huge ego*
Ward, Helen. *The king of the birds*
Wilde, Oscar. *The happy prince*
Wisniewski, David. *Sundiata: lion king of Mali*
Wood, Audrey. *King Bidgood's in the bathtub*
Yep, Laurence. *The shell woman and the king*
Yolen, Jane. *King Long Shanks*

Royalty – pharaohs

Base, Graeme. *The Jewel Fish of Karnak*
Sabuda, Robert. *Tutankhamen's gift*

Royalty – princes

Allchin, Rosalind. *The frog princess*
Anderson, Brian. *The prince's new pet*
Arnold, Tedd. *The twin princes*
Bently, Peter. *The prince and the porker*
Brett, Jan. *Cinders*
Burdett, Lois. *Hamlet for kids*
Carey, Lorraine. *Cinderella's stepsister and the big
    bad wolf*
Cinderella
Climo, Shirley. *The Persian Cinderella*
Coburn, Jewell Reinhart. *Angkat*
    Jouanah
Cole, Babette. *Prince Cinders*
Daly, Jude. *Fair, brown and trembling*
Debecker, Benoît. *The naughty prince*
Demas, Corinne. *The magic apple*
Dodd, Emma. *Cinderelephant*
Dodds, Dayle Ann. *The prince won't go to bed*
The firebird. *The firebird*, ill. by Demi
    The firebird, ill. by Rachel Isadora
    The tale of the firebird
Geras, Adèle. *Sleeping beauty*
    Swan Lake
Gow, Nancy. *Ten big toes and a prince's nose*
Grimm, Jacob and Wilhelm. *The frog prince*, ill. by
    Anne Yvonne Gilbert
    The frog prince, ill. by Todd Ouren
    Iron John, ill. by Trina Schart Hyman
    Iron John, ill. by Winslow Pels
    Rapunzel, ill. by Sarah Gibb
    Rapunzel, ill. by Trina Schart Hyman
    Rapunzel, ill. by Rachel Isadora
    Rapunzel, ill. by Joma
    Rapunzel, ill. by Kris Waldherr
    Rapunzel, ill. by Paul O. Zelinsky
    Rapunzel: a fairy tale
    Rose Red and the bear prince
    Sleeping Beauty, ill. by Maja Dusíková
    Sleeping beauty, ill. by Sarah Gibb
    The sleeping beauty
Gunnufson, Charlotte. *Prince and Pirate*
Helmer, Marilyn. *Three prince charming tales*
Jackson, Ellen. *Cinder Edna*
Kimmel, Eric A. *The three princes*
Lattimore, Deborah Nourse. *Cinderhazel*
Lester, Helen. *Princess Penelope's parrot*
Lunge-Larsen, Lise. *The race of the Birkebeiners*
McCaughrean, Geraldine. *Beauty and the beast*
McLeod, Heather. *Kiss me!*

Manna, Anthony L. *The orphan*
Martin, Rafe. *The storytelling princess*
Milligan, Bryce. *The prince of Ireland and the three magic stallions*
Minters, Frances. *Cinder-Elly*
Osborne, Mary Pope. *Sleeping Bobby*
Perkins, Chloe. *Cinderella*
Perrault, Charles *Cinderella*, ill. by Nicoletta Ceccoli
  Cinderella, ill. by Susan Jeffers
  Cinderella, ill. by Loek Koopmans
  Cinderella, ill. by Barbara McClintock
  Cinderella, ill. by James Marshall
  Cinderella / Cenicienta
  Cinderella: a pop-up fairy tale
  Cinderella: or, the little glass slipper
  Sleeping Beauty
Piumini, Roberto. *Doctor Me Di Cin*
Roberts, Lynn. *Cinderella, an Art Deco love story*
Roscoe, Charlie. *The red prince*
Sanderson, Ruth. *Cinderella*
  The enchanted wood
  Papa Gatto
San Souci, Robert D. *Cinderella Skeleton*
Scieszka, Jon. *The frog prince, continued*
Shepard, Aaron. *One-eye! Two-eyes! Three-eyes!*
Souhami, Jessica. *Rama and the demon king*
Stampler, Ann Redisch. *The rooster prince of Breslov*
Stanley, Fay. *The last princess*
Underwood, Deborah. *Interstellar Cinderella*
Verma, Jatinder Nath. *The story of Divaali*
Wells, Rosemary. *The little lame prince*
Wilson, Tony. *The princess and the packet of frozen peas*
Yolen, Jane. *The firebird*
  Wings

Royalty – princesses

Allchin, Rosalind. *The frog princess*
Allen, Joy. *Princess Palooza*
  Princess party
Alley, Zoe B. *There's a princess in the palace*
Andersen, Hans Christian. *La princesa and the pea*
  The princess and the pea, ill. by Emily Bolam
  The princess and the pea, ill. by Charlene DeLage
  The princess and the pea, ill. by Dorothée Duntze
  The princess and the pea, ill. by Maja Dusíková
  The princess and the pea, ill. by Paul Galdone
  The princess and the pea, ill. by Rachel Isadora
  The princess and the pea, ill. by Bernhard Oberdieck
  The princess and the pea, ill. by Janet Stevens
  The princess and the pea, ill. by Alain Vaës
  The princess and the pea in miniature
Andrews, Julie. *The very fairy princess*
  The very fairy princess: a spooky, sparkly Halloween
  The very fairy princess: graduation girl!
  The very fairy princess: here comes the flower girl!
  The very fairy princess follows her heart
  The very fairy princess sparkles in the snow
Auch, Mary Jane. *The princess and the pizza*
Bar-el, Dan. *Such a prince*
Bardhan-Quallen, Sudipta. *Pirate princess*
  Snoring Beauty
Bartles, Veronica. *The princess and the frogs*
Bateman, Teresa. *The princesses have a ball*
Beaton, Kate. *The princess and the pony*
Bonning, Tony. *Snog the frog*

Calvert, Pam. *Princess Peepers*
  Princess Peepers picks a pet
Clarkson, Stephanie. *Sleeping Cinderella and other princess mix-ups*
Coh, Smiljana. *Princesses on the run*
  The seven princesses
Cole, Babette. *Princess Smartypants*
Coyle, Carmela LaVigna. *Do princesses have best friends forever?*
  Do princesses make happy campers?
  Do princesses really kiss frogs?
Cuyler, Margery. *Princess Bess gets dressed*
Davidson, Ellen Dee. *Princess Justina Albertina*
DeFelice, Cynthia C. *The real, true Dulcie Campbell*
Donaldson, Julia. *A gold star for Zog*
  Zog and the flying doctors
Edwards, Pamela Duncan. *Princess Pigtoria and the pea*
Emmett, Jonathan. *Prince Ribbit*
  The princess and the pig
Falconer, Ian. *Olivia and the fairy princesses*
Ferguson, Sarah. *Tea for Ruby*
Fleming, Candace. *Clever Jack takes the cake*
French, Vivian. *The most wonderful thing in the world*
Funke, Cornelia. *Princess Pigsty*
Gaiman, Neil. *Cinnamon*
Gardner, Carol. *Princess Zelda and the frog*
Goodhart, Pippa. *Arthur's tractor*
Gow, Nancy. *Ten big toes and a prince's nose*
Grambling, Lois G. *The witch who wanted to be a princess*
Greenawalt, Kelly. *Princess Truly in I am Truly*
Grey, Mini. *The very smart pea and the princess-to-be*
Grimm, Jacob and Wilhelm. *The frog prince*, ill. by Anne Yvonne Gilbert
  The frog prince, ill. by Todd Ouren
  The golden goose
  Sleeping Beauty, ill. by Maja Dusíková
  Sleeping beauty, ill. by Sarah Gibb
  The sleeping beauty
  Twelve dancing princesses
  The twelve dancing princesses, ill. by Lucy Corvino
  The twelve dancing princesses, ill. by Kinuko Y. Craft
  The twelve dancing princesses, ill. by Rachel Isadora
  The twelve dancing princesses, ill. by Alison Jay
  The twelve dancing princesses, ill. by Gerald McDermott
  The twelve dancing princesses, ill. by Jane Ray
  The twelve dancing princesses, ill. by Suçie Stevenson
  The twelve princesses
Hale, Bruce. *Snoring Beauty*
Hart, Caryl. *The princess and the Christmas rescue*
  The princess and the peas
Heide, Florence Parry. *Princess Hyacinth*
Hindley, Judy. *Princess Rosa's winter*
Hoffman, Mary. *Princess Grace*
Holabird, Katharine. *Angelina at the palace*
Horowitz, Dave. *Twenty-six princesses*
Howland, Naomi. *Princess says goodnight*
Huck, Charlotte S. *Princess Furball*
Jenkins, Emily. *Princessland*
Jones, Ursula. *The princess who had no kingdom*
Joosse, Barbara. *Evermore Dragon*
  Lovabye Dragon
  Sail away Dragon
Katz, Karen. *Princess Baby*

476 • Subject Guide—Royalty – queens

Princess Baby, night-night
Keller, Emily Snowell. *Sleeping Bunny*
Kimmel, Eric A. *The frog princess: a Tlingit legend from Alaska*
   The three princes
Kleven, Elisa. *The paper princess*
Lammle, Leslie. *Princess wannabe*
LaRochelle, David. *The end*
Lee, Y. J. *The little moon princess*
Lendler, Ian. *An undone fairy tale*
Lester, Helen. *Princess Penelope's parrot*
Levert, Mireille. *The princess who had almost everything*
Lewison, Wendy Cheyette. *The princess and the potty*
Lum, Kate. *Princesses are not just pretty*
   Princesses are not perfect
   Princesses are not quitters!
McCourt, Lisa. *Good night, Princess Pruney Toes*
McDonald, Megan. *The Hinky Pink*
MacHale, D. J. *The monster princess*
Mack, Todd. *Princess Penelope*
McKinlay, Meg. *No bears*
McNaughton, Janet. *Brave Jack and the unicorn*
Martin, Rafe. *The storytelling princess*
Masini, Beatrice. *A brave little princess*
Mayer, Mercer. *Shibumi and the kitemaker*
Melling, David. *Good knight sleep tight*
Metzger, Steve. *Will Princess Isabel ever say please?*
Milne, A. A. *The magic hill*
Milord, Susan. *Willa the wonderful*
Miura, Taro. *The big princess*
Moore, Marian. *Dear Cinderella*
Mortimer, Rachael. *Song for a princess*
Murray, Alison. *Princess Penelope and the runaway kitten*
Numeroff, Laura Joffe. *Ponyella*
O'Malley, Kevin. *Once upon a cool motorcycle dude*
Ørdal, Stina Langlo. *Princess Aasta*
Orr, Wendy. *The princess and her panther*
Osborne, Mary Pope. *Sleeping Bobby*
Perlman, Janet. *The penguin and the pea*
Perrault, Charles. *Sleeping Beauty*
Priceman, Marjorie. *Princess Picky*
Ray, Jane. *The apple-pip princess*
Ringgold, Faith. *The invisible princesses*
Ross, Tony. *I didn't do it!*
   I don't want to go to the hospital!
   I feel sick!
   I want a friend!
   I want a party!
   I want my light on!
   I want my tooth
   I want snow!
   I want to do it myself!
   I want to win!
   I want two birthdays!
Sauer, Tammi. *Princess in training*
Scieszka, Jon. *The frog prince, continued*
Scrimger, Richard. *Princess Bun Bun*
Shannon, Margaret. *The red wolf*
Shepard, Aaron. *The princess mouse*
Shields, Carol Diggory. *I am really a princess*
Spinelli, Eileen. *Princess Pig*
Stanley, Fay. *The last princess*
Strauss, Linda Leopold. *The princess gown*
Thompson, Lauren. *One riddle, one answer*
Thurber, James. *Many moons*, ill. by Marc Simont
   Many moons, ill. by Louis Slobodkin
Tonatiuh, Duncan. *The princess and the warrior*

Underwood, Deborah. *Part-time princess*
Verde, Susan. *The water princess*
Williams, Brenda. *The real princess*
Wilson, Karma. *Princess me*
Wilson, Tony. *The princess and the packet of frozen peas*
Yolen, Jane. *Not all princesses dress in pink*

Royalty – queens

Antony, Steve. *The queen's handbag*
   The Queen's hat
Buehner, Caralyn. *The queen of style*
Burdett, Lois. *Macbeth for kids*
Cullen, Lynn. *Moi and Marie Antoinette*
Ellis, Sarah. *The queen's feet*
Engelbreit, Mary. *Queen of the class*
Falconer, Ian. *Olivia and the fairy princesses*
Foreman, Michael. *Oh! if only . . .*
Hennessy, B. G. *The missing tarts*
Heos, Bridget. *Queen Dog*
McGrory, Anik. *Mouton's impossible dream*
Masini, Beatrice. *A brave little princess*
Moore, Inga. *Captain Cat*
Nobisso, Josephine. *The weight of a Mass*
Oberman, Sheldon. *The wisdom bird*
Osborne, Mary Pope. *The brave little seamstress*
Paterson, John. *Blueberries for the queen*
Paxton, Tom. *Engelbert the elephant*
San Souci, Robert D. *A weave of words*
Wadham, Tim. *The queen of France*
Whelan, Gloria. *Queen Victoria's bathing machine*

Royalty – rajahs

Demi. *One grain of rice*

Royalty – sultans

Farmer, Nancy. *Clever Ali*
Lottridge, Celia Barker. *The little rooster and the diamond button*

Royalty – tsars

Bell, Anthea. *Vasilisa the beautiful*
Gorbachev, Valeri. *The fool of the world and the flying ship: a Ukrainian folk tale*
Hoffman, Mary. *Clever Katya*
Ogburn, Jacqueline K. *The magic nesting doll*
Ransome, Arthur. *The fool of the world and the flying ship*
Sanderson, Ruth. *The golden mare, the firebird, and the magic ring*
San Souci, Robert D. *Peter and the blue witch baby*
Winthrop, Elizabeth. *Vasilissa the beautiful*

Rummage sales *see* Garage sales, rummage sales

Rumors *see* Behavior – gossip, rumors

Running *see* Activities – running; Sports – racing

Running away *see* Behavior – running away

Safety

Austin, Mike. *Rescue Squad No. 9*
Berenstain, Stan and Jan. *The Berenstain bears learn
    about strangers*
Braun, Sebastien. *Whoosh and Chug!*
Brill, Marlene Targ. *Margaret Knight, girl inventor*
Brown, Marc. *Dinosaurs, beware!*
Calmenson, Stephanie. *May I pet your dog?*
Cuyler, Margery. *Please play safe!*
    Stop drop and roll
Ethan, Eric. *Helicopters*
Gordon, Sharon. *Bruises*
    Cuts and scrapes
Hassett, John. *The nine lives of Dudley Dog*
Heos, Bridget. *Be safe around fire*
Houran, Lori Haskins. *I will keep you safe and sound*
International Center for Assault Prevention. *My
    body belongs to me from my head to my toes*
Jacobs, Paul DuBois. *Fire drill*
Kaczman, James. *A bird and his worm*
Kevi. *Don't talk to strangers*
Kurtz, Jane. *Do kangaroos wear seat belts?*
Lindgren, Barbro. *Sam's lamp*
McMullan, Kate. *I'm smart!*
Mayo, Margaret. *Emergency!*
Miller, Edward. *Fireboy to the rescue!*
Murphy, Stuart J. *Freda is found*
Pendziwol, Jean E. *No dragons for tea*
    A treasure at sea for dragon and me
Pfister, Marcus. *Hang on, Hopper!*
Proimos, James. *The best bike ride ever*
Rex, Michael. *My fire engine*
Roche, Denis. *Little Pig is capable*
Salat, Cristina. *Peanut's emergency*
Shaskan, Stephen. *Toad on the road*
Shore, Diane Z. *Look both ways*
Spelman, Cornelia Maude. *Your body belongs to you*
Spinelli, Eileen. *A safe place called home*
Starishevsky, Jill. *My body belongs to me*
Trottier, Maxine. *A safe place*
Yolen, Jane. *How do dinosaurs stay safe?*

Sailors *see also* Careers – military

Ahlberg, Allan. *The baby in the hat*
Brown, Margaret Wise. *Sailor boy jig*
Calhoun, Mary. *Henry the sailor cat*
Crews, Donald. *Sail away*
Flanagan, Alice K. *Riding the ferry with Captain
    Cruz*
Friedman, Ina R. *How my parents learned to eat*
Joosse, Barbara. *Old Robert and the sea-silly cats*
Lendroth, Susan. *Ocean wide, ocean deep*
Lenski, Lois. *The little sailboat*
Lund, Deb. *Dinosailors*
Maass, Robert. *Tugboats*
Manning, Mick. *What a Viking!*

Meister, Cari. *Follow the drinking gourd: an
    Underground Railroad story*
Moore, Inga. *Captain Cat*
O'Neill, Alexis. *Loud Emily*
Rand, Gloria. *Sailing home*
Rosenthal, Eileen. *Bobo the sailor man!*
Shulevitz, Uri. *When I wore my sailor suit*
Van Allsburg, Chris. *The wreck of the Zephyr*
Waddell, Martin. *Sailor Bear*
Winter, Jeanette. *Follow the drinking gourd*
Zeman, Ludmila. *Sindbad*

Sand *see also* Sea & seashore – beaches

Inkpen, Mick. *Sandcastle*
Nolan, Dennis. *Sea of dreams*
Robertson, M. P. *The sandcastle*
Roddie, Shen. *Sandbear*
Yee, Brenda Shannon. *Sand castle*

Sandcastles *see* Sand

Santa Claus

Agee, Jon. *Little Santa*
Allen, Jonathan. *"I'm not Santa!"*
Alsenas, Linas. *Mrs. Claus takes a vacation*
Anderson, Derek. *How the Easter Bunny saved
    Christmas*
Apperley, Dawn. *Santa Claus will come tonight*
Arnold, Katya. *The adventures of Snowwoman*
Augustin, Barbara. *Antonella and her Santa Claus*
Autry, Gene. *Here comes Santa Claus*
Bailey, Linda. *When Santa was a baby*
Bailey, Mary Bryant. *Jeoffry's Christmas*
Barrett, Judi. *Santa from Cincinnati*
Bedford, David. *I've seen Santa!*
Biedrzycki, David. *Santa retires*
Breen, Steve. *The secret of Santa's island*
Brennan-Nelson, Denise. *Good night, reindeer*
Brett, Jan. *The animals' Santa*
    The wild Christmas reindeer
Briggs, Raymond. *Father Christmas*
Brown, Marc. *Arthur's Christmas*
Burgess, Mark. *Where teddy bears come from*
Burningham, John. *Harvey Slumfenburger's
    Christmas present*
Butler, M. Christina. *One special Christmas*
Catalano, Dominic. *Santa and the three bears*
Chung, Arree. *Ninja Claus!*
Conover, Chris. *The Christmas bears*
Conrad, Pam. *The Tub People's Christmas*
Cronin, Doreen. *Click, clack, ho! ho! ho!*
Currey, Anna. *Truffle's Christmas*
David, Lawrence. *Peter Claus and the naughty list*
Demi. *The legend of Saint Nicholas*
dePaola, Tomie. *Get dressed, Santa!*
Donaldson, Julia. *Stick Man*
Dunrea, Olivier. *Merry Christmas, Ollie!*
Duquennoy, Jacques. *North Pole, South Pole*
Duval, Kathy. *The Three Bears' Christmas*
Emmett, Jonathan. *The Santa trap*
Evert, Lori. *The Christmas wish*
Faulkner, Keith. *Charlie Chimp's Christmas*
Fergus, Maureen. *The day Santa stopped believing in
    Harold*
Frazee, Marla. *Santa Claus*
Gammell, Stephen. *Wake up, bear . . . It's Christmas!*
Grün, Anselm. *The legend of Saint Nicholas*

Wolff, Patricia Rae. *A new, improved Santa*
Wood, Audrey. *The Christmas adventure of Space Elf Sam*
Yee, Wong Herbert. *A small Christmas*
Yin. *Dear Santa, please come to the 19th floor*
Yorinks, Arthur. *Christmas in July*

Sasquatch *see* Monsters

Saving things *see* Behavior – saving things

Scarecrows

Brown, Ken. *The scarecrow's hat*
Cazet, Denys. *Nothing at all*
Long, Loren. *Otis and the scarecrow*
Martin, Bill, Jr.. *Barn dance!*
Patten, Brian. *The big snuggle-up*
Rau, Dana Meachen. *Shoo crow, shoo!*
Rylant, Cynthia. *Scarecrow*
San Souci, Robert D. *Feathertop*
Schertle, Alice. *Witch Hazel*
Williams, Linda. *The little old lady who was not afraid of anything*

School

Adams, Diane. *I want to help!*
Ajmera, Maya. *Back to school*
Alexander, Claire. *Back to front and upside down*
Aliki. *Marianthe's story one: painted words; Marianthe's story two: spoken memories*
A play's the thing
Allard, Harry. *Miss Nelson is back*
Miss Nelson is missing!
Alter, Anna. *Abigail spells*
Disappearing Desmond
Ancona, George. *It's our garden*
Anderson, Laurie Halse. *The hair of Zoe Fleefenbacher goes to school*
Andreae, Giles. *Captain Flinn and the pirate dinosaurs*
Captain Flinn and the pirate dinosaurs: missing treasure!
Andrews, Julie. *The very fairy princess: a spooky, sparkly Halloween*
The very fairy princess: graduation girl!
The very fairy princess follows her heart
The very fairy princess sparkles in the snow
Anstee, Ashlyn. *No, no, Gnome!*
Arnold, Caroline. *Hatching chicks in Room 6*
Arnold, Tedd. *Green Wilma*
Asim, Jabari. *Fifty cents and a dream*
Aston, Dianna Hutts. *Not so tall for six*
Baer, Edith. *This is the way we go to school*
Ballard, Robin. *My day, your day*
Barnett, Mac. *Billy Twitters and his big blue whale problem*
Barton, Chris. *Book or bell?*
Bateman, Teresa. *The Bully Blockers Club*
Bean, Jonathan. *This is my home, this is my school*
Beaty, Andrea. *Artist Ted*
Firefighter Ted
Beeny, Emily. *Hector the collector*
Bell, Cece. *Chuck and Woodchuck*
Bercaw, Edna Coe. *Halmoni's day*
Berenstain, Stan and Jan. *The Berenstain bears' report card trouble*

The Berenstain bears' trouble at school
Berenzy, Alix. *Sammy*
Berger, Samantha. *Back to school with Bigfoot*
Bergman, Mara. *Lively Elizabeth!*
Best, Cari. *Beatrice spells some lulus and learns to write a letter*
My three best friends and me, Zulay
Blackstone, Stella. *Bear's school day*
Bliss, Harry. *Bailey*
Bloom, Suzanne. *Piggy Monday*
Bond, Felicia. *The Halloween play*
Borden, Louise. *The day Eddie met the author*
Kindergarten luck
The lost-and-found tooth
Border, Terry. *Milk goes to school*
Bottner, Barbara. *Miss Brooks loves books! (and I don't)*
Priscilla gorilla
Bowen, Anne. *The great math tattle battle*
I know an old teacher
Bracken, Beth. *The little bully*
Too shy for show-and-tell
Brennan-Nelson, Denise. *Willow*
Brenner, Emily. *On the first day of grade school*
Bridges, Shirin Yim. *Ruby's wish*
Brisson, Pat. *I remember Miss Perry*
Bromley, Anne C. *The lunch thief*
Brown, Marc. *Arthur and the true Francine*
Arthur goes to school
Arthur turns green
Arthur's teacher moves in
Arthur's teacher trouble
Arthur's underwear
Arthur's Valentine
The true Francine
Brown, Peter. *My teacher is a monster! (no, I am not)*
Brun-Cosme, Nadine. *Daddy long legs*
Bunting, Eve. *My special day at third street school*
Walking to school
Burnard, Damon. *Dave's haircut*
Burnett, Frances Hodgson. *A little princess*, ill. by Barbara McClintock
A little princess, ill. by Graham Rust
Burningham, John. *John Patrick Norman McHennessy — the boy who was always late*
Bus-a-saurus bop
Bush, Laura. *Read all about it!*
Cali, Davide. *A funny thing happened on the way to school . . .*
Calmenson, Stephanie. *The frog principal*
Ollie's school day
The principal's new clothes
The teeny tiny teacher
Campbell, Bebe Moore. *I get so hungry*
Campbell, K. G. *Dylan the villain*
Capucilli, Alyssa Satin. *Biscuit goes to school*
Biscuit loves school
Carlson, Nancy. *Henry and the bully*
Henry and the Valentine surprise
Henry's amazing imagination!
Henry's 100 days of kindergarten
Hooray for Grandparent's Day!
I don't like to read!
Sit still!
Think big!
Carrick, Carol. *Patrick's dinosaurs on the Internet*
Caseley, Judith. *Bully*
Cash, Rosanne. *Penelope Jane*
Catalanotto, Peter. *Matthew A.B.C.*

Franco, Betsy. *Double play!*
Frankel, Erin. *Nobody!*
Fraser, Mary Ann. *I.Q. gets fit*
  I.Q. goes to school
  I.Q. goes to the library
  I.Q., it's time
French, Simon. *Guess the baby*
Friedman, Darlene. *Star of the Week: a story of love, adoption, and brownies with sprinkles*
Gall, Chris. *Substitute creacher*
Gantos, Jack. *Not so Rotten Ralph*
  Rotten Ralph's show and tell
Garden, Nancy. *Molly's family*
Garland, Michael. *Miss Smith reads again!*
  Miss Smith's incredible storybook
Garton, Sam. *Otter goes to school*
Gerstein, Mordicai. *Minifred goes to school*
Gianferrari, Maria. *Hello goodbye dog*
Giff, Patricia Reilly. *Today was a terrible day*
Giles, Almira Astudillo. *Willie wins*
Gill, Timothy. *Flip and Fin: we rule the school!*
The gingerbread boy. *The Gingerbread Man loose in the school*
Glaser, Linda. *Hannah's way*
Goodman, Susan E. *The first step*
Gorbachev, Valeri. *Turtle's penguin day*
Gran, Julia. *Big bug surprise*
Grandits, John. *Seven rules you absolutely must not break if you want to survive the cafeteria*
Gregory, Nan. *Amber waiting*
Grigsby, Susan. *First peas to the table*
  In the garden with Dr. Carver
Grimes, Nikki. *Danitra Brown, class clown*
Griswell, Kim T. *Rufus goes to school*
Gundersheimer, Karen. *Find cat, wear hat*
Gutman, Anne. *Gaspard and Lisa, friends forever*
  Lisa in the jungle
Guy, Ginger Foglesong. *My school / Mi escuela*
Hader, Berta Hoerner. *The mighty hunter*
Hale, Bruce. *Clark the Shark*
Hale, Sarah Josepha Buell. *Mary had a little lamb*, ill. by Tomie dePaola
  Mary had a little lamb, ill. by Laura Huliska-Beith
  Mary had a little lamb, photos by Bruce McMillan
  Mary had a little lamb, ill. by Salley Mavor
Hamilton, Richard. *Let's take over the kindergarten*
Hanlon, Abby. *Ralph tells a story*
Harley, Bill. *Lost and found*
Harper, Jamie. *Miss Mingo and the fire drill*
Harper, Jessica. *Lizzy's ups and downs*
Hassett, John. *The three silly girls Grubb*
Havill, Juanita. *Jamaica and the substitute teacher*
  Jamaica is thankful
Hayes, Sarah. *Dog day*
Hays, Anna Jane. *Ready, set, preschool!*
Hayward, Linda. *A day in the life of a teacher*
  What homework?
Heck, Ed. *Monkey lost*
Heelan, Jamee Riggio. *Can you hear a rainbow?*
Heiligman, Deborah. *Cool dog, school dog*
Helakoski, Leslie. *The smushy bus*
Helmer, Marilyn. *Recess riddles*
Henkes, Kevin. *Chrysanthemum*
  El gran día de Lily / Lilly's big day
  Lilly's purple plastic purse
Hilton, Perez. *The boy with pink hair*
Hoban, Russell. *Bread and jam for Frances*
Hodge, Deborah. *Lily and the mixed-up letters*
Hoffman, Mary. *Amazing Grace*

  Princess Grace
Holabird, Katharine. *Angelina and Alice*
Holub, Joan. *Groundhog weather school*
  Little red writing
  Tool school
  Twinkle, star of the week
Hopkins, Lee Bennett. *School supplies*
Hopkinson, Deborah. *A letter to my teacher*
  Steamboat school
Horn, Emily. *Excuse me — are you a witch?*
Horton, Joan. *Math attack!*
Howe, James. *The day the teacher went bananas*
Hubbell, Patricia. *Teacher!*
Hughes, Shirley. *Bobbo goes to school*
Hurwitz, Johanna. *Mighty Monty*
Husband, Amy. *Dear Teacher*
Hutchins, Pat. *Three-star Billy*
Ikegami, Aiko. *Friends*
Isadora, Rachel. *Bea at ballet*
Isherwood, Shirley. *Flora the frog*
Iyengar, Malathi Michelle. *Romina's rangoli*
Jacobs, Paul DuBois. *Fire drill*
James, Brian. *Supertwins and the sneaky, slimy book worms*
Janovitz, Marilyn. *We love school!*
Jocelyn, Marthe. *Hannah's Collections*
Johnson, Doug. *Substitute teacher plans*
Johnson, Stephen T. *Alphabet school*
Jones, Christianne C. *Miles McHale, tattletale*
Joosse, Barbara. *Bad dog school*
Joyce, William. *Billy's booger*
Jules, Jacqueline. *Duck for Turkey Day*
Kalz, Jill. *An a-maze-ing school adventure*
Kann, Victoria. *Purplicious*
Katz, Alan. *Don't say that word!*
  That stinks!
Katz, Susan B. *ABC school's for me!*
Kay, Verla. *Hornbooks and inkwells*
Keller, Holly. *That's mine, Horace*
Kelley, True. *Blabber Mouse*
Kent, Allegra. *Ballerina swan*
Ketteman, Helen. *The ghosts go haunting*
Kidslabel. *Spot 7: school*
Kirk, Daniel. *Keisha Ann can!*
Kirk, David. *Truckeroo school*
Kleven, Elisa. *The apple doll*
Klise, Kate. *Little Rabbit and the Night Mare*
Knudsen, Michelle. *Argus*
Koster, Gloria. *The peanut-free cafe*
Krensky, Stephen. *Big bad wolves at school*
  My teacher's secret life
Kroll, Steven. *Patches lost and found*
  Will you be my valentine?
Kroll, Virginia L. *Ryan respects*
Krosoczka, Jarrett J. *Max for president*
Kuefler, Joseph. *Rulers of the playground*
Lakin, Patricia. *Snow day!*
Lambert, Martha Lewis. *I won't get lost*
Laminack, Lester L. *Jake's 100th day of school*
Lamstein, Sarah Marwil. *I like your buttons!*
Langley, Karen. *Shine*
Langreuter, Jutta. *Little Bear and the big fight*
Lasky, Kathryn. *Science fair bunnies*
  Show and tell bunnies
Lauture, Denizé. *Running the road to ABC*
Layne, Steven L. *T is for teachers*
Lears, Laurie. *Becky the brave*
Leedy, Loreen. *Fraction action*
  Messages in the mailbox

Mission — addition

Lefebvre, Jason. *Too much glue*

Lehman, Barbara. *The secret box*

Lehrhaupt, Adam. *Chicken in school*

LeSourd, Nancy. *Christy, Christmastime at Cutter Gap*

Lester, Helen. *Hooway for Wodney Wat*
  Score one for the sloths
  Tackylocks and the three bears
  Three cheers for Tacky
  Wodney Wat's wobot

Lesynski, Loris. *Night school*

Lewis, J. Patrick. *Kindergarten cat*

Lewis, Kim. *My friend Harry*

Lillegard, Dee. *Hello school!*

Lin, Grace. *Lissy's friends*

Lindbergh, Reeve. *The awful aardvarks go to school*

Lipp, Frederick. *Running shoes*

Lithgow, John. *Mahalia Mouse goes to college*

Littlesugar, Amy. *Freedom school, yes!*

Litwin, Eric. *Pete the Cat: rocking in my school shoes*

Ljungkvist, Laura. *Follow the line to school*

Lloyd, Jennifer. *The best thing about kindergarten*

Loehr, Patrick. *Mucumber McGee and the lunch lady's liver*

Loewen, Nancy. *The last day of kindergarten*

London, Jonathan. *Froggy's first kiss*

Ludwig, Trudy. *The invisible boy*

Lundy, Charlotte. *Thank you, Esther*

Lyon, George Ella. *The pirate of kindergarten*

McAllister, Angela. *Take a kiss to school*

McBratney, Sam. *I'm sorry*

McCain, Becky R. *Nobody knew what to do*

McCourt, Lisa. *Chicken soup for little souls: The Goodness Gorillas*
  Chicken soup for little souls: The new kid and the cookie thief
  It's time for school, Stinky Face

McCully, Emily Arnold. *School*

McDonald, Megan. *Beetle McGrady eats bugs!*
  Insects are my life
  It's picture day today!
  Reptiles are my life

McGinty, Alice B. *Eliza's kindergarten pet*

Mackintosh, David. *The Frank show*
  Marshall Armstrong is new to our school

McKissack, Robert L. *Try your best*

MacLachlan, Patricia. *Three names*

McLellan, Gretchen Brandenburg. *Mrs. McBee leaves Room 3*

McMillan, Bruce. *Mouse views*

McMullan, Kate. *I'm smart!*

McNamara, Margaret. *A poem in your pocket*

McNaughton, Colin. *Captain Abdul's pirate school*
  Once upon an ordinary school day
  When I grow up

Madison, Alan. *Velma Gratch and the way cool butterfly*

Malaspina, Ann. *Yasmin's hammer*

Manley, Curtis. *Shawn loves sharks*

Mann, Jennifer K. *I will never get a star on Mrs. Benson's blackboard*

Marciano, John Bemelmans. *Madeline and the old house in Paris*

Marshall, James. *The Cut-Ups crack up*
  The Cut-Ups cut loose

Martin, Ann M. *Rachel Parker, kindergarten show-off*

Marx, Trish. *Kindergarten day USA and China*

Marzollo, Jean. *I spy school days*

Medearis, Michael. *Daisy and the doll*

Menchin, Scott. *Harry goes to dog school*

Michelson, Richard. *Busing Brewster*

Milgrim, David. *Eddie gets ready for school*

Miller, Edward. *Fireboy to the rescue!*

Miller, Margaret. *Now I'm big*

Mills, Claudia. *Ziggy's blue-ribbon day*

Milord, Susan. *Happy one hundredth day!*
  Willa the wonderful

Mitchell, Margaree King. *Susie Mae*

Montanari, Eva. *The crocodile's true colors*

Moon, Nicola. *Something special*

Moore, Julianne. *Freckleface Strawberry and the dodgeball bully*

Moore, Mary-Alice. *The wheels on the school bus*

Moore-Mallinos, Jennifer. *My brother is autistic*

Mora, Pat. *The rainbow tulip*

Mortenson, Greg. *Listen to the wind*

Morton, Carlene. *The library pages*

Moses, Will. *Mary and her little lamb*

Moss, Marissa. *Regina's big mistake*

Moss, Miriam. *Wibble wobble*

Moss, Peggy. *One of us*

Munsch, Robert N. *Get out of bed!*
  Mmm, cookies!
  Show-and-tell
  Stephanie's ponytail
  Thomas' snowsuit
  We share everything!

Murphy, Stuart J. *Get up and go!*
  100 days of cool
  The penny pot

Murray, Alison. *Hickory dickory dog*

Neitzel, Shirley. *I'm not feeling well today*

Neuschwander, Cindy. *Amanda Bean's amazing dream*

Nevius, Carol. *Building with Dad*

Nez, John. *One smart Cookie*

Nichols, Lori. *Maple and Willow apart*

Noble, Trinka Hakes. *Lizzie and the last day of school*

Norac, Carl. *Hello, sweetie pie*

Numeroff, Laura Joffe. *If you take a mouse to school*

O'Brien, Anne Sibley. *I'm new here*

O'Connor, Jane. *Fancy Nancy: poet extraordinaire!*

Ohi, Ruth. *Chicken, Pig, Cow and the class pet*

O'Malley, Kevin. *Straight to the pole*

O'Neill, Alexis. *The Recess Queen*

Ormerod, Jan. *Molly and her dad*
  Ms. MacDonald has a class

Palacios, Argentina. *A Christmas surprise for Chabelita*

Palatini, Margie. *Bedhead*

Parish, Herman. *Amelia Bedelia's first valentine*
  Amelia Bedelia's first vote

Park, Frances. *The royal bee*

Parr, Todd. *Teachers rock!*

Parsley, Elise. *If you ever want to bring an alligator to school, don't!*

Passen, Lisa. *Attack of the 50-foot teacher*
  The incredible shrinking teacher

Pattou, Edith. *Mrs. Spitzer's garden*

Perl, Erica S. *Dotty*
  Ferocious Fluffity

Petrillo, Genevieve. *Keep your ear on the ball*

Pinkwater, Daniel. *Yo-yo man*

Plourde, Lynn. *Book Fair Day*
  Dino pets go to school
  Pajama day
  School picture day

Polacco, Patricia. *An A from Miss Keller*
  The art of Miss Chew
  The junkyard wonders
  The lemonade club
  Mr. Lincoln's way
  Mr. Wayne's masterpiece
  Thank you, Mr. Falker
  Welcome Comfort
Pomeranc, Marion Hess. *The can-do Thanksgiving*
Portis, Antoinette. *Kindergarten diary*
Porto, Tony. *Blue aliens*
  Get red
Poydar, Nancy. *The bad-news report card*
  The biggest test in the universe
  Busy Bea
  No fair science fair
  The perfectly horrible Halloween
  Rhyme time Valentine
  Snip, snip . . . snow!
  Zip, zip . . . homework
Preller, James. *A pirate's guide to recess*
Prelutsky, Jack. *There's no place like school*
  What a day it was at school!
Priceman, Marjorie. *Emeline at the circus*
Primavera, Elise. *Louise the big cheese and the back-to-school smarty-pants*
Pringle, Laurence P. *One room school*
Pulver, Robin. *Author day for room 3T*
  Axle Annie
  Axle Annie and the speed grump
  The case of the incapacitated capitals
  Happy endings
  Mrs. Toggle and the dinosaur
  Mrs. Toggle's beautiful blue shoe
  Mrs. Toggle's zipper
  Never say boo!
  Nobody's mother is in second grade
  Nouns and verbs have a field day
  Punctuation takes a vacation
  Silent letters loud and clear
  Thank you, Miss Doover
Puttock, Simon. *Miss Fox*
Rania, Queen, consort of Abdullah II, King of Jordan. *The sandwich swap*
Rankin, Laura. *Ruthie and the (not so) teeny tiny lie*
Ransome, James. *My teacher*
Rappaport, Doreen. *The school is not white!*
Rathmann, Peggy. *Officer Buckle and Gloria*
  Ruby the copycat
Rawlinson, Julia. *Mule school*
Reagan, Jean. *How to get your teacher ready*
Recorvits, Helen. *Yoon and the jade bracelet*
Reed, Lynn Rowe. *Basil's birds*
  Benny Shark goes to friend school
  Color chaos!
Reid, Barbara. *Perfect snow*
Reiser, Lynn. *Earthdance*
Rey, Margret. *Curious George goes to school*
Reynolds, Aaron. *Superhero School*
Reynolds, Peter H. *Sky color*
Rickert, Janet Elizabeth. *Russ and the almost perfect day*
Rissi, Anica Mrose. *The teacher's pet*
Robb, Diane Burton. *The alphabet war*
Robberecht, Thierry. *Sam tells stories*
Robbins, Jacqui. *The new girl . . . and me*
  Two of a kind
Robertson, David A. *When we were alone*
Roche, Denis. *The best class picture ever*

Mim, gym, and June
Rockwell, Anne. *Becoming butterflies*
  Career day
  Father's Day
  Halloween Day
  Mother's Day
  100 school days
  St. Patrick's Day
  Show and tell day
  Thanksgiving Day
  Valentine's Day
Rogers, Jacqueline. *Kindergarten ABC*
  Tiptoe into kindergarten
Rose, Deborah Lee. *The spelling bee before recess*
  The twelve days of kindergarten
  The twelve days of springtime
Rosen, Michael. *Totally wonderful Miss Plumberry*
Ross, Tony. *Our Kid*
Roth, Carol. *The little school bus*
Rouillard, Wendy. *Barnaby's bunny*
Rumford, James. *Rain school*
Russo, Marisabina. *A very big bunny*
Ruurs, Margriet. *My school in the rain forest*
Ryder, Joanne. *Panda kindergarten*
Rylant, Cynthia. *The ticky-tacky doll*
Saab, Julie. *Little Lola*
Sadler, Marilyn. *Alistair's time machine*
Saltzberg, Barney. *Cornelius P. Mud, are you ready for school?*
  Crazy hair day
  Star of the week
Santoro, Scott. *Which way to witch school?*
Sauer, Tammi. *Ginny Louise and the school showdown*
  Mostly monsterly
Say, Allen. *The favorite daughter*
Schachner, Judith Byron. *Sarabella's thinking cap*
  Skippyjon Jones class action
Schaefer, Carole Lexa. *Kids like us*
Schafer, Milton. *That crazy Barb'ra*
Schertle, Alice. *Jeremy Bean's St. Patrick's Day*
Schmid, Paul. *Hugs from Pearl*
Schreck, Karen Halvorsen. *Lucy's family tree*
Schrock, Jan West. *Give a goat*
Schwartz, Amy. *Oscar*
  Things I learned in second grade
Scieszka, Jon. *Baloney, Henry P.*
Scotton, Rob. *Love, Splat*
  Splat the cat: on with the show
Senisi, Ellen B. *All kinds of friends, even green*
  Just kids
Shannon, David. *David goes to school*
Shaw, Hannah. *School for bandits*
Shea, Bob. *Big plans*
Sheldon, Dyan. *Unicorn dreams*
Shields, Carol Diggory. *Lunch money and other poems about school*
Shipton, Jonathan. *No biting, horrible crocodile!*
Shreeve, Elizabeth. *Oliver at the window*
Sierra, Judy. *The secret science project that almost ate school*
  There's a zoo in room 22
Simms, Laura. *Rotten teeth*
Simon, Norma. *All families are special*
Singer, Marilyn. *First food fight this fall and other school poems*
  I'm your bus
Slade, Suzanne. *With books and bricks*
Slate, Joseph. *Miss Bindergarten celebrates the last day of kindergarten*

Miss Bindergarten celebrates the 100th day of
kindergarten
Miss Bindergarten has a wild day in kindergarten
Miss Bindergarten stays home from kindergarten
Miss Bindergarten takes a field trip with
kindergarten
Smallcomb, Pam. *Earth to Clunk*
Smalls, Irene. *Don't say ain't*
Spinelli, Eileen. *Miss Fox's class gets it wrong*
Miss Fox's class goes green
Miss Fox's class shapes up
Peace Week in Miss Fox's class
Spirin, Gennady. *Philipok*
Stadler, Alexander. *Beverly Billingsly takes a bow*
Stadler, John. *Wilson and Miss Lovely*
Stein, Janet. *This little bunny can bake*
Steptoe, John. *Creativity*
Stevens, Janet. *The little red pen*
Stier, Catherine. *Bugs in my hair?!*
Stoeke, Janet Morgan. *The bus stop*
It's library day
Minerva Louise at school
Sullivan, Deirdre. *Ming goes to school*
Surat, Michele Maria. *Angel child, dragon child*
Swann, Rick. *Our school garden!*
Tavares, Matt. *Becoming Babe Ruth*
Teague, Mark. *The lost and found*
The secret shortcut
Teyssèdre, Fabienne. *Joseph wants to read*
Thoms, Susan Collins. *Cesar takes a break*
Tobin, Jim. *The very inappropriate word*
Tonatiuh, Duncan. *Separate is never equal*
Trent, Tereai. *The girl who buried her dreams in a can*
Tryon, Leslie. *Albert's alphabet*
Patsy says
Tuma, Refe. *What the dinosaurs did at school*
Udry, Janice May. *What Mary Jo shared*
Underwood, Deborah. *A balloon for Isabel*
Here comes teacher cat
Urdahl, Catherine. *Polka-dot fixes kindergarten*
Vail, Rachel. *Flabbersmashed about you*
Van Slyke, Rebecca. *Dad school*
Mom school
Vernick, Audrey. *First grade dropout*
Waber, Bernard. *Evie and Margie*
Wagner, Anke. *Tim's big move!*
Wall, Laura. *Goose goes to school*
Wallace, Nancy Elizabeth. *Ready, set, 100th day!*
Recycle every day!
The Valentine Express
Walton, Rick. *Bunny school*
Watts, Jeri. *A piece of home*
Welch, Willy. *Grumpy Bunnies*
Wells, Rosemary. *Fiona's little lie*
First tomato
Hands off, Harry!
Letters and sounds
McDuff goes to school
Miracle melts down
My kindergarten
Otto runs for President
Otto se presenta para presidente / Otto runs for
President
Yoko
Yoko writes her name
Yoko's show-and-tell
Weston, Carrie. *The new bear at school*
White, Kathryn. *Ruby's school walk*
Whitehead, Jenny. *Lunch box mail and other poems*

Whiting, Sue. *The firefighters*
Wiesner, David. *Sector 7*
Williams, Karen Lynn. *Beatrice's dream*
Wilson, N. D. *Ninja boy goes to school*
Wing, Natasha. *Jalapeño bagels*
Winter, Jeanette. *Malala, a brave girl from Pakistan /*
Iqbal, a brave boy from Pakistan
Nasreen's secret school
Winters, Kari-Lynn. *Gift days*
Winters, Kay. *The bears go to school*
The teeny tiny ghost and the monster
Wolff, Nancy. *It's time for school with Tallulah*
Wolff, Patricia Rae. *The toll-bridge troll*
Wood, Douglas. *What teachers can't do*
Woodson, Jacqueline. *Each kindness*
Wortche, Allison. *Rosie Sprout's time to shine*
Wright, Betty Ren. *The blizzard*
Yaccarino, Dan. *First day on a strange new planet*
Yankovic, Al. *When I grow up*
Yashima, Taro. *Crow boy*
Yolen, Jane. *How do dinosaurs go to school?*
Yousafzai, Malala. *Malala's magic pencil*
Zemach, Kaethe. *Ms. McCaw learns to draw*
Ziefert, Harriet. *Buzzy had a little lamb*
Messy Bessie
Zimmett, Debbie. *Eddie enough*
Zwillich, Julie. *Phoebe sounds it out*

School – field trips

Alberti, Theresa Jarosz. *Out and about at the*
planetarium
Allard, Harry. *Miss Nelson has a field day*
Anstee, Ashlyn. *Are we there, Yeti?*
Beaty, Andrea. *Iggy Peck, architect*
Bemelmans, Ludwig. *Madeline*
Bertram, Debbie. *The best book to read*
Bliss, Harry. *Bailey at the museum*
Bogan, Carmen. *Where's Rodney?*
Bottner, Barbara. *Priscilla gorilla*
Bourgeois, Paulette. *Franklin's class trip*
Bunting, Eve. *One green apple*
Calmenson, Stephanie. *Ollie's class trip*
Caseley, Judith. *Field Day Friday*
Chernesky, Felicia Sanzari. *Sun above and blooms*
below
Cohen, Miriam. *Lost in the museum*
Cole, Joanna. *The magic school bus and the electric*
field trip
The magic school bus and the science fair expedition
The magic school bus at the waterworks
The magic school bus in the time of the dinosaurs
The magic school bus inside a beehive
The magic school bus inside a hurricane
The magic school bus inside the human body
The magic school bus lost in the solar system
The magic school bus on the ocean floor
Cox, Judy. *Pick a pumpkin, Mrs. Millie!*
Cuyler, Margery. *That's good! that's bad! in*
Washington, D.C.
Deady, Kathleen W. *Out and about at the zoo*
Dubois, Muriel L. *Out and about at the fire station*
Ericsson, Jennifer A. *Out and about at the bakery*
Formento, Alison. *These bees count!*
These rocks count!
These seas count!
Garland, Michael. *Miss Smith and the haunted*
library

The gingerbread boy. *The Gingerbread Man loose at the zoo*
  The Gingerbread Man loose on the fire truck
Hanson, Faye. *Midnight at the zoo*
Harper, Jamie. *Miss Mingo weathers the storm*
Holub, Joan. *Apple countdown*
  Pumpkin countdown
Jarman, Julia. *Class Two at the zoo*
Katz, Susan. *Mrs. Brown on exhibit*
Lithgow, John. *Carnival of the animals*
McNamara, Margaret. *The apple orchard riddle*
Mayr, Diane. *Out and about at the apple orchard*
Millman, Isaac. *Moses goes to a concert*
Murphy, Andy. *Out and about at the dairy farm*
Murphy, Stuart J. *Freda is found*
Noble, Trinka Hakes. *The day Jimmy's boa ate the wash*
Parish, Herman. *Amelia Bedelia's first field trip*
Plourde, Lynn. *Field trip day*
Poydar, Nancy. *Fish school*
Rechner, Amy. *Out and about at the aquarium*
Scotton, Rob. *Splat and the cool school trip*
Shea, Kitty. *Out and about at the post office*
  Out and about at the science center
  Out and about at the supermarket
  Out and about at the vet clinic
Slate, Joseph. *Miss Bindergarten takes a field trip with kindergarten*
Spinelli, Eileen. *Miss Fox's class earns a field trip*
Tougas, Chris. *Dojo daytrip*
Watson, Richard Jesse. *The boy who went ape*
Williams, Carol Ann. *Booming Bella*

School – first day

Ahlberg, Janet. *Starting school*
Amado, Elisa. *What are you doing?*
Andrews, Julie. *Dumpy at school*
Anholt, Laurence. *Billy and the big new school*
Argueta, Jorge. *Moony Luna / Luna, Lunita Lunera*
Ashburn, Boni. *The class*
Ashdown, Rebecca. *Bob and Flo*
Audet, Martine. *Martin on the moon*
Auerbach, Adam. *Edda*
Berenstain, Stan and Jan. *The Berenstain bears go to school*
Biggs, Brian. *Tinyville town: time for school*
Black, Harley. *Amazing magic school*
Blake, Stephanie. *I don't want to go to school!*
Bloch, Serge. *Butterflies in my stomach and other school hazards*
Bloom, Suzanne. *The bus for us*
  Nuestro autobús / The bus for us
Borden, Louise. *Off to first grade*
Brillhart, Julie. *Molly rides the school bus*
Brown, Marc. *Monkey: not ready for kindergarten*
Buzzeo, Toni. *Adventure Annie goes to kindergarten*
Capucilli, Alyssa Satin. *Not this bear*
Carlson, Nancy. *First grade, here I come!*
  Look out kindergarten, here I come!
Carlstrom, Nancy White. *It's your first day of school, Annie Claire*
Cazet, Denys. *Never spit on your shoes*
Chapman, Jared. *Steve, raised by wolves*
Chast, Roz. *Marco goes to school*
Child, Lauren. *I am too absolutely small for school*
Cocca-Leffler, Maryann. *Jack's talent*
Cohen, Jeff. *Eva and Sadie and the best classroom ever!*

Cohen, Miriam. *Will I have a friend?*, ill. by Ronald Himler
  Will I have a friend?, ill. by Lillian Hoban
Colandro, Lucille. *There was an old lady who swallowed some books!*
Corey, Shana. *First graders from Mars: Horus's horrible day*
Cork, Barbara Taylor. *Sam starts school*
Cuyler, Margery. *Bonaparte falls apart*
D'Amico, Carmela. *Ella, the elegant elephant*
Danneberg, Julie. *First day jitters*
Davis, Katie. *Kindergarten rocks!*
deGroat, Diane. *Brand-new pencils, brand-new books*
dePaola, Tomie. *Meet the Barkers*
Derby, Sally. *A new school year*
Dewdney, Anna. *Llama Llama misses Mama*
Diesen, Deborah. *The pout-pout fish goes to school*
Dillard, Sarah. *First day at Zoo School*
Dodd, Emma. *Foxy*
Edwards, Becky. *My first day at nursery school*
Edwards, Pamela Duncan. *Dinosaur starts school*
Ehrlich, Nikki. *Twindergarten*
Falwell, Cathryn. *David's drawing*
Ferguson, Sarah. *Emily's first day of school*
Fortenberry, Julie. *Lily's cat mask*
Forward, Toby. *What did you do today?*
Gaiman, Neil. *Chu's first day of school*
Gantos, Jack. *Back to school for Rotten Ralph*
George, Lucy M. *Back to school Tortoise*
Goldfinger, Jennifer P. *Hello, my name is Tiger*
Goodman, Joan Elizabeth. *Bernard goes to school*
Gorbachev, Valeri. *Chicken chickens go to school*
Grandits, John. *Ten rules you absolutely must not break if you want to survive the school bus*
Greenfield, Eloise. *Me and Neesie*
Grindley, Sally. *It's my school*
Grogan, John. *Marley goes to school*
Hale, Nathan. *Yellowbelly and Plum go to school*
Harper, Jamie. *Miss Mingo and the first day of school*
Harper, Jessica. *A place called Kindergarten*
Harris, Robie H. *I am not going to school today*
Hartt-Sussman, Heather. *Noni is nervous*
Hays, Anna Jane. *Kindergarten countdown*
Henkes, Kevin. *Jessica*
  Wemberly worried
Hennessy, B. G. *Mr. Ouchy's first day*
Hest, Amy. *Off to school, Baby Duck*
Hill, Eric. *Spot goes to school*
Hodgkinson, Jo. *A big day for Migs*
Hood, Susan. *Mission: back to school*, ill. by Mary Lundquist
  Mission: back to school, ill. by Mary Lundquist
Jagtenberg, Yvonne. *Jack the wolf*
Janni, Rebecca. *Every cowgirl goes to school*
Janousky, Peggy Robbins. *Move it, Miss Macintosh!*
Johnston, Tony. *First grade, here I come!*
  Off to kindergarten
Kaufmann, Nancy. *Bye, Bye*
Kirk, David. *Little Miss Spider at Sunny Patch School*
Kroll, Virginia L. *On the way to kindergarten*
Krumwiede, Lana. *Just Itzy*
Langreuter, Jutta. *Little Bear goes to kindergarten*
Lasky, Kathryn. *Lunch bunnies*
Latimer, Miriam. *Dear Panda*
Léonard, Marie. *Tibili, the little boy who didn't want to go to school*
Lester, Mike. *A is for salad*
Levitin, Sonia. *When Kangaroo goes to school*
Livingston, A. A. *B. Bear and Lolly: off to school*

London, Jonathan. *Froggy goes to school*
Lorenz, Albert. *The exceptionally, extraordinarily ordinary first day of school*
McCarthy, Jenna. *Lola knows a lot*
McCarty, Peter. *Henry in love*
McGhee, Alison. *Countdown to kindergarten*
McGinty, Alice B. *Eliza's kindergarten surprise*
McQuade, Jacqueline. *At preschool with Teddy Bear*
Mahoney, Daniel J. *Monstergarten*
Marshall, James. *Eugene*
Marshall, Linda Elovitz. *Kindergarten is cool!*
Martin, Bill, Jr.. *Kitty Cat, Kitty Cat, are you going to school?*
Miller, Pat Zietlow. *Sophie's squash go to school*
Millman, Isaac. *Moses goes to school*
Milord, Susan. *Happy school year!*
Mitchard, Jacquelyn. *Ready, set, school!*
Montanari, Eva. *A very full morning*
Moreillon, Judi. *Ready and waiting for you*
Morrow, Tara Jaye. *Panda goes to school*
Neubecker, Robert. *Fall is for school*
   Wow! school!
Novak, Matt. *Jazzbo goes to school*
Onyefulu, Ifeoma. *Deron goes to nursery school*
Ormerod, Jan. *When an elephant comes to school*
Pak, Soyung. *Sumi's first day of school ever*
Parish, Herman. *Amelia Bedelia's first day of school*
Parr, Todd. *Otto goes to school*
Pennypacker, Sara. *Stuart's cape*
Pérez, L. King. *First day in grapes*
Plourde, Lynn. *You're wearing that to school?!*
Poydar, Nancy. *First day, hooray!*
Preller, James. *A pirate's guide to first grade*
Puttock, Simon. *Mouse's first night at Moonlight School*
Quackenbush, Robert M. *First grade jitters*
Rabe, Tish. *On the first day of kindergarten*
Radabaugh, Melinda Beth. *Going to school*
Rankin, Joan. *First day*
Ransom, Candice F. *Amanda Panda quits kindergarten*
Recorvits, Helen. *My name is Yoon*
Rex, Adam. *School's first day of school*
Rim, Sujean. *Birdie's first day of school*
Robbins, Beth. *Tom's first day at school*
Rockwell, Anne. *First day of school*
   Welcome to kindergarten
Rodman, Mary Ann. *First grade stinks!*
Rosenberry, Vera. *Vera's first day of school*
Rouss, Sylvia A. *Sammy Spider's first day of school*
Rubel, Nicole. *Ham and Pickles*
Rusackas, Francesca. *I love you all day long*
Sanders, Rob. *Ruby Rose*
Schaefer, Lola M. *Frankie Stein starts school*
Schmid, Paul. *Oliver and his alligator*
Schwartz, Amy. *Annabelle Swift, kindergartner*
   Polka dots for Poppy
Scotton, Rob. *Splat the cat*
Sierra, Judy. *We love our school!*
Slate, Joseph. *Miss Bindergarten gets ready for kindergarten*
Smalls-Hector, Irene. *Beginning school*
Stampler, Ann Redisch. *Go home, Mrs. Beekman!*
Staub, Leslie. *Time for (Earth) school, Dewey Dew*
Stevenson, James. *That dreadful day*
Stewart, Amber. *Puddle's new school*
Stuve-Bodeen, Stephanie. *Elizabeti's school*
Tanner, Suzy-Jane. *Tinyflock Nursery School*
Taulbert, Clifton L. *Little Cliff's first day of school*

Torrey, Richard. *Ally-Saurus and the first day of school*
Uegaki, Chieri. *Suki's kimono*
Underwood, Deborah. *Super Saurus saves kindergarten*
Vernick, Audrey. *Is your buffalo ready for kindergarten?*
   Second grade holdout
Wells, Rosemary. *Emily's first 100 days of school*
   How many? How much?
   Timothy goes to school
Whybrow, Ian. *Harry and the dinosaurs go to school*
Wild, Margaret. *Tom goes to kindergarten*
Winget, Susan. *Tucker's four-carrot school day*
Winters, Kay. *This school year will be the best!*
Wohnoutka, Mike. *Dad's first day*
Wright, Michael. *Jake starts school*
Yamashita, Haruo. *Seven little mice go to school*
Yankovic, Al. *My new teacher and me!*
Yoon, Salina. *Bear's big day*
Yum, Hyewon. *Mom, it's my first day of kindergarten!*

School – nursery

Alexander, Claire. *Lucy and the bully*
Ashdown, Rebecca. *Bob and Flo*
Bottner, Barbara. *An annoying ABC*
Brandt, Amy. *Benjamin comes back / Benjamin regresa*
   When Katie was our teacher / Cuando Katie era nuestra maestra
Chodos-Irvine, Margaret. *Best best friends*
Codell, Esme Raji. *It's time for preschool!*
Cole, Joanna. *When Mommy and Daddy go to work*
Cousins, Lucy. *Maisy goes to preschool*
Day, Alexandra. *Carl goes to daycare*
Edvall, Lilian. *The rabbit who longed for home*
Edwards, Becky. *My first day at nursery school*
Elliott, David. *Hunter's best friend at school*
Gary, Meredith. *Sometimes you get what you want*
Gerber, Carole. *A band of babies*
Golan, Avirama. *Little Naomi, Little Chick*
Henkes, Kevin. *Wemberly worried*
Hesse, Karen. *My thumb*
Hughes, Shirley. *Alfie and the big boys*
Ismail, Yasmeen. *Specs for Rex*
Katz, Karen. *Rosie goes to preschool*
Korngold, Jamie S. *Sadie and the big mountain*
Kroll, Virginia L. *Everybody has a teddy*
Larsen, Andrew. *Bella and the bunny*
McQuade, Jacqueline. *At preschool with Teddy Bear*
Murkoff, Heidi Eisenberg. *What to expect at preschool*
Onyefulu, Ifeoma. *Deron goes to nursery school*
Rankin, Joan. *First day*
Rockwell, Anne. *My preschool*
   President's Day
Rogers, Fred. *Going to day care*
Schaefer, Carole Lexa. *Someone says*
Schwartz, Amy. *The boys teams*
Senisi, Ellen B. *Hurray for pre-K!*
Shea, Bob. *Dinosaur vs. school*
Sierra, Judy. *Preschool to the rescue*
Sturges, Philemon. *I love school*
Tanner, Suzy-Jane. *Tinyflock Nursery School*
Tougas, Chris. *Dojo Daycare*
   Dojo surprise
Weeks, Sarah. *My somebody special*
Willems, Mo. *Knuffle Bunny too*

School teachers *see* Careers – teachers

Science

Adler, David A. *Magnets push, magnets pull*
  Redwoods are the tallest trees in the world
  Things that float and things that don't
Alberti, Theresa Jarosz. *Out and about at the
  planetarium*
Aliki. *Corn is maize*
  Digging up dinosaurs
  Dinosaurs are different
  Fossils tell of long ago
  The long lost coelacanth and other living fossils
  My feet
  My hands
  My visit to the dinosaurs
  A weed is a flower
  Wild and woolly mammoths
Allen, Judy. *Are you a butterfly?*
  Are you a grasshopper?
  Are you a ladybug?
  Are you a snail?
  Are you an ant?
Allen, Pamela. *Who sank the boat?*
Anderson, Stephen Axel. *I know the moon*
Andros, Camille. *Charlotte the scientist is squished*
Arnold, Caroline. *Too hot? too cold?*
Arnosky, Jim. *All about deer*
  Crinkleroot's guide to knowing butterflies and moths
  Dolphins on the sand
  Gobble it up!
Asch, Frank. *The sun is my favorite star*
Atkins, Jeannine. *Mary Anning and the sea dragon*
Baby animals
Bang, Molly. *Buried sunlight*
  Living sunlight
  My light
  Ocean sunlight
  Rivers of sunlight
Barner, Bob. *Stars, stars, stars*
Barnett, Mac. *Oh no!*
Beaty, Andrea. *Ada Twist, scientist*
Berenstain, Stan and Jan. *The Berenstain bears'
  science fair*
Berger, Melvin. *Brrr! a book about polar animals*
  Buzz! a book about insects
  Dive! a book of deep sea creatures
  Early humans
  Germs make me sick!
  How do airplanes fly?
  How's the weather?
  Look out for turtles!
  Oil spill!
  Spinning spiders
  Switch on, switch off
  Why I sneeze, shiver, hiccup, and yawn
Berne, Jennifer. *Manfish*
Berry, Lynne. *What floats in a moat?*
Boothroyd, Jennifer. *What is a gas?*
Branley, Franklyn M. *Air is all around you*
  Comets
  Down comes the rain
  Earthquakes
  Eclipse
  Flash, crash, rumble, and roll
  Floating in space
  Gravity is a mystery
  Light and darkness

  The planets in our solar system
  Rain and hail
  The sky is full of stars
  Snow is falling
  The sun, our nearest star
  Sunshine makes the seasons
  Tornado alert
  Volcanoes, ill. by Megan Lloyd
  Volcanoes, ill. by Marc Simont
  What makes a magnet?
  What makes day and night
  What the moon is like
Brighton, Catherine. *Galileo's treasure box*
Brown, Don. *Rare treasure*
Carrick, Carol. *Patrick's dinosaurs*
Cash, Megan Montague. *What makes the seasons?*
Cassino, Mark, with Jon Nelson. *The story of snow*
Chapman, Jared. *Pirate, Viking, and Scientist*
Chin, Jason. *Gravity*
Cobb, Vicki. *I fall down*
  I get wet
  I see myself
  Open your eyes
Cole, Joanna. *How you were born*
  The magic school bus and the climate challenge
  The magic school bus and the science fair expedition
  The magic school bus in the time of the dinosaurs
  The magic school bus inside a beehive
  The magic school bus inside a hurricane
  The magic school bus inside the earth
  The magic school bus inside the human body
  The magic school bus lost in the solar system
  The magic school bus on the ocean floor
  My puppy is born
Davies, Jacqueline. *The boy who drew birds*
Davies, Nicola. *Tiny creatures*
Dennard, Deborah. *Lemur landing*
Diffily, Deborah. *Jurassic shark*
Dorros, Arthur. *Ant cities*
  The fungus that ate my school
Dotlich, Rebecca Kai. *What is science?*
Drummond, Allan. *Energy island*
Edwards, Wallace. *The extinct files*
Egan, Tim. *The experiments of Doctor Vermin*
Ferri, Giuliano. *Little Tad grows up*
Gall, Chris. *NanoBots*
Gibbons, Gail. *Dinosaur discoveries*
  Exploring the deep, dark sea
  From seed to plant
  Galaxies, galaxies!
  It's raining!
  Monarch butterfly
  Prehistoric animals
  Sharks
  Soaring with the wind
  Sun up, sun down
Glaser, Linda. *Magnificent monarchs*
Goldin, Augusta. *Ducks don't get wet*
Greenstein, Elaine. *The goose man*
Greenwood, Rosie. *I wonder why volcanoes blow their
  tops*
Harrison, David L. *Caves*
  Earthquakes
Heller, Ruth. *Chickens aren't the only ones*
Hickling, Meg. *Boys, girls and body science*
Hirst, Robin. *My place in space*
Hiscock, Bruce. *Ookpik*
Hodge, Deborah. *Ants*
  Bees

Eagles
Salmon
Holderness, Jackie. *What is a shadow?*
Hollenbeck, Kathleen M. *Islands of ice*
Hopkinson, Deborah. *The humblebee hunter*
Hort, Lenny. *Did dinosaurs eat pizza?*
Jenkins, Priscilla Belz. *A nest full of eggs*
Jenkins, Steve. *How to clean a hippopotamus*
Jolivet, Joëlle. *Almost everything*
Zoo-ology
Jordan, Helene J. *How a seed grows*
Kalz, Jill. *Northern lights*
Karas, G. Brian. *Atlantic*
Kleven, Elisa. *Glasswings*
Knudsen, Michelle. *Argus*
Bugged!
A moldy mystery
Krebs, Laurie. *The beeman*, ill. by Valeria Cis
The beeman, ill. by Melissa Iwai
Kudlinski, Kathleen V. *Boy, were we wrong about dinosaurs!*
Boy, were we wrong about the human body!
Boy, were we wrong about the solar system!
Lasky, Kathryn. *Science fair bunnies*
Lauber, Patricia. *Be a friend to trees*
Snakes are hunters
Who eats what?
Lehn, Barbara. *What is a scientist?*
Locker, Thomas. *Sky tree*
Loewen, Nancy. *Busy buzzers*
Lunde, Darrin. *Hello, bumblebee bat*
Whose poop is that?
Lyon, George Ella. *All the water in the world*
McMillan, Bruce. *Counting wildflowers*
McNamara, Margaret. *How many seeds in a pumpkin?*
McQuade, Jacqueline. *Small babies*
Maestro, Betsy. *How do apples grow?*
Why do leaves change color?
Manning, Mick. *Snap!*
Markle, Sandra. *Creepy, crawly baby bugs*
Sneaky, spinning, baby spiders
Mason, Adrienne. *Lu and Clancy sound off*
Snakes
Mayer, Lynne. *Newton and me*
Meltzer, Brad. *I am Albert Einstein*
Morrison, Gordon. *A drop of water*
Nagda, Anne Whitehead. *World above the clouds*
Offill, Jenny. *11 experiments that failed*
Parker, Michael. *You are a star!*
Parker, Nancy Winslow. *Bugs*
Patkau, Karen. *Creatures*
Paul, Miranda. *Are we pears yet?*
Water is water
Peters, Lisa Westberg. *The sun, the wind and the rain*
Water's way
Pettenati, Jeanne K. *Galileo's journal, 1609–1610*
Pfeffer, Wendy. *From tadpole to frog*
Light is all around us
Wiggling worms at work
Pfister, Marcus. *Ava's poppy*
Polacco, Patricia. *Meteor!*
Posada, Mia. *Dandelions, stars in the grass*
Guess what is growing inside this egg
Poydar, Nancy. *No fair science fair*
Pringle, Laurence P. *Crows*
Snakes
Raab, Brigitte. *Where does pepper come from?*
Rau, Dana Meachen. *Mars*

Reynolds, Aaron. *Carnivores*
Rockwell, Anne. *Clouds*
One bean
What's so bad about gasoline?
Rotter, Charles. *Seals*
Walruses
Ryan, Pam Muñoz. *How do you raise a raisin?*
Ryder, Joanne. *Rainbow wings*
Where butterflies grow
Sabuda, Robert. *Encyclopedia prehistorica: mega-beasts*
Encyclopedia prehistorica: sharks and other seamonsters
Sadler, Marilyn. *Alistair's time machine*
Sayre, April Pulley. *Army ant parade*
Dig, wait, listen
The hungry hummingbird
Schaefer, Lola M. *Lifetime*
Schanzer, Rosalyn. *How Ben Franklin stole the lightning*
Schwartz, David M. *If you hopped like a frog*
Seuling, Barbara. *Flick a switch*
From head to toe
Shea, Kitty. *Out and about at the science center*
Showers, Paul. *A drop of blood*
Ears are for hearing
Hear your heart
Look at your eyes
Sleep is for everyone
Where does the garbage go?
Sierra, Judy. *The secret science project that almost ate school*
Sill, Cathryn. *Wetlands*
Sklansky, Amy E. *Where do chicks come from?*
Steig, William. *The toy brother*
Sykes, Julie. *Little Rocket's special star*
Tagholm, Sally. *The frog*
Tang, Greg. *Math fables too*
Thornhill, Jan. *I am Josephine (and I am a living thing)*
Toft, Kim Michelle. *Neptune's nursery*
Tomecek, Steve. *Dirt*
Tresselt, Alvin R. *Rain drop splash*
Van Woerkom, Dorothy. *Hidden messages*
Vern, Alex. *Where do frogs come from?*
Verstraete, Larry. *S is for scientists*
Voake, Steve. *Insect detective*
Wallace, Nancy Elizabeth. *Pond walk*
Rocks! rocks! rocks!
Ward, Jennifer. *What will grow?*
What will hatch?
Wells, Robert E. *Did a dinosaur drink this water?*
Why do elephants need the sun?
Yolen, Jane. *Welcome to the icehouse*
Zoehfeld, Kathleen Weidner. *How mountains are made*
Secrets of the garden
What lives in a shell?
What's alive?

Scorpions

Emberley, Rebecca. *The crocodile and the scorpion*

Scuba diving *see* Sports – skin diving

Sea & seashore

Ahlberg, Allan. *The baby in the hat*

Aliki. *Those summers*
Arnold, Caroline. *Giant shark*
Arnosky, Jim. *Parrotfish and sunken ships*
   Turtle in the sea
Asch, Frank. *Sand cake*
Ashforth, Camilla. *Willow by the sea*
Austin, Mike. *Rescue Squad No. 9*
Axelrod, Amy. *Pigs on a blanket*
Bailey, Linda. *Stanley at sea*
Baker, Jeannie. *The hidden forest*
Bang, Molly. *Ocean sunlight*
   Yellow ball
Barclay, Jane. *Going on a journey to the sea*
Barner, Bob. *Sea bones*
Beliveau, Kathy. *The yoga game by the sea*
Belton, Robyn. *Herbert*
Berger, Melvin. *Dive! a book of deep sea creatures*
   Oil spill!
Berkes, Marianne. *Seashells by the seashore*
Berne, Jennifer. *Manfish*
Biro, Maureen Boyd. *Walking with Maga*
Blackstone, Stella. *An island in the sun*
   Secret seahorse
Bouler, Olivia. *Olivia's birds*
Brenner, Barbara A. *One small place by the sea*
Brown, Marc. *D. W. all wet*
Brown, Margaret Wise. *Sneakers, the seaside cat*
Browne, Christopher. *Marlo*
Buckingham, Matt. *Bright Stanley*
Bunting, Eve. *Ducky*
Burdett, Lois. *Twelfth night for kids*
Burleigh, Robert. *Solving the puzzle under the sea*
Burnard, Damon. *I spy in the ocean*
Burningham, John. *Come away from the water,*
   Shirley
Butterworth, Chris. *Sea horse*
Buzzeo, Toni. *The sea chest*
Calhoun, Mary. *Henry the sailor cat*
Carle, Eric. *A house for Hermit Crab*
   10 little rubber ducks
Casin, Sheridan. *Little Turtle and the song of the sea*
Catrow, David. *Fun in the sun*
Chin, Jason. *Coral reefs*
Coffey, Maria. *A cat adrift*
Cohen, Miriam. *See you in second grade!*
Cole, Joanna. *The magic school bus on the ocean floor*
Coombs, Kate. *Water sings blue*
Cottle, Joan. *Miles away from home*
Cousins, Lucy. *Hooray for fish!*
   Maisy goes on vacation
Cowell, Cressida. *Hiccup the seasick Viking*
Cuevas, Michelle. *The uncorker of ocean bottles*
Cumberbatch, Judy. *Can you hear the sea?*
Dahl, Michael. *One giant splash*
   Starry arms
Daly, Niki. *Why the sun and moon live in the sky*
Davies, Jacqueline. *The house takes a vacation*
Davies, Nicola. *Oceans and seas*
   One tiny turtle
Day, Jan. *The pirate, Pink*
   Pirate Pink and treasures of the reef
Demas, Corinne. *The boy who was generous with salt*
DiCamillo, Kate. *Louise*
Dickson, Louise. *The vanishing cat*
Domanska, Janina. *If all the seas were one sea*
Dunning, Joan. *Seabird in the forest*
Ehrlich, H. M. *Gotcha, Louie!*
   Louie's goose
Elliott, David. *In the sea*

Engels-Fietzek, Petra. *Sophie and the seagull*
Field, Eugene. *Wynken, Blynken and Nod*
   Wynken, Blynken, and Nod: a Dutch lullaby
Fisher, Leonard Everett. *Sky, sea, the jetty, and me*
Fitzpatrick, Marie-Louise. *You, me and the big blue*
   sea
Ford, Christine. *Ocean's child*
Formento, Alison. *These seas count!*
Franco, Betsy. *A spectacular selection of sea critters*
Frasier, Debra. *Out of the ocean*
Freymann, Saxton. *One lonely seahorse*
Galloway, Ruth. *Fidgety fish*
Gay, Marie-Louise. *Stella, star of the sea*
Geist, Ken. *The three little fish and the big bad shark*
Gibbons, Gail. *Coral reefs*
   Exploring the deep, dark sea
Gibbs, Edward. *I spy under the sea*
Goudey, Alice E. *Houses from the sea*
Grassby, Donna. *A seaside alphabet*
Guiberson, Brenda Z. *Into the sea*
Gutman, Anne. *Gaspard at the seashore*
Hamilton, K. R. *This is the ocean*
Harris, Trudy. *Pattern fish*
Harshman, Terry Webb. *Does a sea cow say moo?*
Hayashi, Leslie Ann. *Fables from the sea*
Heidbreder, Robert. *A sea-wishing day*
Hines, Anna Grossnickle. *Gramma's walk*
Hodgkins, Fran. *Between the tides*
Horowitz, Ruth. *Crab moon*
Hort, Lenny. *We're going on a treasure hunt*
Hughes, Langston. *Sail away*
Hunter, Anne. *What's in the tide pool?*
Inkpen, Mick. *Sandcastle*
Jackson, Ellen. *The seven seas*
Johnson, Angela. *Joshua by the sea*
Karas, G. Brian. *Atlantic*
Kranking, Kathy. *The ocean is . . .*
Kudlinski, Kathleen V. *The seaside switch*
Kuskin, Karla. *I am me*
Lawler, Janet. *Ocean counting*
Lawlor, Laurie. *Rachel Carson and her book that*
   changed the world
Limentani, Alison. *How long is a whale?*
Lionni, Leo. *Swimmy*
Loomis, Christine. *Scuba bunnies*
McCarthy, Meghan. *The adventures of Patty and the*
   big red bus
McCarty, Peter. *Hondo and Fabian*
McCloskey, Robert. *One morning in Maine*
   Time of wonder
MacDonald, Margaret Read. *Surf war!*
McDonald, Megan. *Is this a house for Hermit Crab?*
McNaughton, Colin. *Oomph!*
Mahy, Margaret. *A summery Saturday morning*
Mason, Janeen I. *Ocean commotion*
Munsch, Robert N. *A promise is a promise*
Nelson, Robert Lyn. *Ocean friends*
Neubecker, Robert. *Wow! ocean!*
Nivola, Claire A. *Life in the ocean*
Nolan, Dennis. *Sea of dreams*
O'Connor, George. *Ker-splash!*
Olien, Jessica. *The blobfish book*
Pallotta, Jerry. *Dory story*
   Ocean counting: odd numbers
Peet, Bill. *Cyrus the unsinkable sea serpent*
   Kermit the hermit
Perrin, Martine. *Look who's there!*
Peters, Lisa Westberg. *The sun, the wind and the rain*
Pfeffer, Wendy. *Life in a coral reef*

Pfister, Marcus. *Milo and the mysterious island*
  Rainbow fish ABC
  Rainbow fish and the sea monsters' cave
Pollard, Nik. *The tide*
Preston-Gannon, Frann. *Deep deep sea*
Raff, Courtney Granet. *Giant of the sea*
Rand, Gloria. *Sailing home*
Reiser, Lynn. *Little clam*
Riddell, Chris. *Platypus*
Rockwell, Anne. *Ferryboat ride!*
Roderick, Stacey. *Ocean animals from head to tail*
Roop, Peter. *Down east in the ocean*
Rose, Deborah Lee. *Into the A, B, sea*
  Ocean babies
Rylant, Cynthia. *The whales*
Sabuda, Robert. *Encyclopedia prehistorica: sharks and other seamonsters*
St. Pierre, Stephanie. *What the sea saw*
San Souci, Daniel. *The rabbit and the dragon king*
San Souci, Robert D. *Brave Margaret*
  Nicholas Pipe
Santoro, Lucio. *Wild oceans*
Sarcone-Roach, Julia. *Subway story*
Schwarz, Viviane. *Shark and Lobster's amazing undersea adventure*
Serafini, Frank. *Looking closely along the shore*
Seven, John. *The ocean story*
Shepard, Aaron. *The sea king's daughter*
Sherry, Kevin. *I'm the best artist in the ocean*
  I'm the biggest thing in the ocean
Simmons, Jane. *Ebb and Flo and the greedy gulls*
Sís, Peter. *An ocean world*
  Ship ahoy!
Slate, Jenny. *Marcel the shell with shoes on*
Sperring, Mark. *Mermaid dreams*
Stevenson, James. *July*
  Which one is Whitney?
Stevenson, Robert Louis. *Block city*, ill. by Daniel Kirk
  Block city, ill. by Ashley Wolff
Strauss, Susan. *When woman became the sea*
Sutherland, Marc. *MacMurtrey's wall*
Taylor, Eleanor. *Beep, beep, let's go!*
Thomson, Bill. *The typewriter*
Titherington, Jeanne. *Baby's boat*
Toft, Kim Michelle. *Neptune's nursery*
Tokuda, Wendy. *Humphrey the lost whale*
Townsend, Emily Rose. *Seals*
Tresselt, Alvin R. *Hide and seek fog*
Tucker, Kathy. *Do pirates take baths?*
Turkle, Brinton. *Do not open*
Turnbull, Victoria. *The sea tiger*
Van Dusen, Chris. *Down to the sea with Mr. Magee*
Viva, Frank. *A long way away*
Waddell, Martin. *The big big sea*
  Sailor Bear
Ward, Helen. *Old shell, new shell*
Ward, Jennifer. *Somewhere in the ocean*
Williams, Garth. *Benjamin's treasure*
Winkelman, Barbara Gaines. *Puffer's surprise*
Winton, Tim. *The deep*
Wolkstein, Diane. *The day Ocean came to visit*
Wood, Audrey. *The deep blue sea*
Yaccarino, Dan. *The fantastic undersea life of Jacques Cousteau*
Yee, Brenda Shannon. *Sand castle*
Yoon, Salina. *Penguin on vacation*
Zeman, Ludmila. *Sindbad*
Ziefert, Harriet. *Beach party!*
  Wiggle like an octopus
Zoehfeld, Kathleen Weidner. *What lives in a shell?*

Sea & seashore – beaches

Ashman, Linda. *To the beach!*
Beardshaw, Rosalind. *Grandma's beach*
Berry, Lynne. *Duck dunks*
Bottner, Barbara. *Feet go to sleep*
Breen, Steve. *The secret of Santa's island*
Briant, Ed. *A day at the beach*
Cash, Megan Montague. *I saw the sea and the sea saw me*
Caswell, Deanna. *Beach house*
Clements, Andrew. *Because your daddy loves you*
Cooper, Elisha. *Beach*
Crimi, Carolyn. *There might be lobsters*
Crum, Shutta. *Uh-oh!*
Docherty, Thomas. *To the beach*
Elya, Susan Middleton. *Bebé goes to the beach*
Estefan, Gloria. *Noelle's treasure tale*
Fleming, Candace. *Tippy-tippy-tippy, splash!*
Frazee, Marla. *A couple of boys have the best week ever*
Gaiman, Neil. *Chu's day at the beach*
Gall, Chris. *Dinotrux dig the beach*
Greenberg, Melanie Hope. *Mermaids on parade*
Grey, Mini. *Traction Man and the beach odyssey*
Hill, Eric. *Spot goes to the beach*
Hills, Tad. *Duck and Goose go to the beach*
Hubbell, Patricia. *Sea, sand, me!*
Huneck, Stephen. *Sally goes to the beach*
Hurley, Jorey. *Fetch*
Idle, Molly. *Sea Rex*
Inkpen, Mick. *Kipper's sunny day*
Jay, Alison. *Out of the blue*
Johnson, Crockett. *Magic beach*
Keller, Holly. *Miranda's beach day*
Konagaya, Kiyomi. *Beach feet*
Larsen, Andrew. *The not-so-faraway adventure*
  See you next year
Lee, Suzy. *Wave*
Lies, Brian. *Bats at the beach*
McClure, Nikki. *Waiting for high tide*
Mathers, Petra. *Lottie's new beach towel*
Monroe, Chris. *Monkey with a tool belt and the seaside shenanigans*
Moore, Jodi. *When a dragon moves in*
Murphy, Patti Beling. *Elinor and Violet*
Napoli, Donna Jo. *Hands and hearts*
Naylor, Phyllis Reynolds. *Please do feed the bears*
Oxenbury, Helen. *Tom and Pippo on the beach*
Parsley, Elise. *If you ever want to bring a piano to the beach, don't!*
Pendziwol, Jean E. *A treasure at sea for dragon and me*
Perry, Robert. *Down at the Seaweed Café*
Rau, Dana Meachen. *Stroll by the sea*
Robertson, M. P. *The sandcastle*
Rockwell, Anne. *At the beach*
Roosa, Karen. *Beach day*
Rotner, Shelley. *Senses at the seashore*
Ryan, Pam Muñoz. *Hello, Ocean!*
  Hello Ocean / Hola mar
Sattler, Jennifer. *Pig kahuna: who's that pig?*
  Pig kahuna pirates!
Scheffler, Axel. *Pip and Posy: the new friend*
Sierra, Judy. *Ballyhoo Bay*
Sís, Peter. *Beach ball*
Soman, David. *Ladybug Girl at the beach*

Stein, David Ezra. *Ice boy*
Stevenson, James. *The worst person in the world at Crab Beach*
Stojic, Manya. *Wet pebbles under our feet*
Thaler, Mike. *Pig Little*
Turnbull, Victoria. *Kings of the castle*
Wallace, Nancy Elizabeth. *Shells! shells! shells!*
Walsh, Ellen Stoll. *Hamsters to the rescue*
Watt, Mélanie. *Scaredy Squirrel at the beach*
Waugh, Peter. *The great cannon beach mouse caper*
Weninger, Brigitte. *Miko goes on vacation*
Wiesner, David. *Flotsam*
Williams, Karen Lynn. *A beach tail*
Willis, Jeanne. *I'm sure I saw a dinosaur*
Yektai, Niki. *Bears at the beach*
Yoon, Salina. *At the beach*
Ziefert, Harriet. *Mighty Max*

Sea serpents *see* Monsters; Mythical creatures

Seahorses *see* Fish – seahorses

Seashore *see* Sand; Sea & seashore – beaches

Seasons

Adler, David A. *It's time to sleep, it's time to dream*
Adoff, Arnold. *In for winter, out for spring*
Ammon, Richard. *An Amish year*
Anholt, Catherine. *Sun, snow, stars, sky*
Anno, Mitsumasa. *Anno's counting book*
Arnosky, Jim. *Outdoors on foot*
Austin, Heather. *Visiting Aunt Sylvia's*
Baker, Keith. *Hap-pea all year*
Banks, Kate. *The great blue house*
Barack, Marcy. *Season song*
Berger, Carin. *Forever friends*
Berner, Rotraut Susanne. *In the town all year 'round*
Birnbaum, Abe. *Green eyes*
Bissonette, Aimée. *North woods girl*
Blexbolex. *Seasons*
Branley, Franklyn M. *Sunshine makes the seasons*
Brown, Kerry. *Tupag the dreamer*
Brown, Margaret Wise. *Goodnight songs*
    The little island
    Love songs of the little bear
Browne, Anthony. *Voices in the park*
Bruchac, Joseph. *Thirteen moons on turtle's back*
Bruel, Nick. *A wonderful year*
Brunhoff, Laurent de. *Meet Babar and his family*
Burrowes, Adjoa J. *Grandma's purple flowers*
Carle, Eric. *The tiny seed*
Carlstrom, Nancy White. *How does the wind walk?*
Cash, Megan Montague. *What makes the seasons?*
Clement, Nathan. *Big tractor*
Cooper, Elisha. *Farm*
Costa, Nicoletta. *The little tree that would not share*
Dahl, Michael. *From the garden*
Deady, Kathleen W. *All year long*
Diesen, Deborah. *Bloom*
Duval, Kathy. *A bear's year*
Edwards, Richard. *Copy me, Copycub*
Ehlert, Lois. *Red leaf, yellow leaf*
Ewart, Claire. *The giant*
Farrar, Sid. *The year comes round*
Félix, Lucie. *Apples and robins*

Fisher, Valorie. *Everything I need to know before I'm five*
Fleming, Denise. *In the small, small pond*
Florian, Douglas. *The curious cares of bears*
Fogliano, Julie. *When green becomes tomatoes*
Frisch, Aaron. *The lonely pine*
Geisert, Bonnie. *Mountain town*
George, Jean Craighead. *Dear Rebecca, winter is here*
    Look to the north
George, Kristine O'Connell. *Old Elm speaks*
Gershator, Phillis. *Listen, listen*
Gibbons, Gail. *Farming*
    The reasons for seasons
    The seasons of Arnold's apple tree
Glaser, Linda. *Hello, squirrels!*
Gomi, Taro. *Spring is here*
Gray, Luli. *Ant and Grasshopper*
Greene, Rhonda Gowler. *Daddy is a cozy hug*
    Mommy is a soft, warm kiss
Greenstein, Elaine. *As big as you*
Guenther, James. *Turnagain, Ptarmigan, where did you go?*
Hall, Donald. *Ox-cart man*
Hall, Zoe. *The apple pie tree*
Henkes, Kevin. *In the middle of fall*
    Old Bear
    When spring comes
Hewitt, Sally. *All year round*
    Woods and meadows
Hines, Anna Grossnickle. *Pieces, a year in poems and quilts*
Hoberman, Mary Ann. *Right outside my window*
Horácek, Petr. *A surprise for Tiny Mouse*
Howell, Will C. *I call it sky*
Hubery, Julia. *A friend for all seasons*
Hunter, Anne. *Possum's harvest moon*
Hurley, Jorey. *Nest*
Issa, Kobayashi. *Today and today*
Jackson, Richard. *Snow scene*
Janeczko, Paul B. *Firefly July*
Johnson, Amy Crane. *Cinnamon and the April shower / Canela y el aguacero de abril*
Johnston, Tony. *Sequoia*
Karas, G. Brian. *The village garage*
Katz, Bobbi. *Once around the sun*
Katz, Susan B. *All year round*
Kespert, Deborah. *Rain and shine*
Kinsey-Warnock, Natalie. *From dawn till dusk*
Kirk, Daniel. *The thing about spring*
Kirk, David. *Little bunny, Biddle bunny*
Kleven, Elisa. *Cozy light, cozy night*
Krauss, Ruth. *The growing story*
LaMarche, Jim. *Pond*
Lasky, Kathryn. *Mommy's hands*
Leduc, Emilie. *All year round*
Lemniscates . *Trees*
Lesser, Carolyn. *What a wonderful day to be a cow*
Lin, Grace. *Our seasons*
Lionni, Leo. *A busy year*
Lister, Mary. *The Winter King and the Summer Queen*
Livingston, Myra Cohn. *Calendar*
Lloyd, Megan Wagner. *Fort-building time*
Lobel, Arnold. *Frog and Toad all year*
Locker, Thomas. *Sky tree*
London, Jonathan. *Otters love to play*
    Park beat
Long, Loren. *Little tree*
Lyon, George Ella. *What forest knows*
McClure, Nikki. *Apple*

McGhee, Alison. *Making a friend*
Marshak, S. *The Month-Brothers*
Martin, Bill, Jr.. *I love our Earth*
    The turning of the year
Martin, David. *Shh! bears sleeping*
Marzollo, Jean. *Once upon a springtime*
Matheson, Christie. *Tap the magic tree*
Messinger, Carla. *When the shadbush blooms*
Messner, Kate. *Up in the garden and down in the dirt*
Micklos, John. *One leaf, two leaves, count with me!*
Millard, Glenda. *Isabella's garden*
Murphy, Mary. *Here comes spring, and summer and fall and winter*
Muth, Jon J. *Hi, Koo!*
Naberhaus, Sarvinder. *Boom boom*
Näslund, Gorel Kristina. *Our apple tree*
Nikola-Lisa, W. *The year with Grandma Moses*
Oppenheim, Joanne. *Have you seen trees?*
Paul, Ann Whitford. *The seasons sewn*
Paul, Miranda. *Water is water*
Pfister, Marcus. *Ava's poppy*
Pollock, Penny. *When the moon is full*
Provensen, Alice. *A book of seasons*
    The year at Maple Hill Farm
Raczka, Bob. *Guyku*
Rau, Dana Meachen. *In the yard*
Rockwell, Anne. *Ducklings and pollywogs*
    First comes spring
Rose, Deborah Lee. *All the seasons of the year*
Rosenberry, Vera. *Run, jump, whiz, splash*
Ross, Michael Elsohn. *Earth cycles*
Rotner, Shelley. *Every season*
Ruddell, Deborah. *The popcorn astronauts*
Ryder, Joanne. *Toad by the road*
Saltzberg, Barney. *All around the seasons*
Sayre, April Pulley. *Eat like a bear*
Schertle, Alice. *Such a little mouse*
    Very hairy bear
Schubert, Leda. *Here comes Darrell*
Schulman, Janet. *A bunny for all seasons*
Seven, John. *A year with friends*
Shields, Carol Diggory. *Month by month a year goes round*
Siddals, Mary McKenna. *Bringing the outside in*
    Tell me a season
Sidman, Joyce. *Red sings from treetops*
Singleton, Linda Joy. *Snow dog, sand dog*
Spinelli, Eileen. *Summerbath, winterbath*
Stead, Philip C. *Bear has a story to tell*
Stein, David Ezra. *Leaves*
Stewart, Sarah. *The money tree*
Tafuri, Nancy. *Snowy flowy blowy*
Takabayashi, Mari. *I live in Brooklyn*
Taylor, Theodore. *Hello, Arctic!*
Teckentrup, Britta. *Tree: a peek-through picture book*
Thong, Roseanne. *Gai see*
Train, Mary. *Time for the fair*
Trapani, Iza. *The bear went over the mountain*
Trimble, Marcia. *Flower Green*
Udry, Janice May. *A tree is nice*
Verdet, Andre. *All about time*
Weaver, Jo. *Little One*
Wells, Rosemary. *Night sounds, morning colors*
White, Teagan. *Adventures with barefoot critters*
Wick, Walter. *Can you see what I see? cool collections*
Willems, Mo. *City dog, country frog*
Wilson, Sarah. *Friends and pals and brothers, too*
Wright, Joanna. *Bunnies on ice*
Yolen, Jane. *Sing a season song*

Welcome to the icehouse
Zagwÿn, Deborah Turney. *Turtle spring*
Zoehfeld, Kathleen Weidner. *Secrets of the seasons*

Seasons – fall

Aesop. *The ant and the grasshopper*, ill. by Amy Lowry Poole
    The ant and the grasshopper, ill. by Sara Rojo
Arnosky, Jim. *Every autumn comes the bear*
Berger, Carin. *The little yellow leaf*
Brenner, Tom. *And then comes Halloween*
Bunting, Eve. *Peepers*
    The pumpkin fair
Burg, Ann. *Autumn walk*
Carr, Jan. *Dappled apples*
Chernesky, Felicia Sanzari. *From apple trees to cider, please!*
    Pick a circle, gather squares
Curato, Mike. *Little Elliot, fall friends*
Detlefsen, Lisl H. *Time for cranberries*
Emmett, Jonathan. *Leaf trouble*
Frank, John. *A chill in the air*
Freeman, Don. *One more acorn*
George, Lindsay Barrett. *In the woods*
Gerritsen, Paula. *Nuts*
Gibbons, Gail. *The pumpkin book*
Glaser, Linda. *It's fall*
Goldstone, Bruce. *Awesome autumn*
Hall, Michael. *Wonderfall*
Hall, Zoe. *Fall leaves fall*
Harshman, Marc. *Red are the apples*
Hawk, Fran. *Count down to fall*
Henkes, Kevin. *In the middle of fall*
Hills, Tad. *Duck and Goose find a pumpkin*
Hirschi, Ron. *Fall*
Hoban, Julia. *Amy loves the wind*
Holland, Loretta. *Fall leaves*
Hopkins, Lee Bennett. *Merrily comes our harvest in*
Iwamura, Kazuo. *Hooray for fall!*
Jackson, Ellen. *The autumn equinox*
    November
    October
    September
Jocelyn, Marthe. *Ready for autumn*
Johnston, Tony. *Winter is coming*
Koller, Jackie French. *Nickommoh!*
Lee, Huy Voun. *In the leaves*
Lenski, Lois. *Now it's fall*
Lipson, Eden Ross. *Applesauce season*
Maass, Robert. *A is for autumn*
    When autumn comes
McCarty, Peter. *Fall ball*
McNamara, Margaret. *Fall leaf project*
Maestro, Betsy. *Why do leaves change color?*
Neubecker, Robert. *Fall is for school*
Nidey, Kelli. *When autumn falls*
O'Brien, Anne Sibley. *Hocus pocus, it's fall!*
Pak, Kenard. *Goodbye autumn, hello winter*
    Goodbye summer, hello autumn
Pickering, Jimmy. *It's fall*
Plourde, Lynn. *Bella's fall coat*
    Wild child
Potter, Beatrix. *The tale of Squirrel Nutkin*
Raczka, Bob. *Fall mixed up*
    Who loves the fall?
Rawlinson, Julia. *Fletcher and the falling leaves*
Rim, Sujean. *Birdie's happiest Halloween*
Robbins, Ken. *Autumn leaves*

Pumpkins
Rotner, Shelley. *Hello autumn!*
Rylant, Cynthia. *In November*
Sayre, April Pulley. *Full of fall*
Schnur, Steven. *Autumn*
Schweninger, Ann. *Autumn days*
Shapiro, Jody Fickes. *Up, up, up! It's apple-picking time*
Slegers, Liesbet. *Fall leaves*
Spetter, Jung-Hee. *Lily and Trooper's fall*
Spinelli, Eileen. *I know it's autumn*
   Now it is summer
Stringer, Lauren. *Yellow time*
Tafuri, Nancy. *The busy little squirrel*
Thompson, Lauren. *Mouse's first fall*
Tresselt, Alvin R. *Autumn harvest*
Van Allsburg, Chris. *The stranger*
Watson, Wendy. *Bedtime bunnies*
Wellington, Monica. *My leaf book*
Wilson, Steve. *Hedgehugs: autumn hide-and-squeak*
Wohl, Lauren L. *A teeny tiny Halloween*
Wright, Maureen. *Sneeze, Big Bear, sneeze*
Yee, Wong Herbert. *My autumn book*
Yoon, Salina. *Penguin and Pumpkin*
Ziefert, Harriet. *By the light of the harvest moon*
Zoehfeld, Kathleen Weidner. *Apples, apples*
Zolotow, Charlotte. *Say it!*

Seasons – spring

Arden, Carolyn. *Goose moon*
Bauer, Marion Dane. *In like a lion out like a lamb*
Beck, Andrea. *Elliot gets stuck*
Berenstain, Stan and Jan. *The Berenstain bears and the real Easter eggs*
Berger, Carin. *Finding spring*
Blecha, Aaron. *Good morning, Grizzle Grump!*
Bourgeois, Paulette. *Franklin's baby sister*
Capucilli, Alyssa Satin. *Katy Duck is a caterpillar*
Carr, Jan. *Splish, splash, spring*
Chaconas, Dori. *Looking for Easter*
Chall, Marsha Wilson. *Sugarbush spring*
Chernesky, Felicia Sanzari. *Sun above and blooms below*
Cocca-Leffler, Maryann. *Let it rain*
Colandro, Lucille. *There was an old lady who swallowed a frog!*
Cyrus, Kurt. *Shake a leg, egg!*
De colores / Bright with colors
Ernst, Lisa Campbell. *Wake up, it's Spring!*
Esbaum, Jill. *Everything spring*
Fernandes, Eugenie. *Kitten's spring*
Florian, Douglas. *Handsprings*
Fogliano, Julie. *And then it's spring*
Fontes, Justine Korman. *Signs of spring*
Frost, Helen. *Wake up!*
Gerber, Carole. *Spring blossoms*
Gershator, Phillis. *Who's awake in springtime?*
Glaser, Linda. *It's spring*
Henkes, Kevin. *When spring comes*
Hillenbrand, Will. *Spring is here*
Hirschi, Ron. *Spring*
Hubbell, Patricia. *Hurray for spring!*
Hulme, Joy N. *Easter babies*
Hunter, Anne. *Possum and the peeper*
Iwamura, Kazuo. *Hooray for spring!*
Jackson, Ellen. *April*
   March
   May

The spring equinox
Jocelyn, Marthe. *Ready for spring*
Johnson, Crockett. *Will spring be early or will spring be late?*
Kimura, Ken. *999 frogs wake up*
Kinsey-Warnock, Natalie. *When spring comes*
Kirk, Daniel. *The thing about spring*
Krauss, Ruth. *The happy day*
Lamstein, Sarah Marwil. *Big night for salamanders*
Lindbergh, Reeve. *North country spring*
Lloyd-Jones, Sally. *Bunny's first spring*
Maass, Robert. *When spring comes*
Mansfield, Howard. *Hogwood steps out*
Miller, Edna. *Mousekin's Easter basket*
Minarik, Else Holmelund. *It's spring!*
Na, Il Sung. *Snow rabbit, spring rabbit*
Newman, Lesléa. *Skunk's spring surprise*
O'Brien, Anne Sibley. *Abracadabra, it's spring!*
Peters, Lisa Westberg. *Cold little duck, duck, duck*
Pfister, Marcus. *Hopper*
   Hopper hunts for spring
Pitcher, Caroline. *Are you spring?*
Plourde, Lynn. *Spring's sprung*
Raczka, Bob. *Spring things*
Rawlinson, Julia. *Fletcher and the springtime blossoms*
Ray, Mary Lyn. *Mud*
Rockwell, Anne. *My spring robin*
Rose, Deborah Lee. *The twelve days of springtime*
Rotner, Shelley. *Hello spring!*
Schnur, Steven. *Spring*
   Spring thaw
Schulman, Janet. *Countdown to spring*
Seuling, Barbara. *Spring song*
Shannon, George. *Spring: a haiku story*
Spetter, Jung-Hee. *Lily and Trooper's spring*
Thompson, Lauren. *Mouse's first spring*
Voake, Charlotte. *Tweedle - dee - dee*
von Olfers, Sibylle. *Mother Earth and her children*
Wallace, Nancy Elizabeth. *Paperwhite*
Walters, Catherine. *When will it be spring?*
Wells, Rosemary. *Forest of dreams*
   Max's chocolate chicken
Werber, Yael. *Spring for Sophie*
Wilde, Oscar. *The selfish giant*, ill. by S. Saelig Gallagher
   The selfish giant, ill. by Fabian Negrin
   The selfish giant, ill. by Lisbeth Zwerger
Wood, Audrey. *When the root children wake up*
Yee, Wong Herbert. *Who likes rain?*
Yelchin, Eugene. *Spring hare*

Seasons – summer

Alarcón, Francisco X. *From the bellybutton of the moon and other summer poems / Del ombligo de la luna y otros poemas de verano*
Aliki. *Those summers*
Berenstain, Stan and Jan. *The Berenstain bears go to camp*
Brennan, Linda Crotta. *Marshmallow kisses*
Brenner, Tom. *And then comes summer*
Broach, Elise. *Wet dog!*
Bunting, Eve. *Sunflower house*
Chernesky, Felicia Sanzari. *Cheers for a dozen ears*
Crews, Nina. *One hot summer day*
Crisp, Marty. *Totally polar*
Day, Alexandra. *Carl's summer vacation*
English, Karen. *Hot day on Abbott Avenue*
Florian, Douglas. *Summersaults*

Frampton, David. *Mr. Ferlinghetti's poem*
Franco, Betsy. *Summer beat*
Freedman, Claire. *One magical day*
George, Lindsay Barrett. *Around the pond*
Gershator, Phillis. *Summer is summer*
Glaser, Linda. *It's summer*
Godwin, Laura. *Central Park serenade*
Greenberg, Melanie Hope. *Mermaids on parade*
Hakala, Marjorie Rose. *Mermaid dance*
Hayes, Karel. *The summer visitors*
Heidbreder, Robert. *Song for a summer night*
Henkes, Kevin. *Grandpa and Bo*
Hesse, Karen. *Come on, rain*
Hirschi, Ron. *Summer*
Hughes, Susan. *Earth to Audrey*
Inkpen, Mick. *Hissss!*
Iwamura, Kazuo. *Hooray for summer!*
Jackson, Ellen. *August*
   July
   June
   The summer solstice
Jocelyn, Marthe. *Ready for summer*
Kelley, Marty. *Summer stinks*
Kooser, Ted. *The bell in the bridge*
Korda, Lerryn. *It's vacation time*
Layton, Neal. *Hot, hot, hot*
Lewis, Kim. *One summer day*
Lister, Mary. *The Winter King and the Summer Queen*
London, Jonathan. *Sun dance, water dance*
Maass, Robert. *When summer comes*
McCloskey, Robert. *Time of wonder*
McClure, Nikki. *Mama, is it summer yet?*
Mahy, Margaret. *A summery Saturday morning*
Novak, Matt. *Flip flop bop*
Pak, Kenard. *Goodbye summer, hello autumn*
Paulsen, Gary. *Canoe days*
Payne, Nina. *Summertime waltz*
Perry, Elizabeth. *Think cool thoughts*
Polacco, Patricia. *Mrs. Mack*
Posey, Lee. *Night rabbits*
Poydar, Nancy. *Cool Ali*
Raczka, Bob. *Summer wonders*
Scanlon, Elizabeth Garton. *All the world*
Scheer, Julian. *By the light of the captured moon*
Schnur, Steven. *Summer*
Sís, Peter. *Ice cream summer*
Spetter, Jung-Hee. *Lily and Trooper's summer*
Spinelli, Eileen. *Now it is summer*
Stevenson, James. *July*
Stroud, Bettye. *Down home at Miss Dessa's*
Thomas, Patricia. *Firefly mountain*
Van Leeuwen, Jean. *Touch the sky summer*
Vogel, Vin. *The thing about yetis*
Weisburd, Stefi. *Barefoot: poems for naked feet*
Woodson, Jacqueline. *The other side*
Yee, Wong Herbert. *Summer days and nights*
Yolen, Jane. *Before the storm*
Zagwÿn, Deborah Turney. *The sea house*
Zolotow, Charlotte. *Summer is . . .*

Seasons – winter

Aesop. *The ant and the grasshopper*, ill. by Amy
   Lowry Poole
   The ant and the grasshopper, ill. by Sara Rojo
   The grasshopper and the ants
Alarcón, Francisco X. *Iguanas in the snow and other*
   winter poems / Iguanas en la nieve y otros poemas
   de invierno

Arnold, Marsha Diane. *Waiting for snow*
Arnosky, Jim. *Every autumn comes the bear*
Asch, Frank. *Good night, Baby Bear*
   Mooncake
Ashman, Linda. *William's winter nap*
Baird, Audrey B. *A cold snap!*
Baker, Keith. *No two alike*
Bauer, Marion Dane. *The longest night*
   Winter dance
Bean, Jonathan. *Big snow*
Berger, Carin. *Finding spring*
   A perfect day
Berry, Lynne. *Duck skates*
Blackaby, Susan. *Brownie Groundhog and the*
   February Fox
   Brownie Groundhog and the wintry surprise
Blades, Ann. *Mary of mile 18*
Blumenthal, Deborah. *Ice palace*
Boiger, Alexandra. *Max and Marla*
Brenner, Tom. *And then comes Christmas*
Brett, Jan. *The three snow bears*
Brunelle, Nicholas. *Snow moon*
Burton, Virginia Lee. *Katy and the big snow*
Butler, M. Christina. *One winter's day*
   The smiley snowman
   Snow friends
Caple, Kathy. *Hillary to the rescue*
Carlstrom, Nancy White. *Mama, will it snow*
   tonight?
   The snow speaks
Carnesi, Monica. *Sleepover with Beatrice and Bear*
Carr, Jan. *Frozen noses*
Carrick, Carol. *The polar bears are hungry*
Casanova, Mary. *Utterly otterly night*
Cassino, Mark, with Jon Nelson. *The story of snow*
Chaconas, Dori. *On a wintry morning*
Chernesky, Felicia Sanzari. *Sugar white snow and*
   evergreens
Chessa, Francesca. *Holly's red boots*
Child, Lauren. *Snow is my favorite and my best*
Christelow, Eileen. *The five-dog night*
Cooper, Elisha. *Bear dreams*
Cote, Nancy. *It feels like snow*
Cotten, Cynthia. *Snow ponies*
Crews, Nina. *Snowball*
Cuyler, Margery. *The biggest, best snowman*
Dahl, Michael. *Downhill fun*
   Footprints in the snow
Davies, Benji. *The storm whale in winter*
Denslow, Sharon Phillips. *In the snow*
DePrisco, Dorothea. *Snowbear's winter day*
Dewey, Jennifer Owings. *Once I knew a spider*
Dixon, Ann. *Winter is . . .*
Doodler, Todd H. *Bear in long underwear*
Doyle, Eugenie. *Sleep tight farm*
Ehlert, Lois. *Snowballs*
Emmett, Jonathan. *Diamond in the snow*
Fernandes, Eugenie. *Kitten's winter*
Fisher, Aileen Lucia. *Do rabbits have Christmas?*
Fleming, Denise. *The first day of winter*
   Time to sleep
Ford, Bernette. *First snow*
Frank, John. *A chill in the air*
Fredericks, Anthony D. *In one tidepool*
Frost, Robert. *Stopping by woods on a snowy evening*
Gammell, Stephen. *Is that you, winter?*
Gavin, Ciara. *Bear is not tired*
George, Jean Craighead. *Dear Rebecca, winter is here*
George, William T. *Christmas at Long Pond*

Gerber, Carole. *Winter trees*
Gershator, Phillis. *When it starts to snow*
Ghigna, Charles. *I see winter*
Gibbons, Gail. *It's snowing!*
Glaser, Linda. *It's winter*
   Not a buzz to be found
Goldstone, Bruce. *Wonderful winter*
Gore, Leonid. *Danny's first snow*
Grindley, Sally. *What will I do without you?*
Haas, Rick de. *Peter and the winter sleepers*
Harris, John. *Jingle bells: how the holiday classic came to be*
Hawcock, Claire. *Mine, all mine!*
Hayes, Karel. *The winter visitors*
Helquist, Brett. *Bedtime for Bear*
Henkes, Kevin. *Oh!*
Hest, Amy. *The reader*
Hillenbrand, Will. *Snowman's story*
Hindley, Judy. *Princess Rosa's winter*
Hirschi, Ron. *Winter*
Huneck, Stephen. *Sally's snow adventure*
Hurst, Carol Otis. *Terrible storm*
Iwamura, Kazuo. *Hooray for snow!*
Jackson, Ellen. *December*
   February
   January
   The winter solstice
Jenkins, Emily. *Lemonade in winter*
   Toys meet snow
Jocelyn, Marthe. *Ready for winter*
Judge, Lita. *Red sled*
Kaneko, Yuki. *Into the snow*
Katz, Karen. *Baby loves winter!*
Keats, Ezra Jack. *The snowy day*
Kelley, Marty. *Winter woes*
Kohara, Kazuno. *Here comes Jack Frost*
Krauss, Ruth. *The happy day*
Kuskin, Karla. *Under my hood I have a hat*
Laminack, Lester L. *Snow day!*
Lenski, Lois. *I like winter*
Lester, Helen. *Tacky and the Winter Games*
Lister, Mary. *The Winter King and the Summer Queen*
Lobel, Gillian. *Little Honey Bear and the smiley moon*
London, Jonathan. *Froggy gets dressed*
Maass, Robert. *When winter comes*
McCarty, Peter. *First snow*
McCue, Lisa. *Quiet Bunny and Noisy Puppy*
McCully, Emily Arnold. *First snow*
McDaniels, Preston. *A perfect snowman*
Maclear, Kyo. *The wish tree*
Manushkin, Fran. *How mama brought the spring*
Mayer, Kirsten. *Game of gnomes*
Messner, Kate. *Over and under the snow*
Miller, Edna. *Mousekin's golden house*
Mitton, Tony. *Snowy Bear*
Moffatt, Judith. *Snow shapes*
Morgan, Michaela. *Bunny wishes*
Morpurgo, Michael. *The silver swan*
Munsch, Robert N. *Thomas' snowsuit*
Na, Il Sung. *Snow rabbit, spring rabbit*
Nelson, Steve. *Frosty the snowman*
Neubecker, Robert. *Winter is for snow*
Norman, Kim. *If it's snowy and you know it, clap your paws!*
   Ten on the sled
Pak, Kenard. *Goodbye autumn, hello winter*
Pallotta, Jerry. *Who will see their shadows this year?*
Park, Bomi. *First snow*
Partridge, Elizabeth. *Moon glowing*

Pearson, Tracey Campbell. *Where does Joe go?*
Pendziwol, Jean E. *Once upon a northern night*
Perkins, Lynne Rae. *Snow music*
Pfister, Marcus. *Hopper*
Pickering, Jimmy. *It's winter*
Plourde, Lynn. *A mountain of mittens*
   Winter waits
Porter, Sue. *Parsnip*
Powell, Consie. *The first day of winter*
Poydar, Nancy. *Snip, snip . . . snow!*
Prelutsky, Jack. *It's snowing! It's snowing!*
Quattlebaum, Mary. *Winter friends*
Raczka, Bob. *Snowy, blowy winter*
Rawlinson, Julia. *Fletcher and the snowflake Christmas*
Reiser, Lynn. *My dog Truffle*
Rockwell, Anne. *The first snowfall*
Rolli, Jennifer Hansen. *Claudia and Moth*
Root, Phyllis. *Grandmother Winter*
   Lucia and the light
Rose, Deborah Lee. *The twelve days of winter*
Rule, Rebecca. *The iciest, diciest, scariest sled ride ever!*
Rylant, Cynthia. *Brownie and Pearl see the sights*
   Little penguins
Sabuda, Robert. *Winter in white*
   Winter's tale
Sakai, Komako. *The snow day*
Sayre, April Pulley. *Best in snow*
Schnur, Steven. *Winter*
Selsam, Millicent E. *Keep looking!*
Seuling, Barbara. *Winter lullaby*
Sidman, Joyce. *Winter bees and other poems of the cold*
Silvestro, Annie. *Mice skating*
Slayton, Fran Cannon. *Snowball moon*
Slegers, Liesbet. *Winter snow*
Smee, Nicola. *Jingle-jingle*
Smith, Danna. *Arctic white*
Spetter, Jung-Hee. *Lily and Trooper's winter*
Spinelli, Eileen. *Cold snap*
Steig, William. *Brave Irene*
Stevenson, James. *Brr!*
Stewart, Melissa. *Under the snow*
Stewart, Paul. *A little bit of winter*
Stojic, Manya. *Snow*
Stringer, Lauren. *Winter is the warmest season*
Szekeres, Cyndy. *The mouse that Jack built*
Taylor, Sean. *The snowbear*
Tegen, Katherine Brown. *Snowman magic*
Thomas, Patricia. *Red sled*
Thomas, Peggy. *Snow dance*
Thomas, Shelley Moore. *A cold winter's Good Knight*
Thompson, Lauren. *Mouse's first snow*
Thornhill, Jan. *Winter's coming*
Trasler, Janee. *Mimi and Bear in the snow*
Turkle, Brinton. *Thy friend, Obadiah*
Van Laan, Nancy. *Shingebiss*
   When winter comes: a lullaby
Vigna, Judith. *Boot weather*
Vogel, Vin. *The thing about yetis*
Waber, Bernard. *Bearsie Bear and the surprise sleepover party*
Wahman, Joe. *Snowboy 1, 2, 3*
Wallace, Ivy. *Pookie puts the world right*
Walters, Catherine. *The magical snowman*
   When will it be spring?
Ward, Lindsay. *When Blue met Egg*
Watanabe, Shigeo. *Ice cream is falling!*
Watts, Bernadette. *The smallest snowflake*

Wellington, Monica. *Bunny's first snowflake*
Wells, Rosemary. *Forest of dreams*
Whybrow, Ian. *Bella gets her skates on*
  Harry and the snow king
Wilson, Karma. *Dinos in the snow!*
Winget, Susan. *Sam the Snowman*
Wolff, Ashley. *Baby Bear counts one*
Wright, Maureen. *Sleep, Big Bear, sleep!*
Yamashita, Haruo. *Seven little mice have fun on the ice*
Yee, Wong Herbert. *Tracks in the snow*
Yolen, Jane. *Sleep, black bear, sleep*

Secrets *see* Behavior – secrets

Seeds

Alda, Arlene. *Morning glory Monday*
Anno, Mitsumasa. *Anno's magic seeds*
Aston, Dianna Hutts. *A seed is sleepy*
Bauld, Jane Scoggins. *Journey of the third seed*
Blackstone, Stella. *What's this?*
Buchanan, Jane. *Seed magic*
Carle, Eric. *The tiny seed*
Cave, Kathryn. *One child, one seed*
Christensen, Bonnie. *Plant a little seed*
Edwards, Nancy. *Glenna's seeds*
Galbraith, Kathryn O. *Planting the wild garden*
Geisert, Arthur. *The giant seed*
Gibbons, Gail. *From seed to plant*
Hall, Zoe. *The surprise garden*
Henkes, Kevin. *So happy!*
Himmelman, John. *A dandelion's life*
Honey, Elizabeth. *That's not a daffodil!*
Hood, Susan. *Rooting for you*
Hubbell, Will. *Pumpkin Jack*
John, Jory. *The bad seed*
Jordan, Helene J. *How a seed grows*
Karon, Jan. *The trellis and the seed*
Kim, Sue. *How does a seed grow?*
Kottke, Jan. *From seed to pumpkin*
MacKay, Elly. *If you hold a seed*
Macken, JoAnn Early. *Flip, float, fly*
Matheson, Christie. *Plant the tiny seed*
Middleton, Charlotte. *Nibbles*
Nelson, Kadir. *If you plant a seed*
Pak, Soyung. *A place to grow*
Pallotta, Jerry. *Who will plant a tree?*
Paul, Miranda. *Are we pears yet?*
Peterson, Cris. *Seed soil sun*
Pin, Isabel. *The seed*
Pizzoli, Greg. *The watermelon seed*
Ramirez, Melissa Bourbon. *The flight of the sunflower*
Robbins, Ken. *Seeds*
Rockwell, Anne. *One bean*
Roemer, Heidi Bee. *What kind of seeds are these?*
Santucci, Barbara. *Anna's corn*
Sasso, Sandy Eisenberg. *Naamah, Noah's wife*
Schaefer, Lola M. *This is the sunflower*
Swanson, Susan Marie. *To be like the sun*
Vojtech, Anna. *Surprise in the meadow*
Wallace, Nancy Elizabeth. *Planting seeds*
  Seeds! seeds! seeds!
Walsh, Ellen Stoll. *Dot and Jabber and the great acorn mystery*
Ward, Jennifer. *What will grow?*
Wheeler, Eliza. *Miss Maple's seeds*

Wunderli, Stephen. *Little Boo*

Seeing *see* Anatomy – eyes; Glasses; Disabilities – blindness; Senses – sight

Seeing eye dogs *see* Animals – service animals

Seeking better things *see* Behavior – seeking better things

Self-concept

Ackerman, Karen. *Bean's big day*
Adams, Diane. *I can do it myself!*
Adoff, Jaime. *Small fry*
Agee, Jon. *Lion lessons*
Alexander, Claire. *Small Florence*
Alexie, Sherman. *Thunder Boy Jr.*
Aliki. *All by myself!*
Andrews, Julie. *Simeon's gift*
  The very fairy princess
Aponte, Carlos. *A season to bee*
Appelt, Kathi. *Incredible me!*
Backker, Vera de. *Coco the koala*
Baldacchino, Christine. *Morris Micklewhite and the tangerine dress*
Bansch, Helga. *Odd bird out*
  Rosie the raven
Bar-el, Dan. *Not your typical dragon*
Barbero, Maria. *The bravest mouse*
Barnes, Brynne. *Colors of me*
Barnes, Derrick. *Crown*
Barnes, Laura T. *Ernest and the big itch*
  Teeny tiny Ernest
Barnwell, Ysaye M. *No mirrors in my Nana's house*
Baryshnikov, Mikhail. *Because . . .*
Bea, Holly. *My spiritual alphabet book*
Beaumont, Karen. *Wild about us!*
Beck, Robert. *A bunny in the ballet*
Bell, Cece. *Bee-Wigged*
Belton, Sandra. *Pictures for Miss Josie*
Bishop, Brett. *Clayton's path*
Blume, Judy. *The one in the middle is a green kangaroo*
Bonwill, Ann. *Naughty toes*
Borden, Louise. *A. Lincoln and me*
Boyce, Katie. *Hector the hermit crab*
Bradley, Sandra. *Henry Holton takes the ice*
Brennan, Eileen. *Dirtball Pete*
Bright, Rachel. *The koala who could*
Britt, Paige. *Why am I me?*
Brown, Lisa. *How to be*
Brown, Peter. *Mr. Tiger goes wild*
Brown-Wood, JaNay. *Imani's moon*
Browne, Anthony. *Willy the wimp*
Buchanan, Sue. *Mud Pie Annie*
Budnitz, Paul. *The hole in the middle*
Buehner, Caralyn. *Superdog, the heart of a hero*
Buitrago, Jairo. *Jimmy the greatest*
Bunting, Eve. *One green apple*
Campisi, Stephanie. *The ugly dumpling*
Carle, Eric. *The mixed-up chameleon*
Carlson, Nancy. *ABC, I like me!*
  Armond goes to a party
  I like me
  Think big!

Ismail, Yasmeen. *I'm a girl!*
Jagtenberg, Yvonne. *Jack the wolf*
Jamieson, Victoria. *Olympig!*
Jeffers, Oliver. *The Hueys in It wasn't me*
    The Hueys in The new sweater
John, Jory. *Quit calling me a monster!*
Johnson, Dinah. *Black magic*
Johnston, Tony. *A small thing . . . but big*
Joosse, Barbara. *Grandma calls me Beautiful*
Joslin, Mary. *The shore beyond*
Kasza, Keiko. *The dog who cried wolf*
Keats, Ezra Jack. *Peter's chair*
    Whistle for Willie
Keller, Holly. *Horace*
Kimmel, Elizabeth Cody. *Glamsters*
Kirk, Daniel. *Bigger*
Kirk, David. *Little bird, Biddle bird*
Knudsen, Michelle. *Big Mean Mike*
Krauss, Ruth. *The carrot seed*
Krishnaswami, Uma. *The happiest tree*
Kroll, Virginia L. *Boy, you're amazing!*
Kumin, Maxine. *What color is Caesar?*
Lallemand, Orianne. *The wolf who wanted to change*
    his color
LaMarche, Jim. *Up*
Latifah, Queen. *Queen of the scene*
Lawrence, Michael. *The caterpillar that roared*
Lechelt, Karen. *What do you love about you?*
Lee, Spike. *Giant steps to change the world*
Lewis, Jacqueline Janette. *You are so wonderful*
Lichtenheld, Tom. *Bridget's beret*
Lionni, Leo. *Mr. McMouse*
    Pezzettino
Lithgow, John. *Marsupial Sue*
Lobel, Gillian. *Does anybody love me?*
Look at me!
Lovell, Patty. *Stand tall, Molly Lou Melon*
Lozoff, Bo. *The wonderful life of a fly who couldn't fly*
Ludwig, Trudy. *Better than you*
Lum, Kate. *Princesses are not perfect*
Lundy, Charlotte. *Thank you, Esther*
McAnulty, Stacy. *Beautiful*
    Brave
McCaughrean, Geraldine. *How the reindeer got their*
    antlers
MacDonald, Alan. *The pig in a wig*
McDonnell, Patrick. *Shine!*
McEvoy, Anne. *Betsy B. Little*
McGhee, Alison. *So many days*
MacHale, D. J. *The monster princess*
Mack, Jeff. *The things I can do*
McKee, David. *Elmer and the kangaroo*
McKissack, Robert L. *Try your best*
Maclear, Kyo. *Spork*
McLellan, Stephanie Simpson. *Tweezle into*
    everything
McNamara, Margaret. *A poem in your pocket*
Maloney, Peter. *His mother's nose*
Mandell, B. B. *Samanthasaurus Rex*
Manning, Jane. *Millie Fierce*
Manson, Ainslie. *Ballerinas don't wear glasses*
Manushkin, Fran. *Happy in our skin*
Markes, Julie. *Good thing you're not an octopus!*
Mayer, Kirsten. *Game of gnomes*
Medearis, Angela Shelf. *Annie's gifts*
Medearis, Michael. *Daisy and the doll*
Meng, Cece. *Tough chicks*
Merino, Gemma. *The sheep who hatched an egg*
Meserve, Jessica. *Small sister*

Milgrim, David. *How you got so smart*
Mills, Claudia. *Ziggy's blue-ribbon day*
Milway, Katie Smith. *Cappuccina goes to town*
Minarik, Else Holmelund. *Am I beautiful?*
Monks, Lydia. *The cat barked?*
Monnier, Miriam. *Just right*
Moore, Julianne. *Freckleface Strawberry*
Moss, Marissa. *Regina's big mistake*
Mueller, Doris L. *Small One's adventure*
Munsch, Robert N. *Makeup mess*
Murguia, Bethanie Deeney. *Zoe gets ready*
Murphy, Jill. *A piece of cake*
Neal, Kate Jane. *Words and your heart*
Nelson, Vaunda Micheaux. *Who will I be, Lord?*
Neubecker, Robert. *Courage of the blue boy*
Newman, Lesléa. *Miss Tutu's star*
Nishimura, Kae. *Dinah*
Nolan, Lucy A. *Jack Quack*
Nordling, Lee. *The bramble*
Norman, Kim. *Still a gorilla!*
Obama, Barack. *Of thee I sing*
O'Connor, Jane. *Fancy Nancy*
    Fancy Nancy: ooh la la! it's beauty day
    Fancy Nancy and the posh puppy
    Nancy la elegante / Fancy Nancy
    Ready, set, skip!
Odone, Jamison. *Mole had everything*
Olien, Jessica. *Adrift*
Oram, Hiawyn. *Just Dog*
    The wrong overcoat
Otoshi, Kathryn. *Two*
    Zero
Owen, Karen. *I could be, you could be*
Palacio, R. J. *We're all wonders*
Parr, Todd. *Be who you are*
    It's okay to make mistakes
    The okay book
    The thankful book
Peet, Bill. *Pamela Camel*
Pelley, Kathleen T. *Raj the bookstore tiger*
Perkins, Useni Eugene. *Hey Black Child*
Peters, Bernadette. *Stella is a star!*
Pett, Mark. *The girl who never made mistakes*
Petty, Dev. *I don't want to be a frog*
Petty, Dini. *The queen, the bear and the bumblebee*
Pfister, Marcus. *Just the way you are*
    The little moon raven
Phinn, Gervase. *Who am I?*
Pinkney, Sandra L. *I am Latino*
Polacco, Patricia. *An A from Miss Keller*
    The art of Miss Chew
    The junkyard wonders
Portis, Antoinette. *Now*
Prelutsky, Jack. *Me I am!*
Raczka, Bob. *Niko draws a feeling*
Raschka, Chris. *Arlene sardine*
    Waffle
Razi, Michaele. *Frank the seven-legged spider*
Reynolds, Peter H. *The dot*
    Happy dreamer
    Ish
    My very big little world
Richards, Beah E. *Keep climbing, girls*
Richardson, John. *Grunt*
Robinson, Fiona. *Whale shines*
Rosenthal, Amy Krouse. *Dear Girl,*
    Exclamation mark
    The OK book

One smart cookie: bite-size lessons for the school years and beyond

Rossetti-Shustak, Bernadette. *I love you through and through*

Rotner, Shelley. *What can you do?*

Rubin, C. M. *Eleanor, Ellatony, Ellencake, and me*

Rudolph, Shaina. *All my stripes*

Russo, Marisabina. *A very big bunny*

Saltzberg, Barney. *Star of the week*

Scanlon, Elizabeth Garton. *Noodle and Lou*

Schachner, Judith Byron. *Sarabella's thinking cap*

Schneider, Christine M. *Picky Mrs. Pickle*

Schoonmaker, Elizabeth. *Square cat*

Schotter, Roni. *The boy who loved words*
Doo-Wop Pop

Schreck, Karen Halvorsen. *Lucy's family tree*

Schwartz, Amy. *Dee Dee and me*
Starring Miss Darlene

Schwarz, Viviane. *The adventures of a nose*

Seuss, Dr. *Oh, the places you'll go!*

Shapiro, Esmé. *Ooko*

Sharmat, Marjorie Weinman. *I'm terrific*
The 329th friend

Shea, Bob. *New socks*
Unicorn thinks he's pretty great

Shields, Carol Diggory. *I am really a princess*

Shipton, Jonathan. *What if?*

Shireen, Nadia. *Good little wolf*

Sima, Jessie. *Not quite narwhal*

Simon, Norma. *All kinds of children*
Why am I different?

Singer, Marilyn. *I'm gonna climb a mountain in my patent leather shoes*

Sís, Peter. *Robinson*

Slade-Robinson, Nikki. *Muddle and Mo*

Smallcomb, Pam. *I'm not*

Smith, Jada Pinkett. *Girls hold up this world*

Smith, Lane. *Pinocchio, the boy*

Spinelli, Eileen. *Princess Pig*
When no one is watching

Stanton, Elizabeth Rose. *Henny*

Starishevsky, Jill. *My body belongs to me*

Stein, David Ezra. *Pouch!*

Stewart, Amber. *Little by little*

Stewart, Whitney. *Meditation is an open sky*

Stone, Tanya Lee. *Who says women can't be doctors?*

Swanson, Susan Marie. *The first thing my mama told me*

Terry, Michael. *Rhino's horns*

Thompson, Kay. *Kay Thompson's Eloise's what I absolutely love love love*

Thompson, Lauren. *Wee little chick*

Thornhill, Jan. *I am Josephine (and I am a living thing)*

Tillman, Nancy. *The crown on your head*
You're all kinds of wonderful
You're here for a reason

Timmers, Leo. *Crow*

Turner, Sandy. *Otto's trunk*

Tyler, Michael. *The skin you live in*

Urban, Linda. *Little Red Henry*

Urdahl, Catherine. *Polka-dot fixes kindergarten*

Vail, Rachel. *Piggy Bunny*

Van Dusen, Chris. *King Hugo's huge ego*

van Lieshout, Maria. *Peep!*

Viorst, Judith. *And two boys booed*

Waddell, Martin. *Bee frog*

Waldron, Kevin. *Mr. Peek and the misunderstanding at the zoo*

Wallis, Quvenzhané. *A night out with Mama*

Walton, Jessica. *Introducing Teddy*

Weeks, Sarah. *I'm a pig*

Weigelt, Udo. *Old Beaver*

Wells, Rosemary. *The gulps*

Wiesner, David. *Art and Max*

Willems, Mo. *Edwina, the dinosaur who didn't know she was extinct*

Williams, Carol Ann. *Booming Bella*

Wilson, Gina. *Ignis*

Winthrop, Elizabeth. *Squashed in the middle*

Wolff, Patricia Rae. *A new, improved Santa*

Wong, Benedict Norbert. *Lo and behold*
Lo and behold, good enough to eat

Wong, Liz. *Quackers*

Wormell, Christopher. *Henry and the fox*

Wright, Joanna. *Bunnies on ice*

Yaccarino, Dan. *Morris Mole*
Unlovable

Yankey, Lindsey. *Sun and Moon*

Yerkes, Jennifer. *A funny little bird*

Ziefert, Harriet. *Squarehead*

Self-esteem *see* Self-concept

Self-image *see* Self-concept

Self-reliance *see* Character traits – confidence

Selfishness *see* Character traits – selfishness

Senses

Apperley, Dawn. *Don't wake the baby*

Blackstone, Stella. *Bear's busy family*

Brocket, Jane. *Cold, crunchy, colorful*

Cash, Megan Montague. *I saw the sea and the sea saw me*

Ciboul, Adele. *The five senses*

Cole, Joanna. *The magic school bus explores the senses*

Crummel, Susan Stevens. *Sherlock Bones and the missing cheese*

Goodman, Susan E. *It's a dog's life*

Hartley, Karen. *The sixth sense and other special senses*

Henderson, Kathy. *Look at you!*

Isadora, Rachel. *I hear a pickle*

Jenkins, Steve. *What do you do with a tail like this?*

Lears, Laurie. *Ian's walk*

Leigh, Heather. *Hey little baby!*

Lloyd, Megan Wagner. *Finding wild*

McMillan, Bruce. *Sense suspense*

Miller, Margaret. *My five senses*

Murphy, Mary. *You smell and taste and feel and see and hear*

Raschka, Chris. *Five for a little one*

Reiser, Lynn. *My cat Tuna*
My dog Truffle

Rosenfeld, Dina Herman. *Five alive*

Rotner, Shelley. *Senses at the seashore*
Senses in the city

Ryan, Pam Muñoz. *Hello, Ocean!*
Hello Ocean / Hola mar

Seuss, Dr. *Gerald McBoing Boing*

Shannon, David. *David smells*

Sweeney, Joan. *Me and my senses*

Trapani, Iza. *The bear went over the mountain*
Waters, John F. *Sharks have six senses*
Wells, Rosemary. *Night sounds, morning colors*
Werber, Yael. *Spring for Sophie*
Wood, Douglas. *No one but you*
Ziefert, Harriet. *You can't taste a pickle with your ear*

Senses – hearing

Aliki. *My five senses*
Charlip, Remy. *Handtalk birthday*
Charlip, Remy, et al. *Handtalk*
Hartley, Karen, et al. *Hearing in living things*
Jackson, Richard. *All ears, all eyes*
Miller, Mary Beth. *Handtalk zoo*
Millman, Isaac. *Moses goes to school*
Murphy, Stuart J. *Percy listens up*
Showers, Paul. *Ears are for hearing*
    The listening walk
Soto, Gary. *The old man and his door*
Winnie-the-Pooh's A B C

Senses – sight

Aliki. *My five senses*
Brown, Marc. *Arthur's eyes*
Cobb, Vicki. *Open your eyes*
Gordon, Sharon. *Seeing*
Hartley, Karen. *Seeing in living things*
Hawkes, Kevin. *Remy and Lulu*
Jackson, Richard. *All ears, all eyes*
Keats, Ezra Jack. *Apt. 3*
Lyon, George Ella. *The pirate of kindergarten*
McCarthy, Mary. *A closer look*
Martin, Bill, Jr.. *Knots on a counting rope*
Serafini, Frank. *Looking closely along the shore*
Shannon, George. *White is for blueberry*
Showers, Paul. *Look at your eyes*
Smith, Lane. *Glasses . . . who needs 'em?*
Wenzel, Brendan. *They all saw a cat*
Young, Ed. *Seven blind mice*

Senses – smell

Aliki. *My five senses*
Allen, Jonathan. *Mucky moose*
Gordon, Sharon. *Smelling*
Hartley, Karen. *Smelling in living things*
Kajikawa, Kimiko. *Yoshi's feast*
Keller, Holly. *Nosy Rosie*
Kinerk, Robert. *Timothy Cox will not change his socks*
Mack, Jeff. *Who needs a bath?*
Palatini, Margie. *Gorgonzola*
Posthuma, Sieb. *Benny*
Southwell, Jandelyn. *The little country town*
Ward, B. J. *Farty Marty*

Senses – taste

Aliki. *My five senses*
Bonsignore, Joan. *Stick out your tongue*
Hartley, Karen. *Tasting in living things*

Senses – touch

Adoff, Arnold. *Touch the poem*
Aliki. *My five senses*
Becker, Bonny. *Tickly prickly*
Carle, Eric. *My very first book of touch*
Cottin, Menena. *The black book of colors*

Grant, Jacob. *Through with the zoo*
Hartley, Karen. *Touching in living things*
International Center for Assault Prevention. *My body belongs to me from my head to my toes*
Sherman, Joanne. *Because it's my body*
Starishevsky, Jill. *My body belongs to me*

Sex instruction

Allan, Nicholas. *Where Willy went*
Blackall, Sophie. *The baby tree*
Brown, Laurie Krasny. *What's the big secret?*
Collard, Sneed B. *Making animal babies*
Harris, Robie H. *What's in there?*
Roberts, Jillian. *Where do babies come from? our first talk about birth*
Saltz, Gail. *Amazing you*

Sex roles *see* Gender roles

Shadows

Asch, Frank. *Bear shadow*
Biedrzycki, David. *Groundhog's runaway shadow*
Cendrars, Blaise. *Shadow*
Chorao, Kay. *Shadow night*
Cuevas, Michelle. *Smoot*
DiFiori, Lawrence. *Jackie and the Shadow Snatcher*
Freeman, Don. *Gregory's Shadow*
Hoban, Tana. *Shadows and reflections*
Hodgkinson, Leigh. *Boris and the wrong shadow*
Holderness, Jackie. *What is a shadow?*
Leathers, Philippa. *The black rabbit*
Lee, Suzy. *Shadow*
Lewin, Betsy. *Groundhog day*
MacDonald, Amy. *Quentin Fenton Herter three*
O'Hara, Natalia. *Hortense and the shadow*
Pace, Anne Marie. *Groundhug Day*
Pallotta, Jerry. *Who will see their shadows this year?*
Swinburne, Stephen R. *Guess whose shadow?*
Tompert, Ann. *Nothing sticks like a shadow*
Van Nutt, Julia. *The monster in the shadows*
Walter, Mildred Pitts. *Darkness*
Waring, Geoff. *Oscar and the moth*
Welling, Peter J. *Andrew McGroundhog and his shady shadow*
Willard, Nancy. *Shadow story*

Shaped books *see* Format, unusual

Sharing *see* Behavior – sharing

Shells *see* Sea & seashore

Ships *see* Boats, ships

Shopping

Agee, Jon. *Nothing*
Ahlberg, Allan. *The shopping expedition*
Baker, Jeannie. *Mirror*
Birchall, Mark. *Hen goes shopping*
Birdseye, Tom. *Soap! soap! don't forget the soap!*
Bulion, Leslie. *Fatuma's new cloth*
Burningham, John. *The shopping basket*

Chen, Chih-Yuan. *On my way to buy eggs*
Christelow, Eileen. *Five little monkeys go shopping*
Cocca-Leffler, Maryann. *Bus route to Boston*
Cousins, Lucy. *Maisy goes shopping*
Daly, Niki. *Next stop — Zanzibar Road!*
   Not so fast Songololo
Darbyshire, Kristen. *Put it on the list!*
Day, Alexandra. *Carl goes shopping*
Dewdney, Anna. *Llama Llama mad at Mama*
Dodds, Dayle Ann. *The Kettles get new clothes*
Edens, Cooper. *The Animal Mall*
Elya, Susan Middleton. *Bebé goes shopping*
Empson, Jo. *Chimpanzees for tea!*
Flanagan, Alice K. *A busy day at Mr. Kang's grocery store*
Florence, Tyler. *Tyler makes pancakes!*
Gill, Shelley. *The big buck adventure*
Glass, Eleri. *The red shoes*
Grossman, Patricia. *Saturday market*
Hutchins, Pat. *Don't forget the bacon!*
Ichikawa, Satomi. *My father's shop*
Johnson, Marion. *Caillou, new shoes*
Kaplan, Michael B. *Betty Bunny wants everything*
Korchek, Lori. *Adventures of Cow, too*
Lindbergh, Reeve. *The awful aardvarks shop for school*
Lobel, Arnold. *On Market Street*
London, Jonathan. *Ali, child of the desert*
Long, Kathy. *The runaway shopping cart*
McAllister, Angela. *Trust me, Mom!*
Martin, David. *Five little piggies*
Melvin, Alice. *The high street*
Munsch, Robert N. *Something good*
   Where is Gah-Ning?
Murphy, Jill. *Meltdown!*
Murphy, Stuart J. *Just enough carrots*
Oxenbury, Helen. *Tom and Pippo go shopping*
Potter, Beatrix. *The tale of Little Pig Robinson*
Puttock, Simon. *Goat and Donkey in strawberry sunglasses*
Rader, Laura. *Santa's new suit*
Rockwell, Anne. *At the supermarket*
   Let's go to the hardware store
Russo, Marisabina. *Mama talks too much*
Rylant, Cynthia. *Brownie and Pearl see the sights*
Seibold, J. Otto. *Lost sloth*
Shaw, Nancy. *Sheep in a shop*
Sierra, Judy. *Suppose you meet a dinosaur*
Singer, Marilyn. *Shoe bop!*
Stevens, April. *Edwin speaks up*
Trent, Shanda. *Farmers' market day*
Verdick, Elizabeth. *On-the-go time*
Wells, Rosemary. *Max's bunny business*
   Shopping
Wood, Don. *Merry Christmas, big hungry bear*
Wynne-Jones, Tim. *Secret Agent Man goes shopping for shoes*

Shops *see* Stores

Showing off *see* Behavior – boasting, showing off

Shows *see* Theater

Shyness *see* Character traits – shyness

Siam *see* Foreign lands – Thailand

Sibling rivalry

Alexander, Martha G. *Nobody asked me if I wanted a baby sister*
   When the new baby comes, I'm moving out
Alter, Anna. *Estelle and Lucy*
Atinuke. *Double trouble for Anna Hibiscus!*
Bedford, David. *Ella's games*
Berenstain, Stan and Jan. *The Berenstain bears and the double dare*
   The Berenstain bears get in a fight
Blume, Judy. *The Pain and The Great One*
Blumenthal, Deborah. *Don't let the peas touch!*
Bond, Felicia. *Poinsettia and her family*
Bourgeois, Paulette. *Franklin and Harriet*
Bradman, Tony. *The perfect baby*
Broach, Elise. *What the no-good baby is good for*
Brown, Marc. *D. W. all wet*
Bunting, Eve. *Baby can*
Capucilli, Alyssa Satin. *Katy Duck, big sister*
Carlson, Nancy. *Harriet and Walt*
Child, Lauren. *The new small person*
Cinderella
Climo, Shirley. *The Egyptian Cinderella*
   The Korean Cinderella
   The Persian Cinderella
Coburn, Jewell Reinhart. *Angkat*
   Jouanah
Coh, Smiljana. *The seven princesses*
Cole, Joanna. *The new baby at your house*
Cote, Nancy. *It's all about me!*
Daly, Jude. *Fair, brown and trembling*
Davies, Gill. *Wilbur waited*
deGroat, Diane. *Mother, you're the best! (but Sister, you're a pest!)*
Dempsey, Sheena. *Bye-bye baby brother!*
Dewan, Ted. *Crispin and the 3 little piglets*
Duke, Kate. *The tale of Pip and Squeak*
Feeney, Tatyana. *Little Frog's tadpole trouble*
Frazee, Marla. *The bossier baby*
Gay, Marie-Louise. *Caramba and Henry*
Geras, Adèle. *Sleeping beauty*
Grimm, Jacob and Wilhelm. *The water of life*
Hall, Algy Craig. *Fine as we are*
Hänel, Wolfram. *Little elephant runs away*
Hazen, Barbara Shook. *Who is your favorite monster, Mama?*
Henkes, Kevin. *Julius, the baby of the world*
Hoban, Russell. *A baby sister for Frances*
Holabird, Katharine. *Angelina's baby sister*
Hurwitz, Johanna. *Russell's secret*
Hutchins, Pat. *The very worst monster*
Itaya, Satoshi. *Buttons and Bo*
Jonell, Lynne. *It's my birthday, too!*
Joosse, Barbara. *I love you the purplest*
Joyce, William. *Santa calls*
Kaplan, Bruce Eric. *Meaniehead*
Kassirer, Sue. *Joseph and his coat of many colors*
Keller, Holly. *Geraldine first*
   Geraldine's baby brother
Koller, Jackie French. *Baby for sale*
Kornell, Max. *Me first*
Kroll, Steven. *The squirrels' Thanksgiving*
Lindgren, Barbro. *Benny and the binky*
Lloyd-Jones, Sally. *His Royal Highness, King Baby*
Lobel, Gillian. *Too small for honey cake*
Lowell, Susan. *Cindy Ellen*

McCully, Emily Arnold. *New baby*
Manna, Anthony L. *The orphan*
Michels-Gualtieri, Akaela S. *I was born to be a sister*
Minters, Frances. *Cinder-Elly*
Montanari, Eva. *Tiff, Taff, and Lulu*
Murphy, Stuart J. *Give me half!*
Oelschlager, Vanita. *Made in China*
Orlean, Susan. *Lazy little loafers*
Palatini, Margie. *Goldie is mad*
    Good as Goldie
Pelham, David. *Sam's pizza*
Perkins, Chloe. *Cinderella*
Perrault, Charles *Cinderella*, ill. by Nicoletta
    Ceccoli
    Cinderella, ill. by Susan Jeffers
    Cinderella, ill. by Loek Koopmans
    Cinderella, ill. by Barbara McClintock
    Cinderella, ill. by James Marshall
    Cinderella / Cenicienta
    Cinderella: a pop-up fairy tale
    Cinderella: or, the little glass slipper
Plourde, Lynn. *Spring's sprung*
Polacco, Patricia. *My rotten redheaded older brother*
Pryor, Bonnie. *Amanda and April*
    The porcupine mouse
Raschka, Chris. *The blushful hippopotamus*
Regan, Dian Curtis. *Space Boy and his dog*
    Space Boy and the space pirate
Reynolds, Peter H. *The best kid in the world*
Richardson, John. *Grunt*
Robberecht, Thierry. *Back into Mommy's tummy*
Roberts, Lynn. *Cinderella, an Art Deco love story*
Rogers, Fred. *The new baby*
Rosenberry, Vera. *Vera's baby sister*
Russo, Marisabina. *The big brown box*
Samuels, Barbara. *Faye and Dolores*
    What's so great about Cindy Snappleby?
Sanderson, Ruth. *Cinderella*
San Souci, Robert D. *Cinderella Skeleton*
    Little gold star
Schwartz, Amy. *Annabelle Swift, kindergartner*
Scott, Ann Herbert. *On mother's lap*
Scrimger, Richard. *Eugene's story*
Shields, Carol Diggory. *I wish my brother was a dog*
Skinner, Daphne. *Henry keeps score*
Steig, William. *The toy brother*
Steptoe, John. *Baby says*
Stevenson, James. *That's exactly the way it wasn't*
    Worse than Willy!
Sullivan, Sarah. *Once upon a baby brother*
Viorst, Judith. *I'll fix Anthony*
Waddell, Martin. *Sam Vole and his brothers*
Wahl, Jan. *Mabel ran away with the toys*
Weeks, Sarah. *Sophie Peterman tells the truth!*
Wells, Rosemary. *Max counts his chickens*
    Max's bedtime
    Max's breakfast
    Max's chocolate chicken
    Peabody
    Stanley and Rhoda
Wilson, Troy. *Liam takes a stand*
Wolff, Ashley. *Stella and Roy go camping*
Wynne-Jones, Tim. *The boat in the tree*
Yep, Laurence. *Dragon prince*
Yezerski, Thomas. *Queen of the world*
Young, Ed. *My Mei Mei*
Zolotow, Charlotte. *If it weren't for you*

Siblings *see* Family life – brothers; Family life – brothers & sisters; Family life – sisters; Family life – stepfamilies; Sibling rivalry

Sickness *see* Health & fitness; Illness

Sight *see* Anatomy – eyes; Glasses; Disabilities – blindness; Senses – sight

Sign language

Acredolo, Linda P. *My first baby signs*
Browne, Anthony. *Little Beauty*
Churnin, Nancy. *The William Hoy story*
Domney, Alexis. *Splish, splat!*
Heller, Lora. *Sign language ABC*
Kubler, Annie. *My first signs*
McCully, Emily Arnold. *My heart glow*
Millman, Isaac. *Moses goes to a concert*
Napoli, Donna Jo. *Hands and hearts*
Prochovnic, Dawn Babb. *The big blue bowl*
    Hip hip hooray! It's Family Day!
Uhlberg, Myron. *The printer*
Waller, Curt. *Baby's first signs*
    More baby's first signs
    Winnie-the-Pooh's A B C

Signs

Ashman, Linda. *No dogs allowed*
Gillingham, Sara. *Alpha, Bravo, Charlie: the complete book of nautical codes*
Slawson, Michele Benoit. *Signs for sale*
van Lieshout, Maria. *Backseat A-B-see*
Wells, Rosemary. *Yoko finds her way*

Singers *see* Careers – singers

Sioux Indians *see* Indians of North America – Cheyenne (Sioux); Indians of North America – Dakota (Sioux); Indians of North America – Sioux

Sisters *see* Family life – brothers & sisters; Family life – sisters; Sibling rivalry

Skating *see* Sports – ice skating; Sports – hockey; Sports – roller skating

Sky

Belting, Natalia Maree. *The sun is a golden earring*
Berger, Barbara. *Thunder Bunny*
Branley, Franklyn M. *Comets*
    The sky is full of stars
Cabrera, Jane. *Twinkle, twinkle, little star*
Carle, Eric. *Little cloud*
Carlstrom, Nancy White. *What does the sky say?*
Dayrell, Elphinstone. *Why the sun and the moon live in the sky*
Dean, James. *Pete the Cat: twinkle, twinkle, little star*
Gerson, Mary-Joan. *Why the sky is far away*
Hest, Amy. *On the night of the shooting star*

Hopkinson, Deborah. *Maria's comet*
Luján, Jorge. *Sky blue accident / Accidente celeste*
Otto, Carolyn. *That sky, that rain*
Oughton, Jerrie. *How the stars fell into the sky*
Parker, Michael. *You are a star!*
Ray, Mary Lyn. *Stars*
Reynolds, Peter H. *Sky color*
Sabuda, Robert. *The Blizzard's robe*
Shaw, Charles Green. *It looked like spilt milk*
Taylor, Harriet Peck. *Ulaq and the northern lights*
Taylor, Jane. *Twinkle, twinkle little star,* ill. by
    Heather Collins
    Twinkle, twinkle, little star, ill. by Michael Hague
    Twinkle, twinkle, little star, ill. by Julia Noonan
    Twinkle, twinkle, little star, ill. by Jerry Pinkney
Waboose, Jan Bourdeau. *SkySisters*
Wilson, Karma. *Mama, why?*
Wood, Audrey. *Blue sky*

Slavery

Altman, Linda Jacobs. *The legend of Freedom Hill*
Armand, Glenda. *Love twelve miles long*
Asim, Jabari. *Fifty cents and a dream*
Bauer, Marion Dane. *Harriet Tubman*
Broyles, Anne. *Priscilla and the hollyhocks*
Carbone, Elisa. *Night running*
Cline-Ransome, Lesa. *Before she was Harriet*
    Light in the darkness
    Words set me free
Cole, Henry. *Unspoken*
Cooper, Floyd. *Juneteenth for Mazie*
Edwards, Pamela Duncan. *Barefoot: escape on the
    Underground Railroad*
Evans, Shane W. *Underground: finding the light to
    freedom*
Fradin, Dennis. *The price of freedom*
Grady, Cynthia. *I lay my stitches down*
Grifalconi, Ann. *Ain't nobody a stranger to me*
    The village that vanished
Herkert, Barbara. *Sewing stories*
Hill, Laban Carrick. *Dave the potter*
Hopkinson, Deborah. *Sweet Clara and the freedom
    quilt*
Johnson, Angela. *All different now*
Johnson, D. B. *Henry climbs a mountain*
Johnson, Dolores. *Now let me fly*
Johnson, James Weldon. *Lift every voice and sing*
    Lift ev'ry voice and sing
Johnston, Tony. *The wagon*
Levine, Ellen. *Henry's freedom box*
Levy, Debbie. *We shall overcome*
Lilly, Melinda. *From slavery to freedom*
Lyons, Kelly Starling. *Ellen's broom*
    Hope's gift
McGhee, Alison. *In the hollow of your hand*
McGill, Alice. *Molly Bannaky*
    Way up and over everything
Medearis, Angela Shelf. *The freedom riddle*
Meister, Cari. *Follow the drinking gourd: an
    Underground Railroad story*
Nelson, Vaunda Micheaux. *Almost to freedom*
Nolen, Jerdine. *Big Jabe*
Pinkney, Andrea Davis. *Dear Benjamin Banneker*
    Sojourner Truth's step-stomp stride
Rappaport, Doreen. *Frederick's journey*
    Freedom river
    Freedom ship
Raven, Margot Theis. *Night boat to freedom*

Riggio, Anita. *Secret signs*
Ringgold, Faith. *The invisible princesses*
Robbins, Dean. *Two friends*
Rochelle, Belinda. *Jewels*
Sanders, Nancy. *D is for drinking gourd*
Sanders, Scott R. *A place called Freedom*
Schroeder, Alan. *Minty*
Shange, Ntozake. *Freedom's a-callin me*
Siegelson, Kim L. *In the time of the drums*
Slate, Joseph. *I want to be free*
Smalls-Hector, Irene. *Jenny Reen and the Jack Muh
    Lantern*
Smith, Charles R. *Brick by brick*
Stroud, Bettye. *The leaving*
    The patchwork path
Tate, Don. *It jes' happened*
Turner, Glennette Tilley. *An apple for Harriet
    Tubman*
Uchida, Yoshiko. *The bracelet*
Walker, Sally M. *Freedom song*
Weatherford, Carole Boston. *The Beatitudes*
    Freedom in Congo Square
    Juneteenth jamboree
    *Moses: when Harriet Tubman led her people to
    freedom*
Winter, Jeanette. *Follow the drinking gourd*
Woelfle, Gretchen. *Mumbet's Declaration of
    Independence*
Woodson, Jacqueline. *Show way*
Wright, Courtni Crump. *Journey to freedom*
    Jumping the broom

Sleep

Alexander, Martha G. *I'll protect you from the jungle
    beasts*
Allenby, Victoria. *Nat the cat can sleep like that*
Andersen, Hans Christian. *La princesa and the pea*
    The princess and the pea, ill. by Emily Bolam
    The princess and the pea, ill. by Charlene DeLage
    The princess and the pea, ill. by Dorothée Duntze
    The princess and the pea, ill. by Maja Dusíková
    The princess and the pea, ill. by Paul Galdone
    The princess and the pea, ill. by Rachel Isadora
    The princess and the pea, ill. by Bernhard
    Oberdieck
    The princess and the pea, ill. by Janet Stevens
    The princess and the pea, ill. by Alain Vaës
    The princess and the pea in miniature
Apperley, Dawn. *Don't wake the baby*
Arnold, Tedd. *Five ugly monsters*
Asch, Frank. *Good night, Baby Bear*
Baker, Roberta. *Olive's first sleepover*
Banks, Kate. *Close your eyes*
Batten, Mary. *Please don't wake the animals*
Bauer, Marion Dane. *Sleep, little one, sleep*
Bean, Jonathan. *At night*
Berger, Samantha. *Snoozefest at the Nuzzledome*
Bergman, Mara. *Musical beds*
    Oliver who would not sleep!
Blomgren, Jennifer. *Where do I sleep?*
Bonnett-Rampersaud, Louise. *How do you sleep?*
Bottner, Barbara. *Feet go to sleep*
Branford, Henrietta. *Little Pig Figwort can't get to
    sleep*
Braun, Sebastien. *Back to bed, Ed!*
Brown, Marc. *Monkey: not ready for bedtime*
Brown, Margaret Wise. *The Golden sleepy book*
    Sheep don't count sheep

Waber, Bernard. *Ira sleeps over*
Waddell, Martin. *Can't you sleep, Little Bear?*
 Sleep tight, Little Bear
Walton, Rick. *So many bunnies*
Watt, Mélanie. *Scaredy Squirrel at night*
Weiss, Nicki. *Where does the brown bear go?*
Whatley, Bruce. *Captain Pajamas*
Wheeler, Lisa. *Babies can sleep anywhere*
 Even monsters need to sleep
Wolf, Karina. *The Insomniacs*
Wolff, Ferida. *It is the wind*
Wong, Janet S. *Grump*
Wood, Audrey. *The full moon at the napping house*
 It's Duffy time!
 Moonflute
 The napping house
 The napping house wakes up
Wright, Michael. *Jake stays awake*
Yuly, Toni. *Cat nap*
Ziefert, Harriet. *It's time to go to sleep*
 It's time to take a nap
 Mommy, I want to sleep in your bed!
 What do ducks dream?
Zolotow, Charlotte. *Sleepy book*, ill. by Ilse Plume
 Sleepy book, ill. by Stefano Vitale

Sleep – snoring

Arnold, Marsha Diane. *Roar of a snore*
Bardhan-Quallen, Sudipta. *Snoring Beauty*
Blecha, Aaron. *Goodnight, Grizzle Grump!*
DiPucchio, Kelly. *Dinosnores*
Escoffier, Michaël. *Sleep tight, Charlie*
Hodgkinson, Leigh. *The big monster snorey book*
Long, Kathy. *Christopher sat straight up in bed*
Long, Melinda. *When Papa snores*
Monfreid, Dorothée de. *Shhh! I'm sleeping*
Ohora, Zachariah. *Stop snoring, Bernard!*
Waber, Bernard. *The mouse that snored*

Sleepovers

Beck, Scott. *Monster sleepover!*
Becker, Bonny. *A bedtime for Bear*
Berenstain, Stan and Jan. *The Berenstain bears and the slumber party*
Brown, Marc. *Arthur's first sleepover*
Clarke, Jane. *Dippy's sleepover*
Dean, James. *Pete the Cat and the bedtime blues*
Dewdney, Anna. *Llama Llama Gram and Grandpa*
Ellis, Sarah. *Ben over night*
Gianferrari, Maria. *Penny and Jelly: slumber under the stars*
Giglio, Judy. *The tapping tale*
Greene, Rhonda Gowler. *At grandma's*
Harper, Charise Mericle. *When Randolph turned rotten*
Hill, Eric. *Spot sleeps over*
Jackson, Isaac. *Somebody's new pajamas*
Jennings, Sharon. *Franklin wants a badge*
Joosse, Barbara. *Sleepover at Gramma's house*
Leijten, Aileen. *Hugging hour!*
Long, Kathy. *Christopher sat straight up in bed*
McDonnell, Patrick. *Thank you and good night*
McKissack, Patricia C. *Messy Bessey and the birthday overnight*
Manning, Jane. *Millie Fierce sleeps out*
Mitchard, Jacquelyn. *Ready, set, school!*
Murphy, Stuart J. *Rabbit's pajama party*

Pace, Anne Marie. *Vampirina ballerina hosts a sleepover*
Pearce, Philippa. *Amy's three best things*
Penn, Audrey. *Chester Raccoon and the almost perfect sleepover*
Pinkwater, Daniel. *Sleepover Larry*
Radabaugh, Melinda Beth. *Sleeping over*
Regan, Dian Curtis. *The Snow Blew Inn*
Robberecht, Thierry. *Sam's new friend*
Rodriguez, Bobbie. *Sarah's sleepover*
Russo, Marisabina. *Sophie sleeps over*
Smith, Danna. *Mother Goose's pajama party*
Smith, Maggie. *Pigs in pajamas*
Tyler, Anne. *Timothy Tugbottom says no!*
Vulliamy, Clara. *Small*
Waber, Bernard. *Bearsie Bear and the surprise sleepover party*
Winthrop, Elizabeth. *Squashed in the middle*

Sleight-of-hand *see* Magic

Smallness *see* Character traits – smallness

Smell *see* Anatomy – noses; Senses – smell

Smiles, smiling *see* Anatomy – faces

Snoring *see* Noise, sounds; Sleep – snoring

Snow *see* Weather – blizzards; Weather – snow

Snow plows *see* Machines

Snowmen

Arena, Jen. *One hundred snowmen*
Arnold, Katya. *The adventures of Snowwoman*
Briggs, Raymond. *The snowman*
Britt, Chris. *The most perfect snowman*
Buehner, Caralyn. *Snowmen all year*
 Snowmen at Christmas
 Snowmen at night
Butler, M. Christina. *The smiley snowman*
Carlson, Nancy. *Snowden*
Colandro, Lucille. *There was a cold lady who swallowed some snow!*
Cuyler, Margery. *The biggest, best snowman*
Doodler, Todd H. *Bear in long underwear*
Ehlert, Lois. *Snowballs*
Fleming, Denise. *The first day of winter*
Garland, Michael. *Christmas magic*
Gilmore, Rachna. *Making grizzle grow*
Gorbachev, Valeri. *Pizza-pie snowman*
Hillenbrand, Will. *Snowman's story*
Hoban, Julia. *Amy loves the snow*
Joyce, William. *Snowie Rolie*
Kellogg, Steven. *The mystery of the missing red mitten*
Kirk, Daniel. *Snow family*
LaReau, Kara. *Snowbaby could not sleep*
Lawler, Janet. *Snowzilla*
McDaniels, Preston. *A perfect snowman*
McGhee, Alison. *Making a friend*
Mahoney, Daniel J. *A really good snowman*

Marlow, Layn. *You make me smile*
Miller, Edna. *Mousekin's frosty friend*
Moser, Lisa. *Perfect soup*
Nelson, Steve. *Frosty the snowman*
Peddle, Daniel. *Snow day*
Pittman, Helena Clare. *The snowman's path*
Reid, Barbara. *Perfect snow*
Schaefer, Carole Lexa. *Snow pumpkin*
Scheffler, Axel. *Pip and Posy: the snowy day*
Taylor, Sean. *The snowbear*
Tegen, Katherine Brown. *Snowman magic*
Wahman, Joe. *Snowboy 1, 2, 3*
Walters, Catherine. *The magical snowman*
Whybrow, Ian. *Harry and the snow king*
    Wish, change, friend
Winget, Susan. *Sam the Snowman*
Wright, Maureen. *Sneezy the snowman*

Society Islands *see* Foreign lands – South Sea
    Islands

Soldiers *see* Careers – military

Soldiers, toy *see* Toys – soldiers

Solitude *see* Behavior – solitude

Songs

Alexander, Cecil Frances. *All creatures great and
    small*
    All things bright and beautiful, ill. by Ashley Bryan
    All things bright and beautiful, ill. by Anna
        Vojtech
    All things bright and beautiful, ill. by Anna
        Vojtech
    All things bright and beautiful, ill. by Bruce
        Whatley
Alger, Leclaire Gowans. *All in the morning early*
Allen, Nancy Kelly. *"Happy birthday"*
Alley, R. W. *There once was a witch*
Anderson, Derek. *Over the river*
Arnosky, Jim. *Gobble it up!*
    I'm a turkey!
Ashburn, Boni. *Over at the castle*
Autry, Gene. *Here comes Santa Claus*
Aylesworth, Jim. *Our Abe Lincoln*
Baker, Ken. *Old MacDonald had a dragon*
Baring-Gould, S. *Now the day is over*
Barnwell, Ysaye M. *We are one*
Bateman, Donna M. *Out on the prairie*
Bates, Ivan. *Five little ducks*
Bates, Katharine Lee. *America the beautiful*, ill. by
    Chris Gall
    America the beautiful, ill. by Wendell Minor
    America the beautiful: together we stand
Baum, Maxie. *I have a little dreidel*
Beall, Pamela Conon. *Wee Sing if you're happy and
    you know it*
The bear
Berkes, Marianne. *Over in a river*
Berkner, Laurie. *Pillowland*
    We are the dinosaurs
Berlin, Irving. *Easter parade*
    God bless America
Bonwill, Ann. *The Frazzle family finds a way*

Brantley-Newton, Vanessa. *Let freedom sing*
Brebeuf, Jean de. *The Huron carol*
Brokering, Herbert F. *Earth and all stars*
Brown, Marc. *Play rhymes*
Brown, Margaret Wise. *Goodnight songs*
Bryan, Ashley. *All night, all day*
Burke, Bobby. *Daddy's little girl*
Busse, Sarah Martin. *Banjo granny*
Butler, Geoff. *Ode to Newfoundland*
Butler, John. *Bedtime in the jungle*
Cabrera, Jane. *Here we go round the mulberry bush*
    If you're happy and you know it
    Row, row, row your boat
    Twinkle, twinkle, little star
    The wheels on the bus
Canyon, Christopher. *John Denver's Sunshine on my
    shoulders*
Carle, Eric. *Today is Monday*
Carter, David A. *If you're happy and you know it, clap
    your hands*
    Old MacDonald had a farm: a pop-up book
Catrow, David. *Monster mash*
Chapin, Tom. *The backwards birthday party*
    The library book
Child, Lydia Maria. *Over the river and through the
    wood*
    *Over the river and through the wood: the New
        England boy's song about Thanksgiving Day*
Cleland, Jo. *Getting your zzzzs*
Cohan, George M. *You're a grand old flag*
Colato Laínez, René. *Señor Pancho had a rancho*
Collins, Billy. *Daddy's little boy*
Comden, Betty. *What's new at the zoo?*
Comden, Betty, et al. *Flying to Neverland with Peter
    Pan*
Conahan, Carolyn. *The twelve days of Christmas dogs*
Corr, Christopher. *Whole world*
Creech, Sharon. *Who's that baby?*
Crum, Shutta. *My mountain song*
Dale, Penny. *The boy on the bus*
Dann, Penny. *Eensy weensy spider*
Davenier, Christine. *It's raining, it's pouring*
De colores / Bright with colors
Dealey, Erin. *Deck the walls!*
Dean, James. *Pete the Cat: the wheels on the bus*
    Pete the Cat: twinkle, twinkle, little star
Delacre, Lulu. *Arroz con leche*
    Las Navidades
Demas, Corinne. *Nina's waltz*
Dominguez, Angela. *Maria had a little llama/Maria
    tenia una llama pequena*
Downes, Belinda. *Baby days*
Downing, Johnette. *Down in Louisiana*
    There was an old lady who swallowed some bugs
    Today is Monday in Louisiana
Durango, Julia. *Angels watching over me*
Dylan, Bob. *Blowin' in the wind*
    If not for you
    Man gave names to all the animals
Egielski, Richard. *Itsy bitsy spider*, ill. by Richard
    Egielski
    Itsy bitsy spider, ill. by Richard Egielski
Ehrhardt, Karen. *This jazz man*
Ellwand, David. *Ten in the bed*
Emberley, Barbara. *One wide river to cross*
Emberley, Rebecca. *If you're a monster and you know
    it*
Emberley, Rebecca, et al. *There was an old monster*

Emmett, Jonathan. *She'll be coming 'round the mountain*

The farmer in the dell. *The farmer in the dell*, ill. by John O'Brien

The farmer in the dell, ill. by Alexandra Wallner

Fine, Howard. *A piggie Christmas*

Fitzgerald, Ella. *A-tisket, a-tasket*

Fleming, Candace. *Gabriella's song*

The fox went out on a chilly night

Freed, Arthur. *Singing in the rain*

A frog he would a-wooing go [folk-song] *Frog went a-courtin'*

Frog went a-courting

Froggie went a courting

Froggy went a-courtin'

Gershator, Phillis. *This is the day!*

Go tell Aunt Rhody

Goembel, Ponder. *Animal fair*

Goode, Diane. *Diane Goode's book of silly stories and songs*

Guthrie, Woody. *Bling blang*

My dolly

This land is your land

Hallworth, Grace. *Sing me a story*

Harburg, E. Y. *Over the rainbow*

Harris, John. *Jingle bells: how the holiday classic came to be*

Heras, Theo. *What will we do with the baby-o?*

Here we go round the mulberry bush

Hoberman, Mary Ann. *Bill Grogan's goat*

Mary had a little lamb

Hodges, Margaret. *Silent night: the song and its story*

Hooper, Maureen Brett. *Silent night: a Christmas carol is born*

Hoose, Philip M. *Hey little ant*

House, Catherine. *A stork in a baobab tree*

Hush songs

Isadora, Rachel. *Old Mikamba had a farm*

There was a tree

Ivimey, John William. *The complete story of the three blind mice*

Three blind mice

Jackson, Jill. *Let there be peace on earth*

Jeffers, Susan. *Jingle bells*

Jewel. *Sweet dreams*

Joel, Billy. *New York state of mind*

Johnson, James Weldon. *Lift every voice and sing*

Lift ev'ry voice and sing

Johnson, Paul Brett. *Little Bunny Foo Foo*

On top of spaghetti

Jonas, Ann. *Bird talk*

Judd, Naomi. *Naomi Judd's guardian angels*

Judge, Lita. *Hoot and Peep: a song for snow*

Katz, Karen. *The babies on the bus*

Keats, Ezra Jack. *The little drummer boy*

Kellogg, Steven. *Give the dog a bone*

A-hunting we will go!

I was born about 10,000 years ago

Santa Claus is comin' to town

Yankee Doodle

Kennedy, Jimmy. *The teddy bears' picnic*

Ketteman, Helen. *The ghosts go haunting*

Key, Francis Scott. *The Star Spangled Banner*

The Star-Spangled Banner

Kirk, Daniel. *Go!*

Knick knack paddy whack

Knight, Hilary. *A firefly in a fir tree*

Kovalski, Maryann. *The wheels on the bus*

Kroll, Steven. *By the dawn's early light: the story of the Star Spangled Banner*

Krosoczka, Jarrett J. *Punk Farm on tour*

Langstaff, John M. *Oh, a-hunting we will go*

Over in the meadow

What a morning!

Lendroth, Susan. *Old Manhattan has some farms*

Lennon, John. *Imagine*

Lenski, Lois. *I like winter*

Let it shine

Let me call you sweetheart

Levy, Debbie. *We shall overcome*

Lithgow, John. *I got two dogs*

Marsupial Sue

Never play music right next to the zoo

Little old lady who swallowed a fly. *I know an old lady*

I know an old lady who swallowed a fly, ill. by Stephen Gulbis

I know an old lady who swallowed a fly, ill. by Glen Rounds

I know an old lady who swallowed a fly, ill. by Nadine Bernard Westcott

There once was a cowpoke who swallowed an ant

There was an old lady who swallowed a fly, ill. by Pam Adams

There was an old lady who swallowed a fly, ill. by Rashin Kheiriyeh

There was an old lady who swallowed a fly, ill. by Simms Taback

There was an old monkey who swallowed a frog

There was an old mummy who swallowed a spider

There was an old pirate who swallowed a fish

Lloyd-Jones, Sally. *Old MacNoah had an ark*

Loggins, Kenny. *Footloose*

Long, Ethan. *The croaky pokey!*

Long, Sylvia. *Deck the hall*

McCutcheon, John. *Happy adoption day!*

MacDonald, Margaret Read. *A hen, a chick, and a string guitar*

McGinley-Nally, Sharon. *The friendly beasts*

Margolin, H. Ellen. *Goin' to Boston*

Marley, Cedella. *Every little thing*

One love

Mayo, Margaret. *Wiggle waggle fun*

Meister, Cari. *Follow the drinking gourd: an Underground Railroad story*

Melmed, Laura Krauss. *The first song ever sung*

Milgrim, David. *Young MacDonald*

Miller, J. Philip. *We all sing with the same voice*

Mitchell, Susan K. *The rainforest grew all around*

Mohr, Joseph. *Silent night*

Moore, Mary-Alice. *The wheels on the school bus*

Mora, Pat. *A piñata in a pine tree*

Moses, Will. *Silent night*

Moss, Marissa. *Knick knack paddywack*

Munsch, Robert N. *Mortimer*

Nelson, Kadir. *He's got the whole world in His hands*

Nelson, Steve. *Frosty the snowman*

Newman, Lesléa. *The eight nights of Chanukah*

Norman, Kim. *If it's snowy and you know it, clap your paws!*

Norworth, Jack. *Take me out to the ball game*

Take me out to the ballgame

Old MacDonald had a farm. *Grandma's nursery rhymes: Old MacDonald*

Old MacDonald

Old MacDonald had a farm, ill. by Holly Berry

Old MacDonald had a farm, ill. by Jane Cabrera

Suen, Anastasia. *Man on the moon*
Thomas, Frances. *One day, Daddy*
Timmers, Leo. *Franky*
Tokuda-Hall, Maggie. *Also an octopus*
Underwood, Deborah. *Interstellar Cinderella*
Ungerer, Tomi. *Moon man*
Van Allsburg, Chris. *Zathura*
Van Camp, Katie. *Harry and Horsie*
Van Vleet, Carmella. *To the stars!*
Viva, Frank. *A long way away*
Wakeman, Daniel. *Ben's bunny trouble*
Wallace, Nancy Elizabeth. *Stars! stars! stars!*
Weitekamp, Margaret A. *Pluto's secret*
Wells, Robert E. *What's so special about planet Earth?*
Wethered, Peggy. *Touchdown Mars!*
Wick, Walter. *Can you see what I see? out of this world*
Wiesner, David. *Mr. Wuffles!*
Wood, Audrey. *The Christmas adventure of Space Elf Sam*
Yaccarino, Dan. *First day on a strange new planet*
    New pet
    Zoom! zoom! zoom! I'm off to the moon!
Yolen, Jane. *Moon ball*
Yorinks, Arthur. *Company's coming*
    Company's going
    Quack!
Young, Ned. *Zoomer's out-of-this-world Christmas*

Spectacles *see* Glasses

Speech *see* Disabilities – stuttering; Language

Spelunking *see* Caves

Spiders

Aardema, Verna. *Anansi does the impossible!*
    Anansi finds a fool
    The vingananee and the tree toad
Barton, Bethany. *I'm trying to love spiders*
Berger, Melvin. *Spinning spiders*
Bodkin, Odds. *The Christmas cobwebs*
Carle, Eric. *The very busy spider*
Cronin, Doreen. *Diary of a spider*
Cummings, Troy. *The Eensy Weensy Spider freaks out! (big-time!)*
Dann, Penny. *Eensy weensy spider*
Dewey, Jennifer Owings. *Once I knew a spider*
Dodd, Emma. *I love bugs!*
Egielski, Richard. *Itsy bitsy spider*
Gibbons, Gail. *Spiders*
Himmelman, John. *A house spider's life*
Hopgood, Tim. *Walter's wonderful web*
Howitt, Mary Botham. *Mary Howitt's The spider and the fly*
Jaramillo, Susie. *Elefantitos / little elephants*
Keens-Douglas, Richardo. *Anancy and the haunted house*
Ketteman, Helen. *Armadilly chili*
Kimmel, Eric A. *Anansi and the magic stick*
    Anansi and the moss-covered rock
    Anansi and the talking melon
    Anansi goes fishing
    Anansi's party time
Kirk, David. *Little Miss Spider*
    Little Miss Spider at Sunny Patch School
    Miss Spider's ABC

    Miss Spider's new car
    Miss Spider's tea party
Krumwiede, Lana. *Just Itzy*
Lasky, Kathryn. *Show and tell bunnies*
Lewis, J. Patrick. *The little buggers*
London, Jonathan. *Dream weaver*
McDermott, Gerald. *Anansi the spider*
Markle, Sandra. *Sneaky, spinning, baby spiders*
Mollel, Tololwa M. *Ananse's feast*
Monks, Lydia. *Aaaarrgghh! spider!*
Mother Goose. *Little Miss Muffet*
Murawski, Darlyne A. *Bug faces*
Musgrove, Margaret. *The spider weaver*
Noble, Trinka Hakes. *A Christmas spider's miracle*
Oppenheim, Joanne. *Have you seen bugs?*
Pienkowski, Jan. *Pizza!*
Razi, Michaele. *Frank the seven-legged spider*
Rouss, Sylvia A. *Sammy Spider's first day of school*
    Sammy Spider's first Passover
    Sammy Spider's first Shabbat
    Sammy Spider's first Tu B'Shevat
    Sammy Spider's first Yom Kippur
Shields, Carol Diggory. *The bugliest bug*
Siomades, Lorianne. *The itsy bitsy spider*
Spinelli, Eileen. *Sophie's masterpiece*
Temple, Frances. *Tiger soup*
Trapani, Iza. *The itsy bitsy spider*
Wells, Rosemary. *The itsy-bitsy spider*
Williams, Brenda. *Home for a tiger, home for a bear*

Split page books *see* Format, unusual

Spooks *see* Ghosts; Mythical creatures – goblins

Sports

Adler, David A. *Joe Louis*
Axelrod, Amy. *Pigs on the ball*
Berenstain, Stan and Jan. *The Berenstain bears go out for the team*
    The Berenstain bears' report card trouble
Blumenthal, Deborah. *Ice palace*
Brown, Don. *Bright path*
Carr, Jan. *Frozen noses*
Clayton, Elaine. *A blue ribbon for Sugar*
Deans, Karen. *Playing to win*
Hammerle, Susa. *Let's try horseback riding*
Hayden, Kate. *Horse show*
Lehn, Barbara. *What is an athlete?*
Lester, Helen. *Tacky and the Winter Games*
London, Jonathan. *White water*
McKissack, Robert L. *Try your best*
Macy, Sue. *Miss Mary reporting*
Mills, Claudia. *Ziggy's blue-ribbon day*
Pendziwol, Jean E. *A treasure at sea for dragon and me*
Prelutsky, Jack. *Good sports*
Reiser, Lynn. *Play ball with me!*
Rex, Michael. *Dunk skunk*
Smith, Nikkolas. *The golden girls of Rio*
Snyder, Betsy. *I can play*
Stauffacher, Sue. *Nothing but trouble*
Stockdale, Sean. *Max the champion*
Wheeler, Lisa. *Dino-boarding*
Ziefert, Harriet. *Murphy jumps a hurdle*

Sports – archery

Fisher, Leonard Everett. *William Tell*
San Souci, Robert D. *Robin Hood and the golden arrow*

Sports – baseball

Abbott, Bud. *Who's on first?*
Abrahams, Peter. *Quacky baseball*
Adler, David A. *Campy*
   Satchel Paige
Alborough, Jez. *Hit the ball Duck*
Bildner, Phil. *Shoeless Joe and Black Betsy*
   The shot heard 'round the world
Borden, Louise. *Baseball is . . .*
Burleigh, Robert. *Home run*
   Stealing home
Churnin, Nancy. *The William Hoy story*
Cooper, Elisha. *Ballpark*
Cooper, Floyd. *Willie and the All-Stars*
Cristaldi, Kathryn. *Baseball ballerina*
   Baseball ballerina strikes out
Crowe, Chris. *Just as good*
Curtis, Gavin. *The bat boy and his violin*
Dahl, Michael. *Goodnight baseball*
Day, Alexandra. *Frank and Ernest play ball*
deGroat, Diane. *Homer*
Egan, Tim. *Roasted peanuts*
Ellery, Amanda. *If I were a jungle animal*
Elster, Jean Alicia. *Just call me Joe Joe*
Fauchald, Nick. *Batter up!*
   Nice hit!
Fishman, Cathy Goldberg. *When Jackie and Hank met*
Florian, Douglas. *Poem runs*
Golenbock, Peter. *ABCs of baseball*
   Hank Aaron
Gutman, Dan. *Casey back at bat*
Hernandez, Keith. *First-base hero*
Herzog, Brad. *I spy with my little eye: baseball*
Hopkinson, Deborah. *Girl wonder*
Hubbard, Crystal. *Catching the moon: the story of a young girl's baseball dream*
Hyman, Zachary. *The Bambino and me*
Isadora, Rachel. *Luke goes to bat*
   Nick plays baseball
Jordan, Deloris. *Michael's golden rules*
Keane, Dave. *Daddy adventure day*
Kelly, David A. *Miracle mud*
Kinerk, Robert. *Clorinda plays baseball!*
Kovalski, Maryann. *Take me out to the ball game*
Kraus, Robert. *Mort the sport*
Krensky, Stephen. *Play ball, Jackie!*
Leonetti, Mike. *Swinging for the fences*
Lester, Helen. *Batter up Wombat*
Lewis, J. Patrick. *Tulip at the bat*
Lies, Brian. *Bats at the ballgame*
Lorbiecki, Marybeth. *Jackie's bat*
McCully, Emily Arnold. *Mouse practice*
   Queen of the diamond
McDonough, Yona Zeldis. *Hammerin' Hank*
Mackall, Dandi Daley. *A girl named Dan*
Madison, Alan. *Pecorino plays ball*
Madonna. *Mr. Peabody's apples*
Mammano, Julie. *Rhinos who play baseball*
Mandel, Peter. *Say hey*
Mellage, Nanette. *Coming home*
Meshon, Aaron. *Take me out to the Yakyu*
Michelson, Richard. *Across the alley*

Mochizuki, Ken. *Baseball saved us*
Nevius, Carol. *Baseball hour*
Newman, Jeff. *The boys*
Norworth, Jack. *Take me out to the ball game*
   Take me out to the ballgame
Pallotta, Jerry. *F is for Fenway*
Paxton, Tom. *The jungle baseball game*
Raczka, Bob. *Joy in Mudville*
Rappaport, Doreen. *Dirt on their skirts*
Robinson, Sharon. *Testing the ice*
Rodriguez, Alex. *Out of the ballpark*
Rosenstock, Barb. *The streak*
Skead, Robert. *Something to prove*
Soto, Gary. *Lucky Luis*
Spradlin, Michael P. *Baseball from A to Z*
Stadler, John. *Take me out to the ball game: a pop-up book*
Tavares, Matt. *Becoming Babe Ruth*
   Growing up Pedro
   Henry Aaron's dream
   Mudball
   Oliver's game
   There goes Ted Williams
   Zachary's ball
Thayer, Ernest Lawrence. *Casey at the bat*
   Casey at the bat: a ballad of the Republic, sung in the year 1888, ill. by Christopher Bing
   Casey at the bat: a ballad of the Republic, sung in the year 1888, ill. by Patricia Polacco
Uhlberg, Myron. *Dad, Jackie, and me*
Van Dusen, Chris. *Randy Riley's really big hit*
Van Nutt, Julia. *Skyrockets and snickerdoodles*
Vernick, Audrey. *Brothers at bat*
   She loved baseball
Waber, Bernard. *Gina*
Weatherford, Carole Boston. *Champions on the bench*
Welch, Willy. *Playing right field*
Wheeler, Lisa. *Dino-baseball*
Winter, Jonah. *Joltin' Joe DiMaggio*
Wise, Bill. *Silent star*
Wittenstein, Barry. *Waiting for Pumpsie*
Yolen, Jane. *All star!*
   Moon ball
Zagwÿn, Deborah Turney. *Apple batter*

Sports – basketball

Bateman, Teresa. *The princesses have a ball*
Codell, Esmé Raji. *The basket ball*
Fauchald, Nick. *Jump ball!*
Garland, Michael. *Hooray José!*
Jordan, Deloris. *Dream big*
   Salt in his shoes
Martin, Bill, Jr. *Swish!*
Meunier, Brian. *Bravo, Tavo!*
Paul, Chris. *Long shot*
Rockwell, Anne. *Brendan and Belinda and the slam dunk!*
Wheeler, Lisa. *Dino-basketball*

Sports – bicycling

Aylesworth, Jim. *My sister's rusty bike*
Barton, Byron. *My bike*
Beardshaw, Rosalind. *Grandpa's surprise*
Berry, Lynne. *Ducking for apples*
Best, Cari. *Sally Jean, the Bicycle Queen*
Blackstone, Stella. *Bear on a bike*

Boelts, Maribeth. *A bike like Sergio's*
Bourgeois, Paulette. *Franklin rides a bike*
Braver, Vanita. *Madison and the two wheeler*
Brown, Marc. *D. W. rides again!*
Burleigh, Robert. *Messenger, messenger*
Crews, Donald. *Bicycle race*
Davies, Matt. *Ben rides on*
Doi, Kaya. *Chirri and Chirra*
Edwards, Michelle. *The Hanukkah trike*
Elya, Susan Middleton. *Adiós, tricycle*
Eriksson, Eva. *A crash course for Molly*
Farish, Terry. *Joseph's big ride*
Gerstein, Mordicai. *How to bicycle to the moon to plant sunflowers*
Goldin, David. *Go-Go-Go!*
Hillenbrand, Will. *Off we go! a Bear and Mole story*
Isabella, Jude. *The red bicycle*
Janni, Rebecca. *Every cowgirl loves a rodeo*
Liu, Cynthea. *Bike on, Bear!*
London, Jonathan. *Froggy rides a bike*
   Let's go, Froggy!
Mollel, Tololwa M. *My rows and piles of coins*
Monroe, Chris. *Bug on a bike*
Montanari, Eva. *Dino bikes*
Mortensen, Lori. *Cowpoke Clyde rides the range*
Olaleye, Isaac. *Bikes for rent!*
Pett, Mark. *The girl and the bicycle*
Proimos, James. *The best bike ride ever*
Ransome, James. *New red bike!*
Raschka, Chris. *Everyone can learn to ride a bicycle*
Rey, H. A. *Curious George rides a bike*
Say, Allen. *The bicycle man*
Shannon, David. *Duck on a bike*
Spinelli, Eileen. *A big boy now*
Tessler, Manya. *Yuki's ride home*
Thompson, Laurie Ann. *Emmanuel's dream*
Tutu, Archbishop Desmond. *Desmond and the very mean word*
Viva, Frank. *Along a long road*
Wormell, Christopher. *Blue Rabbit and the runaway wheel*

Sports – bowling

Durand, Hallie. *Mitchell goes bowling*

Sports – boxing

Adler, David A. *Joe Louis*
Buitrago, Jairo. *Jimmy the greatest*
de la Peña, Matt. *A nation's hope*
Lewin, Ted. *At Gleason's gym*
Myers, Walter Dean. *Muhammad Ali: the people's champion*
Olshan, Matthew. *The mighty Lalouche*
Winter, Jonah. *Muhammad Ali: champion of the world*

Sports – camping *see* Camps, camping

Sports – fishing

Aruego, José. *Splash!*
Banks, Kate. *That's Papa's way*
Bootman, Colin. *Fish for the Grand Lady*
Carney, Margaret. *The biggest fish in the lake*
Cook, Bernadine. *The little fish that got away*
Creech, Sharon. *Fishing in the air*
Cronin, Doreen. *Click, clack, splish, splash*

Crowley, Ned. *Nanook and Pryce*
Emmons, Chip. *Sammy wakes his dad*
Farish, Terry. *The cat who liked potato soup*
Frank, John. *How to catch a fish*
Gentle, Victor. *Killer sharks, killer people*
George, William T. *Fishing at Long Pond*
Gibbons, Gail. *Surrounded by sea*
Gourounas, Jean. *Something's fishy*
Gravett, Emily. *Bear and Hare go fishing*
Gréban, Quentin. *Nestor*
Henson, Heather. *Grumpy Grandpa*
Joosse, Barbara. *I love you the purplest*
Krudop, Walter Lyon. *The man who caught fish*
London, Jonathan. *Where the big fish are*
Luenn, Nancy. *Nessa's fish*
McDonald, Rae A. *A fishing surprise*
McKissack, Patricia C. *A million fish . . . more or less*
Martin, David. *Piggy and Dad go fishing*
Mayer, Mercer. *A boy, a dog, a frog and a friend*
   A boy, a dog and a frog
Ness, Evaline. *Sam, Bangs, and moonshine*
Oppel, Kenneth. *Peg and the whale*
Partridge, Elizabeth. *Oranges on Golden Mountain*
Paterson, Brian. *Zigby dives in*
Pendziwol, Jean E. *Me and you and the red canoe*
Phi, Bao. *A different pond*
Potter, Beatrix. *The tale of Mr. Jeremy Fisher*, ill. by David Jorgensen
   The tale of Mr. Jeremy Fisher, ill. by Beatrix Potter
Quigley, Mary. *Granddad's fishing buddy*
Rey, Margret. *Curious George flies a kite*
Roth, Roger. *Fishing for Methuselah*
San Souci, Robert D. *Six foolish fishermen*
Say, Allen. *A river dream*
Selick, Henry. *Moongirl*
Shannon, David. *Jangles*
Sterer, Gideon. *Skyfishing*
Stevenson, Robert Louis. *The moon*
Walsh, Liam Francis. *Fish*
Williams, Garth. *Benjamin's treasure*
Yamashita, Haruo. *Seven little mice have fun on the ice*
Young, Judy. *H is for hook*

Sports – football

Barber, Tiki. *By my brother's side*
   Game day
   Teammates
Bildner, Phil. *The greatest game ever played*
   Turkey Bowl
Dahl, Michael. *Goodnight football*
Fauchald, Nick. *Touchdown!*
Gruska, Denise. *The only boy in ballet class*
McCarty, Peter. *Fall ball*
Manning, Peyton. *Family huddle*
Martin, Bill, Jr.. *Little granny quarterback*
Ransome, James. *Gunner, football hero*
Reynolds, Aaron. *Buffalo wings*
Wheeler, Lisa. *Dino-football*

Sports – golf

Fauchald, Nick. *Tee off!*
Michelson, Richard. *Twice as good*

Sports – gymnastics

Brown, Marc. *D. W. flips!*
Gray, Karlin. *Nadia*

Isadora, Rachel. *Jake at gymnastics*
Lasky, Kathryn. *Tumble bunnies*
Newcome, Zita. *Pop-up toddlerobics*
Roche, Denis. *Mim, gym, and June*
Taylor, Sean. *Boing!*

Sports – hiking *see* Activities – hiking

Sports – hockey

Bailey, Linda. *The farm team*
Bradley, Sandra. *Henry Holton takes the ice*
Carter, Anne Laurel. *The F team*
Fauchald, Nick. *Face off!*
Leonetti, Mike. *Gretzky's game*
MacGregor, Roy. *The highest number in the world*
McMullan, Kate. *I'm cool!*
Mizzoni, Chris. *Clancy with the puck*
Napier, Matt. *Z is for zamboni*
Polacco, Patricia. *Rotten Richie and the ultimate dare*
Stevenson, James. *Sam the Zamboni man*
Sylvester, Kevin. *Splinters*
Wheeler, Lisa. *Dino-hockey*

Sports – hunting

Cuyler, Margery. *We're going on a lion hunt*
Fraser, Mary Ann. *No Yeti yet*
Freedman, Claire. *Follow that bear if you dare!*
Hader, Berta Hoerner. *The mighty hunter*
Haughton, Chris. *Shh! we have a plan*
Judes, Marie-Odile. *Max, the stubborn little wolf*
Kellogg, Steven. *Tallyho, Pinkerton!*
Kroll, Steven. *One tough turkey*
Langstaff, John M. *Oh, a-hunting we will go*
Lowry, Lois. *Crow call*
Miller, Pat. *We're going on a book hunt*
Nolan, Dennis. *Hunters of the great forest*
Peet, Bill. *Buford the little bighorn*
　　The gnats of knotty pine
Rohmer, Harriet, et al. *The invisible hunters*
Rosen, Michael. *We're going on a bear hunt*
Tankard, Jeremy. *Me hungry!*
Winter, Jeanette. *Kali's song*

Sports – ice skating

Bailey, Linda. *The best figure skater in the whole wide world*
Berger, Carin. *A perfect day*
Berry, Lynne. *Duck skates*
Bradley, Sandra. *Henry Holton takes the ice*
Bunge, Daniela. *The scarves*
Carlson, Nancy. *Snowden*
Child, Lauren. *I really, really need actual ice skates*
Emberley, Rebecca. *Mice on ice*
Holabird, Katharine. *Angelina ice skates*
Idle, Molly. *Flora and the penguin*
Isadora, Rachel. *Sophie skates*
Karas, G. Brian. *Skidamarink*
Keller, Holly. *Pearl's new skates*
Lazar, Tara. *Little Red Gliding Hood*
Medearis, Angela Shelf. *Poppa's itchy Christmas*
Silvestro, Annie. *Mice skating*
Spinelli, Eileen. *Callie Cat, ice skater*
Stevenson, James. *Sam the Zamboni man*
Whybrow, Ian. *Bella gets her skates on*
Wright, Joanna. *Bunnies on ice*
Yamaguchi, Kristi. *Dream big, little pig!*

It's a big world, little pig!

Sports – karate

Hellman, Gary. *The karate way*
Mayer, Mercer. *There are monsters everywhere*
Nevius, Carol. *Karate hour*
Rockwell, Anne. *Chip and the karate kick*
Schwartz, Corey Rosen. *The three ninja pigs*

Sports – martial arts

Chung, Arree. *Ninja!*
　　Ninja! attack of the clan
　　Ninja Claus!
DaCosta, Barbara. *Nighttime Ninja*
Davis, Jacky. *Black Belt Bunny*
The gingerbread boy. *The Ninjabread Man*
Ishida, Sanae. *Little Kunoichi, the ninja girl*
Latimer, Alex. *The boy who cried ninja*
McClintock, Barbara. *The five forms*
Mochizuki, Ken. *Be water, my friend*
Novak, Jordan P. *Mosquitoes can't bite ninjas*
Olson, Jennifer Gray. *Ninja Bunny*
　　Ninja Bunny: sister vs. brother
Pingk, Rubin. *Samurai Santa*
Schwartz, Corey Rosen. *Hensel and Gretel*
　　Ninja Red Riding Hood, ill. by Dan Santat
　　Ninja Red Riding Hood, ill. by Dan Santat
　　The three ninja pigs
Tarpley, Todd. *My grandma's a ninja*
Tougas, Chris. *Dojo Daycare*
　　Dojo daytrip
　　Dojo surprise
Tuell, Todd. *Ninja, ninja, never stop!*
Wilson, N. D. *Ninja boy goes to school*
Zeltser, David. *Ninja baby*

Sports – mountain climbing

Becker, Shari. *Maxwell's mountain*
George, Jean Craighead. *Cliff hanger*

Sports – Olympics

Boiger, Alexandra. *Max and Marla*
Gray, Karlin. *Nadia*
Hennessy, B. G. *Olympics!*
Herzog, Brad. *G is for gold medal*
Jamieson, Victoria. *Olympig!*
Jordan, Deloris. *Dream big*
Lang, Heather. *Queen of the track*
Malaspina, Ann. *Touch the sky*
Richards, Jean. *The first Olympic games*
Smith, Nikkolas. *The golden girls of Rio*
Yoo, Paula. *Sixteen years in sixteen seconds*

Sports – racing

Adams, Adrienne. *The great Valentine's Day balloon race*
Aesop. *The hare and the tortoise*, ill. by Paul Galdone
　　The hare and the tortoise, ill. by Carol Jones
　　The hare and the tortoise, ill. by Helen Ward
　　The hare and the tortoise / La liebre y la tortuga
　　Hare and Tortoise
　　The race
　　Road signs
　　The tortoise and the hare, ill. by Jerry Pinkney
　　The tortoise and the hare, ill. by Sara Rojo

The tortoise and the hare: an Aesop fable
Anderson, Peggy Perry. *We go in a circle*
Berenstain, Stan and Jan. *The Berenstain bears and the big road race*
Blake, Robert J. *Painter and Ugly*
Caseley, Judith. *Field Day Friday*
Chriscoe, Sharon. *Race car dreams*
Clement, Nathan. *Speed*
Crews, Donald. *Bicycle race*
Dahl, Michael. *One checkered flag*
Dempsey, Kristy. *Mini racer*
Denise, Anika. *Monster trucks*
Dotlich, Rebecca Kai. *Race car count*
Downard, Barry. *The Race of the Century*
Fliess, Sue. *Race!*
Goldin, David. *Go-Go-Go!*
Golding, Theresa Martin. *Abby's asthma and the big race*
Herzog, Brad. *R is for race*
Kolar, Bob. *Racer dogs*
Lewin, Ted. *Horse song*
Libby, Barbara. *I rode the red horse*
London, Jonathan. *Sled dogs run*
Lord, Cynthia. *Hot Rod Hamster*
Lowell, Susan. *The tortoise and the jackrabbit*
Lynn, Sarah. *1-2-3 va-va-vroom!*
McCarthy, Meghan. *The incredible life of Balto Seabiscuit*
McKee, David. *Elmer and the race*
McMullan, Kate. *I'm fast*
Miranda, Anne. *Vroom, chugga, vroom-vroom*
Mitton, Tony. *The Jungle Run*
Mora, Pat. *The race of toad and deer*
Morrison, Toni. *The tortoise or the hare*
Muth, Jon J. *Mama Lion wins the race*
O'Malley, Kevin. *The great race*
Pizzoli, Greg. *Number one Sam*
Rex, Michael. *My race car*
Reynolds, Peter H. *Going places*
Rudge, Leila. *Gary*
Scieszka, Jon. *Race from A to Z*
Seibert, Patricia. *Mush!*
Shulevitz, Uri. *Troto and the trucks*
Tingle, Tim. *When Turtle grew feathers*
Todd, Mark. *Start your engines*
Trollinger, Patsi B. *Perfect timing*
Van Woerkom, Dorothy. *Harry and Shelburt*
Wheeler, Lisa. *Dino-racing*
Zane, Alexander. *The wheels on the race car*

Sports – roller skating

Ashman, Linda. *Samantha on a roll*
Pilkey, Dav. *The Moonglow Roll-O-Rama*
Saltzberg, Barney. *Hip, hip, hooray day!*

Sports – sailing

Beck, Andrea. *Elliot's shipwreck*
Blackstone, Stella. *An island in the sun*
Crews, Donald. *Sail away*
Haas, Rick de. *Peter and the seal*
Heidbreder, Robert. *A sea-wishing day*
Lund, Deb. *Dinosailors*
McNeil, Florence. *Sail away*
Schubert, Ingrid. *There's always room for one more*
Uhlberg, Myron. *Lemuel, the fool*
Van Dusen, Chris. *Down to the sea with Mr. Magee*
van Lieshout, Maria. *Hopper and Wilson*

Sports – skateboarding

Brimner, Larry Dane. *Cat on wheels*
Carlson, Nancy. *Arnie and the skateboard gang*
Howard, Arthur. *Cosmo zooms*

Sports – skiing

Berger, Carin. *A perfect day*
Calhoun, Mary. *Cross-country cat*
Dahl, Michael. *Downhill fun*
Huneck, Stephen. *Sally's snow adventure*
Peet, Bill. *Buford the little bighorn*
Rueda, Claudia. *Bunny slopes*
Van Dusen, Chris. *Learning to ski with Mr. Magee*

Sports – skin diving

Baker, Jeannie. *The hidden forest*
Loomis, Christine. *Scuba bunnies*

Sports – sledding

Blake, Robert J. *Painter and Ugly*
Boiger, Alexandra. *Max and Marla*
Casanova, Mary. *One-dog sleigh*
Chaconas, Dori. *On a wintry morning*
Curious George goes sledding
Day, Alexandra. *Carl's snowy afternoon*
Fearnley, Jan. *A perfect day for it*
Harper, Lee. *Snow! snow! snow!*
Judge, Lita. *Red sled*
Kortepeter, Paul. *Oliver's red toboggan*
London, Jonathan. *Sled dogs run*
McCarthy, Meghan. *The incredible life of Balto*
Norman, Kim. *Ten on the sled*
Parenteau, Shirley. *Bears in the snow*
Rule, Rebecca. *The iciest, diciest, scariest sled ride ever!*
Seibert, Patricia. *Mush!*
Slayton, Fran Cannon. *Snowball moon*
Smee, Nicola. *Jingle-jingle*
Thomas, Patricia. *Red sled*
Winthrop, Elizabeth. *Sledding*

Sports – soccer

Aesop. *Bat's big game*
Bildner, Phil. *The soccer fence*
Boelts, Maribeth. *Happy like soccer*
Brown, Monica. *Pelé, king of soccer / Pelé, el rey del fútbol*
Browne, Anthony. *Willy the wizard*
Burleigh, Robert. *Goal*
Capucilli, Alyssa Satin. *My first soccer game*
Cline-Ransome, Lesa. *Young Pelé*
Cousins, Lucy. *Maisy plays soccer*
Diehl, David. *Goal! my soccer book*
Elliott, Laura Malone. *Hunter and Stripe and the soccer showdown*
Fauchald, Nick. *Score!*
Finchler, Judy. *You're a good sport, Miss Malarkey*
Flanagan, Alice K. *Coach John and his soccer team*
Fox, Diane. *Tyson the terrible*
Hamm, Mia. *Winners never quit*
Javaherbin, Mina. *Goal!*
  Soccer star
Kaplan, Michael B. *Betty Bunny wants a goal*
Kolar, Bob. *Big kicks*
Lester, Helen. *Hurty feelings*

London, Jonathan. *Froggy plays soccer*
McNaughton, Colin. *Preston's goal!*
Mammano, Julie. *Rhinos who play soccer*
Murphy, Stuart J. *Game time*
Nevius, Carol. *Soccer hour*
Pelé. *For the love of soccer!*
Pinkney, Brian. *On the ball*
Rockwell, Anne. *Morgan plays soccer*
Rodriguez, Edel. *Sergio saves the game!*
Saltzberg, Barney. *Soccer mom from outer space*
Shahan, Sherry. *That's not how you play soccer, Daddy*
Sís, Peter. *Madlenka, soccer star*
Vyner, Tim. *World team*
Watson, Jesse Joshua. *Hope for Haiti*
Weninger, Brigitte. *Davy, soccer star!*
Wheeler, Lisa. *Dino-soccer*

Sports – Special Olympics

Pulver, Robin. *Way to go, Alex!*

Sports – surfing

Alexander, Kwame. *Surf's up*
Dempsey, Kristy. *Surfer chick*
Mammano, Julie. *Rhinos who surf*
Minters, Frances. *Princess Fishtail*
Sattler, Jennifer. *Pig kahuna*

Sports – swimming

Barclay, Jane. *Going on a journey to the sea*
Casteel, Seth. *Puppy pool party!*
Cooper, Susan. *Frog*
Cornwall, Gaia. *Jabari jumps*
Cousins, Lucy. *Maisy learns to swim*
    Maisy's pool
Fuge, Charles. *Swim, Little Wombat, swim!*
Ginsburg, Mirra. *The chick and the duckling*
Gutman, Anne. *Gaspard at the seashore*
Harper, Jamie. *Me too!*
Hest, Amy. *Make the team, Baby Duck*
Kliphuis, Christine. *Robbie and Ronnie*
Koch, Ed. *Eddie's little sister makes a splash*
Lin, Grace. *Olvina swims*
London, Jonathan. *Froggy learns to swim*
Lucke, Deb. *The boy who wouldn't swim*
Lurie, Susan. *Swim, duck, swim!*
McQuinn, Anna. *Leo can swim*
Newman, Jeff. *Reginald*
Pfister, Marcus. *Hang on, Hopper!*
Redeker, Kent. *Don't splash the sasquatch!*
Reiser, Lynn. *Two dogs swimming*
Rice, Eve. *Swim!*
Riley, Linda Capus. *Elephants swim*
Rockwell, Anne. *Katie Catz makes a splash*
Rodriguez, Edel. *Sergio makes a splash*
Rylant, Cynthia. *Brownie and Pearl take a dip*
Schuurmans, Hilde. *Sydney won't swim*
Schwartz, Roslyn. *The mole sisters and the rainy day*
Scotton, Rob. *Splish, splash, splat!*
Shum, Benson. *Holly's day at the pool*
Stanley, Mandy. *At the pool*
Starin, Liz. *Splashdance*
Stewart, Amber. *Little by little*
Volkmann, Roy. *Curious kittens*
Waddell, Martin. *The pig in the pond*
Ward, Nick. *Come on Baby Duck*
Watanabe, Shigeo. *Let's go swimming*

Webster, Christine. *Otter everywhere*
Weninger, Brigitte. *Miko goes on vacation*
Weston, Martha. *Tuck in the pool*
Wheeler, Lisa. *Dino-swimming*
Whelan, Gloria. *Queen Victoria's bathing machine*
Wilson, Karma. *Don't be afraid, Little Pip*
Winton, Tim. *The deep*

Sports – T-ball

London, Jonathan. *Froggy plays T-ball*

Sports – Tae Kwon Do

Pinkney, Brian. *Jojo's flying side kick*

Sports – tennis

McG, Shane. *Tennis, anyone?*

Sports – volleyball

Fauchald, Nick. *Bump! set! spike!*

Sports – wrestling

Boelts, Maribeth. *Big Daddy, frog wrestler*
Morales, Yuyi. *Niño wrestles the world Rudas*
Wheeler, Lisa. *Dino-wrestling*

Sportsmanship

Elliott, Laura Malone. *Hunter and Stripe and the soccer showdown*
Finchler, Judy. *You're a good sport, Miss Malarkey*
Flanagan, Alice K. *Coach John and his soccer team*
Hamm, Mia. *Winners never quit*
Janni, Rebecca. *Every cowgirl loves a rodeo*
Jordan, Deloris. *Michael's golden rules*
Krosoczka, Jarrett J. *Max for president*
Lasky, Kathryn. *Tumble bunnies*
Nordling, Lee. *Belinda the unbeatable*
Pfister, Marcus. *You can't win them all, rainbow fish*
Robberecht, Thierry. *Sam is not a loser*
Rockwell, Anne. *Brendan and Belinda and the slam dunk!*
Rose, Deborah Lee. *The spelling bee before recess*

Squid

Berry, Lynne. *Squid Kid the Magnificent*
Nyeu, Tao. *Squid and Octopus*
Reynolds, Aaron. *President Squid*
Sherry, Kevin. *I'm the best artist in the ocean I'm the biggest thing in the ocean*
Viva, Frank. *A long way away*

Stage *see* Theater

Starfishes

McDonnell, Patrick. *Shine!*

Stars

Barner, Bob. *Stars, stars, stars*
Baumgart, Klaus. *Laura's Christmas star Laura's secret*

Laura's star
Benjamin, A. H. *Mouse, mole and the falling star*
Branley, Franklyn M. *The sky is full of stars*
Bunting, Eve. *Thunder horse*
Cabrera, Jane. *Twinkle, twinkle, little star*
Dean, James. *Pete the Cat: twinkle, twinkle, little star*
Elschner, Geraldine. *Moonchild, star of the sea*
Fancher, Lou. *Star climbing*
Fischer, Scott M. *Twinkle*
Florian, Douglas. *Comets, stars, the moon, and Mars*
Gerber, Carole. *Annie Jump Cannon, astronomer*
Gibbons, Gail. *Stargazers*
Goble, Paul. *The lost children*
Grimm, Jacob and Wilhelm. *The star child*
Hansen, Felicity. *The first bear*
Hest, Amy. *Little chick*
Hoffman, Mary. *Three wise women*
Holub, Joan. *Twinkle, star of the week*
Horácek, Petr. *Suzy Goose and the Christmas star*
    When the moon smiled
Langley, Karen. *Shine*
Lee, Y. J. *The little moon princess*
Lyon, George Ella. *My friend, the starfinder*
McGhee, Alison. *Star bright*
Mackall, Dandi Daley. *Seeing stars*
Marzollo, Jean. *I see a star*
    Little Bear, you're a star!
Meister, Cari. *Follow the drinking gourd: an*
    Underground Railroad story
Mitton, Jacqueline. *Zoo in the sky*
Nelson, S. D. *The Star People*
Norman, Geoffrey. *Stars above us*
Oughton, Jerrie. *How the stars fell into the sky*
Parker, Michael. *You are a star!*
Pettenati, Jeanne K. *Galileo's journal, 1609–1610*
Pfister, Marcus. *The Christmas star*
Puttock, Simon. *A ladder to the stars*
Ray, Mary Lyn. *Stars*
Reynolds, Peter H. *Sydney's star*
Rosenstock, Barb. *Vincent can't sleep*
Sís, Peter. *Starry messenger*
The sun, the moon, and the stars
Sykes, Julie. *Little Rocket's special star*
Taylor, Jane. *Twinkle, twinkle little star*, ill. by
    Heather Collins
    Twinkle, twinkle, little star, ill. by Michael Hague
    Twinkle, twinkle, little star, ill. by Julia Noonan
    Twinkle, twinkle, little star, ill. by Jerry Pinkney
Tazewell, Charles. *The littlest angel*, ill. by Deborah
    Lanino
    The littlest angel, ill. by Paul Micich
    The littlest angel, ill. by Rebecca Thornburgh
Tomecek, Steve. *Stars*
van Lieshout, Maria. *Hopper and Wilson fetch a star*
Wallace, Nancy Elizabeth. *Stars! stars! stars!*
Washington, Ned. *When you wish upon a star*
Wilson-Max, Ken. *Max's starry night*
Winter, Jeanette. *Follow the drinking gourd*

Stealing *see* Behavior – stealing; Crime

Steam shovels *see* Machines

Steamrollers *see* Machines

Step families *see* Divorce; Family life –
    stepfamilies

Stepchildren *see* Divorce; Family life –
    stepfamilies

Stepparents *see* Divorce; Family life –
    stepfamilies

Stones *see* Rocks

Stores

Agee, Jon. *Nothing*
Alakija, Polly. *Catch that goat!*
Averbeck, Jim. *The market bowl*
Bee, William. *Stanley's store*
Berger, Joe. *My special one and only*
Bond, Michael. *Paddington Bear and the Christmas*
    surprise
Brown, Calef. *Pirateria*
Carling, Amelia Lau. *Mama and Papa have a store*
Corey, Shana. *Milly and the Macy's Parade*
Curious George visits a toy store
Daly, Niki. *Next stop — Zanzibar Road!*
Day, Alexandra. *Carl goes shopping*
Dematons, Charlotte. *Let's go*
DiSalvo, DyAnne. *Grandpa's corner store*
Egan, Tim. *The pink refrigerator*
Ehlert, Lois. *Market day*
Elya, Susan Middleton. *Bebé goes shopping*
Empson, Jo. *Chimpanzees for tea!*
Flanagan, Alice K. *A busy day at Mr. Kang's grocery*
    store
    Buying a pet from Ms. Chavez
Florence, Tyler. *Tyler makes pancakes!*
Fraser, Mary Ann. *Pet shop follies*
    Pet shop lullaby
Freeman, Don. *Corduroy*
Gibbons, Gail. *Department store*
Gomi, Taro. *I lost my dad*
Hillenbrand, Will. *All for a dime! a Bear and Mole*
    story
Johnson, Angela. *The Rolling Store*
Juan, Ana. *The pet shop revolution*
Karas, G. Brian. *On the farm, at the market*
Kirsch, Vincent X. *Natalie and Naughtily*
Korchek, Lori. *Adventures of Cow, too*
Krull, Kathleen. *Supermarket*
Lazar, Tara. *The Monstore*
Lewin, Ted. *Big Jimmy's Kum Kau Chinese take out*
    How much?
    Market!
Lewis, J. Patrick. *The fantastic 5 and 10¢ store*
Lobel, Arnold. *On Market Street*
Loupy, Christophe. *Don't worry, Wags*
Masters, Anthony. *Ricky's rat gang*
Meddaugh, Susan. *The witches' supermarket*
Melvin, Alice. *The high street*
Miranda, Anne. *To market, to market*
Modarressi, Mitra. *Yard sale*
Munro, Roxie. *Market maze*
Munsch, Robert N. *Something good*
Murphy, Jill. *Meltdown!*
Murphy, Stuart J. *Just enough carrots*
    Mall mania

Naylor, Phyllis Reynolds. *Sweet strawberries*
Nelson, Vaunda Micheaux. *The book itch*
O'Neill, Alexis. *Estela's swap*
Ormerod, Jan. *The baby swap*
Parks, Carmen. *Farmers market*
Pelley, Kathleen T. *Raj the bookstore tiger*
Pienkowski, Jan. *Bel and Bub and the black hole*
Polacco, Patricia. *Something about Hensley's*
Potter, Beatrix. *Ginger and Pickles*
Rockwell, Anne. *At the supermarket*
   Let's go to the hardware store
Rylant, Cynthia. *Little Whistle*
   Little Whistle's Christmas
   Little Whistle's dinner party
   Little Whistle's medicine
Schaefer, Lola M. *Supermarket*
Schaub, Michelle. *Fresh-picked poetry*
Schiller, Abbie. *When Lyla got lost (and found)*
Schwartz, Joanne. *Our corner grocery store*
Seibold, J. Otto. *Lost sloth*
Shea, Kitty. *Out and about at the supermarket*
Sierra, Judy. *Suppose you meet a dinosaur*
Skolsky, Mindy Warshaw. *Hannah and the whistling
   tea kettle*
Thong, Roseanne. *Gai see*
Trent, Shanda. *Farmers' market day*
Wellington, Monica. *Apple farmer Annie*
Wells, Rosemary. *Max's dragon shirt*
Williams, Karen Lynn. *Tap-tap*
Yin. *Brothers*
Young, Ed. *Donkey trouble*

Stories in rhyme *see* Rhyming text

Strangers *see* Behavior – talking to strangers

Streams *see* Rivers

Streets *see* Roads

String

Baker, Keith. *Just how long can a long string be?!*
Boyle, Bob. *Hugo and the really, really, really long
   string*
Fleischman, Paul. *Lost!*
Geisert, Arthur. *The giant ball of string*

Stubbornness *see* Character traits –
   stubbornness

Submarines *see* Boats, ships

Subway *see* Trains

Sullivan Islands *see* Foreign lands – South Sea
   Islands

Sun

Aesop. *The contest between the Sun and the Wind*
Alda, Arlene. *Hurry Granny Annie*

Asch, Frank. *The sun is my favorite star*
Bang, Molly. *Buried sunlight*
   Living sunlight
   My light
   Ocean sunlight
   Rivers of sunlight
Baylor, Byrd. *The way to start a day*
Branley, Franklyn M. *Eclipse*
   The planets in our solar system
   The sun, our nearest star
   Sunshine makes the seasons
Canyon, Christopher. *John Denver's Sunshine on my
   shoulders*
Daly, Niki. *Why the sun and moon live in the sky*
Dayrell, Elphinstone. *Why the sun and the moon live
   in the sky*
Ellwand, David. *Midas Mouse*
Gerstein, Mordicai. *The night world*
Gibbons, Gail. *Sun up, sun down*
Goudey, Alice E. *The day we saw the sun come up*
Graham, Bob. *How the sun got to Coco's house*
Hines, Anna Grossnickle. *What can you do in the
   sun?*
Kaner, Etta. *Who likes the sun?*
Kleven, Elisa. *Sun bread*
Lobel, Anita. *Hello, day!*
London, Jonathan. *Like butter on pancakes*
McDermott, Gerald. *Musicians of the sun*
Marzollo, Jean. *Sun song*
Peet, Bill. *Cock-a-doodle Dudley*
Peterson, Cris. *Seed soil sun*
Polacco, Patricia. *I can hear the sun*
Root, Phyllis. *Lucia and the light*
San Souci, Robert D. *Peter and the blue witch baby*
Sherman, Pat. *The sun's daughter*
Shulevitz, Uri. *Dawn*
Slate, Joseph. *Story time for Little Porcupine*
Stewart, Melissa. *Beneath the sun*
The sun, the moon, and the stars
Tafuri, Nancy. *What the sun sees / What the moon sees*
Tresselt, Alvin R. *Sun up*
Wells, Robert E. *Why do elephants need the sun?*
Wolkstein, Diane. *The day Ocean came to visit*
Wood, Douglas. *Where the sunrise begins*
Yankey, Lindsey. *Sun and Moon*
Zoehfeld, Kathleen Weidner. *Secrets of the seasons*

Superstition

Hassett, John. *Father Sun, Mother Moon*
Light, Steve. *Lucky Lazlo*
McNaughton, Colin. *Don't step on the crack!*
Rumford, James. *Don't touch my hat!*
Soto, Gary. *Lucky Luis*
Sutton, Jane. *The trouble with cauliflower*

Sustainability *see* Ecology

Swamps

Appelt, Kathi. *Where, where is Swamp Bear?*
Arnosky, Jim. *Raccoon on his own*
   Wild and swampy
Bateman, Donna M. *Deep in the swamp*
Berkes, Marianne. *Marsh music*
Chaconas, Dori. *Virginie's hat*
Crow, Kristyn. *Bedtime at the swamp*
Dennard, Deborah. *Bullfrog at Magnolia Circle*
Downing, Johnette. *Down in Louisiana*

Doyen, Denise. *Once upon a twice*
Fleming, Candace. *Who invited you?*
Huggins, Peter. *Trosclair and the alligator*
Jewell, Nancy. *Alligator wedding*
LeBox, Annette. *Wild bog tea*
Root, Phyllis. *Big belching bog*
Rose, Caroline Starr. *Over in the wetlands*
Salley, Coleen. *Epossumondas plays possum*
San Souci, Robert D. *Little Pierre*
Stewart, Whitney. *A catfish tale*
Thomas, Joyce Carol. *The gospel Cinderella*
Vaughan, Marcia Kapok. *Whistling Dixie*
Weeks, Sarah. *Catfish Kate and the sweet swamp band*
Yolen, Jane. *Welcome to the river of grass*

Swapping *see* Activities – trading

Talent shows *see* Theater

Talking to strangers *see* Behavior – talking to strangers

Tall tales

Aliki. *The story of Johnny Appleseed*
Anderson, Laurie Halse. *The big cheese of Third Street*
Andreasen, Dan. *The giant of Seville*
Aylesworth, Jim. *My sister's rusty bike*
Balcziak, Bill. *John Henry*
  Paul Bunyan
  Pecos Bill
Bateman, Teresa. *Paul Bunyan vs. Hals Halson*
Bertrand, Lynne. *Granite baby*
Cali, Davide. *The truth about my unbelievable summer . . .*
Codell, Esme Raji. *Seed by seed*
Cole, Brock. *Buttons*
Crunk, Tony. *Railroad John and the Red Rock run*
Davol, Marguerite W. *The loudest, fastest, best drummer in Kansas*
Derby, Sally. *Whoosh went the wind!*
Drummond, Allan. *Casey Jones*
Gorbachev, Valeri. *Where is the apple pie?*
Graves, Keith. *Uncle Blubbafink's seriously ridiculous stories*
Greathouse, Carol. *The dinosaur tamer*
Griffin, Kitty. *The foot-stomping adventures of Clementine Sweet*
Hayes, Joe. *The gum-chewing rattler*
Holt, Kimberly Willis. *The adventures of Granny Clearwater and Little Critter*
Isaacs, Anne. *Dust Devil*
  Meanwhile, back at the ranch
  Pancakes for supper!
  Swamp Angel

Johnston, Tony. *Levi Strauss gets a bright idea*
Keats, Ezra Jack. *John Henry*
Kellogg, Steven. *I was born about 10,000 years ago*
  Johnny Appleseed: a tall tale
  Mike Fink
  Paul Bunyan: a tall tale
  Pecos Bill
  Sally Ann Thunder Ann Whirlwind Crockett
Kimmel, Eric A. *The Erie Canal pirates*
  The great Texas hamster drive
Koren, Edward. *Very hairy Harry*
Lester, Julius. *John Henry*
Lindbergh, Reeve. *Johnny Appleseed*
Luckhurst, Matt. *Paul Bunyan and Babe the Blue Ox*
McGill, Alice. *Sure as sunrise*
McKissack, Patricia C. *A million fish . . . more or less*
Madison, Alan. *The littlest grape stomper*
Miller, Bobbi. *Davy Crockett gets hitched*
  Miss Sally Ann and the panther
Mora, Pat. *Doña Flor*
Myers, Anna. *Tumbleweed Baby*
Nolen, Jerdine. *Big Jabe*
  Harvey Potter's balloon farm
  Thunder Rose
Oppel, Kenneth. *Peg and the whale*
Pinkney, Andrea Davis. *Peggony-Po*
Root, Phyllis. *Kiss the cow*
  Paula Bunyan
  Rosie's fiddle
Roth, Roger. *Fishing for Methuselah*
Roth, Susan L. *The biggest frog in Australia*
Rozier, Lucy Margaret. *Jackrabbit McCabe and the electric telegraph*
Rubel, Nicole. *A cowboy named Ernestine*
Schanzer, Rosalyn. *How Ben Franklin stole the lightning*
Schnitzler, Pattie L. *Widdermaker*
Shannon, David. *Jangles*
Shepard, Aaron. *Master man*
Shulevitz, Uri. *What is a wise bird like you doing in a silly tale like this?*
Sís, Peter. *A small tall tale from the far Far North*
Smith, Cynthia Leitich. *Holler Loudly*
Smith, Janice Lee. *Jess and the stinky cowboys*
Stanton, Andy. *Danny McGee drinks the sea*
Swain, Gwenyth. *Johnny Appleseed*
White, Linda Arms. *Comes a wind*
Willey, Margaret. *Clever Beatrice, an Upper Peninsula conte*
Williams, Suzanne. *Library Lil*
Wilson, Karma. *Whopper cake*
Wood, Audrey. *The Bunyans*
Wooldridge, Connie Nordhielm. *The legend of Strap Buckner*
Wright, Catherine. *Steamboat Annie and the thousand-pound catfish*
Yolen, Jane. *Johnny Appleseed: the legend and the truth*

Tardiness *see* Behavior – promptness, tardiness

Tattletale *see* Behavior – gossip, rumors

Taxis

Agee, Jon. *The other side of town*
Barracca, Debra. *A taxi dog Christmas*
Barracca, Sal. *The adventures of taxi dog*

Milusich, Janice. *Off go their engines, off go their lights*
Sehgal, Kabir. *The wheels on the tuk tuk*
Upton, Elizabeth. *Maxi the little taxi*

Teasing *see* Behavior – bullying, teasing

Technology

Alemagna, Beatrice. *On a magical do-nothing day*
Dormer, Frank W. *Click!*
McDonnell, Patrick. *Tek*
Saltzberg, Barney. *Tea with Grandpa*
Willis, Jeanne. *Troll stinks*
Yaccarino, Dan. *Doug unplugged*
    Doug unplugs on the farm

Teddy bears *see* Toys – bears

Teeth

Bate, Lucy. *Little Rabbit's loose tooth*
Beeler, Selby B. *Throw your tooth on the roof*
Bennett, Kelly. *Vampire baby*
Borden, Louise. *The lost-and-found tooth*
Bouchard, Dave. *Fairy*
Bowen, Anne. *Tooth Fairy's first night*
Brockenbrough, Martha. *The Dinosaur Tooth Fairy*
Brown, Heather. *Chomp!*
Brown, Marc. *Arthur's tooth*
Chandra, Deborah. *George Washington's teeth*
Chetkowski, Emily. *Pumpkin smile*
Colato Laínez, René. *The Tooth Fairy meets El Ratón Pérez*
Coombs, Kate. *The tooth fairy wars*
Cousins, Lucy. *Maisy, Charley, and the wobbly tooth*
Davis, Katie. *Mabel the Tooth Fairy and how she got her job*
Diakité, Penda. *I lost my tooth in Africa*
Durant, Alan. *Dear tooth fairy*
Edwards, Pamela Duncan. *Dear Tooth Fairy*
Elya, Susan Middleton. *Tooth on the loose*
Flanagan, Alice K. *Dr. Kanner, dentist with a smile*
Gomi, Taro. *The crocodile and the dentist*
Graham, Bob. *April and Esme, tooth fairies*
Grambling, Lois G. *This whole Tooth Fairy thing's nothing but a big rip-off!*
High, Linda Oatman. *Cool Bopper's choppers*
Hood, Susan. *The Tooth Mouse*
James, Brian. *The Supertwins and tooth trouble*
Jarvis , Peter. *Alan's big, scary teeth*
Jay, Betsy. *Jane vs. the Tooth Fairy*
Kann, Victoria. *Silverlicious*
Kaye, Marilyn. *The real tooth fairy*
Keller, Laurie. *Open wide*
McCloskey, Robert. *One morning in Maine*
MacDonald, Amy. *Cousin Ruth's tooth*
Maconie, Robin. *Alice and her fabulous teeth*
McPhail, David. *The bear's toothache*
Miles, Elizabeth J. *Mouths and teeth*
Miller, Edward. *The tooth book*
Moss, Miriam. *Wibble wobble*
Munsch, Robert N. *Andrew's loose tooth*
Murkoff, Heidi Eisenberg. *What to expect when you go to the dentist*
O'Brien, Patrick. *Megatooth*
Olson, Mary. *Nice try, Tooth Fairy*
Palatini, Margie. *Gone with the wand*

No biting, Louise
Paxton, Tom. *The story of the Tooth Fairy*
Rey, Margret. *Curious George goes to the dentist*
Rockwell, Harlow. *My dentist*
Rosenberry, Vera. *Vera goes to the dentist*
Ross, Tony. *I want my tooth*
Schaefer, Lola M. *Dental office*
    Loose tooth
Simms, Laura. *Rotten teeth*
Sís, Peter. *Madlenka*
Swanson, Diane. *The dentist and you*
Underwood, Deborah. *Here comes the Tooth Fairy Cat*
Vrombaut, An. *Clarabella's teeth*
Wilson, Karma. *Bear's loose tooth*

Telephone, cell phone

Raschka, Chris. *Ring! Yo?*
Whybrow, Ian. *Hello! Is this grandma?*
Willis, Jeanne. *Troll stinks*

Television

Barracca, Debra. *Maxi, the star*
Berenstain, Stan and Jan. *The Berenstain bears and too much TV*
Bergen, Lara Rice. *Blue's world of words*
Biedrzycki, David. *Breaking news: bear alert*
    Breaking news: bears to the rescue
Brown, Marc. *The bionic bunny show*
McCarty, Peter. *Chloe*
McPhail, David. *Fix-it*
Nickle, John. *TV Rex*
Polacco, Patricia. *Aunt Chip and the great Triple Creek dam affair*
Proimos, James. *Todd's TV*
Weigelt, Udo. *Super Guinea Pig to the rescue*

Telling stories *see* Activities – storytelling

Telling time *see* Clocks, watches; Time

Temper tantrums *see* Emotions – anger

Texas

Adler, David A. *A picture book of Sam Houston*
Borgo, Lacy. *Big Mama's baby*
Burell, Sarah. *Diamond Jim Dandy and the sheriff*
Fern, Tracey E. *Buffalo music*
Johnson, Angela. *All different now*
Ketteman, Helen. *The three little gators*
    Waynetta and the cornstalk
Kimmel, Eric A. *The great Texas hamster drive*
    Jack and the giant barbecue
    The lady in the blue cloak
    Little Britches and the rattlers
    The three cabritos
King, M. G. *Librarian on the roof!*
Munro, Roxie. *The inside-outside book of Texas*
Myers, Anna. *Tumbleweed Baby*

Textless *see* Wordless

Theater

Ackerman, Karen. *Bean's big day*
Agee, Jon. *Milo's hat trick*
Aliki. *A play's the thing*
Avi. *Silent movie*
Beeke, Jemma. *The Rickety Barn show*
Behrens, June. *The feast of Thanksgiving*
Berenstain, Stan and Jan. *The Berenstain bears get stage fright*
Boldt, Mike. *Colors versus shapes*
Bond, Felicia. *The Halloween play*
Brown, Don. *Mack made movies*
Brown, Marc. *Arthur's Thanksgiving*
Brownlee, Sophia Grace. *Show time with Sophia Grace and Rosie*
Calhoun, Mary. *Henry the Christmas cat*
Cohen, Miriam. *Starring first grade*
Comden, Betty, et al. *Flying to Neverland with Peter Pan*
Conway, David. *Errol and his extraordinary nose*
Cousins, Lucy. *Maisy goes to the movies*
Crimi, Carolyn. *Rock 'n' roll Mole*
Cronin, Doreen. *Dooby dooby moo*
Curious George goes to a movie
D'Amico, Carmela. *Ella sets the stage*
Davidson, Rebecca Piatt. *All the world's a stage*
deGroat, Diane. *Liar, liar, pants on fire*
DePalma, Mary Newell. *The Nutcracker doll*
dePaola, Tomie. *The night of Las Posadas*
DeRubertis, Barbara. *Alexander Anteater's amazing act*
Dunrea, Olivier. *Appearing tonight! Mary Heather Elizabeth Livingstone*
Edwards, Pamela Duncan. *Bravo, Livingstone Mouse!*
Engelbreit, Mary. *Queen of the class*
Fox, Mem. *Wombat divine*
Francis, Pauline. *Sam stars at Shakespeare's Globe*
A frog he would a-wooing go [folk-song]. *Frog went a-courting*
Geras, Adèle. *Little ballet star*
Gianferrari, Maria. *Penny and Jelly: the school show*
Hartman, Bob. *Granny Mae's Christmas play*
Hoffman, Mary. *Amazing Grace*
Holabird, Katharine. *Angelina ice skates Angelina on stage*
Hopkins, Lee Bennett. *Full moon and star*
Isadora, Rachel. *Lili on stage*
Isherwood, Shirley. *Flora the frog*
Ives, Penny. *Celestine, drama queen*
Jane, Pamela. *Milo and the greatest trick ever*
Keller, Laurie. *The scrambled states of America talent show*
Kontis, Alethea. *AlphaOops!*
Krensky, Stephen. *Shooting for the moon*
LaChanze. *Little diva*
Langley, Karen. *Shine*
Latimer, Alex. *Penguin's hidden talent*
Lawson, Julie. *Arizona Charlie and the Klondike Kid*
Lester, Helen. *Tackylocks and the three bears*
Light, Steve. *Lucky Lazlo*
Lithgow, John. *Marsupial Sue presents "The Runaway Pancake"*
Littlesugar, Amy. *Tree of hope*
Long, Ethan. *The Wing Wing brothers math spectacular!*
McCully, Emily Arnold. *My real family*
McDonald, Megan. *Penguin and Little Blue*

MacKay, Elly. *Waltz of the snowflakes*
McLean, Dirk. *Curtain up!*
McNaughton, Colin. *When I grow up*
Marshall, James. *Swine lake*
Mayhew, James. *Ella Bella ballerina and A Midsummer Night's Dream*
Mills, Elaine. *Marinetta at the ballet*
Ormerod, Jan. *Ms. MacDonald has a class*
Paraskevas, Betty. *Marvin, the tap-dancing horse*
Perlov, Betty Rosenberg. *Rifka takes a bow*
Plourde, Lynn. *You're doing that in the talent show?!*
Polacco, Patricia. *Mr. Wayne's masterpiece*
Potter, Giselle. *The year I didn't go to school*
Primavera, Elise. *Louise, the big cheese*
Rockwell, Anne. *President's Day Thanksgiving Day*
Ruzzier, Sergio. *Amandina*
Say, Allen. *Kamishibai man*
Scanlon, Elizabeth Garton. *Think big!*
Schotter, Roni. *Purim play*
Schwartz, Amy. *Starring Miss Darlene*
Scotton, Rob. *Splat the cat: on with the show*
Sierra, Judy. *Zoozical*
Spinelli, Eileen. *Six hogs on a scooter*
Stadler, Alexander. *Beverly Billingsly takes a bow*
Trimble, Marcia. *Peppy's shadow*
Tryon, Leslie. *Albert's play*
Uegaki, Chieri. *Hana Hashimoto, sixth violin*
Vail, Rachel. *Over the moon*
Viorst, Judith. *And two boys booed*
Waber, Bernard. *Evie and Margie*
Waterton, Betty. *A bumblebee sweater*
Wells, Rosemary. *Felix stands tall*
Whippo, Walt. *Little white duck*
Ziefert, Harriet. *Lights on Broadway*

Therapy animals *see* Animals – service animals

Thieves *see* Crime

Thumb sucking

Cooper, Ilene. *Jake's best thumb*
Dionne, Wanda. *Little Thumb*
Hesse, Karen. *My thumb*
Primavera, Elise. *Thumb love*
Stille, Ljuba. *Mia's thumb*

Thunder *see* Weather – lightning, thunder; Weather – storms

Time

Adler, David A. *Time zones*
Appelt, Kathi. *Bats around the clock*
Axelrod, Amy. *Pigs on a blanket*
Aylesworth, Jim. *The completed hickory dickory dock*
Baker, Keith. *Hickory dickory dock*
Barnett, Mac. *Oh no! Not again!*
Becker, Bonny. *Just a minute*
Bernhard, Durga. *While you are sleeping: a lift-the-flap book of time around the world*
Blackstone, Stella. *Bear takes a trip*
Brown, Ken. *What's the time, Grandma Wolf?*
Carle, Eric. *The grouchy ladybug*
Carlstrom, Nancy White. *It's about time, Jesse Bear*

Charlip, Remy. *Why I will never ever ever ever have enough time to read this book*
Chast, Roz. *Around the clock!*
Cousins, Lucy. *Maisy's first clock*
Fraser, Mary Ann. *I.Q., it's time*
Gibbons, Gail. *Clocks and how they go*
Gliori, Debi. *What's the time, Mr. Wolf?*
Gregory, Nan. *Amber waiting*
Handford, Martin. *Find Waldo now*
   Where's Waldo now?
Harper, Dan. *Telling time with Big Mama Cat*
Harris, Trudy. *The clock struck one*
Hennessy, B. G. *Mr. Ouchy's first day*
Hutchins, Hazel. *A second is a hiccup*
Hutchins, Pat. *Clocks and more clocks*
Jaramillo, Susie. *Little skeletons / Esqueletitos*
Jenkins, Steve. *Just a second*
McCaughrean, Geraldine. *My grandmother's clock*
McMillan, Bruce. *Time to . . .*
Miller, Mary Beth. *Handtalk zoo*
Murphy, Stuart J. *Game time*
   Get up and go!
   It's about time!
   Rodeo time
Older, Jules. *Telling time*
Omololu, Cynthia Jaynes. *When it's six o'clock in San Francisco*
Perrin, Clotilde. *At the same moment, around the world*
Pilegard, Virginia Walton. *The warlord's alarm*
Plourde, Lynn. *Winter waits*
Richards, Kitty. *It's about time, Max!*
Rohmann, Eric. *Time flies*
Rosa-Mendoza, Gladys. *What time is it? / Qué hora es?*
Sadler, Marilyn. *Alistair's time machine*
Schuett, Stacey. *Somewhere in the world right now*
Singer, Marilyn. *Nine o'clock lullaby*
Skinner, Daphne. *All aboard!*
Stanley, Diane. *Joining the Boston Tea Party*
Sweeney, Joan. *Me counting time*
Verdet, Andre. *All about time*
Vyner, Tim. *World team*
Wood, Audrey. *It's Duffy time!*

Tin soldiers *see* Toys – soldiers

Toads *see* Frogs & toads

Toddlers *see* Babies, toddlers

Toilet training

Amant, Kathleen. *On your potty, Little Rabbit*
Apple, Sam. *The saddest toilet in the world*
Bentley, Dawn. *Fuzzy Bear's potty book*
Bolam, Emily. *I go potty*
Cole, Joanna. *My big boy potty*
   My big girl potty
Elya, Susan Middleton. *Oh no, gotta go #2*
Falwell, Cathryn. *P.J. and Puppy*
Ford, Bernette. *No more diapers for Ducky!*
Freeman, Mylo. *Potty*
Gomi, Taro. *Everyone poops*
Hochman, David. *The potty train*
Hodgkinson, Leigh. *Goldilocks and the just right potty*

Jadoul, Emile. *All by myself!*
Katz, Karen. *A potty for me!*
Lewison, Wendy Cheyette. *The princess and the potty*
Lindgren, Barbro. *Sam's potty*
Manushkin, Fran. *Big girl panties*
Miller, Virginia. *On your potty!*
Morgan, Richard. *Zoo poo*
My potty book for boys
My potty book for girls
O'Connell, Rebecca. *Danny is done with diapers*
Oud, Pauline. *Ian's new potty*
   Sarah on the potty
Patricelli, Leslie. *Potty*
Piggy and Bear in their underwear
Richmond, Marianne. *Big girls go potty*
Rogers, Fred. *Going to the potty*
Rogers, Paul. *Ruby's potty*
Scheffler, Axel. *Pip and Posy: the little puddle*
Sears, William, M.D., et al.. *You can go to the potty*
Shea, Bob. *Dinosaur vs. the potty*
Spector, Todd. *How to pee: potty training for boys*
   How to pee: potty training for girls
Vestergaard, Hope. *Potty animals*
Wax, Wendy. *Even firefighters go to the potty*
Willems, Mo. *Time to pee*

Toilets

Apple, Sam. *The saddest toilet in the world*
Harper, Charise Mericle. *Flush!*

Tongue twisters

Agee, Jon. *Orangutan tongs*
Cleary, Brian P. *Six sheep sip thick shakes and other tricky tongue twisters*
Jenkins, Emily. *A greyhound, a groundhog*
Mahy, Margaret. *Simply delicious!*
Pomerantz, Charlotte. *The piggy in the puddle*
Rovetch, Lissa. *Ook the book*

Tools

Araki, Mie. *The magic toolbox*
Barros, Bruna. *The carpenter*
Barton, Byron. *Tools*
Buzzeo, Toni. *Whose tools?*
Carle, Eric. *My very first book of tools*
Clements, Andrew. *Workshop*
Connor, Leslie. *Miss Bridie chose a shovel*
Garcia, Emma. *Tap tap bang bang*
Garland, Sarah. *Eddie's toolbox and how to make and mend things*
Gibbons, Gail. *The art box*
   Tool book
Holub, Joan. *Tool school*
Lord, Janet. *Albert the fix-it man*
Mandel, Peter. *Jackhammer Sam*
Meltzer, Lynn. *The construction crew*
Meshon, Aaron. *Tools rule!*
Miller, Margaret. *Who uses this?*
Miura, Taro. *Tools*
Monroe, Chris. *Monkey with a tool belt and the seaside shenanigans*
Morris, Ann. *Tools*
Neitzel, Shirley. *The house I'll build for the wrens*
Riggs, Kate. *Time to build*
Rockwell, Anne. *Let's go to the hardware store*
Schaefer, Lola M. *Toolbox twins*
Singer, Marilyn. *Let's build a clubhouse*

Sturges, Philemon. *I love tools!*

Tooth fairy *see* Fairies; Teeth

Tortoises *see* Reptiles – turtles, tortoises

Towns *see* Cities, towns

Toy & movable books *see* Format, unusual – toy & movable books

Toys

Abbot, Judi. *Train!*
Adlerman, Daniel. *Africa calling*
Amant, Kathleen. *Little Rabbit gets messy*
 On your potty, Little Rabbit
Ayres, Katherine. *Matthew's truck*
Bardhan-Quallen, Sudipta. *The Mine-o-saur*
Beaumont, Karen. *Crybaby*
 Where's my t-r-u-c-k?
Beck, Andrea. *Elliot bakes a cake*
 Elliot digs for treasure
 Elliot gets stuck
 Elliot's bath
 Elliot's Christmas surprise
 Elliot's noisy night
 Elliot's shipwreck
Bell, Cece. *Sock Monkey boogie-woogie*
 Sock Monkey goes to Hollywood
 Sock Monkey rides again
Berger, Joe. *My special one and only*
Bianco, Margery Williams. *The velveteen rabbit*, ill. by David Jorgensen
 The velveteen rabbit, ill. by Thea Kliros
 The velveteen rabbit, ill. by Komako Sakai
 The velveteen rabbit, ill. by Gennady Spirin
 The velveteen rabbit: or, How toys became real, ill. by Allen Atkinson
 The velveteen rabbit: or, How toys became real, ill. by Steve Johnson
Birchall, Mark. *Rabbit's birthday surprise*
 Rabbit's wooly sweater
Bourgeois, Paulette. *Franklin and Harriet*
 Franklin's class trip
Brisson, Pat. *Hobbledy-clop*
Brown, Alan James. *Love-a-Duck*
Browne, Anthony. *Gorilla*
Bunting, Eve. *Ducky*
Butterworth, Nick. *Albert the bear*
Cabrera, Jane. *Ten in the bed*
Cader, Lisa Lebowitz. *When I wear my crown*
 When I wear my tiara
Capucilli, Alyssa Satin. *Biscuit visits the pumpkin patch*
Carle, Eric. *10 little rubber ducks*
Carlson, Nancy. *Start saving, Henry!*
Castillo, Lauren. *The troublemaker*
Chichester Clark, Emma. *I love you, Blue Kangaroo!*
 Where are you, Blue Kangaroo?
Choldenko, Gennifer. *Dad and the dinosaur*
Church, Caroline Jayne. *I love my bunny*
Collingridge, Richard. *Lionheart*
Conrad, Pam. *The Tub People*
 The Tub People's Christmas
Cooper, Helen. *Tatty-Ratty*

Cowell, Cressida. *Emily Brown and the Thing*
 That rabbit belongs to Emily Brown
Crampton, Gertrude. *Scuffy the tugboat*
Crews, Nina. *Below*
 Sky-high Guy
Crum, Shutta. *Mine!*
Curious George visits a toy store
Daly, Niki. *Old Bob's brown bear*
Danowski, Sonja. *Little night cat*
Deacon, Alexis. *While you are sleeping*
Deedman, Heidi. *Too many toys!*
Denise, Anika. *Bella and Stella come home*
De Sève, Randall. *A fire truck named Red*
 Mi barco / Toy boat
 Toy boat
De Vries, Anke. *Raf*
De Vries, Maggie. *How sleep found Tabitha*
Dewan, Ted. *Baby gets the zapper*
Dierssen, Andreas. *The old red tractor*
Donaldson, Julia. *One Ted falls out of bed*
Dunbar, Polly. *Penguin*
 Pingüino / penguin
Dunrea, Olivier. *Gideon and Otto*
Egielski, Richard. *Slim and Jim*
Ehrlich, H. M. *Louie's goose*
Emberley, Rebecca. *My toys / Mi juguetes*
Engler, Michael. *Elephantastic!*
Ernst, Lisa Campbell. *The letters are lost!*
Falconer, Ian. *Olivia — and the missing toy*
Fearnley, Jan. *Milo Armadillo*
Feiffer, Jules. *I lost my bear*
Ferrell, Sean. *I don't like Koala*
Ferreri, Della Ross. *How will I ever sleep in this bed?*
Ford, Bernette. *No more blanket for Lambkin!*
Ford, Gilbert. *The marvelous thing that came from a spring*
Fox, Christyan. *What color is that, PiggyWiggy?*
Fox, Mem. *Tell me about your day today*
Frazee, Marla. *Santa Claus*
Freedman, Claire. *Night-night, Emily*
Gall, Chris. *Awesome Dawson*
Garton, Sam. *Otter goes to school*
Gerrard, K.A. *My family is a zoo*
Gershator, Phillis. *Moo, moo, brown cow! Have you any milk?*
Graegin, Stephanie. *Little fox in the forest*
Gravett, Emily. *Monkey and me*
Grey, Mini. *Toys in space*
 Traction Man and the beach odyssey
 Traction Man is here
 Traction Man meets Turbodog
Harper, Charise Mericle. *Superlove*
Harris, Robie H. *Turtle and me*
Hayes, Sarah. *Lucy Anna and the Finders*
Heap, Sue. *Mine!*
Heck, Ed. *Monkey lost*
Henderson, Kathy. *Baby knows best*
Henkes, Kevin. *Waiting*
Herman, R. A. *Gomer and Little Gomer*
Hindley, Judy. *Rosy's visitors*
Hissey, Jane. *Hoot*
 Jolly snow
 Old Bear
Hoffman, Eric. *No fair to tigers / No es justo para los tigres*
Hoffmann, E. T. A. *The nutcracker*, ill. by Alison Jay
 The nutcracker, ill. by Niroot Puttapipat
Holmes, Janet A. *Have you seen Duck?*
Hoppe, Paul. *The woods*

Hughes, Shirley. *Bobbo goes to school*
Hutchins, Pat. *Tidy Titch*
Ichikawa, Satomi. *Come fly with me*
   I am Pangoo the penguin
   La La Rose
   My little train
Inches, Alison. *The stuffed animals get ready for bed*
Inkpen, Mick. *Kipper's snowy day*
   Kipper's toybox
   Nothing
   Thing
Inns, Christopher. *Next! please*
Jenkins, Emily. *Toys meet snow*
Jesset, Aurore. *Loopy*
Jocelyn, Marthe. *A day with Nellie*
Jonas, Ann. *Now we can go*
Joyce, William. *The Leaf Men and the brave good bugs*
Kastner, Jill. *Merry Christmas, Princess Dinosaur*
   Princess Dinosaur
Kenney, Sean. *Cool cars and trucks*
   Cool castles
   Cool city
   Cool creations in 101 pieces
   Cool creations in 35 pieces
Kirk, Daniel. *Honk honk! Beep beep!*
   You are not my friend, but I miss you
Kirsch, Vincent X. *Two little boys from Toolittle Toys*
Korchek, Lori. *Adventures of Cow, too*
Kruusval, Catarina. *Franny's friends*
Landström, Lena. *Where is Pim?*
Lane, Adam J. B. *Stop thief!*
LaReau, Kara. *Rocko and Spanky have company*
Lewis, Kim. *Good night, Harry*
   Here we go Harry
   Hooray for Harry
   My friend Harry
Lewis, Paeony. *No more cookies!*
Lindgren, Barbro. *Sam's car*
Lionni, Leo. *Alexander and the wind-up mouse*
London, Jonathan. *My big rig*
Long, Loren. *Drummer boy*
Lucas, David. *Christmas at the toy museum*
Luthardt, Kevin. *Mine*
Lynn, Sarah. *1-2-3 va-va-vroom!*
McAllister, Angela. *The little blue rabbit*
   Mama and Little Joe
McCully, Emily Arnold. *The Christmas gift*
McDonnell, Flora. *I love boats*
McDonnell, Patrick. *Me . . . Jane*
McNeil, Florence. *Sail away*
McPhail, David. *Bella loves Bunny*
   Olivia loves Owl
   Peter loves Penguin
   The puddle
Mann, Jennifer K. *Sam and Jump*
Marks, Jennifer L. *Sorting toys*
Marshall, James. *The Cut-Ups*
Marzollo, Jean. *I spy little wheels*
Masurel, Claire. *Christmas is coming*
   Too big!
Meadows, Michelle. *Pilot pups*
Mills, Elaine. *Marinetta at the ballet*
Milne, A. A. *Eeyore loses a tail*
   Tigger tales
Miyares, Daniel. *Float*
Moore, Clement Clarke. *The teddy bears' night before Christmas*
Morrissey, Dean. *The Christmas ship*
Nash, Sarah. *Purrfect!*

Nash, Scott. *Tuff Fluff*
Newman, Lesléa. *A fire engine for Ruthie*
Ohi, Ruth. *Chicken, Pig, Cow and the class pet*
   Chicken, Pig, Cow horse around
O'Malley, Kevin. *Leo Cockroach . . . toy tester*
Oppenheim, Shulamith Levey. *I love you, Bunny Rabbit*
Ormerod, Jan. *Miss Mouse's day*
Oxenbury, Helen. *Tom and Pippo go shopping*
   Tom and Pippo in the garden
   Tom and Pippo on the beach
   Tom and Pippo see the moon
Patricelli, Leslie. *Binky*
Pelletier, Andrew T. *The amazing adventures of Bathman!*
   The toy farmer
Perez, Monica. *Curious George saves his pennies*
Perkins, Maripat. *Rodeo Red*
Pett, Mark. *The boy and the airplane*
Phillipps, J. C. *Monkey Ono*
Pilutti, Deb. *Ten rules of being a superhero*
Pinkney, Andrea Davis. *Peggony-Po*
Pinkwater, Daniel. *Yo-yo man*
Polacco, Patricia. *Bun Bun Button*
Potter, Beatrix. *The tale of two bad mice*
Priest, Robert H. *The old pirate of Central Park*
Rau, Dana Meachen. *Rubber duck*
Ray, Mary Lyn. *All aboard*
Reiser, Lynn. *Any kind of dog*
Roberts, Bethany. *Cookie angel*
Roques, Dominique. *Sleep tight, Anna Banana!*
Rose, Deborah Lee. *Birthday zoo*
Rosenthal, Eileen. *Bobo the sailor man!*
   I must have Bobo!
   I'll save you Bobo!
Rowand, Phyllis. *It is night*
Rylant, Cynthia. *Little Whistle*
   Little Whistle's Christmas
   Little Whistle's dinner party
   Little Whistle's medicine
Samuels, Barbara. *The trucker*
Scheffler, Axel. *Pip and Posy: the bedtime frog*
Schertle, Alice. *Goodnight, Hattie, my dearie, my dove*
Schmid, Paul. *A pet for Petunia*
Schotter, Roni. *Room for Rabbit*
Schwartz, Amy. *Oscar*
Seuss, Dr. *The king's stilts*
Shannon, David. *Demasiados juguetes / too many toys*
   Too many toys
Shannon, Terry Miller. *Tub toys*
Sif, Birgitta. *Oliver*
Simmons, Jane. *The dreamtime fairies*
Slonim, David. *Oh, Ducky*
Smith, Maggie. *Dear Daisy, get well soon*
   Paisley
Soman, David. *Ladybug Girl and the best ever playdate*
Soto, Gary. *My little car / Mi carrito*
Springstubb, Tricia. *Phoebe and Digger*
Stevenson, Robert Louis. *Block city*, ill. by Daniel Kirk
   Block city, ill. by Ashley Wolff
Stickland, Paul. *Bears*
Tada, Joni Eareckson. *Forever friends*
Taylor, Sean. *The world champion of staying awake*
Thurber, James. *The great Quillow*
Van Camp, Katie. *CookieBot!*
   Harry and Horsie

Van Leeuwen, Jean. *The strange adventures of Blue Dog*
Velasquez, Eric. *Looking for Bongo*
Vogel, Vin. *Bedtime for Yeti*
Vulliamy, Clara. *Ellen and Penguin and the new baby Small*
Waddell, Martin. *Rosie's babies*
  Tom Rabbit
Wagner, Anke. *Tim's big move!*
Weber, Linda Kay. *Louie Larkey and the bad dream patrol*
Weiss, Nicki. *Where does the brown bear go?*
Wells, Rosemary. *Bunny party*
  Max's bedtime
  Max's birthday
  Max's toys
Weninger, Brigitte. *Double birthday*
  Miko goes on vacation
  What's the matter, Davy?
Whybrow, Ian. *Harry and the bucketful of dinosaurs*
  Harry and the dinosaurs at the museum
  Harry and the dinosaurs go to school
  Harry and the dinosaurs say "Raahh"
  Sammy and the robots
Wick, Walter. *Can you see what I see? toyland express*
Willems, Mo. *Knuffle Bunny*
  Knuffle Bunny free
  Knuffle Bunny too
Williams, Karen Lynn. *Galimoto*
Wilson, Karma. *Princess me*
Wisniewski, David. *Sumo Mouse*
Yoon, Salina. *Bear's big day*
Yorinks, Arthur. *Harry and Lulu*
Zagarenski, Pamela. *Henry and Leo*
Ziefert, Harriet. *Bunny's lessons*
  Buzzy had a little lamb
  Lucy rescued

Toys – balloons

Augustin, Barbara. *Antonella and her Santa Claus*
Baker, Alan. *Brown Rabbit's shape book*
Bernstein, Ariel. *I have a balloon*
Briere-Haquet, Alice. *Zebedee's balloon*
Curtis, Jamie Lee. *Where do balloons go?*
De Sève, Randall. *Mathilda and the orange balloon*
Faulkner, Keith. *Pop! went another balloon!*
Gorbachev, Valeri. *Molly who flew away*
Harrison, Hannah E. *Bernice gets carried away*
Johnson, Angela. *The day Ray got away*
Judge, Chris. *Tin*
Kotzwinkle, William. *Walter, the farting dog: trouble at the yard sale*
Lam, Thao. *Skunk on a string*
Lillegard, Dee. *Balloons, balloons, balloons*
Marino, Gianna. *A boy, a ball, and a dog*
Munsch, Robert N. *Where is Gah-Ning?*
Na, Il Sung. *Bird, balloon, Bear*
Nolen, Jerdine. *Harvey Potter's balloon farm*
Polacco, Patricia. *Bun Bun Button*
Previn, Stacey. *Aberdeen*
Rau, Dana Meachen. *Lots of balloons*
Robledo, Honorio. *Nico visits the moon*
Scheffler, Axel. *Pip and Posy: the big balloon*
Schmid, Paul. *Perfectly Percy*
Smith, Danna. *Balloon trees*
Sweet, Melissa. *Balloons over Broadway*
Taylor, Alastair. *Swollobog*
Ward, Lindsay. *Please bring balloons*

Weitzman, Jacqueline Preiss. *You can't take a balloon into the Metropolitan Museum*
  You can't take a balloon into the National Gallery

Toys – balls

Bang, Molly. *Yellow ball*
Cronin, Doreen. *Bounce*
Egielski, Richard. *Three magic balls*
George, Lindsay Barrett. *Maggie's ball*
Hills, Tad. *Duck and Goose*
Kellogg, Steven. *The mystery of the magic green ball*
Lindgren, Barbro. *Sam's ball*
Marino, Gianna. *A boy, a ball, and a dog*
Raschka, Chris. *A ball for Daisy*
Schmid, Paul. *Peanut and Fifi have a ball*
Schubert, Leda. *Winnie plays ball*
Seeger, Laura Vaccaro. *What if?*
Stevens, Janet. *The great fuzz frenzy*
Sullivan, Mary. *Ball*
Tafuri, Nancy. *The ball bounced*
Wright, Cliff. *Bear and ball*

Toys – bears

Alborough, Jez. *My friend bear*
  Where's my teddy?
Alexander, Martha G. *I'll protect you from the jungle beasts*
Allison, Catherine. *Brown paper bear*
Ashforth, Camilla. *Willow at Christmas*
  Willow by the sea
  Willow on the river
Aylesworth, Jim. *Teddy bear tears*
Bart, Kathleen. *Town Teddy and Country Bear go global*
Beck, Ian. *Home before dark*
  Teddy's snowy day
Bentley, Jonathan. *Where is Bear?*
Bond, Michael. *Paddington Bear goes to the hospital*
  Paddington Bear in the garden
Burgess, Mark. *Where teddy bears come from*
Bush, Timothy. *Teddy bear, teddy bear*
Butterworth, Nick. *Albert the bear*
Carmichael, Clay. *Lonesome bear*
Cousins, Lucy. *Maisy's bedtime*
Coyle, Carmela Lavigna. *Do super heroes have teddy bears?*
Crimi, Carolyn. *Principal Fred won't go to bed*
Cusimano, Maryann K. *You are my I love you*
Daly, Niki. *Old Bob's brown bear*
Dewan, Ted. *One true bear*
Docherty, Thomas. *Wash-a-bye Bear*
Dodd, Emma. *Best bear*
Donaldson, Julia. *One Ted falls out of bed*
Doremus, Gaetan. *Bear despair*
Dunn, Jancee. *I'm afraid your teddy is in trouble today*
Ellwand, David. *Ten in the bed*
Feiffer, Jules. *I lost my bear*
Fox, Christyan. *What shape is that, PiggyWiggy?*
Freedman, Claire. *Night-night, Emily*
Freeman, Don. *Beady Bear*
  Corduroy
  Corduroy's busy street and Corduroy goes to the doctor
  A pocket for Corduroy
Garton, Sam. *I am Otter*
  Otter loves Halloween
Gauch, Patricia Lee. *Bravo, Tanya*
  Dance, Tanya

Gretz, Susanna. *Teddy bears cure a cold*
Guy, Ginger Foglesong. *Siesta*
Hächler, Bruno. *What does my teddy bear do all night?*
Hague, Kathleen. *Alphabears*
　Numbears
Hague, Michael. *Teddy bear, teddy bear*
Hale, Nathan. *Yellowbelly and Plum go to school*
Hansen, Felicity. *The first bear*
Harris, Trudy. *Up bear, down bear*
Hegg, Tom. *Peef and his best friend*
Hennessy, B. G. *A Christmas wish for Corduroy*
　Corduroy at the zoo
　Corduroy's birthday
　Corduroy's Christmas
　Corduroy's Easter
　Corduroy's Halloween
Hissey, Jane. *Jolly snow*
　Old Bear
Ichikawa, Satomi. *The first bear in Africa!*
Inches, Alison. *Corduroy writes a letter*
　Corduroy's garden
　Corduroy's hike
James, J. Alison. *The bears' Christmas surprise*
Johnston, Tony. *My best friend Bear*
Kelly, Luke. *Blanket and bear, a remarkable pair*
Kennedy, Jimmy. *The teddy bears' picnic*, ill. by Alexandra Day
　The teddy bears' picnic, ill. by Michael Hague
　The teddy bears' picnic, ill. by Prue Theobalds
Kroll, Virginia L. *Everybody has a teddy*
Lewis, Kim. *First snow*
Lindgren, Barbro. *Sam's teddy bear*
McCue, Lisa. *Corduroy's best Halloween ever!*
McFarland, Lyn Rossiter. *The pirate's parrot*
McGinness, Suzanne. *My bear Griz*
McGrath, Barbara Barbieri. *Teddy bear addition*
　Teddy bear counting
Mack, Jeff. *Hush little polar bear*
McKee, David. *Elmer and the lost teddy*
McPhail, David. *Ben loves Bear*
　The teddy bear
McQuade, Jacqueline. *At preschool with Teddy Bear*
　At the petting zoo with Teddy Bear
　Christmas with Teddy Bear
　Good times with Teddy Bear
Maitland, Barbara. *My bear and me*
Meserve, Jessica. *Bedtime without Arthur*
Meyers, Susan. *Bear in the air*
Milne, A. A. *Eeyore loses a tail*
　Tigger tales
Moore, Clement Clarke. *The teddy bears' night before Christmas*
Murphy, Mary. *Some things change*
Naylor, Phyllis Reynolds. *Please do feed the bears*
Novak, Matt. *Jazzbo and Googy*
Ormondroyd, Edward. *Theodore*
Reynolds, Adrian. *Pete and Polo's farmyard adventure*
Root, Phyllis. *Contrary bear*
Rosen, Michael. *Red Ted and the lost things*
Sava, Donna Lynn. *Teddy bear dreams*
Schertle, Alice. *The adventures of old Bo Bear*
Schneider, Christine M. *I'm bored!*
Seeger, Laura Vaccaro. *Dog and Bear: three to get ready*
　Dog and Bear: tricks and treats
　Dog and Bear: two friends, three stories
　Dog and Bear: two's company
Simon, Charnan. *Messy Molly*

Smee, Nicola. *No bed without Ted*
Stadler, John. *Catilda*
Stead, Philip C. *Jonathan and the big blue boat*
Stephens, Helen. *The big adventure of the Smalls*
Tibo, Gilles. *The grand journey of Mr. Man*
Tildes, Phyllis Limbacher. *Billy's big-boy bed*
Trasler, Janee. *Mimi and Bear in the snow*
Tyger, Rory. *Newton*
Ungerer, Tomi. *Otto: the autobiography of a teddy bear*
Van Laan, Nancy. *Little baby Bobby*
Waber, Bernard. *Ira sleeps over*
Waddell, Martin. *Night night Cuddly Bear*
　Sailor Bear
　Small Bear lost
　When the teddy bears came
Walton, Jessica. *Introducing Teddy*
Weber, Linda Kay. *Louie Larkey and the bad dream patrol*
Weninger, Brigitte. *Good-bye, Daddy!*
Wickstrom, Sylvie. *I love you, Mister Bear*
Wilson, Karma. *Sleepyhead*
Wishinsky, Frieda. *What's up, bear?*
Wright, Dare. *A gift from the lonely doll*
　The lonely doll
Yektai, Niki. *Hi bears, bye bears*
Young, Ruth. *Golden Bear*
Yum, Hyewon. *Last night*
Ziefert, Harriet. *Clara Ann Cookie go to bed!*

Toys – blocks

Banks, Kate. *Max's castle*
Barrett, Mary Brigid. *All fall down*
Dickson, Irene. *Blocks*
Hutchins, Pat. *Changes, changes*

Toys – dolls

Beck, Andrea. *Elliot's emergency*
Bell, Anthea. *Vasilisa the beautiful*
Bertrand, Diane Gonzales. *The last doll / La última muñeca*
Browne, Anthony. *Silly Billy*
Godden, Rumer. *The story of Holly and Ivy*
Greenfield, Eloise. *My doll, Keshia*
Grey, Mini. *Toys in space*
Guthrie, Woody. *My dolly*
Hall, Patricia. *Hooray for reading!*
Hobbie, Holly. *Fanny*
　Fanny and Annabelle
Keller, Holly. *Geraldine's blanket*
Kroll, Steven. *The hand-me-down doll*
Lasky, Kathryn. *Sophie and Rose*
McClintock, Barbara. *Dahlia*
McKissack, Patricia C. *The all-I'll-ever-want Christmas doll*
　Nettie Jo's friends
McPhail, David. *Emma in charge*
Martin, Ann M. *The Doll People's Christmas*
Mayer, Marianna. *Baba Yaga and Vasilisa the Brave*
Medearis, Michael. *Daisy and the doll*
Milgrim, David. *Time to get up, time to go*
Mills, Elaine. *Marinetta at the ballet*
Montanari, Eva. *My first . . .*
Nelson, Vaunda Micheaux. *Almost to freedom*
Newsome, Jill. *Dream dancer*
Norling, Beth. *The stone baby*
O'Connor, Jane. *Fancy Nancy: fanciest doll in the universe*

Ogburn, Jacqueline K. *The magic nesting doll*
Oram, Hiawyn. *Baba Yaga and the wise doll*
Ormerod, Jan. *Miss Mouse takes off*
Parot, Annelore. *Kimonos*
Pattison, Darcy. *The journey of Oliver K. Woodman*
  Searching for Oliver K. Woodman
Pilgrim, Elza. *The china doll*
Polacco, Patricia. *Babushka's doll*
  Betty Doll
Potter, Giselle. *This is my dollhouse*
Randall, Alison L. *The wheat doll*
Ransom, Candice F. *The Christmas dolls*
Russo, Marisabina. *The trouble with baby*
Santiago, Esmeralda. *A doll for Navidades*
Schneider, Josh. *Princess Sparkle-Heart gets a makeover*
Silbaugh, Elizabeth. *Raggedy Ann's birthday party book*
Steig, William. *Yellow and pink*
Stuve-Bodeen, Stephanie. *Elizabeti's doll*
Tada, Joni Eareckson. *Forever friends*
Tudor, Tasha. *The doll's Christmas*
Turner, Ann Warren. *Secrets from the dollhouse*
Wells, Rosemary. *Peabody*
  Yoko's show-and-tell
Winthrop, Elizabeth. *Vasilissa the beautiful*
Wright, Dare. *A gift from the lonely doll*
  The lonely doll
Zolotow, Charlotte. *William's doll*

Toys – rocking horses

Sokol, Edward. *Meet Stinky Magee*

Toys – soldiers

Andersen, Hans Christian. *The steadfast tin soldier*, ill. by Jen Corace
  The steadfast tin soldier, ill. by Charlene DeLage
  The steadfast tin soldier, ill. by Paul Galdone
  The steadfast tin soldier, ill. by Rachel Isadora
  The steadfast tin soldier, ill. by P. J. Lynch
  The steadfast tin soldier, ill. by Fred Marcellino
  The steadfast tin soldier, ill. by JooHee Yoon
Hoffmann, E. T. A *The Nutcracker in Harlem*
Rylant, Cynthia. *Little Whistle's medicine*

Toys – teddy bears *see* Toys – bears

Toys – tin soldiers *see* Toys – soldiers

Toys – trains

Gall, Chris. *The littlest train*
Lewis, Kevin. *Chugga-chugga choo-choo*
Mallat, Kathy. *Trouble on the tracks*
Richards, Laura Elizabeth Howe. *Jiggle joggle jee*

Toys – wagons

Dodd, Lynley. *A dragon in a wagon*
Lindgren, Barbro. *Sam's wagon*
Liwska, Renata. *Red wagon*
Pullen, Zachary. *Friday my Radio Flyer flew*

Tractors

Alborough, Jez. *The gobble gobble moooooo tractor book*
Angleberger, Tom. *McToad mows Tiny Island*
Big noisy trucks and diggers
Blum, Mark. *Big trucks and diggers in 3-D*
Carter, Don. *Old MacDonald drives a tractor*
Clement, Nathan. *Big tractor*
Dierssen, Andreas. *The old red tractor*
Dobbins, Jan. *Driving my tractor*
Garland, Michael. *Grandpa's tractor*
Goodhart, Pippa. *Arthur's tractor*
Hillenbrand, Will. *Down by the barn*
Kilby, Don. *In the country*
Lewis, Kim. *One summer day*
Long, Loren. *Otis*
  Otis and the kittens
  Otis and the puppy
  Otis and the scarecrow
  Otis and the tornado
  An Otis Christmas
Lund, Deb. *Monsters on machines*
Mayo, Margaret. *Dig dig digging*
Meng, Cece. *Tough chicks*
Old MacDonald had a farm. *Old MacDonald's things that go*
Pallotta, Jerry. *The construction alphabet book*
Peterson, Cris. *Fantastic farm machines*
Ransom, Candice F. *Tractor day*
Schubert, Leda. *Here comes Darrell*
Shannon, David. *Duck on a tractor*
Siy, Alexandra. *One tractor*
Swenson, Jamie A. *Big rig*
van Lieshout, Elle. *The wish*

Traffic, traffic signs

Aesop. *Road signs*
Bell, Babs. *The bridge is up!*
Harper, Charise Mericle. *Go! go! go! stop!*
Liu, Julia. *Gus, the dinosaur bus*
Meister, Cari. *Busy, busy city street*
Pearson, Debora. *Alphabeep*
Robbins, Ken. *Trucks, giants of the highway*
Schertle, Alice. *Little Blue Truck leads the way*
Suen, Anastasia. *Red light, green light*

Train engineers *see* Careers – railroad engineers

Trains

Abbot, Judi. *Train!*
Awdry, W. *Happy birthday, Thomas!*
Aylesworth, Jim. *Country crossing*
Barton, Byron. *Trains*
Barton, Chris. *Shark vs. train*
Bee, William. *And the train goes . . .*
Blechman, Nicholas. *Night light*
Bluemle, Elizabeth. *Tap tap boom boom*
Booth, Philip E. *Crossing*
Braun, Sebastien. *Whoosh and Chug!*
C is for caboose
Caswell, Deanna. *Train trip*
Chall, Marsha Wilson. *Prairie train*
Cohen, Deborah Bodin. *Engineer Ari and the Rosh Hashana ride*
Collicutt, Paul. *This train*

Cooper, Elisha. *Train*
Corey, Shana. *The secret subway*
Crews, Donald. *Freight train*
    Inside freight train
    Shortcut
Crunk, Tony. *Railroad John and the Red Rock run*
Curious George takes a train
Dale, Penny. *Dinosaur rescue!*
De Roo, Elena. *The rain train*
Dorfman, Craig. *I knew you could!*
Dotlich, Rebecca Kai. *All aboard!*
Drummond, Allan. *Casey Jones*
Eaton, Jason Carter. *How to train a train*
Emberley, Ed. *Ed Emberley's drawing book of trucks and trains*
Floca, Brian. *Locomotive*
Gall, Chris. *The littlest train*
Garcia, Emma. *Chugga chugga choo choo*
Gibbons, Gail. *Trains*
Goble, Paul. *Death of the iron horse*
Gurney, John Steven. *Dinosaur train*
Harby, Melanie. *All aboard for Dreamland!*
High, Linda Oatman. *Tenth Avenue cowboy*
Highet, Alistair. *The yellow train*
Hill, Lee Sullivan. *Trains*
Hoberman, Mary Ann. *Bill Grogan's goat*
Horácek, Petr. *Choo choo*
Horsbrugh, Wilma. *The train to Glasgow*
Hubbell, Patricia. *Trains: steaming! pulling! huffing!*
Ichikawa, Satomi. *My little train*
Jacobs, Paul DuBois. *Count on the subway*
Johnson, Angela. *I dream of trains*
Kay, Verla. *Iron horses*
    Orphan train
Kelly, Mij. *William and the night train*
Kimmel, Eric A. *Stormy's hat*
Knapman, Timothy. *Follow the track all the way back*
Kulling, Monica. *All aboard! Elijah McCoy's steam engine*
Lakin, Patricia. *Subway sonata*
Lehman, Barbara. *Trainstop*
Lenski, Lois. *The little train*
Light, Steve. *Trains go*
London, Jonathan. *The owl who became the moon*
    A train goes clickety-clack
Lund, Deb. *All aboard the dinotrain*
Macaulay, David. *Black and white*
McCully, Emily Arnold. *An outlaw Thanksgiving*
McMullan, Kate. *I'm fast*
McNamara, Margaret. *The whistle on the train*
McPhail, David. *Moony B. Finch, fastest draw in the West*
Mahy, Margaret. *Mister Whistler*
Maltbie, P. I. *Claude Monet: the painter who stopped the trains*
Miller, Heather Lynn. *Subway ride*
Moser, Lisa. *Railroad Hank*
Moss, Marissa. *True heart*
Neitzel, Shirley. *I'm taking a trip on my train*
Niemann, Christoph. *Subway*
Nobisso, Josephine. *John Blair and the great Hinckley fire*
Oram, Hiawyn. *Going to Grandpa's*
Paul, Miranda. *Trainbots*
Peet, Bill. *The caboose who got loose*
    Smokey
Pinkney, Gloria Jean. *The Sunday outing*
Piper, Watty. *The little engine that could*, ill. by George Hauman

The little engine that could, ill. by Loren Long
Prince, Joshua. *I saw an ant on the railroad track*
Ray, Mary Lyn. *All aboard*
Rex, Michael. *My freight train*
Rinker, Sherri Duskey. *Steam train, dream train*
Rockwell, Anne. *Trains*
    Whoo! whoo! goes the train
Rosenbaum, Andria Warmflash. *Trains don't sleep*
Roth, Carol. *All aboard to work — choo-choo!*
Rylant, Cynthia. *Silver packages*
Sarcone-Roach, Julia. *Subway story*
Siebert, Diane. *Train song*
Sís, Peter. *Train of states*
Skinner, Daphne. *All aboard!*
Smith, Joseph A. *Circus train*
Sobel, June. *The goodnight train*
Spence, Robert, III.. *Clickety clack*
Steele, Philip. *Trains: the slide-out, see-through story of world-famous trains and railroads*
Steggall, Susan. *Rattle and rap*
Stevenson, James. *All aboard!*
Sturges, Philemon. *I love trains*
Stutson, Caroline. *Night train*
Suen, Anastasia. *Subway*
    Window music
Temple, Charles A. *Train*
Thomas, Joyce Carol. *In the land of milk and honey*
Titcomb, Gordon. *The last train*
Tunnell, Michael O. *Mailing May*
Vamos, Samantha R. *Alphabet trains*
Van Allsburg, Chris. *The polar express*
Voake, Charlotte. *Here comes the train*
Wickberg, Susan. *Hey Mr. Choo-Choo, where are you going?*
Wormell, Christopher. *Puff, puff, chugga-chugga*
Yin. *Coolies*
Ziefert, Harriet. *Train song*
Zimmerman, Andrea Griffing. *Train man*
Zullo, Germano. *Line 135*

Trains, toy *see* Toys – trains

Transgender *see* Gender identity; LGBTQ

Transportation

Angleberger, Tom. *McToad mows Tiny Island*
Baer, Edith. *This is the way we go to school*
Barton, Byron. *Airport*
    My bus
Bee, William. *Stanley's colors*
Bell, Babs. *The bridge is up!*
Calmenson, Stephanie. *Late for school!*
Chancellor, Deborah. *Traveling on land*
Colby, Rebecca. *Motor Goose: rhymes that go!*
Collicutt, Paul. *This train*
Cousins, Lucy. *Maisy's book of things that go*
    Stop and go, Maisy
Crews, Donald. *School bus*
    Truck
Dale, Penny. *Dinosaur zoom!*
Davis, Caroline. *My little rowboat*
Demarest, Chris L. *All aboard! a traveling alphabet*
    Lindbergh
Durango, Julia. *Go-go gorillas*
Fecher, Sarah. *On the move*
Flanagan, Alice K. *Riding the ferry with Captain Cruz*

Riding the school bus with Mrs. Kramer
Freymann, Saxton. *Fast food*
Gertsberg, Inna. *The way downtown*
Gibbons, Gail. *New road!*
　Transportation
Hill, Lee Sullivan. *Trains*
Kirk, Daniel. *Go!*
Kittinger, Jo S. *Rosa's bus*
Laden, Nina. *Peek-a-choo-choo!*
Levinson, Riki. *I go with my family to Grandma's*
Lillegard, Dee. *Go! poetry in motion: poems*
Ljungkvist, Laura. *Search and spot go!*
London, Jonathan. *My big rig*
Lord, Janet. *Here comes Grandma!*
Maass, Robert. *Tugboats*
McCourt, Lisa. *I miss you, Stinky Face*
MacDonald, Suse. *Elephants on board*
Mayo, Margaret. *Choo choo clickety-clack*
Miller, Heather Lynn. *Subway ride*
Miranda, Anne. *Vroom, chugga, vroom-vroom*
Mitton, Tony. *Cool cars*
Morris, Ann. *On the go*
Mortensen, Denise Dowling. *Wake up engines*
Munro, Roxie. *Go! go! go!*
Nobles, Kristen M. *Drive this book*
Old MacDonald had a farm. *Old MacDonald had a farm*
　Old MacDonald's things that go
Olivera, Ramon. *ABCs on wheels*
Rau, Dana Meachen. *Riding*
　Ways to go
Reynolds, Luke. *Bedtime blastoff!*
Ringgold, Faith. *If a bus could talk*
Robbins, Ken. *Trucks, giants of the highway*
Rockwell, Anne. *Ferryboat ride!*
　Planes
　Things that go
　Trains
Rosen, Michael. *The bus is for us!*
Rotner, Shelley. *Boats afloat*
Rylant, Cynthia. *Silver packages*
Spinelli, Eileen. *Six hogs on a scooter*
Stanley, Mandy. *On the move*
Steggall, Susan. *Rattle and rap*
　Red car, red bus
Stevenson, James. *No need for Monty*
Stickland, Paul. *Truck jam*
Suen, Anastasia. *Delivery*
　Red light, green light
　Subway
Temple, Charles A. *Train*
Timmers, Leo. *Bang*
Tunnell, Michael O. *Mailing May*
Vetter, Jennifer Riggs. *Down by the station*
Walker, Sally M. *Druscilla's Halloween*
Wellington, Monica. *Truck driver Tom*
Willems, Mo. *The pigeon loves things that go!*
Ziefert, Harriet. *From Kalamazoo to Timbuktu!*

Trees

Ada, Alma Flor. *The Christmas tree / El arbol de Navidad*
Adler, David A. *Redwoods are the tallest trees in the world*
Alexander, Sue. *Behold the trees*
Aliki. *Christmas tree memories*
Altman, Linda Jacobs. *Amelia's road*

Andersen, Hans Christian. *The fir tree*, ill. by Diane Goode
　The fir tree, ill. by Bernadette Watts
Arnold, Tedd. *Dirty Gert*
Arnosky, Jim. *Crinkleroot's guide to knowing the trees*
Aston, Dianna Hutts. *An orange in January*
Atwood, Margaret. *Up in the tree*
Bailey, Mary Bryant. *Jeoffry's Christmas*
Baumgart, Klaus. *Laura's Christmas star*
Beedie, Duncan. *The lumberjack's beard*
Berenstain, Stan and Jan. *The Berenstain bears and the spooky old tree*
　The Berenstain bears' Christmas tree
　The Berenstain bears' that stump must go!
Berger, Carin. *The little yellow leaf*
Bond, Rebecca. *A city Christmas tree*
Bonfield, Chloe. *The perfect tree*
Bosca, Francesca. *The apple king*
Brallier, Jess M. *Tess's tree*
Brown, Margaret Wise. *The little fir tree*
Brown, Ruth. *The old tree*
Bunting, Eve. *Night tree*
Carney, Margaret. *At Grandpa's sugar bush*
Chernesky, Felicia Sanzari. *Sugar white snow and evergreens*
Cherry, Lynne. *The great kapok tree*
Child, Lauren. *What planet are you from Clarice Bean?*
Chin, Jason. *Redwoods*
Codell, Esme Raji. *Seed by seed*
Cole, Henry. *The littlest evergreen*
Conrad, Pam. *The Tub People's Christmas*
Cooke, Trish. *The grandad tree*
Costa, Nicoletta. *The little tree that would not share*
Cousins, Lucy. *Maisy's Christmas tree*
Demas, Corinne. *Two Christmas mice*
DePalma, Mary Newell. *A grand old tree*
dePaola, Tomie. *The family Christmas tree book*
Devernay, Laetitia. *The conductor*
Donaldson, Julia. *Stick Man*
Dunrea, Olivier. *A Christmas tree for Pyn*
Duvall, John. *The great spruce*
Ehlert, Lois. *Red leaf, yellow leaf*
Emmett, Jonathan. *Leaf trouble*
Félix, Lucie. *Apples and robins*
Flanagan, Alice K. *The Zieglers and their apple orchard*
Florian, Douglas. *Poetrees*
Foggo, Cheryl. *Dear baobab*
Formento, Alison. *This tree counts!*
　This tree, 1, 2, 3
Frisch, Aaron. *The lonely pine*
Galbraith, Kathryn O. *Arbor Day square*
Geisert, Arthur. *Nursery crimes*
George, Kristine O'Connell. *Old Elm speaks*
George, William T. *Christmas at Long Pond*
Gerber, Carole. *Spring blossoms*
　Winter trees
Gibbons, Gail. *The missing maple syrup sap mystery*
　The seasons of Arnold's apple tree
　Tell me, tree
Gold-Vukson, Marji E. *Grandpa and me on Tu B'Shevat*
Goldstyn, Jacques. *Bertolt*
Gottesfeld, Jeff. *The tree in the courtyard*
Hall, Michael. *Wonderfall*
Hall, Zoe. *The apple pie tree*
　Fall leaves fall
Harrison, Troon. *The floating orchard*

Trickery *see* Behavior – trickery

Tricks *see* Magic

Triplets *see* Multiple births – triplets

Trucks

Alborough, Jez. *Duck in the truck*
Anderson, Peggy Perry. *Chuck's truck*
Andrews, Julie. *Dumpy at school*
    Dumpy the dump truck
    Dumpy to the rescue!
    Dumpy's apple shop
Armstrong, Jennifer. *Magnus at the fire*
Ashburn, Boni. *Builder Goose*
Austin, Mike. *Fire Engine No. 9*
Ayres, Katherine. *Matthew's truck*
Barton, Byron. *Trucks*
Barton, Chris. *Mighty truck*
    Mighty truck: muddymania!
Beaumont, Karen. *Where's my t-r-u-c-k?*
Big noisy trucks and diggers
Biggs, Brian. *123 beep beep beep!*
Bingham, Caroline. *Big book of rescue vehicles*
Blechman, Nicholas. *Night light*
Blum, Mark. *Big trucks and diggers in 3-D*
Braun, Sebastien. *Digger and Tom!*
Bryant, Megan E. *Dump Truck Duck*
Buzzeo, Toni. *Whose truck?*
Carr, Jan. *Big Truck and Little Truck*
Carter, Don. *Get to work, trucks!*
Clement, Nathan. *Drive*
Coffelt, Nancy. *Pug in a truck*
Crews, Donald. *Truck*
Crowther, Robert. *Amazing pop-up trucks*
Curious George and the dump truck (1984)
    Curious George and the dump truck (1999)
Cuyler, Margery. *The little dump truck*
    The little fire truck
Cyrus, Kurt. *Big rig bugs*
Dale, Penny. *Dinosaur dig!*
Davis, Sarah. *My first trucks*
Day, Alexandra. *Frank and Ernest on the road*
Deneux, Xavier. *Vehicles*
Denise, Anika. *Monster trucks*
Deschamps, Nicola. *Emergency!*
De Sève, Randall. *A fire truck named Red*
Eaton, Jason Carter. *How to track a truck*
Emberley, Ed. *Ed Emberley's drawing book of trucks and trains*
Evans, Nate. *Bang! Boom! Roar!*
Floca, Brian. *Five trucks*
Freedman, Claire. *Beep beep beep: time for sleep!*
Friend, David. *With any luck, I'll drive a truck*
Gall, Chris. *Dinotrux*
    Dinotrux dig the beach
    Revenge of the Dinotrux
Garcia, Emma. *Tip tip dig dig*
Gergely, Tibor. *The great big fire engine book*
Gibbons, Gail. *Emergency!*
    Trucks
Gillingham, Sara. *Trucks*
The gingerbread boy. The Gingerbread Man loose on the fire truck
Goodwin-Sturges, Judy Sue. *Construction Kitties*
Gordon, David. *The three little rigs*

The ugly truckling
Green, Rod. *Giant vehicles*
Greene, Rhonda Growler. *Push! dig! scoop!*
Hamilton, Kersten. *Red truck*
Harper, Charise Mericle. *Go! go! go! stop!*
Hines, Anna Grossnickle. *I am a backhoe*
Holub, Joan. *Mighty dads*
Horvath, James. *Dig, dogs, dig*
Houston, Gloria. *Miss Dorothy and her bookmobile*
Hundal, Nancy. *Number 21*
Hunter, Jana Novotny. *When Daddy's truck picks me up*
Imershein, Betsy. *Trucks*
Jane, Pamela. *Milo and the fire engine parade*
Keller, Joy. *Monster trucks*
Kenney, Sean. *Cool cars and trucks*
Kilby, Don. *At a construction site*
    In the city
    In the country
    On the road
Kirk, Daniel. *Trash trucks!*
Kirk, David. *Truckeroo school*
Koehler, Lora. *The little snowplow*
Lee, Mark. *20 big trucks in the middle of the street*
Levine, Michelle. *Ambulances*
Light, Steve. *Diggers go*
London, Jonathan. *My big rig*
    A truck goes rattley-bumpa
Lord, Cynthia. *Hot Rod Hamster: monster truck mania!*
Low, William. *Machines go to work in the city*
    Trucks to the rescue!
Lyon, George Ella. *Trucks roll!*
Maass, Robert. *Little trucks with big jobs*
MacDonald, Suse. *Elephants on board*
McMullan, Kate. *I stink!*
    I'm brave!
    I'm dirty!
Mayo, Margaret. *Dig dig digging*
    Emergency!
Meister, Cari. *Busy, busy city street*
Milusich, Janice. *Off go their engines, off go their lights*
Miranda, Anne. *Beep! beep!*
Mitchell, Joyce Slayton. *Tractor-trailer trucker*
Mitton, Tony. *Flashing fire engines*
Moore, Patrick. *The mighty street sweeper*
My big book of trucks and diggers
Newman, Lesléa. *A fire engine for Ruthie*
Niemann, Christoph. *That's how!*
Nobles, Kristen M. *Drive this book*
Novesky, Amy. *Love is a truck*
Odanaka, Barbara. *Smash! mash! crash! there goes the trash!*
Odgers, Sally. *Good night, Truck*
Old MacDonald had a farm. *Old MacDonald had a truck*
    Old MacDonald's things that go
Olson-Brown, Ellen. *Hush little digger*
Pallotta, Jerry. *The construction alphabet book*
Patrick, Jean L. S. *If I had a snowplow*
Pearson, Debora. *Alphabeep*
Penn, Audrey. *Kai to the rescue!*
Rex, Michael. *My fire engine*
Rinker, Sherri Duskey. *Goodnight, goodnight, construction site*
    Mighty, mighty construction site
Robbins, Ken. *Trucks, giants of the highway*
Roberts, Cynthia. *Tow trucks*

Rockwell, Anne. *At the firehouse*
  Fire engines
  Good morning, Digger
  Truck stop
  Trucks
Samuels, Barbara. *The trucker*
Santoro, Scott. *Isaac the Ice Cream Truck*
Savage, Stephen. *The mixed-up truck*
  Supertruck
Sayres, Brianna Caplan. *Where do diggers sleep at night?*
Schertle, Alice. *Little Blue Truck*
  Little Blue Truck leads the way
Schotter, Roni. *Go, Little Green Truck!*
Schubert, Leda. *Here comes Darrell*
Scieszka, Jon. *Melvin might?*
  Race from A to Z
  Smash! crash!
  Truckery rhymes
Shoulders, Michael. *D is for dump truck*
Shulevitz, Uri. *Troto and the trucks*
Siebert, Diane. *Truck song*
Sís, Peter. *Fire truck*
  Trucks, trucks, trucks
Skultety, Nancy. *From here to there*
Steggall, Susan. *Colors*
  The diggers are coming!
Stein, Peter. *Little Red's riding 'hood*
  Trucks galore
Stickland, Paul. *Truck jam*
Stoeke, Janet Morgan. *Minerva Louise and the red truck*
Sturges, Philemon. *I love trucks!*
Suen, Anastasia. *Red light, green light*
Sutton, Sally. *Demolition*
  Roadwork
Swenson, Jamie A. *Big rig*
Timmers, Leo. *Who is driving?*
Todd, Mark. *Food trucks!*
  Monster trucks
Vamos, Samantha R. *Alphabet trucks*
Vestergaard, Hope. *Digger, dozer, dumper*
Wellington, Monica. *Truck driver Tom*
Williams, Karen Lynn. *Tap-tap*
Wolf, Sallie. *Truck stuck*
Wood, Audrey. *Alphabet rescue*

Tsunamis

Bauer, Marion Dane. *A mama for Owen*
Hodges, Margaret. *The wave*
Kajikawa, Kimiko. *Tsunami!*
Kroll, Virginia L. *Selvakumar knew better*
Lucas, David. *Whale*
Ohi, Ruth. *Kenta and the big wave*
Winter, Jeanette. *Mama: a true story, in which a baby hippo loses his mama during a tsunami, but finds a new home*

TV *see* Television

Twilight

Berger, Barbara. *Grandfather Twilight*
Shulevitz, Uri. *Dusk*
Simler, Isabelle. *The blue hour*
Udry, Janice May. *The moon jumpers*

Twins *see* Multiple births – twins

U.S. history

Adler, David A.. *Heroes for civil rights*
  A picture book of Abraham Lincoln
  A picture book of Benjamin Franklin
  A picture book of Cesar Chavez
  A picture book of Dolley and James Madison
  A picture book of Eleanor Roosevelt
  A picture book of George Washington
  A picture book of Harry Houdini
  A picture book of John and Abigail Adams
  A picture book of John F. Kennedy
  A picture book of John Hancock
  A picture book of Martin Luther King, Jr
  A picture book of Sam Houston
  A picture book of Samuel Adams
  A picture book of Thomas Jefferson
Aldrin, Buzz. *Look to the stars*
  Reaching for the moon
Alexander, Elizabeth. *Praise song for the day*
Aliki. *The many lives of Benjamin Franklin*
  The story of William Penn
  A weed is a flower
Allegra, Mike. *Sarah gives thanks*
Allen, Kathy. *The U.S. Constitution*
Altman, Susan. *Followers of the north star*
Andersen, Hans Christian. *The tinderbox*
Anderson, Laurie Halse. *Thank you, Sarah*
Angleberger, Tom. *Crankee Doodle*
Appelt, Kathi. *Miss Lady Bird's wildflowers*
Armand, Glenda. *Love twelve miles long*
Armentrout, David. *John Muir*
Asim, Jabari. *Preaching to the chickens*
Aston, Dianna Hutts. *The moon over Star*
Atwell, Debby. *Pearl*
Aulaire, Ingri Mortenson d'. *Abraham Lincoln*
Aylesworth, Jim. *Our Abe Lincoln*
Bandy, Michael S. *Granddaddy's turn*
  White water
Barbour, Karen. *Mr. Williams*
Barnett, Mac. *President Taft is stuck in the bath*
Barretta, Gene. *Now and Ben*
Bartlett, Robert Merrill. *The story of Thanksgiving*
Bartoletti, Susan Campbell. *The Christmas promise*
  The flag maker
Bass, Hester. *Seeds of freedom*
Bates, Katharine Lee. *America the beautiful*, ill. by Chris Gall
  America the beautiful, ill. by Wendell Minor
  America the beautiful: together we stand
Battle-Lavert, Gwendolyn. *Papa's mark*
Bauer, Marion Dane. *Harriet Tubman*
Berlin, Irving. *God bless America*
Bildner, Phil. *The greatest game ever played*
  The hallelujah flight
  Shoeless Joe and Black Betsy

Binns, Tristan Boyer. *The Liberty Bell*
Birtha, Becky. *Grandmama's pride*
    Lucky beans
Blanco, Richard. *One today*
Borden, Louise. A. *Lincoln and me*
    America is . . .
Brantley-Newton, Vanessa. *Let freedom sing*
Brill, Marlene Targ. *Bronco Charlie and the Pony Express*
    Margaret Knight, girl inventor
Brown, Don. *Henry and the cannons*
    One giant leap: the story of Neil Armstrong
    Teedie
    A voice from the wilderness
    A wizard from the start
Brown, Monica. *Side by side / Lado a lado*
Brown, Tami Lewis. *Soar, Elinor!*
Broyles, Anne. *Priscilla and the hollyhocks*
Bruchac, Joseph. *Squanto's journey*
Brunhoff, Laurent de. *Babar's USA*
Bryant, Jen. *Abe's fish*
    A splash of red
Bunting, Eve. *The blue and the gray*
    The cart that carried Martin
    A picnic in October
Burleigh, Robert. *If you spent a day with Thoreau at Walden pond*
    One giant leap
    Stealing home
Carbone, Elisa. *Diana's White House garden*
    Heroes of the surf
    Night running
Chaconas, Dori. *Pennies in a jar*
Chandra, Deborah. *George Washington's teeth*
Cherry, Lynne. *A river ran wild*
Christensen, Bonnie. *Woody Guthrie, poet of the people*
Cline-Ransome, Lesa. *Before she was Harriet*
    Just a lucky so and so
    Light in the darkness
    Words set me free
Clinton, Catherine. *Phillis's big test*
    When Harriet met Sojourner
Clinton, Chelsea. *She persisted*
Cohan, George M. *You're a grand old flag*
Cole, Barbara Hancock. *Anna and Natalie*
Cole, Henry. *Unspoken*
Collins, Suzanne. *Year of the jungle*
Cooney, Barbara. *Eleanor*
Cooper, Floyd. *Juneteenth for Mazie*
    Willie and the All-Stars
Corey, Shana. *Here come the Girl Scouts!*
    The secret subway
    You forgot your skirt, Amelia Bloomer
Cotten, Cynthia. *Abbie in stitches*
    The book boat's in
Cullen, Lynn. *Dear Mr. Washington*
Dalgliesh, Alice. *The Thanksgiving story*
Davies, Jacqueline. *Tricking the Tallyman*
Demarest, Chris L. *Lindbergh*
Demas, Corinne. *Hurricane!*
dePaola, Tomie. *An early American Christmas*
    My first Thanksgiving
Dray, Philip. *Yours for justice, Ida B. Wells*
Drummond, Allan. *Liberty*
Dunlap, Julie. *Louisa May and Mr. Thoreau's flute*
Edwards, David. *The pen that Pa built*
Edwards, Pamela Duncan. *Barefoot: escape on the Underground Railroad*

    Boston Tea Party
    The bus ride that changed history
Esbaum, Jill. *To the big top*
Evans, Shane W. *Underground: finding the light to freedom*
    We march
Falken, Linda. *Can you find it?*
Farris, Christine King. *March on!*
    My brother Martin
Fern, Tracey. *W is for Webster*
Ferris, Jeri Chase. *Noah Webster and his words*
Figley, Marty Rhodes. *The schoolchildren's blizzard*
Fisher, Leonard Everett. *Stars and stripes: our national flag*
Fisher, Mary M. *Rosita's bridge*
Fishman, Cathy Goldberg. *When Jackie and Hank met*
FitzGerald, Dawn. *Vinnie and Abraham*
Fleischman, Paul. *The matchbox diary*
Fleming, Candace. *Imogene's last stand*
Floca, Brian. *Lightship*
    Locomotive
    Moonshot
Fradin, Dennis. *The price of freedom*
Fulton, Kristen. *Long may she wave*
Garland, Michael. *Americana adventure*
    The President and Mom's apple pie
George, Jean Craighead. *The first Thanksgiving*
Gibbons, Gail. *Apples*
Gilchrist, Jan Spivey. *My America*
Giovanni, Nikki. *Lincoln and Douglass*
    Rosa
Glaser, Linda. *Emma's poem*
    Hannah's way
Goodman, Susan E. *The first step*
Gourley, Robbin. *First garden*
Grady, Cynthia. *I lay my stitches down*
Green, Stephanie. *Betsy Ross and the silver thimble*
Greene, Rhonda Gowler. *The very first Thanksgiving Day*
Greenfield, Eloise. *Easter parade*
Greenwood, Mark. *The Mayflower*
Grifalconi, Ann. *Ain't nobody a stranger to me*
Griffin, Kitty. *The ride*
Grigsby, Susan. *First peas to the table*
    In the garden with Dr. Carver
Grimes, Nikki. *Barack Obama*
Hall, Donald. *Lucy's Christmas*
Harness, Cheryl. *Mary Walker wears the pants*
    Our colonial year
Harvey, Jeanne Walker. *Maya Lin: artist-architect of light and lines*
    My hands sing the blues
Haskins, Jim. *Delivering justice*
Haugen, Brenda. *Thanksgiving*
Heard, Georgia. *This place I know*
Hearne, Betsy Gould. *Seven brave women*
Heinz, Brian J. *Nathan of yesteryear and Michael of today*
Helmer, Marilyn. *One splendid tree*
High, Linda Oatman. *The girl on the high-diving horse*
    Tenth Avenue cowboy
Hilliard, Richard. *Godspeed, John Glenn*
Hines, Gary. *A Christmas tree in the White House*
Holbrook, Stewart. *America's Ethan Allen*
Hopkinson, Deborah. *Abe Lincoln crosses a creek*
    Annie and Helen
    Keep on!

She loved baseball
Vila, Laura. *Building Manhattan*
Waldman, Neil. *They came from the Bronx*
Walker, Sally M. *Freedom song*
Wallner, Alexandra. *Betsy Ross*
  Susan B. Anthony
Warren, Sarah. *Dolores Huerta*
Washington, Donna L. *The story of Kwanzaa*
Watkins, Angela Farris. *Love will see you through*
  My Uncle Martin's big heart
  My Uncle Martin's words for America
Watson, Renée. *Harlem's little blackbird*
Weatherford, Carole Boston. *The Beatitudes*
  Before John was a jazz giant
  Champions on the bench
  Freedom in Congo Square
  Freedom on the menu
  Gordon Parks
  I, Matthew Henson
  Juneteenth jamboree
  *Moses: when Harriet Tubman led her people to
    freedom*
  Sugar Hill
Weber, Elka. *The Yankee at the seder*
Wells, Rosemary. *The house in the mail*
Whitaker, Suzanne George. *The daring Miss
    Quimby*
White, Becky. *Betsy Ross*
Wilson, Karma. *How to bake an American pie*
Winnick, Karen B. *Sybil's night ride*
Winter, Jeanette. *The Christmas tree ship*
  Follow the drinking gourd
Winter, Jonah. *Barack*
  Hillary
  Lillian's right to vote
  Muhammad Ali: champion of the world
Winters, Kay. *Abe Lincoln, the boy who loved books*
Wise, Bill. *Silent star*
Wittenstein, Barry. *Waiting for Pumpsie*
Woelfle, Gretchen. *Mumbet's Declaration of
    Independence*
Woodruff, Elvira. *Small beauties*
Woodson, Jacqueline. *Coming on home soon*
  Show way
  This is the rope
Wooldridge, Connie Nordhielm. *When Esther
    Morris headed west*
Wright, Courtni Crump. *Journey to freedom*
  Jumping the broom
Yaccarino, Dan. *All the way to America*
Yamasaki, Katie. *Fish for Jimmy*
Yin. *Brothers*
  Coolies
Yolen, Jane. *Letting Swift River go*
  My brothers' flying machine
  My Uncle Emily
  Naming Liberty

U.S. history – frontier & pioneer life

Aliki. *The story of Johnny Appleseed*
Altman, Linda Jacobs. *The legend of Freedom Hill*
Amsden, Janet. *Grizzly Pete and the ghosts*
Aston, Claire. *Wild West*
Balcziak, Bill. *Paul Bunyan*
  Pecos Bill
Bateman, Teresa. *Paul Bunyan vs. Hals Halson*
Brecon, Connah. *Paws McDraw*
Browning, Diane. *Signed, Abiah Rose*

Brownlow, Mike. *Way out West — with a baby!*
Bunting, Eve. *Washday*
Burell, Sarah. *Diamond Jim Dandy and the sheriff*
Casanova, Mary. *The day Dirk Yeller came to town*
Clement-Davies, David. *Spirit*
Codell, Esme Raji. *Seed by seed*
Crummel, Susan Stevens. *Ten-Gallon Bart and the
    Wild West Show*
Crunk, Tony. *Railroad John and the Red Rock run*
Davis, David. *Fandango stew*
Davis, Kenneth C. *Don't know much about the
    pioneers*
Emmett, Jonathan. *She'll be coming 'round the
    mountain*
Erdrich, Louise. *The range eternal*
Frank, John. *The toughest cowboy, Or, How the Wild
    West was tamed*
Galbraith, Kathryn O. *Arbor Day square*
Gibbons, Gail. *Yippee-yay!*
Glass, Andrew. *Bewildered for three days*
Griffin, Kitty. *Cowboy Sam and those confounded
    secrets*
Hallowell, George. *Wagons ho!*
Helldorfer, M. C. *Hog music*
Holt, Kimberly Willis. *The adventures of Granny
    Clearwater and Little Critter*
Holub, Joan. *Cinderdog and the wicked stepcat*
Hopkins, Jackie Mims. *The gold miner's daughter*
Howard, Ellen. *The log cabin Christmas*
  The log cabin church
  The log cabin quilt
Isaacs, Anne. *Dust Devil*
  Meanwhile, back at the ranch
  Swamp Angel
Jakes, John. *Susanna of the Alamo*
Johnston, Tony. *The cowboy and the black-eyed pea*
  Levi Strauss gets a bright idea
  Sunsets of the West
Kay, Verla. *Gold fever*
  Hornbooks and inkwells
  Whatever happened to the Pony Express?
Kellogg, Steven. *Johnny Appleseed: a tall tale*
  Paul Bunyan: a tall tale
  Pecos Bill
  Sally Ann Thunder Ann Whirlwind Crockett
Kimmel, Eric A. *The great Texas hamster drive*
  Little Red Hot
Kinsey-Warnock, Natalie. *The bear that heard crying*
Lawson, Robert. *They were strong and good*
Levitin, Sonia. *Boom town*
  Nine for California
Lindbergh, Reeve. *Johnny Appleseed*
Lowell, Susan. *The bootmaker and the elves*
  Cindy Ellen
  Dusty Locks and the three bears
Luckhurst, Matt. *Paul Bunyan and Babe the Blue Ox*
MacLachlan, Patricia. *Nora's chicks*
Miller, Bobbi. *Miss Sally Ann and the panther*
Napoli, Donna Jo. *The crossing*
Nolen, Jerdine. *Thunder Rose*
Paul, Ann Whitford. *The seasons sewn*
Randall, Alison L. *The wheat doll*
Reynolds, Aaron. *Pirates vs. cowboys*
Reynolds, Marilynn. *The new land*
  The prairie fire
Root, Phyllis. *Paula Bunyan*
Rounds, Glen. *Cowboys*
  Sod houses on the Great Plains
Rumford, James. *Don't touch my hat!*

Sanders, Scott R. *A place called Freedom*
  Warm as wool
Schnitzler, Pattie L. *Widdermaker*
Shea, Bob. *Kid Sheriff and the terrible Toads*
Smith, Janice Lee. *Jess and the stinky cowboys*
Sneed, Brad. *Deputy Harvey and the ant cow caper*
Sorensen, Henri. *New Hope*
Spradlin, Michael P. *Off like the wind!*
Stein, David Ezra. *Cowboy Ned and Andy*
  Ned's new friend
Strand, Keith. *Grandfather's Christmas tree*
Stutson, Caroline. *Prairie primer A to Z*
Swain, Gwenyth. *Johnny Appleseed*
Turner, Ann Warren. *Dakota dugout*
Van Leeuwen, Jean. *Going west*
  Nothing here but trees
  Papa and the pioneer quilt
Van Steenwyk, Elizabeth. *Prairie Christmas*
Van Woerkom, Dorothy. *Becky and the bear*
Whiteley, Opal Stanley. *Only Opal*
Wilder, Laura Ingalls. *Going to town*
  My little house songbook
  Santa comes to little house
Winter, Jeanette. *Cowboy Charlie*
Wood, Audrey. *The Bunyans*
Wright, Courtni Crump. *Wagon train*
Yolen, Jane. *Elsie's bird*
  Johnny Appleseed: the legend and the truth
Yorinks, Arthur. *Whitefish Will rides again*

Umbrellas

Bridges, Shirin Yim. *The Umbrella Queen*
Franson, Scott E. *Un-brella*
Kramer, Jackie Azúa. *The green umbrella*
Liu, Jae Soo. *Yellow umbrella*
Na, Il Sung. *The thingamabob*
Sáenz, Benjamin Alire. *Grandma Fina and her
  wonderful umbrellas / La abuelita Fina y sus
  sombrillas maravillosas*
Schubert, Ingrid. *The umbrella*
Todd, Barbara. *The rainmaker*
Weeks, Sarah. *Ella, of course!*
Yashima, Taro. *Umbrella*

Uncles *see* Family life – aunts, uncles

Unhappiness *see* Emotions – happiness;
  Emotions – sadness

UNICEF

Castle, Caroline. *For every child*

Unnoticed *see* Behavior – unnoticed, unseen

Unseen *see* Behavior – unnoticed, unseen

Unusual format *see* Format, unusual

Vanity *see* Character traits – vanity

Vikings

Chapman, Jared. *Pirate, Viking, and Scientist*
Cowell, Cressida. *Hiccup the seasick Viking*
Manning, Mick. *What a Viking!*
Schachner, Judith Byron. *Yo, Vikings*
Smallman, Steve. *Dragon stew*

Violence, nonviolence

Adler, David A. *A picture book of Martin Luther King,
  Jr*
Antony, Steve. *Green lizards vs. red rectangles*
Bass, Hester. *Seeds of freedom*
Brown, Monica. *Side by side / Lado a lado*
Bunting, Eve. *The cart that carried Martin*
  Smoky night
Dylan, Bob. *Blowin' in the wind*
Evans, Shane W. *We march*
Farris, Christine King. *March on!*
  My brother Martin
Halperin, Wendy Anderson. *Peace*
Jackson, Jill. *Let there be peace on earth*
Katz, Karen. *Can you say peace?*
Kelley, Kitty. *Martin's dream day*
Kimmel, Elizabeth Cody. *A taste of freedom*
King, Martin Luther, III.. *My daddy, Dr. Martin
  Luther King, Jr.*
King, Martin Luther, Jr.. *I have a dream*
Kittinger, Jo S. *Rosa's bus*
Leaf, Munro. *The story of Ferdinand the bull*
Lennon, John. *Imagine*
Levy, Debbie. *We shall overcome*
McGinty, Alice B. *Gandhi*
Meltzer, Brad. *I am Rosa Parks*
Nelson, Kadir. *Nelson Mandela*
Nettleton, Pamela Hill. *Martin Luther King, Jr*
Peet, Bill. *The pinkish, purplish, bluish egg*
Pinkney, Andrea Davis. *Martin and Mahalia*
Ramsey, Calvin Alexander. *Belle, the last mule at
  Gee's Bend*
Rappaport, Doreen. *Frederick's journey*
  Martin's big words
Ringgold, Faith. *My dream of Martin Luther King*
Roth, Susan L. *Hands around the library*
Smith, Charles R. *Twenty-eight days*
Thompson, Lauren. *The forgiveness garden*
Watkins, Angela Farris. *Love will see you through*
  My Uncle Martin's big heart
  My Uncle Martin's words for America
Weatherford, Carole Boston. *Be a King: Dr. Martin
  Luther King Jr.'s dream and you*
  Voice of freedom
Winter, Jeanette. *Malala, a brave girl from Pakistan /
  Iqbal, a brave boy from Pakistan*
Yousafzai, Malala. *Malala's magic pencil*

Vocabulary *see* Language

Volcanoes

Branley, Franklyn M. *Volcanoes*, ill. by Megan Lloyd
    Volcanoes, ill. by Marc Simont
Geisert, Arthur. *The giant seed*
Greenwood, Rosie. *I wonder why volcanoes blow their tops*
Grifalconi, Ann. *The village of round and square houses*
Kimmel, Eric A. *The two mountains*
Peters, Lisa Westberg. *Volcano wakes up!*
Schaefer, Lola M. *An island grows*
Tonatiuh, Duncan. *The princess and the warrior*

Wagons *see* Toys – wagons

Waiters *see* Careers – waiters, waitresses

Waitresses *see* Careers – waiters, waitresses

War

Antony, Steve. *Green lizards vs. red rectangles*
Bartoletti, Susan Campbell. *The flag maker*
Biden, Jill. *Don't forget, God bless our troops*
Brown, Don. *Henry and the cannons*
Brunhoff, Laurent de. *Babar's battle*
Bunting, Eve. *The blue and the gray*
    Gleam and Glow
    One candle
    So far from the sea
    The wall
Carbone, Elisa. *Diana's White House garden*
Chaconas, Dori. *Pennies in a jar*
Coerr, Eleanor. *Sadako*
Collins, Suzanne. *Year of the jungle*
Deedy, Carmen Agra. *The yellow star*
Demi. *Joan of Arc*
Dennis, Major Brian. *Nubs*
DiLorenzo, Barbara. *Renato and the lion*
Elvgren, Jennifer. *The whispering town*
Fleming, Candace. *Boxes for Katje*
Fullerton, Alma. *A good trade*
Garland, Sherry. *The lotus seed*
Goble, Paul. *Death of the iron horse*
Gottesfeld, Jeff. *The tree in the courtyard*
Greenfield, Eloise. *Easter parade*
Harness, Cheryl. *Mary Walker wears the pants*
Harvey, Jeanne Walker. *Maya Lin: artist-architect of light and lines*
Hearne, Betsy Gould. *Seven brave women*

Heide, Florence Parry. *Sami and the time of the troubles*
Helmer, Marilyn. *One splendid tree*
Holbrook, Stewart. *America's Ethan Allen*
Hopkinson, Deborah. *Knit your bit*
Johnson, Angela. *Wind flyers*
Keefer, Janice Kulyk. *Anna's goat*
Kobald, Irena. *My two blankets*
Lee, Milly. *Nim and the war effort*
Lee-Tai, Amy. *A place where sunflowers grow / Sabaku ni saita himawari*
Littlesugar, Amy. *Lisette's angel*
Longfellow, Henry Wadsworth. *Paul Revere's ride*
    Paul Revere's ride: the landlord's tale
Lyon, George Ella. *Cecil's story*
McCain, Meghan. *My dad, John McCain*
McElroy, Lisa Tucker. *Love, Lizzie*
Mckee, David. *Six men*
McPhail, David. *No!*
McQuinn, Anna. *My friend Jamal*
Mochizuki, Ken. *Baseball saved us*
Moss, Marissa. *Sky high*
Nadel, Carolina. *Daddy's home*
Oberman, Sheldon. *By the Hanukkah light*
O'Brien, Anne Sibley. *A path of stars*
Paterson, John. *Blueberries for the queen*
Pin, Isabel. *The seed*
Poffenberger, Nancy M. *September 11, 2001*
Polacco, Patricia. *The butterfly*
Poole, Josephine. *Joan of Arc*
Preus, Margi. *The Peace Bell*
Pringle, Laurence P. *One room school*
Radunsky, Vladimir. *Manneken pis*
Rappaport, Doreen. *Freedom ship*
    The secret seder
Raven, Margot Theis. *Mercedes and the chocolate pilot*
Rumford, James. *Silent music*
Russo, Marisabina. *I will come back for you*
Ruth, Greg. *Coming home*
Sandman, Rochel. *Perfect porridge*
Sanna, Francesca. *The journey*
Seuss, Dr. *The butter battle book*
Shea, Pegi Deitz. *The whispering cloth*
Tibo, Gilles. *The grand journey of Mr. Man*
Turner, Ann Warren. *When Mr. Jefferson came to Philadelphia*
Ungerer, Tomi. *Otto: the autobiography of a teddy bear*
Vander Zee, Ruth. *Always with you*
Wade, Mary Dodson. *Cinco de Mayo*
Weber, Elka. *The Yankee at the seder*
Wells, Rosemary. *The language of doves*
Wild, Margaret. *The treasure box*
Winnick, Karen B. *Sybil's night ride*
Winter, Jeanette. *The librarian of Basra*
Woodson, Jacqueline. *Coming on home soon*
Yamasaki, Katie. *Fish for Jimmy*
Yolen, Jane. *All those secrets of the world*
Youme. *Mali under the night sky*
Zhang, Song Nan. *The ballad of Mulan*
Ziefert, Harriet. *A new coat for Anna*

Washing machines *see* Machines

Watches *see* Clocks, watches

Water

Atwell, Debby. *River*
Bang, Molly. *Rivers of sunlight*
Base, Graeme. *The water hole*
Cobb, Vicki. *I get wet*
Cole, Joanna. *The magic school bus at the waterworks*
Cullen, Catherine Ann. *Thirsty baby*
Doyle, Malachy. *Splash, Joshua, splash!*
Gibbons, Gail. *It's raining!*
Graham, Joan Bransfield. *Splish splash*
Greenfield, Eloise. *Water, water*
Grobler, Piet. *Hey, frog!*
Hamilton, K. R. *This is the ocean*
Jenkins, Emily. *Water in the park*
Johnson, Neil. *The falling raindrop*
Kalz, Jill. *Water*
Kerley, Barbara. *A cool drink of water*
Kessler, Cristina. *My great-grandmother's gourd*
Lennon, Julian. *Touch the earth*
Locker, Thomas. *Water dance*
Lucado, Max. *All you ever need*
Lyon, George Ella. *All the water in the world*
MacDonald, Margaret Read. *Give up, Gecko!*
McDonnell, Flora. *Splash!*
McGhee, Alison. *Making a friend*
McPhail, David. *Water boy*
Mora, Pat. *Water rolls, water rises / el agua ruda, el agua sube*
Morrison, Gordon. *A drop of water*
Paul, Miranda. *Water is water*
Peters, Lisa Westberg. *Water's way*
Riley, Linda Capus. *Elephants swim*
Ryder, Joanne. *The waterfall's gift*
Salas, Laura Purdie. *Water can be . . .*
Sayre, April Pulley. *Raindrops roll*
Seim, Donna Marie. *Where is Simon, Sandy?*
Seuling, Barbara. *Drip! drop!*
Seven, John. *The ocean story*
Sookocheff, Carey. *Wet*
Stein, David Ezra. *Ice boy*
Strauss, Rochelle. *One well*
Trenc, Milan. *Another night at the museum*
Turk, Evan. *The storyteller*
Verboven, Agnes. *Ducks like to swim*
Verde, Susan. *The water princess*
Wallace, Nancy Elizabeth. *Water! water! water!*
Wells, Robert E. *Did a dinosaur drink this water?*
Weninger, Brigitte. *Precious water*
Yolen, Jane. *Letting Swift River go*
    A mirror to nature

Weapons

Emberley, Barbara. *Drummer Hoff*
Könnecke, Ole. *Anton and the battle*
Krensky, Stephen. *Shooting for the moon*

Weather

Anholt, Catherine. *Sun, snow, stars, sky*
Baird, Audrey B. *A cold snap!*
Barrett, Judi. *Cloudy with a chance of meatballs*
    Cloudy with a chance of meatballs 3
    Pickles to Pittsburgh
Bauer, Marion Dane. *If frogs made the weather*
Berger, Melvin. *How's the weather?*
Blackstone, Stella. *Bear in sunshine*
Branley, Franklyn M. *Down comes the rain*
    Rain and hail

Brown, Margaret Wise. *The little island*
Canyon, Christopher. *John Denver's Sunshine on my shoulders*
Carlstrom, Nancy White. *What does the sky say?*
Chambers, Catherine. *Heat wave*
Cole, Joanna. *The magic school bus and the climate challenge*
Cousins, Lucy. *Maisy's wonderful weather book*
Crews, Donald. *Cloudy day/sunny day*
Denega, Danielle. *Rain or shine*
DeWitt, Lyndia. *What will the weather be?*
Dodds, Dayle Ann. *Hello, sun!*
Gibbons, Gail. *Weather words and what they mean*
Guiberson, Brenda Z. *Earth*
Harper, Jamie. *Miss Mingo weathers the storm*
Henkes, Kevin. *Waiting*
Hill, Eric. *Spot looks at weather*
Hines, Anna Grossnickle. *What can you do in the sun?*
Holub, Joan. *Groundhog weather school*
Howell, Will C. *I call it sky*
Inkpen, Mick. *Kipper's book of weather*
Jackson, Ellen. *April*
    August
    December
    February
    January
    July
    June
    March
    May
    November
    October
    September
Kespert, Deborah. *Rain and shine*
Krupinski, Loretta. *Pirate treasure*
Kudlinski, Kathleen V. *Boy, were we wrong about the weather!*
Let's count the raindrops
Livinson, Nancy Smiler. *North Pole, South Pole*
Locker, Thomas. *Water dance*
McCloskey, Robert. *Time of wonder*
MacLennan, Cathy. *Chicky Chicky Chook Chook*
Marshak, S. *The Month-Brothers*
Michaels, Pat. *W is for wind*
O'Mara, Carmel. *Sunny day*
Peters, Lisa Westberg. *The sun, the wind and the rain*
    Water's way
Rogers, Paul. *What will the weather be like today?*
Ryan, Pam Muñoz. *There was no snow on Christmas Eve*
Schmidt, Karen Lee. *Carl's nose*
Singer, Marilyn. *On the same day in March*
Spinelli, Eileen. *Heat wave*
Stevenson, James. *Heat wave at Mud Flat*
Tresselt, Alvin R. *Sun up*
Vigna, Judith. *Boot weather*
Zolotow, Charlotte. *The storm book*

Weather – blizzards

Cordell, Matthew. *Wolf in the snow*
Crummel, Susan Stevens. *Ten-Gallon Bart beats the heat*
Figley, Marty Rhodes. *The schoolchildren's blizzard*
Friedman, Laurie. *Ruby Valentine saves the day*
Haas, Rick de. *Peter and the winter sleepers*
Hill, Susanna Leonard. *April Fool, Phyllis!*

Hobbie, Holly. *Toot and Puddle, I'll be home for Christmas*
Hurst, Carol Otis. *Terrible storm*
Joosse, Barbara. *A houseful of Christmas*
Regan, Dian Curtis. *The Snow Blew Inn*
Rocco, John. *Blizzard*
Spinelli, Eileen. *Coming through the blizzard*
Wright, Betty Ren. *The blizzard*

Weather – clouds

Arqués, Isabel M. *Ken's cloud*
Carle, Eric. *Little cloud*
Catchpool, Michael. *The cloud spinner*
dePaola, Tomie. *The cloud book*
Holm, Jennifer L. *I'm Grumpy*
Hoshino, Felicia. *Sora and the cloud*
Lichtenheld, Tom. *Cloudette*
Locker, Thomas. *Cloud dance*
Morrison, Toni. *Little Cloud and Lady Wind*
Niemann, Christoph. *The police cloud*
Rockwell, Anne. *Clouds*
Shaw, Charles Green. *It looked like spilt milk*
Wiesner, David. *Sector 7*

Weather – cold

Aillaud, Cindy Lou. *Recess at 20 below*
Chambers, Catherine. *Big freeze*
Powell, Consie. *The first day of winter*
Spinelli, Eileen. *Cold snap*
    Together at Christmas

Weather – droughts

Aardema, Verna. *Bringing the rain to Kapiti Plain*
Conway, David. *Lila and the secret of rain*
Faundez, Anne. *The day the rains fell*
Hamilton, Virginia. *Drylongso*
Kamkwamba, William. *The boy who harnessed the wind*
Kessler, Cristina. *My great-grandmother's gourd*
Lind, Michael. *Bluebonnet girl*
Marino, Gianna. *Meet me at the moon*
Markle, Sandra. *Thirsty, thirsty elephants*
Meunier, Brian. *Bravo, Tavo!*
Peterson, Jeanne Whitehouse. *Don't forget Winona*
Rappaport, Doreen. *The long-haired girl*
Ray, Jane. *The apple-pip princess*
Turk, Evan. *The storyteller*
Young, Ed. *The cat from Hunger Mountain*

Weather – floods

Arenson, Roberta. *Manu and the talking fish*
Auld, Mary. *Noah's ark*
Cousins, Lucy. *Noah's ark*
Cullen, Lynn. *Little Scraggly Hair*
Dubuc, Marianne. *The animals' ark*
Eitzen, Ruth. *Tara's flight*
Emberley, Barbara. *One wide river to cross*
Goble, Paul. *Remaking the earth*
Goldsboro, Bobby. *Noah and the ark; and, David and Goliath*
Goodhart, Pippa. *Noah makes a boat*
Harker, Lesley. *Annie's ark*
Harrison, Troon. *The floating orchard*
Jonas, Ann. *Aardvarks, disembark!*
Kinsey-Warnock, Natalie. *Nora's ark*
Krensky, Stephen. *Noah's bark*

Kurtz, Jane. *River friendly, river wild*
Lloyd-Jones, Sally. *Old MacNoah had an ark*
Lyon, George Ella. *Come a tide*
McCarthy, Michael. *The story of Noah and the ark*
MacDonald, Alan. *Wilfred to the rescue*
McKee, David. *Elmer and the flood*
Maggi, María Elena. *The great canoe*
Oelschlager, Vanita. *I came from the water*
Paley, Joan. *One more river*
Pfeffer, Wendy. *The big flood*
Pinkney, Jerry. *Noah's ark*
Rosen, Michael J. *The dog who walked with God*
Schneider, Josh. *You'll be sorry*
Shapiro, Zachary. *We're all in the same boat*
Singer, Isaac Bashevis. *Why Noah chose the dove*
Spier, Peter. *Noah's ark*
Stewart, Paul. *Rabbit's wish*
Stewig, John Warren. *The animals watched*
Sting [Musician]. *Rock steady*
Tebbs, Victoria. *Noah's Ark story*
Uhlberg, Myron. *A storm called Katrina*
Villa, Alvaro F. *Flood*
Walton, Rick. *Noah's square dance*
Wilson, Anne. *Noah's ark*
Woelfle, Gretchen. *Katje the windmill cat*

Weather – fog

McDonnell, Patrick. *Just like Heaven*
MacLear, Kyo. *The fog*
May, Robert L. *Rudolph the red-nosed reindeer*
Tresselt, Alvin R. *Hide and seek fog*
Trotter, Deborah W. *How do you know?*

Weather – hurricanes

Berne, Jennifer. *Calvin can't fly*
Bildner, Phil. *Marvelous Cornelius*
Cole, Joanna. *The magic school bus inside a hurricane*
Demas, Corinne. *Hurricane!*
Gibbons, Gail. *Hurricanes!*
Lakin, Patricia. *Hurricane!*
Larson, Kirby. *Two Bobbies*
London, Jonathan. *Hurricane!*
Paterson, Diane. *Hurricane wolf*
Rose, Caroline Starr. *Over in the wetlands*
Uhlberg, Myron. *A storm called Katrina*
Watson, Renée. *A place where hurricanes happen*
Zelch, Patti R. *Ready, set . . . wait!*

Weather – lightning, thunder

Atteberry, Kevan. *Puddles!!!*
Bauer, Marion Dane. *Dinosaur thunder*
Bluemle, Elizabeth. *Tap tap boom boom*
Bourgeois, Paulette. *Franklin and the thunderstorm*
Branley, Franklyn M. *Flash, crash, rumble, and roll*
Bryan, Ashley. *The story of lightning and thunder*
Cotten, Cynthia. *Rain play*
Crum, Shutta. *Thunder-Boomer!*
Geisert, Arthur. *Thunderstorm*
Gorbachev, Valeri. *Catty Jane who hated the rain*
    Dragon is coming!
Griessman, Annette. *Like a hundred drums*
Hines, Anna Grossnickle. *Rumble thumble boom!*
Hobbie, Holly. *Toot and Puddle, you are my sunshine*
Hutchins, Hazel. *One dark night*
McPhail, David. *Weezer changes the world*
Mortensen, Denise Dowling. *Ohio thunder*
Polacco, Patricia. *Thunder cake*

Ray, Mary Lyn. *Boom!*
Shepard, Aaron. *Master man*
Swenson, Jamie A. *Boom! boom! boom!*

Weather – mist *see* Weather – fog

Weather – rain

Aardema, Verna. *Bringing the rain to Kapiti Plain*
Alemagna, Beatrice. *On a magical do-nothing day*
Appelt, Kathi. *Rain dance*
Arnosky, Jim. *Rabbits and raindrops*
Arqués, Isabel M. *Ken's cloud*
Ashman, Linda. *Rain!*
Atteberry, Kevan. *Puddles!!!*
Auld, Mary. *Noah's ark*
Baird, Audrey B. *Storm coming!*
Base, Graeme. *The water hole*
Beaumont, Karen. *Move over, Rover*
Bentley, Dawn. *Fuzzy bear*
Bluemle, Elizabeth. *Tap tap boom boom*
Boswell, Addie. *The rain stomper*
Branley, Franklyn M. *Down comes the rain*
    Rain and hail
Bridges, Margaret Park. *I love the rain*
Burningham, John. *Mr. Gumpy's motor car*
Carle, Eric. *Little cloud*
Cocca-Leffler, Maryann. *Let it rain*
Colborn, Mary Palenick. *Rainy day slug*
Colby, Rebecca. *It's raining bats and frogs*
Conway, David. *Lila and the secret of rain*
Cotten, Cynthia. *Rain play*
Cousins, Lucy. *Noah's ark*
Crews, Nina. *You are here*
Crimi, Carolyn. *Tessa's tip-tapping toes*
Cullen, Lynn. *Little Scraggly Hair*
Dawavendewa, Gerald. *The butterfly dance*
De Roo, Elena. *The rain train*
Docherty, Thomas. *To the beach*
Dubuc, Marianne. *The animals' ark*
Edwards, Pamela Duncan. *Warthogs paint*
Ehlert, Lois. *Rain fish*
Emberley, Barbara. *One wide river to cross*
Feiffer, Kate. *My side of the car*
Freed, Arthur. *Singing in the rain*
Freeman, Don. *Dandelion*
Gammell, Stephen. *Mudkin*
Gibbons, Gail. *It's raining!*
Gibson, Amy. *Split! splat!*
Ginsburg, Mirra. *Mushroom in the rain*
Goodhart, Pippa. *Noah makes a boat*
Gorbachev, Valeri. *Catty Jane who hated the rain*
    Nicky and the rainy day
    One rainy day
Gutman, Anne. *Gaspard and Lisa's rainy day*
Hafner, Marylin. *Molly and Emmett's camping adventure*
Harker, Lesley. *Annie's ark*
Harrison, Troon. *The floating orchard*
Herman, Charlotte. *First rain*
Hesse, Karen. *Come on, rain*
Hines, Anna Grossnickle. *What can you do in the rain?*
Hoban, Julia. *Amy loves the rain*
Inkpen, Mick. *Kipper's rainy day*
    Splosh!
Jackson, Richard. *This beautiful day*
Johanasen, Heather. *About the rain forest*

Johnson, Angela. *Rain feet*
Johnson, D. B. *Henry works*
Johnson, Neil. *The falling raindrop*
Jonas, Ann. *Aardvarks, disembark!*
Jones, Elizabeth. *Sunshine and Storm*
Kalan, Robert. *Rain*
Kaner, Etta. *Who likes the rain?*
Keats, Ezra Jack. *A letter to Amy*
Krensky, Stephen. *Noah's bark*
Kurtz, Jane. *Rain romp*
Lakin, Patricia. *Rainy day*
Lee, Jeanne M. *Toad is the uncle of heaven*
Lehman, Barbara. *Rainstorm*
Lewis, Anne Margaret. *Puddle jumpers*
Lewison, Wendy Cheyette. *So many boots*
Lichtenheld, Tom. *Cloudette*
Liu, Jae Soo. *Yellow umbrella*
London, Jonathan. *Duck and Hippo in the rainstorm*
    Puddles
    What the animals were waiting for
McCanna, Tim. *Watersong*
McCarthy, Michael. *The story of Noah and the ark*
McKee, David. *Elmer and the flood*
Macken, JoAnn Early. *Waiting out the storm*
McPhail, David. *The puddle*
Maggi, María Elena. *The great canoe*
Manning, Maurie J. *The aunts go marching*
Markle, Sandra. *Toad weather*
Martin, Bill, Jr.. *Listen to the rain*
Martin, David. *Peep and Ducky: rainy day*
Millard, Glenda. *And red galoshes*
Mitchell, Marianne. *Gullywasher gulch*
Miyares, Daniel. *Float*
Munsch, Robert N. *Mud puddle*
Olaleye, Isaac. *In the Rainfield*
O'Mara, Carmel. *Rainy day*
Otto, Carolyn. *That sky, that rain*
Paley, Joan. *One more river*
Parker, Mary Jessie. *The deep, deep puddle*
Phelan, Matt. *Druthers*
Pinkney, Jerry. *Noah's ark*
Pinkwater, Daniel. *Rainy morning*
Plourde, Lynn. *Pigs in the mud in the middle of the rud*
Prelutsky, Jack. *Rainy rainy Saturday*
Raschka, Chris. *John Coltrane's giant steps*
Ray, Mary Lyn. *Red rubber boot day*
Rosenthal, Amy Krouse. *Uni the unicorn and the dream come true*
Rumford, James. *Rain school*
Russo, Marisabina. *Little Bird takes a bath*
Salzano, Tammi. *One rainy day*
Sayre, April Pulley. *Raindrops roll*
Scheer, Julian. *Rain makes applesauce*
Schwartz, Roslyn. *The mole sisters and the rainy day*
Sehgal, Kabir. *A bucket of blessings*
Serfozo, Mary. *Rain talk*
Shannon, David. *The rain came down*
Shannon, George. *April showers*
Shapiro, Zachary. *We're all in the same boat*
Sheth, Kashmira. *Monsoon afternoon*
Shulevitz, Uri. *Rain rain rivers*
Singer, Isaac Bashevis. *Why Noah chose the dove*
Spalding, Andrea. *It's raining, it's pouring*
Spetter, Jung-Hee. *Lily and Trooper's winter*
Spier, Peter. *Noah's ark*
    Peter Spier's rain
Stevenson, James. *Heat wave at Mud Flat*
Stewart, Melissa. *When rain falls*

Stewig, John Warren. *The animals watched*
Sting [Musician]. *Rock steady*
Stock, Catherine. *Gugu's house*
Stojic, Manya. *Rain*
Sykes, Julie. *Smudge*
Tebbs, Victoria. *Noah's Ark story*
Todd, Barbara. *The rainmaker*
Tresselt, Alvin R. *Rain drop splash*
Usher, Sam. *Rain*
Verboven, Agnes. *Ducks like to swim*
Vincent, Gabrielle. *Ernest and Celestine's picnic*
Walton, Rick. *Noah's square dance*
White, Dianne. *Blue on blue*
Wilson, Anne. *Noah's ark*
Yaccarino, Dan. *Happyland: rainy day*
Yashima, Taro. *Umbrella*
Yee, Wong Herbert. *Who likes rain?*
Yum, Hyewon. *Puddle*
Zolotow, Charlotte. *The quarreling book*
　The storm book

Weather – rainbows

Asch, Frank. *Skyfire*
Auld, Mary. *Noah's ark*
Barry, Frances. *Duckie's rainbow*
Callahan, Sean. *The leprechaun who lost his rainbow*
Cousins, Lucy. *Noah's ark*
Cullen, Lynn. *Little Scraggly Hair*
Goodhart, Pippa. *Noah makes a boat*
Harburg, E. Y. *Over the rainbow*
Hines, Anna Grossnickle. *What can you do in the sun?*
Horácek, Petr. *A surprise for Tiny Mouse*
Krupp, E. C. *The rainbow and you*
Lyon, George Ella. *My friend, the starfinder*
Paley, Joan. *One more river*
Pinkney, Jerry. *Noah's ark*
Pinkney, Sandra L. *A rainbow all around me*
Shannon, David. *The rain came down*
Singer, Isaac Bashevis. *Why Noah chose the dove*
Sting [Musician]. *Rock steady*
Walsh, Melanie. *Ned's rainbow*
Wilson, Anne. *Noah's ark*
Zolotow, Charlotte. *The storm book*

Weather – sandstorms

London, Jonathan. *Ali, child of the desert*

Weather – snow

Aillaud, Cindy Lou. *Recess at 20 below*
Alarcón, Francisco X. *Iguanas in the snow and other winter poems / Iguanas en la nieve y otros poemas de invierno*
Alborough, Jez. *Ice cream bear*
Andrews, Julie. *The very fairy princess sparkles in the snow*
Arnold, Marsha Diane. *Waiting for snow*
Arqués, Isabel M. *Ken's cloud*
Bahr, Mary. *My brother loved snowflakes*
Bean, Jonathan. *Big snow*
Beck, Ian. *Teddy's snowy day*
Berger, Carin. *A perfect day*
Berry, Lynne. *Duck skates*
Bildner, Phil. *Turkey Bowl*
Blackstone, Stella. *Cleo in the snow*
Bradby, Marie. *The longest wait*
Branley, Franklyn M. *Snow is falling*

Brett, Jan. *The three snow bears*
Bruchac, James. *Rabbit's snow dance*
Brunelle, Nicholas. *Snow moon*
Burton, Virginia Lee. *Katy and the big snow*
Butler, M. Christina. *Snow friends*
Butterworth, Nick. *One snowy night*
Bynum, Janie. *Altoona up north*
Carle, Eric. *Dream snow*
Carlstrom, Nancy White. *Mama, will it snow tonight?*
　The snow speaks
Casanova, Mary. *One-dog sleigh*
Cassino, Mark, with Jon Nelson. *The story of snow*
Chessa, Francesca. *Holly's red boots*
Child, Lauren. *Snow is my favorite and my best*
Colandro, Lucille. *There was a cold lady who swallowed some snow!*
Cole, Henry. *Trudy*
Cordell, Matthew. *Wolf in the snow*
Corderoy, Tracey. *Just right for two*
Cote, Nancy. *It feels like snow*
Cotten, Cynthia. *Snow ponies*
Cox, Judy. *Snow day for Mouse*
Crews, Nina. *Snowball*
Crisp, Marty. *Totally polar*
Croll, Carolyn. *The little snowgirl*
Curious George in the snow
Cuyler, Margery. *The biggest, best snowman*
da Costa, Deborah. *Snow in Jerusalem*
Dahl, Michael. *Footprints in the snow*
Day, Alexandra. *Carl's snowy afternoon*
deGroat, Diane. *Jingle bells, homework smells*
Denslow, Sharon Phillips. *In the snow*
DePrisco, Dorothea. *Snowbear's winter day*
Dooley, Norah. *Everybody serves soup*
Dunrea, Olivier. *It's snowing*
Emmett, Jonathan. *Diamond in the snow*
Fallon, Jimmy. *Snowball fight!*
Fearnley, Jan. *A perfect day for it*
Fitch, Sheree. *No two snowflakes*
Fleischman, Paul. *Lost!*
Fleming, Denise. *The first day of winter*
Ford, Bernette. *First snow*
Gammell, Stephen. *Is that you, winter?*
Garland, Michael. *Super snow day seek and find*
Garoche, Camille. *The snow rabbit*
Gay, Marie-Louise. *Stella, queen of the snow*
George, Jean Craighead. *Snow bear*
Gershator, Phillis. *When it starts to snow*
Gibbons, Gail. *It's snowing!*
Gill, Deirdre. *Outside*
Gliori, Debi. *The snow lambs*
Gorbachev, Valeri. *Me too!*
Gore, Leonid. *Danny's first snow*
Gravett, Emily. *Bear and Hare: snow!*
Hächler, Bruno. *Anna's wish*
Hader, Berta Hoerner. *The big snow*
Halpern, Julie. *Toby and the snowflakes*
Harper, Lee. *Snow! snow! snow!*
Hawcock, Claire. *Mine, all mine!*
Heiligman, Deborah. *Snow dog, go dog*
Helquist, Brett. *Bedtime for Bear*
Henkes, Kevin. *Oh!*
Hest, Amy. *Charley's first night*
　The reader
　When Charley met Grampa
Hines, Anna Grossnickle. *What can you do in the snow?*
Hissey, Jane. *Jolly snow*

Hoban, Julia. *Amy loves the snow*
Hobbie, Holly. *Toot and Puddle: let it snow*
    Toot and Puddle, I'll be home for Christmas
Hubbell, Patricia. *Snow happy!*
Huneck, Stephen. *Sally's snow adventure*
Inkpen, Mick. *Kipper's snowy day*
Iwamura, Kazuo. *Hooray for snow!*
Jenkins, Emily. *Toys meet snow*
Jennings, Linda. *Little puppy lost*
Joosse, Barbara. *Snow day!*
Joyce, William. *Snowie Rolie*
Judge, Lita. *Hoot and Peep: a song for snow*
Kaneko, Yuki. *Into the snow*
Katz, Karen. *Baby loves winter!*
Keats, Ezra Jack. *The snowy day*
Keller, Holly. *Geraldine's big snow*
Kneen, Maggie. *The Christmas surprise*
Koehler, Lora. *The little snowplow*
Krauss, Ruth. *The happy day*
Kroll, Virginia L. *Good citizen Sarah*
Lakin, Patricia. *Snow day!*
Laminack, Lester L. *Snow day!*
Landry, Leo. *The snow ghosts*
Lasky, Kathryn. *Lucille's snowsuit*
Lewis, Kim. *First snow*
Lin, Grace. *Robert's snowflakes*
London, Jonathan. *Froggy gets dressed*
Long, Loren. *An Otis Christmas*
McCarty, Peter. *First snow*
McCully, Emily Arnold. *First snow*
    An outlaw Thanksgiving
McGuirk, Leslie. *Tucker flips!*
McKee, David. *Elmer in the snow*
MacLachlan, Patricia. *Snowflakes fall*
McPhail, David. *Peter loves Penguin*
McQuade, Jacqueline. *Snow babies*
Mahoney, Daniel J. *A really good snowman*
Marlow, Layn. *You make me smile*
Martin, Jacqueline Briggs. *Snowflake Bentley*
Marzollo, Jean. *Snow angel*
Mercer, Lynn. *Schubert's snowflakes*
Meschenmoser, Sebastian. *Waiting for winter*
Messner, Kate. *Over and under the snow*
Mitton, Tony. *Snowy Bear*
Munsch, Robert N. *Thomas' snowsuit*
Murphy, Yannick. *Baby Polar*
Neubecker, Robert. *Winter is for snow*
Norman, Kim. *If it's snowy and you know it, clap your*
    paws!
O'Malley, Kevin. *Straight to the pole*
Paradis, Susan. *Snow princess*
Parenteau, Shirley. *Bears in the snow*
Park, Bomi. *First snow*
Patten, Brian. *The big snuggle-up*
Peddle, Daniel. *Snow day*
Pendziwol, Jean E. *Once upon a northern night*
Perkins, Lynne Rae. *Snow music*
Petersen, David. *Snowy Valentine*
Pfister, Marcus. *Penguin Pete and Little Tim*
    Snow puppy
Pickering, Jimmy. *It's winter*
Poydar, Nancy. *Snip, snip . . . snow!*
Pulver, Robin. *Axle Annie*
Raczka, Bob. *Snowy, blowy winter*
Raschka, Chris. *John Coltrane's giant steps*
Reid, Barbara. *Perfect snow*
Reynolds, Aaron. *Snowbots*
Rocco, John. *Blizzard*
Rockwell, Anne. *The first snowfall*

Roode, Daniel. *Little Bea and the snowy day*
Root, Phyllis. *Grandmother Winter*
Rosen, Michael J. *Avalanche*
Rosenberg, Liz. *On Christmas eve*
Ross, Tony. *I want snow!*
Rylant, Cynthia. *Little penguins*
    Snow
Sabuda, Robert. *Winter's tale*
Sakai, Komako. *The snow day*
Sanfield, Steve. *Snow*
Savage, Stephen. *Supertruck*
Sayre, April Pulley. *Best in snow*
Schaefer, Carole Lexa. *Snow pumpkin*
Scheffler, Axel. *Pip and Posy: the snowy day*
Schoenherr, Ian. *Pip and Squeak*
Shulevitz, Uri. *Snow*
Siddals, Mary McKenna. *Millions of snowflakes*
Sidman, Joyce. *Before morning*
Simmons, Jane. *Little Fern's first winter*
Slayton, Fran Cannon. *Snowball moon*
Sloat, Teri. *Pablo in the snow*
Soman, David. *Ladybug Girl and the big snow*
Spetter, Jung-Hee. *Lily and Trooper's winter*
Spinelli, Eileen. *Cold snap*
Spohn, Kate. *Snow play*
Stafford, Liliana. *The snow bear*
Stead, Philip C. *Samson in the snow*
Steffensmeier, Alexander. *Millie in the snow*
Steig, William. *Brave Irene*
Stewart, Melissa. *Under the snow*
Stojic, Manya. *Snow*
Sweeney, Linda Booth. *When the snow falls*
Tegen, Katherine Brown. *Snowman magic*
Thomas, Peggy. *Snow dance*
Thompson, Lauren. *Mouse's first snow*
Trasler, Janee. *Mimi and Bear in the snow*
Tresselt, Alvin R. *White snow, bright snow*
Usher, Sam. *Snow*
Van Laan, Nancy. *Moose tales*
Verdick, Elizabeth. *Small Walt*
Waddell, Martin. *Snow bears*
Wahman, Joe. *Snowboy 1, 2, 3*
Wallace, Nancy Elizabeth. *Snow*
Ward, Lindsay. *When Blue met Egg*
Watanabe, Shigeo. *Ice cream is falling!*
Watts, Bernadette. *The smallest snowflake*
Weller, Frances Ward. *The angel of Mill Street*
Wellington, Monica. *Bunny's first snowflake*
Wells, Rosemary. *Red boots*
Whybrow, Ian. *Harry and the snow king*
Williams, Sam. *Snowy magic*
Wilson, Karma. *Dinos in the snow!*
Winget, Susan. *Sam the Snowman*
Young, Ned. *Zoomer's summer snowstorm*
Zolotow, Charlotte. *Something is going to happen*

Weather – storms

Anholt, Catherine. *Chimp and Zee and the big storm*
Asare, Meshack. *Sosu's call*
Baird, Audrey B. *Storm coming!*
Belton, Robyn. *Herbert*
Berger, Barbara. *Thunder Bunny*
Boswell, Addie. *The rain stomper*
Bourgeois, Paulette. *Franklin and the thunderstorm*
Bradby, Marie. *The longest wait*
Branley, Franklyn M. *Tornado alert*
Bright, Paul. *The bears in the bed and the great big*
    storm

Brown, Alan James. *Hoot and Holler*
Bryan, Ashley. *The story of lightning and thunder*
Burdett, Lois. *The tempest for kids*
Burton, LeVar. *The rhino who swallowed a storm*
Chiew, Suzanne. *When you need a friend*
Claire, Céline. *Shelter*
Crews, Donald. *Sail away*
Crum, Shutta. *Thunder-Boomer!*
D'Amico, Carmela. *Ella sets sail*
Davies, Benji. *The storm whale in winter*
Davol, Marguerite W. *Why butterflies go by on silent wings*
Doyle, Malachy. *Storm cats*
Emmett, Jonathan. *This way, Ruby!*
Ering, Timothy Basil. *The unexpected love story of Alfred Fiddleduckling*
Fisher, Leonard Everett. *Sky, sea, the jetty, and me*
Geisert, Arthur. *Thunderstorm*
George, Jean Craighead. *Cliff hanger*
Gerritsen, Paula. *Nuts*
Gliori, Debi. *Mr. Bear to the rescue*
    The snow lambs
Griessman, Annette. *Like a hundred drums*
Harvey, Brett. *My prairie Christmas*
Haughton, Emma. *Rainy day*
Hines, Anna Grossnickle. *Rumble thumble boom!*
Hobbie, Holly. *Toot and Puddle, I'll be home for Christmas*
    Toot and Puddle, you are my sunshine
Hutchins, Hazel. *One dark night*
Iwamura, Kazuo. *Hooray for summer!*
Jennings, Sharon. *Bearcub and Mama*
Johnson, Amy Crane. *Cinnamon and the April shower / Canela y el aguacero de abril*
Keats, Ezra Jack. *Clementina's cactus*
Kimura, Yuichi. *One stormy night . . .*
Klise, Kate. *Grammy Lamby and the secret handshake*
Krensky, Stephen. *Milo and the really big bunny*
Kuiper, Nannie. *Bravo, brave beavers*
Landström, Olof. *Boo and Baa get wet*
Leeson, Christine. *Molly and the storm*
McBratney, Sam. *Just you and me*
Macken, JoAnn Early. *Waiting out the storm*
McPhail, David. *The Searcher and Old Tree*
Messier, Mireille. *The branch*
Miller, William. *A house by the river*
Miyakoshi, Akiko. *The storm*
Mortensen, Denise Dowling. *Ohio thunder*
Murphy, Yannick. *Baby Polar*
Perrow, Angeli. *Lighthouse dog to the rescue*
Polacco, Patricia. *Thunder cake*
Quackenbush, Robert M. *Batbaby*
Randall, Alison L. *The wheat doll*
Reynolds, Peter H. *Sydney's star*
Root, Phyllis. *Creak! said the bed*
Rosenberg, Liz. *On Christmas eve*
Sadler, Judy Ann. *Sandwiches for Duke*
Sampson, Michael R. *Caddie, the golf dog*
Seeger, Laura Vaccaro. *Walter was worried*
Sidman, Joyce. *Meow ruff*
Stainton, Sue. *The lighthouse cat*
Steig, William. *Brave Irene*
Stolz, Mary. *Storm in the night*
Sutherland, Marc. *MacMurtrey's wall*
Sweeney, Linda Booth. *When the wind blows*
Swenson, Jamie A. *Boom! boom! boom!*
Tafuri, Nancy. *The big storm*
    Will you be my friend?
Trapani, Iza. *Row, row, row your boat*

Van Allsburg, Chris. *The wreck of the Zephyr*
Van Nutt, Julia. *Pumpkins from the sky?*
Viau, Nancy. *Storm song*
Wellington, Monica. *Night rabbits*
White, Dianne. *Blue on blue*
Wiesner, David. *Hurricane*
Williams, Garth. *Benjamin's treasure*
Yolen, Jane. *Before the storm*
Yoon, Salina. *Stormy night*
Young, Ed. *The lost horse*

Weather – thunder *see* Weather – lightning, thunder

Weather – tornadoes

Arnold, Marsha Diane. *The bravest of us all*
Chambers, Catherine. *Tornado*
Drummond, Allan. *Green city*
Fisher, Carolyn. *A twisted tale*
Gibbons, Gail. *Tornadoes!*
Griffin, Kitty. *The foot-stomping adventures of Clementine Sweet*
Lester, Helen. *Batter up Wombat*
Long, Loren. *Otis and the tornado*
Lyon, George Ella. *One lucky girl*
Polacco, Patricia. *The mermaid's purse*
Prigger, Mary Skillings. *Aunt Minnie and the twister*
Sloat, Teri. *Farmer Brown goes round and round*

Weather – wind

Aesop. *The contest between the Sun and the Wind*
Asch, Frank. *Like a windy day*
Bauer, Marion Dane. *The longest night*
Bijsterbosch, Anita. *Whose hat is that?*
Birdsall, Jeanne. *Flora's very windy day*
Brown, Petra. *When the wind blew*
Carlstrom, Nancy White. *How does the wind walk?*
Day, Nancy Raines. *On a windy night*
Derby, Sally. *Whoosh went the wind!*
DiPucchio, Kelly. *What's the magic word?*
Drummond, Allan. *Energy island*
Ehlert, Lois. *Leaf man*
Ets, Marie Hall. *Gilberto and the wind*
Hamilton, Virginia. *Drylongso*
Hines, Anna Grossnickle. *What can you do in the wind?*
Hoban, Julia. *Amy loves the wind*
Huntington, Amy. *One Monday*
Hutchins, Pat. *The wind blew*
Jackson, Alison. *When the wind blew*
Kaner, Etta. *Who likes the wind?*
Keats, Ezra Jack. *A letter to Amy*
Letourneau, Marie. *Argyle Fox*
McKee, David. *Elmer and the wind*
    Elmer takes off
McMillan, Bruce. *How the ladies stopped the wind*
Manceau, Edouard. *Windblown*
Martin, Bill, Jr.. *Old devil wind*
Mitchell, Robin. *Windy*
Moore, Lilian. *While you were chasing a hat*
Morrison, Toni. *Little Cloud and Lady Wind*
Olaleye, Isaac. *In the Rainfield*
Poydar, Nancy. *Rhyme time Valentine*
Ramirez, Melissa Bourbon. *The flight of the sunflower*
Roberts, Bethany. *The wind's garden*

Salzano, Tammi. *One windy day*
Sweeney, Linda Booth. *When the wind blows*
Teague, David. *The red hat*
Thompson, Lauren. *Mouse's first spring*
White, Linda Arms. *Comes a wind*
Wright, Maureen. *Sneeze, Big Bear, sneeze*
Yankey, Lindsey. *Bluebird*
Zolotow, Charlotte. *When the wind stops*

Weather reporters *see* Careers – meteorologists

Weddings

Ammon, Richard. *An Amish wedding*
Andrews, Julie. *The very fairy princess: here comes the flower girl!*
Austrian, J. J. *Worm loves Worm*
Balian, Lorna. *A sweetheart for Valentine*
Barasch, Lynne. *The reluctant flower girl*
Bottner, Barbara. *Flower girl*
Brannen, Sarah S. *Uncle Bobby's wedding*
Broach, Elise. *Wet dog!*
Brown, Marc. *D. W. thinks big*
Bunting, Eve. *My mom's wedding*
Cooper, Floyd. *The ring bearer*
Crunk, Tony. *Railroad John and the Red Rock run*
English, Karen. *Nadia's hands*
Finchler, Judy. *Congratulations, Miss Malarkey!*
Friedman, Laurie. *A style all her own*
A frog he would a-wooing go [folk-song]. *Frog went a-courting*
  Froggie went a courting
  Froggy went a-courtin'
Furgang, Kathy. *Flower girl*
Gantos, Jack. *Wedding bells for Rotten Ralph*
Grimm, Jacob and Wilhelm *The goose girl*
  Snow White and the seven dwarfs
Harper, Charise Mericle. *Superlove*
Hartt-Sussman, Heather. *Nana's getting married*
Henkes, Kevin. *El gran día de Lily / Lilly's big day*
  Lilly's big day
Holabird, Katharine. *Angelina and the royal wedding*
Jaffe, Nina. *The way meat loves salt*
Jewell, Nancy. *Alligator wedding*
Johnson, Angela. *The wedding*
Johnston, Tony. *The cowboy and the black-eyed pea*
Kraegel, Kenneth. *Green pants*
LaTeef, Nelda. *The hunter and the ebony tree*
Lloyd-Jones, Sally. *How to get married by me, the bride*
Look, Lenore. *Uncle Peter's amazing Chinese wedding*
Lyons, Kelly Starling. *Ellen's broom*
Marshall, Janet Perry. *A honey of a day*
Masini, Beatrice. *Here comes the bride*
Mathers, Petra. *Dodo gets married*
Morris, Ann. *Weddings*
Munsch, Robert N. *Ribbon rescue*
Newman, Lesléa. *Donovan's big day*
Nobisso, Josephine. *The weight of a Mass*
O'Connor, Jane. *Fancy Nancy and the wedding of the century*
Pilkey, Dav. *The Silly Gooses*
Polacco, Patricia. *Someone for Mr. Sussman*
Rylant, Cynthia. *The bookshop dog*
Sierra, Judy. *The beautiful butterfly*
Soto, Gary. *Snapshots from the wedding*
Stadler, John. *The cats of Mrs. Calamari*
Stanley, Mandy. *Lettice the flower girl*
Summers, Kate. *Milly's wedding*

Van Laan, Nancy. *La boda*
Wells, Rosemary. *Max and Ruby at the Warthogs' wedding*
Wright, Courtni Crump. *Jumping the broom*
Yep, Laurence. *The Khan's daughter*
Yorinks, Arthur. *Company's going*
Young, Ed. *Mouse match*
Zalben, Jane Breskin. *Beni's first wedding*
Ziefert, Harriet. *Grandma's wedding album*

Weekdays *see* Days of the week, months of the year

West *see* U.S. history – frontier & pioneer life

Wheelchairs *see* Disabilities – physical disabilities

Wheels

Berenstain, Stan and Jan. *Bears on wheels*
Pearson, Debora. *Sophie's wheels*
Prince, April Jones. *What do wheels do all day?*
Rotner, Shelley. *Wheels around*

Whistles

Egielski, Richard. *Three magic balls*
Schaefer, Carole Lexa. *The little French whistle*

Wildlife rescue *see* Character traits – kindness to animals

Willfulness *see* Character traits – willfulness

Wisdom *see* Character traits – wisdom

Wishing *see* Behavior – wishing

Witches

Adams, Adrienne. *A Halloween happening*
  A woggle of witches
Alexander, Sue. *Who goes out on Halloween?*
Alley, R. W. *There once was a witch*
Andersen, Hans Christian. *The tinderbox*, ill. by Warwick Hutton
  The tinderbox, ill. by Barry Moser
Baeten, Lieve. *The clever little witch*
  The curious little witch
  Happy birthday, Little Witch!
Balian, Lorna. *Humbug witch*
Barrett, Judi. *Which witch is which?*
Bateson-Hill, Margaret. *Masha and the firebird*
Bell, Anthea. *Vasilisa the beautiful*
Berry, Lynne. *The curious demise of a contrary cat*
Bridwell, Norman. *The witch grows up*
  The witch next door
Brokamp, Elizabeth. *The picky little witch*
Brown, Lisa. *Vampire boy's good night*
Christian, Cheryl. *Witches*
Cohen, Caron Lee. *Broom, zoom!*
Colby, Rebecca. *It's raining bats and frogs*

Wizards

Brunhoff, Laurent de. *Babar and the succotash bird*
Clibbon, Meg. *Imagine you're a wizard!*
Fox, Mem. *The magic hat*
Morrissey, Dean. *The wizard mouse*
Prelutsky, Jack. *The wizard*
Robertson, M. P. *The dragon snatcher*
Seder, Rufus Butler. *The Wizard of Oz*
Tom Thumb. *The adventures of Tom Thumb*
Walsh, Ellen Stoll. *Mouse magic*
Yolen, Jane. *The firebird*

Woodchucks *see* Animals – groundhogs

Woods *see* Forest, woods

Word games *see* Language

Wordless

Aliki. *Tabby*
Andreasen, Dan. *The treasure bath*
Anno, Mitsumasa. *Anno's Britain*
   Anno's counting book
   Anno's counting house
   Anno's Italy
   Anno's journey
   Anno's U.S.A.
Arnosky, Jim. *Mouse letters*
   Mouse numbers and letters
   Mouse writing
   Mud time and more
Baker, Jeannie. *Mirror*
   Window
Bang, Molly. *The grey lady and the strawberry snatcher*
Barros, Bruna. *The carpenter*
Becker, Aaron. *Journey*
   Quest
   Return
Borando, Silvia. *Now you see me, now you don't*
Boyd, Lizi. *Flashlight*
   Inside outside
Briggs, Raymond. *Father Christmas*
   The snowman
Camcam, Princesse. *Fox's garden*
Carle, Eric. *Do you want to be my friend?*
   I see a song
Ceelen, Vicky. *Baby! baby!*
Cole, Henry. *Spot, the cat*
   Unspoken
Colón, Raúl. *Draw!*
Cordell, Matthew. *Wolf in the snow*
Cosentino, Ralph. *The marvelous misadventures of*
   — Fun-Boy
Crews, Donald. *Truck*
Day, Alexandra. *Carl goes shopping*
   Carl's snowy afternoon
   Follow Carl!
   Good dog, Carl
dePaola, Tomie. *Pancakes for breakfast*
Desrosiers, Sylvie. *Hocus Pocus*
   Hocus Pocus takes the train
Devernay, Laëtitia. *The conductor*
Doremus, Gaëtan. *Bear despair*
Dornbusch, Erica. *Finding Kate's shoes*
Dudley, Rebecca. *Hank finds an egg*

Dupasquier, Philippe. *1 2 3, follow me!*
Emberley, Ed. *Ed Emberley's big green drawing book*
Faller, Regis. *The adventures of Polo*
   Polo
   Polo and Lily
   Polo and the dragon
   Polo and the magician!
Fleischman, Paul. *Sidewalk circus*
Franson, Scott E. *Un-brella*
Frazee, Marla. *The farmer and the clown*
Frazier, Craig. *Bee and Bird*
Garoche, Camille. *The snow rabbit*
Geisert, Arthur. *The giant seed*
   Hogwash
   Ice
   Oops
Goodall, John S. *Creepy castle*
   Shrewbettina's birthday
Gordon, Domenica More. *Archie*
   Archie's vacation
Graegin, Stephanie. *Little fox in the forest*
Gutierrez, Elisa. *Letter lunch*
Hillenbrand, Will. *Snowman's story*
Hoban, Tana. *Black on white*
   Circles, triangles, and squares
   Colors everywhere
   Dig, drill, dump, fill
   Exactly the opposite
   Is it larger? Is it smaller?
   Is it red? Is it yellow? Is it blue?
   Is it rough? Is it smooth? Is it shiny?
   Just look
   Look book
   Look! look! look!
   More, fewer, less
   Shadows and reflections
   Shapes, shapes, shapes
   So many circles, so many squares
   Spirals, curves, fanshapes and lines
   What is that?
   Who are they?
Hogrogian, Nonny. *Cool cat*
Hutchins, Pat. *Changes, changes*
Idle, Molly. *Flora and the chicks*
   Flora and the flamingo
   Flora and the peacocks
   Flora and the penguin
Jay, Alison. *Bee and me*
   Out of the blue
   Welcome to the zoo
Kamm, Katja. *Invisible*
Keats, Ezra Jack. *Clementina's cactus*
   Kitten for a day
Khing, T. T. *Where is the cake?*
   Where is the cake now?
Krans, Kim. *ABC dream*
Lam, Thao. *Skunk on a string*
Lawson, Jonarno. *Sidewalk flowers*
Lee, Suzy. *Lines*
   Mirror
   Wave
Lehman, Barbara. *Museum trip*
   Rainstorm
   Red again
   The red book
   The secret box
   Trainstop
Liu, Jae Soo. *Yellow umbrella*
McCully, Emily Arnold. *The Christmas gift*

First snow
Four hungry kittens
New baby
Picnic
McDonnell, Patrick. *The little red cat who ran away and learned his ABC's (the hard way)*
South
MacKay, Elly. *Waltz of the snowflakes*
Mayer, Mercer. *A boy, a dog, a frog and a friend*
A boy, a dog and a frog
Frog goes to dinner
Frog on his own
Frog, where are you?
Octopus soup
One frog too many
Miyares, Daniel. *Float*
That neighbor kid
Newgarden, Mark. *Bow-Wow bugs a bug*
Bow-Wow's nightmare neighbors
Newman, Jeff. *The boys*
Nickle, John. *Alphabet explosion!*
Nolan, Dennis. *Hunters of the great forest*
Sea of dreams
Nordling, Lee. *Belinda the unbeatable*
Ommen, Sylvia van. *The surprise*
Otoshi, Kathryn. *Draw the line*
Peddle, Daniel. *Snow day*
Pett, Mark. *The boy and the airplane*
The girl and the bicycle
Pinkney, Jerry. *The lion and the mouse*
Polhemus, Coleman. *The crocodile blues*
Raschka, Chris. *A ball for Daisy*
Daisy gets lost
Riphagen, Loes. *Animals home alone*
Rockhill, Dennis. *Polar slumber / Sueño polar*
Rodriguez, Béatrice. *The chicken thief*
Fox and hen together
Rogers, Gregory. *The boy, the bear, the baron, the bard*
The hero of Little Street
Midsummer knight
Rohmann, Eric. *Time flies*
Runton, Andy. *Owly and Wormy: bright lights and starry nights!*
Owly and Wormy: friends all aflutter!
Savage, Stephen. *Where's Walrus?*
Where's Walrus? and Penguin?
Schories, Pat. *Jack and the night visitors*
Jack wants a snack
When Jack goes out
Schubert, Ingrid. *The umbrella*
Sís, Peter. *Dinosaur!*
An ocean world
Ship ahoy!
Sneed, Brad. *Picture a letter*
Spier, Peter. *Noah's ark*
Peter Spier's rain
Staake, Bob. *Bluebird*
Stevenson, James. *Grandpa's great city tour*
Sturm, James. *Birdsong: a story in pictures*
Tafuri, Nancy. *Do not disturb*
Early morning in the barn
Junglewalk
Rabbit's morning
Tanaka, Shinsuke. *Wings*
Thomson, Bill. *Chalk*
Fossil
Tolman, Marije. *The tree house*
Turkle, Brinton. *Deep in the forest*
Valério, Geraldo. *Turn on the night*

Varon, Sara. *Chicken and Cat*
Chicken and Cat clean up
Villa, Alvaro F. *Flood*
Wakeman, Daniel. *Ben's bunny trouble*
Walsh, Liam Francis. *Fish*
Weitzman, Jacqueline Preiss. *You can't take a balloon into the Metropolitan Museum*
You can't take a balloon into the National Gallery
Wiesner, David. *Free fall*
Mr. Wuffles!
Sector 7
Wilson, April. *April Wilson's magpie magic*
Yelchin, Eugene. *Spring hare*
Yum, Hyewon. *Last night*

Working *see* Activities – working; Careers

World

Ajmera, Maya. *Faith*
Global baby boys
Global baby girls
Music everywhere!
Ajmera, Maya, et al. *Healthy kids*
Our grandparents
What we wear
Amnesty International. *We are all born free*
Bart, Kathleen. *Town Teddy and Country Bear go global*
Branley, Franklyn M. *The planets in our solar system*
Brooks, Jeremy. *Let there be peace*
Brunhoff, Laurent de. *Babar's world tour*
Buzzeo, Toni. *Inside the books*
Caldicott, Chris. *World food alphabet*
Carney-Nunes, Charisse. *I dream for you a world*
Come and play
Corr, Christopher. *Whole world*
Curtis, Andrea. *What's for lunch?*
Delacre, Lulu. *How far do you love me?*
Dillon, Leo. *If kids ran the world*
Frank, John. *How to catch a fish*
Gibson, Amy. *By day, by night*
Gliori, Debi. *Goodnight world*
Graham, Bob. *How the sun got to Coco's house*
Halperin, Wendy Anderson. *Peace*
Here we go round the mulberry bush
Hughes, Susan. *Up! how families around the world carry their little ones*
Jackson, Ellen. *Earth Mother*
Jackson, Jill. *Let there be peace on earth*
Katz, Karen. *Can you say peace?*
Kerley, Barbara. *One world, one day*
With a friend by your side
The world is waiting for you
You and me together
Laroche, Giles. *If you lived here*
Lewin, Ted. *How much?*
Ljungkvist, Laura. *Follow the line around the world*
McGinty, Alice B. *Thank you, world*
Meng, Cece. *World pizza*
Miller, Heather Lynn. *Subway ride*
Mora, Pat. *Join hands!*
Ogburn, Jacqueline K. *Little treasures*
Omololu, Cynthia Jaynes. *When it's six o'clock in San Francisco*
Peet, Bill. *Chester the worldly pig*
Perlman, Willa. *Good night, world*

Perrin, Clotilde. *At the same moment, around the world*

Pow, Tom. *Who is the world for?*

Puck. *Babies around the world*

Reynolds, Jan. *Celebrate!*

Ruurs, Margriet. *My librarian is a camel*
  My school in the rain forest

Rylant, Cynthia. *The stars will still shine*

Scanlon, Elizabeth Garton. *All the world*

Schertle, Alice. *We*

Schubert, Ingrid. *The umbrella*

Schuett, Stacey. *Somewhere in the world right now*

Singer, Marilyn. *On the same day in March*

Sirett, Dawn. *Love your world*

Smith, Charles R. *I am the world*

Smith, David J. *This child, every child*

Spier, Peter. *People*

Swanson, Matthew. *Everywhere, wonder*

Valdivia, Paloma. *Up above and down below*

Walker, Rob D. *Mama says*

Weiss, George. *What a wonderful world*, ill. by Ashley Bryan
  What a wonderful world, ill. by Tim Hopgood

Weiss, Nicki. *The world turns round and round*

Willis, Jeanne. *Gorilla! Gorilla!*

Worrying *see* Behavior – worrying

Wrecking machines *see* Machines

Writers *see* Careers – writers; Children as authors

Writing letters *see* Letters, cards

Yeti *see* Monsters

Yoga *see* Health & fitness – exercise; Character traits – patience, impatience

Zodiac

Casey, Dawn. *The great race: the story of the Chinese zodiac*

Chin, Oliver. *The year of the monkey*
  The year of the sheep
  The year of the tiger

Demi. *The dragon's tale and other animal fables of the Chinese zodiac*

Orgel, Doris. *The cat's tale*

Van Woerkom, Dorothy. *The rat, the ox and the zodiac*

Wade, Mary Dodson. *No year of the cat*

Wang, Gabrielle. *The race for the Chinese zodiac*

Whitfield, Susan. *The animals of the Chinese zodiac*

Young, Ed. *Cat and Rat*

Zombies *see* Monsters

Zoos

Aliki. *My visit to the zoo*

Asch, Frank. *The Lending Zoo*

Baby animals at the zoo

Barton, Byron. *Zoo animals*

Beaumont, Karen. *Wild about us!*

Bleiman, Andrew. *ABC zooborns!*
  1-2-3 zooborns!

Bottner, Barbara. *Priscilla gorilla*

Browne, Anthony. *Gorilla*
  Little Beauty

Burningham, John. *The way to the zoo*

Campbell, Rod. *Dear zoo*

Capucilli, Alyssa Satin. *Inside a zoo in the city*

Carle, Eric. *1, 2, 3 to the zoo*

Carrick, Carol. *Patrick's dinosaurs*

Child, Lauren. *But I've used all my pocket change*

Comden, Betty. *What's new at the zoo?*

Curious George visits the zoo

Cuyler, Margery. *That's good! that's bad!*

Deady, Kathleen W. *Out and about at the zoo*

Degman, Lori. *One zany zoo*

Denim, Sue. *The Dumb Bunnies go to the zoo*

De Vicq de Cumptich, Roberto. *Bembo's zoo*

Doodler, Todd H. *The zoo I drew*

Dyer, Heather. *Tina and the penguin*

Dyer, Sarah. *Batty*

Elliott, George. *The boy who loved bananas*

Ellis, Andy. *When Lulu went to the zoo*

Faulconer, Maria. *A mom for Umande*

Feiffer, Kate. *My side of the car*

Fox, Mem. *Zoo-looking*

Garland, Michael. *Last night at the zoo*

Gershator, Phillis. *Zoo day, olé!*

Gibbons, Gail. *Zoo*

The gingerbread boy. *The Gingerbread Man loose at the zoo*

Goodman, Susan E. *What do you do — at the zoo?*

Grant, Jacob. *Through with the zoo*

Green, John Patrick. *Hippopotamister*

Hall, Michael. *My heart is like a zoo*

Hamburg, Jennifer. *A moose that says mooooooooooo*

Hanson, Faye. *Midnight at the zoo*

Harris, Robie H. *Who's in my family?*

Hart, Christopher. *Merwin, master of disguise*

Hatkoff, Isabella, et al. *Knut*

Heap, Sue. *Danny's drawing book*

Heder, Thyra. *Fraidyzoo*

Hennessy, B. G. *Corduroy at the zoo*

Hoban, Tana. *A children's zoo*

Hogg, Gary. *Beautiful Buehla and the zany zoo makeover*

Howe, James. *The day the teacher went bananas*

Hubbell, Patricia. *Bouncing time*
Ichikawa, Satomi. *I am Pangoo the penguin*
Ipcizade, Catherine. *'Twas the Day before Zoo Day*
Jantzen, Doug. *Henry Hyena, why won't you laugh?*
Jarman, Julia. *Class Two at the zoo*
Jay, Alison. *Welcome to the zoo*
Johnson, Mariana Ruiz. *I know a bear*
Judge, Lita. *Pennies for elephants*
Kalz, Jill. *An a-maze-ing zoo adventure*
Kerr, Judith. *One night in the zoo*
Ketteman, Helen. *If Beaver had a fever*
Krull, Kathleen. *What's new? the zoo!*
Kurtz, Jane. *Do kangaroos wear seat belts?*
Levis, Caron. *Ida, always*
Lithgow, John. *Never play music right next to the zoo*
Loggins, Kenny. *Footloose*
Macaulay, David. *How machines work: zoo break!*
McQuade, Jacqueline. *At the petting zoo with Teddy Bear*
Mandel, Peter. *Zoo ah-choooo*
Martin, Bill, Jr.. *Polar bear, polar bear, what do you hear?*
Mattick, Lindsay. *Finding Winnie*
Mead, Alice. *Billy and Emma*
Metzger, Steve. *The dancing clock*
Miller, Mary Beth. *Handtalk zoo*
Mora, Pat. *Marimba!*
Morgan, Richard. *Zoo poo*
Morozumi, Atsuko. *My friend gorilla*
Morris, Richard T. *Bye-bye, baby!*
Morrison, Cathy. *I want a pet!*
Munari, Bruno. *Bruno Munari's zoo*
Munsch, Robert N. *Alligator baby*
Na, Il Sung. *The opposite zoo*
Napoli, Donna Jo. *Bobby the bold*
Norman, Kim. *Still a gorilla!*
Ohora, Zachariah. *Stop snoring, Bernard!*
Ormerod, Jan. *When we went to the zoo*
Park, Linda Sue. *Xander's panda party*
Paxton, Tom. *Going to the zoo*
Pfister, Marcus. *Charlie at the zoo*
Phillips, Betty Lou. *Emily goes wild*
Pichon, Liz. *Penguins*
Pilkey, Dav. *The Dumb Bunnies go to the zoo*

Pinkwater, Daniel. *Bad bears go visiting*
   Bad bears in the big city
   Irving and Muktuk
Plant, David J. *Hungry Roscoe*
Rathmann, Peggy. *Good night, Gorilla*
Rex, Adam. *Pssst!*
Rey, H. A. *Curious George takes a job*
Rice, Eve. *Sam who never forgets*
Richards, Dan. *Can one balloon make an elephant fly?*
Richardson, Justin. *And Tango makes three*
Rockwell, Anne. *Zoo day*
Rose, Deborah Lee. *Birthday zoo*
Ryan, Candace. *Zoo zoom!*
Ryder, Joanne. *Little panda*
   A pair of polar bears
Saudo, Coralie. *My dad at the zoo*
Sauer, Tammi. *Oh, nuts!*
Savage, Stephen. *Where's Walrus?*
   Where's Walrus? and Penguin?
Scotton, Rob. *Splat and the cool school trip*
Sendelbach, Brian. *The underpants zoo*
Seuss, Dr. *If I ran the zoo*
Sierra, Judy. *Wild about books*
   Wild about you!
   Zoozical
Slade, Suzanne. *What's new at the zoo?: an animal adding adventure*
Smith, Marie. *Z is for zookeeper*
Stead, Philip C. *A sick day for Amos McGee*
Tekavec, Heather. *Manners are not for monkeys*
Waber, Bernard. *A lion named Shirley Williamson*
Waldman, Neil. *They came from the Bronx*
Waldron, Kevin. *Mr. Peek and the misunderstanding at the zoo*
   Panda-monium at Peek Zoo
Walker, Sally M. *Winnie*
Wall, Laura. *Goose goes to the zoo*
Wensink, Patrick. *Go go gorillas*
Willis, Jeanne. *The wheels on the bus: a read-along sing-along trip to the zoo*
Wilson, Karma. *Animal strike at the zoo, it's true!*
Wise, William. *Zany zoo*
Ziefert, Harriet. *You and me: we're opposites*

Bibliographic Guide

Arranged alphabetically by author's name in boldface (or by title, if author is unknown), each entry includes title, illustrator, publisher, publication date, and subjects. Joint authors appear as short entries, with the main author name (in parentheses after the title) citing where the complete entry will be found. Where only an author and title are given, complete information is listed under the title as the main entry.

Aardema, Verna. *Anansi does the impossible! an Ashanti tale* ill. by Lisa Desimini. Atheneum, 1997. ISBN 978-0-689-81092-3 Subj: Folk & fairy tales. Foreign lands – Africa. Spiders.

Anansi finds a fool: an Ashanti tale ill. by Bryna Waldman. Dial, 1992. ISBN 978-0-8037-1165-5 Subj: Behavior – trickery. Folk & fairy tales. Mythical creatures. Spiders.

Bimwili and the Zimwi ill. by Susan Meddaugh. Dial, 1985. ISBN 978-0-8037-0213-4 Subj: Folk & fairy tales. Foreign lands – Africa. Foreign lands – Zanzibar. Mythical creatures – trolls.

Borreguita and the coyote ill. by Petra Mathers. Knopf, 1991. ISBN 978-0-679-90921-7 Subj: Animals – coyotes. Animals – sheep. Behavior – trickery. Folk & fairy tales. Foreign lands – Mexico.

Bringing the rain to Kapiti Plain: a Nandi tale ill. by Beatriz A. Vidal. Dial, 1981. ISBN 978-0-8037-0807-5 Subj: Cumulative tales. Folk & fairy tales. Foreign lands – Africa. Rhyming text. Weather – droughts. Weather – rain.

Half-a-ball-of-kenki: an Ashanti tale ill. by Diane Stanley Zuromskis. Warne, 1979. ISBN 978-0-7232-6158-2 Subj: Animals – leopards. Folk & fairy tales. Foreign lands – Africa. Insects – flies.

Jackal's flying lesson: a Khoikhoi tale ill. by Dale Gottlieb. Knopf, 1995. ISBN 978-0-679-95813-0 Subj: Activities – flying. Animals – jackals. Behavior – trickery. Birds. Folk & fairy tales. Foreign lands – Africa. Foreign lands – Namibia.

Ji-nongo-nongo means riddles ill. by Jerry Pinkney. Four Winds, 1978. ISBN 978-0-590-07474-2 Subj: Folk & fairy tales. Foreign lands – Africa. Riddles & jokes.

Koi and the kola nuts ill. by Joe Cepeda. Atheneum, 1999. ISBN 978-0-689-81760-1 Subj: Character traits – kindness to animals. Folk & fairy tales. Foreign lands – Liberia.

The lonely lioness and the ostrich chicks: a Masai tale ill. by Yumi Heo. Owen, 1992. ISBN 978-0-679-96934-1 Subj: Animals – lions. Animals – mongooses. Behavior – needing someone. Birds – ostriches. Emotions – loneliness. Folk & fairy tales. Foreign lands – Africa.

Misoso ill. by Reynold Ruffins. Knopf, 1994. ISBN 978-0-679-93430-1 Subj: Folk & fairy tales. Foreign lands – Africa.

Oh, Kojo! How could you! an Ashanti tale ill. by Marc Brown. Dial, 1984. ISBN 978-0-8037-0007-9 Subj: Folk & fairy tales. Foreign lands – Africa. Humorous stories.

Pedro and the padre ill. by Friso Henstra. Dial, 1991. ISBN 978-0-8037-0523-4 Subj: Character traits – honesty. Folk & fairy tales. Foreign lands – Mexico.

Princess Gorilla and a new kind of water ill. by Victoria Chess. Dial, 1988. ISBN 978-0-8037-0413-8 Subj: Animals. Animals – gorillas. Folk & fairy tales. Foreign lands – Africa.

Rabbit makes a monkey of lion ill. by Jerry Pinkney. Dial, 1988. ISBN 978-0-8037-0298-1 Subj: Animals. Behavior – trickery. Foreign lands – Africa. Jungle.

The riddle of the drum: a tale from Tizapan, Mexico ill. by Tony Chen. Four Winds, 1978. ISBN 978-0-590-07489-6 Subj: Cumulative tales. Folk & fairy tales. Foreign lands – Mexico. Rhyming text. Royalty.

Sebgugugu the glutton: a Bantu tale from Rwanda ill. by Nancy L. Clouse. Eerdmans, 1993. ISBN 978-0-8028-5073-7 Subj: Behavior – greed. Character traits – foolishness. Folk & fairy tales. Foreign lands – Africa. Foreign lands – Rwanda.

Traveling to Tondo: a tale of the Nkundo of Zaire ill. by Will Hillenbrand. Knopf, 1991. ISBN 978-0-679-90081-8 Subj: Activities – traveling. Animals. Folk & fairy tales. Foreign lands – Congo (Democratic Republic). Foreign lands – Zaire.

The vingananee and the tree toad ill. by Ellen Weiss. Warne, 1983. ISBN 978-0-7232-6217-6 Subj: Animals. Folk & fairy tales. Foreign lands – Africa. Foreign lands – Liberia. Spiders.

What's so funny, Ketu? a Nuer tale ill. by Marc Brown. Dial, 1982. ISBN 978-0-8037-9370-5 Subj: Animals. Behavior – secrets. Foreign lands – Africa. Foreign lands – Sudan. Humorous stories. Reptiles – snakes.

Who's in Rabbit's house? ill. by Leo and Diane Dillon. Dial, 1977. ISBN 978-0-8037-9551-8 Subj: Animals. Folk & fairy tales. Foreign lands – Africa. Humorous stories. Insects – butterflies, caterpillars.

Why mosquitoes buzz in people's ears: a West African tale ill. by Leo and Diane Dillon. Dial, 1975. ISBN 978-0-8037-6087-5 Subj: Animals. Caldecott award books. Folk & fairy tales. Foreign lands – Africa. Insects – mosquitoes.

Abbot, Judi. *Train!* ill. by author. Tiger Tales, 2014. ISBN 978-158925163-2 Subj: Activities – playing. Animals – elephants. Toys. Trains.

Abbott, Bud. *Who's on first?* by Bud Abbott and Lou Costello ill. by John Martz. Quirk, 2013. ISBN 978-1-59474-590-4 Subj: Animals – bears. Animals – rabbits. Humorous stories. Sports – baseball.

Abeele, Veronique van den. *Still my Grandma* ill. by Claude K. Dubois. Eerdmans, 2007. ISBN 978-0-8028-5323-3 Subj: Family life – grandmothers. Illness – Alzheimer's.

Aber, Linda Williams. *Carrie measures up!* ill. by Joy Allen. Kane/Miller, 2001. ISBN 978-1-57565-100-2 Subj: Activities – knitting. Concepts – measurement. Family life – grandmothers.

Abercrombie, Barbara. *Bad dog, Dodger* ill. by Adam Gustavson. Margaret K. McElderry, 2002. ISBN 978-0-689-83782-1 Subj: Animals – babies. Animals – dogs. Pets.

The show-and-tell lion ill. by Lynne Cravath. Simon & Schuster, 2006. ISBN 978-0-689-86408-7 Subj: Behavior – lying. Character traits – honesty. Imagination.

Abley, Mark. *Ghost cat* ill. by Karen Reczuch. Douglas & McIntyre, 2001. ISBN 978-0-88899-433-2 Subj: Animals – cats. Death. Emotions – loneliness. Emotions – sadness. Pets.

Abouraya, Karen Leggett. *Hands around the library: protecting Egypt's treasured books* (Roth, Susan L.)

Abraham, Michelle Shapiro. *My cousin Tamar lives in Israel* ill. by Ann Koffsky. URJ Press, 2007. ISBN 978-0-8074-0989-3 Subj: Foreign lands – Israel. Jewish culture.

Abrahams, Peter. *Quacky baseball* ill. by Frank Morrison. HarperCollins, 2011. ISBN 978-0-06-122978-7 Subj: Birds – ducks. Sports – baseball.

Abrams, Douglas Carlton. *Desmond and the very mean word: a story of forgiveness* (Tutu, Archbishop Desmond)

God's dream (Tutu, Archbishop Desmond)

Abrams, Pam. *Now I eat my ABC's* ill. by Bruce Wolf. Scholastic, 2004. ISBN 978-0-439-64942-1 Subj: ABC books. Food. Format, unusual – board books.

Abramson, Jill. *Ready or not, here comes Scout* by Jill Abramson and Jane O'Connor ill. by Deborah Melmon. Viking, 2012. ISBN 978-0-670-01441-5 Subj: Animals – dogs. Behavior – misbehavior.

Acheson, Alison. *Grandpa's music: a story about Alzheimer's* ill. by Bill Farnsworth. Albert Whitman, 2009. ISBN 978-0-8075-3052-8 Subj: Family life – grandfathers. Illness – Alzheimer's. Music.

Ackerman, Karen. *Bean's big day* ill. by Paul Mombourquette. Kids Can, 2004. ISBN 978-1-55337-444-2 Subj: Careers – actors. Cities, towns. Self-concept. Theater.

By the dawn's early light ill. by Catherine Stock. Atheneum, 1994. ISBN 978-0-689-31788-0 Subj: Activities – working. Ethnic groups in the U.S. – African Americans. Family life – grandmothers. Family life – mothers.

Song and dance man ill. by Stephen Gammell. Knopf, 1988. ISBN 978-0-394-99330-0 Subj: Activities – dancing. Caldecott award books. Family life – grandfathers.

Acredolo, Linda P. *My first baby signs* by Linda P. Acredolo and Susan Goodwyn; photos by Penny Gentieu. HarperCollins, 2002. ISBN 978-0-06-009074-6 Subj: Communication. Disabilities – deafness. Format, unusual – board books. Sign language.

Ada, Alma Flor. *The Christmas tree / El arbol de Navidad* ill. by Terry Ybáñez. Hyperion, 1997. ISBN 978-0-7868-0151-0 Subj: Cumulative tales. Foreign languages. Holidays – Christmas. Rhyming text. Trees.

Dear Peter Rabbit ill. by Leslie Tryon. Atheneum, 1994. ISBN 978-0-689-31850-4 Subj: Animals. Folk & fairy tales. Letters, cards.

Friend frog ill. by Lori Lohstoeter. Harcourt, 2000. ISBN 978-0-15-201522-0 Subj: Animals – mice. Friendship. Frogs & toads.

Gathering the sun: an alphabet in Spanish and English ill. by Simon Silva. Lothrop, 1997. ISBN 978-0-688-13904-9 Subj: ABC books. Foreign languages. Poetry.

The gold coin ill. by Neil Waldman. Macmillan, 1991. ISBN 978-0-689-31633-3 Subj: Behavior – stealing. Circular tales. Crime. Cumulative tales. Foreign lands – Central America.

I love Saturdays y domingos ill. by Elivia Savadier. Atheneum, 2002. ISBN 978-0-689-31819-1 Subj: Ethnic groups in the U.S. – Mexican Americans. Family life – grandparents. Foreign languages.

¡Muu, moo! rimas de animales = animal nursery rhymes by Alma Flor Ada and F. Isabel Campoy ill. by Viví Escrivá. HarperCollins, 2010. ISBN 978-0-06-134613-2 Subj: Foreign languages. Nursery rhymes.

Pio peep! by Alma Flor Ada and F. Isabel Campoy ill. by Viví Escrivá. English adaptations by Alice Schertle. HarperCollins, 2003. ISBN 978-0-688-16020-3 Subj: Foreign languages. Nursery rhymes.

The rooster who went to his uncle's wedding ill. by Kathleen Kuchera. Atheneum, 1993. ISBN 978-0-399-22412-6 Subj: Birds – chickens, roosters. Cumulative tales. Folk & fairy tales. Foreign lands.

With love, Little Red Hen ill. by Leslie Tryon. Atheneum, 2001. ISBN 978-0-689-82581-1 Subj: Ethnic groups in the U.S. – Cuban Americans. Letters, cards.

Adams, Adrienne. *The Christmas party* ill. by author. Scribners, 1978. ISBN 978-0-684-15930-0 Subj: Animals – rabbits. Holidays – Christmas. Parties.

The Easter egg artists ill. by author. Scribners, 1976. ISBN 978-0-684-14652-2 Subj: Activities – painting. Activities – vacationing. Animals – rabbits. Holidays – Easter.

The great Valentine's Day balloon race ill. by author. Scribners, 1980. ISBN 978-0-684-16640-7 Subj: Activities – ballooning. Animals – rabbits. Careers – artists. Holidays – Valentine's Day. Sports – racing.

A Halloween happening ill. by author. Scribners, 1981. ISBN 978-0-684-17166-1 Subj: Holidays – Halloween. Parties. Witches.

A woggle of witches ill. by author. Scribners, 1971. ISBN 978-0-684-12506-0 Subj: Holidays – Halloween. Witches.

Adams, Diane. *I can do it myself!* ill. by Nancy Hayashi. Peachtree, 2009. ISBN 978-1-56145-471-6 Subj: Bedtime. Rhyming text. Self-concept.

I want to help! ill. by Nancy Hayashi. Peachtree, 2012. ISBN 978-1-56145-630-7 Subj: Character traits – helpfulness. Rhyming text. School.

Adams, Eric J. *On the day his daddy left* by Eric J. Adams and Kathleen Adams ill. by Layne Johnson. Albert Whitman, 2000. ISBN 978-0-8075-6072-3 Subj: Divorce. Family life.

Adams, Gloria G. *Ah-choo!* (Koehler, Lana Wayne)

Adams, Kathleen. *On the day his daddy left* (Adams, Eric J.)

Adams, Sarah. *Dave and Violet* ill. by author. Frances Lincoln, 2011. ISBN 978-1-84780-052-7 Subj: Character traits – shyness. Dragons. Friendship.

Gary and Ray ill. by author. Frances Lincoln, 2010. ISBN 978-1-84507-955-0 Subj: Animals – gorillas. Birds. Friendship.

Adamson, Ged. *Douglas, you need glasses!* ill. by author. Random House, 2016. ISBN 978-055352243-3 Subj: Animals – dogs. Glasses.

Shark Dog! ill. by author. HarperCollins, 2017. ISBN 978-006245713-4 Subj: Animals – dogs. Fish – sharks. Pets.

Addasi, Maha. *Time to pray* ill. by Ned Gannon. Boyds Mills, 2010. ISBN 978-1-59078-611-6 Subj: Family life – grandmothers. Foreign lands – Middle East. Foreign languages. Religion.

The white nights of Ramadan ill. by Ned Gannon. Boyds Mills, 2008. ISBN 978-1-59078-523-2 Subj: Holidays – Ramadan. Religion – Islam.

Adderson, Caroline. *Norman, speak!* ill. by Qin Leng. Groundwood, 2014. ISBN 978-155498322-3 Subj: Animals – dogs. Character traits – kindness to animals. Foreign languages. Pets.

Addy, Sharon Hart. *Lucky Jake* ill. by Wade Zahares. Houghton, 2007. ISBN 978-0-618-47286-4 Subj: Animals – pigs. Careers – miners. Character traits – luck.

When wishes were horses ill. by Brad Sneed. Houghton, 2002. ISBN 978-0-618-13166-2 Subj: Animals – horses, ponies. Behavior – wishing.

Adedjouma, Davida, ed. *The palm of my heart: poetry by African American children* ill. by R. Gregory Christie. Lee & Low, 1996. ISBN 978-1-880000-41-0 Subj: Children as authors. Ethnic groups in the U.S. – African Americans. Poetry.

Adkins, Jan. *What if you met a knight?* ill. by author. Macmillan, 2006. ISBN 978-1-59643-148-5 Subj: Knights. Middle Ages.

Adler, David A. *Campy: the story of Roy Campanella* ill. by Gordon C. James. Penguin, 2007. ISBN 978-0-670-06041-2 Subj: Disabilities – physical disabilities. Ethnic groups in the U.S. – African Americans. Sports – baseball.

The children's book of Jewish holidays ill. by David Sears. Mesorah, 1987. ISBN 978-0-89906-810-7 Subj: Holidays. Jewish culture.

Circles ill. by Edward Miller. Holiday, 2016. ISBN 978-082343642-2 Subj: Activities. Concepts – shape.

Fun with Roman numerals ill. by Edward Miller. Holiday, 2008. ISBN 978-0-8234-2060-5 Subj: Counting, numbers.

Helen Keller ill. by John Wallner. Holiday, 2003. ISBN 978-0-8234-1606-6 Subj: Character traits – persistence. Disabilities – blindness. Disabilities – deafness.

Heroes for civil rights ill. by Bill Farnsworth. Holiday, 2008. ISBN 978-0-8234-2008-7 Subj: Ethnic groups in the U.S. – African Americans. U.S. history.

Hiding from the Nazis ill. by Karen Ritz. Holiday, 1997. ISBN 978-0-8234-1288-4 Subj: Behavior – hiding. Family life. Holocaust. Jewish culture.

It's time to sleep, it's time to dream ill. by Kay Chorao. Holiday, 2009. ISBN 978-0-8234-1924-1 Subj: Bedtime. Family life. Seasons.

Joe Louis: America's fighter ill. by Terry Widener. Harcourt, 2005. ISBN 978-0-15-216480-5 Subj: Ethnic groups in the U.S. – African Americans. Sports. Sports – boxing.

A little at a time ill. by Paul Tong. Holiday House, 2010. ISBN 978-0-8234-1739-1 Subj: Character traits – questioning. Family life – grandfathers.

Magnets push, magnets pull ill. by Anna Raff. Holiday, 2017. ISBN 978-082343669-9 Subj: Character traits – curiosity. Science.

Millions, billions, and trillions: understanding big numbers ill. by Edward Miller. Holiday House, 2013. ISBN 978-0-8234-2403-0 Subj: Counting, numbers.

Money madness ill. by Edward Miller. Holiday, 2009. ISBN 978-0-8234-1474-1 Subj: Counting, numbers. Money.

Perimeter, area, and volume: a monster book of dimensions ill. by Edward Miller. Holiday House, 2012. ISBN 978-0-8234-2290-6 Subj: Concepts. Concepts – measurement. Monsters.

A picture book of Abraham Lincoln ill. by John Wallner and Alexandra Wallner. Holiday, 1989. ISBN 978-0-8234-0731-6 Subj: U.S. history.

A picture book of Amelia Earhart ill. by Jeff Fisher. Holiday, 1998. ISBN 978-0-8234-1315-7 Subj: Careers – airplane pilots. Gender roles.

A picture book of Benjamin Franklin ill. by John Wallner and Alexandra Wallner. Holiday, 1990. ISBN 978-0-8234-0792-7 Subj: U.S. history.

A picture book of Cesar Chavez by David A. Adler and Michael S. Adler ill. by Marie Olofsdotter. Holiday House, 2010. ISBN 978-0-8234-2202-9 Subj: Behavior – seeking better things. Careers – migrant workers. Ethnic groups in the U.S. – Mexican Americans. Farms. U.S. history.

A picture book of Dolley and James Madison by David A. Adler and Michael S. Adler ill. by Ronald Himler. Holiday, 2009. ISBN 978-0-8234-2009-4 Subj: U.S. history.

A picture book of Eleanor Roosevelt ill. by Robert Casilla. Holiday, 1991. ISBN 978-0-8234-0856-6 Subj: Gender roles. U.S. history.

A picture book of George Washington ill. by John Wallner and Alexandra Wallner. Holiday, 1989. ISBN 978-0-8234-0732-3 Subj: U.S. history.

A picture book of Hanukkah ill. by Linda Heller. Holiday, 1982. ISBN 978-0-8234-0458-2 Subj: Holidays – Hanukkah. Jewish culture. Religion.

A picture book of Harry Houdini by David A. Adler and Michael S. Adler ill. by Matt Collins. Holiday, 2009. ISBN 978-0-8234-2059-9 Subj: Careers – magicians. Magic. U.S. history.

A picture book of Israel ill. with photos. Holiday, 1984. ISBN 978-0-8234-0513-8 Subj: Foreign lands – Israel. Jewish culture. Religion.

A picture book of Jewish holidays ill. by Linda Heller. Holiday, 1981. ISBN 978-0-8234-0396-7 Subj: Holidays. Holidays – Hanukkah. Holidays – Passover. Jewish culture.

A picture book of John and Abigail Adams by David A. Adler and Michael S. Adler ill. by Ronald Himler. Holiday House, 2010. ISBN 978-0-8234-2007-0 Subj: U.S. history.

A picture book of John F. Kennedy ill. by Robert Casilla. Holiday, 1991. ISBN 978-0-8234-0884-9 Subj: U.S. history.

A picture book of John Hancock ill. by Ronald Himler. Holiday House, 2007. ISBN 978-0-8234-2005-6 Subj: U.S. history.

A picture book of Martin Luther King, Jr ill. by Robert Casilla. Holiday, 1989. ISBN 978-0-8234-0770-5 Subj: Ethnic groups in the U.S. – African Americans. Holidays – Martin Luther King, Jr. Day. U.S. history. Violence, nonviolence.

A picture book of Passover ill. by Linda Heller. Holiday, 1982. ISBN 978-0-8234-0439-1 Subj: Holidays – Passover. Jewish culture.

A picture book of Sam Houston by David A. Adler and Michael S. Adler ill. by Matt Collins. Holiday House, 2012. ISBN 978-0-8234-2369-9 Subj: Texas. U.S. history.

A picture book of Samuel Adams by David A. Adler and Michael S. Adler ill. by Ronald Himler. Holiday House, 2005. ISBN 978-0-8234-1846-6 Subj: U.S. history.

A picture book of Thomas Jefferson ill. by John Wallner and Alexandra Wallner. Holiday, 1990. ISBN 978-0-8234-0791-0 Subj: U.S. history.

Place value ill. by Edward Miller. Holiday House, 2016. ISBN 978-082343550-0 Subj: Counting, numbers.

Redwoods are the tallest trees in the world ill. by Kazue Mizumura. Crowell, 1978. ISBN 978-0-690-01368-9 Subj: Forest, woods. Science. Trees.

Satchel Paige: don't look back ill. by Terry Widener. Harcourt, 2007. ISBN 978-0-15-205585-1 Subj: Ethnic groups in the U.S. – African Americans. Sports – baseball.

The story of Hanukkah ill. by Jill Weber. Holiday House, 2011. ISBN 978-0-8234-2295-1 Subj: Holidays – Hanukkah. Jewish culture. Religion.

The story of Passover ill. by Jill Weber. Holiday House, 2014. ISBN 978-082342902-8 Subj: Holidays – Passover. Jewish culture.

Things that float and things that don't ill. by Anna Raff. Holiday House, 2013. ISBN 978-0-8234-2862-5 Subj: Character traits – curiosity. Concepts. Science.

Time zones ill. by Edward Miller. Holiday House, 2010. ISBN 978-0-8234-2201-2 Subj: Time.

Triangles ill. by Edward Miller. Holiday House, 2014. ISBN 978-082342378-1 Subj: Concepts – shape. Counting, numbers.

Adler, Michael S. *A picture book of Cesar Chavez* (Adler, David A.)

A picture book of Dolley and James Madison (Adler, David A.)

A picture book of Harry Houdini (Adler, David A.)

A picture book of John and Abigail Adams (Adler, David A.)

A picture book of Sam Houston (Adler, David A.)

A picture book of Samuel Adams (Adler, David A.)

Adler, Victoria. *All of baby nose to toes* ill. by Hiroe Nakata. Dial, 2009. ISBN 978-0-8037-3217-9 Subj: Babies, toddlers. Rhyming text.

Baby, come away ill. by David Walker. Farrar, 2011. ISBN 978-0-374-30480-5 Subj: Animals. Babies, toddlers.

Adlerman, Daniel. *Africa calling: nightime falling* ill. by Kimberly Adlerman. Whispering Coyote, 1996. ISBN 978-1-879085-98-5 Subj: Animals. Dreams. Foreign lands – Africa. Imagination. Night. Rhyming text. Toys.

Adoff, Arnold. *Black is brown is tan* ill. by Emily Arnold McCully. HarperCollins, 2002. ISBN 978-0-06-028777-1 Subj: Family life. Marriage, interracial. Rhyming text.

Daring Dog and Captain Cat ill. by Joe Cepeda. Simon & Schuster, 2001. ISBN 978-0-689-82599-6 Subj: Animals – cats. Animals – dogs. Night. Pets.

In for winter, out for spring ill. by Jerry Pinkney. Harcourt, 1991. ISBN 978-0-15-238637-5 Subj: Ethnic groups in the U.S. – African Americans. Family life. Poetry. Seasons.

Love letters ill. by Lisa Desimini. Blue Sky, 1997. ISBN 978-0-590-48478-7 Subj: Emotions – love. Letters, cards. Poetry.

Street music: city poems ill. by Karen Barbour. HarperCollins, 1994. ISBN 978-0-06-021523-1 Subj: Cities, towns. Poetry.

Touch the poem ill. by Bill Creevy. Scholastic, 1996. ISBN 978-0-590-47970-7 Subj: Poetry. Senses – touch.

Adoff, Jaime. *Small fry* ill. by Mike Reed. Dutton, 2008. ISBN 978-0-525-46935-3 Subj: Behavior – growing up. Character traits – smallness. Poetry. Self-concept.

Aesop. *Aesop's fables* retold by Beverley Naidoo; ill. by Piet Grobler. Frances Lincoln, 2011. ISBN 978-1-84780-007-7 Subj: Folk & fairy tales. Foreign lands – Africa.

Aesop's fables sel. by Michael Hague; ill. by selector. Henry Holt, 1985. ISBN 978-0-03-002038-4 Subj: Folk & fairy tales.

Aesop's fables sel. by Heidi Holder; ill. by selector. Viking, 1981. ISBN 978-0-670-10643-1 Subj: Folk & fairy tales.

Aesop's fables by John Cech; ill. by Martin Jarrie. Sterling, 2009. ISBN 978-1-4027-5298-8 Subj: Folk & fairy tales.

Aesop's fables ill. by Jerry Pinkney. SeaStar, 2000. ISBN 978-1-58717-003-4 Subj: Folk & fairy tales.

Aesop's fables retold by Fiona Waters; ill. by Fulvio Testa. Trafalgar Square, 2011. ISBN 978-1-84939-049-1 Subj: Folk & fairy tales.

Androcles and the lion retold by Dennis Nolan; ill. by reteller. Harcourt, 1997. ISBN 978-0-15-203355-2 Subj: Animals – lions. Character traits – helpfulness. Character traits – kindness to animals. Folk & fairy tales. Foreign lands – Italy.

Androcles and the lion adapt. by Janet Stevens; ill. by adapter. Holiday, 1989. ISBN 978-0-8234-0768-2 Subj: Animals – lions. Character traits – helpfulness. Character traits – kindness to animals. Folk & fairy tales. Foreign lands – Italy. Religion.

Androcles and the lion: and other Aesop fables adapt. by Tom Paxton; ill. by Robert Rayevsky. Morrow,

1991. ISBN 978-0-688-09683-0 Subj: Animals – lions. Character traits – helpfulness. Character traits – kindness to animals. Folk & fairy tales. Foreign lands – Italy. Rhyming text.

Animal fables from Aesop adapt. by Barbara McClintock; ill. by adapter. Godine, 2000. ISBN 978-1-56792-144-1 Subj: Animals. Folk & fairy tales.

Anno's Aesop: a book of fables by Aesop and Mr. Fox adapt. by Mitsumasa Anno; ill. by adapter. Watts, 1989. ISBN 978-0-531-08374-1 Subj: Animals – foxes. Folk & fairy tales.

The ant and the grasshopper retold by Amy Lowry Poole; ill. by reteller. Holiday, 2000. ISBN 978-0-8234-1477-2 Subj: Activities – working. Folk & fairy tales. Foreign lands – China. Insects – ants. Insects – grasshoppers. Royalty – emperors. Seasons – fall. Seasons – winter.

The ant and the grasshopper retold by Mark White; ill. by Sara Rojo. Picture Window, 2004. ISBN 978-1-4048-0217-9 Subj: Activities – working. Folk & fairy tales. Insects – ants. Insects – grasshoppers. Seasons – fall. Seasons – winter.

Bat's big game retold by Margaret Read MacDonald; ill. by Eugenia Nobati. Albert Whitman, 2008. ISBN 978-0-8075-0587-8 Subj: Animals. Animals – bats. Birds. Folk & fairy tales. Sports – soccer.

Belling the cat retold by Eric Blair; ill. by Diane Silverman. Picture Window, 2004. ISBN 978-1-4048-0321-3 Subj: Animals – cats. Animals – mice. Folk & fairy tales.

Belling the cat and other Aesop fables by Tom Paxton; ill. by Robert Rayevsky. Morrow, 1990. ISBN 978-0-688-08159-1 Subj: Animals. Folk & fairy tales.

The best of Aesop's fables retold by Margaret Clark; ill. by Charlotte Voake. Little, 1990. ISBN 978-0-316-14499-5 Subj: Folk & fairy tales.

The boy who cried wolf retold by Eric Blair; ill. by Diane Silverman. Picture Window, 2004. ISBN 978-1-4048-0319-0 Subj: Animals – wolves. Behavior – lying. Behavior – trickery. Folk & fairy tales.

The contest between the Sun and the Wind: an Aesop's fable retold by Heather Forest; ill. by Susan Gaber. August House, 2008. ISBN 978-0-87483-832-9 Subj: Contests. Folk & fairy tales. Sun. Weather – wind.

The country mouse and the city mouse retold by Eric Blair; ill. by Diane Silverman. Picture Window, 2004. ISBN 978-1-4048-0318-3 Subj: Animals – mice. Cities, towns. Country. Folk & fairy tales.

The crow and the pitcher retold by Eric Blair; ill. by Diane Silverman. Picture Window, 2004. ISBN 978-1-4048-0322-0 Subj: Birds – crows. Character traits – cleverness. Folk & fairy tales. Problem solving.

Doctor Coyote: a Native American Aesop's fables by John Bierhorst; ill. by Wendy Watson. Macmillan, 1987. ISBN 978-0-02-709780-1 Subj: Animals. Animals – coyotes. Folk & fairy tales. Indians of North America – Aztec.

The dog and the wolf retold by Eric Blair; ill. by Diane Silverman. Picture Window, 2004. ISBN 978-1-4048-0323-7 Subj: Animals – dogs. Animals – wolves. Character traits – freedom. Folk & fairy tales.

The donkey in the lion's skin sel. by Eric Blair; ill. by Diane Silverman. Picture Window, 2004. ISBN 978-1-4048-0320-6 Subj: Animals. Animals – donkeys. Animals – foxes. Behavior – trickery. Clothing. Disguises.

Fables from Aesop adapt. by Tom Lynch; ill. by adapter. Viking, 2000. ISBN 978-0-670-88948-8 Subj: Folk & fairy tales.

Feed me! an Aesop fable by William H. Hooks; ill. by Doug Cushman. G. Stevens, 1996. ISBN 978-0-8368-1616-7 Subj: Birds. Folk & fairy tales.

The fox and the grapes retold by Mark White; ill. by Sara Rojo. Picture Window, 2004. ISBN 978-1-4048-0218-6 Subj: Animals – foxes. Folk & fairy tales. Food.

Fox tails: four fables from Aesop ill. by Amy Lowry. Holiday House, 2012. ISBN 978-0-8234-2400-9 Subj: Animals. Animals – foxes. Behavior – trickery. Folk & fairy tales.

The goose that laid the golden egg retold by Mark White; ill. by Sara Rojo. Picture Window, 2004. ISBN 978-1-4048-0219-3 Subj: Behavior – greed. Birds – geese. Careers – farmers. Eggs. Folk & fairy tales.

The grasshopper and the ants retold by Jerry Pinkney; ill. by reteller. Little, Brown, 2015. ISBN 978-031640081-7 Subj: Activities – working. Folk & fairy tales. Insects – ants. Insects – grasshoppers. Seasons – winter.

The hare and the tortoise ill. by Paul Galdone. Whittlesey House, 1962. Subj: Animals – rabbits. Folk & fairy tales. Reptiles – turtles, tortoises. Sports – racing.

The hare and the tortoise retold by Carol Jones; ill. by reteller. Houghton, 1996. ISBN 978-0-395-81368-3 Subj: Animals – rabbits. Folk & fairy tales. Format, unusual – toy & movable books. Reptiles – turtles, tortoises. Sports – racing.

The hare and the tortoise retold by Helen Ward; ill. by reteller. Millbrook, 1999. ISBN 978-0-7613-1318-2 Subj: Animals – rabbits. Folk & fairy tales. Reptiles – turtles, tortoises. Sports – racing.

The hare and the tortoise / La liebre y la tortuga adapt. by Maria Eulalia Valeri; ill. by Max. Chronicle,

2006. ISBN 978-0-8118-5057-5 Subj: Animals – rabbits. Folk & fairy tales. Foreign languages. Reptiles – turtles, tortoises. Sports – racing.

Hare and Tortoise retold by Alison Murray; ill. by reteller. Candlewick, 2016. ISBN 978-076368721-2 Subj: Animals – rabbits. Folk & fairy tales. Reptiles – turtles, tortoises. Sports – racing.

The lion and the mouse by Gail Herman; ill. by Lisa McCue. Random House, 1998. ISBN 978-0-679-98674-4 Subj: Animals – lions. Animals – mice. Character traits – helpfulness. Folk & fairy tales.

The lion and the mouse retold by Mark White; ill. by Sara Rojo. Picture Window, 2004. ISBN 978-1-4048-0216-2 Subj: Animals – lions. Animals – mice. Character traits – helpfulness. Character traits – kindness. Folk & fairy tales.

The lion and the mouse sel. by Bernadette Watts; ill. by selector. NorthSouth, 2000. ISBN 978-0-7358-1221-5 Subj: Animals – lions. Animals – mice. Character traits – helpfulness. Folk & fairy tales.

The lion and the mouse and other Aesop fables retold by Doris Orgel; ill. by Bert Kitchen. DK, 2000. ISBN 978-0-7894-2665-9 Subj: Animals. Folk & fairy tales.

Milly and Tilly: the story of a town mouse and a country mouse by Kate Summers; ill. by Maggie Kneen. Dutton, 1997. ISBN 978-0-525-45801-2 Subj: Animals – mice. Cities, towns. Country. Folk & fairy tales.

Mouse and lion retold by Rand Burkert; ill. by Nancy Ekholm Burkert. Scholastic, 2011. ISBN 978-0-545-10147-9 Subj: Animals – lions. Animals – mice. Character traits – helpfulness. Character traits – kindness. Folk & fairy tales.

The race by Caroline Repchuk; ill. by Alison Jay. Chronicle, 2002. ISBN 978-0-8118-3500-8 Subj: Animals – rabbits. Folk & fairy tales. Reptiles – turtles, tortoises. Rhyming text. Sports – racing.

Road signs: a harey race with a tortoise by Margery Cuyler; ill. by Steve Haskamp. Winslow, 2000. ISBN 978-1-890817-23-7 Subj: Animals. Animals – rabbits. Folk & fairy tales. Reptiles – turtles, tortoises. Sports – racing. Traffic, traffic signs.

Smog, the city dog by Adria Meserve; ill. by author. Chronicle, 2002. ISBN 978-0-8118-3551-0 Subj: Animals – dogs. Behavior – sharing. Folk & fairy tales.

Three Aesop fox fables ill. by Paul Galdone. Seabury Pr., 1971. ISBN 978-0-395-28810-8 Subj: Animals – foxes. Behavior – trickery. Character traits – flattery. Folk & fairy tales.

The tortoise and the hare retold by Jerry Pinkney; ill. by reteller. Little, Brown, 2013. ISBN 978-0-316-18356-7 Subj: Animals – rabbits. Folk & fairy tales. Reptiles – turtles, tortoises. Sports – racing.

The tortoise and the hare retold by Mark White; ill. by Sara Rojo. Picture Window, 2004. ISBN 978-1-4048-0215-5 Subj: Animals – rabbits. Folk & fairy tales. Reptiles – turtles, tortoises. Sports – racing.

The tortoise and the hare: an Aesop fable adapt. by Janet Stevens; ill. by adapter. Holiday, 1984. ISBN 978-0-8234-0510-7 Subj: Animals – rabbits. Folk & fairy tales. Reptiles – turtles, tortoises. Sports – racing.

The town mouse and the country mouse ill. by Lorinda Bryan Cauley. Putnam, 1984. ISBN 978-0-399-21123-2 Subj: Animals – mice. Cities, towns. Country. Folk & fairy tales.

The town mouse and the country mouse adapt. by Janet Stevens; ill. by adapter. Holiday, 1987. ISBN 978-0-8234-0633-3 Subj: Animals – mice. Cities, towns. Country. Folk & fairy tales.

The town mouse and the country mouse: an Aesop fable retold by Helen Ward; ill. by reteller. Candlewick, 2012. ISBN 978-0-7636-6098-7 Subj: Animals – mice. Cities, towns. Country. Folk & fairy tales.

The town mouse and the country mouse: an Aesop fable retold by Bernadette Watts; ill. by reteller. NorthSouth, 1998. ISBN 978-1-55858-988-9 Subj: Animals – mice. Cities, towns. Country. Folk & fairy tales.

Town mouse, country mouse retold by Jan Brett; ill. by reteller. Putnam, 1994. ISBN 978-0-399-22622-9 Subj: Animals – cats. Animals – mice. Birds – owls. Cities, towns. Country. Folk & fairy tales.

Town mouse, country mouse retold by Carol Jones; ill. by reteller. Houghton, 1995. ISBN 978-0-395-71129-3 Subj: Animals – mice. Cities, towns. Country. Folk & fairy tales.

The wolf in sheep's clothing retold by Mark White; ill. by Sara Rojo. Picture Window, 2004. ISBN 978-1-4048-0220-9 Subj: Animals – sheep. Animals – wolves. Behavior – trickery. Clothing. Disguises. Folk & fairy tales.

Agee, Jon. *Dmitri the astronaut* ill. by author. HarperCollins, 1996. ISBN 978-0-06-205075-5 Subj: Animals. Careers – astronauts. Moon. Space & space ships.

The incredible painting of Felix Clousseau ill. by author. Farrar, 1988. ISBN 978-0-374-33633-2 Subj: Activities – painting. Art. Imagination.

It's only Stanley ill. by author. Dial, 2015. ISBN 978-080373907-9 Subj: Animals – dogs. Moon. Noise, sounds. Rhyming text.

Life on Mars ill. by author. Dial, 2017. ISBN 978-039953852-0 Subj: Careers – astronauts. Space & space ships.

Lion lessons ill. by author. Dial, 2016. ISBN 978-080373908-6 Subj: Animals – lions. Character traits – persistence. Self-concept.

Little Santa ill. by author. Dial, 2013. ISBN 978-0-8037-3906-2 Subj: Foreign lands – Arctic. Holidays – Christmas. Santa Claus.

Milo's hat trick ill. by author. Hyperion, 2001. ISBN 978-0-7868-0902-8 Subj: Animals – bears. Careers – magicians. Magic. Theater.

Mr. Putney's quacking dog ill. by author. Scholastic, 2010. ISBN 978-0-545-16203-6 Subj: Animals. Games. Riddles & jokes.

My rhinoceros ill. by author. Scholastic, 2011. ISBN 978-0-545-29441-6 Subj: Animals – rhinoceros. Crime. Pets.

Nothing ill. by author. Hyperion, 2007. ISBN 978-0-7868-3694-9 Subj: Humorous stories. Shopping. Stores.

Orangutan tongs: poems to tangle your tongue ill. by author. Hyperion, 2009. ISBN 978-1-4231-0315-8 Subj: Poetry. Tongue twisters.

The other side of town ill. by author. Scholastic, 2012. ISBN 978-0-545-16204-3 Subj: Aliens. Taxis.

The retired kid ill. by author. Hyperion, 2008. ISBN 978-1-4231-0314-1 Subj: Humorous stories. Old age.

Terrific ill. by author. Hyperion, 2005. ISBN 978-0-7868-5184-3 Subj: Behavior – bad day, bad mood. Behavior – dissatisfaction. Birds – parakeets, parrots.

Z goes home ill. by author. Hyperion, 2003. ISBN 978-0-7868-1987-4 Subj: ABC books.

Agran, Rick. *Pumpkin shivaree* ill. by Sara Anderson. Handprint, 2003. ISBN 978-1-59354-006-7 Subj: Holidays – Halloween. Plants.

Ahlberg, Allan. *The adventures of Bert* by Allan Ahlberg and Raymond Briggs ill. by Raymond Briggs. Farrar, 2001. ISBN 978-0-374-30092-0 Subj: Humorous stories.

The baby in the hat ill. by André Amstutz. Candlewick, 2008. ISBN 978-0-7636-3958-7 Subj: Foreign lands – England. Sailors. Sea & seashore.

The baby's catalogue (Ahlberg, Janet)

A bit more Bert by Allan Ahlberg and Raymond Briggs ill. by Raymond Briggs. Farrar, 2002. ISBN 978-0-374-32489-6 Subj: Humorous stories.

Each peach pear plum: an "I spy" story (Ahlberg, Janet)

Funnybones (Ahlberg, Janet)

The Goldilocks variations: or Who's been snopperink in my woodootog? ill. by Jessica Ahlberg. Candlewick, 2012. ISBN 978-0-7636-6268-4 Subj: Folk & fairy tales. Format, unusual – toy & movable books. Humorous stories.

Half a pig ill. by Jessica Ahlberg. Candlewick, 2004. ISBN 978-0-7636-2373-9 Subj: Animals – pigs. Humorous stories.

Hooray for bread ill. by Bruce Ingman. Candlewick, 2013. ISBN 978-0-7636-6311-7 Subj: Activities – baking, cooking. Food. Rhyming text.

It was a dark and stormy night (Ahlberg, Janet)

Jeremiah in the dark wood (Ahlberg, Janet)

The jolly Christmas postman (Ahlberg, Janet)

The jolly pocket postman (Ahlberg, Janet)

The jolly postman (Ahlberg, Janet)

Peek-a-boo! (Ahlberg, Janet)

The pencil ill. by Bruce Ingman. Candlewick, 2008. ISBN 978-0-7636-3894-8 Subj: Activities – drawing. Emotions – loneliness. Imagination.

Playmates (Ahlberg, Janet)

Previously ill. by Bruce Ingman. Candlewick, 2007. ISBN 978-0-7636-3542-8 Subj: Folk & fairy tales.

The runaway dinner ill. by Bruce Ingman. Candlewick, 2006. ISBN 978-0-7636-3142-0 Subj: Behavior – running away. Food.

The shopping expedition ill. by André Amstutz. Candlewick, 2005. ISBN 978-0-7636-2586-3 Subj: Imagination. Shopping.

The snail house ill. by Gillian Tyler. Candlewick, 2000. ISBN 978-0-7636-0711-1 Subj: Activities – storytelling. Animals – snails. Concepts – size. Family life – grandmothers.

Starting school (Ahlberg, Janet)

Ahlberg, Janet. *The baby's catalogue* by Janet Ahlberg and Allan Ahlberg; ill. by authors. Little, 1983. ISBN 978-0-316-02037-4 Subj: Babies, toddlers. Family life.

Each peach pear plum: an "I spy" story by Janet Ahlberg and Allan Ahlberg; ill. by authors. Viking, 1978. ISBN 978-0-670-28705-5 Subj: Games. Rhyming text.

Funnybones by Janet Ahlberg and Allan Ahlberg; ill. by authors. Greenwillow, 1981. ISBN 978-0-688-84238-3 Subj: Activities – playing. Anatomy – skeletons. Ghosts. Night.

It was a dark and stormy night by Janet Ahlberg and Allan Ahlberg; ill. by authors. Viking, 1993. ISBN 978-0-670-84620-7 Subj: Activities – storytelling. Character traits – cleverness. Crime. Pirates.

Jeremiah in the dark wood by Janet Ahlberg and Allan Ahlberg; ill. by authors. Viking, 1987. ISBN 978-0-670-40637-1 Subj: Behavior – stealing. Forest, woods. Mythical creatures.

The jolly Christmas postman by Janet Ahlberg and Allan Ahlberg; ill. by authors. Little, 1991. ISBN 978-0-316-02033-6 Subj: Careers – postal workers. Format, unusual. Holidays – Christmas. Nursery rhymes. Post office. Rhyming text.

The jolly pocket postman by Janet Ahlberg and Allan Ahlberg; ill. by authors. Little, 1995. ISBN 978-0-316-60202-0 Subj: Careers – postal workers. Format, unusual – toy & movable books. Post office. Rhyming text.

The jolly postman by Janet Ahlberg and Allan Ahlberg; ill. by authors. Little, 1986. ISBN 978-0-316-02036-7 Subj: Careers – postal workers. Format, unusual – toy & movable books. Post office. Rhyming text.

Peek-a-boo! by Janet Ahlberg and Allan Ahlberg; ill. by authors. Viking, 1981. ISBN 978-0-670-54598-8 Subj: Babies, toddlers. Family life. Format, unusual – toy & movable books. Games. Rhyming text.

Playmates by Janet Ahlberg and Allan Ahlberg; ill. by authors. Viking, 1985. ISBN 978-0-670-55988-6 Subj: Activities – playing. Format, unusual – toy & movable books.

Starting school by Janet Ahlberg and Allan Ahlberg; ill. by authors. Viking, 1988. ISBN 978-0-670-82175-4 Subj: School – first day.

Ahlberg, Jessica. *Fairy tales for Mr. Barker: a peek-through story* ill. by author. Candlewick, 2016. ISBN 978-076368124-1 Subj: Animals – dogs. Folk & fairy tales. Format, unusual.

Ahmed, Said Salah. *The lion's share / Qayb Libaax: a Somali folktale* ill. by Kelly Dupre. Minnesota Humanities Commission, 2006. ISBN 978-1-931016-12-4 Subj: Behavior – greed. Folk & fairy tales. Foreign lands – Somalia. Foreign languages.

Aigner-Clark, Julie. *Language nursery* ill. by Nadeem Zaidi. Hyperion, 2001. ISBN 978-0-7868-0810-6 Subj: Foreign languages. Format, unusual – board books.

You are the best medicine ill. by Jana Christy. HarperCollins, 2010. ISBN 978-0-06-195644-7 Subj: Emotions – love. Family life – mothers. Illness – cancer.

Aillaud, Cindy Lou. *Recess at 20 below* photos by author. Alaska Northwest, 2005. ISBN 978-0-88540-609-8 Subj: Alaska. Weather – cold. Weather – snow.

Ainslie, Tamsin. *I can say please* ill. by author. Kane/Miller, 2011. ISBN 978-1-61067-037-1 Subj: Etiquette.

I can say thank you ill. by author. Kane/Miller, 2011. ISBN 978-1-61067-038-8 Subj: Etiquette.

Ainsworth, Kimberly. *Hootenanny! a festive counting book* ill. by Jo Brown. Simon & Schuster, 2011. ISBN 978-1-4424-2273-5 Subj: Birds – owls. Counting, numbers.

Ajmera, Maya. *Animal friends: a global celebration of children and their animals* by Maya Ajmera and John D. Ivanko ill. with photos. Charlesbridge, 2002. ISBN 978-1-57091-502-4 Subj: Animals. Format, unusual – board books. Pets.

Back to school by Maya Ajmera and John D. Ivanko ill. with photos. Charlesbridge, 2001. ISBN 978-1-57091-383-9 Subj: Foreign lands. School.

Come out and play by Maya Ajmera and John D. Ivanko ill. with photos. Charlesbridge, 2001. ISBN 978-1-57091-385-3 Subj: Activities – playing. Foreign lands.

Faith by Maya Ajmera and Cynthia Pon ill. with photos. Charlesbridge, 2009. ISBN 978-1-58089-177-6 Subj: Religion. World.

Global baby boys ill. with photos. Charlesbridge, 2014. ISBN 978-158089440-1 Subj: Babies, toddlers. Format, unusual – board books. World.

Global baby girls ill. with photos. Charlesbridge, 2013. ISBN 978-158089439-5 Subj: Babies, toddlers. Format, unusual – board books. World.

A kid's best friend by Maya Ajmera and Alex Fisher ill. with photos. Charlesbridge, 2002. ISBN 978-1-57091-513-0 Subj: Animals – dogs. Pets.

Music everywhere! ill. with photos. Charlesbridge, 2014. ISBN 978-157091936-7 Subj: Music. Musical instruments. World.

To be a kid by Maya Ajmera and John D. Ivanko ill. with photos. Charlesbridge, 1999. ISBN 978-0-88106-841-2 Subj: Activities. Family life. Foreign lands.

Ajmera, Maya, et al. *Healthy kids.* Charlesbridge, 2013. ISBN 978-1-58089-436-4 Subj: Health & fitness. World.

Our grandparents: a global album. Charlesbridge, 2010. ISBN 978-1-57091-458-4 Subj: Family life – grandparents. World.

What we wear: dressing up around the world. Charlesbridge, 2012. ISBN 978-1-58089-416-6 Subj: Clothing. World.

Akin, Sara Laux. *Three scoops and a fig* ill. by Susan Kathleen Hartung. Peachtree, 2010. ISBN 978-1-56145-522-5 Subj: Ethnic groups in the U.S. – Italian Americans. Family life. Food.

Alakija, Polly. *Catch that goat!* ill. by author. Barefoot, 2002. ISBN 978-1-84148-908-7 Subj: Animals – goats. Counting, numbers. Foreign lands – Africa. Stores.

Counting chickens ill. by author. Frances Lincoln, 2014. ISBN 978-184780437-2 Subj: Birds – chickens, roosters. Character traits – patience, impatience. Counting, numbers. Days of the week, months of the year. Foreign lands – Africa.

Alalou, Ali. *The butter man* (Alalou, Elizabeth)

Alalou, Elizabeth. *The butter man* by Elizabeth Alalou and Ali Alalou ill. by Julie Klear Essakalli. Charlesbridge, 2008. ISBN 978-1-58089-127-1 Subj: Food. Foreign lands – Morocco.

Alarcón, Francisco X. *From the bellybutton of the moon and other summer poems / Del ombligo de la luna y otros poemas de verano* ill. by Maya Christina Gonzalez. Children's Press, 1998. ISBN 978-0-89239-153-0 Subj: Foreign lands – Mexico. Foreign languages. Nature. Poetry. Seasons – summer.

Iguanas in the snow and other winter poems / Iguanas en la nieve y otros poemas de invierno ill. by Maya Christina Gonzalez. Children's Press, 2001. ISBN 978-0-89239-168-4 Subj: Foreign languages. Picture puzzles. Poetry. Reptiles – iguanas. Seasons – winter. Weather – snow.

Alberti, Theresa Jarosz. *Out and about at the planetarium* ill. by Becky Shipe. Picture Window, 2004. ISBN 978-1-4048-0299-5 Subj: Astronomy. School – field trips. Science.

Vietnam ABCs: a book about the people and places of Vietnam ill. by Natascha Alex Blanks. Picture Window, 2007. ISBN 978-1-4048-2251-1 Subj: ABC books. Foreign lands – Vietnam.

Alborough, Jez. *Captain Duck* ill. by author. HarperCollins, 2003. ISBN 978-0-06-052123-3 Subj: Animals. Birds – ducks. Boats, ships. Rhyming text.

Duck in the truck ill. by author. HarperCollins, 2000. ISBN 978-0-06-028685-9 Subj: Animals. Birds – ducks. Rhyming text. Trucks.

Duck's key where can it be? ill. by author. Kane/Miller, 2005. ISBN 978-1-929132-72-0 Subj: Behavior – lost & found possessions. Birds – ducks. Format, unusual – toy & movable books. Rhyming text.

Fix-it Duck ill. by author. HarperCollins, 2002. ISBN 978-0-06-000699-0 Subj: Animals. Birds – ducks. Rhyming text.

The gobble gobble moooooo tractor book ill. by author. Kane/Miller, 2010. ISBN 978-1-935279-66-2 Subj: Animals – sheep. Farms. Tractors.

Hit the ball Duck ill. by author. Kane/Miller, 2006. ISBN 978-1-929132-96-6 Subj: Birds – ducks. Rhyming text. Sports – baseball.

Hug ill. by author. Candlewick, 2000. ISBN 978-0-7636-1287-0 Subj: Animals. Animals – chimpan-zees. Behavior – lost. Behavior – needing someone. Family life – mothers.

Ice cream bear ill. by author. Candlewick, 1997. ISBN 978-0-7636-0293-2 Subj: Animals – bears. Dreams. Food. Rhyming text. Weather – snow.

It's the bear ill. by author. Candlewick, 1994. ISBN 978-1-56402-486-2 Subj: Activities – picnicking. Animals – bears. Behavior – stealing. Emotions – fear. Family life – mothers. Food. Rhyming text.

My friend bear ill. by author. Candlewick, 1998. ISBN 978-0-7636-0583-4 Subj: Animals – bears. Emotions – loneliness. Friendship. Toys – bears.

Six little chicks ill. by author. Barron's, 2013. ISBN 978-1-43800-181-4 Subj: Animals – foxes. Birds – chickens, roosters. Rhyming text.

Super Duck ill. by author. Kane/Miller, 2009. ISBN 978-1-933605-89-0 Subj: Animals. Birds – ducks. Kites.

Tall ill. by author. Candlewick, 2005. ISBN 978-0-7636-2784-3 Subj: Animals. Animals – monkeys. Character traits – smallness. Concepts – size. Format, unusual – board books. Jungle. Rhyming text.

Watch out! Big Bro's coming! ill. by author. Candlewick, 1997. ISBN 978-0-7636-0130-0 Subj: Animals. Animals – mice. Concepts – size. Emotions – fear. Family life – brothers & sisters.

Where's my teddy? ill. by author. Candlewick, 1992. ISBN 978-1-56402-048-2 Subj: Animals – bears. Forest, woods. Rhyming text. Toys – bears.

Yes ill. by author. Candlewick, 2006. ISBN 978-0-7636-3183-3 Subj: Animals – chimpanzees. Bedtime. Behavior – fighting, arguing.

Alborozo, Gabriel. *The mouse and the moon* ill. by author. Henry Holt, 2016. ISBN 978-162779224-0 Subj: Animals – mice. Friendship. Moon.

Alcott, Louisa May. *Little women* retold by Janet Allison Brown; ill. by Dinah Dryhurst. Viking, 2001. ISBN 978-0-670-89912-8 Subj: Family life – sisters.

An old-fashioned Thanksgiving ill. by James Bernardin. HarperCollins, 2005. ISBN 978-0-06-000451-4 Subj: Family life. Family life – grandmothers. Food. Holidays – Thanksgiving.

Alda, Arlene. *Arlene Alda's ABC* photos by author. Tricycle, 1993. ISBN 978-1-883672-01-0 Subj: ABC books.

Arlene Alda's 1 2 3: what do you see? photos by author. Tricycle, 1998. ISBN 978-1-883672-71-3 Subj: Counting, numbers.

Did you say pears? photos by author. Tundra, 2006. ISBN 978-0-88776-739-5 Subj: Language.

Except the color grey. Tundra, 2011. ISBN 978-1-77049-284-4 Subj: Concepts – color.

Hello, good-bye ill. by author. Tundra, 2009. ISBN 978-0-88776-900-9 Subj: Concepts – opposites.

Here a face, there a face photos by author. Tundra, 2008. ISBN 978-0-88776-845-3 Subj: Anatomy – faces. Rhyming text.

Hurry Granny Annie ill. by Eve Aldridge. Tricycle, 1999. ISBN 978-1-883672-72-0 Subj: Behavior – hurrying. Family life – grandmothers. Sun.

Iris has a virus ill. by Lisa Desimini. Tundra, 2008. ISBN 978-0-88776-844-6 Subj: Family life. Illness.

Lulu's piano lesson ill. by Lisa Desimini. Tundra, 2010. ISBN 978-0-88776-930-6 Subj: Activities – playing. Character traits – completing things. Musical instruments – pianos.

Morning glory Monday ill. by Maryann Kovalski. Tundra, 2003. ISBN 978-0-88776-620-6 Subj: Communities, neighborhoods. Ethnic groups in the U.S. – Italian Americans. Family life – mothers. Flowers. Seeds.

Sheep, sheep, sheep, help me fall asleep photos by author. Delacorte, 1992. ISBN 978-0-385-30791-8 Subj: Animals. Animals – sheep. Bedtime. Rhyming text.

Aldrin, Buzz. *Look to the stars* ill. by Wendell Minor. Putnam, 2009. ISBN 978-0-399-24721-7 Subj: Careers – astronauts. Space & space ships. U.S. history.

Reaching for the moon ill. by Wendell Minor. HarperCollins, 2005. ISBN 978-0-06-055446-0 Subj: Careers – astronauts. Moon. Space & space ships. U.S. history.

Aleichem, Sholem. *Hanukah money* ill. by Uri Shulevitz. Greenwillow, 1978. ISBN 978-0-688-84120-1 Subj: Folk & fairy tales. Foreign lands. Holidays – Hanukkah. Jewish culture. Religion.

Alemagna, Beatrice. *On a magical do-nothing day* ill. by author. HarperCollins, 2017. ISBN 978-006265760-2 Subj: Computers. Games. Imagination. Nature. Technology. Weather – rain.

Alexander, Cecil Frances. *All creatures great and small* ill. by Naoko Stoop. Sterling, 2012. ISBN 978-1-4027-8581-8 Subj: Animals. Creation. Format, unusual – board books. Music. Nature. Religion. Songs.

All things bright and beautiful ill. by Ashley Bryan. Simon & Schuster, 2010. ISBN 978-1-4169-8939-4 Subj: Creation. Nature. Religion. Songs.

All things bright and beautiful ill. by Anna Vojtech. NorthSouth, 2004. ISBN 978-0-7358-1892-7 Subj: Creation. Nature. Religion. Songs. Songs.

All things bright and beautiful ill. by Bruce Whatley. HarperCollins, 2001. ISBN 978-0-06-026618-9 Subj: Creation. Nature. Religion. Songs.

Alexander, Claire. *Back to front and upside down* ill. by author. Eerdmans, 2012. ISBN 978-0-8028-5414-8 Subj: Animals. Animals – dogs. Disabilities – dyslexia. Letters, cards. School.

Lucy and the bully ill. by author. Albert Whitman, 2008. ISBN 978-0-8075-4786-1 Subj: Animals. Behavior – bullying, teasing. School – nursery.

Monkey and the little one ill. by author. Sterling, 2015. ISBN 978-145491580-5 Subj: Animals – mice. Animals – monkeys. Friendship.

Small Florence: piggy pop star! ill. by author. Albert Whitman, 2010. ISBN 978-0-8075-7455-3 Subj: Animals – pigs. Behavior – bullying, teasing. Character traits – confidence. Family life – sisters. Self-concept.

Alexander, Elizabeth. *Praise song for the day: a poem for Barack Obama's presidential inauguration* ill. by David Diaz. HarperCollins, 2012. ISBN 978-0-06-192663-1 Subj: Ethnic groups in the U.S. – African Americans. Poetry. U.S. history.

Alexander, Jessica. *Look both ways: a cautionary tale* (Shore, Diane Z.)

This is the dream (Shore, Diane Z.)

This is the Earth (Shore, Diane Z.)

Alexander, Kwame. *Acoustic Rooster and his barnyard band* ill. by Tim Bowers. Sleeping Bear, 2011. ISBN 978-1-58536-688-0 Subj: Birds – chickens, roosters. Careers – musicians. Contests. Musical instruments – bands. Rhyming text.

Animal ark: celebrating our wild world in poetry and pictures by Kwame Alexander and Mary Rand Hess, et al; photos by Joel Sartore. National Geographic, 2017. ISBN 978-142632767-4 Subj: Animals. Animals – endangered animals. Poetry.

Surf's up ill. by Daniel Miyares. NorthSouth, 2016. ISBN 978-073584220-5 Subj: Animals – whales. Books, reading. Friendship. Frogs & toads. Sports – surfing.

Alexander, Lloyd. *Fortune tellers* ill. by Trina Schart Hyman. Dutton, 1992. ISBN 978-0-525-44849-5 Subj: Careers – fortune tellers. Cumulative tales. Foreign lands – Africa. Foreign lands – Cameroon.

The house Gobbaleen ill. by Diane Goode. Dutton, 1995. ISBN 978-0-525-45289-8 Subj: Animals – cats. Behavior – trickery. Character traits – foolishness. Character traits – luck. Monsters. Mythical creatures – goblins.

How the cat swallowed thunder ill. by Judith Byron Schachner. Dutton, 2000. ISBN 978-0-525-46449-

5 Subj: Animals – cats. Behavior – misbehavior. Folk & fairy tales – pourquoi tales.

Alexander, Martha G. *And my mean old mother will be sorry, Blackboard Bear* ill. by author. Candlewick, 2000. ISBN 978-0-7636-0668-8 Subj: Animals – bears. Behavior – running away. Emotions – anger. Imagination – imaginary friends.

Blackboard Bear ill. by author. 2nd ed. Candlewick, 1999. ISBN 978-0-7636-0667-1 Subj: Activities – playing. Animals – bears. Concepts – size. Imagination – imaginary friends.

I sure am glad to see you, Blackboard Bear ill. by author. Dial, 1976. ISBN 978-0-7636-0669-5 Subj: Animals – bears. Behavior – bullying, teasing. Imagination – imaginary friends.

I'll never share you, Blackboard Bear ill. by author. Candlewick, 2003. ISBN 978-0-7636-1590-1 Subj: Activities – drawing. Animals – bears. Behavior – sharing.

I'll protect you from the jungle beasts ill. by author. Dial, 1973. ISBN 978-0-8037-4309-0 Subj: Emotions – fear. Imagination – imaginary friends. Problem solving. Sleep. Toys – bears.

Max and the dumb flower picture by Martha G. Alexander and James Rumford; ill. by Martha G. Alexander. Charlesbridge, 2009. ISBN 978-1-58089-156-1 Subj: Activities – drawing. Art. Character traits – individuality. Holidays – Mother's Day.

Nobody asked me if I wanted a baby sister ill. by author. Dial, 1971. ISBN 978-0-8037-6402-6 Subj: Babies, toddlers. Emotions – envy, jealousy. Family life – new sibling. Family life – sisters. Sibling rivalry.

We're in big trouble, Blackboard Bear ill. by author. Dial, 1980. ISBN 978-0-8037-9742-0 Subj: Animals – bears. Behavior – misbehavior. Imagination – imaginary friends. Night. Problem solving.

When the new baby comes, I'm moving out ill. by author. Dial, 1979. ISBN 978-0-8037-9558-7 Subj: Animals – babies. Emotions – envy, jealousy. Family life – new sibling. Sibling rivalry.

You're a genius, Blackboard Bear ill. by author. Candlewick, 1995. ISBN 978-1-56402-238-7 Subj: Animals – bears. Dreams. Imagination – imaginary friends. Night. Space & space ships.

Alexander, Sue. *Behold the trees* ill. by Leonid Gore. Scholastic, 2001. ISBN 978-0-590-76211-3 Subj: Ecology. Foreign lands – Israel. Trees.

One more time, Mama ill. by David Soman. Marshall Cavendish, 1999. ISBN 978-0-7614-5051-1 Subj: Birth. Family life – mothers. Nature.

Who goes out on Halloween? ill. by G. Brian Karas. Bantam, 1990. ISBN 978-0-553-05891-8 Subj: Holidays – Halloween. Monsters. Mythical creatures – goblins. Rhyming text. Witches.

Alexander, Van. *A-tisket, a-tasket* (Fitzgerald, Ella)

Alexie, Sherman. *Thunder Boy Jr.* ill. by Yuyi Morales. Little, Brown, 2016. ISBN 978-031601372-7 Subj: Family life – fathers. Indians of North America. Names. Self-concept.

Alger, Leclaire Gowans. *All in the morning early* ill. by Evaline Ness. Henry Holt, 1963. Subj: Caldecott award honor books. Folk & fairy tales. Foreign lands – Scotland. Poetry. Songs.

Always room for one more ill. by Nonny Hogrogian. Henry Holt, 1965. ISBN 978-0-8050-0331-4 Subj: Caldecott award books. Cumulative tales. Folk & fairy tales. Foreign lands – Scotland. Homes, houses. Music.

Aliki. *Ah, music!* ill. by author. HarperCollins, 2003. ISBN 978-0-06-028727-6 Subj: Music.

All by myself! ill. by author. HarperCollins, 2000. ISBN 978-0-06-028930-0 Subj: Activities. Character traits – confidence. Character traits – individuality. Self-concept.

At Mary Bloom's ill. by author. Greenwillow, 1976. ISBN 978-0-688-84048-8 Subj: Animals – babies. Animals – mice.

Best friends together again ill. by author. Greenwillow, 1995. ISBN 978-0-688-13754-0 Subj: Friendship. Moving.

Christmas tree memories ill. by author. HarperCollins, 1991. ISBN 978-0-06-020008-4 Subj: Family life. Holidays – Christmas. Memories, memory. Trees.

Communication ill. by author. Greenwillow, 1993. ISBN 978-0-688-11248-6 Subj: Activities – writing. Language.

Corn is maize: the gift of the Indians ill. by author. Crowell, 1976. ISBN 978-0-690-00976-7 Subj: Gardens, gardening. Indians of North America. Plants. Science.

Digging up dinosaurs ill. by author. Rev. ed. Crowell, 1988. ISBN 978-0-690-04716-5 Subj: Activities – digging. Dinosaurs. Humorous stories. Prehistory. Science.

Dinosaur bones ill. by author. HarperCollins, 1988. ISBN 978-0-690-04550-5 Subj: Dinosaurs. Prehistory.

Dinosaurs are different ill. by author. Crowell, 1985. ISBN 978-0-690-04458-4 Subj: Dinosaurs. Prehistory. Science.

Feelings ill. by author. Greenwillow, 1984. ISBN 978-0-688-03832-8 Subj: Emotions. Friendship.

Fossils tell of long ago ill. by author. Rev. ed. Crowell, 1990. ISBN 978-0-690-31379-6 Subj: Dinosaurs. Fossils. Science.

Hello! Good-bye! ill. by author. Greenwillow, 1996. ISBN 978-0-688-14334-3 Subj: Language.

How a book is made ill. by author. HarperCollins, 1986. ISBN 978-0-690-04498-0 Subj: Books, reading. Libraries.

I'm growing! ill. by author. HarperCollins, 1992. ISBN 978-0-06-020245-3 Subj: Behavior – growing up.

Jack and Jake ill. by author. Greenwillow, 1986. ISBN 978-0-688-06100-5 Subj: Behavior – mistakes. Character traits – individuality. Family life. Multiple births – twins.

The long lost coelacanth and other living fossils ill. by author. Crowell, 1973. ISBN 978-0-690-50478-1 Subj: Fish. Fossils. Science.

Manners ill. by author. Greenwillow, 1990. ISBN 978-0-688-09199-6 Subj: Etiquette.

The many lives of Benjamin Franklin ill. by author. Simon & Schuster, 1988. ISBN 978-0-671-66119-9 Subj: U.S. history.

Marianthe's story one: painted words; Marianthe's story two: spoken memories ill. by author. Greenwillow, 1998. ISBN 978-0-688-15662-6 Subj: Family life. Foreign lands. Format, unusual. School.

Milk from cow to carton ill. by author. HarperCollins, 1992. ISBN 978-0-06-020435-8 Subj: Animals – bulls, cows. Careers – farmers. Food.

Mummies made in Egypt ill. by author. Crowell, 1979. ISBN 978-0-690-03859-0 Subj: Death. Foreign lands – Egypt. Religion.

My feet ill. by author. HarperCollins, 1990. ISBN 978-0-690-04815-5 Subj: Anatomy – feet. Science.

My five senses ill. by author. Rev. ed. HarperCollins, 1989. ISBN 978-0-690-04794-3 Subj: Senses – hearing. Senses – sight. Senses – smell. Senses – taste. Senses – touch.

My hands ill. by author. Rev. ed. HarperCollins, 1992. ISBN 978-0-06-445096-6 Subj: Anatomy – hands. Science.

My visit to the aquarium ill. by author. HarperCollins, 1993. ISBN 978-0-06-021459-3 Subj: Animals. Aquariums. Fish. Plants.

My visit to the dinosaurs ill. by author. Rev. ed. Crowell, 1985. ISBN 978-0-690-04423-2 Subj: Dinosaurs. Museums. Prehistory. Science.

My visit to the zoo ill. by author. HarperCollins, 1997. ISBN 978-0-06-024943-4 Subj: Animals. Animals – endangered animals. Birds. Ecology. Zoos.

Overnight at Mary Bloom's ill. by author. Greenwillow, 1987. ISBN 978-0-688-06765-6 Subj: Activities. Activities – playing. Friendship. Night.

A play's the thing ill. by author. HarperCollins, 2005. ISBN 978-0-06-074356-7 Subj: Character traits – cooperation. School. Theater.

Push button ill. by author. HarperCollins, 2010. ISBN 978-0-06-167308-5 Subj: Activities – playing. Rhyming text.

Quiet in the garden ill. by author. Greenwillow, 2009. ISBN 978-0-06-155207-6 Subj: Gardens, gardening. Nature.

The story of Johnny Appleseed ill. by author. Simon & Schuster, 1988. Reprint. Originally published: Englewood Cliffs, N.J.: Prentice-Hall, ©1963. ISBN 978-0-671-66298-1 Subj: Character traits – generosity. Gardens, gardening. Tall tales. U.S. history – frontier & pioneer life.

The story of William Penn ill. by author. Simon & Schuster, 1994. ISBN 978-0-671-88558-8 Subj: Character traits – kindness. U.S. history.

Tabby ill. by author. HarperCollins, 1995. ISBN 978-0-06-024916-8 Subj: Animals – cats. Ethnic groups in the U.S. – Hispanic Americans. Wordless.

Those summers ill. by author. HarperCollins, 1996. ISBN 978-0-06-024938-0 Subj: Family life. Sea & seashore. Seasons – summer.

Three gold pieces: a Greek folk tale ill. by author. Pantheon, 1967. ISBN 978-0-394-91737-5 Subj: Character traits – luck. Folk & fairy tales. Foreign lands – Greece.

The twelve months ill. by adapter. Greenwillow, 1978. ISBN 978-0-688-84164-5 Subj: Behavior – dissatisfaction. Character traits – optimism. Folk & fairy tales. Foreign lands – Greece.

The two of them ill. by author. Greenwillow, 1979. ISBN 978-0-688-84225-3 Subj: Character traits – helpfulness. Character traits – loyalty. Family life – grandfathers.

Use your head, dear ill. by author. Greenwillow, 1983. ISBN 978-0-688-01812-2 Subj: Behavior – forgetfulness. Birthdays. Reptiles – alligators, crocodiles.

We are best friends ill. by author. Greenwillow, 1982. ISBN 978-0-688-00823-9 Subj: Emotions – anger. Emotions – loneliness. Friendship. Moving.

A weed is a flower: the life of George Washington Carver ill. by author. Simon & Schuster, 1988. ISBN 978-0-671-66118-2 Subj: Character traits – perseverance. Ethnic groups in the U.S. – African Americans. Science. U.S. history.

Welcome, little baby ill. by author. Greenwillow, 1987. ISBN 978-0-688-06811-0 Subj: Babies, toddlers. Family life.

Wild and woolly mammoths ill. by author. Harper-Collins, 1996. ISBN 978-0-06-026277-8 Subj: Animals. Science.

Alizadeh, Kate. *Quiet!* ill. by author. Child's Play, 2017. ISBN 978-184643887-5 Subj: Homes, houses. Noise, sounds.

Alko, Selina. *B is for Brooklyn* ill. by author. Henry Holt, 2012. ISBN 978-0-8050-9213-4 Subj: ABC books. Cities, towns. Communities, neighborhoods.

Daddy Christmas and Hanukkah Mama ill. by author. Knopf, 2012. ISBN 978-0-375-86093-5 Subj: Family life – parents. Holidays – Christmas. Holidays – Hanukkah.

Every-day dress-up ill. by author. Random House, 2011. ISBN 978-0-375-86092-8 Subj: Activities – playing. Clothing. Imagination.

I'm your peanut butter big brother ill. by author. Knopf, 2009. ISBN 978-0-375-85627-3 Subj: Babies, toddlers. Ethnic groups in the U.S. Family life – brothers.

Allan, Nicholas. *Where Willy went* ill. by author. Knopf, 2005. ISBN 978-0-375-93030-0 Subj: Sex instruction.

Allard, Harry. *Bumps in the night* ill. by James Marshall. Doubleday, 1979. ISBN 978-0-385-12943-5 Subj: Animals. Ghosts. Noise, sounds.

Miss Nelson has a field day ill. by James Marshall. Houghton, 1985. ISBN 978-0-395-36690-5 Subj: Behavior – secrets. Humorous stories. School – field trips.

Miss Nelson is back by Harry Allard and James Marshall ill. by James Marshall. Houghton, 1982. ISBN 978-0-395-32956-6 Subj: Behavior – misbehavior. Careers – teachers. Humorous stories. School.

Miss Nelson is missing! by Harry Allard and James Marshall ill. by James Marshall. Houghton, 1977. ISBN 978-0-395-25296-3 Subj: Behavior – misbehavior. Careers – teachers. Humorous stories. School.

Starlight goes to town ill. by George Booth. Farrar, 2008. ISBN 978-0-374-37187-6 Subj: Behavior – wishing. Birds – chickens, roosters. Humorous stories.

The Stupids die ill. by James Marshall. Houghton, 1981. ISBN 978-0-395-30347-4 Subj: Behavior – misunderstanding. Humorous stories.

The Stupids have a ball by Harry Allard and James Marshall ill. by James Marshall. Houghton, 1978. ISBN 978-0-395-26497-3 Subj: Family life. Humorous stories. Parties.

The Stupids step out ill. by James Marshall. Houghton, 1974. ISBN 978-0-395-18513-1 Subj: Activities. Family life. Humorous stories.

The Stupids take off by Harry Allard and James Marshall ill. by James Marshall. Houghton, 1989. ISBN 978-0-395-50068-2 Subj: Activities – flying. Family life. Humorous stories.

Allchin, Rosalind. *The frog princess* ill. by author. Kids Can, 2001. ISBN 978-1-55337-000-0 Subj: Frogs & toads. Royalty – princes. Royalty – princesses.

Allegra, Mike. *Sarah gives thanks: how Thanksgiving became a national holiday* ill. by David C. Gardner. Albert Whitman, 2012. ISBN 978-0-8075-7239-9 Subj: Holidays – Thanksgiving. U.S. history.

Allen, Debbie. *Brothers of the knight* ill. by Kadir Nelson. Dial, 1999. ISBN 978-0-8037-2488-4 Subj: Activities – dancing. Family life – brothers. Folk & fairy tales. Foreign lands – Germany.

Dancing in the wings ill. by Kadir Nelson. Dial, 2000. ISBN 978-0-8037-2501-0 Subj: Activities – dancing. Ballet. Ethnic groups in the U.S. – African Americans.

Allen, Elanna. *Itsy Mitsy runs away* ill. by author. Atheneum, 2011. ISBN 978-1-4424-0671-1 Subj: Bedtime. Behavior – running away. Family life – fathers.

Poor little guy ill. by author. Dial, 2016. ISBN 978-052542825-1 Subj: Fish. Octopuses.

Allen, Jonathan. *Don't copy me!* ill. by author. Boxer, 2012. ISBN 978-1-907967-20-7 Subj: Behavior – imitation. Birds – puffins. Birds – seagulls.

"I'm not cute!" ill. by author. Hyperion, 2006. ISBN 978-0-7868-3720-5 Subj: Animals. Birds – owls. Character traits – appearance.

I'm not reading! ill. by author. Boxer , 2013. ISBN 978-1-907967-44-3 Subj: Animals. Birds – chickens, roosters. Birds – owls. Books, reading.

"I'm not Santa!" ill. by author. Hyperion, 2008. ISBN 978-1-4231-1300-3 Subj: Animals – rabbits. Birds – owls. Holidays – Christmas. Santa Claus.

"I'm not scared!" ill. by author. Hyperion, 2007. ISBN 978-0-7868-3722-9 Subj: Birds – owls. Emotions – fear.

The little rabbit who liked to say moo ill. by author. Boxer, 2008. ISBN 978-1-905417-78-0 Subj: Animals. Animals – rabbits. Noise, sounds.

Mucky moose ill. by author. Macmillan, 1991. ISBN 978-0-02-700251-5 Subj: Animals – moose. Animals – wolves. Character traits – cleanliness. Senses – smell.

Allen, Joy. *Princess Palooza* ill. by author. Penguin, 2011. ISBN 978-0-399-25455-0 Subj: Activities – playing. Imagination. Parties. Rhyming text. Royalty – princesses.

Princess party ill. by author. Putnam, 2009. ISBN 978-0-399-25259-4 Subj: Parties. Rhyming text. Royalty – princesses.

Allen, Judy. *Are you a butterfly?* by Judy Allen and Tudor Humphries ill. by Tudor Humphries. Kingfisher, 2000. ISBN 978-0-7534-5240-0 Subj: Insects – butterflies, caterpillars. Science.

Are you a grasshopper? by Judy Allen and Tudor Humphries ill. by Tudor Humphries. Kingfisher, 2002. ISBN 978-0-7534-5366-7 Subj: Insects – grasshoppers. Science.

Are you a ladybug? by Judy Allen and Tudor Humphries ill. by Tudor Humphries. Kingfisher, 2000. ISBN 978-0-7534-5241-7 Subj: Insects – ladybugs. Science.

Are you a snail? by Judy Allen and Tudor Humphries ill. by Tudor Humphries. Kingfisher, 2000. ISBN 978-0-7534-5242-4 Subj: Animals – snails. Science.

Are you an ant? by Judy Allen and Tudor Humphries ill. by Tudor Humphries. Kingfisher, 2002. ISBN 978-0-7534-5365-0 Subj: Insects – ants. Science.

Whales and dolphins ill. by Mike Bostock. Kingfisher, 2008. ISBN 978-0-7534-6225-6 Subj: Animals – dolphins. Animals – whales. Format, unusual – toy & movable books.

Allen, Kathryn Madeline. *I am a baby* photos by Rebecca Gizicki. Albert Whitman, 2016. ISBN 978-080753622-3 Subj: Babies, toddlers. Rhyming text.

A kiss means I love you photos by Eric Futran. Albert Whitman, 2012. ISBN 978-0-8075-4186-9 Subj: Communication. Emotions. Rhyming text.

Show me happy photos by Eric Futran. Albert Whitman, 2015. ISBN 978-080757349-5 Subj: Communication. Emotions. Rhyming text.

Allen, Kathy. *The U.S. Constitution.* Capstone, 2006. ISBN 978-0-7368-9594-1 Subj: U.S. history.

Allen, Nancy Kelly. *"Happy birthday": the story of the world's most popular song* ill. by Gary Undercuffler. Pelican, 2010. ISBN 978-1-58980-675-7 Subj: Birthdays. Songs.

Allen, Pamela. *Who sank the boat?* ill. by author. Coward, 1983. ISBN 978-0-698-20576-5 Subj: Animals. Boats, ships. Rhyming text. Science.

Allen, Susan. *Read anything good lately?* by Susan Allen and Jane Lindaman ill. by Vicky Enright. Millbrook, 2003. ISBN 978-0-7613-2322-8 Subj: ABC books. Books, reading. Language.

Used any numbers lately? by Susan Allen and Jane Lindaman ill. by Vicky Enright. Lerner, 2008. ISBN 978-0-8225-8658-6 Subj: ABC books. Counting, numbers.

Allenby, Victoria. *Nat the cat can sleep like that* ill. by Tara Anderson. Pajama, 2014. ISBN 978-192748552-1 Subj: Animals – cats. Bedtime. Rhyming text. Sleep.

Alley, R. W. *There once was a witch* ill. by R. W. Alley. HarperCollins, 2003. ISBN 978-0-06-000795-9 Subj: Format, unusual – board books. Holidays – Halloween. Music. Songs. Witches.

Alley, Zoe B. *There's a princess in the palace* ill. by R. W. Alley. Roaring Brook, 2010. ISBN 978-1-59643-471-4 Subj: Folk & fairy tales. Royalty – princesses.

There's a wolf at the door ill. by R. W. Alley. Roaring Brook, 2008. ISBN 978-1-59643-275-8 Subj: Animals – wolves. Folk & fairy tales.

Allison, Catherine. *Brown paper bear* ill. by Neil Reed. Scholastic, 2004. ISBN 978-0-439-63900-2 Subj: Toys – bears.

Almond, David. *Kate, the cat and the moon* ill. by Stephen Lambert. Random House, 2005. ISBN 978-0-385-90929-7 Subj: Animals – cats. Imagination. Night.

Alphamals A-Z ill. by Graham Carter. Candlewick/Big Picture, 2017. ISBN 978-076369557-6 Subj: ABC books. Animals.

Alphin, Elaine Marie. *Dinosaur hunter* ill. by Don Bolognese. HarperCollins, 2003. ISBN 978-0-06-028304-9 Subj: Dinosaurs. Fossils.

Alrawi, Karim. *The girl who lost her smile* ill. by Czernecki, Stefan. Winslow, 2000. ISBN 978-1-890817-17-6 Subj: Emotions. Foreign lands – Iraq.

Alsdurf, Phyllis. *It's milking time* ill. by Steve Johnson. Random House, 2012. ISBN 978-0-375-86911-2 Subj: Animals – bulls, cows. Farms.

Alsenas, Linas. *Mrs. Claus takes a vacation* ill. by author. Scholastic, 2006. ISBN 978-0-439-77978-4

Subj: Activities – traveling. Activities – vacationing. Holidays – Christmas. Santa Claus.

Peanut ill. by author. Scholastic, 2007. ISBN 978-0-439-77980-7 Subj: Animals – camels. Animals – elephants. Circus. Old age. Pets.

Alter, Anna. *Abigail spells* ill. by author. Knopf, 2009. ISBN 978-0-375-85617-4 Subj: Animals – bears. Birds – chickens, roosters. Contests. Friendship. School.

Disappearing Desmond ill. by author. Random House, 2010. ISBN 978-0-375-86684-5 Subj: Animals. Behavior – hiding. Character traits – shyness. School.

Estelle and Lucy ill. by author. Greenwillow, 2001. ISBN 978-0-688-17883-3 Subj: Animals – cats. Animals – mice. Concepts – size. Family life – sisters. Sibling rivalry.

A photo for Greta ill. by author. Random House, 2011. ISBN 978-0-375-85618-1 Subj: Careers – photographers. Family life – fathers.

What can you do with an old red shoe? a green activity book about re-use ill. by author. Henry Holt, 2009. ISBN 978-0-8050-8290-6 Subj: Activities – making things. Behavior – seeking better things. Ecology.

Altes, Marta. *My grandpa* ill. by author. Abrams, 2013. ISBN 978-1-4197-0588-5 Subj: Animals – bears. Family life – grandfathers. Old age.

Altman, Alexandra Jessup. *Waiting for Benjamin: a story about autism* ill. by Susan Keeter. Albert Whitman, 2008. ISBN 978-0-8075-7364-8 Subj: Disabilities – autism. Emotions – embarrassment. Family life – brothers.

Altman, Linda Jacobs. *Amelia's road* ill. by Enrique O. Sánchez. Lee & Low, 1993. ISBN 978-1-880000-04-5 Subj: Activities – working. Behavior – seeking better things. Careers – migrant workers. Family life. Homes, houses. Trees.

The legend of Freedom Hill ill. by Cornelius Van Wright and Ying-Hwa Hu. Lee & Low, 2000. ISBN 978-1-58430-003-8 Subj: Ethnic groups in the U.S. – African Americans. Slavery. U.S. history – frontier & pioneer life.

Singing with Momma Lou ill. by author. Lee & Low, 2002. ISBN 978-1-58430-040-3 Subj: Ethnic groups in the U.S. – African Americans. Family life – grandmothers. Illness – Alzheimer's. Old age.

Altman, Susan. *Followers of the north star: rhymes about African American heroes, heroines, and historical times* by Susan Altman and Susan Lechner ill. by Byron Wooden. Children's Press, 1993. ISBN 978-0-516-05151-2 Subj: Ethnic groups in the U.S. – African Americans. Poetry. U.S. history.

Alvarez, Julia. *The secret footprints* ill. by Fabian Negrin. Knopf, 2000. ISBN 978-0-679-99309-4 Subj: Folk & fairy tales. Foreign lands – Dominican Republic. Indians of Central America – Taino.

Where do they go? ill. by Sabra Field. Seven Stories/Triangle Square, 2016. ISBN 978-160980670-5 Subj: Death. Emotions – grief. Rhyming text.

Amado, Elisa. *Tricycle* ill. by Alfonso Ruano. Groundwood, 2007. ISBN 978-0-88899-614-5 Subj: Behavior – stealing. Friendship. Prejudice.

What are you doing? ill. by Manuel Monroy. Groundwood, 2011. ISBN 978-1-55498-070-3 Subj: Books, reading. Foreign lands – Mexico. School – first day.

Aman, Kimiko. *The fox wish* ill. by Komako Sakai. Chronicle, 2017. ISBN 978-145215188-5 Subj: Activities – jumping. Animals – foxes. Behavior – wishing.

Amann, Jürg. *Ten birds* ill. by Helga Gebert. NorthSouth, 2012. ISBN 978-0-7358-4100-0 Subj: Birds. Counting, numbers. Problem solving.

Amant, Kathleen. *Little Rabbit gets messy* ill. by author. Clavis, 2008. ISBN 978-1-60537-017-0 Subj: Animals – rabbits. Behavior – messy. Toys.

On your potty, Little Rabbit ill. by author. Clavis, 2008. ISBN 978-1-60537-015-6 Subj: Animals – rabbits. Toilet training. Toys.

Amato, Mary. *The chicken of the family* ill. by Delphine Durand. Putnam, 2008. ISBN 978-0-399-24196-3 Subj: Behavior – bullying, teasing. Birds – chickens, roosters. Family life – sisters. Farms.

Ambrose, Sophie. *The lonely giant* ill. by author. Candlewick, 2016. ISBN 978-076368225-5 Subj: Ecology. Forest, woods. Giants.

Amenta, Charles A., III. *Russell's world: a story for kids about autism* ill. by Monika Pollak; photos by author. Magination, 2011. ISBN 978-1-4338-0975-0 Subj: Disabilities – autism.

American babies. Charlesbridge, 2010. ISBN 978-1-58089-280-3 Subj: Babies, toddlers. Format, unusual – board books.

American Museum of Natural History. *ABC insects.* Sterling, 2014. ISBN 978-145491194-4 Subj: ABC books. Format, unusual – board books. Insects.

Spot the animals: a lift-the-flap book of colors ill. by Steve Jenkins. Sterling, 2012. ISBN 978-1-4027-7723-3 Subj: Animals. Format, unusual – toy & movable books.

Ammon, Richard. *An Amish Christmas* ill. by Pamela Patrick. Atheneum, 1996. ISBN 978-0-689-

80377-2 Subj: Ethnic groups in the U.S. – Amish. Holidays – Christmas. Religion.

Amish horses ill. by Pamela Patrick. Atheneum, 2001. ISBN 978-0-689-82623-8 Subj: Animals – horses, ponies. Ethnic groups in the U.S. – Amish. Farms.

An Amish wedding ill. by Pamela Patrick. Atheneum, 1998. ISBN 978-0-689-81677-2 Subj: Ethnic groups in the U.S. – Amish. Weddings.

An Amish year ill. by Pamela Patrick. Atheneum, 2000. ISBN 978-0-689-82622-1 Subj: Ethnic groups in the U.S. – Amish. Seasons.

Amnesty International. *We are all born free: the Universal Declaration of Human Rights in pictures* ill. with photos. Frances Lincoln, 2008. ISBN 978-1-84507-650-4 Subj: Character traits – freedom. World.

Amsden, Janet. *Grizzly Pete and the ghosts* ill. by John Beder. Annick, 2002. ISBN 978-1-55037-719-4 Subj: Careers – miners. Ghosts. U.S. history – frontier & pioneer life.

Anastas, Margaret. *A hug for you* ill. by Susan Winter. HarperCollins, 2005. ISBN 978-0-06-623614-8 Subj: Animals. Birds – ducks. Emotions – love. Family life – parents. Friendship. Insects. Rhyming text.

Mommy's best kisses ill. by Susan Winter. HarperCollins, 2003. ISBN 978-0-06-623606-3 Subj: Animals. Emotions – love. Family life – mothers. Rhyming text.

Anaya, Rudolfo A. *Farolitos for Abuelo* ill. by Edward Gonzales. Hyperion, 1998. ISBN 978-0-7868-2186-0 Subj: Death. Ethnic groups in the U.S. – Mexican Americans. Family life – grandfathers. Holidays – Christmas.

Roadrunner's dance ill. by David Diaz. Hyperion, 2000. ISBN 978-0-7868-2209-6 Subj: Animals. Behavior – bullying, teasing. Birds – roadrunners. Creation. Desert. Reptiles – snakes.

Ancona, George. *Barrio: José's neighborhood* ill. by author. Harcourt, 1998. ISBN 978-0-15-201049-2 Subj: Communities, neighborhoods. Ethnic groups in the U.S. – Hispanic Americans.

Handtalk zoo (Miller, Mary Beth)

It's our garden: from seeds to harvest in a school garden photos by author. Candlewick, 2013. ISBN 978-0-7636-5392-7 Subj: Gardens, gardening. School.

Mi música / My music photos by author. Scholastic, 2005. ISBN 978-0-516-25295-7 Subj: Ethnic groups in the U.S. – Hispanic Americans. Foreign languages. Music.

Mis abuelos / My grandparents photos by author. Scholastic, 2005. ISBN 978-0-516-25294-0 Subj:

Ethnic groups in the U.S. – Hispanic Americans. Family life – grandparents. Foreign languages.

Mis comidas / My foods photos by author. Scholastic, 2005. ISBN 978-0-516-25292-6 Subj: Ethnic groups in the U.S. – Hispanic Americans. Food. Foreign languages.

Mis fiestas / My celebrations photos by author. Scholastic, 2005. ISBN 978-0-516-25290-2 Subj: Ethnic groups in the U.S. – Hispanic Americans. Foreign languages. Holidays.

Mis juegos / My games photos by author. Scholastic, 2005. ISBN 978-0-516-25293-3 Subj: Ethnic groups in the U.S. – Hispanic Americans. Foreign languages. Games.

Mis quehaceres / My chores photos by author. Scholastic, 2005. ISBN 978-0-516-25291-9 Subj: Activities – working. Character traits – helpfulness. Ethnic groups in the U.S. – Hispanic Americans. Foreign languages.

Andersen, Hans Christian. *The dinosaur's new clothes* by Diane Goode; ill. by author. Blue Sky, 1999. ISBN 978-0-590-38360-8 Subj: Character traits – pride. Character traits – vanity. Clothing. Dinosaurs. Folk & fairy tales. Imagination. Prehistory. Royalty – emperors.

The emperor's new clothes ill. by Angela Barrett. Candlewick, 1997. ISBN 978-0-7636-0119-5 Subj: Character traits – pride. Character traits – vanity. Clothing. Folk & fairy tales. Imagination. Royalty – emperors.

The emperor's new clothes ill. by Virginia Lee Burton. Houghton, 2004, 1949. ISBN 978-0-618-34420-8 Subj: Character traits – pride. Character traits – vanity. Clothing. Folk & fairy tales. Humorous stories. Imagination. Royalty – emperors.

The emperor's new clothes retold by Riki Levinson; ill. by Robert Byrd. Dutton, 1991. ISBN 978-0-525-44611-8 Subj: Animals. Character traits – pride. Character traits – vanity. Clothing. Folk & fairy tales. Humorous stories. Imagination. Royalty – emperors.

The emperor's new clothes retold by Louise John; ill. by Serena Curmi. Evans Brothers, 2011. ISBN 978-0-237-53895-8 Subj: Character traits – pride. Character traits – vanity. Clothing. Folk & fairy tales. Humorous stories. Imagination. Royalty – emperors.

The emperor's new clothes adapt. by Susan Blackaby; ill. by Charlene DeLage. Picture Window, 2004. ISBN 978-1-4048-0224-7 Subj: Character traits – pride. Character traits – vanity. Clothing. Folk & fairy tales. Humorous stories. Imagination. Royalty – emperors.

The emperor's new clothes adapt. by Jean Van Leeuwen; ill. by Jack Delano and Irene Delano. Random House, 1971. ISBN 978-0-394-82105-4 Subj: Character traits – pride. Character traits – vanity. Clothing. Folk & fairy tales. Humorous stories. Imagination. Royalty – emperors.

The emperor's new clothes ill. by Anne Rockwell. Crowell, 1982. ISBN 978-0-690-04149-1 Subj: Character traits – pride. Character traits – vanity. Clothing. Folk & fairy tales. Humorous stories. Imagination. Royalty – emperors.

The emperor's new clothes adapt. by Janet Stevens; ill. by adapter. Holiday, 1985. ISBN 978-0-8234-0566-4 Subj: Character traits – pride. Character traits – vanity. Clothing. Folk & fairy tales. Humorous stories. Imagination. Royalty – emperors.

The emperor's new clothes adapt. by Eve Tharlet; ill. by adapter. NorthSouth, 2000. ISBN 978-0-7358-1341-0 Subj: Character traits – pride. Character traits – vanity. Clothing. Folk & fairy tales. Foreign lands – China. Humorous stories. Royalty – emperors.

The emperor's new clothes: a tale set in China retold by Demi; ill. by reteller. Margaret K. McElderry, 2000. ISBN 978-0-689-83068-6 Subj: Character traits – pride. Character traits – vanity. Clothing. Folk & fairy tales. Foreign lands – China. Humorous stories. Royalty – emperors.

The fir tree adapt. by Diane Goode; ill. by adapter. Random House, 1988. ISBN 978-0-394-81941-9 Subj: Folk & fairy tales. Holidays – Christmas. Trees.

The fir tree adapt. by Bernadette Watts; ill. by adapter. NorthSouth, 1990. ISBN 978-1-55858-093-0 Subj: Folk & fairy tales. Holidays – Christmas. Trees.

It's perfectly true! adapt. by Janet Stevens; ill. by adapter. Holiday, 1987. ISBN 978-0-8234-0672-2 Subj: Behavior – gossip, rumors. Character traits – vanity. Death. Folk & fairy tales.

La princesa and the pea by Susan Middleton Elya; ill. by Juana Martinez-Neal. Putnam, 2017. ISBN 978-039925156-6 Subj: Folk & fairy tales. Foreign languages. Rhyming text. Royalty – princesses. Sleep.

The little match girl ill. by Rachel Isadora. Putnam, 1987. ISBN 978-0-399-21336-6 Subj: Death. Folk & fairy tales. Holidays – New Year's. Homeless. Poverty.

The little match girl ill. by Blair Lent. Houghton, 1968. ISBN 978-1-56397-470-0 Subj: Death. Folk & fairy tales. Holidays – New Year's. Homeless. Poverty.

The little match girl ill. by Jerry Pinkney. Fogelman, 1999. ISBN 978-0-8037-2314-6 Subj: Death. Folk & fairy tales. Holidays – New Year's. Homeless. Poverty.

The little matchstick girl ill. by Debbie Lavreys. Clavis, 2008. ISBN 978-1-60537-008-8 Subj: Death. Folk & fairy tales. Holidays – New Year's. Homeless. Poverty.

The little mermaid adapt. by Susan Blackaby; ill. by Charlene DeLage. Picture Window, 2004. ISBN 978-1-4048-0221-6 Subj: Folk & fairy tales. Mythical creatures – mermaids, mermen.

The little mermaid ill. by Michael Hague. Henry Holt, 1993. ISBN 978-0-8050-1010-7 Subj: Folk & fairy tales. Mythical creatures – mermaids, mermen.

The little mermaid retold by Rachel Isadora; ill. by reteller. Putnam, 1998. ISBN 978-0-399-22813-1 Subj: Folk & fairy tales. Mythical creatures – mermaids, mermen.

The nightingale ill. by Nancy Ekholm Burkert. HarperCollins, 1965. Subj: Birds – nightingales. Character traits – freedom. Folk & fairy tales. Foreign lands – China. Royalty – emperors.

The nightingale adapt. by Pirkko Vainio; ill. by adapter. NorthSouth, 2011. ISBN 978-0-7358-4029-4 Subj: Birds – nightingales. Character traits – freedom. Folk & fairy tales. Foreign lands – China. Royalty – emperors.

The nightingale ill. by Lisbeth Zwerger. NorthSouth, 1999. ISBN 978-0-7358-1118-8 Subj: Birds – nightingales. Character traits – freedom. Folk & fairy tales. Foreign lands – China. Royalty – emperors.

The penguin and the pea (Perlman, Janet)

The princess and the pea retold by Harriet Ziefert; ill. by Emily Bolam. Viking, 1996. ISBN 978-0-670-86054-8 Subj: Folk & fairy tales. Royalty – princesses. Sleep.

The princess and the pea adapt. by Susan Blackaby; ill. by Charlene DeLage. Picture Window, 2004. ISBN 978-1-4048-0223-0 Subj: Folk & fairy tales. Royalty – princesses. Sleep.

The princess and the pea ill. by Dorothée Duntze. Henry Holt, 1985. ISBN 978-0-8050-0170-9 Subj: Folk & fairy tales. Royalty – princesses. Sleep.

The princess and the pea ill. by Maja Dusíková. Floris, 2012. ISBN 978-0-86315-857-5 Subj: Folk & fairy tales. Royalty – princesses. Sleep.

The princess and the pea ill. by Paul Galdone. Seabury Pr., 1978. ISBN 978-0-8164-3202-8 Subj: Folk & fairy tales. Royalty – princesses. Sleep.

The princess and the pea ill. by Rachel Isadora. Penguin, 2007. ISBN 978-0-399-24611-1 Subj: Folk & fairy tales. Foreign lands – Africa. Royalty – princesses. Sleep.

The princess and the pea retold by John Cech; ill. by Bernhard Oberdieck. Sterling, 2007. ISBN 978-

1-4027-3065-8 Subj: Folk & fairy tales. Royalty – princesses. Sleep.

The princess and the pea adapt. by Janet Stevens; ill. by adapter. Holiday, 1982. ISBN 978-0-8234-0442-1 Subj: Folk & fairy tales. Royalty – princesses. Sleep.

The princess and the pea by Alain Vaës; ill. by author. Little, 2001. ISBN 978-0-316-89633-7 Subj: Behavior – greed. Folk & fairy tales. Humorous stories. Jewelry. Royalty – princesses. Sleep.

The princess and the pea in miniature: after the fairy tale by Hans Christian Andersen adapt. by Lauren Child, photos by Polly Borland. Hyperion, 2006. ISBN 978-0-7868-3886-8 Subj: Folk & fairy tales. Royalty – princesses. Sleep.

The snow queen ill. by Angela Barrett. Candlewick, 1993. ISBN 978-1-56402-215-8 Subj: Character traits – bravery. Emotions – love. Folk & fairy tales.

The snow queen sel. by Neil Philip; ill. by Sally Holmes. Lothrop, 1989. ISBN 978-0-688-09048-7 Subj: Character traits – bravery. Emotions – love. Folk & fairy tales.

The snow queen adapt. by Amy Ehrlich; ill. by Susan Jeffers. Dial, 1982. ISBN 978-0-8037-8029-3 Subj: Character traits – bravery. Emotions – love. Folk & fairy tales.

The snow queen: a retelling of the fairy tale ill. by Bagram Ibatoulline. HarperCollins, 2013. ISBN 978-0-06-220950-4 Subj: Character traits – bravery. Emotions – love. Folk & fairy tales.

The steadfast tin soldier retold by Cynthia Rylant; ill. by Jen Corace. Abrams, 2013. ISBN 978-1-4197-0432-1 Subj: Folk & fairy tales. Toys – soldiers.

The steadfast tin soldier adapt. by Susan Blackaby; ill. by Charlene DeLage. Picture Window, 2004. ISBN 978-1-4048-0226-1 Subj: Folk & fairy tales. Toys – soldiers.

The steadfast tin soldier ill. by Paul Galdone. Houghton, 1979. ISBN 978-0-395-28964-8 Subj: Folk & fairy tales. Toys – soldiers.

The steadfast tin soldier retold by Rachel Isadora; ill. by reteller. Putnam, 1996. ISBN 978-0-399-22676-2 Subj: Folk & fairy tales. Toys – soldiers.

The steadfast tin soldier ill. by P. J. Lynch. Harcourt, 1992. ISBN 978-0-15-200599-3 Subj: Folk & fairy tales. Toys – soldiers.

The steadfast tin soldier retold by Tor Seidler; ill. by Fred Marcellino. HarperCollins, 1992. ISBN 978-0-06-205001-4 Subj: Folk & fairy tales. Toys – soldiers.

The steadfast tin soldier JooHee Yoon; ill. by JooHee Yoon. Enchanted Lion, 2016. ISBN 978-

159270202-2 Subj: Folk & fairy tales. Toys – soldiers.

The swineherd ill. by Lisbeth Zwerger. Morrow, 1982. ISBN 978-0-688-00930-4 Subj: Character traits – cleverness. Character traits – selfishness. Folk & fairy tales.

Sylvia Long's Thumbelina by Sylvia Long; ill. by author. Chronicle, 2010. ISBN 978-0-8118-5522-8 Subj: Character traits – smallness. Folk & fairy tales.

Thumbelina adapt. by Susan Blackaby; ill. by Charlene DeLage. Picture Window, 2004. ISBN 978-1-4048-0225-4 Subj: Character traits – smallness. Folk & fairy tales.

Thumbelina ill. by Demi. Putnam, 1987. ISBN 978-0-396-09241-4 Subj: Character traits – smallness. Folk & fairy tales.

Thumbelina ill. by Arlene Graston. Delacorte, 1997. ISBN 978-0-385-32251-5 Subj: Character traits – smallness. Folk & fairy tales.

Thumbelina retold by Brian Alderson; ill. by Bagram Ibatoulline. Candlewick, 2009. ISBN 978-0-7636-2079-0 Subj: Character traits – smallness. Folk & fairy tales.

Thumbelina retold by Amy Ehrlich; ill. by Susan Jeffers. Dial, 1979. ISBN 978-0-8037-8815-2 Subj: Character traits – smallness. Folk & fairy tales.

Thumbelina retold by Lauren A. Mills; ill. by reteller. Little, Brown, 2005. ISBN 978-0-316-57359-7 Subj: Character traits – smallness. Folk & fairy tales.

Thumbeline ill. by Lisbeth Zwerger. Picture Book Studio, 1985. ISBN 978-0-88708-006-7 Subj: Character traits – smallness. Folk & fairy tales.

The tinderbox ill. by Warwick Hutton. Macmillan, 1988. ISBN 978-0-689-50458-7 Subj: Folk & fairy tales. Magic. Witches.

The tinderbox retold by Stephen Mitchell; ill. by Bagram Ibatoulline. Candlewick, 2007. ISBN 978-0-7636-2078-3 Subj: Careers – military. Folk & fairy tales. Magic.

The tinderbox ill. by Barry Moser. Little, 1990. ISBN 978-0-316-03938-3 Subj: Folk & fairy tales. Magic. U.S. history. Witches.

The ugly duckling ill. by Adrienne Adams. Scribners, 1965. Subj: Birds – ducks. Birds – swans. Character traits – appearance. Character traits – being different. Folk & fairy tales.

The ugly duckling adapt. by Sebastien Braun; ill. by adapter. Boxer, 2010. ISBN 978-1-907152-04-7 Subj: Birds – ducks. Birds – swans. Character traits – appearance. Character traits – being different. Folk & fairy tales.

The ugly duckling ill. by Lorinda Bryan Cauley. Harcourt, 1979. ISBN 978-0-15-292435-5 Subj:

Birds – ducks. Birds – swans. Character traits – appearance. Character traits – being different. Folk & fairy tales.

The ugly duckling adapt. by Susan Blackaby; ill. by Charlene DeLage. Picture Window, 2004. ISBN 978-1-4048-0222-3 Subj: Birds – ducks. Birds – swans. Character traits – appearance. Character traits – being different. Folk & fairy tales.

The ugly duckling ill. by Robert Ingpen. Minedition, 2005. ISBN 978-0-698-40010-8 Subj: Birds – ducks. Birds – swans. Character traits – appearance. Character traits – being different. Folk & fairy tales.

The ugly duckling retold by Rachel Isadora; ill. by reteller. Putnam, 2009. ISBN 978-0-399-25029-3 Subj: Birds – ducks. Birds – swans. Character traits – appearance. Character traits – being different. Folk & fairy tales. Foreign lands – Africa.

The ugly duckling ill. by Steve Johnson and Lou Fancher. Candlewick, 2008. ISBN 978-0-7636-2159-9 Subj: Birds – ducks. Birds – swans. Character traits – appearance. Character traits – being different. Folk & fairy tales.

The ugly duckling adapt. by Jerry Pinkney; ill. by adapter. Morrow, 1999. ISBN 978-0-688-15933-7 Subj: Birds – ducks. Birds – swans. Caldecott award honor books. Character traits – appearance. Character traits – being different. Folk & fairy tales.

The ugly duckling retold by Kevin Crossley-Holland; ill. by Meilo So. Knopf, 2001. ISBN 978-0-375-91319-8 Subj: Birds – ducks. Birds – swans. Character traits – appearance. Character traits – being different. Folk & fairy tales.

The ugly duckling ill. by Pirkko Vainio. North-South, 2009. ISBN 978-0-7358-2226-9 Subj: Birds – ducks. Birds – swans. Character traits – appearance. Character traits – being different. Folk & fairy tales.

The ugly duckling retold by Bernadette Watts; ill. by reteller. NorthSouth, 2000. Subj: Birds – ducks. Birds – swans. Character traits – appearance. Character traits – being different. Folk & fairy tales.

The ugly duckling ill. by Roberta Wilson. Odyssey, 2010. ISBN 978-0-917665-86-8 Subj: Birds – ducks. Birds – swans. Character traits – appearance. Character traits – being different. Folk & fairy tales.

The wild swans ill. by Anne Yvonne Gilbert. Barefoot, 2005. ISBN 978-1-84148-164-7 Subj: Birds – swans. Folk & fairy tales. Magic.

The wild swans retold by Amy Ehrlich; ill. by Susan Jeffers. Dial, 1981. ISBN 978-0-8037-9391-0 Subj: Birds – swans. Folk & fairy tales. Magic.

The woman with the eggs adapt. by Jan Wahl; ill. by Ray Cruz. Crown, 1974. ISBN 978-0-517-51587-7 Subj: Behavior – greed. Eggs. Folk & fairy tales.

Anderson, Airlie. *Cat's colors* ill. by author. Child's Play, 2016. ISBN 978-184643761-8 Subj: Animals – cats. Concepts – color.

Anderson, Brian. *Monster chefs* by Brian Anderson and Liam Anderson; ill. by Brian Anderson. Roaring Brook, 2014. ISBN 978-159643808-8 Subj: Activities – baking, cooking. Careers – chefs, cooks. Monsters. Royalty – kings.

The prince's new pet ill. by author. Roaring Brook, 2011. ISBN 978-1-59643-357-1 Subj: Concepts – color. Pets. Royalty – princes.

Anderson, Christine. *Bedtime!* ill. by Steven Salerno. Penguin, 2005. ISBN 978-0-399-24004-1 Subj: Bedtime.

Anderson, Derek. *Gladys goes out to lunch* ill. by author. Simon & Schuster, 2005. ISBN 978-0-689-85688-4 Subj: Animals – gorillas. Food.

How the Easter Bunny saved Christmas ill. by author. Simon & Schuster, 2006. ISBN 978-0-689-87634-9 Subj: Animals – rabbits. Character traits – helpfulness. Holidays – Christmas. Santa Claus.

Over the river: a turkey's tale ill. by author. Simon & Schuster, 2005. ISBN 978-0-689-87635-6 Subj: Birds – turkeys. Holidays – Thanksgiving. Songs.

Romeo and Lou blast off ill. by author. Simon & Schuster, 2007. ISBN 978-1-4169-3784-5 Subj: Animals – polar bears. Birds – penguins. Friendship. Space & space ships.

Story county: here we come! ill. by author. Scholastic, 2011. ISBN 978-0-545-16844-1 Subj: Animals. Farms.

Ten hungry pigs: an epic lunch adventure ill. by author. Scholastic/Orchard, 2016. ISBN 978-054516848-9 Subj: Animals – pigs. Animals – wolves. Counting, numbers. Disguises. Food. Rhyming text.

Ten pigs: an epic bath adventure ill. by author. Orchard, 2015. ISBN 978-054516846-5 Subj: Activities – bathing. Animals – pigs. Animals – wolves. Counting, numbers. Rhyming text.

Anderson, Laurie Halse. *The big cheese of Third Street* ill. by David Gordon. Simon & Schuster, 2002. ISBN 978-0-689-82464-7 Subj: Behavior – bullying, teasing. Character traits – persistence. Concepts – size. Tall tales.

The hair of Zoe Fleefenbacher goes to school ill. by Ard Hoyt. Simon & Schuster, 2009. ISBN 978-0-689-85809-3 Subj: Behavior – misbehavior. Careers – teachers. Hair. Humorous stories. School.

No time for Mother's Day ill. by Dorothy Donohue. Albert Whitman, 1999. ISBN 978-0-8075-4955-1 Subj: Family life – mothers. Gifts. Holidays – Mother's Day.

Thank you, Sarah: the woman who saved Thanksgiving ill. by Matt Faulkner. Simon & Schuster, 2002. ISBN 978-0-689-84787-5 Subj: Holidays – Thanksgiving. U.S. history.

Turkey pox ill. by Dorothy Donohue. Albert Whitman, 1996. ISBN 978-0-8075-8127-8 Subj: Family life. Family life – grandmothers. Holidays – Thanksgiving. Illness – chicken pox.

Anderson, Lena. *The hedgehog, the pig, and their little friend* ill. by author. Farrar, 2007. ISBN 978-91-29-66742-4 Subj: Animals – hedgehogs. Animals – pigs. Behavior – lost. Rhyming text.

Anderson, Liam. *Monster chefs* (Anderson, Brian)

Anderson, M. T. *Strange Mr. Satie* ill. by Petra Mathers. Viking, 2003. ISBN 978-0-670-03637-0 Subj: Careers – composers. Foreign lands – France.

Anderson, Peggy Perry. *Chuck's band* ill. by author. Houghton, 2008. ISBN 978-0-618-96506-9 Subj: Animals. Farms. Music. Musical instruments – bands. Rhyming text.

Chuck's truck ill. by author. Houghton, 2006. ISBN 978-0-618-66836-6 Subj: Animals. Rhyming text. Trucks.

Joe on the go ill. by author. Houghton, 2007. ISBN 978-0-618-77331-2 Subj: Activities – playing. Family life – grandmothers. Frogs & toads.

Out to lunch ill. by author. Houghton, 1998. ISBN 978-0-395-89826-0 Subj: Behavior – misbehavior. Etiquette. Family life. Frogs & toads. Restaurants. Rhyming text.

Time for bed, the babysitter said ill. by author. Houghton, 1987. ISBN 978-0-395-41851-2 Subj: Activities – babysitting. Bedtime. Frogs & toads.

To the tub ill. by author. Houghton, 1996. ISBN 978-0-395-77614-8 Subj: Activities – bathing. Family life – fathers. Frogs & toads.

We go in a circle ill. by author. Houghton, 2004. ISBN 978-0-618-44756-5 Subj: Animals – horses, ponies. Disabilities. Sports – racing.

Anderson, Stephen Axel. *I know the moon* ill. by Greg Couch. Philomel, 2001. ISBN 978-0-399-23425-5 Subj: Animals. Emotions. Moon. Rhyming text. Science.

Andreae, Giles. *Be brave, little penguin* ill. by Guy Parker-Rees. Orchard, 2017. ISBN 978-133815039-1 Subj: Birds – penguins. Emotions – fear. Rhyming text.

Bustle in the bushes ill. by David Wojtowycz. Tiger Tales, 2012. ISBN 978-1-58925-109-0 Subj: Insects. Poetry.

Captain Flinn and the pirate dinosaurs ill. by Russell Ayto. Simon & Schuster, 2005. ISBN 978-1-4169-0713-8 Subj: Dinosaurs. Imagination. Pirates. School.

Captain Flinn and the pirate dinosaurs: missing treasure! ill. by Russell Ayto. Simon & Schuster, 2008. ISBN 978-1-4169-6745-3 Subj: Dinosaurs. Imagination. Pirates. School.

Cock-a-doodle-doo! ill. by David Wojtowycz. Tiger Tales, 2002. ISBN 978-1-58925-020-8 Subj: Animals. Poetry.

Dinosaurs galore! ill. by David Wojtowycz. Tiger Tales, 2005. ISBN 978-1-58925-044-4 Subj: Dinosaurs. Poetry.

Giraffes can't dance ill. by Guy Parker-Rees. Orchard, 2001. ISBN 978-0-439-28719-7 Subj: Activities – dancing. Animals – giraffes. Character traits – individuality. Rhyming text.

I love my daddy ill. by Emma Dodd. Hyperion, 2012. ISBN 978-1-4231-4328-4 Subj: Family life – fathers. Rhyming text.

I love my mommy ill. by Emma Dodd. Hyperion/Disney, 2011. ISBN 978-1-4231-4327-7 Subj: Family life – mothers. Rhyming text.

Pants by Giles Andreae and Nick Sharratt ill. by Nick Sharratt. Fickling, 2003. ISBN 978-0-385-75014-1 Subj: Clothing – pants. Humorous stories. Rhyming text.

Rumble in the jungle ill. by David Wojtowycz. Little Tiger, 1997. ISBN 978-1-888444-08-7 Subj: Animals. Insects – ants. Jungle. Rhyming text.

There's a house inside my mommy ill. by Vanessa Cabban. Albert Whitman, 2002. ISBN 978-0-8075-7853-7 Subj: Babies, toddlers. Birth. Family life – brothers. Family life – mothers. Rhyming text.

Andreasen, Dan. *The giant of Seville: a "tall" tale based on a true story* ill. by author. Abrams, 2007. ISBN 978-0-8109-0988-5 Subj: Character traits – kindness. Circus. Giants. Tall tales.

Saturday with Daddy ill. by author. Henry Holt, 2013. ISBN 978-0-8050-8687-4 Subj: Animals – elephants. Day. Family life – fathers.

The treasure bath ill. by author. Henry Holt, 2009. ISBN 978-0-8050-8686-7 Subj: Activities – bathing. Imagination. Wordless.

Andres, Kristina. *Elephant in the bathtub* ill. by author. NorthSouth, 2010. ISBN 978-0-7358-2291-7 Subj: Activities – bathing. Animals – elephants.

Good Little Wolf ill. by author. NorthSouth, 2008. ISBN 978-0-7358-2210-8 Subj: Animals – wolves. Behavior.

Andrews, Julie. *Dumpy at school* by Julie Andrews and Emma Walton Hamilton ill. by Tony Walton. Hyperion, 2000. ISBN 978-0-7868-0610-2 Subj: School – first day. Trucks.

Dumpy the dump truck by Julie Andrews and Emma Walton Hamilton ill. by Tony Walton. Hyperion, 2000. ISBN 978-0-7868-2523-3 Subj: Family life – grandfathers. Farms. Trucks.

Dumpy to the rescue! by Julie Andrews and Emma Walton Hamilton ill. by Tony Walton. HarperCollins, 2004. ISBN 978-0-06-052690-0 Subj: Animals – goats. Behavior – lost & found possessions. Family life. Trucks.

Dumpy's apple shop by Julie Andrews and Emma Walton Hamilton ill. by Tony Walton. HarperCollins, 2004. ISBN 978-0-06-052693-1 Subj: Food. Trucks.

Simeon's gift by Julie Andrews and Emma Walton Hamilton ill. by Gennady Spirin. HarperCollins, 2003. ISBN 978-0-06-008915-3 Subj: Careers – musicians. Self-concept.

The very fairy princess by Julie Andrews and Emma Walton Hamilton ill. by Christine Davenier. Little, Brown, 2010. ISBN 978-0-316-04050-1 Subj: Royalty – princesses. Self-concept.

The very fairy princess: a spooky, sparkly Halloween by Julie Andrews and Emma Walton Hamilton ill. by Christine Davenier. Little, Brown, 2015. ISBN 978-031628304-5 Subj: Clothing – costumes. Holidays – Halloween. Royalty – princesses. School.

The very fairy princess: graduation girl! by Julie Andrews and Emma Walton Hamilton ill. by Christine Davenier. Little, Brown, 2014. ISBN 978-031621960-0 Subj: Behavior – worrying. Royalty – princesses. School.

The very fairy princess: here comes the flower girl! by Julie Andrews and Emma Walton Hamilton ill. by Christine Davenier. Little, Brown, 2012. ISBN 978-0-316-18561-5 Subj: Royalty – princesses. Weddings.

The very fairy princess follows her heart by Julie Andrews and Emma Walton Hamilton ill. by Christine Davenier. Little, Brown, 2013. ISBN 978-0-316-18559-2 Subj: Holidays – Valentine's Day. Royalty – princesses. School.

The very fairy princess sparkles in the snow by Julie Andrews and Emma Walton Hamilton ill. by Christine Davenier. Little, Brown, 2013. ISBN 978-0-316-21963-1 Subj: Activities – singing. Royalty – princesses. School. Weather – snow.

Andrews, Sylvia. *Dancing in my bones* ill. by Ellen Mueller. HarperCollins, 2001. ISBN 978-0-694-01316-6 Subj: Activities – dancing. Anatomy. Rhyming text.

Andrews, Troy. *Trombone Shorty* ill. by Bryan Collier. Abrams, 2015. ISBN 978-141971465-8 Subj: Caldecott award honor books. Careers – musicians. Ethnic groups in the U.S. – African Americans. Musical instruments – trombones.

Andrews-Goebel, Nancy. *The pot that Juan built* ill. by David Diaz. Lee & Low, 2002. ISBN 978-1-58430-038-0 Subj: Art. Careers – potters. Rhyming text.

Andros, Camille. *Charlotte the scientist is squished* ill. by Brianne Farley. Houghton Mifflin Harcourt, 2017. ISBN 978-054478583-0 Subj: Animals – rabbits. Careers – scientists. Emotions – loneliness. Family life – brothers & sisters. Problem solving. Science.

Angelou, Maya. *Amazing peace: a Christmas poem* ill. by Steve Johnson and Lou Fancher. Random House, 2008. ISBN 978-0-375-84150-7 Subj: Holidays – Christmas. Poetry.

Angelina of Italy ill. by Lizzy Rockwell. Random House, 2004. ISBN 978-0-375-92832-1 Subj: Food. Foreign lands – Italy.

Kofi and his magic photos by Margaret Courtney-Clarke. Potter, 1996. ISBN 978-0-375-92566-5 Subj: Foreign lands – Ghana. Imagination.

My painted house, my friendly chicken, and me photos by Margaret Courtney-Clarke. Random House, 2003. ISBN 978-0-375-92567-2 Subj: Art. Foreign lands – South Africa. Homes, houses. Poetry.

Angleberger, Tom. *Crankee Doodle* ill. by Cece Bell. Clarion, 2013. ISBN 978-0-547-81854-2 Subj: Animals – horses, ponies. Behavior – fighting, arguing. Humorous stories. U.S. history.

McToad mows Tiny Island ill. by John Hendrix. Abrams, 2015. ISBN 978-141971650-8 Subj: Frogs & toads. Machines. Tractors. Transportation.

Anglund, Joan Walsh. *The brave cowboy* ill. by author. McMeel, 1959. ISBN 978-0-7407-0649-3 Subj: Activities – playing. Character traits – bravery. Cowboys, cowgirls. Games. Imagination.

Christmas is a time of giving ill. by author. Harcourt, 1961. ISBN 978-0-15-217863-5 Subj: Character traits – generosity. Holidays – Christmas.

The cowboy's Christmas ill. by author. Atheneum, 1972. ISBN 978-0-689-30301-2 Subj: Animals – bears. Cowboys, cowgirls. Holidays – Christmas. Imagination – imaginary friends.

A friend is someone who likes you ill. by author. Harcourt, 1958. ISBN 978-0-15-229678-0 Subj: Friendship.

Anholt, Catherine. *Chimp and Zee and the big storm* by Catherine Anholt and Laurence Anholt; ill. by authors. Fogelman, 2002. ISBN 978-0-8037-2700-7 Subj: Animals – chimpanzees. Behavior – lost. Weather – storms.

Chimp and Zee's noisy book by Catherine Anholt and Laurence Anholt; ill. by authors. Fogelman, 2002. ISBN 978-0-8037-2772-4 Subj: Animals. Animals – chimpanzees. Format, unusual – board books. Noise, sounds.

Come back, Jack! by Catherine Anholt and Laurence Anholt; ill. by authors. Candlewick, 1994. ISBN 978-1-56402-313-1 Subj: Behavior – boredom. Books, reading. Nursery rhymes.

Happy birthday, Chimp and Zee by Catherine Anholt and Laurence Anholt; ill. by authors. Frances Lincoln, 2006. ISBN 978-1-84507-507-1 Subj: Animals – chimpanzees. Birthdays. Parties. Rhyming text.

Monkey around with Chimp and Zee [board book] by Catherine Anholt and Laurence Anholt; ill. by authors. Fogelman, 2002. ISBN 978-0-8037-2773-1 Subj: Animals – chimpanzees. Format, unusual – board books.

Sun, snow, stars, sky by Catherine Anholt and Laurence Anholt; ill. by authors. Viking, 1995. ISBN 978-0-670-86196-5 Subj: Seasons. Weather.

What makes me happy? by Catherine Anholt and Laurence Anholt; ill. by authors. Candlewick, 1995. ISBN 978-1-56402-482-4 Subj: Babies, toddlers. Emotions. Rhyming text.

Anholt, Laurence. *Billy and the big new school* ill. by Catherine Anholt. Albert Whitman, 1999. ISBN 978-0-8075-0743-8 Subj: Behavior – growing up. Birds. School – first day.

Chimp and Zee and the big storm (Anholt, Catherine)

Chimp and Zee's noisy book (Anholt, Catherine)

Come back, Jack! (Anholt, Catherine)

Happy birthday, Chimp and Zee (Anholt, Catherine)

Jack and the dreamsack ill. by Ross Collins. Bloomsbury, 2003. ISBN 978-1-58234-786-8 Subj: Dreams. Night.

Monkey around with Chimp and Zee [board book] (Anholt, Catherine)

Seven for a secret ill. by James Coplestone. Frances Lincoln, 2006. ISBN 978-1-84507-300-8 Subj: Death. Emotions – love. Family life – grandfathers. Letters, cards.

Sophie and the new baby ill. by Catherine Anholt. Albert Whitman, 2000. ISBN 978-0-8075-7550-5 Subj: Babies, toddlers. Birth. Family life – new sibling.

Sun, snow, stars, sky (Anholt, Catherine)

Two nests ill. by James Coplestone. Frances Lincoln, 2014. ISBN 978-184780323-8 Subj: Birds. Homes, houses. Rhyming text.

What makes me happy? (Anholt, Catherine)

Animal I spy: what can you spot? ill. by Kate Sheppard. Kingfisher, 2010. ISBN 978-0-7534-6395-6 Subj: Animals. Format, unusual – board books. Picture puzzles.

Animal 123: one to ten and back again ill. by Kate Sheppard. Kingfisher, 2010. ISBN 978-0-7534-6394-9 Subj: Animals. Counting, numbers. Format, unusual – board books. Picture puzzles.

Anno, Mitsumasa. *Anno's alphabet: an adventure in imagination* ill. by author. Crowell, 1975. ISBN 978-0-690-00546-2 Subj: ABC books. Imagination. Optical illusions. Picture puzzles.

Anno's Britain ill. by author. Philomel, 1982. ISBN 978-0-399-20861-4 Subj: Foreign lands – England. Games. Imagination. Wordless.

Anno's counting book ill. by author. Crowell, 1975. ISBN 978-0-690-01288-0 Subj: Counting, numbers. Imagination. Optical illusions. Picture puzzles. Seasons. Wordless.

Anno's counting house ill. by author. Philomel, 1982. ISBN 978-0-399-20896-6 Subj: Counting, numbers. Games. Imagination. Optical illusions. Picture puzzles. Wordless.

Anno's hat tricks ill. by author. Putnam, 1985. ISBN 978-0-399-21212-3 Subj: Counting, numbers. Magic.

Anno's Italy ill. by author. Collins-World, 1980. ISBN 978-0-529-05560-6 Subj: Foreign lands – Italy. Games. Imagination. Optical illusions. Picture puzzles. Wordless.

Anno's journey ill. by author. Putnam, 1981. ISBN 978-0-529-05419-7 Subj: Games. Imagination. Optical illusions. Picture puzzles. Wordless.

Anno's magic seeds ill. by author. Philomel, 1995. ISBN 978-0-399-22538-3 Subj: Counting, numbers. Gardens, gardening. Seeds.

Anno's math games ill. by author. Philomel, 1987. ISBN 978-0-399-21151-5 Subj: Concepts. Counting, numbers. Riddles & jokes.

Anno's math games II ill. by author. Putnam, 1989. ISBN 978-0-399-21615-2 Subj: Concepts. Counting, numbers. Riddles & jokes.

Anno's math games III ill. by author. Putnam, 1991. ISBN 978-0-399-22274-0 Subj: Concepts. Counting, numbers. Riddles & jokes.

Anno's U.S.A. ill. by author. Philomel, 1983. ISBN 978-0-399-20974-1 Subj: Games. Imagination. Wordless.

Annunziata, Jane. *Shy spaghetti and excited eggs: a kid's menu of feelings* (Nemiroff, Marc A.)

Anstee, Ashlyn. *Are we there, Yeti?* ill. by author. Simon & Schuster, 2015. ISBN 978-148143089-0 Subj: Careers – bus drivers. Monsters. School – field trips.

No, no, Gnome! ill. by author. Simon & Schuster, 2016. ISBN 978-148143091-3 Subj: Gardens, gardening. Mythical creatures – gnomes. School.

Antony, Steve. *Betty goes bananas* ill. by author. Random House, 2014. ISBN 978-055350761-4 Subj: Animals – gorillas. Birds – toucans. Emotions – anger. Food.

Green lizards vs. red rectangles ill. by author. Scholastic, 2015. ISBN 978-054584902-9 Subj: Concepts – shape. Reptiles – lizards. Violence, nonviolence. War.

I'll wait, Mr. Panda ill. by author. Scholastic, 2016. ISBN 978-133802836-2 Subj: Animals – pandas. Birds – penguins. Character traits – patience, impatience.

Please, Mr. Panda ill. by author. Scholastic, 2015. ISBN 978-054578892-2 Subj: Animals – pandas. Behavior – sharing. Etiquette.

The queen's handbag ill. by author. Scholastic, 2017. ISBN 978-133803293-2 Subj: Behavior – lost & found possessions. Birds – swans. Clothing – handbags, purses. Foreign lands – Great Britain. Royalty – queens.

The Queen's hat ill. by author. Scholastic, 2015. ISBN 978-054583556-5 Subj: Behavior – lost & found possessions. Clothing – hats. Foreign lands – England. Royalty – queens.

Aoki, Elaine M. *The White Swan express* (Okimoto, Jean Davies)

Aponte, Carlos. *A season to bee* ill. by author. Price Stern Sloan, 2017. ISBN 978-110199570-9 Subj: Clothing. Concepts – color. Insects – bees. Rhyming text. Self-concept.

Appelt, Kathi. *The Alley Cat's Meow* ill. by Jon Goodell. Harcourt, 2002. ISBN 978-0-15-201980-8 Subj: Activities – dancing. Animals – cats. Rhyming text.

Bats around the clock ill. by Melissa Sweet. HarperCollins, 2000. ISBN 978-0-688-16470-6 Subj: Activities – dancing. Animals – bats. Clocks, watches. Music. Rhyming text. Time.

Bats on parade ill. by Melissa Sweet. Morrow, 1999. ISBN 978-0-688-15666-4 Subj: Animals – bats. Counting, numbers. Music. Musical instruments – bands. Parades. Rhyming text.

Brand-new baby blues ill. by Kelly Murphy. HarperCollins, 2010. ISBN 978-0-06-053233-8 Subj: Babies, toddlers. Family life – new sibling. Rhyming text.

Counting crows ill. by Rob Dunlavey. Atheneum, 2015. ISBN 978-144242327-5 Subj: Birds – crows. Counting, numbers. Rhyming text.

Cowboy dreams ill. by Barry Root. HarperCollins, 1999. ISBN 978-0-06-027764-2 Subj: Bedtime. Cowboys, cowgirls. Dreams. Night. Rhyming text.

Elephants aloft ill. by Keith Baker. Harcourt, 1993. ISBN 978-0-15-225384-4 Subj: Activities – ballooning. Animals – elephants. Foreign lands – Africa. Foreign lands – India.

Incredible me! ill. by G. Brian Karas. HarperCollins, 2003. ISBN 978-0-06-028623-1 Subj: Character traits – individuality. Rhyming text. Self-concept.

Merry Christmas, merry crow ill. by Jon Goodell. Harcourt, 2005. ISBN 978-0-15-202651-6 Subj: Birds – crows. Holidays – Christmas. Rhyming text.

Miss Lady Bird's wildflowers: how a first lady changed America ill. by Joy Fisher Hein. HarperCollins, 2005. ISBN 978-0-06-001108-6 Subj: Ecology. Flowers. U.S. history.

Mogie: the heart of the house ill. by Marc Rosenthal. Atheneum, 2014. ISBN 978-144248054-4 Subj: Animals – dogs. Animals – service animals. Illness.

My father's house ill. by Raúl Colón. Penguin, 2007. ISBN 978-0-670-03669-1 Subj: Nature. Poetry. Religion.

Oh my baby, little one ill. by Jane Dyer. Harcourt, 2000. ISBN 978-0-15-200041-7 Subj: Emotions – love. Family life – mothers. Rhyming text.

Rain dance ill. by Emilie Chollat. HarperCollins, 2001. ISBN 978-0-694-01291-6 Subj: Counting, numbers. Rhyming text. Weather – rain.

When Otis courted Mama ill. by Jill McElmurry. Houghton, 2015. ISBN 978-015216688-5 Subj: Animals – coyotes. Divorce. Family life – mothers. Family life – stepfamilies.

Where, where is Swamp Bear? ill. by Megan Halsey. HarperCollins, 2002. ISBN 978-0-688-17103-2 Subj: Animals – bears. Family life – grandfathers. Swamps.

Apperley, Dawn. *Blossom and Boo: a story about best friends* ill. by author. Little, 2000. ISBN 978-0-316-04963-4 Subj: Animals – bears. Animals – rabbits. Friendship.

Blossom and Boo stay up late: a story about bedtime ill. by author. Little, 2002. ISBN 978-0-316-05312-9 Subj: Animals – bears. Animals – rabbits. Bedtime. Night.

Don't wake the baby ill. by author. Bloomsbury, 2001. ISBN 978-0-7475-5003-7 Subj: Animals – squirrels. Babies, toddlers. Family life – new sibling. Humorous stories. Senses. Sleep.

Flip and Flop ill. by author. Orchard, 2001. ISBN 978-0-439-28892-7 Subj: Activities – playing. Birds – penguins. Family life – brothers.

Good night, sleep tight, little bunnies ill. by author. Scholastic, 2002. ISBN 978-0-439-22525-0 Subj: Animals. Bedtime. Birds. Night. Rhyming text.

Santa Claus will come tonight ill. by author. Scholastic, 2002. ISBN 978-0-439-40449-5 Subj: Animals. Holidays – Christmas. Rhyming text. Santa Claus.

Apple, Margot. *Brave Martha* ill. by author. Houghton, 1999. ISBN 978-0-395-59422-3 Subj: Animals – cats. Bedtime. Emotions – fear. Monsters. Night.

Apple, Sam. *The saddest toilet in the world* ill. by Sam Ricks. Aladdin, 2016. ISBN 978-148145122-2 Subj: Behavior – running away. Toilet training. Toilets.

Applegate, Katherine. *Ivan: the remarkable true story of the shopping mall gorilla* ill. by G. Brian Karas. Clarion, 2014. ISBN 978-054425230-1 Subj: Animals – gorillas. Character traits – kindness to animals.

Arabian Nights. *The tale of Ali Baba and the forty thieves: a story from the Arabian nights* retold by Eric A. Kimmel; ill. by Will Hillenbrand. Holiday, 1996. ISBN 978-0-8234-1258-7 Subj: Behavior – stealing. Folk & fairy tales. Foreign lands – Middle East.

Araki, Mie. *The magic toolbox: starring Fred and Lulu* ill. by author. Chronicle, 2003. ISBN 978-0-8118-3564-0 Subj: Animals – rabbits. Animals – rhinoceros. Magic. Tools.

Aralan, Haydé. *Milton* ill. by author. Chronicle, 2000. ISBN 978-0-8118-2762-1 Subj: Animals – cats.

Milton's Christmas ill. by author. Chronicle, 2000. ISBN 978-0-8118-2842-0 Subj: Animals – cats. Behavior – misbehavior. Holidays – Christmas.

Archambault, John. *Chicka chicka boom boom* (Martin, Bill, Jr.)

Here are my hands (Martin, Bill, Jr.)

Knots on a counting rope (Martin, Bill, Jr.)

Listen to the rain (Martin, Bill, Jr.)

The magic pumpkin (Martin, Bill, Jr.)

Archer, Micha. *Daniel finds a poem* ill. by author. Penguin/Nancy Paulsen, 2016. ISBN 978-039916913-7 Subj: Animals. Days of the week, months of the year. Nature. Poetry.

Archer, Peggy. *From dawn to dreams: poems for busy babies* ill. by Hanako Wakiyama. Candlewick, 2007. ISBN 978-0-7636-2467-5 Subj: Babies, toddlers. Poetry.

Name that dog! puppy poems from a to z ill. by Stephanie Buscema. Penguin, 2010. ISBN 978-0-8037-3322-0 Subj: ABC books. Animals – dogs. Poetry.

Turkey surprise ill. by Thor Wickstrom. Penguin, 2005. ISBN 978-0-8037-2969-8 Subj: Birds – turkeys. Family life – brothers & sisters. Holidays – Thanksgiving.

Arden, Carolyn. *Goose moon* ill. by Jim Postier. Boyds Mills, 2004. ISBN 978-0-613-79879-2 Subj: Moon. Seasons – spring.

Aregui, Matthias. *Before after* ill. by Anne-Margot Ramstein. Candlewick, 2014. ISBN 978-076367621-6 Subj: Concepts – change. Nature.

Arena, Jen. *Lady Liberty's holiday* ill. by Matt Hunt. Knopf, 2016. ISBN 978-055352067-5 Subj: Activities – traveling. Activities – vacationing. Behavior – boredom. Holidays – Fourth of July.

Marta! big and small ill. by Angela Dominguez. Roaring Brook, 2016. ISBN 978-162672243-9 Subj: Animals. Concepts – opposites. Ethnic groups in the U.S. – Hispanic Americans. Foreign languages.

One hundred snowmen ill. by Stephen Gilpin. Amazon/Two Lions, 2013. ISBN 978-1-4778-4703-9 Subj: Counting, numbers. Rhyming text. Snowmen.

Arenson, Roberta. *Manu and the talking fish* ill. by author. Barefoot, 2000. ISBN 978-1-84148-032-9 Subj: Fish. Folk & fairy tales. Foreign lands – India. Weather – floods.

Argueta, Jorge. *Arroz con leche / Rice pudding: un poema para cocinar / a cooking poem* ill. by Fernando Vilela. Groundwood, 2010. ISBN 978-0-88899-981-8 Subj: Activities – baking, cooking. Food. Foreign languages. Poetry.

Guacamole: un poema para cocinar / a cooking poem ill. by Margarita Sada. Groundwood, 2012. ISBN 978-1-55498-133-5 Subj: Activities – baking, cooking. Food. Foreign languages. Poetry.

Moony Luna / Luna, Lunita Lunera ill. by Elizabeth Gomez. Children's Book Press, 2005. ISBN 978-0-89239-205-6 Subj: Foreign languages. School – first day.

Salsa: un poema para cocinar / a cooking poem ill. by Duncan Tonatiuh. Groundwood, 2015. ISBN 978-155498442-8 Subj: Activities – baking, cooking. Foreign lands – Latin America. Foreign languages. Poetry.

Sopa de frijoles: un poema para cocinar / Bean soup: a cooking poem ill. by Rafael Yockteng. Groundwood, 2009. ISBN 978-0-88899-881-1 Subj: Activities – baking, cooking. Food. Foreign languages. Poetry.

Tamalitos: un poema para cocinar / a cooking poem ill. by Domi. Groundwood, 2013. ISBN 978-1-55498-300-1 Subj: Activities – baking, cooking. Food. Foreign languages. Poetry.

Trees are hanging from the sky ill. by Rafael Yockteng. Groundwood, 2003. ISBN 978-0-88899-509-4 Subj: Dreams. Foreign lands – El Salvador. Poetry.

Armand, Glenda. *Love twelve miles long* ill. by Colin Bootman. Lee & Low, 2011. ISBN 978-1-60060-245-0 Subj: Ethnic groups in the U.S. – African Americans. Family life – mothers. Slavery. U.S. history.

Armentrout, David. *John Muir* by David Armentrout and Patricia Armentrout ill. with photos. Rourke, 2002. ISBN 978-1-58952-055-4 Subj: Careers – naturalists. Ecology. U.S. history.

Armentrout, Patricia. *John Muir* (Armentrout, David)

Armo, Nancy. *A friend for Mole* ill. by author. Peachtree, 2016. ISBN 978-156145865-3 Subj: Animals – moles. Animals – wolves. Character traits – cooperation. Emotions – fear. Friendship.

Armstrong, Jennifer. *Magnus at the fire* ill. by Owen Smith. Simon & Schuster, 2005. ISBN 978-0-689-83922-1 Subj: Animals – horses, ponies. Careers – firefighters. Trucks.

Once upon a banana ill. by David Small. Simon & Schuster, 2006. ISBN 978-0-689-84251-1 Subj: Food. Humorous stories.

Armstrong, Matthew S. *Jane and Mizmow* ill. by author. HarperCollins, 2011. ISBN 978-0-06-117719-4 Subj: Friendship. Monsters.

Armstrong-Ellis, Carey. *Prudy's problem and how she solved it* ill. by author. Abrams, 2002. ISBN 978-0-8109-0569-6 Subj: Behavior – collecting things. Humorous stories. Museums. Problem solving.

Ten creepy monsters ill. by author. Abrams, 2012. ISBN 978-1-4197-0433-8 Subj: Counting, numbers. Monsters. Rhyming text.

Arnaldo, Monica. *Margo thinks twice* ill. by author. OwlKids, 2016. ISBN 978-177147162-6 Subj: Behavior – worrying. Emotions – fear. Imagination.

Arndt, Michael. *Cat says meow and other animalopoeia* ill. by author. Chronicle, 2014. ISBN 978-145211234-3 Subj: Animals. Noise, sounds.

Arnold, Andrew. *Gryphons aren't so great* (Sturm, James)

Ogres awake! (Sturm, James)

Sleepless knight (Sturm, James)

Arnold, Caroline. *Australian animals* ill. with photos. HarperCollins, 2000. ISBN 978-0-688-16767-7 Subj: Animals. Foreign lands – Australia.

Giant shark: megalodon, prehistoric super predator ill. by Laurie Caple. Clarion, 2000. ISBN 978-0-395-91419-9 Subj: Fish – sharks. Prehistory. Sea & seashore.

Hatching chicks in Room 6 ill. with photos. Charlesbridge, 2017. ISBN 978-158089735-8 Subj: Birds – chickens, roosters. Eggs. School.

A penguin's world ill. by author. Picture Window, 2006. ISBN 978-1-4048-1323-6 Subj: Birds – penguins.

A platypus' world ill. by author. Picture Window, 2008. ISBN 978-1-4048-3985-4 Subj: Animals – platypuses. Foreign lands – Australia.

Too hot? too cold? keeping body temperature just right ill. by Annie Patterson. Charlesbridge, 2013. ISBN 978-1-58089-276-6 Subj: Concepts – cold & heat. Science.

A warmer world: from polar bears to butterflies, how climate change affects wildlife ill. by Jamie Hogan. Charlesbridge, 2012. ISBN 978-1-58089-266-7 Subj: Ecology.

A wombat's world ill. by author. Picture Window, 2008. ISBN 978-1-4048-3986-1 Subj: Animals – wombats. Foreign lands – Australia.

Arnold, Katya, reteller. *The adventures of Snowwoman* ill. by reteller. Based on a story by V. Suteev. Holiday, 1998. ISBN 978-0-8234-1390-4 Subj: Animals. Holidays – Christmas. Santa Claus. Snowmen.

Elephants can paint, too! photos by author. Simon & Schuster, 2005. ISBN 978-0-689-86985-3 Subj: Activities – painting. Animals – elephants. Foreign lands – Thailand.

Let's find it! my first nature guide ill. by author. Holiday, 2002. ISBN 978-0-8234-1539-7 Subj: Animals. Nature. Plants.

Meow! ill. by reteller. Based on a story by V. Suteev. Holiday, 1998. ISBN 978-0-8234-1361-4 Subj: Animals. Animals – cats. Animals – dogs. Noise, sounds.

That apple is mine! ill. by reteller. Based on a story by V. Suteev. Holiday, 2000. ISBN 978-0-8234-

1629-5 Subj: Behavior – sharing. Folk & fairy tales. Foreign lands – Russia.

Arnold, Marsha Diane. *The bravest of us all* ill. by Brad Sneed. Dial, 2000. ISBN 978-0-8037-2409-9 Subj: Character traits – bravery. Emotions – fear. Family life – sisters. Weather – tornadoes.

Lost. found ill. by Matthew Cordell. Roaring Brook/Neal Porter, 2015. ISBN 978-162672017-6 Subj: Animals. Animals – bears. Behavior – lost & found possessions. Clothing – scarves.

Metro cat ill. by Jack E. Davis. Golden, 2001. ISBN 978-0-307-10213-3 Subj: Animals – cats. Foreign lands – France.

Roar of a snore ill. by Pierre Pratt. Penguin, 2006. ISBN 978-0-8037-2936-0 Subj: Bedtime. Noise, sounds. Rhyming text. Sleep – snoring.

Waiting for snow ill. by Renata Liwska. Houghton Mifflin Harcourt, 2016. ISBN 978-054441687-1 Subj: Animals. Character traits – patience, impatience. Forest, woods. Seasons – winter. Weather – snow.

Arnold, Tedd. *Dirty Gert* ill. by author. Holiday House, 2013. ISBN 978-0-8234-2404-7 Subj: Humorous stories. Rhyming text. Trees.

Five ugly monsters ill. by author. Scholastic, 1995. ISBN 978-0-590-22226-6 Subj: Counting, numbers. Monsters. Rhyming text. Sleep.

Green Wilma ill. by author. Dial, 1993. ISBN 978-0-8037-1314-7 Subj: Character traits – being different. Dreams. Frogs & toads. Rhyming text. School.

Green Wilma, frog in space ill. by author. Dial, 2009. ISBN 978-0-8037-2698-7 Subj: Aliens. Frogs & toads. Rhyming text. Space & space ships.

Huggly gets dressed ill. by author. Scholastic, 1997. ISBN 978-0-590-11759-3 Subj: Clothing. Monsters. Night.

Huggly takes a bath ill. by author. Scholastic, 1998. ISBN 978-0-590-91820-6 Subj: Behavior – misbehavior. Monsters. Night.

More parts ill. by author. Dial, 2001. ISBN 978-0-8037-1417-5 Subj: Anatomy. Language. Rhyming text.

No jumping on the bed! ill. by author. Dial, 1987. ISBN 978-0-8037-0038-3 Subj: Bedtime. Behavior – misbehavior. Dreams. Furniture – beds. Imagination.

No more water in the tub! ill. by author. Dial, 1995. ISBN 978-0-8037-1583-7 Subj: Activities – bathing. Cumulative tales. Imagination.

Parts ill. by author. Dial, 1997. ISBN 978-0-8037-2041-1 Subj: Anatomy. Rhyming text.

A pet for Fly Guy ill. by author. Scholastic/Orchard, 2014. ISBN 978-054531615-6 Subj: Humorous stories. Insects – flies. Pets.

The twin princes ill. by author. Penguin, 2007. ISBN 978-0-8037-2696-3 Subj: Birds – chickens, roosters. Contests. Multiple births – twins. Royalty – princes.

Vincent paints his house ill. by author. Holiday House, 2015. ISBN 978-082343210-3 Subj: Activities – painting. Animals. Careers – artists. Concepts – color. Homes, houses.

Arnosky, Jim. *All about deer* ill. by author. Scholastic, 1996. ISBN 978-0-590-46792-6 Subj: Animals – deer. Science.

All about frogs ill. by author. Scholastic, 2002. ISBN 978-0-590-48164-9 Subj: Frogs & toads.

All about manatees ill. by author. Scholastic, 2008. ISBN 978-0-439-90361-5 Subj: Animals – manatees.

All about turkeys ill. by author. Scholastic, 1998. ISBN 978-0-590-48147-2 Subj: Birds – turkeys.

All night near the water ill. by author. Putnam, 1994. ISBN 978-0-399-22629-8 Subj: Birds – ducks. Night.

Armadillo's orange ill. by author. Putnam, 2003. ISBN 978-0-399-23412-5 Subj: Animals – armadillos. Behavior – lost. Friendship. Homes, houses.

At this very moment ill. by author. Penguin, 2011. ISBN 978-0-525-42252-5 Subj: Animals. Nature.

Babies in the bayou ill. by author. Penguin, 2007. ISBN 978-0-399-22653-3 Subj: Animals. Babies, toddlers. Nature.

Beaver pond, moose pond ill. by author. National Geographic, 2000. ISBN 978-0-7922-7692-0 Subj: Animals – beavers. Animals – moose. Lakes, ponds.

Come out, muskrats ill. by author. Lothrop, 1989. ISBN 978-0-688-05458-8 Subj: Animals – muskrats. Nature.

Coyote raid in Cactus Canyon ill. by author. Penguin, 2005. ISBN 978-0-399-23413-2 Subj: Animals – coyotes. Desert. Reptiles – snakes.

Crinkleroot's guide to giving back to nature ill. by author. Putnam, 2012. ISBN 978-0-399-25520-5 Subj: Ecology. Nature.

Crinkleroot's guide to knowing animal habitats ill. by author. Simon & Schuster, 1997. ISBN 978-0-689-80583-7 Subj: Animals. Nature.

Crinkleroot's guide to knowing butterflies and moths ill. by author. Simon & Schuster, 1996. ISBN 978-0-689-80587-5 Subj: Insects – butterflies, caterpillars. Insects – moths. Science.

Crinkleroot's guide to knowing the trees ill. by author. Macmillan, 1992. ISBN 978-0-02-705855-0 Subj: Forest, woods. Nature. Trees.

Crinkleroot's guide to walking in wild places ill. by author. Bradbury, 1990. ISBN 978-0-02-705842-0 Subj: Activities – walking. Nature.

Crinkleroot's 25 birds every child should know ill. by author. Bradbury, 1993. ISBN 978-0-02-705859-8 Subj: Birds. Nature.

Crinkleroot's 25 fish every child should know ill. by author. Bradbury, 1993. ISBN 978-0-02-705844-4 Subj: Fish. Nature.

Crinkleroot's 25 mammals every child should know ill. by author. Bradbury, 1994. ISBN 978-0-02-705845-1 Subj: Animals. Nature.

Crinkleroot's visit to Crinkle Cove ill. by author. Simon & Schuster, 1998. ISBN 978-0-689-81602-4 Subj: Ecology. Nature. Reptiles – snakes.

Deer at the brook ill. by author. Lothrop, 1986. ISBN 978-0-688-04100-7 Subj: Animals – deer.

Dolphins on the sand ill. by author. Putnam, 2008. ISBN 978-0-399-24606-7 Subj: Animals – dolphins. Nature. Science.

Every autumn comes the bear ill. by author. Putnam, 1993. ISBN 978-0-399-22508-6 Subj: Animals. Animals – bears. Hibernation. Seasons – fall. Seasons – winter.

Gobble it up! a fun song about eating! ill. by author. Scholastic, 2008. ISBN 978-0-439-90362-2 Subj: Animals. Food. Rhyming text. Science. Songs.

Grandfather Buffalo ill. by author. Penguin, 2006. ISBN 978-0-399-24169-7 Subj: Animals – buffaloes. Old age.

I see animals hiding ill. by author. Scholastic, 1995. ISBN 978-0-590-48143-4 Subj: Animals. Behavior – hiding. Nature.

I'm a turkey! ill. by author. Scholastic, 2009. ISBN 978-0-439-90364-6 Subj: Birds – turkeys. Rhyming text. Songs.

Little Burro ill. by author. Putnam, 2013. ISBN 978-0-399-25519-9 Subj: Animals – donkeys. Nature.

A manatee morning ill. by author. Simon & Schuster, 2000. ISBN 978-0-689-81604-8 Subj: Animals – manatees. Rhyming text.

Mouse letters: a very first alphabet book ill. by author. Clarion, 1999. ISBN 978-0-03-955538-2 Subj: ABC books. Animals – mice. Wordless.

Mouse numbers and letters ill. by author. Harcourt, 1982. ISBN 978-0-15-256022-5 Subj: ABC books. Animals – mice. Counting, numbers. Wordless.

Mouse writing ill. by author. Harcourt, 1983. ISBN 978-0-15-256028-7 Subj: ABC books. Activities – writing. Animals – mice. Birds. Wordless.

Mud time and more: Nathaniel stories ill. by author. Addison-Wesley, 1979. ISBN 978-0-201-00173-0 Subj: Problem solving. Wordless.

Outdoors on foot ill. by author. Coward, 1978. ISBN 978-0-698-30684-4 Subj: Activities – walking. Humorous stories. Seasons.

Parrotfish and sunken ships: exploring a tropical reef ill. by author. HarperCollins, 2007. ISBN 978-0-688-17123-0 Subj: Boats, ships. Nature. Sea & seashore.

Rabbits and raindrops ill. by author. Putnam, 1997. ISBN 978-0-399-22635-9 Subj: Animals – rabbits. Weather – rain.

Raccoon on his own ill. by author. Putnam, 2001. ISBN 978-0-399-22756-1 Subj: Animals – raccoons. Character traits – curiosity. Swamps.

Raccoons and ripe corn ill. by author. Lothrop, 1987. ISBN 978-0-688-05456-4 Subj: Animals – raccoons. Farms. Food. Night.

Rattlesnake dance ill. by author. Putnam, 2000. ISBN 978-0-399-22755-4 Subj: Activities – dancing. Reptiles – snakes.

Slither and crawl: eye to eye with reptiles ill. by author. Sterling, 2009. ISBN 978-1-4027-3986-6 Subj: Reptiles.

Slow down for manatees ill. by author. Penguin, 2010. ISBN 978-0-399-24170-3 Subj: Animals – manatees. Character traits – kindness to animals.

Turtle in the sea ill. by author. Putnam, 2002. ISBN 978-0-399-22757-8 Subj: Reptiles – turtles, tortoises. Sea & seashore.

Watching foxes ill. by author. Lothrop, 1985. ISBN 978-0-688-04260-8 Subj: Activities – playing. Animals – foxes.

Wild and swampy ill. by author. HarperCollins, 2000. ISBN 978-0-688-17120-9 Subj: Animals. Format, unusual – toy & movable books. Swamps.

Wild tracks! a guide to nature's footprints ill. by author. Sterling, 2008. ISBN 978-1-4027-3985-9 Subj: Animals. Nature.

Aronson, Billy. *Peg and Cat: the pizza problem* (Oxley, Jennifer)

Arqués, Isabel M. *Ken's cloud* ill. by Angela Pelaez. NorthSouth, 2001. ISBN 978-0-7358-1526-1 Subj: Behavior – boredom. Weather – clouds. Weather – rain. Weather – snow.

Arquette, Kerry. *What did you do today?* ill. by Nancy Hayashi. Harcourt, 2002. ISBN 978-0-15-201414-8 Subj: Activities. Animals. Rhyming text.

Arrigan, Mary. *Mario's angels: a story about the artist Giotto* ill. by Gillian McClure. Frances Lincoln,

2006. ISBN 978-1-84507-404-3 Subj: Angels. Art. Careers – artists.

Arro, Lena. *By geezers and galoshes!* ill. by Catarina Kruusval. R&S Books, 2001. ISBN 978-91-29-65348-9 Subj: Boats, ships. Family life – aunts, uncles. Old age. Pirates.

Arsenault, Isabelle. *Colette's lost pet* ill. by author. Random House, 2017. ISBN 978-055353659-1 Subj: Behavior – lying. Friendship. Imagination. Moving.

Artell, Mike. *Jacques and de beanstalk* (Jack and the beanstalk)

Petite Rouge: a Cajun Red Riding Hood ill. by Jim Harris. Dial, 2003. ISBN 978-0-8037-2514-0 Subj: Animals. Folk & fairy tales. Rhyming text.

Artzybasheff, Boris. *Seven Simeons* ill. by author. Viking, 1937. Subj: Caldecott award honor books.

Aruego, Ariane *see* Dewey, Ariane

Aruego, José. *The last laugh* by José Aruego and Ariane Dewey; ill. by authors. Penguin, 2006. ISBN 978-0-8037-3093-9 Subj: Behavior – bullying, teasing. Birds – ducks. Reptiles – snakes.

Splash! by José Aruego and Ariane Dewey; ill. by authors. Harcourt, 2001. ISBN 978-0-15-216256-6 Subj: Animals – bears. Character traits – clumsiness. Sports – fishing.

We hide, you seek by José Aruego and Ariane Dewey; ill. by authors. Greenwillow, 1979. ISBN 978-0-688-84201-7 Subj: Animals. Behavior – hiding. Foreign lands – Africa. Games.

Weird friends: unlikely allies in the animal kingdom by José Aruego and Ariane Dewey; ill. by authors. Harcourt, 2002. ISBN 978-0-15-202128-3 Subj: Animals. Behavior – needing someone. Fish.

Asare, Meshack. *Sosu's call* ill. by author. Kane/Miller, 2002. ISBN 978-1-929132-21-8 Subj: Animals – dogs. Character traits – bravery. Disabilities. Foreign lands – Africa. Weather – storms.

Asbjørnsen, P. C. *The three billy goats Gruff* retold by Stephen Carpenter; ill. by reteller. HarperCollins, 1998. ISBN 978-0-694-01033-2 Subj: Animals – goats. Character traits – cleverness. Cumulative tales. Folk & fairy tales. Mythical creatures – trolls.

The three billy goats Gruff ill. by Paul Galdone. Seabury Pr., 1973. ISBN 978-0-8164-3080-2 Subj: Animals – goats. Character traits – cleverness. Cumulative tales. Folk & fairy tales. Mythical creatures – trolls.

The three billy goats gruff retold by Jerry Pinkney; ill. by reteller. Little, Brown, 2017. ISBN 978-031634157-8 Subj: Animals – goats. Character traits – cleverness. Cumulative tales. Folk & fairy tales. Mythical creatures – trolls.

The three billy goats Gruff retold by Glen Rounds; ill. by reteller. Holiday, 1993. ISBN 978-0-8234-1015-6 Subj: Animals – goats. Character traits – cleverness. Cumulative tales. Folk & fairy tales. Mythical creatures – trolls.

The three billy goats Gruff adapt. by Janet Stevens; ill. by adapter. Harcourt, 1987. ISBN 978-0-15-286396-8 Subj: Animals – goats. Character traits – cleverness. Cumulative tales. Folk & fairy tales. Mythical creatures – trolls.

The three Billygoats Gruff and Mean Calypso Joe by Cathrene Valente Youngquist; ill. by Kristin Sorra. Atheneum, 2002. ISBN 978-0-689-82824-9 Subj: Animals – goats. Character traits – cleverness. Folk & fairy tales. Foreign lands – Caribbean Islands. Mythical creatures – trolls.

Who's that tripping over my bridge? by Coleen Salley; ill. by Amy Jackson Dixon. Pelican, 2002. ISBN 978-1-56554-890-9 Subj: Animals – goats. Character traits – cleverness. Mythical creatures – trolls.

Asch, Devin. *Baby Duck's new friend* (Asch, Frank)

Like a windy day (Asch, Frank)

Asch, Frank. *Baby Bird's first nest* ill. by author. Harcourt, 1999. ISBN 978-0-15-201726-2 Subj: Animals – babies. Birds. Character traits – helpfulness. Frogs & toads.

Baby Duck's new friend by Frank Asch and Devin Asch; ill. by authors. Harcourt, 2001. ISBN 978-0-15-202257-0 Subj: Birds – ducks. Character traits – confidence.

Barnyard lullaby ill. by author. Simon & Schuster, 1998. ISBN 978-0-689-81363-4 Subj: Animals. Careers – farmers. Lullabies. Music. Noise, sounds.

Bear shadow ill. by author. Prentice-Hall, 1985. ISBN 978-0-13-071580-7 Subj: Animals – bears. Shadows.

Bear's bargain ill. by author. Prentice-Hall, 1985. ISBN 978-0-13-071606-4 Subj: Animals – bears. Birds. Emotions – envy, jealousy.

The Daily Comet: boy saves Earth from giant octopus! ill. by Devin Asch. Kids Can, 2010. ISBN 978-1-55453-281-0 Subj: Activities – writing. Humorous stories.

The earth and I ill. by author. Gulliver, 1994. ISBN 978-0-15-200443-9 Subj: Earth. Nature.

Good night, Baby Bear ill. by author. Harcourt, 1998. ISBN 978-0-15-200836-9 Subj: Animals – bears. Bedtime. Family life. Seasons – winter. Sleep.

Goodbye house ill. by author. Prentice-Hall, 1986. ISBN 978-0-13-360272-2 Subj: Animals – bears. Family life. Moving.

Happy birthday, Big Bad Wolf ill. by author. Kids Can, 2011. ISBN 978-1-55337-368-1 Subj: Animals – pigs. Animals – wolves. Birthdays.

Happy birthday, moon! ill. by author. Prentice-Hall, 1982. ISBN 978-0-13-383687-5 Subj: Animals – bears. Birthdays. Moon.

Here comes the cat (Vagin, Vladimir)

Just like daddy ill. by author. Prentice-Hall, 1981. ISBN 978-0-13-514042-0 Subj: Animals – bears. Behavior – imitation. Family life – fathers.

The last puppy ill. by author. Prentice-Hall, 1980. ISBN 978-0-13-524058-8 Subj: Animals – dogs. Pets.

The Lending Zoo ill. by author. Aladdin, 2016. ISBN 978-144246678-4 Subj: Animals – tigers. Careers – librarians. Libraries. Zoos.

Like a windy day by Frank Asch and Devin Asch; ill. by authors. Harcourt, 2002. ISBN 978-0-15-216376-1 Subj: Activities. Weather – wind.

Monsieur Saguette and his baguette ill. by author. Kids Can, 2004. ISBN 978-1-55337-461-9 Subj: Character traits – helpfulness. Food.

Moonbear ill. by author. Simon & Schuster, 1993. ISBN 978-0-671-86743-0 Subj: Animals – bears. Birds. Food. Moon. Night.

Moonbear's books ill. by author. Simon & Schuster, 1993. ISBN 978-0-671-86744-7 Subj: Animals – bears. Books, reading. Format, unusual – board books.

Moonbear's canoe ill. by author. Simon & Schuster, 1993. ISBN 978-0-671-86745-4 Subj: Animals – bears. Canoes & canoeing. Format, unusual – board books.

Moonbear's dream ill. by author. Simon & Schuster, 1999. ISBN 978-0-689-82244-5 Subj: Animals. Animals – bears. Behavior – misbehavior. Birds. Dreams.

Moonbear's friend ill. by author. Simon & Schuster, 1993. ISBN 978-0-671-86746-1 Subj: Animals – bears. Friendship.

Moonbear's pet ill. by author. Simon & Schuster, 1997. ISBN 978-0-689-80794-7 Subj: Animals – bears. Birds. Fish. Friendship. Frogs & toads.

Mooncake ill. by author. Prentice-Hall, 1983. ISBN 978-0-13-601013-5 Subj: Animals – bears. Birds. Moon. Seasons – winter.

Moondance ill. by author. Scholastic, 1993. ISBN 978-0-590-45487-2 Subj: Activities – dancing. Animals – bears. Moon.

Moongame ill. by author. Prentice-Hall, 1984. ISBN 978-0-13-600503-2 Subj: Activities – dancing. Animals – bears. Behavior – hiding. Moon.

Mr. Maxwell's mouse ill. by Devin Asch. Kids Can, 2004. ISBN 978-1-55337-486-2 Subj: Animals – cats. Animals – mice. Problem solving.

Mrs. Marlowe's mice ill. by Devin Asch. Kids Can, 2007. ISBN 978-1-55453-022-9 Subj: Animals – cats. Animals – mice. Behavior – secrets.

Pizza ill. by author. Simon & Schuster, 2015. ISBN 978-144246675-3 Subj: Animals – bears. Food.

Popcorn ill. by author. Parents' Magazine, 1979. ISBN 978-0-8193-1002-6 Subj: Animals – bears. Food. Holidays – Halloween. Parties.

Sand cake ill. by author. Parents' Magazine, 1979. ISBN 978-0-8193-0986-0 Subj: Activities – picnicking. Animals – bears. Humorous stories. Sea & seashore.

Skyfire ill. by author. Simon & Schuster, 1988. ISBN 978-0-671-66692-7 Subj: Animals – bears. Weather – rainbows.

The sun is my favorite star ill. by author. Harcourt, 2000. ISBN 978-0-15-202127-6 Subj: Astronomy. Science. Sun.

Ziggy Piggy and the three little pigs ill. by author. Kids Can, 1998. ISBN 978-1-55074-515-3 Subj: Animals – pigs. Animals – wolves. Character traits – cleverness. Folk & fairy tales.

Ashburn, Boni. *Builder Goose: it's construction rhyme time!* ill. by Sergio De Giorgi. Sterling, 2012. ISBN 978-1-4027-7118-7 Subj: Careers – construction workers. Machines. Nursery rhymes. Trucks.

The class ill. by Kimberly Gee. Simon & Schuster/Beach Lane, 2016. ISBN 978-144242248-3 Subj: Rhyming text. School – first day.

The fort that Jack built ill. by Brett Helquist. Abrams, 2013. ISBN 978-1-41970-795-7 Subj: Activities – playing. Family life. Imagination. Rhyming text.

I had a favorite dress ill. by Julia Denos. Abrams, 2011. ISBN 978-1-4197-0016-3 Subj: Activities – sewing. Clothing – dresses.

Over at the castle ill. by Kelly Murphy. Abrams, 2010. ISBN 978-0-8109-8414-1 Subj: Castles. Counting, numbers. Dragons. Middle Ages. Rhyming text. Songs.

Ashdown, Rebecca. *Bob and Flo* ill. by author. Houghton Mifflin Harcourt, 2015. ISBN 978-054444430-0 Subj: Birds – penguins. Friendship. School – first day. School – nursery.

Bob and Flo play hide-and-seek ill. by author. Houghton Mifflin Harcourt, 2016. ISBN 978-054459631-3 Subj: Behavior – hiding. Birds – penguins. Games.

The Whopper ill. by author. Candlewick/Templar, 2017. ISBN 978-076369291-9 Subj: Behavior – lying. Character traits – honesty. Monsters.

Asher, Sandy. *Chicken story time* ill. by Mark Fearing. Dial, 2016. ISBN 978-080373944-4 Subj: Activities – storytelling. Birds – chickens, roosters. Books, reading. Careers – librarians. Humorous stories. Libraries.

Here comes Gosling! ill. by Keith Graves. Philomel, 2009. ISBN 978-0-399-25085-9 Subj: Activities – picnicking. Animals. Babies, toddlers. Birds – geese. Frogs & toads.

Stella's dancing days ill. by Kathryn Brown. Harcourt, 2001. ISBN 978-0-15-201613-5 Subj: Activities – dancing. Animals – cats.

Too many frogs! ill. by Keith Graves. Penguin, 2005. ISBN 978-0-399-23978-6 Subj: Animals – rabbits. Behavior – solitude. Frogs & toads.

What a party! ill. by Keith Graves. Penguin, 2007. ISBN 978-0-399-24496-4 Subj: Birthdays. Family life – grandfathers. Frogs & toads. Parties.

Ashforth, Camilla. *Willow at Christmas* ill. by author. Candlewick, 2002. ISBN 978-0-7636-1850-6 Subj: Farms. Holidays – Christmas. Toys – bears.

Willow by the sea ill. by author. Candlewick, 2002. ISBN 978-0-7636-1401-0 Subj: Animals. Sea & seashore. Toys – bears.

Willow on the river ill. by author. Candlewick, 2002. ISBN 978-0-7636-1088-3 Subj: Activities – picnicking. Rivers. Toys – bears.

Ashley Bryan's ABC of African American poetry ill. by Ashley Bryan. Atheneum, 1997. ISBN 978-0-689-81209-5 Subj: ABC books. Ethnic groups in the U.S. – African Americans. Poetry.

Ashman, Linda. *All we know* ill. by Jane Dyer. HarperCollins, 2016. ISBN 978-006168958-1 Subj: Family life – mothers. Nature. Rhyming text.

Babies on the go ill. by Jane Dyer. Harcourt, 2003. ISBN 978-0-15-201894-8 Subj: Animals – babies. Rhyming text.

Castles, caves, and honeycombs ill. by Lauren Stringer. Harcourt, 2001. ISBN 978-0-15-202211-2 Subj: Animals. Homes, houses. Rhyming text.

Creaky old house: a topsy-turvy tale of a real fixer-upper ill. by Michael Chesworth. Sterling, 2009. ISBN 978-1-4027-4461-7 Subj: Family life. Homes, houses. Rhyming text.

Desmond and the naughtybugs ill. by Anik McCrory. Penguin, 2006. ISBN 978-0-525-47203-2 Subj: Behavior – misbehavior.

Ella who? ill. by Sara Sanchez. Sterling, 2017. ISBN 978-145491904-9 Subj: Animals – elephants. Behavior – misunderstanding. Friendship. Moving.

The essential worldwide monster guide ill. by David Small. Simon & Schuster, 2003. ISBN 978-0-689-82640-5 Subj: Monsters. Mythical creatures. Poetry.

Henry wants more! ill. by Brooke Boynton Hughes. Random House, 2016. ISBN 978-038538512-1 Subj: Activities. Babies, toddlers. Family life. Rhyming text.

How to make a night ill. by Tricia Tusa. HarperCollins, 2004. ISBN 978-0-06-029014-6 Subj: Bedtime. Night. Rhyming text.

Just another morning ill. by Claudio Muñoz. HarperCollins, 2004. ISBN 978-0-06-029054-2 Subj: Day. Imagination. Rhyming text.

M is for mischief: an A to Z of naughty children ill. by Nancy Carpenter. Dutton, 2008. ISBN 978-0-525-47564-4 Subj: ABC books. Behavior – misbehavior. Rhyming text.

Mama's day ill. by Jan Ormerod. Simon & Schuster, 2006. ISBN 978-0-689-83475-2 Subj: Babies, toddlers. Family life – mothers. Rhyming text.

Maxwell's magic mix-up ill. by Regan Dunnick. Simon & Schuster, 2001. ISBN 978-0-689-83178-2 Subj: Birthdays. Careers – magicians. Parties. Rhyming text.

No dogs allowed ill. by Kristin Sorra. Sterling, 2011. ISBN 978-1-4027-5837-9 Subj: Pets. Restaurants. Signs.

Over the river and through the wood ill. by Kim Smith. Sterling, 2015. ISBN 978-145491024-4 Subj: Activities – traveling. Family life. Holidays – Thanksgiving.

Rain! ill. by Christian Robinson. Harcourt, 2013. ISBN 978-0-547-73395-1 Subj: Activities – playing. Weather – rain.

Rock-a-bye romp ill. by Simona Mulazzani. Penguin/Nancy Paulsen, 2016. ISBN 978-039917150-5 Subj: Animals. Babies, toddlers. Bedtime. Lullabies.

Samantha on a roll ill. by Christine Davenier. Farrar, 2011. ISBN 978-0-374-36399-4 Subj: Rhyming text. Sports – roller skating.

Starry safari ill. by Jeff Mack. Harcourt, 2005. ISBN 978-0-15-204766-5 Subj: Bedtime. Jungle. Rhyming text.

Stella, unleashed: notes from the doghouse ill. by Paul Meisel. Sterling, 2008. ISBN 978-1-4027-3987-3 Subj: Animals – dogs. Family life. Rhyming text.

The tale of Wagmore Gently ill. by John Bendall-Brunello. Dutton, 2002. ISBN 978-0-525-46916-2 Subj: Anatomy – tails. Animals – dogs.

To the beach! ill. by Nadine Bernard Westcott. Harcourt, 2005. ISBN 978-0-15-216490-4 Subj: Behavior – forgetfulness. Family life. Humorous stories. Rhyming text. Sea & seashore – beaches.

What could be better than this ill. by Linda S. Wingerter. Penguin, 2006. ISBN 978-0-525-46954-4 Subj: Emotions – love. Family life – parents.

When I was king ill. by David McPhail. HarperCollins, 2008. ISBN 978-0-06-029051-1 Subj: Babies, toddlers. Family life – new sibling. Rhyming text.

William's winter nap ill. by Chuck Groenink. Disney/Hyperion, 2017. ISBN 978-148472282-4 Subj: Animals. Bedtime. Behavior – sharing. Rhyming text. Seasons – winter.

Asim, Jabari. *Daddy goes to work* ill. by Aaron Boyd. Little, Brown, 2006. ISBN 978-0-316-73575-9 Subj: Activities – working. Ethnic groups in the U.S. – African Americans. Family life – fathers. Rhyming text.

Fifty cents and a dream: young Booker T. Washington ill. by Bryan Collier. Little, Brown, 2012. ISBN 978-0-316-08657-8 Subj: Behavior – seeking better things. Books, reading. Character traits – perseverance. Ethnic groups in the U.S. – African Americans. Prejudice. School. Slavery.

Preaching to the chickens: the story of young John Lewis ill. by E. B. Lewis. Penguin/Nancy Paulsen, 2016. ISBN 978-039916856-7 Subj: Birds – chickens, roosters. Careers – clergy. Character traits – patience, impatience. Character traits – persistence. Ethnic groups in the U.S. – African Americans. Farms. U.S. history.

Aska, Warabe. *Tapicero tap tap* ill. by author. Tundra, 2006. ISBN 978-0-88776-760-9 Subj: Activities – storytelling. Character traits – ambition. Family life – grandfathers. Foreign lands – Spain.

Askani, Tanja. *A friend like you* ill. by author. Scholastic, 2009. ISBN 978-0-545-05851-3 Subj: Animals. Friendship.

Asper-Smith, Sarah. *I would tuck you in* ill. by Mitchell Watley. Sasquatch, 2012. ISBN 978-1-57061-844-4 Subj: Animals – babies. Bedtime.

Aspinall, Sarah. *Penguins love colors* ill. by author. Scholastic/Blue Sky, 2016. ISBN 978-054587654-4 Subj: Activities – painting. Birds – penguins. Concepts – color.

Aston, Claire. *Wild West* ill. by Mark Stacey. Barron's, 2001. ISBN 978-0-7641-5312-9 Subj: U.S. history – frontier & pioneer life.

Aston, Dianna Hutts. *A beetle is shy* ill. by Sylvia Long. Chronicle, 2016. ISBN 978-145212712-5 Subj: Insects – beetles.

A butterfly is patient ill. by Sylvia Long. Chronicle, 2011. ISBN 978-0-8118-6479-4 Subj: Insects – butterflies, caterpillars. Metamorphosis.

An egg is quiet ill. by Sylvia Long. Chronicle, 2006. ISBN 978-0-8118-4428-4 Subj: Eggs.

Loony Little ill. by Kelly Murphy. Candlewick, 2003. ISBN 978-0-7636-1682-3 Subj: Animals. Behavior – gossip, rumors. Birds – loons. Cumulative tales. Foreign lands – Arctic.

Mama Outside, Mama Inside ill. by Susan Gaber. Henry Holt, 2006. ISBN 978-0-8050-7716-2 Subj: Babies, toddlers. Birds. Birth. Family life – mothers.

The moon over Star ill. by Jerry Pinkney. Dial, 2008. ISBN 978-0-8037-3107-3 Subj: Ethnic groups in the U.S. – African Americans. Space & space ships. U.S. history.

A nest is noisy ill. by Sylvia Long. Chronicle, 2015. ISBN 978-145212713-2 Subj: Animals. Birds. Homes, houses.

Not so tall for six ill. by Frank W. Dormer. Charlesbridge, 2008. ISBN 978-1-57091-705-9 Subj: Behavior – bullying, teasing. Character traits – kindness. Character traits – smallness. School.

An orange in January ill. by Julie Maren. Penguin, 2007. ISBN 978-0-8037-3146-2 Subj: Food. Trees.

A rock is lively ill. by Sylvia Long. Chronicle, 2012. ISBN 978-1-4521-0645-8 Subj: Rocks.

A seed is sleepy ill. by Sylvia Long. Chronicle, 2007. ISBN 978-0-8118-5520-4 Subj: Seeds.

Atinuke. *Double trouble for Anna Hibiscus!* ill. by Lauren Tobia. Kane/Miller, 2015. ISBN 978-161067367-9 Subj: Foreign lands – Africa. Multiple births – twins. Sibling rivalry.

Atkins, Jeannine. *Mary Anning and the sea dragon* ill. by Michael Dooling. Farrar, 1999. ISBN 978-0-374-34840-3 Subj: Careers – paleontologists. Dinosaurs. Dragons. Foreign lands – England. Fossils. Science.

Robin's home ill. by Candace Whitman. Farrar, 2001. ISBN 978-0-374-36337-6 Subj: Behavior – growing up. Birds – robins.

Atkinson, Cale. *Explorers of the wild* ill. by author. Disney/Hyperion, 2016. ISBN 978-148472340-1 Subj: Animals – bears. Careers – explorers. Forest, woods.

Atteberry, Kevan. *Bunnies!!!* ill. by author. HarperCollins/Katherine Tegen, 2015. ISBN 978-006230783-5 Subj: Activities – playing. Animals – rabbits. Monsters. Nature.

Puddles!!! ill. by author. HarperCollins/Katherine Tegen, 2016. ISBN 978-006230784-2 Subj: Animals – rabbits. Monsters. Weather – lightning, thunder. Weather – rain.

Atwell, Debby. *Barn* ill. by author. Houghton, 1996. ISBN 978-0-395-78568-3 Subj: Barns.

Pearl ill. by author. Houghton, 2001. ISBN 978-0-395-88416-4 Subj: Family life. U.S. history.

River ill. by author. Houghton, 1999. ISBN 978-0-395-93546-0 Subj: Ecology. Rivers. Water.

The Thanksgiving door ill. by author. Houghton, 2003. ISBN 978-0-618-24036-4 Subj: Holidays – Thanksgiving. Immigrants, immigration.

Atwood, Margaret. *Up in the tree* ill. by author. Groundwood, 2006. ISBN 978-0-88899-729-6 Subj: Trees.

Auch, Herm. *Beauty and the beaks: a turkey's cautionary tale* (Auch, Mary Jane)

Chickerella (Auch, Mary Jane)

The plot chickens (Auch, Mary Jane)

Poultrygeist (Auch, Mary Jane)

The princess and the pizza (Auch, Mary Jane)

Souperchicken (Auch, Mary Jane)

Auch, Mary Jane. *Bantam of the opera* ill. by author. Holiday, 1997. ISBN 978-0-8234-1312-6 Subj: Activities – singing. Birds – chickens, roosters. Humorous stories.

Beauty and the beaks: a turkey's cautionary tale by Mary Jane Auch and Herm Auch; ill. by authors. Holiday House, 2007. ISBN 978-0-8234-1990-6 Subj: Behavior – boasting, showing off. Birds – chickens, roosters. Birds – turkeys. Holidays – Thanksgiving.

The buk buk buk festival ill. by author. Holiday House, 2015. ISBN 978-082343201-1 Subj: Activities – writing. Birds – chickens, roosters. Books, reading. Humorous stories.

Chickerella by Mary Jane Auch and Herm Auch; ill. by authors. Holiday House, 2005. ISBN 978-0-8234-1804-6 Subj: Birds – chickens, roosters. Folk & fairy tales. Humorous stories.

The Easter egg farm ill. by author. Holiday, 1992. ISBN 978-0-8234-0917-4 Subj: Birds – chickens, roosters. Eggs. Holidays – Easter.

Eggs mark the spot ill. by author. Holiday, 1996. ISBN 978-0-8234-1242-6 Subj: Art. Birds – chickens, roosters. Crime. Eggs.

Hen lake ill. by author. Holiday, 1995. ISBN 978-0-8234-1188-7 Subj: Activities – dancing. Ballet. Birds – chickens, roosters. Birds – peacocks, peahens.

The nutquacker ill. by author. Holiday, 1999. ISBN 978-0-8234-1524-3 Subj: Animals. Birds – ducks. Farms. Holidays – Christmas.

Peeping Beauty ill. by author. Holiday, 1993. ISBN 978-0-8234-1001-9 Subj: Activities – dancing. Animals – foxes. Ballet. Birds – chickens, roosters.

The plot chickens by Mary Jane Auch and Herm Auch; ill. by authors. Holiday House, 2009. ISBN 978-0-8234-2087-2 Subj: Activities – writing. Birds – chickens, roosters. Books, reading. Humorous stories.

Poultrygeist by Mary Jane Auch and Herm Auch; ill. by authors. Holiday, 2003. ISBN 978-0-8234-1756-8 Subj: Animals. Behavior. Birds – chickens, roosters. Ghosts. Holidays – Halloween.

The princess and the pizza by Mary Jane Auch and Herm Auch ill. by Herm Auch. Holiday, 2002. ISBN 978-0-8234-1683-7 Subj: Activities – baking, cooking. Folk & fairy tales. Food. Humorous stories. Royalty – princesses.

Souperchicken by Mary Jane Auch and Herm Auch; ill. by authors. Holiday, 2003. ISBN 978-0-8234-1704-9 Subj: Animals. Birds – chickens, roosters. Books, reading.

Audet, Martine. *Martin on the moon* ill. by Luc Melanson. OwlKids, 2012. ISBN 978-1-926973-16-6 Subj: Imagination. School – first day.

Auerbach, Adam. *Edda: a little Valkyrie's first day of school* ill. by author. Henry Holt, 2014. ISBN 978-080509703-0 Subj: Character traits – individuality. Folk & fairy tales. School – first day.

Monkey brother ill. by author. Holt/Christy Ottaviano, 2017. ISBN 978-162779600-2 Subj: Animals – monkeys. Family life – brothers.

Auerbach, Annie. *Splat the cat: on with the show* (Scotton, Rob)

Augustin, Barbara. *Antonella and her Santa Claus* ill. by Gerhard Lahr. Kane/Miller, 2001. ISBN 978-1-929132-13-3 Subj: Letters, cards. Santa Claus. Toys – balloons.

Aulaire, Edgar Parin d'. *Abraham Lincoln* (Aulaire, Ingri Mortenson d')

Aulaire, Ingri Mortenson d'. *Abraham Lincoln* by Ingri Mortenson d' Aulaire and Edgar Parin d' Aulaire ill. by Ingri d' Aulaire and Edgar Parin d' Aulaire. Rev. ed. Doubleday, 1957. ISBN 978-0-385-07674-6 Subj: Caldecott award books. U.S. history.

Auld, Mary. *Daniel in the lions' den* ill. by Diana Mayo. Simon & Schuster, 1999. ISBN 978-0-531-14514-2 Subj: Animals – lions. Religion – Daniel.

David and Goliath ill. by Diana Mayo. Watts, 2000. ISBN 978-0-531-14522-7 Subj: Foreign lands – Israel. Giants. Religion – David.

Exodus from Egypt ill. by Diana Mayo. Watts, 2000. ISBN 978-0-531-14585-2 Subj: Foreign lands – Egypt. Religion – Moses.

My aunt and uncle ill. with photos. G. Stevens, 2004. ISBN 978-0-8368-3923-4 Subj: Family life. Family life – aunts, uncles.

My brother ill. with photos. G. Stevens, 2004. ISBN 978-0-8368-3924-1 Subj: Family life. Family life – brothers.

My dad ill. with photos. G. Stevens, 2004. ISBN 978-0-8368-3925-8 Subj: Family life. Family life – fathers.

My grandparents ill. with photos. G. Stevens, 2004. ISBN 978-0-8368-3926-5 Subj: Family life. Family life – grandparents.

My mom ill. with photos. G. Stevens, 2004. ISBN 978-0-8368-3927-2 Subj: Family life. Family life – mothers.

My sister ill. with photos. G. Stevens, 2004. ISBN 978-0-8368-3928-9 Subj: Family life. Family life – sisters.

Noah's ark ill. by Diana Mayo. Watts, 2000. ISBN 978-0-531-14523-4 Subj: Animals. Boats, ships. Religion – Noah. Weather – floods. Weather – rain. Weather – rainbows.

The story of Jonah ill. by Diana Mayo. Watts, 1999. ISBN 978-0-531-14517-3 Subj: Animals – whales. Religion – Jonah.

Austin, Heather. *Visiting Aunt Sylvia's: a Maine adventure* ill. by author. Down East, 2002. ISBN 978-0-89272-523-6 Subj: Family life – aunts, uncles. Seasons.

Austin, Margot. *A friend for Growl Bear* ill. by David McPhail. HarperCollins, 1999. ISBN 978-0-06-027802-1 Subj: Animals. Animals – bears. Behavior – needing someone.

Austin, Mike. *Countdown with Milo* ill. by author. Blue Apple, 2012. ISBN 978-1-60905-208-9 Subj: Animals – cats. Animals – mice. Counting, numbers. Format, unusual – board books. Space & space ships.

Fire Engine No. 9 ill. by author. Random House, 2015. ISBN 978-055351095-9 Subj: Careers – firefighters. Trucks.

Junkyard ill. by author. Simon & Schuster/Beach Lane, 2014. ISBN 978-144245961-8 Subj: Ecology. Robots.

Monsters love colors ill. by author. HarperCollins, 2013. ISBN 978-0-06-212594-1 Subj: Concepts – color. Monsters.

Rescue Squad No. 9 ill. by author. Random House, 2016. ISBN 978-110193662-7 Subj: Boats, ships. Helicopters. Safety. Sea & seashore.

Austin, Patricia. *The cat who loved Mozart* ill. by Henri Sorensen. Holiday, 2001. ISBN 978-0-8234-1535-9 Subj: Animals – cats. Music. Musical instruments – pianos.

Austin, Richard. *Pocket piggies opposites!* ill. by author. Workman, 2016. ISBN 978-076118548-2 Subj: Animals – pigs. Concepts – opposites. Format, unusual – board books.

Austrian, J. J. *Worm loves Worm* ill. by Mike Curato. HarperCollins/Balzer+Bray, 2016. ISBN 978-006238633-5 Subj: Animals – worms. Emotions – love. Insects. Weddings.

Autry, Gene. *Here comes Santa Claus* by Gene Autry and Oakley Haldeman ill. by Bruce Whatley. Words & music by Gene Autry & Oakley Haldeman. HarperCollins, 2002. ISBN 978-0-06-028269-1 Subj: Animals – dogs. Holidays – Christmas. Music. Santa Claus. Songs.

Averbeck, Jim. *Except if* ill. by author. Simon & Schuster, 2011. ISBN 978-1-4169-9544-9 Subj: Animals. Eggs.

In a blue room ill. by Tricia Tusa. Harcourt, 2008. ISBN 978-0-15-205992-7 Subj: Bedtime. Concepts – color.

The market bowl ill. by author. Charlesbridge, 2013. ISBN 978-1-58089-368-8 Subj: Activities – baking, cooking. Food. Foreign lands – Cameroon. Stores.

Oh no, Little Dragon! ill. by author. Atheneum, 2012. ISBN 978-1-4169-9545-6 Subj: Activities – bathing. Dragons. Family life – mothers.

One word from Sophia ill. by Yasmeen Ismail. Atheneum, 2015. ISBN 978-148140514-0 Subj: Animals – giraffes. Birthdays. Ethnic groups in the U.S. Family life.

Avi. *Silent movie* ill. by C. B. Mordan. Atheneum, 2003. ISBN 978-0-689-84145-3 Subj: Immigrants, immigration. Theater.

Avraham, Kate Aver. *What will you be, Sara Mee?* ill. by Anne Sibley O'Brien. Charlesbridge, 2010. ISBN 978-1-58089-210-0 Subj: Birthdays. Ethnic groups in the U.S. – Korean Americans. Family life. Parties.

Awdry, W. *Happy birthday, Thomas!* ill. by Owain Bell. Based on The Railway Series. Random

House, 2003. ISBN 978-0-679-90809-8 Subj: Birthdays. Parties. Trains.

Axelrod, Amy. *Pigs in the corner: fun with math and dance* ill. by Sharon McGinley-Nally. Simon & Schuster, 2001. ISBN 978-0-689-82470-8 Subj: Activities – dancing. Animals – pigs.

Pigs in the pantry: fun with math and cooking ill. by Sharon McGinley-Nally. Simon & Schuster, 1997. ISBN 978-0-689-80665-0 Subj: Activities – baking, cooking. Animals – pigs. Counting, numbers. Food.

Pigs on a blanket ill. by Sharon McGinley-Nally. Simon & Schuster, 1996. ISBN 978-0-689-80505-9 Subj: Animals – pigs. Behavior – promptness, tardiness. Clocks, watches. Sea & seashore. Time.

Pigs on the ball: fun with math and sports ill. by Sharon McGinley-Nally. Simon & Schuster, 1998. ISBN 978-0-689-81565-2 Subj: Animals – pigs. Concepts – shape. Counting, numbers. Family life. Sports.

Pigs on the move: fun with math and travel ill. by Sharon McGinley-Nally. Simon & Schuster, 1999. ISBN 978-0-689-81070-1 Subj: Activities – traveling. Animals – pigs. Concepts – distance. Concepts – measurement. Holidays – Christmas.

Pigs will be pigs ill. by Sharon McGinley-Nally. Four Winds, 1994. ISBN 978-0-02-765415-8 Subj: Animals – pigs. Family life. Food. Money.

They'll believe me when I'm gone ill. by Jack E. Davis. Dutton, 2003. ISBN 978-0-525-46660-4 Subj: Family life. Humorous stories. Space & space ships.

Aylesworth, Jim. *The burger and the hot dog* ill. by Stephen Gammell. Atheneum, 2001. ISBN 978-0-689-83897-2 Subj: Food. Poetry.

Cock-a-doodle-doo, creak, pop-pop, moo ill. by Brad Sneed. Holiday House, 2012. ISBN 978-0-8234-2356-9 Subj: Animals. Farms. Noise, sounds. Rhyming text.

The completed hickory dickory dock ill. by Eileen Christelow. Macmillan, 1990. ISBN 978-0-689-31606-7 Subj: Animals – mice. Clocks, watches. Counting, numbers. Nursery rhymes. Time.

Country crossing ill. by Ted Rand. Macmillan, 1991. ISBN 978-0-689-31580-0 Subj: Noise, sounds. Trains.

The folks in the valley ill. by Stefano Vitale. HarperCollins, 1992. ISBN 978-0-06-021929-1 Subj: ABC books. Rhyming text.

The full belly bowl ill. by Wendy Anderson Halperin. Atheneum, 1998. ISBN 978-0-689-81033-6 Subj: Folk & fairy tales. Magic.

Little Bitty Mousie ill. by Michael Hague. Walker, 2007. ISBN 978-0-8027-9637-0 Subj: ABC books. Animals – mice. Rhyming text.

The mitten ill. by Barbara McClintock. Scholastic, 2009. ISBN 978-0-439-92544-0 Subj: Animals. Behavior – lost & found possessions. Folk & fairy tales. Foreign lands – Ukraine.

Mother Halverson's new cat ill. by Toni Goffe. Macmillan, 1989. ISBN 978-0-689-31465-0 Subj: Animals – cats. Character traits – practicality.

My grandfather's coat ill. by Barbara McClintock. Scholastic, 2014. ISBN 978-043992545-7 Subj: Careers – tailors. Clothing – coats. Family life – grandfathers. Immigrants, immigration. Jewish culture.

My sister's rusty bike ill. by Richard Hull. Atheneum, 1996. ISBN 978-0-689-31798-9 Subj: Activities – traveling. Rhyming text. Sports – bicycling. Tall tales.

Old Black Fly ill. by Stephen Gammell. Henry Holt, 1992. ISBN 978-0-8050-1401-3 Subj: ABC books. Insects – flies. Rhyming text.

One crow: a counting rhyme ill. by Ruth Young. HarperCollins, 1988. ISBN 978-0-397-32175-9 Subj: Animals. Counting, numbers. Farms. Rhyming text.

Our Abe Lincoln ill. by Barbara McClintock. Scholastic, 2009. ISBN 978-0-439-92548-8 Subj: Songs. U.S. history.

Teddy bear tears ill. by Jo Ellen McAllister Stammen. Atheneum, 1997. ISBN 978-0-689-31776-7 Subj: Bedtime. Emotions – fear. Toys – bears.

Two terrible frights ill. by Eileen Christelow. Atheneum, 1987. ISBN 978-0-689-31327-1 Subj: Animals – mice. Emotions – fear. Night.

Ayres, Katherine. *Matthew's truck* ill. by Hideko Takahashi. Candlewick, 2005. ISBN 978-0-7636-2269-5 Subj: Activities – playing. Toys. Trucks.

Up, down, and around ill. by Nadine Bernard Westcott. Candlewick, 2007. ISBN 978-0-7636-2378-4 Subj: Gardens, gardening. Language. Rhyming text.

Azarian, Mary. *A gardener's alphabet* ill. by author. Houghton, 2000. ISBN 978-0-618-03380-5 Subj: ABC books. Gardens, gardening. Language. Plants.

Azore, Barbara. *Wanda and the frogs* ill. by Georgia Graham. Tundra, 2007. ISBN 978-0-88776-761-6 Subj: Frogs & toads. Humorous stories.

Wanda and the wild hair ill. by Georgia Graham. Tundra, 2005. ISBN 978-0-88776-717-3 Subj: Animals. Character traits – individuality. Cumulative tales. Hair.

Baasansuren, Bolormaa. *My little round house* by Bolormaa Baasansuren and Helen Mixter; ill. by Bolormaa Baasansuren. Groundwood, 2009. ISBN 978-0-88899-934-4 Subj: Foreign lands – Mongolia. Nomads.

Baby animals ill. with photos. DK, 2003. ISBN 978-0-7894-9750-5 Subj: Animals – babies. Format, unusual – toy & movable books. Science.

Baby animals at the zoo. Kingfisher, 2012. ISBN 978-0-7534-6690-2 Subj: Animals – babies. Format, unusual – board books. Zoos.

Babypants, Caspar. *Augie to zebra: an alphabet book!* ill. by Kate Endle. Sasquatch, 2012. ISBN 978-1-57061-750-8 Subj: ABC books. Animals.

Bach, Annie. *Monster party!* ill. by author. Sterling, 2014. ISBN 978-145491051-0 Subj: Birthdays. Monsters. Parties. Rhyming text.

Bachelet, Gilles. *My cat, the silliest cat in the world* ill. by author. Abrams, 2006. ISBN 978-0-8109-4913-3 Subj: Animals – elephants. Humorous stories. Pets.

When the silliest cat was small ill. by author. Abrams, 2007. ISBN 978-0-8109-9415-7 Subj: Animals – elephants. Humorous stories. Pets.

Back, Rachel Tzvia. *The perfect purple feather* (Piven, Hanoch)

Backker, Vera de. *Coco the koala* ill. by author. G. Stevens, 2000. ISBN 978-0-8368-2729-3 Subj: Animals – koalas. Self-concept.

Backx, Patsy. *Josie and Mr. Fernandez* ill. by author. G. Stevens, 2002. ISBN 978-0-8368-3079-8 Subj: Animals – dogs. Behavior – sharing. Food.

Skippy and Jack ill. by author. G. Stevens, 2002. ISBN 978-0-8368-3080-4 Subj: Activities – dancing. Animals – dogs. Rhyming text.

Baddiel, Ivor. *Cock-a-doodle quack! quack!* by Ivor Baddiel and Sophie Jubb ill. by Ailie Busby. Random House, 2007. ISBN 978-0-385-75104-9 Subj: Animals. Animals – babies. Birds – chickens, roosters. Farms. Noise, sounds.

Badescu, Ramona. *Big Rabbit's bad mood* ill. by Delphine Durand. Chronicle, 2009. ISBN 978-0-8118-6666-8 Subj: Animals. Animals – rabbits. Behavior – bad day, bad mood. Birthdays.

Pomelo begins to grow ill. by Benjamin Chaud. Enchanted Lion, 2011. ISBN 978-1-59270-111-7 Subj: Animals – elephants. Behavior – growing up.

Pomelo's opposites ill. by Benjamin Chaud. Enchanted Lion, 2013. ISBN 978-1-59270-132-2 Subj: Animals – elephants. Concepts – opposites.

Badiel, Georgie. *The water princess* (Verde, Susan)

Bae, Hyun-Joo. *New clothes for New Year's day* ill. by author. Kane/Miller, 2007. ISBN 978-1-933605-29-6 Subj: Clothing. Foreign lands – Korea. Holidays – New Year's.

Baehr, Patricia. *Boo Cow* ill. by Margot Apple. Charlesbridge, 2010. ISBN 978-1-58089-108-0 Subj: Animals – bulls, cows. Birds – chickens, roosters. Ghosts.

Baek, Matthew J. *Be gentle with the dog, dear* ill. by author. Dial, 2008. ISBN 978-0-8037-3250-6 Subj: Animals – dogs. Babies, toddlers. Behavior – misbehavior. Character traits – kindness to animals.

Panda and polar bear ill. by author. Dial, 2009. ISBN 978-0-8037-3359-6 Subj: Animals – pandas. Animals – polar bears. Character traits – being different.

Baer, Edith. *This is the way we go to school* ill. by Steve Björkman. Scholastic, 1990. ISBN 978-0-590-43161-3 Subj: Rhyming text. School. Transportation.

Baer, Gene. *Thump thump rat-a-tat-tat* ill. by Lois Ehlert. HarperCollins, 1989. ISBN 978-0-06-020362-7 Subj: Music. Musical instruments – bands. Parades.

Baeten, Lieve. *The clever little witch* ill. by Wietse Fossey. NorthSouth, 2012. ISBN 978-0-7358-4079-9 Subj: Format, unusual. Magic. Witches.

The curious little witch. NorthSouth, 2010. ISBN 978-0-7358-2305-1 Subj: Format, unusual. Witches.

Happy birthday, Little Witch! ill. by author. NorthSouth, 2011. ISBN 978-0-7358-4043-0 Subj: Animals – cats. Behavior – lost. Birthdays. Format, unusual – toy & movable books. Witches.

Bagert, Brod. *Giant children* ill. by Tedd Arnold. Dial, 2002. ISBN 978-0-8037-2556-0 Subj: Poetry.

Shout! little poems that roar ill. by Sachiko Yoshikawa. Penguin, 2007. ISBN 978-0-8037-2972-8 Subj: Poetry.

Bagley, Jessixa. *Before I leave* ill. by author. Roaring Brook/Neal Porter, 2016. ISBN 978-162672040-4 Subj: Animals – anteaters. Animals – hedgehogs. Friendship. Moving.

Boats for Papa ill. by author. Roaring Brook/Neal Porter, 2015. ISBN 978-162672039-8 Subj: Animals – beavers. Boats, ships. Death. Emotions – grief. Family life – mothers.

Laundry day ill. by author. Roaring Brook/Neal Porter, 2017. ISBN 978-162672317-7 Subj: Animals – badgers. Behavior – boredom. Character traits – helpfulness. Laundry.

Baguley, Elizabeth. *A long way from home* ill. by Jane Chapman. Tiger Tales, 2008. ISBN 978-1-58925-074-1 Subj: Animals – rabbits. Bedtime. Behavior – dissatisfaction.

Meggie moon ill. by Gregoire Mabire. Good Books, 2005. ISBN 978-1-56148-474-4 Subj: Activities – playing. Gender roles. Imagination.

Ready, steady, ghost! ill. by Marion Lindsay. Disney/Hyperion, 2014. ISBN 978-142318039-5 Subj: Character traits – smallness. Emotions – fear. Ghosts.

Bahr, Mary. *My brother loved snowflakes* ill. by Laura Jacobsen. Boyds Mills, 2002. ISBN 978-1-56397-689-6 Subj: Careers – meteorologists. Careers – photographers. Weather – snow.

Baicker, Karen. *Pea pod babies* ill. by Sam Williams. Handprint, 2003. ISBN 978-1-59354-003-6 Subj: Babies, toddlers. Character traits – individuality. Gardens, gardening. Rhyming text.

You can do it too! ill. by Ken Wilson-Max. Handprint, 2005. ISBN 978-1-59354-080-7 Subj: Ethnic groups in the U.S. – African Americans. Family life – brothers & sisters. Rhyming text.

Bailey, Ella. *No such thing* ill. by author. Flying Eye, 2014. ISBN 978-190926348-2 Subj: Ghosts. Holidays – Halloween. Rhyming text.

Bailey, Linda. *The best figure skater in the whole wide world* ill. by Alan Daniel and Lea Daniel. Kids Can, 2001. ISBN 978-1-55074-879-6 Subj: Sports – ice skating.

The farm team ill. by Bill Slavin. Kids Can, 2006. ISBN 978-1-55337-850-1 Subj: Animals. Behavior – cheating. Character traits – bravery. Farms. Sports – hockey.

Goodnight, sweet pig ill. by Josée Masse. Kids Can, 2006. ISBN 978-1-55337-844-0 Subj: Animals – pigs. Bedtime. Counting, numbers. Rhyming text.

If kids ruled the world ill. by David Huyck. Kids Can, 2014. ISBN 978-155453591-0 Subj: Imagination.

If you happen to have a dinosaur ill. by Colin Jack. Tundra, 2014. ISBN 978-177049568-5 Subj: Dinosaurs.

Stanley at sea ill. by Bill Slavin. Kids Can, 2008. ISBN 978-1-55453-193-6 Subj: Activities – traveling. Animals – dogs. Sea & seashore.

Stanley's beauty contest ill. by Bill Slavin. Kids Can, 2009. ISBN 978-1-55453-318-3 Subj: Animals – dogs. Contests.

Stanley's little sister ill. by Bill Slavin. Kids Can, 2010. ISBN 978-1-55453-487-6 Subj: Animals – cats. Animals – dogs. Friendship.

Stanley's party ill. by Bill Slavin. Kids Can, 2003. ISBN 978-1-55337-382-7 Subj: Animals – dogs. Parties.

Stanley's wild ride ill. by Bill Slavin. Kids Can, 2006. ISBN 978-1-55337-960-7 Subj: Animals – dogs. Behavior – running away.

Toads on toast ill. by Colin Jack. Kids Can, 2012. ISBN 978-1-55453-662-7 Subj: Activities – baking, cooking. Animals – foxes. Food. Frogs & toads.

When Santa was a baby ill. by Geneviève Godbout. Tundra, 2015. ISBN 978-177049556-2 Subj: Behavior – growing up. Santa Claus.

Bailey, Mary Bryant. *Jeoffry's Christmas* ill. by Elizabeth Sayles. Farrar, 2002. ISBN 978-0-374-33676-9 Subj: Animals – cats. Holidays – Christmas. Rhyming text. Santa Claus. Trees.

Baillie, Allan. *Dragonquest* ill. by Wayne Harris. Candlewick, 2013. ISBN 978-0-7636-6617-0 Subj: Activities – traveling. Dragons. Knights.

Baillie, Marilyn. *Nose to toes* ill. by Marisol Sarrazin. Boyds Mills, 2001. ISBN 978-1-56397-319-2 Subj: Activities – playing. Animals. Imagination. Rhyming text.

Small wonders: baby animals in the wild ill. by Romi Caron. Maple Tree, 2006. ISBN 978-1-987066-72-0 Subj: Animals – babies.

Bair, Sheila. *Isabel's car wash* ill. by Judy Stead. Albert Whitman, 2008. ISBN 978-0-8075-3652-0 Subj: Activities – working. Automobiles. Counting, numbers. Money.

Baird, Audrey B. *A cold snap! frosty poems* ill. by Patrick O'Brien. Wordsong, 2002. ISBN 978-1-56397-633-9 Subj: Poetry. Seasons – winter. Weather.

Storm coming! ill. by Patrick O'Brien. Wordsong, 2001. ISBN 978-1-56397-887-6 Subj: Poetry. Weather – rain. Weather – storms.

Bajaj, Varsha. *This is our baby, born today* ill. by Eliza Wheeler. Penguin/Nancy Paulsen, 2016. ISBN 978-039916684-6 Subj: Animals – babies. Animals – elephants.

Baker, Alan. *Black and White Rabbit's ABC* ill. by author. Kingfisher, 1994. ISBN 978-1-85697-851-4

Subj: ABC books. Activities – painting. Animals – rabbits. Cumulative tales.

Brown Rabbit's shape book ill. by author. Kingfisher, 1994. ISBN 978-1-85697-950-4 Subj: Animals – rabbits. Concepts – shape. Toys – balloons.

Gray Rabbit's one, two, three ill. by author. Kingfisher, 1994. ISBN 978-1-85697-952-8 Subj: Animals. Animals – rabbits. Counting, numbers.

Little Rabbit's first number book ill. by author. Kingfisher, 1998. ISBN 978-0-7534-5167-0 Subj: Animals – rabbits. Counting, numbers.

Little Rabbit's first word book ill. by author. Kingfisher, 1996. ISBN 978-0-7534-5020-8 Subj: Animals – rabbits. Language.

White Rabbit's color book ill. by author. Kingfisher, 1994. ISBN 978-1-85697-953-5 Subj: Activities – painting. Animals – rabbits. Concepts – color.

Baker, Jeannie. *Circle* ill. by author. Candlewick, 2016. ISBN 978-076367966-8 Subj: Birds. Migration.

The hidden forest ill. by author. Greenwillow, 2000. ISBN 978-0-688-15760-9 Subj: Foreign lands – Tasmania. Plants. Sea & seashore. Sports – skin diving.

Mirror ill. by author. Candlewick, 2010. ISBN 978-0-7636-4848-0 Subj: Foreign lands – Australia. Foreign lands – Morocco. Format, unusual – toy & movable books. Mirrors. Shopping. Wordless.

The story of rosy dock ill. by author. Greenwillow, 1995. ISBN 978-0-688-11493-0 Subj: Ecology. Foreign lands – Australia. Plants.

Where the forest meets the sea ill. by author. Greenwillow, 1988. ISBN 978-0-688-06364-1 Subj: Ecology. Foreign lands – Australia. Forest, woods.

Window ill. by author. Greenwillow, 1991. ISBN 978-0-688-08918-4 Subj: Ecology. Foreign lands – Australia. Wordless.

Baker, Keith. *Hap-pea all year* ill. by author. Simon & Schuster/Beach Lane, 2016. ISBN 978-148145854-2 Subj: Days of the week, months of the year. Food. Rhyming text. Seasons.

Hickory dickory dock ill. by author. Harcourt, 2007. ISBN 978-0-15-205818-0 Subj: Animals – mice. Clocks, watches. Time.

Just how long can a long string be?! ill. by author. Scholastic, 2009. ISBN 978-0-545-08661-5 Subj: Birds. Insects – ants. Rhyming text. String.

Little green peas: a big book of colors ill. by author. Simon & Schuster/Beach Lane, 2014. ISBN 978-144247660-8 Subj: Concepts – color. Food. Rhyming text.

LMNO pea-quel ill. by author. Simon & Schuster/Beach Lane, 2017. ISBN 978-148145856-6 Subj: ABC books. Careers. Food. Rhyming text.

LMNO peas ill. by author. Simon & Schuster, 2010. ISBN 978-1-4169-9141-0 Subj: ABC books. Careers. Food. Rhyming text.

My octopus arms ill. by author. Simon & Schuster, 2013. ISBN 978-1-4424-5843-7 Subj: Anatomy. Octopuses. Rhyming text.

No two alike ill. by author. Simon & Schuster, 2011. ISBN 978-1-4424-1742-7 Subj: Birds. Character traits – individuality. Rhyming text. Seasons – winter.

1-2-3 peas ill. by author. Simon & Schuster, 2012. ISBN 978-1-4424-4551-2 Subj: Counting, numbers. Food. Rhyming text.

Potato Joe ill. by author. Harcourt, 2008. ISBN 978-0-15-206230-9 Subj: Counting, numbers. Nursery rhymes.

Baker, Ken. *Brave little monster* ill. by Geoffrey Hayes. HarperCollins, 2001. ISBN 978-0-06-028699-6 Subj: Bedtime. Emotions – fear. Monsters. Night.

Old MacDonald had a dragon ill. by Christopher Santoro. Amazon, 2012. ISBN 978-0-7614-6175-3 Subj: Animals. Careers – farmers. Cumulative tales. Dragons. Farms. Songs.

Baker, Leslie A. *You bad dog!* ill. by author. Dutton, 2003. ISBN 978-0-525-47127-1 Subj: Activities – playing. Animals – dogs. Behavior – misbehavior.

Baker, Liza. *Dinosaur days* color by Sharon Matsumoto; ill. by Andy Chiang. HarperCollins, 2003. ISBN 978-0-06-000541-2 Subj: Activities – drawing. Dinosaurs. Jungle.

I love you because you're you ill. by David McPhail. Scholastic, 2001. ISBN 978-0-439-20638-9 Subj: Animals – foxes. Emotions – love. Family life – mothers. Rhyming text.

Baker, Olaf. *Where the buffaloes begin* ill. by Stephen Gammell. Warne, 1981. ISBN 978-0-670-82760-2 Subj: Animals – buffaloes. Caldecott award honor books. Folk & fairy tales. Indians of North America.

Baker, Roberta. *No ordinary Olive* ill. by Debbie Tilley. Little, 2002. ISBN 978-0-316-07336-3 Subj: Character traits – individuality. Family life – daughters. Family life – parents. Imagination.

Olive's first sleepover ill. by Debbie Tilley. Little, Brown, 2007. ISBN 978-0-316-73418-9 Subj: Bedtime. Emotions – fear. Friendship. Sleep.

Olive's pirate party ill. by Debbie Tilley. Little, Brown, 2005. ISBN 978-0-316-16792-5 Subj: Birthdays. Family life – aunts, uncles. Parties. Pirates.

Bakos, Lisa M. *Too many moose!* ill. by Mark Chambers. Sourcebooks/Jabberwocky, 2016. ISBN

978-149260935-3 Subj: Animals – moose. Pets. Rhyming text.

The wrong side of the bed ill. by Anna Raff. Putnam, 2016. ISBN 978-0-399-16572-6 Subj: Behavior – bad day, bad mood. Humorous stories.

Balcziak, Bill. *John Henry* ill. by Drew Rose. Compass Point, 2003. ISBN 978-0-7565-0457-1 Subj: Character traits – perseverance. Character traits – pride. Ethnic groups in the U.S. – African Americans. Folk & fairy tales. Tall tales.

Paul Bunyan ill. by Patrick Girouard. Compass Point, 2003. ISBN 978-0-7565-0459-5 Subj: Animals – oxen. Careers – lumberjacks. Tall tales. U.S. history – frontier & pioneer life.

Pecos Bill ill. by Roberta Collier-Morales. Compass Point, 2003. ISBN 978-0-7565-0460-1 Subj: Cowboys, cowgirls. Tall tales. U.S. history – frontier & pioneer life.

Baldacchino, Christine. *Morris Micklewhite and the tangerine dress* ill. by Isabelle Malenfant. Groundwood, 2014. ISBN 978-155498347-6 Subj: Clothing – dresses. Gender identity. Self-concept.

Balducci, Rita. *Little Bear's timeless tales* ill. by Amy Flynn. Reader's Digest, 2003. ISBN 978-0-7944-0215-0 Subj: Folk & fairy tales.

Balian, Lorna. *Bah! Humbug?* ill. by author. Abingdon, 1977. ISBN 978-0-687-02345-5 Subj: Holidays – Christmas.

Humbug rabbit ill. by author. Abingdon, 1974. ISBN 978-1-932065-40-4 Subj: Animals – rabbits. Eggs. Family life – grandmothers. Holidays – Easter.

Humbug witch ill. by author. Abingdon, 1965. ISBN 978-1-881772-24-8 Subj: Holidays – Halloween. Witches.

Leprechauns never lie ill. by author. Abingdon, 1980. ISBN 978-0-687-21371-9 Subj: Animals – cats. Folk & fairy tales. Foreign lands – Ireland. Humorous stories. Mythical creatures – leprechauns.

Mother's Mother's Day ill. by author. Abingdon, 1982. ISBN 978-0-685-57645-8 Subj: Animals – mice. Family life – mothers. Holidays – Mother's Day.

Sometimes it's turkey ill. by author. Abingdon, 1973. ISBN 978-0-687-39074-8 Subj: Birds – turkeys. Holidays – Thanksgiving.

A sweetheart for Valentine ill. by author. Abingdon, 1987. ISBN 978-0-687-40771-2 Subj: Giants. Holidays – Valentine's Day. Weddings.

Ballard, Robin. *I used to be the baby* ill. by author. Greenwillow, 2002. ISBN 978-0-06-029586-8 Subj: Babies, toddlers. Family life – brothers.

My day, your day ill. by author. Greenwillow, 2001. ISBN 978-0-688-17796-6 Subj: Activities – working. Day. Family life – parents. School.

Tonight and tomorrow ill. by author. Greenwillow, 2000. ISBN 978-0-688-16790-5 Subj: Bedtime. Night.

Balmes, Santi. *I will fight monsters for you* ill. by Lyona. Albert Whitman, 2015. ISBN 978-080759056-0 Subj: Bedtime. Emotions – fear. Monsters.

Balouch, Kristen, reteller. *The king and the three thieves* ill. by reteller. Viking, 2000. ISBN 978-0-670-88059-1 Subj: Crime. Folk & fairy tales. Foreign lands – Iran. Royalty – kings.

The little little girl with the big big voice ill. by author. Simon & Schuster, 2011. ISBN 978-1-4424-0808-1 Subj: Character traits – smallness. Jungle. Noise, sounds.

Mystery bottle ill. by author. Hyperion, 2006. ISBN 978-0-7868-0999-8 Subj: Family life – grandfathers. Foreign lands – Iran.

Bandy, Michael S. *Granddaddy's turn: a journey to the ballot box* by Michael S. Bandy and Eric Stein ill. by James Ransome. Candlewick, 2015. ISBN 978-076366593-7 Subj: Character traits – persistence. Ethnic groups in the U.S. – African Americans. Family life – grandfathers. Prejudice. U.S. history.

White water by Michael S. Bandy and Eric Stein ill. by Shadra Strickland. Candlewick, 2011. ISBN 978-0-7636-3678-4 Subj: Ethnic groups in the U.S. – African Americans. Prejudice. U.S. history.

Bang, Molly. *All of me! a book of thanks* ill. by author. Scholastic, 2009. ISBN 978-0-545-04424-0 Subj: Anatomy.

Buried sunlight: how fossil fuels have changed the earth by Molly Bang and Penny Chisholm; ill. by Molly Bang. Scholastic/Blue Sky, 2014. ISBN 978-054557785-4 Subj: Earth. Science. Sun.

Dawn ill. by author. Morrow, 1983. ISBN 978-0-688-02404-8 Subj: Activities – weaving. Behavior – secrets. Birds – cranes. Character traits – curiosity. Folk & fairy tales. Foreign lands – Japan.

Goose ill. by author. Blue Sky, 1996. ISBN 978-0-590-89005-2 Subj: Activities – flying. Animals – groundhogs. Birds – geese.

The grey lady and the strawberry snatcher ill. by author. Four Winds, 1980. ISBN 978-0-590-07547-3 Subj: Caldecott award honor books. Imagination. Wordless.

In my heart ill. by author. Little, Brown, 2006. ISBN 978-0-316-79617-0 Subj: Emotions – love. Family life.

Living sunlight: how plants bring the earth to life by Molly Bang and Penny Chrisholm; ill. by Molly Bang. Scholastic, 2009. ISBN 978-0-545-04422-6 Subj: Plants. Science. Sun.

My light ill. by author. Scholastic, 2004. ISBN 978-0-439-48961-4 Subj: Light, lights. Science. Sun.

Ocean sunlight: how tiny plants feed the seas by Molly Bang and Penny Chisholm; ill. by Molly Bang. Scholastic, 2012. ISBN 978-0-545-27322-0 Subj: Plants. Science. Sea & seashore. Sun.

The paper crane ill. by author. Greenwillow, 1985. ISBN 978-0-688-04109-0 Subj: Birds – cranes. Character traits – kindness. Folk & fairy tales.

Rivers of sunlight: how the sun moves water around the earth by Molly Bang and Penny Chisholm; ill. by Molly Bang. Scholastic/Blue Sky, 2017. ISBN 978-054580541-4 Subj: Ecology. Science. Sun. Water.

Ten, nine, eight ill. by author. Greenwillow, 1983. ISBN 978-0-688-00907-6 Subj: Bedtime. Caldecott award honor books. Counting, numbers. Ethnic groups in the U.S. – African Americans. Lullabies. Rhyming text.

When Sophie gets angry — really, really angry . . . ill. by author. Blue Sky, 1999. ISBN 978-0-590-18979-8 Subj: Caldecott award honor books. Emotions – anger. Family life – sisters.

When Sophie's feelings are really, really hurt ill. by author. Scholastic/Blue Sky, 2015. ISBN 978-054578831-1 Subj: Activities – painting. Art. Emotions. Emotions – sadness.

Wiley and the hairy man ill. by adapter. Macmillan, 1976. ISBN 978-0-02-708370-5 Subj: Character traits – cleverness. Ethnic groups in the U.S. – African Americans. Folk & fairy tales. Monsters.

Yellow ball ill. by author. Morrow, 1991. ISBN 978-0-688-06315-3 Subj: Activities – playing. Sea & seashore. Toys – balls.

Banks, Kate. *The bear in the book* ill. by Georg Hallensleben. Farrar, 2012. ISBN 978-0-374-30591-8 Subj: Animals – bears. Bedtime. Books, reading. Family life – mothers. Hibernation.

City cat ill. by Lauren Castillo. Farrar, 2013. ISBN 978-0-374-31321-0 Subj: Activities – traveling. Animals – cats. Foreign lands – Europe. Rhyming text.

Close your eyes ill. by Georg Hallensleben. Farrar, 2002. ISBN 978-0-374-31382-1 Subj: Animals – tigers. Dreams. Family life – mothers. Sleep.

The eraserheads ill. by Boris Kulikov. Farrar, 2010. ISBN 978-0-374-39920-7 Subj: Activities – drawing. Activities – writing. Imagination.

Fox ill. by Georg Hallensleben. Farrar, 2007. ISBN 978-0-374-39967-2 Subj: Animals – foxes. Behavior – growing up.

The great blue house ill. by Georg Hallensleben. Farrar, 2005. ISBN 978-0-374-32769-9 Subj: Homes, houses. Seasons.

How to find an elephant ill. by Boris Kulikov. Farrar/Margaret Ferguson, 2017. ISBN 978-037433508-3 Subj: Animals – elephants. Character traits – curiosity.

Mama's coming home ill. by Tomasz Bogacki. Farrar, 2003. ISBN 978-0-374-34747-5 Subj: Activities – working. Family life. Family life – mothers. Gender roles.

Max's castle ill. by Boris Kulikov. Farrar, 2011. ISBN 978-0-374-39919-1 Subj: Family life – brothers. Imagination. Knights. Language. Toys – blocks.

Max's dragon ill. by Boris Kulikov. Farrar, 2008. ISBN 978-0-374-39921-4 Subj: Activities – playing. Dragons. Imagination. Language.

Max's math ill. by Boris Kulikov. Farrar/Frances Foster, 2015. ISBN 978-037434875-5 Subj: Concepts – shape. Counting, numbers.

Max's words ill. by Boris Kulikov. Farrar, 2006. ISBN 978-0-374-39949-8 Subj: Activities – storytelling. Behavior – collecting things. Language.

The night worker ill. by Georg Hallensleben. Farrar, 2000. ISBN 978-0-374-35520-3 Subj: Activities – working. Careers – construction workers. Family life – fathers.

Pup and bear ill. by Naoko Stoop. Random House, 2017. ISBN 978-039955409-4 Subj: Animals – polar bears. Animals – wolves. Character traits – kindness to animals. Family life – mothers. Foreign lands – Arctic.

That's Papa's way ill. by Lauren Castillo. Farrar, 2009. ISBN 978-0-374-37445-7 Subj: Character traits – individuality. Family life – fathers. Sports – fishing.

This baby ill. by Gabi Swiatkowska. Farrar, 2011. ISBN 978-0-374-37514-0 Subj: Babies, toddlers. Family life – new sibling.

What's coming for Christmas? ill. by Georg Hallensleben. Farrar, 2009. ISBN 978-0-374-39948-1 Subj: Animals. Farms. Holidays – Christmas.

Banks, Merry. *N is for Navidad* (Elya, Susan Middleton)

Bannerman, Helen. *Sam and the tigers: a new telling of Little Black Sambo* (Lester, Julius)

The story of Little Babaji ill. by Fred Marcellino. HarperCollins, 1996. ISBN 978-0-06-205065-6 Subj: Animals – tigers. Character traits – cleverness. Family life. Foreign lands – India.

The story of Little Black Sambo (1996) ill. by author. Applewood, 1996. ISBN 978-1-55709-414-8 Subj:

Animals – tigers. Character traits – cleverness. Family life. Foreign lands – India.

The story of Little Black Sambo (1990) ill. by author. HarperCollins, 1990. ISBN 978-0-397-30006-8 Subj: Animals – tigers. Character traits – cleverness. Family life. Foreign lands – India.

The story of Little Black Sambo (2003) ill. by Christopher Bing. Handprint, 2003. ISBN 978-1-929766-55-0 Subj: Animals – tigers. Character traits – cleverness. Family life. Foreign lands – India.

Bansch, Helga. *At night* ill. by author. Eerdmans, 2016. ISBN 978-080285471-1 Subj: Animals. Bedtime.

Brava, Mimi! ill. by author. NorthSouth, 2010. ISBN 978-0-7358-2322-8 Subj: Activities – dancing. Animals – mice. Ballet.

Odd bird out ill. by author. Gecko, 2011. ISBN 978-1-8774-6708-0 Subj: Birds – ravens. Character traits – being different. Self-concept.

Rosie the raven ill. by author. Annick, 2016. ISBN 978-155451834-0 Subj: Birds – ravens. Character traits – being different. Character traits – individuality. Self-concept.

Bar-el, Dan. *A fish named Glub* ill. by Josée Bisaillon. Kids Can, 2014. ISBN 978-155453812-6 Subj: Dreams. Fish. Memories, memory. Rhyming text.

Not your typical dragon ill. by Tim Bowers. Viking, 2013. ISBN 978-0-670-01402-6 Subj: Character traits – being different. Character traits – individuality. Dragons. Self-concept.

Such a prince ill. by John Manders. Houghton, 2007. ISBN 978-0-618-71468-1 Subj: Fairies. Folk & fairy tales. Royalty – princesses.

Barack, Marcy. *Season song* ill. by Thierry Courtin. HarperCollins, 2002. ISBN 978-0-694-01567-2 Subj: Format, unusual – board books. Rhyming text. Seasons.

Baranski, Joan Sullivan. *Round is a pancake* ill. by Yu-Mei Han. Dutton, 2001. ISBN 978-0-525-46173-9 Subj: Concepts – shape. Food. Rhyming text. Royalty – kings.

Barasch, Lynne. *First come the zebra* ill. by author. Lee & Low, 2009. ISBN 978-1-60060-365-5 Subj: Animals. Behavior – fighting, arguing. Character traits – cooperation. Foreign lands – Kenya.

Hiromi's hands ill. by author. Lee & Low, 2007. ISBN 978-1-58430-275-9 Subj: Careers – chefs, cooks. Ethnic groups in the U.S. – Japanese Americans. Food.

Radio rescue ill. by author. Farrar, 2000. ISBN 978-0-374-36166-2 Subj: Activities. Radios.

The reluctant flower girl ill. by author. HarperCollins, 2001. ISBN 978-0-06-028810-5 Subj: Family life – sisters. Friendship. Weddings.

Barash, Chris. *Is it Hanukkah yet?* ill. by Alessandra Psacharopulo. Albert Whitman, 2015. ISBN 978-080753384-0 Subj: Family life. Holidays – Hanukkah. Rhyming text.

Barba, Ale. *Time out!* ill. by author. Philomel, 2017. ISBN 978-039916304-3 Subj: Animals – pigs. Behavior – misbehavior. Imagination.

When your elephant comes to play ill. by author. Philomel, 2016. ISBN 978-039916312-8 Subj: Activities – playing. Animals – elephants.

Barber, Patti. *First number book* ill. by Mandy Stanley. Kingfisher, 2001. ISBN 978-0-7534-5338-4 Subj: Counting, numbers. Picture puzzles.

Barber, Ronde. *By my brother's side* (Barber, Tiki)

Game day (Barber, Tiki)

Teammates (Barber, Tiki)

Barber, Tiki. *By my brother's side* by Tiki Barber and Ronde Barber ill. by Barry Root. Simon & Schuster, 2004. ISBN 978-0-689-86559-6 Subj: Ethnic groups in the U.S. – African Americans. Family life – brothers. Multiple births – twins. Sports – football.

Game day by Tiki Barber and Ronde Barber ill. by Barry Root. Simon & Schuster, 2005. ISBN 978-1-4169-0093-1 Subj: Ethnic groups in the U.S. – African Americans. Family life – brothers. Multiple births – twins. Sports – football.

Teammates by Tiki Barber and Ronde Barber ill. by Barry Root. Simon & Schuster, 2006. ISBN 978-1-4169-2489-0 Subj: Character traits – perseverance. Ethnic groups in the U.S. – African Americans. Family life – brothers. Multiple births – twins. Sports – football.

Barbero, Maria. *The bravest mouse* ill. by author. NorthSouth, 2002. ISBN 978-0-7358-1709-8 Subj: Animals – cats. Animals – mice. Character traits – bravery. Self-concept.

Barbour, Karen. *Little Nino's pizzeria* ill. by author. Harcourt, 1987. ISBN 978-0-15-247650-2 Subj: Family life. Food.

Mr. Williams ill. by author. Henry Holt, 2005. ISBN 978-0-8050-6773-6 Subj: Careers – farmers. Ethnic groups in the U.S. – African Americans. Farms. Old age. Prejudice. U.S. history.

Barclay, Eric. *Counting dogs* ill. by author. Scholastic, 2015. ISBN 978-054578392-7 Subj: Animals – dogs. Counting, numbers. Format, unusual – board books.

Hiding Phil ill. by author. Scholastic, 2013. ISBN 978-0-545-46477-2 Subj: Animals – elephants. Behavior – hiding things. Family life – brothers & sisters.

I can see just fine ill. by author. Abrams, 2013. ISBN 978-1-4197-0801-5 Subj: Anatomy – eyes. Careers – opticians, optometrists. Glasses.

Barclay, Jane. *Going on a journey to the sea* ill. by Elizabeth Mikau. Lobster, 2002. ISBN 978-1-894222-34-1 Subj: Activities – playing. Sea & seashore. Sports – swimming.

Bardhan-Quallen, Sudipta. *Chicks run wild* ill. by Ward Jenkins. Simon & Schuster, 2011. ISBN 978-1-4424-0673-5 Subj: Bedtime. Behavior – misbehavior. Birds – chickens, roosters. Family life – mothers. Rhyming text.

Flying eagle ill. by Deborah Kogan Ray. Charlesbridge, 2009. ISBN 978-1-57091-671-7 Subj: Birds – eagles. Foreign lands – Tanzania.

Hampire! ill. by Howard Fine. HarperCollins, 2011. ISBN 978-0-06-114239-0 Subj: Animals – pigs. Birds – ducks. Food. Humorous stories. Monsters.

The Mine-o-saur ill. by David Clark. Penguin, 2007. ISBN 978-0-399-24642-5 Subj: Behavior – greed. Behavior – sharing. Dinosaurs. Friendship. Toys.

Pirate princess ill. by Jill McElmurry. HarperCollins, 2012. ISBN 978-0-06-114242-0 Subj: Pirates. Rhyming text. Royalty – princesses.

Snoring Beauty ill. by Jane Manning. HarperCollins, 2014. ISBN 978-006087403-2 Subj: Animals – mice. Rhyming text. Royalty – princesses. Sleep – snoring.

Tyrannosaurus wrecks! ill. by Zachariah OHora. Abrams, 2014. ISBN 978-141971035-3 Subj: Behavior – misbehavior. Dinosaurs. Rhyming text.

Bardill, Linard. *The great golden thing* ill. by Miriam Monnier. NorthSouth, 2002. ISBN 978-0-7358-1594-0 Subj: Animals – bears. Animals – rabbits. Careers – magicians. Flowers. Plants.

Baring-Gould, S. *Now the day is over* ill. by Preston McDaniels. Morehouse, 2001. ISBN 978-0-8192-1868-1 Subj: Bedtime. Religion. Songs.

Barner, Bob. *Animal baths* ill. by author. Chronicle, 2011. ISBN 978-1-4521-0056-2 Subj: Activities – bathing. Animals.

Ants rule: the long and short of it ill. by author. Holiday, 2017. ISBN 978-082343660-6 Subj: Concepts – measurement. Concepts – size. Insects – ants.

Bears! bears! bears! ill. by author. Chronicle, 2010. ISBN 978-0-8118-7057-3 Subj: Animals – bears. Rhyming text.

The Day of the Dead / El Día de los Muertos ill. by author. Holiday House, 2010. ISBN 978-0-8234-2214-2 Subj: Foreign languages. Holidays – Day of the Dead.

Dinosaur bones ill. by author. Chronicle, 2001. ISBN 978-0-8118-3158-1 Subj: Careers – paleontologists. Dinosaurs. Fossils. Rhyming text.

Dinosaurs roar, butterflies soar! ill. by author. Chronicle, 2009. ISBN 978-0-8118-5663-8 Subj: Dinosaurs. Fossils. Insects – butterflies, caterpillars.

Penguins, penguins, everywhere! ill. by author. Chronicle, 2007. ISBN 978-0-8118-5664-5 Subj: Birds – penguins. Rhyming text.

Sea bones ill. by author. Chronicle, 2015. ISBN 978-145212500-8 Subj: Animals. Sea & seashore.

Stars, stars, stars ill. by author. Chronicle, 2002. ISBN 978-0-8118-3159-8 Subj: Astronomy. Planets. Rhyming text. Science. Stars.

Barnes, Brynne. *Colors of me* ill. by Annika M. Nelson. Sleeping Bear, 2011. ISBN 978-1-58536-541-8 Subj: Concepts – color. Rhyming text. Self-concept.

Barnes, Derrick. *Crown: an ode to the fresh cut* ill. by Gordon C James. Bolden, 2017. ISBN 978-157284224-3 Subj: Caldecott award honor books. Careers – barbers. Ethnic groups in the U.S. – African Americans. Hair. Self-concept.

Barnes, Laura T. *Ernest and the big itch* ill. by Carol A. Camburn. Barnsyard, 2002. ISBN 978-0-9674681-2-9 Subj: Animals – donkeys. Birds. Friendship. Self-concept.

Ernest's special Christmas ill. by Carol A. Camburn. Barnsyard, 2003. ISBN 978-0-9674681-3-6 Subj: Animals. Animals – donkeys. Character traits – helpfulness. Friendship.

Teeny tiny Ernest ill. by Carol A. Camburn. Barnsyard, 2000. ISBN 978-0-9674681-1-2 Subj: Animals – donkeys. Concepts – size. Self-concept.

Twist and Ernest ill. by Carol A. Camburn. Barnsyard, 1999. ISBN 978-0-9674681-0-5 Subj: Animals – donkeys. Animals – horses, ponies. Friendship.

Barnett, Mac. *Battle Bunny* (Scieszka, Jon)

Billy Twitters and his big blue whale problem ill. by Adam Rex. Hyperion, 2009. ISBN 978-0-7868-4958-1 Subj: Animals – whales. Behavior – misbehavior. Family life. School.

Chloe and the lion ill. by Adam Rex. Hyperion, 2012. ISBN 978-1-4231-1334-8 Subj: Activities – writing. Books, reading.

Count the monkeys ill. by Kevin Cornell. Disney/Hyperion, 2013. ISBN 978-1-4231-6065-6 Subj:

Animals. Animals – monkeys. Counting, numbers.

Extra yarn ill. by Jon Klassen. HarperCollins, 2012. ISBN 978-0-06-195338-5 Subj: Activities – knitting. Caldecott award honor books. Concepts – color. Humorous stories. Imagination.

Guess again! ill. by Adam Rex. Simon & Schuster, 2009. ISBN 978-1-4169-5566-5 Subj: Format, unusual. Games. Rhyming text.

How this book was made ill. by Adam Rex. Disney/Hyperion, 2016. ISBN 978-142315220-0 Subj: Activities – drawing. Activities – writing. Books, reading. Careers – illustrators. Careers – writers.

I love you like a pig ill. by Greg Pizzoli. HarperCollins/Balzer+Bray, 2017. ISBN 978-006235483-9 Subj: Emotions. Friendship.

Leo: a ghost story ill. by Christian Robinson. Chronicle, 2015. ISBN 978-145213156-6 Subj: Emotions – loneliness. Friendship. Ghosts.

The magic word ill. by Elise Parsley. HarperCollins/Balzer+Bray, 2016. ISBN 978-006235484-6 Subj: Behavior – wishing. Character traits – selfishness. Character traits – willfulness. Etiquette. Language. Magic.

Mustache! ill. by Kevin Cornell. Hyperion/Disney, 2011. ISBN 978-1-4231-1671-4 Subj: Anatomy. Character traits – appearance. Character traits – vanity. Royalty – kings.

Noisy night ill. by Brian Biggs. Roaring Brook, 2017. ISBN 978-159643967-2 Subj: Bedtime. Homes, houses. Night. Noise, sounds.

Oh no! (or how my science project destroyed the world) ill. by Dan Santat. Hyperion/Disney, 2010. ISBN 978-1-4231-2312-5 Subj: Humorous stories. Robots. Science.

Oh no! Not again! (or how I built a time machine to save history) (or at least my history grade) ill. by Dan Santat. Hyperion, 2012. ISBN 978-1-4231-4912-5 Subj: Activities – traveling. Humorous stories. Petroglyphs. Time.

Places to be ill. by Renata Liwska. HarperCollins/Balzer+Bray, 2017. ISBN 978-006228621-5 Subj: Activities – traveling. Animals – bears. Emotions. Friendship.

President Taft is stuck in the bath ill. by Chris Van Dusen. Candlewick, 2014. ISBN 978-076366317-9 Subj: Activities – bathing. Hugging. U.S. history.

Rules of the house ill. by Matthew Myers. Disney/Hyperion, 2016. ISBN 978-142318516-1 Subj: Behavior – misbehavior. Character traits – cleverness. Family life – brothers & sisters. Monsters.

Sam and Dave dig a hole ill. by Jon Klassen. Candlewick, 2014. ISBN 978-076366229-5 Subj: Activities – digging. Caldecott award honor books. Imagination.

The skunk ill. by Patrick McDonnell. Roaring Brook, 2015. ISBN 978-159643966-5 Subj: Animals – skunks. Humorous stories.

Telephone ill. by Jen Corace. Chronicle, 2014. ISBN 978-145211023-3 Subj: Birds. Communication. Language.

Triangle ill. by Jon Klassen. Candlewick, 2017. ISBN 978-076369603-0 Subj: Behavior – misbehavior. Concepts – shape. Humorous stories.

The wolf, the duck, and the mouse ill. by Jon Klassen. Candlewick, 2017. ISBN 978-076367754-1 Subj: Animals – mice. Animals – wolves. Birds – ducks. Humorous stories.

Barnwell, Ysaye M. *No mirrors in my Nana's house* ill. by Synthia Saint James. Harcourt, 1999. ISBN 978-0-15-201825-2 Subj: Ethnic groups in the U.S. – African Americans. Family life – grandmothers. Self-concept.

We are one ill. by Brian Pinkney. Harcourt, 2008. ISBN 978-0-15-205735-0 Subj: Music. Songs.

Barracca, Debra. *The adventures of taxi dog* (Barracca, Sal)

Maxi, the hero by Debra Barracca and Sal Barracca ill. by Mark Buehner. Dial, 1991. ISBN 978-0-8037-0940-9 Subj: Animals – dogs. Cities, towns. Crime. Rhyming text.

Maxi, the star by Debra Barracca and Sal Barracca ill. by Alan Ayers. Dial, 1993. ISBN 978-0-8037-1349-9 Subj: Activities – traveling. Animals – dogs. Rhyming text. Television.

A taxi dog Christmas by Debra Barracca and Sal Barracca ill. by Alan Ayers. Dial, 1994. ISBN 978-0-8037-1368-0 Subj: Animals – dogs. Cities, towns. Holidays – Christmas. Rhyming text. Taxis.

Barracca, Sal. *The adventures of taxi dog* by Sal Barracca and Debra Barracca ill. by Mark Buehner. Dial, 1990. ISBN 978-0-8037-0672-9 Subj: Animals – dogs. Cities, towns. Rhyming text. Taxis.

Maxi, the hero (Barracca, Debra)

Maxi, the star (Barracca, Debra)

A taxi dog Christmas (Barracca, Debra)

Barrett, Judi. *Animals should definitely not act like people* ill. by Ron Barrett. Atheneum, 1980. ISBN 978-0-689-30768-3 Subj: Animals. Behavior – imitation.

Animals should definitely not wear clothing ill. by Ron Barrett. Atheneum, 1970. ISBN 978-0-689-20592-7 Subj: Animals. Behavior – imitation. Clothing.

Cloudy with a chance of meatballs ill. by Ron Barrett. Atheneum, 1978. ISBN 978-0-689-30647-1

Subj: Family life – grandfathers. Food. Imagination. Weather.

Cloudy with a chance of meatballs 3: Planet of the pies ill. by Isidre Monés. Atheneum, 2013. ISBN 978-1-4424-9027-7 Subj: Careers – astronauts. Family life – grandfathers. Food. Planets. Weather.

An excessive alphabet: avalanches of As to zillions of Zs ill. by Ron Barrett. Atheneum/Caitlyn Dlouhy, 2016. ISBN 978-148143986-2 Subj: ABC books. Picture puzzles.

The marshmallow incident ill. by Ron Barrett. Scholastic, 2009. ISBN 978-0-545-04653-4 Subj: Concepts – left & right. Food. Humorous stories.

Never take a shark to the dentist and other things not to do ill. by John Nickle. Atheneum, 2008. ISBN 978-1-4169-0724-4 Subj: Animals. Humorous stories.

Pickles to Pittsburgh: the sequel to Cloudy with a chance of meatballs ill. by Ron Barrett. Atheneum, 1997. ISBN 978-0-689-80104-4 Subj: Family life – grandparents. Food. Weather.

Santa from Cincinnati ill. by Kevin Hawkes. Atheneum, 2012. ISBN 978-1-4424-2993-2 Subj: Holidays – Christmas. Santa Claus.

Which witch is which? ill. by Sharleen Collicott. Atheneum, 2001. ISBN 978-0-689-82940-6 Subj: Rhyming text. Witches.

Barrett, Mary Brigid. *All fall down* ill. by LeUyen Pham. Candlewick, 2014. ISBN 978-076364430-7 Subj: Format, unusual – board books. Games. Toys – blocks.

Pat-a-cake ill. by LeUyen Pham. Candlewick, 2014. ISBN 978-076364358-4 Subj: Format, unusual – board books. Games.

Shoebox Sam ill. by Frank Morrison. Zonderkidz, 2011. ISBN 978-0-310-71549-8 Subj: Careers – shoemakers. Character traits – generosity. Character traits – kindness. Clothing – shoes. Ethnic groups in the U.S. – African Americans. Homeless.

Barrett, Ron. *Cats got talent* ill. by author. Simon & Schuster/Paula Wiseman, 2014. ISBN 978-144249451-0 Subj: Activities – singing. Animals – cats. Friendship.

Barretta, Gene. *Dear deer: a book of homophones* ill. by author. Henry Holt, 2007. ISBN 978-0-8050-8104-6 Subj: Animals. Language.

Neo Leo: the ageless ideas of Leonardo da Vinci ill. by author. Henry Holt, 2009. ISBN 978-0-8050-8703-1 Subj: Careers – inventors. Inventions.

Now and Ben: the modern inventions of Benjamin Franklin ill. by author. Henry Holt, 2006. ISBN 978-0-8050-7917-3 Subj: Careers – inventors. Inventions. U.S. history.

Timeless Thomas: how Thomas Edison changed our lives ill. by author. Henry Holt, 2012. ISBN 978-0-8050-9108-3 Subj: Careers – inventors. Inventions.

Barringer, William. *Gregory and Alexander* ill. by Kim LaFave. Orca, 2003. ISBN 978-1-55143-252-6 Subj: Animals – mice. Friendship. Insects – butterflies, caterpillars. Metamorphosis.

Barron, Rex. *Fed up! a feast of frazzled foods* ill. by author. Putnam, 2000. ISBN 978-0-399-23450-7 Subj: ABC books. Food.

Barron, T. A. *Where is Grandpa?* ill. by Chris Soentpiet. Philomel, 2000. ISBN 978-0-399-23037-0 Subj: Death. Emotions – grief. Family life – grandfathers.

Barros, Bruna. *The carpenter* ill. by author. Gibbs Smith, 2017. ISBN 978-142364676-1 Subj: Careers – carpenters. Imagination. Tools. Wordless.

Barroux. *Welcome* ill. by author. little bee, 2016. ISBN 978-149980444-7 Subj: Animals – polar bears. Immigrants, immigration. Refugees.

Where's the elephant? ill. by author. Candlewick, 2016. ISBN 978-076368110-4 Subj: Animals. Ecology. Jungle.

Barrow, David. *Have you seen Elephant?* ill. by author. Gecko, 2016. ISBN 978-177657008-9 Subj: Animals – elephants. Behavior – hiding. Games.

Barry, Frances. *Duckie's ducklings: a one-to-ten counting book* ill. by author. Candlewick, 2005. ISBN 978-0-7636-2514-6 Subj: Birds – ducks. Counting, numbers.

Duckie's rainbow ill. by author. Candlewick, 2003. ISBN 978-0-7636-2066-0 Subj: Birds – ducks. Concepts – color. Format, unusual – toy & movable books. Weather – rainbows.

Let's look at dinosaurs: a flip-the-flap book ill. by author. Candlewick, 2011. ISBN 978-0-7636-5354-5 Subj: Dinosaurs. Format, unusual – toy & movable books.

Let's save the animals: a flip-the-flap book ill. by author. Candlewick, 2010. ISBN 978-0-7636-4501-4 Subj: Animals – endangered animals. Format, unusual – toy & movable books.

Barry, Holly M. *Helen Keller's best friend Belle* ill. by Jennifer Thermes. Albert Whitman, 2013. ISBN 978-0-8075-3198-3 Subj: Animals – dogs. Disabilities – blindness. Disabilities – deafness.

Bart, Kathleen. *Town Teddy and Country Bear go global* ill. by author. Reverie, 2011. ISBN 978-1-932485-60-8 Subj: Activities – traveling. Toys – bears. World.

Bartles, Veronica. *The princess and the frogs* ill. by Sara Palacios. HarperCollins/Balzer+Bray, 2016. ISBN 978-0-06-236591-0 Subj: Frogs & toads. Royalty – princesses.

Bartlett, Robert Merrill. *The story of Thanksgiving* ill. by Sally Wern Comport. HarperCollins, 2001. ISBN 978-0-06-028779-5 Subj: Holidays – Thanksgiving. Indians of North America – Wampanoag. U.S. history.

Bartoletti, Susan Campbell. *The Christmas promise* ill. by David Christiana. Blue Sky, 2001. ISBN 978-0-590-98451-5 Subj: Family life – daughters. Family life – fathers. Holidays – Christmas. Homeless. Poverty. U.S. history.

The flag maker ill. by Claire A. Nivola. Houghton, 2004. ISBN 978-0-618-26757-6 Subj: Flags. U.S. history. War.

Naamah and the ark at night ill. by Holly Meade. Candlewick, 2011. ISBN 978-0-7636-4242-6 Subj: Animals. Boats, ships. Night. Religion.

Nobody's diggier than a dog ill. by Beppe Giacobbe. Hyperion, 2005. ISBN 978-0-7868-1824-2 Subj: Animals – dogs.

Nobody's nosier than a cat ill. by Beppe Giacobbe. Hyperion, 2003. ISBN 978-0-7868-1614-9 Subj: Animals – cats. Pets. Rhyming text.

Barton, Bethany. *Give bees a chance* ill. by author. Viking, 2017. ISBN 978-067001694-5 Subj: Emotions – fear. Insects – bees.

I'm trying to love spiders: (it isn't easy) ill. by author. Viking, 2015. ISBN 978-067001693-8 Subj: Spiders.

This monster cannot wait! ill. by author. Dial, 2013. ISBN 978-0-8037-3779-2 Subj: Character traits – patience, impatience. Monsters.

This monster needs a haircut ill. by author. Dial, 2012. ISBN 978-0-8037-3733-4 Subj: Hair. Monsters.

Barton, Bob. *Paul Gallico's The small miracle* by Bob Barton and Paul Gallico ill. by Carolyn Croll. Henry Holt, 2003. ISBN 978-0-8050-6745-3 Subj: Animals – donkeys. Foreign lands – Italy. Religion.

Barton, Byron. *Airplanes* ill. by author. Crowell, 1986. ISBN 978-0-690-04532-1 Subj: Airplanes, airports.

Airport ill. by author. Crowell, 1982. ISBN 978-0-690-04169-9 Subj: Airplanes, airports. Careers – airplane pilots. Transportation.

Boats ill. by author. Crowell, 1986. ISBN 978-0-690-04563-5 Subj: Boats, ships.

Bones, bones, dinosaur bones ill. by author. HarperCollins, 1990. ISBN 978-0-690-04827-8 Subj: Dinosaurs. Prehistory.

Building a house ill. by author. Greenwillow, 1981. ISBN 978-0-688-84291-8 Subj: Homes, houses.

Buzz, buzz, buzz ill. by author. Macmillan, 1973. ISBN 978-0-02-708450-4 Subj: Cumulative tales. Insects – bees.

Dinosaurs, dinosaurs ill. by author. HarperCollins, 1989. ISBN 978-0-690-04768-4 Subj: Dinosaurs. Prehistory.

I want to be an astronaut ill. by author. Crowell, 1988. ISBN 978-0-690-04744-8 Subj: Careers – astronauts. Character traits – ambition. Space & space ships.

Machines at work ill. by author. HarperCollins, 1987. ISBN 978-0-690-04573-4 Subj: Activities – working. Machines.

My bike ill. by author. Greenwillow, 2015. ISBN 978-006233699-6 Subj: Circus. Clowns, jesters. Sports – bicycling.

My bus ill. by author. Greenwillow, 2014. ISBN 978-006228736-6 Subj: Animals. Buses. Counting, numbers. Pets. Transportation.

My car ill. by author. Greenwillow, 2001. ISBN 978-0-06-029625-4 Subj: Automobiles.

My house ill. by author. HarperCollins/Greenwillow, 2016. ISBN 978-006233703-0 Subj: Animals – cats. Homes, houses.

Tools ill. by author. HarperCollins, 1995. ISBN 978-0-694-00623-6 Subj: Language. Tools.

Trains ill. by author. Crowell, 1986. ISBN 978-0-690-04534-5 Subj: Trains.

Trucks ill. by author. Crowell, 1986. ISBN 978-0-690-04530-7 Subj: Trucks.

The wee little woman ill. by author. HarperCollins, 1995. ISBN 978-0-06-023388-4 Subj: Animals – cats. Behavior – running away. Behavior – stealing.

Zoo animals ill. by author. HarperCollins, 1995. ISBN 978-0-694-00620-5 Subj: Animals. Zoos.

Barton, Chris. *Book or bell?* ill. by Ashley Spires. Bloomsbury, 2017. ISBN 978-168119729-6 Subj: Books, reading. School.

88 instruments ill. by Louis Thomas. Knopf, 2016. ISBN 978-055353814-4 Subj: Behavior – indecision. Musical instruments.

Mighty truck ill. by Troy Cummings. HarperCollins, 2016. ISBN 978-006234478-6 Subj: Character traits – helpfulness. Trucks.

Mighty truck: muddymania! ill. by Troy Cummings. HarperCollins, 2017. ISBN 978-006234479-3 Subj: Character traits – helpfulness. Trucks.

Shark vs. train ill. by Tom Lichtenheld. Little, Brown, 2010. ISBN 978-0-316-00762-7 Subj: Contests. Fish – sharks. Trains.

That's not Bunny! ill. by Colin Jack. Disney/Hyperion, 2016. ISBN 978-142319086-8 Subj: Animals – rabbits. Behavior – trickery. Birds – hawks.

Barton, Suzanne. *The sleepy songbird* ill. by author. Bloomsbury, 2016. ISBN 978-080273648-2 Subj: Activities – singing. Birds. Character traits – individuality. Music.

Bartone, Elisa. *Peppe the lamplighter* ill. by Ted Lewin. Lothrop, 1993. ISBN 978-0-688-10269-2 Subj: Caldecott award honor books. Cities, towns. Ethnic groups in the U.S. – Italian Americans. Family life – brothers & sisters. Family life – fathers.

Bartram, Simon. *Bob's best-ever friend* ill. by author. Candlewick, 2009. ISBN 978-0-7636-4425-3 Subj: Aliens. Careers – astronauts. Space & space ships.

Man on the moon: a day in the life of Bob ill. by author. Candlewick, 2002. ISBN 978-0-7636-1897-1 Subj: Careers – astronauts. Moon. Mythical creatures. Space & space ships.

Baruzzi, Agnese. *Look, look again* ill. by author. Minedition, 2016. ISBN 978-988834120-7 Subj: Counting, numbers. Format, unusual – toy & movable books.

Opposite surprise ill. by author. Minedition, 2017. ISBN 978-988834137-5 Subj: Concepts – opposites. Format, unusual – toy & movable books.

Baryshnikov, Mikhail. *Because . . .* by Mikhail Baryshnikov and Vladimir Radunsky ill. by Vladimir Radunsky. Simon & Schuster, 2007. ISBN 978-0-689-87582-3 Subj: Activities – dancing. Character traits – being different. Emotions – embarrassment. Family life – grandmothers. Self-concept.

Base, Graeme. *Animalia* ill. by author. Abrams, 1987. ISBN 978-0-8109-1868-9 Subj: ABC books. Animals.

The Jewel Fish of Karnak ill. by author. Abrams, 2011. ISBN 978-1-4197-0086-6 Subj: Crime. Foreign lands – Egypt. Magic. Puzzles. Royalty – pharaohs.

Jungle drums ill. by author. Abrams, 2004. ISBN 978-0-8109-5044-3 Subj: Animals. Animals – warthogs. Behavior – wishing. Foreign lands – Africa. Jungle. Magic. Musical instruments – drums.

The legend of the Golden Snail. Abrams, 2010. ISBN 978-0-8109-8965-8 Subj: Animals – snails. Boats, ships. Imagination.

Little elephants ill. by author. Abrams, 2012. ISBN 978-1-4197-0463-5 Subj: Animals – elephants. Character traits – smallness. Farms. Magic.

The water hole ill. by author. Abrams, 2001. ISBN 978-0-8109-4568-5 Subj: Animals. Counting, numbers. Water. Weather – rain.

Bash, Barbara. *Desert giant: the world of the Saguaro cactus* ill. by author. Little, 1988. ISBN 978-0-316-08301-0 Subj: Desert. Plants.

Urban roosts ill. by author. Little, 1990. ISBN 978-0-316-08306-5 Subj: Birds. Cities, towns. Nature.

Basher, Simon. *ABC kids* ill. by author. Kingfisher, 2011. ISBN 978-0-7534-6495-3 Subj: ABC books. Language.

Go! go! Bobo: shapes ill. by author. Kingfisher, 2011. ISBN 978-0-7534-6494-6 Subj: Concepts – shape. Format, unusual – board books.

Bashevis, Isaac *see* Singer, Isaac Bashevis

Baskin, Leonard. *Hosie's alphabet* ill. by author. Words by Hosea, Tobias & Lisa Baskin. Viking, 1972. ISBN 978-0-670-37958-3 Subj: ABC books. Caldecott award honor books. Children as authors.

Bass, Hester. *Seeds of freedom: the peaceful integration of Huntsville, Alabama* ill. by E. B. Lewis. Candlewick, 2015. ISBN 978-076366919-5 Subj: Ethnic groups in the U.S. – African Americans. Prejudice. U.S. history. Violence, nonviolence.

Bass, Jennifer Vogel. *Edible colors* photos by author. Roaring Brook, 2014. ISBN 978-162672002-2 Subj: Concepts – color. Food.

Edible numbers photos by author. Roaring Brook, 2015. ISBN 978-162672003-9 Subj: Counting, numbers. Food.

Bassède, Francine. *A day with the Bellyflops* ill. by author. Orchard, 2000. ISBN 978-0-531-33242-9 Subj: Animals – pigs. Family life – brothers & sisters. Family life – mothers.

Bastianich, Lidia. *Nonna tell me a story: Lidia's Christmas kitchen* ill. by Laura Logan. Running Press, 2010. ISBN 978-0-7624-3692-7 Subj: Activities – baking, cooking. Ethnic groups in the U.S. – Italian Americans. Family life – grandmothers. Food. Holidays – Christmas.

Nonna's birthday surprise ill. by Renée Graef. Running Press, 2013. ISBN 978-0-7624-4655-1 Subj: Activities – baking, cooking. Birthdays. Ethnic groups in the U.S. – Italian Americans. Family life – grandmothers. Food.

Bastin, Marjolein. *Christmas with Vera* ill. by author. NorthSouth, 2011. ISBN 978-0-7358-4044-7

Subj: Activities – making things. Animals – mice. Holidays – Christmas.

Bataille, Marion. *ABC3D* ill. by author. Roaring Brook, 2008. ISBN 978-1-59643-425-7 Subj: ABC books. Format, unusual – toy & movable books.

Bate, Lucy. *Little Rabbit's loose tooth* ill. by Diane deGroat. Crown, 1975. ISBN 978-0-517-52240-0 Subj: Animals – rabbits. Fairies. Teeth.

Bateman, Donna M. *Deep in the swamp* ill. by Brian Lies. Charlesbridge, 2007. ISBN 978-1-57091-596-3 Subj: Counting, numbers. Ecology. Rhyming text. Swamps.

Out on the prairie ill. by Susan Swan. Charlesbridge, 2012. ISBN 978-1-58089-377-0 Subj: Animals. Ecology. Songs.

Bateman, Teresa. *April foolishness* ill. by Nadine Bernard Westcott. Albert Whitman, 2004. ISBN 978-0-8075-0404-8 Subj: Family life – grandparents. Farms. Holidays – April Fools' Day. Rhyming text.

The Bully Blockers Club ill. by Jackie Urbanovic. Albert Whitman, 2004. ISBN 978-0-8075-0918-0 Subj: Behavior – bullying, teasing. Clubs, gangs. School.

Farm flu ill. by Nadine Bernard Westcott. Albert Whitman, 2001. ISBN 978-0-8075-2274-5 Subj: Animals. Farms. Illness – influenza. Rhyming text.

Fiona's luck ill. by Kelly Murphy. Charlesbridge, 2007. ISBN 978-1-57091-651-9 Subj: Character traits – luck. Foreign lands – Ireland. Mythical creatures – leprechauns.

The frog with the big mouth ill. by Will Terry. Albert Whitman, 2008. ISBN 978-0-8075-2621-7 Subj: Animals. Foreign lands – South America. Frogs & toads. Jungle.

Gus, the pilgrim turkey ill. by Ellen Joy Sasaki. Albert Whitman, 2008. ISBN 978-0-8075-1266-1 Subj: Activities – traveling. Birds – turkeys. Holidays – Thanksgiving.

Hamster Camp: how Harry got fit ill. by Nancy Cote. Albert Whitman, 2005. ISBN 978-0-8075-3139-6 Subj: Animals – hamsters. Camps, camping. Health & fitness – exercise. Magic. Rhyming text.

Harp o' gold ill. by Jill Weber. Holiday, 2001. ISBN 978-0-8234-1523-6 Subj: Folk & fairy tales. Music.

Hunting the daddyosaurus ill. by Benrei Huang. Albert Whitman, 2002. ISBN 978-0-8075-1433-7 Subj: Dinosaurs. Family life – brothers. Family life – fathers. Rhyming text.

Job wanted ill. by Chris Sheban. Holiday House, 2015. ISBN 978-082343391-9 Subj: Animals – dogs. Farms.

Keeper of soles ill. by Yayo. Holiday House, 2006. ISBN 978-0-8234-1734-6 Subj: Behavior – trickery. Careers – shoemakers. Clothing – shoes. Death.

Leprechaun gold ill. by Rosanne Litzinger. Holiday, 1998. ISBN 978-0-8234-1344-7 Subj: Folk & fairy tales. Mythical creatures – leprechauns.

The leprechaun under the bed ill. by Paul Meisel. Holiday House, 2012. ISBN 978-0-8234-2221-0 Subj: Friendship. Mythical creatures – leprechauns.

The merbaby ill. by Patience Brewster. Holiday, 2001. ISBN 978-0-8234-1531-1 Subj: Careers – fishermen. Family life – brothers. Mythical creatures – mermaids, mermen.

Paul Bunyan vs. Hals Halson: the giant lumberjack challenge! ill. by C. B. Canga. Albert Whitman, 2011. ISBN 978-0-8075-6367-0 Subj: Careers – lumberjacks. Contests. Tall tales. U.S. history – frontier & pioneer life.

A plump and perky turkey ill. by Jeff Shelly. Marshall Cavendish, 2004. ISBN 978-0-7714-5188-1 Subj: Birds – turkeys. Holidays – Thanksgiving. Rhyming text.

The princesses have a ball ill. by Lynne Cravath. Albert Whitman, 2002. ISBN 978-0-8075-6626-8 Subj: Folk & fairy tales. Rhyming text. Royalty – princesses. Sports – basketball.

Traveling Tom and the leprechaun ill. by Mélisande Potter. Holiday House, 2007. ISBN 978-0-8234-1976-0 Subj: Folk & fairy tales. Foreign lands – Ireland. Music. Mythical creatures – leprechauns.

Bates, Ivan. *All by myself* ill. by author. HarperCollins, 2000. ISBN 978-0-06-028585-2 Subj: Animals. Animals – elephants. Character traits – individuality.

Five little ducks ill. by adapter. Scholastic, 2006. ISBN 978-0-439-74693-9 Subj: Birds – ducks. Counting, numbers. Songs.

Bates, Katharine Lee. *America the beautiful* ill. by Chris Gall. Little, 2004. ISBN 978-0-316-73743-2 Subj: Music. Poetry. Songs. U.S. history.

America the beautiful ill. by Wendell Minor. Putnam, 2003. ISBN 978-0-399-23885-7 Subj: Music. Poetry. Songs. U.S. history.

America the beautiful: together we stand ill. by Bryan Collier, et al. Scholastic, 2013. ISBN 978-0-545-49207-2 Subj: Music. Poetry. Songs. U.S. history.

Bateson-Hill, Margaret. *Masha and the firebird* by Margaret Bateson-Hill and Anne Wilson ill. by Anne Wilson. Zero to Ten, 2000. ISBN 978-1-84089-134-8 Subj: Eggs. Folk & fairy tales. Foreign lands – Russia. Witches.

Shota and the star quilt Lakota text by Philomine Lakota; ill. by Christine Fowler. Zero to Ten, 2001, 1998. ISBN 978-1-84089-021-1 Subj: Indians of North America – Lakota (Sioux). Quilts.

Batt, Tanya Robyn. *The faerie's gift* ill. by Nicoletta Ceccoli. Barefoot, 2003. ISBN 978-1-84148-998-8 Subj: Activities – working. Fairies. Folk & fairy tales.

Batten, Mary. *Please don't wake the animals: a book about sleep* ill. by Higgins Bond. Peachtree, 2008. ISBN 978-1-56145-393-1 Subj: Animals. Sleep.

Who has a belly button? ill. by Higgins Bond. Peachtree, 2004. ISBN 978-1-56145-235-4 Subj: Anatomy – navels. Animals. Birth.

Battersby, Katherine. *Brave Squish Rabbit* ill. by author. Viking, 2012. ISBN 978-0-670-01268-8 Subj: Animals – rabbits. Character traits – bravery. Character traits – smallness. Emotions – fear.

Squish Rabbit ill. by author. Penguin, 2011. ISBN 978-0-670-01267-1 Subj: Animals – rabbits. Character traits – smallness. Emotions – loneliness. Friendship.

Battle-Lavert, Gwendolyn. *The music in Derrick's heart* ill. by Colin Bootman. Holiday, 2000. ISBN 978-0-8234-1353-9 Subj: Careers – musicians. Ethnic groups in the U.S. – African Americans. Musical instruments – harmonicas.

Papa's mark ill. by Colin Bootman. Holiday, 2003. ISBN 978-0-8234-1650-9 Subj: Activities – writing. Books, reading. Ethnic groups in the U.S. – African Americans. Family life – fathers. U.S. history.

The shaking bag ill. by Aminah Brenda Lynn Robinson. Albert Whitman, 2000. ISBN 978-0-8075-7328-0 Subj: Birds – ravens. Character traits – generosity. Ethnic groups in the U.S. – African Americans.

Battut, Eric. *The fox and the hen* ill. by author. Boxer, 2010. ISBN 978-1-907152-02-3 Subj: Animals. Animals – foxes. Birds – chickens, roosters. Eggs. Farms.

Little Mouse's big secret ill. by author. Sterling, 2011. ISBN 978-1-4027-7462-1 Subj: Animals. Animals – mice. Behavior – secrets. Behavior – sharing.

The little pea ill. by author. Skyhorse/Sky Pony, 2011. ISBN 978-1-61608-482-0 Subj: Character traits – individuality.

Bauer, Marion Dane. *Christmas lights* ill. by Susan Mitchell. Simon & Schuster, 2006. ISBN 978-0-689-86942-6 Subj: Format, unusual – toy & movable books. Holidays – Christmas.

The cutest critter ill. by Stan Tekiela. Adventure, 2010. ISBN 978-1-59193-253-6 Subj: Animals – babies.

Dinosaur thunder ill. by Margaret Chodos-Irvine. Scholastic, 2012. ISBN 978-0-590-45296-0 Subj: Dinosaurs. Emotions – fear. Weather – lightning, thunder.

Frog's best friend ill. by Diane Dawson Hearn. Holiday, 2002. ISBN 978-0-8234-1501-4 Subj: Animals. Friendship. Frogs & toads. Reptiles – turtles, tortoises.

Grandmother's song ill. by Pamela Rossi. Simon & Schuster, 2000. ISBN 978-0-689-82272-8 Subj: Babies, toddlers. Birth. Family life – grandmothers. Family life – mothers.

Halloween forest ill. by John Shelley. Holiday House, 2012. ISBN 978-0-8234-2324-8 Subj: Emotions – fear. Forest, woods. Holidays – Halloween. Rhyming text.

Harriet Tubman ill. by Tammie Lyon. Scholastic, 2010. ISBN 978-0-545-23257-9 Subj: Ethnic groups in the U.S. – African Americans. Prejudice. Slavery. U.S. history.

If frogs made the weather ill. by Dorothy Donohue. Holiday House, 2005. ISBN 978-0-8234-1622-6 Subj: Animals. Weather.

If you had a nose like an elephant's trunk ill. by Susan Winter. Holiday, 2001. ISBN 978-0-8234-1589-2 Subj: Anatomy. Animals.

If you were born a kitten ill. by Jo Ellen McAllister Stammen. Simon & Schuster, 1997. ISBN 978-0-689-80111-2 Subj: Animals. Animals – babies.

I'm not afraid of Halloween! a pop-up and flap book ill. by Rusty Fletcher. Simon & Schuster, 2006. ISBN 978-0-689-85050-9 Subj: Format, unusual – toy & movable books. Holidays – Halloween. Monsters.

In like a lion out like a lamb ill. by Emily Arnold McCully. Holiday House, 2011. ISBN 978-0-8234-2238-8 Subj: Rhyming text. Seasons – spring.

Jason's bears ill. by Kevin Hawkes. Hyperion, 2000. ISBN 978-0-7868-2303-1 Subj: Animals – bears. Emotions – fear. Family life – brothers.

The longest night ill. by Ted Lewin. Holiday, 2009. ISBN 978-0-8234-2054-4 Subj: Animals. Birds. Night. Seasons – winter. Weather – wind.

A mama for Owen ill. by John Butler. Simon & Schuster, 2007. ISBN 978-0-689-85787-4 Subj: Animals – hippopotamuses. Behavior – lost. Family life – mothers. Reptiles – turtles, tortoises. Tsunamis.

My mother is mine ill. by Peter Elwell. Simon & Schuster, 2001. ISBN 978-0-689-82267-4 Subj:

Animals. Family life – mothers. Holidays – Mother's Day. Letters, cards. Rhyming text.

One brown bunny ill. by Ivan Bates. Scholastic, 2009. ISBN 978-0-439-68010-3 Subj: Animals – rabbits. Concepts – color. Counting, numbers. Rhyming text.

Sleep, little one, sleep ill. by author. Simon & Schuster, 1999. ISBN 978-0-689-82250-6 Subj: Animals. Bedtime. Family life – fathers. Sleep.

Thank you for me! ill. by Kristina Stephenson. Simon & Schuster, 2010. ISBN 978-0-689-85788-1 Subj: Anatomy. Rhyming text.

Toes, ears, and nose! a lift-the-flap book ill. by Karen Katz. Simon & Schuster, 2003. ISBN 978-0-689-84712-7 Subj: Anatomy. Format, unusual – toy & movable books.

Uh-oh! a lift-the-flap story ill. by Valeria Petrone. Simon & Schuster, 2002. ISBN 978-0-689-84711-0 Subj: Accidents. Format, unusual – toy & movable books.

Why do kittens purr? ill. by Henry Cole. Simon & Schuster, 2003. ISBN 978-0-689-84179-8 Subj: Animals. Behavior.

Winter dance ill. by Richard Jones. Houghton Mifflin Harcourt, 2017. ISBN 978-054431334-7 Subj: Animals – foxes. Forest, woods. Hibernation. Seasons – winter.

Bauer, Sepp. *The Christmas rose* ill. by Else Wenz-Vieetor. Charlesbridge, 2008. ISBN 978-1-58089-232-2 Subj: Activities – traveling. Foreign lands – Germany. Holidays – Christmas. Illness.

Bauld, Jane Scoggins. *Journey of the third seed* ill. by Cynthia G. Darr. Eakin, 2000. ISBN 978-1-57168-428-8 Subj: Foreign lands – Japan. Gardens, gardening. Royalty – emperors. Seeds.

Baum, Louis. *The mouse who braved bedtime* ill. by Susan Hellard. Bloomsbury, 2006. ISBN 978-1-58234-691-5 Subj: Animals – mice. Bedtime. Emotions – fear. Monsters.

Baum, Maxie. *I have a little dreidel* ill. by Julie Paschkis. Scholastic, 2006. ISBN 978-0-439-64997-1 Subj: Food. Holidays – Hanukkah. Jewish culture. Songs.

Baumgart, Klaus. *Laura's Christmas star* ill. by author. Little Tiger, 1999. ISBN 978-1-888444-59-9 Subj: Holidays – Christmas. Magic. Stars. Trees.

Laura's secret English text by Judy Waite; ill. by author. Tiger Tales, 2003. ISBN 978-1-58925-031-4 Subj: Behavior – wishing. Family life – brothers & sisters. Kites. Magic. Stars.

Laura's star ill. by author. Tiger Tales, 2002. ISBN 978-1-58925-374-2 Subj: Friendship. Stars.

Baumgarten, Bret. *Beautiful hands* (Otoshi, Kathryn)

Bayer, Jane. *A my name is Alice* ill. by Steven Kellogg. Dial, 1984. ISBN 978-0-8037-0124-3 Subj: ABC books. Animals. Names.

Baylor, Byrd. *The desert is theirs* ill. by Peter Parnall. Scribners, 1975. ISBN 978-0-684-14266-1 Subj: Caldecott award honor books. Desert. Ecology. Folk & fairy tales. Indians of North America – Papago. Rhyming text.

Everybody needs a rock ill. by Peter Parnall. Scribners, 1974. ISBN 978-0-684-13899-2 Subj: Rhyming text. Rocks.

Hawk, I'm your brother ill. by Peter Parnall. Scribners, 1976. ISBN 978-0-684-14571-6 Subj: Birds – hawks. Caldecott award honor books. Character traits – freedom. Indians of North America.

The way to start a day ill. by Peter Parnall. Aladdin, 1986, ©1978. ISBN 978-0-684-15651-4 Subj: Caldecott award honor books. Folk & fairy tales. Foreign lands. Religion. Sun.

When clay sings ill. by Tom Bahti. Scribners, 1972. ISBN 978-0-684-12807-8 Subj: Art. Caldecott award honor books. Indians of North America.

Baynton, Martin. *Jane and the dragon* ill. by author. Candlewick, 2007. ISBN 978-0-7636-3570-1 Subj: Clowns, jesters. Dragons. Knights.

Jane and the magician ill. by author. Candlewick, 2007. ISBN 978-0-7636-3571-8 Subj: Careers – magicians. Dragons. Magic.

Bea, Holly. *Bless your heart* ill. by Kim Howard. Kramer, 2001. ISBN 978-0-915811-94-6 Subj: Bedtime. Religion. Rhyming text.

My spiritual alphabet book ill. by Kim Howard. Kramer, 2000. ISBN 978-0-915811-83-0 Subj: ABC books. Religion. Rhyming text. Self-concept.

Beake, Lesley. *Home now* ill. by Karin Littlewood. Charlesbridge, 2007. ISBN 978-1-58089-162-2 Subj: Animals – elephants. Family life – aunts, uncles. Foreign lands – Africa. Illness – AIDS. Moving. Orphans.

Beall, Pamela Conon. *Wee Sing if you're happy and you know it* by Pamela Conon Beall and Susan Hagen Nipp ill. by Hala Wittwer. Price Stern Sloan, 2002. ISBN 978-0-8431-7759-6 Subj: Format, unusual – board books. Insects. Songs.

Beames, Margaret. *Night cat* ill. by Sue Hitchcock. Scholastic, 2003. ISBN 978-0-439-38576-3 Subj: Animals. Animals – cats. Gardens, gardening. Night.

Bean, Jonathan. *At night* ill. by author. Farrar, 2007. ISBN 978-0-374-30446-1 Subj: Bedtime. Night. Sleep.

Big snow ill. by author. Farrar, 2013. ISBN 978-0-374-30696-0 Subj: Seasons – winter. Weather – snow.

Building our house ill. by author. Farrar, 2013. ISBN 978-0-374-38023-6 Subj: Careers – construction workers. Family life. Homes, houses.

This is my home, this is my school ill. by author. Farrar, 2015. ISBN 978-037438020-5 Subj: Family life. Homes, houses. School.

The bear: an American folk song ill. by Kenneth J. Spengler. Mondo, 2002. ISBN 978-1-59034-190-2 Subj: Animals – bears. Birds – eagles. Camps, camping. Music. Songs.

Beard, Alex. *Crocodile's tears* ill. by author. Abrams, 2012. ISBN 978-1-4197-0008-8 Subj: Animals – endangered animals. Ecology. Foreign lands – Africa. Reptiles – alligators, crocodiles.

Beardshaw, Rosalind. *Grandma's beach* ill. by author. Bloomsbury, 2004. ISBN 978-1-58234-935-0 Subj: Family life – grandmothers. Sea & seashore – beaches.

Grandpa's surprise ill. by author. Bloomsbury, 2004. ISBN 978-1-58234-934-3 Subj: Family life – grandfathers. Foreign lands – England. Sports – bicycling.

Beaton, Clare. *At home / A la maison* ill. by author. Barron's, 2001. ISBN 978-0-7641-1693-3 Subj: Foreign languages. Homes, houses.

Clare Beaton's action rhymes ill. by author. Barefoot, 2010. ISBN 978-1-84686-473-5 Subj: Format, unusual – board books. Games.

Clare Beaton's bedtime rhymes ill. by author. Barefoot, 2012. ISBN 978-1-84686-737-8 Subj: Animals. Bedtime. Format, unusual – board books. Nursery rhymes.

Clare Beaton's farmyard rhymes ill. by author. Barefoot, 2012. ISBN 978-1-84686-736-1 Subj: Animals. Farms. Format, unusual – board books. Nursery rhymes.

Clare Beaton's nursery rhymes ill. by author. Barefoot, 2010. ISBN 978-1-84686-472-8 Subj: Format, unusual – board books. Nursery rhymes.

Daisy gets dressed ill. by author. Barefoot, 2005. ISBN 978-1-84148-794-6 Subj: Clothing. Concepts – patterns. Rhyming text.

How loud is a lion? ill. by author. Barefoot, 2002. ISBN 978-1-84148-896-7 Subj: Animals. Jungle. Noise, sounds.

One moose, twenty mice ill. by author. Barefoot, 1999. ISBN 978-1-902283-37-1 Subj: Animals. Animals – cats. Counting, numbers.

Zoë and her zebra ill. by author. Barefoot, 1999. ISBN 978-1-902283-75-3 Subj: ABC books. Language.

Beaton, Kate. *King Baby* ill. by author. Scholastic/Arthur A. Levine, 2016. ISBN 978-054563754-1 Subj: Babies, toddlers. Behavior – bossy. Family life – new sibling.

The princess and the pony ill. by author. Scholastic, 2015. ISBN 978-054563708-4 Subj: Animals – horses, ponies. Royalty – princesses.

Beaty, Andrea. *Ada Twist, scientist* ill. by David Roberts. Abrams, 2016. ISBN 978-141972137-3 Subj: Careers – scientists. Character traits – curiosity. Character traits – perseverance. Character traits – questioning. Ethnic groups in the U.S. – African Americans. Rhyming text. Science.

Artist Ted ill. by Pascal Lemaître. Simon & Schuster, 2012. ISBN 978-1-4169-5374-6 Subj: Animals – bears. Careers – artists. Imagination. School.

Doctor Ted ill. by Pascal Lemaître. Simon & Schuster, 2008. ISBN 978-1-4169-2820-1 Subj: Animals – bears. Careers – doctors. Imagination.

Firefighter Ted ill. by Pascal Lemaître. Simon & Schuster, 2009. ISBN 978-1-4169-2821-8 Subj: Animals – bears. Careers – firefighters. Imagination. School.

Hide and sheep ill. by Bill Mayer. Simon & Schuster, 2011. ISBN 978-1-4169-2544-6 Subj: Animals – sheep. Counting, numbers. Rhyming text.

Hush, Baby Ghostling ill. by Pascal Lemaître. Simon & Schuster, 2009. ISBN 978-1-4169-2545-3 Subj: Bedtime. Emotions – fear. Family life – mothers. Ghosts. Monsters.

Iggy Peck, architect ill. by David Roberts. Abrams, 2007. ISBN 978-0-8109-1106-2 Subj: Buildings. Careers – architects. Rhyming text. School – field trips.

Rosie Revere, engineer ill. by David Roberts. Abrams, 2013. ISBN 978-1-4197-0845-9 Subj: Careers – engineers. Character traits – perseverance. Inventions. Rhyming text.

When giants come to play ill. by Kevin Hawkes. Abrams, 2006. ISBN 978-0-8109-5759-6 Subj: Activities – playing. Giants.

Beaty, Daniel. *Knock knock: my dad's dream for me* ill. by Bryan Collier. Little, Brown, 2013. ISBN 978-0-316-20917-5 Subj: Behavior – growing up. Emotions – sadness. Ethnic groups in the U.S. – African Americans. Family life – fathers. Family life – single-parent families.

Beaumont, Karen. *Crybaby* ill. by Eugene Yelchin. Henry Holt, 2015. ISBN 978-080508974-5 Subj: Animals – dogs. Babies, toddlers. Bedtime. Emotions. Rhyming text. Toys.

Dini Dinosaur ill. by Daniel Roode. Greenwillow, 2012. ISBN 978-0-06-207299-3 Subj: Activities – bathing. Bedtime. Clothing. Dinosaurs. Rhyming text.

Doggone dogs! ill. by David Catrow. Dial, 2008. ISBN 978-0-8037-3157-8 Subj: Animals – dogs. Counting, numbers. Rhyming text.

Duck, duck, goose! a coyote's on the loose! ill. by José Aruego and Ariane Dewey. HarperCollins, 2004. ISBN 978-0-06-050804-3 Subj: Animals. Animals – coyotes. Farms. Rhyming text.

Hats off to you! ill. by LeUyen Pham. Scholastic, 2017. ISBN 978-054547423-8 Subj: Character traits – appearance. Clothing – hats. Rhyming text.

I ain't gonna paint no more! ill. by David Catrow. Harcourt, 2005. ISBN 978-0-15-202488-8 Subj: Activities – painting. Rhyming text.

Move over, Rover ill. by Jane Dyer. Harcourt, 2006. ISBN 978-0-15-201979-2 Subj: Animals – dogs. Behavior – sharing. Rhyming text. Weather – rain.

No sleep for the sheep! ill. by Jackie Urbanovic. Houghton, 2011. ISBN 978-0-15-204969-0 Subj: Animals. Animals – sheep. Bedtime. Farms. Noise, sounds. Rhyming text.

Shoe-la-la! ill. by LeUyen Pham. Scholastic, 2011. ISBN 978-0-545-06705-8 Subj: Character traits – appearance. Clothing – shoes. Rhyming text.

Where's my t-r-u-c-k? ill. by David Catrow. Penguin, 2011. ISBN 978-0-8037-3222-3 Subj: Animals – dogs. Behavior – lost & found possessions. Toys. Trucks.

Who ate all the cookie dough? ill. by Eugene Yelchin. Henry Holt, 2008. ISBN 978-0-8050-8267-8 Subj: Animals. Animals – kangaroos. Behavior – lost & found possessions. Rhyming text.

Wild about us! ill. by Janet Stevens. Houghton Mifflin Harcourt, 2015. ISBN 978-015206294-1 Subj: Animals. Character traits – appearance. Character traits – individuality. Rhyming text. Self-concept. Zoos.

Beautiful moments in the wild: animals and their colors ill. with photos. Moonstone, 2002. ISBN 978-0-9707768-7-7 Subj: Animals. Concepts – color.

Beaver steals fire: a Salish Coyote story ill. by Sam Sandoval. Univ. of Nebraska, 2005. ISBN 978-0-8032-4323-1 Subj: Animals. Animals – coyotes. Behavior – stealing. Behavior – trickery. Fire. Folk & fairy tales. Indians of North America.

Bechtold, Lisze. *Edna's tale* ill. by author. Houghton, 2001. ISBN 978-0-618-09164-5 Subj: Anatomy – tails. Animals – cats.

Sally and the purple socks ill. by author. Philomel, 2008. ISBN 978-0-399-24734-7 Subj: Birds – ducks. Clothing – socks. Concepts – size.

Beck, Andrea. *Elliot bakes a cake* ill. by author. Kids Can, 1999. ISBN 978-1-55074-443-9 Subj: Activities – baking, cooking. Animals. Animals – moose. Birthdays. Toys.

Elliot digs for treasure ill. by author. Kids Can, 2001. ISBN 978-1-55074-806-2 Subj: Animals. Animals – moose. Behavior – hiding things. Gardens, gardening. Maps. Toys.

Elliot gets stuck ill. by author. Kids Can, 2002. ISBN 978-1-55337-014-7 Subj: Animals. Animals – moose. Seasons – spring. Toys.

Elliot's bath ill. by author. Kids Can, 2001. ISBN 978-1-55074-802-4 Subj: Activities – bathing. Animals. Animals – moose. Toys.

Elliot's Christmas surprise ill. by author. Kids Can, 2003. ISBN 978-1-55337-474-9 Subj: Animals. Animals – moose. Friendship. Gifts. Holidays – Christmas. Toys.

Elliot's emergency ill. by author. Kids Can, 1998. ISBN 978-1-55074-441-5 Subj: Activities – sewing. Animals. Animals – moose. Friendship. Toys – dolls.

Elliot's great big lift-the-flap book ill. by author. Kids Can, 2003. ISBN 978-1-55337-373-5 Subj: Animals – moose. Concepts – color. Concepts – shape. Counting, numbers. Format, unusual – toy & movable books.

Elliot's noisy night ill. by author. Kids Can, 2002. ISBN 978-1-55337-011-6 Subj: Animals – moose. Bedtime. Night. Noise, sounds. Toys.

Elliot's shipwreck ill. by author. Kids Can, 2000. ISBN 978-1-55074-698-3 Subj: Activities – playing. Animals. Animals – moose. Boats, ships. Friendship. Sports – sailing. Toys.

Beck, Ian. *Home before dark* ill. by author. Scholastic, 2001. ISBN 978-0-439-17522-7 Subj: Behavior – lost. Toys – bears.

Teddy's snowy day ill. by author. Scholastic, 2002. ISBN 978-0-439-17520-3 Subj: Behavior – lost. Toys – bears. Weather – snow.

Beck, Robert. *A bunny in the ballet* ill. by author. Scholastic/Orchard, 2014. ISBN 978-054542930-6 Subj: Animals – rabbits. Ballet. Character traits – perseverance. Self-concept.

Beck, Scott. *Happy birthday, Monster!* ill. by author. Abrams, 2007. ISBN 978-0-8109-9363-1 Subj: Birthdays. Dragons. Monsters. Parties.

Monster sleepover! ill. by author. Abrams, 2009. ISBN 978-0-8109-4059-8 Subj: Monsters. Sleepovers.

A mud pie for mother ill. by author. Dutton, 2003. ISBN 978-0-525-47040-3 Subj: Animals – pigs. Birthdays. Character traits – generosity. Family life – mothers. Gifts.

Pepito the brave ill. by author. Dutton, 2001. ISBN 978-0-525-46524-9 Subj: Birds. Character traits – bravery. Emotions – fear.

Becker, Aaron. *Journey* ill. by author. Candlewick, 2013. ISBN 978-0-7636-6053-6 Subj: Activities – drawing. Activities – traveling. Caldecott award honor books. Imagination. Magic. Wordless.

Quest ill. by author. Candlewick, 2014. ISBN 978-076366595-1 Subj: Activities – drawing. Activities – traveling. Imagination. Magic. Maps. Wordless.

Return ill. by author. Candlewick, 2016. ISBN 978-076367730-5 Subj: Activities – drawing. Activities – traveling. Family life – fathers. Imagination. Magic. Wordless.

Becker, Bonny. *An ant's day off* ill. by Nina Laden. Simon & Schuster, 2003. ISBN 978-0-689-82274-2 Subj: Animals. Insects – ants.

A bedtime for Bear ill. by Kady MacDonald Denton. Candlewick, 2010. ISBN 978-0-7636-4101-6 Subj: Animals – bears. Animals – mice. Bedtime. Friendship. Sleepovers.

A birthday for Bear ill. by Kady MacDonald Denton. Candlewick, 2009. ISBN 978-0-7636-3746-0 Subj: Animals – bears. Animals – mice. Birthdays. Friendship.

The Christmas crocodile ill. by David Small. Simon & Schuster, 1997. ISBN 978-0-689-81503-4 Subj: Behavior – mistakes. Holidays – Christmas. Reptiles – alligators, crocodiles.

A Christmas for Bear ill. by Kady MacDonald Denton. Candlewick, 2017. ISBN 978-076364923-4 Subj: Animals – bears. Animals – mice. Friendship. Gifts. Holidays – Christmas.

Just a minute ill. by Jack E. Davis. Simon & Schuster, 2003. ISBN 978-0-689-83374-8 Subj: Time.

A library book for Bear ill. by Kady MacDonald Denton. Candlewick, 2014. ISBN 978-076364924-1 Subj: Animals – bears. Animals – mice. Books, reading. Friendship. Libraries.

The sniffles for Bear ill. by Kady MacDonald Denton. Candlewick, 2011. ISBN 978-0-7636-4756-8 Subj: Animals – bears. Animals – mice. Friendship. Illness – cold (disease).

Tickly prickly ill. by Shari Halpern. HarperCollins, 1999. ISBN 978-0-694-01239-8 Subj: Animals. Rhyming text. Senses – touch.

A visitor for Bear ill. by Kady MacDonald Denton. Candlewick, 2008. ISBN 978-0-7636-2807-9 Subj: Animals – bears. Animals – mice. Friendship.

Becker, Helaine. *Mama likes to mambo* ill. by John Beder. Stoddart, 2001. ISBN 978-0-7737-3316-9 Subj: Animals. Foreign lands – Canada. Poetry.

You can read ill. by Mark Hoffmann. Orca, 2017. ISBN 978-145981324-3 Subj: Books, reading.

Becker, John Leonard. *Seven little rabbits* ill. by Barbara Cooney. Walker, 1973. ISBN 978-0-8027-6130-9 Subj: Animals – rabbits. Counting, numbers.

Becker, Shari. *Maxwell's mountain* ill. by Nicole Wong. Charlesbridge, 2006. ISBN 978-1-58089-047-2 Subj: Imagination. Parks. Sports – mountain climbing.

Becker, Shelly. *Even superheroes have bad days* ill. by Eda Kaban. Sterling, 2016. ISBN 978-145491394-8 Subj: Behavior – bad day, bad mood. Rhyming text.

Becker, Suzy. *Manny's cows: the Niagara Falls tale* ill. by author. HarperCollins, 2006. ISBN 978-0-06-054152-1 Subj: Activities – vacationing. Animals – bulls, cows.

Bedard, Michael. *The wolf of Gubbio* ill. by Murray Kimber. Stoddart, 2000. ISBN 978-0-7737-3250-6 Subj: Animals – wolves. Folk & fairy tales. Religion.

Bedford, David. *Big bears can!* ill. by Gaby Hansen. Tiger Tales, 2001. ISBN 978-1-58925-006-2 Subj: Animals – bears. Concepts – size. Family life – brothers.

Ella's games ill. by Peter Kavanagh. Barron's, 2002. ISBN 978-0-7641-5583-3 Subj: Animals – mice. Family life – brothers & sisters. Sibling rivalry.

I've seen Santa! ill. by Tim Warnes. Tiger Tales, 2006. ISBN 978-1-58925-058-1 Subj: Animals – bears. Holidays – Christmas. Santa Claus.

Little Otter's big journey ill. by Susan Winter. Good Books, 2006. ISBN 978-1-56148-548-2 Subj: Animals – otters. Behavior – lost. Family life – mothers.

Mole's in love ill. by Rosalind Beardshaw. Tiger Tales, 2009. ISBN 978-1-58925-084-0 Subj: Animals – moles. Behavior – mistakes. Emotions – love. Glasses.

Shaggy Dog and the terrible itch ill. by Gwyneth Williamson. Barron's, 2001. ISBN 978-0-7641-5391-4 Subj: Activities – bathing. Animals – dogs. Illness.

Touch the sky, my little bear by David Bedford and Jane Chapman ill. by Jane Chapman. Handprint, 2001. ISBN 978-1-929766-20-8 Subj: Animals – polar bears. Behavior – growing up. Family life – mothers.

Two tough crocs ill. by Tom Jellett. Holiday House, 2014. ISBN 978-082343048-2 Subj: Behavior – fighting, arguing. Reptiles – alligators, crocodiles.

The way I love you ill. by Ann James. Simon & Schuster, 2005. ISBN 978-0-689-87625-7 Subj: Animals – dogs. Emotions – love. Pets.

Bee, William. *And the cars go . . .* ill. by author. Candlewick, 2013. ISBN 978-0-7636-6580-7 Subj: Automobiles. Noise, sounds.

And the train goes . . . ill. by author. Candlewick, 2007. ISBN 978-0-7636-3248-9 Subj: Birds – parakeets, parrots. Noise, sounds. Trains.

Digger Dog ill. by Cecilia Johansson. Candlewick/Nosy Crow, 2014. ISBN 978-076366162-5 Subj: Animals – dogs. Machines.

Stanley the builder ill. by author. Peachtree, 2014. ISBN 978-156145801-1 Subj: Animals – hamsters. Careers – construction workers. Homes, houses. Machines.

Stanley the farmer ill. by author. Peachtree, 2015. ISBN 978-156145803-5 Subj: Animals – hamsters. Animals – moles. Careers – farmers. Farms.

Stanley the mailman ill. by author. Peachtree, 2016. ISBN 978-156145867-7 Subj: Animals – hamsters. Careers – postal workers.

Stanley's colors ill. by author. Peachtree, 2016. ISBN 978-156145948-3 Subj: Animals – hamsters. Concepts – color. Format, unusual – board books. Transportation.

Stanley's diner ill. by author. Peachtree, 2015. ISBN 978-156145802-8 Subj: Activities – baking, cooking. Animals – hamsters. Restaurants.

Stanley's garage ill. by author. Peachtree, 2014. ISBN 978-156145804-2 Subj: Animals – hamsters. Automobiles. Careers – mechanics.

Stanley's numbers ill. by author. Peachtree, 2017. ISBN 978-156145976-6 Subj: Activities – picnicking. Animals – hamsters. Counting, numbers. Format, unusual – board books.

Stanley's opposites ill. by author. Peachtree, 2017. ISBN 978-156145977-3 Subj: Animals – hamsters. Concepts – opposites. Format, unusual – board books.

Stanley's store ill. by author. Peachtree, 2017. ISBN 978-156145868-4 Subj: Animals – hamsters. Stores.

Whatever ill. by author. Candlewick, 2005. ISBN 978-0-7636-2886-4 Subj: Animals – tigers. Behavior – indifference. Family life – fathers.

Worst in show ill. by Kate Hindley. Candlewick, 2015. ISBN 978-076367318-5 Subj: Contests. Monsters.

Beebe, Katy. *Brother Hugo and the bear* ill. by S. D. Schindler. Eerdmans, 2014. ISBN 978-080285407-0 Subj: Animals – bears. Books, reading. Careers – clergy.

Beedie, Duncan. *The lumberjack's beard* ill. by author. Candlewick/Templar, 2017. ISBN 978-076369649-8 Subj: Animals. Careers – lumberjacks. Homes, houses. Trees.

Beeke, Jemma. *The Rickety Barn show* ill. by Lynne Chapman. Doubleday, 2001. ISBN 978-0-385-32795-4 Subj: Animals. Farms. Theater.

Beeke, Tiphanie. *Roar like a lion!* ill. by author. Gullane, 2001. ISBN 978-1-86233-143-3 Subj: Animals. Animals – endangered animals. Communication. Noise, sounds.

Beeler, Selby B. *How many Elephants?* ill. by Barney Saltzberg. Candlewick, 2004. ISBN 978-0-7636-1583-3 Subj: Animals – elephants. Counting, numbers. Format, unusual – toy & movable books.

Throw your tooth on the roof: tooth traditions from around the world ill. by G. Brian Karas. Houghton, 1998. ISBN 978-0-395-89108-7 Subj: Folk & fairy tales. Teeth.

Beeny, Emily. *Hector the collector* ill. by Stephanie Graegin. Roaring Brook, 2017. ISBN 978-162672296-5 Subj: Animals. Animals – dogs. Behavior – collecting things. Museums. School.

Begin, Mary Jane. *The sorcerer's apprentice* ill. by author. Little, Brown, 2005. ISBN 978-0-316-73611-4 Subj: Folk & fairy tales. Magic.

Behrens, Janice. *Let's find rain forest animals: up, down, around* ill. with photos. Scholastic, 2007.

ISBN 978-0-531-14874-7 Subj: Animals. Format, unusual. Games. Jungle. Picture puzzles.

Behrens, June. *The feast of Thanksgiving* ill. by Anne Siberell. Children's Press, 1974. ISBN 978-0-516-08725-2 Subj: Holidays – Thanksgiving. Pilgrims. Theater.

Beil, Karen Magnuson. *Jack's house* ill. by Mike Wohnoutka. Holiday House, 2008. ISBN 978-0-8234-1913-5 Subj: Animals – dogs. Careers – construction workers. Cumulative tales. Homes, houses.

Beliveau, Kathy. *The yoga game by the sea* ill. by Denis Holmes. Simply Read, 2014. ISBN 978-192701849-1 Subj: Health & fitness – exercise. Sea & seashore.

Bell, Anthea. *Vasilisa the beautiful* ill. by Anna Morgunova. Minedition, 2015. ISBN 978-988824050-0 Subj: Family life – stepfamilies. Folk & fairy tales. Foreign lands – Russia. Royalty – tsars. Toys – dolls. Witches.

Bell, Babs. *The bridge is up!* ill. by Rob Hefferan. HarperCollins, 2004. ISBN 978-0-06-053794-4 Subj: Automobiles. Bridges. Cumulative tales. Traffic, traffic signs. Transportation.

Sputter, sputter, sput! ill. by Bob Staake. HarperCollins, 2008. ISBN 978-0-06-056222-9 Subj: Automobiles. Rhyming text.

Bell, Cece. *Bee-Wigged* ill. by author. Candlewick, 2008. ISBN 978-0-7636-3614-2 Subj: Character traits – appearance. Disguises. Friendship. Humorous stories. Insects – bees. Self-concept.

Chuck and Woodchuck ill. by author. Candlewick, 2016. ISBN 978-076367524-0 Subj: Animals – groundhogs. Character traits – shyness. Friendship. School.

I yam a donkey! ill. by author. Clarion, 2015. ISBN 978-054408720-0 Subj: Animals – donkeys. Language.

Itty Bitty ill. by author. Candlewick, 2009. ISBN 978-0-7636-3616-6 Subj: Animals – dogs. Character traits – smallness.

Sock Monkey boogie-woogie: a friend is made ill. by author. Candlewick, 2004. ISBN 978-0-7636-2392-0 Subj: Activities – dancing. Animals – monkeys. Careers – actors. Toys.

Sock Monkey goes to Hollywood: a star is bathed ill. by author. Candlewick, 2003. ISBN 978-0-7636-1962-6 Subj: Animals – monkeys. Careers – actors. Character traits – cleanliness. Toys.

Sock Monkey rides again ill. by author. Candlewick, 2007. ISBN 978-0-7636-3089-8 Subj: Animals – monkeys. Careers – actors. Cowboys, cowgirls. Toys.

Belle, Jennifer. *Animal stackers* ill. by David McPhail. Hyperion, 2005. ISBN 978-0-7868-1834-1 Subj: ABC books. Animals. Poetry.

Belloni, Giulia. *Anything is possible* ill. by Marco Trevisan. OwlKids, 2013. ISBN 978-1-926973-91-3 Subj: Animals – sheep. Animals – wolves. Character traits – cooperation. Character traits – perseverance. Friendship.

Belting, Natalia Maree. *The sun is a golden earring* ill. by Bernarda Bryson. Henry Holt, 1962. Subj: Caldecott award honor books. Folk & fairy tales. Sky.

Belton, Robyn. *Herbert: the true story of a brave sea dog* ill. by author. Candlewick, 2010. ISBN 978-0-7636-4741-4 Subj: Animals – dogs. Sea & seashore. Weather – storms.

Belton, Sandra. *Pictures for Miss Josie* ill. by Benny Andrews. Greenwillow, 2003. ISBN 978-0-688-17481-1 Subj: Careers – artists. Ethnic groups in the U.S. – African Americans. Friendship. Self-concept.

Bemelmans, Ludwig. *Madeline* ill. by author. Viking, 1939. Subj: Caldecott award honor books. Foreign lands – France. Hospitals. Orphans. Rhyming text. School – field trips.

Madeline and the bad hat ill. by author. Viking, 1956. Subj: Behavior – animals, dislike of. Behavior – misbehavior. Foreign lands – France. Orphans. Rhyming text.

Madeline and the gypsies ill. by author. Viking, 1959. ISBN 978-0-670-44682-7 Subj: Behavior – lost. Foreign lands – France. Orphans. Rhyming text. Romani.

Madeline in London ill. by author. Viking, 1978, ©1961. ISBN 978-0-14-050199-5 Subj: Animals – horses, ponies. Birthdays. Foreign lands – England. Orphans. Rhyming text.

Madeline's Christmas ill. by author. Viking, 1985. ISBN 978-0-670-80666-9 Subj: Foreign lands – France. Holidays – Christmas. Illness. Magic. Orphans. Rhyming text.

Madeline's rescue ill. by author. Viking, 1978, ©1953. ISBN 978-0-14-050207-7 Subj: Animals – dogs. Caldecott award books. Foreign lands – France. Orphans. Rhyming text.

Bendall-Brunello, Tiziana. *I wish I could read! a story about making friends* ill. by John Bendall-Brunello. Amicus, 2011. ISBN 978-1-60992-109-5 Subj: Animals – pigs. Books, reading. Friendship.

Bender, Rebecca. *Giraffe meets Bird* ill. by author. Pajama, 2015. ISBN 978-192748535-4 Subj: Animals – giraffes. Birds. Character traits – compromising. Character traits – cooperation. Friendship.

Not friends ill. by author. Pajama, 2017. ISBN 978-177278026-0 Subj: Animals – giraffes. Behavior – fighting, arguing. Birds. Friendship.

Benevelli, Alberto. *The colors of the chameleon* ill. by Loretta Serofilloi. G. Stevens, 2002. ISBN 978-0-8368-3042-2 Subj: Animals. Concepts – color. Reptiles – chameleons.

Benjamin, A. H. *Mouse, mole and the falling star* ill. by John Bendall-Brunello. Dutton, 2002. ISBN 978-0-525-46880-6 Subj: Animals – mice. Animals – moles. Behavior – sharing. Friendship. Stars.

Bennett, Artie. *The butt book* ill. by Mike Lester. Bloomsbury, 2010. ISBN 978-1-59990-311-8 Subj: Anatomy. Rhyming text.

Bennett, Barbara. *Lion's precious gift* ill. by Amanda Hall. Barron's, 2002. ISBN 978-0-7641-5533-8 Subj: Animals – lions. Babies, toddlers.

Bennett, Howard J. *Harry goes to the hospital: a story for children about what it's like to be in the hospital* ill. by M. S. Weber. Magination, 2008. ISBN 978-1-4338-0319-2 Subj: Hospitals. Illness.

Bennett, Jill. *Teeny tiny* ill. by Tomie dePaola. Putnam, 1986. ISBN 978-0-399-21293-2 Subj: Folk & fairy tales. Foreign lands – England. Ghosts.

Bennett, Kelly. *Dad and Pop: an ode to fathers and stepfathers* ill. by Paul Meisel. Candlewick, 2010. ISBN 978-0-7636-3379-0 Subj: Family life – fathers. Family life – stepfamilies.

Not Norman ill. by Noah Jones. Candlewick, 2005. ISBN 978-0-7636-2384-5 Subj: Ethnic groups in the U.S. – African Americans. Fish. Friendship. Pets.

Vampire baby ill. by Paul Meisel. Candlewick, 2013. ISBN 978-0-7636-4691-2 Subj: Babies, toddlers. Family life – brothers & sisters. Monsters. Teeth.

Your daddy was just like you ill. by David Walker. Penguin, 2010. ISBN 978-0-399-25258-7 Subj: Behavior. Family life – fathers.

Benson, Kathleen. *Count your way through Afghanistan* (Haskins, Jim)

Count your way through Brazil (Haskins, Jim)

Count your way through Iran (Haskins, Jim)

Bentley, Dawn. *Busy little beaver* ill. by Beth Stover. Soundprints, 2003. ISBN 978-1-59249-011-0 Subj: Animals – beavers. Family life.

Fuzzy bear: a getting dressed book ill. by Krisztina Nagy. Piggy Toes, 1998. Subj: Animals – bears. Clothing. Format, unusual – toy & movable books. Rhyming text. Weather – rain.

Fuzzy Bear's potty book ill. by Krisztina Nagy. Piggy Toes, 2001. ISBN 978-1-58117-161-7 Subj: Animals – bears. Behavior – growing up. Format, unusual – toy & movable books. Rhyming text. Toilet training.

Welcome back, Puffin ill. by Beth Stover. Soundprints, 2003. ISBN 978-1-59249-009-7 Subj: Birds – puffins. Family life.

Bentley, Jonathan. *Little big* ill. by author. Eerdmans, 2015. ISBN 978-080285462-9 Subj: Character traits – smallness. Concepts – size. Family life – brothers. Imagination.

Where is Bear? ill. by author. Doubleday, 2017. ISBN 978-039955593-0 Subj: Animals – bears. Bedtime. Toys – bears.

Bentley, Tadgh. *Little Penguin gets the hiccups* ill. by author. HarperCollins/Balzer+Bray, 2015. ISBN 978-006233536-4 Subj: Birds – penguins. Hiccups.

Bently, Peter. *Captain Jack and the pirates* ill. by Helen Oxenbury. Dial, 2016. ISBN 978-052542950-0 Subj: Imagination. Pirates. Rhyming text.

The great sheep shenanigans ill. by Mei Matsuoka. Andersen, 2012. ISBN 978-0-7613-8990-3 Subj: Animals – sheep. Animals – wolves. Behavior – trickery. Rhyming text.

King Jack and the dragon ill. by Helen Oxenbury. Penguin, 2011. ISBN 978-0-8037-3698-6 Subj: Activities – playing. Emotions – fear. Imagination. Rhyming text.

Meet the parents ill. by Sara Ogilvie. Simon & Schuster/Paula Wiseman, 2014. ISBN 978-148141483-8 Subj: Family life – parents. Rhyming text.

The prince and the porker ill. by David Roberts. Abrams, 2017. ISBN 978-141972312-4 Subj: Animals – pigs. Behavior – misunderstanding. Character traits – appearance. Rhyming text. Royalty – princes.

A recipe for bedtime ill. by Sarah Massini. Penguin/Putnam, 2016. ISBN 978-039917625-8 Subj: Babies, toddlers. Bedtime. Rhyming text.

Those magnificent sheep in their flying machine ill. by David Roberts. Andersen, 2014. ISBN 978-146774935-0 Subj: Activities – flying. Airplanes, airports. Animals – sheep. Rhyming text.

Benton, Jim. *The end (almost)* ill. by author. Scholastic, 2014. ISBN 978-054517731-3 Subj: Activities – storytelling. Animals – bears. Books, reading.

Where did all the dinos go? ill. by author. Scholastic, 2016. ISBN 978-054564789-2 Subj: Dinosaurs. Format, unusual – board books. Rhyming text.

Benzwie, Teresa. *Numbers on the move: 1 2 3 dance and count with me* ill. by Mark Weber. Temple Univ., 2011. ISBN 978-1-4399-0342-1 Subj: Activities – dancing. Counting, numbers.

Bercaw, Edna Coe. *Halmoni's day* ill. by Robert Hunt. Dial, 2000. ISBN 978-0-8037-2445-7 Subj: Ethnic groups in the U.S. – Korean Americans. Family life – grandmothers. School.

Berenstain, Jan. *The Berenstain bears trim the tree* by Jan Berenstain and Michael Berenstain; ill. by authors. HarperCollins, 2007. ISBN 978-0-06-057417-8 Subj: Animals – bears. Format, unusual – toy & movable books. Holidays – Christmas.

Berenstain, Michael. *The Berenstain bears trim the tree* (Berenstain, Jan)

Berenstain, Stan and Jan. *The bear detectives: the case of the missing pumpkin* ill. by Stan and Jan Berenstain. Random House, 1975. ISBN 978-0-394-93127-2 Subj: Animals – bears. Careers – detectives. Mystery stories. Rhyming text.

Bears in the night ill. by Stan and Jan Berenstain. Random House, 1971. ISBN 978-0-394-92286-7 Subj: Animals – bears. Bedtime. Night. Noise, sounds.

Bears on wheels ill. by Stan and Jan Berenstain. Random House, 1969. ISBN 978-0-394-90967-7 Subj: Animals – bears. Counting, numbers. Wheels.

The Berenstain bears and mama's new job ill. by Stan and Jan Berenstain. Random House, 1984. ISBN 978-0-394-96881-0 Subj: Animals – bears. Careers.

The Berenstain bears and the bad dream ill. by Stan and Jan Berenstain. Random House, 1988. ISBN 978-0-394-97341-8 Subj: Animals – bears. Dreams.

The Berenstain bears and the bad habit ill. by Stan and Jan Berenstain. Random House, 1987. ISBN 978-0-394-97340-1 Subj: Animals – bears.

The Berenstain bears and the big road race ill. by Stan and Jan Berenstain. Random House, 1987. ISBN 978-0-394-99134-4 Subj: Animals – bears. Sports – racing.

The Berenstain bears and the double dare ill. by Stan and Jan Berenstain. Random House, 1988. ISBN 978-0-394-99748-3 Subj: Animals – bears. Sibling rivalry.

The Berenstain bears and the ghost of the forest ill. by Stan and Jan Berenstain. Random House, 1988. ISBN 978-0-394-90565-5 Subj: Animals – bears. Forest, woods. Ghosts.

The Berenstain bears and the messy room ill. by Stan and Jan Berenstain. Random House, 1983. ISBN 978-0-394-95639-8 Subj: Animals – bears. Mystery stories.

The Berenstain bears and the missing dinosaur bone ill. by Stan and Jan Berenstain. Random House, 1980. ISBN 978-0-394-94447-0 Subj: Animals – bears. Museums. Mystery stories. Prehistory. Rhyming text.

The Berenstain bears and the missing honey ill. by Stan and Jan Berenstain. Random House, 1987. ISBN 978-0-394-99133-7 Subj: Animals – bears. Mystery stories.

The Berenstain bears and the prize pumpkin ill. by Stan and Jan Berenstain. Random House, 1990. ISBN 978-0-679-90847-0 Subj: Animals – bears. Holidays – Thanksgiving. Plants.

The Berenstain bears and the real Easter eggs ill. by Stan and Jan Berenstain. Random House, 2002. ISBN 978-0-375-91133-0 Subj: Animals – bears. Eggs. Holidays – Easter. Seasons – spring.

The Berenstain bears and the sitter ill. by Stan and Jan Berenstain. Random House, 1981. ISBN 978-0-394-94837-9 Subj: Activities – babysitting. Animals – bears. Magic.

The Berenstain bears and the slumber party ill. by Stan and Jan Berenstain. McKay, 1990. ISBN 978-0-679-90419-9 Subj: Animals – bears. Bedtime. Parties. Sleepovers.

The Berenstain bears and the spooky old tree ill. by Stan and Jan Berenstain. Random House, 1978. ISBN 978-0-394-93910-0 Subj: Animals – bears. Rhyming text. Trees.

The Berenstain bears and the trouble with friends ill. by Stan and Jan Berenstain. Random House, 1987. ISBN 978-0-394-97339-5 Subj: Animals – bears. Friendship.

The Berenstain bears and the truth ill. by Stan and Jan Berenstain. Random House, 1983. ISBN 978-0-394-95640-4 Subj: Animals – bears. Behavior – lying. Behavior – misbehavior. Family life.

The Berenstain bears and the week at grandma's ill. by Stan and Jan Berenstain. Random House, 1986. ISBN 978-0-394-97335-7 Subj: Animals – bears. Family life – grandmothers.

The Berenstain bears and the wild, wild honey ill. by Stan and Jan Berenstain. Random House, 1983. ISBN 978-0-394-85924-8 Subj: Animals – bears. Nature.

The Berenstain bears and too much birthday ill. by Stan and Jan Berenstain. Random House, 1986. ISBN 978-0-394-97332-6 Subj: Animals – bears. Birthdays.

The Berenstain bears and too much junk food ill. by Stan and Jan Berenstain. Random House, 1985. ISBN 978-0-394-97217-6 Subj: Animals – bears. Food.

The Berenstain bears and too much TV ill. by Stan and Jan Berenstain. Random House, 1984. ISBN 978-0-394-96570-3 Subj: Animals – bears. Family life. Television.

The Berenstain bears and too much vacation ill. by Stan and Jan Berenstain. Random House, 1989. ISBN 978-0-394-93014-5 Subj: Activities – vacationing. Animals – bears.

The Berenstain bears blaze a trail ill. by Stan and Jan Berenstain. Random House, 1987. ISBN 978-0-394-99132-0 Subj: Animals – bears.

The Berenstain bears' Christmas tree ill. by Stan and Jan Berenstain. Random House, 1980. ISBN 978-0-394-94566-8 Subj: Animals – bears. Family life. Holidays – Christmas. Rhyming text. Trees.

The Berenstain bears' counting book ill. by Stan and Jan Berenstain. Random House, 1976. ISBN 978-0-394-83246-3 Subj: Animals – bears. Counting, numbers.

The Berenstain bears don't pollute anymore ill. by Stan and Jan Berenstain. Random House, 1991. ISBN 978-0-679-92351-0 Subj: Animals – bears. Ecology.

The Berenstain bears forget their manners ill. by Stan and Jan Berenstain. Random House, 1985. ISBN 978-0-394-97333-3 Subj: Animals – bears. Etiquette. Family life.

The Berenstain bears get in a fight ill. by Stan and Jan Berenstain. Random House, 1982. ISBN 978-0-394-95132-4 Subj: Animals – bears. Behavior – bad day, bad mood. Sibling rivalry.

The Berenstain bears get stage fright ill. by Stan and Jan Berenstain. Random House, 1986. ISBN 978-0-394-97337-1 Subj: Animals – bears. Emotions – fear. Theater.

The Berenstain bears get the gimmies ill. by Stan and Jan Berenstain. Random House, 1988. ISBN 978-0-394-90566-2 Subj: Animals – bears. Behavior – greed.

The Berenstain bears go out for the team ill. by Stan and Jan Berenstain. Random House, 1987. ISBN 978-0-394-97338-8 Subj: Animals – bears. Sports.

The Berenstain bears go to camp ill. by Stan and Jan Berenstain. Random House, 1982. ISBN 978-0-394-95131-7 Subj: Animals – bears. Camps, camping. Seasons – summer.

The Berenstain bears go to school ill. by Stan and Jan Berenstain. Random House, 1978. ISBN 978-0-394-93736-6 Subj: Animals – bears. School – first day.

The Berenstain bears go to the doctor ill. by Stan and Jan Berenstain. Random House, 1981. ISBN 978-0-394-94835-5 Subj: Animals – bears. Careers – doctors.

The Berenstain bears in the dark ill. by Stan and Jan Berenstain. Random House, 1982. Subj: Animals – bears. Family life. Imagination. Night.

The Berenstain bears learn about strangers ill. by Stan and Jan Berenstain. Random House, 1985. ISBN 978-0-394-87334-3 Subj: Animals – bears. Behavior – talking to strangers. Emotions – fear. Family life. Safety.

The Berenstain bears meet Santa Bear ill. by Stan and Jan Berenstain. Random House, 1988. ISBN 978-0-394-89797-4 Subj: Animals – bears. Holidays – Christmas.

The Berenstain bears' moving day ill. by Stan and Jan Berenstain. Random House, 1981. Subj: Animals – bears. Family life. Friendship. Moving.

The Berenstain bears no girls allowed ill. by Stan and Jan Berenstain. Random House, 1986. ISBN 978-0-394-97331-9 Subj: Animals – bears. Clubs, gangs. Family life – brothers & sisters.

The Berenstain bears on the moon ill. by Stan and Jan Berenstain. Random House, 1985. ISBN 978-0-394-97180-3 Subj: Animals – bears. Animals – dogs. Moon. Space & space ships.

The Berenstain bears ready, set, go! ill. by Stan and Jan Berenstain. Random House, 1988. ISBN 978-0-394-90564-8 Subj: Animals – bears.

The Berenstain bears' report card trouble ill. by Stan and Jan Berenstain. Random House, 2000. ISBN 978-0-375-91127-9 Subj: Animals – bears. Family life. School. Sports.

The Berenstain bears' science fair ill. by Stan and Jan Berenstain. Random House, 1977. Subj: Animals – bears. Science.

The Berenstain bears' that stump must go! ill. by Stan and Jan Berenstain. Random House, 2000. ISBN 978-0-679-98963-9 Subj: Animals – bears. Plants. Rhyming text. Trees.

The Berenstain bears trick or treat ill. by Stan and Jan Berenstain. Random House, 1989. ISBN 978-0-679-90091-7 Subj: Animals – bears. Holidays – Halloween.

The Berenstain bears' trouble at school ill. by Stan and Jan Berenstain. Random House, 1987. ISBN 978-0-394-97336-4 Subj: Animals – bears. Behavior. School.

The Berenstain bears' trouble with money ill. by Stan and Jan Berenstain. Random House, 1983. Subj: Animals – bears. Money.

The Berenstain bears' trouble with pets ill. by Stan and Jan Berenstain. Random House, 1990. ISBN 978-0-679-90848-7 Subj: Animals – bears. Pets.

The Berenstain bears visit the dentist ill. by Stan and Jan Berenstain. Random House, 1981. Subj: Animals – bears. Careers – dentists.

The Berenstains' B book ill. by Stan and Jan Berenstain. Random House, 1971. Subj: ABC books. Animals – bears.

He bear, she bear ill. by Stan and Jan Berenstain. Random House, 1974. Subj: Animals – bears. Rhyming text.

Inside outside upside down ill. by Stan and Jan Berenstain. Random House, 1968. Subj: Animals – bears. Concepts.

Old hat, new hat ill. by Stan and Jan Berenstain. Random House, 1970. Subj: Animals – bears. Concepts – shape. Concepts – size.

Berenzy, Alix. *Sammy: the classroom guinea pig* ill. by author. Henry Holt, 2005. ISBN 978-0-8050-4024-1 Subj: Animals – guinea pigs. Pets. School.

Berg, Charles Ramírez. *The gift of the poinsettia / El regalo de la flor de nochebuena* (Mora, Pat)

Bergel, Colin. *Mail by the pail* ill. by Mark Koenig. Wayne State Univ, 2000. ISBN 978-0-8143-2890-3 Subj: Birthdays. Boats, ships. Family life – fathers. Post office.

Bergen, Lara Rice. *Blue's world of words* ill. by Victoria Miller. Simon & Schuster, 2002. ISBN 978-0-689-84741-7 Subj: Animals – dogs. Dictionaries. Language. Television.

Berger, Barbara. *All the way to Lhasa* ill. by author. Philomel, 2002. ISBN 978-0-399-23387-6 Subj: Animals – yaks. Folk & fairy tales. Foreign lands – Tibet.

Angels on a pin ill. by author. Philomel, 2000. ISBN 978-0-399-23247-3 Subj: Cities, towns. Concepts – size.

Grandfather Twilight ill. by author. Putnam, 1986. ISBN 978-0-399-20996-3 Subj: Folk & fairy tales. Moon. Twilight.

Thunder Bunny ill. by author. Penguin, 2007. ISBN 978-0-399-22035-7 Subj: Animals – rabbits. Sky. Weather – storms.

Berger, Carin. *Finding spring* ill. by author. Greenwillow, 2015. ISBN 978-006225019-3 Subj: Animals – bears. Hibernation. Seasons – spring. Seasons – winter.

Forever friends ill. by author. HarperCollins, 2010. ISBN 978-0-06-191528-4 Subj: Animals – rabbits. Birds. Friendship. Seasons.

Good night! Good night! ill. by author. Greenwillow, 2017. ISBN 978-006240884-6 Subj: Activities – playing. Animals – rabbits. Bedtime. Family life – mothers.

The little yellow leaf ill. by author. Greenwillow, 2008. ISBN 978-0-06-145223-9 Subj: Seasons – fall. Trees.

OK go ill. by author. HarperCollins, 2009. ISBN 978-0-06-157666-9 Subj: Ecology.

A perfect day ill. by author. Greenwillow, 2012. ISBN 978-0-06-201580-8 Subj: Activities – playing. Day. Seasons – winter. Sports – ice skating. Sports – skiing. Weather – snow.

Berger, Gilda. *How do airplanes fly?* (Berger, Melvin)

How's the weather? (Berger, Melvin)

Why did the dinosaurs disappear? the great dinosaur mystery (Berger, Melvin)

Berger, Joe. *Bridget Fidget and the most perfect pet!* ill. by author. Dial, 2009. ISBN 978-0-8037-3405-0 Subj: Insects – ladybugs. Pets.

My special one and only ill. by author. Dial, 2012. ISBN 978-0-8037-3410-4 Subj: Animals – cats. Behavior – lost & found possessions. Stores. Toys.

Berger, Lou. *Dream dog* ill. by David Catrow. Random House, 2013. ISBN 978-0-375-86655-5 Subj: Animals – dogs. Family life – fathers. Illness – allergies. Imagination.

Berger, Melvin. *Brrr! a book about polar animals* ill. with photos. Scholastic, 2000. ISBN 978-0-439-20165-0 Subj: Animals. Foreign lands – Arctic. Science.

Buzz! a book about insects ill. with photos. Scholastic, 2000. ISBN 978-0-439-08748-3 Subj: Insects. Science.

Dive! a book of deep sea creatures ill. with photos. Scholastic, 2000. ISBN 978-0-439-08747-6 Subj: Animals. Boats, ships. Fish. Science. Sea & seashore.

Early humans: a pop-up book ill. by Michael Welply. Putnam, 1988. ISBN 978-0-399-21476-9 Subj: Format, unusual – toy & movable books. Science.

Germs make me sick! ill. by Marylin Hafner. Crowell, 1985. ISBN 978-0-690-04429-4 Subj: Illness. Science.

How do airplanes fly? by Melvin Berger and Gilda Berger ill. by Paul Babb. Ideals, 1996. ISBN 978-1-57102-058-1 Subj: Activities – flying. Airplanes, airports. Science.

How's the weather? by Melvin Berger and Gilda Berger ill. by John Emil Cymerman. Ideals, 1996. ISBN 978-0-8249-8641-4 Subj: Science. Weather.

Look out for turtles! ill. by Megan Lloyd. HarperCollins, 1992. ISBN 978-0-06-022540-7 Subj: Nature. Reptiles – turtles, tortoises. Science.

Oil spill! ill. by Paul Mirocha. HarperCollins, 1994. ISBN 978-0-06-022912-2 Subj: Ecology. Oil. Science. Sea & seashore.

Spinning spiders ill. by S. D. Schindler. Harper-Collins, 2003. ISBN 978-0-06-028697-2 Subj: Science. Spiders.

Switch on, switch off ill. by Carolyn Croll. HarperCollins, 1992. ISBN 978-0-690-04786-8 Subj: Light, lights. Science.

Why did the dinosaurs disappear? the great dinosaur mystery by Melvin Berger and Gilda Berger ill. by Susan Harrison. Ideals, 1995. ISBN 978-1-57102-033-8 Subj: Dinosaurs. Prehistory.

Why I sneeze, shiver, hiccup, and yawn ill. by Paul Meisel. rev. ed. HarperCollins, 2000. ISBN 978-0-06-028143-4 Subj: Hiccups. Illness – allergies. Illness – asthma. Science.

Berger, Samantha. *Back to school with Bigfoot* by Samantha Berger and Martha Brockenbrough ill. by David Pressler. Scholastic/Arthur A. Levine, 2017. ISBN 978-054585973-8 Subj: Behavior – worrying. Monsters. School.

Crankenstein ill. by Dan Santat. Little, Brown, 2013. ISBN 978-0-316-12656-4 Subj: Activities – playing. Behavior – dissatisfaction. Emotions.

Martha doesn't say sorry ill. by Bruce Whatley. Little, Brown, 2009. ISBN 978-0-316-06682-2 Subj: Animals – otters. Character traits – stubbornness.

Martha doesn't share! ill. by Bruce Whatley. Little, Brown, 2010. ISBN 978-0-316-07367-7 Subj: Animals – otters. Behavior – sharing.

Monster's new undies ill. by Tad Carpenter. Scholastic/Orchard, 2017. ISBN 978-054587973-6 Subj: Clothing – underwear. Monsters. Rhyming text.

Snoozefest at the Nuzzledome ill. by Kristyna Litten. Dial, 2015. ISBN 978-080374046-4 Subj: Animals – sloths. Fairs, festivals. Rhyming text. Sleep.

Bergman, Mara. *Lively Elizabeth! what happens when you push* ill. by Cassia Thomas. Albert Whitman, 2010. ISBN 978-0-8075-4702-1 Subj: Activities – playing. Behavior – carelessness. School.

Musical beds ill. by Marjolein Pottie. Margaret K. McElderry, 2002. ISBN 978-0-689-84463-8 Subj: Bedtime. Family life. Sleep.

Oliver who would not sleep! ill. by Nick Naland. Scholastic, 2007. ISBN 978-0-439-92826-7 Subj: Bedtime. Imagination. Sleep.

Snip snap! what's that? ill. by Nick Maland. HarperCollins, 2005. ISBN 978-0-06-077754-8 Subj: Emotions – fear. Family life – brothers & sisters. Reptiles – alligators, crocodiles.

Yum yum! What fun! ill. by Nick Maland. Greenwillow, 2009. ISBN 978-0-06-168860-7 Subj: Animals. Food. Rhyming text.

Bergman, Tamar. *Where is?* ill. by Rutu Modan. Houghton, 2002. ISBN 978-0-618-09539-1 Subj: Animals – cats. Family life – grandparents. Family life – mothers.

Bergmann, Andy. *The starry giraffe* ill. by author. Simon & Schuster, 2017. ISBN 978-148149100-6 Subj: Animals – giraffes. Behavior – sharing. Character traits – generosity. Food.

Bergren, Lisa Tawn. *God gave us Easter* ill. by Laura J. Bryant. WaterBrook, 2013. ISBN 978-0-307-73072-5 Subj: Animals – polar bears. Holidays – Easter. Religion.

How big is God? ill. by Laura J. Bryant. HarperCollins, 2008. ISBN 978-0-06-113174-5 Subj: Religion.

Bergstein, Rita M. *Your own big bed* ill. by Susan Kathleen Hartung. Viking, 2008. ISBN 978-0-670-06079-5 Subj: Animals. Behavior – growing up. Furniture – beds.

Berk, Ari. *Nightsong* ill. by Loren Long. Simon & Schuster, 2012. ISBN 978-1-4169-7886-2 Subj: Animals – bats. Behavior – growing up. Nature. Night.

Berkeley, Jon. *Chopsticks* ill. by author. Random House, 2005. ISBN 978-0-375-83309-0 Subj: Activities – flying. Animals – mice. Dragons. Foreign lands – China.

Berkes, Marianne. *Animalogy: animal analogies* ill. by Cathy Morrison. Sylvan Dell, 2011. ISBN 978-1-60718-127-9 Subj: Animals. Language.

Going home: the mystery of animal migration ill. by Jennifer DiRubbio. Dawn, 2010. ISBN 978-1-58469-126-6 Subj: Animals. Migration.

Marsh music ill. by Robert Noreika. Millbrook, 2000. ISBN 978-0-7613-1850-7 Subj: Animals. Birds. Frogs & toads. Noise, sounds. Rhyming text. Swamps.

Over in a river: flowing out to the sea ill. by Jill Dubin. Dawn, 2013. ISBN 978-1-58469-330-7 Subj: Animals. Counting, numbers. Rhyming text. Rivers. Songs.

Over in Australia: amazing animals down under ill. by Jill Dubin. Dawn, 2011. ISBN 978-1-58469-135-8 Subj: Animals. Counting, numbers. Foreign lands – Australia. Rhyming text.

Over in the Arctic: where the cold winds blow ill. by Jill Dubin. Dawn, 2008. ISBN 978-1-58469-109-9 Subj: Animals. Counting, numbers. Foreign lands – Arctic. Rhyming text.

Over in the forest: come and take a peek ill. by Jill Dubin. Dawn, 2012. ISBN 978-1-58469-162-4 Subj: Animals. Counting, numbers. Forest, woods. Rhyming text.

Over in the jungle: a rainforest rhyme ill. by Jeanette Canyon. Dawn, 2007. ISBN 978-1-58469-091-7 Subj: Animals. Counting, numbers. Jungle. Rhyming text.

Over on a mountain: somewhere in the world ill. by Jill Dubin. Dawn, 2015. ISBN 978-158469518-9 Subj: Animals. Counting, numbers. Mountains. Rhyming text.

Seashells by the seashore ill. by Robert Noreika. Dawn, 2002. ISBN 978-1-58469-035-1 Subj: Counting, numbers. Sea & seashore.

Berkner, Laurie. *Pillowland* ill. by Camille Garoche. Simon & Schuster, 2017. ISBN 978-148146467-3 Subj: Bedtime. Songs.

The story of my feelings ill. by Caroline Jayne Church. Scholastic, 2007. ISBN 978-0-439-42915-3 Subj: Emotions. Music.

We are the dinosaurs ill. by Ben Clanton. Simon & Schuster, 2017. ISBN 978-148146463-5 Subj: Dinosaurs. Music. Songs.

Berlin, Irving. *Easter parade* ill. by Lisa McCue. HarperCollins, 2003. ISBN 978-0-06-029126-6 Subj: Animals – rabbits. Holidays – Easter. Music. Songs.

God bless America ill. by Lynn Munsinger. HarperCollins, 2002. ISBN 978-0-06-009789-9 Subj: Music. Songs. U.S. history.

Bernadette *see* Watts, Bernadette

Bernardo, Susan Schaefer. *The rhino who swallowed a storm* (Burton, LeVar)

Berne, Jennifer. *Calvin can't fly: the story of a bookworm birdie* ill. by Keith Bendis. Sterling, 2010. ISBN 978-1-4027-7323-5 Subj: Activities – flying. Birds. Books, reading. Migration. Weather – hurricanes.

Calvin, look out! a bookworm birdie gets glasses ill. by Keith Bendis. Sterling, 2014. ISBN 978-145490910-1 Subj: Birds. Books, reading. Glasses.

Manfish: a story of Jacques Cousteau ill. by Eric Puybaret. Chronicle, 2008. ISBN 978-0-8118-6063-5 Subj: Careers. Nature. Science. Sea & seashore.

On a beam of light: a story of Albert Einstein ill. by Vladimir Radunsky. Chronicle, 2013. ISBN 978-0-8118-7235-5 Subj: Careers – scientists. Character traits – individuality.

Berner, Rotraut Susanne. *In the town all year 'round* ill. by author. Chronicle, 2008. ISBN 978-0-8118-6474-9 Subj: Cities, towns. Picture puzzles. Seasons.

Bernhard, Durga. *Earth, sky, wet, dry: a book of nature opposites* ill. by author. Orchard, 2000. ISBN 978-0-531-33213-9 Subj: Animals. Concepts – opposites. Nature. Plants.

In the fiddle is a song: a lift-the-flap book of hidden potential ill. by author. Chronicle, 2006. ISBN 978-0-8118-4951-7 Subj: Format, unusual – toy & movable books. Rhyming text.

To and fro, fast and slow ill. by author. Walker, 2001. ISBN 978-0-8027-8783-5 Subj: Cities, towns. Concepts – opposites. Country. Divorce. Family life.

While you are sleeping: a lift-the-flap book of time around the world ill. by author. Charlesbridge, 2011. ISBN 978-1-57091-473-7 Subj: Day. Format, unusual – toy & movable books. Night. Time.

Bernheimer, Kate. *The girl in the castle inside the museum* ill. by Nicoletta Ceccoli. Random House, 2008. ISBN 978-0-375-83606-0 Subj: Castles. Emotions – loneliness. Museums.

The girl who wouldn't brush her hair ill. by Jake Parker. Random House, 2013. ISBN 978-0-375-86878-8 Subj: Animals – mice. Character traits – cleanliness. Hair. Hygiene.

The lonely book ill. by Chris Sheban. Random House, 2012. ISBN 978-0-375-86226-7 Subj: Books, reading. Emotions – loneliness. Libraries.

Bernier-Grand, Carmen T. *Our Lady of Guadalupe* ill. by Tonya Engel. Marshall Cavendish, 2012. ISBN 978-0-7614-6135-7 Subj: Foreign lands – Mexico. Religion.

Bernstein, Ariel. *I have a balloon* ill. by Scott Magoon. Simon & Schuster, 2017. ISBN 978-148147251-7 Subj: Animals – monkeys. Behavior – sharing. Birds – owls. Toys – balloons.

Bernstrom, Daniel. *One day in the eucalyptus, eucalyptus tree* ill. by Brendan Wenzel. HarperCollins/Katherine Tegen, 2016. ISBN 978-006235485-3 Subj: Animals. Behavior – greed. Behavior – trickery. Character traits – cleverness. Reptiles – snakes.

Berry, Lynne. *The curious demise of a contrary cat* ill. by Luke LaMarca. Simon & Schuster, 2006. ISBN 978-1-4169-0211-9 Subj: Animals – cats. Parties. Witches.

Duck dunks ill. by Hiroe Nakata. Henry Holt, 2008. ISBN 978-0-8050-8128-2 Subj: Birds – ducks. Counting, numbers. Rhyming text. Sea & seashore – beaches.

Duck skates ill. by Hiroe Nakata. Henry Holt, 2005. ISBN 978-0-8050-7219-8 Subj: Birds – ducks. Rhyming text. Seasons – winter. Sports – ice skating. Weather – snow.

Duck tents ill. by Nakata Hiroe. Henry Holt, 2009. ISBN 978-0-8050-8696-6 Subj: Birds – ducks. Camps, camping. Rhyming text.

Ducking for apples ill. by Hiroe Nakata. Henry Holt, 2010. ɪsʙɴ 978-0-8050-8935-6 Subj: Birds – ducks. Food. Rhyming text. Sports – bicycling.

Pig and Pug ill. by Gemma Correll. Simon & Schuster, 2015. ɪsʙɴ 978-148142131-7 Subj: Animals – dogs. Animals – pigs.

Squid Kid the Magnificent ill. by Luke LaMarca. Disney/Hyperion, 2015. ɪsʙɴ 978-142316119-6 Subj: Family life – brothers & sisters. Magic. Squid.

What floats in a moat? ill. by Matthew Cordell. Simon & Schuster, 2013. ɪsʙɴ 978-1-4169-9763-4 Subj: Animals – goats. Birds – chickens, roosters. Castles. Concepts. Problem solving. Science.

Berry, Matt. *Up on Daddy's shoulders* ill. by Lucy Corvino. Scholastic, 2006. ɪsʙɴ 978-0-439-67045-6 Subj: Concepts – perspective. Family life – fathers.

Bertier, Anne. *Wednesday* ill. by author. Enchanted Lion, 2014. ɪsʙɴ 978-159270152-0 Subj: Activities – playing. Behavior – boasting, showing off. Character traits – cooperation. Concepts – shape. Friendship.

Bertram, Debbie. *The best book to read* by Debbie Bertram and Susan Bloom ill. by Michael Garland. Random House, 2008. ɪsʙɴ 978-0-375-84702-8 Subj: Books, reading. Libraries. Rhyming text. School – field trips.

The best place to read by Debbie Bertram and Susan Bloom ill. by Michael Garland. Random House, 2003. ɪsʙɴ 978-0-375-92293-0 Subj: Books, reading. Family life – mothers. Furniture – chairs. Rhyming text.

The best time to read by Debbie Bertram and Susan Bloom ill. by Michael Garland. Random House, 2005. ɪsʙɴ 978-0-375-93025-6 Subj: Books, reading. Rhyming text.

My new big-kid bed ill. by Taia Morley. Random House, 2017. ɪsʙɴ 978-110193731-0 Subj: Bedtime. Emotions – fear. Furniture – beds. Rhyming text.

Bertrand, Diane Gonzales. *Family / familia* ill. by Pauline Rodriguez Howard. Piñata, 1999. ɪsʙɴ 978-1-55885-269-3 Subj: Ethnic groups in the U.S. – Mexican Americans. Family life. Foreign languages.

The last doll / La última muñeca ill. by Anthony Accardo. Piñata, 2000. ɪsʙɴ 978-1-55885-290-7 Subj: Birthdays. Ethnic groups in the U.S. – Mexican Americans. Foreign languages. Toys – dolls.

The party for Papa Luis / La fiesta para Papa Luis ill. by Alejandro Galindo. Arte Publico/Piñata, 2010. ɪsʙɴ 978-1-55885-532-8 Subj: Birthdays. Cumulative tales. Ethnic groups in the U.S. – Mexican Americans. Language. Parties.

Sofía and the purple dress / Sofía y el vestido morado ill. by Lisa Fields. Arte Publico/Piñata, 2012. ɪsʙɴ 978-1-55885-701-8 Subj: Clothing – dresses. Ethnic groups in the U.S. – Mexican Americans. Family life. Food. Foreign languages. Health & fitness – exercise.

Uncle Chente's picnic / El picnic de Tío Chente ill. by Pauline Rodriguez Howard. Piñata, 2001. ɪsʙɴ 978-1-55885-337-9 Subj: Activities – picnicking. Ethnic groups in the U.S. – Mexican Americans. Family life – aunts, uncles. Foreign languages. Holidays – Fourth of July.

Bertrand, Lynne. *Granite baby* ill. by Kevin Hawkes. Farrar, 2005. ɪsʙɴ 978-0-374-32761-3 Subj: Babies, toddlers. Giants. Rocks. Tall tales.

Best, Cari. *Are you going to be good?* ill. by G. Brian Karas. Farrar, 2005. ɪsʙɴ 978-0-374-30394-5 Subj: Etiquette. Old age. Parties.

Ava and the real Lucille ill. by Madeline Valentine. Farrar, 2012. ɪsʙɴ 978-0-374-39903-0 Subj: Birds – parakeets, parrots. Contests. Family life – sisters. Pets.

Beatrice spells some lulus and learns to write a letter ill. by Giselle Potter. Farrar, 2013. ɪsʙɴ 978-0-374-39904-7 Subj: Activities – writing. Family life – grandmothers. Language. School.

Easy as pie ill. by Melissa Sweet. Farrar, 2010. ɪsʙɴ 978-0-374-39929-0 Subj: Activities – baking, cooking. Food.

If I could drive, Mama ill. by Simone Shin. Farrar/Margaret Ferguson, 2016. ɪsʙɴ 978-037430205-4 Subj: Activities – playing. Automobiles. Babies, toddlers. Family life – mothers. Imagination.

My three best friends and me, Zulay ill. by Vanessa Brantley-Newton. Farrar/Margaret Ferguson, 2015. ɪsʙɴ 978-037438819-5 Subj: Activities – running. Disabilities – blindness. Ethnic groups in the U.S. – African Americans. School.

A perfect day for digging ill. by Christine Davenier. Amazon/Two Lions, 2014. ɪsʙɴ 978-147784706-0 Subj: Activities – playing. Character traits – cleanliness. Gardens, gardening.

Sally Jean, the Bicycle Queen ill. by Christine Davenier. Farrar, 2006. ɪsʙɴ 978-0-374-36386-4 Subj: Behavior – growing up. Character traits – perseverance. Sports – bicycling.

Three cheers for Catherine the Great! ill. by Giselle Potter. DK, 1999. ɪsʙɴ 978-0-7894-2622-2 Subj: Birthdays. Family life – grandmothers. Gifts.

What's so bad about being an only child? ill. by Sophie Blackall. Farrar, 2007. ɪsʙɴ 978-0-374-39943-6 Subj: Family life – only child.

When Catherine the Great and I were eight! ill. by Giselle Potter. Farrar, 2003. ɪsʙɴ 978-0-374-39954-2 Subj: Activities – traveling. Automobiles. Communities, neighborhoods. Concepts – cold & heat. Ethnic groups in the U.S. – Russian Americans. Family life – grandmothers.

When we go walking ill. by Kyrsten Brooker. Amazon/Two Lions, 2013. ISBN 978-1-4778-1648-6 Subj: Activities – walking. Behavior – collecting things. Family life.

The best cat in the world ill. by Ronald Himler. Eerdmans, 2004. ISBN 978-0-8028-5252-6 Subj: Animals – cats. Death. Emotions – grief. Pets.

The best part of me: children talk about their bodies in pictures and words photos by Wendy Ewald. Little, 2002. ISBN 978-0-316-70306-2 Subj: Anatomy. Children as authors. Poetry.

Bestor, Sheri Mabry. *Good trick, walking stick!* ill. by Jonny Lambert. Sleeping Bear, 2016. ISBN 978-158536943-0 Subj: Disguises. Insects.

Bevis, Mary. *Wolf song* ill. by Consie Powell. Raven, 2007. ISBN 978-0-9794202-0-7 Subj: Animals – wolves. Family life – aunts, uncles. Nature.

Bianco, Margery Williams. *The velveteen rabbit* ill. by David Jorgensen. Knopf, 1985. ISBN 978-0-394-87711-2 Subj: Animals – rabbits. Emotions – love. Folk & fairy tales. Magic. Toys.

The velveteen rabbit retold by Thea Kliros; ill. by reteller. HarperCollins, 2003. ISBN 978-0-06-052746-4 Subj: Animals – rabbits. Emotions – love. Folk & fairy tales. Magic. Toys.

The velveteen rabbit retold by Komako Sakai; ill. by reteller. Enchanted Lion, 2012. ISBN 978-1-59270-128-5 Subj: Animals – rabbits. Emotions – love. Folk & fairy tales. Magic. Toys.

The velveteen rabbit ill. by Gennady Spirin. Marshall Cavendish, 2011. ISBN 978-0-7614-5848-7 Subj: Animals – rabbits. Emotions – love. Folk & fairy tales. Magic. Toys.

The velveteen rabbit: or, How toys became real ill. by Allen Atkinson. Knopf, 1983. ISBN 978-0-394-53221-9 Subj: Animals – rabbits. Emotions – love. Folk & fairy tales. Magic. Toys.

The velveteen rabbit: or, How toys became real adapt. by Lou Fancher; ill. by Steve Johnson and Lou Fancher. Atheneum, 2002. ISBN 978-0-689-84134-7 Subj: Animals – rabbits. Emotions – love. Folk & fairy tales. Magic. Toys.

Bibbel, Mark. *Oh, Harry!* ill. by Sarah Massini. Henry Holt, 2003. ISBN 978-0-8050-6851-1 Subj: Animals – cats. Furniture – beds. Pets.

Bibbons, Faye. *The day the picture man came* ill. by Sherry Meidell. Boyds Mills, 2003. ISBN 978-1-56397-161-7 Subj: Careers – photographers. Farms.

Bible. New Testament. *The Lord's prayer* ill. by Tim Ladwig. Eerdmans, 1999. ISBN 978-0-8028-5180-2 Subj: Ethnic groups in the U.S. – African Americans. Religion.

Bible. New Testament. Corinthians 1st, XIII. *Love is* adapt. by Wendy Anderson Halperin; ill. by adapter. Simon & Schuster, 2001. ISBN 978-0-689-82980-2 Subj: Emotions – love. Religion.

Bible. New Testament. Gospels. *Bethlehem: from the authorized version of the King James Bible* ed. by Fiona French; ill. by Fiona French. HarperCollins, 2001. ISBN 978-0-06-029623-0 Subj: Holidays – Christmas. Religion – Nativity.

The Christmas story: from the Gospel according to St. Luke from the King James Bible ill. by James Bernardin. HarperCollins, 2002. ISBN 978-0-06-028883-9 Subj: Holidays – Christmas. Religion – Nativity.

Easter: from the King James Bible ill. by Fiona French. HarperCollins, 2002. ISBN 978-0-06-623929-3 Subj: Holidays – Easter. Religion.

The story of Christmas ill. by Pamela Dalton. Chronicle, 2011. ISBN 978-1-4521-0470-6 Subj: Holidays – Christmas. Religion – Nativity.

Bible. Old Testament. Ecclesiastes. *To every thing there is a season* ill. by Leo and Diane Dillon. Blue Sky, 1998. ISBN 978-0-590-47887-8 Subj: Religion.

To everything there is a season ill. by Jude Daly. Eerdmans, 2006. ISBN 978-0-8028-5286-1 Subj: Religion.

Bible. Old Testament. Genesis. *Genesis* ill. by Ed Young. Geringer, 1997. ISBN 978-0-06-025356-1 Subj: Creation. Religion.

The Genesis of it all retold by Luci Shaw; ill. by Huai-Kuang Miao. Paraclete, 2006. ISBN 978-1-55725-480-1 Subj: Creation. Religion.

Let there be light by Archbishop Desmond Tutu; ill. by Nancy Tillman. Zonderkidz, 2014. ISBN 978-031072785-9 Subj: Creation. Religion.

Bible. Old Testament. Jonah. *The Book of Jonah* adapt. by Peter Spier; ill. by adapter. Doubleday, 1985. ISBN 978-0-385-19335-1 Subj: Animals – whales. Religion – Jonah.

Bible. Old Testament. Psalms. *I will rejoice: celebrating Psalm 118* ill. by Amy Bates. Zondervan, 2007. ISBN 978-0-310-71117-9 Subj: Religion. Rhyming text.

The Lord is my shepherd ill. by Regolo Ricci. Tundra, 2007. ISBN 978-0-88776-776-0 Subj: Religion.

Psalms for young children ill. by Arno. Eerdmans, 2008. ISBN 978-0-8028-5322-6 Subj: Religion.

The twenty-third Psalm: from the King James Bible ill. by Michael Hague. Henry Holt, 1997. ISBN 978-0-8050-3820-0 Subj: Religion.

Bible. Old Testament. Ruth. *Ruth and Naomi: a Bible story* retold by Jean Marzollo; ill. by reteller. Little, Brown, 2005. ISBN 978-0-316-74139-2 Subj: Religion.

Biddulph, Rob. *Blown away* ill. by author. HarperCollins, 2015. ISBN 978-006236724-2 Subj: Activities – flying. Animals. Birds – penguins. Kites. Rhyming text.

The grizzly bear who lost his grrrrr! ill. by author. HarperCollins, 2016. ISBN 978-006236725-9 Subj: Animals – bears. Behavior – stealing. Character traits – cooperation. Contests. Friendship. Rhyming text.

Biden, Jill. *Don't forget, God bless our troops* ill. by Raúl Colón. Simon & Schuster, 2012. ISBN 978-1-4424-5735-5 Subj: Careers – military. Character traits – bravery. Family life. War.

Biedrzycki, David. *Ace Lacewing, Bug Detective: the big swat* ill. by author. Charlesbridge, 2010. ISBN 978-1-57091-747-9 Subj: Careers – detectives. Crime. Insects.

Breaking news: bear alert ill. by author. Charlesbridge, 2014. ISBN 978-158089663-4 Subj: Animals – bears. Humorous stories. Television.

Breaking news: bears to the rescue ill. by author. Charlesbridge, 2016. ISBN 978-158089624-5 Subj: Animals – bears. Crime. Humorous stories. Television.

Groundhog's runaway shadow ill. by author. Charlesbridge, 2016. ISBN 978-158089734-1 Subj: Animals – groundhogs. Friendship. Shadows.

Me and my dragon ill. by author. Charlesbridge, 2011. ISBN 978-1-58089-278-0 Subj: Dragons. Pets.

Me and my dragon: Christmas spirit ill. by author. Charlesbridge, 2015. ISBN 978-158089622-1 Subj: Character traits – generosity. Dragons. Holidays – Christmas. Pets.

Me and my dragon: scared of Halloween ill. by author. Charlesbridge, 2013. ISBN 978-1-58089-658-0 Subj: Clothing – costumes. Dragons. Holidays – Halloween. Pets.

Santa retires ill. by author. Charlesbridge, 2012. ISBN 978-1-58925-640-8 Subj: Holidays – Christmas. Santa Claus.

Bierhorst, John. *Doctor Coyote: a Native American Aesop's fables* (Aesop)

Biers-Ariel, Matt. *Solomon and the trees* ill. by Esti Silverberg-Kiss. UAHC Pr., 2001. ISBN 978-0-8074-0749-3 Subj: Foreign lands – Israel. Holidays. Jewish culture. Royalty – kings.

Big noisy trucks and diggers ill. with photos. Chronicle, 2001. ISBN 978-0-8118-3173-4 Subj: Careers – construction workers. Format, unusual – toy & movable books. Machines. Noise, sounds. Tractors. Trucks.

Biggs, Brian. *123 beep beep beep! a counting book* ill. by author. HarperCollins, 2013. ISBN 978-0-06-195812-0 Subj: Automobiles. Counting, numbers. Format, unusual – board books. Trucks.

Stop! go! a book of opposites ill. by author. HarperCollins, 2013. ISBN 978-0-06-195813-7 Subj: Concepts – opposites. Format, unusual – board books.

Tinyville town: I'm a police officer ill. by author. Abrams/Appleseed, 2017. ISBN 978-141972323-0 Subj: Careers – police officers. Format, unusual – board books.

Tinyville town: I'm a veterinarian ill. by author. Abrams/Appleseed, 2016. ISBN 978-141972135-9 Subj: Careers – veterinarians. Format, unusual – board books.

Tinyville town: time for school ill. by author. Abrams, 2017. ISBN 978-141972566-1 Subj: School – first day.

Tinyville town gets to work ill. by author. Abrams/Appleseed, 2016. ISBN 978-141972133-5 Subj: Bridges. Careers – construction workers. Careers – engineers. Cities, towns. Machines.

Bijsterbosch, Anita. *Whose hat is that?* ill. by author. Clavis, 2014. ISBN 978-160537185-6 Subj: Animals. Clothing – hats. Weather – wind.

Bildner, Phil. *The greatest game ever played: a football story* ill. by Zachary Pullen. Penguin, 2006. ISBN 978-0-399-24171-0 Subj: Family life – fathers. Sports – football. U.S. history.

The hallelujah flight ill. by John Holyfield. Penguin, 2010. ISBN 978-0-399-24789-7 Subj: Activities – flying. Careers – airplane pilots. Ethnic groups in the U.S. – African Americans. U.S. history.

Marvelous Cornelius: Hurricane Katrina and the spirit of New Orleans ill. by John Parra. Chronicle, 2015. ISBN 978-145212578-7 Subj: Character traits – perseverance. Ethnic groups in the U.S. – African Americans. Weather – hurricanes.

Shoeless Joe and Black Betsy ill. by C. F. Payne. Simon & Schuster, 2002. ISBN 978-0-689-82913-0 Subj: Sports – baseball. U.S. history.

The shot heard 'round the world ill. by C. F. Payne. Simon & Schuster, 2005. ISBN 978-0-689-86273-1 Subj: Sports – baseball.

The soccer fence: a story of friendship, hope, and apartheid in South Africa ill. by Jesse Joshua Watson. Putnam, 2014. ISBN 978-039924790-3 Subj: Foreign lands – South Africa. Prejudice. Sports – soccer.

Turkey Bowl ill. by C. F. Payne. Simon & Schuster, 2008. ISBN 978-0-689-87896-1 Subj: Family life. Holidays – Thanksgiving. Sports – football. Weather – snow.

Bileck, Marvin. *Rain makes applesauce* (Scheer, Julian)

Bilgrami, Shaheen. *Amazing dinosaur discovery: a magic skeleton* ill. by Mike Phillips and Phil Garner. Dinosaurs & skeletons ill. by Treve Tamblin. Sterling, 2002. ISBN 978-0-8069-8591-6 Subj: Anatomy. Animals. Dinosaurs. Format, unusual – toy & movable books. Museums. Prehistory.

Farmyard painting party ill. by Patrick Girouard. Sterling, 2002. ISBN 978-1-4027-0205-1 Subj: Activities – painting. Animals. Concepts – color. Farms. Format, unusual – toy & movable books.

Incredible animal discovery ill. by Mike Phillips and Phil Garner. Animals & skeletons ill. by Chris Shields. Sterling, 2002. ISBN 978-0-8069-8593-0 Subj: Anatomy. Animals. Format, unusual – toy & movable books.

Jungle art show ill. by Patrick Girouard. Sterling, 2002. ISBN 978-1-4027-0206-8 Subj: Activities – painting. Animals. Art. Concepts – color. Format, unusual – toy & movable books. Jungle.

Billin-Frye, Paige. *One, two, buckle my shoe* ill. by author. Child's World, 2009. ISBN 978-1-60253-303-5 Subj: Counting, numbers. Nursery rhymes. Rhyming text.

Billingsley, Franny. *Big bad bunny* ill. by G. Brian Karas. Atheneum, 2008. ISBN 978-1-4169-0601-8 Subj: Animals – mice. Behavior – lost. Clothing – costumes. Family life. Imagination.

Billstrom, Dianne. *You can't go to school naked!* ill. by Don Kilpatrick, III. Putnam, 2008. ISBN 978-0-399-24738-5 Subj: Character traits – appearance. Clothing. Rhyming text.

Bingham, Caroline. *Big book of rescue vehicles* ill. with photos. DK, 2000. ISBN 978-0-7894-5454-6 Subj: Careers – firefighters. Careers – lifeguards. Trucks.

DK big book of airplanes ill. with photos. DK, 2001. ISBN 978-0-7894-6521-4 Subj: Airplanes, airports.

Bingham, Kelly. *Circle, square, Moose* ill. by Paul O. Zelinsky. Greenwillow, 2014. ISBN 978-006229003-8 Subj: Animals – moose. Animals – zebras. Behavior – misbehavior. Concepts – shape. Humorous stories.

Z is for Moose ill. by Paul O. Zelinsky. Greenwillow, 2012. ISBN 978-0-06-079984-7 Subj: ABC books. Animals – moose. Animals – zebras. Humorous stories.

Binns, Tristan Boyer. *The Liberty Bell* ill. with photos. Heinemann, 2001. ISBN 978-1-58810-119-8 Subj: U.S. history.

Birchall, Mark. *Hen goes shopping* ill. by author. Dial, 2002. ISBN 978-0-8037-2690-1 Subj: Birds – chickens, roosters. Format, unusual – toy & movable books. Shopping.

Rabbit's birthday surprise ill. by author. Carolrhoda, 2002. ISBN 978-0-87614-910-2 Subj: Animals – rabbits. Behavior – lost & found possessions. Parties. Toys.

Rabbit's wooly sweater ill. by author. Carolrhoda, 2001. ISBN 978-1-57505-465-0 Subj: Animals – rabbits. Behavior. Clothing – sweaters. Toys.

Bird, Betsy. *Giant dance party* ill. by Brandon Dorman. Greenwillow, 2013. ISBN 978-0-06-196083-3 Subj: Activities – dancing. Emotions – fear. Giants.

Birdsall, Jeanne. *Flora's very windy day* ill. by Matt Phelan. Clarion, 2010. ISBN 978-0-618-98676-7 Subj: Family life – brothers & sisters. Weather – wind.

Lucky and Squash ill. by Jane Dyer. HarperCollins, 2012. ISBN 978-0-06-083150-9 Subj: Animals – dogs. Character traits – cleverness. Friendship.

My favorite pets: by Gus W. for Ms. Smolinski's class ill. by Harry Bliss. Knopf, 2016. ISBN 978-038575570-2 Subj: Activities – writing. Animals – sheep. Humorous stories.

Birdseye, Tom. *Look out, Jack! The giant is back* ill. by Will Hillenbrand. Holiday, 2001. ISBN 978-0-8234-1450-5 Subj: Folk & fairy tales. Giants.

Oh yeah! ill. by Ethan Long. Holiday, 2003. ISBN 978-0-8234-1649-3 Subj: Camps, camping. Character traits – bravery. Night.

Soap! soap! don't forget the soap! an Appalachian folktale ill. by Andrew Glass. Holiday, 1993. ISBN 978-0-8234-1005-7 Subj: Behavior – forgetfulness. Cumulative tales. Folk & fairy tales. Shopping.

Birnbaum, Abe. *Green eyes* ill. by author. Golden, 2001. ISBN 978-0-307-20203-1 Subj: Animals – cats. Caldecott award honor books. Seasons.

Biro, Maureen Boyd. *Walking with Maga* ill. by Joyce Wheeler. All About Kids, 2002. ISBN 978-0-9700863-4-1 Subj: Family life – grandmothers. Nature. Old age. Sea & seashore.

Birtha, Becky. *Far apart, close in heart: being a family when a loved one is incarcerated* ill. by Maja Kastelic. Albert Whitman, 2017. ISBN 978-080751275-3 Subj: Behavior – needing someone. Behavior – worrying. Crime. Emotions – anger. Emotions – embarrassment. Emotions – sadness. Family life.

Grandmama's pride ill. by Colin Bootman. Albert Whitman, 2005. ISBN 978-0-8075-3028-3 Subj: Ethnic groups in the U.S. – African Americans. Family life. Prejudice. U.S. history.

Lucky beans ill. by Nicole Tadgell. Albert Whitman, 2010. ISBN 978-0-8075-4782-3 Subj: Character traits – cleverness. Contests. Counting, numbers. Ethnic groups in the U.S. – African Americans. U.S. history.

Bishop, Brett. *Clayton's path* by Brett Bishop and Laura Olson ill. by Mona Eagle. Apogee, 2001. ISBN 978-0-9700035-3-9 Subj: Animals – mules. Disabilities – ADD. Self-concept.

Bishop, Claire Huchet. *The five Chinese brothers* by Claire Huchet Bishop and Kurt Wiese ill. by Kurt Wiese. Coward, 1938. ISBN 978-0-698-20044-9 Subj: Character traits – cleverness. Family life. Folk & fairy tales. Foreign lands – China.

Bishop, Nic. *Penguin day: a family story* photos by author. Scholastic, 2017. ISBN 978-054520636-5 Subj: Birds – penguins. Foreign lands – Antarctic. Nature.

Bishop, Poppy. *Bear's house of books* ill. by Alison Edgson. Tiger Tales, 2017. ISBN 978-168010038-9 Subj: Animals. Books, reading. Etiquette. Libraries.

Bissonette, Aimée. *North woods girl* ill. by Claudia McGehee. Minnesota Historical Society, 2015. ISBN 978-087351966-3 Subj: Activities – hiking. Family life – grandmothers. Forest, woods. Nature. Seasons.

Blabey, Aaron. *Pearl Barley and Charlie Parsley* ill. by author. Front Street, 2008. ISBN 978-1-59078-596-6 Subj: Character traits – individuality. Friendship.

Pig the elf ill. by author. Scholastic, 2017. ISBN 978-133822122-0 Subj: Animals – dogs. Behavior – greed. Character traits – selfishness. Holidays – Christmas. Rhyming text.

Pig the pug ill. by author. Scholastic, 2016. ISBN 978-133811245-0 Subj: Animals – dogs. Behavior – sharing. Character traits – selfishness. Rhyming text.

Pig the winner ill. by author. Scholastic, 2017. ISBN 978-133813638-8 Subj: Animals – dogs. Behavior – greed. Behavior – misbehavior. Emotions – anger. Rhyming text.

Black, Birdie. *Just right for Christmas* ill. by Rosalind Beardshaw. Candlewick, 2012. ISBN 978-0-7636-6174-8 Subj: Family life – fathers. Gifts. Holidays – Christmas. Royalty – kings.

Black, Harley. *Amazing magic school* ill. by Dana Regan. Sterling, 2000. ISBN 978-0-8069-1553-1 Subj: Animals. Art. Concepts – color. Format, unusual – toy & movable books. Magic. School – first day.

Magic art class ill. by author. Sterling, 2000. ISBN 978-0-8069-0600-3 Subj: Activities – painting. Concepts – color. Format, unusual – toy & movable books.

Black, Michael Ian. *Cock-a-doodle-doo-bop!* ill. by Matthew Myers. Simon & Schuster, 2015. ISBN 978-144249510-4 Subj: Birds – chickens, roosters. Farms. Noise, sounds.

I'm bored ill. by Debbie Ridpath Ohi. Simon & Schuster, 2012. ISBN 978-1-4424-1403-7 Subj: Behavior – boredom. Food. Imagination.

Naked! ill. by Debbie Ridpath Ohi. Simon & Schuster, 2014. ISBN 978-144246738-5 Subj: Clothing. Humorous stories.

A pig parade is a terrible idea ill. by Kevin Hawkes. Simon & Schuster, 2010. ISBN 978-1-4169-7922-7 Subj: Animals – pigs. Humorous stories. Parades.

The purple kangaroo ill. by Peter Brown. Simon & Schuster, 2010. ISBN 978-1-4169-5771-3 Subj: Animals – monkeys. Humorous stories. Imagination.

Black, Sonia. *Hanging out with Mom* ill. by George Ford. Scholastic, 2000. ISBN 978-0-590-86636-1 Subj: Family life – mothers. Parks. Rhyming text.

Blackaby, Susan. *Brownie Groundhog and the February Fox* ill. by Carmen Segovia. Sterling, 2011. ISBN 978-1-4027-4336-8 Subj: Animals – foxes. Animals – groundhogs. Behavior – trickery. Friendship. Holidays – Groundhog Day. Seasons – winter.

Brownie Groundhog and the wintry surprise ill. by Carmen Segovia. Sterling, 2013. ISBN 978-1-4027-9836-8 Subj: Animals. Animals. Animals – groundhogs. Friendship. Seasons – winter.

Rembrandt's hat ill. by Mary Newell DePalma. Houghton, 2002. ISBN 978-0-618-11452-8 Subj: Animals – bears. Behavior – lost & found possessions. Clothing – hats.

Blackall, Sophie. *Are you awake?* ill. by author. Henry Holt, 2011. ISBN 978-0-8050-7858-9 Subj: Bedtime. Character traits – questioning. Family life – mothers. Night.

The baby tree ill. by author. Penguin/Nancy Paulsen, 2014. ISBN 978-039925718-6 Subj: Babies, toddlers. Character traits – questioning. Sex instruction.

Blackford, Harriet. *Elephant's story* ill. by Manya Stojic. Sterling, 2008. ISBN 978-1-905417-75-9 Subj: Animals – elephants. Animals – endangered animals. Foreign lands – Africa.

Tiger's story ill. by Manya Stojic. Sterling, 2007. ISBN 978-1-905417-39-1 Subj: Animals – tigers. Behavior – growing up.

Blackstone, Stella. *Alligator alphabet* ill. by Stephanie Bauer. Barefoot, 2005. ISBN 978-1-84148-494-5 Subj: ABC books. Animals. Rhyming text.

Baby talk ill. with photos. Barefoot, 2015. ISBN 978-178285222-3 Subj: Activities – talking. Babies, toddlers. Format, unusual – board books.

Bear at home ill. by Debbie Harter. Barefoot, 2001. ISBN 978-1-84148-436-5 Subj: Animals – bears. Homes, houses. Rhyming text.

Bear at work ill. by Debbie Harter. Barefoot, 2008. ISBN 978-1-84686-110-9 Subj: Animals – bears. Careers. Careers – postal workers. Rhyming text.

Bear in a square ill. by Debbie Harter. Barefoot, 1998. ISBN 978-1-84148-120-3 Subj: Animals – bears. Concepts – shape. Concepts – size. Counting, numbers.

Bear in sunshine ill. by Debbie Harter. Barefoot, 2001. ISBN 978-1-84148-321-4 Subj: Animals – bears. Rhyming text. Weather.

Bear on a bike ill. by Debbie Harter. Barefoot, 1999. ISBN 978-1-84148-121-0 Subj: Animals – bears. Ethnic groups in the U.S. – African Americans. Sports – bicycling.

Bear takes a trip ill. by Debbie Harter. Barefoot, 2012. ISBN 978-1-84686-756-9 Subj: Activities – traveling. Animals – bears. Clocks, watches. Time.

Bear's birthday ill. by Debbie Harter. Barefoot, 2011. ISBN 978-1-84686-515-2 Subj: Animals – bears. Birthdays. Counting, numbers. Parties. Rhyming text.

Bear's busy family ill. by Debbie Harter. Barefoot, 1999. ISBN 978-1-84148-391-7 Subj: Animals – bears. Concepts – color. Rhyming text. Senses.

Bear's school day ill. by Debbie Harter. Barefoot, 2014. ISBN 978-178285085-4 Subj: Animals – bears. Rhyming text. School.

Cleo and Caspar ill. by Caroline Mockford. Barefoot, 2001. ISBN 978-1-84148-440-2 Subj: Animals – cats. Animals – dogs. Friendship. Rhyming text.

Cleo in the snow ill. by Caroline Mockford. Barefoot, 2002. ISBN 978-1-84148-951-3 Subj: Animals – cats. Animals – dogs. Friendship. Rhyming text. Weather – snow.

Cleo on the move ill. by Caroline Mockford. Barefoot, 2002. ISBN 978-1-84148-898-1 Subj: Animals – cats. Animals – dogs. Friendship. Moving. Rhyming text.

Cleo the cat ill. by Caroline Mockford. Barefoot, 2000. ISBN 978-1-84148-259-0 Subj: Animals – cats. Friendship. Rhyming text.

Cleo's alphabet book ill. by Caroline Mockford. Barefoot, 2003. ISBN 978-1-84148-008-4 Subj: ABC books. Animals – cats. Rhyming text.

Cleo's color book ill. by Caroline Mockford. Barefoot, 2006. ISBN 978-1-905236-30-5 Subj: Animals – cats. Concepts – color. Rhyming text.

Cleo's counting book ill. by Caroline Mockford. Barefoot, 2003. ISBN 978-1-84148-207-1 Subj: Animals – cats. Counting, numbers. Rhyming text.

Come here, Cleo ill. by Caroline Mockford. Barefoot, 2001. ISBN 978-1-84148-329-0 Subj: Animals – cats. Rhyming text.

How big is a pig? ill. by Clare Beaton. Barefoot, 2000. ISBN 978-1-84148-077-0 Subj: Activities – storytelling. Animals. Farms. Rhyming text.

I dreamt I was a dinosaur ill. by Clare Beaton. Barefoot, 2005. ISBN 978-1-84148-238-5 Subj: Dinosaurs. Dreams. Rhyming text.

An island in the sun ill. by Nicoletta Ceccoli. Barefoot, 2002. ISBN 978-1-84148-193-7 Subj: Animals – dogs. Cumulative tales. Islands. Rhyming text. Sea & seashore. Sports – sailing.

Making minestrone ill. by Nan Brooks. Barefoot, 2000. ISBN 978-1-84148-211-8 Subj: Activities – baking, cooking. Food.

Octopus opposites ill. by Stephanie Bauer. Barefoot, 2010. ISBN 978-1-84686-328-8 Subj: Animals. Concepts – opposites. Rhyming text.

Secret seahorse ill. by Clare Beaton. Barefoot, 2004. ISBN 978-1-84148-704-5 Subj: Animals. Fish. Fish – seahorses. Foreign lands – South Sea Islands. Rhyming text. Sea & seashore.

Ship shapes ill. by Siobhan Bell. Barefoot, 2006. ISBN 978-1-905236-34-3 Subj: Boats, ships. Concepts – shape. Rhyming text.

What's this? ill. by Caroline Mockford. Barefoot, 2000. ISBN 978-1-84148-018-3 Subj: Flowers. Gardens, gardening. Seeds.

You and me ill. by Giovanni Manna. Barefoot, 2000. ISBN 978-1-84148-263-7 Subj: Activities. Concepts – opposites.

Blackwood, Freya. *Ivy loves to give* ill. by author. Scholastic, 2010. ISBN 978-0-545-23467-2 Subj: Character traits – generosity. Gifts.

Blades, Ann. *Mary of mile 18* ill. by author. Tundra, 2001. ISBN 978-0-88776-581-0 Subj: Animals – dogs. Animals – wolves. Character traits – perseverance. Farms. Foreign lands – Canada. Seasons – winter.

Too small ill. by author. Douglas & McIntyre, 2000. ISBN 978-0-88899-400-4 Subj: Concepts – size. Family life. Foreign lands – Canada. Moving.

Blaich, Ute. *The star* ill. by Julie Wintz-Litty. NorthSouth, 2001. ISBN 978-0-7358-1510-0 Subj: Animals. Birds – owls. Character traits – kindness. Holidays – Christmas. Religion – Nativity.

Blaikie, Lynn. *Beyond the northern lights* ill. by author. Fitzhenry & Whiteside, 2006. ISBN 978-1-55041-123-2 Subj: Foreign lands – Arctic. Nature. Rhyming text.

Blake, Quentin. *Fantastic Daisy Artichoke* ill. by author. Red Fox, 2001. ISBN 978-0-09-940006-6 Subj: Animals. Friendship. Rhyming text.

Mrs. Armitage: queen of the road ill. by author. Peachtree, 2003. ISBN 978-1-56145-287-3 Subj: Animals – dogs. Automobiles. Family life – aunts, uncles. Motorcycles.

Three little monkeys ill. by Emma Chichester Clark. HarperCollins, 2017. ISBN 978-006267067-0 Subj: Animals – monkeys. Behavior – misbehavior. Pets.

Blake, Robert J. *Fledgling* ill. by author. Philomel, 2000. ISBN 978-0-399-23321-0 Subj: Activities – flying. Birds – kestrels. Cities, towns.

Little devils ill. by author. Philomel, 2009. ISBN 978-0-399-24322-6 Subj: Animals – Tasmanian devils. Behavior – lost. Family life – mothers.

Painter and Ugly ill. by author. Penguin, 2011. ISBN 978-0-399-24323-3 Subj: Alaska. Animals – dogs. Friendship. Sports – racing. Sports – sledding.

Blake, Stephanie. *I don't want to go to school!* ill. by author. Random House, 2009. ISBN 978-0-375-85688-4 Subj: Animals – rabbits. Emotions – fear. School – first day.

Blanco, Richard. *One today* ill. by Dav Pilkey. Little, Brown, 2015. ISBN 978-031637144-5 Subj: Poetry. U.S. history.

Blankenship, Lee Ann. *Mr. Tuggle's troubles* ill. by Karen Dugan. Boyds Mills, 2005. ISBN 978-1-59078-196-8 Subj: Behavior – lost & found possessions. Behavior – messy. Character traits – orderliness. Clothing.

Blatt, Jane. *Books always everywhere* ill. by Sarah Massini. Random House, 2014. ISBN 978-038537506-1 Subj: Books, reading. Rhyming text.

Blecha, Aaron. *Good morning, Grizzle Grump!* ill. by author. HarperCollins, 2017. ISBN 978-006229749-5 Subj: Animals – bears. Animals – squirrels. Seasons – spring.

Goodnight, Grizzle Grump! ill. by author. HarperCollins, 2015. ISBN 978-006229746-4 Subj: Animals – bears. Hibernation. Sleep – snoring.

Blechman, Nicholas. *Night light* ill. by author. Scholastic, 2013. ISBN 978-0-545-46263-1 Subj: Airplanes, airports. Automobiles. Counting, numbers. Format, unusual. Light, lights. Rhyming text. Trains. Trucks.

Blegvad, Lenore. *First friends* ill. by Erik Blebgad. HarperCollins, 2000. ISBN 978-0-694-01273-2 Subj: Behavior – sharing. Friendship. Rhyming text.

Bleiman, Andrew. *ABC zooborns!* by Andrew Bleiman and Chris Eastland ill. with photos. Simon & Schuster, 2012. ISBN 978-1-4424-4371-6 Subj: ABC books. Animals. Zoos.

1-2-3 zooborns! by Andrew Bleiman and Chris Eastland ill. with photos. Simon & Schuster, 2015. ISBN 978-148143103-3 Subj: Animals. Counting, numbers. Zoos.

Bless the beasts: children's prayers and poems about animals ill. by Kris Waldherr. SeaStar, 2002. ISBN 978-1-58717-176-5 Subj: Animals. Poetry. Religion.

Blessing, Charlotte. *New old shoes* ill. by Gary R. Phillips. Pleasant St, 2009. ISBN 978-0-9792035-6-5 Subj: Clothing – shoes. Foreign lands – Africa.

Blexbolex. *Seasons* ill. by author. Enchanted Lion, 2010. ISBN 978-1-59270-095-0 Subj: Seasons.

Bley, Anette. *And what comes after a thousand?* ill. by author. Kane/Miller, 2007. ISBN 978-1-933605-27-2 Subj: Death. Emotions – grief. Old age.

A friend ill. by author. Kane/Miller, 2009. ISBN 978-1-935279-00-6 Subj: Friendship.

Bliss, Harry. *Bailey* ill. by author. Scholastic, 2011. ISBN 978-0-545-23344-6 Subj: Animals – dogs. School.

Bailey at the museum ill. by author. Scholastic, 2012. ISBN 978-0-545-23345-3 Subj: Animals – dogs. Museums. School – field trips.

Bloch, Serge. *Butterflies in my stomach and other school hazards* ill. by author. Sterling, 2008. ISBN 978-1-4027-4158-6 Subj: Humorous stories. Language. School – first day.

You are what you eat: and other mealtime hazards ill. by author. Sterling, 2010. ISBN 978-1-4027-7130-9 Subj: Food. Humorous stories. Language.

Block party today ill. by Stéphanie Roth. Knopf, 2004. ISBN 978-0-375-92216-9 Subj: Communities, neighborhoods. Friendship. Parties.

Blomgren, Jennifer. *Where do I sleep?* ill. by Andrea Gabriel. Sasquatch, 2001. ISBN 978-1-57061-258-9 Subj: Animals – babies. Lullabies. Rhyming text. Sleep.

Blood, Charles L. *The goat in the rug* by Charles L. Blood and Martin A. Link ill. by Nancy Winslow Parker. Parents' Magazine, 1976. ISBN 978-0-8193-0828-3 Subj: Activities – weaving. Animals – goats. Indians of North America – Navajo.

Bloom, Becky. *Crackers* ill. by Pascal Biet. Orchard, 2001. ISBN 978-0-531-30326-9 Subj: Activities – working. Animals – cats. Animals – mice. Character traits – kindness.

Mice make trouble ill. by Pascal Biet. Orchard, 2000. ISBN 978-0-531-33253-5 Subj: Activities – drawing. Animals – mice. Magic.

Bloom, C. P. *The Monkey goes bananas* ill. by Peter Raymundo. Abrams, 2014. ISBN 978-141970885-5 Subj: Animals – monkeys. Character traits – persistence. Fish – sharks.

Bloom, Susan. *The best book to read* (Bertram, Debbie)

The best place to read (Bertram, Debbie)

The best time to read (Bertram, Debbie)

Bloom, Suzanne. *Alone together* ill. by author. Boyds Mills, 2014. ISBN 978-162091736-7 Subj: Animals – bears. Animals – foxes. Behavior – solitude. Birds – geese. Character traits – individuality. Friendship.

Bear can dance! ill. by author. Boyds Mills, 2015. ISBN 978-162979442-6 Subj: Activities – dancing. Activities – flying. Animals – bears. Animals – foxes. Birds – geese. Character traits – helpfulness.

The bus for us ill. by author. Boyds Mills, 2001. ISBN 978-1-56397-932-3 Subj: School – first day.

Feeding friendsies ill. by author. Boyds Mills, 2011. ISBN 978-1-59078-529-4 Subj: Food. Imagination.

Fox forgets ill. by author. Boyds Mills, 2013. ISBN 978-1-59078-996-4 Subj: Animals – bears. Animals – foxes. Behavior – forgetfulness. Birds – geese. Memories, memory.

A mighty fine time machine ill. by author. Boyds Mills, 2009. ISBN 978-1-59078-527-0 Subj: Activities – playing. Animals. Imagination.

No place for a pig ill. by author. Boyds Mills, 2003. ISBN 978-1-59078-047-3 Subj: Animals – pigs. Cities, towns. Homes, houses.

Nuestro autobús / The bus for us ill. by author. Boyds Mills, 2008. ISBN 978-1-59078-629-1 Subj: Foreign languages. School – first day.

A number slumber ill. by author. Boyds Mills, 2016. ISBN 978-162979557-7 Subj: Animals. Bedtime. Counting, numbers. Rhyming text.

Oh! what a surprise! ill. by author. Boyds Mills, 2012. ISBN 978-1-59078-892-9 Subj: Animals – bears. Animals – foxes. Birds – geese. Gifts.

Piggy Monday ill. by author. Albert Whitman, 2001. ISBN 978-0-8075-6529-2 Subj: Animals – pigs. Etiquette. School.

A splendid friend, indeed ill. by author. Boyds Mills, 2005. ISBN 978-1-59078-286-6 Subj: Animals – polar bears. Birds – geese. Friendship.

What about Bear? ill. by author. Boyds Mills, 2010. ISBN 978-1-59078-528-7 Subj: Activities – playing. Animals – bears. Animals – foxes. Birds – geese. Friendship.

Blossom tales ill. by Sarah Dillard. Moon Mt, 2002. ISBN 978-0-9677929-8-9 Subj: Flowers. Folk & fairy tales. Foreign lands.

Bloxam, Frances. *Antlers forever!* ill. by Jim Sollers. Down East, 2001. ISBN 978-0-89272-512-0 Subj: Animals – moose. Nature.

Blue, Rose. *Ron's big mission* (Naden, Corinne J.)

Bluemle, Elizabeth. *Dogs on the bed* ill. by Anne Wilsdorf. Candlewick, 2008. ISBN 978-0-7636-2608-2 Subj: Animals – dogs. Bedtime. Furniture – beds. Rhyming text.

How do you wokka-wokka? ill. by Randy Cecil. Candlewick, 2009. ISBN 978-0-7636-3228-1 Subj: Activities – dancing. Communities, neighborhoods. Parties.

My father the dog ill. by Randy Cecil. Candlewick, 2006. ISBN 978-0-7636-2222-0 Subj: Animals – dogs. Family life – fathers.

Tap tap boom boom ill. by G. Brian Karas. Candlewick, 2014. ISBN 978-076365696-6 Subj: Cities, towns. Rhyming text. Trains. Weather – lightning, thunder. Weather – rain.

Blum, Mark. *Big trucks and diggers in 3-D* ill. by author. Chronicle, 2001. ISBN 978-0-8118-3172-7 Subj: Format, unusual – toy & movable books. Machines. Tractors. Trucks.

Blume, Judy. *The one in the middle is a green kangaroo* ill. by Irene Trivas. Macmillan, 1991. ISBN 978-0-02-711055-5 Subj: Family life. Self-concept.

The Pain and The Great One ill. by Irene Trivas. McGraw-Hill, 1974. ISBN 978-0-02-711100-2 Subj: Family life. Sibling rivalry.

Blumenthal, Deborah. *Aunt Claire's yellow beehive hair* ill. by Mary GrandPré. Dial, 2001. ISBN 978-0-8037-2509-6 Subj: Behavior – collecting things. Family life. Memories, memory.

The blue house dog ill. by Adam Gustavson. Peachtree, 2010. ISBN 978-1-56145-537-9 Subj: Animals – dogs. Death. Emotions – grief.

Charlie hits it big ill. by Denise Brunkus. HarperCollins, 2008. ISBN 978-0-06-056353-0 Subj: Animals – guinea pigs. Careers – actors.

Don't let the peas touch! ill. by Timothy Basil Ering. Scholastic, 2004. ISBN 978-0-439-29732-5 Subj: Family life – sisters. Sibling rivalry.

Fancy party gowns: the story of fashion designer Ann Cole Lowe ill. by Laura Freeman. little bee, 2017. ISBN 978-149980239-9 Subj: Careers. Character traits – persistence. Clothing. Ethnic groups in the U.S. – African Americans.

Ice palace ill. by Ted Rand. Clarion, 2003. ISBN 978-0-618-15960-4 Subj: Fairs, festivals. Seasons – winter. Sports.

Bluthenthal, Diana Cain. *I'm not invited?* ill. by author. Atheneum, 2003. ISBN 978-0-689-84141-5 Subj: Emotions. Friendship. Parties.

Boase, Susan. *Lucky boy* ill. by author. Houghton, 2002. ISBN 978-0-618-13175-4 Subj: Animals – dogs. Behavior – needing someone. Emotions – grief.

Boatfield, Jonny. *The twilight book* ill. by author. Bloomsbury, 2000. ISBN 978-0-7475-5083-9 Subj: Books, reading. Games. Mystery stories. Puzzles.

Bober, Suzanne. *In the garden with Van Gogh* (Merberg, Julie)

A magical day with Matisse (Merberg, Julie)

Bock, Lee. *Oh, crumps! / Ay, caramba!* ill. by Morgan Midgett. Raven Tree, 2003. ISBN 978-0-9720192-4-8 Subj: Animals. Careers – farmers. Farms. Foreign languages. Noise, sounds.

Bodkin, Odds. *The Christmas cobwebs* ill. by Terry Widener. Harcourt, 2001. ISBN 978-0-15-201459-9 Subj: Ethnic groups in the U.S. – German Americans. Family life. Holidays – Christmas. Spiders.

The crane wife ill. by Gennady Spirin. Harcourt, 1998. ISBN 978-0-15-201407-0 Subj: Activities – weaving. Birds – cranes. Character traits – kindness to animals. Folk & fairy tales. Foreign lands – Japan.

Boedoe, Geefwee. *Arrowville* ill. by author. Geringer, 2004. ISBN 978-0-06-055599-3 Subj: Prejudice. Rhyming text.

Boelts, Maribeth. *Before you were mine* ill. by David Walker. Penguin, 2007. ISBN 978-0-399-24526-8 Subj: Animals – dogs. Pets.

Big Daddy, frog wrestler ill. by Benrei Huang. Albert Whitman, 2000. ISBN 978-0-8075-0717-9 Subj: Family life – fathers. Frogs & toads. Sports – wrestling.

A bike like Sergio's ill. by Noah Jones. Candlewick, 2016. ISBN 978-076366649-1 Subj: Behavior – indecision. Character traits – honesty. Sports – bicycling.

Happy like soccer ill. by Lauren Castillo. Candlewick, 2012. ISBN 978-0-7636-4616-5 Subj: Behavior – resourcefulness. Communities, neighborhoods. Ethnic groups in the U.S. – African Americans. Family life – aunts, uncles. Poverty. Sports – soccer.

Looking for Sleepy ill. by Bernadette Pons. Albert Whitman, 2004. ISBN 978-0-8075-0447-5 Subj: Animals – bears. Bedtime. Family life – fathers. Family life – sons.

Sweet dreams, Little Bunny! ill. by Kathy Parkinson. Albert Whitman, 2010. ISBN 978-0-8075-4589-8 Subj: Animals – rabbits. Bedtime. Format, unusual – board books.

Those shoes ill. by Noah Jones. Candlewick, 2007. ISBN 978-0-7636-2499-6 Subj: Character traits – appearance. Clothing – shoes. Ethnic groups in the U.S. – African Americans.

You're a brother, Little Bunny! ill. by Kathy Parkinson. Albert Whitman, 2001. ISBN 978-0-8075-9446-9 Subj: Animals – rabbits. Babies, toddlers. Family life – brothers. Family life – brothers & sisters. Family life – new sibling.

Bogacki, Tomasz. *Circus girl* ill. by author. Farrar, 2001. ISBN 978-0-374-31291-6 Subj: Character traits – helpfulness. Circus. Friendship.

My first garden ill. by author. Farrar, 2000. ISBN 978-0-374-32518-3 Subj: Gardens, gardening.

Bogan, Carmen. *Where's Rodney?* ill. by Floyd Cooper. Yosemite Conservancy, 2017. ISBN 978-193023873-2 Subj: Character traits – curiosity. Nature. Parks. School – field trips.

Bogan, Paulette. *Goodnight Lulu* ill. by author. Bloomsbury, 2003. ISBN 978-1-58234-803-2 Subj: Bedtime. Birds – chickens, roosters. Family life – mothers.

Lulu the big little chick ill. by author. Bloomsbury, 2009. ISBN 978-1-59990-343-9 Subj: Behavior – running away. Birds – chickens, roosters. Character traits – smallness. Concepts – size. Family life – mothers.

Momma's magical purse ill. by author. Bloomsbury, 2004. ISBN 978-1-58234-842-1 Subj: Animals – cats. Animals – dogs. Clothing – handbags, purses. Family life – mothers. Magic.

Spike in the city ill. by author. Putnam, 2000. ISBN 978-0-399-23442-2 Subj: Animals – dogs. Behavior – lost & found possessions. Cities, towns.

Virgil and Owen ill. by author. Bloomsbury, 2015. ISBN 978-161963372-8 Subj: Animals – polar bears. Behavior – bossy. Birds – penguins. Friendship.

Virgil and Owen stick together ill. by author. Bloomsbury, 2016. ISBN 978-161963373-5 Subj: Animals – polar bears. Behavior – hurrying. Birds – penguins. Character traits – patience, impatience. Friendship.

Bogart, Jo Ellen. *Big and small, room for all* ill. by Gillian Newland. Tundra, 2009. ISBN 978-0-88776-891-0 Subj: Concepts – size. Nature.

Count your chickens ill. by Lori Joy Smith. Tundra, 2017. ISBN 978-177049792-4 Subj: Birds – chickens, roosters. Counting, numbers. Rhyming text.

Bogue, Gary. *There's an opossum in my backyard* ill. by Chuck Todd. Heyday, 2007. ISBN 978-1-59714-059-1 Subj: Animals – babies. Animals – possums.

Boiger, Alexandra. *Max and Marla* ill. by author. Putnam, 2015. ISBN 978-039917504-6 Subj: Birds – owls. Character traits – persistence. Seasons – winter. Sports – Olympics. Sports – sledding.

Bolam, Emily. *Animals talk* ill. by author. ME Media/Tiger Tales, 2010. ISBN 978-1-58925-855-6 Subj: Animals. Format, unusual – board books. Noise, sounds.

I go potty ill. by author. Scholastic, 2010. ISBN 978-0-531-25233-8 Subj: Format, unusual – board books. Rhyming text. Toilet training.

Bolden, Tonya. *Beautiful moon: a child's prayer* ill. by Eric Velasquez. Abrams, 2014. ISBN 978-141970792-6 Subj: Bedtime. Ethnic groups in the U.S. – African Americans. Moon. Religion.

Rock of ages: a tribute to the Black church ill. by R. Gregory Christie. Knopf, 2001. ISBN 978-0-679-99485-5 Subj: Church. Ethnic groups in the U.S. – African Americans. Poetry. Religion.

Boldt, Claudia. *Odd dog* ill. by author. North-South, 2012. ISBN 978-0-7358-4068-3 Subj: Animals – dogs. Behavior – sharing. Food. Friendship.

Boldt, Mike. *Colors versus shapes* ill. by author. HarperCollins, 2014. ISBN 978-006210303-1 Subj: Concepts – color. Concepts – shape. Theater.

123 versus ABC ill. by author. HarperCollins, 2013. ISBN 978-0-06-210299-7 Subj: ABC books. Counting, numbers. Humorous stories.

Boling, Katharine. *New year be coming! a Gullah year* ill. by Daniel Minter. Albert Whitman, 2002. ISBN 978-0-8075-5590-3 Subj: Days of the week, months of the year. Poetry.

Boling, Ruth L. *Come worship with me* ill. by Tracey Dahle Carrier. Geneva, 2001. ISBN 978-0-664-50045-0 Subj: Days of the week, months of the year. Religion.

Bolliger, Max. *The happy troll* ill. by Peter Sís. Henry Holt, 2005. ISBN 978-0-8050-6982-2 Subj: Activities – singing. Behavior – greed. Mythical creatures – trolls.

Bollinger, Peter. *Algernon Graeves is scary enough* ill. by author. HarperCollins, 2005. ISBN 978-0-06-052269-8 Subj: Clothing – costumes. Holidays – Halloween.

Bond, Felicia. *Big hugs, little hugs* ill. by author. Penguin, 2012. ISBN 978-0-399-25614-1 Subj: Animals. Hugging.

The Halloween play ill. by author. HarperCollins, 1999. ISBN 978-0-06-028684-2 Subj: Animals – mice. Holidays – Halloween. School. Theater.

Poinsettia and her family ill. by author. HarperCollins, 1981. ISBN 978-0-690-04145-3 Subj: Animals – pigs. Behavior. Family life. Moving. Sibling rivalry.

Poinsettia and the firefighters ill. by author. Crowell, 1984. ISBN 978-0-690-04400-3 Subj: Animals – pigs. Bedtime. Night. Noise, sounds.

Bond, Michael. *Paddington Bear* ill. by R. W. Alley. HarperCollins, 1998. ISBN 978-0-06-027854-0 Subj: Animals – bears.

Paddington Bear and the Busy Bee Carnival ill. by R. W. Alley. HarperCollins, 1998. ISBN 978-0-06-027765-9 Subj: Animals – bears. Contests. Fairs, festivals.

Paddington Bear and the Christmas surprise ill. by R. W. Alley. HarperCollins, 1997. ISBN 978-0-694-00897-1 Subj: Animals – bears. Careers. Holidays – Christmas. Stores.

Paddington Bear goes to the hospital by Michael Bond and Karen Jankel ill. by R. W. Alley. HarperCollins, 2001. ISBN 978-0-694-01563-4 Subj: Accidents. Hospitals. Toys – bears.

Paddington Bear in the garden ill. by R. W. Alley. HarperCollins, 2002. ISBN 978-0-06-029696-4 Subj: Gardens, gardening. Toys – bears.

Bond, Rebecca. *Bravo, Maurice!* ill. by author. Little, 2000. ISBN 978-0-316-10545-3 Subj: Careers. Family life. Noise, sounds.

A city Christmas tree ill. by author. Little, Brown, 2005. ISBN 978-0-316-53731-5 Subj: Holidays – Christmas. Trees.

The great doughnut parade ill. by author. Houghton, 2007. ISBN 978-0-618-77705-1 Subj: Cumulative tales. Food. Parades.

Bonfield, Chloe. *The perfect tree* ill. by author. Running Press Kids, 2016. ISBN 978-076245586-7 Subj: Animals. Ecology. Trees.

Bonilla, Rocio. *The highest mountain of books in the world* ill. by author. Peter Pauper, 2016. ISBN 978-144131999-9 Subj: Books, reading. Imagination.

Bonnet, Rosalinde. *Daddy Honk Honk!* ill. by author. Dial, 2017. ISBN 978-039918676-9 Subj: Animals – foxes. Birds – geese. Character traits – kindness to animals.

Bonnett-Rampersaud, Louise. *Bubble and Squeak* ill. by Susan Banta. Marshall Cavendish, 2006. ISBN 978-0-7614-5310-9 Subj: Animals – mice. Bedtime. Emotions – fear. Family life – brothers & sisters.

How do you sleep? ill. by Kristin Kest. Marshall Cavendish, 2005. ISBN 978-0-7614-5231-7 Subj: Animals. Rhyming text. Sleep.

Never ask a bear ill. by Doris Barrette. HarperCollins, 2009. ISBN 978-0-06-112876-9 Subj: Animals – bears. Rhyming text.

Polly Hopper's pouch ill. by Lina Chesak-Librace. Dutton, 2001. ISBN 978-0-525-46525-6 Subj: Animals – kangaroos. Character traits – curiosity. Foreign lands – Australia.

Bonnice, Lindsey. *Libby and Pearl: the best of friends* photos by author. HarperCollins, 2016. ISBN 978-006245927-5 Subj: Animals – pigs. Babies, toddlers. Ethnic groups in the U.S. – African Americans. Friendship.

Bonning, Tony. *Fox tale soup* ill. by Sally Hobson. Simon & Schuster, 2002. ISBN 978-0-689-84900-8 Subj: Animals – foxes. Character traits – cleverness. Farms. Folk & fairy tales. Food.

Snog the frog ill. by Rosalind Beardshaw. Barron's, 2005. ISBN 978-0-7641-5824-7 Subj: Frogs & toads. Royalty – princesses.

Bono, Mary. *Ugh! a bug* ill. by author. Walker, 2002. ISBN 978-0-8027-8800-9 Subj: Insects – ladybugs. Rhyming text.

Bonsignore, Joan. *Stick out your tongue: fantastic facts, features, and functions of animal and human tongues* ill. by John Ward. Peachtree, 2001. ISBN 978-1-56145-230-9 Subj: Anatomy – tongues. Senses – taste.

Bonwill, Ann. *Bug and Bear: a story of true friendship* ill. by Layn Marlow. Marshall Cavendish, 2011. ISBN 978-0-7614-5902-6 Subj: Animals – bears. Friendship. Insects.

The Frazzle family finds a way ill. by Stephen Gammell. Holiday House, 2013. ISBN 978-0-8234-2405-4 Subj: Activities – singing. Behavior – forgetfulness. Family life. Memories, memory. Songs.

I am not a copycat! ill. by Simon Rickerty. Simon & Schuster, 2013. ISBN 978-1-4424-8053-7 Subj: Animals – hippopotamuses. Behavior – imitation. Birds. Friendship.

Naughty toes ill. by Teresa Murfin. Tiger Tales, 2011. ISBN 978-1-58925-103-8 Subj: Activities – dancing. Ballet. Family life – sisters. Self-concept.

Booth, Anne. *The fairiest fairy* ill. by Rosalind Beardshaw. Candlewick/Nosy Crow, 2016. ISBN 978-076368659-8 Subj: Behavior – messy. Character traits – helpfulness. Character traits – kindness. Fairies. Magic. Rhyming text.

Booth, Philip E. *Crossing* ill. by Bagram Ibatoulline. Candlewick, 2001. ISBN 978-0-7636-1420-1 Subj: Poetry. Trains.

Booth, Tom. *Don't blink!* ill. by author. Feiwel & Friends, 2017. ISBN 978-125011736-6 Subj: Animals. Contests.

Boothroyd, Jennifer. *What is a gas?* ill. with photos. Lerner, 2007. ISBN 978-0-8225-6818-6 Subj: Science.

Bootman, Colin. *Fish for the Grand Lady* ill. by author. Holiday House, 2006. ISBN 978-0-8234-1898-5 Subj: Family life – grandmothers. Foreign lands – Trinidad. Sports – fishing.

Borando, Silvia. *Black cat, white cat* ill. by author. Candlewick, 2015. ISBN 978-076368106-7 Subj: Animals – cats. Day. Friendship. Night.

The cat book ill. by author. Candlewick, 2017. ISBN 978-076369472-2 Subj: Animals – cats. Participation.

Now you see me, now you don't ill. by author. Candlewick, 2016. ISBN 978-076368782-3 Subj: Animals. Concepts – color. Disguises. Wordless.

Borchard, Therese Johnson. *Taste and see the goodness of the Lord* ill. by Phyllis V. Saroff. Paulist, 2000. ISBN 978-0-8091-6665-7 Subj: Religion.

Borden, Louise. *A. Lincoln and me* ill. by Ted Lewin. Scholastic, 2000. ISBN 978-0-590-45714-9 Subj: Birthdays. Self-concept. U.S. history.

America is . . . ill. by Stacey Schuett. Margaret K. McElderry, 2002. ISBN 978-0-689-83900-9 Subj: Poetry. U.S. history.

Baseball is . . . ill. by Raúl Colón. Simon & Schuster, 2014. ISBN 978-141695502-3 Subj: Sports – baseball.

Big brothers don't take naps ill. by Emma Dodd. Simon & Schuster, 2011. ISBN 978-1-4169-5503-0 Subj: Family life – brothers. Family life – new sibling.

The day Eddie met the author ill. by Adam Gustavson. Margaret K. McElderry, 2001. ISBN 978-0-689-83405-9 Subj: Books, reading. Careers – writers. School.

Kindergarten luck ill. by Genevieve Godbout. Chronicle, 2015. ISBN 978-145211394-4 Subj: Character traits – luck. Money. School.

The lost-and-found tooth ill. by Adam Gustavson. Simon & Schuster, 2008. ISBN 978-1-4169-1814-1 Subj: School. Teeth.

Off to first grade ill. by Joan Rankin. Simon & Schuster, 2008. ISBN 978-0-689-87395-9 Subj: Behavior – worrying. School – first day.

Thanksgiving is . . . ill. by Steve Björkman. Scholastic, 1997. ISBN 978-0-590-33128-9 Subj: Holidays – Thanksgiving.

Border, Terry. *Merry Christmas, Peanut!* ill. by author. Philomel, 2017. ISBN 978-039917621-0 Subj: Activities – traveling. Family life. Food. Holidays – Christmas. Humorous stories.

Milk goes to school photos by author. Philomel, 2016. ISBN 978-039917619-7 Subj: Behavior – boasting, showing off. Food. School.

Peanut Butter and Cupcake! photos by author. Philomel, 2014. ISBN 978-039916773-7 Subj: Activities – playing. Food. Friendship. Moving.

Borgo, Lacy. *Big Mama's baby* ill. by Nancy Cote. Boyds Mills, 2007. ISBN 978-1-59078-187-6 Subj: Animals – bulls, cows. Family life – grandmothers. Texas.

Boroson, Martin. *Becoming me: a story of creation* ill. by Chris Gilvan-Cartwright. Skylight Paths, 2000. ISBN 978-1-893361-11-9 Subj: Creation. Religion.

Bosca, Francesca. *The apple king* ill. by Giuliano Ferri. NorthSouth, 2001. ISBN 978-0-7358-1397-7 Subj: Animals. Behavior – sharing. Royalty – kings. Trees.

The three grasshoppers ill. by Giuliano Ferri. Purple Bear, 2006. ISBN 978-1-933327-13-6 Subj: Friendship. Insects – grasshoppers. Music.

Boswell, Addie. *The rain stomper* ill. by Eric Velasquez. Marshall Cavendish, 2008. ISBN 978-0-7614-5393-2 Subj: Ethnic groups in the U.S. – African Americans. Parades. Weather – rain. Weather – storms.

Bottner, Barbara. *An annoying ABC* ill. by Michael Emberley. Random House, 2011. ISBN 978-0-375-86708-8 Subj: ABC books. Behavior – misbehavior. School – nursery.

Bootsie Barker bites ill. by Peggy Rathmann. Putnam, 1992. ISBN 978-0-399-22125-5 Subj: Activities – playing. Behavior – bullying, teasing.

Feet go to sleep ill. by Maggie Smith. Knopf, 2015. ISBN 978-044981325-6 Subj: Anatomy. Bedtime. Sea & seashore – beaches. Sleep.

Flower girl ill. by Laura Grier. Marshall Cavendish, 2012. ISBN 978-0-7614-6119-7 Subj: Family life – aunts, uncles. Weddings.

Miss Brooks loves books! (and I don't) ill. by Michael Emberley. Random House, 2010. ISBN 978-0-375-84682-3 Subj: Books, reading. Libraries. School.

Miss Brooks' Story Nook (where tales are told and ogres are welcome) ill. by Michael Emberley. Knopf, 2014. ISBN 978-044981328-7 Subj: Activities – storytelling. Careers – librarians. Libraries.

Pish and Posh by Barbara Bottner and Gerald Kruglik; ill. by Barbara Bottner. Tegen, 2004. ISBN 978-0-06-051417-4 Subj: Behavior – lost & found possessions. Fairies. Magic.

Priscilla gorilla ill. by Michael Emberley. Atheneum/Caitlyn Dlouhy, 2017. ISBN 978-148145897-9 Subj: Animals – gorillas. Character traits – willfulness. School. School – field trips. Zoos.

Raymond and Nelda ill. by Nancy Hayashi. Peachtree, 2007. ISBN 978-1-56145-394-8 Subj: Animals – rabbits. Animals – squirrels. Careers – postal workers. Friendship.

Rosa's room ill. by Beth Spiegel. Peachtree, 2004. ISBN 978-1-56145-302-3 Subj: Family life – mothers. Friendship. Furniture – beds. Moving.

Wallace's lists by Barbara Bottner and Gerald Kruglik ill. by Olof Landström. Tegen, 2004. ISBN 978-0-06-000225-1 Subj: Animals – mice. Character traits – orderliness. Friendship.

Bouchard, Dave. *Fairy* ill. by Dean Griffiths. Orca, 2001. ISBN 978-1-55143-212-0 Subj: Fairies. Teeth.

Nokum is my teacher ill. by Allen Sapp. Fitzhenry & Whiteside, 2007. ISBN 978-0-88995-367-3 Subj: Family life – grandmothers. Foreign languages. Indians of North America – Cree.

The song within my heart ill. by Allen Sapp. Raincoast, 2002. ISBN 978-1-55192-559-2 Subj: Activities – storytelling. Indians of North America. Pow-wows.

Boudreau, Hélène. *I dare you not to yawn* ill. by Serge Bloch. Candlewick, 2013. ISBN 978-0-7636-5070-4 Subj: Bedtime.

Bouler, Olivia. *Olivia's birds: saving the Gulf* ill. by author. Sterling, 2011. ISBN 978-1-4027-8665-5 Subj: Behavior – resourcefulness. Birds. Character traits – generosity. Character traits – helpfulness. Sea & seashore.

Bourgeois, Paulette. *Fire fighters* ill. by Kim La-Fave. Kids Can, 1998. ISBN 978-1-55074-438-5 Subj: Careers – firefighters. Communities, neighborhoods. Fire.

Franklin and Harriet ill. by Brenda Clark. Scholastic, 2001. ISBN 978-0-439-26424-2 Subj: Animals. Character traits – helpfulness. Family life – brothers & sisters. Reptiles – turtles, tortoises. Sibling rivalry. Toys.

Franklin and the thunderstorm ill. by Brenda Clark. Scholastic, 1998. ISBN 978-0-590-02635-2 Subj: Animals. Emotions – fear. Reptiles – turtles, tortoises. Weather – lightning, thunder. Weather – storms.

Franklin in the dark ill. by Brenda Clark. Kids Can, 1986. ISBN 978-0-919964-93-8 Subj: Emotions – fear. Night. Reptiles – turtles, tortoises.

Franklin rides a bike ill. by Brenda Clark. Kids Can, 1997. ISBN 978-1-55074-414-9 Subj: Animals. Reptiles – turtles, tortoises. Sports – bicycling.

Franklin says "I love you" ill. by Brenda Clark. Scholastic, 2002. ISBN 978-1-55337-035-2 Subj: Behavior – worrying. Birthdays. Family life – mothers. Gifts. Reptiles – turtles, tortoises.

Franklin's baby sister ill. by Brenda Clark. Scholastic, 2000. ISBN 978-1-55074-794-2 Subj: Babies, toddlers. Family life – brothers & sisters. Reptiles – turtles, tortoises. Seasons – spring.

Franklin's Christmas gift ill. by Brenda Clark. Kids Can, 1998. ISBN 978-1-55074-466-8 Subj: Gifts. Holidays – Christmas. Reptiles – turtles, tortoises.

Franklin's class trip by Paulette Bourgeois and Sharon Jennings ill. by Brenda Clark. Scholastic, 1999. ISBN 978-0-590-13002-8 Subj: Animals. Dinosaurs. Museums. Reptiles – turtles, tortoises. School – field trips. Toys.

Franklin's new friend ill. by Brenda Clark. Scholastic, 1997. ISBN 978-0-590-02592-8 Subj: Animals – moose. Friendship. Reptiles – turtles, tortoises.

Franklin's secret club ill. by Brenda Clark. Kids Can, 1998. ISBN 978-0-590-13000-4 Subj: Animals. Clubs, gangs. Friendship. Reptiles – turtles, tortoises.

Garbage collectors ill. by Kim LaFave. Kids Can, 1998. ISBN 978-1-55074-440-8 Subj: Careers – sanitation workers. Communities, neighborhoods.

Oma's quilt ill. by Stéphane Jorisch. Kids Can, 2001. ISBN 978-1-55074-777-5 Subj: Family life – grandmothers. Quilts.

Police officers ill. by Kim LaFave. Kids Can, 1999. ISBN 978-1-55074-502-3 Subj: Careers – police officers. Communities, neighborhoods.

Postal workers ill. by Kim LaFave. Kids Can, 1998. ISBN 978-1-55074-504-7 Subj: Birthdays. Careers – postal workers. Communities, neighborhoods.

Bourguignon, Laurence. *Heart in the pocket* ill. by Valérie d'Heur. Eerdmans, 2008. ISBN 978-0-8028-5343-1 Subj: Animals – babies. Animals – kangaroos. Family life – mothers.

Boutignon, Beatrice. *Not all animals are blue: a big book of little differences* ill. by author. Kane/Miller, 2009. ISBN 978-1-933605-96-8 Subj: Animals. Character traits – individuality. Concepts.

Bowen, Anne. *Christmas is coming* ill. by Tomasz Bogacki. Lerner, 2007. ISBN 978-1-57505-934-1 Subj: Holidays – Christmas.

The great math tattle battle ill. by Jaime Zollars. Albert Whitman, 2006. ISBN 978-0-8075-3163-1 Subj: Behavior – gossip, rumors. Counting, numbers. School.

I know an old teacher ill. by Stephen Gammell. Carolrhoda, 2008. ISBN 978-0-8225-7984-7 Subj: Careers – teachers. Cumulative tales. Pets. Rhyming text. School.

I loved you before you were born ill. by Greg Shed. HarperCollins, 2001. ISBN 978-0-06-028721-4 Subj: Babies, toddlers. Family life – grandmothers. Memories, memory.

Scooter in the outside ill. by Abby Carter. Holiday House, 2012. ISBN 978-0-8234-2326-2 Subj: Animals – dogs. Character traits – responsibility. Pets.

Tooth Fairy's first night ill. by Jon Berkeley. Carolrhoda, 2005. ISBN 978-1-57505-753-8 Subj: Fairies. Teeth.

When you visit Grandma and Grandpa ill. by Tomasz Bogacki. Lerner, 2004. ISBN 978-1-57505-610-4 Subj: Babies, toddlers. Family life – brothers & sisters. Family life – grandparents.

Bower, Gary. *Ivy's icicle* ill. by Jan Bower. Tyndale, 2002. ISBN 978-0-8423-7417-0 Subj: Behavior – forgiving. Family life – brothers & sisters. Family life – grandmothers.

Bower, Tamara. *The shipwrecked sailor: an Egyptian tale with hieroglyphs* ill. by author. Atheneum, 2000. ISBN 978-0-689-83046-4 Subj: Folk & fairy tales. Foreign lands – Egypt. Hieroglyphics. Magic. Reptiles – snakes.

Bowers, Tim. *A new home* ill. by author. Harcourt, 2002. ISBN 978-0-15-216564-2 Subj: Animals – squirrels. Friendship. Moving.

Bowie, C. W. *Busy fingers* ill. by Fred Willingham. Whispering Coyote, 2003. ISBN 978-1-58089-036-6 Subj: Anatomy – hands. Rhyming text.

Busy toes ill. by Fred Willingham. Whispering Coyote, 1998. ISBN 978-1-879085-72-5 Subj: Activities. Anatomy – toes. Rhyming text.

Bowles, Paula. *Messy Jesse* ill. by author. Tiger Tales, 2015. ISBN 978-158925133-5 Subj: Animals – dogs. Behavior – messy.

Scary Mary ill. by author. Tiger Tales, 2012. ISBN 978-1-58925-110-6 Subj: Behavior – bullying, teasing. Birds – chickens, roosters. Emotions – loneliness.

Bowman, Patty. *The amazing Hamweenie* ill. by author. Philomel, 2012. ISBN 978-0-399-25688-2 Subj: Animals – cats. Imagination.

Boxall, Ed. *Francis the scaredy cat* ill. by author. Candlewick, 2002. ISBN 978-0-7636-1767-7 Subj: Animals – cats. Emotions – fear. Monsters.

Boyce, Katie. *Hector the hermit crab* ill. by author. Bloomsbury, 2003. ISBN 978-1-58234-800-1 Subj: Character traits – confidence. Crustaceans – crabs. Friendship. Self-concept.

Boyd, Colin. *The bath monster* ill. by Tony Ross. Andersen, 2016. ISBN 978-151240426-5 Subj: Activities – bathing. Monsters.

Boyd, Lizi. *Big bear little chair* ill. by author. Chronicle, 2015. ISBN 978-145214447-4 Subj: Animals. Concepts – opposites. Concepts – size.

Flashlight ill. by author. Chronicle, 2014. ISBN 978-145211894-9 Subj: Light, lights. Night. Wordless.

I love Daddy ill. by author. Candlewick, 2004. ISBN 978-0-7636-2217-6 Subj: Activities. Family life – fathers. Family life – sons. Frogs & toads.

I love Mommy ill. by author. Candlewick, 2004. ISBN 978-0-7636-2216-9 Subj: Activities. Family life – mothers. Family life – sons. Frogs & toads.

Inside outside ill. by author. Chronicle, 2013. ISBN 978-1-4521-0644-1 Subj: Activities – playing. Concepts. Format, unusual. Wordless.

Boyden, Linda. *The blue roses* ill. by Amy Córdova. Lee & Low, 2002. ISBN 978-1-58430-037-3 Subj: Death. Emotions. Family life – grandfathers. Gardens, gardening. Indians of North America.

Boyer, Cécile. *Woof meow tweet-tweet* ill. by author. Seven Footer, 2011. ISBN 978-1-934734-60-5 Subj: Animals – cats. Animals – dogs. Birds.

Boyle, Bob. *Hugo and the really, really, really long string* ill. by author. Random House, 2010. ISBN 978-0-375-83423-3 Subj: Animals. String.

Boynton, Sandra. *Christmas parade* ill. by author. Simon & Schuster, 2012. ISBN 978-1-4424-6813-9 Subj: Animals. Holidays – Christmas. Musical instruments – bands. Parades. Rhyming text.

Dinosaur dance! ill. by author. Simon & Schuster, 2016. ISBN 978-148148099-4 Subj: Activities – dancing. Dinosaurs. Format, unusual – board books. Rhyming text.

Eek! Halloween! ill. by author. Workman, 2016. ISBN 978-076119300-5 Subj: Birds – chickens, roosters. Format, unusual – board books. Holidays – Halloween. Rhyming text.

Happy birthday, Little Pookie ill. by author. Simon & Schuster, 2017. ISBN 978-148149770-1 Subj: Animals – pigs. Birthdays. Family life – mothers. Format, unusual – board books. Rhyming text.

Little Pookie ill. by author. Simon & Schuster, 2017. ISBN 978-148149768-8 Subj: Animals – pigs. Family life – mothers. Format, unusual – board books. Rhyming text.

Night-night, Little Pookie ill. by author. Simon & Schuster, 2017. ISBN 978-148149771-8 Subj: Animals – pigs. Bedtime. Format, unusual – board books. Rhyming text.

Spooky Pookie ill. by author. Simon & Schuster, 2017. ISBN 978-148149767-1 Subj: Animals – pigs. Clothing – costumes. Format, unusual – board books. Holidays – Halloween. Rhyming text.

Yay, you! moving out, moving up, moving on ill. by author. Simon & Schuster, 2001. ISBN 978-0-689-84283-2 Subj: Character traits – individuality. Rhyming text.

Bozik, Chrissy. *The ghosts go scaring* ill. by Patricia Storms. Sky Pony, 2016. ISBN 978-151071228-7 Subj: Counting, numbers. Ghosts. Holidays – Halloween. Rhyming text.

Bracken, Beth. *The little bully* ill. by Jennifer A. Bell. Picture Window, 2012. ISBN 978-1-4048-6795-6 Subj: Animals. Behavior – bullying, teasing. Friendship. School.

Too shy for show-and-tell ill. by Jennifer A. Bell. Picture Window, 2011. ISBN 978-1-4048-6654-6 Subj: Animals – giraffes. Character traits – shyness. School.

Bradbury, Ray. *Switch on the night* ill. by Leo and Diane Dillon. Knopf, 2000, 1993. ISBN 978-0-375-80608-7 Subj: Emotions – fear. Friendship. Night.

Bradby, Marie. *The longest wait* ill. by Peter Catalanotto. Orchard, 1998. ISBN 978-0-531-08721-3 Subj: Careers – postal workers. Weather – snow. Weather – storms.

Momma, where are you from? ill. by Chris Soentpiet. Orchard, 2000. ISBN 978-0-531-33105-7 Subj: Cities, towns. Ethnic groups in the U.S. – African Americans. Family life – mothers.

More than anything else ill. by Chris Soentpiet. Orchard, 1995. ISBN 978-0-531-08764-0 Subj: Behavior – seeking better things. Books, reading. Ethnic groups in the U.S. – African Americans.

Once upon a farm ill. by Ted Rand. Orchard, 2002. ISBN 978-0-439-31766-5 Subj: Ethnic groups in the U.S. – African Americans. Farms. Rhyming text.

Bradford, Karleen. *You can't rush a cat* by Karleen Bradford and Leslie Elizabeth Watts ill. by Leslie Elizabeth Watts. Orca, 2004. ISBN 978-1-55143-247-2 Subj: Animals – cats. Family life – grandfathers.

Bradford, Wade. *Why do I have to make my bed?* ill. by Johanna van der Sterre. Tricycle, 2011. ISBN 978-1-58246-327-8 Subj: Character traits – cleanliness. Family life – mothers.

Bradley, Kimberly Brubaker. *Ballerino Nate* ill. by R. W. Alley. Penguin, 2006. ISBN 978-0-8037-2954-4 Subj: Activities – dancing. Animals – dogs. Ballet. Character traits – being different.

Favorite things ill. by Laura Huliska-Beith. Dial, 2003. ISBN 978-0-8037-2597-3 Subj: Bedtime. Day. Family life – mothers. Imagination.

The perfect pony ill. by Shelagh McNicholas. Penguin, 2007. ISBN 978-0-8037-2851-6 Subj: Animals – horses, ponies.

Pop! a book about bubbles photos by Margaret Miller. HarperCollins, 2001. ISBN 978-0-06-028701-6 Subj: Bubbles.

Bradley, Sandra. *Henry Holton takes the ice* ill. by Sara Palacios. Dial, 2015. ISBN 978-080373856-0 Subj: Character traits – individuality. Self-concept. Sports – hockey. Sports – ice skating.

Bradman, Tony. *Daddy's lullaby* ill. by Jason Cockcroft. Margaret K. McElderry, 2002. ISBN 978-0-689-84295-5 Subj: Family life – fathers. Lullabies.

The perfect baby ill. by Holly Swain. Egmont, 2010. ISBN 978-1-4052-2755-1 Subj: Family life – new sibling. Sibling rivalry.

Braeuner, Shellie. *The great dog wash* ill. by Robert Neubecker. Simon & Schuster, 2009. ISBN 978-1-4169-7116-0 Subj: Animals – dogs. Character traits – cleanliness. Rhyming text.

Braithwaite, Jill. *Police cars* ill. by author. Lerner, 2004. ISBN 978-0-8225-0770-3 Subj: Automobiles. Careers – police officers.

Brallier, Jess M. *Tess's tree* ill. by Peter H. Reynolds. HarperCollins, 2010. ISBN 978-0-06-168752-5 Subj: Trees.

Bram, Elizabeth. *Rufus the writer* ill. by Chuck Groenink. Random House, 2015. ISBN 978-038537853-6 Subj: Activities – trading. Activities – writing. Careers – writers.

Brami, Elisabeth. *Mommy time* by Elisabeth Brami and Anne-Sophie Tschiegg ill. by Anne-Sophie Tschiegg. Kane/Miller, 2002. ISBN 978-1-929132-22-5 Subj: Family life – mothers. Imagination.

Bramsen, Carin. *Hey, duck!* ill. by author. Random House, 2013. ISBN 978-0-375-86990-7 Subj: Animals – cats. Birds – ducks. Friendship. Rhyming text.

Just a duck? ill. by author. Random House, 2015. ISBN 978-038538415-5 Subj: Animals – cats. Birds – ducks. Friendship. Rhyming text.

Brandenberg, Alexa. *Ballerina flying* ill. by author. HarperCollins, 2002. ISBN 978-0-06-029550-9 Subj: Activities – dancing. Ballet.

Brandenberg, Aliki *see* Aliki

Brandle, Bine. *Flusi, the sock monster* ill. by author. Kane/Miller, 2004. ISBN 978-1-929132-69-0 Subj: Behavior – lost & found possessions. Clothing – socks. Monsters.

Brandt, Amy. *Benjamin comes back / Benjamin regresa* ill. by Janice Lee Porter. Redleaf, 2000. ISBN 978-1-884834-79-0 Subj: Family life – mothers. Foreign languages. School – nursery.

When Katie was our teacher / Cuando Katie era nuestra maestra ill. by Janice Lee Porter. Redleaf, 2000. ISBN 978-1-884834-78-3 Subj: Careers – teachers. Foreign languages. School – nursery.

Brandt, Lois. *Maddi's fridge* ill. by Vin Vogel. IPG, 2014. ISBN 978-193626129-1 Subj: Behavior – secrets. Character traits – helpfulness. Character traits – kindness. Food. Poverty.

Branford, Henrietta. *Little Pig Figwort can't get to sleep* ill. by Claudio Muñoz. Clarion, 2000. ISBN 978-0-618-15968-0 Subj: Animals – pigs. Bedtime. Sleep.

Branley, Franklyn M. *Air is all around you* ill. by Holly Keller. Rev. ed. Crowell, 1986. ISBN 978-0-690-04503-1 Subj: Science.

Comets ill. by Giulio Maestro. Crowell, 1984. Subj: Science. Sky.

Down comes the rain ill. by James Graham Hale. HarperCollins, 1997. ISBN 978-0-06-025338-7 Subj: Science. Weather. Weather – rain.

Earthquakes ill. by Richard Rosenblum. HarperCollins, 1990. ISBN 978-0-690-04663-2 Subj: Earth. Science.

Eclipse: darkness in daytime ill. by Donald Crews. Rev. ed. HarperCollins, 1988. ISBN 978-0-690-04619-9 Subj: Science. Sun.

Flash, crash, rumble, and roll ill. by Barbara Emberley and Ed Emberley. Rev. ed. Crowell, 1985. ISBN 978-0-690-04425-6 Subj: Science. Weather – lightning, thunder.

Floating in space ill. by True Kelley. HarperCollins, 1998. ISBN 978-0-06-025433-9 Subj: Careers – astronauts. Science. Space & space ships.

Gravity is a mystery ill. by Don Madden. Rev. ed. Crowell, 1986. ISBN 978-0-690-04527-7 Subj: Science.

The International Space Station ill. by True Kelley. HarperCollins, 2000. ISBN 978-0-06-028703-0 Subj: Space & space ships.

Light and darkness ill. by Stacey Schuett. Rev. ed. HarperCollins, 1998. ISBN 978-0-06-027295-1 Subj: Science.

The planets in our solar system ill. by Don Madden. Crowell, 1981. ISBN 978-0-690-04026-5 Subj: Planets. Science. Space & space ships. Sun. World.

Rain and hail ill. by Harriett Barton. Rev. ed. Crowell, 1983. ISBN 978-0-690-04353-2 Subj: Science. Weather. Weather – rain.

The sky is full of stars ill. by Felicia Bond. Crowell, 1981. ISBN 978-0-690-04123-1 Subj: Science. Sky. Stars.

Snow is falling ill. by Holly Keller. Rev. ed. Crowell, 1986. ISBN 978-0-690-04548-2 Subj: Science. Weather – snow.

The sun, our nearest star ill. by Edward Miller. Rev. & newly ill. ed. HarperCollins, 2002. ISBN 978-0-06-028535-7 Subj: Earth. Science. Sun.

Sunshine makes the seasons ill. by Giulio Maestro. Rev. ed. Crowell, 1985. ISBN 978-0-690-04482-9 Subj: Science. Seasons. Sun.

Tornado alert ill. by Giulio Maestro. Crowell, 1988. ISBN 978-0-690-04688-5 Subj: Science. Weather – storms.

Volcanoes ill. by Megan Lloyd. HarperCollins, 2008. ISBN 978-0-06-028011-6 Subj: Science. Volcanoes.

Volcanoes ill. by Marc Simont. Crowell, 1985. ISBN 978-0-690-04431-7 Subj: Science. Volcanoes.

What makes a magnet? ill. by True Kelley. HarperCollins, 1996. ISBN 978-0-06-026442-0 Subj: Science.

What makes day and night ill. by Arthur Dorros. Rev. ed. Crowell, 1986. ISBN 978-0-690-04524-6 Subj: Earth. Science.

What the moon is like ill. by True Kelley. Rev. ed. Crowell, 1986. ISBN 978-0-690-04512-3 Subj: Moon. Science.

Brannen, Sarah S. *Uncle Bobby's wedding* ill. by author. Putnam, 2008. ISBN 978-0-399-24712-5 Subj: Family life – aunts, uncles. LGBTQ. Weddings.

Brantley-Newton, Vanessa. *Let freedom sing* ill. by author. Blue Apple, 2009. ISBN 978-1-934706-90-9 Subj: Ethnic groups in the U.S. – African Americans. Holidays – Martin Luther King, Jr. Day. Prejudice. Songs. U.S. history.

Brantz, Loryn. *Feminist Baby* ill. by author. Disney/Hyperion, 2017. ISBN 978-148477858-6 Subj: Babies, toddlers. Format, unusual – board books. Gender roles. Rhyming text.

Braun, Eric. *Trust me, Jack's beanstalk stinks: the story of Jack and the beanstalk as told by the giant* ill. by Cristian Bernardini. Picture Window, 2011. ISBN 978-1-4048-6675-1 Subj: Folk & fairy tales. Giants. Humorous stories. Plants.

Braun, Sebastien. *Back to bed, Ed!* ill. by author. Peachtree, 2010. ISBN 978-1-56145-518-8 Subj: Animals – mice. Bedtime. Sleep.

Digger and Tom! ill. by author. HarperCollins, 2013. ISBN 978-0-06-207752-3 Subj: Character traits – cooperation. Character traits – persistence. Machines. Trucks.

I love my daddy ill. by author. HarperCollins, 2004. ISBN 978-0-06-054311-2 Subj: Animals – bears. Day. Family life – fathers. Family life – sons.

I love my mommy ill. by author. HarperCollins, 2004. ISBN 978-0-06-054310-5 Subj: Animals – squirrels. Family life – mothers.

Toot and Pop! ill. by author. HarperCollins, 2012. ISBN 978-0-06-207750-9 Subj: Behavior – boasting, showing off. Boats, ships. Character traits – smallness. Character traits – vanity.

Whoosh and Chug! ill. by author. HarperCollins, 2014. ISBN 978-006207754-7 Subj: Character traits – perseverance. Concepts – speed. Safety. Trains.

Who's hiding? ill. by author. Candlewick, 2013. ISBN 978-0-7636-5932-5 Subj: Behavior – hiding. Format, unusual – toy & movable books. Gardens, gardening.

Braver, Vanita. *Madison and the two wheeler* ill. by Carl DiRocco. Star Bright, 2007. ISBN 978-1-59572-110-5 Subj: Character traits – perseverance. Sports – bicycling.

Braybrooks, Ann. *Plenty of pockets* ill. by Scott Menchin. Harcourt, 2000. ISBN 978-0-15-202173-3 Subj: Character traits – orderliness. Clothing – pockets.

Breathed, Berkeley. *Edwurd Fudwupper fibbed big: explained by Fannie Fudwupper* ill. by author. Little, 2000. ISBN 978-0-316-10675-7 Subj: Aliens. Character traits – honesty. Family life – brothers & sisters.

Mars needs moms! ill. by author. Penguin, 2007. ISBN 978-0-399-24736-1 Subj: Aliens. Family life – mothers.

Brebeuf, Jean de. *The Huron carol* English lyrics by Jesse Edgar Middleton; ill. by Ian Wallace. Groundwood, 2006. ISBN 978-0-88899-711-1 Subj: Foreign lands – Canada. Holidays – Christmas. Religion – Nativity. Songs.

Brecon, Connah. *Paws McDraw: the fastest doodler in the West* ill. by author. Tiger Tales, 2016. ISBN 978-168010035-8 Subj: Activities – drawing. Animals – dogs. U.S. history – frontier & pioneer life.

Breen, Steve. *A perfect mess* ill. by author. Dial, 2016. ISBN 978-080374156-0 Subj: Animals – rhinoceros. Behavior – messy. Character traits – cleanliness.

Pug and Doug ill. by author. Dial, 2013. ISBN 978-0-8037-3521-7 Subj: Animals – dogs. Behavior – misunderstanding. Birthdays. Friendship.

The secret of Santa's island ill. by author. Dial, 2009. ISBN 978-0-8037-3126-4 Subj: Activities – vacationing. Holidays – Christmas. Islands. Santa Claus. Sea & seashore – beaches.

Stick ill. by author. Penguin, 2007. ISBN 978-0-8037-3124-0 Subj: Frogs & toads. Insects – dragonflies.

Violet the pilot ill. by author. Dial, 2008. ISBN 978-0-8037-3125-7 Subj: Activities – flying. Behavior – resourcefulness. Careers – airplane pilots. Character traits – individuality.

Woodpecker wants a waffle ill. by author. HarperCollins, 2016. ISBN 978-006234257-7 Subj: Birds – woodpeckers. Character traits – cleverness. Character traits – persistence. Food.

Brendler, Carol. *Not very scary* ill. by Greg Pizzoli. Farrar, 2014. ISBN 978-037435547-0 Subj: Cumulative tales. Emotions – fear. Holidays – Halloween. Monsters. Parties.

Brennan, Eileen. *Bad Astrid* ill. by Regan Dunnick. Random House, 2013. ISBN 978-0-375-85580-1 Subj: Animals – dogs. Behavior – bullying, teasing. Rhyming text.

Dirtball Pete ill. by author. Random House, 2010. ISBN 978-0-375-83425-7 Subj: Behavior – messy. Character traits – cleanliness. Hygiene. Self-concept.

Brennan, Herbie. *Frankenstella and the video store monster* ill. by Cathy Gale. Bloomsbury, 2002. ISBN 978-1-58234-752-3 Subj: Monsters.

Brennan, Linda Crotta. *Marshmallow kisses* ill. by Mari Takabayashi. Houghton, 2000. ISBN 978-0-395-73872-6 Subj: Rhyming text. Seasons – summer.

Brennan, Rosemarie. *Willow* (Brennan-Nelson, Denise)

Brennan-Nelson, Denise. *Good night, reindeer* ill. by Marco Bucci. Sleeping Bear, 2017. ISBN 978-158536370-4 Subj: Animals – reindeer. Bedtime. Holidays – Christmas. Rhyming text. Santa Claus.

Grady the goose ill. by Michael Glenn Monroe. Sleeping Bear, 2006. ISBN 978-1-58536-282-0 Subj: Behavior – lost. Birds – geese.

He's been a monster all day! ill. by Cyd Moore. Sleeping Bear, 2013. ISBN 978-1-58536-827-3 Subj: Behavior – misbehavior. Monsters. Rhyming text.

J is for jack-o-lantern: a halloween alphabet ill. by Donald Wu. Sleeping Bear, 2009. ISBN 978-1-58536-443-5 Subj: ABC books. Holidays – Halloween.

My grandma likes to say ill. by Jane Monroe Donovan. Sleeping Bear, 2007. ISBN 978-1-58536-284-4 Subj: Language. Rhyming text.

Willow by Denise Brennan-Nelson and Rosemarie Brennan ill. by Cyd Moore. Sleeping Bear, 2008. ISBN 978-1-58536-342-1 Subj: Art. Careers – teachers. Imagination. School.

Brenner, Barbara A. *Beef stew* ill. by Catherine Siracusa. Random House, 2004, ©1990. ISBN 978-0-394-95046-4 Subj: Family life – grandmothers. Food. Friendship.

Good morning, garden ill. by Denise Ortakales. NorthWord, 2004. ISBN 978-1-55971-888-2 Subj: Gardens, gardening. Morning. Rhyming text.

One small place by the sea ill. by Thomas Leonard. HarperCollins, 2004. ISBN 978-0-688-17183-4 Subj: Animals. Ecology. Sea & seashore.

What the elephant told ill. by Akemi Gutierrez. Henry Holt, 2003. ISBN 978-0-8050-6442-1 Subj: Animals – babies. Animals – elephants. Babies, toddlers.

Brenner, Emily. *On the first day of grade school* ill. by Bruce Whatley. HarperCollins, 2004. ISBN 978-0-06-051041-1 Subj: Animals. Careers – teachers. Cumulative tales. Rhyming text. School.

Brenner, Tom. *And then comes Christmas* ill. by Jana Christy. Candlewick, 2014. ISBN 978-076365342-2 Subj: Holidays – Christmas. Seasons – winter.

And then comes Halloween ill. by Holly Meade. Candlewick, 2009. ISBN 978-0-7636-3659-3 Subj: Holidays – Halloween. Seasons – fall.

And then comes summer ill. by Jaime Kim. Candlewick, 2017. ISBN 978-076366071-0 Subj: Seasons – summer.

Brenning, Juli. *Maggi and Milo* ill. by Priscilla Burris. Dial, 2014. ISBN 978-080373795-2 Subj: Animals – dogs. Frogs & toads.

Maggi and Milo make new friends ill. by Priscilla Burris. Dial, 2016. ISBN 978-080373776-1 Subj: Activities – playing. Animals – dogs. Friendship.

Brett, Jan. *The animals' Santa* ill. by author. Putnam, 2014. ISBN 978-039925784-1 Subj: Animals. Animals – rabbits. Holidays – Christmas. Santa Claus.

Annie and the wild animals ill. by author. Houghton, 1985. ISBN 978-0-395-37800-7 Subj: Animals. Animals – cats. Emotions – loneliness. Pets.

Armadillo rodeo ill. by author. Putnam, 1995. ISBN 978-0-399-22803-2 Subj: Animals. Animals – armadillos. Behavior – mistakes. Family life.

Berlioz the bear ill. by author. Putnam, 1991. ISBN 978-0-399-22248-1 Subj: Animals. Animals – bears. Cumulative tales. Music. Musical instruments – bands.

Christmas trolls ill. by author. Putnam, 1993. ISBN 978-0-399-22507-9 Subj: Animals – hedgehogs. Behavior – sharing. Behavior – stealing. Holidays – Christmas. Mythical creatures – trolls.

Cinders: a chicken Cinderella ill. by author. Putnam, 2013. ISBN 978-039925783-4 Subj: Birds – chickens, roosters. Folk & fairy tales. Royalty – princes.

Comet's nine lives ill. by author. Putnam, 1996. ISBN 978-0-399-22931-2 Subj: Animals – cats. Animals – dogs. Behavior – carelessness. Lighthouses.

Daisy comes home ill. by author. Putnam, 2002. ISBN 978-0-399-23618-1 Subj: Behavior – lost. Birds – chickens, roosters. Foreign lands – China.

The Easter egg ill. by author. Penguin, 2010. ISBN 978-0-399-25238-9 Subj: Animals – rabbits. Contests. Eggs. Holidays – Easter.

The first dog ill. by author. Harcourt, 1988. ISBN 978-0-15-227650-8 Subj: Animals – dogs. Animals – wolves. Art. Caves. Pets.

Fritz and the beautiful horses ill. by author. Houghton, 1981. ISBN 978-0-395-30850-9 Subj: Animals – horses, ponies. Behavior – wishing. Character traits – cleverness. Folk & fairy tales.

The hat ill. by author. Putnam, 1997. ISBN 978-0-399-23101-8 Subj: Animals. Animals – hedgehogs. Clothing.

Hedgie blasts off! ill. by author. Penguin, 2006. ISBN 978-0-399-24621-0 Subj: Animals – hedgehogs. Careers – astronauts. Careers – custodians, janitors. Space & space ships.

Hedgie's surprise ill. by author. Putnam, 2000. ISBN 978-0-399-23477-4 Subj: Animals – hedgehogs. Birds – chickens, roosters. Character traits – cleverness. Eggs. Food. Mythical creatures – trolls.

Home for Christmas ill. by author. Penguin, 2011. ISBN 978-0-399-25653-0 Subj: Behavior – running away. Character traits – helpfulness. Holidays – Christmas. Mythical creatures – trolls.

Honey, honey — lion! a story from Africa ill. by author. Penguin, 2005. ISBN 978-0-399-24463-6 Subj: Animals – badgers. Behavior – greed. Birds. Foreign lands – Africa.

The mermaid ill. by author. Putnam, 2017. ISBN 978-039917072-0 Subj: Mythical creatures – mermaids, mermen. Octopuses.

The mitten ill. by author. Putnam, 1989. ISBN 978-0-399-21920-7 Subj: Animals. Behavior – lost & found possessions. Cumulative tales. Folk & fairy tales. Foreign lands – Ukraine.

Mossy ill. by author. Putnam, 2012. ISBN 978-0-399-25782-7 Subj: Character traits – kindness to animals. Ecology. Gardens, gardening. Museums. Nature. Reptiles – turtles, tortoises.

The three little dassies ill. by author. Penguin, 2010. ISBN 978-0-399-25499-4 Subj: Animals. Birds – eagles. Desert. Folk & fairy tales. Foreign lands – Africa. Homes, houses.

The three snow bears ill. by author. Penguin, 2007. ISBN 978-0-399-24792-7 Subj: Animals – polar bears. Folk & fairy tales. Foreign lands – Arctic. Seasons – winter. Weather – snow.

The trouble with trolls ill. by author. Putnam, 1992. ISBN 978-0-399-22336-5 Subj: Animals – dogs. Character traits – cleverness. Clothing. Mythical creatures – trolls.

The turnip ill. by author. Putnam, 2015. ISBN 978-039917070-6 Subj: Animals. Character traits – cooperation. Cumulative tales. Farms. Folk & fairy tales. Foreign lands – Russia. Plants. Problem solving.

Who's that knocking on Christmas eve? ill. by author. Putnam, 2002. ISBN 978-0-399-23873-4 Subj: Foreign lands – Norway. Holidays – Christmas. Mythical creatures – trolls.

The wild Christmas reindeer ill. by author. Putnam, 1990. ISBN 978-0-399-22192-7   Subj: Animals – reindeer. Holidays – Christmas. Santa Claus.

Brett, Jeannie. *Wild about bears* ill. by author. Charlesbridge, 2014. ISBN 978-158089418-0 Subj: Animals – bears.

Brett, Jessica. *Animals on the go* ill. by Richard Cowdrey. Harcourt, 2000. ISBN 978-0-15-202584-7 Subj: Animals.

Brewer, Dan. *Silver seeds* (Paolilli, Paul)

Brewer, Paul. *Lincoln tells a joke: how laughter saved the president (and the country)* (Krull, Kathleen)

Breznak, Irene. *Sneezy Louise* ill. by Janet Pedersen. Random House, 2009. ISBN 978-0-375-85169-8 Subj: Behavior – bad day, bad mood. Etiquette. Illness – cold (disease).

Brian, Janeen. *Where does Thursday go?* ill. by Stephen Michael King. Clarion, 2001. ISBN 978-0-618-21264-4 Subj: Animals – bears. Birds. Days of the week, months of the year.

Briant, Ed. *A day at the beach* ill. by author. HarperCollins, 2005. ISBN 978-0-06-079982-3 Subj: Animals – pandas. Family life – fathers. Sea & seashore – beaches.

Seven stories ill. by author. Macmillan, 2005. ISBN 978-1-59643-056-3 Subj: Books, reading. Folk & fairy tales.

Bridge, Chris. *Andrew's story: a book about a boy who beat cancer* photos by author. Lerner, 2002. ISBN 978-0-8225-2587-5 Subj: Health & fitness. Illness – cancer.

Bridges, Margaret Park. *Am I big or little?* ill. by Tracy Dockray. SeaStar, 2000. ISBN 978-1-58717-020-1 Subj: Concepts – size. Family life – mothers.

Edna elephant ill. by Janie Bynum. Candlewick, 2002. ISBN 978-0-7636-1555-0 Subj: Activities. Animals – elephants.

I love the rain ill. by Christine Davenier. Chronicle, 2005. ISBN 978-1-58717-208-3 Subj: Weather – rain.

Bridges, Shirin Yim. *Mary Wrightly, so politely* ill. by Maria Monescillo. Harcourt, 2013. ISBN 978-0-547-34248-1 Subj: Behavior – unnoticed, unseen. Character traits – assertiveness. Etiquette. Family life. Gifts.

Ruby's wish ill. by Sophie Blackall. Chronicle, 2002. ISBN 978-0-8118-3490-2 Subj: Foreign lands – China. Gender roles. School.

The Umbrella Queen ill. by Taeeun Yoo. Greenwillow, 2008. ISBN 978-0-06-075040-4 Subj: Activities – painting. Character traits – individuality. Foreign lands – Thailand. Umbrellas.

Bridwell, Norman. *Clifford celebrates Hanukkah* ill. by author. Scholastic, 2015. ISBN 978-054582334-0 Subj: Animals – dogs. Holidays – Hanukkah.

Clifford counts bubbles ill. by author. Scholastic, 1992. ISBN 978-0-590-45872-6 Subj: Animals – dogs. Bubbles. Counting, numbers.

Clifford goes to Hollywood ill. by author. Scholastic, 1981. ISBN 978-0-606-03090-8 Subj: Animals – dogs. Character traits – loyalty.

Clifford the champion ill. by author. Scholastic, 2009. ISBN 978-0-545-10146-2 Subj: Animals – dogs. Contests.

Clifford's ABC ill. by author. Scholastic, 1984. ISBN 978-0-590-48694-1 Subj: ABC books. Animals – dogs.

Clifford's good deeds ill. by author. Four Winds, 1975. ISBN 978-0-590-07439-1 Subj: Animals – dogs. Automobiles. Behavior – mistakes. Careers – firefighters. Character traits – helpfulness.

Clifford's Halloween ill. by author. Four Winds, 1967. ISBN 978-0-590-66159-1 Subj: Animals – dogs. Holidays – Halloween.

Clifford's neighborhood ill. by Carolyn Bracken and Ken Edwards. Scholastic, 2002. ISBN 978-0-439-33242-2 Subj: Animals – dogs. Format, unusual – toy & movable books. Rhyming text.

Glow-in-the-dark Halloween ill. by Thompson Bros. Scholastic, 2001. ISBN 978-0-439-30566-2 Subj: Animals – dogs. Format, unusual. Holidays – Halloween.

The witch grows up ill. by author. Scholastic, 1980. ISBN 978-0-590-30045-2 Subj: Humorous stories. Magic. Witches.

The witch next door ill. by author. Four Winds, 1966. ISBN 978-0-590-40433-4 Subj: Witches.

Briere-Haquet, Alice. *Zebedee's balloon* ill. by Olivier Philipponneau. Auzou, 2011. ISBN 978-2-733819-42-5 Subj: Behavior – lost & found possessions. Rhyming text. Toys – balloons.

One very big bear ill. by Olivier Philipponneau. Abrams/Appleseed, 2016. ISBN 978-141972117-5 Subj: Animals. Animals – polar bears. Concepts – size. Counting, numbers.

Briggs, John. *Leaping lemmings!* ill. by Nicola Slater. Sterling, 2016. ISBN 978-145491819-6 Subj: Animals – lemmings. Character traits – being different. Character traits – individuality.

Briggs, Kelly Paul. *Lighthouse lullaby* ill. by author. Down East, 2000. ISBN 978-0-89272-486-4 Subj: Bedtime. Lighthouses. Rhyming text.

Briggs, Raymond. *The adventures of Bert* (Ahlberg, Allan)

A bit more Bert (Ahlberg, Allan)

Father Christmas ill. by author. Random House, 1997. ISBN 978-0-679-88776-8 Subj: Holidays – Christmas. Santa Claus. Wordless.

Jim and the beanstalk ill. by author. Coward, 1970. ISBN 978-0-698-11577-4 Subj: Folk & fairy tales. Giants. Humorous stories. Old age.

The puddleman ill. by author. Red Fox, 2006. ISBN 978-0-09-945642-1 Subj: Activities – walking. Family life – grandfathers. Magic.

The snowman ill. by author. Random House, 1978. ISBN 978-0-394-93973-5 Subj: Friendship. Snowmen. Wordless.

Bright, Paul. *The bears in the bed and the great big storm* ill. by Jane Chapman. Good Books, 2008. ISBN 978-1-56148-636-6 Subj: Animals – bears. Bedtime. Emotions – fear. Weather – storms.

Grumpy Badger's Christmas ill. by Jane Chapman. Good Books, 2009. ISBN 978-1-56148-673-1 Subj: Animals – badgers. Hibernation. Holidays – Christmas.

Quiet! ill. by Guy Parker-Rees. Scholastic, 2003. ISBN 978-0-439-54512-9 Subj: Animals. Animals – lions. Jungle. Noise, sounds.

There's a bison bouncing on the bed! ill. by Chris Chatterton. Tiger Tales, 2016. ISBN 978-168010006-8 Subj: Bedtime. Behavior – misbehavior. Furniture – beds.

Bright, Rachel. *The koala who could* ill. by Jim Field. Scholastic, 2017. ISBN 978-133813908-2 Subj: Animals – koalas. Emotions – fear. Rhyming text. Self-concept.

The lion inside ill. by Jim Field. Scholastic, 2016. ISBN 978-054587350-5 Subj: Animals – lions. Animals – mice. Character traits – smallness. Friendship. Rhyming text.

Love Monster ill. by author. Farrar, 2013. ISBN 978-0-374-34646-1 Subj: Emotions – love. Monsters.

Love Monster and the last chocolate ill. by author. Farrar, 2015. ISBN 978-037434690-4 Subj: Behavior – sharing. Food. Friendship. Monsters.

Love Monster and the perfect present ill. by author. Farrar, 2014. ISBN 978-037434648-5 Subj: Activities – making things. Friendship. Gifts. Monsters.

Love Monster and the scary something ill. by author. Farrar, 2016. ISBN 978-037434691-1 Subj: Bedtime. Emotions – fear. Monsters.

Side by side ill. by Debi Gliori. Scholastic, 2015. ISBN 978-054581326-6 Subj: Animals – mice. Animals – voles. Friendship. Rhyming text.

Bright, Robert. *Georgie* ill. by author. Doubleday, 1944. ISBN 978-0-385-07307-3 Subj: Family life. Farms. Ghosts.

Georgie's Christmas carol ill. by author. Doubleday, 1975. ISBN 978-0-385-02410-5 Subj: Ghosts. Holidays – Christmas.

Georgie's Halloween ill. by author. Doubleday, 1958. Subj: Ghosts. Holidays – Halloween.

Brighton, Catherine. *Galileo's treasure box* ill. by author. Walker, 2001. ISBN 978-0-8027-8768-2 Subj: Science.

Brill, Calista. *Little Wing learns to fly* ill. by Jennifer A. Bell. HarperCollins, 2016. ISBN 978-006236033-5 Subj: Activities – flying. Behavior – lost. Dragons. Family life – mothers.

Tugboat Bill and the river rescue ill. by Tad Carpenter. HarperCollins, 2017. ISBN 978-006236618-4 Subj: Behavior – bullying, teasing. Boats, ships. Character traits – bravery.

Brill, Marlene Targ. *Bronco Charlie and the Pony Express* ill. by Craig Orback. Carolrhoda, 2004. ISBN 978-1-57505-587-9 Subj: Animals – horses, ponies. Careers – postal workers. U.S. history.

Margaret Knight, girl inventor ill. by Joanne Friar. Millbrook, 2001. ISBN 978-0-7613-1756-2 Subj: Activities – weaving. Careers – inventors. Children as inventors. Safety. U.S. history.

Brillhart, Julie. *Molly rides the school bus* ill. by author. Albert Whitman, 2002. ISBN 978-0-8075-5210-0 Subj: Buses. School – first day.

Brimner, Larry Dane. *The big, beautiful, brown box* ill. by Christine Tripp. Children's Press, 2001. ISBN 978-0-516-22160-1 Subj: Activities – playing. Character traits – cooperation.

Cat on wheels ill. by Mary Peterson. Boyds Mills, 2000. ISBN 978-1-56397-747-3 Subj: Animals – cats. Behavior – carelessness. Imagination. Sports – skateboarding.

The littlest wolf ill. by José Aruego and Ariane Dewey. HarperCollins, 2002. ISBN 978-0-06-029040-5 Subj: Animals – wolves. Behavior – growing up.

Trick or treat, Old Armadillo ill. by Dominic Catalano. Boyds Mills, 2010. ISBN 978-1-59078-758-8 Subj: Animals – armadillos. Foreign languages. Holidays – Halloween.

Brion, David. *Space vehicles* (Rockwell, Anne)

Brisson, Pat. *Before we eat: from farm to table* ill. by Mary Azarian. Tilbury, 2014. ISBN 978-088448352-6 Subj: Character traits – helpfulness. Food. Rhyming text.

Hobbledy-clop ill. by Maxie Chambliss. Boyds Mills, 2003. ISBN 978-1-56397-888-3 Subj: Animals. Cumulative tales. Family life – grandmothers. Toys.

I remember Miss Perry ill. by Stéphane Jorisch. Penguin, 2006. ISBN 978-0-8037-2981-0 Subj: Careers – teachers. Death. Emotions – grief. School.

Melissa Parkington's beautiful, beautiful hair ill. by Suzanne Bloom. Boyds Mills, 2006. ISBN 978-1-59078-409-9 Subj: Character traits – appearance. Character traits – generosity. Hair.

Sometimes we were brave ill. by France Brassard. Boyds Mills, 2010. ISBN 978-1-59078-586-7 Subj: Careers – military. Emotions. Family life. Family life – mothers.

Star blanket ill. by Erica Magnus. Boyds Mills, 2003. ISBN 978-1-56397-889-0 Subj: Bedtime. Family life – fathers. Memories, memory.

Britt, Chris. *The most perfect snowman* ill. by author. HarperCollins/Balzer+Bray, 2016. ISBN 978-006237704-3 Subj: Character traits – appearance. Character traits – kindness to animals. Emotions – envy, jealousy. Snowmen.

Britt, Paige. *Why am I me?* ill. by Sean Qualls and Selina Alko. Scholastic, 2017. ISBN 978-133805314-2 Subj: Character traits – individuality. Character traits – questioning. Self-concept.

Broach, Elise. *Gumption!* ill. by Richard Egielski. Simon & Schuster, 2010. ISBN 978-1-4169-1628-4 Subj: Animals. Family life – aunts, uncles. Jungle.

Wet dog! ill. by David Catrow. Penguin, 2005. ISBN 978-0-8037-2809-7 Subj: Animals – dogs. Seasons – summer. Weddings.

What the no-good baby is good for ill. by Abby Carter. Penguin, 2005. ISBN 978-0-399-23877-2 Subj: Babies, toddlers. Family life – brothers & sisters. Family life – new sibling. Sibling rivalry.

When dinosaurs came with everything ill. by David Small. Simon & Schuster, 2007. ISBN 978-0-689-86922-8 Subj: Dinosaurs. Humorous stories.

Brockenbrough, Martha. *Back to school with Bigfoot* (Berger, Samantha)

The Dinosaur Tooth Fairy ill. by Israel Sanchez. Scholastic, 2013. ISBN 978-0-545-24466-4 Subj: Dinosaurs. Fairies. Teeth.

Brocket, Jane. *Circles, stars, and squares: looking for shapes* photos by author. Millbrook, 2012. ISBN 978-0-7613-4611-1 Subj: Concepts – shape.

Cold, crunchy, colorful: using our senses ill. with photos. Lerner/Millbrook, 2014. ISBN 978-146770233-1 Subj: Senses.

Ruby, violet, lime: looking for color photos by author. Millbrook, 2011. ISBN 978-0-7613-4612-8 Subj: Concepts – color. Language.

Spotty, stripy, swirly: what are patterns? ill. by author. Millbrook, 2012. ISBN 978-0-7613-4613-5 Subj: Concepts – patterns.

Brokamp, Elizabeth. *The picky little witch* ill. by Marsha Riti. Pelican, 2011. ISBN 978-1-58980-882-9 Subj: Food. Holidays – Halloween. Witches.

Brokering, Herbert F. *Earth and all stars: hymns and songs for young and old* ill. by author. Augsburg Fortress, 2003. ISBN 978-0-8006-5929-5 Subj: Music. Religion. Songs.

Bromley, Anne C. *The lunch thief* ill. by Robert Casilla. Tilbury House, 2010. ISBN 978-0-88448-311-3 Subj: Behavior – stealing. Character traits – kindness. Homeless. School.

Bromley, Nick. *Open very carefully: a book with bite* ill. by Nicola O'Byrne. Candlewick, 2013. ISBN 978-0-7636-6163-2 Subj: Birds – ducks. Books, reading. Folk & fairy tales. Reptiles – alligators, crocodiles.

Bronson, Linda. *The circus alphabet* ill. by author. Henry Holt, 2001. ISBN 978-0-8050-6294-6 Subj: ABC books. Circus. Rhyming text.

Sleigh bells and snowflakes ill. by compiler. Henry Holt, 2002. ISBN 978-0-8050-6755-2 Subj: Holidays – Christmas. Poetry.

Brooks, Alan. *Frogs jump* ill. by Steven Kellogg. Scholastic, 1996. ISBN 978-0-590-45528-2 Subj: Animals. Counting, numbers.

Brooks, Erik. *Polar opposites* ill. by author. Marshall Cavendish, 2010. ISBN 978-0-7614-5685-8 Subj: Animals – polar bears. Birds – penguins. Character traits – individuality. Concepts – opposites. Foreign lands – Antarctic. Foreign lands – Arctic.

The practically perfect pajamas ill. by author. Winslow, 2000. ISBN 978-1-890817-22-0 Subj: Animals – polar bears. Behavior – bullying, teasing. Clothing – pajamas.

Slow days, fast friends ill. by author. Albert Whitman, 2005. ISBN 978-0-8075-7437-9 Subj: Animals. Friendship.

Brooks, Gwendolyn. *Bronzeville boys and girls* ill. by Faith Ringgold. HarperCollins, 2007. ISBN 978-0-06-029505-9 Subj: Ethnic groups in the U.S. – African Americans. Poetry.

Brooks, Jeremy. *Let there be peace: prayers from around the world* ill. by Jude Daly. Frances Lincoln, 2009. ISBN 978-1-84507-530-9 Subj: Character traits – cooperation. Religion. World.

Brooks, Nigel. *Country mouse cottage: how we lived one hundred years ago* by Nigel Brooks and Abigail Homer; ill. by authors. Walker, 2000. ISBN 978-0-8027-8752-1 Subj: Animals – mice. Country. Foreign lands – England.

Town mouse house: how we lived one hundred years ago by Nigel Brooks and Abigail Homer; ill. by authors. Walker, 2000. ISBN 978-0-8027-8732-3 Subj: Animals – mice. Cities, towns. Foreign lands – England.

Brooks, Ron. *Fox* (Wild, Margaret)

Brosgol, Vera. *Leave me alone!* ill. by author. Roaring Brook, 2016. ISBN 978-162672441-9 Subj: Activities – knitting. Behavior – solitude. Caldecott award honor books. Family life – grandmothers.

The brothers gruesome ill. by Drahos Zak. Houghton, 2000. ISBN 978-0-618-00515-4 Subj: Behavior – greed. Monsters. Rhyming text.

Brown, Alan James. *Hoot and Holler* ill. by Rimantas Rolia. Knopf, 2001. ISBN 978-0-375-91417-1 Subj: Birds – owls. Emotions. Friendship. Weather – storms.

Love-a-Duck ill. by Francesca Chessa. Holiday House, 2010. ISBN 978-0-8234-2263-0 Subj: Activities – bathing. Behavior – lost & found possessions. Birds – ducks. Toys.

Brown, Alison. *Eddie and Dog* ill. by author. Capstone, 2014. ISBN 978-162370114-7 Subj: Animals – dogs. Friendship.

Brown, Calef. *Boy wonders* ill. by author. Simon & Schuster, 2011. ISBN 978-1-4169-7877-0 Subj: Character traits – questioning. Rhyming text.

Pirateria: the wonderful plunderful pirate emporium ill. by author. Atheneum, 2012. ISBN 978-1-4169-7878-7 Subj: Pirates. Rhyming text. Stores.

Tippintown ill. by author. Houghton, 2003. ISBN 978-0-618-14972-8 Subj: Imagination. Rhyming text.

Brown, Don. *Bright path: young Jim Thorpe* ill. by author. Macmillan, 2006. ISBN 978-1-59643-041-9 Subj: Indians of North America. Sports.

Henry and the cannons: an extraordinary true story of the American Revolution ill. by author. Roaring Brook, 2013. ISBN 978-1-59643-266-6 Subj: U.S. history. War.

Mack made movies ill. by author. Roaring Brook, 2003. ISBN 978-0-7613-2504-8 Subj: Careers – motion picture producers. Theater.

Odd boy out: young Albert Einstein ill. by author. Houghton, 2004. ISBN 978-0-618-49298-5 Subj: Behavior – misunderstanding. Careers – scientists. Character traits – individuality.

One giant leap: the story of Neil Armstrong ill. by author. Houghton, 1998. ISBN 978-0-395-88401-0 Subj: Careers – astronauts. U.S. history.

Rare treasure: Mary Anning and her remarkable discoveries ill. by author. Houghton, 1999. ISBN 978-0-395-92286-6 Subj: Careers – paleontologists. Foreign lands – England. Fossils. Gender roles. Science.

Ruth Law thrills a nation ill. by author. Ticknor & Fields, 1993. ISBN 978-0-395-66404-9 Subj: Airplanes, airports. Careers – airplane pilots. Gender roles.

Teedie: the story of young Teddy Roosevelt ill. by author. Houghton, 2009. ISBN 978-0-618-17999-2 Subj: Character traits – perseverance. U.S. history.

Uncommon traveler: Mary Kingsley in Africa ill. by author. Houghton, 2000. ISBN 978-0-618-00273-3 Subj: Careers – explorers. Foreign lands – Africa. Foreign lands – England.

A voice from the wilderness: the story of Anna Howard ill. by author. Houghton, 2001. ISBN 978-0-618-08362-6 Subj: U.S. history.

A wizard from the start: the incredible boyhood and amazing inventions of Thomas Edison ill. by author. Harcourt, 2010. ISBN 978-0-547-19487-5 Subj: Careers – inventors. U.S. history.

Brown, Heather. *Chomp!* ill. by author. Accord, 2012. ISBN 978-1-44941016-2 Subj: Anatomy – mouths. Animals. Format, unusual – toy & movable books. Teeth.

Brown, James. *Farm* ill. by author. Candlewick, 2013. ISBN 978-0-7636-5931-8 Subj: Animals. Farms. Format, unusual – board books.

Brown, Jeff. *Flat Stanley* ill. by Scott Nash. HarperCollins, 2006. ISBN 978-0-06-112904-9 Subj: Character traits – appearance. Family life. Humorous stories. Problem solving.

Flat Stanley ill. by Tomi Ungerer. HarperCollins, 1961. ISBN 978-0-06-020681-9 Subj: Character traits – appearance. Family life. Humorous stories. Problem solving.

Brown, Jo. *Hoppity skip Little Chick* ill. by author. Tiger Tales, 2005. ISBN 978-1-58925-045-1 Subj: Activities – playing. Birds – chickens, roosters.

Where's my mommy? ill. by author. Tiger Tales, 2002. ISBN 978-1-58295-019-2 Subj: Animals. Birds – chickens, roosters. Family life – mothers. Reptiles – alligators, crocodiles.

Brown, Ken. *The scarecrow's hat* ill. by author. Peachtree, 2001. ISBN 978-1-56145-240-8 Subj: Birds – chickens, roosters. Books, reading. Clothing – hats. Scarecrows.

What's the time, Grandma Wolf? ill. by author. Peachtree, 2001. ISBN 978-1-56145-250-7 Subj: Animals. Animals – wolves. Family life – grandmothers. Prejudice. Rhyming text. Time.

Brown, Kerry. *Tupag the dreamer* ill. by Linda Saport. Marshall Cavendish, 2001. ISBN 978-0-7614-5076-4 Subj: Creation. Eskimos. Foreign lands – Arctic. Seasons.

Brown, Laurie Krasny. *The bionic bunny show* (Brown, Marc)

Dinosaurs alive and well by Laurie Krasny Brown and Marc Brown; ill. by authors. Little, 1990. ISBN 978-0-316-10998-7 Subj: Dinosaurs. Health & fitness. Prehistory.

Dinosaurs divorce by Laurie Krasny Brown and Marc Brown ill. by Marc Brown. Atlantic Monthly, 1986. ISBN 978-0-87113-089-1 Subj: Dinosaurs. Divorce. Prehistory.

Dinosaurs to the rescue by Laurie Krasny Brown and Marc Brown ill. by Marc Brown. Little, 1992. ISBN 978-0-316-11087-7 Subj: Dinosaurs. Ecology. Prehistory.

Dinosaurs travel by Laurie Krasny Brown and Marc Brown ill. by Marc Brown. Little, 1988. ISBN 978-0-316-11076-1 Subj: Activities – traveling. Dinosaurs. Prehistory.

How to be a friend: a guide to making friends and keeping them by Laurie Krasny Brown and Marc Brown ill. by Marc Brown. Little, 1998. ISBN 978-0-316-10913-0 Subj: Dinosaurs. Friendship.

Visiting the art museum by Laurie Krasny Brown and Marc Brown; ill. by authors. Dutton, 1986. ISBN 978-0-525-44233-2 Subj: Art. Museums.

What's the big secret? talking about sex with girls and boys by Laurie Krasny Brown and Marc Brown ill. by Marc Brown. Little, 1997. ISBN 978-0-316-10915-4 Subj: Anatomy. Family life. Sex instruction.

When dinosaurs die: a guide to understanding death by Laurie Krasny Brown and Marc Brown ill. by Marc Brown. Little, 1996. ISBN 978-0-316-10917-8 Subj: Death. Dinosaurs. Emotions. Family life. Prehistory.

Brown, Lisa. *The airport book* ill. by author. Roaring Brook/Neal Porter, 2016. ISBN 978-162672091-6 Subj: Activities – traveling. Airplanes, airports.

How to be ill. by author. HarperCollins, 2006. ISBN 978-0-06-054636-6 Subj: Animals. Behavior – imitation. Imagination. Self-concept.

Vampire boy's good night ill. by author. HarperCollins, 2010. ISBN 978-0-06-114011-2 Subj: Holidays – Halloween. Monsters. Witches.

Brown, Marc. *Arthur and the true Francine* ill. by author. Little, 1996. ISBN 978-0-316-11136-2 Subj: Animals. Behavior – lying. School.

Arthur babysits ill. by author. Little, 1992. ISBN 978-0-316-11293-2 Subj: Activities – babysitting. Animals – aardvarks. Multiple births – twins.

Arthur goes to camp ill. by author. Little, 1982. ISBN 978-0-316-11218-5 Subj: Animals. Camps, camping.

Arthur goes to school ill. by author. Random House, 1995. ISBN 978-0-679-86734-0 Subj: Animals – aardvarks. Format, unusual – board books. Format, unusual – toy & movable books. School.

Arthur lost and found ill. by author. Little, 1998. ISBN 978-0-316-10912-3 Subj: Animals – aardvarks. Behavior – lost. Buses. Careers – bus drivers.

Arthur meets the president ill. by author. Little, 1991. ISBN 978-0-316-11265-9 Subj: Activities – traveling. Animals – aardvarks. Family life – sisters.

Arthur tricks the tooth fairy ill. by author. Random House, 1997. ISBN 978-0-679-98464-1 Subj: Animals – aardvarks. Behavior – trickery. Fairies. Family life – brothers & sisters.

Arthur turns green ill. by author. Little, Brown, 2011. ISBN 978-0-316-12924-4 Subj: Animals – aardvarks. Ecology. Family life – brothers & sisters. School.

Arthur writes a story ill. by author. Little, 1996. ISBN 978-0-316-10916-1 Subj: Activities – writing. Animals – aardvarks.

Arthur's animal adventure ill. by author. Random House, 2002. ISBN 978-0-375-80699-5 Subj: ABC books. Animals. Animals – aardvarks. Foreign lands – Australia. Format, unusual – board books.

Arthur's April fool ill. by author. Little, 1983. ISBN 978-0-316-11196-6 Subj: Animals. Holidays – April Fools' Day.

Arthur's baby ill. by author. Little, 1987. ISBN 978-0-316-11123-2 Subj: Animals – aardvarks. Babies, toddlers. Family life – new sibling.

Arthur's birthday ill. by author. Little, 1989. ISBN 978-0-316-11073-0 Subj: Animals – aardvarks. Birthdays. Friendship. Parties.

Arthur's chicken pox ill. by author. Little, 1994. ISBN 978-0-316-11384-7 Subj: Animals – aardvarks. Circus. Family life. Illness – chicken pox.

Arthur's Christmas ill. by author. Little, 1984. ISBN 978-0-316-11180-5 Subj: Animals. Gifts. Holidays – Christmas. Santa Claus.

Arthur's computer disaster ill. by author. Little, 1997. ISBN 978-0-316-11016-7 Subj: Animals – aardvarks. Behavior – misbehavior. Computers.

Arthur's eyes ill. by author. Little, 1979. ISBN 978-0-316-11063-1   Subj: Animals. Glasses. Senses – sight.

Arthur's family vacation ill. by author. Little, 1993. ISBN 978-0-316-11312-0   Subj: Activities – vacationing. Animals – aardvarks. Family life.

Arthur's first sleepover ill. by author. Little, 1994. ISBN 978-0-316-11445-5   Subj: Animals – aardvarks. Behavior – misbehavior. Camps, camping. Family life – brothers & sisters. Monsters. Sleepovers.

Arthur's Halloween ill. by author. Little, 1982. ISBN 978-0-316-11116-4   Subj: Animals. Holidays – Halloween.

Arthur's neighborhood ill. by author. Random House, 1996. ISBN 978-0-679-86737-1   Subj: Animals – aardvarks. Communities, neighborhoods. Format, unusual – toy & movable books.

Arthur's new puppy ill. by author. Little, 1993. ISBN 978-0-316-11355-7   Subj: Animals – aardvarks. Animals – dogs. Pets.

Arthur's nose ill. by author. Little, 1976. ISBN 978-0-316-11884-2   Subj: Anatomy – noses. Animals – aardvarks.

Arthur's perfect Christmas ill. by author. Little, 2000. ISBN 978-0-316-11968-9   Subj: Animals. Animals – aardvarks. Holidays – Christmas.

Arthur's pet business ill. by author. Little, 1990. ISBN 978-0-316-11262-8   Subj: Animals – aardvarks. Animals – dogs. Pets.

Arthur's really helpful word book ill. by author. Random House, 1997. ISBN 978-0-679-98735-2   Subj: Animals – aardvarks. Books, reading. Language.

Arthur's spookiest Halloween ill. by author. Random House, 2003. ISBN 978-0-375-81004-6   Subj: Animals – aardvarks. Format, unusual – toy & movable books. Holidays – Halloween.

Arthur's teacher moves in ill. by author. Little, 2000. ISBN 978-0-316-11979-5   Subj: Animals. Animals – aardvarks. Careers – teachers. School.

Arthur's teacher trouble ill. by author. Little, 1986. ISBN 978-0-87113-091-4   Subj: Animals. School.

Arthur's Thanksgiving ill. by author. Little, 1983. ISBN 978-0-316-11060-0   Subj: Animals. Holidays – Thanksgiving. Theater.

Arthur's tooth ill. by author. Little, 1985. ISBN 978-0-87113-006-8   Subj: Animals. Teeth.

Arthur's TV trouble ill. by author. Little, 1995. ISBN 978-0-316-10919-2   Subj: Animals – aardvarks. Money. Pets.

Arthur's underwear ill. by author. Little, 1999. ISBN 978-0-316-11012-9   Subj: Animals. Animals – aardvarks. Behavior – worrying. Clothing. Emotions – embarrassment. School.

Arthur's Valentine ill. by author. Little, 1980. ISBN 978-0-316-11062-4   Subj: Animals. Holidays – Valentine's Day. School.

The bionic bunny show by Marc Brown and Laurie Krasny Brown; ill. by Marc Brown. Little, 1984. ISBN 978-0-316-11120-1   Subj: Animals. Animals – rabbits. Television.

D. W. all wet ill. by author. Little, 1988. ISBN 978-0-316-11077-8   Subj: Animals – anteaters. Sea & seashore. Sibling rivalry.

D. W. flips! ill. by author. Little, 1987. ISBN 978-0-316-11239-0   Subj: Animals – anteaters. Sports – gymnastics.

D. W., go to your room! ill. by author. Little, 1999. ISBN 978-0-316-10905-5   Subj: Animals – aardvarks. Character traits – meanness. Family life – sisters.

D. W. rides again! ill. by author. Little, 1998. ISBN 978-0-316-11128-7   Subj: Animals – aardvarks. Family life – brothers & sisters. Sports – bicycling.

D. W., the picky eater ill. by author. Little, 1995. ISBN 978-0-316-10957-4   Subj: Animals – aardvarks. Family life. Food.

D. W. thinks big ill. by author. Joy Street, 1993. ISBN 978-031611305-2   Subj: Accidents. Animals – aardvarks. Family life – brothers & sisters. Weddings.

D. W.'s library card ill. by author. Little, 2001. ISBN 978-0-316-11013-6   Subj: Animals – aardvarks. Books, reading. Family life – brothers & sisters.

D. W.'s lost blankie ill. by author. Little, 1998. ISBN 978-0-316-10914-7   Subj: Animals – aardvarks. Behavior – lost & found possessions. Family life.

Dinosaurs alive and well (Brown, Laurie Krasny)

Dinosaurs, beware! a safety guide by Marc Brown and Stephen Krensky; ill. by authors. Little, 1982. ISBN 978-0-316-11228-4   Subj: Dinosaurs. Prehistory. Safety.

Dinosaurs divorce (Brown, Laurie Krasny)

Dinosaurs to the rescue (Brown, Laurie Krasny)

Dinosaurs travel (Brown, Laurie Krasny)

Finger rhymes ill. by author. Dutton, 1980. ISBN 978-0-525-29732-1   Subj: Games. Nursery rhymes. Participation.

Glasses for D. W. ill. by author. Random House, 1995. ISBN 978-0-679-98043-8   Subj: Animals – aardvarks. Family life – brothers & sisters. Glasses.

Hand rhymes ill. by selector. Dutton, 1985. ISBN 978-0-525-44201-1   Subj: Games. Nursery rhymes.

How to be a friend: a guide to making friends and keeping them (Brown, Laurie Krasny)

In New York ill. by author. Knopf, 2014. ISBN 978-037586454-4 Subj: Cities, towns.

Monkey: not ready for bedtime ill. by author. Knopf, 2017. ISBN 978-110193761-7 Subj: Animals – monkeys. Bedtime. Sleep.

Monkey: not ready for kindergarten ill. by author. Knopf, 2015. ISBN 978-055349658-1 Subj: Animals – monkeys. Behavior – worrying. School – first day.

Monkey: not ready for the baby ill. by author. Knopf, 2016. ISBN 978-110193327-5 Subj: Animals – monkeys. Behavior – worrying. Family life – brothers & sisters. Family life – new sibling.

Perfect pigs: an introduction to manners by Marc Brown and Stephen Krensky; ill. by authors. Little, 1983. ISBN 978-0-316-11079-2 Subj: Animals – pigs. Etiquette.

Play rhymes ill. by author. Dutton, 1987. ISBN 978-0-525-44336-0 Subj: Games. Music. Nursery rhymes. Songs.

The true Francine ill. by author. Little, 1987. ISBN 978-0-316-11212-3 Subj: Animals – aardvarks. Behavior. Friendship. School.

Visiting the art museum (Brown, Laurie Krasny)

What's the big secret? talking about sex with girls and boys (Brown, Laurie Krasny)

When dinosaurs die: a guide to understanding death (Brown, Laurie Krasny)

Brown, Marcia, adapt. *Once a mouse . . .* ill. by adapter. Scribners, 1961. ISBN 978-0-684-12662-3 Subj: Animals. Caldecott award books. Character traits – vanity. Concepts – size. Folk & fairy tales. Foreign lands – India. Magic.

Stone soup ill. by author. Scribners, 1947. ISBN 978-0-684-92296-6 Subj: Caldecott award honor books. Careers – military. Character traits – cleverness. Folk & fairy tales. Food. Foreign lands – Russia.

Brown, Margaret Wise. *Another important book* ill. by Chris Raschka. HarperCollins, 1999. ISBN 978-0-06-026283-9 Subj: Behavior – growing up. Rhyming text.

Bunny's noisy book ill. by Lisa McCue. Hyperion, 2000. ISBN 978-0-7868-2428-1 Subj: Animals – rabbits. Careers – seamstresses. Noise, sounds. Quilts.

A child is born ill. by Floyd Cooper. Hyperion, 2000. ISBN 978-0-7868-2564-6 Subj: Holidays – Christmas. Religion – Nativity. Rhyming text.

A child's good morning book ill. by Karen Katz. HarperCollins, 2009. ISBN 978-0-06-128864-7 Subj: Animals. Morning.

Christmas in the barn ill. by Diane Goode. HarperCollins, 2004. ISBN 978-0-06-052635-1 Subj: Farms. Holidays – Christmas. Religion – Nativity. Rhyming text.

The dead bird ill. by Christian Robinson. HarperCollins, 2016. ISBN 978-006028931-7 Subj: Birds. Death. Emotions – grief. Emotions – sadness.

The dirty little boy ill. by Steven Salerno. Winslow, 2001. ISBN 978-1-890817-52-7 Subj: Activities – bathing. Animals. Character traits – cleanliness.

The fathers are coming home ill. by Stephen Savage. Simon & Schuster, 2010. ISBN 978-0-689-83345-8 Subj: Animals. Family life – fathers. Night.

The fierce yellow pumpkin ill. by Richard Egielski. HarperCollins, 2003. ISBN 978-0-06-024481-1 Subj: Behavior – wishing. Holidays – Halloween.

The find it book ill. by Lisa Sheehan. Paragon, 2015. ISBN 978-147237818-7 Subj: Nursery rhymes. Picture puzzles.

The friendly book ill. by Garth Williams. Random House, 2003. ISBN 978-0-307-10643-8 Subj: Animals. Poetry.

Give yourself to the rain ill. by Teri Weidner. Margaret K. McElderry, 2002. ISBN 978-0-689-83344-1 Subj: Poetry.

The golden egg book ill. by Leonard Weisgard. Simon & Schuster, 1947. ISBN 978-0-685-05367-6 Subj: Animals – rabbits. Birds – ducks. Eggs. Holidays – Easter.

The Golden sleepy book ill. by Garth Williams. Random House, 2004. ISBN 978-0-375-92779-9 Subj: Animals. Poetry. Sleep.

Good day, good night ill. by Loren Long. HarperCollins, 2017. ISBN 978-006238310-5 Subj: Animals – rabbits. Bedtime. Day. Rhyming text.

The good little bad little pig ill. by Dan Yaccarino. Hyperion, 2002. ISBN 978-0-7868-2514-1 Subj: Animals – pigs. Pets.

Goodnight moon ill. by Clement Hurd. HarperCollins, 1934. ISBN 978-0-590-73302-1 Subj: Animals – rabbits. Bedtime. Moon.

Goodnight moon ABC: an alphabet book ill. by Clement Hurd. HarperCollins, 2010. ISBN 978-0-06-189484-8 Subj: ABC books. Animals – rabbits. Bedtime. Moon.

Goodnight moon 123: a counting book ill. by Clement Hurd. HarperCollins, 2007. ISBN 978-0-06-112593-5 Subj: Animals – rabbits. Bedtime. Counting, numbers. Moon.

Goodnight songs. illustrated. Sterling, 2014. ISBN 978-145490446-5 Subj: Lullabies. Seasons. Songs.

The little fir tree ill. by Jim LaMarche. HarperCollins, 2005. ISBN 978-0-06-028190-8 Subj: Holidays – Christmas. Trees.

The little island ill. by Leonard Weisgard. Double-day, 1946. Subj: Caldecott award books. Islands. Seasons. Weather.

Love songs of the little bear ill. by Susan Jeffers. Hyperion, 2001. ISBN 978-0-7868-2445-8 Subj: Animals – bears. Poetry. Seasons.

My world ill. by Clement Hurd. HarperCollins, 2002. ISBN 978-0-694-00862-9 Subj: Animals – rabbits. Family life.

My world of color ill. by Loretta Krupinski. Hyperion, 2002. ISBN 978-0-7868-2519-6 Subj: Concepts – color. Rhyming text.

Nibble, nibble ill. by Wendell Minor. HarperCollins, 2007. ISBN 978-0-06-059208-0 Subj: Nature. Poetry.

North, south, east, west ill. by Greg Pizzoli. HarperCollins, 2017. ISBN 978-006026278-5 Subj: Activities – traveling. Birds.

Robin's room ill. by Steve Johnson and Lou Fancher. Hyperion, 2002. ISBN 978-0-7868-2516-5 Subj: Character traits – being different. Family life. Homes, houses.

The runaway bunny ill. by Clement Hurd. HarperCollins, 1972, ©1942. ISBN 978-0-06-020766-3 Subj: Animals – rabbits. Behavior – running away. Family life – mothers. Holidays – Easter.

Sailor boy jig ill. by Dan Andreasen. Margaret K. McElderry, 2002. ISBN 978-0-689-83348-9 Subj: Activities – dancing. Animals – dogs. Concepts. Rhyming text. Sailors.

Sheep don't count sheep ill. by Benrei Huang. Margaret K. McElderry, 2003. ISBN 978-0-689-83346-5 Subj: Animals – sheep. Sleep.

Sleepy ABC ill. by Karen Katz. HarperCollins, 2010. ISBN 978-0-06-128863-0 Subj: ABC books. Bedtime. Rhyming text. Sleep.

Sleepy ABC ill. by Esphyr Slobodkina. HarperCollins, 1994. ISBN 978-0-06-024285-5 Subj: ABC books. Bedtime. Rhyming text. Sleep.

Sneakers, the seaside cat ill. by Anne Mortimer. HarperCollins, 2003. ISBN 978-0-06-028693-4 Subj: Animals – cats. Behavior – misbehavior. Sea & seashore.

Wheel on the chimney by Margaret Wise Brown and Tibor Gergely ill. by Tibor Gergely. Lippincott, 1954. ISBN 978-0-397-30296-3 Subj: Birds – storks. Caldecott award honor books. Character traits – luck. Foreign lands – Hungary.

Where have you been? ill. by Leo and Diane Dillon. HarperCollins, 2004. ISBN 978-0-06-028379-7 Subj: Animals. Rhyming text.

Brown, Monica. *Chavela and the magic bubble* ill. by Magaly Morales. Clarion, 2010. ISBN 978-0-547-24197-5 Subj: Ethnic groups in the U.S. – Mexican Americans. Family life – grandmothers. Magic.

Maya's blanket ill. by David Diaz. Lee & Low, 2015. ISBN 978-089239292-6 Subj: Activities – sewing. Behavior – resourcefulness. Books, reading. Foreign languages.

My name is Gabito / Me llamo Gabito: the life of Gabriel García Márquez / la vida de Gabriel García Márquez ill. by Raul Colón. Northland, 2007. ISBN 978-0-87358-934-5 Subj: Activities – writing. Careers – writers. Foreign lands – Colombia. Foreign languages.

Pelé, king of soccer / Pelé, el rey del fútbol ill. by Rudy Gutierrez. HarperCollins, 2009. ISBN 978-0-06-122779-0 Subj: Foreign lands – Brazil. Foreign languages. Sports – soccer.

Side by side / Lado a lado: the story of Dolores Huerta and Cesar Chavez / la historia de Dolores Huerta y Cesar Chavez ill. by Joe Cepeda. HarperCollins, 2010. ISBN 978-0-06-122781-3 Subj: Ethnic groups in the U.S. – Mexican Americans. Foreign languages. U.S. history. Violence, nonviolence.

Waiting for the Biblioburro ill. by John Parra. Tricycle, 2011. ISBN 978-1-58246-353-7 Subj: Animals – donkeys. Books, reading. Foreign lands – Colombia. Libraries.

Brown, Nacio Herb. *Singing in the rain* (Freed, Arthur)

Brown, Peter. *Children make terrible pets* ill. by author. Little, Brown, 2010. ISBN 978-0-316-01548-6 Subj: Animals – bears. Humorous stories. Pets.

Chowder ill. by author. Little, Brown, 2006. ISBN 978-0-316-01180-8 Subj: Animals – dogs. Character traits – being different.

The curious garden ill. by author. Little, Brown, 2009. ISBN 978-0-316-01547-9 Subj: Cities, towns. Ecology. Gardens, gardening.

Mr. Tiger goes wild ill. by author. Little, Brown, 2013. ISBN 978-0-316-20063-9 Subj: Animals – tigers. Behavior – boredom. Character traits – individuality. Self-concept.

My teacher is a monster! (no, I am not) ill. by author. Little, Brown, 2014. ISBN 978-031607029-4 Subj: Behavior – misunderstanding. Careers – teachers. Monsters. School.

You will be my friend! ill. by author. Little, Brown, 2011. ISBN 978-0-316-07030-0 Subj: Animals – bears. Friendship.

Brown, Petra. *When the wind blew* ill. by author. Sleeping Bear, 2017. ISBN 978-158536969-0 Subj: Animals – bears. Homes, houses. Moving. Weather – wind.

Brown, Ruth. *A dark, dark tale* ill. by author. Dial, 1981. ISBN 978-0-8037-1673-5 Subj: Cumulative tales. Foreign lands – England.

Gracie the lighthouse cat ill. by author. Andersen, 2011. ISBN 978-0-7613-7454-1 Subj: Animals – cats. Behavior – lost. Lighthouses.

Holly, the true story of a cat ill. by author. Henry Holt, 2000. ISBN 978-0-8050-6500-8 Subj: Animals – cats. Holidays – Christmas.

Monkey's friends ill. by author. Kane/Miller, 2012. ISBN 978-1-61067-045-6 Subj: Animals. Animals – monkeys. Format, unusual – toy & movable books.

The old tree: an environmental fable ill. by author. Candlewick, 2007. ISBN 978-0-7636-3461-2 Subj: Ecology. Format, unusual – toy & movable books. Trees.

The tale of two mice: a cat-and-mouse tale ill. by author. Candlewick, 2008. ISBN 978-0-7636-4015-6 Subj: Animals – cats. Animals – mice. Format, unusual.

Brown, Stephanie Gwyn. *Bang! Boom! Roar! a busy crew of dinosaurs* (Evans, Nate)

Brown, Susan Taylor. *Oliver's must-do list* ill. by Mary Sullivan. Boyds Mills, 2005. ISBN 978-1-59078-198-2 Subj: Activities – playing. Animals – rhinoceros. Family life – mothers.

Brown, Tameka Fryer. *Around our way on Neighbors' Day* ill. by Charlotte Riley-Webb. Abrams, 2010. ISBN 978-0-8109-8971-9 Subj: Cities, towns. Communities, neighborhoods. Parties. Rhyming text.

My cold plum lemon pie bluesy mood ill. by Shane W. Evans. Viking, 2013. ISBN 978-0-670-01285-5 Subj: Concepts – color. Emotions. Ethnic groups in the U.S. – African Americans. Rhyming text.

Brown, Tami Lewis. *Soar, Elinor!* ill. by François Roca. Farrar, 2010. ISBN 978-0-374-37115-9 Subj: Activities – flying. Careers – airplane pilots. Gender roles. U.S. history.

Brown-Wood, JaNay. *Grandma's tiny house* ill. by Priscilla Burris. Charlesbridge, 20174. ISBN 978-158089712-9 Subj: Counting, numbers. Ethnic groups in the U.S. – African Americans. Family life – grandmothers. Food. Rhyming text.

Imani's moon ill. by Hazel Mitchell. Charlesbridge, 2014. ISBN 978-193413357-6 Subj: Behavior – bullying, teasing. Character traits – persistence. Character traits – smallness. Foreign lands – Africa. Moon. Self-concept.

Browne, Anthony. *Animal fair* ill. by author. Candlewick, 2002. ISBN 978-0-7636-1831-5 Subj: Animals. Animals – monkeys. Fairs, festivals. Format, unusual – toy & movable books.

Gorilla ill. by author. Candlewick, 2002, 1983. ISBN 978-0-7636-1813-1 Subj: Animals – gorillas. Birthdays. Family life – fathers. Imagination. Toys. Zoos.

How do you feel? ill. by author. Candlewick, 2012. ISBN 978-0-7636-5862-5 Subj: Animals – chimpanzees. Emotions.

I like books ill. by author. Knopf, 1989. ISBN 978-0-394-84186-1 Subj: Animals – chimpanzees. Books, reading.

The little Bear book ill. by author. Candlewick, 2014. ISBN 978-076367007-8 Subj: Activities – drawing. Animals – bears.

Little Beauty ill. by author. Candlewick, 2008. ISBN 978-0-7636-3959-4 Subj: Animals – cats. Animals – gorillas. Sign language. Zoos.

Me and you ill. by author. Farrar, 2010. ISBN 978-0-374-34908-0 Subj: Animals – bears. Behavior – lost. Cities, towns. Folk & fairy tales.

My brother ill. by author. Farrar, 2007. ISBN 978-0-374-35120-5 Subj: Family life – brothers & sisters.

My dad ill. by author. DK, 2000. ISBN 978-0-7894-2681-9 Subj: Family life – fathers.

My mom ill. by author. Farrar, 2005. ISBN 978-0-374-35098-7 Subj: Family life – mothers.

One gorilla: a counting book ill. by author. Candlewick, 2013. ISBN 978-0-7636-6352-0 Subj: Animals – chimpanzees. Animals – gorillas. Animals – lemurs. Animals – monkeys. Animals – orangutans. Counting, numbers.

The shape game ill. by author. Farrar, 2003. ISBN 978-0-374-36764-0 Subj: Art. Careers – illustrators. Careers – writers. Foreign lands – Great Britain. Museums.

Silly Billy ill. by author. Candlewick, 2006. ISBN 978-0-7636-3124-6 Subj: Behavior – worrying. Family life – grandmothers. Toys – dolls.

Voices in the park ill. by author. DK, 1998. ISBN 978-0-7894-2522-5 Subj: Animals – dogs. Animals – gorillas. Parks. Seasons.

What if . . . ? ill. by author. Candlewick, 2014. ISBN 978-076367419-9 Subj: Behavior – worrying. Imagination. Parties.

Willy and Hugh ill. by author. Knopf, 1991. ISBN 978-0-679-91446-4 Subj: Animals – chimpanzees. Animals – gorillas. Friendship.

Willy the champ ill. by author. Knopf, 1986. ISBN 978-0-394-97907-6 Subj: Animals – chimpanzees. Animals – gorillas. Behavior – bullying, teasing.

Willy the dreamer ill. by author. Candlewick, 1998. ISBN 978-0-7636-0378-6 Subj: Animals – chimpanzees. Dreams.

Willy the wimp ill. by author. Knopf, 1985. ISBN 978-0-394-97061-5 Subj: Animals – chimpanzees. Animals – gorillas. Self-concept.

Willy the wizard ill. by author. Knopf, 1995. ISBN 978-0-679-97644-8 Subj: Animals – chimpanzees. Clothing – shoes. Sports – soccer.

Willy's pictures ill. by author. Candlewick, 2000. ISBN 978-0-7636-0962-7 Subj: Animals – chimpanzees. Art. Careers – artists.

Willy's stories ill. by author. Candlewick, 2015. ISBN 978-076367761-9 Subj: Animals – chimpanzees. Books, reading. Imagination. Libraries.

Browne, Christopher. *Marlo* ill. by author. HarperCollins/Balzer+Bray, 2017. ISBN 978-006244113-3 Subj: Activities – bathing. Animals – dogs. Imagination. Sea & seashore.

Browne, Eileen. *Handa's hen* ill. by author. Candlewick, 2011. ISBN 978-0-7636-5361-3 Subj: Animals. Birds – chickens, roosters. Counting, numbers. Foreign lands – Kenya.

Browning, Diane. *Signed, Abiah Rose* ill. by author. Tricycle, 2010. ISBN 978-1-58246-311-7 Subj: Careers – artists. Gender roles. U.S. history – frontier & pioneer life.

Browning, Kurt. *T is for tutu: a ballet alphabet* (Rodriguez, Sonia)

Browning, Robert. *The pied piper of Hamelin* adapt. by Mercer Mayer; ill. by adapter. Adapt. of the poem The pied piper of Hamelin by Robert Browning. Macmillan, 1987. ISBN 978-0-02-765361-8 Subj: Animals – rats. Behavior – trickery. Folk & fairy tales. Foreign lands – Germany.

The pied piper of Hamelin retold by Robert Holden; ill. by Drahos Zak. Houghton, 1998. ISBN 978-0-395-89918-2 Subj: Animals – rats. Behavior – trickery. Folk & fairy tales. Foreign lands – Germany. Poetry.

Brownlee, Sophia Grace. *Show time with Sophia Grace and Rosie* by Sophia Grace Brownlee and Rosie McClelland ill. by Shelagh McNicholas. Orchard, 2014. ISBN 978-054563135-8 Subj: Family life – cousins. Theater.

Tea time with Sophia Grace and Rosie by Sophia Grace Brownlee and Rosie McClelland ill. by Shelagh McNicholas. Scholastic, 2013. ISBN 978-0-545-50214-6 Subj: Family life – cousins. Friendship. Parties.

Brownlow, Mike. *The big white book with almost nothing in it* ill. by author. Ragged Bears, 2001. ISBN 978-1-929927-24-1 Subj: Format, unusual – toy & movable books. Rhyming text.

Mickey Moonbeam ill. by author. Bloomsbury, 2006. ISBN 978-1-58234-704-2 Subj: Concepts – size. Pen pals. Space & space ships.

Way out West — with a baby! ill. by author. Ragged Bears, 2000. ISBN 978-1-929927-04-3 Subj: Babies, toddlers. Cowboys, cowgirls. Rhyming text. U.S. history – frontier & pioneer life.

Broyles, Anne. *Priscilla and the hollyhocks* ill. by Anna Alter. Charlesbridge, 2008. ISBN 978-1-57091-675-5 Subj: Ethnic groups in the U.S. – African Americans. Slavery. U.S. history.

Shy Mama's Halloween ill. by Leane Morin. Tilbury, 2000. ISBN 978-0-88448-218-5 Subj: Ethnic groups in the U.S. – Russian Americans. Family life. Holidays – Halloween. Immigrants, immigration.

Bruce, Lisa. *Engines, engines* by Lisa Bruce and Stephen Waterhouse ill. by Stephen Waterhouse. Bloomsbury, 2000. ISBN 978-0-7475-5013-6 Subj: Counting, numbers. Foreign lands – India. Rhyming text.

Fran's flower ill. by Rosalind Beardshaw. HarperCollins, 2000. ISBN 978-0-06-028621-7 Subj: Flowers. Gardens, gardening. Plants.

Fran's friend ill. by Rosalind Beardshaw. Bloomsbury, 2003. ISBN 978-1-58234-777-6 Subj: Animals – dogs. Friendship. Gifts.

Bruchac, James. *How Chipmunk got his stripes: a tale of bragging and teasing* (Bruchac, Joseph)

Rabbit's snow dance: a traditional Iroquois story by James Bruchac and Joseph Bruchac ill. by Jeff Newman. Dial, 2012. ISBN 978-0-8037-3270-4 Subj: Animals – rabbits. Folk & fairy tales – pourquois tales. Indians of North America – Iroquois. Weather – snow.

Bruchac, Joseph. *Buffalo song* ill. by Bill Farnsworth. Lee & Low, 2008. ISBN 978-1-58430-280-3 Subj: Animals – buffaloes. Indians of North America.

The circle of thanks: Native American poems and songs of Thanksgiving ill. by Murv Jacob. BridgeWater, 1996. ISBN 978-0-8167-4012-3 Subj: Folk & fairy tales. Indians of North America. Nature. Poetry.

Crazy horse's vision ill. by S. D. Nelson. Lee & Low, 2000. ISBN 978-1-880000-94-6 Subj: Indians of North America – Lakota (Sioux).

The great ball game: a Muskogee story ill. by Susan L. Roth. Dial, 1994. ISBN 978-0-8037-1540-0 Subj: Animals. Behavior – fighting, arguing. Birds. Folk & fairy tales. Indians of North America – Creek. Indians of North America – Muskogee.

How Chipmunk got his stripes: a tale of bragging and teasing by Joseph Bruchac and James Bruchac ill. by José Aruego and Ariane Dewey. Dial, 2001. ISBN 978-0-8037-2404-4 Subj: Animals – chipmunks. Folk & fairy tales – pourquoi tales. Indians of North America.

Many nations: an alphabet of Native America ill. by Robert F. Goetzl. BridgeWater, 1997. ISBN 978-0-8167-4389-6 Subj: ABC books. Indians of North America.

My father is taller than a tree ill. by Wendy Anderson Halperin. Penguin, 2010. ISBN 978-0-8037-3173-8 Subj: Family life – fathers. Rhyming text.

Rabbit's snow dance: a traditional Iroquois story (Bruchac, James)

Squanto's journey ill. by Greg Shed. Silver Whistle, 2000. ISBN 978-0-15-201817-7 Subj: Holidays – Thanksgiving. Indians of North America – Wampanoag. Pilgrims. U.S. history.

Thirteen moons on turtle's back by Joseph Bruchac and Jonathan London ill. by Thomas Locker. Putnam, 1992. ISBN 978-0-399-22141-5 Subj: Folk & fairy tales. Indians of North America. Poetry. Seasons.

Bruel, Nick. *Bad Kitty* ill. by author. Macmillan, 2005. ISBN 978-1-59643-069-3 Subj: ABC books. Animals – cats. Behavior – misbehavior. Food.

A Bad Kitty Christmas ill. by author. Roaring Brook, 2011. ISBN 978-1-59643-668-8 Subj: Animals – cats. Behavior – misbehavior. Holidays – Christmas. Rhyming text.

Bad Kitty, scaredy-cat ill. by author. Roaring Brook, 2016. ISBN 978-159643978-8 Subj: ABC books. Animals – cats. Emotions – fear. Holidays – Halloween.

Poor puppy ill. by author. Macmillan, 2007. ISBN 978-1-59643-270-3 Subj: ABC books. Animals – cats. Animals – dogs. Counting, numbers.

A wonderful year ill. by author. Roaring Brook, 2015. ISBN 978-159643611-4 Subj: Seasons.

Bruel, Robert O. *Bob and Otto* ill. by Nick Bruel. Macmillan, 2007. ISBN 978-1-59643-203-1 Subj: Animals – worms. Friendship. Insects – butterflies, caterpillars.

Bruins, David. *The call of the cowboy* ill. by Hilary Leung. Kids Can, 2011. ISBN 978-1-55453-748-8 Subj: Animals – bears. Cowboys, cowgirls. Friendship. Noise, sounds.

Brumbeau, Jeff. *Miss Hunnicutt's hat* ill. by Gail de Marcken. Orchard, 2003. ISBN 978-0-439-31895-2 Subj: Character traits – individuality. Clothing – hats.

Brun-Cosme, Nadine. *Big Wolf and Little Wolf* ill. by Olivier Tallec. Enchanted Lion, 2009. ISBN 978-1-59270-084-4 Subj: Animals – wolves. Emotions – loneliness. Friendship.

Big Wolf and Little Wolf, such a beautiful orange! ill. by Olivier Tallec. Enchanted Lion, 2011. ISBN 978-1-59270-106-3 Subj: Animals – wolves. Behavior – worrying. Friendship.

Daddy long legs ill. by Aurélie Guillerey. Kids Can, 2017. ISBN 978-177138362-2 Subj: Behavior – worrying. Family life – fathers. School.

With Dad, it's like that ill. by Magali Le Huche. Albert Whitman, 2016. ISBN 978-080758731-7 Subj: Family life – fathers.

Brunelle, Nicholas. *Snow moon* ill. by author. Penguin, 2005. ISBN 978-0-670-06024-5 Subj: Bedtime. Birds – owls. Night. Seasons – winter. Weather – snow.

Brunetti, Ivan. *Wordplay* ill. by author. TOON, 2017. ISBN 978-194314517-1 Subj: Format, unusual – graphic novels. Language.

Brunhoff, Jean de. *Babar and Father Christmas* ill. by author. Random House, 1940. ISBN 978-0-394-89265-8 Subj: Animals – elephants. Holidays – Christmas.

Babar and his children ill. by author. Random House, 1938. ISBN 978-0-394-90577-8 Subj: Animals – elephants. Multiple births – triplets.

Babar the king ill. by author. Random House, 1935. ISBN 978-0-394-90580-8 Subj: Animals – elephants. Royalty – kings.

Babar the king [facsimile ed.] ill. by author. Random House, 1986. ISBN 978-0-394-88245-1 Subj: Animals – elephants. Royalty – kings.

The story of Babar, the little elephant ill. by author. Random House, 1984, ©1933. ISBN 978-0-394-86823-3 Subj: Animals – elephants. Behavior – running away. Foreign lands – France.

The travels of Babar ill. by author. Random House, 1934, 1961. ISBN 978-0-394-90576-1 Subj: Activities – traveling. Animals – elephants.

Brunhoff, Laurent de. *B is for Babar: an alphabet book* ill. by author. Abrams, 2012. ISBN 978-1-4197-0298-3 Subj: ABC books. Animals – elephants. Format, unusual – board books.

Babar and the ghost ill. by author. Abrams, 1981. ISBN 978-0-8109-4398-8 Subj: Animals – elephants. Castles. Ghosts.

Babar and the succotash bird ill. by author. Abrams, 2000. ISBN 978-0-8109-5700-8 Subj: Animals – elephants. Birds. Wizards.

Babar and the Wully-Wully ill. by author. Abrams, 1975. ISBN 978-0-8109-4397-1 Subj: Animals – elephants. Pets.

Babar on Paradise Island ill. by author. Abrams, 2014. ISBN 978-141971038-4 Subj: Animals – elephants. Boats, ships. Dragons. Islands.

Babar's ABC ill. by author. Abrams, 1983. ISBN 978-0-8109-5705-3 Subj: ABC books. Animals – elephants.

Babar's battle ill. by author. Random House, 1992. ISBN 978-0-679-91068-8 Subj: Animals – elephants. Animals – rhinoceros. War.

Babar's birthday surprise ill. by author. Random House, 1970. ISBN 978-0-394-90591-4 Subj: Animals – elephants. Birthdays.

Babar's guide to Paris ill. by author. Abrams, 2017. ISBN 978-141972289-9 Subj: Animals – elephants. Foreign lands – France.

Babar's little girl ill. by author. Abrams, 1987. ISBN 978-0-8109-5703-9 Subj: Animals – elephants. Behavior – carelessness. Behavior – lost. Character traits – kindness to animals.

Babar's Museum of Art: (closed Mondays) ill. by author. Abrams, 2003. ISBN 978-0-8109-4597-5 Subj: Animals – elephants. Art. Museums.

Babar's USA ill. by author. Abrams, 2008. ISBN 978-0-8109-7096-0 Subj: Activities – traveling. Animals – elephants. Royalty. U.S. history.

Babar's world tour ill. by author. Abrams, 2005. ISBN 978-0-8109-5780-0 Subj: Activities – traveling. Animals – elephants. World.

Meet Babar and his family ill. by author. Abrams, 2002. ISBN 978-0-8109-0555-9 Subj: Animals – elephants. Family life. Seasons.

Bruno, Elsa Knight. *Punctuation celebration* ill. by Jenny Whitehead. Henry Holt, 2009. ISBN 978-0-8050-7973-9 Subj: Language. Poetry.

Bruss, Deborah. *Book! book! book!* ill. by Tiphanie Beeke. Scholastic, 2001. ISBN 978-0-439-13525-2 Subj: Animals. Books, reading. Libraries. Noise, sounds.

Brutschy, Jennifer. *Just one more story* ill. by Cat Bowman Smith. Orchard, 2001. ISBN 978-0-531-33296-2 Subj: Activities – storytelling. Activities – traveling. Family life – fathers.

Bruzzone, Catherine. *Puppy finds a friend / Cachorrito encuentra un amigo* ill. by John Bendall-Brunello. Barron's, 2000. ISBN 978-0-7641-5283-2 Subj: Activities – playing. Animals – babies. Animals – dogs. Foreign languages. Friendship.

Puppy finds a friend / Le petit chien se trouve un ami ill. by John Bendall-Brunello. Barron's, 2000. ISBN 978-0-7641-5285-6 Subj: Activities – playing. Animals – babies. Animals – dogs. Foreign languages. Friendship.

Bryan, Ashley, selector. *All night, all day: a child's first book of African-American spirituals* ill. by selector. Macmillan, 1991. ISBN 978-0-689-31662-3 Subj: Ethnic groups in the U.S. – African Americans. Music. Musical instruments – guitars. Musical instruments – pianos. Religion. Songs.

Beat the story-drum, pum-pum ill. by adapter. Atheneum, 1980. ISBN 978-0-689-30769-0 Subj: Cumulative tales. Folk & fairy tales. Foreign lands – Africa. Rhyming text.

Beautiful blackbird ill. by author. Atheneum, 2003. ISBN 978-0-689-84731-8 Subj: Birds – blackbirds. Folk & fairy tales. Foreign lands – Zambia.

Can't scare me! ill. by author. Atheneum, 2013. ISBN 978-1-4424-7657-8 Subj: Character traits – curiosity. Family life – grandmothers. Foreign lands – Caribbean Islands. Giants. Rhyming text.

The cat's purr ill. by author. Atheneum, 1985. ISBN 978-0-689-31086-7 Subj: Animals – cats. Animals – rats. Folk & fairy tales. Rhyming text.

Sing to the sun ill. by author. HarperCollins, 1992. ISBN 978-0-06-020833-2 Subj: Foreign lands – Caribbean Islands. Nature. Poetry.

The story of lightning and thunder ill. by author. Atheneum, 1993. ISBN 978-0-689-31836-8 Subj: Folk & fairy tales. Foreign lands – Africa. Weather – lightning, thunder. Weather – storms.

Turtle knows your name ill. by author. Macmillan, 1989. ISBN 978-0-689-31578-7 Subj: Family life – grandmothers. Folk & fairy tales. Names. Reptiles – turtles, tortoises.

Who built the stable? a Nativity poem ill. by author. Atheneum, 2012. ISBN 978-1-4424-0934-7 Subj: Religion – Nativity. Rhyming text.

Bryan, Sean. *A bear and his boy* ill. by Tom Murphy. Arcade, 2007. ISBN 978-1-55970-838-8 Subj: Animals – bears. Rhyming text.

Bryant, Jen. *Abe's fish: a boyhood tale of Abraham Lincoln* ill. by Amy Bates. Sterling, 2009. ISBN 978-1-4027-6252-9 Subj: Behavior – sharing. Character traits – freedom. U.S. history.

The right word: Roget and his thesaurus ill. by Melissa Sweet. Eerdmans, 2014. ISBN 978-080285385-1 Subj: Books, reading. Caldecott award honor books. Language.

A river of words: the story of William Carlos Williams ill. by Melissa Sweet. Eerdmans, 2008. ISBN 978-0-8028-5302-8 Subj: Caldecott award honor books. Poetry.

A splash of red: the life and art of Horace Pippin ill. by Melissa Sweet. Knopf, 2013. ISBN 978-0-375-86712-5 Subj: Art. Careers – artists. Character traits – perseverance. Ethnic groups in the U.S. – African Americans. U.S. history.

Bryant, Megan E. *Alphasaurus* ill. by Luciana Navarro Powell. Chronicle, 2012. ISBN 978-1-4521-0748-6 Subj: ABC books. Dinosaurs. Format, unusual – board books.

Colorasaurus ill. by Luciana Navarro Powell. Chronicle, 2012. ISBN 978-1-4521-0814-8 Subj: Concepts – color. Dinosaurs. Format, unusual – board books.

Countasaurus ill. by Luciana Navarro Powell. Chronicle, 2012. ISBN 978-1-4521-0747-9 Subj: Counting, numbers. Dinosaurs. Format, unusual – board books.

Dump Truck Duck ill. by Jo de Ruiter. Albert Whitman, 2016. ISBN 978-080751736-9 Subj: Birds – ducks. Careers – construction workers. Rhyming text. Trucks.

Shapeasaurus ill. by Luciana Navarro Powell. Chronicle, 2012. ISBN 978-1-4521-0815-5 Subj: Concepts – shape. Dinosaurs. Format, unusual – board books.

Bryne, Gayle. *Sometimes it's grandmas and grandpas, not mommies and daddies* ill. by Mary Haverfield. Abbeville, 2009. ISBN 978-0-7892-1028-9 Subj: Family life – grandparents.

Buchanan, Jane. *Seed magic* ill. by Charlotte Riley-Webb. Peachtree, 2012. ISBN 978-1-56145-622-2 Subj: Birds. Cities, towns. Disabilities – physical disabilities. Ethnic groups in the U.S. – African Americans. Seeds.

Buchanan, Sue. *Mud Pie Annie: God's recipe for doing your best* by Sue Buchanan and Dana Shafer ill. by Joy Allen. Zondervan, 2001. ISBN 978-0-613-71694-9 Subj: Character traits – cleverness. Rhyming text. Self-concept.

Buck, Nola. *A Christmas goodnight* ill. by Sarah Jane Wright. HarperCollins, 2011. ISBN 978-0-06-166491-5 Subj: Holidays – Christmas. Religion. Rhyming text.

Buckingham, Matt. *Bright Stanley* ill. by author. Tiger Tales, 2006. ISBN 978-1-58925-059-8 Subj: Behavior – lost. Fish. Friendship. Sea & seashore.

Buckley, Carol. *Tarra and Bella: the elephant and dog who became best friends* ill. with photos. Putnam, 2009. ISBN 978-0-399-25443-7 Subj: Animals – dogs. Animals – elephants.

Buckley, Michael. *Kel Gilligan's daredevil stunt show* ill. by Dan Santat. Abrams, 2012. ISBN 978-1-4197-0379-9 Subj: Character traits – bravery. Humorous stories.

Buckley, Richard. *The foolish tortoise* ill. by Eric Carle. Picture Book Studio, 1985. ISBN 978-0-88708-002-9 Subj: Behavior – seeking better things. Folk & fairy tales. Reptiles – turtles, tortoises. Rhyming text.

The greedy python ill. by Eric Carle. Picture Book Studio, 1985. ISBN 978-0-88708-001-2 Subj: Behavior – greed. Folk & fairy tales. Reptiles – snakes. Rhyming text.

Budnitz, Paul. *The hole in the middle* ill. by Aya Kakeda. Hyperion/Disney, 2011. ISBN 978-1-4231-3761-0 Subj: Format, unusual. Friendship. Self-concept.

Buehner, Caralyn. *Merry Christmas, Mr. Mouse* ill. by Mark Buehner. Dial, 2015. ISBN 978-080374010-5 Subj: Animals – mice. Holidays – Christmas. Rhyming text.

The queen of style ill. by Mark Buehner. Dial, 2008. ISBN 978-0-8037-2878-3 Subj: Beauty shops. Behavior – boredom. Royalty – queens.

Snowmen all year ill. by Mark Buehner. Penguin, 2010. ISBN 978-0-8037-3383-1 Subj: Magic. Rhyming text. Snowmen.

Snowmen at Christmas ill. by Mark Buehner. Penguin, 2005. ISBN 978-0-8037-2995-7 Subj: Gifts. Holidays – Christmas. Parties. Rhyming text. Snowmen.

Snowmen at night ill. by Mark Buehner. Fogelman, 2002. ISBN 978-0-8037-2550-8 Subj: Night. Rhyming text. Snowmen.

Superdog, the heart of a hero ill. by Mark Buehner. HarperCollins, 2004. ISBN 978-0-06-623621-6 Subj: Animals – dogs. Concepts – size. Self-concept.

Would I ever lie to you? ill. by Jack E. Davis. Penguin, 2007. ISBN 978-0-8037-2793-9 Subj: Behavior – bullying, teasing. Behavior – lying. Family life – cousins. Rhyming text.

Bùi, Tak. *Spot the difference* ill. by author. Tundra, 2012. ISBN 978-1-77049-279-0 Subj: Picture puzzles.

Buitrago, Jairo. *Jimmy the greatest* ill. by Rafael Yockteng. Groundwood, 2012. ISBN 978-1-55498-178-6 Subj: Books, reading. Cities, towns. Poverty. Self-concept. Sports – boxing.

Two white rabbits ill. by Rafael Yockteng. Groundwood, 2015. ISBN 978-155498741-2 Subj: Activities – traveling. Behavior – seeking better things. Counting, numbers. Family life – daughters. Family life – fathers. Immigrants, immigration. Refugees.

Bulion, Leslie. *Fatuma's new cloth* ill. by Nicole Tadgell. Moon Mt, 2002. ISBN 978-0-9677929-7-2

Subj: Family life – mothers. Foreign lands – Africa. Shopping.

Bullard, Lisa. *Marco's Cinco de Mayo* ill. by Holli Conger. Millbrook, 2012. ISBN 978-0-7613-5082-8 Subj: Foreign lands – Mexico. Holidays – Cinco de Mayo.

Rashad's Ramadan and Eid al-Fitr ill. by Holli Conger. Millbrook, 2012. ISBN 978-0-7613-5079-8 Subj: Holidays. Holidays – Ramadan. Religion.

Trick-or-treat on Milton Street ill. by Joni Oeltjenbruns. Carolrhoda, 2001. ISBN 978-1-57505-158-1 Subj: Family life – stepfamilies. Holidays – Halloween. Moving.

Bunge, Daniela. *Cherry time* ill. by author. Minedition, 2007. ISBN 978-0-698-40057-3 Subj: Animals – dogs. Character traits – shyness. Friendship.

The scarves ill. by author. Minedition, 2006. ISBN 978-0-698-40045-0 Subj: Activities – knitting. Clothing – scarves. Family life – grandparents. Sports – ice skating.

Bunting, Eve. *Anna's table* ill. by Taia Morley. NorthWord, 2003. ISBN 978-1-55971-841-7 Subj: Behavior – collecting things. Nature. Poetry.

Baby can ill. by Maxie Chambliss. Boyds Mills, 2007. ISBN 978-1-59078-322-1 Subj: Babies, toddlers. Emotions – love. Family life – new sibling. Sibling rivalry.

The baby shower ill. by Judy Love. Charlesbridge, 2007. ISBN 978-1-58089-139-4 Subj: Animals – babies. Animals – bulls, cows. Gifts. Rhyming text.

Ballywhinney Girl ill. by Emily Arnold McCully. Clarion, 2012. ISBN 978-0-547-55843-1 Subj: Foreign lands – Ireland. Mummies.

Big Bear's big boat ill. by Nancy Carpenter. Clarion, 2013. ISBN 978-0-618-58537-3 Subj: Animals – bears. Boats, ships.

The blue and the gray ill. by Ned Bittinger. Scholastic, 1996. ISBN 978-0-590-60197-9 Subj: Ethnic groups in the U.S. – African Americans. Friendship. U.S. history. War.

The bones of Fred McFee ill. by Kurt Cyrus. Harcourt, 2002. ISBN 978-0-15-202004-0 Subj: Anatomy – skeletons. Holidays – Halloween. Rhyming text.

Butterfly house ill. by Greg Shed. Scholastic, 1999. ISBN 978-0-590-84884-8 Subj: Family life – grandfathers. Insects – butterflies, caterpillars. Metamorphosis. Rhyming text.

Can you do this, Old Badger? ill. by LeUyen Pham. Harcourt, 1999. ISBN 978-0-15-201654-8 Subj: Animals – badgers. Old age.

The cart that carried Martin ill. by Don Tate. Charlesbridge, 2013. ISBN 978-1-58089-387-9 Subj: Ethnic groups in the U.S. – African Americans. Holidays – Martin Luther King, Jr. Day. U.S. history. Violence, nonviolence.

Christmas cricket ill. by Timothy Bush. Clarion, 2002. ISBN 978-0-618-06554-7 Subj: Holidays – Christmas. Insects – crickets.

The days of summer ill. by William Low. Harcourt, 2001. ISBN 978-0-15-201840-5 Subj: Divorce. Family life – grandparents. Family life – sisters.

A day's work ill. by Ronald Himler. Clarion, 1994. ISBN 978-0-395-67321-8 Subj: Activities – working. Character traits – honesty. Ethnic groups in the U.S. – Mexican Americans. Family life – grandfathers. Gardens, gardening.

December ill. by David Diaz. Harcourt, 1997. ISBN 978-0-15-201434-6 Subj: Character traits – helpfulness. Holidays – Christmas. Homeless.

Ducky ill. by David Wisniewski. Clarion, 1997. ISBN 978-0-395-75185-5 Subj: Activities – traveling. Sea & seashore. Toys.

Emma's turtle ill. by Marsha Winborn. Boyds Mills, 2007. ISBN 978-1-59078-350-4 Subj: Behavior – running away. Pets. Reptiles – turtles, tortoises.

Finn McCool and the great fish ill. by Zachary Pullen. Sleeping Bear, 2010. ISBN 978-1-58536-366-7 Subj: Fish. Folk & fairy tales. Foreign lands – Ireland. Giants.

Flower garden ill. by Kathryn Hewitt. Harcourt, 1994. ISBN 978-0-15-228776-4 Subj: Birthdays. Family life – mothers. Flowers. Gardens, gardening. Rhyming text.

Fly away home ill. by Ronald Himler. Houghton, 1991. ISBN 978-0-395-55962-8 Subj: Airplanes, airports. Family life – fathers. Homeless.

Ghost cat ill. by Kevin M. Barry. Sleeping Bear, 2017. ISBN 978-158536993-5 Subj: Animals – cats. Ghosts. Lighthouses.

Ghost's hour, spook's hour ill. by author. Clarion, 1987. ISBN 978-0-89919-484-4 Subj: Animals – dogs. Emotions – fear. Family life. Night.

Girls A to Z ill. by Suzanne Bloom. Boyds Mills, 2002. ISBN 978-1-56397-147-1 Subj: Careers. Names.

Gleam and Glow ill. by Peter Sylvada. Harcourt, 2001. ISBN 978-0-15-202596-0 Subj: Fish. Foreign lands – Bosnia-Herzegovina. War.

Going home ill. by David Diaz. HarperCollins, 1996. ISBN 978-0-06-026296-9 Subj: Ethnic groups in the U.S. – Mexican Americans. Family life. Foreign lands – Mexico. Holidays – Christmas.

Happy birthday, dear duck ill. by Jan Brett. Clarion, 1988. ISBN 978-0-89919-541-4 Subj: Animals. Birds – ducks. Birthdays. Rhyming text.

Have you seen my new blue socks? ill. by Sergio Ruzzier. Clarion, 2013. ISBN 978-0-547-75267-9 Subj: Animals. Behavior – lost & found possessions. Birds – ducks. Clothing – socks. Rhyming text.

Hey diddle diddle ill. by Mary Ann Fraser. Boyds Mills, 2011. ISBN 978-1-59078-768-7 Subj: Animals. Musical instruments. Rhyming text.

How many days to America? a Thanksgiving story ill. by Beth Peck. Clarion, 1988. ISBN 978-0-89919-521-6 Subj: Character traits – freedom. Holidays – Thanksgiving. Pilgrims.

Hurry! hurry! ill. by Jeff Mack. Harcourt, 2007. ISBN 978-0-15-205410-6 Subj: Animals. Birds – chickens, roosters. Farms.

Jin Woo ill. by Chris Soentpiet. Clarion, 2001. ISBN 978-0-395-93872-0 Subj: Adoption. Ethnic groups in the U.S. – Korean Americans. Family life – brothers.

Little Badger, terror of the seven seas ill. by LeUyen Pham. Harcourt, 2001. ISBN 978-0-15-202395-9 Subj: Animals – badgers. Imagination. Pirates.

Little Badger's just-about birthday ill. by LeUyen Pham. Harcourt, 2002. ISBN 978-0-15-202609-7 Subj: Animals. Animals – badgers. Birthdays. Parties.

The memory string ill. by Ted Rand. Clarion, 2000. ISBN 978-0-395-86146-2 Subj: Emotions – grief. Family life – stepfamilies. Memories, memory.

The Mother's Day mice ill. by Jan Brett. Clarion, 1986. ISBN 978-0-89919-387-8 Subj: Animals – mice. Holidays – Mother's Day.

Mouse island ill. by Dominic Catalano. Boyds Mills, 2008. ISBN 978-1-59078-447-1 Subj: Animals – cats. Animals – mice. Friendship. Islands.

Mr. Goat's valentine ill. by Kevin Zimmer. Sleeping Bear, 2016. ISBN 978-158536944-7 Subj: Animals – goats. Gifts. Holidays – Valentine's Day.

My dog Jack is fat ill. by Michael Rex. Marshall Cavendish, 2011. ISBN 978-0-7614-5809-8 Subj: Animals – dogs. Health & fitness.

My mom's wedding ill. by Lisa Papp. Sleeping Bear, 2006. ISBN 978-1-58536-288-2 Subj: Divorce. Family life – mothers. Weddings.

My red balloon ill. by Kay Life. Boyds Mills, 2005. ISBN 978-1-59078-263-7 Subj: Careers – military. Family life – fathers.

My special day at third street school ill. by Suzanne Bloom. Boyds Mills, 2004. ISBN 978-0-613-79887-7 Subj: Careers – writers. School.

Night tree ill. by Ted Rand. Harcourt, 1991. ISBN 978-0-15-257425-3 Subj: Animals. Character traits – kindness to animals. Family life. Holidays – Christmas. Trees.

One candle ill. by Wendy Popp. Cotler, 2002. ISBN 978-0-06-028116-8 Subj: Holidays – Hanukkah. War.

One green apple ill. by Ted Lewin. Houghton, 2006. ISBN 978-0-618-43477-0 Subj: Ethnic groups in the U.S. – Arab Americans. Food. Immigrants, immigration. School – field trips. Self-concept.

Our library ill. by Maggie Smith. Clarion, 2008. ISBN 978-0-618-49458-3 Subj: Animals. Animals – raccoons. Books, reading. Character traits – cooperation. Libraries.

P is for pirate: a pirate alphabet ill. by John Manders. Sleeping Bear, 2014. ISBN 978-158536815-0 Subj: ABC books. Pirates.

Peepers ill. by James Ransome. Harcourt, 2000. ISBN 978-0-15-260297-0 Subj: Activities – traveling. Nature. Seasons – fall.

A perfect Father's Day ill. by Susan Meddaugh. Houghton, 1991. ISBN 978-0-395-52590-6 Subj: Family life – fathers. Holidays – Father's Day.

A picnic in October ill. by Nancy Carpenter. Harcourt, 1999. ISBN 978-0-15-201656-2 Subj: Activities – picnicking. Birthdays. Emotions – embarrassment. Ethnic groups in the U.S. – Italian Americans. Family life – grandmothers. Immigrants, immigration. U.S. history.

Pirate boy ill. by Julie Fortenberry. Holiday House, 2011. ISBN 978-0-8234-2321-7 Subj: Family life – mothers. Imagination. Pirates.

The pumpkin fair ill. by Eileen Christelow. Clarion, 1997. ISBN 978-0-395-70060-0 Subj: Fairs, festivals. Rhyming text. Seasons – fall.

Riding the tiger ill. by David Frampton. Clarion, 2001. ISBN 978-0-395-79731-0 Subj: Animals – tigers. Cities, towns. Clubs, gangs.

Rudi's pond ill. by Ronald Himler. Clarion, 1999. ISBN 978-0-395-89067-7 Subj: Death. Emotions – grief. Friendship.

St. Patrick's Day in the morning ill. by Jan Brett. Houghton, 1980. ISBN 978-0-395-29098-9 Subj: Holidays – St. Patrick's Day.

Scary, scary Halloween ill. by Jan Brett. Houghton, 1986. ISBN 978-0-89919-414-1 Subj: Holidays – Halloween. Monsters. Mythical creatures – goblins. Rhyming text.

Sing a song of piglets: a calendar in verse ill. by Emily Arnold McCully. Clarion, 2002. ISBN 978-0-618-01137-7 Subj: Animals – babies. Animals – pigs. Days of the week, months of the year. Poetry.

Smoky night ill. by David Diaz. Harcourt, 1994. ISBN 978-0-15-269954-3 Subj: Caldecott award books. Cities, towns. Communities, neighborhoods. Emotions – anger. Ethnic groups in the U.S. Violence, nonviolence.

So far from the sea ill. by Chris Soentpiet. Clarion, 1998. ISBN 978-0-395-72095-0 Subj: Ethnic groups in the U.S. – Japanese Americans. Family life – grandfathers. War.

Sunflower house ill. by Kathryn Hewitt. Harcourt, 1996. ISBN 978-0-15-200483-5 Subj: Flowers. Gardens, gardening. Rhyming text. Seasons – summer.

Swan in love ill. by Jo Ellen McAllister Stammen. Atheneum, 2000. ISBN 978-0-689-82080-9 Subj: Animals. Birds – swans. Boats, ships. Emotions – love.

That's what leprechauns do ill. by Emily Arnold McCully. Houghton, 2006. ISBN 978-0-618-35410-8 Subj: Mythical creatures – leprechauns.

Thunder horse ill. by Dennis Nolan. Roaring Brook/Neal Porter, 2017. ISBN 978-162672443-3 Subj: Animals – horses, ponies. Magic. Stars.

A turkey for Thanksgiving ill. by Diane deGroat. Ticknor & Fields, 1991. ISBN 978-0-89919-793-7 Subj: Animals – moose. Birds – turkeys. Holidays – Thanksgiving.

Tweak tweak ill. by Sergio Ruzzier. Clarion, 2011. ISBN 978-0-618-99851-7 Subj: Animals – elephants. Character traits – curiosity. Family life – mothers.

The Valentine bears ill. by Jan Brett. Seabury Pr., 1983. ISBN 978-0-89919-138-6 Subj: Animals – bears. Holidays – Valentine's Day.

Walking to school ill. by Michael Dooling. Clarion, 2008. ISBN 978-0-618-26144-4 Subj: Foreign lands – Ireland. Prejudice. School.

The wall ill. by Ronald Himler. Clarion, 1990. ISBN 978-0-395-51588-4 Subj: Careers – military. Family life. War.

Washday ill. by Brad Sneed. Holiday House, 2014. ISBN 978-082342868-7 Subj: Character traits – cleanliness. Family life – grandmothers. U.S. history – frontier & pioneer life.

We were there: a Nativity story ill. by Wendell Minor. Clarion, 2001. ISBN 978-0-395-82265-4 Subj: Animals. Holidays – Christmas. Religion – Nativity.

The Wednesday surprise ill. by Donald Garrick. Ticknor & Fields, 1989. ISBN 978-0-89919-721-0 Subj: Birthdays. Books, reading. Family life. Family life – grandmothers.

Who was born this special day? by Eve Bunting and Leonid Gore ill. by Leonid Gore. Atheneum, 2001. ISBN 978-0-689-82302-2 Subj: Holidays – Christmas. Poetry. Religion – Nativity.

Whose shoe? ill. by Sergio Ruzzier. Clarion, 2015. ISBN 978-054430210-5 Subj: Animals. Animals – mice. Behavior – lost & found possessions. Clothing – shoes. Rhyming text.

Will it be a baby brother? ill. by Beth Spiegel. Boyds Mills, 2010. ISBN 978-1-59078-439-6 Subj: Babies, toddlers. Family life – new sibling.

Yard sale ill. by Lauren Castillo. Candlewick, 2015. ISBN 978-076366542-5 Subj: Behavior – worrying. Garage sales, rummage sales. Moving.

You were loved before you were born ill. by Karen Barbour. Scholastic, 2008. ISBN 978-0-439-04061-7 Subj: Emotions – love. Family life.

Burach, Ross. *I am not a chair!* ill. by author. HarperCollins, 2017. ISBN 978-006236016-8 Subj: Animals – giraffes. Behavior – bad day, bad mood. Character traits – assertiveness. Humorous stories.

There's a giraffe in my soup ill. by author. HarperCollins, 2016. ISBN 978-006236014-4 Subj: Animals. Food. Humorous stories. Restaurants.

Burdett, Lois. *Hamlet for kids* intro. by Kenneth Branagh. Ill. by children. Firefly, 2000. ISBN 978-1-55209-522-5 Subj: Children as authors. Children as illustrators. Crime. Foreign lands – Denmark. Rhyming text. Royalty – princes.

Macbeth for kids. Ill. by children. Black Moss, 1996. ISBN 978-0-88753-287-0 Subj: Behavior – fighting, arguing. Children as authors. Children as illustrators. Crime. Foreign lands – Scotland. Royalty – kings. Royalty – queens.

A midsummer night's dream for kids. Ill. by children. Firefly, 1997. ISBN 978-1-55209-130-2 Subj: Children as authors. Children as illustrators. Dreams. Rhyming text.

Romeo and Juliet for kids. Ill. by children. Firefly, 1998. ISBN 978-1-55209-244-6 Subj: Behavior – fighting, arguing. Children as authors. Children as illustrators. Emotions – love. Family life. Rhyming text.

The tempest for kids. Ill. by children. Firefly, 1999. ISBN 978-1-55209-355-9 Subj: Children as authors. Children as illustrators. Emotions. Islands. Magic. Rhyming text. Weather – storms.

Twelfth night for kids. Ill. by children. Firefly, 1997. ISBN 978-0-88753-233-7 Subj: Behavior – mistakes. Behavior – trickery. Boats, ships. Character traits. Children as authors. Children as illustrators. Sea & seashore.

Burell, Sarah. *Diamond Jim Dandy and the sheriff* ill. by Bryan Langdo. Sterling, 2010. ISBN 978-1-4027-5737-2 Subj: Babies, toddlers. Reptiles –

snakes. Texas. U.S. history – frontier & pioneer life.

Burfoot, Ella. *How to bake a book* ill. by author. Sourcebooks/Jabberwocky, 2014. ISBN 978-149260651-2 Subj: Activities – baking, cooking. Books, reading. Rhyming text.

Burg, Ann. *Autumn walk* ill. by Kelly Asbury. HarperCollins, 2003. ISBN 978-0-06-009741-7 Subj: Format, unusual – board books. Seasons – fall.

Burg, Sarah Emmanuelle. *Do you still love me?* ill. by author. NorthSouth, 2010. ISBN 978-0-7358-2293-1 Subj: Behavior – fighting, arguing. Behavior – worrying. Family life – parents.

One more egg ill. by author. NorthSouth, 2006. ISBN 978-0-7358-2001-2 Subj: Animals – rabbits. Birds – chickens, roosters. Eggs. Farms. Holidays – Easter.

Burgess, Mark. *Where teddy bears come from* ill. by Russell Ayto. Peachtree, 2009. ISBN 978-1-56145-487-7 Subj: Animals – wolves. Books, reading. Holidays – Christmas. Santa Claus. Toys – bears.

Burke, Bobby. *Daddy's little girl* by Bobby Burke and Horace Gerlach ill. by Maggie Kneen. Words & music by Bobby Burke & Horace Gerlach. HarperCollins, 2004. ISBN 978-0-06-028722-1 Subj: Animals – rabbits. Family life – daughters. Family life – fathers. Music. Songs.

Burks, James. *Beep and Bah* ill. by author. Carolrhoda, 2012. ISBN 978-0-7613-6567-9 Subj: Animals – goats. Behavior – lost & found possessions. Clothing – socks. Robots.

Pigs and a blanket ill. by author. Disney/Hyperion, 2016. ISBN 978-148472523-8 Subj: Animals – pigs. Behavior – sharing. Family life – brothers & sisters.

Burleigh, Robert. *Clang-clang! beep-beep! listen to the city* ill. by Beppe Giacobbe. Simon & Schuster, 2009. ISBN 978-1-4169-4052-4 Subj: Cities, towns. Noise, sounds. Rhyming text.

Edward Hopper paints his world ill. by Wendell Minor. Henry Holt, 2014. ISBN 978-080508752-9 Subj: Art. Careers – artists.

Goal ill. by Stephen T. Johnson. Harcourt, 2001. ISBN 978-0-15-201789-7 Subj: Poetry. Sports – soccer.

Good-bye, Sheepie ill. by Peter Catalanotto. Marshall Cavendish, 2010. ISBN 978-0-7614-5598-1 Subj: Animals – dogs. Death. Family life – fathers. Pets.

Hit the road, Jack ill. by Ross MacDonald. Abrams, 2012. ISBN 978-1-4197-0399-7 Subj: Activities – traveling. Animals – rabbits. Rhyming text.

Home run: the story of Babe Ruth ill. by Mike Wimmer. Silver Whistle, 1998. ISBN 978-0-15-200970-0 Subj: Sports – baseball.

I love going through this book ill. by Dan Yaccarino. Cotler, 2001. ISBN 978-0-06-028806-8 Subj: Books, reading. Rhyming text.

If you spent a day with Thoreau at Walden pond ill. by Wendell Minor. Henry Holt, 2012. ISBN 978-0-8050-9137-3 Subj: Activities – writing. Nature. U.S. history.

Langston's train ride ill. by Leonard Jenkins. Orchard, 2004. ISBN 978-0-439-35239-0 Subj: Careers – poets. Ethnic groups in the U.S. – African Americans.

Lookin' for Bird in the big city ill. by Marek Los. Harcourt, 2000. ISBN 978-0-15-202031-6 Subj: Careers – musicians. Cities, towns. Ethnic groups in the U.S. – African Americans. Music. Musical instruments – trumpets.

Messenger, messenger ill. by Barry Root. Atheneum, 2000. ISBN 978-0-689-82103-5 Subj: Careers – messengers. Cities, towns. Rhyming text. Sports – bicycling.

One giant leap ill. by Mike Wimmer. Philomel, 2009. ISBN 978-0-399-23883-3 Subj: Careers – astronauts. Moon. Space & space ships. U.S. history.

Solving the puzzle under the sea: Marie Tharp maps the ocean floor ill. by Raúl Colón. Simon & Schuster/Paula Wiseman, 2016. ISBN 978-148141600-9 Subj: Careers – cartographers. Careers – geologists. Gender roles. Maps. Sea & seashore.

Stealing home: Jackie Robinson against the odds ill. by Mike Wimmer. Simon & Schuster, 2007. ISBN 978-0-689-86276-2 Subj: Ethnic groups in the U.S. – African Americans. Sports – baseball. U.S. history.

Trapped! a whale's rescue ill. by Wendell Minor. Charlesbridge, 2015. ISBN 978-158089558-3 Subj: Animals – whales. Character traits – kindness to animals.

Zoom! zoom! sounds of things that go in the city ill. by Tad Carpenter. Simon & Schuster/Paula Wiseman, 2014. ISBN 978-144248315-6 Subj: Automobiles. Cities, towns. Machines. Noise, sounds. Rhyming text.

Burnard, Damon. *Dave's haircut* ill. by author. Dutton, 2003. ISBN 978-0-525-46967-4 Subj: Careers – barbers. Hair. School.

I spy in the jungle ill. by Julia Cairns. Chronicle, 2001. ISBN 978-0-8118-2987-8 Subj: Animals. Format, unusual – board books. Games. Jungle.

I spy in the ocean ill. by Julia Cairns. Chronicle, 2001. ISBN 978-0-8118-2988-5 Subj: ABC books.

Animals. Format, unusual – board books. Sea & seashore.

Burnell, Heather Ayris. *Bedtime monster / ¡A dormir, pequeño monstruo!* ill. by Bonnie Adamson. Raven Tree, 2010. ISBN 978-1-932748-80-2 Subj: Bedtime. Emotions – anger. Foreign languages. Monsters.

Burnett, Frances Hodgson. *A little princess* adapt. by Barbara McClintock; ill. by adapter. HarperCollins, 2000. ISBN 978-0-06-029010-8 Subj: Foreign lands – England. Orphans. Poverty. School.

A little princess retold by Janet Allison Brown; ill. by Graham Rust. Viking, 2001. ISBN 978-0-670-89913-5 Subj: Foreign lands – England. Orphans. School.

The secret garden retold by Janet Allison Brown; ill. by Graham Rus. Viking, 2001. ISBN 978-0-670-89911-1 Subj: Disabilities – physical disabilities. Foreign lands – England. Gardens, gardening.

Burningham, John. *Come away from the water, Shirley* ill. by author. Crowell, 1977. ISBN 978-0-690-01361-0 Subj: Imagination. Pirates. Sea & seashore.

Edwardo: the horriblest boy in the whole world ill. by author. Random House, 2007. ISBN 978-0-375-84053-1 Subj: Behavior – misbehavior.

First steps: letters, numbers, colors, opposites ill. by author. Candlewick, 1994. ISBN 978-1-56402-205-9 Subj: ABC books. Concepts. Concepts – color. Concepts – opposites. Counting, numbers.

Harvey Slumfenburger's Christmas present ill. by author. Candlewick, 1993. ISBN 978-1-56402-246-2 Subj: Character traits – helpfulness. Holidays – Christmas. Santa Claus.

It's a secret! ill. by author. Candlewick, 2009. ISBN 978-0-7636-4275-4 Subj: Activities – dancing. Animals – cats. Night.

John Patrick Norman McHennessy — the boy who was always late ill. by author. Crown, 1987. ISBN 978-0-517-56805-7 Subj: Behavior – promptness, tardiness. Imagination. School.

The magic bed ill. by author. Knopf, 2003. ISBN 978-0-375-92423-1 Subj: Dreams. Furniture – beds. Magic.

Motor Miles ill. by author. Candlewick, 2016. ISBN 978-076369064-9 Subj: Activities – driving. Animals – dogs. Automobiles. Behavior – dissatisfaction.

Mr. Gumpy's motor car ill. by author. Macmillan, 1975, 1973. ISBN 978-0-02-716200-4 Subj: Automobiles. Weather – rain.

Mr. Gumpy's outing ill. by author. Macmillan, 1971. ISBN 978-0-03-086613-5 Subj: Animals. Behavior – fighting, arguing. Boats, ships. Cumulative tales.

Picnic ill. by author. Candlewick, 2014. ISBN 978-076366945-4 Subj: Activities – picnicking. Friendship.

The shopping basket ill. by author. Candlewick, 1996. ISBN 978-1-56402-688-0 Subj: Animals. Character traits – cleverness. Humorous stories. Shopping.

There's going to be a baby ill. by Helen Oxenbury. Candlewick, 2010. ISBN 978-0-7636-4907-4 Subj: Babies, toddlers. Family life – new sibling.

Tug-of-war ill. by author. Candlewick, 2013. ISBN 978-0-7636-6575-3 Subj: Animals – elephants. Animals – hippopotamuses. Animals – rabbits. Behavior – bullying, teasing. Behavior – trickery. Games.

The way to the zoo ill. by author. Candlewick, 2014. ISBN 978-076367317-8 Subj: Animals. Imagination. Zoos.

Burns, Diane L., et al *Backyard beasties* ill. by Brian Gable. Carolrhoda, 2004. ISBN 978-1-57505-646-3 Subj: Animals. Riddles & jokes.

Burns, Loree Griffin. *Handle with care: an unusual butterfly journey* ill. with photos. Millbrook, 2014. ISBN 978-076139342-9 Subj: Foreign lands – Costa Rica. Insects – butterflies, caterpillars.

Burrowes, Adjoa J. *Grandma's purple flowers* ill. by author. Lee & Low, 2000. ISBN 978-1-880000-73-1 Subj: Death. Emotions. Family life – grandmothers. Seasons.

Burton, LeVar. *The rhino who swallowed a storm* by LeVar Burton and Susan Schaefer Bernardo ill. by Courtenay Fletcher. Reading Rainbow, 2014. ISBN 978-099053950-6 Subj: Animals – mice. Animals – rhinoceros. Weather – storms.

Burton, Virginia Lee. *Katy and the big snow* ill. by author. Houghton, 1943. ISBN 978-0-606-03726-6 Subj: Cities, towns. Cumulative tales. Machines. Seasons – winter. Weather – snow.

The little house ill. by author. Houghton, 1939. ISBN 978-0-606-01531-8 Subj: Caldecott award books. Cities, towns. Country. Ecology. Homes, houses. Progress.

Mike Mulligan and his steam shovel ill. by author. Houghton, 1967. ISBN 978-0-395-16961-2 Subj: Activities – working. Machines.

Bus-a-saurus bop ill. by David Clark. Bloomsbury, 2003. ISBN 978-1-58234-850-6 Subj: Buses. Rhyming text. School.

Busch, Miriam. *Lion, lion* ill. by Larry Day. HarperCollins/Balzer+Bray, 2014. ISBN 978-006227104-4 Subj: Animals – cats. Animals – lions. Behavior – lost & found possessions. Ethnic groups in the U.S. – African Americans.

Raisin, the littlest cow ill. by Larry Day. HarperCollins/Balzer+Bray, 2017. ISBN 978-006242763-2 Subj: Animals – bulls, cows. Emotions – envy, jealousy. Family life – brothers & sisters. Family life – new sibling.

Bush, Jenna. *Read all about it!* (Bush, Laura)

Bush, Laura. *Read all about it!* by Laura Bush and Jenna Bush ill. by Denise Brunkus. HarperCollins, 2008. ISBN 978-0-06-156075-0 Subj: Books, reading. Libraries. School.

Bush, Timothy. *Ferocious girls, steamroller boys, and other poems in between* ill. by author. Orchard, 2000. ISBN 978-0-531-33250-4 Subj: Poetry.

Teddy bear, teddy bear ill. by author. Greenwillow, 2005. ISBN 978-0-06-057836-7 Subj: Activities. Behavior – lost. Nursery rhymes. Toys – bears.

Bushey, Jeanne. *The polar bear's gift* ill. by Vladyana Krykorka. Red Deer, 2000. ISBN 978-0-88995-220-1 Subj: Animals – polar bears. Character traits – helpfulness. Foreign lands – Canada. Friendship. Indians of North America – Inuit.

Busse, Sarah Martin. *Banjo granny* by Sarah Martin Busse and Jacqueline Briggs Martin ill. by Barry Root. Houghton, 2006. ISBN 978-0-618-33603-6 Subj: Family life – grandmothers. Musical instruments – banjos. Songs.

Bustos, Eduardo. *Going ape!* ill. by Lucho Rodriguez. Tundra, 2012. ISBN 978-1-77049-282-0 Subj: Animals – baboons. Animals – chimpanzees. Animals – gorillas. Animals – monkeys. Animals – orangutans.

Butler, Christina. *One cozy Christmas* ill. by Tina Macnaughton. Tiger Tales, 2017. ISBN 978-168010068-6 Subj: Animals. Animals – hedgehogs. Friendship. Holidays – Christmas.

Butler, Dori Hillestad. *F is for firefighting* ill. by Joan Waites. Pelican, 2007. ISBN 978-1-58980-420-3 Subj: ABC books. Careers – firefighters.

My grandpa had a stroke ill. by Nicole Wong. Magination, 2007. ISBN 978-1-59147-806-5 Subj: Family life – grandfathers. Illness.

Butler, Geoff. *Ode to Newfoundland* ill. by author. Tundra, 2003. ISBN 978-0-88776-631-2 Subj: Foreign lands – Canada. Music. Songs.

Butler, John. *Bedtime in the jungle* ill. by author. Peachtree, 2009. ISBN 978-1-56145-486-0 Subj: Animals. Bedtime. Counting, numbers. Jungle. Songs.

Can you growl like a bear? ill. by author. Peachtree, 2007. ISBN 978-1-56145-396-2 Subj: Animals. Bedtime. Noise, sounds. Rhyming text.

Hush, little ones ill. by author. Peachtree, 2003. ISBN 978-1-56145-269-9 Subj: Animals – babies. Night. Rhyming text. Sleep.

Pi-shu, the little panda ill. by author. Peachtree, 2001. ISBN 978-1-56145-242-2 Subj: Animals – babies. Animals – endangered animals. Animals – pandas.

Ten in the den ill. by author. Peachtree, 2005. ISBN 978-1-56145-344-3 Subj: Animals. Counting, numbers. Nursery rhymes.

Ten in the meadow ill. by author. Peachtree, 2006. ISBN 978-1-56145-372-6 Subj: Activities – playing. Animals. Behavior – hiding. Games.

While you were sleeping ill. by author. Peachtree, 1999. ISBN 978-1-56145-211-8 Subj: Animals. Bedtime. Counting, numbers. Night. Sleep.

Whose baby am I? ill. by author. Viking, 2001. ISBN 978-0-670-89683-7 Subj: Animals – babies.

Butler, Kristi T. *Rip's secret spot* ill. by Joe Cepeda. Harcourt, 2000. ISBN 978-0-15-202640-0 Subj: Animals – dogs. Behavior – lost & found possessions.

Butler, M. Christina. *Mouse and the moon* ill. by Tina Macnaughton. Good Books, 2012. ISBN 978-1-56148-747-9 Subj: Animals. Animals – mice. Friendship. Moon.

One snowy night ill. by Tina Macnaughton. Good Books, 2004. ISBN 978-1-56148-452-2 Subj: Animals. Character traits – generosity. Clothing – hats. Format, unusual – toy & movable books. Gifts. Holidays – Christmas.

One special Christmas ill. by Tina Macnaughton. Tiger Tales, 2013. ISBN 978-1-58925-145-8 Subj: Animals. Animals – hedgehogs. Gifts. Holidays – Christmas. Santa Claus.

One winter's day ill. by Tina Macnaughton. Good Books, 2006. ISBN 978-1-56148-532-1 Subj: Animals. Animals – hedgehogs. Character traits – kindness. Seasons – winter.

The smiley snowman ill. by Tina Macnaughton. Good Books, 2010. ISBN 978-1-56148-696-0 Subj: Animals. Seasons – winter. Snowmen.

Snow friends ill. by Tina Macnaughton. Good Books, 2005. ISBN 978-1-56148-485-0 Subj: Animals – bears. Friendship. Seasons – winter. Weather – snow.

The special blankie ill. by Tina Macnaughton. Good Books, 2010. ISBN 978-1-56148-682-3 Subj: Activities – babysitting. Animals – hedgehogs. Behavior – lost & found possessions.

Butterfield, Moira. *Magic world of learning* created by Jay Young; ill. by Sian Tucker. Sterling, 2001. ISBN 978-0-8069-5587-2 Subj: Format, unusual – toy & movable books. Games.

Butterworth, Chris. *How did that get in my lunchbox? the story of food* ill. by Lucia Gaggiotti. Candlewick, 2011. ISBN 978-0-7636-5005-6 Subj: Food. Health & fitness.

Sea horse: the shyest fish in the sea ill. by John Lawrence. Candlewick, 2006. ISBN 978-0-7636-2989-2 Subj: Fish – seahorses. Sea & seashore.

See what a seal can do ill. by Kate Nelms. Candlewick, 2013. ISBN 978-0-7636-6574-6 Subj: Animals – seals.

Butterworth, Nick. *Albert the bear* ill. by author. HarperCollins, 2002. ISBN 978-0-06-053688-6 Subj: Friendship. Toys. Toys – bears.

Jasper's beanstalk by Nick Butterworth and Mick Inkpen ill. by Mick Inkpen. Bradbury, 1993. ISBN 978-0-02-716231-8 Subj: Animals – cats. Behavior – dissatisfaction. Days of the week, months of the year. Plants.

Jingle bells ill. by author. Orchard, 1998. ISBN 978-0-531-30124-1 Subj: Animals – cats. Animals – mice. Holidays – Christmas. Problem solving.

My dad is awesome ill. by author. Candlewick, 1992. ISBN 978-1-56402-033-8 Subj: Behavior – boasting, showing off. Family life – fathers. Holidays – Father's Day.

One snowy night ill. by author. Little, 1990. ISBN 978-0-316-11918-4 Subj: Animals. Character traits – kindness to animals. Night. Weather – snow.

Buxton, Jane. *The littlest llama* ill. by Jenny Cooper. Sterling, 2008. ISBN 978-1-4027-5277-3 Subj: Activities – playing. Animals – llamas. Foreign lands – South America. Rhyming text.

Buzzeo, Toni. *Adventure Annie goes to kindergarten* ill. by Amy Wummer. Penguin, 2010. ISBN 978-0-8037-3358-9 Subj: School – first day.

Adventure Annie goes to work ill. by Amy Wummer. Dial, 2009. ISBN 978-0-8037-3233-9 Subj: Behavior – lost. Careers. Family life – mothers.

Inside the books: readers and libraries around the world ill. by Jude Daly. Upstart, 2012. ISBN 978-1-60213-058-6 Subj: Books, reading. Libraries. Rhyming text. World.

Just like my Papa ill. by Mike Wohnoutka. Disney/Hyperion, 2013. ISBN 978-1-4231-4263-8 Subj: Animals – babies. Animals – lions. Family life – fathers. Foreign lands – Africa.

Lighthouse Christmas ill. by Nancy Carpenter. Penguin, 2011. ISBN 978-0-8037-3053-3 Subj: Airplanes, airports. Family life – brothers & sisters. Holidays – Christmas. Lighthouses.

My Bibi always remembers ill. by Mike Wohnoutka. Disney/Hyperion, 2014. ISBN 978-142318385-3 Subj: Animals – elephants. Character traits – curiosity. Family life – grandmothers. Foreign lands – Africa.

No T. Rex in the library ill. by Sachiko Yoshikawa. Simon & Schuster, 2010. ISBN 978-1-4169-3927-6 Subj: Behavior – misbehavior. Dinosaurs. Libraries.

One cool friend ill. by David Small. Dial, 2012. ISBN 978-0-8037-3413-5 Subj: Aquariums. Birds – penguins. Caldecott award honor books. Friendship. Humorous stories.

A passion for elephants: the real life adventure of field scientist Cynthia Moss ill. by Holly Berry. Dial, 2015. ISBN 978-080374090-7 Subj: Animals – elephants. Careers – scientists.

Penelope Popper book doctor ill. by Jana Christy. Upstart, 2011. ISBN 978-1-60213-054-8 Subj: Books, reading. Libraries.

The sea chest ill. by Mary GrandPré. Dial, 2002. ISBN 978-0-8037-2703-8 Subj: Islands. Lighthouses. Sea & seashore.

Stay close to Mama ill. by Mike Wohnoutka. Hyperion, 2012. ISBN 978-1-4231-3482-4 Subj: Animals – babies. Animals – giraffes. Family life – mothers. Foreign lands – Africa.

Whose tools? ill. by Jim Datz. Abrams/Appleseed, 2015. ISBN 978-141971431-3 Subj: Careers – construction workers. Format, unusual – toy & movable books. Homes, houses. Tools.

Whose truck? ill. by Jim Datz. Abrams/Appleseed, 2015. ISBN 978-141971612-6 Subj: Format, unusual – board books. Machines. Trucks.

Bynum, Janie. *Altoona up north* ill. by author. Harcourt, 2001. ISBN 978-0-15-202313-3 Subj: Animals – baboons. Concepts – cold & heat. Family life – aunts, uncles. Weather – snow.

Kiki's blankie ill. by author. Sterling, 2009. ISBN 978-1-4027-5910-9 Subj: Animals – monkeys. Behavior – lost & found possessions. Character traits – bravery. Reptiles – alligators, crocodiles.

Nutmeg and Barley: a budding friendship ill. by author. Candlewick, 2006. ISBN 978-0-7636-2382-1 Subj: Animals – mice. Animals – squirrels. Friendship.

Otis ill. by author. Harcourt, 2000. ISBN 978-0-15-202153-5 Subj: Animals – pigs. Character traits – cleanliness. Character traits – individuality. Friendship. Frogs & toads.

Byous, Shawn. *Because I stubbed my toe* ill. by author. Capstone, 2014. ISBN 978-162370088-1

Subj: Accidents. Anatomy – toes. Humorous stories. Rhyming text.

Byrd, Robert. *Brave Chicken Little* (Chicken Little)

Saint Francis and the Christmas donkey ill. by author. Dutton, 2000. ISBN 978-0-525-46480-8 Subj: Animals – donkeys. Holidays – Christmas. Religion – Nativity.

Byrne, Richard. *This book is out of control!* ill. by author. Henry Holt, 2016. ISBN 978-162779933-1 Subj: Animals – dogs. Books, reading.

This book just ate my dog! ill. by author. Henry Holt, 2014. ISBN 978-162779071-0 Subj: Animals – dogs. Books, reading.

We're in the wrong book! ill. by author. Henry Holt, 2016. ISBN 978-162779451-0 Subj: Behavior – lost. Books, reading.

Byun, You. *Dream friends* ill. by author. Penguin/Nancy Paulsen, 2013. ISBN 978-0-399-25739-1 Subj: Dreams. Emotions – loneliness. Friendship. Imagination – imaginary friends. Moving.

C is for caboose: riding the rails from A to Z. Chronicle, 2007. ISBN 978-0-8118-5643-0 Subj: ABC books. Trains.

Cabatingan, Erin. *A is for Musk Ox* ill. by Matthew Myers. Roaring Brook, 2012. ISBN 978-1-59643-676-3 Subj: ABC books. Animals. Animals – muskoxen. Animals – zebras.

Musk Ox counts ill. by Matthew Myers. Roaring Brook, 2013. ISBN 978-1-59643-798-2 Subj: Animals. Animals – muskoxen. Animals – zebras. Counting, numbers.

Cabrera, Jane. *Baa, baa, black sheep* ill. by author. Holiday House, 2015. ISBN 978-082343388-9 Subj: Animals – sheep. Books, reading. Nursery rhymes. Rhyming text.

Bear's good night ill. by author. Candlewick, 2002. ISBN 978-0-7636-1796-7 Subj: Animals – bears. Bedtime. Format, unusual – toy & movable books.

Here we go round the mulberry bush ill. by author. Holiday House, 2010. ISBN 978-0-8234-2288-3 Subj: Animals – dogs. Songs.

If you're happy and you know it ill. by author. Holiday House, 2005. ISBN 978-0-8234-1881-7 Subj: Animals. Emotions – happiness. Music. Songs.

Kitty's cuddles ill. by author. Holiday House, 2007. ISBN 978-0-8234-2066-7 Subj: Animals – cats. Hugging.

The lonesome polar bear ill. by author. Random House, 2002. ISBN 978-0-375-82410-4 Subj: Animals – polar bears. Behavior – needing someone. Friendship.

Mommy, carry me please! ill. by author. Holiday House, 2006. ISBN 978-0-8234-1935-7 Subj: Animals – babies. Family life – mothers.

Monkey's play time ill. by author. Candlewick, 2002. ISBN 978-0-7636-1795-0 Subj: Activities – playing. Animals. Animals – monkeys. Format, unusual – board books.

Old MacDonald had a farm (Old MacDonald had a farm)

One, two, buckle my shoe ill. by author. Holiday, 2009. ISBN 978-0-8234-2230-2 Subj: Birthdays. Counting, numbers. Nursery rhymes. Parties.

Rock-a-bye baby ill. by author. Holiday House, 2017. ISBN 978-082343753-5 Subj: Animals. Bedtime. Nursery rhymes.

Row, row, row your boat ill. by author. Holiday House, 2014. ISBN 978-082343050-5 Subj: Animals. Boats, ships. Rhyming text. Songs.

Ten in the bed ill. by author. Holiday House, 2006. ISBN 978-0-8234-2027-8 Subj: Bedtime. Counting, numbers. Toys.

There was an old woman who lived in a shoe ill. by author. Holiday House, 2016. ISBN 978-082343554-8 Subj: Behavior – resourcefulness. Clothing – shoes. Family life – mothers. Homes, houses. Nursery rhymes. Problem solving. Rhyming text.

Twinkle, twinkle, little star ill. by author. Holiday House, 2012. ISBN 978-0-8234-2519-8 Subj: Animals. Lullabies. Nursery rhymes. Sky. Songs. Stars.

The wheels on the bus ill. by author. Holiday House, 2011. ISBN 978-0-8234-2350-7 Subj: Buses. Foreign lands – Africa. Music. Songs.

Cader, Lisa Lebowitz. *When I wear my crown* ill. by Laura Huliska-Beith. Chronicle, 2002. ISBN 978-0-8118-3484-1 Subj: Activities – playing. Imagination. Toys.

When I wear my tiara ill. by Laura Huliska-Beith. Chronicle, 2002. ISBN 978-0-8118-3485-8 Subj: Activities – playing. Imagination. Toys.

Cadow, Kenneth M. *Alfie runs away* ill. by Lauren Castillo. Farrar, 2010. ISBN 978-0-374-30202-3 Subj: Behavior – running away. Family life – mothers.

Caffey, Donna. *Yikes-lice!* ill. by Patrick Girouard. Albert Whitman, 1998. ISBN 978-0-8075-9374-5 Subj: Family life. Insects – lice. Rhyming text.

Cain, Janan. *The way I feel* ill. by author. Parenting, 2000. ISBN 978-1-884734-71-7 Subj: Emotions. Rhyming text.

Cain, Sheridan. *By the light of the moon* ill. by Gaby Hansen. Tiger Tales, 2007. ISBN 978-1-58925-062-8 Subj: Animals – mice. Bedtime. Moon.

Calcagnino, Steve. *The body book* (Rotner, Shelley)

Caldicott, Chris. *World food alphabet* ill. with photos. Frances Lincoln, 2013. ISBN 978-1-84780-284-2 Subj: ABC books. Food. World.

Calhoun, Mary. *Blue-ribbon Henry* ill. by Erick Ingraham. Morrow, 1998. ISBN 978-0-688-14675-7 Subj: Animals – cats. Character traits – helpfulness. Fairs, festivals.

Cross-country cat ill. by Erick Ingraham. Morrow, 1979. ISBN 978-0-688-32186-4 Subj: Animals – cats. Character traits – cleverness. Sports – skiing.

Henry the Christmas cat ill. by Erick Ingraham. HarperCollins, 2002. ISBN 978-0-688-16561-1 Subj: Animals – cats. Animals – sheep. Holidays – Christmas. Theater.

Henry the sailor cat ill. by Erick Ingraham. Morrow, 1994. ISBN 978-0-688-10841-0 Subj: Animals – cats. Boats, ships. Sailors. Sea & seashore.

High-wire Henry ill. by Erick Ingraham. Morrow, 1991. ISBN 978-0-688-08984-9 Subj: Animals – cats. Animals – dogs. Emotions – envy, jealousy. Pets.

Hot-air Henry ill. by Erick Ingraham. Morrow, 1981. ISBN 978-0-688-00502-3 Subj: Activities – ballooning. Animals – cats.

A shepherd's gift ill. by Raúl Colón. HarperCollins, 2001. ISBN 978-0-688-15177-5 Subj: Careers – shepherds. Gifts. Holidays – Christmas. Orphans. Religion – Nativity.

Cali, Davide. *A funny thing happened on the way to school . . .* ill. by Benjamin Chaud. Chronicle, 2015. ISBN 978-145213168-9 Subj: Behavior – promptness, tardiness. Imagination. School.

I didn't do my homework because . . . ill. by Benjamin Chaud. Chronicle, 2014. ISBN 978-145212551-0 Subj: Behavior – resourcefulness. Homework. Humorous stories. Imagination.

The tiny tale of Little Pea ill. by Sébastien Mourrain. Kids Can, 2017. ISBN 978-177138843-6 Subj: Character traits – smallness. Concepts – size.

The truth about my unbelievable summer . . . ill. by Benjamin Chaud. Chronicle, 2016. ISBN 978-145214483-2 Subj: Activities – vacationing. Humorous stories. Tall tales.

Callahan, Sean. *The leprechaun who lost his rainbow* ill. by Nancy Cote. Albert Whitman, 2009. ISBN 978-0-8075-4454-9 Subj: Family life – grandfathers. Holidays – St. Patrick's Day. Mythical creatures – leprechauns. Weather – rainbows.

Shannon and the world's tallest leprechaun ill. by Kathleen Kemly. Albert Whitman, 2008. ISBN 978-0-8075-7326-6 Subj: Activities – dancing. Behavior – wishing. Concepts – size. Contests. Holidays – St. Patrick's Day. Mythical creatures – leprechauns.

A wild Father's Day ill. by Daniel Howarth. Albert Whitman, 2009. ISBN 978-0-8075-2293-6 Subj: Animals. Holidays – Father's Day. Imagination.

Callan, Lyndall. *Dirt on their skirts* (Rappaport, Doreen)

Callery, Sean. *Hide and seek in the jungle* ill. by Rebecca Robinson. Kingfisher, 2010. ISBN 978-0-7534-6392-5 Subj: Animals. Format, unusual – board books. Jungle.

Calmenson, Stephanie. *Birthday at the Panda Palace* ill. by Doug Cushman. HarperCollins, 2007. ISBN 978-0-06-052663-4 Subj: Animals. Animals – mice. Animals – pandas. Birthdays. Gifts. Rhyming text.

The frog principal ill. by Denise Brunkus. Scholastic, 2001. ISBN 978-0-590-37070-7 Subj: Careers – school principals. Frogs & toads. Magic. School.

Good for you! toddler rhymes for toddler times ill. by Melissa Sweet. HarperCollins, 2001. ISBN 978-0-688-17737-9 Subj: Babies, toddlers. Poetry.

Jazzmatazz! ill. by Bruce Degen. HarperCollins, 2008. ISBN 978-0-06-077289-5 Subj: Animals. Music. Rhyming text.

Late for school! ill. by Sachiko Yoshikawa. Carolrhoda, 2008. ISBN 978-1-57505-935-8 Subj: Behavior – promptness, tardiness. Careers – teachers. Rhyming text. Transportation.

May I pet your dog? the how-to guide for kids meeting dogs (and dogs meeting kids) ill. by Jan Ormerod. Houghton, 2007. ISBN 978-0-618-51034-4 Subj: Animals – dogs. Friendship. Pets. Safety.

No honking allowed ill. by Antongionata Ferrari. Holiday House, 2017. ISBN 978-082343672-9 Subj: Activities – driving. Automobiles. Dinosaurs. Rhyming text.

Ollie's class trip: a yes-and-no book ill. by Abby Carter. Holiday, 2015. ISBN 978-082343432-9 Subj: Aquariums. Character traits – questioning. School – field trips.

Ollie's school day: a yes-and-no book ill. by Abby Carter. Holiday House, 2012. ISBN 978-0-8234-

2377-4 Subj: Character traits – questioning. Day. School.

Oopsy, teacher! ill. by Sachiko Yoshikawa. Carolrhoda, 2012. ISBN 978-0-7613-5894-7 Subj: Behavior – lost & found possessions. Careers – teachers. Humorous stories. Rhyming text.

Perfect puppy ill. by Thomas Yezerski. Clarion, 2001. ISBN 978-0-618-01139-1 Subj: Animals – babies. Animals – dogs. Emotions – love.

The principal's new clothes ill. by Denise Brunkus. Scholastic, 1989. ISBN 978-0-590-41822-5 Subj: Careers – school principals. Careers – tailors. Character traits – pride. Character traits – vanity. Clothing. Folk & fairy tales. School.

The teeny tiny teacher ill. by Denis Roche. Scholastic, 1998. ISBN 978-0-590-37123-0 Subj: Careers – teachers. Folk & fairy tales. Ghosts. School.

Welcome, baby! ill. by Melissa Sweet. HarperCollins, 2002. ISBN 978-0-06-000492-7 Subj: Babies, toddlers. Poetry.

Calvert, Pam. *Princess Peepers* ill. by Tuesday Mourning. Marshall Cavendish, 2008. ISBN 978-0-7614-5437-3 Subj: Behavior – bullying, teasing. Glasses. Royalty – princesses.

Princess Peepers picks a pet ill. by Tuesday Mourning. Marshall Cavendish, 2011. ISBN 978-0-7614-5815-9 Subj: Contests. Dragons. Glasses. Royalty – princesses.

Camcam, Princesse. *Fox's garden* ill. by author. Enchanted Lion, 2014. ISBN 978-159270167-4 Subj: Animals – foxes. Character traits – kindness to animals. Wordless.

Cameron, C. C. *One for me, one for you* ill. by Grace Lin. Roaring Brook, 2003. ISBN 978-0-7613-2807-0 Subj: Behavior – sharing. Counting, numbers. Rhyming text.

Cameron, Eileen. *Canyon* photos by Michael Collier. Mikaya, 2002. ISBN 978-1-931414-03-6 Subj: Canyons. Earth. Poetry. Rivers.

Camp, Lindsay. *The biggest bed in the world* ill. by Jonathan Langley. HarperCollins, 2000. ISBN 978-0-06-028687-3 Subj: Bedtime. Family life. Furniture – beds. Sleep.

Campbell, Ann-Jeanette. *Queenie Farmer had fifteen daughters* ill. by Holly Meade. Silver Whistle, 2002. ISBN 978-0-15-201933-4 Subj: Family life – daughters. Family life – mothers.

Campbell, Bebe Moore. *I get so hungry* ill. by Amy Bates. Putnam, 2008. ISBN 978-0-399-24311-0 Subj: Ethnic groups in the U.S. – African Americans. Health & fitness. School.

Campbell, K. G. *Dylan the villain* ill. by K. G. Campbell. Viking, 2016. ISBN 978-045147642-5 Subj: Contests. Humorous stories. School.

Lester's dreadful sweaters ill. by K. G. Campbell. Kids Can, 2012. ISBN 978-1-55453-770-9 Subj: Activities – knitting. Circus. Clothing – sweaters. Clowns, jesters. Family life – cousins.

The mermaid and the shoe ill. by author. Kids Can, 2014. ISBN 978-155453771-6 Subj: Character traits – curiosity. Character traits – questioning. Clothing – shoes. Mythical creatures – mermaids, mermen.

Campbell, Rod. *Dear zoo* ill. by author. Four Winds, 1984. ISBN 978-0-02-716440-4 Subj: Animals. Format, unusual – toy & movable books. Zoos.

Farm animals ill. by author. Simon & Schuster, 2015. ISBN 978-148144984-7 Subj: Animals. Farms. Format, unusual – board books.

Campbell, Scott. *Hug machine* ill. by author. Atheneum, 2014. ISBN 978-144245935-9 Subj: Hugging.

Campisi, Stephanie. *The ugly dumpling* ill. by Shahar Kober. Mighty Media, 2016. ISBN 978-193806367-1 Subj: Character traits – appearance. Character traits – being different. Food. Restaurants. Self-concept.

Campoy, F. Isabel. *Maybe something beautiful: how art transformed a neighborhood* by F. Isabel Campoy and Theresa Howell ill. by Rafael López. Houghton Mifflin Harcourt, 2016. ISBN 978-054435769-3 Subj: Activities – painting. Art. Communities, neighborhoods.

¡Muu, moo! rimas de animales = animal nursery rhymes (Ada, Alma Flor)

Pio peep! (Ada, Alma Flor)

Rosa Raposa ill. by José Aruego and Ariane Dewey. Harcourt, 2002. ISBN 978-0-15-202161-0 Subj: Animals – foxes. Animals – jaguars. Behavior – trickery. Foreign lands – South America. Jungle.

Cannon, A. E. *Sophie's fish* ill. by Lee White. Viking, 2012. ISBN 978-0-670-01291-6 Subj: Behavior – worrying. Fish. Pets.

Cannon, Janell. *Crickwing* ill. by author. Harcourt, 2000. ISBN 978-0-15-201790-3 Subj: Character traits – helpfulness. Insects – ants. Insects – cockroaches.

Little Yau ill. by author. Harcourt, 2002. ISBN 978-0-15-201791-0 Subj: Disguises. Illness. Plants.

Stellaluna ill. by author. Harcourt, 1993. ISBN 978-0-15-280217-2 Subj: Animals – bats. Birds.

Character traits – being different. Family life – mothers. Friendship.

Verdi ill. by author. Harcourt, 1997. ISBN 978-0-15-201028-7 Subj: Behavior – growing up. Jungle. Reptiles – snakes.

Cantrell, Charlie. *A friend for Einstein: the smallest stallion* by Charlie Cantrell and Rachel Wagner. Hyperion/Disney, 2011. ISBN 978-1-4231-4563-9 Subj: Animals – horses, ponies. Character traits – smallness.

Canyon, Christopher, adapt. *John Denver's Ancient rhymes: a dolphin lullaby* ill. by Christopher Canyon. Dawn, 2004. ISBN 978-1-58469-064-1 Subj: Animals – dolphins. Lullabies. Music.

John Denver's Sunshine on my shoulders ill. by adapter. Dawn, 2003. ISBN 978-0-613-68518-4 Subj: Music. Songs. Sun. Weather.

Caple, Kathy. *Hillary to the rescue* ill. by author. Carolrhoda, 2000. ISBN 978-1-57505-420-9 Subj: Animals – cats. Seasons – winter.

Worm gets a job ill. by author. Candlewick, 2004. ISBN 978-0-7636-1694-6 Subj: Activities – painting. Animals. Animals – worms. Contests. Money.

Capucilli, Alyssa Satin. *Bathtime for Biscuit* ill. by Pat Schories. HarperCollins, 1998. ISBN 978-0-06-027938-7 Subj: Activities – bathing. Animals – dogs. Pets.

Bear hugs ill. by Jim Ishi. Golden, 2000. ISBN 978-0-307-26113-7 Subj: Animals – bears. Emotions – love. Family life. Rhyming text.

Biscuit ill. by Pat Schories. HarperCollins, 1996. ISBN 978-0-06-026198-6 Subj: Animals – dogs. Bedtime.

Biscuit finds a friend ill. by Pat Schories. HarperCollins, 1997. ISBN 978-0-06-027413-9 Subj: Animals – dogs. Birds – ducks. Friendship.

Biscuit gives a gift ill. by Pat Schories. HarperCollins, 2004. ISBN 978-0-06-009467-6 Subj: Animals – dogs. Format, unusual – board books. Holidays.

Biscuit goes to school ill. by Pat Schories. HarperCollins, 2002. ISBN 978-0-06-028683-5 Subj: Animals – dogs. School.

Biscuit loves school ill. by Pat Schories. HarperCollins, 2003. ISBN 978-0-06-009454-6 Subj: Animals – dogs. Format, unusual – toy & movable books. School.

Biscuit visits the pumpkin patch ill. by Pat Schories. HarperCollins, 2004. ISBN 978-0-06-009466-9 Subj: Activities – bathing. Animals. Animals – moose. Toys.

Biscuit wants to play ill. by Pat Schories. HarperCollins, 2001. ISBN 978-0-06-028070-3 Subj: Activities – playing. Animals – babies. Animals – cats. Animals – dogs.

Biscuit wins a prize ill. by Pat Schories. HarperCollins, 2004. ISBN 978-0-06-009457-7 Subj: Animals – dogs. Pets.

Biscuit's big friend ill. by Pat Schories. HarperCollins, 2003. ISBN 978-0-06-029168-6 Subj: Animals – dogs. Friendship.

Biscuit's new trick ill. by Pat Schories. HarperCollins, 2000. ISBN 978-0-06-028068-0 Subj: Animals – babies. Animals – dogs.

Biscuit's picnic ill. by Pat Schories. HarperCollins, 1998. ISBN 978-0-06-028072-7 Subj: Activities – picnicking. Animals – dogs.

Biscuit's Valentine's Day ill. by Pat Schories. HarperCollins, 2001. ISBN 978-0-694-01222-0 Subj: Animals – babies. Animals – dogs. Format, unusual – toy & movable books. Holidays – Valentine's Day.

Happy birthday, Biscuit! ill. by Pat Schories. HarperCollins, 1999. ISBN 978-0-06-028361-2 Subj: Animals – cats. Animals – dogs. Birthdays. Pets.

Happy Hanukkah, Biscuit ill. by Pat Schories. HarperCollins, 2002. ISBN 978-0-694-01525-2 Subj: Animals – dogs. Format, unusual – toy & movable books. Gifts. Holidays – Hanukkah. Jewish culture.

Hello, Biscuit! ill. by Pat Schories. HarperCollins, 1998. ISBN 978-0-06-028071-0 Subj: Animals – dogs. Names.

Hush a bye, baby ill. by Shahrzad Maydani. Simon & Schuster, 2017. ISBN 978-153440139-6 Subj: Babies, toddlers. Bedtime. Family life – fathers. Format, unusual – board books.

I will love you ill. by Lisa Anchin. Scholastic/Cartwheel, 2017. ISBN 978-054580310-6 Subj: Emotions – love. Family life – mothers. Rhyming text.

Inside a zoo in the city ill. by Tedd Arnold. Scholastic, 2000. ISBN 978-0-590-99715-7 Subj: Animals. Cumulative tales. Rebuses. Rhyming text. Zoos.

Katy Duck ill. by Henry Cole. Simon & Schuster, 2007. ISBN 978-1-4169-1901-8 Subj: Activities – dancing. Birds – ducks. Emotions – fear. Format, unusual – board books.

Katy Duck, big sister ill. by Henry Cole. Simon & Schuster, 2007. ISBN 978-1-4169-4209-2 Subj: Activities – dancing. Birds – ducks. Family life – brothers & sisters. Format, unusual – board books. Sibling rivalry.

Katy Duck is a caterpillar ill. by Henry Cole. Simon & Schuster, 2009. ISBN 978-1-4169-6061-4 Subj: Activities – dancing. Birds – ducks. Seasons – spring.

Little spotted cat ill. by Dan Andreasen. Penguin, 2005. ISBN 978-0-8037-2692-5 Subj: Activities – playing. Animals – cats. Sleep.

Merry Christmas, from Biscuit ill. by Pat Schories. HarperCollins, 2001. ISBN 978-0-694-01522-1 Subj: Animals – dogs. Holidays – Christmas.

Mrs. McTats and her houseful of cats ill. by Joan Rankin. Margaret K. McElderry, 2001. ISBN 978-0-689-83185-0 Subj: ABC books. Animals – cats. Counting, numbers. Rhyming text.

My first ballet class photos by Leyah Jensen. Simon & Schuster, 2011. ISBN 978-1-4424-0895-1 Subj: Ballet. Format, unusual – toy & movable books.

My first soccer game: a book with foldout pages photos by Leyah Jensen. Simon & Schuster, 2011. ISBN 978-1-4424-2747-1 Subj: Format, unusual. Sports – soccer.

Not this bear ill. by Lorna Hussey. Henry Holt, 2015. ISBN 978-080509896-9 Subj: Animals – bears. School – first day.

Only my dad and me ill. by Tiphanie Beeke. HarperCollins, 2003. ISBN 978-0-694-52584-3 Subj: Animals – rabbits. Family life – fathers. Format, unusual – toy & movable books.

Only my mom and me ill. by Tiphanie Beeke. HarperCollins, 2003. ISBN 978-0-694-52585-0 Subj: Animals – cats. Family life – mothers. Format, unusual – toy & movable books.

This bear's birthday ill. by Lorna Hussey. Henry Holt, 2017. ISBN 978-162779701-6 Subj: Animals – bears. Behavior – growing up. Birthdays.

Tulip loves Rex ill. by Sarah Massini. HarperCollins/Katherine Tegen, 2014. ISBN 978-006209413-1 Subj: Activities – dancing. Animals – dogs. Character traits – kindness to animals.

What kind of kiss? ill. by Hiroe Nakata. HarperCollins, 2002. ISBN 978-0-694-01573-3 Subj: Animals – bears. Family life – mothers. Kissing. Rhyming text.

Capucilli, Karen. *The jelly bean fun book* ill. with photos. Simon & Schuster, 2001. ISBN 978-0-689-84071-5 Subj: Food. Puzzles.

Caraballo, Samuel. *My big sister / Mi hermana mayor* ill. by Thelma Muraida. Arte Publico, 2012. ISBN 978-1-55885-750-6 Subj: Character traits – kindness. Ethnic groups in the U.S. – Hispanic Americans. Family life – brothers & sisters. Foreign languages.

Carabine, Sue. *A firefighter's night before Christmas* ill. by Shauna Mooney Kawasaki. Gibbs Smith, 2003. ISBN 978-1-58685-269-6 Subj: Careers – firefighters. Holidays – Christmas. Poetry.

Carbone, Elisa. *Diana's White House garden* ill. by Jen Hill. Viking, 2016. ISBN 978-067001649-5 Subj: Gardens, gardening. U.S. history. War.

Heroes of the surf: a rescue story based on true ill. by Nancy Carpenter. Viking, 2012. ISBN 978-0-670-06312-3 Subj: Boats, ships. U.S. history.

Night running: how James escaped with the help of his faithful dog ill. by E. B. Lewis. Knopf, 2008. ISBN 978-0-375-82247-6 Subj: Animals – dogs. Ethnic groups in the U.S. – African Americans. Slavery. U.S. history.

Carey, Lorraine. *Cinderella's stepsister and the big bad wolf* ill. by Migy Blanco. Nosy Crow, 2015. ISBN 978-076368005-3 Subj: Animals – wolves. Family life – stepfamilies. Folk & fairy tales. Royalty – princes.

Carle, Eric. *The artist who painted a blue horse* ill. by author. Penguin, 2011. ISBN 978-0-399-25713-1 Subj: Activities – painting. Animals. Art. Careers – artists. Concepts – color.

Do you want to be my friend? ill. by author. Crowell, 1971. ISBN 978-0-690-24276-8 Subj: Animals – mice. Friendship. Wordless.

Does a kangaroo have a mother, too? ill. by author. HarperCollins, 2000. ISBN 978-0-06-028767-2 Subj: Animals. Family life – mothers.

Draw me a star ill. by author. Philomel, 1992. ISBN 978-0-399-21877-4 Subj: Activities – drawing. Circular tales.

Dream snow ill. by author. Philomel, 2000. ISBN 978-0-399-23579-5 Subj: Farms. Format, unusual – toy & movable books. Holidays – Christmas. Weather – snow.

Friends ill. by author. Philomel, 2013. ISBN 978-0-399-16533-7 Subj: Activities – traveling. Friendship. Moving.

From head to toe ill. by author. HarperCollins, 1997. ISBN 978-0-06-023516-1 Subj: Activities. Anatomy. Animals. Format, unusual – board books.

The grouchy ladybug ill. by author. Crowell, 1977. ISBN 978-0-690-01392-4 Subj: Behavior. Insects – ladybugs. Time.

Have you seen my cat? ill. by author. Watts, 1973. ISBN 978-0-531-02552-9 Subj: Animals – cats. Behavior – lost.

Hello, red fox ill. by author. Simon & Schuster, 1998. ISBN 978-0-689-81775-5 Subj: Animals. Art. Birthdays. Concepts – color. Frogs & toads. Holidays.

A house for Hermit Crab ill. by author. Simon & Schuster, 2004. ISBN 978-0-689-87064-4 Subj: Crustaceans – crabs. Homes, houses. Sea & seashore.

I see a song ill. by author. Crowell, 1973. ISBN 978-0-690-43307-4 Subj: Music. Musical instruments – violins. Wordless.

Little cloud ill. by author. Philomel, 1996. ISBN 978-0-399-23034-9 Subj: Concepts – shape. Imagination. Sky. Weather – clouds. Weather – rain.

The mixed-up chameleon ill. by author. Rev. ed. Crowell, 1984. ISBN 978-0-690-00924-8 Subj: Character traits – being different. Concepts – color. Reptiles – chameleons. Reptiles – lizards. Self-concept.

My apron: a story from my childhood ill. by author. Philomel, 1994. ISBN 978-0-399-22824-7 Subj: Careers – plasterers. Clothing – aprons. Family life – aunts, uncles.

My first peek-a-boo: animals ill. by author. Simon & Schuster, 2017. ISBN 978-153440105-1 Subj: Animals. Format, unusual – board books. Format, unusual – toy & movable books.

My very first book of colors ill. by author. Harper-Collins, 1985. ISBN 978-0-694-00011-1 Subj: Concepts – color. Format, unusual.

My very first book of food ill. by author. Crowell, 1986. ISBN 978-0-694-00130-9 Subj: Food. Format, unusual – toy & movable books.

My very first book of growth ill. by author. Crowell, 1986. ISBN 978-0-694-00094-4 Subj: Behavior – growing up. Format, unusual.

My very first book of heads and tails ill. by author. Crowell, 1986. ISBN 978-0-694-00128-6 Subj: Anatomy. Format, unusual – toy & movable books.

My very first book of homes ill. by author. Crowell, 1986. ISBN 978-0-694-00092-0 Subj: Format, unusual. Homes, houses.

My very first book of motion ill. by author. Crowell, 1986. ISBN 978-0-694-00093-7 Subj: Concepts. Format, unusual.

My very first book of numbers ill. by author. HarperCollins, 1985. ISBN 978-0-694-00012-8 Subj: Counting, numbers. Format, unusual.

My very first book of shapes ill. by author. HarperCollins, 1985. ISBN 978-0-694-00013-5 Subj: Concepts – shape. Format, unusual.

My very first book of sounds ill. by author. Crowell, 1986. ISBN 978-0-694-00131-6 Subj: Format, unusual – toy & movable books. Noise, sounds.

My very first book of tools ill. by author. Crowell, 1986. ISBN 978-0-694-00129-3 Subj: Format, unusual – toy & movable books. Tools.

My very first book of touch ill. by author. Crowell, 1986. ISBN 978-0-694-00095-1 Subj: Format, unusual. Senses – touch.

My very first book of words ill. by author. Harper-Collins, 1985. ISBN 978-0-694-00014-2 Subj: Format, unusual. Language.

The nonsense show ill. by author. Philomel, 2015. ISBN 978-039917687-6 Subj: Humorous stories. Rhyming text.

1, 2, 3 to the zoo: a counting book ill. by author. Philomel, 1996. ISBN 978-0-399-23013-4 Subj: Animals. Counting, numbers. Zoos.

Pancakes, pancakes ill. by author. Knopf, 1970. ISBN 978-0-394-90490-0 Subj: Cumulative tales. Food.

Papa, please get the moon for me ill. by author. Alphabet, 1986. ISBN 978-0-88708-026-5 Subj: Format, unusual – toy & movable books. Moon.

The rooster who set out to see the world ill. by author. Simon & Schuster, 1991. ISBN 978-0-88708-178-1 Subj: Activities – traveling. Birds – chickens, roosters. Counting, numbers.

Rooster's off to see the world ill. by author. Picture Book Studio, 1987. ISBN 978-0-88708-042-5 Subj: Activities – traveling. Birds – chickens, roosters. Counting, numbers.

The secret birthday message ill. by author. Crowell, 1972. ISBN 978-0-690-72348-9 Subj: Birthdays. Format, unusual – toy & movable books.

"Slowly, slowly, slowly," said the sloth ill. by author. Philomel, 2002. ISBN 978-0-399-23954-0 Subj: Animals. Animals – sloths. Jungle.

10 little rubber ducks ill. by author. HarperCollins, 2005. ISBN 978-0-06-074076-4 Subj: Animals. Birds – ducks. Counting, numbers. Format, unusual. Sea & seashore. Toys.

The tiny seed ill. by author. Rev. ed. Picture Book Studio, 1987. ISBN 978-0-88708-015-9 Subj: Plants. Seasons. Seeds.

Today is Monday ill. by author. Philomel, 1993. ISBN 978-0-399-21966-5 Subj: Animals. Days of the week, months of the year. Food. Songs.

The very busy spider ill. by author. Philomel, 1985. ISBN 978-0-399-21166-9 Subj: Animals. Spiders.

The very clumsy click beetle ill. by author. Philomel, 1999. ISBN 978-0-399-23201-5 Subj: Character traits – perseverance. Insects – beetles.

The very hungry caterpillar ill. by author. Collins-World, 1979. ISBN 978-0-529-00776-6 Subj: Days of the week, months of the year. Format, unusual. Insects – butterflies, caterpillars. Metamorphosis.

The very lonely firefly ill. by author. Philomel, 1995. ISBN 978-0-399-22774-5 Subj: Format, unusual – toy & movable books. Insects – fireflies.

The very quiet cricket ill. by author. Putnam, 1990. ISBN 978-0-399-21885-9 Subj: Format, unusual. Insects – crickets. Noise, sounds.

Walter the baker ill. by author. Simon & Schuster, 1995. ISBN 978-0-689-80078-8 Subj: Activities – working. Careers – bakers. Food. Royalty.

Watch out! A giant! ill. by author. Collins-World, 1978. ISBN 978-0-529-05456-2 Subj: Format, unusual – toy & movable books. Giants.

Carle, Eric, et al. *What's your favorite animal?* ill. by author and 14 other illustrators. Henry Holt, 2014. ISBN 978-080509641-5 Subj: Animals. Art.

What's your favorite color?. ill. by author and 14 other illustrators. Henry Holt, 2017. ISBN 978-080509614-9 Subj: Art. Careers – artists. Careers – illustrators. Concepts – color.

Carlin, Deborah. *What's love?* (Rotner, Shelley)

Carlin, Laura. *A world of your own* ill. by author. Phaidon, 2014. ISBN 978-071486362-7 Subj: Activities – drawing. Art. Imagination.

Carlin, Patricia. *Alfie is not afraid* ill. by author. Hyperion/Disney, 2012. ISBN 978-1-4231-4537-0 Subj: Animals – dogs. Camps, camping. Emotions – fear.

Carling, Amelia Lau. *Mama and Papa have a store* ill. by author. Groundwood, 2003. ISBN 978-0-88899-538-4 Subj: Family life. Foreign lands – Guatemala. Immigrants, immigration. Stores.

Carlson, Lori Marie. *Hurray for Three Kings' Day* ill. by Ed Martinez. Morrow, 1998. ISBN 978-0-688-16240-5 Subj: Ethnic groups in the U.S. – Hispanic Americans. Holidays. Religion.

Carlson, Melody. *The day the circus came to town* ill. by Ned Butterfield. Crossway, 2000. ISBN 978-1-58134-158-4 Subj: Circus.

The Easterville miracle ill. by Susan Reagan. Broadman & Holman, 2004. ISBN 978-0-8054-2680-9 Subj: Holidays – Easter. Religion. Rhyming text.

Farmer Brown's field trip ill. by Steve Björkman. Crossway, 2000. ISBN 978-1-58134-142-3 Subj: Careers – farmers. Glasses. Rhyming text.

Forever friends (Tada, Joni Eareckson)

When the creepy things come out ill. by Susan Reagan. Broadman & Holman, 2003. ISBN 978-0-8054-2687-8 Subj: Emotions – fear. Holidays – Halloween. Night. Rhyming text.

Carlson, Nancy. *ABC, I like me!* ill. by author. Viking, 1997. ISBN 978-0-670-87458-3 Subj: ABC books. Language. Self-concept.

Armond goes to a party: a book about Asperger's and friendship by Nancy Carlson and Armond Isaak; ill. by Nancy Carlson. Free Spirit, 2014. ISBN 978-157542466-8 Subj: Character traits – being different. Disabilities – Asperger's. Disabilities – autism. Parties. Self-concept.

Arnie and the skateboard gang ill. by author. Viking, 1995. ISBN 978-0-670-85722-7 Subj: Animals. Animals – cats. Character traits – bravery. Character traits – foolishness. Sports – skateboarding.

First grade, here I come! ill. by author. Penguin, 2006. ISBN 978-0-670-06127-3 Subj: Animals – mice. School – first day.

Get up and go! ill. by author. Penguin, 2006. ISBN 978-0-670-05981-2 Subj: Animals. Animals – pigs. Health & fitness – exercise.

Harriet and George's Christmas treat ill. by author. Carolrhoda, 2001. ISBN 978-1-57505-506-0 Subj: Animals – dogs. Animals – rabbits. Food. Holidays – Christmas.

Harriet and the garden ill. by author. Carolrhoda, 1982. ISBN 978-0-87614-184-7 Subj: Animals – dogs. Problem solving.

Harriet and the roller coaster ill. by author. Carolrhoda, 1982. ISBN 978-0-87614-183-0 Subj: Animals – dogs. Character traits – bravery.

Harriet and Walt ill. by author. Carolrhoda, 1982. ISBN 978-0-87614-185-4 Subj: Animals – dogs. Sibling rivalry.

Harriet's Halloween candy ill. by author. Carolrhoda, 1982. ISBN 978-0-87614-182-3 Subj: Animals – dogs. Behavior – greed.

Henry and the bully ill. by author. Penguin, 2010. ISBN 978-0-670-01148-3 Subj: Animals. Animals – mice. Behavior – bullying, teasing. School.

Henry and the Valentine surprise ill. by author. Viking, 2008. ISBN 978-0-670-06267-6 Subj: Animals – mice. Careers – teachers. Holidays – Valentine's Day. School.

Henry's amazing imagination! ill. by author. Viking, 2008. ISBN 978-0-670-06296-6 Subj: Activities – storytelling. Activities – writing. Imagination. School.

Henry's 100 days of kindergarten ill. by author. Penguin, 2005. ISBN 978-0-670-05977-5 Subj: Animals – mice. Counting, numbers. School.

Hooray for Grandparent's Day! ill. by author. Viking, 2000. ISBN 978-0-670-88876-4 Subj: Family life – grandparents. Friendship. School.

How about a hug? ill. by author. Viking, 2001. ISBN 978-0-670-03506-9 Subj: Animals. Animals – pigs.

I don't like to read! ill. by author. Penguin, 2007. ISBN 978-0-670-06191-4 Subj: Animals – mice. Books, reading. School.

I like me ill. by author. Viking, 1988. ISBN 978-0-670-82062-7 Subj: Character traits – individuality. Self-concept.

It's going to be perfect ill. by author. Viking, 1998. ISBN 978-0-670-87802-4 Subj: Dreams. Family life.

Look out kindergarten, here I come! ill. by author. Viking, 1999. ISBN 978-0-670-88378-3 Subj: Activities. Animals – mice. School – first day.

Louanne Pig in the mysterious Valentine ill. by author. Carolrhoda, 1985. ISBN 978-0-87614-282-0 Subj: Animals – pigs. Holidays – Valentine's Day.

Loudmouth George and the cornet ill. by author. Carolrhoda, 1983. ISBN 978-0-87614-214-1 Subj: Animals – rabbits. Behavior – boasting, showing off.

Loudmouth George and the fishing trip ill. by author. Carolrhoda, 1983. ISBN 978-0-87614-213-4 Subj: Animals – rabbits. Behavior – boasting, showing off.

Loudmouth George and the new neighbors ill. by author. Carolrhoda, 1983. ISBN 978-0-87614-216-5 Subj: Animals – rabbits. Behavior – boasting, showing off. Prejudice.

Loudmouth George and the sixth-grade bully ill. by author. Carolrhoda, 1983. ISBN 978-0-87614-217-2 Subj: Animals – rabbits. Behavior – boasting, showing off. Behavior – bullying, teasing. Behavior – stealing.

Loudmouth George earns his allowance ill. by author. Carolrhoda, 2007. ISBN 978-0-8225-6550-4 Subj: Animals – rabbits. Behavior – misbehavior. Character traits – willfulness.

My best friend moved away ill. by author. Viking, 2001. ISBN 978-0-670-89498-7 Subj: Friendship. Moving.

My family is forever ill. by author. Viking, 2004. ISBN 978-0-670-03650-9 Subj: Adoption. Ethnic groups in the U.S. – Asian Americans. Family life.

Sit still! ill. by author. Viking, 1996. ISBN 978-0-670-85721-0 Subj: Behavior – fidgeting. School.

Smile a lot! ill. by author. Carolrhoda, 2002. ISBN 978-0-87614-869-3 Subj: Character traits – optimism. Frogs & toads.

Snowden ill. by author. Viking, 1997. ISBN 978-0-670-88078-2 Subj: Friendship. Snowmen. Sports – ice skating.

Sometimes you barf ill. by author. Carolrhoda, 2014. ISBN 978-146771412-9 Subj: Emotions – embarrassment. Illness.

Start saving, Henry! ill. by author. Viking, 2009. ISBN 978-0-670-01147-6 Subj: Animals – mice. Behavior – saving things. Money. Toys.

There's a big, beautiful world out there! ill. by author. Viking, 2002. ISBN 978-0-670-03580-9 Subj: Emotions – fear.

Think big! ill. by author. Carolrhoda, 2005. ISBN 978-1-57505-622-7 Subj: Character traits – appearance. Character traits – smallness. Concepts – size. Frogs & toads. School. Self-concept.

Think happy! ill. by author. Carolrhoda, 2009. ISBN 978-0-8225-8940-2 Subj: Animals. Emotions – happiness. Frogs & toads.

Carlstrom, Nancy White. *Before you were born* ill. by Linda Saport. Eerdmans, 2002. ISBN 978-0-8028-5185-7 Subj: Babies, toddlers. Birth. Family life. Family life – parents. Poetry.

Better not get wet, Jesse Bear ill. by Bruce Degen. Macmillan, 1988. ISBN 978-0-02-717280-5 Subj: Animals – bears. Rhyming text.

Does God know how to tie shoes? ill. by Lori McElrath-Eslick. Eerdmans, 1993. ISBN 978-0-8028-5074-4 Subj: Religion.

Guess who's coming, Jesse Bear ill. by Bruce Degen. Simon & Schuster, 1998. ISBN 978-0-689-80702-2 Subj: Animals – bears. Family life – cousins. Rhyming text.

Happy birthday, Jesse Bear! ill. by Bruce Degen. Macmillan, 1994. ISBN 978-0-02-717277-5 Subj: Animals – bears. Birthdays. Parties. Rhyming text.

How do you say it today, Jesse Bear? ill. by Bruce Degen. Macmillan, 1992. ISBN 978-0-02-717276-8 Subj: Animals – bears. Days of the week, months of the year. Rhyming text.

How does the wind walk? ill. by Deborah Kogan Ray. Macmillan, 1993. ISBN 978-0-02-717275-1 Subj: Seasons. Weather – wind.

I'm not moving, Mama! ill. by Thor Wickstrom. Macmillan, 1990. ISBN 978-0-02-717286-7 Subj: Animals – mice. Moving.

It's about time, Jesse Bear ill. by Bruce Degen. Macmillan, 1990. ISBN 978-0-02-717351-2 Subj: Animals – bears. Rhyming text. Time.

It's your first day of school, Annie Claire ill. by Margie Moore. Abrams, 2009. ISBN 978-0-8109-4057-4 Subj: Animals – dogs. Behavior – worrying. Family life – mothers. Rhyming text. School – first day.

Jesse Bear, what will you wear? ill. by Bruce Degen. Macmillan, 1986. ISBN 978-0-02-717350-5 Subj: Animals – bears. Clothing. Family life.

Let's count it out, Jesse Bear ill. by Bruce Degen. Simon & Schuster, 1996. ISBN 978-0-689-80478-6 Subj: Animals – bears. Counting, numbers. Rhyming text.

Mama, will it snow tonight? ill. by Paul Tong. Boyds Mills, 2009. ISBN 978-1-59078-562-1 Subj: Animals – foxes. Animals – rabbits. Family life – mothers. Seasons – winter. Weather – snow.

The snow speaks ill. by Jane Dyer. Little, 1992. ISBN 978-0-316-12861-2 Subj: Country. Seasons – winter. Weather – snow.

Thanksgiving Day at our house ill. by R. W. Alley. Simon & Schuster, 1999. ISBN 978-0-689-80360-4 Subj: Family life. Holidays – Thanksgiving. Poetry.

The way to Wyatt's house ill. by Mary Morgan. Walker, 2000. ISBN 978-0-8027-8742-2 Subj: Animals. Farms. Friendship.

What a scare, Jesse Bear! ill. by Bruce Degen. Simon & Schuster, 1999. ISBN 978-0-689-81961-2 Subj: Animals – bears. Holidays – Halloween. Rhyming text.

What does the sky say? ill. by Tim Ladwig. Eerdmans, 2001. ISBN 978-0-8028-5208-3 Subj: Nature. Poetry. Religion. Sky. Weather.

Where is Christmas, Jesse Bear? ill. by Bruce Degen. Simon & Schuster, 2000. ISBN 978-0-689-81962-9 Subj: Animals – bears. Holidays – Christmas. Rhyming text.

Who said boo? Halloween poems for the very young ill. by R. W. Alley. Simon & Schuster, 1995. ISBN 978-0-689-80308-6 Subj: Holidays – Halloween. Poetry.

Carluccio, Maria. *D is for dress up: the ABCs of what we wear* ill. by author. Chronicle, 2016. ISBN 978-145214025-4 Subj: ABC books. Clothing.

I'm three! Look what I can do ill. by author. Henry Holt, 2010. ISBN 978-0-8050-8313-2 Subj: Behavior – growing up.

The sounds around town ill. by author. Barefoot, 2008. ISBN 978-1-905236-28-2 Subj: Activities. Day. Noise, sounds.

Carman, William. *What's that noise?* ill. by author. Random House, 2002. ISBN 978-0-375-91052-4 Subj: Emotions – fear. Imagination. Night. Noise, sounds. Sleep.

Carmichael, Clay. *Lonesome bear* ill. by author. NorthSouth, 2001. ISBN 978-1-55858-968-1 Subj: Behavior – lost & found possessions. Toys – bears.

Carmody, Isobelle. *Magic night* ill. by Declan Lee. Random House, 2007. ISBN 978-0-375-83918-4 Subj: Animals – cats. Magic. Mythical creatures.

Carnavas, Peter. *The children who loved books* ill. by author. Kane/Miller, 2013. ISBN 978-1-61067-145-3 Subj: Books, reading. Libraries.

Carnesi, Monica. *Little dog lost: the true story of a brave dog named Baltic* ill. by author. Penguin, 2012. ISBN 978-0-399-25666-0 Subj: Animals – dogs. Foreign lands – Poland.

Sleepover with Beatrice and Bear ill. by author. Penguin/Nancy Paulsen, 2014. ISBN 978-039925667-7 Subj: Animals – bears. Animals – rabbits. Friendship. Hibernation. Seasons – winter.

Carney, Margaret. *At Grandpa's sugar bush* ill. by Janet Wilson. Kids Can, 1998. ISBN 978-1-55074-341-8 Subj: Careers – farmers. Food. Foreign lands – Canada. Trees.

The biggest fish in the lake ill. by Janet Wilson. Kids Can, 2001. ISBN 978-1-55074-720-1 Subj: Family life – grandfathers. Sports – fishing.

Where does a tiger-heron spend the night? ill. by Mélanie Watt. Kids Can, 2002. ISBN 978-1-55337-022-2 Subj: Birds. Format, unusual – toy & movable books. Rhyming text.

Carney, Mary Lou. *The yippy, yappy Yorkie in the green doggy sweater* (Macomber, Debbie)

Carney-Nunes, Charisse. *I dream for you a world: a covenant for our children* ill. by Ann Marie Williams. Brand Nu Words, 2007. ISBN 978-0-9748142-3-0 Subj: World.

Carr, Jan. *Big Truck and Little Truck* ill. by Ivan Bates. Scholastic, 2000. ISBN 978-0-439-07177-2 Subj: Farms. Trucks.

Dappled apples ill. by Dorothy Donohue. Holiday, 2001. ISBN 978-0-8234-1583-0 Subj: Rhyming text. Seasons – fall.

Frozen noses ill. by Dorothy Donohue. Holiday, 1999. ISBN 978-0-8234-1462-8 Subj: Activities. Friendship. Seasons – winter. Sports.

Greedy apostrophe: a cautionary tale ill. by Ethan Long. Holiday House, 2007. ISBN 978-0-8234-2006-3 Subj: Behavior – greed. Language.

Splish, splash, spring ill. by Dorothy Donohue. Holiday, 2001. ISBN 978-0-8234-1578-6 Subj: Rhyming text. Seasons – spring.

Sweet hearts ill. by Dorothy Donohue. Holiday, 2003. ISBN 978-0-8234-1732-2 Subj: Animals – pandas. Holidays – Valentine's Day.

Carr, Matt. *Superbat* ill. by author. Scholastic, 2017. ISBN 978-133816052-9 Subj: Animals – bats. Character traits – bravery.

Carrer, Chiara. *Otto Carrotto* ill. by author. Eerdmans, 2011. ISBN 978-0-8028-5393-6 Subj: Animals – rabbits. Character traits – individuality. Food.

Carrick, Carol. *Big old bones: a dinosaur tale* ill. by Donald Carrick. Houghton, 1992. ISBN 978-0-395-61582-9 Subj: Dinosaurs.

Patrick's dinosaurs ill. by Donald Carrick. Houghton, 1983. ISBN 978-0-89919-189-8 Subj: Animals. Dinosaurs. Imagination. Prehistory. Science. Zoos.

Patrick's dinosaurs on the Internet ill. by David Milgrim. Clarion, 1999. ISBN 978-0-395-50949-4 Subj: Computers. Dinosaurs. Imagination. Prehistory. School. Space & space ships.

The polar bears are hungry ill. by Paul Carrick. Clarion, 2002. ISBN 978-0-618-15962-8 Subj: Animals – bears. Animals – polar bears. Seasons – winter.

Valentine ill. by Paddy Bouma. Clarion, 1995. ISBN 978-0-395-66554-1 Subj: Animals – sheep. Family life – grandmothers. Family life – mothers. Holidays – Valentine's Day.

What happened to Patrick's dinosaurs? ill. by Donald Carrick. Houghton, 1986. ISBN 978-0-89919-406-6 Subj: Dinosaurs. Imagination. Prehistory.

Carroll, James Christopher. *The boy and the moon* ill. by author. Sleeping Bear, 2010. ISBN 978-1-58536-521-0 Subj: Moon. Night.

Papa's backpack ill. by author. Sleeping Bear, 2015. ISBN 978-158536613-2 Subj: Animals – bears. Careers – military. Emotions – sadness. Family life – fathers.

Carroll, Lewis. *Jabberwocky* ill. by Christopher Myers. Hyperion, 2007. ISBN 978-1-4231-0372-1 Subj: Humorous stories. Mythical creatures. Poetry.

Carryl, Charles E. *The camel's lament* ill. by Charles Santore. Random House, 2004. ISBN 978-0-375-91426-3 Subj: Animals. Animals – camels. Poetry.

Cartaya, Pablo. *Tina Cocolina: queen of the cupcakes* by Pablo Cartaya and Martin Howard ill. by Kirsten Richards. Random House, 2010. ISBN 978-0-375-85891-8 Subj: Activities – baking, cooking. Character traits – individuality. Contests. Food.

Carter, Alden R. *Big brother Dustin* photos by Dan Young. Albert Whitman, 1998. ISBN 978-0-8075-0715-5 Subj: Babies, toddlers. Disabilities – Down syndrome. Family life – brothers & sisters. Names.

I'm tougher than asthma! by Alden R. Carter and Siri M. Carter; photos by Dan Young. Albert Whitman, 1996. ISBN 978-0-8075-3474-8 Subj: Illness – asthma.

I'm tougher than diabetes! photos by Carol S Carter. Albert Whitman, 2001. ISBN 978-0-8075-1572-3 Subj: Illness – diabetes.

Seeing things my way photos by Carol S. Carter. Albert Whitman, 1998. ISBN 978-0-8075-7296-2 Subj: Disabilities. Illness.

Carter, Anne Laurel. *Circus play* ill. by Joanne Fitzgerald. Orca, 2002. ISBN 978-1-55143-225-0 Subj: Circus. Imagination.

The F team ill. by Rose Cowles. Orca, 2003. ISBN 978-1-55143-241-0 Subj: Behavior – bullying, teasing. Character traits – perseverance. Sports – hockey.

My home bay ill. by Alan Daniel and Lea Daniel. Red Deer, 2004. ISBN 978-0-88995-284-3 Subj: Foreign lands – Canada. Friendship.

Under a prairie sky ill. by Alan Daniel and Lea Daniel. Orca, 2002. ISBN 978-1-55143-226-7 Subj: Careers – police officers. Foreign lands – Canada.

Carter, David A. *Blue 2: a pop-up book for children of all ages* ill. by author. Simon & Schuster, 2007. ISBN 978-1-4169-1781-6 Subj: Format, unusual – toy & movable books. Picture puzzles.

Chanukah bugs: a pop-up celebration ill. by author. Simon & Schuster, 2002. ISBN 978-0-689-81860-8 Subj: Format, unusual – toy & movable books. Holidays – Hanukkah. Insects.

Easter bugs: a springtime pop-up ill. by author. Simon & Schuster, 2001. ISBN 978-0-689-81862-2 Subj: Eggs. Format, unusual – toy & movable books. Holidays – Easter. Insects.

Flapdoodle dinosaurs: a colorful pop-up book ill. by author. Simon & Schuster, 2001. ISBN 978-0-689-84643-4 Subj: Dinosaurs. Format, unusual – toy & movable books. Rhyming text.

How many bugs in a box? ill. by author. Simon & Schuster, 1988. ISBN 978-0-671-64965-4 Subj: Format, unusual – toy & movable books. Insects.

If you're happy and you know it, clap your hands ill. by author. Scholastic, 1997. ISBN 978-0-590-93828-0 Subj: Emotions. Format, unusual. Music. Songs.

In a dark, dark wood: an old tale with a new twist ill. by author. Simon & Schuster, 2002. ISBN 978-0-689-85280-0 Subj: Format, unusual – toy & movable books. Ghosts. Homes, houses.

Old MacDonald had a farm: a pop-up book ill. by author. Scholastic, 2001. ISBN 978-0-439-26468-6 Subj: Animals. Careers – farmers. Cumulative tales. Farms. Format, unusual – toy & movable books. Music. Noise, sounds. Songs.

One red dot: a pop-up book for children of all ages ill. by author. Simon & Schuster, 2005. ISBN 978-0-

689-87769-8 Subj: Counting, numbers. Format, unusual – toy & movable books. Picture puzzles.

Peekaboo bugs: a hide-and-seek book ill. by author. Simon & Schuster, 2002. ISBN 978-0-689-85035-6 Subj: Format, unusual – toy & movable books. Games. Insects.

600 black spots: a pop-up book for children of all ages ill. by author. Simon & Schuster, 2007. ISBN 978-1-4169-4092-0 Subj: Format, unusual – toy & movable books. Picture puzzles.

Whoo? Whoo? ill. by author. Simon & Schuster, 2007. ISBN 978-1-4169-3816-3 Subj: Animals. Character traits – questioning. Format, unusual – toy & movable books. Games. Picture puzzles.

Who's under that hat? ill. by author. Text by Sarah Weeks. Harcourt, 2005. ISBN 978-0-15-205467-0 Subj: Clothing. Format, unusual – toy & movable books. Picture puzzles.

Yellow square: a pop-up book for children of all ages ill. by author. Simon & Schuster, 2008. ISBN 978-1-4169-4093-7 Subj: Format, unusual – toy & movable books. Picture puzzles.

Carter, Don. *Get to work, trucks!* ill. by author. Roaring Brook, 2002. ISBN 978-0-7613-2518-5 Subj: Machines. Trucks.

Heaven's all-star jazz band ill. by author. Knopf, 2002. ISBN 978-0-375-91571-0 Subj: Careers – musicians. Ethnic groups in the U.S. – African Americans. Family life – grandfathers. Music. Musical instruments – bands.

Old MacDonald drives a tractor ill. by author. Macmillan, 2007. ISBN 978-1-59643-023-5 Subj: Careers – farmers. Farms. Rhyming text. Tractors.

Send it! ill. by author. Roaring Brook, 2003. ISBN 978-0-7613-2573-4 Subj: Careers – postal workers. Post office.

Carter, Siri M. *I'm tougher than asthma!* (Carter, Alden R.)

Cartier, Wesley. *Marco's run* ill. by Reynold Ruffins. Harcourt, 2001. ISBN 978-0-15-216243-6 Subj: Activities – running. Concepts – speed. Imagination.

Cartwright, Reg. *What we do* ill. by author. Henry Holt, 2005. ISBN 978-0-8050-7671-4 Subj: Animals. Rhyming text.

Casanova, Mary. *The day Dirk Yeller came to town* ill. by Ard Hoyt. Farrar, 2011. ISBN 978-0-374-31742-3 Subj: Books, reading. Crime. Libraries. U.S. history – frontier & pioneer life.

The hunter ill. by Ed Young. Atheneum, 2000. ISBN 978-0-689-82906-2 Subj: Folk & fairy tales. Foreign lands – China.

One-dog canoe ill. by Ard Hoyt. Kroupa, 2003. ISBN 978-0-374-35638-5 Subj: Animals. Canoes & canoeing. Rhyming text.

One-dog sleigh ill. by Ard Hoyt. Farrar, 2013. ISBN 978-0-374-35639-2 Subj: Animals. Rhyming text. Sports – sledding. Weather – snow.

Some cat! ill. by Ard Hoyt. Farrar, 2012. ISBN 978-0-374-37123-4 Subj: Animals – cats. Animals – dogs.

Some dog! ill. by Ard Hoyt. Farrar, 2007. ISBN 978-0-347-37133-3 Subj: Animals – dogs.

Utterly otterly day ill. by Ard Hoyt. Simon & Schuster, 2008. ISBN 978-1-4169-0868-5 Subj: Animals – otters. Behavior – needing someone. Family life.

Utterly otterly night ill. by Ard Hoyt. Simon & Schuster, 2011. ISBN 978-1-4169-7562-5 Subj: Animals – otters. Night. Seasons – winter.

Case, Chris. *Sophie and the next-door monsters* ill. by author. Walker, 2008. ISBN 978-0-8027-9756-8 Subj: Emotions – fear. Friendship. Monsters.

Caseley, Judith. *Bully* ill. by author. Greenwillow, 2001. ISBN 978-0-688-17868-0 Subj: Behavior – bullying, teasing. School.

Field Day Friday ill. by author. Greenwillow, 2000. ISBN 978-0-688-16762-2 Subj: Friendship. School – field trips. Sports – racing.

In style with Grandma Antoinette ill. by author. Tanglewood, 2005. ISBN 978-0-9749303-4-3 Subj: Beauty shops. Family life – grandmothers.

On the town ill. by author. Greenwillow, 2002. ISBN 978-0-06-029585-1 Subj: Communities, neighborhoods.

Sophie and Sammy's library sleepover ill. by author. Greenwillow, 1993. ISBN 978-0-688-10616-4 Subj: Books, reading. Family life – brothers & sisters. Libraries. Sleep.

Witch mama ill. by author. Greenwillow, 1996. ISBN 978-0-688-14458-6 Subj: Family life. Holidays – Halloween.

Casey, Dawn. *The great race: the story of the Chinese zodiac* ill. by Anne Wilson. Barefoot, 2006. ISBN 978-1-905236-77-0 Subj: Animals. Folk & fairy tales. Zodiac.

Casey, Patricia. *One day at Wood Green Animal Shelter* ill. by author. Candlewick, 2001. ISBN 978-0-7636-1210-8 Subj: Animals.

Casey, Tina. *The runaway Valentine* ill. by Theresa Smythe. Albert Whitman, 2001. ISBN 978-0-8075-7178-1 Subj: Holidays – Valentine's Day.

Cash, Megan Montague. *Bow-Wow bugs a bug* (Newgarden, Mark)

Bow-Wow orders lunch (Newgarden, Mark)

Bow-Wow's nightmare neighbors (Newgarden, Mark)

I saw the sea and the sea saw me ill. by author. Viking, 2001. ISBN 978-0-670-89966-1 Subj: Animals. Rhyming text. Sea & seashore – beaches. Senses.

What makes the seasons? ill. by author. Viking, 2003. ISBN 978-0-670-03598-4 Subj: Animals – cats. Ethnic groups in the U.S. – African Americans. Plants. Science. Seasons.

Cash, Rosanne. *Penelope Jane: a fairy's tale* ill. by G. Brian Karas. Cotler, 2000. ISBN 978-0-06-027544-0 Subj: Fairies. Fire. School.

Casin, Sheridan. *Little Turtle and the song of the sea* ill. by Norma Burgin. Crocodile, 2000. ISBN 978-1-56656-355-0 Subj: Reptiles – turtles, tortoises. Sea & seashore.

Cassie, Brian. *Say it again* ill. by David Mooney. Charlesbridge, 2000. ISBN 978-0-88106-341-7 Subj: Animals. Language.

Cassino, Mark, with Jon Nelson. *The story of snow: the science of winter's wonder* ill. by Nora Aoyagi. Chronicle, 2009. ISBN 978-0-8118-6866-2 Subj: Science. Seasons – winter. Weather – snow.

Castaneda, Omar S. *Abuela's weave* ill. by Enrique O. Sánchez. Lee & Low, 1993. ISBN 978-1-880000-00-7 Subj: Activities – weaving. Fairs, festivals. Family life – grandmothers. Foreign lands – Guatemala.

Casteel, Seth. *Puppy pool party! an underwater dogs adventure* ill. by author ill. with photos. Little, Brown, 2016. ISBN 978-031637633-4 Subj: Animals – dogs. Rhyming text. Sports – swimming.

Underwater dogs: kids edition photos by author. Little, Brown, 2013. ISBN 978-0-316-25558-5 Subj: Activities – photographing. Animals – dogs. Rhyming text.

Castellucci, Cecil. *Grandma's gloves* ill. by Julia Denos. Candlewick, 2010. ISBN 978-0-7636-3168-0 Subj: Death. Family life – grandmothers. Gardens, gardening.

Casterline, L. C. *The sounds of music* ill. by Lane Yerkes. G. Stevens, 2004. ISBN 978-0-8368-4100-8 Subj: Music. Musical instruments.

Castillo, Lauren. *Melvin and the boy* ill. by author. Henry Holt, 2011. ISBN 978-0-8050-8929-5 Subj: Pets. Reptiles – turtles, tortoises.

Nana in the city ill. by author. Houghton, 2014. ISBN 978-054410443-3 Subj: Caldecott award honor books. Cities, towns. Emotions – fear. Family life – grandmothers.

The troublemaker ill. by author. Clarion, 2014. ISBN 978-054772991-6 Subj: Animals – raccoons. Behavior – lost & found possessions. Behavior – misbehavior. Toys.

Castle, Caroline. *For every child: the UN Convention on the Rights of the Child in words and pictures.* Fogelman, 2001. ISBN 978-0-8037-2650-5 Subj: Self-concept. UNICEF.

Naughty! by Caroline Castle and Sam Childs ill. by Sam Childs. Knopf, 2001. ISBN 978-0-375-91359-4 Subj: Activities – playing. Animals – babies. Animals – hippopotamuses. Animals – zebras. Bedtime. Humorous stories.

Caston, Jane. *Will you help Doug find his dog?* ill. by Carmen Saldaña. Barefoot, 2017. ISBN 978-178285320-6 Subj: Animals – dogs. Problem solving.

Caswell, Deanna. *Beach house* ill. by Amy June Bates. Chronicle, 2015. ISBN 978-145212408-7 Subj: Rhyming text. Sea & seashore – beaches.

Boo! haiku ill. by Bob Shea. Abrams/Appleseed, 2016. ISBN 978-141972118-2 Subj: Holidays – Halloween. Poetry.

Train trip ill. by Dan Andreasen. Hyperion/Disney, 2011. ISBN 978-1-4231-1837-4 Subj: Rhyming text. Trains.

Catalano, Dominic. *Mr. Bassett plays* ill. by author. Boyds Mills, 2003. ISBN 978-1-59078-007-7 Subj: Animals – dogs. Friendship.

Santa and the three bears ill. by author. Boyds Mills, 2000. ISBN 978-1-56397-864-7 Subj: Animals – bears. Holidays – Christmas. Santa Claus.

Catalanotto, Peter. *Emily's art* ill. by author. Atheneum, 2001. ISBN 978-0-689-83831-6 Subj: Careers – artists. Contests.

Ivan the terrier ill. by author. Simon & Schuster, 2007. ISBN 978-1-4169-1247-7 Subj: Animals – dogs. Behavior – misbehavior. Folk & fairy tales.

Kitten red, yellow, blue ill. by author. Simon & Schuster, 2005. ISBN 978-0-689-86562-6 Subj: Animals – cats. Careers. Concepts – color.

Matthew A.B.C. ill. by author. Atheneum, 2002. ISBN 978-0-689-84582-6 Subj: ABC books. Names. School. Self-concept.

Question Boy meets Little Miss Know-It-All ill. by author. Atheneum, 2012. ISBN 978-1-4424-0670-4 Subj: Character traits – curiosity. Character traits – questioning.

The secret lunch special by Peter Catalanotto and Pamela Schembri; ill. by Peter Catalanotto. Henry Holt, 2006. ISBN 978-0-8050-7838-1 Subj: Food. Friendship. School.

Catchpool, Michael. *The cloud spinner* ill. by Alison Jay. Knopf, 2012. ISBN 978-0-375-87011-8 Subj: Clothing. Ecology. Royalty – kings. Weather – clouds.

Cate, Annette LeBlanc. *The magic rabbit* ill. by author. Candlewick, 2007. ISBN 978-0-7636-2672-3 Subj: Animals – rabbits. Behavior – lost & found possessions. Careers – magicians. Magic.

Catrow, David. *Fun in the sun* ill. by author. Holiday House, 2015. ISBN 978-082342945-5 Subj: Animals – rabbits. Sea & seashore.

Monster mash ill. by author. Scholastic, 2012. ISBN 978-0-545-21479-7 Subj: Activities – dancing. Monsters. Songs.

Catusanu, Mircea. *The strange case of the missing sheep* ill. by author. Viking, 2009. ISBN 978-0-670-01131-5 Subj: Animals – dogs. Animals – sheep. Animals – wolves. Mystery stories. Sleep.

Caudill, Rebecca. *A pocketful of cricket* ill. by Evaline Ness. Henry Holt, 1964. Subj: Behavior – sharing. Caldecott award honor books. Farms. Insects – crickets. School.

Cauley, Lorinda Bryan. *Clap your hands* ill. by author. Putnam, 1992. ISBN 978-0-399-22118-7 Subj: Activities. Activities – playing. Games. Nursery rhymes.

What do you know! ill. by author. Putnam, 2001. ISBN 978-0-399-23573-3 Subj: Picture puzzles.

Cave, Kathryn. *The boy who became an eagle* ill. by Nick Maland. DK, 2000. ISBN 978-0-7894-2666-6 Subj: Activities – flying. Fairs, festivals.

Henry's song ill. by Sue Hendra. Eerdmans, 2000. ISBN 978-0-8028-5198-7 Subj: Activities – singing. Animals. Character traits – individuality.

One child, one seed: a South African counting book photos by Gisèle Wulfsohn. Henry Holt, 2003. ISBN 978-0-8050-7204-4 Subj: Counting, numbers. Foreign lands – South Africa. Plants. Seeds.

You've got dragons ill. by Nick Maland. Peachtree, 2003. ISBN 978-1-56145-284-2 Subj: Dragons. Emotions – fear.

Cazet, Denys. *Bob and Tom* ill. by author. Simon & Schuster, 2017. ISBN 978-148146140-5 Subj: Birds – turkeys. Humorous stories.

December 24th ill. by author. Bradbury, 1986. ISBN 978-0-02-717950-7 Subj: Animals – rabbits. Birthdays. Family life – grandfathers. Holidays.

Elvis the rooster almost goes to heaven ill. by author. HarperCollins, 2003. ISBN 978-0-06-000501-6 Subj: Birds – chickens, roosters. Humorous stories.

A fish in his pocket ill. by author. Watts, 1987. ISBN 978-0-531-08313-0 Subj: Birthdays. Character traits – kindness. Death. School.

Never poke a squid ill. by author. Orchard, 2000. ISBN 978-0-531-33279-5 Subj: Animals. Friendship. Holidays – Halloween. School.

Never spit on your shoes ill. by author. Orchard, 1990. ISBN 978-0-531-08447-2 Subj: Animals. Animals – cats. School – first day.

Nothing at all ill. by author. Orchard, 1994. ISBN 978-0-531-08672-8 Subj: Animals. Cumulative tales. Farms. Noise, sounds. Rhyming text. Scarecrows.

The octopus ill. by author. HarperCollins, 2005. ISBN 978-0-06-051089-3 Subj: Activities – storytelling. Animals – dogs. Family life – grandparents. Illness – chicken pox. Octopuses.

The perfect pumpkin pie ill. by author. Simon & Schuster, 2005. ISBN 978-0-689-86467-4 Subj: Activities – baking, cooking. Food. Ghosts. Holidays – Halloween.

Snail and Slug ill. by author. Atheneum, 2016. ISBN 978-148144506-1 Subj: Animals – slugs. Animals – snails. Behavior – bullying, teasing. Friendship.

Will you read to me? ill. by author. Simon & Schuster, 2007. ISBN 978-1-4169-0935-4 Subj: Animals – pigs. Books, reading. Self-concept.

Cech, John. *Aesop's fables* (Aesop)

Cecil, Randy. *Gator* ill. by author. Candlewick, 2007. ISBN 978-0-7636-2952-6 Subj: Merry-go-rounds. Parks – amusement. Reptiles – alligators, crocodiles.

Horsefly and Honeybee ill. by author. Henry Holt, 2012. ISBN 978-0-8050-9300-1 Subj: Character traits – cooperation. Frogs & toads. Insects – bees. Insects – flies.

Lucy ill. by author. Candlewick, 2016. ISBN 978-076366808-2 Subj: Animals – dogs. Emotions – fear. Emotions – loneliness.

Cecka, Melanie. *Violet comes to stay* ill. by Emily Arnold McCully. Penguin, 2006. ISBN 978-0-670-06073-3 Subj: Animals – cats. Behavior – misbehavior. Homes, houses.

Violet goes to the country ill. by Emily Arnold McCully. Penguin, 2007. ISBN 978-0-670-06181-5 Subj: Animals – cats. Character traits – curiosity. Country.

Ceelen, Vicky. *Baby! baby!* photos by author. Random House, 2008. ISBN 978-0-375-84207-8 Subj: Animals. Babies, toddlers. Wordless.

Celenza, Anna Harwell. *Duke Ellington's Nutcracker Suite* ill. by Don Tate. Charlesbridge, 2011. ISBN

978-1-57091-700-4 Subj: Careers – musicians. Ethnic groups in the U.S. – African Americans. Music.

The farewell symphony ill. by JoAnn E. Kitchel. Talewinds, 2000. ISBN 978-1-57091-406-5 Subj: Careers – composers. Music.

Cendrars, Blaise. *Shadow* ill. by Marcia Brown. Scribners, 1982. ISBN 978-0-684-17226-2 Subj: Caldecott award books. Folk & fairy tales. Foreign lands – Africa. Poetry. Shadows.

Chacon, Michelle Netten. *How the Indians bought the farm* (Strete, Craig Kee)

Chaconas, Dori. *Christmas mouseling* ill. by Susan Kathleen Hartung. Penguin, 2005. ISBN 978-0-670-05984-3 Subj: Animals – babies. Animals – mice. Family life – mothers. Holidays – Christmas. Religion – Nativity.

Cork and Fuzz: merry merry holly holly ill. by Lisa McCue. Viking, 2015. ISBN 978-045147501-5 Subj: Animals – muskrats. Animals – possums. Friendship. Holidays – Christmas.

Dancing with Katya ill. by Constance R. Bergum. Peachtree, 2006. ISBN 978-1-56145-376-4 Subj: Activities – dancing. Ballet. Family life – brothers & sisters. Illness – poliomyelitis.

Don't slam the door! ill. by Will Hillenbrand. Candlewick, 2010. ISBN 978-0-7636-3709-5 Subj: Animals. Cumulative tales. Humorous stories. Rhyming text.

Dori the contrary hen ill. by Marsha Gray Carrington. Carolrhoda, 2007. ISBN 978-1-57505-749-1 Subj: Birds – chickens, roosters. Character traits – stubbornness. Farms.

Hurry down to Derry Fair ill. by Gillian Tyler. Candlewick, 2011. ISBN 978-0-7636-3208-3 Subj: Fairs, festivals. Family life. Rhyming text.

Looking for Easter ill. by Margie Moore. Albert Whitman, 2008. ISBN 978-0-8075-4749-6 Subj: Animals. Animals – rabbits. Behavior – sharing. Holidays – Easter. Seasons – spring.

On a wintry morning ill. by Stephen T. Johnson. Viking, 2000. ISBN 978-0-670-89245-7 Subj: Family life – fathers. Rhyming text. Seasons – winter. Sports – sledding.

Pennies in a jar ill. by Ted Lewin. Peachtree, 2007. ISBN 978-1-56145-422-8 Subj: Emotions – fear. U.S. history. War.

Virginnie's hat ill. by Holly Meade. Candlewick, 2007. ISBN 978-0-7636-2397-5 Subj: Clothing – hats. Rhyming text. Swamps.

When cows come home for Christmas ill. by Lynne Chapman. Albert Whitman, 2005. ISBN 978-0-8075-8877-2 Subj: Animals – bulls, cows. Holidays – Christmas. Rhyming text.

Chae, In Seon. *How do you count a dozen ducklings?* ill. by Seung Ha Rew. Albert Whitman, 2006. ISBN 978-0-8075-1718-5 Subj: Birds – ducks. Counting, numbers.

Chaikin, Miriam. *Don't step on the sky: a handful of haiku* ill. by Hiroe Nakata. Henry Holt, 2002. ISBN 978-0-8050-6474-2 Subj: Nature. Poetry.

Chall, Marsha Wilson. *Bonaparte* ill. by Wendy Anderson Halperin. DK, 2000. ISBN 978-0-7894-2617-8 Subj: Animals – dogs. Foreign lands – France. School.

Happy birthday, America! ill. by Guy Porfirio. Lothrop, 2000. ISBN 978-0-688-13052-7 Subj: Family life. Holidays – Fourth of July.

One pup's up ill. by Henry Cole. Simon & Schuster, 2010. ISBN 978-1-4169-7960-9 Subj: Animals – dogs. Counting, numbers. Rhyming text.

Pick a pup ill. by Jed Henry. Simon & Schuster, 2011. ISBN 978-1-4169-7961-6 Subj: Animals – dogs. Character traits – kindness to animals. Pets.

Prairie train ill. by John Thompson. HarperCollins, 2003. ISBN 978-0-688-13434-1 Subj: Cities, towns. Country. Family life – grandmothers. Trains.

Sugarbush spring ill. by Jim Daly. Lothrop, 2000. ISBN 978-0-688-14908-6 Subj: Family life. Food. Seasons – spring.

Chamberlain, Margaret. *Please don't tease Tootsie* ill. by author. Dutton, 2008. ISBN 978-0-525-47982-6 Subj: Behavior – misbehavior. Character traits – kindness to animals. Pets. Rhyming text.

Chamberlin, Mary. *Mama Panya's pancakes: a village tale from Kenya* by Mary Chamberlin and Rich Chamberlin ill. by Julia Cairns. Barefoot, 2005. ISBN 978-1-84148-139-5 Subj: Character traits – generosity. Food. Foreign lands – Kenya.

Chamberlin, Rich. *Mama Panya's pancakes: a village tale from Kenya* (Chamberlin, Mary)

Chamberlin-Calamar, Pat. *Alaska's twelve days of summer* ill. by Shannon Cartwright. Sasquatch, 2003. ISBN 978-1-57061-341-8 Subj: Alaska. Animals. Counting, numbers.

Chambers, Angela. *Follow that chicken!* ill. by Simone Abel. Sterling, 2000. ISBN 978-0-8069-0310-1 Subj: Birds – chickens, roosters. Concepts – opposites. Format, unusual – board books. Format, unusual – toy & movable books. Language.

How now, cow? ill. by Simone Abel. Sterling, 2000. ISBN 978-0-8069-0275-3 Subj: Animals – bulls, cows. Format, unusual – board books. Format, unusual – toy & movable books.

Chambers, Catherine. *Big freeze* ill. with photos. Heinemann, 2002. ISBN 978-1-58810-658-2 Subj: Weather – cold.

Heat wave ill. with photos. Heinemann, 2002. ISBN 978-1-58810-657-5 Subj: Concepts – cold & heat. Weather.

Tornado ill. with photos. Heinemann, 2002. ISBN 978-1-58810-652-0 Subj: Weather – tornadoes.

Chambers, Roland. *Rooftop rocket party* ill. by author. Roaring Brook, 2003. ISBN 978-0-7613-2744-8 Subj: Careers – scientists. Moon. Parties. Space & space ships.

Chan, Arlene. *Awakening the dragon: the dragon boat festival* ill. by Song Nan Zhang. Tundra, 2004. ISBN 978-0-88776-656-5 Subj: Boats, ships. Fairs, festivals. Foreign lands – China.

Chan, Chin-Yi. *Good luck horse* ill. by Plao Chan. Whittlesey House, 1943. Subj: Animals – horses, ponies. Caldecott award honor books.

Chan, Ruth. *Georgie's best bad day* ill. by author. Roaring Brook, 2017. ISBN 978-162672270-5 Subj: Animals – cats. Behavior – bad day, bad mood. Friendship.

Where's the party? ill. by author. Roaring Brook, 2016. ISBN 978-162672269-9 Subj: Animals – cats. Friendship. Parties.

Chancellor, Deborah. *Holidays!* ill. with photos. DK, 2000. ISBN 978-0-7894-5710-3 Subj: Holidays.

Maps and mapping ill. with photos. Kingfisher, 2004. ISBN 978-0-7534-5759-7 Subj: Careers – cartographers. Maps.

Traveling on land ill. with photos. Two-Can, 2001. ISBN 978-0-915741-80-9 Subj: Activities – traveling. Transportation.

Chandra, Deborah. *George Washington's teeth* ill. by Brock Cole. Farrar, 2003. ISBN 978-0-374-32534-3 Subj: Teeth. U.S. history.

Chang, Victoria. *Is Mommy?* ill. by Marla Frazee. Simon & Schuster/Beach Lane, 2015. ISBN 978-148140292-7 Subj: Character traits – questioning. Family life – mothers.

Chapin, Tom. *The backwards birthday party* by Tom Chapin and John Forster ill. by Chuck Groenink. Simon & Schuster, 2015. ISBN 978-144246798-9 Subj: Birthdays. Parties. Songs.

The library book by Tom Chapin and Michael L. Mark ill. by Chuck Groenink. Atheneum, 2017. ISBN 978-148146092-7 Subj: Books, reading. Ethnic groups in the U.S. – African Americans. Libraries. Music. Songs.

Chapman, Jane. *I'm not sleepy!* ill. by author. Good Books, 2012. ISBN 978-1-56148-765-3 Subj: Bedtime. Birds – owls. Family life – grandmothers.

Is it Christmas yet? ill. by author. Tiger Tales, 2013. ISBN 978-1-58925-149-6 Subj: Animals – bears. Holidays – Christmas.

No more cuddles! ill. by author. Tiger Tales, 2015. ISBN 978-158925195-3 Subj: Animals. Hugging. Monsters.

Touch the sky, my little bear (Bedford, David)

Very special friends ill. by author. Good Books, 2012. ISBN 978-1-56148-748-6 Subj: Animals. Animals – mice. Friendship.

Chapman, Jared. *Fruits in suits* ill. by author. Abrams/Appleseed, 2017. ISBN 978-141972298-1 Subj: Clothing – suits. Food.

Pirate, Viking, and Scientist ill. by author. Little, Brown, 2014. ISBN 978-031625389-5 Subj: Behavior – resourcefulness. Careers – scientists. Friendship. Pirates. Science. Vikings.

Steve, raised by wolves ill. by author. Little, Brown, 2015. ISBN 978-031625390-1 Subj: Animals – wolves. Character traits – being different. Character traits – individuality. School – first day.

Vegetables in underwear ill. by author. Abrams/Appleseed, 2015. ISBN 978-141971464-1 Subj: Clothing – underwear. Food. Plants.

Chapman, Nancy Kapp. *Doggie dreams* ill. by Lee Chapman. Putnam, 2000. ISBN 978-0-399-23443-9 Subj: Animals – dogs. Dreams. Rhyming text.

Chapman, Susan Margaret. *Too much noise in the library* ill. by Abby Carter. Upstart, 2010. ISBN 978-1-60213-026-5 Subj: Libraries. Noise, sounds.

Chapra, Mimi. *Amelia's show-and-tell fiesta / Amelia y la fiesta de "muestra y cuenta"* ill. by Martha Avilés. HarperCollins, 2004. ISBN 978-0-06-050256-0 Subj: Ethnic groups in the U.S. – Cuban Americans. Foreign languages. School.

Sparky's bark / El ladrido de Sparky ill. by Viví Escrivá. HarperCollins, 2006. ISBN 978-0-06-053172-0 Subj: Activities – vacationing. Animals – dogs. Ethnic groups in the U.S. – Hispanic Americans. Foreign languages.

Charest, Emily MacLachlan. *Before you came* (MacLachlan, Patricia)

Bittle (MacLachlan, Patricia)

Cat talk (MacLachlan, Patricia)

Fiona loves the night (MacLachlan, Patricia)

Painting the wind (MacLachlan, Patricia)

Charles, Veronika Martenova. *The birdman* ill. by Annouchka Gravel Galouchko. Tundra, 2006.

ISBN 978-0-88776-740-1 Subj: Birds. Careers – tailors. Emotions – grief. Foreign lands – India.

The maiden of the mist ill. by author. Stoddart, 2001. ISBN 978-0-7737-3297-1 Subj: Folk & fairy tales. Indians of North America – Seneca.

Charlip, Remy. *Baby hearts and baby flowers* ill. by author. Greenwillow, 2002. ISBN 978-0-06-029591-2 Subj: Babies, toddlers. Bedtime. Rhyming text.

Handtalk birthday: a number and story book in sign language photos by George Ancona. Four Winds, 1987. ISBN 978-0-02-718080-0 Subj: Birthdays. Disabilities – deafness. Language. Senses – hearing.

"Mother, mother I feel sick" by Remy Charlip and Burton Supree; ill. by Remy Charlip. Parents' Magazine, 1966. ISBN 978-1-58246-043-7 Subj: Careers – doctors. Humorous stories. Illness. Rhyming text.

A perfect day ill. by author. HarperCollins, 2007. ISBN 978-0-06-051972-8 Subj: Day. Family life.

Sleepytime rhyme ill. by author. Greenwillow, 1999. ISBN 978-0-688-16272-6 Subj: Babies, toddlers. Family life – mothers. Nursery rhymes. Rhyming text.

Why I will never ever ever ever have enough time to read this book ill. by Jon J Muth. Tricycle, 2000. ISBN 978-1-58246-018-5 Subj: Books, reading. Day. Time.

Charlip, Remy, et al. *Handtalk: an ABC of finger spelling and sign language* ill. by George Ancona. Parents' Magazine, 1974. ISBN 978-0-8193-0706-4 Subj: ABC books. Communication. Disabilities – deafness. Language. Senses – hearing.

Chase, Kit. *Charlie's boat* ill. by author. Putnam, 2017. ISBN 978-039925702-5 Subj: Activities – playing. Animals – elephants. Animals – rabbits. Birds – owls. Friendship.

Oliver's tree ill. by author. Putnam, 2014. ISBN 978-039925700-1 Subj: Animals – elephants. Animals – rabbits. Behavior – resourcefulness. Birds – owls. Friendship. Problem solving.

Chase, Mary. *The wicked, wicked ladies in the haunted house* ill. by Peter Sís. Knopf, 2003. ISBN 978-0-375-92572-6 Subj: Ghosts. Magic. Mythical creatures – leprechauns.

Chast, Roz. *Around the clock!* ill. by author. Simon & Schuster, 2015. ISBN 978-141698476-4 Subj: Clocks, watches. Day. Imagination. Rhyming text. Time.

Marco goes to school ill. by author. Simon & Schuster, 2012. ISBN 978-1-4424-5307-4 Subj: Birds. Friendship. School – first day.

Chataway, Carol. *The perfect pet* ill. by Greg Holfeld. Kids Can, 2001. ISBN 978-1-55337-178-6 Subj: Animals – pigs. Pets.

Chaucer, Geoffrey. *Chanticleer and the fox* adapt. by Barbara Cooney; ill. by adapter. Adapt. of the "Nun's priest's tale" from the Canterbury tales. Crowell, 1958. ISBN 978-0-690-18562-1 Subj: Animals – foxes. Birds – chickens, roosters. Caldecott award books. Character traits – flattery. Farms. Folk & fairy tales.

Chaud, Benjamin. *The bear's sea escape* ill. by author. Chronicle, 2014. ISBN 978-145212743-9 Subj: Animals – bears. Family life – fathers. Hibernation.

The bear's song ill. by author. Chronicle, 2013. ISBN 978-1-4521-1424-8 Subj: Animals – bears. Behavior – lost. Cities, towns. Family life – fathers. Foreign lands – France.

The bear's surprise ill. by author. Chronicle, 2015. ISBN 978-145214028-5 Subj: Animals – bears. Circus. Family life. Family life – new sibling.

Chavarría-Cháirez, Becky. *Magda's piñata magic / Magda y la piñata mágica* ill. by Anne Vega. Piñata, 2001. ISBN 978-1-55885-320-1 Subj: Birthdays. Family life – brothers & sisters. Foreign languages. Parties.

Magda's tortillas / Las tortillas de Magada ill. by Anne Vega. Piñata, 2000. ISBN 978-1-55885-286-0 Subj: Activities – baking, cooking. Birthdays. Concepts – shape. Food. Foreign languages.

Chedru, Delphine. *Spot it! find the hidden creatures* ill. by author. Abrams, 2009. ISBN 978-0-8109-0632-7 Subj: Animals. Picture puzzles.

Spot it again! ill. by author. Abrams, 2011. ISBN 978-0-8109-9736-3 Subj: Format, unusual. Picture puzzles.

Chen, Chih-Yuan. *The best Christmas ever* ill. by author. Heryin, 2005. ISBN 978-0-9762056-2-3 Subj: Animals – bears. Gifts. Holidays – Christmas.

The featherless chicken ill. by author. Heryin, 2006. ISBN 978-0-9762056-9-2 Subj: Birds – chickens, roosters. Character traits – appearance. Character traits – being different. Self-concept.

Guji Guji ill. by author. Kane/Miller, 2004. ISBN 978-1-929132-67-6 Subj: Birds – ducks. Reptiles – alligators, crocodiles.

On my way to buy eggs ill. by author. Kane/Miller, 2003. ISBN 978-1-929132-49-2 Subj: Food. Foreign lands – Taiwan. Imagination. Shopping.

Chen, Kerstin. *Lord of the cranes* ill. by Jian Jiang Chen. NorthSouth, 2000. ISBN 978-0-7358-1193-5 Subj: Birds – cranes. Folk & fairy tales. Foreign lands – China.

Chen, Yong. *A gift* ill. by author. Boyds Mills, 2009. ISBN 978-1-59078-610-9 Subj: Ethnic groups in the U.S. – Chinese Americans. Foreign languages. Holidays – Chinese New Year. Letters, cards.

Cheng, Andrea. *Anna the bookbinder* ill. by Ted Rand. Walker, 2003. ISBN 978-0-8027-8831-3 Subj: Books, reading. Careers – bookbinders. Family life. Family life – fathers. Self-concept.

Grandfather counts ill. by Ange Zhang. Lee & Low, 2000. ISBN 978-1-58430-010-6 Subj: Communication. Ethnic groups in the U.S. – Chinese Americans. Family life – grandfathers. Language.

The lemon sisters ill. by Tatjana Mai-Wyss. Penguin, 2006. ISBN 978-0-399-24023-2 Subj: Birthdays. Family life – brothers & sisters. Memories, memory. Old age.

Cheng, Christopher. *Python* ill. by Mark Jackson. Candlewick, 2013. ISBN 978-0-7636-6396-4 Subj: Foreign lands – Australia. Reptiles – snakes.

Chernaik, Judith, editor. *Carnival of the animals: poems inspired by Saint-Saëns' music* ill. by Satoshi Kitamura. Candlewick, 2006. ISBN 978-0-7636-2960-1 Subj: Animals. Music. Poetry.

Chernesky, Felicia Sanzari. *Cheers for a dozen ears: a summer crop of counting* ill. by Susan Swan. Albert Whitman, 2014. ISBN 978-080751130-5 Subj: Counting, numbers. Farms. Food. Rhyming text. Seasons – summer.

From apple trees to cider, please! ill. by Julia Patton. Albert Whitman, 2015. ISBN 978-080756513-1 Subj: Farms. Food. Rhyming text. Seasons – fall.

Pick a circle, gather squares: a fall harvest of shapes ill. by Susan Swan. Albert Whitman, 2013. ISBN 978-0-8075-6538-4 Subj: Concepts – shape. Farms. Rhyming text. Seasons – fall.

Sugar white snow and evergreens: a winter wonderland of color ill. by Susan Swan. Albert Whitman, 2014. ISBN 978-080757234-4 Subj: Concepts – color. Rhyming text. Seasons – winter. Trees.

Sun above and blooms below: a springtime of opposites ill. by Susan Swan. Albert Whitman, 2015. ISBN 978-080753632-2 Subj: Concepts – opposites. Farms. Rhyming text. School – field trips. Seasons – spring.

Cherry, Lynne. *The great kapok tree: a tale of the Amazon rain forest* ill. by author. Harcourt, 1990. ISBN 978-0-15-200520-7 Subj: Animals. Ecology. Foreign lands – Brazil. Jungle. Trees.

How Groundhog's garden grew ill. by author. Blue Sky, 2003. ISBN 978-0-439-32371-0 Subj: Animals – groundhogs. Animals – squirrels. Food. Gardens, gardening.

A river ran wild ill. by author. Harcourt, 1992. ISBN 978-0-15-200542-9 Subj: Ecology. Nature. Rivers. U.S. history.

Cheshire, Marc. *Here comes Eloise!* by Marc Cheshire and Kay Thompson ill. by Carolyn Bracken. Based on Kay Thompson's Eloise & the art of Hilary Knight. Simon & Schuster, 2005. ISBN 978-0-689-87154-2 Subj: Format, unusual – toy & movable books. Hotels.

Love and kisses, Eloise ill. by Ted Enik. Based on Kay Thompson's Eloise & the art of Hilary Knight. Simon & Schuster, 2005. ISBN 978-0-689-87156-6 Subj: Emotions – love. Holidays – Valentine's Day.

Merry Christmas, Eloise! a lift-the-flap book ill. by Carolyn Bracken. Simon & Schuster, 2006. ISBN 978-0-689-87155-9 Subj: Format, unusual – toy & movable books. Holidays – Christmas.

Chess, Victoria. *The costume party* ill. by author. Kane/Miller, 2005. ISBN 978-1-929132-87-4 Subj: Animals – dogs. Clothing – costumes. Parties.

Chessa, Francesca. *Holly's red boots* ill. by author. Holiday, 2008. ISBN 978-0-8234-2158-9 Subj: Behavior – lost & found possessions. Clothing – boots. Seasons – winter. Weather – snow.

The mysterious package ill. by author. Bloomsbury, 2007. ISBN 978-1-59990-028-5 Subj: Family life – brothers & sisters. Imagination.

Chester, Jonathan. *Busy penguins* (Schindel, John)

Chetkowski, Emily. *Pumpkin smile* ill. by Dawn Peterson. Seven Coin, 2001. ISBN 978-0-9700974-2-2 Subj: Holidays – Halloween. Rhyming text. Self-concept. Teeth.

Chichester Clark, Emma. *Eliza and the moonchild* ill. by author. Trafalgar, 2008. ISBN 978-1-84270-577-3 Subj: Concepts – color. Moon.

Follow the leader! ill. by author. Margaret K. McElderry, 2003. ISBN 978-0-689-84296-2 Subj: Animals. Animals – tigers. Games.

Goldilocks and the three bears (The three bears)

I love you, Blue Kangaroo! ill. by author. Doubleday, 1999. ISBN 978-0-385-32638-4 Subj: Behavior – needing someone. Toys.

Little Miss Muffet counts to ten ill. by author. Andersen, 2010. ISBN 978-1-84270-955-9 Subj: Animals. Counting, numbers. Nursery rhymes. Rhyming text.

Love is my favorite thing ill. by author. Penguin/Nancy Paulsen, 2015. ISBN 978-039917503-9 Subj: Animals – dogs. Emotions – love.

Melrose and Croc: a Christmas to remember ill. by author. Walker, 2006. ISBN 978-0-8027-9597-7 Subj:

Animals – dogs. Emotions – loneliness. Friendship. Holidays – Christmas. Reptiles – alligators, crocodiles.

Piper ill. by author. Eerdmans, 2007. ISBN 978-0-902853-14-1 Subj: Animals – dogs. Behavior – running away. Character traits – kindness to animals.

Plenty of love to go around ill. by author. Penguin/Nancy Paulsen, 2016. ISBN 978-039954666-2 Subj: Animals – cats. Animals – dogs. Emotions – envy, jealousy.

Where are you, Blue Kangaroo? ill. by author. Random House, 2001. ISBN 978-0-385-32797-8 Subj: Animals – kangaroos. Toys.

Will and Squill ill. by author. Carolrhoda, 2006. ISBN 978-1-57505-936-5 Subj: Animals – cats. Animals – squirrels. Babies, toddlers. Friendship. Pets.

Chicken Little. *Brave Chicken Little* by Robert Byrd; ill. by author. Viking, 2014. ISBN 978-067078616-9 Subj: Animals. Behavior – gossip, rumors. Behavior – trickery. Birds – chickens, roosters. Cumulative tales. Folk & fairy tales.

Chicken Little ill. by Sally Hobson. Simon & Schuster, 1994. ISBN 978-0-671-89548-8 Subj: Animals. Behavior – gossip, rumors. Behavior – trickery. Birds – chickens, roosters. Cumulative tales. Folk & fairy tales.

Henny Penny retold by Harriet Ziefert; ill. by Emily Bolam. Viking, 1997. ISBN 978-0-670-86810-0 Subj: Animals. Behavior – gossip, rumors. Behavior – trickery. Birds – chickens, roosters. Cumulative tales. Folk & fairy tales.

Henny Penny ill. by Paul Galdone. Seabury Pr., 1968. Subj: Animals. Behavior – gossip, rumors. Behavior – trickery. Birds – chickens, roosters. Cumulative tales. Folk & fairy tales.

Henny Penny retold by Vivian French; ill. by Sophie Windham. Bloomsbury, 2006. ISBN 978-1-58234-706-6 Subj: Animals. Behavior – gossip, rumors. Behavior – trickery. Birds – chickens, roosters. Cumulative tales. Folk & fairy tales.

Henny-Penny retold by Jane Wattenberg; ill. by reteller. Scholastic, 2000. ISBN 978-0-439-07817-7 Subj: Animals. Behavior – gossip, rumors. Behavior – trickery. Birds – chickens, roosters. Cumulative tales. Folk & fairy tales.

The sky is falling by Betty Miles; ill. by Cynthia Fisher. Simon & Schuster, 1998. ISBN 978-0-689-81790-8 Subj: Animals. Behavior – gossip, rumors. Behavior – trickery. Birds – chickens, roosters. Cumulative tales. Folk & fairy tales.

Chiew, Suzanne. *When you need a friend* ill. by Caroline Pedler. Tiger Tales, 2015. ISBN 978-158925173-1 Subj: Animals. Animals – bad-

gers. Character traits – helpfulness. Friendship. Homes, houses. Weather – storms.

Child, Lauren. *Absolutely one thing: featuring Charlie and Lola* ill. by author. Candlewick, 2016. ISBN 978-076368728-1 Subj: Counting, numbers. Family life – brothers & sisters.

Beware of the storybook wolves ill. by author. Scholastic, 2001. ISBN 978-0-439-20500-9 Subj: Animals – wolves. Folk & fairy tales. Mythical creatures.

But, excuse me, that is my book ill. by author. Penguin, 2005. ISBN 978-0-8037-3096-0 Subj: Books, reading. Family life – brothers & sisters. Libraries.

But I've used all my pocket change ill. by author. Dial, 2012. ISBN 978-0-8037-3728-0 Subj: Behavior – saving things. Character traits – generosity. Family life – brothers & sisters. Money. Zoos.

Charlie and Lola's numbers ill. by author. Candlewick, 2007. ISBN 978-0-7636-3534-3 Subj: Counting, numbers. Family life – brothers & sisters. Format, unusual – board books.

Charlie and Lola's opposites ill. by author. Candlewick, 2007. ISBN 978-0-7636-3535-0 Subj: Concepts – opposites. Family life – brothers & sisters. Format, unusual – board books.

Clarice Bean, guess who's babysitting? ill. by author. Candlewick, 2001. ISBN 978-0-7636-1373-0 Subj: Activities – babysitting. Careers – firefighters. Family life – aunts, uncles.

Clarice Bean, that's me ill. by author. Candlewick, 1999. ISBN 978-0-7636-0961-0 Subj: Family life.

I am not sleepy and I will not go to bed ill. by author. Candlewick, 2001. ISBN 978-0-7636-1570-3 Subj: Animals. Bedtime.

I am too absolutely small for school ill. by author. Candlewick, 2004. ISBN 978-0-7636-2403-3 Subj: Family life – brothers & sisters. School – first day.

I completely know about guinea pigs ill. by author. Dial, 2008. ISBN 978-0-8037-3295-7 Subj: Animals – guinea pigs. Behavior – lost & found possessions. Family life – brothers & sisters.

I really, really need actual ice skates ill. by author. Penguin, 2010. ISBN 978-0-8037-3451-7 Subj: Family life – brothers & sisters. Money. Sports – ice skating.

I will never not ever eat a tomato ill. by author. Candlewick, 2000. ISBN 978-0-7636-1188-0 Subj: Family life – brothers & sisters. Food. Imagination.

Maude: the not-so-noticeable Shrimpton ill. by Trisha Krauss. Candlewick, 2013. ISBN 978-0-7636-6515-9 Subj: Animals – tigers. Character traits – being different. Character traits – shyness. Family life.

My best, best friend ill. by author and Tiger Aspect Productions. Penguin, 2011. ISBN 978-0-8037-3586-6 Subj: Family life – brothers & sisters. Friendship.

My dream bed ill. by author. Scholastic, 2002. ISBN 978-0-439-30912-7 Subj: Format, unusual – toy & movable books. Furniture – beds. Sleep.

The new small person ill. by author. Candlewick, 2015. ISBN 978-076367810-4 Subj: Emotions – envy, jealousy. Ethnic groups in the U.S. – African Americans. Family life – brothers. Sibling rivalry.

Say cheese! ill. by author. Penguin, 2007. ISBN 978-0-8037-3095-3 Subj: Character traits – cleanliness. Family life – brothers & sisters. School.

Snow is my favorite and my best ill. by author. Penguin, 2006. ISBN 978-0-8037-3174-5 Subj: Family life – brothers & sisters. Seasons – winter. Weather – snow.

That pesky rat ill. by author. Candlewick, 2002. ISBN 978-0-7636-1873-5 Subj: Animals – rats. Names. Pets.

What planet are you from Clarice Bean? ill. by author. Candlewick, 2002. ISBN 978-0-7636-1696-0 Subj: Ecology. Family life. Humorous stories. Trees.

Who wants to be a poodle: I don't ill. by author. Candlewick, 2009. ISBN 978-0-7636-4610-3 Subj: Animals – dogs. Behavior – dissatisfaction. Character traits – individuality.

Who's afraid of the big bad book? ill. by author. Hyperion, 2003. ISBN 978-0-7868-0926-4 Subj: Books, reading. Folk & fairy tales.

Child, Lydia Maria. *Over the river and through the wood* ill. by Brinton Turkle. First pub. in 1844 as The boy's Thanksgiving Day in the 2d vol. of the author's Flowers for children. Coward, 1974. ISBN 978-0-698-30553-3 Subj: Family life – grandparents. Farms. Holidays – Thanksgiving. Songs.

Over the river and through the wood: the New England boy's song about Thanksgiving Day ill. by Matt Tavares. Candlewick, 2011. ISBN 978-0-7636-2790-4 Subj: Family life – grandparents. Farms. Holidays – Thanksgiving. Songs.

A children's treasury of prayers ill. by Linda Bleck. Sterling, 2006. ISBN 978-1-4027-2982-9 Subj: Religion.

A child's calendar ill. by Trina Schart Hyman. Holiday, 1999. ISBN 978-0-8234-1445-1 Subj: Caldecott award honor books. Calendars. Days of the week, months of the year. Poetry.

Childs, Sam. *Naughty!* (Castle, Caroline)

Chin, Jason. *Coral reefs* ill. by author. Roaring Brook, 2011. ISBN 978-1-59643-563-6 Subj: Books, reading. Ecology. Imagination. Sea & seashore.

Grand Canyon ill. by author. Roaring Brook, 2017. ISBN 9781596439504 Subj: Activities – hiking. Caldecott award honor books. Canyons. Careers – geologists. Nature.

Gravity ill. by author. Roaring Brook, 2014. ISBN 978-159643717-3 Subj: Science.

Redwoods ill. by author. Roaring Brook, 2009. ISBN 978-1-59643-430-1 Subj: Imagination. Trees.

Chin, Joel. *The falling raindrop* (Johnson, Neil)

Chin, Oliver. *The year of the monkey: tales from the Chinese zodiac* ill. by Kenji Ono. Immedium, 2016. ISBN 978-159702118-0 Subj: Animals – monkeys. Foreign languages. Zodiac.

The year of the sheep: tales from the Chinese zodiac ill. by Alina Chau. Immedium, 2015. ISBN 978-159702104-3 Subj: Animals – sheep. Character traits – cooperation. Zodiac.

The year of the tiger: tales from the Chinese zodiac ill. by Justin Roth. Immedium, 2010. ISBN 978-1-59702-020-6 Subj: Animals. Animals – tigers. Zodiac.

Chin-Lee, Cynthia. *A is for Asia* ill. by Yumi Heo. Orchard, 1997. ISBN 978-0-531-33011-1 Subj: ABC books. Foreign lands – Asia.

Chinn, Karen. *Sam and the lucky money* ill. by Cornelius Van Wright and Ying-Hwa Hu. Lee & Low, 1995. ISBN 978-1-880000-13-7 Subj: Character traits – generosity. Ethnic groups in the U.S. – Chinese Americans. Holidays – Chinese New Year. Homeless.

Chisholm, Penny. *Buried sunlight: how fossil fuels have changed the earth* (Bang, Molly)

Ocean sunlight: how tiny plants feed the seas (Bang, Molly)

Rivers of sunlight: how the sun moves water around the earth (Bang, Molly)

Chitwood, Suzanne Tanner. *Wake up, big barn!* ill. by author. Scholastic, 2002. ISBN 978-0-439-26627-7 Subj: Animals. Farms. Rhyming text.

Chivers, Natalie. *Rhino's great big itch!* ill. by author. Good Books, 2010. ISBN 978-1-56148-684-7 Subj: Animals. Animals – rhinoceros. Birds. Problem solving.

Chocolate, Deborah. *El barrio* ill. by David Diaz. Henry Holt, 2009. ISBN 978-0-8050-7457-4 Subj: Cities, towns. Communities, neighborhoods. Ethnic groups in the U.S. – Hispanic Americans.

Kente colors ill. by John Ward. Walker, 1996. ISBN 978-0-8027-8389-9 Subj: Clothing. Concepts – color. Foreign lands – Africa. Holidays – Kwanzaa.

Kwanzaa ill. by Melodye Benson Rosales. Children's Press, 1990. ISBN 978-0-516-03991-6 Subj: Ethnic groups in the U.S. – African Americans. Family life. Holidays – Kwanzaa.

Chodos-Irvine, Margaret. *Best best friends* ill. by author. Harcourt, 2006. ISBN 978-0-15-205694-0 Subj: Birthdays. Friendship. School – nursery.

Ella Sarah gets dressed ill. by author. Harcourt, 2003. ISBN 978-0-15-216413-3 Subj: Caldecott award honor books. Character traits – individuality. Clothing. Family life. Friendship. Parties.

Choi, Sook Nyul. *Halmoni and the picnic* ill. by Karen Dugan. Houghton, 1993. ISBN 978-0-395-61626-0 Subj: Ethnic groups in the U.S. – Korean Americans. Family life – grandmothers.

Choi, Yangsook. *Behind the mask* ill. by author. Farrar, 2006. ISBN 978-0-374-30522-2 Subj: Ethnic groups in the U.S. – Korean Americans. Family life – grandfathers. Holidays – Halloween. Masks.

The name jar ill. by author. Knopf, 2001. ISBN 978-0-375-90613-8 Subj: Ethnic groups in the U.S. – Korean Americans. Names. School.

Choldenko, Gennifer. *Dad and the dinosaur* ill. by Dan Santat. Putnam, 2017. ISBN 978-039924353-0 Subj: Behavior – lost & found possessions. Dinosaurs. Emotions – fear. Family life – fathers. Toys.

A giant crush ill. by Melissa Sweet. Penguin, 2011. ISBN 978-0-399-24352-3 Subj: Character traits – shyness. Holidays – Valentine's Day. School.

How to make friends with a giant ill. by Amy Walrod. Penguin, 2006. ISBN 978-0-399-23779-9 Subj: Character traits – appearance. Concepts – size. Friendship. School.

Louder, Lili ill. by S. D. Schindler. Penguin, 2007. ISBN 978-0-399-24252-6 Subj: Behavior – bossy. Character traits – shyness. Friendship. School.

Putting the monkeys to bed ill. by Jack E. Davis. Putnam, 2015. ISBN 978-039924623-4 Subj: Animals – monkeys. Bedtime. Sleep.

Chorao, Kay, compiler. *The baby's bedtime book* ill. by compiler. Dutton, 1984. ISBN 978-0-525-44149-6 Subj: Nursery rhymes. Poetry.

Bad boy, good boy ill. by author. Abrams, 2013. ISBN 978-1-4197-0520-5 Subj: Animals – dogs. Behavior – misbehavior.

The Christmas story ill. by adapter. Holiday, 1996. ISBN 978-0-8234-1251-8 Subj: Holidays – Christmas. Religion – Nativity.

Knock at the door and other baby action rhymes ill. by author. Dutton, 1999. ISBN 978-0-525-45969-9 Subj: Animals – cats. Babies, toddlers. Nursery rhymes. Rhyming text.

Pig and Crow ill. by author. Henry Holt, 2000. ISBN 978-0-8050-5863-5 Subj: Activities – trading. Animals – pigs. Behavior. Birds – crows.

Shadow night ill. by author. Dutton, 2001. ISBN 978-0-525-46685-7 Subj: Emotions – fear. Family life. Shadows.

Chou, Yih-Fen. *Mimi loves to mimic* ill. by Chih-Yuan Chen. Heryin, 2010. ISBN 978-0-9787550-8-9 Subj: Behavior – imitation. Character traits – curiosity.

Mimi says no ill. by Chih-Yuan Chen. Heryin, 2010. ISBN 978-0-9787550-7-2 Subj: Character traits – assertiveness. Character traits – stubbornness.

Choung, Euh-hee. *Minji's Salon* ill. by author. Kane/Miller, 2008. ISBN 978-1-933605-67-8 Subj: Beauty shops. Ethnic groups in the U.S. – Korean Americans. Imagination.

Chriscoe, Sharon. *Race car dreams* ill. by Dave Mottram. Running Press, 2016. ISBN 978-076245964-3 Subj: Automobiles. Bedtime. Dreams. Rhyming text. Sports – racing.

Chrisholm, Penny. *Living sunlight: how plants bring the earth to life* (Bang, Molly)

Christelow, Eileen. *The desperate dog writes again* ill. by author. Clarion, 2010. ISBN 978-0-547-24205-7 Subj: Activities – writing. Animals – dogs. Humorous stories. Letters, cards.

Don't wake up Mama! another five little monkeys story ill. by author. Clarion, 1992. ISBN 978-0-395-60176-1 Subj: Activities – baking, cooking. Animals – monkeys. Birthdays. Family life – mothers. Food.

The five-dog night ill. by author. Clarion, 1993. ISBN 978-0-395-62399-2 Subj: Animals – dogs. Seasons – winter.

Five little monkeys go shopping ill. by author. Houghton, 2007. ISBN 978-0-618-82161-7 Subj: Animals – monkeys. Counting, numbers. Shopping.

Five little monkeys jumping on the bed ill. by author. Houghton, 1991. ISBN 978-0-395-55701-3 Subj: Animals – monkeys. Bedtime. Behavior – misbehavior. Counting, numbers. Nursery rhymes. Poetry.

Five little monkeys reading in bed ill. by author. Clarion, 2011. ISBN 978-0-547-38610-2 Subj: Animals – monkeys. Bedtime. Books, reading. Rhyming text.

Five little monkeys sitting in a tree ill. by author. Houghton, 1991. ISBN 978-0-395-54434-1 Subj: Activities – picnicking. Animals – monkeys. Behavior – misbehavior. Counting, numbers. Reptiles – alligators, crocodiles. Rhyming text.

Five little monkeys trick-or-treat ill. by author. Clarion, 2013. ISBN 978-0-547-85893-7 Subj: Activities – babysitting. Animals – monkeys. Behavior – trickery. Clothing – costumes. Holidays – Halloween.

Five little monkeys wash the car ill. by author. Clarion, 2000. ISBN 978-0-395-92566-9 Subj: Animals – monkeys. Automobiles. Reptiles – alligators, crocodiles. Rhyming text.

Five little monkeys with nothing to do ill. by author. Clarion, 1996. ISBN 978-0-395-75830-4 Subj: Animals – monkeys. Behavior – boredom. Family life.

The great pig escape ill. by author. Clarion, 1994. ISBN 978-0-395-66973-0 Subj: Animals – pigs. Behavior – running away. Careers – farmers.

The great pig search ill. by author. Clarion, 2001. ISBN 978-0-618-04910-3 Subj: Animals – pigs. Behavior – running away.

Jerome camps out ill. by author. Clarion, 1998. ISBN 978-0-395-75831-1 Subj: Behavior – bullying, teasing. Camps, camping. Reptiles – alligators, crocodiles.

Letters from a desperate dog ill. by author. Houghton, 2006. ISBN 978-0-618-51003-0 Subj: Activities – writing. Animals – dogs. Behavior – misbehavior. Careers – artists. Humorous stories. Letters, cards.

Not until Christmas, Walter! ill. by author. Clarion, 1997. ISBN 978-0-395-82273-9 Subj: Animals – dogs. Holidays – Christmas.

What do authors do? ill. by author. Clarion, 1995. ISBN 978-0-395-71124-8 Subj: Careers – artists. Careers – writers.

Where's the big bad wolf? ill. by author. Clarion, 2002. ISBN 978-0-618-18194-0 Subj: Animals. Animals – wolves. Careers – detectives. Humorous stories. Mystery stories.

Christensen, Bonnie. *Plant a little seed* ill. by author. Roaring Brook, 2012. ISBN 978-1-59643-550-6 Subj: Communities, neighborhoods. Gardens, gardening. Seeds.

Woody Guthrie, poet of the people ill. by author. Knopf, 2001. ISBN 978-0-375-91113-2 Subj: Careers – musicians. Music. U.S. history.

Christian, Cheryl. *Witches* ill. by Wish Williams. Star Bright, 2011. ISBN 978-1-59572-283-6 Subj: Holidays – Halloween. Rhyming text. Witches.

Christian, Mary Blount. *If not for the calico cat* ill. by Sebastià Serra. Penguin, 2007. ISBN 978-0-525-47779-2 Subj: Animals – cats. Boats, ships. Character traits – luck. Foreign lands – Japan.

Christian, Peggy. *If you find a rock* photos by Barbara Hirsch Lember. Harcourt, 2000. ISBN 978-0-15-239339-7 Subj: Rocks.

Christie, R. Gregory. *Mousetropolis* ill. by author. Holiday House, 2015. ISBN 978-082342319-4 Subj: Animals – mice. Cities, towns. Country. Folk & fairy tales.

Christopher, Neil. *On the shoulder of a giant: an Inuit folktale* ill. by Jim Nelson. Inhabit, 2015. ISBN 978-177227002-0 Subj: Folk & fairy tales. Giants. Indians of North America – Inuit.

Chrustowski, Rick. *Bee dance* ill. by author. Henry Holt, 2015. ISBN 978-080509919-5 Subj: Communication. Insects – bees.

Bright beetle ill. by author. Henry Holt, 2000. ISBN 978-0-8050-6058-4 Subj: Insects – ladybugs.

Hop frog ill. by author. Henry Holt, 2003. ISBN 978-0-8050-6688-3 Subj: Frogs & toads.

My Little Fox ill. by author. Simon & Schuster/Beach Lane, 2017. ISBN 978-148146961-6 Subj: Animals – foxes. Behavior – growing up. Rhyming text.

Turtle crossing ill. by author. Henry Holt, 2006. ISBN 978-0-8050-7498-7 Subj: Nature. Reptiles – turtles, tortoises.

Chukovskii, Kornei Ivanovich. *Good morning, chick* adapt. by Mirra Ginsburg; ill. by Byron Barton. Greenwillow, 1980. ISBN 978-0-688-84284-0 Subj: Birds – chickens, roosters. Noise, sounds.

Chung, Arree. *Ninja!* ill. by author. Henry Holt, 2014. ISBN 978-080509911-9 Subj: Activities – playing. Imagination. Sports – martial arts.

Ninja! attack of the clan ill. by author. Henry Holt, 2016. ISBN 978-080509916-4 Subj: Imagination. Sports – martial arts.

Ninja Claus! ill. by author. Henry Holt, 2017. ISBN 978-162779552-4 Subj: Holidays – Christmas. Santa Claus. Sports – martial arts.

Out! ill. by author. Henry Holt, 2017. ISBN 978-162779553-1 Subj: Animals – dogs. Babies, toddlers. Behavior – misbehavior.

Chung, Hyechong. *K is for Korea* ill. by Prodeepta Das. Frances Lincoln, 2008. ISBN 978-1-84507-789-1 Subj: ABC books. Foreign lands – Korea.

Church, Caroline Jayne. *Digby takes charge* ill. by author. Simon & Schuster, 2007. ISBN 978-1-4169-3441-7 Subj: Animals – dogs. Animals – sheep. Behavior – misbehavior. Character traits – kindness to animals. Farms.

I love my bunny ill. by author. Scholastic/Cartwheel, 2016. ISBN 978-054583596-1 Subj: Animals – rabbits. Format, unusual – board books. Rhyming text. Toys.

I love my robot ill. by author. Scholastic/Cartwheel, 2016. ISBN 978-054583593-0 Subj: Format, unusual – board books. Rhyming text. Robots.

Little Apple Goat ill. by author. Eerdmans, 2007. ISBN 978-0-8028-5320-2 Subj: Animals – goats. Food.

One more hug for Madison ill. by author. Scholastic, 2010. ISBN 978-0-545-16179-4 Subj: Animals – mice. Bedtime. Family life – mothers. Hugging.

One smart goose ill. by author. Scholastic, 2005. ISBN 978-0-439-68765-2 Subj: Animals – foxes. Behavior – bullying, teasing. Birds – geese. Character traits – cleanliness. Farms.

Ping Pong Pig ill. by author. Holiday House, 2008. ISBN 978-0-8234-2176-3 Subj: Activities – flying. Animals – pigs. Farms.

Ruff! and the wonderfully amazing busy day ill. by author. HarperCollins, 2013. ISBN 978-0-06-201498-6 Subj: Animals – dogs. Animals – mice. Birds – ducks. Character traits – kindness. Friendship.

Churchill, Vicki. *Sometimes I like to curl up in a ball* ill. by Charles Fuge. Sterling, 2001. ISBN 978-0-8069-7943-4 Subj: Animals – wombats. Rhyming text.

Churnin, Nancy. *The William Hoy story: how a deaf baseball player changed the game* ill. by Jez Tuya. Albert Whitman, 2016. ISBN 978-080759192-5 Subj: Disabilities – deafness. Sign language. Sports – baseball.

Chwast, Seymour. *Get dressed!* ill. by author. Abrams, 2012. ISBN 978-1-4197-0107-8 Subj: Clothing. Format, unusual – board books. Format, unusual – toy & movable books. Imagination.

Harry, I need you! ill. by author. Houghton, 2002. ISBN 978-0-618-17917-6 Subj: Animals – babies. Animals – cats. Imagination.

The miracle of Hanukkah ill. by author. Blue Apple, 2006. ISBN 978-1-59354-157-6 Subj: Holidays – Hanukkah. Jewish culture.

Ciboul, Adele. *The five senses* ill. by Clementine Collinet and Benoit Debecker, et al. Firefly, 2006.

ISBN 978-1-55407-007-7 Subj: Format, unusual – toy & movable books. Senses.

Cinderella ill. by Kinuko Y. Craft. SeaStar, 2000. ISBN 978-1-58717-005-8 Subj: Family life – stepfamilies. Folk & fairy tales. Royalty – princes. Sibling rivalry.

Ciraolo, Simona. *The lines on Nana's face* ill. by author. Flying Eye, 2016. ISBN 978-190926398-7 Subj: Anatomy – skin. Family life – grandmothers. Memories, memory. Old age.

Claflin, Willy. *The uglified ducky: a Maynard Moose tale* ill. by James Stimson. August House, 2008. ISBN 978-0-87483-858-9 Subj: Alaska. Animals – moose. Birds – ducks. Character traits – appearance. Character traits – being different. Folk & fairy tales.

Claire, Céline. *Shelter* ill. by Qin Leng. Kids Can, 2017. ISBN 978-177138927-3 Subj: Animals. Behavior – sharing. Character traits – kindness to animals. Forest, woods. Weather – storms.

Clanton, Ben. *Boo who?* ill. by author. Candlewick, 2017. ISBN 978-076368824-0 Subj: Activities – playing. Friendship. Ghosts.

It came in the mail ill. by author. Simon & Schuster, 2016. ISBN 978-148140360-3 Subj: Careers – postal workers. Dragons. Letters, cards.

Mo's mustache ill. by author. Tundra, 2013. ISBN 978-1-77049-538-8 Subj: Behavior – imitation. Character traits – individuality. Monsters. Self-concept.

Rex wrecks it! ill. by author. Candlewick, 2014. ISBN 978-076366501-2 Subj: Activities – playing. Behavior – misbehavior. Character traits – cooperation. Dinosaurs.

Rot, the cutest in the world! ill. by author. Atheneum, 2017. ISBN 978-148146762-9 Subj: Character traits – appearance. Contests. Food. Self-concept.

Vote for me! ill. by author. Kids Can, 2012. ISBN 978-1-55453-822-5 Subj: Animals – donkeys. Animals – elephants. Behavior – fighting, arguing. Behavior – name calling. Character traits – ambition.

Clark, Ann Nolan. *In my mother's house* ill. by Velino Herrera. Viking, 1941. Subj: Caldecott award honor books. Family life. Indians of North America – Tewa.

Clark, Karen Henry. *Sweet moon baby: an adoption tale* ill. by Patrice Barton. Random House, 2010. ISBN 978-0-375-85709-6 Subj: Adoption. Foreign lands – China. Moon.

Clark, Katie. *Seagull Sam* ill. by Amy Huntington. Down East, 2007. ISBN 978-0-89272-715-5 Subj:

Birds – seagulls. Character traits – smallness. Family life – brothers & sisters. Kites.

Clark, Leslie Ann. *Peepsqueak!* ill. by author. HarperCollins, 2012. ISBN 978-0-06-207801-8 Subj: Activities – flying. Animals. Animals – babies. Birds – chickens, roosters. Farms.

Clark, Mary Higgins. *Ghost ship: a Cape Cod story* ill. by Wendell Minor. Simon & Schuster, 2007. ISBN 978-1-4169-3514-8 Subj: Boats, ships. Ghosts.

Clarke, Ginjer L. *Platypus!* ill. by Paul Mirocha. Random House, 2004. ISBN 978-0-375-92417-0 Subj: Animals – platypuses.

Sharks! ill. by Steven James Petruccio. Grosset, 2001. ISBN 978-0-448-42588-7 Subj: Fish – sharks.

Clarke, Jane. *The best of both nests* ill. by Anne Kennedy. Albert Whitman, 2007. ISBN 978-0-8075-0668-4 Subj: Behavior – worrying. Birds – storks. Divorce.

Dancing with the Dinosaurs ill. by Lee Wildish. Charlesbridge, 2012. ISBN 978-1-936140-67-1 Subj: Activities – dancing. Dinosaurs. Rhyming text.

Dippy's sleepover ill. by Mary McQuillan. Barron's, 2006. ISBN 978-0-7641-3425-8 Subj: Behavior – bedwetting. Dinosaurs. Sleepovers.

Gilbert the hero ill. by Charles Fuge. Sterling, 2011. ISBN 978-1-4027-8040-0 Subj: Activities – playing. Family life – brothers. Fish – sharks.

Old MacDonald's things that go (Old MacDonald had a farm)

Stuck in the mud ill. by Garry Parsons. Walker, 2008. ISBN 978-0-8027-9758-2 Subj: Birds – chickens, roosters. Character traits – helpfulness. Cumulative tales. Farms. Rhyming text.

Trumpet: the little elephant with a big temper ill. by Charles Fuge. Simon & Schuster, 2010. ISBN 978-1-4169-0482-3 Subj: Animals – elephants. Birthdays. Emotions – anger. Parties.

Who woke the baby? ill. by Charles Fuge. Candlewick/Nosy Crow, 2016. ISBN 978-076368662-8 Subj: Animals – babies. Animals – gorillas. Cumulative tales. Insects – butterflies, caterpillars.

Clarkson, Stephanie. *Sleeping Cinderella and other princess mix-ups* ill. by Brigette Barrager. Orchard, 2015. ISBN 978-054556564-6 Subj: Behavior – dissatisfaction. Folk & fairy tales. Rhyming text. Royalty – princesses.

Clavel, Bernard. *Castle of books* ill. by Yan Nascimbene. Chronicle, 2001. ISBN 978-0-8118-3501-5 Subj: Castles. Family life. Poetry.

Clayton, Dallas. *A is for awesome* ill. by author. Candlewick, 2014. ISBN 978-076365745-1 Subj: ABC books.

An awesome book! ill. by author. HarperCollins, 2012. ISBN 978-0-06-211468-6 Subj: Imagination. Rhyming text.

An awesome book of love! ill. by author. HarperCollins, 2013. ISBN 978-0-06-211666-6 Subj: Emotions – love. Rhyming text.

Lily the unicorn ill. by author. HarperCollins, 2014. ISBN 978-006211668-0 Subj: Birds – penguins. Emotions – fear. Friendship. Mythical creatures – unicorns.

Clayton, Elaine. *A blue ribbon for Sugar* ill. by author. Macmillan, 2006. ISBN 978-1-59643-157-7 Subj: Animals – horses, ponies. Contests. Sports.

Cleary, Beverly. *The hullabaloo ABC* ill. by Ted Rand. Rev. ed. Morrow, 1998. ISBN 978-0-688-15183-6 Subj: ABC books. Farms. Noise, sounds. Rhyming text.

Cleary, Brian P. *Eight wild nights: a family Hanukkah tale* ill. by David Udovic. Lerner, 2006. ISBN 978-1-58013-152-0 Subj: Holidays – Hanukkah. Rhyming text.

If it rains pancakes: haiku and lantern poems ill. by Andy Rowland. Millbrook, 2014. ISBN 978-146771609-3 Subj: Poetry.

A lime, a mime, a pool of slime: more about nouns ill. by Brian Gable. Lerner, 2006. ISBN 978-1-57505-937-2 Subj: Language. Rhyming text.

Peanut butter and jellyfishes: a very silly alphabet book ill. by Betsy E Snyder. Lerner, 2007. ISBN 978-0-8225-6188-0 Subj: ABC books. Language. Picture puzzles. Rhyming text.

Six sheep sip thick shakes and other tricky tongue twisters ill. by Steve Mack. Millbrook, 2011. ISBN 978-1-58013-585-6 Subj: Tongue twisters.

Cleland, Jo. *Getting your zzzzs.* Rourke, 2012. ISBN 978-1-61810-085-6 Subj: Health & fitness. Sleep. Songs.

Clement, Nathan. *Big tractor* ill. by author. Boyds Mills, 2015. ISBN 978-162091790-9 Subj: Farms. Seasons. Tractors.

Drive ill. by author. Front Street, 2008. ISBN 978-1-59078-517-1 Subj: Careers – truck drivers. Trucks.

Job site ill. by author. Boyds Mills, 2011. ISBN 978-1-59078-769-4 Subj: Careers – construction workers. Machines.

Speed ill. by author. Boyds Mills, 2013. ISBN 978-1-59078-937-7 Subj: Careers – race car drivers. Sports – racing.

Clement-Davies, David. *Spirit: stallion of the Cimarron* ill. by William Maughan. Dutton, 2002. ISBN 978-0-525-46735-9 Subj: Animals – horses, ponies. Indians of North America. U.S. history – frontier & pioneer life.

Clements, Andrew. *Because your daddy loves you* ill. by R. W. Alley. Houghton, 2005. ISBN 978-0-618-00361-7 Subj: Emotions – love. Family life – fathers. Sea & seashore – beaches.

Because your mommy loves you ill. by R. W. Alley. Clarion, 2012. ISBN 978-0-547-25522-4 Subj: Camps, camping. Emotions – love. Family life – mothers.

Big Al and Shrimpy ill. by Yoshi. Simon & Schuster, 2002. ISBN 978-0-689-84247-4 Subj: Concepts – size. Fish. Friendship.

Brave Norman ill. by Ellen Beier. Simon & Schuster, 2001. ISBN 978-0-689-82914-7 Subj: Animals – dogs. Disabilities – blindness.

Bright Christmas: an angel remembers ill. by Kate Kiesler. Clarion, 1996. ISBN 978-0-395-72096-7 Subj: Angels. Holidays – Christmas. Religion – Nativity.

Circus family dog ill. by Sue Truesdell. Clarion, 2000. ISBN 978-0-395-78648-2 Subj: Animals – dogs. Circus.

Dogku ill. by Tim Bowers. Simon & Schuster, 2007. ISBN 978-0-689-85823-9 Subj: Animals – dogs. Pets. Poetry.

Dolores and the big fire ill. by Ellen Beier. Simon & Schuster, 2002. ISBN 978-0-689-82916-1 Subj: Animals – cats. Pets.

The handiest things in the world photos by Raquel Jaramillo. Simon & Schuster, 2010. ISBN 978-1-4169-6166-6 Subj: Anatomy – hands. Rhyming text.

A million dots ill. by Mike Reed. Simon & Schuster, 2006. ISBN 978-0-689-85824-6 Subj: Counting, numbers.

Naptime for Slippers ill. by Janie Bynum. Penguin, 2005. ISBN 978-0-525-47287-2 Subj: Animals – dogs. Sleep.

Slippers at home ill. by Janie Bynum. Dutton, 2004. ISBN 978-0-525-47138-7 Subj: Animals – babies. Animals – dogs. Homes, houses.

Slippers at School ill. by Janie Bynum. Penguin, 2005. ISBN 978-0-525-47189-9 Subj: Animals – dogs. School.

Slippers loves to run ill. by Janie Bynum. Penguin, 2006. ISBN 978-0-525-47648-1 Subj: Animals – dogs. Family life. Hugging. Pets.

Tara and Tiree, fearless friends ill. by Ellen Beier. Simon & Schuster, 2002. ISBN 978-0-689-82917-8 Subj: Animals – dogs. Foreign lands – Canada. Pets.

Workshop ill. by David Wisniewski. Clarion, 1998. ISBN 978-0-395-85579-9 Subj: Merry-go-rounds. Tools.

Clemesha, David. *My dog Toby* (Zimmerman, Andrea Griffing)

Trashy town (Zimmerman, Andrea Griffing)

Cleminson, Katie. *Magic box: a magical story* ill. by author. Hyperion, 2009. ISBN 978-1-4231-2109-1 Subj: Animals – polar bears. Behavior – wishing. Birthdays. Magic.

Otto the book bear ill. by author. Hyperion, 2012. ISBN 978-1-4231-4562-2 Subj: Animals – bears. Books, reading. Libraries.

Clibbon, Lucy. *Imagine you're a fairy!* (Clibbon, Meg)

Imagine you're a mermaid! (Clibbon, Meg)

Imagine you're a pirate! (Clibbon, Meg)

Imagine you're a wizard! (Clibbon, Meg)

Clibbon, Meg. *Imagine you're a fairy!* by Meg Clibbon and Lucy Clibbon ill. by Lucy Clibbon. Annick, 2002. ISBN 978-1-55037-743-9 Subj: Fairies. Imagination.

Imagine you're a mermaid! by Meg Clibbon and Lucy Clibbon ill. by Lucy Clibbon. Annick, 2002. ISBN 978-1-55037-791-0 Subj: Imagination. Mythical creatures – mermaids, mermen.

Imagine you're a pirate! by Meg Clibbon and Lucy Clibbon ill. by Lucy Clibbon. Annick, 2002. ISBN 978-1-55037-741-5 Subj: Imagination. Pirates.

Imagine you're a wizard! by Meg Clibbon and Lucy Clibbon ill. by Lucy Clibbon. Annick, 2002. ISBN 978-1-55037-793-4 Subj: Imagination. Wizards.

Clifton, Lucille. *Everett Anderson's goodbye* ill. by Ann Grifalconi. Henry Holt, 1983, 1988. ISBN 978-0-8050-0800-5 Subj: Death. Emotions – grief. Emotions – love. Ethnic groups in the U.S. – African Americans. Family life. Rhyming text.

One of the problems of Everett Anderson ill. by Ann Grifalconi. Henry Holt, 2001. ISBN 978-0-8050-5201-5 Subj: Child abuse. Ethnic groups in the U.S. – African Americans. Rhyming text.

Three wishes ill. by Michael Hays. Doubleday, 1992. ISBN 978-0-385-30497-9 Subj: Behavior – wishing. Ethnic groups in the U.S. – African Americans. Friendship.

Clifton-Brown, Holly. *Annie Hoot and the knitting extravaganza* ill. by author. Andersen, 2010. ISBN 978-0-7613-6444-3 Subj: Activities – knitting. Activities – traveling. Birds – owls.

Climo, Liz. *Rory the dinosaur: me and my dad* ill. by author. Little, Brown, 2015. ISBN 978-031627728-0 Subj: Dinosaurs. Family life – fathers.

Rory the dinosaur needs a Christmas tree ill. by author. Little, Brown, 2017. ISBN 978-031631523-4 Subj: Dinosaurs. Family life – fathers. Holidays – Christmas. Problem solving.

Rory the dinosaur wants a pet ill. by author. Little, Brown, 2016. ISBN 978-031627729-7 Subj: Dinosaurs. Pets.

Climo, Shirley. *The Egyptian Cinderella* ill. by Ruth Heller. HarperCollins, 1989. ISBN 978-0-690-04824-7 Subj: Family life – stepfamilies. Folk & fairy tales. Foreign lands – Egypt. Royalty. Sibling rivalry.

The Irish Cinderlad ill. by Loretta Krupinski. HarperCollins, 1996. ISBN 978-0-06-024397-5 Subj: Animals – bulls, cows. Folk & fairy tales. Foreign lands – Ireland.

The Korean Cinderella ill. by Ruth Heller. HarperCollins, 1993. ISBN 978-0-06-020433-4 Subj: Family life – stepfamilies. Folk & fairy tales. Foreign lands – Korea. Royalty. Sibling rivalry.

The Persian Cinderella ill. by Robert Florczak. HarperCollins, 1999. ISBN 978-0-06-026765-0 Subj: Fairies. Family life – stepfamilies. Folk & fairy tales. Foreign lands – Persia. Royalty – princes. Sibling rivalry.

Tuko and the birds: a tale from the Philippines ill. by Francisco X. Mora. Henry Holt, 2008. ISBN 978-0-8050-6559-6 Subj: Birds. Folk & fairy tales. Foreign lands – Philippines.

Cline-Ransome, Lesa. *Before she was Harriet* ill. by James Ransome. Holiday, 2017. ISBN 978-082342047-6 Subj: Ethnic groups in the U.S. – African Americans. Prejudice. Slavery. U.S. history.

Freedom's school ill. by James Ransome. Disney/Jump at the Sun, 2015. ISBN 978-142316103-5 Subj: Ethnic groups in the U.S. – African Americans. School.

Just a lucky so and so: the story of Louis Armstrong ill. by James Ransome. Holiday, 2016. ISBN 978-082343428-2 Subj: Careers – musicians. Ethnic groups in the U.S. – African Americans. Musical instruments – trumpets. U.S. history.

Light in the darkness: a story about how slaves learned in secret ill. by James Ransome. Disney/Jump at the Sun, 2013. ISBN 978-1-4231-3495-4 Subj: Books, reading. Ethnic groups in the U.S. – African Americans. Slavery. U.S. history.

Quilt alphabet ill. by James Ransome. Holiday, 2001. ISBN 978-0-8234-1453-6 Subj: ABC books. Country. Poetry. Quilts. Rhyming text.

Quilt counting ill. by James Ransome. SeaStar, 2002. ISBN 978-1-58717-178-9 Subj: Counting, numbers. Country. Quilts. Rhyming text.

Whale trails, before and now ill. by G. Brian Karas. Henry Holt, 2015. ISBN 978-080509642-2 Subj: Animals – endangered animals. Animals – whales.

Words set me free: the story of young Frederick Douglass ill. by James Ransome. Simon & Schuster, 2012. ISBN 978-1-4169-5903-8 Subj: Activities – writing. Books, reading. Ethnic groups in the U.S. – African Americans. Slavery. U.S. history.

Young Pelé: soccer's first star ill. by James Ransome. Random House, 2007. ISBN 978-0-375-83599-5 Subj: Foreign lands – Brazil. Sports – soccer.

Clinton, Catherine. *Phillis's big test* ill. by Sean Qualls. Houghton, 2008. ISBN 978-0-618-73739-0 Subj: Activities – writing. Careers – writers. Ethnic groups in the U.S. – African Americans. Poetry. U.S. history.

When Harriet met Sojourner ill. by Shane W. Evans. HarperCollins, 2007. ISBN 978-0-06-050425-0 Subj: Ethnic groups in the U.S. – African Americans. U.S. history.

Clinton, Chelsea. *She persisted: 13 American women who changed the world* ill. by Alexandra Boiger. Philomel, 2017. ISBN 978-152474172-3 Subj: Character traits – persistence. Gender roles. U.S. history.

Clinton, Hillary Rodham. *It takes a village* ill. by Marla Frazee. Simon & Schuster, 2017. ISBN 978-148143087-6 Subj: Character traits – helpfulness. Character traits – hopefulness. Communities, neighborhoods. Concepts – change.

Cneut, Carll. *The amazing love story of Mr. Morf* ill. by author. Clarion, 2003. ISBN 978-0-618-33170-3 Subj: Animals. Animals – dogs. Circus. Friendship. Insects – fleas.

Coat, Janik. *Hippopposites* ill. by author. Abrams, 2012. ISBN 978-1-4197-0151-1 Subj: Animals – hippopotamuses. Concepts – opposites.

Rhymoceros ill. by author. Abrams/Appleseed, 2015. ISBN 978-141971514-3 Subj: Animals – rhinoceros. Format, unusual – board books. Rhyming text.

Coats, Lucy. *Captain Beastlie's pirate party* ill. by Chris Mould. Candlewick/Nosy Crow, 2014. ISBN 978-076367399-4 Subj: Behavior – messy. Birthdays. Hygiene. Pirates.

Neil's numberless world ill. by Neal Layton. DK, 2000. ISBN 978-0-7894-6354-8 Subj: Birthdays. Clocks, watches. Counting, numbers. Magic.

Cobb, Abigail Jane. *Meet my grandmother. She's a children's book author* (McElroy, Lisa Tucker)

Cobb, Annie. *The long wait* ill. by Liza Woodruff. Kane, 2000. ISBN 978-1-57565-094-4 Subj: Counting, numbers. Parks – amusement.

Cobb, Rebecca. *Missing Mommy: a book about bereavement* ill. by author. Henry Holt, 2013. ISBN 978-0-8050-9507-4 Subj: Death. Emotions – grief. Emotions – sadness. Family life – mothers.

Cobb, Vicki. *I fall down* ill. by Julia Gorton. HarperCollins, 2004. ISBN 978-0-688-17843-7 Subj: Concepts – weight. Science.

I get wet ill. by Julia Gorton. HarperCollins, 2002. ISBN 978-0-688-17839-0 Subj: Science. Water.

I see myself ill. by Julia Gorton. HarperCollins, 2002. ISBN 978-0-688-17837-6 Subj: Mirrors. Science.

Open your eyes ill. by Cynthia C. Lewis. Millbrook, 2002. ISBN 978-0-7613-1705-0 Subj: Anatomy – eyes. Science. Senses – sight.

Coburn, Jewell Reinhart. *Angkat: the Cambodian Cinderella* ill. by Eddie Flotte. Shen's, 1998. ISBN 978-1-885008-09-1 Subj: Family life – stepfamilies. Folk & fairy tales. Foreign lands – Cambodia. Royalty – princes. Sibling rivalry.

Jouanah: a Hmong Cinderella ill. by Anne Sibley O'Brien. Adapt. by Jewell Reinhart Coburn and Tzexa Cherta Lee. Shen's, 1996. ISBN 978-1-885008-01-5 Subj: Family life – stepfamilies. Folk & fairy tales. Foreign lands. Royalty – princes. Sibling rivalry.

Cocca-Leffler, Maryann. *Bravery soup* ill. by author. Albert Whitman, 2002. ISBN 978-0-8075-0870-1 Subj: Animals – bears. Animals – foxes. Animals – raccoons. Emotions – fear.

Bus route to Boston ill. by author. Boyds Mills, 2000. ISBN 978-1-56397-723-7 Subj: Activities – traveling. Buses. Cities, towns. Shopping.

A homemade together Christmas ill. by author. Albert Whitman, 2015. ISBN 978-080753366-6 Subj: Activities – making things. Animals – pigs. Gifts. Holidays – Christmas.

Jack's talent ill. by author. Farrar, 2007. ISBN 978-0-374-33681-3 Subj: Behavior – worrying. School – first day. Self-concept.

Janine ill. by author. Albert Whitman, 2015. ISBN 978-080753754-1 Subj: Behavior – bullying, teasing. Character traits – individuality. Character traits – kindness. Disabilities. Self-concept.

Janine and the field day finish ill. by author. Albert Whitman, 2016. ISBN 978-080753756-5 Subj: Character traits – individuality. Character traits – kindness. Contests. Disabilities. Self-concept.

Jungle Halloween ill. by author. Albert Whitman, 2000. ISBN 978-0-8075-4056-5 Subj: Animals. Holidays – Halloween. Rhyming text.

Let it rain ill. by author. Scholastic, 2013. ISBN 978-0-545-45343-1 Subj: Activities. Rhyming text. Seasons – spring. Weather – rain.

Mr. Tanen's ties rule! ill. by author. Albert Whitman, 2005. ISBN 978-0-8075-5308-4 Subj: Careers – school principals. Clothing – neckties. School.

Princess K.I.M. and the lie that grew ill. by author. Albert Whitman, 2009. ISBN 978-0-8075-4178-4 Subj: Behavior – lying. Character traits – honesty. School. Self-concept.

Princess Kim and too much truth ill. by author. Albert Whitman, 2011. ISBN 978-0-8075-6618-3 Subj: Character traits – honesty. School.

Rain brings frogs: a little book of hope ill. by author. HarperCollins, 2011. ISBN 978-0-06-196106-9 Subj: Character traits – hopefulness. Character traits – optimism.

Theo's mood ill. by author. Albert Whitman, 2013. ISBN 978-0-8075-7778-3 Subj: Babies, toddlers. Emotions. Family life – new sibling. School.

Time to say bye-bye ill. by author. Viking, 2012. ISBN 978-0-670-01309-8 Subj: Activities. Babies, toddlers. Bedtime. Day.

A vacation for Pooch ill. by author. Henry Holt, 2013. ISBN 978-0-8050-9106-9 Subj: Activities – vacationing. Animals – dogs. Family life – grandfathers. Farms.

Cochran, Bill. *The forever dog* ill. by Dan Andreasen. HarperCollins, 2007. ISBN 978-0-06-053939-9 Subj: Animals – dogs. Death. Emotions – grief. Pets.

My parents are divorced, my elbows have nicknames, and other facts about me ill. by Steve Björkman. HarperCollins, 2009. ISBN 978-0-06-053942-9 Subj: Character traits – individuality. Divorce. Self-concept.

Cocoretto . *Toot! toot! guess the instrument!* ill. by author. Child's Play, 2016. ISBN 978-184643749-6 Subj: Format, unusual – board books. Format, unusual – toy & movable books. Musical instruments.

Cocovini, Abby. *What's inside your tummy, Mommy?* ill. by author. Henry Holt, 2008. ISBN 978-0-8050-8760-4 Subj: Babies, toddlers. Birth. Family life – mothers.

Codell, Esme Raji. *It's time for preschool!* ill. by Sue Ramá. Greenwillow, 2012. ISBN 978-0-06-145518-6 Subj: School – nursery.

Seed by seed: the legend and legacy of Johnny "Appleseed" Chapman ill. by Lynne Rae Perkins. Greenwillow, 2012. ISBN 978-0-06-145515-5 Subj: Activities – traveling. Gardens, gardening. Tall tales. Trees. U.S. history – frontier & pioneer life.

The basket ball ill. by Jennifer Plecas. Abrams, 2011. ISBN 978-1-4197-0007-1 Subj: Gender roles. Sports – basketball.

Coelho, Joseph. *Luna loves library day* ill. by Fiona Lumbers. Kane/Miller, 2017. ISBN 978-161067675-5 Subj: Books, reading. Divorce. Family life. Libraries.

Coerr, Eleanor. *Circus day in Japan* ill. by author. Tuttle, 2010. ISBN 978-4-8053-1059-5 Subj: Circus. Foreign lands – Japan. Foreign languages.

Sadako ill. by Ed Young. Putnam, 1993. ISBN 978-0-399-21771-5 Subj: Birds – cranes. Death. Foreign lands – Japan. Illness. War.

Coffelt, Nancy. *Aunt Ant leaves through the leaves: a story with homophones and homonyms* ill. by author. Holiday House, 2012. ISBN 978-0-8234-2353-8 Subj: Activities – baking, cooking. Animals. Character traits – helpfulness. Language.

Big, bigger, biggest! ill. by author. Henry Holt, 2009. ISBN 978-0-8050-8089-6 Subj: Animals. Language.

Catch that baby! ill. by Scott Nash. Simon & Schuster, 2011. ISBN 978-1-4169-9148-9 Subj: Activities – bathing. Babies, toddlers. Humorous stories.

Fred stays with me! ill. by Tricia Tusa. Little, Brown, 2007. ISBN 978-0-316-88269-9 Subj: Animals – dogs. Divorce. Family life.

Pug in a truck ill. by author. Houghton, 2006. ISBN 978-0-618-56319-7 Subj: Animals – dogs. Careers – truck drivers. Trucks.

Coffey, Maria. *A cat adrift* ill. by Eugenie Fernandes. Annick, 2002. ISBN 978-1-55037-727-9 Subj: Animals – cats. Animals – rats. Sea & seashore.

Coh, Smiljana. *Princesses on the run* ill. by author. Running Press, 2013. ISBN 978-0-7624-4612-4 Subj: Behavior – boredom. Behavior – running away. Royalty – princesses.

The seven princesses ill. by author. Running Press Kids, 2016. ISBN 978-076245587-4 Subj: Behavior – fighting, arguing. Emotions – anger. Family life – sisters. Royalty – princesses. Sibling rivalry.

Cohan, George M. *You're a grand old flag* ill. by Warren Kimble. Walker, 2007. ISBN 978-0-8027-9575-5 Subj: Flags. Songs. U.S. history.

Cohen, Caron Lee. *Broom, zoom!* ill. by Sergio Ruzzier. Simon & Schuster, 2010. ISBN 978-1-4169-9113-7 Subj: Character traits – cleanliness. Character traits – cooperation. Friendship. Monsters. Witches.

Digger Pig and the turnip ill. by Christopher Denise. Harcourt, 2000. ISBN 978-0-15-202524-3 Subj: Animals. Behavior – sharing. Character traits – laziness. Cumulative tales. Folk & fairy tales.

Happy to you! ill. by Rosanne Litzinger. Clarion, 2001. ISBN 978-0-689-82421-0 Subj: Babies, toddlers. Emotions – happiness. Family life – mothers.

Martin and the giant lions ill. by Elizabeth Sayles. Clarion, 2002. ISBN 978-0-618-04908-0 Subj: Animals – lions. Dreams. Imagination. Night. Parks.

The mud pony: a traditional Skidi Pawnee tale ill. by Shonto Begay. Scholastic, 1988. ISBN 978-0-590-41525-5 Subj: Animals – horses, ponies. Folk & fairy tales. Indians of North America – Pawnee.

Cohen, Daniel. *Apatosaurus* ill. with photos. Bridgestone, 2001. ISBN 978-0-7368-0616-9 Subj: Dinosaurs. Fossils.

Pteranodon ill. with photos. Bridgestone, 2001. ISBN 978-0-7368-0612-1 Subj: Dinosaurs. Fossils.

Stegosaurus ill. with photos. Bridgestone, 2001. ISBN 978-0-7368-0618-3 Subj: Dinosaurs. Fossils.

Triceratops ill. with photos. Bridgestone, 2001. ISBN 978-0-7368-0619-0 Subj: Dinosaurs. Fossils.

Tyrannosaurus rex ill. with photos. Bridgestone, 2001. ISBN 978-0-7368-0620-6 Subj: Dinosaurs. Fossils.

Velociraptor ill. with photos. Bridgestone, 2001. ISBN 978-0-7368-0621-3 Subj: Dinosaurs. Fossils.

Cohen, Deborah Bodin. *Engineer Ari and the Rosh Hashana ride* ill. by Shahar Kober. Lerner, 2008. ISBN 978-0-8225-8648-7 Subj: Behavior – boasting, showing off. Foreign lands – Israel. Holidays – Rosh Hashanah. Trains.

Papa Jethro ill. by author. Kar-Ben, 2007. ISBN 978-1-58013-250-3 Subj: Family life – grandfathers. Jewish culture. Religion.

The seventh day ill. by Melanie W. Hall. Kar-Ben, 2005. ISBN 978-0-929371-24-5 Subj: Creation. Religion.

Cohen, Jeff. *Eva and Sadie and the best classroom ever!* ill. by Elanna Allen. HarperCollins, 2015. ISBN 978-006224938-8 Subj: Family life – sisters. School – first day.

Eva and Sadie and the worst haircut ever! ill. by Elanna Allen. HarperCollins, 2014. ISBN 978-006224906-7 Subj: Character traits – appearance. Family life – sisters. Hair.

Cohen, Laurie. *The flea* ill. by Marjorie Béal. OwlKids, 2014. ISBN 978-177147056-8 Subj: Character traits – smallness. Concepts – size. Insects – fleas.

Cohen, Miriam. *Bee my Valentine!* ill. by Lillian Hoban. Greenwillow, 1978. ISBN 978-0-688-84129-4 Subj: Holidays – Valentine's Day. School.

Best friends ill. by Lillian Hoban. Aladdin, 1989, ©1971. ISBN 978-0-689-71334-7 Subj: Friendship. School.

Don't eat too much turkey! ill. by Lillian Hoban. Greenwillow, 1987. ISBN 978-0-688-07142-4 Subj: Behavior – sharing. School.

First grade takes a test ill. by Ronald Himler. Star Bright, 2006. ISBN 978-1-59572-054-2 Subj: Friendship. School.

First grade takes a test ill. by Lillian Hoban. Greenwillow, 1980. ISBN 978-0-688-84265-9 Subj: Friendship. School.

It's George! ill. by Lillian Hoban. Greenwillow, 1988. ISBN 978-0-688-06813-4 Subj: Character traits – being different. School.

Jim meets the thing ill. by Lillian Hoban. Greenwillow, 1981. ISBN 978-0-688-00617-4 Subj: Behavior – growing up. Emotions – fear. Monsters. School.

Jim's dog Muffins ill. by Ronald Himler. Star Bright, 2008. ISBN 978-1-59572-099-3 Subj: Animals – dogs. Death. Emotions – grief. Pets.

Jim's dog Muffins ill. by Lillian Hoban. Greenwillow, 1984. ISBN 978-0-688-02565-6 Subj: Animals – dogs. Death. Emotions – grief. Pets.

Lost in the museum ill. by Lillian Hoban. Greenwillow, 1979. ISBN 978-0-688-84187-4 Subj: Behavior – lost. Museums. School – field trips.

No good in art ill. by Lillian Hoban. Greenwillow, 1980. ISBN 978-0-688-80234-9 Subj: Art. School. Self-concept.

The real-skin rubber monster mask ill. by Lillian Hoban. Greenwillow, 1990. ISBN 978-0-688-09123-1 Subj: Emotions – fear. Holidays – Halloween. Masks. School.

See you in second grade! ill. by Lillian Hoban. Greenwillow, 1989. ISBN 978-0-688-07139-4 Subj: Friendship. School. Sea & seashore.

Starring first grade ill. by Lillian Hoban. Greenwillow, 1985. ISBN 978-0-688-04030-7 Subj: Behavior – misbehavior. School. Theater.

Tough Jim ill. by Lillian Hoban. Macmillan, 1974. ISBN 978-0-02-722760-4 Subj: Behavior – bullying, teasing. Parties. School.

When will I read? ill. by Lillian Hoban. Greenwillow, 1977. ISBN 978-0-688-84073-0 Subj: Books, reading. School.

Will I have a friend? ill. by Ronald Himler. Star Bright, 2009. ISBN 978-1-59572-069-6 Subj: Ethnic groups in the U.S. Friendship. School – first day.

Will I have a friend? ill. by Lillian Hoban. Macmillan, 1967. ISBN 978-0-689-71333-0 Subj: Ethnic groups in the U.S. Friendship. School – first day.

Cohen, Peter Zachary. *Boris's glasses* ill. by Olof Landström. Farrar, 2003. ISBN 978-91-29-65942-9 Subj: Animals. Animals – hamsters. Glasses.

Cohn, Diana. *Dream carver* ill. by Amy Córdova. Chronicle, 2002. ISBN 978-0-8118-1244-3 Subj: Animals. Art. Careers – woodcarvers. Foreign lands – Mexico.

Cohn, Scotti. *One wolf howls* ill. by Susan Detwiler. Sylvan Dell, 2009. ISBN 978-1-934359-92-1 Subj: Animals – wolves. Counting, numbers. Days of the week, months of the year.

Colandro, Lucille. *There was a cold lady who swallowed some snow!* ill. by Jared D Lee. Scholastic, 2003. ISBN 978-0-439-47109-1 Subj: Cumulative tales. Rhyming text. Snowmen. Weather – snow.

There was an old lady who swallowed a clover! ill. by Jared D Lee. Scholastic, 2012. ISBN 978-0-545-35222-2 Subj: Cumulative tales. Holidays – St. Patrick's Day. Mythical creatures – leprechauns. Rhyming text.

There was an old lady who swallowed a frog! ill. by Jared D Lee. Scholastic, 2014. ISBN 978-054569138-3 Subj: Cumulative tales. Gardens, gardening. Rhyming text. Seasons – spring.

There was an old lady who swallowed some books! ill. by Jared D Lee. Scholastic, 2012. ISBN 978-0-545-40287-3 Subj: Books, reading. Cumulative tales. Rhyming text. School – first day.

Colato Laínez, René. *Mamá the alien / Mamá la extraterrestre* ill. by Laura Lacámara. Lee & Low, 2016. ISBN 978-089239298-8 Subj: Ethnic groups in the U.S. – Hispanic Americans. Family life – mothers. Foreign languages. Immigrants, immigration.

My shoes and I ill. by Fabricio Vanden Broeck. Boyds Mills, 2010. ISBN 978-1-59078-385-6 Subj: Clothing – shoes. Family life – fathers. Foreign lands – El Salvador. Immigrants, immigration.

Playing lotería / El juego de la lotería ill. by Jill Arena. Luna Rising, 2005. ISBN 978-0-87358-881-2 Subj: Fairs, festivals. Family life – grandmothers. Foreign lands – Mexico. Foreign languages.

Señor Pancho had a rancho ill. by Elwood H. Smith. Holiday House, 2013. ISBN 978-0-8234-2632-4 Subj: Animals. Farms. Foreign languages. Noise, sounds. Songs.

The Tooth Fairy meets El Ratón Pérez ill. by Tom Lintern. Tricycle, 2010. ISBN 978-1-58246-296-7 Subj: Ethnic groups in the U.S. – Mexican Americans. Fairies. Teeth.

Colborn, Mary Palenick. *Rainy day slug* ill. by Lorie Ann Grover. Sasquatch, 2000. ISBN 978-1-57061-238-1 Subj: Animals – slugs. Rhyming text. Weather – rain.

Colby, Rebecca. *It's raining bats and frogs* ill. by Steven Henry. Feiwel & Friends, 2015. ISBN 978-125004992-6 Subj: Holidays – Halloween. Parades. Weather – rain. Witches.

Motor Goose: rhymes that go! ill. by Jef Kaminsky. Feiwel & Friends, 2017. ISBN 978-125010193-8 Subj: Nursery rhymes. Transportation.

Cole, Babette. *Lady Lupin's book of etiquette* ill. by author. Peachtree, 2001. ISBN 978-1-56145-257-6 Subj: Animals – babies. Animals – dogs. Etiquette.

Prince Cinders ill. by author. Putnam, 1988. ISBN 978-0-399-21502-5 Subj: Folk & fairy tales. Magic. Royalty – princes.

Princess Smartypants ill. by author. Putnam, 1987. ISBN 978-0-399-21409-7 Subj: Pets. Problem solving. Royalty – princesses.

Truelove ill. by author. Dial, 2002. ISBN 978-0-8037-2717-5 Subj: Animals – dogs. Babies, toddlers. Emotions – love. Humorous stories.

Cole, Barbara Hancock. *Anna and Natalie* ill. by Ronald Himler. Star Bright, 2007. ISBN 978-1-59572-105-1 Subj: Animals – dogs. Contests. Disabilities – blindness. Letters, cards. School. U.S. history.

Cole, Brock. *Buttons* ill. by author. Farrar, 2000. ISBN 978-0-374-31001-1 Subj: Clothing. Family life – daughters. Family life – fathers. Humorous stories. Tall tales.

Good enough to eat ill. by author. Farrar, 2007. ISBN 978-0-374-32737-8 Subj: Character traits – cleverness. Homeless. Mythical creatures – ogres.

Larky Mavis ill. by author. Farrar, 2001. ISBN 978-0-374-34365-1 Subj: Angels. Babies, toddlers.

The money we'll save ill. by author. Farrar, 2011. ISBN 978-0-374-35011-6 Subj: Birds – turkeys. Family life. Holidays – Christmas.

Cole, Henry. *Big bug* ill. by author. Simon & Schuster, 2014. ISBN 978-144249897-6 Subj: Concepts – size. Farms.

Eddie the bully ill. by author. little bee, 2016. ISBN 978-149980181-1 Subj: Animals. Behavior – bullying, teasing. Birds – chickens, roosters. Character traits – kindness. School.

The littlest evergreen ill. by author. HarperCollins, 2011. ISBN 978-0-06-114519-0 Subj: Ecology. Holidays – Christmas. Trees.

On Meadowview Street ill. by author. HarperCollins, 2007. ISBN 978-0-06-056481-0 Subj: Cities, towns. Ecology. Nature.

Spot, the cat ill. by author. Simon & Schuster/ Little Simon, 2016. ISBN 978-148144225-1 Subj: Animals – cats. Behavior – lost & found possessions. Cities, towns. Picture puzzles. Wordless.

Trudy ill. by author. Greenwillow, 2009. ISBN 978-0-06-154267-1 Subj: Animals – goats. Pets. Weather – snow.

Unspoken: a story from the Underground Railroad ill. by author. Scholastic, 2012. ISBN 978-0-545-39997-5 Subj: Ethnic groups in the U.S. – African Americans. Slavery. U.S. history. Wordless.

Cole, Joanna. *Bony-legs* ill. by Dirk Zimmer. Four Winds, 1983. ISBN 978-0-590-07882-5 Subj: Folk & fairy tales. Foreign lands – Russia. Magic. Witches.

Bully trouble ill. by Marylin Hafner. Random House, 2003. ISBN 978-0-394-94949-9 Subj: Behavior – bullying, teasing.

How I was adopted: Samantha's story ill. by Maxie Chambliss. Morrow, 1995. ISBN 978-0-688-11930-0 Subj: Adoption. Family life.

How you were born photos by Margaret Miller. Rev. and expanded ed. Morrow, 1993. ISBN 978-0-688-12059-7 Subj: Babies, toddlers. Birth. Family life. Science.

I'm a big brother ill. by Maxie Chambliss. Morrow, 1997. ISBN 978-0-688-14507-1 Subj: Babies, toddlers. Family life – brothers.

I'm a big sister ill. by Maxie Chambliss. Morrow, 1997. ISBN 978-0-688-14509-5 Subj: Babies, toddlers. Family life – sisters.

I'm a big sister ill. by Rosalinda Kightley. HarperCollins, 2010. ISBN 978-0-06-190062-4 Subj: Family life – new sibling. Family life – sisters.

The magic school bus and the climate challenge ill. by Bruce Degen. Scholastic, 2010. ISBN 978-0-590-10826-3 Subj: Ecology. Science. Weather.

The magic school bus and the electric field trip ill. by Bruce Degen. Scholastic, 1997. ISBN 978-0-590-44682-2 Subj: Careers – electricians. School – field trips.

The magic school bus and the science fair expedition ill. by Bruce Degen. Scholastic, 2006. ISBN 978-0-590-10824-9 Subj: Buses. Careers – teachers. Magic. School – field trips. Science.

The magic school bus at the waterworks ill. by Bruce Degen. Scholastic, 1986. ISBN 978-0-590-40361-0 Subj: School – field trips. Water.

The magic school bus explores the senses ill. by Bruce Degen. Scholastic, 1999. ISBN 978-0-590-44697-6 Subj: School. Senses.

The magic school bus in the time of the dinosaurs ill. by Bruce Degen. Scholastic, 1994. ISBN 978-0-590-44688-4 Subj: Buses. Careers – teachers. Dinosaurs. Magic. Prehistory. School – field trips. Science.

The magic school bus inside a beehive ill. by Bruce Degen. Scholastic, 1990. ISBN 978-0-590-44684-6 Subj: Buses. Careers – teachers. Insects – bees. Magic. School – field trips. Science.

The magic school bus inside a hurricane ill. by Bruce Degen. Scholastic, 1995. ISBN 978-0-590-44686-0 Subj: School – field trips. Science. Weather – hurricanes.

The magic school bus inside the earth ill. by Bruce Degen. Scholastic, 1987. ISBN 978-0-590-40759-5 Subj: Careers – geologists. Earth. Rocks. Science.

The magic school bus inside the human body ill. by Bruce Degen. Scholastic, 1989. ISBN 978-0-590-41426-5 Subj: Anatomy. School – field trips. Science.

The magic school bus lost in the solar system ill. by Bruce Degen. Scholastic, 1990. ISBN 978-0-590-41428-9 Subj: Buses. Careers – teachers. Magic. School – field trips. Science. Space & space ships.

The magic school bus on the ocean floor ill. by Bruce Degen. Scholastic, 1992. ISBN 978-0-590-41430-2 Subj: Buses. Careers – teachers. Magic. School – field trips. Science. Sea & seashore.

My big boy potty ill. by Maxie Chambliss. Harper-Collins, 2000. ISBN 978-0-688-17042-4 Subj: Behavior – growing up. Toilet training.

My big girl potty ill. by Maxie Chambliss. Harper-Collins, 2000. ISBN 978-0-688-17041-7 Subj: Behavior – growing up. Toilet training.

My friend the doctor ill. by Maxie Chambliss. HarperCollins, 2005. ISBN 978-0-06-050500-4 Subj: Careers – doctors. Health & fitness.

My new kitten photos by Margaret Miller. Morrow, 1995. ISBN 978-0-688-12902-6 Subj: Animals – cats. Friendship.

My puppy is born photos by Margaret Miller. Morrow, 1991. ISBN 978-0-688-09771-4 Subj: Animals – dogs. Birth. Science.

The new baby at your house photos by Hella Hammid. Morrow, 1998. ISBN 978-0-688-05807-4 Subj: Babies, toddlers. Emotions – envy, jealousy. Family life – new sibling. Sibling rivalry.

Sharing is fun ill. by Maxie Chambliss. Harper-Collins, 2004. ISBN 978-0-06-050499-1 Subj: Activities – playing. Behavior – sharing. Format, unusual – board books.

When Mommy and Daddy go to work ill. by Maxie Chambliss. HarperCollins, 2001. ISBN 978-0-688-17044-8 Subj: Family life – parents. School – nursery.

When you were inside mommy ill. by Maxie Chambliss. HarperCollins, 2001. ISBN 978-0-688-17043-1 Subj: Babies, toddlers. Birth. Family life – mothers.

Cole, Kenneth, Dr. *No bad news* photos by John Ruebartsch. Albert Whitman, 2001. ISBN 978-0-8075-4743-4 Subj: Careers – barbers. Cities, towns. Communities, neighborhoods. Ethnic groups in the U.S. – African Americans.

Cole, Rachael. *City moon* ill. by Blanca Gómez. Random House, 2017. ISBN 978-055349707-6 Subj: Bedtime. Character traits – questioning. Cities, towns. Moon. Night.

Coles, Robert. *The story of Ruby Bridges* ill. by George Ford. Scholastic, 1995. ISBN 978-0-590-43967-1 Subj: Character traits – bravery. Ethnic groups in the U.S. – African Americans. Prejudice. School.

Colfer, Eoin. *Imaginary Fred* ill. by Oliver Jeffers. HarperCollins, 2015. ISBN 978-000812614-8 Subj: Emotions – loneliness. Friendship. Imagination – imaginary friends.

Collard, Sneed B. *Animals asleep* ill. by Anik McGrory. Houghton, 2004. ISBN 978-0-618-27697-4 Subj: Animals. Sleep.

Beaks! ill. by Robin Brickman. Charlesbridge, 2002. ISBN 978-1-57091-387-7 Subj: Anatomy. Birds.

Leaving home ill. by Joan Dunning. Houghton, 2002. ISBN 978-0-618-11454-2 Subj: Animals – babies. Behavior. Behavior – growing up.

Making animal babies ill. by Steve Jenkins. Houghton, 2000. ISBN 978-0-395-95317-4 Subj: Animals. Sex instruction.

A platypus, probably ill. by Andrew Plant. Charlesbridge, 2005. ISBN 978-1-57091-583-3 Subj: Animals – platypuses.

Colleen, Marcie. *Love, triangle* ill. by Bob Shea. HarperCollins/Balzer+Bray, 2017. ISBN 978-006241084-9 Subj: Concepts – shape. Emotions – envy, jealousy. Friendship.

Collet, Géraldine. *All by myself!* ill. by Coralie Saudo. OwlKids, 2011. ISBN 978-1-926973-12-8 Subj: Behavior – worrying. Birds – chickens, roosters. Family life – mothers.

Collicott, Sharleen. *Mildred and Sam* ill. by author. Geringer, 2003. ISBN 978-0-06-026682-0 Subj: Animals – mice. Babies, toddlers. Family life. Homes, houses.

Toestomper and the bad butterflies ill. by author. Houghton, 2003. ISBN 978-0-618-14092-3 Subj: Behavior. Insects – butterflies, caterpillars. Metamorphosis. Pets.

Toestomper and the caterpillars ill. by author. Houghton, 1999. ISBN 978-0-395-91168-6 Subj: Animals. Behavior – bullying, teasing. Character traits – kindness to animals. Clubs, gangs. Insects – butterflies, caterpillars.

Collicutt, Paul. *This car* ill. by author. Farrar, 2002. ISBN 978-0-374-39965-8 Subj: Automobiles.

This rocket ill. by author. Farrar, 2005. ISBN 978-0-374-37484-6 Subj: Space & space ships.

This train ill. by author. Farrar, 1999. ISBN 978-0-374-37493-8 Subj: Trains. Transportation.

Collier, Bryan. *Uptown* ill. by author. Henry Holt, 2000. ISBN 978-0-8050-5721-8 Subj: Cities, towns. Ethnic groups in the U.S. – African Americans.

Collier, Kelly. *A horse named Steve* ill. by author. Kids Can, 2017. ISBN 978-177138736-1 Subj: Animals – horses, ponies. Behavior – boasting, showing off. Self-concept.

Collingridge, Richard. *Lionheart* ill. by author. Fickling, 2016. ISBN 978-054583321-9 Subj: Animals – lions. Emotions – fear. Imagination. Toys.

Collington, Peter. *Clever cat* ill. by author. Random House, 2000. ISBN 978-0-375-90477-6 Subj: Animals – cats. Character traits – cleverness. Character traits – individuality. Humorous stories.

Collins, Billy. *Daddy's little boy* ill. by Maggie Kneen. HarperCollins, 2004. ISBN 978-0-06-029003-0 Subj: Animals – bears. Family life – fathers. Family life – sons. Music. Songs.

Collins, Pat Lowery. *The deer watch* ill. by David Slonim. Candlewick, 2013. ISBN 978-0-7636-4890-9 Subj: Animals – deer. Family life – fathers. Forest, woods. Nature.

I am a dancer ill. by Mark Graham. Lerner, 2008. ISBN 978-0-8225-6369-3 Subj: Activities – dancing.

Collins, Ross. *Alvie eats soup* ill. by author. Scholastic, 2002. ISBN 978-0-439-27265-0 Subj: Family life – grandmothers. Food.

Dear Vampa ill. by author. HarperCollins, 2009. ISBN 978-0-06-135534-9 Subj: Humorous stories. Letters, cards. Monsters. Mythical creatures – werewolves.

Doodleday ill. by author. Albert Whitman, 2011. ISBN 978-0-8075-1683-6 Subj: Activities – drawing. Behavior – misbehavior. Family life – mothers.

There's a bear on my chair ill. by author. Nosy Crow, 2016. ISBN 978-076368942-1 Subj: Animals – mice. Animals – polar bears. Furniture – chairs. Rhyming text.

Collins, Sheila Hebert. *'T Pousette et 't Poulette: a Cajun Hansel and Gretel* ill. by Patrick Soper. Pelican, 2001. ISBN 978-1-56554-764-3 Subj: Ethnic groups in the U.S. – Cajuns. Folk & fairy tales.

Collins, Suzanne. *When Charlie McButton lost power* ill. by Mike Lester. Penguin, 2005. ISBN 978-0-399-24000-3 Subj: Computers. Family life – brothers & sisters. Rhyming text.

Year of the jungle ill. by James Proimos. Scholastic, 2013. ISBN 978-0-545-42516-2 Subj: Careers – military. Emotions – fear. Family life – fathers. U.S. history. War.

Colón, Raúl. *Draw!* ill. by author. Simon & Schuster/Paula Wiseman, 2014. ISBN 978-144249493-0 Subj: Activities – drawing. Animals. Illness. Imagination. Wordless.

Combs, Kathy. *Cowboy Sam and those confounded secrets* (Griffin, Kitty)

The foot-stomping adventures of Clementine Sweet (Griffin, Kitty)

Comden, Betty. *What's new at the zoo?* by Betty Comden and Adolph Green ill. by Travis Foster. Blue Apple, 2011. ISBN 978-1-60905-088-7 Subj: Animals. Format, unusual – toy & movable books. Songs. Zoos.

Comden, Betty, et al. *Flying to Neverland with Peter Pan: a lyrical journey with songs from the Broadway musical* ill. by Amy Bates. Blue Apple, 2012. ISBN 978-1-60905-249-2 Subj: Activities – flying. Imagination. Music. Songs. Theater.

Come and play: children of our world having fun. Bloomsbury, 2008. ISBN 978-1-59990-245-6 Subj: Activities – playing. Poetry. World.

Compestine, Ying Chang. *Boy dumplings* ill. by James Yamasaki. Holiday, 2009. ISBN 978-0-8234-1955-5 Subj: Activities – baking, cooking. Food. Foreign lands – China. Ghosts.

Crouching tiger ill. by Yan Nascimbene. Candlewick, 2011. ISBN 978-0-7636-4642-4 Subj: Ethnic groups in the U.S. – Chinese Americans. Family life – grandfathers. Holidays – Chinese New Year. Self-concept.

D is for dragon dance ill. by YongSheng Xuan. Holiday House, 2006. ISBN 978-0-8234-1887-9 Subj: ABC books. Foreign lands – China. Holidays – Chinese New Year.

The real story of stone soup ill. by Stéphane Jorisch. Penguin, 2007. ISBN 978-0-525-47493-7 Subj: Character traits – cleverness. Folk & fairy tales. Food. Foreign lands – China.

The runaway rice cake ill. by Tungwai Chau. Simon & Schuster, 2001. ISBN 978-0-689-82972-7 Subj: Character traits – generosity. Food. Foreign lands – China. Holidays – Chinese New Year.

The runaway wok: a Chinese New Year tale ill. by Sebastià Serra. Penguin, 2011. ISBN 978-0-525-42068-2 Subj: Activities – baking, cooking. Foreign lands – China. Holidays – Chinese New Year. Magic.

The story of chopsticks ill. by YongSheng Xuan. Holiday, 2001. ISBN 978-0-8234-1526-7 Subj: Food. Foreign lands – China.

The story of noodles ill. by YongSheng Xuan. Holiday, 2002. ISBN 978-0-8234-1600-4 Subj: Activities – baking, cooking. Food. Foreign lands – China.

The story of paper ill. by YongSheng Xuan. Holiday, 2003. ISBN 978-0-8234-1705-6 Subj: Foreign lands – China. Paper. School.

Compos, Tito. *Muffler man / El hombre mofle* ill. by Lamberto Alvarez and Beto Alvarez. Piñata, 2001. ISBN 978-1-55885-318-8 Subj: Art. Ethnic groups in the U.S. – Mexican Americans. Family life – fathers. Family life – sons. Foreign languages.

Compton, Joanne. *Ashpet: an Appalachian tale* ill. by Kenn Compton. Holiday, 1994. ISBN 978-0-8234-1106-1 Subj: Character traits – kindness. Folk & fairy tales.

Conahan, Carolyn. *The big wish* ill. by author. Chronicle, 2011. ISBN 978-0-8118-7040-5 Subj: Behavior – wishing. Character traits – cooperation. Contests.

The twelve days of Christmas dogs ill. by author. Penguin, 2005. ISBN 978-0-525-47486-9 Subj: Animals – dogs. Holidays – Christmas. Songs.

Connor, Leslie. *Miss Bridie chose a shovel* ill. by Mary Azarian. Houghton, 2004. ISBN 978-0-618-30564-3 Subj: Ethnic groups in the U.S. – Irish Americans. Immigrants, immigration. Tools.

Conover, Chris. *The Christmas bears* ill. by author. Farrar, 2008. ISBN 978-0-374-33275-4 Subj: Animals – bears. Holidays – Christmas. Rhyming text. Santa Claus.

The lion's share ill. by author. Farrar, 2000. ISBN 978-0-374-34532-7 Subj: Activities – flying. Animals. Animals – lions. Books, reading. Mythical creatures.

Conrad, Donna. *See you soon, Moon* ill. by Don Carter. Random House, 2001. ISBN 978-0-375-90656-5 Subj: Activities – traveling. Family life – grandmothers. Moon. Night.

Conrad, Pam. *The Tub People* ill. by Richard Egielski. HarperCollins, 1989. ISBN 978-0-06-021341-1 Subj: Activities – bathing. Toys.

The Tub People's Christmas ill. by Richard Egielski. Geringer, 1999. ISBN 978-0-06-026029-3 Subj: Holidays – Christmas. Santa Claus. Toys. Trees.

Consentino, Ralph. *The story of Honk-Honk-Ashoo and Swella-Bow-Wow* ill. by author. Penguin, 2005. ISBN 978-0-670-05997-3 Subj: Animals – dogs. Friendship.

Conway, David. *Errol and his extraordinary nose* ill. by Roberta Angaramo. Holiday House, 2010. ISBN 978-0-8234-2262-3 Subj: Anatomy – noses. Animals – elephants. School. Self-concept. Theater.

The great fairy tale disaster ill. by Melanie Williamson. Tiger Tales, 2012. ISBN 978-1-58925-111-3 Subj: Animals – wolves. Folk & fairy tales. Humorous stories.

The great nursery rhyme disaster ill. by Melanie Williamson. Tiger Tales, 2009. ISBN 978-1-58925-080-2 Subj: Humorous stories. Nursery rhymes.

Lila and the secret of rain ill. by Jude Daly. Frances Lincoln, 2008. ISBN 978-1-84507-407-4 Subj: Foreign lands – Kenya. Weather – droughts. Weather – rain.

The most important gift of all ill. by Karin Littlewood. School Specialty/Gingham Dog, 2006. ISBN 978-0-7696-4618-3 Subj: Animals. Emotions – love. Family life – new sibling. Foreign lands – Africa. Gifts.

Cook, Bernadine. *The little fish that got away* ill. by Crockett Johnson. HarperCollins, 2005. ISBN 978-0-06-055714-0 Subj: Fish. Sports – fishing.

Cook, Grace, selector. *Two little eyes and other action rhymes* ill. by Carol Thompson. Candlewick, 2000. ISBN 978-0-7636-0952-8 Subj: Counting, numbers. Participation. Rhyming text.

Cook, Julia. *The "D" word: divorce* ill. by Phillip W. Rodgers. National Center for Youth Issues, 2011. ISBN 978-1-931636-76-6 Subj: Divorce.

Cook, Lisa Broadie. *Peanut butter and homework sandwiches* ill. by Jack E. Davis. Penguin, 2011. ISBN 978-0-399-24533-6 Subj: Careers – teachers. Homework. School.

Cooke, Trish. *The grandad tree* ill. by Sharon Wilson. Candlewick, 2000. ISBN 978-0-7636-0815-6 Subj: Death. Emotions – grief. Family life – grandfathers. Memories, memory. Nature. Trees.

So much ill. by Helen Oxenbury. Candlewick, 1994. ISBN 978-1-56402-344-5 Subj: Babies, toddlers. Birthdays. Cumulative tales. Family life.

Coombs, Kate. *Hans my hedgehog: a tale from the Brothers Grimm* (Grimm, Jacob and Wilhelm)

The secret-keeper ill. by Heather Solomon. Simon & Schuster, 2006. ISBN 978-0-689-83963-4 Subj: Behavior – secrets.

The tooth fairy wars ill. by Jake Parker. Atheneum, 2014. ISBN 978-141697915-9 Subj: Fairies. Teeth.

Water sings blue ill. by Meilo So. Chronicle, 2012. ISBN 978-0-8118-7284-3 Subj: Poetry. Sea & seashore.

Cooney, Barbara. *Eleanor* ill. by author. Viking, 1996. ISBN 978-0-670-86159-0 Subj: Family life. U.S. history.

Miss Rumphius ill. by author. Viking, 1982. ISBN 978-0-670-47958-0 Subj: Activities – traveling. Flowers.

The story of Christmas ill. by Loretta Krupinski. HarperCollins, 1995. ISBN 978-0-06-023434-8 Subj: Holidays. Holidays – Christmas. Religion – Nativity.

Cooper, Elisha. *Ballpark* ill. by author. Greenwillow, 1998. ISBN 978-0-688-15755-5 Subj: Sports – baseball.

Beach ill. by author. Scholastic, 2006. ISBN 978-0-439-68785-0 Subj: Sea & seashore – beaches.

Bear dreams ill. by author. HarperCollins, 2006. ISBN 978-0-06-087428-5 Subj: Animals – bears. Hibernation. Seasons – winter.

Beaver is lost ill. by author. Random House, 2010. ISBN 978-0-375-85765-2 Subj: Animals – beavers. Behavior – lost.

Big cat, little cat ill. by author. Roaring Brook, 2017. ISBN 978-162672371-9 Subj: Animals – cats. Caldecott award honor books. Death. Friendship. Pets.

Building ill. by author. Greenwillow, 1999. ISBN 978-0-688-16494-2 Subj: Buildings. Careers – architects.

Eight, an animal alphabet ill. by author. Scholastic/Orchard, 2015. ISBN 978-054547083-4 Subj: ABC books. Animals. Counting, numbers.

Farm ill. by author. Scholastic, 2010. ISBN 978-0-545-07075-1 Subj: Farms. Seasons.

A good night walk ill. by author. Scholastic, 2005. ISBN 978-0-439-68783-6 Subj: Activities – walking. Communities, neighborhoods.

Homer ill. by author. Greenwillow, 2012. ISBN 978-0-06-201248-7 Subj: Animals – dogs.

Ice cream ill. by author. Greenwillow, 2002. ISBN 978-0-06-001424-7 Subj: Food.

Magic thinks big ill. by author. Greenwillow, 2004. ISBN 978-0-06-058165-7 Subj: Animals – cats. Behavior – indecision.

Train ill. by author. Scholastic, 2013. ISBN 978-0-545-38495-7 Subj: Activities – traveling. Trains.

Cooper, Floyd. *Coming home: from the life of Langston Hughes* ill. by author. Philomel, 1994. ISBN 978-0-399-22682-3 Subj: Ethnic groups in the U.S. – African Americans. Family life. Poetry.

Juneteenth for Mazie ill. by author. Capstone, 2015. ISBN 978-162370170-3 Subj: Character traits – freedom. Ethnic groups in the U.S. – African Americans. Holidays – Juneteenth. Prejudice. Slavery. U.S. history.

Max and the tag-along moon ill. by author. Philomel, 2013. ISBN 978-0-399-23342-5 Subj: Ethnic groups in the U.S. – African Americans. Family life – grandfathers. Moon.

The ring bearer ill. by author. Philomel, 2017. ISBN 978-039916740-9 Subj: Ethnic groups in the U.S. – African Americans. Family life – stepfamilies. Weddings.

Willie and the All-Stars ill. by author. Philomel, 2008. ISBN 978-0-399-23340-1 Subj: Ethnic groups in the U.S. – African Americans. Prejudice. Sports – baseball. U.S. history.

Cooper, Helen. *Delicious! a pumpkin soup story* ill. by author. Farrar, 2007. ISBN 978-0-374-31756-0 Subj: Activities – baking, cooking. Animals. Animals – cats. Animals – squirrels. Birds – ducks. Friendship.

Dog biscuit ill. by author. Farrar, 2009. ISBN 978-0-374-31812-3 Subj: Animals – dogs. Behavior – worrying. Food. Humorous stories.

A pipkin of pepper ill. by author. Farrar, 2005. ISBN 978-0-374-35953-9 Subj: Activities – baking, cooking. Animals. Animals – cats. Animals – squirrels. Birds – ducks. Friendship.

Tatty-Ratty ill. by author. Farrar, 2002. ISBN 978-0-374-37386-3 Subj: Animals – rabbits. Behavior – lost & found possessions. Imagination. Toys.

Cooper, Ilene. *The golden rule* ill. by Gabi Swiatkowska. Abrams, 2007. ISBN 978-0-8109-0960-1 Subj: Behavior.

Jake's best thumb ill. by Claudio Muñoz. Dutton, 2008. ISBN 978-0-525-47788-4 Subj: Behavior – bullying, teasing. School. Thumb sucking.

Cooper, Susan. *Frog* ill. by Jane Browne. Margaret K. McElderry, 2002. ISBN 978-0-689-84302-0 Subj: Frogs & toads. Sports – swimming.

Copeland, Cynthia L. *What are you waiting for?* ill. by Mike Gordon. Millbrook, 2003. ISBN 978-0-7613-2804-9 Subj: Careers – construction workers. Machines.

Copeland, Misty. *Firebird* ill. by Christopher Myers. Putnam, 2014. ISBN 978-039916615-0 Subj:

Ballet. Careers – dancers. Ethnic groups in the U.S. – African Americans.

Coppinger, Tom. *Curse in reverse* ill. by Dirk Zimmer. Atheneum, 2003. ISBN 978-0-689-83096-9 Subj: Folk & fairy tales. Witches.

Cora, Cat. *A suitcase surprise for Mommy* ill. by Joy Allen. Penguin, 2011. ISBN 978-0-8037-3332-9 Subj: Activities – traveling. Emotions – sadness. Family life – mothers.

Cordell, Matthew. *Another brother* ill. by author. Feiwel & Friends, 2012. ISBN 978-0-312-64324-9 Subj: Animals – sheep. Behavior – imitation. Family life – brothers.

Dream ill. by author. Disney/Hyperion, 2017. ISBN 978-148477340-6 Subj: Animals – babies. Animals – gorillas. Character traits – hopefulness. Imagination.

Trouble gum ill. by author. Feiwel & Friends, 2009. ISBN 978-0-312-38774-7 Subj: Animals – pigs. Behavior – boredom. Behavior – misbehavior. Family life – brothers.

Wish ill. by author. Disney/Hyperion, 2015. ISBN 978-148470875-0 Subj: Animals – babies. Animals – elephants. Behavior – wishing. Character traits – hopefulness. Family life.

Wolf in the snow ill. by author. Feiwel & Friends, 2017. ISBN 978-125007636-6 Subj: Animals – wolves. Behavior – lost. Caldecott award books. Character traits – cooperation. Character traits – kindness to animals. Weather – blizzards. Weather – snow. Wordless.

Corderoy, Tracey. *Hubble bubble, Granny trouble* ill. by Joe Berger. Candlewick, 2012. ISBN 978-0-7636-5904-2 Subj: Character traits – individuality. Family life – grandmothers. Rhyming text. Witches.

I want my daddy ill. by Alison Edgson. Tiger Tales, 2015. ISBN 978-158925177-9 Subj: Animals – mice. Family life – fathers.

I want my mommy! ill. by Alison Edgson. Tiger Tales, 2013. ISBN 978-1-58925-130-4 Subj: Animals – mice. Family life – grandmothers.

It's Christmas! ill. by Tim Warnes. Tiger Tales, 2017. ISBN 978-168010067-9 Subj: Animals – rhinoceros. Family life. Holidays – Christmas.

Just right for two ill. by Rosalind Beardshaw. Nosy Crow, 2014. ISBN 978-076367344-4 Subj: Animals – dogs. Animals – mice. Behavior – collecting things. Emotions – loneliness. Friendship. Weather – snow.

The little white owl ill. by Jane Chapman. Good Books, 2010. ISBN 978-1-56148-693-9 Subj: Birds – owls. Character traits – being different. Friendship.

The magical snow garden ill. by Jane Chapman. Tiger Tales, 2014. ISBN 978-158925162-5 Subj: Birds – penguins. Character traits – perseverance. Gardens, gardening.

Monty and Milli: the totally amazing magic trick ill. by Tim Warnes. Good Books, 2012. ISBN 978-1-56148-742-4 Subj: Animals – mice. Family life – brothers & sisters. Magic.

Now! ill. by Tim Warnes. Tiger Tales, 2016. ISBN 978-168010033-4 Subj: Activities – vacationing. Animals – rhinoceros. Character traits – patience, impatience. Family life.

Cordsen, Carol Foskett. *Market day* ill. by Douglas B. Jones. Dutton, 2008. ISBN 978-0-525-47883-6 Subj: Animals – bulls, cows. Behavior – forgetfulness. Careers – farmers. Farms. Rhyming text.

The milkman ill. by Douglas B. Jones. Penguin, 2005. ISBN 978-0-525-47208-7 Subj: Activities – working. Careers. Food. Rhyming text.

Corey, Dorothy. *You go away* ill. by Lisa Fox. Albert Whitman, 2010. ISBN 978-0-8075-9440-7 Subj: Behavior – worrying. Family life.

Corey, Shana. *Ballerina bear* ill. by Pamela Paparone. Random House, 2002. ISBN 978-0-375-91416-4 Subj: Activities – dancing. Animals – bears. Ballet. Character traits – confidence.

Boats! ill. by Mike Reed. Random House, 2003. ISBN 978-0-375-90221-5 Subj: Boats, ships. Rhyming text.

First graders from Mars: Horus's horrible day ill. by Mark Teague. Scholastic, 2001. ISBN 978-0-439-26220-0 Subj: Aliens. Behavior – bad day, bad mood. Humorous stories. School – first day. Space & space ships.

First graders from Mars: Nergal and the Great Space Race ill. by Mark Teague. Scholastic, 2002. ISBN 978-0-439-26633-8 Subj: Aliens. Health & fitness. Humorous stories. School. Self-concept. Space & space ships.

First graders from Mars: Tera, star student ill. by Mark Teague. Scholastic, 2002. ISBN 978-0-439-26634-5 Subj: Aliens. Behavior. Humorous stories. School. Space & space ships.

First graders from Mars: The problem with Pelly ill. by Mark Teague. Scholastic, 2002. ISBN 978-0-439-26632-1 Subj: Aliens. Character traits – individuality. Humorous stories. Self-concept. Space & space ships.

Here come the Girl Scouts! the amazing all-true story of Juliette "Daisy" Gordon Low and her great adventure ill. by Hadley Hooper. Scholastic, 2012. ISBN 978-0-545-34278-0 Subj: Clubs, gangs. U.S. history.

Milly and the Macy's Parade ill. by Brett Helquist. Scholastic, 2002. ISBN 978-0-439-29754-7 Subj:

Cities, towns. Holidays – Christmas. Holidays – Thanksgiving. Immigrants, immigration. Parades. Stores.

The secret subway ill. by Red Nose Studio. Random House, 2016. ISBN 978-037587071-2 Subj: Cities, towns. Trains. U.S. history.

You forgot your skirt, Amelia Bloomer ill. by Chesley McLaren. Scholastic, 2000. ISBN 978-0-439-07819-1 Subj: Clothing. Gender roles. U.S. history.

Cork, Barbara Taylor. *Katie goes to the hospital* ill. by Siobhan Dodds. McGraw-Hill, 2002. ISBN 978-1-57768-986-7 Subj: Hospitals. Illness.

Sam starts school ill. by Nicola Smee. McGraw-Hill, 2002. ISBN 978-1-57768-989-8 Subj: School – first day.

Cornell, Kevin. *Go to sleep, monster!* ill. by author. HarperCollins/Balzer+Bray, 2016. ISBN 978-006234915-6 Subj: Bedtime. Emotions – fear. Monsters. Sleep.

Cornwall, Gaia. *Jabari jumps* ill. by author. Candlewick, 2017. ISBN 978-076367838-8 Subj: Character traits – bravery. Emotions – fear. Ethnic groups in the U.S. – African Americans. Sports – swimming.

Corpi, Lucha. *Where fireflies dance / Ahí, donde bailan las luciérnagas* ill. by Mira Reisberg. Children's Book Press, 1997. ISBN 978-0-89239-145-5 Subj: Careers – writers. Family life. Family life – brothers & sisters. Foreign lands – Mexico. Foreign languages.

Corr, Christopher. *Deep in the woods: a folk tale* ill. by author. Frances Lincoln, 2017. ISBN 978-184780726-7 Subj: Animals. Character traits – cooperation. Cumulative tales. Folk & fairy tales. Foreign lands – Russia. Homes, houses.

Whole world ill. by author. Barefoot, 2007. ISBN 978-1-84686-043-0 Subj: Ecology. Nature. Songs. World.

Cort, Ben. *Pigs can't fly!* ill. by author. Barron's, 2002. ISBN 978-0-7641-5532-1 Subj: Animals – pigs. Behavior – imitation. Emotions – loneliness.

Cosentino, Ralph. *The marvelous misadventures of — Fun-Boy* ill. by author. Penguin, 2006. ISBN 978-0-670-05961-4 Subj: Humorous stories. Imagination. Wordless.

Costa, Maria S. *How to find a friend* ill. by Maria S. Costa. Clarion, 2017. ISBN 978-054492678-3 Subj: Animals – rabbits. Animals – squirrels. Friendship.

Costa, Nicoletta. *The little tree that would not share* ill. by author. Holiday, 2016. ISBN 978-082343549-4 Subj: Behavior – sharing. Character traits – vanity. Seasons. Trees.

Costain, Meredith. *Daddies are awesome* ill. by Polona Lovsin. Henry Holt, 2016. ISBN 978-162779452-7 Subj: Animals – dogs. Family life – fathers. Rhyming text.

Costanza, Stephen. *Vivaldi and the invisible orchestra* ill. by author. Henry Holt, 2012. ISBN 978-0-8050-7801-5 Subj: Careers – composers. Foreign lands – Italy. Imagination. Music. Musical instruments – orchestras.

Coste, Marion. *Finding Joy* ill. by Yong Chen. Boyds Mills, 2006. ISBN 978-1-59078-192-0 Subj: Adoption. Family life. Foreign lands – China.

Costello, David Hyde. *I can help* ill. by author. Farrar, 2010. ISBN 978-0-374-33526-7 Subj: Animals. Birds – ducks. Character traits – helpfulness.

Little Pig joins the band ill. by author. Charlesbridge, 2011. ISBN 978-1-58089-264-3 Subj: Animals – pigs. Careers – conductors (music). Character traits – smallness. Musical instruments – bands.

Little Pig saves the ship ill. by author. Charlesbridge, 2017. ISBN 978-158089715-0 Subj: Animals – pigs. Boats, ships. Character traits – smallness. Family life – grandfathers.

Costello, Emily. *Realm of the panther* ill. by Wes Siegrist. Soundprints, 2000. ISBN 978-1-56899-847-3 Subj: Animals – babies. Animals – cougars. Jungle.

Costello, Lou. *Who's on first?* (Abbott, Bud)

Côté, Geneviève. *Bob's hungry ghost* ill. by author. Tundra, 2014. ISBN 978-177049713-9 Subj: Friendship. Ghosts. Pets.

Goodnight, you ill. by author. Kids Can, 2014. ISBN 978-177138050-8 Subj: Animals – pigs. Animals – rabbits. Camps, camping. Emotions – fear.

Me and you ill. by author. Kids Can, 2009. ISBN 978-1-55453-446-3 Subj: Animals – pigs. Animals – rabbits. Character traits – being different. Character traits – individuality.

Mr. King's machine ill. by author. Kids Can, 2016. ISBN 978-177138021-8 Subj: Activities – making things. Animals – cats. Character traits – cooperation. Ecology. Insects – butterflies, caterpillars. Machines.

Mr. King's things ill. by author. Kids Can, 2012. ISBN 978-1-55453-700-6 Subj: Behavior – collecting things. Ecology. Monsters.

Starring me and you ill. by author. Kids Can, 2014. ISBN 978-189478639-3 Subj: Animals – pigs. Animals – rabbits. Character traits – compromising. Emotions. Friendship.

What elephant? ill. by author. Kids Can, 2006. ISBN 978-1-55337-875-4 Subj: Animals – elephants.

With you always, Little Monday ill. by author. Harcourt, 2007. ISBN 978-0-15-205997-2 Subj: Animals. Animals – rabbits. Behavior – lost. Family life – mothers. Moon.

Without you ill. by author. Kids Can, 2011. ISBN 978-1-55453-620-7 Subj: Animals – pigs. Animals – rabbits. Behavior – fighting, arguing. Friendship.

Cote, Nancy. *It feels like snow* ill. by author. Boyds Mills, 2003. ISBN 978-1-59078-054-1 Subj: Behavior – sharing. Seasons – winter. Weather – snow.

It's all about me! ill. by author. Penguin, 2005. ISBN 978-0-399-24280-9 Subj: Family life – new sibling. Self-concept. Sibling rivalry.

Jackson's blanket ill. by author. Putnam, 2008. ISBN 978-0-399-24694-4 Subj: Behavior – growing up. Rhyming text.

Cotner, June, compiler. *Amazing graces: prayers and poems for children* ill. by Jan Palmer. HarperCollins, 2001. ISBN 978-0-688-15567-4 Subj: Poetry. Religion.

Cotten, Cynthia. *Abbie in stitches* ill. by Beth Peck. Farrar, 2006. ISBN 978-0-374-30004-3 Subj: Activities – sewing. U.S. history.

At the edge of the woods ill. by Reg Cartwright. Henry Holt, 2002. ISBN 978-0-8050-6354-7 Subj: Animals. Counting, numbers. Forest, woods. Plants. Rhyming text.

The book boat's in ill. by Frané Lessac. Holiday House, 2013. ISBN 978-0-8234-2521-1 Subj: Boats, ships. Books, reading. Libraries. U.S. history.

Rain play ill. by Javaka Steptoe. Henry Holt, 2008. ISBN 978-0-8050-6795-8 Subj: Activities – playing. Parks. Rhyming text. Weather – lightning, thunder. Weather – rain.

Snow ponies ill. by Jason Cockcroft. Henry Holt, 2001. ISBN 978-0-8050-6063-8 Subj: Animals – horses, ponies. Seasons – winter. Weather – snow.

This is the stable ill. by Delana Bettoli. Henry Holt, 2006. ISBN 978-0-8050-7556-4 Subj: Religion – Nativity.

Cotter, Bill. *Beard in a box* ill. by author. Knopf, 2016. ISBN 978-055350835-2 Subj: Anatomy – faces. Behavior – cheating. Family life – fathers.

Cotterill, Samantha. *No more bows* ill. by author. HarperCollins, 2017. ISBN 978-006240870-9 Subj: Animals – dogs. Behavior – running away.

Character traits – appearance. Clothing – neckties. Emotions – embarrassment.

Cottin, Menena. *The black book of colors* ill. by Rosana Faria. Groundwood, 2008. ISBN 978-0-88899-873-6 Subj: Concepts – color. Disabilities – blindness. Senses – touch.

Cottle, Joan. *Miles away from home* ill. by author. Harcourt, 2001. ISBN 978-0-15-202212-9 Subj: Activities – vacationing. Animals – dogs. Behavior – misunderstanding. Sea & seashore.

Cotton, Katie. *Counting lions: portraits from the wild* ill. by Stephen Walton. Candlewick, 2015. ISBN 978-076368207-1 Subj: Animals – endangered animals. Counting, numbers.

The road home ill. by Sarah Jacoby. Abrams, 2017. ISBN 978-141972374-2 Subj: Animals. Family life – mothers. Homes, houses. Rhyming text.

Coudray, Jean-Luc. *A goofy guide to penguins* ill. by Philippe Coudray. TOON, 2016. ISBN 978-193517996-2 Subj: Birds – penguins. Format, unusual – graphic novels. Humorous stories.

Counter, Samantha Kurtzman. *When Lyla got lost (and found)* (Schiller, Abbie)

Couric, Katie. *The brand new kid* ill. by Marjorie Priceman. Doubleday, 2000. ISBN 978-0-385-50030-2 Subj: Behavior – bullying, teasing. Ethnic groups in the U.S. – Hungarian Americans. Prejudice. Rhyming text. School.

Court, Rob. *Color.* Child's World, 2003. ISBN 978-1-56766-069-2 Subj: Art. Concepts – color.

Cousins, Lucy. *Count with Maisy* ill. by author. Candlewick, 1999. ISBN 978-0-7636-0234-5 Subj: Animals – mice. Counting, numbers. Format, unusual – board books.

Count with Maisy, cheep, cheep, cheep! ill. by author. Candlewick, 2015. ISBN 978-076367643-8 Subj: Animals – mice. Birds – chickens, roosters. Counting, numbers. Format, unusual – toy & movable books.

Doctor Maisy ill. by author. Candlewick, 2001. ISBN 978-0-7636-1612-0 Subj: Activities – playing. Animals. Animals – mice. Birds.

Ha ha, Maisy! ill. by author. Candlewick, 2005. ISBN 978-0-7636-2633-4 Subj: Animals – mice. Format, unusual – toy & movable books.

Happy birthday, Maisy ill. by author. Candlewick, 1998. ISBN 978-0-7636-0577-3 Subj: Animals. Animals – mice. Birthdays. Format, unusual – toy & movable books.

Happy Easter, Maisy! ill. by author. Candlewick, 2007. ISBN 978-0-7636-3230-4 Subj: Animals –

mice. Format, unusual – board books. Holidays – Easter.

Hooray for birds! ill. by author. Candlewick, 2017. ISBN 978-076369265-0 Subj: Birds. Rhyming text.

Hooray for fish! ill. by author. Candlewick, 2005. ISBN 978-0-7636-2741-6 Subj: Family life – mothers. Fish. Rhyming text. Sea & seashore.

I'm the best ill. by author. Candlewick, 2010. ISBN 978-0-7636-4684-4 Subj: Animals. Animals – dogs. Behavior – boasting, showing off. Character traits – pride. Character traits – vanity. Friendship.

Maisy at the fair ill. by author. Candlewick, 2001. ISBN 978-0-7636-1500-0 Subj: Animals. Animals – mice. Fairs, festivals.

Maisy at the farm ill. by author. Candlewick, 1998. ISBN 978-0-7636-0576-6 Subj: Animals – mice. Farms. Format, unusual – toy & movable books.

Maisy big, Maisy small ill. by author. Candlewick, 2007. ISBN 978-0-7636-3406-3 Subj: Animals – mice. Concepts – opposites.

Maisy, Charley, and the wobbly tooth ill. by author. Candlewick, 2006. ISBN 978-0-7636-2904-5 Subj: Animals. Animals – mice. Careers – dentists. Reptiles – alligators, crocodiles. Teeth.

Maisy cleans up ill. by author. Candlewick, 2002. ISBN 978-0-7636-1711-0 Subj: Animals – mice. Friendship. Reptiles – alligators, crocodiles.

Maisy dresses up ill. by author. Candlewick, 1999. ISBN 978-0-7636-0885-9 Subj: Animals. Animals – mice. Clothing – costumes. Parties.

Maisy goes on a plane ill. by author. Candlewick, 2015. ISBN 978-076367825-8 Subj: Activities – traveling. Airplanes, airports. Animals – mice.

Maisy goes on vacation ill. by author. Candlewick, 2010. ISBN 978-0-7636-4752-0 Subj: Activities – vacationing. Animals – mice. Sea & seashore.

Maisy goes shopping ill. by author. Candlewick, 2001. ISBN 978-0-7636-1501-7 Subj: Animals – mice. Reptiles – alligators, crocodiles. Shopping.

Maisy goes to London ill. by author. Candlewick, 2016. ISBN 978-076368399-3 Subj: Activities – traveling. Animals – mice. Foreign lands – England.

Maisy goes to preschool ill. by author. Candlewick, 2009. ISBN 978-0-7636-4254-9 Subj: Animals – mice. School – nursery.

Maisy goes to the hospital ill. by author. Candlewick, 2007. ISBN 978-0-7636-3377-6 Subj: Animals – mice. Hospitals.

Maisy goes to the library ill. by author. Candlewick, 2005. ISBN 978-0-7636-2669-3 Subj: Animals – mice. Books, reading. Libraries.

Maisy goes to the movies ill. by author. Candlewick, 2014. ISBN 978-076366950-8 Subj: Animals – mice. Theater.

Maisy goes to the museum ill. by author. Candlewick, 2008. ISBN 978-0-7636-3838-2 Subj: Animals – mice. Museums.

Maisy learns to swim ill. by author. Candlewick, 2013. ISBN 978-0-7636-6480-0 Subj: Animals – mice. Sports – swimming.

Maisy makes gingerbread ill. by author. Candlewick, 1999. ISBN 978-0-7636-0887-3 Subj: Activities – baking, cooking. Animals – mice. Food.

Maisy makes lemonade ill. by author. Candlewick, 2002. ISBN 978-0-7636-1728-8 Subj: Animals – elephants. Animals – mice. Behavior – sharing. Character traits – helpfulness.

Maisy plays soccer ill. by author. Candlewick, 2014. ISBN 978-076367228-7 Subj: Animals – mice. Friendship. Sports – soccer.

Maisy's amazing big book of learning ill. by author. Candlewick, 2011. ISBN 978-0-7636-5481-8 Subj: Animals. Animals – mice. Concepts. Format, unusual – toy & movable books.

Maisy's amazing big book of words ill. by author. Candlewick, 2007. ISBN 978-0-7636-0794-4 Subj: Animals – mice. Format, unusual – toy & movable books. Language.

Maisy's bedtime ill. by author. Candlewick, 1999. ISBN 978-0-7636-0884-2 Subj: Animals. Animals – mice. Bedtime. Dreams. Toys – bears.

Maisy's book of things that go ill. by author. Candlewick, 2010. ISBN 978-0-7636-4614-1 Subj: Animals. Animals – mice. Format, unusual – toy & movable books. Transportation.

Maisy's Christmas tree ill. by author. Candlewick, 2014. ISBN 978-076367457-1 Subj: Animals – mice. Format, unusual – board books. Holidays – Christmas. Trees.

Maisy's colors ill. by author. Candlewick, 1997. ISBN 978-0-7636-0159-1 Subj: Animals – mice. Concepts – color.

Maisy's farm ill. by author. Candlewick, 2001. ISBN 978-0-7636-1294-8 Subj: Animals. Animals – mice. Farms. Format, unusual – toy & movable books.

Maisy's field day ill. by author. Candlewick, 2016. ISBN 978-076368441-9 Subj: Animals – mice. Contests. Friendship. School.

Maisy's first clock ill. by author. Candlewick, 2002. ISBN 978-0-7636-1788-2 Subj: Animals – mice. Format, unusual – toy & movable books. Time.

Maisy's Halloween ill. by author. Candlewick, 2004. ISBN 978-0-7636-2579-5 Subj: Animals. Animals – mice. Format, unusual – board books. Holidays – Halloween.

Maisy's morning on the farm ill. by author. Candlewick, 2001. ISBN 978-0-7636-1610-6 Subj: Animals. Animals – mice. Farms.

Maisy's noisy day ill. by author. Candlewick, 2002. ISBN 978-0-7636-1917-6 Subj: Animals. Animals – mice. Format, unusual – board books. Noise, sounds.

Maisy's pirate treasure hunt ill. by author. Candlewick, 2004. ISBN 978-0-7636-2469-9 Subj: Animals – mice. Format, unusual – toy & movable books.

Maisy's pool ill. by author. Candlewick, 1999. ISBN 978-0-7636-0886-6 Subj: Animals. Animals – mice. Sports – swimming.

Maisy's rainbow dream ill. by author. Candlewick, 2003. ISBN 978-0-7636-2195-7 Subj: Animals – mice. Concepts – color. Dreams.

Maisy's twinkly, crinkly counting book ill. by author. Candlewick, 2004. ISBN 978-0-7636-2273-2 Subj: Animals – mice. Counting, numbers. Format, unusual – toy & movable books.

Maisy's wonderful weather book ill. by author. Candlewick, 2006. ISBN 978-0-7636-2987-8 Subj: Animals – mice. Format, unusual – toy & movable books. Weather.

More fun with Maisy! ill. by author. Candlewick, 2005. ISBN 978-0-7636-2632-7 Subj: Animals – mice. Format, unusual – toy & movable books.

Noah's ark ill. by author. Candlewick, 1993. ISBN 978-1-56402-213-4 Subj: Animals. Boats, ships. Religion – Noah. Weather – floods. Weather – rain. Weather – rainbows.

Peck, peck, peck ill. by author. Candlewick, 2013. ISBN 978-0-7636-6621-7 Subj: Birds – woodpeckers. Family life – fathers. Rhyming text.

Stop and go, Maisy ill. by author. Candlewick, 2005. ISBN 978-0-7636-2668-6 Subj: Animals – mice. Format, unusual – toy & movable books. Transportation.

Sweet dreams, Maisy ill. by author. Candlewick, 2005. ISBN 978-0-7636-2874-1 Subj: Animals – mice. Bedtime.

With love from Maisy ill. by author. Candlewick, 2005. ISBN 978-0-7636-2513-9 Subj: Animals – mice. Format, unusual – toy & movable books. Gifts.

Cousteau, Philippe. *Follow the moon home: a tale of one idea, twenty kids, and a hundred sea turtles* by Philippe Cousteau and Deborah Hopkinson ill. by Meilo So. Chronicle, 2016. ISBN 978-145211241-1 Subj: Character traits – kindness to animals. Ecology. Nature. Problem solving. Reptiles – turtles, tortoises.

Covell, David. *Rat and Roach: friends to the end* ill. by author. Viking, 2012. ISBN 978-0-670-01409-5 Subj: Animals – rats. Friendship. Insects – cockroaches.

Rat and Roach rock on! ill. by author. Viking, 2013. ISBN 978-0-670-01410-1 Subj: Animals – rats. Character traits – compromising. Emotions – fear. Friendship. Insects – cockroaches. Musical instruments – bands.

Coville, Bruce. *The prince of butterflies* ill. by John Clapp. Harcourt, 2002. ISBN 978-0-15-201454-4 Subj: Animals – endangered animals. Insects – butterflies, caterpillars.

Cowan, Charlotte. *Katie caught a cold* ill. by Katy Bratun. Hippocratic, 2008. ISBN 978-0-9753516-3-5 Subj: Animals. Animals – bears. Illness – cold (disease).

Peeper has a fever ill. by Susan Banta. Hippocratic, 2008. ISBN 978-0-9753516-2-8 Subj: Animals. Frogs & toads. Illness.

Sadie's sore throat ill. by Katy Bratun. Hippocratic, 2008. ISBN 978-0-9753516-4-2 Subj: Animals. Animals – giraffes. Illness.

Cowcher, Helen. *Desert elephants* ill. by author. Farrar, 2011. ISBN 978-0-374-31774-4 Subj: Animals – elephants. Character traits – cooperation. Character traits – kindness to animals. Foreign lands – Mali. Migration.

Cowell, Cressida. *Emily Brown and the Thing* ill. by Neal Layton. IPG/Hodder & Stoughton, 2012. ISBN 978-1-84616-694-5 Subj: Animals – rabbits. Bedtime. Toys.

Hiccup the seasick Viking ill. by author. Orchard, 2000. ISBN 978-0-531-30278-1 Subj: Character traits – bravery. Emotions – fear. Illness. Sea & seashore. Vikings.

That rabbit belongs to Emily Brown ill. by Neal Layton. Hyperion, 2007. ISBN 978-1-4231-0645-6 Subj: Animals – rabbits. Toys.

What shall we do with the Boo-Hoo Baby? ill. by author. Scholastic, 2003. ISBN 978-0-439-44266-4 Subj: Animals. Babies, toddlers. Behavior. Emotions.

Cowen-Fletcher, Jane. *Hello, puppy!* ill. by author. Candlewick, 2010. ISBN 978-0-7636-4303-4 Subj: Animals – babies. Animals – dogs. Pets.

Mama zooms ill. by author. Scholastic, 1993. ISBN 978-0-590-45774-3 Subj: Disabilities – physical disabilities. Family life – mothers.

Cowley, Joy. *Chameleon, chameleon* photos by Nic Bishop. Scholastic, 2005. ISBN 978-0-439-66653-4 Subj: Reptiles – chameleons.

Gracias, the Thanksgiving turkey ill. by Joe Cepeda. Scholastic, 1996. ISBN 978-0-590-46976-0 Subj: Birds – turkeys. Careers – truck drivers. Ethnic groups in the U.S. – Puerto Rican Americans. Family life – fathers. Holidays – Thanksgiving.

Mrs. Goodstory ill. by Erica Dornbusch. Boyds Mills, 2001. ISBN 978-1-56397-774-9 Subj: Books, reading. Imagination.

Mrs. Wishy-Washy's Christmas ill. by Elizabeth Fuller. Penguin, 2005. ISBN 978-0-399-24344-8 Subj: Animals. Farms. Holidays – Christmas. Rhyming text.

Where horses run free ill. by Layne Johnson. Boyds Mills, 2003. ISBN 978-1-59078-062-6 Subj: Animals – horses, ponies. Cowboys, cowgirls.

Cox, Judy. *Carmen learns English* ill. by Angela Dominguez. Holiday House, 2010. ISBN 978-0-8234-2174-9 Subj: Ethnic groups in the U.S. – Mexican Americans. Family life – sisters. Foreign languages. School.

Cinco de Mouse-o! ill. by Jeffrey Ebbeler. Holiday House, 2010. ISBN 978-0-8234-2194-7 Subj: Animals – mice. Holidays – Cinco de Mayo.

Go to sleep, Groundhog ill. by Paul Meisel. Holiday, 2004. ISBN 978-0-8234-1645-5 Subj: Animals – groundhogs. Hibernation. Holidays – Groundhog Day.

Happy birthday, Mrs. Millie! ill. by Joe Mathieu. Marshall Cavendish, 2012. ISBN 978-0-7614-6126-5 Subj: Birthdays. Careers – teachers. Humorous stories. Parties. School.

Haunted house, haunted Mouse ill. by Jeffrey Ebbeler. Holiday House, 2011. ISBN 978-0-8234-2315-6 Subj: Animals – mice. Holidays – Halloween.

My family plays music ill. by Elbrite Brown. Holiday, 2003. ISBN 978-0-8234-1591-5 Subj: Careers – musicians. Family life. Musical instruments.

One is a feast for Mouse: a Thanksgiving tale ill. by Jeffrey Ebbeler. Holiday, 2008. ISBN 978-0-8234-1977-7 Subj: Animals – cats. Animals – mice. Behavior – greed. Holidays – Thanksgiving.

Pick a pumpkin, Mrs. Millie! ill. by Joe Mathieu. Marshall Cavendish, 2009. ISBN 978-0-7614-5573-8 Subj: Careers – teachers. Humorous stories. School – field trips.

Sheep won't sleep: counting by 2s, 5s, and 10s ill. by Nina Cuneo. Holiday House, 2017. ISBN 978-082343701-6 Subj: Animals. Bedtime. Counting, numbers.

Snow day for Mouse ill. by Jeffrey Ebbeler. Holiday House, 2012. ISBN 978-0-8234-2408-5 Subj: Animals – mice. Rhyming text. Weather – snow.

Cox, Lynne. *Elizabeth, queen of the seas* ill. by Brian Floca. Random House, 2014. ISBN 978-037585888-8 Subj: Animals – seals. Character traits – kindness to animals.

Cox, Phil Roxbee. *Fox on a box* ill. by Stephen Cartwright. Scholastic, 2004. ISBN 978-0-7945-0443-4 Subj: Animals – foxes. Format, unusual – toy & movable books. Language. Rhyming text.

Goose on the loose ill. by Stephen Cartwright. Scholastic, 2001. ISBN 978-0-613-75091-2 Subj: Birds – geese. Format, unusual – toy & movable books. Language. Rhyming text.

Shark in the park ill. by Stephen Cartwright. Scholastic, 2002. ISBN 978-0-439-52876-4 Subj: Fish – sharks. Format, unusual – toy & movable books. Language. Rhyming text.

Coxe, Molly. *Bunny and the beast* ill. by Pamela Silin-Palmer. Random House, 2001. ISBN 978-0-375-80468-7 Subj: Animals. Folk & fairy tales. Foreign lands – France.

Coy, John. *Their great gift: courage, sacrifice, and hope in a new land.* Carolrhoda, 2016. ISBN 978-146778054-4 Subj: Immigrants, immigration.

Two old potatoes and me ill. by Carolyn Fisher. Knopf, 2003. ISBN 978-0-375-92180-3 Subj: Divorce. Family life – daughters. Family life – fathers. Food.

Vroomaloom zoom ill. by Joe Cepeda. Crown, 2000. ISBN 978-0-517-80010-2 Subj: Activities – traveling. Automobiles. Bedtime. Imagination. Noise, sounds.

Coyle, Carmela LaVigna. *Do princesses have best friends forever?* ill. by Mike Gordon and Carl Gordon. Taylor Trade, 2010. ISBN 978-1-58979-542-6 Subj: Friendship. Rhyming text. Royalty – princesses.

Do princesses make happy campers? ill. by Mike Gordon. Taylor Trade, 2015. ISBN 978-163076054-0 Subj: Camps, camping. Character traits – questioning. Rhyming text. Royalty – princesses.

Do princesses really kiss frogs? ill. by Mike Gordon and Carl Gordon. Rising Moon, 2005. ISBN 978-0-87358-880-5 Subj: Activities – hiking. Character traits – questioning. Family life – fathers. Royalty – princesses.

Do super heroes have teddy bears? ill. by Mike Gordon. Taylor Trade, 2012. ISBN 978-1-58979-693-5 Subj: Character traits – questioning. Imagination. Rhyming text. Toys – bears.

Craft, Mahlon F. *Beauty and the beast* ill. by Kinuko Y. Craft. HarperCollins, 2016. ISBN 978-006053919-1 Subj: Character traits – appearance. Character traits – loyalty. Emotions – love. Folk & fairy tales. Magic.

Craig, Lindsey. *Dancing feet!* ill. by Marc Brown. Random House, 2010. ISBN 978-0-375-86181-9 Subj: Activities – dancing. Animals. Rhyming text.

Farmyard beat ill. by Marc Brown. Random House, 2011. ISBN 978-0-375-86455-1 Subj: Animals. Bedtime. Farms. Noise, sounds. Rhyming text.

Crampton, Gertrude. *Scuffy the tugboat* ill. by Tibor Gergely. Random House, 2003. ISBN 978-0-307-10547-9 Subj: Activities – traveling. Boats, ships. Rivers. Toys.

Crandall, Court. *Hugville* ill. by Joe Murray. Random House, 2005. ISBN 978-0-375-82418-0 Subj: Hugging. Rhyming text.

Crane, Carol. *D is for dancing dragon: a China alphabet* ill. by Zong-Zhou Wang. Sleeping Bear, 2006. ISBN 978-1-58536-273-8 Subj: ABC books. Foreign lands – China.

Crawford, Laura. *In arctic waters* ill. by Ben Hodson. Random House, 2007. ISBN 978-0-9768823-4-3 Subj: Animals. Foreign lands – Arctic. Rhyming text.

Crawford, Sheryl Ann. *The baby who changed the world* ill. by Sonya Wilson. Faith Kids, 2000. ISBN 978-0-7814-3431-7 Subj: Animals. Animals – donkeys. Religion – Nativity.

Crawley, Dave. *Cat poems* ill. by Tamara Petrosino. Boyds Mills, 2005. ISBN 978-1-59078-287-3 Subj: Animals – cats. Poetry.

Creech, Sharon. *A fine, fine school* ill. by Harry Bliss. HarperCollins, 2001. ISBN 978-0-06-027737-6 Subj: Careers – school principals. School.

Fishing in the air ill. by Chris Raschka. HarperCollins, 2000. ISBN 978-0-06-028112-0 Subj: Family life – fathers. Family life – sons. Imagination. Sports – fishing.

Who's that baby? new-baby songs ill. by David Diaz. HarperCollins, 2005. ISBN 978-0-06-052940-6 Subj: Babies, toddlers. Poetry. Songs.

Cressy, Judith. *Can you find it?.* Ill. with paintings. Abrams, 2002. ISBN 978-0-8109-3279-1 Subj: Art. Museums. Picture puzzles.

Can you find it, too?. Ill. with paintings. Abrams, 2004. ISBN 978-0-8109-5046-7 Subj: Art. Museums. Picture puzzles.

Crews, Donald. *Bicycle race* ill. by author. Greenwillow, 1985. ISBN 978-0-688-05172-3 Subj: Counting, numbers. Sports – bicycling. Sports – racing.

Carousel ill. by author. Greenwillow, 1982. ISBN 978-0-688-00909-0 Subj: Merry-go-rounds.

Cloudy day/sunny day ill. by author. Harcourt, 1999. ISBN 978-0-15-201997-6 Subj: Activities – playing. Ethnic groups in the U.S. – African Americans. Weather.

Flying ill. by author. Greenwillow, 1986. ISBN 978-0-688-04319-3 Subj: Activities – flying. Airplanes, airports.

Freight train ill. by author. Greenwillow, 1978. ISBN 978-0-688-80165-6 Subj: Caldecott award honor books. Trains.

Harbor ill. by author. Greenwillow, 1982. ISBN 978-0-688-00862-8 Subj: Boats, ships.

Inside freight train ill. by author. HarperCollins, 2001. ISBN 978-0-688-17087-5 Subj: Format, unusual – toy & movable books. Trains.

Light ill. by author. Greenwillow, 1981. ISBN 978-0-688-00310-4 Subj: Concepts. Light, lights.

Night at the fair ill. by author. Greenwillow, 1998. ISBN 978-0-688-11484-8 Subj: Fairs, festivals. Night.

Parade ill. by author. Greenwillow, 1983. ISBN 978-0-688-01996-9 Subj: Cities, towns. Parades.

Sail away ill. by author. Greenwillow, 1995. ISBN 978-0-688-11054-3 Subj: Boats, ships. Family life. Sailors. Sports – sailing. Weather – storms.

School bus ill. by author. Greenwillow, 1984. ISBN 978-0-688-02808-4 Subj: Buses. School. Transportation.

Shortcut ill. by author. Greenwillow, 1992. ISBN 978-0-688-06436-5 Subj: Ethnic groups in the U.S. – African Americans. Trains.

Ten black dots ill. by author. Rev. ed. Greenwillow, 1986. ISBN 978-0-688-06068-8 Subj: Concepts – shape. Counting, numbers.

Truck ill. by author. Greenwillow, 1980. ISBN 978-0-688-84244-4 Subj: Caldecott award honor books. Transportation. Trucks. Wordless.

We read: A to Z ill. by author. Harper & Row, 1967. ISBN 978-0-688-03844-1 Subj: ABC books. Concepts.

Crews, Nina. *Below* photos by author. Henry Holt, 2006. ISBN 978-0-8050-7728-5 Subj: Activities – playing. Imagination. Toys.

A ghost story ill. by author. Greenwillow, 2001. ISBN 978-0-688-17674-7 Subj: Ethnic groups in the U.S. – African Americans. Family life. Family life – aunts, uncles. Ghosts.

A high, low, near, far, loud, quiet story ill. by author. Greenwillow, 1999. ISBN 978-0-688-16795-0 Subj: Activities. Concepts – opposites. Family life – brothers & sisters.

I'll catch the moon ill. by author. Greenwillow, 1996. ISBN 978-0-688-14135-6 Subj: Imagination. Moon. Night.

One hot summer day ill. by author. Greenwillow, 1995. ISBN 978-0-688-13394 8 Subj: Cities, towns. Ethnic groups in the U.S. – African Americans. Seasons – summer.

Sky-high Guy ill. by author. Henry Holt, 2010. ISBN 978-0-8050-8764-2 Subj: Activities – playing. Family life – brothers. Toys.

Snowball ill. by author. Greenwillow, 1997. ISBN 978-0-688-14929-1 Subj: Activities – playing. Seasons – winter. Weather – snow.

You are here ill. by author. Greenwillow, 1998. ISBN 978-0-688-15753-1 Subj: Ethnic groups in the U.S. – African Americans. Family life. Imagination. Weather – rain.

Crimi, Carolyn. *Dear Tabby* ill. by David Roberts. HarperCollins, 2011. ISBN 978-0-06-114245-1 Subj: Activities – writing. Animals. Animals – cats. Letters, cards.

Don't need friends ill. by Lynn Munsinger. Doubleday, 1999. ISBN 978-0-385-32643-8 Subj: Animals. Animals – dogs. Animals – rats. Behavior – needing someone. Friendship.

Henry and the Buccaneer Bunnies ill. by John Manders. Candlewick, 2005. ISBN 978-0-7636-2449-1 Subj: Animals – rabbits. Books, reading. Pirates.

Henry and the Crazed Chicken Pirates ill. by John Manders. Candlewick, 2009. ISBN 978-0-7636-3601-2 Subj: Activities – writing. Animals – rabbits. Birds – chickens, roosters. Books, reading. Pirates.

The Louds move in! ill. by Regan Dunnick. Marshall Cavendish, 2006. ISBN 978-0-7614-5221-8 Subj: Humorous stories. Noise, sounds.

Principal Fred won't go to bed ill. by Donald Wu. Marshall Cavendish, 2010. ISBN 978-0-7614-5709-1 Subj: Bedtime. Behavior – lost & found possessions. Careers – school principals. Rhyming text. Toys – bears.

Pugs in a Bug ill. by Stephanie Buscema. Dial, 2012. ISBN 978-0-8037-3320-6 Subj: Animals – dogs. Automobiles. Counting, numbers. Parades. Rhyming text.

Rock 'n' roll Mole ill. by Lynn Munsinger. Penguin, 2011. ISBN 978-0-8037-3166-0 Subj: Animals – moles. Emotions – fear. Music. Theater.

Tessa's tip-tapping toes ill. by Marsha Gray Carrington. Scholastic, 2002. ISBN 978-0-439-31768-9 Subj: Activities – dancing. Activities – singing. Animals – cats. Animals – mice. Weather – rain.

There might be lobsters ill. by Laurel Molk. Candlewick, 2017. ISBN 978-076367542-4 Subj: Animals – dogs. Emotions – fear. Sea & seashore – beaches.

Where's my mummy? ill. by John Manders. Candlewick, 2008. ISBN 978-0-7636-3196-3 Subj: Bed-

time. Emotions – fear. Family life – mothers. Mummies.

Crisp, Marty. *Black and white* ill. by Sherry Neidigh. Rising Moon, 2000. ISBN 978-0-87358-756-3 Subj: Animals. Animals – dogs. Farms. Pets.

The most precious gift: a story of the Nativity ill. by Floyd Cooper. Penguin, 2006. ISBN 978-0-399-24296-0 Subj: Animals – dogs. Religion – Nativity.

Totally polar ill. by Viv Eisner. Rising Moon, 2001. ISBN 978-0-87358-789-1 Subj: Humorous stories. Imagination. Rhyming text. Seasons – summer. Weather – snow.

Cristaldi, Kathryn. *Baseball ballerina* ill. by Abby Carter. Random House, 2003. ISBN 978-0-679-91734-2 Subj: Activities – dancing. Ballet. Gender roles. Sports – baseball.

Baseball ballerina strikes out ill. by Abby Carter. Random House, 2000. ISBN 978-0-679-99132-8 Subj: Activities – dancing. Ballet. Behavior – bullying, teasing. Sports – baseball.

Crocker, Nancy. *Betty Lou Blue* ill. by Boris Kulikov. Penguin, 2006. ISBN 978-0-8037-2937-7 Subj: Anatomy – feet. Behavior – bullying, teasing. Character traits – appearance. Rhyming text.

Croll, Carolyn. *The little snowgirl* ill. by author. Putnam, 1989. ISBN 978-0-399-21691-6 Subj: Folk & fairy tales. Foreign lands – Russia. Holidays – Christmas. Weather – snow.

Cronin, B. B. *The lost house* ill. by author. Viking, 2016. ISBN 978-110199921-9 Subj: Behavior – lost & found possessions. Behavior – messy. Concepts – color. Family life – grandfathers. Picture puzzles.

The lost picnic: a seek and find book ill. by author. Viking, 2017. ISBN 978-110199922-6 Subj: Activities – picnicking. Behavior – lost & found possessions. Family life – grandfathers. Picture puzzles.

Cronin, Doreen. *Bloom* ill. by David Small. Atheneum, 2016. ISBN 978-144240620-9 Subj: Behavior – messy. Fairies. Folk & fairy tales. Magic. Royalty. Self-concept.

Boom Snot Twitty ill. by Renata Liwska. Viking, 2014. ISBN 978-067078575-9 Subj: Animals. Friendship.

Boom, Snot, Twitty, this way that way ill. by Renata Liwska. Viking, 2015. ISBN 978-067078577-3 Subj: Animals. Friendship.

Bounce ill. by Scott Menchin. Simon & Schuster, 2007. ISBN 978-1-4169-1627-7 Subj: Activities – jumping. Activities – playing. Animals – dogs. Rhyming text. Toys – balls.

Click, clack, boo! a tricky treat ill. by Betsy Lewin. Atheneum, 2013. ISBN 978-1-4424-6553-4 Subj: Animals. Farms. Holidays – Halloween. Parties.

Click, clack, ho! ho! ho! ill. by Betsy Lewin. Atheneum, 2015. ISBN 978-144249673-6 Subj: Animals. Birds – ducks. Farms. Holidays – Christmas. Santa Claus.

Click, clack, moo ill. by Betsy Lewin. Simon & Schuster, 2000. ISBN 978-0-689-83213-0 Subj: Activities – writing. Animals – bulls, cows. Behavior – dissatisfaction. Birds. Caldecott award honor books. Careers – farmers. Farms.

Click, clack, moo I love you! ill. by Betsy Lewin. Simon & Schuster, 2017. ISBN 978-148144496-5 Subj: Activities – dancing. Animals. Birds – ducks. Farms. Holidays – Valentine's Day.

Click, clack, peep! ill. by Betsy Lewin. Atheneum, 2015. ISBN 978-148142411-0 Subj: Animals – babies. Birds – ducks. Farms. Sleep.

Click, clack, quackity-quack: an alphabetical adventure ill. by Betsy Lewin. Simon & Schuster, 2005. ISBN 978-0-689-87715-5 Subj: ABC books. Activities – picnicking. Activities – writing. Animals. Birds – ducks. Farms.

Click, clack, splish, splash: a counting adventure ill. by Betsy Lewin. Simon & Schuster, 2006. ISBN 978-0-689-87716-2 Subj: Animals. Counting, numbers. Farms. Rhyming text. Sports – fishing.

Click, clack, surprise! ill. by Betsy Lewin. Atheneum/Caitlyn Dlouhy, 2016. ISBN 978-148147031-5 Subj: Animals. Birds – ducks. Birthdays. Farms.

Diary of a fly ill. by Harry Bliss. HarperCollins, 2007. ISBN 978-0-06-000156-8 Subj: Activities – writing. Insects – flies.

Diary of a spider ill. by Harry Bliss. HarperCollins, 2005. ISBN 978-0-06-000154-4 Subj: Activities – writing. Spiders.

Diary of a worm ill. by Harry Bliss. Cotler, 2003. ISBN 978-0-06-000151-3 Subj: Activities – writing. Animals – worms.

Dooby dooby moo ill. by Betsy Lewin. Simon & Schuster, 2006. ISBN 978-0-689-84507-9 Subj: Animals. Careers – farmers. Farms. Theater.

Duck for President ill. by Betsy Lewin. Simon & Schuster, 2004. ISBN 978-0-689-86377-6 Subj: Animals. Birds – ducks. Character traits – ambition. Farms. Humorous stories.

Giggle, giggle, quack ill. by Betsy Lewin. Simon & Schuster, 2002. ISBN 978-0-689-84506-2 Subj: Animals. Birds – ducks. Farms.

M.O.M. (Mom Operating Manual) ill. by Laura Cornell. Simon & Schuster, 2011. ISBN 978-1-4169-6150-5 Subj: Family life – mothers. Humorous stories.

Rescue bunnies ill. by Scott Menchin. HarperCollins, 2010. ISBN 978-0-06-112871-4 Subj: Animals – giraffes. Animals – rabbits.

Smick! ill. by Juana Medina. Viking, 2015. ISBN 978-067078578-0 Subj: Animals – dogs. Birds – chickens, roosters. Friendship.

Stretch ill. by Scott Menchin. Atheneum, 2009. ISBN 978-1-4169-5341-8 Subj: Animals – dogs. Health & fitness – exercise. Rhyming text.

Thump, quack, moo: a whacky adventure ill. by Betsy Lewin. Atheneum, 2008. ISBN 978-1-4169-1630-7 Subj: Animals. Birds – ducks. Careers – farmers. Farms.

Wiggle ill. by Scott Menchin. Atheneum, 2005. ISBN 978-0-689-86375-2 Subj: Activities. Animals – dogs. Participation. Rhyming text.

Crosby, Jeff. *Wiener Wolf* ill. by author. Hyperion/Disney, 2011. ISBN 978-1-4231-3983-6 Subj: Animals – dogs. Animals – wolves. Behavior – dissatisfaction.

Crossley-Holland, Kevin. *How many miles to Bethlehem?* ill. by Peter Malone. Scholastic, 2004. ISBN 978-0-439-67642-7 Subj: Holidays – Christmas. Religion – Nativity.

The Riddlemaster ill. by Stéphane Jorisch. Tradewind, 2016. ISBN 978-192689011-1 Subj: Books, reading. Riddles & jokes.

Crouse, Livingstone. *Kisses for kindergarten* ill. by Macky Pamintuan. Silver Dolphin, 2017. ISBN 978-162686703-1 Subj: Animals – dogs. Rhyming text. School.

Crow, Kristyn. *Bedtime at the swamp* ill. by Macky Pamintuan. HarperCollins, 2008. ISBN 978-0-06-083951-2 Subj: Bedtime. Monsters. Rhyming text. Swamps.

Cool Daddy Rat ill. by Mike Lester. Putnam, 2008. ISBN 978-0-399-24375-2 Subj: Animals – rats. Music. Rhyming text.

Hello, Hippo! Goodbye, Bird! ill. by Poly Bernatene. Knopf, 2016. ISBN 978-055350990-8 Subj: Animals – hippopotamuses. Birds. Character traits – persistence. Friendship.

The middle-child blues ill. by David Catrow. Putnam, 2009. ISBN 978-0-399-24735-4 Subj: Activities – singing. Family life – brothers & sisters. Rhyming text.

Skeleton cat ill. by Dan Drall. Scholastic, 2012. ISBN 978-0-545-15385-0 Subj: Anatomy – skeletons. Animals – cats. Musical instruments – drums. Rhyming text.

Zombelina ill. by Molly Idle. Walker, 2013. ISBN 978-0-8027-2803-6 Subj: Ballet. Careers – dancers. Monsters. Rhyming text.

Zombelina: school days ill. by Molly Idle. Bloomsbury, 2017. ISBN 978-161963641-5 Subj: Monsters. Rhyming text. School.

Crowe, Carole. *Turtle girl* ill. by Jim Postier. Boyds Mills, 2008. ISBN 978-1-59078-262-0 Subj: Death. Ecology. Family life – grandmothers. Reptiles – turtles, tortoises.

Crowe, Caroline. *Pirates in pajamas* ill. by Tom Knight. Tiger Tales, 2015. ISBN 978-158925190-8 Subj: Bedtime. Pirates. Rhyming text.

Crowe, Chris. *Just as good: how Larry Doby changed America's game* ill. by Mike Benny. Candlewick, 2012. ISBN 978-0-7636-5026-1 Subj: Ethnic groups in the U.S. – African Americans. Prejudice. Sports – baseball.

Crowley, Ned. *Nanook and Pryce: gone fishing* ill. by Larry Day. HarperCollins, 2009. ISBN 978-0-06-133641-6 Subj: Activities – traveling. Foreign lands – Arctic. Rhyming text. Sports – fishing.

Crowther, Kitty. *Jack and Jim* ill. by author. Hyperion, 2000. ISBN 978-0-7868-2527-1 Subj: Birds. Friendship. Prejudice.

Scritch scratch scraww plop ill. by author. Enchanted Lion, 2015. ISBN 978-159270179-7 Subj: Bedtime. Emotions – fear. Family life – fathers. Frogs & toads. Noise, sounds.

Crowther, Robert. *Amazing pop-up trucks* ill. by author. Candlewick, 2011. ISBN 978-0-7636-5587-7 Subj: Format, unusual – toy & movable books. Trucks.

Colors ill. by author. Candlewick, 2001. ISBN 978-0-7636-1404-1 Subj: Concepts – color. Format, unusual – toy & movable books.

Opposites ill. by author. Candlewick, 2005. ISBN 978-0-7636-2783-6 Subj: Concepts – opposites. Format, unusual – toy & movable books.

Robert Crowther's pop-up dinosaur ABC ill. by author. Candlewick, 2015. ISBN 978-076367296-6 Subj: ABC books. Dinosaurs. Format, unusual – toy & movable books.

Shapes ill. by author. Candlewick, 2002. ISBN 978-0-7636-1889-6 Subj: Concepts – shape. Format, unusual – toy & movable books.

Cruickshank, Margrit. *We're going to feed the ducks* ill. by Rosie Reeve. G. Stevens, 2004. ISBN 978-0-8368-4027-8 Subj: Animals. Birds. Birds – ducks. Food.

Cruikshank, Beth. *Farley follows his nose* (Johnston, Lynn)

Cruise, Robin. *Bartleby speaks!* ill. by Kevin Hawkes. Farrar, 2009. ISBN 978-0-374-30514-7 Subj: Activities – talking. Behavior – growing up. Communication.

Little Mama forgets ill. by Staccy Dressen-McQueen. Farrar, 2006. ISBN 978-0-374-34613-3 Subj: Behavior – forgetfulness. Ethnic groups in the U.S. – Mexican Americans. Family life – grandmothers. Memories, memory. Old age.

Only you ill. by Margaret Chodos-Irvine. Harcourt, 2007. ISBN 978-0-15-216604-5 Subj: Emotions – love. Family life. Rhyming text.

Crum, Shutta. *All on a sleepy night* ill. by Sylvie Daigneault. Stoddart, 2001. ISBN 978-0-7737-3315-2 Subj: Bedtime. Family life – grandparents. Rhyming text.

The bravest of the brave ill. by Tim Bowers. Knopf, 2005. ISBN 978-0-375-92637-2 Subj: Animals. Animals – skunks. Character traits – bravery. Counting, numbers. Emotions – fear. Forest, woods. Rhyming text.

Dozens of cousins ill. by David Catrow. Clarion, 2013. ISBN 978-0-618-15874-4 Subj: Activities – picnicking. Activities – playing. Family life. Family life – cousins.

A family for Old Mill Farm ill. by Niki Daly. Houghton, 2007. ISBN 978-0-618-42846-5 Subj: Animals. Homes, houses. Moving. Rhyming text.

Fox and Fluff ill. by John Bendall-Brunello. Albert Whitman, 2002. ISBN 978-0-8075-2544-9 Subj: Animals – foxes. Birds – chickens, roosters. Family life – fathers.

Mine! ill. by Patrice Barton. Random House, 2011. ISBN 978-0-375-86711-8 Subj: Babies, toddlers. Behavior – sharing. Toys.

Mouseling's words ill. by Ryan O'Rourke. Clarion, 2017. ISBN 978-054430216-7 Subj: Animals – mice. Books, reading.

My mountain song ill. by Ted Rand. Clarion, 2004. ISBN 978-0-618-15970-3 Subj: Family life – cousins. Family life – grandparents. Farms. Songs.

Thunder-Boomer! ill. by Carol Thompson. Clarion, 2009. ISBN 978-0-618-61865-1 Subj: Animals – cats. Farms. Weather – lightning, thunder. Weather – storms.

Uh-oh! ill. by Patrice Barton. Knopf, 2015. ISBN 978-038575268-8 Subj: Activities – playing. Babies, toddlers. Sea & seashore – beaches.

Who took my hairy toe? ill. by Katya Krénina. Albert Whitman, 2001. ISBN 978-0-8075-5972-7 Subj: Anatomy – toes. Folk & fairy tales. Holidays – Halloween. Monsters.

Crummel, Susan Stevens. *And the dish ran away with the spoon* (Stevens, Janet)

Cook-a-doodle-doo! (Stevens, Janet)

Find a cow now! (Stevens, Janet)

The great fuzz frenzy (Stevens, Janet)

Help me, Mr. Mutt! expert answers for dogs with people problems (Stevens, Janet)

The little red pen (Stevens, Janet)

My big dog (Stevens, Janet)

Sherlock Bones and the missing cheese ill. by Dorothy Donohue. Amazon, 2012. ISBN 978-0-7614-6186-9 Subj: Animals – dogs. Careers – detectives. Crime. Senses.

Ten-Gallon Bart ill. by Dorothy Donohue. Marshall Cavendish, 2006. ISBN 978-0-7614-5246-1 Subj: Animals – dogs. Animals – goats. Careers – sheriffs.

Ten-Gallon Bart and the Wild West Show ill. by Dorothy Donohue. Marshall Cavendish, 2008. ISBN 978-0-7614-5391-8 Subj: Animals – dogs. U.S. history – frontier & pioneer life.

Ten-Gallon Bart beats the heat ill. by Dorothy Donohue. Marshall Cavendish, 2010. ISBN 978-0-7614-5634-6 Subj: Alaska. Animals – dogs. Weather – blizzards.

Tumbleweed stew ill. by Janet Stevens. Harcourt, 2000. ISBN 978-0-15-202628-8 Subj: Animals – rabbits. Behavior – trickery.

Crumpacker, Bunny. *Alexander's pretending day* ill. by Dan Andreasen. Penguin, 2005. ISBN 978-0-525-46936-0 Subj: Character traits – questioning. Family life – mothers. Imagination.

Crunk, Tony. *Big Mama* ill. by Margot Apple. Farrar, 2000. ISBN 978-0-374-30688-5 Subj: Family life – grandmothers. Orphans.

Grandpa's overalls ill. by Scott Nash. Orchard, 2001. ISBN 978-0-531-33321-1 Subj: Animals – dogs. Careers – farmers. Clothing – pants. Family life – grandfathers. Farms.

Railroad John and the Red Rock run ill. by Michael Austin. Peachtree, 2006. ISBN 978-1-56145-363-4 Subj: Tall tales. Trains. U.S. history – frontier & pioneer life. Weddings.

Cuetara, Mittie. *Baby business* ill. by author. Dutton, 2003. ISBN 978-0-525-47026-7 Subj: Babies, toddlers. Poetry.

Cuevas, Michelle. *Smoot: a rebellious shadow* ill. by Sydney Smith. Dial, 2017. ISBN 978-052542969-2 Subj: Behavior – boredom. Self-concept. Shadows.

The uncorker of ocean bottles ill. by Erin E. Stead. Dial, 2016. ISBN 978-080373868-3 Subj: Emotions – loneliness. Friendship. Sea & seashore.

Cullen, Catherine Ann. *The magical, mystical, marvelous coat* ill. by David Christiana. Little, 2001.

ISBN 978-0-316-16334-7 Subj: Clothing. Magic. Rhyming text.

Thirsty baby ill. by David McPhail. Little, 2003. ISBN 978-0-316-16357-6 Subj: Babies, toddlers. Folk & fairy tales. Rhyming text. Water.

Cullen, Lynn. *Dear Mr. Washington* ill. by Nancy Carpenter. Dial, 2015. ISBN 978-080373038-0 Subj: Behavior – misbehavior. Etiquette. Family life – brothers & sisters. Letters, cards. U.S. history.

Little Scraggly Hair: a dog on Noah's Ark ill. by Jacqueline Rogers. Holiday, 2003. ISBN 978-0-8234-1772-8 Subj: Anatomy – noses. Animals. Animals – dogs. Boats, ships. Religion – Noah. Weather – floods. Weather – rain. Weather – rainbows.

The mightiest heart ill. by Laurel Long. Dial, 1998. ISBN 978-0-8037-2293-4 Subj: Animals – dogs. Character traits – loyalty. Folk & fairy tales. Foreign lands – Wales.

Moi and Marie Antoinette ill. by Amy Young. Bloomsbury, 2006. ISBN 978-1-58234-958-9 Subj: Animals – dogs. Royalty – queens.

Cumberbatch, Judy. *Can you hear the sea?* ill. by Ken Wilson-Max. Bloomsbury, 2006. ISBN 978-1-58234-703-5 Subj: Family life – grandfathers. Foreign lands – Ghana. Noise, sounds. Sea & seashore.

Cumming, Hannah. *The red boat* ill. by author. Child's Play, 2012. ISBN 978-1-84643-493-8 Subj: Boats, ships. Character traits – confidence. Emotions – loneliness. Imagination. Moving.

Cummings, E. E. *Fairy tales* ill. by Meilo So. Liveright, 2004. ISBN 978-0-87140-658-3 Subj: Folk & fairy tales.

Cummings, Pat. *Ananse and the lizard* ill. by author. Henry Holt, 2002. ISBN 978-0-8050-6476-6 Subj: Animals. Folk & fairy tales – pourquoi tales. Foreign lands – Ghana. Reptiles – lizards.

Angel baby ill. by author. Lothrop, 2000. ISBN 978-0-688-14822-5 Subj: Babies, toddlers. Ethnic groups in the U.S. – African Americans. Family life – brothers & sisters. Rhyming text.

Clean your room, Harvey Moon! ill. by author. Bradbury, 1991. ISBN 978-0-02-725511-9 Subj: Character traits – cleanliness. Ethnic groups in the U.S. – African Americans. Rhyming text.

My aunt came back ill. by author. HarperCollins, 1998. ISBN 978-0-694-01059-2 Subj: Activities – traveling. Ethnic groups in the U.S. – African Americans. Family life – aunts, uncles. Rhyming text.

Cummings, Phil. *Boom bah!* ill. by Nina Rycroft. Kane/Miller, 2010. ISBN 978-1-935279-22-8 Subj:

Animals. Music. Musical instruments. Noise, sounds.

Newspaper hats ill. by Owen Swan. Charlesbridge, 2016. ISBN 978-158089783-9 Subj: Activities – making things. Family life – grandfathers. Illness – dementia. Memories, memory. Old age.

Cummings, Troy. *The Eensy Weensy Spider freaks out! (big-time!)* ill. by author. Random House, 2010. ISBN 978-0-375-86582-4 Subj: Nursery rhymes. Self-concept. Spiders.

Cummins, Julie. *Country kid, city kid* ill. by Ted Rand. Henry Holt, 2002. ISBN 978-0-8050-6467-4 Subj: Camps, camping. Cities, towns. Country. Farms.

Cummins, Lucy Ruth. *A hungry lion; or, a dwindling assortment of animals* ill. by author. Atheneum, 2016. ISBN 978-148144889-5 Subj: Animals. Animals – lions. Birthdays.

Cumpiano, Ina. *Quinito, day and night / Quinito, dia y noche* ill. by José Ramírez. Children's Press, 2008. ISBN 978-0-89239-226-1 Subj: Concepts – opposites. Ethnic groups in the U.S. – Hispanic Americans. Family life. Foreign languages.

Quinito's neighborhood / El vecindario de Quinito ill. by Jose Ramirez. Children's Book Press, 2005. ISBN 978-0-89239-209-4 Subj: Communities, neighborhoods. Ethnic groups in the U.S. – Hispanic Americans. Foreign languages.

Cunnane, Kelly. *Chirchir is singing* ill. by Jude Daly. Random House, 2011. ISBN 978-0-375-86198-7 Subj: Activities – singing. Character traits – helpfulness. Family life. Foreign lands – Kenya.

Deep in the Sahara ill. by Hoda Hadadi. Random House, 2013. ISBN 978-0-375-87034-7 Subj: Clothing. Foreign lands – Mauritania. Religion – Islam.

For you are a Kenyan child ill. by Ana Juan. Simon & Schuster, 2006. ISBN 978-0-689-86194-9 Subj: Foreign lands – Kenya.

Curato, Mike. *Little Elliot, big city* ill. by author. Henry Holt, 2014. ISBN 978-080509825-9 Subj: Animals – elephants. Animals – mice. Character traits – helpfulness. Character traits – smallness. Cities, towns. Friendship.

Little Elliot, big family ill. by author. Henry Holt, 2015. ISBN 978-080509826-6 Subj: Animals – elephants. Animals – mice. Emotions – loneliness. Family life.

Little Elliot, big fun ill. by author. Henry Holt, 2016. ISBN 978-080509827-3 Subj: Animals – elephants. Animals – mice. Emotions – fear. Friendship. Parks – amusement.

Little Elliot, fall friends ill. by author. Holt/Godwin, 2017. ISBN 978-162779640-8 Subj: Animals – elephants. Animals – mice. Behavior – hiding. Country. Friendship. Seasons – fall.

Curious George and the dump truck (1984). Ill. from the Curious George film series. Houghton, 1984. ISBN 978-0-395-36635-6 Subj: Animals – monkeys. Character traits – curiosity. Trucks.

Curious George and the dump truck (1999). Ill. in the style of H. A. Rey by Vipah Interactive. The 1984 ed. of this title has a different story line. Houghton, 1999. ISBN 978-0-395-97832-0 Subj: Animals – monkeys. Birds – ducks. Parks. Trucks.

Curious George and the hot air balloon. Ill. in the style of H. A. Rey by Vipah Interactive. Houghton, 1998. ISBN 978-0-395-92338-2 Subj: Activities – ballooning. Animals – monkeys. Behavior.

Curious George and the pizza. Ill. from the Curious George film series. Houghton, 1985. ISBN 978-0-395-39039-9 Subj: Animals – monkeys. Character traits – curiosity. Food.

Curious George and the puppies. Ill. in the style of H. A. Rey by Vipah Interactive. Houghton, 1998. ISBN 978-0-395-92334-4 Subj: Animals – dogs. Animals – monkeys. Behavior – misbehavior. Money.

Curious George at the fire station. Ill. from the Curious George film series. Houghton, 1985. ISBN 978-0-395-39037-5 Subj: Animals – monkeys. Careers – firefighters. Character traits – curiosity.

Curious George goes camping. Ill. in the style of H. A. Rey by Vipah Interactive. Houghton, 1999. ISBN 978-0-395-97831-3 Subj: Animals – monkeys. Camps, camping.

Curious George goes hiking. Ill. from the Curious George film series. Houghton, 1985. ISBN 978-0-395-39038-2 Subj: Activities – hiking. Animals – monkeys. Character traits – curiosity.

Curious George goes sledding. Ill. from the Curious George film series. Houghton, 1984. ISBN 978-0-395-36637-0 Subj: Animals – monkeys. Character traits – curiosity. Sports – sledding.

Curious George goes to a chocolate factory. Based on the original character by Margret and H. A. Rey; ill. in the style of H. A. Rey by Vipah Interactive. Houghton, 1998. ISBN 978-0-395-91216-4 Subj: Animals – monkeys. Behavior – misbehavior. Food.

Curious George goes to a movie. Based on the original character by Margret and H. A. Rey: ill. in the style of H. A. Rey by Vipah Interactive. Houghton, 1998. ISBN 978-0-395-91901-9 Subj: Animals – monkeys. Behavior – misbehavior. Theater.

Curious George goes to the aquarium. Ill. from the Curious George film series. Houghton, 1984. ISBN 978-0-395-36634-9 Subj: Animals – monkeys. Aquariums. Character traits – curiosity. Fish.

Curious George goes to the circus. Ill. from the Curious George film series. Houghton, 1984. ISBN 978-0-395-36636-3 Subj: Animals – monkeys. Character traits – curiosity. Circus.

Curious George in the big city. Ill. in the style of H. A. Rey by Martha Weston. Houghton, 2001. ISBN 978-0-618-15252-0 Subj: Animals – monkeys. Character traits – curiosity. Cities, towns.

Curious George in the snow: based on the original character by Margret and H. A. Rey. Ill. in the style of H. A. Rey by Vipah Interactive. Houghton, 1998. ISBN 978-0-395-91902-6 Subj: Animals – monkeys. Behavior – misbehavior. Weather – snow.

Curious George makes pancakes. Ill. in the style of H. A. Rey by Vipah Interactive. Houghton, 1998. ISBN 978-0-395-92337-5 Subj: Animals – monkeys. Food. Hospitals.

Curious George takes a train. Ill. in the style of H. A. Rey by Martha Weston. Houghton, 2002. ISBN 978-0-618-06566-0 Subj: Animals – monkeys. Character traits – curiosity. Trains.

Curious George visits a toy store. Ill. in the style of H. A. Rey by Martha Weston. Houghton, 2002. ISBN 978-0-618-06398-7 Subj: Animals – monkeys. Character traits – curiosity. Stores. Toys.

Curious George visits the zoo. Ill. from the Curious George film series. Houghton, 1985. ISBN 978-0-395-39036-8 Subj: Animals – monkeys. Character traits – curiosity. Zoos.

Curious George's 1 to 10 and back again ill. by H. A. Rey. Houghton, 2001. ISBN 978-0-618-12074-1 Subj: Animals – monkeys. Counting, numbers. Format, unusual – board books.

Curlee, Lynn. *Skyscraper* ill. by author. Simon & Schuster, 2007. ISBN 978-0-689-84489-8 Subj: Buildings. Cities, towns.

Currey, Anna. *Truffle's Christmas* ill. by author. Orchard, 2000. ISBN 978-0-531-30289-7 Subj: Animals – mice. Holidays – Christmas. Santa Claus.

Curtis, Andrea. *What's for lunch? how schoolchildren eat around the world* ill. by Sophie Casson. Red Deer, 2012. ISBN 978-0-88995-482-3 Subj: Food. School. World.

Curtis, Gavin. *The bat boy and his violin* ill. by E. B. Lewis. Simon & Schuster, 1998. ISBN 978-0-689-80099-3 Subj: Ethnic groups in the U.S. –

African Americans. Music. Musical instruments – violins. Sports – baseball.

Curtis, Jamie Lee. *Big words for little people* ill. by Laura Cornell. HarperCollins, 2008. ISBN 978-0-06-112760-1 Subj: Language. Rhyming text. Self-concept.

I'm gonna like me ill. by Laura Cornell. Cotler, 2002. ISBN 978-0-06-028762-7 Subj: Behavior. Rhyming text. Self-concept.

Is there really a human race? ill. by Laura Cornell. HarperCollins, 2006. ISBN 978-0-06-075346-7 Subj: Character traits – curiosity. Rhyming text.

It's hard to be five: learning how to work my control panel ill. by Laura Cornell. Cotler, 2004. ISBN 978-0-06-008096-9 Subj: Behavior – growing up. Rhyming text.

My brave year of firsts: tries, sighs, and high fives ill. by Laura Cornell. HarperCollins, 2012. ISBN 978-0-06-144155-4 Subj: Behavior – growing up. Character traits – bravery. Character traits – confidence. Character traits – perseverance. Rhyming text.

My mommy hung the moon: a love story ill. by Laura Cornell. HarperCollins, 2010. ISBN 978-0-06-029016-0 Subj: Family life – mothers. Rhyming text.

Tell me again about the night I was born ill. by Laura Cornell. HarperCollins, 1996. ISBN 978-0-06-024529-0 Subj: Adoption. Babies, toddlers. Family life.

This is me: a story of who we are and where we came from ill. by Laura Cornell. Workman, 2016. ISBN 978-076118011-1 Subj: Immigrants, immigration. Rhyming text. Self-concept.

Today I feel silly and other moods that make my day ill. by Laura Cornell. HarperCollins, 1998. ISBN 978-0-06-024561-0 Subj: Emotions. Family life. Format, unusual – toy & movable books. Rhyming text.

When I was little: a four-year-old's memoir of her youth ill. by Laura Cornell. HarperCollins, 1993. ISBN 978-0-06-021079-3 Subj: Babies, toddlers. Behavior – growing up.

Where do balloons go? ill. by Laura Cornell. HarperCollins, 2000. ISBN 978-0-06-027981-3 Subj: Rhyming text. Toys – balloons.

Curtis, Jennifer Keats. *Seahorses* ill. by Chad Wallace. Henry Holt, 2012. ISBN 978-0-8050-9239-4 Subj: Fish – seahorses.

Cushman, Doug. *Christmas Eve good night* ill. by author. Henry Holt, 2011. ISBN 978-0-8050-6603-6 Subj: Bedtime. Holidays – Christmas. Rhyming text.

Halloween good night ill. by author. Henry Holt, 2010. ISBN 978-0-8050-8928-8 Subj: Bedtime. Holidays – Halloween. Monsters. Rhyming text.

Space cat ill. by author. HarperCollins, 2004. ISBN 978-0-06-008966-5 Subj: Animals – cats. Robots. Space & space ships.

Cusimano, Maryann K. *You are my I love you* ill. by Satomi Ichikawa. Philomel, 2001. ISBN 978-0-399-23392-0 Subj: Family life – parents. Rhyming text. Toys – bears.

You are my wish ill. by Satomi Ichikawa. Penguin, 2010. ISBN 978-0-399-24752-1 Subj: Animals – bears. Family life – grandparents. Rhyming text.

You are my wonders ill. by Satomi Ichikawa. Philomel, 2012. ISBN 978-0-399-25293-8 Subj: Animals. Careers – teachers. Rhyming text. School.

Cutbill, Andy. *The cow that laid an egg* ill. by Russell Ayto. HarperCollins, 2008. ISBN 978-0-06-137295-7 Subj: Animals – bulls, cows. Eggs. Humorous stories.

First week at cow school ill. by Russell Ayto. HarperCollins, 2012. ISBN 978-0-00-727338-6 Subj: Animals – bulls, cows. Humorous stories. School.

Cutler, Jane. *Guttersnipe* ill. by Emily Arnold McCully. Farrar, 2009. ISBN 978-0-374-32813-9 Subj: Character traits – perseverance. Character traits – responsibility. Foreign lands – Canada. Immigrants, immigration. Jewish culture. Poverty.

Cutlip, Kimbra L. *Firefighter's night before Christmas* ill. by James Rice. Pelican, 2002. ISBN 978-1-58980-054-0 Subj: Careers – firefighters. Holidays – Christmas. Poetry.

Cuyler, Margery. *The biggest, best snowman* ill. by Will Hillenbrand. Scholastic, 1998. ISBN 978-0-590-13922-9 Subj: Animals. Concepts – size. Seasons – winter. Snowmen. Weather – snow.

Bonaparte falls apart ill. by Will Terry. Crown, 2017. ISBN 978-110193768-6 Subj: Anatomy – skeletons. Monsters. School – first day. Self-concept.

Bullies never win ill. by Arthur Howard. Simon & Schuster, 2009. ISBN 978-0-689-86187-1 Subj: Behavior – bullying, teasing. Behavior – worrying. Friendship. School. Self-concept.

The bumpy little pumpkin ill. by Will Hillenbrand. Scholastic, 2005. ISBN 978-0-439-52835-1 Subj: Family life – brothers & sisters. Holidays – Halloween.

Groundhog stays up late ill. by Jean Cassels. Walker, 2005. ISBN 978-0-8027-8939-6 Subj: Animals – groundhogs. Hibernation. Holidays – Groundhog Day.

Guinea pigs add up ill. by Tracey Campbell Pearson. Walker, 2010. ISBN 978-0-8027-9795-7 Subj: Animals – guinea pigs. Counting, numbers. Pets. Rhyming text. School.

Hooray for Reading Day! ill. by Arthur Howard. Simon & Schuster, 2008. ISBN 978-0-689-86188-8 Subj: Behavior – worrying. Books, reading. School.

I repeat, don't cheat! ill. by Arthur Howard. Simon & Schuster, 2010. ISBN 978-1-4169-7167-2 Subj: Behavior – cheating. Behavior – lying. Character traits – honesty. Friendship. School.

Kindness is cooler, Mrs. Ruler ill. by Sachiko Yohikawa. Simon & Schuster, 2007. ISBN 978-0-689-87344-7 Subj: Careers – teachers. Character traits – kindness. School.

The little dump truck ill. by Bob Kolar. Henry Holt, 2009. ISBN 978-0-8050-8281-4 Subj: Rhyming text. Trucks.

The little fire truck ill. by Bob Kolar. Holt/Christy Ottaviano, 2017. ISBN 978-162779805-1 Subj: Careers – firefighters. Rhyming text. Trucks.

The little school bus ill. by Bob Kolar. Holt/Christy Ottaviano, 2014. ISBN 978-080509435-0 Subj: Buses. Rhyming text. School.

Monster mess! ill. by S. D. Schindler. Simon & Schuster, 2008. ISBN 978-0-689-86405-6 Subj: Behavior – messy. Character traits – cleanliness. Monsters. Rhyming text.

100th day worries ill. by Arthur Howard. Simon & Schuster, 2000. ISBN 978-0-689-82979-6 Subj: Counting, numbers. School.

Please play safe! Penguin's guide to playground safety ill. by Will Hillenbrand. Scholastic, 2006. ISBN 978-0-439-52832-0 Subj: Activities – playing. Birds – penguins. Safety.

Princess Bess gets dressed ill. by Heather Maione. Simon & Schuster, 2009. ISBN 978-1-4169-3833-0 Subj: Clothing. Rhyming text. Royalty – princesses.

Road signs: a harey race with a tortoise (Aesop)

Skeleton for dinner ill. by Will Terry. Albert Whitman, 2013. ISBN 978-0-8075-7398-3 Subj: Anatomy – skeletons. Behavior – misunderstanding. Rhyming text. Witches.

Skeleton hiccups ill. by S. D. Schindler. Simon & Schuster, 2002. ISBN 978-0-689-84770-7 Subj: Anatomy – skeletons. Ghosts. Hiccups.

Stop drop and roll ill. by Arthur Howard. Simon & Schuster, 2001. ISBN 978-0-689-84355-6 Subj: Behavior – worrying. Emotions – fear. Fire. Safety. School.

That's good! that's bad! ill. by David Catrow. Henry Holt, 1991. ISBN 978-0-8050-1535-5 Subj: Animals. Zoos.

That's good! that's bad! in Washington, D.C. ill. by Michael Garland. Henry Holt, 2007. ISBN 978-0-8050-7727-8 Subj: Geography. School – field trips.

We're going on a lion hunt ill. by Joe Mathieu. Marshall Cavendish, 2008. ISBN 978-0-7614-5454-0 Subj: Animals – lions. Games. Participation. School. Sports – hunting.

Cyrus, Kurt. *Big rig bugs* ill. by author. Walker, 2010. ISBN 978-0-8027-8674-6 Subj: Insects. Rhyming text. Trucks.

Billions of bricks ill. by author. Holt/Christy Ottaviano, 2016. ISBN 978-162779273-8 Subj: Buildings. Careers – construction workers. Counting, numbers. Rhyming text.

Invisible lizard ill. by Andy Atkins. Sleeping Bear, 2017. ISBN 978-158536378-0 Subj: Friendship. Jungle. Reptiles – chameleons.

Motor Dog ill. by David Gordon. Disney/Hyperion, 2014. ISBN 978-142316822-5 Subj: Animals – dogs. Rhyming text. Robots.

Shake a leg, egg! ill. by author. Simon & Schuster/Beach Lane, 2017. ISBN 978-148145848-1 Subj: Birds – geese. Eggs. Rhyming text. Seasons – spring.

Tadpole Rex ill. by author. Harcourt, 2008. ISBN 978-0-15-205990-3 Subj: Dinosaurs. Frogs & toads. Rhyming text.

The voyage of turtle Rex ill. by author. Harcourt, 2011. ISBN 978-0-547-42924-3 Subj: Dinosaurs. Reptiles – turtles, tortoises. Rhyming text.

Czajak, Paul. *Monster needs a Christmas tree* ill. by Wendy Grieb. Scarletta, 2014. ISBN 978-193806346-6 Subj: Holidays – Christmas. Monsters. Rhyming text.

Monster needs your vote ill. by Wendy Grieb. Mighty Media, 2015. ISBN 978-193806363-3 Subj: Character traits – ambition. Character traits – assertiveness. Monsters. Rhyming text.

Czech, Jan M. *An American face* ill. by Frances Clancy. Child & Family, 2000. ISBN 978-0-87868-718-3 Subj: Adoption. Ethnic groups in the U.S. – Korean Americans.

Czekaj, Jef. *A call for a new alphabet* ill. by author. Charlesbridge, 2011. ISBN 978-1-58089-228-5 Subj: ABC books. Humorous stories.

Cat secrets ill. by author. HarperCollins, 2011. ISBN 978-0-06-192088-2 Subj: Animals – cats. Humorous stories.

Hip and Hop, don't stop! ill. by author. Hyperion/Disney, 2010. ISBN 978-1-4231-1664-6 Subj: Animals – rabbits. Contests. Music. Reptiles – turtles, tortoises.

Oink-a-doodle-moo ill. by author. HarperCollins, 2012. ISBN 978-0-06-206011-2 Subj: Animals. Circular tales. Farms. Noise, sounds.

Yes, yes, Yaul! a Hip and Hop book ill. by author. Hyperion/Disney, 2012. ISBN 978-1-4231-4682-7 Subj: Animals – polar bears. Animals – rabbits. Behavior. Music. Reptiles – turtles, tortoises.

Czernecki, Stefan. *Huevos rancheros* ill. by author. Crocodile, 2002. ISBN 978-1-56656-428-1 Subj: Animals – coyotes. Birds – chickens, roosters. Character traits – cleverness.

Paper lanterns ill. by author. Talewinds, 2000. ISBN 978-1-57091-410-2 Subj: Character traits – persistence. Foreign lands – China. Paper.

DaCosta, Barbara. *Mighty Moby* ill. by Ed Young. Little, Brown, 2017. ISBN 978-031629936-7 Subj: Activities – bathing. Animals – whales. Bedtime. Imagination.

Nighttime Ninja ill. by Ed Young. Little, Brown, 2012. ISBN 978-0-316-20384-5 Subj: Bedtime. Ethnic groups in the U.S. – Japanese Americans. Family life – mothers. Imagination. Night. Sports – martial arts.

da Costa, Deborah. *Hanukkah moon* ill. by Gosia Mosz. Kar-Ben, 2007. ISBN 978-1-58013-244-2 Subj: Ethnic groups in the U.S. – Mexican Americans. Family life. Holidays – Hanukkah. Holidays – Rosh Kodesh.

Snow in Jerusalem ill. by Cornelius Van Wright and Ying-Hwa Hu. Albert Whitman, 2001. ISBN 978-0-8075-7521-5 Subj: Animals – cats. Foreign lands – Israel. Weather – snow.

Daddo, Andrew. *Goodnight, me* ill. by Emma Quay. Bloomsbury, 2007. ISBN 978-1-59990-153-4 Subj: Animals – orangutans. Bedtime.

Dahl, Michael. *Bear says "thank you"* ill. by Oriol Vidal. Picture Window, 2012. ISBN 978-1-4048-6786-4 Subj: Animals – bears. Etiquette. Family life – mothers. Format, unusual – board books.

Bedtime for Batman ill. by Ethen Beavers. Capstone, 2016. ISBN 978-162370732-3 Subj: Bedtime. Imagination.

Downhill fun ill. by Todd Ouren. Picture Window, 2004. ISBN 978-1-4048-0579-8 Subj: Counting, numbers. Picture puzzles. Seasons – winter. Sports – skiing.

Eggs and legs ill. by Todd Ouren. Picture Window, 2005. ISBN 978-1-4048-0945-1 Subj: Counting, numbers. Eggs. Picture puzzles.

Footprints in the snow ill. by Todd Ouren. Picture Window, 2004. ISBN 978-1-4048-0946-8 Subj: Counting, numbers. Picture puzzles. Seasons – winter. Weather – snow.

From the garden ill. by Todd Ouren. Picture Window, 2004. ISBN 978-1-4048-0578-1 Subj: Counting, numbers. Food. Gardens, gardening. Picture puzzles. Seasons.

Good morning, Superman ill. by Omar Lozano. Capstone, 2017. ISBN 978-162370850-4 Subj: Imagination. Morning.

Goodnight baseball ill. by Christina Forshay. Capstone, 2013. ISBN 978-1-62370-000-3 Subj: Bedtime. Family life – fathers. Rhyming text. Sports – baseball.

Goodnight football ill. by Christina Forshay. Capstone, 2014. ISBN 978-162370106-2 Subj: Bedtime. Rhyming text. Sports – football.

Hands down ill. by Todd Ouren. Picture Window, 2004. ISBN 978-1-4048-0948-2 Subj: Counting, numbers. Picture puzzles.

Hippo says "excuse me." ill. by Oriol Vidal. Picture Window, 2012. ISBN 978-1-4048-6787-1 Subj: Animals. Animals – hippopotamuses. Etiquette. Format, unusual – board books.

If you were an adjective ill. by Sara Gray. Picture Window, 2006. ISBN 978-1-4048-1356-4 Subj: Language.

Lots of ladybugs! ill. by Todd Ouren. Picture Window, 2005. ISBN 978-1-4048-0944-4 Subj: Counting, numbers. Insects – ladybugs.

Nap time for Kitty ill. by Oriol Vidal. Capstone, 2011. ISBN 978-1-4048-5216-7 Subj: Animals – cats. Format, unusual – board books. Sleep.

On the launch pad ill. by Todd Ouren. Picture Window, 2004. ISBN 978-1-4048-0581-1 Subj: Counting, numbers. Space & space ships.

One big building ill. by Todd Ouren. Picture Window, 2004. ISBN 978-1-4048-0580-4 Subj: Counting, numbers. Machines. Picture puzzles.

One checkered flag ill. by Todd Ouren. Picture Window, 2004. ISBN 978-1-4048-0576-7 Subj: Automobiles. Counting, numbers. Sports – racing.

One giant splash ill. by Todd Ouren. Picture Window, 2004. ISBN 978-1-4048-0577-4 Subj: Animals. Counting, numbers. Fish. Sea & seashore.

Pie for piglets ill. by Todd Ouren. Picture Window, 2005. ISBN 978-1-4048-0943-7 Subj: Animals – pigs. Counting, numbers.

Starry arms ill. by Todd Ouren. Picture Window, 2004. ISBN 978-1-4048-0947-5 Subj: Animals. Counting, numbers. Sea & seashore.

Dahl, Roald. *The enormous crocodile* ill. by Quentin Blake. Knopf, 1978. ISBN 978-0-394-93594-2 Subj: Animals. Reptiles – alligators, crocodiles.

The giraffe and the pelly and me ill. by Quentin Blake. Farrar, 1985. ISBN 978-0-374-32602-9 Subj: Activities – working. Animals. Careers – window cleaners. Crime.

Dahlie, Elizabeth. *Bernelly and Harriet: the country mouse and the city mouse* ill. by author. Little, 2002. ISBN 978-0-316-60811-4 Subj: Animals – mice. Cities, towns. Country. Family life – cousins. Folk & fairy tales.

Dakos, Kalli. *Our principal promised to kiss a pig* by Kalli Dakos and Alicia DesMarteau ill. by Carl DiRocco. Albert Whitman, 2004. ISBN 978-0-8075-6629-9 Subj: Animals – pigs. Books, reading. Careers – school principals. School.

Dale, Penny. *The boy on the bus* ill. by author. Candlewick, 2007. ISBN 978-0-7636-3381-3 Subj: Animals. Buses. Songs.

Dinosaur dig! ill. by author. Candlewick, 2011. ISBN 978-0-7636-5871-7 Subj: Careers – construction workers. Counting, numbers. Dinosaurs. Trucks.

Dinosaur rescue! ill. by author. Candlewick, 2013. ISBN 978-0-7636-6829-7 Subj: Dinosaurs. Trains.

Dinosaur rocket! ill. by author. Candlewick, 2015. ISBN 978-076367999-6 Subj: Dinosaurs. Moon. Space & space ships.

Dinosaur zoom! ill. by author. Candlewick, 2012. ISBN 978-0-7636-6448-0 Subj: Automobiles. Birthdays. Dinosaurs. Parties. Transportation.

Dalgleish, Sharon. *Working dogs* ill. with photos. Chelsea, 2005. ISBN 978-0-7910-8275-1 Subj: Animals – dogs. Animals – service animals. Farms.

Dalgliesh, Alice. *The Thanksgiving story* ill. by Helen Moore Sewell. Scribners, 1987, ©1954. ISBN 978-0-684-18999-4 Subj: Caldecott award honor books. Holidays – Thanksgiving. Pilgrims. U.S. history.

Dallas-Conte, Juliet. *Cock-a-moo-moo* ill. by Alison Bartlett. Little, 2001. ISBN 978-0-316-60505-2 Subj: Animals. Birds – chickens, roosters. Farms. Noise, sounds.

Daly, Catherine. *Whiskers* ill. by Thomas Leonard. Golden, 2000. ISBN 978-0-307-46214-5 Subj: Animals. Hair.

Daly, Cathleen. *Emily's blue period* ill. by Lisa Brown. Roaring Brook, 2014. ISBN 978-159643469-1 Subj: Art. Divorce. Emotions.

Prudence wants a pet ill. by Stephen Michael King. Roaring Brook, 2011. ISBN 978-1-59643-468-4 Subj: Character traits – persistence. Imagination. Pets.

Daly, Jude. *Fair, brown and trembling: an Irish Cinderella story* ill. by author. Farrar, 2000. ISBN 978-0-374-32247-2 Subj: Family life – stepfamilies. Folk & fairy tales. Foreign lands – Ireland. Royalty – princes. Sibling rivalry.

Daly, Niki. *The dinosaurs are back and it's all your fault, Edward!* (Hartmann, Wendy)

Happy birthday, Jamela! ill. by author. Farrar, 2006. ISBN 978-0-374-32842-9 Subj: Birthdays. Clothing – shoes. Foreign lands – South Africa.

The herd boy ill. by author. Eerdmans, 2012. ISBN 978-0-8028-5417-9 Subj: Careers – shepherds. Character traits – ambition. Character traits – hopefulness. Foreign lands – South Africa.

Jamela's dress ill. by author. Farrar, 1999. ISBN 978-0-374-33667-7 Subj: Clothing – dresses. Foreign lands – South Africa.

Next stop — Zanzibar Road! ill. by author. Clarion, 2012. ISBN 978-0-547-68852-7 Subj: Animals. Animals – elephants. Foreign lands – Africa. Shopping. Stores.

No more kisses for Bernard! ill. by author. Frances Lincoln, 2012. ISBN 978-1-84780-105-0 Subj: Family life – aunts, uncles. Kissing.

Not so fast Songololo ill. by author. Atheneum, 1986. ISBN 978-0-689-50367-2 Subj: Cities, towns. Family life – grandmothers. Foreign lands – Africa. Foreign lands – South Africa. Shopping.

Old Bob's brown bear ill. by author. Farrar, 2002. ISBN 978-0-374-35612-5 Subj: Family life – grandfathers. Toys. Toys – bears.

Once upon a time ill. by author. Farrar, 2003. ISBN 978-0-374-35633-0 Subj: Books, reading. Foreign lands – South Africa. Friendship. School.

Pretty Salma: a Little Red Riding Hood story from Africa ill. by author. Houghton, 2007. ISBN 978-0-618-72345-4 Subj: Animals – dogs. Behavior – trickery. Folk & fairy tales. Foreign lands – Africa.

Ruby sings the blues ill. by author. Bloomsbury, 2005. ISBN 978-1-58234-995-4 Subj: Activities – singing. Music. Noise, sounds.

A song for Jamela ill. by author. Frances Lincoln, 2010. ISBN 978-1-84507-871-3 Subj: Beauty shops. Foreign lands – South Africa.

Thank you, Jackson ill. by Jude Daly. Frances Lincoln, 2015. ISBN 978-184780484-6 Subj: Animals – donkeys. Character traits – kindness to animals. Etiquette. Foreign lands – South Africa.

Welcome to Zanzibar Road ill. by author. Houghton, 2006. ISBN 978-0-618-64926-6 Subj: Animals. Animals – elephants. Birds – chickens, roosters. Emotions – loneliness. Foreign lands – Africa. Homes, houses.

What's cooking, Jamela? ill. by author. Farrar, 2001. ISBN 978-0-374-35602-6 Subj: Birds – chickens, roosters. Emotions. Foreign lands – South Africa. Holidays – Christmas. Pets.

Why the sun and moon live in the sky ill. by author. Lothrop, 1995. ISBN 978-0-688-13332-0 Subj: Folk & fairy tales. Foreign lands – Nigeria. Moon. Sea & seashore. Sun.

D'Amico, Carmela. *Ella sets sail* by Carmela D'Amico and Steven D'Amico ill. by Steven D'Amico. Scholastic, 2008. ISBN 978-0-439-83155-0 Subj: Animals – elephants. Character traits – luck. Fairs, festivals. Weather – storms.

Ella sets the stage by Carmela D'Amico and Steven D'Amico ill. by Steven D'Amico. Scholastic, 2006. ISBN 978-0-439-83152-9 Subj: Animals – elephants. Character traits – shyness. School. Theater.

Ella takes the cake by Carmela D'Amico and Steven D'Amico ill. by Steven D'Amico. Scholastic, 2005. ISBN 978-0-439-62794-8 Subj: Animals – elephants. Character traits – helpfulness.

Ella, the elegant elephant by Carmela D'Amico and Steven D'Amico ill. by Steven D'Amico. Scholastic, 2004. ISBN 978-0-439-62792-4 Subj: Animals – elephants. Behavior – bullying, teasing. Clothing – hats. Moving. School – first day.

Suki and Mirabella by Carmela D'Amico and Steven D'Amico ill. by Steven D'Amico. Dial, 2013. ISBN 978-0-8037-3740-2 Subj: Animals – rabbits. Behavior – bossy. Family life – cousins.

Suki the very loud bunny by Carmela D'Amico and Steven D'Amico ill. by Steven D'Amico. Penguin, 2011. ISBN 978-0-525-42230-3 Subj: Animals – rabbits. Behavior – lost.

D'Amico, Steven. *Ella sets sail* (D'Amico, Carmela)

Ella sets the stage (D'Amico, Carmela)

Ella takes the cake (D'Amico, Carmela)

Ella, the elegant elephant (D'Amico, Carmela)

Suki and Mirabella (D'Amico, Carmela)

Suki the very loud bunny (D'Amico, Carmela)

Damjan, Mischa. *The little seahorse and the Christmas pearl* ill. by Alexander Reichstein. NorthSouth, 2001. ISBN 978-0-7358-1506-3 Subj: Fish – seahorses. Holidays – Christmas. Religion – Nativity.

Daniels, Teri. *G-Rex* ill. by Tracey Campbell Pearson. Orchard, 2000. ISBN 978-0-531-33243-6 Subj: Dinosaurs. Family life – brothers.

Just enough ill. by Harley Jessup. Viking, 2000. ISBN 978-0-670-88873-3 Subj: Rhyming text. Self-concept.

Math man ill. by Timothy Bush. Orchard, 2001. ISBN 978-0-439-29308-2 Subj: Counting, numbers. School.

Dann, Penny. *Eensy weensy spider* ill. by author. Barron's, 2003. ISBN 978-0-7641-5662-5 Subj: Format, unusual – board books. Games. Nursery rhymes. Songs. Spiders.

Danneberg, Julie. *The big test* ill. by Judy Love. Charlesbridge, 2011. ISBN 978-1-58089-360-2 Subj: Emotions – fear. School.

Cowboy Slim ill. by Margot Apple. Charlesbridge, 2006. ISBN 978-1-58089-045-8 Subj: Activities – writing. Cowboys, cowgirls. Poetry. Self-concept.

First day jitters ill. by Judy Love. Charlesbridge, 2000. ISBN 978-1-58089-054-0 Subj: Careers – teachers. School – first day.

First year letters ill. by Judy Love. Charlesbridge, 2003. ISBN 978-1-58089-084-7 Subj: Careers – teachers. Letters, cards. School.

Last day blues ill. by Judy Love. Charlesbridge, 2006. ISBN 978-1-58089-046-5 Subj: Careers – teachers. Gifts. School.

Danowski, Sonja. *Little night cat* ill. by author. NorthSouth, 2016. ISBN 978-073584266-3 Subj: Character traits – generosity. Family life – mothers. Toys.

Danticat, Edwidge. *Eight days: a story of Haiti* ill. by Alix Delinois. Scholastic, 2010. ISBN 978-0-545-27849-2 Subj: Character traits – bravery. Earthquakes. Foreign lands – Haiti.

D'Antonio, Nancy. *Our baby from China* ill. by author. Albert Whitman, 1997. ISBN 978-0-8075-6162-1 Subj: Adoption. Ethnic groups in the U.S. – Chinese Americans. Family life. Foreign lands – China.

Danylyshyn, Greg. *A crash of rhinos: and other wild animal groups* ill. by Stephan Lomp. Simon & Schuster/Little Simon, 2016. ISBN 978-148143150-7 Subj: Animals. Language. Rhyming text.

Darbyshire, Kristen. *Put it on the list!* ill. by author. Dutton, 2009. ISBN 978-0-525-47906-2 Subj: Activities – writing. Birds – chickens, roosters. Family life. Shopping.

D'Arc, Karen Scourby. *My grandmother is a singing Yaya* ill. by Diane Palmisciano. Orchard, 2001.

ISBN 978-0-531-33323-5 Subj: Activities – singing. Ethnic groups in the U.S. – Greek Americans. Family life – grandmothers.

Darrow, Sharon. *Old Thunder and Miss Raney* ill. by Kathryn Brown. DK, 2000. ISBN 978-0-7894-2619-2 Subj: Animals – horses, ponies. Contests. Fairs, festivals. Food.

Yafi's family: an Ethiopian boy's journey of love, loss, and adoption (Pettitt, Linda)

Daugherty, James Henry. *Andy and the lion* ill. by author. Viking, 1938. ISBN 978-0-670-12433-6 Subj: Animals – lions. Caldecott award honor books. Character traits – kindness to animals. Humorous stories. Libraries.

D'Aulaire, Edgar Parin *see* Aulaire, Edgar Parin d'

D'Aulaire, Ingri Mortenson *see* Aulaire, Ingri Mortenson d'

Davenier, Christine. *It's raining, it's pouring* ill. by author. Imagine, 2012. ISBN 978-1-936140-77-0 Subj: Games. Rhyming text. Songs.

Davey, Owen. *Night Knight* ill. by author. Candlewick, 2012. ISBN 978-0-7636-5838-0 Subj: Bedtime. Imagination. Knights.

Davick, Linda. *I love you, nose! I love you, toes!* ill. by author. Simon & Schuster, 2013. ISBN 978-1-4424-6037-9 Subj: Anatomy. Rhyming text.

David, Lawrence. *Full moon* (Wilcox, Brian)

The land of the hungry armadillos ill. by Frédérique Bertrand. Doubleday, 2000. ISBN 978-0-385-32698-8 Subj: Animals – armadillos. Behavior – greed. Family life – brothers & sisters. Monsters.

Peter Claus and the naughty list ill. by Delphine Durand. Doubleday, 2001. ISBN 978-0-385-32654-4 Subj: Behavior. Holidays – Christmas. Santa Claus.

Superhero Max ill. by Tara Calahan King. Doubleday, 2002. ISBN 978-0-385-32746-6 Subj: Clothing – costumes. Holidays – Halloween.

David, Ryan. *The magic raincoat* ill. by Sibylla Benatova. Boyds Mills, 2007. ISBN 978-1-932425-68-0 Subj: Clothing – coats. Magic.

Davidson, Ellen Dee. *Princess Justina Albertina: a cautionary tale* ill. by Michael Chesworth. Charlesbridge, 2007. ISBN 978-1-57091-652-6 Subj: Character traits – selfishness. Character traits – willfulness. Pets. Royalty – princesses.

Davidson, Leslie A. *In the red canoe* ill. by Laura Bifano. Orca, 2016. ISBN 978-145980973-4 Subj: Canoes & canoeing. Family life – grandfathers. Nature. Rhyming text.

700 • Bibliographic Guide

Davidson, Rebecca Piatt. *All the world's a stage* ill. by Anita Lobel. Greenwillow, 2003. ISBN 978-0-06-029627-8 Subj: Careers – writers. Cumulative tales. Rhyming text. Theater.

Davies, Benji. *The storm whale* ill. by author. Henry Holt, 2014. ISBN 978-080509967-6 Subj: Animals – whales. Behavior – solitude. Emotions – loneliness. Family life – fathers.

The storm whale in winter ill. by author. Henry Holt, 2017. ISBN 978-125011186-9 Subj: Animals – whales. Behavior – solitude. Emotions – loneliness. Family life – fathers. Seasons – winter. Weather – storms.

Davies, Gill. *Can't, don't, won't* by Gill Davies and Rachael O'Neill ill. by Rachael O'Neill. Sterling, 2001. ISBN 978-0-8069-7841-3 Subj: Behavior – misbehavior. Behavior – running away. Birds – penguins. Character traits – laziness.

Tiny's big wish by Gill Davies and Rachael O'Neill ill. by Rachael O'Neill. Sterling, 2001. ISBN 978-0-8069-7839-0 Subj: Animals – elephants. Behavior – growing up.

Wilbur waited by Gill Davies and Rachael O'Neill ill. by Rachael O'Neill. Sterling, 2001. ISBN 978-0-8069-7843-7 Subj: Animals – tigers. Babies, toddlers. Family life – brothers & sisters. Family life – new sibling. Sibling rivalry.

Davies, Jacqueline. *The boy who drew birds: a story of John James Audubon* ill. by Melissa Sweet. Houghton, 2004. ISBN 978-0-618-24343-3 Subj: Birds. Careers – artists. Careers – naturalists. Careers – ornithologists. Science.

The house takes a vacation ill. by Lee White. Marshall Cavendish, 2007. ISBN 978-0-7314-5331-4 Subj: Activities – vacationing. Homes, houses. Sea & seashore.

The night is singing ill. by Kyrsten Brooker. Penguin, 2006. ISBN 978-0-8037-3004-5 Subj: Bedtime. Country. Lullabies. Night. Noise, sounds. Rhyming text.

Panda pants ill. by Sydney Hanson. Knopf, 2016. ISBN 978-055353576-1 Subj: Animals – pandas. Clothing – pants.

Tricking the Tallyman ill. by S. D. Schindler. Knopf, 2009. ISBN 978-0-375-83909-2 Subj: Counting, numbers. U.S. history.

Davies, Matt. *Ben draws trouble* ill. by author. Roaring Brook, 2015. ISBN 978-159643795-1 Subj: Activities – drawing. Behavior – lost & found possessions. School.

Ben rides on ill. by author. Roaring Brook, 2013. ISBN 978-1-59643-794-4 Subj: Behavior – bullying, teasing. Crime. Sports – bicycling.

Davies, Nicola. *Bat loves the night* ill. by Sarah Fox-Davies. Candlewick, 2001. ISBN 978-0-7636-1202-3 Subj: Animals – bats. Night.

Dolphin baby! ill. by Brita Granström. Candlewick, 2012. ISBN 978-0-7636-5548-8 Subj: Animals – babies. Animals – dolphins.

I (don't) like snakes ill. by Luciano Lozano. Candlewick, 2015. ISBN 978-076367831-9 Subj: Emotions – fear. Reptiles – snakes.

Ice bear: in the steps of the polar bear ill. by Gary Blythe. Candlewick, 2005. ISBN 978-0-7636-2759-1 Subj: Animals – polar bears.

Just ducks! ill. by Salvatore Rubbino. Candlewick, 2012. ISBN 978-0-7636-5936-3 Subj: Birds – ducks. Nature.

Many: the diversity of life on earth ill. by Emily Sutton. Candlewick, 2017. ISBN 978-076369483-8 Subj: Ecology.

Oceans and seas ill. with photos. Kingfisher, 2004. ISBN 978-0-7534-5758-0 Subj: Ecology. Sea & seashore.

One tiny turtle ill. by Jane Chapman. Candlewick, 2001. ISBN 978-0-7636-1549-9 Subj: Reptiles – turtles, tortoises. Sea & seashore.

The pond ill. by Cathy Fisher. IPG/Graffeg, 2017. ISBN 978-191205070-3 Subj: Death. Emotions – grief. Lakes, ponds. Nature.

The promise ill. by Laura Carlin. Candlewick, 2014. ISBN 978-076366633-0 Subj: Behavior – stealing. Character traits – hopefulness.

Tiny creatures: the world of microbes ill. by Emily Sutton. Candlewick, 2014. ISBN 978-076367315-4 Subj: Science.

White owl, barn owl ill. by Michael Foreman. Candlewick, 2007. ISBN 978-0-7636-3364-6 Subj: Birds – owls. Family life – grandfathers. Night.

Davies, Sarah. *Happy to be girls* ill. by Jenny Mattheson. Penguin, 2005. ISBN 978-0-399-23983-0 Subj: Rhyming text. Self-concept.

Davies, Stephen. *All aboard for the Bobo Road* ill. by Christopher Corr. Andersen, 2016. ISBN 978-151241598-8 Subj: Activities – traveling. Buses. Counting, numbers. Foreign lands – Burkina Faso.

Don't spill the milk! ill. by Christopher Corr. Andersen, 2013. ISBN 978-1-46772-028-1 Subj: Character traits – responsibility. Emotions – love. Foreign lands – Africa.

Davis, Anne. *No dogs allowed!* ill. by author. HarperCollins, 2011. ISBN 978-0-06-075353-5 Subj: Animals – cats. Animals – dogs. Character traits – kindness to animals. Friendship.

Davis, Aubrey. *Bagels from Benny* ill. by Dusan Petricic. Kids Can, 2003. ISBN 978-1-55337-417-6 Subj: Family life – grandfathers. Folk & fairy tales. Food. Foreign lands – Spain. Jewish culture. Religion.

A hen for Izzy Pippik ill. by Marie Lafrance. Kids Can, 2012. ISBN 978-1-55453-243-8 Subj: Behavior – lost & found possessions. Birds – chickens, roosters. Character traits – perseverance. Folk & fairy tales.

Kishka for Koppel ill. by Sheldon Cohen. Orca, 2011. ISBN 978-1-55469-299-6 Subj: Behavior – wishing. Character traits – foolishness. Folk & fairy tales. Jewish culture.

Davis, Bart. *Touch the earth* (Lennon, Julian)

Davis, Caroline. *My little rocking horse lullabies* ill. by author. Simon & Schuster, 2002. ISBN 978-0-689-84687-8 Subj: Format, unusual – board books. Lullabies.

My little rowboat ill. by author. Simon & Schuster, 2002. ISBN 978-0-689-84686-1 Subj: Format, unusual – board books. Nursery rhymes. Transportation.

Davis, David. *Fandango stew* ill. by Ben Galbraith. Sterling, 2011. ISBN 978-1-4027-6527-8 Subj: Behavior – trickery. Character traits – cleverness. Folk & fairy tales. Food. U.S. history – frontier & pioneer life.

Jazz cats ill. by Chuck Galey. Pelican, 2001. ISBN 978-1-56554-859-6 Subj: Animals – cats. Music. Rhyming text.

Davis, Jacky. *The amazing adventures of Bumblebee Boy* (Soman, David)

Black Belt Bunny ill. by Jay Fleck. Dial, 2017. ISBN 978-052542902-9 Subj: Animals – rabbits. Food. Health & fitness. Self-concept. Sports – martial arts.

Ladybug Girl (Soman, David)

Ladybug Girl and Bingo (Soman, David)

Ladybug Girl and Bumblebee Boy (Soman, David)

Ladybug Girl and the best ever playdate (Soman, David)

Ladybug Girl and the big snow (Soman, David)

Ladybug Girl and the Bug Squad (Soman, David)

Ladybug Girl and the dress-up dilemma (Soman, David)

Ladybug Girl at the beach (Soman, David)

Ladybug Girl's day out with Grandpa (Soman, David)

Davis, Jerry. *Little Chicken's big day* by Jerry Davis and Katie Davis ill. by Katie Davis. Simon &

Schuster, 2011. ISBN 978-1-4424-1401-3 Subj: Behavior – lost. Birds – chickens, roosters. Family life – mothers.

Davis, Jill. *Orangutans are ticklish: fun facts from an animal photographer* photos by Steve Grubman. Random House, 2010. ISBN 978-0-375-85886-4 Subj: Activities – photographing. Animals. Careers – photographers.

Davis, Jon. *Small Blue and the deep dark night* ill. by author. Houghton, 2014. ISBN 978-054416466-6 Subj: Animals – bears. Animals – rabbits. Emotions – fear.

Davis, Kate. *Barnyard babies* ill. by C. D. Hullinger. Innovative KIDS, 2001. ISBN 978-1-58476-061-0 Subj: Animals – babies. Format, unusual – toy & movable books. Picture puzzles.

Davis, Kathryn Gibbs. *Mr. Ferris and his wheel* ill. by Gilbert Ford. Houghton, 2014. ISBN 978-054795922-1 Subj: Careers – engineers. Careers – inventors. Fairs, festivals. Inventions. Machines. Parks – amusement.

Davis, Katie. *Kindergarten rocks!* ill. by author. Harcourt, 2005. ISBN 978-0-15-204932-4 Subj: Emotions – fear. School – first day.

Little Chicken's big day (Davis, Jerry)

Mabel the Tooth Fairy and how she got her job ill. by author. Harcourt, 2003. ISBN 978-0-15-216307-5 Subj: Careers – dentists. Fairies. Humorous stories. Teeth.

Scared stiff ill. by author. Harcourt, 2001. ISBN 978-0-15-202305-8 Subj: Emotions – fear. Witches.

Who hoots? ill. by author. Harcourt, 2002. ISBN 978-0-15-216616-8 Subj: Animals. Noise, sounds.

Davis, Kenneth C. *Don't know much about the pioneers* ill. by Renée Williams-Andriani. HarperCollins, 2003. ISBN 978-0-06-028618-7 Subj: Activities – traveling. U.S. history – frontier & pioneer life.

Davis, Lee. *Feeding time* photos by author. DK, 2001. ISBN 978-0-7894-7358-5 Subj: Animals. Food.

Davis, Nancy. *A garden of opposites* ill. by author. Random House, 2009. ISBN 978-0-375-85666-2 Subj: Concepts – opposites. Format, unusual – toy & movable books. Gardens, gardening.

Davis, Patricia Anne. *Brian's bird* ill. by Layne Johnson. Albert Whitman, 2000. ISBN 978-0-8075-0881-7 Subj: Birds – parakeets, parrots. Disabilities – blindness. Family life – brothers. Pets.

Davis, Sarah. *My first trucks* ill. with photos. DK, 2015. ISBN 978-146542904-9 Subj: Format, unusual – board books. Trucks.

Davol, Marguerite W. *The loudest, fastest, best drummer in Kansas* ill. by Cat Bowman Smith. Orchard, 2000. ISBN 978-0-531-33191-0 Subj: Musical instruments – drums. Noise, sounds. Tall tales.

The snake's tales ill. by Yumi Heo. Orchard, 2002. ISBN 978-0-439-31769-6 Subj: Activities – storytelling. Reptiles – snakes.

Why butterflies go by on silent wings ill. by Rob Roth. Orchard, 2001. ISBN 978-0-531-33322-8 Subj: Insects – butterflies, caterpillars. Noise, sounds. Weather – storms.

Dawavendewa, Gerald. *The butterfly dance* ill. by author. Abbeville, 2001. ISBN 978-0-7892-0161-4 Subj: Activities – dancing. Indians of North America – Hopi. Weather – rain.

Dawes, Kwame Senu Neville. *I saw your face* ill. by Tom Feelings. Penguin, 2005. ISBN 978-0-8037-1894-4 Subj: Art. Ethnic groups in the U.S. – African Americans. Foreign lands – Africa. Poetry.

Day, Alexandra. *Carl goes shopping* ill. by author. Farrar, 1989. ISBN 978-0-374-31110-0 Subj: Animals – dogs. Shopping. Stores. Wordless.

Carl goes to daycare ill. by author. Farrar, 1993. ISBN 978-0-374-31093-6 Subj: Activities – playing. Animals – dogs. School – nursery.

Carl's birthday ill. by author. Farrar, 1995. ISBN 978-0-374-31144-5 Subj: Activities – babysitting. Animals – dogs. Behavior – misbehavior. Birthdays.

Carl's Halloween ill. by author. Farrar, 2015. ISBN 978-037431082-0 Subj: Animals – dogs. Clothing – costumes. Holidays – Halloween.

Carl's sleepy afternoon ill. by author. Farrar, 2005. ISBN 978-0-374-31088-2 Subj: Activities. Animals – dogs.

Carl's snowy afternoon ill. by author. Farrar, 2009. ISBN 978-0-374-31086-8 Subj: Animals – dogs. Sports – sledding. Weather – snow. Wordless.

Carl's summer vacation ill. by author. Farrar, 2008. ISBN 978-0-374-31085-1 Subj: Activities – vacationing. Animals – dogs. Lakes, ponds. Seasons – summer.

The fairy dogfather ill. by author. Laughing Elephant/Green Tiger, 2012. ISBN 978-1-59583-455-3 Subj: Animals – dogs. Humorous stories.

Follow Carl! ill. by author. Farrar, 1998. ISBN 978-0-374-34380-4 Subj: Activities – babysitting. Activities – playing. Animals – dogs. Parties. Wordless.

Frank and Ernest ill. by author. Scholastic, 1988. ISBN 978-0-590-41557-6 Subj: Animals – bears. Animals – elephants. Character traits – helpfulness. Language.

Frank and Ernest on the road ill. by author. Scholastic, 1994. ISBN 978-0-590-45048-5 Subj: Animals – bears. Animals – elephants. Careers – truck drivers. Language. Trucks.

Frank and Ernest play ball ill. by author. Scholastic, 1990. ISBN 978-0-590-42548-3 Subj: Animals – bears. Animals – elephants. Dictionaries. Language. Sports – baseball.

Good dog, Carl ill. by author. Green Tiger, 1985. ISBN 978-0-88138-062-0 Subj: Activities – babysitting. Animals – dogs. Wordless.

Special deliveries by Alexandra Day and Cooper Edens; ill. by Alexandra Day. HarperCollins, 2001. ISBN 978-0-06-205152-3 Subj: Animals. Careers – postal workers. Pets.

Day, Jan. *The pirate, Pink* ill. by Janeen I. Mason. Pelican, 2001. ISBN 978-1-56554-879-4 Subj: Family life – daughters. Family life – fathers. Pirates. Sea & seashore.

Pirate Pink and treasures of the reef ill. by Janeen I. Mason. Pelican, 2003. ISBN 978-1-58980-086-1 Subj: Family life – daughters. Family life – fathers. Pirates. Sea & seashore.

Day, Marie. *Edward the "crazy man"* ill. by author. Annick, 2002. ISBN 978-1-55037-721-7 Subj: Friendship. Homeless. Illness – mental illness.

Day, Nancy Raines. *A is for alliguitar: musical alphabeasts* ill. by Herb Leonhard. Pelican, 2012. ISBN 978-1-4556-1557-5 Subj: ABC books. Musical instruments. Rhyming text.

A kitten's year ill. by Anne Mortimer. HarperCollins, 2000. ISBN 978-0-06-027231-9 Subj: Animals – cats. Days of the week, months of the year.

The lion's whiskers: an Ethiopian folktale ill. by Ann Grifalconi. Scholastic, 1995. ISBN 978-0-590-45803-0 Subj: Animals – lions. Family life – stepfamilies. Folk & fairy tales. Foreign lands – Ethiopia.

On a windy night ill. by George Bates. Abrams, 2010. ISBN 978-0-8109-3900-4 Subj: Emotions – fear. Holidays – Halloween. Weather – wind.

What in the world? numbers in nature ill. by Kurt Cyrus. Simon & Schuster, 2015. ISBN 978-148140060-2 Subj: Counting, numbers. Nature. Rhyming text.

Day, Trevor. *Youch! it bites! real-life monsters up close* ill. with photos. Simon & Schuster, 2000. ISBN 978-0-689-83416-5 Subj: Animals. Format, unusual – toy & movable books. Monsters. Plants.

Dayrell, Elphinstone. *Why the sun and the moon live in the sky: an African folktale* ill. by Blair Lent. Houghton, 1968. Subj: Caldecott award honor books. Folk & fairy tales. Foreign lands – Africa. Moon. Sky. Sun.

Daywalt, Drew. *BB-8 on the run* ill. by Matthew Myers. Disney/Lucasfilm, 2017. ISBN 978-148470508-7 Subj: Aliens. Character traits – helpfulness. Robots. Space & space ships.

The day the crayons came home ill. by Oliver Jeffers. Philomel, 2015. ISBN 978-039917275-5 Subj: Behavior – lost & found possessions. Concepts – color. Letters, cards.

The day the crayons quit ill. by Oliver Jeffers. Philomel, 2013. ISBN 978-0-399-25537-3 Subj: Behavior – dissatisfaction. Concepts – color. Letters, cards.

The legend of rock paper scissors ill. by Adam Rex. HarperCollins/Balzer+Bray, 2017. ISBN 978-006243889-8 Subj: Games. Humorous stories.

De colores / Bright with colors ill. by David Diaz. Marshall Cavendish, 2008. ISBN 978-0-7614-5431-1 Subj: Foreign languages. Seasons – spring. Songs.

Deacon, Alexis. *Cheese belongs to you!* ill. by Viviane Schwarz. Candlewick, 2013. ISBN 978-0-7636-6608-8 Subj: Animals – rats. Behavior – sharing. Character traits – selfishness. Cumulative tales. Food.

A place to call home ill. by Viviane Schwarz. Candlewick, 2011. ISBN 978-0-7636-5360-6 Subj: Activities – traveling. Animals – hamsters. Homes, houses.

Slow Loris ill. by author. Kane/Miller, 2002. ISBN 978-1-929132-27-0 Subj: Animals. Animals – lorises.

While you are sleeping ill. by author. Farrar, 2006. ISBN 978-0-374-38330-5 Subj: Holidays – Christmas. Night. Sleep. Toys.

Deady, Kathleen W. *All year long* ill. by Linda Bronson. Carolrhoda, 2004. ISBN 978-1-57505-537-4 Subj: Rhyming text. Seasons.

It's time! ill. by Jill Newton. HarperCollins, 2002. ISBN 978-0-694-01565-8 Subj: Animals. Animals – babies. Animals – dogs. Farms. Rhyming text.

Out and about at the zoo ill. by Anne McMullen. Picture Window, 2003. ISBN 978-1-4048-0041-0 Subj: Animals. School – field trips. Zoos.

Deak, Erzsi. *Pumpkin time!* ill. by Doug Cushman. Sourcebooks/Jabberwocky, 2014. ISBN 978-140229526-3 Subj: Animals. Farms. Gardens, gardening.

Dealey, Erin. *Deck the walls! a wacky Christmas carol* ill. by Nick Ward. Sleeping Bear, 2013. ISBN 978-1-58536-857-0 Subj: Food. Holidays – Christmas. Songs.

Goldie Locks has chicken pox ill. by Hanako Wakiyama. Atheneum, 2002. ISBN 978-0-689-82981-9 Subj: Family life – brothers & sisters. Illness – chicken pox. Rhyming text.

K is for kindergarten ill. by Joseph Cowman. Sleeping Bear, 2017. ISBN 978-158536995-9 Subj: ABC books. School.

Dean, James. *Pete the Cat: the wheels on the bus* ill. by Eric Litwin. HarperCollins, 2013. ISBN 978-0-06-219871-6 Subj: Animals – cats. Buses. Music. School. Songs.

Pete the Cat: twinkle, twinkle, little star ill. by author. HarperCollins, 2014. ISBN 978-006230416-2 Subj: Animals – cats. Nursery rhymes. Sky. Songs. Stars.

Pete the Cat: Valentine's Day is cool ill. by author. HarperCollins, 2013. ISBN 978-0-06-219865-5 Subj: Animals – cats. Holidays – Valentine's Day.

Pete the Cat and his magic sunglasses by James Dean and Kim Dean; ill. by James Dean. HarperCollins, 2013. ISBN 978-006227556-1 Subj: Animals – cats. Behavior – bad day, bad mood. Glasses.

Pete the Cat and the bedtime blues by James Dean and Kim Dean; ill. by James Dean. HarperCollins, 2015. ISBN 978-006230430-8 Subj: Animals – cats. Bedtime. Sleepovers.

Pete the Cat and the missing cupcakes (Dean, Kim)

Pete the Cat and the new guy by James Dean and Kim Dean; ill. by James Dean. HarperCollins, 2014. ISBN 978-006227560-8 Subj: Animals – cats. Animals – platypuses. Character traits – being different. Rhyming text.

Dean, Kim. *Pete the Cat and his magic sunglasses* (Dean, James)

Pete the Cat and the bedtime blues (Dean, James)

Pete the Cat and the missing cupcakes by Kim Dean and James Dean ill. by James Dean. HarperCollins, 2016. ISBN 978-006230434-6 Subj: Animals – cats. Counting, numbers. Food. Mystery stories. Rhyming text.

Pete the Cat and the new guy (Dean, James)

De Anda, Diane. *Dancing Miranda / Baila, Miranda, baila* ill. by Lamberto Alvarez. Piñata, 2001. ISBN 978-1-55885-323-2 Subj: Activities – dancing. Disabilities – physical disabilities. Ethnic groups in the U.S. – Hispanic Americans. Family life – daughters. Family life – mothers. Foreign languages. Illness – poliomyelitis.

A day without sugar / Un dia sin azucar ill. by Janet Montecalvo. Arte Publico/Piñata, 2012. ISBN

978-1-55885-702-5 Subj: Ethnic groups in the U.S. – Hispanic Americans. Family life – aunts, uncles. Food. Foreign languages. Health & fitness. Illness – diabetes.

The patchwork garden / pedacitos de huerto ill. by Oksana Kemarskaya. Arte Publico, 2013. ISBN 978-1-55885-763-6 Subj: Communities, neighborhoods. Family life – grandmothers. Foreign languages. Gardens, gardening.

Deans, Karen. *Playing to win: the story of Althea Gibson* ill. by Elbrite Brown. Holiday House, 2007. ISBN 978-0-8234-1926-5 Subj: Ethnic groups in the U.S. – African Americans. Sports.

DeBear, Kirsten. *Be quiet, Marina!* photos by Laura Dwight. Star Bright, 2001. ISBN 978-1-887734-79-0 Subj: Activities – playing. Disabilities – cerebral palsy. Disabilities – Down syndrome. Friendship.

Debecker, Benoit. *The naughty prince* ill. by author. Abrams, 2001. ISBN 978-0-8109-4304-9 Subj: Behavior – misbehavior. Character traits – meanness. Frogs & toads. Royalty – princes. Space & space ships.

De Beer, Hans. *Little Polar Bear and the big balloon* ill. by author. NorthSouth, 2002. ISBN 978-0-7358-1533-9 Subj: Activities – ballooning. Activities – flying. Animals – polar bears. Birds – puffins.

Little Polar Bear and the submarine ill. by author. NorthSouth, 2011. ISBN 978-0-7358-4030-0 Subj: Animals – polar bears. Boats, ships.

Little Polar Bear and the whales ill. by author. NorthSouth, 2009. ISBN 978-0-7358-2209-2 Subj: Animals – polar bears. Animals – whales. Foreign lands – Arctic.

Oh no, Ono! ill. by author. NorthSouth, 2004. ISBN 978-0-7358-1938-2 Subj: Animals – dogs. Character traits – curiosity. Farms. Humorous stories.

De Brunhoff, Jean *see* Brunhoff, Jean de

De Brunhoff, Laurent *see* Brunhoff, Laurent de

Dee, Ruby. *Two ways to count to ten: a Liberian folktale* ill. by Susan Meddaugh. Henry Holt, 1988. ISBN 978-0-8050-0407-6 Subj: Character traits – cleverness. Folk & fairy tales. Foreign lands – Africa.

Deedman, Heidi. *Too many toys!* ill. by author. Candlewick, 2015. ISBN 978-076367861-6 Subj: Behavior – sharing. Gifts. Problem solving. Toys.

Deedy, Carmen Agra. *Martina the beautiful cockroach: a Cuban folktale* ill. by Michael Austin. Peachtree, 2007. ISBN 978-1-56145-399-3 Subj:

Animals – mice. Folk & fairy tales. Foreign lands – Cuba. Insects – cockroaches.

Return of the library dragon ill. by Michael P. White. Peachtree, 2012. ISBN 978-1-56145-621-5 Subj: Books, reading. Careers – librarians. Dragons. Libraries. School.

The rooster who would not be quiet! ill. by Eugene Yelchin. Scholastic, 2017. ISBN 978-054572288-9 Subj: Birds – chickens, roosters. Noise, sounds.

The yellow star: the legend of King Christian X of Denmark ill. by Henri Sorensen. Peachtree, 2000. ISBN 978-1-56145-208-8 Subj: Character traits – bravery. Foreign lands – Denmark. Royalty – kings. War.

Deegan, Kim. *My first book of numbers* ill. by author. Bloomsbury, 2002. ISBN 978-1-58234-755-4 Subj: Counting, numbers. Format, unusual – board books.

My first book of opposites ill. by author. Bloomsbury, 2002. ISBN 978-1-58234-756-1 Subj: Concepts – opposites. Format, unusual – board books.

DeFelice, Cynthia C. *Cold feet* ill. by Robert Andrew Parker. DK, 2000. ISBN 978-0-7894-2636-9 Subj: Behavior – trickery. Careers – musicians. Clothing – boots. Musical instruments – bagpipes.

Nelly May has her say ill. by Henry Cole. Farrar, 2013. ISBN 978-0-374-39899-6 Subj: Folk & fairy tales. Foreign lands – England. Humorous stories. Language.

One potato, two potato ill. by Andrea U'Ren. Farrar, 2006. ISBN 978-0-374-35640-8 Subj: Food. Humorous stories. Magic.

The real, true Dulcie Campbell ill. by R. W. Alley. Farrar, 2002. ISBN 978-0-374-36220-1 Subj: Books, reading. Family life. Royalty – princesses.

Degen, Bruce. *I gotta draw* ill. by author. HarperCollins, 2012. ISBN 978-0-06-028417-6 Subj: Activities – drawing. Animals – dogs. Art. School.

deGennaro, Sue. *The pros and cons of being a frog* ill. by author. Simon & Schuster/Paula Wiseman, 2016. ISBN 978-148147130-5 Subj: Character traits – being different. Character traits – individuality. Clothing – costumes. Friendship.

Degman, Lori. *One zany zoo* ill. by Colin Jack. Simon & Schuster, 2010. ISBN 978-1-4169-8990-5 Subj: Counting, numbers. Rhyming text. Zoos.

deGroat, Diane. *Ants in your pants, worms in your plants! (Gilbert goes green)* ill. by author. HarperCollins, 2011. ISBN 978-0-06-176511-7 Subj: Animals – possums. Ecology. Holidays – Earth Day. School.

April Fool! watch out at school! ill. by author. HarperCollins, 2009. ISBN 978-0-06-143042-8 Subj: Holidays – April Fools' Day. Riddles & jokes. School.

Brand-new pencils, brand-new books ill. by author. HarperCollins, 2005. ISBN 978-0-06-072615-7 Subj: Animals – possums. School – first day.

Good night, sleep tight, don't let the bedbugs bite ill. by author. SeaStar, 2002. ISBN 978-1-58717-129-1 Subj: Animals – possums. Camps, camping. Ghosts.

Happy birthday to you, you belong in a zoo ill. by author. Morrow, 1999. ISBN 978-0-688-16545-1 Subj: Animals. Birthdays. Friendship. Gifts. Parties.

Homer by Diane deGroat and Shelley Rotner; ill. by Diane deGroat. Scholastic, 2012. ISBN 978-0-545-33272-9 Subj: Animals – dogs. Dreams. Sports – baseball.

Jingle bells, homework smells ill. by author. HarperCollins, 2000. ISBN 978-0-688-17544-3 Subj: Animals. Animals – possums. Holidays – Christmas. Homework. School. Weather – snow.

Last one in is a rotten egg! ill. by author. HarperCollins, 2007. ISBN 978-0-06-089294-4 Subj: Animals – possums. Behavior – bossy. Behavior – sharing. Family life – cousins. Holidays – Easter.

Liar, liar, pants on fire ill. by author. SeaStar, 2003. ISBN 978-1-58717-215-1 Subj: Animals – possums. Behavior – lying. Character traits – honesty. School. Self-concept. Theater.

Lola the elf ill. by author. Night Sky, 2002. ISBN 978-1-59014-081-9 Subj: Animals – possums. Character traits – helpfulness. Format, unusual – toy & movable books. Holidays – Christmas. Mythical creatures – elves.

Mother, you're the best! (but Sister, you're a pest!) ill. by author. HarperCollins, 2008. ISBN 978-0-06-123899-4 Subj: Animals – possums. Character traits – helpfulness. Family life – brothers & sisters. Holidays – Mother's Day. Sibling rivalry.

No more pencils, no more books, no more teacher's dirty looks! ill. by author. HarperCollins, 2006. ISBN 978-0-06-079114-8 Subj: Careers – teachers. Friendship. School.

Roses are pink, your feet really stink ill. by author. Morrow, 1996. ISBN 978-0-688-13605-5 Subj: Animals. Behavior – misbehavior. Holidays – Valentine's Day. School.

Trick or treat, smell my feet ill. by author. Morrow, 1998. ISBN 978-0-688-15767-8 Subj: Animals. Clothing – costumes. Family life – brothers & sisters. Holidays – Halloween. School.

De Kinder, Jan. *Red* ill. by author. Eerdmans, 2015. ISBN 978-080285446-9 Subj: Behavior – bullying, teasing. Character traits – being different. School.

Del Rizzo, Suzanne. *My beautiful birds* ill. by author. Pajama, 2017. ISBN 978-177278010-9 Subj: Birds. Foreign lands – Syria. Refugees.

de la Peña, Matt. *Last stop on Market Street* ill. by Christian Robinson. Putnam, 2015. ISBN 978-039925774-2 Subj: Buses. Caldecott award honor books. Character traits – helpfulness. Character traits – kindness. Cities, towns. Ethnic groups in the U.S. Family life – grandmothers.

Miguel and the grand harmony ill. by Ana Ramírez. Disney, 2017. ISBN 978-148478149-4 Subj: Careers – musicians. Character traits – hopefulness. Family life. Foreign lands – Mexico. Music.

A nation's hope: the story of boxing legend Joe Louis ill. by Kadir Nelson. Penguin, 2011. ISBN 978-0-8037-3167-7 Subj: Ethnic groups in the U.S. – African Americans. Sports – boxing.

Delacre, Lulu. *Arroz con leche: popular songs and rhymes from Latin America* ill. by author. Scholastic, 1989. ISBN 978-0-590-42442-4 Subj: Foreign languages. Games. Music. Poetry. Songs.

How far do you love me? ill. by author. Lee & Low, 2013. ISBN 978-1-60060-882-7 Subj: Emotions – love. Nature. World.

Las Navidades: popular Christmas songs from Latin America ill. by selector. Scholastic, 1990. ISBN 978-0-590-43548-2 Subj: Foreign languages. Holidays – Christmas. Music. Poetry. Songs.

¡Olinguito, de la A a la Z! / Olinguito, from A to Z! descubriendo el bosque nublado / unveiling the cloud forest ill. by author. Lee & Low, 2016. ISBN 978-089239327-5 Subj: Ecology. Foreign lands – Ecuador. Foreign languages. Forest, woods.

Delacroix, Sibylle. *Blanche hates the night* ill. by author. Owl, 2016. ISBN 978-177147158-9 Subj: Bedtime. Behavior – misbehavior. Night.

Prickly Jenny ill. by author. OwlKids, 2015. ISBN 978-177147129-9 Subj: Behavior – bad day, bad mood.

Delaporte, Bérengère. *Stripes the tiger* (Leroy, Jean)

Superfab saves the day by Bérengère DeLaporte and Jean Leroy; ill. by Bérengère DeLaporte. OwlKids, 2014. ISBN 978-177147076-6 Subj: Animals – rabbits. Character traits – vanity. Clothing – costumes.

de Las Casas, Dianne. *Blue frog: the legend of chocolate* ill. by Holly Stone-Barker. Pelican, 2011. ISBN 978-1-4556-1459-2 Subj: Folk & fairy tales. Food. Foreign lands – Mexico. Indians of North America – Aztec.

The house that Witchy built ill. by Holly Stone-Barker. Pelican, 2011. ISBN 978-1-58980-965-9 Subj: Cumulative tales. Holidays – Halloween. Witches.

The Little "Read" Hen ill. by Holly Stone-Barker. Pelican, 2013. ISBN 978-1-4556-1702-9 Subj: Activities – writing. Animals. Birds – chickens, roosters. Folk & fairy tales. Language.

Mama's bayou ill. by Holly Stone-Barker. Pelican, 2010. ISBN 978-1-58980-787-7 Subj: Family life – mothers. Lullabies. Rhyming text.

There's a dragon in the library ill. by Marita Gentry. Pelican, 2011. ISBN 978-1-58980-844-7 Subj: Books, reading. Dragons. Libraries.

Delaunois, Angèle. *Magic little words* ill. by Manon Gauthier. OwlKids, 2015. ISBN 978-177147106-0 Subj: Etiquette. Language.

Delessert, Etienne. *A was an apple pie: an English nursery rhyme* ill. by author. Creative Editions, 2005. ISBN 978-1-56846-196-0 Subj: ABC books. Nursery rhymes.

Alert! ill. by author. Houghton, 2007. ISBN 978-0-618-73474-0 Subj: Animals – moles. Behavior – collecting things. Crime.

Full color ill. by author. Creative Editions, 2008. ISBN 978-1-56846-206-6 Subj: Concepts – color.

Hungry for numbers ill. by author. Creative Editions, 2006. ISBN 978-1-56846-198-4 Subj: Counting, numbers. Food.

The seven dwarfs ill. by author. Creative Editions, 2001. ISBN 978-0-439-27863-8 Subj: Dwarfs, midgets. Folk & fairy tales. Foreign lands – Germany. Forest, woods. Royalty.

de Lestrade, Agnès. *Phileas's fortune: a story about self-expression* ill. by Valeria Docampo. Magination, 2010. ISBN 978-1-4338-0790-9 Subj: Communication. Language.

Demarest, Chris L. *All aboard! a traveling alphabet* ill. by Bill Mayer. Simon & Schuster, 2008. ISBN 978-0-689-85249-7 Subj: ABC books. Transportation.

Alpha Bravo Charlie: the military alphabet ill. by author. Simon & Schuster, 2005. ISBN 978-0-689-86928-0 Subj: ABC books. Careers – military.

Firefighters A to Z ill. by author. Margaret K. McElderry, 2000. ISBN 978-0-689-83798-2 Subj: ABC books. Careers – firefighters. Fire. Rhyming text.

Hotshots! ill. by author. Margaret K. McElderry, 2003. ISBN 978-0-689-84816-2 Subj: Careers – firefighters. Fire. Forest, woods. Rhyming text.

Lindbergh ill. by author. Crown, 1993. ISBN 978-0-517-58719-5 Subj: Activities – flying. Airplanes, airports. Transportation. U.S. history.

Smokejumpers one to ten ill. by author. Margaret K. McElderry, 2002. ISBN 978-0-689-84120-0 Subj: Activities – flying. Careers – firefighters. Counting, numbers. Forest, woods.

Demas, Corinne. *Always in trouble* ill. by Noah Jones. Scholastic, 2009. ISBN 978-0-545-02453-2 Subj: Animals – dogs. Behavior – misbehavior. Humorous stories.

Are pirates polite? by Corinne Demas and Artemis Roehrig ill. by David Catrow. Scholastic/Orchard, 2016. ISBN 978-054562874-7 Subj: Etiquette. Pirates. Rhyming text.

The boy who was generous with salt ill. by Michael Hays. Marshall Cavendish, 2002. ISBN 978-0-7614-5099-3 Subj: Birthdays. Careers – chefs, cooks. Careers – fishermen. Sea & seashore.

The disappearing island ill. by Ted Lewin. Simon & Schuster, 2000. ISBN 978-0-689-80539-4 Subj: Birthdays. Boats, ships. Family life – grandmothers. Islands.

Halloween surprise ill. by R. W. Alley. Walker, 2011. ISBN 978-0-8027-8612-8 Subj: Clothing – costumes. Holidays – Halloween.

Here comes trouble! ill. by Noah Jones. Scholastic, 2013. ISBN 978-0-545-35906-1 Subj: Animals – cats. Animals – dogs. Friendship.

Hurricane! ill. by Lenice Strohmeier. Marshall Cavendish, 2000. ISBN 978-0-7614-5052-8 Subj: U.S. history. Weather – hurricanes.

The magic apple ill. by Alexi Natchev. Golden, 2001. ISBN 978-0-307-46334-0 Subj: Character traits – generosity. Family life – sisters. Folk & fairy tales. Royalty – princes.

Nina's waltz ill. by Deborah Lanino. Orchard, 2000. ISBN 978-0-531-33281-8 Subj: Contests. Family life – fathers. Music. Songs.

Pirates go to school ill. by John Manders. Scholastic, 2011. ISBN 978-0-545-20629-7 Subj: Pirates. Rhyming text. School.

Two Christmas mice ill. by Stéphanie Roth. Holiday House, 2005. ISBN 978-0-8234-1785-8 Subj: Animals – mice. Holidays – Christmas. Trees.

Valentine surprise ill. by R. W. Alley. Walker, 2008. ISBN 978-0-8027-9664-6 Subj: Activities – making things. Concepts – shape. Days of the week, months of the year. Holidays – Valentine's Day.

Dematons, Charlotte. *Let's go* ill. by author. Front Street, 2001. ISBN 978-1-886910-65-2 Subj: Imagination. Stores.

Demers, Dominique. *Every single night* ill. by Nicolas Debon. Groundwood, 2006. ISBN 978-0-

88899-699-2 Subj: Animals. Bedtime. Family life – fathers. Sleep.

Old Thomas and the little fairy English text by Sheila Fischman; ill. by Stéphane Poulin. Dominique & Friends, 2000. ISBN 978-1-894363-45-7 Subj: Animals – dogs. Careers – fishermen. Emotions – anger. Fairies.

Demi. *The boy who painted dragons* ill. by author. Simon & Schuster, 2007. ISBN 978-1-4169-2469-2 Subj: Activities – painting. Careers – artists. Character traits – bravery. Dragons. Emotions – fear.

The dragon's tale and other animal fables of the Chinese zodiac ill. by reteller. Henry Holt, 1996. ISBN 978-0-8050-3446-2 Subj: Dragons. Folk & fairy tales. Foreign lands – China. Zodiac.

The empty pot ill. by author. Henry Holt, 1990. ISBN 978-0-8050-1217-0 Subj: Character traits – honesty. Folk & fairy tales. Foreign lands – China. Gardens, gardening. Royalty – emperors.

Florence Nightingale ill. by author. Henry Holt, 2014. ISBN 978-080509729-0 Subj: Careers – nurses. Gender roles.

The girl who drew a phoenix ill. by author. Simon & Schuster, 2008. ISBN 978-1-4169-5347-0 Subj: Activities – drawing. Foreign lands – China. Mythical creatures – phoenix.

The greatest treasure ill. by author. Scholastic, 1998. ISBN 978-0-590-31339-1 Subj: Folk & fairy tales. Foreign lands – China.

Joan of Arc ill. by author. Marshall Cavendish, 2011. ISBN 978-0-7614-5953-8 Subj: Foreign lands – France. Religion. War.

The legend of Saint Nicholas ill. by author. Margaret K. McElderry, 2003. ISBN 978-0-689-84681-6 Subj: Holidays – Christmas. Santa Claus.

The magic pillow ill. by author. Simon & Schuster, 2008. ISBN 978-1-4169-2470-8 Subj: Dreams. Foreign lands – China. Magic.

One grain of rice: a mathematical folktale ill. by author. Scholastic, 1997. ISBN 978-0-590-93998-0 Subj: Character traits – cleverness. Character traits – selfishness. Counting, numbers. Folk & fairy tales. Royalty – rajahs.

The shady tree ill. by author. Henry Holt, 2016. ISBN 978-162779769-6 Subj: Behavior – sharing. Folk & fairy tales. Foreign lands – China.

Dempsey, Kristy. *A dance like starlight: one ballerina's dream* ill. by Floyd Cooper. Philomel, 2014. ISBN 978-039925284-6 Subj: Ballet. Careers – dancers. Ethnic groups in the U.S. – African Americans. Prejudice.

A hop is up ill. by Lori Richmond. Bloomsbury, 2016. ISBN 978-161963390-2 Subj: Activities – playing. Participation. Rhyming text.

Mini racer ill. by Bridget Strevens-Marzo. Bloomsbury, 2010. ISBN 978-1-59990-170-1 Subj: Animals. Rhyming text. Sports – racing.

Surfer chick ill. by author. Abrams, 2012. ISBN 978-1-4197-0188-7 Subj: Birds – chickens, roosters. Character traits – confidence. Character traits – perseverance. Sports – surfing.

Ten little fingers, two small hands ill. by Jane Massey. little bee, 2016. ISBN 978-149980229-0 Subj: Anatomy – hands. Babies, toddlers. Counting, numbers. Rhyming text.

Ten little toes, two small feet ill. by Jane Massey. little bee, 2016. ISBN 978-149980236-8 Subj: Anatomy – feet. Anatomy – toes. Babies, toddlers. Counting, numbers. Rhyming text.

Dempsey, Sheena. *Bye-bye baby brother!* ill. by author. Candlewick, 2013. ISBN 978-0-7636-6241-7 Subj: Babies, toddlers. Family life – brothers. Family life – new sibling. Sibling rivalry.

Denchfield, Nick. *Charlie Chick* ill. by Ant Parker. Harcourt, 2007. ISBN 978-0-15-206013-8 Subj: Birds – chickens, roosters. Format, unusual – toy & movable books.

Denega, Danielle. *Numbers* ill. by Donald Grant. Scholastic, 2001. ISBN 978-0-439-29728-8 Subj: Counting, numbers. Format, unusual – toy & movable books.

Rain or shine ill. by Pierre-Marie Valat. Scholastic, 2001. ISBN 978-0-439-29730-1 Subj: Format, unusual – toy & movable books. Weather.

Deneux, Xavier. *Vehicles* ill. by author. Chronicle, 2015. ISBN 978-145214516-7 Subj: Automobiles. Buses. Format, unusual – toy & movable books. Space & space ships. Trucks.

Denim, Sue. *The Dumb Bunnies* ill. by Dav Pilkey. Blue Sky, 1994. ISBN 978-0-590-47798-7 Subj: Animals – rabbits. Family life.

The Dumb Bunnies' Easter ill. by Dav Pilkey. Blue Sky, 1995. ISBN 978-0-590-20241-1 Subj: Animals – rabbits. Family life. Holidays – Christmas. Holidays – Easter.

The Dumb Bunnies go to the zoo ill. by Dav Pilkey. Blue Sky, 1997. ISBN 978-0-590-84735-3 Subj: Animals. Animals – rabbits. Family life. Zoos.

Make way for Dumb Bunnies ill. by Dav Pilkey. Blue Sky, 1996. ISBN 978-0-590-58286-5 Subj: Activities. Animals – rabbits. Family life.

Denise, Anika. *Baking day at Grandma's* ill. by Christopher Denise. Philomel, 2014. ISBN 978-039924244-1 Subj: Activities – baking, cooking. Animals – bears. Emotions – love. Family life – grandmothers. Rhyming text.

Bella and Stella come home ill. by Christopher Denise. Penguin, 2010. ISBN 978-0-399-24243-4 Subj: Moving. Toys.

Monster trucks ill. by Nate Wragg. HarperCollins, 2016. ISBN 978-006234522-6 Subj: Monsters. Sports – racing. Trucks.

Pigs love potatoes ill. by Christopher Denise. Penguin, 2007. ISBN 978-0-399-24036-2 Subj: Activities – baking, cooking. Animals – pigs. Counting, numbers. Food. Rhyming text.

Dennard, Deborah. *Bullfrog at Magnolia Circle* ill. by Kristin Kest. Soundprints, 2002. ISBN 978-1-931465-04-5 Subj: Animals. Frogs & toads. Insects. Swamps.

Hedgehog haven ill. by Robert Hynes. Soundprints, 2001. ISBN 978-1-56899-987-6 Subj: Animals – hedgehogs. Country. Ecology. Foreign lands – England. Format, unusual.

Koala country ill. by James McKinnon. Soundprints, 2000. ISBN 978-1-56899-887-9 Subj: Animals. Animals – koalas. Foreign lands – Australia. Forest, woods.

Lemur landing ill. by Kristin Kest. Soundprints, 2001. ISBN 978-1-56899-978-4 Subj: Animals – lemurs. Foreign lands – Madagascar. Forest, woods. Science.

Dennis, Major Brian. *Nubs: the true story of a mutt, a marine and a miracle* by Major Brian Dennis and Kirby Larson. Little, Brown, 2009. ISBN 978-0-316-05318-1 Subj: Animals – dogs. Careers – military. Character traits – kindness to animals. Foreign lands – Iraq. War.

DeNoble, Augustine. *Brother Joseph* ill. by Judith Brown. Ignatius, 2000. ISBN 978-1-883937-40-9 Subj: Careers – artists. Careers – clergy.

Denos, Julia. *Windows* ill. by E. B. Goodale. Candlewick, 2017. ISBN 978-076369035-9 Subj: Activities – walking. Character traits – curiosity. Communities, neighborhoods.

Denslow, Sharon Phillips. *In the snow* ill. by Nancy Tafuri. HarperCollins, 2005. ISBN 978-0-06-059684-2 Subj: Animals. Seasons – winter. Weather – snow.

DePalma, Mary Newell. *Bow-wow wiggle-waggle* ill. by author. Eerdmans, 2012. ISBN 978-0-8028-5408-7 Subj: Animals – dogs. Rhyming text.

A grand old tree ill. by author. Scholastic, 2005. ISBN 978-0-439-62334-6 Subj: Ecology. Nature. Trees.

The Nutcracker doll ill. by author. Scholastic, 2007. ISBN 978-0-439-80242-0 Subj: Activities – dancing. Ballet. Holidays – Christmas. Theater.

The perfect gift ill. by author. Scholastic, 2010. ISBN 978-0-545-15402-2 Subj: Animals. Birds – parakeets, parrots. Books, reading. Family life – grandmothers. Gifts.

The strange egg ill. by author. Houghton, 2001. ISBN 978-0-618-09507-0 Subj: Animals – monkeys. Birds. Eggs. Friendship.

Two little birds ill. by author. Eerdmans, 2014. ISBN 978-080285421-6 Subj: Birds. Migration.

Uh-oh! ill. by author. Eerdmans, 2011. ISBN 978-0-8028-5372-1 Subj: Behavior – misbehavior. Dinosaurs.

dePaola, Tomie. *Angels, angels everywhere* ill. by author. Penguin, 2005. ISBN 978-0-399-24370-7 Subj: Angels.

The art lesson ill. by author. Putnam, 1989. ISBN 978-0-399-21688-6 Subj: Art. Family life. School.

The baby sister ill. by author. Putnam, 1996. ISBN 978-0-399-22908-4 Subj: Babies, toddlers. Family life – grandmothers. Family life – new sibling. Family life – sisters.

Baby's first Christmas ill. by author. Putnam, 1988. ISBN 978-0-399-21591-9 Subj: Babies, toddlers. Holidays – Christmas.

Big Anthony and the magic ring ill. by author. Harcourt, 1979. ISBN 978-0-15-207124-0 Subj: Character traits – appearance. Magic.

Big Anthony, his story ill. by author. Putnam, 1998. ISBN 978-0-399-23189-6 Subj: Folk & fairy tales. Foreign lands – Italy. Witches.

Bill and Pete ill. by author. Putnam, 1978. ISBN 978-0-399-20646-7 Subj: Birds – plovers. Foreign lands – Africa. Humorous stories. Reptiles – alligators, crocodiles. School.

Bill and Pete go down the Nile ill. by author. Putnam, 1987. ISBN 978-0-399-21395-3 Subj: Behavior – stealing. Birds – plovers. Foreign lands – Egypt. Museums. Reptiles – alligators, crocodiles. School.

Bill and Pete to the rescue ill. by author. Putnam, 1998. ISBN 978-0-399-23208-4 Subj: Animals. Birds – plovers. Reptiles – alligators, crocodiles.

The birds of Bethlehem ill. by author. Penguin, 2012. ISBN 978-0-399-25780-3 Subj: Birds. Religion – Nativity.

Boss for a day ill. by author. Grosset, 2002. ISBN 978-0-448-42618-1 Subj: Activities – working. Animals – dogs. Behavior – bossy. Family life – brothers & sisters. Multiple births – twins.

Brava Strega Nona! a heartwarming pop-up book ill. by author. Putnam, 2008. ISBN 978-0-399-24453-7 Subj: Foreign languages. Format, unusual – toy & movable books. Magic. Witches.

Charlie needs a cloak ill. by author. Prentice-Hall, 1973. ISBN 978-0-13-128355-8 Subj: Animals – mice. Animals – sheep. Clothing – coats. Problem solving.

The cloud book ill. by author. Holiday, 1975. ISBN 978-0-8234-0531-2 Subj: Weather – clouds.

The clown of God: an old story ill. by author. Harcourt, 1978. ISBN 978-0-15-219175-7 Subj: Foreign lands – Italy. Holidays – Christmas. Religion.

An early American Christmas ill. by author. Holiday, 1987. ISBN 978-0-8234-0617-3 Subj: Holidays – Christmas. U.S. history.

The family Christmas tree book ill. by author. Holiday, 1980. ISBN 978-0-8234-0416-2 Subj: Family life. Holidays – Christmas. Trees.

Favorite nursery tales ill. by adapter. Putnam, 1986. ISBN 978-0-399-21319-9 Subj: Folk & fairy tales. Nursery rhymes.

Fin M'Coul: the giant of Knockmany Hill ill. by author. Holiday, 1981. ISBN 978-0-8234-0384-4 Subj: Folk & fairy tales. Foreign lands – Ireland. Giants.

Get dressed, Santa! ill. by author. Grosset, 1996. ISBN 978-0-448-41258-0 Subj: Format, unusual – board books. Holidays – Christmas. Rhyming text. Santa Claus.

Hide-and-seek all week ill. by author. Grosset, 2001. ISBN 978-0-448-42545-0 Subj: Animals – dogs. Games. Multiple births – twins. School.

Jack ill. by author. Penguin/Nancy Paulsen, 2014. ISBN 978-039916154-4 Subj: Animals. Cumulative tales. Homes, houses.

Jamie O'Rourke and the big potato ill. by author. Putnam, 1992. ISBN 978-0-399-22257-3 Subj: Character traits – laziness. Folk & fairy tales. Foreign lands – Ireland. Mythical creatures – leprechauns.

Jamie O'Rourke and the pooka ill. by author. Putnam, 2000. ISBN 978-0-399-23467-5 Subj: Character traits – laziness. Foreign lands – Ireland. Mythical creatures – goblins. Mythical creatures – pooka spirit.

Jingle, the Christmas clown ill. by author. Putnam, 1992. ISBN 978-0-399-22338-9 Subj: Animals. Circus. Clowns, jesters. Foreign lands – Italy. Holidays – Christmas.

The knight and the dragon ill. by author. Putnam, 1980. ISBN 978-0-606-03327-5 Subj: Dragons. Knights. Libraries.

The Lady of Guadalupe ill. by author. Holiday, 1980. ISBN 978-0-8234-0373-8 Subj: Foreign lands – Mexico. Religion.

The legend of Old Befana ill. by author. Harcourt, 1980. ISBN 978-0-15-243816-6 Subj: Folk & fairy tales. Foreign lands – Italy. Religion.

The legend of the bluebonnet ill. by author. Putnam, 1983. ISBN 978-0-399-20937-6 Subj: Flowers. Folk & fairy tales. Indians of North America – Comanche.

The legend of the Indian paintbrush ill. by author. Putnam, 1987. ISBN 978-0-399-21534-6 Subj: Activities – painting. Flowers. Folk & fairy tales. Indians of North America – Great Plains.

Let the whole earth sing praise ill. by author. Penguin, 2011. ISBN 978-0-399-25478-9 Subj: Creation. Religion.

Little Grunt and the big egg: a prehistoric fairy tale ill. by author. Penguin, 2006. ISBN 978-0-399-24529-9 Subj: Dinosaurs. Folk & fairy tales. Pets.

Look and be grateful ill. by author. Holiday House, 2015. ISBN 978-082343443-5 Subj: Behavior – sharing. Character traits – kindness. Character traits – wisdom. Nature. Religion.

Marcos: red, yellow, blue ill. by author. Putnam, 2003. ISBN 978-0-399-24010-2 Subj: Concepts – color. Family life – brothers & sisters. Foreign languages. Format, unusual – board books. Multiple births – twins.

Meet the Barkers: Morgan and Moffat go to school ill. by author. Putnam, 2001. ISBN 978-0-399-23708-9 Subj: Animals – dogs. Family life – brothers & sisters. Multiple births – twins. School – first day.

Merry Christmas, Strega Nona ill. by author. Harcourt, 1986. ISBN 978-0-15-253183-6 Subj: Foreign lands – Italy. Holidays – Christmas. Humorous stories. Magic. Witches.

My first Thanksgiving ill. by author. Putnam, 1992. ISBN 978-0-399-22327-3 Subj: Friendship. Holidays – Thanksgiving. U.S. history.

My mother is so smart ill. by author. Penguin, 2010. ISBN 978-0-399-25442-0 Subj: Family life – mothers.

Nana Upstairs and Nana Downstairs ill. by author. Putnam, 1998. ISBN 978-0-399-23108-7 Subj: Death. Emotions – grief. Family life – grandmothers. Family life – great-grandparents. Old age.

A new Barker in the house ill. by author. Putnam, 2002. ISBN 978-0-399-23865-9 Subj: Adoption. Animals – dogs. Ethnic groups in the U.S. – Hispanic Americans. Family life – brothers & sisters. Multiple births – twins.

The night of Las Posadas ill. by author. Putnam, 1999. ISBN 978-0-399-23400-2 Subj: Holidays – Christmas. Religion. Theater.

Now one foot, now the other ill. by author. Putnam, 1981. ISBN 978-0-399-20774-7 Subj: Family life – grandfathers. Illness.

Oliver Button is a sissy ill. by author. Harcourt, 1979. ISBN 978-0-15-257852-7 Subj: Activities – dancing. Ballet. Character traits – individuality.

Pancakes for breakfast ill. by author. Harcourt, 1978. ISBN 978-0-15-259455-8 Subj: Activities – baking, cooking. Food. Wordless.

Patrick: patron saint of Ireland ill. by author. Holiday, 1992. ISBN 978-0-8234-0924-2 Subj: Foreign lands – Ireland. Religion.

The popcorn book ill. by author. Holiday, 1978. ISBN 978-0-8234-0314-1 Subj: Activities – baking, cooking. Food.

The quicksand book ill. by author. Holiday, 1977. ISBN 978-0-8234-0291-5 Subj: Behavior – carelessness.

The song of Francis ill. by author. Putnam, 2009. ISBN 978-0-399-25210-5 Subj: Activities – singing. Birds. Religion.

The story of the three wise kings ill. by author. Putnam, 1983. ISBN 978-0-399-20998-7 Subj: Holidays – Christmas. Religion – Nativity.

Strega Nona: an old tale ill. by author. Prentice-Hall, 1975. ISBN 978-0-13-851600-0 Subj: Behavior – forgetfulness. Caldecott award honor books. Humorous stories. Magic. Witches.

Strega Nona does it again ill. by author. Penguin/Nancy Paulsen, 2013. ISBN 978-039925781-0 Subj: Behavior – bossy. Character traits – vanity. Witches.

Strega Nona meets her match ill. by author. Putnam, 1993. ISBN 978-0-399-22421-8 Subj: Folk & fairy tales. Humorous stories. Magic. Witches.

Strega Nona takes a vacation ill. by author. Putnam, 2000. ISBN 978-0-399-23562-7 Subj: Activities – vacationing. Bubbles. Witches.

Strega Nona's gift ill. by author. Penguin, 2011. ISBN 978-0-399-25649-3 Subj: Holidays. Magic. Witches.

Strega Nona's harvest ill. by author. Putnam, 2009. ISBN 978-0-399-25291-4 Subj: Gardens, gardening. Humorous stories. Magic. Witches.

Strega Nona's magic lessons ill. by author. Harcourt, 1982. ISBN 978-0-15-281785-5 Subj: Behavior – carelessness. Humorous stories. Magic. Witches.

Tom ill. by author. Putnam, 1993. ISBN 978-0-399-22417-1 Subj: Family life – grandfathers. Friendship. Names.

Tomie de Paola's Mother Goose by Tomie dePaola and Mother Goose ill. by selector. Putnam, 1985. ISBN 978-0-399-21258-1 Subj: Nursery rhymes.

Tony's bread ill. by author. Putnam, 1989. ISBN 978-0-399-21693-0 Subj: Careers – bakers. Folk & fairy tales. Food. Foreign lands – Italy.

DePrisco, Dorothea. *Snowbear's winter day* ill. by Dagmar Fehlau. Piggy Toes, 2002. ISBN 978-1-58117-133-4 Subj: Activities – playing. Animals. Animals – bears. Forest, woods. Format, unusual – toy & movable books. Seasons – winter. Weather – snow.

What will I become? ill. by Annie Lunsford. Piggy Toes, 2002. ISBN 978-1-58117-160-0 Subj: Animals – babies. Format, unusual – toy & movable books.

Who lives here? ill. by Annie Lunsford. Piggy Toes, 2002. ISBN 978-1-58117-159-4 Subj: Animals. Format, unusual – toy & movable books. Homes, houses.

Derby, Sally. *A new school year: stories in six voices* ill. by Mika Song. Charlesbridge, 2017. ISBN 978-158089730-3 Subj: Poetry. School – first day.

No mush today ill. by Nicole Tadgell. Lee & Low, 2008. ISBN 978-1-60060-238-2 Subj: Ethnic groups in the U.S. – African Americans. Family life – grandmothers. Family life – new sibling.

Two fools and a horse ill. by Robert Rayevsky. Marshall Cavendish, 2002. ISBN 978-0-7614-5119-8 Subj: Behavior – lost & found possessions. Careers – peddlers. Crime.

Whoosh went the wind! ill. by Vincent Nguyen. Marshall Cavendish, 2006. ISBN 978-0-7614-5309-3 Subj: School. Tall tales. Weather – wind.

De Regniers, Beatrice Schenk. *May I bring a friend?* ill. by Beni Montresor. Atheneum, 1964. ISBN 978-0-689-20615-3 Subj: Animals. Caldecott award books. Friendship. Humorous stories. Rhyming text. Royalty.

What did you put in your pocket? ill. by Michael Grejniec. HarperCollins, 2003. ISBN 978-0-06-029029-0 Subj: Animals. Clothing. Cumulative tales. Days of the week, months of the year. Food.

Dernavich, Drew. *It's not easy being Number Three* ill. by author. Henry Holt, 2016. ISBN 978-162779208-0 Subj: Counting, numbers.

De Roo, Elena. *The rain train* ill. by Brian Lovelock. Candlewick, 2011. ISBN 978-0-7636-5313-2 Subj: Night. Trains. Weather – rain.

Derrick, David G., Jr. *I'm the scariest thing in the jungle!* ill. by author. Immedium, 2013. ISBN 978-1-59702087-9 Subj: Animals – tigers. Emotions – fear. Reptiles – alligators, crocodiles.

Derrick, Patricia. *Riley the rhinoceros* ill. by J.-P. Loppo Martinez. KSB Promotions, 2007. ISBN

978-1-933818-15-3 Subj: Animals. Animals – rhinoceros. Jungle.

DeRubertis, Barbara. *Alexander Anteater's amazing act* ill. by R. W. Alley. Kane, 2010. ISBN 978-1-57565-304-4 Subj: ABC books. Animals – anteaters. School. Theater.

Bobby Baboon's banana be-bop ill. by R. W. Alley. Kane, 2010. ISBN 978-1-57565-305-1 Subj: ABC books. Animals – baboons. Counting, numbers. School.

Corky Cub's crazy caps ill. by R. W. Alley. Kane, 2010. ISBN 978-1-57565-306-8 Subj: ABC books. Animals – bears. Clothing – hats. Friendship.

Dilly Dog's dizzy dancing ill. by R. W. Alley. Kane, 2010. ISBN 978-1-57565-307-5 Subj: ABC books. Activities – dancing. Animals – dogs. School.

Desbordes, Astrid. *Edmond, the moonlit party* ill. by Marc Boutavant. Enchanted Lion, 2015. ISBN 978-159270174-2 Subj: Animals – bears. Animals – squirrels. Birds – owls. Character traits – individuality. Character traits – shyness. Parties.

Deschamps, Nicola, ed. *Duckling* photos by Jane Burton. DK, 2002. ISBN 978-0-7894-7856-6 Subj: Birds – ducks. Counting, numbers. Format, unusual – board books.

Emergency! photos by Richard Leeney, et al. DK, 2001. ISBN 978-0-7894-7414-8 Subj: Careers – firefighters. Fire. Format, unusual – board books. Trucks.

De Sève, Randall. *A fire truck named Red* ill. by Bob Staake. Farrar, 2016. ISBN 978-037430073-9 Subj: Family life – grandfathers. Toys. Trucks.

Mathilda and the orange balloon ill. by Jen Corace. HarperCollins, 2010. ISBN 978-0-06-172685-9 Subj: Animals – sheep. Self-concept. Toys – balloons.

Mi barco / Toy boat ill. by Loren Long. Juventud, 2007. ISBN 978-84-26-13657-2 Subj: Behavior – lost & found possessions. Foreign languages. Toys.

Toy boat ill. by Loren Long. Penguin, 2007. ISBN 978-0-399-24374-5 Subj: Behavior – lost & found possessions. Toys.

Desimini, Lisa. *Dot the Firedog* ill. by author. Blue Sky, 2001. ISBN 978-0-439-23322-4 Subj: Animals – dogs. Careers – firefighters.

DesMarteau, Alicia. *Our principal promised to kiss a pig* (Dakos, Kalli)

Desmoinaux, Christel. *"Hallo-what?"* ill. by author. Margaret K. McElderry, 2003. ISBN 978-0-689-84795-0 Subj: Holidays – Halloween. Witches.

Mrs. Hen's big surprise ill. by author. Margaret K. McElderry, 2000. ISBN 978-0-689-83403-5 Subj: Animals. Birds – chickens, roosters. Dinosaurs. Eggs.

Desmond, Jenni. *Red cat blue cat* ill. by author. Blue Apple, 2012. ISBN 978-1-60905-248-5 Subj: Animals – cats. Behavior – fighting, arguing. Emotions – envy, jealousy. Self-concept.

DeSpain, Pleasant. *The dancing turtle: a folktale from Brazil* ill. by David Boston. August House, 1998. ISBN 978-0-87483-502-1 Subj: Behavior – trickery. Folk & fairy tales. Foreign lands – Brazil. Reptiles – turtles, tortoises.

Desrosiers, Sylvie. *Hocus Pocus* by Sylvie Desrosiers and Rémy Simard. Kids Can, 2011. ISBN 978-1-55453-577-4 Subj: Animals – dogs. Animals – rabbits. Character traits – cleverness. Wordless.

Hocus Pocus takes the train ill. by Rémy Simard. Kids Can, 2013. ISBN 978-1-55453-956-7 Subj: Animals – rabbits. Behavior – lost & found possessions. Careers – magicians. Format, unusual – graphic novels. Wordless.

Detlefsen, Lisl H. *Time for cranberries* ill. by Jed Henry. Roaring Brook, 2015. ISBN 978-162672098-5 Subj: Farms. Food. Holidays – Thanksgiving. Seasons – fall.

de Varennes, Monique. *The jewel box ballerinas* ill. by Ana Juan. Random House, 2007. ISBN 978-0-375-83605-3 Subj: Friendship. Magic.

Devernay, Laetitia. *The conductor* ill. by author. Chronicle, 2011. ISBN 978-1-4521-0491-1 Subj: Careers – conductors (music). Imagination. Trees. Wordless.

De Vicq de Cumptich, Roberto. *Bembo's zoo* ill. by author. Henry Holt, 2000. ISBN 978-0-8050-6382-0 Subj: ABC books. Animals. Zoos.

Devine, Monica. *Carry me, Mama* ill. by Pauline Paquin. Stoddart, 2001. ISBN 978-0-7737-3317-6 Subj: Activities – walking. Behavior – growing up. Family life.

Devlin, Harry. *Cranberry autumn* (Devlin, Wende)

Cranberry Christmas (Devlin, Wende)

Cranberry Easter (Devlin, Wende)

Cranberry Thanksgiving (Devlin, Wende)

Cranberry Valentine (Devlin, Wende)

Devlin, Jane. *Hattie the bad* ill. by Joe Berger. Penguin, 2010. ISBN 978-0-8037-3447-0 Subj: Behavior – misbehavior.

Devlin, Wende. *Cranberry autumn* by Wende Devlin and Harry Devlin ill. by Harry Devlin. Four

Winds, 1993. ISBN 978-0-02-729936-6 Subj: Character traits – helpfulness. Family life – grandmothers. Garage sales, rummage sales.

Cranberry Christmas by Wende Devlin and Harry Devlin; ill. by authors. Parents' Magazine, 1976. ISBN 978-0-8193-0845-0 Subj: Behavior – sharing. Character traits – helpfulness. Holidays – Christmas.

Cranberry Easter by Wende Devlin and Harry Devlin ill. by Harry Devlin. Four Winds, 1990. ISBN 978-0-02-729935-9 Subj: Behavior – worrying. Holidays – Easter.

Cranberry Halloween ill. by Harry Devlin. Four Winds, 1982. ISBN 978-0-590-07854-2 Subj: Behavior – stealing. Holidays – Halloween.

Cranberry Thanksgiving by Wende Devlin and Harry Devlin ill. by Harry Devlin. Parents' Magazine, 1971. ISBN 978-0-8193-0499-5 Subj: Holidays – Thanksgiving.

Cranberry Valentine by Wende Devlin and Harry Devlin; ill. by authors. Four Winds, 1986. ISBN 978-0-02-729200-8 Subj: Character traits – shyness. Holidays – Valentine's Day.

DeVorkin, David. *Pluto's secret: an icy world's tale of discovery* (Weitekamp, Margaret A.)

De Vries, Anke. *Raf* ill. by Charlotte Dematons. Boyds Mills, 2009. ISBN 978-1-59078-749-6 Subj: Animals – giraffes. Behavior – lost & found possessions. Foreign lands – Africa. Letters, cards. Toys.

De Vries, Maggie. *How sleep found Tabitha* ill. by Sheena Lott. Orca, 2002. ISBN 978-1-55143-193-2 Subj: Bedtime. Imagination. Sleep. Toys.

Dewan, Ted. *Baby gets the zapper* ill. by author. Random House, 2002. ISBN 978-0-385-74618-2 Subj: Activities – playing. Babies, toddlers. Imagination. Toys.

Crispin and the 3 little piglets ill. by author. Doubleday, 2003. ISBN 978-0-385-74633-5 Subj: Animals – pigs. Babies, toddlers. Family life – brothers & sisters. Family life – new sibling. Sibling rivalry.

Crispin, the pig who had it all ill. by author. Doubleday, 2000. ISBN 978-0-385-32540-0 Subj: Activities – playing. Animals – pigs. Holidays – Christmas.

One true bear ill. by author. Walker, 2009. ISBN 978-0-8027-8495-7 Subj: Careers – military. Character traits – kindness. Toys – bears.

Dewdney, Anna. *Grumpy Gloria* ill. by author. Penguin, 2006. ISBN 978-0-670-06123-5 Subj: Animals – dogs. Emotions. Rhyming text.

Little Excavator ill. by author. Viking, 2017. ISBN 978-110199920-2 Subj: Character traits – smallness. Machines. Rhyming text. Self-concept.

Llama Llama and the bully goat ill. by author. Viking, 2013. ISBN 978-0-670-01395-1 Subj: Animals – goats. Animals – llamas. Behavior – bullying, teasing. Rhyming text. School.

Llama Llama Gram and Grandpa ill. by author. Viking, 2015. ISBN 978-067001396-8 Subj: Animals – llamas. Family life – grandparents. Sleepovers.

Llama Llama home with Mama ill. by author. Penguin, 2011. ISBN 978-0-670-01232-9 Subj: Animals – llamas. Family life – mothers. Illness. Rhyming text.

Llama Llama mad at Mama ill. by author. Penguin, 2007. ISBN 978-0-670-06240-9 Subj: Animals – llamas. Emotions – anger. Family life – mothers. Rhyming text. Shopping.

Llama Llama misses Mama ill. by author. Viking, 2009. ISBN 978-0-670-06198-3 Subj: Animals – llamas. Emotions. Family life – mothers. Rhyming text. School – first day.

Llama, Llama red pajama ill. by author. Penguin, 2005. ISBN 978-0-670-05983-6 Subj: Animals – llamas. Bedtime. Family life – mothers. Rhyming text.

Llama Llama time to share ill. by author. Viking, 2012. ISBN 978-0-670-01233-6 Subj: Animals – llamas. Behavior – sharing. Rhyming text.

Nelly Gnu and Daddy too ill. by author. Viking, 2014. ISBN 978-067001227-5 Subj: Activities – playing. Animals – gnus. Family life – fathers. Rhyming text.

Nobunny's perfect ill. by author. Viking, 2008. ISBN 978-0-670-06288-1 Subj: Animals – rabbits. Behavior – misbehavior. Etiquette. Rhyming text.

Roly Poly pangolin ill. by author. Penguin, 2010. ISBN 978-0-670-01160-5 Subj: Animals – anteaters. Animals – endangered animals. Emotions – fear. Friendship. Rhyming text.

Dewey, Ariane. *The last laugh* (Aruego, José)

Splash! (Aruego, José)

We hide, you seek (Aruego, José)

Weird friends: unlikely allies in the animal kingdom (Aruego, José)

Dewey, Jennifer Owings. *Once I knew a spider* ill. by Jean Cassels. Walker, 2002. ISBN 978-0-8027-8700-2 Subj: Family life. Seasons – winter. Spiders.

DeWitt, Lyndia. *What will the weather be?* ill. by Carolyn Croll. HarperCollins, 1991. ISBN 978-0-06-021597-2 Subj: Weather.

Diakité, Baba Wagué. *The hatseller and the monkeys: a West African folktale* ill. by author. Scholastic, 1999. ISBN 978-0-590-96069-4 Subj: Animals – monkeys. Careers – peddlers. Clothing – hats. Folk & fairy tales. Foreign lands – Africa. Participation.

The hunterman and the crocodiles ill. by author. Scholastic, 1997. ISBN 978-0-590-89828-7 Subj: Behavior – lying. Folk & fairy tales. Foreign lands – Africa.

The magic gourd ill. by author. Scholastic, 2003. ISBN 978-0-439-43960-2 Subj: Animals – rabbits. Behavior – greed. Folk & fairy tales. Foreign lands – Mali. Royalty – kings.

Mee-an and the magic serpent: a folktale from Mali ill. by author. Groundwood, 2007. ISBN 978-0-88899-719-7 Subj: Folk & fairy tales. Foreign lands – Mali. Magic. Reptiles – snakes.

Diakité, Penda. *I lost my tooth in Africa* ill. by Baba Wagué Diakité. Scholastic, 2006. ISBN 978-0-439-66226-0 Subj: Birds – chickens, roosters. Foreign lands – Mali. Teeth.

Díaz, Katacha. *Badger at Sandy Ridge Road* ill. by Kristin Kest. Soundprints, 2005. ISBN 978-1-59249-420-0 Subj: Animals. Animals – badgers.

Carolina's gift ill. by Gredna Landolt. Soundprints, 2002. ISBN 978-1-56899-695-0 Subj: Birthdays. Family life – grandmothers. Foreign lands – Peru. Gifts.

DiCamillo, Kate. *Great joy* ill. by Bagram Ibatoulline. Candlewick, 2007. ISBN 978-0-7636-2920-5 Subj: Animals – monkeys. Character traits – helpfulness. Emotions. Holidays – Christmas. Homeless.

La la la ill. by Jaime Kim. Candlewick, 2017. ISBN 978-076365833-5 Subj: Activities – singing. Character traits – perseverance. Emotions – loneliness. Moon.

Louise: the adventures of a chicken ill. by Harry Bliss. HarperCollins, 2008. ISBN 978-0-06-075554-6 Subj: Birds – chickens, roosters. Pirates. Sea & seashore.

Dick Whittington and his cat. *Dick Whittington and his cat* retold by Marcia Brown; ill. by reteller. Scribners, 1950. Subj: Activities – trading. Animals – cats. Caldecott award honor books. Folk & fairy tales. Foreign lands – England. Middle Ages.

Dick Whittington and his cat retold by Margaret Hodges; ill. by Mélisande Potter. Holiday House, 2006. ISBN 978-0-8234-1987-6 Subj: Animals – cats. Folk & fairy tales. Foreign lands – England. Middle Ages.

Dickens, Charles. *The animals' Christmas carol* (Smath, Jerry)

Dickinson, Rebecca. *Over in the Hollow* ill. by Stephan Britt. Chronicle, 2009. ISBN 978-0-8118-5035-3 Subj: Counting, numbers. Holidays – Halloween. Monsters. Rhyming text.

Dickson, Irene. *Blocks* ill. by author. Candlewick/Nosy Crow, 2016. ISBN 978-076368656-7 Subj: Babies, toddlers. Behavior – sharing. Toys – blocks.

Dickson, Louise. *The vanishing cat* ill. by Pat Cupples. Kids Can, 2001. ISBN 978-1-55337-026-0 Subj: Activities – traveling. Animals – cats. Animals – dogs. Boats, ships. Careers – detectives. Magic. Sea & seashore.

Dicmas, Courtney. *Harold finds a voice* ill. by author. Child's Play, 2013. ISBN 978-1-84643-550-8 Subj: Behavior – imitation. Birds – parakeets, parrots. Character traits – individuality. Foreign lands – France.

Diehl, David. *Goal! my soccer book* ill. by author. Sterling, 2008. ISBN 978-1-60059-241-6 Subj: Format, unusual – board books. Sports – soccer.

Dierssen, Andreas. *The old red tractor* ill. by Daniel Sohr. NorthSouth, 2006. ISBN 978-0-7358-2088-3 Subj: Emotions – envy, jealousy. Problem solving. Toys. Tractors.

Timid Timmy ill. by Felix Scheinberger. NorthSouth, 2003. ISBN 978-0-7358-1812-5 Subj: Animals – rabbits. Character traits – bravery. Character traits – honesty.

Timmy's new friend ill. by Felix Scheinberger. NorthSouth, 2004. ISBN 978-0-7358-1921-4 Subj: Animals – bears. Animals – rabbits. Behavior – forgiving. Friendship.

Diesen, Deborah. *The barefooted, bad-tempered baby brigade* ill. by Tracy Dockray. Tricycle, 2010. ISBN 978-1-58246-274-5 Subj: Babies, toddlers. Humorous stories. Rhyming text.

Bloom ill. by Mary Lundquist. Farrar, 2017. ISBN 978-037430250-4 Subj: Behavior – growing up. Family life – mothers. Gardens, gardening. Seasons.

The not very merry pout-pout fish ill. by Dan Hanna. Farrar, 2015. ISBN 978-037435549-4 Subj: Fish. Gifts. Holidays – Christmas. Rhyming text.

Picture day perfection ill. by Dan Santat. Abrams, 2013. ISBN 978-1-4197-0844-2 Subj: Activities – photographing. Behavior – messy. School.

The pout-pout fish ill. by Dan Hanna. Farrar, 2008. ISBN 978-0-374-36096-2 Subj: Emotions – sadness. Fish. Friendship. Rhyming text.

The pout-pout fish, far, far from home ill. by Dan Hanna. Farrar, 2017. ISBN 978-037430194-1 Subj:

Activities – traveling. Activities – vacationing. Fish. Rhyming text.

The pout-pout fish goes to school ill. by Dan Hanna. Farrar, 2014. ISBN 978-037436095-5 Subj: Behavior – worrying. Character traits – confidence. Fish. Rhyming text. School – first day. Self-concept.

The pout-pout fish in the big-big dark ill. by Dan Hanna. Farrar, 2010. ISBN 978-0-374-30798-1 Subj: Behavior – lost & found possessions. Emotions – fear. Fish. Rhyming text.

Dieterlé, Nathalie. *I am the king!* ill. by author. Orchard, 2001. ISBN 978-0-531-30324-5 Subj: Animals – rabbits. Behavior – misbehavior. Family life. Royalty – kings.

Diffily, Deborah. *Jurassic shark* ill. by Karen Carr. HarperCollins, 2004. ISBN 978-0-06-008250-5 Subj: Fish – sharks. Fossils. Science.

DiFiori, Lawrence. *Jackie and the Shadow Snatcher* ill. by author. Random House, 2006. ISBN 978-0-375-97515-8 Subj: Behavior – lost & found possessions. Crime. Shadows.

Diggs, Taye. *Chocolate me!* ill. by Shane W. Evans. Feiwel & Friends, 2011. ISBN 978-0-312-60326-7 Subj: Behavior – bullying, teasing. Character traits – individuality. Ethnic groups in the U.S. – African Americans. Family life – mothers. Self-concept.

Mixed me! ill. by Shane W Evans. Feiwel & Friends, 2015. ISBN 978-125004719-9 Subj: Ethnic groups in the U.S. Rhyming text. Self-concept.

Dijkstra, Lida. *Cute* ill. by Marije Tolman. Boyds Mills, 2007. ISBN 978-1-59078-505-8 Subj: Animals – rabbits. Self-concept.

Dijs, Carla. *Mommy, what if —?* ill. by author. Simon & Schuster, 2002. ISBN 978-0-689-84692-2 Subj: Animals. Animals – elephants. Family life – mothers. Format, unusual – toy & movable books.

Dillard, Sarah. *First day at Zoo School* ill. by author. Sleeping Bear, 2014. ISBN 978-158536890-7 Subj: Animals – pandas. Reptiles – alligators, crocodiles. School – first day.

Diller, Kevin. *Hello, my name is Octicorn* ill. by Justin Lowe. HarperCollins/Balzer+Bray, 2016. ISBN 978-006238793-6 Subj: Character traits – being different. Character traits – individuality. Mythical creatures – unicorns. Octopuses. Self-concept.

Dillon, Diane. *If kids ran the world* (Dillon, Leo)

Jazz on a Saturday night (Dillon, Leo)

Dillon, Jana. *Lucky O'Leprechaun comes to America* ill. by author. Pelican, 2000. ISBN 978-1-56554-816-9 Subj: Ethnic groups in the U.S. – Irish Americans. Family life – aunts, uncles. Humorous stories. Mythical creatures – leprechauns.

Lucky O'Leprechaun in school ill. by author. Pelican, 2003. ISBN 978-1-58980-035-9 Subj: Moon. Mythical creatures – leprechauns. School. Space & space ships.

Dillon, Leo. *If kids ran the world* by Leo Dillon and Diane Dillon ill. by Leo and Diane Dillon. Scholastic/Blue Sky, 2014. ISBN 978-054544196-4 Subj: Behavior. Character traits – helpfulness. World.

Jazz on a Saturday night by Leo Dillon and Diane Dillon ill. by Leo and Diane Dillon. Scholastic, 2007. ISBN 978-0-590-47893-9 Subj: Careers – musicians. Music.

DiLorenzo, Barbara. *Renato and the lion* ill. by author. Viking, 2017. ISBN 978-045147641-8 Subj: Animals – lions. Foreign lands – Italy. Museums. War.

Dionne, Wanda. *Little Thumb* ill. by Jana Dillon. Pelican, 2000. ISBN 978-1-56554-754-4 Subj: Rhyming text. Thumb sucking.

Diouf, Sylviane A,. *Bintou's braids* ill. by Shane W. Evans. Chronicle, 2001. ISBN 978-0-8118-2514-6 Subj: Foreign lands – Africa. Hair.

DiPucchio, Kelly. *Alfred Zector, book collector* ill. by Macky Pamintuan. HarperCollins, 2010. ISBN 978-0-06-000581-8 Subj: Behavior – collecting things. Books, reading. Rhyming text.

Antoinette ill. by Christian Robinson. Atheneum, 2017. ISBN 978-148145783-5 Subj: Animals – dogs. Character traits – being different. Character traits – individuality. Self-concept.

Crafty Chloe ill. by Heather Ross. Simon & Schuster, 2012. ISBN 978-1-4424-2123-3 Subj: Activities – making things. Birthdays. Gifts.

Crafty Chloe: dress-up mess-up ill. by Heather Ross. Simon & Schuster, 2013. ISBN 978-1-4424-2124-0 Subj: Activities – making things. Clothing – costumes. Friendship. Parades.

Dinosnores ill. by Ponder Goembel. HarperCollins, 2005. ISBN 978-0-06-051578-2 Subj: Dinosaurs. Noise, sounds. Rhyming text. Sleep – snoring.

Dog days of school ill. by Brian Biggs. Disney/Hyperion, 2014. ISBN 978-078685493-6 Subj: Animals – dogs. Behavior – dissatisfaction. Behavior – wishing. Humorous stories.

Dragon was terrible ill. by Greg Pizzoli. Farrar, 2016. ISBN 978-037430049-4 Subj: Behavior –

misbehavior. Books, reading. Dragons. Emotions – anger.

Everyone loves Bacon ill. by Eric Wight. Farrar, 2015. ISBN 978-037430052-4 Subj: Character traits – vanity. Food.

Everyone loves Cupcake ill. by Eric Wight. Farrar, 2016. ISBN 978-037430293-1 Subj: Character traits – appearance. Character traits – vanity. Food.

Gaston ill. by Christian Robinson. Atheneum, 2014. ISBN 978-144245102-5 Subj: Animals – dogs. Character traits – being different. Character traits – individuality. Self-concept.

Gilbert goldfish wants a pet ill. by Bob Shea. Penguin, 2011. ISBN 978-0-8037-3394-7 Subj: Fish. Pets.

Grace for president ill. by LeUyen Pham. Hyperion, 2008. ISBN 978-0-7868-3919-3 Subj: Behavior – seeking better things. Careers. Character traits – ambition. Gender roles. School.

Littles: and how they grow ill. by A. G. Ford. Doubleday, 2017. ISBN 978-039955526-8 Subj: Babies, toddlers. Family life. Rhyming text.

The sandwich swap (Rania, Queen, consort of Abdullah II, King of Jordan)

Super Manny stands up! ill. by Stephanie Graegin. Atheneum, 2017. ISBN 978-148145960-0 Subj: Animals – raccoons. Imagination.

What's the magic word? ill. by Marsha Winborn. HarperCollins, 2005. ISBN 978-0-06-000579-5 Subj: Animals. Birds. Weather – wind.

Zombie in love ill. by Scott Campbell. Simon & Schuster, 2011. ISBN 978-1-4424-0270-6 Subj: Emotions – loneliness. Humorous stories. Monsters.

Zombie in love 2 + 1 ill. by Scott Campbell. Atheneum, 2015. ISBN 978-144245937-3 Subj: Babies, toddlers. Humorous stories. Monsters.

DiSalvo, DyAnne. *A castle on Viola Street* ill. by author. HarperCollins, 2001. ISBN 978-0-688-17691-4 Subj: Character traits – generosity. Homes, houses.

Grandpa's corner store ill. by author. HarperCollins, 2000. ISBN 978-0-688-16717-2 Subj: Communities, neighborhoods. Family life – grandfathers. Stores.

DiSiena, Laura Lyn. *Dinosaurs live on! and other fun facts* by Laura Lyn DiSiena and Hannah Eliot ill. by Aaron Spurgeon. Simon & Schuster, 2015. ISBN 978-148142425-7 Subj: Dinosaurs. Fossils.

Ditchfield, Christin. *Cowlick!* ill. by Rosalind Beardshaw. Random House, 2007. ISBN 978-0-375-83540-7 Subj: Animals – bulls, cows. Character traits – appearance. Hair. Humorous stories.

DiTerlizzi, Angela. *Baby love* ill. by Brooke Boynton Hughes. Simon & Schuster/Beach Lane, 2015. ISBN 978-144243392-2 Subj: Babies, toddlers. Emotions – love. Family life – parents. Rhyming text.

I wanna be a cowgirl ill. by Elizabet Vukovic. Simon & Schuster, 2017. ISBN 978-148145299-1 Subj: Cowboys, cowgirls. Imagination. Rhyming text.

Say what? ill. by Joey Chou. Simon & Schuster, 2011. ISBN 978-1-4169-8694-2 Subj: Animals. Noise, sounds. Rhyming text.

Some bugs ill. by Brendan Wenzel. Simon & Schuster/Beach Lane, 2014. ISBN 978-144245880-2 Subj: Insects. Rhyming text.

Some pets ill. by Brendan Wenzel. Simon & Schuster/Beach Lane, 2016. ISBN 978-148144402-6 Subj: Pets. Rhyming text.

DiTerlizzi, Tony. *G is for one gzonk! an alpha-number-bet book* ill. by author. Simon & Schuster, 2006. ISBN 978-0-689-85290-9 Subj: ABC books. Counting, numbers. Rhyming text.

Jimmy Zangwow's out-of-this-world, moon pie adventure ill. by author. Simon & Schuster, 2000. ISBN 978-0-689-82215-5 Subj: Food. Imagination. Moon. Space & space ships.

Ted ill. by author. Simon & Schuster, 2001. ISBN 978-0-689-83235-2 Subj: Family life – fathers. Imagination – imaginary friends.

Divakaruni, Chitra Banerjee. *Grandma and the great gourd: a Bengali folktale* ill. by Susy Pilgrim Waters. Roaring Brook, 2013. ISBN 978-1-59643-378-6 Subj: Behavior – resourcefulness. Behavior – trickery. Family life – grandmothers. Folk & fairy tales. Foreign lands – India.

Diviny, Sean. *Halloween Motel* ill. by Joe Rocco. HarperCollins, 2000. ISBN 978-0-06-028816-7 Subj: Ghosts. Holidays – Halloween. Hotels. Monsters. Rhyming text.

Dixon, Amy Jackson. *Cajun night after Christmas* (Moss, Jenny Jackson)

Dixon, Ann. *Waiting for Noël* ill. by Mark Graham. Eerdmans, 2000. ISBN 978-0-8028-5192-5 Subj: Babies, toddlers. Birth. Birthdays. Family life. Holidays – Christmas.

Winter is . . . ill. by Mindy Dwyer. Alaska Northwest, 2002. ISBN 978-0-88240-543-8 Subj: Family life – brothers & sisters. Rhyming text. Seasons – winter.

Dobbins, Jan. *Driving my tractor* ill. by David Sim. Barefoot, 2009. ISBN 978-1-84686-358-5 Subj: Animals. Counting, numbers. Rhyming text. Tractors.

Docherty, Helen. *The Snatchabook* ill. by author. Sourcebooks/Jabberwocky, 2013. ISBN 978-1-4022-9082-4 Subj: Animals. Bedtime. Books, reading. Crime. Forest, woods. Rhyming text.

The storybook knight ill. by Thomas Docherty. Sourcebooks/Jabberwocky, 2016. ISBN 978-149263814-8 Subj: Animals – mice. Books, reading. Dragons. Knights. Rhyming text.

Docherty, Thomas. *Big scary monster* ill. by author. Candlewick, 2010. ISBN 978-0-7636-4787-2 Subj: Behavior – bullying, teasing. Concepts – size. Monsters.

To the beach ill. by author. Candlewick, 2009. ISBN 978-0-7636-4429-1 Subj: Activities – traveling. Imagination. Sea & seashore – beaches. Weather – rain.

Wash-a-bye Bear ill. by author. Candlewick, 2013. ISBN 978-0-7636-6486-2 Subj: Laundry. Rhyming text. Toys – bears.

Dockray, Tracy. *The lost and found pony* ill. by author. Feiwel & Friends, 2011. ISBN 978-0-312-59259-2 Subj: Animals – horses, ponies. Character traits – kindness to animals. Circus.

Dodd, Emma. *Always* ill. by author. Candlewick/Templar, 2014. ISBN 978-076367544-8 Subj: Animals – elephants. Emotions – love. Rhyming text.

Best bear ill. by author. Good Books, 2008. ISBN 978-1-56148-638-0 Subj: Bedtime. Rhyming text. Toys – bears.

Cinderelephant ill. by author. Scholastic, 2013. ISBN 978-0-545-53285-3 Subj: Animals – elephants. Folk & fairy tales. Royalty – princes.

Dog's ABC ill. by author. Dutton, 2000. ISBN 978-0-525-46837-0 Subj: ABC books. Animals – dogs.

Dog's colorful day ill. by author. Dutton, 2001. ISBN 978-0-525-46528-7 Subj: Animals – dogs. Concepts – color. Counting, numbers.

Dog's noisy day ill. by author. Dutton, 2003. ISBN 978-0-525-47015-1 Subj: Animals. Animals – dogs. Farms. Noise, sounds.

The entertainer ill. by author. little bee, 2015. ISBN 978-149980078-4 Subj: Animals – bears. Birthdays. Parties. Rhyming text.

Everything ill. by author. Candlewick/Templar, 2015. ISBN 978-076367128-0 Subj: Animals – koalas. Emotions – love. Family life – mothers. Rhyming text.

Forever ill. by author. Candlewick, 2013. ISBN 978-0-7636-7132-7 Subj: Animals – polar bears. Emotions – love. Family life – mothers.

Foxy ill. by author. HarperCollins, 2012. ISBN 978-0-06-201419-1 Subj: Animals – foxes. Behavior – mistakes. Behavior – worrying. Magic. School – first day.

Foxy in love ill. by author. HarperCollins, 2013. ISBN 978-0-06-201422-1 Subj: Animals – foxes. Emotions – love. Holidays – Valentine's Day. Magic.

Happy ill. by author. Candlewick/Nosy Crow, 2015. ISBN 978-076368008-4 Subj: Birds – owls. Emotions – love. Family life – mothers. Rhyming text.

I am small ill. by author. Scholastic, 2011. ISBN 978-0-545-35370-0 Subj: Birds – penguins. Character traits – smallness. Family life.

I don't want a cool cat! ill. by author. Little, Brown, 2010. ISBN 978-0-316-03674-0 Subj: Animals – cats. Rhyming text.

I don't want a posh dog ill. by author. Little, Brown, 2009. ISBN 978-0-316-03390-9 Subj: Animals – dogs. Character traits – assertiveness. Pets. Rhyming text.

I love bugs! ill. by author. Holiday House, 2010. ISBN 978-0-8234-2280-7 Subj: Insects. Rhyming text. Spiders.

Just like you ill. by author. Dutton, 2008. ISBN 978-0-525-47933-8 Subj: Animals – bears. Family life – fathers. Rhyming text.

Love ill. by author. Nosy Crow, 2016. ISBN 978-076368941-4 Subj: Animals – rabbits. Emotions – love. Rhyming text.

Meow said the cow ill. by author. Scholastic, 2011. ISBN 978-0-545-31861-7 Subj: Animals. Farms. Magic. Noise, sounds.

More and more ill. by author. Candlewick/Templar, 2014. ISBN 978-076367543-1 Subj: Animals – monkeys. Emotions – love. Rhyming text.

No matter what ill. by author. Dutton, 2008. ISBN 978-0-525-47932-1 Subj: Animals – elephants. Emotions – love. Family life – mothers. Rhyming text.

What pet to get? ill. by author. Scholastic, 2008. ISBN 978-0-545-03570-5 Subj: Family life. Imagination. Pets.

When I grow up ill. by author. Candlewick/Templar, 2015. ISBN 978-076367985-9 Subj: Animals – bears. Behavior – growing up. Rhyming text.

Dodd, Lynley. *A dragon in a wagon* ill. by author. G. Stevens, 2000. ISBN 978-0-8368-2687-6 Subj: Animals – dogs. Imagination. Rhyming text. Toys – wagons.

Find me a tiger ill. by author. G. Stevens, 2001. ISBN 978-0-8368-2781-1 Subj: Animals. Behavior – hiding. Rhyming text.

Dodds, Dayle Ann. *Hello, sun!* ill. by Sachiko Yoshikawa. Penguin, 2005. ISBN 978-0-8037-2895-0 Subj: Clothing. Rhyming text. Weather.

The Kettles get new clothes ill. by Jill McElmurry. Candlewick, 2002. ISBN 978-0-7636-1091-3 Subj: Animals – dogs. Clothing. Shopping.

Pet wash ill. by Tor Freeman. Candlewick, 2001. ISBN 978-0-7636-0989-4 Subj: Activities – bathing. Animals. Pets. Rhyming text.

The prince won't go to bed ill. by Kyrsten Brooker. Farrar, 2007. ISBN 978-0-374-36108-2 Subj: Bedtime. Behavior – misbehavior. Rhyming text. Royalty – princes.

Teacher's pets ill. by Marylin Hafner. Candlewick, 2006. ISBN 978-0-7636-2252-7 Subj: Careers – teachers. Pets. School.

Where's Pup? ill. by Pierre Pratt. Dial, 2003. ISBN 978-0-8037-2744-1 Subj: Animals – dogs. Circus. Clowns, jesters. Format, unusual – toy & movable books. Rhyming text.

Dodgson, Charles Lutwidge *see* Carroll, Lewis

Doepker, David. *Animal babies* ill. with photos. Sterling, 2004. ISBN 978-1-4027-1717-8 Subj: Animals – babies. Format, unusual – board books.

Farm babies ill. with photos. Sterling, 2004. ISBN 978-1-4027-1714-7 Subj: Animals – babies. Farms. Format, unusual – board books. Noise, sounds.

Doerrfeld, Cori. *Maggie and Wendel: imagine everything!* ill. by author. Simon & Schuster, 2016. ISBN 978-148143974-9 Subj: Activities – playing. Animals – elephants. Family life – brothers & sisters. Imagination.

Penny loves pink ill. by author. Little, Brown, 2011. ISBN 978-0-316-05458-4 Subj: Babies, toddlers. Concepts – color. Family life – brothers & sisters. Family life – new sibling.

Doi, Kaya. *Chirri and Chirra* ill. by author. Enchanted Lion, 2016. ISBN 978-159270199-5 Subj: Forest, woods. Nature. Sports – bicycling.

Dolan, Elys. *The mystery of the haunted farm* ill. by author. Candlewick/Nosy Crow, 2016. ISBN 978-076368658-1 Subj: Farms. Monsters. Mystery stories.

Nuts in space ill. by author. Candlewick, 2015. ISBN 978-076367609-4 Subj: Aliens. Food. Humorous stories. Space & space ships.

Weasels ill. by author. Candlewick, 2014. ISBN 978-076367100-6 Subj: Animals – weasels. Humorous stories.

Dolenz, Micky. *Gakky Two-Feet* ill. by David Clark. Penguin, 2006. ISBN 978-0-399-24468-1 Subj: Behavior – bullying, teasing. Character traits – individuality. Prehistory.

Dollinger, Renate. *The rabbi who flew* ill. by author. Booksmythe, 2001. ISBN 978-0-945585-20-6 Subj: Activities – flying. Careers – clergy. Careers – shoemakers. Jewish culture.

Domanska, Janina. *If all the seas were one sea* ill. by author. Macmillan, 1971. ISBN 978-0-02-732540-9 Subj: Caldecott award honor books. Nursery rhymes. Sea & seashore.

Domeniconi, David. *M is for masterpiece: an art alphabet* ill. by Will Bullas. Sleeping Bear, 2006. ISBN 978-1-58536-276-9 Subj: ABC books. Art.

Dominguez, Angela. *How do you say? / ¿Cómo se dice?* ill. by author. Henry Holt, 2016. ISBN 978-162779496-1 Subj: Animals – giraffes. Foreign languages. Friendship.

Knit together ill. by author. Dial, 2015. ISBN 978-080374099-0 Subj: Activities – drawing. Activities – knitting. Character traits – cooperation. Family life – daughters. Family life – mothers.

Let's go, Hugo! ill. by author. Dial, 2013. ISBN 978-0-8037-3864-5 Subj: Activities – flying. Birds. Emotions – fear. Foreign lands – France.

Maria had a little llama/Maria tenia una llama pequena ill. by author. Henry Holt, 2013. ISBN 978-0-8050-9333-9 Subj: Animals – llamas. Foreign lands – Peru. Foreign languages. Rhyming text. School. Songs.

Sing, don't cry ill. by author. Henry Holt, 2017. ISBN 978-162779839-6 Subj: Activities – singing. Activities – storytelling. Careers – musicians. Character traits – optimism. Family life – grandfathers. Foreign lands – Mexico. Music.

Domney, Alexis. *Splish, splat!* ill. by Alice Crawford. Second Story, 2011. ISBN 978-1-897187-88-3 Subj: Careers – artists. Disabilities – deafness. Sign language.

Donahue, Shari Faden. *The zebra-striped whale with the polka-dot tail* ill. by author. Arimax, 2001. ISBN 978-0-9634287-3-8 Subj: Animals. Imagination. Rhyming text.

Donaldson, Julia. *Charlie Cook's favorite book* ill. by Axel Scheffler. Penguin, 2006. ISBN 978-0-8037-3142-4 Subj: Books, reading. Rhyming text.

The fish who cried wolf ill. by Axel Scheffler. Scholastic, 2008. ISBN 978-0-439-92825-0 Subj: Activities – storytelling. Fish. Imagination. Rhyming text.

The Giant Jumperee ill. by Helen Oxenbury. Dial, 2017. ISBN 978-073522797-2 Subj: Animals. Cumulative tales. Frogs & toads. Rhyming text.

A gold star for Zog ill. by Axel Scheffler. Scholastic, 2012. ISBN 978-0-545-41724-2 Subj: Dragons. Knights. Rhyming text. Royalty – princesses. School.

The Highway Rat ill. by Axel Scheffler. Scholastic, 2013. ISBN 978-0-545-47758-1 Subj: Animals – rats. Crime. Rhyming text.

One mole digging a hole ill. by Nick Sharratt. Macmillan UK, 2010. ISBN 978-0-230-70647-7 Subj: Counting, numbers. Gardens, gardening. Rhyming text.

One Ted falls out of bed ill. by Anna Currey. Henry Holt, 2006. ISBN 978-0-8050-7787-2 Subj: Bedtime. Counting, numbers. Toys. Toys – bears.

Room on the broom ill. by Axel Scheffler. Dial, 2001. ISBN 978-0-8037-2657-4 Subj: Animals. Behavior – lost & found possessions. Dragons. Rhyming text. Witches.

Stick Man ill. by Axel Scheffler. Scholastic, 2009. ISBN 978-0-545-15761-2 Subj: Holidays – Christmas. Rhyming text. Santa Claus. Trees.

Superworm ill. by Axel Scheffler. Scholastic, 2014. ISBN 978-054559176-8 Subj: Animals – worms. Character traits – helpfulness. Insects. Rhyming text.

Tabby McTat, the musical cat ill. by Axel Scheffler. Scholastic, 2012. ISBN 978-0-545-45168-0 Subj: Animals – cats. Music. Rhyming text.

Tyrannosaurus Drip ill. by David Roberts. Feiwel & Friends, 2008. ISBN 978-0-312-37747-2 Subj: Dinosaurs. Humorous stories. Rhyming text. Self-concept.

What the ladybug heard ill. by Lydia Monks. Henry Holt, 2010. ISBN 978-0-8050-9028-4 Subj: Animals. Farms. Insects – ladybugs. Noise, sounds. Rhyming text.

Where's my mom? ill. by Axel Scheffler. Dial, 2008. ISBN 978-0-8037-3228-5 Subj: Animals. Animals – monkeys. Family life – mothers. Insects – butterflies, caterpillars. Rhyming text.

Zog and the flying doctors ill. by Axel Scheffler. Scholastic/Arthur A. Levine, 2017. ISBN 978-133813417-9 Subj: Careers – doctors. Dragons. Gender roles. Rhyming text. Royalty – princesses.

Doner, Kim. *On a road in Africa* ill. by author. Tricycle, 2008. ISBN 978-1-58246-230-1 Subj: Animals. Foreign lands – Kenya. Rhyming text.

Donnelly, Jennifer. *Humble pie* ill. by Stephen Gammell. Atheneum, 2002. ISBN 978-0-689-84435-5 Subj: Behavior. Behavior – greed. Folk & fairy tales. Food.

Donnelly, Liza. *Dinosaurs' Halloween* ill. by author. Scholastic, 1987. ISBN 978-0-590-41025-0 Subj: Cities, towns. Dinosaurs. Holidays – Halloween. Prehistory.

A hippo in our yard ill. by author. Holiday House, 2016. ISBN 978-082343564-7 Subj: Animals. Behavior – indifference.

Donnio, Sylviane. *I'd really like to eat a child* ill. by Dorothée de Monfreid. Random House, 2007. ISBN 978-0-375-83761-6 Subj: Food. Reptiles – alligators, crocodiles.

Donofrio, Beverly. *Mary and the mouse, the mouse and Mary* ill. by Barbara McClintock. Random House, 2007. ISBN 978-0-375-83609-1 Subj: Animals – mice. Friendship.

Where's Mommy? ill. by Barbara McClintock. Random House, 2014. ISBN 978-037584423-2 Subj: Animals – mice. Friendship.

Donohue, Dorothy. *Veggie soup* ill. by author. Winslow, 2000. ISBN 978-1-890817-21-3 Subj: Activities – baking, cooking. Animals. Animals – rabbits. Food. Friendship.

Donohue, Moira Rose. *Alfie the apostrophe* ill. by JoAnn Adinolfi. Albert Whitman, 2006. ISBN 978-0-8075-0255-6 Subj: Language.

Donovan, Gail. *The copycat fish* ill. by David Austin Clar. Night Sky, 2001. ISBN 978-1-59014-018-5 Subj: Fish. Format, unusual. School.

A fishy story ill. by David Austin Clar. Night Sky, 2001. ISBN 978-1-59014-019-2 Subj: Character traits – honesty. Fish. Format, unusual. School.

Hidden treasures ill. by David Austin Clar. Night Sky, 2001. ISBN 978-1-59014-021-5 Subj: Fish. School.

Lost at sea ill. by David Austin Clar. Night Sky, 2001. ISBN 978-1-59014-020-8 Subj: Behavior – lost. Fish. Format, unusual. School.

Donovan, Sandy. *Bob the Alien discovers the Dewey Decimal System* ill. by Martin Haake. Picture Window, 2010. ISBN 978-1-4048-5757-5 Subj: Aliens. Books, reading.

Bored Bella learns about fiction and nonfiction ill. by Leeza Hernandez. Picture Window, 2010. ISBN 978-1-4048-5758-2 Subj: Behavior – boredom. Books, reading.

Karl and Carolina uncover the parts of a book ill. by Michael Mullan. Picture Window, 2010. ISBN 978-1-4048-5760-5 Subj: Books, reading.

Pingpong Perry experiences how a book is made ill. by Jamey Christoph. Picture Window, 2010. ISBN 978-1-4048-5759-9 Subj: Books, reading.

Doodler, Todd H. *Bear in long underwear* ill. by author. Blue Apple, 2011. ISBN 978-1-60905-100-6 Subj: Animals – bears. Seasons – winter. Snowmen.

Veggies with wedgies ill. by author. Simon & Schuster, 2014. ISBN 978-144249340-7 Subj: Clothing – underwear. Farms. Food. Humorous stories.

The zoo I drew ill. by author. Random House, 2009. ISBN 978-0-375-85201-5 Subj: ABC books. Rhyming text. Zoos.

Dooley, Norah. *Everybody brings noodles* ill. by Peter J. Thornton. Carolrhoda, 2002. ISBN 978-0-87614-455-8 Subj: Communities, neighborhoods. Ethnic groups in the U.S. Food. Foreign lands. Parties.

Everybody cooks rice ill. by Peter J. Thornton. Carolrhoda, 1991. ISBN 978-0-87614-412-1 Subj: Ethnic groups in the U.S. Family life. Food.

Everybody serves soup ill. by Peter J. Thornton. Carolrhoda, 2000. ISBN 978-1-57505-422-3 Subj: Activities – baking, cooking. Ethnic groups in the U.S. Food. Gifts. Weather – snow.

Dooley, Virginia. *Tubes in my ears: my trip to the hospital* ill. by Miriam Katin. Mondo, 1996. ISBN 978-1-57255-118-3 Subj: Hospitals. Illness.

Doolittle, Bev. *Reading the wild* ill. by Elise Maclay. Greenwich Workshop, 2001. ISBN 978-0-86713-061-4 Subj: Animals. Birds. Nature.

Doray, Malika. *One more Wednesday* ill. by author. Greenwillow, 2001. ISBN 978-0-06-029590-5 Subj: Animals. Death. Emotions – grief. Family life – grandmothers. Memories, memory.

Doremus, Gaetan. *Bear despair* ill. by author. Enchanted Lion, 2012. ISBN 978-1-59270-125-4 Subj: Animals. Animals – bears. Toys – bears. Wordless.

Dorfman, Craig. *I knew you could!* ill. by Christina Ong. Platt, 2003. ISBN 978-0-448-43148-2 Subj: Rhyming text. Self-concept. Trains.

Dormer, Frank W. *Click!* ill. by Frank W. Dormer. Viking, 2016. ISBN 978-045147644-9 Subj: Animals – cats. Animals – dogs. Computers. Technology.

Firefighter Duckies! ill. by Frank W. Dormer. Atheneum, 2017. ISBN 978-148146090-3 Subj: Birds – ducks. Careers – firefighters. Character traits – helpfulness.

The obstinate pen ill. by author. Henry Holt, 2012. ISBN 978-0-8050-9295-0 Subj: Activities – drawing. Activities – writing. Character traits – stubbornness.

Socksquatch ill. by author. Henry Holt, 2010. ISBN 978-0-8050-8952-3 Subj: Clothing – socks. Monsters.

The sword in the stove ill. by Frank W. Dormer. Atheneum, 2016. ISBN 978-148143167-5 Subj: Behavior – lost. Humorous stories. Knights.

Dornbusch, Erica. *Finding Kate's shoes* ill. by author. Firefly, 2001. ISBN 978-1-55037-671-5 Subj: Behavior – lost & found possessions. Clothing – shoes. Family life – mothers. Imagination. Wordless.

Dorros, Alex. *Número uno* by Alex Dorros and Arthur Dorros ill. by Susan Guevara. Abrams, 2007. ISBN 978-0-8109-5764-0 Subj: Behavior – fighting, arguing. Character traits – cooperation. Contests. Foreign languages. Humorous stories.

Dorros, Arthur. *Abuela* ill. by Elisa Kleven. Dutton, 1991. ISBN 978-0-525-44750-4 Subj: Activities – flying. Cities, towns. Ethnic groups in the U.S. Family life – grandmothers. Foreign languages.

Abuelo ill. by Raúl Colón. HarperCollins, 2014. ISBN 978-006168627-6 Subj: Family life – grandfathers. Foreign lands – Argentina. Foreign languages.

Ant cities ill. by author. Crowell, 1987. ISBN 978-0-690-04570-3 Subj: Insects – ants. Science.

City chicken ill. by Henry Cole. HarperCollins, 2003. ISBN 978-0-06-028483-1 Subj: Animals. Birds – chickens, roosters. Cities, towns. Country. Humorous stories.

The fungus that ate my school ill. by David Catrow. Scholastic, 2000. ISBN 978-0-590-47704-8 Subj: School. Science.

Julio's magic ill. by Ann Grifalconi. HarperCollins, 2005. ISBN 978-0-06-029005-4 Subj: Activities – wood carving. Careers – woodcarvers. Contests. Foreign lands – Mexico. Friendship.

Mama and me ill. by Rudy Gutierrez. HarperCollins, 2011. ISBN 978-0-06-058160-2 Subj: Ethnic groups in the U.S. – Hispanic Americans. Family life – mothers. Foreign languages.

Número uno (Dorros, Alex)

Papa and me ill. by Rudy Gutierrez. HarperCollins, 2008. ISBN 978-0-06-058156-5 Subj: Ethnic groups in the U.S. – Hispanic Americans. Family life – fathers. Family life – sons. Foreign languages.

Radio Man / Don Radio: a story in English and Spanish. Text in English and Spanish. HarperCollins, 1993. ISBN 978-0-06-021548-4 Subj: Careers – migrant workers. Communication. Ethnic groups in the U.S. – Mexican Americans. Farms. Foreign languages. Radios.

Tonight is carnaval ill. with photos. Dutton, 1991. ISBN 978-0-525-44641-5 Subj: Fairs, festivals. Farms. Foreign lands – Peru.

When the pigs took over ill. by Diane Greenseid. Dutton, 2002. ISBN 978-0-525-42030-9 Subj: Animals – pigs. Animals – snails. Ethnic groups in the U.S. – Mexican Americans. Humorous stories. Restaurants.

Dotlich, Rebecca Kai. *All aboard!* ill. by Mike Lowery. Knopf, 2014. ISBN 978-038575420-0 Subj: Rhyming text. Trains.

A family like yours ill. by Tammie Lyon. Boyds Mills, 2002. ISBN 978-1-56397-916-3 Subj: Family life. Poetry.

In the spin of things ill. by Karen Dugan. Boyds Mills, 2003. ISBN 978-1-56397-145-7 Subj: Concepts – motion. Poetry.

The knowing book ill. by Matthew Cordell. Boyds Mills, 2016. ISBN 978-159078926-1 Subj: Animals – rabbits. Character traits – curiosity.

Mama loves ill. by Kathryn Brown. HarperCollins, 2004. ISBN 978-0-06-029408-3 Subj: Animals – pigs. Family life – mothers.

One day, the end: short, very short, shorter-than-ever stories ill. by Fred Koehler. Boyds Mills, 2015. ISBN 978-162091451-9 Subj: Activities – storytelling. Activities – writing. Books, reading.

Papa loves ill. by Kathryn Brown. HarperCollins, 2003. ISBN 978-0-06-029406-9 Subj: Animals – pigs. Family life – fathers.

Race car count ill. by Michael H. Slack. Henry Holt, 2015. ISBN 978-162779009-3 Subj: Automobiles. Counting, numbers. Rhyming text. Sports – racing.

What can a crane pick up? ill. by Mike Lowery. Knopf, 2012. ISBN 978-0-375-86726-2 Subj: Machines. Rhyming text.

What is a triangle? photos by Maria Ferrari. HarperCollins, 2000. ISBN 978-0-694-01392-0 Subj: Concepts – shape.

What is round? photos by Maria Ferrari. HarperCollins, 1999. ISBN 978-0-694-01208-4 Subj: Concepts – shape. Rhyming text.

What is science? ill. by Sachiko Yoshikawa. Henry Holt, 2006. ISBN 978-0-8050-7394-2 Subj: Poetry. Science.

What is square? photos by Maria Ferrari. HarperCollins, 1999. ISBN 978-0-694-01207-7 Subj: Concepts – shape. Rhyming text.

Doughty, Rebecca. *Oh no! Time to go! a book of goodbyes* ill. by author. Random House, 2009. ISBN 978-0-375-84981-7 Subj: Emotions. Family life. Rhyming text.

Douglas, Ann. *Before you were born* ill. by Eugenie Fernandes. Firefly, 2000. ISBN 978-1-894379-01-4 Subj: Babies, toddlers. Birth. Family life. Family life – mothers.

Douglas, Erin. *Get that pest!* ill. by Wong Herbert Yee. Harcourt, 2000. ISBN 978-0-15-202548-9 Subj: Careers – farmers. Crime. Eggs. Farms.

Douglas, Richardo Keens *see* Keens-Douglas, Richardo

Dowley, Tim. *The shepherds' tale* by Tim Dowley and Peter Wyart ill. by Martin Pierce. Kregel, 2002. ISBN 978-0-8254-7257-2 Subj: Format, unusual – toy & movable books. Holidays – Christmas. Religion – Nativity.

The wise men's tale by Tim Dowley and Peter Wyart ill. by Martin Pierce. Kregel, 2002. ISBN 978-0-8254-7256-5 Subj: Format, unusual – toy & movable books. Holidays – Christmas. Religion – Nativity.

Downard, Barry, reteller. *The Race of the Century* ill. by reteller. Simon & Schuster, 2008. ISBN 978-1-4169-2509-5 Subj: Animals – rabbits. Humorous stories. Reptiles – turtles, tortoises. Sports – racing.

Downes, Belinda. *Baby days: a quilt of rhymes and pictures* ill. by author. Candlewick, 2006. ISBN 978-0-7636-2786-7 Subj: Babies, toddlers. Poetry. Quilts. Songs.

Downey, Lisa. *The pirates of plagiarism* (Fox, Kathleen)

Downey, Lynn. *The flea's sneeze* ill. by Karla Firehammer. Henry Holt, 2000. ISBN 978-0-8050-6103-1 Subj: Animals. Farms. Insects – fleas. Rhyming text. Sleep.

Matilda's humdinger ill. by Tim Bowers. Random House, 2006. ISBN 978-0-375-92403-3 Subj: Activities – storytelling. Animals. Animals – cats. Careers – waiters, waitresses. Restaurants.

The tattletale ill. by Pamela Paparone. Henry Holt, 2006. ISBN 978-0-8050-7152-8 Subj: Animals – pigs. Behavior – gossip, rumors. Family life – brothers & sisters.

This is the earth that God made ill. by Benrei Huang. Augsburg Fortress, 2000. ISBN 978-0-8066-3960-4 Subj: Creation. Cumulative tales. Religion. Rhyming text.

Downie, Mary Alice. *A pioneer ABC* ill. by Mary Jane Gerber. Tundra, 2005. ISBN 978-0-88776-688-6 Subj: ABC books. Foreign lands – Canada.

Downing, Johnette. *Amazon alphabet* ill. by author. Pelican, 2011. ISBN 978-1-58980-879-9 Subj: ABC books. Foreign lands – South America. Jungle. Rivers.

Down in Louisiana: traditional song ill. by Deborah Ousley Kadair. Pelican, 2007. ISBN 978-1-58980-451-7 Subj: Animals. Counting, numbers. Songs. Swamps.

There was an old lady who swallowed some bugs ill. by adapter. Pelican, 2010. ISBN 978-1-58980-858-4 Subj: Cumulative tales. Folk & fairy tales. Frogs & toads. Insects. Songs.

Today is Monday in Louisiana ill. by Deborah Ousley Kadair. Pelican, 2006. ISBN 978-1-58980-406-7 Subj: Days of the week, months of the year. Food. Songs.

Downing, Julie. *No hugs till Saturday* ill. by author. Clarion, 2008. ISBN 978-0-618-91078-6 Subj: Days of the week, months of the year. Dragons. Family life. Hugging.

Downs, Mike. *Pig giggles and rabbit rhymes* ill. by David Sheldon. Chronicle, 2002. ISBN 978-0-8118-3114-7 Subj: Animals. Humorous stories. Riddles & jokes.

You see a circus, I see — ill. by Anik McGrory. Charlesbridge, 2005. ISBN 978-1-58089-097-7 Subj: Circus. Family life. Rhyming text.

Dowson, Nick. *Tigress* ill. by Jane Chapman. Candlewick, 2004. ISBN 978-0-7636-2325-8 Subj: Animals – babies. Animals – tigers. Behavior – growing up. Family life – mothers.

Tracks of a panda ill. by Yu Rong. Candlewick, 2007. ISBN 978-0-7636-3146-8 Subj: Animals – pandas.

Doyen, Denise. *Once upon a twice* ill. by Barry Moser. Random House, 2009. ISBN 978-0-375-85612-9 Subj: Animals – mice. Character traits – bravery. Night. Swamps.

Doyle, Charlotte Lackner. *The bouncing, dancing, galloping ABC* ill. by Julia Gorton. Penguin, 2006. ISBN 978-0-399-23778-2 Subj: ABC books. Activities – playing. Rhyming text.

Doyle, Eugenie. *Sleep tight farm: a farm prepares for winter* ill. by Becca Stadtlander. Chronicle, 2016. ISBN 978-145212901-3 Subj: Farms. Seasons – winter.

Doyle, Malachy. *Baby see, baby do!* ill. by Britta Teckentrup. Putnam, 2002. ISBN 978-0-399-23728-7 Subj: Animals – babies. Babies, toddlers. Format, unusual – toy & movable books.

Cow ill. by Angelo Rinaldi. Margaret K. McElderry, 2002. ISBN 978-0-689-84462-1 Subj: Animals – bulls, cows. Farms.

Get happy ill. by Caroline Uff. Walker, 2011. ISBN 978-0-8027-2271-3 Subj: Behavior. Emotions – happiness. Rhyming text.

Horse ill. by Angelo Rinaldi. Simon & Schuster, 2008. ISBN 978-1-4169-2467-8 Subj: Animals – horses, ponies. Farms.

Hungry! hungry! hungry! ill. by Paul Hess. Peachtree, 2000. ISBN 978-1-56145-241-5 Subj: Food. Monsters. Mythical creatures – goblins.

Sleepy Pendoodle ill. by Julie Vivas. Candlewick, 2002. ISBN 978-0-7636-1561-1 Subj: Animals – dogs. Pets.

Splash, Joshua, splash! ill. by Ken Wilson-Max. Bloomsbury, 2004. ISBN 978-1-58234-837-7 Subj: Family life – grandmothers. Water.

Storm cats ill. by Stuart Trotter. Margaret K. McElderry, 2002. ISBN 978-0-689-84464-5 Subj: Animals – cats. Friendship. Rhyming text. Weather – storms.

Too noisy! ill. by Ed Vere. Candlewick, 2012. ISBN 978-0-7636-6226-4 Subj: Behavior – lost. Behavior – solitude. Family life. Noise, sounds.

Well, a crocodile can! ill. by Britta Teckentrup. Millbrook, 2000. ISBN 978-0-7613-1032-7 Subj: Activities. Animals. Behavior. Format, unusual – toy & movable books.

Drachman, Eric. *Leo the lightning bug* ill. by James Muscarello. Kidwick, 2001. ISBN 978-0-9703809-0-6 Subj: Insects – fireflies. Self-concept.

Dragonwagon, Crescent. *All the awake animals are almost asleep* ill. by David McPhail. Little, Brown, 2012. ISBN 978-0-316-07045-4 Subj: ABC books. Animals. Bedtime. Rhyming text.

Drawson, Blair. *All along the river* ill. by author. Douglas & McIntyre, 2003. ISBN 978-0-88899-546-9 Subj: Canoes & canoeing. Family life – grandfathers. Imagination. Rivers.

Dray, Philip. *Yours for justice, Ida B. Wells: the daring life of a crusading journalist* ill. by Stephen Alcorn. Peachtree, 2008. ISBN 978-1-56145-417-4 Subj: Careers – journalists. Ethnic groups in the U.S. – African Americans. Gender roles. Prejudice. U.S. history.

Drehsen, Britta. *Flip-o-storic* ill. by Sara Ball. Abbeville, 2011. ISBN 978-0-7892-1099-9 Subj: Dinosaurs. Format, unusual – toy & movable books.

Drescher, Henrik. *Hubert the Pudge: a vegetarian tale* ill. by author. Candlewick, 2006. ISBN 978-0-7636-1992-3 Subj: Food. Health & fitness.

Driscoll, Amanda. *Duncan the story dragon* ill. by author. Knopf, 2015. ISBN 978-038575507-8 Subj: Books, reading. Dragons. Problem solving.

Wally does not want a haircut ill. by author. Knopf, 2016. ISBN 978-055353579-2 Subj: Animals – sheep. Hair.

Druce, Arden. *Halloween night* ill. by David Wenzel. Rising Moon, 2001. ISBN 978-0-87358-797-6

Subj: Holidays – Halloween. Rhyming text. Riddles & jokes.

Drummond, Allan. *Casey Jones* ill. by author. Farrar, 2001. ISBN 978-0-374-31175-9 Subj: Careers – engineers. Rhyming text. Tall tales. Trains.

Energy island: how one community harnessed the wind and changed their world ill. by author. Farrar, 2011. ISBN 978-0-374-32184-0 Subj: Foreign lands – Denmark. Science. Weather – wind.

Green city: how one community survived a tornado and rebuilt for a sustainable future ill. by author. Farrar, 2016. ISBN 978-037437999-5 Subj: Behavior – resourcefulness. Behavior – seeking better things. Buildings. Character traits – perseverance. Ecology. Weather – tornadoes.

Liberty ill. by author. Farrar, 2002. ISBN 978-0-374-34385-9 Subj: Character traits – freedom. U.S. history.

Tin Lizzie ill. by author. Farrar, 2008. ISBN 978-0-374-32000-3 Subj: Automobiles. Family life – grandfathers.

Drummond, Ree. *Charlie and the new baby* ill. by Diane deGroat. HarperCollins, 2014. ISBN 978-006229750-1 Subj: Animals – bulls, cows. Animals – dogs. Careers – ranchers. Emotions – envy, jealousy.

Charlie goes to school ill. by Diane deGroat. HarperCollins, 2013. ISBN 978-0-06-221920-6 Subj: Animals. Animals – dogs. School.

Charlie the ranch dog ill. by Diane deGroat. HarperCollins, 2011. ISBN 978-0-06-199655-9 Subj: Animals – dogs. Careers – ranchers.

Duble, Kathleen Benner. *Pilot mom* ill. by Alan Marks. Charlesbridge, 2003. ISBN 978-1-57091-555-0 Subj: Careers – airplane pilots. Careers – military. Family life – daughters. Family life – mothers.

Dubois, Muriel L. *Out and about at the fire station* ill. by Anne McMullen. Picture Window, 2003. ISBN 978-1-4048-0039-7 Subj: Careers – firefighters. Fire. School – field trips.

Du Bois, William Pène. *Bear party* ill. by author. Viking, 1951. ISBN 978-0-14-050793-5 Subj: Animals. Animals – koalas. Caldecott award honor books. Emotions – anger. Parties.

Lion ill. by author. Viking, 1957. ISBN 978-0-670-42950-9 Subj: Animals – lions. Caldecott award honor books.

Dubosarsky, Ursula. *Rex* ill. by David Mackintosh. Macmillan, 2006. ISBN 978-1-59643-186-7 Subj: Activities – writing. Imagination. Pets. Reptiles – chameleons. School.

The terrible plop ill. by Andrew Joyner. Farrar, 2009. ISBN 978-0-374-37428-0 Subj: Animals – rabbits. Behavior – mistakes. Emotions – fear. Rhyming text.

Dubuc, Marianne. *Animal masquerade* ill. by author. Kids Can, 2012. ISBN 978-1-55453-782-2 Subj: Animals. Fairs, festivals.

The animals' ark ill. by author. Kids Can, 2016. ISBN 978-177138623-4 Subj: Animals. Behavior – boredom. Boats, ships. Character traits – cooperation. Religion – Noah. Weather – floods. Weather – rain.

The lion and the bird ill. by author. Enchanted Lion, 2014. ISBN 978-159270151-3 Subj: Animals – lions. Birds. Character traits – kindness to animals. Friendship.

Lucy and company ill. by author. Kids Can, 2016. ISBN 978-177138662-3 Subj: Activities – picnicking. Animals. Friendship.

Mr. Postmouse takes a trip ill. by author. Kids Can, 2017. ISBN 978-177138354-7 Subj: Activities – vacationing. Animals – mice. Careers – postal workers.

Mr. Postmouse's rounds ill. by author. Kids Can, 2015. ISBN 978-177138572-5 Subj: Animals – mice. Careers – postal workers.

DuBurke, Randy. *The moon ring* ill. by author. Chronicle, 2002. ISBN 978-0-8118-3487-2 Subj: Ethnic groups in the U.S. – African Americans. Family life – grandmothers. Magic. Moon.

Dudás, Gergely. *Bear's merry book of hidden things* ill. by author. HarperCollins, 2017. ISBN 978-006257078-9 Subj: Animals – bears. Holidays – Christmas. Picture puzzles.

Duddle, Jonny. *Gigantosaurus* ill. by author. Candlewick, 2014. ISBN 978-076367131-0 Subj: Behavior – lying. Dinosaurs. Rhyming text.

The king of space: soon the whole universe will know my name! ill. by author. Candlewick, 2013. ISBN 978-0-7636-6435-0 Subj: Robots. Space & space ships.

The pirate cruncher ill. by author. Candlewick, 2010. ISBN 978-0-7636-4876-3 Subj: Mythical creatures. Pirates. Rhyming text.

The pirates next door: starring the Jolley-Rogers ill. by author. Candlewick, 2012. ISBN 978-0-7636-5842-7 Subj: Pirates. Rhyming text.

Dudley, Rebecca. *Hank finds an egg* ill. by author. Peter Pauper, 2013. ISBN 978-1-4413-1158-0 Subj: Animals. Birds – hummingbirds. Character traits – kindness. Character traits – persistence. Eggs. Wordless.

Hank has a dream ill. by author. Peter Pauper, 2014. ISBN 978-144131572-4 Subj: Activities – flying. Dreams.

Duffield, Katy. *Aliens get the sniffles too! ahhh-choo!* ill. by K. G. Campbell. Candlewick, 2017. ISBN 978-076366502-9 Subj: Aliens. Illness – cold (disease).

Farmer McPeepers and his missing milk cows ill. by Steve Gray. Rising Moon, 2003. ISBN 978-0-87358-825-6 Subj: Animals – bulls, cows. Careers – farmers. Farms. Glasses. Humorous stories.

Dugan, Joanne. *ABC NYC: a book about seeing New York City* photos by author. Abrams, 2005. ISBN 978-0-8109-5854-8 Subj: ABC books. Cities, towns.

Duke, Kate. *In the rainforest* ill. by author. Harper-Collins, 2014. ISBN 978-006028259-2 Subj: Animals. Jungle. Plants.

One guinea pig is not enough ill. by author. Dutton, 1998. ISBN 978-0-525-45918-7 Subj: Activities – playing. Animals – guinea pigs. Counting, numbers.

Ready for pumpkins ill. by author. Knopf, 2012. ISBN 978-0-375-87068-2 Subj: Animals – guinea pigs. Gardens, gardening. Pets. Plants. School.

The tale of Pip and Squeak ill. by author. Penguin, 2007. ISBN 978-0-525-47777-8 Subj: Animals – mice. Family life – brothers & sisters. Sibling rivalry.

Twenty is too many ill. by author. Dutton, 2000. ISBN 978-0-525-42026-2 Subj: Animals – guinea pigs. Boats, ships. Counting, numbers.

Duke, Shirley Smith. *No bows!* ill. by Jenny Mattheson. Peachtree, 2006. ISBN 978-1-56145-356-6 Subj: Character traits – appearance. Character traits – individuality.

Dumont, Jean-François. *The chickens build a wall* ill. by author. Eerdmans, 2013. ISBN 978-0-8028-5422-3 Subj: Animals – hedgehogs. Birds – chickens, roosters. Character traits – being different.

The geese march in step ill. by author. Eerdmans, 2014. ISBN 978-080285443-8 Subj: Birds – geese. Character traits – being different. Character traits – individuality. Self-concept.

The sheep go on strike ill. by author. Eerdmans, 2014. ISBN 978-080285470-4 Subj: Animals – sheep. Character traits – compromising. Farms.

Dunbar, Joyce. *The monster who ate darkness* ill. by Jimmy Liao. Candlewick, 2008. ISBN 978-0-7636-3859-7 Subj: Bedtime. Emotions – fear. Monsters. Night.

Pat-a-cake baby ill. by Polly Dunbar. Candlewick, 2015. ISBN 978-076367577-6 Subj: Activities – baking, cooking. Babies, toddlers. Rhyming text.

Shoe baby ill. by Polly Dunbar. Candlewick, 2005. ISBN 978-0-7636-2779-9 Subj: Activities – traveling. Babies, toddlers. Clothing – shoes. Rhyming text.

The very small ill. by Debi Gliori. Harcourt, 2000. ISBN 978-0-15-202346-1 Subj: Animals – bears. Behavior – lost. Behavior – sharing. Concepts – size.

Where's my sock? ill. by Sanja Rescek. Scholastic, 2006. ISBN 978-0-439-74831-5 Subj: Behavior – lost & found possessions. Clothing – socks.

Dunbar, Polly. *Arthur's dream boat* ill. by author. Candlewick, 2012. ISBN 978-0-7636-5867-0 Subj: Boats, ships. Character traits – appearance. Dreams.

Dog Blue ill. by author. Candlewick, 2004. ISBN 978-0-7636-2476-7 Subj: Animals – dogs. Concepts – color. Imagination.

Flyaway Katie ill. by author. Candlewick, 2004. ISBN 978-0-7636-2366-1 Subj: Concepts – color. Emotions. Imagination.

Happy Hector ill. by author. Candlewick, 2008. ISBN 978-0-7636-4110-8 Subj: Animals – pigs. Behavior – sharing. Friendship.

Hello Tilly ill. by author. Candlewick, 2008. ISBN 978-0-7636-4109-2 Subj: Animals. Friendship.

Penguin ill. by author. Candlewick, 2007. ISBN 978-0-7636-3404-9 Subj: Birds – penguins. Toys.

Pingüino / penguin ill. by author. Serres, 2008. ISBN 978-84-79-01859-7 Subj: Birds – penguins. Foreign languages. Toys.

Pretty Pru ill. by author. Candlewick, 2009. ISBN 978-0-7636-4272-3 Subj: Animals. Character traits – appearance. Clothing – handbags, purses. Friendship.

Where's Tumpty? ill. by author. Candlewick, 2009. ISBN 978-0-7636-4273-0 Subj: Activities – playing. Animals. Animals – elephants. Behavior – hiding. Friendship.

Duncan, Alice Faye. *Honey baby sugar child* ill. by Susan Keeter. Simon & Schuster, 2005. ISBN 978-0-689-84678-6 Subj: Emotions – love. Ethnic groups in the U.S. – African Americans. Family life – mothers.

Duncan, Lois. *I walk at night* ill. by Steve Johnson and Lou Fancher. Viking, 2000. ISBN 978-0-670-87513-9 Subj: Activities – walking. Animals – cats. Night. Rhyming text.

Song of the circus ill. by Meg Cundiff. Philomel, 2002. ISBN 978-0-399-23397-5 Subj: Animals – tigers. Character traits – bravery. Circus. Rhyming text.

Dungy, Tony. *You can do it!* ill. by Amy Bates. Simon & Schuster, 2008. ISBN 978-1-4169-5461-3 Subj: Behavior – growing up. Careers – dentists. Character traits – ambition. Ethnic groups in the U.S. – African Americans. Family life. Religion.

Dunklee, Annika. *My name is Elizabeth!* ill. by Matthew Forsythe. Kids Can, 2011. ISBN 978-1-55453-560-6 Subj: Character traits – assertiveness. Names.

Dunlap, Cirocco. *This book will not be fun* ill. by Olivier Tallec. Random House, 2017. ISBN 978-039955061-4 Subj: Activities – dancing. Animals – mice. Books, reading.

Dunlap, Julie. *Louisa May and Mr. Thoreau's flute* by Julie Dunlap and Marybeth Lorbiecki ill. by Mary Azarian. Dial, 2002. ISBN 978-0-8037-2470-9 Subj: Careers – writers. U.S. history.

Dunn, Jancee. *I'm afraid your teddy is in trouble today* ill. by Scott Nash. Candlewick, 2017. ISBN 978-076367537-0 Subj: Behavior – misbehavior. Careers – police officers. Parties. Toys – bears.

Dunn, Todd. *We go together* ill. by Miki Sakamoto. Sterling, 2007. ISBN 978-1-4027-3260-7 Subj: Concepts. Rhyming text.

Dunnick, Regan. *Sweet dreams, Douglas* ill. by author. Junior League of Houston, 2002. ISBN 978-0-9632421-3-6 Subj: Animals. Animals – dogs. Bedtime. Dreams. Imagination.

Dunning, Joan. *Seabird in the forest: the mystery of the marbled murrelet.* Boyds Mills, 2011. ISBN 978-1-59078-715-1 Subj: Birds. Sea & seashore.

Dunrea, Olivier. *Appearing tonight! Mary Heather Elizabeth Livingstone* ill. by author. Farrar, 2000. ISBN 978-0-374-30455-3 Subj: Careers – actors. Theater.

Bear Noel ill. by author. Farrar, 2000. ISBN 978-0-374-40001-9 Subj: Animals. Animals – bears. Cumulative tales. Holidays – Christmas.

A Christmas tree for Pyn ill. by author. Penguin, 2011. ISBN 978-0-399-24506-0 Subj: Family life – fathers. Gifts. Holidays – Christmas. Trees.

Gemma and Gus ill. by author. Houghton Mifflin Harcourt, 2015. ISBN 978-054786851-6 Subj: Birds – geese. Family life – brothers & sisters.

Gideon ill. by author. Houghton Mifflin, 2012. ISBN 978-0-618-43661-3 Subj: Activities – playing. Birds – geese. Farms. Sleep.

Gideon and Otto ill. by author. Houghton Mifflin, 2012. ISBN 978-0-618-43662-0 Subj: Behavior – lost & found possessions. Birds – geese. Toys.

Gossie's busy day: a first tab book ill. by author. Houghton, 2007. ISBN 978-0-618-82148-8 Subj: Birds – geese. Format, unusual – toy & movable books.

It's snowing ill. by author. Farrar, 2002. ISBN 978-0-374-39992-4 Subj: Babies, toddlers. Family life – mothers. Weather – snow.

Jasper and Joop ill. by author. Houghton Mifflin, 2013. ISBN 978-0-547-86762-5 Subj: Behavior – messy. Birds – geese. Character traits – cleanliness. Friendship.

Little cub ill. by author. Philomel, 2012. ISBN 978-0-399-24235-9 Subj: Animals – babies. Animals – bears. Emotions – fear. Emotions – loneliness.

Me and Annie McPhee ill. by Will Hillenbrand. Philomel, 2016. ISBN 978-039916808-6 Subj: Animals. Animals – monkeys. Counting, numbers. Cumulative tales. Rhyming text.

Merry Christmas, Ollie! ill. by author. Houghton, 2008. ISBN 978-0-618-53242-1 Subj: Birds – geese. Holidays – Christmas. Santa Claus.

Old Bear and his cub ill. by author. Penguin, 2010. ISBN 978-0-399-24507-7 Subj: Animals – bears. Emotions – love. Family life – fathers.

Ollie ill. by author. Houghton, 2003. ISBN 978-0-618-33928-0 Subj: Birds – geese. Character traits – patience, impatience. Eggs. Family life – new sibling.

Ollie the stomper ill. by author. Houghton, 2003. ISBN 978-0-618-33930-3 Subj: Birds – geese. Clothing – boots.

Ollie's Easter eggs ill. by author. Houghton Mifflin, 2010. ISBN 978-0-618-53243-8 Subj: Behavior – hiding things. Birds – geese. Eggs. Holidays – Easter.

Ollie's Halloween ill. by author. Harcourt, 2010. ISBN 978-0-618-53241-4 Subj: Birds – geese. Holidays – Halloween.

Peedie ill. by author. Houghton, 2004. ISBN 978-0-618-35652-2 Subj: Birds – geese. Clothing – hats. Memories, memory.

Dupasquier, Philippe. *1 2 3, follow me!* ill. by author. Candlewick, 2002. ISBN 978-0-7636-1797-4 Subj: Animals. Counting, numbers. Format, unusual – board books. Wordless.

Dupre, Kelly. *The raven's gift* ill. by author. Houghton, 2001. ISBN 978-0-618-01171-1 Subj: Activities – traveling. Birds – ravens. Foreign lands – Greenland.

Duquennoy, Jacques. *North Pole, South Pole* ill. by author. Raincoast, 2000. ISBN 978-1-55192-411-3 Subj: Birds – penguins. Foreign lands – Antarctic. Foreign lands – Arctic. Holidays – Christmas. Santa Claus.

Du Quette, Keith. *Little Monkey lost* ill. by author. Penguin, 2007. ISBN 978-0-399-24294-6 Subj: Animals – monkeys. Behavior – lost. Jungle.

They call me Woolly: what animal names can tell us ill. by author. Putnam, 2002. ISBN 978-0-399-23445-3 Subj: Animals. Language. Names.

Durand, Hallie. *Catch that cookie!* ill. by David Small. Dial, 2014. ISBN 978-052542835-0 Subj: Behavior – running away. Folk & fairy tales. School.

Mitchell goes bowling ill. by Tony Fucile. Candlewick, 2013. ISBN 978-0-7636-6049-9 Subj: Family life – fathers. Sports – bowling.

Mitchell's license ill. by Tony Fucile. Candlewick, 2011. ISBN 978-0-7636-4496-3 Subj: Activities – playing. Bedtime. Family life – fathers.

Durango, Julia. *Angels watching over me* ill. by Elisa Kleven. Simon & Schuster, 2007. ISBN 978-0-689-86252-6 Subj: Angels. Songs.

Cha-cha chimps ill. by Eleanor Taylor. Simon & Schuster, 2006. ISBN 978-0-689-86456-8 Subj: Activities – dancing. Animals – chimpanzees. Counting, numbers. Rhyming text.

Dream hop ill. by Jared D Lee. Simon & Schuster, 2005. ISBN 978-0-689-87163-4 Subj: Bedtime. Dreams. Nightmares. Sleep.

Go-go gorillas ill. by Eleanor Taylor. Simon & Schuster, 2010. ISBN 978-1-4169-3779-1 Subj: Animals – gorillas. Rhyming text. Transportation.

The one day house ill. by Bianca Diaz. Charlesbridge, 2017. ISBN 978-158089709-9 Subj: Character traits – helpfulness. Communities, neighborhoods. Homes, houses.

Pest fest ill. by Kurt Cyrus. Simon & Schuster, 2007. ISBN 978-0-689-85569-6 Subj: Contests. Insects.

Yum! yuck! a foldout book of people sounds (Park, Linda Sue)

Durant, Alan. *Big Bad Bunny* ill. by Guy Parker-Rees. Dutton, 2001. ISBN 978-0-525-46667-3 Subj: Animals – rabbits. Behavior – misbehavior. Crime.

Brown Bear gets in shape ill. by Annabel Hudson. Kingfisher, 2004. ISBN 978-0-7534-5797-9 Subj: Animals – bears. Animals – chimpanzees. Animals – rabbits.

Burger boy ill. by Mei Matsuoka. Houghton, 2006. ISBN 978-0-618-71466-7 Subj: Food. Humorous stories.

Dear tooth fairy ill. by Vanessa Cabban. Candlewick, 2003. ISBN 978-0-7636-2175-9 Subj: Fairies. Format, unusual – toy & movable books. Letters, cards. Teeth.

A dinosaur called Tiny ill. by Jo Simpson. HarperCollins, 2008. ISBN 978-0-06-136633-8 Subj: Character traits – smallness. Concepts – size. Dinosaurs.

I love you, little monkey ill. by Katharine McEwen. Simon & Schuster, 2007. ISBN 978-1-4169-2481-4 Subj: Animals – monkeys. Emotions – love.

Dutton, Sandra. *Dear Miss Perfect: a beast's guide to proper behavior* ill. by author. Houghton, 2007. ISBN 978-0-618-67717-7 Subj: Animals. Behavior. Etiquette.

Duval, Kathy. *A bear's year* ill. by Gerry Turley. Random House, 2015. ISBN 978-038537011-0 Subj: Animals – bears. Rhyming text. Seasons.

Take me to your BBQ ill. by Adam McCauley. Disney/Hyperion, 2013. ISBN 978-1-4231-2255-5 Subj: Activities – dancing. Aliens. Food. Rhyming text.

The Three Bears' Christmas ill. by Paul Meisel. Holiday House, 2005. ISBN 978-0-8234-1871-8 Subj: Animals – bears. Holidays – Christmas. Santa Claus.

The Three Bears' Halloween ill. by Paul Meisel. Holiday House, 2007. ISBN 978-0-8234-2032-2 Subj: Animals – bears. Holidays – Halloween.

Duvall, Deborah L. *The opossum's tale: a grandmother story* ill. by Murv Jacob. Univ. of New Mexico, 2005. ISBN 978-0-8263-3694-1 Subj: Anatomy – tails. Animals – possums. Folk & fairy tales. Indians of North America – Cherokee.

Duvall, John. *The great spruce* ill. by Rebecca Gibbon. Putnam, 2016. ISBN 978-039916084-4 Subj: Ecology. Family life – grandfathers. Holidays – Christmas. Trees.

Duvoisin, Roger Antoine. *Petunia* ill. by author. 50th anniversary ed. Knopf, 1977. ISBN 978-0-394-90865-6 Subj: Animals. Birds – geese. Books, reading. Character traits – pride. Farms. Friendship. Humorous stories.

Dwyer, Mindy. *Quilt of dreams* ill. by author. Alaska Northwest, 2000. ISBN 978-0-88240-522-3 Subj: Family life – grandmothers. Family life – mothers. Quilts.

Dyckman, Ame. *Boy + Bot* ill. by Dan Yaccarino. Knopf, 2012. ISBN 978-0-375-86756-9 Subj: Friendship. Robots.

Horrible Bear! ill. by Zachariah OHora. Little, Brown, 2016. ISBN 978-031628283-3 Subj: Accidents. Animals – bears. Behavior – forgiving. Behavior – misbehavior. Kites.

Read the book, lemmings! ill. by Zachariah OHora. Little, Brown, 2017. ISBN 978-031634348-0 Subj:

Animals – foxes. Animals – lemmings. Books, reading.

Tea party rules ill. by K. G. Campbell. Viking, 2013. ISBN 978-0-670-78501-8 Subj: Animals – bears. Etiquette. Parties.

Wolfie the bunny ill. by Zachariah OHora. Little, Brown, 2015. ISBN 978-031622614-1 Subj: Adoption. Animals – rabbits. Animals – wolves.

You don't want a unicorn! ill. by Liz Climo. Little, Brown, 2017. ISBN 978-031634347-3 Subj: Behavior – wishing. Mythical creatures – unicorns. Pets.

Dyer, Heather. *Tina and the penguin* ill. by Mireille Levert. Kids Can, 2002. ISBN 978-1-55074-947-2 Subj: Behavior – running away. Birds – penguins. Foreign lands – Antarctic. Zoos.

Dyer, Jane. *Little Brown Bear and the bundle of joy* ill. by author. Little, Brown, 2005. ISBN 978-0-316-17469-5 Subj: Animals – bears. Babies, toddlers. Family life – new sibling.

Dyer, Sarah. *Batty* ill. by author. Frances Lincoln, 2011. ISBN 978-1-84780-084-8 Subj: Animals – bats. Character traits – being different. Zoos.

Clementine and Mungo ill. by author. Bloomsbury, 2004. ISBN 978-1-58234-883-4 Subj: Animals. Family life – brothers & sisters. Monsters.

Monster day at work ill. by author. Frances Lincoln, 2010. ISBN 978-1-84780-069-5 Subj: Family life – fathers. Monsters.

Dylan, Bob. *Blowin' in the wind* ill. by Jon J Muth. Sterling, 2011. ISBN 978-1-4027-8002-8 Subj: Music. Songs. Violence, nonviolence.

If not for you ill. by David Walker. Simon & Schuster, 2016. ISBN 978-145164881-2 Subj: Animals – dogs. Emotions – love. Family life – fathers. Songs.

Man gave names to all the animals ill. by Jim Arnosky. Sterling, 2010. ISBN 978-1-4027-6858-3 Subj: Animals. Songs.

Eachus, Jennifer. *I'm sorry* (McBratney, Sam)

Earnhardt, Donna W. *Being Frank* ill. by Andrea Castellani. Flashlight, 2012. ISBN 978-1-93626-119-2 Subj: Character traits – honesty. Character traits – kindness. Family life – grandfathers.

Eastland, Chris. *ABC zooborns!* (Bleiman, Andrew)

1-2-3 zooborns! (Bleiman, Andrew)

Eastman, P. D. *The alphabet book* ill. by author. Random House, 2000. ISBN 978-0-375-80603-2 Subj: ABC books.

Eastwick, Ivy O. *Some folks like cats, and other poems* comp. by Walter B. Barbe; ill. by Mary Kurnick Maass. Boyds Mills, 2002. ISBN 978-1-56397-450-2 Subj: Poetry.

Eaton, Jason Carter. *The catawampus cat* ill. by Gus Gordon. Crown, 2017. ISBN 978-055350971-7 Subj: Animals – cats. Character traits – being different. Character traits – individuality. Cities, towns.

The day my runny nose ran away ill. by Ethan Long. Dutton, 2002. ISBN 978-0-525-47013-7 Subj: Anatomy – noses. Behavior – running away.

Great, now we've got barbarians! ill. by Mark Fearing. Candlewick, 2017. ISBN 978-076366827-3 Subj: Behavior – messy. Character traits – cleanliness. Character traits – orderliness. Family life – mothers.

How to track a truck ill. by John Rocco. Candlewick, 2016. ISBN 978-076368065-7 Subj: Pets. Trucks.

How to train a train ill. by John Rocco. Candlewick, 2013. ISBN 978-0-7636-6307-0 Subj: Pets. Trains.

Eaton, Maxwell. *Best buds* ill. by author. Random House, 2006. ISBN 978-0-375-93803-0 Subj: Animals – pigs. Food. Friendship.

I'm awake! ill. by author. Knopf, 2017. ISBN 978-037584575-8 Subj: Animals – hamsters. Family life – fathers. Morning.

The mystery ill. by author. Knopf, 2008. ISBN 978-0-375-83807-1 Subj: Activities – painting. Animals – pigs. Friendship.

Superheroes ill. by author. Random House, 2007. ISBN 978-0-375-83805-7 Subj: Activities – playing. Animals – pigs. Friendship.

Two dumb ducks ill. by author. Random House, 2010. ISBN 978-0-375-84576-5 Subj: Behavior – bullying, teasing. Behavior – name calling. Birds – ducks. Birds – seagulls.

Eclare, Melanie. *A handful of sunshine* ill. with photos. Ragged Bears, 2000. ISBN 978-1-929927-14-2 Subj: Flowers. Gardens, gardening.

A harvest of color: growing a vegetable garden ill. with photos. Ragged Bears, 2002. ISBN 978-1-929927-31-9 Subj: Communities, neighborhoods. Food. Gardens, gardening.

Edens, Cooper. *The Animal Mall* by Cooper Edens and Daniel Lane ill. by Edward Miller. Dial, 2000. ISBN 978-0-8037-1984-2 Subj: Animals. Rhyming text. Shopping.

Special deliveries (Day, Alexandra)

Edgemon, Darcie. *Seamore, the very forgetful porpoise* ill. by J. Otto Seibold. HarperCollins, 2008. ISBN 978-0-06-085075-3 Subj: Animals – dolphins. Behavior – forgetfulness. Behavior – lost & found possessions. Friendship.

Edgett, Ken. *Touchdown Mars! an ABC adventure* (Wethered, Peggy)

Edvall, Lilian. *The rabbit who longed for home* ill. by Anna-Clara Tidholm. R&S Books, 2001. ISBN 978-91-29-65391-5 Subj: Animals – rabbits. Emotions. School – nursery.

Edwards, Becky. *My first day at nursery school* ill. by Anthony Flintoft. Bloomsbury, 2002. ISBN 978-1-58234-761-5 Subj: Emotions. School – first day. School – nursery.

Edwards, David. *The pen that Pa built* ill. by Ashley Wolff. Ten Speed, 2007. ISBN 978-1-58246-153-3 Subj: Animals – sheep. Cumulative tales. Farms. Rhyming text. U.S. history.

Edwards, Karl Newsom. *Fly!* ill. by author. Knopf, 2015. ISBN 978-038539283-9 Subj: Insects – flies. Self-concept.

I got a new friend ill. by author. Knopf, 2017. ISBN 978-039955700-2 Subj: Animals – dogs. Friendship. Pets.

Edwards, Michelle. *The Hanukkah trike* ill. by Kathryn Mitter. Albert Whitman, 2010. ISBN 978-0-8075-3126-6 Subj: Holidays – Hanukkah. Jewish culture. Sports – bicycling.

A hat for Mrs. Goldman: a story about knitting and love ill. by G. Brian Karas. Random House, 2016. ISBN 978-055349710-6 Subj: Activities – knitting. Character traits – generosity. Character traits – persistence. Clothing – hats. Ethnic groups in the U.S. – Mexican Americans. Jewish culture. Old age.

Max makes a cake ill. by Charles Santoso. Random House, 2014. ISBN 978-044981431-4 Subj: Activities – baking, cooking. Food. Holidays – Passover. Jewish culture.

Papa's latkes ill. by Stacey Schuett. Candlewick, 2004. ISBN 978-0-7636-0779-1 Subj: Emotions – grief. Family life – fathers. Family life – single-parent families. Holidays – Hanukkah. Jewish culture.

Room for the baby ill. by Jana Christy. Random House, 2012. ISBN 978-0-375-87090-3 Subj: Activities – sewing. Holidays – Hanukkah. Jewish culture.

What's that noise? by Michelle Edwards and Phyllis Root ill. by Paul Meisel. Candlewick, 2002. ISBN 978-0-7636-1350-1 Subj: Emotions – fear. Family life – brothers. Night. Noise, sounds.

Edwards, Nancy. *Glenna's seeds* ill. by Sarah K. Hoctor. Child & Family, 2001. ISBN 978-0-87868-788-6 Subj: Character traits – kindness. Communities, neighborhoods. Ethnic groups in the U.S. Seeds.

Edwards, Nicola. *Goodnight Baxter* ill. by author. Running Press, 2004. ISBN 978-0-7624-1725-4 Subj: Animals – babies. Animals – dogs. Bedtime. Emotions – love. Friendship.

Edwards, Pamela Duncan. *Barefoot: escape on the Underground Railroad* ill. by Henry Cole. HarperCollins, 1997. ISBN 978-0-06-027137-4 Subj: Behavior – running away. Ethnic groups in the U.S. – African Americans. Slavery. U.S. history.

Boston Tea Party ill. by Henry Cole. Putnam, 2001. ISBN 978-0-399-23357-9 Subj: U.S. history.

Bravo, Livingstone Mouse! ill. by Henry Cole. Hyperion, 2000. ISBN 978-0-7868-0307-1 Subj: Activities – dancing. Animals. Animals – mice. Insects. Theater.

The bus ride that changed history: the story of Rosa Parks ill. by Danny Shanahan. Houghton, 2005. ISBN 978-0-618-44911-8 Subj: Ethnic groups in the U.S. – African Americans. Prejudice. U.S. history.

Clara Caterpillar ill. by Henry Cole. HarperCollins, 2001. ISBN 978-0-06-028996-6 Subj: Insects – butterflies, caterpillars. Metamorphosis.

Dear Tooth Fairy ill. by Marie-Louise Fitzpatrick. Tegen, 2003. ISBN 978-0-06-623973-6 Subj: Fairies. Letters, cards. Teeth.

Dinosaur starts school ill. by Deborah Allwright. Albert Whitman, 2009. ISBN 978-0-8075-1600-3 Subj: Behavior – worrying. Dinosaurs. School – first day.

Gigi and Lulu's gigantic fight ill. by Henry Cole. Tegen, 2004. ISBN 978-0-06-050753-4 Subj: Behavior – fighting, arguing. Friendship. School. Self-concept.

The grumpy morning ill. by Darcia Labrosse. Hyperion, 1998. ISBN 978-0-7868-2279-9 Subj: Animals. Behavior – promptness, tardiness. Farms. Rhyming text.

Honk! ill. by Henry Cole. Hyperion, 1998. ISBN 978-0-7868-2384-0 Subj: Activities – dancing. Ballet. Birds – swans.

Jack and Jill's treehouse ill. by Henry Cole. HarperCollins, 2008. ISBN 978-0-06-009077-7 Subj:

Buildings. Cumulative tales. Homes, houses. Rebuses.

The leprechaun's gold ill. by Henry Cole. Tegen, 2004. ISBN 978-0-06-623975-0 Subj: Behavior – greed. Careers – harpists. Foreign lands – Ireland. Musical instruments – harps. Mythical creatures – leprechauns.

McGillycuddy could ill. by Sue Porter. Tegen, 2005. ISBN 978-0-06-029001-6 Subj: Animals. Animals – kangaroos. Farms.

The mixed-up rooster ill. by Megan Lloyd. HarperCollins, 2006. ISBN 978-0-06-028999-7 Subj: Birds – chickens, roosters. Character traits – being different.

Ms. Bitsy Bat's kindergarten ill. by Henry Cole. Hyperion, 2005. ISBN 978-0-7868-0669-0 Subj: Animals. Animals – bats. Careers – teachers. School.

Muldoon ill. by Henry Cole. Hyperion, 2002. ISBN 978-0-7868-2305-5 Subj: Animals – dogs. Humorous stories.

The neat line: scribbling through Mother Goose ill. by Diana Cain Bluthenthal. HarperCollins, 2005. ISBN 978-0-06-623971-2 Subj: Activities – drawing. Books, reading. Nursery rhymes.

The old house ill. by Henry Cole. Penguin, 2007. ISBN 978-0-525-47796-9 Subj: Friendship. Homes, houses.

Princess Pigtoria and the pea ill. by Henry Cole. Scholastic, 2010. ISBN 978-0-545-15625-7 Subj: Animals – pigs. Folk & fairy tales. Humorous stories. Royalty – princesses.

Roar ill. by Henry Cole. HarperCollins, 2000. ISBN 978-0-06-028385-8 Subj: Animals. Animals – lions. Counting, numbers. Jungle. Rhyming text.

Rosie's roses ill. by Henry Cole. HarperCollins, 2003. ISBN 978-0-06-028998-0 Subj: Birthdays. Family life – aunts, uncles. Flowers – roses. Gifts.

Rude mule ill. by Barbara Nascimbeni. Henry Holt, 2002. ISBN 978-0-8050-7007-1 Subj: Animals – mules. Behavior. Etiquette.

Slop goes the soup ill. by Henry Cole. Hyperion, 2001. ISBN 978-0-7868-2411-3 Subj: Animals – warthogs. Character traits – clumsiness. Noise, sounds.

Some smug slug ill. by Henry Cole. HarperCollins, 1996. ISBN 978-0-06-024792-8 Subj: Animals. Animals – slugs.

Wake-up kisses ill. by Henry Cole. HarperCollins, 2002. ISBN 978-0-06-623977-4 Subj: Animals – babies. Night. Rhyming text.

Warthogs in a box ill. by Henry Cole. Disney, 2002. ISBN 978-0-7868-0894-6 Subj: Animals – warthogs. Format, unusual – board books. Friendship.

Warthogs in the kitchen: a sloppy counting book ill. by Henry Cole. Hyperion, 1998. ISBN 978-0-7868-2351-2 Subj: Activities – baking, cooking. Animals – warthogs. Counting, numbers. Rhyming text.

Warthogs paint ill. by Henry Cole. Hyperion, 2001. ISBN 978-0-7868-2412-0 Subj: Activities – painting. Animals – warthogs. Concepts – color. Rhyming text. Weather – rain.

While the world is sleeping ill. by Daniel Kirk. Scholastic, 2010. ISBN 978-0-545-01756-5 Subj: Animals. Bedtime. Birds – owls. Night. Rhyming text.

The worrywarts ill. by Henry Cole. HarperCollins, 1999. ISBN 978-0-06-028150-2 Subj: Activities – walking. Animals. Behavior – worrying.

The Wright brothers ill. by Henry Cole. Hyperion, 2003. ISBN 978-0-7868-2682-7 Subj: Activities – flying. Airplanes, airports. Careers – airplane pilots. Cumulative tales.

Edwards, Richard. *Always Copycub* ill. by Susan Winter. HarperCollins, 2001. ISBN 978-0-06-029691-9 Subj: Animals – bears. Behavior – lost. Games.

Copy me, Copycub ill. by Susan Winter. HarperCollins, 1999. ISBN 978-0-06-028571-5 Subj: Animals – bears. Family life – mothers. Seasons.

Good night, Copycub ill. by Susan Winter. HarperCollins, 2004. ISBN 978-0-06-056671-5 Subj: Animals. Animals – bears. Bedtime. Sleep.

Edwards, Wallace. *The extinct files: my science project* ill. by author. Kids Can, 2006. ISBN 978-1-55337-971-3 Subj: Dinosaurs. Humorous stories. Science.

Edwardson, Debby Dahl. *Whale snow* ill. by Annie Patterson. Talewinds, 2003. ISBN 978-1-57091-393-8 Subj: Animals – whales. Eskimos. Indians of North America – Inuit.

Eeckhout, Emmanuelle. *There's no such thing as ghosts!* ill. by author. Kane/Miller, 2008. ISBN 978-1-933605-91-3 Subj: Ghosts.

Egan, Kate. *Kate and Nate are running late!* ill. by Dan Yaccarino. Feiwel & Friends, 2012. ISBN 978-1-250-00080-4 Subj: Behavior – hurrying. Behavior – promptness, tardiness. Family life – single-parent families.

Egan, Tim. *Dodsworth in London* ill. by author. Houghton, 2009. ISBN 978-0-547-13816-9 Subj: Activities – traveling. Animals. Birds – ducks. Foreign lands – England.

Dodsworth in New York ill. by author. Houghton, 2007. ISBN 978-0-618-77708-2 Subj: Activities

– traveling. Animals. Behavior – hiding. Birds – ducks. Humorous stories.

Dodsworth in Paris ill. by author. Houghton, 2008. ISBN 978-0-618-98062-8 Subj: Activities – traveling. Animals. Birds – ducks. Foreign lands – France.

Dodsworth in Rome ill. by author. Harcourt, 2011. ISBN 978-0-547-39006-2 Subj: Activities – traveling. Animals. Birds – ducks. Foreign lands – Italy.

The experiments of Doctor Vermin ill. by author. Houghton, 2002. ISBN 978-0-618-13224-9 Subj: Animals – pigs. Animals – wolves. Careers – chefs, cooks. Emotions – fear. Holidays – Halloween. Science.

A mile from Ellington Station ill. by author. Houghton, 2001. ISBN 978-0-618-00393-8 Subj: Animals – bears. Animals – dogs. Emotions – envy, jealousy.

The pink refrigerator ill. by author. Houghton, 2007. ISBN 978-0-618-63154-4 Subj: Animals. Character traits – laziness. Stores.

Roasted peanuts ill. by author. Houghton, 2006. ISBN 978-0-618-33718-7 Subj: Animals – cats. Animals – horses, ponies. Friendship. Sports – baseball.

Serious farm ill. by author. Houghton, 2003. ISBN 978-0-618-22694-8 Subj: Animals. Careers – farmers. Farms.

The trial of Cardigan Jones ill. by author. Houghton, 2004. ISBN 978-0-618-40237-3 Subj: Animals. Animals – moose. Crime. Food.

Egielski, Richard. *Itsy bitsy spider* ill. by author. Atheneum, 2012. ISBN 978-1-4169-9895-2 Subj: Character traits – persistence. Format, unusual – toy & movable books. Nursery rhymes. Songs. Songs. Spiders.

St. Francis and the wolf ill. by author. HarperCollins, 2005. ISBN 978-0-06-623870-8 Subj: Animals – wolves. Foreign lands – Italy. Religion.

The sleepless little vampire ill. by author. Scholastic, 2011. ISBN 978-0-545-14597-8 Subj: Bedtime. Cumulative tales. Monsters.

Slim and Jim ill. by author. HarperCollins, 2002. ISBN 978-0-06-028353-7 Subj: Animals – cats. Animals – mice. Animals – rats. Toys.

Three magic balls ill. by author. HarperCollins, 2000. ISBN 978-0-06-026033-0 Subj: Activities – whistling. Magic. Toys – balls. Whistles.

Ehlert, Lois. *Boo to you!* ill. by author. Simon & Schuster, 2009. ISBN 978-1-4169-8625-6 Subj: Animals – cats. Animals – mice. Parties. Rhyming text.

Circus ill. by author. HarperCollins, 1992. ISBN 978-0-06-020253-8 Subj: Circus.

Color farm ill. by author. HarperCollins, 1990. ISBN 978-0-397-32441-5 Subj: Concepts – color. Concepts – shape. Format, unusual.

Color zoo ill. by author. HarperCollins, 1990. ISBN 978-0-397-32260-2 Subj: Caldecott award honor books. Concepts – color. Concepts – shape. Format, unusual.

Cuckoo, a Mexican folktale / Cucú: un cuento folklórico mexicano ill. by author. Harcourt, 1997. ISBN 978-0-15-200274-9 Subj: Birds. Birds – cuckoos. Character traits – bravery. Fire. Folk & fairy tales. Foreign lands – Mexico. Foreign languages. Indians of Central America – Maya.

Eating the alphabet ill. by author. Harcourt, 1996. ISBN 978-0-15-201036-2 Subj: ABC books. Food.

Feathers for lunch ill. by author. Harcourt, 1990. ISBN 978-0-15-230550-5 Subj: Animals – cats. Birds. Rhyming text.

Fish eyes: a book you can count on ill. by author. Harcourt, 1990. ISBN 978-0-15-201618-0 Subj: Concepts – color. Counting, numbers. Fish. Rhyming text.

Growing vegetable soup ill. by author. Harcourt, 1987. ISBN 978-0-15-232575-6 Subj: Food. Gardens, gardening.

Hands ill. by author. Harcourt, 1997. ISBN 978-0-15-201506-0 Subj: Activities – making things. Anatomy – hands. Family life. Format, unusual – toy & movable books.

Holey Moley ill. by author. Simon & Schuster/ Beach Lane, 2015. ISBN 978-144249301-8 Subj: Animals – moles. Gardens, gardening. Rhyming text.

In my world ill. by author. Harcourt, 2002. ISBN 978-0-15-216269-6 Subj: Concepts. Format, unusual. Picture puzzles.

Leaf man ill. by author. Harcourt, 2005. ISBN 978-0-15-205304-8 Subj: Format, unusual. Plants. Weather – wind.

Lots of spots ill. by author. Simon & Schuster, 2010. ISBN 978-1-4424-0289-8 Subj: Animals. Disguises. Rhyming text.

Market day ill. by author. Harcourt, 2000. ISBN 978-0-15-202158-0 Subj: Farms. Rhyming text. Stores.

Mole's hill: a woodland tale ill. by author. Harcourt, 1994. ISBN 978-0-15-255116-2 Subj: Animals – foxes. Animals – moles. Folk & fairy tales. Indians of North America – Seneca.

Moon rope / Un lazo a la luna ill. by adapter. Harcourt, 1992. ISBN 978-0-15-255343-2 Subj: Animals – foxes. Animals – moles. Folk & fairy tales. Foreign lands – Peru. Foreign languages. Moon.

Nuts to you! ill. by author. Harcourt, 1993. ISBN 978-0-15-257647-9 Subj: Animals – squirrels. Rhyming text.

Oodles of animals ill. by author. Harcourt, 2008. ISBN 978-0-15-206274-3 Subj: Animals. Character traits – individuality. Rhyming text.

Planting a rainbow ill. by author. Harcourt, 1988. ISBN 978-0-15-262609-9 Subj: Flowers. Gardens, gardening.

Rain fish ill. by author. Simon & Schuster/Beach Lane, 2016. ISBN 978-148146152-8 Subj: Activities – making things. Fish. Imagination. Weather – rain.

Red leaf, yellow leaf ill. by author. Harcourt, 1991. ISBN 978-0-15-266197-7 Subj: Seasons. Trees.

Rrralph ill. by author. Simon & Schuster, 2011. ISBN 978-1-4424-1305-4 Subj: Animals – dogs. Humorous stories.

The scraps book: notes from a colorful life ill. by author. Simon & Schuster/Beach Lane, 2014. ISBN 978-144243571-1 Subj: Art. Books, reading. Careers – artists.

Snowballs ill. by author. Harcourt, 1995. ISBN 978-0-15-200074-5 Subj: Seasons – winter. Snowmen.

Top cat ill. by author. Harcourt, 1998. ISBN 978-0-15-201739-2 Subj: Animals – cats. Behavior – sharing. Rhyming text.

Wag a tail ill. by author. Harcourt, 2007. ISBN 978-0-15-205843-2 Subj: Animals – dogs.

Waiting for wings ill. by author. Harcourt, 2001. ISBN 978-0-15-202608-0 Subj: Format, unusual – toy & movable books. Insects – butterflies, caterpillars. Rhyming text.

Ehrhardt, Karen. *This jazz man* ill. by R. G. Roth. Harcourt, 2006. ISBN 978-0-15-205307-9 Subj: Ethnic groups in the U.S. – African Americans. Music. Rhyming text. Songs.

Ehrlich, Amy. *Baby Dragon* ill. by Will Hillenbrand. Candlewick, 2008. ISBN 978-0-7636-2840-6 Subj: Character traits – patience, impatience. Dragons. Family life – mothers.

Ehrlich, Fred. *A bunny is funny* (Ziefert, Harriet)

Does a baboon sleep in a bed? ill. by Emily Bolam. Blue Apple, 2006. ISBN 978-1-59354-142-2 Subj: Animals. Sleep.

Does a camel cook? ill. by Emily Bolam. Blue Apple, 2007. ISBN 978-1-59354-588-8 Subj: Animals. Food.

Does a chimp wear clothes? ill. by Emily Bolam. Blue Apple, 2005. ISBN 978-1-59354-110-1 Subj: Animals. Clothing.

Does a duck have a daddy? ill. by Emily Bolam. Blue Apple, 2004. ISBN 978-1-59354-032-6 Subj: Animals. Family life – fathers.

Does a giraffe drive? ill. by Emily Bolam. Blue Apple, 2007. ISBN 978-1-59354-614-4 Subj: Animals. Concepts – motion.

Does a mouse have a mommy? ill. by Emily Bolam. Blue Apple, 2004. ISBN 978-1-59354-034-0 Subj: Animals. Family life – mothers.

Does a seal smile? ill. by Emily Bolam. Blue Apple, 2006. ISBN 978-1-59354-168-2 Subj: Anatomy – faces. Animals. Communication.

Does an elephant take a bath? ill. by Emily Bolam. Blue Apple, 2005. ISBN 978-1-59354-111-8 Subj: Activities – bathing. Animals. Character traits – cleanliness.

Ehrlich, H. M. *Gotcha, Louie!* ill. by Emily Bolam. Houghton, 2002. ISBN 978-0-618-19549-7 Subj: Activities – playing. Family life – mothers. Sea & seashore.

Louie's goose ill. by Emily Bolam. Houghton, 2000. ISBN 978-0-618-03023-1 Subj: Sea & seashore. Toys.

Ehrlich, Nikki. *Twindergarten* ill. by Zoey Abbott Wagner. HarperCollins, 2017. ISBN 978-006256423-8 Subj: Behavior – worrying. Character traits – kindness. Multiple births – twins. School – first day.

Eichenberg, Fritz. *Ape in cape* ill. by author. Harcourt, 1952. ISBN 978-0-15-203722-2 Subj: ABC books. Caldecott award honor books.

Eilenberg, Max. *Cowboy Kid* ill. by Sue Heap. Candlewick, 2000. ISBN 978-0-7636-1058-6 Subj: Bedtime. Family life – fathers.

Squeak's good idea ill. by Patrick Benson. Candlewick, 2001. ISBN 978-0-7636-1591-8 Subj: Activities – picnicking. Animals – elephants.

Einhorn, Edward. *Fractions in disguise: A math adventure* ill. by David Clark. Charlesbridge, 2014. ISBN 978-157091773-8 Subj: Counting, numbers.

A very improbable story ill. by Adam Gustavson. Charlesbridge, 2008. ISBN 978-1-57091-871-1 Subj: Animals – cats. Concepts. Games. Problem solving.

Eisner, Will. *Sundiata* ill. by author. NBM, 2003. ISBN 978-1-56163-332-6 Subj: Disabilities. Folk & fairy tales. Foreign lands – Africa. Foreign lands – Mali. Royalty – kings.

Eitzen, Ruth. *Tara's flight* ill. by Allan Eitzen. Boyds Mills, 2008. ISBN 978-1-59078-563-8 Subj: Birds – pigeons. Religion – Noah. Weather – floods.

Eldarova, Sofia. *Builder mouse* ill. by author. Clarion, 2016. ISBN 978-054435766-2 Subj: Animals – mice. Art. Careers – architects. Food.

Elffers, Joost. *Baby food* (Freymann, Saxton)

Do you love me? ill. by author. HarperCollins, 2008. ISBN 978-0-06-166799-2 Subj: Emotions – love. Rhyming text.

Dog food (Freymann, Saxton)

Dr. Pompo's nose (Freymann, Saxton)

Fast food (Freymann, Saxton)

Food for thought: the complete book of concepts for growing minds (Freymann, Saxton)

Food play (Freymann, Saxton)

How are you peeling? foods with moods (Freymann, Saxton)

One lonely seahorse (Freymann, Saxton)

Eliot, Hannah. *Dinosaurs live on! and other fun facts* (DiSiena, Laura Lyn)

Elissa, Barbara. *The remarkable journey of Josh's kippah* ill. by Farida Zaman. Lerner/Kar-Ben, 2010. ISBN 978-0-8225-9911-1 Subj: Activities – traveling. Jewish culture.

Elkin, Mark. *Samuel's baby* ill. by Amy Wummer. Tricycle, 2010. ISBN 978-1-58246-301-8 Subj: Babies, toddlers. Family life – new sibling. School.

Ellery, Amanda. *If I had a dragon* ill. by Tom Ellery. Simon & Schuster, 2006. ISBN 978-1-4169-0924-8 Subj: Activities – playing. Dragons. Family life – brothers & sisters. Imagination.

If I were a jungle animal ill. by Tom Ellery. Simon & Schuster, 2009. ISBN 978-1-4169-3778-4 Subj: Animals. Imagination. Jungle. Sports – baseball.

Elliot, David. *Henry's map* ill. by author. Philomel, 2013. ISBN 978-0-399-16072-1 Subj: Animals – pigs. Character traits – orderliness. Farms. Maps.

Elliott, David. *And here's to you!* ill. by Randy Cecil. Candlewick, 2004. ISBN 978-0-7636-1427-0 Subj: Animals. Birds. Rhyming text.

Baabwaa and Wooliam ill. by Melissa Sweet. Candlewick, 2017. ISBN 978-076366074-1 Subj: Animals – sheep. Animals – wolves. Books, reading. Friendship.

Finn throws a fit! ill. by Timothy Basil Ering. Candlewick, 2009. ISBN 978-0-7636-2356-2 Subj: Behavior – misbehavior. Emotions – anger.

Hazel Nutt, Alien Hunter ill. by True Kelley. Holiday, 2004. ISBN 978-0-8234-1843-5 Subj: Humorous stories. Space & space ships.

Hazel Nutt, mad scientist ill. by True Kelley. Holiday, 2003. ISBN 978-0-8234-1711-7 Subj: Careers – scientists. Humorous stories. Monsters. Music.

Hunter's best friend at school ill. by Lynn Munsinger. HarperCollins, 2002. ISBN 978-0-06-000231-2 Subj: Animals – raccoons. Behavior. Friendship. School – nursery.

In the sea ill. by Holly Meade. Candlewick, 2012. ISBN 978-0-7636-4498-7 Subj: Animals. Poetry. Sea & seashore.

In the wild ill. by Holly Meade. Candlewick, 2010. ISBN 978-0-7636-4497-0 Subj: Animals. Poetry.

Knitty Kitty ill. by Christopher Denise. Candlewick, 2008. ISBN 978-0-7636-3169-7 Subj: Activities – knitting. Animals – cats. Family life.

Nobody's perfect ill. by Sam Zuppardi. Candlewick, 2015. ISBN 978-076366699-6 Subj: Character traits – patience, impatience. Character traits – perfectionism. Family life.

On the farm ill. by Holly Meade. Candlewick, 2008. ISBN 978-0-7636-3322-6 Subj: Farms.

On the wing ill. by Becca Stadtlander. Candlewick, 2014. ISBN 978-076365324-8 Subj: Birds. Poetry.

One little chicken: a counting book ill. by Ethan Long. Holiday House, 2007. ISBN 978-0-8234-1983-8 Subj: Activities – dancing. Birds – chickens, roosters. Counting, numbers. Rhyming text.

This Orq. (He #1!) ill. by Lori Nichols. Boyds Mills, 2016. ISBN 978-162979336-8 Subj: Animals – woolly mammoths. Cave dwellers. Character traits – helpfulness. Inventions. Pets.

This Orq. (He cave boy.) ill. by Lori Nichols. Boyds Mills, 2014. ISBN 978-162091521-9 Subj: Animals – woolly mammoths. Cave dwellers. Pets.

This Orq. (He say "ugh!") ill. by Lori Nichols. Boyds Mills, 2015. ISBN 978-162091789-3 Subj: Animals – woolly mammoths. Behavior – bullying, teasing. Cave dwellers. Pets.

The two Tims ill. by Gabriel Alborozo. Candlewick, 2016. ISBN 978-076367264-5 Subj: Friendship.

Elliott, Devlin. *Naughty Mabel* (Lane, Nathan)

Naughty Mabel sees it all (Lane, Nathan)

Elliott, George. *The boy who loved bananas* ill. by Andrej Krystoforski. Kids Can, 2005. ISBN 978-1-55337-744-3 Subj: Animals – monkeys. Behavior – imitation. Food. Humorous stories. Zoos.

Elliott, Laura Malone. *Hunter and Stripe and the soccer showdown* ill. by Lynn Munsinger. HarperCollins, 2005. ISBN 978-0-06-052759-4 Subj: Animals – raccoons. Friendship. Sports – soccer. Sportsmanship.

Hunter's big sister ill. by Lynn Munsinger. Harper-Collins, 2007. ISBN 978-0-06-000233-6 Subj: Animals – raccoons. Family life – brothers & sisters.

A string of hearts ill. by Lynn Munsinger. HarperCollins, 2010. ISBN 978-0-06-000085-1 Subj: Animals. Friendship. Holidays – Valentine's Day.

Thanksgiving Day thanks ill. by Lynn Munsinger. HarperCollins, 2013. ISBN 978-0-06-000236-7 Subj: Animals. Holidays – Thanksgiving. School.

Elliott, Rebecca. *Dalmatian in a digger* ill. by author. Capstone, 2017. ISBN 978-162370802-3 Subj: Animals – dogs. Careers – construction workers. Machines.

Just because ill. by author. Lion, 2011. ISBN 978-0-7459-6267-2 Subj: Disabilities – physical disabilities. Family life – brothers & sisters.

Elliott, Zetta. *Melena's jubilee: the story of a fresh start* ill. by Aaron Boyd. Tilbury, 2016. ISBN 978-088448443-1 Subj: Character traits – generosity. Character traits – kindness. Character traits – optimism. Ethnic groups in the U.S. – African Americans.

Ellis, Andy. *When Lulu went to the zoo* ill. by author. Andersen, 2010. ISBN 978-0-7613-5499-4 Subj: Zoos.

Ellis, Carson. *Du iz tak?* ill. by author. Candlewick, 2016. ISBN 978-076366530-2 Subj: Caldecott award honor books. Gardens, gardening. Insects. Language.

Home ill. by author. Candlewick, 2015. ISBN 978-076366529-6 Subj: Homes, houses.

Ellis, Gerry. *Natumi takes the lead: the true story of an orphan elephant who finds family* by Gerry Ellis and Amy Novesky; ill. by Gerry Ellis. ill. with photos by Gerry Ellis. National Geographic, 2016. ISBN 978-142632561-8 Subj: Animals – babies. Animals – elephants. Foreign lands – Kenya. Nature. Orphans.

Ellis, Sarah. *Ben over night* ill. by Kim LaFave. Fitzhenry & Whiteside, 2005. ISBN 978-1-55041-807-1 Subj: Emotions – fear. Sleepovers.

Ben says goodbye ill. by Kim LaFave. Pajama, 2016. ISBN 978-192748579-8 Subj: Emotions – loneliness. Friendship. Moving.

Big Ben ill. by Kim Lafave. Fitzhenry & Whiteside, 2001. ISBN 978-1-55041-679-4 Subj: Family life – brothers & sisters.

The queen's feet ill. by Dusan Petricic. Red Deer, 2006. ISBN 978-0-88995-320-8 Subj: Anatomy – feet. Royalty – queens.

Salmon forest (Suzuki, David)

Ellis, Veronica Freeman. *Afro-Bets, first book about Africa* ill. by George Ford. Just Us, 1989. ISBN 978-0-940975-12-5 Subj: Foreign lands – Africa.

Ellwand, David. *Alfred's camera: a collection of picture puzzles* ill. by author. Dutton, 1998. ISBN 978-0-525-45978-1 Subj: Animals – dogs. Behavior – lost & found possessions. Picture puzzles.

Alfred's party ill. by author. Dutton, 2000. ISBN 978-0-525-46385-6 Subj: Animals – dogs. Behavior – lost & found possessions. Birthdays. Picture puzzles.

Cinderlily libretto by Christine Tagg; ill. by author. Candlewick, 2003. ISBN 978-0-7636-2328-9 Subj: Ballet. Flowers. Folk & fairy tales. Foreign lands – France. Rhyming text.

Midas Mouse photos by author. Lothrop, 2000. ISBN 978-0-688-16745-5 Subj: Animals – mice. Behavior – wishing. Sun.

Ten in the bed photos by author. Handprint, 2000. ISBN 978-1-929766-49-9 Subj: Counting, numbers. Format, unusual – board books. Music. Songs. Toys – bears.

Elschner, Geraldine. *Fritz's fish* ill. by Daniela Bunge. Penguin, 2006. ISBN 978-0-698-40028-3 Subj: Fish. Pets.

Like a wolf ill. by Antoine Guilloppe. Minedition, 2015. ISBN 978-988824044-9 Subj: Adoption. Animals – dogs. Character traits – kindness to animals.

Mark's messy room ill. by Alexandra Junge. Minedition, 2006. ISBN 978-0-698-40047-4 Subj: Animals – cats. Behavior – messy. Character traits – cleanliness.

Max's magic seeds ill. by Jean-Pierre Corderoch. Penguin, 2007. ISBN 978-0-698-40059-7 Subj: Behavior – boredom. Flowers. Magic. School.

Moonchild, star of the sea ill. by Lieselotte Schwarz. NorthSouth, 2002. ISBN 978-0-7358-1665-7 Subj: Earth. Moon. Stars.

Pashmina the little Christmas goat ill. by Angela Kehlenbeck. Penguin, 2006. ISBN 978-0-698-40046-7 Subj: Animals – goats. Holidays – Christmas.

Elsdale, Bob. *Mac side up* ill. by author. Dutton, 2000. ISBN 978-0-525-46467-9 Subj: Animals – cats. Animals – ferrets. Humorous stories. Pets.

Elster, Jean Alicia. *Just call me Joe Joe* ill. by Nicole Tadgell. Judson, 2001. ISBN 978-0-8170-1398-1 Subj: Ethnic groups in the U.S. – African Americans. Self-concept. Sports – baseball.

Elvgren, Jennifer. *Josias, hold the book* ill. by Nicole Tadgell. Boyds Mills, 2006. ISBN 978-1-59078-

318-4 Subj: Family life. Food. Foreign lands – Haiti. Gardens, gardening. School.

The whispering town ill. by Fabio Santomauro. Lerner/Kar-Ben, 2014. ISBN 978-146771194-4 Subj: Character traits – bravery. Character traits – freedom. Foreign lands – Denmark. Jewish culture. War.

Elwell, Peter. *Adios Oscar! a butterfly fable* ill. by author. Scholastic, 2009. ISBN 978-0-545-07159-8 Subj: Insects – butterflies, caterpillars. Migration. Self-concept.

Ely, Lesley. *Looking after Louis* ill. by Polly Dunbar. Albert Whitman, 2004. ISBN 978-0-8075-4746-5 Subj: Disabilities – autism. School.

Elya, Susan Middleton. *Adiós, tricycle* ill. by Elisabeth Schlossberg. Putnam, 2009. ISBN 978-0-399-24522-0 Subj: Animals – pigs. Ethnic groups in the U.S. – Hispanic Americans. Foreign languages. Garage sales, rummage sales. Rhyming text. Sports – bicycling.

Bebé goes shopping ill. by Steven Salerno. Harcourt, 2006. ISBN 978-0-15-205426-7 Subj: Babies, toddlers. Foreign languages. Rhyming text. Shopping. Stores.

Bebé goes to the beach ill. by Steven Salerno. Harcourt, 2008. ISBN 978-0-15-206000-8 Subj: Babies, toddlers. Foreign languages. Rhyming text. Sea & seashore – beaches.

Cowboy Jose ill. by Tim Raglin. Penguin, 2005. ISBN 978-0-399-23570-2 Subj: Cowboys, cowgirls. Foreign languages. Rhyming text. Rodeos.

Eight animals bake a cake ill. by Lee Chapman. Putnam, 2002. ISBN 978-0-399-23468-2 Subj: Activities – baking, cooking. Animals. Foreign languages. Rhyming text.

Eight animals on the town ill. by Lee Chapman. Putnam, 2000. ISBN 978-0-399-23437-8 Subj: Animals. Counting, numbers. Foreign languages. Rhyming text.

F is for fiesta ill. by G. Brian Karas. Penguin, 2006. ISBN 978-0-399-24225-0 Subj: ABC books. Birthdays. Foreign languages. Parties. Rhyming text.

Fairy trails: a story told in English and Spanish ill. by Mercedes McDonald. Bloomsbury, 2005. ISBN 978-1-58234-927-5 Subj: Books, reading. Foreign languages.

Fire! ¡Fuego! Brave bomberos ill. by Dan Santat. Bloomsbury, 2012. ISBN 978-1-59990-461-0 Subj: Careers – firefighters. Fire. Foreign languages. Rhyming text.

La Madre Goose: nursery rhymes for los niños (Mother Goose)

La princesa and the pea (Andersen, Hans Christian)

Little Roja Riding Hood ill. by Susan Guevara. Putnam, 2014. ISBN 978-039924767-5 Subj: Animals – wolves. Family life – grandmothers. Folk & fairy tales. Foreign languages. Rhyming text.

N is for Navidad by Susan Middleton Elya and Merry Banks ill. by Joe Cepeda. Chronicle, 2007. ISBN 978-0-8118-5205-0 Subj: ABC books. Family life. Foreign lands – Mexico. Foreign languages. Holidays – Christmas.

No more, por favor ill. by David Walker. Penguin, 2010. ISBN 978-0-399-24766-8 Subj: Animals. Family life – parents. Food. Foreign languages. Jungle. Rhyming text.

Oh no, gotta go #2 ill. by Lynne Avril. Penguin, 2007. ISBN 978-0-399-24308-0 Subj: Activities – picnicking. Foreign languages. Rhyming text. Toilet training.

Rubia and the three osos ill. by Melissa Sweet. Hyperion/Disney, 2010. ISBN 978-1-4231-1252-5 Subj: Animals – bears. Folk & fairy tales. Foreign languages. Rhyming text.

Say hola to Spanish ill. by Loretta Lopez. Lee & Low, 1996. ISBN 978-1-880000-29-8 Subj: Foreign languages.

Sophie's trophy ill. by Viviana Garofoli. Penguin, 2006. ISBN 978-0-399-24199-4 Subj: Activities – singing. Family life – brothers & sisters. Foreign languages. Frogs & toads. Self-concept.

Tooth on the loose ill. by Jenny Mattheson. Putnam, 2008. ISBN 978-0-399-24459-9 Subj: Ethnic groups in the U.S. – Hispanic Americans. Foreign languages. Gifts. Rhyming text. Teeth.

A year full of holidays ill. by Diana Cain Bluthenthal. Penguin, 2010. ISBN 978-0-399-23733-1 Subj: Days of the week, months of the year. Holidays. Rhyming text.

Emberley, Barbara. *Drummer Hoff* ill. by Ed Emberley. Adapt. from a folk verse. Prentice-Hall, 1967. ISBN 978-0-13-220822-2 Subj: Caldecott award books. Careers – military. Cumulative tales. Poetry. Weapons.

Night's nice ill. by Ed Emberley. Little, Brown, 2008. ISBN 978-0-316-06623-5 Subj: Night. Poetry.

One wide river to cross ill. by Ed Emberley. Adapt. of the American folk song. Prentice-Hall, 1966. ISBN 978-0-316-23445-0 Subj: Animals. Caldecott award honor books. Folk & fairy tales. Poetry. Religion – Noah. Songs. Weather – floods. Weather – rain.

Emberley, Ed. *Chicken Little* (Emberley, Rebecca)

Ed Emberley's big green drawing book ill. by author. Little, 1979. ISBN 978-0-316-23595-2 Subj: Art. Wordless.

Ed Emberley's big orange drawing book ill. by author. Little, 1980. ISBN 978-0-316-23418-4 Subj: Art.

Ed Emberley's big purple drawing book ill. by author. Little, 1981. ISBN 978-0-316-23422-1 Subj: Art.

Ed Emberley's bye-bye, big bad bullybug! ill. by author. Little, Brown, 2007. ISBN 978-0-316-01762-6 Subj: Behavior – bullying, teasing. Format, unusual – toy & movable books. Monsters.

Ed Emberley's drawing book: make a world ill. by author. Little, 1972. ISBN 978-0-316-23598-3 Subj: Art.

Ed Emberley's drawing book of trucks and trains ill. by author. Little, 2002. ISBN 978-0-316-23898-4 Subj: Activities – drawing. Trains. Trucks.

Ed Emberley's fingerprint drawing book ill. by author. Little, 2000. ISBN 978-0-316-23638-6 Subj: Activities – drawing. Anatomy – hands.

Glad monster, sad monster: a book about feelings ill. by author. Little, 1997. ISBN 978-0-316-57395-5 Subj: Emotions. Format, unusual – toy & movable books. Masks. Monsters.

Go away, big green monster! ill. by author. Little, 1992. ISBN 978-0-316-23653-9 Subj: Bedtime. Emotions – fear. Format, unusual – toy & movable books. Monsters.

If you're a monster and you know it (Emberley, Rebecca)

Nighty night Little Green Monster ill. by author. Little, Brown, 2013. ISBN 978-0-316-21041-6 Subj: Bedtime. Format, unusual – toy & movable books. Monsters.

The red hen by Ed Emberley and Rebecca Emberley; ill. by Ed Emberley. Roaring Brook, 2010. ISBN 978-1-59643-492-9 Subj: Activities – baking, cooking. Animals. Behavior – sharing. Birds – chickens, roosters. Character traits – helpfulness. Cumulative tales. Folk & fairy tales.

Ten little beasties (Emberley, Rebecca)

Thanks, Mom! ill. by author. Little, 2003. ISBN 978-0-316-24022-2 Subj: Animals. Animals – mice. Circus. Family life – mothers. Food.

Where's my sweetie pie? ill. by author. Little, Brown, 2010. ISBN 978-0-316-01891-3 Subj: Animals. Format, unusual – board books. Format, unusual – toy & movable books.

The wing on a flea ill. by author. Little, 2001. ISBN 978-0-316-23487-0 Subj: Concepts – shape. Rhyming text.

Emberley, Rebecca. *The ant and the grasshopper* ill. by Ed Emberley. Roaring Brook, 2012. ISBN 978-1-59643-493-6 Subj: Activities – working. Insects – ants. Insects – grasshoppers. Music. Musical instruments – bands.

Chicken Little by Rebecca Emberley and Ed Emberley; ill. by authors. Roaring Brook, 2009. ISBN 978-1-59643-464-6 Subj: Animals. Behavior – gossip, rumors. Behavior – trickery. Birds – chickens, roosters. Cumulative tales. Folk & fairy tales.

The crocodile and the scorpion ill. by Ed Emberley. Roaring Brook, 2013. ISBN 978-1-59643-494-3 Subj: Behavior – trickery. Folk & fairy tales. Reptiles – alligators, crocodiles. Scorpions.

If you're a monster and you know it by Rebecca Emberley and Ed Emberley; ill. by Rebecca Emberley. Scholastic, 2010. ISBN 978-0-545-21829-0 Subj: Emotions – happiness. Monsters. Songs.

Mice on ice ill. by Ed Emberley. Holiday House, 2012. ISBN 978-0-8234-2576-1 Subj: Animals – cats. Animals – mice. Rhyming text. Sports – ice skating.

My animals / Mis animales ill. by author. Little, 2002. ISBN 978-0-316-17343-8 Subj: Animals. Foreign languages. Format, unusual – board books.

My big book of Spanish words ill. by author. Little, Brown, 2008. ISBN 978-0-316-11803-3 Subj: Foreign languages.

My city / Mi cuidad ill. by author. Little, 2005. ISBN 978-0-316-00051-2 Subj: Cities, towns. Foreign languages. Format, unusual – board books.

My clothes / Mi ropa ill. by author. Little, 2002. ISBN 978-0-316-17454-1 Subj: Clothing. Foreign languages. Format, unusual – board books.

My colors / Mis colores ill. by author. Little, 2000. ISBN 978-0-316-23347-7 Subj: Concepts – color. Foreign languages. Format, unusual – board books.

My food / Mi comida ill. by author. Little, 2002. ISBN 978-0-316-17718-4 Subj: Food. Foreign languages. Format, unusual – board books.

My garden / Mi jardin ill. by author. Little, 2005. ISBN 978-0-316-00049-9 Subj: Foreign languages. Format, unusual – board books. Gardens, gardening.

My house / Mi casa ill. by author. Little, 1990. ISBN 978-0-316-23637-9 Subj: Foreign languages. Format, unusual – board books. Homes, houses.

My numbers / Mis números ill. by author. Little, 2000. ISBN 978-0-316-23350-7 Subj: Counting, numbers. Foreign languages. Format, unusual – board books.

My opposites / Mis opuestos ill. by author. Little, 2000. ISBN 978-0-316-23345-3 Subj: Concepts – opposites. Foreign languages. Format, unusual – board books.

My room / Mi cuarto ill. by author. Little, 2005. ISBN 978-0-316-00052-9 Subj: Foreign languages. Format, unusual – board books. Homes, houses.

My school / Mi escuela ill. by author. Little, 2005. ISBN 978-0-316-00050-5 Subj: Foreign languages. Format, unusual – board books. School.

My shapes / Mis formas ill. by author. Little, 2000. ISBN 978-0-316-23355-2 Subj: Concepts – shape. Foreign languages. Format, unusual – board books.

My toys / Mi juguetes ill. by author. Little, 2002. ISBN 978-0-316-17494-7 Subj: Foreign languages. Format, unusual – board books. Toys.

The red hen (Emberley, Ed)

Spare parts ill. by Ed Emberley. Roaring Brook/ Neal Porter, 2015. ISBN 978-159643723-4 Subj: Emotions – loneliness. Friendship. Rhyming text. Robots.

Ten little beasties by Rebecca Emberley and Ed Emberley; ill. by authors. Roaring Brook, 2011. ISBN 978-1-59643-627-5 Subj: Counting, numbers. Monsters.

Three cool kids ill. by author. Little, 1995. ISBN 978-0-316-23666-9 Subj: Animals – goats. Animals – rats. Cities, towns. Folk & fairy tales.

Emberley, Rebecca, et al. *There was an old monster* ill. by author and Ed Emberley. Scholastic, 2009. ISBN 978-0-545-10145-5 Subj: Cumulative tales. Monsters. Songs.

Emerman, Ellen. *Is it Shabbos yet?* ill. by Tova Leff. Hachai, 2001. ISBN 978-1-929628-02-5 Subj: Holidays. Jewish culture. Religion.

Just right: the story of a Jewish home ill. by Sarah Kranz. Hachai, 1999. ISBN 978-0-922613-91-5 Subj: Family life. Homes, houses. Jewish culture.

Emmett, Jonathan. *The best gift of all* ill. by Vanessa Cabban. Candlewick, 2008. ISBN 978-0-7636-3860-3 Subj: Animals. Animals – moles. Friendship. Gifts. Illness – cold (disease).

Bringing down the moon ill. by Vanessa Cabban. Candlewick, 2001. ISBN 978-0-7636-1577-2 Subj: Animals. Animals – moles. Moon.

Diamond in the snow ill. by Vanessa Cabban. Candlewick, 2007. ISBN 978-0-7636-3117-8 Subj: Animals – moles. Seasons – winter. Weather – snow.

I love you always and forever ill. by Daniel Howarth. Scholastic, 2007. ISBN 978-0-439-91654-7 Subj: Animals – mice. Behavior – growing up. Emotions – love.

Leaf trouble ill. by Caroline Jayne Church. Scholastic, 2009. ISBN 978-0-545-16070-4 Subj: Animals – squirrels. Seasons – fall. Trees.

No place like home ill. by Vanessa Cabban. Candlewick, 2005. ISBN 978-0-7636-2554-2 Subj: Animals. Animals – moles. Homes, houses.

Prince Ribbit ill. by Poly Bernatene. Peachtree, 2017. ISBN 978-156145761-8 Subj: Folk & fairy tales. Frogs & toads. Royalty – princesses.

The princess and the pig ill. by Poly Bernatene. Walker, 2011. ISBN 978-0-8027-2334-5 Subj: Animals – pigs. Royalty – princesses.

Ruby in her own time ill. by Rebecca Harry. Scholastic, 2004. ISBN 978-0-439-57915-5 Subj: Birds – ducks. Character traits – smallness.

The Santa trap ill. by Poly Bernatene. Peachtree, 2012. ISBN 978-1-56145-670-3 Subj: Behavior – misbehavior. Holidays – Christmas. Santa Claus.

She'll be coming 'round the mountain ill. by Deborah Allwright. Simon & Schuster, 2007. ISBN 978-1-4169-3652-7 Subj: Songs. U.S. history – frontier & pioneer life.

Someone bigger ill. by Adrian Reynolds. Clarion, 2004. ISBN 978-0-618-44397-0 Subj: Concepts – size. Kites. Rhyming text.

This way, Ruby! ill. by Rebecca Harry. Scholastic, 2007. ISBN 978-0-439-87992-7 Subj: Behavior – lost. Birds – ducks. Character traits – smallness. Weather – storms.

Emmons, Chip. *Sammy wakes his dad* ill. by Shirley Venit Anger. Star Bright, 2002. ISBN 978-1-887734-87-5 Subj: Disabilities – physical disabilities. Family life – fathers. Sports – fishing.

Empson, Jo. *Chimpanzees for tea!* ill. by author. Philomel, 2016. ISBN 978-014135643-3 Subj: Behavior – forgetfulness. Memories, memory. Shopping. Stores.

Little home bird ill. by author. Child's Play, 2016. ISBN 978-184643889-9 Subj: Birds. Homes, houses. Migration.

Rabbityness ill. by author. Child's Play, 2012. ISBN 978-1-84643-492-1 Subj: Animals – rabbits. Behavior – lost. Character traits – being different.

Enderle, Dotti. *The Library Gingerbread Man* (The gingerbread boy)

Enderle, Judith Ross. *Smile, Principessa!* by Judith Ross Enderle and Stephanie Jacob Gordon ill. by Serena Curmi. Simon & Schuster, 2007. ISBN 978-1-4169-1004-6 Subj: Emotions – envy, jealousy. Family life – new sibling.

Enersen, Adele. *Vincent and the night* ill. by author. Dial, 2015. ISBN 978-080374106-5 Subj: Babies, toddlers. Bedtime. Behavior – misbehavior. Imagination. Night.

When my baby dreams ill. by author. HarperCollins, 2012. ISBN 978-0-06-207175-0 Subj: Babies, toddlers. Dreams. Sleep.

Engelbreit, Mary. *Mary Engelbreit's A merry little Christmas: celebrate from a to z* ill. by author. HarperCollins, 2006. ISBN 978-0-06-074159-4 Subj: ABC books. Animals – mice. Holidays – Christmas. Rhyming text.

A night of great joy ill. by author. Zonderkidz, 2016. ISBN 978-031074354-5 Subj: Holidays – Christmas. Religion – Nativity.

Queen of Christmas ill. by author. HarperCollins, 2003. ISBN 978-0-06-008176-8 Subj: Gifts. Holidays – Christmas.

Queen of Halloween ill. by author. HarperCollins, 2008. ISBN 978-0-06-008190-4 Subj: Emotions – fear. Holidays – Halloween.

Queen of the class ill. by author. HarperCollins, 2004. ISBN 978-0-06-008179-9 Subj: Royalty – queens. School. Theater.

Engels-Fietzek, Petra. *Sophie and the seagull* ill. by Julia Ginsbach. G. Stevens, 2002. ISBN 978-0-8368-3174-0 Subj: Birds – seagulls. Friendship. Sea & seashore.

Engle, Margarita. *All the way to Havana* ill. by Mike Curato. Henry Holt, 2017. ISBN 978-162779642-2 Subj: Automobiles. Behavior – resourcefulness. Character traits – perseverance. Family life. Foreign lands – Cuba.

Drum dream girl: how one girl's courage changed music ill. by Rafael López. Houghton Mifflin Harcourt, 2015. ISBN 978-054410229-3 Subj: Foreign lands – Cuba. Gender roles. Music. Musical instruments – drums.

Orangutanka ill. by Renee Kurilla. Henry Holt, 2015. ISBN 978-080509839-6 Subj: Animals – orangutans. Poetry.

The sky painter ill. by Aliona Bereghici. Amazon/Two Lions, 2015. ISBN 978-147782633-1 Subj: Activities – painting. Art. Birds. Careers – artists. Nature. Poetry.

Summer birds: the butterflies of Maria Merian ill. by Julie Paschkis. Henry Holt, 2010. ISBN 978-0-8050-8937-0 Subj: Activities – painting. Art. Insects – butterflies, caterpillars.

Tiny rabbit's big wish ill. by David Walker. Houghton, 2014. ISBN 978-054785286-7 Subj: Animals – rabbits. Character traits – smallness. Concepts – size. Self-concept.

Engler, Michael. *Elephantastic!* ill. by Joelle Tourlonias. Peter Pauper, 2015. ISBN 978-144130841-2 Subj: Animals – elephants. Friendship. Imagination. Toys.

English, Karen. *The baby on the way* ill. by Sean Qualls. Farrar, 2005. ISBN 978-0-374-37361-0 Subj: Babies, toddlers. Ethnic groups in the U.S. – African Americans. Family life – grandmothers.

Hot day on Abbott Avenue ill. by Javaka Steptoe. Clarion, 2004. ISBN 978-0-395-98527-4 Subj: Activities – jumping. Ethnic groups in the U.S. – African Americans. Friendship. Seasons – summer.

Nadia's hands ill. by Jonathan Weiner. Boyds Mills, 1999. ISBN 978-1-56397-667-4 Subj: Ethnic groups in the U.S. – Pakistani Americans. Family life. Self-concept. Weddings.

Speak English for us, Marisol ill. by Enrique O. Sánchez. Albert Whitman, 2000. ISBN 978-0-8075-7554-3 Subj: Ethnic groups in the U.S. – Hispanic Americans. Foreign languages.

Erdrich, Liselotte. *Bears make rock soup and other stories* ill. by Lisa Fifield. Children's Book Press, 2002. ISBN 978-0-89239-172-1 Subj: Animals. Indians of North America – Great Plains.

Erdrich, Louise. *The range eternal* ill. by Steve Johnson and Lou Fancher. Hyperion, 2002. ISBN 978-0-7868-0220-3 Subj: Activities – baking, cooking. U.S. history – frontier & pioneer life.

Ericsson, Jennifer A. *Home to me, home to you* ill. by Ashley Wolff. Little, Brown, 2005. ISBN 978-0-316-60922-7 Subj: Activities – working. Careers. Family life – mothers.

Out and about at the bakery ill. by Anne McMullen. Picture Window, 2003. ISBN 978-1-4048-0037-3 Subj: Activities – baking, cooking. Careers – bakers. School – field trips.

A piece of chalk ill. by Michelle Shapiro. Macmillan, 2007. ISBN 978-1-59643-057-0 Subj: Activities – drawing. Concepts – color.

She did it! ill. by Nadine Bernard Westcott. Farrar, 2002. ISBN 978-0-374-36776-3 Subj: Behavior – messy. Family life – sisters. Rhyming text.

Whoo goes there? ill. by Bert Kitchen. Roaring Brook, 2009. ISBN 978-1-59643-371-7 Subj: Animals. Birds – owls. Nature.

Eriksson, Eva. *A crash course for Molly* ill. by author. Farrar, 2005. ISBN 978-91-29-66156-9 Subj: Animals. Family life – grandmothers. Sports – bicycling.

Ering, Timothy Basil. *The unexpected love story of Alfred Fiddleduckling* ill. by author. Candlewick, 2017. ISBN 978-076366432-9 Subj: Birds – ducks. Boats, ships. Musical instruments – violins. Weather – storms.

Erlbruch, Wolf. *The big question* by Wolf Erlbruch and Michael Reynolds; ill. by Wolf Erlbruch. Europa, 2005. ISBN 978-1-933372-03-7 Subj: Character traits – questioning. Self-concept.

Ernst, Lisa Campbell. *The gingerbread girl* (The gingerbread boy)

The Gingerbread Girl goes animal crackers ill. by author. Penguin, 2011. ISBN 978-0-525-42259-4 Subj: Animals – foxes. Behavior – running away. Cumulative tales. Food.

Goldilocks returns ill. by author. Simon & Schuster, 2000. ISBN 978-0-689-82537-8 Subj: Animals – bears. Folk & fairy tales. Humorous stories.

The letters are lost! ill. by author. Viking, 1996. ISBN 978-0-670-86336-5 Subj: ABC books. Toys.

Little Red Riding Hood: a newfangled prairie tale ill. by author. Simon & Schuster, 1995. ISBN 978-0-689-80145-7 Subj: Activities – baking, cooking. Animals – wolves. Behavior – talking to strangers. Family life – grandmothers. Folk & fairy tales.

Round like a ball! ill. by author. Blue Apple, 2008. ISBN 978-1-934706-01-5 Subj: Earth. Rhyming text.

Stella Louella's runaway book ill. by author. Simon & Schuster, 1998. ISBN 978-0-689-81883-7 Subj: Behavior – lost & found possessions. Careers – librarians. Cumulative tales. Libraries.

Sylvia Jean, drama queen ill. by author. Penguin, 2005. ISBN 978-0-525-46962-9 Subj: Animals – pigs. Clothing – costumes. Self-concept.

Sylvia Jean, scout supreme ill. by author. Penguin, 2010. ISBN 978-0-525-47873-7 Subj: Animals – pigs. Character traits – helpfulness. Clubs, gangs. Disguises.

This is the van that Dad cleaned ill. by author. Simon & Schuster, 2005. ISBN 978-0-689-86190-1 Subj: Automobiles. Character traits – cleanliness. Family life – fathers. Rhyming text.

Wake up, it's Spring! ill. by author. HarperCollins, 2004. ISBN 978-0-06-008986-3 Subj: Animals. Nature. Seasons – spring.

Esbaum, Jill. *Estelle takes a bath* ill. by Mary Newell DePalma. Henry Holt, 2006. ISBN 978-0-8050-7741-4 Subj: Activities – bathing. Animals – mice. Rhyming text.

Everything spring. National Geographic, 2010. ISBN 978-1-4263-0607-5 Subj: Seasons – spring.

Frankenbunny ill. by Alice Brereton. Sterling, 2017. ISBN 978-145492172-1 Subj: Animals – rabbits. Character traits – bravery. Character traits – cleverness. Emotions – fear. Family life – brothers. Monsters.

I am cow, hear me moo! ill. by Gus Gordon. Dial, 2014. ISBN 978-080373524-8 Subj: Animals –

bulls, cows. Character traits – bravery. Emotions – fear. Rhyming text.

I hatched! ill. by Jen Corace. Dial, 2014. ISBN 978-080373688-7 Subj: Birds. Rhyming text.

Stanza ill. by Jack E. Davis. Harcourt, 2009. ISBN 978-0-15-205998-9 Subj: Activities – writing. Animals – dogs. Behavior – misbehavior. Contests. Poetry. Rhyming text. Self-concept.

To the big top ill. by David Gordon. Farrar, 2008. ISBN 978-0-374-39934-4 Subj: Character traits – helpfulness. Circus. Friendship. U.S. history.

Tom's tweet ill. by Dan Santat. Random House, 2011. ISBN 978-0-375-85171-1 Subj: Animals – cats. Birds. Emotions – loneliness. Friendship.

Eschbacher, Roger. *Nonsense! He yelled* ill. by Adrian Johnson. Dial, 2002. ISBN 978-0-8037-2582-9 Subj: ABC books. Rhyming text.

Road trip ill. by Thor Wickstrom. Penguin, 2006. ISBN 978-0-8037-2927-8 Subj: Activities – traveling. Family life. Rhyming text.

Eskelson, Laura. *The copper braid of Shannon O'Shea* ill. by Pam Newton. Dutton, 2003. ISBN 978-0-525-46138-8 Subj: Foreign lands – Ireland. Hair. Mythical creatures.

Escoffier, Michael. *The day I lost my superpowers* ill. by Kris DiGiacomo. Enchanted Lion, 2014. ISBN 978-159270144-5 Subj: Activities – playing. Imagination.

Rabbit and the Not-So-Big-Bad Wolf ill. by Kris DiGiacomo. Holiday House, 2013. ISBN 978-0-8234-2813-7 Subj: Animals – rabbits. Animals – wolves.

Take away the A ill. by Kris DiGiacomo. Enchanted Lion, 2014. ISBN 978-159270156-8 Subj: ABC books. Language.

Where's the baboon? ill. by Kris DiGiacomo. Enchanted Lion, 2015. ISBN 978-159270189-6 Subj: Humorous stories. Language.

Brief thief ill. by Kris DiGiacomo. Enchanted Lion, 2013. ISBN 978-1-59270-131-5 Subj: Clothing – underwear. Crime. Reptiles – iguanas.

Have you seen my trumpet? ill. by Kris DiGiacomo. Enchanted Lion, 2016. ISBN 978-159270201-5 Subj: Animals. Language.

Me first! ill. by Kris DiGiacomo. Enchanted Lion, 2013. ISBN 978-1-59270-136-0 Subj: Behavior – bossy. Birds – ducks. Family life – brothers & sisters.

Sleep tight, Charlie ill. by Kris DiGiacomo. Princeton Architectural, 2017. ISBN 978-161689599-0 Subj: Animals – rabbits. Bedtime. Noise, sounds. Sleep – snoring.

Esenwine, Matt Forrest. *Flashlight night* ill. by Fred Koehler. Boyds Mills, 2017. ISBN 978-162979493-

8 Subj: Activities – storytelling. Imagination. Night. Rhyming text.

Esham, Barbara. *Last to finish: a story about the smartest boy in math class* ill. by Mike Gordon. Mainstream, 2008. ISBN 978-1-60336-456-0 Subj: Character traits – confidence. Counting, numbers. School.

Estefan, Gloria. *Noelle's treasure tale: a new magically mysterious adventure* ill. by Michael Garland. HarperCollins, 2006. ISBN 978-0-06-112614-7 Subj: Animals – dogs. Rhyming text. Sea & seashore – beaches.

Estes, Allison. *Izzy and Oscar* by Allison Estes and Dan Stark ill. by Tracy Dockray. Sourcebooks/Jabberwocky, 2015. ISBN 978-149260150-0 Subj: Octopuses. Pets. Pirates.

Ethan, Eric. *Helicopters* ill. with photos. G. Stevens, 2002. ISBN 978-0-8368-3046-0 Subj: Character traits – helpfulness. Helicopters. Safety.

Ets, Marie Hall. *Gilberto and the wind* ill. by author. Viking, 1978, ©1963. ISBN 978-0-670-34025-5 Subj: Ethnic groups in the U.S. – Mexican Americans. Weather – wind.

In the forest ill. by author. Viking, 1944. ISBN 978-0-670-39687-0 Subj: Activities – picnicking. Animals. Caldecott award honor books. Forest, woods. Imagination. Parades.

Just me ill. by author. Viking, 1978, ©1965. ISBN 978-0-670-41109-2 Subj: Animals. Caldecott award honor books. Participation.

Mister Penny ill. by author. Viking, 1935. Subj: Animals. Caldecott award honor books. Farms.

Mr. Penny's race horse ill. by author. Viking, 1956. Subj: Animals – horses, ponies. Caldecott award honor books. Fairs, festivals. Farms.

Mr. T. W. Anthony Woo ill. by author. Viking, 1951. Subj: Animals – cats. Animals – dogs. Animals – mice. Caldecott award honor books.

Nine days to Christmas ill. by author. Viking, 1959. ISBN 978-0-670-51350-5 Subj: Caldecott award books. Ethnic groups in the U.S. – Mexican Americans. Foreign lands – Mexico. Holidays – Christmas. Parties.

Play with me ill. by author. Viking, 1955. ISBN 978-0-670-55977-0 Subj: Activities – playing. Animals. Behavior. Caldecott award honor books.

Eure, Wesley. *A fish out of water.* Designed and ill. by Meredith College Art Department. Pelican, 2000. ISBN 978-1-56554-850-3 Subj: Animals. Birds. Character traits – compromising. Emotions – love. Fish.

Evans, Cambria. *Bone soup* ill. by author. Houghton, 2008. ISBN 978-0-618-80908-0 Subj: Folk & fairy tales. Food. Ghosts. Monsters.

Martha Moth makes socks ill. by author. Houghton, 2006. ISBN 978-0-618-55745-5 Subj: Birthdays. Clothing – socks. Gifts. Insects – moths. Parties.

Evans, Dilys, compiler. *Fairies, trolls and goblins galore* ill. by Jacqueline Rogers. Simon & Schuster, 2000. ISBN 978-0-689-82352-7 Subj: Fairies. Mythical creatures. Poetry.

Evans, Kristina. *What's special about me, Mama?* ill. by Javaka Steptoe. Hyperion/Disney, 2011. ISBN 978-0-7868-5274-1 Subj: Character traits – individuality. Emotions – love. Ethnic groups in the U.S. – African Americans. Family life – mothers. Self-concept.

Evans, Lezlie. *The bunnies' picnic* ill. by Kay Chorao. Hyperion, 2007. ISBN 978-0-7868-1612-5 Subj: Activities – baking, cooking. Activities – picnicking. Animals – rabbits. Food. Rhyming text.

The bunnies' trip ill. by Kay Chorao. Hyperion, 2008. ISBN 978-0-7868-1898-3 Subj: Activities – traveling. Animals – rabbits. Rhyming text.

Can you count ten toes? count to 10 in 10 different languages ill. by Denis Roche. Houghton, 1999. ISBN 978-0-395-90499-2 Subj: Counting, numbers. Foreign languages. Rhyming text.

Can you greet the whole wide world? twelve common phrases in twelve different languages ill. by Denis Roche. Houghton, 2006. ISBN 978-0-618-56327-2 Subj: Foreign languages.

Finding Christmas ill. by Yee Von Chan. Albert Whitman, 2017. ISBN 978-080752433-6 Subj: Animals. Birds – sparrows. Character traits – kindness to animals. Holidays – Christmas. Illness.

Who loves the little lamb? ill. by David McPhail. Hyperion/Disney, 2010. ISBN 978-1-4231-1659-2 Subj: Animals – babies. Emotions – love. Family life – mothers. Rhyming text.

Evans, Nate. *Bang! Boom! Roar! a busy crew of dinosaurs* by Nate Evans and Stephanie Gwyn Brown ill. by Christopher Santoro. HarperCollins, 2012. ISBN 978-0-06-087960-0 Subj: ABC books. Careers – construction workers. Dinosaurs. Rhyming text. Trucks.

The Jellybeans and the big art adventure (Numeroff, Laura Joffe)

The Jellybeans and the big book bonanza (Numeroff, Laura Joffe)

The Jellybeans and the big camp kickoff (Numeroff, Laura Joffe)

The Jellybeans and the big dance (Numeroff, Laura Joffe)

Ponyella (Numeroff, Laura Joffe)

Sherman Crunchley (Numeroff, Laura Joffe)

Evans, Richard Paul. *The light of Christmas* ill. by Daniel Craig. Simon & Schuster, 2002. ISBN 978-0-689-83468-4 Subj: Character traits – kindness. Holidays – Christmas.

The spyglass ill. by Jonathan Linton. Simon & Schuster, 2001. ISBN 978-0-689-83466-0 Subj: Character traits – ambition. Royalty – kings.

The tower ill. by Jonathan Linton. Simon & Schuster, 2001. ISBN 978-0-689-83467-7 Subj: Character traits – pride. Character traits – vanity.

Evans, Shane W. *Underground: finding the light to freedom* ill. by Shane W. Evans. Roaring Brook, 2011. ISBN 978-1-59643-538-4 Subj: Character traits – freedom. Ethnic groups in the U.S. – African Americans. Slavery. U.S. history.

We march ill. by Shane W. Evans. Roaring Brook, 2012. ISBN 978-1-59643-539-1 Subj: Ethnic groups in the U.S. – African Americans. Holidays – Martin Luther King, Jr. Day. U.S. history. Violence, nonviolence.

Everitt, Betsy. *Mean soup* ill. by author. Harcourt, 1992. ISBN 978-0-15-253146-1 Subj: Activities – baking, cooking. Behavior – bad day, bad mood. Emotions – anger. Food. School.

Eversole, Robyn. *East Dragon, West Dragon* ill. by Scott Campbell. Atheneum, 2012. ISBN 978-0-689-85828-4 Subj: Dragons. Prejudice.

Evert, Lori. *The Christmas wish* photos by Per Breiehagen. Random House, 2013. ISBN 978-0-375-97173-0 Subj: Activities – traveling. Animals. Holidays – Christmas. Santa Claus.

Ewart, Claire. *The giant* ill. by author. Walker, 2003. ISBN 978-0-8027-8837-5 Subj: Emotions – grief. Family life – fathers. Farms. Seasons.

Ewert, Marcus. *Mummy cat* ill. by Lisa Brown. Clarion, 2015. ISBN 978-054434082-4 Subj: Animals – cats. Foreign lands – Egypt. Mummies. Rhyming text.

Fackelmayer, Regina. *The gifts* ill. by Christa Unzner. NorthSouth, 2009. ISBN 978-0-7358-2265-8

Subj: Character traits – helpfulness. Character traits – kindness. Holidays – Christmas.

Fagan, Cary. *Ella May and the wishing stone* ill. by Geneviève Côté. Tundra, 2011. ISBN 978-1-77049-225-7 Subj: Behavior – wishing. Friendship.

Mr. Zinger's hat ill. by Dusan Petricic. Tundra, 2012. ISBN 978-1-77049-253-0 Subj: Activities – storytelling. Careers – writers. Circular tales. Clothing – hats. Imagination.

Oy, feh, so? ill. by Gary Clement. Groundwood, 2013. ISBN 978-1-55498-148-9 Subj: Family life – aunts, uncles. Jewish culture.

Faglia, Matteo. *Happy birthday, I'm 1* ill. by Luana Rinaldo. Kane/Miller, 2001. ISBN 978-1-929132-07-2 Subj: Animals – rabbits. Birthdays. Food. Format, unusual – board books.

Happy birthday, I'm 2 ill. by Silvia Vignale. Kane/Miller, 2001. ISBN 978-1-929132-08-9 Subj: Animals – dogs. Birthdays. Food. Format, unusual – board books.

Happy birthday, I'm 3 ill. by Sophie Fatus. Kane/Miller, 2001. ISBN 978-1-929132-09-6 Subj: Animals – cats. Birthdays. Food. Format, unusual – board books.

Happy birthday, I'm 4 ill. by Antonella Abbatiello. Kane/Miller, 2001. ISBN 978-1-929132-10-2 Subj: Animals – bears. Birthdays. Food. Format, unusual – board books.

Fairgray, Richard. *Gorillas in our midst* by Richard Fairgray and Terry Jones; ill. by Richard Fairgray. Sky Pony, 2015. ISBN 978-163220607-7 Subj: Animals – gorillas. Disguises. Picture puzzles.

Falatko, Julie. *Snappsy the alligator (did not ask to be in this book)* ill. by Tim Miller. Viking, 2016. ISBN 978-045146945-8 Subj: Books, reading. Humorous stories. Reptiles – alligators, crocodiles.

Snappsy the alligator and his best friend forever (probably) ill. by Tim Miller. Viking, 2017. ISBN 978-042528865-8 Subj: Birds – chickens, roosters. Friendship. Reptiles – alligators, crocodiles.

Falconer, Ian. *Olivia* ill. by author. Atheneum, 2000. ISBN 978-0-689-82953-6 Subj: Activities. Animals – pigs. Behavior. Caldecott award honor books.

Olivia and the fairy princesses ill. by author. Atheneum, 2012. ISBN 978-1-4442-5027-1 Subj: Animals – pigs. Character traits – individuality. Royalty – princesses. Royalty – queens. Self-concept.

Olivia — and the missing toy ill. by author. Atheneum, 2003. ISBN 978-0-689-85291-6 Subj: Animals – pigs. Behavior – lost & found possessions. Format, unusual – board books. Toys.

Olivia counts ill. by author. Atheneum, 2002. ISBN 978-0-689-85087-5 Subj: Animals – babies. Animals – pigs. Counting, numbers. Format, unusual – board books.

Olivia forms a band ill. by author. Simon & Schuster, 2006. ISBN 978-1-4169-2454-8 Subj: Animals – pigs. Music.

Olivia goes to Venice ill. by author. Simon & Schuster, 2010. ISBN 978-1-4169-9674-3 Subj: Activities – vacationing. Animals – pigs. Foreign lands – Italy.

Olivia saves the circus ill. by author. Atheneum, 2001. ISBN 978-0-689-82954-3 Subj: Animals – pigs. Circus. School.

Olivia the spy ill. by author. Atheneum/Caitlyn Dlouhy, 2017. ISBN 978-148145795-8 Subj: Animals – pigs. Behavior – misunderstanding. Behavior – secrets. Behavior – worrying.

Olivia's opposites ill. by author. Atheneum, 2002. ISBN 978-0-689-85088-2 Subj: Animals – babies. Animals – pigs. Behavior. Concepts – opposites. Format, unusual – board books.

Falken, Linda. *Can you find it?*. Abrams, 2010. ISBN 978-0-8109-8890-3 Subj: Art. Picture puzzles. U.S. history.

Falkenstern, Lisa. *A dragon moves in* ill. by author. Marshall Cavendish, 2011. ISBN 978-0-7614-5947-7 Subj: Animals – hedgehogs. Animals – rabbits. Dragons. Homes, houses.

Professor Whiskerton presents Steampunk ABC ill. by author. Amazon/Two Lions, 2014. ISBN 978-147784722-0 Subj: ABC books. Animals – mice. Inventions.

Faller, Regis. *The adventures of Polo* ill. by author. Macmillan, 2006. ISBN 978-1-59643-160-7 Subj: Activities – traveling. Animals – dogs. Imagination. Wordless.

Polo: the runaway book ill. by author. Macmillan, 2007. ISBN 978-1-59643-189-8 Subj: Activities – traveling. Animals – dogs. Imagination. Wordless.

Polo and Lily ill. by author. Roaring Brook, 2009. ISBN 978-1-59643-496-7 Subj: Animals – dogs. Animals – rabbits. Friendship. Wordless.

Polo and the dragon ill. by author. Roaring Brook, 2009. ISBN 978-1-59643-498-1 Subj: Animals – dogs. Dragons. Imagination. Wordless.

Polo and the magician! ill. by author. Roaring Brook, 2009. ISBN 978-1-59643-497-4 Subj: Activities – traveling. Animals – dogs. Careers – magicians. Circus. Wordless.

Fallon, Jimmy. *Snowball fight!* ill. by Adam Stower. Penguin, 2005. ISBN 978-0-525-47456-2 Subj: Rhyming text. Weather – snow.

Falwell, Cathryn. *Christmas for 10* ill. by author. Clarion, 1998. ISBN 978-0-395-85581-2 Subj: Counting, numbers. Ethnic groups in the U.S. – African Americans. Holidays – Christmas. Rhyming text.

David's drawing ill. by author. Lee & Low, 2001. ISBN 978-1-58430-031-1 Subj: Activities – drawing. Ethnic groups in the U.S. – African Americans. Friendship. School – first day.

Feast for ten ill. by author. Clarion, 1993. ISBN 978-0-395-62037-3 Subj: Activities – baking, cooking. Counting, numbers. Ethnic groups in the U.S. – African Americans. Family life. Rhyming text.

Gobble gobble ill. by author. Dawn, 2011. ISBN 978-158469-148-8; Subj: Birds – turkeys. Rhyming text.

Mystery vine: a pumpkin surprise ill. by author. HarperCollins, 2009. ISBN 978-0-06-177198-9 Subj: Food. Gardens, gardening. Rhyming text.

P.J. and Puppy ill. by author. Clarion, 1997. ISBN 978-0-395-56918-4 Subj: Animals – dogs. Family life – mothers. Pets. Toilet training.

Pond babies ill. by author. Down East, 2011. ISBN 978-0-89272-920-3 Subj: Animals – babies. Lakes, ponds.

Rainbow Stew ill. by author. Lee & Low, 2013. ISBN 978-1-60060-847-6 Subj: Activities – baking, cooking. Family life – grandfathers. Food. Rhyming text.

Scoot! ill. by author. Greenwillow, 2008. ISBN 978-0-06-128882-1 Subj: Lakes, ponds. Reptiles – turtles, tortoises. Rhyming text.

Shape capers ill. by author. HarperCollins, 2007. ISBN 978-0-06-123700-3 Subj: Concepts – shape. Rhyming text.

Turtle splash! ill. by author. Greenwillow, 2001. ISBN 978-0-06-029463-2 Subj: Counting, numbers. Reptiles – turtles, tortoises. Rhyming text.

We have a baby ill. by author. Clarion, 1993. ISBN 978-0-395-62038-0 Subj: Babies, toddlers. Family life.

Word wizard ill. by author. Clarion, 1998. ISBN 978-0-395-85580-5 Subj: Imagination. Language.

Fan, Terry. *The Night Gardener* ill. by Eric Fan. Simon & Schuster, 2016. ISBN 978-148143978-7 Subj: Gardens, gardening. Night. Orphans.

Fancher, Lou. *Star climbing* ill. by Steve Johnson. HarperCollins, 2006. ISBN 978-0-06-073902-7 Subj: Bedtime. Imagination. Stars.

Farber, Norma. *How the hibernators came to Bethlehem* ill. by Barbara Cooney. Walker, 2006. ISBN

978-0-8027-9610-3 Subj: Animals. Holidays – Christmas. Poetry. Religion.

Fardell, John. *Jeremiah Jellyfish flies high!* ill. by author. IPG/Andersen, 2012. ISBN 978-1-84939-147-4 Subj: Activities – flying. Airplanes, airports. Animals.

Farish, Terry. *The cat who liked potato soup* ill. by Barry Root. Candlewick, 2003. ISBN 978-0-7636-0834-7 Subj: Animals – cats. Food. Friendship. Pets. Sports – fishing.

Joseph's big ride ill. by Ken Daley. Annick, 2016. ISBN 978-155451806-7 Subj: Foreign lands – Africa. Friendship. Immigrants, immigration. Refugees. Sports – bicycling.

Luis paints the world ill. by Oliver Dominguez. Carolrhoda, 2016. ISBN 978-146775796-6 Subj: Art. Careers – military. Ethnic groups in the U.S. – Dominican Americans. Family life – brothers. Foreign languages.

Farley, Brianne. *Ike's incredible ink* ill. by author. Candlewick, 2013. ISBN 978-0-7636-6296-7 Subj: Activities – writing.

Farley, Carol J. *The king's secret* ill. by Robert Jew. HarperCollins, 2001. ISBN 978-0-688-12777-0 Subj: ABC books. Behavior – secrets. Foreign lands – Korea. Foreign languages. Royalty – kings.

Farmer, Bonnie. *Isaac's dreamcatcher* ill. by Anouk Perusse-Bell. Lobster, 2001. ISBN 978-1-894222-46-4 Subj: Dreams. Emotions – fear. Indians of North America.

The farmer in the dell. *The farmer in the dell* ill. by John O'Brien. Boyds Mills, 2000. ISBN 978-1-56397-775-6 Subj: Careers – farmers. Farms. Games. Music. Songs.

The farmer in the dell ill. by Alexandra Wallner. Holiday, 1998. ISBN 978-0-8234-1382-9 Subj: Careers – farmers. Farms. Games. Music. Songs.

Farmer, Nancy. *Clever Ali* ill. by Gail de Marcken. Scholastic, 2006. ISBN 978-0-439-37014-1 Subj: Birds – pigeons. Family life – fathers. Foreign lands – Egypt. Royalty – sultans.

Farrar, Sid. *The year comes round: haiku through the seasons* ill. by Ilse Plume. Albert Whitman, 2012. ISBN 978-0-8075-8129-2 Subj: Nature. Poetry. Seasons.

Farrell, Darren. *Stop following me, Moon!* ill. by author. Dial, 2016. ISBN 978-080374159-1 Subj: Animals – bears. Behavior – greed. Behavior – sharing. Moon.

Thank you, Octopus ill. by author. Dial, 2014. ISBN 978-080373438-8 Subj: Bedtime. Octopuses.

Farrington, Susan. *What I love about you* ill. by author. HarperCollins/Balzer+Bray, 2016. ISBN 978-006239353-1 Subj: Babies, toddlers. Emotions – love. Family life – parents.

Farris, Christine King. *March on! the day my brother Martin changed the world* ill. by London Ladd. Scholastic, 2008. ISBN 978-0-545-03537-8 Subj: Ethnic groups in the U.S. – African Americans. Holidays – Martin Luther King, Jr. Day. Prejudice. U.S. history. Violence, nonviolence.

My brother Martin: a sister remembers growing up with the Rev. Dr. Martin Luther King ill. by Chris Soentpiet. Simon & Schuster, 2003. ISBN 978-0-689-84387-7 Subj: Ethnic groups in the U.S. – African Americans. Family life – brothers & sisters. Holidays – Martin Luther King, Jr. Day. Prejudice. U.S. history. Violence, nonviolence.

Faruqi, Reem. *Lailah's lunchbox* ill. by Lea Lyon. Tilbury, 2015. ISBN 978-088448431-8 Subj: Ethnic groups in the U.S. Holidays – Ramadan. Moving. Religion – Islam. School.

Fauchald, Nick. *Batter up! you can play softball* ill. by Ronnie Rooney. Picture Window, 2006. ISBN 978-1-4048-1152-2 Subj: Sports – baseball.

Bump! set! spike! you can play volleyball ill. by Ronnie Rooney. Picture Window, 2006. ISBN 978-1-4048-1153-9 Subj: Sports – volleyball.

Face off! you can play hockey ill. by Ronnie Rooney. Picture Window, 2006. ISBN 978-1-4048-1154-6 Subj: Sports – hockey.

Jump ball! you can play basketball ill. by Bill Dickson. Picture Window, 2004. ISBN 978-1-4048-0261-2 Subj: Sports – basketball.

Nice hit! you can play baseball ill. by Bill Dickson. Picture Window, 2004. ISBN 978-1-4048-0259-9 Subj: Sports – baseball.

Score! you can play soccer ill. by Bill Dickson. Picture Window, 2004. ISBN 978-1-4048-0262-9 Subj: Sports – soccer.

Tee off! you can play golf ill. by Ronnie Rooney. Picture Window, 2006. ISBN 978-1-4048-1155-3 Subj: Sports – golf.

Touchdown! you can play football ill. by Bill Dickson. Picture Window, 2004. ISBN 978-1-4048-0260-5 Subj: Sports – football.

Faulconer, Maria. *A mom for Umande* ill. by Susan Kathleen Hartung. Dial, 2014. ISBN 978-080373762-4 Subj: Animals – babies. Animals – gorillas. Character traits – kindness to animals. Zoos.

Faulkenberry, Lauren. *What do animals do on the weekend?* ill. by author. Novello, 2002. ISBN 978-0-9708972-4-4 Subj: ABC books. Activities. Animals.

Faulkner, Keith. *Charlie Chimp's Christmas* ill. by Jonathan Lambert. Barron's, 2002. ISBN 978-0-7641-5556-7 Subj: Animals – chimpanzees. Format, unusual – toy & movable books. Holidays – Christmas. Santa Claus.

Do you have my quack? ill. by Rob Hefferan. Scholastic, 2001. ISBN 978-0-439-24085-7 Subj: Animals. Birds – ducks. Farms. Format, unusual – toy & movable books. Noise, sounds.

The giraffe who cock-a-doodle-doo'd ill. by Jonathan Lambert. Dial, 2002. ISBN 978-0-8037-2739-7 Subj: Animals. Format, unusual – toy & movable books. Jungle.

Jumbled jungle ill. by Jonathan Lambert. Scholastic, 2001. ISBN 978-0-439-30903-5 Subj: Animals. Format, unusual – toy & movable books. Jungle.

The monster who loved books ill. by Jonathan Lambert. Orchard, 2002. ISBN 978-0-439-34099-1 Subj: Books, reading. Format, unusual – toy & movable books. Monsters.

Pop! went another balloon! ill. by Rory Tyger. Dutton, 2002. ISBN 978-0-525-47122-6 Subj: Counting, numbers. Format, unusual – toy & movable books. Toys – balloons.

Rexerella ill. by Graham Kennedy. Paper engineering by Jonathan Lambert. Simon & Schuster, 2002. ISBN 978-0-689-85355-5 Subj: Dinosaurs. Format, unusual – toy & movable books.

The scared little bear ill. by Jonathan Lambert. 1st American Ed. Scholastic, 2000. ISBN 978-0-531-30267-5 Subj: Bedtime. Emotions – fear. Format, unusual – toy & movable books.

The tallest shortest longest greenest brownest animal in the jungle! ill. by Rory Tyger. Dutton, 2002. ISBN 978-0-525-46868-4 Subj: Animals. Format, unusual – toy & movable books. Friendship. Jungle.

A trick or a treat? ill. by Manhar Chauhan. Dutton, 2001. ISBN 978-0-525-46765-6 Subj: Format, unusual – toy & movable books. Holidays – Halloween. Night. Picture puzzles.

Faundez, Anne. *The day the rains fell* ill. by Karin Littlewood. IPG/Tamarind, 2010. ISBN 978-1-84853-015-7 Subj: Foreign lands – Africa. Weather – droughts.

Fearing, Mark. *The great Thanksgiving escape* ill. by author. Candlewick, 2014. ISBN 978-076366306-3 Subj: Family life. Holidays – Thanksgiving.

Fearnley, Jan. *Arthur and the meanies* ill. by author. Egmont UK, 2011. ISBN 978-1-4052-5380-2 Subj: Animals. Animals – elephants. Behavior – bullying, teasing. Friendship.

Just like you ill. by author. Candlewick, 2001. ISBN 978-0-7636-1322-8 Subj: Animals – babies. Animals – mice. Bedtime. Family life – parents.

Martha in the middle ill. by author. Candlewick, 2008. ISBN 978-0-7636-3800-9 Subj: Animals – mice. Behavior – running away. Family life – brothers & sisters. Frogs & toads.

Milo Armadillo ill. by author. Candlewick, 2009. ISBN 978-0-7636-4575-5 Subj: Animals – armadillos. Family life – grandmothers. Toys.

Mr. Wolf and the three bears ill. by author. Harcourt, 2002. ISBN 978-0-15-216423-2 Subj: Activities – baking, cooking. Animals – bears. Animals – wolves. Birthdays.

Mr. Wolf's pancakes ill. by author. Tiger Tales, 2001. ISBN 978-1-888444-76-6 Subj: Activities – baking, cooking. Animals – wolves. Food.

A perfect day for it ill. by author. Harcourt, 2002. ISBN 978-0-15-216634-2 Subj: Animals. Animals – bears. Friendship. Sports – sledding. Weather – snow.

The search for the perfect child ill. by author. Candlewick, 2006. ISBN 978-0-7636-3231-1 Subj: Animals – dogs. Behavior. Character traits – perfectionism.

A special something ill. by author. Hyperion, 2000. ISBN 978-0-7868-0589-1 Subj: Babies, toddlers. Birth. Family life. Family life – new sibling. Imagination.

Watch out! ill. by author. Candlewick, 2004. ISBN 978-0-7636-2318-0 Subj: Animals – mice. Behavior. Family life – mothers.

Fearrington, Ann. *Who sees the lighthouse?* ill. by Giles Laroche. Putnam, 2002. ISBN 978-0-399-23703-4 Subj: Counting, numbers. Lighthouses. Rhyming text.

Fecher, Sarah. *On the move* by Sarah Fecher and Deborah Kespert ill. by Gaëtan Evrard. Story by Belinda Webster; computer Ill. by Jon Stuart. Two-Can, 2000. ISBN 978-1-58728-605-6 Subj: Transportation.

Feder, Sandra. *The moon inside* ill. by Aimée Sicuro. Groundwood, 2016. ISBN 978-155498823-5 Subj: Bedtime. Emotions – fear. Moon. Night.

Federle, Tim. *Tommy can't stop!* ill. by Mark Fearing. Disney/Hyperion, 2015. ISBN 978-142316917-8 Subj: Activities – dancing. Family life.

Federspiel, Jurg. *Alligator Mike* ill. by Petra Rappo. NorthSouth, 2007. ISBN 978-0-7358-2124-8 Subj: Character traits – kindness to animals. Reptiles – alligators, crocodiles.

Feelings, Muriel. *Jambo means hello: Swahili alphabet book* ill. by Tom Feelings. Dial, 1974. ISBN 978-0-8037-4346-5 Subj: ABC books. Caldecott award honor books. Foreign lands – Africa. Foreign languages.

Moja means one: Swahili counting book ill. by Tom Feelings. Dial, 1972. ISBN 978-0-8037-5711-0 Subj: Caldecott award honor books. Counting, numbers. Foreign lands – Africa. Foreign languages.

Feeney, Tatyana. *Little Frog's tadpole trouble* ill. by author. Knopf, 2014. ISBN 978-038575372-2 Subj: Family life – brothers & sisters. Family life – new sibling. Frogs & toads. Sibling rivalry.

Little Owl's orange scarf ill. by author. Knopf, 2013. ISBN 978-0-449-81411-6 Subj: Behavior – lost & found possessions. Birds – owls. Clothing – scarves. Family life – mothers.

Small Bunny's blue blanket ill. by author. Knopf, 2012. ISBN 978-0-375-87087-3 Subj: Animals – rabbits. Laundry.

Small Elephant's bathtime ill. by author. Knopf, 2015. ISBN 978-055349721-2 Subj: Activities – bathing. Animals – elephants. Behavior – misbehavior.

Feiffer, Jules. *Bark, George* ill. by author. Harper-Collins, 1999. ISBN 978-0-06-205185-1 Subj: Animals – dogs. Humorous stories. Noise, sounds.

The daddy mountain ill. by author. Hyperion, 2004. ISBN 978-0-7868-0912-7 Subj: Family life – daughters. Family life – fathers.

I lost my bear ill. by author. Morrow, 1998. ISBN 978-0-688-15148-5 Subj: Behavior – lost & found possessions. Family life. Toys. Toys – bears.

Rupert can dance ill. by author. Farrar, 2014. ISBN 978-037436363-5 Subj: Activities – dancing. Animals – cats.

Feiffer, Kate. *But I wanted a baby brother!* ill. by Diane Goode. Simon & Schuster, 2010. ISBN 978-1-4169-3941-2 Subj: Babies, toddlers. Family life – brothers & sisters.

Double pink ill. by Bruce Ingman. Simon & Schuster, 2005. ISBN 978-0-689-87190-0 Subj: Concepts – color.

Henry, the dog with no tail ill. by Jules Feiffer. Simon & Schuster, 2007. ISBN 978-1-4169-1614-7 Subj: Anatomy – tails. Animals – dogs. Language. Self-concept.

My mom is trying to ruin my life ill. by Diane Goode. Simon & Schuster, 2009. ISBN 978-1-4169-4100-2 Subj: Emotions – embarrassment. Family life – parents. Humorous stories.

My side of the car ill. by Jules Feiffer. Candlewick, 2011. ISBN 978-0-7636-4405-5 Subj: Family life – fathers. Weather – rain. Zoos.

No go sleep! ill. by Jules Feiffer. Simon & Schuster, 2012. ISBN 978-1-4424-1683-3 Subj: Babies, toddlers. Bedtime. Family life. Night.

President Pennybaker ill. by Diane Goode. Simon & Schuster, 2008. ISBN 978-1-4169-1354-2 Subj: Animals – dogs. Behavior – seeking better things. Character traits – ambition.

Which puppy? ill. by Jules Feiffer. Simon & Schuster, 2009. ISBN 978-1-4169-9147-2 Subj: Animals. Animals – dogs. Ethnic groups in the U.S. – African Americans. Family life. Pets.

Feldman, Eve B. *Billy and Milly, short and silly* ill. by Tuesday Mourning. Putnam, 2009. ISBN 978-0-399-24651-7 Subj: Language. Rhyming text.

Félix, Lucie. *Apples and robins* ill. by author. Chronicle, 2016. ISBN 978-145213264-8 Subj: Concepts – color. Concepts – shape. Format, unusual – toy & movable books. Seasons. Trees.

Felix, Monique. *The rumor* ill. by author. Creative Education, 2011. ISBN 978-1-56846-219-6 Subj: Animals. Animals – wolves. Behavior – gossip, rumors. Communication.

Fenske, Jonathan. *Barnacle is bored* ill. by author. Scholastic, 2016. ISBN 978-054586504-3 Subj: Behavior – boredom. Crustaceans. Emotions – envy, jealousy. Fish.

Fenton, Joe. *Boo!* ill. by author. Simon & Schuster, 2010. ISBN 978-1-4169-7936-4 Subj: Disguises. Ghosts.

Ferber, Brenda A. *The yuckiest, stinkiest, best Valentine ever* ill. by Tedd Arnold. Dial, 2012. ISBN 978-0-8037-3505-7 Subj: Emotions – love. Holidays – Valentine's Day. Humorous stories.

Fergus, Maureen. *Buddy and Earl* ill. by Carey Sookocheff. Groundwood, 2015. ISBN 978-155498712-2 Subj: Animals – dogs. Animals – hedgehogs. Behavior – boredom. Friendship. Imagination.

Buddy and Earl and the great big baby ill. by Carey Sookocheff. Groundwood, 2016. ISBN 978-155498716-0 Subj: Animals – dogs. Animals – hedgehogs. Babies, toddlers.

Buddy and Earl go exploring ill. by Carey Sookocheff. Groundwood, 2016. ISBN 978-155498714-6 Subj: Animals – dogs. Animals – hedgehogs. Friendship. Imagination.

Buddy and Earl go to school ill. by Carey Sookocheff. Groundwood, 2017. ISBN 978-155498927-0 Subj: Animals – dogs. Animals – hedgehogs. School.

The day my mom came to kindergarten ill. by Mike Lowery. Kids Can, 2013. ISBN 978-1-55453-698-6 Subj: Behavior – misbehavior. Family life – mothers. School.

The day Santa stopped believing in Harold ill. by Cale Atkinson. Tundra, 2016. ISBN 978-177049824-

2 Subj: Ethnic groups in the U.S. Holidays – Christmas. Humorous stories. Santa Claus.

Ferguson, Sarah. *Ballerina Rosie* ill. by Diane Goode. Simon & Schuster, 2012. ISBN 978-1-4424-3066-2 Subj: Ballet. Careers – dancers. Self-concept.

Emily's first day of school ill. by Ian Cunliffe. Sterling, 2010. ISBN 978-1-4027-7392-1 Subj: School – first day.

Tea for Ruby ill. by Robin Preiss-Glasser. Simon & Schuster, 2008. ISBN 978-1-4169-5419-4 Subj: Etiquette. Royalty – princesses.

Fern, Tracey E. *Buffalo music* ill. by Lauren Castillo. Clarion, 2008. ISBN 978-0-618-72341-6 Subj: Animals – buffaloes. Texas.

W is for Webster: Noah Webster and his American dictionary ill. by Boris Kulikov. Farrar/Margaret Ferguson, 2015. ISBN 978-037438240-7 Subj: Careers – teachers. Dictionaries. Language. U.S. history.

Fernandes, Eugenie. *Big week for little mouse* ill. by Kim Fernandes. Kids Can, 2004. ISBN 978-1-55337-665-1 Subj: Animals – mice. Birthdays. Concepts – opposites. Days of the week, months of the year. Rhyming text.

Busy little mouse ill. by Kim Fernandes; photos by Pat Lacroix. Kids Can, 2002. ISBN 978-1-55074-776-8 Subj: Animals. Animals – mice. Farms. Noise, sounds. Rhyming text.

Kitten's spring ill. by author. Kids Can, 2010. ISBN 978-1-55453-340-4 Subj: Animals – babies. Animals – cats. Farms. Rhyming text. Seasons – spring.

Kitten's winter ill. by author. Kids Can, 2011. ISBN 978-1-55453-343-5 Subj: Animals. Animals – cats. Rhyming text. Seasons – winter.

Sleepy little mouse ill. by Kim Fernandes. Kids Can, 2000. ISBN 978-1-55074-701-0 Subj: Animals – mice. Behavior. Emotions. Sleep.

Ferrell, Sean. *I don't like Koala* ill. by Charles Santoso. Atheneum, 2015. ISBN 978-148140068-8 Subj: Animals – koalas. Toys.

The Snurtch ill. by Charles Santoso. Atheneum, 2016. ISBN 978-148145656-2 Subj: Behavior – misbehavior. Imagination – imaginary friends.

Ferreri, Della Ross. *How will I ever sleep in this bed?* ill. by Capucine Mazille. Sterling, 2005. ISBN 978-1-4027-1492-4 Subj: Bedtime. Furniture – beds. Rhyming text. Toys.

Ferri, Giuliano. *Little Tad grows up* ill. by author. Penguin, 2007. ISBN 978-0-698-40060-3 Subj: Behavior – growing up. Frogs & toads. Nature. Science.

Peekaboo ill. by author. Minedition, 2015. ISBN 978-988824093-7 Subj: Animals. Format, unusual – board books. Format, unusual – toy & movable books.

Ferris, Jeri Chase. *Noah Webster and his words* ill. by Vincent X. Kirsch. Houghton Mifflin, 2012. ISBN 978-0-547-39055-0 Subj: Careers – teachers. Dictionaries. Language. U.S. history.

Ferry, Beth. *Land shark* ill. by Ben Mantle. Chronicle, 2015. ISBN 978-145212458-2 Subj: Animals – dogs. Birthdays. Fish – sharks. Pets.

Pirate's perfect pet ill. by Matthew Myers. Candlewick, 2016. ISBN 978-076367288-1 Subj: Animals. Birds – parakeets, parrots. Pets. Pirates.

A small blue whale ill. by Lisa Mundorff. Knopf, 2017. ISBN 978-152471337-9 Subj: Animals – whales. Birds – penguins. Character traits – kindness to animals. Emotions – loneliness. Friendship.

Stick and Stone ill. by Tom Lichtenheld. Harcourt, 2015. ISBN 978-054403256-9 Subj: Emotions – loneliness. Friendship. Rhyming text. Rocks.

Feutl, Rita. *Room enough for Daisy* (Waldman, Debby)

Ficocelli, Elizabeth. *Kid tea* ill. by Glin Dibley. Marshall Cavendish, 2007. ISBN 978-0-7614-5333-8 Subj: Activities – bathing. Concepts – color. Days of the week, months of the year. Rhyming text.

Field, Eugene. *Wynken, Blynken and Nod* ill. by Johanna Westerman. NorthSouth, 1995. ISBN 978-1-55858-423-5 Subj: Poetry. Sea & seashore. Sleep.

Wynken, Blynken, and Nod: a Dutch lullaby ill. by Giselle Potter. Random House, 2008. ISBN 978-0-375-84196-5 Subj: Poetry. Sea & seashore. Sleep.

Field, Rachel Lyman. *Grace for an island meal* ill. by Cynthia Jabar. Farrar, 2006. ISBN 978-0-374-32759-0 Subj: Islands. Poetry. Religion.

Prayer for a child ill. by Elizabeth Orton Jones. Macmillan, 1944. ISBN 978-0-02-735190-3 Subj: Caldecott award books. Religion.

Fielding, Beth. *Animal eyes.* EarlyLight, 2011. ISBN 978-0-9797455-5-3 Subj: Anatomy – eyes. Animals.

Animal tails ill. with photos. EarlyLight, 2011. ISBN 978-0-9797455-8-4 Subj: Anatomy – tails. Animals.

Fields, Terri. *One good deed* ill. by Deborah Melmon. Kar-Ben, 2015. ISBN 978-146773478-3 Subj: Character traits – kindness. Jewish culture.

Fierstein, Harvey. *The sissy duckling* ill. by Henry Cole. Simon & Schuster, 2002. ISBN 978-0-689-83566-7 Subj: Birds – ducks. Gender roles. Self-concept.

Figley, Marty Rhodes. *Emily and Carlo* ill. by Catherine Stock. Charlesbridge, 2012. ISBN 978-1-58089-274-2 Subj: Animals – dogs. Poetry.

The schoolchildren's blizzard ill. by Shelly O. Haas. Carolrhoda, 2004. ISBN 978-1-57505-586-2 Subj: Careers – teachers. Family life – sisters. U.S. history. Weather – blizzards.

Filleul, Liz. *Tumbler* ill. by Susan Field. Augsburg Fortress, 2001. ISBN 978-0-8066-4268-0 Subj: Careers – acrobats. Religion.

Fillion, Kate. *The darkest dark* (Hadfield, Chris)

Finch, Mary. *The little red hen* (The little red hen)

Finchler, Judy. *Congratulations, Miss Malarkey!* by Judy Finchler and Kevin O'Malley ill. by Kevin O'Malley. Walker, 2009. ISBN 978-0-8027-9835-0 Subj: Careers – teachers. School. Weddings.

Miss Malarkey leaves no reader behind by Judy Finchler and Kevin O'Malley ill. by Kevin O'Malley. Walker, 2006. ISBN 978-0-8027-8084-3 Subj: Books, reading. Careers – teachers. School.

Miss Malarkey won't be in today ill. by Kevin O'Malley. Walker, 2000. ISBN 978-0-8027-8653-1 Subj: Careers – teachers. Illness. School.

Testing Miss Malarkey ill. by Kevin O'Malley. Walker, 2000. ISBN 978-0-8027-8739-2 Subj: Careers – teachers. School.

You're a good sport, Miss Malarkey ill. by Kevin O'Malley. Walker, 2002. ISBN 978-0-8027-8816-0 Subj: Careers – coaches. Careers – teachers. Sports – soccer. Sportsmanship.

Findlay, Lisa. *What's in Oscar's trashcan?* ill. by Joe Ewers. Random House, 2002. ISBN 978-0-375-81580-5 Subj: Behavior – lost & found possessions. Format, unusual – toy & movable books. Puppets.

Fine, Edith Hope. *Water, weed, and wait* by Edith Hope Fine and Angela Demos Halpin ill. by Colleen M. Madden. Tricycle, 2010. ISBN 978-1-58246-320-9 Subj: Gardens, gardening. School.

Fine, Howard. *A piggie Christmas* ill. by author. Hyperion, 2000. ISBN 978-0-7868-2505-9 Subj: Animals – pigs. Holidays – Christmas. Music. Songs.

Finlay, Lizzie. *Little Croc's purse* ill. by author. Eerdmans, 2011. ISBN 978-0-8028-5392-9 Subj: Behavior – bullying, teasing. Character traits – honesty. Clothing – handbags, purses. Money. Reptiles – alligators, crocodiles.

Finn, Isobel. *The very lazy ladybug* ill. by Jack Tickle. Tiger Tales, 2001. ISBN 978-1-58925-007-9 Subj: Activities – flying. Animals. Character traits – laziness. Insects – ladybugs.

The firebird. *The firebird* retold by Demi; ill. by reteller. Henry Holt, 1994. ISBN 978-0-8050-3244-4 Subj: Ballet. Behavior – stealing. Folk & fairy tales. Foreign lands – Russia. Magic. Mythical creatures. Royalty – princes.

The firebird adapt. by Rachel Isadora; ill. by adapter. Putnam, 1994. ISBN 978-0-399-22510-9 Subj: Ballet. Behavior – stealing. Folk & fairy tales. Foreign lands – Russia. Magic. Mythical creatures. Royalty – princes.

The tale of the firebird ill. by Gennady Spirin. Philomel, 2002. ISBN 978-0-399-23584-9 Subj: Ballet. Behavior – stealing. Folk & fairy tales. Foreign lands – Russia. Magic. Mythical creatures. Royalty – princes.

Firmin, Josie. *My week* ill. by author. Candlewick, 2001. ISBN 978-0-7636-1548-2 Subj: Days of the week, months of the year. Format, unusual – toy & movable books.

Fischer, Ellen. *Latke, the lucky dog* ill. by Tiphanie Beeke. Kar-Ben, 2014. ISBN 978-076139038-1 Subj: Animals – dogs. Character traits – kindness to animals. Holidays – Hanukkah.

Fischer, Scott M. *Jump!* ill. by author. Simon & Schuster, 2010. ISBN 978-1-4169-7884-8 Subj: Activities – jumping. Animals. Rhyming text.

Twinkle ill. by author. Simon & Schuster, 2007. ISBN 978-1-4169-3980-1 Subj: Format, unusual – toy & movable books. Poetry. Space & space ships. Stars.

Fisher, Aileen Lucia. *Do rabbits have Christmas?* ill. by Sarah Fox-Davies. Henry Holt, 2007. ISBN 978-0-8050-7491-8 Subj: Animals. Holidays – Christmas. Nature. Poetry. Seasons – winter.

Know what I saw? ill. by Deborah Durland DeSaix. Macmillan, 2005. ISBN 978-1-59643-055-6 Subj: Animals. Counting, numbers. Rhyming text.

The story goes on ill. by Mique Moriuchi. Macmillan, 2005. ISBN 978-1-59643-037-2 Subj: Nature. Poetry.

You don't look like your mother ill. by Lilith Jones. Mondo, 2002. ISBN 978-1-58653-856-9 Subj: Animals – babies. Birds – robins. Rhyming text.

Fisher, Alex. *A kid's best friend* (Ajmera, Maya)

Fisher, Carolyn. *A twisted tale* ill. by author. Knopf, 2002. ISBN 978-0-375-91540-6 Subj: Animals. Farms. Humorous stories. Weather – tornadoes.

Fisher, Doris. *Happy birthday to whooo? a baby animal riddle book* ill. by Lisa Downey. Sylvan Dell, 2006. ISBN 978-0-9768823-1-2 Subj: Animals – babies. Riddles & jokes.

My even day by Doris Fisher and Dani Sneed ill. by Karen Lee. Sylvan Dell, 2007. ISBN 978-0-9777423-3-2 Subj: Counting, numbers. Rhyming text.

One odd day by Doris Fisher and Dani Sneed ill. by Karen Lee. Sylvan Dell, 2006. ISBN 978-0-9768823-3-6 Subj: Counting, numbers. Rhyming text.

Fisher, Jeff. *The hair scare* ill. by author. Bloomsbury, 2005. ISBN 978-1-58234-672-4 Subj: Hair. Royalty – kings.

Fisher, Leonard Everett. *Cyclops* ill. by author. Holiday, 1991. ISBN 978-0-8234-0891-7 Subj: Folk & fairy tales. Mythical creatures.

David and Goliath ill. by adapter. Holiday, 1993. ISBN 978-0-8234-0997-6 Subj: Foreign lands – Israel. Giants. Religion – David.

Gutenberg ill. by author. Macmillan, 1993. ISBN 978-0-02-735238-2 Subj: Careers – printers. Communication. Inventions.

The seven days of creation ill. by author. Adapt. from the Bible. Holiday, 1981. ISBN 978-0-8234-0398-1 Subj: Creation. Religion.

Sky, sea, the jetty, and me ill. by author. Marshall Cavendish, 2001. ISBN 978-0-7614-5082-5 Subj: Sea & seashore. Weather – storms.

Stars and stripes: our national flag ill. by author. Holiday, 1993. ISBN 978-0-8234-1053-8 Subj: Flags. U.S. history.

Theseus and the Minotaur ill. by author. Holiday, 1988. ISBN 978-0-8234-0703-3 Subj: Folk & fairy tales. Mythical creatures. Royalty.

William Tell ill. by author. Farrar, 1996. ISBN 978-0-374-38436-4 Subj: Folk & fairy tales. Foreign lands – Switzerland. Sports – archery.

Fisher, Mary M. *Rosita's bridge* ill. by Barbara Mathews Whitehead. Maverick, 2001. ISBN 978-1-893271-18-0 Subj: Careers – singers. Ethnic groups in the U.S. – Mexican Americans. U.S. history.

Fisher, Valorie. *Ellsworth's extraordinary electric ears and other amazing alphabet anecdotes* ill. with photos. Atheneum, 2003. ISBN 978-0-689-85030-1 Subj: ABC books.

Everything I need to know before I'm five ill. by author. Random House, 2011. ISBN 978-0-375-86865-8 Subj: Concepts. Counting, numbers. Seasons.

How high can a dinosaur count? and other math mysteries ill. by author. Random House, 2006. ISBN 978-0-375-83608-4 Subj: Counting, numbers. Puzzles.

I can do it myself ill. by author. Random House, 2014. ISBN 978-044981593-9 Subj: Concepts. Counting, numbers. Self-concept.

My big brother ill. with photos. Atheneum, 2002. ISBN 978-0-689-84327-3 Subj: Family life – brothers.

Fishman, Anna Schnur. *Tashlich at Turtle Rock* (Schnur, Susan)

Fishman, Cathy Goldberg. *On Hanukkah* ill. by Melanie W. Hall. Atheneum, 1998. ISBN 978-0-689-80643-8 Subj: Holidays – Hanukkah. Jewish culture. Religion.

On Passover ill. by Melanie W. Hall. Atheneum, 1997. ISBN 978-0-689-80528-8 Subj: Holidays – Passover. Jewish culture. Religion.

On Purim ill. by Melanie W. Hall. Atheneum, 2000. ISBN 978-0-689-82392-3 Subj: Family life. Holidays – Purim. Jewish culture.

On Rosh Hashanah and Yom Kippur ill. by Melanie W. Hall. Atheneum, 1997. ISBN 978-0-689-80526-4 Subj: Holidays – Rosh Hashanah. Holidays – Yom Kippur. Jewish culture. Religion.

On Shabbat ill. by Melanie W. Hall. Atheneum, 2001. ISBN 978-0-689-83894-1 Subj: Family life. Holidays. Jewish culture. Religion.

When Jackie and Hank met ill. by Mark Elliott. Amazon Children's, 2012. ISBN 978-0-7614-6140-1 Subj: Ethnic groups in the U.S. – African Americans. Jewish culture. Prejudice. Sports – baseball. U.S. history.

Fisman, Karen. *Nonna's Hanukkah surprise* ill. by Martha Avilés. Kar-Ben, 2015. ISBN 978-146773476-9 Subj: Behavior – lost & found possessions. Family life – grandmothers. Holidays – Hanukkah.

Fitch, Florence Mary. *A book about God* ill. by Henri Sorensen. Lothrop, 1999. ISBN 978-0-688-16129-3 Subj: Religion.

Fitch, Sheree. *No two snowflakes* ill. by Janet Wilson. Orca, 2001. ISBN 978-1-55143-206-9 Subj: Poetry. Weather – snow.

Fitz-Gibbon, Sally. *On Uncle John's farm* ill. by Brian Deines. Fitzhenry & Whiteside, 2005. ISBN 978-1-55041-691-6 Subj: Careers – farmers. Farms.

Two shoes, blue shoes, new shoes! ill. by Farida Zaman. Fitzhenry & Whiteside, 2003. ISBN 978-1-55041-729-6 Subj: Activities. Clothing – shoes.

FitzGerald, Dawn. *Vinnie and Abraham* ill. by Catherine Stock. Charlesbridge, 2007. ISBN 978-1-57091-658-8 Subj: Art. U.S. history.

Fitzgerald, Ella. *A-tisket, a-tasket* by Ella Fitzgerald and Van Alexander ill. by Ora Eitan. Philomel, 2003. ISBN 978-0-399-23206-0 Subj: Behavior – lost & found possessions. Music. Songs.

Fitzgerald, Joanne. *This is me and where I am* ill. by author. Fitzhenry & Whiteside, 2004. ISBN 978-1-55041-819-4 Subj: Cities, towns. Homes, houses.

Yum! yum! delicious nursery rhymes ill. by author. Fitzhenry & Whiteside, 2007. ISBN 978-1-55041-888-0 Subj: Animals. Food. Nursery rhymes.

Fitzpatrick, Marie-Louise. *I'm a tiger, too!* ill. by author. Roaring Brook, 2002. ISBN 978-0-7613-2410-2 Subj: Activities – playing. Animals. Imagination. Rhyming text.

Lizzy and Skunk ill. by author. DK, 2000. ISBN 978-0-7894-6163-6 Subj: Behavior – lost. Emotions – fear. Puppets.

You, me and the big blue sea ill. by author. Roaring Brook, 2002. ISBN 978-0-7613-2806-3 Subj: Activities – traveling. Boats, ships. Family life – mothers. Memories, memory. Sea & seashore.

FitzSimmons, David. *Curious critters* photos by author. Wild Iris, 2011. ISBN 978-1-936607-69-3 Subj: Animals. Frogs & toads. Nature. Reptiles.

Curious critters, vol. 2 photos by author. Wild Iris, 2014. ISBN 978-193660770-9 Subj: Animals. Frogs & toads. Nature. Reptiles.

Salamander dance ill. by Michael DiGiorgio. Wild Iris, 2016. ISBN 978-193660700-6 Subj: Nature. Reptiles – salamanders.

Five little pumpkins ill. by Ben Mantle. Tiger Tales, 2010. ISBN 978-1-58925-856-3 Subj: Counting, numbers. Format, unusual – board books. Holidays – Halloween. Plants. Rhyming text. Witches.

Five little pumpkins ill. by Iris Van Rynbach. Boyds Mills, 1995. ISBN 978-1-56397-452-6 Subj: Counting, numbers. Holidays – Halloween. Plants. Rhyming text.

Five little pumpkins ill. by Dan Yaccarino. HarperCollins, 1998. ISBN 978-0-694-01177-3 Subj: Counting, numbers. Format, unusual – board books. Holidays – Halloween. Plants. Rhyming text. Witches.

Flack, Marjorie. *Ask Mr. Bear* ill. by author. Macmillan, 1932. ISBN 978-0-02-735390-7 Subj: Animals. Animals – bears. Birthdays. Emotions – love. Family life – mothers.

The story about Ping by Marjorie Flack and Kurt Wiese ill. by Kurt Wiese. Viking, 1933. Subj:

Behavior – misbehavior. Birds – ducks. Foreign lands – China.

Flaherty, A. W. *The luck of the Loch Ness monster: a tale of picky eating* ill. by Scott Magoon. Houghton, 2007. ISBN 978-0-618-55644-1 Subj: Food. Monsters.

Flake, Sharon G. *You are not a cat!* ill. by Anna Raff. Boyds Mills, 2016. ISBN 978-159078980-3 Subj: Animals – cats. Birds – ducks. Humorous stories.

Flanagan, Alice K. *Ask Nurse Pfaff, she'll help you!* photos by Christine Osinski. Children's Press, 1997. ISBN 978-0-516-20495-6 Subj: Careers – nurses. Hospitals.

A busy day at Mr. Kang's grocery store photos by Christine Osinski. Children's Press, 1996. ISBN 978-0-516-20047-7 Subj: Careers – storekeepers. Communities, neighborhoods. Ethnic groups in the U.S. – Korean Americans. Shopping. Stores.

Buying a pet from Ms. Chavez photos by Romie Flanagan. Children's Press, 1998. ISBN 978-0-516-20773-5 Subj: Careers – storekeepers. Communities, neighborhoods. Pets. Stores.

Call Mr. Vasquez, he'll fix it! photos by Christine Osinski. Children's Press, 1996. ISBN 978-0-516-20045-3 Subj: Careers – custodians, janitors. Careers – handymen. Homes, houses.

Chinese New Year ill. by Svetlana Zhurkina. Compass Point, 2004. ISBN 978-0-7565-0479-3 Subj: Ethnic groups in the U.S. – Chinese Americans. Fairs, festivals. Holidays – Chinese New Year.

Choosing eyeglasses with Mrs. Koutris photos by Romie Flanagan. Children's Press, 1998. ISBN 978-0-516-20775-9 Subj: Careers – opticians, optometrists. Careers – storekeepers. Glasses.

Christmas ill. by Viki Woodworth. Compass Point, 2002. ISBN 978-0-7565-0085-6 Subj: Holidays – Christmas.

Cinco de Mayo ill. by Patrick Girouard. Compass Point, 2004. ISBN 978-0-7565-0480-9 Subj: Ethnic groups in the U.S. – Mexican Americans. Foreign lands – Mexico. Holidays – Cinco de Mayo.

Coach John and his soccer team photos by Christine Osinski. Children's Press, 1998. ISBN 978-0-516-20777-3 Subj: Careers – coaches. Communities, neighborhoods. Sports – soccer. Sportsmanship.

A day in court with Mrs. Trinh photos by Christine Osinski. Children's Press, 1997. ISBN 978-0-516-20008-8 Subj: Careers – lawyers. Crime.

Dr. Friedman helps animals photos by Christine Osinski. Children's Press, 1999. ISBN 978-0-516-21138-1 Subj: Animals. Careers – veterinarians.

Dr. Kanner, dentist with a smile photos by Christine Osinski. Children's Press, 1997. ISBN 978-0-516-20493-2 Subj: Careers – dentists. Teeth.

Exploring parks with Ranger Dockett photos by Christine Osinski. Children's Press, 1997. ISBN 978-0-516-20496-3 Subj: Careers – park rangers. Parks.

Flying an agricultural plane with Mr. Miller photos by Romie Flanagan. Children's Press, 1999. ISBN 978-0-516-21132-9 Subj: Airplanes, airports. Careers – airplane pilots. Farms.

Halloween ill. by Patrick Girouard. Compass Point, 2002. ISBN 978-0-7565-0086-3 Subj: Holidays – Halloween.

Here comes Mr. Eventoff with the mail! photos by Christine Osinski. Children's Press, 1998. ISBN 978-0-516-20776-6 Subj: Careers – postal workers. Communities, neighborhoods. Letters, cards.

Learning about bees from Mr. Krebs photos by Christine Osinski. Children's Press, 1999. ISBN 978-0-516-21136-7 Subj: Careers – beekeepers. Insects – bees.

Learning is fun with Mrs. Perez photos by Romie Flanagan. Children's Press, 1998. ISBN 978-0-516-20774-2 Subj: Careers – teachers. Foreign languages. School.

Mr. Paul and Mr. Luecke build communities photos by Romie Flanagan. Children's Press, 1999. ISBN 978-0-516-21131-2 Subj: Careers – construction workers. Homes, houses.

Mr. Santizo's tasty treats! photos by Romie Flanagan. Children's Press, 1998. ISBN 978-0-516-20771-1 Subj: Careers – bakers. Ethnic groups in the U.S. – Guatemalan Americans.

Mr. Yee fixes cars photos by Romie Flanagan. Children's Press, 1998. ISBN 978-0-516-20772-8 Subj: Automobiles. Careers – mechanics.

Mrs. Scott's beautiful art photos by Romie Flanagan. Children's Press, 1999. ISBN 978-0-516-21135-0 Subj: Careers – artists. Indians of North America – Cherokee.

Ms. Davison, our librarian photos by Christine Osinski. Children's Press, 1996. ISBN 978-0-516-20009-5 Subj: Books, reading. Careers – librarians. Communities, neighborhoods. Libraries.

Ms. Murphy fights fires photos by Christine Osinski. Children's Press, 1997. ISBN 978-0-516-20494-9 Subj: Careers – firefighters. Communities, neighborhoods. Fire.

Officer Brown keeps neighborhoods safe photos by Christine Osinski. Children's Press, 1998. ISBN 978-0-516-20780-3 Subj: Careers – police officers. Communities, neighborhoods. Crime.

Passover ill. by Ann Koffsky. Compass Point, 2004. ISBN 978-0-7565-0481-6 Subj: Holidays – Passover. Jewish culture.

Raising cows on the Koebels' farm photos by Romie Flanagan. Children's Press, 1999. ISBN 978-0-516-21133-6 Subj: Animals – bulls, cows. Careers – farmers. Farms.

Riding the ferry with Captain Cruz photos by Christine Osinski. Children's Press, 1996. ISBN 978-0-516-20046-0 Subj: Boats, ships. Sailors. Transportation.

Riding the school bus with Mrs. Kramer photos by Christine Osinski. Children's Press, 1998. ISBN 978-0-516-20779-7 Subj: Careers – bus drivers. Communities, neighborhoods. School. Transportation.

Thanksgiving ill. by Kathie Kelleher. Compass Point, 2002. ISBN 978-0-7565-0087-0 Subj: Holidays – Thanksgiving.

Valentine's Day ill. by Shelly Dieterichs. Compass Point, 2002. ISBN 978-0-7565-0088-7 Subj: Holidays – Valentine's Day.

A visit to the Gravesens' farm photos by Christine Osinski. Children's Press, 1998. ISBN 978-0-516-20778-0 Subj: Careers – farmers. Communities, neighborhoods. Family life. Farms.

The Wilsons, a house-painting team photos by Christine Osinski. Children's Press, 1996. ISBN 978-0-516-20216-7 Subj: Activities – painting. Careers – artists. Homes, houses.

The Zieglers and their apple orchard photos by Romie Flanagan. Children's Press, 1999. ISBN 978-0-516-21134-3 Subj: Careers – farmers. Farms. Food. Trees.

Flattinger, Hubert. *Stormy night* ill. by Nathalie Duroussy. NorthSouth, 2002. ISBN 978-0-7358-1667-1 Subj: Bedtime. Emotions – fear. Family life – mothers.

Fleischer-Camp, Dean. *Marcel the shell with shoes on: things about me* (Slate, Jenny)

Fleischman, Paul. *First light, first life: a worldwide creation story* ill. by Julie Paschkis. Henry Holt, 2016. ISBN 978-162779101-4 Subj: Creation. Folk & fairy tales. Foreign lands.

Glass slipper, gold sandal: a worldwide Cinderella ill. by Julie Paschkis. Henry Holt, 2007. ISBN 978-0-8050-7953-1 Subj: Folk & fairy tales. Foreign lands. Royalty.

Lost! a story in string ill. by C. B. Mordan. Henry Holt, 2000. ISBN 978-0-8050-5583-2 Subj: Behavior – lost. String. Weather – snow.

The matchbox diary ill. by Bagram Ibatoulline. Candlewick, 2013. ISBN 978-0-7636-4601-1 Subj: Behavior – collecting things. Ethnic groups in the U.S. – Italian Americans. Family life – great-grandparents. Immigrants, immigration. Memories, memory. U.S. history.

Sidewalk circus ill. by Kevin Hawkes. Candlewick, 2004. ISBN 978-0-7636-1107-1 Subj: Circus. Cities, towns. Wordless.

Weslandia ill. by Kevin Hawkes. Candlewick, 1999. ISBN 978-0-7636-0006-8 Subj: Gardens, gardening. Plants.

Fleming, Candace. *Boxes for Katje* ill. by Stacey Dressen-McQueen. Farrar, 2003. ISBN 978-0-374-30922-0 Subj: Character traits – generosity. Foreign lands – Holland. War.

Bulldozer helps out ill. by Eric Rohmann. Atheneum/Caitlyn Dlouhy, 2017. ISBN 978-148145894-8 Subj: Animals – cats. Machines.

Bulldozer's big day ill. by Eric Rohmann. Atheneum, 2015. ISBN 978-148140097-8 Subj: Birthdays. Machines. Parties.

Clever Jack takes the cake ill. by G. Brian Karas. Random House, 2010. ISBN 978-0-375-84979-4 Subj: Activities – storytelling. Birthdays. Folk & fairy tales. Food. Royalty – princesses.

Emma's circus ill. by Christine Davenier. Farrar/Margaret Ferguson, 2017. ISBN 978-037439907-8 Subj: Animals. Circus. Farms.

Gabriella's song ill. by Giselle Potter. Atheneum, 1997. ISBN 978-0-689-80973-6 Subj: Foreign lands – Italy. Music. Songs.

Gator gumbo ill. by Sally Anne Lambert. Farrar, 2004. ISBN 978-0-374-38050-2 Subj: Animals. Food. Reptiles – alligators, crocodiles.

Go sleep in your own bed ill. by Lori Nichols. Random House, 2017. ISBN 978-037586648-7 Subj: Bedtime. Farms.

Imogene's last stand ill. by Nancy Carpenter. Random House, 2009. ISBN 978-0-375-83607-7 Subj: Character traits – assertiveness. Self-concept. U.S. history.

Muncha! muncha! muncha! ill. by G. Brian Karas. Atheneum, 2002. ISBN 978-0-689-83152-2 Subj: Animals – rabbits. Gardens, gardening.

Oh, no! ill. by Eric Rohmann. Random House, 2012. ISBN 978-0-375-84271-9 Subj: Animals. Cumulative tales.

Papa's mechanical fish ill. by Boris Kulikov. Farrar, 2013. ISBN 978-0-374-39908-5 Subj: Boats, ships. Careers – inventors. Family life. Inventions.

Seven hungry babies ill. by Eugene Yelchin. Simon & Schuster, 2010. ISBN 978-1-4169-5402-6 Subj: Babies, toddlers. Birds. Counting, numbers. Rhyming text.

Sunny Boy! the life and times of a tortoise ill. by Anne Wilsdorf. Farrar, 2005. ISBN 978-0-374-37297-2 Subj: Reptiles – turtles, tortoises.

Tippy-tippy-tippy, hide! ill. by G. Brian Karas. Simon & Schuster, 2007. ISBN 978-0-689-87479-6 Subj: Animals – rabbits. Behavior – hiding.

Tippy-tippy-tippy, splash! ill. by G. Brian Karas. Atheneum, 2014. ISBN 978-141695403-3 Subj: Animals – rabbits. Sea & seashore – beaches.

When Agnes caws ill. by Giselle Potter. Atheneum, 1999. ISBN 978-0-689-81471-6 Subj: Birds. Foreign lands – Himalayas. Noise, sounds.

Who invited you? ill. by George Booth. Atheneum, 2001. ISBN 978-0-689-83153-9 Subj: Animals. Counting, numbers. Rhyming text. Swamps.

Fleming, Denise. *Alphabet under construction* ill. by author. Henry Holt, 2002. ISBN 978-0-8050-6848-1 Subj: ABC books. Activities – making things. Animals – mice.

Barnyard banter ill. by author. Henry Holt, 1994. ISBN 978-0-8050-1957-5 Subj: Animals. Farms. Noise, sounds. Rhyming text.

Beetle bop ill. by author. Harcourt, 2007. ISBN 978-0-15-205936-1 Subj: Insects – beetles. Rhyming text.

Buster ill. by author. Henry Holt, 2003. ISBN 978-0-8050-6279-3 Subj: Animals – cats. Animals – dogs. Behavior – running away. Emotions – envy, jealousy. Pets.

Buster goes to Cowboy Camp ill. by author. Henry Holt, 2008. ISBN 978-0-8050-7892-3 Subj: Animals – dogs. Camps, camping. Cowboys, cowgirls.

Count! ill. by author. Henry Holt, 1992. ISBN 978-0-8050-1595-9 Subj: Animals. Counting, numbers.

The cow who clucked ill. by author. Henry Holt, 2006. ISBN 978-0-8050-7365-2 Subj: Animals. Animals – bulls, cows. Noise, sounds.

The everything book ill. by author. Henry Holt, 2000. ISBN 978-0-8050-6292-2 Subj: Concepts. Nursery rhymes.

The first day of winter ill. by author. Henry Holt, 2005. ISBN 978-0-8050-7384-3 Subj: Counting, numbers. Rhyming text. Seasons – winter. Snowmen. Weather – snow.

5 little ducks ill. by author. Simon & Schuster/Beach Lane, 2016. ISBN 978-148142422-6 Subj: Birds – ducks. Counting, numbers. Days of the week, months of the year.

Go, shapes, go! ill. by author. Simon & Schuster/Beach Lane, 2014. ISBN 978-144248240-1 Subj: Animals – mice. Concepts – shape.

In the small, small pond ill. by author. Henry Holt, 1993. ISBN 978-0-8050-2264-3 Subj: Animals. Caldecott award honor books. Frogs & toads. Lakes, ponds. Rhyming text. Seasons.

In the tall, tall grass ill. by author. Henry Holt, 1991. ISBN 978-0-8050-1635-2 Subj: Insects – butterflies, caterpillars. Nature.

Lunch ill. by author. Henry Holt, 1992. ISBN 978-0-8050-1636-9 Subj: Animals – mice. Concepts – color. Food.

Maggie and Michael get dressed ill. by author. Henry Holt, 2016. ISBN 978-080508794-9 Subj: Activities – playing. Animals – dogs. Clothing. Concepts – color.

Mama cat has three kittens ill. by author. Henry Holt, 1998. ISBN 978-0-8050-5745-4 Subj: Animals – babies. Animals – cats. Character traits – being different. Family life – brothers & sisters.

Shout! shout it out! ill. by author. Henry Holt, 2011. ISBN 978-0-8050-9237-0 Subj: ABC books. Animals – mice. Counting, numbers. Language.

Sleepy, oh so sleepy ill. by author. Henry Holt, 2010. ISBN 978-0-8050-8126-8 Subj: Animals. Bedtime. Family life – mothers.

Time to sleep ill. by author. Henry Holt, 1997. ISBN 978-0-8050-3762-3 Subj: Animals – bears. Hibernation. Seasons – winter.

Underground ill. by author. Simon & Schuster, 2012. ISBN 978-1-4424-5882-6 Subj: Animals. Nature. Rhyming text.

Where once there was a wood ill. by author. Henry Holt, 1996. ISBN 978-0-8050-3761-6 Subj: Animals. Nature. Plants.

Fleming, Meg. *I heart you* ill. by Sarah Jane Wright. Simon & Schuster, 2016. ISBN 978-144248895-3 Subj: Animals. Emotions – love. Family life – parents. Rhyming text.

Ready, set, build! ill. by Peter Jarvis. little bee, 2017. ISBN 978-149980175-0 Subj: Careers – construction workers. Rhyming text.

Flesher, Vivienne. *Alfred's nose* photos by author. HarperCollins, 2008. ISBN 978-0-06-084313-7 Subj: Anatomy – noses. Animals – dogs. Clothing – costumes. Self-concept.

Fletcher, Ashlee. *My dog, my cat* ill. by author. Tanglewood, 2011. ISBN 978-1-933718-22-4 Subj: Animals – cats. Animals – dogs.

Fletcher, Ralph. *The circus surprise* ill. by Vladimir Vagin. Clarion, 2001. ISBN 978-0-395-98029-3 Subj: Behavior – lost. Circus. Clowns, jesters.

Grandpa never lies ill. by Harvey Stevenson. Clarion, 2000. ISBN 978-0-395-79770-9 Subj: Death. Emotions – grief. Family life – grandfathers. Family life – grandmothers. Poetry.

Hello, harvest moon ill. by Kate Kiesler. Clarion, 2003. ISBN 978-0-618-16451-6 Subj: Moon. Nature. Night.

The Sandman ill. by Richard Cowdrey. Henry Holt, 2008. ISBN 978-0-8050-7726-1 Subj: Dragons. Sleep.

Fletcher, Tom. *The dinosaur that pooped a planet!* by Tom Fletcher and Dougie Poynter ill. by Garry Parsons. Aladdin, 2017. ISBN 978-148149866-1 Subj: Dinosaurs. Humorous stories. Space & space ships.

There's a monster in your book ill. by Greg Abbott. Random House, 2017. ISBN 978-152476456-2 Subj: Books, reading. Monsters. Participation.

Fliess, Sue. *Books for me!* ill. by Mike Laughead. Amazon/Two Lions, 2015. ISBN 978-147782036-0 Subj: Animals – hippopotamuses. Books, reading. Libraries. Rhyming text.

Calling all cars ill. by Sarah Beise. Sourcebooks/Jabberwocky, 2016. ISBN 978-149261881-2 Subj: Automobiles. Rhyming text.

A fairy friend ill. by Claire Keane. Holt/Christy Ottaviano, 2016. ISBN 978-162779081-9 Subj: Fairies. Magic. Rhyming text.

A gluten-free birthday for me! ill. by Jennifer Morris. Albert Whitman, 2013. ISBN 978-0-8075-2955-3 Subj: Birthdays. Food. Illness – allergies. Parties. Rhyming text.

Race! ill. by Edwardian Taylor. little bee, 2017. ISBN 978-149980237-5 Subj: Automobiles. Rhyming text. Sports – racing.

Shoes for me! ill. by Mike Laughead. Marshall Cavendish, 2011. ISBN 978-0-7614-5825-8 Subj: Animals – hippopotamuses. Clothing – shoes. Rhyming text.

Floca, Brian. *Five trucks* ill. by author. Simon & Schuster, 2014. ISBN 978-148140593-5 Subj: Airplanes, airports. Trucks.

Lightship ill. by author. Simon & Schuster, 2007. ISBN 978-1-4169-2436-4 Subj: Boats, ships. U.S. history.

Locomotive ill. by author. Atheneum, 2013. ISBN 978-1-4169-9415-2 Subj: Caldecott award books. Trains. U.S. history.

Moonshot: the flight of Apollo 11 ill. by author. Atheneum, 2009. ISBN 978-1-4169-5046-2 Subj: Careers – astronauts. Moon. Space & space ships. U.S. history.

Florence, Tyler. *Tyler makes pancakes!* ill. by Craig Frazier. HarperCollins, 2012. ISBN 978-0-06-

204752-6 Subj: Activities – baking, cooking. Food. Shopping. Stores.

Tyler makes spaghetti! ill. by Craig Frazier. HarperCollins, 2013. ISBN 978-0-06-204756-4 Subj: Activities – baking, cooking. Food. Restaurants.

Florian, Douglas. *Bow wow meow meow, it's rhyming cats and dogs* ill. by author. Harcourt, 2003. ISBN 978-0-15-216395-2 Subj: Animals – cats. Animals – dogs. Poetry.

Comets, stars, the moon, and Mars: space poems and paintings ill. by author. Harcourt, 2007. ISBN 978-0-15-205372-7 Subj: Moon. Planets. Poetry. Stars.

The curious cares of bears ill. by Sonia Sánchez. little bee, 2017. ISBN 978-149980462-1 Subj: Animals – bears. Rhyming text. Seasons.

Dinothesaurus: prehistoric poems and paintings ill. by author. Atheneum, 2009. ISBN 978-1-4169-7978-4 Subj: Dinosaurs. Poetry. Prehistory.

Handsprings ill. by author. HarperCollins, 2006. ISBN 978-0-06-009281-8 Subj: Poetry. Seasons – spring.

How to draw a dragon ill. by author. Simon & Schuster/Beach Lane, 2015. ISBN 978-144247399-7 Subj: Activities – drawing. Dragons. Rhyming text.

I love my hat ill. by Paige Keiser. Amazon/Two Lions, 2014. ISBN 978-147784780-0 Subj: Animals. Careers – farmers. Clothing. Rhyming text.

Insectlopedia ill. by author. Harcourt, 1998. ISBN 978-0-15-201306-6 Subj: Insects. Poetry.

Lizards, frogs, and polliwogs ill. by author. Harcourt, 2001. ISBN 978-0-15-202591-5 Subj: Amphibians. Frogs & toads. Poetry. Reptiles.

A pig is big ill. by author. Greenwillow, 2000. ISBN 978-0-688-17126-1 Subj: Concepts – size. Rhyming text.

Poem runs: baseball poems and paintings ill. by author. Harcourt, 2012. ISBN 978-0-547-68838-1 Subj: Poetry. Sports – baseball.

Poetrees ill. by author. Simon & Schuster, 2010. ISBN 978-1-4169-8672-0 Subj: Poetry. Trees.

Shiver me timbers! pirate poems & paintings ill. by Robert Neubecker. Simon & Schuster, 2012. ISBN 978-1-4424-1321-4 Subj: Pirates. Poetry.

Summersaults ill. by author. Greenwillow, 2002. ISBN 978-0-06-029268-3 Subj: Poetry. Seasons – summer.

Unbeelievables: honeybee poems and paintings ill. by author. Simon & Schuster, 2012. ISBN 978-1-4424-2652-8 Subj: Insects – bees. Poetry.

The wonderful habits of rabbits ill. by Sonia Sanchez. little bee, 2016. ISBN 978-149980104-0 Subj: Animals – rabbits. Poetry.

Zoo's who: poems and paintings ill. by author. Harcourt, 2005. ISBN 978-0-15-204639-2 Subj: Animals. Poetry.

Flory, Neil. *The short giraffe* ill. by Mark Cleary. Albert Whitman, 2014. ISBN 978-080757346-4 Subj: Animals – giraffes. Character traits – cooperation. Character traits – smallness. Problem solving.

Flournoy, Valerie. *The patchwork quilt* ill. by Jerry Pinkney. Dial, 1985. ISBN 978-0-8037-0098-7 Subj: Ethnic groups in the U.S. – African Americans. Family life – grandmothers. Quilts.

Floyd, Madeleine. *Cold paws, warm heart* ill. by author. Candlewick, 2005. ISBN 978-0-7636-2761-4 Subj: Animals – polar bears. Concepts – cold & heat. Emotions – loneliness. Friendship.

Flynn, Kitson. *Carrot in my pocket* ill. by Denise Ortakales. Moon Mt, 2001. ISBN 978-0-9677929-6-5 Subj: Animals. Behavior – lost & found possessions. Farms. Rhyming text.

Foges, Clare. *Kitchen disco* ill. by Al Murphy. Faber and Faber, 2017. ISBN 978-057133697-5 Subj: Activities – dancing. Food. Music. Rhyming text.

Foggo, Cheryl. *Dear baobab* ill. by Qin Leng. Second Story, 2011. ISBN 978-1-897187-91-3 Subj: Adoption. Emotions – loneliness. Family life. Family life – aunts, uncles. Foreign lands – Africa. Trees.

Fogliano, Julie. *And then it's spring* ill. by Erin E. Stead. Roaring Brook, 2012. ISBN 978-1-59643-624-4 Subj: Gardens, gardening. Seasons – spring.

If you want to see a whale ill. by Erin E. Stead. Roaring Brook, 2013. ISBN 978-1-59643-731-9 Subj: Animals – whales. Character traits – patience, impatience. Imagination.

Old dog baby baby ill. by Chris Raschka. Roaring Brook/Neal Porter, 2016. ISBN 978-159643853-8 Subj: Animals – dogs. Babies, toddlers. Rhyming text.

When green becomes tomatoes ill. by Julie Morstad. Roaring Brook/Neal Porter, 2016. ISBN 978-159643852-1 Subj: Poetry. Seasons.

When's my birthday? ill. by Christian Robinson. Roaring Brook/Neal Porter, 2017. ISBN 978-162672293-4 Subj: Birthdays.

Foley, Greg. *Don't worry Bear* ill. by author. Viking, 2008. ISBN 978-0-670-06245-4 Subj: Animals. Animals – bears. Behavior – worrying. Insects – butterflies, caterpillars. Metamorphosis.

Good luck Bear ill. by author. Viking, 2009. ISBN 978-0-670-06258-4 Subj: Animals. Animals – bears. Character traits – luck.

I miss you Mouse ill. by author. Penguin, 2010. ISBN 978-0-670-01238-1 Subj: Animals – bears. Animals – mice. Format, unusual – toy & movable books. Friendship.

Make a wish Bear ill. by author. Viking, 2012. ISBN 978-0-670-01239-8 Subj: Animals – bears. Behavior – wishing. Friendship.

Purple Little Bird ill. by author. HarperCollins, 2011. ISBN 978-0-06-200828-2 Subj: Animals. Birds. Concepts – color. Homes, houses.

Thank you, Bear ill. by author. Penguin, 2007. ISBN 978-0-670-06165-5 Subj: Animals. Animals – bears. Animals – mice. Friendship. Gifts.

Willoughby and the lion ill. by author. HarperCollins, 2009. ISBN 978-0-06-154750-8 Subj: Animals – lions. Behavior – wishing. Friendship. Magic.

Willoughby and the moon ill. by author. HarperCollins, 2010. ISBN 978-0-06-154753-9 Subj: Animals – snails. Emotions – fear. Moon.

Folgueira, Rodrigo. *Ribbit!* ill. by Poly Bernatene. Knopf, 2013. ISBN 978-0-307-98146-2 Subj: Animals – pigs. Behavior – needing someone. Friendship. Frogs & toads. Lakes, ponds.

Fontes, Justine Korman. *Black meets White* ill. by Geoff Waring. Candlewick, 2005. ISBN 978-0-7636-1933-6 Subj: Concepts – color. Format, unusual – toy & movable books.

Signs of spring ill. by Rob Hefferan. Mondo, 2002. ISBN 978-1-59034-180-3 Subj: Animals – mice. School. Seasons – spring.

Ford, Bernette. *Ballet Kitty* ill. by Sam Williams. Boxer, 2007. ISBN 978-1-905417-56-8 Subj: Animals – cats. Ballet.

Bright eyes, brown skin (Hudson, Cheryl Willis)

First snow ill. by Sebastien Braun. Holiday House,, 2005. ISBN 978-0-8234-1937-1 Subj: Animals – rabbits. Night. Seasons – winter. Weather – snow.

No more biting for Billy Goat! ill. by Sam Williams. Boxer, 2013. ISBN 978-1-907967-31-3 Subj: Animals – goats. Behavior – misbehavior.

No more blanket for Lambkin! ill. by Sam Williams. Boxer, 2009. ISBN 978-1-906250-28-7 Subj: Animals – sheep. Birds – ducks. Friendship. Laundry. Toys.

No more bottles for Bunny! ill. by Sam Williams. Boxer, 2007. ISBN 978-1-905417-34-6 Subj: Animals – rabbits. Behavior – growing up. Parties.

No more diapers for Ducky! ill. by Sam Williams. Sterling, 2007. ISBN 978-1-905417-38-4 Subj: Birds – ducks. Format, unusual – board books. Toilet training.

No more pacifier for Piggy! ill. by Sam Williams. Sterling, 2008. ISBN 978-1-905417-89-6 Subj: Animals – pigs. Babies, toddlers. Behavior – growing up.

Ford, Christine. *Ocean's child* by Christine Ford and Trish Holland ill. by David Diaz. Golden, 2009. ISBN 978-0-375-84752-3 Subj: Animals. Bedtime. Canoes & canoeing. Family life – mothers. Foreign lands – Arctic. Indians of North America – Inuit. Sea & seashore.

Ford, Gilbert. *Flying lessons* ill. by author. Hyperion/Disney, 2010. ISBN 978-1-4231-1997-5 Subj: Airplanes, airports. Birds – doves. Character traits – being different.

The marvelous thing that came from a spring: the accidental invention of the toy that swept the nation ill. by author. Atheneum, 2016. ISBN 978-148145065-2 Subj: Careers – inventors. Inventions. Toys.

Ford, Juwanda G. *K is for Kwanzaa: a Kwanzaa alphabet book* ill. by Ken Wilson-Max. Scholastic, 1997. ISBN 978-0-590-92200-5 Subj: ABC books. Ethnic groups in the U.S. – African Americans. Holidays – Kwanzaa.

Together for Kwanzaa ill. by Shelly Hehenberger. Random House, 2000. ISBN 978-0-375-90329-8 Subj: Ethnic groups in the U.S. – African Americans. Family life – brothers & sisters. Holidays – Kwanzaa.

Ford, Lauren. *The ageless story* ill. by author. Dodd, 1939. Subj: Caldecott award honor books.

Ford, Miela. *Follow the leader* photos by author. Greenwillow, 1996. ISBN 978-0-688-14655-9 Subj: Activities – playing. Animals – polar bears.

Mom and me ill. by author. Greenwillow, 1998. ISBN 978-0-688-15890-3 Subj: Activities – playing. Animals – polar bears. Family life – mothers. Foreign lands – Arctic.

Sunflower ill. by Sally Noll. Greenwillow, 1995. ISBN 978-0-688-13302-3 Subj: Flowers. Gardens, gardening. Nature. Plants.

Fore, S. J. *Read to Tiger* ill. by R. W. Alley. Penguin, 2010. ISBN 978-0-670-01140-7 Subj: Animals – tigers. Books, reading.

Tiger can't sleep ill. by R. W. Alley. Penguin, 2006. ISBN 978-0-670-06078-8 Subj: Animals – tigers. Bedtime. Emotions – fear.

Foreman, George. *Let George do it!* by George Foreman and Fran Manushkin ill. by Whitney Martin. Simon & Schuster, 2005. ISBN 978-0-689-87807-7 Subj: Birthdays. Family life. Humorous stories. Names. Parties.

Foreman, Jack. *Say hello* ill. by Michael Foreman. Candlewick, 2008. ISBN 978-0-7636-3657-9 Subj:

Animals – dogs. Emotions – loneliness. Rhyming text.

Foreman, Michael. *Cat in the manger* ill. by author. Henry Holt, 2001. ISBN 978-0-8050-6677-7 Subj: Animals – cats. Holidays – Christmas. Memories, memory. Religion.

Fortunately, unfortunately ill. by author. Andersen, 2011. ISBN 978-0-7613-7460-2 Subj: Activities – traveling. Behavior – resourcefulness.

Friends ill. by author. Andersen, 2012. ISBN 978-1-46770317-8 Subj: Animals – cats. Fish. Friendship.

I love you, too! ill. by author. Andersen, 2014. ISBN 978-146773451-6 Subj: Animals – bears. Bedtime. Emotions – love. Family life – fathers.

The littlest dinosaur ill. by author. Walker, 2008. ISBN 978-0-8027-9759-9 Subj: Character traits – bravery. Character traits – smallness. Dinosaurs. Friendship.

Mia's story: a sketchbook of hopes and dreams ill. by author. Candlewick, 2006. ISBN 978-0-7636-3063-8 Subj: Animals – dogs. Flowers. Foreign lands – Chile.

Oh! if only . . . ill. by author. Andersen, 2013. ISBN 978-1-46771-213-2 Subj: Animals – dogs. Emotions – embarrassment. Royalty – queens.

Tufty: the little lost duck who found love ill. by author. Andersen, 2016. ISBN 978-151240425-8 Subj: Behavior – lost. Birds – ducks. Character traits – kindness to animals.

Forest, Heather, reteller. *Stone soup* ill. by Susan Gaber. August House, 1998. ISBN 978-0-87483-498-7 Subj: Behavior – sharing. Character traits – cleverness. Folk & fairy tales. Food.

Forler, Nan. *Bird child* ill. by François Thisdale. Tundra, 2009. ISBN 978-0-88776-894-1 Subj: Activities – flying. Behavior – bullying, teasing. Self-concept.

Forman, Ruth. *Young Cornrows callin out the moon: poem* ill. by Cbabi Bayoc. Children's Book Press, 2007. ISBN 978-0-89239-218-6 Subj: Communities, neighborhoods. Ethnic groups in the U.S. – African Americans. Poetry.

Formento, Alison. *These bees count!* ill. by Sarah Snow. Albert Whitman, 2012. ISBN 978-0-8075-7868-1 Subj: Counting, numbers. Insects – bees. School – field trips.

These rocks count! ill. by Sarah Snow. Albert Whitman, 2014. ISBN 978-080757870-4 Subj: Counting, numbers. Rocks. School – field trips.

These seas count! ill. by Sarah Snow. Albert Whitman, 2013. ISBN 978-0-8075-7871-1 Subj: Counting, numbers. Ecology. School – field trips. Sea & seashore.

This tree counts! ill. by Sarah Snow. Albert Whitman, 2010. ISBN 978-0-8075-7890-2 Subj: Counting, numbers. Nature. School. Trees.

This tree, 1, 2, 3 ill. by Sarah Snow. Albert Whitman, 2011. ISBN 978-0-8075-7891-9 Subj: Counting, numbers. Format, unusual – board books. Nature. School. Trees.

Forss, Sarah. *Alphasaurs and other prehistoric types* (Werner, Sharon)

Forster, John. *The backwards birthday party* (Chapin, Tom)

Fortenberry, Julie. *Lily's cat mask* ill. by author. Viking, 2017. ISBN 978-042528799-6 Subj: Family life – fathers. Masks. School – first day.

Forward, Toby. *Ben's Christmas carol* ill. by Ruth Brown. Dutton, 1996. ISBN 978-0-525-45593-6 Subj: Animals – mice. Behavior – greed. Behavior – sharing. Holidays – Christmas.

What did you do today? ill. by Carol Thompson. Clarion, 2004. ISBN 978-0-618-49586-3 Subj: School – first day.

Fosberry, Jennifer. *Isabella: girl on the go* ill. by Mike Litwin. Sourcebooks/Jabberwocky, 2012. ISBN 978-1-4022-6648-5 Subj: Activities – playing. Imagination.

Isabella star of the story ill. by Mike Litwin. Sourcebooks/Jabberwocky, 2013. ISBN 978-1-4022-7936-2 Subj: Books, reading. Imagination. Libraries.

Foster, John. *Pet poems* ill. by Korky Paul. Oxford Univ., 2000. ISBN 978-0-19-276191-0 Subj: Animals. Pets. Poetry.

Foster, Travis. *Give me back my book!* ill. by Ethan Long. Chronicle, 2017. ISBN 978-145216040-5 Subj: Behavior – fighting, arguing. Books, reading.

Fox, Christyan. *Astronaut PiggyWiggy* by Christyan Fox and Diane Fox; ill. by Christyan Fox. Handprint, 2002. ISBN 978-1-929766-41-3 Subj: Animals – pigs. Careers – astronauts. Imagination.

Count to ten, PiggyWiggy! by Christyan Fox and Diane Fox; ill. by Christyan Fox. Handprint, 2001. ISBN 978-1-929766-18-5 Subj: Activities – baking, cooking. Animals – pigs. Counting, numbers. Food. Format, unusual – board books.

Fire fighter PiggyWiggy by Christyan Fox and Diane Fox; ill. by Christyan Fox. Handprint, 2001. ISBN 978-1-929766-16-1 Subj: Animals – pigs. Careers – firefighters. Imagination.

Tyson the terrible (Fox, Diane)

What color is that, PiggyWiggy? by Christyan Fox and Diane Fox; ill. by Christyan Fox. Handprint, 2001. ISBN 978-1-929766-17-8 Subj: Animals – pigs. Clowns, jesters. Concepts – color. Format, unusual – board books. Toys.

What shape is that, PiggyWiggy? by Christyan Fox and Diane Fox; ill. by Christyan Fox. Handprint, 2002. ISBN 978-1-929766-44-4 Subj: Animals – pigs. Format, unusual – board books. Toys – bears.

Fox, Diane. *Astronaut PiggyWiggy* (Fox, Christyan)

The cat, the dog, Little Red, the exploding eggs, the wolf, and Grandma ill. by Christyan Fox. Scholastic, 2014. ISBN 978-054569481-0 Subj: Animals – cats. Animals – dogs. Books, reading. Folk & fairy tales. Humorous stories.

Count to ten, PiggyWiggy! (Fox, Christyan)

Fire fighter PiggyWiggy (Fox, Christyan)

Tyson the terrible by Diane Fox and Christyan Fox; ill. by authors. Bloomsbury, 2007. ISBN 978-1-58234-734-9 Subj: Dinosaurs. Emotions – fear. Format, unusual – toy & movable books. Friendship. Sports – soccer.

What color is that, PiggyWiggy? (Fox, Christyan)

What shape is that, PiggyWiggy? (Fox, Christyan)

Fox, Kathleen. *The pirates of plagiarism* by Kathleen Fox and Lisa Downey ill. by Lisa Downey. Upstart, 2010. ISBN 978-1-60213-053-1 Subj: Behavior – cheating. Books, reading. Libraries. Pirates.

Fox, Lee. *Ella Kazoo will not brush her hair* ill. by Jennifer Plecas. Walker, 2010. ISBN 978-0-8027-8836-8 Subj: Hair. Hygiene. Rhyming text.

Fox, Mem. *Baby bedtime* ill. by Emma Quay. Simon & Schuster/Beach Lane, 2014. ISBN 978-148142097-6 Subj: Animals – elephants. Babies, toddlers. Bedtime.

Boo to a goose ill. by David Miller. Dial, 1998. ISBN 978-0-8037-2274-3 Subj: Birds – geese. Rhyming text.

The goblin and the empty chair ill. by Leo Dillon. Simon & Schuster, 2009. ISBN 978-1-4169-8585-3 Subj: Character traits – appearance. Emotions – loneliness. Mythical creatures – goblins. Self-concept.

Good night, sleep tight ill. by Judy Horacek. Scholastic, 2013. ISBN 978-0-545-53370-6 Subj: Activities – babysitting. Bedtime. Nursery rhymes. Rhyming text.

Harriet, you'll drive me wild ill. by Marla Frazee. Harcourt, 2000. ISBN 978-0-15-201977-8 Subj: Character traits – clumsiness. Emotions – anger. Family life – mothers.

Hattie and the fox ill. by Patricia Mullins. Bradbury, 1987. ISBN 978-0-02-735470-6 Subj: Animals. Birds – chickens, roosters. Cumulative tales. Farms.

Hello, baby! ill. by Steve Jenkins. Simon & Schuster, 2009. ISBN 978-1-4169-8513-6 Subj: Animals. Babies, toddlers. Rhyming text.

Hunwick's egg ill. by Pamela Lofts. Harcourt, 2005. ISBN 978-0-15-216318-1 Subj: Animals – bandicoots. Eggs. Friendship.

Koala Lou ill. by Pamela Lofts. Harcourt, 1989. ISBN 978-0-15-200502-3 Subj: Animals – koalas. Emotions – love. Family life – mothers.

Let's count goats! ill. by Jan Thomas. Simon & Schuster, 2010. ISBN 978-1-4424-0598-1 Subj: Animals – goats. Counting, numbers. Rhyming text.

The magic hat ill. by Tricia Tusa. Harcourt, 2002. ISBN 978-0-15-201025-6 Subj: Magic. Rhyming text. Wizards.

Nellie Belle ill. by Mike Austin. Simon & Schuster/Beach Lane, 2015. ISBN 978-141699005-5 Subj: Animals – dogs. Character traits – willfulness. Rhyming text.

Night noises ill. by Terry Denton. Harcourt, 1989. ISBN 978-0-15-200543-6 Subj: Animals – dogs. Birthdays. Night. Noise, sounds. Sleep.

A particular cow ill. by Terry Denton. Harcourt, 2006. ISBN 978-0-15-200250-3 Subj: Animals – bulls, cows. Humorous stories.

Possum magic ill. by Julie Vivas. Abingdon, 1987. ISBN 978-0-687-31732-5 Subj: Activities – traveling. Animals – possums. Behavior – wishing. Food. Foreign lands – Australia.

Shoes from grandpa ill. by Patricia Mullins. Watts, 1990. ISBN 978-0-531-08448-9 Subj: Behavior – growing up. Clothing. Cumulative tales. Family life – grandfathers. Rhyming text.

Sleepy bears ill. by Kerry Argent. Harcourt, 1999. ISBN 978-0-15-202016-3 Subj: Animals – bears. Lullabies. Rhyming text. Sleep.

Sophie ill. by Aminah Brenda Lynn Robinson. Harcourt, 1994. ISBN 978-0-15-277160-7 Subj: Birth. Death. Emotions – love. Family life – grandfathers.

Tell me about your day today ill. by Lauren Stringer. Simon & Schuster, 2012. ISBN 978-1-4169-9006-2 Subj: Bedtime. Imagination. Toys.

Ten little fingers and ten little toes ill. by Helen Oxenbury. Harcourt, 2008. ISBN 978-0-15-206057-2 Subj: Anatomy – hands. Anatomy – toes. Babies, toddlers. Rhyming text.

This and that ill. by Judy Horacek. Scholastic, 2017. ISBN 978-133803780-7 Subj: Activities – storytelling. Animals – mice. Bedtime. Family life – mothers. Rhyming text.

Time for bed ill. by Jane Dyer. Harcourt, 1993. ISBN 978-0-15-288183-2 Subj: Animals. Bedtime. Family life. Rhyming text.

Tough Boris ill. by Kathryn Brown. Harcourt, 1994. ISBN 978-0-15-289612-6 Subj: Birds – parakeets, parrots. Pirates.

Two little monkeys ill. by Jill Barton. Simon & Schuster, 2012. ISBN 978-1-4169-8687-4 Subj: Animals – leopards. Animals – monkeys. Rhyming text.

Where is the green sheep? ill. by Judy Horacek. Harcourt, 2004. ISBN 978-0-15-204907-2 Subj: Animals – sheep. Rhyming text.

Where the giant sleeps ill. by Vladimir Radunsky. Harcourt, 2007. ISBN 978-0-15-205785-5 Subj: Bedtime. Rhyming text. Sleep.

Wilfrid Gordon McDonald Partridge ill. by Julie Vivas. Kane/Miller, 1985. ISBN 978-0-916291-04-4 Subj: Behavior – forgetfulness. Old age.

Wombat divine ill. by Kerry Argent. Harcourt, 1996. ISBN 978-0-15-201416-2 Subj: Animals. Animals – wombats. Holidays – Christmas. Theater.

Yoo-hoo, Ladybug! ill. by Laura Ljungkvist. Simon & Schuster, 2013. ISBN 978-1-4424-3400-4 Subj: Insects – ladybugs. Picture puzzles. Rhyming text.

Zoo-looking ill. by Candace Whitman. Mondo, 1996. ISBN 978-1-57255-010-0 Subj: Animals. Rhyming text. Zoos.

Fox, Paula. *Traces* ill. by Karla Kuskin. Front Street, 2008. ISBN 978-1-932425-43-7 Subj: Nature. Poetry.

The fox went out on a chilly night ill. by Peter Spier. Doubleday, 1961. ISBN 978-0-385-00231-8 Subj: Animals – foxes. Caldecott award honor books. Folk & fairy tales. Songs.

Fradin, Dennis. *The price of freedom: how one town stood up to slavery* by Dennis Fradin and Judith Bloom Fradin ill. by Eric Velasquez. Walker, 2013. ISBN 978-0-8027-2166-2 Subj: Character traits – assertiveness. Character traits – bravery. Ethnic groups in the U.S. – African Americans. Slavery. U.S. history.

Fradin, Judith Bloom. *The price of freedom: how one town stood up to slavery* (Fradin, Dennis)

Fraggalosch, Audrey. *Great grizzly wilderness* ill. by Donald G. Eberhart. Soundprints, 2000. ISBN 978-1-56899-838-1 Subj: Animals – bears. Family life.

Grizzly bear family ill. by Donald G. Eberhart. Soundprints, 2003. ISBN 978-1-59249-048-6 Subj: Animals – bears. Behavior – growing up. Family life – mothers. Hibernation.

Trails above the tree line ill. by Higgins Bond. Soundprints, 2002. ISBN 978-1-56899-941-8 Subj: Animals – babies. Animals – sheep. Family life – mothers.

Frame, Jeron Ashford. *Yesterday I had the blues* ill. by Donald G. Eberhart. Tricycle, 2003. ISBN 978-1-58246-084-0 Subj: Emotions. Ethnic groups in the U.S. – African Americans. Family life.

Frampton, David. *Mr. Ferlinghetti's poem* ill. by author. Eerdmans, 2006. ISBN 978-0-8028-5290-8 Subj: Careers – firefighters. Poetry. Seasons – summer.

My beastie book of ABC ill. by author. HarperCollins, 2002. ISBN 978-0-06-028823-5 Subj: ABC books. Animals. Poetry.

The whole night through ill. by author. HarperCollins, 2002. ISBN 978-0-06-028826-6 Subj: Animals – leopards. Jungle. Lullabies. Rhyming text. Sleep.

Franceschelli, Christopher. *Alphablock* ill. by Peskimo. Abrams, 2013. ISBN 978-1-4197-0936-4 Subj: ABC books. Format, unusual – toy & movable books.

Cityblock ill. by Peskimo. Abrams/Appleseed, 2016. ISBN 978-141972189-2 Subj: Cities, towns. Format, unusual – toy & movable books.

Countablock ill. by Peskimo. Abrams/Appleseed, 2014. ISBN 978-141971374-3 Subj: Counting, numbers. Format, unusual – toy & movable books.

Dinoblock ill. by Peskimo. Abrams/Appleseed, 2015. ISBN 978-141971674-4 Subj: Dinosaurs. Format, unusual – board books.

(Oliver) ill. by Gaby Kooijman, et al. Lemniscaat, 2011. ISBN 978-1-9359-5401-9 Subj: Birds – chickens, roosters. Eggs. Format, unusual.

Francis, Lee DeCora. *Kunu's basket: a story from Indian Island* ill. by Susan Drucker. Tilbury, 2012. ISBN 978-0-88448-330-4 Subj: Activities – weaving. Character traits – perseverance. Family life – grandfathers. Indians of North America.

Francis, Panama. *David gets his drum* by Panama Francis and Bob Reiser ill. by Eric Velasquez. Marshall Cavendish, 2002. ISBN 978-0-7614-5088-7 Subj: Careers – musicians. Family life. Musical instruments – drums.

Francis, Pauline. *Sam stars at Shakespeare's Globe* ill. by Jane Tattersfield. Frances Lincoln, 2006. ISBN 978-1-84507-406-7 Subj: Careers – actors. Foreign lands – England. Theater.

Franco, Betsy. *Bees, snails, and peacock tails: patterns and shapes--naturally* ill. by Steve Jenkins. Simon

& Schuster, 2008. ISBN 978-1-4169-0386-4 Subj: Concepts – shape. Nature. Poetry.

Birdsongs ill. by Steve Jenkins. Simon & Schuster, 2007. ISBN 978-0-689-87777-3 Subj: Birds. Counting, numbers.

A curious collection of cats: concrete poems ill. by Michael Wertz. Tricycle, 2009. ISBN 978-1-58246-248-6 Subj: Animals – cats. Poetry.

A dazzling display of dogs: concrete poems ill. by Michael Wertz. Tricycle, 2011. ISBN 978-1-58246-343-8 Subj: Animals – dogs. Poetry.

Double play! monkeying around with addition ill. by Doug Cushman. Tricycle, 2011. ISBN 978-1-58246-384-1 Subj: Animals – monkeys. Counting, numbers. Rhyming text. School.

Pond circle ill. by Stefano Vitale. Simon & Schuster, 2009. ISBN 978-1-4169-4021-0 Subj: Animals. Ecology. Lakes, ponds.

A spectacular selection of sea critters: concrete poems ill. by Michael Wertz. Millbrook, 2015. ISBN 978-146772152-3 Subj: Animals. Poetry. Sea & seashore.

Summer beat ill. by Charlotte Middleton. Simon & Schuster, 2007. ISBN 978-1-4169-1237-8 Subj: Activities. Seasons – summer.

Why the frog has big eyes ill. by Joung Un Kim. Harcourt, 2000. ISBN 978-0-15-202536-6 Subj: Folk & fairy tales. Frogs & toads.

Frank, John. *A chill in the air: nature poems for fall and winter* ill. by Mike Reed. Simon & Schuster, 2003. ISBN 978-0-689-83923-8 Subj: Poetry. Seasons – fall. Seasons – winter.

How to catch a fish ill. by Peter Sylvada. Macmillan, 2007. ISBN 978-1-59643-163-8 Subj: Foreign lands. Poetry. Sports – fishing. World.

The toughest cowboy, Or, How the Wild West was tamed ill. by Zachary Pullen. Simon & Schuster, 2004. ISBN 978-0-689-83462-2 Subj: Animals – dogs. Cowboys, cowgirls. Humorous stories. U.S. history – frontier & pioneer life.

Frankel, Erin. *Dare!* ill. by Paula Heaphy. Free Spirit, 2012. ISBN 978-1-57542-399-9 Subj: Behavior – bullying, teasing. Emotions – fear. Self-concept.

Nobody! a story about overcoming bullying in schools ill. by Paula Heaphy. Free Spirit, 2015. ISBN 978-157542495-8 Subj: Behavior – bullying, teasing. School. Self-concept.

Tough! ill. by Paula Heaphy. Free Spirit, 2012. ISBN 978-1-57542-400-2 Subj: Behavior – bullying, teasing. Friendship. Self-concept.

Weird! ill. by Paula Heaphy. Free Spirit, 2012. ISBN 978-1-57542-398-2 Subj: Behavior – bullying, teasing. Character traits – individuality. Self-concept.

Franson, Scott E. *Un-brella* ill. by author. Macmillan, 2007. ISBN 978-1-59643-179-9 Subj: Magic. Umbrellas. Wordless.

Frantz, Jennifer. *Totem poles* ill. by Allan Eitzen. Grosset, 2001. ISBN 978-0-448-42476-7 Subj: Indians of North America – Haida.

Fraser, Mary Ann. *Heebie-Jeebie Jamboree* ill. by author. Boyds Mills, 2011. ISBN 978-1-59078-857-8 Subj: Fairs, festivals. Family life – brothers & sisters. Holidays – Halloween.

How animal babies stay safe ill. by author. HarperCollins, 2002. ISBN 978-0-06-028804-4 Subj: Animals – babies. Family life – parents.

I.Q. gets fit ill. by author. Walker, 2007. ISBN 978-0-8027-9558-8 Subj: Animals – mice. Health & fitness. Pets. School.

I.Q. goes to school ill. by author. Walker, 2002. ISBN 978-0-8027-8813-9 Subj: Animals – mice. Pets. School.

I.Q. goes to the library ill. by author. Walker, 2003. ISBN 978-0-8027-8877-1 Subj: Animals – mice. Libraries. Pets. School.

I.Q., it's time ill. by author. Walker, 2005. ISBN 978-0-8027-8978-5 Subj: Animals – mice. Clocks, watches. Pets. School. Time.

Mermaid sister ill. by author. Bloomsbury, 2008. ISBN 978-0-8027-9746-9 Subj: Family life – sisters. Mythical creatures – mermaids, mermen.

No Yeti yet ill. by author. Peter Pauper, 2015. ISBN 978-144130855-9 Subj: Family life – brothers. Monsters. Sports – hunting.

Pet shop follies ill. by author. Boyds Mills, 2010. ISBN 978-1-59078-619-2 Subj: Character traits – cooperation. Pets. Stores.

Pet shop lullaby ill. by author. Boyds Mills, 2009. ISBN 978-1-59078-618-5 Subj: Animals – hamsters. Bedtime. Pets. Stores.

Where are the night animals? ill. by author. HarperCollins, 1999. ISBN 978-0-06-027718-5 Subj: Animals. Night.

Frasier, Debra. *A birthday cake is no ordinary cake* ill. by author. Harcourt, 2006. ISBN 978-0-15-205742-8 Subj: Birthdays. Calendars.

A fabulous fair alphabet ill. by author. Simon & Schuster, 2010. ISBN 978-1-4169-9817-4 Subj: ABC books. Fairs, festivals.

On the day you were born ill. by author. Harcourt, 1991. ISBN 978-0-15-257995-1 Subj: Babies, toddlers. Birth. Poetry.

Out of the ocean ill. by author. Harcourt, 1998. ISBN 978-0-15-258849-6 Subj: Family life – mothers. Sea & seashore.

Spike: ugliest dog in the universe ill. by author. Simon & Schuster, 2013. ISBN 978-1-4424-1452-5 Subj: Animals – dogs. Character traits – bravery. Contests.

Fraustino, Lisa Rowe. *The hickory chair* ill. by Benny Andrews. Scholastic, 2000. ISBN 978-0-590-52248-9 Subj: Death. Disabilities – blindness. Family life – grandmothers.

Frazee, Marla. *Boot and Shoe* ill. by author. Simon & Schuster, 2012. ISBN 978-1-4424-2247-6 Subj: Animals – dogs. Animals – squirrels. Friendship.

The boss baby ill. by author. Simon & Schuster, 2010. ISBN 978-1-4424-0167-9 Subj: Babies, toddlers. Behavior – bossy.

The bossier baby ill. by author. Simon & Schuster/Beach Lane, 2016. ISBN 978-148147162-6 Subj: Babies, toddlers. Behavior – bossy. Emotions – envy, jealousy. Family life – brothers & sisters. Family life – new sibling. Sibling rivalry.

A couple of boys have the best week ever ill. by author. Harcourt, 2008. ISBN 978-0-15-206020-6 Subj: Activities – vacationing. Caldecott award honor books. Family life – grandparents. Humorous stories. Sea & seashore – beaches.

The farmer and the clown ill. by author. Simon & Schuster/Beach Lane, 2014. ISBN 978-144249744-3 Subj: Behavior – lost. Careers – farmers. Circus. Clowns, jesters. Wordless.

Hush, little baby: a folk song with pictures ill. by author. Harcourt, 2007. ISBN 978-0-15-205887-6 Subj: Babies, toddlers. Character traits – generosity. Cumulative tales. Format, unusual – board books. Lullabies. Music.

Roller coaster ill. by author. Harcourt, 2003. ISBN 978-0-15-204554-8 Subj: Emotions – fear. Parks – amusement.

Santa Claus: the world's number one toy expert ill. by author. Harcourt, 2005. ISBN 978-0-15-204970-6 Subj: Gifts. Holidays – Christmas. Santa Claus. Toys.

Walk on! a guide for babies of all ages ill. by author. Harcourt, 2006. ISBN 978-0-15-205573-8 Subj: Activities – walking. Babies, toddlers. Behavior – growing up. Self-concept.

Frazier, Craig. *Bee and Bird* ill. by author. Roaring Brook, 2011. ISBN 978-1-59643-660-2 Subj: Birds. Insects – bees. Wordless.

Lots of dots ill. by author. Chronicle, 2010. ISBN 978-0-8118-7715-2 Subj: Concepts – shape. Rhyming text.

Frederick, Heather Vogel. *Babyberry pie* ill. by Amy Schwartz. Harcourt, 2010. ISBN 978-0-15-205927-9 Subj: Babies, toddlers. Bedtime. Rhyming text.

Hide and squeak. Simon & Schuster, 2011. ISBN 978-0-689-85570-2 Subj: Animals – mice. Bedtime. Family life – fathers. Rhyming text.

Frederick-Frost, Alexis. *Gryphons aren't so great* (Sturm, James)

Ogres awake! (Sturm, James)

Sleepless knight (Sturm, James)

Fredericks, Anthony D. *In one tidepool: crabs, snails, and salty tails* ill. by Jennifer DiRubbio. Dawn, 2002. ISBN 978-1-58469-039-9 Subj: Animals. Birds – geese. Forest, woods. Seasons – winter.

Fredrickson, Lane. *Monster trouble!* ill. by Michael Robertson. Sterling, 2015. ISBN 978-145491345-0 Subj: Bedtime. Ethnic groups in the U.S. – African Americans. Kissing. Monsters.

Watch your tongue, Cecily Beasley ill. by Jon Davis. Sterling, 2012. ISBN 978-1-4027-7089-0 Subj: Behavior – misbehavior. Birds. Etiquette. Rhyming text.

Freed, Arthur. *Singing in the rain* by Arthur Freed and Nacio Herb Brown ill. by Tim Hopgood. Henry Holt, 2017. ISBN 978-125012770-9 Subj: Songs. Weather – rain.

Freedman, Claire. *Beep beep beep: time for sleep!* ill. by Richard Smythe. Simon & Schuster, 2017. ISBN 978-148149011-5 Subj: Bedtime. Careers – construction workers. Machines. Trucks.

Dinosaurs love underpants ill. by Ben Cort. Simon & Schuster, 2010. ISBN 978-1-4169-8938-7 Subj: Clothing – underwear. Dinosaurs. Rhyming text.

Follow that bear if you dare! ill. by Alison Edgson. Good Books, 2008. ISBN 978-1-56148-588-8 Subj: Animals – bears. Animals – rabbits. Sports – hunting.

Hushabye Lily ill. by John Bendall-Brunello. Orchard, 2003. ISBN 978-0-439-47106-0 Subj: Animals – rabbits. Bedtime. Noise, sounds.

Night-night, Emily ill. by Jane Massey. Tiger Tales, 2003. ISBN 978-1-58925-032-1 Subj: Bedtime. Behavior – lost & found possessions. Toys. Toys – bears.

One magical day ill. by Tina Macnaughton. Good Books, 2007. ISBN 978-1-56148-567-3 Subj: Animals. Day. Rhyming text. Seasons – summer.

One magical morning ill. by Louise Ho. Good Books, 2005. ISBN 978-1-56148-472-0 Subj: Animals. Animals – bears. Family life – mothers. Morning. Rhyming text.

Pirates love underpants ill. by Ben Cort. Aladdin, 2013. ISBN 978-1-4424-8512-9 Subj: Clothing – underwear. Pirates. Rhyming text.

Snuggle up, sleepy ones ill. by Tina Macnaughton. Good Books, 2005. ISBN 978-1-56148-475-1 Subj: Animals. Bedtime. Rhyming text. Sleep.

Spider sandwiches ill. by Sue Hendra and Paul Linnet. Bloomsbury, 2014. ISBN 978-161963364-3 Subj: Food. Monsters. Rhyming text.

Where's your smile, crocodile? ill. by Sean Julian. Peachtree, 2001. ISBN 978-1-56145-251-4 Subj: Animals. Emotions. Reptiles – alligators, crocodiles.

Freedman, Deborah. *Blue chicken* ill. by author. Penguin, 2011. ISBN 978-0-670-01293-0 Subj: Activities – painting. Birds – chickens, roosters. Careers – artists. Character traits – helpfulness. Concepts – color.

By Mouse and Frog ill. by author. Viking, 2015. ISBN 978-067078490-5 Subj: Animals – mice. Careers – writers. Character traits – compromising. Character traits – cooperation. Frogs & toads.

Scribble ill. by author. Random House, 2007. ISBN 978-0-375-83966-5 Subj: Activities – drawing. Family life – brothers & sisters. Imagination.

Shy ill. by author. Viking, 2016. ISBN 978-045147496-4 Subj: Animals – giraffes. Birds. Books, reading. Character traits – shyness. Emotions – fear. Friendship.

The Story of Fish and Snail ill. by author. Viking, 2013. ISBN 978-0-670-78489-9 Subj: Activities – storytelling. Animals – snails. Books, reading. Fish. Libraries.

This house, once ill. by author. Atheneum, 2017. ISBN 978-148144284-8 Subj: Homes, houses. Nature.

Freeman, Don. *Beady Bear* ill. by author. Viking, 1954. ISBN 978-0-670-15056-4 Subj: Behavior – running away. Toys – bears.

Bearymore ill. by author. Viking, 1976. ISBN 978-0-670-15174-5 Subj: Animals – bears. Circus. Hibernation.

Corduroy ill. by author. Viking, 1968. ISBN 978-0-670-24133-0 Subj: Clothing. Emotions – love. Ethnic groups in the U.S. – African Americans. Stores. Toys – bears.

Corduroy's busy street and Corduroy goes to the doctor ill. by author. Live Oak Media, 1989. ISBN 978-0-87499-133-8 Subj: Careers – doctors. Communities, neighborhoods. Format, unusual – board books. Toys – bears.

Dandelion ill. by author. Viking, 1964. ISBN 978-0-670-25532-0 Subj: Animals – lions. Character traits – appearance. Parties. Weather – rain.

Earl the squirrel ill. by author. Penguin, 2005. ISBN 978-0-670-06019-1 Subj: Animals – squirrels.

Gregory's Shadow ill. by author. Viking, 2000. ISBN 978-0-670-89328-7 Subj: Animals – groundhogs. Holidays – Groundhog Day. Shadows.

One more acorn by Don Freeman and Roy Freeman; ill. by Don Freeman and Jody Wheeler. Penguin, 2010. ISBN 978-0-670-01083-7 Subj: Animals – squirrels. Seasons – fall.

A pocket for Corduroy ill. by author. Viking, 1978. ISBN 978-0-670-56172-8 Subj: Clothing. Ethnic groups in the U.S. – African Americans. Laundry. Toys – bears.

Quiet! There's a canary in the library ill. by author. Golden Gate, 1969. ISBN 978-0-516-08737-5 Subj: Birds – canaries. Emotions – embarrassment. Imagination. Libraries.

Freeman, Mylo. *Potty* ill. by author. Tricycle, 2002. ISBN 978-1-58246-070-3 Subj: Animals. Behavior – growing up. Jungle. Toilet training.

Freeman, Roy. *One more acorn* (Freeman, Don)

Freeman, Tor. *Hooray! I'm five today!* ill. by author. Candlewick, 2004. ISBN 978-0-7636-2452-1 Subj: Animals. Birthdays. Parties.

Olive and the bad mood ill. by author. Candlewick, 2013. ISBN 978-0-7636-6657-6 Subj: Animals – cats. Behavior – bad day, bad mood. Behavior – sharing. Friendship.

Olive and the big secret ill. by author. Candlewick, 2012. ISBN 978-0-7636-6149-6 Subj: Animals. Animals – cats. Behavior – secrets.

Olive and the embarrassing gift ill. by author. Candlewick/Templar, 2014. ISBN 978-076367406-9 Subj: Animals. Clothing – hats. Emotions – embarrassment. Friendship. Gifts.

French, Jackie. *Christmas wombat* ill. by Bruce Whatley. Harcourt, 2012. ISBN 978-0-547-86872-1 Subj: Animals – wombats. Holidays – Christmas.

Diary of a baby wombat ill. by Bruce Whatley. Clarion, 2010. ISBN 978-0-547-43005-8 Subj: Activities – writing. Animals – babies. Animals – wombats.

Diary of a wombat ill. by Bruce Whatley. Clarion, 2003. ISBN 978-0-618-38136-4 Subj: Activities – writing. Animals – wombats.

Josephine wants to dance ill. by Bruce Whatley. Abrams, 2007. ISBN 978-0-8109-9431-7 Subj: Activities – dancing. Animals – kangaroos. Ballet. Foreign lands – Australia.

Pete the sheep-sheep ill. by Bruce Whatley. Houghton, 2005. ISBN 978-0-618-56862-8 Subj: Animals – dogs. Animals – sheep. Humorous stories.

French, Simon. *Guess the baby* ill. by Donna Rawlins. Clarion, 2002. ISBN 978-0-618-25989-2 Subj: Babies, toddlers. School.

French, Vivian. *Growing frogs* ill. by Alison Bartlett. Candlewick, 2000. ISBN 978-0-7636-0317-5 Subj: Animals – babies. Frogs & toads.

The most wonderful thing in the world ill. by Angela Barrett. Candlewick, 2015. ISBN 978-076367501-1 Subj: Character traits – wisdom. Folk & fairy tales. Royalty – princesses.

A present for mom ill. by Dana Kubick. Candlewick, 2002. ISBN 978-0-7636-1587-1 Subj: Animals – cats. Gifts. Holidays – Mother's Day.

Yucky worms ill. by Jessica Ahlberg. Candlewick, 2010. ISBN 978-0-7636-4446-8 Subj: Animals – worms. Family life – grandmothers. Gardens, gardening.

Freschet, Gina. *Beto and the bone dance* ill. by author. Farrar, 2001. ISBN 978-0-374-31720-1 Subj: Ethnic groups in the U.S. – Mexican Americans. Holidays – Day of the Dead.

Naty's parade ill. by author. Farrar, 2000. ISBN 978-0-374-35500-5 Subj: Behavior – lost. Holidays. Parades.

Freymann, Saxton. *Baby food* by Saxton Freymann and Joost Elffers; ill. by Saxton Freymann. Scholastic, 2006. ISBN 978-0-439-11021-1 Subj: Animals – babies. Food. Format, unusual – board books.

Dog food by Saxton Freymann and Joost Elffers; ill. by Saxton Freymann. Scholastic, 2006. ISBN 978-0-439-11020-4 Subj: Animals – dogs. Food. Format, unusual – board books.

Dr. Pompo's nose by Saxton Freymann and Joost Elffers; ill. by authors. Scholastic, 2000. ISBN 978-0-439-11013-6 Subj: Anatomy – noses. Rhyming text.

Fast food by Saxton Freymann and Joost Elffers; ill. by Saxton Freymann. Scholastic, 2006. ISBN 978-0-439-11019-8 Subj: Food. Transportation.

Food for thought: the complete book of concepts for growing minds by Saxton Freymann and Joost Elffers; ill. by Saxton Freymann. Scholastic, 2005. ISBN 978-0-439-11018-1 Subj: ABC books. Concepts – color. Concepts – opposites. Concepts – shape. Counting, numbers. Food. Format, unusual – board books.

Food play by Saxton Freymann and Joost Elffers; ill. by Saxton Freymann. Chronicle, 2006. ISBN 978-0-8118-5705-5 Subj: Food.

How are you peeling? foods with moods by Saxton Freymann and Joost Elffers; ill. by Saxton Freymann. Scholastic, 2004. ISBN 978-0-439-59841-5 Subj: Emotions. Food.

One lonely seahorse by Saxton Freymann and Joost Elffers; ill. by authors. Scholastic, 2000. ISBN 978-0-439-11014-3 Subj: Counting, numbers. Fish – seahorses. Friendship. Rhyming text. Sea & seashore.

Friday, Mary Ellen. *It's a bad day* ill. by Glin Dibley. Rising Moon, 2006. ISBN 978-0-87358-904-8 Subj: Behavior – bad day, bad mood. Character traits – luck.

Friedlaender, Linda K. *Look! look! look!* (Wallace, Nancy Elizabeth)

Friedland, Katy. *Art museum opposites* by Katy Friedland and Marla K. Shoemaker. Temple Univ., 2010. ISBN 978-1-4399-0523-4 Subj: Art. Concepts – opposites. Museums.

Friedman, Caitlin. *How do you feed a hungry giant? a munch-and-sip pop-up book* ill. by Shaw Nielsen. Workman, 2011. ISBN 978-0-7611-5752-6 Subj: Food. Format, unusual – toy & movable books. Giants.

Friedman, Darlene. *Star of the Week: a story of love, adoption, and brownies with sprinkles* ill. by Roger Roth. HarperCollins, 2009. ISBN 978-0-06-114136-2 Subj: Adoption. Ethnic groups in the U.S. – Chinese Americans. School.

Friedman, Ina R. *How my parents learned to eat* ill. by Allen Say. Houghton, 1984. ISBN 978-0-395-35379-0 Subj: Family life. Sailors.

Friedman, Laurie. *Love, Ruby Valentine* ill. by Lynne Cravath. Carolrhoda, 2006. ISBN 978-1-57505-899-3 Subj: Gifts. Holidays – Valentine's Day.

Ruby Valentine and the sweet surprise ill. by Lynne Avril. Carolrhoda, 2014. ISBN 978-076138873-9 Subj: Animals – cats. Birds – parakeets, parrots. Holidays – Valentine's Day. Pets. Rhyming text.

Ruby Valentine saves the day ill. by Lynne Avril. Carolrhoda, 2010. ISBN 978-0-7613-4213-7 Subj: Holidays – Valentine's Day. Parties. Rhyming text. Weather – blizzards.

A style all her own ill. by Sharon Watts. Lerner, 2005. ISBN 978-1-57505-599-2 Subj: Character traits – individuality. Clothing – dresses. Weddings.

Thanksgiving rules ill. by Teresa Murfin. Carolrhoda, 2009. ISBN 978-0-8225-7983-0 Subj: Holidays – Thanksgiving. Rhyming text.

Friedman, Mel. *Kitten castle* by Mel Friedman and Ellen Weiss ill. by Lynn Adams. Kane, 2001. ISBN 978-1-57565-103-3 Subj: Animals – babies. Animals – cats. Concepts – shape.

Friedrich, Molly. *You're not my real mother!* ill. by Christy Hale. Little, Brown, 2004. ISBN 978-0-316-60553-3 Subj: Adoption. Family life. Self-concept.

Friedrich, Otto. *The Easter bunny that overslept* (Friedrich, Priscilla)

Friedrich, Priscilla. *The Easter bunny that overslept* by Priscilla Friedrich and Otto Friedrich ill. by Adrienne Adams. Lothrop, 1957. ISBN 978-0-688-01541-1 Subj: Holidays – Easter.

Friend, Catherine. *Eddie the raccoon* ill. by Wong Herbert Yee. Candlewick, 2004. ISBN 978-0-7636-2334-0 Subj: Activities. Animals – raccoons.

Funny Ruby ill. by Rachel Merriman. Candlewick, 2000. ISBN 978-0-7636-1066-1 Subj: Activities. Animals – sheep.

The perfect nest ill. by John Manders. Candlewick, 2007. ISBN 978-0-7636-2430-9 Subj: Animals – cats. Behavior – trickery. Birds. Eggs. Farms.

Friend, David. *With any luck, I'll drive a truck* ill. by Michael Rex. Penguin/Nancy Paulsen, 2016. ISBN 978-039916956-4 Subj: Activities – playing. Rhyming text. Trucks.

Fries, Claudia. *A pig is moving in* ill. by author. Orchard, 2000. ISBN 978-0-531-33307-5 Subj: Animals. Communities, neighborhoods. Homes, houses. Prejudice.

Frisch, Aaron. *The lonely pine* ill. by Etienne Delessert. Creative Editions, 2011. ISBN 978-1-56846-214-1 Subj: Nature. Seasons. Trees.

Frith, Margaret. *Frida Kahlo: the artist who painted herself* ill. by Tomie dePaola. Grosset, 2003. ISBN 978-0-448-43239-7 Subj: Careers – artists. Foreign lands – Mexico.

Frith, Nicholas John. *Hector and Hummingbird* ill. by author. Scholastic/Arthur A. Levine, 2016. ISBN 978-054585701-7 Subj: Animals – bears. Behavior – solitude. Birds – hummingbirds. Friendship.

Fritts, Mary Bahr. *If Nathan were here* ill. by Karen Jerome. Eerdmans, 2000. ISBN 978-0-8028-5187-1 Subj: Death. Emotions – grief. Friendship.

A frog he would a-wooing go [folk-song]. *Frog went a-courtin'* retold by John M. Langstaff; ill. by Feodor Rojankovsky. Harcourt, 1955. ISBN 978-0-15-230214-6 Subj: Animals. Caldecott award books. Frogs & toads. Songs.

Frog went a-courting: a musical play in six acts retold by Dominic Catalano; ill. by reteller. Boyds Mills, 1998. ISBN 978-1-56397-637-7 Subj: Animals. Frogs & toads. Music. Songs. Theater. Weddings.

Froggie went a courting adapt. by Marjorie Priceman; ill. by adapter. Little, 1999. ISBN 978-0-316-71227-9 Subj: Animals. Frogs & toads. Songs. Weddings.

Froggy went a-courtin' adapt. by Gillian Tyler; ill. by adapter. Candlewick, 2005. ISBN 978-0-7636-2306-7 Subj: Animals. Frogs & toads. Songs. Weddings.

Fromental, Jean-Luc. *Bonesville* ill. by Joëlle Jolivet. Abrams, 2016. ISBN 978-141972277-6 Subj: Anatomy – skeletons. Mystery stories.

365 penguins by Jean-Luc Fromental and Joëlle Jolivet; ill. by authors. Abrams, 2006. ISBN 978-0-8109-4460-2 Subj: Birds – penguins. Counting, numbers. Holidays – New Year's.

Fronis, Aly. *If you're spooky and you know it* ill. by Jannie Ho. little bee, 2016. ISBN 978-149980165-1 Subj: Format, unusual – board books. Holidays – Halloween. Monsters. Rhyming text.

Frost, Helen. *Among a thousand fireflies* ill. by Rick Lieder. Candlewick, 2016. ISBN 978-076367642-1 Subj: Insects – fireflies. Poetry.

Monarch and milkweed ill. by Leonid Gore. Atheneum, 2008. ISBN 978-1-4169-0085-6 Subj: Insects – butterflies, caterpillars. Metamorphosis. Migration.

Step gently out photos by Rick Lieder. Candlewick, 2012. ISBN 978-0-7636-5601-0 Subj: Insects. Nature. Poetry.

Sweep up the sun photos by Rick Lieder. Candlewick, 2015. ISBN 978-076366904-1 Subj: Birds. Nature. Poetry.

Wake up! photos by Rick Lieder. Candlewick, 2017. ISBN 978-076368149-4 Subj: Animals – babies. Poetry. Seasons – spring.

Frost, Robert. *Stopping by woods on a snowy evening* ill. by Susan Jeffers. Dutton, 1978. ISBN 978-0-525-40115-5 Subj: Forest, woods. Poetry. Seasons – winter.

Fruisen, Catherine Myler. *My mother's pearls* ill. by author. Star Bright, 2005. ISBN 978-1-59572-005-4 Subj: Family life – daughters. Family life – mothers. Jewelry.

Fry, Jenny. *Building numbers* ill. by Jacqueline East. Barron's, 2002. ISBN 978-0-7641-5499-7 Subj: Counting, numbers. Machines.

Fry, Stella. *Grandpa's garden* ill. by Sheila Moxley. Barefoot, 2012. ISBN 978-1-84686-053-9 Subj: Family life – grandfathers. Gardens, gardening.

Fucile, Tony. *Let's do nothing!* ill. by author. Candlewick, 2009. ISBN 978-0-7636-3440-7 Subj: Activities – playing.

Poor Louie ill. by author. Candlewick, 2017. ISBN 978-076365828-1 Subj: Animals – dogs. Babies, toddlers. Family life – new sibling.

Fuge, Charles. *Astonishing animal ABC* ill. by author. Sterling, 2011. ISBN 978-1-4027-8645-7 Subj: ABC books. Animals. Rhyming text.

I know a rhino ill. by author. Sterling, 2002. ISBN 978-1-4027-0137-5 Subj: Activities – playing. Animals. Imagination. Rhyming text.

Swim, Little Wombat, swim! ill. by author. Sterling, 2005. ISBN 978-1-4027-2375-9 Subj: Animals – platypuses. Animals – wombats. Friendship. Sports – swimming.

Three little dinosaurs ill. by author. Sterling, 2012. ISBN 978-1-4027-9645-6 Subj: Activities – flying. Dinosaurs.

Where to, Little Wombat? ill. by author. Sterling, 2006. ISBN 978-1-4027-3698-8 Subj: Animals – wombats. Format, unusual – board books. Homes, houses.

Yip! snap! yap! ill. by author. Tricycle, 2001. ISBN 978-1-58246-046-8 Subj: Animals – dogs. Noise, sounds.

Fuller, Sandy F. *The Blues go birding across America* (Malnor, Carol L.)

My cat, coon cat ill. by Jeannie Brett. Islandport, 2011. ISBN 978-1-934031-32-2 Subj: Animals – cats.

Fullerton, Alma. *A good trade* ill. by Karen Patkau. Pajama Press, 2012. ISBN 978-0-9869495-9-3 Subj: Clothing – shoes. Foreign lands – Uganda. Poverty. War.

Fulton, Kristen. *Long may she wave: the true story of Caroline Pickersgill and her star-spangled creation* ill. by Holly Berry. Simon & Schuster/Margaret K. McElderry, 2017. ISBN 978-148146096-5 Subj: Activities – sewing. Flags. U.S. history.

Funk, Josh. *Dear dragon* ill. by Rodolfo Montalvo. Viking, 2016. ISBN 978-045147230-4 Subj: Dragons. Letters, cards. Pen pals. Rhyming text.

Pirasaurs! ill. by Michael H. Slack. Scholastic/Orchard, 2016. ISBN 978-054575049-3 Subj: Dinosaurs. Pirates. Rhyming text.

Funke, Cornelia. *The book no one ever read* ill. by author. Breathing Books, 2017. ISBN 978-098916569-3 Subj: Books, reading. Libraries.

Pirate girl ill. by Kerstin Meyer. Scholastic, 2005. ISBN 978-0-439-71672-7 Subj: Pirates.

Princess Pigsty ill. by Kerstin Meyer. Scholastic, 2007. ISBN 978-0-439-98855-1 Subj: Behavior – misbehavior. Character traits – cleanliness. Royalty – princesses. Self-concept.

The wildest brother ill. by Kerstin Meyer. Scholastic, 2006. ISBN 978-0-439-82862-8 Subj: Emotions – fear. Family life – brothers & sisters. Monsters.

Furgang, Kathy. *Flower girl* ill. by Harley Jessup. Viking, 2002. ISBN 978-0-670-88950-1 Subj: Weddings.

Furrow, Elena. *Ready to dream* (Napoli, Donna Jo)

Furrow, Eva. *Bobby the bold* (Napoli, Donna Jo)

Take your time: a tale of Harriet, the Galápagos tortoise by Eva Furrow and Donna Jo Napoli ill. by Laurel Molk. Henry Holt, 2017. ISBN 978-080509521-0 Subj: Character traits – confidence. Concepts – speed. Foreign lands – Galapagos Islands. Reptiles – turtles, tortoises. Self-concept.

Furstinger, Nancy. *Maggie's second chance: a gentle dog's rescue* ill. by Joe Hyatt. Gryphon, 2011. ISBN 978-0-940719-11-8 Subj: Animals – dogs. Character traits – kindness to animals.

Fyleman, Rose. *Mice* ill. by Lois Ehlert. Simon & Schuster, 2012. ISBN 978-1-4424-5684-6 Subj: Animals – mice. Rhyming text.

Gabriel, Ashala. *Night night toes* ill. by Sue Porter. Simon & Schuster, 2002. ISBN 978-0-689-85089-9 Subj: Animals – bears. Bedtime. Format, unusual – toy & movable books. Night.

Gadot, A. S. *The first gift* ill. by Marie Lafrance. Lerner, 2006. ISBN 978-1-58013-146-9 Subj: Jewish culture. Names. Religion.

Tower of Babel ill. by Cecilia Rebora. Lerner/Kar-Ben, 2010. ISBN 978-0-8225-9917-3 Subj: Religion.

Gág, Wanda. *Millions of cats* ill. by author. Coward, 1928. ISBN 978-0-698-20091-3 Subj: Animals – cats. Character traits – practicality. Cumulative tales.

Gaiman, Neil. *Chu's day* ill. by Adam Rex. HarperCollins, 2013. ISBN 978-0-06-201781-9 Subj: Animals – pandas. Illness.

Chu's day at the beach ill. by Adam Rex. HarperCollins, 2015. ISBN 978-006222399-9 Subj: Animals – pandas. Sea & seashore – beaches.

Chu's first day of school ill. by Adam Rex. HarperCollins, 2014. ISBN 978-006222397-5 Subj: Animals – pandas. Behavior – worrying. Illness. School – first day.

Cinnamon ill. by Divya Srinivasan. HarperCollins, 2017. ISBN 978-006239961-8 Subj: Animals – tigers. Disabilities. Royalty – princesses.

Crazy hair ill. by Dave McKean. HarperCollins, 2009. ISBN 978-0-06-057908-1 Subj: Character traits – appearance. Hair. Humorous stories. Rhyming text.

The dangerous alphabet ill. by Gris Grimly. HarperCollins, 2008. ISBN 978-0-06-078333-4 Subj: ABC books. Emotions – fear. Monsters. Pirates. Rhyming text.

Instructions ill. by Charles Vess. HarperCollins, 2010. ISBN 978-0-06-196030-7 Subj: Activities – traveling. Self-concept.

Gainer, Cindy. *I'm like you, you're like me: a book about understanding and appreciating each other* ill. by Miki Sakamoto. Free Spirit, 2011. ISBN 978-1-57542-383-8 Subj: Character traits – cooperation. Character traits – individuality. Character traits – kindness.

Gal, Susan. *Day by day* ill. by author. Knopf, 2012. ISBN 978-0-375-86959-4 Subj: Animals – pigs. Communities, neighborhoods. Family life.

Night lights ill. by author. Knopf, 2009. ISBN 978-0-375-85862-8 Subj: Bedtime. Family life – mothers. Light, lights. Night.

Please take me for a walk ill. by author. Random House, 2010. ISBN 978-0-375-85863-5 Subj: Animals – dogs.

Galbraith, Kathryn O. *Arbor Day square* ill. by Cyd Moore. Peachtree, 2010. ISBN 978-1-56145-517-1 Subj: Family life – fathers. Holidays. Trees. U.S. history – frontier & pioneer life.

Boo, bunny! ill. by Jeff Mack. Harcourt, 2008. ISBN 978-0-15-216246-7 Subj: Animals – rabbits. Emotions – fear. Holidays – Halloween. Rhyming text.

Planting the wild garden ill. by Wendy Anderson Halperin. Peachtree, 2011. ISBN 978-1-56145-563-8 Subj: Nature. Seeds.

Two bunny buddies ill. by Joe Cepeda. Houghton, 2014. ISBN 978-054417652-2 Subj: Animals – rabbits. Behavior – fighting, arguing. Friendship.

Galdone, Joanna. *The tailypo: a ghost story* ill. by Paul Galdone. Seabury Pr., 1977. ISBN 978-0-8164-3191-5 Subj: Ghosts.

Galdone, Paul, adapt. *Cat goes fiddle-i-fee* ill. by adapter. Clarion, 1985. ISBN 978-0-89919-336-6 Subj: Animals. Cumulative tales. Farms. Noise, sounds. Nursery rhymes.

The magic porridge pot ill. by author. Seabury Pr., 1976. ISBN 978-0-8164-3173-1 Subj: Behavior – forgetfulness. Behavior – sharing. Folk & fairy tales. Food. Magic.

The teeny-tiny woman: a ghost story ill. by adapter. Clarion, 1984. ISBN 978-0-89919-270-3 Subj: Emotions. Folk & fairy tales. Ghosts.

What's in fox's sack? ill. by author. Houghton, 1982. ISBN 978-0-89919-062-4 Subj: Character traits – cleverness. Folk & fairy tales.

Galindo, Mary Sue. *Icy watermelon / Sandía fría* ill. by Pauline Rodriguez Howard. Piñata, 2001. ISBN 978-1-55885-306-5 Subj: Ethnic groups in the U.S. – Mexican Americans. Family life – grandparents. Foreign languages.

Galindo, Renata. *My new mom and me* ill. by author. Random House, 2016. ISBN 978-055352134-4 Subj: Adoption. Animals – cats. Animals – dogs. Family life – mothers.

Galing, Ed. *Tony* ill. by Erin E. Stead. Roaring Brook/Neal Porter, 2017. ISBN 978-162672308-5 Subj: Animals – horses, ponies. Character traits – kindness to animals.

Galko, Francine. *Cave animals* ill. with photos. Heinemann, 2003. ISBN 978-1-4034-0176-2 Subj: Animals. Caves. Ecology.

Gall, Chris. *Awesome Dawson* ill. by author. Little, Brown, 2013. ISBN 978-0-316-21330-1 Subj: Behavior – collecting things. Careers – inventors. Ecology. Robots. Toys.

Dinotrux ill. by author. Little, Brown, 2009. ISBN 978-0-316-02777-9 Subj: Dinosaurs. Trucks.

Dinotrux dig the beach ill. by author. Little, Brown, 2015. ISBN 978-031637553-5 Subj: Dinosaurs. Sea & seashore – beaches. Trucks.

Dog vs. Cat ill. by author. Little, Brown, 2014. ISBN 978-031623801-4 Subj: Animals – cats. Animals – dogs. Character traits – being different. Friendship.

The littlest train ill. by author. Little, Brown, 2017. ISBN 978-031639286-0 Subj: Activities – traveling. Toys – trains. Trains.

NanoBots ill. by author. Little, Brown, 2016. ISBN 978-031637552-8 Subj: Careers – inventors. Character traits – helpfulness. Character traits – smallness. Concepts – size. Robots. Science.

Revenge of the Dinotrux ill. by author. Little, Brown, 2012. ISBN 978-0-316-13288-6 Subj: Behavior – misbehavior. Books, reading. Dinosaurs. Museums. Trucks.

Substitute creacher ill. by author. Little, Brown, 2011. ISBN 978-0-316-08915-9 Subj: Careers – teachers. Monsters. Rhyming text. School.

There's nothing to do on Mars ill. by author. Little, Brown, 2008. ISBN 978-0-316-16684-3 Subj: Behavior – boredom. Space & space ships.

Gallaher, Jason. *Whobert Whover, owl detective* ill. by Jess Pauwels. Simon & Schuster/Margaret K. McElderry, 2017. ISBN 978-148146271-6 Subj: Animals – possums. Birds – owls. Careers – detectives. Mystery stories.

Gallico, Paul. *Paul Gallico's The small miracle* (Barton, Bob)

Gallion, Sue Lowell. *Pug and Pig trick-or-treat* ill. by Joyce Wan. Beach Lane, 2017. ISBN 978-148144977-9 Subj: Animals – dogs. Animals – pigs. Clothing – costumes. Holidays – Halloween.

Pug meets Pig ill. by Joyce Wan. Simon & Schuster, 2016. ISBN 978-148142066-2 Subj: Animals – dogs. Animals – pigs. Behavior – dissatisfaction.

Gallo, Frank. *Bird calls* ill. by Lori Lohstoeter. Sounds recorded by Michael DiGiorgio. Innovative KIDS, 2001. ISBN 978-1-58476-064-1 Subj: Birds. Format, unusual – toy & movable books. Noise, sounds.

Night sounds ill. by Lori Lohstoeter. Sounds recorded by Michael DiGiorgio. Innovative KIDS, 2001. ISBN 978-1-58476-065-8 Subj: Animals. Format, unusual – toy & movable books. Night. Noise, sounds.

Galloway, Ruth. *Clumsy crab* ill. by author. Tiger Tales, 2005. ISBN 978-1-58925-050-5 Subj: Crustaceans – crabs. Self-concept.

Fidgety fish ill. by author. Tiger Tales, 2001. ISBN 978-1-58925-012-3 Subj: Caves. Fish. Sea & seashore.

Galvin, Laura Gates. *Bumblebee at Apple Tree Lane* ill. by Kristin Kest. Soundprints, 2000. ISBN 978-1-56899-820-6 Subj: Insects – bees.

River Otter at Autumn Lane ill. by Christopher Leeper. Soundprints, 2002. ISBN 978-1-931465-62-5 Subj: Animals – otters. Behavior – growing up. Family life.

Gamble, Isobel. *Who's that?* by Isobel Gamble and Tim Warnes ill. by Tim Warnes. Barron's, 2001. ISBN 978-0-7641-5335-8 Subj: Animals. Bedtime. Format, unusual – toy & movable books. Homes, houses. Sleep.

Gammell, Stephen. *How about going for a ride* ill. by author. Harcourt, 2001. ISBN 978-0-15-202682-0 Subj: Activities – traveling. Automobiles. Family life – brothers & sisters.

Is that you, winter? ill. by author. Silver Whistle, 1997. ISBN 978-0-15-201415-5 Subj: Behavior – bad day, bad mood. Seasons – winter. Weather – snow.

Mudkin ill. by author. Carolrhoda, 2011. ISBN 978-0-7613-5790-2 Subj: Activities – playing. Imagination. Weather – rain.

Wake up, bear . . . It's Christmas! ill. by author. Morrow, 1990. ISBN 978-0-688-09934-3 Subj: Animals – bears. Hibernation. Holidays – Christmas. Santa Claus.

Gannij, Joan. *Elusive moose* ill. by Clare Beaton. Barefoot, 2006. ISBN 978-1-905236-75-6 Subj: Animals – moose. Picture puzzles.

Hidden hippo ill. by Clare Beaton. Barefoot, 2008. ISBN 978-1-84686-170-3 Subj: Animals. Foreign lands – Africa. Rhyming text.

Gantos, Jack. *Back to school for Rotten Ralph* ill. by Nicole Rubel. HarperCollins, 1998. ISBN 978-0-06-027532-7 Subj: Animals – cats. Character traits – selfishness. Emotions – envy, jealousy. Emotions – fear. Friendship. School – first day.

Happy birthday, Rotten Ralph ill. by Nicole Rubel. Houghton, 1990. ISBN 978-0-395-53766-4 Subj: Animals – cats. Behavior – misbehavior. Birthdays.

The nine lives of Rotten Ralph ill. by Nicole Rubel. Houghton, 2009. ISBN 978-0-618-80046-9 Subj: Animals – cats. Behavior – misbehavior.

Not so Rotten Ralph ill. by Nicole Rubel. Houghton, 1994. ISBN 978-0-395-62302-2 Subj: Animals – cats. Behavior – misbehavior. School.

Rotten Ralph ill. by Nicole Rubel. Houghton, 1976. ISBN 978-0-395-24276-6 Subj: Animals – cats. Behavior – misbehavior.

Rotten Ralph's rotten Christmas ill. by Nicole Rubel. Houghton, 1984. ISBN 978-0-395-35380-6 Subj: Animals – cats. Character traits – meanness. Emotions – envy, jealousy. Holidays – Christmas.

Rotten Ralph's rotten romance ill. by Nicole Rubel. Houghton, 1997. ISBN 978-0-395-73978-5 Subj: Animals – cats. Behavior – misbehavior. Holidays – Valentine's Day. Parties.

Rotten Ralph's show and tell ill. by Nicole Rubel. Houghton, 1989. ISBN 978-0-395-44312-5 Subj: Animals – cats. Character traits – meanness. School.

Rotten Ralph's trick or treat ill. by Nicole Rubel. Houghton, 1986. ISBN 978-0-395-38943-0 Subj: Animals – cats. Character traits – meanness. Holidays – Halloween.

Wedding bells for Rotten Ralph ill. by Nicole Rubel. HarperCollins, 1999. ISBN 978-0-06-027534-1 Subj: Animals – cats. Behavior – misbehavior. Weddings.

Worse than Rotten Ralph ill. by Nicole Rubel. Houghton, 1978. ISBN 978-0-395-28106-2 Subj: Animals – cats. Behavior – misbehavior. Character traits – meanness.

García, Cheo. *Pick a pet* (Rotner, Shelley)

Garcia, Emma. *Chugga chugga choo choo* ill. by author. Sterling, 2017. ISBN 978-191071623-6 Subj: Birds. Counting, numbers. Trains.

Tap tap bang bang ill. by author. Boxer, 2010. ISBN 978-1-907152-00-9 Subj: Noise, sounds. Tools.

Tip tip dig dig ill. by author. Boxer, 2007. ISBN 978-1-905417-59-9 Subj: Trucks.

Gardella, Tricia. *Blackberry booties* ill. by Glo Coalson. Orchard, 2000. ISBN 978-0-531-33184-2 Subj: Activities – trading. Gifts. Problem solving.

Garden, Nancy. *Molly's family* ill. by Sharon Wooding. Farrar, 2004. ISBN 978-0-374-35002-4 Subj: Adoption. Behavior – bullying, teasing. Family life – mothers. School.

Gardeski, Christina Mia. *Diwali* ill. with photos. Children's Press, 2001. ISBN 978-0-516-22372-8 Subj: Foreign lands – India. Holidays – Diwali. Religion – Hinduism.

Gardiner, Lindsey. *Good night, Poppy and Max* ill. by author. Little, 2002. ISBN 978-0-316-60122-1 Subj: Animals – dogs. Bedtime. Counting, numbers. Format, unusual – board books.

Here come Poppy and Max ill. by author. Little, 2000. ISBN 978-0-316-60346-1 Subj: Activities – playing. Animals – dogs. Imagination.

If you're happy and you know it! (Ormerod, Jan)

When Poppy and Max grow up ill. by author. Little, 2001. ISBN 978-0-316-60342-3 Subj: Activities – playing. Animals – dogs. Careers. Imagination.

Gardner, Carol. *Princess Zelda and the frog* photos by Shane Young. Feiwel & Friends, 2011. ISBN 978-0-312-60325-0 Subj: Animals – dogs. Frogs & toads. Royalty – princesses.

Gardner, Sally. *Mama, don't go out tonight* ill. by author. Bloomsbury, 2002. ISBN 978-1-58234-790-5 Subj: Activities – babysitting. Family life – mothers. Imagination.

Garelli, Cristina. *Farm friends clean up* ill. by Francesca Chessa. Crown, 2000. ISBN 978-0-517-80082-9 Subj: Animals. Character traits – cleanliness. Farms. Hygiene.

Garhan Attebury, Nancy. *Out and about at city hall* ill. by Zachary Trover. Picture Window, 2006. ISBN 978-1-4048-1146-1 Subj: Cities, towns.

Out and about at the bank ill. by Zachary Trover. Picture Window, 2006. ISBN 978-1-4048-1147-8 Subj: Money.

Out and about at the hospital ill. by Zachary Trover. Picture Window, 2006. ISBN 978-1-4048-1148-5 Subj: Hospitals. Illness.

Out and about at the United States Mint ill. by Zachary Trover. Picture Window, 2006. ISBN 978-1-4048-1151-5 Subj: Money.

Garland, Michael. *Americana adventure: a look again book* ill. by author. Dutton, 2008. ISBN 978-0-525-47945-1 Subj: Family life – aunts, uncles. Picture puzzles. U.S. history.

Birds make nests ill. by author. Holiday, 2017. ISBN 978-082343662-0 Subj: Birds. Homes, houses.

Christmas City ill. by author. Dutton, 2002. ISBN 978-0-525-46904-9 Subj: Holidays – Christmas. Picture puzzles. Rhyming text.

Christmas magic ill. by author. Dutton, 2001. ISBN 978-0-525-46797-7 Subj: Holidays – Christmas. Snowmen.

Grandpa's tractor ill. by author. Boyds Mills, 2011. ISBN 978-1-59078-762-5 Subj: Family life – grandfathers. Farms. Memories, memory. Tractors.

The great Easter egg hunt ill. by author. Penguin, 2005. ISBN 978-0-525-47357-2 Subj: Holidays – Easter. Picture puzzles. Rhyming text.

Hooray José! ill. by author. Marshall Cavendish, 2007. ISBN 978-0-7614-5345-1 Subj: Animals – mice. Character traits – perseverance. Concepts – size. Rhyming text. Sports – basketball.

How many mice? ill. by author. Penguin, 2007. ISBN 978-0-525-47833-1 Subj: Animals – mice. Counting, numbers.

Icarus Swinebuckle ill. by author. Albert Whitman, 2000. ISBN 978-0-8075-3495-3 Subj: Activities – flying. Animals – pigs.

King Puck ill. by author. HarperCollins, 2007. ISBN 978-0-06-084809-5 Subj: Animals – goats. Books, reading. Fairies. Foreign lands – Ireland. Magic.

Last night at the zoo ill. by author. Boyds Mills, 2001. ISBN 978-1-56397-759-6 Subj: Animals. Behavior – running away. Rhyming text. Zoos.

Miss Smith and the haunted library ill. by author. Dutton, 2009. ISBN 978-0-525-42139-9 Subj: Books, reading. Careers – teachers. Libraries. Magic. School – field trips.

Miss Smith reads again! ill. by author. Penguin, 2006. ISBN 978-0-525-47722-8 Subj: Books, reading. Careers – teachers. Dinosaurs. Magic. School.

Miss Smith's incredible storybook ill. by author. Dutton, 2003. ISBN 978-0-525-47133-2 Subj: Books, reading. Careers – teachers. Magic. School.

The President and Mom's apple pie ill. by author. Dutton, 2003. ISBN 978-0-525-46887-5 Subj: Food. U.S. history.

Super snow day seek and find ill. by author. Penguin, 2010. ISBN 978-0-525-42245-7 Subj: Family life – aunts, uncles. Picture puzzles. Weather – snow.

Tugboat ill. by author. Holiday House, 2014. ISBN 978-082342866-3 Subj: Boats, ships.

Garland, Sally Anne. *Share* ill. by author. OwlKids, 2014. ISBN 978-177147005-6 Subj: Activities – playing. Animals – rabbits. Behavior – sharing. Family life – cousins. Rhyming text.

Garland, Sarah. *Eddie's toolbox and how to make and mend things* ill. by author. Frances Lincoln, 2011. ISBN 978-1-84780-053-4 Subj: Character traits – helpfulness. Communities, neighborhoods. Friendship. Tools.

Garland, Sherry. *The lotus seed* ill. by Tatsuro Kiuchi. Harcourt, 1993. ISBN 978-0-15-249465-0 Subj: Ethnic groups in the U.S. – Vietnamese Americans. Family life – grandmothers. Foreign lands – Vietnam. War.

My father's boat ill. by Ted Rand. Scholastic, 1998. ISBN 978-0-590-47867-0 Subj: Boats, ships. Careers – fishermen. Ethnic groups in the U.S. – Vietnamese Americans.

Garner, Alan. *Little red hen* (The little red hen)

Garoche, Camille. *The snow rabbit* ill. by author. Enchanted Lion, 2015. ISBN 978-159270181-0 Subj: Animals – rabbits. Disabilities – physical disabilities. Family life – sisters. Magic. Weather – snow. Wordless.

Garriel, Barbara S. *I know a shy fellow who swallowed a cello* ill. by John O'Brien. Boyds Mills, 2004. ISBN 978-1-56397-962-0 Subj: Cumulative tales. Humorous stories. Musical instruments – cellos. Rhyming text.

Garton, Sam. *I am Otter* ill. by author. HarperCollins/Balzer+Bray, 2014. ISBN 978-006224775-9 Subj: Animals – otters. Behavior – lost & found possessions. Behavior – messy. Friendship. Toys – bears.

Otter goes to school ill. by author. HarperCollins/Balzer+Bray, 2016. ISBN 978-006235225-5 Subj: Animals – otters. Careers – teachers. School. Toys.

Otter in space ill. by author. HarperCollins/Balzer+Bray, 2015. ISBN 978-006224776-6 Subj: Animals – otters. Imagination. Museums. Space & space ships.

Otter loves Easter! ill. by author. HarperCollins/Balzer+Bray, 2017. ISBN 978-006236667-2 Subj: Animals – otters. Behavior – sharing. Character traits – willfulness. Holidays – Easter.

Otter loves Halloween ill. by author. HarperCollins/Balzer+Bray, 2015. ISBN 978-006236666-5 Subj: Animals – otters. Emotions – fear. Holidays – Halloween. Toys – bears.

Gary, Meredith. *Sometimes you get what you want* ill. by Lisa Brown. HarperCollins, 2008. ISBN 978-0-06-114015-0 Subj: Behavior. Family life – brothers & sisters. School – nursery.

Garza, Cynthia Leonor. *Lucía the luchadora* ill. by Alyssa Bermudez. POW!, 2017. ISBN 978-157687827-9 Subj: Character traits – assertiveness. Character traits – cleverness. Foreign lands – Mexico. Gender roles. Masks.

Gassman, Julie. *Crabby pants* ill. by Richard Watson. Picture Window, 2010. ISBN 978-1-4048-6165-7 Subj: Behavior – misbehavior. Clothing – pants. Emotions – anger.

Gauch, Patricia Lee. *Bravo, Tanya* ill. by Satomi Ichikawa. Putnam, 1992. ISBN 978-0-399-22145-3 Subj: Activities – dancing. Ballet. Toys – bears.

Dance, Tanya ill. by Satomi Ichikawa. Putnam, 1989. ISBN 978-0-399-21521-6 Subj: Activities – dancing. Ballet. Behavior – imitation. Toys – bears.

Presenting Tanya, the Ugly Duckling ill. by Satomi Ichikawa. Philomel, 1999. ISBN 978-0-399-23200-8 Subj: Activities – dancing. Ballet. Self-concept.

Tanya and Emily in a dance for two ill. by Satomi Ichikawa. Philomel, 1994. ISBN 978-0-399-22688-5 Subj: Activities – dancing. Ballet. Friendship.

Gavin, Ciara. *Bear is not tired* ill. by author. Knopf, 2016. ISBN 978-038575476-7 Subj: Animals – bears. Birds – ducks. Family life. Hibernation. Seasons – winter.

Bear likes jam ill. by author. Knopf, 2017. ISBN 978-039955179-6 Subj: Animals – bears. Birds – ducks. Food. Health & fitness.

Room for Bear ill. by author. Knopf, 2015. ISBN 978-038575473-6 Subj: Animals – bears. Birds – ducks. Concepts – size. Homes, houses.

Gavril, David. *Penelope Nuthatch and the big surprise* ill. by author. Abrams, 2006. ISBN 978-0-8109-5762-6 Subj: Behavior – worrying. Birds. Parks – amusement.

Gay, Marie-Louise. *Any questions?* ill. by author. Groundwood, 2014. ISBN 978-155498382-7 Subj: Activities – storytelling. Books, reading. Careers

– writers. Character traits – questioning. Imagination.

Caramba ill. by author. Groundwood, 2005. ISBN 978-0-88899-667-1 Subj: Animals – cats. Imagination.

Caramba and Henry ill. by author. Groundwood, 2011. ISBN 978-1-55498-097-0 Subj: Animals – cats. Family life – brothers. Sibling rivalry.

Good morning Sam ill. by author. Douglas & McIntyre, 2003. ISBN 978-0-88899-528-5 Subj: Clothing. Family life – brothers & sisters. Humorous stories. Morning.

On my island ill. by author. Douglas & McIntyre, 2000. ISBN 978-0-88899-396-0 Subj: Animals. Behavior – boredom. Islands.

Read me a story, Stella ill. by author. Groundwood, 2013. ISBN 978-1-55498-216-5 Subj: Activities. Books, reading. Family life – brothers & sisters.

Roslyn Rutabaga and the biggest hole on earth! ill. by author. Groundwood, 2010. ISBN 978-0-88899-994-8 Subj: Activities – digging. Animals – rabbits. Family life – fathers.

Short stories for little monsters ill. by author. Groundwood, 2017. ISBN 978-155498896-9 Subj: Humorous stories. Imagination.

Stella, fairy of the forest ill. by author. Douglas & McIntyre, 2002. ISBN 978-0-88899-448-6 Subj: Animals. Fairies. Family life – brothers & sisters. Forest, woods.

Stella, queen of the snow ill. by author. Douglas & McIntyre, 2000. ISBN 978-0-88899-404-2 Subj: Activities – playing. Family life – brothers & sisters. Weather – snow.

Stella, star of the sea ill. by author. Douglas & McIntyre, 1999. ISBN 978-0-88899-337-3 Subj: Family life – brothers & sisters. Sea & seashore.

What are you doing, Sam? ill. by author. Groundwood, 2006. ISBN 978-0-88899-734-0 Subj: Animals – dogs. Behavior – messy. Family life – brothers & sisters. Pets.

When Stella was very, very small ill. by author. Groundwood, 2009. ISBN 978-0-88899-906-1 Subj: Behavior – growing up. Character traits – smallness. Family life – brothers & sisters. Imagination.

Gay, Michel. *Zee is not scared* ill. by author. Clarion, 2004. ISBN 978-0-618-43931-7 Subj: Animals – zebras. Bedtime. Emotions – fear. Family life – parents.

Gehl, Laura. *One big pair of underwear* ill. by Tom Lichtenheld. Simon & Schuster/Beach Lane, 2014. ISBN 978-144245336-4 Subj: Animals. Behavior – sharing. Counting, numbers. Rhyming text.

Peep and Egg: I'm not hatching ill. by Joyce Wan. Farrar, 2016. ISBN 978-037430121-7 Subj: Behavior – worrying. Birds – chickens, roosters. Eggs. Emotions – fear.

Peep and Egg: I'm not taking a bath ill. by Joyce Wan. Farrar, 2017. ISBN 978-037430327-3 Subj: Activities – bathing. Birds – chickens, roosters.

Peep and Egg: I'm not trick-or-treating ill. by Joyce Wan. Farrar, 2016. ISBN 978-037430122-4 Subj: Birds – chickens, roosters. Emotions – fear. Holidays – Halloween.

Gehrmann, Katja. *Goose the bear* ill. by author. Sky Pony, 2014. ISBN 978-162636384-7 Subj: Animals – bears. Birds – geese. Character traits – being different.

Geisel, Theodor Seuss *see* Seuss, Dr.

Geisert, Arthur. *Country road ABC: an illustrated journey through America's farmland* ill. by author. Harcourt, 2010. ISBN 978-0-547-19469-1 Subj: ABC books. Farms.

Desert town (Geisert, Bonnie)

The giant ball of string ill. by author. Houghton, 2002. ISBN 978-0-618-13221-8 Subj: Animals – pigs. Behavior – lost & found possessions. Character traits – cooperation. String.

The giant seed ill. by author. Enchanted Lion, 2012. ISBN 978-1-59270-115-5 Subj: Animals – pigs. Behavior – resourcefulness. Seeds. Volcanoes. Wordless.

Hogwash ill. by author. Houghton, 2008. ISBN 978-0-618-77332-9 Subj: Activities – bathing. Animals – pigs. Character traits – cleanliness. Machines. Wordless.

Ice ill. by author. Enchanted Lion, 2011. ISBN 978-1-59270-098-1 Subj: Animals – pigs. Character traits – cleverness. Character traits – cooperation. Wordless.

Lights out ill. by author. Houghton, 2005. ISBN 978-0-618-47892-7 Subj: Animals – pigs. Bedtime. Character traits – cleverness. Emotions – fear. Inventions.

Mountain town (Geisert, Bonnie)

Mystery ill. by author. Houghton, 2003. ISBN 978-0-618-27293-8 Subj: Animals – pigs. Careers – detectives. Crime. Family life – grandfathers. Museums. Mystery stories. Picture puzzles.

Nursery crimes ill. by author. Houghton, 2001. ISBN 978-0-618-06487-8 Subj: Animals – pigs. Crime. Farms. Holidays – Thanksgiving. Mystery stories. Trees.

Oops ill. by author. Houghton, 2006. ISBN 978-0-618-60904-8 Subj: Animals – pigs. Wordless.

Pigaroons ill. by author. Houghton, 2004. ISBN 978-0-618-41058-3 Subj: Animals – pigs. Crime. Fairs, festivals.

Thunderstorm ill. by author. Enchanted Lion, 2013. ISBN 978-1-59270-133-9 Subj: Weather – lightning, thunder. Weather – storms.

Geisert, Bonnie. *Desert town* by Bonnie Geisert and Arthur Geisert ill. by Arthur Geisert. Houghton, 2001. ISBN 978-0-395-95387-7 Subj: Cities, towns. Desert.

Mountain town by Bonnie Geisert and Arthur Geisert ill. by Arthur Geisert. Houghton, 2000. ISBN 978-0-395-95390-7 Subj: Cities, towns. Mountains. Seasons.

Geist, Ken. *The three little fish and the big bad shark* ill. by Julia Gorton. Scholastic, 2007. ISBN 978-0-439-71962-9 Subj: Fish. Fish – sharks. Sea & seashore.

Who's who? ill. by Henry Cole. Feiwel & Friends, 2012. ISBN 978-0-312-64437-6 Subj: Animals. Multiple births – twins. Rhyming text.

Gellman, Ellie B. *Netta and her plant* ill. by Natascia Ugliano. Lerner/Kar-Ben, 2014. ISBN 978-146770422-9 Subj: Holidays – Tu B'Shevat. Jewish culture. Plants.

Genechten, Guido van. *Because you are my friend* ill. by author. Clavis, 2011. ISBN 978-1-60537-095-8 Subj: Animals – polar bears. Family life – mothers. Friendship.

The big woods orchestra ill. by author. Clavis, 2012. ISBN 978-1-60537-113-9 Subj: Birds. Forest, woods. Music. Nature.

Flop-Ear ill. by author. Barron's, 2001. ISBN 978-0-7641-1762-6 Subj: Anatomy – ears. Animals – rabbits. Character traits – individuality.

Guess what? ill. by author. Clavis, 2012. ISBN 978-1-60537-116-0 Subj: Animals. Format, unusual – toy & movable books.

Guess where? ill. by author. Clavis, 2012. ISBN 978-1-60537-115-3 Subj: Animals. Format, unusual – toy & movable books.

Kai-Mook ill. by author. Clavis, 2011. ISBN 978-1-60537-096-5 Subj: Animals – babies. Animals – elephants.

No ghost under my bed ill. by author. Clavis, 2010. ISBN 978-1-60537-069-9 Subj: Bedtime. Birds – penguins. Emotions – fear.

Ricky and the squirrel ill. by author. Clavis, 2010. ISBN 978-1-60537-078-1 Subj: Animals – rabbits. Animals – squirrels. Death.

Ricky is brave ill. by author. Clavis, 2011. ISBN 978-1-60537-097-2 Subj: Animals – rabbits. Camps, camping. Character traits – bravery. Emotions – fear.

Gentieu, Penny. *Baby! Talk!* ill. by author. Crown, 1999. ISBN 978-0-517-80028-7 Subj: Activities. Babies, toddlers.

Grow! babies! ill. by author. Crown, 2000. ISBN 978-0-517-80029-4 Subj: Babies, toddlers. Behavior – growing up.

Gentle, Victor. *Baby sharks* by Victor Gentle and Janet Perry Marshall ill. with photos. G. Stevens, 2001. ISBN 978-0-8368-2824-5 Subj: Animals – babies. Fish – sharks.

Killer sharks, killer people by Victor Gentle and Janet Perry Marshall ill. with photos. G. Stevens, 2001. ISBN 978-0-8368-2826-9 Subj: Fish – sharks. Sports – fishing.

Orcas, killer whales by Victor Gentle and Janet Perry Marshall ill. with photos. G. Stevens, 2001. ISBN 978-0-8368-2883-2 Subj: Animals – whales.

Shark camouflage and armor by Victor Gentle and Janet Perry Marshall ill. with photos. G. Stevens, 2001. ISBN 978-0-8368-2827-6 Subj: Disguises. Fish – sharks.

Very big sharks by Victor Gentle and Janet Perry Marshall ill. with photos. G. Stevens, 2001. ISBN 978-0-8368-2828-3 Subj: Fish – sharks.

The world's strangest shark by Victor Gentle and Janet Perry Marshall ill. with photos. G. Stevens, 2001. ISBN 978-0-8368-2829-0 Subj: Fish – sharks.

Geoghegan, Adrienne. *All your own teeth* ill. by Cathy Gale. Dial, 2001. ISBN 978-0-8037-2655-0 Subj: Activities – painting. Animals. Jungle.

George, Bobby. *Montessori number work* by Bobby George and June George ill. by Alyssa Nassner. Abrams, 2012. ISBN 978-1-4197-0412-3 Subj: Counting, numbers. Format, unusual – board books.

My first book of patterns by Bobby George and June George ill. by Boyoun Kim. Phaidon, 2017. ISBN 978-071487249-0 Subj: Concepts – patterns. Concepts – shape. Format, unusual – board books.

George, Jean Craighead. *The buffalo are back* ill. by Wendell Minor. Penguin, 2010. ISBN 978-0-525-42215-0 Subj: Animals – buffaloes. Animals – endangered animals. Ecology.

Cliff hanger ill. by Wendell Minor. HarperCollins, 2002. ISBN 978-0-06-000261-9 Subj: Animals – dogs. Family life – fathers. Mountains. Sports – mountain climbing. Weather – storms.

Dear Rebecca, winter is here ill. by Loretta Krupinski. HarperCollins, 1993. ISBN 978-0-06-021140-

0 Subj: Family life – grandmothers. Nature. Seasons. Seasons – winter.

The eagles are back ill. by Wendell Minor. Dial, 2013. ISBN 978-0-8037-3771-6 Subj: Animals – endangered animals. Birds – eagles. Ecology.

Everglades ill. by Wendell Minor. HarperCollins, 1995. ISBN 978-0-06-021229-2 Subj: Ecology. Nature. Rivers.

The first Thanksgiving ill. by Thomas Locker. Philomel, 1993. ISBN 978-0-399-21991-7 Subj: Holidays – Thanksgiving. Pilgrims. U.S. history.

Frightful's daughter ill. by Daniel San Souci. Dutton, 2002. ISBN 978-0-525-46907-0 Subj: Birds – falcons.

Frightful's daughter meets the Baron Weasel ill. by Daniel San Souci. Penguin, 2007. ISBN 978-0-525-47202-5 Subj: Animals – weasels. Birds – falcons.

Galápagos George ill. by Wendell Minor. HarperCollins, 2014. ISBN 978-006028793-1 Subj: Foreign lands – Galapagos Islands. Reptiles – turtles, tortoises.

The last polar bear ill. by Wendell Minor. HarperCollins, 2009. ISBN 978-0-06-124067-6 Subj: Animals – polar bears. Ecology. Foreign lands – Arctic.

Look to the north: a wolf pup diary ill. by Lucia Washburn. HarperCollins, 1997. ISBN 978-0-06-023640-3 Subj: Animals – babies. Animals – wolves. Behavior – growing up. Seasons.

Luck ill. by Wendell Minor. HarperCollins, 2006. ISBN 978-0-06-008201-7 Subj: Birds – cranes. Migration.

Morning, noon, and night ill. by Wendell Minor. HarperCollins, 1999. ISBN 978-0-06-023628-1 Subj: Activities. Animals. Day.

Nutik and Amaroq play ball ill. by Ted Rand. HarperCollins, 2001. ISBN 978-0-06-028166-3 Subj: Animals – wolves. Eskimos. Foreign lands – Arctic.

Nutik, the wolf pup ill. by Ted Rand. HarperCollins, 2001. ISBN 978-0-06-028164-9 Subj: Animals – wolves. Eskimos. Family life – brothers & sisters. Foreign lands – Arctic.

Snow bear ill. by Wendell Minor. Hyperion, 1999. ISBN 978-0-7868-0456-6 Subj: Activities – playing. Animals – polar bears. Eskimos. Foreign lands – Arctic. Weather – snow.

The wolves are back ill. by Wendell Minor. Dutton, 2008. ISBN 978-0-525-47947-5 Subj: Animals – endangered animals. Animals – wolves. Ecology.

George, June. *Montessori number work* (George, Bobby)

My first book of patterns (George, Bobby)

George, Kallie. *Secrets I know* ill. by Paola Zakimi. Random House, 2017. ISBN 978-110193893-5 Subj: Behavior – secrets. Friendship.

George, Kristine O'Connell. *Emma dilemma: big sister poems* ill. by Nancy Carpenter. Clarion, 2011. ISBN 978-0-618-42842-7 Subj: Family life – sisters. Poetry.

The great frog race and other poems ill. by Kate Kiesler. Clarion, 1997. ISBN 978-0-395-77607-0 Subj: Counting, numbers. Nature. Poetry.

Little Dog and Duncan ill. by June Otani. Clarion, 2002. ISBN 978-0-618-11758-1 Subj: Animals – dogs. Poetry.

Old Elm speaks ill. by Kate Kiesler. Clarion, 1998. ISBN 978-0-395-87611-4 Subj: Poetry. Seasons. Trees.

Up! ill. by Hiroe Nakata. Houghton, 2005. ISBN 978-0-618-06489-2 Subj: Concepts – up & down. Family life – fathers. Rhyming text.

George, Lindsay Barrett. *Around the pond: who's been here?* ill. by author. Greenwillow, 1996. ISBN 978-0-688-14377-0 Subj: Animals. Lakes, ponds. Nature. Seasons – summer.

Beaver at Long Pond (George, William T.)

In the garden: who's been here? ill. by author. HarperCollins, 2006. ISBN 978-0-06-078762-2 Subj: Animals. Gardens, gardening. Nature. Problem solving.

In the woods: who's been here? ill. by author. Greenwillow, 1995. ISBN 978-0-688-12319-2 Subj: Activities – walking. Animals. Forest, woods. Nature. Problem solving. Seasons – fall.

Maggie's ball ill. by author. HarperCollins, 2010. ISBN 978-0-06-172166-3 Subj: Animals – dogs. Behavior – lost & found possessions. Toys – balls.

My bunny and me ill. by author. Greenwillow, 2001. ISBN 978-0-688-16075-3 Subj: Animals – rabbits. Imagination.

The secret ill. by author. HarperCollins, 2005. ISBN 978-0-06-029600-1 Subj: Animals. Behavior – secrets. Emotions – love.

That pup! ill. by author. HarperCollins, 2011. ISBN 978-0-06-200413-0 Subj: Animals – dogs. Animals – squirrels.

George, Lucy M. *Back to school Tortoise* ill. by Merel Eyckerman. Albert Whitman, 2011. ISBN 978-0-8075-0510-6 Subj: Behavior – worrying. Careers – teachers. Reptiles – turtles, tortoises. School – first day.

George, Margaret. *Lucille lost: a true adventure* by Margaret George and Christopher J. Murphy ill. by Debra Bandelin and Bob Dacey. Penguin, 2006. ISBN 978-0-670-06093-1 Subj: Behavior –

lost & found possessions. Reptiles – turtles, tortoises.

George, William T. *Beaver at Long Pond* by William T. George and Lindsay Barrett George ill. by Lindsay Barrett George. Greenwillow, 1988. ISBN 978-0-688-07107-3 Subj: Animals – beavers. Nature. Night.

Box turtle at Long Pond ill. by Lindsay Barrett George. Greenwillow, 1989. ISBN 978-0-688-08185-0 Subj: Nature. Reptiles – turtles, tortoises.

Christmas at Long Pond ill. by Lindsay Barrett George. Greenwillow, 1992. ISBN 978-0-688-09215-3 Subj: Animals. Family life – fathers. Forest, woods. Holidays – Christmas. Nature. Seasons – winter. Trees.

Fishing at Long Pond ill. by Lindsay Barrett George. Greenwillow, 1991. ISBN 978-0-688-09402-7 Subj: Animals. Family life – grandfathers. Sports – fishing.

Geraghty, Paul. *Help me!* ill. by author. IPG/Andersen, 2012. ISBN 978-1-84939-027-9 Subj: Animals. Foreign lands – Africa. Nature.

The hoppameleon ill. by author. Barron's, 2001. ISBN 978-0-7641-5406-5 Subj: Animals. Friendship. Frogs & toads. Self-concept.

Gerardi, Jan. *The little recycler* ill. by author. Random House, 2013. ISBN 978-0-375-86172-7 Subj: Ecology. Format, unusual – board books.

Geras, Adèle. *The Cats of Cuckoo Square, Geejay the Hero* ill. by Tony Ross. Dell, 2003. ISBN 978-0-385-90082-9 Subj: Communities, neighborhoods. Illness – allergies.

Giselle ill. by Emma Chichester Clark. David & Charles, 2000. ISBN 978-1-86233-226-3 Subj: Activities – dancing. Ballet.

Little ballet star ill. by Shelagh McNicholas. Dial, 2008. ISBN 978-0-8037-3237-7 Subj: Ballet. Family life – aunts, uncles. Theater.

My wishes for you ill. by Cliff Wright. Simon & Schuster, 2002. ISBN 978-0-689-85333-3 Subj: Animals. Animals – rabbits. Behavior – wishing. Day. Family life – parents.

The nutcracker ill. by Emma Chichester Clark. David & Charles, 2000. ISBN 978-1-86233-236-2 Subj: Activities – dancing. Animals – mice. Ballet. Careers – toy makers. Folk & fairy tales. Holidays – Christmas. Imagination. Royalty.

Rebecca's Passover ill. by Sheila Moxley. Frances Lincoln, 2004. ISBN 978-1-84507-155-4 Subj: Holidays – Passover. Jewish culture.

Sleep tight, Ginger Kitten ill. by Catherine Walters. Dutton, 2001. ISBN 978-0-525-46771-7 Subj: Animals – cats. Rhyming text. Sleep.

Sleeping beauty ill. by Emma Chichester Clark. David & Charles, 2000. ISBN 978-1-86233-246-1 Subj: Activities – dancing. Ballet. Family life – stepfamilies. Folk & fairy tales. Royalty – princes. Sibling rivalry.

Swan Lake ill. by Emma Chichester Clark. David & Charles, 2000. ISBN 978-1-86233-231-7 Subj: Activities – dancing. Ballet. Birds – swans. Careers – magicians. Folk & fairy tales. Magic. Metamorphosis. Royalty – princes.

Time for ballet ill. by Shelagh McNicholas. Dial, 2004. ISBN 978-0-8037-2978-0 Subj: Activities – dancing. Ballet.

Gerber, Carole. *Annie Jump Cannon, astronomer* ill. by Christina Wald. Pelican, 2011. ISBN 978-1-58980-911-6 Subj: Careers – astronomers. Gender roles. Stars.

A band of babies ill. by Jane Dyer. HarperCollins, 2017. ISBN 978-006168955-0 Subj: Activities – playing. Babies, toddlers. Musical instruments – bands. Rhyming text. School – nursery.

Little red bat ill. by Christina Wald. Sylvan Dell, 2010. ISBN 978-1-60718-069-2 Subj: Animals – bats. Hibernation. Migration.

Seeds, bees, butterflies, and more! poems for two voices ill. by Eugene Yelchin. Henry Holt, 2013. ISBN 978-0-8050-9211-0 Subj: Insects. Nature. Plants. Poetry.

Spring blossoms ill. by Leslie Evans. Charlesbridge, 2013. ISBN 978-1-58089-412-8 Subj: Flowers. Rhyming text. Seasons – spring. Trees.

Ten busy brooms ill. by Michael Fleming. Doubleday, 2016. ISBN 978-055353341-5 Subj: Counting, numbers. Holidays – Halloween. Rhyming text. Witches.

Tuck-in time ill. by Tracey Campbell Pearson. Farrar, 2014. ISBN 978-037437860-8 Subj: Babies, toddlers. Bedtime. Family life – parents.

Winter trees ill. by Leslie Evans. Charlesbridge, 2008. ISBN 978-1-58089-168-4 Subj: Seasons – winter. Trees.

Gerdner, Linda. *Grandfather's story cloth / Yawg daim paj ntaub dab neeg* by Linda Gerdner and Sarah Langford ill. by Stuart Loughridge. Shen's, 2008. ISBN 978-1-885008-34-3 Subj: Ethnic groups in the U.S. – Hmong Americans. Family life – grandfathers. Illness – Alzheimer's. Memories, memory. Quilts.

Gergely, Tibor. *The great big fire engine book* ill. by author. 1st Random House ed. Golden, 2003. ISBN 978-0-307-90321-1 Subj: Careers – firefighters. Format, unusual – board books. Trucks.

Wheel on the chimney (Brown, Margaret Wise)

Geringer, Laura. *Boom boom go away!* ill. by Bagram Ibatoulline. Simon & Schuster, 2010. ISBN 978-0-689-85093-6 Subj: Bedtime. Musical instruments. Rhyming text.

Gerlach, Horace. *Daddy's little girl* (Burke, Bobby)

Germein, Katrina. *My dad thinks he's funny* ill. by Tom Jellett. Candlewick, 2013. ISBN 978-0-7636-6522-7 Subj: Family life – fathers.

Gerrard, K.A. *My family is a zoo* ill. by Emma Dodd. Bloomsbury, 2016. ISBN 978-161963851-8 Subj: Animals. Family life. Rhyming text. Toys.

Gerritsen, Paula. *Nuts* ill. by author. Boyds Mills, 2006. ISBN 978-1-932425-66-6 Subj: Animals – mice. Seasons – fall. Weather – storms.

Gershator, David. *Summer is summer* (Gershator, Phillis)

Gershator, Phillis. *Listen, listen* ill. by Alison Jay. Barefoot, 2007. ISBN 978-1-84686-084-3 Subj: Nature. Noise, sounds. Rhyming text. Seasons.

Moo, moo, brown cow! Have you any milk? ill. by Giselle Potter. Random House, 2011. ISBN 978-0-375-86744-6 Subj: Animals. Bedtime. Farms. Rhyming text. Toys.

Only one cowry: Dahomean tale ill. by David Soman. Orchard, 2000. ISBN 978-0-531-33288-7 Subj: Folk & fairy tales. Foreign lands – Africa. Royalty – kings.

Sky sweeper ill. by Holly Meade. Farrar, 2007. ISBN 978-0-374-37007-7 Subj: Activities – working. Foreign lands – Japan. Gardens, gardening. Self-concept.

Summer is summer by Phillis Gershator and David Gershator ill. by Sophie Blackall. Henry Holt, 2006. ISBN 978-0-8050-7444-4 Subj: Rhyming text. Seasons – summer.

This is the day! ill. by Marjorie Priceman. Houghton, 2007. ISBN 978-0-618-49746-1 Subj: Babies, toddlers. Days of the week, months of the year. Family life – mothers. Songs.

Time for a bath ill. by David Walker. Sterling, 2014. ISBN 978-145491032-9 Subj: Activities – bathing. Animals – rabbits. Behavior – messy. Rhyming text.

Time for a hug by Phillis Gershator and Mim Green ill. by David Walker. Sterling, 2012. ISBN 978-1-4027-7862-9 Subj: Animals – rabbits. Family life – mothers. Hugging. Rhyming text.

When it starts to snow ill. by Martin Matje. Henry Holt, 1998. ISBN 978-0-8050-5404-0 Subj: Animals. Rhyming text. Seasons – winter. Weather – snow.

Who's awake in springtime? by Phillis Gershator and Mim Green ill. by Emilie Chollat. Henry Holt, 2010. ISBN 978-0-8050-6390-5 Subj: Animals. Bedtime. Cumulative tales. Rhyming text. Seasons – spring.

Who's in the farmyard? ill. by Jill McDonald. Barefoot, 2012. ISBN 978-1-84686-574-9 Subj: Animals. Farms. Noise, sounds. Rhyming text.

Who's in the forest? ill. by Jill McDonald. Barefoot, 2010. ISBN 978-1-84686-476-6 Subj: Animals. Forest, woods. Rhyming text.

Zoo day, olé! a counting book ill. by Santiago Cohen. Marshall Cavendish, 2009. ISBN 978-0-7614-5462-5 Subj: Counting, numbers. Foreign languages. Zoos.

Zzzng! zzzng! zzzng! a Yoruba tale ill. by Theresa Smith. Orchard, 1998. ISBN 978-0-531-08873-9 Subj: Folk & fairy tales. Foreign lands – Africa. Insects – mosquitoes.

Gerson, Mary-Joan. *Why the sky is far away* ill. by Carla Golembe. Little, 1992. ISBN 978-0-316-30852-6 Subj: Behavior – greed. Folk & fairy tales. Foreign lands – Nigeria. Sky.

Gerstein, Mordicai. *The absolutely awful alphabet* ill. by author. Harcourt, 1999. ISBN 978-0-15-201494-0 Subj: ABC books. Animals. Monsters.

A book ill. by author. Roaring Brook, 2009. ISBN 978-1-59643-251-2 Subj: Activities – writing. Books, reading. Imagination.

The boy and the whale ill. by author. Roaring Brook, 2017. ISBN 978-162672505-8 Subj: Animals – whales. Careers – fishermen. Character traits – kindness to animals. Family life – fathers.

The first drawing ill. by author. Little, Brown, 2013. ISBN 978-0-316-20478-1 Subj: Activities – drawing. Imagination. Petroglyphs. Prehistory.

How to bicycle to the moon to plant sunflowers: a simple but brilliant plan in 24 easy steps ill. by author. Roaring Brook, 2013. ISBN 978-1-59643-512-4 Subj: Activities – traveling. Imagination. Moon. Sports – bicycling.

Leaving the nest ill. by author. Farrar, 2007. ISBN 978-0-374-34369-9 Subj: Animals. Behavior – growing up. Family life – mothers. Self-concept.

The man who walked between the towers ill. by author. Roaring Brook, 2003. ISBN 978-0-7613-2868-1 Subj: Activities. Caldecott award books. Careers – aerialists. Format, unusual – toy & movable books.

Minifred goes to school ill. by author. HarperCollins, 2009. ISBN 978-0-06-075889-9 Subj: Animals – cats. Behavior – misbehavior. Character traits – being different. School.

The night world ill. by author. Little, Brown, 2015. ISBN 978-031618822-7 Subj: Animals – cats. Morning. Night. Sun.

You can't have too many friends! ill. by author. Holiday House, 2014. ISBN 978-082342393-4 Subj: Birds – ducks. Friendship. Humorous stories. Royalty – kings.

Gertsberg, Inna. *The way downtown: adventures in public transit* ill. by Mike Lowery. Kids Can, 2017. ISBN 978-177138552-7 Subj: Cities, towns. Maps. Transportation.

Gervais, Bernadette. *Out of sight* (Pittau, Francisco)

Geser, Gretchen. *One bright ring* ill. by author. Henry Holt, 2013. ISBN 978-0-8050-9279-0 Subj: Behavior – lost & found possessions. Character traits – honesty. Cities, towns. Counting, numbers.

Ghahremani, Susie. *Stack the cats* ill. by author. Abrams/Appleseed, 2017. ISBN 978-141972349-0 Subj: Animals – cats. Counting, numbers.

Ghazi, Suhaib Hamid. *Ramadan* ill. by Omar Rayyan. Holiday, 1996. ISBN 978-0-8234-1254-9 Subj: Holidays – Ramadan. Religion. Religion – Islam.

Ghigna, Charles. *I see winter* ill. by Ag Jatkowska. Picture Window, 2011. ISBN 978-1-4048-6588-4 Subj: Rhyming text. Seasons – winter.

Gianferrari, Maria. *Coyote moon* ill. by Bagram Ibatoulline. Roaring Brook, 2016. ISBN 978-162672041-1 Subj: Animals – coyotes. Cities, towns.

Hello goodbye dog ill. by Patrice Barton. Roaring Brook, 2017. ISBN 978-162672177-7 Subj: Animals – dogs. Animals – service animals. Character traits – helpfulness. Character traits – kindness to animals. Disabilities – physical disabilities. School.

Penny and Jelly: the school show ill. by Thyra Heder. Houghton Mifflin Harcourt, 2015. ISBN 978-054423014-9 Subj: Animals – dogs. Friendship. Theater.

Penny and Jelly: slumber under the stars ill. by Thyra Heder. Houghton Mifflin Harcourt, 2016. ISBN 978-054428005-2 Subj: Animals – dogs. Problem solving. Sleepovers.

Gibala-Broxholm, Scott. *Maddie's monster dad* ill. by author. Marshall Cavendish, 2011. ISBN 978-0-7614-5846-3 Subj: Activities – playing. Family life – fathers. Imagination. Monsters.

Gibbons, Gail. *Alligators and crocodiles* ill. by author. Holiday House, 2010. ISBN 978-0-8234-2234-0 Subj: Reptiles – alligators, crocodiles.

Apples ill. by author. Holiday, 2000. ISBN 978-0-8234-1497-0 Subj: Activities – baking, cooking. Food. U.S. history.

The art box ill. by author. Holiday, 1998. ISBN 978-0-8234-1386-7 Subj: Art. Careers – artists. Tools.

Bats ill. by author. Holiday, 1999. ISBN 978-0-8234-1457-4 Subj: Animals – bats. Behavior. Night.

Beavers ill. by author. Holiday House, 2013. ISBN 978-0-8234-2412-2 Subj: Animals – beavers. Nature.

The berry book ill. by author. Holiday, 2002. ISBN 978-0-8234-1697-4 Subj: Activities – baking, cooking. Food. Plants.

Boat book ill. by author. Holiday, 1983. ISBN 978-0-8234-0478-0 Subj: Boats, ships.

Cats ill. by author. Holiday, 1996. ISBN 978-0-8234-1253-2 Subj: Animals – cats.

Check it out! the book about libraries ill. by author. Harcourt, 1985. ISBN 978-0-15-216400-3 Subj: Libraries.

Clocks and how they go ill. by author. Crowell, 1979. ISBN 978-0-690-03974-0 Subj: Clocks, watches. Time.

Coral reefs ill. by author. Holiday House, 2007. ISBN 978-0-8234-2080-3 Subj: Ecology. Sea & seashore.

Corn ill. by author. Holiday, 2008. ISBN 978-0-8234-2169-5 Subj: Food. Gardens, gardening.

County fair ill. by author. Little, 1994. ISBN 978-0-316-30951-6 Subj: Country. Fairs, festivals.

Deadline! from news to newspaper ill. by author. HarperCollins, 1987. ISBN 978-0-690-04602-1 Subj: Activities – working. Paper.

Department store ill. by author. Crowell, 1984. ISBN 978-0-690-04367-9 Subj: Stores.

Dinosaur discoveries ill. by author. Holiday House, 2005. ISBN 978-0-8234-1971-5 Subj: Dinosaurs. Science.

Dinosaurs! ill. by author. Holiday, 2008. ISBN 978-0-8234-2143-5 Subj: Dinosaurs. Prehistory.

Dogs ill. by author. Holiday, 1996. ISBN 978-0-8234-1226-6 Subj: Animals – dogs.

Ducks ill. by author. Holiday, 2001. ISBN 978-0-8234-1567-0 Subj: Birds – ducks.

Easter ill. by author. Holiday, 1989. ISBN 978-0-8234-0737-8 Subj: Holidays – Easter.

Elephants of Africa ill. by author. Holiday House, 2008. ISBN 978-0-8234-2168-8 Subj: Animals – elephants. Foreign lands – Africa.

Emergency! ill. by author. Holiday, 1994. ISBN 978-0-8234-1128-3 Subj: Careers. Character traits – helpfulness. Trucks.

Exploring the deep, dark sea ill. by author. Little, 1999. ISBN 978-0-316-30945-5 Subj: Boats, ships. Ecology. Science. Sea & seashore.

Farming ill. by author. Holiday, 1988. ISBN 978-0-8234-0682-1 Subj: Careers. Farms. Seasons.

Fill it up! all about service stations ill. by author. Crowell, 1985. ISBN 978-0-690-04440-9 Subj: Automobiles. Careers.

Fire! Fire! ill. by author. Crowell, 1984. ISBN 978-0-690-04416-4 Subj: Careers – firefighters.

Flying ill. by author. Holiday, 1986. ISBN 978-0-8234-0599-2 Subj: Activities – ballooning. Activities – flying. Airplanes, airports.

Frogs ill. by author. Holiday, 1993. ISBN 978-0-8234-1052-1 Subj: Frogs & toads.

From seed to plant ill. by author. Holiday, 1991. ISBN 978-0-8234-0872-6 Subj: Plants. Science. Seeds.

The fruits we eat ill. by author. Holiday House, 2015. ISBN 978-082343204-2 Subj: Food. Gardens, gardening.

Galaxies, galaxies! ill. by author. Holiday House, 2006. ISBN 978-0-8234-2002-5 Subj: Science. Space & space ships.

Giant pandas ill. by author. Holiday, 2002. ISBN 978-0-8234-1761-2 Subj: Animals – endangered animals. Animals – pandas. Foreign lands – China.

Gorillas ill. by author. Holiday House, 2011. ISBN 978-0-8234-2236-4 Subj: Animals – gorillas.

Grizzly bears ill. by author. Holiday, 2003. ISBN 978-0-8234-1793-3 Subj: Animals – bears. Animals – endangered animals.

Groundhog Day ill. by author. Holiday House, 2007. ISBN 978-0-8234-2003-2 Subj: Holidays – Groundhog Day.

Gulls — gulls — gulls ill. by author. Holiday, 1997. ISBN 978-0-8234-1323-2 Subj: Birds – seagulls.

Halloween ill. by author. Holiday, 1984. ISBN 978-0-8234-0524-4 Subj: Holidays – Halloween.

Halloween is . . . ill. by author. Holiday, 2002. ISBN 978-0-8234-1758-2 Subj: Holidays – Halloween.

Happy birthday! ill. by author. Holiday, 1986. ISBN 978-0-8234-0614-2 Subj: Birthdays.

The honey makers ill. by author. Morrow, 1997. ISBN 978-0-688-11387-2 Subj: Food. Insects – bees.

How a house is built ill. by author. Holiday, 1990. ISBN 978-0-8234-0841-2 Subj: Activities – making things. Homes, houses.

Hurricanes! ill. by author. Holiday, 2009. ISBN 978-0-8234-2233-3 Subj: Weather – hurricanes.

Ice cream: the full scoop ill. by author. Holiday House, 2006. ISBN 978-0-8234-2000-1 Subj: Food.

It's raining! ill. by author. Holiday House, 2014. ISBN 978-082342924-0 Subj: Science. Water. Weather – rain.

It's snowing! ill. by author. Holiday House, 2011. ISBN 978-0-8234-2237-1 Subj: Seasons – winter. Weather – snow.

Knights in shining armor ill. by author. Little, 1995. ISBN 978-0-316-30948-6 Subj: Knights. Middle Ages.

Ladybugs ill. by author. Holiday House, 2012. ISBN 978-0-8234-2368-2 Subj: Insects – ladybugs.

The milk makers ill. by author. Macmillan, 1985. ISBN 978-0-02-736640-2 Subj: Farms. Food.

The missing maple syrup sap mystery: or, How maple syrup is made ill. by author. Warne, 1979. ISBN 978-0-7232-6167-4 Subj: Activities. Food. Mystery stories. Trees.

Monarch butterfly ill. by author. Holiday, 1989. ISBN 978-0-8234-0773-6 Subj: Insects – butterflies, caterpillars. Metamorphosis. Science.

Nature's green umbrella: tropical rain forests ill. by author. Morrow, 1994. ISBN 978-0-688-12353-6 Subj: Animals. Ecology. Jungle. Plants.

New road! ill. by author. Crowell, 1983. ISBN 978-0-690-04343-3 Subj: Transportation.

Owls ill. by author. Holiday House, 2005. ISBN 978-0-8234-1880-0 Subj: Birds – owls.

Paper, paper everywhere ill. by author. Harcourt, 1983. ISBN 978-0-15-259488-6 Subj: Paper.

Penguins! ill. by author. Holiday, 1998. ISBN 978-0-8234-1388-1 Subj: Birds – penguins. Foreign lands – Antarctic.

Pigs ill. by author. Holiday, 1999. ISBN 978-0-8234-1441-3 Subj: Animals – pigs.

The planets ill. by author. Rev. ed. Holiday House, 2005. ISBN 978-0-8234-1957-9 Subj: Astronomy. Planets.

Playgrounds ill. by author. Holiday, 1985. ISBN 978-0-8234-0553-4 Subj: Activities – playing.

Polar bears ill. by author. Holiday, 2001. ISBN 978-0-8234-1593-9 Subj: Animals – polar bears.

The post office book: mail and how it moves ill. by author. Crowell, 1982. ISBN 978-0-690-04199-6 Subj: Careers – postal workers. Communication. Post office.

The pottery place ill. by author. Harcourt, 1987. ISBN 978-0-15-263265-6 Subj: Careers.

Prehistoric animals ill. by author. Holiday, 1988. ISBN 978-0-8234-0707-1 Subj: Animals. Prehistory. Science.

Puff — flash — bang! a book about signals ill. by author. Morrow, 1993. ISBN 978-0-688-07378-7 Subj: Communication.

The pumpkin book ill. by author. Holiday, 1999. ISBN 978-0-8234-1465-9 Subj: Gardens, gardening. Seasons – fall.

The quilting bee ill. by author. HarperCollins, 2004. ISBN 978-0-688-16398-3 Subj: Activities – sewing. Quilts.

The reasons for seasons ill. by author. Holiday, 1995. ISBN 978-0-8234-1174-0 Subj: Seasons.

Recycle! ill. by author. Little, 1992. ISBN 978-0-316-30971-4 Subj: Ecology.

Say woof! the day of a country veterinarian ill. by author. Macmillan, 1992. ISBN 978-0-02-736781-2 Subj: Animals. Careers – veterinarians. Illness.

The seasons of Arnold's apple tree ill. by author. Harcourt, 1988. ISBN 978-0-15-271246-4 Subj: Food. Seasons. Trees.

Sharks ill. by author. Holiday, 1992. ISBN 978-0-8234-0960-0 Subj: Fish – sharks. Science.

Snakes ill. by author. Holiday, 2008. ISBN 978-0-8234-2122-0 Subj: Reptiles – snakes.

Soaring with the wind: the bald eagle ill. by author. Morrow, 1998. ISBN 978-0-688-13731-1 Subj: Birds – eagles. Science.

Spiders ill. by author. Holiday, 1993. ISBN 978-0-8234-1006-4 Subj: Spiders.

Stargazers ill. by author. Holiday, 1992. ISBN 978-0-8234-0983-9 Subj: Astronomy. Stars.

Sun up, sun down ill. by author. Harcourt, 1983. ISBN 978-0-15-282781-6 Subj: Science. Sun.

Surrounded by sea ill. by author. Little, 1991. ISBN 978-0-316-30961-5 Subj: Careers – fishermen. Islands. Sports – fishing.

Tell me, tree ill. by author. Little, 2002. ISBN 978-0-316-30903-5 Subj: Trees.

Thanksgiving Day ill. by author. Holiday, 1983. ISBN 978-0-8234-0489-6 Subj: Holidays – Thanksgiving. Pilgrims.

The too-great bread bake book ill. by author. Warne, 1980. ISBN 978-0-7232-6182-7 Subj: Activities – baking, cooking.

Tool book ill. by author. Holiday, 1982. ISBN 978-0-8234-0444-5 Subj: Tools.

Tornadoes! ill. by author. Holiday, 2009. ISBN 978-0-8234-2216-0 Subj: Weather – tornadoes.

Trains ill. by author. Holiday, 1987. ISBN 978-0-8234-0640-1 Subj: Trains.

Transportation: how people get around ill. by author. Holiday, 2017. ISBN 978-082343425-1 Subj: Transportation.

Trucks ill. by author. Crowell, 1981. ISBN 978-0-690-04119-4 Subj: Trucks.

Tunnels ill. by author. Holiday, 1984. ISBN 978-0-8234-0507-7 Subj: Activities – digging.

Up goes the skyscraper! ill. by author. Four Winds, 1986. ISBN 978-0-02-736780-5 Subj: Buildings. Cities, towns.

Valentine's Day is — ill. by author. Holiday House, 2006. ISBN 978-0-8234-1852-7 Subj: Holidays – Valentine's Day.

The vegetables we eat ill. by author. Holiday House, 2007. ISBN 978-0-8234-2001-8 Subj: Food. Plants.

Weather words and what they mean ill. by author. Holiday, 1990. ISBN 978-0-8234-0805-4 Subj: Language. Weather.

Whales ill. by author. Holiday, 1991. ISBN 978-0-8234-0900-6 Subj: Animals – whales.

Yippee-yay! a book about cowboys and cowgirls ill. by author. Little, 1998. ISBN 978-0-316-30944-8 Subj: Animals – bulls, cows. Cowboys, cowgirls. Rodeos. U.S. history – frontier & pioneer life.

Zoo ill. by author. Crowell, 1987. ISBN 978-0-690-04633-5 Subj: Activities – working. Animals. Zoos.

Gibbs, Edward. *I spy on the farm* ill. by author. Candlewick, 2013. ISBN 978-0-7636-6431-2 Subj: Animals. Concepts – color. Farms. Format, unusual – toy & movable books.

I spy pets ill. by author. Candlewick, 2013. ISBN 978-0-7636-6622-4 Subj: Format, unusual – toy & movable books. Pets.

I spy under the sea ill. by author. Candlewick, 2012. ISBN 978-0-7636-5952-3 Subj: Animals. Counting, numbers. Format, unusual – toy & movable books. Sea & seashore.

I spy with my little eye ill. by author. Candlewick, 2011. ISBN 978-0-7636-5284-5 Subj: Animals. Concepts – color. Format, unusual – toy & movable books.

Gibbs, Lynne. *Don't slurp your soup!* ill. by John Eastwood. McGraw-Hill, 2003. ISBN 978-1-57768-556-2 Subj: Etiquette.

Gibert, Bruno. *The king is naked!* ill. by author. Clarion, 2004. ISBN 978-0-618-41067-5 Subj: Animals. Animals – lions. Clothing. Jungle. Royalty – kings.

Gibfried, Diane. *Brother Juniper* ill. by Meilo So. Houghton, 2006. ISBN 978-0-618-54361-8 Subj: Character traits – generosity. Foreign lands – Italy. Religion.

Gibson, Amy. *By day, by night* ill. by Meilo So. Boyds Mills, 2014. ISBN 978-159078991-9 Subj: Activities. Rhyming text. World.

Catching kisses ill. by Maria van Lieshout. Feiwel & Friends, 2013. ISBN 978-0-312-37647-5 Subj: Kissing.

Split! splat! ill. by Steve Björkman. Scholastic, 2012. ISBN 978-0-439-58753-2 Subj: Activities – playing. Animals – dogs. Rhyming text. Weather – rain.

Gibson, Ginger Foglesong. *Tiptoe Joe* ill. by Laura Rankin. Greenwillow, 2013. ISBN 978-0-06-177203-0 Subj: Animals. Animals – babies. Animals – bears. Noise, sounds.

Gibson, Karen Bush. *Child care workers* ill. with photos. Bridgestone, 2001. ISBN 978-0-7368-0622-0 Subj: Careers. Communities, neighborhoods.

Emergency medical technicians ill. with photos. Bridgestone, 2001. ISBN 978-0-7368-0623-7 Subj: Careers. Communities, neighborhoods.

Pharmacists ill. with photos. Bridgestone, 2001. ISBN 978-0-7368-0624-4 Subj: Careers – pharmacists. Communities, neighborhoods.

Truck drivers ill. with photos. Bridgestone, 2001. ISBN 978-0-7368-0625-1 Subj: Careers – truck drivers. Communities, neighborhoods.

Gifaldi, David. *Ben, king of the river* ill. by Layne Johnson. Albert Whitman, 2001. ISBN 978-0-8075-0635-6 Subj: Camps, camping. Disabilities – mental disabilities. Family life – brothers.

Giff, Patricia Reilly. *Good luck, Ronald Morgan* ill. by Susanna Natti. Viking, 1996. ISBN 978-0-670-86303-7 Subj: Animals – cats. Animals – dogs. Pets.

Today was a terrible day ill. by Susanna Natti. Viking, 1980. ISBN 978-0-670-81830-3 Subj: Behavior – bad day, bad mood. School.

Gifford, Peggy. *The great big green* ill. by Lisa Desimini. Boyds Mills, 2014. ISBN 978-162091629-2 Subj: Earth. Nature.

Giganti, Paul. *Each orange had eight slices* ill. by Donald Crews. Greenwillow, 1992. ISBN 978-0-688-10429-0 Subj: Counting, numbers.

How many blue birds flew away? a counting book with a difference ill. by Donald Crews. HarperCollins, 2005. ISBN 978-0-06-000763-8 Subj: Counting, numbers.

How many snails? a counting book ill. by Donald Crews. Greenwillow, 1988. ISBN 978-0-688-06370-2 Subj: Counting, numbers.

Giglio, Judy. *The tapping tale* ill. by Joe Cepeda. Harcourt, 2000. ISBN 978-0-15-202572-4 Subj: Animals – dogs. Noise, sounds. Sleepovers.

Gigot, Jami. *Mae and the moon* ill. by author. Ripple Grove, 2015. ISBN 978-099138662-8 Subj: Imagination. Moon.

Gilani-Williams, Fawzia. *Nabeel's new pants: an Eid tale* ill. by Proiti Roy. Marshall Cavendish, 2010. ISBN 978-0-7614-5629-2 Subj: Clothing – pants. Family life. Foreign lands – Turkey. Holidays – Ramadan. Religion.

Gilbert, Jane. *Indescribably Arabella* ill. by author. Atheneum, 2003. ISBN 978-0-689-85321-0 Subj: Character traits – individuality.

Gilchrist, Jan Spivey. *My America* ill. by Ashley Bryan and Jan Spivey Gilchrist. HarperCollins, 2007. ISBN 978-0-06-079105-6 Subj: Poetry. U.S. history.

Giles, Almira Astudillo. *Willie wins* ill. by Carl Angel. Lee & Low, 2001. ISBN 978-1-58430-023-6 Subj: Ethnic groups in the U.S. – Filipino Americans. Family life – fathers. School.

Gill, Deirdre. *Outside* ill. by author. Houghton, 2014. ISBN 978-054791065-9 Subj: Activities – playing. Imagination. Weather – snow.

Gill, Shelley. *The big buck adventure* by Shelley Gill and Deborah Tobola ill. by Grace Lin. Charlesbridge, 2000. ISBN 978-0-88106-294-6 Subj: Counting, numbers. Money. Shopping.

The egg ill. by Jo-Ellen Bosson. Charlesbridge, 2001. ISBN 978-1-57091-377-8 Subj: Eggs. Nature.

Up on Denali ill. by Shannon Cartwright. Sasquatch, 2006. ISBN 978-1-57061-366-1 Subj: Alaska. Mountains.

Gill, Timothy. *Flip and Fin: super sharks to the rescue!* ill. by Neil Numberman. Greenwillow, 2016. ISBN 978-006224301-0 Subj: Character traits – helpfulness. Family life – brothers. Fish – sharks. Humorous stories. Multiple births – twins.

Flip and Fin: we rule the school! ill. by Neil Numberman. HarperCollins/Greenwillow, 2014. ISBN 978-006224300-3 Subj: Family life – brothers. Fish – sharks. Multiple births – twins. Riddles & jokes. School.

Gill-Brown, Vanessa. *Rufferella* ill. by Mandy Stanley. Scholastic, 2001. ISBN 978-0-439-25617-9 Subj: Animals – dogs. Behavior – imitation.

Gillard, Denise. *Music from the sky* ill. by Stephen Taylor. Douglas & McIntyre, 2001. ISBN 978-0-88899-311-3 Subj: Family life – grandfathers. Musical instruments – flutes.

Gillham, Bill. *How many sharks in the bath?* ill. by Christyan Fox. Frances Lincoln, 2005. ISBN 978-1-84507-288-9 Subj: Animals. Counting, numbers.

Gilliland, Judith Heide. *The day of Ahmed's secret* (Heide, Florence Parry)

Sami and the time of the troubles (Heide, Florence Parry)

Gillingham, Sara. *Alpha, Bravo, Charlie: the complete book of nautical codes* ill. by author. Phaidon, 2016. ISBN 978-071487143-1 Subj: ABC books. Flags. Signs.

Friends ill. by author. Chronicle, 2015. ISBN 978-145214188-6 Subj: Babies, toddlers. Format, unusual – board books. Format, unusual – toy & movable books. Friendship.

Trucks ill. by author. Chronicle, 2015. ISBN 978-145214187-9 Subj: Format, unusual – board books. Format, unusual – toy & movable books. Trucks.

Gillmor, Don. *Yuck, a love story* ill. by Marie-Louise Gay. Stoddart, 2000. ISBN 978-0-7737-3218-6 Subj: Birthdays. Friendship. Moon.

Gilman, Rita Golden. *Mole in a hole* ill. by Holly Hannon. Random House, 2003. ISBN 978-0-679-99037-6 Subj: Animals. Animals – moles. Rebuses. Rhyming text.

Rice is life ill. by Yangsook Choi. Henry Holt, 2000. ISBN 978-0-8050-5719-5 Subj: Animals. Food. Foreign lands – Indonesia. Poetry.

Gilmore, Rachna. *Making grizzle grow* ill. by Leslie Elizabeth Watts. Fitzhenry & Whiteside, 2008. ISBN 978-1-55041-885-9 Subj: Emotions – anger. Family life – daughters. Family life – fathers. Imagination. Snowmen.

The gingerbread boy. *Can't catch me* by John Hassett and Ann Hassett; ill. by authors. Houghton, 2006. ISBN 978-0-618-70490-3 Subj: Behavior – running away. Cumulative tales.

Gingerbread baby retold by Jan Brett; ill. by reteller. Putnam, 1999. ISBN 978-0-399-23444-6 Subj: Behavior – running away. Cumulative tales. Folk & fairy tales. Food. Format, unusual – toy & movable books.

The gingerbread boy retold by Harriet Ziefert; ill. by Emily Bolam. Viking, 1995. ISBN 978-0-670-86052-4 Subj: Behavior – running away. Cumulative tales. Folk & fairy tales.

The gingerbread boy retold by Richard Egielski; ill. by reteller. Geringer, 1997. ISBN 978-0-06-026031-6 Subj: Behavior – running away. Cumulative tales. Folk & fairy tales. Food.

The gingerbread boy ill. by Paul Galdone. Seabury Pr., 1975. ISBN 978-0-8164-3132-8 Subj: Behavior – running away. Cumulative tales. Folk & fairy tales. Food. Rhyming text.

The Gingerbread Cowboy ill. by Holly Berry. HarperCollins, 2006. ISBN 978-0-06-077863-7 Subj: Animals – coyotes. Behavior – running away. Cowboys, cowgirls. Cumulative tales. Folk & fairy tales. Food.

The gingerbread girl by Lisa Campbell Ernst; ill. by author. Penguin, 2006. ISBN 978-0-525-47667-2 Subj: Behavior – running away. Cumulative tales. Folk & fairy tales. Food.

The gingerbread man retold by Carol Jones; ill. by reteller. Houghton, 2002. ISBN 978-0-618-18822-2 Subj: Behavior – running away. Cumulative tales. Folk & fairy tales. Food.

The gingerbread man retold by Eric A. Kimmel; ill. by Megan Lloyd. Holiday, 1993. ISBN 978-0-8234-0824-5 Subj: Behavior – running away. Cumulative tales. Folk & fairy tales.

The gingerbread man retold by Jim Aylesworth; ill. by Barbara McClintock. Scholastic, 1998. ISBN 978-0-590-97219-2 Subj: Behavior – running away. Cumulative tales. Folk & fairy tales. Food.

The gingerbread man by Béatrice Rodriguez; ill. by author. NorthSouth, 2012. ISBN 978-0-7358-4086-7 Subj: Behavior – running away. Cumulative tales. Folk & fairy tales. Food.

The Gingerbread Man loose at Christmas by Laura Murray; ill. by Mike Lowery. Putnam, 2015. ISBN 978-039916866-6 Subj: Behavior – sharing. Folk & fairy tales. Food. Gifts. Holidays – Christmas. Rhyming text.

The Gingerbread Man loose at the zoo by Laura Murray; ill. by Mike Lowery. Putnam, 2016. ISBN 978-039916867-3 Subj: Folk & fairy tales. Food. Rhyming text. School – field trips. Zoos.

The Gingerbread Man loose in the school by Laura Murray; ill. by Mike Lowery. Penguin, 2011. ISBN 978-0-399-25052-1 Subj: Behavior – running away. Cumulative tales. Folk & fairy tales. Food. Rhyming text. School.

The Gingerbread Man loose on the fire truck by Laura Murray; ill. by Mike Lowery. Putnam, 2013. ISBN 978-0-399-25779-7 Subj: Behavior – running away. Folk & fairy tales. Food. Rhyming text. School – field trips. Trucks.

The Library Gingerbread Man by Dotti Enderle; ill. by Colleen M. Madden. Upstart, 2010. ISBN 978-1-60213-048-7 Subj: Behavior – running away. Cumulative tales. Food. Libraries.

The Ninjabread Man by C.J Leigh; ill. by Chris Gall. Scholastic/Orchard, 2016. ISBN 978-054581430-0 Subj: Cumulative tales. Folk & fairy tales. Food. Sports – martial arts.

The pancake boy adapt. by Lorinda Bryan Cauley; ill. by adapter. Putnam, 1988. ISBN 978-0-399-21505-6 Subj: Behavior – running away. Cumulative tales. Folk & fairy tales. Food.

Señorita Gordita by Helen Ketteman; ill. by Will Terry. Albert Whitman, 2012. ISBN 978-0-8075-7302-0 Subj: Behavior – running away. Cumulative tales. Folk & fairy tales. Food. Foreign languages.

Whiff, sniff, nibble and chew: the Gingerbread boy retold by Charlotte Pomerantz; ill. by Monica Incisa. Greenwillow, 1984. ISBN 978-0-688-02552-6 Subj: Behavior – running away. Cumulative tales. Folk & fairy tales. Rhyming text.

Ginkel, Anne. *I've got an elephant* ill. by Janie Bynum. Peachtree, 2006. ISBN 978-1-56145-373-3 Subj: Animals – elephants. Counting, numbers. Emotions – loneliness. Rhyming text.

Ginsburg, Mirra. *Across the stream* ill. by Nancy Tafuri. Greenwillow, 1982. ISBN 978-0-688-01206-9 Subj: Animals – foxes. Birds – chickens, roosters. Birds – ducks. Dreams.

Asleep, asleep ill. by Nancy Tafuri. Greenwillow, 1992. ISBN 978-0-688-09154-5 Subj: Bedtime. Lullabies. Night.

The chick and the duckling ill. by José Aruego and Ariane Dewey. Macmillan, 1972. ISBN 978-0-02-735940-4 Subj: Birds – chickens, roosters. Birds – ducks. Sports – swimming.

Clay boy ill. by Joseph A. Smith. Adapt. from a Russian folk tale. Greenwillow, 1997. ISBN 978-0-688-14410-4 Subj: Activities – making things. Folk & fairy tales. Foreign lands – Russia.

Mushroom in the rain ill. by José Aruego and Ariane Dewey. Macmillan, 1988, 1974. ISBN 978-0-02-736241-1 Subj: Animals. Animals – foxes. Plants. Weather – rain.

Giogas, Valarie. *In my backyard* ill. by Katherine Zecca. Sylvan Dell, 2007. ISBN 978-0-9777423-1-8 Subj: Animals. Counting, numbers. Nature. Rhyming text.

Giovanni, Nikki. *Lincoln and Douglass: an American friendship* ill. by Bryan Collier. Henry Holt, 2008. ISBN 978-0-8050-8264-7 Subj: Ethnic groups in the U.S. – African Americans. Friendship. U.S. history.

Rosa ill. by Bryan Collier. Henry Holt, 2005. ISBN 978-0-8050-7106-1 Subj: Caldecott award honor books. Character traits – bravery. Ethnic groups in the U.S. – African Americans. Prejudice. U.S. history.

The sun is so quiet ill. by Ashley Bryan. Henry Holt, 1996. ISBN 978-0-8050-4119-4 Subj: Ethnic groups in the U.S. – African Americans. Nature. Poetry.

Girnis, Margaret. *ABC for you and me* photos by Shirley Leaman Green. Albert Whitman, 2000. ISBN 978-0-8075-0101-6 Subj: ABC books. Disabilities – Down syndrome.

1, 2, 3 for you and me photos by Shirley Leaman Green. Albert Whitman, 2001. ISBN 978-0-8075-6107-2 Subj: Counting, numbers. Disabilities – Down syndrome.

Glaser, Byron. *Bonz, inside-out* by Byron Glaser and Sandra Higashi; ill. by authors. Abrams, 2003. ISBN 978-0-8109-4599-9 Subj: Anatomy – skeletons.

Glaser, Jason. *Pinkeye* ill. with photos. Capstone, 2006. ISBN 978-0-7368-4292-1 Subj: Anatomy – eyes. Health & fitness. Illness.

Glaser, Linda. *Emma's poem: the voice of the Statue of Liberty* ill. by Claire A. Nivola. Houghton Mifflin, 2010. ISBN 978-0-547-17184-5 Subj: Poetry. U.S. history.

Garbage helps our garden grow: a compost story ill. by Shelley Rotner. Millbrook, 2010. ISBN 978-0-7613-4911-2 Subj: Ecology. Gardens, gardening.

Hannah's way ill. by Adam Gustavson. Lerner/Kar-Ben, 2012. ISBN 978-0-7613-5138-2 Subj: Friendship. Jewish culture. Moving. School. U.S. history.

Hello, squirrels! scampering through the seasons ill. by Gay W. Holland. Lerner, 2006. ISBN 978-0-7613-2887-2 Subj: Animals – squirrels. Seasons.

Hoppy Passover! ill. by Daniel Howarth. Albert Whitman, 2011. ISBN 978-0-8075-3380-2 Subj: Animals – rabbits. Holidays – Passover. Jewish culture.

It's fall ill. by Susan Swan. Millbrook, 2001. ISBN 978-0-7613-1758-6 Subj: Nature. Seasons – fall.

It's spring ill. by Susan Swan. Millbrook, 2002. ISBN 978-0-7613-1760-9 Subj: Nature. Seasons – spring.

It's summer ill. by Susan Swan. Millbrook, 2003. ISBN 978-0-7613-1757-9 Subj: Nature. Seasons – summer.

It's winter ill. by Susan Swan. Millbrook, 2002. ISBN 978-0-7613-1759-3 Subj: Nature. Seasons – winter.

Magnificent monarchs ill. by Gay W. Holland. Millbrook, 2000. ISBN 978-0-7613-1700-5 Subj: Insects – butterflies, caterpillars. Science.

Mrs. Greenberg's messy Hanukkah ill. by Nancy Cote. Albert Whitman, 2004. ISBN 978-0-8075-

5297-1 Subj: Activities – baking, cooking. Character traits – orderliness. Food. Holidays – Hanukkah. Jewish culture.

Not a buzz to be found: insects in winter ill. by Jaime Zollars. Millbrook, 2011. ISBN 978-0-7613-5644-8 Subj: Insects. Seasons – winter.

Our big home ill. by Elisa Kleven. Millbrook, 2000. ISBN 978-0-7613-1650-3 Subj: Earth. Nature.

Stone soup with matzoh balls: a Passover tale in Chelm ill. by Maryam Tabatabaei. Albert Whitman, 2014. ISBN 978-080757620-5 Subj: Character traits – cleverness. Folk & fairy tales. Food. Holidays – Passover. Jewish culture.

Glass, Andrew. *Bewildered for three days: as to why Daniel Boone never wore his coonskin cap* ill. by author. Holiday, 2000. ISBN 978-0-8234-1446-8 Subj: Animals – bears. Animals – raccoons. U.S. history – frontier & pioneer life.

The wondrous whirligig: the Wright Brothers' first flying machine ill. by author. Holiday, 2003. ISBN 978-0-8234-1717-9 Subj: Activities – flying. Careers – inventors. Helicopters.

Glass, Beth Raisner. *Blue-ribbon dad* ill. by Margie Moore. Abrams, 2011. ISBN 978-0-8109-9727-1 Subj: Animals – squirrels. Family life – fathers. Rhyming text.

Noises at night by Beth Raisner Glass and Susan Lubner ill. by Bruce Whatley. Abrams, 2005. ISBN 978-0-8109-5750-3 Subj: Bedtime. Noise, sounds. Rhyming text.

Glass, Eleri. *The red shoes* ill. by Ashley Spires. PGW, 2008. ISBN 978-1-894965-78-1 Subj: Character traits – appearance. Clothing – shoes. Shopping.

Glass, Julie. *A dollar for Penny* ill. by Joy Allen. Random House, 2000. ISBN 978-0-679-98973-8 Subj: Birthdays. Money. Rhyming text.

Glassman, Peter. *My dad's job* ill. by Timothy Bush. Simon & Schuster, 2003. ISBN 978-0-689-82890-4 Subj: Careers. Family life – fathers. Imagination.

Gleeson, Libby. *Clancy and Millie and the very fine house* ill. by Freya Blackwood. Little Hare, 2010. ISBN 978-1-921541-19-3 Subj: Friendship. Homes, houses. Imagination. Moving.

Cuddle time ill. by Julie Vivas. Candlewick, 2004. ISBN 978-0-7636-2320-3 Subj: Family life. Morning.

Half a world away ill. by Freya Blackwood. Scholastic, 2007. ISBN 978-0-439-88977-3 Subj: Friendship. Moving.

Glenn, Sharlee. *Just what Mama needs* ill. by Amiko Hirao. Harcourt, 2008. ISBN 978-0-15-205759-6 Subj: Days of the week, months of the year. Family life – mothers. Imagination.

Glicksman, Caroline. *Eric the math bear* ill. by author. Knopf, 2003. ISBN 978-0-375-92432-3 Subj: Animals – bears. Counting, numbers. Crime.

Gliori, Debi. *Can I have a hug?* ill. by author. Orchard, 2002. ISBN 978-0-439-27602-3 Subj: Animals – bears. Format, unusual – board books.

Dragon's extraordinary egg ill. by author. Walker, 2014. ISBN 978-080273759-5 Subj: Adoption. Birds – penguins. Character traits – being different. Dragons.

Flora's blanket ill. by author. Orchard, 2001. ISBN 978-0-531-30305-4 Subj: Animals – rabbits. Bedtime. Behavior – lost & found possessions.

Flora's surprise ill. by author. Orchard, 2003. ISBN 978-0-439-45590-9 Subj: Animals – rabbits. Gardens, gardening. Homes, houses.

Goodnight world ill. by author. Bloomsbury, 2017. ISBN 978-168119363-2 Subj: Bedtime. Rhyming text. World.

Little Owl's egg ill. by Alison Brown. Bloomsbury, 2017. ISBN 978-168119324-3 Subj: Birds – owls. Eggs. Family life – mothers. Family life – new sibling.

Mr. Bear to the rescue ill. by author. Orchard, 2000. ISBN 978-0-531-30276-7 Subj: Animals. Animals – bears. Forest, woods. Homes, houses. Weather – storms.

Mr. Bear's new baby ill. by author. Orchard, 1999. ISBN 978-0-531-30152-4 Subj: Animals – bears. Babies, toddlers. Family life.

No matter what ill. by author. Harcourt, 1999. ISBN 978-0-15-202061-3 Subj: Animals – foxes. Emotions – love. Family life. Rhyming text.

Penguin post ill. by author. Harcourt, 2001. ISBN 978-0-15-216765-3 Subj: Babies, toddlers. Birds – penguins. Post office.

Polar Bolero ill. by author. Harcourt, 2001. ISBN 978-0-15-202436-9 Subj: Activities – dancing. Animals – polar bears. Bedtime. Rhyming text.

The scariest thing of all ill. by author. Walker, 2012. ISBN 978-0-8027-2391-8 Subj: Animals – rabbits. Character traits – bravery. Emotions – fear.

The snow lambs ill. by author. Scholastic, 1996. ISBN 978-0-590-20304-3 Subj: Animals – dogs. Animals – sheep. Weather – snow. Weather – storms.

Stormy weather ill. by author. Walker, 2009. ISBN 978-0-8027-9419-2 Subj: Animals – foxes. Bedtime. Family life – mothers. Rhyming text.

The trouble with dragons ill. by author. Walker, 2008. ISBN 978-0-8027-9789-6 Subj: Dragons. Ecology.

What can I give him? ill. by author. Holiday, 1998. ISBN 978-0-8234-1392-8 Subj: Gifts. Holidays – Christmas. Religion – Nativity. Rhyming text.

What's the time, Mr. Wolf? ill. by author. Walker, 2012. ISBN 978-0-8027-3432-7 Subj: Animals – pigs. Animals – wolves. Birthdays. Nursery rhymes. Time.

Where did that baby come from? ill. by author. Harcourt, 2005. ISBN 978-0-15-205373-4 Subj: Animals – tigers. Babies, toddlers. Family life – new sibling. Rhyming text.

Go tell Aunt Rhody ill. by Aliki. Macmillan, 1974. ISBN 978-0-02-700410-6 Subj: Family life – aunts, uncles. Folk & fairy tales. Games. Songs.

Goble, Paul. *Adopted by the eagles: a Plains Indian story of friendship and treachery* ill. by author. Bradbury, 1994. ISBN 978-0-02-736575-7 Subj: Animals – horses, ponies. Birds – eagles. Folk & fairy tales. Indians of North America – Lakota (Sioux).

Beyond the ridge ill. by author. Bradbury, 1988. ISBN 978-0-02-736581-8 Subj: Death. Indians of North America – Great Plains.

Buffalo woman ill. by author. Bradbury, 1984. ISBN 978-0-02-737720-0 Subj: Folk & fairy tales. Indians of North America.

Crow chief: a Plains Indian story ill. by author. Orchard, 1992. ISBN 978-0-531-08547-9 Subj: Birds – crows. Folk & fairy tales. Indians of North America – Crow.

Death of the iron horse ill. by author. Bradbury, 1987. ISBN 978-0-02-737830-6 Subj: Indians of North America – Cheyenne (Sioux). Trains. War.

The dream wolf ill. by author. Rev. ed of The friendly wolf. Bradbury, 1990. ISBN 978-0-02-736585-6 Subj: Folk & fairy tales. Indians of North America – Great Plains.

The gift of the sacred dog ill. by author. Bradbury, 1980. ISBN 978-0-87888-165-9 Subj: Animals – horses, ponies. Folk & fairy tales. Gifts. Indians of North America – Great Plains.

The girl who loved wild horses ill. by author. Dutton, 1978. ISBN 978-0-87888-121-5 Subj: Animals – horses, ponies. Caldecott award books. Indians of North America.

The great race of the birds and animals ill. by author. Bradbury, 1991. ISBN 978-0-689-71452-8 Subj: Animals. Birds. Creation. Folk & fairy tales. Indians of North America – Cheyenne (Sioux).

Her seven brothers ill. by author. Bradbury, 1988. ISBN 978-0-02-737960-0 Subj: Animals – buffaloes. Folk & fairy tales. Indians of North America – Cheyenne (Sioux).

Iktomi and the berries: a Plains Indian story ill. by author. Orchard, 1989. ISBN 978-0-531-08419-9 Subj: Folk & fairy tales. Indians of North America – Great Plains.

Iktomi and the boulder: a Plains Indian story ill. by author. Watts, 1988. ISBN 978-0-531-08360-4 Subj: Birthdays. Character traits – conceit. Folk & fairy tales. Indians of North America – Dakota (Sioux). Indians of North America – Great Plains. Rocks.

Iktomi and the buffalo skull: a Plains Indian story ill. by author. Orchard, 1991. ISBN 978-0-531-08511-0 Subj: Behavior – trickery. Character traits – conceit. Folk & fairy tales. Indians of North America – Great Plains.

Iktomi and the buzzard: a Plains Indian story ill. by author. Orchard, 1994. ISBN 978-0-531-08662-9 Subj: Behavior – trickery. Birds – buzzards. Folk & fairy tales. Indians of North America – Dakota (Sioux). Indians of North America – Great Plains.

Iktomi and the coyote: a Plains Indian story ill. by author. Orchard, 1998. ISBN 978-0-531-33108-8 Subj: Behavior – trickery. Folk & fairy tales. Indians of North America – Great Plains. Mythical creatures.

Iktomi and the ducks: a Plains Indian story ill. by author. Orchard, 1990. ISBN 978-0-531-08483-0 Subj: Animals – coyotes. Behavior – trickery. Birds – ducks. Folk & fairy tales. Indians of North America – Great Plains.

The legend of the White Buffalo Woman ill. by author. National Geographic, 1998. ISBN 978-0-7922-7074-4 Subj: Folk & fairy tales. Indians of North America – Lakota (Sioux).

The lost children: the boys who were neglected ill. by author. Bradbury, 1993. ISBN 978-0-02-736555-9 Subj: Character traits – meanness. Folk & fairy tales. Indians of North America – Blackfoot. Indians of North America – Siksika. Orphans. Stars.

Love flute ill. by author. Bradbury, 1992. ISBN 978-0-02-736261-9 Subj: Character traits – shyness. Emotions – love. Folk & fairy tales. Indians of North America – Dakota (Sioux).

Mystic horse ill. by author. HarperCollins, 2003. ISBN 978-0-06-029814-2 Subj: Animals – horses, ponies. Folk & fairy tales. Indians of North America – Great Plains. Indians of North America – Pawnee.

Remaking the earth: a creation story from the Great Plains of North America ill. by author. Orchard, 1996. ISBN 978-0-531-08874-6 Subj: Creation. Folk & fairy tales. Indians of North America – Great Plains. Weather – floods.

The return of the buffaloes: a Plains Indian story about famine and renewal of the earth ill. by author. National Geographic, 1996. ISBN 978-0-7922-2714-4 Subj: Animals – buffaloes. Folk & fairy tales.

Food. Indians of North America – Great Plains. Indians of North America – Lakota (Sioux).

Star boy ill. by author. Bradbury, 1983. ISBN 978-0-02-722660-7 Subj: Activities – dancing. Character traits – appearance. Folk & fairy tales. Indians of North America – Siksika.

Godard, Alex. *Mama, across the sea* adapt. from the French by George Wen; ill. by author. Henry Holt, 2000. ISBN 978-0-8050-6161-1 Subj: Behavior – needing someone. Family life – grandmothers. Family life – mothers. Foreign lands – Caribbean Islands.

Godden, Rumer. *The story of Holly and Ivy* ill. by Barbara Cooney. Penguin, 2006. ISBN 978-0-670-06219-5 Subj: Holidays – Christmas. Orphans. Toys – dolls.

Godin, Thelma Lynne. *The hula-hoopin' queen* ill. by Vanessa Brantley-Newton. Lee & Low, 2014. ISBN 978-160060846-9 Subj: Birthdays. Character traits – responsibility. Contests. Ethnic groups in the U.S. – African Americans. Parties.

Godkin, Celia. *Wolf island* ill. by author. Fitzhenry & Whiteside, 2006. ISBN 978-1-55455-007-4 Subj: Animals – wolves. Islands.

Godwin, Jane. *Bear make den* by Jane Godwin and Michael Wagner ill. by Andrew Joyner. Candlewick, 2017. ISBN 978-076369061-8 Subj: Animals – bears. Homes, houses.

Godwin, Laura. *Barnyard prayers* ill. by Brian Selznick. Hyperion, 2000. ISBN 978-0-7868-0355-2 Subj: Animals. Poetry. Religion.

Central Park serenade ill. by Barry Root. HarperCollins, 2002. ISBN 978-0-06-025892-4 Subj: Cities, towns. Parks. Rhyming text. Seasons – summer.

The Doll People's Christmas (Martin, Ann M.)

Little white dog ill. by Dan Yaccarino. Hyperion, 1998. ISBN 978-0-7868-2256-0 Subj: Animals. Concepts – color. Concepts – shape. Imagination. Rhyming text.

One moon, two cats ill. by Yoko Tanaka. Simon & Schuster, 2011. ISBN 978-1-4424-1202-6 Subj: Animals – cats. Cities, towns. Farms. Rhyming text.

Owl sees owl ill. by Rob Dunlavey. Random House, 2016. ISBN 978-05534978-2-3 Subj: Birds – owls. Night.

This is the firefighter ill. by Julian Hector. Hyperion, 2009. ISBN 978-1-4231-0800-9 Subj: Careers – firefighters. Rhyming text.

What the baby hears ill. by Mary Morgan. Hyperion, 2002. ISBN 978-0-7868-2484-7 Subj: Animals – babies. Family life – parents. Noise, sounds. Rhyming text.

Goembel, Ponder, adapt. *Animal fair* ill. by adapter. Marshall Cavendish, 2010. ISBN 978-0-7614-5642-1 Subj: Animals. Fairs, festivals. Rhyming text. Songs.

Goetz, Steve. *Old MacDonald had a truck* (Old MacDonald had a farm)

Going, K. L. *Bumpety, dunkety, thumpety-thump!* ill. by Simone Shin. Simon & Schuster/Beach Lane, 2017. ISBN 978-144243415-8 Subj: Family life – brothers & sisters. Noise, sounds. Rhyming text.

Dog in charge ill. by Dan Santat. Dial, 2012. ISBN 978-0-8037-3479-1 Subj: Animals – cats. Animals – dogs. Behavior – misbehavior.

Golan, Avirama. *Little Naomi, Little Chick* ill. by Raaya Karas. Eerdmans, 2013. ISBN 978-0-8028-5427-8 Subj: Birds – chickens, roosters. Farms. School – nursery.

Gold, August. *Does God hear my prayer?* ill. by Diane Hardy Waller. Skylight Paths, 2005. ISBN 978-1-59473-102-0 Subj: Religion.

Gold-Vukson, Marji E. *The colors of my Jewish Year* ill. by author. Kar-Ben, 1998. ISBN 978-1-58013-011-0 Subj: Concepts – color. Format, unusual – board books. Jewish culture. Religion.

Grandpa and me on Tu B'Shevat ill. by Leslie Evans. Kar-Ben, 2004. ISBN 978-1-58013-122-3 Subj: Cumulative tales. Family life – grandfathers. Holidays. Jewish culture. Religion. Rhyming text. Trees.

Goldberg, Myla. *Catching the moon* ill. by Chris Sheban. Scholastic, 2007. ISBN 978-0-439-57686-4 Subj: Moon.

Goldberg, Whoopi. *Whoopi's big book of manners* ill. by Olo. Hyperion, 2006. ISBN 978-0-7868-5295-6 Subj: Etiquette.

Goldfinger, Jennifer P. *A fish named Spot* ill. by author. Little, 2001. ISBN 978-0-316-32047-4 Subj: Fish. Pets.

Hello, my name is Tiger ill. by Jennifer P. Goldfinger. HarperCollins, 2016. ISBN 978-006239951-9 Subj: Character traits – shyness. Clothing – costumes. School – first day.

My dog Lyle ill. by author. Houghton, 2007. ISBN 978-0-618-63983-0 Subj: Animals – dogs. Pets.

Goldhor, Susan Henne. *Franny B. Kranny, there's a bird in your hair* (Lerner, Harriet Goldhor)

Goldie, Sonia. *Ghosts* ill. by Marc Boutavant. Enchanted Lion, 2013. ISBN 978-1-59270-142-1 Subj: Ghosts.

Goldin, Augusta. *Ducks don't get wet* ill. by Leonard P. Kessler. Crowell, 1989. ISBN 978-0-690-04782-0 Subj: Birds – ducks. Science.

Goldin, Barbara Diamond. *Cakes and miracles: a Purim tale* ill. by Jaime Zollars. Marshall Cavendish, 2010. ISBN 978-0-7614-5701-5 Subj: Activities – baking, cooking. Disabilities – blindness. Holidays – Purim. Jewish culture.

A mountain of blintzes ill. by Anik McGrory. Harcourt, 2001. ISBN 978-0-15-201902-0 Subj: Food. Holidays – Shavuot. Jewish culture. Religion.

Night lights ill. by Laura Sucher. UAHC Pr., 2002. ISBN 978-0-8074-0803-2 Subj: Emotions – fear. Holidays – Sukkot. Jewish culture.

Goldin, David. *Go-Go-Go!* ill. by author. Abrams, 2000. ISBN 978-0-8109-4141-0 Subj: Animals. Sports – bicycling. Sports – racing.

Golding, Theresa Martin. *Abby's asthma and the big race* ill. by Margeaux Lucas. Albert Whitman, 2009. ISBN 978-0-8075-0465-9 Subj: Activities – running. Illness – asthma. Sports – racing.

Memorial Day surprise ill. by Alexandra Artigas. Boyds Mills, 2004. ISBN 978-1-59078-048-0 Subj: Ethnic groups in the U.S. Family life – grandfathers. Holidays – Memorial Day.

Goldman, Judy. *Uncle Monarch and the Day of the Dead* ill. by Rene King Moreno. Boyds Mills, 2008. ISBN 978-1-59078-425-9 Subj: Death. Family life – aunts, uncles. Foreign lands – Mexico. Holidays – Day of the Dead. Insects – butterflies, caterpillars.

Goldsaito, Katrina. *The sound of silence* ill. by Julia Kuo. Little, Brown, 2016. ISBN 978-031620337-1 Subj: Foreign lands – Japan. Noise, sounds.

Goldsboro, Bobby. *Jonah and the whale; and, Daniel in the lion's den* ill. by Toni Donelow Stewart. New Canaan, 2003. ISBN 978-1-889658-28-5 Subj: Animals – lions. Animals – whales. Religion – Daniel. Religion – Jonah.

Noah and the ark; and, David and Goliath ill. by Toni Donelow Stewart. New Canaan, 2003. ISBN 978-1-889658-27-8 Subj: Animals – mice. Birds – ducks. Boats, ships. Foreign lands – Israel. Giants. Religion – David. Religion – Noah. Weather – floods.

Goldstone, Bruce. *Awesome autumn* ill. with photos. Henry Holt, 2012. ISBN 978-0-8050-9210-3 Subj: Seasons – fall.

Great estimations ill. with photos. Henry Holt, 2006. ISBN 978-0-8050-7446-8 Subj: Concepts. Counting, numbers.

I see a pattern here ill. with photos. Henry Holt, 2015. ISBN 978-080509209-7 Subj: Concepts – patterns.

That's a possibility! a book about what might happen ill. with photos. Henry Holt, 2013. ISBN 978-0-8050-8998-1 Subj: Concepts. Counting, numbers.

Wonderful winter ill. with photos. Henry Holt, 2016. ISBN 978-080509981-2 Subj: Seasons – winter.

Goldstyn, Jacques. *Bertolt* ill. by author. Enchanted Lion, 2017. ISBN 978-159270229-9 Subj: Character traits – individuality. Death. Emotions – loneliness. Trees.

Golenbock, Peter. *ABCs of baseball* ill. by Dan Andreasen. Dial, 2012. ISBN 978-0-8037-3711-2 Subj: ABC books. Sports – baseball.

Hank Aaron ill. by Paul Lee. Harcourt, 2001. ISBN 978-0-15-202093-4 Subj: Character traits – bravery. Ethnic groups in the U.S. – African Americans. Sports – baseball.

Golio, Gary. *Bird and Diz* ill. by Ed Young. Candlewick, 2015. ISBN 978-076366660-6 Subj: Careers – musicians. Ethnic groups in the U.S. – African Americans. Music.

Gollub, Matthew. *Cool melons — turn to frogs: the life and poems of Issa* ill. by Kazuko G. Stone. Lee & Low, 1998. ISBN 978-1-880000-71-7 Subj: Careers – poets. Foreign lands – Japan. Poetry.

Gobble, quack, moon ill. by Judy Love. Tortuga, 2002. ISBN 978-1-889910-20-8 Subj: Activities – dancing. Animals. Animals – bulls, cows. Moon. Music.

The Jazz Fly: starring the Jazz Bugs ill. by Karen Hanke. Tortuga, 2000. ISBN 978-1-889910-17-8 Subj: Animals. Insects – flies. Music. Musical instruments – drums. Rhyming text.

Jazz Fly 2: the jungle pachanga ill. by Karen Hanke. Tortuga, 2010. ISBN 978-1-889910-44-4 Subj: Foreign languages. Insects – flies. Jungle. Music. Rhyming text.

Ten oni drummers ill. by Kazuko G. Stone. Lee & Low, 2000. ISBN 978-1-58430-011-3 Subj: Counting, numbers. Foreign lands – Japan. Foreign languages. Rhyming text.

Golson, Terry. *Tillie lays an egg* ill. by Ben Fink. Scholastic, 2009. ISBN 978-0-545-00537-1 Subj: Birds – chickens, roosters. Eggs. Farms.

Gomez, Rebecca J. *Hensel and Gretel: ninja chicks* (Schwartz, Corey Rosen)

Gomi, Taro. *The crocodile and the dentist* ill. by author. Millbrook, 1994. ISBN 978-1-56294-555-8

Subj: Careers – dentists. Reptiles – alligators, crocodiles. Teeth.

Everyone poops ill. by author. Kane/Miller, 1993. ISBN 978-0-916291-45-7 Subj: Nature. Toilet training.

The great day ill. by author. Chronicle, 2014. ISBN 978-145211125-4 Subj: Activities – playing. Day.

I know numbers! ill. by author. Chronicle, 2017. ISBN 978-145215918-8 Subj: Counting, numbers.

I lost my dad ill. by author. Kane/Miller, 2001. ISBN 978-1-929132-04-1 Subj: Behavior – lost. Family life – fathers. Stores.

Over the ocean ill. by author. Chronicle, 2016. ISBN 978-145214515-0 Subj: Imagination.

Spring is here ill. by author. Chronicle, 1989. ISBN 978-0-87701-626-7 Subj: Animals – bulls, cows. Seasons.

Gonyea, Mark. *A book about color* ill. by author. Henry Holt, 2010. ISBN 978-0-8050-9055-0 Subj: Concepts – color.

The spooky box ill. by author. Henry Holt, 2013. ISBN 978-0-8050-8813-7 Subj: Character traits – questioning. Emotions – fear. Format, unusual – toy & movable books.

Gonzales, Mark. *Yo soy Muslim* ill. by Mehrdokht Amini. Simon & Schuster/Salaam Reads, 2017. ISBN 978-148148936-2 Subj: Family life – fathers. Foreign lands – Mexico. Religion – Islam. Self-concept.

Gonzalez, Lucia. *The storyteller's candle / La velita de los cuentos* ill. by Lulu Delacre. Children's Book Press, 2008. ISBN 978-0-89239-222-3 Subj: Activities – storytelling. Careers – librarians. Ethnic groups in the U.S. – Puerto Rican Americans. Foreign languages. Libraries.

Good, Jason. *Must. push. buttons!* ill. by Jarrett J. Krosoczka. Bloomsbury, 2015. ISBN 978-161963095-6 Subj: Babies, toddlers. Behavior.

Good, Merle, et al. *Dan's pants* ill. by Cheryl Benner. Good Books, 2000. ISBN 978-1-56148-307-5 Subj: Clothing – pants. Rhyming text.

Good morning ill. by Summer Durantz. Simon & Schuster, 2002. ISBN 978-0-689-85099-8 Subj: Format, unusual – board books. Morning.

Goodall, Jane. *The eagle and the wren* ill. by Alexander Reichstein. NorthSouth, 2000. ISBN 978-0-7358-1380-9 Subj: Birds. Character traits – cooperation. Folk & fairy tales.

Goodall, John S. *Creepy castle* ill. by author. Rev. jacket ed. Margaret K. McElderry, 1998. ISBN 978-0-689-82205-6 Subj: Animals – mice. Format, unusual. Knights. Monsters. Wordless.

Shrewbettina's birthday ill. by author. Rev. jacket ed. Margaret K. McElderry, 1998. ISBN 978-0-689-82206-3 Subj: Animals – shrews. Birthdays. Format, unusual. Wordless.

Goode, Diane. *Diane Goode's book of silly stories and songs* ill. by author. Dutton, 1992. ISBN 978-0-525-44967-6 Subj: Folk & fairy tales. Humorous stories. Music. Songs.

The dinosaur's new clothes (Andersen, Hans Christian)

Mama's perfect present ill. by author. Dutton, 1996. ISBN 978-0-525-45493-9 Subj: Animals – dogs. Birthdays. Family life – brothers & sisters. Family life – mothers. Foreign lands – France.

The most perfect spot ill. by author. HarperCollins, 2006. ISBN 978-0-06-072697-3 Subj: Activities – picnicking. Animals – dogs. Family life – mothers.

Tiger trouble ill. by author. Blue Sky, 2001. ISBN 978-0-439-20866-6 Subj: Animals – dogs. Animals – tigers. Cities, towns. Crime. Homes, houses.

Goodhart, Pippa. *Arthur's tractor: a fairy tale with mechanical parts* ill. by Colin Paine. Bloomsbury, 2003. ISBN 978-1-58234-847-6 Subj: Careers – farmers. Dragons. Humorous stories. Royalty – princesses. Tractors.

Little Nelly's big book ill. by Andy Rowland. Bloomsbury, 2012. ISBN 978-1-59990-779-6 Subj: Animals – elephants. Animals – mice. Books, reading. Concepts – size. Self-concept.

My very own space ill. by Rebecca Crane. Flying Eye, 2017. ISBN 978-191117112-6 Subj: Animals – rabbits. Behavior – sharing. Behavior – solitude. Rhyming text.

Noah makes a boat ill. by Bernard Lodge. Houghton, 1997. ISBN 978-0-395-86957-4 Subj: Animals. Boats, ships. Religion – Noah. Weather – floods. Weather – rain. Weather – rainbows.

Pudgy, a puppy to love ill. by Caroline Jayne Church. Scholastic, 2003. ISBN 978-0-439-45699-9 Subj: Animals – babies. Animals – dogs. Behavior – needing someone. Behavior – running away. Friendship.

Three little ghosties ill. by AnnaLaura Cantone. Bloomsbury, 2007. ISBN 978-1-58234-711-0 Subj: Ghosts.

You choose ill. by Nick Sharratt. Kane/Miller, 2012. ISBN 978-1-61067-076-0 Subj: Character traits – individuality. Character traits – questioning. Self-concept.

Goodings, Christina. *Creation story* ill. by Melanie Mitchell. Lion, 2010. ISBN 978-0-7459-6089-0 Subj: Creation. Religion.

Lost sheep story ill. by Melanie Mitchell. Lion, 2010. ISBN 978-0-7459-6087-6 Subj: Animals – sheep. Behavior – lost. Religion.

Goodings, Lennie. *When you grow up* ill. by Jenny Jones. Fogelman, 2001. ISBN 978-0-8037-2677-2 Subj: Animals – bears. Behavior – growing up. Careers. Family life – mothers.

Goodman, Emily. *Plant secrets* ill. by Phyllis Limbacher Tildes. Charlesbridge, 2009. ISBN 978-1-58089-204-9 Subj: Plants.

Goodman, Joan Elizabeth. *Ballet Bunnies* ill. by author. Marshall Cavendish, 2008. ISBN 978-0-7614-5392-5 Subj: Animals – rabbits. Ballet.

Bernard goes to school ill. by Dominic Catalano. Boyds Mills, 2001. ISBN 978-1-56397-958-3 Subj: Animals – elephants. School – first day.

Goodman, Susan E. *Chopsticks for my noodle soup: Eliza's life in Malaysia* photos by Michael Doolittle. Millbrook, 2000. ISBN 978-0-7613-1552-0 Subj: Family life. Foreign lands – Malaysia.

The first step: how one girl put segregation on trial ill. by E. B. Lewis. Bloomsbury, 2016. ISBN 978-080273739-7 Subj: Ethnic groups in the U.S. – African Americans. Prejudice. School. U.S. history.

It's a dog's life ill. by David Slonim. Roaring Brook, 2012. ISBN 978-1-59643-448-6 Subj: Animals – dogs. Senses.

What do you do — at the zoo? ill. by Steve Pica. Millbrook, 2002. ISBN 978-0-7613-2755-4 Subj: Animals. Careers – zookeepers. Zoos.

Goodrich, Carter. *A creature was stirring: one boy's night before Christmas* (Moore, Clement Clarke)

Mister Bud wears the cone ill. by author. Simon & Schuster, 2014. ISBN 978-144248088-9 Subj: Animals – dogs. Behavior – misbehavior.

Say hello to Zorro! ill. by author. Simon & Schuster, 2011. ISBN 978-1-4169-3893-4 Subj: Animals – dogs.

We forgot Brock! ill. by author. Simon & Schuster, 2015. ISBN 978-144248090-2 Subj: Behavior – lost. Friendship. Imagination – imaginary friends.

Zorro gets an outfit ill. by author. Simon & Schuster, 2012. ISBN 978-1-4424-3535-3 Subj: Animals – dogs. Clothing – costumes. Emotions – embarrassment.

Goodwin-Sturges, Judy Sue. *Construction Kitties* ill. by Shari Halpern. Henry Holt, 2013. ISBN 978-0-8050-9105-2 Subj: Animals – cats. Careers – construction workers. Trucks.

Goodwyn, Susan. *My first baby signs* (Acredolo, Linda P.)

Goossens, Philippe. *Knock! knock! knock! who's there?* ill. by author. NorthSouth, 2013. ISBN 978-0-7358-4122-2 Subj: Animals – bears. Emotions – fear. Friendship. Night.

Gorbachev, Valeri. *The best cat* ill. by author. Candlewick, 2010. ISBN 978-0-7636-3675-3 Subj: Animals – cats. Family life – brothers & sisters. Pets.

Big Little Elephant ill. by author. Harcourt, 2005. ISBN 978-0-15-205195-2 Subj: Activities – playing. Animals – elephants. Concepts – size. Emotions – loneliness. Friendship.

Big Little Hippo ill. by author. Sterling, 2017. ISBN 978-145491906-3 Subj: Animals – hippopotamuses. Character traits – smallness. Concepts – size. Insects – beetles.

Cats are cats ill. by author. Holiday House, 2014. ISBN 978-082343052-9 Subj: Animals – cats. Animals – tigers. Pets.

Catty Jane who hated the rain ill. by author. Boyds Mills, 2012. ISBN 978-1-59078-700-7 Subj: Animals – cats. Friendship. Weather – lightning, thunder. Weather – rain.

Catty Jane who loved to dance ill. by author. Boyds Mills, 2013. ISBN 978-1-59078-982-7 Subj: Activities – dancing. Animals – cats. Ballet. Friendship.

Chicken chickens ill. by author. NorthSouth, 2001. ISBN 978-0-7358-1542-1 Subj: Activities – playing. Animals. Birds – chickens, roosters. Character traits – confidence. Parks.

Chicken chickens go to school ill. by author. NorthSouth, 2003. ISBN 978-0-7358-1767-8 Subj: Animals. Birds – chickens, roosters. Character traits – shyness. Friendship. School – first day.

Christopher counting ill. by author. Philomel, 2008. ISBN 978-0-399-24629-6 Subj: Animals – rabbits. Counting, numbers.

Dragon is coming! ill. by author. Harcourt, 2009. ISBN 978-0-15-205196-9 Subj: Animals. Animals – mice. Behavior – gossip, rumors. Cumulative tales. Emotions – fear. Weather – lightning, thunder.

The fool of the world and the flying ship: a Ukrainian folk tale ill. by adapter. Star Bright, 1998. ISBN 978-1-887734-19-6 Subj: Activities – flying. Boats, ships. Character traits – cleverness. Folk & fairy tales. Foreign lands – Ukraine. Royalty – tsars.

Heron and Turtle ill. by author. Penguin, 2006. ISBN 978-0-399-24321-9 Subj: Birds – herons. Friendship. Reptiles – turtles, tortoises.

How to be friends with a dragon ill. by author. Albert Whitman, 2012. ISBN 978-0-8075-3432-8 Subj: Dragons. Etiquette. Family life – brothers & sisters.

Me too! ill. by author. Holiday House, 2013. ISBN 978-0-8234-2744-4 Subj: Animals – bears. Animals – chipmunks. Friendship. Weather – snow.

The missing chick ill. by author. Candlewick, 2009. ISBN 978-0-7636-3676-0 Subj: Behavior – lost. Birds – chickens, roosters. Careers – firefighters. Careers – police officers.

Molly who flew away ill. by author. Philomel, 2009. ISBN 978-0-399-25211-2 Subj: Animals. Animals – mice. Fairs, festivals. Toys – balloons.

Nicky and the big, bad wolves ill. by author. North-South, 1998. ISBN 978-1-55858-918-6 Subj: Animals – rabbits. Animals – wolves. Bedtime. Dreams. Emotions – fear.

Nicky and the fantastic birthday gift ill. by author. NorthSouth, 2000. ISBN 978-0-7358-1379-3 Subj: Animals – rabbits. Birthdays. Family life – mothers.

Nicky and the rainy day ill. by author. NorthSouth, 2002. ISBN 978-0-7358-1645-9 Subj: Animals – rabbits. Family life – brothers & sisters. Weather – rain.

One rainy day ill. by author. Philomel, 2002. ISBN 978-0-399-23628-0 Subj: Animals. Animals – goats. Animals – pigs. Counting, numbers. Weather – rain.

Pizza-pie snowman ill. by author. Holiday House, 2016. ISBN 978-082343654-5 Subj: Animals – pigs. Character traits – completing things. Character traits – responsibility. Food. Snowmen.

Red red red ill. by author. Penguin, 2007. ISBN 978-0-399-24628-9 Subj: Animals. Character traits – curiosity. Concepts – color. Reptiles – turtles, tortoises.

Shhh! ill. by author. Penguin, 2011. ISBN 978-0-399-25429-1 Subj: Family life – brothers. Noise, sounds. Sleep.

That's what friends are for ill. by author. Penguin, 2005. ISBN 978-0-399-23966-3 Subj: Animals – goats. Animals – pigs. Friendship.

Turtle's penguin day ill. by author. Knopf, 2008. ISBN 978-0-375-84374-7 Subj: Birds – penguins. Imagination. Reptiles – turtles, tortoises. School.

What's the big idea, Molly? ill. by author. Penguin, 2010. ISBN 978-0-399-25428-4 Subj: Activities – writing. Animals. Animals – mice. Birthdays. Gifts.

When someone is afraid ill. by Kostya Gorbachev. Star Bright, 2005. ISBN 978-1-932065-99-2 Subj: Dreams. Emotions – fear.

Where is the apple pie? ill. by author. Philomel, 1999. ISBN 978-0-399-23385-2 Subj: Animals. Character traits – questioning. Circular tales. Tall tales.

Whose hat is it? ill. by author. HarperCollins, 2004. ISBN 978-0-06-053435-6 Subj: Animals. Behavior – lost & found possessions. Clothing – hats. Reptiles – turtles, tortoises.

Gordon, David. *Extremely cute animals operating heavy machinery* ill. by author. Simon & Schuster, 2016. ISBN 978-141692441-8 Subj: Activities – playing. Animals. Behavior – bullying, teasing. Machines.

The three little rigs ill. by author. Geringer, 2005. ISBN 978-0-06-058119-0 Subj: Family life – brothers. Machines. Trucks.

The ugly truckling ill. by author. Geringer, 2004. ISBN 978-0-06-054601-4 Subj: Airplanes, airports. Family life – brothers & sisters. Self-concept. Trucks.

Gordon, Domenica More. *Archie* ill. by author. Bloomsbury, 2012. ISBN 978-1-59990-936-3 Subj: Activities – sewing. Animals – dogs. Clothing. Wordless.

Archie's vacation ill. by author. Bloomsbury, 2014. ISBN 978-161963190-8 Subj: Animals – dogs. Behavior – worrying. Wordless.

Gordon, Gus. *Herman and Rosie* ill. by author. Roaring Brook, 2013. ISBN 978-1-59643-856-9 Subj: Animals – deer. Cities, towns. Emotions – loneliness. Friendship. Music. Reptiles – alligators, crocodiles.

Somewhere else ill. by author. Roaring Brook/ Neal Porter, 2017. ISBN 978-162672349-8 Subj: Activities – ballooning. Activities – flying. Activities – traveling. Animals – bears. Birds. Problem solving.

Gordon, Sharon. *Asthma* ill. with photos. Children's Press, 2003. ISBN 978-0-516-22582-1 Subj: Health & fitness. Illness – asthma.

Bruises ill. with photos. Children's Press, 2002. ISBN 978-0-516-22568-5 Subj: Health & fitness. Safety.

Cuts and scrapes ill. with photos. Children's Press, 2002. ISBN 978-0-516-22566-1 Subj: Health & fitness. Safety.

Pinkeye ill. with photos. Children's Press, 2003. ISBN 978-0-516-22583-8 Subj: Anatomy – eyes. Health & fitness. Illness.

Seeing ill. with photos. Children's Press, 2001. ISBN 978-0-516-22291-2 Subj: Anatomy – eyes. Health & fitness. Senses – sight.

Smelling ill. with photos. Children's Press, 2001. ISBN 978-0-516-22292-9 Subj: Anatomy – noses. Health & fitness. Senses – smell.

Gordon, Stephanie Jacob. *Smile, Principessa!* (Enderle, Judith Ross)

Gore, Emily. *And Nick* ill. by author. Atheneum, 2015. ISBN 978-141695506-1 Subj: Animals – mice. Character traits – individuality. Character traits – smallness. Family life – brothers.

Gore, Leonid. *Danny's first snow* ill. by author. Simon & Schuster, 2007. ISBN 978-1-4169-1330-6 Subj: Animals – rabbits. Seasons – winter. Weather – snow.

Mommy, where are you? ill. by author. Atheneum, 2009. ISBN 978-1-4169-5505-4 Subj: Animals – mice. Family life – mothers. Format, unusual – toy & movable books.

When I grow up ill. by author. Scholastic, 2009. ISBN 978-0-545-08597-7 Subj: Behavior – growing up. Family life – fathers.

Who was born this special day? (Bunting, Eve)

The wonderful book ill. by author. Scholastic, 2010. ISBN 978-0-545-08598-4 Subj: Animals. Books, reading. Forest, woods.

Worms for lunch? ill. by author. Scholastic, 2011. ISBN 978-0-545-24338-4 Subj: Animals. Food. Format, unusual.

Gormley, Greg. *Dog in boots* ill. by Roberta Angaramo. Holiday House, 2011. ISBN 978-0-8234-2347-7 Subj: Animals – dogs. Clothing – shoes.

Goss, Gary. *Where does food come from?* (Rotner, Shelley)

Got, Yves. *Sam loves kisses* ill. by author. Chronicle, 2002. ISBN 978-0-8118-3505-3 Subj: Emotions. Format, unusual – board books. Kissing.

Sam's big book of words ill. by author. Chronicle, 2001. ISBN 978-0-8118-3088-1 Subj: Animals – rabbits. Dictionaries. Language.

Sam's little sister ill. by author. Chronicle, 2002. ISBN 978-0-8118-3504-6 Subj: Animals – rabbits. Family life – brothers & sisters. Format, unusual – board books.

Gottesfeld, Jeff. *The tree in the courtyard: looking through Anne Frank's window* ill. by Peter McCarty. Knopf, 2016. ISBN 978-038575397-5 Subj: Behavior – hiding. Foreign lands – Holland. Jewish culture. Trees. War.

Gottfried, Maya. *Good dog* ill. by Robert Rahway Zakanitch. Knopf, 2005. ISBN 978-0-375-93049-2 Subj: Animals – dogs. Pets. Poetry.

Last night I dreamed a circus ill. by Robert Rahway Zakanitch. Random House, 2003. ISBN 978-0-375-92388-3 Subj: Circus. Dreams.

Our farm: by the animals of Farm Sanctuary ill. by Robert Rahway Zakanitch. Random House, 2010. ISBN 978-0-375-86118-5 Subj: Animals. Character traits – kindness to animals. Farms. Poetry.

Goudey, Alice E. *The day we saw the sun come up* ill. by Adrienne Adams. Scribners, 1961. Subj: Caldecott award honor books. Family life. Sun.

Houses from the sea ill. by Adrienne Adams. Scribners, 1959. Subj: Caldecott award honor books. Sea & seashore.

Gourley, Robbin. *Bring me some apples and I'll make you a pie: a story about Edna Lewis* ill. by author. Clarion, 2009. ISBN 978-0-618-15836-2 Subj: Activities – baking, cooking. Ethnic groups in the U.S. – African Americans. Family life. Farms. Food.

First garden: the White House garden and how it grew ill. by author. Clarion, 2011. ISBN 978-0-547-48224-8 Subj: Food. Gardens, gardening. Plants. U.S. history.

Gourounas, Jean. *Something's fishy* ill. by author. Phaidon, 2017. ISBN 978-071487531-6 Subj: Behavior – bad day, bad mood. Birds – penguins. Sports – fishing.

Gow, Nancy. *Ten big toes and a prince's nose.* Sterling, 2010. ISBN 978-1-4027-6396-0 Subj: Anatomy – feet. Anatomy – noses. Rhyming text. Royalty – princes. Royalty – princesses. Self-concept.

Gower, Catherine. *Long-Long's new year: a story about the Chinese spring festival* ill. by He Zhihong. Periplus/Tuttle, 2005. ISBN 978-0-8048-3666-1 Subj: Family life – grandfathers. Holidays – Chinese New Year.

Graber, Janet. *Jacob and the polar bears* ill. by Sandra Salzillo-Shields. Moon Mt, 2002. ISBN 978-1-931659-00-0 Subj: Animals – polar bears. Clothing – pajamas. Humorous stories. Night.

Grabill, Rebecca. *Halloween good night* ill. by Ella Okstad. Simon & Schuster, 2017. ISBN 978-148145061-4 Subj: Counting, numbers. Holidays – Halloween. Monsters. Rhyming text.

Grady, Cynthia. *I lay my stitches down: poems of American slavery* ill. by Michele Wood. Eerdmans, 2012. ISBN 978-0-8028-5386-8 Subj: Character traits – freedom. Ethnic groups in the U.S. – African Americans. Poetry. Slavery. U.S. history.

Graegin, Stephanie. *Little fox in the forest* ill. by author. Random House, 2017. ISBN 978-055353789-5 Subj: Animals – foxes. Behavior – sharing. Character traits – generosity. Toys. Wordless.

Graff, Lisa. *It is not time for sleeping* ill. by Lauren Castillo. Clarion, 2016. ISBN 978-054431930-1 Subj: Bedtime. Family life.

Graham, Bob. *April and Esme, tooth fairies* ill. by author. Candlewick, 2010. ISBN 978-0-7636-4683-7 Subj: Fairies. Family life – sisters. Teeth.

A bus called Heaven ill. by author. Candlewick, 2012. ISBN 978-0-7636-5893-9 Subj: Buses. Character traits – cooperation. Communities, neighborhoods.

Dimity Dumpty: the story of Humpty's little sister ill. by author. Candlewick, 2007. ISBN 978-0-7636-3078-2 Subj: Character traits – shyness. Circus. Eggs. Family life – brothers & sisters.

How the sun got to Coco's house ill. by author. Candlewick, 2015. ISBN 978-076368109-8 Subj: Day. Sun. World.

How to heal a broken wing ill. by author. Candlewick, 2008. ISBN 978-0-7636-3903-7 Subj: Birds. Character traits – kindness to animals.

Jethro Byrd, fairy child ill. by author. Candlewick, 2002. ISBN 978-0-7636-1772-1 Subj: Activities – picnicking. Fairies.

"Let's get a pup!" said Kate ill. by author. Candlewick, 2001. ISBN 978-0-7636-1452-2 Subj: Animals – dogs. Family life. Pets.

Max ill. by author. Candlewick, 2000. ISBN 978-0-7636-1138-5 Subj: Activities – flying. Imagination. Mythical creatures.

Oscar's half birthday ill. by author. Candlewick, 2005. ISBN 978-0-7636-2699-0 Subj: Activities – picnicking. Birthdays. Ethnic groups in the U.S. Family life.

The silver button ill. by author. Candlewick, 2013. ISBN 978-0-7636-6437-4 Subj: Activities – walking. Babies, toddlers. Cities, towns.

"The trouble with dogs," said Dad ill. by author. Candlewick, 2007. ISBN 978-0-7636-3316-5 Subj: Animals – dogs. Pets.

Graham, Elspeth. *Cloud tea monkeys* (Peet, Mal)

Graham, Joan Bransfield. *Flicker flash* ill. by Nancy Davis. Houghton, 1999. ISBN 978-0-395-90501-2 Subj: Light, lights. Poetry.

The poem that will not end ill. by Kyrsten Brooker. Amazon/Two Lions, 2014. ISBN 978-147784715-2 Subj: Activities – writing. Poetry. Rhyming text.

Splish splash ill. by Steven Scott. Houghton, 1994. ISBN 978-0-395-70128-7 Subj: Poetry. Water.

Graham, Tom. *Five little firefighters* ill. by author. Henry Holt, 2008. ISBN 978-0-8050-8697-3 Subj: Careers – firefighters. Character traits – helpfulness.

Graham-Barber, Lynda. *Spy hops and belly flops* ill. by Brian Lies. Houghton, 2004. ISBN 978-0-618-22291-9 Subj: Animals. Behavior. Forest, woods. Rhyming text.

Graham-Yooll, Liz. *Timothy Tib* ill. by author. Ragged Bears, 2001. ISBN 978-1-929927-25-8 Subj: Animals – cats. Rhyming text.

Grahame, Kenneth. *The reluctant dragon* abridged by Inga Moore; ill. by abridger. Candlewick, 2004. ISBN 978-0-7636-2199-5 Subj: Dragons. Knights. Poetry.

The wind in the willows retold by Janet Allison Brown; ill. by Joanne Moss. Viking, 2001. ISBN 978-0-670-89914-2 Subj: Animals. Animals – badgers. Animals – moles. Animals – rats. Foreign lands – England. Frogs & toads.

A wind in the willows Christmas ill. by Michael Hague. SeaStar, 2000. ISBN 978-1-58717-007-2 Subj: Animals. Animals – moles. Animals – rats. Holidays – Christmas. Homes, houses.

Gralley, Jean. *Very boring alligator* ill. by author. Henry Holt, 2001. ISBN 978-0-8050-6328-8 Subj: Reptiles – alligators, crocodiles. Rhyming text.

Gramatky, Hardie. *Little Toot* ill. by author. Putnam, 1939. Subj: Boats, ships. Character traits – ambition.

Grambling, Lois G. *Big Dog* ill. by Andrew L. San Diego. Marshall Cavendish, 2001. ISBN 978-0-7614-5045-0 Subj: Animals – dogs. Dinosaurs. Pets.

Can I bring Woolly to the library, Ms. Reeder? ill. by Judy Love. Charlesbridge, 2012. ISBN 978-1-58089-281-0 Subj: Animals – woolly mammoths. Careers – librarians. Libraries. Problem solving.

Grandma tells a story ill. by Fred Willingham. Whispering Coyote, 2001. ISBN 978-1-58089-057-1 Subj: Babies, toddlers. Birth. Family life – grandparents.

Here comes T. Rex Cottontail ill. by Jack E. Davis. HarperCollins, 2007. ISBN 978-0-06-053129-4 Subj: Animals – rabbits. Character traits – helpfulness. Dinosaurs. Eggs. Holidays – Easter.

Miss Hildy's missing cape caper ill. by Bridget Starr Taylor. Random House, 2000. ISBN 978-0-375-90196-6 Subj: Birds – flamingos. Holidays – Halloween. Mystery stories.

My mom is a firefighter ill. by Jane Manning. HarperCollins, 2007. ISBN 978-0-06-058640-9 Subj: Careers – firefighters. Family life – mothers.

T. Rex and the Mother's Day hug ill. by Jack E. Davis. HarperCollins, 2008. ISBN 978-0-06-053126-3 Subj: Dinosaurs. Holidays – Mother's Day. Hugging.

T. Rex trick-or-treats ill. by Jack E. Davis. HarperCollins, 2005. ISBN 978-0-06-050253-9 Subj: Dinosaurs. Holidays – Halloween.

This whole Tooth Fairy thing's nothing but a big rip-off! ill. by Thomas Payne. Marshall Cavendish,

2002. ISBN 978-0-7614-5104-4 Subj: Animals. Animals – hippopotamuses. Fairies. Teeth.

The witch who wanted to be a princess ill. by Judy Love. Whispering Coyote, 2002. ISBN 978-1-58089-062-5 Subj: Character traits – honesty. Folk & fairy tales. Royalty – princesses. Self-concept. Witches.

Gran, Julia. *Big bug surprise* ill. by author. Scholastic, 2007. ISBN 978-0-439-67609-0 Subj: Insects. Insects – bees. School.

Grandits, John. *Seven rules you absolutely must not break if you want to survive the cafeteria* ill. by Michael Austin. Clarion, 2017. ISBN 978-054469951-9 Subj: Insects. School.

Ten rules you absolutely must not break if you want to survive the school bus ill. by Michael Austin. Clarion, 2011. ISBN 978-0-618-78822-4 Subj: Buses. Emotions – fear. Family life – brothers. School – first day.

GrandPre, Mary. *Cleonardo, the little inventor* ill. by author. Scholastic/Arthur A. Levine, 2016. ISBN 978-043935764-7 Subj: Careers – inventors. Children as inventors. Contests. Family life – fathers. Gender roles. Inventions.

Granfield, Linda. *The legend of the panda* ill. by Song Nan Zhang. Tundra, 1998. ISBN 978-0-88776-421-9 Subj: Animals – pandas. Folk & fairy tales. Foreign lands – China.

What am I? ill. by Jennifer Herbert. Tundra, 2007. ISBN 978-0-88776-812-5 Subj: Riddles & jokes.

Graniczewski, Wojciech. *Found alphabet* (Shindler, Ramon)

Granowsky, Alvin. *At the park*. Ill. with photos & ill. Copper Beech, 2001. ISBN 978-0-7613-2167-5 Subj: Animals – dogs. Family life – fathers. Family life – sons. Parks. Pets.

Can I help? ill. by author. Copper Beech, 2001. ISBN 978-0-7613-2172-9 Subj: Activities – picnicking. Character traits – helpfulness. Parties.

Diggers and cranes ill. by author. Copper Beech, 2000. ISBN 978-0-7613-1222-2 Subj: Machines.

Dinosaurs ill. by author. Copper Beech, 2000. ISBN 978-0-7613-1217-8 Subj: Dinosaurs.

Granström, Brita. *Snap!* (Manning, Mick)

Woolly mammoth (Manning, Mick)

Grant, Brianna K. *We are girls who love to run / Somos chicas y a nosotras nos encanta correr* ill. by Nicholas A. Wright. Balanced Steps, 2008. ISBN 978-0-9798511-1-7 Subj: Activities – running. Foreign languages. Gender roles. Self-concept.

Grant, Holly. *Wee Sister Strange* ill. by K. G. Campbell. Random House, 2017. ISBN 978-055350879-6 Subj: Bedtime. Character traits – smallness. Forest, woods. Night. Rhyming text.

Grant, Jacob. *Cat knit* ill. by author. Feiwel & Friends, 2016. ISBN 978-125005150-9 Subj: Activities – knitting. Animals – cats. Emotions – envy, jealousy. Friendship.

Little Bird's bad word ill. by author. Feiwel & Friends, 2015. ISBN 978-125005149-3 Subj: Behavior – misbehavior. Birds. Family life – fathers. Language.

Through with the zoo ill. by author. Feiwel & Friends, 2017. ISBN 978-125010814-2 Subj: Animals – goats. Behavior – running away. Senses – touch. Zoos.

Grant, Joan. *Cat and Fish* ill. by Neil Curtis. Simply Read, 2005. ISBN 978-1-894965-14-9 Subj: Animals – cats. Fish. Friendship.

Grant, Rose Marie. *Andiamo, Weasel* ill. by Jon Goodell. Knopf, 2002. ISBN 978-0-375-90607-7 Subj: Animals – weasels. Animals – wolves. Birds – crows. Character traits – confidence. Foreign lands – Italy. Self-concept.

Grassby, Donna. *A seaside alphabet* ill. by Susan Tooke. Tundra, 2000. ISBN 978-0-88776-516-2 Subj: Foreign lands – Canada. Sea & seashore.

Gravdahl, John. *Curious catwalk* ill. by author. Propeller, 2003. ISBN 978-0-9678577-8-7 Subj: Animals – cats. Character traits – curiosity. Rhyming text.

Gravel, Elise. *The cranky ballerina* ill. by author. HarperCollins/Katherine Tegen, 2016. ISBN 978-006235124-1 Subj: Ballet. Behavior – bad day, bad mood. Careers – dancers.

I want a monster! ill. by author. HarperCollins/Katherine Tegen, 2016. ISBN 978-006241533-2 Subj: Monsters. Pets.

Graves, Keith. *Chicken Big* ill. by author. Chronicle, 2010. ISBN 978-0-8118-7237-9 Subj: Birds – chickens, roosters. Character traits – being different. Concepts – size.

Loretta, ace Pinky Scout ill. by author. Scholastic, 2002. ISBN 978-0-439-36831-5 Subj: Self-concept.

The monsterator ill. by author. Roaring Brook, 2014. ISBN 978-159643855-2 Subj: Format, unusual – toy & movable books. Holidays – Halloween. Monsters. Rhyming text.

Pet boy ill. by author. Chronicle, 2000. ISBN 978-0-8118-2672-3 Subj: Behavior – boredom. Character traits – responsibility. Pets. Rhyming text.

Second banana ill. by author. Roaring Brook, 2015. ISBN 978-159643883-5 Subj: Animals – gorillas. Animals – monkeys. Circus.

Uncle Blubbafink's seriously ridiculous stories ill. by author. Scholastic, 2001. ISBN 978-0-439-24083-3 Subj: Tall tales.

The unexpectedly bad hair of Barcelona Smith ill. by author. Penguin, 2006. ISBN 978-0-399-24273-1 Subj: Behavior – worrying. Hair.

Gravett, Emily. *Again!* ill. by author. Simon & Schuster, 2013. ISBN 978-1-4424-5231-2 Subj: Bedtime. Books, reading. Dragons.

Bear and Hare: share! ill. by author. Simon & Schuster, 2016. ISBN 978-148146217-4 Subj: Animals – bears. Animals – rabbits. Behavior – sharing. Character traits – selfishness. Friendship.

Bear and Hare: snow! ill. by author. Simon & Schuster, 2015. ISBN 978-148144514-6 Subj: Animals – bears. Animals – rabbits. Friendship. Weather – snow.

Bear and Hare go fishing ill. by author. Simon & Schuster, 2015. ISBN 978-148142289-5 Subj: Animals – bears. Animals – rabbits. Friendship. Sports – fishing.

Bear and Hare—where's Bear? ill. by author. Simon & Schuster, 2016. ISBN 978-148145615-9 Subj: Animals – bears. Animals – rabbits. Behavior – hiding. Counting, numbers. Friendship.

Blue chameleon ill. by author. Simon & Schuster, 2011. ISBN 978-1-4424-1958-2 Subj: Concepts – color. Concepts – shape. Reptiles – chameleons.

Dogs ill. by author. Simon & Schuster, 2010. ISBN 978-1-4169-8703-1 Subj: Animals – dogs.

Little Mouse's big book of beasts ill. by author. Simon & Schuster, 2016. ISBN 978-148143929-9 Subj: Animals. Animals – mice. Character traits – cleverness. Emotions – fear. Format, unusual – toy & movable books.

Little Mouse's big book of fears ill. by author. Simon & Schuster, 2008. ISBN 978-141695930-4 Subj: Animals – mice. Emotions – fear. Format, unusual – toy & movable books.

Matilda's cat ill. by author. Simon & Schuster, 2014. ISBN 978-144247527-4 Subj: Animals – cats. Pets.

Meerkat mail ill. by author. Simon & Schuster, 2007. ISBN 978-1-416-93473-8 Subj: Activities – traveling. Animals – meerkats. Foreign lands – Africa. Format, unusual – toy & movable books. Letters, cards.

Monkey and me ill. by author. Simon & Schuster, 2008. ISBN 978-1-4169-5457-6 Subj: Activities – playing. Animals. Animals – monkeys. Rhyming text. Toys.

The odd egg ill. by author. Simon & Schuster, 2009. ISBN 978-1-4169-6872-6 Subj: Birds – ducks. Eggs. Reptiles – alligators, crocodiles.

Orange pear apple bear ill. by author. Simon & Schuster, 2007. ISBN 978-1-4169-3999-3 Subj: Animals – bears. Concepts – color. Concepts – shape.

The rabbit problem ill. by author. Simon & Schuster, 2010. ISBN 978-1-4424-1255-2 Subj: Animals – rabbits. Counting, numbers. Days of the week, months of the year. Format, unusual – toy & movable books.

Spells ill. by author. Simon & Schuster, 2009. ISBN 978-1-4169-8270-8 Subj: Books, reading. Format, unusual. Frogs & toads. Imagination. Magic.

Tidy ill. by author. Simon & Schuster, 2017. ISBN 978-148148019-2 Subj: Animals – badgers. Character traits – cleanliness. Character traits – orderliness. Rhyming text.

Wolf won't bite! ill. by author. Simon & Schuster, 2012. ISBN 978-1-4424-2763-1 Subj: Animals – pigs. Animals – wolves. Circus.

Wolves ill. by author. Simon & Schuster, 2006. ISBN 978-1-4169-1491-4 Subj: Animals – rabbits. Animals – wolves. Humorous stories.

Gray, Karlin. *Nadia: the girl who couldn't sit still* ill. by Christine Davenier. Houghton Mifflin Harcourt, 2016. ISBN 978-054431960-8 Subj: Character traits – persistence. Foreign lands – Romania. Sports – gymnastics. Sports – Olympics.

Gray, Kes. *Eat your peas* ill. by Nick Sharratt. DK, 2000. ISBN 978-0-7894-2667-3 Subj: Character traits – persistence. Family life – daughters. Family life – mothers. Food.

Frog on a log? ill. by Jim Field. Scholastic, 2015. ISBN 978-054568791-1 Subj: Animals – cats. Frogs & toads. Rhyming text.

The "Get well soon" book ill. by Mary McQuillan. Millbrook, 2000. ISBN 978-0-7613-1922-1 Subj: Animals. Illness.

006 and a half ill. by Nick Sharratt. Abrams, 2007. ISBN 978-0-8109-1719-4 Subj: Behavior – secrets. Family life – daughters. Family life – mothers.

Gray, Luli. *Ant and Grasshopper* ill. by Giuliano Ferri. Simon & Schuster, 2011. ISBN 978-1-4169-5140-7 Subj: Activities – singing. Activities – working. Folk & fairy tales. Friendship. Insects – ants. Insects – grasshoppers. Seasons.

Gray, Nigel. *Time to play!* ill. by Bob Graham. Candlewick, 2008. ISBN 978-0-7636-4013-2 Subj: Activities – playing. Family life. Format, unusual – toy & movable books. Imagination.

Gray, Rita. *Have you heard the nesting bird?* ill. by Kenard Pak. Houghton, 2014. ISBN 978-054410580-5 Subj: Birds. Nature. Rhyming text.

Nonna's porch ill. by Terry Widener. Hyperion, 2004. ISBN 978-0-7868-1613-2 Subj: Country. Family life – grandmothers.

The wild little horse ill. by Ashley Wolff. Penguin, 2005. ISBN 978-0-525-47455-5 Subj: Animals – horses, ponies. Rhyming text.

Gray, Samantha. *Birds* by Samantha Gray and Sarah Walker ill. with photos. DK, 2002. ISBN 978-0-7894-8550-2 Subj: Birds.

Gray Smith, Monique. *My heart fills with happiness* ill. by Julie Flett. Orca, 2016. ISBN 978-145980957-4 Subj: Emotions – happiness. Format, unusual – board books.

Greathouse, Carol. *The dinosaur tamer* ill. by John Shroades. Dutton, 2009. ISBN 978-0-525-47866-9 Subj: Cowboys, cowgirls. Dinosaurs. Tall tales.

Gréban, Quentin. *Nestor* ill. by author. Mondo, 2001. ISBN 978-1-58653-855-2 Subj: Animals – babies. Animals – elephants. Animals – monkeys. Sports – fishing.

Green, Adolph. *What's new at the zoo?* (Comden, Betty)

Green, Alison. *The fox in the dark* ill. by Deborah Allwright. Tiger Tales, 2010. ISBN 978-1-58925-091-8 Subj: Animals. Emotions – fear.

Green, Dan. *Wild alphabet: an A to Zoo pop-up book* ill. by Mike Haines. Kingfisher, 2010. ISBN 978-0-7534-6472-4 Subj: ABC books. Animals. Format, unusual – toy & movable books.

Green, Emily K. *Bumblebees* ill. with photos. Scholastic, 2006. ISBN 978-0-531-17859-1 Subj: Insects – bees.

Crickets ill. with photos. Scholastic, 2006. ISBN 978-0-531-17861-4 Subj: Insects – crickets.

Grasshoppers ill. with photos. Scholastic, 2006. ISBN 978-0-531-17864-5 Subj: Insects – grasshoppers.

Walkingsticks ill. with photos. Scholastic, 2006. ISBN 978-0-531-17865-2 Subj: Insects.

Green, Jen. *Birds* ill. with photos. Copper Beech, 2000. ISBN 978-0-7613-1216-1 Subj: Birds.

Our new baby ill. by Christopher O'Neill. Copper Beech, 1998. ISBN 978-0-7613-0871-3 Subj: Babies, toddlers. Family life – brothers & sisters.

Reptiles ill. with photos. Copper Beech, 2000. ISBN 978-0-7613-1214-7 Subj: Reptiles.

Green, John Patrick. *Hippopotamister* ill. by author. First Second, 2016. ISBN 978-162672200-2 Subj: Animals – hippopotamuses. Animals – red pandas. Careers. Format, unusual – graphic novels. Zoos.

Green, Mim. *Time for a hug* (Gershator, Phillis)

Who's awake in springtime? (Gershator, Phillis)

Green, Rod. *Giant vehicles* ill. by Stephen Biesty. Candlewick/Templar, 2014. ISBN 978-076367404-5 Subj: Airplanes, airports. Format, unusual – toy & movable books. Machines. Space & space ships. Trucks.

Green, Stephanie. *Betsy Ross and the silver thimble* ill. by Diana Magnuson. Aladdin, 2002. ISBN 978-0-689-84967-1 Subj: Activities – sewing. Careers – tailors. Flags. U.S. history.

Not just another moose ill. by Andrea Wallace. Marshall Cavendish, 2000. ISBN 978-0-7614-5061-0 Subj: Animals – moose. Humorous stories. Self-concept.

Greenawalt, Kelly. *Princess Truly in I am Truly* ill. by Amariah Rauscher. Orchard, 2017. ISBN 978-133816720-7 Subj: Character traits – assertiveness. Character traits – cleverness. Character traits – confidence. Ethnic groups in the U.S. – African Americans. Rhyming text. Royalty – princesses. Self-concept.

Greenaway, Theresa. *Centipedes and millipedes* ill. by Dick Twinney and Stefan Chabluk; photos by Chris Fairclough. Raintree, 2000. ISBN 978-0-7398-1829-9 Subj: Crustaceans – centipedes, millipedes. Pets.

Greenberg, David. *Crocs!* ill. by Lynn Munsinger. Little, Brown, 2008. ISBN 978-0-316-07306-6 Subj: Humorous stories. Reptiles – alligators, crocodiles. Rhyming text.

Don't forget your etiquette! the essential guide to misbehavior ill. by Nadine Bernard Westcott. Farrar, 2006. ISBN 978-0-374-34990-5 Subj: Etiquette. Poetry.

Skunks ill. by Lynn Munsinger. Little, 2001. ISBN 978-0-316-32606-3 Subj: Animals – skunks. Rhyming text.

Greenberg, Jan. *Ballet for Martha: making Appalachian Spring* by Jan Greenberg and Sandra Jordan ill. by Brian Floca. Roaring Brook, 2010. ISBN 978-1-59643-338-0 Subj: Activities – dancing. Ballet. Music.

Greenberg, Melanie Hope. *Mermaids on parade* ill. by author. Putnam, 2008. ISBN 978-0-399-24708-8 Subj: Parades. Sea & seashore – beaches. Seasons – summer.

Greene, Carol. *Where is that cat?* ill. by Loretta Krupinski. Hyperion, 1999. ISBN 978-0-7868-2399-4 Subj: Animals – cats. Behavior – hiding.

Greene, Rhonda Gowler. *At grandma's* ill. by Karla Firehammer. Henry Holt, 2003. ISBN 978-0-8050-6336-3 Subj: Family life – grandmothers. Rhyming text. Sleepovers.

Barnyard song ill. by Robert Bender. Atheneum, 1997. ISBN 978-0-689-80758-9 Subj: Animals. Farms. Illness. Noise, sounds. Rhyming text.

The beautiful world that God made ill. by Anne Wilson. Eerdmans, 2002. ISBN 978-0-8028-5213-7 Subj: Creation. Earth.

Daddy is a cozy hug ill. by Maggie Smith. Walker, 2010. ISBN 978-0-8027-9728-5 Subj: Family life – fathers. Rhyming text. Seasons.

Eek! creak! snicker, sneak ill. by Joseph A. Smith. Atheneum, 2002. ISBN 978-0-689-83047-1 Subj: Behavior – trickery. Emotions – fear. Monsters. Rhyming text.

Firebears: the rescue team ill. by Dan Andreasen. Henry Holt, 2005. ISBN 978-0-8050-7010-1 Subj: Animals – bears. Careers – firefighters.

Jamboree day ill. by Jason Wolff. Orchard, 2001. ISBN 978-0-439-29310-5 Subj: Animals. Jungle. Parties. Rhyming text.

Mommy is a soft, warm kiss ill. by Maggie Smith. Walker, 2010. ISBN 978-0-8027-9729-2 Subj: Family life – mothers. Rhyming text. Seasons.

No pirates allowed! said Library Lou ill. by Brian Ajhar. Sleeping Bear, 2013. ISBN 978-1-58536-796-2 Subj: Books, reading. Careers – librarians. Libraries. Pirates. Rhyming text.

Noah and the mighty ark ill. by Santiago Cohen. Zondervan, 2007. ISBN 978-0-310-71097-4 Subj: Animals. Boats, ships. Religion – Noah.

Push! dig! scoop! a construction counting rhyme ill. by Daniel Kirk. Bloomsbury, 2016. ISBN 978-080273506-5 Subj: Careers – construction workers. Counting, numbers. Rhyming text. Trucks.

The stable where Jesus was born ill. by Susan Gaber. Atheneum, 1999. ISBN 978-0-689-81258-3 Subj: Holidays – Christmas. Religion – Nativity. Rhyming text.

The very first Thanksgiving Day ill. by Susan Gaber. Atheneum, 2002. ISBN 978-0-689-83301-4 Subj: Holidays – Thanksgiving. Pilgrims. Rhyming text. U.S. history.

Greene, Sheppard M. *We all sing with the same voice* (Miller, J. Philip)

Greenfield, Eloise. *Angels* ill. by Jan Spivey Gilchrist. Jump at the Sun, 1998. ISBN 978-0-7868-0442-9 Subj: Angels. Ethnic groups in the U.S. – African Americans. Poetry.

Big friend, little friend ill. by Jan Spivey Gilchrist. Black Butterfly, 1991. ISBN 978-0-86316-204-6 Subj: Activities – playing. Ethnic groups in the U.S. – African Americans. Format, unusual – board books. Friendship. Poetry.

Brothers and sisters: family poems ill. by Jan Spivey Gilchrist. HarperCollins, 2009. ISBN 978-0-06-056284-7 Subj: Ethnic groups in the U.S. – African Americans. Family life – brothers & sisters. Poetry.

Daydreamers ill. by Tom Feelings. Dial, 1981. ISBN 978-0-8037-2134-0 Subj: Ethnic groups in the U.S. – African Americans. Poetry.

Easter parade ill. by Jan Spivey Gilchrist. Hyperion, 1997. ISBN 978-0-7868-0326-2 Subj: Ethnic groups in the U.S. – African Americans. Family life – cousins. Holidays – Easter. Parades. U.S. history. War.

First pink light ill. by Moneta Barnett. Crowell, 1976. ISBN 978-0-690-01087-9 Subj: Ethnic groups in the U.S. – African Americans. Family life – fathers.

The friendly four ill. by Jan Spivey Gilchrist. HarperCollins, 2006. ISBN 978-0-06-000760-7 Subj: Activities – playing. Imagination. Poetry.

Grandpa's face ill. by Floyd Cooper. Putnam, 1988. ISBN 978-0-399-21525-4 Subj: Character traits – appearance. Family life – grandfathers.

I can draw a weeposaur and other dinosaurs ill. by Jan Spivey Gilchrist. Greenwillow, 2001. ISBN 978-0-688-17635-8 Subj: Dinosaurs. Imagination. Mythical creatures. Poetry.

I make music ill. by Jan Spivey Gilchrist. Black Butterfly, 1991. ISBN 978-0-86316-205-3 Subj: Ethnic groups in the U.S. – African Americans. Family life. Format, unusual – board books. Music. Poetry.

In the land of words ill. by Jan Spivey Gilchrist. HarperCollins, 2004. ISBN 978-0-06-028994-2 Subj: Poetry.

Me and Neesie ill. by Jan Spivey Gilchrist. HarperCollins, 2005. ISBN 978-0-06-000702-7 Subj: Ethnic groups in the U.S. – African Americans. Family life. Imagination – imaginary friends. School – first day.

My doll, Keshia ill. by Jan Spivey Gilchrist. Black Butterfly, 1991. ISBN 978-0-86316-203-9 Subj: Activities – playing. Ethnic groups in the U.S. – African Americans. Format, unusual – board books. Poetry. Toys – dolls.

Nathaniel talking ill. by Jan Spivey Gilchrist. Black Butterfly, 1988. ISBN 978-0-86316-200-8 Subj: Ethnic groups in the U.S. – African Americans. Poetry.

Night on Neighborhood Street ill. by Jan Spivey Gilchrist. Dial, 1991. ISBN 978-0-8037-0778-8 Subj:

Cities, towns. Communities, neighborhoods. Ethnic groups in the U.S. – African Americans. Night. Poetry.

Water, water ill. by Jan Spivey Gilchrist. HarperCollins, 1999. ISBN 978-0-694-01247-3 Subj: Ethnic groups in the U.S. – African Americans. Rhyming text. Water.

Greenfield, Howard. *Waking up is hard to do* (Sedaka, Neil)

Greenfield, Monica. *Waiting for Christmas* ill. by Jan Spivey Gilchrist. Scholastic, 1996. ISBN 978-0-590-52700-2 Subj: Ethnic groups in the U.S. – African Americans. Family life. Holidays – Christmas.

Greenstein, Elaine. *As big as you* ill. by author. Knopf, 2002. ISBN 978-0-375-91353-2 Subj: Babies, toddlers. Behavior – growing up. Family life – mothers. Seasons.

Dreaming: a countdown to sleep ill. by author. Scholastic, 2000. ISBN 978-0-439-06302-9 Subj: Bedtime. Counting, numbers.

The goose man: the story of Konrad Lorenz ill. by author. Clarion, 2010. ISBN 978-0-547-08459-6 Subj: Birds – geese. Careers – scientists. Foreign lands – Austria. Science.

Greenwood, Mark. *Drummer boy of John John* ill. by Frané Lessac. Lee & Low, 2012. ISBN 978-1-60060-652-6 Subj: Fairs, festivals. Foreign lands – Trinidad. Musical instruments – drums.

The Mayflower ill. by Frané Lessac. Holiday House, 2014. ISBN 978-082342943-1 Subj: Boats, ships. Pilgrims. U.S. history.

Greenwood, Rosie. *I wonder why volcanoes blow their tops* ill. by author. Kingfisher, 2004. ISBN 978-0-7534-5751-1 Subj: Science. Volcanoes.

Gregorowski, Christopher. *Fly, eagle, fly! an African fable* ill. by Niki Daly. Margaret K. McElderry, 2000. ISBN 978-0-689-82398-5 Subj: Activities – flying. Birds – eagles. Folk & fairy tales. Foreign lands – Africa. Self-concept.

Gregory, Nan. *Amber waiting* ill. by Kady MacDonald Denton. Red Deer, 2003. ISBN 978-0-88995-258-4 Subj: Behavior – promptness, tardiness. School. Time.

How Smudge came ill. by Ron Lightburn. Walker, 1997. ISBN 978-0-88995-143-3 Subj: Animals – dogs. Character traits – loyalty. Disabilities – Down syndrome. Pets.

Pink ill. by author. Groundwood, 2007. ISBN 978-0-88899-781-4 Subj: Behavior – greed. Concepts – color. Family life.

Wild Girl and Gran ill. by Ron Lightburn. Red Deer, 2000. ISBN 978-0-88995-221-8 Subj: Death.

Emotions – grief. Family life – grandmothers. Foreign lands – Canada. Friendship. Imagination.

Gretz, Susanna. *Rabbit food* ill. by author. Candlewick, 1999. ISBN 978-0-7636-0731-9 Subj: Animals – rabbits. Family life – aunts, uncles. Food.

Riley and Rose in the picture ill. by author. Candlewick, 2005. ISBN 978-0-7636-2681-5 Subj: Activities – drawing. Animals – cats. Animals – dogs. Behavior – fighting, arguing. Friendship.

Teddy bears cure a cold by Susanna Gretz and Alison Sage; ill. by Susanna Gretz. Four Winds, 1985. ISBN 978-0-590-07949-5 Subj: Illness. Toys – bears.

Grey, Mini. *The adventures of the dish and the spoon* ill. by author. Random House, 2006. ISBN 978-0-375-93691-3 Subj: Crime. Humorous stories. Nursery rhymes.

Ginger bear ill. by author. Random House, 2007. ISBN 978-0-375-84253-5 Subj: Activities – baking, cooking. Emotions – loneliness. Food. Friendship.

Hermelin the detective mouse ill. by author. Knopf, 2014. ISBN 978-038575433-0 Subj: Animals – mice. Behavior – lost & found possessions. Careers – detectives. Communities, neighborhoods.

Space Dog ill. by author. Knopf, 2015. ISBN 978-055351058-4 Subj: Animals – cats. Animals – dogs. Animals – mice. Careers – astronauts. Friendship. Space & space ships.

Three by the sea ill. by author. Random House, 2011. ISBN 978-0-375-86784-2 Subj: Animals. Character traits – cooperation. Friendship.

Toys in space ill. by author. Knopf, 2013. ISBN 978-0-307-97812-7 Subj: Activities – storytelling. Night. Toys. Toys – dolls.

Traction Man and the beach odyssey ill. by author. Knopf, 2012. ISBN 978-0-375-86952-5 Subj: Sea & seashore – beaches. Toys.

Traction Man is here ill. by author. Knopf, 2005. ISBN 978-0-375-93191-8 Subj: Clothing – costumes. Family life. Toys.

Traction Man meets Turbodog ill. by author. Knopf, 2008. ISBN 978-0-375-85583-2 Subj: Behavior – lost & found possessions. Imagination. Toys.

The very smart pea and the princess-to-be ill. by author. Knopf, 2003. ISBN 978-0-375-92626-6 Subj: Folk & fairy tales. Plants. Royalty – princesses. Sleep.

Griessman, Annette. *The fire* ill. by Leonid Gore. Penguin, 2005. ISBN 978-0-399-24019-5 Subj: Ethnic groups in the U.S. – Hispanic Americans. Family life. Fire.

Like a hundred drums ill. by Julie Monks. Houghton, 2006. ISBN 978-0-618-55878-0 Subj: Animals. Family life – grandmothers. Weather – lightning, thunder. Weather – storms.

Grifalconi, Ann. *Ain't nobody a stranger to me* ill. by Jerry Pinkney. Hyperion, 2007. ISBN 978-0-7868-1857-0 Subj: Character traits – freedom. Ethnic groups in the U.S. – African Americans. Family life – grandfathers. Slavery. U.S. history.

Tiny's hat ill. by author. HarperCollins, 1999. ISBN 978-0-06-027655-3 Subj: Clothing – hats. Emotions – grief. Ethnic groups in the U.S. – African Americans. Family life – fathers.

The village of round and square houses ill. by author. Little, 1986. ISBN 978-0-316-32862-3 Subj: Caldecott award honor books. Folk & fairy tales. Foreign lands – Africa. Volcanoes.

The village that vanished ill. by Kadir Nelson. Dial, 2002. ISBN 978-0-8037-2623-9 Subj: Behavior – hiding. Ethnic groups in the U.S. – African Americans. Foreign lands – Africa. Slavery.

Griff. *Shark-mad Stanley* ill. by author. Hyperion, 2000. ISBN 978-0-7868-0594-5 Subj: Fish – sharks. Imagination. Pets.

Griffin, Kitty. *Cowboy Sam and those confounded secrets* by Kitty Griffin and Kathy Combs ill. by Mike Wohnoutka. Clarion, 2001. ISBN 978-0-618-08854-6 Subj: Behavior – secrets. Humorous stories. U.S. history – frontier & pioneer life.

The foot-stomping adventures of Clementine Sweet by Kitty Griffin and Kathy Combs ill. by Mike Wohnoutka. Clarion, 2004. ISBN 978-0-618-24746-2 Subj: Behavior. Humorous stories. Tall tales. Weather – tornadoes.

The ride: the legend of Betsy Dowdy ill. by Marjorie Priceman. Simon & Schuster, 2010. ISBN 978-1-4169-2816-4 Subj: Character traits – bravery. U.S. history.

Griffin, Molly Beth. *Loon baby* ill. by Anne Hunter. Houghton Mifflin, 2011. ISBN 978-0-547-25487-6 Subj: Behavior – worrying. Birds – loons.

Griffith, Helen V. *Moonlight* ill. by Laura Dronzek. HarperCollins, 2012. ISBN 978-0-06-203285-0 Subj: Animals – rabbits. Bedtime. Moon. Rhyming text.

Grigsby, Susan. *First peas to the table: how Thomas Jefferson inspired a school garden* ill. by Nicole Tadgell. Albert Whitman, 2012. ISBN 978-0-8075-2452-7 Subj: Contests. Food. Gardens, gardening. School. U.S. history.

In the garden with Dr. Carver ill. by Nicole Tadgell. Albert Whitman, 2010. ISBN 978-0-8075-3630-8 Subj: Ethnic groups in the U.S. – African Americans. Gardens, gardening. Plants. School. U.S. history.

Grimes, Nikki. *At break of day* ill. by Paul Morin. Eerdmans, 1995. ISBN 978-0-8028-5104-8 Subj: Creation. Religion.

Barack Obama: son of promise, child of hope ill. by Bryan Collier. Simon & Schuster, 2008. ISBN 978-1-4169-7144-3 Subj: Ethnic groups in the U.S. – African Americans. U.S. history.

Danitra Brown, class clown ill. by E. B. Lewis. HarperCollins, 2005. ISBN 978-0-688-17290-9 Subj: Ethnic groups in the U.S. – African Americans. Friendship. Poetry. School.

Minnie's new friend ill. by Peter Emslie and Darren Hunt. Western, 1992. ISBN 978-0-307-11524-9 Subj: Animals. Friendship.

A pocketful of poems ill. by Javaka Steptoe. Clarion, 2001. ISBN 978-0-395-93868-3 Subj: Cities, towns. Nature. Poetry.

Shoe magic ill. by Terry Widener. Orchard, 2000. ISBN 978-0-531-33286-3 Subj: Clothing – shoes. Poetry.

Voices of Christmas ill. by Eric Velasquez. Zondervan, 2009. ISBN 978-0-310-71192-6 Subj: Holidays – Christmas. Poetry. Religion – Nativity.

Welcome, Precious ill. by Bryan Collier. Scholastic, 2006. ISBN 978-0-439-55702-3 Subj: Babies, toddlers. Ethnic groups in the U.S. – African Americans.

When Daddy prays ill. by Tim Ladwig. Eerdmans, 2002. ISBN 978-0-8028-5152-9 Subj: Ethnic groups in the U.S. – African Americans. Family life – fathers. Poetry. Religion.

When Gorilla goes walking ill. by Shane W. Evans. Scholastic, 2007. ISBN 978-0-439-31770-2 Subj: Animals – cats. Ethnic groups in the U.S. – African Americans. Friendship. Pets. Poetry.

Grimm, Edward. *The doorman* ill. by Ted Lewin. Orchard, 2000. ISBN 978-0-531-33280-1 Subj: Careers – doormen. Death. Emotions – grief. Homes, houses.

Grimm, Jacob and Wilhelm. *As luck would have it: from the Brothers Grimm* ill. by Daniel San Souci. August House, 2008. ISBN 978-0-87483-833-6 Subj: Animals – bears. Folk & fairy tales. Foreign lands – Germany. Humorous stories.

Battle of the beasts: a tale of epic proportions from the brothers Grimm retold by Diz Wallis; ill. by reteller. Ragged Bears, 2000. ISBN 978-1-929927-15-9 Subj: Animals. Behavior – fighting, arguing. Birds. Folk & fairy tales.

The brave little tailor retold by Olga Dugina and Andrej Dugin; ill. by retellers. Abrams, 2000. ISBN 978-0-8109-4113-7 Subj: Careers – tailors.

Character traits – bravery. Folk & fairy tales. Foreign lands – Germany. Giants.

The brave little tailor retold by Eric Blair; ill. by David Shaw. Picture Window, 2004. ISBN 978-1-4048-0315-2 Subj: Careers – tailors. Character traits – bravery. Folk & fairy tales. Foreign lands – Germany. Giants.

The Bremen town band retold by Brian Wildsmith; ill. by reteller. Oxford Univ., 1999. ISBN 978-0-19-279034-7 Subj: Animals. Careers – musicians. Crime. Folk & fairy tales. Old age.

The Bremen town musicians retold by Eric Blair; ill. by Bill Dickson. Picture Window, 2004. ISBN 978-1-4048-0310-7 Subj: Animals. Careers – musicians. Crime. Folk & fairy tales. Old age.

The Bremen town musicians retold by Ilse Plume; ill. by reteller. Doubleday, 1980. ISBN 978-0-385-15162-7 Subj: Animals. Careers – musicians. Crime. Folk & fairy tales. Old age.

The Bremen town musicians ill. by Bernadette Watts. NorthSouth, 1992. ISBN 978-1-55858-148-7 Subj: Animals. Careers – musicians. Crime. Folk & fairy tales. Old age.

The Bremen town musicians ill. by Lisbeth Zwerger. Penguin, 2007. ISBN 978-0-698-40042-9 Subj: Animals. Careers – musicians. Crime. Folk & fairy tales. Old age.

Doctor All-Knowing: a folk tale from the Brothers Grimm retold by Doris Orgel; ill. by Alexandra Boiger. Atheneum, 2008. ISBN 978-1-4169-1246-0 Subj: Careers – doctors. Folk & fairy tales. Poverty.

The elves and the shoemaker retold by John Cech; ill. by Kirill Chelushkin. Sterling, 2007. ISBN 978-1-4027-3067-2 Subj: Careers – shoemakers. Character traits – helpfulness. Folk & fairy tales. Foreign lands – Germany. Mythical creatures – elves.

The elves and the shoemaker ill. by Paul Galdone. Clarion, 1984. ISBN 978-0-89919-226-0 Subj: Careers – shoemakers. Character traits – helpfulness. Folk & fairy tales. Foreign lands – Germany. Mythical creatures – elves.

The elves and the shoemaker ill. by Margaret Walty. Barefoot, 1998. ISBN 978-1-901223-69-9 Subj: Careers – shoemakers. Character traits – helpfulness. Folk & fairy tales. Foreign lands – Germany. Mythical creatures – elves.

The fisherman and his wife retold by Rosemary Wells; ill. by Eleanor Hubbard. Dial, 1998. ISBN 978-0-8037-1851-7 Subj: Animals – cats. Behavior – greed. Folk & fairy tales.

The fisherman and his wife retold by Rachel Isadora; ill. by reteller. Putnam, 2008. ISBN 978-0-399-24771-2 Subj: Behavior – greed. Folk & fairy tales. Foreign lands – Africa.

The fisherman and his wife retold by Eric Blair; ill. by Todd Ouren. Picture Window, 2004. ISBN 978-1-4048-0317-6 Subj: Behavior – greed. Folk & fairy tales.

The fisherman and the turtle adapt. by Eric A. Kimmel; ill. by Martha Avilés. Marshall Cavendish, 2008. ISBN 978-0-7614-5387-1 Subj: Behavior – greed. Folk & fairy tales. Foreign lands – Mexico.

The frog prince retold by Kathy-Jo Wargin; ill. by Anne Yvonne Gilbert. Mitten, 2007. ISBN 978-1-58726-279-1 Subj: Folk & fairy tales. Frogs & toads. Kissing. Royalty – princes. Royalty – princesses.

The frog prince retold by Eric Blair; ill. by Todd Ouren. Picture Window, 2004. ISBN 978-1-4048-0313-8 Subj: Folk & fairy tales. Frogs & toads. Royalty – princes. Royalty – princesses.

The glass mountain adapt. by Diane Wolkstein; ill. by Louisa Bauer. Morrow, 1999. ISBN 978-0-688-14848-5 Subj: Folk & fairy tales. Mythical creatures – trolls.

The golden goose retold by Dennis McDermott; ill. by reteller. Morrow, 2000. ISBN 978-0-688-11403-9 Subj: Behavior – greed. Birds – geese. Character traits – kindness. Folk & fairy tales. Royalty – princesses.

The goose girl: a story from the Brothers Grimm retold by Eric A. Kimmel; ill. by Robert Sauber. Holiday, 1995. ISBN 978-0-8234-1074-3 Subj: Folk & fairy tales. Royalty. Weddings.

Hans my hedgehog: a tale from the Brothers Grimm by Kate Coombs; ill. by John Nickle. Atheneum, 2012. ISBN 978-1-4169-1533-1 Subj: Animals – hedgehogs. Folk & fairy tales. Foreign lands – Germany. Music. Royalty.

Hansel and Gretel retold by Cynthia Rylant; ill. by Jen Corace. Hyperion, 2008. ISBN 978-1-4231-1186-3 Subj: Behavior – lost. Folk & fairy tales. Forest, woods. Witches.

Hansel and Gretel retold by Holly Hobbie; ill. by reteller. Little, Brown, 2015. ISBN 978-031607017-1 Subj: Behavior – lost. Folk & fairy tales. Forest, woods. Witches.

Hansel and Gretel retold by Rachel Isadora; ill. by reteller. Putnam, 2009. ISBN 978-0-399-25028-6 Subj: Behavior – lost. Folk & fairy tales. Foreign lands – Africa. Forest, woods. Witches.

Hansel and Gretel retold by Amy Ehrlich; ill. by Susan Jeffers. Penguin, 2011. ISBN 978-0-525-42221-1 Subj: Behavior – lost. Folk & fairy tales. Forest, woods. Witches.

Hansel and Gretel retold by James Marshall; ill. by reteller. Dial, 1990. ISBN 978-0-8037-0828-0 Subj: Behavior – lost. Folk & fairy tales. Forest, woods. Witches.

Hansel and Gretel retold by Jane Ray; ill. by reteller. Candlewick, 1997. ISBN 978-0-7636-0358-8 Subj: Behavior – lost. Folk & fairy tales. Forest, woods. Witches.

Hansel and Gretel retold by Eric Blair; ill. by Claudia Wolf. Picture Window, 2004. ISBN 978-1-4048-0316-9 Subj: Behavior – lost. Folk & fairy tales. Forest, woods. Witches.

Hansel and Gretel retold by Rika Lesser; ill. by Paul O. Zelinsky. Dodd, 1984. ISBN 978-0-396-08449-5 Subj: Behavior – lost. Caldecott award honor books. Folk & fairy tales. Forest, woods. Witches.

Hansel and Gretel ill. by Lisbeth Zwerger. Morrow, 1980. ISBN 978-0-688-32198-7 Subj: Behavior – lost. Folk & fairy tales. Forest, woods. Witches.

Hansel and Gretel / Hansel y Gretel adapt. by Elisabet Abeya; ill. by Cristina Losantos. Chronicle, 2005. ISBN 978-0-8118-4793-3 Subj: Behavior – lost. Folk & fairy tales. Foreign languages. Forest, woods. Witches.

Hansel and Gretel: a retelling from the original tale by the Brothers Grimm retold by Will Moses; ill. by reteller. Penguin, 2006. ISBN 978-0-399-24234-2 Subj: Behavior – lost. Folk & fairy tales. Forest, woods. Witches.

Iron John adapt. by Eric A. Kimmel; ill. by Trina Schart Hyman. Holiday, 1994. ISBN 978-0-8234-1073-6 Subj: Folk & fairy tales. Foreign lands – Germany. Royalty – kings. Royalty – princes.

Iron John retold by Marianna Mayer; ill. by Winslow Pels. Morrow, 1998. ISBN 978-0-688-11555-5 Subj: Folk & fairy tales. Foreign lands – Germany. Royalty – kings. Royalty – princes.

Jorinda and Jorindel retold by Bernadette Watts; ill. by reteller. NorthSouth, 2005. ISBN 978-0-7358-1987-0 Subj: Folk & fairy tales. Witches.

Little red cap ill. by Lisbeth Zwerger. Morrow, 1983. ISBN 978-0-688-01715-6 Subj: Animals – wolves. Behavior – talking to strangers. Folk & fairy tales.

Little Red Riding Hood retold by Lari Don; ill. by Célia Chauffrey. Barefoot, 2012. ISBN 978-1-84686-766-8 Subj: Animals – wolves. Behavior – talking to strangers. Folk & fairy tales.

Little Red Riding Hood retold by Margaret Hilert; ill. by Gwen Connelly. Follett, 1982. ISBN 978-0-695-41543-3 Subj: Animals – wolves. Behavior – talking to strangers. Folk & fairy tales.

Little Red Riding Hood retold by Trina Schart Hyman; ill. by reteller. Holiday, 1983. ISBN 978-0-8234-0470-4 Subj: Animals – wolves. Behavior – talking to strangers. Caldecott award honor books. Folk & fairy tales.

Little Red Riding Hood retold by Jerry Pinkney; ill. by reteller. Little, Brown, 2007. ISBN 978-0-316-01355-0 Subj: Animals – wolves. Behavior – talking to strangers. Folk & fairy tales.

Little Red Riding Hood adapt. by Gennady Spirin; ill. by adapter. Marshall Cavendish, 2010. ISBN 978-0-7614-5704-6 Subj: Animals – wolves. Behavior – talking to strangers. Folk & fairy tales.

Little Red Riding Hood ill. by Bernadette Watts. NorthSouth, 2009. ISBN 978-0-7358-2256-6 Subj: Animals – wolves. Behavior – talking to strangers. Folk & fairy tales.

Little Red Riding Hood retold by Andrea Wisnewski; ill. by reteller. Godine, 2007. ISBN 978-1-56792-303-2 Subj: Animals – wolves. Behavior – talking to strangers. Folk & fairy tales.

Musicians of Bremen retold by Niroot Puttapipat; ill. by reteller. Candlewick, 2005. ISBN 978-0-7636-2758-4 Subj: Animals. Careers – musicians. Crime. Folk & fairy tales. Old age.

Musicians of Bremen / Los musicos de Bremner: a bilingual book adapt. by Roser Ros; ill. by Pep Montserrat. Chronicle, 2005. ISBN 978-0-8118-4795-7 Subj: Animals. Careers – musicians. Crime. Folk & fairy tales. Foreign languages. Old age.

Princess Sophie and the six swans: a tale from the Brothers Grimm retold by Kim Jacobs. Wisdom Tales, 2017. ISBN 978-193778667-0 Subj: Birds – swans. Family life – brothers & sisters. Folk & fairy tales. Magic.

The rabbit's bride retold by Holly Meade; ill. by reteller. Marshall Cavendish, 2001. ISBN 978-0-7614-5081-8 Subj: Animals – rabbits. Character traits – cleverness. Folk & fairy tales. Foreign lands – Germany.

Rapunzel adapt. by Allison Sage; ill. by Sarah Gibb. Albert Whitman, 2011. ISBN 978-0-8075-6804-0 Subj: Folk & fairy tales. Hair. Royalty – princes. Witches.

Rapunzel retold by Barbara Rogasky; ill. by Trina Schart Hyman. Holiday, 1982. ISBN 978-0-8234-0454-4 Subj: Folk & fairy tales. Hair. Royalty – princes. Witches.

Rapunzel retold by Rachel Isadora; ill. by reteller. Putnam, 2008. ISBN 978-0-399-24772-9 Subj: Folk & fairy tales. Foreign lands – Africa. Hair. Royalty – princes. Witches.

Rapunzel adapt. by Francesc Bofill; ill. by Joma. Chronicle, 2006. ISBN 978-0-8118-5059-9 Subj: Folk & fairy tales. Hair. Royalty – princes. Witches.

Rapunzel retold by Amy Ehrlich; ill. by Kris Waldherr. Dial, 1989. ISBN 978-0-8037-0655-2 Subj: Folk & fairy tales. Hair. Royalty – princes. Witches.

Rapunzel retold by Paul O. Zelinsky; ill. by reteller. Dutton, 1997. ISBN 978-0-525-45607-0 Subj: Caldecott award books. Folk & fairy tales. Hair. Royalty – princes. Witches.

Rapunzel: a fairy tale ill. by Maja Dusíková. NorthSouth, 1997. ISBN 978-1-55858-685-7 Subj: Folk & fairy tales. Hair. Royalty – princes. Witches.

Rose Red and the bear prince adapt. by Dan Andreasen; ill. by adapter. HarperCollins, 2000. ISBN 978-0-06-027967-7 Subj: Animals – bears. Dwarfs, midgets. Folk & fairy tales. Magic. Royalty – princes.

Rumpelstiltskin adapt. by Paul Galdone; ill. by adapter. Houghton, 1985. ISBN 978-0-89919-266-6 Subj: Behavior – boasting, showing off. Folk & fairy tales. Magic. Riddles & jokes. Royalty.

Rumpelstiltskin retold by Eric Blair; ill. by David Shaw. Picture Window, 2004. ISBN 978-1-4048-0311-4 Subj: Behavior – boasting, showing off. Folk & fairy tales. Magic. Riddles & jokes. Royalty.

Rumpelstiltskin adapt. by Paul O. Zelinsky; ill. by adapter. Dutton, 1986. ISBN 978-0-525-44265-3 Subj: Behavior – boasting, showing off. Folk & fairy tales. Magic. Riddles & jokes. Royalty.

Seven at one blow: a tale from the Brothers Grimm retold by Eric A. Kimmel; ill. by Megan Lloyd. Holiday, 1998. ISBN 978-0-8234-1383-6 Subj: Careers – tailors. Character traits – bravery. Folk & fairy tales. Foreign lands – Germany. Giants.

The shoemaker and his elves retold by Eric Blair; ill. by Bill Dickson. Picture Window, 2004. ISBN 978-1-4048-0314-5 Subj: Careers – shoemakers. Character traits – helpfulness. Folk & fairy tales. Foreign lands – Germany. Mythical creatures – elves.

The shoemaker and the elves ill. by Adrienne Adams. Macmillan, 1972. ISBN 978-0-684-12982-2 Subj: Careers – shoemakers. Character traits – helpfulness. Folk & fairy tales. Foreign lands – Germany. Mythical creatures – elves.

The shoemaker and the elves retold by Ilse Plume; ill. by reteller. Harcourt, 1991. ISBN 978-0-15-274050-4 Subj: Careers – shoemakers. Character traits – helpfulness. Folk & fairy tales. Foreign lands – Germany. Mythical creatures – elves.

The six swans retold by Robert D. San Souci; ill. by Daniel San Souci. Simon & Schuster, 1989. ISBN 978-0-671-65848-9 Subj: Birds – swans. Family life – brothers & sisters. Folk & fairy tales. Magic.

Sleeping Beauty ill. by Maja Dusíková. NorthSouth, 2012. ISBN 978-0-7358-4087-4 Subj: Fairies. Folk & fairy tales. Royalty – princes. Royalty – princesses. Sleep.

Sleeping beauty retold by Sarah Gibb; ill. by reteller. Albert Whitman, 2015. ISBN 978-080757351-8 Subj: Fairies. Folk & fairy tales. Royalty – princes. Royalty – princesses. Sleep. Witches.

The sleeping beauty retold by Trina Schart Hyman; ill. by reteller. Little, 1977. ISBN 978-0-316-38702-6 Subj: Fairies. Folk & fairy tales. Royalty – princes. Royalty – princesses. Sleep. Witches.

Snow White retold by Melinda Copper; ill. by reteller. Penguin, 2005. ISBN 978-0-525-47474-6 Subj: Animals. Dwarfs, midgets. Emotions – envy, jealousy. Folk & fairy tales. Magic. Witches.

Snow White ill. by Quentin Gréban. NorthSouth, 2009. ISBN 978-0-7358-2257-3 Subj: Dwarfs, midgets. Emotions – envy, jealousy. Folk & fairy tales. Magic. Witches.

Snow White ill. by Trina Schart Hyman. Little, 1999, 1974. ISBN 978-0-316-35450-9 Subj: Dwarfs, midgets. Emotions – envy, jealousy. Folk & fairy tales. Magic. Witches.

Snow White ill. by Charles Santore. Sterling, 2010. ISBN 978-1-4027-7157-6 Subj: Dwarfs, midgets. Emotions – envy, jealousy. Folk & fairy tales. Magic.

Snow White and the seven dwarfs ill. by Wanda Gág. Coward, 1938. Subj: Caldecott award honor books. Dwarfs, midgets. Emotions – envy, jealousy. Folk & fairy tales. Magic. Weddings.

Snow White and the seven dwarfs retold by Laura Ljungkvist; ill. by reteller. Abrams, 2003. ISBN 978-0-8109-4241-7 Subj: Dwarfs, midgets. Emotions – envy, jealousy. Folk & fairy tales. Magic. Witches.

The star child adapt. by J. Alison James; ill. by Bernadette Watts. NorthSouth, 2010. ISBN 978-0-7358-2330-3 Subj: Behavior – sharing. Character traits – generosity. Folk & fairy tales. Stars.

The story of Little Red Riding Hood ill. by Christopher Bing. Chronicle, 2010. ISBN 978-0-8118-6886-7 Subj: Animals – wolves. Behavior – talking to strangers. Folk & fairy tales.

The three spinning fairies retold by Lisa Campbell Ernst; ill. by reteller. Dutton, 2002. ISBN 978-0-525-46826-4 Subj: Character traits – laziness. Fairies. Folk & fairy tales. Foreign lands – Germany.

Twelve dancing princesses retold by Brigette Barrager; ill. by reteller. Chronicle, 2011. ISBN 978-0-8118-7696-4 Subj: Activities – dancing. Folk & fairy tales. Royalty – princesses.

The twelve dancing princesses retold by John Cech; ill. by Lucy Corvino. Sterling, 2009. ISBN 978-1-4027-4435-8 Subj: Activities – dancing. Folk & fairy tales. Royalty – princesses.

The twelve dancing princesses retold by Marianna Mayer; ill. by Kinuko Y. Craft. Morrow, 1989.

ISBN 978-0-688-02026-2 Subj: Activities – dancing. Folk & fairy tales. Royalty – princesses.

The twelve dancing princesses ill. by Rachel Isadora. Penguin, 2007. ISBN 978-0-399-24744-6 Subj: Activities – dancing. Folk & fairy tales. Foreign lands – Africa. Royalty – princesses.

The twelve dancing princesses retold by Alison Jay; ill. by reteller. little bee, 2016. ISBN 978-149980329-7 Subj: Activities – dancing. Folk & fairy tales. Royalty – princesses.

The twelve dancing princesses retold by Marianna Mayer; ill. by Gerald McDermott. Morrow, 1988. Subj: Activities – dancing. Folk & fairy tales. Royalty – princesses.

The twelve dancing princesses retold by Jane Ray; ill. by reteller. Dutton, 1996. ISBN 978-0-525-45595-0 Subj: Activities – dancing. Folk & fairy tales. Royalty – princesses.

The twelve dancing princesses retold by Suçie Stevenson; ill. by reteller. Yearling, 1995. ISBN 978-0-385-32167-9 Subj: Activities – dancing. Folk & fairy tales. Royalty – princesses.

The twelve princesses retold by Gordon Fitchett; ill. by reteller. Fogelman, 2000. ISBN 978-0-8037-2474-7 Subj: Activities – dancing. Birds – ducks. Folk & fairy tales. Royalty – princesses.

The water of life adapt. by Barbara Rogasky; ill. by Trina Schart Hyman. Holiday, 1986. ISBN 978-0-8234-0552-7 Subj: Character traits – pride. Folk & fairy tales. Magic. Royalty. Sibling rivalry.

Grindley, Sally. *Can we play too, Piglittle?* ill. by Andy Ellis. Barron's, 2000. ISBN 978-0-7641-1582-0 Subj: Activities – playing. Animals – pigs. Behavior – sharing. Character traits – selfishness.

The giant postman ill. by Wendy Smith. Kingfisher, 2000. ISBN 978-0-7534-5319-3 Subj: Careers – postal workers. Concepts – size. Friendship.

It's my school ill. by Margaret Chamberlain. Walker, 2006. ISBN 978-0-8027-8086-7 Subj: Family life – brothers & sisters. School – first day.

Little Elephant Thunderfoot ill. by John Butler. Peachtree, 1999. ISBN 978-1-56145-180-7 Subj: Animals – babies. Animals – elephants.

Mucky Duck ill. by Neal Layton. Bloomsbury, 2003. ISBN 978-1-58234-821-6 Subj: Activities. Birds – ducks. Character traits – cleanliness.

A new room for William ill. by Carol Thompson. Candlewick, 2000. ISBN 978-0-7636-1196-5 Subj: Divorce. Family life. Homes, houses. Moving.

Silly Goose and Dizzy Duck play hide-and-seek ill. by Adrian Reynolds. DK, 1999. ISBN 978-0-7894-4844-6 Subj: Animals – foxes. Birds – ducks. Birds – geese. Games.

The sorcerer's apprentice ill. by Thomas Taylor. Fogelman, 2002. ISBN 978-0-8037-2726-7 Subj: Folk & fairy tales. Magic.

The sulky vulture ill. by Michael Terry. Bloomsbury, 2003. ISBN 978-1-58234-794-3 Subj: Behavior – bad day, bad mood. Behavior – dissatisfaction. Birds – vultures.

What are friends for? ill. by Penny Dann. Kingfisher, 1998. ISBN 978-0-7534-5108-3 Subj: Animals – bears. Animals – foxes. Friendship.

What will I do without you? ill. by Penny Dann. Kingfisher, 1999. ISBN 978-0-7534-5110-6 Subj: Animals – bears. Animals – foxes. Animals – squirrels. Friendship. Hibernation. Seasons – winter.

Where are my chicks? ill. by Jill Newton. Fogelman, 1999. ISBN 978-0-8037-2497-6 Subj: Animals. Behavior – lost. Birds – chickens, roosters. Counting, numbers.

Who is it? ill. by Rosalind Beardshaw. Peachtree, 2000. ISBN 978-1-56145-224-8 Subj: Folk & fairy tales. Problem solving. Riddles & jokes.

Grist, Julie. *Flying, just plane fun* ill. by author. Spoonbender, 2003. ISBN 978-0-9725750-0-3 Subj: Activities – flying. Airplanes, airports. Family life – grandfathers.

Griswell, Kim T. *Rufus blasts off!* ill. by Valeri Gorbachev. Sterling, 2017. ISBN 978-145492099-1 Subj: Animals – pigs. Books, reading. Space & space ships.

Rufus goes to school ill. by Valeri Gorbachev. Sterling, 2013. ISBN 978-1-4549-0416-8 Subj: Animals – pigs. Books, reading. Careers – school principals. School.

Rufus goes to sea ill. by Valeri Gorbachev. Sterling, 2015. ISBN 978-145491052-7 Subj: Animals – pigs. Books, reading. Pirates.

Gritton, Steve. *The trouble with sisters and robots* ill. by author. Albert Whitman, 2009. ISBN 978-0-8075-8090-5 Subj: Family life – sisters. Robots.

Grobler, Piet. *Hey, frog!* ill. by author. Front Street, 2002. ISBN 978-1-886910-84-3 Subj: Animals. Behavior – greed. Frogs & toads. Water.

Grogan, John. *Bad dog, Marley!* ill. by Richard Cowdrey. HarperCollins, 2007. ISBN 978-0-06-117114-7 Subj: Animals – dogs. Behavior – misbehavior.

Marley goes to school ill. by Richard Cowdrey. HarperCollins, 2009. ISBN 978-0-06-156151-1 Subj: Animals – dogs. School – first day.

Trick or treat, Marley! ill. by Richard Cowdrey. HarperCollins, 2011. ISBN 978-0-06-185755-3 Subj: Animals – dogs. Holidays – Halloween.

A very Marley Christmas ill. by Richard Cowdrey. HarperCollins, 2008. ISBN 978-0-06-137292-6 Subj: Animals – dogs. Holidays – Christmas.

Groner, Judyth Saypol. *My first Hebrew word book* ill. by Pepi Marzel. Kar-Ben, 2005. ISBN 978-1-58013-126-1 Subj: Foreign languages. Jewish culture. Language.

Gross, Benedikt. *ABC: the alphabet from the sky* by Benedikt Gross and Joey Lee; ill. by Benedikt Gross. Price Stern Sloan, 2016. ISBN 978-110199581-5 Subj: ABC books. Picture puzzles.

Grossman, Bill. *My little sister ate one hare* ill. by Kevin Hawkes. Crown, 1996. ISBN 978-0-517-59601-2 Subj: Counting, numbers. Rhyming text.

My little sister hugged an ape ill. by Kevin Hawkes. Knopf, 2004. ISBN 978-0-517-80018-8 Subj: ABC books. Emotions. Family life – sisters. Rhyming text.

Timothy Tunny swallowed a bunny ill. by Kevin Hawkes. Geringer, 2000. ISBN 978-0-06-028758-0 Subj: Humorous stories. Poetry.

Grossman, Patricia. *Saturday market* by Patricia Grossman and Enrique O. Sánchez ill. by Enrique O. Sánchez. Lothrop, 1994. ISBN 978-0-688-12177-8 Subj: Foreign lands – Mexico. Indians of North America – Zapotec. Shopping.

Grossman, Virginia. *Ten little rabbits* ill. by Sylvia Long. Chronicle, 1991. ISBN 978-0-87701-552-9 Subj: Animals – rabbits. Counting, numbers. Indians of North America. Rhyming text.

Grossmann-Hensel, Katharina. *Papa is a pirate* ill. by author. NorthSouth, 2009. ISBN 978-0-7358-2237-5 Subj: Family life – fathers. Pirates.

Groundhog at Evergreen Road ill. by Higgins Bond. Soundprints, 2003. ISBN 978-1-59249-022-6 Subj: Animals – groundhogs. Behavior – growing up. Homes, houses.

Grover, Jan Zitz. *A home for Dakota* ill. by Nancy Lane. Gryphon, 2008. ISBN 978-0-940719-05-7 Subj: Animals – dogs. Character traits – kindness to animals.

Grün, Anselm. *Jesus* ill. by Giuliano Ferri. Eerdmans, 2014. ISBN 978-080285438-4 Subj: Religion.

The legend of Saint Nicholas ill. by Giuliano Ferri. Eerdmans, 2014. ISBN 978-080285434-6 Subj: Holidays – Christmas. Religion. Santa Claus.

Grupper, Jonathan. *Destination — Rocky Mountains* ill. with photos. National Geographic, 2001. ISBN 978-0-7922-7722-4 Subj: Animals. Ecology. Mountains. Nature.

Destination, rain forest ill. with photos. National Geographic, 1997. ISBN 978-0-7922-7018-8 Subj: Ecology. Jungle. Nature.

Gruska, Denise. *The only boy in ballet class* ill. by Amy Wummer. Gibbs Smith, 2007. ISBN 978-1-4236-0220-0 Subj: Activities – dancing. Ballet. Prejudice. Sports – football.

Guarino, Deborah. *Is your mama a llama?* ill. by Steven Kellogg. Scholastic, 1989. ISBN 978-0-590-41387-9 Subj: Animals. Animals – llamas. Rhyming text.

Guarnaccia, Steven. *The three little pigs: an architectural tale* ill. by author. Abrams, 2010. ISBN 978-0-8109-8941-2 Subj: Animals – pigs. Animals – wolves. Careers – architects. Character traits – cleverness. Folk & fairy tales.

Guback, Georgia. *Luka's quilt* ill. by author. Greenwillow, 1994. ISBN 978-0-688-12155-6 Subj: Family life – grandmothers. Hawaii. Quilts.

Gude, Paul. *When Elephant met Giraffe* ill. by author. Disney/Hyperion, 2014. ISBN 978-142316303-9 Subj: Animals – elephants. Animals – giraffes. Character traits – compromising. Friendship. Noise, sounds.

Gudeon, Adam. *Me and Meow* ill. by author. HarperCollins, 2011. ISBN 978-0-06-199821-8 Subj: Activities – playing. Animals – cats.

Guenther, James. *Turnagain, Ptarmigan, where did you go?* ill. by Shannon Cartwright. Sasquatch, 2000. ISBN 978-1-57061-237-4 Subj: Alaska. Birds – ptarmigans. Rhyming text. Seasons.

Guest, C. Z. *Tiny green thumbs* ill. by Loretta Krupinski. Hyperion, 2000. ISBN 978-0-7868-0516-7 Subj: Animals – mice. Animals – rabbits. Family life – grandmothers. Gardens, gardening.

Guest, Elissa Haden. *Harriet's had enough!* ill. by Paul Meisel. Candlewick, 2009. ISBN 978-0-7636-3454-4 Subj: Animals – raccoons. Character traits – orderliness. Family life.

Gugler, Laurel Dee. *There's a billy goat in the garden* ill. by Clare Beaton. Barefoot, 2003. ISBN 978-1-84148-089-3 Subj: Animals. Animals – goats. Folk & fairy tales. Foreign lands – Puerto Rico. Insects – bees.

Guiberson, Brenda Z. *Cactus hotel* ill. by Megan Lloyd. Henry Holt, 1991. ISBN 978-0-8050-1333-7 Subj: Desert. Ecology. Plants.

Earth: feeling the heat ill. by Chad Wallace. Henry Holt, 2010. ISBN 978-0-8050-7719-3 Subj: Earth. Ecology. Weather.

The emperor lays an egg ill. by Joan Paley. Henry Holt, 2001. ISBN 978-0-8050-6204-5 Subj: Birds – penguins. Family life.

Frog song ill. by Gennady Spirin. Henry Holt, 2013. ISBN 978-0-8050-9254-7 Subj: Frogs & toads. Noise, sounds.

Ice bears ill. by Ilya Spirin. Henry Holt, 2008. ISBN 978-0-8050-7607-3 Subj: Animals – polar bears. Foreign lands – Arctic.

Into the sea ill. by Alix Berenzy. Henry Holt, 1996. ISBN 978-0-8050-2263-6 Subj: Nature. Reptiles – turtles, tortoises. Sea & seashore.

Moon bear ill. by Ed Young. Henry Holt, 2010. ISBN 978-0-8050-8977-6 Subj: Animals – bears. Animals – endangered animals.

Mud city: a flamingo story ill. by author. Henry Holt, 2005. ISBN 978-0-8050-7177-1 Subj: Birds – flamingos. Nature.

Guidone, Thea. *Drum city* ill. by Vanessa Brantley Newton. Tricycle, 2010. ISBN 978-1-58246-308-7 Subj: Musical instruments – drums. Parades. Rhyming text.

Guion, Melissa. *Baby penguins everywhere!* ill. by author. Philomel, 2012. ISBN 978-0-399-25535-9 Subj: Animals – babies. Behavior – solitude. Birds – penguins.

Baby penguins love their Mama ill. by author. Philomel, 2014. ISBN 978-039916365-4 Subj: Birds – penguins. Days of the week, months of the year. Family life – mothers.

Gukova, Julia. *All mixed-up!* ill. by author. North-South, 2000. ISBN 978-0-7358-1300-7 Subj: Format, unusual – toy & movable books. Picture puzzles. Witches.

Gulbis, Stephen. *Cowgirl Rosie and her five baby bison* ill. by author. Little, 2001. ISBN 978-0-316-64712-0 Subj: Animals – babies. Animals – buffaloes. Behavior – lost & found possessions. Cowboys, cowgirls. Rhyming text.

Gundersheimer, Karen. *Find cat, wear hat* ill. by author. Scholastic, 1995. ISBN 978-0-590-48061-1 Subj: Activities – playing. Format, unusual – board books. Noise, sounds. Rhyming text. School.

Gunnufson, Charlotte. *Halloween hustle* ill. by Kevan Atteberry. Amazon/Two Lions, 2013. ISBN 978-1-4778-1723-0 Subj: Activities – dancing. Anatomy – skeletons. Holidays – Halloween. Monsters. Rhyming text.

Prince and Pirate ill. by Mike Lowery. Putnam, 2017. ISBN 978-039917604-3 Subj: Behavior – fighting, arguing. Fish. Pirates. Royalty – princes.

Gunzi, Christiane. *Colors* ill. by author. Two-Can, 2001. ISBN 978-1-58728-236-2 Subj: Concepts – color.

Numbers ill. by author. Two-Can, 2001. ISBN 978-1-58728-237-9 Subj: Counting, numbers.

Shapes ill. by author. Two-Can, 2001. ISBN 978-1-58728-238-6 Subj: Concepts – shape.

Sizes ill. by author. Two-Can, 2001. ISBN 978-1-58728-239-3 Subj: Concepts – size.

Gurney, John Steven. *Dinosaur train* ill. by author. HarperCollins, 2002. ISBN 978-0-06-029246-1 Subj: Bedtime. Dinosaurs. Trains.

Gutch, Michael. *Sticky, sticky, stuck!* ill. by Steve Björkman. HarperCollins, 2013. ISBN 978-0-06-199818-8 Subj: Computers. Cumulative tales. Family life.

Guthrie, James. *Last song* ill. by Eric Rohmann. Roaring Brook, 2010. ISBN 978-1-59643-508-7 Subj: Animals – squirrels. Bedtime. Lullabies. Poetry.

Guthrie, Woody. *Bling blang* ill. by Vladimir Radunsky. Candlewick, 2000. ISBN 978-0-7636-0769-2 Subj: Homes, houses. Music. Songs.

My dolly ill. by Vladimir Radunsky. Candlewick, 2001. ISBN 978-0-7636-0770-8 Subj: Music. Songs. Toys – dolls.

This land is your land ill. by Kathy Jakobsen. With a tribute by Pete Seeger. Little, 1998. ISBN 978-0-316-39215-0 Subj: Music. Songs.

Gutierrez, Akemi. *The mummy and other adventures of Sam and Alice* ill. by author. Houghton, 2005. ISBN 978-0-618-50761-0 Subj: Activities – playing. Family life – brothers & sisters.

Gutierrez, Elisa. *Letter lunch* ill. by author. Owl-Kids, 2014. ISBN 978-177147000-1 Subj: ABC books. Food. Wordless.

Gutman, Anne. *Gaspard and Lisa, friends forever* by Anne Gutman and Georg Hallensleben ill. by Georg Hallensleben. Knopf, 2003. ISBN 978-0-375-82253-7 Subj: Animals – dogs. Friendship. School.

Gaspard and Lisa's Christmas surprise by Anne Gutman and Georg Hallensleben ill. by Georg Hallensleben. Knopf, 2002. ISBN 978-0-375-82229-2 Subj: Animals – dogs. Gifts. Holidays – Christmas.

Gaspard and Lisa's rainy day by Anne Gutman and Georg Hallensleben ill. by Georg Hallensleben. Knopf, 2003. ISBN 978-0-375-82252-0 Subj: Animals – dogs. Behavior – boredom. Behavior – misbehavior. Friendship. Weather – rain.

Gaspard at the seashore by Anne Gutman and Georg Hallensleben ill. by Georg Hallensleben. Knopf, 2002. ISBN 978-0-375-81118-0 Subj: Animals – dogs. Camps, camping. Sea & seashore. Sports – swimming.

Gaspard in the hospital by Anne Gutman and Georg Hallensleben ill. by Georg Hallensleben. Knopf, 2001. ISBN 978-0-375-81116-6 Subj: Animals – dogs. Hospitals.

Gaspard on vacation by Anne Gutman and Georg Hallensleben ill. by Georg Hallensleben. Knopf, 2001. ISBN 978-0-375-81115-9 Subj: Activities – vacationing. Animals – dogs. Boats, ships. Foreign lands – Italy.

Lisa in New York by Anne Gutman and Georg Hallensleben ill. by Georg Hallensleben. Knopf, 2002. ISBN 978-0-375-81119-7 Subj: Animals – dogs. Behavior – lost. Family life – aunts, uncles.

Lisa in the jungle by Anne Gutman and Georg Hallensleben ill. by Georg Hallensleben. Knopf, 2003. ISBN 978-0-375-82254-4 Subj: Animals – dogs. Character traits – honesty. Jungle. School.

Lisa's airplane trip by Anne Gutman and Georg Hallensleben ill. by Georg Hallensleben. Knopf, 2001. ISBN 978-0-375-81114-2 Subj: Activities – traveling. Airplanes, airports. Animals – dogs.

Lisa's baby sister by Anne Gutman and Georg Hallensleben ill. by Georg Hallensleben. Knopf, 2003. ISBN 978-0-375-82251-3 Subj: Animals – dogs. Babies, toddlers. Behavior. Family life – new sibling. Family life – sisters.

Gutman, Dan. *Casey back at bat* ill. by Steve Johnson and Lou Fancher. HarperCollins, 2007. ISBN 978-0-06-056025-6 Subj: Poetry. Sports – baseball.

Rappy the raptor ill. by Tim Bowers. HarperCollins, 2015. ISBN 978-006229180-6 Subj: Character traits – individuality. Dinosaurs. Rhyming text. Self-concept.

Guy, Ginger Foglesong. *¡Bravo!* ill. by Rene King Moreno. HarperCollins, 2010. ISBN 978-0-06-173180-8 Subj: Activities – playing. Foreign languages. Language.

Fiesta ill. by Rene King Moreno. Greenwillow, 1996. ISBN 978-0-688-14332-9 Subj: Counting, numbers. Fairs, festivals. Foreign lands – Mexico. Foreign languages.

My grandma / Mi abuelita ill. by Viví Escrivá. HarperCollins, 2007. ISBN 978-0-06-079098-1 Subj: Family life. Foreign languages.

My school / Mi escuela ill. by Viví Escrivá. HarperCollins, 2006. ISBN 978-0-06-079101-8 Subj: Foreign languages. School.

Perros! perros! dogs! dogs! a story in English and Spanish ill. by Sharon Glick. HarperCollins, 2006.

ISBN 978-0-06-083574-3 Subj: Animals – dogs. Concepts – opposites. Foreign languages.

Siesta ill. by René King Moreno. HarperCollins, 2005. ISBN 978-0-06-056063-8 Subj: Family life – brothers & sisters. Foreign languages. Sleep. Toys – bears.

Gwynne, Fred. *A chocolate moose for dinner* ill. by author. Messner, 1981. ISBN 978-0-671-43706-0 Subj: Imagination. Language.

A little pigeon toad ill. by author. Simon & Schuster, 1988. ISBN 978-0-671-66659-0 Subj: Imagination. Language.

Haas, Irene. *Bess and Bella* ill. by author. Simon & Schuster, 2006. ISBN 978-1-4169-0013-9 Subj: Birds. Emotions – loneliness. Friendship.

Haas, Jessie. *Appaloosa zebra* ill. by Margot Apple. Greenwillow, 2002. ISBN 978-0-688-17881-9 Subj: ABC books. Animals – horses, ponies.

Hurry! ill. by Joseph A. Smith. Greenwillow, 2000. ISBN 978-0-688-16889-6 Subj: Careers – farmers. Family life – grandparents.

Haas, Rick de. *Peter and the seal* ill. by author. NorthSouth, 2012. ISBN 978-0-7358-4061-4 Subj: Animals – seals. Boats, ships. Sports – sailing.

Peter and the winter sleepers ill. by author. NorthSouth, 2011. ISBN 978-0-7358-4033-1 Subj: Animals. Lighthouses. Seasons – winter. Weather – blizzards.

Haber, Tiffany Strelitz. *The monster who lost his mean* ill. by Kirstie Edmunds. Henry Holt, 2012. ISBN 978-0-8050-9375-9 Subj: Behavior – bullying, teasing. Monsters. Rhyming text. Self-concept.

Ollie and Claire ill. by Matthew Cordell. Philomel, 2013. ISBN 978-0-399-25603-5 Subj: Animals – dogs. Behavior – boredom. Friendship. Rhyming text.

Hächler, Bruno. *Anna's wish* ill. by Friederike Rave. NorthSouth, 2008. ISBN 978-0-7358-2207-8 Subj: Behavior – wishing. Holidays – Christmas. Weather – snow.

What does my teddy bear do all night? ill. by Birte Müller. Minedition, 2005. ISBN 978-0-698-40029-0 Subj: Bedtime. Rhyming text. Toys – bears.

Hacohen, Dean. *Tuck me in!* by Dean Hacohen and Sherry Scharschmidt; ill. by Dean Hacohen. Candlewick, 2010. ISBN 978-0-7636-4728-5 Subj: Animals. Bedtime. Format, unusual – toy & movable books.

Who's hungry? ill. by Sherry Scharschmidt. Candlewick, 2015. ISBN 978-076366586-9 Subj: Animals. Food. Format, unusual – toy & movable books.

Hader, Berta Hoerner. *The big snow* by Berta Hoerner Hader and Elmer Hader; ill. by authors. Macmillan, 1948. Subj: Caldecott award books. Weather – snow.

Cock-a-doodle doo: the story of a little red rooster by Berta Hoerner Hader and Elmer Hader; ill. by authors. Macmillan, 1939. Subj: Birds – chickens, roosters. Birds – ducks. Caldecott award honor books. Farms.

The mighty hunter by Berta Hoerner Hader and Elmer Hader; ill. by authors. Macmillan, 1943. Subj: Caldecott award honor books. Ecology. Indians of North America. School. Sports – hunting.

Hader, Elmer. *The big snow* (Hader, Berta Hoerner)

Cock-a-doodle doo: the story of a little red rooster (Hader, Berta Hoerner)

The mighty hunter (Hader, Berta Hoerner)

Hadfield, Chris. *The darkest dark* by Chris Hadfield and Kate Fillion ill. by Eric Fan. Little, Brown, 2016. ISBN 978-031639472-7 Subj: Bedtime. Careers – astronauts. Emotions – fear. Space & space ships.

Hafner, Marylin. *Molly and Emmett's camping adventure* ill. by author. McGraw-Hill, 2001. ISBN 978-1-57768-894-5 Subj: Animals – cats. Camps, camping. Weather – rain.

Molly and Emmett's surprise garden ill. by author. McGraw-Hill, 2000. ISBN 978-1-57768-895-2 Subj: Animals – cats. Food. Gardens, gardening.

Hager, Sarah. *Dancing Matilda* ill. by Kelly Murphy. HarperCollins, 2005. ISBN 978-0-06-051453-2 Subj: Activities – dancing. Rhyming text.

Hague, Kathleen. *Alphabears: an ABC book* ill. by Michael Hague. Henry Holt, 1984. Subj: ABC books. Rhyming text. Toys – bears.

Calendarbears: a book of months ill. by Michael Hague. Henry Holt, 1997. ISBN 978-0-8050-3818-7 Subj: Animals – bears. Calendars. Days of the week, months of the year. Rhyming text.

Good night, fairies ill. by Michael Hague. SeaStar, 2002. ISBN 978-1-58717-134-5 Subj: Bedtime. Fairies. Family life – mothers.

Numbears: a counting book ill. by Michael Hague. Henry Holt, 1986. ISBN 978-0-03-007194-2 Subj: Counting, numbers. Toys – bears.

Ten little bears: a counting rhyme ill. by Michael Hague. Morrow, 1999. ISBN 978-0-688-16383-9 Subj: Animals – bears. Counting, numbers. Rhyming text.

Hague, Michael, compiler. *Animal friends: a collection of poems for children* ill. by compiler. Henry Holt, 2007. ISBN 978-0-8050-3817-0 Subj: Animals. Poetry.

The nutcracker text by Sarah L. Thomson; ill. by author. SeaStar, 2003. ISBN 978-1-58717-255-7 Subj: Activities – dancing. Animals – mice. Ballet. Careers – toy makers. Folk & fairy tales. Holidays – Christmas. Imagination. Royalty.

Teddy bear, teddy bear ill. by author. Morrow, 1993. ISBN 978-0-688-12085-6 Subj: Games. Nursery rhymes. Toys – bears.

Haines, Mike. *Countdown to bedtime* ill. by David Melling. Hyperion, 2001. ISBN 978-0-7868-0741-3 Subj: Animals – porcupines. Animals – raccoons. Bedtime. Format, unusual – toy & movable books.

Hakala, Marjorie Rose. *Mermaid dance* ill. by Mark Jones. Blue Apple, 2009. ISBN 978-1-934706-47-3 Subj: Mythical creatures – mermaids, mermen. Seasons – summer.

Hakte, Ben. *Julia's house for lost creatures* ill. by Ben Hatke. First Second, 2014. ISBN 978-159643866-8 Subj: Behavior – lost. Behavior – resourcefulness. Character traits – responsibility. Homes, houses. Mythical creatures.

Haldeman, Oakley. *Here comes Santa Claus* (Autry, Gene)

Hale, Bruce. *Big Bad Baby* ill. by Steve Breen. Dial, 2014. ISBN 978-080373585-9 Subj: Babies, toddlers. Behavior – misbehavior.

Clark the Shark ill. by Guy Francis. HarperCollins, 2013. ISBN 978-0-06-219226-4 Subj: Behavior – misbehavior. Fish – sharks. School.

Santa on the loose! ill. by David Garbot. HarperFestival, 2012. ISBN 978-0-06-202262-2 Subj: Holidays – Christmas. Picture puzzles. Santa Claus.

Snoring Beauty ill. by Howard Fine. Harcourt, 2008. ISBN 978-0-15-216314-3 Subj: Dragons. Folk & fairy tales. Humorous stories. Royalty – princesses.

Hale, Christy. *Dreaming up: a celebration of building* ill. by author. Lee & Low, 2012. ISBN 978-1-60060-651-9 Subj: Activities – playing. Art. Buildings.

Hale, Dean. *Scapegoat: the story of a goat named Oat and a chewed-up coat.* Bloomsbury, 2011. ISBN 978-1-59990-468-9 Subj: Animals – goats. Behavior – lying.

Hale, Nathan. *Yellowbelly and Plum go to school* ill. by author. Penguin, 2007. ISBN 978-0-399-24624-1 Subj: School – first day. Toys – bears.

Hale, Sarah Josepha Buell. *Mary had a little lamb* ill. by Tomie dePaola. Holiday, 1984. ISBN 978-0-8234-0509-1 Subj: Animals – sheep. Music. Nursery rhymes. School.

Mary had a little lamb ill. by Laura Huliska-Beith. Marshall Cavendish, 2011. ISBN 978-0-7614-5824-1 Subj: Animals – sheep. Music. Nursery rhymes. School.

Mary had a little lamb photos by Bruce McMillan. Scholastic, 1990. ISBN 978-0-590-43773-8 Subj: Animals – sheep. Music. Nursery rhymes. School.

Mary had a little lamb ill. by Salley Mavor. Orchard, 1995. ISBN 978-0-531-08725-1 Subj: Animals – sheep. Nursery rhymes. School.

Haley, Alex. *Young Martin's promise* (Myers, Walter Dean)

Haley, Amanda. *It's a baby's world* ill. by author. Little, 2001. ISBN 978-0-316-34596-5 Subj: Activities. Babies, toddlers. Day.

Haley, Gail E. *A story, a story* ill. by author. Aladdin, 1988, ©1970. ISBN 978-0-689-71201-2 Subj: Caldecott award books. Folk & fairy tales. Foreign lands – Africa.

Two bad boys: a very old Cherokee tale ill. by author. Dutton, 1996. ISBN 978-0-525-45311-6 Subj: Activities – working. Creation. Indians of North America – Cherokee.

Halfmann, Janet. *Eggs 1, 2, 3: who will the babies be?* ill. by Betsy Thompson. Blue Apple, 2012. ISBN 978-1-60905-191-4 Subj: Animals – babies. Counting, numbers. Eggs. Format, unusual.

Hall, Algy Craig. *Dino bites!* ill. by author. Boxer, 2013. ISBN 978-1-907967-50-4 Subj: Concepts – size. Cumulative tales. Dinosaurs. Rhyming text.

Fine as we are ill. by author. Boxer, 2008. ISBN 978-1-905417-72-8 Subj: Family life – new sibling. Frogs & toads. Sibling rivalry.

Mammoth and me ill. by author. Sterling, 2012. ISBN 978-1-9079-6722-1 Subj: Animals – woolly mammoths. Friendship.

Hall, Donald. *Lucy's Christmas* ill. by Michael McCurdy. Harcourt, 1994. ISBN 978-0-15-276870-6 Subj: Activities – making things. Family life. Holidays – Christmas. U.S. history.

Ox-cart man ill. by Barbara Cooney. Viking, 1979. ISBN 978-0-670-53328-2 Subj: Activities – working. Caldecott award books. Farms. Seasons.

Hall, Kathy *see* McMullan, Kate

Hall, Kirsten. *The jacket* ill. by Dasha Tolstikova. Enchanted Lion, 2014. ISBN 978-159270168-1 Subj: Activities – making things. Animals – dogs. Books, reading.

Hall, Marcellus. *Everyone sleeps* ill. by author. Penguin/Nancy Paulsen, 2013. ISBN 978-0-399-25793-3 Subj: Animals – dogs. Bedtime. Rhyming text. Sleep.

Hall, Margaret. *Corn* ill. with photos. Heinemann, 2003. ISBN 978-1-58810-617-9 Subj: Activities – baking, cooking. Farms. Food.

Peanuts ill. with photos. Heinemann, 2003. ISBN 978-1-58810-619-3 Subj: Activities – baking, cooking. Farms. Food.

Hall, Michael. *Cat tale* ill. by author. Greenwillow, 2012. ISBN 978-0-06-191516-1 Subj: Animals – cats. Language. Rhyming text.

Frankencrayon ill. by author. Greenwillow, 2016. ISBN 978-006225211-1 Subj: Books, reading. Humorous stories. Monsters.

It's an orange aardvark! ill. by author. Greenwillow, 2014. ISBN 978-006225206-7 Subj: Concepts – color. Format, unusual – toy & movable books. Imagination. Insects – ants.

Little i ill. by author. Greenwillow, 2017. ISBN 978-006238300-6 Subj: ABC books. Behavior – lost & found possessions. Language. Rhyming text.

My heart is like a zoo ill. by author. HarperCollins, 2010. ISBN 978-0-06-191510-9 Subj: Animals. Concepts – shape. Emotions. Rhyming text. Zoos.

Perfect square ill. by author. HarperCollins, 2011. ISBN 978-0-06-191513-0 Subj: Character traits – individuality. Concepts – shape. Emotions – happiness. Self-concept.

Red: a crayon's story ill. by author. Greenwillow, 2015. ISBN 978-006225207-4 Subj: Character traits – appearance. Character traits – being different. Concepts – color. Self-concept.

Wonderfall ill. by author. Greenwillow, 2016. ISBN 978-006238298-6 Subj: Animals. Seasons – fall. Trees.

Hall, Mikele. *Mommy works, Daddy works* (Pedersen, Marika)

Hall, Pamela. *Miss you like crazy* ill. by Jennifer A. Bell. Tanglewood, 2014. ISBN 978-193371891-0 Subj: Animals – squirrels. Family life – mothers.

Hall, Patricia. *Hooray for reading!* ill. by Kathryn Mitter. Simon & Schuster, 2002. ISBN 978-0-689-85206-0 Subj: Books, reading. Toys – dolls.

Hall, Richard. *Humphrey the lost whale* (Tokuda, Wendy)

Hall, Zoe. *The apple pie tree* ill. by Shari Halpern. Scholastic, 1996. ISBN 978-0-590-62382-7 Subj: Food. Nature. Seasons. Trees.

Fall leaves fall ill. by Shari Halpern. Scholastic, 2000. ISBN 978-0-590-10079-3 Subj: Seasons – fall. Trees.

It's pumpkin time! ill. by Shari Halpern. Scholastic, 1994. ISBN 978-0-590-47833-5 Subj: Holidays – Halloween. Plants.

The surprise garden ill. by Shari Halpern. Blue Sky, 1998. ISBN 978-0-590-10075-5 Subj: Gardens, gardening. Seeds.

Hallensleben, Georg. *Gaspard and Lisa, friends forever* (Gutman, Anne)

Gaspard and Lisa's Christmas surprise (Gutman, Anne)

Gaspard and Lisa's rainy day (Gutman, Anne)

Gaspard at the seashore (Gutman, Anne)

Gaspard in the hospital (Gutman, Anne)

Gaspard on vacation (Gutman, Anne)

Lisa in New York (Gutman, Anne)

Lisa in the jungle (Gutman, Anne)

Lisa's airplane trip (Gutman, Anne)

Lisa's baby sister (Gutman, Anne)

Halloweena ill. by Victoria Roberts. Atheneum, 2002. ISBN 978-0-689-82825-6 Subj: Holidays – Halloween. Witches.

Hallowell, George. *Wagons ho!* by George Hallowell and Joan Holub ill. by Lynne Avril. Albert Whitman, 2011. ISBN 978-0-8075-8612-9 Subj: Moving. U.S. history – frontier & pioneer life.

Halls, Kelly Milner. *Dinosaur parade: a spectacle of prehistoric proportions* ill. by Rick C. Spears. Sterling, 2008. ISBN 978-1-60059-267-6 Subj: Dinosaurs. Rhyming text.

I bought a baby chicken ill. by Karen Stormer Brooks. Boyds Mills, 2000. ISBN 978-1-56397-800-5 Subj: Animals – babies. Birds – chickens, roosters. Counting, numbers.

Hallworth, Grace. *Sing me a story* ill. by John Clementson. August House, 2002. ISBN 978-0-87483-672-1 Subj: Activities – dancing. Folk & fairy tales. Foreign lands – Caribbean Islands. Music. Songs.

Halperin, Wendy Anderson. *Peace* ill. by author. Atheneum, 2013. ISBN 978-068982552-1 Subj: Violence, nonviolence. World.

Halpern, Julie. *Toby and the snowflakes* ill. by Matthew Cordell. Houghton, 2004. ISBN 978-0-618-42004-9 Subj: Activities – playing. Emotions – loneliness. Friendship. Weather – snow.

Halpern, Shari. *Dinosaur parade* ill. by author. Henry Holt, 2014. ISBN 978-080509242-4 Subj: Dinosaurs. Rhyming text.

Halpin, Angela Demos. *Water, weed, and wait* (Fine, Edith Hope)

Hambleton, Laura. *Monkey business: fun with idioms* by Laura Hambleton and Sedat Turhan ill. by Hervé Tullet. Milet, 2007. ISBN 978-1-84059-499-7 Subj: Language.

Hamburg, Jennifer. *Monkey and Duck quack up!* ill. by Edwin Fotheringham. Scholastic, 2015. ISBN 978-054564514-0 Subj: Animals – monkeys. Birds – ducks. Contests. Rhyming text.

A moose that says mooooooooooo ill. by Sue Truesdell. Farrar, 2013. ISBN 978-0-374-35058-1 Subj: Animals. Imagination. Rhyming text. Zoos.

Hamilton, Arlene. *Only a cow* ill. by Dean Griffiths. Fitzhenry & Whiteside, 2006. ISBN 978-1-55041-871-2 Subj: Animals – bulls, cows. Animals – horses, ponies. Emotions – envy, jealousy. Fairs, festivals.

Hamilton, Emma Walton. *Dumpy at school* (Andrews, Julie)

Dumpy the dump truck (Andrews, Julie)

Dumpy to the rescue! (Andrews, Julie)

Dumpy's apple shop (Andrews, Julie)

Simeon's gift (Andrews, Julie)

The very fairy princess (Andrews, Julie)

The very fairy princess: a spooky, sparkly Halloween (Andrews, Julie)

The very fairy princess: graduation girl! (Andrews, Julie)

The very fairy princess: here comes the flower girl! (Andrews, Julie)

The very fairy princess follows her heart (Andrews, Julie)

The very fairy princess sparkles in the snow (Andrews, Julie)

Hamilton, K. R. *This is the ocean* ill. by Lorianne Siomades. Boyds Mills, 2001. ISBN 978-1-56397-890-6 Subj: Rhyming text. Sea & seashore. Water.

Hamilton, Kersten. *Firefighters to the rescue!* ill. by Rich Davis. Penguin, 2005. ISBN 978-0-670-03503-8 Subj: Careers – firefighters.

Police officers on patrol ill. by R. W. Alley. Viking, 2009. ISBN 978-0-670-06315-4 Subj: Careers – police officers. Rhyming text.

Red truck ill. by Valeria Petrone. Viking, 2008. ISBN 978-0-670-06275-1 Subj: Character traits – helpfulness. Rhyming text. Trucks.

Hamilton, Libby. *The monstrous book of monsters* ill. by Jonny Duddle and Aleksei Bitskoff. Candlewick, 2011. ISBN 978-0-7636-5756-7 Subj: Format, unusual – toy & movable books. Monsters.

Hamilton, Martha. *The ghost catcher: a Bengali folktale* by Martha Hamilton and Mitch Weiss ill. by Kristen Balouch. August House, 2008. ISBN 978-0-87483-835-0 Subj: Careers – barbers. Character traits – generosity. Folk & fairy tales. Foreign lands – India. Ghosts.

The hidden feast: a folktale from the American South by Martha Hamilton and Mitch Weiss ill. by Don Tate. August House, 2006. ISBN 978-0-87483-758-2 Subj: Animals. Etiquette. Farms. Folk & fairy tales.

Priceless gifts: a folktale from Italy by Martha Hamilton and Mitch Weiss ill. by John Kanzler. August House, 2007. ISBN 978-0-87483-788-9 Subj: Animals – cats. Animals – rats. Folk & fairy tales. Foreign lands – Italy. Gifts.

Hamilton, Richard. *Let's take over the kindergarten* ill. by Sue Heap. Bloomsbury, 2007. ISBN 978-1-58234-707-3 Subj: Rhyming text. School.

Polly's picnic ill. by Sophy Williams. Bloomsbury, 2003. ISBN 978-1-58234-819-3 Subj: Activities – picnicking. Animals. Behavior – sharing. Rhyming text.

Hamilton, Virginia. *Drylongso* ill. by Jerry Pinkney. Harcourt, 1992. ISBN 978-0-15-224241-1 Subj: Ecology. Ethnic groups in the U.S. – African Americans. Farms. Weather – droughts. Weather – wind.

The girl who spun gold ill. by Leo and Diane Dillon. Blue Sky, 2000. ISBN 978-0-590-47378-1 Subj: Activities – weaving. Behavior – greed. Folk & fairy tales. Foreign lands – West Indies.

Jaguarundi ill. by Floyd Cooper. Blue Sky, 1995. ISBN 978-0-590-47366-8 Subj: Animals. Animals – endangered animals. Animals – jaguars. Behavior – seeking better things. Ecology.

Hamm, Mia. *Winners never quit* ill. by Carol Thompson. HarperCollins, 2004. ISBN 978-0-06-074051-1 Subj: Sports – soccer. Sportsmanship.

Hammerle, Susa. *Let's try horseback riding* ill. by Kyrima Trapp. NorthSouth, 2006. ISBN 978-0-7358-2093-7 Subj: Animals – horses, ponies. Sports.

Hammersmith, Craig. *Patterns* ill. with photos. Compass Point, 2003. ISBN 978-0-7565-0452-6 Subj: Concepts.

Watch it grow ill. with photos. Compass Point, 2002. ISBN 978-0-7565-0246-1 Subj: Nature. Plants.

What is a family? ill. with photos. Compass Point, 2003. ISBN 978-0-7565-0367-3 Subj: Family life.

Hammerstein, Oscar. *My favorite things* (Rodgers, Richard)

Hammill, Matt. *Sir Reginald's logbook* ill. by author. Kids Can, 2008. ISBN 978-1-55453-202-5 Subj: Humorous stories. Imagination.

Hample, Stoo. *I will kiss you (lots and lots and lots!)* ill. by author. Candlewick, 2005. ISBN 978-0-7636-2787-4 Subj: Animals – rabbits. Emotions – love. Family life – mothers. Kissing. Rhyming text.

Hamsa, Bobbie. *Fast-draw Freddie* ill. by Susan Miller. Rev. ed. Children's Press, 2000. ISBN 978-0-516-22153-3 Subj: Activities – drawing. Rhyming text.

Han, Eun-sun. *The flying birds* ill. by Ju-kyoung Kim. IPG/TanTan, 2015. ISBN 978-193924805-3 Subj: Birds. Counting, numbers. Homes, houses.

Hancocks, Helen. *Penguin in peril* ill. by author. Candlewick/Templar, 2014. ISBN 978-076367159-4 Subj: Animals – cats. Behavior – stealing. Birds – penguins. Crime.

Handford, Martin. *Find Waldo now* ill. by author. Little, 1994. ISBN 978-0-316-34232-2 Subj: Activities – traveling. Games. Picture puzzles. Time.

The great Waldo search ill. by author. Little, 1989. ISBN 978-0-316-34282-7 Subj: Activities – traveling. Games. Picture puzzles.

Where's Waldo? ill. by author. Candlewick, 1997. ISBN 978-0-7636-0310-6 Subj: Activities – traveling. Behavior – lost & found possessions. Foreign lands. Games. Picture puzzles.

Where's Waldo? In Hollywood ill. by author. Candlewick, 1993. ISBN 978-1-56402-294-3 Subj: Activities – traveling. Games.

Where's Waldo? The fantastic journey ill. by author. Candlewick, 1997. ISBN 978-0-7636-0309-0 Subj: Activities – traveling. Games. Imagination.

Where's Waldo? The wonder book ill. by author. Candlewick, 1997. ISBN 978-0-7636-0312-0 Subj: Activities – traveling. Behavior – lost & found possessions. Games.

Where's Waldo now? ill. by author. Candlewick, 1997. ISBN 978-0-7636-0308-3 Subj: Activities – traveling. Games. Time.

Handforth, Thomas. *Mei Li* ill. by author. Doubleday, 1938. ISBN 978-0-385-07401-8 Subj: Caldecott award books. Foreign lands – China. Holidays – Chinese New Year.

Hänel, Wolfram. *Little elephant runs away* ill. by Cristina Kadmon. NorthSouth, 2001. ISBN 978-0-7358-1444-8 Subj: Behavior – lost. Behavior – running away. Family life – brothers & sisters. Sibling rivalry.

Little elephant's song ill. by Cristina Kadmon. NorthSouth, 2000. ISBN 978-0-7358-1298-7 Subj: Animals – elephants. Behavior – growing up. Family life. Noise, sounds.

Hanft, Josh. *The miracles of Passover* ill. by Seymour Chwast. Blue Apple, 2007. ISBN 978-1-59354-600-7 Subj: Holidays – Passover. Jewish culture.

Hanlon, Abby. *Ralph tells a story* ill. by author. Amazon, 2012. ISBN 978-0-7614-6180-7 Subj: Activities – storytelling. Activities – writing. School. Self-concept.

Hannert, Todd. *Morning dance* ill. by author. Chronicle, 2001. ISBN 978-0-8118-2812-3 Subj: Activities – dancing. Morning.

Hannigan, Katherine. *Gwendolyn Grace* ill. by author. HarperCollins/Greenwillow, 2015. ISBN 978-006234519-6 Subj: Activities – playing. Character traits – patience, impatience. Family life. Noise, sounds. Reptiles – alligators, crocodiles.

Hansen, Felicity. *The first bear* ill. by Anthony Carnabuci. Barefoot, 2000. ISBN 978-1-84148-012-1 Subj: Animals – bears. Creation. Stars. Toys – bears.

Hansen, P. *My granny's purse.* Workman, 2003. ISBN 978-0-7611-2978-3 Subj: Clothing – handbags, purses. Family life – grandmothers. Format, unusual – toy & movable books.

Hanson, Faye. *Midnight at the zoo* ill. by author. Candlewick/Templar, 2017. ISBN 978-076368908-7 Subj: School – field trips. Zoos.

The wonder ill. by author. Candlewick/Templar, 2015. ISBN 978-076367957-6 Subj: Careers – artists. Dreams. Imagination.

Hanson, Mary Elizabeth. *The difference between babies and cookies* ill. by Debbie Tilley. Harcourt, 2002. ISBN 978-0-15-202406-2 Subj: Babies, toddlers. Family life – new sibling. Family life – sisters.

The old man and the flea ill. by David Webber Merrell. Rising Moon, 2001. ISBN 978-0-87358-776-1 Subj: Insects – fleas. Pets.

Hanson, Regina. *A season for mangoes* ill. by Eric Velasquez. Clarion, 2004. ISBN 978-0-618-15972-7 Subj: Activities – storytelling. Death. Emotions – grief. Family life – grandmothers. Foreign lands – Jamaica. Memories, memory.

Hanson, Warren. *Bugtown Boogie* ill. by Steve Johnson and Lou Fancher. HarperCollins, 2008. ISBN 978-0-06-059937-9 Subj: Activities – dancing. Insects. Parties. Rhyming text.

It's Monday, Mrs. Jolly Bones! ill. by Tricia Tusa. Simon & Schuster, 2013. ISBN 978-1-4424-1229-3 Subj: Careers – housekeepers. Character traits – cleanliness. Days of the week, months of the year. Humorous stories.

Hapka, Cathy. *Margret and H. A. Rey's Merry Christmas, Curious George.* Houghton, 2006. ISBN 978-0-618-69237-8 Subj: Animals – monkeys. Character traits – curiosity. Holidays – Christmas. Hospitals. Humorous stories.

Harburg, E. Y. *Over the rainbow* ill. by Eric Puybaret. Imagine, 2010. ISBN 978-1-936140-00-8 Subj: Songs. Weather – rainbows.

Harby, Melanie. *All aboard for Dreamland!* ill. by Geraldo Valério. Simon & Schuster, 2008. ISBN 978-1-4169-6127-7 Subj: Bedtime. Rhyming text. Trains.

Hardin, Melinda. *Hero dad* ill. by Bryan Langdo. Marshall Cavendish, 2010. ISBN 978-0-7614-5713-8 Subj: Careers – military. Family life – fathers.

Hardy, Sarah Frances. *Puzzled by pink* ill. by author. Viking, 2012. ISBN 978-0-670-01320-3 Subj: Birthdays. Character traits – individuality. Family life – sisters. Parties.

Hargrove, Linda. *Wings across the moon* ill. by Joung Un Kim. HarperCollins, 2001. ISBN 978-0-694-01280-0 Subj: Animals. Moon. Night. Rhyming text.

Haring, Kay A. *Keith Haring: the boy who just kept drawing* ill. by Robert Neubecker. Dial, 2017. ISBN 978-052542819-0 Subj: Activities – drawing. Art. Careers – artists. Illness – AIDS.

Harjo, Joy. *The good luck cat* ill. by Paul Lee. Harcourt, 2000. ISBN 978-0-15-232197-0 Subj: Animals – cats. Character traits – luck. Indians of North America.

Harker, Lesley. *Annie's ark* ill. by author. Scholastic, 2002. ISBN 978-0-439-36823-0 Subj: Animals. Boats, ships. Religion – Noah. Weather – floods. Weather – rain.

Harley, Bill. *Bear's all-night party* ill. by Melissa Ferreira. August House, 2001. ISBN 978-0-87483-572-4 Subj: Animals. Animals – bears. Moon. Parties.

Dear Santa: the letters of James B. Dobbins ill. by R. W. Alley. HarperCollins, 2005. ISBN 978-0-06-623779-4 Subj: Behavior. Holidays – Christmas. Letters, cards. Santa Claus.

Dirty Joe, the pirate: a true story ill. by Jack E. Davis. HarperCollins, 2008. ISBN 978-0-06-623780-0 Subj: Clothing. Family life – brothers & sisters. Pirates. Rhyming text.

Lost and found ill. by Adam Gustavson. Peachtree, 2012. ISBN 978-1-56145-628-4 Subj: Behavior – lost & found possessions. Careers – custodians, janitors. Clothing – hats. Family life – grandmothers. School.

Harline, Leigh. *When you wish upon a star* (Washington, Ned)

Harness, Cheryl. *Mary Walker wears the pants: the true story of the doctor, reformer, and civil war hero* ill. by Carlo Molinari. Albert Whitman, 2013. ISBN 978-0-8075-4990-2 Subj: Careers – doctors. Character traits – assertiveness. Character traits – being different. Gender roles. U.S. history. War.

Our colonial year ill. by author. Simon & Schuster, 2005. ISBN 978-0-689-83479-0 Subj: Days of the week, months of the year. U.S. history.

Papa's Christmas gift: around the world on the night before Christmas ill. by author. Simon & Schuster, 1995. ISBN 978-0-689-80344-4 Subj: Holidays – Christmas. Poetry.

Harper, Anita. *It's not fair!* ill. by Mary McQuillan. Holiday House, 2007. ISBN 978-0-8234-2094-0 Subj: Animals – cats. Emotions – envy, jealousy. Family life – brothers & sisters. Family life – new sibling.

Harper, Charise Mericle. *Amy and Ivan* ill. by author. Ten Speed, 2006. ISBN 978-1-58246-134-2 Subj: Birds. Counting, numbers. Format, unusual – toy & movable books. Gifts.

The best birthday ever! by me (Lana Kittie) ill. by author. Hyperion/Disney, 2011. ISBN 978-1-4231-3776-4 Subj: Animals – cats. Birthdays. Etiquette. Imagination.

A big surprise for Little Card ill. by Anna Raff. Candlewick, 2016. ISBN 978-076367485-4 Subj: Books, reading. Libraries.

Cupcake: a journey to special ill. by author. Hyperion/Disney, 2010. ISBN 978-1-4231-1897-8 Subj: Character traits – appearance. Food. Friendship. Self-concept.

Flush! the scoop on poop throughout the ages ill. by author. Little, Brown, 2007. ISBN 978-0-316-01064-1 Subj: Health & fitness. Toilets.

Go! go! go! stop! ill. by author. Knopf, 2014. ISBN 978-037586924-2 Subj: Machines. Traffic, traffic signs. Trucks.

Henry's heart ill. by author. Henry Holt, 2011. ISBN 978-0-8050-8989-9 Subj: Anatomy. Animals – dogs. Emotions. Health & fitness. Pets.

Imaginative inventions ill. by author. Little, 2001. ISBN 978-0-316-34725-9 Subj: Inventions.

Mimi and Lulu: three sweet stories, one forever friendship ill. by author. HarperCollins, 2009. ISBN 978-0-06-175583-5 Subj: Activities – playing. Friendship.

The Monster Show ill. by author. Houghton, 2004. ISBN 978-0-618-38797-7 Subj: Monsters.

Pink me up ill. by author. Random House, 2010. ISBN 978-0-375-85607-5 Subj: Activities – picnicking. Animals – rabbits. Concepts – color. Family life – fathers.

Superlove ill. by Mark Chambers. Knopf, 2014. ISBN 978-037586923-5 Subj: Animals – cats. Imagination. Toys. Weddings.

There was a bold lady who wanted a star ill. by author. Little, 2002. ISBN 978-0-316-14673-9 Subj: Cumulative tales. Folk & fairy tales. Rhyming text.

The trouble with normal ill. by author. Houghton, 2003. ISBN 978-0-618-15626-9 Subj: Animals – squirrels. Homes, houses.

When I grow up ill. by author. Chronicle, 2001. ISBN 978-0-8118-2905-2 Subj: Behavior – growing up.

When Randolph turned rotten ill. by author. Random House, 2007. ISBN 978-0-375-84071-5 Subj: Animals – beavers. Birds – geese. Birthdays. Friendship. Parties. Self-concept. Sleepovers.

Harper, Dan. *Sit, Truman* ill. by Barry Moser and Cara Moser. Harcourt, 2001. ISBN 978-0-15-202616-5 Subj: Activities. Animals – dogs.

Telling time with Big Mama Cat ill. by Barry Moser and Cara Moser. Harcourt, 1998. ISBN 978-0-15-201738-5 Subj: Animals – cats. Clocks, watches. Format, unusual – toy & movable books. Time.

Harper, Jamie. *Don't grown-ups ever have fun?* ill. by author. Little, 2003. ISBN 978-0-316-14664-7 Subj: Behavior. Family life – parents.

Me too! ill. by author. Little, Brown, 2005. ISBN 978-0-316-60552-6 Subj: Behavior – imitation. Family life – brothers & sisters. Sports – swimming.

Miles to go ill. by author. Candlewick, 2010. ISBN 978-0-7636-3598-5 Subj: Automobiles. Imagination.

Miss Mingo and the fire drill ill. by author. Candlewick, 2009. ISBN 978-0-7636-3597-8 Subj: Animals. Birds – flamingos. Careers – firefighters. School.

Miss Mingo and the first day of school ill. by author. Candlewick, 2006. ISBN 978-0-7636-2410-1 Subj: Animals. Birds – flamingos. Careers – teachers. School – first day.

Miss Mingo weathers the storm ill. by author. Candlewick, 2012. ISBN 978-0-7636-4931-9 Subj: Activities – hiking. Animals. School – field trips. Weather.

Night night, Baby Bundt ill. by author. Candlewick, 2007. ISBN 978-0-7636-3239-7 Subj: Bedtime. Format, unusual – board books.

Splish splash, Baby Bundt ill. by author. Candlewick, 2007. ISBN 978-0-7636-3240-3 Subj: Activities – bathing. Format, unusual – board books.

Harper, Jessica. *I'm not going to chase the cat today* ill. by Lindsay Harper DuPont. HarperCollins, 2000. ISBN 978-0-688-17637-2 Subj: Animals – cats. Animals – dogs. Animals – mice. Parties. Rhyming text.

Lizzy's do's and don'ts ill. by Lindsay Harper DuPont. HarperCollins, 2002. ISBN 978-0-06-623861-6 Subj: Behavior. Family life – mothers. Rhyming text.

Lizzy's ups and downs ill. by Lindsay Harper DuPont. HarperCollins, 2004. ISBN 978-0-06-052064-9 Subj: Emotions. Family life – mothers. Rhyming text. School.

Nora's room ill. by Lindsay Harper DuPont. HarperCollins, 2001. ISBN 978-0-06-029137-2 Subj: Imagination. Noise, sounds. Rhyming text.

A place called Kindergarten ill. by G. Brian Karas. Penguin, 2006. ISBN 978-0-399-24226-7 Subj: Animals. Farms. School – first day.

Harper, Jo. *I could eat you up!* ill. by Kay Chorao. Holiday House, 2007. ISBN 978-0-8234-1733-9 Subj: Animals. Family life – parents. Language.

Ollie Jolly, rodeo clown ill. by Amy Meissner. WestWinds, 2002. ISBN 978-1-55868-552-9 Subj: Clowns, jesters. Cowboys, cowgirls. Rodeos.

Harper, Lee. *The Emperor's cool clothes* ill. by author. Marshall Cavendish, 2011. ISBN 978-0-7614-5948-4 Subj: Birds – penguins. Character traits – appearance. Character traits – vanity. Clothing. Folk & fairy tales. Humorous stories.

Snow! snow! snow! ill. by author. Simon & Schuster, 2009. ISBN 978-1-4169-8454-2 Subj: Animals – dogs. Family life – fathers. Sports – sledding. Weather – snow.

Harpham, Wendy Schlessel. *The hope tree* (Numeroff, Laura Joffe)

Harrington, Janice N. *Busy-busy Little Chick* ill. by Brian Pinkney. Farrar, 2013. ISBN 978-0-374-34746-8 Subj: Birds – chickens, roosters. Folk & fairy tales. Foreign lands – Africa. Homes, houses.

The chicken-chasing queen of Lamar County ill. by Shelley Jackson. Farrar, 2007. ISBN 978-0-374-31251-0 Subj: Birds – chickens, roosters. Ethnic groups in the U.S. – African Americans. Farms.

Roberto walks home ill. by Jody Wheeler. Viking, 2008. ISBN 978-0-670-06316-1 Subj: Emotions – anger. Ethnic groups in the U.S. – Hispanic Americans. Family life – brothers.

Harrington, Tim. *Nose to toes, you are yummy!* ill. by author. HarperCollins/Balzer+Bray, 2015. ISBN 978-006232816-8 Subj: Anatomy. Animals. Participation. Rhyming text.

This little piggy ill. by author. HarperCollins, 2013. ISBN 978-0-06-221808-7 Subj: Anatomy – toes. Counting, numbers. Nursery rhymes.

Harris, Joel Chandler. *Jump! the adventures of Brer Rabbit* adapt. by Van Dyke Parks and Malcolm Jones; ill. by Barry Moser. Harcourt, 1986. ISBN 978-0-15-241350-7 Subj: Animals. Folk & fairy tales.

Jump again! more adventures of Brer Rabbit adapt. by Van Dyke Parks; ill. by Barry Moser. Harcourt, 1987. ISBN 978-0-15-241352-1 Subj: Animals. Folk & fairy tales.

Harris, John. *A giraffe goes to Paris* (Holmes, Mary Tavener)

Jingle bells: how the holiday classic came to be ill. by Adam Gustavson. Peachtree, 2011. ISBN 978-1-56145-590-4 Subj: Music. Seasons – winter. Songs.

Harris, Peter. *The night pirates* ill. by Deborah Allwright. Scholastic, 2006. ISBN 978-0-439-79959-1 Subj: Bedtime. Night. Pirates.

Perfect Prudence ill. by Deborah Allwright. Gingham Dog, 2003. ISBN 978-1-57768-437-4 Subj: Character traits – perfectionism.

Harris, Robie H. *The day Leo said I hate you!* ill. by Molly Bang. Little, Brown, 2008. ISBN 978-0-316-06580-1 Subj: Behavior – fighting, arguing. Emotions – anger. Emotions – hate. Family life – mothers.

Don't forget to come back ill. by Harry Bliss. Candlewick, 2004. ISBN 978-0-7636-1782-0 Subj: Activities – babysitting. Behavior. Family life.

Go! go! Maria! ill. by Michael Emberley. Margaret K. McElderry, 2003. ISBN 978-0-689-83258-1 Subj: Behavior – growing up. Family life.

Goodbye, Mousie ill. by Jan Ormerod. Margaret K. McElderry, 2001. ISBN 978-0-689-83217-8 Subj: Animals – mice. Death. Emotions – grief. Pets.

Hi, new baby ill. by Michael Emberley. Candlewick, 2000. ISBN 978-0-7636-0539-1 Subj: Babies, toddlers. Family life – brothers & sisters. Family life – new sibling.

I am not going to school today ill. by Jan Ormerod. Margaret K. McElderry, 2001. ISBN 978-0-689-83913-9 Subj: School – first day.

I love messes! ill. by Nicole Hollander. Little, Brown, 2005. ISBN 978-0-316-10946-8 Subj: Behavior – messy. Character traits – cleanliness. Character traits – orderliness.

I'm all dressed! ill. by Nicole Hollander. Little, Brown, 2005. ISBN 978-0-316-10948-2 Subj: Character traits – individuality. Clothing.

Mail Harry to the moon! ill. by Michael Emberley. Little, Brown, 2008. ISBN 978-0-316-15376-8 Subj: Family life – brothers. Family life – new sibling. Imagination.

Maybe a bear ate it! ill. by Michael Emberley. Scholastic, 2007. ISBN 978-0-439-92961-5 Subj: Animals. Bedtime. Books, reading. Imagination.

Turtle and me ill. by Tor Freeman. little bee, 2015. ISBN 978-149980046-3 Subj: Friendship. Reptiles – turtles, tortoises. Toys.

What's in there? all about before you were born ill. by Nadine Bernard Westcott. Candlewick, 2013. ISBN 978-0-7636-3630-2 Subj: Babies, toddlers. Birth. Family life – new sibling. Sex instruction.

What's so yummy? all about eating well and feeling good ill. by Nadine Bernard Westcott. Candlewick, 2014. ISBN 978-076363632-6 Subj: Food. Health & fitness.

When lions roar ill. by Chris Raschka. Scholastic, 2013. ISBN 978-0-545-11283-3 Subj: Emotions – fear. Noise, sounds.

Who has what? all about girls' bodies and boys' bodies ill. by Nadine Bernard Westcott. Candlewick, 2011. ISBN 978-0-7636-2931-1 Subj: Anatomy.

Who we are! all about being the same and being different ill. by Nadine Bernard Westcott. Candlewick, 2016. ISBN 978-076366903-4 Subj: Character traits – being different. Character traits – individuality. Ethnic groups in the U.S. Self-concept.

Who's in my family? all about our families ill. by Nadine Bernard Westcott. Candlewick, 2012. ISBN 978-0-7636-3631-9 Subj: Character traits – being different. Ethnic groups in the U.S. Family life. Zoos.

Harris, Teresa E. *Summer Jackson: grown up* ill. by A. G. Ford. HarperCollins, 2011. ISBN 978-0-06-185757-7 Subj: Behavior – growing up. Ethnic groups in the U.S. – African Americans. Family life.

Harris, Trudy. *The clock struck one: a time-telling tale* ill. by Carrie Hartman. Millbrook, 2009. ISBN 978-0-8225-9067-5 Subj: Animals. Nursery rhymes. Time.

Jenny found a penny ill. by John Hovell. Lerner, 2007. ISBN 978-0-8225-6725-7 Subj: Counting, numbers. Money. Rhyming text.

100 days of school ill. by Beth Griffis Johnson. Millbrook, 1999. ISBN 978-0-7613-1271-0 Subj: Counting, numbers. Rhyming text.

Pattern bugs ill. by Anne Canevari Green. Millbrook, 2001. ISBN 978-0-7613-2107-1 Subj: Concepts – patterns. Insects. Language. Rhyming text.

Pattern fish ill. by Anne Canevari Green. Millbrook, 2000. ISBN 978-0-7613-1712-8 Subj: Concepts – patterns. Fish. Rhyming text. Sea & seashore.

Say something, Perico ill. by Cecilia Rébora. Lerner/Kar-Ben, 2011. ISBN 978-0-7613-5231-0 Subj: Birds – parakeets, parrots. Foreign languages.

Tally cat keeps track ill. by Andrew N. Harris. Millbrook, 2010. ISBN 978-0-7613-4451-3 Subj: Animals – cats. Counting, numbers. Friendship.

Twenty hungry piggies ill. by Andrew N. Harris. Lerner, 2007. ISBN 978-0-8225-6370-9 Subj: Animals – pigs. Counting, numbers. Nursery rhymes. Rhyming text.

Up bear, down bear ill. by Ora Eitan. Houghton, 2001. ISBN 978-0-395-97767-5 Subj: Concepts – up & down. Format, unusual – board books. Toys – bears.

Harrison, Carol. *Dinosaurs everywhere!* ill. by Richard Courtney. Scholastic, 1998. ISBN 978-0-590-00089-5 Subj: Dinosaurs. Prehistory.

Harrison, David L. *The alligator in the closet and other poems around the house* ill. by Jane Kendall. Boyds Mills, 2003. ISBN 978-1-56397-994-1 Subj: Homes, houses. Poetry.

The book of giant stories ill. by Philippe Fix. Boyds Mills, 2001. ISBN 978-1-56397-976-7 Subj: Folk & fairy tales. Giants.

Caves ill. by Cheryl Nathan. Boyds Mills, 2001. ISBN 978-1-56397-915-6 Subj: Caves. Science.

Dylan, the eagle-hearted chicken ill. by Karen Stormer Brooks. Boyds Mills, 2002. ISBN 978-1-56397-982-8 Subj: Behavior – imitation. Birds – chickens, roosters. Birds – eagles.

Earthquakes ill. by Cheryl Nathan. Boyds Mills, 2004. ISBN 978-1-59078-243-9 Subj: Earthquakes. Science.

Farmer's garden ill. by Arden Johnson-Petrov. Boyds Mills, 2000. ISBN 978-1-56397-776-3 Subj: Animals – dogs. Gardens, gardening. Poetry.

A perfect home for a family ill. by Roberta Angaramo. Holiday House, 2013. ISBN 978-0-8234-2338-5 Subj: Animals. Animals – raccoons. Homes, houses.

Piggy Wiglet ill. by Karen Stormer Brooks. Boyds Mills, 2007. ISBN 978-1-59078-386-3 Subj: Animals – pigs. Behavior – running away. Rhyming text.

Rivers ill. by Cheryl Nathan. Boyds Mills, 2002. ISBN 978-1-56397-968-2 Subj: Rivers.

Harrison, Hannah E. *Bernice gets carried away* ill. by author. Dial, 2015. ISBN 978-080373916-1 Subj: Animals – cats. Behavior – bad day, bad mood. Birthdays. Parties. Toys – balloons.

Extraordinary Jane ill. by author. Dial, 2014. ISBN 978-080373914-7 Subj: Animals – dogs. Circus. Self-concept.

My friend Maggie ill. by Hannah E. Harrison. Dial, 2016. ISBN 978-052542916-6 Subj: Animals – beavers. Animals – elephants. Behavior – bullying, teasing. Friendship. Self-concept.

Harrison, Joanna. *Grizzly dad* ill. by author. Random House, 2009. ISBN 978-0-385-75173-5 Subj: Animals – bears. Behavior – bad day, bad mood. Family life – fathers.

Harrison, Troon. *Aaron's awful allergies* ill. by Eugenie Fernandes. Kids Can, 1998. ISBN 978-1-55074-299-2 Subj: Illness – allergies. Pets.

Courage to fly ill. by Zhong-Yang Huang. Red Deer, 2002. ISBN 978-0-88995-273-7 Subj: Character traits – bravery. Cities, towns. Ethnic groups in the U.S. – African Americans. Friendship. Moving.

The floating orchard ill. by Miranda Jones. Tundra, 2000. ISBN 978-0-88776-439-4 Subj: Boats, ships. Magic. Trees. Weather – floods. Weather – rain.

Harry, Rebecca. *Snow Bunny's Christmas wish* ill. by author. Scholastic, 2013. ISBN 978-0-545-54103-9 Subj: Animals – rabbits. Character traits – kindness. Holidays – Christmas. Santa Claus.

Harshman, Marc. *All the way to morning* ill. by Felipe Dávalos. Marshall Cavendish, 1999. ISBN 978-0-7614-5042-9 Subj: Bedtime. Night. Noise, sounds. Sleep.

Only one neighborhood ill. by Barbara Garrison. Penguin, 2007. ISBN 978-0-525-47468-5 Subj: Communities, neighborhoods. Counting, numbers.

Red are the apples by Marc Harshman and Cheryl Ryan ill. by Wade Zahares. Gulliver, 2001. ISBN 978-0-15-201917-4 Subj: Concepts – color. Gardens, gardening. Rhyming text. Seasons – fall.

Harshman, Terry Webb. *Does a sea cow say moo?* ill. by George McClements. Bloomsbury, 2008. ISBN 978-1-58234-740-0 Subj: Language. Rhyming text. Sea & seashore.

Hart, Caryl. *The princess and the Christmas rescue* ill. by Sarah Warburton. Candlewick/Nosy Crow, 2017. ISBN 978-076369632-0 Subj: Holidays – Christmas. Inventions. Rhyming text. Royalty – princesses. Santa Claus.

The princess and the peas ill. by Sarah Warburton. Candlewick, 2013. ISBN 978-0-7636-6532-6 Subj: Food. Rhyming text. Royalty – princesses.

Hart, Christopher. *Merwin, master of disguise* ill. by author. Watson-Guptill, 2002. ISBN 978-0-8230-3049-1 Subj: Animals – elephants. Humorous stories. Zoos.

Hartland, Jessie. *Bon appetit! the delicious life of Julia Child* ill. by author. Random House, 2012. ISBN 978-0-375-86944-0 Subj: Activities – baking, cooking. Careers – chefs, cooks. Food. Foreign lands – France.

How the dinosaur got to the museum ill. by author. Blue Apple, 2011. ISBN 978-1-60905-090-0 Subj: Careers – paleontologists. Dinosaurs. Museums.

How the meteorite got to the museum ill. by author. Blue Apple, 2013. ISBN 978-1-60905-252-2 Subj: Museums. Space & space ships.

How the sphinx got to the museum ill. by author. Blue Apple, 2010. ISBN 978-1-60905-032-0 Subj: Art. Foreign lands – Egypt. Museums.

Night shift ill. by author. Bloomsbury, 2007. ISBN 978-1-59990-025-4 Subj: Activities – working. Careers. Night.

Hartley, Karen. *Seeing in living things* by Karen Hartley and Chris Marco; photos by Philip Taylor. Heinemann, 2000. ISBN 978-1-57572-247-4 Subj: Anatomy – eyes. Senses – sight.

The sixth sense and other special senses by Karen Hartley and Chris Marco; photos by Philip Taylor. Heinemann, 2000. ISBN 978-1-57572-248-1 Subj: Animals. Senses.

Smelling in living things by Karen Hartley and Chris Marco; photos by Philip Taylor. Heinemann, 2000. ISBN 978-1-57572-249-8 Subj: Anatomy – noses. Senses – smell.

Tasting in living things by Karen Hartley and Chris Marco; photos by Philip Taylor. Heinemann,

2000. ISBN 978-1-57572-250-4 Subj: Anatomy – tongues. Senses – taste.

Touching in living things by Karen Hartley and Chris Marco; photos by Philip Taylor. Heinemann, 2000. ISBN 978-1-57572-251-1 Subj: Senses – touch.

Hartley, Karen, et al. *Hearing in living things* ill. with photos. Heinemann, 2000. ISBN 978-1-57572-246-7 Subj: Anatomy – ears. Senses – hearing.

Hartman, Bob. *Dinner in the lions' den* ill. by Tim Raglin. Penguin, 2007. ISBN 978-0-399-24674-6 Subj: Animals – lions. Religion – Daniel.

Granny Mae's Christmas play ill. by Lynne Cravath. Augsburg Fortress, 2001. ISBN 978-0-8066-4063-1 Subj: Family life. Family life – grandmothers. Holidays – Christmas. Religion – Nativity. Theater.

The wolf who cried boy ill. by Tim Raglin. Putnam, 2002. ISBN 978-0-399-23578-8 Subj: Animals – wolves. Food.

Hartman, Gail. *As the crow flies* ill. by Harvey Stevenson. Bradbury, 1991. ISBN 978-0-02-743005-9 Subj: Animals. Maps.

Hartmann, Wendy. *The dinosaurs are back and it's all your fault, Edward!* by Wendy Hartmann and Niki Daly ill. by Niki Daly. Margaret K. McElderry, 1997. ISBN 978-0-689-81152-4 Subj: Dinosaurs. Eggs. Family life – brothers. Prehistory.

Hartt-Sussman, Heather. *Here comes Hortense!* ill. by Georgia Graham. Tundra, 2012. ISBN 978-1-77049-221-9 Subj: Emotions – envy, jealousy. Family life – grandmothers. Parks – amusement.

Nana's getting married ill. by Georgia Graham. Tundra, 2010. ISBN 978-0-88776-911-5 Subj: Family life – grandmothers. Weddings.

Noni is nervous ill. by Geneviève Côté. Tundra, 2013. ISBN 978-1-77049-323-0 Subj: Behavior – worrying. School – first day.

Seamus's short story ill. by Milan Pavlovic. Groundwood, 2017. ISBN 978-155498793-1 Subj: Character traits – smallness. Clothing – shoes. Concepts – size.

Harvey, Amanda. *Dog days* ill. by author. Random House, 2003. ISBN 978-0-385-90860-3 Subj: Animals – cats. Animals – dogs. Pets.

Dog-eared ill. by author. Doubleday, 2002. ISBN 978-0-385-72911-6 Subj: Anatomy – ears. Animals – dogs. Pets. Self-concept.

Dog gone ill. by author. Random House, 2004. ISBN 978-0-385-90870-2 Subj: Animals – dogs. Pets.

Harvey, Brett. *My prairie Christmas* ill. by Deborah Kogan Ray. Holiday, 1990. ISBN 978-0-8234-0827-6 Subj: Holidays – Christmas. Weather – storms.

Harvey, Damian. *Just the thing!* ill. by Lynne Chapman. School Specialty/Gingham Dog, 2005. ISBN 978-0-7696-4300-7 Subj: Animals – gorillas. Problem solving.

Harvey, Jayne. *Busy bugs* ill. by Bernard Adnet. Grosset, 2003. ISBN 978-0-448-43234-2 Subj: Concepts – patterns. Counting, numbers. Insects. Rhyming text.

Harvey, Jeanne Walker. *Maya Lin: artist-architect of light and lines* ill. by Dow Phumiruk. Holt/Christy Ottaviano, 2017. ISBN 978-125011249-1 Subj: Art. Careers – architects. Careers – artists. Character traits – assertiveness. Ethnic groups in the U.S. – Chinese Americans. U.S. history. War.

My hands sing the blues: Romare Bearden's childhood journey ill. by Elizabeth Zunon. Marshall Cavendish, 2011. ISBN 978-0-7614-5810-4 Subj: Art. Careers – artists. Ethnic groups in the U.S. – African Americans. U.S. history.

Harvey, Matthea. *Cecil the pet glacier* ill. by Giselle Potter. Random House, 2012. ISBN 978-0-375-86773-6 Subj: Behavior – lost & found possessions. Foreign lands – Norway. Pets.

Haseley, Dennis. *The invisible moose* ill. by Steven Kellogg. Penguin, 2006. ISBN 978-0-8037-2892-9 Subj: Animals – moose. Character traits – shyness.

A story for Bear ill. by Jim LaMarche. Harcourt, 2002. ISBN 978-0-15-200239-8 Subj: Animals – bears. Books, reading.

Twenty heartbeats ill. by Ed Young. Roaring Brook, 2008. ISBN 978-1-59643-238-3 Subj: Activities – painting. Animals – horses, ponies. Art. Careers – artists.

Haskins, Jim. *Count your way through Afghanistan* by Jim Haskins and Kathleen Benson ill. by Megan Moore. Lerner, 2006. ISBN 978-1-57505-880-1 Subj: Counting, numbers. Foreign lands – Afghanistan. Foreign languages.

Count your way through Africa ill. by Barbara Knutson. Carolrhoda, 1989. ISBN 978-0-87614-347-6 Subj: Counting, numbers. Foreign lands – Africa. Foreign languages.

Count your way through Brazil by Jim Haskins and Kathleen Benson ill. by Liz Brenner Dodson. Carolrhoda, 1996. ISBN 978-0-87614-873-0 Subj: Counting, numbers. Foreign lands – Brazil. Foreign languages.

Count your way through Canada ill. by Steve Michaels. Carolrhoda, 1989. ISBN 978-0-87614-

350-6 Subj: Counting, numbers. Foreign lands – Canada.

Count your way through China ill. by Dennis Hockerman. Carolrhoda, 1987. ISBN 978-0-87614-302-5 Subj: Counting, numbers. Foreign lands – China. Foreign languages.

Count your way through France ill. by Andrea Shine. Carolrhoda, 1996. ISBN 978-0-87614-874-7 Subj: Counting, numbers. Foreign lands – France. Foreign languages.

Count your way through Germany ill. by Helen Byers. Carolrhoda, 1992. ISBN 978-0-87614-407-7 Subj: Counting, numbers. Foreign lands – Germany. Foreign languages.

Count your way through Greece ill. by Janice Lee Porter. Carolrhoda, 1996. ISBN 978-0-87614-875-4 Subj: Counting, numbers. Foreign lands – Greece. Foreign languages.

Count your way through India ill. by Liz Brenner Dodson. Carolrhoda, 1990. ISBN 978-0-87614-414-5 Subj: Counting, numbers. Foreign lands – India. Foreign languages.

Count your way through Iran by Jim Haskins and Kathleen Benson ill. by Farida Zaman. Lerner, 2006. ISBN 978-1-57505-881-8 Subj: Counting, numbers. Foreign lands – Iran. Foreign languages.

Count your way through Ireland ill. by Beth Wright. Carolrhoda, 1996. ISBN 978-0-87614-872-3 Subj: Counting, numbers. Foreign lands – Ireland.

Count your way through Israel ill. by Rick Hanson. Carolrhoda, 1990. ISBN 978-0-87614-415-2 Subj: Counting, numbers. Foreign lands – Israel. Foreign languages.

Count your way through Italy ill. by Beth Wright. Carolrhoda, 1990. ISBN 978-0-87614-406-0 Subj: Counting, numbers. Foreign lands – Italy. Foreign languages.

Count your way through Japan ill. by Martin Skoro. Carolrhoda, 1987. ISBN 978-0-87614-301-8 Subj: Counting, numbers. Foreign lands – Japan. Foreign languages.

Count your way through Korea ill. by Dennis Hockerman. Carolrhoda, 1989. ISBN 978-0-87614-348-3 Subj: Counting, numbers. Foreign lands – Korea. Foreign languages.

Count your way through Mexico ill. by Helen Byers. Carolrhoda, 1989. ISBN 978-0-87614-349-0 Subj: Counting, numbers. Foreign lands – Mexico. Foreign languages.

Count your way through Russia ill. by Vera Mednikov. Carolrhoda, 1987. ISBN 978-0-87614-303-2 Subj: Counting, numbers. Foreign lands – Russia. Foreign languages.

Count your way through the Arab world ill. by Dana Gustafson. Carolrhoda, 1987. ISBN 978-0-87616-304-7 Subj: Counting, numbers. Foreign lands – Arabia. Foreign languages.

Delivering justice: W. W. Law and the fight for civil rights ill. by Benny Andrews. Candlewick, 2006. ISBN 978-0-7636-2592-4 Subj: Ethnic groups in the U.S. – African Americans. Prejudice. U.S. history.

Hasler, Eveline. *A tale of two brothers* ill. by Kathi Bhend. NorthSouth, 2006. ISBN 978-0-7358-2102-6 Subj: Character traits – kindness. Character traits – meanness. Family life – brothers & sisters. Folk & fairy tales. Foreign lands – Switzerland.

Hassett, Ann. *Can't catch me* (The gingerbread boy)

Father Sun, Mother Moon (Hassett, John)

The finest Christmas tree by Ann Hassett and John Hassett; ill. by authors. Houghton, 2005. ISBN 978-0-618-50901-0 Subj: Holidays – Christmas. Santa Claus. Trees.

Mouse in the house (Hassett, John)

The nine lives of Dudley Dog (Hassett, John)

The three silly girls Grubb (Hassett, John)

Too many frogs! by Ann Hassett and John Hassett ill. by John Hassett. Harcourt, 2011. ISBN 978-0-547-36299-1 Subj: Activities – baking, cooking. Family life – grandmothers. Frogs & toads.

Hassett, John. *Can't catch me* (The gingerbread boy)

Father Sun, Mother Moon by John Hassett and Ann Hassett; ill. by authors. Houghton, 2001. ISBN 978-0-395-97565-7 Subj: Concepts – color. Superstition.

The finest Christmas tree (Hassett, Ann)

Mouse in the house by John Hassett and Ann Hassett; ill. by authors. Houghton, 2004. ISBN 978-0-618-35317-0 Subj: Animals. Character traits – orderliness. Family life – grandmothers.

The nine lives of Dudley Dog by John Hassett and Ann Hassett; ill. by John Hassett. Houghton, 2008. ISBN 978-0-618-81153-3 Subj: Animals – cats. Animals – dogs. Safety.

The three silly girls Grubb by John Hassett and Ann Hassett; ill. by authors. Houghton, 2002. ISBN 978-0-618-14183-8 Subj: Behavior – bullying, teasing. Folk & fairy tales. School.

Too many frogs! (Hassett, Ann)

Hatanaka, Kellen. *Drive: a look at roadside opposites* ill. by author. Groundwood, 2015. ISBN 978-

155498731-3 Subj: Activities – driving. Concepts – opposites.

Work: an occupational ABC ill. by author. Groundwood, 2014. ISBN 978-155498409-1 Subj: ABC books. Careers.

Hatch, Elizabeth. *Halloween night* ill. by Jimmy Pickering. Random House, 2005. ISBN 978-0-385-90887-0 Subj: Cumulative tales. Holidays – Halloween. Rhyming text.

Hatke, Ben. *Nobody likes a goblin* ill. by author. First Second, 2016. ISBN 978-162672081-7 Subj: Friendship. Mythical creatures – goblins.

Hatkoff, Craig. *Good-bye tonsils* (Hatkoff, Juliana Lee)

Hatkoff, Craig, et al. *Leo the snow leopard: the true story of an amazing rescue.* Scholastic, 2010. ISBN 978-0-545-22927-2 Subj: Animals – endangered animals. Animals – leopards.

Looking for Miza: the true story of the mountain gorilla family who rescued one of their own photos by Peter Greste. Scholastic, 2008. ISBN 978-0-545-08540-3 Subj: Animals – endangered animals. Animals – gorillas. Behavior – lost. Foreign lands – Congo (Democratic Republic).

Winter's tail: how one little dolphin learned to swim again ill. with photos. Scholastic, 2009. ISBN 978-0-545-12335-8 Subj: Anatomy – tails. Animals – dolphins. Character traits – kindness to animals.

Hatkoff, Isabella, et al. *Knut: how one little polar bear captivated the world* ill. with photos. Scholastic, 2007. ISBN 978-0-545-04716-6 Subj: Animals – polar bears. Zoos.

Hatkoff, Juliana Lee. *Good-bye tonsils* by Juliana Lee Hatkoff and Craig Hatkoff ill. by Marilyn Mets. Viking, 2001. ISBN 978-0-670-89775-9 Subj: Hospitals. Illness – tonsillectomy.

Haugen, Brenda. *Thanksgiving* ill. by Todd Ouren. Picture Window, 2004. ISBN 978-1-4048-0191-2 Subj: Holidays – Thanksgiving. U.S. history.

Haughton, Chris. *Goodnight everyone* ill. by author. Candlewick, 2016. ISBN 978-076369079-3 Subj: Animals. Animals – bears. Bedtime.

Little Owl lost ill. by author. Candlewick, 2010. ISBN 978-0-7636-5022-3 Subj: Behavior – lost. Birds – owls.

Oh no, George! ill. by author. Candlewick, 2012. ISBN 978-0-7636-5546-4 Subj: Animals – dogs. Behavior – misbehavior. Pets.

Shh! we have a plan ill. by author. Candlewick, 2014. ISBN 978-076367293-5 Subj: Birds. Sports – hunting.

Haughton, Emma. *Rainy day* ill. by Angelo Rinaldi. Carolrhoda, 2000. ISBN 978-1-57505-452-0 Subj: Activities – walking. Divorce. Family life – fathers. Weather – storms.

Hausman, Gerald. *Coyote walks on two legs* ill. by Floyd Cooper. Philomel, 1993. ISBN 978-0-399-22018-0 Subj: Animals – coyotes. Behavior – greed. Behavior – trickery. Character traits – vanity. Folk & fairy tales. Indians of North America – Navajo.

Eagle boy ill. by Cara Moser and Barry Moser. HarperCollins, 1996. ISBN 978-0-06-021101-1 Subj: Birds – eagles. Folk & fairy tales. Indians of North America – Navajo.

Hautzig, Deborah. *Beauty and the beast* ill. by Kathy Mitchell. Random House, 1995. ISBN 978-0-679-95296-1 Subj: Character traits – loyalty. Emotions – love. Folk & fairy tales. Magic.

Havill, Juanita. *Call the horse lucky* ill. by Nancy Lane. Gryphon, 2010. ISBN 978-0-940719-10-1 Subj: Animals – horses, ponies. Character traits – kindness to animals.

Jamaica and Brianna ill. by Anne Sibley O'Brien. Houghton, 1993. ISBN 978-0-395-64489-8 Subj: Clothing – boots. Emotions – envy, jealousy. Ethnic groups in the U.S. – African Americans. Ethnic groups in the U.S. – Asian Americans. Friendship.

Jamaica and the substitute teacher ill. by Anne Sibley O'Brien. Houghton, 1999. ISBN 978-0-395-90503-6 Subj: Behavior – cheating. Behavior – misbehavior. Careers – teachers. Ethnic groups in the U.S. – African Americans. School. Self-concept.

Jamaica is thankful ill. by Anne Sibley O'Brien. Houghton, 2009. ISBN 978-0-618-98231-8 Subj: Animals – cats. Ethnic groups in the U.S. – African Americans. Family life – brothers & sisters. Illness – allergies. School.

Jamaica Tag-Along ill. by Anne Sibley O'Brien. Houghton, 1989. ISBN 978-0-395-49602-2 Subj: Activities – playing. Ethnic groups in the U.S. – African Americans. Family life – brothers & sisters. Friendship.

Jamaica's blue marker ill. by Anne Sibley O'Brien. Houghton, 1995. ISBN 978-0-395-72036-3 Subj: Emotions – sadness. Ethnic groups in the U.S. – African Americans. Moving.

Jamaica's find ill. by Anne Sibley O'Brien. Houghton, 1986. ISBN 978-0-395-39376-5 Subj: Behavior – lost & found possessions. Character traits – honesty. Ethnic groups in the U.S. – African Americans.

Just like a baby ill. by Christine Davenier. Chronicle, 2009. ISBN 978-0-8118-5026-1 Subj: Babies, toddlers. Careers. Family life.

Hawcock, Claire. *Mine, all mine!* ill. by Chiara Pasqualotto. Boxer, 2009. ISBN 978-1-906250-76-8 Subj: Animals – squirrels. Behavior – sharing. Seasons – winter. Weather – snow.

Hawk, Fran. *Count down to fall* ill. by Sherry Neidigh. Sylvan Dell, 2009. ISBN 978-1-934359-94-5 Subj: Counting, numbers. Seasons – fall.

Hawkes, Kevin. *Remy and Lulu* ill. by author and Hannah E. Harrison. Knopf, 2014. ISBN 978-044981085-9 Subj: Activities – painting. Animals – dogs. Careers – artists. Foreign lands – France. Senses – sight.

The wicked big toddlah ill. by author. Random House, 2007. ISBN 978-0-375-82427-2 Subj: Babies, toddlers. Giants. Humorous stories.

The wicked big toddlah goes to New York ill. by author. Random House, 2011. ISBN 978-0-375-86188-8 Subj: Activities – traveling. Babies, toddlers. Behavior – lost. Giants. Humorous stories.

Hawkins, Colin. *Creepy castle* by Colin Hawkins and Jacqui Hawkins ill. by Jacqui Hawkins. Barron's, 2001. ISBN 978-0-7641-5438-6 Subj: Castles. Format, unusual – toy & movable books. Ghosts. Monsters.

Fairytale news by Colin Hawkins and Jacqui Hawkins ill. by Jacqui Hawkins. Candlewick, 2004. ISBN 978-0-7636-2166-7 Subj: Careers – journalists. Folk & fairy tales.

One, two, guess who? by Colin Hawkins and Jacqui Hawkins ill. by Jacqui Hawkins. Barron's, 2001. ISBN 978-0-7641-5341-9 Subj: Counting, numbers. Folk & fairy tales. Format, unusual – toy & movable books. Rhyming text.

Hawkins, Emily. *Little snow goose* ill. by Maggie Kneen. Dutton, 2009. ISBN 978-0-525-42166-5 Subj: Animals – foxes. Birds – geese. Character traits – responsibility. Friendship.

Hawkins, Jacqui. *Creepy castle* (Hawkins, Colin)

Fairytale news (Hawkins, Colin)

One, two, guess who? (Hawkins, Colin)

Hawthorne, Nathaniel. *King Midas and the golden touch* adapt. by Kathryn Hewitt; ill. by adapter. Harcourt, 1987. ISBN 978-0-15-242800-6 Subj: Behavior – greed. Folk & fairy tales. Royalty – kings.

Hayashi, Leslie Ann. *Fables from the sea* ill. by Kathleen Wong Bishop. Univ. of Hawaii Pr., 2000. ISBN 978-0-8248-2224-8 Subj: Animals. Hawaii. Sea & seashore.

Hayden, Kate. *Horse show* ill. with photos. DK, 2001. ISBN 978-0-7894-7372-1 Subj: Animals – horses, ponies. Sports.

Hayes, Geoffrey. *The bunny's night-light: a glow-in-the-dark search* ill. by author. Random House, 2012. ISBN 978-0-375-86926-6 Subj: Animals – rabbits. Bedtime. Light, lights.

Patrick at the circus ill. by author. Hyperion, 2002. ISBN 978-0-7868-2595-0 Subj: Animals – bears. Circus. Clowns, jesters.

Hayes, Joe. *Don't say a word, Mamá/No digas nada, Mamá* ill. by Esau Andrade. Cinco Puntos, 2013. ISBN 978-1-935955-29-0 Subj: Character traits – generosity. Ethnic groups in the U.S. – Hispanic Americans. Family life – sisters. Foreign languages. Gardens, gardening.

The gum-chewing rattler ill. by Antonio Castro Lopez. Cinco Puntos, 2006. ISBN 978-0-938317-99-9 Subj: Reptiles – snakes. Tall tales.

Juan Verdades, the man who could not tell a lie ill. by Joseph Daniel Fiedler. Orchard, 2001. ISBN 978-0-439-29311-2 Subj: Behavior – lying. Folk & fairy tales. Foreign languages.

Little Gold Star / Estrellita de oro ill. by Gloria Osuna Perez and Lucia Angela Perez. Cinco Puntos, 2000. ISBN 978-0-938317-49-4 Subj: Birds – hawks. Folk & fairy tales. Foreign languages. Magic.

Hayes, Karel. *The summer visitors* ill. by author. Down East, 2011. ISBN 978-0-89272-918-0 Subj: Animals – bears. Seasons – summer.

The winter visitors ill. by author. Down East, 2007. ISBN 978-0-89272-750-6 Subj: Animals – bears. Seasons – winter.

Hayes, Sarah. *Dog day* ill. by Hannah Broadway. Farrar, 2008. ISBN 978-0-374-31810-9 Subj: Animals – dogs. Careers – teachers. School.

Lucy Anna and the Finders ill. by author. Candlewick, 2000. ISBN 978-0-7636-1200-9 Subj: Behavior – lost & found possessions. Behavior – resourcefulness. Mythical creatures. Toys.

Hayles, Marsha. *Bunion Burt* ill. by Jack E. Davis. Simon & Schuster, 2009. ISBN 978-1-4169-4132-3 Subj: Anatomy – feet. Clothing – shoes. Rhyming text.

The feathered crown ill. by Bernadette Pons. Henry Holt, 2002. ISBN 978-0-8050-6421-6 Subj: Birds. Gifts. Holidays – Christmas. Religion – Nativity. Rhyming text.

He saves the day ill. by Lynne Cravath. Putnam, 2001. ISBN 978-0-399-23363-0 Subj: Activities. Imagination. Rhyming text.

Pajamas anytime ill. by Hiroe Nakata. Penguin, 2005. ISBN 978-0-399-23871-0 Subj: Clothing – pajamas. Days of the week, months of the year. Rhyming text.

A pet of a pet ill. by Scott Nash. Dial, 2001. ISBN 978-0-8037-2512-6 Subj: Animals. Farms. Pets. Self-concept.

Haynes, Max. *Grandma's gone to live in the stars* ill. by author. Albert Whitman, 2000. ISBN 978-0-8075-3026-9 Subj: Death. Emotions – grief. Family life – grandmothers.

Hays, Anna Jane. *Kindergarten countdown* ill. by Linda Davick. Random House, 2007. ISBN 978-0-375-84252-8 Subj: Counting, numbers. Rhyming text. School – first day.

The pup speaks up ill. by Valeria Petrone. Random House, 2003. ISBN 978-0-375-91232-0 Subj: Animals. Animals – dogs. Noise, sounds. Pets.

Ready, set, preschool! ill. by True Kelley. Random House, 2005. ISBN 978-0-375-92519-1 Subj: Concepts. Games. School.

Hayward, Linda. *A day in the life of a builder* ill. with photos. DK, 2001. ISBN 978-0-7894-7364-6 Subj: Careers – construction workers. Homes, houses.

A day in the life of a dancer ill. with photos. DK, 2001. ISBN 978-0-7894-7370-7 Subj: Activities – dancing. Ballet. Careers – dancers.

A day in the life of a firefighter ill. with photos. DK, 2001. ISBN 978-0-613-35098-3 Subj: Careers – firefighters. Fire.

A day in the life of a teacher ill. with photos. DK, 2001. ISBN 978-0-7894-7368-4 Subj: Careers – teachers. School.

I am a book ill. by Carol Nicklaus. Lerner, 2005. ISBN 978-0-7613-1826-2 Subj: Books, reading.

The King's chorus ill. by Jennifer P. Goldfinger. Houghton, 2006. ISBN 978-0-618-51618-6 Subj: Animals. Birds – chickens, roosters. Farms. Morning.

Pepe and Papa ill. by Laura Huliska-Beith. Golden, 2001. ISBN 978-0-307-46114-8 Subj: Folk & fairy tales. Humorous stories.

What homework? ill. by Page Eastburn O'Rourke. Kane, 2002. ISBN 978-1-57565-116-3 Subj: Plants. School.

Hazen, Barbara Shook. *Katie's wish* ill. by Emily Arnold McCully. Dial, 2003. ISBN 978-0-8037-2478-5 Subj: Ethnic groups in the U.S. – Irish Americans. Family life – fathers. Family life – grandparents. Foreign lands – Ireland.

Who is your favorite monster, Mama? ill. by Maryann Kovalski. Hyperion, 2006. ISBN 978-0-7868-1810-5 Subj: Family life. Monsters. Sibling rivalry.

Head, Judith. *Mud soup* ill. by Susan Guevara. Random House, 2003. ISBN 978-0-375-91087-6 Subj: Activities – baking, cooking. Ethnic groups in the U.S. – Mexican Americans. Food. Foreign languages.

Headley, Justina Chen. *The patch* ill. by Mitch Vane. Charlesbridge, 2006. ISBN 978-1-58089-049-6 Subj: Activities – dancing. Ballet. Glasses. Self-concept.

Heap, Sue. *Danny's drawing book* ill. by author. Candlewick, 2008. ISBN 978-0-7636-3654-8 Subj: Activities – drawing. Foreign lands – Africa. Imagination. Zoos.

Four friends in the garden ill. by author. Candlewick, 2004. ISBN 978-0-7636-2371-5 Subj: Animals – bears. Animals – rabbits. Animals – sheep. Friendship. Gardens, gardening. Insects – butterflies, caterpillars.

Mine! ill. by author. Candlewick, 2014. ISBN 978-076366888-4 Subj: Behavior – sharing. Toys.

What shall we play? ill. by author. Candlewick, 2002. ISBN 978-0-7636-1685-4 Subj: Activities – playing. Imagination.

Heapy, Teresa. *Very little Red Riding Hood* ill. by Sue Heap. Houghton, 2014. ISBN 978-054428000-7 Subj: Animals – wolves. Behavior – talking to strangers. Character traits – smallness. Family life – grandmothers. Folk & fairy tales.

Heard, Georgia, selector. *This place I know.* Ill. by eighteen renowned picture book artists. Candlewick, 2002. ISBN 978-0-7636-1924-4 Subj: Emotions – fear. Emotions – grief. Poetry. U.S. history.

Hearne, Betsy Gould. *Seven brave women* ill. by Bethanne Andersen. Greenwillow, 1997. ISBN 978-0-688-14503-3 Subj: Character traits – bravery. Family life. Immigrants, immigration. U.S. history. War.

Heath, Amy. *Sofie's role* ill. by Sheila Hamanaka. Four Winds, 1992. ISBN 978-0-02-743505-4 Subj: Activities – baking, cooking. Careers – bakers. Ethnic groups in the U.S. – African Americans. Family life. Holidays – Christmas.

Heck, Ed. *Monkey lost* ill. by author. Simon & Schuster, 2005. ISBN 978-0-689-04633-9 Subj: Animals – monkeys. Behavior – lost. School. Toys.

Hector, Julian. *The gentleman bug* ill. by author. Simon & Schuster, 2010. ISBN 978-1-4169-9467-1 Subj: Books, reading. Insects. Self-concept.

Heder, Thyra. *Alfie: (the turtle that disappeared)* ill. by author. Abrams, 2017. ISBN 978-141972529-6 Subj: Birthdays. Ethnic groups in the U.S. – African Americans. Hibernation. Pets. Reptiles – turtles, tortoises.

The bear report ill. by author. Abrams, 2015. ISBN 978-141970783-4 Subj: Animals – polar bears. Foreign lands – Arctic. Homework.

Fraidyzoo ill. by author. Abrams, 2013. ISBN 978-1-4197-0776-6 Subj: ABC books. Emotions – fear. Zoos.

Heelan, Jamee Riggio. *Can you hear a rainbow?* ill. by Nicola Simmonds. Peachtree, 2002. ISBN 978-1-56145-268-2 Subj: Communication. Disabilities – deafness. Language. School.

The making of my special hand, Madison's story ill. by Nicola Simmonds. Peachtree, 1998. ISBN 978-1-56145-186-9 Subj: Disabilities – physical disabilities.

Rolling along, the story of Taylor and his wheelchair ill. by Nicola Simmonds. Peachtree, 2000. ISBN 978-1-56145-219-4 Subj: Disabilities – cerebral palsy. Disabilities – physical disabilities.

Hegarty, Patricia. *Bug Bear* ill. by Carmen Saldaña. Tiger Tales, 2017. ISBN 978-168010053-2 Subj: Animals – bears. Insects. Rhyming text.

Good night farm ill. by Thomas Elliott. Tiger Tales, 2016. ISBN 978-158925233-2 Subj: Bedtime. Farms. Format, unusual – board books. Rhyming text.

Hegg, Tom. *Peef and his best friend* ill. by Warren Hanson. Waldman, 2001. ISBN 978-0-931674-49-5 Subj: Friendship. Rhyming text. Toys – bears.

Heidbreder, Robert. *Black and bittern was night* ill. by John Martz. Kids Can, 2013. ISBN 978-1-55453-302-2 Subj: Anatomy – skeletons. Holidays – Halloween. Rhyming text.

Drumheller dinosaur dance ill. by Bill Slavin. Kids Can, 2004. ISBN 978-1-55337-393-3 Subj: Activities – dancing. Dinosaurs.

I wished for a unicorn ill. by Kady MacDonald Denton. Kids Can, 2000. ISBN 978-1-55074-543-6 Subj: Activities – playing. Behavior – wishing. Imagination. Mythical creatures – unicorns. Rhyming text.

Lickety-split ill. by Dusan Petricic. Kids Can, 2007. ISBN 978-1-55337-710-8 Subj: Language.

Noisy poems for a busy day ill. by Lori Joy Smith. Kids Can, 2012. ISBN 978-1-55453-706-8 Subj: Activities. Day. Noise, sounds. Poetry.

A sea-wishing day ill. by Kady MacDonald Denton. Kids Can, 2007. ISBN 978-1-55337-707-8 Subj: Rhyming text. Sea & seashore. Sports – sailing.

Song for a summer night: a lullaby ill. by Qin Leng. Groundwood, 2015. ISBN 978-155498493-0 Subj: Lullabies. Night. Rhyming text. Seasons – summer.

Heide, Florence Parry. *Always listen to your mother* by Florence Parry Heide and Roxanne Heide Pierce ill. by Kyle M. Stone. Hyperion/Disney, 2010. ISBN 978-1-4231-1395-9 Subj: Behavior – misbehavior. Character traits – cooperation. Humorous stories.

The day of Ahmed's secret by Florence Parry Heide and Judith Heide Gilliland ill. by Ted Lewin. Lothrop, 1990. ISBN 978-0-688-08895-8 Subj: Activities – working. Activities – writing. Behavior – secrets. Foreign lands – Egypt.

How to be a hero ill. by Chuck Groenink. Chronicle, 2016. ISBN 978-145212710-1 Subj: Behavior – dissatisfaction. Character traits – ambition. Humorous stories. Imagination.

The one and only Marigold ill. by Jill McElmurry. Random House, 2009. ISBN 978-0-375-84031-9 Subj: Animals – monkeys. Character traits – individuality. Friendship.

Princess Hyacinth: the surprising tale of a girl who floated ill. by Lane Smith. Random House, 2009. ISBN 978-0-375-84501-7 Subj: Activities – flying. Behavior – boredom. Kites. Royalty – princesses.

A promise is a promise ill. by Tony Auth. Candlewick, 2007. ISBN 978-0-7636-2285-5 Subj: Pets.

Sami and the time of the troubles by Florence Parry Heide and Judith Heide Gilliland ill. by Ted Lewin. Clarion, 1992. ISBN 978-0-395-55964-2 Subj: Family life. Foreign lands – Lebanon. War.

Some things are scary ill. by Jules Feiffer. Candlewick, 2000. ISBN 978-0-7636-1222-1 Subj: Emotions – fear.

Heide, Iris van der. *The red chalk* ill. by Marije Tolman. Boyds Mills, 2006. ISBN 978-1-932425-79-6 Subj: Activities – playing. Activities – trading. Behavior – boredom.

A strange day ill. by Marijke ten Cate. Boyds Mills, 2007. ISBN 978-1-932425-94-9 Subj: Character traits – helpfulness. Contests. Letters, cards.

Heiligman, Deborah. *Babies* ill. by Laura Freeman. National Geographic, 2002. ISBN 978-0-7922-8205-1 Subj: Babies, toddlers. Behavior – growing up.

The boy who loved math: the improbable life of Paul Erdös ill. by LeUyen Pham. Roaring Brook, 2013. ISBN 978-1-59643-307-6 Subj: Careers – mathematicians. Character traits – individuality. Counting, numbers. Foreign lands – Hungary.

Cool dog, school dog ill. by Tim Bowers. Marshall Cavendish, 2009. ISBN 978-0-7614-5561-5 Subj: Animals – dogs. Rhyming text. School.

Fun dog, sun dog ill. by Tim Bowers. Marshall Cavendish, 2005. ISBN 978-0-7614-5162-4 Subj: Animals – dogs. Pets.

Honeybees ill. by Carla Golembe. National Geographic, 2002. ISBN 978-0-7922-6678-5 Subj: Insects – bees.

Snow dog, go dog ill. by Tim Bowers. Amazon/Two Lions, 2013. ISBN 978-1-4778-1724-7 Subj: Animals – dogs. Behavior – lost. Rhyming text. Weather – snow.

Heim, Alastair. *Love you too* ill. by Alisa Coburn. little bee, 2016. ISBN 978-149980174-3 Subj: Animals – pigs. Family life – fathers. Rhyming text.

Heine, Theresa. *Chandra's magic light: a story in Nepal* ill. by Judith Gueyfier. Barefoot, 2014. ISBN 978-184686493-3 Subj: Behavior – resourcefulness. Family life – sisters. Foreign lands – Nepal. Light, lights. Money.

Heinz, Brian J. *Butternut Hollow Pond* ill. by Bob Marstall. Millbrook, 2000. ISBN 978-0-7613-0268-1 Subj: Animals. Ecology. Lakes, ponds.

Mocha Dick: the legend and fury ill. by Randall Enos. Creative Company, 2014. ISBN 978-156846242-4 Subj: Animals – whales.

The monsters' test ill. by Sal Murdocca. Millbrook, 1996. ISBN 978-0-7613-0095-3 Subj: Holidays – Halloween. Monsters. Rhyming text. Witches.

Nathan of yesteryear and Michael of today ill. by Joanne Friar. Lerner, 2006. ISBN 978-0-7613-2893-3 Subj: U.S. history.

Red Fox at McCloskey's farm ill. by Chris Sheban. Creative Editions, 2006. ISBN 978-1-56846-195-3 Subj: Animals – foxes. Farms. Rhyming text.

The wolves ill. by Bernie Fuchs. Dial, 1996. ISBN 978-0-8037-1736-7 Subj: Animals – endangered animals. Animals – wolves. Nature.

Helakoski, Leslie. *Big chickens* ill. by Henry Cole. Penguin, 2006. ISBN 978-0-525-47575-0 Subj: Animals – wolves. Birds – chickens, roosters. Emotions – fear. Farms.

Big chickens fly the coop ill. by Henry Cole. Dutton, 2008. ISBN 978-0-525-47915-4 Subj: Birds – chickens, roosters. Farms. Humorous stories.

Big chickens go to town ill. by Henry Cole. Penguin, 2010. ISBN 978-0-525-42162-7 Subj: Birds – chickens, roosters. Cities, towns. Emotions – fear.

Big pigs ill. by author. Boyds Mills, 2014. ISBN 978-162091023-8 Subj: Animals – pigs. Behavior – messy. Concepts – size.

Doggone feet! ill. by author. Boyds Mills, 2013. ISBN 978-1-59078-933-9 Subj: Animals – dogs. Family life. Pets. Rhyming text.

Fair cow ill. by author. Marshall Cavendish, 2010. ISBN 978-0-7614-5684-1 Subj: Animals – bulls, cows. Character traits – individuality. Fairs, festivals.

The smushy bus ill. by Sal Murdocca. Millbrook, 2002. ISBN 978-0-7613-1398-4 Subj: Buses. Careers – bus drivers. Counting, numbers. School.

Woolbur ill. by Lee Harper. HarperCollins, 2008. ISBN 978-0-06-084726-5 Subj: Animals – sheep. Behavior. Character traits – individuality.

Helberg, Berit. *Sniffer and Tinni: a true tale of amazing friendship* ill. by Torgeir Berge. ill. with photos by Torgeir Berge. Sterling, 2016. ISBN 978-145491870-7 Subj: Animals – dogs. Animals – foxes. Friendship.

The Helen Oxenbury nursery collection ill. by Helen Oxenbury. Knopf, 2004. ISBN 978-0-375-92992-2 Subj: Folk & fairy tales. Nursery rhymes. Poetry.

Heling, Kathryn. *Clothesline clues to jobs people do* by Kathryn Heling and Deborah Hembrook ill. by Andy Robert Davies. Charlesbridge, 2012. ISBN 978-1-58089-251-3 Subj: Careers. Clothing.

Mouse makes magic by Kathryn Heling and Deborah Hembrook ill. by Patrick Joseph. Random House, 2003. ISBN 978-0-375-92184-1 Subj: Animals – mice. Language.

Mouse's hide-and-seek words by Kathryn Heling and Deborah Hembrook ill. by Patrick Joseph. Random House, 2003. ISBN 978-0-375-92185-8 Subj: Animals – mice. Language. Rhyming text.

Helldorfer, M. C. *Hog music* ill. by S. D. Schindler. Viking, 2000. ISBN 978-0-670-87182-7 Subj: Activities – traveling. Family life – aunts, uncles. Gifts. U.S. history – frontier & pioneer life.

Heller, Linda. *How Dalia put a big yellow comforter inside a tiny blue box: and other wonders of tzedakah* ill. by Stacey Dressen-McQueen. Tricycle, 2011. ISBN 978-1-58246-378-0 Subj: Character traits – generosity. Family life – brothers & sisters. Jewish culture.

Heller, Lora. *Sign language ABC* ill. by author. Sterling, 2012. ISBN 978-1-4027-6392-2 Subj: ABC books. Sign language.

Heller, Nicholas. *Elwood and the witch* ill. by Joseph A. Smith. Greenwillow, 2000. ISBN 978-0-689-16946-5 Subj: Activities – flying. Animals – pigs. Moon. Witches.

Ogres! ogres! ogres! a feasting frenzy from A to Z ill. by Joseph A. Smith. Greenwillow, 1999. ISBN 978-0-688-16987-9 Subj: Food. Monsters. Mythical creatures – ogres.

This little piggy ill. by Sonja Lamut. Greenwillow, 1997. ISBN 978-0-688-15175-1 Subj: Bedtime. Family life – grandmothers. Nursery rhymes.

Heller, Ruth. *A cache of jewels and other collective nouns* ill. by author. Grosset, 1989. ISBN 978-0-448-19211-6 Subj: Language. Rhyming text.

Chickens aren't the only ones ill. by author. Grosset, 1981. ISBN 978-0-448-01872-0 Subj: Eggs. Science.

Color, color, color, color ill. by author. Putnam, 1995. ISBN 978-0-399-22815-5 Subj: Concepts – color. Rhyming text.

Fantastic! wow! and unreal! a book about interjections and conjunctions ill. by author. Grosset, 1998. ISBN 978-0-448-41862-9 Subj: Language. Rhyming text.

Kites sail high: a book about verbs ill. by author. Grosset, 1988. ISBN 978-0-448-10480-5 Subj: Language. Rhyming text.

Many luscious lollipops: a book about adjectives ill. by author. Sandcastle Books, 1992. ISBN 978-0-448-03151-4 Subj: Language. Rhyming text.

Merry-go-round ill. by author. Sandcastle Books, 1992. ISBN 978-0-448-40085-3 Subj: Language. Rhyming text.

Mine, all mine: a book about pronouns ill. by author. Grosset, 1997. ISBN 978-0-448-41606-9 Subj: Language. Rhyming text.

The reason for a flower ill. by author. Grosset, 1983. ISBN 978-0-448-14495-5 Subj: Flowers. Rhyming text.

Hellman, Gary. *The karate way* ill. by author. Doubleday, 2001. ISBN 978-0-385-32742-8 Subj: Self-concept. Sports – karate.

Hellums, Julia Pemberton. *Hold the anchovies!* (Rotner, Shelley)

Helmer, Diana Star. *The cat who came for tacos* ill. by Viví Escrivá. Albert Whitman, 2003. ISBN 978-0-8075-5106-6 Subj: Animals – cats. Etiquette.

Helmer, Marilyn. *Critter riddles* ill. by Eric Parker. Kids Can, 2003. ISBN 978-1-55337-445-9 Subj: Humorous stories. Riddles & jokes.

Funtime riddles ill. by Jane Kurisu. Kids Can, 2004. ISBN 978-1-55337-579-1 Subj: Riddles & jokes.

One splendid tree ill. by Dianne Eastman. Kids Can, 2005. ISBN 978-1-55337-683-5 Subj: Family life. Holidays – Christmas. Trees. U.S. history. War.

Recess riddles ill. by Jane Kurisu. Kids Can, 2004. ISBN 978-1-55337-577-7 Subj: Riddles & jokes. School.

Spooky riddles ill. by Eric Parker. Kids Can, 2003. ISBN 978-1-55337-447-3 Subj: Monsters. Riddles & jokes.

Three barnyard tales ill. by Laura Watson. Kids Can, 2002. ISBN 978-1-55074-796-6 Subj: Animals. Birds. Folk & fairy tales.

Three cat and mouse tales ill. by Josée Masse. Kids Can, 2004. ISBN 978-1-55074-943-4 Subj: Animals – cats. Animals – mice. Folk & fairy tales.

Three prince charming tales ill. by Kasia Charko. Kids Can, 2000. ISBN 978-1-55074-761-4 Subj: Folk & fairy tales. Royalty – princes.

Three royal tales ill. by Dianna Bonder. Kids Can, 2003. ISBN 978-1-55074-939-7 Subj: Folk & fairy tales. Royalty.

Three tales of enchantment ill. by Kasia Charko. Kids Can, 2001. ISBN 978-1-55074-843-7 Subj: Folk & fairy tales. Magic.

Three tales of three ill. by Chris Jackson. Kids Can, 2000. ISBN 978-1-55074-759-1 Subj: Animals. Folk & fairy tales.

Three tales of trickery ill. by Noushin Pajouhesh. Kids Can, 2002. ISBN 978-1-55074-937-3 Subj: Behavior – trickery. Folk & fairy tales.

Three teeny tiny tales ill. by Veselina Tomova. Kids Can, 2001. ISBN 978-1-55074-841-3 Subj: Concepts – size. Folk & fairy tales.

Three tuneful tales ill. by Kasia Charko. Kids Can, 2003. ISBN 978-1-55074-941-0 Subj: Folk & fairy tales. Music.

Yucky riddles ill. by Eric Parker. Kids Can, 2003. ISBN 978-1-55337-448-0 Subj: Riddles & jokes.

Yummy riddles ill. by Eric Parker. Kids Can, 2003. ISBN 978-1-55337-446-6 Subj: Food. Riddles & jokes.

Helmore, Jim. *Oh no, monster tomato!* ill. by Karen Wall. Egmont UK, 2011. ISBN 978-1-4052-4741-2 Subj: Contests. Gardens, gardening. Plants.

Helquist, Brett. *Bedtime for Bear* ill. by author. HarperCollins, 2010. ISBN 978-0-06-050205-8 Subj: Animals – bears. Hibernation. Seasons – winter. Weather – snow.

Grumpy Goat ill. by author. HarperCollins, 2013. ISBN 978-0-06-113953-6 Subj: Animals – goats. Behavior – dissatisfaction. Farms. Friendship.

Roger, the jolly pirate ill. by author. HarperCollins, 2004. ISBN 978-0-06-623806-7 Subj: Humorous stories. Pirates.

Hembrook, Deborah. *Clothesline clues to jobs people do* (Heling, Kathryn)

Mouse makes magic (Heling, Kathryn)

Mouse's hide-and-seek words (Heling, Kathryn)

Hemingway, Edward. *Bad apple: a tale of friendship* ill. by author. Putnam, 2012. ISBN 978-0-399-25191-7 Subj: Animals – worms. Food. Friendship.

Bump in the night ill. by author. Putnam, 2008. ISBN 978-0-399-24761-3 Subj: Bedtime. Monsters.

Field guide to the Grumpasaurus ill. by author. Clarion, 2016. ISBN 978-054454665-3 Subj: Behavior – misbehavior. Emotions – anger.

Henderson, Alicia Terry. *Call me black, call me beautiful* ill. by Jennifer C. Kindert. Royal Regal, 2002. ISBN 978-0-9719490-1-0 Subj: Character traits – individuality. Ethnic groups in the U.S. – African Americans. Self-concept.

Henderson, Kathy. *And the good brown earth* ill. by author. Candlewick, 2004. ISBN 978-0-7636-2301-2 Subj: Family life – grandmothers. Gardens, gardening.

Baby knows best ill. by Brita Granström. Little, 2001. ISBN 978-0-316-60580-9 Subj: Babies, toddlers. Rhyming text. Toys.

Hush, baby, hush! lullabies from around the world ill. by Pam Smy. Frances Lincoln, 2011. ISBN 978-1-84507-967-3 Subj: Foreign languages. Lullabies.

Look at you! a baby body book ill. by Paul Howard. Candlewick, 2006. ISBN 978-0-7636-2745-4 Subj: Anatomy. Babies, toddlers. Senses.

Hendra, Sue. *Barry, the fish with fingers* ill. by author. Random House, 2010. ISBN 978-0-375-85894-9 Subj: Anatomy – hands. Fish.

Norman the slug with the silly shell ill. by author. Aladdin, 2017. ISBN 978-148149032-0 Subj: Animals – slugs. Character traits – being different. Self-concept.

Henkes, Kevin. *Bailey goes camping* ill. by author. Greenwillow, 1985. ISBN 978-0-688-05702-2 Subj: Animals – rabbits. Camps, camping. Family life.

The biggest boy ill. by Nancy Tafuri. Greenwillow, 1995. ISBN 978-0-688-12830-2 Subj: Concepts – shape. Concepts – size.

Birds ill. by Laura Dronzek. Greenwillow, 2009. ISBN 978-0-06-136304-7 Subj: Birds. Concepts – color. Concepts – shape. Concepts – size.

Chester's way ill. by author. Greenwillow, 1988. ISBN 978-0-688-07608-5 Subj: Animals – mice. Behavior – bullying, teasing.

Chrysanthemum ill. by author. Greenwillow, 1991. ISBN 978-0-688-09700-4 Subj: Animals – mice. Names. School.

Circle dogs ill. by Dan Yaccarino. Greenwillow, 1998. ISBN 978-0-688-15447-9 Subj: Animals – dogs. Concepts – shape.

Egg ill. by author. Greenwillow, 2017. ISBN 978-006240872-3 Subj: Birds. Eggs. Friendship. Reptiles – alligators, crocodiles.

Good-bye, Curtis ill. by Marisabina Russo. Greenwillow, 1995. ISBN 978-0-688-12828-9 Subj: Careers – postal workers. Communities, neighborhoods.

A good day ill. by author. HarperCollins, 2007. ISBN 978-0-06-114019-8 Subj: Animals. Behavior – bad day, bad mood.

El gran día de Lily / Lilly's big day ill. by author. Greenwillow, 2008. ISBN 978-0-06-136316-0 Subj: Animals – mice. Careers – teachers. Foreign languages. School. Weddings.

Grandpa and Bo ill. by author. Greenwillow, 1986. ISBN 978-0-688-04957-7 Subj: Family life – grandfathers. Seasons – summer.

In the middle of fall ill. by Laura Dronzek. Greenwillow, 2017. ISBN 978-006257311-7 Subj: Nature. Seasons. Seasons – fall.

Jessica ill. by author. Greenwillow, 1989. ISBN 978-0-688-07830-0 Subj: Friendship. Imagination – imaginary friends. School – first day.

Julius, the baby of the world ill. by author. Greenwillow, 1990. ISBN 978-0-688-08944-3 Subj: Animals – mice. Family life. Sibling rivalry.

Kitten's first full moon ill. by author. Greenwillow, 2004. ISBN 978-0-06-058829-8 Subj: Animals – babies. Animals – cats. Behavior – misunderstanding. Caldecott award books. Moon.

Lilly's big day ill. by author. HarperCollins, 2006. ISBN 978-0-06-074236-2 Subj: Animals – mice. Careers – teachers. Character traits – assertiveness. Emotions – anger. Weddings.

Lilly's chocolate heart ill. by author. HarperCollins, 2004. ISBN 978-0-06-056066-9 Subj: Animals – mice. Format, unusual – board books. Holidays – Valentine's Day.

Lilly's purple plastic purse ill. by author. Greenwillow, 1996. ISBN 978-0-688-12898-2 Subj: Animals – mice. Careers – teachers. Clothing – handbags, purses. Emotions – anger. School.

Little white rabbit ill. by author. HarperCollins, 2011. ISBN 978-0-06-200642-4 Subj: Animals – rabbits. Character traits – curiosity. Imagination.

My garden ill. by author. HarperCollins, 2010. ISBN 978-0-06-171517-4 Subj: Gardens, gardening. Imagination.

Oh! ill. by Laura Dronzek. Greenwillow, 1999. ISBN 978-0-688-17054-7 Subj: Activities – playing. Animals. Rhyming text. Seasons – winter. Weather – snow.

Old Bear ill. by author. Greenwillow, 2008. ISBN 978-0-06-155205-2 Subj: Animals – bears. Dreams. Hibernation. Seasons.

Owen ill. by author. Greenwillow, 1993. ISBN 978-0-688-11450-3 Subj: Animals – mice. Behavior – growing up. Caldecott award honor books.

Sheila Rae, the brave ill. by author. Greenwillow, 1987. ISBN 978-0-688-07156-1 Subj: Animals – mice. Behavior – lost. Character traits – bravery. Family life – sisters.

Sheila Rae's peppermint stick ill. by author. HarperCollins, 2001. ISBN 978-0-06-029451-9 Subj: Animals – mice. Behavior – sharing. Family life – sisters. Food. Format, unusual – board books.

Shhhh ill. by author. Greenwillow, 1989. ISBN 978-0-688-07986-4 Subj: Family life. Morning. Sleep.

So happy! ill. by Anita Lobel. HarperCollins, 2005. ISBN 978-0-06-056484-1 Subj: Animals – rabbits. Plants. Seeds.

Waiting ill. by author. Greenwillow, 2015. ISBN 978-006236843-0 Subj: Animals. Caldecott award honor books. Character traits – patience, impatience. Toys. Weather.

A weekend with Wendell ill. by author. Greenwillow, 1986. ISBN 978-0-688-06326-9 Subj: Activities – playing. Animals – mice. Behavior – misbehavior. Character traits – selfishness.

Wemberly worried ill. by author. Greenwillow, 2000. ISBN 978-0-688-17028-8 Subj: Animals – mice. Behavior – worrying. School – first day. School – nursery.

When spring comes ill. by Laura Dronzek. Greenwillow, 2016. ISBN 978-006233139-7 Subj: Animals – cats. Seasons. Seasons – spring.

Henn, Sophy. *Pass it on* ill. by author. Philomel, 2017. ISBN 978-039954775-1 Subj: Behavior – sharing. Character traits – kindness. Emotions – happiness.

Pom Pom Panda gets the grumps ill. by author. Philomel, 2015. ISBN 978-039917159-8 Subj: Animals – pandas. Behavior – bad day, bad mood. Emotions – anger.

Hennessy, B. G. *Because of you: a book of kindness* ill. by Hiroe Nakata. Candlewick, 2005. ISBN 978-0-7636-1926-8 Subj: Character traits – kindness.

The boy who cried wolf ill. by Boris Kulikov. Simon & Schuster, 2006. ISBN 978-0-689-87433-8 Subj: Animals – wolves. Behavior – lying. Behavior – trickery. Folk & fairy tales.

Busy Dinah Dinosaur ill. by Ana Martin Larrañaga. Candlewick, 2000. ISBN 978-0-7636-1140-8 Subj: Activities. Dinosaurs. Prehistory.

A Christmas wish for Corduroy ill. by Jody Wheeler. Viking, 2014. ISBN 978-067078550-6 Subj: Clothing. Holidays – Christmas. Santa Claus. Toys – bears.

Corduroy at the zoo ill. by Lisa McCue. Based on the character by Don Freeman. Viking, 2000. ISBN 978-0-670-89288-4 Subj: Animals. Format, unusual – toy & movable books. Toys – bears. Zoos.

Corduroy's birthday ill. by Lisa McCue. Based on the character by Don Freeman. Viking, 1997. ISBN 978-0-670-87065-3 Subj: Birthdays. Format, unusual – toy & movable books. Parties. Toys – bears.

Corduroy's Christmas ill. by Lisa McCue. Based on the character by Don Freeman. Viking, 1992. ISBN 978-0-670-84477-7 Subj: Format, unusual – toy & movable books. Holidays – Christmas. Toys – bears.

Corduroy's Easter ill. by Lisa McCue. Based on the character by Don Freeman. Viking, 1998. ISBN 978-0-670-88101-7 Subj: Format, unusual – toy & movable books. Holidays – Easter. Toys – bears.

Corduroy's Halloween ill. by Lisa McCue. Based on the character by Don Freeman. Viking, 1995. ISBN 978-0-670-86193-4 Subj: Clothing – costumes. Format, unusual – toy & movable books. Holidays – Halloween. Toys – bears.

The dinosaur who lived in my backyard ill. by Susan Davis. Viking, 1988. ISBN 978-0-670-81685-9 Subj: Dinosaurs. Imagination. Prehistory.

The first night ill. by Lou Fancher and Steve Johnson. Viking, 1993. ISBN 978-0-670-83026-8 Subj: Holidays – Christmas. Religion.

Meet Dinah Dinosaur ill. by Ana Martin Larrañaga. Candlewick, 2000. ISBN 978-0-7636-1133-0 Subj: Dinosaurs. Prehistory.

The missing tarts ill. by Tracey Campbell Pearson. Viking, 1989. ISBN 978-0-670-82039-9 Subj: Behavior – stealing. Nursery rhymes. Rhyming text. Royalty – queens.

Mr. Ouchy's first day ill. by Paul Meisel. Penguin, 2006. ISBN 978-0-399-24248-9 Subj: Careers – teachers. Counting, numbers. School – first day. Time.

Olympics! ill. by Michael Chesworth. Viking, 1996. ISBN 978-0-670-86522-2 Subj: Sports – Olympics.

One little, two little, three little pilgrims ill. by Lynne Cravath. Viking, 1999. ISBN 978-0-670-87779-9 Subj: Counting, numbers. Indians of North America – Wampanoag. Pilgrims.

Road builders ill. by Simms Taback. Viking, 1994. ISBN 978-0-670-83390-0 Subj: Careers – construction workers. Machines. Roads.

Henrichs, Wendy. *I am Tama, lucky cat: a Japanese legend* ill. by Yoshiko Jaeggi. Peachtree, 2011. ISBN 978-1-56145-589-8 Subj: Animals – cats. Folk & fairy tales. Foreign lands – Japan.

When Anju loved being an elephant ill. by John Butler. Sleeping Bear, 2011. ISBN 978-1-58536-533-3 Subj: Animals – elephants. Character traits –

kindness to animals. Circus. Foreign lands – Indonesia.

Henry, Jed. *Cheer up, Mouse!* ill. by author. Houghton Mifflin, 2013. ISBN 978-0-547-68107-8 Subj: Animals. Animals – mice. Emotions – sadness. Friendship. Hugging.

Good night, Mouse! ill. by author. Houghton Mifflin, 2013. ISBN 978-0-547-98156-7 Subj: Animals – mice. Bedtime. Friendship. Sleep.

I speak dinosaur ill. by author. Abrams, 2012. ISBN 978-1-4197-0233-4 Subj: Behavior – misbehavior. Dinosaurs. Etiquette. Language.

Henry, Rohan. *The gift box* ill. by author. Abrams, 2012. ISBN 978-1-4197-0167-2 Subj: Animals – dogs. Animals – elephants. Friendship.

Henry, Steve. *Here is Big Bunny* ill. by author. Holiday House, 2016. ISBN 978-082343458-9 Subj: Animals – rabbits. Cities, towns. Concepts – size.

Nobody asked me! ill. by author. HarperCollins, 2001. ISBN 978-0-688-17866-6 Subj: Animals – cats. Family life – brothers. Family life – new sibling.

Henson, Heather. *Grumpy Grandpa* ill. by Ross MacDonald. Atheneum, 2009. ISBN 978-1-4169-0811-1 Subj: Family life – grandfathers. Old age. Sports – fishing.

Henterly, Jamichael. *Good night, garden gnome* ill. by author. Dial, 2001. ISBN 978-0-8037-2531-7 Subj: Gardens, gardening. Mythical creatures – gnomes.

Heo, Yumi. *Father's rubber shoes* ill. by author. Orchard, 1995. ISBN 978-0-531-08723-7 Subj: Careers – storekeepers. Clothing – shoes. Ethnic groups in the U.S. – Korean Americans. Family life – fathers.

The green frogs ill. by author. Houghton, 1996. ISBN 978-0-395-68378-1 Subj: Behavior – misbehavior. Folk & fairy tales. Foreign lands – Korea. Frogs & toads.

Lady Hahn and her seven friends ill. by author. Henry Holt, 2012. ISBN 978-0-8050-4127-9 Subj: Activities – sewing. Behavior – boasting, showing off. Behavior – fighting, arguing. Careers – seamstresses. Character traits – vanity. Foreign lands – Korea.

One afternoon ill. by author. Orchard, 1994. ISBN 978-0-531-08695-7 Subj: Cities, towns. Communities, neighborhoods. Family life – mothers. Noise, sounds.

One Sunday morning ill. by author. Orchard, 1999. ISBN 978-0-531-33156-9 Subj: Cities, towns. Family life – fathers. Noise, sounds. Parks.

Ten days and nine nights: an adoption story ill. by author. Random House, 2009. ISBN 978-0-375-84718-9 Subj: Adoption. Ethnic groups in the U.S. – Korean Americans. Family life.

Heos, Bridget. *Be safe around fire* ill. by Silvia Baroncelli. Amicus, 2014. ISBN 978-160753444-0 Subj: Fire. Safety.

Mustache Baby ill. by Joy Ang. Clarion, 2013. ISBN 978-0-547-77357-5 Subj: Babies, toddlers. Behavior. Character traits – appearance. Self-concept.

Mustache Baby meets his match ill. by Joy Ang. Clarion, 2015. ISBN 978-054436375-5 Subj: Babies, toddlers. Character traits – appearance. Contests.

Queen Dog ill. by Alejandro O'Keeffe. Disney/Hyperion, 2017. ISBN 978-148472852-9 Subj: Animals – dogs. Babies, toddlers. Family life – new sibling. Royalty – queens.

Shell, beak, tusk: shared traits and the wonders of adaptation ill. with photos. Houghton Mifflin Harcourt, 2017. ISBN 978-054481166-9 Subj: Animals. Evolution. Nature.

What to expect when you're expecting hatchlings: a guide for crocodilian parents (and curious kids) ill. by Stéphane Jorisch. Millbrook, 2012. ISBN 978-0-7613-5860-2 Subj: Animals – babies. Reptiles – alligators, crocodiles.

What to expect when you're expecting joeys: a guide for marsupial parents (and curious kids) ill. by Stéphane Jorisch. Millbrook, 2011. ISBN 978-0-7613-5859-6 Subj: Animals – babies. Animals – marsupials.

Hepworth, Catherine. *ANTics! an alphabetical anthology* ill. by author. Putnam, 1992. ISBN 978-0-399-21862-0 Subj: ABC books. Insects – ants.

Heras, Theo. *Baby cakes* ill. by Renné Benoit. Pajama, 2017. ISBN 978-177278030-7 Subj: Activities – baking, cooking. Babies, toddlers. Food.

What will we do with the baby-o? ill. by Jennifer Herbert. Tundra, 2004. ISBN 978-0-88776-689-3 Subj: Rhyming text. Songs.

Herbert, Gail. *Mattland* (Hutchins, Hazel)

Here we go round the mulberry bush ill. by Sophie Fatus. Barefoot, 2007. ISBN 978-1-84686-035-5 Subj: Music. Songs. World.

Herkert, Barbara. *Birds in your backyard* ill. by author. Dawn, 2001. ISBN 978-1-58469-026-9 Subj: Activities. Birds.

Sewing stories: Harriet Powers' journey from slave to artist ill. by Vanessa Brantley-Newton. Knopf, 2015. ISBN 978-038575462-0 Subj: Activities – sewing. Art. Ethnic groups in the U.S. – African Americans. Quilts. Slavery.

Herman, Charlotte. *First rain* ill. by Kathryn Mitter. Albert Whitman, 2010. ISBN 978-0-8075-2453-4 Subj: Foreign lands – Israel. Jewish culture. Weather – rain.

The memory cupboard ill. by Ben F. Stahl. Albert Whitman, 2003. ISBN 978-0-8075-5055-7 Subj: Family life. Family life – grandmothers. Holidays – Thanksgiving.

Herman, Gail. *The lion and the mouse* (Aesop)

Herman, R. A. *Gomer and Little Gomer* ill. by Steve Haskamp. Penguin, 2005. ISBN 978-0-525-47359-6 Subj: Animals – dogs. Toys.

Hernandez, Keith. *First-base hero* ill. by John Manders. Golden, 2002. ISBN 978-0-307-10626-1 Subj: Format, unusual – toy & movable books. Sports – baseball.

Hernandez, Leeza. *Cat napped* ill. by author. Putnam, 2014. ISBN 978-039916438-5 Subj: Animals – cats. Behavior – lost & found possessions. Character traits – kindness to animals.

Dog gone! ill. by author. Putnam, 2012. ISBN 978-0-399-25447-5 Subj: Animals – dogs. Behavior – lost & found possessions. Behavior – running away.

Herrera, Juan Felipe. *Grandma and Me at the flea / Los meros meros remateros* ill. by Anita de Lucio-Brock. Children's Book Press, 2002. ISBN 978-0-89239-171-4 Subj: Communities, neighborhoods. Ethnic groups in the U.S. – Mexican Americans. Family life – grandmothers. Foreign languages.

Hershenhorn, Esther. *Fancy that* ill. by Megan Lloyd. Holiday, 2003. ISBN 978-0-8234-1605-9 Subj: Careers – artists. Family life – brothers & sisters. Orphans.

Herthel, Jessica. *I am Jazz* by Jessica Herthel and Jazz Jennings ill. by Shelagh McNicholas. Dial, 2014. ISBN 978-080374107-2 Subj: Character traits – being different. Gender identity.

Hertz, Grete Janus. *Olie's bedtime walk* ill. by Nynke Mare Talsma. Star Bright, 2002. ISBN 978-1-887734-90-5 Subj: Activities – walking. Activities – working. Night. Sleep.

Herzog, Brad. *G is for gold medal: an Olympics alphabet* ill. by Doug Bowles. Sleeping Bear, 2011. ISBN 978-1-58536-462-6 Subj: ABC books. Sports – Olympics.

I spy with my little eye: baseball ill. by David Milne. Sleeping Bear, 2011. ISBN 978-1-58536-496-1 Subj: Picture puzzles. Sports – baseball.

R is for race: a stock car alphabet ill. by Jane Gilltrap Bready. Sleeping Bear, 2006. ISBN 978-1-58536-272-1 Subj: ABC books. Automobiles. Sports – racing.

Herzog, Kenny. *Phil Pickle* ill. by Kelly Canby. Peter Pauper, 2016. ISBN 978-144131933-3 Subj: Careers – actors. Character traits – ambition. Food. Humorous stories.

Hess, Mary Rand, et al. *Animal ark: celebrating our wild world in poetry and pictures* (Alexander, Kwame)

Hesse, Karen. *Come on, rain* ill. by Jon J Muth. Scholastic, 1999. ISBN 978-0-590-33125-8 Subj: Activities – dancing. Ethnic groups in the U.S. – African Americans. Family life – daughters. Family life – mothers. Seasons – summer. Weather – rain.

My thumb ill. by Rich Deas. Feiwel & Friends, 2016. ISBN 978-031267120-4 Subj: Rhyming text. School – nursery. Thumb sucking.

Spuds ill. by Wendy Watson. Scholastic, 2008. ISBN 978-0-439-87993-4 Subj: Character traits – honesty. Country. Emotions – love. Family life. Food.

Hesselberth, Joyce. *Shape shift* ill. by author. Holt/Christy Ottaviano, 2016. ISBN 978-162779057-4 Subj: Concepts – shape. Imagination.

Hest, Amy. *Are you sure, Mother Bear?* ill. by Lauren Tobia. Candlewick, 2016. ISBN 978-076367207-2 Subj: Animals – bears. Family life – mothers. Hibernation.

The babies are coming! ill. by Chloë Cheese. Crown, 1997. ISBN 978-0-517-70944-3 Subj: Activities – storytelling. Babies, toddlers. Libraries.

Baby Duck and the bad eyeglasses ill. by Jill Barton. Candlewick, 1996. ISBN 978-1-56402-680-4 Subj: Birds – ducks. Family life – grandfathers. Glasses.

Baby Duck and the cozy blanket ill. by Jill Barton. Candlewick, 2002. ISBN 978-0-7636-1582-6 Subj: Birds – ducks. Format, unusual – board books.

Buster and the baby ill. by Polly Dunbar. Candlewick, 2017. ISBN 978-076368787-8 Subj: Activities – playing. Animals – dogs. Babies, toddlers. Bedtime.

Charley's first night ill. by Helen Oxenbury. Candlewick, 2012. ISBN 978-0-7636-4055-2 Subj: Animals – dogs. Character traits – kindness to animals. Pets. Sleep. Weather – snow.

The dog who belonged to no one ill. by Amy Bates. Abrams, 2008. ISBN 978-0-8109-9483-6 Subj: Animals – dogs. Emotions – loneliness.

The Friday nights of Nana ill. by Claire A. Nivola. Candlewick, 2001. ISBN 978-0-7636-0658-9 Subj: Family life – grandmothers. Jewish culture. Religion.

Guess who, Baby Duck ill. by Jill Barton. Candlewick, 2004. ISBN 978-0-7636-1981-7 Subj: Activities – photographing. Birds – ducks. Family life – grandfathers. Illness – cold (disease).

Kiss good night ill. by Anita Jeram. Candlewick, 2001. ISBN 978-0-7636-0780-7 Subj: Animals – bears. Bedtime. Family life – mothers. Kissing.

Little chick ill. by Anita Jeram. Candlewick, 2009. ISBN 978-0-7636-2890-1 Subj: Birds – chickens, roosters. Gardens, gardening. Kites. Stars.

Mabel dancing ill. by Christine Davenier. Candlewick, 2000. ISBN 978-0-7636-0746-3 Subj: Activities – dancing. Bedtime. Family life – parents. Parties.

Make the team, Baby Duck ill. by Jill Barton. Candlewick, 2002. ISBN 978-0-7636-1541-3 Subj: Birds – ducks. Character traits – confidence. Family life – grandfathers. Sports – swimming.

My old pal, Oscar ill. by Amy Bates. Abrams, 2016. ISBN 978-141971901-1 Subj: Animals – dogs. Death. Emotions – grief. Pets.

Nana's birthday party ill. by Amy Schwartz. Morrow, 1993. ISBN 978-0-688-07498-2 Subj: Birthdays. Careers – artists. Cities, towns. Family life – cousins. Family life – grandmothers.

Off to school, Baby Duck ill. by Jill Barton. Candlewick, 1999. ISBN 978-0-7636-0244-4 Subj: Babies, toddlers. Birds – ducks. Emotions – fear. Family life – grandfathers. School – first day.

On the night of the shooting star ill. by Jenni Desmond. Candlewick, 2017. ISBN 978-076369154-7 Subj: Animals – dogs. Animals – rabbits. Friendship. Sky.

The purple coat ill. by Amy Schwartz. Four Winds, 1986. ISBN 978-0-02-743640-2 Subj: Careers – tailors. Clothing – coats. Concepts – color. Family life. Family life – grandfathers.

The reader ill. by Lauren Castillo. Amazon Children's, 2012. ISBN 978-0-7614-6184-5 Subj: Animals – dogs. Books, reading. Seasons – winter. Weather – snow.

When Charley met Grampa ill. by Helen Oxenbury. Candlewick, 2013. ISBN 978-0-7636-5314-9 Subj: Animals – dogs. Family life – grandfathers. Pets. Weather – snow.

When you meet a bear on Broadway ill. by Elivia Savadier. Farrar, 2009. ISBN 978-0-374-40015-6 Subj: Animals – bears. Behavior – lost. Cities, towns. Family life – mothers.

You can do it, Sam ill. by Anita Jeram. Candlewick, 2003. ISBN 978-0-7636-1934-3 Subj: Animals – bears. Character traits – confidence. Family life – mothers. Food.

You're the boss, Baby Duck ill. by Jill Barton. Candlewick, 1997. ISBN 978-1-56402-667-5 Subj: Babies, toddlers. Birds – ducks. Emotions – envy, jealousy. Family life – brothers & sisters. Family life – grandfathers. Self-concept.

Hester, Denia Lewis. *Grandma Lena's big ol' turnip* ill. by Jackie Urbanovic. Albert Whitman, 2005. ISBN 978-0-8075-3027-6 Subj: Character traits – cooperation. Cumulative tales. Ethnic groups in the U.S. – African Americans. Farms. Food. Problem solving.

Hewett, Joan. *A flamingo chick grows up* photos by Richard Hewett. Carolrhoda, 2001. ISBN 978-1-57505-164-2 Subj: Animals – babies. Behavior – growing up. Birds – flamingos.

A giraffe calf grows up photos by Richard Hewett. Carolrhoda, 2004. ISBN 978-1-57505-197-0 Subj: Animals – babies. Animals – giraffes. Behavior – growing up.

A harbor seal pup grows up photos by Richard Hewett. Carolrhoda, 2002. ISBN 978-1-57505-166-6 Subj: Animals – babies. Animals – seals. Behavior – growing up.

A kangaroo joey grows up photos by Richard Hewett. Carolrhoda, 2002. ISBN 978-1-57505-165-9 Subj: Animals – babies. Animals – kangaroos. Behavior – growing up.

A koala joey grows up photos by Richard Hewett. Carolrhoda, 2004. ISBN 978-1-57505-198-7 Subj: Animals – babies. Animals – koalas. Behavior – growing up.

A monkey baby grows up photos by Richard Hewett. Carolrhoda, 2004. ISBN 978-1-57505-199-4 Subj: Animals – babies. Animals – monkeys. Behavior – growing up.

A penguin chick grows up photos by Richard Hewett. Carolrhoda, 2004. ISBN 978-1-57505-200-7 Subj: Animals – babies. Behavior – growing up. Birds – penguins.

A tiger cub grows up photos by Richard Hewett. Carolrhoda, 2002. ISBN 978-1-57505-163-5 Subj: Animals – babies. Animals – tigers. Behavior – growing up.

Hewitt, Kathryn. *No dogs here!* ill. by author. Penguin, 2005. ISBN 978-0-525-47200-1 Subj: Animals – dogs. Days of the week, months of the year.

Hewitt, Sally. *All year round* ill. by Tony Kenyon and Mike Atkinson. Copper Beech, 2000. ISBN 978-0-7613-1208-6 Subj: Animals. Ecology. Nature. Seasons.

Animal homes story by Inga Phipps; ill. by Fiametta Dogi. Two-Can, 2000. ISBN 978-1-58728-600-1 Subj: Animals. Homes, houses.

Face to face safari ill. by Chris Gilvan-Cartwright. Abrams, 2003. ISBN 978-0-8109-4261-5 Subj: Animals. Format, unusual – toy & movable books. Jungle.

Woods and meadows ill. by Tony Kenyon and Mike Atkinson. Copper Beech, 2000. ISBN 978-0-7613-1207-9 Subj: Animals. Ecology. Forest, woods. Nature. Seasons.

Heyer, Marilee. *The weaving of a dream: a Chinese folktale* ill. by author. Viking, 1986. ISBN 978-0-670-80555-6 Subj: Activities – weaving. Folk & fairy tales. Foreign lands – China.

Heyward, Du Bose. *The country bunny and the little gold shoes* ill. by Marjorie Flack. Houghton, 1974, ©1939. ISBN 978-0-395-18557-5 Subj: Animals – rabbits. Character traits – kindness. Holidays – Easter.

Hiatt, Fred. *Baby talk* ill. by Mark Graham. Margaret K. McElderry, 1999. ISBN 978-0-689-82146-2 Subj: Babies, toddlers. Family life – brothers. Language.

Hickling, Meg. *Boys, girls and body science* ill. by Kim LaFave. Harbour, 2002. ISBN 978-1-55017-236-2 Subj: Anatomy. Science.

Hickman, Martha Whitmore. *A baby born in Bethlehem* ill. by Giuliano Ferri. Albert Whitman, 1999. ISBN 978-0-8075-5522-4 Subj: Holidays – Christmas. Religion – Nativity.

Hickman, Pamela. *It's moving day!* ill. by Geraldo Valério. Kids Can, 2008. ISBN 978-1-55453-074-8 Subj: Animals. Homes, houses.

Hickox, Rebecca. *The golden sandal* ill. by Will Hillenbrand. Holiday, 1998. ISBN 978-0-8234-1331-7 Subj: Clothing. Family life – stepfamilies. Folk & fairy tales. Foreign lands – Iraq.

Hicks, Barbara Jean. *I like black and white* ill. by Lila Prap. Tiger Tales, 2006. ISBN 978-1-58925-057-4 Subj: Concepts – color. Rhyming text.

Jitterbug jam: a monster tale ill. by Alexis Deacon. Farrar, 2005. ISBN 978-0-374-33685-1 Subj: Bedtime. Emotions – fear. Monsters.

Monsters don't eat broccoli ill. by Sue Hendra. Knopf, 2009. ISBN 978-0-375-85686-0 Subj: Food. Imagination. Monsters. Rhyming text.

The secret life of Walter Kitty ill. by Dan Santat. Random House, 2007. ISBN 978-0-375-83196-6 Subj: Animals – cats. Humorous stories.

Higashi, Sandra. *Bonz, inside-out* (Glaser, Byron)

Higgins, Ryan T. *Be quiet!* ill. by author. Disney/Hyperion, 2017. ISBN 978-148473162-8 Subj: Activities – talking. Animals – mice. Books, reading. Character traits – patience, impatience. Noise, sounds.

Hotel Bruce ill. by author. Disney/Hyperion, 2016. ISBN 978-148474362-1 Subj: Animals – bears. Animals – mice. Behavior – bad day, bad mood. Birds – geese. Hotels.

Mother Bruce ill. by author. Disney/Hyperion, 2015. ISBN 978-148473088-1 Subj: Animals – bears. Behavior – bad day, bad mood. Birds – geese. Eggs.

Wilfred ill. by author. Dial, 2013. ISBN 978-0-8037-3732-7 Subj: Friendship. Giants. Hair.

High, Linda Oatman. *Cool Bopper's choppers* ill. by John O'Brien. Boyds Mills, 2007. ISBN 978-1-59078-379-5 Subj: Music. Musical instruments – saxophones. Teeth.

The girl on the high-diving horse ill. by Ted Lewin. Philomel, 2003. ISBN 978-0-399-23649-5 Subj: Animals – horses, ponies. Careers – photographers. Family life – fathers. Parks. U.S. history.

The last chimney of Christmas eve ill. by Kestutis Kasparavicius. Boyds Mills, 2001. ISBN 978-1-56397-804-3 Subj: Careers. Holidays – Christmas. Santa Claus.

Tenth Avenue cowboy ill. by Bill Farnsworth. Eerdmans, 2008. ISBN 978-0-8028-5330-1 Subj: Behavior – bullying, teasing. Cities, towns. Cowboys, cowgirls. Trains. U.S. history.

Under New York ill. by Robert Rayevsky. Holiday, 2001. ISBN 978-0-8234-1551-9 Subj: Cities, towns. Concepts – opposites.

Winter shoes for Shadow Horse ill. by Ted Lewin. Boyds Mills, 2001. ISBN 978-1-56397-472-4 Subj: Animals – horses, ponies. Careers – blacksmiths. Family life – fathers.

Highet, Alistair. *The yellow train* based on a story by Fred Bernard; ill. by François Roca. Creative Editions, 2000. ISBN 978-1-56846-128-1 Subj: Careers – engineers. Family life – grandfathers. Trains.

Hill, Elizabeth Starr. *Evan's corner* ill. by Sandra Speidel. Rev. ed. Viking, 1991. ISBN 978-0-670-82830-2 Subj: Character traits – helpfulness. Ethnic groups in the U.S. – African Americans. Family life.

Hill, Eric. *Spot at home* ill. by author. Putnam, 1991. ISBN 978-0-399-21774-6 Subj: Animals – dogs. Format, unusual – board books.

Spot at play ill. by author. Putnam, 1985. ISBN 978-0-399-21228-4 Subj: Activities – playing. Animals. Animals – dogs.

Spot at the fair ill. by author. Putnam, 1985. ISBN 978-0-399-21229-1 Subj: Animals. Animals – dogs. Fairs, festivals. Format, unusual – board books.

Spot bakes a cake ill. by author. Putnam, 1994. ISBN 978-0-399-22701-1 Subj: Activities – baking, cooking. Animals – dogs. Birthdays. Food. Format, unusual – toy & movable books.

Spot counts from 1 to 10 ill. by author. Putnam, 1989. ISBN 978-0-399-21672-5 Subj: Animals. Animals – dogs. Counting, numbers. Format, unusual – board books.

Spot goes to a party ill. by author. Putnam, 1992. ISBN 978-0-399-22409-6 Subj: Animals – dogs. Cowboys, cowgirls. Format, unusual – toy & movable books. Parties.

Spot goes to school ill. by author. Putnam, 1984. ISBN 978-0-399-21073-0 Subj: Animals – dogs. Format, unusual – toy & movable books. School – first day.

Spot goes to the beach ill. by author. Putnam, 1985. ISBN 978-0-399-21247-5 Subj: Activities – playing. Animals – dogs. Family life. Format, unusual – toy & movable books. Sea & seashore – beaches.

Spot goes to the circus ill. by author. Putnam, 1986. ISBN 978-0-399-21317-5 Subj: Animals – dogs. Circus. Format, unusual – board books.

Spot goes to the farm ill. by author. Putnam, 1987. ISBN 978-0-399-21434-9 Subj: Animals. Animals – dogs. Farms. Format, unusual – board books. Machines.

Spot goes to the park ill. by author. Putnam, 1991. ISBN 978-0-399-21833-0 Subj: Activities – playing. Animals – dogs. Format, unusual – toy & movable books. Parks.

Spot looks at colors ill. by author. Putnam, 1986. ISBN 978-0-399-21349-6 Subj: Animals – dogs. Concepts – color. Format, unusual – board books.

Spot looks at opposites ill. by author. Putnam, 1989. ISBN 978-0-399-21681-7 Subj: Animals – dogs. Concepts – opposites. Format, unusual – board books.

Spot looks at shapes ill. by author. Putnam, 1986. ISBN 978-0-399-21350-2 Subj: Animals – dogs. Concepts – shape. Format, unusual – board books.

Spot looks at weather ill. by author. Putnam, 1989. ISBN 978-0-399-21673-2 Subj: Animals – dogs. Format, unusual – board books. Weather.

Spot on the farm ill. by author. Putnam, 1985. ISBN 978-0-399-21230-7 Subj: Animals. Animals – dogs. Farms. Format, unusual – board books.

Spot sleeps over ill. by author. Putnam, 1990. ISBN 978-0-399-21815-6 Subj: Activities – playing. Animals – dogs. Format, unusual – toy & movable books. Friendship. Sleepovers.

Spot visits his grandparents ill. by author. Putnam, 1996. ISBN 978-0-399-23033-2 Subj: Animals

– dogs. Family life – grandparents. Format, unusual – board books.

Spot's baby sister ill. by author. Putnam, 1989. ISBN 978-0-399-21640-4 Subj: Animals – dogs. Animals – hippopotamuses. Format, unusual – toy & movable books. Reptiles – alligators, crocodiles.

Spot's big book of words / El libro grande de las palabras de Spot ill. by author. Rev. ed. Putnam, 1989. ISBN 978-0-399-21689-3 Subj: Animals – dogs. Foreign languages. Language.

Spot's birthday party ill. by author. Putnam, 1982. ISBN 978-0-399-20903-1 Subj: Birthdays. Folk & fairy tales. Format, unusual – toy & movable books.

Spot's first Christmas ill. by author. Putnam, 1983. ISBN 978-0-399-20963-5 Subj: Animals – dogs. Format, unusual – toy & movable books. Holidays – Christmas.

Spot's first Easter ill. by author. Putnam, 1988. ISBN 978-0-399-21435-6 Subj: Animals – dogs. Eggs. Format, unusual – toy & movable books. Holidays – Easter.

Spot's first walk ill. by author. Putnam, 1981. ISBN 978-0-399-20838-6 Subj: Activities – walking. Animals – dogs. Format, unusual – toy & movable books.

Spot's first words ill. by author. Putnam, 1986. ISBN 978-0-399-21348-9 Subj: Animals – dogs. Format, unusual – board books. Language.

Spot's magical Christmas ill. by author. Putnam, 1995. ISBN 978-0-399-22912-1 Subj: Animals – dogs. Format, unusual – board books. Holidays – Christmas. Santa Claus.

Where's Spot? ill. by author. Putnam, 1980. ISBN 978-0-399-20758-7 Subj: Behavior – lost. Folk & fairy tales. Format, unusual – toy & movable books.

Hill, Frances. *The bug cemetery* ill. by Vera Rosenberry. Henry Holt, 2002. ISBN 978-0-8050-6370-7 Subj: Death. Emotions – grief. Pets.

Hill, Isabel. *Building stories* photos by author. Star Bright, 2011. ISBN 978-1-59572-279-9 Subj: Buildings. Rhyming text.

Hill, Laban Carrick. *Dave the potter: artist, poet, slave* ill. by Bryan Collier. Little, Brown, 2010. ISBN 978-0-316-10731-0 Subj: Art. Caldecott award honor books. Careers – potters. Ethnic groups in the U.S. – African Americans. Slavery.

Hill, Lee Sullivan. *Earthmovers* ill. with photos. Lerner, 2003. ISBN 978-0-8225-0689-8 Subj: Careers – construction workers. Machines.

Homes keep us warm ill. with photos. Carolrhoda, 2001. ISBN 978-1-57505-430-8 Subj: Homes, houses.

Motorcycles ill. with photos. Lerner, 2004. ISBN 978-0-8225-0695-9 Subj: Motorcycles.

Trains photos by Howard Ande. Lerner, 2003. ISBN 978-0-8225-0692-8 Subj: Trains. Transportation.

Hill, Mary. *Let's make pizza* ill. with photos. Children's Press, 2002. ISBN 978-0-516-23959-0 Subj: Activities – baking, cooking. Food.

Let's make tacos ill. with photos. Children's Press, 2002. ISBN 978-0-516-23957-6 Subj: Activities – baking, cooking. Food.

Hill, Meggan. *Nico and Lola: kindness shared between a boy and a dog* photos by Susan M. Graunke. HarperCollins, 2010. ISBN 978-0-06-199043-4 Subj: Animals – dogs. Character traits – kindness to animals.

Hill, Ros. *Shamoo: a whale of a cow* ill. by author. Simon & Schuster, 2005. ISBN 978-0-689-04634-6 Subj: Animals – bulls, cows. Animals – whales.

Hill, Susanna Leonard. *April Fool, Phyllis!* ill. by Jeffrey Ebbeler. Holiday House, 2011. ISBN 978-0-8234-2270-8 Subj: Animals – groundhogs. Holidays – April Fools' Day. Weather – blizzards.

Can't sleep without sheep ill. by Mike Wohnoutka. Walker, 2010. ISBN 978-0-8027-2066-5 Subj: Animals. Animals – sheep. Bedtime. Counting, numbers. Sleep.

The house that Mack built ill. by Ken Wilson-Max. Simon & Schuster, 2002. ISBN 978-0-689-84813-1 Subj: Cumulative tales. Format, unusual – toy & movable books. Homes, houses. Nursery rhymes. Rhyming text.

Not yet, Rose ill. by Nicole Rutten. Eerdmans, 2009. ISBN 978-0-8028-5326-4 Subj: Animals – hamsters. Babies, toddlers. Family life – new sibling.

Punxsutawney Phyllis ill. by Jeffrey Ebbeler. Holiday House, 2005. ISBN 978-0-8234-1872-5 Subj: Animals – groundhogs. Gender roles. Holidays – Groundhog Day.

Hillenbrand, Jane. *What a treasure!* ill. by Will Hillenbrand. Holiday House, 2006. ISBN 978-0-8234-1896-1 Subj: Animals – moles. Character traits – confidence. Character traits – pride.

Hillenbrand, Will. *All for a dime! a Bear and Mole story* ill. by author. Holiday House, 2015. ISBN 978-082342946-2 Subj: Animals – bears. Animals – moles. Animals – skunks. Stores.

Down by the barn ill. by author. Amazon/Two Lions, 2014. ISBN 978-147784731-2 Subj: Animals. Farms. Tractors.

Fiddle-i-fee ill. by author. Harcourt, 2002. ISBN 978-0-15-201945-7 Subj: Animals. Babies, toddlers. Cumulative tales. Farms. Nursery rhymes.

Kite day ill. by author. Holiday House, 2012. ISBN 978-0-8234-1603-5 Subj: Animals – bears. Animals – moles. Kites.

Louie! ill. by author. Philomel, 2009. ISBN 978-0-399-24707-1 Subj: Activities – drawing. Animals – pigs. Art.

Mother Goose picture puzzles ill. by author. Marshall Cavendish, 2011. ISBN 978-0-7614-5808-1 Subj: Nursery rhymes. Picture puzzles.

My book box ill. by author. Harcourt, 2006. ISBN 978-0-15-202029-3 Subj: Animals – elephants. Books, reading.

Off we go! a Bear and Mole story ill. by author. Holiday House, 2013. ISBN 978-0-8234-2520-4 Subj: Animals – bears. Animals – moles. Sports – bicycling.

Snowman's story ill. by author. Amazon/Two Lions, 2014. ISBN 978-147784787-9 Subj: Animals – rabbits. Clothing – hats. Seasons – winter. Snowmen. Wordless.

Spring is here ill. by author. Holiday House, 2011. ISBN 978-0-8234-1602-8 Subj: Animals – bears. Animals – moles. Seasons – spring.

Hilliard, Richard. *Godspeed, John Glenn* ill. by author. Boyds Mills, 2006. ISBN 978-1-59078-384-9 Subj: Careers – astronauts. U.S. history.

Hills, Tad. *Duck and Goose* ill. by author. Random House, 2006. ISBN 978-0-375-93611-1 Subj: Birds – ducks. Birds – geese. Friendship. Toys – balls.

Duck and Goose find a pumpkin ill. by author. Random House, 2009. ISBN 978-0-375-85813-0 Subj: Birds – ducks. Birds – geese. Format, unusual – board books. Seasons – fall.

Duck and Goose go to the beach ill. by author. Random House, 2014. ISBN 978-038537235-0 Subj: Birds – ducks. Birds – geese. Friendship. Sea & seashore – beaches.

Duck and Goose, honk! quack! boo! ill. by author. Random House, 2017. ISBN 978-152470175-8 Subj: Birds – ducks. Birds – geese. Clothing – costumes. Holidays – Halloween.

Duck and Goose, how are you feeling? ill. by author. Schwartz & Wade, 2009. ISBN 978-0-375-84629-8 Subj: Birds – ducks. Birds – geese. Emotions. Format, unusual – board books.

Duck and Goose, 1, 2, 3 ill. by author. Schwartz & Wade, 2008. ISBN 978-0-375-85621-1 Subj: Birds – ducks. Birds – geese. Counting, numbers. Format, unusual – board books.

Duck, Duck, Goose ill. by author. Random House, 2007. ISBN 978-0-375-84068-5 Subj: Birds – ducks. Birds – geese. Friendship.

How Rocket learned to read ill. by author. Random House, 2010. ISBN 978-0-375-85899-4 Subj: Animals – dogs. Birds. Books, reading.

R is for Rocket ill. by author. Random House, 2015. ISBN 978-055352228-0 Subj: ABC books. Animals – dogs.

Rocket writes a story ill. by author. Random House, 2012. ISBN 978-0-375-87086-6 Subj: Activities – writing. Animals – dogs. Birds. Birds – owls. Books, reading.

Rocket's mighty words ill. by author. Random House, 2013. ISBN 978-0-385-37233-6 Subj: Animals – dogs. Birds. Format, unusual – board books. Language.

What's up, Duck? a book of opposites ill. by author. Random House, 2008. ISBN 978-0-375-84738-7 Subj: Birds – ducks. Birds – geese. Concepts – opposites. Format, unusual – board books.

Hilton, Perez. *The boy with pink hair* ill. by Jen Hill. Penguin, 2011. ISBN 978-0-451-23420-9 Subj: Behavior – bullying, teasing. Character traits – being different. Hair. School. Self-concept.

Himes, Rachel. *Princess and the peas* ill. by author. Charlesbridge, 2017. ISBN 978-158089718-1 Subj: Activities – baking, cooking. Contests. Ethnic groups in the U.S. – African Americans. Folk & fairy tales. Food.

Himmelman, John. *Chickens to the rescue* ill. by author. Henry Holt, 2006. ISBN 978-0-8050-7951-7 Subj: Birds – chickens, roosters. Character traits – helpfulness. Farms.

Cows to the rescue ill. by author. Henry Holt, 2011. ISBN 978-0-8050-9249-3 Subj: Animals – bulls, cows. Fairs, festivals. Farms. Humorous stories.

A dandelion's life ill. by author. Children's Press, 1998. ISBN 978-0-516-21177-0 Subj: Flowers. Plants. Seeds.

Duck to the rescue ill. by author. Henry Holt, 2014. ISBN 978-080509485-5 Subj: Birds – ducks. Humorous stories.

A house spider's life ill. by author. Children's Press, 1999. ISBN 978-0-516-21185-5 Subj: Spiders.

Katie and the puppy next door ill. by author. Henry Holt, 2013. ISBN 978-0-8050-9484-8 Subj: Animals – dogs. Behavior – sharing.

Katie loves the kittens ill. by author. Henry Holt, 2008. ISBN 978-0-8050-8682-9 Subj: Animals – cats. Animals – dogs. Character traits – patience, impatience. Friendship.

A luna moth's life ill. by author. Children's Press, 1998. ISBN 978-0-516-20821-3 Subj: Insects – moths.

A monarch butterfly's life ill. by author. Children's Press, 1999. ISBN 978-0-516-21147-3 Subj: Insects – butterflies, caterpillars.

Mouse in a meadow ill. by author. Charlesbridge, 2005. ISBN 978-1-57091-520-8 Subj: Animals. Ecology. Plants.

Noisy bird sing-along ill. by author. Dawn, 2015. ISBN 978-158469513-4 Subj: Birds. Noise, sounds.

Noisy bug sing-along ill. by author. Dawn, 2013. ISBN 978-1-58469-192-1 Subj: Insects. Noise, sounds.

Noisy frog sing-along ill. by author. Dawn, 2013. ISBN 978-1-58469-339-0 Subj: Frogs & toads. Noise, sounds.

Pigs to the rescue ill. by author. Henry Holt, 2010. ISBN 978-0-8050-8683-6 Subj: Animals – pigs. Character traits – helpfulness. Farms.

A pill bug's life ill. by author. Children's Press, 1999. ISBN 978-0-516-21165-7 Subj: Crustaceans.

Ten little hot dogs ill. by author. Marshall Cavendish, 2010. ISBN 978-0-7614-5797-8 Subj: Animals – dogs. Counting, numbers.

There's a bug on my book! ill. by author. Dawn, 2017. ISBN 978-158469588-2 Subj: Insects.

Tudley didn't know ill. by author. Sylvan Dell, 2006. ISBN 978-0-9764943-6-2 Subj: Character traits – individuality. Friendship. Reptiles – turtles, tortoises.

A wood frog's life ill. by author. Children's Press, 1998. ISBN 978-0-516-21178-7 Subj: Forest, woods. Frogs & toads. Nature.

Hindley, Judy. *Baby talk* ill. by Brita Granström. Candlewick, 2006. ISBN 978-0-7636-2971-7 Subj: Activities – talking. Babies, toddlers. Rhyming text.

The best thing about a puppy ill. by Patricia Casey. Candlewick, 1998. ISBN 978-0-7636-0596-4 Subj: Animals – babies. Animals – dogs. Pets.

Do like a duck does ill. by Ivan Bates. Candlewick, 2002. ISBN 978-0-7636-1668-7 Subj: Animals – foxes. Birds – ducks. Rhyming text.

Does a cow say boo? ill. by Brita Granström. Candlewick, 2002. ISBN 978-0-7636-1718-9 Subj: Animals. Farms. Noise, sounds.

Eyes, nose, fingers and toes ill. by Brita Granström. Candlewick, 1999. ISBN 978-0-7636-0440-0 Subj: Anatomy. Rhyming text.

Princess Rosa's winter ill. by Margaret Chamberlain. Kingfisher, 2005. ISBN 978-0-7534-5859-4

Subj: Middle Ages. Royalty – princesses. Seasons – winter.

Rosy's visitors ill. by Helen Craig. Candlewick, 2002. ISBN 978-0-7636-1769-1 Subj: Homes, houses. Imagination. Toys.

Sleepy places ill. by Tor Freeman. Candlewick, 2006. ISBN 978-0-7636-2983-0 Subj: Animals. Bedtime. Rhyming text. Sleep.

What's in baby's morning ill. by Jo Burroughes. Candlewick, 2004. ISBN 978-0-7636-2372-2 Subj: Activities. Babies, toddlers. Family life.

Hines, Anna Grossnickle. *Big like me* ill. by author. Greenwillow, 1989. ISBN 978-0-688-08355-7 Subj: Babies, toddlers. Behavior – growing up. Family life.

Daddy makes the best spaghetti ill. by author. Clarion, 1986. ISBN 978-0-89919-388-5 Subj: Family life. Family life – fathers. Gender roles.

Even if I spill my milk? ill. by author. Clarion, 1994. ISBN 978-0-395-65010-3 Subj: Character traits – questioning. Emotions. Family life.

Gramma's walk ill. by author. Greenwillow, 1993. ISBN 978-0-688-11481-7 Subj: Disabilities – physical disabilities. Family life – grandmothers. Imagination. Nature. Sea & seashore.

I am a backhoe ill. by author. Tricycle, 2010. ISBN 978-1-58246-306-3 Subj: Activities – playing. Imagination. Machines. Trucks.

I am a Tyrannosaurus ill. by author. Tricycle, 2011. ISBN 978-1-58246-413-8 Subj: Dinosaurs. Imagination.

Miss Emma's wild garden ill. by author. Greenwillow, 1997. ISBN 978-0-688-14693-1 Subj: Animals. Birds. Flowers. Gardens, gardening. Insects. Plants.

My grandma is coming to town ill. by Melissa Sweet. Candlewick, 2003. ISBN 978-0-7636-1237-5 Subj: Family life – grandmothers.

My own big bed ill. by Mary Watson. Greenwillow, 1998. ISBN 978-0-688-15600-8 Subj: Emotions – fear. Furniture – beds.

No, no Jack! ill. by Pierre Pratt. Dial, 2002. ISBN 978-0-8037-2612-3 Subj: Animals – dogs. Behavior – hiding things. Format, unusual – toy & movable books.

1, 2, buckle my shoe (Mother Goose)

Pieces, a year in poems and quilts ill. by author. Greenwillow, 2001. ISBN 978-0-688-16964-0 Subj: Nature. Poetry. Quilts. Seasons.

Rumble thumble boom! ill. by author. Greenwillow, 1992. ISBN 978-0-688-10912-7 Subj: Bedtime. Emotions – fear. Weather – lightning, thunder. Weather – storms.

The secret keeper ill. by author. Greenwillow, 1990. ISBN 978-0-688-08946-7 Subj: Behavior – secrets. Family life. Holidays – Christmas.

What can you do in the rain? ill. by Thea Kliros. Greenwillow, 1999. ISBN 978-0-688-16077-7 Subj: Activities. Format, unusual – board books. Weather – rain.

What can you do in the snow? ill. by Thea Kliros. Greenwillow, 1999. ISBN 978-0-688-16078-4 Subj: Activities. Format, unusual – board books. Weather – snow.

What can you do in the sun? ill. by Thea Kliros. Greenwillow, 1999. ISBN 978-0-688-16080-7 Subj: Activities. Format, unusual – board books. Sun. Weather. Weather – rainbows.

What can you do in the wind? ill. by Thea Kliros. Greenwillow, 1999. ISBN 978-0-688-16079-1 Subj: Activities. Format, unusual – board books. Games. Weather – wind.

What Joe saw ill. by author. Greenwillow, 1994. ISBN 978-0-688-13124-1 Subj: Behavior – promptness, tardiness. Character traits – individuality.

When the goblins came knocking ill. by author. Greenwillow, 1995. ISBN 978-0-688-13736-6 Subj: Holidays – Halloween. Memories, memory. Rhyming text.

When we married Gary ill. by author. Greenwillow, 1996. ISBN 978-0-688-14277-3 Subj: Emotions – love. Family life – stepfamilies.

Whose shoes? ill. by LeUyen Pham. Harcourt, 2001. ISBN 978-0-15-201773-6 Subj: Animals – mice. Clothing – shoes. Family life. Format, unusual – toy & movable books.

Hines, Gary. *A Christmas tree in the White House* ill. by Alexandra Wallner. Henry Holt, 1998. ISBN 978-0-8050-5076-9 Subj: Ecology. Holidays – Christmas. Trees. U.S. history.

Hirsch, Rebecca E. *Plants can't sit still* ill. by Mia Posada. Lerner/Millbrook, 2016. ISBN 978-146778031-5 Subj: Nature. Plants.

Hirschi, Ron. *Fall* photos by Thomas D. Mangelsen. Dutton, 1991. ISBN 978-0-525-65053-9 Subj: Animals. Seasons – fall.

Our three bears photos by Thomas D. Mangelsen. Boyds Mills, 2008. ISBN 978-1-59078-015-2 Subj: Animals – bears. Nature.

Spring photos by Thomas D. Mangelsen. Dutton, 1990. ISBN 978-0-525-65037-9 Subj: Animals. Seasons – spring.

Summer photos by Thomas D. Mangelsen. Dutton, 1991. ISBN 978-0-525-65054-6 Subj: Animals. Nature. Seasons – summer.

When morning comes photos by Thomas D. Mangelsen. Boyds Mills, 2000. ISBN 978-1-56397-767-1 Subj: Animals. Birds. Morning.

When night comes photos by Thomas D. Mangelsen. Boyds Mills, 2000. ISBN 978-1-56397-766-4 Subj: Animals. Birds. Night.

Winter photos by Thomas D. Mangelsen. Dutton, 1990. ISBN 978-0-525-65026-3 Subj: Animals. Seasons – winter.

Hirsh, Marilyn. *Potato pancakes all around: a Hanukkah tale* ill. by author. Bonim Books, 1978. ISBN 978-0-88482-762-7 Subj: Food. Holidays – Hanukkah. Jewish culture. Religion.

Hirst, Robin. *My place in space* by Robin Hirst and Sally Hirst ill. by Roland Harvey and Joe Levine. Watts, 1990. ISBN 978-0-531-08459-5 Subj: Astronomy. Buses. Science. Space & space ships.

Hirst, Sally. *My place in space* (Hirst, Robin)

Hiscock, Bruce. *Coyote and badger: desert hunters of the Southwest* ill. by author. Boyds Mills, 2001. ISBN 978-1-56397-848-7 Subj: Animals. Animals – badgers. Animals – coyotes. Character traits – cooperation. Desert.

Ookpik: the travels of a snowy owl ill. by author. Boyds Mills, 2008. ISBN 978-1-59078-461-7 Subj: Birds – owls. Nature. Science.

Hiskey, Iris. *The secret of the first one up* ill. by Renée Graef. NorthWord, 2003. ISBN 978-1-55971-867-7 Subj: Animals – groundhogs. Holidays – Groundhog Day.

Hissey, Jane. *Hoot* ill. by author. Random House, 1997. Subj: Bedtime. Birds – owls. Night. Toys.

Jolly snow. Book House Scribblers, 2014. ISBN 978-190897302-3 Subj: Animals. Toys. Toys – bears. Weather – snow.

Old Bear ill. by author. Philomel, 1986. ISBN 978-0-399-21401-1 Subj: Friendship. Toys. Toys – bears.

Hittleman, Carol G., selector. *A grand celebration: grandparents in poetry* sel. by Daniel R. Hittleman; ill. by Kay Life. Boyds Mills, 2002. ISBN 978-1-56397-901-9 Subj: Family life – grandparents. Poetry.

Ho, Jannie. *Bear and Chicken* ill. by author. Running Press, 2017. ISBN 978-076246266-7 Subj: Animals – bears. Birds – chickens, roosters. Character traits – helpfulness. Character traits – kindness to animals.

Ho, Minfong. *Brother Rabbit: a Cambodian tale* ill. by Jennifer Hewitson. Lothrop, 1997. ISBN 978-0-688-12553-0 Subj: Animals. Animals – rabbits. Folk & fairy tales. Foreign lands – Cambodia.

Hush! a Thai lullaby ill. by Holly Meade. Orchard, 1996. ISBN 978-0-531-08850-0 Subj: Animals. Caldecott award honor books. Family life – mothers. Foreign lands – Thailand. Lullabies. Noise, sounds.

Hoban, Julia. *Amy loves the rain* ill. by Lillian Hoban. HarperCollins, 1989. ISBN 978-0-06-022358-8 Subj: Family life. Weather – rain.

Amy loves the snow ill. by Lillian Hoban. HarperCollins, 1989. ISBN 978-0-06-022395-3 Subj: Family life. Snowmen. Weather – snow.

Amy loves the sun ill. by Lillian Hoban. HarperCollins, 1988. ISBN 978-0-06-022397-7 Subj: Family life. Flowers.

Amy loves the wind ill. by Lillian Hoban. HarperCollins, 1988. ISBN 978-0-06-022403-5 Subj: Seasons – fall. Weather – wind.

Hoban, Russell. *Ace Dragon Ltd* ill. by Quentin Blake. Candlewick, 2015. ISBN 978-076367482-3 Subj: Dragons.

A baby sister for Frances ill. by Lillian Hoban. HarperCollins, 1964. ISBN 978-0-06-022336-6 Subj: Animals – badgers. Behavior – running away. Emotions – envy, jealousy. Family life. Sibling rivalry.

A bargain for Frances ill. by Lillian Hoban. HarperCollins, 1992. ISBN 978-0-06-022330-4 Subj: Animals – badgers. Friendship.

Bedtime for Frances ill. by Garth Williams. HarperCollins, 1995. ISBN 978-0-06-022351-9 Subj: Animals – badgers. Bedtime. Emotions – fear.

Best friends for Frances ill. by Lillian Hoban. HarperCollins, 1994. ISBN 978-0-06-022328-1 Subj: Animals – badgers. Family life – brothers. Family life – sisters. Friendship.

A birthday for Frances ill. by Lillian Hoban. HarperCollins, 1995. ISBN 978-0-06-022339-7 Subj: Animals – badgers. Birthdays. Emotions – envy, jealousy.

Bread and jam for Frances ill. by Lillian Hoban. HarperCollins, 1993. ISBN 978-0-06-022360-1 Subj: Animals – badgers. Food. School.

Rosie's magic horse ill. by Quentin Blake. Candlewick, 2013. ISBN 978-0-7636-6400-8 Subj: Animals – horses, ponies. Dreams. Magic.

Hoban, Tana. *A B see!* photos by author. Greenwillow, 1982. ISBN 978-0-688-00833-8 Subj: ABC books.

All about where photos by author. Greenwillow, 1991. ISBN 978-0-688-09698-4 Subj: Concepts. Language.

Black on white photos by author. Greenwillow, 1993. ISBN 978-0-688-11918-8 Subj: Concepts. Wordless.

A children's zoo photos by author. Greenwillow, 1985. ISBN 978-0-688-05204-1   Subj: Animals. Birds. Zoos.

Circles, triangles, and squares photos by author. Macmillan, 1974. ISBN 978-0-02-744830-6 Subj: Concepts – shape. Wordless.

Colors everywhere photos by author. Greenwillow, 1994. ISBN 978-0-688-12763-3 Subj: Concepts – color. Wordless.

Construction zone photos by author. Greenwillow, 1997. ISBN 978-0-688-12285-0 Subj: Activities – making things. Machines.

Count and see photos by author. Macmillan, 1972. ISBN 978-0-02-744800-9 Subj: Counting, numbers.

Cubes, cones, cylinders and spheres photos by author. Greenwillow, 2000. ISBN 978-0-688-15326-7 Subj: Concepts – shape.

Dig, drill, dump, fill photos by author. Greenwillow, 1975. ISBN 978-0-688-84016-7 Subj: Activities – digging. Machines. Wordless.

Dots, spots, speckles, and stripes photos by author. Greenwillow, 1987. ISBN 978-0-688-06863-9 Subj: Concepts. Concepts – color. Concepts – shape.

Exactly the opposite photos by author. Greenwillow, 1990. ISBN 978-0-688-08862-0 Subj: Concepts – opposites. Wordless.

I read signs photos by author. Greenwillow, 1983. ISBN 978-0-688-02318-8 Subj: Books, reading. Communication.

I read symbols photos by author. Greenwillow, 1983. ISBN 978-0-688-02332-4 Subj: Books, reading. Communication.

I walk and read photos by author. Greenwillow, 1984. ISBN 978-0-688-02576-2 Subj: Activities – walking. Books, reading.

Is it larger? Is it smaller? photos by author. Greenwillow, 1985. ISBN 978-0-688-04028-4 Subj: Concepts – size. Wordless.

Is it red? Is it yellow? Is it blue? photos by author. Greenwillow, 1978. ISBN 978-0-688-84171-3 Subj: Cities, towns. Concepts – color. Concepts – shape. Concepts – size. Wordless.

Is it rough? Is it smooth? Is it shiny? photos by author. Greenwillow, 1984. ISBN 978-0-688-03824-3 Subj: Concepts. Wordless.

Just look photos by author. Greenwillow, 1996. ISBN 978-0-688-14041-0 Subj: Format, unusual – toy & movable books. Wordless.

Let's count photos by author. Greenwillow, 1999. ISBN 978-0-688-16009-8 Subj: Counting, numbers.

Look book photos by author. Greenwillow, 1997. ISBN 978-0-688-14972-7 Subj: Format, unusual – toy & movable books. Nature. Wordless.

Look! look! look! photos by author. Greenwillow, 1988. ISBN 978-0-688-07240-7 Subj: Concepts. Format, unusual. Wordless.

Look up, look down photos by author. Greenwillow, 1992. ISBN 978-0-688-10578-5 Subj: Concepts – up & down.

More, fewer, less photos by author. Greenwillow, 1998. ISBN 978-0-688-15694-7 Subj: Concepts. Counting, numbers. Wordless.

Of colors and things photos by author. Greenwillow, 1989. ISBN 978-0-688-07535-4 Subj: Concepts – color.

Over, under and through photos by author. Aladdin, 1987. ISBN 978-0-689-71111-4 Subj: Concepts.

Shadows and reflections photos by author. Greenwillow, 1990. ISBN 978-0-688-07090-8 Subj: Shadows. Wordless.

Shapes, shapes, shapes photos by author. Greenwillow, 1985. ISBN 978-0-688-05833-3 Subj: Concepts – shape. Wordless.

So many circles, so many squares photos by author. Greenwillow, 1998. ISBN 978-0-688-15166-9 Subj: Concepts – shape. Wordless.

Spirals, curves, fanshapes and lines photos by author. Greenwillow, 1992. ISBN 978-0-688-11229-5 Subj: Concepts – shape. Concepts – size. Wordless.

26 letters and 99 cents photos by author. Greenwillow, 1987. ISBN 978-0-688-06362-7 Subj: ABC books. Counting, numbers. Format, unusual.

What is that? photos by author. Greenwillow, 1994. ISBN 978-0-688-12920-0 Subj: Format, unusual – board books. Wordless.

Where is it? photos by author. Macmillan, 1974. ISBN 978-0-02-744070-6 Subj: Animals – rabbits. Participation. Rhyming text.

White on black photos by author. Greenwillow, 1993. ISBN 978-0-688-11919-5 Subj: Concepts. Format, unusual – board books.

Who are they? photos by author. Greenwillow, 1994. ISBN 978-0-688-12921-7 Subj: Animals. Format, unusual – board books. Wordless.

Hobbie, Holly. *A cat named Swan* ill. by author. Random House, . ISBN 978-055353744-4 Subj: Animals – cats. Character traits – kindness to animals. Pets.

Everything but the horse ill. by author. Little, Brown, 2010. ISBN 978-0-316-07019-5 Subj: Animals – horses, ponies. Birthdays. Farms. Moving.

Fanny ill. by author. Little, Brown, 2008. ISBN 978-0-316-16687-4 Subj: Character traits – individuality. Toys – dolls.

Fanny and Annabelle ill. by author. Little, Brown, 2009. ISBN 978-0-316-16688-1 Subj: Activities – writing. Character traits – honesty. Toys – dolls.

Gem ill. by author. Little, Brown, 2012. ISBN 978-0-316-20334-0 Subj: Ecology. Frogs & toads.

Toot and Puddle ill. by author. Little, 1997. ISBN 978-0-316-36552-9 Subj: Activities – traveling. Animals – pigs. Friendship. Letters, cards.

Toot and Puddle: let it snow ill. by author. Little, Brown, 2007. ISBN 978-0-316-16686-7 Subj: Animals – pigs. Friendship. Gifts. Holidays – Christmas. Weather – snow.

Toot and Puddle: wish you were here ill. by author. Little, Brown, 2005. ISBN 978-0-316-36602-1 Subj: Activities – traveling. Animals – pigs. Friendship. Illness. Plants.

Toot and Puddle, a present for Toot ill. by author. Little, 1998. ISBN 978-0-316-36556-7 Subj: Animals – pigs. Birthdays. Gifts.

Toot and Puddle, I'll be home for Christmas ill. by author. Little, 2001. ISBN 978-0-316-36623-6 Subj: Activities – traveling. Animals – pigs. Holidays – Christmas. Weather – blizzards. Weather – snow. Weather – storms.

Toot and Puddle, Puddle's ABC ill. by author. Little, 2000. ISBN 978-0-316-36593-2 Subj: ABC books. Animals – pigs.

Toot and Puddle, top of the world ill. by author. Little, 2002. ISBN 978-0-316-36513-0 Subj: Activities – traveling. Animals – pigs. Foreign lands – France. Foreign lands – Nepal. Friendship.

Toot and Puddle, you are my sunshine ill. by author. Little, 1999. ISBN 978-0-316-36562-8 Subj: Animals – pigs. Emotions. Friendship. Weather – lightning, thunder. Weather – storms.

Hoberman, Mary Ann. *All kinds of families* ill. by Marc Boutavant. Little, Brown, 2009. ISBN 978-0-316-14633-3 Subj: Family life. Rhyming text.

And to think that we thought that we'd never be friends ill. by Kevin Hawkes. Crown, 1999. ISBN 978-0-517-80070-6 Subj: Family life – brothers & sisters. Friendship. Rhyming text.

Bill Grogan's goat ill. by Nadine Bernard Westcott. Little, 2002. ISBN 978-0-316-36232-0 Subj: Animals – goats. Music. Songs. Trains.

A house is a house for me ill. by Betty Fraser. Viking, 1978. ISBN 978-0-670-38016-9 Subj: Homes, houses. Rhyming text.

I like old clothes ill. by Patrice Barton. Knopf, 2012. ISBN 978-0-375-86951-8 Subj: Clothing. Rhyming text.

I'm going to Grandma's ill. by Tiphanie Beeke. Harcourt, 2007. ISBN 978-0-15-216592-5 Subj: Family life – grandparents. Night. Quilts. Rhyming text.

"It's simple," said Simon ill. by Meilo So. Knopf, 2001. ISBN 978-0-375-91201-6 Subj: Animals. Animals – tigers. Humorous stories.

The looking book ill. by Laura Huliska-Beith. Little, 2002. ISBN 978-0-316-36328-0 Subj: Animals – cats. Behavior – lost & found possessions. Counting, numbers. Rhyming text.

Mary had a little lamb ill. by Nadine Bernard Westcott. Little, 2003. ISBN 978-0-316-60687-5 Subj: Animals – sheep. Nursery rhymes. Songs.

Miss Mary Mack ill. by Nadine Bernard Westcott. Little, 1998. ISBN 978-0-316-93118-2 Subj: Animals – elephants. Nursery rhymes.

Mrs. O'Leary's cow ill. by Jenny Mattheson. Little, Brown, 2007. ISBN 978-0-316-14840-5 Subj: Animals – bulls, cows. Fire. Rhyming text.

One of each ill. by Marjorie Priceman. Little, 1997. ISBN 978-0-316-36731-8 Subj: Animals – dogs. Behavior – sharing. Friendship. Rhyming text.

Right outside my window ill. by Nicholas Wilton. Mondo, 2002. ISBN 978-1-59034-194-0 Subj: Rhyming text. Seasons.

The seven silly eaters ill. by Marla Frazee. Harcourt, 1997. ISBN 978-0-15-200096-7 Subj: Birthdays. Family life – brothers & sisters. Family life – mothers. Food. Rhyming text.

The two sillies ill. by Lynne Cravath. Harcourt, 2000. ISBN 978-0-15-202221-1 Subj: Animals – cats. Animals – mice. Rhyming text.

Hochman, David. *The potty train* by David Hochman and Ruth Kennison ill. by Derek Anderson. Simon & Schuster, 2008. ISBN 978-1-4169-2833-1 Subj: Toilet training.

Hodge, Deborah. *Ants* ill. by Julian Mulock. Kids Can, 2004. ISBN 978-1-55337-066-6 Subj: Insects – ants. Science.

Bees ill. by Julian Mulock. Kids Can, 2004. ISBN 978-1-55337-065-9 Subj: Insects – bees. Science.

Eagles ill. by Nancy Gray Ogle. Kids Can, 2000. ISBN 978-1-55074-715-7 Subj: Birds – eagles. Science.

Emma's story ill. by Song Nan Zhang. Tundra, 2003. ISBN 978-0-88776-632-9 Subj: Adoption. Family life. Foreign lands – Canada. Foreign lands – China. Self-concept.

Lily and the mixed-up letters ill. by France Brassard. Tundra, 2007. ISBN 978-0-88776-757-9 Subj: Books, reading. Character traits – perseverance. Disabilities – dyslexia. School. Self-concept.

Salmon ill. by Nancy Gray Ogle. Kids Can, 2002. ISBN 978-1-55074-961-8 Subj: Fish. Science.

Watch me grow! a down-to-earth look at growing food in the city photos by Brian Harris. Kids Can, 2011. ISBN 978-1-55453-618-4 Subj: Cities, towns. Gardens, gardening.

Hodge, Marie. *Are you sleepy yet, Petey?* ill. by Renée Graef. Sterling, 2005. ISBN 978-1-4027-1265-4 Subj: Animals – dogs. Bedtime.

Hodges, Margaret. *Moses* ill. by Barry Moser. Harcourt, 2006. ISBN 978-0-15-200946-5 Subj: Religion – Moses.

Saint George and the dragon ill. by Trina Schart Hyman. Little, 1984. ISBN 978-0-316-36789-9 Subj: Caldecott award books. Dragons. Folk & fairy tales. Foreign lands – England. Middle Ages.

Silent night: the song and its story ill. by Tim Ladwig. Eerdmans, 1997. ISBN 978-0-8028-5138-3 Subj: Family life. Holidays – Christmas. Music. Songs.

The wave ill. by Blair Lent. Houghton, 1964. ISBN 978-0-395-06817-5 Subj: Caldecott award honor books. Folk & fairy tales. Foreign lands – Japan. Tsunamis.

Hodgkins, Fran. *Between the tides* ill. by Jim Sollers. Down East, 2007. ISBN 978-0-89272-727-8 Subj: Sea & seashore.

The cat of Strawberry Hill: a true story ill. by Lesia Sochor. Down East, 2005. ISBN 978-0-89272-684-4 Subj: Animals – cats. Behavior – lost.

How people learned to fly ill. by True Kelley. HarperCollins, 2007. ISBN 978-0-06-029558-5 Subj: Activities – flying. Airplanes, airports.

Who's been here? a tale in tracks ill. by Karel Hayes. Down East, 2008. ISBN 978-0-89272-714-8 Subj: Animals. Nature.

Hodgkinson, Jo. *A big day for Migs* ill. by author. Andersen, 2014. ISBN 978-146775014-1 Subj: Animals – mice. Behavior – misbehavior. Character traits – shyness. Rhyming text. School – first day.

Hodgkinson, Leigh. *The big monster snorey book* ill. by author. Candlewick/Nosy Crow, 2016. ISBN 978-076368660-4 Subj: Bedtime. Character traits – cleverness. Monsters. Noise, sounds. Sleep – snoring.

Boris and the snoozebox ill. by author. Tiger Tales, 2008. ISBN 978-1-58925-071-0 Subj: Activities – traveling. Animals – cats. Letters, cards.

Boris and the wrong shadow ill. by author. Tiger Tales, 2009. ISBN 978-1-58925-082-6 Subj: Animals – cats. Animals – mice. Shadows.

Goldilocks and just one bear ill. by author. Candlewick, 2012. ISBN 978-0-7636-6172-4 Subj:

Animals – bears. Behavior – misbehavior. Cities, towns. Folk & fairy tales. Humorous stories.

Goldilocks and the just right potty ill. by author. Nosy Crow, 2017. ISBN 978-076369799-0 Subj: Toilet training.

Limelight Larry ill. by author. Tiger Tales, 2011. ISBN 978-1-58925-102-1 Subj: Animals. Behavior – boasting, showing off. Birds – peacocks, peahens.

A place to read ill. by author. Bloomsbury, 2017. ISBN 978-168119323-6 Subj: Books, reading. Rhyming text.

Smile! ill. by author. HarperCollins, 2010. ISBN 978-0-06-185269-5 Subj: Anatomy – faces. Behavior – bad day, bad mood. Behavior – lost & found possessions. Emotions. Family life.

Troll swap ill. by author. Candlewick/Nosy Crow, 2014. ISBN 978-076367101-3 Subj: Behavior – messy. Character traits – individuality. Character traits – orderliness. Mythical creatures – trolls.

Hodson, Sally. *Granny's clan: a tale of wild orcas* ill. by Ann Jones. Dawn, 2012. ISBN 978-1-58469-172-3 Subj: Animals – whales.

Hoe, Susan. *Which shoes would you choose?* ill. by Mircea Catusanu. Innovative KIDS, 2002. ISBN 978-1-58476-102-0 Subj: Clothing – shoes. Format, unusual – board books.

Hoefler, Kate. *Real cowboys* ill. by Jonathan Bean. Houghton Mifflin Harcourt, 2016. ISBN 978-054414892-5 Subj: Careers – ranchers. Cowboys, cowgirls.

Hoffman, Don. *Billy is a big boy* ill. by Todd Dakins. Popcorn, 2000. ISBN 978-0-9702518-0-0 Subj: Behavior – growing up.

A counting book with Billy and Abigail ill. by Todd Dakins. Dalmation, 2004. ISBN 978-1-4037-0543-3 Subj: Counting, numbers. Format, unusual – board books. Rhyming text.

Good morning, good night Billy and Abigail ill. by Todd Dakins. Dalmation, 2004. ISBN 978-1-4037-0542-6 Subj: Family life. Format, unusual – board books. Morning. Night. Rhyming text.

Hoffman, Elizabeth Stokes. *Miss Renée's mice* ill. by Dawn Peterson. Down East, 2001. ISBN 978-0-89272-505-2 Subj: Animals – mice. Homes, houses.

Miss Renée's mice go to an exhibition ill. by Dawn Peterson. Down East, 2003. ISBN 978-0-89272-581-6 Subj: Animals – mice. Country. Fairs, festivals.

Hoffman, Eric. *A dark, dark cave* ill. by Corey R. Tabor. Viking, 2016. ISBN 978-067001636-5 Subj: Activities – playing. Family life. Imagination. Rhyming text.

No fair to tigers / No es justo para los tigres ill. by Janice Lee Porter. Redleaf, 1999. ISBN 978-1-884834-62-2 Subj: Animals – tigers. Disabilities – physical disabilities. Foreign languages. Toys.

Play Lady / La Señora Juguetona ill. by Suzanne Tornquist. Redleaf, 1999. ISBN 978-1-884834-61-5 Subj: Crime. Foreign languages. Gardens, gardening. Prejudice.

Hoffman, Ian. *Jacob's new dress* (Hoffman, Sarah)

Hoffman, Mary. *Amazing Grace* ill. by Caroline Binch. Dial, 1991. ISBN 978-0-8037-1040-5 Subj: Ethnic groups in the U.S. – African Americans. School. Self-concept. Theater.

Clever Katya ill. by Marie Cameron. Barefoot, 1998. ISBN 978-1-901223-64-4 Subj: Animals – horses, ponies. Folk & fairy tales. Foreign lands – Russia. Riddles & jokes. Royalty – tsars.

Grace at Christmas ill. by Cornelius Van Wright and Ying-Hwa Hu. Penguin, 2011. ISBN 978-0-8037-3577-4 Subj: Ethnic groups in the U.S. – African Americans. Family life. Holidays – Christmas.

Miracles: wonders Jesus worked ill. by Jackie Morris. Fogelman, 2001. ISBN 978-0-8037-2610-9 Subj: Religion.

Parables, stories Jesus told ill. by Jackie Morris. Fogelman, 2000. ISBN 978-0-8037-2560-7 Subj: Religion.

Princess Grace ill. by Cornelius Van Wright. Dial, 2008. ISBN 978-0-8037-3260-5 Subj: Ethnic groups in the U.S. – African Americans. Parades. Royalty – princesses. School.

Three wise women ill. by Lynne Russell. Fogelman, 1999. ISBN 978-0-8037-2466-2 Subj: Character traits – wisdom. Holidays – Christmas. Religion – Nativity. Stars.

Hoffman, Sarah. *Jacob's new dress* by Sarah Hoffman and Ian Hoffman ill. by Chris Case. Albert Whitman, 2014. ISBN 978-080756373-1 Subj: Behavior – bullying, teasing. Clothing – dresses. Gender identity. Gender roles. Self-concept.

Hoffmann, E. T. A. *The nutcracker* adapt. by Janet Schulman; ill. by Renée Graef. HarperCollins, 1999. ISBN 978-0-06-027814-4 Subj: Activities – dancing. Animals – mice. Ballet. Careers – toy makers. Folk & fairy tales. Holidays – Christmas. Imagination. Royalty.

The nutcracker by Alison Jay; ill. by author. Penguin, 2010. ISBN 978-0-8037-3285-8 Subj: Activities – dancing. Animals – mice. Ballet. Folk & fairy tales. Holidays – Christmas. Imagination. Royalty. Toys.

The nutcracker retold by Stephanie Spinner; ill. by Peter Malone. Knopf, 2008. ISBN 978-0-375-

84464-5 Subj: Activities – dancing. Animals – mice. Ballet. Careers – toy makers. Folk & fairy tales. Holidays – Christmas. Imagination. Royalty.

The nutcracker retold by Kate Davies; ill. by Niroot Puttapipat. Candlewick, 2016. ISBN 978-076368125-8 Subj: Animals – mice. Careers – toy makers. Folk & fairy tales. Format, unusual – toy & movable books. Holidays – Christmas. Imagination. Royalty. Toys.

The nutcracker ill. by Maurice Sendak. Crown, 1984. ISBN 978-0-517-55285-8 Subj: Activities – dancing. Animals – mice. Ballet. Careers – toy makers. Folk & fairy tales. Holidays – Christmas. Imagination. Royalty.

The nutcracker retold by Anthea Bell; ill. by Lisbeth Zwerger. Picture Book Studio, 1987. ISBN 978-0-88708-051-7 Subj: Activities – dancing. Animals – mice. Ballet. Careers – toy makers. Folk & fairy tales. Holidays – Christmas. Imagination. Royalty.

The Nutcracker and the Mouse King adapt. by Wren Maysen; ill. by Gail de Marcken. Scholastic, 2009. ISBN 978-0-545-03773-0 Subj: Activities – dancing. Animals – mice. Ballet. Careers – toy makers. Folk & fairy tales. Holidays – Christmas. Imagination. Royalty.

The nutcracker ballet retold by Vladimir Vagin; ill. by reteller. Scholastic, 1995. ISBN 978-0-590-47220-3 Subj: Activities – dancing. Animals – mice. Ballet. Careers – toy makers. Folk & fairy tales. Holidays – Christmas. Imagination. Royalty.

The Nutcracker in Harlem retold by T. E. McMorrow; ill. by James Ransome. HarperCollins, 2017. ISBN 978-006117598-5 Subj: Activities – dancing. Animals – mice. Dreams. Ethnic groups in the U.S. – African Americans. Family life. Holidays – Christmas. Toys – soldiers.

Hofmann-Maniyar, Ariane. *That's NOT how you do it!* ill. by author. Child's Play, 2017. ISBN 978-184643929-2 Subj: Animals. Behavior – bossy. Character traits – being different. Character traits – individuality. Friendship.

Hofmeyr, Dianne. *The star-bearer* ill. by Jude Daly. Farrar, 2001. ISBN 978-0-374-37181-4 Subj: Creation. Foreign lands – Egypt.

Hogg, Gary. *Beautiful Buehla and the zany zoo makeover* ill. by Victoria Chess. HarperCollins, 2006. ISBN 978-0-06-009420-1 Subj: Animals. Character traits – appearance. Zoos.

Look what the cat dragged in! ill. by Mike Wohnoutka. Penguin, 2005. ISBN 978-0-525-46984-1 Subj: Animals – cats. Character traits – laziness. Pets.

Hogrogian, Nonny. *The contest* ill. by author. Greenwillow, 1976. ISBN 978-0-688-84042-6 Subj: Caldecott award honor books. Crime. Folk & fairy tales. Foreign lands – Armenia.

Cool cat ill. by author. Roaring Brook, 2009. ISBN 978-1-59643-429-5 Subj: Activities – painting. Animals – cats. Art. Wordless.

The first Christmas ill. by author. Greenwillow, 1995. ISBN 978-0-688-13580-5 Subj: Holidays – Christmas. Religion – Nativity.

One fine day ill. by author. Macmillan, 1971. ISBN 978-0-606-01196-9 Subj: Animals – foxes. Caldecott award books. Cumulative tales.

The tiger of Turkestan ill. by author. Hampton Roads, 2002. ISBN 978-1-57174-308-4 Subj: Animals – tigers. Character traits – individuality.

Hohn, Nadia L. *Malaika's costume* ill. by Irene Luxbacher. Groundwood, 2016. ISBN 978-155498754-2 Subj: Activities – making things. Clothing – costumes. Fairs, festivals. Family life – grandmothers. Foreign lands – Caribbean Islands.

Höjer, Dan. *Heart of mine* by Dan Höjer and Lotta Höjer; ill. by authors. R&S Books, 2001. ISBN 978-91-29-65301-4 Subj: Adoption. Babies, toddlers. Family life. Foreign lands.

Höjer, Lotta. *Heart of mine* (Höjer, Dan)

Holabird, Katharine. *Angelina and Alice* ill. by Helen Craig. Potter/Crown, 1987. ISBN 978-0-517-56074-7 Subj: Animals – mice. Friendship. School.

Angelina and Henry ill. by Helen Craig. Pleasant, 2002. ISBN 978-1-58485-523-1 Subj: Animals – mice. Behavior – lost. Camps, camping. Family life – aunts, uncles. Forest, woods.

Angelina and the princess ill. by Helen Craig. Crown, 1984. ISBN 978-0-517-55273-5 Subj: Activities – dancing. Animals – mice. Ballet.

Angelina and the royal wedding ill. by Helen Craig. Penguin, 2010. ISBN 978-0-670-01213-8 Subj: Animals – mice. Weddings.

Angelina at the fair ill. by Helen Craig. Crown, 1985. ISBN 978-0-517-55744-0 Subj: Animals – mice. Fairs, festivals. Friendship.

Angelina at the palace ill. by Helen Craig. Penguin, 2005. ISBN 978-0-670-06048-1 Subj: Animals – mice. Ballet. Royalty – princesses.

Angelina ballerina ill. by Helen Craig. 3rd ed. Pleasant, 2004. ISBN 978-1-58485-952-9 Subj: Activities – dancing. Animals – mice. Ballet.

Angelina dances ill. by Helen Craig. Random House, 1992. ISBN 978-0-679-83484-7 Subj: Activities – dancing. Animals – mice. Ballet. Format, unusual – board books.

Angelina ice skates ill. by Helen Craig. 2nd ed. Pleasant, 2001. ISBN 978-1-58485-146-2 Subj: Animals – mice. Holidays – New Year's. Sports – ice skating. Theater.

Angelina on stage ill. by Helen Craig. Crown, 1986. ISBN 978-0-517-56073-0 Subj: Activities – dancing. Animals – mice. Ballet. Theater.

Angelina, star of the show ill. by Helen Craig. Viking, 2008. ISBN 978-0-670-01108-7 Subj: Activities – dancing. Animals – mice. Behavior – misbehavior. Boats, ships. Family life – grandparents.

Angelina's baby sister ill. by Helen Craig. Pleasant, 2000. ISBN 978-1-58485-132-5 Subj: Animals – mice. Babies, toddlers. Family life – new sibling. Family life – sisters. Sibling rivalry.

Angelina's ballet class ill. by Catherine Kanner. Based on the illustrations of Helen Craig. Pleasant, 2001. ISBN 978-0-613-49711-4 Subj: Activities – dancing. Animals – mice. Ballet.

Angelina's big city ballet ill. by Helen Craig. Viking, 2014. ISBN 978-067001560-3 Subj: Animals – mice. Ballet. Family life – cousins.

Angelina's Christmas ill. by Helen Craig. Crown, 1986. ISBN 978-0-517-55823-2 Subj: Animals – mice. Careers – postal workers. Family life – cousins. Holidays – Christmas.

Angelina's Cinderella ill. by Helen Craig. Viking, 2015. ISBN 978-045147359-2 Subj: Activities – traveling. Animals – mice. Ballet.

Angelina's Halloween ill. by Helen Craig. Pleasant, 2000. ISBN 978-1-58485-152-3 Subj: Animals – mice. Holidays – Halloween.

Christmas in Mouseland. Based on the illustrations of Helen Craig. Penguin, 2007. ISBN 978-0-448-44663-9 Subj: Activities – dancing. Animals – mice. Ballet. Holidays – Christmas.

Christmas with Angelina ill. by Helen Craig. Random House, 1992. ISBN 978-0-679-83485-4 Subj: Animals – mice. Holidays – Christmas.

Holbrook, Stewart. *America's Ethan Allen* ill. by Lynd Ward. Houghton, 1949. ISBN 978-0-395-24449-4 Subj: Caldecott award honor books. U.S. history. War.

Holderness, Jackie. *What is a shadow?* ill. by author. Copper Beech, 2002. ISBN 978-0-7613-2821-6 Subj: Light, lights. Science. Shadows.

Hole, Stian. *Anna's heaven* ill. by author. Eerdmans, 2014. ISBN 978-080285441-4 Subj: Death. Emotions – grief. Family life – fathers. Imagination. Religion.

Holland, Loretta. *Fall leaves* ill. by Elly MacKay. Houghton, 2014. ISBN 978-054410664-2 Subj: Language. Seasons – fall.

Holland, Mary. *Otis the owl* photos by author. Arbordale, 2017. ISBN 978-162855939-2 Subj: Birds – owls. Nature.

Holland, Simon. *Space* ill. with photos. DK, 2001. ISBN 978-0-7894-8182-5 Subj: Astronomy. Space & space ships.

Holland, Trish. *Ocean's child* (Ford, Christine)

Hollenbeck, Kathleen M. *Islands of ice* ill. by John Paul Genzo. Soundprints, 2001. ISBN 978-1-56899-965-4 Subj: Animals – seals. Science.

Holling, Holling C. *Paddle-to-the-sea* ill. by author. Houghton, 1941. ISBN 978-0-395-15082-5 Subj: Caldecott award honor books. Foreign lands – Canada. Rivers.

Holm, Jennifer L. *I'm Grumpy* by Jennifer L. Holm and Matthew Holm ill. by Jennifer L. Holm. Random House, 2016. ISBN 978-055353344-6 Subj: Behavior – bad day, bad mood. Format, unusual – board books. Weather – clouds.

Holm, Matthew. *I'm Grumpy* (Holm, Jennifer L.)

Holm, Sharon Lane. *Zoe's hats* ill. by author. Boyds Mills, 2003. ISBN 978-1-59078-042-8 Subj: Clothing – hats. Concepts – color. Concepts – patterns.

Holmberg, Bo R. *A day with Dad* ill. by Eva Eriksson. Candlewick, 2008. ISBN 978-0-7636-3221-2 Subj: Divorce. Family life – fathers.

Holmes, Anita. *Can you find us?* ill. with photos. Benchmark, 2001. ISBN 978-0-7614-1108-6 Subj: Animals. Disguises.

Flowers and friends ill. with photos. Benchmark, 2001. ISBN 978-0-7614-1113-0 Subj: Flowers. Friendship. Gardens, gardening.

Insect detector ill. with photos. Benchmark, 2001. ISBN 978-0-7614-1110-9 Subj: Insects.

Where robins fly ill. with photos. Benchmark, 2001. ISBN 978-0-7614-1109-3 Subj: Birds – robins.

Who dug that hole? ill. with photos. Marshall Cavendish, 2001. ISBN 978-0-7614-1112-3 Subj: Animals. Homes, houses.

Holmes, Janet A. *Have you seen Duck?* ill. by Jonathan Bentley. Scholastic, 2011. ISBN 978-0-545-22488-8 Subj: Behavior – lost & found possessions. Birds – ducks. Toys.

Me and you ill. by Judith Rossell. NorthSouth, 2009. ISBN 978-0-7358-2250-4 Subj: Activities – playing. Animals – mice. Animals – rabbits. Friendship.

Holmes, Mary Tavener. *A giraffe goes to Paris* by Mary Tavener Holmes and John Harris ill. by Jon Cannell. Marshall Cavendish, 2010. ISBN 978-0-7614-5595-0 Subj: Activities – traveling. Animals – giraffes. Foreign lands – France.

Holmquist, Delano. *SantaSaurus* ill. by Chuck Galey. Pelican, 2002. ISBN 978-1-56554-933-3 Subj: Character traits – kindness. Dinosaurs. Holidays – Christmas. Santa Claus.

Holt, Kimberly Willis. *The adventures of Granny Clearwater and Little Critter* ill. by Laura Huliska-Beith. Henry Holt, 2010. ISBN 978-0-8050-7899-2 Subj: Behavior – lost. Family life – grandmothers. Tall tales. U.S. history – frontier & pioneer life.

Dinner with the Highbrows ill. by Kyrsten Brooker. Henry Holt, 2014. ISBN 978-080508088-9 Subj: Etiquette. Food. Humorous stories.

Skinny brown dog ill. by Donald Saaf. Henry Holt, 2007. ISBN 978-0-8050-7587-8 Subj: Animals – dogs. Careers – bakers.

Waiting for Gregory ill. by Gabi Swiatkowska. Henry Holt, 2006. ISBN 978-0-8050-7388-1 Subj: Babies, toddlers. Birth. Family life – cousins.

Holt, Sharon. *Did my mother do that?* ill. by Brian Lovelock. Candlewick, 2010. ISBN 978-0-7636-4685-1 Subj: Animals – babies. Bedtime. Birth.

Holub, Joan. *Apple countdown* ill. by Jan Smith. Albert Whitman, 2009. ISBN 978-0-8075-0398-0 Subj: Counting, numbers. Food. Rhyming text. School – field trips. Trees.

Cinderdog and the wicked stepcat ill. by author. Albert Whitman, 2001. ISBN 978-0-8075-1178-7 Subj: Animals – cats. Animals – dogs. Cowboys, cowgirls. U.S. history – frontier & pioneer life.

Geogra-fleas ill. by Regan Dunnick. Albert Whitman, 2004. ISBN 978-0-8075-2818-1 Subj: Geography. Riddles & jokes.

Groundhog weather school ill. by Kristin Sorra. Putnam, 2009. ISBN 978-0-399-24659-3 Subj: Animals – groundhogs. Holidays – Groundhog Day. School. Weather.

The Halloween Queen ill. by Theresa Smythe. Albert Whitman, 2004. ISBN 978-0-8075-3138-9 Subj: Holidays – Halloween. Parties. Rhyming text.

Little red writing ill. by Melissa Sweet. Chronicle, 2013. ISBN 978-0-81187-869-2 Subj: Activities – writing. Humorous stories. Language. School.

Mighty dads ill. by James Dean. Scholastic, 2014. ISBN 978-054560968-5 Subj: Family life – fathers. Machines. Rhyming text. Trucks.

The pizza that we made ill. by Lynne Cravath. Viking, 2001. ISBN 978-0-670-03520-5 Subj: Activities – baking, cooking. Food. Rhyming text.

Pumpkin countdown ill. by Jan Smith. Albert Whitman, 2012. ISBN 978-0-8075-6660-2 Subj:

Counting, numbers. Farms. Food. School – field trips.

Scat cats ill. by Rich Davis. Viking, 2001. ISBN 978-0-670-89279-2 Subj: Animals – cats. Rhyming text.

Tool school ill. by James Dean. Scholastic, 2017. ISBN 978-054568520-7 Subj: Character traits – cooperation. Rhyming text. School. Tools.

Turkeys never gobble ill. by Jennifer Beck Harris. HarperCollins, 2002. ISBN 978-0-06-008091-4 Subj: Animals. Etiquette. Format, unusual – board books. Holidays – Thanksgiving. Rhyming text.

Twinkle, star of the week ill. by Paul Nicholls. Albert Whitman, 2010. ISBN 978-0-8075-8131-5 Subj: Behavior – wishing. School. Stars.

Vincent van Gogh: sunflowers and swirly stars. Ill. with art reproductions. Grosset, 2001. ISBN 978-0-448-42612-9 Subj: Art. Careers – artists.

Wagons ho! (Hallowell, George)

Why do cats meow? ill. by Anna DiVito. Dial, 2001. ISBN 978-0-8037-2503-4 Subj: Animals – cats. Character traits – questioning.

Why do dogs bark? ill. by Anna DiVito. Dial, 2001. ISBN 978-0-8037-2504-1 Subj: Animals – dogs. Character traits – questioning.

Zero the hero ill. by Tom Lichtenheld. Henry Holt, 2012. ISBN 978-0-8050-9384-1 Subj: Counting, numbers. Humorous stories.

Homer, Abigail. *Country mouse cottage: how we lived one hundred years ago* (Brooks, Nigel)

Town mouse house: how we lived one hundred years ago (Brooks, Nigel)

Honey, Elizabeth. *The moon in the man* ill. by author. Allen & Unwin, 2002. ISBN 978-1-86508-455-8 Subj: Nursery rhymes. Poetry.

That's not a daffodil! ill. by author. IPG/Allen & Unwin, 2012. ISBN 978-1-7423-7248-8 Subj: Gardens, gardening. Imagination. Plants. Seeds.

Hong, Chen Jiang. *The magic horse of Han Gan* ill. by author. Enchanted Lion, 2006. ISBN 978-1-59270-063-9 Subj: Activities – painting. Animals – horses, ponies. Art. Careers – artists. Folk & fairy tales. Foreign lands – China. Magic.

Hong, Jess. *Lovely* ill. by author. Creston, 2017. ISBN 978-193954737-8 Subj: Character traits – being different. Character traits – individuality. Self-concept.

Hong, Nari. *Days with Dad* ill. by author. Enchanted Lion, 2017. ISBN 978-159270233-6 Subj: Disabilities – physical disabilities. Family life – fathers.

Hood, Morag. *Carrot and pea: an unlikely friendship* ill. by author. Houghton Mifflin Harcourt, 2017. ISBN 978-054486842-7 Subj: Character traits – being different. Character traits – individuality. Food.

Hood, Susan. *Double take! a new look at opposites* ill. by Jay Fleck. Candlewick Studio, 2017. ISBN 978-076367291-1 Subj: Concepts – opposites. Rhyming text.

The fix-it man ill. by Arree Chung. HarperCollins, 2016. ISBN 978-006237085-3 Subj: Behavior – resourcefulness. Careers – inventors. Inventions. Problem solving. Rhyming text.

Just say boo! ill. by Jed Henry. HarperCollins, 2012. ISBN 978-0-06-201029-2 Subj: Etiquette. Holidays – Halloween. Rhyming text.

Leaps and bounce ill. by Matthew Cordell. Disney/Hyperion, 2016. ISBN 978-142315234-7 Subj: Format, unusual. Frogs & toads. Rhyming text.

Look! I can read! ill. by Amy Wummer. Grosset, 2000. ISBN 978-0-448-42282-4 Subj: Books, reading. Ethnic groups in the U.S. – African Americans. Rhyming text.

Meet Trouble ill. by Kristina Stephenson. Grosset, 2001. ISBN 978-0-448-42455-2 Subj: Animals – cats. Behavior – misbehavior.

Mission: back to school: top-secret information ill. by Mary Lundquist. Random House, 2016. ISBN 978-038538471-1 Subj: School – first day.

Mission: new baby ill. by Mary Lundquist. Random House, 2015. ISBN 978-038537672-3 Subj: Babies, toddlers. Family life – brothers & sisters.

Rooting for you ill. by Matthew Cordell. Disney/Hyperion, 2014. ISBN 978-142315230-9 Subj: Plants. Seeds.

Spike, the mixed-up monster ill. by Melissa Sweet. Simon & Schuster, 2012. ISBN 978-1-4424-0601-8 Subj: Animals. Foreign languages. Reptiles. Reptiles – salamanders.

Tickly toes ill. by Barroux. Kids Can, 2014. ISBN 978-189478652-2 Subj: Anatomy – toes. Babies, toddlers. Format, unusual – board books. Rhyming text.

The Tooth Mouse ill. by Janice Nadeau. Kids Can, 2012. ISBN 978-1-55453-565-1 Subj: Animals – mice. Character traits – bravery. Character traits – cleverness. Character traits – honesty. Teeth.

Hooks, Bell. *Be boy buzz* ill. by Chris Raschka. Hyperion, 2002. ISBN 978-0-7868-2633-9 Subj: Activities. Ethnic groups in the U.S. – African Americans. Gender roles.

Grump groan growl ill. by Chris Raschka. Hyperion, 2008. ISBN 978-0-7868-0816-8 Subj: Emotions – anger.

Happy to be nappy ill. by Chris Raschka. Hyperion, 1999. ISBN 978-0-7868-2377-2 Subj: Ethnic groups in the U.S. – African Americans. Hair.

Hooks, William H. *A dozen dizzy dogs* ill. by Gary Baseman. G. Stevens, 1997. ISBN 978-0-8368-1748-5 Subj: Animals – dogs. Counting, numbers. Rhyming text.

Feed me! an Aesop fable (Aesop)

The legend of the Christmas rose ill. by Richard Williams. HarperCollins, 1998. ISBN 978-0-06-027103-9 Subj: Family life – brothers & sisters. Flowers – roses. Foreign lands – Sweden. Holidays – Christmas. Religion – Nativity.

Moss gown ill. by Donald Carrick. Clarion, 1987. ISBN 978-0-89919-460-8 Subj: Family life – fathers. Folk & fairy tales. Magic.

Hooper, Maureen Brett. *Silent night: a Christmas carol is born* ill. by Kasi Kubiak. Boyds Mills, 2001. ISBN 978-1-56397-782-4 Subj: Holidays – Christmas. Music. Songs.

Hooper, Meredith. *Celebrity cat* ill. by Bee Willey. Frances Lincoln, 2006. ISBN 978-1-84507-290-2 Subj: Animals – cats. Art. Museums.

Dogs' Night ill. by Allan Curless and Mark Burgess. Millbrook, 2000. ISBN 978-0-7613-1824-8 Subj: Animals – dogs. Art. Museums.

River story ill. by Bee Willey. Candlewick, 2000. ISBN 978-0-7636-0792-0 Subj: Rivers.

Hooper, Patricia. *Where do you sleep, little one?* ill. by John Winch. Holiday, 2001. ISBN 978-0-8234-1668-4 Subj: Animals. Poetry. Sleep.

Hoose, Hannah. *Hey little ant* (Hoose, Philip M.)

Hoose, Philip M. *Hey little ant* by Philip M. Hoose and Hannah Hoose ill. by Debbie Tilley. Tricycle, 1998. ISBN 978-1-883672-54-6 Subj: Character traits – kindness to animals. Insects – ants. Music. Songs.

Hop a little, jump a little! ill. by Annie Kubler. Child's Play, 2010. ISBN 978-1-84643-341-2 Subj: Activities. Babies, toddlers. Format, unusual – board books. Rhyming text.

Hopgood, Tim. *Walter's wonderful web* ill. by author. Farrar, 2016. ISBN 978-037430352-5 Subj: Concepts – shape. Spiders.

Wow! said the owl ill. by author. Farrar, 2009. ISBN 978-0-374-38518-7 Subj: Birds – owls. Character traits – curiosity. Concepts – color. Day. Night.

Hopkins, H. Joseph. *The tree lady: the true story of how one tree-loving woman changed a city forever* ill. by Jill McElmurry. Simon & Schuster, 2013. ISBN 978-1-4424-1402-0 Subj: Character traits – persistence. Cities, towns. Gardens, gardening. Gender roles. Trees.

Hopkins, Jackie Mims. *The gold miner's daughter: a melodramatic fairytale* ill. by Jon Goodell. Peachtree, 2006. ISBN 978-1-56145-362-7 Subj: Folk & fairy tales. U.S. history – frontier & pioneer life.

Prairie chicken little ill. by Henry Cole. Peachtree, 2013. ISBN 978-1-56145-694-9 Subj: Animals – coyotes. Behavior – gossip, rumors. Birds – chickens, roosters. Cumulative tales. Folk & fairy tales.

Hopkins, Lee Bennett. *All God's children* ill. by Amanda Schaffer. Harcourt, 1998. ISBN 978-0-15-201499-5 Subj: Poetry. Religion.

Alphathoughts ill. by Marla Baggetta. Wordsong, 2003. ISBN 978-1-56397-979-8 Subj: ABC books. Poetry.

April, bubbles, chocolate: an ABC of poetry ill. by Barry Root. Simon & Schuster, 1994. ISBN 978-0-671-75911-7 Subj: ABC books. Poetry.

Behind the museum door ill. by Stacey Dressen-McQueen. Abrams, 2007. ISBN 978-0-8109-1204-5 Subj: Art. Museums. Poetry.

Christmas presents: holiday poetry ill. by Melanie W. Hall. HarperCollins, 2004. ISBN 978-0-06-008055-6 Subj: Holidays – Christmas. Poetry.

City I love ill. by Marcellus Hall. Abrams, 2009. ISBN 978-0-8109-8327-4 Subj: Cities, towns. Poetry.

Full moon and star ill. by Marcellus Hall. Abrams, 2011. ISBN 978-1-4197-0013-2 Subj: Activities – writing. Character traits – cooperation. Friendship. Theater.

Good books, good times ill. by Harvey Stevenson. HarperCollins, 1990. ISBN 978-0-06-022528-5 Subj: Books, reading. Poetry.

Good rhymes, good times ill. by Frané Lessac. HarperCollins, 1995. ISBN 978-0-06-023500-0 Subj: Poetry.

Hanukkah lights ill. by Melanie W. Hall. HarperCollins, 2004. ISBN 978-0-06-008052-5 Subj: Holidays – Hanukkah. Jewish culture. Poetry. Religion.

Incredible inventions ill. by Julia Sarcone-Roach. Greenwillow, 2009. ISBN 978-0-06-087245-8 Subj: Inventions. Poetry.

Jumping off library shelves: a book of poems ill. by Jane Manning. Boyds Mills, 2015. ISBN 978-159078924-7 Subj: Books, reading. Libraries. Poetry.

Manger ill. by Helen Cann. Eerdmans, 2014. ISBN 978-080285419-3 Subj: Poetry. Religion – Nativity.

Merrily comes our harvest in ill. by Ben Shecter. Harcourt, 1978. ISBN 978-0-15-253179-9 Subj: Holidays – Thanksgiving. Poetry. Seasons – fall.

Nasty bugs: poems ill. by Will Terry. Dial, 2012. ISBN 978-0-8037-3716-7 Subj: Insects. Poetry.

Ragged shadows: poems of Halloween night ill. by Giles Laroche. Little, 1993. ISBN 978-0-316-37276-3 Subj: Holidays – Halloween. Poetry.

School supplies ill. by Renee Flower. Simon & Schuster, 1996. ISBN 978-0-671-51172-2 Subj: Poetry. School.

Yummy! eating through a day ill. by Renée Flower. Simon & Schuster, 2000. ISBN 978-0-689-81755-7 Subj: Food. Poetry.

Hopkinson, Deborah. *Abe Lincoln crosses a creek: a tall, thin tale (introducing his forgotten frontier friend)* ill. by John Hendrix. Random House, 2008. ISBN 978-0-375-83768-5 Subj: Character traits – bravery. Friendship. U.S. history.

Annie and Helen ill. by Raúl Colón. Random House, 2012. ISBN 978-0-375-85706-5 Subj: Careers – teachers. Disabilities – blindness. Disabilities – deafness. U.S. history.

Bluebird summer ill. by Bethanne Andersen. Greenwillow, 2001. ISBN 978-0-688-17399-9 Subj: Death. Emotions. Family life – grandfathers. Farms. Memories, memory.

Fannie in the kitchen ill. by Nancy Carpenter. Atheneum, 2001. ISBN 978-0-689-81965-0 Subj: Activities – baking, cooking.

Follow the moon home: a tale of one idea, twenty kids, and a hundred sea turtles (Cousteau, Philippe)

Girl wonder ill. by Terry Widener. Atheneum, 2003. ISBN 978-0-689-83300-7 Subj: Sports – baseball.

The humblebee hunter: inspired by the life and experiments of Charles Darwin and his children ill. by Jen Corace. Hyperion, 2010. ISBN 978-1-4231-1356-0 Subj: Foreign lands – England. Insects – bees. Science.

Keep on! the story of Matthew Henson, co-discoverer of the North Pole ill. by Stephen Alcorn. Peachtree, 2009. ISBN 978-1-56145-473-0 Subj: Careers – explorers. Ethnic groups in the U.S. – African Americans. Foreign lands – Arctic. U.S. history.

Knit your bit: a World War I story ill. by Steven Guarnaccia. Putnam, 2013. ISBN 978-0-399-25241-9 Subj: Activities – knitting. Clothing. Gender roles. U.S. history. War.

A letter to my teacher ill. by Nancy Carpenter. Random House, 2017. ISBN 978-037586845-0 Subj: Careers – teachers. Letters, cards. School.

Maria's comet ill. by Deborah Lanino. Atheneum, 1999. ISBN 978-0-689-81501-0 Subj: Careers – astronomers. Family life. Sky.

Steamboat school: inspired by a true story : St. Louis, Missouri: 1847 ill. by Ron Husband. Disney/Jump at the Sun, 2016. ISBN 978-142312196-1 Subj: Behavior – resourcefulness. Careers – teachers. Character traits – bravery. Ethnic groups in the U.S. – African Americans. School. U.S. history.

Sweet Clara and the freedom quilt ill. by author. Knopf, 1993. ISBN 978-0-679-92311-4 Subj: Activities – sewing. Behavior – seeking better things. Ethnic groups in the U.S. – African Americans. Quilts. Slavery.

Hoppe, Paul. *Hat* ill. by author. Bloomsbury, 2009. ISBN 978-1-59990-247-0 Subj: Behavior – lost & found possessions. Clothing – hats. Imagination.

The woods ill. by author. Chronicle, 2011. ISBN 978-0-8118-7547-9 Subj: Bedtime. Behavior – lost & found possessions. Character traits – bravery. Emotions – fear. Toys.

Horacek, Judy. *Yellow is my color star* ill. by author. Simon & Schuster, 2014. ISBN 978-144249299-8 Subj: Concepts – color. Rhyming text.

Horácek, Petr. *Animal opposites: a pop-up book* ill. by author. Candlewick, 2013. ISBN 978-0-7636-6776-4 Subj: Animals. Concepts – opposites. Format, unusual – toy & movable books.

Beep beep ill. by author. Candlewick, 2008. ISBN 978-0-7636-3482-7 Subj: Automobiles. Format, unusual – board books.

Blue Penguin ill. by author. Candlewick, 2016. ISBN 978-076369251-3 Subj: Birds – penguins. Character traits – being different. Emotions – loneliness. Friendship.

Butterfly butterfly: a book of colors ill. by author. Candlewick, 2007. ISBN 978-0-7636-3343-1 Subj: Concepts – color. Format, unusual. Nature.

Choo choo ill. by author. Candlewick, 2008. ISBN 978-0-7636-3477-3 Subj: Format, unusual – board books. Noise, sounds. Trains.

Flip's day ill. by author. Candlewick, 2002. ISBN 978-0-7636-1798-1 Subj: Birds – penguins. Format, unusual – toy & movable books.

The fly ill. by author. Candlewick, 2015. ISBN 978-076367480-9 Subj: Insects – flies.

Jonathan and Martha ill. by author. Phaidon, 2012. ISBN 978-0-7148-6351-1 Subj: Animals – worms. Behavior – fighting, arguing. Behavior – sharing. Format, unusual.

Look out, Suzy Goose ill. by author. Candlewick, 2008. ISBN 978-0-7636-3803-0 Subj: Animals. Behavior – solitude. Birds – geese. Character traits – individuality. Noise, sounds.

The mouse who ate the moon ill. by author. Candlewick, 2014. ISBN 978-076367059-7 Subj: Animals – mice. Format, unusual – toy & movable books. Moon.

The mouse who reached the sky ill. by author. Candlewick, 2016. ISBN 978-076367916-3 Subj: Animals – mice. Character traits – cooperation. Character traits – helpfulness. Format, unusual – toy & movable books.

My elephant ill. by author. Candlewick, 2009. ISBN 978-0-7636-4566-3 Subj: Animals – elephants. Behavior – misbehavior. Family life – grandparents. Imagination.

One spotted giraffe ill. by author. Candlewick, 2012. ISBN 978-0-7636-6157-1 Subj: Animals. Counting, numbers. Format, unusual – toy & movable books.

Puffin Peter ill. by author. Candlewick, 2013. ISBN 978-0-7636-6572-2 Subj: Animals – whales. Behavior – lost. Birds – puffins. Friendship.

Silly Suzy Goose ill. by author. Candlewick, 2006. ISBN 978-0-7636-3040-9 Subj: Animals. Animals – lions. Birds – geese. Character traits – individuality. Self-concept.

Strawberries are red ill. by author. Candlewick, 2001. ISBN 978-0-7636-1461-4 Subj: Concepts – color. Food. Format, unusual – toy & movable books.

A surprise for Tiny Mouse ill. by author. Candlewick, 2015. ISBN 978-076367967-5 Subj: Animals – mice. Format, unusual – board books. Format, unusual – toy & movable books. Seasons. Weather – rainbows.

Suzy Goose and the Christmas star ill. by author. Candlewick, 2009. ISBN 978-0-7636-4487-1 Subj: Animals. Behavior – lost. Birds – geese. Holidays – Christmas. Stars.

Time for bed ill. by author. Candlewick, 2014. ISBN 978-076366779-5 Subj: Babies, toddlers. Bedtime. Format, unusual – board books.

What is black and white? ill. by author. Candlewick, 2001. ISBN 978-0-7636-1460-7 Subj: Concepts – color.

When the moon smiled ill. by author. Candlewick, 2004. ISBN 978-0-7636-2209-1 Subj: Animals. Counting, numbers. Moon. Night. Stars.

Horn, Emily. *Excuse me — are you a witch?* ill. by Pawel Pawlak. Whispering Coyote, 2003. ISBN 978-1-58089-093-9 Subj: Animals – cats. Libraries. School. Witches.

Horn, Peter. *The best father of all* ill. by Cristina Kadmon. NorthSouth, 2003. ISBN 978-0-7358-1680-0 Subj: Animals. Family life – fathers. Reptiles – turtles, tortoises.

When I grow up . . . ill. by Cristina Kadmon. NorthSouth, 1999. ISBN 978-0-7358-1149-2 Subj: Behavior – growing up. Family life – fathers. Reptiles – turtles, tortoises.

Horn, Sandra Ann. *Babushka* ill. by Sophie Fatus. Barefoot, 2002. ISBN 978-1-84148-353-5 Subj: Folk & fairy tales. Foreign lands – Russia. Holidays – Christmas. Religion – Nativity.

The dandelion wish ill. by Jason Cockcroft. DK, 2000. ISBN 978-0-7894-6326-5 Subj: Behavior – wishing. Fairs, festivals. Plants.

Horning, Sandra. *The giant hug* ill. by Valeri Gorbachev. Knopf, 2005. ISBN 978-0-375-92477-4 Subj: Animals – pigs. Careers – postal workers. Cumulative tales. Family life – grandmothers. Hugging. Post office.

Hornsey, Chris. *Why do I have to eat off the floor?* ill. by Gwen Perkins. Walker, 2007. ISBN 978-0-8027-9617-2 Subj: Animals – dogs. Character traits – questioning. Humorous stories.

Horowitz, Dave. *Buy my hats!* ill. by author. Penguin, 2010. ISBN 978-0-399-25275-4 Subj: Animals. Careers – salespeople. Clothing – hats. Friendship.

Chico the brave. Penguin, 2012. ISBN 978-0-399-25636-3 Subj: Animals – llamas. Birds – chickens, roosters. Character traits – bravery. Emotions – fear. Foreign lands – Peru.

Duck, duck, moose ill. by author. Putnam, 2009. ISBN 978-0-399-24782-8 Subj: Activities – traveling. Animals – moose. Birds – ducks.

Humpty Dumpty climbs again ill. by author. Putnam, 2008. ISBN 978-0-399-24773-6 Subj: Character traits – bravery. Eggs. Humorous stories. Nursery rhymes. Rhyming text.

A monkey among us ill. by author. HarperCollins, 2004. ISBN 978-0-06-054335-8 Subj: Animals – giraffes. Animals – hippopotamuses. Animals – monkeys. Rhyming text.

Soon, Baboon, soon ill. by author. Penguin, 2005. ISBN 978-0-399-24268-7 Subj: Animals. Animals – baboons. Character traits – patience, impatience. Music. Musical instruments. Rhyming text.

Twenty-six pirates ill. by author. Penguin/Nancy Paulsen, 2013. ISBN 978-0-399-25777-3 Subj: ABC books. Pirates. Rhyming text.

Twenty-six princesses ill. by author. Putnam, 2008. ISBN 978-0-399-24607-4 Subj: ABC books. Rhyming text. Royalty – princesses.

The ugly pumpkin ill. by author. Penguin, 2005. ISBN 978-0-399-24267-0 Subj: Food. Holidays –

Halloween. Holidays – Thanksgiving. Rhyming text.

Horowitz, Ruth. *Are we still friends?* ill. by Blanca Gómez. Scholastic, 2017. ISBN 978-054564521-8 Subj: Animals – bears. Animals – mice. Behavior – misunderstanding. Friendship. Insects – bees.

Crab moon ill. by Kate Kiesler. Candlewick, 2000. ISBN 978-0-7636-0709-8 Subj: Animals. Crustaceans – crabs. Sea & seashore.

Horrocks, Anita. *Silas' seven grandparents* ill. by Helen Flook. Orca, 2010. ISBN 978-1-55143-561-9 Subj: Family life – grandparents. Family life – stepfamilies.

Horsbrugh, Wilma. *The train to Glasgow* ill. by Paul Cox. Clarion, 2004. ISBN 978-0-618-38143-2 Subj: Cumulative tales. Rhyming text. Trains.

Horse, Harry. *Little Rabbit lost* ill. by author. Peachtree, 2002. ISBN 978-1-56145-273-6 Subj: Animals – rabbits. Behavior – lost. Parks – amusement.

Little Rabbit runaway ill. by author. Peachtree, 2005. ISBN 978-1-56145-343-6 Subj: Animals – rabbits. Behavior – running away.

Little Rabbit's new baby ill. by author. Peachtree, 2008. ISBN 978-1-56145-431-0 Subj: Animals – rabbits. Babies, toddlers. Family life – new sibling. Multiple births – triplets.

Hort, Lenny. *Did dinosaurs eat pizza? mysteries science hasn't solved* ill. by John O'Brien. Henry Holt, 2006. ISBN 978-0-8050-6757-6 Subj: Dinosaurs. Science.

Tie your socks and clap your feet ill. by Stephen Kroninger. Atheneum, 2000. ISBN 978-0-689-83195-9 Subj: Humorous stories. Poetry.

We're going on a treasure hunt photos by Tom Arma. Abrams, 2003. ISBN 978-0-8109-4654-5 Subj: Animals. Babies, toddlers. Clothing – costumes. Games. Sea & seashore.

We're going on safari photos by Tom Arma. Abrams, 2002. ISBN 978-0-8109-0574-0 Subj: Animals. Babies, toddlers. Clothing – costumes.

Horton, Joan. *Hippopotamus stew: and other silly animal poems* ill. by JoAnn Adinolfi. Henry Holt, 2006. ISBN 978-0-8050-7350-8 Subj: Animals. Poetry.

Math attack! ill. by Kyrsten Brooker. Farrar, 2009. ISBN 978-0-374-34861-8 Subj: Behavior – worrying. Counting, numbers. Rhyming text. School.

Working mummies ill. by Drazen Kozjan. Farrar, 2012. ISBN 978-0-374-38524-8 Subj: Careers. Family life – mothers. Monsters. Mummies. Rhyming text.

Horvath, David. *Bossy bear* ill. by author. Hyperion, 2007. ISBN 978-1-4231-0336-3 Subj: Animals – bears. Behavior – bossy.

Just like Bossy Bear ill. by author. Hyperion, 2009. ISBN 978-1-4231-1097-2 Subj: Animals – bears. Behavior – bossy. Reptiles – turtles, tortoises.

Horvath, James. *Dig, dogs, dig: a construction tail* ill. by author. HarperCollins, 2013. ISBN 978-0-06-218964-6 Subj: Animals – dogs. Careers – construction workers. Machines. Rhyming text. Trucks.

Work, dogs, work: a highway tail ill. by author. HarperCollins, 2014. ISBN 978-006218970-7 Subj: Animals – dogs. Careers – construction workers. Rhyming text. Roads.

Horwood, Annie. *Butterfly, butterfly what colors do you see?* ill. by author. Simon & Schuster, 2001. ISBN 978-0-689-84075-3 Subj: Concepts – color. Format, unusual – toy & movable books. Insects – butterflies, caterpillars.

Hosford, Kate. *Big birthday* ill. by Holly Clifton-Brown. Carolrhoda, 2012. ISBN 978-0-7613-5410-9 Subj: Behavior – dissatisfaction. Birthdays. Character traits – individuality. Rhyming text.

Big bouffant ill. by Holly Clifton-Brown. Carolrhoda, 2011. ISBN 978-0-7613-5409-3 Subj: Character traits – appearance. Character traits – individuality. Hair. Rhyming text.

Infinity and me ill. by Gabi Swiatkowska. Carolrhoda, 2012. ISBN 978-0-7613-6726-0 Subj: Character traits – smallness. Concepts – size. Counting, numbers.

Hoshino, Felicia. *Sora and the cloud* ill. by author. Immedium, 2012. ISBN 978-1-59702-027-5 Subj: Foreign languages. Imagination. Weather – clouds.

Hosta, Dar. *I love the night* ill. by author. Brown Dog, 2003. ISBN 978-0-9721967-0-3 Subj: Animals. Night.

Houblon, Marie. *A world of colors: seeing colors in a new way* ill. with photos. National Geographic, 2009. ISBN 978-1-4263-0556-6 Subj: Concepts – color.

Houran, Lori Haskins. *Dig those dinosaurs* ill. by Francisca Marquez. Albert Whitman, 2013. ISBN 978-0-8075-1579-2 Subj: Careers – paleontologists. Dinosaurs. Fossils. Rhyming text.

A dozen cousins ill. by Sam Usher. Sterling, 2015. ISBN 978-145491062-6 Subj: Behavior – misbehavior. Family life – cousins. Rhyming text.

How to spy on a shark ill. by Francisca Marquez. Albert Whitman, 2015. ISBN 978-080753402-1 Subj: Careers – scientists. Fish – sharks. Robots.

I will keep you safe and sound ill. by Petra Brown. Scholastic, 2013. ISBN 978-0-545-19751-9 Subj: Animals – babies. Family life – parents. Rhyming text. Safety.

A trip into space: an adventure to the International Space Station ill. by Francisca Marquez. Albert Whitman, 2014. ISBN 978-080758091-2 Subj: Careers – astronauts. Space & space ships.

House, Catherine. *A stork in a baobab tree: an African twelve days of Christmas* ill. by Polly Alakija. Frances Lincoln, 2011. ISBN 978-1-84780-116-6 Subj: Cumulative tales. Foreign lands – Africa. Holidays – Christmas. Music. Songs.

The house that Jack built. *The house that Jack built* ill. by Diana Mayo. Barefoot, 2001. ISBN 978-1-84148-251-4 Subj: Cumulative tales. Nursery rhymes.

The house that Jack built retold by Jeanette Winter; ill. by reteller. Dial, 2000. ISBN 978-0-8037-2524-9 Subj: Cumulative tales. Nursery rhymes. Rebuses.

This is the house that Jack built ill. by Simms Taback. Putnam, 2002. ISBN 978-0-399-23488-0 Subj: Cumulative tales. Nursery rhymes.

Houston, Gloria. *Miss Dorothy and her bookmobile* ill. by Susan Condie Lamb. HarperCollins, 2011. ISBN 978-0-06-029155-6 Subj: Books, reading. Libraries. Trucks.

My Great-Aunt Arizona ill. by Susan Condie Lamb. HarperCollins, 1992. ISBN 978-0-06-022607-7 Subj: Careers – teachers. Family life – aunts, uncles.

The year of the perfect Christmas tree: an Appalachian story ill. by Barbara Cooney. Dial, 1988. ISBN 978-0-8037-0300-1 Subj: Family life. Holidays – Christmas. Trees.

Hout, Mies van. *Friends* ill. by Mies van Hout. Lemniscaat, 2013. ISBN 978-1-9359-5423-1 Subj: Friendship. Monsters.

Happy ill. by Mies van Hout. Lemniscaat, 2012. ISBN 978-1-935954-14-9 Subj: Emotions. Fish.

Hovland, Henrik. *John Jensen feels different* ill. by Torill Kove. Eerdmans, 2012. ISBN 978-0-8028-5399-8 Subj: Character traits – appearance. Character traits – individuality. Reptiles – alligators, crocodiles. Self-concept.

How much does God love me? ill. by Rory Tyger. Barron's, 2001. ISBN 978-0-7641-5405-8 Subj: Format, unusual – toy & movable books. Religion.

Howard, Arthur. *Cosmo zooms* ill. by author. Harcourt, 1999. ISBN 978-0-15-201788-0 Subj: Animals – dogs. Self-concept. Sports – skateboarding.

Hoodwinked ill. by author. Harcourt, 2001. ISBN 978-0-15-202656-1 Subj: Pets. Witches.

My dream dog ill. by author. Simon & Schuster/Beach Lane, 2016. ISBN 978-148145838-2 Subj: Animals – dogs. Dreams.

When I was five ill. by author. Harcourt, 1996. ISBN 978-0-15-200261-9 Subj: Behavior – growing up. Friendship.

Howard, Elizabeth Fitzgerald. *Aunt Flossie's hats (and crab cakes later)* ill. by James Ransome. Houghton, 1991. ISBN 978-0-395-54682-6 Subj: Clothing – hats. Ethnic groups in the U.S. – African Americans. Family life – aunts, uncles.

Chita's Christmas tree ill. by Floyd Cooper. Bradbury, 1989. ISBN 978-0-02-744621-0 Subj: Ethnic groups in the U.S. – African Americans. Holidays – Christmas.

Virgie goes to school with us boys ill. by E. B. Lewis. Simon & Schuster, 1999. ISBN 978-0-689-80076-4 Subj: Ethnic groups in the U.S. – African Americans. Gender roles. U.S. history.

Howard, Ellen. *The log cabin Christmas* ill. by Ronald Himler. Holiday, 2000. ISBN 978-0-8234-1381-2 Subj: Family life. Holidays – Christmas. U.S. history – frontier & pioneer life.

The log cabin church ill. by Ronald Himler. Holiday, 2002. ISBN 978-0-8234-1740-7 Subj: Church. Family life. Religion. U.S. history – frontier & pioneer life.

The log cabin quilt ill. by Ronald Himler. Holiday, 1996. ISBN 978-0-8234-1247-1 Subj: Family life – grandmothers. Quilts. U.S. history – frontier & pioneer life.

Howard, Ginger. *William's house* ill. by Larry Day. Millbrook, 2001. ISBN 978-0-7613-1674-9 Subj: Homes, houses. U.S. history.

Howard, Martin. *Tina Cocolina: queen of the cupcakes* (Cartaya, Pablo)

Howard, Reginald. *The big, big wall* ill. by José Aruego and Ariane Dewey. Harcourt, 2000. ISBN 978-0-15-216504-8 Subj: Eggs. Friendship. Rhyming text.

Howatt, Sandra J. *Sleepyheads* ill. by Joyce Wan. Simon & Schuster/Beach Lane, 2014. ISBN 978-144242266-7 Subj: Animals – babies. Bedtime. Rhyming text. Sleep.

Howe, James. *Big Bob, Little Bob* ill. by Laura Ellen Anderson. Candlewick, 2016. ISBN 978-076364436-9 Subj: Character traits – being different. Character traits – individuality. Friendship. Gender identity.

Brontorina ill. by Randy Cecil. Candlewick, 2010. ISBN 978-0-7636-4437-6 Subj: Ballet. Concepts – size. Dinosaurs.

The day the teacher went bananas ill. by Lillian Hoban. Dutton, 1984. ISBN 978-0-525-44107-6 Subj: Animals – gorillas. School. Zoos.

Horace and Morris but mostly Dolores ill. by Amy Walrod. Atheneum, 1999. ISBN 978-0-689-31874-0 Subj: Animals – mice. Clubs, gangs. Friendship.

Horace and Morris join the chorus (but what about Dolores?) ill. by Amy Walrod. Atheneum, 2002. ISBN 978-0-689-83939-9 Subj: Activities – singing. Animals – mice. Character traits – persistence. Emotions – anger. Friendship.

Horace and Morris say cheese (which makes Dolores sneeze!) ill. by Amy Walrod. Atheneum, 2005. ISBN 978-0-689-83940-5 Subj: Animals – mice. Food. Illness – allergies.

Houndsley and Catina ill. by Marie-Louise Gay. Candlewick, 2006. ISBN 978-0-7636-2404-0 Subj: Activities – baking, cooking. Activities – writing. Animals – cats. Animals – dogs. Friendship.

Houndsley and Catina and the birthday surprise ill. by Marie-Louise Gay. Candlewick, 2006. ISBN 978-0-7636-2405-7 Subj: Animals – cats. Animals – dogs. Birthdays. Friendship. Parties.

I wish I were a butterfly ill. by Ed Young. Harcourt, 1987. ISBN 978-0-15-200470-5 Subj: Behavior – wishing. Emotions – envy, jealousy.

Otter and odder: a love story ill. by Chris Raschka. Candlewick, 2012. ISBN 978-0-7636-4174-0 Subj: Animals – otters. Character traits – being different. Emotions – love. Fish.

There's a dragon in my sleeping bag ill. by David S. Rose. Atheneum, 1994. ISBN 978-0-689-31873-3 Subj: Dragons. Family life – brothers. Imagination – imaginary friends.

There's a monster under my bed ill. by David S. Rose. Atheneum, 1986. ISBN 978-0-689-31178-9 Subj: Emotions – fear. Furniture – beds. Monsters. Night.

Howell, Theresa. *Maybe something beautiful: how art transformed a neighborhood* (Campoy, F. Isabel)

Howell, Will C. *I call it sky* ill. by John Ward. Walker, 1999. ISBN 978-0-8027-8678-4 Subj: Friendship. Nature. Seasons. Weather.

Zoo flakes ABC ill. by author. Walker, 2002. ISBN 978-0-8027-8826-9 Subj: ABC books. Activities – making things. Animals. Art. Paper.

Howie, Betsy. *The Block Mess Monster* ill. by C. B. Decker. Henry Holt, 2008. ISBN 978-0-8050-7940-1 Subj: Character traits – cleanliness. Family life – mothers. Monsters.

Howitt, Mary Botham. *Mary Howitt's The spider and the fly* ill. by Tony DiTerlizzi. Simon & Schuster, 2002. ISBN 978-0-689-85289-3 Subj: Caldecott award honor books. Insects – flies. Poetry. Spiders.

Howland, Naomi. *ABCDrive!* ill. by author. Clarion, 1994. ISBN 978-0-395-66414-8 Subj: ABC books. Activities – traveling. Automobiles.

Latkes, latkes, good to eat: a Chanukah story ill. by author. Clarion, 1999. ISBN 978-0-395-89903-8 Subj: Folk & fairy tales. Foreign lands – Russia. Holidays – Hanukkah. Jewish culture. Magic.

The matzah man ill. by author. Clarion, 2002. ISBN 978-0-618-11750-5 Subj: Behavior – running away. Cumulative tales. Food. Holidays – Passover. Jewish culture.

Princess says goodnight ill. by David Small. HarperCollins, 2010. ISBN 978-0-06-145525-4 Subj: Bedtime. Rhyming text. Royalty – princesses.

Hru, Dakari. *Joshua's Masai mask* ill. by Anna Rich. Lee & Low, 1993. ISBN 978-1-880000-02-1 Subj: Behavior – wishing. Ethnic groups in the U.S. – African Americans. Magic. Masks.

Tickle, tickle ill. by Ken Wilson-Max. Roaring Brook, 2002. ISBN 978-0-7613-1537-7 Subj: Activities – playing. Babies, toddlers. Family life – fathers. Games. Rhyming text.

Hruby, Emily. *Counting in the garden* ill. by Patrick Hruby. AMMO, 2011. ISBN 978-1-934429-70-9 Subj: Animals. Counting, numbers. Gardens, gardening.

Hubbard, Crystal. *Catching the moon: the story of a young girl's baseball dream* ill. by Randy DuBurke. Lee & Low, 2005. ISBN 978-1-58430-243-8 Subj: Character traits – perseverance. Ethnic groups in the U.S. – African Americans. Gender roles. Sports – baseball. U.S. history.

Hubbard, Patricia. *My crayons talk* ill. by G. Brian Karas. Henry Holt, 1996. ISBN 978-0-8050-3529-2 Subj: Concepts – color. Rhyming text.

Trick or treat countdown ill. by Michael Letzig. Holiday, 1999. ISBN 978-0-8234-1367-6 Subj: Counting, numbers. Holidays – Halloween. Rhyming text.

Hubbard, Woodleigh Marx. *All that you are* ill. by author. Putnam, 2000. ISBN 978-0-399-23364-7 Subj: Character traits – optimism. Self-concept.

Whoa, jealousy ill. by Madeleine Houston. Putnam, 2002. ISBN 978-0-399-23435-4 Subj: Behavior. Emotions – envy, jealousy.

Hubbell, Patricia. *Airplanes: soaring! diving! turning!* ill. by Megan Halsey. Marshall Cavendish,

2008. ISBN 978-0-7614-5388-8 Subj: Airplanes, airports. Rhyming text.

Black earth, gold sun ill. by Mary Newell DePalma. Marshall Cavendish, 2001. ISBN 978-0-7614-5090-0 Subj: Gardens, gardening. Poetry.

Boats: speeding! sailing! cruising! ill. by Megan Halsey. Marshall Cavendish, 2009. ISBN 978-0-7614-5524-0 Subj: Boats, ships. Rhyming text.

Boo! Halloween poems and limericks ill. by Jeff Spackman. Marshall Cavendish, 1998. ISBN 978-0-7614-5023-8 Subj: Holidays – Halloween. Poetry.

Bouncing time ill. by Melissa Sweet. HarperCollins, 2000. ISBN 978-0-688-17376-0 Subj: Babies, toddlers. Family life. Poetry. Zoos.

Cars: rushing! honking! zooming! ill. by Megan Halsey. Marshall Cavendish, 2006. ISBN 978-0-7614-5296-6 Subj: Automobiles. Rhyming text.

Check it out! reading, finding, helping ill. by Nancy Speir. Marshall Cavendish, 2011. ISBN 978-0-7614-5803-6 Subj: Books, reading. Libraries. Rhyming text.

City kids ill. by Teresa Flavin. Marshall Cavendish, 2001. ISBN 978-0-7614-5079-5 Subj: Cities, towns. Poetry.

Earthmates ill. by Jean Cassels. Marshall Cavendish, 2000. ISBN 978-0-7614-5062-7 Subj: Animals. Poetry.

Firefighters! speeding! spraying! saving! ill. by Viviana Garofoli. Marshall Cavendish, 2007. ISBN 978-0-7614-5337-6 Subj: Careers – firefighters. Rhyming text.

Horses: trotting! prancing! racing! ill. by Joe Mathieu. Marshall Cavendish, 2011. ISBN 978-0-7614-5949-1 Subj: Animals – horses, ponies. Rhyming text.

Hurray for spring! ill. by Taia Morley. NorthWord, 2005. ISBN 978-1-55971-913-1 Subj: Rhyming text. Seasons – spring.

My first airplane ride ill. by Nancy Speir. Marshall Cavendish, 2008. ISBN 978-0-7614-5436-6 Subj: Activities – traveling. Airplanes, airports. Noise, sounds. Rhyming text.

Police: hurrying! helping! saving! ill. by Viviana Garofoli. Marshall Cavendish, 2008. ISBN 978-0-7614-5421-2 Subj: Careers – police officers. Rhyming text.

Pots and pans ill. by Diane deGroat. HarperCollins, 1998. ISBN 978-0-694-01072-1 Subj: Activities – playing. Format, unusual – board books. Noise, sounds. Rhyming text.

Rabbit moon ill. by Wendy Watson. Marshall Cavendish, 2002. ISBN 978-0-7614-5103-7 Subj: Animals – rabbits. Days of the week, months of the year. Holidays. Rhyming text.

Sea, sand, me! ill. by Lisa Campbell Ernst. HarperCollins, 2001. ISBN 978-0-688-17379-1 Subj: Family life – mothers. Rhyming text. Sea & seashore – beaches.

Shaggy dogs, waggy dogs ill. by Donald Wu. Marshall Cavendish, 2011. ISBN 978-0-7614-5957-6 Subj: Animals – dogs. Rhyming text.

Sidewalk trip ill. by Mari Takabayashi. HarperCollins, 1999. ISBN 978-0-694-01174-2 Subj: Activities – walking. Cities, towns. Communities, neighborhoods. Family life – mothers. Rhyming text.

Snow happy! ill. by Hiroe Nakata. Tricycle, 2010. ISBN 978-1-58246-329-2 Subj: Activities – playing. Rhyming text. Weather – snow.

Teacher! sharing, helping, caring ill. by Nancy Speir. Marshall Cavendish, 2009. ISBN 978-0-7614-5574-5 Subj: Careers – teachers. Rhyming text. School.

Trains: steaming! pulling! huffing! ill. by Megan Halsey and Sean Addy. Marshall Cavendish, 2005. ISBN 978-0-7614-5194-5 Subj: Rhyming text. Trains.

Wrapping paper romp ill. by Jennifer Plecas. HarperCollins, 1998. ISBN 978-0-694-01098-1 Subj: Animals – cats. Babies, toddlers. Format, unusual – board books. Gifts. Holidays – Halloween. Rhyming text.

Hubbell, Will. *Pumpkin Jack* ill. by author. Albert Whitman, 2000. ISBN 978-0-8075-6665-7 Subj: Holidays – Halloween. Plants. Seeds.

Huber, Raymond. *Flight of the honey bee* ill. by Brian Lovelock. Candlewick, 2013. ISBN 978-0-7636-6760-3 Subj: Insects – bees. Nature.

Hubery, Julia. *A friend for all seasons* ill. by Mei Matsuoka. Simon & Schuster, 2007. ISBN 978-1-4169-2685-6 Subj: Animals – raccoons. Seasons. Trees.

Huck, Charlotte S. *A creepy countdown* ill. by Joseph A. Smith. Greenwillow, 1998. ISBN 978-0-688-15461-5 Subj: Counting, numbers. Holidays – Halloween. Rhyming text.

Princess Furball ill. by Anita Lobel. Greenwillow, 1989. ISBN 978-0-688-07838-6 Subj: Character traits – cleverness. Folk & fairy tales. Royalty – princesses.

Hucke, Johannes. *Pip in the Grand Hotel* ill. by Daniel Muller. NorthSouth, 2009. ISBN 978-0-7358-2225-2 Subj: Animals – mice. Hotels.

Huddy, Delia. *The Christmas Eve tree* ill. by Emily Sutton. Candlewick, 2016. ISBN 978-076367917-0 Subj: Holidays – Christmas. Homeless. Trees.

Hudelhoff, Allen H. *Cats and kids* ill. by Anne Canevari Green. Millbrook, 2002. ISBN 978-0-7613-2668-7 Subj: Activities – playing. Animals – cats. Character traits – cooperation.

Hudes, Quiara Alegría. *Welcome to my neighborhood! a barrio ABC* ill. by Shino Arihara. Scholastic, 2010. ISBN 978-0-545-09424-5 Subj: ABC books. Communities, neighborhoods. Ethnic groups in the U.S. – Hispanic Americans. Foreign languages. Rhyming text.

Hudson, Cheryl Willis. *Bright eyes, brown skin* by Cheryl Willis Hudson and Bernette Ford ill. by George Ford. Just Us, 1990. ISBN 978-0-940975-10-1 Subj: Ethnic groups in the U.S. – African Americans. Poetry.

Construction zone photos by Richard Sobol. Candlewick, 2006. ISBN 978-0-7636-2684-6 Subj: Buildings. Careers – construction workers. Machines.

My friend Maya loves to dance ill. by Eric Velasquez. Abrams, 2010. ISBN 978-0-8109-8328-1 Subj: Activities – dancing. Disabilities – physical disabilities. Ethnic groups in the U.S. – African Americans. Rhyming text.

Hudson, Katy. *Bear and Duck* ill. by author. HarperCollins, 2015. ISBN 978-006232051-3 Subj: Animals – bears. Birds – ducks. Friendship. Self-concept.

Hudson, Wade. *Pass it on: African-American poetry for children* ill. by Floyd Cooper. Scholastic, 1993. ISBN 978-0-590-45770-5 Subj: Ethnic groups in the U.S. – African Americans. Poetry.

Hueston, M. P. *The all-American jump and jive jig* ill. by Amanda Haley. Sterling, 2010. ISBN 978-1-4027-5143-1 Subj: Activities – dancing. Rhyming text. U.S. history.

Huget, Jennifer LaRue. *The beginner's guide to running away from home* ill. by Red Nose Studio. Schwartz & Wade, 2013. ISBN 978-0-375-86739-2 Subj: Behavior – running away. Family life. Family life – new sibling.

The best birthday party ever ill. by LeUyen Pham. Random House, 2011. ISBN 978-0-375-84763-9 Subj: Birthdays. Parties.

How to clean your room in ten easy steps ill. by Edward Koren. Random House, 2010. ISBN 978-0-375-84410-2 Subj: Character traits – cleanliness. Humorous stories.

Thanks a lot, Emily Post! ill. by Alexandra Boiger. Random House, 2009. ISBN 978-0-375-83853-8 Subj: Behavior. Etiquette. Family life – mothers.

Huggins, Peter. *Trosclair and the alligator* ill. by Lindsey Gardiner. Star Bright, 2006. ISBN 978-1-932065-98-5 Subj: Reptiles – alligators, crocodiles. Swamps.

Hughes, Langston. *Carol of the brown king: nativity poems* ill. by Ashley Bryan. Atheneum, 1998. ISBN 978-0-689-81877-6 Subj: Ethnic groups in the U.S. – African Americans. Holidays – Christmas. Poetry. Religion – Nativity.

I, too, am America ill. by Bryan Collier. Simon & Schuster, 2012. ISBN 978-1-4424-2008-3 Subj: Ethnic groups in the U.S. – African Americans. Poetry.

Lullaby (for a Black mother) ill. by Sean Qualls. Harcourt, 2013. ISBN 978-0-547-36265-6 Subj: Ethnic groups in the U.S. – African Americans. Family life – mothers. Lullabies. Poetry.

My people ill. by Charles R. Smith. Atheneum, 2009. ISBN 978-1-4169-3540-7 Subj: Character traits – pride. Ethnic groups in the U.S. – African Americans. Poetry. Self-concept.

The Negro speaks of rivers ill. by E. B. Lewis. Disney/Jump at the Sun, 2009. ISBN 978-0-7868-1867-9 Subj: Ethnic groups in the U.S. – African Americans. Poetry.

Sail away ill. by Ashley Bryan. Atheneum, 2015. ISBN 978-148143085-2 Subj: Poetry. Sea & seashore.

The sweet and sour animal book ill. by Harlem School of the Arts students. Oxford Univ., 1994. ISBN 978-0-19-509185-4 Subj: ABC books. Animals. Art. Children as illustrators. Poetry.

That is my dream! ill. by Daniel Miyares. Random House, 2017. ISBN 978-039955017-1 Subj: Ethnic groups in the U.S. – African Americans. Poetry. Prejudice.

Hughes, Laura. *We're going on an egg hunt* ill. by author. Bloomsbury, 2017. ISBN 978-168119314-4 Subj: Animals – rabbits. Eggs. Format, unusual – toy & movable books. Holidays – Easter.

Hughes, Sarah. *Let's play hopscotch* ill. with photos. Children's Press, 2000. ISBN 978-0-516-23112-9 Subj: Activities – playing. Games.

Let's play jacks ill. with photos. Children's Press, 2000. ISBN 978-0-516-23113-6 Subj: Activities – playing. Games.

Hughes, Shirley. *Alfie and the big boys* ill. by author. Random House, 2008. ISBN 978-0-370-32884-3 Subj: Foreign lands – England. School – nursery.

Alfie and the birthday surprise ill. by author. Lothrop, 1998. ISBN 978-0-688-15187-4 Subj: Animals – cats. Birthdays. Gifts. Parties.

Alfie gets in first ill. by author. Lothrop, 1982. ISBN 978-0-688-00849-9 Subj: Cumulative tales. Homes, houses.

Alfie's ABC ill. by author. Lothrop, 1998. ISBN 978-0-688-16126-2 Subj: ABC books. Family life – brothers & sisters.

Annie Rose is my little sister ill. by author. Candlewick, 2003. ISBN 978-0-7636-1959-6 Subj: Activities. Family life – brothers & sisters.

Bobbo goes to school ill. by author. Candlewick, 2013. ISBN 978-0-7636-6524-1 Subj: Behavior – lost & found possessions. School. Toys.

The Christmas Eve ghost ill. by author. Candlewick, 2010. ISBN 978-0-7636-4472-7 Subj: Holidays – Christmas. Prejudice. Religion.

Don't want to go! ill. by author. Candlewick, 2010. ISBN 978-0-7636-5091-9 Subj: Activities – babysitting. Emotions – anger. Emotions – fear.

Giving ill. by author. Candlewick, 1993. ISBN 978-1-56402-129-8 Subj: Character traits – generosity. Family life.

Olly and me ill. by author. Candlewick, 2004. ISBN 978-0-7636-2374-6 Subj: Babies, toddlers. Family life. Family life – brothers & sisters. Poetry.

Olly and me 1-2-3 ill. by author. Candlewick, 2009. ISBN 978-0-7636-4016-3 Subj: Counting, numbers. Family life – brothers & sisters.

Out and about ill. by author. Lothrop, 1988. ISBN 978-0-688-07691-7 Subj: Family life. Foreign lands – England. Rhyming text.

Rhymes for Annie Rose ill. by author. Lothrop, 1995. ISBN 978-0-688-14220-9 Subj: Family life – brothers & sisters. Rhyming text.

Hughes, Susan. *Earth to Audrey* ill. by Stéphane Poulin. Kids Can, 2005. ISBN 978-1-55337-843-3 Subj: Character traits – individuality. Friendship. Imagination. Seasons – summer.

Up! how families around the world carry their little ones ill. by Ashley Barron. OwlKids, 2017. ISBN 978-177147176-3 Subj: Babies, toddlers. World.

Hughes, Ted. *My brother Bert* ill. by Tracey Campbell Pearson. Farrar, 2009. ISBN 978-0-374-39982-5 Subj: Behavior – collecting things. Pets. Rhyming text.

Hughes, Vi. *Aziz, the story teller* ill. by Stefan Czernecki. Crocodile, 2001. ISBN 978-1-56656-456-4 Subj: Activities – storytelling. Family life – fathers.

Hulbert, Laura. *Who has these feet?* ill. by Erik Brooks. Henry Holt, 2011. ISBN 978-0-8050-8907-3 Subj: Anatomy – feet. Animals.

Who has this tail? ill. by Erik Brooks. Henry Holt, 2012. ISBN 978-0-8050-9429-9 Subj: Anatomy – tails. Animals.

Huling, Jan. *Ol' Bloo's boogie-woogie band and blues ensemble* ill. by Henri Sorensen. Peachtree, 2010. ISBN 978-1-56145-436-5 Subj: Animals. Careers – musicians. Crime. Folk & fairy tales. Old age.

Puss in cowboy boots ill. by Phil Huling. Simon & Schuster, 2002. ISBN 978-0-689-83119-5 Subj: Animals – cats. Character traits – cleverness. Clothing – boots. Folk & fairy tales. Foreign lands – France. Royalty – kings.

Hull, Rod. *Mr. Betts and Mr. Potts* ill. by Jo Davies. Barefoot, 2000. ISBN 978-1-84148-106-7 Subj: Animals. Careers – veterinarians. Illness. Pets. Rhyming text.

Hulme, Joy N. *Easter babies: a springtime counting book* ill. by Dan Andreasen. Sterling, 2010. ISBN 978-1-4027-6352-6 Subj: Animals – babies. Counting, numbers. Farms. Holidays – Easter. Rhyming text. Seasons – spring.

Hume, Lachie. *Clancy the courageous cow* ill. by author. HarperCollins, 2007. ISBN 978-0-06-117249-6 Subj: Animals – bulls, cows. Character traits – appearance. Character traits – individuality. Prejudice.

Hume, Stephen Eaton. *Red moon follows truck* ill. by Leslie Elizabeth Watts. Orca, 2001. ISBN 978-1-55143-218-2 Subj: Activities – traveling. Animals – dogs. Camps, camping. Foreign lands – Canada. Moving.

Humphries, Tudor. *Are you a butterfly?* (Allen, Judy)

Are you a grasshopper? (Allen, Judy)

Are you a ladybug? (Allen, Judy)

Are you a snail? (Allen, Judy)

Are you an ant? (Allen, Judy)

Hundal, Nancy. *Camping* ill. by Brian Deines. Fitzhenry & Whiteside, 2002. ISBN 978-1-55041-668-8 Subj: Activities – vacationing. Camps, camping. Family life. Poetry.

Number 21 ill. by Brian Deines. Fitzhenry & Whiteside, 2001. ISBN 978-1-55041-543-8 Subj: Family life – fathers. Trucks.

Twilight fairies ill. by Don Kilby. Fitzhenry & Whiteside, 2002. ISBN 978-1-55041-645-9 Subj: Fairies.

Huneck, Stephen. *Sally gets a job* ill. by author. Abrams, 2008. ISBN 978-0-8109-9493-5 Subj: Animals – dogs. Imagination.

Sally goes to heaven ill. by author. Abrams, 2014. ISBN 978-141970969-2 Subj: Animals – dogs. Death. Pets.

Sally goes to the beach ill. by author. Abrams, 2000. ISBN 978-0-8109-4186-1 Subj: Animals – dogs. Sea & seashore – beaches.

Sally goes to the farm ill. by author. Abrams, 2002. ISBN 978-0-8109-4498-5 Subj: Animals. Animals – dogs. Farms.

Sally goes to the mountains ill. by author. Abrams, 2001. ISBN 978-0-8109-4485-5 Subj: Animals – dogs. Camps, camping. Mountains.

Sally's great balloon adventure ill. by author. Abrams, 2010. ISBN 978-0-8109-8331-1 Subj: Activities – ballooning. Animals – dogs.

Sally's snow adventure ill. by author. Abrams, 2006. ISBN 978-0-8109-7061-8 Subj: Animals – dogs. Behavior – lost. Seasons – winter. Sports – skiing. Weather – snow.

Hunt, Joyce. *Keep looking!* (Selsam, Millicent E.)

Hunter, Anne. *Cricket song* ill. by author. Houghton Mifflin Harcourt, 2016. ISBN 978-054458259-0 Subj: Animals. Bedtime. Noise, sounds.

Possum and the peeper ill. by author. Houghton, 1998. ISBN 978-0-395-84631-5 Subj: Animals. Animals – possums. Frogs & toads. Seasons – spring.

Possum's harvest moon ill. by author. Houghton, 1996. ISBN 978-0-395-73575-6 Subj: Animals. Animals – possums. Moon. Parties. Seasons.

What's in the meadow? ill. by author. Houghton, 2000. ISBN 978-0-618-01512-2 Subj: Animals. Birds. Insects.

What's in the tide pool? ill. by author. Houghton, 2000. ISBN 978-0-618-01510-8 Subj: Animals. Sea & seashore.

Hunter, Dette. *38 ways to entertain your babysitter* ill. by Stephen MacEachern. Annick, 2003. ISBN 978-1-55037-795-8 Subj: Activities – babysitting. Activities – baking, cooking. Activities – making things. Games.

38 ways to entertain your grandparents ill. by Deirdre Betteridge. Annick, 2002. ISBN 978-1-55037-749-1 Subj: Activities – baking, cooking. Activities – making things. Family life – grandparents. Games.

Hunter, Jana Novotny. *Little ones do* ill. by Sally Anne Lambert. Dutton, 2001. ISBN 978-0-525-46690-1 Subj: Dragons. Family life – parents. Rhyming text.

My tail's not tired ill. by Paula Bowles. Child's Play, 2017. ISBN 978-184643985-8 Subj: Bedtime. Monsters.

When Daddy's truck picks me up ill. by Carol Thompson. Albert Whitman, 2006. ISBN 978-0-8075-8914-4 Subj: Family life – fathers. Rhyming text. Trucks.

Hunter, Sally. *Humphrey's bedtime* ill. by author. Henry Holt, 2001. ISBN 978-0-8050-6903-7 Subj: Animals – elephants. Bedtime. Family life – brothers & sisters.

Humphrey's birthday ill. by author. Henry Holt, 2003. ISBN 978-0-8050-7421-5 Subj: Animals – elephants. Birthdays. Parties.

Humphrey's Christmas ill. by author. Henry Holt, 2002. ISBN 978-0-8050-7176-4 Subj: Animals – elephants. Family life – brothers & sisters. Holidays – Christmas.

Humphrey's corner ill. by author. Henry Holt, 2001. ISBN 978-0-8050-6786-6 Subj: Activities – playing. Animals – elephants. Family life – mothers.

Hunter, Tom. *Build it up and knock it down* ill. by James Yang. HarperCollins, 2002. ISBN 978-0-694-01568-9 Subj: Concepts – opposites. Friendship. Language.

Huntington, Amy. *One Monday* ill. by author. Orchard, 2001. ISBN 978-0-439-29304-4 Subj: Farms. Weather – wind.

Hurd, Thacher. *Art dog* ill. by author. HarperCollins, 1996. ISBN 978-0-06-024425-5 Subj: Activities – painting. Animals – dogs. Art. Museums. Mystery stories.

Bad frogs ill. by author. Candlewick, 2009. ISBN 978-0-7636-3253-3 Subj: Behavior – misbehavior. Frogs & toads. Rhyming text.

Cat's pajamas ill. by author. HarperCollins, 2001. ISBN 978-0-694-01058-5 Subj: Animals – cats. Format, unusual – board books. Language. Rhyming text.

Little Mouse's big Valentine ill. by author. HarperCollins, 1990. ISBN 978-0-06-026193-1 Subj: Animals – mice. Holidays – Valentine's Day.

Mama don't allow ill. by author. HarperCollins, 1984. ISBN 978-0-06-022690-9 Subj: Animals – possums. Music. Musical instruments – bands. Reptiles – alligators, crocodiles.

Moo Cow Kaboom! ill. by author. HarperCollins, 2003. ISBN 978-0-06-050502-8 Subj: Animals – bulls, cows. Farms. Space & space ships.

Santa Mouse and the ratdeer ill. by author. HarperCollins, 1998. ISBN 978-0-06-027694-2 Subj: Accidents. Animals – mice. Behavior – bad day, bad mood. Holidays – Christmas. Santa Claus.

Sleepy Cadillac: a bedtime drive ill. by author. HarperCollins, 2005. ISBN 978-0-06-073021-5 Subj: Automobiles. Bedtime. Sleep.

The weaver ill. by Elisa Kleven. Farrar, 2010. ISBN 978-0-374-38254-4 Subj: Activities – weaving. Dreams.

Zoom City ill. by author. HarperCollins, 1998. ISBN 978-0-694-01057-8 Subj: Automobiles. Cities, towns.

Hurley, Jorey. *Fetch* ill. by author. Simon & Schuster/Paula Wiseman, 2015. ISBN 978-144248969-1 Subj: Animals – dogs. Sea & seashore – beaches.

Hop ill. by author. Simon & Schuster/Paula Wiseman, 2016. ISBN 978-148143272-6 Subj: Animals – rabbits. Nature.

Nest ill. by author. Simon & Schuster/Paula Wiseman, 2014. ISBN 978-144248971-4 Subj: Birds – robins. Nature. Seasons.

Ribbit ill. by author. Simon & Schuster/Paula Wiseman, 2017. ISBN 978-148143274-0 Subj: Frogs & toads. Nature.

Hurst, Carol Otis. *Rocks in his head* ill. by James Stevenson. Greenwillow, 2001. ISBN 978-0-06-029404-5 Subj: Behavior – collecting things. Rocks. U.S. history.

Terrible storm ill. by S. D. Schindler. HarperCollins, 2007. ISBN 978-0-06-009001-2 Subj: Family life – grandfathers. Seasons – winter. Weather – blizzards.

Hurst, Margaret M. *Grannie and the Jumbie* ill. by author. HarperCollins, 2001. ISBN 978-0-06-623633-9 Subj: Folk & fairy tales. Foreign lands – Caribbean Islands.

Hurston, Zora Neale. *The six fools* adapt. by Joyce Carol Thomas; ill. by Ann Tanksley. HarperCollins, 2006. ISBN 978-0-06-000647-1 Subj: Character traits – foolishness. Ethnic groups in the U.S. – African Americans. Folk & fairy tales.

Hurwitz, Johanna. *Ethan out and about* ill. by Brian Floca. Candlewick, 2002. ISBN 978-0-7636-1098-2 Subj: Animals. Family life – fathers. Food.

Mighty Monty ill. by Anik McGrory. Candlewick, 2008. ISBN 978-0-7636-2977-9 Subj: Character traits – shyness. Illness – asthma. School.

Russell's secret ill. by Heather Maione. HarperCollins, 2001. ISBN 978-0-688-17575-7 Subj: Babies, toddlers. Family life – brothers & sisters. Sibling rivalry.

Hurwitz, Laura. *Polar bear puzzle* (Lumry, Amanda)

Safari in South Africa (Lumry, Amanda)

Husband, Amy. *Dear Teacher* ill. by author. Sourcebooks, 2010. ISBN 978-1-4022-4268-7 Subj: Imagination. Letters, cards. School.

The noisy foxes ill. by author. little bee, 2015. ISBN 978-149980154-5 Subj: Animals – foxes. Noise, sounds.

Hush, little baby ill. by Marla Frazee. Browndeer, 1999. ISBN 978-0-15-201429-2 Subj: Babies, toddlers. Character traits – generosity. Cumulative tales. Lullabies. Music.

Hush songs: African American lullabies col., ed., & commentary by Joyce Carol Thomas; ill. by Brenda Joysmith. Jump at the Sun, 2000. ISBN 978-0-7868-2488-5 Subj: Ethnic groups in the U.S. – African Americans. Lullabies. Music. Songs.

Hutchins, Hazel. *Beneath the bridge* ill. by Ruth Ohi. Annick, 2004. ISBN 978-1-55037-859-7 Subj: Activities – traveling. Boats, ships. Dreams. Rhyming text.

I'd know you anywhere ill. by Ruth Ohi. Annick, 2002. ISBN 978-1-55037-747-7 Subj: Disguises. Family life – fathers.

Mattland by Hazel Hutchins and Gail Herbert ill. by Dusan Petricic. Annick, 2008. ISBN 978-1-55451-121-1 Subj: Character traits – cooperation. Friendship.

One dark night ill. by Susan Kathleen Hartung. Viking, 2001. ISBN 978-0-670-89246-4 Subj: Animals – babies. Animals – cats. Family life – grandparents. Weather – lightning, thunder. Weather – storms.

A second is a hiccup: a child's book of time ill. by Kady MacDonald Denton. Scholastic, 2007. ISBN 978-0-439-83106-2 Subj: Time.

The sidewalk rescue ill. by Ruth Ohi. Annick, 2004. ISBN 978-1-55037-831-3 Subj: Activities – drawing. Art.

Snap! ill. by Dusan Petricic. Annick, 2015. ISBN 978-155451770-1 Subj: Art. Concepts – color. Imagination.

Two so small ill. by Ruth Ohi. Firefly, 2000. ISBN 978-1-55037-651-7 Subj: Babies, toddlers. Concepts – size. Format, unusual – toy & movable books. Giants.

Up dog ill. by Fanny. Annick, 2012. ISBN 978-155451-389-5 Subj: Animals – dogs. Format, unusual – board books.

Hutchins, Pat. *Barn dance!* ill. by author. HarperCollins, 2007. ISBN 978-0-06-089122-0 Subj: Activities – dancing. Animals. Farms.

Bumpety bump ill. by author. HarperCollins, 2006. ISBN 978-0-06-056000-3 Subj: Birds – chickens, roosters. Family life – grandfathers. Farms. Rhyming text.

Changes, changes ill. by author. Macmillan, 1971. ISBN 978-0-02-745870-1 Subj: Toys – blocks. Wordless.

Clocks and more clocks ill. by author. Macmillan, 1994. ISBN 978-0-02-745921-0 Subj: Clocks, watches. Humorous stories. Time.

Don't forget the bacon! ill. by author. Greenwillow, 1975. ISBN 978-0-688-84019-8 Subj: Behavior – forgetfulness. Cumulative tales. Food. Humorous stories. Shopping.

The doorbell rang ill. by author. Greenwillow, 1986. ISBN 978-0-688-05252-2 Subj: Behavior – sharing. Family life. Friendship.

Good-night Owl ill. by author. Macmillan, 1991. ISBN 978-0-689-71541-9 Subj: Birds – owls. Cumulative tales. Noise, sounds. Participation. Sleep.

Happy birthday, Sam ill. by author. Greenwillow, 1978. ISBN 978-0-688-84160-7 Subj: Birthdays. Family life – grandfathers.

It's my birthday! ill. by author. Greenwillow, 1999. ISBN 978-0-688-09664-9 Subj: Behavior – sharing. Birthdays. Family life. Gifts. Monsters.

Little pink pig ill. by author. Greenwillow, 1994. ISBN 978-0-688-12015-3 Subj: Animals. Animals – pigs. Bedtime. Behavior – promptness, tardiness.

My best friend ill. by author. Greenwillow, 1993. ISBN 978-0-688-11486-2 Subj: Ethnic groups in the U.S. – African Americans. Friendship.

One hunter ill. by author. Greenwillow, 1982. ISBN 978-0-688-00615-0 Subj: Animals. Counting, numbers.

Rosie's walk ill. by author. Macmillan, 1968. ISBN 978-0-02-745850-3 Subj: Animals – foxes. Birds – chickens, roosters. Farms. Humorous stories.

Shrinking mouse ill. by author. Greenwillow, 1997. ISBN 978-0-688-13962-9 Subj: Animals. Concepts – perspective. Concepts – size.

Silly Billy! ill. by author. Greenwillow, 1992. ISBN 978-0-688-10818-2 Subj: Family life – brothers & sisters. Monsters.

The surprise party ill. by author. Macmillan, 1986, 1969. ISBN 978-0-02-745930-2 Subj: Animals. Behavior – gossip, rumors. Parties.

Ten red apples ill. by author. Greenwillow, 2000. ISBN 978-0-688-16798-1 Subj: Animals. Counting, numbers. Food. Noise, sounds. Rhyming text.

Three-star Billy ill. by author. Greenwillow, 1994. ISBN 978-0-688-13079-4 Subj: Behavior – misbehavior. Monsters. School.

Tidy Titch ill. by author. Greenwillow, 1991. ISBN 978-0-688-09964-0 Subj: Behavior. Family life. Toys.

Titch ill. by author. Macmillan, 1971. Subj: Concepts – size. Cumulative tales. Family life. Plants.

Titch and Daisy ill. by author. Greenwillow, 1996. ISBN 978-0-688-13960-5 Subj: Behavior – hiding. Character traits – shyness. Friendship. Parties.

The very worst monster ill. by author. Greenwillow, 1985. ISBN 978-0-688-04011-6 Subj: Monsters. Sibling rivalry.

What game shall we play? ill. by author. Greenwillow, 1990. ISBN 978-0-688-09197-2 Subj: Animals. Games.

Where, oh where, is Rosie's chick? ill. by author. Simon & Schuster, 2016. ISBN 978-148146071-2 Subj: Animals – foxes. Behavior – lost. Birds – chickens, roosters. Family life – mothers. Farms.

Where's the baby? ill. by author. Greenwillow, 1988. ISBN 978-0-688-05934-7 Subj: Babies, toddlers. Behavior – lost. Behavior – misbehavior. Character traits – cleanliness. Monsters.

Which witch is which? ill. by author. Greenwillow, 1989. ISBN 978-0-688-06358-0 Subj: Games. Holidays – Halloween. Multiple births – twins. Parties. Rhyming text.

The wind blew ill. by author. Macmillan, 1974. ISBN 978-0-02-745910-4 Subj: Rhyming text. Weather – wind.

You'll soon grow into them, Titch ill. by author. Greenwillow, 1983. ISBN 978-0-688-01771-2 Subj: Clothing. Family life.

Hyde, Heidi Smith. *Emanuel and the Hanukkah rescue* ill. by Jamel Akib. Lerner/Kar-Ben, 2012. ISBN 978-0-7613-6625-6 Subj: Boats, ships. Holidays – Hanukkah. Jewish culture.

Mendel's accordion ill. by Johanna van der Sterre. Lerner, 2007. ISBN 978-1-58013-212-1 Subj: Immigrants, immigration. Jewish culture. Music. Musical instruments – accordions.

Shanghai Sukkah ill. by Jing Jing Tsong. Kar-Ben, 2015. ISBN 978-146773474-5 Subj: Foreign lands – China. Friendship. Holidays – Sukkot. Immigrants, immigration. Jewish culture. Refugees.

Hyde, Margaret E. *Matisse for kids.* Penguin, 2004. ISBN 978-1-58980-204-9 Subj: Art. Careers – artists. Format, unusual – board books.

Van Gogh for kids. Penguin, 2004. ISBN 978-1-58980-207-0 Subj: Art. Careers – artists. Format, unusual – board books.

Hyman, Trina Schart. *A little alphabet* ill. by author. SeaStar, 2000. Originally pub. Little, Brown, ©1980. ISBN 978-1-58717-008-9 Subj: ABC books. Language.

Hyman, Zachary. *The Bambino and me* ill. by Zachary Pullen. Tundra, 2014. ISBN 978-177049627-9 Subj: Sports – baseball.

I invited a dragon to dinner ill. by Chris L. Demarest. Philomel, 2002. ISBN 978-0-399-23567-2 Subj: Humorous stories. Poetry.

Ichikawa, Satomi. *Come fly with me* ill. by author. Philomel, 2008. ISBN 978-0-399-24679-1 Subj: Activities – flying. Airplanes, airports. Animals – dogs. Foreign lands – France. Imagination. Toys.

The first bear in Africa! ill. by author. Philomel, 2001. ISBN 978-0-399-23485-9 Subj: Behavior – lost & found possessions. Foreign lands – Africa. Toys – bears.

I am Pangoo the penguin ill. by author. Penguin, 2006. ISBN 978-0-399-23313-5 Subj: Behavior – running away. Birds – penguins. Toys. Zoos.

La La Rose ill. by author. Philomel, 2004. ISBN 978-0-399-24029-4 Subj: Animals – rabbits. Behavior – lost. Foreign lands – France. Parks. Toys.

My father's shop ill. by author. Kane/Miller, 2006. ISBN 978-1-929132-99-7 Subj: Family life – fathers. Foreign lands – Morocco. Shopping.

My little train ill. by author. Penguin, 2010. ISBN 978-0-399-25453-6 Subj: Animals. Imagination. Toys. Trains.

What the little fir tree wore to the Christmas party ill. by author. Philomel, 2001. ISBN 978-0-399-23746-1 Subj: Holidays – Christmas. Trees.

Idle, Molly. *Camp Rex* ill. by author. Viking, 2014. ISBN 978-067078573-5 Subj: Camps, camping. Dinosaurs.

Flora and the chicks ill. by author. Chronicle, 2017. ISBN 978-145214657-7 Subj: Birds – chickens, roosters. Counting, numbers. Format, unusual – toy & movable books. Wordless.

Flora and the flamingo ill. by author. Chronicle, 2013. ISBN 978-1-4521-1006-6 Subj: Activities – dancing. Birds – flamingos. Caldecott award honor books. Format, unusual – toy & movable books. Friendship. Wordless.

Flora and the ostrich: an opposites book ill. by author. Chronicle, 2017. ISBN 978-145214658-4 Subj: Birds – ostriches. Concepts – opposites. Format, unusual – toy & movable books.

Flora and the peacocks ill. by author. Chronicle, 2016. ISBN 978-145213816-9 Subj: Activities – dancing. Birds – peacocks, peahens. Emotions – envy, jealousy. Format, unusual – toy & movable books. Wordless.

Flora and the penguin ill. by author. Chronicle, 2014. ISBN 978-145212891-7 Subj: Birds – penguins. Character traits – kindness. Format, unusual – toy & movable books. Sports – ice skating. Wordless.

Santa Rex ill. by author. Viking, 2017. ISBN 978-042529011-8 Subj: Dinosaurs. Holidays – Christmas. Santa Claus.

Sea Rex ill. by author. Viking, 2015. ISBN 978-067078574-2 Subj: Dinosaurs. Sea & seashore – beaches.

Tea Rex ill. by author. Viking, 2013. ISBN 978-0-670-01430-9 Subj: Dinosaurs. Etiquette. Parties.

Iijima, Geneva Cobb. *The way we do it in Japan* ill. by Paige Billin-Frye. Albert Whitman, 2002. ISBN 978-0-8075-7822-3 Subj: Family life – parents. Foreign lands – Japan. Foreign languages.

Ikegami, Aiko. *Friends* ill. by author. Albert Whitman, 2016. ISBN 978-080752550-0 Subj: Animals. Character traits – being different. Emotions – loneliness. Friendship. School.

Imai, Ayano. *Chester* ill. by author. Minedition, 2007. ISBN 978-0-698-40062-7 Subj: Animals – dogs. Behavior – running away. Pets.

Mr. Brown's fantastic hat ill. by author. Minedition, 2014. ISBN 978-988824084-5 Subj: Animals – bears. Birds. Clothing – hats. Emotions – loneliness. Friendship.

The 108th sheep ill. by author. Tiger Tales, 2007. ISBN 978-1-58925-063-5 Subj: Animals – sheep. Bedtime. Counting, numbers.

Puss and boots ill. by author. Minedition, 2014. ISBN 978-988824071-5 Subj: Animals – cats. Behavior – resourcefulness. Careers – shoemakers. Character traits – cleverness. Folk & fairy tales. Monsters.

Imbody, Amy. *Snug as a bug?* ill. by Mike Gordon. Zondervan, 2001. ISBN 978-0-310-70063-0 Subj: Bedtime. Rhyming text.

Imershein, Betsy. *Trucks* photos by author. Simon & Schuster, 2000. ISBN 978-0-689-82887-4 Subj: Format, unusual – board books. Trucks.

In daddy's arms I am tall ill. by Javaka Steptoe. Lee & Low, 1997. ISBN 978-1-880000-31-1 Subj: Ethnic groups in the U.S. – African Americans. Family life – fathers. Poetry.

Inches, Alison. *Corduroy writes a letter* ill. by Allan Eitzen. Based on the character created by Don Freeman. Viking, 2002. ISBN 978-0-670-03548-9 Subj: Activities – writing. Letters, cards. Toys – bears.

Corduroy's garden ill. by Allan Eitzen. Based on the character created by Don Freeman. Viking, 2002. ISBN 978-0-670-03547-2 Subj: Gardens, gardening. Plants. Toys – bears.

Corduroy's hike ill. by Allan Eitzen. Based on the character created by Don Freeman. Viking, 2001. ISBN 978-0-670-88945-7 Subj: Activities – walking. Behavior – lost. Toys – bears.

I'm not little! ill. by Glenn Thomas. little bee, 2017. ISBN 978-149980377-8 Subj: Character traits – smallness. Emotions – anger. Monsters.

The stuffed animals get ready for bed ill. by Bryan Langdo. Harcourt, 2006. ISBN 978-0-15-216466-9 Subj: Bedtime. Rhyming text. Toys.

Ingalls, Ann. *The little piano girl: the story of Mary Lou Williams, jazz legend* by Ann Ingalls and Maryann Macdonald ill. by Giselle Potter. Houghton Mifflin, 2010. ISBN 978-0-618-95974-7 Subj: Careers – musicians. Ethnic groups in the U.S. – African Americans. Music. Musical instruments – pianos.

Inkpen, Deborah. *Harriet and the little fat fairy* ill. by author. Barron's, 2002. ISBN 978-0-7641-5562-8 Subj: Animals – hamsters. Fairies. Holidays – Christmas. Pets.

Inkpen, Mick. *The great pet sale* ill. by author. Orchard, 1999. ISBN 978-0-531-30130-2 Subj: Animals. Money. Pets.

Hissss! ill. by author. Harcourt, 2000. ISBN 978-0-15-202415-4 Subj: Animals – dogs. Seasons – summer.

Honk! ill. by author. Harcourt, 1998. ISBN 978-0-15-202284-6 Subj: Animals – dogs. Birds – geese. Noise, sounds.

I will love you anyway ill. by Chloë Inkpen. Aladdin, 2016. ISBN 978-148147099-5 Subj: Animals – dogs. Behavior – misbehavior.

Jasper's beanstalk (Butterworth, Nick)

Kipper ill. by author. Little, 1992. ISBN 978-0-316-41883-6 Subj: Animals – dogs. Behavior – imitation. Sleep.

Kipper and Roly ill. by author. Harcourt, 2001. ISBN 978-0-15-216344-0 Subj: Animals – dogs. Animals – hamsters. Animals – pigs. Birthdays. Gifts. Pets.

Kipper's A to Z ill. by author. Harcourt, 2000. ISBN 978-0-15-202594-6 Subj: ABC books. Animals. Animals – dogs. Animals – pigs.

Kipper's birthday ill. by author. Harcourt, 1993. ISBN 978-0-15-200503-0 Subj: Animals – dogs. Behavior – mistakes. Birthdays. Parties.

Kipper's book of colors ill. by author. Harcourt, 1995. ISBN 978-0-15-200647-1 Subj: Animals – dogs. Concepts – color.

Kipper's book of numbers ill. by author. Harcourt, 1995. ISBN 978-0-15-200646-4 Subj: Animals. Animals – dogs. Counting, numbers.

Kipper's book of opposites ill. by author. Harcourt, 1995. ISBN 978-0-15-200668-6 Subj: Animals – dogs. Concepts – opposites. Language.

Kipper's book of weather ill. by author. Harcourt, 1995. ISBN 978-0-15-200644-0 Subj: Animals – dogs. Weather.

Kipper's Christmas eve ill. by author. Harcourt, 1999. ISBN 978-0-15-202660-8 Subj: Animals – dogs. Format, unusual – toy & movable books. Friendship. Holidays – Christmas.

Kipper's monster ill. by author. Harcourt, 2002. ISBN 978-0-15-216614-4 Subj: Animals – dogs. Camps, camping. Monsters.

Kipper's rainy day ill. by Stuart Trotter. Based on the books by Mick Inkpen. Harcourt, 2001. ISBN 978-0-15-216351-8 Subj: Animals – dogs. Format, unusual – toy & movable books. Weather – rain.

Kipper's snowy day ill. by author. Harcourt, 1996. ISBN 978-0-15-201362-2 Subj: Activities – playing. Animals – dogs. Friendship. Toys. Weather – snow.

Kipper's sunny day ill. by Stuart Trotter. Based on the books by Mick Inkpen. Harcourt, 2002. ISBN 978-0-15-216357-0 Subj: Animals – dogs. Format, unusual – toy & movable books. Sea & seashore – beaches.

Kipper's toybox ill. by author. Harcourt, 1992. ISBN 978-0-15-200501-6 Subj: Animals – dogs. Animals – mice. Counting, numbers. Toys.

Meow! ill. by author. Harcourt, 2000. ISBN 978-0-15-202666-0 Subj: Animals. Animals – cats. Animals – dogs.

Nothing ill. by author. Orchard, 1998. ISBN 978-0-531-30076-3 Subj: Names. Self-concept. Toys.

Picnic ill. by author. Harcourt, 2001. ISBN 978-0-15-216319-8 Subj: Activities – picnicking. Animals. Animals – dogs.

Sandcastle ill. by author. Harcourt, 1998. ISBN 978-0-15-202296-9 Subj: Sand. Sea & seashore.

Splosh! ill. by author. Harcourt, 1998. ISBN 978-0-15-202299-0 Subj: Animals – dogs. Weather – rain.

Swing! ill. by author. Harcourt, 2000. ISBN 978-0-15-202672-1 Subj: Activities – playing. Animals – dogs. Friendship.

Thing ill. by author. Harcourt, 2001. ISBN 978-0-15-216326-6 Subj: Animals – dogs. Bubbles. Toys.

Wibbly Pig can make a tent ill. by author. Golden, 1995. ISBN 978-0-307-16628-9 Subj: Activities – making things. Activities – playing. Animals –

pigs. Camps, camping. Format, unusual – board books.

Wibbly Pig is upset ill. by author. Golden, 1995. ISBN 978-0-307-16629-6 Subj: Animals – pigs. Emotions. Format, unusual – board books.

Wibbly Pig likes bananas ill. by author. Golden, 1995. ISBN 978-0-307-16630-2 Subj: Animals – pigs. Food. Format, unusual – board books.

Wibbly Pig opens his presents ill. by author. Golden, 1995. ISBN 978-0-307-16627-2 Subj: Animals – pigs. Format, unusual – board books. Gifts.

Inns, Christopher. *Next! please* ill. by author. Tricycle, 2001. ISBN 978-1-58246-038-3 Subj: Illness. Toys.

International Center for Assault Prevention. *My body belongs to me from my head to my toes* ill. by Dagmar Geisler. Sky Pony, 2014. ISBN 978-162636345-8 Subj: Child abuse. Health & fitness. Safety. Self-concept. Senses – touch.

Intrater, Roberta Grobel. *Peek-a-boo!* ill. by author. Scholastic, 1997. ISBN 978-0-590-05896-4 Subj: Babies, toddlers. Family life. Format, unusual – board books. Games.

Smile! ill. by author. Scholastic, 1997. ISBN 978-0-590-05899-5 Subj: Babies, toddlers. Family life. Format, unusual – board books.

Intriago, Patricia. *Dot* ill. by author. Farrar, 2011. ISBN 978-0-374-31835-2 Subj: Concepts – opposites.

Ipcizade, Catherine. *'Twas the Day before Zoo Day* ill. by Ben Hodson. Sylvan Dell, 2008. ISBN 978-1-934359-08-2 Subj: Animals. Rhyming text. Zoos.

Irving, John. *A sound like someone trying not to make a sound* ill. by Tatjana Hauptmann. Random House, 2004. ISBN 978-0-385-90910-5 Subj: Animals – mice. Bedtime. Family life – fathers. Monsters. Noise, sounds.

Irving, Washington. *The legend of Sleepy Hollow* retold by Diane Wolkstein; ill. by R. W. Alley. Morrow, 1987. ISBN 978-0-688-06533-1 Subj: Folk & fairy tales. Holidays – Halloween.

The legend of Sleepy Hollow retold by Robert D. San Souci; ill. by Daniel San Souci. Doubleday, 1986. ISBN 978-0-385-23397-2 Subj: Folk & fairy tales. Holidays – Halloween.

Irwin, Michael. *Bears in my bed* ill. by author. Bennett, 2000. ISBN 978-0-8069-7535-1 Subj: Animals – bears. Imagination. Rhyming text.

Isaacs, Anne. *Dust Devil* ill. by Paul O. Zelinsky. Random House, 2010. ISBN 978-0-375-86722-4 Subj: Animals – horses, ponies. Tall tales. U.S. history – frontier & pioneer life.

Meanwhile, back at the ranch ill. by Kevin Hawkes. Random House, 2014. ISBN 978-037586745-3 Subj: Humorous stories. Tall tales. U.S. history – frontier & pioneer life.

Pancakes for supper! ill. by Mark Teague. Scholastic, 2006. ISBN 978-0-439-64483-9 Subj: Animals. Character traits – cleverness. Food. Tall tales.

Swamp Angel ill. by Paul O. Zelinsky. Dutton, 1994. ISBN 978-0-525-45271-3 Subj: Caldecott award honor books. Tall tales. U.S. history – frontier & pioneer life.

Isaak, Armond. *Armond goes to a party: a book about Asperger's and friendship* (Carlson, Nancy)

Isabella, Jude. *The red bicycle: the extraordinary story of one ordinary bicycle* ill. by Simone Shin. Kids Can, 2015. ISBN 978-177138023-2 Subj: Character traits – helpfulness. Ecology. Foreign lands – Burkina Faso. Money. Sports – bicycling.

Isadora, Rachel. *ABC pop!* ill. by author. Viking, 1999. ISBN 978-0-670-88329-5 Subj: ABC books. Art.

At the crossroads ill. by author. Greenwillow, 1991. ISBN 978-0-688-05271-3 Subj: Emotions. Family life. Foreign lands – South Africa.

Bea at ballet ill. by author. Penguin, 2012. ISBN 978-0-399-25409-3 Subj: Ballet. School.

Bea in The Nutcracker ill. by author. Penguin/ Nancy Paulsen, 2015. ISBN 978-039925231-0 Subj: Activities – dancing. Babies, toddlers. Ballet.

Ben's trumpet ill. by author. Greenwillow, 1979. ISBN 978-0-688-80194-6 Subj: Caldecott award honor books. Ethnic groups in the U.S. – African Americans. Music. Musical instruments – trumpets.

Bring on that beat ill. by author. Putnam, 2001. ISBN 978-0-399-23232-9 Subj: Ethnic groups in the U.S. – African Americans. Music. Rhyming text.

Caribbean dream ill. by author. Putnam, 1998. ISBN 978-0-399-23230-5 Subj: Dreams. Foreign lands – Caribbean Islands. Islands.

Happy belly, happy smile ill. by author. Harcourt, 2009. ISBN 978-0-15-206546-1 Subj: Ethnic groups in the U.S. – Chinese Americans. Family life – grandfathers. Food. Restaurants.

I hear a pickle: (and smell, see, touch, and taste it, too!) ill. by author. Penguin/Nancy Paulsen, 2016. ISBN 978-039916049-3 Subj: Senses.

I just want to say good night ill. by author. Penguin/Nancy Paulsen, 2017. ISBN 978-039917384-4 Subj: Bedtime. Foreign lands – Africa.

Jake at gymnastics ill. by author. Penguin/Nancy Paulsen, 2014. ISBN 978-039916048-6 Subj: Sports – gymnastics.

Lili at ballet ill. by author. Putnam, 1993. ISBN 978-0-399-22423-2 Subj: Activities – dancing. Ballet.

Lili on stage ill. by author. Putnam, 1995. ISBN 978-0-399-22637-3 Subj: Activities – dancing. Ballet. Careers – dancers. Theater.

Listen to the city ill. by author. Putnam, 2000. ISBN 978-0-399-23047-9 Subj: Cities, towns. Noise, sounds.

Luke goes to bat ill. by author. Penguin, 2005. ISBN 978-0-399-23604-4 Subj: Character traits – perseverance. Ethnic groups in the U.S. – African Americans. Family life – grandmothers. Sports – baseball.

Nick plays baseball ill. by author. Putnam, 2001. ISBN 978-0-399-23231-2 Subj: Sports – baseball.

Not just tutus ill. by author. Putnam, 2003. ISBN 978-0-399-23603-7 Subj: Activities – dancing. Ballet. Rhyming text.

Old Mikamba had a farm ill. by author. Penguin/Nancy Paulsen, 2013. ISBN 978-0-399-25740-7 Subj: Animals. Cumulative tales. Farms. Foreign lands – Africa. Songs.

123 pop! ill. by author. Viking, 2000. ISBN 978-0-670-88859-7 Subj: Counting, numbers.

Over the green hills ill. by author. Greenwillow, 1992. ISBN 978-0-688-10510-5 Subj: Activities – traveling. Communities, neighborhoods. Family life – grandmothers. Foreign lands – South Africa.

Peekaboo bedtime ill. by author. Putnam, 2008. ISBN 978-0-399-24384-4 Subj: Bedtime. Ethnic groups in the U.S. – African Americans. Games.

Peekaboo morning ill. by author. Putnam, 2002. ISBN 978-0-399-23602-0 Subj: Ethnic groups in the U.S. – African Americans. Games.

Say hello! ill. by author. Penguin, 2010. ISBN 978-0-399-25230-3 Subj: Cities, towns. Communities, neighborhoods. Foreign languages.

Sophie skates ill. by author. Putnam, 1999. ISBN 978-0-399-23046-2 Subj: Sports – ice skating.

A South African night ill. by author. Greenwillow, 1998. ISBN 978-0-688-11390-2 Subj: Animals. Foreign lands – Africa. Foreign lands – South Africa. Jungle. Night.

There was a tree ill. by author. Penguin, 2012. ISBN 978-0-399-25741-4 Subj: Cumulative tales. Foreign lands – Africa. Nature. Songs.

Twelve days of Christmas (The twelve days of Christmas. English folk song)

Uh-oh! ill. by author. Harcourt, 2008. ISBN 978-0-15-205765-7 Subj: Behavior – misbehavior. Ethnic groups in the U.S. – African Americans.

What a family! ill. by author. Penguin, 2006. ISBN 978-0-399-24254-0 Subj: Family life.

Yo, Jo! ill. by author. Harcourt, 2007. ISBN 978-0-15-205783-1 Subj: Communities, neighborhoods. Ethnic groups in the U.S. – African Americans. Family life – brothers & sisters. Family life – grandfathers. Language.

Isern, Susanna. *The lonely mailman* ill. by Daniel Montero Galan. Cuento de Luz, 2017. ISBN 978-841614798-4 Subj: Animals – badgers. Careers – postal workers. Character traits – kindness. Emotions – loneliness. Letters, cards.

Middle bear ill. by Manon Gauthier. Kids Can, 2017. ISBN 978-177138842-9 Subj: Character traits – perseverance. Family life – brothers. Self-concept.

Isherwood, Shirley. *Flora the frog* ill. by Anna C. Leplar. Peachtree, 2000. ISBN 978-1-56145-223-1 Subj: Frogs & toads. School. Theater.

Ishida, Sanae. *Little Kunoichi, the ninja girl* ill. by author. Sasquatch, 2015. ISBN 978-157061954-0 Subj: Character traits – cooperation. Character traits – persistence. Contests. Sports – martial arts.

Ismail, Yasmeen. *I'm a girl!* ill. by author. Bloomsbury, 2016. ISBN 978-161963975-1 Subj: Animals – donkeys. Character traits – individuality. Gender roles. Self-concept.

Imagine that! ill. by author. Bloomsbury, 2017. ISBN 978-168119362-5 Subj: Activities – playing. Animals – bears. Family life – grandfathers. Imagination. Rhyming text.

Specs for Rex ill. by author. Bloomsbury, 2015. ISBN 978-161963710-8 Subj: Animals – lions. Glasses. School – nursery.

Time for bed, Fred! ill. by author. Bloomsbury, 2014. ISBN 978-080273597-3 Subj: Animals – dogs. Bedtime. Behavior – misbehavior.

Isol. *Petit, the monster* ill. by author. Groundwood, 2010. ISBN 978-0-88899-947-4 Subj: Behavior – misbehavior.

Isop, Laurie. *How do you hug a porcupine?* ill. by Gwen Millward. Simon & Schuster, 2011. ISBN 978-1-4424-1291-0 Subj: Animals. Hugging. Rhyming text.

Issa, Kai Jackson. *Howard Thurman's great hope* ill. by Arthur L. Dawson. Lee & Low, 2008. ISBN 978-1-60060-249-8 Subj: Ethnic groups in the U.S. – African Americans. Prejudice. U.S. history.

Issa, Kobayashi. *Today and today* ill. by G. Brian Karas. Scholastic, 2007. ISBN 978-0-439-59078-5 Subj: Foreign lands – Japan. Nature. Poetry. Seasons.

Itaya, Satoshi. *Buttons and Bo* ill. by author. North-South, 2004. ISBN 978-0-7358-1883-5 Subj: Animals – bears. Behavior – lost. Family life – brothers. Forest, woods. Sibling rivalry.

Ivanko, John D. *Animal friends: a global celebration of children and their animals* (Ajmera, Maya)

Back to school (Ajmera, Maya)

Come out and play (Ajmera, Maya)

To be a kid (Ajmera, Maya)

I've seen the promised land ill. by Leonard Jenkins. HarperCollins, 2004. ISBN 978-0-06-027704-8 Subj: Careers – clergy. Ethnic groups in the U.S. – African Americans. Religion. U.S. history.

Ives, Penny. *Celestine, drama queen* ill. by author. Scholastic, 2009. ISBN 978-0-545-08149-8 Subj: Birds – ducks. Emotions – fear. Theater.

Rabbit pie ill. by author. Penguin, 2006. ISBN 978-0-670-05951-5 Subj: Animals – rabbits. Bedtime.

Ivey, Randall. *Jay and the bounty of books* ill. by Chuck Galey. Pelican, 2007. ISBN 978-1-58980-372-5 Subj: Books, reading. Giants. Libraries.

Ivimey, John William. *The complete story of the three blind mice* ill. by Paul Galdone. Clarion, 1987. ISBN 978-0-89919-481-3 Subj: Animals – mice. Music. Nursery rhymes. Songs.

Three blind mice ill. by Victoria Chess. Little, 1990. ISBN 978-0-316-13867-3 Subj: Animals – mice. Music. Nursery rhymes. Songs.

Iwai, Melissa. *Pizza day* ill. by author. Holt/Christy Ottaviano, 2017. ISBN 978-162779790-0 Subj: Activities – baking, cooking. Family life – fathers. Food. Gardens, gardening.

Soup day ill. by author. Henry Holt, 2010. ISBN 978-0-8050-9004-8 Subj: Activities – baking, cooking. Family life – mothers. Food.

Iwamura, Kazuo. *Bedtime in the forest* ill. by author. NorthSouth, 2010. ISBN 978-0-7358-2310-5 Subj: Animals – squirrels. Bedtime. Birds – owls.

Hooray for fall! ill. by author. NorthSouth, 2009. ISBN 978-0-7358-2252-8 Subj: Animals – squirrels. Seasons – fall.

Hooray for snow! ill. by author. NorthSouth, 2009. ISBN 978-0-7358-2219-1 Subj: Animals – squirrels. Birds. Seasons – winter. Weather – snow.

Hooray for spring! ill. by author. NorthSouth, 2009. ISBN 978-0-7358-2228-3 Subj: Animals – squirrels. Seasons – spring.

Hooray for summer! ill. by author. NorthSouth, 2010. ISBN 978-0-7358-2285-6 Subj: Animals – squirrels. Seasons – summer. Weather – storms.

Iyengar, Malathi Michelle. *Romina's rangoli* ill. by Jennifer Wanardi. Shen's, 2007. ISBN 978-1-885008-32-9 Subj: Character traits – individuality. Ethnic groups in the U.S. – East Indian Americans. Ethnic groups in the U.S. – Mexican Americans. School.

Tan to tamarind: poems about the color brown ill. by Jamel Akib. Children's Book Press, 2009. ISBN 978-0-89239-227-8 Subj: Anatomy – skin. Concepts – color. Poetry.

Jack and the beanstalk. *Jack and the beanstalk* retold by Anthea Bell; ill. by Aljoscha Blau. NorthSouth, 2000. ISBN 978-0-7358-1375-5 Subj: Folk & fairy tales. Foreign lands – England. Giants. Plants.

Jack and the beanstalk retold by Maggie Moore; ill. by Steve Cox. Picture Window, 2003. ISBN 978-1-4048-0059-5 Subj: Folk & fairy tales. Giants. Plants.

Jack and the beanstalk retold by Nina Crews; ill. by reteller. Henry Holt, 2011. ISBN 978-0-8050-8765-9 Subj: Cities, towns. Folk & fairy tales. Giants. Plants.

Jack and the beanstalk ill. by Julek Heller. Doubleday, 1992. ISBN 978-0-385-30693-5 Subj: Folk & fairy tales. Giants. Plants.

Jack and the beanstalk retold by John Howe; ill. by reteller. Little, 1989. ISBN 978-0-316-37579-5 Subj: Folk & fairy tales. Giants. Plants.

Jack and the beanstalk retold by Steven Kellogg; ill. by reteller. Morrow, 1991. ISBN 978-0-688-10251-7 Subj: Folk & fairy tales. Giants. Plants.

Jack and the beanstalk retold by Albert Lorenz; ill. by reteller. Abrams, 2002. ISBN 978-0-8109-1160-4 Subj: Folk & fairy tales. Giants. Plants.

Jack and the beanstalk retold by Richard Walker; ill. by Niamh Sharkey. Barefoot, 1999. ISBN 978-1-902283-13-5 Subj: Folk & fairy tales. Giants. Plants.

Jack and the beanstalk retold by Ann Keay Beneduce; ill. by Gennady Spirin. Philomel, 1999. ISBN 978-0-399-23118-6 Subj: Folk & fairy tales. Giants. Plants.

Jack and the beanstalk retold by E. Nesbit; ill. by Matt Tavares. Candlewick, 2006. ISBN 978-0-7636-2124-7 Subj: Folk & fairy tales. Giants. Plants.

Jack and the beanstalk and the french fries by Mark Teague; ill. by author. Scholastic/Orchard, 2017. ISBN 978-054591431-4 Subj: Folk & fairy tales. Food. Gardens, gardening. Giants. Plants.

Jacques and de beanstalk by Mike Artell; ill. by Jim Harris. Penguin, 2010. ISBN 978-0-8037-2816-5 Subj: Folk & fairy tales. Giants. Plants. Rhyming text.

Jackson, Alison. *The ballad of Valentine* ill. by Tricia Tusa. Dutton, 2002. ISBN 978-0-525-46720-5 Subj: Holidays – Valentine's Day. Rhyming text.

I know an old lady who swallowed a pie ill. by Judith Byron Schachner. Dutton, 1997. ISBN 978-0-525-45645-2 Subj: Cumulative tales. Folk & fairy tales. Food. Holidays – Thanksgiving. Humorous stories. Rhyming text.

If the shoe fits ill. by Karla Firehammer. Henry Holt, 2001. ISBN 978-0-8050-6466-7 Subj: Homes, houses. Nursery rhymes. Rhyming text.

Thea's tree ill. by Janet Pedersen. Dutton, 2008. ISBN 978-0-525-47443-2 Subj: Folk & fairy tales. Letters, cards. Plants.

When the wind blew ill. by Doris Barrette. Henry Holt, 2014. ISBN 978-080508688-1 Subj: Behavior – lost & found possessions. Nursery rhymes. Rhyming text. Weather – wind.

Jackson, Byron. *The saggy baggy elephant* (Jackson, Kathryn)

Jackson, Chris. *The Gaggle sisters river tour* ill. by author. Lobster, 2002. ISBN 978-1-894222-58-7 Subj: Birds – geese. Character traits – pride. Family life – sisters.

Jackson, Ellen. *Abe Lincoln loved animals* ill. by Doris Ettlinger. Albert Whitman, 2008. ISBN 978-0-8075-0123-8 Subj: Character traits – kindness to animals. Pets. U.S. history.

April ill. by Kay Life. Charlesbridge, 2002. ISBN 978-0-88106-908-2 Subj: Days of the week, months of the year. Holidays. Seasons – spring. Weather.

August ill. by Pat DeWitt and Robin DeWitt. Charlesbridge, 2002. ISBN 978-0-88106-921-1 Subj: Days of the week, months of the year. Holidays. Seasons – summer. Weather.

The autumn equinox ill. by Jan Davey Ellis. Millbrook, 2000. ISBN 978-0-7613-1354-0 Subj: Fairs, festivals. Holidays. Seasons – fall.

Beastly babies ill. by Brendan Wenzel. Simon & Schuster/Beach Lane, 2015. ISBN 978-144240834-0 Subj: Animals – babies. Rhyming text.

Cinder Edna ill. by Kevin O'Malley. Lothrop, 1994. ISBN 978-0-688-12323-9 Subj: Folk & fairy tales. Royalty – princes.

December ill. by Pat DeWitt and Robin DeWitt. Charlesbridge, 2002. ISBN 978-0-88106-958-7 Subj: Days of the week, months of the year. Holidays. Seasons – winter. Weather.

Earth Mother ill. by Leo and Diane Dillon. Walker, 2005. ISBN 978-0-8027-8993-8 Subj: Ecology. Nature. World.

February ill. by Pat DeWitt and Robin DeWitt. Charlesbridge, 2002. ISBN 978-0-88106-996-9 Subj: Days of the week, months of the year. Holidays. Seasons – winter. Weather.

January ill. by Pat DeWitt and Robin DeWitt. Charlesbridge, 2002. ISBN 978-0-88106-995-2 Subj: Days of the week, months of the year. Holidays. Seasons – winter. Weather.

July ill. by Pat DeWitt and Robin DeWitt. Charlesbridge, 2002. ISBN 978-0-88106-920-4 Subj: Days of the week, months of the year. Holidays. Seasons – summer. Weather.

June ill. by Kay Life. Charlesbridge, 2002. ISBN 978-0-88106-919-8 Subj: Days of the week, months of the year. Holidays. Seasons – summer. Weather.

March ill. by Kay Life. Charlesbridge, 2002. ISBN 978-0-88106-905-1 Subj: Days of the week, months of the year. Holidays. Seasons – spring. Weather.

May ill. by Kay Life. Charlesbridge, 2002. ISBN 978-0-88106-918-1 Subj: Days of the week, months of the year. Holidays. Seasons – spring. Weather.

November ill. by Pat DeWitt and Robin DeWitt. Charlesbridge, 2002. ISBN 978-0-88106-927-3 Subj: Days of the week, months of the year. Holidays. Seasons – fall. Weather.

October ill. by Pat DeWitt and Robin DeWitt. Charlesbridge, 2002. ISBN 978-0-88106-923-5 Subj: Days of the week, months of the year. Holidays. Seasons – fall. Weather.

Octopuses one to ten ill. by Robin Page. Simon & Schuster/Beach Lane, 2016. ISBN 978-148143182-8 Subj: Counting, numbers. Octopuses.

September ill. by Pat DeWitt and Robin DeWitt. Charlesbridge, 2002. ISBN 978-0-88106-922-8 Subj: Days of the week, months of the year. Holidays. Seasons – fall. Weather.

The seven seas ill. by Bill Slavin and Esperança Melo. Eerdmans, 2011. ISBN 978-0-8028-5341-7 Subj: Animals – rabbits. Concepts – color. Geography. Imagination. Rhyming text. Sea & seashore.

Sometimes bad things happen photos by Shelley Rotner. Millbrook, 2002. ISBN 978-0-7613-2810-0 Subj: Behavior – bad day, bad mood. Character traits – helpfulness. Emotions. Emotions – happiness.

The spring equinox ill. by Jan Davey Ellis. Millbrook, 2002. ISBN 978-0-7613-1955-9 Subj: Holidays. Seasons – spring.

The summer solstice ill. by Jan Davey Ellis. Millbrook, 2001. ISBN 978-0-7613-1623-7 Subj: Holidays. Seasons – summer.

The winter solstice ill. by Jan Davey Ellis. Millbrook, 1994. ISBN 978-1-56294-400-1 Subj: Holidays. Seasons – winter.

Jackson, Emma. *A home for Dixie: the true story of a rescued puppy* photos by Bob Carey. Collins, 2008. ISBN 978-0-06-144962-8 Subj: Animals – dogs. Character traits – kindness to animals.

Jackson, Gwen. *Lump Lump and the blanket of dreams: inspired by Navajo culture and folklore* ill. by Lissa Calvert. Friesen, 2016. ISBN 978-146026438-6 Subj: Animals – bears. Hibernation. Indians of North America – Navajo.

Jackson, Isaac. *Somebody's new pajamas* ill. by David Soman. Dial, 1996. ISBN 978-0-8037-1549-3 Subj: Clothing – pajamas. Ethnic groups in the U.S. – African Americans. Family life. Friendship. Sleepovers.

Jackson, Jill. *Let there be peace on earth: and let it begin with me* by Jill Jackson and Sy Miller ill. by David Diaz. Tricycle, 2009. ISBN 978-1-58246-285-1 Subj: Character traits – cooperation. Songs. Violence, nonviolence. World.

Jackson, Kathryn. *The golden circus book* ill. by Alice Provensen and Martin Provensen. Random House, 2005. ISBN 978-0-375-83215-4 Subj: Circus. Format, unusual – board books.

Pantaloon ill. by Steven Salerno. Random House, 2010. ISBN 978-0-375-85624-2 Subj: Activities – baking, cooking. Animals – dogs. Careers – bakers. Character traits – helpfulness.

The saggy baggy elephant by Kathryn Jackson and Byron Jackson ill. by Tenggren. Golden, 2003. ISBN 978-0-375-92590-0 Subj: Animals – elephants. Behavior – worrying.

Jackson, Richard. *All ears, all eyes* ill. by Katherine Tillotson. Atheneum/Caitlyn Dlouhy, 2017. ISBN 978-148141571-2 Subj: Animals. Bedtime. Forest, woods. Night. Noise, sounds. Rhyming text. Senses – hearing. Senses – sight.

Have a look, says Book ill. by Kevin Hawkes. Atheneum, 2016. ISBN 978-148142105-8 Subj: Books, reading. Rhyming text.

In plain sight ill. by Jerry Pinkney. Roaring Brook/Neal Porter, 2016. ISBN 978-162672255-2 Subj: Behavior – hiding things. Ethnic groups in the U.S. – African Americans. Family life – grandfathers. Games. Picture puzzles.

Snow scene ill. by Laura Vaccaro Seeger. Roaring Brook/Neal Porter, 2017. ISBN 978-162672680-2 Subj: Character traits – questioning. Rhyming text. Seasons.

This beautiful day ill. by Suzy Lee. Atheneum/Caitlyn Dlouhy, 2017. ISBN 978-148144139-1 Subj: Activities – playing. Rhyming text. Weather – rain.

Jackson, Shelley. *Mimi's Dada Catifesto* ill. by author. Clarion, 2010. ISBN 978-0-547-12681-4 Subj: Animals – cats. Art.

Jackson, Shirley. *9 magic wishes* ill. by Miles Hyman. Farrar, 2001. ISBN 978-0-374-35525-8 Subj: Behavior – wishing. Magic.

Jacobs, Francine. *Lonesome George, the giant tortoise* ill. by Jean Cassels. Walker, 2003. ISBN 978-0-8027-8865-8 Subj: Animals – endangered animals. Foreign lands – Galapagos Islands. Reptiles – turtles, tortoises.

Jacobs, Joseph. *King of the cats: a ghost story* adapt. by Paul Galdone; ill. by adapter. Houghton, 1980. ISBN 978-0-395-29030-9 Subj: Animals – cats. Folk & fairy tales. Ghosts.

The three sillies adapt. by Steven Kellogg; ill. by adapter. Candlewick, 1999. ISBN 978-0-7636-0811-8 Subj: Animals. Animals – pigs. Character traits – foolishness. Folk & fairy tales.

Jacobs, Julie. *My heart is a magic house* ill. by Bernadette Pons. Albert Whitman, 2007. ISBN 978-0-8075-5335-0 Subj: Behavior – worrying. Emotions – love. Family life – new sibling.

Jacobs, Paul DuBois. *Abiyoyo returns* (Seeger, Pete)

Count on the subway by Paul DuBois Jacobs and Jennifer Swender ill. by Dan Yaccarino. Knopf, 2014. ISBN 978-030797923-0 Subj: Counting, numbers. Rhyming text. Trains.

The deaf musicians (Seeger, Pete)

Fire drill by Paul DuBois Jacobs and Jennifer Swender ill. by Huy Voun Lee. Henry Holt, 2010. ISBN 978-0-8050-8953-0 Subj: Fire. Rhyming text. Safety. School.

Some friends to feed: the story of Stone Soup (Seeger, Pete)

Jadoul, Emile. *All by myself!* ill. by author. Eerdmans, 2012. ISBN 978-0-8028-5411-7 Subj: Behavior – growing up. Birds – penguins. Family life. Toilet training.

Good night, Chickie ill. by author. Eerdmans, 2011. ISBN 978-0-8028-5378-3 Subj: Bedtime. Behavior – worrying. Birds – chickens, roosters. Family life – mothers.

No room for baby!. Kids Can, 2017. ISBN 978-177138841-2 Subj: Birds – penguins. Family life – new sibling.

Jaffe, Nina. *The golden flower: a Taino myth from Puerto Rico* ill. by Enrique O. Sánchez. Simon & Schuster, 1996. ISBN 978-0-02-747585-2 Subj: Creation. Folk & fairy tales. Foreign lands – Puerto Rico. Indians of North America – Taino.

In the month of Kislev: a story for Hanukkah ill. by Louise August. Viking, 1992. ISBN 978-0-670-82863-0 Subj: Folk & fairy tales. Holidays – Hanukkah. Jewish culture.

Tales for the seventh day ill. by Kelly Stribling Sutherland. Scholastic, 2000. ISBN 978-0-590-12054-8 Subj: Folk & fairy tales. Jewish culture. Religion.

The way meat loves salt: a Cinderella tale from the Jewish tradition ill. by Louise August. Henry Holt, 1998. ISBN 978-0-8050-4384-6 Subj: Emotions – love. Family life – fathers. Folk & fairy tales. Foreign lands – Europe. Jewish culture. Weddings.

Jagtenberg, Yvonne. *Jack the wolf* ill. by author. Roaring Brook, 2002. ISBN 978-0-7613-2855-1 Subj: Animals – wolves. Humorous stories. School – first day. Self-concept.

Jack's kite ill. by author. Roaring Brook, 2004. ISBN 978-0-7613-2940-4 Subj: Camps, camping. Kites.

Jack's rabbit ill. by author. Roaring Brook, 2003. ISBN 978-0-7613-2916-9 Subj: Activities – drawing. Animals – rabbits. Behavior – running away. Pets.

Jahn-Clough, Lisa. *Alicia's best friends* ill. by author. Houghton, 2003. ISBN 978-0-618-23951-1 Subj: Friendship.

Felicity and Cordelia: a tale of two bunnies ill. by author. Farrar, 2011. ISBN 978-0-374-32300-4 Subj: Activities – ballooning. Activities – traveling. Animals – rabbits. Friendship.

Little dog ill. by author. Houghton, 2006. ISBN 978-0-618-57405-6 Subj: Animals – dogs. Careers – artists.

Missing Molly ill. by author. Houghton, 2000. ISBN 978-0-618-00980-0 Subj: Behavior – hiding. Friendship. Games.

On the hill ill. by author. Houghton, 2004. ISBN 978-0-618-40741-5 Subj: Animals. Emotions – loneliness. Homes, houses.

Simon and Molly plus Hester ill. by author. Houghton, 2001. ISBN 978-0-618-08220-9 Subj: Friendship.

Jakes, John. *Susanna of the Alamo* ill. by Paul Bacon. Harcourt, 1986. ISBN 978-0-15-200595-5 Subj: Character traits – bravery. U.S. history – frontier & pioneer life.

Jalali, Reza. *Moon watchers: Shirin's Ramadan miracle* ill. by Anne Sibley O'Brien. Tilbury House, 2010. ISBN 978-0-88448-321-2 Subj: Family life – brothers & sisters. Holidays – Ramadan. Religion.

James, Ann. *Bird and Bear* ill. by author. little bee, 2015. ISBN 978-149980037-1 Subj: Animals – bears. Birds. Friendship.

James, Betsy. *Tadpoles* ill. by author. Dutton, 1999. ISBN 978-0-525-46197-5 Subj: Animals – babies. Behavior. Frogs & toads.

James, Brian. *Supertwins and the sneaky, slimy book worms* ill. by Chris L. Demarest. Scholastic, 2004. ISBN 978-0-613-72181-3 Subj: Animals – worms. Family life – brothers & sisters. Multiple births – twins. School.

The Supertwins and tooth trouble ill. by Chris L. Demarest. Scholastic, 2003. ISBN 978-0-439-46624-0 Subj: Crime. Fairies. Family life – brothers & sisters. Multiple births – twins. Teeth.

The Supertwins meet the bad dogs from space ill. by Chris L. Demarest. Scholastic, 2003. ISBN 978-0-439-46623-3 Subj: Animals – dogs. Family life – brothers & sisters. Multiple births – twins. Mythical creatures.

Supertwins meet the dangerous dino-robots ill. by Chris L. Demarest. Scholastic, 2003. ISBN 978-0-439-46625-7 Subj: Careers – scientists. Dinosaurs. Family life – brothers & sisters. Multiple births – twins. Robots.

James, J. Alison, adapt. *The bears' Christmas surprise* ill. by Angela Kehlenbeck. NorthSouth, 2000. ISBN 978-0-7358-1364-9 Subj: Emotions – loneliness. Holidays – Christmas. Toys – bears.

James, Simon. *Baby Brains and RoboMom* ill. by author. Candlewick, 2008. ISBN 978-0-7636-3463-6 Subj: Babies, toddlers. Humorous stories. Inventions. Robots.

The birdwatchers ill. by author. Candlewick, 2002. ISBN 978-0-7636-1676-2 Subj: Birds. Family life – grandfathers.

Dear Mr. Blueberry ill. by author. Macmillan, 1991. ISBN 978-0-689-50529-4 Subj: Animals – whales. Careers – teachers. Imagination. Letters, cards.

George flies south ill. by author. Candlewick, 2011. ISBN 978-0-7636-5724-6 Subj: Activities – flying. Behavior – growing up. Birds.

Little One Step ill. by author. Candlewick, 2003. ISBN 978-0-7636-2070-7 Subj: Birds – ducks. Family life – brothers. Games.

Nurse Clementine ill. by author. Candlewick, 2013. ISBN 978-0-7636-6382-7 Subj: Careers – nurses. Family life.

Rex ill. by author. Candlewick, 2016. ISBN 978-076367294-2 Subj: Dinosaurs. Family life – fathers.

Jamieson, Victoria. *Olympig! the triumphant story of an underdog* ill. by author. Dial, 2012. ISBN 978-0-8037-3536-1 Subj: Animals. Animals – pigs. Self-concept. Sports – Olympics.

Jamison, Jocelyn. *Drac's night out* ill. by Bill Basso. Price Stern Sloan, 2001. ISBN 978-0-8431-4393-5 Subj: Monsters.

Jane, Pamela. *Little elfie one* ill. by Jane Manning. HarperCollins/Balzer+Bray, 2015. ISBN 978-006220673-2 Subj: Counting, numbers. Holidays – Christmas. Rhyming text.

Little goblins ten ill. by Jane Manning. HarperCollins, 2011. ISBN 978-0-06-176798-2 Subj: Counting, numbers. Holidays – Halloween. Monsters. Mythical creatures.

Milo and the fire engine parade ill. by Meredith Johnson. Mondo, 2002. ISBN 978-1-59034-192-6 Subj: Animals – dogs. Careers – firefighters. Parades. Trucks.

Milo and the greatest trick ever ill. by Meredith Johnson. Mondo, 2002. ISBN 978-1-59034-187-2 Subj: Animals – cats. Magic. Theater.

Monster countdown ill. by Nick Zarin-Ackerman. Mondo, 2001. ISBN 978-1-58653-857-6 Subj: Counting, numbers. Monsters. Rhyming text.

Monster mischief ill. by Vera Rosenberry. Atheneum, 2001. ISBN 978-0-689-80471-7 Subj: Holidays – Halloween. Monsters. Rhyming text.

Janeczko, Paul B. *Firefly July: a year of very short poems* ill. by Melissa Sweet. Candlewick, 2014. ISBN 978-076364842-8 Subj: Poetry. Seasons.

Janice. *Little Bear marches in the St. Patrick's Day parade* ill. by Mariana. Lothrop, 1967. Subj: Animals – bears. Holidays – St. Patrick's Day. Parades.

Little Bear's Christmas ill. by Mariana. Lothrop, 1964. ISBN 978-0-688-51076-3 Subj: Animals – bears. Character traits – generosity. Hibernation. Holidays – Christmas.

Little Bear's Thanksgiving ill. by Mariana. Lothrop, 1967. ISBN 978-0-688-51078-7 Subj: Animals – bears. Holidays – Thanksgiving.

Janisch, Heinz. *The merry pranks of Till Eulenspiegel* ill. by Lisbeth Zwerger. NorthSouth, 2001. ISBN 978-1-55858-806-6 Subj: Behavior – trickery. Folk & fairy tales. Foreign lands – Germany.

Jankel, Karen. *Paddington Bear goes to the hospital* (Bond, Michael)

Janni, Rebecca. *Every cowgirl goes to school* ill. by Lynne Avril. Dial, 2013. ISBN 978-0-8037-3937-6 Subj: Cowboys, cowgirls. Friendship. School – first day.

Every cowgirl loves a rodeo. Dial, 2012. ISBN 978-0-8037-3734-1 Subj: Cowboys, cowgirls. Fairs, festivals. Rodeos. Sports – bicycling. Sportsmanship.

Every cowgirl needs a horse ill. by Lynne Avril. Penguin, 2010. ISBN 978-0-525-42164-1 Subj: Birthdays. Cowboys, cowgirls. Imagination.

Every cowgirl needs dancing boots ill. by Lynne Avril. Penguin, 2011. ISBN 978-0-525-42341-6 Subj: Activities – dancing. Character traits – compromising. Cowboys, cowgirls. Emotions – loneliness. Friendship.

Janousky, Peggy Robbins. *Move it, Miss Macintosh!* ill. by Meghan Lands. Annick, 2016. ISBN 978-155451863-0 Subj: Careers – teachers. School – first day.

Janovitz, Marilyn. *A, B, see!* ill. by author. Chronicle, 2005. ISBN 978-0-8118-4673-8 Subj: ABC books. Animals. Format, unusual – toy & movable books.

Baby, Baby, Baby! ill. by author. Sourcebooks, 2010. ISBN 978-1-4022-4414-8 Subj: Babies, toddlers. Format, unusual – board books.

Play baby play! ill. by author. Sourcebooks, 2012. ISBN 978-1-4022-6224-1 Subj: Activities – playing. Babies, toddlers. Rhyming text.

We love school! ill. by author. NorthSouth, 2007. ISBN 978-0-7358-2112-5 Subj: Animals – cats. Rhyming text. School.

Janowitz, Tama. *Hear that?* ill. by Tracy Dockray. SeaStar, 2001. ISBN 978-1-58717-075-1 Subj: Family life – mothers. Noise, sounds.

Jantzen, Doug. *Henry Hyena, why won't you laugh?* ill. by Jean Claude. Aladdin, 2015. ISBN 978-148142822-4 Subj: Animals – hyenas. Behavior – bullying, teasing. Character traits – kindness. Rhyming text. Zoos.

Jaramillo, Susie. *Elefantitos / little elephants* ill. by author. Encantos, 2016. ISBN 978-099699591-7 Subj: Animals – elephants. Foreign languages.

Format, unusual – board books. Nursery rhymes. Spiders.

Little skeletons / Esqueletitos : countdown to midnight / un libro para contar en el Día de los Muertos ill. by author. Encantos, 2017. ISBN 978-194563506-9 Subj: Anatomy – skeletons. Clocks, watches. Foreign languages. Format, unusual – toy & movable books. Holidays – Day of the Dead. Time.

Jarka, Jeff. *Love that kitty! the story of a boy who wanted to be a cat* ill. by author. Henry Holt, 2010. ISBN 978-0-8050-9053-6 Subj: Animals – cats. Family life. Imagination. Pets.

Love that puppy! the story of a boy who wanted to be a dog ill. by author. Henry Holt, 2009. ISBN 978-0-8050-8741-3 Subj: Animals – dogs. Family life. Imagination. Pets.

Jarman, Julia. *Class Two at the zoo* ill. by Lynne Chapman. Carolrhoda, 2007. ISBN 978-0-8225-7132-2 Subj: Reptiles – snakes. Rhyming text. School – field trips. Zoos.

Two shy pandas ill. by Susan Varley. Andersen, 2013. ISBN 978-1-46771-141-8 Subj: Animals – pandas. Character traits – shyness. Rhyming text.

Jarrett, Clare. *Arabella Miller's tiny caterpillar* ill. by author. Candlewick, 2008. ISBN 978-0-7636-3660-9 Subj: Insects – butterflies, caterpillars. Metamorphosis. Rhyming text.

The best picnic ever ill. by author. Candlewick, 2004. ISBN 978-0-7636-2370-8 Subj: Activities – picnicking. Activities – playing. Animals.

Jarvis , Peter. *Alan's big, scary teeth* ill. by Peter Jarvis. Candlewick, 2016. ISBN 978-076368120-3 Subj: Behavior – secrets. Reptiles – alligators, crocodiles. Teeth.

Lazy Dave ill. by Peter Jarvis. HarperCollins, 2015. ISBN 978-006235598-0 Subj: Animals – dogs. Sleep.

Jaspersohn, William. *The two brothers* ill. by Michael A. Donato. Vermont Folklife Center, 2000. ISBN 978-0-916718-16-9 Subj: Ethnic groups in the U.S. – German Americans. Family life – brothers. Farms. Immigrants, immigration.

Javaherbin, Mina. *Elephant in the dark* ill. by Eugene Yelchin. Scholastic, 2015. ISBN 978-054563670-4 Subj: Animals – elephants. Folk & fairy tales. Foreign lands – India.

Goal! ill. by A. G. Ford. Candlewick, 2010. ISBN 978-0-7636-4571-7 Subj: Behavior – bullying, teasing. Foreign lands – South Africa. Friendship. Sports – soccer.

The secret message ill. by Bruce Whatley. Hyperion/Disney, 2010. ISBN 978-1-4231-1044-6 Subj:

Birds – parakeets, parrots. Folk & fairy tales. Foreign lands – Iran.

Soccer star ill. by Renato Alarcao. Candlewick, 2014. ISBN 978-076366056-7 Subj: Family life – brothers & sisters. Foreign lands – Brazil. Poverty. Sports – soccer.

Javernick, Ellen. *The birthday pet* ill. by Kevin O'Malley. Marshall Cavendish, 2009. ISBN 978-0-7614-5522-6 Subj: Pets. Reptiles – turtles, tortoises.

What if everybody did that? ill. by Colleen M. Madden. Marshall Cavendish, 2010. ISBN 978-0-7614-5686-5 Subj: Behavior. Character traits.

Jay, Alison. *Bee and me* ill. by author. Candlewick, 2017. ISBN 978-076369010-6 Subj: Cities, towns. Friendship. Insects – bees. Wordless.

Christmastime ill. by author. Dial, 2012. ISBN 978-0-8037-3804-1 Subj: Holidays – Christmas. Language. Picture puzzles.

The nutcracker (Hoffmann, E. T. A)

1 2 3: a child's first counting book ill. by author. Penguin, 2007. ISBN 978-0-525-47836-2 Subj: Counting, numbers. Dreams. Folk & fairy tales.

Out of the blue ill. by author. Barefoot, 2014. ISBN 978-178285042-7 Subj: Character traits – kindness to animals. Sea & seashore – beaches. Wordless.

Red green blue: a first book of colors ill. by author. Penguin, 2010. ISBN 978-0-525-42303-4 Subj: Concepts – color. Nursery rhymes. Picture puzzles. Rhyming text.

Welcome to the zoo ill. by author. Dial, 2008. ISBN 978-0-8037-3177-6 Subj: Animals. Wordless. Zoos.

Jay, Betsy. *Jane vs. the Tooth Fairy* ill. by Lori Osiecki. Rising Moon, 2000. ISBN 978-0-87358-739-6 Subj: Fairies. Teeth.

Jeffers, Oliver. *A child of books* by Oliver Jeffers and Sam Winston; ill. by Oliver Jeffers. Candlewick, 2016. ISBN 978-076369077-9 Subj: Books, reading. Imagination.

The great paper caper ill. by author. Philomel, 2009. ISBN 978-0-399-25097-2 Subj: Activities – making things. Animals. Animals – bears. Ecology. Paper. Trees.

The heart and the bottle ill. by author. Penguin, 2010. ISBN 978-0-399-25452-9 Subj: Death. Emotions – grief. Emotions – loneliness.

Here we are: notes for living on planet earth ill. by author. Philomel, 2017. ISBN 978-039916789-8 Subj: Earth. Ecology.

The Hueys in It wasn't me ill. by author. Philomel, 2014. ISBN 978-000742067-4 Subj: Behavior –

fighting, arguing. Character traits – individuality. Self-concept.

The Hueys in None the number: a counting adventure ill. by author. Philomel, 2014. ISBN 978-039925769-8 Subj: Counting, numbers.

The Hueys in The new sweater ill. by author. Philomel, 2012. ISBN 978-0-399-25767-4 Subj: Character traits – individuality. Clothing – sweaters. Self-concept.

The Hueys in What's the opposite? ill. by author. Philomel, 2016. ISBN 978-039925770-4 Subj: Concepts – opposites.

The incredible book eating boy ill. by author. Penguin, 2007. ISBN 978-0-399-24749-1 Subj: Books, reading. Food.

Lost and found ill. by author. Penguin, 2006. ISBN 978-0-399-24503-9 Subj: Behavior – lost. Birds – penguins. Emotions – loneliness. Foreign lands – Antarctic. Friendship.

Stuck ill. by author. Penguin, 2011. ISBN 978-0-399-25737-7 Subj: Humorous stories. Kites. Trees.

This moose belongs to me ill. by author. Philomel, 2012. ISBN 978-0-399-16103-2 Subj: Animals – moose. Pets.

Up and down. Penguin, 2010. ISBN 978-0-399-25545-8 Subj: Activities – flying. Birds – penguins. Friendship.

The way back home ill. by author. Philomel, 2008. ISBN 978-0-399-25074-3 Subj: Aliens. Character traits – helpfulness. Friendship. Moon. Space & space ships.

Jeffers, Susan. *Forest of dreams* (Wells, Rosemary)

Jingle bells ill. by author. HarperCollins, 2017. ISBN 978-006236020-5 Subj: Holidays – Christmas. Music. Songs.

My Chincoteague pony ill. by author. Hyperion, 2008. ISBN 978-1-4231-0023-2 Subj: Animals – horses, ponies.

The twelve days of Christmas ill. by author. HarperCollins, 2013. ISBN 978-0-06-206615-2 Subj: Gifts. Holidays – Christmas. Magic. Santa Claus.

Jeffs, Stephanie. *Jenny: coming to terms with the death of a sibling* ill. by Jacqui Thomas. Abingdon, 2006. ISBN 978-0-687-49709-6 Subj: Death. Emotions – grief. Family life – brothers & sisters. Illness. Religion.

Josh: coming to terms with the death of a friend ill. by Jacqui Thomas. Abingdon, 2006. ISBN 978-0-687-49719-5 Subj: Death. Emotions – grief. Friendship. Religion.

Jenkins, Emily. *Daffodil* ill. by Tomasz Bogacki. Farrar, 2004. ISBN 978-0-374-31676-1 Subj: Character traits – individuality. Clothing – dresses. Family life – sisters. Multiple births – triplets.

Daffodil, crocodile ill. by Tomasz Bogacki. Farrar, 2007. ISBN 978-0-374-39944-3 Subj: Character traits – individuality. Family life – sisters. Imagination. Multiple births – triplets.

A fine dessert: four centuries, four families, one delicious treat ill. by Sophie Blackall. Random House, 2015. ISBN 978-037586832-0 Subj: Activities – baking, cooking. Food. U.S. history.

Five creatures ill. by Tomasz Bogacki. Farrar, 2001. ISBN 978-0-374-32341-7 Subj: Animals – cats. Family life.

The fun book of scary stuff ill. by Hyewon Yum. Farrar/Frances Foster, 2015. ISBN 978-037430000-5 Subj: Animals – dogs. Emotions – fear.

A greyhound, a groundhog ill. by Chris Appelhans. Random House, 2017. ISBN 978-055349805-9 Subj: Animals – dogs. Animals – groundhogs. Rhyming text. Tongue twisters.

Lemonade in winter: a book about two kids counting money ill. by G. Brian Karas. Random House, 2012. ISBN 978-0-375-85883-3 Subj: Counting, numbers. Family life – brothers & sisters. Money. Seasons – winter.

Love you when you whine ill. by Sergio Ruzzier. Farrar, 2006. ISBN 978-0-374-34652-2 Subj: Animals – cats. Behavior – misbehavior. Emotions – love. Family life – mothers.

Num, num, num! a Bea and Haha book ill. by Tomasz Bogacki. Farrar, 2006. ISBN 978-0-374-30583-3 Subj: Animals – ferrets. Animals – hippopotamuses. Format, unusual – board books. Friendship.

Plonk, plonk, plonk! a Bea and Haha book ill. by Tomasz Bogacki. Farrar, 2006. ISBN 978-0-374-30585-7 Subj: Animals – ferrets. Animals – hippopotamuses. Format, unusual – board books. Friendship. Music.

Princessland ill. by Yoko Tanaka. Farrar, 2017. ISBN 978-037436115-0 Subj: Animals – cats. Behavior – bad day, bad mood. Behavior – boredom. Imagination. Royalty – princesses.

Skunkdog ill. by Pierre Pratt. Farrar, 2008. ISBN 978-0-374-37009-1 Subj: Animals – dogs. Animals – skunks. Friendship.

Small medium large ill. by Tomasz Bogacki. Star Bright, 2011. ISBN 978-1-59572-278-2 Subj: Concepts – size. Language.

That new animal ill. by Pierre Pratt. Farrar, 2005. ISBN 978-0-374-37443-3 Subj: Animals – dogs. Babies, toddlers.

Tiger and Badger ill. by Marie-Louise Gay. Candlewick, 2016. ISBN 978-076366604-0 Subj:

Animals – badgers. Animals – tigers. Behavior – fighting, arguing. Friendship.

Toys meet snow: being the wintertime adventures of a curious stuffed buffalo, a sensitive plush stingray, and a book-loving rubber ball ill. by Paul O. Zelinsky. Random House, 2015. ISBN 978-038537330-2 Subj: Activities – playing. Seasons – winter. Toys. Weather – snow.

Up, up, up! a Bea and Haha book ill. by Tomasz Bogacki. Farrar, 2006. ISBN 978-0-374-30584-0 Subj: Animals – ferrets. Animals – hippopotamuses. Character traits – helpfulness. Format, unusual – board books. Friendship.

Water in the park: a book about water and the times of the day ill. by Stephanie Graegin. Random House, 2013. ISBN 978-0-375-87002-6 Subj: Day. Parks. Water.

What happens on Wednesdays ill. by Lauren Castillo. Farrar, 2007. ISBN 978-0-374-38303-9 Subj: Day. Family life.

Jenkins, Martin. *Can we save the tiger?* ill. by Vicky White. Candlewick, 2011. ISBN 978-0-7636-4909-8 Subj: Animals – endangered animals. Nature.

Fabulous frogs ill. by Tim Hopgood. Candlewick, 2016. ISBN 978-076368100-5 Subj: Frogs & toads.

Jenkins, Priscilla Belz. *Falcons nest on skyscrapers* ill. by Megan Lloyd. HarperCollins, 1996. ISBN 978-0-06-021105-9 Subj: Animals – endangered animals. Birds – falcons. Cities, towns.

A nest full of eggs ill. by Lizzy Rockwell. HarperCollins, 1995. ISBN 978-0-06-023442-3 Subj: Birds – robins. Eggs. Science.

Jenkins, Steve. *Actual size* ill. by author. Houghton, 2004. ISBN 978-0-618-37594-3 Subj: Anatomy. Animals. Concepts – size.

Almost gone: the world's rarest animals ill. by author. HarperCollins, 2006. ISBN 978-0-06-053600-8 Subj: Animals – endangered animals.

Animals in flight by Steve Jenkins and Robin Page; ill. by Steve Jenkins. Houghton, 2001. ISBN 978-0-618-12351-3 Subj: Activities – flying. Animals. Birds. Dinosaurs. Insects.

Animals upside down: a pull, pop, lift and learn book! by Steve Jenkins and Robin Page; ill. by Steve Jenkins. Houghton Mifflin, 2013. ISBN 978-0-547-34127-9 Subj: Animals. Format, unusual – toy & movable books.

Big and little ill. by author. Houghton, 1996. ISBN 978-0-395-72664-8 Subj: Animals. Concepts – size.

Biggest, strongest, fastest ill. by author. Ticknor & Fields, 1995. ISBN 978-0-395-69701-6 Subj: Animals. Concepts.

Creature features: 25 animals explain why they look the way they do by Steve Jenkins and Robin Page; ill. by Steve Jenkins. Houghton, 2014. ISBN 978-054423351-5 Subj: Anatomy. Animals. Character traits – appearance.

Dogs and cats ill. by author. Houghton, 2007. ISBN 978-0-618-50767-2 Subj: Animals – cats. Animals – dogs. Format, unusual.

Eye to eye: how animals see the world ill. by author. Houghton, 2014. ISBN 978-054795907-8 Subj: Anatomy – eyes. Animals.

Flying frogs and walking fish: leaping lemurs, tumbling toads, jet-propelled jellyfish, and more surprising ways that animals move by Steve Jenkins and Robin Page; ill. by Steve Jenkins. Houghton Mifflin Harcourt, 2016. ISBN 978-054463090-1 Subj: Animals. Nature.

Hottest, coldest, highest, deepest ill. by author. Houghton, 1998. ISBN 978-0-395-89999-1 Subj: Earth. Geography.

How many ways can you catch a fly? (Page, Robin)

How to clean a hippopotamus: a look at unusual animal partnerships by Steve Jenkins and Robin Page; ill. by Steve Jenkins. Houghton Mifflin, 2010. ISBN 978-0-547-24515-7 Subj: Animals. Nature. Science.

How to swallow a pig: step-by-step advice from the animal kingdom by Steve Jenkins and Robin Page; ill. by Steve Jenkins. Houghton Mifflin Harcourt, 2015. ISBN 978-054431365-1 Subj: Animals. Character traits – questioning. Nature.

I see a kookaburra by Steve Jenkins and Robin Page; ill. by Steve Jenkins. Houghton, 2005. ISBN 978-0-618-50764-1 Subj: Animals. Ecology. Picture puzzles.

Just a second: a different way to look at time ill. by author. Houghton Mifflin, 2011. ISBN 978-0-618-70896-3 Subj: Nature. Time.

Living color ill. by author. Houghton, 2007. ISBN 978-0-618-70897-0 Subj: Animals. Concepts – color.

Move! by Steve Jenkins and Robin Page; ill. by Steve Jenkins. Houghton, 2006. ISBN 978-0-618-64637-1 Subj: Animals. Concepts – motion. Language.

My first day: what animals do on day one by Steve Jenkins and Robin Page; ill. by Steve Jenkins. Houghton Mifflin, 2013. ISBN 978-0-547-73851-2 Subj: Animals – babies.

Never smile at a monkey: and 17 other important things to remember ill. by author. Houghton, 2009. ISBN 978-0-618-96620-2 Subj: Animals.

Perros y gatos / dogs and cats ill. by author. Juventud, 2008. ISBN 978-84-26-13669-5 Subj: Animals – cats. Animals – dogs. Foreign languages. Format, unusual.

Prehistoric actual size ill. by author. Houghton, 2005. ISBN 978-0-618-53578-1 Subj: Anatomy. Animals. Concepts – size. Prehistory.

Sisters and brothers: sibling relationships in the animal world (Page, Robin)

Slap, squeak, and scatter ill. by author. Houghton, 2001. ISBN 978-0-618-03376-8 Subj: Animals. Communication. Noise, sounds.

Time for a bath by Steve Jenkins and Robin Page; ill. by Steve Jenkins. Houghton Mifflin, 2011. ISBN 978-0-547-25037-3 Subj: Activities – bathing. Animals.

Time to eat by Steve Jenkins and Robin Page; ill. by Steve Jenkins. Houghton Mifflin, 2011. ISBN 978-0-547-25032-8 Subj: Animals. Food.

Time to sleep by Steve Jenkins and Robin Page; ill. by Steve Jenkins. Houghton Mifflin, 2011. ISBN 978-0-547-25040-3 Subj: Animals. Sleep.

What do you do when something wants to eat you? ill. by author. Houghton, 1997. ISBN 978-0-395-82514-3 Subj: Animals.

What do you do with a tail like this? ill. by author. Houghton, 2003. ISBN 978-0-618-25628-0 Subj: Anatomy. Animals. Caldecott award honor books. Games. Senses.

Who am I? an animal guessing game by Steve Jenkins and Robin Page; ill. by Steve Jenkins. Houghton Mifflin Harcourt, 2017. ISBN 978-054493539-6 Subj: Animals. Character traits – questioning.

Jenks, Deneen. *Flowers from Mariko* (Noguchi, Rick)

Jennewein, Lenore. *Chick-o-Saurus Rex* ill. by Daniel Jennewein. Simon & Schuster, 2013. ISBN 978-1-4424-5186-5 Subj: Animals. Behavior – bullying, teasing. Birds – chickens, roosters. Character traits – bravery. Dinosaurs.

Jennings, Jazz. *I am Jazz* (Herthel, Jessica)

Jennings, Linda. *Hide and seek birthday treat* ill. by Joanne Partis. Barron's, 2001. ISBN 978-0-7641-5336-5 Subj: Animals. Animals – leopards. Behavior – hiding. Birthdays. Games. Jungle. Parties. Rhyming text.

Little puppy lost ill. by Alison Edgson. Good Books, 2008. ISBN 978-1-56148-635-9 Subj: Animals – dogs. Behavior – lost. Weather – snow.

Jennings, Patrick. *Bat and Rat* ill. by Matthew Cordell. Abrams, 2012. ISBN 978-1-4197-0160-3 Subj: Animals – bats. Animals – rats. Friendship. Music.

Naughty Claudine's Christmas ill. by Suzanne Kaufman. Random House, 2017. ISBN 978-110193734-1 Subj: Behavior – misbehavior. Holidays – Christmas.

Jennings, Sharon. *Bearcub and Mama* ill. by Mélanie Watt. Kids Can, 2005. ISBN 978-1-55337-566-1 Subj: Animals – bears. Family life – mothers. Family life – sons. Weather – storms.

C'mere, boy! ill. by Ashley Spires. Kids Can, 2010. ISBN 978-1-55453-440-1 Subj: Animals – dogs. Humorous stories.

Franklin forgives ill. by Céléste Gagnon, et al. Based on the Franklin books by Paulette Bourgeois & Brenda Clark. Kids Can, 2004. ISBN 978-0-439-62159-5 Subj: Animals. Behavior – forgiving. Reptiles – turtles, tortoises.

Franklin goes to the hospital ill. by Brenda Clark. Based on the Franklin books by Paulette Bourgeois & Brenda Clark. Kids Can, 2000. ISBN 978-1-55074-732-4 Subj: Hospitals. Illness. Reptiles – turtles, tortoises.

Franklin makes a deal ill. by Sean Jeffrey, et al. Based on the Franklin books by Paulette Bourgeois & Brenda Clark. Kids Can, 2003. ISBN 978-1-55337-469-5 Subj: Activities – trading. Animals. Reptiles – turtles, tortoises.

Franklin wants a badge ill. by Sean Jeffrey, et al. Based on the Franklin books by Paulette Bourgeois & Brenda Clark. Kids Can, 2003. ISBN 978-1-55337-467-1 Subj: Animals. Friendship. Reptiles – turtles, tortoises. Sleepovers.

Franklin's class trip (Bourgeois, Paulette)

Franklin's Thanksgiving ill. by Brenda Clark. Based on the Franklin books by Paulette Bourgeois & Brenda Clark. Scholastic, 2001. ISBN 978-1-55074-798-0 Subj: Family life – grandparents. Holidays – Thanksgiving. Reptiles – turtles, tortoises.

The happily ever afternoon ill. by Ron Lightburn. Annick, 2006. ISBN 978-1-55037-945-7 Subj: Imagination.

No monsters here ill. by Ruth Ohi. Fitzhenry & Whiteside, 2004. ISBN 978-1-55041-787-6 Subj: Bedtime. Emotions – fear. Family life – fathers.

Priscilla and Rosy ill. by Linda Hendry. Fitzhenry & Whiteside, 2001. ISBN 978-1-55041-676-3 Subj: Animals – rats. Character traits – loyalty. Friendship.

Priscilla's paw de deux ill. by Linda Hendry. Fitzhenry & Whiteside, 2002. ISBN 978-1-55041-718-0 Subj: Activities – dancing. Animals – cats. Animals – rats. Ballet. Character traits – cooperation. Emotions – fear.

Jensen, Dana. *A meal of the stars: poems up and down* ill. by Tricia Tusa. Houghton Mifflin, 2012. ISBN 978-0-547-39007-9 Subj: Poetry.

Jensen, Sara. *Be glad your dad . . . is not an octopus!* (Logelin, Matthew)

Jenson-Elliott, Cindy. *Antsy Ansel: Ansel Adams, a life in nature* ill. by Christy Hale. Henry Holt, 2016. ISBN 978-162779082-6 Subj: Activities – photographing. Art. Careers – photographers. Nature.

Dig in! ill. by Mary Peterson. Simon & Schuster, 2016. ISBN 978-144241261-3 Subj: Activities – digging.

Jeppson, Ann-Sofie. *Here comes Pontus* ill. by Catarina Kruusval. R&S Books, 2000. ISBN 978-91-29-64561-3 Subj: Animals – horses, ponies. Farms.

You're growing up, Pontus ill. by Catarina Kruusval. Farrar, 2001. ISBN 978-91-29-65393-9 Subj: Animals – horses, ponies. Behavior – growing up.

Jeram, Anita. *I love my little storybook* ill. by author. Candlewick, 2002. ISBN 978-0-7636-1698-4 Subj: Animals – rabbits. Books, reading. Imagination.

Jessell, Tim. *Falcon* ill. by author. Random House, 2012. ISBN 978-0-375-86866-5 Subj: Activities – flying. Birds – falcons. Imagination.

Jesset, Aurore. *Loopy* ill. by Barbara Korthues. NorthSouth, 2008. ISBN 978-0-7358-2175-0 Subj: Behavior – lost & found possessions. Toys.

Jewel. *Sweet dreams* ill. by Amy Bates. Simon & Schuster, 2013. ISBN 978-1-4424-8931-8 Subj: Bedtime. Lullabies. Rhyming text. Songs.

That's what I'd do ill. by Amy Bates. Simon & Schuster, 2012. ISBN 978-1-4424-5813-0 Subj: Bedtime. Family life – mothers. Lullabies.

Jewell, Nancy. *Alligator wedding* ill. by J. Rutland. Henry Holt, 2010. ISBN 978-0-8050-6819-1 Subj: Reptiles – alligators, crocodiles. Rhyming text. Swamps. Weddings.

Jeyaveeran, Ruth. *The road to Mumbai* ill. by author. Houghton, 2004. ISBN 978-0-618-43419-0 Subj: Animals – monkeys. Foreign lands – India. Imagination.

Jiang, Ji-li. *Lotus and Feather* ill. by Julie Downing. Disney/Hyperion, 2016. ISBN 978-142312754-3 Subj: Birds – cranes. Character traits – kindness to animals. Emotions – loneliness. Family life – grandfathers.

The magical Monkey King, mischief in heaven ill. by Hui Hui Su-Kennedy. HarperCollins, 2002. ISBN 978-0-06-029544-8 Subj: Animals – monkeys. Folk & fairy tales. Foreign lands – China.

Red kite, blue kite ill. by Greg Ruth. Disney/Hyperion, 2013. ISBN 978-1-4231-2753-6 Subj: Family life – fathers. Foreign lands – China. Kites.

Jiménez, Francisco. *The Christmas gift / El regalo de Navidad* ill. by Claire B. Cotts. Houghton, 2000. ISBN 978-0-395-92869-1 Subj: Character traits – kindness. Ethnic groups in the U.S. – Mexican Americans. Foreign languages. Holidays – Christmas. Immigrants, immigration.

Jin, Susie Lee. *Mine!* ill. by author. Simon & Schuster, 2016. ISBN 978-148142772-2 Subj: Animals – rabbits. Behavior – fighting, arguing. Behavior – sharing. Character traits – selfishness.

Jobling, Curtis. *Frankenstein's cat* ill. by author. Simon & Schuster, 2001. ISBN 978-0-689-84695-3 Subj: Animals – cats. Animals – dogs. Humorous stories.

Jocelyn, Marthe. *ABC x 3: english, espanol, francais* ill. by Tom Slaughter. Tundra, 2005. ISBN 978-0-88776-707-4 Subj: ABC books. Foreign languages.

A day with Nellie ill. by author. Tundra, 2002. ISBN 978-0-88776-600-8 Subj: Activities – playing. Toys.

Eats ill. by Tom Slaughter. Tundra, 2007. ISBN 978-0-88776-820-0 Subj: Animals. Food.

Hannah and the seven dresses ill. by author. Dutton, 1999. ISBN 978-0-525-46113-5 Subj: Birthdays. Clothing – dresses.

Hannah's Collections ill. by author. Dutton, 2000. ISBN 978-0-525-46442-6 Subj: Behavior – collecting things. School.

Mayfly ill. by author. Tundra, 2004. ISBN 978-0-88776-676-3 Subj: Activities – vacationing. Cities, towns. Country. Homes, houses.

Ones and twos by Marthe Jocelyn and Nell Jocelyn; ill. by Marthe Jocelyn. Tundra, 2011. ISBN 978-1-77049-220-2 Subj: Counting, numbers. Friendship. Rhyming text.

Ready for autumn ill. by author. Tundra, 2008. ISBN 978-0-88776-861-3 Subj: Clothing. Format, unusual – board books. Seasons – fall.

Ready for spring ill. by author. Tundra, 2008. ISBN 978-0-88776-849-1 Subj: Clothing. Format, unusual – board books. Seasons – spring.

Ready for summer ill. by author. Tundra, 2008. ISBN 978-0-88776-860-6 Subj: Clothing. Format, unusual – board books. Seasons – summer.

Ready for winter ill. by author. Tundra, 2008. ISBN 978-0-88776-848-4 Subj: Clothing. Format, unusual – board books. Seasons – winter.

Same same ill. by Tom Slaughter. Tundra, 2009. ISBN 978-0-88776-885-9 Subj: Concepts.

Where do you look? by Marthe Jocelyn and Nell Jocelyn; ill. by Marthe Jocelyn. Tundra, 2013. ISBN 978-1-77049-376-6 Subj: Language.

Jocelyn, Nell. *Ones and twos* (Jocelyn, Marthe)

Where do you look? (Jocelyn, Marthe)

Joel, Billy. *New York state of mind* ill. by Izak. Scholastic, 2005. ISBN 978-0-439-55382-7 Subj: Cities, towns. Songs.

Johanasen, Heather. *About the rain forest* by Heather Johanasen and Sindy McKay ill. with photos. Treasure Bay, 2000. ISBN 978-1-891327-23-0 Subj: Ecology. Jungle. Weather – rain.

Johansen, Hanna. *The duck and the owl* ill. by Kathi Bhend. Godine, 2005. ISBN 978-1-56792-285-1 Subj: Birds – ducks. Birds – owls. Friendship.

Johansen, K. V. *Pippin and Pudding* ill. by Bernice Lum. Kids Can, 2001. ISBN 978-1-55074-631-0 Subj: Animals – cats. Animals – dogs. Friendship.

Pippin and the bones ill. by Bernice Lum. Kids Can, 2000. ISBN 978-1-55074-629-7 Subj: Anatomy – skeletons. Fossils. Museums.

Pippin takes a bath ill. by Bernice Lum. Kids Can, 1999. ISBN 978-1-55074-627-3 Subj: Activities – bathing. Animals – dogs.

John, Jory. *The bad seed* ill. by Pete Oswald. HarperCollins, 2017. ISBN 978-006246776-8 Subj: Behavior – bad day, bad mood. Behavior – misbehavior. Emotions – anger. Seeds.

Come home already! ill. by Benji Davies. HarperCollins, 2017. ISBN 978-006237097-6 Subj: Animals – bears. Birds – ducks. Camps, camping. Friendship.

Goodnight already! ill. by Benji Davies. HarperCollins, 2014. ISBN 978-006228620-8 Subj: Animals – bears. Bedtime. Birds – ducks.

I love you already! ill. by Benji Davies. HarperCollins, 2015. ISBN 978-006237095-2 Subj: Animals – bears. Birds – ducks. Character traits – individuality. Friendship.

I will chomp you! ill. by Bob Shea. Random House, 2015. ISBN 978-038538986-0 Subj: Books, reading. Food. Monsters.

Penguin problems ill. by Lane Smith. Random House, 2016. ISBN 978-055351337-0 Subj: Behavior – bad day, bad mood. Behavior – dissatisfaction. Birds – penguins.

Quit calling me a monster! ill. by Bob Shea. Random House, 2016. ISBN 978-038538990-7 Subj: Monsters. Self-concept.

Johnson, Amy Crane. *Cinnamon and the April shower / Canela y el aguacero de abril* ill. by Robb Mommaerts. Raven Tree, 2003. ISBN 978-0-9720192-2-4 Subj: Animals. Birds – ravens. Foreign languages. Forest, woods. Seasons. Weather – storms.

Mason moves away / Mason se muda ill. by Robb Mommaerts. Raven Tree, 2004. ISBN 978-0-9720192-3-1 Subj: Animals – beavers. Birds – ravens. Ecology. Foreign languages. Moving.

Johnson, Angela. *All different now: Juneteenth, the first day of freedom* ill. by E. B. Lewis. Simon & Schuster, 2014. ISBN 978-068987376-8 Subj: Ethnic groups in the U.S. – African Americans. Slavery. Texas. U.S. history.

Daddy calls me man ill. by Rhonda Mitchell. Orchard, 1997. ISBN 978-0-531-33042-5 Subj: Careers – artists. Ethnic groups in the U.S. – African Americans. Family life. Poetry.

The day Ray got away ill. by Luke LaMarca. Simon & Schuster, 2010. ISBN 978-0-689-87375-1 Subj: Behavior – running away. Parades. Toys – balloons.

Do like Kyla ill. by James Ransome. Watts, 1990. ISBN 978-0-531-08452-6 Subj: Ethnic groups in the U.S. – African Americans. Family life – brothers & sisters.

Down the winding road ill. by Shane W. Evans. DK, 2000. ISBN 978-0-7894-2596-6 Subj: Country. Ethnic groups in the U.S. – African Americans. Family life. Friendship.

The girl who wore snakes ill. by James Ransome. Orchard, 1993. ISBN 978-0-531-08641-4 Subj: Animals. Ethnic groups in the U.S. – African Americans. Family life – aunts, uncles. Pets. Reptiles – snakes.

I dream of trains ill. by Loren Long. Simon & Schuster, 2003. ISBN 978-0-689-82609-2 Subj: Activities – working. Dreams. Family life – fathers. Trains.

Joshua by the sea ill. by Rhonda Mitchell. Orchard, 1994. ISBN 978-0-531-06846-5 Subj: Ethnic groups in the U.S. – African Americans. Format, unusual – board books. Sea & seashore.

Joshua's night whispers ill. by Rhonda Mitchell. Orchard, 1994. ISBN 978-0-531-06847-2 Subj: Ethnic groups in the U.S. – African Americans. Family life – fathers. Format, unusual – board books. Night. Noise, sounds.

Julius ill. by Dav Pilkey. Orchard, 1993. ISBN 978-0-531-08615-5 Subj: Animals – pigs. Ethnic groups in the U.S. – African Americans. Family life – grandfathers. Pets.

The leaving morning ill. by David Soman. Orchard, 1992. ISBN 978-0-531-08592-9 Subj: Emotions. Ethnic groups in the U.S. – African Americans. Family life. Moving.

Lily Brown's paintings ill. by E. B. Lewis. Scholastic, 2007. ISBN 978-0-439-78225-8 Subj: Activities – painting. Ethnic groups in the U.S. – African Americans. Imagination.

Lottie Paris and the best place ill. by Scott M. Fischer. Simon & Schuster, 2013. ISBN 978-0-689-87378-2 Subj: Books, reading. Ethnic groups in the U.S. – African Americans. Friendship. Libraries.

Lottie Paris lives here ill. by Scott M. Fischer. Simon & Schuster, 2011. ISBN 978-0-689-87377-5 Subj: Activities. Behavior. Day. Ethnic groups in the U.S. – African Americans. Family life – fathers. Imagination.

One of three ill. by David Soman. Watts, 1991. ISBN 978-0-531-08555-4 Subj: Ethnic groups in the U.S. – African Americans. Family life – sisters.

Rain feet ill. by Rhonda Mitchell. Orchard, 1994. ISBN 978-0-531-06849-6 Subj: Ethnic groups in the U.S. – African Americans. Format, unusual – board books. Weather – rain.

The Rolling Store ill. by Peter Catalanotto. Orchard, 1997. ISBN 978-0-531-33015-9 Subj: Careers – peddlers. Ethnic groups in the U.S. – African Americans. Family life – grandfathers. Memories, memory. Stores.

Shoes like Miss Alice's ill. by Ken Page. Orchard, 1995. ISBN 978-0-531-08664-3 Subj: Activities – babysitting. Clothing – shoes. Ethnic groups in the U.S. – African Americans.

A sweet smell of roses ill. by Eric Velasquez. Simon & Schuster, 2005. ISBN 978-0-689-83252-9 Subj: Ethnic groups in the U.S. – African Americans. Family life – sisters. Holidays – Martin Luther King, Jr. Day. U.S. history.

Tell me a story, Mama ill. by David Soman. Watts, 1989. ISBN 978-0-531-08394-9 Subj: Family life – mothers.

Those building men ill. by Mike Benny. Blue Sky, 1999. ISBN 978-0-590-66521-6 Subj: Activities – making things. Careers – construction workers.

Violet's music ill. by Laura Huliska-Beith. Dial, 2004. ISBN 978-0-8037-2740-3 Subj: Careers – musicians. Music. Musical instruments – bands.

The wedding ill. by David Soman. Orchard, 1999. ISBN 978-0-531-33139-2 Subj: Ethnic groups in the U.S. – African Americans. Family life – sisters. Weddings.

When I am old with you ill. by David Soman. Watts, 1990. ISBN 978-0-531-08484-7 Subj: Ethnic groups in the U.S. – African Americans. Family life – grandfathers. Old age.

Wind flyers ill. by Loren Long. Simon & Schuster, 2007. ISBN 978-0-689-84879-7 Subj: Activities – flying. Careers – airplane pilots. Ethnic groups

in the U.S. – African Americans. U.S. history. War.

Johnson, Crockett. *Harold and the purple crayon* ill. by author. HarperCollins, 1955. ISBN 978-0-06-022936-8 Subj: Art. Humorous stories. Imagination.

Harold at the North Pole: a Christmas journey with the purple crayon ill. by author. HarperCollins, 1958. ISBN 978-0-06-028074-1 Subj: Holidays – Christmas. Humorous stories. Imagination. Santa Claus.

Magic beach ill. by author. Boyds Mills, 2005. ISBN 978-1-932425-27-7 Subj: Imagination. Sea & seashore – beaches.

A picture for Harold's room ill. by author. HarperCollins, 1960. ISBN 978-0-06-023006-7 Subj: Art. Humorous stories. Imagination.

Will spring be early or will spring be late? ill. by author. Crowell, 1959. ISBN 978-0-690-89423-3 Subj: Animals – groundhogs. Holidays – Groundhog Day. Seasons – spring.

Johnson, D. B. *Eddie's kingdom* ill. by author. Houghton, 2005. ISBN 978-0-618-56299-2 Subj: Activities – drawing. Behavior – fighting, arguing. Communities, neighborhoods. Homes, houses.

Four legs bad, two legs good! ill. by author. Houghton, 2007. ISBN 978-0-618-80909-7 Subj: Animals. Character traits – laziness. Farms.

Henry builds a cabin ill. by author. Houghton, 2002. ISBN 978-0-618-13201-0 Subj: Animals – bears. Homes, houses. U.S. history.

Henry climbs a mountain ill. by author. Houghton, 2003. ISBN 978-0-618-26902-0 Subj: Animals – bears. Character traits – being different. Imagination. Mountains. Slavery.

Henry hikes to Fitchburg ill. by author. Houghton, 2000. ISBN 978-0-395-96867-3 Subj: Activities – hiking. Activities – walking. U.S. history.

Henry works ill. by author. Houghton, 2004. ISBN 978-0-618-42003-2 Subj: Activities – walking. Activities – working. Activities – writing. Animals – bears. Nature. Weather – rain.

Henry's night by D. B. Johnson and Linda Michelin ill. by D. B. Johnson. Houghton, 2009. ISBN 978-0-547-05663-0 Subj: Animals – bears. Bedtime. Night. Sleep.

Magritte's marvelous hat ill. by D. B. Johnson. Houghton Mifflin, 2012. ISBN 978-0-547-55864-6 Subj: Animals – dogs. Art. Careers – artists. Clothing – hats. Foreign lands – France.

Palazzo inverso ill. by author. Harcourt, 2010. ISBN 978-0-15-23999-6 Subj: Art. Buildings. Careers – artists. Format, unusual.

Johnson, David. *Snow sounds: an onomatopoeic story* ill. by author. Houghton, 2006. ISBN 978-0-618-47310-6 Subj: Holidays – Christmas. Noise, sounds.

Johnson, Dinah. *Black magic* ill. by R. Gregory Christie. Henry Holt, 2010. ISBN 978-0-8050-7833-6 Subj: Ethnic groups in the U.S. – African Americans. Self-concept.

Quinnie Blue ill. by James Ransome. Henry Holt, 2000. ISBN 978-0-8050-4378-5 Subj: Ethnic groups in the U.S. – African Americans. Family life – grandmothers.

Johnson, Dolores. *Now let me fly: the story of a slave family* ill. by author. Macmillan, 1993. ISBN 978-0-02-747699-6 Subj: Ethnic groups in the U.S. – African Americans. Slavery. U.S. history.

Johnson, Doug. *Substitute teacher plans* ill. by Tammy Smith. Henry Holt, 2002. ISBN 978-0-8050-6520-6 Subj: Activities. Careers – teachers. Humorous stories. School.

Johnson, G. Francis. *Has anybody lost a glove?* ill. by Dimitrea Tokunbo. Boyds Mills, 2004. ISBN 978-1-59078-041-1 Subj: Behavior – lost & found possessions. Clothing – gloves, mittens. Communities, neighborhoods.

Johnson, Gillian. *My sister Gracie* ill. by author. Tundra, 2000. ISBN 978-0-88776-514-8 Subj: Animals – dogs. Family life – brothers & sisters. Rhyming text.

Johnson, Grace. *The candle in the window* ill. by Mark Elliott. Fleming H. Revell, 2003. ISBN 978-0-8007-1815-2 Subj: Careers – shoemakers. Character traits – kindness. Foreign lands – Germany. Holidays – Christmas. Religion.

Johnson, James Weldon. *The Creation* ill. by James Ransome. Holiday, 1994. ISBN 978-0-8234-1069-9 Subj: Creation. Ethnic groups in the U.S. – African Americans. Poetry. Religion.

Lift every voice and sing ill. by Bryan Collier. HarperCollins, 2007. ISBN 978-0-06-054147-7 Subj: Ethnic groups in the U.S. – African Americans. Music. Slavery. Songs.

Lift ev'ry voice and sing ill. by Jan Spivey Gilchrist. Scholastic, 1995. ISBN 978-0-590-46982-1 Subj: Ethnic groups in the U.S. – African Americans. Music. Slavery. Songs.

Johnson, Jen Cullerton. *Seeds of change: planting a path to peace* ill. by Sonia Lynn Sadler. Lee & Low, 2010. ISBN 978-1-60060-367-9 Subj: Character traits – responsibility. Ecology. Foreign lands – Kenya. Trees.

Johnson, Lindan Lee. *The dream jar* ill. by Serena Curmi. Houghton, 2005. ISBN 978-0-618-17698-4

Subj: Bedtime. Dreams. Family life – brothers & sisters. Nightmares.

Johnson, Mariana Ruiz. *I know a bear* ill. by author. Random House, 2014. ISBN 978-038538614-2 Subj: Animals – bears. Character traits – kindness to animals. Zoos.

Johnson, Marion. *Caillou, new shoes* adapt. by Éric Sévigny; ill. by CINAR Animation. Chouette, 2002. ISBN 978-2-89450-327-0 Subj: Behavior – growing up. Clothing – shoes. Family life – mothers. Shopping.

Johnson, Neil. *The falling raindrop* by Neil Johnson and Joel Chin; ill. by authors. Tricycle, 2010. ISBN 978-1-58246-312-4 Subj: Behavior – worrying. Water. Weather – rain.

Johnson, Paul Brett. *Bearhide and crow* ill. by author. Holiday, 2000. ISBN 978-0-8234-1470-3 Subj: Activities – trading. Behavior – greed. Birds – crows. Humorous stories.

The cow who wouldn't come down ill. by author. Orchard, 1993. ISBN 978-0-531-08631-5 Subj: Activities – flying. Animals – bulls, cows. Farms.

The goose who went off in a huff ill. by author. Orchard, 2001. ISBN 978-0-439-40842-4 Subj: Animals – babies. Animals – elephants. Birds – geese. Family life – mothers. Humorous stories.

Jack outwits the giants ill. by author. Margaret K. McElderry, 2002. ISBN 978-0-689-83902-3 Subj: Behavior – trickery. Folk & fairy tales. Giants.

Little Bunny Foo Foo: told and sung by the Good Fairy ill. by author. Scholastic, 2004. ISBN 978-0-439-37301-2 Subj: Animals – rabbits. Behavior – misbehavior. Fairies. Humorous stories. Music. Songs.

Lost ill. by Celeste Lewis. Orchard, 1996. ISBN 978-0-531-08851-7 Subj: Animals – dogs. Behavior – lost. Camps, camping. Desert. Pets.

Mr. Persnickety and Cat Lady ill. by author. Orchard, 2000. ISBN 978-0-531-33283-2 Subj: Animals – cats. Animals – mice. Communities, neighborhoods. Problem solving.

Old Dry Fry ill. by author. Scholastic, 1999. ISBN 978-0-590-37658-7 Subj: Careers – clergy. Folk & fairy tales.

On top of spaghetti lyrics by Tom Glazer; ill. by author. Scholastic, 2006. ISBN 978-0-439-74944-2 Subj: Animals. Food. Songs.

The pig who ran a red light ill. by author. Orchard, 1999. ISBN 978-0-531-33136-1 Subj: Activities. Animals – pigs. Behavior.

Johnson, Rebecca. *The proud pelican's secret* photos by Steve Parish. Gareth Stevens, 2005. ISBN 978-

0-8368-5974-4 Subj: Birds – pelicans. Character traits – appearance. Character traits – pride.

Sea turtle's clever plan photos by Steve Parish. Gareth Stevens, 2005. ISBN 978-0-8368-5975-1 Subj: Character traits – cleverness. Reptiles – turtles, tortoises.

Tree frog hears a sound photos by Steve Parish. Gareth Stevens, 2005. ISBN 978-0-8368-5976-8 Subj: Frogs & toads. Jungle.

Johnson, Stephen T. *Alphabet city* ill. by author. Viking, 1995. ISBN 978-0-670-85631-2 Subj: ABC books. Caldecott award honor books. Cities, towns. Concepts.

Alphabet school ill. by author. Simon & Schuster, 2015. ISBN 978-141692521-7 Subj: ABC books. School.

City by numbers ill. by author. Viking, 1998. ISBN 978-0-670-87251-0 Subj: Counting, numbers.

My little blue robot ill. by author. Harcourt, 2002. ISBN 978-0-15-216524-6 Subj: Activities – making things. Format, unusual – toy & movable books. Robots.

Johnson, Suzanne C. *Fribbity ribbit* ill. by Debbie Tilley. Knopf, 2001. ISBN 978-0-375-91199-6 Subj: Family life. Frogs & toads. Humorous stories.

Johnson-Davies, Denys. *Goha, the wise fool* ill. by Hany el Saed Ahmed and Hag Hamdy Mohamed Fattouh. Penguin, 2005. ISBN 978-0-399-24222-9 Subj: Character traits – cleverness. Character traits – foolishness. Folk & fairy tales. Foreign lands – Middle East.

Johnston, Lynn. *Farley follows his nose* by Lynn Johnston and Beth Cruikshank; ill. by Lynn Johnston. Bowen, 2009. ISBN 978-0-06-170234-1 Subj: Animals – dogs. Behavior – lost. Behavior – running away.

Johnston, Tony. *The badger and the magic fan* ill. by Tomie dePaola. Putnam, 1990. ISBN 978-0-399-21945-0 Subj: Anatomy – noses. Animals – badgers. Behavior – trickery. Folk & fairy tales. Foreign lands – Japan. Magic.

The barn owls ill. by Deborah Kogan Ray. Charlesbridge, 2000. ISBN 978-0-88106-981-5 Subj: Barns. Birds – owls. Poetry.

Big red apple ill. by Judith Hoffman Corwin. Scholastic, 1999. ISBN 978-0-439-09860-1 Subj: Circular tales. Plants. Trees.

Bigfoot Cinderrrrrella ill. by James Warhola. Putnam, 1998. ISBN 978-0-399-23021-9 Subj: Folk & fairy tales. Forest, woods. Mythical creatures.

The cat with seven names ill. by Christine Davenier. Charlesbridge, 2013. ISBN 978-1-58089-381-7 Subj: Animals – cats. Communities, neighborhoods. Emotions – loneliness.

Chicken in the kitchen ill. by Eleanor Taylor. Simon & Schuster, 2005. ISBN 978-0-689-85641-9 Subj: Birds – chickens, roosters. Rhyming text.

The cowboy and the black-eyed pea ill. by Warren Ludwig. Putnam, 1992. ISBN 978-0-399-22330-3 Subj: Cowboys, cowgirls. Folk & fairy tales. U.S. history – frontier & pioneer life. Weddings.

Day of the Dead ill. by Jeanette Winter. Harcourt, 1997. ISBN 978-0-15-222863-7 Subj: Foreign lands – Mexico. Holidays – Day of the Dead.

Desert dog ill. by Robert Weatherford. Sierra Club, 2001. ISBN 978-0-87156-979-0 Subj: Animals – dogs. Animals – goats. Desert. Rhyming text.

Desert song ill. by Ed Young. Sierra Club, 2000. ISBN 978-0-87156-491-7 Subj: Animals. Desert. Night.

Farmer Mack measures his pig ill. by Megan Lloyd. HarperCollins, 1986. ISBN 978-0-06-023018-0 Subj: Animals – pigs. Behavior – boasting, showing off. Farms.

First grade, here I come! ill. by David Walker. Scholastic, 2015. ISBN 978-054520143-8 Subj: Animals – mice. School – first day.

The ghost of Nicholas Greebe ill. by S. D. Schindler. Dial, 1996. ISBN 978-0-8037-1649-0 Subj: Anatomy – skeletons. Animals – dogs. Ghosts.

Go track a yak ill. by Tim Raglin. Simon & Schuster, 2003. ISBN 978-0-689-83789-0 Subj: Animals – yaks. Family life – parents. Folk & fairy tales. Humorous stories. Witches.

The iguana brothers, a perfect day ill. by Mark Teague. Blue Sky, 1995. ISBN 978-0-590-47468-9 Subj: Family life – brothers. Foreign lands – Mexico. Reptiles – iguanas.

A Kenya Christmas ill. by Leonard Jenkins. Holiday, 2003. ISBN 978-0-8234-1623-3 Subj: Family life – aunts, uncles. Foreign lands – Kenya. Holidays – Christmas. Santa Claus.

Laugh-out-loud baby ill. by Stephen Gammell. Simon & Schuster, 2012. ISBN 978-1-4424-1380-1 Subj: Babies, toddlers. Family life. Parties.

Levi Strauss gets a bright idea: a fairly fabricated story of a pair of pants ill. by Stacy Innerst. Harcourt, 2011. ISBN 978-0-15-206145-6 Subj: Activities – sewing. Clothing – pants. Tall tales. U.S. history – frontier & pioneer life.

Little Rabbit goes to sleep ill. by Harvey Stevenson. HarperCollins, 1994. ISBN 978-0-06-021241-4 Subj: Animals – rabbits. Bedtime. Emotions – fear. Family life – grandfathers. Night. Sleep.

My abuelita ill. by Yuyi Morales. Harcourt, 2009. ISBN 978-0-15-216330-3 Subj: Activities – storytelling. Ethnic groups in the U.S. – Mexican Americans. Family life – grandmothers. Foreign languages.

My best friend Bear ill. by Joy Allen. Rising Moon, 2001. ISBN 978-0-87358-775-4 Subj: Activities – sewing. Family life – mothers. Toys – bears.

My Mexico / México mío ill. by F. John Sierra. Putnam, 1996. ISBN 978-0-399-22275-7 Subj: Foreign lands – Mexico. Foreign languages. Poetry.

Noel ill. by Cheng-Khee Chee. Carolrhoda, 2005. ISBN 978-1-57505-752-1 Subj: Holidays – Christmas.

Off to kindergarten ill. by Melissa Sweet. Houghton, 2007. ISBN 978-0-439-73090-7 Subj: Rhyming text. School – first day.

P is for piñata: a Mexico alphabet ill. by John Parra. Sleeping Bear, 2008. ISBN 978-1-58536-144-1 Subj: ABC books. Foreign lands – Mexico.

The quilt story ill. by Tomie dePaola. Putnam, 1984. ISBN 978-0-399-21009-9 Subj: Family life. Moving. Quilts.

Sequoia ill. by Wendell Minor. Roaring Brook, 2014. ISBN 978-159643727-2 Subj: Nature. Poetry. Seasons. Trees.

A small thing . . . but big ill. by Hadley Hooper. Roaring Brook/Neal Porter, 2016. ISBN 978-162672256-9 Subj: Animals – dogs. Emotions – fear. Friendship. Old age. Self-concept.

Soup bone ill. by Margot Tomes. Harcourt, 1990. ISBN 978-0-15-277255-0 Subj: Anatomy – skeletons. Friendship. Holidays – Halloween.

Sunsets of the West ill. by Ted Lewin. Putnam, 2002. ISBN 978-0-399-22659-5 Subj: Family life. Moving. U.S. history – frontier & pioneer life.

The tale of Rabbit and Coyote ill. by Tomie dePaola. Putnam, 1994. ISBN 978-0-399-22258-0 Subj: Animals – coyotes. Animals – rabbits. Folk & fairy tales. Foreign lands – Mexico. Indians of North America – Zapotec.

That summer ill. by Barry Moser. Harcourt, 2002. ISBN 978-0-15-201585-5 Subj: Death. Emotions – grief. Family life. Family life – brothers. Quilts.

The vanishing pumpkin ill. by Tomie dePaola. Putnam, 1983. ISBN 978-0-399-20991-8 Subj: Holidays – Halloween. Witches.

The wagon ill. by James Ransome. Tambourine, 1996. ISBN 978-0-688-13537-9 Subj: Ethnic groups in the U.S. – African Americans. Slavery. U.S. history.

The whole green world ill. by Elisa Kleven. Farrar, 2005. ISBN 978-0-374-38400-5 Subj: Ecology. Nature. Rhyming text.

Winter is coming ill. by Jim LaMarche. Simon & Schuster, 2014. ISBN 978-144247251-8 Subj: Animals. Forest, woods. Seasons – fall.

Jolivet, Joëlle. *Almost everything* ill. by author. Macmillan, 2005. ISBN 978-1-59643-090-7 Subj: Nature. Science.

365 penguins (Fromental, Jean-Luc)

Zoo-ology ill. by author. Roaring Brook, 2003. ISBN 978-0-7613-2780-6 Subj: Animals. Science.

Jonas, Ann. *Aardvarks, disembark!* ill. by author. Greenwillow, 1990. ISBN 978-0-688-07207-0 Subj: ABC books. Animals. Animals – endangered animals. Boats, ships. Religion – Noah. Weather – floods. Weather – rain.

Bird talk ill. by author. Greenwillow, 1999. ISBN 978-0-688-14173-8 Subj: Birds. Noise, sounds. Songs.

Color dance ill. by author. Greenwillow, 1989. ISBN 978-0-688-05990-3 Subj: Activities – dancing. Concepts – color.

Holes and peeks ill. by author. Greenwillow, 1984. ISBN 978-0-688-02538-0 Subj: Emotions – fear. Problem solving.

Now we can go ill. by author. Greenwillow, 1986. ISBN 978-0-688-04803-7 Subj: Toys.

The quilt ill. by author. Greenwillow, 1984. ISBN 978-0-688-03826-7 Subj: Bedtime. Dreams. Quilts.

Reflections ill. by author. Greenwillow, 1987. ISBN 978-0-688-06141-8 Subj: Concepts. Format, unusual.

Round trip ill. by author. Greenwillow, 1983. ISBN 978-0-688-01781-1 Subj: Activities – traveling. Cities, towns.

Splash! ill. by author. Greenwillow, 1995. ISBN 978-0-688-11052-9 Subj: Animals. Counting, numbers. Ethnic groups in the U.S. – African Americans. Fish.

The thirteenth clue ill. by author. Greenwillow, 1992. ISBN 978-0-688-09742-4 Subj: Birthdays. Format, unusual. Mystery stories. Parties.

The trek ill. by author. Greenwillow, 1985. ISBN 978-0-688-04799-3 Subj: Activities – walking. Animals. Games. Imagination.

Two bear cubs ill. by author. Greenwillow, 1982. ISBN 978-0-688-01408-7 Subj: Animals – bears. Behavior – lost. Family life – mothers.

Watch William walk ill. by author. Greenwillow, 1997. ISBN 978-0-688-14175-2 Subj: Activities – walking. Animals – dogs. Birds – ducks. Language.

When you were a baby ill. by author. Greenwillow, 1982. ISBN 978-0-688-00864-2 Subj: Activities. Behavior – growing up.

Where can it be? ill. by author. Greenwillow, 1986. ISBN 978-0-688-05246-1 Subj: Behavior – lost & found possessions. Format, unusual – toy & movable books.

Jonathan, Langley. *Missing* ill. by author. Marshall Cavendish, 2000. ISBN 978-0-7614-5078-8 Subj: Animals – cats. Behavior – lost.

Jonell, Lynne. *Bravemole* ill. by author. Putnam, 2002. ISBN 978-0-399-23962-5 Subj: Behavior – needing someone. Family life – mothers.

I need a snake ill. by Petra Mathers. Putnam, 1998. ISBN 978-0-399-23176-6 Subj: Family life – mothers. Pets. Reptiles – snakes.

It's my birthday, too! ill. by Petra Mathers. Putnam, 1999. ISBN 978-0-399-23323-4 Subj: Animals – dogs. Birthdays. Family life – brothers. Parties. Sibling rivalry.

Mom pie ill. by Petra Mathers. Putnam, 2001. ISBN 978-0-399-23422-4 Subj: Behavior – needing someone. Family life – mothers.

When Mommy was mad ill. by Petra Mathers. Putnam, 2002. ISBN 978-0-399-23433-0 Subj: Emotions – anger. Family life – mothers.

Jones, Christianne C. *Lacey Walker, nonstop talker* ill. by Richard Watson. Picture Window, 2012. ISBN 978-1-4048-6796-3 Subj: Activities – talking. Birds – owls. Etiquette.

Miles McHale, tattletale ill. by Elina Ellis. Capstone, 2017. ISBN 978-151580753-7 Subj: Behavior – gossip. School.

The Santa shimmy ill. by Emma Randall. Picture Window, 2015. ISBN 978-147956494-1 Subj: Format, unusual – board books. Participation. Rhyming text. Santa Claus.

Jones, Elizabeth. *Sunshine and Storm* ill. by James Coplestone. Ragged Bears, 2001. ISBN 978-1-929927-27-2 Subj: Animals – cats. Animals – dogs. Emotions – anger. Friendship. Weather – rain.

Jones, Stella J. *Glitter* ill. by Judi Abbot. Tiger Tales, 2017. ISBN 978-168010039-6 Subj: Animals – rhinoceros. Art. Behavior – messy.

The very grumpy day ill. by Alison Edgson. Tiger Tales, 2016. ISBN 978-168010012-9 Subj: Animals. Behavior – bad day, bad mood. Cumulative tales.

Jones, Sylvie. *Who's in the tub?* ill. by Pascale Constantin. Blue Apple, 2007. ISBN 978-1-59354-612-0 Subj: Activities – bathing. Animals. Imagination. Rhyming text.

Jones, Terry. *Gorillas in our midst* (Fairgray, Richard)

Jones, Ursula. *Beauty and the beast* ill. by Sarah Gibb. Albert Whitman, 2014. ISBN 978-080750600-4 Subj: Character traits – appearance. Character traits – loyalty. Emotions – love. Folk & fairy tales. Magic.

The princess who had no kingdom ill. by Sarah Gibb. Albert Whitman, 2014. ISBN 978-080756630-5 Subj: Clowns, jesters. Folk & fairy tales. Royalty – princesses.

The witch's children ill. by Russell Ayto. Henry Holt, 2003. ISBN 978-0-8050-7205-1 Subj: Magic. Parks. Witches.

Jonovitz, Marilyn. *Good morning, Little Fox* ill. by author. NorthSouth, 2001. ISBN 978-0-7358-1441-7 Subj: Animals – foxes. Family life – fathers. Family life – sons. Food.

Maybe, my baby ill. by author. NorthSouth, 2003. ISBN 978-0-7358-1763-0 Subj: Animals – babies. Family life – parents. Sleep.

Three little kittens ill. by author. NorthSouth, 2002. ISBN 978-0-7358-1643-5 Subj: Animals – cats. Behavior – lost & found possessions. Clothing – gloves, mittens. Nursery rhymes.

Joosse, Barbara. *Bad dog school* ill. by Jennifer Plecas. Clarion, 2004. ISBN 978-0-618-13331-4 Subj: Animals – dogs. Pets. School.

Dog parade ill. by Eugene Yelchin. Harcourt, 2011. ISBN 978-0-15-206690-1 Subj: Animals – dogs. Clothing – costumes. Parades.

Evermore Dragon ill. by Randy Cecil. Candlewick, 2015. ISBN 978-076366882-2 Subj: Behavior – hiding. Dragons. Friendship. Games. Royalty – princesses.

Friends (mostly) ill. by Tomaso Milian. HarperCollins, 2010. ISBN 978-0-06-088221-1 Subj: Friendship.

Ghost wings ill. by Giselle Potter. Chronicle, 2001. ISBN 978-0-8118-2164-3 Subj: Death. Family life – grandmothers. Foreign lands – Mexico. Holidays – Day of the Dead. Insects – butterflies, caterpillars. Memories, memory.

Grandma calls me Beautiful ill. by Barbara Lavallee. Chronicle, 2008. ISBN 978-0-8118-5815-1 Subj: Activities – storytelling. Emotions – love. Family life – grandmothers. Hawaii. Self-concept.

Higgledy-piggledy chicks ill. by Rick Chrustowski. HarperCollins, 2010. ISBN 978-0-06-075042-8 Subj: Animals – babies. Birds – chickens, roosters. Farms.

Hooray Parade ill. by Hyewon Yum. Viking, 2013. ISBN 978-0-670-01334-0 Subj: Family life – grandmothers. Parades. Puppets. Rhyming text.

A houseful of Christmas ill. by Betsy Lewin. Henry Holt, 2001. ISBN 978-0-8050-6391-2 Subj: Family life. Family life – grandmothers. Holidays – Christmas. Sleep. Weather – blizzards.

I love you the purplest ill. by Mary Whyte. Chronicle, 1996. ISBN 978-0-8118-0718-0 Subj: Family life – brothers. Family life – mothers. Sibling rivalry. Sports – fishing.

Lovabye Dragon ill. by Randy Cecil. Candlewick, 2012. ISBN 978-0-7636-5408-5 Subj: Bedtime. Dragons. Emotions – loneliness. Friendship. Royalty – princesses.

Love is a good thing to feel ill. by Jennifer Plecas. Philomel, 2008. ISBN 978-0-399-25168-9 Subj: Emotions – love.

Mama, do you love me? ill. by Barbara Lavallee. Chronicle, 1991. ISBN 978-0-87701-759-2 Subj: Emotions – love. Eskimos. Family life – mothers.

Nikolai, the only bear ill. by Renata Liwska. Penguin, 2005. ISBN 978-0-399-23884-0 Subj: Adoption. Animals – bears. Foreign lands – Russia. Orphans.

Nugget and Darling ill. by Sue Truesdell. Clarion, 1997. ISBN 978-0-395-64571-0 Subj: Animals – cats. Animals – dogs. Character traits – kindness to animals. Emotions – envy, jealousy.

Old Robert and the sea-silly cats ill. by Jan Jutte. Philomel, 2012. ISBN 978-0-399-25430-7 Subj: Activities – playing. Animals – cats. Sailors.

Papa do you love me? ill. by Barbara Lavallee. Chronicle, 2005. ISBN 978-0-8118-4265-5 Subj: Emotions – love. Family life – fathers. Foreign lands – Africa.

Please is a good word to say ill. by Jennifer Plecas. Penguin, 2007. ISBN 978-0-399-24217-5 Subj: Behavior – misbehavior. Etiquette.

Roawr! ill. by Jan Jutte. Philomel, 2009. ISBN 978-0-399-24777-4 Subj: Animals – bears. Bedtime. Imagination.

Sail away Dragon ill. by Randy Cecil. Candlewick, 2017. ISBN 978-076367313-0 Subj: Activities – traveling. Dragons. Royalty – princesses.

Sleepover at Gramma's house ill. by Jan Jutte. Penguin, 2010. ISBN 978-0-399-25261-7 Subj: Activities – playing. Animals – elephants. Family life – grandmothers. Sleepovers.

Snow day! ill. by Jennifer Plecas. Clarion, 1995. ISBN 978-0-395-66588-6 Subj: Family life. Weather – snow.

Wind-wild dog ill. by Kate Kiesler. Henry Holt, 2006. ISBN 978-0-8050-7053-8 Subj: Alaska. Animals – dogs.

Jordan, Deloris. *Baby blessings: a prayer for the day you are born* ill. by James Ransome. Simon & Schuster, 2010. ISBN 978-1-4169-5362-3 Subj: Emotions – love. Ethnic groups in the U.S. – African Americans. Family life – parents. Religion.

Dream big: Michael Jordan and the pursuit of Olympic gold ill. by Barry Root. Simon & Schuster, 2012. ISBN 978-1-4424-1269-9 Subj: Character traits – perseverance. Ethnic groups in the U.S. – African Americans. Sports – basketball. Sports – Olympics.

Michael's golden rules by Deloris Jordan and Roslyn M. Jordan; intro. by Michael Jordan; ill. by Kadir Nelson. Simon & Schuster, 2007. ISBN 978-0-689-87016-3 Subj: Character traits – persistence. Ethnic groups in the U.S. – African Americans. Family life – aunts, uncles. Sports – baseball. Sportsmanship.

Salt in his shoes: Michael Jordan in pursuit of a dream by Deloris Jordan and Roslyn M. Jordan ill. by Kadir Nelson. Simon & Schuster, 2000. ISBN 978-0-689-83371-7 Subj: Careers. Concepts – size. Family life. Sports – basketball.

Jordan, Helene J. *How a seed grows* ill. by Loretta Krupinski. Rev. ed. HarperCollins, 1992. ISBN 978-0-06-020185-2 Subj: Gardens, gardening. Nature. Science. Seeds.

Jordan, Laurie. *Yawning yoga* ill. by Diana Mayo. Little Pickle, 2017. ISBN 978-193977510-8 Subj: Bedtime. Character traits – patience, impatience. Health & fitness – exercise.

Jordan, Mary Ellen. *Lazy Daisy, cranky Frankie* ill. by Andrew Weldon. Albert Whitman, 2013. ISBN 978-0-8075-4400-6 Subj: Animals. Character traits – laziness. Farms. Humorous stories. Rhyming text.

Jordan, Roslyn M. *Michael's golden rules* (Jordan, Deloris)

Salt in his shoes: Michael Jordan in pursuit of a dream (Jordan, Deloris)

Jordan, Sandra. *Ballet for Martha: making Appalachian Spring* (Greenberg, Jan)

Frog hunt photos by author. Roaring Brook, 2002. ISBN 978-0-7613-2652-6 Subj: Animals. Frogs & toads. Lakes, ponds.

Mr. and Mrs. Portly and their little dog Snack ill. by Christine Davenier. Farrar, 2009. ISBN 978-0-374-35089-5 Subj: Animals – dogs. Art. Character traits – bravery. Crime. Pets.

Jorgensen, Gail. *Crocodile beat* ill. by Patricia Mullins. Bradbury, 1989. ISBN 978-0-02-748010-8 Subj: Animals. Rhyming text.

Gotcha! ill. by Kerry Argent. Scholastic, 1997. ISBN 978-0-590-96208-7 Subj: Animals. Animals – bears. Birthdays. Insects – flies.

Jorgensen, Richard. *Reading with Dad* ill. by Warren Hanson. Waldman, 2000. ISBN 978-0-931674-41-9 Subj: Behavior – growing up. Books, reading. Family life – fathers. Rhyming text.

Joseph, Lynn. *Coconut kind of day* ill. by Sandra Speidel. Lothrop, 1992. ISBN 978-0-688-09120-0 Subj: Foreign lands – Trinidad. Islands. Poetry.

Fly, Bessie, fly ill. by Yvonne Buchanan. Simon & Schuster, 1998. ISBN 978-0-689-81339-9 Subj: Airplanes, airports. Careers – airplane pilots. Ethnic groups in the U.S. – African Americans.

An island Christmas ill. by Catherine Stock. Clarion, 1992. ISBN 978-0-395-58761-4 Subj: Foreign lands – Trinidad. Holidays – Christmas.

Joslin, Mary. *On that Christmas night* ill. by Helen Cann. Good Books, 2005. ISBN 978-1-56148-494-2 Subj: Holidays – Christmas. Religion – Nativity.

The shore beyond ill. by Alison Jay. Good Books, 2000. ISBN 978-1-56148-316-7 Subj: Activities – traveling. Behavior – growing up. Self-concept.

Joubert, Beverly. *African animal alphabet* by Beverly Joubert and Dereck Joubert; photos by Beverly Joubert. National Geographic, 2011. ISBN 978-1-4263-0781-2 Subj: ABC books. Animals. Foreign lands – Africa.

Joubert, Dereck. *African animal alphabet* (Joubert, Beverly)

Joyce, Susan. *ABC nature riddles* ill. by Doug DuBosque. Peel Productions, 2000. ISBN 978-0-939217-53-3 Subj: ABC books. Language. Nature. Rhyming text. Riddles & jokes.

ABC school riddles ill. by Freddie Levin. Peel Productions, 2001. ISBN 978-0-939217-54-0 Subj: ABC books. Rhyming text. Riddles & jokes.

Joyce, William. *A bean, a stalk, and a boy named Jack* ill. by author and Kenny Callicutt. Atheneum, 2014. ISBN 978-144247350-8 Subj: Folk & fairy tales. Giants. Magic. Plants.

Bently and egg ill. by author. HarperCollins, 1992. ISBN 978-0-06-020386-3 Subj: Birds – ducks. Character traits – helpfulness. Eggs. Frogs & toads. Reptiles – turtles, tortoises.

Big time Olie ill. by author. Geringer, 2002. ISBN 978-0-06-008811-8 Subj: Behavior – growing up. Concepts – size. Family life. Problem solving.

Billy's booger ill. by author. Atheneum, 2015. ISBN 978-144247351-5 Subj: Activities – writing. Books, reading. Careers – writers. Careers – writers. Contests. Imagination. School.

A day with Wilbur Robinson ill. by author. HarperCollins, 2006. ISBN 978-0-06-089098-8 Subj: Family life.

Dinosaur Bob: and his adventures with the family Lazardo ill. by author. Expanded ed. HarperCollins, 1995. ISBN 978-0-06-021075-5 Subj: Activities – vacationing. Dinosaurs. Family life. Pets. Prehistory.

The fantastic flying books of Mr. Morris Lessmore ill. by author. Atheneum, 2012. ISBN 978-1-4424-5702-7 Subj: Activities – flying. Books, reading. Libraries.

George shrinks ill. by author. HarperCollins, 1985. ISBN 978-0-06-023071-5 Subj: Activities – babysitting. Concepts – size. Family life.

Jack Frost ill. by author. Atheneum, 2015. ISBN 978-144243043-3 Subj: Character traits – bravery. Imagination.

The Leaf Men and the brave good bugs ill. by author. HarperCollins, 1996. ISBN 978-0-06-027238-8 Subj: Character traits – helpfulness. Gardens, gardening. Insects. Mythical creatures – elves. Old age. Toys.

The Man in the Moon ill. by author. Simon & Schuster, 2011. ISBN 978-1-4424-3041-9 Subj: Imagination. Moon.

The Numberlys ill. by author and Christina Ellis. Atheneum, 2014. ISBN 978-144247343-0 Subj: ABC books. Counting, numbers. Format, unusual.

Rolie Polie Olie ill. by author. Geringer, 1999. ISBN 978-0-06-027164-0 Subj: Concepts – shape. Rhyming text. Robots.

The Sandman: the story of Sanderson Mansnoozie ill. by author. Atheneum, 2012. ISBN 978-1-4424-3042-6 Subj: Bedtime. Dreams. Moon. Sleep.

Santa calls ill. by author. HarperCollins, 1993. ISBN 978-0-06-021134-9 Subj: Activities – flying. Family life – brothers & sisters. Friendship. Santa Claus. Sibling rivalry.

Sleepy time Olie ill. by author. Geringer, 2001. ISBN 978-0-06-029614-8 Subj: Bedtime. Inventions. Rhyming text. Robots.

Snowie Rolie ill. by author. Geringer, 2000. ISBN 978-0-06-029286-7 Subj: Robots. Snowmen. Weather – snow.

Joyner, Andrew. *The pink hat* ill. by author. Random House, 2017. ISBN 978-152477226-0 Subj: Character traits – assertiveness. Clothing – hats. Gender roles.

Juan, Ana. *The pet shop revolution* ill. by author. Scholastic, 2011. ISBN 978-0-545-12810-0 Subj: Animals. Character traits – kindness to animals. Pets. Stores.

Jubb, Sophie. *Cock-a-doodle quack! quack!* (Baddiel, Ivor)

Judd, Naomi. *Naomi Judd's guardian angels* ill. by Dan Andreasen. HarperCollins, 2000. ISBN 978-0-06-027208-1 Subj: Angels. Family life – great-grandparents. Music. Songs.

Judes, Marie-Odile. *Max, the stubborn little wolf* ill. by Martine Bourre. HarperCollins, 2001. ISBN 978-0-06-029417-5 Subj: Animals – wolves. Careers. Family life – fathers. Sports – hunting.

Judge, Chris. *Tin* ill. by author. Andersen, 2014. ISBN 978-146775013-4 Subj: Family life – brothers & sisters. Robots. Toys – balloons.

Judge, Lita. *Born in the wild: baby mammals and their parents* ill. by author. Roaring Brook, 2014. ISBN 978-159643925-2 Subj: Animals – babies.

Flight school ill. by author. Atheneum, 2014. ISBN 978-144248177-0 Subj: Activities – flying. Birds – penguins. Character traits – perseverance.

Good morning to me! ill. by author. Simon & Schuster, 2015. ISBN 978-148140369-6 Subj: Birds – parakeets, parrots. Morning. Noise, sounds.

Hoot and Peep ill. by author. Dial, 2016. ISBN 978-052542837-4 Subj: Birds – owls. Character traits – individuality. Family life – brothers & sisters. Noise, sounds.

Hoot and Peep: a song for snow ill. by author. Dial, 2017. ISBN 978-110199451-1 Subj: Birds – owls. Family life – brothers & sisters. Noise, sounds. Songs. Weather – snow.

How big were dinosaurs? ill. by author. Roaring Brook, 2013. ISBN 978-1-59643-719-7 Subj: Concepts – size. Dinosaurs.

Pennies for elephants ill. by author. Hyperion, 2009. ISBN 978-1-4231-1390-4 Subj: Animals – elephants. U.S. history. Zoos.

Red hat ill. by author. Atheneum, 2013. ISBN 978-1-4424-4232-0 Subj: Animals. Clothing – hats. Forest, woods.

Red sled ill. by author. Simon & Schuster, 2011. ISBN 978-1-4424-2007-6 Subj: Animals. Seasons – winter. Sports – sledding.

Jukes, Mavis. *You're a bear* ill. by Steve Johnson and Lou Fancher. Knopf, 2003. ISBN 978-0-375-90267-3 Subj: Animals – bears. Imagination. Night. Rhyming text.

Jules, Jacqueline. *Abraham's search for God* ill. by Natascia Ugliano. Kar-Ben, 2007. ISBN 978-1-58013-243-5 Subj: Religion.

Benjamin and the silver goblet ill. by Natascia Ugliano. Lerner, 2009. ISBN 978-0-8225-8757-6 Subj: Religion.

Duck for Turkey Day ill. by Kathryn Mitter. Albert Whitman, 2009. ISBN 978-0-8075-1734-5 Subj: Ethnic groups in the U.S. – Vietnamese Americans. Holidays – Thanksgiving. School.

Feathers for peacock ill. by Helen Cann. Wisdom Tales, 2016. ISBN 978-193778653-3 Subj: Birds. Birds – peacocks, peahens. Character traits – generosity. Folk & fairy tales.

No English ill. by Amy Huntington. Mitten, 2007. ISBN 978-1-58726-474-0 Subj: Character traits – kindness. Emotions – loneliness. Friendship. Immigrants, immigration.

Picnic at Camp Shalom ill. by Deborah Melmon. Lerner/Kar-Ben, 2011. ISBN 978-0-7613-6661-4 Subj: Camps, camping. Friendship. Jewish culture.

Julian, Alison. *Brave as a bunny can be* ill. by author. Waldman, 2001. ISBN 978-0-931674-46-4 Subj: Animals – rabbits. Character traits – bravery. Emotions – fear. Family life.

Julian, Sean. *Sloppy wants a hug* ill. by author. NorthSouth, 2017. ISBN 978-073584273-1 Subj: Dragons. Hugging.

Jullien, Jean. *Before and after* ill. by author. Phaidon, 2017. ISBN 978-071487408-1 Subj: Concepts. Concepts – change. Format, unusual – board books. Format, unusual – toy & movable books.

Jurmain, Suzanne Tripp. *Nice work, Franklin!* ill. by Larry Day. Dial, 2016. ISBN 978-080373800-3 Subj: Disabilities – physical disabilities. U.S. history.

Worst of friends: Thomas Jefferson, John Adams, and the true story of an American feud ill. by Larry Day. Penguin, 2011. ISBN 978-0-525-47903-1 Subj: Friendship. U.S. history.

Just like father ill. by John Huxtable. Based on the books by Hans de Beer. Sterling, 2003. ISBN 978-1-4027-1289-0 Subj: Animals – polar bears. Family life – fathers. Format, unusual – board books.

Juster, Norton. *The hello, goodbye window* ill. by Chris Raschka. Hyperion, 2005. ISBN 978-0-7868-0914-1 Subj: Caldecott award books. Family life – grandparents.

Neville ill. by G. Brian Karas. Random House, 2011. ISBN 978-0-375-86765-1 Subj: Behavior – resourcefulness. Emotions – loneliness. Moving.

The odious ogre ill. by Jules Feiffer. Scholastic, 2010. ISBN 978-0-545-16202-9 Subj: Character traits – kindness. Mythical creatures – ogres.

Sourpuss and sweetie pie ill. by Chris Raschka. Scholastic, 2008. ISBN 978-0-439-92943-1 Subj: Behavior – misbehavior. Emotions – love. Family life – grandparents.

Kabakov, Vladimir. *R is for Russia* photos by Prodeepta Das. Frances Lincoln, 2011. ISBN 978-1-84780-102-9 Subj: ABC books. Foreign lands – Russia.

Kaczman, James. *A bird and his worm* ill. by author. Houghton, 2002. ISBN 978-0-618-09460-8 Subj: Activities – traveling. Animals – worms. Behavior – talking to strangers. Birds. Character traits – being different. Safety.

Kahng, Kim. *The loathsome dragon* (Wiesner, David)

Kaiser, Ruth. *The smiley book of colors* ill. by author. Random House, 2012. ISBN 978-0-375-86983-9 Subj: Concepts – color. Emotions – happiness.

Kajikawa, Kimiko. *Close to you: how animals bond* ill. by author. Henry Holt, 2008. ISBN 978-0-8050-8123-7 Subj: Animals – babies. Nature.

Sweet dreams: how animals sleep ill. by author. Henry Holt, 1999. ISBN 978-0-8050-5890-1 Subj: Animals. Sleep.

Tsunami! ill. by Ed Young. Philomel, 2009. ISBN 978-0-399-25006-4 Subj: Character traits – wisdom. Folk & fairy tales. Foreign lands – Japan. Tsunamis.

Yoshi's feast ill. by Yumi Heo. DK, 2000. ISBN 978-0-7894-2607-9 Subj: Activities – dancing. Folk & fairy tales. Foreign lands – Japan. Friendship. Senses – smell.

Kako, Satoshi. *Little Daruma and little Daikoku* ill. by author. Tuttle, 2003. ISBN 978-0-8048-3351-6 Subj: Character traits – cooperation. Foreign lands – Japan. Friendship. Magic.

Little Daruma and little Kaminari ill. by author. Tuttle, 2002. ISBN 978-0-8048-3348-6 Subj: Behavior – lost & found possessions. Foreign lands – Japan. Friendship.

Kalan, Robert. *Blue sea* ill. by Donald Crews. Greenwillow, 1979. ISBN 978-0-688-84184-3 Subj: Concepts – size. Fish.

Jump, frog, jump! ill. by Byron Barton. Greenwillow, 1981. ISBN 978-0-688-84271-0 Subj: Cumulative tales. Frogs & toads.

Moving day ill. by Yossi Abolafia. Greenwillow, 1996. ISBN 978-0-688-13949-0 Subj: Crustaceans – crabs. Cumulative tales. Moving. Rhyming text.

Rain ill. by Donald Crews. Greenwillow, 1978. ISBN 978-0-688-84139-3 Subj: Weather – rain.

Kallok, Emma. *Gem* ill. by Joel Bower. Tricycle, 2001. ISBN 978-1-58246-027-7 Subj: Babies, toddlers. Birth. Children as authors. Ethnic groups in the U.S. Family life – new sibling. Musical instruments – saxophones.

Kalman, Maira. *Looking at Lincoln* ill. by author. Penguin, 2012. ISBN 978-0-399-24039-3 Subj: U.S. history.

Thomas Jefferson: life, liberty, and the pursuit of everything ill. by author. Penguin/Nancy Paulsen, 2014. ISBN 978-039924040-9 Subj: U.S. history.

What Pete ate from A-Z ill. by author. Putnam, 2001. ISBN 978-0-399-23362-3 Subj: ABC books. Animals – dogs.

Kalz, Jill. *An a-maze-ing amusement park adventure* ill. by Mattia Cerato. Capstone, 2010. ISBN 978-1-4048-6023-0 Subj: Mazes. Parks – amusement.

An a-maze-ing farm adventure ill. by Mattia Cerato. Picture Window, 2010. ISBN 978-1-4048-6038-4 Subj: Farms. Mazes.

An a-maze-ing school adventure ill. by Mattia Cerato. Picture Window, 2010. ISBN 978-1-4048-6039-1 Subj: Mazes. School.

An a-maze-ing zoo adventure ill. by Mattia Cerato. Picture Window, 2010. ISBN 978-1-4048-6024-7 Subj: Mazes. Zoos.

Fruits ill. with photos. Smart Apple Media, 2003. ISBN 978-1-58340-299-3 Subj: Food. Health & fitness.

Northern lights ill. with photos. Creative Editions, 2004. ISBN 978-1-58341-326-5 Subj: Northern lights. Science.

Water ill. with photos. Smart Apple Media, 2003. ISBN 978-1-58340-302-0 Subj: Water.

Kamine, Jane. *Mommy's hands* (Lasky, Kathryn)

Kamish, Daniel. *Diggy Dan* by Daniel Kamish and David Kamish; ill. by Daniel Kamish. Random House, 2001. ISBN 978-0-375-90576-6 Subj: Character traits – cleanliness. Character traits – orderliness. Children as illustrators. Imagination.

Kamish, David. *Diggy Dan* (Kamish, Daniel)

Kamkwamba, William. *The boy who harnessed the wind* by William Kamkwamba and Bryan Mealer ill. by Elizabeth Zunon. Dial, 2012. ISBN 978-0-8037-3511-8 Subj: Behavior – resourcefulness. Foreign lands – Malawi. Weather – droughts.

Kamm, Katja. *Invisible* ill. by author. NorthSouth, 2006. ISBN 978-0-7358-2052-4 Subj: Art. Picture puzzles. Wordless.

Kaneko, Yuki. *Into the snow* ill. by Masamitsu Saito. Enchanted Lion, 2016. ISBN 978-159270188-9 Subj: Activities – playing. Seasons – winter. Weather – snow.

Kaner, Etta. *And the winner is . . . : amazing animal athletes* ill. by David Anderson. Kids Can, 2013. ISBN 978-1-55453-904-8 Subj: Animals. Contests.

Who likes the rain? ill. by Marie Lafrance. Kids Can, 2007. ISBN 978-1-55337-841-9 Subj: Format, unusual – toy & movable books. Weather – rain.

Who likes the sun? ill. by Marie Lafrance. Kids Can, 2007. ISBN 978-1-55337-840-2 Subj: Format, unusual – toy & movable books. Sun.

Who likes the wind? ill. by Marie Lafrance. Kids Can, 2006. ISBN 978-1-55337-839-6 Subj: Format, unusual – toy & movable books. Weather – wind.

Kanevsky, Polly. *Sleepy boy* ill. by Stephanie Anderson. Simon & Schuster, 2006. ISBN 978-0-689-86735-4 Subj: Animals – lions. Bedtime. Family life – fathers. Sleep.

Kang, A. N. *Papillon goes to the vet* ill. by A. N. Kang. Disney/Hyperion, 2017. ISBN 978-148472881-9 Subj: Activities – flying. Animals – cats. Careers – veterinarians. Hiccups.

The very fluffy kitty, Papillon ill. by A. N. Kang. Disney/Hyperion, 2016. ISBN 978-148471798-1 Subj: Activities – flying. Animals – cats. Humorous stories.

Kang, Anna. *Can I tell you a secret?* ill. by Christopher Weyant. HarperCollins, 2016. ISBN 978-006239684-6 Subj: Behavior – secrets. Emotions – fear. Frogs & toads.

I am (not) scared ill. by Christopher Weyant. Amazon/Two Lions, 2017. ISBN 978-150393745-1 Subj: Animals. Emotions – fear. Parks – amusement.

That's not mine ill. by Christopher Weyant. Amazon/Two Lions, 2015. ISBN 978-147782639-3 Subj: Animals. Behavior – fighting, arguing. Behavior – sharing.

You are (not) small ill. by Christopher Weyant. Amazon/Two Lions, 2014. ISBN 978-147784772-5 Subj: Animals. Behavior – fighting, arguing. Character traits – smallness. Concepts – size.

Kangas, Juli. *The surprise visitor* ill. by author. Penguin, 2005. ISBN 978-0-8037-2989-6 Subj: Animals. Animals – mice. Eggs.

Kann, Elizabeth. *Pinkalicious* (Kann, Victoria)

Purplicious (Kann, Victoria)

Kann, Victoria. *Emeraldalicious* ill. by author. HarperCollins, 2013. ISBN 978-0-06-178126-1 Subj: Ecology. Gardens, gardening. Magic. Parks.

Pinkalicious by Victoria Kann and Elizabeth Kann; ill. by Victoria Kann. HarperCollins, 2006. ISBN 978-0-06-077639-8 Subj: Concepts – color. Food.

Purplicious by Victoria Kann and Elizabeth Kann; ill. by Victoria Kann. HarperCollins, 2007. ISBN 978-0-06-124405-6 Subj: Character traits – individuality. Concepts – color. School.

Silverlicious ill. by author. HarperCollins, 2011. ISBN 978-0-06-178123-0 Subj: Fairies. Family life – brothers & sisters. Teeth.

Kanninen, Barbara. *A story with pictures* ill. by Lynn Rowe Reed. Holiday House, 2007. ISBN 978-0-8234-2049-0 Subj: Books, reading. Careers – illustrators. Careers – writers. Imagination.

Kaplan, Bruce Eric. *Meaniehead* ill. by author. Simon & Schuster, 2014. ISBN 978-144248542-6 Subj: Behavior – fighting, arguing. Family life – brothers & sisters. Sibling rivalry.

Monsters eat whiny children ill. by author. Simon & Schuster, 2010. ISBN 978-1-4169-8689-8 Subj: Behavior – misbehavior. Family life – brothers & sisters. Monsters.

Kaplan, Michael B. *Betty Bunny didn't do it* ill. by Stéphane Jorisch. Dial, 2013. ISBN 978-0-8037-3858-4 Subj: Animals – rabbits. Behavior – lying. Character traits – honesty. Family life.

Betty Bunny loves chocolate cake ill. by Stéphane Jorisch. Penguin, 2011. ISBN 978-0-8037-3407-4 Subj: Animals – rabbits. Character traits – patience, impatience. Food.

Betty Bunny loves Easter ill. by Stéphane Jorisch. Dial, 2015. ISBN 978-080374061-7 Subj: Animals – rabbits. Eggs. Holidays – Easter.

Betty Bunny wants a goal ill. by Stéphane Jorisch. Dial, 2014. ISBN 978-080373859-1 Subj: Animals – rabbits. Character traits – perseverance. Family life. Sports – soccer.

Betty Bunny wants everything ill. by Stéphane Jorisch. Dial, 2012. ISBN 978-0-8037-3408-1 Subj: Animals – rabbits. Behavior – greed. Emotions – anger. Family life. Shopping.

Kaplanoglou, Mania. *Mama Bear, Little Bear* ill. by Giuliano Ferri. Minedition, 2016. ISBN 978-988834122-1 Subj: Animals – bears. Family life – mothers.

Karas, G. Brian. *As an oak tree grows* ill. by author. Penguin/Nancy Paulsen, 2014. ISBN 978-039925233-4 Subj: Ecology. Trees.

Atlantic ill. by author. Putnam, 2002. ISBN 978-0-399-23632-7 Subj: Science. Sea & seashore.

Bebe's bad dream ill. by author. Greenwillow, 2000. ISBN 978-0-688-16183-5 Subj: Aliens. Family life – brothers & sisters. Nightmares.

On Earth ill. by author. Penguin, 2005. ISBN 978-0-399-24025-6 Subj: Earth.

On the farm, at the market ill. by author. Henry Holt, 2016. ISBN 978-080509372-8 Subj: Careers – farmers. Farms. Stores.

Skidamarink ill. by author. HarperCollins, 2002. ISBN 978-0-694-01595-5 Subj: Animals – polar bears. Birds – penguins. Emotions – love. Format, unusual – toy & movable books. Rhyming text. Sports – ice skating.

The village garage ill. by author. Henry Holt, 2010. ISBN 978-0-8050-8716-1 Subj: Careers. Cities, towns. Seasons.

Karon, Jan. *The trellis and the seed* ill. by Robert Gantt Steele. Viking, 2003. ISBN 978-0-670-89289-1 Subj: Behavior – growing up. Flowers. Seeds.

Kasbarian, Lucine, reteller. *The greedy sparrow: an Armenian tale* ill. by Maria Zaikina. Marshall Cavendish, 2011. ISBN 978-0-7614-5821-2 Subj: Behavior – greed. Behavior – trickery. Birds – sparrows. Folk & fairy tales.

Kasparavicius, Kestutis. *The bear family's world tour Christmas* ill. by author. Abrams, 2002. ISBN 978-0-8109-0573-3 Subj: Activities – traveling. Animals – bears. Holidays – Christmas.

Kassirer, Sue. *Joseph and his coat of many colors* ill. by Danuta Jarecka. Simon & Schuster, 1997. ISBN 978-0-689-81227-9 Subj: Clothing – coats. Religion. Sibling rivalry.

Math fair blues ill. by Jerry Smath. Kane, 2001. ISBN 978-0-613-39339-3 Subj: Concepts – shape. Counting, numbers. Fairs, festivals. Musical instruments – bands.

What's next, Nina? ill. by Page Eastburn O'Rourke. Kane, 2001. ISBN 978-1-57565-106-4 Subj: Concepts – patterns. Family life – sisters. Jewelry. Parties.

Kastner, Jill. *Merry Christmas, Princess Dinosaur* ill. by author. Greenwillow, 2002. ISBN 978-0-06-000472-9 Subj: Dinosaurs. Holidays – Christmas. Toys.

Princess Dinosaur ill. by author. Greenwillow, 2001. ISBN 978-0-688-17046-2 Subj: Animals – dogs. Dinosaurs. Toys.

Kasza, Keiko. *Badger's fancy meal* ill. by author. Penguin, 2007. ISBN 978-0-399-24603-6 Subj: Animals – badgers. Food.

The dog who cried wolf ill. by author. Penguin, 2005. ISBN 978-0-399-24247-2 Subj: Animals – dogs. Animals – wolves. Self-concept.

Don't laugh, Joe ill. by author. Putnam, 1997. ISBN 978-0-399-23036-3 Subj: Animals – bears. Animals – possums. Behavior.

Dorothy and Mikey ill. by author. Putnam, 2000. ISBN 978-0-399-23356-2 Subj: Activities – playing. Animals – hippopotamuses. Friendship.

Finders keepers ill. by author. Putnam, 2015. ISBN 978-039916898-7 Subj: Animals. Animals – squirrels. Behavior – lost & found possessions. Clothing – hats.

Grandpa Toad's last secret ill. by author. Putnam, 1995. ISBN 978-0-399-22610-6 Subj: Family life – grandfathers. Frogs & toads. Monsters.

The mightiest ill. by author. Putnam, 2001. ISBN 978-0-399-23586-3 Subj: Animals – bears. Animals – elephants. Animals – lions. Giants.

A mother for Choco ill. by author. Putnam, 1992. ISBN 978-0-399-21841-5 Subj: Adoption. Animals. Birds. Emotions – love. Family life – mothers.

My lucky birthday ill. by author. Penguin, 2013. ISBN 978-0-399-25763-6 Subj: Animals – pigs. Behavior – trickery. Birthdays. Reptiles – alligators, crocodiles.

Ready for anything ill. by author. Putnam, 2009. ISBN 978-0-399-25235-8 Subj: Activities – picnicking. Animals – raccoons. Behavior – worrying. Birds – ducks. Character traits – kindness.

Silly Goose's big story ill. by author. Putnam, 2012. ISBN 978-0-399-25542-7 Subj: Activities – storytelling. Animals. Birds – geese. Friendship.

The wolf's chicken stew ill. by author. Putnam, 1987. ISBN 978-0-399-21400-4 Subj: Animals – wolves. Birds – chickens, roosters. Character traits – generosity. Food.

Kato, Yukiko. *In the meadow* ill. by Komako Sakai. Enchanted Lion, 2011. ISBN 978-1-59270-108-7 Subj: Behavior – lost. Nature.

Katschke, Judy. *Take a hike, Snoopy* ill. by Nick LoBianco and Peter LoBianco. Simon & Schuster, 2002. ISBN 978-0-689-84938-1 Subj: Activities – hiking. Animals – dogs. Birds. Camps, camping.

Katz, Alan. *Don't say that word!* ill. by David Catrow. Simon & Schuster, 2007. ISBN 978-0-689-86971-6 Subj: Etiquette. Humorous stories. Rhyming text. School.

That stinks! a punny show-and-tell ill. by Stephen Gilpin. Simon & Schuster, 2016. ISBN 978-141697880-0 Subj: Humorous stories. Language. School.

Katz, Bobbi. *Nothing but a dog* ill. by Jane Manning. Penguin, 2010. ISBN 978-0-525-47858-4 Subj: Animals – dogs. Pets.

Once around the sun ill. by LeUyen Pham. Harcourt, 2006. ISBN 978-0-15-216397-6 Subj: Days of the week, months of the year. Poetry. Seasons.

Katz, Jon. *Lenore finds a friend: a true story from Bedlam Farm* ill. by author. Henry Holt, 2012. ISBN 978-0-8050-9220-2 Subj: Animals – dogs. Farms. Friendship.

Meet the dogs of Bedlam Farm photos by author. Henry Holt, 2011. ISBN 978-0-8050-9219-6 Subj: Animals – dogs. Farms.

Katz, Karen. *The babies on the bus* ill. by author. Henry Holt, 2011. ISBN 978-0-8050-9011-6 Subj: Babies, toddlers. Buses. Music. Songs.

Baby loves winter! ill. by author. Simon & Schuster, 2013. ISBN 978-1-4424-5213-8 Subj: Babies, toddlers. Format, unusual – board books. Seasons – winter. Weather – snow.

Can you say peace? ill. by author. Henry Holt, 2006. ISBN 978-0-8050-7893-0 Subj: Foreign languages. Violence, nonviolence. World.

The colors of us ill. by author. Henry Holt, 1999. ISBN 978-0-8050-5864-2 Subj: Character traits – individuality. Concepts – color. Ethnic groups in the U.S.

Counting kisses ill. by author. Margaret K. McElderry, 2001. ISBN 978-0-689-83470-7 Subj: Counting, numbers. Kissing.

Daddy hugs 1 2 3 ill. by author. Simon & Schuster, 2005. ISBN 978-0-689-87771-1 Subj: Counting, numbers. Emotions – love. Family life – fathers. Hugging.

Mommy hugs ill. by author. Simon & Schuster, 2006. ISBN 978-0-689-87772-8 Subj: Emotions – love. Family life – mothers. Hugging.

My first Ramadan ill. by author. Henry Holt, 2007. ISBN 978-0-8050-7894-7 Subj: Holidays – Ramadan. Religion. Religion – Islam.

Now I'm big ill. by author. Simon & Schuster, 2013. ISBN 978-1-4169-3547-6 Subj: Babies, toddlers. Behavior – growing up.

Over the moon ill. by author. Henry Holt, 1997. ISBN 978-0-8050-5013-4 Subj: Adoption. Babies, toddlers.

A potty for me! a lift-the-flap instruction manual ill. by author. Simon & Schuster, 2005. ISBN 978-0-689-87423-9 Subj: Format, unusual – toy & movable books. Toilet training.

Princess Baby ill. by author. Random House, 2008. ISBN 978-0-375-84119-4 Subj: Babies, toddlers. Names. Royalty – princesses.

Princess Baby, night-night ill. by author. Random House, 2009. ISBN 978-0-375-84462-1 Subj: Babies, toddlers. Bedtime. Royalty – princesses.

Rosie goes to preschool ill. by author. Random House, 2015. ISBN 978-038537917-5 Subj: School – nursery.

Ten tiny babies ill. by author. Simon & Schuster, 2008. ISBN 978-1-4169-3546-9 Subj: Babies, toddlers. Counting, numbers. Rhyming text.

Ten tiny tickles ill. by author. Simon & Schuster, 2005. ISBN 978-0-689-85976-2 Subj: Babies, toddlers. Counting, numbers.

Twelve hats for Lena ill. by author. Margaret K. McElderry, 2002. ISBN 978-0-689-84873-5 Subj: Clothing – hats. Days of the week, months of the year. Rhyming text.

Where is baby's mommy? ill. by author. Simon & Schuster, 2000. ISBN 978-0-689-83561-2 Subj: Babies, toddlers. Family life – mothers. Format, unusual – toy & movable books. Games.

Katz, Susan. *Mrs. Brown on exhibit* ill. by R. W. Alley. Simon & Schuster, 2002. ISBN 978-0-689-82970-3 Subj: Museums. Poetry. School – field trips.

Oh, Theodore! guinea pig poems ill. by Stacey Schuett. Houghton, 2007. ISBN 978-0-618-70222-0 Subj: Animals – guinea pigs. Pets. Poetry.

When the shadbush blooms (Messinger, Carla)

Katz, Susan B. *ABC, baby me!* ill. by Alicia Padrón. Random House, 2010. ISBN 978-0-375-86679-1 Subj: ABC books. Babies, toddlers. Format, unusual – board books.

ABC school's for me! ill. by Lynn Munsinger. Scholastic, 2015. ISBN 978-054553092-7 Subj: ABC books. Animals – bears. Rhyming text. School.

All year round ill. by Eiko Ojala. Scholastic/Orchard, 2016. ISBN 978-054574100-2 Subj: Concepts – shape. Days of the week, months of the year. Rhyming text. Seasons.

Katzler, Eva. *Florentine and Pig* ill. by Jess Mikhail. Bloomsbury, 2012. ISBN 978-1-59990-847-2 Subj: Activities – baking, cooking. Activities – picnicking. Animals – pigs. Friendship.

Katzman, Nicole. *Nathan blows out the Hanukkah candles* (Lehman-Wilzig, Tami)

Kaufman, Jeanne. *Young Henry and the dragon* ill. by Daria Tessler. Shenanigan, 2011. ISBN 978-1-934860-11-3 Subj: Dragons. Fire. Middle Ages. Rhyming text.

Kaufmann, Nancy. *Bye, Bye* ill. by Jung-Hee Spetter. Front Street, 2003. ISBN 978-1-886910-95-9

Subj: Animals. Animals – pigs. Family life – fathers. School – first day.

Kavanagh, Peter. *I love my mama* ill. by Jane Chapman. Simon & Schuster, 2003. ISBN 978-0-689-85691-4 Subj: Activities. Animals – elephants. Day. Family life – mothers. Rhyming text.

Kawata, Ken. *Animal tails* ill. by Masayuki Yabuuchi. Kane/Miller, 2001. ISBN 978-1-929132-05-8 Subj: Anatomy – tails. Animals.

Kay, Julia. *Gulliver Snip* ill. by author. Henry Holt, 2008. ISBN 978-0-8050-7992-0 Subj: Activities – bathing. Imagination. Pirates. Rhyming text.

Kay, Verla. *Broken Feather* ill. by Stephen Alcorn. Putnam, 2002. ISBN 978-0-399-23550-4 Subj: Indians of North America – Nez Perce. Poetry. U.S. history.

Civil War drummer boy ill. by Larry Day. Putnam, 2012. ISBN 978-0-399-23992-2 Subj: Musical instruments – drums. Rhyming text. U.S. history.

Covered wagons, bumpy trails ill. by S. D. Schindler. Putnam, 2000. ISBN 978-0-399-22928-2 Subj: Activities – traveling. Homes, houses. Rhyming text. U.S. history.

Gold fever ill. by S. D. Schindler. Putnam, 1999. ISBN 978-0-399-23027-1 Subj: Careers – miners. Rhyming text. U.S. history – frontier & pioneer life.

Hornbooks and inkwells ill. by S. D. Schindler. Penguin, 2011. ISBN 978-0-399-23870-3 Subj: Rhyming text. School. U.S. history – frontier & pioneer life.

Iron horses ill. by Michael McCurdy. Putnam, 1999. ISBN 978-0-399-23119-3 Subj: Rhyming text. Trains. U.S. history.

Orphan train ill. by Ken Stark. Putnam, 2003. ISBN 978-0-399-23613-6 Subj: Family life – brothers & sisters. Orphans. Rhyming text. Trains. U.S. history.

Whatever happened to the Pony Express? ill. by Kimberly Bulcken Root and Barry Root. Penguin, 2010. ISBN 978-0-399-24483-4 Subj: Animals – horses, ponies. Careers – postal workers. Rhyming text. U.S. history – frontier & pioneer life.

Kaye, Marilyn. *The real tooth fairy* ill. by Helen Cogancherry. Harcourt, 1990. ISBN 978-0-15-265780-2 Subj: Fairies. Teeth.

Keane, Claire. *Little big girl* ill. by author. Dial, 2016. ISBN 978-080373912-3 Subj: Babies, toddlers. Character traits – smallness. Family life – brothers & sisters. Family life – new sibling.

Once upon a cloud ill. by author. Dial, 2015. ISBN 978-080373911-6 Subj: Gifts. Imagination.

Keane, Dave. *Daddy adventure day* ill. by Sue Ramá. Penguin, 2011. ISBN 978-0-399-24627-2 Subj: Family life – fathers. Sports – baseball.

Sloppy Joe ill. by Denise Brunkus. HarperCollins, 2009. ISBN 978-0-06-171020-9 Subj: Behavior – messy. Character traits – cleanliness. Character traits – individuality. Family life. Illness.

Who wants a tortoise? ill. by K. G. Campbell. Knopf, 2016. ISBN 978-038575417-0 Subj: Behavior – dissatisfaction. Birthdays. Pets. Reptiles – turtles, tortoises.

Keane, Michael. *The night Santa got lost: how NORAD saved Christmas* ill. by Michael Garland. Regnery, 2012. ISBN 978-1-5969-8810-1 Subj: Behavior – lost. Careers – military. Holidays – Christmas. Santa Claus.

Keating, Jess. *Shark lady: the true story of how Eugenie Clark became the ocean's most fearless scientist* ill. by Marta Álvarez Miguéns. Sourcebooks/Jabberwocky, 2017. ISBN 978-149264204-6 Subj: Careers – scientists. Character traits – persistence. Fish – sharks. Gender roles.

Keats, Ezra Jack. *Apt. 3* ill. by author. Macmillan, 1971. ISBN 978-0-689-71059-9 Subj: Cities, towns. Disabilities – blindness. Ethnic groups in the U.S. – African Americans. Family life. Music. Musical instruments – harmonicas. Senses – sight.

Clementina's cactus ill. by author. Viking, 1999. ISBN 978-0-670-88545-9 Subj: Desert. Plants. Weather – storms. Wordless.

Dreams ill. by author. Macmillan, 1974. ISBN 978-0-02-749610-9 Subj: Dreams. Ethnic groups in the U.S. – African Americans. Imagination. Night. Sleep.

Goggles ill. by author. Macmillan, 1969. ISBN 978-0-02-749590-4 Subj: Behavior – bullying, teasing. Caldecott award honor books. Cities, towns. Ethnic groups in the U.S. – African Americans. Problem solving.

Hi, cat! ill. by author. Viking, 1999. ISBN 978-0-670-88546-6 Subj: Animals – cats. Cities, towns. Ethnic groups in the U.S. – African Americans.

Jennie's hat ill. by author. HarperCollins, 1966. ISBN 978-0-06-023114-9 Subj: Behavior – dissatisfaction. Character traits – kindness to animals. Clothing – hats.

John Henry ill. by author. HarperCollins, 1965. ISBN 978-0-394-99052-1 Subj: Character traits – perseverance. Character traits – pride. Ethnic groups in the U.S. – African Americans. Folk & fairy tales. Tall tales.

Kitten for a day ill. by author. Watts, 1974. ISBN 978-0-531-02714-1 Subj: Animals – cats. Animals – dogs. Wordless.

A letter to Amy ill. by author. HarperCollins, 1968. ISBN 978-0-06-023109-5 Subj: Ethnic groups in the U.S. – African Americans. Friendship. Letters, cards. Parties. Weather – rain. Weather – wind.

The little drummer boy ill. by author. Words & music by Katherine Davis, Henry Onorati & Harry Simeonne. Aladdin, 1987, ©1968. ISBN 978-0-689-71158-9 Subj: Gifts. Holidays – Christmas. Music. Musical instruments – drums. Religion – Nativity. Songs.

Louie ill. by author. Greenwillow, 1975. ISBN 978-0-688-84002-0 Subj: Character traits – shyness. Ethnic groups in the U.S. – African Americans. Puppets.

Louie's search ill. by author. Four Winds, 1989, ©1980. ISBN 978-0-689-71354-5 Subj: Behavior – needing someone. Family life.

Maggie and the pirate ill. by author. Four Winds, 1979. ISBN 978-0-590-07602-9 Subj: Death. Pets. Pirates.

My dog is lost! ill. by author. Viking, 1999. ISBN 978-0-670-88550-3 Subj: Animals – dogs. Behavior – lost. Careers – police officers. Ethnic groups in the U.S. Ethnic groups in the U.S. – Puerto Rican Americans. Foreign languages.

One red sun: a counting book ill. by author. Viking, 1999. ISBN 978-0-670-88478-0 Subj: Counting, numbers. Format, unusual – board books.

Pet show! ill. by author. Puffin, 2001, ©1972. ISBN 978-0-670-03504-5 Subj: Animals. Cities, towns. Communities, neighborhoods. Ethnic groups in the U.S. – African Americans. Pets.

Peter's chair ill. by author. HarperCollins, 1967. ISBN 978-0-06-023112-5 Subj: Babies, toddlers. Behavior – sharing. Ethnic groups in the U.S. – African Americans. Family life – new sibling. Friendship. Furniture – chairs. Self-concept.

The snowy day ill. by author. Viking, 1962. Subj: Activities – playing. Caldecott award books. Ethnic groups in the U.S. – African Americans. Seasons – winter. Weather – snow.

The trip ill. by author. Greenwillow, 1978. ISBN 978-0-688-84123-2 Subj: Emotions – loneliness. Ethnic groups in the U.S. – African Americans. Holidays – Halloween. Imagination. Moving.

Whistle for Willie ill. by author. Viking, 1964. Subj: Activities – whistling. Animals – dogs. Ethnic groups in the U.S. – African Americans. Problem solving. Self-concept.

Keefer, Janice Kulyk. *Anna's goat* ill. by Janet Wilson. Orca, 2000. ISBN 978-1-55143-153-6 Subj: Animals – goats. Family life – sisters. Foreign lands – Europe. War.

Keeler, Patricia A. *A huge hog is a big pig* (McCall, Francis X.)

Keely, Cheryl. *Here to there and me to you* ill. by Celia Krampien. Sleeping Bear, 2017. ISBN 978-158536996-6 Subj: Bridges.

Keens-Douglas, Richardo. *Anancy and the haunted house* ill. by Stéphane Jorisch. Annick, 2002. ISBN 978-1-55037-737-8 Subj: Folk & fairy tales. Holidays – Halloween. Homes, houses. Spiders.

Keep, Linda Lowery. *Day of the Dead* ill. by Barbara Knutson. Carolrhoda, 2004. ISBN 978-0-87614-914-0 Subj: Foreign lands – Mexico. Holidays – Day of the Dead.

Keillor, Garrison. *Daddy's girl* ill. by Robin Preiss-Glasser. Hyperion, 2005. ISBN 978-0-7868-1986-7 Subj: Family life – fathers. Rhyming text.

Keister, Douglas. *Fernando's gift / El regalo de Fernando* ill. with photos. Sierra Club, 1995. ISBN 978-0-87156-414-6 Subj: Ecology. Family life. Foreign lands – Costa Rica. Foreign languages. Forest, woods. Gifts. Trees.

To grandmother's house: a visit to old-town Beijing photos by author. Gibbs Smith, 2008. ISBN 978-1-4236-0283-5 Subj: Family life – grandmothers. Foreign lands – China. Homes, houses.

Keller, Emily Snowell. *Sleeping Bunny* ill. by author. Random House, 2003. ISBN 978-0-375-91541-3 Subj: Animals. Animals – rabbits. Folk & fairy tales. Royalty – princesses.

Keller, Holly. *Brave Horace* ill. by author. Greenwillow, 1998. ISBN 978-0-688-15408-0 Subj: Animals – leopards. Character traits – bravery. Emotions – fear. Parties.

Cecil's garden ill. by author. Greenwillow, 2002. ISBN 978-0-06-029594-3 Subj: Animals. Animals – rabbits. Behavior – fighting, arguing.

Geraldine and Mrs. Duffy ill. by author. Greenwillow, 2000. ISBN 978-0-688-16888-9 Subj: Activities – babysitting. Animals – pigs. Family life – brothers & sisters.

Geraldine first ill. by author. Greenwillow, 1996. ISBN 978-0-688-14150-9 Subj: Animals – pigs. Family life. Sibling rivalry.

Geraldine's baby brother ill. by author. Greenwillow, 1994. ISBN 978-0-688-12006-1 Subj: Animals – pigs. Babies, toddlers. Emotions – envy, jealousy. Family life – new sibling. Sibling rivalry.

Geraldine's big snow ill. by author. Greenwillow, 1988. ISBN 978-0-688-07514-9 Subj: Animals – pigs. Weather – snow.

Geraldine's blanket ill. by author. Greenwillow, 1984. ISBN 978-0-688-02540-3 Subj: Animals – pigs. Family life. Toys – dolls.

Help! a story of friendship ill. by author. HarperCollins, 2007. ISBN 978-0-06-123913-7 Subj: Animals. Animals – mice. Behavior – resourcefulness. Emotions – fear. Friendship. Reptiles – snakes.

Henry's Fourth of July ill. by author. Greenwillow, 1985. ISBN 978-0-688-04013-0 Subj: Activities – picnicking. Animals – possums. Holidays – Fourth of July.

Henry's happy birthday ill. by author. Greenwillow, 1990. ISBN 978-0-688-09451-5 Subj: Animals – possums. Birthdays. Parties.

Horace ill. by author. Greenwillow, 1991. ISBN 978-0-688-09832-2 Subj: Adoption. Animals – leopards. Character traits – being different. Self-concept.

Jacob's tree ill. by author. Greenwillow, 1999. ISBN 978-0-688-15996-2 Subj: Animals – bears. Behavior – growing up. Concepts – size. Family life.

Merry Christmas, Geraldine ill. by author. Greenwillow, 1997. ISBN 978-0-688-14501-9 Subj: Animals – pigs. Character traits – stubbornness. Holidays – Christmas.

Miranda's beach day ill. by author. HarperCollins, 2009. ISBN 978-0-06-158298-1 Subj: Family life – mothers. Sea & seashore – beaches.

Nosy Rosie ill. by author. HarperCollins, 2006. ISBN 978-0-06-078758-5 Subj: Animals – foxes. Behavior – bullying, teasing. Character traits – helpfulness. Senses – smell.

Pearl's new skates ill. by author. HarperCollins, 2005. ISBN 978-0-06-056281-6 Subj: Animals – rabbits. Character traits – persistence. Sports – ice skating.

Sophie's window ill. by author. HarperCollins, 2005. ISBN 978-0-06-056283-0 Subj: Animals – dogs. Birds – pigeons. Emotions – fear. Friendship.

That's mine, Horace ill. by author. Greenwillow, 2000. ISBN 978-0-688-17159-9 Subj: Animals. Behavior. Character traits – honesty. School.

Keller, John G. *The rubber-legged ducky* ill. by Henry Cole. Harcourt, 2008. ISBN 978-0-15-205289-8 Subj: Animals – foxes. Birds – ducks. Character traits – being different. Character traits – individuality.

Keller, Joy. *Monster trucks* ill. by Misa Saburi. Henry Holt, 2017. ISBN 978-162779617-0 Subj: Bedtime. Careers – construction workers. Monsters. Rhyming text. Trucks.

Keller, Laurie. *Arnie the doughnut* ill. by author. Henry Holt, 2003. ISBN 978-0-8050-6283-0 Subj: Food. Humorous stories.

Do unto otters: a book about manners ill. by author. Henry Holt, 2007. ISBN 978-0-8050-7996-8 Subj: Animals. Behavior. Etiquette. Language.

Grandpa Gazillion's number yard ill. by author. Henry Holt, 2005. ISBN 978-0-8050-6282-3 Subj: Counting, numbers. Humorous stories. Rhyming text.

Open wide: tooth school inside ill. by author. Henry Holt, 2000. ISBN 978-0-8050-6192-5 Subj: Careers – dentists. Health & fitness. Teeth.

The scrambled states of America ill. by author. Henry Holt, 1998. ISBN 978-0-8050-5802-4 Subj: Geography. Maps. U.S. history.

The scrambled states of America talent show ill. by author. Henry Holt, 2008. ISBN 978-0-8050-7997-5 Subj: Geography. Maps. Theater. U.S. history.

Keller, Shana. *Ticktock Banneker's clock* ill. by David C. Gardner. Sleeping Bear, 2016. ISBN 978-158536956-0 Subj: Careers – inventors. Character traits – perseverance. Clocks, watches. Ethnic groups in the U.S. – African Americans. U.S. history.

Kelley, Ellen A. *My life as a chicken* ill. by Michael H. Slack. Harcourt, 2007. ISBN 978-0-15-205306-2 Subj: Birds – chickens, roosters. Humorous stories.

Kelley, Kitty. *Martin's dream day* ill. by Stanley Tretick. Atheneum, 2017. ISBN 978-148146766-7 Subj: Careers – clergy. Ethnic groups in the U.S. – African Americans. Holidays – Martin Luther King, Jr. Day. Prejudice. U.S. history. Violence, nonviolence.

Kelley, Marty. *The rules* ill. by author. Zino, 2000. ISBN 978-1-55933-284-2 Subj: Behavior. Rhyming text.

Summer stinks ill. by author. Zino, 2001. ISBN 978-1-55933-291-0 Subj: ABC books. Rhyming text. Seasons – summer.

Twelve terrible things ill. by author. Tricycle, 2008. ISBN 978-1-58246-229-5 Subj: Humorous stories.

Winter woes ill. by author. Zino, 2005. ISBN 978-1-55933-306-1 Subj: Behavior – worrying. Rhyming text. Seasons – winter.

Kelley, True. *Blabber Mouse* ill. by author. Dutton, 2001. ISBN 978-0-525-46742-7 Subj: Animals – mice. Behavior – secrets. School.

Claude Monet ill. by author. Grosset, 2001. ISBN 978-0-448-42613-6 Subj: Activities – painting. Careers – artists. Foreign lands – France.

The dog who saved Santa ill. by author. Holiday, 2008. ISBN 978-0-8234-2120-6 Subj: Animals – dogs. Holidays – Christmas. Santa Claus.

I've got chicken pox ill. by author. Dutton, 1994. ISBN 978-0-525-45185-3 Subj: Illness – chicken pox.

Kellogg, Steven. *Aster Aardvark's alphabet adventures* ill. by author. Morrow, 1987. ISBN 978-0-688-07257-5 Subj: ABC books. Animals. Animals – aardvarks. Birds.

A beasty story (Martin, Bill, Jr.)

Best friends ill. by author. Dial, 1986. ISBN 978-0-8037-0101-4 Subj: Animals – dogs. Emotions – envy, jealousy. Friendship.

Can I keep him? ill. by author. Dial, 1971. ISBN 978-0-8037-0989-8 Subj: Family life. Pets.

Chicken Little ill. by author. Morrow, 1985. ISBN 978-0-688-05691-9 Subj: Animals. Behavior – trickery. Birds – chickens, roosters. Folk & fairy tales.

The Christmas witch ill. by author. Dial, 1992. ISBN 978-0-8037-1269-0 Subj: Holidays – Christmas. Witches.

Give the dog a bone ill. by author. SeaStar, 2000. ISBN 978-1-58717-002-7 Subj: Animals – dogs. Counting, numbers. Songs.

A-hunting we will go! ill. by author. Morrow, 1998. ISBN 978-0-688-14945-1 Subj: Bedtime. Songs.

I was born about 10,000 years ago: a tall tale ill. by author. Morrow, 1996. ISBN 978-0-688-13412-9 Subj: Folk & fairy tales. Songs. Tall tales.

The island of the skog ill. by author. Dial, 1973. ISBN 978-0-8037-3840-9 Subj: Animals – mice. Boats, ships. Islands. Monsters.

Johnny Appleseed: a tall tale ill. by author. Morrow, 1988. ISBN 978-0-688-06418-1 Subj: Activities – traveling. Gardens, gardening. Tall tales. Trees. U.S. history – frontier & pioneer life.

Mike Fink: a tall tale ill. by author. Morrow, 1992. ISBN 978-0-688-07004-5 Subj: Boats, ships. Rivers. Tall tales. U.S. history.

The mysterious tadpole ill. by author. Dial, 1977. ISBN 978-0-8037-6246-6 Subj: Frogs & toads. Monsters. Pets.

The mystery of the flying orange pumpkin ill. by author. Dial, 1980. ISBN 978-0-8037-6116-2 Subj: Holidays – Halloween. Mystery stories.

The mystery of the magic green ball ill. by author. Dial, 1978. ISBN 978-0-8037-6215-2 Subj: Behavior – lost & found possessions. Mystery stories. Romani. Toys – balls.

The mystery of the missing red mitten ill. by author. Dial, 2000. ISBN 978-0-8037-2566-9 Subj: Behavior – lost & found possessions. Clothing – gloves, mittens. Mystery stories. Snowmen.

The mystery of the stolen blue paint ill. by author. Dial, 1982. ISBN 978-0-8037-5659-5 Subj: Mystery stories.

Paul Bunyan: a tall tale ill. by reteller. Morrow, 1984. ISBN 978-0-688-03850-2 Subj: Animals – oxen. Careers – lumberjacks. Tall tales. U.S. history – frontier & pioneer life.

Pecos Bill ill. by reteller. Morrow, 1986. ISBN 978-0-688-05872-2 Subj: Cowboys, cowgirls. Tall tales. U.S. history – frontier & pioneer life.

A penguin pup for Pinkerton ill. by author. Dial, 2001. ISBN 978-0-8037-2536-2 Subj: Animals – dogs. Birds – penguins. Eggs.

The Pied Piper's magic ill. by author. Dial, 2009. ISBN 978-0-8037-2818-9 Subj: Animals – rats. Folk & fairy tales. Magic.

Pinkerton, behave! ill. by author. Dial, 2014. ISBN 978-080374130-0 Subj: Animals – dogs. Behavior – misbehavior.

Prehistoric Pinkerton ill. by author. Dial, 1987. ISBN 978-0-8037-0323-0 Subj: Animals – dogs. Behavior – misbehavior. Dinosaurs. Museums. Prehistory.

Ralph's secret weapon ill. by author. Dial, 1983. ISBN 978-0-8037-7087-4 Subj: Activities – vacationing. Imagination.

A rose for Pinkerton ill. by author. Dial, 1981. ISBN 978-0-8037-7503-9 Subj: Animals – cats. Animals – dogs. Behavior – imitation.

Sally Ann Thunder Ann Whirlwind Crockett ill. by author. Morrow, 1995. ISBN 978-0-688-14043-4 Subj: Tall tales. U.S. history – frontier & pioneer life.

Santa Claus is comin' to town lyrics by Haven Gillespi; ill. by author. HarperCollins, 2004. ISBN 978-0-06-623849-4 Subj: Holidays – Christmas. Santa Claus. Songs.

Tallyho, Pinkerton! ill. by author. Dial, 1982. ISBN 978-0-8037-8743-8 Subj: Animals – cats. Animals – dogs. Sports – hunting.

Yankee Doodle ill. by author. Four Winds, 1980, ©1976. ISBN 978-0-590-07782-8 Subj: Music. Songs. U.S. history.

Kelly, David A. *Miracle mud: Lena Blackburne and the secret mud that changed baseball* ill. by Oliver Dominguez. Millbrook, 2013. ISBN 978-0-7613-8092-4 Subj: Careers – inventors. Inventions. Sports – baseball.

Kelly, Irene. *Even an octopus needs a home* ill. by author. Holiday House, 2011. ISBN 978-0-8234-2235-7 Subj: Animals. Homes, houses.

Even an ostrich needs a nest: where birds begin ill. by author. Holiday, 2009. ISBN 978-0-8234-2102-2 Subj: Birds. Homes, houses.

It's a butterfly's life ill. by author. Holiday House, 2007. ISBN 978-0-8234-1860-2 Subj: Insects – butterflies, caterpillars.

Kelly, L. J. R. *Sometimes it's storks* ill. by Hilts Brothers. Putnam, 2017. ISBN 978-039925682-0 Subj: Animals. Babies, toddlers. Behavior – lost. Birds – storks. Rhyming text.

Kelly, Luke. *Blanket and bear, a remarkable pair* ill. by Yoko Tanaka. Putnam, 2013. ISBN 978-0-399-25681-3 Subj: Behavior – growing up. Behavior – lost & found possessions. Rhyming text. Toys – bears.

Kelly, Mark. *Mousetronaut: based on a (partially) true story* ill. by C. F. Payne. Simon & Schuster, 2012. ISBN 978-1-4424-5824-6 Subj: Animals – mice. Careers – astronauts. Character traits – bravery. Space & space ships.

Mousetronaut goes to Mars ill. by C. F. Payne. Simon & Schuster, 2013. ISBN 978-1-4424-8426-9 Subj: Animals – mice. Careers – astronauts. Space & space ships.

Kelly, Mij. *Achoo! good manners can be contagious!* ill. by Mary McQuillan. Barron's, 2009. ISBN 978-0-7641-6969-4 Subj: Animals. Behavior. Etiquette. Health & fitness. Hygiene. Rhyming text.

A bed of your own! ill. by Mary McQuillan. Barron's, 2011. ISBN 978-0-7641-4768-5 Subj: Animals. Bedtime. Farms. Rhyming text.

Friendly Day ill. by Charles Fuge. Barron's, 2013. ISBN 978-1-43800-345-0 Subj: Animals. Character traits – kindness. Rhyming text.

One more sheep ill. by Russell Ayto. Peachtree, 2006. ISBN 978-1-56145-378-8 Subj: Animals – sheep. Animals – wolves. Behavior – trickery. Rhyming text.

Where's my darling daughter? ill. by Katharine McEwen. Good Books, 2006. ISBN 978-1-56148-537-6 Subj: Animals. Behavior – lost. Farms. Rhyming text.

William and the night train ill. by Alison Jay. Farrar, 2001. ISBN 978-0-374-38437-1 Subj: Activities – traveling. Bedtime. Trains.

Kelly, Scott. *My journey to the stars* ill. by André Ceolin. Crown, 2017. ISBN 978-152476377-0 Subj: Behavior – growing up. Careers – astronauts. Space & space ships.

Kelly, Sheila M. *The A.D.D. book for kids* (Rotner, Shelley)

All kinds of friends (Rotner, Shelley)

Families (Rotner, Shelley)

Feeling thankful (Rotner, Shelley)

I'm adopted! (Rotner, Shelley)

Lots of grandparents (Rotner, Shelley)

Lots of moms (Rotner, Shelley)

Shades of people (Rotner, Shelley)

What can you do? (Rotner, Shelley)

Kempter, Christa. *Dear Little Lamb* ill. by Frauke Weldin. NorthSouth, 2006. ISBN 978-0-7358-2086-9 Subj: Activities – writing. Animals – sheep. Animals – wolves. Letters, cards. Pen pals.

Wally and Mae ill. by Frauke Weldin. NorthSouth, 2008. ISBN 978-0-7358-2208-5 Subj: Animals – bears. Animals – rabbits. Character traits – cleanliness.

When Mama can't sleep ill. by Natascha Rosenberg. NorthSouth, 2011. ISBN 978-0-7358-4015-7 Subj: Bedtime. Behavior – worrying. Family life. Family life – mothers.

Kenah, Katharine. *The dream shop* ill. by Peter Catalanotto. HarperCollins, 2002. ISBN 978-0-688-17901-4 Subj: Dreams. Night.

Ferry tail ill. by Nicole Wong. Sleeping Bear, 2014. ISBN 978-158536829-7 Subj: Animals – dogs. Behavior – running away. Boats, ships.

Predator attack! ill. with photos. McGraw-Hill, 2004. ISBN 978-0-7696-3176-9 Subj: Animals.

The very stuffed turkey ill. by Binny Talib. Scholastic, 2015. ISBN 978-054576109-3 Subj: Birds – turkeys. Food. Friendship. Holidays – Thanksgiving.

Kennedy, Anne Vittur. *The farmer's away! baa! neigh!* ill. by Anne Kennedy. Candlewick, 2014. ISBN 978-076366679-8 Subj: Animals. Farms. Noise, sounds. Rhyming text.

Ragweed's farm dog handbook ill. by Anne Kennedy. Candlewick, 2015. ISBN 978-076367417-5 Subj: Animals – dogs. Farms.

Kennedy, Cindy. *The star of Christmas* ill. by Dennis Bredow. Zondervan, 2002. ISBN 978-0-310-70504-8 Subj: Foreign lands – England. Holidays – Christmas.

Kennedy, Jimmy. *The teddy bears' picnic* ill. by Alexandra Day. Green Tiger, 1983. ISBN 978-0-88138-010-1 Subj: Activities – picnicking. Toys – bears.

The teddy bears' picnic ill. by Michael Hague. Henry Holt, 1992. ISBN 978-0-8050-1008-4 Subj: Activities – picnicking. Poetry. Songs. Toys – bears.

The teddy bears' picnic ill. by Prue Theobalds. HarperCollins, 1987. ISBN 978-0-87226-153-2 Subj: Activities – picnicking. Poetry. Toys – bears.

Kennedy, Kim. *Hee-Haw-Dini and the Great Zambini* ill. by Doug Kennedy. Abrams, 2009. ISBN 978-0-8109-7025-0 Subj: Animals – donkeys.

Animals – mice. Careers – magicians. Character traits – persistence.

Pirate Pete's giant adventure ill. by Doug Kennedy. Abrams, 2006. ISBN 978-0-8109-5965-1 Subj: Birds – parakeets, parrots. Giants. Magic. Pirates.

Kenney, Sean. *Cool cars and trucks* ill. with photos. Henry Holt, 2009. ISBN 978-0-8050-8761-1 Subj: Activities – making things. Automobiles. Imagination. Toys. Trucks.

Cool castles ill. with photos. Henry Holt, 2012. ISBN 978-0-8050-9539-5 Subj: Activities – making things. Castles. Imagination. Toys.

Cool city photos by John E. Barrett. Henry Holt, 2011. ISBN 978-0-8050-8762-8 Subj: Activities – making things. Cities, towns. Imagination. Toys.

Cool creations in 101 pieces ill. with photos. Holt/Christy Ottaviano, 2014. ISBN 978-162779017-8 Subj: Activities – making things. Imagination. Toys.

Cool creations in 35 pieces ill. with photos. Henry Holt, 2013. ISBN 978-0-8050-9692-7 Subj: Activities – making things. Imagination. Toys.

Kennison, Ruth. *The potty train* (Hochman, David)

Kensington, Mary Jane. *Dear Cinderella* (Moore, Marian)

Kent, Allegra. *Ballerina gets ready* ill. by Catherine Stock. Holiday, 2016. ISBN 978-082343563-0 Subj: Ballet. Careers – dancers.

Ballerina swan ill. by Emily Arnold McCully. Holiday House, 2012. ISBN 978-0-8234-2373-6 Subj: Ballet. Birds – swans. School.

Kenyon, Tony. *Hyacinth Hop has the hic-hops* ill. by author. Ragged Bears, 2000. ISBN 978-1-929927-06-7 Subj: Animals – rabbits. Hiccups.

Kepes, Juliet. *Five little monkeys* ill. by author. Houghton, 1952. Subj: Animals. Animals – monkeys. Caldecott award honor books.

Kerby, Johanna. *Little pink pup* photos by author. Penguin, 2010. ISBN 978-0-399-25435-2 Subj: Animals – dogs. Animals – pigs. Pets.

Kerby, Mona. *Owney, the mail-pouch pooch* ill. by Lynne Barasch. Farrar, 2008. ISBN 978-0-374-35685-9 Subj: Activities – traveling. Animals – dogs. Careers – postal workers.

Kerley, Barbara. *Brave like me* ill. with photos. National Geographic, 2016. ISBN 978-142632361-4 Subj: Careers – military. Character traits – bravery. Character traits – perseverance.

A cool drink of water ill. by author. National Geographic, 2002. ISBN 978-0-7922-6723-2 Subj: Water.

A home for Mr. Emerson ill. by Edwin Fotheringham. Scholastic, 2014. ISBN 978-054535088-4 Subj: Books, reading. Careers – writers. U.S. history.

One world, one day ill. with photos. National Geographic, 2009. ISBN 978-1-4263-0460-6 Subj: Day. World.

What to do about Alice? how Alice Roosevelt broke the rules, charmed the world, and drove her father Teddy crazy! ill. by Edwin Fotheringham. Scholastic, 2008. ISBN 978-0-439-92231-9 Subj: Behavior – misbehavior. Character traits – confidence. U.S. history.

With a friend by your side ill. with photos. National Geographic, 2015. ISBN 978-142631905-1 Subj: Friendship. World.

The world is waiting for you ill. with photos. National Geographic, 2013. ISBN 978-1-4263-1114-7 Subj: Activities. Behavior – growing up. Careers. World.

You and me together: moms, dads, and kids around the world ill. with photos. National Geographic, 2005. ISBN 978-0-7922-8298-3 Subj: Family life – parents. World.

Kern, Noris. *I love you with all my heart* ill. by author. Chronicle, 1998. ISBN 978-0-8118-2031-8 Subj: Animals – polar bears. Emotions – love. Family life – mothers.

Kerner, Susan. *Always by my side* ill. by Ian P. Benfold Haywood. Star Bright, 2013. ISBN 978-1-59572-336-9 Subj: Death. Emotions – grief. Emotions – sadness. Family life. Rhyming text.

Kerr, Judith. *One night in the zoo* ill. by author. Kane/Miller, 2010. ISBN 978-1-935279-37-2 Subj: Counting, numbers. Rhyming text. Zoos.

Kespert, Deborah. *On the move* (Fecher, Sarah)

Rain and shine ill. by Fran Jordan. Two-Can, 2000. ISBN 978-1-58728-609-4 Subj: Careers – meteorologists. Seasons. Weather.

Kessler, Cristina. *The best beekeeper of Lalibela: a tale from Africa* ill. by Leonard Jenkins. Holiday House, 2006. ISBN 978-0-8234-1858-9 Subj: Careers – beekeepers. Character traits – perseverance. Foreign lands – Ethiopia. Gender roles. Insects – bees.

Jubela ill. by Jo Ellen McAllister Stammen. Simon & Schuster, 2001. ISBN 978-0-689-81895-0 Subj: Animals – babies. Animals – rhinoceros. Foreign lands – Africa. Orphans.

My great-grandmother's gourd ill. by Walter Lyon Krudop. Orchard, 2000. ISBN 978-0-531-33284-9 Subj: Family life – grandmothers. Foreign lands – Sudan. Trees. Water. Weather – droughts.

Ketcham, Sallie. *The Christmas bird* ill. by Stacey Schuett. Augsburg Fortress, 2000. ISBN 978-0-8066-3871-3 Subj: Birds – robins. Folk & fairy tales. Foreign lands – England. Holidays – Christmas. Religion – Nativity.

Ketteman, Helen. *Armadillo tattletale* ill. by Keith Graves. Scholastic, 2000. ISBN 978-0-590-99723-2 Subj: Animals – armadillos. Behavior – gossip, rumors.

Armadilly chili ill. by Will Terry. Albert Whitman, 2004. ISBN 978-0-8075-0457-4 Subj: Animals – armadillos. Behavior – sharing. Birds – bluebirds. Character traits – laziness. Food. Friendship. Frogs & toads. Spiders.

At the old haunted house ill. by Nate Wragg. Two Lions, 2014. ISBN 978-147784769-5 Subj: Counting, numbers. Holidays – Halloween. Homes, houses. Rhyming text.

Bubba the cowboy prince: a fractured Texas tale ill. by James Warhola. Scholastic, 1997. ISBN 978-0-590-25506-6 Subj: Animals – bulls, cows. Cowboys, cowgirls. Folk & fairy tales. Humorous stories. Parties.

The ghosts go haunting ill. by Adam Record. Albert Whitman, 2014. ISBN 978-080752852-5 Subj: Ghosts. Holidays – Halloween. Monsters. School. Songs. Witches.

Goodnight, Little Monster ill. by Bonnie Leick. Marshall Cavendish, 2010. ISBN 978-0-7614-5683-4 Subj: Bedtime. Monsters. Rhyming text.

If Beaver had a fever ill. by Kevin O'Malley. Marshall Cavendish, 2011. ISBN 978-0-7614-5951-4 Subj: Animals – bears. Careers – doctors. Family life – mothers. Illness. Rhyming text. Zoos.

Señorita Gordita (The gingerbread boy)

There once was a cowpoke who swallowed an ant (Little old lady who swallowed a fly)

The three little gators ill. by Will Terry. Albert Whitman, 2009. ISBN 978-0-8075-7824-7 Subj: Folk & fairy tales. Homes, houses. Reptiles – alligators, crocodiles. Texas.

Waynetta and the cornstalk: a Texas fairy tale ill. by Diane Greenseid. Albert Whitman, 2007. ISBN 978-0-8075-8687-7 Subj: Folk & fairy tales. Giants. Plants. Texas.

Kevi. *Don't talk to strangers* ill. by JibJab Media. Scholastic, 2003. ISBN 978-0-439-31385-8 Subj: Behavior – talking to strangers. Safety.

Key, Francis Scott. *The Star Spangled Banner* ill. by Dana Regan. Random House, 2002. ISBN 978-0-375-91596-3 Subj: Flags. Songs. U.S. history.

The Star-Spangled Banner ill. by Peter Spier. Doubleday, 1973. ISBN 978-0-385-07746-0 Subj: Flags. Songs. U.S. history.

Khalsa, Dayal Kaur. *Green cat* ill. by author. Tundra, 2002. ISBN 978-0-88776-586-5 Subj: Animals – cats. Rhyming text.

Khan, Hena. *The night of the moon: a Muslim holiday story* ill. by Julie Paschkis. Chronicle, 2008. ISBN 978-0-8118-6062-8 Subj: Ethnic groups in the U.S. – Lebanese Americans. Holidays – Ramadan. Religion – Islam.

Khan, Rukhsana. *Big red lollipop* ill. by Sophie Blackall. Penguin, 2010. ISBN 978-0-670-06287-4 Subj: Birthdays. Ethnic groups in the U.S. – Pakistani Americans. Family life – sisters. Parties.

King for a day ill. by Christiane Krömer. Lee & Low, 2013. ISBN 978-1-60060-659-5 Subj: Contests. Disabilities – physical disabilities. Fairs, festivals. Foreign lands – Pakistan. Kites.

Kheiriyeh, Rashin. *There was an old lady who swallowed a fly* (Little old lady who swallowed a fly)

Kherdian, David. *Come back, Moon* ill. by Nonny Hogrogian. Simon & Schuster, 2013. ISBN 978-1-4424-5887-1 Subj: Animals. Animals – bears. Forest, woods. Moon.

Khing, T. T. *Where is the cake?* ill. by T. T. Khing. Abrams, 2007. ISBN 978-0-8109-1798-9 Subj: Animals. Behavior – stealing. Food. Picture puzzles. Wordless.

Where is the cake now? ill. by T. T. Khing. Abrams, 2009. ISBN 978-0-8109-8926-9 Subj: Animals. Behavior – stealing. Food. Picture puzzles. Wordless.

Kidslabel. *Spot 7: Christmas* ill. with photos. Chronicle, 2006. ISBN 978-0-8118-5323-1 Subj: Holidays – Christmas. Picture puzzles.

Spot 7: school ill. with photos. Chronicle, 2006. ISBN 978-0-8118-5324-8 Subj: Picture puzzles. School.

Kiernan, Pat. *Good morning, city* ill. by Pascal Campion. Farrar, 2016. ISBN 978-037430346-4 Subj: Cities, towns. Morning.

Kilaka, John. *True friends: a tale from Tanzania* ill. by author. Groundwood, 2006. ISBN 978-0-88899-698-5 Subj: Animals – elephants. Animals – rats. Folk & fairy tales. Foreign lands – Tanzania. Friendship.

Kilby, Don. *At a construction site* ill. by author. Kids Can, 2003. ISBN 978-1-55337-378-0 Subj: Careers – construction workers. Machines. Trucks.

In the city ill. by author. Kids Can, 2004. ISBN 978-1-55337-471-8 Subj: Cities, towns. Machines. Trucks.

In the country ill. by author. Kids Can, 2004. ISBN 978-1-55337-472-5 Subj: Country. Machines. Tractors. Trucks.

On the road ill. by author. Kids Can, 2003. ISBN 978-1-55337-379-7 Subj: Roads. Trucks.

Killen, Nicola. *The little reindeer* ill. by author. Simon & Schuster/Paula Wiseman, 2017. ISBN 978-148148686-6 Subj: Animals – reindeer. Holidays – Christmas.

Not me! ill. by author. Egmont, 2010. ISBN 978-1-4052-4829-7 Subj: Behavior – messy. Character traits – responsibility.

Killion, Bette. *Just think!* ill. by Linda Bronson. HarperCollins, 2001. ISBN 978-0-694-01315-9 Subj: Concepts. Family life – mothers. Rhyming text.

Kilodavis, Cheryl. *My princess boy* ill. by Suzanne DeSimone. Simon & Schuster, 2010. ISBN 978-1-4424-2988-8 Subj: Behavior – bullying, teasing. Character traits – being different. Character traits – individuality. Gender roles.

Kim, Aram. *Cat on the bus* ill. by author. Holiday, 2016. ISBN 978-082343647-7 Subj: Animals – cats. Character traits – kindness to animals. Ethnic groups in the U.S. – Asian Americans.

No kimchi for me! ill. by author. Holiday House, 2017. ISBN 978-082343762-7 Subj: Animals – cats. Ethnic groups in the U.S. – Korean Americans. Family life – brothers & sisters. Food.

Kim, Hanmin. *Tiptoe tapirs* ill. by author. Holiday, 2015. ISBN 978-082343395-7 Subj: Animals – tapirs. Folk & fairy tales. Jungle. Noise, sounds.

Kim, Julie. *Where's Halmoni?* ill. by author. Sasquatch/Little Bigfoot, 2017. ISBN 978-163217077-4 Subj: Behavior – lost. Family life – brothers & sisters. Family life – grandmothers. Folk & fairy tales. Foreign lands – Korea. Format, unusual – graphic novels.

Kim, Sue. *How does a seed grow?* ill. by Tilde. Simon & Schuster, 2010. ISBN 978-1-4169-9435-0 Subj: Format, unusual – board books. Plants. Seeds.

Kimmel, Elizabeth Cody. *Glamsters* ill. by Jackie Urbanovic. Hyperion, 2008. ISBN 978-1-4231-1148-1 Subj: Animals – hamsters. Self-concept.

My penguin Osbert ill. by H. B. Lewis. Candlewick, 2004. ISBN 978-0-7636-1699-1 Subj: Birds – penguins. Gifts. Holidays – Christmas. Humorous stories.

My penguin Osbert in love ill. by H. B. Lewis. Candlewick, 2009. ISBN 978-0-7636-3032-4 Subj: Birds – penguins. Emotions – love. Foreign lands – Antarctic. Helicopters.

A taste of freedom: Gandhi and the Great Salt March ill. by Giuliano Ferri. Bloomsbury, 2014. ISBN 978-080279467-3 Subj: Behavior – seeking better things. Character traits – perseverance. Foreign lands – India. Violence, nonviolence.

Kimmel, Eric A. *Anansi and the magic stick* ill. by Janet Stevens. Holiday, 2001. ISBN 978-0-8234-1443-7 Subj: Animals – hyenas. Folk & fairy tales. Foreign lands – Africa. Magic. Spiders.

Anansi and the moss-covered rock ill. by Janet Stevens. Holiday, 1990. ISBN 978-0-8234-0689-0 Subj: Animals. Behavior – trickery. Folk & fairy tales. Spiders.

Anansi and the talking melon ill. by Janet Stevens. Holiday, 1994. ISBN 978-0-8234-1104-7 Subj: Animals. Animals – elephants. Behavior – trickery. Folk & fairy tales. Foreign lands – Africa. Spiders.

Anansi goes fishing ill. by Janet Stevens. Holiday, 1992. ISBN 978-0-8234-0918-1 Subj: Behavior – trickery. Folk & fairy tales. Foreign lands – Africa. Reptiles – turtles, tortoises. Spiders.

Anansi's party time ill. by Janet Stevens. Holiday, 2008. ISBN 978-0-8234-1922-7 Subj: Behavior – trickery. Folk & fairy tales. Foreign lands – Africa. Reptiles – turtles, tortoises. Spiders.

The birds' gift: a Ukrainian Easter story ill. by Katya Krenina. Holiday, 1999. ISBN 978-0-8234-1384-3 Subj: Birds. Character traits – kindness to animals. Eggs. Folk & fairy tales. Foreign lands – Ukraine. Holidays – Easter.

The Chanukkah guest ill. by Giyora Karmi. Holiday, 1990. ISBN 978-0-8234-0788-0 Subj: Holidays – Hanukkah. Jewish culture. Religion.

Easy work! an old tale ill. by Andrew Glass. Holiday, 1998. ISBN 978-0-8234-1349-2 Subj: Folk & fairy tales. Foreign lands – Norway.

The Erie Canal pirates ill. by Andrew Glass. Holiday, 2002. ISBN 978-0-8234-1657-8 Subj: Boats, ships. Folk & fairy tales. Music. Pirates. Rhyming text. Tall tales.

The frog princess: a Tlingit legend from Alaska ill. by Rosanne Litzinger. Holiday House, 2006. ISBN 978-0-8234-1618-9 Subj: Folk & fairy tales. Frogs & toads. Indians of North America – Tlingit. Royalty – princesses.

Gershon's monster: a story for the Jewish New Year ill. by Jon J Muth. Scholastic, 2000. ISBN 978-0-439-10839-3 Subj: Folk & fairy tales. Holidays – Rosh Hashanah. Jewish culture. Religion.

The great Texas hamster drive ill. by Bruce Whatley. Marshall Cavendish, 2007. ISBN 978-0-7614-5357-4 Subj: Animals – hamsters. Tall tales. Texas. U.S. history – frontier & pioneer life.

Hanukkah bear ill. by Mike Wohnoutka. Holiday House, 2013. ISBN 978-0-8234-2855-7 Subj: Animals – bears. Food. Holidays – Hanukkah. Jewish culture.

Hershel and the Hanukkah goblins ill. by Trina Schart Hyman. Holiday, 1989. ISBN 978-0-8234-0769-9 Subj: Caldecott award honor books. Holidays – Hanukkah. Jewish culture. Mythical creatures – goblins. Religion.

I took my frog to the library ill. by Blanche Sims. Viking, 1990. ISBN 978-0-670-82418-2 Subj: Animals. Libraries. Pets.

Jack and the giant barbecue ill. by John Manders. Amazon Children's, 2012. ISBN 978-0-7614-6128-9 Subj: Activities – baking, cooking. Food. Giants. Texas.

Joha makes a wish: a Middle Eastern tale ill. by Omar Rayyan. Marshall Cavendish, 2010. ISBN 978-0-7614-5599-8 Subj: Behavior – wishing. Foreign lands – Middle East. Magic.

Joseph and the Sabbath fish ill. by Martina Peluso. Lerner/Kar-Ben, 2011. ISBN 978-0-7613-5908-1 Subj: Folk & fairy tales. Jewish culture. Religion.

The lady in the blue cloak: legends from the Texas missions ill. by Susan Guevara. Holiday House, 2006. ISBN 978-0-8234-1738-4 Subj: Religion. Texas.

Little Britches and the rattlers ill. by Vincent Nguyen. Marshall Cavendish, 2008. ISBN 978-0-7614-5432-8 Subj: Cowboys, cowgirls. Reptiles – snakes. Texas.

Little Red Hot ill. by Laura Huliska-Beith. Amazon/Two Lions, 2013. ISBN 978-1-4778-1638-7 Subj: Animals – wolves. Folk & fairy tales. Food. U.S. history – frontier & pioneer life.

The magic dreidels ill. by Katya Krénina. Holiday, 1996. ISBN 978-0-8234-1256-3 Subj: Folk & fairy tales. Holidays – Hanukkah. Jewish culture.

Medio Pollito: a Spanish tale ill. by Valeria Docampo. Marshall Cavendish, 2010. ISBN 978-0-7614-5705-3 Subj: Birds – chickens, roosters. Folk & fairy tales. Foreign lands – Spain.

The mysterious guests: a Sukkot story ill. by Katya Krenina. Holiday, 2008. ISBN 978-0-8234-1893-0 Subj: Character traits – selfishness. Holidays – Sukkot.

Pumpkinhead ill. by Steve Haskamp. Winslow, 2001. ISBN 978-1-890817-33-6 Subj: Activities – traveling. Anatomy – heads. Animals – squirrels. Plants.

Rattlestiltskin ill. by Erin Camarca. Westwinds, 2016. ISBN 978-194332838-3 Subj: Behavior –

boasting, showing off. Folk & fairy tales. Food. Foreign languages. Names.

Rip Van Winkle's return ill. by Leonard Everett Fisher. Farrar, 2007. ISBN 978-0-374-36308-6 Subj: Behavior – lost. Folk & fairy tales. Mythical creatures – elves. Sleep.

Robin Hook, pirate hunter! ill. by Michael Dooling. Scholastic, 2001. ISBN 978-0-590-68199-5 Subj: Pirates.

The runaway tortilla ill. by Randy Cecil. Winslow, 2000. ISBN 978-1-890817-18-3 Subj: Behavior – running away. Cumulative tales. Folk & fairy tales.

Simon and the bear: a Hanukkah tale ill. by Matthew Trueman. Hyperion, 2014. ISBN 978-142314355-0 Subj: Animals – polar bears. Holidays – Hanukkah. Jewish culture.

Stormy's hat: just right for a railroad man ill. by Andrea U'Ren. Farrar, 2008. ISBN 978-0-374-37262-0 Subj: Activities – sewing. Careers – railroad engineers. Clothing – hats. Trains.

The three cabritos ill. by Stephen Gilpin. Marshall Cavendish, 2007. ISBN 978-0-7614-5343-7 Subj: Animals – goats. Character traits – cleverness. Folk & fairy tales. Magic. Monsters. Music. Texas.

The three little tamales ill. by Valeria Docampo. Marshall Cavendish, 2009. ISBN 978-0-7614-5519-6 Subj: Animals – wolves. Behavior – running away. Folk & fairy tales. Food.

The three princes ill. by Leonard Everett Fisher. Holiday, 1994. ISBN 978-0-8234-1115-3 Subj: Folk & fairy tales. Foreign lands – Arabia. Royalty – princes. Royalty – princesses.

The two mountains: an Aztec legend ill. by Leonard Everett Fisher. Holiday, 2000. ISBN 978-0-8234-1504-5 Subj: Folk & fairy tales. Foreign lands – Mexico. Indians of North America – Aztec. Mountains. Volcanoes.

Zigazak! ill. by Jon Goodell. Doubleday, 2001. ISBN 978-0-385-32652-0 Subj: Careers – clergy. Holidays – Hanukkah. Jewish culture.

Kimmel, Haven. *Orville, a dog story* ill. by Robert Andrew Parker. Clarion, 2003. ISBN 978-0-618-15955-0 Subj: Animals – dogs. Emotions. Farms.

Kimmelman, Leslie. *Dance, sing, remember* ill. by Ora Eitan. HarperCollins, 2000. ISBN 978-0-06-027726-0 Subj: Holidays. Jewish culture. Religion.

Everybody bonjours! ill. by Sarah McMenemy. Knopf, 2008. ISBN 978-0-375-84443-0 Subj: Foreign lands – France. Foreign languages. Rhyming text.

Hanukkah lights, Hanukkah nights ill. by John Himmelman. HarperCollins, 1992. ISBN 978-0-

06-020369-6 Subj: Family life. Holidays – Hanukkah. Jewish culture. Religion.

Hooray! it's Passover! ill. by John Himmelman. HarperCollins, 1996. ISBN 978-0-06-024674-7 Subj: Family life. Holidays – Passover. Jewish culture. Religion.

How do I love you? ill. by Lisa McCue. HarperCollins, 2005. ISBN 978-0-06-001200-7 Subj: Counting, numbers. Emotions – love. Family life. Reptiles – alligators, crocodiles. Rhyming text.

The Little Red Hen and the Passover matzah (The little red hen)

Round the turkey ill. by Nancy Cote. Albert Whitman, 2002. ISBN 978-0-8075-7131-6 Subj: Family life. Holidays – Thanksgiving. Rhyming text.

The runaway latkes ill. by Paul Yalowitz. Albert Whitman, 2000. ISBN 978-0-8075-7176-7 Subj: Behavior – running away. Holidays – Hanukkah. Jewish culture. Religion.

The Shabbat puppy ill. by Jaime Zollars. Marshall Cavendish, 2012. ISBN 978-0-7614-6145-6 Subj: Activities – walking. Animals – dogs. Family life – grandfathers. Jewish culture. Religion.

Sound the shofar! a story for Rosh Hashanah and Yom Kippur ill. by John Himmelman. HarperCollins, 1998. ISBN 978-0-06-027498-6 Subj: Family life – aunts, uncles. Holidays – Rosh Hashanah. Holidays – Yom Kippur. Jewish culture. Religion.

The three bully goats ill. by Will Terry. Albert Whitman, 2011. ISBN 978-0-8075-7900-8 Subj: Animals – babies. Animals – goats. Behavior – bullying, teasing. Mythical creatures – ogres.

Trick ARRR treat: a pirate Halloween ill. by Jorge Monlongo. Albert Whitman, 2015. ISBN 978-080758061-5 Subj: Holidays – Halloween. Pirates. Rhyming text.

Kimura, Ken. *999 frogs and a little brother* ill. by Yasunari Murakami. NorthSouth, 2015. ISBN 978-073584202-1 Subj: Character traits – smallness. Concepts – size. Friendship. Frogs & toads.

999 frogs wake up ill. by Yasunari Murakami. NorthSouth, 2013. ISBN 978-0-7358-4108-6 Subj: Frogs & toads. Reptiles – snakes. Seasons – spring.

999 tadpoles ill. by Yasunari Murakami. NorthSouth, 2011. ISBN 978-0-7358-4013-3 Subj: Birds – hawks. Frogs & toads.

Kimura, Yuichi. *One stormy night . . .* ill. by Hiroshi Abe. Kodansha, 2003. ISBN 978-4-7700-2970-6 Subj: Animals – goats. Animals – wolves. Emotions – fear. Foreign lands – Japan. Friendship. Weather – storms.

One sunny day . . . ill. by Hiroshi Abe. Kodansha, 2003. ISBN 978-4-7700-2971-3 Subj: Animals – goats. Animals – wolves. Emotions – fear. Foreign lands – Japan. Friendship. Nature.

Kinch, Devon. *Pretty Penny cleans up* ill. by author. Random House, 2012. ISBN 978-0-375-86736-1 Subj: Animals – dogs. Money.

Pretty Penny makes ends meet ill. by author. Random House, 2013. ISBN 978-0-375-86737-8 Subj: Character traits – helpfulness. Counting, numbers. Jewelry. Money.

Kindermans, Martine. *You and me* by Martine Kindermans and Sasha Quinton; ill. by Martine Kindermans. Penguin, 2006. ISBN 978-0-399-24471-1 Subj: Birds – geese. Emotions – love. Family life – mothers. Rhyming text.

Kinerk, Robert. *Clorinda* ill. by Steven Kellogg. Simon & Schuster, 2003. ISBN 978-0-689-86449-0 Subj: Activities – dancing. Animals – bulls, cows. Ballet. Character traits – perseverance. Rhyming text.

Clorinda plays baseball! ill. by Steven Kellogg. Simon & Schuster, 2012. ISBN 978-0-689-86865-8 Subj: Animals – bulls, cows. Character traits – helpfulness. Friendship. Rhyming text. Sports – baseball.

Clorinda takes flight ill. by Steven Kellogg. Simon & Schuster, 2007. ISBN 978-0-689-86864-1 Subj: Activities – flying. Animals. Animals – bulls, cows. Character traits – perseverance. Rhyming text.

Timothy Cox will not change his socks ill. by Stephen Gammell. Simon & Schuster, 2005. ISBN 978-0-689-87181-8 Subj: Animals – dogs. Character traits – perseverance. Clothing – socks. Rhyming text. Senses – smell.

King, Dedie. *I see the sun in Afghanistan* ill. by Judith Inglese. Satya House, 2011. ISBN 978-0-9818720-8-7 Subj: Family life. Foreign lands – Afghanistan. Foreign languages.

I see the sun in Russia ill. by Judith Inglese. Satya, 2012. ISBN 978-1-93587-408-9 Subj: Family life. Foreign lands – Russia. Foreign languages.

King, M. G. *Librarian on the roof! a true story* ill. by Stephen Gilpin. Albert Whitman, 2010. ISBN 978-0-8075-4512-6 Subj: Careers – librarians. Libraries. Texas.

King, Martin Luther, III. *My daddy, Dr. Martin Luther King, Jr.* ill. by A. G. Ford. Amistad, 2013. ISBN 978-0-06-028075-8 Subj: Ethnic groups in the U.S. – African Americans. Family life – fathers. Holidays – Martin Luther King, Jr. Day. Prejudice. U.S. history. Violence, nonviolence.

King, Martin Luther, Jr. *I have a dream* ill. by Kadir Nelson. Random House, 2012. ISBN 978-0-375-85887-1 Subj: Dreams. Ethnic groups in the U.S.

– African Americans. Holidays – Martin Luther King, Jr. Day. Prejudice. U.S. history. Violence, nonviolence.

King, Stephen Michael. *Emily loves to bounce* ill. by author. Philomel, 2003. ISBN 978-0-399-23886-4 Subj: Activities – jumping. Activities – playing. Rhyming text.

Mutt dog! ill. by author. Harcourt, 2005. ISBN 978-0-15-205561-5 Subj: Animals – dogs. Homeless.

You: a story of love and friendship ill. by author. HarperCollins, 2011. ISBN 978-0-06-206014-3 Subj: Animals – dogs. Birds. Friendship.

King, Thomas. *Coyote sings to the moon* ill. by Johnny Wales. WestWinds, 2001. ISBN 978-1-55868-642-7 Subj: Animals. Animals – coyotes. Creation. Folk & fairy tales. Moon.

King-Chai, Sharon. *Lucy Ladybug* ill. by author. Random House, 2016. ISBN 978-055351005-8 Subj: Character traits – appearance. Character traits – being different. Character traits – generosity. Emotions – loneliness. Insects – ladybugs.

Kinkade, Sheila. *My family* photos by Elaine Little. Charlesbridge, 2006. ISBN 978-1-57091-662-5 Subj: Family life. Foreign lands.

Kinney, Jessica. *The pig scramble* ill. by Sarah S. Brannen. Islandport, 2011. ISBN 978-1-934031-61-2 Subj: Animals – pigs. Contests. Fairs, festivals.

Kinsey, Helen. *The bear that heard crying* (Kinsey-Warnock, Natalie)

Kinsey-Warnock, Natalie. *The bear that heard crying* by Natalie Kinsey-Warnock and Helen Kinsey ill. by Ted Rand. Cobblehill, 1993. ISBN 978-0-525-65103-1 Subj: Animals – bears. Behavior – lost. U.S. history – frontier & pioneer life.

A Christmas like Helen's ill. by Mary Azarian. Houghton, 2004. ISBN 978-0-618-23137-9 Subj: Family life. Farms. Holidays – Christmas.

A farm of her own ill. by Kathleen Kolb. Dutton, 2001. ISBN 978-0-525-46507-2 Subj: Family life – aunts, uncles. Family life – cousins. Farms.

From dawn till dusk ill. by Mary Azarian. Houghton, 2002. ISBN 978-0-618-18655-6 Subj: Family life. Farms. Seasons.

Nora's ark ill. by Emily Arnold McCully. HarperCollins, 2005. ISBN 978-0-06-029517-2 Subj: Family life – grandparents. Farms. U.S. history. Weather – floods.

When spring comes ill. by Stacey Schuett. Dutton, 1993. ISBN 978-0-525-45008-5 Subj: Family life – fathers. Farms. Seasons – spring.

Kipling, Rudyard. *The beginning of the armadillos* ill. by Lorinda Bryan Cauley. Harcourt, 1985. ISBN 978-0-15-206380-1 Subj: Animals – armadillos.

The elephant's child ill. by Lorinda Bryan Cauley. Harcourt, 1983. ISBN 978-0-15-225385-1 Subj: Animals. Animals – elephants. Character traits – curiosity. Foreign lands – Africa.

How the camel got his hump ill. by Lisbeth Zwerger. NorthSouth, 2001. ISBN 978-0-7358-1483-7 Subj: Animals. Animals – camels. Behavior – misbehavior. Folk & fairy tales – pourquoi tales. Foreign lands – Africa.

How the elephant got his trunk retold by Jean Richards; ill. by Norman Gorbaty. Henry Holt, 2003. ISBN 978-0-8050-6699-9 Subj: Anatomy – noses. Animals. Animals – elephants. Character traits – curiosity. Folk & fairy tales – pourquoi tales. Foreign lands – Africa. Reptiles – alligators, crocodiles.

How the leopard got his spots ill. by Lori Lohstoeter. Picture Book Studio, 1989. ISBN 978-0-88708-112-5 Subj: Animals – leopards. Folk & fairy tales – pourquoi tales.

The jungle book retold by Laura Driscoll; ill. by Migy Blanco. HarperCollins, 2016. ISBN 978-006237087-7 Subj: Animals. Behavior – growing up. Jungle.

Rikki-tikki-tavi ill. by Lambert Davis. Harcourt, 1992. ISBN 978-0-15-267015-3 Subj: Animals – mongooses. Character traits – bravery. Character traits – cleverness. Foreign lands – India. Reptiles – snakes.

Rikki-tikki-tavi adapt. by Jerry Pinkney; ill. by adapter. Morrow, 1997. ISBN 978-0-688-14321-3 Subj: Animals – mongooses. Character traits – bravery. Character traits – cleverness. Foreign lands – India. Reptiles – snakes.

Kirby, Pamela F. *What bluebirds do* ill. with photos. Boyds Mills, 2009. ISBN 978-1-59078-614-7 Subj: Birds – bluebirds.

Kirk, Daniel. *Bigger* ill. by author. Putnam, 1998. ISBN 978-0-399-23127-8 Subj: Behavior – growing up. Concepts – size. Self-concept.

Bus stop, bus go ill. by author. Putnam, 2001. ISBN 978-0-399-23333-3 Subj: Animals – hamsters. Buses. Rhyming text.

Go! ill. by author. Hyperion, 2001. ISBN 978-0-7868-0305-7 Subj: Music. Songs. Transportation.

Honk honk! Beep beep! ill. by author. Hyperion/Disney, 2010. ISBN 978-1-4231-2486-3 Subj: Activities – traveling. Automobiles. Imagination. Rhyming text. Toys.

Hush, little alien ill. by author. Hyperion, 1999. ISBN 978-0-7868-2469-4 Subj: Aliens. Bedtime. Lullabies.

Jack and Jill ill. by author. Putnam, 2003. ISBN 978-0-399-23553-5 Subj: Behavior – wishing. Humorous stories. Nursery rhymes.

Keisha Ann can! ill. by author. Putnam, 2008. ISBN 978-0-399-24179-6 Subj: Character traits – pride. Ethnic groups in the U.S. – African Americans. Rhyming text. School.

Library mouse ill. by author. Abrams, 2007. ISBN 978-0-8109-9346-4 Subj: Activities – writing. Animals – mice. Books, reading. Careers – writers. Character traits – shyness. Libraries.

Library mouse: a friend's tale ill. by author. Abrams, 2009. ISBN 978-0-8109-8927-6 Subj: Activities – writing. Animals – mice. Books, reading. Careers – writers. Character traits – shyness. Libraries.

Library mouse: a museum adventure ill. by author. Abrams, 2012. ISBN 978-1-4197-0173-3 Subj: Activities – writing. Animals – cats. Animals – mice. Art. Careers – artists. Careers – explorers. Museums.

Library mouse: a world to explore ill. by author. Abrams, 2010. ISBN 978-0-8109-8968-9 Subj: Animals – mice. Careers – explorers. Character traits – bravery. Emotions – fear. Friendship. Libraries.

Library mouse: home sweet home ill. by author. Abrams, 2013. ISBN 978-1-4197-0544-1 Subj: Animals – mice. Books, reading. Buildings. Homes, houses. Libraries.

Moondogs ill. by author. Putnam, 1999. ISBN 978-0-399-23128-5 Subj: Animals – dogs. Moon. Rhyming text. Space & space ships.

Rhino in the house: the true story of saving Samia ill. by author. Abrams, 2017. ISBN 978-141972316-2 Subj: Animals – endangered animals. Animals – rhinoceros. Character traits – kindness to animals. Foreign lands – Kenya.

Snow family ill. by author. Hyperion, 2000. ISBN 978-0-7868-2244-7 Subj: Family life – parents. Rhyming text. Snowmen.

Ten thank-you letters ill. by author. Penguin/Nancy Paulsen, 2014. ISBN 978-039916937-3 Subj: Animals – pigs. Animals – rabbits. Character traits. Character traits – kindness. Letters, cards.

Ten things I love about you ill. by author. Penguin/Nancy Paulsen, 2012. ISBN 978-0-399-25288-4 Subj: Activities – writing. Animals – pigs. Animals – rabbits. Friendship.

The thing about spring ill. by author. Abrams, 2015. ISBN 978-141971492-4 Subj: Animals. Concepts – change. Seasons. Seasons – spring.

Trash trucks! ill. by author. Putnam, 1997. ISBN 978-0-399-22927-5 Subj: Careers – sanitation workers. Rhyming text. Trucks.

You are not my friend, but I miss you ill. by author. Abrams, 2014. ISBN 978-141971236-4 Subj: Behavior – sharing. Friendship. Toys.

Kirk, David. *Little bird, Biddle bird* ill. by author. Scholastic, 2001. ISBN 978-0-439-26092-3 Subj: Birds. Food. Rhyming text. Self-concept.

Little bunny, Biddle bunny ill. by author. Scholastic, 2002. ISBN 978-0-439-33819-6 Subj: Animals – rabbits. Rhyming text. Seasons.

Little Miss Spider ill. by author. Scholastic, 1999. ISBN 978-0-439-08389-8 Subj: Emotions – love. Family life – mothers. Rhyming text. Spiders.

Little Miss Spider at Sunny Patch School ill. by author. Scholastic, 2000. ISBN 978-0-439-08727-8 Subj: Insects. Rhyming text. School – first day. Spiders.

Little pig, Biddle pig ill. by author. Scholastic, 2001. ISBN 978-0-439-30575-4 Subj: Animals – pigs. Character traits – cleanliness. Rhyming text.

Miss Spider's ABC ill. by author. Scholastic, 1998. ISBN 978-0-590-28279-6 Subj: ABC books. Birthdays. Insects. Rhyming text. Spiders.

Miss Spider's new car ill. by author. Scholastic, 1997. ISBN 978-0-590-30713-0 Subj: Automobiles. Insects. Rhyming text. Spiders.

Miss Spider's tea party ill. by author. Scholastic, 1994. ISBN 978-0-590-47724-6 Subj: Emotions – fear. Parties. Rhyming text. Spiders.

Oh so brave dragon ill. by author. Feiwel & Friends, 2014. ISBN 978-125001689-8 Subj: Character traits – bravery. Dragons. Emotions – fear. Friendship.

Oh So Tiny bunny ill. by author. Feiwel & Friends, 2013. ISBN 978-1-250-01688-1 Subj: Animals – babies. Animals – rabbits. Character traits – smallness. Dreams.

Truckeroo school ill. by author. Feiwel & Friends, 2017. ISBN 978-125001690-4 Subj: Monsters. Rhyming text. School. Trucks.

Kirk, Katie. *Eli, no!* ill. by author. Abrams, 2011. ISBN 978-0-8109-8964-1 Subj: Animals – dogs. Behavior – misbehavior.

Kirsch, Vincent X. *Forsythia and me* ill. by author. Farrar, 2011. ISBN 978-0-374-32438-4 Subj: Behavior – sharing. Character traits – helpfulness. Friendship.

Freddie and Gingersnap ill. by author. Hyperion/Disney, 2013. ISBN 978-1-4231-5958-2 Subj: Dinosaurs. Dragons. Friendship.

Natalie and Naughtily ill. by author. Bloomsbury, 2008. ISBN 978-1-59990-269-2 Subj: Character traits – helpfulness. Family life – sisters. Multiple births – twins. Stores.

Two little boys from Toolittle Toys ill. by author. Bloomsbury, 2010. ISBN 978-1-59990-428-3 Subj: Family life – brothers. Toys.

Kirwan, Wednesday. *Baby loves to boogie!* ill. by author. Simon & Schuster, 2014. ISBN 978-148140383-2 Subj: Activities – dancing. Animals – babies. Babies, toddlers. Format, unusual – board books.

Minerva the monster ill. by author. Sterling, 2008. ISBN 978-1-4027-5718-1 Subj: Animals – dogs. Family life.

Nobody notices Minerva ill. by author. Sterling, 2007. ISBN 978-1-4027-4728-1 Subj: Animals – dogs. Behavior – misbehavior. Family life.

Kishira, Mayuko. *Who's next door?* ill. by Jun Takabatake. OwlKids, 2014. ISBN 978-177147071-1 Subj: Birds – chickens, roosters. Birds – owls. Problem solving.

Kitamura, Satoshi. *Comic adventures of Boots* ill. by author. Farrar, 2002. ISBN 978-0-374-31455-2 Subj: Animals – cats.

Me and my cat? ill. by author. Farrar, 2000. ISBN 978-0-374-34906-6 Subj: Animals – cats. Magic. Witches.

Pablo the artist ill. by author. Farrar, 2006. ISBN 978-0-374-35687-3 Subj: Animals – elephants. Art. Careers – artists. Friendship.

Kittinger, Jo S. *The house on Dirty-Third Street* ill. by Thomas Gonzalez. Peachtree, 2012. ISBN 978-1-56145-619-2 Subj: Character traits – hopefulness. Communities, neighborhoods. Homes, houses. Religion.

Rosa's bus: the ride to civil rights ill. by Steven Walker. Calkins Creek, 2010. ISBN 978-1-59078-722-9 Subj: Ethnic groups in the U.S. – African Americans. Prejudice. Transportation. U.S. history. Violence, nonviolence.

Kladstrup, Kristin. *The gingerbread pirates* ill. by Matt Tavares. Candlewick, 2009. ISBN 978-0-7636-3223-6 Subj: Food. Holidays – Christmas. Pirates.

Klassen, Jon. *I want my hat back* ill. by author. Candlewick, 2011. ISBN 978-0-7636-5598-3 Subj: Animals – bears. Behavior – lost & found possessions. Clothing – hats.

This is not my hat ill. by author. Candlewick, 2012. ISBN 978-0-7636-5599-0 Subj: Caldecott award books. Clothing – hats. Crime. Fish. Humorous stories.

We found a hat ill. by author. Candlewick, 2016. ISBN 978-076365600-3 Subj: Behavior – lost & found possessions. Clothing – hats. Reptiles – turtles, tortoises.

Klausmeier, Jesse. *Open this little book* ill. by Suzy Lee. Chronicle, 2013. ISBN 978-0-8118-6783-2 Subj: Animals. Books, reading. Character traits – cooperation. Concepts – color. Format, unusual – toy & movable books. Giants.

Kleber, Dori. *More-igami* ill. by G. Brian Karas. Candlewick, 2016. ISBN 978-076366819-8 Subj: Activities – making things. Character traits – patience, impatience. Character traits – perseverance. Paper.

Klein, Tali. *Hop! Plop!* (Schwartz, Corey Rosen)

Kleven, Elisa. *The apple doll* ill. by author. Farrar, 2007. ISBN 978-0-374-30380-8 Subj: Activities – making things. Food. School.

A carousel tale ill. by author. Tricycle, 2009. ISBN 978-1-58246-239-4 Subj: Anatomy – tails. Art. Merry-go-rounds. Reptiles – alligators, crocodiles.

Cozy light, cozy night ill. by author. Creston, 2013. ISBN 978-1-939547-02-6 Subj: Rhyming text. Seasons.

The dancing deer and the foolish hunter ill. by author. Dutton, 2002. ISBN 978-0-525-46832-5 Subj: Activities – dancing. Animals – deer. Birds. Ecology. Forest, woods.

Ernst ill. by author. Tricycle, 2002. ISBN 978-1-58246-053-6 Subj: Birthdays. Reptiles – alligators, crocodiles.

The friendship wish ill. by author. Penguin, 2011. ISBN 978-0-525-42374-4 Subj: Angels. Animals – dogs. Emotions – loneliness. Friendship. Moving.

Glasswings: a butterfly's story ill. by author. Dial, 2013. ISBN 978-0-8037-3742-6 Subj: Behavior – lost. Cities, towns. Ecology. Insects – butterflies, caterpillars. Science.

A monster in the house ill. by author. Dutton, 1998. ISBN 978-0-525-45973-6 Subj: Babies, toddlers. Family life – brothers. Monsters.

The paper princess ill. by author. Dutton, 1994. ISBN 978-0-525-45231-7 Subj: Activities – drawing. Activities – flying. Paper. Royalty – princesses.

The puddle pail ill. by author. Dutton, 1997. ISBN 978-0-525-45803-6 Subj: Behavior – collecting things. Family life – brothers. Reptiles – alligators, crocodiles.

Sun bread ill. by author. Dutton, 2001. ISBN 978-0-525-46674-1 Subj: Animals. Careers – bakers. Food. Rhyming text. Sun.

Welcome home, Mouse ill. by author. Tricycle, 2010. ISBN 978-1-58246-277-6 Subj: Animals – elephants. Animals – mice. Character traits – clumsiness. Friendship. Homes, houses.

The wishing ball ill. by author. Farrar, 2006. ISBN 978-0-374-38449-4 Subj: Animals – cats. Behavior – wishing. Birds – crows. Reptiles – alligators, crocodiles.

Kleven, Sandy. *The right touch: a read aloud story to help prevent child sexual abuse* ill. by Jody Bergsma. Illumination, 1997. ISBN 978-0-935699-10-4 Subj: Child abuse. Family life.

Kling, Kevin. *Big little brother* ill. by Chris Monroe. Borealis, 2011. ISBN 978-0-87351-844-4 Subj: Behavior – bullying, teasing. Family life – brothers.

Klinting, Lars. *What do you want?* ill. by author. Groundwood, 2006. ISBN 978-0-88899-636-7 Subj: Behavior – wishing.

Kliphuis, Christine. *Robbie and Ronnie* ill. by Charlotte Dematons. NorthSouth, 2002. ISBN 978-0-7358-1627-5 Subj: Behavior – bullying, teasing. Concepts – size. Friendship. Sports – swimming.

Klise, Kate. *Grammy Lamby and the secret handshake* ill. by M. Sarah Klise. Henry Holt, 2012. ISBN 978-0-8050-9313-1 Subj: Animals – sheep. Character traits – helpfulness. Family life – grandmothers. Weather – storms.

Imagine Harry ill. by M. Sarah Klise. Harcourt, 2007. ISBN 978-0-15-205704-6 Subj: Animals – rabbits. Imagination – imaginary friends.

Little Rabbit and the Meanest Mother on Earth ill. by M. Sarah Klise. Harcourt, 2010. ISBN 978-0-15-206201-9 Subj: Animals – rabbits. Behavior – messy. Circus. Family life – mothers.

Little Rabbit and the Night Mare ill. by M. Sarah Klise. Harcourt, 2008. ISBN 978-0-15-205717-6 Subj: Animals – rabbits. Behavior – worrying. Emotions – fear. Nightmares. School.

Stand straight, Ella Kate: the true story of a real giant ill. by M. Sarah Klise. Penguin, 2010. ISBN 978-0-8037-3404-3 Subj: Character traits – being different. Concepts – size. Giants.

Stay: a girl, a dog, a bucket list ill. by M. Sarah Klise. Feiwel & Friends, 2017. ISBN 978-125010714-5 Subj: Animals – dogs. Character traits – kindness to animals. Old age. Pets.

Why do you cry? not a sob story ill. by M. Sarah Klise. Henry Holt, 2006. ISBN 978-0-8050-7319-5 Subj: Animals. Animals – rabbits. Emotions.

Kloske, Geoffrey. *Once upon a time, the end (asleep in 60 seconds)* ill. by Barry Blitt. Simon & Schuster, 2005. ISBN 978-0-689-86619-7 Subj: Bedtime. Books, reading. Folk & fairy tales.

Klostermann, Penny Parker. *A cooked-up fairy tale* ill. by Ben Mantle. Random House, 2017. ISBN 978-110193232-2 Subj: Activities – baking, cooking. Folk & fairy tales.

There was an old dragon who swallowed a knight ill. by Ben Mantle. Random House, 2015. ISBN 978-038539080-4 Subj: Cumulative tales. Dragons. Knights. Middle Ages.

Knapman, Timothy. *Can't catch me!* ill. by Simona Ciraolo. Candlewick, 2017. ISBN 978-076369496-8 Subj: Animals – cats. Animals – mice. Behavior – boasting, showing off. Behavior – trickery.

Dinosaurs don't have bedtimes! ill. by Nikki Dyson. Candlewick, 2016. ISBN 978-076368927-8 Subj: Bedtime. Behavior – misbehavior. Dinosaurs. Imagination.

Follow the track all the way back ill. by Ben Mantle. Candlewick, 2017. ISBN 978-076369573-6 Subj: Trains.

A monster moved in! ill. by Loretta Schauer. Tiger Tales, 2015. ISBN 978-158925176-2 Subj: Behavior – boredom. Imagination. Monsters.

Soon ill. by Patrick Benson. Candlewick, 2015. ISBN 978-076367478-6 Subj: Animals – elephants. Family life – mothers.

Superhero dad ill. by Joe Berger. Nosy Crow, 2016. ISBN 978-076368657-4 Subj: Family life – fathers.

Time now to dream ill. by Helen Oxenbury. Candlewick, 2017. ISBN 978-076369078-6 Subj: Animals – wolves. Emotions – fear. Family life – brothers & sisters. Family life – mothers. Forest, woods.

Knapp, Ruthie. *Who stole Mona Lisa?* ill. by Jill McElmurry. Bloomsbury, 2010. ISBN 978-1-59990-058-2 Subj: Activities – painting. Art. Crime.

Kneen, Maggie. *Chocolate moose* ill. by author. Penguin, 2011. ISBN 978-0-525-42202-0 Subj: Activities – baking, cooking. Animals – mice. Animals – moose. Careers – bakers.

The Christmas surprise ill. by author. Chronicle, 2001. ISBN 978-0-8118-3210-6 Subj: Animals – pigs. Holidays – Christmas. Rhyming text. Weather – snow.

Knick knack paddy whack ill. by Christiane Engel. Barefoot, 2008. ISBN 978-1-84686-144-4 Subj: Activities – making things. Counting, numbers. Cumulative tales. Songs.

Knight, Hilary. *A firefly in a fir tree* ill. by author. Tegen, 2004. ISBN 978-0-06-000992-2 Subj: Animals – mice. Holidays – Christmas. Music. Nature. Songs.

Hilary Knight's the owl and the pussy-cat by Hilary Knight and Edward Lear; ill. by Hilary Knight. Based on The owl and the pussy-cat by Edward Lear. Macmillan, 1983. ISBN 978-0-02-750900-7 Subj: Imagination. Magic. Poetry.

Knight, Margy Burns. *Africa is not a country* by Margy Burns Knight and Mark Melnicove ill. by Anne Sibley O'Brien. Millbrook, 2000. ISBN 978-0-7613-1266-6 Subj: Foreign lands – Africa.

Talking walls ill. by Anne Sibley O'Brien. Tilbury, 1992. ISBN 978-0-88448-102-7 Subj: Foreign lands.

Knister. *Sophie's dance* ill. by Mandy Schlunt. Minedition, 2007. ISBN 978-0-698-40056-6 Subj: Activities – dancing. Family life – grandmothers.

Knowlton, Laurie Lazzaro. *Why cowgirls are such sweet talkers* ill. by James Rice. Pelican, 2000. ISBN 978-1-56554-698-1 Subj: Behavior. Cowboys, cowgirls.

Knudsen, Michelle. *Argus* ill. by Andréa Wesson. Candlewick, 2011. ISBN 978-0-7636-3790-3 Subj: Birds – chickens, roosters. Dragons. School. Science.

Big Mean Mike ill. by Scott Magoon. Candlewick, 2012. ISBN 978-0-7636-4990-6 Subj: Animals – dogs. Animals – rabbits. Character traits – kindness to animals. Self-concept.

Bugged! ill. by Blanche Sims. Kane, 2008. ISBN 978-1-57565-259-7 Subj: Insects – mosquitoes. Problem solving. Science.

Library lion ill. by Kevin Hawkes. Candlewick, 2006. ISBN 978-0-7636-2262-6 Subj: Animals – lions. Character traits – helpfulness. Libraries.

Marilyn's monster ill. by Matt Phelan. Candlewick, 2015. ISBN 978-076366011-6 Subj: Friendship. Monsters.

A moldy mystery ill. by Barry Gott. Kane, 2006. ISBN 978-1-57565-167-5 Subj: Family life – brothers & sisters. Science.

Knutson, Barbara. *Love and roast chicken* ill. by author. Lerner, 2004. ISBN 978-1-57505-657-9 Subj: Animals – guinea pigs. Behavior – trickery. Folk & fairy tales. Foreign lands – South America. Indians of South America.

Ko, Sangmi. *A dog wearing shoes* ill. by author. Random House, 2015. ISBN 978-038538396-7 Subj: Animals – dogs. Behavior – lost & found possessions. Character traits – kindness to animals. Clothing – shoes.

Kobald, Irena. *My two blankets* ill. by Freya Blackwood. Houghton Mifflin Harcourt, 2015. ISBN 978-054443228-4 Subj: Emotions – sadness. Immigrants, immigration. War.

Koch, Ed. *Eddie's little sister makes a splash* by Ed Koch and Pat Koch ill. by James Warhola. Penguin, 2007. ISBN 978-0-399-24310-3 Subj: Activities – vacationing. Family life – brothers & sisters. Sports – swimming.

Koch, Pat. *Eddie's little sister makes a splash* (Koch, Ed)

Kochan, Vera. *What if your best friend were blue?* ill. by Viviana Garofoli. Marshall Cavendish, 2011. ISBN 978-0-7614-5897-5 Subj: Character traits – appearance. Character traits – being different. Friendship. Prejudice.

Koda-Callan, Elizabeth. *The squiggly Wigglys* ill. by author. Workman, 2003. ISBN 978-0-7611-2821-2 Subj: Family life. Food. Format, unusual – toy & movable books. Parties. Rhyming text.

Koehler, Fred. *How to cheer up Dad* ill. by author. Dial, 2014. ISBN 978-080373922-2 Subj: Animals – elephants. Behavior – bad day, bad mood. Behavior – misbehavior. Family life – fathers.

Super Jumbo ill. by author. Dial, 2016. ISBN 978-080373923-9 Subj: Activities – playing. Animals – elephants. Character traits – helpfulness.

Koehler, Lana Wayne. *Ah-choo!* by Lana Wayne Koehler and Gloria G. Adams ill. by Ken Min. Sterling, 2016. ISBN 978-145491415-0 Subj: Illness – allergies. Pets. Rhyming text.

Koehler, Lora. *The little snowplow* ill. by Jake Parker. Candlewick, 2015. ISBN 978-076367074-0 Subj: Character traits – persistence. Character traits – smallness. Machines. Trucks. Weather – snow.

Kohara, Kazuno. *Ghosts in the house!* ill. by author. Roaring Brook, 2008. ISBN 978-1-59643-427-1 Subj: Ghosts. Homes, houses. Witches.

Here comes Jack Frost ill. by author. Roaring Brook, 2009. ISBN 978-1-59643-442-2 Subj: Emotions – loneliness. Mythical creatures. Seasons – winter.

The Midnight Library ill. by author. Roaring Brook, 2014. ISBN 978-159643985-6 Subj: Animals. Books, reading. Libraries.

Kohuth, Jane. *Duck sock hop* ill. by Jane Porter. Dial, 2012. ISBN 978-0-8037-3712-9 Subj: Activities – dancing. Birds – ducks. Clothing – socks. Rhyming text.

Kolanovic, Dubravka. *Everyone needs a friend* ill. by author. Price Stern Sloan, 2010. ISBN 978-0-8431-9918-5 Subj: Animals – mice. Animals – wolves. Emotions – loneliness. Friendship.

Kolar, Bob. *Big kicks* ill. by author. Candlewick, 2008. ISBN 978-0-7636-3390-5 Subj: Animals – bears. Sports – soccer.

Racer dogs ill. by author. Dutton, 2003. ISBN 978-0-525-45939-2 Subj: Animals – dogs. Automobiles. Sports – racing.

Koller, Jackie French. *Baby for sale* ill. by Janet Pedersen. Marshall Cavendish, 2002. ISBN 978-0-7614-5106-8 Subj: Babies, toddlers. Family life – brothers & sisters. Sibling rivalry.

Bouncing on the bed ill. by Anna Grossnickle Hines. Orchard, 1999. ISBN 978-0-531-33138-5 Subj: Activities. Rhyming text.

Nickommoh! a Thanksgiving celebration ill. by Marcia Sewall. Atheneum, 1999. ISBN 978-0-689-81094-7 Subj: Holidays – Thanksgiving. Indians of North America – Narragansett. Seasons – fall.

No such thing ill. by Betsy Lewin. Boyds Mills, 1997. ISBN 978-1-56397-490-8 Subj: Bedtime. Emotions – fear. Family life – mothers. Monsters.

One monkey too many ill. by Lynn Munsinger. Harcourt, 1999. ISBN 978-0-15-200006-6 Subj: Animals – monkeys. Counting, numbers. Rhyming text.

Konagaya, Kiyomi. *Beach feet* ill. by Masamitsu Saito. Enchanted Lion, 2012. ISBN 978-1-59270-121-6 Subj: Anatomy – feet. Sea & seashore – beaches.

Könnecke, Ole. *Anthony and the girls* ill. by author. Farrar, 2006. ISBN 978-0-374-30376-1 Subj: Activities – playing. Behavior – indifference. Emotions.

Anton and the battle ill. by author. Gecko, 2013. ISBN 978-1-87757-926-4 Subj: Animals – dogs. Behavior – fighting, arguing. Weapons.

Anton can do magic ill. by author. Gecko, 2011. ISBN 978-1-8774-6737-0 Subj: Clothing – hats. Humorous stories. Magic.

The big book of words and pictures ill. by author. Gecko, 2012. ISBN 978-1-87757-905-9 Subj: Format, unusual – board books. Language.

You can do it, Bert! ill. by author. Gecko, 2015. ISBN 978-192727103-2 Subj: Birds. Character traits – confidence.

Kono, Erin Eitter. *Caterina and the perfect party* ill. by author. Dial, 2013. ISBN 978-0-8037-3902-4 Subj: Birds. Character traits – perfectionism. Parties.

Every color ill. by author. Dial, 2016. ISBN 978-080374132-4 Subj: Activities – traveling. Animals – polar bears. Concepts – color.

Hula lullaby ill. by author. Little, Brown, 2005. ISBN 978-0-316-73591-9 Subj: Bedtime. Family life – mothers. Hawaii. Lullabies. Rhyming text.

Kontis, Alethea. *Alpha oops! The day Z went first* ill. by Bob Kolar. Candlewick, 2006. ISBN 978-0-7636-2728-7 Subj: ABC books.

AlphaOops! H is for Halloween ill. by Bob Kolar. Candlewick, 2010. ISBN 978-0-7636-3966-2 Subj: ABC books. Holidays – Halloween. Theater.

Kooser, Ted. *The bell in the bridge* ill. by Barry Root. Candlewick, 2016. ISBN 978-076366481-7 Subj: Bridges. Emotions – loneliness. Family life – grandparents. Noise, sounds. Seasons – summer.

House held up by trees: not far from here, I have seen a house held up by the hands of trees, this is its story ill. by Jon Klassen. Candlewick, 2012. ISBN 978-0-7636-5107-7 Subj: Homes, houses. Trees.

Kopelke, Lisa. *Excuse me!* ill. by author. Simon & Schuster, 2003. ISBN 978-0-689-85111-7 Subj: Behavior. Etiquette. Frogs & toads.

Koponen, Libby. *Mmm . . . let's eat!* ill. by Betsy Thompson. Blue Apple, 2013. ISBN 978-1-60905-292-8 Subj: Animals. Food. Format, unusual – toy & movable books.

Korchek, Lori. *Adventures of Cow, too* photos by Marshall Taylor. Ten Speed, 2007. ISBN 978-1-58246-189-2 Subj: Animals – bulls, cows. Shopping. Stores. Toys.

Korda, Lerryn. *Into the wild* ill. by author. Candlewick, 2010. ISBN 978-0-7636-4812-1 Subj: Animals. Camps, camping. Friendship.

It's vacation time ill. by author. Candlewick, 2010. ISBN 978-0-7636-4813-8 Subj: Activities – vacationing. Animals. Friendship. Seasons – summer.

Koren, Edward. *Very hairy Harry* ill. by author. Cotler, 2003. ISBN 978-0-06-050908-8 Subj: Careers – barbers. Hair. Tall tales.

Korman, Susan. *Box turtle at Silver Pond Lane* ill. by Stephen Marchesi. Soundprints, 2000. ISBN 978-1-56899-860-2 Subj: Reptiles – turtles, tortoises.

Kornell, Max. *Bear with me* ill. by author. Penguin, 2011. ISBN 978-0-399-25257-0 Subj: Animals – bears. Behavior – dissatisfaction. Family life.

Me first ill. by author. Penguin/Nancy Paulsen, 2014. ISBN 978-039915997-8 Subj: Animals – donkeys. Behavior – fighting, arguing. Family life – brothers & sisters. Sibling rivalry.

Korngold, Jamie S. *Sadie and the big mountain* ill. by Julie Fortenberry. Lerner/Kar-Ben, 2012. ISBN 978-0-7613-6492-4 Subj: Activities – hiking. Holidays – Shavuot. Jewish culture. School – nursery.

Sadie's sukkah breakfast ill. by Julie Fortenberry. Lerner/Kar-Ben, 2011. ISBN 978-0-7613-5647-9 Subj: Holidays – Sukkot. Jewish culture.

Kortepeter, Paul. *Oliver's red toboggan* ill. by Susan Wheeler. Penguin, 2006. ISBN 978-0-525-47752-5 Subj: Animals – rabbits. Behavior – fighting, arguing. Behavior – sharing. Family life – brothers & sisters. Sports – sledding.

Kosofsky, Chaim. *Much, much better* ill. by Jessica Schiffman. Hachai, 2006. ISBN 978-1-929628-22-3 Subj: Family life. Folk & fairy tales. Foreign lands – Iraq. Jewish culture.

Kostecki-Shaw, Jenny Sue. *My travelin' eye* ill. by author. Henry Holt, 2008. ISBN 978-0-8050-8169-5 Subj: Anatomy – eyes. Character traits – individuality. Health & fitness.

Same, same but different ill. by author. Henry Holt, 2011. ISBN 978-0-8050-8946-2 Subj: Foreign lands – India. Friendship. Pen pals.

Koster, Gloria. *Little Red Ruthie: a Hanukkah tale* ill. by Sue Eastland. Albert Whitman, 2017. ISBN 978-080754646-8 Subj: Animals – wolves. Family life – grandmothers. Folk & fairy tales. Food. Holidays – Hanukkah.

The peanut-free cafe ill. by Maryann Cocca-Leffler. Albert Whitman, 2006. ISBN 978-0-8075-6386-1 Subj: Food. Illness – allergies. School.

Kottke, Jan. *From seed to pumpkin* ill. by author. Children's Press, 2000. ISBN 978-0-516-23309-3 Subj: Plants. Seeds.

Kotzwinkle, William. *Walter, the farting dog* by William Kotzwinkle and Glenn Murray ill. by Audrey Colman. Frog, Ltd, 2001. ISBN 978-1-58394-053-2 Subj: Animals – dogs.

Walter, the farting dog: rough weather ahead by William Kotzwinkle and Glenn Murray ill. by Audrey Colman. Dutton, 2005. ISBN 978-0-525-47218-6 Subj: Activities – flying. Animals – dogs. Insects – butterflies, caterpillars.

Walter, the farting dog: trouble at the yard sale by William Kotzwinkle and Glenn Murray ill. by Audrey Colman. Dutton, 2004. ISBN 978-0-525-47217-9 Subj: Animals – dogs. Clowns, jesters. Crime. Garage sales, rummage sales. Toys – balloons.

Kovacs, Deborah. *Katie Copley* ill. by Jared T. Williams. Godine, 2007. ISBN 978-1-56792-332-2 Subj: Animals – dogs. Animals – service animals. Behavior – lost & found possessions. Hotels.

Kovalski, Maryann. *Omar's Halloween* ill. by author. Fitzhenry & Whiteside, 2006. ISBN 978-1-55041-559-9 Subj: Clothing – costumes. Holidays – Halloween.

Take me out to the ball game ill. by author. Fitzhenry & Whiteside, 2004. ISBN 978-1-55041-897-2 Subj: Family life – grandmothers. Music. Sports – baseball.

The wheels on the bus ill. by author. Little, 1987. ISBN 978-0-316-50256-6 Subj: Buses. Family life – grandmothers. Music. Musical instruments – guitars. Songs.

Kozielski, Dolores. *On Halloween night* (Wolff, Ferida)

Kraegel, Kenneth. *Green pants* ill. by author. Candlewick, 2017. ISBN 978-076368840-0 Subj: Character traits – individuality. Clothing – pants. Weddings.

King Arthur's very great grandson ill. by author. Candlewick, 2012. ISBN 978-0-7636-5311-8 Subj: Dragons. Friendship. Knights. Monsters. Mythical creatures.

Kraft, Betsy Harvey. *The fantastic Ferris wheel: the story of inventor George Ferris* ill. by Steven Salerno. Holt/Christy Ottaviano, 2015. ISBN 978-162779072-7 Subj: Careers – engineers. Careers – inventors. Fairs, festivals. Inventions. Machines. Parks – amusement.

Krall, Dan. *The great lollipop caper* ill. by author. Simon & Schuster, 2013. ISBN 978-1-4424-4460-7 Subj: Crime. Food. Humorous stories.

Sick Simon ill. by author. Simon & Schuster, 2015. ISBN 978-144249097-0 Subj: Character traits – cleanliness. Health & fitness. Illness – cold (disease).

Kramer, Andrew. *Pajama pirates* ill. by Leslie Lammle. HarperCollins, 2010. ISBN 978-0-06-125194-8 Subj: Bedtime. Pirates. Rhyming text.

Kramer, Jackie Azúa. *The green umbrella* ill. by Maral Sassouni. NorthSouth, 2017. ISBN 978-073584218-2 Subj: Animals. Animals – elephants. Imagination. Umbrellas.

Kranking, Kathy. *The ocean is . . .* photos by Norbert Wu. Henry Holt, 2003. ISBN 978-0-8050-7097-2 Subj: Animals. Plants. Rhyming text. Sea & seashore.

Krans, Kim. *ABC dream* ill. by author. Random House, 2016. ISBN 978-055353929-5 Subj: ABC books. Picture puzzles. Wordless.

1, 2, 3 dream ill. by author. Random House, 2016. ISBN 978-055353932-5 Subj: Animals. Counting, numbers.

Krasnesky, Thad. *That cat can't stay* ill. by David Parkins. Flashlight, 2010. ISBN 978-0-9799746-5-6 Subj: Animals – cats. Rhyming text.

Kraus, Robert. *Another mouse to feed* ill. by José Aruego and Ariane Dewey. Simon & Schuster, 1989. ISBN 978-0-671-66522-7 Subj: Animals – mice. Family life.

Come out and play, little mouse ill. by José Aruego and Ariane Dewey. Delmar, 1991. ISBN 978-0-8273-4504-1 Subj: Activities – playing. Animals – cats. Animals – mice. Behavior – trickery.

Leo the late bloomer ill. by José Aruego. Simon & Schuster, 1987. ISBN 978-0-671-96078-0 Subj: Animals – tigers. Behavior – growing up.

Little Louie the baby bloomer ill. by José Aruego and Ariane Dewey. HarperCollins, 1998. ISBN 978-0-06-026294-5 Subj: Animals – tigers. Family life – brothers.

Milton the early riser ill. by José Aruego and Ariane Dewey. Simon & Schuster, 1987. ISBN 978-0-671-66272-1 Subj: Animals – pandas. Sleep.

Mort the sport ill. by John Himmelman. Orchard, 2000. ISBN 978-0-531-33247-4 Subj: Games. Musical instruments – violins. Sports – baseball.

Mouse in love ill. by Ariane Dewey and José Aruego. Orchard, 2000. ISBN 978-0-531-33297-9 Subj: Animals – mice. Communities, neighborhoods. Emotions – love. Rhyming text.

Where are you going, little mouse? ill. by José Aruego and Ariane Dewey. Greenwillow, 1986. ISBN 978-0-688-04295-0 Subj: Animals – mice. Behavior – running away. Behavior – seeking better things.

Whose mouse are you? ill. by José Aruego. Aladdin, 1986. ISBN 978-0-02-751190-1 Subj: Animals – mice. Rhyming text.

Krause, Ute. *Oscar and the very hungry dragon* ill. by author. NorthSouth, 2010. ISBN 978-0-7358-2306-8 Subj: Activities – baking, cooking. Behavior – trickery. Character traits – cleverness. Dragons. Restaurants.

Krauss, Ruth. *And I love you* ill. by Steven Kellogg. Scholastic, 2010. ISBN 978-0-439-02459-4 Subj: Animals – cats. Emotions – love. Family life.

Bears ill. by Maurice Sendak. HarperCollins, 2005. ISBN 978-0-06-075716-8 Subj: Animals – bears. Poetry.

The carrot seed ill. by Crockett Johnson. Scholastic, 1974, ©1945. ISBN 978-0-06-023351-8 Subj: Character traits – optimism. Gardens, gardening. Plants. Self-concept.

Goodnight, goodnight, sleepyhead ill. by Jane Dyer. HarperCollins, 2004. ISBN 978-0-06-028895-2 Subj: Bedtime. Rhyming text.

The growing story ill. by Helen Oxenbury. HarperCollins, 2007. ISBN 978-0-06-024716-4 Subj: Animals – babies. Behavior – growing up. Seasons.

The happy day ill. by Marc Simont. HarperCollins, 1949. ISBN 978-0-06-023396-9 Subj: Caldecott award honor books. Hibernation. Seasons – spring. Seasons – winter. Weather – snow.

A hole is to dig: a first book of first definitions ill. by Maurice Sendak. HarperCollins, 1952. ISBN 978-0-06-023406-5 Subj: Activities – digging. Language.

A very special house ill. by Maurice Sendak. HarperCollins, 1953. ISBN 978-0-06-023456-0 Subj: Caldecott award honor books. Homes, houses. Imagination.

You're just what I need ill. by Julia Noonan. HarperCollins, 1998. ISBN 978-0-06-027515-0 Subj: Emotions. Family life – mothers. Games.

Krebs, Laurie. *The beeman* ill. by Valeria Cis. Barefoot, 2008. ISBN 978-1-84686-146-8 Subj: Careers – beekeepers. Family life – grandfathers. Insects – bees. Rhyming text. Science.

The beeman ill. by Melissa Iwai. National Geographic, 2002. ISBN 978-0-7922-7224-3 Subj: Careers – beekeepers. Family life – grandfathers. Insects – bees. Rhyming text. Science.

Off we go to Mexico: an adventure in the sun ill. by Christopher Corr. Barefoot, 2006. ISBN 978-1-905236-40-4 Subj: Activities – traveling. Foreign lands – Mexico. Foreign languages. Rhyming text.

Up and down the Andes: a Peruvian festival tale ill. by Aurelia Fronty. Barefoot, 2008. ISBN 978-1-84686-203-8 Subj: Foreign lands – Peru. Indians of South America. Rhyming text.

We all went on safari ill. by Julia Cairns. Barefoot, 2003. ISBN 978-1-84148-478-5 Subj: Counting, numbers. Foreign lands – Tanzania. Foreign languages.

We're riding on a caravan: an adventure on the Silk Road ill. by Helen Cann. Barefoot, 2005. ISBN 978-1-84148-343-6 Subj: Activities – traveling. Foreign lands – China.

We're roaming in the rainforest: an Amazon adventure ill. by Anne Wilson. Barefoot, 2010. ISBN 978-1-84686-331-8 Subj: Animals. Jungle. Rhyming text.

We're sailing down the Nile: a journey through Egypt ill. by Anne Wilson. Barefoot, 2007. ISBN 978-1-84686-040-9 Subj: Activities – traveling. Foreign lands – Egypt. Rhyming text.

We're sailing to Galapagos: a week in the Pacific ill. by Grazia Restelli. Barefoot, 2005. ISBN 978-1-84148-902-5 Subj: Activities – traveling. Animals. Foreign lands – Galapagos Islands. Rhyming text.

Kreisler, Ken. *Everybody works* (Rotner, Shelley)

Krensky, Stephen. *Ben Franklin and his first kite* ill. by Bert Dodson. Aladdin, 2002. ISBN 978-0-689-84985-5 Subj: Careers – inventors. Careers – scientists. Kites. U.S. history.

Big bad wolves at school ill. by Brad Sneed. Simon & Schuster, 2007. ISBN 978-0-689-38799-9 Subj: Animals – wolves. School.

The crimson comet (Morrissey, Dean)

Dinosaurs, beware! a safety guide (Brown, Marc)

Dinosaurs in disguise ill. by Lynn Munsinger. Houghton Mifflin Harcourt, 2016. ISBN 978-054447271-6 Subj: Dinosaurs. Disguises. Humorous stories.

Hanukkah at Valley Forge ill. by Greg Harlin. Penguin, 2006. ISBN 978-0-525-47738-9 Subj: Holidays – Hanukkah. U.S. history.

How Santa got his job ill. by S. D. Schindler. Simon & Schuster, 1998. ISBN 978-0-689-80697-1 Subj: Careers. Holidays – Christmas. Santa Claus.

How Santa lost his job ill. by S. D. Schindler. Simon & Schuster, 2001. ISBN 978-0-689-83173-7 Subj: Careers. Holidays – Christmas. Mythical creatures – elves. Santa Claus.

I am so brave! ill. by Sara Gillingham. Abrams/Appleseed, 2014. ISBN 978-141970937-1 Subj: Babies, toddlers. Behavior – growing up. Ethnic groups in the U.S. – African Americans. Format, unusual – board books. Rhyming text.

I know a lot! ill. by Sara Gillingham. Abrams, 2013. ISBN 978-1-4197-0938-8 Subj: Character traits – confidence. Concepts – opposites. Ethnic groups in the U.S. – African Americans. Format, unusual – board books. Rhyming text.

The last Christmas tree ill. by Pascal Campion. Dial, 2014. ISBN 978-080373757-0 Subj: Character traits – hopefulness. Holidays – Christmas. Trees.

A man for all seasons: the life of George Washington Carver ill. by Wil Clay. Collins, 2008. ISBN 978-0-06-027885-4 Subj: Careers – scientists. Ethnic groups in the U.S. – African Americans. U.S. history.

Milo and the really big bunny ill. by Melissa Suber. Simon & Schuster, 2006. ISBN 978-0-689-87345-4 Subj: Animals – rabbits. Character traits – appearance. Holidays – Easter. Weather – storms.

Mother's Day surprise ill. by Kathi Ember. Marshall Cavendish, 2010. ISBN 978-0-7614-5633-9 Subj: Animals. Gifts. Holidays – Mother's Day. Reptiles – snakes.

My teacher's secret life ill. by JoAnn Adinolfi. Simon & Schuster, 1996. ISBN 978-0-689-80271-3 Subj: Careers – teachers. Communities, neighborhoods. School.

Noah's bark ill. by Rogé. Carolrhoda, 2010. ISBN 978-0-8225-7645-7 Subj: Animals. Boats, ships. Noise, sounds. Religion – Noah. Weather – floods. Weather – rain.

Perfect pigs: an introduction to manners (Brown, Marc)

Play ball, Jackie! ill. by Joe Morse. Millbrook, 2011. ISBN 978-0-8225-9030-9 Subj: Ethnic groups in the U.S. – African Americans. Prejudice. Sports – baseball.

Shooting for the moon ill. by Bernie Fuchs. Kroupa, 2001. ISBN 978-0-374-36843-2 Subj: Theater. U.S. history. Weapons.

Sisters of Scituate Light ill. by Stacey Schuett. Dutton, 2008. ISBN 978-0-525-47792-1 Subj: Character traits – bravery. Family life – sisters. Lighthouses. U.S. history.

Spark the firefighter ill. by Amanda Haley. Dutton, 2008. ISBN 978-0-525-47887-4 Subj: Careers – firefighters. Dragons. Emotions – fear.

Too many leprechauns: or how that pot o' gold got to the end of the rainbow ill. by Dan Andreasen. Simon & Schuster, 2007. ISBN 978-0-689-85112-4 Subj: Folk & fairy tales. Foreign lands – Ireland. Mythical creatures – leprechauns.

We just had a baby ill. by Amélie Graux. Capstone, 2016. ISBN 978-162370603-6 Subj: Babies, toddlers. Family life – brothers & sisters. Family life – new sibling.

What a mess! ill. by Joe Mathieu. Random House, 2001. ISBN 978-0-375-90220-8 Subj: Character traits – cleanliness.

The youngest fairy godmother ever ill. by Diana Cain Bluthenthal. Simon & Schuster, 2000. ISBN 978-0-689-82011-3 Subj: Behavior – wishing. Fairies.

Krieb, Mr. *We're off to find the witch's house* ill. by R. W. Alley. Penguin, 2005. ISBN 978-0-525-47003-8 Subj: Holidays – Halloween. Rhyming text.

Krilanovich, Nadia. *Chicken, chicken, duck!* ill. by author. Tricycle, 2011. ISBN 978-1-58246-385-8 Subj: Animals. Birds. Farms. Games. Noise, sounds.

Moon child ill. by Elizabeth Sayles. Tricycle, 2010. ISBN 978-1-58246-325-4 Subj: Animals. Bedtime. Moon.

Krishnaswami, Uma. *Bringing Asha home* ill. by Jamel Akib. Lee & Low, 2006. ISBN 978-1-58430-259-9 Subj: Adoption. Babies, toddlers. Ethnic groups in the U.S. – East Indian Americans. Family life.

Chachaji's cup ill. by Soumya Sitaraman. Children's Book Press, 2003. ISBN 978-0-89239-178-3 Subj: Ethnic groups in the U.S. – East Indian Americans. Family life – aunts, uncles. Memories, memory.

The happiest tree: a yoga story ill. by Ruth Jeyaveeran. Lee & Low, 2005. ISBN 978-1-58430-237-7

Subj: Ethnic groups in the U.S. – East Indian Americans. Health & fitness. Self-concept.

Holi ill. with photos. Children's Press, 2003. ISBN 978-0-516-22863-1 Subj: Fairs, festivals. Religion.

Out of the way! Out of the way! ill. by Uma Krishnaswamy. Groundwood, 2012. ISBN 978-1-55498-130-4 Subj: Roads. Trees.

Remembering Grandpa ill. by Layne Johnson. Boyds Mills, 2007. ISBN 978-1-59078-424-2 Subj: Animals – rabbits. Death. Emotions – grief. Family life – grandparents.

Kroll, Steven. *The big bunny and the Easter eggs* ill. by Janet Stevens. Holiday, 1982. ISBN 978-0-8234-0436-0 Subj: Animals – rabbits. Holidays – Easter. Illness.

The big bunny and the magic show ill. by Janet Stevens. Holiday, 1986. ISBN 978-0-8234-0589-3 Subj: Animals – rabbits. Holidays – Easter. Magic.

By the dawn's early light: the story of the Star Spangled Banner ill. by Dan Andreasen. Scholastic, 1994. ISBN 978-0-590-45054-6 Subj: Flags. Music. Songs. U.S. history.

The hand-me-down doll ill. by Dan Andreasen. Marshall Cavendish, 2012. ISBN 978-0-7614-6124-1 Subj: Emotions – loneliness. Toys – dolls.

The Hanukkah mice ill. by Michelle Shapiro. Marshall Cavendish, 2008. ISBN 978-0-7614-5428-1 Subj: Animals – mice. Holidays – Hanukkah.

Happy Father's Day ill. by Marylin Hafner. Holiday, 1987. ISBN 978-0-523-40671-8 Subj: Family life – fathers. Holidays – Father's Day.

Happy Mother's Day ill. by Marylin Hafner. Holiday, 1985. ISBN 978-0-8234-0504-6 Subj: Family life. Holidays – Mother's Day.

It's April Fools' Day! ill. by Jeni Bassett. Holiday, 1990. ISBN 978-0-8234-0747-7 Subj: Animals – cats. Behavior – bullying, teasing. Holidays – April Fools' Day.

It's Groundhog Day! ill. by Jeni Bassett. Holiday, 1987. ISBN 978-0-8234-0643-2 Subj: Activities – picnicking. Animals. Holidays – Groundhog Day.

Jungle bullies ill. by Vincent Nguyen. Marshall Cavendish, 2006. ISBN 978-0-7614-5297-3 Subj: Animals. Behavior – bullying, teasing. Behavior – sharing. Jungle.

Lewis and Clark: explorers of the American West ill. by Richard Williams. Holiday, 1994. ISBN 978-0-8234-1034-7 Subj: Careers – explorers. U.S. history.

Mary McLean and the St. Patrick's Day parade ill. by Michael Dooling. Scholastic, 1991. ISBN 978-0-590-43701-1 Subj: Cities, towns. Ethnic groups in the U.S. – Irish Americans. Holidays – St. Patrick's Day. Parades.

Oh, Tucker! ill. by Scott Nash. Candlewick, 1998. ISBN 978-0-7636-0429-5 Subj: Animals – dogs. Character traits – clumsiness.

Oh, what a Thanksgiving! ill. by S. D. Schindler. Scholastic, 1988. ISBN 978-0-590-40613-0 Subj: Holidays – Thanksgiving. Imagination. U.S. history.

One tough turkey: a Thanksgiving story ill. by John Wallner. Holiday, 1982. ISBN 978-0-8234-0457-5 Subj: Birds – turkeys. Holidays – Thanksgiving. Pilgrims. Sports – hunting.

Patches: an art story ill. by Barry Gott. Winslow, 2001. ISBN 978-1-890817-53-4 Subj: Activities – drawing. Animals – guinea pigs. Behavior – lost & found possessions. Children as authors. Children as illustrators.

Patches lost and found ill. by Barry Gott. Marshall Cavendish, 2005. ISBN 978-0-7614-5217-1 Subj: Activities – drawing. Animals – guinea pigs. Behavior – lost & found possessions. Pets. School.

Pooch on the loose: a Christmas adventure ill. by Michael Garland. Marshall Cavendish, 2005. ISBN 978-0-7614-5239-3 Subj: Animals – dogs. Behavior – lost. Holidays – Christmas.

Santa's crash-bang Christmas ill. by Tomie dePaola. Holiday, 1977. ISBN 978-0-8234-0302-8 Subj: Holidays – Christmas. Santa Claus.

The squirrels' Thanksgiving ill. by Jeni Bassett. Holiday, 1991. ISBN 978-0-8234-0823-8 Subj: Animals – squirrels. Family life. Holidays – Thanksgiving. Sibling rivalry.

Stuff! reduce, reuse, recycle ill. by Steve Cox. Marshall Cavendish, 2009. ISBN 978-0-7614-5570-7 Subj: Animals – pack rats. Behavior – collecting things. Ecology. Garage sales, rummage sales.

Super-dragon ill. by Douglas Holgate. Marshall Cavendish, 2011. ISBN 978-0-7614-5819-7 Subj: Activities – flying. Contests. Dragons.

That makes me mad ill. by Christine Davenier. SeaStar, 2002. ISBN 978-1-58717-184-0 Subj: Behavior. Emotions – anger. Family life – mothers.

The Tyrannosaurus game ill. by S. D. Schindler. Marshall Cavendish, 2010. ISBN 978-0-7614-5603-2 Subj: Activities – storytelling. Dinosaurs. Games. Imagination.

Will you be my valentine? ill. by Lillian Hoban. Holiday, 1993. ISBN 978-0-8234-0925-9 Subj: Activities – making things. Behavior – indifference. Holidays – Valentine's Day. School.

Kroll, Virginia L. *Africa brothers and sisters* ill. by Vanessa French. Four Winds, 1993. ISBN 978-0-02-751166-6 Subj: Ethnic groups in the U.S. – African Americans. Family life – fathers. Foreign lands – Africa.

Boy, you're amazing! ill. by Sachiko Yoshikawa. Albert Whitman, 2004. ISBN 978-0-8075-0868-8 Subj: Activities. Rhyming text. Self-concept.

Can you dance, Dalila? ill. by Nancy Carpenter. Simon & Schuster, 1996. ISBN 978-0-689-80551-6 Subj: Activities – dancing. Ballet. Ethnic groups in the U.S. – African Americans.

Cristina keeps a promise ill. by Enrique O. Sánchez. Albert Whitman, 2006. ISBN 978-0-8075-1350-7 Subj: Behavior. Character traits – responsibility.

Equal shmequal: a math adventure ill. by Philomena O'Neill. Charlesbridge, 2005. ISBN 978-1-57091-891-9 Subj: Counting, numbers.

Everybody has a teddy ill. by Sophie Allsopp. Sterling, 2007. ISBN 978-1-4027-3580-6 Subj: Rhyming text. School – nursery. Toys – bears.

Faraway drums ill. by Floyd Cooper. Little, 1998. ISBN 978-0-316-50449-2 Subj: Cities, towns. Ethnic groups in the U.S. – African Americans. Family life – sisters. Foreign lands – Africa. Imagination.

Forgiving a friend ill. by Paige Billin-Frye. Albert Whitman, 2005. ISBN 978-0-8075-0618-9 Subj: Behavior – forgiving. Friendship.

Girl, you're amazing! ill. by Mélisande Potter. Albert Whitman, 2001. ISBN 978-0-8075-2930-0 Subj: Gender roles. Rhyming text.

Good citizen Sarah ill. by Nancy Cote. Albert Whitman, 2007. ISBN 978-0-8075-2992-8 Subj: Behavior. Character traits – helpfulness. Weather – snow.

Good neighbor Nicholas ill. by Nancy Cote. Albert Whitman, 2006. ISBN 978-0-8075-2998-0 Subj: Behavior. Character traits – kindness.

Hands! ill. by Cathryn Falwell. Boyds Mills, 1997. ISBN 978-1-56397-051-1 Subj: Anatomy – hands.

Honest Ashley ill. by Nancy Cote. Albert Whitman, 2006. ISBN 978-0-8075-3371-0 Subj: Character traits – honesty. Homework.

Jaha and Jamil went down the hill: an African Mother Goose ill. by Katherine Roundtree. Charlesbridge, 1995. ISBN 978-0-88106-867-2 Subj: Foreign lands – Africa. Nursery rhymes.

Jason takes responsibility ill. by Nancy Cote. Albert Whitman, 2005. ISBN 978-0-8075-2537-1 Subj: Birthdays. Character traits – responsibility. Family life – grandmothers.

Makayla cares about others ill. by Nancy Cote. Albert Whitman, 2007. ISBN 978-0-8075-4945-2 Subj: Character traits – helpfulness. Emotions – fear.

Masai and I ill. by Nancy Carpenter. Four Winds, 1992. ISBN 978-0-02-751165-9 Subj: Ethnic groups in the U.S. – African Americans. Family life. Foreign lands – Africa.

On the way to kindergarten ill. by Elisabeth Schlossberg. Penguin, 2006. ISBN 978-0-399-24168-0 Subj: Animals – bears. Behavior – growing up. Rhyming text. School – first day.

Pink paper swans ill. by Nancy L. Clouse. Eerdmans, 1994. ISBN 978-0-8028-5081-2 Subj: Ethnic groups in the U.S. – Japanese Americans. Illness. Paper.

Really rabbits ill. by Philomena O'Neill. Charlesbridge, 2006. ISBN 978-1-57091-897-1 Subj: Animals – rabbits. Character traits – cleanliness. Pets.

Ryan respects ill. by Paige Billin-Frye. Albert Whitman, 2006. ISBN 978-0-8075-6946-7 Subj: Behavior – bullying, teasing. School.

Selvakumar knew better ill. by Xiaojun Li. Shen's, 2006. ISBN 978-1-885008-29-9 Subj: Animals – dogs. Foreign lands – India. Tsunamis.

The Thanksgiving bowl ill. by Philomena O'Neill. Pelican, 2007. ISBN 978-1-58980-365-7 Subj: Family life – grandmothers. Holidays – Thanksgiving.

Uno, dos, tres, posada! let's celebrate Christmas ill. by Loretta Lopez. Penguin, 2006. ISBN 978-0-670-05923-2 Subj: Counting, numbers. Ethnic groups in the U.S. – Hispanic Americans. Holidays – Christmas. Rhyming text.

Kromhout, Rindert. *Little Donkey and the babysitter* ill. by Annemarie van Haeringen. NorthSouth, 2006. ISBN 978-0-7358-2057-9 Subj: Activities – babysitting. Animals – donkeys. Birds – chickens, roosters.

Little Donkey and the birthday present ill. by Annemarie van Haeringen. NorthSouth, 2007. ISBN 978-0-7358-2132-3 Subj: Animals – donkeys. Animals – yaks. Birthdays. Character traits – generosity. Gifts.

Kropf, Latifa Berry. *It's Hanukkah time!* photos by Tod Cohen. Kar-Ben, 2004. ISBN 978-1-58013-120-9 Subj: Family life – grandparents. Holidays – Hanukkah. Jewish culture. Parties. Religion.

It's seder time! photos by Tod Cohen. Kar-Ben, 2004. ISBN 978-1-58013-092-9 Subj: Holidays – Passover. Holidays – Seder. Jewish culture. Religion.

It's Shofar time! ill. by Tod Cohen. Kar-Ben, 2006. ISBN 978-1-58013-158-2 Subj: Holidays – Rosh Hashanah. Jewish culture. Religion.

Krosoczka, Jarrett J. *Annie was warned* ill. by author. Knopf, 2003. ISBN 978-0-375-91567-3 Subj: Holidays – Halloween. Homes, houses.

Baghead ill. by author. Dragonfly, 2004. ISBN 978-0-375-91566-6 Subj: Hair. Humorous stories.

Bubble bath pirates ill. by author. Viking, 2003. ISBN 978-0-670-03599-1 Subj: Activities – bathing. Family life – mothers. Pirates.

Giddy up, Cowgirl ill. by author. Penguin, 2006. ISBN 978-0-670-06050-4 Subj: Character traits – helpfulness. Family life – daughters. Family life – mothers.

Good night, Monkey Boy ill. by author. Knopf, 2001. 978-0-375-91121-7 Subj: Bedtime. Family life – mothers. Family life – sons.

It's tough to lose your balloon ill. by author. Knopf, 2015. ISBN 978-038575479-8 Subj: Character traits – optimism. Emotions. Problem solving.

Max for president ill. by author. Knopf, 2004. ISBN 978-0-375-92428-6 Subj: Friendship. School. Sportsmanship.

My buddy, Slug ill. by author. Random House, 2006. ISBN 978-0-375-83342-7 Subj: Animals – slugs. Emotions. Friendship.

Naptastrophe! ill. by Jarrett J. Krosoczka. Knopf, 2017. ISBN 978-038575483-5 Subj: Animals – rabbits. Behavior – bad day, bad mood. Emotions – anger. Sleep.

Ollie the purple elephant ill. by author. Random House, 2011. ISBN 978-0-375-86654-8 Subj: Activities – dancing. Animals – cats. Animals – elephants. Circus. Family life.

Punk Farm ill. by author. Random House, 2005. ISBN 978-0-375-92429-3 Subj: Animals. Farms. Music.

Punk Farm on tour ill. by author. Random House, 2007. ISBN 978-0-375-83343-4 Subj: Animals. Farms. Songs.

Krudop, Walter Lyon. *The man who caught fish* ill. by author. Farrar, 2000. ISBN 978-0-374-34786-4 Subj: Behavior – greed. Folk & fairy tales. Foreign lands – Thailand. Royalty – kings. Sports – fishing.

Kruglik, Gerald. *Pish and Posh* (Bottner, Barbara)

Wallace's lists (Bottner, Barbara)

Krulik, Nancy E. *Is it Hanukkah yet?* ill. by DyAnne DiSalvo. Random House, 2003. ISBN 978-0-375-90286-4 Subj: Holidays – Hanukkah. Jewish culture. Religion.

Krull, Kathleen. *Big wig* ill. by Peter Malone. Scholastic, 2011. ISBN 978-0-439-67640-3 Subj: Hair.

The boy on Fairfield Street: how Ted Geisel grew up to become Dr. Seuss ill. by Steve Johnson and Lou Fancher. Decorative ill. by Dr. Seuss. Random House, 2004. ISBN 978-0-375-92298-5 Subj: Books, reading. Careers – illustrators. Careers – writers.

Hillary Rodham Clinton: dreams taking flight ill. by Amy June Bates. Simon & Schuster, 2015. ISBN 978-1-4814-5113-0 Subj: Character traits – persistence. Gender roles. U.S. history.

Lincoln tells a joke: how laughter saved the president (and the country) by Kathleen Krull and Paul Brewer ill. by Stacy Innerst. Harcourt, 2010. ISBN 978-0-15-206639-0 Subj: Riddles & jokes. U.S. history.

M is for music ill. by Stacy Innerst. Harcourt, 2003. ISBN 978-0-15-201438-4 Subj: ABC books. Music.

Pocahontas: princess of the New World ill. by David Diaz. Walker, 2007. ISBN 978-0-8027-9555-7 Subj: Indians of North America – Powhatan. U.S. history.

Supermarket ill. by Melanie Hope Greenberg. Holiday, 2001. ISBN 978-0-8234-1546-5 Subj: Food. Stores.

What's new? the zoo! a zippy history of zoos ill. by Marcellus Hall. Scholastic, 2014. ISBN 978-054513571-9 Subj: Zoos.

Krumwiede, Lana. *Just Itzy* ill. by Greg Pizzoli. Candlewick, 2015. ISBN 978-076365811-3 Subj: Character traits – confidence. Character traits – perseverance. Nursery rhymes. School – first day. Spiders.

Krupinski, Loretta. *Christmas in the city* ill. by author. Hyperion, 2002. ISBN 978-0-7868-2652-0 Subj: Animals – mice. Cities, towns. Holidays – Christmas. Trees.

Pirate treasure ill. by author. Penguin, 2006. ISBN 978-0-525-47579-8 Subj: Animals – mice. Farms. Pirates. Weather.

Krupp, E. C. *The rainbow and you* ill. by Robin Rector Krupp. HarperCollins, 2000. ISBN 978-0-688-15602-2 Subj: Weather – rainbows.

Kruusval, Catarina. *Franny's friends* ill. by author. Farrar, 2008. ISBN 978-91-29-66836-0 Subj: Activities – picnicking. Behavior – lost & found possessions. Imagination. Toys.

Krykorka, Ian. *Carl, the Christmas carp* ill. by Vladyana Krykorka. Orca, 2006. ISBN 978-1-55143-329-5 Subj: Fish. Foreign lands – Czechoslovakia. Holidays – Christmas.

Kubler, Annie. *My first signs* ill. by author. Child's Play, 2005. ISBN 978-1-904550-39-6 Subj: Language. Sign language.

Kudlinski, Kathleen V. *Boy, were we wrong about dinosaurs!* ill. by S. D. Schindler. Penguin, 2005. ISBN 978-0-525-46978-0 Subj: Dinosaurs. Science.

Boy, were we wrong about the human body! ill. by Debbie Tilley. Dial, 2015. ISBN 978-080373792-1 Subj: Anatomy. Science.

Boy, were we wrong about the solar system! ill. by John Rocco. Dutton, 2008. ISBN 978-0-525-46979-7 Subj: Science. Space & space ships.

Boy, were we wrong about the weather! ill. by Sebastià Serra. Dial, 2015. ISBN 978-080373793-8 Subj: Careers – meteorologists. Careers – scientists. Weather.

The seaside switch ill. by Lindy Burnett. North-Word, 2007. ISBN 978-1-55971-964-3 Subj: Ecology. Sea & seashore.

The sunset switch ill. by Lindy Burnett. North-Word, 2005. ISBN 978-1-55971-916-2 Subj: Animals. Night.

What do roots do? ill. by David Schuppert. North-Word, 2005. ISBN 978-1-55971-896-7 Subj: Plants.

Kuefler, Joseph. *Beyond the pond* ill. by author. HarperCollins/Balzer+Bray, 2015. ISBN 978-006236427-2 Subj: Imagination. Lakes, ponds. Nature.

Rulers of the playground ill. by author. HarperCollins/Balzer+Bray, 2017. ISBN 978-006242432-7 Subj: Activities – playing. Behavior – fighting, arguing. School.

Kuhlman, Evan. *Hank's big day: the story of a bug* ill. by Chuck Groenink. Random House, 2016. ISBN 978-055351150-5 Subj: Activities – playing. Character traits – smallness. Friendship. Insects.

Kuhlmann, Torben. *Moletown* ill. by author. NorthSouth, 2015. ISBN 978-073584208-3 Subj: Animals – moles. Cities, towns. Ecology.

Kuiper, Nannie. *Bailey the bear cub* ill. by Jeska Verstegen. NorthSouth, 2002. ISBN 978-0-7358-1625-1 Subj: Animals – babies. Animals – bears. Behavior – growing up. Family life – mothers.

Bravo, brave beavers ill. by Jeska Verstegen. North-South, 2004. ISBN 978-0-7358-1916-0 Subj: Animals – beavers. Character traits – cooperation. Family life. Weather – storms.

Kuklin, Susan. *Families* photos by author. Hyperion, 2006. ISBN 978-0-7868-0822-9 Subj: Emotions – love. Family life.

Kulka, Joe. *My crocodile does not bite* ill. by author. Carolrhoda, 2013. ISBN 978-0-7613-8937-8 Subj: Behavior – boasting, showing off. Contests. Pets. Reptiles – alligators, crocodiles.

Wolf's coming ill. by author. Carolrhoda, 2007. ISBN 978-1-57505-930-3 Subj: Animals – wolves. Birthdays.

Kulling, Monica. *All aboard! Elijah McCoy's steam engine* ill. by Bill Slavin. Tundra, 2010. ISBN 978-0-88776-945-0 Subj: Careers – inventors. Ethnic groups in the U.S. – African Americans. Inventions. Trains.

Grant and Tillie go walking ill. by Sydney Smith. Groundwood, 2015. ISBN 978-155498446-6 Subj: Activities – painting. Animals – bulls, cows. Art. Careers – artists.

Kumin, Maxine. *Mites to astodons: a book of animal poems* ill. by Pamela Zagarenski. Houghton, 2006. ISBN 978-0-618-50753-5 Subj: Animals. Poetry.

Oh, Harry! ill. by Barry Moser. Roaring Brook, 2011. ISBN 978-1-59643-439-4 Subj: Animals – horses, ponies. Behavior – misbehavior. Rhyming text.

What color is Caesar? ill. by Alison Friend. Candlewick, 2010. ISBN 978-0-7636-3432-2 Subj: Animals – dogs. Concepts – color. Self-concept.

Kunhardt, Katharine. *Let's count the puppies* photos by author. HarperCollins, 2004. ISBN 978-0-06-054337-2 Subj: Animals – babies. Animals – dogs. Counting, numbers.

Kunkel, Jeff, ed. *Noah, build your boat: Old Testament stories and pictures by kids.* Augsburg Fortress, 2002. ISBN 978-0-8066-4402-8 Subj: Children as authors. Children as illustrators. Religion.

Kurtz, Jane. *Do kangaroos wear seat belts?* ill. by Jane Manning. Penguin, 2005. ISBN 978-0-525-47358-9 Subj: Animals. Safety. Zoos.

Faraway home ill. by E. B. Lewis. Harcourt, 2000. ISBN 978-0-15-200036-3 Subj: Ethnic groups in the U.S. – African Americans. Family life – fathers. Foreign lands – Ethiopia. Memories, memory.

In the small, small night ill. by Rachel Isadora. HarperCollins, 2005. ISBN 978-0-06-623813-5 Subj: Activities – storytelling. Bedtime. Character traits – perseverance. Family life – brothers & sisters. Folk & fairy tales. Foreign lands – Ghana. Immigrants, immigration.

Rain romp: stomping away a grouchy day ill. by Dyanna Wolcott. Greenwillow, 2002. ISBN 978-0-06-029806-7 Subj: Behavior. Family life – parents. Rhyming text. Weather – rain.

River friendly, river wild ill. by Neil Brennan. Simon & Schuster, 2000. ISBN 978-0-689-82049-6 Subj: Family life. Rivers. U.S. history. Weather – floods.

Kurtz, Kevin. *A day in the salt marsh* ill. by Consie Powell. Sylvan Dell, 2007. ISBN 978-0-9768823-5-0 Subj: Ecology. Nature. Rhyming text.

Kushner, Donn. *Peter's pixie* ill. by Sylvie Daigneault. Tundra, 2003. ISBN 978-0-88776-603-9 Subj: Family life – brothers. Family life – new sibling. Magic. Mythical creatures – pixies.

Kushner, Karen. *Because Nothing Looks Like God* (Kushner, Lawrence)

Kushner, Lawrence. *Because Nothing Looks Like God* by Lawrence Kushner and Karen Kushner ill. by Dawn Majewski. Jewish Lights, 2000. ISBN 978-1-58023-092-6 Subj: Religion.

Kushner, Tony. *Brundibar* ill. by Maurice Sendak. Hyperion, 2003. ISBN 978-0-7868-0904-2 Subj: Activities – singing. Behavior – bullying, teasing. Family life – brothers & sisters.

Kuskin, Karla. *A boy had a mother who bought him a hat* ill. by Kevin Hawkes. HarperCollins, 2010. ISBN 978-0-06-075330-6 Subj: Family life – mothers. Rhyming text.

A great miracle happened there: a Chanukah story ill. by Robert Andrew Parker. Willa Perlman Books, 1993. ISBN 978-0-06-023618-2 Subj: Family life. Holidays – Hanukkah. Jewish culture. Religion.

Green as a bean ill. by Melissa Iwai. HarperCollins, 2007. ISBN 978-0-06-075334-4 Subj: Character traits – questioning. Rhyming text.

I am me ill. by Dyanna Wolcott. Simon & Schuster, 2000. ISBN 978-0-689-81473-0 Subj: Character traits – individuality. Family life. Sea & seashore.

The Philharmonic gets dressed ill. by Marc Simont. HarperCollins, 1982. ISBN 978-0-06-023622-9 Subj: Clothing. Musical instruments – orchestras.

So, what's it like to be a cat? ill. by Betsy Lewin. Simon & Schuster, 2005. ISBN 978-0-689-84733-2 Subj: Animals – cats. Rhyming text.

Toots the cat ill. by Lisze Bechtold. Henry Holt, 2005. ISBN 978-0-8050-6841-2 Subj: Animals – cats. Poetry.

Under my hood I have a hat ill. by Fumi Kosaka. Geringer, 2004. ISBN 978-0-06-057243-3 Subj: Clothing. Rhyming text. Seasons – winter.

Kusugak, Michael. *A promise is a promise* (Munsch, Robert N.)

Kuszyk, R. Nicholas. *R Robot saves lunch* ill. by author. Putnam, 2009. ISBN 978-0-399-24757-6 Subj: Humorous stories. Robots.

Kutner, Merrily. *Z is for zombie* ill. by John Manders. Albert Whitman, 1999. ISBN 978-0-8075-9490-2 Subj: ABC books. Holidays – Halloween. Rhyming text.

The Zombie Nite Cafe ill. by Ethan Long. Holiday House, 2007. ISBN 978-0-8234-1963-0 Subj: Monsters. Restaurants. Rhyming text.

Kvasnosky, Laura McGee. *Little Wolf's first howling* ill. by author. Candlewick, 2017. ISBN 978-076368971-1 Subj: Animals – wolves. Behavior – imitation. Character traits – individuality. Family life – fathers. Noise, sounds.

Really truly Bingo ill. by author. Candlewick, 2008. ISBN 978-0-7636-3210-6 Subj: Activities – playing. Animals – dogs. Behavior – boredom. Imagination – imaginary friends.

Kwan, James. *Dear Yeti* ill. by author. Farrar, 2015. ISBN 978-037430045-6 Subj: Activities – hiking. Character traits – helpfulness. Letters, cards. Monsters.

Kwon, Yoon-duck. *My cat copies me* ill. by author. Kane/Miller, 2007. ISBN 978-1-933605-26-5 Subj: Animals – cats. Imagination. Pets.

Kyle, Tracey. *Gazpacho for Nacho* ill. by Carolina Farias. Amazon/Two Lions, 2014. ISBN 978-147781727-8 Subj: Activities – baking, cooking. Ethnic groups in the U.S. – Hispanic Americans. Food. Foreign languages. Rhyming text.

Lach, William. *I am not a dinosaur!* ill. by Jonny Lambert. Sterling, 2016. ISBN 978-145491491-4 Subj: Dinosaurs. Fossils. Prehistory.

LaChanze. *Little diva* ill. by Brian Pinkney. Feiwel & Friends, 2010. ISBN 978-0-312-37010-7 Subj: Careers – actors. Family life – mothers. Theater.

Lachenmeyer, Nathaniel. *The origami master* ill. by Aki Sogabe. Albert Whitman, 2008. ISBN 978-0-8075-6134-8 Subj: Activities – making things. Birds. Foreign lands – Japan.

Lachtman, Ofelia Dumas. *Pepita takes time / Pepita, siempre tarde* Spanish by Alejandra Balestra; ill. by Alex Pardo DeLange. Piñata, 2001. ISBN 978-1-55885-304-1 Subj: Behavior – promptness, tardiness. Ethnic groups in the U.S. – Hispanic Americans. Foreign languages.

Lackner, Michelle Myers. *Toil in the soil* ill. by Daniel Powers. Millbrook, 2001. ISBN 978-0-7613-1807-1 Subj: Animals – worms.

Lacombe, Benjamin. *Cherry and Olive* ill. by author. Walker, 2007. ISBN 978-0-8027-9707-0 Subj: Animals – dogs. Behavior – bullying, teasing. Emotions – loneliness.

Lacome, Julie. *Ruthie's big old coat* ill. by author. Candlewick, 2000. ISBN 978-0-7636-0969-6 Subj: Activities – playing. Animals – rabbits. Clothing – coats.

Laden, Nina. *Are we there yet?* ill. by Adam McCauley. Chronicle, 2016. ISBN 978-145213155-9 Subj: Activities – traveling. Imagination.

Bad dog ill. by author. Walker, 2000. ISBN 978-0-8027-8748-4 Subj: Animals – dogs. Behavior – misbehavior. Humorous stories.

Clowns on vacation ill. by author. Walker, 2002. ISBN 978-0-8027-8781-1 Subj: Activities – vacationing. Clowns, jesters. Rhyming text.

Once upon a memory ill. by Renata Liwska. Little, Brown, 2013. ISBN 978-0-316-20816-1 Subj: Behavior – growing up. Character traits – questioning. Memories, memory.

Peek-a-who? ill. by author. Chronicle, 2000. ISBN 978-0-8118-2602-0 Subj: Format, unusual – board books. Rhyming text.

Peek-a-choo-choo! ill. by author. Chronicle, 2016. ISBN 978-145215473-2 Subj: Format, unusual – board books. Rhyming text. Transportation.

Roberto, the insect architect ill. by author. Chronicle, 2000. ISBN 978-0-8118-2465-1 Subj: Careers – architects. Insects – termites.

Laird, Elizabeth. *A book of promises* ill. by Michael Frith. DK, 2000. ISBN 978-0-7894-2547-8 Subj: Emotions – love. Family life.

Lairla, Sergio. *Abel and the wolf* ill. by Alessandra Roberti. NorthSouth, 2004. ISBN 978-0-7358-1903-0 Subj: Animals – wolves. Emotions. Forest, woods. Friendship.

Lakin, Patricia. *Camping day* ill. by Scott Nash. Dial, 2009. ISBN 978-0-8037-3309-1 Subj: Camps, camping. Friendship. Reptiles – alligators, crocodiles.

Clarence the copy cat ill. by John Manders. Doubleday, 2002. ISBN 978-0-385-32747-3 Subj: Animals – cats. Animals – mice. Libraries.

Fat chance Thanksgiving ill. by Stacey Schuett. Albert Whitman, 2001. ISBN 978-0-8075-2288-2 Subj: Books, reading. Communities, neighborhoods. Holidays – Thanksgiving. Homes, houses.

Hurricane! ill. by Vanessa Lubach. Millbrook, 2000. ISBN 978-0-7613-1616-9 Subj: Family life – fathers. Weather – hurricanes.

Rainy day ill. by Scott Nash. Penguin, 2007. ISBN 978-0-8037-3092-2 Subj: Activities – playing.

Behavior – boredom. Books, reading. Libraries. Reptiles – alligators, crocodiles. Weather – rain.

Snow day! ill. by Scott Nash. Dial, 2002. ISBN 978-0-8037-2642-0 Subj: School. Weather – snow.

Subway sonata ill. by Heather Maione. Millbrook, 2001. ISBN 978-0-7613-1464-6 Subj: Careers – artists. Cities, towns. Trains.

Lallemand, Orianne. *The wolf who wanted to change his color* ill. by Eleonore Thuillier. Auzou, 2012. ISBN 978-2-7338-1945-6 Subj: Animals – wolves. Concepts – color. Self-concept.

Lam, Maple. *My little sister and me* ill. by author. HarperCollins, 2016. ISBN 978-006239697-6 Subj: Activities – walking. Family life – brothers & sisters.

Lam, Thao. *Skunk on a string* ill. by author. OwlKids, 2016. ISBN 978-177147131-2 Subj: Activities – flying. Animals – skunks. Toys – balloons. Wordless.

LaMarche, Jim. *Lost and found: three dog stories* ill. by author. Chronicle, 2009. ISBN 978-0-8118-6401-5 Subj: Animals – dogs. Behavior – lost. Behavior – lost & found possessions.

Pond ill. by author. Simon & Schuster/Paula Wiseman, 2016. ISBN 978-148144735-5 Subj: Character traits – cooperation. Ecology. Lakes, ponds. Nature. Seasons.

The raft ill. by author. HarperCollins, 2000. ISBN 978-0-688-13978-0 Subj: Animals. Boats, ships. Family life – grandmothers. Rivers.

Up ill. by author. Chronicle, 2006. ISBN 978-0-8118-4445-1 Subj: Careers – fishermen. Character traits – smallness. Family life – brothers & sisters. Magic. Self-concept.

Lamb, Albert. *The abandoned lighthouse* ill. by David McPhail. Roaring Brook, 2011. ISBN 978-1-59643-525-4 Subj: Animals – bears. Boats, ships. Lighthouses.

Sam's winter hat ill. by David McPhail. Scholastic, 2006. ISBN 978-0-439-79304-9 Subj: Animals – bears. Behavior – lost & found possessions. Clothing – hats.

Tell me the day backwards ill. by David McPhail. Candlewick, 2011. ISBN 978-0-7636-5055-1 Subj: Animals – bears. Bedtime. Day. Family life – mothers.

Lamb, Rosy. *Paul meets Bernadette* ill. by author. Candlewick, 2013. ISBN 978-0-7636-6130-4 Subj: Character traits – curiosity. Fish. Imagination.

Lamba, Baldev. *Green green: a community gardening story* (Lamba, Marie)

Lamba, Marie. *Green green: a community gardening story* by Marie Lamba and Baldev Lamba ill. by Sonia Sánchez. Farrar, 2017. ISBN 978-037432797-2 Subj: Cities, towns. Communities, neighborhoods. Gardens, gardening. Rhyming text.

Lambert, Jonny. *The great aaa-ooo!* ill. by author. Tiger Tales, 2016. ISBN 978-168010032-7 Subj: Animals. Noise, sounds.

The only lonely panda ill. by author. Tiger Tales, 2017. ISBN 978-168010065-5 Subj: Animals – pandas. Emotions – loneliness. Friendship.

Tiger tiger ill. by author. Tiger Tales, 2017. ISBN 978-168010044-0 Subj: Activities – playing. Animals – tigers.

Lambert, Martha Lewis. *I won't get lost* ill. by Kate Duke. HarperCollins, 2003. ISBN 978-0-06-028961-4 Subj: Behavior – lost. Dragons. School.

Why do you love me? (Schlessinger, Laura)

Laminack, Lester L. *Jake's 100th day of school* ill. by Judy Love. Peachtree, 2006. ISBN 978-1-56145-355-9 Subj: Counting, numbers. School.

Saturdays and teacakes ill. by Chris Soentpiet. Peachtree, 2004. ISBN 978-1-56145-303-0 Subj: Activities – baking, cooking. Character traits – helpfulness. Family life – grandmothers.

Snow day! ill. by Adam Gustavson. Peachtree, 2007. ISBN 978-1-56145-418-1 Subj: Careers – teachers. Seasons – winter. Weather – snow.

Three hens and a peacock ill. by Henry Cole. Peachtree, 2011. ISBN 978-1-56145-564-5 Subj: Behavior – dissatisfaction. Birds – chickens, roosters. Birds – peacocks, peahens. Farms.

Lamm, C. Drew. *Gauchada* ill. by Fabian Negrin. Knopf, 2001. ISBN 978-0-375-91267-2 Subj: Foreign lands – Argentina. Jewelry.

Pirates ill. by Stacey Schuett. Hyperion, 2001. ISBN 978-0-7868-0392-7 Subj: Books, reading. Emotions – fear. Family life – brothers & sisters. Pirates.

Lammle, Leslie. *Princess wannabe* ill. by author. HarperCollins, 2014. ISBN 978-006125197-9 Subj: Books, reading. Imagination. Royalty – princesses.

Lamstein, Sarah Marwil. *Big night for salamanders* ill. by Carol Benioff. Boyds Mills, 2010. ISBN 978-1-932425-98-7 Subj: Character traits – kindness to animals. Ecology. Migration. Nature. Reptiles – salamanders. Seasons – spring.

I like your buttons! ill. by Nancy Cote. Albert Whitman, 1999. ISBN 978-0-8075-3510-3 Subj: Character traits – kindness. School.

Landa, Norbert. *The great monster hunt* ill. by Tim Warnes. Good Books, 2010. ISBN 978-1-56148-681-6 Subj: Animals. Emotions – fear. Imagination.

Little Bear and the wishing tree ill. by Simon Mendez. Good Books, 2007. ISBN 978-1-56148-566-6 Subj: Animals – bears. Behavior – sharing. Behavior – wishing. Emotions – anger. Family life – brothers & sisters. Trees.

Landau, Orna. *Leopardpox!* ill. by Omer Hoffmann. Clarion, 2015. ISBN 978-054429001-3 Subj: Animals – leopards. Character traits – appearance. Character traits – being different. Family life – mothers.

Landman, Tanya. *Mary's penny* ill. by Richard Holland. Candlewick, 2010. ISBN 978-0-7636-4768-1 Subj: Farms. Gender roles.

Landolf, Diane Wright. *What a good big brother!* ill. by Steve Johnson. Random House, 2009. ISBN 978-0-375-84258-0 Subj: Babies, toddlers. Family life – brothers & sisters.

Landry, Leo. *Eat your peas, Ivy Louise!* ill. by author. Houghton, 2005. ISBN 978-0-618-44886-9 Subj: Circus. Food. Imagination.

The snow ghosts ill. by author. Houghton, 2003. ISBN 978-0-618-19655-5 Subj: Ghosts. Weather – snow.

Space boy ill. by author. Houghton, 2007. ISBN 978-0-618-60568-2 Subj: Bedtime. Space & space ships.

Trick or treat ill. by author. Houghton Mifflin, 2012. ISBN 978-0-547-24969-8 Subj: Clothing – costumes. Ghosts. Holidays – Halloween. Parties.

Landström, Lena. *Boo and Baa get wet* (Landström, Olof)

Boo and Baa have company by Lena Landström and Olof Landström ill. by Olof Landström. Farrar, 2006. ISBN 978-91-29-66546-8 Subj: Animals – sheep. Humorous stories.

Boo and Baa in the woods (Landström, Olof)

A hippo's tale ill. by author. Farrar, 2007. ISBN 978-91-29-66603-8 Subj: Activities – bathing. Animals – hippopotamuses. Animals – monkeys. Foreign lands – Africa.

The little hippos' adventure ill. by author. Farrar, 2002. ISBN 978-91-29-65500-1 Subj: Animals – hippopotamuses.

Pom and Pim ill. by Olof Landström. Gecko, 2014. ISBN 978-187757966-0 Subj: Activities – playing. Character traits – luck. Friendship. Imagination.

Where is Pim? ill. by Olof Landström. Gecko, 2015. ISBN 978-192727173-5 Subj: Activities – playing. Behavior – lost & found possessions. Friendship. Toys.

Landström, Olof. *Boo and Baa get wet* by Olof Landström and Lena Landström; ill. by authors. Farrar, 2000. ISBN 978-91-29-64752-5 Subj: Animals – sheep. Humorous stories. Weather – storms.

Boo and Baa have company (Landström, Lena)

Boo and Baa in the woods by Olof Landström and Lena Landström; ill. by authors. Farrar, 2000. ISBN 978-91-29-64754-9 Subj: Activities – picnicking. Animals – sheep. Forest, woods. Humorous stories. Insects – ants.

Lane, Adam J. B. *Stop thief!* ill. by author. Roaring Brook, 2012. ISBN 978-1-59643-693-0 Subj: Behavior – growing up. Crime. Toys.

Lane, Daniel. *The Animal Mall* (Edens, Cooper)

Lane, Nathan. *Naughty Mabel* by Nathan Lane and Devlin Elliott ill. by Dan Krall. Simon & Schuster, 2015. ISBN 978-148143022-7 Subj: Animals – dogs. Behavior – misbehavior. Etiquette.

Naughty Mabel sees it all by Nathan Lane and Devlin Elliott ill. by Dan Krall. Simon & Schuster, 2016. ISBN 978-148143024-1 Subj: Animals – dogs. Glasses.

Lang, Glenna. *Looking out for Sarah* ill. by author. Talewinds, 2001. ISBN 978-0-88106-647-0 Subj: Animals – dogs. Animals – service animals. Disabilities – blindness.

Lang, Heather. *Fearless flyer: Ruth Law and her flying machine* ill. by Raul Colón. Boyds Mills, 2016. ISBN 978-162091650-6 Subj: Activities – flying. Airplanes, airports. Careers – airplane pilots. Character traits – persistence. Gender roles.

Queen of the track: Alice Coachman, Olympic high-jump champion ill. by Floyd Cooper. Boyds Mills, 2012. ISBN 978-1-59078-850-9 Subj: Ethnic groups in the U.S. – African Americans. Sports – Olympics. U.S. history.

Swimming with sharks: the daring discoveries of Eugenie Clark ill. by Jordi Solano. Albert Whitman, 2016. ISBN 978-080752187-8 Subj: Careers – scientists. Character traits – persistence. Ethnic groups in the U.S. – Japanese Americans. Fish – sharks. Gender roles.

Lang, Suzanne. *Families, families, families!* ill. by Max Lang. Random House, 2015. ISBN 978-055349938-4 Subj: Animals. Family life. Rhyming text.

Langdo, Bryan. *The dog who loved the good life* ill. by author. Henry Holt, 2001. ISBN 978-0-8050-6494-0 Subj: Animals – dogs.

Tornado Slim and the magic cowboy hat ill. by author. Marshall Cavendish, 2011. ISBN 978-0-7614-5962-0 Subj: Clothing – hats. Cowboys, cowgirls. Magic.

Lange, Willem. *John and Tom* ill. by Bert Dodson. Vermont Folklife Center, 2001. ISBN 978-0-916718-17-6 Subj: Accidents. Animals – horses, ponies. Careers – lumberjacks.

Langen, Annette. *I won't comb my hair!* ill. by Frauke Bahr. NorthSouth, 2010. ISBN 978-0-7358-2315-0 Subj: Character traits – appearance. Character traits – stubbornness. Hair.

Langford, Sarah. *Grandfather's story cloth / Yawg daim paj ntaub dab neeg* (Gerdner, Linda)

Langley, Jonathan. *Shine* (Langley, Karen)

Langley, Karen. *Shine* by Karen Langley and Jonathan Langley ill. by Jonathan Langley. Marshall Cavendish, 2002. ISBN 978-0-7614-5127-3 Subj: Family life – fathers. Holidays – Christmas. School. Stars. Theater.

Langreuter, Jutta. *Little Bear and the big fight* by Jutta Langreuter and Vera Sobat ill. by Vera Sobat. Millbrook, 1998. ISBN 978-0-7613-0403-6 Subj: Animals – bears. Behavior – misbehavior. Emotions – anger. Friendship. School.

Little Bear brushes his teeth by Jutta Langreuter and Vera Sobat ill. by Vera Sobat. Millbrook, 1997. ISBN 978-0-7613-0190-5 Subj: Animals – bears. Family life. Hygiene.

Little Bear goes to kindergarten by Jutta Langreuter and Vera Sobat ill. by Vera Sobat. Millbrook, 1997. ISBN 978-0-7613-0191-2 Subj: Animals – bears. Friendship. School – first day.

Little Bear won't go to bed ill. by Vera Sobat. Millbrook, 2000. ISBN 978-0-7613-1872-9 Subj: Animals – bears. Bedtime.

Langsen, Richard C. *When someone in the family drinks too much* ill. by Nicole Rubel. Dial, 1996. ISBN 978-0-8037-1687-2 Subj: Animals – bears. Family life. Illness – alcoholism.

Langstaff, John M. *Oh, a-hunting we will go* ill. by Nancy Winslow Parker. Atheneum, 1974. ISBN 978-0-689-50007-7 Subj: Folk & fairy tales. Music. Songs. Sports – hunting.

Over in the meadow ill. by Feodor Rojankovsky. Includes Over in the meadow (for voice and piano) by Marshall Woodbridge. Harcourt, 1957. ISBN 978-0-15-258854-0 Subj: Animals. Counting, numbers. Folk & fairy tales. Songs.

What a morning! the Christmas story in Black spirituals ill. by Ashley Bryan. Musical arrangements by John Andrew Ross. Margaret K. McElderry, 1987. ISBN 978-0-689-50422-8 Subj: Holidays – Christmas. Music. Religion. Songs.

Langton, Jane. *Saint Francis and the wolf* ill. by Ilse Plume. Godine, 2007. ISBN 978-1-56792-320-9

Subj: Animals – wolves. Folk & fairy tales. Religion.

Lansky, Vicki. *It's not your fault, KoKo Bear: a read-together book for parents and young children during divorce* ill. by Jane Prince. Book Peddlers, 1998. ISBN 978-0-916773-46-5 Subj: Animals – bears. Divorce. Family life.

LaReau, Kara. *Mr. Prickles: a quill-fated love story* ill. by Scott Magoon. Roaring Brook, 2011. ISBN 978-1-59643-483-7 Subj: Animals – porcupines. Emotions – loneliness. Friendship.

No slurping, no burping! a tale of table manners ill. by Lorelay Bove. Disney/Hyperion, 2014. ISBN 978-142315733-5 Subj: Behavior – misbehavior. Etiquette. Family life – fathers. Food. Humorous stories.

Otto: the boy who loved cars ill. by Scott Magoon. Roaring Brook, 2011. ISBN 978-1-59643-484-4 Subj: Automobiles. Humorous stories.

Rocko and Spanky have company ill. by Jenna LaReau. Harcourt, 2006. ISBN 978-0-15-216618-2 Subj: Animals – monkeys. Multiple births – twins. Toys.

Snowbaby could not sleep ill. by Jim Ishikawa. Little, Brown, 2005. ISBN 978-0-316-60703-2 Subj: Bedtime. Emotions – loneliness. Snowmen.

Ugly fish ill. by Scott Magoon. Harcourt, 2006. ISBN 978-0-15-205082-5 Subj: Behavior – bullying, teasing. Behavior – sharing. Character traits – appearance. Emotions – loneliness. Fish.

Larios, Julie. *Imaginary menagerie: a book of curious creatures* ill. by Julie Paschkis. Harcourt, 2008. ISBN 978-0-15-206325-2 Subj: Mythical creatures. Poetry.

Yellow elephant: a bright bestiary ill. by Julie Paschkis. Harcourt, 2006. ISBN 978-0-15-205422-9 Subj: Animals. Concepts – color. Poetry.

Laroche, Giles. *If you lived here: houses of the world* ill. by author. Harcourt, 2011. ISBN 978-0-547-23892-0 Subj: Homes, houses. World.

LaRochelle, David. *The end* ill. by Richard Egielski. Scholastic, 2007. ISBN 978-0-439-64011-4 Subj: Folk & fairy tales. Humorous stories. Royalty – princesses.

The haunted hamburger and other ghostly stories ill. by Paul Meisel. Penguin, 2011. ISBN 978-0-525-42272-3 Subj: Activities – storytelling. Bedtime. Family life – brothers & sisters. Ghosts.

How Martha saved her parents from green beans ill. by Mark Fearing. Dial, 2013. ISBN 978-0-8037-3766-2 Subj: Family life. Food. Humorous stories.

It's a tiger ill. by Jeremy Tankard. Chronicle, 2012. ISBN 978-0-8118-6925-6 Subj: Activities – storytelling. Animals. Animals – tigers. Imagination.

Monster and son ill. by Joey Chou. Chronicle, 2016. ISBN 978-145212937-2 Subj: Family life – fathers. Monsters. Rhyming text.

Moo! ill. by Mike Wohnoutka. Walker, 2013. ISBN 978-0-8027-3409-9 Subj: Animals – bulls, cows. Automobiles. Behavior – misbehavior.

1+1=5: and other unlikely additions ill. by Brenda Sexton. Sterling, 2010. ISBN 978-1-4027-5995-6 Subj: Counting, numbers. Imagination.

L'Arronge, Lilli. *Me tall, you small* ill. by author. OwlKids, 2017. ISBN 978-177147194-7 Subj: Concepts – opposites. Family life – parents.

Larsen, Andrew. *Bella and the bunny* ill. by Kate Endle. Kids Can, 2007. ISBN 978-1-55337-970-6 Subj: Animals – rabbits. Clothing – sweaters. School – nursery.

The imaginary garden ill. by Irene Luxbacher. Kids Can, 2009. ISBN 978-1-55453-279-7 Subj: Activities – painting. Art. Family life – grandfathers. Gardens, gardening. Imagination.

In the tree house ill. by Dusan Petricic. Kids Can, 2013. ISBN 978-1-55453-635-1 Subj: Family life – brothers. Homes, houses. Trees.

The man who loved libraries: the story of Andrew Carnegie ill. by Katty Maurey. OwlKids, 2017. ISBN 978-177147267-8 Subj: Books, reading. Careers. Character traits – generosity. Immigrants, immigration. Libraries.

The not-so-faraway adventure ill. by Irene Luxbacher. Kids Can, 2016. ISBN 978-177138097-3 Subj: Birthdays. Family life – grandfathers. Sea & seashore – beaches.

See you next year ill. by Todd Stewart. OwlKids, 2015. ISBN 978-192697399-9 Subj: Activities – vacationing. Sea & seashore – beaches.

A squiggly story ill. by Mike Lowery. Kids Can, 2016. ISBN 978-177138016-4 Subj: Activities – drawing. Activities – writing. Character traits – cleverness. Family life – brothers & sisters.

Larsen, Mylisa. *How to put your parents to bed* ill. by Babette Cole. HarperCollins/Katherine Tegen, 2016. ISBN 978-006232064-3 Subj: Bedtime. Family life – parents.

If I were a kangaroo: a bedtime tale ill. by Anna Raff. Viking, 2017. ISBN 978-045146958-8 Subj: Animals – babies. Bedtime. Rhyming text.

Larson, Bonnie. *When animals were people / Cuando los animales eran personas* ill. by Modesto Rivera Lemus. Clear Light, 2002. ISBN 978-1-57416-051-2 Subj: Animals. Folk & fairy tales – pourquoi tales. Foreign lands – Mexico. Foreign languages. Indians of North America – Huichol.

Larson, Kirby. *The magic kerchief* ill. by Rosanne Litzinger. Holiday, 2000. ISBN 978-0-8234-1473-4 Subj: Clothing. Folk & fairy tales. Magic.

Nubs: the true story of a mutt, a marine and a miracle (Dennis, Major Brian)

Two Bobbies: a true story of Hurricane Katrina, friendship, and survival by Kirby Larson and Mary Nethery ill. by Jean Cassels. Walker, 2008. ISBN 978-0-8027-9754-4 Subj: Animals – cats. Animals – dogs. Weather – hurricanes.

Lasky, Kathryn. *Baby love* ill. by Jennifer Plecas. Candlewick, 2001. ISBN 978-1-56402-679-8 Subj: Babies, toddlers.

The emperor's old clothes ill. by David Catrow. Harcourt, 1999. ISBN 978-0-15-200384-5 Subj: Careers – farmers. Clothing. Folk & fairy tales. Humorous stories. Royalty – emperors.

Fourth of July bear ill. by Helen Cogancherry. Morrow, 1991. ISBN 978-0-688-08288-8 Subj: Animals – bears. Friendship. Holidays – Fourth of July. Parades.

Lucille camps in ill. by Marylin Hafner. Knopf, 2003. ISBN 978-0-517-80042-3 Subj: Animals – pigs. Camps, camping. Family life.

Lucille's snowsuit ill. by Marylin Hafner. Crown, 2000. ISBN 978-0-517-80038-6 Subj: Animals – pigs. Clothing. Family life – brothers & sisters. Weather – snow.

Lunch bunnies ill. by Marylin Hafner. Little, 1996. ISBN 978-0-316-51525-2 Subj: Animals – rabbits. Behavior – worrying. School – first day.

Mommy's hands by Kathryn Lasky and Jane Kamine ill. by Darcia Labrosse. Hyperion, 2002. ISBN 978-0-7868-2225-6 Subj: Anatomy – hands. Family life – mothers. Seasons.

Pirate Bob ill. by David Clark. Charlesbridge, 2006. ISBN 978-1-57091-595-6 Subj: Behavior – greed. Pirates.

Science fair bunnies ill. by Marylin Hafner. Candlewick, 2000. ISBN 978-0-7636-0729-6 Subj: Animals – rabbits. Fairs, festivals. School. Science.

Show and tell bunnies ill. by Marylin Hafner. Candlewick, 1998. ISBN 978-0-7636-0396-0 Subj: Animals – rabbits. School. Spiders.

Sophie and Rose ill. by Wendy Anderson Halperin. Candlewick, 1998. ISBN 978-0-7636-0459-2 Subj: Family life. Toys – dolls.

Starring Lucille ill. by Marylin Hafner. Crown, 2001. ISBN 978-0-517-80039-3 Subj: Activities – dancing. Animals – pigs. Ballet. Birthdays. Family life – brothers & sisters.

Tumble bunnies ill. by Marylin Hafner. Candlewick, 2005. ISBN 978-0-7636-2265-7 Subj: Animals – rabbits. Sports – gymnastics. Sportsmanship.

Lass, Bonnie. *Who took the cookies from the cookie jar?* by Bonnie Lass and Philemon Sturges ill. by Ashley Wolff. Little, 2000. ISBN 978-0-316-82016-5 Subj: Animals. Food. Insects – ants. Mystery stories. Rhyming text.

LaTeef, Nelda. *The hunter and the ebony tree* ill. by author. Moon Mt, 2002. ISBN 978-0-9677929-9-6 Subj: Folk & fairy tales. Foreign lands – Africa. Weddings.

Latham, Irene. *Dear Wandering Wildebeest: and other poems from the Water Hole* ill. by Anna Wadham. Lerner/Millbrook, 2014. ISBN 978-146771232-3 Subj: Animals. Foreign lands – Africa. Poetry.

Latifah, Queen. *Queen of the scene* ill. by Frank Morrison. HarperCollins, 2006. ISBN 978-0-06-077857-6 Subj: Character traits – confidence. Ethnic groups in the U.S. – African Americans. Rhyming text. Self-concept.

Latimer, Alex. *The boy who cried ninja* ill. by author. Peachtree, 2011. ISBN 978-0-56145-579-9 Subj: Behavior – lying. Character traits – honesty. Sports – martial arts.

Lion vs Rabbit ill. by author. Peachtree, 2013. ISBN 978-1-56145-709-0 Subj: Animals. Animals – lions. Animals – rabbits. Behavior – bullying, teasing. Behavior – trickery. Foreign lands – Africa.

Penguin's hidden talent ill. by author. Peachtree, 2012. ISBN 978-1-56145-629-1 Subj: Animals. Behavior – resourcefulness. Birds – penguins. Character traits – assertiveness. Theater.

Pig and small ill. by author. Peachtree, 2014. ISBN 978-156145797-7 Subj: Animals – pigs. Character traits – smallness. Concepts – size. Friendship. Insects.

Stay! a top dog story ill. by author. Peachtree, 2015. ISBN 978-156145884-4 Subj: Activities – vacationing. Animals – dogs. Family life – grandfathers. Letters, cards.

Latimer, Miriam. *Dear Panda* ill. by author. OwlKids, 2014. ISBN 978-177147078-0 Subj: Animals – pandas. Behavior – worrying. Friendship. Letters, cards. School – first day.

Latter, Jill. *Mama Hen's big day* ill. by author. NorthSouth, 2013. ISBN 978-0-7358-4109-3 Subj: Birds – chickens, roosters. Eggs.

Lattimore, Deborah Nourse. *Cinderhazel: the Cinderella of Halloween* ill. by author. Scholastic, 1997. ISBN 978-0-590-20232-9 Subj: Character traits – cleanliness. Royalty – princes. Witches.

Lauber, Patricia. *Be a friend to trees* ill. by Holly Keller. HarperCollins, 1994. ISBN 978-0-06-021529-3 Subj: Ecology. Science. Trees.

An octopus is amazing ill. by Holly Keller. Crowell, 1990. ISBN 978-0-690-04862-9 Subj: Octopuses.

Snakes are hunters ill. by Holly Keller. HarperCollins, 1988. ISBN 978-0-690-04630-4 Subj: Reptiles – snakes. Science.

What you never knew about tubs, toilets and showers ill. by John Manders. Simon & Schuster, 2001. ISBN 978-0-689-82420-3 Subj: Activities – bathing. Character traits – cleanliness.

Who eats what? ill. by Holly Keller. HarperCollins, 1995. ISBN 978-0-06-022982-5 Subj: Ecology. Food. Science.

You're aboard spaceship Earth ill. by Holly Keller. HarperCollins, 1996. ISBN 978-0-06-024408-8 Subj: Earth. Space & space ships.

Lauture, Denizé. *Running the road to ABC* ill. by Reynold Ruffins. Simon & Schuster, 1996. ISBN 978-0-689-80507-3 Subj: ABC books. Foreign lands – Haiti. School.

Laverde, Arlene. *Alaska's three pigs* ill. by Mindy Dwyer. Sasquatch, 2000. ISBN 978-1-57061-229-9 Subj: Alaska. Animals – pigs. Folk & fairy tales. Homes, houses.

Lavis, Steve. *Cock-a-doodle-doo: a farmyard counting book* ill. by author. Dutton, 1997. ISBN 978-0-525-67542-6 Subj: Animals. Counting, numbers. Noise, sounds.

Jump! ill. by author. Lodestar, 1998. ISBN 978-0-525-67578-5 Subj: Activities. Animals. Behavior – imitation. Birds.

On the farm ill. by author. Ragged Bears, 2001. ISBN 978-1-929927-23-4 Subj: Animals. Farms. Format, unusual – toy & movable books.

Law, Diane. *Come out and play: count around the world in five languages* ill. by author. NorthSouth, 2006. ISBN 978-0-7358-2060-9 Subj: Counting, numbers. Foreign languages.

Lawler, Janet. *A father's song* ill. by Lucy Corvino. Sterling, 2006. ISBN 978-1-4027-2501-2 Subj: Activities – playing. Emotions – love. Family life – fathers. Rhyming text.

Love is real ill. by Anna Brown. HarperCollins, 2014. ISBN 978-006224170-2 Subj: Animals. Emotions – love. Rhyming text.

A mother's song ill. by Kathleen Kemly. Sterling, 2010. ISBN 978-1-4027-6968-9 Subj: Family life – mothers. Nature. Rhyming text.

Ocean counting ill. with photos. National Geographic, 2013. ISBN 978-1-4263-1116-1 Subj: Animals. Counting, numbers. Sea & seashore.

Snowzilla ill. by Amanda Haley. Amazon, 2012. ISBN 978-0-7614-6188-3 Subj: Rhyming text. Snowmen.

Tyrannoclaus ill. by John Shroades. HarperCollins, 2009. ISBN 978-0-06-117054-6 Subj: Dinosaurs. Holidays – Christmas. Rhyming text. Santa Claus.

Lawlor, Laurie. *Muddy as a duck puddle and other American similes* ill. by Ethan Long. Holiday House, 2010. ISBN 978-0-8234-2229-6 Subj: ABC books. Language.

Old Crump ill. by John Winch. Holiday, 2002. ISBN 978-0-8234-1608-0 Subj: Activities – traveling. Animals – oxen. Desert. Moving. U.S. history.

Rachel Carson and her book that changed the world ill. by Laura Beingessner. Holiday House, 2012. ISBN 978-0-8234-2370-5 Subj: Careers – scientists. Ecology. Gender roles. Sea & seashore.

Lawrence, Jennifer B. *Sad doggy* ill. by Timothy Basil Ering. Piggy Toes, 2001. ISBN 978-1-58117-066-5 Subj: Animals – dogs. Emotions – sadness. Format, unusual – toy & movable books. Rhyming text.

Lawrence, John. *This little chick* ill. by author. Candlewick, 2002. ISBN 978-0-7636-1716-5 Subj: Animals. Animals – babies. Birds – chickens, roosters. Noise, sounds. Rhyming text.

Lawrence, Mary. *What's that sound?* ill. by Lynn Adams. Kane, 2002. ISBN 978-1-57565-118-7 Subj: Country. Family life. Noise, sounds.

Lawrence, Michael. *Baby loves* ill. by Adrian Reynolds. DK, 1999. ISBN 978-0-7894-3410-4 Subj: Babies, toddlers. Emotions – love. Format, unusual – board books.

The caterpillar that roared ill. by Alison Bartlett. DK, 2000. ISBN 978-0-7894-5618-2 Subj: Animals. Behavior – imitation. Insects – butterflies, caterpillars. Self-concept.

Lawson, Dorie McCullough. *Tex* photos by author. Trafalgar Square, 2011. ISBN 978-1-57076-501-8 Subj: Careers – ranchers. Cowboys, cowgirls. Dreams. Imagination.

Lawson, Janet. *Audrey and Barbara* ill. by author. Atheneum, 2002. ISBN 978-0-689-83896-5 Subj: Animals – cats. Imagination.

Lawson, JonArno. *Leap!* ill. by Josée Bisaillon. Kids Can, 2017. ISBN 978-177138678-4 Subj: Animals. Circular tales. Insects. Rhyming text.

Sidewalk flowers ill. by Sydney Smith. Groundwood, 2015. ISBN 978-155498431-2 Subj: Activities – walking. Family life – fathers. Flowers. Wordless.

Lawson, Julie. *Arizona Charlie and the Klondike Kid* ill. by Kasia Charko. Orca, 2003. ISBN 978-1-55143-250-2 Subj: Cowboys, cowgirls. Crime. Foreign lands – Canada. Theater.

Lawson, Robert. *They were strong and good* ill. by author. Viking, 1940. ISBN 978-0-670-69949-0 Subj: Caldecott award books. Family life. U.S. history – frontier & pioneer life.

Layne, Deborah Dover. *T is for teachers: a school alphabet* (Layne, Steven L.)

Layne, Steven L. *Love the baby* ill. by Ard Hoyt. Pelican, 2007. ISBN 978-1-58980-392-3 Subj: Animals – rabbits. Babies, toddlers. Emotions – envy, jealousy. Family life – new sibling.

My brother Dan's delicious ill. by Chuck Galey. Pelican, 2003. ISBN 978-1-58980-071-7 Subj: Emotions – fear. Family life – brothers. Monsters.

T is for teachers: a school alphabet by Steven L. Layne and Deborah Dover Layne ill. by Doris Ettlinger. Sleeping Bear, 2005. ISBN 978-1-58536-159-5 Subj: ABC books. Careers – teachers. School.

Layton, Neal. *Hot, hot, hot* ill. by author. Candlewick, 2004. ISBN 978-0-7636-2148-3 Subj: Animals. Behavior – resourcefulness. Seasons – summer.

Smile if you're human ill. by author. Dial, 1998. ISBN 978-0-8037-2381-8 Subj: Aliens. Animals. Animals – gorillas. Family life.

The tree ill. by author. Candlewick, 2017. ISBN 978-076368952-0 Subj: Animals. Ecology. Homes, houses. Nature. Trees.

Lazar, Tara. *Little Red Gliding Hood* ill. by Troy Cummings. Random House, 2015. ISBN 978-038537006-6 Subj: Animals – wolves. Contests. Folk & fairy tales. Sports – ice skating.

The Monstore ill. by James Burks. Simon & Schuster, 2013. ISBN 978-1-4424-2017-5 Subj: Family life – brothers & sisters. Monsters. Stores.

Normal Norman ill. by S. britt. Sterling, 2016. ISBN 978-145491321-4 Subj: Animals – gorillas. Careers – scientists. Character traits – individuality. Humorous stories.

7 ate 9: the untold story ill. by Ross MacDonald. Disney/Hyperion, 2017. ISBN 978-148471779-0 Subj: Careers – detectives. Counting, numbers. Humorous stories. Mystery stories.

Lazo, Caroline. *Someday when my cat can talk* ill. by Kyrsten Brooker. Random House, 2008. ISBN 978-0-375-83754-8 Subj: Activities – traveling. Animals – cats. Imagination. Rhyming text.

Lê, Minh. *Let me finish!* ill. by Isabel Roxas. Disney/Hyperion, 2016. ISBN 978-148472173-5 Subj: Animals. Books, reading.

Leaf, Munro. *The story of Ferdinand the bull* ill. by Robert Lawson. Viking, 1936. Subj: Animals – bulls, cows. Character traits – individuality. Foreign lands – Spain. Violence, nonviolence.

Wee Gillis ill. by Robert Lawson. Puffin, 1985, ©1938. ISBN 978-0-14-050535-1 Subj: Caldecott award honor books. Foreign lands – Scotland.

Lear, Edward. *Hilary Knight's the owl and the pussycat* (Knight, Hilary)

The owl and the pussycat ill. by Jan Brett. Putnam, 1991. ISBN 978-0-399-21925-2 Subj: Animals – cats. Birds – owls. Poetry.

The owl and the pussycat ill. by Paul Galdone. Houghton, 1987. ISBN 978-0-89919-505-6 Subj: Animals – cats. Birds – owls. Poetry.

The owl and the pussycat ill. by Anne Mortimer. HarperCollins, 2006. ISBN 978-0-06-027229-6 Subj: Animals – cats. Birds – owls. Poetry.

The Quangle Wangle's hat ill. by Louise Voce. Candlewick, 2005. ISBN 978-0-7636-1289-4 Subj: Clothing – hats. Humorous stories. Poetry.

Lears, Laurie. *Becky the brave: a story about epilepsy* ill. by Gail Piazza. Albert Whitman, 2002. ISBN 978-0-8075-0601-1 Subj: Character traits – bravery. Family life – sisters. Illness – epilepsy. School.

Ben has something to say: a story about stuttering ill. by Karen Ritz. Albert Whitman, 2000. ISBN 978-0-8075-0633-2 Subj: Animals – dogs. Disabilities – stuttering. Emotions – fear.

Ian's walk: a story about autism ill. by Karen Ritz. Albert Whitman, 1998. ISBN 978-0-8075-3480-9 Subj: Behavior – lost. Disabilities – autism. Family life – brothers & sisters. Senses.

Megan's birthday tree: a story about open adoption ill. by Bill Farnsworth. Albert Whitman, 2005. ISBN 978-0-8075-5036-6 Subj: Adoption. Birthdays. Family life. Moving. Trees.

Nathan's wish: a story about cerebral palsy ill. by Stacey Schuett. Albert Whitman, 2005. ISBN 978-0-8075-7101-9 Subj: Birds – owls. Disabilities – cerebral palsy.

Waiting for Mr. Goose ill. by Karen Ritz. Albert Whitman, 1999. ISBN 978-0-8075-8628-0 Subj: Birds – geese. Character traits – kindness to animals. Disabilities.

Leathers, Philippa. *The black rabbit* ill. by author. Candlewick, 2013. ISBN 978-0-7636-5714-7 Subj: Animals – rabbits. Shadows.

How to catch a mouse ill. by author. Candlewick, 2015. ISBN 978-076366912-6 Subj: Animals – cats. Animals – mice.

LeBox, Annette. *Salmon Creek* ill. by Karen Reczuch. Douglas & McIntyre, 2002. ISBN 978-0-88899-458-5 Subj: Fish. Poetry.

Wild bog tea ill. by Harvey Chan. Douglas & McIntyre, 2001. ISBN 978-0-88899-406-6 Subj: Family life – grandfathers. Nature. Swamps.

Lechelt, Karen. *What do you love about you?* ill. by author. Bloomsbury, 2016. ISBN 978-168119093-8 Subj: Character traits – individuality. Self-concept.

Lechner, Susan. *Followers of the north star: rhymes about African American heroes, heroines, and historical times* (Altman, Susan)

Leduc, Emilie. *All year round* ill. by Shelley Tanaka. Groundwood, 2015. ISBN 978-155498411-4 Subj: Days of the week, months of the year. Seasons.

Ledwon, Peter. *Midnight math twelve terrific math games* ill. by Marilyn Mets. Holiday, 2000. ISBN 978-0-8234-1530-4 Subj: Animals. Counting, numbers. Games.

Lee. *The lost kitten* ill. by Komako Sakai. Gecko, 2017. ISBN 978-177657126-0 Subj: Animals – cats. Behavior – lost.

Lee, Chinlun. *Good dog, Paw* ill. by author. Candlewick, 2004. ISBN 978-0-7636-2178-0 Subj: Animals. Animals – dogs. Careers – veterinarians. Emotions – love.

The very kind rich lady and her one hundred dogs ill. by author. Candlewick, 2001. ISBN 978-0-7636-1290-0 Subj: Animals – dogs. Pets.

Lee, Dennis. *Bubblegum delicious* ill. by David McPhail. HarperCollins, 2001. ISBN 978-0-06-623709-1 Subj: Foreign lands – Canada. Poetry.

Lee, H. Chuku. *Beauty and the beast: a retelling* ill. by Pat Cummings. Amistad, 2014. ISBN 978-068814819-5 Subj: Character traits – appearance. Character traits – loyalty. Emotions – love. Folk & fairy tales. Foreign lands – Africa. Magic.

Lee, Ho Baek. *While we were out* ill. by author. Kane/Miller, 2002. ISBN 978-1-929132-44-7 Subj: Activities. Animals – rabbits. Pets.

Lee, Huy Voun. *In the leaves* ill. by author. Henry Holt, 2005. ISBN 978-0-8050-6764-4 Subj: Farms. Foreign languages. Seasons – fall.

1, 2, 3 go! ill. by author. Henry Holt, 2000. ISBN 978-0-8050-6205-2 Subj: Counting, numbers. Foreign languages.

Lee, Jeanne M. *Silent lotus* ill. by author. Farrar, 1991. ISBN 978-0-374-36911-8 Subj: Activities – dancing. Disabilities – deafness. Disabilities – physical disabilities. Foreign lands – Cambodia.

The song of Mu Lan ill. by author. Front Street, 1995. ISBN 978-1-886910-00-3 Subj: Careers – military. Character traits – bravery. Folk & fairy tales. Foreign lands – China.

Toad is the uncle of heaven: a Vietnamese folk tale ill. by reteller. Henry Holt, 1985. ISBN 978-0-03-004652-0 Subj: Animals. Folk & fairy tales. Foreign lands – Vietnam. Frogs & toads. Royalty. Weather – rain.

Lee, Joey. *ABC: the alphabet from the sky* (Gross, Benedikt)

Lee, Mark. *20 big trucks in the middle of the street* ill. by Kurt Cyrus. Candlewick, 2013. ISBN 978-0-7636-5809-0 Subj: Counting, numbers. Trucks.

Lee, Michelle. *Play with me!* ill. by author. Putnam, 2017. ISBN 978-039954601-3 Subj: Activities – playing. Animals – bears. Animals – pigs. Character traits – compromising.

Lee, Milly. *Earthquake* ill. by Yangsook Choi. Farrar, 2001. ISBN 978-0-374-39964-1 Subj: Earthquakes. Ethnic groups in the U.S. – Chinese Americans. U.S. history.

Landed ill. by Yangsook Choi. Farrar, 2006. ISBN 978-0-374-34314-9 Subj: Ethnic groups in the U.S. – Chinese Americans. Immigrants, immigration.

Nim and the war effort ill. by Yangsook Choi. Farrar, 1997. ISBN 978-0-374-22262-8 Subj: Ethnic groups in the U.S. – Chinese Americans. Family life. U.S. history. War.

Lee, Quinlan B. *Crazy Christmas chaos* ill. by Clive Scruton. HarperCollins, 2002. ISBN 978-0-694-01683-9 Subj: Holidays – Christmas. Santa Claus.

Lee, Spike. *Giant steps to change the world* by Spike Lee and Tonya Lewis Lee ill. by Sean Qualls. Simon & Schuster, 2011. ISBN 978-0-689-86815-3 Subj: Character traits. Character traits – perseverance. Self-concept.

Please, puppy, please by Spike Lee and Tonya Lewis Lee ill. by Kadir Nelson. Simon & Schuster, 2005. ISBN 978-0-689-86804-7 Subj: Animals – dogs. Ethnic groups in the U.S. – African Americans. Pets.

Lee, Stan. *Stan Lee's superhero Christmas* ill. by Tim Jessell. Tegen, 2004. ISBN 978-0-06-056560-2 Subj: Holidays – Christmas. Santa Claus.

Lee, Suzy. *Lines* ill. by author. Simon & Schuster/Little Simon, 2017. ISBN 978-148149074-0 Subj: Activities – drawing. Wordless.

Mirror ill. by author. Seven Footer, 2010. ISBN 978-1-934734-39-1 Subj: Mirrors. Wordless.

Shadow ill. by author. Chronicle, 2010. ISBN 978-0-8118-7280-5 Subj: Imagination. Shadows.

Wave ill. by author. Chronicle, 2008. ISBN 978-0-8118-5924-0 Subj: Sea & seashore – beaches. Wordless.

Lee, Tae-Jun. *Waiting for Mama: a bilingual picture book* ill. by Dong-Seong Kim. NorthSouth, 2007. ISBN 978-0-7358-2143-9 Subj: Family life – mothers. Foreign lands – Korea. Language.

Lee, Tonya Lewis. *Giant steps to change the world* (Lee, Spike)

Please, puppy, please (Lee, Spike)

Lee, Y. J. *The little moon princess* ill. by author. HarperCollins, 2010. ISBN 978-0-06-154736-2 Subj: Birds – sparrows. Royalty – princesses. Stars.

Lee-Tai, Amy. *A place where sunflowers grow / Sabaku ni saita himawari* ill. by Felicia Hoshino. Children's Book Press, 2006. ISBN 978-0-89239-215-5 Subj: Art. Ethnic groups in the U.S. – Japanese Americans. Flowers. Foreign languages. U.S. history. War.

Leedahl, Shelley A. *The bone talker* ill. by Bill Slavin. Red Deer, 2000. ISBN 978-0-88995-214-0 Subj: Activities – sewing. Communities, neighborhoods. Family life – grandmothers. Memories, memory. Old age. Quilts.

Leedy, Loreen. *Crazy like a fox: a simile story* ill. by author. Holiday House, 2008. ISBN 978-0-8234-1719-3 Subj: Animals – foxes. Birthdays. Language.

The dragon Halloween party ill. by author. Holiday, 1986. ISBN 978-0-8234-0611-1 Subj: Dragons. Holidays – Halloween. Parties. Rhyming text.

The dragon Thanksgiving feast ill. by author. Holiday, 1990. ISBN 978-0-8234-0828-3 Subj: Dragons. Food. Holidays – Thanksgiving. Rhyming text.

The edible pyramid: good eating every day ill. by author. Rev. ed. Holiday House, 2007. ISBN 978-0-8234-2074-2 Subj: Food. Health & fitness.

Follow the money ill. by author. Holiday, 2002. ISBN 978-0-8234-1587-8 Subj: Money.

Fraction action ill. by author. Holiday, 1994. ISBN 978-0-8234-1109-2 Subj: Animals. Counting, numbers. School.

The Furry News ill. by author. Holiday, 1990. ISBN 978-0-8234-0793-4 Subj: Activities – writing. Animals. Careers – journalists. Communication. Communities, neighborhoods.

The great graph contest ill. by author. Holiday House, 2005. ISBN 978-0-8234-1710-0 Subj: Animals – snails. Contests. Counting, numbers. Frogs & toads. Reptiles – lizards.

The great trash bash ill. by author. Holiday, 1991. ISBN 978-0-8234-0869-6 Subj: Animals. Ecology.

It's probably Penny ill. by author. Henry Holt, 2007. ISBN 978-0-8050-7389-8 Subj: Animals – dogs.

Jack and the hungry giant eat right with MyPlate ill. by author. Holiday House, 2013. ISBN 978-0-8234-2602-7 Subj: Food. Giants. Health & fitness.

Mapping Penny's world ill. by author. Henry Holt, 2000. ISBN 978-0-8050-6178-9 Subj: Animals – dogs. Maps.

Messages in the mailbox ill. by author. Holiday, 1991. ISBN 978-0-8234-0889-4 Subj: Activities – writing. Letters, cards. School.

Missing math: a number mystery ill. by author. Marshall Cavendish, 2008. ISBN 978-0-7614-5385-7 Subj: Animals. Counting, numbers. Mystery stories.

Mission — addition ill. by author. Holiday, 1997. ISBN 978-0-8234-1307-2 Subj: Animals. Counting, numbers. School.

Postcards from Pluto ill. by author. Holiday, 1993. ISBN 978-0-8234-1000-2 Subj: Astronomy. Space & space ships.

Seeing symmetry ill. by author. Holiday House, 2012. ISBN 978-0-8234-2360-6 Subj: Concepts.

There's a frog in my throat: 312 animal sayings from the horse's mouth by Loreen Leedy and Pat Street; ill. by Loreen Leedy. Winslow, 2001. ISBN 978-1-890817-24-4 Subj: Animals. Language.

2 x 2 = boo! a set of spooky multiplication stories ill. by author. Holiday, 1995. ISBN 978-0-8234-1190-0 Subj: Counting, numbers. Holidays – Halloween. Witches.

Leeson, Christine. *Molly and the storm* ill. by Gaby Hansen. Tiger Tales, 2003. ISBN 978-1-58925-027-7 Subj: Animals. Animals – mice. Friendship. Weather – storms.

Lefebvre, Jason. *Too much glue* ill. by Zac Retz. Flashlight, 2013. ISBN 978-1-936261-27-7 Subj: Art. School.

Le Guin, Ursula K. *Cat dreams* ill. by S. D. Schindler. Scholastic, 2009. ISBN 978-0-545-04216-1 Subj: Animals – cats. Dreams. Rhyming text.

Lehman, Barbara. *Museum trip* ill. by author. Houghton, 2006. ISBN 978-0-618-58125-2 Subj: Imagination. Museums. Wordless.

Rainstorm ill. by author. Houghton, 2007. ISBN 978-0-618-75639-1 Subj: Imagination. Weather – rain. Wordless.

Red again ill. by author. Houghton Mifflin Harcourt, 2017. ISBN 978-054481859-0 Subj: Books, reading. Friendship. Wordless.

The red book ill. by author. Houghton, 2004. ISBN 978-0-618-42858-8 Subj: Books, reading. Caldecott award honor books. Friendship. Wordless.

The secret box ill. by author. Houghton Mifflin, 2011. ISBN 978-0-547-23868-5 Subj: Behavior – secrets. Imagination. School. Wordless.

Trainstop ill. by author. Houghton, 2008. ISBN 978-0-618-75640-7 Subj: Character traits – helpfulness. Imagination. Trains. Wordless.

Lehman-Wilzig, Tami. *Keeping the promise: a Torah's journey* ill. by Craig Orback. Kar-Ben, 2004. ISBN 978-1-58013-117-9 Subj: Holocaust. Jewish culture. Religion.

Nathan blows out the Hanukkah candles by Tami Lehman-Wilzig and Nicole Katzman ill. by Jeremy Tugeau. Lerner/Kar-Ben, 2011. ISBN 978-0-7613-6657-7 Subj: Disabilities – autism. Family life – brothers. Holidays – Hanukkah. Jewish culture.

Lehn, Barbara. *What is a scientist?* photos by Carol Krauss. Millbrook, 1998. ISBN 978-0-7613-1272-7 Subj: Careers – scientists. Science.

What is a teacher? photos by Carol Krauss. Millbrook, 2000. ISBN 978-0-7613-1713-5 Subj: Careers – teachers.

What is an athlete? photos by Carol Krauss. Millbrook, 2002. ISBN 978-0-7613-2258-0 Subj: Sports.

Lehrhaupt, Adam. *Chicken in school* ill. by Shahar Kober. HarperCollins, 2017. ISBN 978-006236413-5 Subj: Animals – pigs. Birds – chickens, roosters. Farms. Imagination. School.

Chicken in space ill. by Shahar Kober. HarperCollins, 2016. ISBN 978-006236412-8 Subj: Activities – flying. Animals – pigs. Birds – chickens, roosters. Character traits – confidence. Farms. Imagination.

I will not eat you ill. by Scott Magoon. Simon & Schuster/Paula Wiseman, 2016. ISBN 978-148142933-7 Subj: Animals. Dragons.

Please, open this book! ill. by Matthew Forsythe. Simon & Schuster/Paula Wiseman, 2015. ISBN 978-144245071-4 Subj: Animals. Books, reading. Humorous stories.

This is a good story ill. by Magali Le Huche. Simon & Schuster/Paula Wiseman, 2017. ISBN 978-148142935-1 Subj: Activities – drawing. Activities – storytelling. Activities – writing. Books, reading. Careers – illustrators. Careers – writers. Children as authors. Children as illustrators.

Warning: do not open this book! ill. by Matthew Forsythe. Simon & Schuster, 2013. ISBN 978-1-4424-3582-7 Subj: Animals – monkeys. Birds – toucans. Books, reading. Reptiles – alligators, crocodiles.

Wordplay ill. by Jared Chapman. Scholastic/Arthur A. Levine, 2017. ISBN 978-054593428-2 Subj: Humorous stories. Language.

Leigh, C.J. *The Ninjabread Man* (The gingerbread boy)

Leigh, Heather. *Hey little baby!* ill. by Geneviève Côté. Simon & Schuster, 2012. ISBN 978-1-4169-8979-0 Subj: Babies, toddlers. Senses.

Leijten, Aileen. *Hugging hour!* ill. by author. Philomel, 2009. ISBN 978-0-399-24680-7 Subj: Behavior – worrying. Family life – grandmothers. Sleepovers.

Leiner, Katherine. *Mama does the mambo* ill. by Edel Rodriguez. Hyperion, 2001. ISBN 978-0-7868-0646-1 Subj: Activities – dancing. Emotions – grief. Foreign lands – Cuba.

Leiter, Richard. *The flying hand of Marco B.* ill. by Shahar Kober. Sleeping Bear, 2015. ISBN 978-158536888-4 Subj: Activities – flying. Automobiles. Imagination. Rhyming text.

Lemke, Donald. *Book-o-beards: a wearable book* ill. by Bob Lentz. Capstone, 2015. ISBN 978-162370183-3 Subj: Format, unusual – board books. Format, unusual – toy & movable books. Hair. Masks. Rhyming text.

Lemniscates. *Silence* ill. by author. Magination, 2012. ISBN 978-1-4338-1137-1 Subj: Behavior – solitude. Character traits – patience, impatience. Noise, sounds.

Trees ill. by Lemniscates. Candlewick Studio, 2017. ISBN 978-076369001-4 Subj: Seasons. Trees.

Lendler, Ian. *Saturday* ill. by Serge Bloch. Roaring Brook/Neal Porter, 2016. ISBN 978-159643965-8 Subj: Activities – playing. Family life.

An undone fairy tale ill. by Whitney Martin. Simon & Schuster, 2005. ISBN 978-0-689-86677-7 Subj: Folk & fairy tales. Food. Humorous stories. Royalty – princesses.

Lendroth, Susan. *Calico Dorsey: mail dog of the mining camps* ill. by Adam Gustavson. Tricycle, 2010. ISBN 978-1-58246-318-6 Subj: Animals – dogs. Careers – postal workers. Post office. U.S. history.

Ocean wide, ocean deep ill. by Raul Allen. Tricycle, 2008. ISBN 978-1-58246-232-5 Subj: Family life. Rhyming text. Sailors. U.S. history.

Old Manhattan has some farms: e-i-e-i-grow! ill. by Kate Endle. Charlesbridge, 2014. ISBN 978-158089572-9   Subj: Cities, towns. Cumulative tales. Farms. Gardens, gardening. Songs.

Le Neouanic, Lionel. *Little smudge* ill. by author. Boxer, 2006. ISBN 978-1-905417-22-3 Subj: Character traits – being different. Concepts – shape. Emotions – loneliness. Friendship.

L'Engle, Madeleine. *The other dog* ill. by Christine Davenier. SeaStar, 2001. ISBN 978-1-58717-041-6 Subj: Animals – dogs. Babies, toddlers.

Lennon, John. *Imagine* ill. by Jean Jullien. Clarion, 2017. ISBN 978-132880865-3   Subj: Character traits – hopefulness. Songs. Violence, nonviolence.

Lennon, Julian. *Touch the earth* by Julian Lennon and Bart Davis ill. by Smiljana Coh. Skyhorse/Sky Pony, 2017. ISBN 978-151072083-1 Subj: Ecology. Water.

Lenski, Lois. *The Easter Rabbit's parade* ill. by author. Random House, 2004. ISBN 978-0-375-92748-5   Subj: Animals. Holidays – Easter. Parades.

I like winter ill. by author. Random House, 2000, ©1950. ISBN 978-0-375-91068-5   Subj: Music. Poetry. Seasons – winter. Songs.

The little airplane ill. by author. Random House, 2003, ©1938. ISBN 978-0-375-91079-1   Subj: Airplanes, airports. Careers – airplane pilots.

The little family ill. by author. Random House, 2002, ©1932. ISBN 978-0-375-91077-7   Subj: Family life.

The little fire engine ill. by author. Random House, 2000, ©1946. ISBN 978-0-375-82263-6   Subj: Careers – firefighters.

The little sailboat ill. by author. Random House, 2003. ISBN 978-0-375-91078-4   Subj: Animals – dogs. Boats, ships. Sailors.

The little train ill. by author. Random House, 2002, ©1940. ISBN 978-0-375-82264-3   Subj: Careers – railroad engineers. Trains.

Now it's fall ill. by author. Random House, 2000, ©1948. ISBN 978-0-375-91069-2   Subj: Poetry. Seasons – fall.

Papa Small ill. by author. Random House, 2004, ©1951. ISBN 978-0-375-92749-2   Subj: Family life. Family life – fathers.

Policeman Small ill. by author. Random House, 2001, ©1962. ISBN 978-0-375-91072-2   Subj: Careers – police officers. Cities, towns.

Lent, Blair. *Ruby and Fred* ill. by author. Henry Holt, 2000. ISBN 978-0-8050-6117-8   Subj: Animals – cats. Animals – dogs. Birds.

Leodhas, Sorche Nic *see* Alger, Leclaire Gowans

Léonard, Marie. *Tibili, the little boy who didn't want to go to school* ill. by Andrée Prigent. Kane/Miller, 2002. ISBN 978-1-929132-20-1 Subj: Animals. Books, reading. Foreign lands – Africa. School – first day.

Leonetti, Mike. *Gretzky's game* ill. by Greg Banning. Raincoast, 2006. ISBN 978-1-55192-851-7 Subj: Sports – hockey.

Swinging for the fences: Hank Aaron and me ill. by David Kim. Chronicle, 2008. ISBN 978-0-8118-5662-1   Subj: Character traits – patience, impatience. Sports – baseball.

Lepp, Bil. *The King of Little Things* ill. by David Wenzel. Peachtree, 2013. ISBN 978-1-56145-708-3 Subj: Behavior – greed. Character traits – smallness. Concepts – size. Royalty – kings.

Lerch. *Swim! swim!* ill. by author. Scholastic, 2010. ISBN 978-0-545-09419-1   Subj: Emotions – loneliness. Fish. Friendship.

Lerman, Josh. *How to raise Mom and Dad: instructions from someone who figured it out* ill. by Greg Clarke. Dutton, 2009. ISBN 978-0-525-47870-6 Subj: Family life – parents. Humorous stories.

Lerner, Harriet Goldhor. *Franny B. Kranny, there's a bird in your hair* by Harriet Goldhor Lerner and Susan Henne Goldhor ill. by Helen Oxenbury. HarperCollins, 2000. ISBN 978-0-06-024683-9 Subj: Birds. Family life. Hair.

Leroy, Jean. *Stripes the tiger* by Jean Leroy and Bérengère Delaporte ill. by Bérengère Delaporte. Peter Pauper, 2016. ISBN 978-144132184-8 Subj: Animals – cats. Animals – tigers. Imagination.

Superfab saves the day (DeLaporte, Bérengère)

A well-mannered young wolf ill. by Matthieu Maudet. Eerdmans, 2016. ISBN 978-080285479-7 Subj: Animals – wolves. Behavior – trickery. Etiquette.

LeSieg, Theo *see* Seuss, Dr.

Leslie, Amanda. *Alfie and Betty Bug* ill. by author. Handprint, 2001. ISBN 978-1-929766-33-8 Subj: Animals. Animals – elephants. Format, unusual – toy & movable books. Insects.

Are chickens stripy? ill. by author. Handprint, 2000. ISBN 978-1-929766-09-3   Subj: Animals. Birds – chickens, roosters. Format, unusual – toy & movable books.

Do crocodiles moo? ill. by author. Handprint, 2000. ISBN 978-1-929766-08-6 Subj: Animals. Concepts – color. Format, unusual – toy & movable books. Noise, sounds.

Flappy, waggy, wiggly ill. by author. Dutton, 1999. ISBN 978-0-525-46182-1 Subj: Animals. Format, unusual – toy & movable books.

Who's that scratching at my door? ill. by author. Handprint, 2001. ISBN 978-1-929766-19-2 Subj: Activities – playing. Animals. Animals – dogs. Format, unusual – toy & movable books.

LeSourd, Nancy. *Christy, Christmastime at Cutter Gap* by Nancy LeSourd and Catherine Marshall ill. by Bill Farnsworth. Based on the novel by Catherine Marshall. Zondervan, 2003. ISBN 978-0-310-70571-0 Subj: Holidays – Christmas. Religion. School.

Lessac, Frané. *Island Counting 123* ill. by author. Candlewick, 2005. ISBN 978-0-7636-1960-2 Subj: Counting, numbers. Foreign lands – Caribbean Islands. Rhyming text.

Lesser, Carolyn. *What a wonderful day to be a cow* ill. by Melissa Bay Mathis. Knopf, 1995. ISBN 978-0-679-92430-2 Subj: Animals. Days of the week, months of the year. Farms. Poetry. Seasons.

Lester, Alison. *Ernie dances to the didgeridoo* ill. by author. Houghton, 2001. ISBN 978-0-618-10442-0 Subj: Australian aborigines. Foreign lands – Australia. Letters, cards.

Noni the pony ill. by author. Simon & Schuster, 2012. ISBN 978-1-4424-5959-5 Subj: Animals. Animals – horses, ponies. Farms. Rhyming text.

Running with the horses ill. by author. NorthSouth, 2011. ISBN 978-0-7358-4002-7 Subj: Animals – horses, ponies. Character traits – bravery. Character traits – loyalty. Foreign lands – Austria.

Sophie Scott goes south ill. by author. Houghton Mifflin, 2013. ISBN 978-054408895-5 Subj: Activities – traveling. Foreign lands – Antarctic.

Lester, Helen. *All for me and none for all* ill. by Lynn Munsinger. Houghton Mifflin, 2012. ISBN 978-0-547-68834-3 Subj: Animals – pigs. Behavior – greed. Behavior – sharing.

Author: a true story ill. by author. Houghton, 1997. ISBN 978-0-395-82744-4 Subj: Careers – writers. Disabilities.

Batter up Wombat ill. by Lynn Munsinger. Houghton, 2006. ISBN 978-0-618-73784-0 Subj: Animals – wombats. Sports – baseball. Weather – tornadoes.

Boris and the worrisome wakies ill. by Lynn Munsinger. Houghton Mifflin Harcourt, 2017. ISBN 978-054464094-8 Subj: Animals – badgers. Bedtime. Sleep.

Happy birdday, Tacky! ill. by Lynn Munsinger. Houghton Mifflin, 2013. ISBN 978-0-547-91228-8 Subj: Birds – penguins. Birthdays. Parties.

Hooway for Wodney Wat ill. by Lynn Munsinger. Houghton, 1999. ISBN 978-0-395-92392-4 Subj: Animals. Animals – rats. Behavior – bullying, teasing. Disabilities. School.

Hurty feelings ill. by Lynn Munsinger. Houghton, 2004. ISBN 978-0-618-41082-8 Subj: Animals – elephants. Animals – hippopotamuses. Behavior. Emotions. Sports – soccer.

It wasn't my fault ill. by Lynn Munsinger. Houghton, 1985. ISBN 978-0-395-35629-6 Subj: Animals. Cumulative tales.

Listen, Buddy ill. by Lynn Munsinger. Houghton, 1995. ISBN 978-0-395-72361-6 Subj: Animals – rabbits.

The loch mess monster ill. by Lynn Munsinger. Houghton, 2014. ISBN 978-054409990-6 Subj: Behavior – messy. Foreign lands – Scotland. Humorous stories. Monsters.

Me first ill. by Lynn Munsinger. Houghton, 1992. ISBN 978-0-395-58706-5 Subj: Animals – pigs. Behavior. Character traits – selfishness. Witches.

A porcupine named Fluffy ill. by Lynn Munsinger. Houghton, 1986. ISBN 978-0-395-36895-4 Subj: Animals – porcupines. Names.

Princess Penelope's parrot ill. by Lynn Munsinger. Houghton, 1996. ISBN 978-0-395-78320-7 Subj: Birds – parakeets, parrots. Character traits – selfishness. Emotions – anger. Royalty – princes. Royalty – princesses.

The revenge of the magic chicken ill. by Lynn Munsinger. Houghton, 1990. ISBN 978-0-395-50929-6 Subj: Birds – chickens, roosters. Magic.

Score one for the sloths ill. by Lynn Munsinger. Houghton, 2001. ISBN 978-0-618-10857-2 Subj: Animals – pigs. Animals – sloths. Character traits – ambition. Character traits – laziness. School.

The sheep in wolf's clothing ill. by Lynn Munsinger. Houghton, 2007. ISBN 978-0-618-86844-5 Subj: Animals – sheep. Animals – wolves. Clothing. Disguises.

Something might happen ill. by Lynn Munsinger. Houghton, 2003. ISBN 978-0-618-25406-4 Subj: Animals – lemurs. Behavior – worrying. Emotions – fear. Family life – aunts, uncles.

Tacky and the Emperor ill. by Lynn Munsinger. Houghton, 2000. ISBN 978-0-395-98120-7 Subj: Birds – penguins. Clothing.

Tacky and the haunted igloo ill. by Lynn Munsinger. Houghton Mifflin Harcourt, 2015. ISBN 978-054433994-1 Subj: Birds – penguins. Clothing – costumes. Emotions – fear. Holidays – Halloween. Homes, houses.

Tacky and the Winter Games ill. by Lynn Munsinger. Houghton, 2005. ISBN 978-0-618-55659-5 Subj: Birds – penguins. Seasons – winter. Sports.

Tacky goes to camp ill. by Lynn Munsinger. Houghton, 2009. ISBN 978-0-618-98812-9 Subj: Birds – penguins. Camps, camping.

Tacky in trouble ill. by Lynn Munsinger. Houghton, 1998. ISBN 978-0-395-86113-4 Subj: Animals – elephants. Behavior. Birds – penguins.

Tacky the penguin ill. by Lynn Munsinger. Houghton, 1988. ISBN 978-0-395-45536-4 Subj: Animals – wolves. Birds – penguins. Character traits – individuality.

Tackylocks and the three bears ill. by Lynn Munsinger. Houghton, 2002. ISBN 978-0-618-22490-6 Subj: Birds – penguins. School. Theater.

Tacky's Christmas ill. by Lynn Munsinger. Houghton Mifflin, 2010. ISBN 978-0-547-17208-8 Subj: Birds – penguins. Holidays – Christmas. Santa Claus.

Three cheers for Tacky ill. by Lynn Munsinger. Houghton, 1994. ISBN 978-0-395-66841-2 Subj: Birds – penguins. Character traits – individuality. Cheerleading. Friendship. School.

Wodney Wat's wobot ill. by Lynn Munsinger. Harcourt, 2011. ISBN 978-0-547-36756-9 Subj: Animals. Animals – rats. Behavior – bullying, teasing. Disabilities. Robots. School.

Lester, J. D. *Mommy calls me Monkeypants* ill. by Hiroe Nakata. Robin Corey, 2009. ISBN 978-0-375-84502-4 Subj: Babies, toddlers. Format, unusual – board books. Names. Rhyming text.

Lester, Julius. *Ackamarackus: Julius Lester's sumptuously silly fantastically funny fables* ill. by Emilie Chollat. Scholastic, 2001. ISBN 978-0-590-48913-3 Subj: Animals. Folk & fairy tales.

Albidaro and the mischievous dream ill. by Jerry Pinkney. Fogelman, 2000. ISBN 978-0-8037-1987-3 Subj: Animals. Behavior. Dreams.

Black cowboy, wild horses ill. by Jerry Pinkney. Dial, 1998. ISBN 978-0-8037-1788-6 Subj: Animals – horses, ponies. Cowboys, cowgirls. Ethnic groups in the U.S. – African Americans.

The hungry ghosts ill. by Geraldo Valério. Dial, 2009. ISBN 978-0-8037-2513-3 Subj: Ghosts.

John Henry ill. by Jerry Pinkney. Dial, 1994. ISBN 978-0-8037-1607-0 Subj: Caldecott award honor books. Character traits – perseverance. Character traits – pride. Ethnic groups in the U.S. – African Americans. Folk & fairy tales. Tall tales.

Let's talk about race ill. by Karen Barbour. HarperCollins, 2005. ISBN 978-0-06-028598-2 Subj: Ethnic groups in the U.S. Prejudice.

Sam and the tigers: a new telling of Little Black Sambo by Julius Lester and Helen Bannerman ill. by Jerry Pinkney. Dial, 1996. ISBN 978-0-8037-2029-9 Subj: Animals – tigers. Character traits – cleverness. Clothing. Family life. Foreign lands – India. Humorous stories.

Shining ill. by Terea D. Shaffer. Silver Whistle, 2000. ISBN 978-0-15-200773-7 Subj: Disabilities. Foreign lands – Africa.

What a truly cool world ill. by Joe Cepeda. Scholastic, 1999. ISBN 978-0-590-86468-8 Subj: Angels. Creation. Ethnic groups in the U.S. – African Americans. Religion.

Why heaven is far away ill. by Joe Cepeda. Scholastic, 2002. ISBN 978-0-439-17871-6 Subj: Angels. Ethnic groups in the U.S. – African Americans. Folk & fairy tales – pourquoi tales. Religion. Reptiles – snakes.

Lester, Mike. *A is for salad* ill. by author. Putnam, 2000. ISBN 978-0-399-23388-3 Subj: ABC books. School – first day.

Lesynski, Loris. *Night school* ill. by author. Firefly, 2001. ISBN 978-1-55037-585-5 Subj: Bedtime. Monsters. Night. School.

Rocksy ill. by author. Annick, 2002. ISBN 978-1-55037-751-4 Subj: Behavior – wishing. Rhyming text. Rocks.

Let it shine: three favorite spirituals ill. by Ashley Bryan. Simon & Schuster, 2007. ISBN 978-0-689-84732-5 Subj: Religion. Songs.

Let me call you sweetheart ill. by Amanda Haley. HarperCollins, 2002. ISBN 978-0-694-01556-6 Subj: Animals – dogs. Holidays – Valentine's Day. Pets. Songs.

Let there be light: poems and prayers for repairing the world comp. by Jane Breskin Zalben; ill. by compiler. Dutton, 2002. ISBN 978-0-525-46995-7 Subj: Poetry. Religion.

Letourneau, Marie. *Argyle Fox* ill. by author. Tanglewood, 2017. ISBN 978-193910009-2 Subj: Animals – foxes. Character traits – stubbornness. Weather – wind.

Let's count the raindrops ill. by Fumi Kosaka. Viking, 2001. ISBN 978-0-670-89689-9 Subj: Poetry. Weather.

Leuck, Laura. *Goodnight, baby monster* ill. by Nigel McMullen. HarperCollins, 2002. ISBN 978-0-06-029152-5 Subj: Bedtime. Monsters. Rhyming text.

I love my pirate papa ill. by Kyle M. Stone. Harcourt, 2007. ISBN 978-0-15-205664-3 Subj: Family life – fathers. Pirates. Rhyming text.

My beastly brother ill. by Scott Nash. HarperCollins, 2003. ISBN 978-0-06-029548-6 Subj: Family life – brothers. Monsters. Rhyming text.

My monster mama loves me so ill. by Mark Buehner. Lothrop, 1999. ISBN 978-0-688-16867-4 Subj: Family life – mothers. Monsters. Rhyming text.

One witch ill. by S. D. Schindler. Walker, 2003. ISBN 978-0-8027-8860-3 Subj: Counting, numbers. Holidays – Halloween. Rhyming text. Witches.

Levenson, George. *Pumpkin circle: the story of a garden* photos by Shmuel Thaler. Tricycle, 1999. ISBN 978-1-58246-004-8 Subj: Gardens, gardening. Rhyming text.

Levert, Mireille. *Eddie Longpants* ill. by author. Groundwood, 2005. ISBN 978-0-88899-671-8 Subj: Behavior – bullying, teasing. Character traits – being different.

An island in the soup ill. by author. Douglas & McIntyre, 2001. ISBN 978-0-88899-403-5 Subj: Food. Imagination.

The princess who had almost everything ill. by Josée Masse. Tundra, 2008. ISBN 978-0-88776-887-3 Subj: Behavior – boredom. Imagination. Royalty – princesses.

Levine, Abby. *Daddies give you horsey rides* ill. by John Bendall-Brunello. Albert Whitman, 2004. ISBN 978-0-8075-1429-0 Subj: Activities. Family life – fathers. Rhyming text.

Gretchen Groundhog, it's your day! ill. by Nancy Cote. Albert Whitman, 1998. ISBN 978-0-8075-3058-0 Subj: Animals – groundhogs. Holidays – Groundhog Day.

This is the matzah ill. by Paige Billin-Frye. Albert Whitman, 2005. ISBN 978-0-8075-7885-8 Subj: Holidays – Passover. Holidays – Seder. Jewish culture. Rhyming text.

This is the pumpkin ill. by Paige Billin-Frye. Albert Whitman, 1997. ISBN 978-0-8075-7886-5 Subj: Cumulative tales. Holidays – Halloween. Rhyming text.

This is the turkey ill. by Paige Billin-Frye. Albert Whitman, 2000. ISBN 978-0-8075-7888-9 Subj: Family life. Holidays – Thanksgiving. Rhyming text.

Levine, Arthur A. *Monday is one day* ill. by Julian Hector. Scholastic, 2011. ISBN 978-0-439-78924-0 Subj: Activities – working. Counting, numbers. Days of the week, months of the year. Family life. Rhyming text.

What a beautiful morning ill. by Katie Kath. Running Press, 2016. ISBN 978-076245906-3 Subj: Family life – grandfathers. Illness – dementia. Memories, memory. Old age.

Levine, Deb. *Parker picks* ill. by Pedro Martin. Simon & Schuster, 2002. ISBN 978-0-689-83456-1 Subj: Anatomy – noses. Behavior.

Levine, Ellen. *Henry's freedom box* ill. by Kadir Nelson. Scholastic, 2007. ISBN 978-0-439-77733-9 Subj: Caldecott award honor books. Character traits – freedom. Ethnic groups in the U.S. – African Americans. Slavery. U.S. history.

Seababy: a little otter returns home ill. by Jon Van Zyle. Walker, 2012. ISBN 978-0-8027-9808-4 Subj: Animals – babies. Animals – otters. Aquariums. Behavior – lost.

Levine, Gail Carson. *Betsy Red Hoodie* ill. by Scott Nash. HarperCollins, 2010. ISBN 978-0-06-146870-4 Subj: Animals – sheep. Animals – wolves. Birthdays. Careers – shepherds. Family life – grandmothers. Folk & fairy tales. Parties.

Betsy who cried wolf ill. by Scott Nash. HarperCollins, 2002. ISBN 978-0-06-028764-1 Subj: Animals – sheep. Animals – wolves. Careers – shepherds.

Forgive me, I meant to do it: false apology poems ill. by Matthew Cordell. HarperCollins, 2012. ISBN 978-0-06-178725-6 Subj: Behavior. Folk & fairy tales. Poetry.

Levine, Joan. *Topsy-turvy bedtime* ill. by Tony Auth. Candlewick, 2008. ISBN 978-0-7636-3008-9 Subj: Bedtime.

Levine, Michelle. *Ambulances* ill. with photos. Lerner, 2004. ISBN 978-0-8225-0769-7 Subj: Careers – emergency medical technicians. Trucks.

Red foxes ill. with photos. Lerner, 2004. ISBN 978-0-8225-3774-8 Subj: Animals – foxes.

Levine, Sara. *Bone by bone: comparing animal skeletons* ill. by T. S. Spookytooth. Millbrook, 2013. ISBN 978-0-7613-8464-9 Subj: Anatomy – skeletons. Animals.

Levins, Sandra. *Do you sing Twinkle? a story about remarriage and new family* ill. by Bryan Langdo. Magination, 2009. ISBN 978-1-4338-0539-4 Subj: Divorce. Family life – stepfamilies.

Levinson, Nancy Smiler. *Death Valley* ill. by Diane Dawson Hearn. Holiday, 2001. ISBN 978-0-8234-1566-3 Subj: Desert. Ecology.

Rain forests ill. by Diane Dawson Hearn. Holiday, 2008. ISBN 978-0-8234-1899-2 Subj: Ecology. Jungle.

Levinson, Riki. *I go with my family to Grandma's* ill. by Diane Goode. Dutton, 1990. ISBN 978-0-525-44261-5 Subj: Activities – photographing. Family life. Family life – grandmothers. Transportation.

Watch the stars come out ill. by Diane Goode. Dutton, 1985. ISBN 978-0-525-44205-9 Subj: Family life. Family life – grandmothers. U.S. history.

Levinthal, David. *Who pushed Humpty Dumpty? and other notorious nursery tale mysteries* ill. by John Nickle. Random House, 2012. ISBN 978-0-375-84195-8 Subj: Careers – detectives. Folk & fairy tales. Mystery stories. Nursery rhymes.

Levis, Caron. *Ida, always* ill. by Charles Santoso. Atheneum, 2016. ISBN 978-148142640-4 Subj: Animals – polar bears. Death. Emotions – grief. Friendship. Zoos.

May I have a word? ill. by Andy Rash. Farrar, 2017. ISBN 978-037434880-9 Subj: ABC books. Language.

Stuck with the Blooz ill. by Jon Davis. Harcourt, 2012. ISBN 978-0-547-74560-2 Subj: Emotions – sadness. Monsters.

Levitin, Sonia. *Boom town* ill. by Cat Bowman Smith. Orchard, 1998. ISBN 978-0-531-33043-2 Subj: Careers – bakers. Careers – miners. Cities, towns. U.S. history – frontier & pioneer life.

Nine for California ill. by Cat Bowman Smith. Orchard, 1996. ISBN 978-0-531-08877-7 Subj: Activities – traveling. Family life. U.S. history – frontier & pioneer life.

When Elephant goes to a party ill. by Jeff Seaver. Rising Moon, 2001. ISBN 978-0-87358-751-8 Subj: Animals – elephants. Etiquette. Humorous stories. Parties.

When Kangaroo goes to school ill. by Jeff Seaver. Rising Moon, 2001. ISBN 978-0-87358-791-4 Subj: Animals – kangaroos. Etiquette. School – first day.

Levy, Debbie. *We shall overcome: the story of a song* ill. by Vanessa Brantley Newton. Disney/Jump at the Sun, 2013. ISBN 978-1-4231-1954-8 Subj: Ethnic groups in the U.S. – African Americans. Prejudice. Slavery. Songs. Violence, nonviolence.

Levy, Janice. *Celebrate! It's cinco de mayo! / Celebremos! Es el cinco de mayo!* ill. by Loretta Lopez. Albert Whitman, 2007. ISBN 978-0-8075-1176-3 Subj: Foreign lands – Mexico. Foreign languages. Holidays – Cinco de Mayo.

Thomas the toadilly terrible bully ill. by Bill Slavin. Eerdmans, 2014. ISBN 978-080285373-8 Subj: Behavior – bullying, teasing. Friendship. Frogs & toads.

Lewandowski, Frrich. *It's Christmas again* ill. by Kathryn H. Delisle. Ambassador, 2000. ISBN 978-1-929039-04-3 Subj: Animals. Holidays – Christmas. Religion – Nativity.

Lewin, Betsy. *Good night, Knight* ill. by author. Holiday House, 2015. ISBN 978-082343206-6 Subj: Animals – horses, ponies. Food. Knights.

Groundhog day ill. by author. Scholastic, 2000. ISBN 978-0-439-10802-7 Subj: Animals – groundhogs. Holidays – Groundhog Day. Shadows.

Horse song: the Naadam of Mongolia (Lewin, Ted)

Thumpy Feet ill. by author. Holiday House, 2013. ISBN 978-0-8234-2901-1 Subj: Activities – playing. Animals – cats.

Where is Tippy Toes? ill. by author. Simon & Schuster, 2010. ISBN 978-1-4169-3808-8 Subj: Animals – cats. Format, unusual – toy & movable books. Rhyming text.

Lewin, Hugh. *Jafta* ill. by Lisa Kopper. Carolrhoda, 1983. ISBN 978-0-87614-207-3 Subj: Emotions. Family life. Foreign lands – Africa.

Jafta — the homecoming ill. by Lisa Kopper. Knopf, 1994. ISBN 978-0-679-84722-9 Subj: Emotions. Family life – fathers. Foreign lands – South Africa.

Jafta's father ill. by Lisa Kopper. Carolrhoda, 1983. ISBN 978-0-87614-209-7 Subj: Family life – fathers. Foreign lands – Africa.

Jafta's mother ill. by Lisa Kopper. Carolrhoda, 1983. ISBN 978-0-87614-208-0 Subj: Family life – mothers. Foreign lands – Africa.

Lewin, Ted. *Amazon boy* ill. by author. Macmillan, 1993. ISBN 978-0-02-757383-1 Subj: Birthdays. Boats, ships. Cities, towns. Ecology. Foreign lands – Brazil. Rivers.

At Gleason's gym ill. by author. Macmillan, 2007. ISBN 978-1-59643-231-4 Subj: Sports – boxing.

Big Jimmy's Kum Kau Chinese take out ill. by author. HarperCollins, 2002. ISBN 978-0-688-16027-2 Subj: Activities – baking, cooking. Family life – fathers. Family life – sons. Restaurants. Stores.

Fair! ill. by author. Lothrop, 1997. ISBN 978-0-688-12851-7 Subj: Country. Fairs, festivals.

Horse song: the Naadam of Mongolia by Ted Lewin and Betsy Lewin; ill. by authors. Lee & Low, 2008. ISBN 978-1-58430-277-3 Subj: Animals – horses, ponies. Foreign lands – Mongolia. Sports – racing.

How much? visiting markets around the world ill. by author. HarperCollins, 2006. ISBN 978-0-688-17553-5 Subj: Stores. World.

Market! ill. by author. Lothrop, 1996. ISBN 978-0-688-12162-4 Subj: Foreign lands. Stores.

Lewis, Anne Margaret. *Fly blanky fly* ill. by Elisa Chevarri. HarperCollins, 2012. ISBN 978-0-06-199996-3 Subj: Bedtime. Imagination.

Puddle jumpers ill. by Nancy Cote. Sky Pony, 2016. ISBN 978-163450185-9 Subj: Family life – mothers. Imagination. Rhyming text. Weather – rain.

What am I? Christmas ill. by Tom Mills. Albert Whitman, 2011. ISBN 978-0-8075-8958-8 Subj: Format, unusual – toy & movable books. Holidays – Christmas.

Lewis, J. Patrick. *Arithme-tickle* ill. by Frank Remkiewicz. Harcourt, 2002. ISBN 978-0-15-216418-8 Subj: Counting, numbers. Rhyming text. Riddles & jokes.

Big is big and little little: a book of contrasts ill. by Bob Barner. Holiday House, 2007. ISBN 978-0-8234-1909-8 Subj: Concepts – opposites. Language. Rhyming text.

The bookworm's feast ill. by John O'Brien. Dial, 1999. ISBN 978-0-8037-1693-3 Subj: Games. Humorous stories. Poetry.

Doodle dandies: poems that take shape ill. by Lisa Desimini. Atheneum, 1998. ISBN 978-0-689-81075-6 Subj: Poetry.

Earth and me, our family tree ill. by Christopher Canyon. Dawn, 2002. ISBN 978-1-58469-031-3 Subj: Animals. Earth. Nature. Rhyming text.

Earth and you, a closer view ill. by Christopher Canyon. Dawn, 2001. ISBN 978-1-58469-016-0 Subj: Earth. Ecology. Geography. Nature. Rhyming text.

Face bug ill. by Kelly Murphy; photos by Frederic B. Siskind. Boyds Mills, 2013. ISBN 978-1-59078-925-4 Subj: Insects. Poetry.

The fantastic 5 and 10¢ store: a rebus adventure ill. by Valorie Fisher. Random House, 2010. ISBN 978-0-375-85878-9 Subj: Rebuses. Rhyming text. Stores.

Good mousekeeping ill. by Lisa Desimini. Atheneum, 2001. ISBN 978-0-689-83161-4 Subj: Animals. Homes, houses. Poetry.

A hippopotamusn't ill. by Victoria Chess. Dial, 1990. ISBN 978-0-8037-0519-7 Subj: Animals. Poetry.

The house of Boo ill. by Katya Krénina. Atheneum, 1998. ISBN 978-0-689-80356-7 Subj: Ghosts. Holidays – Halloween. Rhyming text.

Kindergarten cat ill. by Ailie Busby. Random House, 2010. ISBN 978-0-375-84475-1 Subj: Animals – cats. Rhyming text. School.

The little buggers: insect and spider poems ill. by Victoria Chess. Dial, 1998. ISBN 978-0-8037-1770-1 Subj: Insects. Poetry. Spiders.

Long was the winter road they traveled: a tale of the nativity ill. by Drew Bairley. Dial, 1997. ISBN 978-0-8037-1815-9 Subj: Animals. Holidays – Christmas. Poetry. Religion – Nativity.

M is for monster: a fantastic creatures alphabet ill. by Gerald Kelley. Sleeping Bear, 2014. ISBN 978-158536818-1 Subj: ABC books. Monsters.

Riddle-icious ill. by Debbie Tilley. Knopf, 1996. ISBN 978-0-679-94011-1 Subj: Poetry. Riddles & jokes.

Riddle-lightful: oodles of little riddle-poems ill. by Debbie Tilley. Knopf, 1998. ISBN 978-0-679-98760-4 Subj: Rhyming text. Riddles & jokes.

Tulip at the bat ill. by Amiko Hirao. Little, Brown, 2007. ISBN 978-0-316-61280-7 Subj: Animals. Humorous stories. Rhyming text. Sports – baseball.

What's looking at you, kid? ill. by Renée Graef. Sleeping Bear, 2012. ISBN 978-1-58536-793-1 Subj: Animals. Rhyming text.

World Rat Day: poems about real holidays you've never heard of ill. by Anna Raff. Candlewick, 2013. ISBN 978-0-7636-5402-3 Subj: Holidays. Poetry.

Lewis, Jacqueline Janette. *You are so wonderful* ill. by Jeremy Tugeau. Augsburg Fortress, 2003. ISBN 978-0-8066-4553-7 Subj: Creation. Religion. Rhyming text. Self-concept.

Lewis, Jill. *Don't read this book!* ill. by Deborah Allwright. Tiger Tales, 2010. ISBN 978-1-58925-094-9 Subj: Folk & fairy tales. Royalty – kings.

Lewis, Kevin. *Chugga-chugga choo-choo* ill. by Daniel Kirk. Hyperion, 1999. ISBN 978-0-7868-2379-6 Subj: Rhyming text. Toys – trains.

Dinosaur dinosaur ill. by Daniel Kirk. Scholastic, 2006. ISBN 978-0-439-60371-3 Subj: Dinosaurs. Rhyming text.

The lot at the end of my block ill. by Reg Cartwright. Hyperion, 2001. ISBN 978-0-7868-2512-7 Subj: Buildings. Careers – construction workers. Cumulative tales. Rhyming text.

Not inside this house! ill. by David Ercolini. Scholastic, 2011. ISBN 978-0-439-43981-7 Subj: Animals. Character traits – curiosity. Humorous stories. Nature. Rhyming text.

The runaway pumpkin ill. by S. D. Schindler. Orchard, 2003. ISBN 978-0-439-43974-9 Subj: Holidays – Halloween. Rhyming text.

Lewis, Kim. *Emma's lamb* ill. by author. Four Winds, 1991. ISBN 978-0-02-758821-7 Subj: Animals – sheep. Behavior – needing someone. Farms.

First snow ill. by author. Candlewick, 1993. ISBN 978-1-56402-194-6 Subj: Animals – dogs. Animals – sheep. Behavior – lost & found possessions. Farms. Toys – bears. Weather – snow.

Floss ill. by author. Candlewick, 1992. ISBN 978-1-56402-010-9 Subj: Activities – playing. Activities – working. Animals – dogs.

Friends ill. by author. Candlewick, 1997. ISBN 978-0-7636-0346-5 Subj: Emotions – anger. Farms. Friendship.

Good night, Harry ill. by author. Candlewick, 2004. ISBN 978-0-7636-2206-0 Subj: Animals – elephants. Bedtime. Friendship. Sleep. Toys.

Here we go Harry ill. by author. Candlewick, 2005. ISBN 978-0-7636-2549-8 Subj: Activities – flying. Animals. Animals – elephants. Friendship. Toys.

Hooray for Harry ill. by author. Candlewick, 2006. ISBN 978-0-7636-2962-5 Subj: Animals – elephants. Behavior – lost & found possessions. Friendship. Sleep. Toys.

Just like Floss ill. by author. Candlewick, 1998. ISBN 978-0-7636-0684-8 Subj: Animals – babies. Animals – dogs. Farms.

Little Baa ill. by author. Candlewick, 2001. ISBN 978-0-7636-1447-8 Subj: Animals – babies. Animals – sheep. Farms.

Little calf ill. by author. Candlewick, 2000. ISBN 978-0-7636-0899-6 Subj: Animals – babies. Animals – bulls, cows. Farms.

Little lamb ill. by author. Candlewick, 2000. ISBN 978-0-7636-0900-9 Subj: Animals – babies. Animals – sheep. Farms.

Little puppy ill. by author. Candlewick, 2000. ISBN 978-0-7636-0901-6 Subj: Animals – babies. Animals – dogs. Farms.

My friend Harry ill. by author. Candlewick, 1995. ISBN 978-1-56402-617-0 Subj: Animals – elephants. School. Toys.

One summer day ill. by author. Candlewick, 1996. ISBN 978-1-56402-883-9 Subj: Activities – walking. Country. Seasons – summer. Tractors.

A puppy for Annie ill. by author. Candlewick, 2006. ISBN 978-0-7636-3200-7 Subj: Animals – dogs. Pets.

Seymour and Henry ill. by author. Candlewick, 2009. ISBN 978-0-7636-4243-3 Subj: Activities – playing. Behavior – hiding. Birds – ducks. Family life – mothers.

The shepherd boy ill. by author. Four Winds, 1990. ISBN 978-0-02-758581-0 Subj: Animals – sheep. Careers – shepherds.

Lewis, Paeony. *I'll always love you* ill. by Penny Ives. Tiger Tales, 2002. ISBN 978-0-613-52270-0 Subj: Animals – bears. Behavior – worrying. Family life – mothers.

No more cookies! ill. by Brita Granström. Scholastic, 2005. ISBN 978-0-439-68332-6 Subj: Food. Toys.

No more yawning! ill. by Brita Granström. Scholastic, 2008. ISBN 978-0-545-02957-5 Subj: Bedtime.

Lewis, Rob. *Friends* ill. by author. Henry Holt, 2001. ISBN 978-0-8050-6691-3 Subj: Animals – rabbits. Communities, neighborhoods. Friendship.

Lewis, Rose A. *Every year on your birthday* ill. by Jane Dyer. Little, Brown, 2007. ISBN 978-0-316-52552-7 Subj: Adoption. Birthdays. Ethnic groups in the U.S. – Chinese Americans.

I love you like crazy cakes ill. by Jane Dyer. Little, 2002. ISBN 978-0-316-52576-3 Subj: Adoption. Babies, toddlers. Family life. Foreign lands – China.

Orange Peel's pocket ill. by Grace Zong. Abrams, 2010. ISBN 978-0-8109-8394-6 Subj: Adoption. Clothing. Ethnic groups in the U.S. – Chinese Americans.

Sweet dreams ill. by Jen Corace. Abrams, 2012. ISBN 978-1-4197-0189-4 Subj: Bedtime. Lullabies. Nature. Rhyming text.

Lewis, Wendy A. *In Abby's hands* ill. by Marilyn Mets and Peter Ledwon. Red Deer, 2003. ISBN 978-0-88995-282-9 Subj: Animals – dogs. Character traits – confidence.

Lewison, Wendy Cheyette. *"Buzz," said the bee* ill. by Hans Wilhelm. Scholastic, 1992. ISBN 978-0-590-44185-8 Subj: Animals. Cumulative tales. Noise, sounds. Rhyming text.

Going to sleep on the farm ill. by Juan Wijngaard. Dial, 1992. ISBN 978-0-8037-1097-9 Subj: Animals. Bedtime. Cumulative tales. Farms. Rhyming text. Sleep.

Mud ill. by Maryann Cocca-Leffler. Random House, 2001. ISBN 978-0-679-80251-8 Subj: Activities – playing. Rhyming text.

The princess and the potty ill. by Rick Brown. Simon & Schuster, 1994. ISBN 978-0-671-87284-7 Subj: Behavior – growing up. Royalty – princesses. Toilet training.

So many boots ill. by Tony Griego. Scholastic, 2000. ISBN 978-0-439-09865-6 Subj: Clothing – boots. Insects. Rhyming text. Weather – rain.

Two is for twins ill. by Hiroe Nakata. Penguin, 2006. ISBN 978-0-670-06128-0 Subj: Counting, numbers. Multiple births – twins. Rhyming text.

Lia, Simone. *Red's great chase* ill. by author. Dutton, 2000. ISBN 978-0-525-46213-2 Subj: Activities – playing. Monsters.

Liao, Jimmy. *The sound of colors: a journey of the imagination* ill. by author. Little, Brown, 2005. ISBN 978-0-316-93992-8 Subj: Disabilities – blindness. Imagination.

Libby, Barbara. *I rode the red horse: Secretariat's Belmont race* ill. by author. Eclipse, 2003. ISBN 978-

1-58150-096-7 Subj: Animals – horses, ponies. Sports – racing.

Libney, Varda. *What I like about Passover* ill. by author. Simon & Schuster, 2002. ISBN 978-0-689-84491-1 Subj: Format, unusual – board books. Holidays – Passover. Jewish culture. Religion.

Lichtenheld, Tom. *Bridget's beret* ill. by author. Henry Holt, 2010. ISBN 978-0-8050-8775-8 Subj: Activities – drawing. Careers – artists. Clothing – hats. Self-concept.

Cloudette ill. by author. Henry Holt, 2011. ISBN 978-0-8050-8776-5 Subj: Character traits – smallness. Concepts – size. Weather – clouds. Weather – rain.

E-mergency! by Tom Lichtenheld and Ezra Fields Meyer; ill. by Tom Lichtenheld. Chronicle, 2011. ISBN 978-0-8118-7898-2 Subj: ABC books. Humorous stories.

Everything I know about monsters ill. by author. Simon & Schuster, 2002. ISBN 978-0-689-84381-5 Subj: Monsters.

Everything I know about pirates ill. by author. Simon & Schuster, 2000. ISBN 978-0-689-82625-2 Subj: Pirates.

What's with this room? ill. by author. Little, Brown, 2005. ISBN 978-0-316-59286-4 Subj: Behavior – messy. Character traits – cleanliness. Humorous stories.

Liebman, Daniel. *I want to be a builder* ill. with photos. Firefly, 2003. ISBN 978-1-55297-758-3 Subj: Careers – construction workers.

I want to be a cowboy ill. with photos. Firefly, 1999. ISBN 978-1-55209-447-1 Subj: Careers. Cowboys, cowgirls.

I want to be a doctor ill. with photos. Firefly, 2000. ISBN 978-1-55209-463-1 Subj: Careers – doctors.

I want to be a firefighter ill. with photos. Firefly, 1999. ISBN 978-1-55209-448-8 Subj: Careers – firefighters. Communities, neighborhoods. Fire.

I want to be a librarian ill. with photos. Firefly, 2001. ISBN 978-1-55297-691-3 Subj: Careers – librarians.

I want to be a mechanic ill. with photos. Firefly, 2003. ISBN 978-1-55297-695-1 Subj: Careers – mechanics.

I want to be a musician ill. with photos. Firefly, 2003. ISBN 978-1-55297-760-6 Subj: Careers – musicians.

I want to be a nurse ill. with photos. Firefly, 2001. ISBN 978-1-55209-568-3 Subj: Careers – nurses.

I want to be a police officer ill. with photos. Firefly, 2000. ISBN 978-1-55209-467-9 Subj: Careers – police officers. Communities, neighborhoods.

I want to be a teacher ill. with photos. Firefly, 2001. ISBN 978-1-55209-572-0 Subj: Careers – teachers.

I want to be a truck driver ill. with photos. Firefly, 2001. ISBN 978-1-55209-576-8 Subj: Careers – truck drivers.

I want to be a vet ill. with photos. Firefly, 2000. ISBN 978-1-55209-471-6 Subj: Careers – veterinarians.

I want to be a zookeeper ill. with photos. Firefly, 2003. ISBN 978-1-55297-699-9 Subj: Careers – zookeepers.

Liersch, Anne. *Nell and Fluffy* ill. by Christa Unzner. NorthSouth, 2001. ISBN 978-0-7358-1424-0 Subj: Animals – guinea pigs. Character traits – responsibility. Pets.

Lies, Brian. *Bats at the ballgame* ill. by author. Harcourt, 2010. ISBN 978-0-547-24970-4 Subj: Animals – bats. Rhyming text. Sports – baseball.

Bats at the beach ill. by author. Houghton, 2006. ISBN 978-0-618-55744-8 Subj: Activities – picnicking. Animals – bats. Rhyming text. Sea & seashore – beaches.

Bats at the library ill. by author. Houghton, 2008. ISBN 978-0-618-99923-1 Subj: Animals – bats. Books, reading. Libraries. Rhyming text.

Bats in the band ill. by author. Houghton Mifflin Harcourt, 2014. ISBN 978-054410569-0 Subj: Animals – bats. Music. Rhyming text.

Gator dad ill. by author. Houghton Mifflin Harcourt, 2016. ISBN 978-054453433-9 Subj: Family life – fathers. Reptiles – alligators, crocodiles.

Light, Kelly. *Louise and Andie: the art of friendship* ill. by author. HarperCollins/Balzer+Bray, 2016. ISBN 978-006234440-3 Subj: Art. Behavior – misunderstanding. Character traits – cooperation. Friendship.

Louise loves art ill. by author. HarperCollins/Balzer+Bray, 2014. ISBN 978-006224817-6 Subj: Activities – drawing. Art. Family life – brothers & sisters.

Light, Steve. *The bunny burrow buyer's book: a tale of rabbit real estate* ill. by author. POW!, 2016. ISBN 978-157687752-4 Subj: Animals – rabbits. Homes, houses. Moving.

The Christmas giant ill. by author. Candlewick, 2010. ISBN 978-0-7636-4692-9 Subj: Friendship. Giants. Holidays – Christmas. Mythical creatures – elves. Trees.

Diggers go ill. by author. Chronicle, 2013. ISBN 978-1-4521-1864-2 Subj: Format, unusual – board books. Machines. Trucks.

Have you seen my dragon? ill. by author. Candlewick, 2014. ISBN 978-076366648-4 Subj: Cities, towns. Counting, numbers. Dragons.

Have you seen my lunch box? ill. by author. Candlewick, 2017. ISBN 978-076369068-7 Subj: Behavior – lost & found possessions. Format, unusual – board books. Picture puzzles.

Have you seen my monster? ill. by author. Candlewick, 2015. ISBN 978-076367513-4 Subj: Behavior – lost & found possessions. Concepts – shape. Fairs, festivals. Monsters.

Lucky Lazlo ill. by author. Candlewick, 2016. ISBN 978-076368825-7 Subj: Animals – cats. Superstition. Theater.

Planes go ill. by author. Chronicle, 2014. ISBN 978-145212899-3 Subj: Airplanes, airports. Format, unusual – board books.

The shoemaker extraordinaire ill. by author. Abrams, 2003. ISBN 978-0-8109-4236-3 Subj: Careers – shoemakers. Clothing – shoes. Folk & fairy tales. Giants.

Swap! ill. by author. Candlewick, 2016. ISBN 978-076367990-3 Subj: Activities – trading. Boats, ships. Friendship. Pirates.

Trains go ill. by author. Chronicle, 2012. ISBN 978-0-8118-7942-2 Subj: Format, unusual – board books. Noise, sounds. Trains.

Zephyr takes flight ill. by author. Candlewick, 2012. ISBN 978-0-7636-5695-9 Subj: Activities – flying. Imagination.

Lillegard, Dee. *Balloons, balloons, balloons* ill. by Bernadette Pons. Penguin, 2007. ISBN 978-0-525-45940-8 Subj: Animals – rabbits. Rhyming text. Toys – balloons.

The Big Bug Ball ill. by Rex Barron. Putnam, 1999. ISBN 978-0-399-23121-6 Subj: Activities – dancing. Parties. Rhyming text.

Go! poetry in motion: poems ill. by Valeri Gorbachev. Random House, 2006. ISBN 978-0-375-92387-6 Subj: Concepts – motion. Poetry. Transportation.

Hello school! ill. by Don Carter. Knopf, 2001. ISBN 978-0-375-91020-3 Subj: Poetry. School.

Tortoise brings the mail ill. by Jillian Lund. Dutton, 1997. ISBN 978-0-525-45156-3 Subj: Animals. Careers – postal workers. Letters, cards. Reptiles – turtles, tortoises.

Wake up house! rooms full of poems ill. by Don Carter. Knopf, 2000. ISBN 978-0-679-98351-4 Subj: Furniture. Homes, houses. Poetry.

Lilly, Melinda. *From slavery to freedom* ill. by Lori McElrath-Eslick. Rourke, 2003. ISBN 978-1-58952-363-0 Subj: Slavery. U.S. history.

Limentani, Alison. *How long is a whale?* ill. by author. Boxer, 2017. ISBN 978-191071621-2 Subj: Animals. Concepts – measurement. Counting, numbers. Sea & seashore.

How much does a ladybug weigh? ill. by author. Boxer, 2016. ISBN 978-191071611-3 Subj: Animals. Concepts – weight. Counting, numbers. Insects.

Lin, Grace. *Dim sum for everyone* ill. by author. Knopf, 2001. ISBN 978-0-375-91082-1 Subj: Activities – baking, cooking. Ethnic groups in the U.S. – Chinese Americans. Food. Restaurants.

Fortune cookie fortunes ill. by author. Knopf, 2004. ISBN 978-0-375-91521-5 Subj: Character traits – luck. Ethnic groups in the U.S. – Chinese Americans. Food.

Kite flying ill. by author. Knopf, 2002. ISBN 978-0-375-91520-8 Subj: Kites.

Lissy's friends ill. by author. Penguin, 2007. ISBN 978-0-670-06072-6 Subj: Activities – making things. Character traits – shyness. Friendship. School.

Okie-dokie, Artichokie ill. by author. Viking, 2003. ISBN 978-0-670-03623-3 Subj: Animals – giraffes. Animals – monkeys. Friendship. Holidays – Christmas. Homes, houses. Noise, sounds.

Olvina flies ill. by author. Henry Holt, 2003. ISBN 978-0-8050-6711-8 Subj: Activities – traveling. Airplanes, airports. Animals – pigs. Birds – chickens, roosters. Emotions – fear.

Olvina swims ill. by author. Henry Holt, 2007. ISBN 978-0-8050-7661-5 Subj: Birds – chickens, roosters. Birds – penguins. Emotions – fear. Hawaii. Sports – swimming.

Our food: a healthy serving of science and poems by Grace Lin and Ranida T. McKneally ill. by Grace Zong. Charlesbridge, 2016. ISBN 978-158089590-3 Subj: Food. Health & fitness. Poetry.

Our seasons by Grace Lin and Ranida T. McKneally; ill. by Grace Lin. Charlesbridge, 2006. ISBN 978-1-57091-360-0 Subj: Seasons.

The red thread: an adoption fairy tale ill. by author. Albert Whitman, 2007. ISBN 978-0-8075-6922-1 Subj: Adoption. Folk & fairy tales. Foreign lands – China. Royalty.

Robert's snowflakes: artists' snowflakes for cancer's cure. Comp. by Grace Lin & Robert Mercer. Penguin, 2005. ISBN 978-0-670-06044-3 Subj: Art. Illness – cancer. Poetry. Weather – snow.

Thanking the moon: celebrating the Mid-Autumn Moon Festival ill. by author. Random House, 2010. ISBN 978-0-375-86101-7 Subj: Ethnic groups in the U.S. – Chinese Americans. Fairs, festivals. Family life. Food. Holidays. Moon.

The ugly vegetables ill. by author. Charlesbridge, 1999. ISBN 978-0-88106-336-3 Subj: Ethnic groups in the U.S. – Chinese Americans. Flowers. Food. Gardens, gardening.

Linch, Tanya. *My duck* ill. by author. Scholastic, 2000. ISBN 978-0-439-20670-9 Subj: Activities – writing. Birds – ducks. Careers – teachers.

Lind, Michael. *Bluebonnet girl* ill. by Kate Kiesler. Henry Holt, 2003. ISBN 978-0-8050-6573-2 Subj: Behavior – greed. Flowers. Folk & fairy tales. Indians of North America – Comanche. Weather – droughts.

Lindaman, Jane. *Read anything good lately?* (Allen, Susan)

Used any numbers lately? (Allen, Susan)

Zip it! ill. by Nancy Carlson. Carolrhoda, 2012. ISBN 978-0-7613-5592-2 Subj: Clothing. Family life – fathers. Humorous stories.

Lindbergh, Reeve. *The awful aardvarks go to school* ill. by Tracey Campbell Pearson. Viking, 1997. ISBN 978-0-670-85920-7 Subj: ABC books. Animals – aardvarks. Behavior – misbehavior. Rhyming text. School.

The awful aardvarks shop for school ill. by Tracey Campbell Pearson. Viking, 2000. ISBN 978-0-670-88763-7 Subj: Animals – aardvarks. Behavior – misbehavior. Rhyming text. Shopping.

Bridget and the gray wolves ill. by Pija Lindenbaum. R&S Books, 2001. ISBN 978-91-29-65395-3 Subj: Animals – wolves. Behavior – lost. Emotions – fear.

The circle of days ill. by Cathie Felstead. Candlewick, 1998. ISBN 978-0-7636-0357-1 Subj: Creation. Religion.

The day the goose got loose ill. by Steven Kellogg. Dial, 1990. ISBN 978-0-8037-0409-1 Subj: Animals. Behavior – misbehavior. Birds – geese. Farms.

The hippie grandmother ill. by Abby Carter. Candlewick, 2002. ISBN 978-0-7636-0671-8 Subj: Family life – grandmothers. Rhyming text.

Homer the library cat ill. by Anne Wilsdorf. Candlewick, 2011. ISBN 978-0-7636-3448-3 Subj: Animals – cats. Libraries. Rhyming text.

Johnny Appleseed ill. by Kathy Jakobsen. Little, 1990. ISBN 978-0-316-52618-0 Subj: Activities – traveling. Gardens, gardening. Rhyming text. Tall tales. Trees. U.S. history – frontier & pioneer life.

Midnight farm ill. by Susan Jeffers. Dial, 1987. ISBN 978-0-8037-0333-9 Subj: Animals. Counting, numbers. Farms. Night.

My little grandmother often forgets ill. by Kathryn Brown. Candlewick, 2007. ISBN 978-0-7636-1989-3 Subj: Behavior – forgetfulness. Family life – grandmothers. Memories, memory. Old age.

Nobody owns the sky: the story of "brave Bessie" Coleman ill. by Pamela Paparone. Candlewick, 1996.

ISBN 978-1-56402-533-3 Subj: Activities – flying. Airplanes, airports. Ethnic groups in the U.S. – African Americans. Rhyming text.

North country spring ill. by Liz Sivertson. Houghton, 1997. ISBN 978-0-395-82819-9 Subj: Animals. Nature. Rhyming text. Seasons – spring.

On morning wings ill. by Holly Meade. Candlewick, 2002. ISBN 978-0-7636-1106-4 Subj: Religion. Rhyming text.

Our nest ill. by Jill McElmurry. Candlewick, 2004. ISBN 978-0-7636-1286-3 Subj: Homes, houses. Rhyming text.

Lindenbaum, Pija. *Mini Mia and her darling uncle* ill. by author. R&S Books, 2007. ISBN 978-91-29-66734-9 Subj: Emotions – envy, jealousy. Family life – aunts, uncles.

Linders, Clara. *The very best door of all* by Clara Linders and Marijke ten Cate ill. by Marijke ten Cate. Front Street, 2001. ISBN 978-1-886910-64-5 Subj: Animals – badgers. Animals – porcupines. Birthdays. Friendship. Gifts.

Lindgren, Astrid. *Pippi Longstocking's after-Christmas party* ill. by Michael Chesworth. Viking, 1996. ISBN 978-0-679-86790-6 Subj: Character traits – assertiveness. Foreign lands – Sweden. Holidays – Christmas. Parties.

Lindgren, Barbro. *Benny and the binky* ill. by Olof Landström. Farrar, 2002. ISBN 978-91-29-65497-4 Subj: Animals – pigs. Babies, toddlers. Sibling rivalry.

Benny's had enough ill. by Olof Landström. R&S Books, 1999. ISBN 978-91-29-64563-7 Subj: Animals – pigs. Behavior – running away. Family life – mothers.

Oink, oink, Benny ill. by Olof Landström. Farrar, 2008. ISBN 978-91-29-66855-1 Subj: Animals – pigs. Behavior – misbehavior. Family life – brothers.

Sam's ball ill. by Eva Eriksson. Morrow, 1983. ISBN 978-0-688-02359-1 Subj: Animals – cats. Toys – balls.

Sam's bath ill. by Eva Eriksson. Morrow, 1983. ISBN 978-0-688-02362-1 Subj: Activities – bathing. Animals – dogs.

Sam's car ill. by Eva Eriksson. Morrow, 1982. ISBN 978-0-688-01263-2 Subj: Behavior – sharing. Toys.

Sam's cookie ill. by Eva Eriksson. Morrow, 1982. ISBN 978-0-688-01267-0 Subj: Behavior – sharing. Pets.

Sam's lamp ill. by Eva Eriksson. Morrow, 1983. ISBN 978-0-688-02356-0 Subj: Safety.

Sam's potty ill. by Eva Eriksson. Morrow, 1986. ISBN 978-0-688-06603-1 Subj: Behavior – growing up. Toilet training.

Sam's teddy bear ill. by Eva Eriksson. Morrow, 1982. ISBN 978-0-688-01270-0 Subj: Toys – bears.

Sam's wagon ill. by Eva Eriksson. Morrow, 1986. ISBN 978-0-688-05803-6 Subj: Animals – dogs. Toys – wagons.

Lindsay, Jeanne Warren. *Do I have a daddy?* ill. by Jami Moffett. Morning Glory, 2000. ISBN 978-1-885356-62-8 Subj: Family life. Family life – fathers. Family life – mothers.

Liniers. *What there is before there is anything there: a scary story* ill. by author. House of Anansi/Groundwood, 2014. ISBN 978-155498385-8 Subj: Emotions – fear.

Link, Martin A. *The goat in the rug* (Blood, Charles L.)

Lionni, Leo. *Alexander and the wind-up mouse* ill. by author. Pantheon, 1969. ISBN 978-0-394-90914-1 Subj: Animals – mice. Caldecott award honor books. Emotions – envy, jealousy. Friendship. Toys.

The alphabet tree ill. by author. Knopf, 2004. ISBN 978-0-394-91016-1 Subj: ABC books. Activities – writing. Insects – butterflies, caterpillars.

The biggest house in the world ill. by author. Pantheon, 1968. ISBN 978-0-394-90944-8 Subj: Animals. Behavior – greed.

A busy year ill. by author. Knopf, 1992. ISBN 978-0-679-92464-7 Subj: Animals – mice. Nature. Seasons. Trees.

A color of his own ill. by author. Delmar, 1990. ISBN 978-0-8273-4114-2 Subj: Character traits – individuality. Concepts – color. Reptiles – lizards.

A color of his own [Spanish-English bilingual edition] ill. by author. Knopf, 2016. ISBN 978-055353873-1 Subj: Character traits – individuality. Concepts – color. Foreign languages. Reptiles – lizards.

Cornelius ill. by author. Pantheon, 1983. ISBN 978-0-394-95419-6 Subj: Character traits – being different. Reptiles – alligators, crocodiles.

An extraordinary egg ill. by author. Knopf, 1994. ISBN 978-0-679-95840-6 Subj: Eggs. Friendship. Frogs & toads. Reptiles – alligators, crocodiles.

Fish is fish ill. by author. Pantheon, 1970. ISBN 978-0-394-90440-5 Subj: Behavior – misunderstanding. Fish. Friendship. Frogs & toads.

Frederick ill. by author. Random House, 1973, ©1967. ISBN 978-0-394-82614-1 Subj: Animals – mice. Caldecott award honor books. Music.

Frederick's fables ill. by author. Pantheon, 1985. ISBN 978-0-394-87710-5 Subj: Animals.

Geraldine, the music mouse ill. by author. Pantheon, 1979. ISBN 978-0-394-94238-4 Subj: Animals – mice. Music. Musical instruments – flutes.

The greentail mouse ill. by author. Pantheon, 1973. ISBN 978-0-394-92678-0 Subj: Animals – mice. Mardi Gras.

Inch by inch ill. by author. Astor-Honor, 1960. ISBN 978-0-8392-3010-6 Subj: Birds. Caldecott award honor books. Concepts – measurement. Insects.

It's mine! a fable ill. by author. Knopf, 1986. ISBN 978-0-394-97000-4 Subj: Behavior – fighting, arguing. Frogs & toads.

Let's make rabbits ill. by author. Knopf, 1992. Originally published: New York: Pantheon Books, ©1982. ISBN 978-0-679-82640-8 Subj: Activities. Animals – rabbits. Art. Imagination.

Little blue and little yellow ill. by author. Mulberry, 1994. ISBN 978-0-688-13285-9 Subj: Concepts – color. Friendship.

Matthew's dream ill. by author. Knopf, 1991. ISBN 978-0-679-91075-6 Subj: Animals – mice. Careers – artists. Museums.

Mr. McMouse ill. by author. Knopf, 1992. ISBN 978-0-679-93890-3 Subj: Animals – mice. Friendship. Self-concept.

Nicolas, where have you been? ill. by author. Knopf, 1987. ISBN 978-0-394-98370-7 Subj: Animals – mice. Friendship.

Pezzettino ill. by author. Pantheon, 1975. ISBN 978-0-394-93156-2 Subj: Character traits – individuality. Concepts – shape. Self-concept.

Six crows ill. by author. Knopf, 1988. ISBN 978-0-394-99572-4 Subj: Birds – crows. Birds – owls. Farms.

Swimmy ill. by author. Random House, 1973, ©1963. ISBN 978-0-394-82620-2 Subj: Caldecott award honor books. Fish. Sea & seashore.

Theodore and the talking mushroom ill. by author. Pantheon, 1971. ISBN 978-0-394-82312-6 Subj: Animals – mice. Character traits – optimism.

Tico and the golden wings ill. by author. Knopf, 1975, ©1964. ISBN 978-0-394-83078-0 Subj: Birds. Character traits – generosity. Character traits – individuality. Character traits – questioning. Folk & fairy tales.

Tillie and the wall ill. by author. Knopf, 1989. ISBN 978-0-394-92155-6 Subj: Animals – mice. Behavior – seeking better things.

Lipan, Sabine. *Mom, there's a bear at the door* ill. by Manuela Olten. Eerdmans, 2016. ISBN 978-

080285460-5 Subj: Animals – bears. Family life – mothers.

Lipkind, William. *Finders keepers* by William Lipkind and Nicolas Mordvinoff ill. by Nicolas Mordvinoff. Harcourt, 1951. ISBN 978-0-15-227529-7 Subj: Animals – dogs. Caldecott award books. Character traits – selfishness.

Lipp, Frederick. *The caged birds of Phnom Penh* ill. by Ronald Himler. Holiday, 2001. ISBN 978-0-8234-1534-2 Subj: Behavior – wishing. Birds. Foreign lands – Canada.

Running shoes ill. by Jason Gaillard. Charlesbridge, 2008. ISBN 978-1-58089-175-2 Subj: Clothing – shoes. Foreign lands – Cambodia. Poverty. School.

Lipson, Eden Ross. *Applesauce season* ill. by Mordicai Gerstein. Roaring Brook, 2009. ISBN 978-1-59643-216-1 Subj: Activities – baking, cooking. Food. Seasons – fall.

Lipton, Leonard. *Puff, the magic dragon* (Yarrow, Peter)

Lish, Ted. *The three little puppies and the big bad flea* ill. by Charles Jordan. Munchweiler, 2001. ISBN 978-0-7940-0001-1 Subj: Animals – dogs. Family life – mothers. Homes, houses. Insects – fleas.

Lister, Mary. *The Winter King and the Summer Queen* ill. by Diana Mayo. Barefoot, 2002. ISBN 978-1-84148-357-3 Subj: Behavior – sharing. Seasons. Seasons – summer. Seasons – winter.

Litchfield, David. *The bear and the piano* ill. by author. Clarion, 2016. ISBN 978-054467454-7 Subj: Animals – bears. Emotions – loneliness. Friendship. Music. Musical instruments – pianos.

Lithgow, John. *Carnival of the animals* ill. by Boris Kulikov. Simon & Schuster, 2004. ISBN 978-0-689-86721-7 Subj: Animals. Imagination. Museums. Rhyming text. School – field trips.

I got two dogs ill. by Robert Neubecker. Simon & Schuster, 2008. ISBN 978-1-4169-5881-9 Subj: Animals – dogs. Songs.

I'm a manatee ill. by Ard Hoyt. Simon & Schuster, 2003. ISBN 978-0-689-85427-9 Subj: Animals – manatees. Imagination. Rhyming text.

Mahalia Mouse goes to college ill. by Igor Oleynikov. Simon & Schuster, 2007. ISBN 978-1-4169-2715-0 Subj: Animals – mice. Rhyming text. School.

Marsupial Sue ill. by Jack E. Davis. Simon & Schuster, 2001. ISBN 978-0-689-84394-5 Subj: Animals – kangaroos. Rhyming text. Self-concept. Songs.

Marsupial Sue presents "The Runaway Pancake" ill. by Jack E. Davis. Simon & Schuster, 2005. ISBN 978-0-689-87847-3 Subj: Animals – kangaroos. Theater.

Micawber ill. by C. F. Payne. Simon & Schuster, 2002. ISBN 978-0-689-83341-0 Subj: Animals – squirrels. Careers – artists. Museums. Rhyming text.

Never play music right next to the zoo ill. by Leeza Hernandez. Simon & Schuster, 2013. ISBN 978-1-4424-6743-9 Subj: Animals. Dreams. Music. Musical instruments. Songs. Zoos.

The remarkable Farkle McBride ill. by C. F. Payne. Simon & Schuster, 2000. ISBN 978-0-689-83340-3 Subj: Careers – conductors (music). Careers – musicians. Format, unusual – toy & movable books. Musical instruments. Rhyming text.

Litten, Kristyna. *Blue and Bertie* ill. by author. Simon & Schuster/Paula Wiseman, 2016. ISBN 978-148146154-2 Subj: Animals – giraffes. Behavior – lost. Character traits – being different. Friendship.

Little Bear's Valentine ill. by Heather Green. HarperCollins, 2003. ISBN 978-0-06-052244-5 Subj: Animals. Animals – bears. Family life – mothers. Holidays – Valentine's Day.

Little, Jean. *Pippin the Christmas pig* ill. by H. Werner Zimmermann. Scholastic, 2004. ISBN 978-0-439-65062-5 Subj: Animals. Animals – pigs. Gifts. Holidays – Christmas.

Little old lady who swallowed a fly. *I know an old lady* retold by G. Brian Karas; ill. by reteller. Scholastic, 1994. ISBN 978-0-590-46575-5 Subj: Cumulative tales. Folk & fairy tales. Foreign lands – England. Insects – flies. Rhyming text. Songs. Witches.

I know an old lady who swallowed a fly ill. by Stephen Gulbis. Scholastic, 2001. ISBN 978-0-439-24328-5 Subj: Cumulative tales. Folk & fairy tales. Foreign lands – England. Format, unusual – toy & movable books. Insects – flies. Songs.

I know an old lady who swallowed a fly retold by Glen Rounds; ill. by reteller. Holiday, 1990. ISBN 978-0-8234-0814-6 Subj: Cumulative tales. Folk & fairy tales. Foreign lands – England. Insects – flies. Songs.

I know an old lady who swallowed a fly retold by Nadine Bernard Westcott; ill. by reteller. Little, 1980. ISBN 978-0-316-93128-1 Subj: Cumulative tales. Folk & fairy tales. Foreign lands – England. Insects – flies. Songs.

There once was a cowpoke who swallowed an ant by Helen Ketteman; ill. by Will Terry. Albert Whitman, 2014. ISBN 978-080757850-6 Subj: Cowboys, cowgirls. Cumulative tales. Folk & fairy tales. Insects – ants. Songs.

There was an old lady who swallowed a fly ill. by Pam Adams. Child's Play, 1990. ISBN 978-0-85953-021-7 Subj: Cumulative tales. Folk & fairy tales. Foreign lands – Canada. Format, unusual – toy & movable books. Insects – flies. Songs.

There was an old lady who swallowed a fly by Rashin Kheiriyeh; ill. by author. NorthSouth, 2014. ISBN 978-0-735-84183-3 Subj: Cumulative tales. Folk & fairy tales. Insects – flies. Songs.

There was an old lady who swallowed a fly retold by Simms Taback; ill. by reteller. Viking, 1997. ISBN 978-0-670-86939-8 Subj: Caldecott award honor books. Cumulative tales. Folk & fairy tales. Format, unusual. Insects – flies. Rhyming text. Songs.

There was an old monkey who swallowed a frog by Jennifer Ward; ill. by Steve Gray. Marshall Cavendish, 2010. ISBN 978-0-7614-5580-6 Subj: Animals. Cumulative tales. Folk & fairy tales. Frogs & toads. Rhyming text. Songs.

There was an old mummy who swallowed a spider by Jennifer Ward; ill. by Steve Gray. Two Lions, 2015. ISBN 978-147782637-9 Subj: Cumulative tales. Holidays – Halloween. Mummies. Songs.

There was an old pirate who swallowed a fish by Jennifer Ward; ill. by Steve Gray. Amazon, 2012. ISBN 978-0-7614-6196-8 Subj: Cumulative tales. Fish. Pirates. Songs.

The little red hen. *The little red hen* ill. by Byron Barton. HarperCollins, 1993. ISBN 978-0-06-021676-4 Subj: Activities – baking, cooking. Animals. Behavior – sharing. Birds – chickens, roosters. Character traits – laziness. Cumulative tales. Farms. Folk & fairy tales.

The little red hen retold by Harriet Ziefert; ill. by Emily Bolam. Viking, 1995. ISBN 978-0-670-86050-0 Subj: Activities – baking, cooking. Animals. Behavior – sharing. Birds – chickens, roosters. Character traits – laziness. Cumulative tales. Farms. Folk & fairy tales.

The little red hen ill. by Paul Galdone. Seabury Pr., 1973. ISBN 978-0-8164-3099-4 Subj: Activities – baking, cooking. Animals. Behavior – sharing. Birds – chickens, roosters. Character traits – laziness. Cumulative tales. Farms. Folk & fairy tales.

Little red hen by Alan Garner; ill. by Norman Messenger. DK, 1997. ISBN 978-0-7894-1171-6 Subj: Activities – baking, cooking. Animals. Behavior – sharing. Birds – chickens, roosters. Character traits – laziness. Cumulative tales. Farms. Folk & fairy tales.

The little red hen retold by Jerry Pinkney; ill. by reteller. Penguin, 2006. ISBN 978-0-8037-2935-3 Subj: Activities – baking, cooking. Animals.

Behavior – sharing. Birds – chickens, roosters. Character traits – laziness. Cumulative tales. Farms. Folk & fairy tales.

The little red hen by Mary Finch; ill. by Kate Slater. Barefoot, 2013. ISBN 978-1-84686-575-6 Subj: Activities – baking, cooking. Animals. Behavior – sharing. Birds – chickens, roosters. Character traits – laziness. Cumulative tales. Farms. Folk & fairy tales. Plants.

The little red hen retold by John Escott; ill. by Annie West. Gingham Dog, 2003. ISBN 978-1-57768-492-3 Subj: Activities – baking, cooking. Animals. Behavior – sharing. Birds – chickens, roosters. Character traits – laziness. Cumulative tales. Farms. Folk & fairy tales.

The little red hen retold by Margot Zemach; ill. by reteller. Farrar, 1983. ISBN 978-0-374-34621-8 Subj: Activities – baking, cooking. Animals. Behavior – sharing. Birds – chickens, roosters. Character traits – laziness. Cumulative tales. Farms. Folk & fairy tales.

The little red hen: an old fable retold by Heather Forest; ill. by Susan Gaber. August House, 2006. ISBN 978-0-87483-795-7 Subj: Activities – baking, cooking. Animals. Behavior – sharing. Birds – chickens, roosters. Character traits – laziness. Cumulative tales. Folk & fairy tales. Plants.

The Little Red Hen and the Passover matzah by Leslie Kimmelman; ill. by Paul Meisel. Holiday House, 2010. ISBN 978-0-8234-1952-4 Subj: Activities – baking, cooking. Animals. Behavior – sharing. Birds – chickens, roosters. Character traits – laziness. Folk & fairy tales. Holidays – Passover. Jewish culture.

The Little Red Hen makes a pizza retold by Philemon Sturges; ill. by Amy Walrod. Dutton, 1999. ISBN 978-0-525-45953-8 Subj: Activities – baking, cooking. Animals. Behavior – sharing. Birds – chickens, roosters. Character traits – laziness. Cumulative tales. Farms. Folk & fairy tales.

Littlesugar, Amy. *Clown child* ill. by Kimberly Bulcken Root. Penguin, 2006. ISBN 978-0-399-23106-3 Subj: Circus. Clowns, jesters.

Freedom school, yes! ill. by Floyd Cooper. Philomel, 2001. ISBN 978-0-399-23006-6 Subj: Ethnic groups in the U.S. – African Americans. School.

Lisette's angel ill. by Max Ginsburg. Dial, 2002. ISBN 978-0-8037-2435-8 Subj: Careers – military. Foreign lands – France. War.

Tree of hope ill. by Floyd Cooper. Philomel, 1999. ISBN 978-0-399-23300-5 Subj: Careers – actors. Ethnic groups in the U.S. – African Americans. Poverty. Theater. U.S. history.

Litton, Jonathan. *Big fish little fish* ill. by Fhiona Galloway. Tiger Tales, 2016. ISBN 978-158925215-

8 Subj: Concepts – opposites. Format, unusual – board books.

Snip snap: pop-up fun ill. by Kasia Nowowiejska. Tiger Tales, 2015. ISBN 978-158925548-7 Subj: Animals. Format, unusual – toy & movable books. Rhyming text.

Litwin, Eric. *Groovy Joe: dance party countdown* ill. by Tom Lichtenheld. Orchard, 2017. ISBN 978-054588379-5 Subj: Animals – dogs. Counting, numbers. Music. Musical instruments – guitars. Parties.

Groovy Joe: ice cream and dinosaurs ill. by Tom Lichtenheld. Scholastic/Orchard, 2016. ISBN 978-054588378-8 Subj: Animals – dogs. Behavior – sharing. Dinosaurs. Food. Music. Rhyming text.

The Nuts: bedtime at the Nut house ill. by Scott Magoon. Little, Brown, 2014. ISBN 978-031632244-7 Subj: Activities – playing. Bedtime. Humorous stories. Rhyming text.

The Nuts: keep rolling! ill. by Scott Magoon. Little, Brown, 2017. ISBN 978-031632251-5 Subj: Character traits – smallness. Concepts – size. Humorous stories. Rhyming text.

The Nuts: sing and dance in your polka-dot pants ill. by Scott Magoon. Little, Brown, 2015. ISBN 978-031632250-8 Subj: Activities – dancing. Activities – playing. Activities – singing. Humorous stories. Rhyming text.

Pete the Cat: I love my white shoes ill. by James Dean. HarperCollins, 2010. ISBN 978-0-06-190622-0 Subj: Animals – cats. Clothing – shoes. Concepts – color.

Pete the Cat: rocking in my school shoes ill. by James Dean. HarperCollins, 2011. ISBN 978-0-06-191024-1 Subj: Activities – singing. Animals – cats. Clothing – shoes. Rhyming text. School.

Pete the Cat and his four groovy buttons ill. by James Dean. HarperCollins, 2012. ISBN 978-0-06-211058-9 Subj: Activities – singing. Animals – cats. Clothing. Counting, numbers.

Pete the Cat saves Christmas ill. by James Dean. HarperCollins, 2012. ISBN 978-0-06-211062-6 Subj: Animals – cats. Holidays – Christmas. Rhyming text. Santa Claus.

Liu, Cynthea. *Bike on, Bear!* ill. by Kristyna Litten. Aladdin, 2015. ISBN 978-148140507-2 Subj: Animals – bears. Character traits – persistence. Sports – bicycling.

Liu, Jae Soo. *Yellow umbrella* ill. by author. Kane/Miller, 2002. ISBN 978-1-929132-36-2 Subj: Concepts – color. Music. Umbrellas. Weather – rain. Wordless.

Liu, Julia. *Gus, the dinosaur bus* ill. by Bei Lynn. Houghton Mifflin, 2013. ISBN 978-0-547-90573-0 Subj: Buses. Dinosaurs. Traffic, traffic signs.

Liu, Sylvia. *A morning with grandpa* ill. by Christina Forshay. Lee & Low, 2016. ISBN 978-162014192-2 Subj: Ethnic groups in the U.S. – Asian Americans. Family life – grandfathers. Health & fitness – exercise.

Livingston, A. A. *B. Bear and Lolly: catch that cookie!* ill. by Joey Chou. HarperCollins, 2015. ISBN 978-006219791-7 Subj: Activities – baking, cooking. Animals – bears. Folk & fairy tales. Food.

B. Bear and Lolly: off to school ill. by Joey Chou. HarperCollins, 2014. ISBN 978-00621978-8-7 Subj: Animals – bears. Folk & fairy tales. Friendship. School – first day.

Livingston, Irene. *Finklehopper Frog* ill. by Brian Lies. Tricycle, 2003. ISBN 978-1-58246-075-8 Subj: Activities – running. Animals – rabbits. Character traits – individuality. Frogs & toads. Rhyming text.

Finklehopper Frog cheers ill. by Brian Lies. Ten Speed, 2005. ISBN 978-1-58246-138-0 Subj: Activities – picnicking. Animals – rabbits. Friendship. Frogs & toads. Rhyming text.

Livingston, Myra Cohn. *Abraham Lincoln: a man for all the people* ill. by Samuel Byrd. Holiday, 1993. ISBN 978-0-8234-1049-1 Subj: Poetry. U.S. history.

Calendar ill. by Will Hillenbrand. Holiday House, 2007. ISBN 978-0-8234-1725-4 Subj: Calendars. Days of the week, months of the year. Poetry. Seasons.

Celebrations ill. by Leonard Everett Fisher. Holiday, 1985. ISBN 978-0-8234-0550-3 Subj: Holidays. Poetry.

Keep on singing: a ballad of Marian Anderson ill. by Samuel Byrd. Holiday, 1994. ISBN 978-0-8234-1098-9 Subj: Ethnic groups in the U.S. – African Americans. Poetry. U.S. history.

Valentine poems ill. by Patience Brewster. Holiday, 1987. ISBN 978-0-8234-0587-9 Subj: Animals. Holidays – Valentine's Day.

Livingstone, Star. *Harley* ill. by Molly Bang. Sea-Star, 2001. ISBN 978-1-58717-049-2 Subj: Animals – llamas. Animals – sheep.

Livinson, Nancy Smiler. *North Pole, South Pole* ill. by Diane Dawson Hearn. Holiday, 2002. ISBN 978-0-8234-1737-7 Subj: Animals. Foreign lands – Antarctic. Foreign lands – Arctic. Weather.

Liwska, Renata. *Little panda* ill. by author. Houghton, 2008. ISBN 978-0-618-96627-1 Subj: Animals – pandas. Family life – grandfathers.

Red wagon ill. by author. Penguin, 2011. ISBN 978-0-399-25237-2 Subj: Activities – playing. Animals. Animals – foxes. Imagination. Toys – wagons.

Ljungkvist, Laura. *Follow the line* ill. by author. Penguin, 2006. ISBN 978-0-670-06049-8 Subj: Counting, numbers. Imagination. Picture puzzles.

Follow the line around the world ill. by author. Viking, 2008. ISBN 978-0-670-06334-5 Subj: Animals. Geography. World.

Follow the line through the house ill. by author. Penguin, 2007. ISBN 978-0-670-06225-6 Subj: Homes, houses. Imagination. Picture puzzles. Rhyming text.

Follow the line to school ill. by author. Penguin, 2011. ISBN 978-0-670-01226-8 Subj: Picture puzzles. School.

Pepi sings a new song ill. by author. Simon & Schuster, 2010. ISBN 978-1-4169-9138-0 Subj: Activities – singing. Birds – parakeets, parrots. Foreign languages.

Search and spot: animals! ill. by author. Houghton Mifflin Harcourt, 2015. ISBN 978-054454005-7 Subj: Animals. Picture puzzles.

Search and spot go! ill. by author. Houghton Mifflin Harcourt, 2016. ISBN 978-054457042-9 Subj: Picture puzzles. Transportation.

Toni's topsy-turvy telephone day ill. by author. Abrams, 2001. ISBN 978-0-8109-4486-2 Subj: Food. Humorous stories. Parties.

Llewellyn, Claire. *Crocodile* ill. by Simon Mendez. NorthWord, 2004. ISBN 978-1-55971-900-1 Subj: Animals – babies. Format, unusual. Reptiles – alligators, crocodiles.

Duck ill. by Simon Mendez. NorthWord, 2004. ISBN 978-1-55971-878-3 Subj: Animals – babies. Birds – ducks. Format, unusual.

Ladybug ill. by Simon Mendez. NorthWord, 2004. ISBN 978-1-55971-892-9 Subj: Format, unusual. Insects – ladybugs.

Tree ill. by Simon Mendez. NorthWord, 2004. ISBN 978-1-55971-879-0 Subj: Food. Format, unusual. Trees.

Lloyd, David. *Polly Molly Woof Woof* ill. by Charlotte Hard. Candlewick, 2000. ISBN 978-0-7636-0755-5 Subj: Animals – dogs. Emotions – happiness.

Lloyd, Jennifer. *The best thing about kindergarten* ill. by Qin Leng. Simply Read, 2013. ISBN 978-1-897476-82-6 Subj: Memories, memory. School.

Lloyd, Megan Wagner. *Finding wild* ill. by Abigail Halpin. Knopf, 2016. ISBN 978-110193281-0 Subj: Nature. Senses.

Fort-building time ill. by Abigail Halpin. Knopf, 2017. ISBN 978-039955655-5 Subj: Activities – making things. Activities – playing. Seasons.

Lloyd, Sam. *Chief Rhino to the rescue!* ill. by author. Henry Holt, 2009. ISBN 978-0-8050-8821-2 Subj: Animals – rhinoceros. Careers – firefighters. Character traits – bravery.

Doctor Meow's big emergency ill. by author. Henry Holt, 2008. ISBN 978-0-8050-8819-9 Subj: Animals – cats. Careers – doctors. Hospitals.

Mr. Pusskins: a love story ill. by author. Simon & Schuster, 2006. ISBN 978-1-4169-2517-0 Subj: Animals – cats. Behavior – running away.

Mr. Pusskins and Little Whiskers: another love story ill. by author. Atheneum, 2008. ISBN 978-1-4169-5796-6 Subj: Animals – cats.

Lloyd-Jones, Sally. *Being a pig is nice: a child's-eye view of manners* ill. by Dan Krall. Random House, 2009. ISBN 978-0-375-84187-3 Subj: Animals. Behavior. Etiquette.

Bunny's first spring ill. by David McPhail. Zonderkidz, 2015. ISBN 978-031073386-7 Subj: Animals – rabbits. Seasons – spring.

His Royal Highness, King Baby: a terrible true story ill. by David Roberts. Candlewick, 2017. ISBN 978-076369793-8 Subj: Babies, toddlers. Emotions – envy, jealousy. Family life – brothers & sisters. Family life – new sibling. Royalty – kings. Sibling rivalry.

The house that's your home ill. by Jane Dyer. Random House, 2015. ISBN 978-037585884-0 Subj: Family life. Homes, houses.

How to be a baby — by me, the big sister ill. by Sue Heap. Random House, 2007. ISBN 978-0-375-83843-9 Subj: Babies, toddlers. Family life – brothers & sisters.

How to get a job — by me, the boss ill. by Sue Heap. Random House, 2011. ISBN 978-0-375-86664-7 Subj: Careers.

How to get married by me, the bride ill. by Sue Heap. Random House, 2009. ISBN 978-0-375-84118-7 Subj: Weddings.

Just because you're mine ill. by Frank Endersby. HarperCollins, 2012. ISBN 978-0-06-201476-4 Subj: Animals – squirrels. Bedtime. Emotions – love. Family life.

Old MacNoah had an ark ill. by Jill Newton. HarperCollins, 2008. ISBN 978-0-06-055717-1 Subj: Animals. Boats, ships. Cumulative tales. Music. Noise, sounds. Religion – Noah. Songs. Weather – floods.

Poor Doreen: a fishy tale ill. by Alexandra Boiger. Random House, 2014. ISBN 978-037586918-1 Subj: Activities – traveling. Character traits – optimism. Fish.

Song of the stars: a Christmas story ill. by Alison Jay. Zonderkidz, 2011. ISBN 978-0-310-72291-5 Subj: Holidays – Christmas. Religion – Nativity.

Time to say goodnight ill. by Jane Chapman. HarperCollins, 2006. ISBN 978-0-06-054328-0 Subj: Animals. Bedtime. Rhyming text.

The ultimate guide to grandmas and grandpas! ill. by Michael Emberley. HarperCollins, 2008. ISBN 978-0-06-075687-1 Subj: Animals. Family life – grandparents.

Lo, Ginnie. *Auntie Yang's great soybean picnic* ill. by Beth Lo. Lee & Low, 2012. ISBN 978-1-60060-442-3 Subj: Activities – picnicking. Ethnic groups in the U.S. – Chinese Americans. Family life. Family life – aunts, uncles. Food.

Lobe, Mira. *Hoppelpopp and the best bunny* ill. by Angelika Kaufmann. Holiday House, 2015. ISBN 978-082343287-5 Subj: Animals – rabbits. Character traits – cooperation. Contests. Family life – brothers & sisters.

Lobel, Anita. *Alison's zinnia* ill. by author. Greenwillow, 1990. ISBN 978-0-688-08866-8 Subj: ABC books. Flowers.

Animal antics: A to Z ill. by author. HarperCollins, 2005. ISBN 978-0-06-051815-8 Subj: ABC books. Animals. Circus.

Hello, day! ill. by author. Greenwillow, 2008. ISBN 978-0-06-078765-3 Subj: Animals. Day. Sun.

Lena's sleep sheep ill. by author. Knopf, 2013. ISBN 978-0-449-81025-5 Subj: Animals – sheep. Bedtime. Clothing – costumes. Moon.

Nini here and there ill. by author. HarperCollins, 2007. ISBN 978-0-06-078767-7 Subj: Animals – cats. Moving.

Nini lost and found ill. by author. Random House, 2010. ISBN 978-0-375-85880-2 Subj: Animals – cats. Behavior – lost & found possessions.

One lighthouse, one moon ill. by author. Greenwillow, 2000. ISBN 978-0-688-15540-7 Subj: Animals – cats. Counting, numbers. Days of the week, months of the year. Lighthouses.

Playful pigs from A to Z ill. by author. Knopf, 2015. ISBN 978-055350832-1 Subj: ABC books. Activities – playing. Animals – pigs.

Taking care of Mama Rabbit ill. by author. Knopf, 2014. ISBN 978-038575368-5 Subj: Animals – rabbits. Family life. Family life – mothers. Illness.

Ten hungry rabbits: counting and color concepts ill. by author. Knopf, 2012. ISBN 978-0-375-86864-1 Subj: Animals – rabbits. Concepts – color. Counting, numbers. Food. Gardens, gardening.

Lobel, Arnold. *Days with Frog and Toad* ill. by author. HarperCollins, 1979. ISBN 978-0-06-023964-0 Subj: Friendship. Frogs & toads.

Fables ill. by author. HarperCollins, 1980. ISBN 978-0-06-023974-9 Subj: Animals. Caldecott award books.

Frog and Toad all year ill. by author. HarperCollins, 1976. ISBN 978-0-06-023951-0 Subj: Friendship. Frogs & toads. Seasons.

Frog and Toad are friends ill. by author. HarperCollins, 1970. ISBN 978-0-06-023958-9 Subj: Caldecott award honor books. Friendship. Frogs & toads.

The Frog and Toad pop-up book ill. by author. HarperCollins, 1986. ISBN 978-0-06-023986-2 Subj: Format, unusual – toy & movable books. Frogs & toads.

Frog and Toad together ill. by author. HarperCollins, 1971. ISBN 978-0-06-023959-6 Subj: Friendship. Frogs & toads.

The frogs and toads all sang ill. by author and Adrianne Lobel. HarperCollins, 2009. ISBN 978-0-06-180022-1 Subj: Frogs & toads. Rhyming text.

Ming Lo moves the mountain ill. by author. Greenwillow, 1982. ISBN 978-0-688-00611-2 Subj: Foreign lands – China. Moving.

Odd owls and stout pigs: a book of nonsense ill. by Adrianne Lobel. HarperCollins, 2009. ISBN 978-0-06-180054-2 Subj: Animals – pigs. Birds – owls. Rhyming text.

On Market Street ill. by Anita Lobel. Greenwillow, 1981. ISBN 978-0-688-84309-0 Subj: ABC books. Caldecott award honor books. Rhyming text. Shopping. Stores.

Lobel, Gillian. *Does anybody love me?* ill. by Rosalind Beardshaw. Good Books, 2002. ISBN 978-1-56148-368-6 Subj: Behavior – running away. Family life – grandfathers. Family life – parents. Self-concept.

Little Honey Bear and the smiley moon ill. by Tim Warnes. Good Books, 2006. ISBN 978-1-56148-533-8 Subj: Animals. Animals – bears. Behavior – lost. Family life – mothers. Moon. Seasons – winter.

Too small for honey cake ill. by Sebastien Braun. Harcourt, 2006. ISBN 978-0-15-206097-8 Subj: Animals – foxes. Babies, toddlers. Family life. Sibling rivalry.

Locker, Thomas. *Cloud dance* ill. by author. Harcourt, 2000. ISBN 978-0-15-202231-0 Subj: Weather – clouds.

Mountain dance ill. by author. Harcourt, 2001. ISBN 978-0-15-202622-6 Subj: Mountains. Poetry.

Sky tree ill. by author and Candace Christiansen. HarperCollins, 1995. ISBN 978-0-06-024884-0 Subj: Science. Seasons. Trees.

Water dance ill. by author. Harcourt, 2002. ISBN 978-0-15-216396-9 Subj: Nature. Poetry. Water. Weather.

Where the river begins ill. by author. Dial, 1984. ISBN 978-0-89370-090-4 Subj: Family life – grandfathers. Rivers.

Lodding, Linda Ravin. *A gift for Mama* ill. by Alison Jay. Knopf, 2014. ISBN 978-038575331-9 Subj: Activities – trading. Circular tales. Foreign lands – Austria. Gifts.

Little red riding sheep ill. by Cale Atkinson. Atheneum, 2017. ISBN 978-148145748-4 Subj: Activities – storytelling. Animals – sheep.

Painting Pepette ill. by Claire Fletcher. little bee, 2016. ISBN 978-149980136-1 Subj: Activities – painting. Animals – rabbits. Art. Careers – artists. Foreign lands – France.

Lodge, Bernard. *How scary* ill. by author. Houghton, 2001. ISBN 978-0-618-11547-1 Subj: Counting, numbers. Monsters.

Shoe Shoe Baby ill. by Katherine Lodge. Random House, 2000. ISBN 978-0-375-81084-8 Subj: Clothing – shoes.

Lodge, Jo. *Happy birthday, Moo Moo* ill. by author. Little, 2001. ISBN 978-0-316-66644-2 Subj: Animals. Birthdays. Format, unusual – toy & movable books. Parties.

Happy Snappy! a Mr.Croc book about feelings ill. by author. IPG/Hodder, 2012. ISBN 978-0-3409-8879-4 Subj: Emotions. Format, unusual – board books. Format, unusual – toy & movable books. Reptiles – alligators, crocodiles.

Moo Moo goes to the city ill. by author. Little, 2002. ISBN 978-0-316-65582-8 Subj: Animals – bulls, cows. Cities, towns. Format, unusual – toy & movable books.

Loehr, Patrick. *Mucumber McGee and the lunch lady's liver* ill. by author. HarperCollins, 2008. ISBN 978-0-06-082330-6 Subj: Food. Humorous stories. Rhyming text. School.

Loewen, Nancy. *Busy buzzers* ill. by Brandon Reibeling. Picture Window, 2004. ISBN 978-1-4048-0143-1 Subj: Insects – bees. Science.

Hungry hoppers ill. by Brandon Reibeling. Picture Window, 2004. ISBN 978-1-4048-0146-2 Subj: Insects – grasshoppers.

The last day of kindergarten ill. by Sachiko Yoshikawa. Marshall Cavendish, 2011. ISBN 978-0-7614-5807-7 Subj: School.

Living lights ill. by Brandon Reibeling. Picture Window, 2004. ISBN 978-1-4048-0145-5 Subj: Insects – fireflies.

Night fliers ill. by Brandon Reibeling. Picture Window, 2004. ISBN 978-1-4048-0144-8 Subj: Insects – moths.

Spotted beetles ill. by Melissa Voda. Picture Window, 2004. ISBN 978-1-4048-0142-4 Subj: Insects – ladybugs.

Tiny workers ill. by Brandon Reibeling. Picture Window, 2004. ISBN 978-1-4048-0141-7 Subj: Insects – ants.

Logan, Bob. *Rocket town* ill. by author. Sourcebooks, 2011. ISBN 978-1-4022-4186-4 Subj: Format, unusual – board books. Space & space ships.

Logelin, Matthew. *Be glad your dad . . . is not an octopus!* by Matthew Logelin and Sara Jensen ill. by Jared Chapman. Little, Brown, 2016. ISBN 978-031625438-0 Subj: Animals. Family life – fathers. Humorous stories.

Loggins, Kenny. *Footloose* by Kenny Loggins and Dean Pitchford ill. by Tim Bowers. Quarto/Moondance, 2016. ISBN 978-163322118-5 Subj: Activities – dancing. Animals. Songs. Zoos.

Logue, Mary. *Sleep like a tiger* ill. by Pamela Zagarenski. Houghton Mifflin, 2012. ISBN 978-0-547-64102-7 Subj: Animals. Bedtime. Caldecott award honor books. Sleep.

Lohans, Alison. *Waiting for the sun* ill. by Marilyn Mets and Peter Ledwon. Red Deer, 2002. ISBN 978-0-88995-240-9 Subj: Babies, toddlers. Birth. Family life – new sibling.

Loki. *Jake Greenthumb* ill. by Jason Gaillard. Mondo, 2002. ISBN 978-1-59034-186-5 Subj: Character traits – helpfulness. Gardens, gardening. Plants.

Lomas Garza, Carmen. *In my family* ill. by author. Children's Book Press, 1996. ISBN 978-0-89239-138-7 Subj: Ethnic groups in the U.S. – Hispanic Americans. Family life. Foreign languages.

Lombardi, Kristine A. *The grumpy pets* ill. by Kristine A. Lombardi. Abrams, 2016. ISBN 978-141971888-5 Subj: Behavior – bad day, bad mood. Pets.

Lomp, Stephan. *Mamasaurus* ill. by author. Chronicle, 2016. ISBN 978-145214424-5 Subj: Behavior – lost. Dinosaurs. Family life – mothers.

Londner, Renee. *Stones for Grandpa* ill. by Martha Avilés. Lerner/Kar-Ben, 2013. ISBN 978-0-7613-7495-4 Subj: Death. Family life – grandfathers. Jewish culture.

London, Jonathan. *Ali, child of the desert* ill. by Ted Lewin. Lothrop, 1997. ISBN 978-0-688-12561-5 Subj: Behavior – lost. Desert. Foreign lands – Morocco. Shopping. Weather – sandstorms.

Baby whale's journey ill. by Jon Van Zyle. Chronicle, 1999. ISBN 978-0-8118-2496-5 Subj: Animals – babies. Animals – whales.

Count the ways, Little Brown Bear ill. by Margie Moore. Dutton, 2002. ISBN 978-0-525-46097-8 Subj: Animals – bears. Counting, numbers. Emotions – love. Family life – mothers.

Crunch munch ill. by Michael Rex. Silver Whistle, 2001. ISBN 978-0-15-202603-5 Subj: Animals. Food.

Do your ABC's, Little Brown Bear ill. by Margie Moore. Penguin, 2005. ISBN 978-0-525-47360-2 Subj: ABC books. Animals – bears. Family life – fathers.

Dream weaver ill. by Rocco Baviera. Silver Whistle, 1997. ISBN 978-0-15-200944-1 Subj: Nature. Spiders.

Duck and Hippo in the rainstorm ill. by Andrew Joyner. Amazon/Two Lions, 2017. ISBN 978-150393723-9 Subj: Animals – hippopotamuses. Birds – ducks. Friendship. Weather – rain.

Duck and Hippo lost and found ill. by Andrew Joyner. Amazon/Two Lions, 2017. ISBN 978-154204562-9 Subj: Activities – picnicking. Animals – hippopotamuses. Behavior – lost. Birds – ducks. Friendship.

Fireflies, fireflies, light my way ill. by Linda Messier. Viking, 1996. ISBN 978-0-670-85442-4 Subj: Animals. Indians of North America. Lullabies. Night. Rhyming text.

Flamingo sunset ill. by Kristina Rodanas. Marshall Cavendish, 2008. ISBN 978-0-7614-5384-9 Subj: Birds – flamingos. Nature.

Froggy eats out ill. by Frank Remkiewicz. Viking, 2001. ISBN 978-0-670-89686-8 Subj: Behavior – misbehavior. Family life – parents. Food. Frogs & toads. Restaurants.

Froggy gets a doggy ill. by Frank Remkiewicz. Viking, 2014. ISBN 978-067001428-6 Subj: Animals – dogs. Frogs & toads.

Froggy gets dressed ill. by Frank Remkiewicz. Viking, 1992. ISBN 978-0-670-84249-0 Subj: Clothing. Frogs & toads. Hibernation. Seasons – winter. Weather – snow.

Froggy goes to bed ill. by Frank Remkiewicz. Viking, 2000. ISBN 978-0-670-88860-3 Subj: Bedtime. Frogs & toads.

Froggy goes to camp ill. by Frank Remkiewicz. Viking, 2008. ISBN 978-0-670-01098-1 Subj: Camps, camping. Frogs & toads.

Froggy goes to Hawaii ill. by Frank Remkiewicz. Penguin, 2011. ISBN 978-0-670-01221-3 Subj: Activities – traveling. Frogs & toads. Hawaii.

Froggy goes to school ill. by Frank Remkiewicz. Viking, 1996. ISBN 978-0-670-86726-4 Subj: Clothing. Dreams. Frogs & toads. School – first day.

Froggy goes to the doctor ill. by Frank Remkiewicz. Viking, 2002. ISBN 978-0-670-03578-6 Subj: Careers – doctors. Frogs & toads. Humorous stories.

Froggy goes to the library ill. by Frank Remkiewicz. Viking, 2016. ISBN 978-067001573-3 Subj: Behavior – misbehavior. Books, reading. Frogs & toads. Libraries.

Froggy learns to swim ill. by Frank Remkiewicz. Viking, 1995. ISBN 978-0-670-85551-3 Subj: Emotions – fear. Frogs & toads. Sports – swimming.

Froggy plays in the band ill. by Frank Remkiewicz. Viking, 2002. ISBN 978-0-670-03532-8 Subj: Animals. Contests. Frogs & toads. Musical instruments – bands. Parades.

Froggy plays soccer ill. by Frank Remkiewicz. Viking, 1999. ISBN 978-0-670-88257-1 Subj: Animals. Frogs & toads. Sports – soccer.

Froggy plays T-ball ill. by Frank Remkiewicz. Penguin, 2007. ISBN 978-0-670-06187-7 Subj: Frogs & toads. Sports – T-ball.

Froggy rides a bike ill. by Frank Remkiewicz. Penguin, 2006. ISBN 978-0-670-06099-3 Subj: Frogs & toads. Sports – bicycling.

Froggy's birthday wish ill. by Frank Remkiewicz. Viking, 2015. ISBN 978-067001572-6 Subj: Birthdays. Frogs & toads. Parties.

Froggy's first Christmas ill. by Frank Remkiewicz. Viking, 2000. ISBN 978-0-670-89220-4 Subj: Animals. Frogs & toads. Holidays – Christmas.

Froggy's first kiss ill. by Frank Remkiewicz. Viking, 1998. ISBN 978-0-670-87064-6 Subj: Emotions – love. Frogs & toads. Holidays – Valentine's Day. School.

Froggy's Halloween ill. by Frank Remkiewicz. Viking, 1999. ISBN 978-0-670-88449-0 Subj: Clothing – costumes. Frogs & toads. Holidays – Halloween.

Gone again ptarmigan ill. by Jon Van Zyle. National Geographic, 2001. ISBN 978-0-7922-7561-9 Subj: Animals. Birds – ptarmigans. Ecology. Foreign lands – Arctic.

Here comes Doctor Hippo ill. by Gilles Eduar. Boyds Mills, 2012. ISBN 978-1-59078-851-6 Subj: Animals – hippopotamuses. Careers – doctors. Family life – mothers. Imagination.

Here comes firefighter Hippo ill. by Gilles Eduar. Boyds Mills, 2013. ISBN 978-1-59078-968-1 Subj: Animals – hippopotamuses. Careers – firefighters. Imagination.

Hippos are huge! ill. by Matthew Trueman. Candlewick, 2015. ISBN 978-076366592-0 Subj: Animals – hippopotamuses. Foreign lands – Africa.

Honey Paw and Lightfoot ill. by Jon Van Zyle. Chronicle, 1994. ISBN 978-0-8118-0533-9 Subj: Animals – bears. Nature.

Hurricane! ill. by Henri Sorensen. Lothrop, 1998. ISBN 978-0-688-12978-1 Subj: Family life. Foreign lands – Puerto Rico. Weather – hurricanes.

Ice Bear and Little Fox ill. by Daniel San Souci. Dutton, 1998. ISBN 978-0-525-45907-1 Subj: Animals – foxes. Animals – polar bears. Foreign lands – Arctic. Indians of North America – Inuit.

I'm a truck driver ill. by David Parkins. Henry Holt, 2010. ISBN 978-0-8050-7989-0 Subj: Careers – truck drivers. Rhyming text.

Jackrabbit ill. by Deborah Kogan Ray. Crown, 1996. ISBN 978-0-517-59658-6 Subj: Animals – rabbits. Character traits – kindness to animals.

Let's go, Froggy! ill. by Frank Remkiewicz. Viking, 1994. ISBN 978-0-670-85055-6 Subj: Activities – picnicking. Behavior – lost & found possessions. Frogs & toads. Sports – bicycling.

Like butter on pancakes ill. by G. Brian Karas. Viking, 1995. ISBN 978-0-670-85130-0 Subj: Farms. Sun.

Little lost tiger ill. by Ilya Spirin. Amazon Children's, 2012. ISBN 978-0-7614-6130-2 Subj: Animals – tigers. Behavior – lost. Fire. Foreign lands – Russia. Nature.

Little penguin: the Emperor of Antarctica ill. by Julie Olson. Marshall Cavendish, 2011. ISBN 978-0-7614-5954-5 Subj: Animals – babies. Birds – penguins. Foreign lands – Antarctic.

Little Puffin's first flight ill. by Jon Van Zyle. Alaska Northwest, 2015. ISBN 978-194182140-4 Subj: Alaska. Birds – puffins.

Little swan ill. by Kristina Rodanas. Marshall Cavendish, 2009. ISBN 978-0-7614-5523-3 Subj: Birds – swans. Nature.

Loon Lake ill. by Susan Ford. Chronicle, 2001. ISBN 978-0-8118-2003-5 Subj: Animals. Birds – loons. Canoes & canoeing. Family life – fathers. Family life – sons. Lakes, ponds.

Moshi moshi ill. by Yoshi Miyake. Millbrook, 1998. ISBN 978-0-7613-0110-3 Subj: Activities – traveling. Family life – brothers. Foreign lands – Japan.

Mustang canyon ill. by Daniel San Souci. Dutton, 2000. ISBN 978-0-525-45596-7 Subj: Animals – horses, ponies. Canyons.

My big rig ill. by Viviana Garofoli. Marshall Cavendish, 2007. ISBN 978-0-7614-5346-8 Subj: Imagination. Toys. Transportation. Trucks.

Ollie's first year ill. by Jon Van Zyle. Univ. of Alaska/Snowy Owl, 2014. ISBN 978-160223229-7 Subj: Animals – otters. Nature.

Otters love to play ill. by Meilo So. Candlewick, 2016. ISBN 978-076366913-3 Subj: Activities – playing. Animals – otters. Seasons.

The owl who became the moon ill. by Ted Rand. Dutton, 1993. ISBN 978-0-525-45054-2 Subj: Animals. Birds – owls. Night. Trains.

Panther, shadow of the swamp ill. by Paul Morin. Candlewick, 2000. ISBN 978-1-56402-623-1 Subj: Animals – cougars.

Park beat: rhyming through the seasons ill. by Woodleigh Marx Hubbard. HarperCollins, 2000. ISBN 978-0-688-13995-7 Subj: Rhyming text. Seasons.

A plane goes ka-zoom! ill. by Denis Roche. Henry Holt, 2010. ISBN 978-0-8050-8970-7 Subj: Airplanes, airports. Rhyming text.

Puddles ill. by G. Brian Karas. Viking, 1997. ISBN 978-0-670-87218-3 Subj: Activities – playing. Clothing – boots. Weather – rain.

Pup the sea otter ill. by Sean London. Graphic Arts/Westwinds, 2017. ISBN 978-194332887-1 Subj: Animals – otters. Behavior – growing up. Nature.

Red wolf country ill. by Daniel San Souci. Dutton, 1996. ISBN 978-0-525-45191-4 Subj: Animals – wolves. Nature.

The seasons of Little Wolf ill. by Jon Van Zyle. WestWinds, 2014. ISBN 978-194182106-0 Subj: Animals – wolves. Nature.

Sled dogs run ill. by Jon Van Zyle. Walker, 2005. ISBN 978-0-8027-8958-7 Subj: Alaska. Animals – dogs. Sports – racing. Sports – sledding.

Snuggle wuggle ill. by Michael Rex. Silver Whistle, 2000. ISBN 978-0-15-202159-7 Subj: Animals – babies.

The sugaring-off party ill. by Gilles Pelletier. Dutton, 1995. ISBN 978-0-525-45187-7 Subj: Family life – grandmothers. Food. Foreign lands – Canada. Trees.

Sun dance, water dance ill. by Greg Couch. Dutton, 2001. ISBN 978-0-525-46682-6 Subj: Activities – playing. Poetry. Seasons – summer.

Thirteen moons on turtle's back (Bruchac, Joseph)

A train goes clickety-clack ill. by Denis Roche. Henry Holt, 2007. ISBN 978-0-8050-7972-2 Subj: Noise, sounds. Rhyming text. Trains.

A truck goes rattley-bumpa ill. by Denis Roche. Henry Holt, 2005. ISBN 978-0-8050-7233-4 Subj: Noise, sounds. Rhyming text. Trucks.

What do you love? ill. by Karen Lee Schmidt. Harcourt, 2000. ISBN 978-0-15-201919-8 Subj: Animals – dogs. Emotions – love. Family life – mothers. Rhyming text.

What the animals were waiting for ill. by Paul Morin. Scholastic, 2002. ISBN 978-0-439-33630-7 Subj: Animals. Foreign lands – Africa. Weather – rain.

Where the big fish are ill. by Adam Gustavson. Candlewick, 2001. ISBN 978-0-7636-0922-1 Subj: Boats, ships. Character traits – perseverance. Fish. Sports – fishing.

White water ill. by Jill Kastner. Viking, 2001. ISBN 978-0-670-89286-0 Subj: Rivers. Sports.

Who bop ill. by Henry Cole. HarperCollins, 2000. ISBN 978-0-06-027918-9 Subj: Activities – dancing. Animals. Rhyming text.

Wiggle, waggle ill. by Michael Rex. Harcourt, 1999. ISBN 978-0-15-201940-2 Subj: Activities – walking. Animals. Noise, sounds.

Loney, Andrea J. *Bunnybear* ill. by Carmen Saldaña. Albert Whitman, 2017. ISBN 978-080750938-8 Subj: Animals – bears. Animals – rabbits. Character traits – being different. Character traits – individuality. Prejudice.

Long, Ethan. *Bird and Birdie in a fine day* ill. by author. Tricycle, 2010. ISBN 978-1-58246-321-6 Subj: Birds. Friendship.

The book that Zack wrote ill. by author. Blue Apple, 2011. ISBN 978-1-60905-060-3 Subj: Activities – writing. Books, reading. Cumulative tales. Format, unusual.

Chamelia ill. by author. Little, Brown, 2011. ISBN 978-0-316-08612-7 Subj: Character traits – appearance. Character traits – individuality. Clothing. Reptiles – chameleons.

The croaky pokey! ill. by author. Holiday House, 2011. ISBN 978-0-8234-2291-3 Subj: Frogs & toads. Songs.

Fright club ill. by author. Bloomsbury, 2015. ISBN 978-161963337-7 Subj: Clubs, gangs. Holidays – Halloween. Monsters.

In, over, and on (the farm) ill. by author. Putnam, 2015. ISBN 978-039916907-6 Subj: Animals. Farms. Language.

Lion and Tiger and Bear: Tag! You're it! ill. by author. Abrams, 2016. ISBN 978-141971896-0 Subj: Activities – painting. Animals – bears. Animals – lions. Animals – tigers. Games.

Me and my big mouse ill. by author. Amazon/Two Lions, 2014. ISBN 978-147784728-2 Subj: Animals – mice. Concepts – size. Pets.

Ms. Spell ill. by author. Holiday House, 2015. ISBN 978-082343292-9 Subj: Humorous stories. Language.

My dad, my hero ill. by author. Sourcebooks, 2011. ISBN 978-1-4022-4239-7 Subj: Family life – fathers.

One drowsy dragon ill. by author. Scholastic, 2010. ISBN 978-0-545-16557-0 Subj: Counting, numbers. Dragons. Sleep.

Snickerdoodle takes the cake ill. by author. Holiday, 2017. ISBN 978-082343784-9 Subj: Activities – baking, cooking. Animals. Birthdays. Character traits – responsibility. Character traits – selfishness. Food.

Soup for one ill. by author. Running Press, 2012. ISBN 978-0-7624-4354-3 Subj: Counting, numbers. Food. Insects – flies. Rhyming text.

Up, tall and high ill. by author. Putnam, 2012. ISBN 978-0-399-25611-0 Subj: Birds. Concepts – size. Format, unusual – toy & movable books. Language.

Valensteins: (a love story) ill. by author. Bloomsbury, 2017. ISBN 978-161963433-6 Subj: Clubs, gangs. Emotions – love. Holidays – Valentine's Day. Monsters.

The Wing Wing brothers carnival de math ill. by author. Holiday House, 2013. ISBN 978-0-8234-2604-1 Subj: Birds – ducks. Counting, numbers. Family life – brothers.

The Wing Wing brothers geometry palooza! ill. by author. Holiday House, 2014. ISBN 978-082342951-6 Subj: Birds – ducks. Counting, numbers. Family life – brothers.

The Wing Wing brothers math spectacular! ill. by author. Holiday House, 2012. ISBN 978-0-8234-2320-0 Subj: Birds – ducks. Counting, numbers. Family life – brothers. Theater.

Long, Heather. *Max and Milo go to sleep!* ill. by Ethan Long. Simon & Schuster, 2013. ISBN 978-1-4424-5143-8 Subj: Animals – beavers. Bedtime. Family life – brothers.

Long, Kathy. *Christopher sat straight up in bed* ill. by Patricia Cantor. Eerdmans, 2013. ISBN 978-0-8028-5359-2 Subj: Bedtime. Family life – grandparents. Noise, sounds. Sleep – snoring. Sleepovers.

The runaway shopping cart ill. by Susan Estelle Kwas. Penguin, 2007. ISBN 978-0-525-47187-5 Subj: Behavior – running away. Cumulative tales. Shopping.

Long, Loren. *Drummer boy* ill. by author. Philomel, 2008. ISBN 978-0-399-25174-0 Subj: Behavior – lost. Careers – musicians. Holidays – Christmas. Musical instruments – drums. Toys.

Little tree ill. by author. Philomel, 2015. ISBN 978-039916397-5 Subj: Animals. Concepts – change. Seasons. Trees.

Otis ill. by author. Philomel, 2009. ISBN 978-0-399-25248-8 Subj: Farms. Tractors.

Otis and the kittens ill. by author. Philomel, 2016. ISBN 978-039916398-2 Subj: Animals – cats. Careers – firefighters. Character traits – bravery. Farms. Fire. Tractors.

Otis and the puppy ill. by author. Philomel, 2013. ISBN 978-0-399-25469-7 Subj: Animals – dogs. Behavior – lost & found possessions. Farms. Friendship. Tractors.

Otis and the scarecrow ill. by author. Philomel, 2014. ISBN 978-039916396-8 Subj: Farms. Scarecrows. Tractors.

Otis and the tornado ill. by author. Penguin, 2011. ISBN 978-0-399-25477-2 Subj: Farms. Tractors. Weather – tornadoes.

An Otis Christmas ill. by author. Philomel, 2013. ISBN 978-0-399-16395-1 Subj: Animals – horses, ponies. Character traits – bravery. Farms. Holidays – Christmas. Tractors. Weather – snow.

Long, Matty. *Super Happy Magic Forest* ill. by author. Scholastic, 2016. ISBN 978-054586059-8 Subj: Activities – traveling. Behavior – lost & found possessions. Mythical creatures.

Long, Melinda. *Hiccup snickup* ill. by Thor Wickstrom. Simon & Schuster, 2001. ISBN 978-0-689-82245-2 Subj: Family life. Hiccups.

How I became a pirate ill. by David Shannon. Harcourt, 2003. ISBN 978-0-15-201848-1 Subj: Imagination. Pirates.

Pirates don't change diapers ill. by David Shannon. Harcourt, 2007. ISBN 978-0-15-205353-6 Subj: Pirates.

When Papa snores ill. by Holly Meade. Simon & Schuster, 2000. ISBN 978-0-689-81943-8 Subj: Family life – grandparents. Sleep – snoring.

Long, Steffanie. *Such a silly baby!* by Steffanie Long and Richard Lorig ill. by Amanda Shepherd. Chronicle, 2008. ISBN 978-0-8118-5134-3 Subj: Animals. Babies, toddlers. Humorous stories. Rhyming text.

Long, Sylvia. *Deck the hall* ill. by author. Chronicle, 2000. ISBN 978-0-8118-2821-5 Subj: Animals – rabbits. Foreign lands – England. Holidays – Christmas. Music. Songs.

Sylvia Long's Thumbelina (Andersen, Hans Christian)

Longfellow, Henry Wadsworth. *Hiawatha* ill. by Susan Jeffers. Dial, 1983. ISBN 978-0-8037-0014-7 Subj: Indians of North America – Iroquois. Poetry.

Paul Revere's ride ill. by Nancy Winslow Parker. Mulberry, 1993. ISBN 978-0-688-12387-1 Subj: Poetry. U.S. history. War.

Paul Revere's ride: the landlord's tale ill. by Charles Santore. HarperCollins, 2003. ISBN 978-0-688-16552-9 Subj: Poetry. U.S. history. War.

Longstreth, Galen Goodwin. *Yes, let's* ill. by Maris Wicks. Tanglewood, 2013. ISBN 978-1-933718-87-3 Subj: Activities – hiking. Activities – picnicking. Family life. Rhyming text.

Loo, Sanne te. *Ping-Li's kite* ill. by author. Front Street, 2002. ISBN 978-1-886910-75-1 Subj: Folk & fairy tales. Foreign lands – China.

Look at me! ill. by Rachel Fuller. Child's Play, 2010. ISBN 978-1-84643-278-1 Subj: Format, unusual – board books. Self-concept.

Look, Lenore. *Brush of the gods* ill. by Meilo So. Random House, 2013. ISBN 978-0-375-87001-9 Subj: Activities – painting. Art. Careers – artists. Foreign lands – China.

Henry's first-moon birthday ill. by Yumi Heo. Atheneum, 2001. ISBN 978-0-689-82294-0 Subj: Babies, toddlers. Birthdays. Ethnic groups in the U.S. – Chinese Americans. Family life – brothers & sisters. Family life – grandmothers.

Love as strong as ginger ill. by Stephen T. Johnson. Atheneum, 1999. ISBN 978-0-689-81248-4 Subj: Activities – working. Ethnic groups in the U.S. – Chinese Americans. Family life – grandmothers.

Polka Dot Penguin Pottery ill. by Yumi Heo. Random House, 2011. ISBN 978-0-375-86332-5 Subj: Activities – writing. Ethnic groups in the U.S. – Chinese Americans. Family life – grandparents.

Uncle Peter's amazing Chinese wedding ill. by Yumi Heo. Simon & Schuster, 2006. ISBN 978-0-689-84458-4 Subj: Ethnic groups in the U.S. – Chinese Americans. Family life – aunts, uncles. Weddings.

Loomis, Christine. *Across America, I love you* ill. by Kate Kiesler. Hyperion, 2000. ISBN 978-0-7868-2314-7 Subj: Family life. Nature. U.S. history.

Astro Bunnies ill. by Ora Eitan. Putnam, 1998. ISBN 978-0-399-23175-9 Subj: Animals – rabbits. Rhyming text. Space & space ships.

The best Father's Day present ever ill. by Pamela Paparone. Penguin, 2007. ISBN 978-0-399-24253-3 Subj: Animals – snails. Family life – fathers. Holidays – Father's Day.

Cowboy bunnies ill. by Ora Eitan. Putnam, 1997. ISBN 978-0-399-22625-0 Subj: Activities – playing. Animals – rabbits. Country. Cowboys, cowgirls. Rhyming text.

Hattie hippo ill. by Robert Neubecker. Scholastic, 2006. ISBN 978-0-439-54340-8 Subj: Animals – hippopotamuses.

Scuba bunnies ill. by Ora Eitan. Putnam, 2004. ISBN 978-0-399-23465-1 Subj: Animals. Animals – rabbits. Rhyming text. Sea & seashore. Sports – skin diving.

López, Susana. *The best family in the world* ill. by Ulises Wensell. Kane/Miller, 2010. ISBN 978-1-935279-47-1 Subj: Adoption. Family life.

Lorbiecki, Marybeth. *Jackie's bat* ill. by Brian Pinkney. Simon & Schuster, 2006. ISBN 978-0-689-84102-6 Subj: Ethnic groups in the U.S. – African Americans. Prejudice. Sports – baseball.

Louisa May and Mr. Thoreau's flute (Dunlap, Julie)

Lord, Cynthia. *Happy birthday, Hamster* ill. by Derek Anderson. Scholastic, 2011. ISBN 978-0-545-25522-6 Subj: Animals – hamsters. Birthdays. Parties.

Hot Rod Hamster ill. by Derek Anderson. Scholastic, 2010. ISBN 978-0-545-03530-9 Subj: Animals – dogs. Animals – hamsters. Animals – mice. Automobiles. Sports – racing.

Hot Rod Hamster: monster truck mania! ill. by Derek Anderson. Scholastic, 2014. ISBN 978-054546261-7 Subj: Animals – hamsters. Fairs, festivals. Rhyming text. Trucks.

Lord, Janet. *Albert the fix-it man* ill. by Julie Paschkis. Peachtree, 2008. ISBN 978-1-56145-433-4 Subj: Character traits – helpfulness. Communities, neighborhoods. Tools.

Here comes Grandma! ill. by Julie Paschkis. Henry Holt, 2005. ISBN 978-0-8050-7666-0 Subj: Family life – grandmothers. Transportation.

Where is Catkin? ill. by Julie Paschkis. Peachtree, 2010. ISBN 978-1-56145-523-2 Subj: Animals – cats.

Lorenz, Albert. *The exceptionally, extraordinarily ordinary first day of school* ill. by author. Abrams, 2010. ISBN 978-0-8109-8960-3 Subj: Moving. School – first day.

Lorig, Richard. *Such a silly baby!* (Long, Steffanie)

Loth, Sebastian. *Clementine* ill. by author. NorthSouth, 2011. ISBN 978-0-7358-4009-6 Subj: Activities – traveling. Animals – snails. Concepts – shape. Format, unusual. Moon.

Remembering Crystal ill. by author. NorthSouth, 2010. ISBN 978-0-7358-2300-6 Subj: Birds – geese. Death. Reptiles – turtles, tortoises.

Zelda the Varigoose ill. by author. NorthSouth, 2012. ISBN 978-0-7358-4076-8 Subj: Birds –

geese. Format, unusual. Imagination. Rhyming text.

Lottridge, Celia Barker. *Berta, a remarkable dog* ill. by Elsa Myotte. Groundwood, 2002. ISBN 978-0-88899-461-5 Subj: Adoption. Animals. Animals – dogs. Behavior – needing someone. Farms.

The little rooster and the diamond button ill. by Joanne Fitzgerald. Douglas & McIntyre, 2001. ISBN 978-0-88899-443-1 Subj: Birds – chickens, roosters. Clothing. Folk & fairy tales. Foreign lands – Hungary. Royalty – sultans.

One watermelon seed ill. by Karen Patkau. Fitzhenry & Whiteside, 2008. ISBN 978-1-55455-034-0 Subj: Concepts – color. Counting, numbers. Gardens, gardening.

Louie, Ai-Ling. *Yeh Shen: a Cinderella story from China* ill. by Ed Young. Putnam, 1990. ISBN 978-0-399-20900-0 Subj: Folk & fairy tales. Foreign lands – China.

Louie, Therese On. *Raymond's perfect present* ill. by Suling Wang. Lee & Low, 2002. ISBN 978-1-58430-055-7 Subj: Birds. Communities, neighborhoods. Ethnic groups in the U.S. – Chinese Americans. Flowers. Gifts. Illness.

Louis, Catherine. *Liu and the bird: a journey in Chinese calligraphy* ill. by author. NorthSouth, 2006. ISBN 978-0-7358-2050-0 Subj: Activities – traveling. Activities – writing. Foreign lands – China.

Louise, Tina. *When I grow up* ill. by Oliver Corwin. Abrams, 2007. ISBN 978-0-8109-3948-6 Subj: Animals. Behavior – growing up.

Loupy, Christophe. *Don't worry, Wags* ill. by Eve Tharlet. NorthSouth, 2003. ISBN 978-0-7358-1850-7 Subj: Animals – dogs. Behavior – lost. Behavior – worrying. Stores.

Wiggles ill. by Eve Tharlet. NorthSouth, 2005. ISBN 978-0-7358-1981-8 Subj: Animals – dogs. Character traits – curiosity. Farms.

Loux, Lynn C. *The day I could fly* ill. by Guy Porfirio. NorthWord, 2003. ISBN 978-1-55971-866-0 Subj: Activities – flying. Birds – crows. Imagination.

Lovell, Patty. *Have fun, Molly Lou Melon* ill. by David Catrow. Putnam, 2012. ISBN 978-0-399-25406-2 Subj: Activities – making things. Family life – grandmothers. Friendship. Imagination.

Stand tall, Molly Lou Melon ill. by David Catrow. Putnam, 2001. ISBN 978-0-399-23416-3 Subj: Behavior – bullying, teasing. Family life – grandmothers. Self-concept.

Low, Alice. *Aunt Lucy went to buy a hat* ill. by Laura Huliska-Beith. HarperCollins, 2004. ISBN 978-

0-06-008972-6 Subj: Behavior – lost & found possessions. Clothing – hats. Humorous stories. Rhyming text.

Low, Joseph. *Mice twice* ill. by author. Aladdin, 1986, ©1980. ISBN 978-0-689-71060-5 Subj: Animals – mice. Caldecott award honor books.

Low, William. *Daytime nighttime* ill. by author. Henry Holt, 2014. ISBN 978-080509751-1 Subj: Animals. Day. Nature. Night.

Machines go to work ill. by author. Henry Holt, 2009. ISBN 978-0-8050-8759-8 Subj: Format, unusual – toy & movable books. Machines.

Machines go to work in the city ill. by author. Henry Holt, 2012. ISBN 978-0-8050-9050-5 Subj: Cities, towns. Format, unusual – toy & movable books. Machines. Trucks.

Trucks to the rescue! ill. by author. Henry Holt, 2017. ISBN 978-162779575-3 Subj: Format, unusual – board books. Trucks.

Lowell, Susan. *The bootmaker and the elves* ill. by Tom Curry. Orchard, 1997. ISBN 978-0-531-33044-9 Subj: Careers – shoemakers. Character traits – helpfulness. Clothing – boots. Cowboys, cowgirls. Folk & fairy tales. Humorous stories. Mythical creatures – elves. U.S. history – frontier & pioneer life.

Cindy Ellen: a wild western Cinderella ill. by Jane Manning. HarperCollins, 2000. ISBN 978-0-06-027447-4 Subj: Fairies. Family life – stepfamilies. Folk & fairy tales. Sibling rivalry. U.S. history – frontier & pioneer life.

Dusty Locks and the three bears ill. by Randy Cecil. Henry Holt, 2001. ISBN 978-0-8050-5862-8 Subj: Animals – bears. U.S. history – frontier & pioneer life.

The elephant quilt! stitch by stitch to California! ill. by Stacey Dressen-McQueen. Farrar, 2008. ISBN 978-0-374-38223-0 Subj: Quilts. U.S. history.

Josefina javelina: a hairy tale ill. by Bruce MacPherson. Rising Moon, 2005. ISBN 978-0-87358-790-7 Subj: Animals – coyotes. Animals – pigs. Ballet.

Little Red Cowboy Hat ill. by Randy Cecil. Henry Holt, 1997. ISBN 978-0-8050-3508-7 Subj: Animals – bulls, cows. Animals – wolves. Clothing – hats. Family life – grandmothers. Folk & fairy tales.

The three little javelinas ill. by Jim Harris. Northland, 1992. ISBN 978-0-87358-542-2 Subj: Animals – coyotes. Animals – pigs. Character traits – cleverness. Folk & fairy tales.

The tortoise and the jackrabbit ill. by Jim Harris. Northland, 1994. ISBN 978-0-87358-586-6 Subj: Animals. Animals – rabbits. Desert. Folk & fairy tales. Reptiles – turtles, tortoises. Sports – racing.

Lowry, Lois. *Crow call* ill. by Bagram Ibatoulline. Scholastic, 2009. ISBN 978-0-545-03035-9 Subj: Birds – crows. Family life – fathers. Sports – hunting.

Lozoff, Bo. *The wonderful life of a fly who couldn't fly* ill. by Beth Stover. Hampton Roads, 2002. ISBN 978-1-57174-286-5 Subj: Insects – flies. Self-concept.

Lubner, Susan. *Noises at night* (Glass, Beth Raisner)

Ruthie Bon Bair, do not go to bed with wringing wet hair! ill. by Bruce Whatley. Abrams, 2006. ISBN 978-0-8109-5470-0 Subj: Behavior – bad day, bad mood. Hair. Humorous stories. Rhyming text.

Lucado, Max. *Alabaster's song: Christmas through the eyes of an angel* ill. by Michael Garland. Word, 1996. ISBN 978-0-8499-1307-5 Subj: Activities – singing. Angels. Holidays – Christmas.

All you ever need ill. by Douglas Klauba. Crossway, 2000. ISBN 978-1-58134-134-8 Subj: Behavior. Character traits – generosity. Water.

Jacob's gift ill. by Robert Hunt. Tommy Nelson, 1998. ISBN 978-0-8499-5830-4 Subj: Careers – carpenters. Religion – Nativity.

Lucas, David. *Cake girl* ill. by author. Farrar, 2009. ISBN 978-0-374-39909-2 Subj: Birthdays. Emotions – loneliness. Friendship. Witches.

Christmas at the toy museum ill. by author. Candlewick, 2012. ISBN 978-0-7636-5868-7 Subj: Holidays – Christmas. Museums. Toys.

Halibut Jackson ill. by author. Knopf, 2004. ISBN 978-0-375-92690-7 Subj: Character traits – individuality. Character traits – shyness. Clothing.

Nutmeg ill. by author. Random House, 2006. ISBN 978-0-375-93519-0 Subj: Imagination. Magic. Mythical creatures – genies.

The robot and the bluebird ill. by author. Farrar, 2008. ISBN 978-0-374-36330-7 Subj: Birds – bluebirds. Character traits. Robots.

The skeleton pirate ill. by author. Candlewick, 2013. ISBN 978-0-7636-6107-6 Subj: Anatomy – skeletons. Animals – whales. Mythical creatures – mermaids, mermen. Pirates.

Something to do ill. by author. Philomel, 2009. ISBN 978-0-399-25247-1 Subj: Activities – drawing. Animals – bears. Imagination.

Whale ill. by author. Random House, 2007. ISBN 978-0-375-84338-9 Subj: Animals – whales. Tsunamis.

Luciani, Brigitte. *Those messy Hempels* ill. by Vannessa Hié. NorthSouth, 2004. ISBN 978-0-7358-1910-8 Subj: Behavior – lost & found possessions. Character traits – cleanliness. Food.

Lucke, Deb. *The boy who wouldn't swim* ill. by author. Clarion, 2008. ISBN 978-0-618-91484-5 Subj: Emotions – fear. Family life – brothers & sisters. Sports – swimming.

Sneezenesia ill. by author. Clarion, 2010. ISBN 978-0-547-33006-8 Subj: Anatomy – noses. Humorous stories. Memories, memory. Noise, sounds.

Luckhurst, Matt. *Paul Bunyan and Babe the Blue Ox: the great pancake adventure* ill. by author. Abrams, 2012. ISBN 978-1-4197-0420-8 Subj: Animals – oxen. Careers – lumberjacks. Food. Tall tales. U.S. history – frontier & pioneer life.

Ludwig, Trudy. *Better than you* ill. by Adam Gustavson. Random House, 2011. ISBN 978-1-58246-380-3 Subj: Behavior – boasting, showing off. Friendship. Self-concept.

The invisible boy ill. by Patrice Barton. Knopf, 2013. ISBN 978-1-58246-450-3 Subj: Activities – drawing. Behavior – unnoticed, unseen. Emotions – loneliness. Friendship. School.

Luenn, Nancy. *A gift for Abuelita* ill. by Robert Chapman. Rising Moon, 1998. ISBN 978-0-87358-688-7 Subj: Death. Ethnic groups in the U.S. – Mexican Americans. Family life – grandmothers. Foreign languages. Holidays – Day of the Dead.

Mother earth ill. by Neil Waldman. Atheneum, 1992. ISBN 978-0-689-31668-5 Subj: Earth. Ecology.

Nessa's fish ill. by Neil Waldman. Atheneum, 1990. ISBN 978-0-689-31477-3 Subj: Eskimos. Family life – grandmothers. Indians of North America. Sports – fishing.

Nessa's story ill. by Neil Waldman. Atheneum, 1994. ISBN 978-0-689-31782-8 Subj: Eskimos. Family life – grandmothers. Foreign lands – Arctic. Imagination.

Otter play ill. by Anna Vojtech. Atheneum, 1998. ISBN 978-0-689-81126-5 Subj: Activities – playing. Animals – otters.

Squish! a wetland walk ill. by Ronald Himler. Atheneum, 1994. ISBN 978-0-689-31842-9 Subj: Activities – walking. Ecology. Nature.

Luján, Jorge. *Beyond my hand* ill. by Georgina Quintana. Groundwood, 2002. ISBN 978-0-88899-460-8 Subj: Poetry.

Colors! / ¡Colores! ill. by Piet Grobler. Groundwood, 2008. ISBN 978-0-88899-863-7 Subj: Concepts – color. Foreign languages. Poetry.

Moví la mano / I moved my hand ill. by Mandana Sadat. Groundwood, 2014. ISBN 978-155498485-5 Subj: Activities – storytelling. Foreign languages. Imagination. Magic. Poetry.

Sky blue accident / Accidente celeste ill. by Piet Grobler. Groundwood, 2007. ISBN 978-0-88899-805-7 Subj: Accidents. Foreign languages. Sky.

Stephen and the beetle ill. by Chiara Carrer. Groundwood, 2012. ISBN 978-1-55498-192-2 Subj: Character traits – kindness to animals. Insects – beetles.

Lukasewich, Lori. *The night fire* ill. by author. Stoddart, 2001. ISBN 978-0-7737-3296-4 Subj: Careers – firefighters. Rhyming text.

Lullaby moons and a silver spoon ill. by Brooke Dyer. Little, 2003. ISBN 978-0-316-17474-9 Subj: Lullabies. Night. Poetry.

Lum, Kate. *Princesses are not just pretty* ill. by Sue Hellard. Bloomsbury, 2014. ISBN 978-159990778-9 Subj: Character traits – helpfulness. Character traits – vanity. Contests. Royalty – princesses.

Princesses are not perfect ill. by Susan Hellard. Bloomsbury, 2010. ISBN 978-1-59990-432-0 Subj: Royalty – princesses. Self-concept.

Princesses are not quitters! ill. by Susan Hellard. Bloomsbury, 2003. ISBN 978-1-58234-762-2 Subj: Activities – working. Royalty – princesses.

What! cried Granny ill. by Adrian Johnson. Dial, 1999. ISBN 978-0-8037-2382-5 Subj: Activities – making things. Bedtime. Family life – grandmothers. Furniture – beds.

Lumbard, Alexis York. *Everyone prays: celebrating faith around the world* ill. by Alireza Sadeghian. Wisdom Tales, 2014. ISBN 978-193778619-9 Subj: Religion.

Lumry, Amanda. *Polar bear puzzle* by Amanda Lumry and Laura Hurwitz. Eaglemont, 2007. ISBN 978-1-60040-004-9 Subj: Animals – polar bears. Ecology. Foreign lands – Canada.

Safari in South Africa by Amanda Lumry and Laura Hurwitz ill. by Sarah McIntyre. Eaglemont, 2003. ISBN 978-0-9662257-8-5 Subj: Animals. Ecology. Foreign lands – South Africa.

Lund, Deb. *All aboard the dinotrain* ill. by Howard Fine. Harcourt, 2006. ISBN 978-0-15-205237-9 Subj: Dinosaurs. Rhyming text. Trains.

Dinosailors ill. by Howard Fine. Harcourt, 2003. ISBN 978-0-15-204609-5 Subj: Dinosaurs. Rhyming text. Sailors. Sports – sailing.

Dinosoaring ill. by Howard Fine. Harcourt, 2012. ISBN 978-0-15-206016-9 Subj: Activities – flying. Airplanes, airports. Dinosaurs. Rhyming text.

Monsters on machines ill. by Robert Neubecker. Harcourt, 2008. ISBN 978-0-15-205365-9 Subj: Careers – construction workers. Machines. Monsters. Rhyming text. Tractors.

Tell me my story, Mama ill. by Hiroe Nakata. HarperCollins, 2004. ISBN 978-0-06-028877-8 Subj: Babies, toddlers. Birth. Family life – parents.

Lunde, Darrin. *Hello, baby beluga* ill. by Patricia J. Wynne. Charlesbridge, 2011. ISBN 978-1-57091-739-4 Subj: Animals – whales.

Hello, bumblebee bat ill. by Patricia J. Wynne. Charlesbridge, 2007. ISBN 978-1-57091-374-7 Subj: Animals – bats. Animals – endangered animals. Science.

Meet the meerkat ill. by Patricia J. Wynne. Charlesbridge, 2007. ISBN 978-1-58089-110-3 Subj: Animals – meerkats.

Monkey colors ill. by Patricia J. Wynne. Charlesbridge, 2012. ISBN 978-1-57091-741-7 Subj: Animals – monkeys.

Whose poop is that? ill. by Kelsey Oseid. Charlesbridge, 2017. ISBN 978-157091798-1 Subj: Animals. Science.

Lunde, Stein Erik. *My father's arms are a boat* ill. by Oyvind Torseter. Enchanted Lion, 2013. ISBN 978-1-59270-124-7 Subj: Death. Emotions – grief. Family life – fathers.

Lundgren, Mary Beth. *Seven scary monsters* ill. by Howard Fine. Clarion, 2003. ISBN 978-0-395-88913-8 Subj: Bedtime. Monsters. Rhyming text.

Lundquist, Mary. *Cat and Bunny* ill. by author. HarperCollins/Balzer+Bray, 2015. ISBN 978-006228780-9 Subj: Activities – playing. Animals – cats. Animals – rabbits. Friendship.

Lundy, Charlotte. *Thank you, Esther* ill. by Evelyn Diane Overcash. Bay Light, 2002. ISBN 978-0-9670280-4-0 Subj: Religion. School. Self-concept.

Thank you, Ruth and Naomi ill. by Miriam Sagasti. Bay Light, 2004. ISBN 978-0-9741817-0-7 Subj: Friendship. Religion.

Lunge-Larsen, Lise. *Noah's mittens: the story of felt* ill. by Matthew Trueman. Houghton, 2006. ISBN 978-0-618-32950-2 Subj: Animals – sheep. Clothing. Religion – Noah.

The race of the Birkebeiners ill. by Mary Azarian. Houghton, 2001. ISBN 978-0-618-10313-3 Subj: Folk & fairy tales. Foreign lands – Norway. Royalty – princes.

Lupton, David. *Goodbye, Brecken: a story about the death of a pet* ill. by author. Magination, 2013. ISBN 978-1-4338-1290-3 Subj: Animals – dogs. Death. Pets.

Lupton, Hugh. *Pirican Pic and Pirican Mor* ill. by Yumi Heo. Barefoot, 2003. ISBN 978-1-84148-070-1 Subj: Cumulative tales. Folk & fairy tales. Foreign lands – Scotland.

Lurie, Susan. *Swim, duck, swim!* ill. by Murray Head. Feiwel & Friends, 2014. ISBN 978-125004642-0 Subj: Birds – ducks. Rhyming text. Sports – swimming.

Will you be my friend? ill. by Murray Head. Feiwel & Friends, 2016. ISBN 978-125004643-7 Subj: Animals – mice. Character traits – shyness. Friendship. Rhyming text.

Luthardt, Kevin. *Flying* ill. by author. Peachtree, 2009. ISBN 978-1-56145-430-3 Subj: Character traits – questioning. Ethnic groups in the U.S. – African Americans. Family life – fathers.

Hats ill. by author. Albert Whitman, 2004. ISBN 978-0-8075-3171-6 Subj: Clothing – hats. Friendship.

Mine ill. by author. Atheneum, 2001. ISBN 978-0-689-83237-6 Subj: Behavior – sharing. Family life – brothers. Toys.

You're weird! ill. by author. Penguin, 2005. ISBN 978-0-8037-2986-5 Subj: Animals – rabbits. Behavior – name calling. Friendship. Reptiles – turtles, tortoises.

Luxbacher, Irene. *Mattoo, let's play!* ill. by author. Kids Can, 2010. ISBN 978-1-55453-424-1 Subj: Animals – cats.

Mr. Frank ill. by author. Groundwood, 2014. ISBN 978-155498435-0 Subj: Activities – sewing. Careers – tailors. Clothing. Family life. Memories, memory.

Luyken, Corinna. *The book of mistakes* ill. by author. Dial, 2017. ISBN 978-073522792-7 Subj: Activities – drawing. Behavior – mistakes. Careers – illustrators. Imagination.

Luzzati, Emanuele. *Three little owls* by Emanuele Luzzati and John Yeoman ill. by Quentin Blake. Tate, 2014. ISBN 978-184976080-5 Subj: Activities – traveling. Birds – owls. Holidays – Christmas. Rhyming text.

Lynch, Jane. *Marlene, Marlene, Queen of Mean* ill. by Tricia Tusa. Random House, 2014. ISBN 978-038537908-3 Subj: Behavior – bullying, teasing. Rhyming text.

Lynn, Sarah. *1-2-3 va-va-vroom! a counting book* ill. by Daniel Griffo. Amazon, 2012. ISBN 978-0-7614-6162-3 Subj: Activities – playing. Automobiles. Counting, numbers. Imagination. Sports – racing. Toys.

Tip-tap pop ill. by Valeria Docampo. Marshall Cavendish, 2010. ISBN 978-0-7614-5712-1 Subj: Activities – dancing. Family life – grandfathers. Memories, memory.

Lyon, Benn. *Boats float!* (Lyon, George Ella)

Lyon, George Ella. *All the water in the world* ill. by Katherine Tillotson. Atheneum, 2011. ISBN 978-1-4169-7130-6 Subj: Science. Water.

Boats float! by George Ella Lyon and Benn Lyon ill. by Mick Wiggins. Atheneum, 2015. ISBN 978-148140380-1 Subj: Boats, ships. Rhyming text.

Book ill. by Peter Catalanotto. DK, 1999. ISBN 978-0-7894-2560-7 Subj: Books, reading. Poetry.

Cecil's story ill. by Peter Catalanotto. Watts, 1991. ISBN 978-0-531-08512-7 Subj: Emotions – fear. Family life. Illness. U.S. history. War.

Come a tide ill. by Stephen Gammell. Watts, 1990. ISBN 978-0-531-08454-0 Subj: Family life. Weather – floods.

Counting on the woods photos by Ann W. Olson. DK, 1998. ISBN 978-0-7894-2480-8 Subj: Counting, numbers. Forest, woods. Nature. Poetry.

Mama is a miner ill. by Peter Catalanotto. Orchard, 1994. ISBN 978-0-531-08703-9 Subj: Activities – working. Careers – miners. Family life – mothers. Gender roles. Rhyming text.

Mother to tigers ill. by Peter Catalanotto. Atheneum, 2003. ISBN 978-0-689-84221-4 Subj: Animals. Careers – zookeepers.

My friend, the starfinder ill. by Stephen Gammell. Atheneum, 2008. ISBN 978-1-4169-2738-9 Subj: Activities – storytelling. Stars. Weather – rainbows.

No dessert forever! ill. by Peter Catalanotto. Simon & Schuster, 2006. ISBN 978-1-4169-0385-7 Subj: Behavior – fighting, arguing. Emotions – anger. Family life.

One lucky girl ill. by Irene Trivas. DK, 2000. ISBN 978-0-7894-2613-0 Subj: Family life. Homes, houses. Weather – tornadoes.

The pirate of kindergarten ill. by Lynne Avril. Simon & Schuster, 2010. ISBN 978-1-4169-5024-0 Subj: Anatomy – eyes. School. Senses – sight.

Planes fly! ill. by Mick Wiggins. Atheneum, 2013. ISBN 978-1-4424-5025-7 Subj: Airplanes, airports. Rhyming text.

Sleepsong ill. by Peter Catalanotto. Atheneum, 2009. ISBN 978-0-689-86973-0 Subj: Animals. Babies, toddlers. Bedtime. Rhyming text.

Trucks roll! ill. by Craig Frazier. Simon & Schuster, 2007. ISBN 978-1-4169-2435-7 Subj: Rhyming text. Trucks.

What forest knows ill. by August Hall. Atheneum, 2014. ISBN 978-144246775-0 Subj: Forest, woods. Nature. Seasons. Trees.

Who came down that road? ill. by Peter Catalanotto. Orchard, 1992. ISBN 978-0-531-08587-5 Subj: Imagination. Roads.

You and me and home sweet home ill. by Stephanie Anderson. Atheneum, 2009. ISBN 978-0-689-87589-2 Subj: Communities, neighborhoods. Ethnic groups in the U.S. – African Americans. Homes, houses.

Lyon, Tammie. *Olive and Snowflake* ill. by author. Marshall Cavendish, 2011. ISBN 978-0-7614-5955-2 Subj: Animals – dogs. Behavior – worrying. Pets.

Lyons, Kelly Starling. *Ellen's broom* ill. by Daniel Minter. Putnam, 2012. ISBN 978-0-399-25003-3 Subj: Ethnic groups in the U.S. – African Americans. Slavery. U.S. history. Weddings.

Hope's gift ill. by Don Tate. Putnam, 2012. ISBN 978-0-399-16001-1 Subj: Character traits – freedom. Ethnic groups in the U.S. – African Americans. Slavery. U.S. history.

One million men and me ill. by Peter Ambush. Just Us, 2007. ISBN 978-1-933491-07-3 Subj: Ethnic groups in the U.S. – African Americans. U.S. history.

One more dino on the floor ill. by Luke Flowers. Albert Whitman, 2016. ISBN 978-080751598-3 Subj: Activities – dancing. Counting, numbers. Dinosaurs. Rhyming text.

Tea cakes for Tosh ill. by E. B. Lewis. Putnam, 2012. ISBN 978-0-399-25213-6 Subj: Activities – baking, cooking. Ethnic groups in the U.S. – African Americans. Family life – grandmothers. Memories, memory. Old age.

Maass, Robert. *A is for autumn* photos by author. Henry Holt, 2011. ISBN 978-0-8050-9093-2 Subj: ABC books. Seasons – fall.

Garbage ill. by author. Henry Holt, 2000. ISBN 978-0-8050-5951-9 Subj: Careers – sanitation workers. Ecology.

Garden ill. by author. Henry Holt, 1998. ISBN 978-0-8050-5477-4 Subj: Gardens, gardening. Plants.

Little trucks with big jobs photos by author. Henry Holt, 2007. ISBN 978-0-8050-7748-3 Subj: Trucks.

Tugboats ill. by author. Henry Holt, 1997. ISBN 978-0-8050-3116-4 Subj: Boats, ships. Sailors. Transportation.

When autumn comes photos by author. Henry Holt, 1990. ISBN 978-0-8050-1259-0 Subj: Seasons – fall.

When spring comes photos by author. Henry Holt, 1994. ISBN 978-0-8050-2085-4 Subj: Seasons – spring.

When summer comes photos by author. Henry Holt, 1993. ISBN 978-0-8050-2087-8 Subj: Seasons – summer.

When winter comes photos by author. Henry Holt, 1993. ISBN 978-0-8050-2086-1 Subj: Seasons – winter.

McAlister, Caroline. *Holy Molé! a folktale from Mexico* ill. by Stefan Czernecki. August House, 2007. ISBN 978-0-87483-775-9 Subj: Activities – baking, cooking. Folk & fairy tales. Food. Foreign lands – Mexico.

McAllister, Angela. *Found you, Little Wombat!* ill. by Charles Fuge. Sterling, 2004. ISBN 978-1-4027-1599-0 Subj: Animals – wombats. Behavior – lost.

Harry's box ill. by Jenny Jones. Bloomsbury, 2003. ISBN 978-1-58234-772-1 Subj: Activities – playing. Animals – dogs. Imagination.

The little blue rabbit ill. by Jason Cockcroft. Bloomsbury, 2003. ISBN 978-1-58234-834-6 Subj: Animals – rabbits. Behavior – needing someone. Emotions. Toys.

Little Mist ill. by Sarah Fox-Davies. Random House, 2011. ISBN 978-0-375-86788-0 Subj: Animals – babies. Animals – leopards.

Mama and Little Joe ill. by Terry Milne. Simon & Schuster, 2007. ISBN 978-1-4169-1631-4 Subj: Animals – kangaroos. Behavior – lost. Emotions – love. Toys.

My mom has x-ray vision ill. by Alex T. Smith. Tiger Tales, 2011. ISBN 978-1-58925-097-0 Subj: Family life – mothers. Humorous stories.

Night-night, little one ill. by Maggie Kneen. Random House, 2003. ISBN 978-0-385-90861-0 Subj: Animals – rabbits. Bedtime. Family life – mothers.

Take a kiss to school ill. by Susan Hellard. Bloomsbury, 2006. ISBN 978-1-58234-702-8 Subj: Animals – moles. Kissing. School.

Trust me, Mom! ill. by Ross Collins. Bloomsbury, 2005. ISBN 978-1-58234-955-8 Subj: Behavior – resourcefulness. Emotions – fear. Family life – mothers. Monsters. Shopping.

Yuck! That's not a monster ill. by Alison Edgson. Good Books, 2010. ISBN 978-1-56148-683-0 Subj: Character traits – being different. Character traits – individuality. Family life. Monsters.

McAnulty, Stacy. *Beautiful* ill. by Joanne Lew-Vriethoff. Running Press, 2016. ISBN 978-076245781-6 Subj: Character traits – appearance. Character traits – assertiveness. Character traits – confidence. Character traits – individuality. Clothing. Self-concept.

Brave ill. by Joanne Lew-Vriethoff. Running Press, 2017. ISBN 978-076245782-3 Subj: Character traits – bravery. Self-concept.

Dear Santasaurus ill. by Jef Kaminsky. Boyds Mills, 2013. ISBN 978-1-59078-876-9 Subj: Activities – writing. Behavior – misbehavior. Dinosaurs. Holidays – Christmas. Letters, cards. Santa Claus.

Excellent Ed ill. by Julia Sarcone-Roach. Knopf, 2016. ISBN 978-055351023-2 Subj: Animals – dogs. Family life.

Mr. Fuzzbuster knows he's the favorite ill. by Edward Hemingway. Amazon/Two Lions, 2017. ISBN 978-150394838-9 Subj: Animals – cats. Pets.

McArthur, Meher. *An ABC of what art can be* ill. by Esther Pearl Watson. Getty Museum, 2010. ISBN 978-0-89236-999-7 Subj: ABC books. Art. Rhyming text.

Macaulay, David. *Angelo* ill. by author. Houghton, 2002. ISBN 978-0-618-16826-2 Subj: Birds – pigeons. Character traits – kindness to animals. Friendship.

Black and white ill. by author. Houghton, 1990. ISBN 978-0-395-52151-9 Subj: Animals – bulls, cows. Caldecott award books. Family life. Trains.

Castle ill. by author. Houghton, 1977. ISBN 978-0-395-25784-5 Subj: Caldecott award honor books.

Cathedral ill. by author. Houghton, 1973. ISBN 978-0-395-17513-2 Subj: Caldecott award honor books.

How machines work: zoo break! ill. by author. DK, 2015. ISBN 978-146544012-9 Subj: Animals – shrews. Animals – sloths. Behavior – resourcefulness. Format, unusual – toy & movable books. Machines. Zoos.

McBratney, Sam. *The caterpillow fight* ill. by Jill Barton. Candlewick, 1996. ISBN 978-1-56402-804-4 Subj: Bedtime. Behavior – misbehavior. Insects – butterflies, caterpillars. Rhyming text.

The dark at the top of the stairs ill. by Ivan Bates. Candlewick, 1996. ISBN 978-1-56402-640-8 Subj: Animals – cats. Animals – mice. Bedtime. Character traits – curiosity. Emotions – fear.

Guess how much I love you ill. by Anita Jeram. Candlewick, 1995. ISBN 978-1-56402-473-2 Subj: Animals – rabbits. Bedtime. Emotions – love. Family life – fathers.

I'll always be your friend ill. by Kim Lewis. HarperCollins, 2001. ISBN 978-0-06-029485-4 Subj: Animals – foxes. Emotions – anger. Family life – mothers.

I'm sorry by Sam McBratney and Jennifer Eachus; ed. by Robert Warren; ill. by Jennifer Eachus. HarperCollins, 2000. ISBN 978-0-06-028686-6 Subj: Behavior – fighting, arguing. Emotions – anger. Friendship. School.

In the light of the moon and other bedtime stories ill. by Kady MacDonald Denton. Kingfisher, 2001. ISBN 978-0-7534-5224-0 Subj: Bedtime.

Just you and me ill. by Ivan Bates. Candlewick, 1998. ISBN 978-0-7636-0436-3 Subj: Animals. Birds – geese. Weather – storms.

Once there was a Hoodie ill. by Paul Hess. Putnam, 2001. ISBN 978-0-399-23581-8 Subj: Behavior – needing someone. Emotions – happiness. Mythical creatures.

There, there ill. by Ivan Bates. Candlewick, 2013. ISBN 978-0-7636-6702-3 Subj: Animals – bears. Emotions – love. Family life – fathers. Hugging.

Yes we can! ill. by Charles Fuge. HarperCollins, 2007. ISBN 978-0-06-121515-5 Subj: Animals – kangaroos. Behavior – bullying, teasing. Character traits – individuality. Friendship.

McBrier, Page. *Beatrice's goat* ill. by Lori Lohstoeter. Atheneum, 2001. ISBN 978-0-689-82460-9 Subj: Animals – goats. Behavior – resourcefulness. Behavior – seeking better things. Foreign lands – Uganda.

McCain, Becky R. *Grandmother's dreamcatcher* ill. by Stacey Schuett. Albert Whitman, 1998. ISBN 978-0-8075-3031-3 Subj: Activities – making things. Dreams. Family life – grandmothers. Indians of North America – Chippewa.

Nobody knew what to do: a story about bullying ill. by Todd Leonard. Albert Whitman, 2001. ISBN 978-0-8075-5711-2 Subj: Behavior – bullying, teasing. School.

McCain, Meghan. *My dad, John McCain* ill. by Dan Andreasen. Aladdin, 2008. ISBN 978-1-4169-7528-1 Subj: Family life – fathers. U.S. history. War.

McCall, Bruce. *Marveltown* ill. by author. Farrar, 2008. ISBN 978-0-374-39925-2 Subj: Careers – inventors. Robots.

McCall, Francis X. *A huge hog is a big pig* by Francis X. McCall and Patricia A. Keeler ill. with photos. Greenwillow, 2002. ISBN 978-0-06-029766-4 Subj: Animals. Games. Rhyming text.

McCanna, Tim. *Bitty Bot* ill. by Tad Carpenter. Simon & Schuster/Paula Wiseman, 2016. ISBN 978-148144929-8 Subj: Bedtime. Rhyming text. Robots. Space & space ships.

Watersong ill. by Richard Smythe. Simon & Schuster/Paula Wiseman, 2017. ISBN 978-148146881-7 Subj: Animals – foxes. Nature. Noise, sounds. Rhyming text. Weather – rain.

McCardie, Amanda. *Our very own dog* ill. by Salvatore Rubbino. Candlewick, 2017. ISBN 978-076368948-3 Subj: Animals – dogs. Character traits – kindness to animals. Pets.

McCarney, Rosemary. *Where will I live?* ill. with photos. Second Story, 2017. ISBN 978-177260028-5 Subj: Behavior – worrying. Homes, houses. Refugees.

Maccarone, Grace. *Cars! cars! cars!* ill. by David A. Carter. Scholastic, 1995. ISBN 978-0-590-47572-3 Subj: Automobiles. Rhyming text.

A child was born ill. by Sam Williams. Scholastic, 2000. ISBN 978-0-439-18296-6 Subj: Holidays – Christmas. Religion – Nativity. Rhyming text.

A child's good night prayer ill. by Sam Williams. Scholastic, 2001. ISBN 978-0-439-23505-1 Subj: Bedtime. Religion.

Miss Lina's ballerinas ill. by Christine Davenier. Feiwel & Friends, 2010. ISBN 978-0-312-38243-8 Subj: Ballet. Counting, numbers. Problem solving. Rhyming text.

Miss Lina's ballerinas and the prince ill. by Christine Davenier. Feiwel & Friends, 2011. ISBN 978-0-312-64963-0 Subj: Activities – dancing. Ballet. Character traits – shyness. Rhyming text.

Miss Lina's ballerinas and the wicked wish ill. by Christine Davenier. Feiwel & Friends, 2012. ISBN 978-1-250-00580-9 Subj: Activities – dancing. Ballet. Rhyming text.

Oink! moo! how do you do? ill. by Hans Wilhelm. Scholastic, 1994. ISBN 978-0-590-48161-8 Subj: Animals. Careers – farmers. Farms. Noise, sounds. Rhyming text.

The three bears ABC: an alphabet book ill. by Hollie Hibbert. Albert Whitman, 2013. ISBN 978-0-8075-7904-6 Subj: ABC books. Animals – bears. Folk & fairy tales.

The three little pigs count to 100 ill. by Pistacchio. Albert Whitman, 2015. ISBN 978-080757901-5 Subj: Animals – pigs. Concepts – shape. Counting, numbers. Folk & fairy tales.

McCarthy, Conor Clarke. *Just add one Chinese sister* (McMahon, Patricia)

McCarthy, Jenna. *Lola knows a lot* ill. by Sara Palacios. HarperCollins/Balzer+Bray, 2016. ISBN

978-006225017-9 Subj: Behavior – worrying. Character traits – confidence. Family life – sisters. School – first day.

Lola's rules for friendship ill. by Sara Palacios. HarperCollins/Balzer+Bray, 2017. ISBN 978-006225018-6 Subj: Friendship. Moving.

Poppy Louise is not afraid of anything ill. by Molly Idle. Random House, 2017. ISBN 978-038539086-6 Subj: Emotions – fear. Family life – sisters.

McCarthy, Mary. *A closer look* ill. by author. HarperCollins, 2007. ISBN 978-0-06-124073-7 Subj: Concepts. Nature. Senses – sight.

McCarthy, Meghan. *The adventures of Patty and the big red bus* ill. by author. Knopf, 2005. ISBN 978-0-375-92939-7 Subj: Activities – traveling. Buses. Family life – sisters. Imagination. Moon. Mountains. Sea & seashore. Space & space ships.

Astronaut handbook ill. by author. Knopf, 2008. ISBN 978-0-375-84459-1 Subj: Careers – astronauts.

City hawk: the story of Pale Male ill. by author. Simon & Schuster, 2007. ISBN 978-1-4169-3359-5 Subj: Birds – hawks. Cities, towns.

Earmuffs for everyone! how Chester Greenwood became known as the inventor of earmuffs ill. by author. Simon & Schuster/Paula Wiseman, 2015. ISBN 978-148140637-6 Subj: Anatomy – ears. Careers – inventors. Inventions.

George upside down ill. by author. Viking, 2003. ISBN 978-0-670-03608-0 Subj: Behavior. Character traits – individuality.

The incredible life of Balto ill. by author. Random House, 2011. ISBN 978-0-375-84460-7 Subj: Alaska. Animals – dogs. Sports – racing. Sports – sledding.

Seabiscuit: the wonder horse ill. by author. Simon & Schuster, 2008. ISBN 978-1-4169-3360-1 Subj: Animals – horses, ponies. Sports – racing.

McCarthy, Michael. *The story of Daniel in the lions' den* ill. by Giuliano Ferri. Barefoot, 2005. ISBN 978-1-84148-209-5 Subj: Animals – lions. Religion – Daniel. Rhyming text.

The story of Noah and the ark ill. by Giuliano Ferri. Barefoot, 2001. ISBN 978-1-84148-361-0 Subj: Animals. Boats, ships. Religion – Noah. Rhyming text. Weather – floods. Weather – rain.

McCarty, Peter. *Baby steps* ill. by author. Henry Holt, 2000. ISBN 978-0-8050-5953-3 Subj: Babies, toddlers. Behavior – growing up.

Bunny dreams ill. by author. Henry Holt, 2016. ISBN 978-080509687-3 Subj: Animals – rabbits. Bedtime. Dreams.

Chloe ill. by author. HarperCollins, 2012. ISBN 978-0-06-114291-8 Subj: Animals – rabbits. Family life. Imagination. Television.

Fabian escapes ill. by author. Henry Holt, 2007. ISBN 978-0-8050-7713-1 Subj: Animals – cats. Animals – dogs.

Fall ball ill. by author. Henry Holt, 2013. ISBN 978-0-8050-9253-0 Subj: Seasons – fall. Sports – football.

First snow ill. by author. HarperCollins/Balzer+Bray, 2015. ISBN 978-006218996-7 Subj: Activities – playing. Animals – dogs. Family life – cousins. Seasons – winter. Weather – snow.

Henry in love ill. by author. HarperCollins, 2010. ISBN 978-0-06-114288-8 Subj: Animals – cats. Animals – rabbits. Emotions – love. School – first day.

Hondo and Fabian ill. by author. Henry Holt, 2002. ISBN 978-0-8050-6352-3 Subj: Animals – cats. Animals – dogs. Caldecott award honor books. Sea & seashore.

Jeremy draws a monster ill. by author. Henry Holt, 2009. ISBN 978-0-8050-6934-1 Subj: Activities – drawing. Emotions – loneliness. Monsters.

Little bunny on the move ill. by author. Henry Holt, 1999. ISBN 978-0-8050-4620-5 Subj: Activities – traveling. Animals. Animals – rabbits. Homes, houses.

The monster returns ill. by author. Henry Holt, 2012. ISBN 978-0-8050-9030-7 Subj: Activities – drawing. Friendship. Monsters.

Moon plane ill. by author. Henry Holt, 2006. ISBN 978-0-8050-7943-2 Subj: Activities – flying. Airplanes, airports. Imagination. Moon.

McCaughrean, Geraldine. *Beauty and the beast* ill. by Gary Blythe. Carolrhoda, 2000. ISBN 978-1-57505-491-9 Subj: Emotions – love. Folk & fairy tales. Foreign lands – France. Royalty – princes.

Father and son: a nativity story ill. by Fabian Negrin. Hyperion, 2006. ISBN 978-1-4231-0344-8 Subj: Family life – fathers. Holidays – Christmas. Religion – Nativity.

Grandma Chickenlegs ill. by Moira Kemp. Carolrhoda, 2000. ISBN 978-1-57505-415-5 Subj: Family life – stepfamilies. Folk & fairy tales. Foreign lands – Russia. Magic. Witches.

How the reindeer got their antlers ill. by Heather Holland. Holiday, 2000. ISBN 978-0-8234-1562-5 Subj: Animals – reindeer. Character traits – individuality. Character traits – pride. Holidays – Christmas. Santa Claus. Self-concept.

My grandmother's clock ill. by Stephen Lambert. Clarion, 2002. ISBN 978-0-618-21695-6 Subj: Clocks, watches. Family life – grandmothers. Time.

One bright Penny ill. by Paul Howard. Viking, 2002. ISBN 978-0-670-03588-5 Subj: Behavior – trickery. Family life – fathers. Money.

McClatchy, Lisa. *Dear Tyrannosaurus Rex* ill. by John Manders. Random House, 2010. ISBN 978-0-375-85608-2 Subj: Birthdays. Dinosaurs. Letters, cards. Parties.

McCleery, Peter. *Bob and Joss get lost!* ill. by Vin Vogel. HarperCollins, 2017. ISBN 978-006241531-8 Subj: Behavior – boredom. Behavior – lost. Behavior – worrying. Boats, ships.

McClelland, Rosie. *Show time with Sophia Grace and Rosie* (Brownlee, Sophia Grace)

Tea time with Sophia Grace and Rosie (Brownlee, Sophia Grace)

McClements, George. *Baron von Baddie and the ice ray incident* ill. by author. Harcourt, 2008. ISBN 978-0-15-206138-8 Subj: Behavior – misbehavior. Humorous stories.

Dinosaur Woods: can seven clever critters save their forest home? ill. by author. Simon & Schuster, 2009. ISBN 978-1-4169-8626-3 Subj: Animals. Dinosaurs. Ecology. Forest, woods.

Night of the Veggie Monster ill. by author. Bloomsbury, 2008. ISBN 978-1-59990-061-2 Subj: Behavior – misbehavior. Food.

Ridin' dinos with Buck Bronco ill. by author. Harcourt, 2007. ISBN 978-0-15-205989-7 Subj: Cowboys, cowgirls. Dinosaurs.

McClintock, Barbara. *Adele and Simon* ill. by author. Farrar, 2006. ISBN 978-0-374-38044-1 Subj: Behavior – lost & found possessions. Family life – brothers & sisters. Foreign lands – France.

Adele and Simon in America ill. by author. Farrar, 2008. ISBN 978-0-374-39924-5 Subj: Activities – traveling. Behavior – lost & found possessions. Family life – aunts, uncles. Family life – brothers & sisters.

Dahlia ill. by author. Farrar, 2002. ISBN 978-0-374-31678-5 Subj: Activities – playing. Family life – aunts, uncles. Toys – dolls.

Emma and Julia love ballet ill. by author. Scholastic, 2016. ISBN 978-043989401-2 Subj: Ballet. Ethnic groups in the U.S. – African Americans.

The five forms ill. by author. Farrar, 2017. ISBN 978-162672216-3 Subj: Animals. Magic. Sports – martial arts.

Lost and found: Adele and Simon in China ill. by author. Farrar, 2016. ISBN 978-037439923-8 Subj: Activities – traveling. Behavior – lost & found possessions. Family life – brothers & sisters. Foreign lands – China.

Molly and the magic wishbone ill. by author. Farrar, 2000. ISBN 978-0-374-34999-8 Subj: Behavior – wishing. Fairies. Family life – brothers & sisters.

McCloskey, Kevin. *The real poop on pigeons!* ill. by author. TOON, 2016. ISBN 978-193517993-1 Subj: Birds – pigeons. Format, unusual – graphic novels.

McCloskey, Robert. *Blueberries for Sal* ill. by author. Viking, 1948. ISBN 978-0-670-17591-8 Subj: Animals – bears. Behavior – lost. Caldecott award honor books. Family life. Food.

Lentil ill. by author. Viking, 1940. ISBN 978-0-670-42357-6 Subj: Music. Musical instruments – harmonicas. Noise, sounds. Problem solving.

Make way for ducklings ill. by author. Viking, 1941. ISBN 978-0-670-45149-4 Subj: Birds – ducks. Caldecott award books. Careers – police officers. Cities, towns.

One morning in Maine ill. by author. Viking, 1952. ISBN 978-0-670-52627-7 Subj: Caldecott award honor books. Family life. Sea & seashore. Teeth.

Time of wonder ill. by author. Viking, 1957. ISBN 978-0-670-71512-1 Subj: Caldecott award books. Islands. Sea & seashore. Seasons – summer. Weather.

McClure, Gillian. *Tom Finger* ill. by author. Bloomsbury, 2002. ISBN 978-1-58234-782-0 Subj: Animals – cats. Gifts. Pets.

McClure, Nikki. *Apple* ill. by author. Abrams, 2012. ISBN 978-1-4197-0378-2 Subj: Food. Nature. Seasons. Trees.

How to be a cat ill. by author. Abrams, 2013. ISBN 978-1-4197-0528-1 Subj: Animals – babies. Animals – cats.

In ill. by author. Abrams/Appleseed, 2015. ISBN 978-141971486-3 Subj: Activities – playing. Birds – owls. Imagination.

Mama, is it summer yet? ill. by author. Abrams, 2010. ISBN 978-0-8109-8468-4 Subj: Character traits – questioning. Seasons – summer.

Waiting for high tide ill. by author. Abrams, 2016. ISBN 978-141971656-0 Subj: Activities – making things. Family life. Sea & seashore – beaches.

McClure, Wendy. *The princess and the peanut allergy* ill. by Tammie Lyon. Albert Whitman, 2009. ISBN 978-0-8075-6623-7 Subj: Birthdays. Illness – allergies. Parties.

McClurkan, Rob. *Aw, nuts!* ill. by author. HarperCollins, 2014. ISBN 978-006231729-2 Subj: Animals – squirrels. Behavior – greed.

Playdates rule! ill. by author. Bloomsbury, 2017. ISBN 978-168119369-4 Subj: Activities – playing. Animals – elephants. Friendship.

McCormack, Caren McNelly. *The fiesta dress: a quinceañera tale* ill. by Martha Avilés. Marshall Cavendish, 2009. ISBN 978-0-7614-5467-0 Subj: Birthdays. Clothing – dresses. Ethnic groups in the U.S. – Hispanic Americans. Family life – sisters. Parties.

McCormick, Wendy. *Daddy, will you miss me?* ill. by Jennifer Eachus. Simon & Schuster, 1999. ISBN 978-0-689-81898-1 Subj: Behavior – needing someone. Emotions – loneliness. Family life – fathers. Foreign lands – Africa.

The night you were born ill. by Sophy Williams. Peachtree, 2000. ISBN 978-1-56145-225-5 Subj: Babies, toddlers. Family life – aunts, uncles. Family life – brothers & sisters. Family life – new sibling.

McCourt, Lisa. *Chicken soup for little souls: Della Splatnuk birthday girl* ill. by Pat Grant Porter. Health Communications, 1999. ISBN 978-1-55874-600-8 Subj: Birthdays. Friendship. Parties. Prejudice.

Chicken soup for little souls: The best night out with Dad ill. by Bert Dodson. Health Communications, 1997. ISBN 978-1-55874-508-7 Subj: Character traits – generosity. Circus. Family life – fathers.

Chicken soup for little souls: The Goodness Gorillas ill. by Pat Grant Porter. Health Communications, 1997. ISBN 978-1-55874-505-6 Subj: Character traits – kindness. Clubs, gangs. School.

Chicken soup for little souls: The never-forgotten doll ill. by Mary O'Keefe Young. Health Communications, 1997. ISBN 978-1-55874-507-0 Subj: Activities – babysitting. Behavior – lost & found possessions. Birthdays. Character traits – kindness. Gifts.

Chicken soup for little souls: The new kid and the cookie thief ill. by Mary O'Keefe Young. Health Communications, 1998. ISBN 978-1-55874-588-9 Subj: Character traits – shyness. Friendship. School.

Good night, Princess Pruney Toes ill. by Cyd Moore. BridgeWater, 2001. ISBN 978-0-8167-5205-8 Subj: Bedtime. Family life – daughters. Family life – fathers. Imagination. Royalty – princesses.

Happy Halloween, Stinky Face ill. by Cyd Moore. Scholastic, 2007. ISBN 978-0-439-77977-7 Subj: Family life – mothers. Holidays – Halloween. Imagination.

I love you, Stinky Face ill. by Cyd Moore. Troll, 1997. ISBN 978-0-8167-4392-6 Subj: Bedtime. Emotions – love. Family life – mothers. Imagination.

I miss you, Stinky Face ill. by Cyd Moore. BridgeWater, 1999. ISBN 978-0-8167-5647-6 Subj: Activities – traveling. Family life – mothers. Transportation.

It's time for school, Stinky Face ill. by Cyd Moore. BridgeWater, 2000. ISBN 978-0-8167-6961-2 Subj: Family life – mothers. Imagination. School.

Merry Christmas, Stinky Face ill. by Cyd Moore. Scholastic, 2003. ISBN 978-0-439-63577-6 Subj: Family life – mothers. Holidays – Christmas. Imagination.

McCue, Lisa. *Corduroy's best Halloween ever!* ill. by author. Based on the character by Don Freeman. Grosset, 2001. ISBN 978-0-448-42499-6 Subj: Clothing – costumes. Holidays – Halloween. Toys – bears.

Quiet Bunny ill. by author. Sterling, 2009. ISBN 978-1-4027-5719-8 Subj: Animals – rabbits. Character traits – individuality. Noise, sounds.

Quiet Bunny and Noisy Puppy ill. by author. Sterling, 2011. ISBN 978-1-4027-8559-7 Subj: Animals – dogs. Animals – rabbits. Friendship. Seasons – winter.

McCullough, Sharon Pierce. *Bunbun at bedtime* ill. by author. Barefoot, 2001. ISBN 978-1-84148-438-9 Subj: Animals – rabbits. Bedtime.

Bunbun, the middle one ill. by author. Barefoot, 2001. ISBN 978-1-84148-377-1 Subj: Animals – rabbits. Family life – brothers & sisters.

McCully, Emily Arnold. *The Christmas gift* ill. by author. HarperCollins, 1988. ISBN 978-0-06-024212-1 Subj: Animals – mice. Family life – grandfathers. Gifts. Holidays – Christmas. Toys. Wordless.

Clara: the (mostly) true story of the rhinoceros who dazzled kings, inspired artists, and won the hearts of everyone . . . while she ate her way up and down a continent! ill. by author. Random House, 2016. ISBN 978-055352246-4 Subj: Animals – rhinoceros. Character traits – kindness to animals.

First snow ill. by author. HarperCollins, 1985. ISBN 978-0-06-623853-1 Subj: Activities – playing. Animals – mice. Seasons – winter. Weather – snow. Wordless.

Four hungry kittens ill. by author. Dial, 2001. ISBN 978-0-8037-2505-8 Subj: Animals – cats. Wordless.

Hurry! ill. by author. Harcourt, 2000. ISBN 978-0-15-201579-4 Subj: Animals – endangered animals. Behavior – hurrying.

Marvelous Mattie: how Margaret E. Knight became an inventor ill. by author. Farrar, 2006. ISBN 978-0-374-34810-6 Subj: Careers – scientists. Inventions. Problem solving.

Mirette and Bellini cross Niagara Falls ill. by author. Putnam, 2000. ISBN 978-0-399-23348-7 Subj: Careers – aerialists. Ethnic groups in the U.S. – French Americans. Immigrants, immigration.

Mirette on the high wire ill. by author. Putnam, 1992. ISBN 978-0-399-22130-9 Subj: Caldecott award books. Careers – aerialists. Emotions – fear. Foreign lands – France.

Monk camps out ill. by author. Scholastic, 2000. ISBN 978-0-439-09976-9 Subj: Animals – mice. Camps, camping. Family life.

Mouse practice ill. by author. Scholastic, 1999. ISBN 978-0-590-68220-6 Subj: Animals – mice. Character traits – persistence. Sports – baseball.

My heart glow: Alice Cogswell, Thomas Gallaudet, and the birth of American sign language ill. by author. Hyperion, 2008. ISBN 978-1-4231-0028-7 Subj: Disabilities – deafness. Sign language. U.S. history.

My real family ill. by author. Browndeer, 1994. ISBN 978-0-15-277698-5 Subj: Adoption. Animals – bears. Animals – sheep. Behavior – running away. Family life. Theater.

New baby ill. by author. HarperCollins, 1988. ISBN 978-0-06-024131-5 Subj: Animals – mice. Sibling rivalry. Wordless.

An outlaw Thanksgiving ill. by author. Dial, 1998. ISBN 978-0-8037-2198-2 Subj: Crime. Holidays – Thanksgiving. Trains. U.S. history. Weather – snow.

Picnic ill. by author. HarperCollins, 1984. ISBN 978-0-06-024099-8 Subj: Activities – picnicking. Animals – mice. Behavior – lost. Wordless.

The pirate queen ill. by author. Putnam, 1995. ISBN 978-0-399-22657-1 Subj: Boats, ships. Foreign lands – Ireland. Pirates.

Popcorn at the palace ill. by author. Browndeer, 1997. ISBN 978-0-15-277699-2 Subj: Family life – fathers. Food. Foreign lands – England.

Queen of the diamond: the Lizzie Murphy story ill. by author. Farrar, 2015. ISBN 978-037430007-4 Subj: Gender roles. Sports – baseball.

School ill. by author. HarperCollins, 2005. ISBN 978-0-06-623856-2 Subj: Animals – mice. School.

The secret cave: discovering Lascaux ill. by author. Farrar, 2010. ISBN 978-0-374-36694-0 Subj: Art. Caves. Prehistory.

Strongheart: the world's first movie star dog ill. by author. Henry Holt, 2014. ISBN 978-080509448-0 Subj: Animals – dogs. Careers – actors.

Wonder horse: the true story of the world's smartest horse ill. by author. Henry Holt, 2010. ISBN 978-0-8050-8793-2 Subj: Animals – horses, ponies. Careers – veterinarians. Ethnic groups in the U.S. – African Americans. Prejudice.

McCurdy, Michael. *An Algonquian year: the year according to the full moon* ill. by author. Houghton, 2000. ISBN 978-0-618-00705-9 Subj: Days of the week, months of the year. Food. Indians of North America – Algonquin.

McCutcheon, John. *Happy adoption day!* ill. by Julie Paschkis. Little, 1996. ISBN 978-0-316-55455-8 Subj: Adoption. Family life. Songs.

McDaniels, Preston. *A perfect snowman* ill. by author. Simon & Schuster, 2007. ISBN 978-1-4169-1026-8 Subj: Behavior – sharing. Seasons – winter. Snowmen.

McDermott, Gerald. *Anansi the spider: a tale from the Ashanti* ill. by author. Henry Holt, 1972. ISBN 978-0-03-080236-2 Subj: Caldecott award honor books. Folk & fairy tales. Foreign lands – Africa. Moon. Spiders.

Arrow to the sun: a Pueblo Indian tale ill. by author. Viking, 1974. ISBN 978-0-670-13369-7 Subj: Caldecott award books. Folk & fairy tales. Indians of North America – Pueblo.

Coyote: a trickster tale from the American Southwest ill. by author. Harcourt, 1994. ISBN 978-0-15-220724-3 Subj: Activities – flying. Animals – coyotes. Birds – crows. Folk & fairy tales. Indians of North America – Southwest.

Daniel O'Rourke: an Irish tale ill. by author. Viking, 1986. ISBN 978-0-670-80924-0 Subj: Dreams. Folk & fairy tales. Foreign lands – Ireland. Mythical creatures – pooka spirit.

Jabutí the tortoise ill. by author. Harcourt, 2001. ISBN 978-0-15-200496-5 Subj: Behavior – trickery. Folk & fairy tales – pourquoi tales. Foreign lands – South America. Reptiles – turtles, tortoises.

Monkey: a trickster tale from India ill. by author. Harcourt, 2011. ISBN 978-0-15-216596-3 Subj: Animals – monkeys. Behavior – trickery. Character traits – cleverness. Folk & fairy tales. Foreign lands – India.

Musicians of the sun ill. by author. Simon & Schuster, 1997. ISBN 978-0-689-80706-0 Subj: Folk & fairy tales. Foreign lands – Mexico. Indians of North America – Aztec. Music. Sun.

Pig-Boy: a trickster tale from Hawai'i ill. by author. Harcourt, 2009. ISBN 978-0-15-216590-1 Subj: Animals – pigs. Behavior – trickery. Folk & fairy tales. Hawaii.

Raven: a trickster tale from the Pacific Northwest ill. by author. Harcourt, 1993. ISBN 978-0-15-265661-4 Subj: Behavior – trickery. Birds – ravens. Caldecott award honor books. Folk & fairy tales. Indians of North America.

Tim O'Toole and the wee folk ill. by author. Viking, 1990. ISBN 978-0-670-80393-4 Subj: Behavior – trickery. Cities, towns. Folk & fairy tales. Magic.

Zomo the rabbit ill. by author. Harcourt, 1992. ISBN 978-0-15-299967-4 Subj: Animals – rabbits. Behavior – trickery. Foreign lands – Africa.

MacDonald, Alan. *Beware of the bears!* ill. by Gwyneth Williamson. Little Tiger, 1998. ISBN 978-1-888444-28-5 Subj: Animals – bears. Character traits – orderliness.

The pig in a wig ill. by Paul Hess. Peachtree, 1999. ISBN 978-1-56145-197-5 Subj: Animals – pigs. Hair. Self-concept.

Wilfred to the rescue: stories from Brambly Hedge ill. by Lizzie Sanders. Simon & Schuster, 2006. ISBN 978-1-4169-0901-9 Subj: Animals. Animals – mice. Behavior – lost. Foreign lands – England. Weather – floods.

MacDonald, Amy. *Cousin Ruth's tooth* ill. by Marjorie Priceman. Houghton, 1996. ISBN 978-0-395-71253-5 Subj: Behavior – growing up. Behavior – lost & found possessions. Family life. Rhyming text. Teeth.

Please, Malese! a trickster tale from Haiti ill. by Emily Lisker. DK, 2001. ISBN 978-0-7894-2647-5 Subj: Behavior – trickery. Folk & fairy tales. Foreign lands – Haiti.

Quentin Fenton Herter three ill. by Giselle Potter. Farrar, 2002. ISBN 978-0-374-36170-9 Subj: Behavior. Behavior – misbehavior. Humorous stories. Rhyming text. Shadows.

Rachel Fister's blister ill. by Marjorie Priceman. Houghton, 1990. ISBN 978-0-395-52152-6 Subj: Illness. Rhyming text.

MacDonald, Elizabeth. *The wolf is coming!* ill. by Ken Brown. Dutton, 1998. ISBN 978-0-525-45952-1 Subj: Animals. Animals – rabbits. Animals – wolves. Cumulative tales.

MacDonald, Golden *see* Brown, Margaret Wise

MacDonald, Margaret Read. *Conejito: a folktale from Panama* ill. by Geraldo Valério. August House, 2006. ISBN 978-0-87483-779-7 Subj: Animals – rabbits. Behavior – trickery. Folk & fairy tales. Foreign lands – Panama. Foreign languages.

Fat cat ill. by Julie Paschkis. August House, 2001. ISBN 978-0-87483-616-5 Subj: Animals – cats. Animals – mice. Folk & fairy tales. Foreign lands – Denmark.

The girl who wore too much Thai text by Supaporn Vathanaprida; ill. by Yvonne Davis. August House, 1998. ISBN 978-0-87483-503-8 Subj: Character traits – vanity. Clothing. Folk & fairy tales. Foreign lands – Thailand.

Give up, Gecko! a folktale from Uganda ill. by Deborah Melmon. Amazon/Two Lions, 2013. ISBN 978-1-4778-1635-6 Subj: Animals. Character traits – perseverance. Folk & fairy tales. Foreign lands – Uganda. Reptiles. Water.

The great smelly, slobbery small-toothed dog ill. by Julie Paschkis. Random House, 2007. ISBN 978-0-87483-808-4 Subj: Animals – dogs. Character traits – appearance. Emotions – love. Folk & fairy tales. Magic.

A hen, a chick, and a string guitar ill. by Sophie Fatus. Barefoot, 2005. ISBN 978-1-84148-796-0 Subj: Animals. Counting, numbers. Cumulative tales. Folk & fairy tales. Songs.

How many donkeys? an Arabic counting tale by Margaret Read MacDonald and Nadia Jameel Taibah ill. by Carol Liddiment. Albert Whitman, 2009. ISBN 978-0-8075-3424-3 Subj: Counting, numbers. Folk & fairy tales. Foreign lands – Saudi Arabia. Foreign languages.

Little Rooster's diamond button ill. by Will Terry. Albert Whitman, 2007. ISBN 978-0-8075-4644-4 Subj: Behavior – greed. Birds – chickens, roosters. Clothing. Folk & fairy tales. Foreign lands – Hungary. Royalty – kings.

Mabela the clever ill. by Tim Coffey. Albert Whitman, 2001. ISBN 978-0-8075-4902-5 Subj: Animals – cats. Animals – mice. Folk & fairy tales. Foreign lands – Africa.

The old woman who lived in a vinegar bottle ill. by Nancy Dunaway Fowlkes. August House, 1995. ISBN 978-0-87483-415-4 Subj: Behavior – dissatisfaction. Folk & fairy tales. Foreign lands – England.

Pickin' peas ill. by Pat Cummings. HarperCollins, 1998. ISBN 978-0-06-027970-7 Subj: Animals – rabbits. Behavior – trickery. Ethnic groups in the U.S. – African Americans. Folk & fairy tales. Gardens, gardening.

Slop! a Welsh folktale ill. by Yvonne Davis. Fulcrum Kids, 1997. ISBN 978-1-55591-352-6 Subj: Character traits – kindness. Fairies. Folk & fairy tales. Foreign lands – Wales.

The squeaky door ill. by Mary Newell DePalma. HarperCollins, 2006. ISBN 978-0-06-028373-5 Subj: Animals. Bedtime. Cumulative tales. Emotions – fear. Family life – grandmothers. Folk & fairy tales. Noise, sounds.

Surf war! a folktale from the Marshall Islands ill. by Geraldo Valério. August House, 2009. ISBN 978-0-87483-889-3 Subj: Ecology. Folk & fairy tales. Foreign lands. Sea & seashore.

Teeny Weeny Bop ill. by Diane Greenseid. Albert Whitman, 2006. ISBN 978-0-8075-7992-3 Subj: Cumulative tales. Folk & fairy tales.

Too many fairies: a Celtic tale ill. by Susan Mitchell. Marshall Cavendish, 2010. ISBN 978-0-7614-5604-9 Subj: Fairies. Folk & fairy tales.

Tuck-me-in tales ill. by Yvonne Davis. August House, 1996. ISBN 978-0-87483-461-1 Subj: Bedtime. Folk & fairy tales.

Tunjur! Tunjur! Tunjur! a Palestinian folktale ill. by Alik Arzoumanian. Marshall Cavendish, 2006. ISBN 978-0-7614-5225-6 Subj: Behavior – stealing. Folk & fairy tales. Foreign lands – Palestine.

MacDonald, Maryann. *The Christmas cat* ill. by Amy Bates. Dial, 2013. ISBN 978-0-8037-3498-2 Subj: Animals – cats. Religion – Nativity.

How to hug ill. by Jana Christy. Marshall Cavendish, 2011. ISBN 978-0-7614-5804-3 Subj: Hugging.

The little piano girl: the story of Mary Lou Williams, jazz legend (Ingalls, Ann)

The pink party ill. by Judy Stead. Marshall Cavendish, 2011. ISBN 978-0-7614-5814-2 Subj: Concepts – color. Emotions – envy, jealousy. Friendship.

McDonald, Megan. *Ant and Honey Bee, what a pair!* ill. by G. Brian Karas. Candlewick, 2005. ISBN 978-0-7636-1265-8 Subj: Clothing – costumes. Insects – ants. Insects – bees. Parties.

Beetle McGrady eats bugs! ill. by Jane Manning. HarperCollins, 2005. ISBN 978-0-06-001355-4 Subj: Character traits – bravery. Food. Insects. School.

The great pumpkin switch ill. by Ted Lewin. Watts, 1992. ISBN 978-0-531-08600-1 Subj: Family life – grandfathers. Mystery stories. Plants.

Hen hears gossip ill. by Joung Un Kim. Greenwillow, 2008. ISBN 978-0-06-113876-8 Subj: Animals. Behavior – gossip, rumors. Birds – chickens, roosters.

The Hinky Pink: an old tale ill. by Brian Floca. Atheneum, 2008. ISBN 978-0-689-87588-5 Subj: Activities – sewing. Clothing – dresses. Folk & fairy tales. Mythical creatures – goblins. Royalty – princesses.

Insects are my life ill. by Paul Brett Johnson. Orchard, 1995. ISBN 978-0-531-08724-4 Subj: Behavior – collecting things. Family life. Insects. School.

Is this a house for Hermit Crab? ill. by S. D. Schindler. Watts, 1990. ISBN 978-0-531-08455-7 Subj: Crustaceans – crabs. Sea & seashore.

It's picture day today! ill. by Katherine Tillotson. Atheneum, 2009. ISBN 978-1-4169-2434-0 Subj: Activities – making things. Art. Rhyming text. School.

Penguin and Little Blue ill. by Katherine Tillotson. Atheneum, 2003. ISBN 978-0-689-84415-7 Subj: Birds – penguins. Foreign lands – Antarctic. Theater.

Reptiles are my life ill. by Paul Brett Johnson. Orchard, 2001. ISBN 978-0-439-29306-8 Subj: Friendship. Insects. Reptiles. School.

Shoe dog ill. by Katherine Tillotson. Atheneum/Richard Jackson, 2014. ISBN 978-141697932-6 Subj: Animals – dogs. Character traits – kindness to animals. Clothing – shoes. Pets.

When the library lights go out ill. by Katherine Tillotson. Simon & Schuster, 2005. ISBN 978-0-689-86170-3 Subj: Animals. Behavior – lost. Libraries. Light, lights. Puppets.

Whoo-oo is it? ill. by S. D. Schindler. Watts, 1992. ISBN 978-0-531-08574-5 Subj: Birds – owls. Night. Noise, sounds.

McDonald, Rae A. *A fishing surprise* ill. by Kathleen Kemly. NorthWord, 2007. ISBN 978-1-55971-977-3 Subj: Family life – brothers & sisters. Food. Rhyming text. Sports – fishing.

MacDonald, Ross. *Achoo! Bang! Crash!* ill. by author. Roaring Brook, 2003. ISBN 978-0-7613-2900-8 Subj: ABC books. Language. Noise, sounds.

Another perfect day ill. by author. Roaring Brook, 2002. ISBN 978-0-7613-2659-5 Subj: Dreams.

Bad baby ill. by author. Macmillan, 2005. ISBN 978-1-59643-064-8 Subj: Babies, toddlers. Concepts – size. Family life – brothers & sisters. Family life – new sibling.

MacDonald, Suse. *Alphabatics* ill. by author. Bradbury, 1986. ISBN 978-0-02-761520-3 Subj: ABC books. Caldecott award honor books.

Circus opposites: an interactive extravaganza! ill. by author. Simon & Schuster, 2010. ISBN 978-1-4169-7154-2 Subj: Circus. Concepts – opposites. Format, unusual – toy & movable books.

Edward Lear's A was once an apple pie ill. by adapter. Scholastic, 2005. ISBN 978-0-439-66056-3 Subj: ABC books. Poetry.

Elephants on board ill. by author. Harcourt, 1999. ISBN 978-0-15-200951-9 Subj: Animals – elephants. Circus. Machines. Rhyming text. Transportation. Trucks.

Fish, swish! splash, dash! counting round and round ill. by author. Simon & Schuster, 2007. ISBN 978-1-4169-3605-3 Subj: Counting, numbers. Fish. Format, unusual.

Look whooo's counting ill. by author. Scholastic, 2000. ISBN 978-0-590-68320-3 Subj: Animals. Counting, numbers. Picture puzzles.

Shape by shape ill. by author. Simon & Schuster, 2009. ISBN 978-1-4169-7147-4 Subj: Concepts – shape. Dinosaurs. Format, unusual.

McDonnell, Christine. *Dog wants to play* ill. by Jeff Mack. Viking, 2009. ISBN 978-0-670-01126-1 Subj: Activities – playing. Animals. Animals – dogs.

Goyangi means cat ill. by Steve Johnson and Lou Fancher. Penguin, 2011. ISBN 978-0-670-01179-7 Subj: Adoption. Animals – cats. Behavior – lost & found possessions. Emotions – loneliness. Ethnic groups in the U.S. – Korean Americans.

McDonnell, Flora. *Flora McDonnell's ABC* ill. by author. Candlewick, 1997. ISBN 978-0-7636-0118-8 Subj: ABC books.

Giddy-up! Let's ride! ill. by author. Candlewick, 2002. ISBN 978-0-7636-1778-3 Subj: Animals. Animals – horses, ponies.

I love animals ill. by author. Candlewick, 1994. ISBN 978-1-56402-387-2 Subj: Animals. Character traits – kindness to animals. Farms.

I love boats ill. by author. Candlewick, 1995. ISBN 978-1-56402-539-5 Subj: Activities – bathing. Boats, ships. Toys.

Sparky ill. by author. Candlewick, 2004. ISBN 978-0-7636-2208-4 Subj: Animals – dogs. Pets.

Splash! ill. by author. Candlewick, 1999. ISBN 978-0-7636-0481-3 Subj: Animals. Animals – elephants. Water.

McDonnell, Patrick. *Art* ill. by author. Little, Brown, 2006. ISBN 978-0-316-11491-2 Subj: Activities – drawing. Art. Rhyming text.

The gift of nothing ill. by author. Little, Brown, 2005. ISBN 978-0-316-11488-2 Subj: Animals – cats. Animals – dogs. Friendship. Gifts.

Just like Heaven ill. by author. Little, Brown, 2006. ISBN 978-0-316-11493-6 Subj: Animals – cats. Animals – dogs. Weather – fog.

The little red cat who ran away and learned his ABC's (the hard way) ill. by author. Little, Brown, 2017. ISBN 978-031650246-7 Subj: ABC books. Animals – cats. Behavior – running away. Wordless.

Me . . . Jane ill. by author. Little, Brown, 2011. ISBN 978-0-316-04546-9 Subj: Animals. Animals – chimpanzees. Caldecott award honor books. Careers – scientists. Nature. Toys.

The monsters' monster ill. by author. Little, Brown, 2012. ISBN 978-0-316-04547-6 Subj: Behavior – misbehavior. Monsters.

A perfectly messed-up story ill. by author. Little, Brown, 2014. ISBN 978-031622258-7 Subj: Behavior – messy. Books, reading. Character traits – orderliness. Emotions – anger.

Shine! ill. by Naoko Stoop. Little, Brown/Megan Tingley, 2017. ISBN 978-031626278-1 Subj: Behavior – dissatisfaction. Self-concept. Starfishes.

South ill. by author. Little, Brown, 2008. ISBN 978-0-316-00509-8 Subj: Animals – cats. Birds. Emotions – loneliness. Wordless.

Tek: the modern cave boy ill. by author. Little, Brown, 2016. ISBN 978-031633805-9 Subj: Cave dwellers. Prehistory. Technology.

Thank you and good night ill. by author. Little, Brown, 2015. ISBN 978-031633801-1 Subj: Bedtime. Character traits – kindness. Friendship. Sleepovers.

Wag! ill. by author. Little, Brown, 2009. ISBN 978-0-316-04548-3 Subj: Anatomy – tails. Animals – cats. Animals – dogs.

McDonough, Yona Zeldis. *Hammerin' Hank: the life of Hank Greenberg* ill. by Malcah Zeldis. Walker, 2006. ISBN 978-0-8027-8997-6 Subj: Jewish culture. Sports – baseball.

McElligott, Matthew. *Backbeard and the birthday suit: the hairiest pirate who ever lived* ill. by author. Walker, 2006. ISBN 978-0-8027-8065-2 Subj: Birthdays. Character traits – cleanliness. Clothing. Hair. Parties. Pirates.

Bean thirteen ill. by author. Penguin, 2007. ISBN 978-0-399-24535-0 Subj: Counting, numbers. Insects.

Even aliens need snacks ill. by author. Walker, 2012. ISBN 978-0-8027-2398-7 Subj: Activities – baking, cooking. Aliens. Food.

Even monsters need haircuts ill. by author. Walker, 2010. ISBN 978-0-8027-8819-1 Subj: Careers – barbers. Monsters.

The lion's share ill. by author. Walker, 2009. ISBN 978-0-8027-9768-1 Subj: Animals – lions. Behavior – misbehavior. Counting, numbers. Etiquette. Insects – ants.

McElmurry, Jill. *I'm not a baby!* ill. by author. Random House, 2006. ISBN 978-0-375-93614-2 Subj: Babies, toddlers. Behavior – growing up. Humorous stories.

Mad about plaid ill. by author. Morrow, 2000. ISBN 978-0-688-16952-7 Subj: Behavior – lost & found possessions. Clothing – handbags, purses. Concepts – patterns.

Mario makes a move ill. by author. Random House, 2012. ISBN 978-0-375-86854-2 Subj: Activities – dancing. Animals – squirrels.

Mess pets ill. by author. SeaStar, 2002. ISBN 978-1-58717-175-8 Subj: Character traits – cleanliness. Character traits – orderliness. Family life – sisters. Health & fitness. Multiple births – twins.

McElroy, Lisa Tucker. *Love, Lizzie: letters to a military mom* ill. by Diane Paterson. Albert Whitman, 2005. ISBN 978-0-8075-4777-9 Subj: Careers – military. Emotions – loneliness. Family life – mothers. Letters, cards. War.

Meet my grandmother. She's a children's book author by Lisa Tucker McElroy and Abigail Jane Cobb; photos by Joel Benjamin. Millbrook, 2001. ISBN 978-0-7613-1972-6 Subj: Activities – writing. Careers – writers. Family life – grandmothers.

McEvoy, Anne. *Betsy B. Little* ill. by Jacqueline Rogers. HarperCollins, 2009. ISBN 978-0-06-059337-7 Subj: Animals – giraffes. Ballet. Concepts – size. Rhyming text. Self-concept.

McFarland, Clive. *A bed for Bear* ill. by author. HarperCollins, 2014. ISBN 978-006223705-7 Subj: Animals. Animals – bears. Bedtime. Forest, woods. Hibernation.

Caterpillar dreams ill. by author. HarperCollins, 2017. ISBN 978-006238636-6 Subj: Insects – butterflies, caterpillars.

The fox and the wild ill. by author. Candlewick/Templar, 2017. ISBN 978-076369648-1 Subj: Animals – foxes. Cities, towns. Forest, woods.

McFarland, Lyn Rossiter. *Mouse went out to get a snack* ill. by Jim McFarland. Farrar, 2005. ISBN 978-0-374-37672-7 Subj: Animals – mice. Counting, numbers. Food.

The pirate's parrot ill. by Jim McFarland. Tricycle, 2000. ISBN 978-1-58246-014-7 Subj: Behavior – fighting, arguing. Behavior – mistakes. Birds – parakeets, parrots. Pirates. Toys – bears.

Widget and the puppy ill. by Jim McFarland. Farrar, 2004. ISBN 978-0-374-38429-6 Subj: Animals – cats. Animals – dogs. Behavior – lost.

McFarlane, Sheryl. *In the city* ill. by Kim LaFave. Fitzhenry & Whiteside, 2004. ISBN 978-1-55041-812-5 Subj: Cities, towns. Format, unusual – board books. Noise, sounds.

On the farm ill. by Kim LaFave. Fitzhenry & Whiteside, 2004. ISBN 978-1-55041-814-9 Subj: Animals. Farms. Format, unusual – board books. Noise, sounds.

McG, Shane. *Tennis, anyone?* ill. by author. Carolrhoda, 2007. ISBN 978-0-8225-6901-5 Subj: Sports – tennis.

McGaw, Wayne T. *T-boy of the bayou* ill. by George Crespo. Carolrhoda, 2002. ISBN 978-0-87614-648-4 Subj: Birds – herons. Careers – fishermen. Crustaceans – shrimp. Fish. Magic.

McGee, Joe. *Peanut butter and brains: a zombie culinary tale* ill. by Charles Santoso. Abrams/Appleseed, 2015. ISBN 978-141971247-0 Subj: Food. Monsters.

McGee, Marni. *The colt and the king* ill. by John Winch. Holiday, 2002. ISBN 978-0-8234-1695-0 Subj: Animals – donkeys. Holidays. Religion.

The noisy farm ill. by Leonie Shearing. Bloomsbury, 2004. ISBN 978-1-58234-879-7 Subj: Animals. Day. Farms. Noise, sounds.

Sleepy me ill. by Sam Williams. Simon & Schuster, 2001. ISBN 978-0-689-82378-7 Subj: Bedtime. Family life – fathers. Rhyming text.

Wake up, me! ill. by Sam Williams. Simon & Schuster, 2002. ISBN 978-0-689-83163-8 Subj: Behavior. Family life – parents. Morning. Rhyming text.

Winston the book wolf ill. by Ian Beck. Walker, 2006. ISBN 978-0-8027-9569-4 Subj: Animals – wolves. Books, reading. Libraries.

McGhee, Alison. *Always* ill. by Pascal Lemaître. Simon & Schuster, 2009. ISBN 978-1-4169-7481-9 Subj: Animals – dogs. Character traits – loyalty. Pets.

Bye-bye, crib ill. by Ross MacDonald. Simon & Schuster, 2008. ISBN 978-1-4169-1621-5 Subj: Behavior – growing up. Furniture – beds.

The case of the missing donut ill. by Isabel Roxas. Dial, 2013. ISBN 978-0-8037-3925-3 Subj: Activities – playing. Food. Humorous stories.

Countdown to kindergarten ill. by Harry Bliss. Harcourt, 2002. ISBN 978-0-15-202516-8 Subj: Emotions – fear. School – first day.

In the hollow of your hand ill. by Michael Cummings. Houghton, 2000. ISBN 978-0-395-85755-7 Subj: Ethnic groups in the U.S. – African Americans. Lullabies. Slavery. Sleep.

Little boy ill. by Peter H. Reynolds. Atheneum, 2008. ISBN 978-1-4169-5872-7 Subj: Behavior – growing up. Family life – fathers.

Making a friend ill. by Marc Rosenthal. Simon & Schuster, 2011. ISBN 978-1-4169-8998-1 Subj: Friendship. Seasons. Snowmen. Water.

Only a witch can fly ill. by Taeeun Yoo. Feiwel & Friends, 2009. ISBN 978-0-312-37503-4 Subj: Activities – flying. Character traits – persistence. Holidays – Halloween. Poetry.

Percy, dog of destiny ill. by Jennifer K. Mann. Boyds Mills, 2017. ISBN 978-159078984-1 Subj: Activities – playing. Animals – dogs. Parks.

So many days ill. by Taeeun Yoo. Simon & Schuster, 2010. ISBN 978-1-4169-5857-4 Subj: Self-concept.

Someday ill. by Peter H. Reynolds. Simon & Schuster, 2006. ISBN 978-1-4169-2811-9 Subj: Behavior – growing up. Family life – mothers.

Song of middle C ill. by Scott Menchin. Candlewick, 2009. ISBN 978-0-7636-3013-3 Subj: Emotions – fear. Imagination. Music. Musical instruments – pianos.

Star bright: a Christmas story ill. by Peter H. Reynolds. Atheneum, 2014. ISBN 978-141695858-1 Subj: Angels. Gifts. Holidays – Christmas. Religion – Nativity. Stars.

The sweetest witch around ill. by Harry Bliss. Simon & Schuster/Paula Wiseman, 2014. ISBN 978-144247833-6 Subj: Character traits – bravery. Character traits – curiosity. Family life – sisters. Holidays – Halloween. Witches.

Tell me a tattoo story ill. by Eliza Wheeler. Chronicle, 2016. ISBN 978-145211937-3 Subj: Activities – storytelling. Anatomy – skin. Art. Family life – fathers.

A very brave witch ill. by Harry Bliss. Simon & Schuster, 2006. ISBN 978-0-689-86730-9 Subj: Character traits – bravery. Holidays – Halloween. Witches.

McGill, Alice. *Molly Bannaky* ill. by Chris Soentpiet. Houghton, 1999. ISBN 978-0-395-72287-9 Subj: Books, reading. Ethnic groups in the U.S. – African Americans. Farms. Immigrants, immigration. Marriage, interracial. Slavery. U.S. history.

Sure as sunrise: stories of Bruh Rabbit and his walkin' talkin' friends ill. by Don Tate. Houghton, 2004. ISBN 978-0-618-21196-8 Subj: Animals. Ethnic groups in the U.S. – African Americans. Folk & fairy tales. Tall tales.

Way up and over everything ill. by Jude Daly. Houghton, 2008. ISBN 978-0-618-38796-0 Subj: Activities – flying. Ethnic groups in the U.S. – African Americans. Folk & fairy tales. Slavery.

McGill, Erin. *I do not like Al's hat* ill. by author. Greenwillow, 2017. ISBN 978-006245576-5 Subj: Animals – rabbits. Careers – magicians. Humorous stories.

McGinley, Phyllis. *The year without a Santa Claus* ill. by John Manders. Marshall Cavendish, 2010. ISBN 978-0-7614-5799-2 Subj: Character traits – generosity. Gifts. Holidays – Christmas. Rhyming text. Santa Claus.

McGinley-Nally, Sharon. *The friendly beasts* ill. by author. Greenwillow, 2000. ISBN 978-0-688-17422-4 Subj: Animals. Holidays – Christmas. Music. Religion – Nativity. Songs.

McGinness, Suzanne. *My bear Griz* ill. by author. Frances Lincoln, 2011. ISBN 978-1-84780-113-5 Subj: Animals – bears. Toys – bears.

McGinty, Alice B. *Eliza's kindergarten pet* ill. by Nancy Speir. Marshall Cavendish, 2010. ISBN 978-0-7614-5702-2 Subj: Animals – guinea pigs. Behavior – lost & found possessions. Behavior – worrying. School.

Eliza's kindergarten surprise ill. by Nancy Speir. Marshall Cavendish, 2007. ISBN 978-0-7614-5351-2 Subj: Behavior – collecting things. Family life – mothers. School – first day.

Gandhi: a march to the sea ill. by Thomas Gonzalez. Amazon/Two Lions, 2013. ISBN 978-1-4778-1644-8 Subj: Behavior – seeking better things. Character traits – perseverance. Foreign lands – India. Violence, nonviolence.

Ten little lambs ill. by Melissa Sweet. Dial, 2002. ISBN 978-0-8037-2596-6 Subj: Animals – sheep. Counting, numbers. Night. Rhyming text. Sleep.

Thank you, world ill. by Wendy Anderson Halperin. Penguin, 2007. ISBN 978-0-8037-2705-2 Subj: Rhyming text. World.

McGough, Roger. *What on earth can it be?* ill. by Lydia Monks. Simon & Schuster, 2002. ISBN 978-0-689-85351-7 Subj: Humorous stories. Poetry. Rhyming text.

McGovern, Ann. *Too much noise* ill. by Simms Taback. Houghton, 1967. ISBN 978-0-590-02435-8 Subj: Humorous stories. Noise, sounds.

McGowan, Jayme. *One bear extraordinaire* ill. by author. Abrams, 2015. ISBN 978-141971654-6 Subj: Animals. Animals – bears. Music. Musical instruments – bands.

McGowan, Michael. *Sunday is for God* ill. by Steve Johnson and Lou Fancher. Random House, 2010. ISBN 978-0-375-84188-0 Subj: Church. Days of the week, months of the year. Ethnic groups in the U.S. – African Americans. Family life. Religion.

McGrath, Barbara Barbieri. *Kellogg's froot loops color fun book* ill. by Frank Mazzola. HarperCollins, 2001. ISBN 978-0-694-01577-1 Subj: Concepts – color. Food. Format, unusual – board books. Picture puzzles. Rhyming text.

Kellogg's froot loops counting fun book ill. by Rob Bolster and Frank Mazzola, Jr. HarperCollins, 2000. ISBN 978-0-694-01506-1 Subj: Counting, numbers. Food. Rhyming text.

The little gray bunny ill. by Violet Kim. Charlesbridge, 2013. ISBN 978-1-58089-394-7 Subj: Animals. Animals – rabbits. Character traits – laziness. Farms. Holidays – Easter.

The little green witch ill. by Martha G. Alexander. Charlesbridge, 2005. ISBN 978-1-58089-042-7 Subj: Character traits – laziness. Plants. Witches.

Teddy bear addition ill. by Tim Nihoff. Charlesbridge, 2014. ISBN 978-158089424-1 Subj: Counting, numbers. Rhyming text. Toys – bears.

Teddy bear counting ill. by Tim Nihoff. Charlesbridge, 2010. ISBN 978-1-58089-215-5 Subj: Concepts – color. Concepts – shape. Counting, numbers. Rhyming text. Toys – bears.

McGraw, Sheila. *Pussycats everywhere* ill. by author. Firefly, 2000. ISBN 978-1-55209-346-7 Subj: Animals – cats. Behavior – lost. Humorous stories.

MacGregor, Roy. *The highest number in the world* ill. by Geneviève Després. Tundra, 2014. ISBN 978-177049575-3 Subj: Family life – grandmothers. Foreign lands – Canada. Gender roles. Sports – hockey.

McGrory, Anik. *Kidogo* ill. by author. Bloomsbury, 2005. ISBN 978-1-58234-974-9 Subj: Animals – elephants. Character traits – smallness. Concepts – size. Foreign lands – Africa.

Mouton's impossible dream ill. by author. Harcourt, 2000. ISBN 978-0-15-202195-5 Subj: Activities – ballooning. Animals – sheep. Behavior – wishing. Birds. Royalty – queens.

McGuinness-Kelly, Tracy-Lee. *Bad Cat puts on his top hat* ill. by author. Little, 2005. ISBN 978-0-316-60547-2 Subj: Animals – cats. Behavior – trickery.

McGuirk, Leslie. *Ho, ho, ho, Tucker!* ill. by author. Candlewick, 2005. ISBN 978-0-7636-2582-5 Subj: Animals – dogs. Holidays – Christmas. Santa Claus.

If rocks could sing: a discovered alphabet ill. by author. Tricycle, 2011. ISBN 978-1-58246-370-4 Subj: ABC books. Rocks.

Lucky Tucker ill. by author. Candlewick, 2008. ISBN 978-0-7636-3389-9 Subj: Animals – dogs. Character traits – luck. Holidays – St. Patrick's Day.

Snail boy ill. by author. Candlewick, 2003. ISBN 978-0-7636-1259-7 Subj: Animals – snails. Behavior – needing someone. Concepts – size.

Tucker flips! ill. by author. Dutton, 1999. ISBN 978-0-525-46259-0 Subj: Activities – playing. Animals – dogs. Weather – snow.

Tucker off his rocker ill. by author. Dutton, 2000. ISBN 978-0-525-46398-6 Subj: Activities. Animals – dogs.

Tucker over the top ill. by author. Dutton, 2000. ISBN 978-0-525-46465-5 Subj: Animals – dogs. Circus.

Tucker's spooky Halloween ill. by author. Candlewick, 2007. ISBN 978-0-7636-3181-9 Subj: Animals – dogs. Clothing – costumes. Holidays – Halloween.

Machado, Ana Maria. *What a party!* ill. by Helene Moreau. Groundwood, 2013. ISBN 978-1-55498-

168-7 Subj: Birthdays. Communities, neighborhoods. Food. Parties.

Wolf wanted ill. by Laurent Cardon. Groundwood, 2010. ISBN 978-0-88899-880-4 Subj: Animals – wolves. Folk & fairy tales.

MacHale, D. J. *The monster princess* ill. by Alexandra Boiger. Simon & Schuster, 2010. ISBN 978-1-4169-4809-4 Subj: Monsters. Royalty – princesses. Self-concept.

McHenry, E. B. *Has anyone seen Winnie and Jean?* ill. by author. Bloomsbury, 2007. ISBN 978-1-58234-999-2 Subj: Animals – dogs. Behavior – lost. Behavior – running away.

Poodlena ill. by author. Bloomsbury, 2004. ISBN 978-1-58234-824-7 Subj: Activities – playing. Animals – dogs. Character traits – cleanliness. Rhyming text.

Mack, Jeff. *Ah ha!* ill. by author. Chronicle, 2013. ISBN 978-1-4521-1265-7 Subj: Cumulative tales. Frogs & toads.

Duck in the fridge ill. by author. Amazon/Two Lions, 2014. ISBN 978-147784776-3 Subj: Animals. Bedtime. Behavior – misbehavior. Birds – ducks. Books, reading. Family life – fathers.

Frog and Fly: six slurpy stories ill. by author. Philomel, 2012. ISBN 978-0-399-25617-2 Subj: Frogs & toads. Humorous stories. Insects – flies.

Good news, bad news ill. by author. Chronicle, 2012. ISBN 978-1-4521-0110-1 Subj: Activities – picnicking. Animals – mice. Animals – rabbits. Behavior – bad day, bad mood. Character traits – optimism.

Hush little polar bear ill. by author. Roaring Brook, 2008. ISBN 978-1-59643-368-7 Subj: Bedtime. Dreams. Rhyming text. Toys – bears.

Look! ill. by author. Philomel, 2015. ISBN 978-039916205-3 Subj: Animals – gorillas. Books, reading.

Mine! ill. by author. Chronicle, 2017. ISBN 978-145215234-9 Subj: Animals – mice. Behavior – fighting, arguing.

Playtime? ill. by author. Philomel, 2016. ISBN 978-039917598-5 Subj: Activities – playing. Animals – gorillas. Bedtime. Humorous stories.

The things I can do ill. by author. Roaring Brook, 2013. ISBN 978-1-59643-675-6 Subj: Books, reading. Character traits – confidence. Rhyming text. Self-concept.

Who needs a bath? ill. by author. HarperCollins, 2015. ISBN 978-006222028-8 Subj: Activities – bathing. Animals – bears. Animals – skunks. Parties. Senses – smell.

Who wants a hug? ill. by author. HarperCollins, 2015. ISBN 978-006222026-4 Subj: Animals – bears. Animals – skunks. Hugging.

Mack, Todd. *Princess Penelope* ill. by Julia Gran. Scholastic, 2003. ISBN 978-0-439-22436-9 Subj: Family life – parents. Royalty – princesses.

Mackall, Dandi Daley. *A girl named Dan* ill. by Renée Graef. Sleeping Bear, 2008. ISBN 978-1-58536-351-3 Subj: Gender roles. Sports – baseball. U.S. history.

Off to Bethlehem! ill. by R. W. Alley. HarperCollins, 2002. ISBN 978-0-694-01505-4 Subj: Religion – Nativity. Rhyming text.

Seeing stars ill. by Claudine Gevry. Simon & Schuster, 2006. ISBN 978-1-4169-0361-1 Subj: Stars.

The story of the Easter robin ill. by Anna Vojtech. Zonderkidz, 2010. ISBN 978-0-310-71331-9 Subj: Birds – robins. Family life – grandmothers. Holidays – Easter. Religion.

There's a baby in there! ill. by Carlynn Whitt. Amazon, 2012. ISBN 978-0-7614-6191-3 Subj: Babies, toddlers. Birth. Family life – new sibling.

MacKay, Elly. *If you hold a seed* ill. by author. Running Press, 2013. ISBN 978-0-7624-4721-3 Subj: Character traits – patience, impatience. Seeds. Trees.

Waltz of the snowflakes ill. by author. Running Press, 2017. ISBN 978-076245338-2 Subj: Ballet. Family life – grandmothers. Holidays – Christmas. Theater. Wordless.

McKay, Hilary. *Pirates ahoy!* ill. by Alex Ayliffe. Margaret K. McElderry, 2000. ISBN 978-0-689-83114-0 Subj: Activities – playing. Family life – cousins. Family life – grandmothers. Imagination.

McKay, Jodi. *Where are the words?* ill. by Denise Holmes. Albert Whitman, 2016. ISBN 978-080758733-1 Subj: Language.

McKay, Sindy. *About the rain forest* (Johanasen, Heather)

McKee, David. *Elmer* ill. by author. Lothrop, 1989. ISBN 978-0-688-09172-9 Subj: Animals – elephants. Character traits – being different.

Elmer again ill. by author. Lothrop, 1991. ISBN 978-0-688-11597-5 Subj: Animals – elephants. Behavior – boredom.

Elmer and Butterfly ill. by author. Andersen, 2015. ISBN 978-146776326-4 Subj: Animals – elephants. Character traits – helpfulness. Insects – butterflies, caterpillars.

Elmer and Grandpa Eldo ill. by author. Andersen, 2016. ISBN 978-151240569-9 Subj: Animals – elephants. Family life – grandfathers. Memories, memory.

Elmer and Rose ill. by author. Andersen, 2010. ISBN 978-0-7613-5493-2 Subj: Animals – elephants. Character traits – being different. Character traits – individuality.

Elmer and Snake ill. by author. Andersen, 2013. ISBN 978-1-46772-033-5 Subj: Animals – elephants. Behavior – trickery. Reptiles – snakes. Riddles & jokes.

Elmer and Super El ill. by author. Andersen, 2012. ISBN 978-0-7613-8989-7 Subj: Activities – sewing. Animals. Animals – elephants. Clothing.

Elmer and the big bird ill. by author. Andersen, 2012. ISBN 978-1-46770319-2 Subj: Animals – elephants. Behavior – bullying, teasing. Birds. Character traits – cooperation.

Elmer and the flood ill. by author. Andersen, 2015. ISBN 978-146779312-4 Subj: Animals – elephants. Behavior – resourcefulness. Behavior – solitude. Weather – floods. Weather – rain.

Elmer and the hippos ill. by author. Andersen, 2010. ISBN 978-0-7613-6442-9 Subj: Animals – elephants. Animals – hippopotamuses. Character traits – cooperation. Problem solving.

Elmer and the kangaroo ill. by author. HarperCollins, 2000. ISBN 978-0-688-17951-9 Subj: Animals – elephants. Animals – kangaroos. Self-concept.

Elmer and the lost teddy ill. by author. Lothrop, 1999. ISBN 978-0-688-16912-1 Subj: Animals – elephants. Behavior – lost & found possessions. Toys – bears.

Elmer and the monster ill. by author. Andersen, 2014. ISBN 978-146774200-9 Subj: Animals – elephants. Emotions – fear. Monsters.

Elmer and the race ill. by author. Andersen, 2016. ISBN 978-151246124-4 Subj: Animals – elephants. Behavior – cheating. Contests. Sports – racing.

Elmer and the whales ill. by author. Andersen, 2014. ISBN 978-146773453-0 Subj: Animals – elephants. Animals – whales. Family life – cousins.

Elmer and the wind ill. by author. Lothrop, 1998. Subj: Activities – flying. Animals – elephants. Weather – wind.

Elmer and Wilbur ill. by author. Lothrop, 1996. ISBN 978-0-688-14934-5 Subj: Animals – elephants. Behavior – lost. Friendship.

Elmer in the snow ill. by author. Lothrop, 1995. ISBN 978-0-688-14596-5 Subj: Activities – playing. Animals – elephants. Friendship. Weather – snow.

Elmer takes off ill. by author. Lothrop, 1998. ISBN 978-0-688-15785-2 Subj: Activities – flying. Animals – elephants. Weather – wind.

Elmer's Christmas ill. by author. Lerner/Kar-Ben, 2011. ISBN 978-0-7613-8088-7 Subj: Animals – elephants. Holidays – Christmas.

Elmer's special day ill. by author. Andersen, 2009. ISBN 978-0-7613-5154-2 Subj: Animals. Animals – elephants. Parades.

Six men ill. by author. NorthSouth, 2011. ISBN 978-0-7358-4050-8 Subj: War.

McKellar, Danica. *Goodnight, numbers* ill. by Alicia Padrón. Crown, 2017. ISBN 978-110193378-7 Subj: Bedtime. Counting, numbers.

McKelvey, Douglas Kaine. *Locust pocus* ill. by Richard Egielski. Philomel, 2001. ISBN 978-0-399-23452-1 Subj: Insects. Rhyming text.

Macken, JoAnn Early. *Baby says "moo!"* ill. by David Walker. Hyperion/Disney, 2011. ISBN 978-1-4231-3400-8 Subj: Babies, toddlers. Noise, sounds. Rhyming text.

Flip, float, fly: seeds on the move ill. by Pamela Paparone. Holiday, 2008. ISBN 978-0-8234-2043-8 Subj: Seeds.

Waiting out the storm ill. by Susan Gaber. Candlewick, 2010. ISBN 978-0-7636-3378-3 Subj: Family life – mothers. Rhyming text. Weather – rain. Weather – storms.

McKenna, Martin. *The octopuppy* ill. by author. Scholastic, 2015. ISBN 978-054575140-7 Subj: Humorous stories. Octopuses. Pets.

McKenna, Sharon. *Good morning, sunshine: a grandpa story* ill. by author. Red Cygnet, 2007. ISBN 978-1-60108-003-5 Subj: Family life – grandfathers.

McKinlay, Meg. *No bears* ill. by Leila Rudge. Candlewick, 2012. ISBN 978-0-7636-5890-8 Subj: Activities – storytelling. Animals – bears. Royalty – princesses.

McKinlay, Penny. *Flabby Tabby* ill. by Britta Teckentrup. Frances Lincoln, 2006. ISBN 978-1-84507-090-8 Subj: Animals – cats. Health & fitness – exercise.

McKinley, Cindy. *One smile* ill. by Mary Gregg Byrne. Illumination, 2002. ISBN 978-0-935699-23-4 Subj: Character traits – kindness. Circular tales.

MacKinnon, Debbie. *Eye spy shapes* photos by Anthea Sieveking. Charlesbridge, 2000. ISBN 978-0-88106-135-2 Subj: Concepts – shape. Format, unusual.

Mackintosh, David. *The Frank show* ill. by author. Abrams, 2012. ISBN 978-1-4197-0393-5 Subj: Careers – military. Family life – grandfathers. School.

Lucky ill. by author. Abrams, 2014. ISBN 978-141970809-1 Subj: Family life. Imagination.

Marshall Armstrong is new to our school ill. by author. Abrams, 2011. ISBN 978-1-4197-0036-1 Subj: Birthdays. Character traits – individuality. Parties. School.

McKissack, Fredrick. *Messy Bessey* (McKissack, Patricia C.)

Messy Bessey / Ada, la desordenada (McKissack, Patricia C.)

Messy Bessey and the birthday overnight (McKissack, Patricia C.)

Messy Bessey's closet (McKissack, Patricia C.)

Messy Bessey's family reunion (McKissack, Patricia C.)

Messy Bessey's holidays (McKissack, Patricia C.)

McKissack, Patricia C. *The all-I'll-ever-want Christmas doll* ill. by Jerry Pinkney. Random House, 2007. ISBN 978-0-375-93759-0 Subj: Behavior – sharing. Family life – brothers & sisters. Holidays – Christmas. Toys – dolls. U.S. history.

Flossie and the fox ill. by Rachel Isadora. Dial, 1986. ISBN 978-0-8037-0251-6 Subj: Animals – foxes. Ethnic groups in the U.S. – African Americans.

Goin' someplace special ill. by Jerry Pinkney. Atheneum, 2001. ISBN 978-0-689-81885-1 Subj: Ethnic groups in the U.S. – African Americans. Prejudice. U.S. history.

The honest-to-goodness truth ill. by Giselle Potter. Atheneum, 2000. ISBN 978-0-689-82668-9 Subj: Behavior – lying. Character traits – honesty. Ethnic groups in the U.S. – African Americans.

Ma Dear's aprons ill. by Floyd Cooper. Atheneum, 1997. ISBN 978-0-689-81051-0 Subj: Careers – housekeepers. Clothing – aprons. Ethnic groups in the U.S. – African Americans.

Messy Bessey by Patricia C. McKissack and Fredrick McKissack ill. by Dana Regan. Children's Press, 1999. ISBN 978-0-516-21650-8 Subj: Behavior – messy. Character traits – cleanliness. Character traits – orderliness. Ethnic groups in the U.S. – African Americans.

Messy Bessey / Ada, la desordenada by Patricia C. McKissack and Fredrick McKissack ill. by Richard Hackney. Children's Press, 1988. ISBN 978-0-516-32083-0 Subj: Behavior – messy. Character traits – cleanliness. Ethnic groups in the U.S. – African Americans. Foreign languages.

Messy Bessey and the birthday overnight by Patricia C. McKissack and Fredrick McKissack ill. by Dana Regan. Children's Press, 1998. ISBN 978-0-516-20828-2 Subj: Birthdays. Character traits – cleanliness. Character traits – helpfulness. Friendship. Rhyming text. Sleepovers.

Messy Bessey's closet by Patricia C. McKissack and Fredrick McKissack ill. by Richard Hackney. Children's Press, 1989. ISBN 978-0-516-02091-4 Subj: Behavior – messy. Ethnic groups in the U.S. – African Americans. Rhyming text.

Messy Bessey's family reunion by Patricia C. McKissack and Fredrick McKissack ill. by Dana Regan. Children's Press, 2000. ISBN 978-0-516-20830-5 Subj: Character traits – cleanliness. Ethnic groups in the U.S. – African Americans. Family life. Parks.

Messy Bessey's holidays by Patricia C. McKissack and Fredrick McKissack ill. by Dana Regan. Children's Press, 1999. ISBN 978-0-516-20829-9 Subj: Activities – baking, cooking. Character traits – cleanliness. Ethnic groups in the U.S. – African Americans. Holidays – Christmas. Holidays – Hanukkah. Holidays – Kwanzaa. Rhyming text.

A million fish . . . more or less ill. by Dena Schutzer. Knopf, 1992. ISBN 978-0-679-90692-6 Subj: Folk & fairy tales. Sports – fishing. Tall tales.

Mirandy and Brother Wind ill. by Jerry Pinkney. Knopf, 1988. ISBN 978-0-394-88765-4 Subj: Activities – dancing. Caldecott award honor books. Ethnic groups in the U.S. – African Americans. Folk & fairy tales.

Nettie Jo's friends ill. by Scott Cook. Knopf, 1989. ISBN 978-0-394-99158-0 Subj: Clothing. Family life. Toys – dolls.

Ol' Clip-Clop: a ghost story ill. by Eric Velasquez. Holiday House, 2013. ISBN 978-0-8234-2265-4 Subj: Careers – lawyers. Character traits – meanness. Ghosts. U.S. history.

Precious and the Boo Hag by Patricia C. McKissack and Onawumi Jean Moss ill. by Kyrsten Brooker. Simon & Schuster, 2005. ISBN 978-0-689-85194-0 Subj: Character traits – bravery. Ethnic groups in the U.S. – African Americans. Illness. Monsters.

Stitchin' and pullin': a Gee's Bend quilt ill. by Cozbi A. Cabrera. Random House, 2008. ISBN 978-0-375-83163-8 Subj: Ethnic groups in the U.S. – African Americans. Family life. Quilts. U.S. history.

McKissack, Robert L. *Try your best* ill. by Joe Cepeda. Harcourt, 2004. ISBN 978-0-15-205089-4 Subj: Careers – teachers. School. Self-concept. Sports.

McKneally, Ranida T. *Our food: a healthy serving of science and poems* (Lin, Grace)

Our seasons (Lin, Grace)

McKy, Katie. *Pumpkin town! (or, nothing is better and worse than pumpkins)* ill. by Pablo Bernasconi. Houghton, 2006. ISBN 978-0-618-60569-9 Subj: Family life – brothers & sisters. Plants.

MacLachlan, Patricia. *All the places to love* ill. by Mike Wimmer. HarperCollins, 1994. ISBN 978-0-06-021099-1 Subj: Babies, toddlers. Birth. Country. Family life. Farms.

Before you came by Patricia MacLachlan and Emily MacLachlan Charest ill. by David Diaz. HarperCollins, 2011. ISBN 978-0-06-051234-7 Subj: Babies, toddlers. Family life – mothers.

Bittle by Patricia MacLachlan and Emily MacLachlan Charest ill. by Dan Yaccarino. Cotler, 2004. ISBN 978-0-06-000962-5 Subj: Animals – cats. Animals – dogs. Babies, toddlers. Pets.

Cat talk by Patricia MacLachlan and Emily MacLachlan Charest ill. by Barry Moser. Amistad, 2013. ISBN 978-0-06-027978-3 Subj: Animals – cats. Poetry.

Fiona loves the night by Patricia MacLachlan and Emily MacLachlan Charest ill. by Amanda Shepherd. HarperCollins, 2007. ISBN 978-0-06-057031-6 Subj: Nature. Night.

The iridescence of birds: a book about Henri Matisse ill. by Hadley Hooper. Roaring Brook/ Neal Porter, 2014. ISBN 978-159643948-1 Subj: Art. Careers – artists.

Lala salama: a Tanzanian lullaby ill. by Elizabeth Zunon. Candlewick, 2011. ISBN 978-0-7636-4747-6 Subj: Family life – mothers. Foreign lands – Tanzania. Lullabies.

The moon's almost here ill. by Tomie dePaola. Simon & Schuster/Margaret K. McElderry, 2016. ISBN 978-148142062-4 Subj: Bedtime. Rhyming text.

Nora's chicks ill. by Kathryn Brown. Candlewick, 2013. ISBN 978-0-7636-4753-7 Subj: Birds – chickens, roosters. Emotions – loneliness. Friendship. Immigrants, immigration. U.S. history – frontier & pioneer life.

Painting the wind by Patricia MacLachlan and Emily MacLachlan Charest ill. by Katy Schneider. Cotler, 2003. ISBN 978-0-06-029799-2 Subj: Activities – painting. Careers – artists. Islands.

The sick day ill. by Jane Dyer. Random House, 2001. ISBN 978-0-385-90007-2 Subj: Family life – fathers. Illness.

Snowflakes fall ill. by Steven Kellogg. Random House, 2013. ISBN 978-0-385-37693-8 Subj: Character traits – hopefulness. Memories, memory. Poetry. Weather – snow.

Someone like me ill. by Chris Sheban. Roaring Brook/Neal Porter, 2017. ISBN 978-162672334-4 Subj: Careers – writers. Memories, memory.

Three names ill. by Alexander Pertzoff. HarperCollins, 1991. ISBN 978-0-06-024036-3 Subj: Animals – dogs. Family life – great-grandparents. Names. School.

Who loves me? ill. by Amanda Shepherd. Cotler, 2005. ISBN 978-0-06-027977-6 Subj: Animals – cats. Animals – dogs. Emotions – love. Family life.

You were the first ill. by Stephanie Graegin. Little, Brown, 2013. ISBN 978-0-316-18533-2 Subj: Babies, toddlers. Family life.

Your moon, my moon: a grandmother's words to a faraway child ill. by Bryan Collier. Simon & Schuster, 2011. ISBN 978-1-4169-7950-0 Subj: Family life – grandmothers. Foreign lands – Africa.

McLaren, Chesley. *Zat cat! a haute couture tail* ill. by author. Scholastic, 2002. ISBN 978-0-439-27316-9 Subj: Animals – cats. Foreign lands – France. Rhyming text.

McLaren, Meg. *Pigeon P.I.* ill. by author. Clarion, 2017. ISBN 978-132871561-6 Subj: Birds – pigeons. Careers – detectives. Crime. Mystery stories.

Rabbit magic ill. by author. Clarion, 2017. ISBN 978-054478469-7 Subj: Animals – rabbits. Careers – magicians. Magic.

McLarey, Kristina Thermaenius. *When you take a pig to a party* by Kristina Thermaenius McLarey and Myra McLarey ill. by Marjory Wunsch. Orchard, 2000. ISBN 978-0-531-33257-3 Subj: Animals – pigs. Humorous stories. Parties.

McLarey, Myra. *When you take a pig to a party* (McLarey, Kristina Thermaenius)

McLaughlin, Lauren. *Mitzi Tulane, preschool detective, in The secret ingredient* ill. by Debbie Ridpath Ohi. Random House, 2017. ISBN 978-044981916-6 Subj: Activities – baking, cooking. Careers – detectives. Food. Health & fitness. Mystery stories.

Mitzi Tulane, preschool detective, in What's that smell ill. by Debbie Ridpath Ohi. Random House, 2016. ISBN 978-044981915-9 Subj: Birthdays. Careers – detectives. Mystery stories. Parties.

Wonderful you: an adoption story ill. by Meilo So. Random House, 2017. ISBN 978-055351001-0 Subj: Adoption. Family life. Rhyming text.

McLean, Dirk. *Curtain up!* ill. by France Brassard. Tundra, 2010. ISBN 978-0-88776-899-6 Subj: Careers – actors. Theater.

Play mas'! a carnival ABC ill. by author. Tundra, 2000. ISBN 978-0-88776-486-8 Subj: ABC books.

Fairs, festivals. Foreign lands – Caribbean Islands. Foreign languages. Language.

McLean, Janet. *Let's go, baby-o!* ill. by Andrew McLean. IPG/Allen & Unwin, 2012. ISBN 978-1-7423-7564-9 Subj: Activities – playing. Babies, toddlers. Participation. Rhyming text.

MacLean, Kerry Lee. *Peaceful piggy meditation* ill. by author. Albert Whitman, 2004. ISBN 978-0-8075-6380-9 Subj: Animals – pigs. Careers – artists. Careers – writers.

MacLear, Kyo. *The fog* ill. by Kenard Pak. Tundra, 2017. ISBN 978-177049492-3 Subj: Birds. Ecology. Islands. Weather – fog.

Spork ill. by Isabelle Arsenault. Kids Can, 2010. ISBN 978-1-55337-736-8 Subj: Character traits – being different. Character traits – individuality. Self-concept.

Virginia Wolf ill. by Isabelle Arsenault. Kids Can, 2012. ISBN 978-1-55453-649-8 Subj: Emotions. Family life – sisters.

The wish tree ill. by Chris Turnham. Chronicle, 2016. ISBN 978-145215065-9 Subj: Animals. Behavior – wishing. Character traits – helpfulness. Seasons – winter.

McLellan, Gretchen Brandenburg. *Mrs. McBee leaves Room 3* ill. by Grace Zong. Peachtree, 2017. ISBN 978-156145944-5 Subj: Careers – teachers. School.

McLellan, Stephanie Simpson. *The chicken cat* ill. by Sean Cassidy. Fitzhenry & Whiteside, 2000. ISBN 978-1-55041-531-5 Subj: Activities – flying. Animals – babies. Animals – cats. Birds – chickens, roosters. Ethnic groups in the U.S. – African Americans. Friendship.

Tweezle into everything ill. by Dean Griffiths. Pajama, 2014. ISBN 978-192748547-7 Subj: Character traits – helpfulness. Family life. Self-concept.

MacLennan, Cathy. *Chicky Chicky Chook Chook* ill. by author. Sterling, 2007. ISBN 978-1-905417-40-7 Subj: Activities – playing. Animals. Rhyming text. Weather.

McLeod, Bob. *Super hero ABC* ill. by author. HarperCollins, 2006. ISBN 978-0-06-074514-1 Subj: ABC books.

McLeod, Elaine. *Lessons from Mother Earth* ill. by Colleen Wood. Douglas & McIntyre, 2002. ISBN 978-0-88899-312-0 Subj: Family life – grandmothers. Gardens, gardening. Indians of North America. Nature.

MacLeod, Elizabeth. *What did dinosaurs eat?* ill. by Gordon Sauvé. Kids Can, 2001. ISBN 978-1-55337-460-2 Subj: Dinosaurs.

McLeod, Heather. *Kiss me! (I'm a prince!)* ill. by Brooke Kerrigan. Fitzhenry & Whiteside, 2011. ISBN 978-1-55455-161-3 Subj: Folk & fairy tales. Frogs & toads. Kissing. Royalty – princes.

McLerran, Alice. *Roxaboxen* ill. by Barbara Cooney. Lothrop, 1991. ISBN 978-0-688-07593-4 Subj: Activities – playing. Desert. Imagination.

McLimans, David. *Gone wild* ill. by author. Walker, 2006. ISBN 978-0-8027-9563-2 Subj: ABC books. Animals – endangered animals. Caldecott award honor books.

McMahon, Patricia. *Just add one Chinese sister* by Patricia McMahon and Conor Clarke McCarthy ill. by Karen Jerome. Boyds Mills, 2005. ISBN 978-1-56397-989-7 Subj: Adoption. Ethnic groups in the U.S. – Chinese Americans.

McMillan, Bruce. *Counting wildflowers* photos by author. Lothrop, 1986. ISBN 978-0-688-02860-2 Subj: Counting, numbers. Flowers. Science.

Days of the ducklings photos by author. Houghton, 2001. ISBN 978-0-618-04878-6 Subj: Birds – ducks. Ecology. Foreign lands – Iceland. Islands.

Dry or wet? photos by author. Lothrop, 1988. ISBN 978-0-688-07101-1 Subj: Concepts.

Eating fractions photos by author. Scholastic, 1991. ISBN 978-0-590-43770-7 Subj: Counting, numbers.

Fire engine shapes photos by author. Lothrop, 1988. ISBN 978-0-688-07843-0 Subj: Concepts – shape.

Growing colors photos by author. Lothrop, 1988. ISBN 978-0-688-07845-4 Subj: Concepts – color.

How the ladies stopped the wind ill. by Gunnella. Houghton, 2007. ISBN 978-0-618-77330-5 Subj: Behavior – resourcefulness. Foreign lands – Iceland. Weather – wind.

Jelly beans for sale photos by author. Scholastic, 1996. ISBN 978-0-590-86584-5 Subj: Counting, numbers. Money.

Mouse views: what the class pet saw photos by author. Holiday, 1993. ISBN 978-0-8234-1008-8 Subj: Animals – mice. Picture puzzles. School.

Nights of the pufflings photos by author. Houghton, 1995. ISBN 978-0-395-70810-1 Subj: Birds – puffins. Character traits – kindness to animals. Foreign lands – Iceland.

One, two, one pair! photos by author. Scholastic, 1991. ISBN 978-0-590-43767-7 Subj: Concepts. Counting, numbers.

The problem with chickens ill. by Gunnella. Houghton, 2005. ISBN 978-0-618-58581-6 Subj: Behavior – resourcefulness. Birds – chickens, roosters.

Character traits – cleverness. Foreign lands – Iceland.

Puffins climb, penguins rhyme photos by author. Harcourt, 1995. ISBN 978-0-15-200362-3 Subj: Birds – penguins. Birds – puffins. Rhyming text.

Sense suspense: a guessing game for the five senses photos by author. Scholastic, 1994. ISBN 978-0-590-47904-2 Subj: Concepts. Foreign lands – Caribbean Islands. Senses.

Time to . . . photos by author. Lothrop, 1989. ISBN 978-0-688-08856-9 Subj: Clocks, watches. Time.

McMullan, Kate. *Baby Goose* ill. by Pascal Lemaître. Hyperion, 2002. ISBN 978-0-7868-2380-2 Subj: Nursery rhymes.

Bulldog's big day ill. by Pascal Lemaître. Scholastic, 2011. ISBN 978-0-545-17155-7 Subj: Activities – baking, cooking. Animals – dogs. Careers. Careers – bakers.

I stink! ill. by Jim McMullan. Colter, 2002. ISBN 978-0-06-029849-4 Subj: Careers – sanitation workers. Trucks.

If you were my bunny ill. by David McPhail. Scholastic, 1996. ISBN 978-0-590-52749-1 Subj: Animals – babies. Babies, toddlers. Bedtime. Family life – mothers. Lullabies.

I'm bad! ill. by Jim McMullan. HarperCollins, 2008. ISBN 978-0-06-122971-8 Subj: Dinosaurs. Prehistory.

I'm big! ill. by Jim McMullan. HarperCollins, 2010. ISBN 978-0-06-122974-9 Subj: Behavior – lost. Dinosaurs.

I'm brave! ill. by Jim McMullan. HarperCollins/Balzer+Bray, 2014. ISBN 978-006220318-2 Subj: Careers – firefighters. Character traits – bravery. Trucks.

I'm cool! ill. by Jim McMullan. HarperCollins/Balzer+Bray, 2015. ISBN 978-006230629-6 Subj: Machines. Sports – hockey.

I'm dirty! ill. by Jim McMullan. HarperCollins, 2006. ISBN 978-0-06-009294-8 Subj: Careers – construction workers. Counting, numbers. Trucks.

I'm fast ill. by Jim McMullan. HarperCollins, 2012. ISBN 978-0-06-192085-1 Subj: Automobiles. Contests. Sports – racing. Trains.

I'm smart! ill. by Jim McMullan. HarperCollins/Balzer+Bray, 2017. ISBN 978-006244923-8 Subj: Buses. Safety. School.

Mama's kisses ill. by Tao Nyeu. Dial, 2017. ISBN 978-052542832-9 Subj: Animals. Bedtime. Family life – mothers. Jungle. Rhyming text.

Papa's song ill. by Jim McMullan. Farrar, 2000. ISBN 978-0-374-35732-0 Subj: Animals – bears. Babies, toddlers. Family life – fathers. Sleep.

Rock-a-baby band ill. by Janie Bynum. Little, 2003. ISBN 978-0-316-60858-9 Subj: Babies, toddlers. Music. Musical instruments – bands. Rhyming text.

Supercat ill. by Pascal Lemaître. Workman, 2002. ISBN 978-0-7611-2644-7 Subj: Animals. Animals – babies. Animals – cats. Format, unusual – board books.

Supercat to the rescue ill. by Pascal Lemaître. Workman, 2003. ISBN 978-0-7611-2734-5 Subj: Animals – cats. Animals – mice. Babies, toddlers.

McNamara, Margaret. *The apple orchard riddle* ill. by G. Brian Karas. Schwartz & Wade, 2013. ISBN 978-0-375-84744-8 Subj: Food. Riddles & jokes. School – field trips.

Apples A to Z ill. by Jake Parker. Scholastic, 2012. ISBN 978-0-439-72808-9 Subj: ABC books. Animals. Food.

Fall leaf project ill. by Mike Gordon. Simon & Schuster, 2006. ISBN 978-1-4169-1538-6 Subj: Nature. Seasons – fall.

George Washington's birthday: a mostly true tale ill. by Barry Blitt. Random House, 2012. ISBN 978-0-375-84499-7 Subj: Birthdays. U.S. history.

How many seeds in a pumpkin? ill. by G. Brian Karas. Random House, 2007. ISBN 978-0-375-84014-2 Subj: Counting, numbers. Food. Science.

A poem in your pocket ill. by G. Brian Karas. Random House, 2015. ISBN 978-030797947-6 Subj: Activities – writing. Careers – writers. Poetry. School. Self-concept.

The three little aliens and the big bad robot ill. by Mark Fearing. Random House, 2011. ISBN 978-0-375-86689-0 Subj: Aliens. Humorous stories. Planets. Robots. Space & space ships.

The whistle on the train ill. by Richard Egielski. Hyperion, 2008. ISBN 978-0-7868-4890-4 Subj: Format, unusual – toy & movable books. Trains.

McNaughton, Colin. *Boo!* ill. by author. Harcourt, 1996. ISBN 978-0-15-200834-5 Subj: Animals – pigs. Disguises.

Captain Abdul's little treasure ill. by author. Candlewick, 2006. ISBN 978-0-7636-3045-4 Subj: Babies, toddlers. Pirates.

Captain Abdul's pirate school ill. by author. Candlewick, 1994. ISBN 978-1-56402-429-9 Subj: Behavior – misbehavior. Pirates. School.

Don't step on the crack! ill. by author. Dial, 2001. ISBN 978-0-8037-2611-6 Subj: Superstition.

Here come the aliens! ill. by author. Candlewick, 1995. ISBN 978-1-56402-642-2 Subj: Aliens. Space & space ships.

Not last night but the night before ill. by Emma Chichester Clark. Candlewick, 2009. ISBN 978-0-7636-4420-8 Subj: Birthdays. Books, reading. Imagination. Rhyming text.

Once upon an ordinary school day ill. by Satoshi Kitamura. Farrar, 2005. ISBN 978-0-374-35634-7 Subj: Careers – teachers. School.

Oomph! ill. by author. Harcourt, 2001. ISBN 978-0-15-216463-8 Subj: Animals – pigs. Animals – wolves. Emotions – love. Sea & seashore.

Oops! ill. by author. Harcourt, 1997. ISBN 978-0-15-201588-6 Subj: Animals – pigs. Animals – wolves. Character traits – cleverness.

Preston's goal! ill. by author. Harcourt, 1998. ISBN 978-0-15-201816-0 Subj: Animals – pigs. Animals – wolves. Character traits – clumsiness. Humorous stories. Sports – soccer.

Suddenly! ill. by author. Harcourt, 1995. ISBN 978-0-15-200308-1 Subj: Animals – pigs. Animals – wolves. Humorous stories.

We're off to look for aliens ill. by author. Candlewick, 2008. ISBN 978-0-7636-3636-4 Subj: Aliens. Rhyming text.

When I grow up ill. by author. Candlewick, 2005. ISBN 978-0-7636-2675-4 Subj: Careers. Rhyming text. School. Theater.

McNaughton, Janet. *Brave Jack and the unicorn* ill. by Susan Tooke. Tundra, 2005. ISBN 978-0-88776-677-0 Subj: Character traits – kindness. Folk & fairy tales. Foreign lands – Canada. Magic. Mythical creatures – unicorns. Royalty – princesses.

McNulty, Stacy. *101 reasons why I'm not taking a bath* ill. by Joy Ang. Random House, 2016. ISBN 978-038539189-4 Subj: Activities – bathing. Character traits – cleanliness. Hygiene.

McNeil, Florence. *Sail away* ill. by David McPhail. Orca, 2000. ISBN 978-1-55143-147-5 Subj: Boats, ships. Imagination. Pirates. Sports – sailing. Toys.

McNeil, Kelli. *Sleepy toes* ill. by Cori Doerrfeld. Scholastic/Cartwheel, 2017. ISBN 978-133803072-3 Subj: Anatomy. Bedtime. Format, unusual – board books.

McNiff, Dawn. *Mommy's little monster* ill. by Kate Willis-Crowley. Scholastic, 2013. ISBN 978-0-545-48057-4 Subj: Activities – babysitting. Family life – mothers. Mythical creatures – trolls.

McNulty, Faith. *If you decide to go to the moon* ill. by Steven Kellogg. Scholastic, 2005. ISBN 978-0-590-48359-9 Subj: Moon. Space & space ships.

Macomber, Debbie. *The yippy, yappy Yorkie in the green doggy sweater* by Debbie Macomber and

Mary Lou Carney ill. by Sally Anne Lambert. HarperCollins, 2012. ISBN 978-0-06-165096-3 Subj: Animals – dogs. Behavior – running away. Moving.

Maconie, Robin. *Alice and her fabulous teeth* ill. by Catherine Myler Fruisen. Cedco, 2000. ISBN 978-0-7683-2176-0 Subj: Dreams. Fairies. Mythical creatures – elves. Rhyming text. Teeth.

McPhail, David. *Andrew draws* ill. by author. Holiday House, 2014. ISBN 978-082343063-5 Subj: Activities – drawing. Imagination.

Baby Pig Pig talks ill. by author. Charlesbridge, 2014. ISBN 978-158089597-2 Subj: Animals – babies. Animals – pigs. Format, unusual – board books.

Bad dog ill. by author. Holiday House, 2014. ISBN 978-082342852-6 Subj: Animals – dogs. Behavior – misbehavior.

The bear's toothache ill. by author. Puffin, 1978, ©1972. ISBN 978-0-14-050263-3 Subj: Animals – bears. Character traits – kindness to animals. Illness. Teeth.

Beatrix Potter and her paint box ill. by author. Henry Holt, 2015. ISBN 978-080509170-0 Subj: Activities – drawing. Activities – painting. Art. Careers – artists. Careers – writers. Nature.

Bella loves Bunny ill. by author. Abrams, 2013. ISBN 978-1-4197-0543-4 Subj: Animals – rabbits. Format, unusual – board books. Friendship. Toys.

Ben loves Bear ill. by author. Abrams, 2013. ISBN 978-1-4197-0386-7 Subj: Format, unusual – board books. Friendship. Toys – bears.

Big Brown Bear goes to town ill. by author. Harcourt, 2006. ISBN 978-1-4156-7142-9 Subj: Animals – bears. Animals – rats. Friendship.

Big Brown Bear's birthday surprise ill. by author. Harcourt, 2007. ISBN 978-0-15-206098-5 Subj: Animals – bears. Animals – rats. Birthdays. Friendship.

Big Brown Bear's up and down day ill. by author. Harcourt, 2003. ISBN 978-0-15-216407-2 Subj: Animals – bears. Animals – rats. Friendship.

Boy on the brink ill. by author. Henry Holt, 2006. ISBN 978-0-8050-7618-9 Subj: Dreams. Imagination.

Brothers ill. by author. Harcourt, 2014. ISBN 978-054430200-6 Subj: Character traits – individuality. Emotions – love. Family life – brothers.

Budgie and Boo ill. by author. Abrams, 2009. ISBN 978-0-8109-8324-3 Subj: Animals – bears. Animals – rabbits. Friendship.

Crash! the cat ill. by author. Holiday House, 2016. ISBN 978-082343649-1 Subj: Animals – cats.

Character traits – clumsiness. Family life – sisters.

Drawing lessons from a bear ill. by author. Little, 2000. ISBN 978-0-316-56345-1 Subj: Activities – drawing. Animals – bears. Careers – artists.

Edward and the pirates ill. by author. Little, 1997. ISBN 978-0-316-56344-4 Subj: Books, reading. Imagination. Pirates.

Edward in the jungle ill. by author. Little, 2001. ISBN 978-0-316-56391-8 Subj: Animals. Imagination. Jungle.

Emma in charge ill. by author. Penguin, 2005. ISBN 978-0-525-47411-1 Subj: Activities – playing. Animals – bears. Imagination. Toys – dolls.

Emma's pet ill. by author. Dutton, 1987. ISBN 978-0-525-44210-3 Subj: Activities – vacationing. Animals – bears. Behavior – needing someone. Family life. Pets.

Emma's vacation ill. by author. Dutton, 1987. ISBN 978-0-525-44315-5 Subj: Activities – vacationing. Animals – bears. Family life.

The family tree ill. by author. Henry Holt, 2012. ISBN 978-0-8050-9057-4 Subj: Ecology. Trees.

Farm morning ill. by author. Harcourt, 1985. ISBN 978-0-15-227299-9 Subj: Animals. Birds. Farms.

Fix-it ill. by author. Dutton, 1984. ISBN 978-0-525-44093-2 Subj: Books, reading. Television.

Henry Bear's Christmas ill. by author. Atheneum, 2001. ISBN 978-0-689-82198-1 Subj: Animals – bears. Animals – raccoons. Holidays – Christmas. Trees.

Henry Bear's park ill. by author. Atheneum, 2001. ISBN 978-0-689-83967-2 Subj: Activities – ballooning. Animals – bears. Family life – fathers. Parks.

I promise ill. by author. Little, Brown, 2017. ISBN 978-031629787-5 Subj: Animals – bears. Emotions – love. Family life – mothers.

Lost ill. by author. Little, 1990. ISBN 978-0-316-56329-1 Subj: Animals – bears. Behavior – lost.

Mole music ill. by author. Henry Holt, 1999. ISBN 978-0-8050-2819-5 Subj: Animals – moles. Music. Musical instruments – violins.

Moony B. Finch, fastest draw in the West ill. by author. Artists & Writers Guild, 1994. ISBN 978-0-307-17554-0 Subj: Activities – drawing. Crime. Imagination. Magic. Trains.

No! ill. by author. Roaring Brook, 2009. ISBN 978-1-59643-288-8 Subj: Character traits. War.

Olivia loves Owl ill. by author. Abrams/Appleseed, 2016. ISBN 978-141972127-4 Subj: Activities – playing. Birds – owls. Format, unusual – board books. Friendship. Toys.

Peter loves Penguin ill. by author. Abrams/Appleseed, 2014. ISBN 978-141971337-8 Subj: Birds – penguins. Format, unusual – board books. Friendship. Toys. Weather – snow.

Pig Pig and the magic photo album ill. by author. Dutton, 1986. ISBN 978-0-525-44238-7 Subj: Activities – photographing. Animals – pigs. Imagination.

Pig Pig gets a job ill. by author. Dutton, 1990. ISBN 978-0-525-44619-4 Subj: Activities – working. Animals – pigs. Careers.

Pig Pig goes to camp ill. by author. Dutton, 1983. ISBN 978-0-525-44064-2 Subj: Animals – pigs. Camps, camping.

Pig Pig grows up ill. by author. Dutton, 1980. ISBN 978-0-525-37027-7 Subj: Animals – pigs. Behavior – growing up.

Pig Pig meets the lion ill. by author. Charlesbridge, 2012. ISBN 978-1-58089-358-9 Subj: Animals – lions. Animals – pigs. Friendship. Language.

Pig Pig returns ill. by author. Charlesbridge, 2011. ISBN 978-1-58089-356-5 Subj: Activities – traveling. Animals – pigs. Behavior – worrying.

Pig Pig rides ill. by author. Dutton, 1982. ISBN 978-0-525-44024-6 Subj: Activities – playing. Animals – pigs. Imagination.

Pigs ahoy ill. by author. Dutton, 1995. ISBN 978-0-525-45334-5 Subj: Animals – pigs. Boats, ships. Rhyming text.

Pigs aplenty, pigs galore! ill. by author. Dutton, 1993. ISBN 978-0-525-45079-5 Subj: Animals – pigs. Food. Rhyming text.

The puddle ill. by author. Farrar, 1998. ISBN 978-0-374-36148-8 Subj: Animals. Toys. Weather – rain.

Santa's book of names ill. by author. Little, 1993. ISBN 978-0-316-56335-2 Subj: Books, reading. Character traits – helpfulness. Holidays – Christmas. Santa Claus.

The Searcher and Old Tree ill. by author. Charlesbridge, 2008. ISBN 978-1-58089-223-0 Subj: Animals – raccoons. Trees. Weather – storms.

Something special ill. by author. Little, 1988. ISBN 978-0-316-56324-6 Subj: Activities – painting. Animals – raccoons.

Sylvie and True ill. by author. Farrar, 2007. ISBN 978-0-374-37364-1 Subj: Animals – rabbits. Friendship. Reptiles – snakes.

The teddy bear ill. by author. Henry Holt, 2002. ISBN 978-0-8050-6414-8 Subj: Behavior – lost & found possessions. Emotions – love. Homeless. Toys – bears.

Those can-do pigs ill. by author. Dutton, 1996. ISBN 978-0-525-45495-3 Subj: Activities. Animals – pigs. Rhyming text.

Tinker and Tom and the Star Baby ill. by author. Little, 1998. ISBN 978-0-316-56349-9 Subj: Aliens. Animals – bears. Imagination. Space & space ships.

Waddles ill. by author. Abrams, 2011. ISBN 978-0-8109-8415-8 Subj: Animals – raccoons. Birds – ducks. Friendship.

Water boy ill. by author. Abrams, 2007. ISBN 978-0-8109-1784-2 Subj: Emotions – fear. Magic. Water.

Weezer changes the world ill. by author. Simon & Schuster, 2009. ISBN 978-1-4169-9000-0 Subj: Animals – dogs. Behavior – seeking better things. Concepts – change. Weather – lightning, thunder.

McPike, Elizabeth. *Little bitty friends* ill. by Patrice Barton. Putnam, 2016. ISBN 978-039917255-7 Subj: Animals – babies. Babies, toddlers. Nature. Rhyming text.

Little sleepyhead ill. by Patrice Barton. Putnam, 2015. ISBN 978-039916240-4 Subj: Babies, toddlers. Bedtime. Rhyming text.

McQuade, Jacqueline. *At preschool with Teddy Bear* ill. by author. Dial, 1999. ISBN 978-0-8037-2394-8 Subj: Family life – fathers. Format, unusual – board books. School – first day. School – nursery. Toys – bears.

At the petting zoo with Teddy Bear ill. by author. Dial, 1999. ISBN 978-0-8037-2395-5 Subj: Animals. Format, unusual – board books. Toys – bears. Zoos.

Big babies ill. by author. Sterling, 2000. ISBN 978-0-8069-7537-5 Subj: Animals. Animals – babies. Names.

Christmas with Teddy Bear ill. by author. Dial, 1996. ISBN 978-0-8037-2075-6 Subj: Holidays – Christmas. Toys – bears.

Farm babies ill. by author. Sterling, 2000. ISBN 978-0-8069-7539-9 Subj: Animals – babies. Farms.

Good times with Teddy Bear ill. by author. Dial, 1997. ISBN 978-0-8037-2076-3 Subj: Activities. Animals – cats. Family life. Toys – bears.

Small babies ill. by author. Sterling, 2000. ISBN 978-0-8069-7541-2 Subj: Animals. Animals – babies. Science.

Snow babies ill. by author. Sterling, 2000. ISBN 978-1-85602-366-5 Subj: Animals. Animals – babies. Foreign lands – Antarctic. Foreign lands – Arctic. Weather – snow.

McQuinn, Anna. *Leo can swim* ill. by Ruth Hearson. Charlesbridge, 2016. ISBN 978-158089725-9 Subj: Babies, toddlers. Family life – fathers. Sports – swimming.

Leo loves baby time ill. by Ruth Hearson. Charlesbridge, 2014. ISBN 978-158089665-8 Subj: Activities – playing. Activities – storytelling. Babies, toddlers. Ethnic groups in the U.S. – African Americans. Libraries.

Lola at the library ill. by Rosalind Beardshaw. Charlesbridge, 2006. ISBN 978-1-58089-113-4 Subj: Books, reading. Ethnic groups in the U.S. – African Americans. Libraries.

Lola gets a cat ill. by Rosalind Beardshaw. Charlesbridge, 2017. ISBN 978-158089736-5 Subj: Animals – cats. Character traits – kindness to animals. Ethnic groups in the U.S. – African Americans. Pets.

Lola loves stories ill. by Rosalind Beardshaw. Charlesbridge, 2010. ISBN 978-1-58089-258-2 Subj: Activities – playing. Activities – storytelling. Books, reading. Ethnic groups in the U.S. – African Americans. Imagination.

Lola plants a garden ill. by Rosalind Beardshaw. Charlesbridge, 2014. ISBN 978-158089694-8 Subj: Ethnic groups in the U.S. – African Americans. Flowers. Gardens, gardening.

Lola reads to Leo ill. by Rosalind Beardshaw. Charlesbridge, 2012. ISBN 978-1-58089-403-6 Subj: Babies, toddlers. Books, reading. Ethnic groups in the U.S. – African Americans. Family life – brothers & sisters. Family life – new sibling.

My friend Jamal ill. by author. Annick, 2008. ISBN 978-1-55451-123-5 Subj: Foreign lands – Somalia. Friendship. Immigrants, immigration. War.

My friend Mei Jing ill. by Ben Frey. Annick, 2009. ISBN 978-1-55451-153-2 Subj: Ethnic groups in the U.S. – African Americans. Ethnic groups in the U.S. – Chinese Americans. Friendship.

The sleep sheep ill. by Hannah Shaw. Scholastic, 2010. ISBN 978-0-545-23145-9 Subj: Animals – sheep. Bedtime. Counting, numbers. Sleep.

McReynolds, Linda. *Eight days gone* ill. by Ryan O'Rourke. Charlesbridge, 2012. ISBN 978-1-58089-364-0 Subj: Careers – astronauts. Moon. Rhyming text. Space & space ships. U.S. history.

Macy, Sue. *Miss Mary reporting: the true story of sportswriter Mary Garber* ill. by C. F. Payne. Simon & Schuster/Paula Wiseman, 2016. ISBN 978-148140120-3 Subj: Careers – writers. Gender roles. Sports.

Maddern, Eric. *Nail soup* ill. by Paul Hess. Frances Lincoln, 2007. ISBN 978-1-84507-479-1 Subj: Character traits – cleverness. Folk & fairy tales. Foreign lands – Sweden.

Mader, C. Roger. *Lost cat* ill. by author. Houghton Mifflin, 2013. ISBN 978-0-547-97458-3 Subj: Animals – cats. Behavior – lost. Clothing – shoes. Pets.

Tiptop cat ill. by author. Houghton, 2014. ISBN 978-054414799-7 Subj: Animals – cats. Character traits – bravery. Emotions – fear. Foreign lands – France.

Madison, Alan. *The littlest grape stomper* ill. by Giselle Potter. Random House, 2007. ISBN 978-0-375-83675-6 Subj: Anatomy – toes. Food. Tall tales.

Pecorino plays ball ill. by AnnaLaura Cantone. Simon & Schuster, 2006. ISBN 978-0-689-86522-0 Subj: Humorous stories. Sports – baseball.

Pecorino's first concert ill. by AnnaLaura Cantone. Simon & Schuster, 2005. ISBN 978-0-689-85952-6 Subj: Humorous stories. Music. Musical instruments.

Velma Gratch and the way cool butterfly ill. by Kevin Hawkes. Random House, 2007. ISBN 978-0-375-83597-1 Subj: Insects – butterflies, caterpillars. Migration. School.

Madonna. *Mr. Peabody's apples* ill. by Loren Long. Viking, 2003. ISBN 978-0-670-05883-9 Subj: Behavior – gossip, rumors. Character traits – honesty. Food. Sports – baseball.

Yakov and the seven thieves ill. by Gennady Spirin. Callaway, 2004. ISBN 978-0-670-05887-7 Subj: Careers – shoemakers. Crime. Illness. Religion.

Madrigal, Antonio Hernandez. *Erandi's braids* ill. by Tomie dePaola. Putnam, 1999. ISBN 978-0-399-23212-1 Subj: Birthdays. Family life – mothers. Foreign lands – Mexico. Hair.

Maestro, Betsy. *Bats* ill. by Giulio Maestro. Scholastic, 1994. ISBN 978-0-590-46150-4 Subj: Animals – bats.

Coming to America ill. by Susannah Ryan. Scholastic, 1996. ISBN 978-0-590-44151-3 Subj: Ethnic groups in the U.S.

Dollars and cents for Harriet ill. by Giulio Maestro. Crown, 1988. ISBN 978-0-517-56958-0 Subj: Counting, numbers. Money.

How do apples grow? ill. by Giulio Maestro. HarperCollins, 1992. ISBN 978-0-06-020056-5 Subj: Food. Science. Trees.

The story of the Statue of Liberty by Betsy Maestro and Giulio Maestro ill. by Giulio Maestro. Lothrop, 1986. ISBN 978-0-688-05773-2 Subj: Art. U.S. history.

Why do leaves change color? ill. by Loretta Krupinski. HarperCollins, 1994. ISBN 978-0-06-022874-3 Subj: Nature. Science. Seasons – fall. Trees.

Maestro, Giulio. *The story of the Statue of Liberty* (Maestro, Betsy)

Magerl, Caroline. *Rose and the wish thing: a journey of friendship* ill. by author. Doubleday, 2016. ISBN 978-055353617-1 Subj: Behavior – wishing. Emotions – loneliness. Friendship. Imagination – imaginary friends. Moving.

Maggi, María Elena. *The great canoe* ill. by Gloria Calderón. Douglas & McIntyre, 2001. ISBN 978-0-88899-444-8 Subj: Animals. Canoes & canoeing. Folk & fairy tales. Indians of South America – Karina. Weather – floods. Weather – rain.

Magliaro, Elaine. *Things to do* ill. by Catia Chien. Chronicle, 2017. ISBN 978-145211124-7 Subj: Activities. Nature. Rhyming text.

Magloff, Lisa. *Bear* ill. by author. DK, 2003. ISBN 978-0-7566-0194-2 Subj: Animals – babies. Animals – bears. Behavior – growing up.

Butterfly ill. with photos. DK, 2003. ISBN 978-0-7566-0193-5 Subj: Animals – babies. Behavior – growing up. Insects – butterflies, caterpillars.

Duckling ill. with photos. DK, 2003. ISBN 978-0-7894-9628-7 Subj: Animals – babies. Behavior – growing up. Birds – ducks.

Elephant ill. with photos. DK, 2005. ISBN 978-0-7566-1155-2 Subj: Animals – babies. Animals – elephants. Behavior – growing up.

Frog ill. with photos. DK, 2003. ISBN 978-0-7894-9629-4 Subj: Animals – babies. Behavior – growing up. Frogs & toads.

Kitten ill. with photos. DK, 2005. ISBN 978-0-7566-1156-9 Subj: Animals – babies. Animals – cats. Behavior – growing up.

Penguin ill. with photos. DK, 2004. ISBN 978-0-7566-0263-5 Subj: Animals – babies. Behavior – growing up. Birds – penguins.

Rabbit ill. with photos. DK, 2004. ISBN 978-0-7566-0262-8 Subj: Animals – babies. Animals – rabbits. Behavior – growing up.

Magnier, Thierry. *Isabelle and the angel* ill. by Georg Hallensleben. Chronicle, 2000. ISBN 978-0-8118-2526-9 Subj: Angels. Animals – pigs. Careers – artists. Museums.

Magoon, Scott. *The boy who cried bigfoot!* ill. by author. Simon & Schuster, 2013. ISBN 978-1-4424-1257-6 Subj: Behavior – lying. Crime. Mythical creatures.

Breathe ill. by author. Simon & Schuster/Paula Wiseman, 2014. ISBN 978-144241258-3 Subj: Animals – babies. Animals – whales.

Hugo and Miles in I've painted everything! ill. by author. Houghton, 2007. ISBN 978-0-618-64638-8 Subj: Animals – dogs. Animals – elephants. Art. Foreign lands – France.

Magruder, Nilah. *How to find a fox* ill. by author. Feiwel & Friends, 2016. ISBN 978-125008656-3 Subj: Activities – photographing. Animals – foxes. Character traits – patience, impatience.

Maguire, Gregory. *Crabby Cratchitt* ill. by Andrew Glass. Clarion, 2000. ISBN 978-0-395-60485-4 Subj: Birds – chickens, roosters. Careers – farmers. Farms. Rhyming text.

Maguire, John. *People* ill. by Pauline Bewick. Collins, 2001. ISBN 978-1-903464-06-9 Subj: Character traits – individuality. Poetry.

Mahoney, Daniel J. *Monstergarten* ill. by Jef Kaminsky. Feiwel & Friends, 2013. ISBN 978-1-250-01441-2 Subj: Behavior – worrying. Monsters. School – first day.

The perfect clubhouse ill. by author. Clarion, 2004. ISBN 978-0-618-34672-1 Subj: Animals. Character traits – cooperation. Clubs, gangs. Friendship.

A really good snowman ill. by author. Houghton, 2005. ISBN 978-0-618-47554-4 Subj: Animals – bears. Character traits – helpfulness. Contests. Family life – brothers & sisters. Snowmen. Weather – snow.

The Saturday escape ill. by author. Clarion, 2002. ISBN 978-0-618-13326-0 Subj: Activities – storytelling. Animals. Behavior. Books, reading. Character traits – responsibility. Libraries.

Mahy, Margaret. *Boom Baby boom, boom* ill. by Patricia MacCarthy. Viking, 1997. ISBN 978-0-670-87314-2 Subj: Animals. Babies, toddlers. Family life – mothers. Food. Noise, sounds.

Bubble trouble ill. by Polly Dunbar. Clarion, 2009. ISBN 978-0-547-07421-4 Subj: Bubbles. Humorous stories. Rhyming text.

The Christmas tree tangle ill. by Anthony Kerins. Margaret K. McElderry, 1994. ISBN 978-0-689-50616-1 Subj: Animals. Animals – cats. Cumulative tales. Holidays – Christmas. Rhyming text. Trees.

Down the back of the chair ill. by Polly Dunbar. Houghton, 2006. ISBN 978-0-618-69395-5 Subj: Behavior – lost & found possessions. Furniture – chairs. Poverty. Rhyming text.

Down the dragon's tongue ill. by Patricia MacCarthy. Orchard, 2000. ISBN 978-0-531-30272-9 Subj: Family life – fathers. Multiple births – twins. Parks.

The great white man-eating shark ill. by Jonathan Allen. Dial, 1990. ISBN 978-0-8037-0749-8 Subj: Behavior – trickery. Fish – sharks.

The green bath ill. by Steven Kellogg. Scholastic, 2013. ISBN 978-0-545-20667-9 Subj: Activities – bathing. Imagination.

The man from the land of Fandango ill. by Polly Dunbar. Clarion, 2012. ISBN 978-0-547-81988-4 Subj: Humorous stories. Imagination. Rhyming text.

Mister Whistler ill. by Gavin Bishop. Gecko, 2013. ISBN 978-1-87746-791-2 Subj: Activities – dancing. Activities – whistling. Behavior – lost & found possessions. Trains.

The rattlebang picnic ill. by Steven Kellogg. Dial, 1994. ISBN 978-0-8037-1319-2 Subj: Activities – picnicking. Automobiles. Family life.

The seven Chinese brothers ill. by Jean Tseng and Mou-Sien Tseng. Scholastic, 1990. ISBN 978-0-590-42055-6 Subj: Character traits – cleverness. Family life. Folk & fairy tales. Foreign lands – China.

17 kings and 42 elephants ill. by Patricia MacCarthy. Dial, 1987. ISBN 978-0-8037-0458-9 Subj: Animals. Jungle. Rhyming text. Royalty – kings.

Simply delicious! ill. by Jonathan Allen. Orchard, 1999. ISBN 978-0-531-33181-1 Subj: Animals. Food. Jungle. Tongue twisters.

A summery Saturday morning ill. by Selina Young. Viking, 1998. ISBN 978-0-670-87943-4 Subj: Animals. Birds – geese. Humorous stories. Rhyming text. Sea & seashore. Seasons – summer.

Maidment, Stella. *Cowboy puzzles* ill. by Daniela Dogliani. Amicus, 2012. ISBN 978-1-60992-271-9 Subj: Behavior – lost & found possessions. Cowboys, cowgirls. Puzzles.

Maier, Inger. *Ben's flying flowers* ill. by Maria Bogade. Magination, 2012. ISBN 978-1-4338-1133-3 Subj: Death. Emotions – grief. Emotions – sadness. Illness. Insects – butterflies, caterpillars.

Mair, Samia J. *The perfect gift* ill. by Craig Howarth. Kube, 2010. ISBN 978-0-86037-438-1 Subj: Family life – brothers & sisters. Gifts. Holidays. Plants. Religion – Islam.

Maitland, Barbara. *Moo in the morning* ill. by Andrew Kulman. Farrar, 2000. ISBN 978-0-374-35038-3 Subj: Animals. Cities, towns. Farms. Noise, sounds.

My bear and me ill. by Lisa Flather. Margaret K. McElderry, 1999. ISBN 978-0-689-82085-4 Subj: Activities. Bedtime. Toys – bears.

Maizes, Sarah. *On my way to bed* ill. by Michael Paraskevas. Walker, 2013. ISBN 978-0-8027-2366-6 Subj: Bedtime. Imagination.

On my way to the bath ill. by Michael Paraskevas. Walker, 2012. ISBN 978-0-8027-2364-2 Subj: Activities – bathing. Imagination.

Major, Kevin. *Aunt Olga's Christmas postcards* ill. by Bruce Roberts. Groundwood, 2005. ISBN 978-0-88899-593-3 Subj: Behavior – collecting things. Family life – aunts, uncles. Holidays – Christmas. Letters, cards.

Eh to zed? ill. by Alan Daniel. Red Deer, 2002. ISBN 978-0-88995-272-0 Subj: ABC books. Foreign lands – Canada.

Mak, Kam. *My Chinatown* ill. by author. HarperCollins, 2002. ISBN 978-0-06-029191-4 Subj: Cities, towns. Ethnic groups in the U.S. – Chinese Americans. Immigrants, immigration. Poetry.

Makhijani, Pooja. *Mama's saris* ill. by Elena Gomez. Little, Brown, 2007. ISBN 978-0-316-01105-1 Subj: Clothing. Ethnic groups in the U.S. – East Indian Americans. Family life – daughters. Family life – mothers.

Making faces: a first book of emotions photos by Molly Magnuson. Abrams/Appleseed, 2017. ISBN 978-141972383-4 Subj: Babies, toddlers. Emotions. Format, unusual – board books.

Malaspina, Ann. *Finding Lincoln* ill. by Colin Bootman. Albert Whitman, 2009. ISBN 978-0-8075-2435-0 Subj: Ethnic groups in the U.S. – African Americans. Libraries. Prejudice. U.S. history.

Phillis sings out freedom: the story of George Washington and Phillis Wheatley ill. by Susan Keeter. Albert Whitman, 2010. ISBN 978-0-8075-6545-2 Subj: Careers – poets. Ethnic groups in the U.S. – African Americans. U.S. history.

Touch the sky: Alice Coachman, Olympic high jumper ill. by Eric Velasquez. Albert Whitman, 2012. ISBN 978-0-8075-8035-6 Subj: Character traits – perseverance. Ethnic groups in the U.S. – African Americans. Sports – Olympics. U.S. history.

Yasmin's hammer ill. by Doug Chayka. Lee & Low, 2010. ISBN 978-1-60060-359-4 Subj: Foreign lands – Bangladesh. School.

Malbrough, Mike. *Marigold bakes a cake* ill. by author. Philomel, 2017. ISBN 978-152473738-2 Subj: Activities – baking, cooking. Animals – cats. Behavior – messy. Birds. Character traits – orderliness. Character traits – perfectionism.

Malkin, Michele. *Pinky's sweet tooth* ill. by author. Dutton, 2003. ISBN 978-0-525-47088-5 Subj: Activities – baking, cooking. Reptiles – alligators, crocodiles.

Mallat, Kathy. *Just ducky* ill. by author. Walker, 2001. ISBN 978-0-8027-8824-5 Subj: Activities –

playing. Birds – ducks. Friendship. Optical illusions.

Papa pride ill. by author. Walker, 2005. ISBN 978-0-8027-8964-8 Subj: Animals – wolves. Family life – fathers. Rhyming text.

Trouble on the tracks ill. by author. Walker, 2001. ISBN 978-0-8027-8773-6 Subj: Activities – playing. Animals – cats. Toys – trains.

Malnor, Carol L. *The Blues go birding across America* by Carol L. Malnor and Sandy F. Fuller ill. by Louise Schroeder. Dawn, 2010. ISBN 978-1-58469-124-2 Subj: Birds. Holidays – Fourth of July.

Malone, Cheryl Lawton. *Dario and the whale* ill. by Bistra Masseva. Albert Whitman, 2016. ISBN 978-080751463-4 Subj: Animals – whales. Careers – migrant workers. Foreign lands – Brazil. Immigrants, immigration.

Maloney, Brenna. *Ready Rabbit gets ready!* photos by Chuck Kennedy. Viking, 2015. ISBN 978-067001549-8 Subj: Animals – rabbits. Character traits – willfulness. Imagination.

Maloney, Peter. *Belly button boy* by Peter Maloney and Felicia Zekauskas; ill. by authors. Dial, 2000. ISBN 978-0-8037-2542-3 Subj: Anatomy – navels. Character traits – cleanliness. Rhyming text.

His mother's nose by Peter Maloney and Felicia Zekauskas; ill. by authors. Dial, 2001. ISBN 978-0-8037-2545-4 Subj: Anatomy. Character traits – individuality. Family life. Self-concept.

One foot two feet: an exceptional counting book by Peter Maloney and Felicia Zekauskas; ill. by authors. Penguin, 2011. ISBN 978-0-399-25446-8 Subj: Concepts. Counting, numbers.

Maltbie, P. I. *Claude Monet: the painter who stopped the trains* ill. by Joseph A. Smith. Abrams, 2010. ISBN 978-0-8109-8961-0 Subj: Art. Careers – artists. Trains.

Mamada, Mineko. *Which is round? which is bigger?* ill. by author. Kids Can, 2013. ISBN 978-1-55453-973-4 Subj: Character traits – questioning. Concepts. Problem solving.

Mammano, Julie. *Rhinos who play baseball* ill. by author. Chronicle, 2003. ISBN 978-0-8118-3605-0 Subj: Animals – rhinoceros. Sports – baseball.

Rhinos who play soccer ill. by author. Chronicle, 2001. ISBN 978-0-8118-2779-9 Subj: Animals – rhinoceros. Sports – soccer.

Rhinos who rescue ill. by author. Chronicle, 2007. ISBN 978-0-8118-5419-1 Subj: Animals – rhinoceros. Careers – firefighters.

Rhinos who surf ill. by author. Chronicle, 1996. ISBN 978-0-8118-1000-5 Subj: Animals – rhinoceros. Sports – surfing.

Manceau, Edouard. *Tickle monster* ill. by author. Abrams/Appleseed, 2015. ISBN 978-141971731-4 Subj: Bedtime. Emotions – fear. Monsters.

Windblown ill. by author. OwlKids, 2013. ISBN 978-1-926973-77-7 Subj: Animals. Concepts – shape. Imagination. Weather – wind.

Mandel, Peter. *Jackhammer Sam* ill. by David Catrow. Roaring Brook, 2011. ISBN 978-1-59643-034-1 Subj: Careers – construction workers. Rhyming text. Tools.

Say hey: a song of Willie Mays ill. by Don Tate. Hyperion, 2000. ISBN 978-0-7868-2417-5 Subj: Ethnic groups in the U.S. – African Americans. Rhyming text. Sports – baseball.

Zoo ah-choooo ill. by Elwood H. Smith. Holiday House, 2012. ISBN 978-0-8234-2317-0 Subj: Illness – cold (disease). Noise, sounds. Zoos.

Mandell, B. B. *Samanthasaurus Rex* ill. by Suzanne Kaufman. HarperCollins/Balzer+Bray, 2016. ISBN 978-006234873-9 Subj: Character traits – being different. Character traits – individuality. Dinosaurs. Family life. Self-concept.

Mandell, Muriel, adapt. *A donkey reads: adapted from a Turkish folktale* ill. by André Letria. Star Bright, 2011. ISBN 978-1-59572-256-0 Subj: Animals – donkeys. Character traits – cleverness. Folk & fairy tales. Foreign lands – Turkey.

Manders, John. *The really awful musicians* ill. by author. Clarion, 2011. ISBN 978-0-547-32820-1 Subj: Careers – musicians. Music. Royalty – kings.

Mangan, Anne. *The monkey who wanted the moon* ill. by Catherine Walters. Crocodile, 2001. ISBN 978-1-56656-376-5 Subj: Animals – monkeys. Behavior – greed. Jungle. Moon.

Manley, Curtis. *Shawn loves sharks* ill. by Tracy Subisak. Roaring Brook, 2017. ISBN 978-162672134-0 Subj: Animals – seals. Fish – sharks. Friendship. School.

The summer Nick taught his cats to read ill. by Kate Berube. Simon & Schuster/Paula Wiseman, 2016. ISBN 978-148143569-7 Subj: Animals – cats. Books, reading.

Mann, Jennifer K. *I will never get a star on Mrs. Benson's blackboard* ill. by author. Candlewick/Nosy Crow, 2015. ISBN 978-076366514-2 Subj: Careers – teachers. Character traits – individuality. School.

Sam and Jump ill. by Jennifer K. Mann. Candlewick, 2016. ISBN 978-076367947-7 Subj: Animals – rabbits. Behavior – lost & found possessions. Behavior – worrying. Friendship. Toys.

Two speckled eggs ill. by author. Candlewick, 2014. ISBN 978-076366168-7 Subj: Birthdays. Character traits – being different. Friendship. Parties.

Manna, Anthony L. *The orphan: a Cinderella story from Greece* by Anthony L. Manna and Soula Mitakidou ill. by Giselle Potter. Random House, 2011. ISBN 978-0-375-86691-3 Subj: Family life – stepfamilies. Folk & fairy tales. Foreign lands – Greece. Orphans. Royalty – princes. Sibling rivalry.

Manners mash-up: a goofy guide to good behavior ill. by Tedd Arnold, et al. Penguin, 2011. ISBN 978-0-8037-3480-7 Subj: Etiquette.

Manning, Eli, et al. *Family huddle* (Manning, Peyton)

Manning, Jane. *Cat nights* ill. by author. HarperCollins, 2008. ISBN 978-0-06-113888-1 Subj: Animals – cats. Character traits – individuality. Witches.

Millie Fierce ill. by author. Philomel, 2012. ISBN 978-0-399-25642-4 Subj: Behavior – misbehavior. Self-concept.

Millie Fierce sleeps out ill. by author. Philomel, 2014. ISBN 978-039916093-6 Subj: Camps, camping. Character traits – assertiveness. Sleepovers.

My first baby games ill. by author. HarperCollins, 2001. ISBN 978-0-694-01435-4 Subj: Babies, toddlers. Games.

Manning, Maurie J. *The aunts go marching* ill. by author. Boyds Mills, 2003. ISBN 978-1-59078-026-8 Subj: Counting, numbers. Cumulative tales. Family life – aunts, uncles. Rhyming text. Weather – rain.

Kitchen dance ill. by author. Clarion, 2008. ISBN 978-0-618-99110-5 Subj: Activities – dancing. Bedtime. Ethnic groups in the U.S. – Hispanic Americans. Family life.

Laundry day ill. by author. Clarion, 2012. ISBN 978-0-547-24196-8 Subj: Behavior – lost & found possessions. Communities, neighborhoods. U.S. history.

Manning, Mick. *Cock-a-doodle hooooooo!* ill. by Brita Granström. Good Books, 2007. ISBN 978-1-56148-568-0 Subj: Birds – chickens, roosters. Birds – owls. Character traits – helpfulness. Farms.

Dino-dinners ill. by Brita Granström. Holiday House, 2007. ISBN 978-0-8234-2089-6 Subj: Dinosaurs.

Snap! by Mick Manning and Brita Granström; ill. by authors. Frances Lincoln, 2006. ISBN 978-1-84507-408-1 Subj: Food. Science.

Supermom ill. by Brita Granström. Albert Whitman, 2001. ISBN 978-0-8075-7666-3 Subj: Animals. Family life – mothers.

What a Viking! ill. by Brita Granström. R&S Books, 2000. ISBN 978-91-29-64883-6 Subj: Foreign lands – Scandinavia. Sailors. Vikings.

Woolly mammoth by Mick Manning and Brita Granström ill. by Brita Granström. Frances Lincoln, 2009. ISBN 978-1-84507-860-7 Subj: Animals – woolly mammoths.

Manning, Peyton. *Family huddle* by Peyton Manning and Eli Manning, et al ill. by Jim Madsen. Scholastic, 2009. ISBN 978-0-545-15377-5 Subj: Family life. Sports – football.

Mannis, Celeste Davidson. *One leaf rides the wind* ill. by Susan Kathleen Hartung. Viking, 2002. ISBN 978-0-670-03525-0 Subj: Counting, numbers. Gardens, gardening. Nature. Poetry.

Mansfield, Andy. *One lonely fish* ill. by Thomas Flintham. Bloomsbury, 2017. ISBN 978-168119201-7 Subj: Counting, numbers. Fish.

Mansfield, Howard. *Hogwood steps out: a good, good pig story* ill. by Barry Moser. Roaring Brook, 2008. ISBN 978-1-59643-269-7 Subj: Animals – pigs. Behavior – misbehavior. Farms. Seasons – spring.

Manson, Ainslie. *Ballerinas don't wear glasses* ill. by Dean Griffiths. Orca, 2000. ISBN 978-1-55143-176-5 Subj: Activities – dancing. Ballet. Family life – brothers & sisters. Self-concept.

Mantchev, Lisa. *Sister day!* ill. by Sonia Sánchez. Simon & Schuster, 2017. ISBN 978-148143795-0 Subj: Activities – making things. Family life – sisters.

Someday, narwhal ill. by Hyewon Yum. Simon & Schuster/Paula Wiseman, 2017. ISBN 978-148147970-7 Subj: Animals – narwhals. Behavior – boredom. Character traits – kindness to animals. Friendship.

Strictly no elephants ill. by Taeeun Yoo. Simon & Schuster/Paula Wiseman, 2015. ISBN 978-148141647-4 Subj: Animals – elephants. Character traits – being different. Pets.

Manuel, Lynn. *Camels always do* ill. by Kasia Charko. Orca, 2004. ISBN 978-1-55143-284-7 Subj: Animals – camels. Foreign lands – British Columbia.

The trouble with Tilly Trumble ill. by Diane Greenseid. Abrams, 2006. ISBN 978-0-8109-5972-9 Subj: Animals – dogs. Behavior – collecting things. Furniture – chairs.

Manushkin, Fran. *Bamboo for me, bamboo for you!* ill. by Purificación Hernández. Simon & Schuster,

2017. ISBN 978-148145063-8 Subj: Animals – pandas. Plants. Rhyming text.

Big girl panties ill. by Valeria Petrone. Random House, 2012. ISBN 978-0-307-93152-8 Subj: Toilet training.

Happy in our skin ill. by Lauren Tobia. Candlewick, 2015. ISBN 978-076367002-3 Subj: Anatomy – skin. Ethnic groups in the U.S. Family life. Rhyming text. Self-concept.

Hooray for Hanukkah! ill. by author. Random House, 2001. ISBN 978-0-375-91043-2 Subj: Holidays – Hanukkah. Jewish culture. Religion.

How mama brought the spring ill. by Holly Berry. Dutton, 2008. ISBN 978-0-525-42027-9 Subj: Family life – grandmothers. Food. Foreign lands – Belarus. Seasons – winter.

Latkes and applesauce ill. by Robin Spowart. Scholastic, 1990. ISBN 978-0-590-42261-1 Subj: Holidays – Hanukkah. Jewish culture. Religion.

Let George do it! (Foreman, George)

Miriam's cup: a Passover story ill. by Bob Dacey. Scholastic, 1998. ISBN 978-0-590-67720-2 Subj: Holidays – Passover. Jewish culture. Religion.

The shivers in the fridge ill. by Paul O. Zelinsky. Penguin, 2006. ISBN 978-0-525-46943-8 Subj: Imagination.

Many, Paul. *Dad's bald head* ill. by Kevin O'Malley. Walker, 2007. ISBN 978-0-8027-9579-3 Subj: Family life – fathers. Hair.

The great pancake escape ill. by Scott Goto. Walker, 2002. ISBN 978-0-8027-8796-5 Subj: Activities – baking, cooking. Careers – magicians. Food. Magic. Rhyming text.

Manzano, Sonia. *A box full of kittens* ill. by Matt Phelan. Simon & Schuster, 2007. ISBN 978-0-689-83089-1 Subj: Animals – cats. Babies, toddlers. Character traits – helpfulness. Ethnic groups in the U.S. – Puerto Rican Americans.

Miracle on 133rd Street ill. by Marjorie Priceman. Atheneum, 2015. ISBN 978-068987887-9 Subj: Activities – baking, cooking. Character traits – cooperation. Communities, neighborhoods. Ethnic groups in the U.S. – Puerto Rican Americans. Holidays – Christmas.

No dogs allowed ill. by Jon J Muth. Atheneum, 2004. ISBN 978-0-689-83088-4 Subj: Activities – picnicking. Animals – dogs. Automobiles. Ethnic groups in the U.S. – Puerto Rican Americans. Family life.

Maples in the mist: children's poems from the Tang Dynasty ill. by Jean Tseng and Mou-Sien Tseng. Lothrop, 1996. ISBN 978-0-688-12044-3 Subj: Foreign lands – China. Poetry.

Mara, Nichole. *So many feet* ill. by Alexander Vidal. Abrams/Appleseed, 2017. ISBN 978-141972318-6 Subj: Anatomy – feet. Animals. Format, unusual – board books.

Marcellino, Fred. *I, crocodile* ill. by author. HarperCollins, 1999. ISBN 978-0-06-205199-8 Subj: Food. Foreign lands – Egypt. Foreign lands – France. Humorous stories. Reptiles – alligators, crocodiles. Royalty – emperors.

Marcero, Deborah. *Ursa's light* ill. by author. Peter Pauper, 2016. ISBN 978-144131881-7 Subj: Activities – flying. Animals – bears. Character traits – perseverance. Dreams.

Marchon, Benoit. *Spoonful!* ill. by Soledad Bravi. Harcourt, 2013. ISBN 978-0-547-89313-6 Subj: Food. Format, unusual – board books.

Marciano, John Bemelmans. *Delilah* ill. by author. Viking, 2002. ISBN 978-0-670-03523-6 Subj: Animals – babies. Animals – sheep. Careers – farmers. Character traits – individuality. Farms. Friendship.

Madeline and the cats of Rome ill. by author. Viking, 2008. ISBN 978-0-670-06297-3 Subj: Animals – cats. Crime. Foreign lands – Italy. Orphans. Rhyming text.

Madeline and the old house in Paris ill. by author. Viking, 2013. ISBN 978-0-670-78485-1 Subj: Foreign lands – France. Ghosts. Orphans. Rhyming text. School.

Madeline at the White House ill. by author. Penguin, 2011. ISBN 978-0-670-01228-2 Subj: Holidays – Easter. Orphans. U.S. history.

Madeline says merci ill. by author. Viking, 2001. ISBN 978-0-670-03505-2 Subj: Etiquette. Rhyming text.

Marco, Chris. *Seeing in living things* (Hartley, Karen)

The sixth sense and other special senses (Hartley, Karen)

Smelling in living things (Hartley, Karen)

Tasting in living things (Hartley, Karen)

Touching in living things (Hartley, Karen)

Marcotte, Danielle. *Mom, dad, our books, and me* ill. by Josee Bisaillon. OwlKids, 2016. ISBN 978-177147201-2 Subj: Books, reading. Family life.

Marcus, Kimberly. *Scritch-scratch a perfect match* ill. by Mike Lester. Penguin, 2011. ISBN 978-0-399-25004-0 Subj: Animals – dogs. Insects – fleas. Rhyming text.

Marcus, Leonard S. *Oscar: the big adventures of a little sock monkey* (Schwartz, Amy)

Margalith, Joan. *The babies are landing* ill. by Linda Bronson. Chronicle, 2000. ISBN 978-0-8118-2674-7 Subj: Babies, toddlers. Rhyming text.

Margolin, H. Ellen. *Goin' to Boston* ill. by Emily Bolam. Handprint, 2002. ISBN 978-1-929766-45-1 Subj: Activities – traveling. Cumulative tales. Music. Songs.

Mariconda, Barbara. *Sort it out!* ill. by Sherry Rogers. Sylvan Dell, 2008. ISBN 978-1-934359-11-2 Subj: Animals – pack rats. Behavior – collecting things. Character traits – orderliness. Counting, numbers. Rhyming text.

Marin, Cheech. *Cheech and the spooky ghost bus* ill. by Orlando L. Ramirez. HarperCollins, 2009. ISBN 978-0-06-113211-7 Subj: Careers – bus drivers. Ghosts.

Marino, Gianna. *A boy, a ball, and a dog* ill. by author. Roaring Brook/Neal Porter, 2016. ISBN 978-162672287-3 Subj: Animals – dogs. Toys – balloons. Toys – balls.

Following Papa's song ill. by author. Viking, 2014. ISBN 978-067001315-9 Subj: Animals – whales. Behavior – worrying. Family life – fathers. Migration.

I am the Mountain Mouse: four furry tales, one crazy mouse! ill. by author. Viking, 2016. ISBN 978-045146955-7 Subj: Animals – mice. Behavior – boasting, showing off. Character traits – conceit.

Meet me at the moon ill. by author. Viking, 2012. ISBN 978-0-670-01313-5 Subj: Animals – elephants. Family life – mothers. Foreign lands – Africa. Weather – droughts.

Night animals ill. by author. Viking, 2015. ISBN 978-045146954-0 Subj: Animals. Animals – possums. Emotions – fear. Night.

One too many: a seek and find counting book ill. by author. Chronicle, 2010. ISBN 978-0-8118-6908-9 Subj: Animals. Counting, numbers. Picture puzzles.

Too tall houses ill. by author. Viking, 2012. ISBN 978-0-670-01314-2 Subj: Animals – rabbits. Birds – owls. Character traits – cooperation. Homes, houses. Problem solving.

Zoopa: an animal alphabet ill. by author. Chronicle, 2005. ISBN 978-0-8118-4789-6 Subj: ABC books. Animals. Food.

Mark, Michael L. *The library book* (Chapin, Tom)

Markel, Michelle. *Balderdash! John Newbery and the boisterous birth of children's books* ill. by Nancy Carpenter. Chronicle, 2017. ISBN 978-081187922-4

Subj: Books, reading. Careers – printers. Careers – publishers.

Brave girl: Clara and the Shirtwaist Makers' Strike of 1909 ill. by Melissa Sweet. HarperCollins, 2013. ISBN 978-0-06-180442-7 Subj: Activities – working. Behavior – seeking better things. Character traits – bravery. Clothing. U.S. history.

The fantastic jungles of Henri Rousseau ill. by Amanda Hall. Eerdmans, 2012. ISBN 978-0-8028-5364-6 Subj: Art. Careers – artists. Character traits – perseverance. Foreign lands – France.

Tyrannosaurus math ill. by Doug Cushman. Tricycle, 2009. ISBN 978-1-58246-282-0 Subj: Counting, numbers. Dinosaurs.

Markell, Denis. *Hush, Little Monster* ill. by Melissa Iwai. Simon & Schuster, 2012. ISBN 978-1-4424-4195-8 Subj: Family life – fathers. Lullabies. Monsters. Rhyming text.

Markes, Julie. *Good thing you're not an octopus!* ill. by Maggie Smith. HarperCollins, 2001. ISBN 978-0-06-028466-4 Subj: Activities. Animals. Self-concept.

Shhhhh! Everybody's sleeping ill. by David Parkins. HarperCollins, 2005. ISBN 978-0-06-053791-3 Subj: Bedtime. Rhyming text. Sleep.

Sidewalk ABC ill. by Jennifer Markes. HarperCollins, 2001. ISBN 978-0-694-01455-2 Subj: ABC books. Format, unusual – board books.

Sidewalk 1 2 3 ill. by Jennifer Markes. HarperCollins, 2001. ISBN 978-0-694-01500-9 Subj: Counting, numbers. Format, unusual – board books.

Thanks for Thanksgiving ill. by Doris Barrette. HarperCollins, 2004. ISBN 978-0-06-051097-8 Subj: Holidays – Thanksgiving. Rhyming text.

Markham, Beryl. *The good lion* ill. by Don Brown. Houghton, 2005. ISBN 978-0-618-56306-7 Subj: Animals – lions. Foreign lands – Africa.

Markle, Sandra. *Bats: biggest! littlest!.* Boyds Mills, 2013. ISBN 978-1-59078-952-0 Subj: Animals – bats. Concepts – size.

Build, beaver, build! life at the longest beaver dam ill. by Deborah Hocking. Lerner/Millbrook, 2016. ISBN 978-146774900-8 Subj: Animals – beavers. Nature.

Butterfly tree ill. by Leslie Wu. Peachtree, 2011. ISBN 978-1-56145-539-3 Subj: Insects – butterflies, caterpillars. Migration.

Creepy, crawly baby bugs ill. with photos. Walker, 1996. ISBN 978-0-8027-8444-5 Subj: Animals – babies. Insects. Science.

Family pack ill. by Alan Marks. Charlesbridge, 2011. ISBN 978-1-58089-217-9 Subj: Animals – endangered animals. Animals – wolves.

Finding home ill. by Alan Marks. Charlesbridge, 2008. ISBN 978-1-58089-122-6 Subj: Animals – koalas. Fire. Foreign lands – Australia.

Hip-pocket papa ill. by Alan Marks. Charlesbridge, 2010. ISBN 978-1-57091-708-0 Subj: Foreign lands – Australia. Frogs & toads.

How many baby pandas? ill. with photos. Walker, 2009. ISBN 978-0-8027-9783-4 Subj: Animals – pandas. Counting, numbers. Foreign lands – China.

Insects: biggest! littlest! photos by Simon Pollard. Boyds Mills, 2009. ISBN 978-1-59078-512-6 Subj: Insects.

Little lost bat ill. by Alan Marks. Charlesbridge, 2006. ISBN 978-1-57091-656-4 Subj: Animals – bats. Nature.

A mother's journey ill. by Alan Marks. Charlesbridge, 2005. ISBN 978-1-57091-621-2 Subj: Birds – penguins. Family life.

Sharks: biggest! littlest! ill. with photos. Boyds Mills, 2008. ISBN 978-1-59078-513-3 Subj: Concepts – size. Fish – sharks.

Sneaky, spinning, baby spiders ill. with photos. Walker, 2008. ISBN 978-0-8027-9697-4 Subj: Science. Spiders.

Thirsty, thirsty elephants ill. by Fabricio Vanden Broeck. Charlesbridge, 2017. ISBN 978-158089634-4 Subj: Animals – elephants. Family life – grandmothers. Foreign lands – Tanzania. Nature. Weather – droughts.

Toad weather ill. by Thomas Gonzalez. Peachtree, 2015. ISBN 978-156145818-9 Subj: Frogs & toads. Migration. Weather – rain.

Waiting for ice ill. by Alan Marks. Charlesbridge, 2012. ISBN 978-1-58089-255-1 Subj: Animals – polar bears. Ecology.

Marks, Jennifer L. *Sorting by size* ill. with photos. Capstone, 2006. ISBN 978-0-7368-6740-5 Subj: Concepts – size.

Sorting money ill. with photos. Capstone, 2006. ISBN 978-0-7368-6738-2 Subj: Money.

Sorting toys ill. with photos. Capstone, 2006. ISBN 978-0-7368-6737-5 Subj: Toys.

Marley, Cedella, reteller. *Every little thing* ill. by Vanessa Brantley Newton. Chronicle, 2012. ISBN 978-1-4521-0697-7 Subj: Activities – playing. Birds. Day. Songs.

One love: based on the song by Bob Marley ill. by Vanessa Brantley Newton. Chronicle, 2011. ISBN 978-1-4521-0224-5 Subj: Emotions – love. Songs.

Marlow, Layn. *Hurry up and slow down* ill. by author. Holiday, 2009. ISBN 978-0-8234-2178-7 Subj: Animals – rabbits. Bedtime. Behavior – hurrying. Reptiles – turtles, tortoises.

You make me smile ill. by author. Holiday House, 2013. ISBN 978-0-8234-2922-6 Subj: Snowmen. Weather – snow.

Marlowe, Pete. *One Arabian morning* ill. by Charles Bell. Annick, 2000. ISBN 978-1-55037-659-3 Subj: Foreign lands. Imagination. Royalty.

Marlowe, Sara. *No ordinary apple: a story about eating mindfully* ill. by Philip Pascuzzo. Wisdom, 2013. ISBN 978-1-61429-076-6 Subj: Behavior. Character traits – patience, impatience. Character traits – wisdom. Food.

Marsalis, Wynton. *Squeak, rumble, whomp! whomp! whomp! a sonic adventure* ill. by Paul Rogers. Candlewick, 2012. ISBN 978-0-7636-3991-4 Subj: Careers – musicians. Communities, neighborhoods. Ethnic groups in the U.S. – African Americans. Music. Musical instruments. Noise, sounds.

Marsh, T. J. *Somewhere in the ocean* (Ward, Jennifer)

Marshak, S. *The Month-Brothers: a Slavic tale* ill. by Diane Stanley. Morrow, 1983. ISBN 978-0-688-01510-7 Subj: Foreign lands – Czechoslovakia. Rhyming text. Seasons. Weather.

Marshall, Catherine. *Christy, Christmastime at Cutter Gap* (LeSourd, Nancy)

Marshall, Edward. *Space case* ill. by James Marshall. Dial, 1980. ISBN 978-0-8037-8007-1 Subj: Holidays – Halloween. Robots. Space & space ships.

Marshall, James. *The Cut-Ups* ill. by author. Viking, 1984. ISBN 978-0-670-25195-7 Subj: Behavior – misbehavior. Humorous stories. Toys.

The Cut-Ups at Camp Custer ill. by author. Viking, 1989. ISBN 978-0-670-82051-1 Subj: Behavior – misbehavior. Camps, camping. Humorous stories.

The Cut-Ups carry on ill. by author. Viking, 1990. ISBN 978-0-670-81645-3 Subj: Activities – dancing. Contests. Humorous stories.

The Cut-Ups crack up ill. by author. Viking, 1992. ISBN 978-0-670-84486-9 Subj: Automobiles. Behavior – misbehavior. Humorous stories. School.

The Cut-Ups cut loose ill. by author. Viking, 1987. ISBN 978-0-670-80740-6 Subj: Behavior – misbehavior. Friendship. Humorous stories. School.

Eugene ill. by author. Houghton, 2000. ISBN 978-0-618-07319-1 Subj: Animals. Careers – teachers. Format, unusual – board books. Reptiles – turtles, tortoises. School – first day.

George and Martha ill. by author. Houghton, 1972. ISBN 978-0-395-13732-1 Subj: Animals – hippopotamuses. Friendship.

George and Martha back in town ill. by author. Houghton, 1984. ISBN 978-0-395-35386-8 Subj: Animals – hippopotamuses. Behavior – misbehavior. Friendship.

George and Martha encore ill. by author. Houghton, 1973. ISBN 978-0-395-17512-5 Subj: Activities – dancing. Animals – hippopotamuses. Friendship.

George and Martha one fine day ill. by author. Houghton, 1978. ISBN 978-0-395-27154-4 Subj: Animals – hippopotamuses. Friendship.

George and Martha rise and shine ill. by author. Houghton, 1976. ISBN 978-0-395-24738-9 Subj: Animals – hippopotamuses. Friendship.

George and Martha 'round and 'round ill. by author. Houghton, 1988. ISBN 978-0-395-46763-3 Subj: Activities – vacationing. Animals – hippopotamuses. Friendship. Imagination.

George and Martha, tons of fun ill. by author. Houghton, 1980. ISBN 978-0-395-29524-3 Subj: Animals – hippopotamuses. Character traits – vanity.

Merry Christmas, space case ill. by author. Dial, 1986. ISBN 978-0-8037-0216-5 Subj: Holidays – Christmas. Space & space ships.

Miss Nelson is back (Allard, Harry)

Miss Nelson is missing! (Allard, Harry)

Pocketful of nonsense ill. by author. Artists & Writers Guild, 1993. ISBN 978-0-307-17552-6 Subj: Poetry.

Portly McSwine ill. by author. Houghton, 1979. ISBN 978-0-395-28003-4 Subj: Animals – pigs. Behavior – worrying.

Red Riding Hood ill. by reteller. Dial, 1987. ISBN 978-0-8037-0345-2 Subj: Animals – wolves. Behavior – talking to strangers. Folk & fairy tales.

The Stupids have a ball (Allard, Harry)

The Stupids take off (Allard, Harry)

Swine lake ill. by Maurice Sendak. HarperCollins, 1999. ISBN 978-0-06-205171-4 Subj: Activities – dancing. Animals – pigs. Animals – wolves. Ballet. Theater.

Wings: a tale of two chickens ill. by author. Viking, 1986. ISBN 978-0-670-80961-5 Subj: Animals – foxes. Birds – chickens, roosters. Books, reading.

Yummers! ill. by author. Houghton, 1973. ISBN 978-0-395-14757-3 Subj: Animals – pigs. Food. Illness.

Yummers too: the second course ill. by author. Houghton, 1986. ISBN 978-0-395-38990-4 Subj: Animals – pigs. Behavior – greed. Food. Reptiles – turtles, tortoises.

Marshall, Janet Perry. *Baby sharks* (Gentle, Victor)

A honey of a day ill. by author. Greenwillow, 2000. ISBN 978-0-688-16917-6 Subj: Animals. Flowers. Weddings.

Killer sharks, killer people (Gentle, Victor)

Orcas, killer whales (Gentle, Victor)

Shark camouflage and armor (Gentle, Victor)

Very big sharks (Gentle, Victor)

The world's strangest shark (Gentle, Victor)

Marshall, Linda Elovitz. *Grandma Rose's magic* ill. by Ag Jatkowska. Lerner/Kar-Ben, 2012. ISBN 978-0-7613-5215-0 Subj: Activities – sewing. Character traits – generosity. Family life – grandmothers. Jewish culture.

Kindergarten is cool! ill. by Chris Chatterton. Scholastic/Cartwheel, 2016. ISBN 978-054565266-7 Subj: Rhyming text. School – first day.

The passover lamb ill. by Tatjana Mai-Wyss. Random House, 2013. ISBN 978-0-307-93177-1 Subj: Animals – sheep. Character traits – questioning. Farms. Holidays – Passover. Holidays – Seder. Jewish culture.

Rainbow weaver / Tejedora del arcoíris ill. by Elisa Chavarri. Lee & Low, 2016. ISBN 978-089239374-9 Subj: Activities – weaving. Behavior – resourcefulness. Character traits – perseverance. Foreign lands – Guatemala. Foreign languages. Indians of Central America – Maya.

Talia and the rude vegetables ill. by Francesca Assirelli. Lerner/Kar-Ben, 2011. ISBN 978-0-7613-5217-4 Subj: Food. Gardens, gardening. Holidays – Rosh Hashanah.

Marshall, Natalie. *Five little ducks: a fingers and toes nursery rhyme book* ill. by author. Scholastic, 2017. ISBN 978-133809116-8 Subj: Birds – ducks. Counting, numbers. Format, unusual – board books. Rhyming text.

Martin, Ann M. *The Doll People's Christmas* by Ann M. Martin and Laura Godwin ill. by Brett Helquist. Disney/Hyperion, 2016. ISBN 978-148472339-5 Subj: Holidays – Christmas. Toys – dolls.

Rachel Parker, kindergarten show-off ill. by Nancy Poydar. Holiday, 1992. ISBN 978-0-8234-0935-8 Subj: Behavior – boasting, showing off. Character traits – conceit. Emotions – envy, jealousy. Ethnic groups in the U.S. – African Americans. Friendship. School.

Martin, Bernard H. *Chicken Chuck* (Martin, Bill, Jr.)

Martin, Bill, Jr. *Adam, Adam, what do you see?* by Bill Martin, Jr. and Michael R. Sampson ill. by Cathie Felstead. Tommy Nelson, 2000. ISBN 978-0-8499-7614-8 Subj: Religion. Rhyming text.

Baby bear, baby bear, what do you see? ill. by Eric Carle. Henry Holt, 2007. ISBN 978-0-8050-8336-1 Subj: Animals. Animals – bears. Cumulative tales. Rhyming text.

Barn dance! ill. by Ted Rand. Henry Holt, 1986. ISBN 978-0-8050-0089-4 Subj: Activities – dancing. Barns. Country. Dreams. Night. Rhyming text. Scarecrows.

A beasty story by Bill Martin, Jr. and Steven Kellogg ill. by Steven Kellogg. Harcourt, 1999. ISBN 978-0-15-201683-8 Subj: Animals – mice. Forest, woods. Monsters.

Brown bear, brown bear, what do you see? ill. by Eric Carle. Henry Holt, 1992. ISBN 978-0-8050-1744-1 Subj: Animals – bears. Concepts – color. Cumulative tales. Rhyming text.

Chicka chicka boom boom by Bill Martin, Jr. and John Archambault ill. by Lois Ehlert. Simon & Schuster, 1989. ISBN 978-0-617-67949-3 Subj: ABC books. Rhyming text. Trees.

Chicken Chuck by Bill Martin, Jr. and Bernard H. Martin ill. by Steven Salerno. Winslow, 2000. ISBN 978-1-890817-31-2 Subj: Animals. Animals – horses, ponies. Birds – chickens, roosters. Character traits – individuality. Circus. Farms.

Fire! Fire! said Mrs. McGuire ill. by Richard Egielski. Harcourt, 1996. ISBN 978-0-15-227562-4 Subj: Birthdays. Careers – firefighters. Fire. Nursery rhymes.

"Fire! Fire!" said Mrs. McGuire ill. by Vladimir Radunsky. Harcourt, 2006. ISBN 978-0-15-205725-1 Subj: Birthdays. Careers – firefighters. Fire. Nursery rhymes.

Here are my hands by Bill Martin, Jr. and John Archambault ill. by Ted Rand. Henry Holt, 1998. ISBN 978-0-8050-5911-3 Subj: Anatomy. Rhyming text.

I love our Earth by Bill Martin, Jr. and Michael R. Sampson ill. by Dan Lipow. Charlesbridge, 2006. ISBN 978-1-58089-106-6 Subj: Earth. Nature. Seasons.

I pledge allegiance commentary by Michael R. Sampson; ill. by Chris Raschka. Candlewick, 2002. ISBN 978-076361648-9 Subj: Flags. U.S. history.

Kitty Cat, Kitty Cat, are you going to school? by Bill Martin, Jr. and Michael R. Sampson ill. by Laura J. Bryant. Amazon/Two Lions, 2013. ISBN 978-1-4778-1722-3 Subj: Animals – cats. Rhyming text. School – first day.

Kitty Cat, Kitty Cat, are you going to sleep? by Bill Martin, Jr. and Michael R. Sampson ill. by Laura

J. Bryant. Marshall Cavendish, 2011. ISBN 978-0-7614-5946-0 Subj: Animals – cats. Bedtime. Rhyming text.

Kitty Cat, Kitty Cat, are you waking up? by Bill Martin, Jr. and Michael R. Sampson ill. by Laura J. Bryant. Marshall Cavendish, 2008. ISBN 978-0-7614-5438-0 Subj: Animals – cats. Rhyming text.

Knots on a counting rope by Bill Martin, Jr. and John Archambault ill. by Ted Rand. Henry Holt, 1987. ISBN 978-0-8050-0571-4 Subj: Character traits – bravery. Disabilities – blindness. Emotions – love. Family life – grandfathers. Indians of North America. Senses – sight.

Listen to our world by Bill Martin, Jr. and Michael Sampson ill. by Melissa Sweet. Simon & Schuster/Paula Wiseman, 2016. ISBN 978-144245472-9 Subj: Animals. Nature. Noise, sounds.

Listen to the rain by Bill Martin, Jr. and John Archambault ill. by James R. Endicott. Henry Holt, 1988. ISBN 978-0-8050-0682-7 Subj: Rhyming text. Weather – rain.

Little granny quarterback by Bill Martin, Jr. and Michael R. Sampson ill. by Michael Chesworth. Boyds Mills, 2001. ISBN 978-1-56397-930-9 Subj: Dreams. Family life – grandmothers. Old age. Rhyming text. Sports – football.

The little squeegy bug by Bill Martin, Jr. and Michael R. Sampson ill. by Pat Corrigan. Winslow, 2001. ISBN 978-1-890817-90-9 Subj: Insects.

Maestro plays ill. by Vladimir Radunsky. Henry Holt, 1994. ISBN 978-0-8050-1746-5 Subj: Careers – musicians. Rhyming text.

The magic pumpkin by Bill Martin, Jr. and John Archambault ill. by Robert J. Lee. Henry Holt, 1989. ISBN 978-0-8050-1134-0 Subj: Holidays – Halloween. Magic. Rhyming text.

Old devil wind ill. by Barry Root. Harcourt, 1993. ISBN 978-0-15-257768-1 Subj: Cumulative tales. Ghosts. Holidays – Halloween. Weather – wind.

Polar bear, polar bear, what do you hear? ill. by Eric Carle. Henry Holt, 1991. ISBN 978-0-8050-1759-5 Subj: Animals. Noise, sounds. Rhyming text. Zoos.

Rock it, sock it, number line by Bill Martin, Jr. and Michael R. Sampson ill. by Heather Cahoon. Henry Holt, 2001. ISBN 978-0-8050-6304-2 Subj: Counting, numbers. Food. Parties. Plants. Royalty.

Spunky Little Monkey by Bill Martin, Jr. and Michael Sampson ill. by Brian Won. Scholastic, 2017. ISBN 978-054577643-1 Subj: Activities – dancing. Animals – monkeys. Health & fitness – exercise. Participation. Rhyming text.

Swish! by Bill Martin, Jr. and Michael R. Sampson ill. by Michael Chesworth. Henry Holt, 1997.

ISBN 978-0-8050-4498-0 Subj: Sports – basketball.

Ten little caterpillars ill. by Lois Ehlert. Simon & Schuster, 2011. ISBN 978-1-4424-3385-4 Subj: Counting, numbers. Insects – butterflies, caterpillars. Metamorphosis. Rhyming text.

Trick or treat? by Bill Martin, Jr. and Michael R. Sampson ill. by Paul Meisel. Simon & Schuster, 2002. ISBN 978-0-689-84968-8 Subj: Behavior – trickery. Food. Holidays – Halloween. Magic.

The turning of the year ill. by Greg Shed. Harcourt, 1998. ISBN 978-0-15-201085-0 Subj: Days of the week, months of the year. Rhyming text. Seasons.

Martin, David. *All for pie, pie for all* ill. by Valeri Gorbachev. Candlewick, 2006. ISBN 978-0-7636-2393-7 Subj: Activities – baking, cooking. Animals – cats. Animals – mice. Behavior – sharing. Food. Insects – ants.

Five little piggies ill. by Susan Meddaugh. Candlewick, 1998. ISBN 978-1-56402-918-8 Subj: Animals – pigs. Family life. Shopping.

Hanukkah lights ill. by Melissa Sweet. Candlewick, 2009. ISBN 978-0-7636-3029-4 Subj: Format, unusual – board books. Holidays – Hanukkah. Rhyming text.

Let's have a tree party! ill. by John Manders. Candlewick, 2012. ISBN 978-0-7636-3704-0 Subj: Animals. Forest, woods. Rhyming text. Trees.

Little Bunny and the magic Christmas tree ill. by Valeri Gorbachev. Candlewick, 2011. ISBN 978-0-7636-3693-7 Subj: Animals – rabbits. Character traits – smallness. Holidays – Christmas.

Monkey business ill. by Scott Nash. Candlewick, 2000. ISBN 978-0-7636-1178-1 Subj: Animals – monkeys. Birthdays. Family life – mothers.

Monkey trouble ill. by Scott Nash. Candlewick, 2000. ISBN 978-0-7636-1179-8 Subj: Animals – monkeys. Behavior – misbehavior.

Peep and Ducky ill. by David Walker. Candlewick, 2013. ISBN 978-0-7636-5039-1 Subj: Activities – playing. Birds – bluebirds. Birds – ducks. Friendship. Rhyming text.

Peep and Ducky: rainy day ill. by David Walker. Candlewick, 2015. ISBN 978-076366884-6 Subj: Activities – playing. Birds – bluebirds. Birds – ducks. Friendship. Rhyming text. Weather – rain.

Piggy and Dad ill. by Frank Remkiewicz. Candlewick, 2001. ISBN 978-0-7636-1326-6 Subj: Activities. Animals – pigs. Family life – fathers.

Piggy and Dad go fishing ill. by Frank Remkiewicz. Candlewick, 2005. ISBN 978-0-7636-2506-1 Subj: Animals – pigs. Animals – worms. Family life – fathers. Fish. Sports – fishing.

Shh! bears sleeping ill. by Steve Johnson. Viking, 2016. ISBN 978-067001718-8 Subj: Animals – bears. Hibernation. Rhyming text. Seasons.

We've all got bellybuttons ill. by Randy Cecil. Candlewick, 2005. ISBN 978-0-7636-1775-2 Subj: Anatomy. Anatomy – navels. Animals. Rhyming text.

Martin, Emily Winfield. *Day dreamers: a journey of imagination* ill. by author. Random House, 2014. ISBN 978-038537670-9 Subj: Dreams. Imagination. Mythical creatures. Rhyming text.

Dream animals ill. by author. Random House, 2013. ISBN 978-0-449-81080-4 Subj: Animals. Bedtime. Dreams. Rhyming text.

The littlest family's big day ill. by author. Random House, 2016. ISBN 978-055351101-7 Subj: Animals – bears. Character traits – smallness. Concepts – size. Family life.

The wonderful things you will be ill. by author. Random House, 2015. ISBN 978-038537671-6 Subj: Character traits. Family life – parents. Rhyming text.

Martin, Francesca. *Clever Tortoise: a traditional African tale* ill. by author. Candlewick, 2000. ISBN 978-0-7636-0506-3 Subj: Animals. Folk & fairy tales. Foreign lands – Tanzania. Reptiles – turtles, tortoises.

Martín, Hugo C. *Pablo's Christmas* ill. by Lee Chapman. Sterling, 2006. ISBN 978-1-4027-2560-9 Subj: Activities – wood carving. Family life. Farms. Foreign lands – Mexico. Holidays – Christmas.

Martin, Jacqueline Briggs. *Alice Waters and the trip to delicious* ill. by Hayelin Choi. Readers to Eaters, 2014. ISBN 978-098366156-6 Subj: Activities – baking, cooking. Careers – chefs, cooks. Food. Health & fitness.

Banjo granny (Busse, Sarah Martin)

Chicken joy on Redbean Road: a bayou country romp ill. by Melissa Sweet. Houghton, 2007. ISBN 978-0-618-50759-7 Subj: Activities – singing. Birds – chickens, roosters. Farms. Food. Illness. Music.

The chiru of High Tibet: a true story ill. by Linda S. Wingerter. Harcourt, 2010. ISBN 978-0-618-58130-6 Subj: Animals – endangered animals. Foreign lands – Tibet.

Creekfinding: a true story ill. by Claudia McGehee. Univ. of Minnesota, 2017. ISBN 978-081669802-8 Subj: Ecology. Nature. Rivers.

Farmer Will Allen and the growing table ill. by Eric-Shabazz Larkin. Readers to Eaters, 2013. ISBN 978-0-98366-153-5 Subj: Behavior – seeking better things. Cities, towns. Communities, neighborhoods. Ethnic groups in the U.S. – African Americans. Gardens, gardening.

On Sand Island ill. by David Johnson. Houghton, 2003. ISBN 978-0-618-23151-5 Subj: Activities – trading. Boats, ships. Family life. Islands. Lakes, ponds.

Snowflake Bentley ill. by Mary Azarian. Houghton, 1998. ISBN 978-0-395-86162-2 Subj: Caldecott award books. Careers – photographers. Careers – scientists. Nature. U.S. history. Weather – snow.

The water gift and the pig of the pig ill. by Linda S. Wingerter. Houghton, 2002. ISBN 978-0-618-07436-5 Subj: Animals – pigs. Family life – grandfathers. Orphans.

Martín Larrañaga, Ana. *Pepo and Lolo and the red apple* ill. by author. Candlewick, 2004. ISBN 978-0-7636-2036-3 Subj: Animals – pigs. Birds – chickens, roosters. Character traits – cooperation. Food.

Pepo and Lolo are friends ill. by author. Candlewick, 2004. ISBN 978-0-7636-1982-4 Subj: Animals – pigs. Birds – chickens, roosters. Friendship.

Woo! the not-so-scary Ghost ill. by author. Scholastic, 2000. ISBN 978-0-439-16958-5 Subj: Behavior – running away. Emotions – fear. Ghosts.

Martin, Rafe. *The language of birds* ill. by Susan Gaber. Putnam, 2000. ISBN 978-0-399-22925-1 Subj: Character traits – kindness to animals. Folk & fairy tales. Foreign lands – Russia.

The rough-face girl ill. by David Shannon. Putnam, 1992. ISBN 978-0-399-21859-0 Subj: Family life – sisters. Folk & fairy tales. Indians of North America – Algonquin.

The Shark God ill. by David Shannon. Scholastic, 2001. ISBN 978-0-590-39500-7 Subj: Character traits – kindness to animals. Fish – sharks. Folk & fairy tales. Hawaii. Royalty – kings.

The storytelling princess ill. by Kimberly Bulcken Root. Putnam, 2001. ISBN 978-0-399-22924-4 Subj: Activities – storytelling. Royalty – princes. Royalty – princesses.

Will's mammoth ill. by Stephen Gammell. Putnam, 1989. ISBN 978-0-399-21627-5 Subj: Animals. Imagination.

Martin, Ruth. *Moon dreams* ill. by Olivier Latyk. Candlewick, 2010. ISBN 978-0-7636-5012-4 Subj: Day. Dreams. Moon. Night.

Santa's on his way ill. by Sophy Williams. Candlewick, 2011. ISBN 978-0-7636-5555-6 Subj: Format, unusual – toy & movable books. Holidays – Christmas. Santa Claus.

Martin, Sarah Catherine. *Old Mother Hubbard* retold by Jane Cabrera; ill. by reteller. Based on

The comic adventures of Old Mother Hubbard and her dog, originally published in London, 1805, by John Harris. Holiday, 2001. ISBN 978-0-8234-1659-2 Subj: Animals – dogs. Nursery rhymes.

Old Mother Hubbard and her wonderful dog ill. by James Marshall. Farrar, 1991. ISBN 978-0-374-35621-7 Subj: Animals – dogs. Nursery rhymes.

Martin, Stephen W. *Charlotte and the rock* ill. by Samantha Cotterill. Dial, 2017. ISBN 978-110199389-7 Subj: Character traits – optimism. Dinosaurs. Pets. Rocks.

Martin-James, Kathleen. *Soaring bald eagles* ill. with photos. Lerner, 2001. ISBN 978-0-8225-3636-9 Subj: Birds – eagles.

Martinez, Libby. *I pledge allegiance* (Mora, Pat)

Martins, Isabel Minhós. *Little lamb, have you any wool?* ill. by Yara Kono. OwlKids, 2012. ISBN 978-1-926973-14-2 Subj: Activities – knitting. Animals – sheep. Behavior – sharing. Character traits – cooperation. Clothing. Friendship.

My neighbor is a dog ill. by Madalena Matoso. OwlKids, 2013. ISBN 978-1-926973-68-5 Subj: Animals. Animals – dogs. Character traits – being different. Prejudice.

Marx, Patricia. *Dot in Larryland: the big little book of an odd-sized friendship* ill. by Roz Chast. Bloomsbury, 2009. ISBN 978-1-59990-181-7 Subj: Character traits – smallness. Concepts – size. Emotions – loneliness. Friendship. Humorous stories.

Marx, Trish. *Kindergarten day USA and China: a flip-me-over book* photos by Ellen B. Senisi. Charlesbridge, 2010. ISBN 978-1-58089-219-3 Subj: Foreign lands – China. Format, unusual. School.

Marzollo, Jean. *Baby's alphabet* photos by Nancy Sheehan. Roaring Brook, 2002. ISBN 978-0-7613-2760-8 Subj: ABC books. Babies, toddlers.

Daniel in the lion's den ill. by reteller. Little, 2003. ISBN 978-0-316-74132-3 Subj: Animals – lions. Religion – Daniel.

Do you know new? ill. by Mari Takabayashi. HarperCollins, 1997. ISBN 978-0-694-00870-4 Subj: Babies, toddlers. Format, unusual – board books. Rhyming text.

Help me learn addition ill. by Chad Phillips. Holiday House, 2012. ISBN 978-0-8234-2398-9 Subj: Counting, numbers.

Help me learn numbers 0–20 photos by Chad Phillips. Holiday House, 2011. ISBN 978-0-8234-2334-7 Subj: Counting, numbers.

Help me learn subtraction ill. by Chad Phillips. Holiday House, 2012. ISBN 978-0-8234-2401-6 Subj: Counting, numbers.

I love you: a rebus poem ill. by Suse MacDonald. Scholastic, 2000. ISBN 978-0-590-37656-3 Subj: Concepts. Emotions – love. Poetry. Rebuses.

I see a star ill. by Suse MacDonald. Scholastic, 2002. ISBN 978-0-439-26616-1 Subj: Holidays – Christmas. Rebuses. Stars.

I spy: a book of picture riddles photos by Walter Wick. Scholastic, 1992. ISBN 978-0-590-45087-4 Subj: Picture puzzles. Rhyming text.

I spy A to Z: a book of picture riddles photos by Walter Wick. Scholastic, 2009. ISBN 978-0-545-10782-2 Subj: ABC books. Picture puzzles.

I spy Christmas: a book of picture riddles photos by Walter Wick. Scholastic, 1992. ISBN 978-0-590-45846-7 Subj: Holidays – Christmas. Picture puzzles. Rhyming text. Riddles & jokes.

I spy extreme challenger! a book of picture riddles photos by Walter Wick. Scholastic, 2000. ISBN 978-0-439-19900-1 Subj: Picture puzzles. Rhyming text. Riddles & jokes.

I spy fantasy: a book of picture riddles photos by Walter Wick. Scholastic, 1994. ISBN 978-0-590-46295-2 Subj: Imagination. Picture puzzles. Rhyming text. Riddles & jokes.

I spy gold challenger! a book of picture riddles photos by Walter Wick. Scholastic, 1998. ISBN 978-0-590-04296-3 Subj: Picture puzzles. Rhyming text. Riddles & jokes.

I spy little animals photos by Walter Wick. Scholastic, 1998. ISBN 978-0-590-11711-1 Subj: Animals. Format, unusual – board books. Picture puzzles. Rhyming text.

I spy little book photos by Walter Wick. Scholastic, 1997. ISBN 978-0-590-34129-5 Subj: Format, unusual – board books. Picture puzzles. Rhyming text.

I spy little bunnies photos by Walter Wick. Scholastic, 2001. ISBN 978-0-439-22158-0 Subj: Animals – rabbits. Picture puzzles. Rhyming text.

I spy little Christmas photos by Walter Wick. Scholastic, 1999. ISBN 978-0-439-08331-7 Subj: Holidays – Christmas. Picture puzzles. Rhyming text.

I spy little letters photos by Walter Wick. Scholastic, 2000. ISBN 978-0-439-11496-7 Subj: ABC books. Picture puzzles. Rhyming text.

I spy little numbers photos by Walter Wick. Scholastic, 1999. ISBN 978-0-590-68714-0 Subj: Counting, numbers. Picture puzzles. Rhyming text.

I spy little wheels photos by Walter Wick. Scholastic, 1998. ISBN 978-0-590-04706-7 Subj: Format, unusual – board books. Picture puzzles. Rhyming text. Toys.

I spy, mystery photos by Walter Wick. Scholastic, 1993. ISBN 978-0-590-46294-5 Subj: Picture puzzles. Rhyming text. Riddles & jokes.

I spy school days: a book of picture riddles photos by Walter Wick. Scholastic, 1995. ISBN 978-0-590-48135-9 Subj: Picture puzzles. Rhyming text. Riddles & jokes. School.

I spy spooky night: a book of picture riddles photos by Walter Wick. Scholastic, 1996. ISBN 978-0-590-48137-3 Subj: Ghosts. Holidays – Halloween. Picture puzzles. Rhyming text. Riddles & jokes.

I spy super challenger! a book of picture riddles photos by Walter Wick. Scholastic, 1997. ISBN 978-0-590-34128-8 Subj: Picture puzzles. Rhyming text. Riddles & jokes.

I spy treasure hunt: a book of picture riddles photos by Walter Wick. Scholastic, 2007. ISBN 978-0-439-02674-1 Subj: Mystery stories. Picture puzzles. Pirates. Rhyming text. Riddles & jokes.

I spy ultimate challenger! a book of picture riddles photos by Walter Wick. Scholastic, 2003. ISBN 978-0-439-45401-8 Subj: Picture puzzles. Rhyming text. Riddles & jokes.

I spy, year-round challenger! photos by Walter Wick. Scholastic, 2001. ISBN 978-0-439-31634-7 Subj: Days of the week, months of the year. Picture puzzles. Rhyming text. Riddles & jokes.

Little Bear, you're a star! A Greek myth about the constellations ill. by reteller. Little, Brown, 2005. ISBN 978-0-316-74135-4 Subj: Animals – bears. Stars.

The little plant doctor: a story about George Washington Carver ill. by Ken Wilson-Max. Holiday House, 2011. ISBN 978-0-8234-2325-5 Subj: Careers – scientists. Ethnic groups in the U.S. – African Americans. U.S. history.

Mama, Mama ill. by Laura Regan. HarperCollins, 1999. ISBN 978-0-694-01245-9 Subj: Animals. Family life – mothers. Format, unusual – board books. Rhyming text.

Miriam and her brother Moses ill. by reteller. Little, 2003. ISBN 978-0-316-74131-6 Subj: Religion. Religion – Moses.

Once upon a springtime ill. by Jacqueline Rogers. Scholastic, 1997. ISBN 978-0-590-46017-0 Subj: Animals – deer. Seasons.

Papa, Papa ill. by Simone Kaplan. HarperCollins, 2000. ISBN 978-0-694-01246-6 Subj: Animals. Family life – fathers. Format, unusual – board books. Rhyming text.

Pierre the penguin: a true story ill. by Laura Regan. Sleeping Bear, 2010. ISBN 978-1-58536-485-5 Subj: Birds – penguins. Character traits – kindness to animals. Rhyming text.

Pretend you're a cat ill. by Jerry Pinkney. Dial, 1990. ISBN 978-0-8037-0774-0 Subj: Animals. Behavior – imitation. Imagination. Rhyming text.

Snow angel ill. by Jacqueline Rogers. Scholastic, 1995. ISBN 978-0-590-48748-1 Subj: Angels. Behavior – lost. Weather – snow.

Sun song ill. by Laura Regan. HarperCollins, 1995. ISBN 978-0-06-020788-5 Subj: Animals. Plants. Rhyming text. Sun.

Ten cats have hats: a counting book ill. by David McPhail. Scholastic, 1994. ISBN 978-0-590-46968-5 Subj: Animals. Counting, numbers. Rhyming text.

Ten little Christmas presents ill. by author. Scholastic, 2008. ISBN 978-0-545-02791-5 Subj: Animals. Counting, numbers. Gifts. Holidays – Christmas.

Thanksgiving cats ill. by Hans Wilhelm. Scholastic, 1999. ISBN 978-0-590-03714-3 Subj: Animals – cats. Holidays – Thanksgiving. Rhyming text.

Valentine cats ill. by Hans Wilhelm. Scholastic, 1996. ISBN 978-0-590-47596-9 Subj: Animals – cats. Holidays – Valentine's Day. Rhyming text.

Masini, Beatrice. *A brave little princess* ill. by Octavia Monaco. Barefoot, 2000. ISBN 978-1-84148-267-5 Subj: Character traits – bravery. Concepts – patterns. Folk & fairy tales. Problem solving. Royalty – princesses. Royalty – queens.

Here comes the bride ill. by AnnaLaura Cantone. Tundra, 2010. ISBN 978-0-88776-898-9 Subj: Activities – sewing. Clothing – dresses. Weddings.

Mason, Adrienne. *Lu and Clancy sound off* ill. by Pat Cupples. Kids Can, 2002. ISBN 978-1-55337-058-1 Subj: Animals – dogs. Careers – detectives. Noise, sounds. Science.

Lu and Clancy's spy stuff ill. by Pat Cupples. Kids Can, 2000. ISBN 978-1-55074-693-8 Subj: Animals – dogs. Careers – detectives. Disguises.

Snakes ill. by Nancy Gray Ogle. Kids Can, 2005. ISBN 978-1-55337-627-9 Subj: Reptiles – snakes. Science.

Mason, Janeen I. *Ocean commotion: life on the reef* ill. by author. Pelican, 2010. ISBN 978-1-58980-783-9 Subj: Crustaceans – crabs. Sea & seashore.

Mason, Margaret H. *These hands* ill. by Floyd Cooper. Harcourt, 2011. ISBN 978-0-547-21566-2 Subj: Anatomy – hands. Ethnic groups in the U.S. – African Americans. Family life – grandfathers. Prejudice.

Massie, Felix. *Dogs in cars* ill. by Emmanuelle Walker. Flying Eye, 2016. ISBN 978-190926387-1 Subj: ABC books. Animals – dogs. Counting, numbers.

Massini, Sarah. *Love always everywhere* ill. by author. Random House, 2014. ISBN 978-038537552-8 Subj: Emotions – love. Rhyming text.

Trixie ten ill. by author. Henry Holt, 2013. ISBN 978-0-8050-9520-3 Subj: Behavior – running away. Family life – brothers & sisters. Noise, sounds.

Masters, Anthony. *Ricky's rat gang* ill. by Chris Fisher. Kingfisher, 2004. ISBN 978-0-7534-5800-6 Subj: Animals – mice. Behavior – bullying, teasing. Stores.

Masurel, Claire. *A cat and a dog* ill. by Bob Kolar. NorthSouth, 2001. ISBN 978-1-55858-950-6 Subj: Animals – cats. Animals – dogs. Behavior – fighting, arguing. Friendship.

Christmas is coming ill. by Marie H. Henry. Chronicle, 1998. ISBN 978-0-8118-2106-3 Subj: Behavior – sharing. Holidays – Christmas. Toys.

Domino ill. by David Walker. Candlewick, 2007. ISBN 978-0-7636-2862-8 Subj: Animals – dogs. Character traits – smallness.

Too big! ill. by Hanako Wakiyama. Chronicle, 1999. ISBN 978-0-8118-2090-5 Subj: Concepts – size. Dinosaurs. Toys.

Two homes ill. by Kady MacDonald Denton. Candlewick, 2001. ISBN 978-0-7636-0511-7 Subj: Divorce. Emotions – love. Family life – parents. Homes, houses.

Matheis, Mickie. *Bedtime for Boo* ill. by Bonnie Leick. Random House, 2012. ISBN 978-0-375-86991-4 Subj: Bedtime. Ghosts. Noise, sounds.

Mathers, Petra. *A cake for Herbie* ill. by author. Atheneum, 2000. ISBN 978-0-689-83017-4 Subj: Animals. Birds – ducks. Contests. Poetry.

Dodo gets married ill. by author. Atheneum, 2001. ISBN 978-0-689-83018-1 Subj: Birds – dodos. Weddings.

Herbie's secret Santa ill. by author. Atheneum, 2002. ISBN 978-0-689-83550-6 Subj: Birds. Careers – bakers. Character traits – honesty. Friendship. Holidays – Christmas.

Lottie's new beach towel ill. by author. Atheneum, 1998. ISBN 978-0-689-81606-2 Subj: Birds – chickens, roosters. Character traits – cleverness. Gifts. Sea & seashore – beaches.

Lottie's new friend ill. by author. Atheneum, 1999. ISBN 978-0-689-82014-4 Subj: Birds. Emotions – envy, jealousy. Friendship.

When Aunt Mattie got her wings ill. by author. Simon & Schuster/Beach Lane, 2014. ISBN 978-148141044-1 Subj: Birds – chickens, roosters. Birds – ducks. Death. Memories, memory.

Matheson, Christie. *Plant the tiny seed* ill. by author. Greenwillow, 2017. ISBN 978-006239339-5 Subj: Activities. Gardens, gardening. Rhyming text. Seeds.

Tap the magic tree ill. by author. Greenwillow, 2013. ISBN 978-0-06-227445-8 Subj: Activities. Rhyming text. Seasons. Trees.

Touch the brightest star ill. by author. Greenwillow, 2015. ISBN 978-006227447-2 Subj: Bedtime. Night. Participation.

Mathews, Judith, reteller. *Nathaniel Willy, scared silly* also retold by Fay Robinson; ill. by Alexi Natchev. Bradbury, 1994. ISBN 978-0-02-765285-7 Subj: Animals. Bedtime. Emotions – fear. Family life – grandmothers. Folk & fairy tales. Rhyming text.

Matsuoka, Mei. *Footprints in the snow* ill. by author. Henry Holt, 2008. ISBN 978-0-8050-8792-5 Subj: Activities – writing. Animals – wolves. Friendship.

Matteson, George. *The Christmas tugboat: how the Rockefeller Center Christmas tree came to New York City* by George Matteson and Adele Ursone ill. by James Ransome. Clarion, 2012. ISBN 978-0-618-99215-7 Subj: Boats, ships. Family life. Holidays – Christmas. Trees.

Matthews, Tina. *Out of the egg* ill. by author. Houghton, 2007. ISBN 978-0-618-73741-3 Subj: Birds – chickens, roosters. Folk & fairy tales.

Matthies, Janna. *The goodbye cancer garden* ill. by Kristi Valiant. Albert Whitman, 2011. ISBN 978-0-8075-2994-2 Subj: Family life – mothers. Gardens, gardening. Illness – cancer.

Peter, the knight with asthma ill. by Anthony Lewis. Albert Whitman, 2009. ISBN 978-0-8075-6517-9 Subj: Illness – asthma. Knights.

Mattick, Lindsay. *Finding Winnie: the true story of the world's most famous bear* ill. by Sophie Blackall. Little, Brown, 2015. ISBN 978-031632490-8 Subj: Animals – bears. Books, reading. Caldecott award books. Zoos.

Maturana, Andrea. *Life without Nico* ill. by Francisco Javier Olea. Kids Can, 2016. ISBN 978-177138611-1 Subj: Emotions – loneliness. Friendship. Moving.

Mauner, Claudia. *Zoe Sophia in New York: the mystery of the Pink Phoenix papers* by Claudia Mauner and Elisa Smalley; ill. by Claudia Mauner. Chronicle, 2006. ISBN 978-0-8118-4877-0 Subj: Family life. Museums. Mystery stories.

Zoe Sophia's scrapbook by Claudia Mauner and Elisa Smalley; ill. by Claudia Mauner. Chronicle, 2003. ISBN 978-0-8118-3606-7 Subj: Activities – traveling. Animals – dogs. Behavior – lost. Family life – aunts, uncles. Foreign lands – Italy.

Maurer, Tracy. *Growing flowers* ill. with photos. Rourke, 2001. ISBN 978-1-55916-251-7 Subj: Flowers. Gardens, gardening.

May, Eleanor. *Albert is not scared* ill. by Deborah Melmon. Kane, 2013. ISBN 978-1-57565-629-8 Subj: Animals – mice. Concepts – left & right. Concepts – up & down. Emotions – fear. Parks – amusement.

Albert the muffin-maker ill. by Deborah Melmon. Kane, 2014. ISBN 978-157565631-1 Subj: Activities – baking, cooking. Animals – mice. Counting, numbers.

Albert's amazing snail ill. by Deborah Melmon. Kane, 2012. ISBN 978-1-57565-448-5 Subj: Animals – mice. Animals – snails. Character traits – patience, impatience. Concepts. Language.

The mousier the merrier ill. by Deborah Melmon. Kane, 2012. ISBN 978-1-57565-447-8 Subj: Animals – mice. Counting, numbers.

May, Kathy. *Molasses man* ill. by Felicia Marshall. Holiday, 2000. ISBN 978-0-8234-1438-3 Subj: Ethnic groups in the U.S. – African Americans. Family life. Family life – grandfathers.

May, Robert L. *Rudolph shines again* ill. by Antonio Caparo. Simon & Schuster, 2015. ISBN 978-144247498-7 Subj: Animals – rabbits. Animals – reindeer. Behavior – lost. Character traits – helpfulness. Holidays – Christmas. Rhyming text.

Rudolph the red-nosed reindeer ill. by David Wenzel. Grosset, 2001. ISBN 978-0-448-42534-4 Subj: Anatomy – noses. Animals – reindeer. Holidays – Christmas. Mythical creatures – elves. Rhyming text. Santa Claus. Weather – fog.

Mayer, Kirsten. *Game of gnomes* ill. by Laura K. Horton. Imprint, 2017. ISBN 978-125012394-7 Subj: Character traits – appearance. Contests. Games. Mythical creatures – gnomes. Seasons – winter. Self-concept.

Go big or go gnome! ill. by Laura K. Horton. Imprint, 2017. ISBN 978-125011127-2 Subj: Careers – barbers. Character traits – appearance. Mythical creatures – gnomes.

Mayer, Lynne. *Newton and me* ill. by Sherry Rogers. Sylvan Dell, 2010. ISBN 978-1-60718-067-8 Subj: Rhyming text. Science.

Mayer, Marianna. *Baba Yaga and Vasilisa the Brave* ill. by Kinuko Y. Craft. Morrow, 1994. ISBN 978-0-688-08501-8 Subj: Folk & fairy tales. Foreign lands – Russia. Royalty. Toys – dolls. Witches.

Beauty and the beast ill. by Mercer Mayer. SeaStar, 2000. ISBN 978-1-58717-018-8 Subj: Animals. Character traits – appearance. Character traits – loyalty. Emotions – love. Folk & fairy tales. Magic.

One frog too many (Mayer, Mercer)

Pegasus ill. by Kinuko Y. Craft. Morrow, 1998. ISBN 978-0-688-13382-5 Subj: Folk & fairy tales. Foreign lands – Greece. Monsters. Mythical creatures – Pegasus.

Perseus ill. by Joel Spector. Fogelman, 2002. ISBN 978-0-8037-2619-2 Subj: Folk & fairy tales. Foreign lands – Greece. Religion.

The prince and the pauper ill. by Gary A. Lippincott. Dial, 1999. ISBN 978-0-8037-2099-2 Subj: Behavior – growing up. Behavior – misunderstanding. Character traits – individuality. Royalty – kings.

The unicorn and the lake ill. by Michael Hague. Dial, 1982. ISBN 978-0-8037-9338-5 Subj: Character traits – bravery. Mythical creatures – unicorns.

Mayer, Mercer. *A boy, a dog, a frog and a friend* ill. by author. Dial, 1971. ISBN 978-0-8037-0755-9 Subj: Animals – dogs. Friendship. Frogs & toads. Sports – fishing. Wordless.

A boy, a dog and a frog ill. by author. Dial, 1967. ISBN 978-0-8037-0767-2 Subj: Animals – dogs. Friendship. Frogs & toads. Sports – fishing. Wordless.

The bravest knight ill. by author. Penguin, 2007. ISBN 978-0-8037-3206-3 Subj: Imagination. Knights. Monsters. Mythical creatures. Mythical creatures – trolls.

Bun Bun's birthday ill. by author. Random House, 1996. ISBN 978-0-679-87368-6 Subj: Behavior – growing up. Behavior – misunderstanding. Birthdays.

Frog goes to dinner ill. by author. Dial, 1974. ISBN 978-0-8037-3381-7 Subj: Food. Frogs & toads. Wordless.

Frog on his own ill. by author. Dial, 1973. ISBN 978-0-8037-2695-6 Subj: Frogs & toads. Wordless.

Frog, where are you? ill. by author. Dial, 1969. ISBN 978-0-8037-2732-8 Subj: Friendship. Frogs & toads. Wordless.

Just big enough ill. by author. HarperCollins, 2004. ISBN 978-0-06-053964-1 Subj: Behavior – bullying, teasing. Behavior – growing up. Concepts – size. Family life – grandfathers. Problem solving.

Just for you ill. by author. Golden, 1975. ISBN 978-0-307-12542-2 Subj: Character traits – helpfulness. Emotions – love. Family life – mothers.

Just me and my dad ill. by author. Golden, 1977. ISBN 978-0-307-61839-9 Subj: Camps, camping. Family life – fathers.

The little drummer mouse: a Christmas story ill. by author. Penguin, 2006. ISBN 978-0-8037-3147-9 Subj: Animals – mice. Holidays – Christmas. Music. Musical instruments – drums. Religion – Nativity.

Liza Lou and the Yeller Belly Swamp ill. by author. Parents' Magazine, 1976. ISBN 978-0-8193-0802-3 Subj: Character traits – bravery. Ethnic groups in the U.S. – African Americans. Monsters.

Octopus soup ill. by author. Marshall Cavendish, 2011. ISBN 978-0-7614-5812-8 Subj: Octopuses. Wordless.

One frog too many by Mercer Mayer and Marianna Mayer; ill. by Mercer Mayer. Dial, 1975. ISBN 978-0-8037-4858-3 Subj: Emotions – envy, jealousy. Frogs & toads. Wordless.

Shibumi and the kitemaker ill. by author. Marshall Cavendish, 1999. ISBN 978-0-7614-5054-2 Subj: Family life – fathers. Foreign lands – Japan. Kites. Royalty – emperors. Royalty – princesses.

There are monsters everywhere ill. by author. Penguin, 2005. ISBN 978-0-8037-0621-7 Subj: Emotions – fear. Monsters. Sports – karate.

There's a nightmare in my closet ill. by author. Dial, 1990. ISBN 978-0-8037-0843-3 Subj: Bedtime. Emotions – fear. Monsters.

There's an alligator under my bed ill. by author. Dial, 1987. ISBN 978-0-8037-0375-9 Subj: Bedtime. Emotions – fear. Reptiles – alligators, crocodiles.

Too many dinosaurs ill. by author. Holiday House, 2011. ISBN 978-0-8234-2316-3 Subj: Dinosaurs. Pets.

What do you do with a kangaroo? ill. by author. Four Winds, 1973. ISBN 978-0-590-72851-5 Subj: Animals. Humorous stories. Problem solving.

You're the scaredy cat ill. by author. Parents' Magazine, 1974. ISBN 978-0-8193-0763-7 Subj: Camps, camping. Emotions – fear. Night.

Mayer, Pamela. *The Grandma cure* ill. by John Nez. Penguin, 2005. ISBN 978-0-525-47559-0 Subj: Behavior – fighting, arguing. Family life – grandmothers. Illness – cold (disease).

The scariest monster in the whole wide world ill. by Lydia Monks. Putnam, 2001. ISBN 978-0-399-23459-0 Subj: Clothing – costumes. Family life – grandmothers. Holidays – Halloween. Monsters.

Mayhew, James. *Ella Bella ballerina and A Midsummer Night's Dream* ill. by author. Barron's, 2015. ISBN 978-076416797-3 Subj: Ballet. Music. Theater.

Ella Bella ballerina and Swan Lake ill. by author. Barron's, 2011. ISBN 978-0-7641-6407-1 Subj: Ballet. Music.

Ella Bella ballerina and The Nutcracker ill. by author. Barron's, 2012. ISBN 978-0-7641-6581-8 Subj: Activities – dancing. Ballet. Holidays – Christmas. Imagination. Music.

Ella Bella ballerina and The sleeping beauty ill. by author. Barron's, 2008. ISBN 978-0-7641-6118-6 Subj: Ballet. Music.

Katie and the Mona Lisa ill. by author. Orchard, 1999. ISBN 978-0-531-30177-7 Subj: Art. Careers – artists. Museums.

Katie and the sunflowers ill. by author. Orchard, 2001. ISBN 978-0-531-30325-2 Subj: Art. Family life – grandmothers. Imagination. Museums.

Katie meets the Impressionists ill. by author. Orchard, 1999. ISBN 978-0-531-30151-7 Subj: Art. Careers – artists. Museums.

The knight who took all day ill. by author. Scholastic, 2005. ISBN 978-0-439-74829-2 Subj: Dragons. Knights.

Where's my hug? ill. by Susan Hellard. Bloomsbury, 2008. ISBN 978-1-59990-225-8 Subj: Cumulative tales. Family life. Hugging.

Maynard, Bill. *Santa's time off* ill. by Tom Browning. Putnam, 1997. ISBN 978-0-399-23138-4 Subj: Activities – vacationing. Rhyming text. Santa Claus.

Maynor, Megan. *Ella and Penguin: stick together* ill. by Rosalinde Bonnet. HarperCollins, 2016. ISBN 978-006233088-8 Subj: Birds – penguins. Emotions – fear.

Mayo, Margaret. *Choo choo clickety-clack* ill. by Alex Ayliffe. Carolrhoda, 2005. ISBN 978-1-57505-819-1 Subj: Format, unusual – board books. Noise, sounds. Transportation.

Dig dig digging ill. by Alex Ayliffe. Henry Holt, 2002. ISBN 978-0-8050-6840-5 Subj: Rhyming text. Tractors. Trucks.

Emergency! ill. by Alex Ayliffe. Carolrhoda, 2002. ISBN 978-0-87614-922-5 Subj: Careers – emergency medical technicians. Careers – firefighters. Rhyming text. Safety. Trucks.

Roar! ill. by Alex Ayliffe. Carolrhoda, 2007. ISBN 978-0-7613-9473-0 Subj: Animals.

Stomp, dinosaur, stomp! ill. by Alex Ayliffe. Walker, 2010. ISBN 978-0-8027-2195-2 Subj: Activities. Dinosaurs. Rhyming text.

Wiggle waggle fun. Ill. by 24 illustrators. Knopf, 2002. ISBN 978-0-375-91529-1 Subj: Poetry. Rhyming text. Songs.

Zoom, rocket, zoom! ill. by Alex Ayliffe. Walker, 2012. ISBN 978-0-8027-2790-9 Subj: Careers – astronauts. Space & space ships.

Mayper, Monica. *Come and see: a Christmas story* ill. by Stacey Schuett. HarperCollins, 1999. ISBN 978-0-06-023527-7 Subj: Holidays – Christmas. Religion – Nativity.

Mayr, Diane. *Littlebat's Halloween story* ill. by Gideon Kendall. Albert Whitman, 2001. ISBN 978-0-8075-7629-8 Subj: Activities – storytelling. Animals – bats. Holidays – Halloween. Libraries.

Out and about at the apple orchard ill. by Anne McMullen. Picture Window, 2003. ISBN 978-1-4048-0036-6 Subj: Farms. Food. School – field trips. Trees.

Run, Turkey, run ill. by Laura Rader. Walker, 2007. ISBN 978-0-8027-9630-1 Subj: Behavior – hiding. Birds – turkeys. Holidays – Thanksgiving.

Mazer, Anne. *The salamander room* ill. by Steve Johnson. Knopf, 1991. ISBN 978-0-394-92945-3 Subj: Ecology. Imagination. Pets. Reptiles – salamanders.

Mazer, Norma Fox. *Has anyone seen my Emily Greene?* ill. by Christine Davenier. Candlewick, 2007. ISBN 978-0-7636-1384-6 Subj: Behavior – hiding. Family life – fathers. Rhyming text.

Mazzola, Frank. *Counting is for the birds* ill. by author. Charlesbridge, 1997. ISBN 978-0-88106-952-5 Subj: Birds. Counting, numbers. Rhyming text.

Mead, Alice. *Billy and Emma* ill. by Christy Hale. Farrar, 2000. ISBN 978-0-374-30705-9 Subj: Birds. Birds – macaws. Crime. Friendship. Zoos.

Meade, Holly. *If I never forever endeavor* ill. by author. Candlewick, 2011. ISBN 978-0-7636-4071-2 Subj: Activities – flying. Birds. Character traits – assertiveness. Character traits – bravery. Rhyming text.

Inside, inside, inside ill. by author. Marshall Cavendish, 2005. ISBN 978-0-7614-5125-9 Subj: Family life – brothers & sisters. Games.

John Willy and Freddy McGee ill. by author. Marshall Cavendish, 1998. ISBN 978-0-7614-5033-7 Subj: Animals – guinea pigs. Behavior – running away. Character traits – freedom.

A place to sleep ill. by author. Marshall Cavendish, 2001. ISBN 978-0-7614-5096-2 Subj: Animals. Bedtime. Rhyming text. Sleep.

Meade, Rita. *Edward gets messy* ill. by Olga Stern. Simon & Schuster, 2016. ISBN 978-148143777-6 Subj: Animals – pigs. Character traits – cleanliness. Character traits – orderliness.

Meadows, Michelle. *Hibernation station* ill. by Kurt Cyrus. Simon & Schuster, 2010. ISBN 978-1-4169-3788-3 Subj: Animals. Hibernation. Rhyming text. Sleep.

Itsy-bitsy baby mouse ill. by Matthew Cordell. Simon & Schuster, 2012. ISBN 978-1-4169-3786-9 Subj: Animals – mice. Behavior – lost. Rhyming text.

Piggies in pajamas ill. by Ard Hoyt. Simon & Schuster, 2013. ISBN 978-1-4169-4982-4 Subj: Animals – pigs. Bedtime. Rhyming text.

Piggies in the kitchen ill. by Ard Hoyt. Simon & Schuster, 2011. ISBN 978-1-4169-3787-6 Subj: Activities – baking, cooking. Animals – pigs. Rhyming text.

Pilot pups ill. by Dan Andreasen. Simon & Schuster, 2008. ISBN 978-1-4169-2484-5 Subj: Airplanes, airports. Animals – dogs. Careers – airplane pilots. Rhyming text. Toys.

Super bugs ill. by Bill Mayer. Scholastic/Orchard, 2016. ISBN 978-054568756-0 Subj: Character traits – helpfulness. Insects. Rhyming text.

Traffic pups ill. by Dan Andreasen. Simon & Schuster, 2011. ISBN 978-1-4169-2485-2 Subj: Animals – dogs. Careers – police officers. Motorcycles.

Mealer, Bryan. *The boy who harnessed the wind* (Kamkwamba, William)

Meddaugh, Susan. *The best place* ill. by author. Houghton, 1999. ISBN 978-0-395-97994-5 Subj: Animals. Animals – wolves. Behavior – dissatisfaction. Homes, houses.

Cinderella's rat ill. by author. Houghton, 1997. ISBN 978-0-395-86833-1 Subj: Animals – rats. Family life – brothers & sisters. Humorous stories. Magic.

Harry on the rocks ill. by author. Houghton, 2003. ISBN 978-0-618-27603-5 Subj: Boats, ships. Dragons. Eggs. Islands.

Hog-eye ill. by author. Houghton, 1995. ISBN 978-0-395-74276-1 Subj: Activities – baking, cooking. Animals – pigs. Animals – wolves. Books, reading.

Just Teenie ill. by author. Houghton, 2006. ISBN 978-0-618-68565-3 Subj: Character traits – appearance. Concepts – size. Plants.

Martha and Skits ill. by author. Houghton, 2000. ISBN 978-0-618-05776-4 Subj: Activities – talking. Animals – dogs. Behavior – growing up.

Martha blah blah ill. by author. Houghton, 1996. ISBN 978-0-395-79755-6 Subj: Activities – talking. Animals – dogs. Food.

Martha calling ill. by author. Houghton, 1994. ISBN 978-0-395-69825-9 Subj: Activities – talking. Activities – vacationing. Animals – dogs.

Martha says it with flowers ill. by author. Houghton Mifflin, 2010. ISBN 978-0-547-21058-2 Subj: Activities – talking. Animals – dogs. Birthdays. Family life – grandmothers. Gifts.

Martha speaks ill. by author. Houghton, 1992. ISBN 978-0-395-63313-7 Subj: Activities – talking. Animals – dogs.

Martha walks the dog ill. by author. Houghton, 1998. ISBN 978-0-395-90494-7 Subj: Activities – talking. Animals – dogs. Behavior – bullying, teasing. Birds – parakeets, parrots.

Perfectly Martha ill. by author. Houghton, 2004. ISBN 978-0-618-37857-9 Subj: Activities – talking. Animals – dogs. Careers – detectives.

Tree of birds ill. by author. Houghton, 1990. ISBN 978-0-395-53147-1 Subj: Birds. Character traits – kindness to animals.

The witches' supermarket ill. by author. Houghton, 1991. ISBN 978-0-395-57034-0 Subj: Animals – dogs. Holidays – Halloween. Stores. Witches.

The witch's walking stick ill. by author. Houghton, 2005. ISBN 978-0-618-52948-3 Subj: Behavior – wishing. Magic. Witches.

Medearis, Angela Shelf. *Annie's gifts* ill. by Anna Rich. Just Us, 1994. ISBN 978-0-940975-30-9 Subj: Ethnic groups in the U.S. – African Americans. Gifts. Self-concept.

Daisy and the doll (Medearis, Michael)

Dancing with the Indians ill. by Samuel Byrd. Holiday, 1991. ISBN 978-0-8234-0893-1 Subj: Activities – dancing. Ethnic groups in the U.S. – African Americans. Indians of North America – Seminole. Rhyming text.

The freedom riddle ill. by John Ward. Dutton, 1995. ISBN 978-0-525-67469-6 Subj: Ethnic groups in the U.S. – African Americans. Folk & fairy tales. Riddles & jokes. Slavery. U.S. history.

The ghost of Sifty-Sifty Sam ill. by Jacqueline Rogers. Scholastic, 1997. ISBN 978-0-590-48290-5 Subj: Careers – chefs, cooks. Ethnic groups in the U.S. – African Americans. Ghosts. Homes, houses. Rhyming text.

Poppa's itchy Christmas ill. by John Ward. Holiday, 1998. ISBN 978-0-8234-1298-3 Subj: Clothing. Holidays – Christmas. Sports – ice skating.

Poppa's new pants ill. by John Ward. Holiday, 1995. ISBN 978-0-8234-1155-9 Subj: Behavior – mistakes. Clothing. Clothing – pants. Ethnic groups in the U.S. – African Americans.

Rum-a-tum-tum ill. by James Ransome. Holiday, 1997. ISBN 978-0-8234-1143-6 Subj: Communities, neighborhoods. Ethnic groups in the U.S. – African Americans. Noise, sounds. Rhyming text.

Seven spools of thread: a Kwanzaa story ill. by Daniel Minter. Albert Whitman, 2000. ISBN 978-0-8075-7315-0 Subj: Activities – weaving. Folk & fairy tales. Foreign lands – Ghana. Holidays – Kwanzaa.

The singing man: adapted from a West African folktale ill. by Terea D. Shaffer. Holiday, 1994. ISBN

978-0-8234-1103-0 Subj: Folk & fairy tales. Foreign lands – Nigeria. Music.

Tailypo: a newfangled tall tale ill. by Sterling Brown. Holiday, 1996. ISBN 978-0-8234-1249-5 Subj: Ethnic groups in the U.S. – African Americans. Folk & fairy tales. Monsters.

Too much talk ill. by Stefano Vitale. Candlewick, 1995. ISBN 978-1-56402-323-0 Subj: Cumulative tales. Folk & fairy tales. Foreign lands – Ghana. Royalty – kings.

Medearis, Michael. *Daisy and the doll* by Michael Medearis and Angela Shelf Medearis ill. by Larry Johnson. Vermont Folklife Center, 2000. ISBN 978-0-916718-15-2 Subj: Ethnic groups in the U.S. – African Americans. Prejudice. School. Self-concept. Toys – dolls.

Medina, Juana. *ABC pasta: an entertaining alphabet* ill. by author. Viking, 2017. ISBN 978-110199978-3 Subj: ABC books. Food.

One big salad: a delicious counting book ill. by author. Viking, 2016. ISBN 978-110199974-5 Subj: Animals. Counting, numbers. Food.

Medina, Meg. *Mango, Abuela, and me* ill. by Angela Dominguez. Candlewick, 2015. ISBN 978-076366900-3 Subj: Birds – parakeets, parrots. Family life – grandmothers. Foreign languages.

Tía Isa wants a car ill. by Claudio Muñoz. Candlewick, 2011. ISBN 978-0-7636-4156-6 Subj: Automobiles. Behavior – resourcefulness. Ethnic groups in the U.S. – Hispanic Americans. Family life – aunts, uncles. Money.

Medina, Sarah. *Sad* ill. by Jo Brooker. Heinemann, 2007. ISBN 978-1-4034-9293-7 Subj: Emotions – sadness.

Medina, Tony. *Christmas makes me think* ill. by Chandra Cox. Lee & Low, 2001. ISBN 978-1-58430-024-3 Subj: Behavior – sharing. Ethnic groups in the U.S. – African Americans. Holidays – Christmas. Religion.

DeShawn days ill. by R. Gregory Christie. Lee & Low, 2001. ISBN 978-1-58430-022-9 Subj: Cities, towns. Ethnic groups in the U.S. – African Americans. Family life. Poetry.

Medoff, Francine. *The mouse in the matzah factory* ill. by Nicole in den Bosch. Kar-Ben, 2003. ISBN 978-1-58013-048-6 Subj: Animals – mice. Food. Jewish culture.

Meggs, Libby Phillips. *Go home! the true story of James the cat* ill. by author. Albert Whitman, 2000. ISBN 978-0-8075-2975-1 Subj: Animals – cats. Behavior – needing someone. Homeless.

Meisel, Paul. *Good night, bat! good morning, squirrel!* ill. by author. Boyds Mills, 2016. ISBN 978-162979495-2 Subj: Activities – writing. Animals – bats. Animals – squirrels. Behavior – misunderstanding. Friendship.

My awesome summer, by P. Mantis ill. by author. Holiday, 2017. ISBN 978-082343671-2 Subj: Insects. Nature.

Zara's hats ill. by author. Dutton, 2003. ISBN 978-0-525-45465-6 Subj: Behavior – resourcefulness. Clothing – hats. Family life – fathers.

Meister, Cari. *Busy, busy city street* ill. by Steven Guarnaccia. Viking, 2000. ISBN 978-0-670-88944-0 Subj: Automobiles. Cities, towns. Noise, sounds. Rhyming text. Traffic, traffic signs. Trucks.

Follow the drinking gourd: an Underground Railroad story ill. by Robert Squier. Picture Window, 2012. ISBN 978-1-4048-7375-9 Subj: Ethnic groups in the U.S. – African Americans. Sailors. Slavery. Songs. Stars. U.S. history.

Melanson, Luc. *Topsy-Turvy Town* ill. by author. Tundra, 2010. ISBN 978-0-88776-920-7 Subj: Imagination.

Mellage, Nanette. *Coming home* ill. by Cornelius Van Wright and Ying-Hwa Hu. BridgeWater, 2001. ISBN 978-0-8167-7009-0 Subj: Careers. Ethnic groups in the U.S. – African Americans. Sports – baseball.

Melling, David. *Don't worry, Douglas!* ill. by author. Tiger Tales, 2011. ISBN 978-1-58925-106-9 Subj: Animals – bears. Character traits – helpfulness. Clothing – hats.

Good knight sleep tight ill. by author. Barron's, 2006. ISBN 978-0-7641-5878-0 Subj: Knights. Royalty – princesses.

Hugless Douglas ill. by author. Tiger Tales, 2010. ISBN 978-1-58925-098-7 Subj: Animals – bears. Hugging.

The Scallywags ill. by author. Barron's, 2006. ISBN 978-0-7641-5991-6 Subj: Animals – wolves. Etiquette. Humorous stories.

Melmed, Laura Krauss. *Capital! Washington D.C. from A to Z* ill. by Frané Lessac. HarperCollins, 2003. ISBN 978-0-688-17562-7 Subj: ABC books. Cities, towns. Rhyming text.

Eight winter nights: a family Hanukkah book ill. by Elisabeth Schlossberg. Chronicle, 2010. ISBN 978-0-8118-5552-5 Subj: Holidays – Hanukkah. Jewish culture. Rhyming text.

The first song ever sung ill. by Ed Young. Lothrop, 1993. ISBN 978-0-688-08231-4 Subj: Bedtime. Foreign lands – Japan. Poetry. Songs.

Fright night flight ill. by Henry Cole. HarperCollins, 2002. ISBN 978-0-06-029702-2 Subj: Holidays – Halloween. Rhyming text. Witches.

A hug goes around ill. by Betsy Lewin. HarperCollins, 2002. ISBN 978-0-688-14681-8 Subj: Day. Emotions. Family life. Rhyming text.

I love you as much . . . ill. by Henri Sorensen. 1st Tupelo board books ed. Tupelo, 1998. ISBN 978-0-688-15978-8 Subj: Animals. Family life – mothers. Format, unusual – board books. Rhyming text.

Jumbo's lullaby ill. by Henri Sorensen. Lothrop, 1999. ISBN 978-0-688-16996-1 Subj: Animals – elephants. Bedtime. Dreams. Foreign lands – Africa. Lullabies. Rhyming text.

Little Oh ill. by Jim LaMarche. Lothrop, 1997. ISBN 978-0-688-14209-4 Subj: Behavior – lost. Family life. Paper.

Moishe's miracle ill. by David Slonim. HarperCollins, 2000. ISBN 978-0-688-14683-2 Subj: Folk & fairy tales. Holidays – Hanukkah. Jewish culture. Magic.

New York, New York! the Big Apple from A to Z ill. by Frané Lessac. HarperCollins, 2005. ISBN 978-0-06-054876-6 Subj: ABC books. Cities, towns.

The rainbabies ill. by Jim LaMarche. Lothrop, 1992. ISBN 978-0-688-10756-7 Subj: Babies, toddlers. Folk & fairy tales.

This first Thanksgiving ill. by Mark Buehner. HarperCollins, 2001. ISBN 978-0-688-14555-2 Subj: Counting, numbers. Holidays – Thanksgiving. Poetry.

Melnicove, Mark. *Africa is not a country* (Knight, Margy Burns)

Meltzer, Amy. *A mezuzah on the door* ill. by Janice Fried. Kar-Ben, 2007. ISBN 978-1-58013-249-7 Subj: Jewish culture. Moving.

The Shabbat Princess ill. by Martha Avilés. Lerner/Kar-Ben, 2011. ISBN 978-0-7613-5142-9 Subj: Family life. Jewish culture.

Meltzer, Brad. *I am Albert Einstein* ill. by Christopher Eliopoulos. Dial, 2014. ISBN 978-080374084-6 Subj: Careers – scientists. Character traits – curiosity. Character traits – individuality. Science.

I am Rosa Parks ill. by Christopher Eliopoulos. Dial, 2014. ISBN 978-080374085-3 Subj: Ethnic groups in the U.S. – African Americans. Prejudice. U.S. history. Violence, nonviolence.

Meltzer, Lynn. *The construction crew* ill. by Carrie Eko-Burgess. Henry Holt, 2011. ISBN 978-0-8050-8884-7 Subj: Careers – construction workers. Machines. Rhyming text. Tools.

Melvin, Alice. *Counting birds* ill. by author. Abrams, 2010. ISBN 978-1-85437-855-2 Subj: Birds. Counting, numbers. Rhyming text.

The high street ill. by author. Abrams, 2011. ISBN 978-1-85437-943-6 Subj: Cumulative tales. Shopping. Stores.

Membrino, Anna. *I want to be a ballerina* ill. by Smiljana Coh. Random House, 2014. ISBN 978-037597330-7 Subj: Ballet. Careers – dancers. Family life – sisters.

Mena, Pato. *The perfect siesta* ill. by author. NubeOcho, 2017. ISBN 978-849454153-7 Subj: Animals. Jungle. Sleep.

Menchin, Scott. *Grandma in blue with red hat* ill. by Harry Bliss. Abrams, 2015. ISBN 978-141971484-9 Subj: Art. Family life – grandmothers. Museums.

Harry goes to dog school ill. by author. HarperCollins, 2012. ISBN 978-0-06-195801-4 Subj: Animals – dogs. Imagination. School.

Taking a bath with the dog and other things that make me happy ill. by author. Candlewick, 2007. ISBN 978-0-7636-2919-9 Subj: Character traits – questioning. Emotions – happiness.

What are you waiting for? ill. by Matt Phelan. Roaring Brook/Neal Porter, 2017. ISBN 978-162672152-4 Subj: Animals – badgers. Animals – rabbits. Character traits – patience, impatience. Character traits – questioning.

What if everything had legs? ill. by author. Candlewick, 2011. ISBN 978-0-7636-4220-4 Subj: Anatomy. Character traits – questioning. Imagination.

Mendes, Valerie. *Look at me, Grandma!* ill. by Claire Fletcher. Scholastic, 2001. ISBN 978-0-439-29654-0 Subj: Babies, toddlers. Dreams. Family life – aunts, uncles. Family life – brothers & sisters. Family life – grandmothers. Family life – new sibling.

Meng, Cece. *Always remember* ill. by Jago. Philomel, 2016. ISBN 978-039916809-3 Subj: Death. Memories, memory. Reptiles – turtles, tortoises.

Bedtime is canceled ill. by Aurelie Neyret. Clarion, 2012. ISBN 978-0-547-63668-9 Subj: Bedtime.

I will not read this book ill. by Joy Ang. Clarion, 2011. ISBN 978-0-547-04971-7 Subj: Bedtime. Books, reading. Family life.

Tough chicks ill. by Melissa Suber. Clarion, 2009. ISBN 978-0-618-82415-1 Subj: Animals. Birds – chickens, roosters. Self-concept. Tractors.

The wonderful thing about hiccups ill. by Janet Pedersen. Houghton, 2007. ISBN 978-0-618-59544-0 Subj: Animals – hippopotamuses. Family life – brothers & sisters. Hiccups. Libraries.

World pizza ill. by Ellen Shi. Sterling, 2017. ISBN 978-145491946-9 Subj: Food. World.

Menotti, Andrea. *How many jelly beans? a giant book of giant numbers!* ill. by Yancey Labat. Chronicle, 2012. ISBN 978-1-4521-0206-1 Subj: Counting, numbers. Food. Format, unusual.

Merberg, Julie. *In the garden with Van Gogh* by Julie Merberg and Suzanne Bober. Chronicle, 2002. ISBN 978-0-8118-3415-5 Subj: Art. Careers – artists. Format, unusual – board books. Rhyming text.

A magical day with Matisse by Julie Merberg and Suzanne Bober. Chronicle, 2002. ISBN 978-0-8118-3414-8 Subj: Art. Careers – artists. Format, unusual – board books. Rhyming text.

Mercer, Lynn. *Schubert's snowflakes* ill. by author. Sagebrush, 2001. ISBN 978-0-9535413-6-2 Subj: Animals – polar bears. Weather – snow.

Meres, Jonathan. *The big bad rumor* ill. by Jacqueline East. Orchard, 2000. ISBN 978-0-531-30292-7 Subj: Animals. Behavior – gossip, rumors. Birds. Communication.

Merino, Gemma. *The cow who climbed a tree* ill. by author. Albert Whitman, 2016. ISBN 978-080751298-2 Subj: Animals – bulls, cows. Behavior – disbelief. Character traits – curiosity. Character traits – individuality. Family life – brothers & sisters.

The crocodile who didn't like water ill. by author. NorthSouth, 2014. ISBN 978-073584163-5 Subj: Character traits – being different. Dragons. Reptiles – alligators, crocodiles.

The sheep who hatched an egg ill. by author. Albert Whitman, 2017. ISBN 978-080757338-9 Subj: Animals – sheep. Birds. Character traits – appearance. Emotions – embarrassment. Self-concept.

Merlin, Christophe. *Under the hood* ill. by author. Candlewick, 2011. ISBN 978-0-7636-5535-8 Subj: Animals – bears. Automobiles. Careers – mechanics. Format, unusual – toy & movable books.

Merriam, Eve. *Bam, bam, bam* ill. by Dan Yaccarino. Henry Holt, 1995. ISBN 978-0-8050-3527-8 Subj: Buildings. Cities, towns. Machines. Poetry.

Blackberry ink ill. by Hans Wilhelm. Morrow, 1985. ISBN 978-0-688-04151-9 Subj: Poetry.

Halloween ABC ill. by Lane Smith. Macmillan, 1987. ISBN 978-0-02-766870-4 Subj: ABC books. Holidays – Halloween. Poetry.

Low song ill. by Pamela Paparone. Margaret K. McElderry, 2001. ISBN 978-0-689-82820-1 Subj: Nature. Rhyming text.

12 ways to get to 11 ill. by Bernie Karlin. Simon & Schuster, 1993. ISBN 978-0-671-75544-7 Subj: Counting, numbers.

Where's that cat? by Eve Merriam and Pamela Pollack ill. by Joanna Harrison. Margaret K. McElderry, 2000. ISBN 978-0-689-82904-8 Subj: Animals – cats. Parks. Rhyming text.

Merski, P. K. *Roaring, boring, Alice* ill. by Mark Weber. Skeezel, 2004. ISBN 978-0-9747217-0-5 Subj: Animals – mice. Foreign lands – Arctic. Northern lights. Rhyming text.

Merz, Jennifer J. *Playground day* ill. by author. Houghton, 2007. ISBN 978-0-618-81696-5 Subj: Activities – playing. Animals. Behavior – imitation. Imagination. Rhyming text.

Meschenmoser, Sebastian. *Gordon and Tapir* ill. by author. NorthSouth, 2016. ISBN 978-073584253-3 Subj: Animals – tapirs. Behavior – messy. Birds – penguins. Character traits – being different. Character traits – cleanliness. Friendship.

Pug Man's 3 wishes ill. by author. NorthSouth, 2016. ISBN 978-073584261-8 Subj: Animals – dogs. Behavior – bad day, bad mood. Behavior – wishing.

Waiting for winter ill. by author. Kane/Miller, 2009. ISBN 978-1-935279-04-4 Subj: Animals. Weather – snow.

Meserve, Adria. *No room for Napoleon* ill. by author. Farrar, 2006. ISBN 978-0-374-35536-4 Subj: Animals – dogs. Behavior – sharing. Character traits – selfishness. Friendship. Homes, houses.

Smog, the city dog (Aesop)

Meserve, Jessica. *Bedtime without Arthur* ill. by author. Andersen, 2010. ISBN 978-0-7613-5497-0 Subj: Bedtime. Behavior – lost & found possessions. Emotions – fear. Family life – brothers & sisters. Toys – bears.

Small sister ill. by author. Houghton, 2007. ISBN 978-0-618-77658-0 Subj: Character traits – smallness. Family life – brothers & sisters. Self-concept.

Meshon, Aaron. *The best days are dog days* ill. by author. Dial, 2016. ISBN 978-052542817-6 Subj: Activities – playing. Animals – dogs.

Take me out to the Yakyu ill. by author. Atheneum, 2013. ISBN 978-1-4424-4177-4 Subj: Ethnic groups in the U.S. – Japanese Americans. Family life – grandfathers. Foreign lands – Japan. Foreign languages. Sports – baseball.

Tools rule! ill. by author. Atheneum, 2014. ISBN 978-144249601-9 Subj: Activities – making things. Character traits – cooperation. Tools.

Messer, Claire. *Grumpy pants* ill. by author. Albert Whitman, 2016. ISBN 978-080753075-7 Subj: Activities – bathing. Bedtime. Behavior – bad day, bad mood. Birds – penguins.

Messier, Mireille. *The branch* ill. by Pierre Pratt. Kids Can, 2016. ISBN 978-177138564-0 Subj: Activities – making things. Character traits – cooperation. Trees. Weather – storms.

Messinger, Carla. *When the shadbush blooms* by Carla Messinger and Susan Katz ill. by David Kanietakeron Fadden. Ten Speed, 2007. ISBN 978-1-58246-192-2 Subj: Family life. Indians of North America – Lenape. Seasons. U.S. history.

Messner, Kate. *How to read a story* ill. by Mark Siegel. Chronicle, 2015. ISBN 978-145211233-6 Subj: Behavior – sharing. Books, reading.

Over and under the snow ill. by Christopher Silas Neal. Chronicle, 2011. ISBN 978-0-8118-6784-9 Subj: Animals. Hibernation. Nature. Seasons – winter. Weather – snow.

Rolling Thunder ill. by Greg Ruth. Scholastic, 2017. ISBN 978-054547012-4 Subj: Careers – military. Family life – grandfathers. Holidays – Memorial Day. Motorcycles. Rhyming text. U.S. history.

Tree of wonder: the many marvelous lives of a rainforest tree ill. by Simona Mulazzani. Chronicle, 2015. ISBN 978-145211248-0 Subj: Animals. Ecology. Jungle. Nature. Trees.

Up in the garden and down in the dirt ill. by Christopher Silas Neal. Chronicle, 2015. ISBN 978-145211936-6 Subj: Gardens, gardening. Seasons.

Metaxas, Eric. *It's time to sleep, my love* ill. by Nancy Tillman. Feiwel & Friends, 2008. ISBN 978-0-312-38371-8 Subj: Animals. Bedtime. Lullabies. Sleep.

Squanto and the miracle of Thanksgiving ill. by Shannon Stirnweis. Nelson, 1999. ISBN 978-0-8499-5864-9 Subj: Holidays – Thanksgiving. Indians of North America – Wampanoag. Pilgrims. U.S. history.

Metropolitan Museum of Art, NY. *Museum shapes.* Little, Brown, 2005. ISBN 978-0-316-05698-4 Subj: Art. Concepts – shape. Museums.

Metz, Lorijo. *Floridius Bloom and the planet of Gloom* ill. by Matt Phelan. Penguin, 2007. ISBN 978-0-8037-3084-7 Subj: Behavior – greed. Friendship. Monsters.

Metzger, Steve. *The dancing clock* ill. by John Nez. Tiger Tales, 2011. ISBN 978-1-58925-100-7 Subj: Animals – monkeys. Clocks, watches. Zoos.

Detective Blue ill. by Tedd Arnold. Scholastic, 2011. ISBN 978-0-545-17286-8 Subj: Careers – detectives. Humorous stories. Nursery rhymes.

Pluto visits Earth! ill. by Jared D Lee. Scholastic, 2012. ISBN 978-0-545-24934-8 Subj: Planets. Space & space ships.

This is the house that monsters built ill. by Jared D Lee. Scholastic/Cartwheel, 2016. ISBN 978-054561112-1 Subj: Cumulative tales. Monsters. Rhyming text.

Waiting for Santa ill. by Alison Edgson. Tiger Tales, 2015. ISBN 978-158925199-1 Subj: Animals. Holidays – Christmas. Santa Claus.

Will Princess Isabel ever say please? ill. by Amanda Haley. Holiday House, 2012. ISBN 978-0-8234-2323-1 Subj: Etiquette. Royalty – princesses.

Meunier, Brian. *Bravo, Tavo!* ill. by Perky Edgerton. Penguin, 2007. ISBN 978-0-525-47478-4 Subj: Clothing – shoes. Foreign lands – Mexico. Sports – basketball. Weather – droughts.

Meyer, Ezra Fields. *E-mergency!* (Lichtenheld, Tom)

Meyer, Susan Lynn. *New shoes* ill. by Eric Velasquez. Holiday House, 2015. ISBN 978-082342528-0 Subj: Clothing – shoes. Ethnic groups in the U.S. – African Americans. Prejudice. U.S. history.

Meyers, Susan. *Bear in the air* ill. by Amy Bates. Abrams, 2010. ISBN 978-0-8109-8398-4 Subj: Behavior – lost & found possessions. Rhyming text. Toys – bears.

Everywhere babies ill. by Marla Frazee. Harcourt, 2004. ISBN 978-0-15-205315-4 Subj: Activities. Babies, toddlers. Rhyming text.

Kittens! kittens! kittens! ill. by David Walker. Abrams, 2007. ISBN 978-0-8109-1218-2 Subj: Animals – cats. Rhyming text.

Puppies! puppies! puppies! ill. by David Walker. Abrams, 2005. ISBN 978-0-8109-5856-2 Subj: Animals – dogs. Rhyming text.

Rock-a-bye room ill. by Amy Bates. Abrams, 2013. ISBN 978-1-4197-0537-3 Subj: Babies, toddlers. Bedtime. Rhyming text.

This is the way a baby rides ill. by Hiroe Nakata. Abrams, 2005. ISBN 978-0-8109-5763-3 Subj: Animals. Babies, toddlers. Behavior – imitation. Rhyming text.

Michaels, Pat. *W is for wind: a weather alphabet* ill. by Melanie Rose. Sleeping Bear, 2005. ISBN 978-1-58536-237-0 Subj: ABC books. Weather.

Michelin, Linda. *Henry's night* (Johnson, D. B.)

Zuzu's wishing cake ill. by D. B. Johnson. Houghton, 2006. ISBN 978-0-618-64640-1 Subj: Activities – making things. Behavior – wishing. Food. Friendship. Moving.

Michels-Gualtieri, Akaela S. *I was born to be a sister* ill. by Marcy Ramsey. Platypus Media, 2001. ISBN 978-1-930775-03-9 Subj: Babies, toddlers. Children as authors. Family life – brothers & sisters. Sibling rivalry.

Michelson, Richard. *Across the alley* ill. by E. B. Lewis. Penguin, 2006. ISBN 978-0-399-23970-0 Subj: Ethnic groups in the U.S. – African Americans. Friendship. Jewish culture. Music. Prejudice. Sports – baseball.

Busing Brewster ill. by R. G. Roth. Random House, 2010. ISBN 978-0-375-83334-2 Subj: Ethnic groups in the U.S. – African Americans. Prejudice. School. U.S. history.

Oh no, not ghosts! ill. by Adam McCauley. Harcourt, 2006. ISBN 978-0-15-205186-0 Subj: Emotions – fear. Family life – brothers & sisters. Rhyming text.

Ten times better ill. by author. Marshall Cavendish, 2001. ISBN 978-0-7614-5070-2 Subj: Animals. Counting, numbers. Format, unusual – toy & movable books. Rhyming text.

Too young for Yiddish ill. by Neil Waldman. Talewinds, 2002. ISBN 978-0-88106-118-5 Subj: Family life – grandfathers. Jewish culture. Language.

Twice as good: the story of William Powell and Clearview, the only golf course designed, built, and owned by an African American ill. by Eric Velasquez. Sleeping Bear, 2012. ISBN 978-1-58536-466-4 Subj: Ethnic groups in the U.S. – African Americans. Prejudice. Sports – golf. U.S. history.

Micklethwait, Lucy. *In the picture.* Frances Lincoln, 2010. ISBN 978-1-84507-636-8 Subj: Art. Picture puzzles.

Micklos, John. *Daddy poems* foreword by Jim Trelease; ill. by Robert Casilla. Boyds Mills, 2000. ISBN 978-1-56397-735-0 Subj: Family life – fathers. Poetry.

Mommy poems ill. by Lori McElrath-Eslick. Boyds Mills, 2001. ISBN 978-1-56397-849-4 Subj: Family life – mothers. Poetry.

One leaf, two leaves, count with me! ill. by Clive McFarland. Penguin/Nancy Paulsen, 2017. ISBN 978-039954471-2 Subj: Counting, numbers. Rhyming text. Seasons. Trees.

Micucci, Charles. *The life and times of corn* ill. by author. Houghton, 2009. ISBN 978-0-618-50751-1 Subj: Food. Plants.

Middleton, Charlotte. *Nibbles: a green tale* ill. by author. Marshall Cavendish, 2010. ISBN 978-0-7614-5791-6 Subj: Animals – guinea pigs. Ecology. Gardens, gardening. Libraries. Seeds.

Nibbles' garden: another green tale ill. by author. Marshall Cavendish, 2012. ISBN 978-0-7614-6134-0 Subj: Animals – guinea pigs. Gardens, gardening. Insects – butterflies, caterpillars. Metamorphosis.

Middleton, Julie. *Are the dinosaurs dead, Dad?* ill. by Russell Ayto. Peachtree, 2013. ISBN 978-1-56145-690-1 Subj: Dinosaurs. Family life – fathers. Museums.

Migy. *And away we go!* ill. by author. Henry Holt, 2014. ISBN 978-080509901-0 Subj: Activities – ballooning. Animals. Animals – foxes.

Miles, Betty. *The sky is falling* (Chicken Little)

Miles, Elizabeth J. *Ears* ill. with photos. Heinemann, 2003. ISBN 978-1-4034-0014-7 Subj: Anatomy – ears. Animals.

Mouths and teeth ill. with photos. Heinemann, 2003. ISBN 978-1-4034-0018-5 Subj: Anatomy – mouths. Animals. Teeth.

Noses ill. with photos. Heinemann, 2003. ISBN 978-1-4034-0019-2 Subj: Anatomy – noses. Animals.

Wings, fins, and flippers ill. with photos. Heinemann, 2003. ISBN 978-1-4034-0023-9 Subj: Anatomy – fins. Anatomy – wings. Animals.

Miles, Victoria. *Old Mother Bear* ill. by Molly Bang. Chronicle, 2007. ISBN 978-0-8118-5033-9 Subj: Animals – bears. Foreign lands – Canada. Nature.

Milgrim, David. *Amelia makes a movie* ill. by author. Putnam, 2008. ISBN 978-0-399-24670-8 Subj: Careers – actors. Careers – motion picture producers. Family life – brothers & sisters.

Another day in the Milky Way ill. by author. Penguin, 2007. ISBN 978-0-399-24548-0 Subj: Dreams. Space & space ships.

Best baby ever ill. by author. Putnam, 2009. ISBN 978-0-399-25204-4 Subj: Babies, toddlers. Family life – parents.

Cows can't fly ill. by author. Viking, 1998. ISBN 978-0-670-87475-0 Subj: Animals – bulls, cows. Imagination. Rhyming text.

Dog brain ill. by author. Viking, 1996. ISBN 978-0-670-86935-0 Subj: Animals – dogs. Behavior – misbehavior.

Eddie gets ready for school ill. by author. Scholastic, 2011. ISBN 978-0-545-27329-9 Subj: Character traits – assertiveness. Character traits – confidence. Humorous stories. School.

Here in space ill. by author. BridgeWater, 1997. ISBN 978-0-8167-4393-3 Subj: Earth. Rhyming text.

How you got so smart ill. by author. Penguin, 2010. ISBN 978-0-399-25260-0 Subj: Behavior – growing up. Rhyming text. Self-concept.

My friend Lucky ill. by author. Atheneum, 2002. ISBN 978-0-689-84253-5 Subj: Animals – dogs. Concepts – opposites. Language.

Santa Duck ill. by author. Putnam, 2008. ISBN 978-0-399-25018-7 Subj: Animals. Birds – ducks. Holidays – Christmas. Santa Claus.

Santa Duck and his merry helpers ill. by author. Penguin, 2010. ISBN 978-0-399-25473-4 Subj: Birds – ducks. Family life – brothers & sisters. Holidays – Christmas. Santa Claus.

Some monsters are different ill. by author. Henry Holt, 2013. ISBN 978-0-8050-9519-7 Subj: Character traits – being different. Character traits – individuality. Monsters.

Time to get up, time to go ill. by author. Houghton, 2006. ISBN 978-0-618-51998-9 Subj: Activities – playing. Gender roles. Toys – dolls.

Why Benny barks ill. by author. Random House, 1994. ISBN 978-0-679-86157-7 Subj: Animals – dogs. Noise, sounds. Rhyming text.

Wild feelings ill. by author. Henry Holt, 2015. ISBN 978-080509587-6 Subj: Animals. Clothing – costumes. Emotions.

Young MacDonald ill. by author. Penguin, 2006. ISBN 978-0-525-47570-5 Subj: Animals. Careers – inventors. Farms. Inventions. Music. Songs.

Milhander, Laura Aron. *Not for all the hamantaschen in town* ill. by Inna Chernyak. Kar-Ben, 2016. ISBN 978-146775928-1 Subj: Animals – pigs. Animals – wolves. Folk & fairy tales. Holidays – Purim. Jewish culture.

Milhous, Katherine. *The egg tree* ill. by author. Aladdin, 1992, ©1950. ISBN 978-0-689-71568-6 Subj: Caldecott award books. Eggs. Holidays – Easter.

Milich, Zoran. *The city ABC book* ill. by author. Kids Can, 2001. ISBN 978-1-55074-942-7 Subj: ABC books. Cities, towns.

City colors ill. by author. Kids Can, 2004. ISBN 978-1-55337-542-5 Subj: Cities, towns. Concepts – color.

City 1 2 3 ill. by author. Kids Can, 2005. ISBN 978-1-55337-540-1 Subj: Cities, towns. Counting, numbers.

City signs ill. by author. Kids Can, 2002. ISBN 978-1-55337-003-1 Subj: Cities, towns. Communication.

Millard, Glenda. *And red galoshes: a story about a rainy day* ill. by Jonathan Bentley. IPG/Little Hare, 2013. ISBN 978-1-921541-46-9 Subj: Clothing – boots. Rhyming text. Weather – rain.

Isabella's garden ill. by Rebecca Cool. Candlewick, 2012. ISBN 978-0-7636-6016-1 Subj: Cumulative tales. Gardens, gardening. Rhyming text. Seasons.

Millen, C. M. *Blue bowl down* ill. by Holly Meade. Candlewick, 2004. ISBN 978-0-7636-1817-9 Subj: Activities – baking, cooking. Food. Lullabies. Rhyming text.

Miller, Bobbi. *Davy Crockett gets hitched* ill. by Megan Lloyd. Holiday, 2009. ISBN 978-0-8234-1837-4 Subj: Tall tales. U.S. history.

Miss Sally Ann and the panther ill. by Megan Lloyd. Holiday House, 2012. ISBN 978-0-8234-1833-6 Subj: Tall tales. U.S. history – frontier & pioneer life.

Miller, David. *Just like you and me* ill. by author. Dial, 1999. ISBN 978-0-8037-2586-7 Subj: Animals.

Miller, Debbie S. *Are trees alive?* ill. by Stacey Schuett. Walker, 2002. ISBN 978-0-8027-8801-6 Subj: Ecology. Forest, woods. Trees.

A caribou journey ill. by Jon Van Zyle. Little, 1994. ISBN 978-0-316-57380-1 Subj: Alaska. Animals – reindeer. Nature.

River of life ill. by Jon Van Zyle. Clarion, 2000. ISBN 978-0-395-96790-4 Subj: Alaska. Ecology. Rivers.

Woolly mammoth journey ill. by Jon Van Zyle. Little, 2001. ISBN 978-0-316-57212-5 Subj: Animals – woolly mammoths.

Miller, Edna. *Mousekin's Christmas eve* ill. by author. Prentice-Hall, 1965. ISBN 978-0-13-604454-3 Subj: Animals – mice. Holidays – Christmas.

Mousekin's Easter basket ill. by author. Prentice-Hall, 1987. ISBN 978-0-13-604141-2 Subj: Animals – mice. Holidays – Easter. Seasons – spring.

Mousekin's frosty friend ill. by author. Simon & Schuster, 1990. ISBN 978-0-671-70445-2 Subj: Animals – mice. Character traits – kindness to animals. Food. Snowmen.

Mousekin's golden house ill. by author. Prentice-Hall, 1964. ISBN 978-0-13-604232-7 Subj: Animals – mice. Hibernation. Holidays – Halloween. Seasons – winter.

Mousekin's Thanksgiving ill. by author. Prentice-Hall, 1985. ISBN 978-0-13-604299-0 Subj: Animals. Animals – mice. Forest, woods. Holidays – Thanksgiving.

Miller, Edward. *Fireboy to the rescue! a fire safety book* ill. by author. Holiday House, 2010. ISBN 978-0-8234-2222-7 Subj: Careers – firefighters. Safety. School.

The tooth book: a guide to healthy teeth and gums ill. by author. Holiday, 2008. ISBN 978-0-8234-2092-6 Subj: Health & fitness. Teeth.

Miller, Elizabeth I. *Just like home / Como en mi tierra* ill. by Mira Reisberg. Albert Whitman, 1999. ISBN 978-0-8075-4068-8 Subj: Ethnic groups in the U.S. – Hispanic Americans. Foreign languages. Homes, houses. Immigrants, immigration.

Miller, Heather Lynn. *Subway ride* ill. by Sue Ramá. Charlesbridge, 2009. ISBN 978-1-58089-111-0 Subj: Trains. Transportation. World.

This is your life cycle ill. by Michael Chesworth. Clarion, 2008. ISBN 978-0-618-72485-7 Subj: Insects – dragonflies.

Miller, J. Philip. *We all sing with the same voice* by J. Philip Miller and Sheppard M. Greene ill. by Paul Meisel. HarperCollins, 2001. ISBN 978-0-06-027475-7 Subj: Ethnic groups in the U.S. Music. Rhyming text. Songs.

Miller, John. *Winston and George* ill. by Giuliano Cucco. Enchanted Lion, 2014. ISBN 978-159270145-2 Subj: Behavior – lying. Behavior – trickery. Birds – plovers. Reptiles – alligators, crocodiles.

Miller, Margaret. *Baby faces* ill. by author. Simon & Schuster, 1998. ISBN 978-0-689-81911-7 Subj: Anatomy – faces. Babies, toddlers. Format, unusual – board books.

Big and little ill. by author. Greenwillow, 1998. ISBN 978-0-688-14749-5 Subj: Concepts – opposites. Concepts – size.

Can you guess? ill. by author. Greenwillow, 1993. ISBN 978-0-688-11181-6 Subj: Character traits – questioning.

Guess who? photos by author. Simon & Schuster, 1996. ISBN 978-0-688-12784-8 Subj: Format, unusual – board books.

I love colors ill. by author. Simon & Schuster, 1999. ISBN 978-0-689-82356-5 Subj: Animals. Babies, toddlers. Concepts – color. Family life. Format, unusual – board books.

My five senses photos by author. Simon & Schuster, 1994. ISBN 978-0-671-79168-1 Subj: Senses.

Now I'm big photos by author. Greenwillow, 1996. ISBN 978-0-688-14078-6 Subj: Babies, toddlers. Concepts – size. School.

What's on my head? ill. by author. Simon & Schuster, 1998. ISBN 978-0-689-81912-4 Subj: Anatomy – heads. Clothing – hats. Format, unusual – board books.

Who uses this? photos by author. Greenwillow, 1990. ISBN 978-0-688-08279-6 Subj: Careers. Tools.

Whose hat? photos by author. Greenwillow, 1988. ISBN 978-0-688-06907-0 Subj: Careers. Clothing – hats.

Whose shoe? photos by author. Greenwillow, 1991. ISBN 978-0-688-10009-4 Subj: Clothing – shoes. Games.

Miller, Mary Beth. *Handtalk zoo* by Mary Beth Miller and George Ancona; photos by George Ancona. Macmillan, 1989. ISBN 978-0-02-700801-2 Subj: Animals. Communication. Disabilities – deafness. Language. Senses – hearing. Time. Zoos.

Miller, Pat. *The hole story of the doughnut* ill. by Vincent X. Kirsch. Houghton Mifflin Harcourt, 2016. ISBN 978-054431961-5 Subj: Activities – baking, cooking. Careers – chefs, cooks. Food.

Squirrel's New Year's resolution ill. by Kathi Ember. Albert Whitman, 2010. ISBN 978-0-8075-7591-8 Subj: Animals. Animals – squirrels. Character traits – helpfulness. Holidays – New Year's.

Substitute Groundhog ill. by Kathi Ember. Albert Whitman, 2006. ISBN 978-0-8075-7643-4 Subj: Animals. Animals – groundhogs. Holidays – Groundhog Day. Illness.

We're going on a book hunt ill. by Nadine Bernard Westcott. Upstart, 2008. ISBN 978-1-60213-034-0 Subj: Books, reading. Libraries. Rhyming text. Sports – hunting.

Miller, Pat Zietlow. *The quickest kid in Clarksville* ill. by Frank Morrison. Chronicle, 2016. ISBN 978-145212936-5 Subj: Activities – running. Character traits – cooperation. Ethnic groups in the U.S. – African Americans. Prejudice.

Sharing the bread: an old-fashioned Thanksgiving story ill. by Jill McElmurry. Random House, 2015. ISBN 978-030798182-0 Subj: Activities – baking, cooking. Behavior – sharing. Family life. Food. Holidays – Thanksgiving. Rhyming text. U.S. history.

Sophie's squash ill. by Anne Wilsdorf. Random House, 2013. ISBN 978-0-307-978-96-7 Subj: Food. Friendship. Gardens, gardening.

Sophie's squash go to school ill. by Anne Wilsdorf. Random House, 2016. ISBN 978-055350944-1

Subj: Character traits – shyness. Character traits – stubbornness. Friendship. School – first day.

Wherever you go ill. by Eliza Wheeler. Little, Brown, 2015. ISBN 978-031640002-2 Subj: Activities – traveling. Animals – rabbits. Rhyming text.

Miller, Ruth. *The bear on the bed* ill. by Bill Slavin. Kids Can, 2002. ISBN 978-1-55337-036-9 Subj: Animals – bears. Rhyming text.

I went to the farm ill. by Per-Henrik Gurth. Kids Can, 2000. ISBN 978-1-55074-705-8 Subj: Activities – playing. Animals. Farms. Rhyming text.

Miller, Sara Swan. *Cat in the bag* ill. by Benton Mahan. Children's Press, 2001. ISBN 978-0-516-22014-7 Subj: Activities – traveling. Animals – cats.

Miller, Sy. *Let there be peace on earth: and let it begin with me* (Jackson, Jill)

Miller, Tim. *Moo Moo in a tutu* ill. by author. HarperCollins/Balzer+Bray, 2017. ISBN 978-006241440-3 Subj: Animals – bulls, cows. Ballet. Birds – ducks. Character traits – ambition.

Miller, Virginia. *Be gentle!* ill. by author. Candlewick, 1997. ISBN 978-0-7636-0251-2 Subj: Animals – bears. Animals – cats. Pets.

I love you just the way you are ill. by author. Candlewick, 1998. ISBN 978-0-7636-0664-0 Subj: Animals – bears. Behavior – bad day, bad mood.

In a minute! ill. by author. Candlewick, 2000. ISBN 978-0-7636-1270-2 Subj: Activities – playing. Animals – bears.

On your potty! ill. by author. Greenwillow, 1991. ISBN 978-0-688-10618-8 Subj: Animals – bears. Behavior – growing up. Etiquette. Toilet training.

Ten red apples ill. by author. Candlewick, 2002. ISBN 978-0-7636-1901-5 Subj: Animals – bears. Animals – cats. Counting, numbers. Food.

Miller, William. *The bus ride* ill. by John Ward. Intro. by Rosa Parks. Lee & Low, 1998. ISBN 978-1-880000-60-1 Subj: Ethnic groups in the U.S. – African Americans. Prejudice. U.S. history.

A house by the river ill. by Cornelius Van Wright and Ying-Hwa Hu. Lee & Low, 1997. ISBN 978-1-880000-48-9 Subj: Emotions – fear. Ethnic groups in the U.S. – African Americans. Family life – mothers. Homes, houses. Weather – storms.

Jenny and the peddler ill. by Rod Brown. Dial, 2000. ISBN 978-0-8037-2046-6 Subj: Careers – peddlers. Country. Ethnic groups in the U.S. – African Americans. Jewish culture.

The piano ill. by Susan Keeter. Lee & Low, 2000. ISBN 978-1-880000-98-4 Subj: Ethnic groups in the U.S. – African Americans. Music. Musical instruments – pianos. Old age.

Rent party jazz ill. by Charlotte Riley-Webb. Lee & Low, 2001. ISBN 978-1-58430-025-0 Subj: Ethnic groups in the U.S. – African Americans. Music. U.S. history.

Richard Wright and the library card ill. by R. Gregory Christie. Lee & Low, 1997. ISBN 978-1-880000-57-1 Subj: Books, reading. Ethnic groups in the U.S. – African Americans. Libraries.

Milligan, Bryce. *Brigid's cloak* ill. by Helen Cann. Eerdmans, 2002. ISBN 978-0-8028-5224-3 Subj: Clothing – coats. Folk & fairy tales. Foreign lands – Ireland. Religion – Nativity.

The prince of Ireland and the three magic stallions ill. by Preston McDaniels. Holiday, 2003. ISBN 978-0-8234-1573-1 Subj: Emotions – envy, jealousy. Folk & fairy tales. Foreign lands – Ireland. Royalty – princes.

Millman, Isaac. *Moses goes to a concert* ill. by author. Farrar, 1998. ISBN 978-0-374-35067-3 Subj: Communication. Disabilities – deafness. Language. Music. Musical instruments – orchestras. School – field trips. Sign language.

Moses goes to school ill. by author. Farrar, 2000. ISBN 978-0-374-35069-7 Subj: Disabilities – deafness. Language. School – first day. Senses – hearing.

Moses goes to the circus ill. by author. Farrar, 2003. ISBN 978-0-374-35064-2 Subj: Circus. Communication. Disabilities – deafness. Language.

Millner, Denene. *Early Sunday morning* ill. by Vanessa Brantley-Newton. Bolden, 2017. ISBN 978-157284211-3 Subj: Activities – singing. Behavior – worrying. Character traits – kindness. Church. Ethnic groups in the U.S. – African Americans.

Mills, Claudia. *Ziggy's blue-ribbon day* ill. by R. W. Alley. Farrar, 2005. ISBN 978-0-374-32352-3 Subj: Activities – drawing. School. Self-concept. Sports.

Mills, Elaine. *Marinetta at the ballet* ill. by author. Andersen, 2001. ISBN 978-1-59019-439-3 Subj: Ballet. Theater. Toys. Toys – dolls.

Mills, Judith Christine. *The painted chest* ill. by author. Key Porter Kids, 2000. ISBN 978-1-55263-015-0 Subj: Activities – dancing. Activities – playing. Activities – working. Music.

Mills, Lauren A. *The rag coat* ill. by author. Little, 1991. ISBN 978-0-316-57407-5 Subj: Behavior – sharing. Clothing. Friendship. Poverty.

Milne, A. A. *Eeyore loses a tail* ill. by Ernest H. Shepard. Dutton, 2001. ISBN 978-0-525-46703-8 Subj: Anatomy – tails. Toys. Toys – bears.

The magic hill ill. by Isabel Bodor Brown. Dutton, 2000. ISBN 978-0-525-46147-0 Subj: Flowers. Folk & fairy tales. Royalty – princesses.

Tigger tales ill. by Ernest H. Shepard. Dutton, 2002. ISBN 978-0-525-46941-4 Subj: Toys. Toys – bears.

Milord, Susan. *The ghost on the hearth* ill. by Lydia Dabcovich. Vermont Folklife Center, 2003. ISBN 978-0-916718-18-3 Subj: Farms. Foreign lands – Canada. Ghosts.

Happy one hundredth day! ill. by Mary Newell De-Palma. Scholastic, 2011. ISBN 978-0-439-88281-1 Subj: Birthdays. Books, reading. Counting, numbers. School.

Happy school year! ill. by Mary Newell DePalma. Scholastic, 2008. ISBN 978-0-439-88280-4 Subj: Behavior – worrying. Emotions – fear. School – first day.

If I could: a mother's promise ill. by Christopher De-nise. Candlewick, 2008. ISBN 978-0-7636-2348-7 Subj: Animals – raccoons. Emotions – love. Family life – mothers. Rhyming text.

Love that baby ill. by author. Houghton, 2005. ISBN 978-0-618-56323-4 Subj: Babies, toddlers. Emotions – love.

Willa the wonderful ill. by author. Houghton, 2003. ISBN 978-0-618-27522-9 Subj: Animals – pigs. Fairies. Royalty – princesses. School.

Milusich, Janice. *Off go their engines, off go their lights* ill. by David Gordon. Dutton, 2008. ISBN 978-0-525-47940-6 Subj: Automobiles. Night. Rhyming text. Taxis. Trucks.

Milway, Katie Smith. *Cappuccina goes to town* ill. by Eugenie Fernandes. Kids Can, 2002. ISBN 978-1-55074-807-9 Subj: Animals – bulls, cows. Cities, towns. Farms. Self-concept.

The good garden: how one family went from hunger to having enough ill. by Sylvie Daigneault. Kids Can, 2010. ISBN 978-1-55453-488-3 Subj: Food. Foreign lands – Honduras. Gardens, gardening.

Mimi's village and how basic health care transformed it ill. by Eugenie Fernandes. Kids Can, 2012. ISBN 978-1-55453-722-8 Subj: Character traits – cleanliness. Foreign lands – Kenya. Health & fitness. Illness.

One hen: how one small loan made a big difference ill. by Eugenie Fernandes. Kids Can, 2008. ISBN 978-1-55453-028-1 Subj: Behavior – seeking better things. Birds – chickens, roosters. Foreign lands – Ghana. Money. Poverty.

Minarik, Else Holmelund. *Am I beautiful?* ill. by Yossi Abolafia. Greenwillow, 1992. ISBN 978-0-688-09912-1 Subj: Animals. Animals – hippopotamuses. Family life – mothers. Self-concept.

It's spring! ill. by Margaret Bloy Graham. Greenwillow, 1989. ISBN 978-0-688-07620-7 Subj: Animals – cats. Seasons – spring.

Little Bear's new friend ill. by Heather Green. HarperCollins, 2002. ISBN 978-0-06-623688-9 Subj: Animals – bears. Behavior – lost. Friendship.

Minor, Florence. *Christmas tree!* (Minor, Wendell)

How to be a bigger bunny ill. by Wendell Minor. HarperCollins/Katherine Tegen, 2017. ISBN 978-006235255-2 Subj: Animals – rabbits. Behavior – growing up. Character traits – bravery.

If you were a penguin ill. by Wendell Minor. HarperCollins, 2009. ISBN 978-0-06-113097-7 Subj: Birds – penguins. Rhyming text.

Minor, Wendell. *Christmas tree!* by Wendell Minor and Florence Minor; ill. by authors. HarperCollins, 2005. ISBN 978-0-06-056035-5 Subj: Holidays – Christmas. Rhyming text. Trees.

Daylight starlight wildlife ill. by author. Penguin/Nancy Paulsen, 2015. ISBN 978-039924662-3 Subj: Animals. Day. Night.

How big could your pumpkin grow? ill. by author. Penguin/Nancy Paulsen, 2013. ISBN 978-0-399-24684-5 Subj: Food. Imagination. U.S. history.

My farm friends ill. by author. Penguin, 2011. ISBN 978-0-399-24477-3 Subj: Animals. Farms. Rhyming text.

Pumpkin heads ill. by author. Blue Sky, 2000. ISBN 978-0-590-52105-5 Subj: Holidays – Halloween.

Yankee Doodle America: the spirit of 1776 from A to Z ill. by author. Penguin, 2006. ISBN 978-0-399-24003-4 Subj: ABC books. U.S. history.

Minshull, Evelyn White. *Eaglet's world* ill. by Andrea Gabriel. Albert Whitman, 2002. ISBN 978-0-8075-8929-8 Subj: Activities – flying. Behavior – growing up. Birds – eagles.

Minters, Frances. *Cinder-Elly* ill. by G. Brian Karas. Viking, 1994. ISBN 978-0-670-84417-3 Subj: Folk & fairy tales. Rhyming text. Royalty – princes. Sibling rivalry.

Princess Fishtail ill. by G. Brian Karas. Viking, 2002. ISBN 978-0-670-03529-8 Subj: Humorous stories. Mythical creatures – mermaids, mermen. Mythical creatures – trolls. Rhyming text. Sports – surfing.

Sleepless Beauty ill. by G. Brian Karas. Viking, 1996. ISBN 978-0-670-87033-2 Subj: Folk & fairy tales. Rhyming text. Witches.

Too big, too small, just right ill. by Janie Bynum. Harcourt, 2001. ISBN 978-0-15-202157-3 Subj: Animals – rabbits. Concepts – opposites. Rhyming text.

Miranda, Anne. *Alphabet fiesta.* ill. by young children. Turtle, 2001. ISBN 978-1-890515-29-4 Subj: ABC books. Animals. Animals – zebras. Birthdays. Children as illustrators. Parties.

Beep! beep! ill. by David Murphy. Turtle, 1999. ISBN 978-1-890515-14-0 Subj: Automobiles. Imagination. Noise, sounds. Rhyming text. Trucks.

Monster math ill. by Polly Powell. Harcourt, 1999. ISBN 978-0-15-201835-1 Subj: Birthdays. Counting, numbers. Monsters. Parties. Rhyming text.

Pignic ill. by Rosekrans Hoffman. Boyds Mills, 1996. ISBN 978-1-56397-558-5 Subj: ABC books. Activities – picnicking. Animals – pigs.

To market, to market ill. by Janet Stevens. Harcourt, 1997. ISBN 978-0-15-200035-6 Subj: Animals. Animals – pigs. Nursery rhymes. Stores.

Vroom, chugga, vroom-vroom ill. by David Murphy. Turtle, 1998. ISBN 978-1-890515-07-2 Subj: Automobiles. Counting, numbers. Sports – racing. Transportation.

Mitakidou, Soula. *The orphan: a Cinderella story from Greece* (Manna, Anthony L.)

Mitchard, Jacquelyn. *Baby bat's lullaby* ill. by Julia Noonan. HarperCollins, 2004. ISBN 978-0-06-050761-9 Subj: Animals – bats. Bedtime. Family life – mothers. Lullabies.

Ready, set, school! ill. by Paul Ratz de Tagyos. HarperCollins, 2007. ISBN 978-0-06-050766-4 Subj: Animals – raccoons. Family life – parents. School – first day. Sleepovers.

Mitchell, Adrian. *Nobody rides the unicorn* ill. by Stephen Lambert. Scholastic, 2000. ISBN 978-0-439-11204-8 Subj: Mythical creatures – unicorns. Royalty – kings.

Mitchell, Brian Stokes. *Lights on Broadway: a theatrical tour from A to Z* (Ziefert, Harriet)

Mitchell, Hazel. *Toby* ill. by author. Candlewick, 2016. ISBN 978-076368093-0 Subj: Animals – dogs. Character traits – kindness to animals. Emotions – loneliness.

Mitchell, Joyce Slayton. *Tractor-trailer trucker: a powerful truck book* photos by Steven Borns. Tricycle, 2000. ISBN 978-1-58246-010-9 Subj: Careers – truck drivers. Trucks.

Mitchell, Lori. *Different just like me* ill. by author. Charlesbridge, 1999. ISBN 978-0-88106-975-4 Subj: Character traits – individuality. Family life – grandmothers.

Mitchell, Margaree King. *Granddaddy's gift* ill. by Larry Johnson. BridgeWater, 1996. ISBN 978-0-8167-4010-9 Subj: Character traits – bravery. Ethnic groups in the U.S. – African Americans. Family life – grandfathers. U.S. history.

Susie Mae ill. by Melodye Benson Rosales. Lothrop, 2000. ISBN 978-0-688-15222-2 Subj: Ethnic groups in the U.S. – African Americans. Prejudice. School.

Uncle Jed's barbershop ill. by James Ransome. Simon & Schuster, 1993. ISBN 978-0-671-76969-7 Subj: Careers – barbers. Character traits – perseverance. Ethnic groups in the U.S. – African Americans. Family life – aunts, uncles.

When Grandmama sings ill. by James Ransome. HarperCollins, 2012. ISBN 978-0-688-17563-4 Subj: Activities – singing. Ethnic groups in the U.S. – African Americans. Family life – grandmothers. Prejudice. U.S. history.

Mitchell, Marianne. *Gullywasher gulch* ill. by Normand Chartier. Boyds Mills, 2002. ISBN 978-1-56397-123-5 Subj: Character traits – generosity. Weather – rain.

Joe Cinders ill. by Bryan Langdo. Henry Holt, 2002. ISBN 978-0-8050-6529-9 Subj: Clothing – boots. Cowboys, cowgirls. Folk & fairy tales.

Mitchell, Rhonda. *The talking cloth* ill. by author. Orchard, 1997. ISBN 978-0-531-33004-3 Subj: Ethnic groups in the U.S. – African Americans. Family life – aunts, uncles. Foreign lands – Africa.

Mitchell, Robin. *Windy* by Robin Mitchell and Judith Steedman; photos by Mia Cunningham. Simply Read, 2002. ISBN 978-0-9688768-2-4 Subj: Kites. Weather – wind.

Mitchell, Susan K. *The rainforest grew all around* ill. by Connie McLennan. Random House, 2007. ISBN 978-0-9768823-6-7 Subj: Animals. Jungle. Plants. Songs.

Mitter, Matt. *ABC: alphabet rhymes* ill. by Doug Cushman. G. Stevens, 2004. ISBN 978-0-8368-4095-7 Subj: ABC books. Animals. Rhyming text.

Once upon a rhyme ill. by Susan Banta. G. Stevens, 2004. ISBN 978-0-8368-4096-4 Subj: Animals. Humorous stories. Rebuses. Rhyming text.

1, 2, 3, counting rhymes ill. by Doug Cushman. G. Stevens, 2004. ISBN 978-0-8368-4094-0 Subj: Animals. Counting, numbers. Farms. Rhyming text.

Mitton, Jacqueline. *Zoo in the sky: a book of animal constellations* ill. by Christina Balit. Star maps by Wil Tirion. National Geographic, 1998. ISBN 978-0-7922-7069-0 Subj: Stars.

Mitton, Tony. *All afloat on Noah's boat!* ill. by Guy Parker-Rees. Scholastic, 2007. ISBN 978-0-439-

87397-0 Subj: Animals. Boats, ships. Religion – Noah. Rhyming text.

Cool cars ill. by Ant Parker. Houghton, 2005. ISBN 978-0-7534-5802-0 Subj: Automobiles. Rhyming text. Transportation.

Dinosaurumpus ill. by Guy Parker-Rees. Orchard, 2003. ISBN 978-0-439-39514-4 Subj: Activities – dancing. Dinosaurs. Rhyming text.

Down by the cool of the pool ill. by Guy Parker-Rees. Orchard, 2002. ISBN 978-0-439-30915-8 Subj: Activities – dancing. Animals. Frogs & toads. Lakes, ponds. Rhyming text.

Farmer Joe and the music show ill. by Guy Parker-Rees. Scholastic, 2009. ISBN 978-0-545-12493-5 Subj: Animals. Farms. Music. Rhyming text.

Flashing fire engines by Tony Mitton and Ant Parker ill. by Ant Parker. Kingfisher, 1998. ISBN 978-0-7534-5104-5 Subj: Careers – firefighters. Noise, sounds. Rhyming text. Trucks.

The Jungle Run ill. by Guy Parker-Rees. Scholastic, 2012. ISBN 978-0-545-39256-3 Subj: Activities – running. Animals. Jungle. Rhyming text. Sports – racing.

Playful little penguins ill. by Guy Parker-Rees. Walker, 2007. ISBN 978-0-8027-9710-0 Subj: Animals – seals. Behavior – lost. Birds – penguins. Rhyming text.

Riddledy piggledy ill. by Paddy Mounter. Fickling, 2003. ISBN 978-0-385-75033-2 Subj: Nursery rhymes. Riddles & jokes.

Rumble, roar, dinosaur! more prehistoric poems with lift-the-flap surprises! ill. by Lynne Chapman. Kingfisher, 2010. ISBN 978-0-7534-1932-8 Subj: Dinosaurs. Format, unusual – toy & movable books.

Snowy Bear ill. by Alison Brown. Bloomsbury, 2015. ISBN 978-161963905-8 Subj: Animals – bears. Rhyming text. Seasons – winter. Weather – snow.

A very curious bear ill. by Paul Howard. Random House, 2009. ISBN 978-0-375-85083-7 Subj: Animals – bears. Character traits – curiosity. Character traits – questioning. Rhyming text.

Miura, Taro. *The big princess* ill. by author. Candlewick, 2015. ISBN 978-076367459-5 Subj: Concepts – size. Royalty – princesses.

The tiny king ill. by author. Candlewick, 2013. ISBN 978-0-7636-6687-3 Subj: Character traits – smallness. Emotions – happiness. Royalty – kings.

Tools ill. by author. Chronicle, 2006. ISBN 978-0-8118-5519-8 Subj: Tools.

Mixter, Helen. *My little round house* (Baasansuren, Bolormaa)

Miyakoshi, Akiko. *The storm* ill. by author. Kids Can, 2016. ISBN 978-177138559-6 Subj: Imagination. Weather – storms.

The tea party in the woods ill. by author. Kids Can, 2015. ISBN 978-177138107-9 Subj: Animals. Forest, woods. Parties.

The way home in the night ill. by author. Kids Can, 2017. ISBN 978-177138663-0 Subj: Animals – rabbits. Bedtime. Cities, towns. Family life – mothers.

Miyares, Daniel. *Bring me a rock!* ill. by author. Simon & Schuster, 2016. ISBN 978-148144602-0 Subj: Character traits – smallness. Insects. Royalty – kings.

Float ill. by author. Simon & Schuster, 2015. ISBN 978-148141524-8 Subj: Behavior – lost & found possessions. Boats, ships. Toys. Weather – rain. Wordless.

Pardon me! ill. by author. Simon & Schuster, 2014. ISBN 978-144248997-4 Subj: Behavior – sharing. Birds. Humorous stories. Reptiles – alligators, crocodiles.

That neighbor kid ill. by author. Simon & Schuster, 2017. ISBN 978-148144979-3 Subj: Character traits – cooperation. Friendship. Homes, houses. Trees. Wordless.

Mizzoni, Chris. *Clancy with the puck* ill. by author. Raincoast, 2007. ISBN 978-1-55192-804-3 Subj: Rhyming text. Sports – hockey.

Mobin-Uddin, Asma. *The best Eid ever* ill. by Laura Jacobsen. Boyds Mills, 2007. ISBN 978-1-59078-431-0 Subj: Holidays. Religion – Islam.

A party in Ramadan ill. by Laura Jacobsen. Boyds Mills, 2009. ISBN 978-1-59078-604-8 Subj: Holidays – Ramadan. Religion – Islam.

Mochizuki, Ken. *Baseball saved us* ill. by Dom Lee. Lee & Low, 1993. ISBN 978-1-880000-01-4 Subj: Ethnic groups in the U.S. – Japanese Americans. Sports – baseball. U.S. history. War.

Be water, my friend: the early years of Bruce Lee ill. by Dom Lee. Lee & Low, 2006. ISBN 978-1-58430-265-0 Subj: Ethnic groups in the U.S. – Chinese Americans. Sports – martial arts.

Modan, Rutu. *Maya makes a mess* ill. by author. TOON, 2012. ISBN 978-1-93517-917-7 Subj: Behavior – messy. Etiquette. Food. Format, unusual – graphic novels.

Modarressi, Mitra. *Owlet's first flight* ill. by author. Putnam, 2012. ISBN 978-0-399-25526-7 Subj: Activities – flying. Birds – owls. Emotions – fear. Rhyming text.

Stay awake, Sally ill. by author. Penguin, 2007. ISBN 978-0-399-24545-9 Subj: Animals – raccoons. Bedtime. Family life – parents. Rhyming text.

Taking care of Mama ill. by author. Penguin, 2010. ISBN 978-0-399-25216-7 Subj: Animals – raccoons. Family life – mothers. Illness.

Yard sale ill. by author. DK, 2000. ISBN 978-0-7894-2651-2 Subj: Communities, neighborhoods. Magic. Stores.

Modell, Frank. *Goodbye old year, hello new year* ill. by author. Greenwillow, 1984. ISBN 978-0-688-03939-4 Subj: Holidays – New Year's.

Ice cream soup ill. by author. Greenwillow, 1988. ISBN 978-0-688-07771-6 Subj: Birthdays. Parties.

Look out, it's April Fools' Day ill. by author. Greenwillow, 1985. ISBN 978-0-688-04017-8 Subj: Holidays – April Fools' Day. Riddles & jokes.

One zillion valentines ill. by author. Greenwillow, 1981. ISBN 978-0-688-00569-6 Subj: Character traits – practicality. Holidays – Valentine's Day.

Modesitt, Jeanne. *Little Bunny's Easter surprise* ill. by Robin Spowart. Simon & Schuster, 1999. ISBN 978-0-689-82491-3 Subj: Animals – rabbits. Behavior – hiding things. Holidays – Easter.

Little Mouse's happy birthday ill. by Robin Spowart. Boyds Mills, 2007. ISBN 978-1-59078-272-9 Subj: Animals – mice. Birthdays. Family life.

Oh, what a beautiful day! a counting book ill. by Robin Spowart. Boyds Mills, 2009. ISBN 978-1-56397-409-0 Subj: Animals. Counting, numbers. Day. Rhyming text.

Modugno, Maria. *Santa Claus and the three bears* ill. by Jane Dyer. HarperCollins, 2013. ISBN 978-0-06-170023-1 Subj: Animals – polar bears. Holidays – Christmas. Santa Claus.

Moerbeek, Kees. *The diary of Hansel and Gretel* ill. by author. Simon & Schuster, 2002. ISBN 978-0-689-84602-1 Subj: Behavior – lost. Folk & fairy tales. Forest, woods. Format, unusual – toy & movable books. Witches.

Moers, Hermann. *Rufus and Max* ill. by Philippe Goossens. NorthSouth, 2003. ISBN 978-0-7358-1798-2 Subj: Activities – playing. Animals – dogs. Imagination.

Moffatt, Judith. *The pumpkin man* ill. by author. Scholastic, 1998. ISBN 978-0-590-63865-4 Subj: Holidays – Halloween. Rhyming text.

Snow shapes ill. by author. Scholastic, 2000. ISBN 978-0-439-09858-8 Subj: Activities – making things. Art. Paper. Seasons – winter.

Trick-or-treat faces: a glowing book you can read in the dark! ill. by author. Scholastic, 2000. ISBN 978-0-439-18299-7 Subj: Format, unusual. Holidays – Halloween. Monsters. Rhyming text.

Mohammed, Khadra. *Four feet, two sandals* (Williams, Karen Lynn)

My name is Sangoel (Williams, Karen Lynn)

Mohr, Joseph, verses. *Silent night* ill. by Susan Jeffers. Orig. title: Stille Nacht, heilige Nacht. Dutton, 1984. ISBN 978-0-525-44144-1 Subj: Holidays – Christmas. Songs.

Molchadsky, Yael. *The chameleon that saved Noah's ark* ill. by Orit Bergman. Penguin/Nancy Paulsen, 2016. ISBN 978-110199676-8 Subj: Animals. Religion – Noah. Reptiles – chameleons.

Molk, Laurel. *Eeny, Meeny, Miney, Mo and Flo!* ill. by author. Viking, 2015. ISBN 978-067001538-2 Subj: Animals – mice. Family life – brothers & sisters. Rhyming text.

Good job, Oliver! ill. by author. Crown, 1999. ISBN 978-0-517-70976-4 Subj: Animals – rabbits. Gardens, gardening.

Mollel, Tololwa M. *Ananse's feast: an Ashanti tale* ill. by Andrew Glass. Clarion, 1997. ISBN 978-0-395-67402-4 Subj: Behavior – trickery. Country. Folk & fairy tales. Foreign lands – Ghana. Reptiles – turtles, tortoises. Spiders.

The flying tortoise: an Igbo tale ill. by Barbara Spurll. Oxford Univ., 1993. ISBN 978-0-395-68845-8 Subj: Behavior – greed. Behavior – trickery. Folk & fairy tales. Foreign lands – Nigeria. Reptiles – turtles, tortoises.

Kele's secret ill. by Catherine Stock. Dutton, 1997. ISBN 978-0-525-67500-6 Subj: Birds – chickens, roosters. Family life – grandparents. Foreign lands – Tanzania.

Kitoto the mighty ill. by Kristi Frost. Stoddart, 1998. ISBN 978-0-7737-3019-9 Subj: Animals – mice. Folk & fairy tales. Foreign lands – Africa.

My rows and piles of coins ill. by E. B. Lewis. Clarion, 1999. ISBN 978-0-395-75186-2 Subj: Foreign lands – Tanzania. Money. Sports – bicycling.

Orphan boy ill. by Paul Morin. Clarion, 1991. ISBN 978-0-89919-985-6 Subj: Folk & fairy tales. Foreign lands – Kenya. Magic. Orphans.

Rhinos for lunch and elephants for supper ill. by Barbara Spurll. Houghton, 1992. ISBN 978-0-395-60734-3 Subj: Animals. Cumulative tales. Emotions – fear. Foreign lands – Kenya.

Song bird ill. by Rosanne Litzinger. Clarion, 1999. ISBN 978-0-395-82908-0 Subj: Birds. Folk & fairy tales. Foreign lands – Tanzania. Magic. Monsters.

Subira subira ill. by Linda Saport. Clarion, 2000. ISBN 978-0-395-91809-8 Subj: Character traits –

patience, impatience. Folk & fairy tales. Foreign lands – Tanzania.

To dinner, for dinner ill. by Synthia Saint James. Holiday, 2000. ISBN 978-0-8234-1527-4 Subj: Animals. Animals – leopards. Animals – rabbits. Foreign lands – Africa.

Monari, Manuela. *Zero kisses for me!* ill. by Virginie Soumagnac. Tundra, 2010. ISBN 978-1-77049-208-0 Subj: Animals – bears. Bedtime. Kissing.

Monfreid, Dorothée de. *The cake* ill. by author. Gecko, 2014. ISBN 978-187757945-5 Subj: Animals. Behavior – fighting, arguing. Food.

Dark night ill. by author. Random House, 2009. ISBN 978-0-375-85687-7 Subj: Animals. Emotions – fear. Night.

Shhh! I'm sleeping ill. by author. Gecko, 2016. ISBN 978-192727195-7 Subj: Animals – dogs. Format, unusual – board books. Sleep. Sleep – snoring.

Monk, Isabell. *Blackberry stew* ill. by Janice Lee Porter. Carolrhoda, 2005. ISBN 978-1-57505-605-0 Subj: Death. Emotions – grief. Emotions – sadness. Family life – grandfathers. Memories, memory.

Family ill. by Janice Lee Porter. Carolrhoda, 2001. ISBN 978-1-57505-485-8 Subj: Ethnic groups in the U.S. – African Americans. Family life. Food.

Hope ill. by Janice Lee Porter. Carolrhoda, 1999. ISBN 978-1-57505-230-4 Subj: Ethnic groups in the U.S. – African Americans. Family life – aunts, uncles. Names.

Monks, Lydia. *Aaaarrgghh! spider!* ill. by author. Houghton, 2004. ISBN 978-0-618-43250-9 Subj: Pets. Spiders.

The cat barked? ill. by author. Dial, 1999. ISBN 978-0-8037-2338-2 Subj: Animals – cats. Animals – dogs. Rhyming text. Self-concept.

Monnier, Miriam. *Just right* ill. by author. North-South, 2001. ISBN 978-0-7358-1522-3 Subj: Behavior – growing up. Family life – mothers. Self-concept.

Monroe, Chris. *Bug on a bike* ill. by author. Carolrhoda, 2014. ISBN 978-146772154-7 Subj: Birthdays. Cumulative tales. Insects. Rhyming text. Sports – bicycling.

Cookie, the walker ill. by author. Carolrhoda, 2013. ISBN 978-0-7613-5617-2 Subj: Activities – walking. Animals – dogs. Character traits – being different.

Monkey with a tool belt and the seaside shenanigans ill. by author. Carolrhoda, 2011. ISBN 978-0-7613-5616-5 Subj: Animals – elephants. Animals – monkeys. Sea & seashore – beaches. Tools.

Sneaky sheep ill. by author. Carolrhoda, 2010. ISBN 978-0-7613-5615-8 Subj: Animals – dogs. Animals – sheep. Behavior – misbehavior.

Monson, A. M. *Wanted . . . best friend* ill. by Lynn Munsinger. Dial, 1997. ISBN 978-0-8037-1485-4 Subj: Animals – cats. Animals – mice. Friendship. Games.

Monster, be good! ill. by Natalie Marshall. Blue Apple, 2013. ISBN 978-1-60905-314-7 Subj: Behavior. Etiquette. Monsters.

Montalván, Luis Carlos. *Tuesday tucks me in: the loyal bond between a soldier and his service dog* by Luis Carlos Montalván and Bret Witter ill. with photos. Roaring Brook, 2014. ISBN 978-159643891-0 Subj: Animals – dogs. Animals – service animals. Careers – military. Disabilities.

Montanari, Donata. *Children around the world* ill. by author. Kids Can, 2001. ISBN 978-1-55337-064-2 Subj: Etiquette. Foreign lands.

Montanari, Eva. *The crocodile's true colors* ill. by author. Watson-Guptill, 2002. ISBN 978-0-8230-2435-3 Subj: Animals. Concepts. Foreign lands – Africa. Reptiles – alligators, crocodiles. School.

Dino bikes ill. by author. NorthSouth, 2004. ISBN 978-0-7358-1918-4 Subj: Behavior – bullying, teasing. Dinosaurs. Sports – bicycling.

My first . . . ill. by author. Houghton, 2007. ISBN 978-0-618-64644-9 Subj: Books, reading. Gifts. Toys – dolls.

Tiff, Taff, and Lulu ill. by author. Houghton, 2004. ISBN 978-0-618-40238-0 Subj: Family life – sisters. Sibling rivalry.

A very full morning ill. by author. Houghton, 2006. ISBN 978-0-618-56318-0 Subj: Animals – rabbits. Behavior – worrying. Careers – teachers. School – first day.

Montanari, Susan McElroy. *My dog's a chicken* ill. by Anne Wilsdorf. Random House, 2016. ISBN 978-038538490-2 Subj: Birds – chickens, roosters. Family life. Farms. Pets.

Montenegro, Laura Nyman. *A bird about to sing* ill. by author. Houghton, 2003. ISBN 978-0-618-18865-9 Subj: Character traits – shyness. Poetry.

Montes, Marisa. *Egg-napped!* ill. by Marsha Winborn. HarperCollins, 2002. ISBN 978-0-06-028951-5 Subj: Animals. Behavior – lost & found possessions. Birds – geese. Eggs. Rhyming text.

Juan Bobo goes to work: a Puerto Rican folktale ill. by Joe Cepeda. Morrow, 2000. ISBN 978-0-688-16234-4 Subj: Folk & fairy tales. Foreign lands – Puerto Rico.

Los gatos black on Halloween ill. by Yuyi Morales. Henry Holt, 2006. ISBN 978-0-8050-7429-1 Subj: Animals – cats. Foreign languages. Holidays – Day of the Dead. Holidays – Halloween. Monsters. Rhyming text.

Montgomery, Michael G., compiler. *Over the candlestick: classic nursery rhymes and the real stories behind them* also comp. by Wayne Montgomery; ill. by Michael G. Montgomery. Peachtree, 2002. ISBN 978-1-56145-259-0 Subj: Nursery rhymes.

Montijo, Rhode. *The Halloween Kid* ill. by author. Simon & Schuster, 2010. ISBN 978-1-4169-3575-9 Subj: Cowboys, cowgirls. Holidays – Halloween.

Montserrat, Pep. *Ms. Rubinstein's beauty* ill. by author. Sterling, 2006. ISBN 978-1-4027-3063-4 Subj: Character traits – appearance. Character traits – individuality. Circus.

Moodie, Fiona. *Noko and the night monster* ill. by author. Marshall Cavendish, 2001. ISBN 978-0-7614-5093-1 Subj: Animals – aardvarks. Animals – porcupines. Emotions – fear. Monsters. Night.

Moon, Nicola. *Lucy's picture* ill. by Alex Ayliffe. Dial, 1995. ISBN 978-0-8037-1833-3 Subj: Activities – making things. Art. Disabilities – blindness. Family life – grandfathers.

Something special ill. by Alex Ayliffe. Peachtree, 1997. ISBN 978-1-56145-137-1 Subj: Babies, toddlers. Family life – brothers & sisters. School.

Tick-tock, drip-drop ill. by Eleanor Taylor. Bloomsbury, 2004. ISBN 978-1-58234-944-2 Subj: Animals – moles. Animals – rabbits. Bedtime. Noise, sounds. Sleep.

Moore, Clement Clarke. *A creature was stirring: one boy's night before Christmas* by Clement Clarke Moore and Carter Goodrich ill. by Carter Goodrich. Simon & Schuster, 2006. ISBN 978-0-689-86399-8 Subj: Holidays – Christmas. Poetry. Santa Claus.

The night before Christmas ill. by Jan Brett. Putnam, 1998. ISBN 978-0-399-23190-2 Subj: Holidays – Christmas. Poetry. Santa Claus.

The night before Christmas ill. by Tomie dePaola. Holiday, 1980. ISBN 978-0-8234-0414-8 Subj: Holidays – Christmas. Poetry. Santa Claus.

The night before Christmas ill. by Mary Engelbreit. HarperCollins, 2002. ISBN 978-0-06-008161-4 Subj: Holidays – Christmas. Poetry. Santa Claus.

The night before Christmas ill. by David Ercolini. Scholastic/Orchard, 2015. ISBN 978-054539112-2 Subj: Holidays – Christmas. Poetry. Santa Claus.

The night before Christmas ill. by Holly Hobbie. Little, Brown, 2013. ISBN 978-0-316-07018-8 Subj: Holidays – Christmas. Poetry. Santa Claus.

The night before Christmas retold by Rachel Isadora; ill. by reteller. Putnam, 2009. ISBN 978-0-399-25408-6 Subj: Animals – mice. Foreign lands – Africa. Holidays – Christmas. Poetry. Santa Claus.

The night before Christmas ill. by Raquel Jaramillo. Atheneum, 2001. ISBN 978-0-689-84053-1 Subj: Holidays – Christmas. Poetry. Santa Claus.

The night before Christmas ill. by Anita Lobel. Knopf, 1984. ISBN 978-0-394-96863-6 Subj: Holidays – Christmas. Poetry. Santa Claus.

The night before Christmas ill. by James Marshall. Scholastic, 1989. ISBN 978-0-590-33805-9 Subj: Holidays – Christmas. Poetry. Santa Claus.

The night before Christmas ill. by Will Moses. Penguin, 2006. ISBN 978-0-399-23745-4 Subj: Holidays – Christmas. Poetry. Santa Claus.

The night before Christmas ill. by Ted Rand. North-South, 1995. ISBN 978-1-55858-466-2 Subj: Holidays – Christmas. Poetry. Santa Claus.

The night before Christmas ill. by Barbara Reid. Albert Whitman, 2014. ISBN 978-080755625-2 Subj: Animals – mice. Holidays – Christmas. Poetry. Santa Claus.

The night before Christmas ill. by Ruth Sanderson. Little, 1997. ISBN 978-0-316-57963-6 Subj: Holidays – Christmas. Poetry. Santa Claus.

The night before Christmas ill. by Gennady Spirin. Marshall Cavendish, 2006. ISBN 978-0-7614-5298-0 Subj: Holidays – Christmas. Poetry. Santa Claus.

The night before Christmas ill. by Tasha Tudor. Little, 1999. ISBN 978-0-316-85579-2 Subj: Holidays – Christmas. Poetry. Santa Claus.

The night before Christmas ill. by Richard Jesse Watson. HarperCollins, 2006. ISBN 978-0-06-075742-7 Subj: Holidays – Christmas. Poetry. Santa Claus.

The night before Christmas ill. by Wendy Watson. Houghton, 1990. ISBN 978-0-395-53624-7 Subj: Holidays – Christmas. Poetry. Santa Claus.

The night before Christmas ill. by Bruce Whatley. HarperCollins, 1999. ISBN 978-0-06-026609-7 Subj: Holidays – Christmas. Poetry. Santa Claus.

The night before Christmas ill. by Lisbeth Zwerger. Penguin, 2005. ISBN 978-0-698-40030-6 Subj: Holidays – Christmas. Poetry. Santa Claus.

The night before Christmas comp. by Cooper Edens and Harold Darling. Ill. by various 19th- & 20th-century artists. A classic illustrated ed. Chronicle, 1998. ISBN 978-0-8118-1712-7 Subj: Holidays – Christmas. Poetry. Santa Claus.

The night before Christmas: a pop-up ill. by Robert Sabuda. Simon & Schuster, 2002. ISBN 978-0-689-83899-6 Subj: Format, unusual – toy & movable books. Holidays – Christmas. Poetry. Santa Claus.

The teddy bears' night before Christmas photos by Monica Stevenson. Scholastic, 1999. ISBN 978-0-590-03243-8 Subj: Holidays – Christmas. Poetry. Santa Claus. Toys. Toys – bears.

'Twas the night before Christmas adapt. by Daniel Kirk; ill. by adapter. Abrams, 2015. ISBN 978-1-419-71233-3 Subj: Animals – mice. Holidays – Christmas. Poetry. Santa Claus.

'Twas the night before Christmas ill. by Matt Tavares. Candlewick, 2002. ISBN 978-0-7636-1585-7 Subj: Holidays – Christmas. Poetry. Santa Claus.

'Twas the night before Christmas ill. by Christopher Wormell. Running Press, 2010. ISBN 978-0-7624-2717-8 Subj: Holidays – Christmas. Poetry. Santa Claus.

Moore, Elaine. *Roly-poly puppies* ill. by Jacqueline Rogers. Scholastic, 1996. ISBN 978-0-590-46665-3 Subj: Animals – dogs. Counting, numbers. Rhyming text.

Moore, Eva. *Lucky ducklings* ill. by Nancy Carpenter. Scholastic, 2013. ISBN 978-0-439-44861-1 Subj: Birds – ducks. Character traits – kindness to animals. Family life – mothers.

Moore, Genevieve. *Catherine's story* ill. by Karin Littlewood. Frances Lincoln, 2010. ISBN 978-1-84507-655-9 Subj: Disabilities – physical disabilities. Family life – fathers. Family life – single-parent families.

Moore, Inga. *Captain Cat* ill. by author. Candlewick, 2013. ISBN 978-0-7636-6151-9 Subj: Animals – cats. Animals – rats. Islands. Royalty – queens. Sailors.

A house in the woods ill. by author. Candlewick, 2011. ISBN 978-0-7636-5277-7 Subj: Animals. Homes, houses.

Moore, Jodi. *When a dragon moves in* ill. by Howard McWilliam. Flashlight, 2011. ISBN 978-0-979974-67-0 Subj: Dragons. Imagination. Sea & seashore – beaches.

Moore, Julianne. *Freckleface Strawberry* ill. by LeUyen Pham. Bloomsbury, 2007. ISBN 978-1-59990-107-7 Subj: Anatomy. Friendship. Self-concept.

Freckleface Strawberry: best friends forever ill. by LeUyen Pham. Bloomsbury, 2011. ISBN 978-1-59990-551-8 Subj: Anatomy. Friendship. Gender roles.

Freckleface Strawberry and the dodgeball bully ill. by LeUyen Pham. Bloomsbury, 2009. ISBN 978-1-59990-316-3 Subj: Behavior – bullying, teasing. Games. School.

Moore, Lilian. *Beware, take care: fun and spooky poems* ill. by Howard Fine. Henry Holt, 2006. ISBN 978-0-8050-6917-4 Subj: Dragons. Emotions – fear. Ghosts. Monsters. Poetry.

While you were chasing a hat ill. by Rosanne Litzinger. HarperCollins, 2001. ISBN 978-0-694-01342-5 Subj: Clothing – hats. Family life – grandfathers. Weather – wind.

Moore, Liz. *Zizi and Tish* ill. by Liz Milkau. Orca, 2003. ISBN 978-1-55143-254-0 Subj: Emotions – envy, jealousy. Family life – sisters.

Moore, Maggie. *The three little pigs* (The three little pigs)

Moore, Marian. *Dear Cinderella* by Marian Moore and Mary Jane Kensington ill. by Julie Olson. Scholastic, 2012. ISBN 978-0-545-34220-9 Subj: Folk & fairy tales. Letters, cards. Pen pals. Royalty – princesses.

Moore, Mary-Alice. *The wheels on the school bus* ill. by Laura Huliska-Beith. HarperCollins, 2006. ISBN 978-0-06-059427-5 Subj: Buses. Music. School. Songs.

Moore, Patrick. *The mighty street sweeper* ill. by author. Henry Holt, 2006. ISBN 978-0-8050-7789-6 Subj: Trucks.

Moore, Raina. *How do you say good night?* ill. by Robin Luebs. HarperCollins, 2008. ISBN 978-0-06-083163-9 Subj: Animals. Bedtime. Family life. Rhyming text.

Moore, Suzi. *Whoops!* ill. by Russell Ayto. Candlewick/Templar, 2016. ISBN 978-076368180-7 Subj: Animals – cats. Animals – dogs. Animals – mice. Magic. Noise, sounds. Rhyming text.

Moore-Mallinos, Jennifer. *It's ok to be me! just like you, I can do almost anything!* ill. by Marta Fabrega. Barron's, 2007. ISBN 978-0-7641-3584-2 Subj: Disabilities – physical disabilities.

Mom has cancer! ill. by Marta Fàbrega. Barron's, 2008. ISBN 978-0-7641-4074-7 Subj: Family life – mothers. Illness – cancer.

My brother is autistic ill. by Marta Fàbrega. Barron's, 2008. ISBN 978-0-7641-4044-0 Subj: Disabilities – autism. Emotions – embarrassment. Family life – brothers. School.

When my parents forgot how to be friends ill. by Marta Fabrega. Barron's, 2005. ISBN 978-0-7641-3172-1 Subj: Divorce. Family life.

Moorman, Margaret. *Light the lights!* ill. by author. Scholastic, 1994. ISBN 978-0-590-47003-2 Subj: Family life. Holidays – Christmas. Holidays – Hanukkah. Religion.

Mora, Pat. *Abuelos* ill. by Amelia Lau Carling. Groundwood, 2008. ISBN 978-0-88899-716-6 Subj: Behavior. Ethnic groups in the U.S. – Hispanic Americans. Mythical creatures.

The bakery lady / La señora de la panadería ill. by Pablo Torrecilla. Piñata, 2001. ISBN 978-1-55885-343-0 Subj: Activities – baking, cooking. Ethnic groups in the U.S. – Mexican Americans. Food. Foreign languages. Holidays.

The beautiful lady: Our Lady of Guadalupe ill. by Steve Johnson and Lou Fancher. Knopf, 2012. ISBN 978-0-375-86838-2 Subj: Foreign lands – Mexico. Indians of North America – Aztec. Religion.

A birthday basket for Tía ill. by Cecily Lang. Macmillan, 1992. ISBN 978-0-02-767400-2 Subj: Animals – cats. Birthdays. Ethnic groups in the U.S. – Mexican Americans. Family life – aunts, uncles. Gifts.

Book fiesta! celebrate Children's Day/Book Day / Celebremos El día de los niños/El día de los libros: a bilingual picture book ill. by Rafael López. HarperCollins, 2009. ISBN 978-0-06-128877-7 Subj: Books, reading. Foreign languages. Holidays.

Confetti ill. by Enrique O. Sánchez. Lee & Low, 1996. ISBN 978-1-880000-25-0 Subj: Ethnic groups in the U.S. – Mexican Americans. Foreign languages. Poetry.

Delicious hullabaloo / Pachanga deliciosa ill. by Francisco X. Mora. Piñata, 1998. ISBN 978-1-55885-246-4 Subj: Animals. Desert. Foreign languages. Night. Parties. Poetry. Reptiles – lizards.

The desert is my mother / El desierto es mi madre ill. by Daniel Lechón. Piñata, 1994. ISBN 978-1-55885-121-4 Subj: Desert. Foreign languages. Poetry.

Doña Flor: a tall tale about a giant woman with a great big heart ill. by Raúl Colón. Random House, 2005. ISBN 978-0-679-98002-5 Subj: Animals – cougars. Giants. Tall tales.

The gift of the poinsettia / El regalo de la flor de nochebuena by Pat Mora and Charles Ramírez Berg ill. by Charles Ramírez Berg. Piñata, 1995. ISBN 978-1-55885-137-5 Subj: Foreign lands – Mexico. Foreign languages. Gifts. Holidays – Christmas.

Gracias / Thanks ill. by John Parra. Lee & Low, 2009. ISBN 978-1-60060-258-0 Subj: Character traits. Ethnic groups in the U.S. – Hispanic Americans. Foreign languages.

Here, kitty, kitty! / ¡Ven, gatita, ven! ill. by Maribel Suárez. HarperCollins, 2008. ISBN 978-0-06-085044-9 Subj: Animals – cats. Foreign languages.

I pledge allegiance by Pat Mora and Libby Martinez ill. by Patrice Barton. Knopf, 2014. ISBN 978-030793181-8 Subj: Ethnic groups in the U.S.

– Mexican Americans. Family life. Foreign languages. Immigrants, immigration. U.S. history.

Join hands! ill. by George Ancona. Charlesbridge, 2008. ISBN 978-1-58089-202-5 Subj: Activities. Friendship. World.

Let's eat! / A comer! ill. by Maribel Suárez. HarperCollins, 2008. ISBN 978-0-06-085038-8 Subj: Family life. Food. Foreign languages.

A library for Juana: the world of Sor Juana Inés ill. by Beatriz A. Vidal. Knopf, 2002. ISBN 978-0-375-80643-8 Subj: Books, reading. Careers – nuns. Careers – writers. Foreign lands – Mexico. Libraries.

Listen to the desert / Oye al desierto ill. by Francisco X. Mora. Clarion, 1994. ISBN 978-0-395-67292-1 Subj: Animals. Desert. Foreign languages. Noise, sounds. Poetry.

Love to mamá ill. by Paula Barragán. Lee & Low, 2001. ISBN 978-1-58430-019-9 Subj: Family life – grandmothers. Family life – mothers. Foreign languages. Poetry.

Marimba! animales from A to Z ill. by Doug Cushman. Houghton, 2006. ISBN 978-0-618-19453-7 Subj: ABC books. Animals. Foreign languages. Parties. Rhyming text. Zoos.

The night the moon fell: a Maya myth retold ill. by Domi. Douglas & McIntyre, 2000. ISBN 978-0-88899-398-4 Subj: Folk & fairy tales. Foreign lands – Mexico. Indians of Central America – Maya. Moon.

One, two, three / Uno, dos, tres ill. by Barbara Lavallee. Clarion, 1996. ISBN 978-0-395-67294-5 Subj: Birthdays. Counting, numbers. Foreign languages. Rhyming text.

Pablo's tree ill. by Cecily Lang. Macmillan, 1994. ISBN 978-0-02-767401-9 Subj: Adoption. Birthdays. Ethnic groups in the U.S. – Mexican Americans. Family life – grandfathers.

A piñata in a pine tree: a Latino twelve days of Christmas ill. by Magaly Morales. Clarion, 2009. ISBN 978-0-618-84198-1 Subj: Cumulative tales. Foreign lands – Latin America. Foreign languages. Holidays – Christmas. Music. Songs.

The race of toad and deer ill. by Maya Itzna Brooks. Orchard, 1995. ISBN 978-0-531-08777-0 Subj: Animals. Behavior – trickery. Folk & fairy tales. Foreign lands – Guatemala. Foreign languages. Sports – racing.

The rainbow tulip ill. by Elizabeth Sayles. Viking, 1999. ISBN 978-0-670-87291-6 Subj: Character traits – being different. Ethnic groups in the U.S. – Mexican Americans. Holidays – May Day. Parades. School.

The remembering day / El día de los muertos ill. by Robert Casilla. Arte Publico, 2015. ISBN 978-155885805-3 Subj: Death. Family life – grandmothers. Foreign lands – Mexico. Foreign languages. Gardens, gardening. Holidays – Day of the Dead. Memories, memory.

The song of Francis and the animals ill. by David Frampton. Eerdmans, 2005. ISBN 978-0-8028-5253-3 Subj: Animals. Character traits – kindness to animals. Religion.

Sweet dreams / Dulces suenos ill. by Maribel Suárez. HarperCollins, 2008. ISBN 978-0-06-085041-8 Subj: Animals. Bedtime. Family life – grandmothers. Foreign languages.

This big sky ill. by Steve Jenkins. Scholastic, 1998. ISBN 978-0-590-37120-9 Subj: Animals. Desert. Poetry.

Tomás and the library lady ill. by Raúl Colón. Knopf, 1997. ISBN 978-0-679-90401-4 Subj: Books, reading. Careers – librarians. Careers – migrant workers. Ethnic groups in the U.S. – Mexican Americans. Libraries.

Water rolls, water rises / el agua ruda, el agua sube ill. by Meilo So. Lee & Low, 2014. ISBN 978-089239325-1 Subj: Foreign languages. Poetry. Water.

Yum! mmmm! que rico! Americas' sproutings ill. by Rafael López. Lee & Low, 2007. ISBN 978-1-58430-271-1 Subj: Food. Language. Poetry.

Morales, Melita. *Jam and honey* ill. by Laura J. Bryant. Tricycle, 2011. ISBN 978-1-58246-299-8 Subj: Insects – bees. Rhyming text.

Morales, Yuyi. *Just a minute: a trickster tale and counting book* ill. by author. Chronicle, 2003. ISBN 978-0-8118-3758-3 Subj: Behavior – trickery. Counting, numbers. Folk & fairy tales. Foreign lands – Mexico.

Just in case: a trickster tale and Spanish alphabet book ill. by author. Roaring Brook, 2008. ISBN 978-1-59643-329-8 Subj: ABC books. Anatomy – skeletons. Behavior – trickery. Birthdays. Folk & fairy tales. Foreign languages. Gifts.

Little night ill. by author. Macmillan, 2007. ISBN 978-1-59643-088-4 Subj: Bedtime. Night.

Niño wrestles the world ill. by author. Roaring Brook, 2013. ISBN 978-1-59643-604-6 Subj: Ethnic groups in the U.S. – Mexican Americans. Family life – brothers & sisters. Foreign languages. Sports – wrestling.

Rudas: Niño's horrendous hermanitas ill. by author. Roaring Brook/Neal Porter, 2016. ISBN 978-162672240-8 Subj: Ethnic groups in the U.S. – Mexican Americans. Family life – brothers & sisters. Foreign languages. Sports – wrestling.

Viva Frida ill. by Tim O'Meara. Roaring Brook, 2014. ISBN 978-159643603-9 Subj: Art. Caldecott award honor books. Careers – artists. Foreign lands – Mexico. Foreign languages.

Moran, Alex. *Boots for Beth* ill. by Lisa Campbell Ernst. Harcourt, 2002. ISBN 978-0-15-216558-1 Subj: Animals. Animals – pigs. Clothing – boots.

Come here, tiger ill. by Lisa Campbell Ernst. Harcourt, 2001. ISBN 978-0-15-216218-4 Subj: Animals. Animals – cats. Pets.

Sam and Jack ill. by Tim Bowers. Harcourt, 2001. ISBN 978-0-15-216240-5 Subj: Animals – cats. Animals – mice. Friendship.

Morck, Irene. *Old bird* by Irene Morck and Muriel Wood ill. by Muriel Wood. Fitzhenry & Whiteside, 2003. ISBN 978-1-55041-695-4 Subj: Activities – working. Animals – horses, ponies. Friendship.

Mordvinoff, Nicolas. *Finders keepers* (Lipkind, William)

Moreillon, Judi. *Ready and waiting for you* ill. by Catherine Stock. Eerdmans, 2013. ISBN 978-0-8028-5355-4 Subj: Rhyming text. School – first day.

Moreton, Daniel, reteller. *La Cucaracha Martina: a Caribbean folktale* ill. by reteller. Turtle, 1997. ISBN 978-1-890515-03-4 Subj: Animals. Cities, towns. Folk & fairy tales. Foreign lands – Caribbean Islands. Foreign languages. Insects – cockroaches. Noise, sounds.

Morgan, Mary. *Dragon pizzeria* ill. by author. Knopf, 2008. ISBN 978-0-375-82309-1 Subj: Dragons. Folk & fairy tales. Food. Nursery rhymes.

My good night book ill. by author. Dutton, 2003. ISBN 978-0-525-46987-2 Subj: Bedtime. Format, unusual – toy & movable books. Night. Rhyming text.

Morgan, Michaela. *Brave, brave mouse* ill. by Michelle Cartlidge. Albert Whitman, 2004. ISBN 978-0-8075-0869-5 Subj: Animals – mice. Character traits – bravery. Emotions – fear. Rhyming text.

Bunny wishes ill. by Caroline Jayne Church. Scholastic, 2007. ISBN 978-0-439-91812-1 Subj: Animals – mice. Animals – rabbits. Behavior – wishing. Friendship. Seasons – winter.

Dear bunny: a bunny love story ill. by Caroline Jayne Church. Scholastic, 2006. ISBN 978-0-439-74833-9 Subj: Activities – writing. Animals – mice. Animals – rabbits. Character traits – shyness. Emotions – love. Friendship.

Morgan, Richard. *Zoo poo* ill. by author. Barron's, 2004. ISBN 978-0-613-81357-0 Subj: Behavior – growing up. Toilet training. Zoos.

Morgan-Vanroyen, Mary. *Curious Rosie* ill. by author. Hyperion, 2000. ISBN 978-0-7868-0477-1

Subj: Animals – mice. Character traits – curiosity.

Gentle Rosie ill. by author. Hyperion, 1999. ISBN 978-0-7868-0474-0 Subj: Animals – mice. Behavior.

Patient Rosie ill. by author. Hyperion, 2000. ISBN 978-0-7868-0476-4 Subj: Animals – mice. Character traits – patience, impatience.

Sleep tight, little mouse ill. by author. Knopf, 2003. ISBN 978-0-375-92308-1 Subj: Animals – mice. Bedtime. Family life – mothers.

Wild Rosie ill. by author. Hyperion, 1999. ISBN 978-0-7868-0475-7 Subj: Activities – playing. Animals – mice. Behavior.

Morison, Toby. *Little Louie takes off* ill. by author. Walker, 2007. ISBN 978-0-8027-9645-5 Subj: Activities – flying. Birds – penguins. Emotions – loneliness.

Morlock, Lisa. *Track that scat!* ill. by Carrie Anne Bradshaw. Sleeping Bear, 2012. ISBN 978-1-58536-536-4 Subj: Animals. Nature.

Moroney, Trace. *When I'm feeling angry* ill. by author. School Specialty/Gingham Dog, 2006. ISBN 978-0-7696-4424-0 Subj: Animals – rabbits. Emotions – anger.

When I'm feeling happy ill. by author. School Specialty/Gingham Dog, 2006. ISBN 978-0-7696-4425-7 Subj: Animals – rabbits. Emotions – happiness.

When I'm feeling sad ill. by author. School Specialty/Gingham Dog, 2006. ISBN 978-0-7696-4426-4 Subj: Animals – rabbits. Emotions – sadness.

When I'm feeling scared ill. by author. School Specialty/Gingham Dog, 2006. ISBN 978-0-7696-4427-1 Subj: Animals – rabbits. Emotions – fear.

Morozumi, Atsuko. *Helping daddy* ill. by author. Knopf, 2000. ISBN 978-0-375-80593-6 Subj: Family life. Format, unusual – board books.

In the park ill. by author. Knopf, 2000. ISBN 978-0-375-80591-2 Subj: Format, unusual – board books. Parks.

My friend gorilla ill. by author. Farrar, 1998. ISBN 978-0-374-35458-9 Subj: Animals – gorillas. Foreign lands – Africa. Friendship. Pets. Zoos.

One gorilla ill. by author. Farrar, 1990. ISBN 978-0-374-35644-6 Subj: Animals. Animals – gorillas. Counting, numbers.

Playing ill. by author. Knopf, 2000. ISBN 978-0-375-80592-9 Subj: Activities – playing. Format, unusual – board books.

Time for bed ill. by author. Knopf, 2000. ISBN 978-0-375-80594-3 Subj: Bedtime. Format, unusual – board books.

Morpurgo, Michael. *On angel wings* ill. by Quentin Blake. Candlewick, 2007. ISBN 978-0-7636-3466-7 Subj: Angels. Holidays – Christmas. Religion – Nativity.

The silver swan ill. by Christian Birmingham. Fogelman, 2000. ISBN 978-0-8037-2543-0 Subj: Birds – swans. Seasons – winter.

Wombat goes walkabout ill. by Christian Birmingham. Candlewick, 2000. ISBN 978-0-7636-1168-2 Subj: Animals. Animals – wombats. Behavior – lost. Foreign lands – Australia.

Morris, Ann. *Bread, bread, bread* photos by Ken Heyman. Lothrop, 1989. ISBN 978-0-688-06335-1 Subj: Food.

Families ill. with photos. HarperCollins, 2000. ISBN 978-0-688-17199-5 Subj: Character traits – individuality. Family life.

Grandma Esther remembers photos by Peter Linenthal. Millbrook, 2002. ISBN 978-0-7613-2318-1 Subj: Family life – grandmothers. Holocaust. Jewish culture. Memories, memory.

Grandma Francisca remembers photos by Peter Linenthal. Millbrook, 2002. ISBN 978-0-7613-2315-0 Subj: Ethnic groups in the U.S. – Hispanic Americans. Family life – grandmothers. Memories, memory.

Grandma Lai Goon remembers photos by Peter Linenthal. Millbrook, 2002. ISBN 978-0-7613-2314-3 Subj: Ethnic groups in the U.S. – Chinese Americans. Family life – grandmothers. Foreign lands – China. Memories, memory.

Grandma Lois remembers photos by Peter Linenthal. Millbrook, 2002. ISBN 978-0-7613-2316-7 Subj: Ethnic groups in the U.S. – African Americans. Family life – grandmothers. Memories, memory. Prejudice.

Grandma Maxine remembers photos by Peter Linenthal. Millbrook, 2002. ISBN 978-0-7613-2317-4 Subj: Family life – grandmothers. Indians of North America – Shoshone. Memories, memory.

Hats, hats, hats photos by Ken Heyman. Lothrop, 1989. ISBN 978-0-688-06339-9 Subj: Clothing – hats.

Houses and homes photos by Ken Heyman. Lothrop, 1992. ISBN 978-0-688-10169-5 Subj: Foreign lands. Homes, houses.

Light the candle! bang the drum! ill. by Peter Linenthal. Dutton, 1997. ISBN 978-0-525-45639-1 Subj: Holidays.

Loving photos by Ken Heyman. Lothrop, 1990. ISBN 978-0-688-06341-2 Subj: Emotions – love. Family life. Foreign lands.

The mommy book photos by Ken Heyman. Silver Pr., 1996. ISBN 978-0-382-24693-7 Subj: Family life – mothers.

On the go photos by Ken Heyman. Lothrop, 1990. ISBN 978-0-688-06337-5 Subj: Foreign lands. Transportation.

Play photos by Ken Heyman. Lothrop, 1998. ISBN 978-0-688-14553-8 Subj: Activities – playing. Foreign lands. Imagination.

Shoes, shoes, shoes photos by Ken Heyman. Lothrop, 1995. ISBN 978-0-688-13667-3 Subj: Clothing – shoes. Rhyming text.

Tools photos by Ken Heyman. Lothrop, 1992. ISBN 978-0-688-10171-8 Subj: Tools.

Weddings photos by Ken Heyman. Lothrop, 1995. ISBN 978-0-688-13273-6 Subj: Clothing. Weddings.

Work photos by Ken Heyman. Lothrop, 1998. ISBN 978-0-688-14867-6 Subj: Activities – working. Careers. Foreign lands.

Morris, Bob. *Crispin the Terrible* ill. by Dasha Ziborova. Callaway, 2000. ISBN 978-0-935112-44-3 Subj: Animals – cats. Imagination.

Morris, Carla. *The boy who was raised by librarians* ill. by Brad Sneed. Peachtree, 2007. ISBN 978-1-56145-391-7 Subj: Books, reading. Careers – librarians. Libraries.

Morris, Dewi. *Sandy's street* ill. by author. Little, 2001. ISBN 978-0-316-83609-8 Subj: Animals – cats. Format, unusual – toy & movable books. Roads.

Morris, Jackie. *I am Cat* ill. by author. Frances Lincoln, 2013. ISBN 978-1-84780-135-7 Subj: Animals – cats.

Morris, Jennifer E. *May I please have a cookie?* ill. by Jennifer Morris. Scholastic, 2005. ISBN 978-0-439-73819-4 Subj: Etiquette. Food. Reptiles – alligators, crocodiles.

Morris, Richard T. *Bye-bye, baby!* ill. by Larry Day. Walker, 2009. ISBN 978-0-8027-9772-8 Subj: Babies, toddlers. Family life – new sibling. Zoos.

This is a moose ill. by Tom Lichtenheld. Little, Brown, 2014. ISBN 978-031621360-8 Subj: Animals – moose. Humorous stories.

Morrison, Cathy. *I want a pet!* ill. by author. Tiger Tales, 2012. ISBN 978-1-58925-113-7 Subj: Pets. Rhyming text. Zoos.

Morrison, Gordon. *A drop of water* ill. by author. Houghton, 2006. ISBN 978-0-618-58557-1 Subj: Science. Water.

Morrison, Slade. *Little Cloud and Lady Wind* (Morrison, Toni)

Peeny butter fudge (Morrison, Toni)

Please, Louise (Morrison, Toni)

The tortoise or the hare (Morrison, Toni)

Morrison, Toni. *The book of mean people* ill. by Pascal Lemaître. Hyperion, 2002. ISBN 978-0-7868-2471-7 Subj: Behavior – bullying, teasing. Behavior – fighting, arguing. Character traits – meanness. Emotions – anger.

Little Cloud and Lady Wind by Toni Morrison and Slade Morrison ill. by Sean Qualls. Simon & Schuster, 2010. ISBN 978-1-4169-8523-5 Subj: Character traits – individuality. Weather – clouds. Weather – wind.

Peeny butter fudge by Toni Morrison and Slade Morrison ill. by Joe Cepeda. Simon & Schuster, 2009. ISBN 978-1-4169-8332-3 Subj: Activities – playing. Ethnic groups in the U.S. – African Americans. Family life – grandmothers. Food. Rhyming text.

Please, Louise by Toni Morrison and Slade Morrison ill. by Shadra Strickland. Simon & Schuster, 2014. ISBN 978-141698338-5 Subj: Books, reading. Emotions – fear. Libraries. Rhyming text.

The tortoise or the hare by Toni Morrison and Slade Morrison ill. by Joe Cepeda. Simon & Schuster, 2010. ISBN 978-1-4169-8334-7 Subj: Animals – rabbits. Folk & fairy tales. Reptiles – turtles, tortoises. Sports – racing.

Morrissey, Dean. *The Christmas ship* ill. by author. HarperCollins, 2000. ISBN 978-0-06-028576-0 Subj: Boats, ships. Gifts. Holidays – Christmas. Magic. Santa Claus. Toys.

The crimson comet by Dean Morrissey and Stephen Krensky; ill. by Dean Morrissey. HarperCollins, 2006. ISBN 978-0-06-008070-9 Subj: Bedtime. Family life – brothers & sisters. Moon. Space & space ships.

The wizard mouse ill. by author. HarperCollins, 2011. ISBN 978-0-06-008066-2 Subj: Animals – mice. Magic. Wizards.

Morrow, Barbara Olenyik. *Mr. Mosquito put on his tuxedo* ill. by Ponder Goembel. Holiday, 2009. ISBN 978-0-8234-2072-8 Subj: Insects. Insects – mosquitoes. Parties. Rhyming text.

Morrow, Tara Jaye. *Mommy loves her baby; Daddy loves his baby* ill. by Tiphanie Beeke. HarperCollins, 2003. ISBN 978-0-06-029078-8 Subj: Animals. Babies, toddlers. Emotions – love. Family life – parents. Format, unusual. Rhyming text.

Panda goes to school ill. by Aaron Boyd. Sterling, 2007. ISBN 978-1-4027-4313-9 Subj: Animals – pandas. Family life – mothers. School – first day.

Morstad, Julie. *How to* ill. by author. Simply Read, 2013. ISBN 978-1-897476-57-4 Subj: Activities – playing. Behavior. Character traits. Imagination.

Mortensen, Denise Dowling. *Bug Patrol* ill. by Cece Bell. Clarion, 2013. ISBN 978-0-618-79024-1 Subj: Careers – police officers. Insects. Rhyming text.

Ohio thunder ill. by Kate Kiesler. Houghton, 2006. ISBN 978-0-618-59542-6 Subj: Farms. Weather – lightning, thunder. Weather – storms.

Wake up engines ill. by Melissa Iwai. Houghton, 2007. ISBN 978-0-618-51736-7 Subj: Morning. Rhyming text. Transportation.

Mortensen, Lori. *Chicken Lily* ill. by Nina Victor Crittenden. Henry Holt, 2016. ISBN 978-162779120-5 Subj: Birds – chickens, roosters. Character traits – shyness. Emotions – fear. Poetry.

Cindy Moo ill. by Jeff Mack. HarperCollins, 2012. ISBN 978-0-06-204393-1 Subj: Animals – bulls, cows. Character traits – persistence. Moon. Nursery rhymes. Rhyming text.

Cowpoke Clyde and Dirty Dawg ill. by Michael Austin. Clarion, 2013. ISBN 978-0-547-23993-4 Subj: Activities – bathing. Animals – dogs. Cowboys, cowgirls.

Cowpoke Clyde rides the range ill. by Michael Austin. Clarion, 2016. ISBN 978-054437030-2 Subj: Cowboys, cowgirls. Rhyming text. Sports – bicycling.

Mousequerade ball: a counting tale ill. by Betsy Lewin. Bloomsbury, 2016. ISBN 978-161963422-0 Subj: Animals – mice. Counting, numbers. Rhyming text.

Mortenson, Greg. *Listen to the wind: the story of Dr. Greg and three cups of tea* by Greg Mortenson and Susan L. Roth ill. by Susan L. Roth. Dial, 2009. ISBN 978-0-8037-3058-8 Subj: Behavior – seeking better things. Character traits – completing things. Character traits – perseverance. Foreign lands – Pakistan. Gender roles. School.

Mortimer, Anne. *Bunny's Easter egg* ill. by author. HarperCollins, 2010. ISBN 978-0-06-126664-2 Subj: Animals – rabbits. Eggs. Holidays – Easter. Sleep.

Pumpkin cat ill. by author. HarperCollins, 2011. ISBN 978-0-06-187485-7 Subj: Animals – cats. Animals – mice. Gardens, gardening. Holidays – Halloween.

Mortimer, Rachael. *Red Riding Hood and the sweet little wolf* ill. by Liz Pichon. Tiger Tales, 2013. ISBN 978-1-58925-117-5 Subj: Animals – wolves. Character traits – being different. Family life – grandmothers. Folk & fairy tales.

Song for a princess ill. by Maddy McClellan. Scholastic, 2010. ISBN 978-0-545-24835-8 Subj: Activities – storytelling. Birds. Communication. Emotions – loneliness. Language. Royalty – princesses.

The three Billy Goats Fluff ill. by Liz Pichon. Tiger Tales, 2011. ISBN 978-1-58925-101-4 Subj: Activities – knitting. Animals – goats. Mythical creatures – trolls.

Morton, Carlene. *The library pages* ill. by Valeria Docampo. Upstart, 2010. ISBN 978-1-60213-045-6 Subj: Holidays – April Fools' Day. Libraries. School.

Morton, Lone. *Hurry up, Molly / Apúrate, Molly* ill. by Gill Scriven. Barron's, 2000. ISBN 978-0-7641-5286-3 Subj: Bedtime. Family life – fathers. Foreign languages.

Hurry up, Molly / Dépêche-toi, Molly ill. by Gill Scriven. Barron's, 2000. ISBN 978-0-7641-5287-0 Subj: Bedtime. Family life – fathers. Foreign languages.

Morton-Shaw, Christine. *Wake up, sleepy bear!* by Christine Morton-Shaw and Greg Shaw ill. by John Butler. Penguin, 2006. ISBN 978-0-670-06175-4 Subj: Animals – babies. Rhyming text.

Mosca, Julia Finley. *The girl who thought in pictures: the story of Dr. Temple Grandin* ill. by Daniel Rieley. The Innovation Press, 2017. ISBN 978-194314730-4 Subj: Careers – scientists. Character traits – being different. Disabilities – autism. Rhyming text.

Mosel, Arlene. *The funny little woman* ill. by Blair Lent. Dutton, 1972. ISBN 978-0-525-30265-0 Subj: Caldecott award books. Foreign lands – Japan. Monsters.

Tikki Tikki Tembo ill. by Blair Lent. Henry Holt, 1968. ISBN 978-0-8050-0662-9 Subj: Folk & fairy tales. Foreign lands – China. Names.

Moseley, Keith. *Where's the dinosaur?* ill. by author. Sterling, 2012. ISBN 978-1-4027-8894-9 Subj: Activities – ballooning. Counting, numbers. Dinosaurs. Family life – grandfathers. Picture puzzles.

Moser, Barry. *Psalm 23* ill. by author. Zondervan, 2008. ISBN 978-0-310-71085-1 Subj: Careers – shepherds. Foreign lands – Caribbean Islands. Religion.

Moser, Lisa. *Cowboy Boyd and Mighty Calliope* ill. by Sebastiaan Van Doninck. Random House, 2013. ISBN 978-0-375-87056-9 Subj: Animals – rhinoceros. Careers – ranchers. Cowboys, cowgirls.

Perfect soup ill. by Ben Mantle. Random House, 2010. ISBN 978-0-375-86014-0 Subj: Animals – mice. Cumulative tales. Food. Snowmen.

Railroad Hank ill. by Benji Davies. Random House, 2012. ISBN 978-0-375-86849-8 Subj: Careers – railroad engineers. Family life – grandmothers. Farms. Humorous stories. Trains.

Stories from Bug Garden ill. by Gwen Millward. Candlewick, 2016. ISBN 978-076366534-0 Subj: Gardens, gardening. Insects. Poetry.

Watermelon wishes ill. by Stacey Schuett. Houghton, 2006. ISBN 978-0-618-56433-0 Subj: Behavior – wishing. Family life – grandfathers. Food.

Moses, Will. *Mary and her little lamb: the true story of the famous nursery rhyme* ill. by author. Penguin, 2011. ISBN 978-0-399-25154-2 Subj: Animals – sheep. Farms. Nursery rhymes. School. U.S. history.

Raining cats and dogs: a collection of irresistible idioms and illustrations to tickle the funny bones of young people ill. by author. Philomel, 2008. ISBN 978-0-399-24233-5 Subj: Language.

Silent night ill. by author. Philomel, 1997. ISBN 978-0-399-23100-1 Subj: Babies, toddlers. Family life. Holidays – Christmas. Songs.

Moss, Jenny Jackson. *Cajun night after Christmas* by Jenny Jackson Moss and Amy Jackson Dixon ill. by James Rice. Pelican, 2000. ISBN 978-1-56554-779-7 Subj: Ethnic groups in the U.S. Holidays – Christmas. Poetry. Reptiles – alligators, crocodiles. Santa Claus.

Moss, Lloyd. *Our marching band* ill. by Diana Cain Bluthenthal. Putnam, 2001. ISBN 978-0-399-23335-7 Subj: Music. Musical instruments – bands. Rhyming text.

Zin! zin! zin! A violin ill. by Marjorie Priceman. Simon & Schuster, 1995. ISBN 978-0-671-88239-6 Subj: Caldecott award honor books. Counting, numbers. Music. Musical instruments – violins. Rhyming text.

Moss, Marissa. *Knick knack paddywack* ill. by author. Houghton, 1992. ISBN 978-0-395-54701-4 Subj: Activities – making things. Animals – dogs. Counting, numbers. Cumulative tales. Songs. Space & space ships.

Regina's big mistake ill. by author. Houghton, 1990. ISBN 978-0-395-55330-5 Subj: Activities – drawing. Art. Careers – artists. School. Self-concept.

Sky high: the true story of Maggie Gee ill. by Carl Angel. Tricycle, 2009. ISBN 978-1-58246-280-6 Subj: Careers – airplane pilots. Ethnic groups in the U.S. – Chinese Americans. Gender roles. U.S. history. War.

True heart ill. by C. F. Payne. Silver Whistle, 1999. ISBN 978-0-15-201344-8 Subj: Careers – engineers. Gender roles. Trains.

Moss, Miriam. *A babysitter for Billy Bear* ill. by Anna Currey. Dial, 2008. ISBN 978-0-8037-3269-8 Subj: Activities – babysitting. Animals – bears. Behavior – worrying.

Bad hare day ill. by Lynne Chapman. Bloomsbury, 2003. ISBN 978-1-58234-785-1 Subj: Animals. Animals – rabbits. Behavior – misbehavior. Family life – aunts, uncles. Hair.

Bare bear ill. by Mary McQuillan. Holiday House, 2005. ISBN 978-0-8234-1934-0 Subj: Animals – bears. Behavior – lost & found possessions. Clothing. Rhyming text.

I'll be your friend, Smudge ill. by Lynne Chapman. Gullane, 2001. ISBN 978-1-86233-207-2 Subj: Animals – mice. Birthdays. Friendship. Moving.

It's my turn, Smudge ill. by Lynne Chapman. Gullane, 2001. ISBN 978-1-86233-287-4 Subj: Animals – mice. Behavior – sharing.

Matty in a mess! ill. by Jane Simmons. Andersen, 2010. ISBN 978-1-84270-812-5 Subj: Animals – bears. Animals – cats. Behavior – messy. Character traits – cleanliness.

Matty takes off! ill. by Jane Simmons. Andersen, 2010. ISBN 978-1-84270-758-6 Subj: Activities – traveling. Animals – bears. Animals – cats. Behavior – lost & found possessions.

A new house for Smudge ill. by Lynne Chapman. Gullane, 2001. ISBN 978-1-86233-202-7 Subj: Animals – mice. Homes, houses. Moving.

Smudge's grumpy day ill. by Lynne Chapman. Gullane, 2001. ISBN 978-1-86233-282-9 Subj: Behavior – bad day, bad mood. Behavior – running away. Emotions – anger.

The snow bear ill. by Maggie Kneen. Dutton, 2000. ISBN 978-0-525-46658-1 Subj: Activities – playing. Animals – polar bears. Behavior – lost. Family life – mothers. Foreign lands – Arctic.

This is the mountain ill. by Adrienne Kennaway. Frances Lincoln, 2011. ISBN 978-1-84507-984-0 Subj: Foreign lands – Africa. Mountains.

This is the oasis ill. by Adrienne Kennaway. Kane/Miller, 2005. ISBN 978-1-929132-76-8 Subj: Desert. Foreign lands – Africa.

This is the tree ill. by Adrienne Kennaway. Kane/Miller, 2000. ISBN 978-0-916291-98-3 Subj: Animals. Ecology. Foreign lands – Africa. Trees.

Wibble wobble ill. by Joanna Mockler. Tiger Tales, 2001. ISBN 978-1-58925-013-0 Subj: Behavior – lost & found possessions. School. Teeth.

Moss, Onawumi Jean. *Precious and the Boo Hag* (McKissack, Patricia C.)

Moss, P. Buckley. *Reuben and the quilt* ill. by author. Text by Merle Good. Good Books, 1999. ISBN 978-1-56148-234-4 Subj: Crime. Ethnic groups in the U.S. – Amish. Quilts.

Moss, Peggy. *One of us* ill. by Penny Weber. Tilbury House, 2010. ISBN 978-0-88448-322-9 Subj: Character traits – individuality. Friendship. Moving. School.

Say something ill. by Lea Lyon. Tilbury, 2004. ISBN 978-0-88448-261-1 Subj: Behavior – bullying, teasing.

Moss, Thylias. *I want to be* ill. by Jerry Pinkney. Dial, 1993. ISBN 978-0-8037-1287-4 Subj: Behavior – growing up. Ethnic groups in the U.S. – African Americans.

Most, Bernard. *ABC T-Rex* ill. by author. Harcourt, 2000. ISBN 978-0-15-202007-1 Subj: ABC books. Dinosaurs.

Cock-a-doodle-moo! ill. by author. Harcourt, 1996. ISBN 978-0-15-201252-6 Subj: Animals. Birds – chickens, roosters. Careers – farmers. Farms. Morning.

The cow that went oink ill. by author. Harcourt, 1990. ISBN 978-0-15-220195-1 Subj: Animals. Noise, sounds.

A dinosaur named after me ill. by author. Harcourt, 1991. ISBN 978-0-15-223494-2 Subj: Dinosaurs. Names. Prehistory.

Dinosaur questions ill. by author. Harcourt, 1995. ISBN 978-0-15-292885-8 Subj: Dinosaurs. Prehistory.

How big were the dinosaurs? ill. by author. Harcourt, 1994. ISBN 978-0-15-236800-5 Subj: Concepts – size. Dinosaurs. Prehistory.

If the dinosaurs came back ill. by author. Harcourt, 1995. ISBN 978-0-15-238020-5 Subj: Dinosaurs. Imagination. Prehistory.

A pair of protoceratops ill. by author. Harcourt, 1998. ISBN 978-0-15-201443-8 Subj: Activities. Dinosaurs.

A trio of triceratops ill. by author. Harcourt, 1998. ISBN 978-0-15-201448-3 Subj: Activities. Dinosaurs.

Whatever happened to the dinosaurs? ill. by author. Harcourt, 1995. ISBN 978-0-15-200378-4 Subj: Dinosaurs. Prehistory.

Z-Z-Zoink! ill. by author. Harcourt, 1999. ISBN 978-0-15-292845-2 Subj: Animals – pigs. Birds – owls. Noise, sounds. Sleep.

Mother Goose. *Arnold Lobel book of Mother Goose* ill. by Arnold Lobel. Knopf, 1997. ISBN 978-0-679-98736-9 Subj: Nursery rhymes. Poetry.

Baa baa black sheep (Trapani, Iza)

The baby's lap book ill. by Kay Chorao. Dutton, 1990. ISBN 978-0-525-44604-0 Subj: Nursery rhymes.

The cat and the fiddle: a treasury of nursery rhymes ill. by Jackie Morris. Frances Lincoln, 2011. ISBN 978-1-84507-987-4 Subj: Nursery rhymes.

The Chinese Mother Goose rhymes by Robert Wyndham; ill. by Ed Young. Sel. & ed. by Robert Wyndham. Putnam, 1982. ISBN 978-0-399-20866-9 Subj: Nursery rhymes.

Hey, diddle, diddle comp. by Linda Bronson; ill. by compiler. Henry Holt, 2003. ISBN 978-0-8050-6754-5 Subj: Animals. Moon. Nursery rhymes.

Hey, diddle, diddle [board book] ill. by Heather Collins. Kids Can, 2003. ISBN 978-1-55337-078-9 Subj: Animals. Format, unusual – board books. Moon. Nursery rhymes.

Hickory, dickory, dock ill. by Heather Collins. Kids Can, 1997. ISBN 978-1-55074-408-8 Subj: Format, unusual – board books. Nursery rhymes.

Hickory, dickory, dock adapt. by Robin Muller; ill. by Suzanne Duranceau. Scholastic, 1994. ISBN 978-0-590-47278-4 Subj: Animals. Clocks, watches. Parties. Rhyming text.

Hickory dickory dock and other nursery rhymes ill. by Carol Jones. Houghton, 1992. ISBN 978-0-395-60834-0 Subj: Format, unusual. Nursery rhymes.

Humpty Dumpty ill. by Annie Kubler. Child's Play, 2010. ISBN 978-1-84643-339-9 Subj: Eggs. Format, unusual – board books. Nursery rhymes. Rhyming text.

Humpty Dumpty and other rhymes ed. by Iona Opie; ill. by Rosemary Wells. Candlewick, 1997. ISBN 978-0-7636-0353-3 Subj: Format, unusual – board books. Nursery rhymes.

Ian Penney's book of nursery rhymes ill. by Ian Penney. Abrams, 1994. ISBN 978-0-8109-3733-8 Subj: Nursery rhymes.

Jack and Jill [board book] ill. by Heather Collins. Kids Can, 2003. ISBN 978-1-55337-075-8 Subj: Format, unusual – board books. Nursery rhymes.

James Marshall's Mother Goose ill. by James Marshall. Farrar, 1979. ISBN 978-0-374-33653-0 Subj: Nursery rhymes.

La Madre Goose: nursery rhymes for los niños by Susan Middleton Elya; ill. by Juana Martinez-Neal. Putnam, 2016. ISBN 978-039925157-3 Subj: Foreign languages. Nursery rhymes.

Little Boy Blue and other rhymes ed. by Iona Opie; ill. by Rosemary Wells. Candlewick, 1997. ISBN 978-0-7636-0354-0 Subj: Format, unusual – board books. Nursery rhymes.

Little Miss Muffet [board book] ill. by Heather Collins. Kids Can, 2003. ISBN 978-1-55337-076-5 Subj: Format, unusual – board books. Nursery rhymes.

Little Miss Muffet adapt. by Tracey Campbell Pearson; ill. by adapter. Farrar, 2005. ISBN 978-0-374-

30862-9 Subj: Format, unusual – board books. Nursery rhymes. Spiders.

Mother Goose sel. by Scott Cook; ill. by selector. Knopf, 1994. ISBN 978-0-679-90949-1 Subj: Nursery rhymes.

Mother Goose sel. by Michael Hague; ill. by selector. Henry Holt, 1984. ISBN 978-0-03-070723-0 Subj: Nursery rhymes.

Mother Goose ill. by Tasha Tudor. Walck, 1944. Subj: Caldecott award honor books. Nursery rhymes.

Mother Goose numbers on the loose adapt. by Leo and Diane Dillon; ill. by adapters. Harcourt, 2007. ISBN 978-0-15-205676-6 Subj: Counting, numbers. Nursery rhymes.

Mother Goose remembers ill. by Clare Beaton. Barefoot, 2000. ISBN 978-1-84148-073-2 Subj: Nursery rhymes.

The movable Mother Goose (Sabuda, Robert)

My first real Mother Goose [board book] ill. by Blanche Fisher Wright. Scholastic, 2000. ISBN 978-0-439-14671-5 Subj: Format, unusual – board books. Nursery rhymes.

1, 2, buckle my shoe by Anna Grossnickle Hines; ill. by author. Harcourt, 2008. ISBN 978-0-15-206305-4 Subj: Counting, numbers. Nursery rhymes. Rhyming text.

One, two, buckle my shoe [board book] ill. by Heather Collins. Kids Can, 1997. ISBN 978-1-55074-410-1 Subj: Format, unusual – board books. Nursery rhymes.

Over the candlestick: classic nursery rhymes and the real stories behind them (Montgomery, Michael G.)

Pat-a-cake adapt. by R. A. Herman; ill. by Olga Ivanov and Aleksey Ivanov. Handprint, 2005. ISBN 978-1-59354-039-5 Subj: Activities – baking, cooking. Format, unusual – board books. Games. Nursery rhymes.

Pat-a-cake ill. by Annie Kubler. Child's Play, 2010. ISBN 978-1-84643-338-2 Subj: Activities – baking, cooking. Format, unusual – board books. Nursery rhymes. Rhyming text.

Pat-a-cake [board book] ill. by Heather Collins. Kids Can, 2003. ISBN 978-1-55337-077-2 Subj: Format, unusual – board books. Nursery rhymes.

Pussycat, pussycat and other rhymes ed. by Iona Opie; ill. by Rosemary Wells. Candlewick, 1997. ISBN 978-0-7636-0355-7 Subj: Format, unusual – board books. Nursery rhymes.

Richard Scarry's best Mother Goose ever ill. by Richard Scarry. Golden, 1970. ISBN 978-0-307-15578-8 Subj: Nursery rhymes.

Rock-a-bye baby [board book] ill. by Heather Collins. Kids Can, 2000. ISBN 978-1-55074-572-6 Subj: Format, unusual – board books. Nursery rhymes.

Snuggle up with Mother Goose ed. by Iona Opie; ill. by Rosemary Wells. Candlewick, 2015. ISBN 978-076367867-8 Subj: Format, unusual – board books. Nursery rhymes.

This little piggy [board book] ill. by Heather Collins. Kids Can, 1997. ISBN 978-1-55074-404-0 Subj: Format, unusual – board books. Nursery rhymes.

The three jovial huntsmen ill. by Susan Jeffers. Bradbury, 1973. ISBN 978-0-87888-023-2 Subj: Caldecott award honor books. Nursery rhymes.

The three little kittens ill. by Paul Galdone. Clarion, 1986. ISBN 978-0-89919-426-4 Subj: Animals – cats. Behavior – lost & found possessions. Clothing – gloves, mittens. Nursery rhymes.

Three little kittens (Siomades, Lorianne)

Tomie de Paola's Mother Goose (dePaola, Tomie)

Wee Willie Winkie [board book] ill. by Heather Collins. Kids Can, 2000. ISBN 978-1-55074-568-9 Subj: Format, unusual – board books. Nursery rhymes.

Wee Willie Winkie and other rhymes ed. by Iona Opie; ill. by Rosemary Wells. Candlewick, 1997. ISBN 978-0-7636-0356-4 Subj: Format, unusual – board books. Nursery rhymes.

Wendy Watson's Mother Goose ill. by Wendy Watson. Lothrop, 1989. ISBN 978-0-688-05708-4 Subj: Nursery rhymes.

Will Moses Mother Goose ill. by Will Moses. Philomel, 2003. ISBN 978-0-399-23744-7 Subj: Nursery rhymes.

Mould, Wendy. *Ants in my pants* ill. by author. Clarion, 2001. ISBN 978-0-618-09640-4 Subj: Clothing. Humorous stories. Imagination.

Moulton, Mark Kimball. *Reindeer Christmas* ill. by Karen Hillard Good. Simon & Schuster, 2008. ISBN 978-1-4169-6108-6 Subj: Animals – reindeer. Holidays – Christmas. Rhyming text.

The very best pumpkin ill. by Karen Hillard Good. Simon & Schuster, 2010. ISBN 978-1-4169-8288-3 Subj: Farms. Friendship. Gardens, gardening.

Moundlic, Charlotte. *The scar* ill. by Olivier Tallec. Candlewick, 2011. ISBN 978-0-7636-5341-5 Subj: Death. Emotions – grief. Family life – mothers.

Moüy, Iris de. *Naptime* ill. by author. House of Anansi/Groundwood, 2014. ISBN 978-155498487-9 Subj: Animals. Behavior – fighting, arguing. Sleep.

Moxley, Sheila. *ABCD an alphabet book of cats and dogs* ill. by author. Little, 2001. ISBN 978-0-316-

59240-6 Subj: ABC books. Animals – cats. Animals – dogs.

Mozelle, Shirley. *The bear upstairs* ill. by Doug Cushman. Henry Holt, 2005. ISBN 978-0-8050-6820-7 Subj: Activities – baking, cooking. Animals – bears. Noise, sounds.

The kitchen talks ill. by Petra Mathers. Henry Holt, 2006. ISBN 978-0-8050-7143-6 Subj: Food. Homes, houses. Poetry.

The pig is in the pantry, the cat is on the shelf ill. by Jennifer Plecas. Clarion, 2000. ISBN 978-0-395-78627-7 Subj: Animals. Behavior – misbehavior. Farms. Homes, houses. Pets.

Mraz, David. *Little Goose* ill. by Margot Apple. Tricycle, 2009. ISBN 978-1-58246-190-8 Subj: Birds – geese. Family life – mothers.

Muecke, Anne. *The dinosaurs' night before Christmas* ill. by Nathan Hale. Chronicle, 2008. ISBN 978-0-8118-6322-3 Subj: Dinosaurs. Holidays – Christmas. Rhyming text.

Mueller, Dagmar H. *David's world: a picture book about living with autism* ill. by Verena Ballhaus. Skyhorse/Sky Pony, 2012. ISBN 978-1-61608-962-7 Subj: Disabilities – autism.

Mueller, Doris L. *Small One's adventure* ill. by Parker Fulton. All About Kids, 2003. ISBN 978-0-9710278-1-7 Subj: Animals – elephants. Behavior – growing up. Concepts – size. Self-concept.

Mühle, Jörg. *Tickle my ears* ill. by author. Gecko, 2016. ISBN 978-177657076-8 Subj: Animals – rabbits. Bedtime. Format, unusual – board books. Participation.

Muir, Leslie. *C.R. Mudgeon* ill. by Julian Hector. Simon & Schuster, 2012. ISBN 978-1-4169-7906-7 Subj: Animals – hedgehogs. Animals – squirrels. Friendship.

The little bitty bakery ill. by Betsy Lewin. Hyperion/Disney, 2011. ISBN 978-1-4231-1640-0 Subj: Activities – baking, cooking. Animals – elephants. Animals – mice. Birthdays. Rhyming text.

Muldrow, Diane. *We planted a tree* ill. by Bob Staake. Random House, 2010. ISBN 978-0-375-86432-2 Subj: Ecology. Trees.

Müller, Birte. *Finn cooks* ill. by author. North-South, 2004. ISBN 978-0-7358-1936-8 Subj: Activities – baking, cooking. Family life – mothers. Food. Health & fitness.

I can dress myself! ill. by author. NorthSouth, 2007. ISBN 978-0-7358-2128-6 Subj: Animals – rabbits. Clothing.

Muller, Gerda. *How does my garden grow?* ill. by author. Floris, 2014. ISBN 978-178250037-7 Subj: Family life – grandfathers. Foreign lands – France. Gardens, gardening.

Muller, Robin. *Badger's new house* ill. by author. Henry Holt, 2002. ISBN 978-0-8050-6383-7 Subj: Animals – badgers. Animals – mice. Homes, houses.

The lucky old woman ill. by author. Kids Can, 1987. ISBN 978-0-921103-07-3 Subj: Folk & fairy tales.

Mullins, Patricia. *One horse waiting for me* ill. by author. Simon & Schuster, 1998. ISBN 978-0-689-81381-8 Subj: Animals – horses, ponies. Counting, numbers.

V for vanishing: an alphabet of endangered animals ill. by author. HarperCollins, 1994. ISBN 978-0-06-023557-4 Subj: ABC books. Animals – endangered animals.

Mulryan, Doreen. *Lucky Ducky* ill. by author. Abrams, 2016. ISBN 978-141971467-2 Subj: Birds – ducks. Character traits – luck. Friendship.

Munari, Bruno. *ABC* ill. by author. Collins-World, 1960. Subj: ABC books.

Bruno Munari's zoo ill. by author. Collins-World, 1963. Subj: Animals. Birds. Zoos.

Muncaster, Harriet. *I am a witch's cat* ill. by author. HarperCollins, 2014. ISBN 978-006222914-4 Subj: Animals – cats. Witches.

Munro, Roxie. *Amazement Park* ill. by author. Chronicle, 2005. ISBN 978-0-8118-4581-6 Subj: Picture puzzles.

Busy builders ill. by author. Marshall Cavendish, 2012. ISBN 978-0-7614-6105-0 Subj: Insects.

Circus ill. by author. Chronicle, 2006. ISBN 978-0-8118-5209-8 Subj: Circus. Format, unusual – toy & movable books. Picture puzzles. Rhyming text.

Desert days, desert nights ill. by author. Bright Sky, 2010. ISBN 978-1-933979-77-9 Subj: Day. Desert. Ecology. Night.

Ecomazes: twelve Earth adventures ill. by author. Sterling, 2010. ISBN 978-1-4027-6393-9 Subj: Earth. Ecology. Mazes. Picture puzzles.

Go! go! go! with more than 70 flaps to uncover and discover ill. by author. Sterling, 2009. ISBN 978-1-4027-3773-2 Subj: Concepts – speed. Format, unusual – toy & movable books. Transportation.

Hatch! ill. by author. Marshall Cavendish, 2011. ISBN 978-0-7614-5882-1 Subj: Birds. Character traits – questioning. Eggs.

The inside-outside book of libraries ill. by author. Dutton, 1996. ISBN 978-0-525-45608-7 Subj: Libraries.

The inside-outside book of London ill. by author. Dutton, 1989. ISBN 978-0-525-44522-7 Subj: Cities, towns. Foreign lands – England.

The inside-outside book of New York City ill. by author. Dodd, 1985. ISBN 978-0-396-08513-3 Subj: Cities, towns.

The inside-outside book of Paris ill. by author. Dutton, 1992. ISBN 978-0-525-44863-1 Subj: Cities, towns. Foreign lands – France.

The inside-outside book of Texas ill. by author. SeaStar, 2001. ISBN 978-1-58717-050-8 Subj: Activities – traveling. Cities, towns. Country. Cowboys, cowgirls. Museums. Texas. U.S. history.

The inside-outside book of Washington, D.C. ill. by author. Dutton, 1987. ISBN 978-0-525-44298-1 Subj: Activities – traveling. Cities, towns. Museums.

Inside-outside dinosaurs ill. by author. Marshall Cavendish, 2009. ISBN 978-0-7614-5624-7 Subj: Dinosaurs.

Market maze ill. by author. Holiday House, 2015. ISBN 978-082343092-5 Subj: Farms. Mazes. Picture puzzles. Stores.

Mazescapes ill. by author. SeaStar, 2001. ISBN 978-1-58717-060-7 Subj: Activities – traveling. Cities, towns. Country. Games. Mazes. Picture puzzles.

Mazeways: A to Z ill. by author. Sterling, 2007. ISBN 978-1-4027-3774-9 Subj: Mazes. Picture puzzles.

Rodeo ill. by author. Bright Sky, 2007. ISBN 978-1-933979-03-8 Subj: Rodeos.

Munsch, Robert N. *Aaron's hair* ill. by Alan Daniel and Lea Daniel. Scholastic, 2000. ISBN 978-0-439-19258-3 Subj: Behavior – running away. Emotions. Hair.

Alligator baby ill. by Michael Martchenko. Scholastic, 1997. ISBN 978-0-590-21101-7 Subj: Animals. Babies, toddlers. Family life – brothers & sisters. Family life – new sibling. Zoos.

Andrew's loose tooth ill. by Michael Martchenko. Scholastic, 1998. ISBN 978-0-590-21102-4 Subj: Behavior – growing up. Fairies. Teeth.

Angela's airplane ill. by Michael Martchenko. Firefly, 1988. ISBN 978-1-55037-027-0 Subj: Activities – flying. Airplanes, airports. Behavior – misbehavior.

David's father ill. by Michael Martchenko. Firefly, 1983. ISBN 978-0-920236-62-8 Subj: Character traits – kindness. Giants.

The fire station ill. by Michael Martchenko. Firefly, 1991. ISBN 978-1-55037-170-3 Subj: Careers – firefighters.

Get out of bed! ill. by Alan Daniel. Scholastic, 1998. ISBN 978-0-590-21103-1 Subj: School. Sleep.

I have to go! ill. by Michael Martchenko. Firefly, 1987. ISBN 978-0-920303-77-1 Subj: Behavior – growing up. Family life.

Love you forever ill. by Sheila McGraw. Firefly, 1994, 1986. ISBN 978-0-920668-36-8 Subj: Emotions – love. Family life – mothers. Foreign lands – Canada.

Makeup mess ill. by Michael Martchenko. Scholastic, 2001. ISBN 978-0-439-18771-8 Subj: Beauty shops. Character traits – appearance. Self-concept.

Mmm, cookies! ill. by Michael Martchenko. Scholastic, 2000. ISBN 978-0-590-89603-0 Subj: Behavior – trickery. Family life. Food. School.

Moira's birthday ill. by Michael Martchenko. Firefly, 1987. ISBN 978-0-920303-85-6 Subj: Behavior – misbehavior. Birthdays. Parties.

More pies ill. by Michael Martchenko. Cartwheel, 2002. ISBN 978-0-439-18773-2 Subj: Contests. Food.

Mortimer ill. by Michael Martchenko. Firefly, 1985. ISBN 978-0-920303-12-2 Subj: Bedtime. Noise, sounds. Songs.

Mud puddle ill. by author. Firefly, 1982. ISBN 978-0-920236-47-5 Subj: Activities – playing. Character traits – cleanliness. Foreign lands – Canada. Weather – rain.

The paper bag princess ill. by Michael Martchenko. Firefly, 1980. ISBN 978-0-920236-82-6 Subj: Character traits – appearance. Dragons.

Pigs ill. by Michael Martchenko. Firefly, 1989. ISBN 978-1-55037-039-3 Subj: Animals – pigs.

A promise is a promise by Robert N. Munsch and Michael Kusugak ill. by Vladyana Krykorka. Firefly, 1988. ISBN 978-1-55037-009-6 Subj: Eskimos. Folk & fairy tales. Foreign lands – Canada. Sea & seashore.

Purple, green and yellow ill. by Hélène Desputeaux. Firefly, 1992. ISBN 978-1-55037-255-7 Subj: Concepts – color.

Ribbon rescue ill. by Eugenie Fernandes. Scholastic, 1999. ISBN 978-0-590-89012-0 Subj: Character traits – generosity. Clothing – dresses. Weddings.

Show-and-tell ill. by Michael Martchenko. Firefly, 1991. ISBN 978-1-55037-195-6 Subj: School.

Something good ill. by Michael Martchenko. Firefly, 1990. ISBN 978-1-55037-099-7 Subj: Family life – fathers. Shopping. Stores.

Stephanie's ponytail ill. by Michael Martchenko. Firefly, 1996. ISBN 978-1-55037-485-8 Subj: Behavior – imitation. Character traits – appearance. Cumulative tales. Hair. School.

Thomas' snowsuit ill. by Michael Martchenko. Firefly, 1985. ISBN 978-0-920303-32-0 Subj: Careers – teachers. Clothing. Foreign lands – Canada. School. Seasons – winter. Weather – snow.

Up, up, down! ill. by Michael Martchenko. Scholastic, 2001. ISBN 978-0-439-18770-1 Subj: Activities. Trees.

Wait and see ill. by Michael Martchenko. Firefly, 1993. ISBN 978-1-55037-335-6 Subj: Behavior – wishing. Birthdays. Foreign lands – Canada. Friendship.

We share everything! ill. by Michael Martchenko. Scholastic, 1999. ISBN 978-0-590-89600-9 Subj: Behavior – sharing. School.

Where is Gah-Ning? ill. by Hélène Desputeaux. Annick, 1994. ISBN 978-1-55037-982-2 Subj: Family life – fathers. Foreign lands – Canada. Shopping. Toys – balloons.

Zoom ill. by Michael Martchenko. Cartwheel, 2003. ISBN 978-0-439-18774-9 Subj: Concepts – speed. Disabilities – physical disabilities.

Munson, Derek. *Enemy pie* ill. by Tara Calahan King. Chronicle, 2000. ISBN 978-0-8118-2778-2 Subj: Family life – fathers. Food. Friendship.

Muntean, Michaela. *Do not open this book!* ill. by Pascal Lemaître. Scholastic, 2006. ISBN 978-0-439-66037-2 Subj: Activities – writing. Animals – pigs. Books, reading. Humorous stories.

Murawski, Darlyne A. *Bug faces* ill. with photos. National Geographic, 2000. ISBN 978-0-7922-7557-2 Subj: Insects. Spiders.

Murguia, Bethanie Deeney. *The best parts of Christmas* ill. by author. Candlewick, 2015. ISBN 978-076367556-1 Subj: Holidays – Christmas. Trees.

Cockatoo, too ill. by author. little bee, 2016. ISBN 978-149980102-6 Subj: Birds. Birds – cockatoos. Language.

I feel five! ill. by author. Candlewick, 2014. ISBN 978-076366291-2 Subj: Behavior – growing up. Birthdays.

Princess! Fairy! Ballerina! ill. by author. Scholastic/Arthur A. Levine, 2016. ISBN 978-054573240-6 Subj: Activities – playing. Behavior – fighting, arguing. Friendship. Imagination.

Snippet the early riser ill. by author. Knopf, 2013. ISBN 978-1-58246-460-2 Subj: Animals – snails. Family life. Morning. Problem solving. Sleep.

The too-scary story ill. by author. Scholastic/Arthur A. Levine, 2017. ISBN 978-054573242-0

Subj: Activities – storytelling. Bedtime. Family life – fathers. Imagination.

Toucans, too ill. by author. little bee, 2017. ISBN 978-149980421-8 Subj: Birds – cockatoos. Birds – toucans. Language. Rhyming text.

Zoe gets ready ill. by author. Scholastic, 2012. ISBN 978-0-545-34215-5 Subj: Character traits – appearance. Character traits – individuality. Clothing. Self-concept.

Zoe's jungle ill. by author. Scholastic/Arthur A. Levine, 2014. ISBN 978-054555869-3 Subj: Activities – playing. Family life – sisters. Imagination.

Zoe's room (no sisters allowed) ill. by author. Scholastic, 2013. ISBN 978-0-545-45781-1 Subj: Family life – sisters.

Murkoff, Heidi Eisenberg. *What to expect at a play date* ill. by Laura Rader. HarperCollins, 2001. ISBN 978-0-694-01330-2 Subj: Activities – playing. Behavior. Friendship.

What to expect at preschool ill. by Laura Rader. HarperCollins, 2001. ISBN 978-0-694-01326-5 Subj: Activities. Friendship. School – nursery.

What to expect when the new baby comes home ill. by Laura Rader. HarperCollins, 2001. ISBN 978-0-694-01327-2 Subj: Babies, toddlers. Family life – brothers & sisters. Family life – new sibling.

What to expect when you go to the dentist ill. by Laura Rader. HarperCollins, 2002. ISBN 978-0-694-01328-9 Subj: Careers – dentists. Health & fitness. Teeth.

What to expect when you go to the doctor ill. by Laura Rader. HarperCollins, 2000. ISBN 978-0-694-01324-1 Subj: Careers – doctors. Health & fitness.

Murphy, Andy. *Out and about at the dairy farm* ill. by Anne McMullen. Picture Window, 2003. ISBN 978-1-4048-0038-0 Subj: Animals – bulls, cows. Farms. Machines. School – field trips.

Murphy, Christopher J. *Lucille lost: a true adventure* (George, Margaret)

Murphy, Elspeth Campbell. *Happy Easter, God* ill. by Jim Lewis. Bethany Backyard, 2001. ISBN 978-0-7642-2386-0 Subj: Holidays – Easter. Poetry. Religion.

Murphy, Jill. *All for one* ill. by author. Candlewick, 1999. ISBN 978-0-7636-0785-2 Subj: Activities – playing. Friendship. Monsters.

Meltdown! ill. by author. Candlewick, 2016. ISBN 978-076368926-1 Subj: Animals – rabbits. Babies, toddlers. Emotions – anger. Family life – mothers. Shopping. Stores.

Mr. Large in charge ill. by author. Candlewick, 2007. ISBN 978-0-7636-3504-6 Subj: Animals – elephants. Family life – fathers. Illness.

Peace at last ill. by author. Dial, 1980. ISBN 978-0-8037-6758-4 Subj: Animals – bears. Noise, sounds. Sleep.

A piece of cake ill. by author. Candlewick, 1997. ISBN 978-0-7636-0572-8 Subj: Animals – elephants. Food. Self-concept.

A quiet night in ill. by author. Candlewick, 1994. ISBN 978-1-56402-248-6 Subj: Animals – elephants. Bedtime. Family life.

Murphy, Jim. *Fergus and the Night-Demon: an Irish ghost story* ill. by John Manders. Houghton, 2006. ISBN 978-0-618-33955-6 Subj: Character traits – laziness. Emotions – fear. Foreign lands – Ireland. Ghosts.

Murphy, Kelly. *The boll weevil ball* ill. by author. Henry Holt, 2002. ISBN 978-0-8050-6712-5 Subj: Activities – dancing. Concepts – size. Insects – beetles.

Murphy, Liz. *ABC doctor: staying healthy from A to Z* ill. by author. Blue Apple, 2007. ISBN 978-1-59354-593-2 Subj: ABC books. Careers – doctors. Health & fitness.

Murphy, Mary. *The Alphabet Keeper* ill. by author. Knopf, 2003. ISBN 978-0-375-92347-0 Subj: ABC books. Character traits – freedom.

Caterpillar's wish ill. by author. DK, 1999. ISBN 978-0-7894-2593-5 Subj: Behavior – wishing. Insects – butterflies, caterpillars. Metamorphosis.

Crocopotamus ill. by author. Candlewick, 2016. ISBN 978-076368102-9 Subj: Animals. Format, unusual – board books. Format, unusual – toy & movable books.

Good night like this ill. by author. Candlewick, 2016. ISBN 978-076367970-5 Subj: Animals. Bedtime. Format, unusual – toy & movable books. Rhyming text.

Here comes spring, and summer and fall and winter ill. by author. DK, 1999. ISBN 978-0-7894-3484-5 Subj: Animals – dogs. Seasons.

How kind ill. by author. Candlewick, 2002. ISBN 978-0-7636-1732-5 Subj: Animals. Character traits – kindness. Circular tales. Farms.

I feel happy, and sad, and angry, and glad ill. by author. DK, 2000. ISBN 978-0-7894-2680-2 Subj: Animals – dogs. Emotions.

I like it when . . . ill. by author. Harcourt, 1997. ISBN 978-0-15-200039-4 Subj: Activities. Birds – penguins. Family life – parents.

A kiss like this ill. by author. Candlewick, 2012. ISBN 978-0-7636-61823. Subj: Animals – babies. Format, unusual – toy & movable books. Kissing.

Koala and the flower ill. by author. Roaring Brook, 2002. ISBN 978-0-7613-2674-8 Subj: Animals. Animals – koalas. Character traits – curiosity. Character traits – questioning. Flowers. Libraries.

Panda Foo and the new friend ill. by author. Candlewick, 2007. ISBN 978-0-7636-3405-6 Subj: Activities – picnicking. Animals – pandas. Friendship.

Please be quiet! ill. by author. Houghton, 1999. ISBN 978-0-395-97113-0 Subj: Birds – penguins. Family life – mothers. Noise, sounds.

Quick Duck! ill. by author. Candlewick, 2013. ISBN 978-0-7636-6022-2 Subj: Birds – ducks. Concepts. Format, unusual – board books.

Say hello like this! ill. by author. Candlewick, 2014. ISBN 978-076366951-5 Subj: Animals. Format, unusual – toy & movable books. Noise, sounds.

Slow snail ill. by author. Candlewick, 2013. ISBN 978-0-7636-6023-9 Subj: Animals – snails. Concepts. Format, unusual – board books.

Some things change ill. by author. Houghton, 2001. ISBN 978-0-618-00334-1 Subj: Activities. Birds – penguins. Concepts – change. Toys – bears.

You smell and taste and feel and see and hear ill. by author. DK, 1997. ISBN 978-0-7894-2471-6 Subj: Animals – dogs. Senses.

Murphy, Patricia J. *Mama, look!* ill. by David Diaz. little bee, 2017. ISBN 978-149980080-7 Subj: Activities – walking. Family life – mothers. Nature.

Murphy, Patti Beling. *Elinor and Violet* ill. by author. Little, 2003. ISBN 978-0-316-91034-7 Subj: Behavior – misbehavior. Birds – chickens, roosters. Family life – grandmothers. Friendship. Sea & seashore – beaches.

Murphy, Sally. *Pearl verses the world* ill. by Heather Potter. Candlewick, 2011. ISBN 978-0-7636-4821-3 Subj: Death. Emotions – grief. Emotions – loneliness. Family life – grandmothers. Poetry.

Murphy, Stuart J. *Animals on board* ill. by R. W. Alley. HarperCollins, 1998. ISBN 978-0-06-027443-6 Subj: Animals. Counting, numbers. Merry-go-rounds. Rhyming text.

Beep beep, vroom vroom! ill. by Chris L. Demarest. HarperCollins, 2000. ISBN 978-0-06-028017-8 Subj: Automobiles. Counting, numbers.

The best bug parade ill. by Holly Keller. HarperCollins, 1996. ISBN 978-0-06-025872-6 Subj: Counting, numbers. Insects.

The best vacation ever ill. by Nadine Bernard Westcott. HarperCollins, 1997. ISBN 978-0-06-026767-

4 Subj: Activities – vacationing. Family life. Problem solving. Rhyming text.

Betcha! ill. by S. D. Schindler. HarperCollins, 1997. ISBN 978-0-06-026769-8 Subj: Counting, numbers. Friendship.

Bigger, better, best ill. by Marsha Winborn. HarperCollins, 2002. ISBN 978-0-06-028919-5 Subj: Concepts – measurement. Concepts – size.

Bug dance ill. by Christopher Santoro. HarperCollins, 2002. ISBN 978-0-06-446252-5 Subj: Counting, numbers. Insects.

Captain Invincible and the space shapes ill. by Rémy Simard. HarperCollins, 2001. ISBN 978-0-06-028023-9 Subj: Concepts – shape. Counting, numbers.

Circus shapes ill. by Edward Miller. HarperCollins, 1998. ISBN 978-0-06-027437-5 Subj: Circus. Concepts – shape. Rhyming text.

Dave's down-to-earth rock shop ill. by Cat Bowman Smith. HarperCollins, 2000. ISBN 978-0-06-028019-2 Subj: Counting, numbers.

Dinosaur deals ill. by Kevin O'Malley. HarperCollins, 2001. ISBN 978-0-06-028927-0 Subj: Activities – trading. Counting, numbers. Dinosaurs.

Earth Day — hooray! ill. by Renée Williams-Andriani. HarperCollins, 2004. ISBN 978-0-06-000127-8 Subj: Counting, numbers. Ecology. Holidays.

Elevator magic ill. by G. Brian Karas. HarperCollins, 1997. ISBN 978-0-06-446709-4 Subj: Counting, numbers. Elevators, escalators. Rhyming text.

Every buddy counts ill. by Fiona Dunbar. HarperCollins, 1997. ISBN 978-0-06-026773-5 Subj: Counting, numbers. Rhyming text.

A fair bear share ill. by John Speirs. HarperCollins, 1998. ISBN 978-0-06-446714-8 Subj: Activities – baking, cooking. Animals – bears. Counting, numbers. Food.

Freda is found ill. by Tim Jones. Charlesbridge, 2011. ISBN 978-1-58089-462-3 Subj: Animals. Behavior – lost. Safety. School – field trips.

Game time ill. by Cynthia Jabar. HarperCollins, 2000. ISBN 978-0-06-028025-3 Subj: Clocks, watches. Sports – soccer. Time.

Get up and go! ill. by Diane Greenseid. HarperCollins, 1996. ISBN 978-0-06-025882-5 Subj: Animals – dogs. Morning. Rhyming text. School. Time.

Give me half! ill. by G. Brian Karas. HarperCollins, 1996. ISBN 978-0-06-025874-0 Subj: Behavior – sharing. Counting, numbers. Friendship. Sibling rivalry.

The greatest gymnast of all ill. by Cynthia Jabar. HarperCollins, 1998. ISBN 978-0-06-027609-6 Subj: Concepts. Counting, numbers.

Henry the fourth ill. by Scott Nash. HarperCollins, 1999. ISBN 978-0-06-027611-9 Subj: Animals – dogs. Counting, numbers.

It's about time! ill. by John Speirs. HarperCollins, 2005. ISBN 978-0-06-055768-3 Subj: Clocks, watches. Day. Night. Time.

Jack the builder ill. by Michael Rex. HarperCollins, 2006. ISBN 978-0-06-055775-1 Subj: Counting, numbers. Imagination.

Just enough carrots ill. by Frank Remkiewicz. HarperCollins, 1997. ISBN 978-0-06-026779-7 Subj: Animals – rabbits. Counting, numbers. Food. Shopping. Stores.

Leaping lizards ill. by JoAnn Adinolfi. HarperCollins, 2005. ISBN 978-0-06-000130-8 Subj: Counting, numbers. Reptiles – lizards.

Left, right, Emma! ill. by Tim Jones. Charlesbridge, 2012. ISBN 978-1-58089-472-2 Subj: Concepts – left & right.

Let's fly a kite ill. by Brian Floca. HarperCollins, 2000. ISBN 978-0-06-028035-2 Subj: Behavior – sharing. Concepts. Kites.

Mall mania ill. by Renée Williams-Andriani. HarperCollins, 2006. ISBN 978-0-06-055776-8 Subj: Counting, numbers. Stores.

Missing mittens ill. by G. Brian Karas. HarperCollins, 2001. ISBN 978-0-06-028027-7 Subj: Concepts. Counting, numbers.

Monster musical chairs ill. by Scott Nash. HarperCollins, 2000. ISBN 978-0-06-028021-5 Subj: Counting, numbers. Games.

More or less ill. by David Wenzel. HarperCollins, 2005. ISBN 978-0-06-053165-2 Subj: Activities – picnicking. Counting, numbers. Games.

100 days of cool ill. by John Bendall-Brunello. HarperCollins, 2004. ISBN 978-0-06-000121-6 Subj: Counting, numbers. School.

A pair of socks ill. by Lois Ehlert. HarperCollins, 1996. ISBN 978-0-06-025880-1 Subj: Clothing – socks.

The penny pot ill. by Lynne Cravath. HarperCollins, 1998. ISBN 978-0-06-027607-2 Subj: Counting, numbers. Fairs, festivals. Money. School.

Pepper's journal ill. by Marsha Winborn. HarperCollins, 2000. ISBN 978-0-06-027619-5 Subj: Animals – babies. Animals – cats. Calendars.

Percy listens up ill. by Tim Jones. Charlesbridge, 2012. ISBN 978-1-58089-468-5 Subj: Noise, sounds. Senses – hearing.

Polly's pen pal ill. by Rémy Simard. HarperCollins, 2005. ISBN 978-0-06-053168-3 Subj: Concepts – measurement. Pen pals.

Probably pistachio ill. by Marsha Winborn. HarperCollins, 2001. ISBN 978-0-06-028029-1 Subj: Behavior – bad day, bad mood. Concepts.

Rabbit's pajama party ill. by Frank Remkiewicz. HarperCollins, 1999. ISBN 978-0-06-027617-1 Subj: Animals – rabbits. Family life – mothers. Rhyming text. Sleepovers.

Ready, set, hop! ill. by John Buller. HarperCollins, 1996. ISBN 978-0-06-025878-8 Subj: Activities – jumping. Counting, numbers. Frogs & toads.

Rodeo time ill. by David Wenzel. HarperCollins, 2006. ISBN 978-0-06-055778-2 Subj: Rodeos. Time.

Same old horse ill. by Steve Björkman. HarperCollins, 2005. ISBN 978-0-06-055770-6 Subj: Animals – horses, ponies. Character traits – persistence. Counting, numbers. Rhyming text.

Seaweed soup ill. by Frank Remkiewicz. HarperCollins, 2001. ISBN 978-0-06-446736-0 Subj: Behavior – sharing. Counting, numbers. Food.

Sluggers' car wash ill. by Barney Saltzberg. HarperCollins, 2002. ISBN 978-0-06-028921-8 Subj: Activities – working. Counting, numbers. Money.

The sundae scoop ill. by Cynthia Jabar. HarperCollins, 2003. ISBN 978-0-06-028924-9 Subj: Counting, numbers.

Too many kangaroo things to do! ill. by Kevin O'Malley. HarperCollins, 1996. ISBN 978-0-06-025884-9 Subj: Animals – kangaroos. Birthdays. Counting, numbers. Parties.

Treasure map ill. by Tricia Tusa. HarperCollins, 2004. ISBN 978-0-06-028036-9 Subj: Clubs, gangs. Maps. Problem solving.

Write on, Carlos! ill. by Tim Jones. Charlesbridge, 2011. ISBN 978-1-58089-464-7 Subj: Activities – writing. Animals. Names.

Murphy, Yannick. *Ahwoooooooo!* ill. by Claudio Muñoz. Houghton, 2006. ISBN 978-0-618-11762-8 Subj: Animals – wolves. Family life – grandfathers. Noise, sounds.

Baby Polar ill. by Kristen Balouch. Clarion, 2009. ISBN 978-0-618-99850-0 Subj: Animals – polar bears. Family life – mothers. Weather – snow. Weather – storms.

Murray, Alison. *Apple pie ABC* ill. by author. Hyperion/Disney, 2011. ISBN 978-1-4231-3694-1 Subj: ABC books. Activities – baking, cooking. Animals – dogs.

Hickory dickory dog ill. by author. Candlewick, 2014. ISBN 978-076366826-6 Subj: Animals – dogs. Rhyming text. School.

The house that Zack built ill. by author. Candlewick, 2016. ISBN 978-076367844-9 Subj: Cumulative tales. Farms. Insects – flies. Rhyming text.

Little Mouse ill. by author. Disney/Hyperion, 2013. ISBN 978-1-4231-4330-7 Subj: Bedtime. Family life – mothers. Names.

One two that's my shoe! ill. by author. Hyperion/Disney, 2012. ISBN 978-1-4231-4329-1 Subj: Animals – dogs. Counting, numbers. Rhyming text.

Princess Penelope and the runaway kitten ill. by author. Candlewick, 2013. ISBN 978-0-7636-6952-2 Subj: Animals – cats. Behavior – boredom. Royalty – princesses.

Murray, Andrew. *Have you seen Chester?* ill. by Nicola Slater. HarperCollins, 2003. ISBN 978-0-06-057187-0 Subj: Animals – cats. Animals – dogs. Behavior – fighting, arguing. Behavior – running away.

Murray, Diana. *City shapes* ill. by Bryan Collier. Little, Brown, 2016. ISBN 978-031637092-9 Subj: Birds – pigeons. Cities, towns. Concepts – shape. Ethnic groups in the U.S. – African Americans. Rhyming text.

Ned the knitting pirate ill. by Leslie Lammle. Roaring Brook, 2016. ISBN 978-159643890-3 Subj: Activities – knitting. Monsters. Pirates. Rhyming text.

Murray, Glenn. *Walter, the farting dog* (Kotzwinkle, William)

Walter, the farting dog: rough weather ahead (Kotzwinkle, William)

Walter, the farting dog: trouble at the yard sale (Kotzwinkle, William)

Murray, Laura. *The Gingerbread Man loose at Christmas* (The gingerbread boy)

The Gingerbread Man loose at the zoo (The gingerbread boy)

The Gingerbread Man loose in the school (The gingerbread boy)

The Gingerbread Man loose on the fire truck (The gingerbread boy)

Murray, Marjorie Dennis. *Halloween night* ill. by Brandon Dorman. HarperCollins, 2008. ISBN 978-0-06-135186-0 Subj: Holidays – Halloween. Parties. Rhyming text.

Little Wolf and the moon ill. by Stacey Shuett. Marshall Cavendish, 2002. ISBN 978-0-7614-5100-6 Subj: Animals – babies. Animals – wolves. Moon.

Murray, Martine. *A moose called Mouse* ill. by author. Allen & Unwin, 2001. ISBN 978-1-86508-495-4 Subj: Animals – moose. Friendship. Games. Nature. Night.

Musgrove, Margaret. *Ashanti to Zulu* ill. by Leo and Diane Dillon. Dial, 1976. ISBN 978-0-8037-0358-2 Subj: ABC books. Caldecott award books. Foreign lands – Africa.

The spider weaver: a legend of kente cloth ill. by Julia Cairns. Blue Sky, 2001. ISBN 978-0-590-98787-5 Subj: Activities – weaving. Careers – weavers. Folk & fairy tales. Foreign lands – Ghana. Spiders.

Muth, Jon J. *Hi, Koo! a year of seasons* ill. by author. Scholastic, 2014. ISBN 978-054516668-3 Subj: Animals – pandas. Poetry. Seasons.

Mama Lion wins the race ill. by author. Scholastic, 2017. ISBN 978-054585282-1 Subj: Animals. Animals – lions. Character traits – helpfulness. Sports – racing.

Stone soup ill. by reteller. Scholastic, 2003. ISBN 978-0-439-33909-4 Subj: Careers – clergy. Character traits – cleverness. Folk & fairy tales. Food. Foreign lands – China.

The three questions ill. by author. Scholastic, 2002. ISBN 978-0-439-19996-4 Subj: Animals. Behavior.

Zen ghosts ill. by author. Scholastic, 2010. ISBN 978-0-439-63430-4 Subj: Activities – storytelling. Animals – pandas. Family life – brothers & sisters. Ghosts. Holidays – Halloween.

Zen shorts ill. by author. Scholastic, 2005. ISBN 978-0-439-33911-7 Subj: Activities – storytelling. Animals – pandas. Caldecott award honor books. Family life – brothers & sisters. Folk & fairy tales.

Zen socks ill. by author. Scholastic, 2015. ISBN 978-054516669-0 Subj: Activities – storytelling. Animals – pandas. Behavior – greed. Behavior – sharing. Character traits – kindness. Character traits – patience, impatience. Family life – brothers & sisters.

Zen ties ill. by author. Scholastic, 2008. ISBN 978-0-439-63425-0 Subj: Animals – pandas. Character traits – helpfulness. Family life – brothers & sisters. Old age.

My big book of trucks and diggers. Chronicle, 2011. ISBN 978-0-8118-7892-0 Subj: Format, unusual – board books. Machines. Trucks.

My new baby ill. by Rachel Fuller. Child's Play, 2010. ISBN 978-1-84643-276-7 Subj: Family life – new sibling. Format, unusual – board books.

My potty book for boys ill. with photos. DK, 2001. ISBN 978-0-7894-4889-7 Subj: Behavior – growing up. Toilet training.

My potty book for girls ill. with photos. DK, 2001. ISBN 978-0-7894-4845-3 Subj: Behavior – growing up. Toilet training.

Myer, Andy. *Delia's dull day: an incredibly boring story* ill. by author. Sleeping Bear, 2012. ISBN 978-1-58536-804-4 Subj: Behavior – boredom. Humorous stories.

Myers, Anna. *Tumbleweed Baby* ill. by Charles Vess. Abrams, 2014. ISBN 978-141971232-6 Subj: Babies, toddlers. Family life. Tall tales. Texas.

Myers, Christopher. *My pen* ill. by author. Disney/Hyperion, 2015. ISBN 978-142310371-4 Subj: Activities – drawing. Imagination.

Sparrows ill. by author. Hyperion, 2001. ISBN 978-0-7868-2373-4 Subj: Birds. Birds – sparrows. Cities, towns. Ethnic groups in the U.S. – African Americans. Homeless.

Wings ill. by author. Scholastic, 2000. ISBN 978-0-590-03377-0 Subj: Activities – flying. Anatomy – wings. Character traits – being different.

Myers, Tim. *Basho and the fox* ill. by Oki S. Han. Marshall Cavendish, 2000. ISBN 978-0-7614-5068-9 Subj: Animals – foxes. Poetry.

Down at the Dino Wash Deluxe ill. by Macky Pamintuan. Sterling, 2013. ISBN 978-1-4027-7798-1 Subj: Activities – bathing. Character traits – cleanliness. Dinosaurs.

Looking for Luna ill. by Mike Reed. Marshall Cavendish, 2009. ISBN 978-0-7614-5564-6 Subj: Animals – cats. Behavior – lost & found possessions. Family life – fathers. Rhyming text.

Myers, Walter Dean. *The blues of Flats Brown* ill. by Nina Laden. Holiday, 2000. ISBN 978-0-8234-1480-2 Subj: Animals – dogs. Music. Musical instruments – guitars.

Brown angels ill. with photos. HarperCollins, 1993. ISBN 978-0-06-022918-4 Subj: Angels. Ethnic groups in the U.S. – African Americans. Poetry.

Harlem: a poem ill. by Christopher Myers. Scholastic, 1997. ISBN 978-0-590-54340-8 Subj: Caldecott award honor books. Careers – illustrators. Careers – writers. Cities, towns. Ethnic groups in the U.S. – African Americans. Poetry.

Looking for the easy life ill. by Lee Harper. HarperCollins, 2011. ISBN 978-0-06-054375-4 Subj: Animals – monkeys. Behavior – seeking better things.

Muhammad Ali: the people's champion ill. by Alix Delinois. HarperCollins, 2010. ISBN 978-0-06-029131-0 Subj: Ethnic groups in the U.S. – African Americans. Prejudice. Sports – boxing. U.S. history.

The story of the three kingdoms ill. by Ashley Bryan. HarperCollins, 1995. ISBN 978-0-06-024287-9 Subj: Animals. Nature.

Young Martin's promise by Walter Dean Myers and Alex Haley ill. by Barbara Higgins Bond. Alex Haley, general editor. Raintree, 1993. ISBN 978-0-8114-7210-4 Subj: Ethnic groups in the U.S. – African Americans. Holidays – Martin Luther King, Jr. Day. U.S. history.

Myller, Rolf. *How big is a foot?* ill. by author. Atheneum, 1962. ISBN 978-0-689-20298-8 Subj: Birthdays. Concepts – measurement. Humorous stories. Royalty – kings.

Myra, Harold Lawrence. *Thanksgiving: what makes it special?* ill. by Jane Kurisu. Nelson, 2002. ISBN 978-1-4003-0006-8 Subj: Holidays – Thanksgiving. Religion.

Myron, Vicki. *Dewey: there's a cat in the library!* by Vicki Myron and Bret Witter ill. by Steve James. Little, Brown, 2009. ISBN 978-0-316-06874-1 Subj: Animals – cats. Libraries.

Mystery manor ill. by Phil Wilson. Design by Willabel L. Tong; paper engineering by José R. Seminario. Piggy Toes, 2000. ISBN 978-1-58117-108-2 Subj: Animals – dogs. Format, unusual – toy & movable books. Ghosts. Monsters. Witches.

Na, Il Sung. *Bird, balloon, Bear* ill. by author. Knopf, 2017. ISBN 978-039955155-0 Subj: Animals – bears. Birds. Character traits – shyness. Emotions – loneliness. Toys – balloons.

A book of sleep ill. by author. Knopf, 2009. ISBN 978-0-375-86223-6 Subj: Animals. Birds – owls. Night. Sleep.

Hide and seek ill. by author. Knopf, 2012. ISBN 978-0-375-87078-1 Subj: Animals. Animals – elephants. Behavior – hiding. Games. Reptiles – chameleons.

The opposite zoo ill. by author. Knopf, 2016. ISBN 978-055351127-7 Subj: Animals. Animals – monkeys. Concepts – opposites. Zoos.

Snow rabbit, spring rabbit: a book of changing seasons ill. by author. Random House, 2011. ISBN 978-0-375-86786-6 Subj: Animals. Animals – rabbits. Seasons – spring. Seasons – winter.

The thingamabob ill. by author. Random House, 2010. ISBN 978-0-375-86106-2 Subj: Animals – elephants. Imagination. Umbrellas.

Welcome home, Bear: a book of animal habitats ill. by author. Knopf, 2015. ISBN 978-038575375-3 Subj: Activities – traveling. Animals – bears. Homes, houses.

Naberhaus, Sarvinder. *Blue sky white stars* ill. by Kadir Nelson. Dial, 2017. ISBN 978-080373700-6 Subj: Character traits – pride. Flags. U.S. history.

Boom boom ill. by Margaret Chodos-Irvine. Simon & Schuster/Beach Lane, 2014. ISBN 978-144243412-7 Subj: Noise, sounds. Rhyming text. Seasons.

Lines ill. by Melinda Beck. Simon & Schuster/Little Simon, 2017. ISBN 978-148149074-0 Subj: Concepts – shape. Format, unusual – board books.

Nadel, Carolina. *Daddy's home* ill. by author. Mookind, 2011. ISBN 978-0-9792761-4-9 Subj: Careers – military. Emotions – anger. Family life – fathers. War.

Naden, Corinne J. *Ron's big mission* by Corinne J. Naden and Rose Blue ill. by Don Tate. Dutton, 2009. ISBN 978-0-525-47849-2 Subj: Careers – astronauts. Ethnic groups in the U.S. – African Americans. Libraries. Prejudice. U.S. history.

Nadimi, Suzan. *The rich man and the parrot* ill. by Ande Cook. Albert Whitman, 2007. ISBN 978-0-8075-5059-5 Subj: Behavior – trickery. Birds – parakeets, parrots. Character traits – freedom. Folk & fairy tales. Foreign lands – Persia.

Nagda, Anne Whitehead. *A home for panda* ill. by Jim Effler. Soundprints, 2003. ISBN 978-1-59249-045-5 Subj: Animals – pandas. Foreign lands – China. Homes, houses.

A tiger tale ill. by Paul Kratter. Soundprints, 2003. ISBN 978-1-59249-042-4 Subj: Animals – tigers. Foreign lands – Nepal.

World above the clouds ill. by Paul Kratter. Soundprints, 2000. ISBN 978-1-56899-878-7 Subj: Animals – leopards. Foreign lands – Himalayas. Mountains. Science.

Nagel, Karen. *Shapes that roll* ill. by Steve Wilson. Blue Apple, 2009. ISBN 978-1-934706-81-7 Subj: Concepts – shape.

Nahas, Sylvaine. *Nicolo's unicorn* ill. by Bimba Landmann. Watson-Guptill, 2001. ISBN 978-0-8230-5580-7 Subj: Dreams. Mythical creatures – unicorns.

Nakagawa, Chihiro. *Who made this cake?* ill. by Junji Koyose. Front Street, 2008. ISBN 978-1-59078-595-9 Subj: Activities – baking, cooking. Character traits – smallness. Machines.

Nakagawa, Rieko. *Guri and Gura* by Rieko Nakagawa and Yuriko Yamawaki ill. by Yuriko Yamawaki. Tuttle, 2002. ISBN 978-0-8048-3352-3 Subj: Activities – baking, cooking. Animals – mice. Behavior – sharing. Eggs. Food. Problem solving.

Guri and Gura's special gift by Rieko Nakagawa and Yuriko Yamawaki ill. by Yuriko Yamawaki. Tuttle, 2002. ISBN 978-0-8048-3357-8 Subj: Activities – baking, cooking. Animals – mice. Behavior – sharing. Food.

Nakamura, Katherine Riley. *Song of night* ill. by Linnea Asplind Riley. Blue Sky, 2002. ISBN 978-0-439-26678-9 Subj: Animals. Animals – babies. Bedtime.

Nakawaki, Hatsue. *Wait! wait!* ill. by Komako Sakai. Enchanted Lion, 2013. ISBN 978-1-59270-138-4 Subj: Animals. Family life – fathers.

Namioka, Lensey. *Hungriest boy in the world* ill. by Aki Sogabe. Holiday, 2001. ISBN 978-0-8234-1542-7 Subj: Food. Foreign lands – Japan. Monsters.

Nanji, Shenaaz. *An alien in my house* ill. by Chum McLeod. Second Story, 2003. ISBN 978-1-896764-77-1 Subj: Character traits – being different. Family life – grandfathers. Old age.

Treasure for lunch ill. by Yvonne Cathcart. Second Story, 2000. ISBN 978-1-896764-32-0 Subj: Behavior – sharing. Food.

Napier, Matt. *Z is for zamboni* ill. by Melanie Rose. Sleeping Bear, 2002. ISBN 978-1-58536-065-9 Subj: ABC books. Sports – hockey.

Napoli, Donna Jo. *Albert* ill. by Jim LaMarche. Harcourt, 2001. ISBN 978-0-15-201572-5 Subj: Birds. Homes, houses.

Bobby the bold by Donna Jo Napoli and Eva Furrow ill. by Ard Hoyt. Penguin, 2006. ISBN 978-0-8037-2990-2 Subj: Animals – bonobos. Animals – chimpanzees. Character traits – appearance. Character traits – being different. Hair. Zoos.

The crossing ill. by Jim Madsen. Simon & Schuster, 2011. ISBN 978-1-4169-9474-9 Subj: Indians of North America – Shoshone. U.S. history – frontier & pioneer life.

Flamingo dream ill. by Cathie Felstead. Greenwillow, 2002. ISBN 978-0-688-17863-5 Subj: Death. Emotions. Emotions – grief. Family life – fathers. Illness – cancer.

Hands and hearts: with 15 words in American Sign Language ill. by Amy June Bates. Abrams, 2014. ISBN 978-141971022-3 Subj: Family life – mothers. Sea & seashore – beaches. Sign language.

Mama Miti: Wangari Maathai and the trees of Kenya ill. by Kadir Nelson. Simon & Schuster, 2010.

ISBN 978-1-4169-3505-6 Subj: Character traits – responsibility. Ecology. Foreign lands – Kenya. Trees.

Ready to dream by Donna Jo Napoli and Elena Furrow ill. by Bronwyn Bancroft. Bloomsbury, 2009. ISBN 978-1-59990-049-0 Subj: Art. Careers – artists. Dreams. Foreign lands – Australia.

Rocky, the cat who barks ill. by Tamara Petrosino. Dutton, 2002. ISBN 978-0-525-46544-7 Subj: Animals – cats. Animals – dogs. Friendship.

Take your time: a tale of Harriet, the Galápagos tortoise (Furrow, Eva)

The wishing club: a story about fractions ill. by Anna Currey. Henry Holt, 2007. ISBN 978-0-8050-7665-3 Subj: Behavior – wishing. Counting, numbers. Family life – brothers & sisters.

Narahashi, Keiko. *Two girls can!* ill. by author. Margaret K. McElderry, 2000. ISBN 978-0-689-82618-4 Subj: Friendship.

Nargi, Lela. *The honeybee man* ill. by Kyrsten Brooker. Random House, 2011. ISBN 978-0-375-84980-0 Subj: Careers – beekeepers. Insects – bees.

Nash, Ogden. *The adventures of Isabel* ill. by James Marshall. Little, 1991. ISBN 978-0-316-59874-3 Subj: Animals – bears. Character traits – bravery. Emotions – fear. Giants. Poetry. Witches.

The adventures of Isabel ill. by Bridget Starr Taylor. Sourcebooks/Jabberwocky, 2008. ISBN 978-1-4022-1027-3 Subj: Animals – bears. Character traits – bravery. Emotions – fear. Giants. Poetry. Witches.

Custard the dragon and the wicked knight ill. by Lynn Munsinger. Little, 1996. ISBN 978-0-316-59882-8 Subj: Character traits – bravery. Dragons. Knights. Poetry.

Nash, Sarah. *Purrfect!* ill. by Pamela Venus. Tamarind, 2010. ISBN 978-1-870516-86-0 Subj: Ethnic groups in the U.S. – African Americans. Toys.

Nash, Scott. *Tuff Fluff: the case of Duckie's missing brain* ill. by author. Candlewick, 2004. ISBN 978-0-7636-1882-7 Subj: Activities – storytelling. Careers – detectives. Mystery stories. Toys.

Näslund, Gorel Kristina. *Our apple tree* ill. by Kristina Digman. Macmillan, 2005. ISBN 978-1-59643-052-5 Subj: Food. Seasons. Trees.

Nastro, Caroline. *The bear who couldn't sleep* ill. by Vanya Nastanlieva. NorthSouth, 2016. ISBN 978-073584268-7 Subj: Animals – bears. Cities, towns. Hibernation.

Nathan, Emma. *What do you call a group of turkeys?* ill. with photos. Blackbirch, 2000. ISBN 978-1-

56711-357-0 Subj: Birds. Birds – turkeys. Language.

National Geographic Society [U.S.]. *National Geographic our world: a child's first picture atlas* ill. with photos. National Geographic, 2000. ISBN 978-0-7922-7576-3 Subj: Geography. Maps.

National Wildlife Federation. *My first book of animal opposites* ill. with photos. Imagine!, 2016. ISBN 978-162354062-3 Subj: Animals. Concepts – opposites. Format, unusual – board books.

My first book of baby animals ill. with photos. Imagine, 2014. ISBN 978-162354028-9 Subj: Animals – babies. Format, unusual – board books.

Naylor, Phyllis Reynolds. *Keeping a Christmas secret* ill. by Lena Shiffman. Macmillan, 1993. ISBN 978-0-689-71760-4 Subj: Behavior – secrets. Gifts. Holidays – Christmas.

King of the playground ill. by Nola Langner Malone. Atheneum, 1991. ISBN 978-0-689-31558-9 Subj: Activities – playing. Behavior – bullying, teasing. Friendship.

Please do feed the bears ill. by Ana López-Escrivá. Atheneum, 2002. ISBN 978-0-689-82561-3 Subj: Activities – picnicking. Animals – bears. Sea & seashore – beaches. Toys – bears.

Sweet strawberries ill. by Rosalind Charney Kaye. Atheneum, 1999. ISBN 978-0-689-81338-2 Subj: Behavior. Food. Stores.

Nazoa, Aquiles. *A small Nativity* ill. by Ana Palmero Caceres. Groundwood, 2007. ISBN 978-0-88899-839-2 Subj: Foreign lands – Venezuela. Holidays – Christmas. Religion – Nativity.

Neal, Christopher Silas. *Everyone* ill. by author. Candlewick, 2016. ISBN 978-076367683-4 Subj: Emotions.

I won't eat that ill. by author. Candlewick, 2017. ISBN 978-076367909-5 Subj: Animals – cats. Food.

Neal, Kate Jane. *Words and your heart* ill. by author. Feiwel & Friends, 2017. ISBN 978-125016872-6 Subj: Character traits – kindness. Self-concept.

Nedwidek, John. *Ducks don't wear socks* ill. by Lee White. Viking, 2008. ISBN 978-0-670-06136-5 Subj: Birds – ducks. Clothing. Humorous stories.

Neitzel, Shirley. *The bag I'm taking to Grandma's* ill. by Nancy Winslow Parker. Greenwillow, 1995. ISBN 978-0-688-12961-3 Subj: Activities – traveling. Cumulative tales. Rebuses. Rhyming text.

The dress I'll wear to the party ill. by Nancy Winslow Parker. Greenwillow, 1992. ISBN 978-0-688-09960-2 Subj: Clothing. Cumulative tales. Rebuses. Rhyming text.

The house I'll build for the wrens ill. by Nancy Winslow Parker. Greenwillow, 1997. ISBN 978-0-688-14974-1 Subj: Activities – making things. Birds. Cumulative tales. Homes, houses. Rebuses. Rhyming text. Tools.

I'm not feeling well today ill. by Nancy Winslow Parker. Greenwillow, 2001. ISBN 978-0-688-17381-4 Subj: Cumulative tales. Illness. Rebuses. Rhyming text. School.

I'm taking a trip on my train ill. by Nancy Winslow Parker. Greenwillow, 1999. ISBN 978-0-688-15834-7 Subj: Activities – playing. Cumulative tales. Imagination. Rebuses. Rhyming text. Trains.

The jacket I wear in the snow ill. by Nancy Winslow Parker. Greenwillow, 1989. ISBN 978-0-688-08030-3 Subj: Clothing. Cumulative tales. Rhyming text.

We're making breakfast for mother ill. by Nancy Winslow Parker. Greenwillow, 1997. ISBN 978-0-688-14576-7 Subj: Family life – mothers. Food. Rebuses. Rhyming text.

Who will I be? a Halloween rebus story ill. by Nancy Winslow Parker. HarperCollins, 2005. ISBN 978-0-06-056068-3 Subj: Clothing – costumes. Holidays – Halloween. Rebuses. Rhyming text.

Nelson, Kadir. *Baby Bear* ill. by author. HarperCollins/Balzer+Bray, 2014. ISBN 978-006224172-6 Subj: Animals. Animals – bears. Behavior – lost.

He's got the whole world in His hands ill. by author. Penguin, 2005. ISBN 978-0-8037-2850-9 Subj: Religion. Songs.

If you plant a seed ill. by author. HarperCollins/Balzer+Bray, 2015. ISBN 978-006229889-8 Subj: Animals. Character traits – cooperation. Character traits – kindness. Gardens, gardening. Seeds.

Nelson Mandela ill. by author. HarperCollins, 2013. ISBN 978-0-06-178374-6 Subj: Foreign lands – South Africa. Prejudice. Violence, nonviolence.

Nelson, Marilyn. *Beautiful ballerina* ill. by Susan Kuklin. Scholastic, 2009. ISBN 978-0-545-08920-3 Subj: Ballet.

Ostrich and Lark ill. by Kuru Art Project. Boyds Mills, 2012. ISBN 978-1-59078-702-1 Subj: Birds – larks. Birds – ostriches. Foreign lands – Africa.

Snook alone ill. by Timothy Basil Ering. Candlewick, 2010. ISBN 978-0-7636-2667-9 Subj: Animals – dogs. Character traits – loyalty. Friendship. Religion.

Nelson, Robert Lyn. *Ocean friends* ill. by author. NorthWord, 2003. ISBN 978-1-55971-840-0 Subj: Animals. Animals – dolphins. Sea & seashore.

Nelson, S. D. *Gift horse: a Lakota story* ill. by author. Abrams, 1999. ISBN 978-0-8109-4127-4 Subj: Animals – horses, ponies. Behavior – growing up. Indians of North America – Dakota (Sioux).

Quiet hero: the Ira Hayes story ill. by author. Lee & Low, 2006. ISBN 978-1-58430-263-6 Subj: Careers – military. Indians of North America – Pima. U.S. history.

The Star People ill. by author. Abrams, 2003. ISBN 978-0-8109-4584-5 Subj: Family life – brothers & sisters. Family life – grandmothers. Fire. Indians of North America – Lakota. Stars.

Nelson, Steve. *Frosty the snowman* by Steve Nelson and Jack Rollins ill. by Wade Zahares. Imagine, 2013. ISBN 978-1-62354-012-8 Subj: Music. Seasons – winter. Snowmen. Songs.

Nelson, Vaunda Micheaux. *Almost to freedom* ill. by Colin Bootman. Carolrhoda, 2003. ISBN 978-1-57505-342-4 Subj: Character traits – freedom. Ethnic groups in the U.S. – African Americans. Slavery. Toys – dolls.

The book itch: freedom, truth, and Harlem's greatest bookstore ill. by R. Gregory Christie. Carolrhoda, 2015. ISBN 978-076133943-4 Subj: Books, reading. Ethnic groups in the U.S. – African Americans. Stores.

Don't call me Grandma ill. by Elizabeth Zunon. Carolrhoda, 2016. ISBN 978-146774208-5 Subj: Ethnic groups in the U.S. – African Americans. Family life – great-grandparents. Old age.

Who will I be, Lord? ill. by Sean Qualls. Random House, 2009. ISBN 978-0-375-84342-6 Subj: Ethnic groups in the U.S. – African Americans. Religion. Self-concept.

Nelson-Schmidt, Michelle. *Cats, cats!* ill. by author. Kane/Miller, 2011. ISBN 978-1-61067-042-5 Subj: Animals – cats. Format, unusual. Pets.

Dogs, dogs! ill. by author. Kane/Miller, 2011. ISBN 978-1-61067-041-8 Subj: Animals – dogs. Format, unusual. Pets.

Nemiroff, Marc A. *Shy spaghetti and excited eggs: a kid's menu of feelings* by Marc A. Nemiroff and Jane Annunziata ill. by Christine Battuz. Magination, 2011. ISBN 978-1-4338-0956-9 Subj: Emotions.

Nesbitt, Kenn. *More bears!* ill. by Troy Cummings. Sourcebooks, 2010. ISBN 978-1-4022-3835-2 Subj: Animals – bears. Careers – writers. Humorous stories.

Ness, Evaline. *Sam, Bangs, and moonshine* ill. by author. Henry Holt, 1966. ISBN 978-0-606-01326-0 Subj: Caldecott award books. Imagination. Sports – fishing.

Nethery, Mary. *Two Bobbies: a true story of Hurricane Katrina, friendship, and survival* (Larson, Kirby)

Nettleton, Pamela Hill. *Abraham Lincoln* ill. by Becky Shipe. Picture Window, 2004. ISBN 978-1-4048-0185-1 Subj: U.S. history.

Benjamin Franklin ill. by Jeff Yesh. Picture Window, 2004. ISBN 978-1-4048-0186-8 Subj: Careers – inventors. Careers – printers. Careers – scientists. U.S. history.

George Washington ill. by Jeff Yesh. Picture Window, 2004. ISBN 978-1-4048-0184-4 Subj: Careers. Careers – farmers. Careers – military. U.S. history.

Martin Luther King, Jr ill. by Garry Nichols. Picture Window, 2004. ISBN 978-1-4048-0188-2 Subj: Careers – clergy. Ethnic groups in the U.S. – African Americans. Holidays – Martin Luther King, Jr. Day. Religion. U.S. history. Violence, nonviolence.

Pocahontas ill. by Jeff Yesh. Picture Window, 2004. ISBN 978-1-4048-0187-5 Subj: Indians of North America – Powhatan. U.S. history.

Sally Ride ill. by Becky Shipe. Picture Window, 2004. ISBN 978-1-4048-0189-9 Subj: Careers – astronauts. U.S. history.

Neubecker, Robert. *Beasty bath* ill. by author. Scholastic, 2005. ISBN 978-0-439-64000-8 Subj: Activities – bathing. Imagination. Monsters. Rhyming text.

Courage of the blue boy ill. by author. Ten Speed, 2006. ISBN 978-1-58246-182-3 Subj: Activities – traveling. Animals – bulls, cows. Concepts – color. Self-concept.

Fall is for school ill. by author. Disney/Hyperion, 2017. ISBN 978-148473254-0 Subj: Family life – brothers & sisters. Rhyming text. School – first day. Seasons – fall.

Linus the vegetarian T. rex ill. by author. Simon & Schuster, 2013. ISBN 978-1-4169-8512-9 Subj: Dinosaurs. Food. Museums.

What little boys are made of ill. by author. HarperCollins, 2012. ISBN 978-0-06-202355-1 Subj: Activities – playing. Imagination. Rhyming text.

Winter is for snow ill. by author. Disney/Hyperion, 2013. ISBN 978-1-4231-7831-6 Subj: Family life – brothers & sisters. Rhyming text. Seasons – winter. Weather – snow.

Wow! America! ill. by author. Hyperion, 2006. ISBN 978-0-7868-3816-5 Subj: U.S. history.

Wow! city! ill. by author. Hyperion, 2004. ISBN 978-0-7868-0951-6 Subj: Cities, towns.

Wow! ocean! ill. by author. Hyperion/Disney, 2011. ISBN 978-1-4231-3113-7 Subj: Sea & seashore.

Wow! school! ill. by author. Hyperion, 2007. ISBN 978-0-7868-3896-7 Subj: School – first day.

Neugebauer, Charise. *The real winner* ill. by Barbara Nascimbeni. NorthSouth, 2000. ISBN 978-0-7358-1253-6 Subj: Animals – hippopotamuses. Animals – raccoons. Contests.

Neuschwander, Cindy. *Amanda Bean's amazing dream* ill. by Liza Woodruff. Scholastic, 1998. ISBN 978-0-590-30012-4 Subj: Counting, numbers. Dreams. School.

Pastry school in Paris: an adventure in capacity ill. by Bryan Langdo. Henry Holt, 2009. ISBN 978-0-8050-8314-9 Subj: Activities – baking, cooking. Concepts. Family life – brothers & sisters. Foreign lands – France. Multiple births – twins.

Sir Cumference and all the king's tens: a math adventure ill. by Wayne Geehan. Charlesbridge, 2009. ISBN 978-1-57091-727-1 Subj: Birthdays. Counting, numbers. Knights. Royalty.

Nevius, Carol. *Baseball hour* ill. by Bill Thomson. Marshall Cavendish, 2008. ISBN 978-0-7614-5380-2 Subj: Rhyming text. Sports – baseball.

Building with Dad ill. by Bill Thomson. Marshall Cavendish, 2006. ISBN 978-0-7614-5312-3 Subj: Careers – construction workers. Rhyming text. School.

Karate hour ill. by Bill Thomson. Marshall Cavendish, 2004. ISBN 978-0-7614-5169-3 Subj: Rhyming text. Sports – karate.

Soccer hour ill. by Bill Thomson. Marshall Cavendish, 2011. ISBN 978-0-7614-5689-6 Subj: Rhyming text. Sports – soccer.

Newberry, Clare Turlay. *April's kittens* ill. by author. HarperCollins, 1940. ISBN 978-0-06-024401-9 Subj: Animals – cats. Caldecott award honor books. Pets.

Barkis ill. by author. HarperCollins, 1938. Subj: Animals – dogs. Caldecott award honor books. Pets.

Marshmallow ill. by author. HarperCollins, 1942. Subj: Animals – cats. Animals – rabbits. Caldecott award honor books. Friendship.

Newbery, Linda. *Posy* ill. by Catherine Rayner. Atheneum, 2009. ISBN 978-1-4169-7112-2 Subj: Animals – cats. Rhyming text.

Newcome, Zita. *Pop-up toddlerobics* ill. by author. Candlewick, 2002. ISBN 978-0-7636-1838-4 Subj: Activities – playing. Health & fitness. Rhyming text. Sports – gymnastics.

Newgarden, Mark. *Bow-Wow bugs a bug* by Mark Newgarden and Megan Montague Cash; ill. by authors. Harcourt, 2007. ISBN 978-0-15-205813-5 Subj: Animals – dogs. Insects. Wordless.

Bow-Wow orders lunch by Mark Newgarden and Megan Montague Cash; ill. by authors. Harcourt, 2007. ISBN 978-0-15-205829-6 Subj: Animals – dogs. Food. Format, unusual – board books.

Bow-Wow's nightmare neighbors by Mark Newgarden and Megan Montague Cash; ill. by Mark Newgarden. Roaring Brook, 2014. ISBN 978-159643640-4 Subj: Animals – cats. Animals – dogs. Character traits – bravery. Ghosts. Wordless.

Newhouse, Maxwell. *The house that Max built* ill. by author. Tundra, 2008. ISBN 978-0-88776-774-6 Subj: Buildings. Careers – construction workers. Homes, houses.

Newman, Barbara Johansen. *Glamorous glasses* ill. by author. Boyds Mills, 2012. ISBN 978-1-59078-878-3 Subj: Character traits – appearance. Family life – cousins. Glasses.

Newman, Jeff. *The boys* ill. by author. Simon & Schuster, 2010. ISBN 978-1-4169-5012-7 Subj: Character traits – shyness. Days of the week, months of the year. Old age. Sports – baseball. Wordless.

Hippo! No, rhino! ill. by author. Little, Brown, 2006. ISBN 978-0-316-15573-1 Subj: Animals – rhinoceros. Humorous stories.

Reginald ill. by author. Doubleday, 2003. ISBN 978-0-385-74634-2 Subj: Animals. Animals – bulls, cows. Jungle. Sports – swimming.

Newman, Lesléa. *Cats, cats, cats* ill. by Erika Oller. Simon & Schuster, 2001. ISBN 978-0-689-83077-8 Subj: Animals – cats. Night. Rhyming text.

Daddy, Papa, and me ill. by Carol Thompson. Tricycle, 2009. ISBN 978-1-58246-262-2 Subj: Family life – fathers. Family life – same-sex parents. Format, unusual – board books. LGBTQ.

Daddy's song ill. by Karen Ritz. Henry Holt, 2007. ISBN 978-0-8050-6975-4 Subj: Bedtime. Emotions – love. Family life – fathers. Lullabies. Rhyming text.

Dogs, dogs, dogs ill. by Erika Oller. Simon & Schuster, 2002. ISBN 978-0-698-84492-6 Subj: Activities. Animals – dogs. Counting, numbers. Rhyming text.

Donovan's big day ill. by Mike Dutton. Tricycle, 2011. ISBN 978-1-58246-332-2 Subj: Family life – mothers. LGBTQ. Weddings.

The eight nights of Chanukah ill. by Elivia Savadier. Abrams, 2005. ISBN 978-0-8109-5785-5 Subj: Holidays – Hanukkah. Jewish culture. Songs.

A fire engine for Ruthie ill. by Cyd Moore. Clarion, 2004. ISBN 978-0-618-15989-5 Subj: Activities – playing. Toys. Trucks.

Heather has two mommies ill. by Laura Cornell. Candlewick, 2015. ISBN 978-076366631-6 Subj: Family life – daughters. Family life – mothers. Family life – same-sex parents. LGBTQ.

Here is the world: a year of Jewish holidays ill. by Susan Gal. Abrams, 2014. ISBN 978-141971185-5 Subj: Holidays. Jewish culture.

Just like Mama ill. by Julia Gorton. Abrams, 2010. ISBN 978-0-8109-8393-9 Subj: Family life – mothers. Rhyming text.

Ketzel, the cat who composed ill. by Amy June Bates. Candlewick, 2015. ISBN 978-076366555-5 Subj: Animals – cats. Careers – composers. Character traits – kindness to animals. Friendship. Music. Musical instruments – pianos.

Matzo ball moon ill. by Elaine Greenstein. Clarion, 1998. ISBN 978-0-395-71530-7 Subj: Family life – grandmothers. Food. Holidays – Passover. Jewish culture. Religion.

Miss Tutu's star ill. by Carey Armstrong-Ellis. Abrams, 2010. ISBN 978-0-8109-8396-0 Subj: Ballet. Emotions – fear. Self-concept.

Mommy, Mama, and Me ill. by Carol Thompson. Tricycle, 2009. ISBN 978-1-58246-263-9 Subj: Family life – mothers. Family life – same-sex parents. Format, unusual – board books. LGBTQ.

Pigs, pigs, pigs ill. by Erika Oller. Simon & Schuster, 2003. ISBN 978-0-689-84979-4 Subj: Animals – pigs. Careers – entertainers. Rhyming text.

Runaway dreidel ill. by Kyrsten Brooker. Henry Holt, 2002. ISBN 978-0-8050-6237-3 Subj: Games. Holidays – Hanukkah. Jewish culture. Rhyming text.

Skunk's spring surprise ill. by Valeri Gorbachev. Harcourt, 2007. ISBN 978-0-15-205683-4 Subj: Animals. Animals – skunks. Friendship. Rhyming text. Seasons – spring.

Sparkle boy ill. by Maria Mola. Lee & Low, 2017. ISBN 978-162014285-1 Subj: Behavior – bullying, teasing. Family life – brothers & sisters. Gender identity.

A sweet Passover ill. by David Slonim. Abrams, 2012. ISBN 978-0-8109-9737-0 Subj: Activities – baking, cooking. Family life – grandfathers. Food. Holidays – Passover. Jewish culture.

Newman, Marjorie. *Just like me* ill. by Ken Wilson-Max. Walker, 2006. ISBN 978-0-8027-8080-5 Subj: Babies, toddlers. Family life – brothers & sisters. Family life – new sibling.

Mole and the baby bird ill. by Patrick Benson. Bloomsbury, 2002. ISBN 978-1-58234-784-4 Subj: Animals – moles. Birds. Emotions – love.

Newman, Marlene. *Myron's magic cow* ill. by Jago. Barefoot, 2005. ISBN 978-1-84148-496-9 Subj:

Animals – bulls, cows. Behavior – wishing. Folk & fairy tales. Magic.

Newman, Nanette. *What will you be, Grandma?* ill. by Emma Chichester Clark. Candlewick, 2012. ISBN 978-0-7636-6099-4 Subj: Family life – grandmothers. Imagination.

Newman, Tracy. *Shabbat hiccups* ill. by Ilana Exelby. Albert Whitman, 2016. ISBN 978-080757312-9 Subj: Hiccups. Jewish culture.

Newsome, Jill. *Dream dancer* ill. by Claudio Muñoz. HarperCollins, 2002. ISBN 978-0-06-000932-8 Subj: Activities – dancing. Ballet. Family life – grandmothers. Illness. Toys – dolls.

Newton, Jill. *Crash bang donkey!* ill. by author. Albert Whitman, 2010. ISBN 978-0-8075-1330-9 Subj: Animals – donkeys. Farms. Musical instruments. Noise, sounds.

Neyer, Andrew. *Letters are for learning* ill. by author. Blue Manatee, 2015. ISBN 978-193666937-0 Subj: ABC books. Format, unusual – board books.

Nez, John. *One smart Cookie* ill. by author. Albert Whitman, 2006. ISBN 978-0-8075-6099-0 Subj: Animals – dogs. Books, reading. Fire. School.

Nic Leodhas, Sorche *see* Alger, Leclaire Gowans

Nichol, Barbara. *Trunks all aboard* ill. by Sir William Cornelius Van Horne. Tundra, 2001. ISBN 978-0-88776-536-0 Subj: ABC books. Animals – elephants. Rhyming text.

Nicholls, Judith. *Billywise* ill. by Jason Cockcroft. Bloomsbury, 2002. ISBN 978-1-58234-778-3 Subj: Behavior – growing up. Birds – owls. Family life – mothers.

Someone I like: poems about people ill. by Giovanni Manna. Barefoot, 2000. ISBN 978-1-84148-004-6 Subj: Emotions. Family life. Friendship. Poetry.

Nichols, Grace. *Whoa, Baby, whoa!* ill. by Eleanor Taylor. Bloomsbury, 2012. ISBN 978-1-59990-742-0 Subj: Babies, toddlers.

Nichols, Lori. *Maple* ill. by author. Penguin/Nancy Paulsen, 2014. ISBN 978-039916085-1 Subj: Family life – new sibling. Friendship. Trees.

Maple and Willow apart ill. by author. Penguin/Nancy Paulsen, 2015. ISBN 978-039916753-9 Subj: Emotions – loneliness. Family life – sisters. School.

Maple and Willow together ill. by author. Penguin/Nancy Paulsen, 2014. ISBN 978-039916283-1 Subj: Behavior – fighting, arguing. Family life – sisters. Friendship. Nature.

Maple and Willow's Christmas tree ill. by author. Penguin/Nancy Paulsen, 2016. ISBN 978-039916756-0 Subj: Character traits – cleverness. Family life – sisters. Holidays – Christmas. Illness – allergies. Trees.

Nickle, John. *Alphabet explosion! Search and count from alien to zebra* ill. by author. Random House, 2006. ISBN 978-0-375-83598-8 Subj: ABC books. Counting, numbers. Picture puzzles. Wordless.

The ant bully ill. by author. Scholastic, 1999. ISBN 978-0-590-39591-5 Subj: Behavior – bullying, teasing. Concepts – size. Insects – ants.

TV Rex ill. by author. Scholastic, 2001. ISBN 978-0-439-12043-2 Subj: Emotions – grief. Family life – grandfathers. Imagination. Television.

Nidey, Kelli. *When autumn falls* ill. by Susan Swan. Albert Whitman, 2004. ISBN 978-0-8075-0490-1 Subj: Poetry. Seasons – fall.

Niekerk, Clarabelle van. *Understanding Sam and Asperger syndrome* by Clarabelle van Niekerk and Liezl Venter; ill. by Clarabelle van Niekerk. Skeezel, 2008. ISBN 978-0-9747217-1-2 Subj: Disabilities – Asperger's.

Nielsen, Laura. *Mrs. Muddle's holidays* ill. by Thomas Yezerski. Farrar, 2008. ISBN 978-0-374-35094-9 Subj: Communities, neighborhoods. Holidays.

Niemann, Christoph. *The pet dragon: a story about adventure, friendship, and Chinese characters* ill. by author. Greenwillow, 2008. ISBN 978-0-06-157776-5 Subj: Activities – writing. Dragons. Foreign lands – China. Foreign languages. Pets.

The police cloud ill. by author. Random House, 2007. ISBN 978-0-375-83963-4 Subj: Careers – police officers. Weather – clouds.

The potato king ill. by author. OwlKids, 2015. ISBN 978-177147139-8 Subj: Behavior – trickery. Food. Foreign lands. Royalty – kings.

Subway ill. by author. HarperCollins, 2010. ISBN 978-0-06-157779-6 Subj: Cities, towns. Family life – fathers. Rhyming text. Trains.

That's how! ill. by author. HarperCollins, 2011. ISBN 978-0-06-201963-9 Subj: Imagination. Machines. Trucks.

Nieminen, Lotta. *Pancakes! an interactive recipe book* ill. by author. Phaidon, 2016. ISBN 978-071487283-4 Subj: Activities – baking, cooking. Food. Format, unusual – board books. Participation.

Nijssen, Elfi. *Laurie* ill. by Eline van Lindenhuizen. Clavis, 2010. ISBN 978-1-60537-072-9 Subj: Disabilities – deafness.

Nikola-Lisa, W. *Bein' with you this way* ill. by Michael Bryant. Lee & Low, 1994. ISBN 978-1-880000-05-2 Subj: Activities – playing. Ethnic groups in the U.S. Ethnic groups in the U.S. – African Americans. Friendship. Poetry.

Can you top that? ill. by Hector Viveros Lee. Lee & Low, 2000. ISBN 978-1-880000-99-1 Subj: Activities – drawing. Animals. Counting, numbers.

Hallelujah! a Christmas celebration ill. by Synthia Saint James. Atheneum, 1999. ISBN 978-0-689-81673-4 Subj: Ethnic groups in the U.S. – African Americans. Holidays – Christmas. Religion – Nativity.

Magic in the margins: a medieval tale of bookmaking ill. by Bonnie Christensen. Houghton, 2007. ISBN 978-0-618-49642-6 Subj: Animals – mice. Art. Books, reading. Middle Ages.

One hole in the road ill. by Dan Yaccarino. Henry Holt, 1996. ISBN 978-0-8050-4285-6 Subj: Counting, numbers. Machines. Roads.

One, two, three Thanksgiving! ill. by Robin Kramer. Albert Whitman, 1991. ISBN 978-0-8075-6109-6 Subj: Counting, numbers. Family life. Holidays – Thanksgiving.

Shake dem Halloween bones ill. by Mike Reed. Houghton, 1997. ISBN 978-0-395-73095-9 Subj: Holidays – Halloween. Parties. Rhyming text.

Summer sun risin' ill. by Don Tate. Lee & Low, 2002. ISBN 978-1-58430-034-2 Subj: Ethnic groups in the U.S. – African Americans. Family life. Farms. Rhyming text.

To hear the angels sing ill. by Jill Weber. Holiday, 2002. ISBN 978-0-8234-1627-1 Subj: Holidays – Christmas. Religion – Nativity. Rhyming text.

The year with Grandma Moses ill. by Grandma Moses. Henry Holt, 2000. ISBN 978-0-8050-6243-4 Subj: Art. Careers – artists. Seasons.

Nimmo, Jenny. *Esmeralda and the children next door* ill. by Paul Howard. Houghton, 2000. ISBN 978-0-618-02902-0 Subj: Circus. Concepts – size. Friendship. Illness.

Something wonderful ill. by Debbie Boon. Harcourt, 2001. ISBN 978-0-15-216486-7 Subj: Birds – chickens, roosters. Character traits – being different.

Niner, Holly L. *I can't stop! a story about Tourette Syndrome* ill. by Meryl Treatner. Albert Whitman, 2005. ISBN 978-0-8075-3620-9 Subj: Disabilities.

Mr. Worry ill. by Greg Swearingen. Albert Whitman, 2004. ISBN 978-0-8075-5182-0 Subj: Behavior. Illness – mental illness.

Nipp, Susan Hagen. *Wee Sing if you're happy and you know it* (Beall, Pamela Conon)

Nishimura, Kae. *Bunny Lune* ill. by author. Houghton, 2007. ISBN 978-0-618-71606-7 Subj: Animals – rabbits. Moon.

Dinah ill. by author. Clarion, 2004. ISBN 978-0-618-33612-8 Subj: Animals – cats. Behavior – lost. Humorous stories. Self-concept.

Nishizuka, Koko. *The beckoning cat: based on a Japanese folktale* ill. by Rosanne Litzinger. Holiday, 2009. ISBN 978-0-8234-2051-3 Subj: Animals – cats. Character traits – luck. Folk & fairy tales. Foreign lands – Japan.

Nivola, Claire A. *The forest* ill. by author. Farrar, 2002. ISBN 978-0-374-32452-0 Subj: Animals – mice. Emotions – fear. Forest, woods.

Life in the ocean: the story of oceanographer Sylvia Earle ill. by author. Farrar, 2012. ISBN 978-0-374-38068-7 Subj: Careers – oceanographers. Ecology. Sea & seashore.

Orani: my father's village ill. by author. Farrar, 2011. ISBN 978-0-374-35657-6 Subj: Foreign lands – Italy. Memories, memory.

Planting the trees of Kenya: the story of Wangari Maathai ill. by author. Farrar, 2008. ISBN 978-0-374-39918-4 Subj: Ecology. Foreign lands – Kenya. Trees.

Nobisso, Josephine. *Grandpa loved* ill. by Maureen Hyde. 2nd ed. Gingerbread House, 2000. ISBN 978-0-940112-01-8 Subj: Death. Emotions – grief. Emotions – love. Family life – grandfathers.

John Blair and the great Hinckley fire ill. by Ted Rose. Houghton, 2000. ISBN 978-0-618-01560-3 Subj: Character traits – bravery. Ethnic groups in the U.S. – African Americans. Fire. Trains.

The moon's lullaby ill. by Glo Coalson. Orchard, 2001. ISBN 978-0-439-29312-9 Subj: Activities. Bedtime. Night. Sleep.

The weight of a Mass ill. by Katalin Szegedi. Gingerbread House, 2002. ISBN 978-0-940112-09-4 Subj: Religion. Royalty – kings. Royalty – queens. Weddings.

The yawn ill. by Glo Coalson. Orchard, 2001. ISBN 978-0-531-33319-8 Subj: Sleep.

Noble, Sheilagh. *More* ill. by author. Zero to Ten, 2000. ISBN 978-1-84089-127-0 Subj: Animals – dogs. Family life – mothers. Parks.

Noble, Trinka Hakes. *A Christmas spider's miracle* ill. by Stephen Costanza. Sleeping Bear, 2011. ISBN 978-1-58536-602-6 Subj: Folk & fairy tales. Holidays – Christmas. Spiders.

The day Jimmy's boa ate the wash ill. by Steven Kellogg. Dial, 1980. ISBN 978-0-8037-1724-4 Subj: Activities. Humorous stories. Reptiles – snakes. School – field trips.

Jimmy's boa and the big splash birthday bash ill. by Steven Kellogg. Dial, 1989. ISBN 978-0-8037-0540-1 Subj: Birthdays. Humorous stories. Pets. Reptiles – snakes.

Jimmy's boa bounces back ill. by Steven Kellogg. Dial, 1984. ISBN 978-0-8037-0049-9 Subj: Humorous stories. Reptiles – snakes.

Lizzie and the last day of school ill. by Kris Aro McLeod. Sleeping Bear, 2015. ISBN 978-158536895-2 Subj: School.

Nobleman, Marc Tyler. *The chupacabra ate the candelabra* ill. by Ana Aranda. Penguin/Nancy Paulsen, 2017. ISBN 978-039917443-8 Subj: Animals – goats. Food. Mythical creatures.

Nobles, Kristen M. *Drive this book* ill. by author. Chronicle, 2001. ISBN 978-0-8118-2861-1 Subj: Automobiles. Format, unusual – toy & movable books. Noise, sounds. Transportation. Trucks.

Noda, Takayo. *Dear world* ill. by author. Dial, 2002. ISBN 978-0-8037-2644-4 Subj: Nature. Poetry.

Song of the flowers ill. by author. Penguin, 2006. ISBN 978-0-8037-2934-6 Subj: Flowers. Lullabies.

Nogales, Jill. *Zebra on the go* ill. by Lorraine Rocha. Peachtree, 2017. ISBN 978-156145911-7 Subj: Animals – lions. Animals – zebras. Character traits – kindness to animals. Circus. Rhyming text.

Noguchi, Rick. *Flowers from Mariko* by Rick Noguchi and Deneen Jenks ill. by Michelle Reiko Kumata. Lee & Low, 2001. ISBN 978-1-58430-032-8 Subj: Ethnic groups in the U.S. – Japanese Americans. Gardens, gardening. U.S. history.

Nolan, Dennis. *Hunters of the great forest* ill. by author. Roaring Brook, 2014. ISBN 978-159643896-5 Subj: Sports – hunting. Wordless.

Sea of dreams ill. by author. Roaring Brook, 2011. ISBN 978-1-59643-470-7 Subj: Sand. Sea & seashore. Wordless.

Nolan, Janet. *A Father's Day thank you* ill. by Kathi Ember. Albert Whitman, 2007. ISBN 978-0-8075-2291-2 Subj: Animals – bears. Art. Family life – fathers. Gifts. Holidays – Father's Day.

The firehouse light ill. by Marie Lafrance. Tricycle, 2010. ISBN 978-1-58246-298-1 Subj: Careers – firefighters. Fire. U.S. history.

The St. Patrick's Day shillelagh ill. by Ben F. Stahl. Albert Whitman, 2002. ISBN 978-0-8075-7344-0 Subj: Activities – storytelling. Ethnic groups in the U.S. – Irish Americans. Foreign lands – Ireland. Holidays – St. Patrick's Day. Immigrants, immigration.

Nolan, Lucy A. *Jack Quack* ill. by Andréa Wesson. Marshall Cavendish, 2001. ISBN 978-0-7614-5091-

7 Subj: Animals – babies. Birds – ducks. Self-concept.

Nolan, Nina. *Mahalia Jackson: walking with kings and queens* ill. by John Holyfield. Amistad, 2015. ISBN 978-006087944-0 Subj: Careers – singers. Ethnic groups in the U.S. – African Americans. Music.

Nolen, Jerdine. *Big Jabe* ill. by Kadir Nelson. Lothrop, 2000. ISBN 978-0-688-13663-5 Subj: Ethnic groups in the U.S. – African Americans. Slavery. Tall tales.

Harvey Potter's balloon farm ill. by Mark Buehner. Lothrop, 1994. ISBN 978-0-688-07888-1 Subj: Farms. Magic. Tall tales. Toys – balloons.

Hewitt Anderson's great big life ill. by Kadir Nelson. Simon & Schuster, 2005. ISBN 978-0-689-86866-5 Subj: Character traits – smallness. Concepts – size. Family life. Giants.

In my momma's kitchen ill. by Colin Bootman. Lothrop, 1999. ISBN 978-0-688-12761-9 Subj: Activities – baking, cooking. Family life. Homes, houses.

Irene's wish ill. by A. G Ford. Simon & Schuster/ Paula Wiseman, 2014. ISBN 978-068986300-4 Subj: Behavior – wishing. Ethnic groups in the U.S. – African Americans. Family life – fathers. Gardens, gardening.

Pitching in for Eubie ill. by E. B. Lewis. Harper-Collins, 2007. ISBN 978-0-06-056960-0 Subj: Character traits – helpfulness. Ethnic groups in the U.S. – African Americans. Family life.

Plantzilla goes to camp ill. by David Catrow. Simon & Schuster, 2005. ISBN 978-0-689-86803-0 Subj: Behavior – bullying, teasing. Camps, camping. Humorous stories. Letters, cards. Plants.

Raising dragons ill. by Elise Primavera. Silver Whistle, 1998. ISBN 978-0-15-201288-5 Subj: Careers. Dragons. Eggs. Farms. Friendship.

Thunder Rose ill. by Kadir Nelson. Harcourt, 2003. ISBN 978-0-15-216472-0 Subj: Ethnic groups in the U.S. – African Americans. Tall tales. U.S. history – frontier & pioneer life.

Noll, Amanda. *I need my monster* ill. by Howard Mc-William. Flashlight, 2009. ISBN 978-0-9799746-2-5 Subj: Bedtime. Monsters.

Noonan, Diana. *The crocodile* ill. with photos. Chelsea, 2003. ISBN 978-0-7910-6964-6 Subj: Animals – endangered animals. Reptiles – alligators, crocodiles.

Noonan, Julia. *Bath day* ill. by author. Scholastic, 2000. ISBN 978-0-439-11492-9 Subj: Activities – bathing. Animals – dogs. Rhyming text.

Breakfast time ill. by author. Scholastic, 2000. ISBN 978-0-439-11490-5 Subj: Animals – dogs. Food. Rhyming text.

Hare and Rabbit, friends forever ill. by author. Scholastic, 2000. ISBN 978-0-439-08753-7 Subj: Animals – rabbits. Character traits – cleanliness. Circus. Friendship.

Mouse by mouse ill. by author. Dutton, 2003. ISBN 978-0-525-46864-6 Subj: Animals – mice. Counting, numbers. Format, unusual – toy & movable books. Rhyming text.

Norac, Carl. *Hello, sweetie pie* ill. by Claude K. Dubois. Random House, 2000. ISBN 978-0-385-32733-6 Subj: Animals – hamsters. Names. School.

I love to cuddle ill. by Claude K. Dubois. Double-day, 1999. ISBN 978-0-385-32646-9 Subj: Animals – hamsters. Emotions – loneliness. Format, unusual – board books.

I love you so much ill. by Claude K. Dubois. Dou-bleday, 1997. ISBN 978-0-385-32512-7 Subj: Animals – hamsters. Emotions – love. Family life.

Monster, don't eat me! ill. by Carll Cneut. Ground-wood, 2007. ISBN 978-0-88899-800-2 Subj: Animals – pigs. Behavior – greed. Food. Monsters.

My daddy is a giant ill. by Ingrid Godon. Clarion, 2005. ISBN 978-0-618-44399-4 Subj: Concepts – size. Family life – fathers.

My mommy is magic ill. by Ingrid Godon. Hough-ton, 2007. ISBN 978-0-618-75766-4 Subj: Family life – mothers. Magic.

Nordling, Lee. *Belinda the unbeatable* ill. by Scott Roberts. Lerner/Graphic Universe, 2017. ISBN 978-151241331-1 Subj: Format, unusual – graphic novels. Friendship. Games. Sportsmanship. Wordless.

The bramble ill. by Bruce Zick. Carolrhoda, 2013. ISBN 978-0-7613-5856-5 Subj: Format, unusual – graphic novels. Monsters. Self-concept.

Shehewe ill. by Meritxell Bosch. Lerner/Graphic Universe, 2015. ISBN 978-146774574-1 Subj: Activities – playing. Format, unusual – graphic novels. Gender roles. Parks.

Norling, Beth. *Sister night and sister day* ill. by author. Retelling of the Grimm's fairy tale Mother Holle. Allen & Unwin, 2000. ISBN 978-1-86448-863-0 Subj: Family life – sisters. Folk & fairy tales. Foreign lands – Germany. Multiple births – twins.

The stone baby ill. by author. Lothian, 2004. ISBN 978-0-7344-0353-7 Subj: Activities – traveling. Birds. Emotions. Toys – dolls.

Norman, Geoffrey. *Stars above us* ill. by E. B. Lewis. Putnam, 2009. ISBN 978-0-399-24724-8 Subj:

Careers – military. Emotions – fear. Family life – fathers. Stars.

Norman, Kim. *I know a wee piggy* ill. by Henry Cole. Dial, 2012. ISBN 978-0-8037-3735-8 Subj: Animals – pigs. Concepts – color. Cumulative tales. Fairs, festivals. Rhyming text.

If it's snowy and you know it, clap your paws! ill. by Liza Woodruff. Sterling, 2013. ISBN 978-1-4549-0384-0 Subj: Animals. Rhyming text. Seasons – winter. Songs. Weather – snow.

Puddle pug ill. by Keika Yamaguchi. Sterling, 2014. ISBN 978-145490436-6 Subj: Animals – dogs. Animals – pigs. Behavior – lost.

Still a gorilla! ill. by author. Orchard Scholastic, 2016. ISBN 978-054575791-1 Subj: Animals – gorillas. Rhyming text. Self-concept. Zoos.

Ten on the sled ill. by Liza Woodruff. Sterling, 2010. ISBN 978-1-4027-7076-0 Subj: Animals. Counting, numbers. Rhyming text. Seasons – winter. Sports – sledding.

Norris, Kathleen. *The holy twins: Benedict and Scholastica* ill. by Tomie dePaola. Putnam, 2001. ISBN 978-0-399-23424-8 Subj: Careers – clergy. Careers – nuns. Family life – brothers & sisters. Foreign lands – Italy. Multiple births – twins. Religion.

Norris, Leslie. *Albert and the angels* ill. by Mordicai Gerstein. Farrar, 2000. ISBN 978-0-374-30192-7 Subj: Angels. Animals – dogs. Behavior – lost & found possessions. Holidays – Christmas.

North, Sherry. *Because I am your daddy* ill. by Marcellus Hall. Abrams, 2010. ISBN 978-0-8109-8392-2 Subj: Family life – fathers. Rhyming text.

Because you are my baby ill. by Marcellus Hall. Abrams, 2008. ISBN 978-0-8109-9482-9 Subj: Babies, toddlers. Emotions – love. Family life – mothers. Rhyming text.

Champ's story: dogs get cancer too! ill. by Kathleen Rietz. Sylvan Dell, 2010. ISBN 978-1-60718-077-7 Subj: Animals – dogs. Illness – cancer.

Northey, Lawrence. *I'm a hop hop hoppity frog* ill. by Julie Northey. Stoddart, 2002. ISBN 978-0-7737-3335-0 Subj: Frogs & toads. Poetry. Rhyming text.

Norwich, William D. *Molly and the magic dress* ill. by M. Scott Miller. Doubleday, 2002. ISBN 978-0-385-32745-9 Subj: Animals – cats. Clothing – dresses. Emotions – loneliness. Imagination. Magic.

Norworth, Jack. *Take me out to the ball game* ill. by Amiko Hirao. Imagine, 2011. ISBN 978-1-936140-26-8 Subj: Songs. Sports – baseball.

Take me out to the ballgame: the sensational baseball song ill. by Jim Burke. Little, Brown, 2006. ISBN 978-0-316-75819-2 Subj: Songs. Sports – baseball.

Noullet, Georgette. *Bed hog* ill. by David Slonim. Marshall Cavendish, 2011. ISBN 978-0-7614-5823-4 Subj: Animals – dogs. Sleep.

Novak, B. J. *The book with no pictures.* Dial, 2014. ISBN 978-080374171-3 Subj: Books, reading. Humorous stories.

Novak, Jordan P. *Mosquitoes can't bite ninjas* ill. by Jordan P. Novak. Bloomsbury, 2017. ISBN 978-168119215-4 Subj: Insects – mosquitoes. Sports – martial arts.

Novak, Matt. *The everything machine* ill. by author. Roaring Brook, 2009. ISBN 978-1-59643-268-4 Subj: Character traits – cleanliness. Humorous stories. Machines.

Flip flop bop ill. by author. Macmillan, 2005. ISBN 978-1-59643-049-5 Subj: Clothing – shoes. Rhyming text. Seasons – summer.

Jazzbo and Googy ill. by author. Hyperion, 2000. ISBN 978-0-7868-2340-6 Subj: Animals – bears. Animals – pigs. Friendship. Toys – bears.

Jazzbo goes to school ill. by author. Hyperion, 1999. ISBN 978-0-7868-2339-0 Subj: Animals – bears. School – first day.

The last Christmas present ill. by author. Orchard, 1993. ISBN 978-0-531-08645-2 Subj: Holidays – Christmas. Mythical creatures – elves. Santa Claus.

No zombies allowed ill. by author. Atheneum, 2001. ISBN 978-0-689-84130-9 Subj: Holidays – Halloween. Parties. Witches.

The Pillow War ill. by author. Orchard, 1998. ISBN 978-0-531-33048-7 Subj: Animals – dogs. Behavior – fighting, arguing. Family life – brothers & sisters. Rhyming text. Sleep.

The Robobots ill. by author. DK, 1999. ISBN 978-0-7894-2566-9 Subj: Communities, neighborhoods. Robots.

Too many bunnies ill. by author. Macmillan, 2005. ISBN 978-1-59643-038-9 Subj: Animals – rabbits. Format, unusual – toy & movable books.

A wish for you ill. by author. HarperCollins, 2010. ISBN 978-0-06-155202-1 Subj: Babies, toddlers. Family life. Rhyming text.

Novesky, Amy. *Georgia in Hawaii: when Georgia O'Keeffe painted what she pleased* ill. by Yuyi Morales. Harcourt, 2012. ISBN 978-0-15-205420-5 Subj: Careers – artists. Character traits – assertiveness. Hawaii.

Love is a truck ill. by Sara Gillingham. Cameron Kids, 2016. ISBN 978-193735986-7 Subj: Format, unusual – board books. Trucks.

Natumi takes the lead: the true story of an orphan elephant who finds family (Ellis, Gerry)

Noyes, Deborah. *When I met the wolf girls* ill. by August Hall. Houghton, 2007. ISBN 978-0-618-60567-5 Subj: Foreign lands – India. Orphans.

Numberman, Neil. *Do not build a Frankenstein!* ill. by author. HarperCollins, 2009. ISBN 978-0-06-156816-9 Subj: Humorous stories. Monsters. Moving.

Numeroff, Laura Joffe. *The Chicken sisters* ill. by Sharleen Collicott. Geringer, 1997. ISBN 978-0-06-026680-6 Subj: Animals. Birds – chickens, roosters. Family life – sisters. Farms.

Chimps don't wear glasses ill. by Joe Mathieu. Simon & Schuster, 1995. ISBN 978-0-671-87007-2 Subj: Activities. Animals. Imagination. Rhyming text.

Happy Valentine's Day, Mouse! ill. by Felicia Bond. HarperCollins/Balzer+Bray, 2015. ISBN 978-006242740-3 Subj: Animals – mice. Format, unusual – board books. Friendship. Holidays – Valentine's Day.

The hope tree by Laura Joffe Numeroff and Wendy Schlessel Harpham ill. by David McPhail. Simon & Schuster, 1999. ISBN 978-0-689-84526-0 Subj: Animals. Emotions. Family life – mothers. Illness – cancer.

If you give a cat a cupcake ill. by Felicia Bond. HarperCollins, 2008. ISBN 978-0-06-028324-7 Subj: Animals – cats. Character traits – kindness to animals. Circular tales.

If you give a dog a donut ill. by Felicia Bond. HarperCollins, 2011. ISBN 978-0-06-026683-7 Subj: Animals – dogs. Character traits – kindness to animals. Circular tales.

If you give a moose a muffin ill. by Felicia Bond. HarperCollins, 1991. ISBN 978-0-06-024406-4 Subj: Animals – moose. Character traits – kindness to animals. Circular tales.

If you give a mouse a cookie ill. by Felicia Bond. HarperCollins, 1985. ISBN 978-0-06-024587-0 Subj: Animals – mice. Behavior – imitation. Character traits – kindness to animals. Circular tales.

If you give a pig a pancake ill. by Felicia Bond. Geringer, 1998. ISBN 978-0-06-026687-5 Subj: Animals – pigs. Character traits – kindness to animals. Circular tales.

If you give a pig a party ill. by Felicia Bond. HarperCollins, 2005. ISBN 978-0-06-028327-8 Subj: Animals – pigs. Circular tales. Parties.

If you take a mouse to school ill. by Felicia Bond. Geringer, 2002. ISBN 978-0-06-028329-2 Subj: Animals – mice. School.

If you take a mouse to the movies ill. by Felicia Bond. Geringer, 2000. ISBN 978-0-06-027868-7 Subj: Activities. Animals – mice. Holidays – Christmas.

The Jellybeans and the big art adventure by Laura Joffe Numeroff and Nate Evans ill. by Lynn Munsinger. Abrams, 2012. ISBN 978-1-4197-0171-9 Subj: Activities – painting. Animals. Character traits – cooperation. Friendship.

The Jellybeans and the big book bonanza by Laura Joffe Numeroff and Nate Evans ill. by Lynn Munsinger. Abrams, 2010. ISBN 978-0-8109-8412-7 Subj: Animals. Books, reading. Friendship. Libraries.

The Jellybeans and the big camp kickoff by Laura Joffe Numeroff and Nate Evans ill. by Lynn Munsinger. Abrams, 2011. ISBN 978-0-8109-9765-3 Subj: Animals. Camps, camping. Character traits – cooperation. Friendship.

The Jellybeans and the big dance by Laura Joffe Numeroff and Nate Evans ill. by Lynn Munsinger. Abrams, 2008. ISBN 978-0-8109-9352-5 Subj: Animals. Ballet. Character traits – cooperation.

Laura Numeroff's 10-step guide to living with your monster ill. by Nate Evans. Geringer, 2002. ISBN 978-0-06-623823-4 Subj: Humorous stories. Monsters. Pets.

Merry Christmas, Mouse! ill. by Felicia Bond. HarperCollins, 2007. ISBN 978-0-06-134499-2 Subj: Animals – mice. Counting, numbers. Holidays – Christmas.

Nighty-night, Cooper ill. by Lynn Munsinger. Houghton Mifflin, 2013. ISBN 978-0-547-40205-5 Subj: Animals – kangaroos. Bedtime. Family life – mothers. Lullabies.

Otis and Sydney and the best birthday ever ill. by Dan Andreasen. Abrams, 2010. ISBN 978-0-8109-8959-7 Subj: Animals – bears. Birthdays. Friendship. Parties.

Ponyella by Laura Joffe Numeroff and Nate Evans ill. by Lynn Munsinger. Hyperion/Disney, 2011. ISBN 978-1-4231-0259-5 Subj: Animals – horses, ponies. Fairies. Folk & fairy tales. Royalty – princesses.

Sherman Crunchley by Laura Joffe Numeroff and Nate Evans ill. by Tim Bowers. Dutton, 2003. ISBN 978-0-525-47130-1 Subj: Animals – dogs. Careers – police officers. Character traits – individuality. Clothing – hats.

Sometimes I wonder if poodles like noodles ill. by Tim Bowers. Simon & Schuster, 1999. ISBN 978-0-689-80563-9 Subj: Humorous stories. Poetry.

What brothers do best ill. by Lynn Munsinger. Chronicle, 2012. ISBN 978-1-4521-1073-8 Subj:

Family life – brothers. Format, unusual – board books.

What brothers do best; What sisters do best ill. by Lynn Munsinger. Chronicle, 2009. ISBN 978-0-8118-6545-6 Subj: Character traits – helpfulness. Family life – brothers & sisters.

What daddies do best ill. by Lynn Munsinger. Simon & Schuster, 2002. ISBN 978-0-689-84466-9 Subj: Animals – foxes. Buildings. Cities, towns. Family life – fathers. Gender roles.

What grandmas do best; What grandpas do best ill. by Lynn Munsinger. Simon & Schuster, 2000. ISBN 978-0-689-80552-3 Subj: Animals. Family life – grandfathers. Family life – grandmothers. Format, unusual.

What mommies do best ill. by Lynn Munsinger. Simon & Schuster, 1998. ISBN 978-0-689-80577-6 Subj: Activities – picnicking. Animals – mice. Gender roles.

What puppies do best ill. by Lynn Munsinger. Chronicle, 2011. ISBN 978-0-8118-6601-9 Subj: Activities. Animals – babies. Animals – dogs.

When sheep sleep ill. by David McPhail. Abrams, 2006. ISBN 978-0-8109-5469-4 Subj: Animals. Animals – sheep. Bedtime. Counting, numbers. Rhyming text.

Why a disguise? ill. by David McPhail. Simon & Schuster, 1996. ISBN 978-0-671-87006-5 Subj: Character traits – appearance.

Would I trade my parents? ill. by James Bernardin. Abrams, 2009. ISBN 978-0-8109-0637-2 Subj: Family life – parents.

Nunes, Susan Miho. *The last dragon* ill. by Chris Soentpiet. Clarion, 1995. ISBN 978-0-395-67020-0 Subj: Dragons. Ethnic groups in the U.S. – Chinese Americans. Family life – aunts, uncles.

Nye, Naomi Shihab. *Come with me: poems for a journey* ill. by Dan Yaccarino. Greenwillow, 2000. ISBN 978-0-688-15947-4 Subj: Activities – traveling. Poetry.

Sitti's secrets ill. by Nancy Carpenter. Four Winds, 1994. ISBN 978-0-02-768460-5 Subj: Ethnic groups in the U.S. – Arab Americans. Family life – grandmothers. Foreign lands – Palestine. Foreign languages.

Nyeu, Tao. *Bunny days* ill. by author. Penguin, 2010. ISBN 978-0-8037-3330-5 Subj: Animals – babies. Animals – bears. Animals – rabbits.

Squid and Octopus: friends for always ill. by author. Dial, 2012. ISBN 978-0-8037-3565-1 Subj: Friendship. Octopuses. Squid.

Nygaard, Elizabeth. *Snake alley band* ill. by Betsy Lewin. Doubleday, 1998. ISBN 978-0-385-32323-

9 Subj: Animals. Music. Musical instruments – bands. Noise, sounds. Reptiles – snakes.

Ó Flatharta, Antoine. *Hurry and the monarch* ill. by Meilo So. Knopf, 2005. ISBN 978-0-375-93003-4 Subj: Friendship. Insects – butterflies, caterpillars. Migration. Reptiles – turtles, tortoises.

Obama, Barack. *Change has come: an artist celebrates our American spirit* ill. by Kadir Nelson. Simon & Schuster, 2009. ISBN 978-1-4169-8955-4 Subj: Ethnic groups in the U.S. – African Americans. U.S. history.

Of thee I sing: a letter to my daughters ill. by Loren Long. Random House, 2010. ISBN 978-0-375-83527-8 Subj: Character traits. Self-concept. U.S. history.

Obed, Ellen Bryan. *Who would like a Christmas tree?* ill. by Anne Hunter. Houghton, 2009. ISBN 978-0-547-04625-9 Subj: Days of the week, months of the year. Holidays – Christmas. Trees.

Oberman, Sheldon. *The always prayer shawl* ill. by Ted Lewin. Boyds Mills, 1994. ISBN 978-1-878093-22-6 Subj: Clothing. Family life – grandfathers. Immigrants, immigration. Jewish culture.

By the Hanukkah light ill. by Neil Waldman. Boyds Mills, 1997. ISBN 978-1-56397-658-2 Subj: Family life – grandfathers. Holidays – Hanukkah. Holocaust. War.

The wisdom bird: a tale of Solomon and Sheba ill. by Neil Waldman. Boyds Mills, 2000. ISBN 978-1-56397-816-6 Subj: Birds. Character traits – wisdom. Folk & fairy tales. Foreign lands – Africa. Foreign lands – Israel. Royalty – kings. Royalty – queens.

Oborne, Martine. *One beautiful baby* ill. by Ingrid Godon. Little, 2002. ISBN 978-0-316-06562-7 Subj: Babies, toddlers.

O'Brien, Anne Sibley. *Abracadabra, it's spring!* ill. by Susan Gal. Abrams/Appleseed, 2016. ISBN 978-141971891-5 Subj: Format, unusual – toy & movable books. Nature. Rhyming text. Seasons – spring.

Hocus pocus, it's fall! ill. by Susan Gal. Abrams/Appleseed, 2016. ISBN 978-141972125-0 Subj: Format, unusual – toy & movable books. Nature. Rhyming text. Seasons – fall.

I'm new here ill. by author. Charlesbridge, 2015. ISBN 978-158089612-2 Subj: Ethnic groups in the U.S. – Guatemalan Americans. Ethnic groups in the U.S. – Korean Americans. Ethnic groups in the U.S. – Somali Americans. Immigrants, immigration. School.

A path of stars ill. by author. Charlesbridge, 2012. ISBN 978-1-57091-735-6 Subj: Character traits – perseverance. Death. Emotions – grief. Ethnic groups in the U.S. – Cambodian Americans. Family life – grandmothers. Memories, memory. War.

O'Brien, Patrick. *Captain Raptor and the space pirates* (O'Malley, Kevin)

Gigantic! how big were the dinosaurs? ill. by author. Henry Holt, 1999. ISBN 978-0-8050-5738-6 Subj: Concepts – size. Dinosaurs.

Megatooth ill. by author. Henry Holt, 2001. ISBN 978-0-8050-6214-4 Subj: Fish – sharks. Teeth.

Sabertooth ill. by author. Henry Holt, 2008. ISBN 978-0-8050-7105-4 Subj: Animals – tigers. Dinosaurs. Prehistory.

You are the first kid on Mars ill. by author. Putnam, 2009. ISBN 978-0-399-24634-0 Subj: Planets. Space & space ships.

O'Callahan, Jay. *Raspberries!* ill. by Will Moses. Philomel, 2009. ISBN 978-0-399-25181-8 Subj: Careers – bakers. Character traits – kindness. Character traits – perseverance. Food.

Ochiltree, Dianne. *It's a firefly night* ill. by Betsy E Snyder. Blue Apple, 2013. ISBN 978-1-60905-291-1 Subj: Family life – fathers. Insects – fireflies. Night. Rhyming text.

Molly, by golly! the legend of Molly Williams, America's first female firefighter ill. by Kathleen Kemly. Boyds Mills, 2012. ISBN 978-1-59078-721-2 Subj: Careers – chefs, cooks. Careers – firefighters. Ethnic groups in the U.S. – African Americans. Gender roles. U.S. history.

Pillow pup ill. by Mireille d' Allancé. Margaret K. McElderry, 2002. ISBN 978-0-689-83408-0 Subj: Activities – playing. Animals – dogs. Rhyming text.

O'Connell, Jennifer. *It's Halloween night!* ill. by Jennifer Morris. Scholastic, 2012. ISBN 978-0-545-40283-5 Subj: Clothing – costumes. Holidays – Halloween.

O'Connell, Rebecca. *Baby parade* ill. by Susie Poole. Albert Whitman, 2013. ISBN 978-0-8075-0509-0 Subj: Babies, toddlers. Family life.

Baby party ill. by Susie Poole. Albert Whitman, 2015. ISBN 978-080750512-0 Subj: Babies, toddlers. Concepts – shape. Parties.

Danny is done with diapers: a potty ABC ill. by Amanda Gulliver. Albert Whitman, 2010. ISBN 978-0-8075-1466-5 Subj: ABC books. Toilet training.

O'Connor, George. *If I had a raptor* ill. by author. Candlewick, 2014. ISBN 978-076366012-3 Subj: Dinosaurs. Ethnic groups in the U.S. – African Americans. Pets.

If I had a triceratops ill. by author. Candlewick, 2015. ISBN 978-076366013-0 Subj: Dinosaurs. Pets.

Ker-splash! ill. by author. Simon & Schuster, 2005. ISBN 978-0-689-87682-0 Subj: Activities – playing. Behavior – bullying, teasing. Imagination. Sea & seashore.

Sally and the Some-Thing ill. by author. Macmillan, 2006. ISBN 978-1-59643-141-6 Subj: Friendship. Monsters.

Uncle Bigfoot ill. by author. Roaring Brook, 2008. ISBN 978-1-59643-271-0 Subj: Anatomy – feet. Character traits – being different. Family life – aunts, uncles. Giants.

O'Connor, Jane. *Bonjour, butterfly* ill. by Robin Preiss-Glasser. HarperCollins, 2008. ISBN 978-0-06-123588-7 Subj: Birthdays. Insects – butterflies, caterpillars. Parties.

Fancy Nancy ill. by Robin Preiss-Glasser. HarperCollins, 2006. ISBN 978-0-06-054209-2 Subj: Clothing. Family life. Self-concept.

Fancy Nancy: aspiring artist ill. by Robin Preiss-Glasser. HarperCollins, 2011. ISBN 978-0-06-191526-0 Subj: Activities – drawing. Art. Language.

Fancy Nancy: explorer extraordinaire! ill. by Robin Preiss-Glasser. HarperCollins, 2009. ISBN 978-0-06-168486-9 Subj: Birds. Clubs, gangs. Insects. Language. Nature.

Fancy Nancy: fanciest doll in the universe ill. by Robin Preiss-Glasser. HarperCollins, 2013. ISBN 978-0-06-170384-3 Subj: Behavior – misbehavior. Family life – sisters. Toys – dolls.

Fancy Nancy: ooh la la! it's beauty day ill. by Robin Preiss-Glasser. HarperCollins, 2010. ISBN 978-0-06-191525-3 Subj: Beauty shops. Birthdays. Language. Self-concept.

Fancy Nancy: poet extraordinaire! ill. by Robin Preiss-Glasser. HarperCollins, 2010. ISBN 978-0-06-189643-9 Subj: Activities – writing. Poetry. School.

Fancy Nancy and the fabulous fashion boutique ill. by Robin Preiss-Glasser. HarperCollins, 2010. ISBN 978-0-06-123592-4 Subj: Character traits – generosity. Family life – sisters. Language. Money.

Fancy Nancy and the posh puppy ill. by Robin Preiss-Glasser. HarperCollins, 2012. ISBN 978-0-06-

221052-4 Subj: Animals – dogs. Character traits – appearance. Family life. Self-concept.

Fancy Nancy and the wedding of the century ill. by Robin Preiss Glasser. HarperCollins, 2014. ISBN 978-006208319-7 Subj: Character traits – compromising. Weddings.

Fancy Nancy splendiferous Christmas ill. by Robin Preiss-Glasser. HarperCollins, 2009. ISBN 978-0-06-123590-0 Subj: Family life. Holidays – Christmas. Language.

Fancy Nancy's collection of fancy words: from accessories to zany ill. by Robin Preiss-Glasser. HarperCollins, 2008. ISBN 978-0-06-154923-6 Subj: ABC books. Language.

Nancy la elegante / Fancy Nancy ill. by Robin Preiss-Glasser. HarperCollins, 2008. ISBN 978-0-06-143528-7 Subj: Clothing. Family life. Foreign languages. Self-concept.

The perfect puppy for me ill. by Jessie Hartland. Viking, 2003. ISBN 978-0-670-03614-1 Subj: Animals – dogs. Pets.

Ready or not, here comes Scout (Abramson, Jill)

Ready, set, skip! ill. by Ann James. Penguin, 2007. ISBN 978-0-670-06216-4 Subj: Activities. Character traits – persistence. Rhyming text. Self-concept.

The snow globe family ill. by S. D. Schindler. Penguin, 2006. ISBN 978-0-399-24242-7 Subj: Family life.

O'Connor, Teddy. *A new brain for Igor* ill. by Bill Basso. Random House, 2003. ISBN 978-0-375-90626-8 Subj: Anatomy – brain. Careers – scientists.

Odanaka, Barbara. *A crazy day at the Critter Café* ill. by Lee White. Simon & Schuster, 2009. ISBN 978-1-4169-3914-6 Subj: Animals. Restaurants. Rhyming text.

Smash! mash! crash! there goes the trash! ill. by Will Hillenbrand. Simon & Schuster, 2006. ISBN 978-0-689-85160-5 Subj: Animals – pigs. Careers – sanitation workers. Rhyming text. Trucks.

Oddino, Licia. *Finn and the fairies* ill. by Alessandra Toni. Purple Bear, 2006. ISBN 978-1-933327-17-4 Subj: Careers – tailors. Fairies.

Odgers, Sally. *Good night, Truck* ill. by Heath McKenzie. Feiwel & Friends, 2016. ISBN 978-125007019-7 Subj: Bedtime. Machines. Rhyming text. Trucks.

Odone, Jamison. *Honey badgers* ill. by author. Boyds Mills, 2007. ISBN 978-1-932425-51-2 Subj: Animals – badgers. Orphans.

Mole had everything ill. by author. Blue Apple, 2012. ISBN 978-1-60905-224-9 Subj: Animals – moles. Behavior – seeking better things. Character traits – orderliness. Self-concept.

Oelschlager, Vanita. *Bonyo Bonyo: the true story of a brave boy from Kenya* ill. by Kristin Blackwood. Vanita, 2010. ISBN 978-0-9819714-3-8 Subj: Careers – doctors. Foreign lands – Kenya.

I came from the water: one Haitian boy's incredible tale of survival ill. by Mike Blanc. Vanita, 2012. ISBN 978-0-9832904-4-5 Subj: Earthquakes. Foreign lands – Haiti. Illness. Orphans. Weather – floods.

Made in China: a story of adoption ill. by Kristin Blackwood. Vanita, 2008. ISBN 978-0-9800162-3-9 Subj: Adoption. Ethnic groups in the U.S. – Chinese Americans. Family life. Rhyming text. Sibling rivalry.

A tale of two daddies ill. by Kristin Blackwood. Vanita, 2010. ISBN 978-0-9819714-5-2 Subj: Family life – fathers. LGBTQ.

A tale of two mommies ill. by Mike Blanc. Vanita, 2011. ISBN 978-0-9826366-6-4 Subj: Family life – mothers. LGBTQ.

Ofanansky, Allison. *Harvest of light* ill. by Eliyahu Alpern. Lerner, 2008. ISBN 978-0-8225-7389-0 Subj: Food. Foreign lands – Israel. Holidays – Hanukkah.

Offill, Jenny. *11 experiments that failed* ill. by Nancy Carpenter. Random House, 2011. ISBN 978-0-375-84762-2 Subj: Careers – scientists. Character traits – questioning. Science.

17 things I'm not allowed to do anymore ill. by Nancy Carpenter. Random House, 2006. ISBN 978-0-375-83596-4 Subj: Behavior – misbehavior.

Sparky! ill. by Chris Appelhans. Random House, 2014. ISBN 978-037587023-1 Subj: Animals – sloths. Pets.

While you were napping ill. by Barry Blitt. Random House, 2014. ISBN 978-037586572-5 Subj: Family life – brothers & sisters. Imagination. Sleep.

Ogburn, Jacqueline K. *The bake shop ghost* ill. by Marjorie Priceman. Houghton, 2005. ISBN 978-0-618-44557-8 Subj: Careers – bakers. Food. Ghosts.

Little treasures ill. by Chris Raschka. Houghton Mifflin, 2012. ISBN 978-0-547-42862-8 Subj: Foreign languages. Language. World.

The magic nesting doll ill. by Laurel Long. Dial, 2000. ISBN 978-0-8037-2414-3 Subj: Family life – grandmothers. Folk & fairy tales. Magic. Royalty – tsars. Toys – dolls.

Oh, Jiwon. *Cat and mouse* ill. by author. HarperCollins, 2003. ISBN 978-0-06-052744-0 Subj: Animals – cats. Animals – mice. Friendship.

O'Hair, Margaret. *My kitten* ill. by Tammie Lyon. Marshall Cavendish, 2011. ISBN 978-0-7614-5811-1 Subj: Animals – babies. Animals – cats. Rhyming text.

My pup ill. by Tammie Lyon. Marshall Cavendish, 2008. ISBN 978-0-7614-5389-5 Subj: Animals – dogs. Rhyming text.

Star baby ill. by Erin Eitter Kono. Houghton, 2005. ISBN 978-0-618-30668-8 Subj: Babies, toddlers. Rhyming text.

Sweet baby feet ill. by Tracy Dockray. Farrar, 2012. ISBN 978-0-374-37348-1 Subj: Anatomy – feet. Babies, toddlers. Rhyming text.

O'Hara, Natalia. *Hortense and the shadow* ill. by Lauren O'Hara. Little, Brown, 2017. ISBN 978-031644079-0 Subj: Imagination. Shadows.

Ohi, Debbie Ridpath. *Sam and Eva* ill. by author. Simon & Schuster, 2017. ISBN 978-148141628-3 Subj: Activities – drawing. Character traits – cooperation. Imagination.

Where are my books? ill. by author. Simon & Schuster, 2015. ISBN 978-144246741-5 Subj: Animals – squirrels. Behavior – lost & found possessions. Books, reading.

Ohi, Ruth. *And you can come too* ill. by author. Annick, 2005. ISBN 978-1-55037-905-1 Subj: Activities – playing. Behavior – running away. Family life.

Chicken, Pig, Cow and the class pet ill. by author. Annick, 2011. ISBN 978-1-55451-347-5 Subj: Animals – bulls, cows. Animals – hamsters. Animals – pigs. Birds – chickens, roosters. School. Toys.

Chicken, Pig, Cow horse around ill. by author. Annick, 2010. ISBN 978-1-55451-245-4 Subj: Animals – bulls, cows. Animals – horses, ponies. Animals – pigs. Birds – chickens, roosters. Toys.

Chicken, Pig, Cow's first fight ill. by author. Annick, 2012. ISBN 978-1-55451-371-0 Subj: Animals – bulls, cows. Animals – pigs. Behavior – fighting, arguing. Birds – chickens, roosters.

Clara and the Bossy ill. by author. Annick, 2006. ISBN 978-1-55037-943-3 Subj: Animals – guinea pigs. Behavior – bossy. Friendship.

The couch was a castle ill. by author. Annick, 2006. ISBN 978-1-55451-014-6 Subj: Animals – guinea pigs. Family life – brothers & sisters. Imagination.

Kenta and the big wave ill. by author. Annick, 2013. ISBN 978-1-55451-577-6 Subj: Behavior – lost & found possessions. Foreign lands – Japan. Tsunamis.

Me and my brother ill. by author. Annick, 2007. ISBN 978-1-55451-091-7 Subj: Family life – brothers & sisters. Rhyming text.

Me and my sister ill. by author. Annick, 2005. ISBN 978-1-55037-892-4 Subj: Family life – brothers & sisters. Rhyming text.

Pants off first ill. by author. Fitzhenry & Whiteside, 2001. ISBN 978-1-55041-667-1 Subj: Bedtime. Clothing. Family life – mothers. Format, unusual – board books. Pets.

A trip with Grandma ill. by author. Annick, 2007. ISBN 978-1-55451-072-6 Subj: Activities – traveling. Animals – guinea pigs. Behavior – worrying. Family life – brothers & sisters. Family life – grandmothers.

Ohmura, Tomoko. *The long, long line* ill. by author. OwlKids, 2013. ISBN 978-1-926973-92-0 Subj: Animals. Concepts – size. Counting, numbers.

OHora, Zachariah. *My cousin Momo* ill. by author. Dial, 2015. ISBN 978-080374011-2 Subj: Animals – squirrels. Character traits – being different. Character traits – individuality. Family life – cousins.

No fits, Nilson! ill. by author. Dial, 2013. ISBN 978-0-8037-3852-2 Subj: Animals – gorillas. Emotions – anger.

The not so quiet library ill. by author. Dial, 2016. ISBN 978-080374140-9 Subj: Animals – bears. Books, reading. Careers – librarians. Libraries. Monsters.

Stop snoring, Bernard! ill. by author. Henry Holt, 2011. ISBN 978-0-8050-9002-4 Subj: Animals – otters. Sleep – snoring. Zoos.

O'Keefe, Susan Heyboer. *Baby day* ill. by Robin Spowart. Boyds Mills, 2006. ISBN 978-1-59078-981-0 Subj: Activities – playing. Animals – bears. Babies, toddlers. Family life. Rhyming text.

Good night, God bless ill. by Hideko Takahashi. Henry Holt, 1999. ISBN 978-0-8050-6008-9 Subj: Bedtime. Religion. Rhyming text.

Hungry monster ABC ill. by Lynn Munsinger. Little, Brown, 2007. ISBN 978-0-316-15574-8 Subj: ABC books. Monsters. Rhyming text.

Love me, love you ill. by Robin Spowart. Boyds Mills, 2001. ISBN 978-1-56397-837-1 Subj: Animals – rabbits. Emotions – love. Family life – mothers. Rhyming text.

One hungry monster ill. by Lynn Munsinger. Little, 1989. ISBN 978-0-316-63385-7 Subj: Counting, numbers. Food. Monsters. Poetry.

Okimoto, Jean Davies. *The White Swan express* by Jean Davies Okimoto and Elaine M. Aoki ill. by Meilo So. Clarion, 2002. ISBN 978-0-618-16453-0 Subj: Adoption. Babies, toddlers. Ethnic groups in the U.S. – Chinese Americans. Family life – parents. Foreign lands – China.

Olaleye, Isaac. *Bikes for rent!* ill. by Chris L. Demarest. Orchard, 2001. ISBN 978-0-531-33290-0 Subj: Foreign lands – Nigeria. Sports – bicycling.

Bitter bananas ill. by Ed Young. Caroline House, 1994. ISBN 978-1-56397-039-9 Subj: Animals – baboons. Character traits – cleverness. Food. Foreign lands – Africa. Foreign lands – Nigeria. Problem solving.

The distant talking drum ill. by Frané Lessac. Wordsong, 1995. ISBN 978-1-56397-095-5 Subj: Foreign lands – Nigeria. Poetry.

In the Rainfield: who is the greatest? ill. by Ann Grifalconi. Blue Sky, 2000. ISBN 978-0-590-48363-6 Subj: Contests. Folk & fairy tales. Foreign lands – Nigeria. Nature. Weather – rain. Weather – wind.

Lake of the Big Snake ill. by Claudia Shepard. Boyds Mills, 1998. ISBN 978-1-56397-096-2 Subj: Foreign lands – Africa. Forest, woods. Reptiles – snakes.

Old MacDonald had a farm. *Grandma's nursery rhymes: Old MacDonald* ill. by Petra Brown. Sleeping Bear, 2015. ISBN 978-158536609-5 Subj: Animals. Careers – farmers. Cumulative tales. Farms. Format, unusual – board books. Music. Songs.

Old MacDonald retold by Rosemary Wells; ill. by reteller. Scholastic, 1998. ISBN 978-0-590-76985-3 Subj: Animals. Careers – farmers. Cumulative tales. Farms. Songs.

Old MacDonald had a farm ill. by Holly Berry. NorthSouth, 1994. ISBN 978-1-55858-282-8 Subj: Animals. Careers – farmers. Cumulative tales. Farms. Music. Songs.

Old MacDonald had a farm by Jane Cabrera; ill. by author. Holiday, 2008. ISBN 978-0-8234-2141-1 Subj: Animals. Careers – farmers. Cumulative tales. Farms. Music. Songs.

Old MacDonald had a farm ill. by Carol Jones. Houghton, 1989. ISBN 978-0-395-49212-3 Subj: Animals. Careers – farmers. Cumulative tales. Farms. Format, unusual. Music. Songs.

Old MacDonald had a farm ill. by Tracey Campbell Pearson. Dial, 1984. ISBN 978-0-8037-0070-3 Subj: Animals. Careers – farmers. Cumulative tales. Farms. Music. Songs.

Old MacDonald had a farm ill. by Glen Rounds. Holiday, 1989. ISBN 978-0-8234-0739-2 Subj: Animals. Careers – farmers. Cumulative tales. Farms. Music. Songs.

Old MacDonald had a farm retold by Jessica Souhami; designed by Paul McAlinden; ill. by reteller. Orchard, 1996. ISBN 978-0-531-09493-8 Subj: Animals. Careers – farmers. Cumulative tales. Farms. Format, unusual – toy & movable books. Songs. Transportation.

Old MacDonald had a farm ill. by Prue Theobalds. Peter Bedrick, 1991. ISBN 978-0-87226-452-6 Subj: Animals. Careers – farmers. Cumulative tales. Farms. Music. Songs.

Old MacDonald had a truck by Steve Goetz; ill. by Eda Kaban. Chronicle, 2016. ISBN 978-145213260-0 Subj: Animals. Careers – farmers. Cumulative tales. Farms. Machines. Songs. Trucks.

Old MacDonald's things that go by Jane Clarke; ill. by Migy Blanco. Candlewick/Nosy Crow, 2017. ISBN 978-076369326-8 Subj: Farms. Rhyming text. Songs. Tractors. Transportation. Trucks.

Pete the Cat: Old MacDonald had a farm ill. by James Dean. HarperCollins, 2014. ISBN 978-006219873-0 Subj: Animals. Careers – farmers. Cumulative tales. Farms. Music. Songs.

The old woman and her pig. *The old woman and her pig* adapt. by Eric A. Kimmel; ill. by Giyora Karmi. Holiday, 1992. ISBN 978-0-8234-0970-9 Subj: Cumulative tales. Folk & fairy tales.

The old woman and her pig: an Appalachian folktale retold by Margaret Read MacDonald; ill. by John Kanzler. HarperCollins, 2007. ISBN 978-0-06-028090-1 Subj: Cumulative tales. Folk & fairy tales.

Older, Effin. *My two grandmothers* ill. by Nancy Hayashi. Harcourt, 2000. ISBN 978-0-15-200785-0 Subj: Family life – grandmothers. Holidays – Christmas. Holidays – Hanukkah. Parties.

Older, Jules. *Telling time: how to tell time on digital and analog clocks* ill. by Megan Halsey. Charlesbridge, 2000. ISBN 978-0-88106-396-7 Subj: Clocks, watches. Time.

Oldland, Nicholas. *Big bear hug* ill. by author. Kids Can, 2009. ISBN 978-1-55453-464-7 Subj: Animals – bears. Ecology. Hugging. Trees.

The busy beaver ill. by author. Kids Can, 2011. ISBN 978-1-55453-749-5 Subj: Animals – beavers. Behavior – carelessness.

Dinosaur countdown ill. by author. Kids Can, 2012. ISBN 978-1-55453-834-8 Subj: Counting, numbers. Dinosaurs.

Making the moose out of life ill. by author. Kids Can, 2010. ISBN 978-1-55453-580-4 Subj: Animals – moose. Friendship. Reptiles – turtles, tortoises.

Up the creek ill. by author. Kids Can, 2013. ISBN 978-1-894786-32-4 Subj: Animals. Canoes & canoeing.

Walk on the wild side ill. by author. Kids Can, 2015. ISBN 978-177138109-3 Subj: Activities – hiking. Animals – bears. Animals – beavers. Animals – moose. Contests. Friendship.

O'Leary, Sara. *A family is a family is a family* ill. by Qin Leng. Groundwood, 2016. ISBN 978-155498794-8 Subj: Foster children, foster homes.

This is Sadie ill. by Julie Morstad. Tundra, 2015. ISBN 978-177049532-6 Subj: Activities – storytelling. Books, reading. Imagination.

When you were small ill. by Julie Morstad. Simply Read, 2006. ISBN 978-1-894965-36-1 Subj: Character traits – smallness. Concepts – size. Family life – fathers. Imagination.

Olfers, Sibylle Von. *When the root children wake up* (Wood, Audrey)

Olien, Jessica. *Adrift: an odd couple of polar bears* ill. by author. HarperCollins/Balzer+Bray, 2017. ISBN 978-006245177-4 Subj: Animals – polar bears. Character traits – individuality. Friendship. Self-concept.

The blobfish book ill. by author. HarperCollins/Balzer+Bray, 2016. ISBN 978-006239415-6 Subj: Character traits – appearance. Fish. Sea & seashore.

Shark Detective! ill. by author. HarperCollins/Balzer+Bray, 2015. ISBN 978-006235714-4 Subj: Animals – cats. Behavior – lost & found possessions. Careers – detectives. Fish – sharks. Mystery stories.

Oliver, Lin. *Little poems for tiny ears* ill. by Tomie dePaola. Penguin/Nancy Paulsen, 2014. ISBN 978-039916605-1 Subj: Babies, toddlers. Poetry.

Oliver, Narelle. *Twilight hunt: a seek-and-find book* ill. by author. Star Bright, 2007. ISBN 978-1-59572-107-5 Subj: Behavior – hiding. Birds – owls. Disguises. Nature. Picture puzzles.

Olivera, Ramon. *ABCs on wheels* ill. by author. Simon & Schuster/Little Simon, 2016. ISBN 978-148143244-3 Subj: ABC books. Automobiles. Transportation.

ABCs on wings ill. by author. Simon & Schuster, 2015. ISBN 978-148143242-9 Subj: ABC books. Airplanes, airports.

Oller, Erika. *The cabbage soup solution* ill. by author. Dutton, 2004. ISBN 978-0-525-47005-2 Subj: Animals – cats. Animals – rabbits. Farms. Food. Humorous stories.

Olofsson, Helena. *The little jester* ill. by author. R&S Books, 2002. ISBN 978-91-29-65499-8 Subj: Books, reading. Careers – clergy. Clowns, jesters. Foreign lands – France. Middle Ages.

Olsen, Sylvia. *Yetsa's sweater* ill. by Joan Larson. Sono Nis, 2006. ISBN 978-1-55039-155-8 Subj: Animals – sheep. Clothing – sweaters. Foreign lands – British Columbia. Indians of North America.

Olshan, Matthew. *The mighty Lalouche* ill. by Sophie Blackall. Random House, 2013. ISBN 978-0-375-86225-0 Subj: Careers – postal workers. Foreign lands – France. Sports – boxing.

A voyage in the clouds: the (mostly) true story of the first international flight by balloon in 1785 ill. by Sophie Blackall. Farrar, 2016. ISBN 978-037432954-9 Subj: Activities – ballooning.

Olson, David J. *The thunderstruck stork* ill. by Lynn Munsinger. Albert Whitman, 2007. ISBN 978-0-8075-7910-7 Subj: Animals. Animals – babies. Birds – storks. Rhyming text.

Olson, Jennifer Gray. *Me and Mr. Fluffernutter* ill. by author. Knopf, 2017. ISBN 978-038575496-5 Subj: Animals – cats. Friendship.

Ninja Bunny ill. by author. Knopf, 2015. ISBN 978-038575493-4 Subj: Animals – rabbits. Friendship. Sports – martial arts.

Ninja Bunny: sister vs. brother ill. by author. Knopf, 2016. ISBN 978-039955074-4 Subj: Animals – rabbits. Family life – brothers & sisters. Sports – martial arts.

Olson, Julie. *Tickle, tickle! itch, twitch!* ill. by author. Marshall Cavendish, 2010. ISBN 978-0-7614-5714-5 Subj: Animals – groundhogs. Animals – mice.

Olson, Laura. *Clayton's path* (Bishop, Brett)

Olson, Mary. *An alligator ate my brother* ill. by Tammie Lyon. Boyds Mills, 2000. ISBN 978-1-56397-803-6 Subj: Family life – brothers. Reptiles – alligators, crocodiles.

Nice try, Tooth Fairy ill. by Katherine Tillotson. Simon & Schuster, 2000. ISBN 978-0-689-82422-7 Subj: Fairies. Letters, cards. Teeth.

Olson, Nathan. *Animal patterns* ill. with photos. Capstone, 2006. ISBN 978-0-7368-6728-3 Subj: Animals. Concepts – patterns.

Olson-Brown, Ellen. *Hush little digger* ill. by Lee White. Ten Speed, 2006. ISBN 978-1-58246-160-1 Subj: Machines. Music. Trucks.

Ooh la la polka-dot boots ill. by Christiane Engel. Tricycle, 2010. ISBN 978-1-58246-287-5 Subj: Clothing – boots. Format, unusual. Rhyming text.

O'Malley, Kevin. *Animal crackers fly the coop* ill. by author. Walker, 2010. ISBN 978-0-8027-9837-4 Subj: Animals. Humorous stories. Language.

Bud ill. by author. Walker, 2000. ISBN 978-0-8027-8719-4 Subj: Animals – rhinoceros. Character traits – orderliness. Family life – grandfathers. Gardens, gardening.

Captain Raptor and the moon mystery ill. by Patrick O'Brien. Walker, 2005. ISBN 978-0-8027-8935-8 Subj: Aliens. Dinosaurs. Space & space ships.

Captain Raptor and the space pirates by Kevin O'Malley and Patrick O'Brien ill. by Patrick O'Brien. Walker, 2007. ISBN 978-0-8027-9571-7 Subj: Dinosaurs. Pirates. Space & space ships.

Congratulations, Miss Malarkey! (Finchler, Judy)

Gimme cracked corn and I will share ill. by author. Walker, 2007. ISBN 978-0-8027-9684-4 Subj: Birds – chickens, roosters. Humorous stories.

The great race ill. by author. Walker, 2011. ISBN 978-0-8027-2158-7 Subj: Animals – rabbits. Folk & fairy tales. Reptiles – turtles, tortoises. Sports – racing.

Humpty Dumpty egg-splodes ill. by author. Walker, 2001. ISBN 978-0-8027-8757-6 Subj: Character traits – meanness. Emotions – anger. Nursery rhymes.

Leo Cockroach . . . toy tester ill. by author. Walker, 1999. ISBN 978-0-8027-8690-6 Subj: Insects – cockroaches. Toys.

Little Buggy ill. by author. Harcourt, 2002. ISBN 978-0-15-216339-6 Subj: Activities – flying. Family life – fathers. Insects – ladybugs.

Little Buggy runs away ill. by author. Harcourt, 2003. ISBN 978-0-15-216550-5 Subj: Behavior – fighting, arguing. Behavior – running away. Family life – fathers. Insects – ants. Insects – ladybugs.

Miss Malarkey leaves no reader behind (Finchler, Judy)

Once upon a cool motorcycle dude ill. by author and Carol Heyer, et al. Walker, 2005. ISBN 978-0-8027-8949-5 Subj: Activities – writing. Giants. Motorcycles. Royalty – princesses.

Once upon a royal superbaby ill. by author and Carol Heyer. Walker, 2010. ISBN 978-0-8027-2164-8 Subj: Activities – writing. Babies, toddlers. Royalty.

The perfect dog ill. by author. Crown, 2016. ISBN 978-110193441-8 Subj: Animals – dogs. Pets.

Roller coaster ill. by author. Lothrop, 1995. ISBN 978-0-688-13972-8 Subj: Fairs, festivals.

Straight to the pole ill. by author. Walker, 2003. ISBN 978-0-8027-8868-9 Subj: Imagination. School. Weather – snow.

Velcome ill. by author. Walker, 1997. ISBN 978-0-8027-8629-6 Subj: Activities – storytelling. Holidays – Halloween. Monsters.

O'Mara, Carmel. *Good morning* ill. by author. Harcourt, 2000. ISBN 978-0-15-202135-1 Subj: Activities. Animals – bears. Family life – parents. Morning.

Good night ill. by author. Harcourt, 2000. ISBN 978-0-15-202136-8 Subj: Activities. Animals – bears. Family life – parents.

Rainy day ill. by author. Harcourt, 2001. ISBN 978-0-15-201934-1 Subj: Activities – playing. Animals – bears. Animals – rabbits. Format, unusual – board books. Friendship. Weather – rain.

Sunny day ill. by author. Harcourt, 2001. ISBN 978-0-15-202066-8 Subj: Activities – playing. Animals – bears. Animals – rabbits. Format, unusual – board books. Weather.

Ommen, Sylvia van. *The surprise* ill. by author. Boyds Mills, 2007. ISBN 978-1-932425-85-7 Subj: Animals – giraffes. Animals – sheep. Gifts. Wordless.

Omololu, Cynthia Jaynes. *When it's six o'clock in San Francisco: a trip through time zones* ill. by Randy DuBurke. Clarion, 2009. ISBN 978-0-618-76827-1 Subj: Time. World.

One, two, skip a few! ill. by Roberta Arenson. Barefoot, 1998. ISBN 978-1-901223-99-6 Subj: Counting, numbers. Nursery rhymes. Rhyming text.

O'Neill, Alexis. *Estela's swap* ill. by Enrique O. Sánchez. Lee & Low, 2002. ISBN 978-1-58430-044-1 Subj: Activities – trading. Ethnic groups in the U.S. – Mexican Americans. Family life – fathers. Money. Stores.

Loud Emily ill. by Nancy Carpenter. Simon & Schuster, 1998. ISBN 978-0-689-81078-7 Subj: Animals – whales. Boats, ships. Noise, sounds. Sailors.

The Recess Queen ill. by Laura Huliska-Beith. Scholastic, 2002. ISBN 978-0-439-20637-2 Subj: Behavior – bullying, teasing. School.

O'Neill, Gemma. *Monty's magnificent mane* ill. by author. Candlewick, 2015. ISBN 978-076367593-6 Subj: Animals – lions. Animals – meerkats. Character traits – appearance. Friendship. Reptiles – alligators, crocodiles.

Oh dear, Geoffrey! ill. by author. Candlewick, 2014. ISBN 978-076366659-0 Subj: Animals – giraffes. Character traits – clumsiness. Foreign lands – Africa. Friendship.

O'Neill, Rachael. *Can't, don't, won't* (Davies, Gill)

Tiny's big wish (Davies, Gill)

Wilbur waited (Davies, Gill)

O'Neill, Richard. *Yokki and the Parno Gry* by Richard O'Neill and Katharine Quarmby ill. by Marieke Nelissen. Child's Play, 2017. ISBN 978-184643927-8 Subj: Animals – horses, ponies. Folk & fairy tales. Magic. Romani.

Onishi, Satoru. *Who's hiding* ill. by author. Kane/Miller, 2007. ISBN 978-1-933605-24-1 Subj: Animals. Disguises. Picture puzzles.

Onyefulu, Ifeoma. *An African Christmas* photos by author. Frances Lincoln, 2005. ISBN 978-1-84507-387-9 Subj: Foreign lands – Africa. Holidays – Christmas.

Deron goes to nursery school photos by author. Frances Lincoln, 2010. ISBN 978-1-84507-864-5 Subj: Foreign lands – Ghana. School – first day. School – nursery.

Grandma comes to stay photos by author. Frances Lincoln, 2010. ISBN 978-1-84507-865-7 Subj: Family life – grandmothers. Foreign lands – Ghana.

Ife's first haircut photos by author. Frances Lincoln, 2014. ISBN 978-184780364-1 Subj: Foreign lands – Nigeria. Hair.

Ogbo: sharing life in an African village photos by author. Gulliver, 1996. ISBN 978-0-15-200498-9 Subj: Foreign lands – Nigeria.

Omer's favorite place photos by author. Frances Lincoln, 2011. ISBN 978-1-84780-241-5 Subj: Activities – playing. Family life. Foreign lands – Ethiopia.

Saying goodbye photos by author. Millbrook, 2001. ISBN 978-0-7613-1965-8 Subj: Death. Emotions – grief. Foreign lands – Nigeria.

A triangle for Adaora photos by author. Dutton, 2000. ISBN 978-0-525-46382-5 Subj: Concepts – shape. Foreign lands – Africa.

Onyefulu, Obi. *Chinye* ill. by Evie Safarewicz. Viking, 1994. ISBN 978-0-670-85115-7 Subj: Folk & fairy tales. Foreign lands – Africa.

Oppel, Kenneth. *The king's taster* ill. by Steve Johnson and Lou Fancher. HarperCollins, 2009. ISBN 978-0-06-075372-6 Subj: Animals – dogs. Food. Royalty.

Peg and the whale ill. by Terry Widener. Simon & Schuster, 2000. ISBN 978-0-689-82423-4 Subj: Animals – whales. Boats, ships. Sports – fishing. Tall tales.

Oppenheim, Joanne. *The Christmas witch* ill. by Annie Mitra. G. Stevens, 1997. ISBN 978-0-8368-1697-6 Subj: Folk & fairy tales. Holidays – Christmas. Religion – Nativity. Witches.

Have you seen bugs? ill. by Ron Broda. Scholastic, 1997. ISBN 978-0-590-05963-3 Subj: Insects. Rhyming text. Spiders.

Have you seen trees? ill. by Jean Tseng and Mou-Sien Tseng. Scholastic, 1995. ISBN 978-0-590-46691-2 Subj: Poetry. Seasons. Trees.

Oppenheim, Shulamith Levey. *Ali and the magic stew* ill. by Winslow Pels. Boyds Mills, 2002. ISBN 978-1-56397-869-2 Subj: Careers – beggars. Family life – fathers. Foreign lands – Iran. Illness.

Fireflies for Nathan ill. by John Ward. Tambourine, 1994. ISBN 978-0-688-12148-8 Subj: Ethnic groups in the U.S. – African Americans. Family life – grandparents. Insects – fireflies.

I love you, Bunny Rabbit ill. by Cyd Moore. Boyds Mills, 1995. ISBN 978-1-56397-322-2 Subj: Emotions – love. Toys.

Oram, Hiawyn. *Baba Yaga and the wise doll* ill. by Ruth Brown. Dutton, 1998. ISBN 978-0-525-45947-7 Subj: Behavior – trickery. Folk & fairy tales. Foreign lands – Russia. Toys – dolls. Witches.

Badger's bad mood ill. by Susan Varley. Scholastic, 1998. ISBN 978-0-590-18920-0 Subj: Animals. Animals – badgers. Animals – moles. Behavior – bad day, bad mood. Friendship.

Gerda the goose ill. by David Melling. Barron's, 2000. ISBN 978-0-7641-1484-7 Subj: Birds – geese.

Going to Grandpa's ill. by Frédéric Joos. Dutton, 2001. ISBN 978-0-525-46701-4 Subj: Animals – bears. Family life – grandfathers. Trains.

Just Dog ill. by Lisa Flather. Chronicle, 1998. ISBN 978-0-8118-2247-3 Subj: Animals – cats. Animals – dogs. Self-concept.

Kiss it better ill. by Frédéric Joos. Dutton, 2000. ISBN 978-0-525-46386-3 Subj: Animals – bears. Behavior – bad day, bad mood. Emotions – love. Kissing.

My friend Fred ill. by Rosie Reeve. Tiger Tales, 2012. ISBN 978-1-58925-105-2 Subj: Animals – dogs. Behavior – sharing. Friendship.

The wrong overcoat ill. by Mark Birchall. Carolrhoda, 2000. ISBN 978-1-57505-453-7 Subj: Animals – chimpanzees. Character traits – individuality. Clothing – coats. Self-concept.

Ørdal, Stina Langlo. *Princess Aasta* ill. by author. Bloomsbury, 2002. ISBN 978-1-58234-783-7 Subj: Animals – bears. Animals – polar bears. Behavior – resourcefulness. Friendship. Royalty – kings. Royalty – princesses.

Orgel, Doris. *The cat's tale: why the years are named for animals* ill. by Meilo So. Roaring Brook, 2008. ISBN 978-1-59643-202-4 Subj: Animals. Folk & fairy tales. Foreign lands – China. Zodiac.

Orgill, Roxane. *If I only had a horn* ill. by Leonard Jenkins. Houghton, 1997. ISBN 978-0-395-75919-6 Subj: Careers – musicians. Ethnic groups in the U.S. – African Americans. Musical instruments – bands. Musical instruments – trumpets. U.S. history.

Skit-scat raggedy cat: Ella Fitzgerald ill. by Sean Qualls. Candlewick, 2010. ISBN 978-0-7636-1733-2 Subj: Careers – singers. Ethnic groups in the U.S. – African Americans. Music.

Orlean, Susan. *Lazy little loafers* ill. by G. Brian Karas. Abrams, 2008. ISBN 978-0-8109-7027-4 Subj: Babies, toddlers. Humorous stories. Sibling rivalry.

Orloff, Karen Kaufman. *I wanna go home* ill. by David Catrow. Putnam, 2014. ISBN 978-039925407-9 Subj: Family life – grandparents. Letters, cards. Old age.

I wanna new room ill. by David Catrow. Penguin, 2010. ISBN 978-0-399-25405-5 Subj: Behavior – sharing. Family life. Homes, houses. Letters, cards.

Miles of smiles ill. by Luciano Lozano. Sterling, 2016. ISBN 978-145491699-4 Subj: Anatomy – faces. Character traits – kindness.

Ormerod, Jan. *The baby swap* ill. by Andrew Joyner. Simon & Schuster, 2015. ISBN 978-148141914-7 Subj: Activities – trading. Emotions – envy, jealousy. Family life – brothers & sisters. Family life – new sibling. Reptiles – alligators, crocodiles. Stores.

If you're happy and you know it! by Jan Ormerod and Lindsey Gardiner ill. by Lindsey Gardiner. Star Bright, 2003. ISBN 978-1-932065-07-7 Subj: Animals. Emotions – happiness. Rhyming text.

Maudie and Bear ill. by Freya Blackwood. Putnam, 2012. ISBN 978-0-399-25709-4 Subj: Animals – bears. Friendship.

Miss Mouse takes off ill. by author. HarperCollins, 2001. ISBN 978-0-688-17871-0 Subj: Activities – traveling. Airplanes, airports. Toys – dolls.

Miss Mouse's day ill. by author. HarperCollins, 2001. ISBN 978-0-688-16334-1 Subj: Activities – playing. Animals – mice. Toys.

Molly and her dad ill. by Carol Thompson. Roaring Brook, 2008. ISBN 978-1-59643-285-7 Subj: Family life – fathers. School.

Ms. MacDonald has a class ill. by author. Clarion, 1996. ISBN 978-0-395-77611-7 Subj: Animals. Cumulative tales. Farms. Rhyming text. School. Songs. Theater.

When an elephant comes to school ill. by author. Scholastic, 2005. ISBN 978-0-439-73967-2 Subj: Animals – elephants. School – first day.

When we went to the zoo ill. by author. Lothrop, 1991. ISBN 978-0-688-09879-7 Subj: Animals. Zoos.

Who's whose? ill. by author. Lothrop, 1998. ISBN 978-0-688-14679-5 Subj: Activities. Family life.

Ormondroyd, Edward. *Theodore* ill. by Juli Kangas. Dial, 2009. ISBN 978-0-8037-3163-9 Subj: Character traits – appearance. Character traits – kindness. Laundry. Toys – bears.

Orona-Ramirez, Kristy. *Kiki's journey* ill. by Jonathan Day. Children's Book Press, 2006. ISBN 978-0-89239-214-8 Subj: Activities – traveling. Family life. Indians of North America – Tewa.

Orozco, Jose-Luis. *Pancho Claus* ill. by Ashley Wolff. Dial, 2013. ISBN 978-0-8037-3756-3 Subj: Foreign languages. Holidays – Christmas. Rhyming text. Santa Claus.

Rin, rin, rin / do, re, mi: libro ilustrado en Español e Inglés / a picture book in Spanish and English ill. by David Diaz. Scholastic, 2005. ISBN 978-0-439-64941-4 Subj: Books, reading. Counting, numbers. Foreign languages.

Orr, Wendy. *The princess and her panther* ill. by Lauren Stringer. Simon & Schuster, 2010. ISBN 978-1-4169-9780-1 Subj: Animals – leopards. Camps, camping. Family life – sisters. Imagination. Royalty – princesses.

Osborne, Mary Pope. *The brave little seamstress* ill. by Giselle Potter. Atheneum, 2002. ISBN 978-0-689-84486-7 Subj: Careers – tailors. Character traits – bravery. Folk & fairy tales. Giants. Royalty – kings. Royalty – queens.

Happy birthday, America ill. by Peter Catalanotto. Roaring Brook, 2003. ISBN 978-0-7613-2761-5 Subj: Family life. Holidays – Fourth of July.

Kate and the beanstalk ill. by Giselle Potter. Atheneum, 2000. ISBN 978-0-689-82550-7 Subj: Folk & fairy tales. Giants. Plants.

New York's bravest ill. by Steve Johnson and Lou Fancher. Knopf, 2002. ISBN 978-0-375-92196-4 Subj: Careers – firefighters. Character traits – bravery. Cities, towns.

Sleeping Bobby ill. by Giselle Potter. Simon & Schuster, 2005. ISBN 978-0-689-87668-4 Subj: Folk & fairy tales. Royalty – princes. Royalty – princesses. Sleep.

Oskarsson, Bardur. *The flat rabbit* ill. by author. Owl, 2014. ISBN 978-177147059-9 Subj: Animals – rabbits. Death. Kites.

Osofsky, Audrey. *Dreamcatcher* ill. by Ed Young. Watts, 1992. ISBN 978-0-531-08588-2 Subj: Babies, toddlers. Dreams. Family life. Folk & fairy tales. Indians of North America – Ojibwa.

Oswald, Pete. *Mingo the flamingo* ill. by Justin K Thompson. HarperCollins, 2017. ISBN 978-006239198-8 Subj: Birds – flamingos. Character traits – being different. Character traits – helpfulness. Farms. Migration.

Otoshi, Kathryn. *Beautiful hands* by Kathryn Otoshi and Bret Baumgarten; ill. by Kathryn Otoshi. Blue Dot, 2015. ISBN 978-099079930-6 Subj: Anatomy – hands. Art. Character traits – helpfulness. Character traits – optimism.

Draw the line ill. by author. Roaring Brook, 2017. ISBN 978-162672563-8 Subj: Activities – drawing. Behavior – fighting, arguing. Behavior – forgiving. Wordless.

One ill. by author. KO Kids, 2008. ISBN 978-0-9723946-4-2 Subj: Behavior – bullying, teasing. Character traits – bravery. Concepts – color. Counting, numbers. Emotions.

Two ill. by author. KO Kids, 2014. ISBN 978-097239466-6 Subj: Behavior – fighting, arguing. Counting, numbers. Friendship. Self-concept.

Zero ill. by author. KO Kids, 2010. ISBN 978-0-9723946-3-5 Subj: Character traits – cooperation. Counting, numbers. Self-concept.

Otsuka, Yuzo, reteller. *Suho's white horse: a Mongolian legend* ill. by Suekichi Akaba. R.I.C., 2007. ISBN 978-1-74126-021-2 Subj: Animals – horses, ponies. Emotions – love. Folk & fairy tales. Foreign lands – Mongolia. Musical instruments – violins.

Otten, Charlotte F. *January rides the wind: a book of months* ill. by Todd L. W. Doney. Lothrop, 1997. ISBN 978-0-688-12557-8 Subj: Days of the week, months of the year. Poetry.

Otto, Carolyn. *Dinosaur chase* ill. by Thacher Hurd. HarperCollins, 1991. ISBN 978-0-06-021614-6 Subj: Bedtime. Dinosaurs. Poetry. Prehistory.

Our puppies are growing ill. by Mary Morgan. HarperCollins, 1998. ISBN 978-0-06-027272-2 Subj: Animals – babies. Animals – dogs. Behavior – growing up.

That sky, that rain ill. by Megan Lloyd. HarperCollins, 1990. ISBN 978-0-690-04765-3 Subj: Family life – grandfathers. Farms. Sky. Weather – rain.

What color is camouflage? ill. by Megan Lloyd. HarperCollins, 1996. ISBN 978-0-06-027099-5 Subj: Animals. Character traits – appearance.

Oud, Pauline. *Ian's new potty* ill. by author. Clavis, 2011. ISBN 978-1-60537-103-0 Subj: Behavior – growing up. Toilet training.

Sarah on the potty ill. by author. Clavis, 2014. ISBN 978-160537175-7 Subj: Toilet training.

Oughton, Jerrie. *How the stars fell into the sky* ill. by Lisa Desimini. Houghton, 1992. ISBN 978-0-395-58798-0 Subj: Folk & fairy tales. Indians of North America – Navajo. Sky. Stars.

The magic weaver of rugs ill. by Lisa Desimini. Houghton, 1994. ISBN 978-0-395-66140-6 Subj: Activities – weaving. Folk & fairy tales. Indians of North America – Navajo.

Our children can soar: a celebration of Rosa, Barack, and the pioneers of change ill. by Cozbi A. Cabrera. Bloomsbury, 2009. ISBN 978-1-59990-418-4 Subj: Character traits – hopefulness. Ethnic groups in the U.S. – African Americans. U.S. history.

Over in the meadow ill. by Ezra Jack Keats. Four Winds, 1971. Subj: Animals. Counting, numbers. Folk & fairy tales. Rhyming text. Songs.

Overend, Jenni. *Welcome with love* ill. by Julie Vivas. Kane/Miller, 2000. ISBN 978-0-916291-96-9 Subj: Babies, toddlers. Birth. Family life.

Owen, Ann. *Caring for your pet* ill. by Eric Thomas. Picture Window, 2004. ISBN 978-1-4048-0087-8 Subj: Careers – veterinarians. Pets.

Delivering your mail ill. by Eric Thomas. Picture Window, 2004. ISBN 978-1-4048-0091-5 Subj: Careers – postal workers. Letters, cards.

Keeping you healthy ill. by Eric Thomas. Picture Window, 2004. ISBN 978-1-4048-0085-4 Subj: Careers – doctors. Health & fitness.

Keeping you safe ill. by Eric Thomas. Picture Window, 2003. ISBN 978-1-4048-0089-2 Subj: Careers – police officers.

Protecting your home ill. by Eric Thomas. Picture Window, 2004. ISBN 978-1-4048-0088-5 Subj: Careers – firefighters. Fire.

Taking your places ill. by Eric Thomas. Picture Window, 2004. ISBN 978-1-4048-0090-8 Subj: Buses. Careers – bus drivers. Communities, neighborhoods.

Owen, Karen. *I could be, you could be* ill. by Barroux. Barefoot, 2011. ISBN 978-1-84686-405-6 Subj: Rhyming text. Self-concept.

Owens, Mary Beth. *Panda whispers* ill. by author. Penguin, 2007. ISBN 978-0-525-47171-4 Subj: Animals. Bedtime. Dreams. Rhyming text.

Oxenbury, Helen. *It's my birthday* ill. by author. Candlewick, 1994. ISBN 978-1-56402-412-1 Subj: Activities – baking, cooking. Animals. Birthdays. Cumulative tales. Food.

Pig tale ill. by author. Simon & Schuster, 2005. ISBN 978-1-4169-0277-5 Subj: Animals – pigs. Behavior – greed. Rhyming text.

Tom and Pippo go shopping ill. by author. Macmillan, 1989. ISBN 978-0-689-71278-4 Subj: Animals – monkeys. Shopping. Toys.

Tom and Pippo in the garden ill. by author. Macmillan, 1989. ISBN 978-0-689-71275-3 Subj: Animals – monkeys. Gardens, gardening. Toys.

Tom and Pippo on the beach ill. by author. Candlewick, 1993. ISBN 978-1-56402-181-6 Subj: Animals – monkeys. Sea & seashore – beaches. Toys.

Tom and Pippo see the moon ill. by author. Macmillan, 1989. ISBN 978-0-689-71277-7 Subj: Animals – monkeys. Moon. Space & space ships. Toys.

Oxley, Jennifer. *The chicken problem* ill. by Billy Aronson. Random House, 2012. ISBN 978-0-375-86989-1 Subj: Animals – cats. Birds – chickens, roosters. Counting, numbers. Farms. Problem solving.

Peg and Cat: the pizza problem by Jennifer Oxley and Billy Aronson ill. by Amy De Lay. Candlewick, 2016. ISBN 978-076367559-2 Subj: Counting, numbers. Food. Problem solving.

Oyibo, Papa. *Big brother, little sister* ill. by John Clementson. Barefoot, 2000. ISBN 978-1-84148-117-3 Subj: Animals – elephants. Animals – mice. Character traits – helpfulness. Friendship.

Pace, Anne Marie. *Groundhug Day* ill. by Christopher Denise. Disney/Hyperion, 2017. ISBN 978-148475356-9 Subj: Animals – groundhogs. Animals – moose. Holidays – Valentine's Day. Shadows.

Vampirina ballerina ill. by LeUyen Pham. Disney/Hyperion, 2012. ISBN 978-1-4231-5753-3 Subj: Ballet. Careers – dancers. Character traits – perseverance. Monsters.

Vampirina ballerina hosts a sleepover ill. by LeUyen Pham. Hyperion/Disney, 2013. ISBN 978-1-4231-7570-4 Subj: Ballet. Careers – dancers. Monsters. Sleepovers.

Pacilio, V. J. *Ling Cho and his three friends* ill. by Scott Cook. Farrar, 2000. ISBN 978-0-374-34545-7 Subj: Behavior – sharing. Foreign lands – China. Friendship. Rhyming text.

Packard, Edward. *Big numbers: and pictures that show just how big they are!* ill. by Sal Murdocca. Millbrook, 2000. ISBN 978-0-7613-1570-4 Subj: Concepts – size. Counting, numbers.

Page, Gail. *Bobo and the new neighbor* ill. by author. Bloomsbury, 2008. ISBN 978-1-59990-009-4 Subj: Animals – dogs. Humorous stories.

How to be a good cat ill. by author. Bloomsbury, 2011. ISBN 978-1-59990-474-0 Subj: Animals – cats. Animals – dogs.

Page, Robin. *Animals in flight* (Jenkins, Steve)

Animals upside down: a pull, pop, lift and learn book! (Jenkins, Steve)

Creature features: 25 animals explain why they look the way they do (Jenkins, Steve)

Flying frogs and walking fish: leaping lemurs, tumbling toads, jet-propelled jellyfish, and more surprising ways that animals move (Jenkins, Steve)

How many ways can you catch a fly? by Robin Page and Steve Jenkins ill. by Steve Jenkins. Houghton, 2008. ISBN 978-0-618-96634-9 Subj: Animals.

How to clean a hippopotamus: a look at unusual animal partnerships (Jenkins, Steve)

How to swallow a pig: step-by-step advice from the animal kingdom (Jenkins, Steve)

I see a kookaburra (Jenkins, Steve)

Move! (Jenkins, Steve)

My first day: what animals do on day one (Jenkins, Steve)

Sisters and brothers: sibling relationships in the animal world by Robin Page and Steve Jenkins ill. by Steve Jenkins. Houghton, 2008. ISBN 978-0-618-37596-7 Subj: Animals. Nature.

Time for a bath (Jenkins, Steve)

Time to eat (Jenkins, Steve)

Time to sleep (Jenkins, Steve)

Who am I? an animal guessing game (Jenkins, Steve)

Pajalunga, Lorena V. *Yoga for kids* ill. by Anna Forlati. Albert Whitman, 2015. ISBN 978-080759172-7 Subj: Animals. Health & fitness – exercise.

Pak, Kenard. *Goodbye autumn, hello winter* ill. by author. Holt/Godwin, 2017. ISBN 978-162779416-9 Subj: Nature. Seasons – fall. Seasons – winter.

Goodbye summer, hello autumn ill. by author. Henry Holt, 2016. ISBN 978-162779415-2 Subj: Nature. Seasons – fall. Seasons – summer.

Pak, Soyung. *Dear Juno* ill. by Susan Kathleen Hartung. Viking, 1999. ISBN 978-0-670-88252-6 Subj: Ethnic groups in the U.S. – Korean Americans. Family life – grandmothers. Foreign languages. Letters, cards.

A place to grow ill. by Marcelino Truong. Scholastic, 2002. ISBN 978-0-439-13015-8 Subj: Ethnic groups in the U.S. – Korean Americans. Family life – fathers. Gardens, gardening. Immigrants, immigration. Seeds.

Sumi's first day of school ever ill. by Joung Un Kim. Viking, 2003. ISBN 978-0-670-03522-9 Subj: Ethnic groups in the U.S. – Korean Americans. School – first day.

Palacio, R. J. *We're all wonders* ill. by R. J. Palacio. Knopf, 2017. ISBN 978-152476649-8 Subj: Behavior – bullying, teasing. Character traits – appearance. Disabilities – physical disabilities. Imagination. Self-concept.

Palacios, Argentina. *A Christmas surprise for Chabelita* ill. by Lori Lohstoeter. BridgeWater, 1993. ISBN 978-0-8167-3131-2 Subj: Family life – grandparents. Family life – mothers. Foreign lands – Panama. School.

Palatini, Margie. *Bad boys get cookie!* ill. by Henry Cole. HarperCollins, 2006. ISBN 978-0-06-074437-3 Subj: Animals – wolves. Food.

Bad boys get henpecked! ill. by Henry Cole. HarperCollins, 2009. ISBN 978-0-06-074433-5 Subj: Animals – wolves. Birds – chickens, roosters.

Bedhead ill. by Jack E. Davis. Simon & Schuster, 2000. ISBN 978-0-689-82397-8 Subj: Hair. School.

Boo-hoo moo ill. by Keith Graves. HarperCollins, 2009. ISBN 978-0-06-114375-5 Subj: Animals – bulls, cows. Humorous stories. Noise, sounds.

The cheese ill. by Steve Johnson and Lou Fancher. HarperCollins, 2007. ISBN 978-0-06-052630-6 Subj: Careers – farmers. Farms. Games. Music. Songs.

Ding dong ding dong ill. by Howard Fine. Hyperion, 1999. ISBN 978-0-7868-2367-3 Subj: Animals – gorillas. Careers – salespeople. Humorous stories.

Earthquack ill. by Barry Moser. Simon & Schuster, 2002. ISBN 978-0-689-84280-1 Subj: Animals. Birds – ducks. Earthquakes. Humorous stories.

Goldie and the three hares ill. by Jack E. Davis. HarperCollins, 2011. ISBN 978-0-06-125314-0 Subj: Animals – rabbits. Behavior – misbehavior.

Goldie is mad ill. by author. Hyperion, 2001. ISBN 978-0-7868-2490-8 Subj: Babies, toddlers. Emotions – anger. Family life – brothers & sisters. Sibling rivalry.

Gone with the wand: a fairy's tale ill. by Brian Ajhar. Scholastic, 2009. ISBN 978-0-439-72768-6 Subj: Behavior – bad day, bad mood. Fairies. Magic. Teeth.

Good as Goldie ill. by author. Hyperion, 2000. ISBN 978-0-7868-2435-9 Subj: Behavior – dissatisfaction. Family life – brothers & sisters. Sibling rivalry.

Gorgonzola: a very stinkysaurus ill. by Tim Bowers. HarperCollins, 2007. ISBN 978-0-06-073897-6 Subj: Birds. Dinosaurs. Hygiene. Senses – smell.

Hogg, Hogg, and Hog ill. by author. Simon & Schuster, 2011. ISBN 978-1-4424-0322-2 Subj: Animals – pigs. Character traits – ambition. Cities, towns.

Lousy rotten stinkin' grapes ill. by Barry Moser. Simon & Schuster, 2009. ISBN 978-0-689-80246-1 Subj: Animals – foxes. Folk & fairy tales. Food.

Moo who? ill. by Keith Graves. Tegen, 2004. ISBN 978-0-06-000106-3 Subj: Animals. Animals – bulls, cows. Noise, sounds.

Moosetache ill. by Henry Cole. Hyperion, 1997. ISBN 978-0-7868-2246-1 Subj: Animals – moose. Hair.

No biting, Louise ill. by Matthew Reinhart. HarperCollins, 2007. ISBN 978-0-06-052627-6 Subj: Reptiles – alligators, crocodiles. Teeth.

No nap! yes nap! ill. by Dan Yaccarino. Little, Brown, 2014. ISBN 978-031624821-1 Subj: Babies, toddlers. Behavior – misbehavior. Rhyming text. Sleep.

Oink? ill. by Henry Cole. Simon & Schuster, 2006. ISBN 978-0-689-86258-8 Subj: Animals – pigs. Farms. Humorous stories.

The perfect pet ill. by Bruce Whatley. HarperCollins, 2003. ISBN 978-0-06-000109-4 Subj: Character traits – persistence. Insects. Pets.

Piggie pie ill. by Howard Fine. Clarion, 1995. ISBN 978-0-395-71691-5 Subj: Animals – pigs. Animals – wolves. Character traits – appearance. Holidays – Halloween. Witches.

Shelly ill. by Guy Francis. Penguin, 2006. ISBN 978-0-525-47565-1 Subj: Behavior – bossy. Birds – chickens, roosters. Character traits – smallness.

Stuff ill. by Noah Jones. HarperCollins, 2011. ISBN 978-0-06-171921-9 Subj: Animals – rabbits. Behavior – collecting things. Friendship.

Three French hens ill. by Richard Egielski. Hyperion, 2005. ISBN 978-0-7868-5167-6 Subj: Animals – foxes. Birds – chickens, roosters. Foreign lands – France. Humorous stories. Songs.

The three silly billies ill. by Barry Moser. Simon & Schuster, 2005. ISBN 978-0-689-85862-8 Subj: Animals – goats. Books, reading. Humorous stories. Mythical creatures – trolls.

Tub-boo-boo ill. by Glin Dibley. Simon & Schuster, 2001. ISBN 978-0-689-82394-7 Subj: Activities – bathing. Family life. Family life – brothers.

Under a pig tree: a history of the noble fruit ill. by Chuck Groenink. Abrams, 2015. ISBN 978-141971488-7 Subj: Activities – writing. Animals – pigs. Books, reading. Careers – writers. Food. Humorous stories.

The web files ill. by Richard Egielski. Hyperion, 2001. ISBN 978-0-7868-2366-6 Subj: Careers – detectives. Farms. Humorous stories. Nursery rhymes.

Zak's lunch ill. by Howard Fine. Clarion, 1998. ISBN 978-0-395-81674-5 Subj: Family life – mothers. Food. Imagination.

Zoom Broom ill. by Howard Fine. Hyperion, 1998. ISBN 978-0-7868-0322-4 Subj: Animals – foxes. Witches.

Paley, Joan, adapt. *One more river* ill. by adapter. Little, 2002. ISBN 978-0-316-60702-5 Subj: Animals. Boats, ships. Counting, numbers. Religion – Noah. Songs. Weather – floods. Weather – rain. Weather – rainbows.

Pallotta, Jerry. *The airplane alphabet book* by Jerry Pallotta and Fred Stillwell ill. by Rob Bolster. Charlesbridge, 1997. ISBN 978-0-88106-907-8 Subj: ABC books. Airplanes, airports.

Butterfly counting ill. by Shennen Bersani. Charlesbridge, 2015. ISBN 978-157091414-0 Subj: Counting, numbers. Insects – butterflies, caterpillars.

The construction alphabet book ill. by Rob Bolster. Charlesbridge, 2006. ISBN 978-1-57091-437-9 Subj: ABC books. Machines. Tractors. Trucks.

The crayon counting book (Ryan, Pam Muñoz)

Dory story ill. by David Biedrzycki. Talewinds, 2000. ISBN 978-0-88106-075-1 Subj: Activities – bathing. Animals. Boats, ships. Fish. Imagination. Nature. Sea & seashore.

F is for Fenway: America's oldest major league ballpark ill. by John S. Dykes. Sleeping Bear, 2012. ISBN 978-1-58536-788-7 Subj: ABC books. Sports – baseball.

A giraffe did one ill. by Tatjana Mai-Wyss. Sleeping Bear, 2012. ISBN 978-1-58536-641-5 Subj: Animals. Behavior – misbehavior. Rhyming text.

The jet alphabet book ill. by Rob Bolster. Charlesbridge, 1999. ISBN 978-0-88106-916-7 Subj: ABC books. Airplanes, airports.

Ocean counting: odd numbers ill. by Shennen Bersani. Charlesbridge, 2005. ISBN 978-0-88106-151-2 Subj: Animals. Counting, numbers. Sea & seashore.

Twizzlers percentages book ill. by Rob Bolster. Scholastic, 2001. ISBN 978-0-439-25407-6 Subj: Aliens. Counting, numbers. Space & space ships.

Who will plant a tree? ill. by Thomas Leonard. Sleeping Bear, 2010. ISBN 978-1-58536-502-9 Subj: Seeds. Trees.

Who will see their shadows this year? ill. by David Biedrzycki. Scholastic, 2013. ISBN 978-0-545-47275-3 Subj: Animals. Animals – groundhogs. Holidays – Groundhog Day. Seasons – winter. Shadows.

Pamintuan, Macky. *Twelve haunted rooms of Halloween* ill. by author. Sterling, 2011. ISBN 978-1-4027-7935-0 Subj: Animals – bears. Counting, numbers. Holidays – Halloween. Picture puzzles. Rhyming text.

Pandell, Karen. *I love you sun, I love you moon* ill. by Tomie dePaola. Putnam, 1994. ISBN 978-0-399-22628-1 Subj: Ecology. Nature.

Pandya, Meenal. *Here comes Diwali* recipes by Laxmi Jain; ill. by author. MeeRa, 2000. ISBN 978-0-9635539-3-5 Subj: Holidays. Holidays – Diwali. Religion – Hinduism.

Pantone: colors ill. by Helen Dardik. Abrams, 2012. ISBN 978-1-4197-0180-1 Subj: Concepts – color. Format, unusual – board books.

Panzieri, Lucia. *The kindhearted crocodile* ill. by Anton Gionata Ferrari. Holiday House, 2013. ISBN 978-0-8234-2767-3 Subj: Behavior – hiding. Books, reading. Character traits – helpfulness. Pets. Reptiles – alligators, crocodiles.

Paola, Tomie de *see* dePaola, Tomie

Paolilli, Paul. *Silver seeds* by Paul Paolilli and Dan Brewer ill. by Steve Johnson and Lou Fancher. Viking, 2001. ISBN 978-0-670-88941-9 Subj: Imagination. Nature. Poetry.

Papineau, Lucie. *Lulu's pajamas* ill. by Stéphane Jorisch. Kids Can, 2009. ISBN 978-1-55453-371-8 Subj: Animals – mice. Bedtime. Character traits – cleanliness. Clothing – pajamas.

Papp, Lisa. *Madeline Finn and the library dog* ill. by author. Peachtree, 2016. ISBN 978-156145910-0 Subj: Animals – dogs. Animals – service animals. Books, reading. Character traits – confidence. Character traits – patience, impatience. Libraries.

Paquette, Ammi-Joan. *Bunny Bus* ill. by Lesley Breen Withrow. Farrar, 2017. ISBN 978-037430225-2 Subj: Animals. Animals – rabbits. Buses. Holidays – Easter. Parades. Rhyming text.

Ghost in the house ill. by Adam Record. Candlewick, 2013. ISBN 978-0-7636-5529-7 Subj: Counting, numbers. Cumulative tales. Ghosts. Rhyming text.

The tiptoe guide to tracking fairies ill. by Christa Unzner. Tanglewood, 2009. ISBN 978-1-933718-20-0 Subj: Behavior – hiding. Fairies. Nature.

Parachini, Jodie. *This is a serious book* ill. by Daniel Rieley. Greenwillow, 2016. ISBN 978-006247052-2 Subj: Animals. Books, reading. Humorous stories.

Paradis, Susan. *My Daddy* ill. by author. Front Street, 1998. ISBN 978-1-886910-30-0 Subj: Activities. Family life – fathers.

My mommy ill. by author. Front Street, 2002. ISBN 978-1-886910-73-7 Subj: Emotions – love. Family life – mothers.

Snow princess ill. by author. Boyds Mills, 2005. ISBN 978-1-932425-31-4 Subj: Family life – fathers. Imagination. Weather – snow.

Paraskevas, Betty. *Chocolate at the Four Seasons* ill. by Michael Paraskevas. Little, Brown, 2007. ISBN 978-0-306-01375-8 Subj: Animals – dogs. Character traits – shyness. Hotels.

Maggie and the Ferocious Beast, the big carrot ill. by Michael Paraskevas. Simon & Schuster, 2000. ISBN 978-0-689-82490-6 Subj: Activities – digging. Animals – mice. Animals – pigs. Animals – rabbits. Character traits – helpfulness. Gardens, gardening. Monsters.

Maggie and the Ferocious Beast, the big scare ill. by Michael Paraskevas. Simon & Schuster, 1999. ISBN 978-0-689-82489-0 Subj: Animals – mice. Animals – pigs. Emotions – fear. Monsters.

Marvin, the tap-dancing horse ill. by Michael Paraskevas. Simon & Schuster, 2001. ISBN 978-0-689-82153-0 Subj: Activities – dancing. Animals – horses, ponies. Fairs, festivals. Friendship. Theater.

Nibbles O'Hare ill. by Michael Paraskevas. Simon & Schuster, 2001. ISBN 978-0-689-82865-2 Subj: Animals – rabbits. Holidays – Easter.

Parenteau, Shirley. *Bears and a birthday* ill. by David Walker. Candlewick, 2015. ISBN 978-076367152-5 Subj: Activities – baking, cooking. Animals – bears. Birthdays. Rhyming text.

Bears in a band ill. by David Walker. Candlewick, 2016. ISBN 978-076368147-0 Subj: Animals – bears. Music. Musical instruments – bands. Noise, sounds.

Bears in beds ill. by David Walker. Candlewick, 2012. ISBN 978-0-7636-5338-5 Subj: Animals – bears. Bedtime. Rhyming text.

Bears in the bath ill. by David Walker. Candlewick, 2014. ISBN 978-076366418-3 Subj: Activities – bathing. Animals – bears. Rhyming text.

Bears in the snow ill. by David Walker. Candlewick, 2016. ISBN 978-076368148-7 Subj: Animals – bears. Behavior – sharing. Rhyming text. Sports – sledding. Weather – snow.

Bears on chairs ill. by David Walker. Candlewick, 2009. ISBN 978-0-7636-3588-6 Subj: Animals – bears. Behavior – sharing. Furniture – chairs. Problem solving. Rhyming text.

One frog sang ill. by Cynthia Jabar. Candlewick, 2006. ISBN 978-0-7636-2394-4 Subj: Counting, numbers. Frogs & toads.

Parish, Herman. *Amelia Bedelia's first apple pie* ill. by Lynne Avril. HarperCollins, 2010. ISBN 978-0-06-196409-1 Subj: Activities – baking, cooking. Family life – grandparents. Humorous stories.

Amelia Bedelia's first day of school ill. by Lynne Avril. Greenwillow, 2009. ISBN 978-0-06-154455-2 Subj: Humorous stories. School – first day.

Amelia Bedelia's first field trip ill. by Lynne Avril. HarperCollins, 2011. ISBN 978-0-06-196413-8 Subj: Farms. Humorous stories. School – field trips.

Amelia Bedelia's first library card ill. by Lynne Avril. HarperCollins, 2013. ISBN 978-0-06-209512-1 Subj: Books, reading. Language. Libraries.

Amelia Bedelia's first valentine ill. by Lynne Avril. Greenwillow, 2009. ISBN 978-0-06-154458-3 Subj: Holidays – Valentine's Day. Humorous stories. School.

Amelia Bedelia's first vote ill. by Lynne Avril. HarperCollins, 2012. ISBN 978-0-06-209405-6 Subj: Behavior – seeking better things. Language. School.

Go west, Amelia Bedelia! ill. by Lynn Sweat. HarperCollins, 2011. ISBN 978-0-06-084361-8 Subj: Careers – ranchers. Family life – aunts, uncles. Humorous stories.

Park, Bomi. *First snow* ill. by author. Chronicle, 2016. ISBN 978-145215472-5 Subj: Babies, toddlers. Seasons – winter. Weather – snow.

Park, Frances. *Good-bye, 382 Shin Dang Dong* ill. by Yangsook Choi. National Geographic, 2002. ISBN 978-0-7922-7985-3 Subj: Ethnic groups in the U.S. – Korean Americans. Foreign lands – Korea. Moving.

The Have a Good Day Cafe by Frances Park and Ginger Park ill. by Katherine Potter. Lee & Low, 2005. ISBN 978-1-58430-171-4 Subj: Ethnic groups in the U.S. – Korean Americans. Family life – grandmothers. Immigrants, immigration. Restaurants.

My freedom trip by Frances Park and Ginger Park ill. by Debra Reid Jenkins. Boyds Mills, 1998. ISBN 978-1-56397-468-7 Subj: Character traits – freedom. Foreign lands – Korea (North). Immigrants, immigration.

The royal bee by Frances Park and Ginger Park ill. by Christopher Zhong-Yuan Zhang. Boyds Mills, 2000. ISBN 978-1-56397-614-8 Subj: Contests. Foreign lands – Korea. Poverty. School.

Where on earth is my bagel? by Frances Park and Ginger Park ill. by Grace Lin. Lee & Low, 2001. ISBN 978-1-58430-033-5 Subj: Activities – baking, cooking. Food. Foreign lands – Korea. Imagination.

Park, Ginger. *The Have a Good Day Cafe* (Park, Frances)

My freedom trip (Park, Frances)

The royal bee (Park, Frances)

Where on earth is my bagel? (Park, Frances)

Park, Linda Sue. *Bee-bim bop!* ill. by Ho Baek Lee. Houghton, 2005. ISBN 978-0-618-26511-4 Subj: Activities – baking, cooking. Food. Foreign lands – Korea. Rhyming text.

The firekeeper's son ill. by Julie Downing. Clarion, 2003. ISBN 978-0-618-13337-6 Subj: Character traits – responsibility. Family life – fathers. Foreign lands – Korea.

The third gift ill. by Bagram Ibatoulline. Clarion, 2011. ISBN 978-0-547-20195-5 Subj: Family life – fathers. Holidays – Christmas. Religion.

What does Bunny see? s book of colors and flowers ill. by Maggie Smith. Houghton, 2005. ISBN 978-0-618-23485-1 Subj: Animals – rabbits. Concepts – color. Flowers. Gardens, gardening. Rhyming text.

Xander's panda party ill. by Matt Phelan. Houghton Mifflin, 2013. ISBN 978-0-547-55865-3 Subj: Animals. Animals – pandas. Parties. Rhyming text. Zoos.

Yaks yak: animal word pairs ill. by Jennifer Black Reinhardt. Clarion, 2016. ISBN 978-054439101-7 Subj: Animals. Language.

Yum! yuck! a foldout book of people sounds by Linda Sue Park and Julia Durango ill. by Sue Ramá. Charlesbridge, 2005. ISBN 978-1-57091-659-5 Subj: Foreign languages. Format, unusual – toy & movable books. Noise, sounds.

Parker, Ant. *Flashing fire engines* (Mitton, Tony)

Parker, Danny. *Parachute* ill. by Matt Ottley. Eerdmans, 2016. ISBN 978-080285469-8 Subj: Character traits – kindness to animals. Emotions – fear.

Parker, Kim. *Counting in the garden* ill. by author. Scholastic, 2005. ISBN 978-0-439-69452-0 Subj: Animals. Counting, numbers. Gardens, gardening.

Parker, Marjorie Blain. *Colorful dreamer: the story of artist Henri Matisse* ill. by Holly Berry. Dial, 2012.

ISBN 978-0-8037-3758-7 Subj: Activities – painting. Art. Careers – artists. Foreign lands – France.

Jasper's day ill. by Janet Wilson. Kids Can, 2002. ISBN 978-1-55074-957-1 Subj: Animals – dogs. Death. Emotions – grief. Memories, memory.

Mama's little duckling ill. by Mike Wohnoutka. Dutton, 2008. ISBN 978-0-525-47950-5 Subj: Behavior – growing up. Birds – ducks. Family life – mothers.

A paddling of ducks: animals in groups from A to Z ill. by Joseph Kelly. Kids Can, 2010. ISBN 978-1-55337-682-8 Subj: ABC books. Animals. Language.

When dads don't grow up ill. by R. W. Alley. Dial, 2012. ISBN 978-0-8037-3717-4 Subj: Behavior – growing up. Family life – fathers.

Your kind of mommy ill. by Cyd Moore. Penguin, 2007. ISBN 978-0-525-46989-6 Subj: Animals. Family life – mothers. Rhyming text.

Parker, Mary Jessie. *The deep, deep puddle* ill. by Deborah Zemke. Dial, 2013. ISBN 978-0-8037-3765-5 Subj: Counting, numbers. Weather – rain.

Parker, Michael. *You are a star!* ill. by Judith Rossell. Walker, 2012. ISBN 978-0-8027-2841-8 Subj: Astronomy. Science. Sky. Stars.

Parker, Nancy Winslow. *Bugs* by Nancy Winslow Parker and Joan Richards Wright; ill. by Nancy Winslow Parker. Greenwillow, 1987. ISBN 978-0-688-06624-6 Subj: Insects. Science.

Parker, Robert Andrew. *Piano starts here: the young Art Tatum* ill. by author. Random House, 2008. ISBN 978-0-375-83965-8 Subj: Careers – musicians. Ethnic groups in the U.S. – African Americans. U.S. history.

Parker, Victoria. *Bearum scarum* ill. by Emily Bolam. Viking, 2002. ISBN 978-0-670-03546-5 Subj: Animals. Animals – bears. Counting, numbers. Jungle. Rhyming text.

Parkhurst, Carolyn. *Cooking with Henry and Elliebelly* ill. by Dan Yaccarino. Feiwel & Friends, 2010. ISBN 978-0-312-54848-3 Subj: Activities – baking, cooking. Family life – brothers & sisters. Imagination.

Parkinson, Curtis. *Emily's eighteen aunts* ill. by Andrea Wayne-von Königslöw. Stoddart, 2002. ISBN 978-0-7737-3336-7 Subj: Character traits – individuality. Family life – aunts, uncles. Humorous stories.

Parkinson, Kathy, adapt. *The enormous turnip* ill. by adapter. Albert Whitman, 1985. ISBN 978-0-8075-2062-8 Subj: Behavior – sharing. Character traits – cooperation. Cumulative tales. Folk &

fairy tales. Foreign lands – Russia. Plants. Problem solving.

Parks, Carmen. *Farmers market* ill. by Ed Martinez. Harcourt, 2002. ISBN 978-0-15-216680-9 Subj: Careers – farmers. Country. Family life – parents. Stores.

Parlato, Stephen. *The world that loved books* ill. by author. Simply Read, 2003. ISBN 978-1-894965-04-0 Subj: Books, reading. Imagination.

Parnell, Peter. *And Tango makes three* (Richardson, Justin)

Christian, the hugging lion (Richardson, Justin)

Parot, Annelore. *Kimonos* ill. by author. Chronicle, 2011. ISBN 978-1-4521-0493-5 Subj: Foreign lands – Japan. Format, unusual – toy & movable books. Toys – dolls.

Parr, Todd. *Be who you are* ill. by author. Little, Brown, 2016. ISBN 978-031626523-2 Subj: Character traits – individuality. Self-concept.

The best friends book ill. by author. Little, 2000. ISBN 978-0-316-69201-4 Subj: Friendship.

Big and little ill. by author. Little, 2001. ISBN 978-0-316-69291-5 Subj: Concepts – size. Format, unusual – board books. Language.

Black and white ill. by author. Little, 2001. ISBN 978-0-316-69225-0 Subj: Concepts – color. Format, unusual – board books. Language.

The daddy book ill. by author. Little, 2002. ISBN 978-0-316-60799-5 Subj: Family life – fathers.

Do's and don'ts ill. by author. Little, 1999. ISBN 978-0-316-69213-7 Subj: Behavior. Etiquette.

The earth book ill. by author. Little, Brown, 2010. ISBN 978-0-316-04265-9 Subj: Earth. Ecology.

The feel good book ill. by author. Little, 2002. ISBN 978-0-316-07206-9 Subj: Emotions – happiness.

The feelings book ill. by author. Little, 2000. ISBN 978-0-316-69131-4 Subj: Emotions.

The goodbye book ill. by author. Little, Brown, 2015. ISBN 978-031640497-6 Subj: Emotions – grief. Emotions – sadness.

The grandma book ill. by author. Little, Brown, 2006. ISBN 978-0-316-05802-5 Subj: Family life – grandmothers.

The grandpa book ill. by author. Little, Brown, 2006. ISBN 978-0-316-05801-8 Subj: Family life – grandfathers.

The I love you book ill. by author. Little, Brown, 2009. ISBN 978-0-316-01985-9 Subj: Emotions – love.

It's okay to make mistakes ill. by author. Little, Brown, 2014. ISBN 978-031623053-7 Subj: Behavior – mistakes. Self-concept.

The mommy book ill. by author. Little, 2002. ISBN 978-0-316-60827-5 Subj: Family life – mothers.

The okay book ill. by author. Little, 1999. ISBN 978-0-316-69220-5 Subj: Character traits – individuality. Self-concept.

Otto goes to school ill. by author. Little, Brown, 2005. ISBN 978-0-316-83533-6 Subj: Animals – dogs. School – first day.

Reading makes you feel good ill. by author. Little, Brown, 2005. ISBN 978-0-316-16004-9 Subj: Books, reading.

Teachers rock! ill. by author. Little, Brown/Megan Tingley, 2016. ISBN 978-031626512-6 Subj: Careers – teachers. School.

The thankful book ill. by author. Little, Brown, 2012. ISBN 978-0-316-18101-3 Subj: Character traits. Self-concept.

Things that make you feel good, things that make you feel bad ill. by author. Little, 1999. ISBN 978-0-316-69270-0 Subj: Emotions.

This is my hair ill. by author. Little, 1999. ISBN 978-0-316-69236-6 Subj: Hair.

Underwear do's and don'ts ill. by author. Little, 2000. ISBN 978-0-316-69151-2 Subj: Clothing. Humorous stories.

We belong together: a book about adoption and families ill. by author. Little, Brown, 2005. ISBN 978-0-316-01668-1 Subj: Adoption. Family life.

Parsley, Elise. *If you ever want to bring a circus to the library, don't!* ill. by author. Little, Brown, 2017. ISBN 978-031637661-7 Subj: Circus. Humorous stories. Libraries.

If you ever want to bring a piano to the beach, don't! ill. by author. Little, Brown, 2016. ISBN 978-031637659-4 Subj: Humorous stories. Musical instruments – pianos. Sea & seashore – beaches.

If you ever want to bring an alligator to school, don't! ill. by author. Little, Brown, 2015. ISBN 978-031637657-0 Subj: Behavior – misbehavior. Humorous stories. Reptiles – alligators, crocodiles. School.

Partis, Joanne. *Stripe* ill. by author. Carolrhoda, 2000. ISBN 978-1-57505-450-6 Subj: Animals – babies. Animals – tigers. Behavior – misbehavior.

Stripe's naughty sister ill. by author. Carolrhoda, 2002. ISBN 978-0-87614-466-4 Subj: Animals – tigers. Family life – brothers & sisters.

Partridge, Elizabeth. *Big Cat Pepper* ill. by Lauren Castillo. Bloomsbury, 2009. ISBN 978-1-59990-

024-7 Subj: Animals – cats. Death. Pets. Rhyming text.

Moon glowing ill. by Joan Paley. Dutton, 2002. ISBN 978-0-525-46873-8 Subj: Animals. Hibernation. Rhyming text. Seasons – winter.

Oranges on Golden Mountain ill. by Aki Sogabe. Dutton, 2001. ISBN 978-0-525-46453-2 Subj: Ethnic groups in the U.S. – Chinese Americans. Family life – aunts, uncles. Foreign lands – China. Immigrants, immigration. Sports – fishing.

Pig's eggs ill. by Martha Weston. Golden, 2000. ISBN 978-0-307-10232-4 Subj: Activities – painting. Animals – pigs. Birds – chickens, roosters. Eggs.

Paschkis, Julie. *Apple cake: a recipe for love* ill. by author. Harcourt, 2012. ISBN 978-0-547-80745-4 Subj: Activities – baking, cooking. Books, reading. Emotions – love.

Magic spell ill. by author. Simon & Schuster, 2017. ISBN 978-148142210-9 Subj: Careers – magicians. Character traits – cooperation. Character traits – patience, impatience. Language. Magic.

Mooshka: a quilt story ill. by author. Peachtree, 2012. ISBN 978-1-56145-620-8 Subj: Activities – storytelling. Behavior – sharing. Family life – new sibling. Quilts.

P. Zonka lays an egg ill. by author. Peachtree, 2015. ISBN 978-156145819-6 Subj: Birds – chickens, roosters. Character traits – being different. Concepts – color. Eggs.

Pasquali, Elena. *Ituku's Christmas journey* ill. by Dubravka Kolanovic. Good Books, 2005. ISBN 978-1-56148-495-9 Subj: Holidays – Christmas. Indians of North America – Inuit. Religion – Nativity.

Passen, Lisa. *Attack of the 50-foot teacher* ill. by author. Henry Holt, 2000. ISBN 978-0-8050-6100-0 Subj: Aliens. Careers – teachers. Concepts – size. Holidays – Halloween. School.

The incredible shrinking teacher ill. by author. Henry Holt, 2002. ISBN 978-0-8050-6452-0 Subj: Careers – teachers. Concepts – size. Humorous stories. Parties. School.

Patent, Dorothy Hinshaw. *Bold and bright, black-and-white animals* ill. by Kendahl Jan Jubb. Walker, 1998. ISBN 978-0-8027-8673-9 Subj: Animals. Concepts – color.

Fabulous fluttering tropical butterflies ill. by Kendahl Jan Jubb. Walker, 2003. ISBN 978-0-8027-8839-9 Subj: Insects – butterflies, caterpillars.

Slinky, scaly, slithery snakes ill. by Kendahl Jan Jubb. Walker, 2000. ISBN 978-0-8027-8744-6 Subj: Reptiles – snakes.

Paterson, Brian. *Zigby camps out* ill. by author. HarperCollins, 2002. ISBN 978-0-06-052921-5 Subj: Animals. Animals – meerkats. Animals – zebras. Birds – guinea fowl. Camps, camping. Jungle.

Zigby dives in ill. by author. HarperCollins, 2004. ISBN 978-0-06-053799-9 Subj: Animals – zebras. Octopuses. Sports – fishing.

Zigby hunts for treasure ill. by author. HarperCollins, 2003. ISBN 978-0-06-052922-2 Subj: Animals – meerkats. Animals – zebras. Canoes & canoeing. Jungle. Maps.

Paterson, Diane. *Hurricane wolf* ill. by author. Albert Whitman, 2006. ISBN 978-0-8075-3438-0 Subj: Family life. Weather – hurricanes.

Paterson, John. *Blueberries for the queen* by John Paterson and Katherine Paterson ill. by Susan Jeffers. HarperCollins, 2004. ISBN 978-0-06-623943-9 Subj: Food. Royalty – queens. U.S. history. War.

Paterson, Katherine. *Blueberries for the queen* (Paterson, John)

Brother Sun, Sister Moon: Saint Francis of Assisi's canticle of the creatures ill. by Pamela Dalton. Chronicle, 2011. ISBN 978-0-8118-7734-3 Subj: Nature. Religion.

The light of the world: the life of Jesus for children ill. by François Roca. Scholastic, 2008. ISBN 978-0-545-01172-3 Subj: Religion.

The tale of the Mandarin ducks ill. by Leo and Diane Dillon. Dutton, 1990. ISBN 978-0-525-67283-8 Subj: Birds – ducks. Folk & fairy tales. Foreign lands – Japan.

Patkau, Karen. *Creatures: yesterday and today* ill. by author. Tundra, 2008. ISBN 978-0-88776-833-0 Subj: Animals. Prehistory. Science.

Patricelli, Leslie. *Baby happy, baby sad* ill. by author. Candlewick, 2008. ISBN 978-0-7636-3245-8 Subj: Babies, toddlers. Emotions. Format, unusual – board books.

Be quiet, Mike! ill. by author. Candlewick, 2011. ISBN 978-0-7636-4477-2 Subj: Animals – monkeys. Musical instruments – drums. Noise, sounds.

Binky ill. by author. Candlewick, 2005. ISBN 978-0-7636-2364-7 Subj: Babies, toddlers. Format, unusual – board books. Toys.

The birthday box ill. by author. Candlewick, 2007. ISBN 978-0-7636-2825-3 Subj: Birthdays. Imagination.

Blankie ill. by author. Candlewick, 2005. ISBN 978-0-7636-2363-0 Subj: Babies, toddlers. Format, unusual – board books.

Boo! ill. by author. Candlewick, 2015. ISBN 978-076366320-9   Subj: Clothing – costumes. Format, unusual – board books. Holidays – Halloween.

Fa la la ill. by author. Candlewick, 2012. ISBN 978-0-7636-3247-2   Subj: Babies, toddlers. Format, unusual – board books. Holidays – Christmas.

Faster! faster! ill. by author. Candlewick, 2012. ISBN 978-0-7636-5473-3 Subj: Animals. Concepts – speed. Family life – fathers. Imagination.

Hair ill. by author. Candlewick, 2017. ISBN 978-076367931-6   Subj: Format, unusual – board books. Hair.

Higher! higher! ill. by author. Candlewick, 2009. ISBN 978-0-7636-3241-0   Subj: Activities – swinging. Imagination.

Hop! hop! ill. by author. Candlewick, 2015. ISBN 978-076366319-3   Subj: Animals – rabbits. Concepts – color. Eggs. Format, unusual – board books. Holidays – Easter.

Nighty-night ill. by author. Candlewick, 2017. ISBN 978-076367932-3   Subj: Babies, toddlers. Bedtime. Format, unusual – board books.

No no, yes yes ill. by author. Candlewick, 2008. ISBN 978-0-7636-3244-1   Subj: Babies, toddlers. Behavior. Format, unusual – board books.

The Patterson puppies and the midnight monster party ill. by author. Candlewick, 2010. ISBN 978-0-7636-3243-4   Subj: Animals – dogs. Bedtime. Emotions – fear. Monsters.

Potty ill. by author. Candlewick, 2010. ISBN 978-0-7636-4476-5   Subj: Toilet training.

Tubby ill. by author. Candlewick, 2010. ISBN 978-0-7636-4567-0   Subj: Activities – bathing. Activities – playing.

Patrick, Jean L. S. *If I had a snowplow* ill. by Karen Dugan. Boyds Mills, 2001. ISBN 978-1-56397-746-6   Subj: Family life – mothers. Machines. Rhyming text. Trucks.

Patschke, Steve. *The spooky book* ill. by Matthew McElligott. Walker, 1999. ISBN 978-0-8027-8693-7   Subj: Books, reading. Emotions – fear. Homes, houses.

Patten, Brian. *The big snuggle-up* ill. by Nicola Bayley. Kane/Miller, 2011. ISBN 978-1-61067-036-4   Subj: Animals. Behavior – sharing. Character traits – generosity. Rhyming text. Scarecrows. Weather – snow.

Patterson, Rebecca. *My no, no, no day!* ill. by author. Viking, 2012. ISBN 978-0-670-01405-7   Subj: Behavior – bad day, bad mood. Behavior – misbehavior. Emotions.

Pattison, Darcy. *Desert baths* ill. by Kathleen Rietz. Sylvan Dell, 2012. ISBN 978-1-607185-25-3   Subj: Activities – bathing. Animals. Desert.

The journey of Oliver K. Woodman ill. by Joe Cepeda. Harcourt, 2003. ISBN 978-0-15-202329-4   Subj: Activities – traveling. Letters, cards. Toys – dolls.

Searching for Oliver K. Woodman ill. by Joe Cepeda. Harcourt, 2005. ISBN 978-0-15-205184-6   Subj: Activities – traveling. Letters, cards. Toys – dolls.

Patton, Julia. *The very very very long dog* ill. by author. Sourcebooks/Jabberwocky, 2017. ISBN 978-149265445-2 Subj: Animals – dogs. Cities, towns. Humorous stories.

Pattou, Edith. *Mrs. Spitzer's garden* ill. by Tricia Tusa. Gift edition. Harcourt, 2007. ISBN 978-0-15-205802-9   Subj: Careers – teachers. Gardens, gardening. School.

Patz, Nancy. *Babies can't eat kimchee!* by Nancy Patz and Susan L. Roth; ill. by authors. Bloomsbury, 2007. ISBN 978-1-59990-017-9   Subj: Babies, toddlers. Behavior – growing up. Ethnic groups in the U.S. – Korean Americans. Family life – brothers & sisters. Family life – new sibling. Food.

Paul, Alison. *The crow (a not so scary story)* ill. by author. Houghton, 2007. ISBN 978-0-618-66380-4 Subj: Birds – crows. Emotions – fear. Language.

The plan ill. by Barbara Lehman. Houghton Mifflin Harcourt, 2015. ISBN 978-054428333-6 Subj: Activities – flying. Airplanes, airports. Behavior – resourcefulness. Emotions – sadness. Family life – daughters. Family life – fathers.

Paul, Ann Whitford. *Count on Culebra: go from 1 to 10 in Spanish* ill. by Ethan Long. Holiday, 2008. ISBN 978-0-8234-2124-4   Subj: Counting, numbers. Desert. Foreign languages. Reptiles – iguanas. Reptiles – snakes.

Eight hands round ill. by Jeanette Winter. HarperCollins, 1991. ISBN 978-0-06-024704-1   Subj: ABC books. Quilts.

Everything to spend the night . . . from A to Z ill. by Maggie Smith. DK, 1999. ISBN 978-0-7894-2511-9   Subj: ABC books. Bedtime. Family life – grandfathers. Rhyming text.

Fiesta fiasco ill. by Ethan Long. Holiday House, 2007. ISBN 978-0-8234-2037-7   Subj: Animals. Birthdays. Desert. Foreign languages. Gifts.

Hello toes! Hello feet! ill. by Nadine Bernard Westcott. DK, 1998. ISBN 978-0-7894-2481-5   Subj: Activities – playing. Anatomy – feet. Anatomy – toes. Animals – dogs. Clothing – shoes.

If animals kissed goodnight ill. by David Walker. Farrar, 2008. ISBN 978-0-374-38051-9   Subj: Animals. Bedtime. Rhyming text.

If animals said I love you ill. by David Walker. Farrar, 2017. ISBN 978-037430602-1 Subj: Animals. Emotions – love. Rhyming text.

Mañana Iguana ill. by Ethan Long. Holiday House, 2004. ISBN 978-0-8234-1808-4 Subj: Character traits – laziness. Desert. Foreign languages. Parties. Reptiles – iguanas.

The seasons sewn ill. by Michael McCurdy. Browndeer, 1996. ISBN 978-0-15-276918-5 Subj: Activities – sewing. Quilts. Seasons. U.S. history – frontier & pioneer life.

Tortuga in trouble ill. by Ethan Long. Holiday, 2009. ISBN 978-0-8234-2180-0 Subj: Animals – coyotes. Desert. Family life – grandmothers. Folk & fairy tales. Foreign languages. Reptiles – turtles, tortoises.

Word builder ill. by Kurt Cyrus. Simon & Schuster, 2009. ISBN 978-1-4169-3981-8 Subj: Careers – construction workers. Language.

Paul, Chris. *Long shot: never too small to dream big* ill. by Frank Morrison. Simon & Schuster, 2009. ISBN 978-1-4169-5079-0 Subj: Character traits – persistence. Character traits – smallness. Ethnic groups in the U.S. – African Americans. Sports – basketball.

Paul, Ellis. *The night the lights went out on Christmas* ill. by Scott Brundage. Albert Whitman, 2015. ISBN 978-080754543-0 Subj: Contests. Holidays – Christmas. Light, lights. Rhyming text.

Paul, Korky. *Tiny* (Rogers, Paul)

Paul, Miranda. *Are we pears yet?* ill. by Carin Berger. Roaring Brook, 2017. ISBN 978-162672351-1 Subj: Character traits – patience, impatience. Nature. Science. Seeds.

One plastic bag: Isatou Ceesay and the recycling women of the Gambia ill. by Elizabeth Zunon. Lerner/ Millbrook, 2015. ISBN 978-146771608-6 Subj: Behavior – seeking better things. Ecology. Foreign lands – Gambia. Money.

10 little ninjas ill. by Nate Wragg. Knopf, 2016. ISBN 978-055353497-9 Subj: Bedtime. Counting, numbers. Imagination. Rhyming text.

Trainbots ill. by Shane McG. little bee, 2016. ISBN 978-149980167-5 Subj: Robots. Trains.

Water is water ill. by Jason Chin. Roaring Brook, 2015. ISBN 978-159643984-9 Subj: Science. Seasons. Water.

Whose hands are these? : a community helper guessing book ill. by Luciana Navarro Powell. Lerner, 2016. ISBN 978-146775214-5 Subj: Careers. Character traits – helpfulness. Rhyming text.

Paul, Ruth. *Bad dog, Flash* ill. by author. Sourcebooks/Jabberwocky, 2014. ISBN 978-149260153-1 Subj: Animals – dogs. Behavior – misbehavior.

Go home Flash ill. by author. Sourcebooks/Jabberwocky, 2015. ISBN 978-149261523-1 Subj: Animals – dogs. Behavior – misbehavior.

Hedgehog's magic tricks ill. by author. Candlewick, 2013. ISBN 978-0-7636-6385-8 Subj: Animals. Animals – hedgehogs. Careers – magicians. Friendship.

Pauli, Lorenz. *The fox in the library* ill. by Kathrin Schärer. NorthSouth, 2013. ISBN 978-0-7358-4150-5 Subj: Animals – foxes. Animals – mice. Behavior – trickery. Birds – chickens, roosters. Books, reading. Libraries.

Paulsen, Gary. *Canoe days* ill. by Ruth Wright Paulsen. Doubleday, 1999. ISBN 978-0-385-32524-0 Subj: Birds. Canoes & canoeing. Fish. Insects. Seasons – summer.

Worksong ill. by Ruth Wright Paulsen. Harcourt, 1997. ISBN 978-0-15-200980-9 Subj: Activities – working. Careers. Rhyming text.

Pavlova, Anna. *I dreamed I was a ballerina.* Ill. with art by Edgar Degas. Atheneum, 2001. ISBN 978-0-689-84676-2 Subj: Activities – dancing. Ballet. Careers – dancers. Character traits – ambition. Foreign lands – Russia.

Paxton, Tom. *Belling the cat and other Aesop fables* (Aesop)

Engelbert the elephant ill. by Steven Kellogg. Morrow, 1990. ISBN 978-0-688-08936-8 Subj: Activities – dancing. Animals – elephants. Etiquette. Parties. Royalty – queens.

Going to the zoo ill. by Karen Lee Schmidt. Morrow, 1996. ISBN 978-0-688-13801-1 Subj: Animals. Music. Songs. Zoos.

The jungle baseball game ill. by Karen Lee Schmidt. Morrow, 1999. ISBN 978-0-688-13980-3 Subj: Animals – hippopotamuses. Animals – monkeys. Sports – baseball.

The story of Santa Claus ill. by Michael Dooling. Morrow, 1995. ISBN 978-0-688-11365-0 Subj: Folk & fairy tales. Holidays – Christmas. Santa Claus.

The story of the Tooth Fairy ill. by Robert Sauber. Morrow, 1996. ISBN 978-0-688-12988-0 Subj: Fairies. Folk & fairy tales. Friendship. Teeth.

Paye, Won-Ldy. *Head, body, legs* retold by Won-Ldy Paye and Margaret H. Lippert; ill. by Julie Paschkis. Henry Holt, 2002. ISBN 978-0-8050-6570-1 Subj: Character traits – cooperation. Folk & fairy tales. Foreign lands – Liberia.

Mrs. Chicken and the hungry crocodile retold by Won-Ldy Paye and Margaret H. Lippert; ill. by Julie Paschkis. Henry Holt, 2003. ISBN 978-0-8050-7047-7 Subj: Birds – chickens, roosters. Folk & fairy tales. Foreign lands – Liberia. Reptiles – alligators, crocodiles.

Payne, Emmy. *Katy no-pocket* ill. by H. A. Rey. Houghton, 1944. ISBN 978-0-395-52141-0 Subj: Animals – kangaroos. Clothing – aprons. Clothing – pockets. Problem solving.

Payne, Nina. *Summertime waltz* ill. by Gabi Swiatkowska. Farrar, 2005. ISBN 978-0-374-37291-0 Subj: Seasons – summer.

Peaceful moments in the wild: animals and their homes ill. with photos. Moonstone, 2001. ISBN 978-0-9707768-1-5 Subj: Animals. Homes, houses.

Peacock, Carol Antoinette. *Mommy far, Mommy near* ill. by Shawn Costello Brownell. Albert Whitman, 2000. ISBN 978-0-8075-5234-6 Subj: Adoption. Emotions. Ethnic groups in the U.S. – Chinese Americans. Family life – mothers.

Pilgrim cat ill. by Doris Ettlinger. Albert Whitman, 2004. ISBN 978-0-8075-6532-2 Subj: Animals – cats. Boats, ships. Pilgrims. U.S. history.

Pearce, Clemency. *Frangoline and the midnight dream* ill. by Rebecca Elliott. Scholastic, 2011. ISBN 978-0-545-31426-8 Subj: Behavior – misbehavior. Moon. Night. Rhyming text.

Three little words ill. by Rosalind Beardshaw. Doubleday, 2014. ISBN 978-038537001-1 Subj: Animals. Emotions – love. Rhyming text.

Pearce, Philippa. *Amy's three best things* ill. by Helen Craig. Candlewick, 2013. ISBN 978-0-7636-6314-8 Subj: Family life – grandmothers. Imagination. Sleepovers.

Pearle, Ida. *A child's day: an alphabet of play* ill. by author. Harcourt, 2008. ISBN 978-0-15-206552-2 Subj: ABC books. Activities.

The moon is going to Addy's house ill. by author. Dial, 2015. ISBN 978-080374054-9 Subj: Bedtime. Moon.

Pearlman, Robb. *Groundhog's day off* ill. by Brett Helquist. Bloomsbury, 2015. ISBN 978-161963289-9 Subj: Activities – vacationing. Animals – groundhogs. Behavior – dissatisfaction. Holidays – Groundhog Day. Humorous stories.

Pearson, Debora. *Alphabeep* ill. by Edward Miller. Holiday, 2003. ISBN 978-0-8234-1722-3 Subj: ABC books. Automobiles. Traffic, traffic signs. Trucks.

Big city song ill. by Lynn Rowe Reed. Holiday House, 2006. ISBN 978-0-8234-1988-3 Subj: Cities, towns. Noise, sounds. Rhyming text.

Leo's tree ill. by Nora Hilb. Annick, 2004. ISBN 978-1-55037-844-3 Subj: Behavior – growing up. Poetry. Trees.

Sophie's wheels ill. by Nora Hilb. Annick, 2006. ISBN 978-1-55451-038-2 Subj: Behavior – growing up. Wheels.

Pearson, Julie. *Elliot* ill. by Manon Gauthier. Pajama, 2016. ISBN 978-192748585-9 Subj: Animals – rabbits. Behavior – needing someone. Foster children, foster homes.

Pearson, Peter. *How to eat an airplane* ill. by Mircea Catusanu. HarperCollins/Katherine Tegen, 2016. ISBN 978-006232062-9 Subj: Airplanes, airports. Etiquette. Humorous stories.

Pearson, Susan, selector. *The drowsy hours: poems for bedtime* ill. by Peter Malone. HarperCollins, 2002. ISBN 978-0-06-029421-2 Subj: Bedtime. Lullabies. Night. Poetry. Sleep.

Hooray for feet! ill. by Roxanna Baer-Block. Blue Apple, 2005. ISBN 978-1-59354-093-7 Subj: Anatomy – feet. Rhyming text.

How to teach a slug to read ill. by David Slonim. Marshall Cavendish, 2011. ISBN 978-0-7614-5805-0 Subj: Animals – slugs. Books, reading.

Slugs in love ill. by Kevin O'Malley. Marshall Cavendish, 2006. ISBN 978-0-7614-5311-6 Subj: Activities – writing. Animals – slugs. Character traits – shyness. Emotions – love. Poetry.

We're going on a ghost hunt ill. by S. D. Schindler. Amazon Children's, 2012. ISBN 978-0-7614-6307-8 Subj: Ghosts. Holidays – Halloween. Imagination.

Pearson, Tracey Campbell. *Bob* ill. by author. Farrar, 2002. ISBN 978-0-374-39957-3 Subj: Animals. Birds – chickens, roosters. Humorous stories. Noise, sounds.

Diddle diddle dumpling ill. by author. Farrar, 2005. ISBN 978-0-374-30861-2 Subj: Format, unusual – board books. Nursery rhymes.

Elephant's story ill. by author. Farrar, 2013. ISBN 978-0-374-39913-9 Subj: Animals. Animals – elephants. Books, reading. Language.

Hector Protector [board book] ill. by author. Farrar, 2004. ISBN 978-0-374-30860-5 Subj: Format, unusual – board books. Nursery rhymes.

The purple hat ill. by author. Farrar, 1997. ISBN 978-0-374-36153-2 Subj: Birds. Clothing – hats. Forest, woods.

Where does Joe go? ill. by author. Farrar, 1999. ISBN 978-0-374-38319-0 Subj: Restaurants. Rhyming text. Santa Claus. Seasons – winter.

Peck, Jan. *The giant carrot* ill. by Barry Root. Dial, 1998. ISBN 978-0-8037-1824-1 Subj: Behavior – sharing. Folk & fairy tales. Food. Foreign lands – Russia.

Giant peach yodel! ill. by Barry Root. Pelican, 2012. ISBN 978-1-58980-980-2 Subj: Character traits – cooperation. Cumulative tales. Folk & fairy tales. Food. Problem solving.

Pirate treasure hunt! ill. by Adrian Tans. Pelican, 2008. ISBN 978-1-58980-549-1 Subj: Imagination. Pirates.

Way up high in a tall green tree ill. by Valeria Petrone. Simon & Schuster, 2005. ISBN 978-1-4169-0071-9 Subj: Animals. Bedtime. Imagination. Jungle. Rhyming text.

Peck, Richard. *Monster night at Grandma's house* ill. by Don Freeman. Dial, 2003. ISBN 978-0-8037-2904-9 Subj: Bedtime. Emotions – fear. Family life – grandmothers. Monsters. Night.

Peddicord, Jane Ann. *That special little baby* ill. by Meilo So. Harcourt, 2007. ISBN 978-0-15-205430-4 Subj: Babies, toddlers. Rhyming text.

Peddle, Daniel. *Snow day* ill. by author. Doubleday, 2000. ISBN 978-0-385-32693-3 Subj: Nature. Snowmen. Weather – snow. Wordless.

Pedersen, Janet. *Houdini the amazing caterpillar* ill. by author. Clarion, 2008. ISBN 978-0-618-89332-4 Subj: Insects – butterflies, caterpillars. Metamorphosis.

Millie wants to play ill. by author. Candlewick, 2004. ISBN 978-0-7636-1993-0 Subj: Animals – bulls, cows. Morning. Noise, sounds.

Pedersen, Judy. *When night time comes near* ill. by author. Viking, 2000. ISBN 978-0-670-88259-5 Subj: Bedtime. Communities, neighborhoods. Night.

Pedersen, Marika. *Mommy works, Daddy works* by Marika Pedersen and Mikele Hall ill. by Deirdre Betteridge. Annick, 2000. ISBN 978-1-55037-657-9 Subj: Activities – working. Family life – parents.

Peek, Merle, adapt. *Mary wore her red dress and Henry wore his green sneakers* ill. by adapter. Clarion, 1985. ISBN 978-0-89919-324-3 Subj: Animals. Animals – bears. Birthdays. Concepts – color. Songs.

Roll over! a counting song ill. by author. Houghton, 1981. ISBN 978-0-395-29438-3 Subj: Counting, numbers. Songs.

Peet, Amanda. *Dear Santa, Love Rachel Rosenstein* by Amanda Peet and Andrea Troyer ill. by Christine Davenier. Knopf, 2015. ISBN 978-055351061-4 Subj: Holidays – Christmas. Jewish culture. Letters, cards. Santa Claus.

Peet, Bill. *The ant and the elephant* ill. by author. Little, 1972. ISBN 978-0-395-13734-5 Subj: Animals. Animals – elephants. Character traits – helpfulness. Character traits – selfishness. Cumulative tales. Insects – ants.

Big bad Bruce ill. by author. Houghton, 1977. ISBN 978-0-395-25150-8 Subj: Animals – bears. Behavior – bullying, teasing. Forest, woods. Humorous stories. Witches.

Bill Peet: an autobiography ill. by author. Houghton, 1989. ISBN 978-0-395-50932-6 Subj: Caldecott award honor books. Careers – illustrators. Careers – writers.

Buford the little bighorn ill. by author. Houghton, 1967. Subj: Animals – sheep. Character traits – individuality. Humorous stories. Sports – hunting. Sports – skiing.

The caboose who got loose ill. by author. Houghton, 1971. ISBN 978-0-395-12578-6 Subj: Behavior – dissatisfaction. Ecology. Trains.

Chester the worldly pig ill. by author. Houghton, 1965. Subj: Animals – pigs. Circus. Humorous stories. World.

Cock-a-doodle Dudley ill. by author. Houghton, 1990. ISBN 978-0-395-55331-2 Subj: Animals. Birds – chickens, roosters. Farms. Sun.

Countdown to Christmas ill. by author. Houghton, 1972. ISBN 978-0-87464-199-8 Subj: Holidays – Christmas. Humorous stories. Magic. Progress. Santa Claus.

Cowardly Clyde ill. by author. Houghton, 1979. ISBN 978-0-395-27802-4 Subj: Animals – horses, ponies. Character traits – bravery. Humorous stories. Knights.

Cyrus the unsinkable sea serpent ill. by author. Houghton, 1975. ISBN 978-0-395-20272-2 Subj: Character traits – helpfulness. Monsters. Mythical creatures. Sea & seashore.

Eli ill. by author. Houghton, 1978. ISBN 978-0-606-03378-7 Subj: Animals – lions. Birds – vultures. Friendship. Humorous stories.

Ella ill. by author. Houghton, 1964. ISBN 978-0-395-17577-4 Subj: Animals – elephants. Behavior – lost. Character traits – conceit. Circus. Rhyming text.

Encore for Eleanor ill. by author. Houghton, 1981. ISBN 978-0-395-29860-2 Subj: Animals – elephants. Art.

Farewell to Shady Glade ill. by author. Houghton, 1966. ISBN 978-0-395-18975-7 Subj: Animals. Ecology. Progress.

Fly, Homer, fly ill. by author. Houghton, 1969. Subj: Birds – pigeons. Cities, towns. Ecology.

The gnats of knotty pine ill. by author. Houghton, 1975. ISBN 978-0-395-21405-3 Subj: Animals. Ecology. Insects – gnats. Sports – hunting.

How Droofus the dragon lost his head ill. by author. Houghton, 1971. ISBN 978-0-395-15085-6 Subj: Dragons. Knights. Royalty – kings.

Hubert's hair-raising adventures ill. by author. Houghton, 1959. Subj: Animals – lions. Careers – barbers. Humorous stories. Rhyming text.

Huge Harold ill. by author. Houghton, 1961. ISBN 978-0-395-32923-8 Subj: Animals – rabbits. Character traits – kindness to animals. Concepts – size. Humorous stories. Rhyming text.

Jennifer and Josephine ill. by author. Houghton, 1967. ISBN 978-0-395-18225-3 Subj: Animals – cats. Automobiles. Humorous stories.

Jethro and Joel were a troll ill. by author. Houghton, 1987. ISBN 978-0-395-43081-1 Subj: Humorous stories. Magic. Mythical creatures – trolls.

Kermit the hermit ill. by author. Houghton, 1965. ISBN 978-0-395-15084-9 Subj: Behavior – greed. Crustaceans – crabs. Humorous stories. Rhyming text. Sea & seashore.

The kweeks of Kookatumdee ill. by author. Houghton, 1985. ISBN 978-0-395-37902-8 Subj: Activities – flying. Behavior – greed. Birds. Rhyming text.

The luckiest one of all ill. by author. Houghton, 1982. ISBN 978-0-395-31863-8 Subj: Behavior – dissatisfaction. Emotions – envy, jealousy. Rhyming text.

Merle the high flying squirrel ill. by author. Houghton, 1974. ISBN 978-0-395-18452-3 Subj: Activities – flying. Animals – squirrels. Humorous stories. Kites. Trees.

No such things ill. by author. Houghton, 1983. ISBN 978-0-395-33888-9 Subj: Animals. Mythical creatures. Rhyming text.

Pamela Camel ill. by author. Houghton, 1984. ISBN 978-0-395-35975-4 Subj: Animals – camels. Behavior – running away. Self-concept.

The pinkish, purplish, bluish egg ill. by author. Houghton, 1963. ISBN 978-0-395-18472-1 Subj: Birds. Birds – doves. Eggs. Mythical creatures. Rhyming text. Violence, nonviolence.

Randy's dandy lions ill. by author. Houghton, 1964. ISBN 978-0-395-18507-0 Subj: Animals – lions. Circus. Humorous stories. Rhyming text.

Smokey ill. by author. Houghton, 1962. ISBN 978-0-395-15992-7 Subj: Old age. Rhyming text. Trains.

The spooky tail of Prewitt Peacock ill. by author. Houghton, 1973. ISBN 978-0-395-15494-6 Subj: Birds – peacocks, peahens. Character traits – being different. Character traits – individuality.

The Whingdingdilly ill. by author. Houghton, 1970. ISBN 978-0-395-24729-7 Subj: Animals – dogs. Behavior – dissatisfaction. Character traits – optimism. Witches.

The wump world ill. by author. Houghton, 1970. ISBN 978-0-395-19841-4 Subj: Ecology. Progress. Space & space ships.

Zella, Zack, and Zodiac ill. by author. Houghton, 1986. ISBN 978-0-395-40567-3 Subj: Animals – zebras. Behavior – needing someone. Birds – ostriches. Rhyming text.

Peet, Mal. *Cloud tea monkeys* by Mal Peet and Elspeth Graham ill. by Juan Wijngaard. Candlewick, 2010. ISBN 978-0-7636-4453-6 Subj: Animals – monkeys. Character traits – kindness to animals. Family life – mothers. Foreign lands – Himalayas. Illness.

Peete, Holly Robinson. *My brother Charlie* by Holly Robinson Peete and Ryan Elizabeth Peete ill. by Shane W. Evans. Scholastic, 2010. ISBN 978-0-545-09466-5 Subj: Disabilities – autism. Ethnic groups in the U.S. – African Americans. Family life – brothers & sisters. Multiple births – twins.

Peete, Ryan Elizabeth. *My brother Charlie* (Peete, Holly Robinson)

Pegram, Laura. *Daughter's Day blues* ill. by Cornelius Van Wright and Ying-Hwa Hu. Dial, 2000. ISBN 978-0-8037-1557-8 Subj: Ethnic groups in the U.S. – African Americans. Family life – brothers & sisters. Family life – grandmothers.

Pelé. *For the love of soccer!* ill. by Frank Morrison. Hyperion/Disney, 2010. ISBN 978-1-4231-1538-0 Subj: Sports – soccer.

Pelham, David. *A is for animals* ill. by author. Simon & Schuster, 1991. ISBN 978-0-671-72495-5 Subj: ABC books. Animals. Format, unusual – toy & movable books.

Crawlies creep ill. by author. Dutton, 1996. ISBN 978-0-525-45576-9 Subj: Animals. Format, unusual – toy & movable books.

Sam's pizza ill. by author. Dutton, 1996. ISBN 978-0-525-45594-3 Subj: Activities – baking, cooking. Family life – brothers & sisters. Food. Format, unusual – toy & movable books. Rhyming text. Sibling rivalry.

Sam's sandwich ill. by author. Dutton, 1991. ISBN 978-0-525-44751-1 Subj: Family life – brothers & sisters. Food. Format, unusual – toy & movable books. Rhyming text.

Pellant, Chris. *The best book of fossils, rocks, and minerals* ill. by author. Kingfisher, 2000. ISBN 978-0-7534-5274-5 Subj: Fossils. Rocks.

Pelletier, Andrew T. *The amazing adventures of Bathman!* ill. by Peter Elwell. Penguin, 2005. ISBN 978-0-525-47164-6 Subj: Activities – bathing. Toys.

The toy farmer ill. by Scott Nash. Penguin, 2007. ISBN 978-0-525-47649-8 Subj: Careers – farmers. Farms. Magic. Toys.

Pelletier, David. *The graphic alphabet* ill. by author. Orchard, 1996. ISBN 978-0-531-36001-9 Subj: ABC books. Caldecott award honor books. Concepts.

Pelley, Kathleen T. *Inventor McGregor* ill. by Michael Chesworth. Farrar, 2006. ISBN 978-0-374-33606-6 Subj: Careers – inventors. Family life.

Magnus Maximus, a marvelous measurer ill. by S. D. Schindler. Farrar, 2010. ISBN 978-0-374-34725-3 Subj: Concepts – measurement. Counting, numbers.

Raj the bookstore tiger ill. by Paige Keiser. Charlesbridge, 2011. ISBN 978-1-58089-230-8 Subj: Animals – cats. Self-concept. Stores.

Pelton, Mindy L. *When Dad's at sea* ill. by Robert Gantt Steele. Albert Whitman, 2004. ISBN 978-0-8075-6339-7 Subj: Behavior – needing someone. Boats, ships. Careers – airplane pilots. Careers – military. Family life – fathers.

Pendziwol, Jean E. *Me and you and the red canoe.* Groundwood, 2017. ISBN 978-155498847-1 Subj: Canoes & canoeing. Family life – brothers & sisters. Sports – fishing.

No dragons for tea: fire safety for kids (and dragons) ill. by Martine Gourbault. Kids Can, 1999. ISBN 978-1-55074-569-6 Subj: Dragons. Fire. Friendship. Rhyming text. Safety.

Once upon a northern night ill. by Isabelle Arsenault. Groundwood, 2013. ISBN 978-1-55498-138-0 Subj: Night. Seasons – winter. Weather – snow.

The red sash ill. by Nicolas Debon. Groundwood, 2005. ISBN 978-0-88899-589-6 Subj: Careers – fur traders. Foreign lands – Canada. Indians of North America – Metis.

The tale of Sir Dragon: dealing with bullies for kids (and dragons) ill. by Martine Gourbault. Kids Can, 2007. ISBN 978-1-55453-135-6 Subj: Behavior – bullying, teasing. Dragons. Rhyming text.

A treasure at sea for dragon and me ill. by Martine Gourbault. Kids Can, 2005. ISBN 978-1-55337-721-4 Subj: Dragons. Rhyming text. Safety. Sea & seashore – beaches. Sports.

Penfold, Alexandra. *We are brothers, we are friends* ill. by Eda Kaban. Farrar, 2017. ISBN 978-037430201-6 Subj: Family life – brothers. Family life – new sibling.

Penn, Audrey. *A bedtime kiss for Chester Raccoon* ill. by Barbara L. Gibson. Tanglewood, 2011. ISBN 978-1-933718-52-1 Subj: Animals – raccoons. Bedtime. Emotions – fear. Format, unusual – board books. Rhyming text.

Chester Raccoon and the almost perfect sleepover ill. by Barbara Gibson. Tanglewood, 2017. ISBN 978-193910011-5 Subj: Animals – raccoons. Sleepovers.

A color game for Chester Raccoon ill. by Barbara L. Gibson. Tanglewood, 2012. ISBN 978-1-933718-58-3 Subj: Animals – raccoons. Concepts – color. Format, unusual – board books.

Kai to the rescue! ill. by Mike Yamada. Scholastic/Orchard, 2016. ISBN 978-054581636-6 Subj: Behavior – bullying, teasing. Careers – firefighters. Character traits – smallness. Fire. Trucks.

Penner, Fred. *The cat came back* ill. by Renee Reichert. Macmillan, 2005. ISBN 978-1-59643-030-3 Subj: Animals – cats. Character traits – persistence. Songs.

Pennypacker, Sara. *Meet the Dullards* ill. by Daniel Salmieri. HarperCollins/Balzer+Bray, 2015. ISBN 978-006219856-3 Subj: Behavior – boredom. Family life. Humorous stories. Moving.

Pierre in love ill. by Petra Mathers. Scholastic, 2007. ISBN 978-0-439-51740-9 Subj: Animals – mice. Animals – rabbits. Ballet. Careers – fishermen. Emotions – love.

Stuart's cape ill. by Martin Matje. Orchard, 2002. ISBN 978-0-439-30180-0 Subj: Behavior – worrying. Imagination. Moving. School – first day.

Peppa Pig and the vegetable garden. Candlewick, 2014. ISBN 978-076366987-4 Subj: Activities – baking, cooking. Animals – pigs. Gardens, gardening.

Percival, Tom. *Herman's letter* ill. by author. Bloomsbury, 2014. ISBN 978-161963423-7 Subj: Animals – bears. Animals – raccoons. Friendship. Letters, cards. Moving. Moving. Pen pals.

Perdorno, Willie. *Visiting Langston* ill. by Bryan Collier. Henry Holt, 2002. ISBN 978-0-8050-6744-6 Subj: Careers – poets. Ethnic groups in the U.S. – African Americans. Poetry.

Perepeczko, Jenny. *Moses: the true story of an elephant baby* ill. by author. Atheneum, 2014. ISBN 978-144249603-3 Subj: Animals – elephants. Character traits – kindness to animals.

Peretz, Isaac Loeb. *The magician* (Shulevitz, Uri)

Pérez, Amada Irma. *My diary from here to there / Mi diario de aquí hasta allá* ill. by Maya Christina Gonzalez. Children's Book Press, 2002. ISBN 978-0-89239-175-2 Subj: Ethnic groups in the U.S. – Mexican Americans. Family life. Foreign languages. Immigrants, immigration. Moving.

My very own room / Mi propio cuartito ill. by Maya Christina Gonzalez. Lee & Low, 2000. ISBN 978-0-89239-164-6 Subj: Ethnic groups in the U.S. – Mexican Americans. Family life. Foreign languages. Homes, houses.

Pérez, L. King. *First day in grapes* ill. by Robert Casilla. Lee & Low, 2002. ISBN 978-1-58430-045-8 Subj: Careers – migrant workers. Character traits – confidence. Ethnic groups in the U.S. – Mexican Americans. School – first day.

Perez, Monica. *Curious George plants a tree* ill. by Anna Grossnickle Hines. Houghton, 2009. ISBN 978-0-547-15087-1 Subj: Animals – monkeys. Ecology. Trees.

Curious George saves his pennies ill. by Mary O'Keefe Young. Houghton Mifflin, 2013. ISBN 978-0-547-63231-5 Subj: Animals – monkeys. Behavior – saving things. Money. Toys.

Pericoli, Matteo. *See the city* ill. by author. Knopf, 2004. ISBN 978-0-375-82469-2 Subj: Activities – drawing. Cities, towns. Format, unusual.

Tommaso and the missing line ill. by author. Knopf, 2008. ISBN 978-0-375-84102-6 Subj: Activities – drawing. Behavior – lost & found possessions. Foreign lands – Italy. Imagination.

The true story of Stellina ill. by author. Random House, 2006. ISBN 978-0-375-93273-1 Subj: Birds – finches. Character traits – kindness to animals.

Perkins, Chloe. *Cinderella* ill. by Sandra Equihua. Simon & Schuster/Little Simon, 2016. ISBN 978-148147915-8 Subj: Family life – stepfamilies. Folk & fairy tales. Foreign lands – Mexico. Format, unusual – board books. Royalty – princes. Sibling rivalry.

Perkins, Lynne Rae. *The broken cat* ill. by author. Greenwillow, 2002. ISBN 978-0-06-029264-5 Subj: Animals – cats. Careers – veterinarians. Family life. Illness. Memories, memory.

The cardboard piano ill. by author. Greenwillow, 2008. ISBN 978-0-06-154265-7 Subj: Friendship. Musical instruments – pianos.

Frank and Lucky get schooled ill. by author. Greenwillow, 2016. ISBN 978-006237345-8 Subj: Animals – dogs. Character traits – curiosity. Character traits – kindness to animals. Pets.

Home lovely ill. by author. Greenwillow, 1995. ISBN 978-0-688-13688-8 Subj: Family life. Gardens, gardening.

Pictures from our vacation ill. by author. HarperCollins, 2007. ISBN 978-0-06-085098-2 Subj: Activities – photographing. Activities – vacationing. Family life. Foreign lands – Canada.

Snow music ill. by author. Greenwillow, 2003. ISBN 978-0-06-623956-9 Subj: Animals – dogs. Behavior – lost & found possessions. Noise, sounds. Seasons – winter. Weather – snow.

Perkins, Maripat. *Rodeo Red* ill. by Molly Idle. Peachtree, 2015. ISBN 978-156145816-5 Subj: Cowboys, cowgirls. Family life – brothers & sisters. Family life – new sibling. Toys.

Perkins, Useni Eugene. *Hey Black Child* ill. by Bryan Collier. Little, Brown, 2017. ISBN 978-031636030-2 Subj: Ethnic groups in the U.S. – African Americans. Poetry. Self-concept.

Perl, Erica S. *Chicken Butt's back!* ill. by Henry Cole. Abrams, 2011. ISBN 978-0-8109-9729-5 Subj: Birds – chickens, roosters. Humorous stories. Language.

Dotty ill. by Julia Denos. Abrams, 2010. ISBN 978-0-8109-8962-7 Subj: Emotions – anger. Imagination – imaginary friends. School.

Ferocious Fluffity: a mighty bite-y class pet ill. by Henry Cole. Abrams, 2016. ISBN 978-141972182-3 Subj: Animals – hamsters. Pets. Rhyming text. School.

Goatilocks and the three bears (The three bears)

Ninety-three in my family ill. by Mike Lester. Abrams, 2006. ISBN 978-0-8109-5760-2 Subj: Counting, numbers. Family life. Rhyming text.

Totally tardy Marty ill. by Jarrett J. Krosoczka. Abrams, 2015. ISBN 978-141971661-4 Subj: Behavior – promptness, tardiness. Friendship.

Perlman, Janet. *The delicious bug* ill. by author. Kids Can, 2009. ISBN 978-1-55337-996-6 Subj: Behavior – sharing. Insects. Reptiles – chameleons.

The Emperor Penguin's new clothes ill. by author. Viking, 1995. ISBN 978-0-670-85864-4 Subj: Birds – penguins. Character traits – pride. Character traits – vanity. Clothing. Folk & fairy tales. Imagination. Royalty – emperors.

The penguin and the pea by Janet Perlman and Hans Christian Anderson ill. by reteller. Kids Can, 2004. ISBN 978-1-55074-832-1 Subj: Birds –

penguins. Folk & fairy tales. Royalty – princesses. Sleep.

Perlman, Willa. *Good night, world* ill. by Carolyn Fisher. Simon & Schuster, 2011. ISBN 978-1-4424-0197-4 Subj: Bedtime. Rhyming text. World.

Perlov, Betty Rosenberg. *Rifka takes a bow* ill. by Cosei Kawa. Lerner/Kar-Ben, 2013. ISBN 978-0-7613-8127-3 Subj: Jewish culture. Theater.

Perrault, Charles. *Cinderella* retold by Sarah L. Thomson; ill. by Nicoletta Ceccoli. Amazon Children's, 2012. ISBN 978-0-7614-6170-8 Subj: Family life – stepfamilies. Folk & fairy tales. Royalty – princes. Sibling rivalry.

Cinderella retold by Amy Ehrlich; ill. by Susan Jeffers. Dial, 1985. ISBN 978-0-8037-0206-6 Subj: Family life – stepfamilies. Folk & fairy tales. Royalty – princes. Sibling rivalry.

Cinderella ill. by Loek Koopmans. NorthSouth, 1999. ISBN 978-0-7358-1052-5 Subj: Family life – stepfamilies. Folk & fairy tales. Royalty – princes. Sibling rivalry.

Cinderella retold by Barbara McClintock; ill. by reteller. Scholastic, 2005. ISBN 978-0-439-56145-7 Subj: Family life – stepfamilies. Folk & fairy tales. Royalty – princes. Sibling rivalry.

Cinderella retold by Barbara Karlin; ill. by James Marshall. Little, 1989. ISBN 978-0-316-54654-6 Subj: Family life – stepfamilies. Folk & fairy tales. Royalty – princes. Sibling rivalry.

Cinderella / Cenicienta adapt. by Francesc Boada; ill. by Monse Fransoy. Chronicle, 2001. ISBN 978-0-8118-3084-3 Subj: Family life – stepfamilies. Folk & fairy tales. Foreign lands – France. Foreign languages. Royalty – princes. Sibling rivalry.

Cinderella: a pop-up fairy tale retold by Matthew Reinhart; ill. by reteller. Simon & Schuster, 2005. ISBN 978-1-4169-0501-1 Subj: Family life – stepfamilies. Folk & fairy tales. Format, unusual – toy & movable books. Royalty – princes. Sibling rivalry.

Cinderella: or, the little glass slipper ill. by Marcia Brown. Aladdin, 1988, ©1954. ISBN 978-0-689-71261-6 Subj: Caldecott award books. Family life – stepfamilies. Folk & fairy tales. Royalty – princes. Sibling rivalry.

Puss in boots ill. by Marcia Brown. Scribners, 1952. Subj: Animals – cats. Caldecott award honor books. Character traits – cleverness. Folk & fairy tales. Royalty – kings.

Puss in boots adapt. by Lorinda Bryan Cauley; ill. by adapter. Harcourt, 1986. ISBN 978-0-15-264227-3 Subj: Animals – cats. Character traits – cleverness. Folk & fairy tales. Royalty – kings.

Puss in boots ill. by Paul Galdone. Seabury Pr., 1976. ISBN 978-0-8164-3159-5 Subj: Animals – cats. Character traits – cleverness. Folk & fairy tales. Royalty – kings.

Puss in boots retold by Steve Light; ill. by reteller. Abrams, 2002. ISBN 978-0-8109-4368-1 Subj: Animals – cats. Character traits – cleverness. Clothing – boots. Folk & fairy tales. Royalty – kings.

Puss in boots retold by Kurt Baumann; ill. by Giuliano Lunelli. NorthSouth, 1999. ISBN 978-0-7358-1159-1 Subj: Animals – cats. Character traits – cleverness. Folk & fairy tales. Royalty – kings.

Puss in boots ill. by Fred Marcellino. Farrar, 1990. ISBN 978-0-374-36160-0 Subj: Animals – cats. Caldecott award honor books. Character traits – cleverness. Folk & fairy tales. Royalty – kings.

Puss in boots retold by John Cech; ill. by Bernhard Oberdieck. Sterling, 2010. ISBN 978-1-4027-4436-5 Subj: Animals – cats. Character traits – cleverness. Folk & fairy tales. Royalty – kings.

Puss in boots retold by Jerry Pinkney; ill. by reteller. Dial, 2012. ISBN 978-0-8037-1642-1 Subj: Animals – cats. Character traits – cleverness. Clothing – boots. Folk & fairy tales. Royalty – kings.

Puss in boots retold by Lincoln Kirstein; ill. by Alain Vaës. Little, 1992. ISBN 978-0-316-89506-4 Subj: Animals – cats. Character traits – cleverness. Folk & fairy tales. Royalty – kings.

Sleeping Beauty Cynthia Rylant; ill. by Erin McGuire. Disney/Hyperion, 2017. ISBN 978-142312108-4 Subj: Fairies. Folk & fairy tales. Royalty – princes. Royalty – princesses. Sleep.

Perret, Delphine. *The Big Bad Wolf and me* ill. by author. Sterling, 2006. ISBN 978-1-4027-3725-1 Subj: Animals – wolves. Pets.

The Big Bad Wolf goes on vacation ill. by author. Sterling, 2013. ISBN 978-1-4027-8633-4 Subj: Activities – vacationing. Animals – wolves. Family life – grandfathers.

Pedro and George ill. by author. Atheneum, 2015. ISBN 978-148142925-2 Subj: Family life – cousins. Humorous stories. Reptiles – alligators, crocodiles.

Perrin, Clotilde. *At the same moment, around the world* ill. by author. Chronicle, 2014. ISBN 978-145212208-3 Subj: Time. World.

Perrin, Martine. *Cock-a-doodle who?* ill. by author. Albert Whitman, 2012. ISBN 978-0-8075-1107-7 Subj: Animals. Farms. Format, unusual. Rhyming text.

Look who's there! ill. by author. Albert Whitman, 2011. ISBN 978-0-8075-7676-2 Subj: Animals. Format, unusual – toy & movable books. Sea & seashore.

Perrow, Angeli. *Lighthouse dog to the rescue* ill. by Emily Harris. Down East, 2000. ISBN 978-0-89272-487-1 Subj: Animals – dogs. Lighthouses. Weather – storms.

Many hands: a Penobscot Indian story ill. by Heather Austin. Down East, 2010. ISBN 978-0-89272-782-7 Subj: Activities – weaving. Family life – grandmothers. Indians of North America.

Sirius, the dog star ill. by Emily Harris. Down East, 2002. ISBN 978-0-89272-545-8 Subj: Animals – dogs. Behavior – resourcefulness. Boats, ships.

Perry, Andrea. *The Bicklebys' birdbath* ill. by Roberta Angaramo. Simon & Schuster, 2010. ISBN 978-1-4169-0624-7 Subj: Birds. Cumulative tales. Rhyming text.

Here's what you do when you can't find your shoe ill. by Alan Snow. Atheneum, 2003. ISBN 978-0-689-83067-9 Subj: Inventions. Poetry.

Perry, Elizabeth. *Think cool thoughts* ill. by Linda Bronson. Houghton, 2005. ISBN 978-0-618-23493-6 Subj: Ethnic groups in the U.S. – African Americans. Family life – aunts, uncles. Seasons – summer.

Perry, John. *The book that eats people* ill. by Mark Fearing. Tricycle, 2009. ISBN 978-1-58246-268-4 Subj: Books, reading.

Perry, Michael. *Daniel's ride* ill. by Lee Ballard. Free Will, 2001. ISBN 978-0-9701771-9-3 Subj: Automobiles. Family life – brothers.

Perry, Phyllis J. *Pandas' earthquake escape* ill. by Susan Detwiler. Sylvan Dell, 2010. ISBN 978-1-60718-071-5 Subj: Animals – pandas. Earthquakes. Foreign lands – China.

Perry, Robert. *Down at the Seaweed Café* ill. by Greta Guzek. Raincoast, 2002. ISBN 978-1-55192-473-1 Subj: Restaurants. Rhyming text. Sea & seashore – beaches.

Petach, Heidi. *Goldilocks and the three hares* ill. by author. Putnam, 1995. ISBN 978-0-399-22828-5 Subj: Animals – rabbits. Folk & fairy tales.

Wee three pigs ill. by author. Grosset, 2002. ISBN 978-0-448-42528-3 Subj: Animals – pigs. Holidays – Christmas. Homes, houses.

Peters, Bernadette. *Stella is a star!* ill. by Liz Murphy. Blue Apple, 2010. ISBN 978-1-60905-008-5 Subj: Animals – dogs. Ballet. Disguises. Self-concept.

Peters, Lisa Westberg. *Cold little duck, duck, duck* ill. by Sam Williams. Greenwillow, 2000. ISBN 978-0-688-16179-8 Subj: Birds – ducks. Imagination. Seasons – spring.

Frankie works the night shift ill. by Jennifer Taylor. HarperCollins, 2010. ISBN 978-0-06-009095-1 Subj: Animals – cats. Counting, numbers. Night.

October smiled back ill. by Ed Young. Henry Holt, 1996. ISBN 978-0-8050-1776-2 Subj: Days of the week, months of the year. Rhyming text.

Sleepyhead bear ill. by Ian Schoenherr. HarperCollins, 2006. ISBN 978-0-06-059675-0 Subj: Animals – bears. Insects. Rhyming text. Sleep.

The sun, the wind and the rain ill. by Ted Rand. Henry Holt, 1988. ISBN 978-0-8050-0699-5 Subj: Nature. Science. Sea & seashore. Weather.

Volcano wakes up! ill. by Steve Jenkins. Henry Holt, 2010. ISBN 978-0-8050-8287-6 Subj: Poetry. Volcanoes.

Water's way ill. by Ted Rand. Arcade, 1991. ISBN 978-1-55970-062-7 Subj: Nature. Science. Water. Weather.

Peters, Stephanie True. *Raggedy Ann and Andy and the magic potion* ill. by Reg Sandland. Adapt. by Stephanie True Peters from the stories by Johnny Gruelle. Simon & Schuster, 2001. ISBN 978-0-689-83180-5 Subj: Fairies. Magic. Toys – dolls.

Petersen, David. *Snowy Valentine* ill. by author. HarperCollins, 2011. ISBN 978-0-06-146378-5 Subj: Animals. Animals – rabbits. Holidays – Valentine's Day. Weather – snow.

Petersham, Maud. *An American ABC* by Maud Petersham and Miska Petersham; ill. by authors. Macmillan, 1941. Subj: ABC books. Caldecott award honor books. U.S. history.

The rooster crows by Maud Petersham and Miska Petersham; ill. by authors. Macmillan, 1945. ISBN 978-0-02-773100-2 Subj: Caldecott award books. Nursery rhymes.

Petersham, Miska. *An American ABC* (Petersham, Maud)

The rooster crows (Petersham, Maud)

Peterson, Cris. *Amazing grazing* photos by Alvis Upitis. Boyds Mills, 2002. ISBN 978-1-56397-942-2 Subj: Animals – bulls, cows. Careers – ranchers. Ecology.

Extra cheese, please! photos by Alvis Upitis. Boyds Mills, 1994. ISBN 978-1-56397-177-8 Subj: Animals – bulls, cows. Careers – farmers. Farms. Food.

Fantastic farm machines ill. by David R. Lundquist. Boyds Mills, 2006. ISBN 978-1-59078-271-2 Subj: Farms. Machines. Tractors.

Seed soil sun: Earth's recipe for food photos by David R. Lundquist. Boyds Mills, 2010. ISBN 978-1-59078-713-7 Subj: Gardens, gardening. Plants. Seeds. Sun.

Peterson, Jeanne Whitehouse. *Don't forget Winona* ill. by Kimberly Bulcken Root. Cotler, 2004. ISBN 978-0-06-027198-5 Subj: Family life. Family life – sisters. U.S. history. Weather – droughts.

My mama sings ill. by Sandra Speidel. HarperCollins, 1994. ISBN 978-0-06-023859-9 Subj: Activities – singing. Ethnic groups in the U.S. – African Americans. Family life – mothers. Music.

Peterson, Mary. *Piggies in the pumpkin patch* by Mary Peterson and Jennifer Rofé; ill. by Mary Peterson. Charlesbridge, 2010. ISBN 978-1-57091-460-7 Subj: Animals – pigs. Farms.

Peterson, Melissa. *Hanna's Christmas* ill. by Melissa Iwai. HarperCollins, 2001. ISBN 978-0-694-01371-5 Subj: Ethnic groups in the U.S. – Swedish Americans. Format, unusual – board books. Holidays – Christmas.

Petricic, Dusan. *My family tree and me* ill. by author. Kids Can, 2015. ISBN 978-177138049-2 Subj: Ethnic groups in the U.S. Ethnic groups in the U.S. – Chinese Americans. Family life.

Petrillo, Genevieve. *Keep your ear on the ball* ill. by Lea Lyon. Tilbury, 2007. ISBN 978-0-88448-296-3 Subj: Character traits – helpfulness. Disabilities – blindness. Games. School.

Pett, Mark. *The boy and the airplane* ill. by author. Simon & Schuster, 2013. ISBN 978-1-4424-5123-0 Subj: Airplanes, airports. Behavior – lost & found possessions. Gifts. Problem solving. Toys. Wordless.

The girl and the bicycle ill. by author. Simon & Schuster, 2014. ISBN 978-144248319-4 Subj: Problem solving. Sports – bicycling. Wordless.

The girl who never made mistakes by Mark Pett and Gary Rubinstein; ill. by Mark Pett. Sourcebooks, 2011. ISBN 978-1-4022-5544-1 Subj: Behavior – worrying. Character traits – perfectionism. Self-concept.

Lizard from the park ill. by author. Simon & Schuster, 2015. ISBN 978-144248321-7 Subj: Dinosaurs. Friendship. Pets.

Pettenati, Jeanne K. *Galileo's journal, 1609–1610* ill. by Paolo Rui. Charlesbridge, 2006. ISBN 978-1-57091-879-7 Subj: Astronomy. Careers – astronomers. Careers – scientists. Science. Stars.

Pettitt, Linda. *Yafi's family: an Ethiopian boy's journey of love, loss, and adoption* by Linda Pettitt and Sharon Darrow ill. by Jan Spivey Gilchrist. Amharic Kids, 2010. ISBN 978-0-9797481-4-1 Subj: Adoption. Foreign lands – Australia. Foreign lands – Ethiopia.

Petty, Dev. *I don't want to be a frog* ill. by Mike Boldt. Doubleday, 2015. ISBN 978-038537866-6 Subj: Animals. Behavior – dissatisfaction. Frogs & toads. Self-concept.

I don't want to be big ill. by Mike Boldt. Doubleday, 2016. ISBN 978-110193920-8 Subj: Behavior – growing up. Frogs & toads.

There's nothing to do! ill. by Mike Boldt. Doubleday, 2017. ISBN 978-039955803-0 Subj: Behavior – boredom. Frogs & toads.

Petty, Dini. *The queen, the bear and the bumblebee* ill. by Rose Cowles. Beyond Words, 2000. ISBN 978-1-58270-036-6 Subj: Animals – bears. Behavior – wishing. Friendship. Insects – bees. Self-concept. Space & space ships.

Petz, Moritz. *Wish you were here* ill. by Quentin Gréban. NorthSouth, 2005. ISBN 978-0-7358-2005-0 Subj: Animals – hedgehogs. Animals – mice. Friendship.

Pfeffer, Wendy. *The big flood* ill. by Vanessa Lubach. Millbrook, 2001. ISBN 978-0-7613-1653-4 Subj: Farms. Rivers. U.S. history. Weather – floods.

Dolphin talk ill. by Helen Davie. HarperCollins, 2003. ISBN 978-0-06-028802-0 Subj: Animals – dolphins. Communication. Noise, sounds.

From tadpole to frog ill. by Holly Keller. HarperCollins, 1994. ISBN 978-0-06-023117-0 Subj: Frogs & toads. Nature. Science.

Life in a coral reef ill. by Steve Jenkins. Collins, 2009. ISBN 978-0-06-029553-0 Subj: Nature. Sea & seashore.

Light is all around us ill. by Paul Meisel. HarperCollins, 2014. ISBN 978-006029121-1 Subj: Light, lights. Science.

Mallard duck at Meadow View Pond ill. by Taylor Oughton. Soundprints, 2001. ISBN 978-1-56899-956-2 Subj: Animals – babies. Behavior – growing up. Birds – ducks. Family life. Lakes, ponds.

What's it like to be a fish? ill. by Holly Keller. HarperCollins, 1996. ISBN 978-0-06-024429-3 Subj: Fish. Pets.

Wiggling worms at work ill. by Steve Jenkins. HarperCollins, 2004. ISBN 978-0-06-028449-7 Subj: Animals – worms. Science.

Pfister, Marcus. *Animal ABC* ill. by author. NorthSouth, 2013. ISBN 978-0-7358-4136-9 Subj: ABC books. Animals.

Ava's poppy ill. by author. NorthSouth, 2012. ISBN 978-0-7358-4057-7 Subj: Flowers. Science. Seasons.

Bertie: just like daddy ill. by author. NorthSouth, 2009. ISBN 978-0-7358-2224-5 Subj: Animals – hippopotamuses. Behavior – imitation. Family life – fathers.

Bertie at bedtime ill. by author. NorthSouth, 2008. ISBN 978-0-7358-2194-1 Subj: Animals – hippopotamuses. Bedtime.

Charlie at the zoo ill. by author. NorthSouth, 2004. ISBN 978-0-7358-2144-6 Subj: Animals. Birds – ducks. Format, unusual. Zoos.

The Christmas star ill. by author. NorthSouth, 1993. ISBN 978-1-55858-204-0 Subj: Holidays – Christmas. Religion – Nativity. Stars.

Dazzle the dinosaur ill. by author. NorthSouth, 1994. ISBN 978-1-55858-338-2 Subj: Dinosaurs. Prehistory.

Good night, little rainbow fish ill. by author. NorthSouth, 2012. ISBN 978-0-7358-4082-9 Subj: Bedtime. Fish. Sleep.

Hang on, Hopper! ill. by Rosemary Lanning. NorthSouth, 1995. ISBN 978-1-55858-404-4 Subj: Animals – rabbits. Safety. Sports – swimming.

Happy birthday, Bertie! ill. by author. NorthSouth, 2010. ISBN 978-0-7358-2280-1 Subj: Animals – hippopotamuses. Birthdays. Parties.

The happy hedgehog ill. by author. NorthSouth, 2000. ISBN 978-0-7358-1165-2 Subj: Animals – hedgehogs. Family life – grandfathers.

Hopper ill. by author. NorthSouth, 1991. ISBN 978-1-55858-106-7 Subj: Animals – rabbits. Seasons – spring. Seasons – winter.

Hopper hunts for spring ill. by author. NorthSouth, 1992. ISBN 978-1-55858-139-5 Subj: Animals. Animals – rabbits. Frogs & toads. Seasons – spring.

Hopper's treetop adventure ill. by author. NorthSouth, 1997. ISBN 978-1-55858-681-9 Subj: Animals – rabbits. Animals – squirrels. Nature. Trees.

How Leo learned to be king ill. by author. NorthSouth, 1998. ISBN 978-1-55858-914-8 Subj: Animals. Animals – lions. Behavior. Royalty – kings.

Just the way you are ill. by author. NorthSouth, 2002. ISBN 978-0-7358-1615-2 Subj: Animals. Format, unusual – toy & movable books. Parties. Self-concept.

The little moon raven ill. by author. Minedition, 2014. ISBN 978-988824081-4 Subj: Behavior – bullying, teasing. Birds – ravens. Character traits – bravery. Moon. Self-concept.

Make a wish, Honey Bear! ill. by author. NorthSouth, 1999. ISBN 978-0-7358-1244-4 Subj: Animals – bears. Behavior – wishing. Birthdays.

Milo and the magical stones ill. by author. NorthSouth, 1997. ISBN 978-1-55858-682-6 Subj: Animals – mice. Behavior. Format, unusual – toy & movable books. Magic.

Milo and the mysterious island ill. by author. NorthSouth, 2000. ISBN 978-0-7358-1352-6 Subj: Animals – mice. Islands. Prejudice. Sea & seashore.

Penguin Pete and Little Tim ill. by author. NorthSouth, 1994. ISBN 978-1-55858-302-3 Subj: Activities – walking. Birds – penguins. Family life – fathers. Weather – snow.

Questions, questions ill. by author. NorthSouth, 2011. ISBN 978-0-7358-4000-3 Subj: Animals – hippopotamuses. Character traits – questioning. Nature. Rhyming text.

The rainbow fish ill. by author. NorthSouth, 1992. ISBN 978-0-7358-1748-7 Subj: Behavior – sharing. Character traits – appearance. Emotions – loneliness. Fish.

Rainbow fish ABC ill. by author. NorthSouth, 2002. ISBN 978-0-7358-1714-2 Subj: ABC books. Fish. Sea & seashore.

Rainbow fish and the big blue whale ill. by author. NorthSouth, 1998. ISBN 978-0-7358-1010-5 Subj: Animals – whales. Behavior – fighting, arguing. Fish.

Rainbow fish and the sea monsters' cave ill. by author. NorthSouth, 2001. ISBN 978-0-7358-1537-7 Subj: Caves. Fish. Monsters. Sea & seashore.

Rainbow fish to the rescue! ill. by author. NorthSouth, 1995. ISBN 978-1-55858-487-7 Subj: Character traits – appearance. Emotions – fear. Fish. Fish – sharks. Friendship.

Snow puppy ill. by author. NorthSouth, 2011. ISBN 978-0-7358-4031-7 Subj: Animals – dogs. Behavior – lost. Weather – snow.

Wake up, Santa Claus! ill. by author. NorthSouth, 1996. ISBN 978-1-55858-606-2 Subj: Behavior – hurrying. Dreams. Holidays – Christmas. Santa Claus.

Where is my friend? ill. by author. Henry Holt, 1986. ISBN 978-0-03-008033-3 Subj: Animals – porcupines. Format, unusual – board books. Friendship.

You can't win them all, rainbow fish ill. by author. NorthSouth, 2017. ISBN 978-073584287-8 Subj: Behavior – hiding. Emotions – anger. Fish. Games. Sportsmanship.

Pham, LeUyen. *All the things I love about you* ill. by author. HarperCollins, 2010. ISBN 978-0-06-199029-8 Subj: Emotions – love. Family life – mothers.

The bear who wasn't there ill. by author. Roaring Brook, 2016. ISBN 978-159643970-2 Subj: Animals. Animals – bears. Behavior – lost. Birds – ducks. Books, reading.

Big sister, little sister ill. by author. Hyperion, 2005. ISBN 978-0-7868-5182-9 Subj: Character traits – individuality. Family life – brothers & sisters.

A piece of cake ill. by author. HarperCollins/Balzer+Bray, 2014. ISBN 978-006199264-3 Subj: Activities – trading. Animals. Animals – mice. Birthdays. Character traits – cooperation. Food.

There's no such thing as little ill. by author. Knopf, 2015. ISBN 978-038539150-4 Subj: Character traits – smallness. Concepts. Format, unusual – toy & movable books.

Phelan, Matt. *Druthers* ill. by author. Candlewick, 2014. ISBN 978-076365955-4 Subj: Activities – playing. Behavior – boredom. Family life – fathers. Imagination. Weather – rain.

Phi, Bao. *A different pond* ill. by Thi Bui. Capstone, 2017. ISBN 978-162370803-0 Subj: Behavior – resourcefulness. Caldecott award honor books. Ethnic groups in the U.S. – Vietnamese Americans. Family life – fathers. Immigrants, immigration. Sports – fishing.

Philip, Neil, selector. *The fish is me* ill. by Claire Henley. Clarion, 2002. ISBN 978-0-618-15939-0 Subj: Activities – bathing. Poetry.

Hot potato: mealtime rhymes ill. by Claire Henley. Clarion, 2004. ISBN 978-0-618-31554-3 Subj: Food. Poetry.

Noah and the devil ill. by Isabelle Brent. Clarion, 2001. ISBN 978-0-618-11754-3 Subj: Boats, ships. Devil. Folk & fairy tales. Foreign lands – Romania. Religion – Noah.

Philip, Simon. *I don't know what to call my cat* ill. by Ella Bailey. Houghton Mifflin Harcourt, 2017. ISBN 978-054497143-1 Subj: Animals – cats. Animals – gorillas. Names.

You must bring a hat! ill. by Kate Hindley. Sterling, 2017. ISBN 978-145492688-7 Subj: Clothing – hats. Parties.

Phillipps, J. C. *Monkey Ono* ill. by author. Viking, 2013. ISBN 978-0-670-78505-6 Subj: Animals – monkeys. Behavior – resourcefulness. Toys.

The Simples love a picnic ill. by author. Houghton, 2014. ISBN 978-054416667-7 Subj: Activities – picnicking. Family life.

Phillips, Betty Lou. *Emily goes wild* ill. by Sharon Watts. Gibbs Smith, 2003. ISBN 978-1-58685-268-9 Subj: Animals – monkeys. Behavior – misbehavior. Pets. Zoos.

Phillips, Christopher. *Ceci Ann's day of why* ill. by Shino Arihara. Ten Speed, 2006. ISBN 978-1-58246-171-7 Subj: Character traits – questioning. Ethnic groups in the U.S. – African Americans. Rhyming text.

Phillips, Mildred. *And the cow said, "moo"!* ill. by Sonja Lamut. Greenwillow, 2000. ISBN 978-0-688-16803-2 Subj: Animals. Farms. Noise, sounds.

Philpot, Graham. *Find Anthony Ant* (Philpot, Lorna)

Where is Little Harry? ill. by author. Candlewick, 2001. ISBN 978-0-7636-1439-3 Subj: Animals – pigs. Behavior – hiding. Format, unusual – toy & movable books. Games.

Philpot, Lorna. *Find Anthony Ant* by Lorna Philpot and Graham Philpot; ill. by Lorna Philpot. Sterling, 2006. ISBN 978-1-905417-10-0 Subj: Counting, numbers. Insects – ants. Mazes. Picture puzzles. Puzzles.

Phinn, Gervase. *Who am I?* ill. by Tony Ross. Andersen, 2012. ISBN 978-0-7613-8996-5 Subj: Character traits – individuality. Reptiles – chameleons. Self-concept.

Pia Toya: a Goshute Indian legend. Retold & Ill. by the children & teachers of Ibapah Elementary school. Univ. of Utah Pr., 2000. ISBN 978-0-87480-661-8 Subj: Animals – coyotes. Birds – hawks. Children as authors. Children as illustrators. Creation. Folk & fairy tales. Indians of North America – Goshute. Indians of North America – Great Basin.

Pichard, Alexandra. *Pen pals* ill. by author. Aladdin, 2017. ISBN 978-148147247-0 Subj: Activities – writing. Insects – ants. Letters, cards. Octopuses. Pen pals.

Pichon, Liz. *Penguins* ill. by author. Scholastic, 2008. ISBN 978-0-545-02215-6 Subj: Activities – photographing. Birds – penguins. Zoos.

The three horrid little pigs ill. by author. Tiger Tales, 2008. ISBN 978-1-58925-077-2 Subj: Animals – pigs. Animals – wolves. Behavior – misbehavior. Humorous stories.

The very ugly bug ill. by author. Tiger Tales, 2005. ISBN 978-1-58925-048-2 Subj: Character traits – appearance. Insects.

Pickering, Jimmy. *It's fall* ill. by author. Smallfellow, 2002. ISBN 978-1-931290-15-9 Subj: Animals – dogs. Poetry. Rhyming text. Seasons – fall.

It's winter ill. by author. Smallfellow, 2002. ISBN 978-1-931290-16-6 Subj: Animals – dogs. Poetry. Seasons – winter. Weather – snow.

Skelly the skeleton girl ill. by author. Simon & Schuster, 2007. ISBN 978-1-4169-1192-0 Subj: Anatomy – skeletons. Animals – dogs. Monsters.

Pickthall, Marjorie L. C. *The worker in sandalwood: a Christmas Eve miracle* ill. by Frances Tyrrell. Dutton, 1994. ISBN 978-0-525-45332-1 Subj: Careers – carpenters. Foreign lands – Canada. Holidays – Christmas.

Pienkowski, Jan. *Bel and Bub and the baby bird* ill. by author. DK, 2000. ISBN 978-0-7894-6526-9 Subj: Angels. Birds.

Bel and Bub and the bad snowball ill. by author. DK, 2000. ISBN 978-0-7894-6529-0 Subj: Angels. Behavior – bullying, teasing. Emotions – anger.

Bel and Bub and the big brown box ill. by author. DK, 2000. ISBN 978-0-7894-6527-6 Subj: Angels. Behavior – sharing.

Bel and Bub and the black hole ill. by author. DK, 2000. ISBN 978-0-7894-6528-3 Subj: Angels. Character traits – bravery. Dragons. Friendship. Stores.

Easter ill. by author. Knopf, 1989. ISBN 978-0-394-82455-0 Subj: Holidays – Easter. Religion.

Good night, a pop-up lullaby ill. by author. Paper engineering by Helen Balmer & Martin Taylor. Candlewick, 1999. ISBN 978-0-7636-0763-0 Subj: Format, unusual – toy & movable books. Lullabies.

Haunted house ill. by Jane Walmsley. Dutton, 1979. ISBN 978-0-525-46802-8 Subj: Format, unusual – toy & movable books. Ghosts. Homes, houses. Monsters.

Pizza! ill. by author and David Walser. Paper engineering by Helen Balmer & Martin Taylor. Candlewick, 2001. ISBN 978-0-7636-1626-7 Subj: Animals. Food. Format, unusual – toy & movable books. Insects. Royalty – kings. Spiders.

Piepmeier, Charlotte. *Lucy's journey to the wild west* ill. by author. Azro, 2002. ISBN 978-1-929115-07-5 Subj: Activities – traveling. Animals – dogs. Geography. Maps. Moving. U.S. history.

Pierce, Christa. *Did you know that I love you?* ill. by author. HarperCollins, 2014. ISBN 978-006229744-0 Subj: Animals – foxes. Birds. Emotions – love. Rhyming text.

Pierce, Roxanne Heide. *Always listen to your mother* (Heide, Florence Parry)

Pierce, Terry, editor. *Counting your way: number nursery rhymes* ill. by Andrea Petrlik Huseinovic. Picture Window, 2007. ISBN 978-1-4048-2346-4 Subj: Counting, numbers. Nursery rhymes.

My busy green garden ill. by Carol Schwartz. Tilbury House, 2017. ISBN 978-088448495-0 Subj: Birds. Cumulative tales. Gardens, gardening. Insects.

Piernas-Davenport, Gail. *Shanté Keys and the New Year's peas* ill. by Marion Eldridge. Albert Whitman, 2007. ISBN 978-0-8075-7330-3 Subj: Ethnic groups in the U.S. – African Americans. Family life. Food. Holidays – New Year's.

Piers, Helen. *Who's in my bed?* ill. by Dave Saunders. Marshall Cavendish, 1999. ISBN 978-0-7614-5046-7 Subj: Animals. Bedtime. Character traits – orderliness. Cumulative tales. Farms. Format, unusual – toy & movable books.

Piggy and Bear in their underwear ill. by Dara Goldman. Innovative KIDS, 2002. ISBN 978-1-58476-101-3 Subj: Behavior – growing up. Clothing – underwear. Format, unusual – toy & movable books. Toilet training.

Pignataro, Anna. *Our love grows* ill. by author. Sourcebooks/Jabberwocky, 2016. ISBN 978-149263418-8 Subj: Animals – pandas. Behavior – growing up. Emotions – love. Family life – mothers.

Pilcher, Steve. *Over there* ill. by author. Disney/Hyperion, 2014. ISBN 978-142314793-0 Subj: Animals – moles. Animals – shrews. Emotions – loneliness. Friendship.

Pilegard, Virginia Walton. *The warlord's alarm: a mathematical adventure* ill. by Nicolas Debon. Pelican, 2006. ISBN 978-1-58980-378-7 Subj: Clocks, watches. Foreign lands – China. Time.

The warlord's beads ill. by Nicolas Debon. Pelican, 2001. ISBN 978-1-56554-863-3 Subj: Counting, numbers. Foreign lands – China.

The warlord's puzzle ill. by Nicolas Debon. Pelican, 2000. ISBN 978-1-56554-495-6 Subj: Concepts – shape. Folk & fairy tales. Foreign lands – China.

Pilgrim, Elza. *The china doll* ill. by Carmen Segovia. Sterling, 2006. ISBN 978-1-4027-2223-3 Subj: Birthdays. Gifts. Toys – dolls.

Pilkey, Dav. *Dragon's fat cat* ill. by author. Orchard, 1992. ISBN 978-0-531-08582-0 Subj: Animals – cats. Dragons.

Dragon's merry Christmas ill. by author. Orchard, 1991. ISBN 978-0-531-08557-8 Subj: Character traits – generosity. Dragons. Holidays – Christmas.

The Dumb Bunnies ill. by author. Blue Sky, 2007, ©1994. ISBN 978-0-545-03938-3 Subj: Animals – rabbits. Character traits – foolishness. Family life. Humorous stories.

The Dumb Bunnies' Easter ill. by author. Blue Sky, 2009, ©1995. ISBN 978-0-545-03946-8 Subj: Animals – rabbits. Character traits – foolishness. Family life. Holidays – Christmas. Holidays – Easter. Humorous stories.

The Dumb Bunnies go to the zoo ill. by author. Blue Sky, 2009, ©1997. ISBN 978-0-545-03937-6 Subj: Animals – rabbits. Character traits – foolishness. Family life. Humorous stories. Zoos.

A friend for Dragon ill. by author. Orchard, 1991. ISBN 978-0-531-05934-0 Subj: Dragons. Emotions – loneliness. Friendship. Reptiles – snakes.

The Hallo-wiener ill. by author. Blue Sky, 1995. ISBN 978-0-590-41703-7 Subj: Animals – dogs. Family life. Holidays – Halloween.

Make way for Dumb Bunnies ill. by author. Blue Sky, 2007, ©1996. ISBN 978-0-545-03939-0 Subj: Activities. Animals – rabbits. Character traits – foolishness. Family life. Humorous stories.

The Moonglow Roll-O-Rama ill. by author. Orchard, 1995. ISBN 978-0-531-08726-8 Subj: Animals. Night. Rhyming text. Sports – roller skating.

The paperboy ill. by author. Orchard, 1996. ISBN 978-0-531-08856-2 Subj: Activities – working. Caldecott award honor books. Morning.

The Silly Gooses ill. by author. Blue Sky, 1997. ISBN 978-0-590-94733-6 Subj: Behavior. Birds – geese. Humorous stories. Weddings.

'Twas the night before Thanksgiving ill. by author. Watts, 1990. ISBN 978-0-531-08505-9 Subj: Birds – turkeys. Holidays – Thanksgiving. Rhyming text.

When cats dream ill. by author. Watts, 1992. ISBN 978-0-531-08597-4 Subj: Animals – cats. Art. Dreams.

Pilutti, Deb. *Bear and Squirrel are friends . . . yes, really!* ill. by author. Simon & Schuster/Paula Wiseman, 2015. ISBN 978-148142913-9 Subj: Animals – bears. Animals – squirrels. Friendship.

Ten rules of being a superhero ill. by author. Henry Holt, 2014. ISBN 978-080509759-7 Subj: Activities – playing. Humorous stories. Imagination. Toys.

Pin, Isabel. *The seed* ill. by author. NorthSouth, 2001. ISBN 978-0-7358-1408-0 Subj: Insects. Seeds. War.

Pinczes, Elinor J. *Inchworm and a half* ill. by Randall Enos. Houghton, 2001. ISBN 978-0-395-82849-6 Subj: Animals – worms. Concepts – measurement. Counting, numbers. Food. Gardens, gardening. Rhyming text.

My full moon is square ill. by Randall Enos. Houghton, 2002. ISBN 978-0-618-15489-0 Subj: Books, reading. Frogs & toads. Insects – fireflies. Rhyming text.

A remainder of one ill. by Bonnie MacKain. Houghton, 1995. ISBN 978-0-395-69455-8 Subj: Counting, numbers. Insects. Rhyming text.

Pinder, Eric. *How to share with a bear* ill. by Stephanie Graegin. Farrar, 2015. ISBN 978-037430019-7 Subj: Animals – bears. Behavior – sharing. Clothing – costumes. Family life – brothers.

If all the animals came inside ill. by Marc Brown. Little, Brown, 2012. ISBN 978-0-316-09883-0 Subj: Animals. Imagination. Rhyming text.

Pinfold, Levi. *Black dog* ill. by author. Candlewick, 2012. ISBN 978-0-7636-6097-0 Subj: Animals – dogs. Concepts – size. Emotions – fear. Family life.

The Django ill. by author. Candlewick, 2010. ISBN 978-0-7636-4788-9 Subj: Behavior – misbehavior. Imagination – imaginary friends. Musical instruments – banjos. Romani.

Greenling ill. by author. Candlewick/Templar, 2016. ISBN 978-076367598-1 Subj: Gardens, gardening. Rhyming text.

Pingk, Rubin. *Samurai Santa: a very Ninja Christmas* ill. by author. Simon & Schuster, 2015. ISBN 978-148143057-9 Subj: Holidays – Christmas. Santa Claus. Sports – martial arts.

Pinkney, Andrea Davis. *Alvin Ailey* ill. by Brian Pinkney. Hyperion, 1993. ISBN 978-1-56282-414-3 Subj: Activities – dancing. Careers – dancers. Ethnic groups in the U.S. – African Americans.

Bill Pickett, rodeo ridin' cowboy ill. by Brian Pinkney. Harcourt, 1996. ISBN 978-0-15-200100-1 Subj: Cowboys, cowgirls. Ethnic groups in the U.S. – African Americans.

Boycott blues: how Rosa Parks inspired a nation ill. by Brian Pinkney. Greenwillow, 2008. ISBN 978-0-06-082118-0 Subj: Ethnic groups in the U.S. – African Americans. Prejudice. U.S. history.

Dear Benjamin Banneker ill. by Brian Pinkney. Harcourt, 1994. ISBN 978-0-15-200417-0 Subj: Careers – astronomers. Ethnic groups in the U.S. – African Americans. Slavery. U.S. history.

Duke Ellington: the piano prince and his orchestra ill. by Brian Pinkney. Hyperion, 1998. ISBN 978-0-7868-2150-1 Subj: Caldecott award honor books. Careers – musicians. Ethnic groups in the U.S. – African Americans. Music. Musical instruments – pianos.

Martin and Mahalia: his words, her song ill. by Brian Pinkney. Little, Brown, 2013. ISBN 978-0-316-07013-3 Subj: Careers – singers. Ethnic groups in the U.S. – African Americans. Holidays – Martin Luther King, Jr. Day. U.S. history. Violence, nonviolence.

Mim's Christmas jam ill. by Brian Pinkney. Harcourt, 2001. ISBN 978-0-15-201918-1 Subj: Ethnic groups in the U.S. – African Americans. Family life. Food. Holidays – Christmas.

Peggony-Po: a whale of a tale ill. by Brian Pinkney. Hyperion, 2006. ISBN 978-0-7868-1958-4 Subj: Animals – whales. Tall tales. Toys.

Sit-in: how four friends stood up by sitting down ill. by Brian Pinkney. Little, Brown, 2010. ISBN 978-

0-316-07016-4 Subj: Ethnic groups in the U.S. – African Americans. Prejudice. U.S. history.

Sojourner Truth's step-stomp stride ill. by Brian Pinkney. Jump at the Sun, 2009. ISBN 978-0-7868-0767-3 Subj: Character traits – freedom. Ethnic groups in the U.S. – African Americans. Slavery. U.S. history.

Pinkney, Brian. *The adventures of sparrowboy* ill. by author. Simon & Schuster, 1997. ISBN 978-0-689-81071-8 Subj: Activities – flying. Behavior – bullying, teasing. Communities, neighborhoods. Ethnic groups in the U.S. – African Americans. Humorous stories.

Cosmo and the robot ill. by author. Greenwillow, 2000. ISBN 978-0-688-15941-2 Subj: Monsters. Planets. Robots. Space & space ships.

Hush, little baby ill. by adapter. HarperCollins, 2006. ISBN 978-0-06-055994-6 Subj: Babies, toddlers. Character traits – generosity. Cumulative tales. Lullabies. Music.

Jojo's flying side kick ill. by author. Simon & Schuster, 1995. ISBN 978-0-671-88111-5 Subj: Character traits – perseverance. Family life. Sports – Tae Kwon Do.

On the ball ill. by author. Disney/Hyperion, 2015. ISBN 978-148472329-6 Subj: Imagination. Sports – soccer.

Pinkney, Gloria Jean. *Back home* ill. by Jerry Pinkney. Dial, 1992. ISBN 978-0-8037-1169-3 Subj: Ethnic groups in the U.S. – African Americans. Family life. Farms.

Music from our Lord's holy heaven ill. by Jerry Pinkney and Brian Pinkney, et al. HarperCollins, 2005. ISBN 978-0-06-000769-0 Subj: Music. Religion. Songs.

The Sunday outing ill. by Jerry Pinkney. Dial, 1994. ISBN 978-0-8037-1199-0 Subj: Activities – traveling. Ethnic groups in the U.S. – African Americans. Family life. Farms. Trains.

Pinkney, Jerry. *The lion and the mouse* ill. by author. Little, Brown, 2009. ISBN 978-0-316-01356-7 Subj: Animals – lions. Animals – mice. Caldecott award books. Character traits – helpfulness. Folk & fairy tales. Wordless.

Noah's ark ill. by author. SeaStar, 2002. ISBN 978-1-58717-202-1 Subj: Animals. Boats, ships. Caldecott award honor books. Religion – Noah. Weather – floods. Weather – rain. Weather – rainbows.

Three little kittens ill. by author. Penguin, 2010. ISBN 978-0-8037-3533-0 Subj: Animals – cats. Behavior – lost & found possessions. Clothing – gloves, mittens. Nursery rhymes.

Pinkney, Sandra L. *I am Latino: the beauty in me* photos by Myles C. Pinkney. Little, Brown, 2007.

ISBN 978-0-316-16009-4 Subj: Ethnic groups in the U.S. – Hispanic Americans. Self-concept.

A rainbow all around me photos by Myles C. Pinkney. Scholastic, 2002. ISBN 978-0-439-30928-8 Subj: Anatomy – skin. Concepts – color. Ethnic groups in the U.S. Weather – rainbows.

Read and rise photos by Myles C. Pinkney. Foreword by Maya Angelou. Scholastic, 2006. ISBN 978-0-439-30929-5 Subj: Books, reading. Ethnic groups in the U.S. – African Americans.

Shades of black photos by Myles C. Pinkney. Scholastic, 2000. ISBN 978-0-439-14892-4 Subj: Ethnic groups in the U.S. – African Americans.

Pinkwater, Daniel. *At the Hotel Larry* ill. by Jill Pinkwater. Marshall Cavendish, 1997. ISBN 978-0-7614-5005-4 Subj: Animals – polar bears. Careers – lifeguards. Hotels. Humorous stories.

Bad bear detectives: an Irving and Muktuk story ill. by Jill Pinkwater. Houghton, 2006. ISBN 978-0-618-43125-0 Subj: Animals – polar bears. Behavior – stealing. Careers – detectives. Humorous stories.

Bad bears and a bunny ill. by Jill Pinkwater. Houghton, 2005. ISBN 978-0-618-33926-6 Subj: Animals – polar bears. Animals – rabbits. Behavior. Hotels. Humorous stories. Parties.

Bad bears go visiting ill. by Jill Pinkwater. Houghton, 2007. ISBN 978-0-618-43126-7 Subj: Animals – polar bears. Humorous stories. Zoos.

Bad bears in the big city ill. by Jill Pinkwater. Houghton, 2003. ISBN 978-0-618-25208-4 Subj: Animals – polar bears. Behavior – misbehavior. Cities, towns. Food. Humorous stories. Zoos.

Bear and Bunny ill. by Will Hillenbrand. Candlewick, 2015. ISBN 978-076367153-2 Subj: Animals – bears. Animals – rabbits. Friendship. Frogs & toads. Pets.

Bear in love ill. by Will Hillenbrand. Candlewick, 2012. ISBN 978-0-7636-4569-4 Subj: Animals – bears. Animals – rabbits. Behavior – sharing. Food. Friendship.

Bear's Picture ill. by D. B. Johnson. Houghton, 2008. ISBN 978-0-618-75923-1 Subj: Animals – bears. Art. Careers – artists. Concepts – color.

Beautiful Yetta: the Yiddish chicken ill. by Jill Pinkwater. Feiwel & Friends, 2010. ISBN 978-0-312-55824-6 Subj: Behavior – lost. Birds – chickens, roosters. Birds – parakeets, parrots. Cities, towns. Foreign languages.

Beautiful Yetta's Hanukkah kitten ill. by Jill Pinkwater. Feiwel & Friends, 2014. ISBN 978-031262134-6 Subj: Animals – cats. Birds – chickens, roosters. Foreign languages. Holidays – Hanukkah.

Bongo Larry ill. by Jill Pinkwater. Marshall Cavendish, 1998. ISBN 978-0-7614-5020-7 Subj:

Animals – bears. Animals – polar bears. Careers – musicians. Humorous stories. Musical instruments – drums.

Dancing Larry ill. by Jill Pinkwater. Marshall Cavendish, 2006. ISBN 978-0-7614-5220-1 Subj: Activities – dancing. Animals – polar bears. Ballet. Humorous stories.

I am the dog ill. by Jack E. Davis. HarperCollins, 2010. ISBN 978-0-06-055505-4 Subj: Animals – dogs. Humorous stories.

Ice-cream Larry ill. by Jill Pinkwater. Marshall Cavendish, 1999. ISBN 978-0-7614-5043-6 Subj: Animals – polar bears. Behavior – misbehavior. Food. Humorous stories.

Irving and Muktuk ill. by Jill Pinkwater. Houghton, 2001. ISBN 978-0-618-09334-2 Subj: Animals – polar bears. Animals – rabbits. Behavior – misbehavior. Zoos.

The picture of Morty and Ray ill. by Jack E. Davis. HarperCollins, 2003. ISBN 978-0-06-623786-2 Subj: Activities – painting. Behavior – misbehavior. Humorous stories.

Rainy morning ill. by Jill Pinkwater. Atheneum, 1998. ISBN 978-0-689-81143-2 Subj: Animals. Character traits – kindness to animals. Circus. Food. Homes, houses. Weather – rain.

Sleepover Larry ill. by Jill Pinkwater. Marshall Cavendish, 2007. ISBN 978-0-7614-5314-7 Subj: Animals – polar bears. Humorous stories. Sleepovers.

Wolf Christmas ill. by Jill Pinkwater. Marshall Cavendish, 1998. ISBN 978-0-7614-5030-6 Subj: Animals – wolves. Holidays – Christmas.

Yo-yo man ill. by Jack E. Davis. HarperCollins, 2007. ISBN 978-0-06-055502-3 Subj: Behavior – bullying, teasing. School. Toys.

Young Larry ill. by Jill Pinkwater. Marshall Cavendish, 1997. ISBN 978-0-7614-5004-7 Subj: Animals – polar bears. Behavior – growing up. Careers – lifeguards. Family life – brothers. Family life – mothers. Foreign lands – Canada. Humorous stories.

Pinto, Sara. *Apples and oranges: going bananas with pairs* ill. by author. Bloomsbury, 2008. ISBN 978-1-59990-103-9 Subj: Concepts. Imagination.

Piper, Sophie. *I can say a prayer* ill. by Emily Bolam. IPG/Lion, 2011. ISBN 978-0-7459-6233-7 Subj: Religion.

Piper, Watty. *The little engine that could* ill. by George Hauman and Doris Hauman. Retold from *The pony engine,* by Mable C. Bragg. This version first pub. in 1955. 60th anniversary ed. Platt, 1990. ISBN 978-0-448-40041-9 Subj: Character traits – perseverance. Trains.

The little engine that could ill. by Loren Long. Penguin, 2005. ISBN 978-0-399-24467-4 Subj: Character traits – perseverance. Trains.

Pippin-Mathur, Courtney. *Maya was grumpy* ill. by author. Flashlight, 2013. ISBN 978-1-9362611-3-0 Subj: Behavior – bad day, bad mood. Family life – grandmothers.

Pirner, Connie White. *Even little kids get diabetes* ill. by Nadine Bernard Westcott. Albert Whitman, 1991. ISBN 978-0-8075-2158-8 Subj: Hospitals. Illness – diabetes.

Pitcher, Caroline. *Are you spring?* ill. by Cliff Wright. DK, 2000. ISBN 978-0-7894-5614-4 Subj: Animals. Animals – bears. Seasons – spring.

Mariana and the merchild: a folk tale from Chile ill. by Jackie Morris. Eerdmans, 2000. ISBN 978-0-8028-5204-5 Subj: Folk & fairy tales. Foreign lands – Chile. Mythical creatures – mermaids, mermen.

Nico's octopus ill. by Nilesh Mistry. Crocodile, 2003. ISBN 978-1-56656-483-0 Subj: Death. Octopuses. Pets.

Pitchford, Dean. *Footloose* (Loggins, Kenny)

Pitman, Gayle E. *This day in June* ill. by Kristyna Litten. Magination, 2014. ISBN 978-143381658-1 Subj: LGBTQ. Parades. Rhyming text.

Pittau, Francisco. *Out of sight* by Francisco Pittau and Bernadette Gervais; ill. by authors. Chronicle, 2010. ISBN 978-0-8118-7712-1 Subj: Animals. Format, unusual – toy & movable books.

Pittman, Helena Clare. *The angel tree* ill. by Jo Ellen McAllister Stammen. Dial, 1998. ISBN 978-0-8037-1941-5 Subj: Angels. Communities, neighborhoods. Friendship. Holidays – Christmas. Trees.

The snowman's path ill. by Raúl Colón. Dial, 2000. ISBN 978-0-8037-2170-8 Subj: Friendship. Snowmen.

Pitzer, Susanna. *Not afraid of dogs* ill. by Larry Day. Walker, 2006. ISBN 978-0-8027-8067-6 Subj: Animals – dogs. Behavior – animals, dislike of. Emotions – fear.

Piumini, Roberto. *Doctor Me Di Cin* ill. by Piet Grobler. Front Street, 2001. ISBN 978-1-886910-67-6 Subj: Careers – doctors. Foreign lands – China. Royalty – princes.

Piven, Hanoch. *Let's make faces* ill. by author. Simon & Schuster, 2013. ISBN 978-1-4169-1532-4 Subj: Anatomy – faces. Art. Imagination.

The perfect purple feather by Hanoch Piven and Rachel Tzvia Back; photos by Adi Gilad. Silhouettes by Janet Stein; photos by Adi Gilad. Little, 2002. ISBN 978-0-316-76657-9 Subj: Animals. Feathers. Rhyming text.

Pizzoli, Greg. *Good night Owl* ill. by author. Disney/Hyperion, 2016. ISBN 978-148471275-7 Subj: Bedtime. Birds – owls. Noise, sounds.

Number one Sam ill. by author. Disney/Hyperion, 2014. ISBN 978-142317111-9 Subj: Animals – dogs. Automobiles. Contests. Sports – racing.

Templeton gets his wish ill. by author. Disney/Hyperion, 2015. ISBN 978-148471274-0 Subj: Animals – cats. Behavior – wishing. Emotions – loneliness. Family life.

The watermelon seed ill. by author. Disney/Hyperion, 2013. ISBN 978-1-4231-7101-0 Subj: Behavior – worrying. Imagination. Reptiles – alligators, crocodiles. Seeds.

Plant, David J. *Hungry Roscoe* ill. by David J. Plant. Flying Eye, 2015. ISBN 978-190926353-6 Subj: Animals – raccoons. Zoos.

Platt, Cynthia. *A little bit of love* ill. by Hannah Whitty. Tiger Tales, 2011. ISBN 978-1-58925-095-6 Subj: Activities – baking, cooking. Animals – mice. Family life – mothers.

Player, Micah. *Chloe, instead* ill. by author. Chronicle, 2012. ISBN 978-0-8118-7865-4 Subj: Character traits – individuality. Family life – sisters.

Plecas, Jennifer. *Olive's perfect world: a friendship story* ill. by author. Philomel, 2013. ISBN 978-0-399-25287-7 Subj: Animals – cats. Emotions – sadness. Friendship.

Pretend ill. by author. Penguin, 2011. ISBN 978-0-399-23430-9 Subj: Family life – fathers. Imagination.

Plourde, Lynn. *Bella's fall coat* ill. by Susan Gal. Disney/Hyperion, 2016. ISBN 978-148472697-6 Subj: Behavior – growing up. Clothing – coats. Family life – grandmothers. Seasons – fall.

Book Fair Day ill. by Thor Wickstrom. Penguin, 2006. ISBN 978-0-525-47696-2 Subj: Books, reading. School.

Dad, aren't you glad? ill. by Amy Wummer. Penguin, 2005. ISBN 978-0-525-47362-6 Subj: Family life – fathers. Kissing.

Dino pets ill. by Gideon Kendall. Penguin, 2007. ISBN 978-0-525-47778-5 Subj: Dinosaurs. Pets. Rhyming text.

Dino pets go to school ill. by Gideon Kendall. Penguin, 2011. ISBN 978-0-525-42232-7 Subj: Dinosaurs. Pets. Rhyming text. School.

Field trip day ill. by Thor Wickstrom. Penguin, 2010. ISBN 978-0-525-47994-9 Subj: Farms. School – field trips.

Grandpappy snippy snappies ill. by Christopher Santoro. HarperCollins, 2009. ISBN 978-0-06-028050-5 Subj: Careers – farmers. Clothing. Humorous stories. Rhyming text.

Margaret Chase Smith: a woman for president ill. by David McPhail. Charlesbridge, 2008. ISBN 978-1-58089-234-6 Subj: Gender roles. U.S. history.

Merry Moosey Christmas ill. by Russ Cox. Islandport, 2014. ISBN 978-193901738-3 Subj: Animals – moose. Animals – reindeer. Holidays – Christmas. Santa Claus.

A mountain of mittens ill. by Mitch Vane. Charlesbridge, 2007. ISBN 978-1-57091-585-7 Subj: Behavior – lost & found possessions. Clothing – gloves, mittens. Seasons – winter.

Only cows allowed! ill. by Rebecca Harrison Reed. Down East, 2011. ISBN 978-0-89272-790-2 Subj: Animals. Animals – bulls, cows. Farms. Humorous stories.

Pajama day ill. by Thor Wickstrom. Penguin, 2005. ISBN 978-0-525-47355-8 Subj: Behavior – forgetfulness. Clothing – pajamas. School.

Pigs in the mud in the middle of the rud ill. by John Schoenherr. Blue Sky, 1997. ISBN 978-0-590-56863-0 Subj: Animals – pigs. Character traits – stubbornness. Humorous stories. Poetry. Roads. Weather – rain.

School picture day ill. by Thor Wickstrom. Dutton, 2002. ISBN 978-0-525-46886-8 Subj: Activities – photographing. School.

Spring's sprung ill. by Greg Couch. Simon & Schuster, 2002. ISBN 978-0-689-84229-0 Subj: Family life – sisters. Rhyming text. Seasons – spring. Sibling rivalry.

Wild child ill. by Greg Couch. Simon & Schuster, 1999. ISBN 978-0-689-81552-2 Subj: Bedtime. Mythical creatures. Rhyming text. Seasons – fall.

Winter waits ill. by Greg Couch. Simon & Schuster, 2001. ISBN 978-0-689-83268-0 Subj: Mythical creatures. Rhyming text. Seasons – winter. Time.

You're doing that in the talent show?! ill. by Sue Cornelison. Disney/Hyperion, 2016. ISBN 978-148471491-1 Subj: Animals – hippopotamuses. Animals – mice. Friendship. Theater.

You're wearing that to school?! ill. by Sue Cornelison. Disney/Hyperion, 2013. ISBN 978-1-4231-5510-2 Subj: Animals – hippopotamuses. Animals – mice. Character traits – individuality. Clothing. School – first day.

A pocketful of stars: poems about the night ill. by Emma Shaw-Smith. Barefoot, 2000. ISBN 978-1-902283-84-5 Subj: Night. Poetry.

Podwal, Mark H. *The menorah story* ill. by author. Greenwillow, 1998. ISBN 978-0-688-15759-3 Subj: Holidays – Hanukkah. Jewish culture. Religion.

A sweet year ill. by author. Random House, 2003. ISBN 978-0-385-90869-6 Subj: Food. Holidays. Jewish culture. Religion.

Poffenberger, Nancy M. *September 11, 2001* ill. by the Lotspeich School students. Fun, 2002. ISBN 978-0-938293-12-5 Subj: Cities, towns. Crime. U.S. history. War.

Poh, Jennifer. *Herbie's big adventure* ill. by author. Capstone, 2016. ISBN 978-162370766-8 Subj: Animals – hedgehogs. Behavior – growing up. Family life – mothers.

Polacco, Patricia. *An A from Miss Keller* ill. by author. Putnam, 2015. ISBN 978-039916691-4 Subj: Activities – writing. Careers – teachers. Death. Emotions – grief. School. Self-concept.

Appelemando's dreams ill. by author. Putnam, 1991. ISBN 978-0-399-21800-2 Subj: Dreams. Imagination.

The art of Miss Chew ill. by author. Putnam, 2012. ISBN 978-0-399-25703-2 Subj: Art. Careers – teachers. Character traits – individuality. Disabilities. School. Self-concept.

Aunt Chip and the great Triple Creek dam affair ill. by author. Philomel, 1996. ISBN 978-0-399-22943-5 Subj: Books, reading. Libraries. Television.

Babushka's doll ill. by author. Simon & Schuster, 1990. ISBN 978-0-671-68343-6 Subj: Toys – dolls.

Babushka's Mother Goose ill. by author. Philomel, 1995. ISBN 978-0-399-22747-9 Subj: Family life – grandmothers. Folk & fairy tales. Foreign lands – Russia. Nursery rhymes.

Because of Thursday ill. by author. Simon & Schuster/Paula Wiseman, 2016. ISBN 978-148142140-9 Subj: Animals – cats. Days of the week, months of the year. Food. Restaurants.

Betty Doll ill. by author. Philomel, 2001. ISBN 978-0-399-23638-9 Subj: Family life – mothers. Illness – cancer. Memories, memory. Toys – dolls.

The blessing cup ill. by author. Simon & Schuster, 2013. ISBN 978-1-4424-5047-9 Subj: Family life. Immigrants, immigration. Jewish culture.

Bun Bun Button ill. by author. Penguin, 2011. ISBN 978-0-399-25472-7 Subj: Behavior – lost & found possessions. Character traits – luck. Family life – grandmothers. Toys. Toys – balloons.

The butterfly ill. by author. Philomel, 2000. ISBN 978-0-399-23170-4 Subj: Behavior – hiding. Behavior – secrets. Character traits – freedom. Foreign lands – France. Insects – butterflies, caterpillars. War.

Chicken Sunday ill. by author. Putnam, 1992. ISBN 978-0-399-22133-0 Subj: Eggs. Ethnic groups in the U.S. – African Americans. Family life – grandmothers. Friendship. Holidays – Easter. Religion.

Clara and Davie: the true story of young Clara Barton ill. by author. Scholastic, 2014. ISBN 978-054535477-6 Subj: Careers – nurses. U.S. history.

Emma Kate ill. by author. Penguin, 2005. ISBN 978-0-399-24452-0 Subj: Animals – elephants. Friendship. Imagination.

Fiona's lace ill. by author. Simon & Schuster/Paula Wiseman, 2014. ISBN 978-144248724-6 Subj: Character traits – perseverance. Ethnic groups in the U.S. – Irish Americans. Immigrants, immigration.

Gifts of the heart ill. by author. Penguin, 2013. ISBN 978-0-399-16094-3 Subj: Careers – housekeepers. Family life. Gifts. Holidays – Christmas. Magic. Santa Claus.

Ginger and Petunia ill. by author. Penguin, 2007. ISBN 978-0-399-24539-8 Subj: Animals – pigs. Pets.

I can hear the sun ill. by author. Philomel, 1996. ISBN 978-0-399-22520-8 Subj: Birds – geese. Character traits – being different. Ethnic groups in the U.S. – African Americans. Homeless. Sun.

In Enzo's splendid gardens ill. by author. Philomel, 1997. ISBN 978-0-399-23107-0 Subj: Accidents. Cumulative tales. Food. Humorous stories. Insects – bees. Restaurants.

In our mothers' house ill. by author. Philomel, 2009. ISBN 978-0-399-25076-7 Subj: Ethnic groups in the U.S. Family life – mothers. Family life – same-sex parents. LGBTQ.

The junkyard wonders ill. by author. Penguin, 2010. ISBN 978-0-399-25078-1 Subj: Careers – teachers. Disabilities. Inventions. School. Self-concept.

Just plain Fancy ill. by author. Bantam, 1990. ISBN 978-0-553-07062-0 Subj: Birds – peacocks, peahens. Eggs. Farms.

The keeping quilt ill. by author. Simon & Schuster, 1998. ISBN 978-0-689-82090-8 Subj: Immigrants, immigration. Jewish culture. Quilts.

The lemonade club ill. by author. Penguin, 2007. ISBN 978-0-399-24540-4 Subj: Careers – teachers. Illness – cancer. School.

Luba and the wren ill. by author. Philomel, 1999. ISBN 978-0-399-23168-1 Subj: Behavior – wishing. Birds – wrens. Folk & fairy tales. Foreign lands – Ukraine. Magic.

The mermaid's purse ill. by author. Putnam, 2016. ISBN 978-039916692-1 Subj: Books, reading. Libraries. Weather – tornadoes.

Meteor! ill. by author. Dodd, 1987. ISBN 978-0-396-08910-0 Subj: Country. Science.

Mommies say shhh! ill. by author. Penguin, 2005. ISBN 978-0-399-24341-7 Subj: Animals. Family life – mothers. Noise, sounds.

Mr. Lincoln's way ill. by author. Philomel, 2001. ISBN 978-0-399-23754-6 Subj: Behavior – bullying, teasing. Birds. Careers – school principals. Prejudice. School.

Mr. Wayne's masterpiece ill. by author. Putnam, 2014. ISBN 978-039916095-0 Subj: Careers – teachers. Character traits – shyness. Emotions – fear. School. Theater.

Mrs. Katz and Tush ill. by author. Bantam, 1992. ISBN 978-0-553-08122-0 Subj: Animals – cats. Ethnic groups in the U.S. – African Americans. Friendship. Jewish culture. Pets.

Mrs. Mack ill. by author. Philomel, 1998. ISBN 978-0-399-23167-4 Subj: Animals – horses, ponies. Memories, memory. Seasons – summer.

My ol' man ill. by author. Philomel, 1995. ISBN 978-0-399-22822-3 Subj: Family life – fathers. Imagination. Magic. Rocks.

My rotten redheaded older brother ill. by author. Simon & Schuster, 1994. ISBN 978-0-671-72751-2 Subj: Family life – brothers & sisters. Family life – grandparents. Sibling rivalry.

Oh, look! ill. by author. Philomel, 2004. ISBN 978-0-399-24223-6 Subj: Animals – goats. Fairs, festivals. Mythical creatures – trolls.

Picnic at Mudsock Meadow ill. by author. Putnam, 1992. ISBN 978-0-399-21811-8 Subj: Activities – picnicking. Holidays – Halloween.

Rechenka's eggs ill. by author. Putnam, 1988. ISBN 978-0-399-21501-8 Subj: Birds – geese. Eggs. Folk & fairy tales.

Remembering Vera ill. by author. Simon & Schuster, 2017. ISBN 978-148144227-5 Subj: Animals – dogs. Careers – military. Character traits – bravery. Character traits – kindness to animals.

Rotten Richie and the ultimate dare ill. by author. Penguin, 2006. ISBN 978-0-399-24531-2 Subj: Ballet. Behavior – bullying, teasing. Contests. Family life – brothers & sisters. Sports – hockey.

Some birthday! ill. by author. Simon & Schuster, 1991. ISBN 978-0-671-72750-5 Subj: Birthdays. Family life – fathers. Monsters. Parties.

Someone for Mr. Sussman ill. by author. Philomel, 2008. ISBN 978-0-399-25075-0 Subj: Family life – grandmothers. Jewish culture. Weddings.

Something about Hensley's ill. by author. Penguin, 2006. ISBN 978-0-399-24538-1 Subj: Family life – single-parent families. Stores.

Thank you, Mr. Falker ill. by author. Philomel, 1998. ISBN 978-0-399-23166-7 Subj: Books, reading. Careers – teachers. Disabilities. School.

Thunder cake ill. by author. Putnam, 1990. ISBN 978-0-399-22231-3 Subj: Emotions – fear. Family life – grandmothers. Weather – lightning, thunder. Weather – storms.

Tikvah means hope ill. by author. Doubleday, 1994. ISBN 978-0-385-32059-7 Subj: Animals – cats. Fire. Holidays – Sukkot. Jewish culture.

The trees of the dancing goats ill. by author. Simon & Schuster, 1996. ISBN 978-0-689-80862-3 Subj: Ethnic groups in the U.S. – Russian Americans. Family life – grandparents. Holidays – Christmas. Holidays – Hanukkah. Jewish culture.

Welcome Comfort ill. by author. Philomel, 1999. ISBN 978-0-399-23169-8 Subj: Holidays – Christmas. Orphans. Santa Claus. School.

Poletti, Frances. *Miss Todd and her wonderful flying machine* by Frances Poletti and Kristina Yee ill. by Kristina Yee, et al. Compendium, 2015. ISBN 978-193829876-9 Subj: Airplanes, airports. Careers – airplane pilots. Gender roles.

Polhemus, Coleman. *The crocodile blues* ill. by author. Candlewick, 2007. ISBN 978-0-7636-3543-5 Subj: Eggs. Reptiles – alligators, crocodiles. Wordless.

Politi, Leo. *Juanita* ill. by author. Scribners, 1948. Subj: Caldecott award honor books. Ethnic groups in the U.S. – Mexican Americans.

Pedro, the angel of Olvera Street ill. by author. Scribners, 1946. Subj: Caldecott award honor books. Ethnic groups in the U.S. – Mexican Americans. Holidays – Christmas.

Song of the swallows ill. by author. Scribners, 1949. ISBN 978-0-684-18831-7 Subj: Birds – swallows. Caldecott award books. Ethnic groups in the U.S. – Mexican Americans. Missions.

Pollack, Pamela. *Where's that cat?* (Merriam, Eve)

Pollard, Nik. *The river* ill. by author. Roaring Brook, 2003. ISBN 978-0-7613-2858-2 Subj: Rhyming text. Rivers.

The tide ill. by author. Roaring Brook, 2002. ISBN 978-0-7613-2467-6 Subj: Nature. Sea & seashore.

Pollock, Penny. *The turkey girl: a Zuni Cinderella story* ill. by Ed Young. Little, 1996. ISBN 978-0-316-71314-6 Subj: Birds – turkeys. Character traits – loyalty. Folk & fairy tales. Indians of North America – Zuni.

When the moon is full ill. by Mary Azarian. Little, 2001. ISBN 978-0-316-71317-7 Subj: Folk & fairy tales. Indians of North America. Moon. Poetry. Seasons.

Pomeranc, Marion Hess. *The American Wei* ill. by DyAnne DiSalvo. Albert Whitman, 1998. ISBN 978-0-8075-0312-6 Subj: Ethnic groups in the U.S. – Chinese Americans. Fairies. Immigrants, immigration.

The can-do Thanksgiving ill. by Nancy Cote. Albert Whitman, 1998. ISBN 978-0-8075-1054-4 Subj: Food. Holidays – Thanksgiving. School.

Pomerantz, Charlotte. *All asleep* ill. by Nancy Tafuri. Greenwillow, 1984. ISBN 978-0-688-03762-8 Subj: Bedtime. Lullabies. Poetry.

Flap your wings and try ill. by Nancy Tafuri. Greenwillow, 1989. ISBN 978-0-688-08020-4 Subj: Activities – flying. Birds. Rhyming text.

Here comes Henny ill. by Nancy Winslow Parker. Greenwillow, 1994. ISBN 978-0-688-12356-7 Subj: Birds – chickens, roosters. Rhyming text.

The mousery ill. by Kurt Cyrus. Harcourt, 2000. ISBN 978-0-15-202304-1 Subj: Animals – mice. Character traits – generosity. Orphans. Rhyming text.

One duck, another duck ill. by José Aruego and Ariane Dewey. Greenwillow, 1984. ISBN 978-0-688-03745-1 Subj: Birds – ducks. Counting, numbers.

The piggy in the puddle ill. by James Marshall. Macmillan, 1974. ISBN 978-0-02-774900-7 Subj: Animals – pigs. Rhyming text. Tongue twisters.

You're not my best friend anymore ill. by David Soman. Dial, 1998. ISBN 978-0-8037-1560-8 Subj: Birthdays. Friendship. Gifts.

Pomeroy, Diana. *One potato* ill. by author. Harcourt, 1996. ISBN 978-0-15-200300-5 Subj: Counting, numbers. Food.

Wildflower ABC ill. by author. Harcourt, 1997. ISBN 978-0-15-201041-6 Subj: ABC books. Activities. Flowers.

Pomranz, Craig. *Made by Raffi* ill. by Margaret Chamberlain. Frances Lincoln, 2014. ISBN 978-184780433-4 Subj: Activities – knitting. Character traits – being different. Character traits – shyness. Gender roles.

Pon, Cynthia. *Faith* (Ajmera, Maya)

Poole, Amy Lowry. *How the rooster got his crown* ill. by author. Holiday, 1999. ISBN 978-0-8234-1389-8 Subj: Birds – chickens, roosters. Creation. Folk & fairy tales – pourquoi tales. Foreign lands – China.

The pea blossom ill. by reteller. Based on the Hans Christian Andersen story: Five peas in a pod. Holiday House, 2005. ISBN 978-0-8234-1864-0 Subj: Folk & fairy tales. Foreign lands – China. Plants.

Poole, Josephine. *Joan of Arc* ill. by Angela Barrett. Knopf, 1998. ISBN 978-0-679-99041-3 Subj: Foreign lands – France. Religion. War.

Porter, Pamela. *Yellow moon, apple moon* ill. by Matt James. Groundwood, 2008. ISBN 978-0-88899-809-5 Subj: Bedtime. Moon. Rhyming text.

Porter, Sue. *Parsnip* ill. by author. DK, 1997. ISBN 978-0-7894-2470-9 Subj: Animals – babies. Animals – sheep. Format, unusual – toy & movable books. Seasons – winter.

Portis, Antoinette. *Best frints in the whole universe* ill. by author. Roaring Brook/Neal Porter, 2016. ISBN 978-162672136-4 Subj: Aliens. Friendship.

Froodle ill. by author. Roaring Brook, 2014. ISBN 978-159643922-1 Subj: Birds. Character traits – individuality. Humorous stories. Noise, sounds. Songs.

Kindergarten diary ill. by author. HarperCollins, 2010. ISBN 978-0-06-145691-6 Subj: School.

No es una caja / not a box ill. by author. Barcelona, 2008. ISBN 978-84-96-95722-0 Subj: Activities – playing. Animals – rabbits. Foreign languages. Imagination.

Not a box ill. by author. HarperCollins, 2006. ISBN 978-0-06-112322-1 Subj: Activities – playing. Animals – rabbits. Imagination.

Not a stick ill. by author. HarperCollins, 2008. ISBN 978-0-06-112325-2 Subj: Activities – playing. Animals – pigs. Imagination.

Now ill. by author. Roaring Brook/Neal Porter, 2017. ISBN 978-162672137-1 Subj: Character traits – individuality. Character traits – patience, impatience. Character traits – wisdom. Emotions – happiness. Self-concept.

A penguin story ill. by author. HarperCollins, 2009. ISBN 978-0-06-145688-6 Subj: Birds – penguins. Character traits – being different. Concepts – color.

Princess Super Kitty ill. by author. HarperCollins, 2011. ISBN 978-0-06-182725-9 Subj: Activities – playing. Imagination.

Wait ill. by author. Roaring Brook/Neal Porter, 2015. ISBN 978-159643921-4 Subj: Behavior – hurrying. Character traits – patience, impatience. Family life – mothers.

Portnoy, Mindy Avra. *A tale of two seders* ill. by Valeria Cis. Lerner/Kar-Ben, 2010. ISBN 978-0-8225-9907-4 Subj: Divorce. Family life. Holidays – Passover.

Where do people go when they die? ill. by Shelly O. Haas. Kar-Ben, 2004. ISBN 978-1-58013-081-3 Subj: Death. Family life.

Porto, Tony. *Blue aliens.* Conceived & designed by 3CD (Tony Porto, Mitch Rice, Glenn Deutsch). Little, 2003. ISBN 978-0-316-61359-0 Subj: Aliens. Concepts – color. School.

Get red. Conceived & designed by 3CD (Tony Porto, Mitch Rice, Glenn Deutsch). Little, 2002. ISBN 978-0-316-60940-1 Subj: Aliens. Concepts – color. School.

Posada, Mia. *Dandelions, stars in the grass* ill. by author. Carolrhoda, 2000. ISBN 978-1-57505-383-7 Subj: Flowers. Plants. Science.

Guess what is growing inside this egg ill. by author. Lerner, 2007. ISBN 978-0-8225-6192-7 Subj: Eggs. Science.

Ladybugs ill. by author. Carolrhoda, 2002. ISBN 978-0-87614-334-6 Subj: Insects – ladybugs. Rhyming text.

Robins ill. by author. Carolrhoda, 2004. ISBN 978-1-57505-615-9 Subj: Birds – robins. Rhyming text.

Who was here? discovering wild animal tracks ill. by author. Millbrook, 2014. ISBN 978-146771871-4 Subj: Animals. Nature. Rhyming text.

Posey, Lee. *Night rabbits* ill. by Michael G. Montgomery. Peachtree, 1999. ISBN 978-1-56145-164-7 Subj: Animals – rabbits. Family life – fathers. Homes, houses. Night. Seasons – summer.

Post, Peggy. *Emily's everyday manners* by Peggy Post and Cindy Post Senning ill. by Steve Björkman. HarperCollins, 2006. ISBN 978-0-06-076177-6 Subj: Etiquette.

Emily's out and about book (Senning, Cindy Post)

Postgate, Daniel. *The richest crocodile in the world* ill. by author. Collins, 2003. ISBN 978-0-00-710388-1 Subj: Friendship. Reptiles – alligators, crocodiles.

Smelly Bill ill. by author. NorthSouth, 2007. ISBN 978-0-7358-2135-4 Subj: Animals – dogs. Rhyming text.

Smelly Bill: love stinks ill. by author. Albert Whitman, 2010. ISBN 978-0-8075-7464-5 Subj: Activities – bathing. Animals – dogs. Rhyming text.

The snagglegrollop ill. by Nick Price. Scholastic, 2009. ISBN 978-0-545-10470-8 Subj: Family life. Friendship. Imagination. Pets.

Posthuma, Sieb. *Benny* ill. by author. Kane/Miller, 2002. ISBN 978-1-929132-43-0 Subj: Animals – dogs. Family life – mothers. Illness – cold (disease). Senses – smell.

Potter, Alicia. *Miss Hazeltine's Home for Shy and Fearful Cats* ill. by Birgitta Sif. Knopf, 2015. ISBN 978-

038575334-0 Subj: Animals – cats. Character traits – shyness. Emotions – fear.

Mrs. Harkness and the panda ill. by Melissa Sweet. Knopf, 2012. ISBN 978-0-375-84448-5 Subj: Animals – pandas. Character traits – perseverance. Foreign lands – China.

Potter, Beatrix. *Appley Dapply's nursery rhymes* ill. by author. Warne, 1917. ISBN 978-0-7232-0613-2 Subj: Animals. Nursery rhymes.

Cecily Parsley's nursery rhymes ill. by author. Warne, 1922. ISBN 978-0-7232-0614-9 Subj: Animals. Nursery rhymes.

The complete adventures of Peter Rabbit ill. by author. Warne, 1982. ISBN 978-0-7232-6165-0 Subj: Animals – rabbits. Behavior – misbehavior.

Ginger and Pickles ill. by author. First pub. in 1909. Warne, 1937. Subj: Animals. Stores.

More tales from Beatrix Potter ill. by author. Warne, 1987. ISBN 978-0-7232-3366-4 Subj: Animals.

Peter Rabbit's ABC ill. by author. Warne, 1999, ©1987. ISBN 978-0-7232-3423-4 Subj: ABC books. Animals.

Peter Rabbit's one two three ill. by author. Warne, 1999, ©1988. ISBN 978-0-7232-3424-1 Subj: Animals – rabbits. Counting, numbers.

The pie and the patty-pan ill. by author. First pub. in 1905. Warne, 1933. Subj: Animals – cats. Animals – dogs. Behavior – trickery.

Rolly-polly pudding ill. by author. First pub. in 1908. Warne, 1936. Subj: Animals – cats.

The sly old cat ill. by author. Warne, 1971. ISBN 978-0-7232-1420-5 Subj: Animals – cats. Animals – rats. Character traits – cleverness. Etiquette. Parties.

The story of fierce bad rabbit ill. by author. Warne, 1906. Subj: Animals – rabbits.

The story of Miss Moppet ill. by author. Warne, 1906. ISBN 978-0-7232-0612-5 Subj: Animals – cats. Behavior – trickery.

The tailor of Gloucester ill. by author. Warne, 1931. Subj: Animals – mice. Careers – tailors. Character traits – helpfulness.

The tale of Benjamin Bunny ill. by author. Warne, 1904. ISBN 978-0-7232-0595-1 Subj: Animals – rabbits. Behavior – misbehavior.

The tale of Jemima Puddle-Duck ill. by author. First pub. in 1910. Warne, 1936. Subj: Birds – ducks. Eggs.

The tale of Johnny Town-Mouse ill. by author. Warne, 1918. ISBN 978-0-7232-0604-0 Subj: Animals – mice.

The tale of Little Pig Robinson ill. by author. Warne, 1930. Subj: Animals – pigs. Behavior – talking to strangers. Boats, ships. Shopping.

The tale of Mr. Jeremy Fisher ill. by David Jorgensen. Picture Book Studio, 1989. ISBN 978-0-88708-094-4 Subj: Frogs & toads. Sports – fishing.

The tale of Mr. Jeremy Fisher ill. by author. Warne, 1934. ISBN 978-0-7232-6231-2 Subj: Frogs & toads. Sports – fishing.

The tale of Mr. Tod ill. by author. First pub. in 1911. Warne, 1939. Subj: Animals – badgers. Animals – foxes. Animals – rabbits.

The tale of Mrs. Tiggy-Winkle ill. by author. Warne, 1905. Subj: Animals – hedgehogs. Clothing.

The tale of Mrs. Tittlemouse ill. by author. Warne, 1910. ISBN 978-0-7232-6235-0 Subj: Animals – mice. Character traits – cleanliness.

The tale of Peter Rabbit ill. by Margot Apple. Troll, 1979. ISBN 978-0-89375-124-1 Subj: Animals – rabbits. Behavior – misbehavior.

The tale of Peter Rabbit ill. by author. Warne, 1902. ISBN 978-0-7232-0592-0 Subj: Animals – rabbits. Behavior – misbehavior. Farms.

The tale of Peter Rabbit and other stories ill. by Allen Atkinson. Knopf, 1982. ISBN 978-0-394-52845-8 Subj: Animals.

The tale of Pigling Bland ill. by author. Warne, 1941, 1913. ISBN 978-0-7232-0606-4 Subj: Animals – pigs.

The tale of Squirrel Nutkin ill. by author. Warne, 1903. ISBN 978-0-7232-0593-7 Subj: Animals – squirrels. Birds – owls. Riddles & jokes. Seasons – fall.

The tale of the faithful dove ill. by Marie Angel. Warne, 1970. Subj: Birds – doves. Character traits – loyalty.

The tale of the Flopsy Bunnies ill. by author. Warne, 1909, 1937. ISBN 978-0-7232-0601-9 Subj: Animals – rabbits. Character traits – cleverness.

The tale of the Flopsy Bunnies ill. by Wendy Rasmussen. Child's World, 2009. ISBN 978-1-60253-297-7 Subj: Animals – rabbits. Character traits – cleverness.

The tale of Timmy Tiptoes ill. by author. Warne, 1911, 1939. ISBN 978-0-7232-0603-3 Subj: Animals – squirrels.

The tale of Tom Kitten ill. by author. Warne, 1907. ISBN 978-0-7232-0599-9 Subj: Animals – cats. Humorous stories.

The tale of Tuppeny ill. by Marie Angel. Warne, 1971. Subj: Animals – guinea pigs.

The tale of two bad mice ill. by author. Warne, 1904, 1934. Subj: Animals – mice. Behavior – misbehavior. Toys.

The two bad mice: pop-up book ill. by author. Warne, 1986. ISBN 978-0-7232-3360-2 Subj: Animals – mice. Behavior – misbehavior. Format, unusual – toy & movable books.

Where's Peter Rabbit? ill. by Colin Twinn. Warne, 1988. ISBN 978-0-7232-3519-4 Subj: Animals – rabbits. Behavior – misbehavior. Format, unusual.

Yours affectionately, Peter Rabbit: miniature letters ill. by author. Warne, 1984. ISBN 978-0-7232-3178-3 Subj: Animals. Communication.

Potter, Giselle. *Tell me what to dream about* ill. by author. Random House, 2015. ISBN 978-038537423-1 Subj: Bedtime. Dreams. Family life – sisters. Imagination.

This is my dollhouse ill. by author. Random House, 2016. ISBN 978-055352153-5 Subj: Activities – making things. Homes, houses. Imagination. Toys – dolls.

The year I didn't go to school ill. by author. Atheneum, 2002. ISBN 978-0-689-84730-1 Subj: Activities – traveling. Foreign lands – Italy. Puppets. Theater.

Poulin, Andrée. *Pablo finds a treasure* ill. by Isabelle Malenfant. Annick, 2016. ISBN 978-155451867-8 Subj: Behavior – bullying, teasing. Poverty.

Pow, Tom. *Tell me one thing, Dad* ill. by Ian Andrew. Candlewick, 2004. ISBN 978-0-7636-2474-3 Subj: Bedtime. Emotions – love. Family life – daughters. Family life – fathers. Games.

Who is the world for? ill. by Robert Ingpen. Candlewick, 2000. ISBN 978-0-7636-1280-1 Subj: Animals. Family life – parents. World.

Powell, Alma. *America's promise* ill. by Marsha Winborn. HarperCollins, 2003. ISBN 978-0-06-052173-8 Subj: Clubs, gangs. Communities, neighborhoods.

Powell, Consie. *Amazing apples* ill. by author. Albert Whitman, 2003. ISBN 978-0-8075-0399-7 Subj: Careers – farmers. Food. Poetry. Trees.

The first day of winter ill. by author. Albert Whitman, 2005. ISBN 978-0-8075-2450-3 Subj: Nature. Seasons – winter. Weather – cold.

Old dog Cora and the Christmas tree ill. by author. Albert Whitman, 1999. ISBN 978-0-8075-5968-0 Subj: Animals – dogs. Family life. Holidays – Christmas. Old age. Trees.

Powell, Polly. *Just dessert* ill. by author. Harcourt, 1996. ISBN 978-0-15-200383-8 Subj: Emotions – fear. Food. Imagination. Night.

Powell-Tuck, Maudie. *The messy book* ill. by Richard Smythe. Tiger Tales, 2016. ISBN 978-168010037-2

Subj: Animals – cats. Animals – dogs. Behavior – messy. Character traits – cleanliness.

Pirates aren't afraid of the dark! ill. by Alison Edgson. Tiger Tales, 2014. ISBN 978-158925165-6 Subj: Camps, camping. Emotions – fear. Family life – brothers & sisters. Pirates.

Poydar, Nancy. *The bad-news report card* ill. by author. Holiday House, 2006. ISBN 978-0-8234-1992-0 Subj: Behavior – worrying. School.

The biggest test in the universe ill. by author. Holiday House, 2005. ISBN 978-0-8234-1944-9 Subj: Behavior – worrying. School.

Busy Bea ill. by author. Margaret K. McElderry, 1994. ISBN 978-0-689-50592-8 Subj: Behavior – lost & found possessions. Ethnic groups in the U.S. – African Americans. Family life – grandmothers. School.

Cool Ali ill. by author. Margaret K. McElderry, 1996. ISBN 978-0-689-80755-8 Subj: Activities – drawing. Cities, towns. Concepts – shape. Concepts – size. Seasons – summer.

First day, hooray! ill. by author. Holiday, 1999. ISBN 978-0-8234-1437-6 Subj: Careers – bus drivers. Careers – school principals. Careers – teachers. School – first day.

Fish school ill. by author. Holiday, 2009. ISBN 978-0-8234-2140-4 Subj: Aquariums. Fish. Pets. School – field trips.

Mailbox magic ill. by author. Holiday, 2000. ISBN 978-0-8234-1525-0 Subj: Character traits – patience, impatience. Letters, cards.

No fair science fair ill. by author. Holiday House, 2011. ISBN 978-0-8234-2269-2 Subj: Character traits – persistence. School. Science.

The perfectly horrible Halloween ill. by author. Holiday, 2001. ISBN 978-0-8234-1592-2 Subj: Clothing – costumes. Holidays – Halloween. Problem solving. School.

Rhyme time Valentine ill. by author. Holiday, 2003. ISBN 978-0-8234-1684-4 Subj: Ethnic groups in the U.S. – African Americans. Holidays – Valentine's Day. Rhyming text. School. Weather – wind.

Snip, snip . . . snow! ill. by author. Holiday, 1997. ISBN 978-0-8234-1328-7 Subj: Activities – playing. Nature. School. Seasons – winter. Weather – snow.

Zip, zip . . . homework ill. by author. Holiday, 2008. ISBN 978-0-8234-2090-2 Subj: Behavior – lying. Character traits – honesty. School.

Poynter, Dougie. *The dinosaur that pooped a planet!* (Fletcher, Tom)

Prap, Lila. *Animal lullabies* ill. by author. NorthSouth, 2006. ISBN 978-0-7358-2097-5 Subj: Animals. Lullabies. Rhyming text.

Animals speak ill. by author. NorthSouth, 2006. ISBN 978-0-7358-2058-6 Subj: Animals. Foreign languages.

Daddies ill. by author. NorthSouth, 2007. ISBN 978-0-7358-2140-8 Subj: Animals. Bedtime. Family life – fathers. Rhyming text.

Dinosaurs?! ill. by author. NorthSouth, 2010. ISBN 978-0-7358-2284-9 Subj: Dinosaurs.

Doggy whys ill. by author. NorthSouth, 2011. ISBN 978-0-7358-4014-0 Subj: Animals – cats. Animals – dogs. Pets.

Prasadam-Halls, Smriti. *I love you night and day* ill. by Alison Brown. Bloomsbury, 2014. ISBN 978-161963222-6 Subj: Animals – bears. Animals – rabbits. Emotions – love. Rhyming text.

T. Veg: the story of a carrot-crunching dinosaur ill. by Katherina Manolessou. Abrams, 2017. ISBN 978-141972494-7 Subj: Character traits – being different. Character traits – individuality. Dinosaurs. Food. Rhyming text.

Preller, James. *Cardinal and sunflower* ill. by Huy Voun Lee. HarperCollins, 1998. ISBN 978-0-06-026223-5 Subj: Birds – cardinals. Flowers. Nature.

A pirate's guide to first grade ill. by Greg Ruth. Feiwel & Friends, 2010. ISBN 978-0-312-36928-6 Subj: Pirates. School – first day.

A pirate's guide to recess ill. by Greg Ruth. Feiwel & Friends, 2013. ISBN 978-1-250-00515-1 Subj: Pirates. School.

Prelutsky, Jack. *Awful Ogre running wild* ill. by Paul O. Zelinsky. Greenwillow, 2008. ISBN 978-0-06-623866-1 Subj: Mythical creatures – ogres. Poetry.

Awful Ogre's awful day ill. by Paul O. Zelinsky. Greenwillow, 2001. ISBN 978-0-688-07779-2 Subj: Mythical creatures – ogres. Poetry.

The baby uggs are hatching ill. by James Stevenson. Greenwillow, 1982. ISBN 978-0-688-00923-6 Subj: Humorous stories. Imagination. Monsters. Poetry.

Behold the bold umbrellaphant and other poems ill. by Carin Berger. HarperCollins, 2006. ISBN 978-0-06-054318-1 Subj: Animals. Imagination. Poetry.

Beneath a blue umbrella ill. by Garth Williams. Greenwillow, 1990. ISBN 978-0-688-06429-7 Subj: Animals. Poetry.

Circus ill. by Arnold Lobel. Macmillan, 1974. ISBN 978-0-02-775060-7 Subj: Circus. Poetry.

For laughing out louder: more poems to tickle your funnybone ill. by Marjorie Priceman. Knopf, 1995. ISBN 978-0-679-87063-0 Subj: Poetry.

The frogs wore red suspenders ill. by Petra Mathers. Greenwillow, 2002. ISBN 978-0-688-16720-2 Subj: Poetry.

Good sports: rhymes about running, jumping, throwing, and more ill. by Chris Raschka. Random House, 2007. ISBN 978-0-375-83700-5 Subj: Poetry. Sports.

Halloween countdown ill. by Dan Yaccarino. HarperCollins, 2002. ISBN 978-0-06-000512-2 Subj: Counting, numbers. Format, unusual – board books. Ghosts. Holidays – Halloween. Poetry.

Imagine that! poems of never-was ill. by Kevin Hawkes. Knopf, 1998. ISBN 978-0-679-98206-7 Subj: Imagination. Poetry.

It's snowing! It's snowing! winter poems ill. by Yossi Abolafia. HarperCollins, 2006. ISBN 978-0-06-053715-9 Subj: Poetry. Seasons – winter.

Me I am! ill. by Christine Davenier. Farrar, 2007. ISBN 978-0-374-64902-9 Subj: Character traits – individuality. Poetry. Self-concept.

The mean old mean hyena ill. by Arnold Lobel. Greenwillow, 1978. ISBN 978-0-688-84163-8 Subj: Animals – hyenas. Character traits – meanness. Rhyming text.

Monday's troll ill. by Peter Sís. Greenwillow, 1996. ISBN 978-0-688-09644-1 Subj: Fairies. Mythical creatures – trolls. Poetry. Witches.

The pack rat's day and other poems ill. by Margaret Bloy Graham. Macmillan, 1974. ISBN 978-0-02-775050-8 Subj: Animals. Poetry.

The queen of Eene ill. by Victoria Chess. Greenwillow, 1978. ISBN 978-0-688-84144-7 Subj: Humorous stories. Poetry.

Rainy rainy Saturday ill. by Marylin Hafner. Greenwillow, 1980. ISBN 978-0-688-84252-9 Subj: Poetry. Weather – rain.

The Random House book of poetry for children ill. by Arnold Lobel. Random House, 1983. ISBN 978-0-394-95010-5 Subj: Humorous stories. Poetry.

Read-aloud rhymes for the very young ill. by Marc Brown. Knopf, 1986. ISBN 978-0-394-97218-3 Subj: Poetry.

Ride a purple pelican ill. by Garth Williams. Greenwillow, 1986. ISBN 978-0-688-04031-4 Subj: Imagination. Poetry.

The snopp on the sidewalk and other poems ill. by Byron Barton. Greenwillow, 1977. ISBN 978-0-688-84084-6 Subj: Humorous stories. Imagination. Poetry.

Stardines swim high across the sky: and other poems ill. by Carin Berger. Greenwillow, 2013. ISBN 978-0-06-201464-1 Subj: Animals. Imagination. Poetry.

The terrible tiger ill. by Arnold Lobel. Macmillan, 1970. ISBN 978-0-689-71300-2 Subj: Animals – tigers. Cumulative tales. Rhyming text.

There's no place like school ill. by Jane Manning. HarperCollins, 2010. ISBN 978-0-06-082338-2 Subj: Poetry. School.

Tyrannosaurus was a beast ill. by Arnold Lobel. Greenwillow, 1988. ISBN 978-0-688-06443-3 Subj: Dinosaurs. Poetry.

What a day it was at school! ill. by Doug Cushman. HarperCollins, 2006. ISBN 978-0-06-082335-1 Subj: Poetry. School.

Wild witches' ball ill. by Kelly Asbury. HarperCollins, 2004. ISBN 978-0-06-052972-7 Subj: Counting, numbers. Holidays – Halloween. Rhyming text. Witches.

The wizard ill. by Brandon Dorman. HarperCollins, 2007. ISBN 978-0-06-124076-8 Subj: Magic. Rhyming text. Wizards.

Preston, Tim. *Pumpkin moon* ill. by Simon Bartram. Dutton, 2001. ISBN 978-0-525-46713-7 Subj: Holidays – Halloween. Moon.

Preston-Gannon, Frann. *Deep deep sea* ill. by author. IPG/Pavilion, 2015. ISBN 978-184365268-7 Subj: Counting, numbers. Format, unusual – board books. Sea & seashore.

Dinosaur farm ill. by author. Sterling, 2014. ISBN 978-145491132-6 Subj: Careers – farmers. Dinosaurs. Farms.

How to lose a lemur ill. by author. Sterling, 2014. ISBN 978-145491131-9 Subj: Animals – lemurs. Behavior – lost. Friendship.

Pepper and Poe ill. by author. Scholastic/Orchard, 2015. ISBN 978-054568357-9 Subj: Animals – cats. Days of the week, months of the year.

Sloth slept on ill. by author. Sterling, 2015. ISBN 978-145491611-6 Subj: Animals – sloths. Sleep.

What a hoot! ill. by author. POW!, 2015. ISBN 978-157687758-6 Subj: Birds – owls. Concepts – opposites. Format, unusual – board books. Rhyming text.

Preus, Margi. *The Peace Bell* ill. by Hideko Takahashi. Henry Holt, 2008. ISBN 978-0-8050-7800-8 Subj: Family life – grandmothers. Foreign lands – Japan. Friendship. Holidays – New Year's. U.S. history. War.

Previn, Stacey. *Aberdeen* ill. by author. Viking, 2016. ISBN 978-045147148-2 Subj: Activities – flying. Animals – mice. Toys – balloons.

Find spot! ill. by author. Little, Brown, 2014. ISBN 978-031621332-5 Subj: Concepts – patterns.

Concepts – shape. Format, unusual – toy & movable books. Rhyming text.

Prevot, Franck. *Wangari Maathai: the woman who planted millions of trees* ill. by Aurelia Fronty. Charlesbridge, 2014. ISBN 978-158089626-9 Subj: Ecology. Foreign lands – Kenya. Trees.

Price, Ben Joel. *Earth space moon base* ill. by author. Random House, 2014. ISBN 978-038537311-1 Subj: Animals – monkeys. Careers – astronauts. Rhyming text. Robots. Space & space ships.

Price, Hope Lynne. *These hands* ill. by Bryan Collier. Hyperion, 1999. ISBN 978-0-7868-2320-8 Subj: Anatomy – hands. Ethnic groups in the U.S. – African Americans. Family life – mothers. Rhyming text.

Price, Kathy. *The Bourbon Street musicians* ill. by Andrew Glass. Clarion, 2002. ISBN 978-0-618-04076-6 Subj: Animals. Careers – musicians. Crime. Folk & fairy tales. Old age.

Price, Leontyne. *Aïda* ill. by Leo and Diane Dillon. Retells the story of Giuseppe Verdi's opera. Harcourt, 1990. ISBN 978-0-15-200405-7 Subj: Emotions – love. Foreign lands – Egypt. Music. Royalty.

Price, Mara. *Grandma's chocolate / El chocolate de Abuelita* ill. by Lisa Fields. Arte Publico/Piñata, 2010. ISBN 978-1-55885-587-8 Subj: Ethnic groups in the U.S. – Mexican Americans. Family life – grandmothers. Foreign languages. Gifts. Indians of Central America – Maya.

Priceman, Marjorie. *Emeline at the circus* ill. by author. Knopf, 1999. ISBN 978-0-679-87685-4 Subj: Careers – teachers. Circus. School.

Hot air: the (mostly) true story of the first hot-air balloon ride ill. by author. Simon & Schuster, 2005. ISBN 978-0-689-82642-9 Subj: Activities – ballooning. Caldecott award honor books. Careers – inventors. Inventions.

How to make a cherry pie and see the U.S.A. ill. by author. Knopf, 2008. ISBN 978-0-375-81255-2 Subj: Activities – baking, cooking. Activities – traveling. Food.

How to make an apple pie and see the world ill. by author. Knopf, 1994. ISBN 978-0-679-93705-0 Subj: Activities – baking, cooking. Activities – traveling. Food.

It's me, Marva! ill. by author. Knopf, 2001. ISBN 978-0-679-98993-6 Subj: Careers – inventors. Concepts – color. Optical illusions.

My nine lives / by Clio ill. by author. Atheneum, 1998. ISBN 978-0-689-81135-7 Subj: Animals – cats. Memories, memory.

Princess Picky ill. by author. Roaring Brook, 2002. ISBN 978-0-7613-2418-8 Subj: Activities – flying. Character traits – stubbornness. Food. Royalty – princesses.

Priest, Robert H. *The old pirate of Central Park* ill. by author. Houghton, 1999. ISBN 978-0-395-90505-0 Subj: Activities – playing. Boats, ships. Toys.

The pirate's eye ill. by author. Houghton, 2005. ISBN 978-0-618-43990-4 Subj: Activities – drawing. Anatomy – eyes. Behavior – lost & found possessions. Character traits – generosity. Pirates.

Prigger, Mary Skillings. *Aunt Minnie and the twister* ill. by Betsy Lewin. Clarion, 2002. ISBN 978-0-618-11136-7 Subj: Family life – aunts, uncles. Farms. Homes, houses. Weather – tornadoes.

Aunt Minnie McGranahan ill. by Betsy Lewin. Clarion, 1999. ISBN 978-0-618-60488-3 Subj: Character traits – orderliness. Family life – aunts, uncles. Family life – brothers & sisters. Orphans.

Primavera, Elise. *Auntie Claus* ill. by author. Harcourt, 1999. ISBN 978-0-15-201909-9 Subj: Family life – aunts, uncles. Foreign lands – Arctic. Holidays – Christmas. Santa Claus.

Auntie Claus and the key to Christmas ill. by author. Harcourt, 2002. ISBN 978-0-15-202441-3 Subj: Family life – aunts, uncles. Foreign lands – Arctic. Holidays – Christmas. Santa Claus.

The house at the end of Ladybug Lane ill. by Valeria Docampo. Random House, 2012. ISBN 978-0-375-85584-9 Subj: Behavior – wishing. Character traits – cleanliness. Character traits – individuality. Insects – ladybugs.

Louise, the big cheese: divine diva ill. by Diane Goode. Simon & Schuster, 2009. ISBN 978-1-4169-7180-1 Subj: Friendship. Theater.

Louise the big cheese and the back-to-school smartypants ill. by Diane Goode. Simon & Schuster, 2011. ISBN 978-1-4424-0600-1 Subj: Careers – teachers. Character traits – ambition. School.

Louise the big cheese and the la-di-da shoes ill. by Diane Goode. Simon & Schuster, 2010. ISBN 978-1-4169-7181-8 Subj: Character traits – appearance. Character traits – vanity. Clothing – shoes.

Louise the big cheese and the Ooh-la-la Charm School ill. by Diane Goode. Simon & Schuster, 2012. ISBN 978-1-4424-0599-8 Subj: Character traits – ambition. Etiquette. Friendship.

Thumb love ill. by author. Random House, 2010. ISBN 978-0-375-84481-2 Subj: Humorous stories. Thumb sucking.

Prince, April Jones. *Goldenlocks and the three pirates* ill. by Steven Salerno. Farrar/Margaret Ferguson, 2017. ISBN 978-037430074-6 Subj: Boats, ships. Character traits – helpfulness. Folk & fairy tales. Pirates.

Twenty-one elephants and still standing ill. by François Roca. Houghton, 2005. ISBN 978-0-618-44887-6 Subj: Animals – elephants. Bridges.

What do wheels do all day? ill. by Giles Laroche. Houghton, 2006. ISBN 978-0-618-56307-4 Subj: Rhyming text. Wheels.

Prince, Joshua. *I saw an ant in a parking lot* ill. by Macky Pamintuan. Sterling, 2007. ISBN 978-1-4027-3823-4 Subj: Humorous stories. Insects – ants. Rhyming text.

I saw an ant on the railroad track ill. by Macky Pamintuan. Sterling, 2006. ISBN 978-1-4027-2183-0 Subj: Humorous stories. Insects – ants. Rhyming text. Trains.

Pringle, Laurence P. *Bear hug* ill. by Kate Salley Palmer. Boyds Mills, 2003. ISBN 978-1-56397-876-0 Subj: Animals – bears. Camps, camping. Family life – fathers.

Crows ill. by Bob Marstall. Boyds Mills, 2002. ISBN 978-1-56397-899-9 Subj: Birds – crows. Science.

Everybody has a bellybutton ill. by Clare Wood. Boyds Mills, 1997. ISBN 978-1-56397-009-2 Subj: Anatomy – navels. Birth. Family life.

Jesse builds a road ill. by Leslie Holt Morrill. Macmillan, 1989. ISBN 978-0-02-775311-0 Subj: Imagination. Machines. Roads.

Naming the cat ill. by Katherine Potter. Walker, 1997. ISBN 978-0-8027-8622-7 Subj: Animals – cats. Names. Pets.

Octopus hug ill. by Kate Salley Palmer. Boyds Mills, 1993. ISBN 978-1-56397-034-4 Subj: Activities – playing. Family life.

One room school ill. by Barbara Garrison. Boyds Mills, 1998. ISBN 978-1-56397-583-7 Subj: School. U.S. history. War.

The secret life of the woolly bear caterpillar ill. by Joan Paley. Boyds Mills, 2014. ISBN 978-162091000-9 Subj: Insects – butterflies, caterpillars. Insects – moths.

Snakes ill. by Meryl Henderson. Boyds Mills, 2004. ISBN 978-1-59078-003-9 Subj: Reptiles – snakes. Science.

Pritchett, Andy. *Stick!* ill. by author. Candlewick, 2013. ISBN 978-0-7636-6616-3 Subj: Activities – playing. Animals. Animals – dogs.

Pritchett, Dylan. *The first music* ill. by Erin Bennett Banks. August House, 2006. ISBN 978-0-87483-776-6 Subj: Foreign lands – Africa. Jungle. Music.

Prochovnic, Dawn Babb. *The big blue bowl: sign language for food* ill. by Stephanie Bauer. Abdo, 2009. ISBN 978-1-60270-668-2 Subj: Food. Rhyming text. Sign language.

Hip hip hooray! It's Family Day! sign language for family ill. by Stephanie Bauer. Abdo, 2012. ISBN 978-1-61641-837-3 Subj: Family life. Rhyming text. Sign language.

Proimos, James. *The best bike ride ever* ill. by Johanna Wright. Dial, 2012. ISBN 978-0-8037-3850-8 Subj: Accidents. Imagination. Safety. Sports – bicycling.

Joe's wish ill. by author. Harcourt, 1998. ISBN 978-0-15-201831-3 Subj: Behavior – wishing. Family life – grandfathers. Old age.

The loudness of Sam ill. by author. Harcourt, 1999. ISBN 978-0-15-202087-3 Subj: Cities, towns. Emotions. Family life – aunts, uncles.

Paulie Pastrami achieves world peace ill. by author. Little, Brown, 2009. ISBN 978-0-316-03292-6 Subj: Behavior – seeking better things. Behavior – sharing. Character traits – kindness. Food.

Todd's TV ill. by author. HarperCollins, 2010. ISBN 978-0-06-170985-2 Subj: Family life – parents. Television.

Waddle! waddle! ill. by author. Scholastic, 2015. ISBN 978-054541846-1 Subj: Activities – dancing. Birds – penguins. Friendship.

Prokofiev, Sergei Sergeievitch. *Peter and the wolf* ill. by Charles Mikolaycak. Viking, 1982. ISBN 978-0-670-54919-1 Subj: Animals – wolves. Character traits – cleverness. Folk & fairy tales. Foreign lands – Russia. Music. Musical instruments.

Peter and the wolf ill. by Josef Palecek. Picture Book Studio, 1987. ISBN 978-0-88708-049-4 Subj: Animals – wolves. Character traits – cleverness. Folk & fairy tales. Foreign lands – Russia. Music. Musical instruments.

Peter and the wolf retold by Chris Raschka; ill. by reteller. Simon & Schuster, 2008. ISBN 978-0-689-85652-5 Subj: Animals – wolves. Character traits – cleverness. Folk & fairy tales. Foreign lands – Russia. Music. Musical instruments.

Peter and the wolf retold by Vladimir Vagin; ill. by reteller. Scholastic, 2000. ISBN 978-0-590-38608-1 Subj: Animals – wolves. Character traits – cleverness. Folk & fairy tales. Foreign lands – Russia. Music. Musical instruments.

Prosek, James. *Bird, butterfly, eel* ill. by author. Simon & Schuster, 2009. ISBN 978-0-689-86829-0 Subj: Birds. Fish. Insects – butterflies, caterpillars. Migration.

Protopopescu, Orel. *Thelonious Mouse* ill. by Anne Wilsdorf. Farrar, 2011. ISBN 978-0-374-37447-1 Subj: Animals – cats. Animals – mice. Music.

Two sticks ill. by Anne Wilsdorf. Farrar, 2007. ISBN 978-0-374-38022-9 Subj: Musical instruments – drums. Reptiles – alligators, crocodiles. Rhyming text.

Provencher, Rose-Marie. *Mouse cleaning* ill. by Bernadette Pons. Henry Holt, 2001. ISBN 978-0-8050-6240-3 Subj: Animals – mice. Behavior – messy. Character traits – cleanliness. Homes, houses.

Provensen, Alice. *A book of seasons* by Alice Provensen and Martin Provensen; ill. by authors. Random House, 1976. ISBN 978-0-394-83242-5 Subj: Seasons.

The glorious flight: across the channel with Louis Blériot by Alice Provensen and Martin Provensen; ill. by authors. Viking, 1983. ISBN 978-0-14-050729-4 Subj: Activities – flying. Airplanes, airports. Caldecott award books.

Klondike gold ill. by author. Simon & Schuster, 2005. ISBN 978-0-689-84885-8 Subj: Careers – miners. Foreign lands – Yukon Territory.

Murphy in the city ill. by author. Simon & Schuster, 2015. ISBN 978-144241971-1 Subj: Animals – dogs. Cities, towns.

Town and country by Alice Provensen and Martin Provensen; ill. by authors. Crown, 1984. ISBN 978-0-15-200182-7 Subj: Cities, towns. Country.

The year at Maple Hill Farm by Alice Provensen and Martin Provensen; ill. by authors. Atheneum, 1978. ISBN 978-0-689-20494-4 Subj: Animals. Days of the week, months of the year. Farms. Seasons.

Provensen, Martin. *A book of seasons* (Provensen, Alice)

The glorious flight: across the channel with Louis Blériot (Provensen, Alice)

Town and country (Provensen, Alice)

The year at Maple Hill Farm (Provensen, Alice)

Pryor, Bonnie. *Amanda and April* ill. by Diane deGroat. Morrow, 1986. ISBN 978-0-688-05870-8 Subj: Animals – pigs. Family life – sisters. Parties. Sibling rivalry.

The dream jar ill. by Mark Graham. Morrow, 1996. ISBN 978-0-688-13062-6 Subj: Activities – working. Cities, towns. Ethnic groups in the U.S. – Russian Americans. Family life. Immigrants, immigration.

The house on Maple Street ill. by Beth Peck. Morrow, 1987. ISBN 978-0-688-06381-8 Subj: U.S. history.

Merry Christmas, Amanda and April ill. by Diane deGroat. Morrow, 1990. ISBN 978-0-688-07545-3 Subj: Animals – pigs. Family life – sisters. Holidays – Christmas.

The porcupine mouse ill. by Mary Jane Begin. Morrow, 1988. ISBN 978-0-688-07154-7 Subj: Animals – mice. Character traits – bravery. Emotions – fear. Sibling rivalry.

Pryor, Katherine. *Zora's zucchini* ill. by Anna Raff. Readers to Eaters, 2015. ISBN 978-098366157-3 Subj: Activities – trading. Behavior – resourcefulness. Food. Gardens, gardening.

Puck. *Babies around the world* ill. by Violet Lemay. Duo Press, 2017. ISBN 978-193809387-6 Subj: Babies, toddlers. Foreign languages. Format, unusual – board books. World.

Puckett, Kelley. *Batman's dark secret* ill. by Jon J Muth. Scholastic, 2016. ISBN 978-054586755-9 Subj: Character traits – bravery. Emotions – fear. Orphans.

Pullen, Zachary. *Friday my Radio Flyer flew* ill. by author. Simon & Schuster, 2008. ISBN 978-1-4169-3983-2 Subj: Family life – fathers. Toys – wagons.

Pullman, Philip. *Puss in boots: the adventures of that most enterprising feline* ill. by Ian Beck. Knopf, 2000. ISBN 978-0-375-81354-2 Subj: Animals – cats. Character traits – cleverness. Folk & fairy tales. Foreign lands – France. Royalty – kings.

Pulver, Robin. *Alicia's tutu* ill. by Mark Graham. Dial, 1997. ISBN 978-0-8037-1933-0 Subj: Activities – dancing. Ballet. Behavior – wishing. Family life. Family life – grandmothers. Furniture – beds.

Author day for room 3T ill. by Chuck Richards. Houghton, 2005. ISBN 978-0-618-35406-1 Subj: Careers – writers. School.

Axle Annie ill. by Tedd Arnold. Dial, 1999. ISBN 978-0-8037-2096-1 Subj: Careers – bus drivers. School. Weather – snow.

Axle Annie and the speed grump ill. by Tedd Arnold. Penguin, 2005. ISBN 978-0-8037-2787-8 Subj: Accidents. Activities – driving. Careers – bus drivers. School.

The case of the incapacitated capitals ill. by Lynn Rowe Reed. Holiday House, 2012. ISBN 978-0-8234-2402-3 Subj: Activities – writing. Careers – teachers. Language. School.

Christmas for a kitten ill. by Layne Johnson. Albert Whitman, 2003. ISBN 978-0-8075-1151-0 Subj: Animals – cats. Holidays – Christmas. Santa Claus.

Christmas kitten, home at last ill. by Layne Johnson. Albert Whitman, 2010. ISBN 978-0-8075-

1157-2 Subj: Animals – cats. Holidays – Christmas. Illness – allergies. Santa Claus.

Happy endings: a story about suffixes ill. by Lynn Rowe Reed. Holiday House, 2011. ISBN 978-0-8234-2296-8 Subj: Language. School.

Mrs. Toggle and the dinosaur ill. by R. W. Alley. Four Winds, 1991. ISBN 978-0-02-775452-0 Subj: Careers – teachers. Dinosaurs. Prehistory. School.

Mrs. Toggle's beautiful blue shoe ill. by R. W. Alley. Four Winds, 1991. ISBN 978-0-02-775456-8 Subj: Careers – teachers. Clothing – shoes. School.

Mrs. Toggle's zipper ill. by R. W. Alley. Four Winds, 1990. ISBN 978-0-02-775451-3 Subj: Careers – teachers. Clothing – coats. Humorous stories. School.

Never say boo! ill. by Deb Lucke. Holiday, 2009. ISBN 978-0-8234-2110-7 Subj: Character traits – being different. Ghosts. School.

Nobody's mother is in second grade ill. by G. Brian Karas. Dial, 1992. ISBN 978-0-8037-1211-9 Subj: Family life – mothers. Plants. School.

Nouns and verbs have a field day ill. by Lynn Rowe Reed. Holiday House, 2006. ISBN 978-0-8234-1982-1 Subj: Language. School.

Punctuation takes a vacation ill. by Lynn Rowe Reed. Holiday House, 2003. ISBN 978-0-8234-1687-5 Subj: Activities – vacationing. Language. School.

Saturday is Dadurday ill. by R. W. Alley. Walker, 2013. ISBN 978-0-8027-8691-3 Subj: Emotions – sadness. Family life – fathers. Problem solving.

Silent letters loud and clear ill. by Lynn Rowe Reed. Holiday, 2008. ISBN 978-0-8234-2127-5 Subj: Language. School.

Thank you, Miss Doover ill. by Stephanie Roth Sisson. Holiday House, 2010. ISBN 978-0-8234-2046-9 Subj: Activities – writing. Letters, cards. School.

Way to go, Alex! ill. by Elizabeth Wolf. Albert Whitman, 1999. ISBN 978-0-8075-1583-9 Subj: Disabilities. Family life – brothers & sisters. Sports – Special Olympics.

Pumphrey, Jerome. *Creepy things are scaring me* ill. by Rosanne Litzinger. HarperCollins, 2003. ISBN 978-0-06-028963-8 Subj: Bedtime. Emotions – fear. Rhyming text.

Purcell, Rebecca. *Super Chicken* ill. by author. Scholastic, 2013. ISBN 978-0-545-45170-3 Subj: Activities – playing. Birds – chickens, roosters. Format, unusual – board books. Imagination.

Purmell, Ann. *Apple cider making days* ill. by Joanne Friar. Millbrook, 2002. ISBN 978-0-7613-2364-8

Subj: Careers – farmers. Family life – grandfathers. Farms. Food.

Christmas tree farm ill. by Jill Weber. Holiday House, 2006. ISBN 978-0-8234-1886-2 Subj: Activities – working. Careers – farmers. Farms. Holidays – Christmas. Trees.

Maple syrup season ill. by Jill Weber. Holiday, 2008. ISBN 978-0-8234-1891-6 Subj: Family life. Food. Trees.

Where wild babies sleep ill. by Lorianne Siomades. Boyds Mills, 2003. ISBN 978-1-59078-049-7 Subj: Animals – babies. Bedtime. Night. Sleep.

Puttock, Simon. *The baby that roared* ill. by Nadia Shireen. Candlewick, 2012. ISBN 978-0-7636-5903-5 Subj: Animals. Animals – deer. Babies, toddlers. Monsters.

Big bad wolf is good ill. by Lynne Chapman. Sterling, 2002. ISBN 978-0-8069-0027-8 Subj: Animals. Animals – wolves. Behavior. Friendship.

Goat and Donkey in strawberry sunglasses ill. by Russell Julian. Good Books, 2007. ISBN 978-1-56148-572-7 Subj: Animals – donkeys. Animals – goats. Friendship. Shopping.

Goat and Donkey in the great outdoors ill. by Russell Julian. Good Books, 2007. ISBN 978-1-56148-573-4 Subj: Activities – vacationing. Animals – donkeys. Animals – goats. Friendship.

A ladder to the stars ill. by Alison Jay. Henry Holt, 2001. ISBN 978-0-8050-6783-5 Subj: Activities – dancing. Behavior – wishing. Old age. Stars.

Little lost cowboy ill. by Caroline Jayne Church. Egmont, 2011. ISBN 978-1-60684-259-1 Subj: Animals – coyotes. Behavior – lost.

Miss Fox ill. by Holly Swain. Frances Lincoln, 2006. ISBN 978-1-84507-475-3 Subj: Animals – foxes. Animals – sheep. Careers – teachers. School.

Mouse's first night at Moonlight School ill. by Ali Pye. Candlewick/Nosy Crow, 2015. ISBN 978-076367607-0 Subj: Animals – mice. Character traits – shyness. School – first day.

Squeaky clean ill. by Mary McQuillan. Little, 2002. ISBN 978-0-316-78816-8 Subj: Activities – bathing. Animals – pigs. Hygiene.

A story for Hippo ill. by Alison Jay. Scholastic, 2001. ISBN 978-0-439-26219-4 Subj: Animals – hippopotamuses. Animals – monkeys. Death. Emotions – grief. Friendship.

Yours truly, Louisa ill. by Jo Kiddie. HarperCollins, 2009. ISBN 978-0-06-136634-5 Subj: Activities – writing. Animals – pigs. Character traits – cleanliness. Farms. Letters, cards.

Pym, Tasha. *Have you ever seen a sneep?* ill. by Joel Stewart. Farrar, 2009. ISBN 978-0-374-32868-9 Subj: Imagination. Rhyming text.

Quackenbush, Robert M. *Batbaby* ill. by author. Random House, 1997. ISBN 978-0-679-98541-9 Subj: Animals – bats. Animals – squirrels. Bedtime. Weather – storms.

First grade jitters ill. by Yan Nascimbene. HarperCollins, 2010. ISBN 978-0-06-077632-9 Subj: Behavior – worrying. School – first day.

Quarmby, Katharine. *Yokki and the Parno Gry* (O'Neill, Richard)

Quattlebaum, Mary. *Jo MacDonald had a garden* ill. by Laura J. Bryant. Dawn, 2012. ISBN 978-1-58469-164-8 Subj: Ecology. Gardens, gardening. Songs.

Jo MacDonald hiked in the woods ill. by Laura J. Bryant. Dawn, 2013. ISBN 978-1-58469-334-5 Subj: Activities – hiking. Animals. Forest, woods. Rhyming text. Songs.

Jo MacDonald saw a pond ill. by Laura J. Bryant. Dawn, 2011. ISBN 978-1-58469-150-1 Subj: Lakes, ponds. Songs.

Pirate vs. pirate: the terrific tale of a big, blustery maritime match ill. by Alexandra Boiger. Hyperion/Disney, 2011. ISBN 978-1-4231-2201-2 Subj: Contests. Emotions – love. Pirates.

The shine man ill. by Tim Ladwig. Eerdmans, 2001. ISBN 978-0-8028-5181-9 Subj: Careers – shoe shiners. Character traits – generosity. Holidays – Christmas. Poverty. U.S. history.

Sparks fly high: the legend of Dancing Point ill. by Leonid Gore. Farrar, 2006. ISBN 978-0-374-34452-8 Subj: Activities – dancing. Character traits – pride. Contests. Devil. Folk & fairy tales.

Winter friends ill. by Hiroe Nakata. Random House, 2005. ISBN 978-0-385-90868-9 Subj: Behavior – lost & found possessions. Clothing – gloves, mittens. Friendship. Poetry. Seasons – winter.

Quigley, Mary. *Granddad's fishing buddy* ill. by Stéphane Jorisch. Penguin, 2007. ISBN 978-0-8037-2942-1 Subj: Birds – herons. Family life – grandfathers. Sports – fishing.

Quinton, Sasha. *You and me* (Kindermans, Martine)

Raab, Brigitte. *Where does pepper come from? and other fun facts* ill. by Manuela Olten. NorthSouth, 2006. ISBN 978-0-7358-2070-8 Subj: Character traits – questioning. Science.

Rabe, Tish. *On the first day of kindergarten* ill. by Laura Hughes. HarperCollins, 2016. ISBN 978-006234834-0 Subj: Counting, numbers. Cumulative tales. School – first day.

Rabinowitz, Alan. *A boy and a jaguar* ill. by Catia Chien. Houghton, 2014. ISBN 978-054787507-1 Subj: Animals – jaguars. Careers – scientists. Disabilities – stuttering. Ecology.

Raczka, Bob. *Art is . . .* ill. with photos. Millbrook, 2003. ISBN 978-0-7613-2874-2 Subj: Art. Rhyming text.

Fall mixed up ill. by Chad Cameron. Carolrhoda, 2011. ISBN 978-0-7613-4606-7 Subj: Picture puzzles. Rhyming text. Seasons – fall.

Guyku: a year of haiku for boys ill. by Peter H. Reynolds. Harcourt, 2010. ISBN 978-0-547-24003-9 Subj: Poetry. Seasons.

Joy in Mudville ill. by Glin Dibley. Carolrhoda, 2014. ISBN 978-076136015-5 Subj: Gender roles. Rhyming text. Sports – baseball.

Niko draws a feeling ill. by Simone Shin. Carolrhoda, 2017. ISBN 978-146779843-3 Subj: Activities – drawing. Art. Emotions. Self-concept.

No one saw: ordinary things through the eyes of an artist. Ill. with famous 20th-century works of art. Millbrook, 2002. ISBN 978-0-7613-2370-9 Subj: Art. Careers – artists.

Santa Clauses: short poems from the North Pole ill. by Chuck Groenink. Carolrhoda, 2014. ISBN 978-146771805-9 Subj: Holidays – Christmas. Poetry. Santa Claus.

Snowy, blowy winter ill. by Judy Stead. Albert Whitman, 2008. ISBN 978-0-8075-7526-0 Subj: Rhyming text. Seasons – winter. Weather – snow.

Spring things ill. by Judy Stead. Albert Whitman, 2007. ISBN 978-0-8075-7596-3 Subj: Nature. Rhyming text. Seasons – spring.

Summer wonders ill. by Judy Stead. Albert Whitman, 2009. ISBN 978-0-8075-7653-3 Subj: Rhyming text. Seasons – summer.

3-D ABC: a sculptural alphabet ill. with photos. Lerner, 2006. ISBN 978-0-7613-9456-3 Subj: ABC books.

Who loves the fall? ill. by Judy Stead. Albert Whitman, 2007. ISBN 978-0-8075-9037-9 Subj: Rhyming text. Seasons – fall.

Radabaugh, Melinda Beth. *Getting a haircut* ill. with photos. Heinemann, 2003. ISBN 978-1-4034-0225-7 Subj: Careers – barbers. Hair.

Going to a restaurant ill. with photos. Heinemann, 2003. ISBN 978-1-4034-0226-4 Subj: Careers – chefs, cooks. Careers – waiters, waitresses. Food. Restaurants.

Going to school ill. with photos. Heinemann, 2003. ISBN 978-1-4034-0227-1 Subj: Careers – teachers. School – first day.

Going to the library ill. with photos. Heinemann, 2003. ISBN 978-1-4034-0230-1 Subj: Books, reading. Careers – librarians. Libraries.

Sleeping over ill. with photos. Heinemann, 2003. ISBN 978-1-4034-0231-8 Subj: Parties. Sleepovers.

Radcliffe, Theresa. *Bashi, elephant baby* ill. by John Butler. Viking, 1997. ISBN 978-0-670-87054-7 Subj: Animals – babies. Animals – elephants. Family life – mothers. Foreign lands – Africa.

Nanu, penguin chick ill. by John Butler. Viking, 2000. ISBN 978-0-670-88638-8 Subj: Birds – penguins. Foreign lands – Antarctic.

Rader, Laura. *Santa's new suit* ill. by author. HarperCollins, 2000. ISBN 978-0-06-028439-8 Subj: Clothing – suits. Holidays – Christmas. Humorous stories. Shopping.

Tea for me, tea for you ill. by author. HarperCollins, 2003. ISBN 978-0-06-008634-3 Subj: Animals – pigs. Counting, numbers. Food. Parties. Rhyming text.

Radunsky, Vladimir. *Alphabetabum* (Raschka, Chris)

Because . . . (Baryshnikov, Mikhail)

Manneken pis ill. by author. Atheneum, 2002. ISBN 978-0-689-83193-5 Subj: Folk & fairy tales. Foreign lands – Belgium. War.

One: a nice story about an awful braggart ill. by author. Viking, 2003. ISBN 978-0-670-03564-9 Subj: Animals – armadillos. Character traits – pride. Character traits – vanity.

Ten: a wonderful story ill. by author. Viking, 2002. ISBN 978-0-670-03563-2 Subj: Animals – armadillos. Babies, toddlers. Birth.

You? ill. by author. Harcourt, 2009. ISBN 978-0-15-205177-8 Subj: Animals – dogs. Emotions – loneliness.

Radzinski, Kandy. *Where to sleep* ill. by author. Sleeping Bear, 2009. ISBN 978-1-58536-436-7 Subj: Animals – cats. Rhyming text. Sleep.

Rael, Elsa Okon. *Rivka's first Thanksgiving* ill. by Maryann Kovalski. Margaret K. McElderry, 2001. ISBN 978-0-689-83901-6 Subj: Holidays – Thanksgiving. Immigrants, immigration. Jewish culture.

Raff, Courtney Granet. *Giant of the sea* ill. by Shawn Gould. Soundprints, 2002. ISBN 978-1-931465-71-7 Subj: Animals – whales. Family life – mothers. Sea & seashore.

Raffi. *Baby beluga* ill. by Ashley Wolff. Words & music by author. Crown, 1990. ISBN 978-0-517-57840-7 Subj: Animals – endangered animals. Animals – whales. Foreign lands – Arctic. Music. Songs.

Down by the bay ill. by Nadine Bernard Westcott. Words & music by author. Crown, 1987. ISBN 978-0-517-56644-2 Subj: Music. Songs.

Everything grows photos by Bruce McMillan. Words & music by author. Crown, 1989. ISBN 978-0-517-57275-7 Subj: Music. Songs.

Like me and you ill. by Lillian Hoban. Words & music by Raffi & Debi Pike. Crown, 1994. ISBN 978-0-517-59588-6 Subj: Foreign lands. Letters, cards. Music. Songs.

One light, one sun ill. by Eugenie Fernandes. Words & music by author. Crown, 1988. ISBN 978-0-517-56785-2 Subj: Family life. Music. Songs.

Rise and shine ill. by Eugenie Fernandes. Words & music by Raffi, & Bonnie & Bert Simpson. Crown, 1996. ISBN 978-0-517-70940-5 Subj: Morning. Music. Songs.

Shake my sillies out ill. by David Allender. Words & music by author. Crown, 1987. ISBN 978-0-517-56646-6 Subj: Music. Songs.

Wheels on the bus ill. by Sylvie Wickstrom. Words & music by author. Crown, 1988. ISBN 978-0-517-56784-5 Subj: Foreign lands – France. Music. Songs.

Rahaman, Vashanti. *Divali rose* ill. by Jamel Akib. Boyds Mills, 2008. ISBN 978-1-59078-524-9 Subj: Character traits – honesty. Family life – grandfathers. Foreign lands – Trinidad. Holidays – Diwali. Prejudice. Religion – Hinduism.

O Christmas tree ill. by Frané Lessac. Boyds Mills, 1996. ISBN 978-1-56397-237-9 Subj: Foreign lands – Caribbean Islands. Foreign lands – West Indies. Holidays – Christmas. Islands.

Read for me, Mama ill. by Lori McElrath-Eslick. Boyds Mills, 1997. ISBN 978-1-56397-313-0 Subj: Books, reading. Family life – mothers. Libraries.

Ramadier, Cédric. *Help! the wolf is coming!* ill. by Vincent Bourgeau. Gecko, 2015. ISBN 978-192727184-1 Subj: Animals – wolves. Format, unusual – board books. Participation.

Shh! this book is sleeping ill. by Vincent Bourgeau. Random House, 2016. ISBN 978-055353875-5 Subj: Bedtime. Books, reading. Format, unusual – board books.

Ramirez, Melissa Bourbon. *The flight of the sunflower* ill. by Nadine Takvorian. All About Kids, 2002. ISBN 978-0-9700863-0-3 Subj: Flowers. Seeds. Weather – wind.

Ramos, Jorge. *I'm just like my mom / Me parezco tanto a mi mamá; I'm just like my dad / Me parezco tanto a mi papá* ill. by Akemi Gutierrez. HarperCollins, 2008. ISBN 978-0-06-123968-7 Subj: Family life – parents. Format, unusual.

Ramos, Mario. *I am so handsome* ill. by author. Gecko, 2012. ISBN 978-1-87757-919-6 Subj: Animals – wolves. Character traits – pride. Character traits – vanity. Folk & fairy tales.

I am so strong ill. by author. Gecko, 2011. ISBN 978-0-9582-7877-5 Subj: Animals – wolves. Behavior – bullying, teasing. Dragons.

Ramsden, Ashley, reteller. *Seven fathers* ill. by Ed Young. Roaring Brook, 2011. ISBN 978-1-59643-544-5 Subj: Behavior – lost. Character traits – persistence. Folk & fairy tales. Old age.

Ramsey, Calvin Alexander. *Belle, the last mule at Gee's Bend: a civil rights story* by Calvin Alexander Ramsey and Bettye Stroud ill. by John Holyfield. Candlewick, 2011. ISBN 978-0-7636-4058-3 Subj: Animals – mules. Ethnic groups in the U.S. – African Americans. U.S. history. Violence, nonviolence.

Ruth and the Green Book ill. by Floyd Cooper. Carolrhoda, 2010. ISBN 978-0-7613-5255-6 Subj: Activities – traveling. Ethnic groups in the U.S. – African Americans. Prejudice. U.S. history.

Rand, Betseygail. *Big Bunny* by Betseygail Rand and Colleen Rand ill. by C. S. W. Rand. Tricycle, 2011. ISBN 978-1-58246-376-6 Subj: Animals – rabbits. Behavior – running away. Concepts – size. Eggs. Holidays – Easter.

Rand, Colleen. *Big Bunny* (Rand, Betseygail)

Rand, Gloria. *Baby in a basket* ill. by Ted Rand. Cobblehill, 1997. ISBN 978-0-525-65233-5 Subj: Accidents. Alaska. Babies, toddlers. Family life. U.S. history.

Little Flower ill. by R. W. Alley. Henry Holt, 2002. ISBN 978-0-8050-6480-3 Subj: Accidents. Animals – pigs. Pets.

A pen pal for Max ill. by Ted Rand. Henry Holt, 2005. ISBN 978-0-8050-7586-1 Subj: Foreign lands – Chile. Friendship. Letters, cards. Pen pals.

Prince William ill. by Ted Rand. Henry Holt, 1992. ISBN 978-0-8050-1841-7 Subj: Alaska. Animals – mice. Ecology. Oil.

Sailing home ill. by Ted Rand. NorthSouth, 2001. ISBN 978-0-7358-1540-7 Subj: Boats, ships. Family life. Sailors. Sea & seashore.

Randall, Alison L. *The wheat doll* ill. by Bill Farnsworth. Peachtree, 2008. ISBN 978-1-56145-456-3 Subj: Behavior – lost & found possessions. Toys – dolls. U.S. history – frontier & pioneer life. Weather – storms.

Randall, Angel. *Snow angels* by Angel Randall and Chris Schoebinger ill. by Brandon Dorman. Shadow Mountain, 2011. ISBN 978-1-60641-046-2 Subj: Angels. Character traits – helpfulness.

Randall, Ronne. *The Hanukkah mice* ill. by Maggie Kneen. Chronicle, 2002. ISBN 978-0-8118-3623-4 Subj: Animals – mice. Holidays – Hanukkah. Jewish culture. Rhyming text.

Rania, Queen, consort of Abdullah II, King of Jordan. *The sandwich swap* by Rania, Queen, consort of Abdullah II, King of Jordan and Kelly DiPucchio ill. by Tricia Tusa. Hyperion/Disney, 2010. ISBN 978-1-4231-2484-9 Subj: Character traits – being different. Food. Friendship. School.

Rankin, Joan. *First day* ill. by author. Margaret K. McElderry, 2002. ISBN 978-0-689-84563-5 Subj: Animals. Animals – dogs. School – first day. School – nursery.

Wow! It's great being a duck ill. by author. Margaret K. McElderry, 1998. ISBN 978-0-689-81756-4 Subj: Animals – foxes. Birds – ducks.

You're somebody special, Walliwigs! ill. by author. Margaret K. McElderry, 1999. ISBN 978-0-689-82230-8 Subj: Animals. Birds – chickens, roosters. Birds – parakeets, parrots. Character traits – being different. Character traits – individuality. Emotions – love.

Rankin, Laura. *Fluffy and Baron* ill. by author. Penguin, 2006. ISBN 978-0-8037-2953-7 Subj: Animals – dogs. Birds – ducks. Friendship.

The handmade counting book ill. by author. Dial, 1998. ISBN 978-0-8037-2311-5 Subj: Counting, numbers. Disabilities – deafness. Language.

My turn! ill. by author. Bloomsbury, 2016. ISBN 978-159990174-9 Subj: Activities – playing. Animals – goats. Animals – sheep. Behavior – bossy. Character traits – cooperation. Friendship.

Ruthie and the (not so) teeny tiny lie ill. by author. Bloomsbury, 2007. ISBN 978-1-59990-010-0 Subj: Animals – foxes. Behavior – lying. Character traits – honesty. School.

Ruthie and the (not so) very busy day ill. by author. Bloomsbury, 2014. ISBN 978-159990052-0 Subj: Animals – foxes. Behavior – bad day, bad mood. Emotions – anger.

Ransom, Candice F. *Amanda Panda quits kindergarten* ill. by Christine Grove. Doubleday, 2017. ISBN 978-039955455-1 Subj: Animals – pandas. School – first day.

The Christmas dolls ill. by Moira Fain. Walker, 1998. ISBN 978-0-8027-8661-6 Subj: Family life – mothers. Holidays – Christmas. Toys – dolls.

Mother Teresa ill. by Elaine Verstraete. Carolrhoda, 2001. ISBN 978-1-57505-441-4 Subj: Careers – nuns. Religion.

The promise quilt ill. by Ellen Beier. Walker, 1999. ISBN 978-0-8027-8695-1 Subj: Activities – making things. Activities – sewing. Quilts. U.S. history.

Tractor day ill. by Laura J. Bryant. Walker, 2007. ISBN 978-0-8027-8090-4 Subj: Farms. Rhyming text. Tractors.

Ransom, Jeanie Franz. *Don't squeal unless it's a big deal: a tale of tattletales* ill. by Jackie Urbanovic. Magination, 2006. ISBN 978-1-59147-239-1 Subj: Animals – pigs. Behavior – fighting, arguing. Behavior – gossip, rumors.

I don't want to talk about it ill. by Kathryn Kunz Finney. Magination, 2000. ISBN 978-1-55798-664-1 Subj: Divorce. Emotions – love. Family life – parents.

What do parents do? (. . . When you're not home) ill. by Cyd Moore. Peachtree, 2007. ISBN 978-1-56145-409-9 Subj: Family life – parents. Humorous stories.

Ransome, Arthur. *The fool of the world and the flying ship* ill. by Uri Shulevitz. Farrar, 1968. ISBN 978-0-374-32442-1 Subj: Activities – flying. Boats, ships. Caldecott award books. Character traits – cleverness. Folk & fairy tales. Foreign lands – Ukraine. Royalty – tsars.

Ransome, James. *Gunner, football hero* ill. by author. Holiday House, 2010. ISBN 978-0-8234-2053-7 Subj: Sports – football.

My teacher ill. by author. Dial, 2012. ISBN 978--08037-3259-9 Subj: Careers – teachers. School.

New red bike! ill. by author. Holiday House, 2011. ISBN 978-0-8234-2226-5 Subj: Behavior – sharing. Sports – bicycling.

Rao, Sandhya. *My mother's sari* ill. by Nina Sabnani. NorthSouth, 2006. ISBN 978-0-7358-2101-9 Subj: Clothing. Ethnic groups in the U.S. – East Indian Americans. Family life – daughters. Family life – mothers.

Raposo, Joe. *Sing!* ill. by Tom Lichtenheld. Henry Holt, 2013. ISBN 978-0-8050-9071-0 Subj: Activities – singing. Music. Songs.

Rappaport, Doreen. *Abe's honest words: the life of Abraham Lincoln* ill. by Kadir Nelson. Hyperion, 2008. ISBN 978-1-4231-0408-7 Subj: Language. U.S. history.

Dirt on their skirts by Doreen Rappaport and Lyndall Callan ill. by E. B. Lewis. Dial, 2000. ISBN 978-0-8037-2042-8 Subj: Sports – baseball.

Eleanor, quiet no more: the life of Eleanor Roosevelt ill. by Gary Kelley. Hyperion, 2009. ISBN 978-0-7868-5141-6 Subj: Character traits – perseverance. Character traits – shyness. U.S. history.

Frederick's journey: the life of Frederick Douglass ill. by London Ladd. Disney/Jump at the Sun, 2015. ISBN 978-142311438-3 Subj: Ethnic groups in the U.S. – African Americans. Slavery. U.S. history. Violence, nonviolence.

Freedom river ill. by Bryan Collier. Hyperion, 2000. ISBN 978-0-7868-0350-7 Subj: Character traits – bravery. Character traits – freedom. Ethnic groups in the U.S. – African Americans. Slavery. U.S. history.

Freedom ship ill. by Curtis James. Hyperion, 2006. ISBN 978-0-7868-0645-4 Subj: Boats, ships. Character traits – freedom. Ethnic groups in the U.S. – African Americans. Slavery. U.S. history. War.

Helen's big world: the life of Helen Keller ill. by Matt Tavares. Disney/Hyperion, 2012. ISBN 978-0-7868-0890-8 Subj: Careers – teachers. Disabilities – blindness. Disabilities – deafness. U.S. history.

Jack's path of courage: the life of John F. Kennedy ill. by Matt Tavares. Hyperion/Disney, 2010. ISBN 978-1-4231-2272-2 Subj: Character traits – bravery. U.S. history.

Lady Liberty: a biography ill. by Matt Tavares. Candlewick, 2008. ISBN 978-0-7636-2530-6 Subj: Careers – sculptors. U.S. history.

The long-haired girl ill. by Ming-Yi Yang. Dial, 1995. ISBN 978-0-8037-1412-0 Subj: Behavior – secrets. Character traits – bravery. Folk & fairy tales. Foreign lands – China. Weather – droughts.

Martin's big words ill. by Bryan Collier. Hyperion, 2001. ISBN 978-0-7868-2591-2 Subj: Caldecott award honor books. Careers – clergy. Ethnic groups in the U.S. – African Americans. Holidays – Martin Luther King, Jr. Day. Language. Prejudice. U.S. history. Violence, nonviolence.

The new king ill. by E. B. Lewis. Dial, 1995. ISBN 978-0-8037-1461-8 Subj: Death. Emotions – grief. Family life – fathers. Folk & fairy tales. Foreign lands – Madagascar. Royalty.

The school is not white! a true story of the civil rights movement ill. by Curtis James. Hyperion, 2005. ISBN 978-0-7868-1838-9 Subj: Ethnic groups in the U.S. – African Americans. Prejudice. School.

The secret seder ill. by Emily Arnold McCully. Hyperion, 2005. ISBN 978-0-7868-0777-2 Subj: Character traits – bravery. Foreign lands – France. Holidays – Passover. Jewish culture. War.

To dare mighty things: the life of Theodore Roosevelt ill. by C. F. Payne. Hyperion/Disney, 2013. ISBN 978-1-4231-2488-7 Subj: Character traits – ambition. Character traits – perseverance. U.S. history.

We are the many ill. by Cornelius Van Wright and Ying-Hwa Hu. HarperCollins, 2002. ISBN 978-0-06-001139-0 Subj: Indians of North America. U.S. history.

Raschka, Chris. *Alphabetabum* by Chris Raschka and Vladimir Radunsky ill. with photos. New York Review, 2014. ISBN 978-159017817-1 Subj: ABC books. Poetry.

Arlene sardine ill. by author. Orchard, 1998. ISBN 978-0-531-33111-8 Subj: Fish. Food. Self-concept.

A ball for Daisy ill. by author. Random House, 2011. ISBN 978-0-375-85861-1 Subj: Animals – dogs. Caldecott award books. Toys – balls. Wordless.

The blushful hippopotamus ill. by author. Orchard, 1996. ISBN 978-0-531-08882-1 Subj: Animals – hippopotamuses. Emotions – embarrassment. Family life – brothers & sisters. Sibling rivalry.

Can't sleep ill. by author. Orchard, 1995. ISBN 978-0-531-08779-4 Subj: Animals – dogs. Bedtime. Emotions – fear. Moon. Night.

Charlie Parker played be bop ill. by author. Watts, 1992. ISBN 978-0-531-08599-8 Subj: Careers – musicians. Ethnic groups in the U.S. – African Americans. Music. Musical instruments – saxophones.

The cosmobiography of Sun Ra: the sound of joy is enlightening ill. by author. Candlewick, 2014. ISBN 978-076365806-9 Subj: Ethnic groups in the U.S. – African Americans. Music.

Cowy cow ill. by author. Abrams/Appleseed, 2014. ISBN 978-141971055-1 Subj: Animals – bulls, cows. Humorous stories. Imagination.

Crabby crab ill. by author. Abrams/Appleseed, 2014. ISBN 978-141971056-8 Subj: Character traits – appearance. Crustaceans – crabs. Humorous stories.

Daisy gets lost ill. by author. Random House, 2013. ISBN 978-0-449-81741-4 Subj: Animals – dogs. Behavior – lost. Emotions – fear. Wordless.

Everyone can learn to ride a bicycle ill. by author. Random House, 2013. ISBN 978-0-375-87007-1 Subj: Character traits – persistence. Family life – fathers. Sports – bicycling.

Five for a little one ill. by author. Simon & Schuster, 2006. ISBN 978-0-689-84599-4 Subj: Animals – rabbits. Counting, numbers. Senses.

Give and take ill. by author. Atheneum, 2014. ISBN 978-144241655-0 Subj: Careers – farmers. Farms. Problem solving.

Hip Hop Dog ill. by Vladimir Radunsky. HarperCollins, 2010. ISBN 978-0-06-123963-2 Subj: Animals – dogs. Music. Rhyming text.

John Coltrane's giant steps ill. by author. Atheneum, 2002. ISBN 978-0-689-84598-7 Subj: Animals – cats. Music. Musical instruments – bands. Weather – rain. Weather – snow.

Little black crow ill. by author. Simon & Schuster, 2010. ISBN 978-0-689-84601-4 Subj: Birds – crows. Character traits – questioning. Imagination. Rhyming text.

Moosey Moose ill. by author. Hyperion, 2000. ISBN 978-0-7868-0581-5 Subj: Animals. Animals – moose. Clothing – pants.

Mysterious Thelonious ill. by author. Orchard, 1997. ISBN 978-0-531-33057-9 Subj: Careers – musicians. Concepts – color. Ethnic groups in the U.S. – African Americans.

New York is English, Chattanooga is Creek ill. by author. Simon & Schuster, 2005. ISBN 978-0-689-84600-7 Subj: Cities, towns. Names. Parties. U.S. history.

The purple balloon ill. by author. Random House, 2007. ISBN 978-0-375-84146-0 Subj: Death. Emotions – grief. Illness.

Ring! Yo? ill. by author. DK, 2000. ISBN 978-0-7894-2614-7 Subj: Emotions. Friendship. Telephone, cell phone.

Sluggy Slug ill. by author. Hyperion, 2000. ISBN 978-0-7868-0584-6 Subj: Animals – slugs.

Talk to me about the alphabet ill. by author. Henry Holt, 2003. ISBN 978-0-8050-6782-8 Subj: ABC books. Noise, sounds.

Waffle ill. by author. Atheneum, 2001. ISBN 978-0-689-83838-5 Subj: Behavior – worrying. Character traits – bravery. Emotions – fear. Self-concept.

Whaley Whale ill. by author. Hyperion, 2000. ISBN 978-0-7868-0583-9 Subj: Animals – whales. Behavior – hiding.

Wormy Worm ill. by author. Hyperion, 2000. ISBN 978-0-7868-0582-2 Subj: Animals – worms.

Yo! Yes? ill. by author. Orchard, 1993. ISBN 978-0-531-08619-3 Subj: Caldecott award honor books. Emotions. Ethnic groups in the U.S. – African Americans. Friendship.

Rash, Andy. *Agent A to Agent Z* ill. by author. Scholastic, 2004. ISBN 978-0-439-36882-7 Subj: ABC books. Careers – detectives. Rhyming text.

Archie the daredevil penguin ill. by author. Viking, 2015. ISBN 978-045147123-9 Subj: Birds – penguins. Emotions – fear. Inventions.

Are you a horse? ill. by author. Scholastic, 2009. ISBN 978-0-439-72417-3 Subj: Animals. Cowboys, cowgirls.

Rasmussen, Halfdan. *The ladder* ill. by Pierre Pratt. Candlewick, 2006. ISBN 978-0-7636-2282-4 Subj: Format, unusual. Imagination. Rhyming text.

Rathmann, Peggy. *Good night, Gorilla* ill. by author. Putnam, 1994. ISBN 978-0-399-22445-4 Subj: Animals. Careers – zookeepers. Night. Zoos.

Officer Buckle and Gloria ill. by author. Putnam, 1995. ISBN 978-0-399-22616-8 Subj: Animals – dogs. Behavior – sharing. Caldecott award books. Careers – police officers. School.

Ruby the copycat ill. by author. Scholastic, 1991. ISBN 978-0-590-43747-9 Subj: Animals – cats. Behavior – imitation. School.

10 minutes till bedtime ill. by author. Putnam, 1998. ISBN 978-0-399-23103-2 Subj: Animals – hamsters. Bedtime. Pets.

Rau, Dana Meachen. *Chilly Charlie* ill. by Martin Lemelman. Children's Press, 2001. ISBN 978-0-516-22210-3 Subj: Concepts – cold & heat. Rhyming text.

Clown around ill. by Nate Evans. Compass Point, 2001. ISBN 978-0-7565-0074-0 Subj: Circus. Clowns, jesters. Rhyming text.

Dr. Seuss ill. with photos. Children's Press, 2003. ISBN 978-0-516-22593-7 Subj: Careers – illustrators. Careers – writers.

Explore in a cave photos by Romie Flanagan. Rourke, 2000. ISBN 978-1-57103-318-5 Subj: Caves.

Flying ill. with photos. Benchmark, 2006. ISBN 978-0-7614-2319-5 Subj: Activities – flying. Rebuses.

I'll make you a card ill. by Jan Bryan-Hunt. Compass Point, 2002. ISBN 978-0-7565-0172-3 Subj: Days of the week, months of the year. Holidays. Letters, cards. Rhyming text.

In the yard ill. by Elizabeth Wolf. Compass Point, 2001. ISBN 978-0-7565-0116-7 Subj: Character traits – helpfulness. Family life – parents. Seasons.

Lots of balloons ill. by Jayoung Cho. Compass Point, 2001. ISBN 978-0-7565-0117-4 Subj: Concepts – color. Toys – balloons.

Mars photos by author. Compass Point, 2002. ISBN 978-0-7565-0199-0 Subj: Planets. Science.

Neil Armstrong ill. with photos. Children's Press, 2003. ISBN 978-0-516-22592-0 Subj: Careers – astronauts. Space & space ships.

Rectangles ill. with photos. Marshall Cavendish, 2006. ISBN 978-0-7614-2282-2 Subj: Concepts – shape.

Riding ill. with photos. Benchmark, 2006. ISBN 978-0-7614-2317-1 Subj: Rebuses. Transportation.

Rolling ill. with photos. Benchmark, 2006. ISBN 978-0-7614-2314-0 Subj: Concepts – motion. Rebuses.

Rubber duck ill. by Patrick Girouard. Compass Point, 2002. ISBN 978-0-7565-0121-1 Subj: Rhyming text. Toys.

The secret code ill. by Bari Weissman. Children's Press, 1998. ISBN 978-0-516-20700-1 Subj: Books, reading. Disabilities – blindness.

Shoo crow, shoo! ill. by Mary Rojas. Compass Point, 2001. ISBN 978-0-7565-0072-6 Subj: Rhyming text. Scarecrows.

Stroll by the sea photos by author. Rourke, 2000. ISBN 978-1-57103-320-8 Subj: Nature. Sea & seashore – beaches.

Ways to go ill. by Jane Conteh-Morgan. Compass Point, 2001. ISBN 978-0-7565-0071-9 Subj: Transportation.

Rausch, Molly. *My cold went on vacation* ill. by Nora Krug. Penguin, 2011. ISBN 978-0-399-25474-1 Subj: Humorous stories. Illness – cold (disease).

Rauss, Ron. *Can I just take a nap?* ill. by Rob Shepperson. Simon & Schuster, 2012. ISBN 978-1-4424-3497-4 Subj: Noise, sounds. Rhyming text. Sleep.

Rave, Friederike. *Outfoxing the fox* ill. by author. NorthSouth, 2010. ISBN 978-0-7358-2295-5 Subj: Animals – foxes. Birds – chickens, roosters.

Raven, Margot Theis. *Mercedes and the chocolate pilot* ill. by Gijsbert van Frankenhuyzen. Sleeping Bear, 2002. ISBN 978-1-58536-069-7 Subj: Airplanes, airports. Careers – airplane pilots. Foreign lands – Germany. War.

Night boat to freedom ill. by E. B. Lewis. Farrar, 2006. ISBN 978-0-374-31266-4 Subj: Ethnic groups in the U.S. – African Americans. Slavery. U.S. history.

Ravishankar, Anushka. *Elephants never forget!* ill. by Christiane Pieper. Houghton, 2008. ISBN 978-81-86-21104-5 Subj: Animals – buffaloes. Animals – elephants.

Rawlinson, Julia. *Fletcher and the falling leaves* ill. by Tiphanie Beeke. HarperCollins, 2006. ISBN 978-0-06-113401-2 Subj: Animals – foxes. Seasons – fall. Trees.

Fletcher and the snowflake Christmas ill. by Tiphanie Beeke. HarperCollins, 2010. ISBN 978-0-06-199033-5 Subj: Animals – foxes. Friendship. Holidays – Christmas. Santa Claus. Seasons – winter.

Fletcher and the springtime blossoms ill. by Tiphanie Beeke. Greenwillow, 2009. ISBN 978-0-06-168855-3 Subj: Animals – foxes. Flowers. Seasons – spring.

Mule school ill. by Lynne Chapman. Good Books, 2008. ISBN 978-1-56148-597-0 Subj: Animals – mules. Character traits – being different. School.

A surprise for Rosie ill. by Tim Warnes. Tiger Tales, 2005. ISBN 978-1-58925-046-8 Subj: Activities – ballooning. Animals – rabbits.

Rawson, Katherine. *If you were a parrot* ill. by Sherry Rogers. Sylvan Dell, 2006. ISBN 978-0-9764943-9-3 Subj: Birds – parakeets, parrots.

Ray, Deborah Kogan. *Lily's garden* ill. by author. Roaring Brook, 2002. ISBN 978-0-7613-2653-3 Subj: Food. Gardens, gardening. Letters, cards.

Ray, Jane. *The apple-pip princess* ill. by author. Candlewick, 2008. ISBN 978-0-7636-3747-7 Subj: Folk & fairy tales. Food. Royalty – princesses. Trees. Weather – droughts.

The dollhouse fairy ill. by author. Candlewick, 2010. ISBN 978-0-7636-4411-6 Subj: Behavior – worrying. Fairies. Family life – fathers. Illness.

Ray, Karen. *Sleep song* ill. by Rhonda Mitchell. Orchard, 1995. ISBN 978-0-531-08728-2 Subj: Activities. Bedtime. Games. Rhyming text.

Ray, Mary Lyn. *All aboard* ill. by Amiko Hirao. Little, 2002. ISBN 978-0-316-73507-0 Subj: Animals – rabbits. Toys. Trains.

Basket moon ill. by Barbara Cooney. Little, 1999. ISBN 978-0-316-73521-6 Subj: Activities – making things. Careers. Family life – fathers. Mountains.

Boom! ill. by Steven Salerno. Disney/Hyperion, 2013. ISBN 978-1-4231-6238-4 Subj: Animals –

dogs. Character traits – bravery. Emotions – fear. Weather – lightning, thunder.

Christmas farm ill. by Barry Root. Harcourt, 2008. ISBN 978-0-15-216290-0 Subj: Holidays – Christmas. Trees.

Deer dancer ill. by Lauren Stringer. Simon & Schuster/Beach Lane, 2014. ISBN 978-144243421-9 Subj: Activities – dancing. Animals – deer.

Go to sleep, little farm ill. by Christopher Silas Neal. Houghton, 2014. ISBN 978-054415014-0 Subj: Bedtime. Farms. Rhyming text.

Goodnight, good dog ill. by Rebecca Malone. Houghton, 2015. ISBN 978-054428612-2 Subj: Animals – dogs. Bedtime.

A lucky author has a dog ill. by Steven Henry. Scholastic, 2015. ISBN 978-054551876-5 Subj: Animals – dogs. Careers – writers.

Mud ill. by Lauren Stringer. Harcourt, 1996. ISBN 978-0-15-256263-2 Subj: Poetry. Seasons – spring.

Red rubber boot day ill. by Lauren Stringer. Harcourt, 2000. ISBN 978-0-15-213756-4 Subj: Activities – playing. Clothing – boots. Weather – rain.

Shaker boy ill. by Jeanette Winter. Harcourt, 1994. ISBN 978-0-15-276921-5 Subj: Ethnic groups in the U.S. – Shakers. Music. Religion. Songs. U.S. history.

Stars ill. by Marla Frazee. Simon & Schuster, 2011. ISBN 978-1-4424-2249-1 Subj: Concepts – shape. Night. Sky. Stars.

A violin for Elva ill. by Tricia Tusa. Houghton, 2015. ISBN 978-015225483-4 Subj: Character traits – persistence. Musical instruments – violins. Old age.

Raye, Rebekah. *The very best bed* ill. by author. Tilbury, 2006. ISBN 978-0-88448-284-0 Subj: Animals. Animals – squirrels. Bedtime. Homes, houses.

Rayner, Catherine. *Abigail* ill. by author. Tiger Tales, 2013. ISBN 978-1-58925-147-2 Subj: Animals. Animals – giraffes. Counting, numbers.

Augustus and his smile ill. by author. Good Books, 2006. ISBN 978-1-56148-510-9 Subj: Anatomy – faces. Animals – tigers. Emotions – happiness.

The bear who shared ill. by author. Penguin, 2011. ISBN 978-0-8037-3576-7 Subj: Animals – bears. Animals – mice. Animals – raccoons. Behavior – sharing. Friendship.

Ernest, the moose who doesn't fit ill. by author. Farrar, 2010. ISBN 978-0-374-32217-5 Subj: Animals – moose. Behavior – resourcefulness. Concepts – size. Format, unusual – toy & movable books.

Solomon Crocodile ill. by author. Farrar, 2011. ISBN 978-0-374-38064-9 Subj: Activities – playing. Friendship. Reptiles – alligators, crocodiles.

Razi, Michaele. *Frank the seven-legged spider* ill. by author. Little Bigfoot, 2017. ISBN 978-163217128-3 Subj: Disabilities – physical disabilities. Self-concept. Spiders.

Reagan, Jean. *How to babysit a grandma* ill. by Lee Wildish. Knopf, 2014. ISBN 978-038575384-5 Subj: Activities – babysitting. Family life – grandmothers.

How to babysit a grandpa ill. by Lee Wildish. Knopf, 2012. ISBN 978-0-375-86713-2 Subj: Activities – babysitting. Family life – grandfathers.

How to catch Santa ill. by Lee Wildish. Knopf, 2015. ISBN 978-055349839-4 Subj: Holidays – Christmas. Santa Claus.

How to get your teacher ready ill. by Lee Wildish. Knopf, 2017. ISBN 978-055353825-0 Subj: Careers – teachers. School.

How to raise a mom ill. by Lee Wildish. Knopf, 2017. ISBN 978-055353829-8 Subj: Family life – mothers.

How to surprise a dad ill. by Lee Wildish. Knopf, 2015. ISBN 978-055349836-3 Subj: Family life – fathers. Parties.

Reasoner, Charles. *Animal babies!* ill. by author. Rourke, 2011. ISBN 978-1-61236-054-6 Subj: Animals – babies.

One blue fish: a colorful counting book ill. by author. Simon & Schuster, 2010. ISBN 978-1-4169-9672-9 Subj: Concepts – color. Counting, numbers. Format, unusual – toy & movable books.

Peek-a-boo monsters ill. by author and Marina LeRay. Capstone, 2013. ISBN 978-1-47952-170-8 Subj: Format, unusual – board books. Monsters. Rhyming text.

Rechner, Amy. *Out and about at the aquarium* ill. by Becky Shipe. Picture Window, 2004. ISBN 978-1-4048-0298-8 Subj: Animals. Aquariums. Fish. School – field trips.

Recorvits, Helen. *My name is Yoon* ill. by Gabi Swiatkowska. Farrar, 2003. ISBN 978-0-374-35114-4 Subj: Ethnic groups in the U.S. – Korean Americans. Immigrants, immigration. Names. School – first day.

Yoon and the Christmas mitten ill. by Gabi Swiatkowska. Farrar, 2006. ISBN 978-0-374-38688-7 Subj: Ethnic groups in the U.S. – Korean Americans. Holidays – Christmas. Immigrants, immigration.

Yoon and the jade bracelet ill. by Gabi Swiatkowska. Farrar, 2008. ISBN 978-0-374-38689-4 Subj: Behavior – bullying, teasing. Ethnic groups in the U.S. – Korean Americans. Jewelry. School.

Redding, Sue. *Up above and down below* ill. by author. Chronicle, 2006. ISBN 978-0-8118-4876-3 Subj: Concepts – up & down. Rhyming text.

Redeker, Kent. *Don't splash the sasquatch!* ill. by Bob Staake. Disney/Hyperion, 2016. ISBN 978-142315233-0 Subj: Imagination. Monsters. Sports – swimming.

Don't squish the sasquatch! ill. by Bob Staake. Disney/Hyperion, 2012. ISBN 978-1-4231-5232-3 Subj: Buses. Humorous stories. Monsters.

Redmond, E. S. *The Unruly Queen* ill. by E. S. Redmond. Candlewick, 2012. ISBN 978-0-7636-3445-2 Subj: Behavior – misbehavior. Rhyming text.

Reed, Liz. *Sweet competition* ill. by Jimmy Reed. HarperCollins, 2016. ISBN 978-006240359-9 Subj: Character traits – cooperation. Contests. Food. Multiple births – twins.

Reed, Lynn Rowe. *Basil's birds* ill. by author. Marshall Cavendish, 2010. ISBN 978-0-7614-5627-8 Subj: Birds. Careers – custodians, janitors. School.

Bear's big breakfast ill. by Brett Helquist. HarperCollins/Balzer+Bray, 2016. ISBN 978-006226455-8 Subj: Animals – bears. Food.

Benny Shark goes to friend school ill. by Rhode Montijo. Amazon/Two Lions, 2017. ISBN 978-147782803-8 Subj: Behavior – bullying, teasing. Fish – sharks. Friendship. School.

Color chaos! ill. by author. Holiday House, 2010. ISBN 978-0-8234-2257-9 Subj: Concepts – color. School.

Pedro, his perro, and the alphabet sombrero ill. by author. Hyperion, 1995. ISBN 978-0-7868-2058-0 Subj: ABC books. Animals – dogs. Birthdays. Clothing – hats. Foreign languages.

Please don't upset P.U. Zorilla! ill. by author. Random House, 2006. ISBN 978-0-375-93654-8 Subj: Animals – skunks. Careers.

Roscoe and the pelican rescue ill. by author. Holiday House, 2011. ISBN 978-0-8234-2352-1 Subj: Birds – pelicans. Character traits – kindness to animals. Ecology.

Thelonius Turkey lives! (on Felicia Ferguson's farm) ill. by author. Random House, 2005. ISBN 978-0-375-93126-0 Subj: Birds – turkeys. Farms. Holidays – Thanksgiving.

Reed, Neil. *The midnight unicorn* ill. by author. Sterling, 2006. ISBN 978-1-4027-3218-8 Subj: Imagination. Mythical creatures – unicorns.

Reed-Jones, Carol. *The tree in the ancient forest* ill. by Christopher Canyon. Dawn, 1995. ISBN 978-1-883220-32-7 Subj: Ecology. Forest, woods. Trees.

Rees, Douglas. *Jeannette Claus saves Christmas* ill. by Olivier Latyk. Simon & Schuster, 2010. ISBN 978-1-4169-2686-3 Subj: Behavior – resourcefulness. Holidays – Christmas. Illness. Santa Claus.

Tyrannosaurus Rex vs. Edna the very first chicken ill. by Jed Henry. Henry Holt, 2017. ISBN 978-162779510-4 Subj: Birds – chickens, roosters. Dinosaurs.

Reeve, Rosie. *Training Tallulah* ill. by author. Walker, 2014. ISBN 978-080273590-4 Subj: Animals – cats. Humorous stories.

Reeves, Howard W. *There was an old witch* ill. by David Catrow. Hyperion, 1998. ISBN 978-0-7868-2387-1 Subj: Holidays – Halloween. Rhyming text. Witches.

Regan, Dana. *Monkey see, monkey do* ill. by author. Grosset, 2000. ISBN 978-0-448-42414-9 Subj: Animals – monkeys. Rhyming text.

Regan, Dian Curtis. *Barnyard slam* ill. by Paul Meisel. Holiday House, 2009. ISBN 978-0-8234-1907-4 Subj: Animals. Farms. Poetry.

How do you know it's Halloween? ill. by Fumi Kosaka. Simon & Schuster, 2002. ISBN 978-0-689-84570-3 Subj: Format, unusual – toy & movable books. Holidays – Halloween. Humorous stories. Riddles & jokes.

The Snow Blew Inn ill. by Doug Cushman. Holiday House, 2011. ISBN 978-0-8234-2351-4 Subj: Animals. Animals – cats. Sleepovers. Weather – blizzards.

Space Boy and his dog ill. by Robert Neubecker. Boyds Mills, 2015. ISBN 978-159078955-1 Subj: Animals – dogs. Family life – brothers & sisters. Imagination. Sibling rivalry. Space & space ships.

Space Boy and the space pirate ill. by Robert Neubecker. Boyds Mills, 2016. ISBN 978-159078956-8 Subj: Family life – brothers & sisters. Imagination. Pirates. Sibling rivalry. Space & space ships.

Regan, Lara Jo. *What is Mr. Winkle?* photos by author. Random House, 2001. ISBN 978-0-375-81554-6 Subj: Animals – dogs. Humorous stories.

A Winkle in time photos by Michael Regan. Random House, 2003. ISBN 978-0-375-92487-3 Subj: Activities. Animals – dogs.

Reibstein, Mark. *Wabi Sabi* ill. by Ed Young. Little, Brown, 2008. ISBN 978-0-316-11825-5 Subj: Activities – traveling. Animals. Animals – cats. Character traits – questioning.

Reich, Kass. *Up hamster, down hamster* ill. by author. Orca, 2015. ISBN 978-145981013-6 Subj: Animals – hamsters. Concepts – opposites. Format, unusual – board books.

Reich, Susanna. *Minette's feast: the delicious story of Julia Child and her cat* ill. by Amy Bates. Abrams, 2012. ISBN 978-1-4197-0177-1 Subj: Activities – baking, cooking. Animals – cats. Careers – chefs, cooks. Food. Foreign lands – France.

Reichert, Amy. *Take your mama to work today* ill. by Alexandra Boiger. Atheneum, 2012. ISBN 978-1-4169-7095-8 Subj: Activities – working. Careers. Family life – mothers. Humorous stories.

Reid, Barbara. *The party* ill. by author. Scholastic, 1999. ISBN 978-0-590-97801-9 Subj: Family life. Parties. Rhyming text.

Perfect snow ill. by author. Albert Whitman, 2011. ISBN 978-0-8075-6492-9 Subj: Character traits – cooperation. School. Snowmen. Weather – snow.

Picture a tree ill. by author. Albert Whitman, 2013. ISBN 978-0-8075-6526-1 Subj: Trees.

Reid, Margarette S. *Lots and lots of coins* ill. by True Kelley. Penguin, 2011. ISBN 978-0-525-47879-9 Subj: Behavior – collecting things. Counting, numbers. Money.

Reider, Katja. *The big little sneeze* ill. by Wolfgang Slawski. NorthSouth, 2002. ISBN 978-0-7358-1629-9 Subj: Animals. Animals – bears. Character traits – helpfulness. Illness.

Snail started it! by Katja Reider and Angela von Roehl ill. by Angela von Roehl. NorthSouth, 1999. ISBN 978-1-55858-707-6 Subj: Animals. Animals – snails. Behavior. Cumulative tales.

Reidy, Hannah. *All sorts of clothes* ill. by Emma Dodd. Picture Window, 2005. ISBN 978-1-4048-1063-1 Subj: Clothing.

Reidy, Jean. *All through my town* ill. by Leo Timmers. Bloomsbury, 2013. ISBN 978-1-59990-785-7 Subj: Animals – rabbits. Cities, towns. Rhyming text.

Busy builders, busy week! ill. by Leo Timmers. Bloomsbury, 2016. ISBN 978-161963556-2 Subj: Animals. Careers – construction workers. Communities, neighborhoods. Days of the week, months of the year. Rhyming text.

Light up the night ill. by Margaret Chodos-Irvine. Hyperion/Disney, 2011. ISBN 978-1-4231-2024-7 Subj: Bedtime. Cumulative tales. Imagination. Rhyming text. Space & space ships.

Time out for monsters! ill. by Robert Neubecker. Hyperion/Disney, 2012. ISBN 978-1-4231-3127-4 Subj: Activities – drawing. Behavior – misbehavior. Imagination.

Too pickley! ill. by Geneviève Leloup. Bloomsbury, 2010. ISBN 978-1-59990-309-5 Subj: Behavior. Food. Rhyming text.

Too purpley! ill. by Geneviève Leloup. Bloomsbury, 2010. ISBN 978-1-59990-307-1 Subj: Behavior – indecision. Character traits – appearance. Clothing. Rhyming text.

Reinen, Judy. *Bow wow* ill. with photos. Little, 2001. ISBN 978-0-316-83290-8 Subj: Activities. Animals – dogs.

Meow ill. with photos. Little, 2001. ISBN 978-0-316-83342-4 Subj: Activities. Animals – cats.

Reiner, Carl. *Tell me a scary story — but not too scary!* ill. by James Bennett. Little, 2003. ISBN 978-0-316-83329-5 Subj: Ghosts. Monsters.

Reinhardt, Jennifer Black. *Blue Ethel* ill. by author. Farrar/Margaret Ferguson, 2017. ISBN 978-037430382-2 Subj: Animals – cats. Character traits – appearance. Concepts – change.

Reinhart, Matthew. *Animal popposites* ill. by author. Simon & Schuster, 2002. ISBN 978-0-689-84423-2 Subj: Animals. Concepts – opposites. Format, unusual – toy & movable books. Language.

Encyclopedia prehistorica: dinosaurs (Sabuda, Robert)

Encyclopedia prehistorica: mega-beasts (Sabuda, Robert)

Encyclopedia prehistorica: sharks and other seamonsters (Sabuda, Robert)

Fairies and magical creatures by Matthew Reinhart and Robert Sabuda; ill. by authors. Candlewick, 2008. ISBN 978-0-7636-3172-7 Subj: Fairies. Format, unusual – toy & movable books. Mythical creatures.

Gods and heroes by Matthew Reinhart and Robert Sabuda; ill. by authors. Candlewick, 2010. ISBN 978-0-7636-3171-0 Subj: Format, unusual – toy & movable books. Mythical creatures.

Reisberg, Joanne A. *Zachary Zormer shape transformer: a math adventure* ill. by David Hohn. Charlesbridge, 2006. ISBN 978-1-57091-875-9 Subj: Concepts – shape. Counting, numbers.

Reiser, Bob. *David gets his drum* (Francis, Panama)

Reiser, Lynn. *Any kind of dog* ill. by author. Greenwillow, 1992. ISBN 978-0-688-10915-8 Subj: Animals – dogs. Family life – mothers. Imagination. Pets. Toys.

Christmas counting ill. by author. Greenwillow, 1992. ISBN 978-0-688-10677-5 Subj: Counting, numbers. Cumulative tales. Holidays – Christmas. Trees.

Earthdance ill. by author. Greenwillow, 1999. ISBN 978-0-688-16327-3 Subj: Earth. Plants. School.

Hardworking puppies ill. by author. Harcourt, 2006. ISBN 978-0-15-205404-5 Subj: Animals – dogs. Careers. Counting, numbers.

Little clam ill. by author. Greenwillow, 1998. ISBN 978-0-688-15909-2 Subj: Activities – storytelling. Animals. Bedtime. Sea & seashore.

My baby and me photos by Penny Gentieu. Knopf, 2008. ISBN 978-0-375-85205-3 Subj: Babies, toddlers. Family life – brothers & sisters. Rhyming text.

My cat Tuna ill. by author. Greenwillow, 2001. ISBN 978-0-688-16874-2 Subj: Animals – cats. Format, unusual – toy & movable books. Senses.

My dog Truffle ill. by author. Greenwillow, 2001. ISBN 978-0-688-16875-9 Subj: Animals – dogs. Format, unusual – toy & movable books. Seasons – winter. Senses.

My way / A mi manera: a Margaret and Margarita story / un cuento de Margarita y Margaret ill. by author. HarperCollins, 2007. ISBN 978-0-06-084101-0 Subj: Foreign languages. Friendship.

Play ball with me! ill. by author. Random House, 2006. ISBN 978-0-375-83244-4 Subj: Format, unusual – toy & movable books. Sports.

The surprise family ill. by author. Greenwillow, 1994. ISBN 978-0-688-11672-9 Subj: Birds – chickens, roosters. Birds – ducks. Emotions – love.

Two dogs swimming ill. by author. HarperCollins, 2005. ISBN 978-0-06-008648-0 Subj: Animals – dogs. Sports – swimming.

Two mice in three fables ill. by author. Greenwillow, 1995. ISBN 978-0-688-13390-0 Subj: Animals – mice. Friendship.

Reiss, Mike. *The boy who wouldn't share* ill. by David Catrow. HarperCollins, 2008. ISBN 978-0-06-059132-8 Subj: Behavior – greed. Family life – brothers & sisters. Rhyming text.

How Murray saved Christmas ill. by David Catrow. Price Stern Sloan, 2000. ISBN 978-0-8431-7610-0 Subj: Holidays – Christmas. Rhyming text. Santa Claus.

Late for school ill. by Michael Austin. Peachtree, 2003. ISBN 978-1-56145-286-6 Subj: Behavior – promptness, tardiness. Cities, towns. Humorous stories. Rhyming text.

Merry un-Christmas ill. by David Catrow. HarperCollins, 2006. ISBN 978-0-06-059126-7 Subj: Holidays – Christmas. Humorous stories.

Santa claustrophobia ill. by David Catrow. Price Stern Sloan, 2002. ISBN 978-0-8431-7756-5 Subj: Activities – vacationing. Holidays. Holidays –

Christmas. Humorous stories. Rhyming text. Santa Claus.

Reitman, Andrea. *Mouse in the house* ill. by Karen Bell. Paper engineering by Renée Jablow. Piggy Toes, 2001. ISBN 978-1-58117-156-3 Subj: Animals – mice. Format, unusual – toy & movable books. Rhyming text.

Rempt, Fiona. *Snail's birthday wish* ill. by Noelle Smit. Boxer, 2007. ISBN 978-1-905417-52-0 Subj: Animals. Animals – snails. Birthdays. Gifts.

Rennert, Laura Joy. *Buying, training and caring for your dinosaur* ill. by Marc Brown. Knopf, 2009. ISBN 978-0-375-83679-4 Subj: Dinosaurs. Humorous stories. Pets.

Repchuk, Caroline. *The race* (Aesop)

Rex, Adam. *Moonday* ill. by author. Disney/Hyperion, 2013. ISBN 978-1-4231-1920-3 Subj: Moon.

Nothing rhymes with orange ill. by author. Chronicle, 2017. ISBN 978-145215443-5 Subj: Character traits – being different. Emotions – loneliness. Food. Rhyming text.

Pssst! ill. by author. Harcourt, 2007. ISBN 978-0-15-205817-3 Subj: Zoos.

School's first day of school ill. by Christian Robinson. Roaring Brook/Neal Porter, 2016. ISBN 978-159643964-1 Subj: Behavior – worrying. Buildings. School – first day.

XO, Ox: a love story ill. by Scott Campbell. Roaring Brook/Neal Porter, 2017. ISBN 978-162672288-0 Subj: Animals – gazelles. Animals – oxen. Character traits – persistence. Letters, cards.

Rex, Michael. *Brooms are for flying* ill. by author. Henry Holt, 2000. ISBN 978-0-8050-6410-0 Subj: Holidays – Halloween. Witches.

Dunk skunk ill. by author. Penguin, 2005. ISBN 978-0-399-24281-6 Subj: Animals. Rhyming text. Sports.

Furious George goes bananas: a primate parody ill. by author. Penguin, 2010. ISBN 978-0-399-25433-8 Subj: Animals – gorillas. Humorous stories.

Goodnight goon: a petrifying parody ill. by author. Putnam, 2008. ISBN 978-0-399-24534-3 Subj: Bedtime. Humorous stories. Monsters. Rhyming text.

My fire engine ill. by author. Henry Holt, 1999. ISBN 978-0-8050-5391-3 Subj: Careers – firefighters. Fire. Imagination. Safety. Trucks.

My freight train ill. by author. Henry Holt, 2002. ISBN 978-0-8050-6682-1 Subj: Careers – railroad engineers. Trains.

My race car ill. by author. Henry Holt, 2000. ISBN 978-0-8050-6101-7 Subj: Automobiles. Careers – race car drivers. Sports – racing.

The pie is cherry ill. by author. Henry Holt, 2001. ISBN 978-0-8050-6717-0 Subj: Activities – baking, cooking. Food.

Runaway mummy: a petrifying parody ill. by author. Putnam, 2009. ISBN 978-0-399-25203-7 Subj: Behavior – running away. Family life – mothers. Mummies.

You can do anything, Daddy! ill. by author. Penguin, 2007. ISBN 978-0-399-24298-4 Subj: Bedtime. Family life – fathers. Humorous stories.

Rey, H. A. *Billy's picture* (Rey, Margret)

Cecily G and the nine monkeys ill. by author. Houghton, 1989, ©1942. ISBN 978-0-395-18430-1 Subj: Animals – giraffes. Animals – monkeys. Humorous stories.

Curious George ill. by author. Houghton, 1941. Subj: Animals – monkeys. Careers – firefighters. Character traits – curiosity. Humorous stories.

Curious George gets a medal ill. by author. Houghton, 1957. Subj: Animals – monkeys. Character traits – curiosity. Humorous stories. Space & space ships.

Curious George goes to the hospital (Rey, Margret)

Curious George learns the alphabet ill. by author. Houghton, 1963. ISBN 978-0-395-16031-2 Subj: ABC books. Animals – monkeys. Character traits – curiosity.

Curious George rides a bike ill. by author. Houghton, 1952. ISBN 978-0-395-16964-3 Subj: Animals – monkeys. Character traits – curiosity. Circus. Humorous stories. Sports – bicycling.

Curious George takes a job ill. by author. Houghton, 1947. Subj: Animals – monkeys. Careers – window cleaners. Character traits – curiosity. Humorous stories. Zoos.

Elizabite: adventures of a carnivorous plant ill. by author. Houghton, 1999. ISBN 978-0-395-97702-6 Subj: Humorous stories. Plants. Rhyming text.

The original Curious George ill. by author. Printed from H. A. Rey's original watercolors. Houghton, 1998. ISBN 978-0-395-92272-9 Subj: Animals – monkeys. Careers – firefighters. Character traits – curiosity. Humorous stories.

Rey, Margret. *Billy's picture* by Margret Rey and H. A. Rey ill. by H. A. Rey. HarperCollins, 1948. Subj: Activities – drawing. Animals. Art. Humorous stories.

Curious George and the dinosaur ed. by Alan J. Shalleck. Houghton, 1989. ISBN 978-0-395-51942-4 Subj: Animals – monkeys. Dinosaurs. Prehistory.

Curious George flies a kite ill. by H. A. Rey. Houghton, 1958. Subj: Animals – monkeys. Character traits – curiosity. Humorous stories. Kites. Sports – fishing.

Curious George goes to an ice cream shop ed. by Alan J. Shalleck. Houghton, 1989. ISBN 978-0-395-51943-1 Subj: Animals – monkeys. Food.

Curious George goes to school ed. by Alan J. Shalleck. Houghton, 1989. ISBN 978-0-395-51944-8 Subj: Animals – monkeys. School.

Curious George goes to the dentist ed. by Alan J. Shalleck. Houghton, 1989. ISBN 978-0-395-51941-7 Subj: Animals – monkeys. Careers – dentists. Teeth.

Curious George goes to the hospital by Margret Rey and H. A. Rey ill. by H. A. Rey. In collaboration with the Children's Hospital Medical Center, Boston. Houghton, 1966. Subj: Animals – monkeys. Behavior – lost. Character traits – curiosity. Hospitals. Humorous stories.

Pretzel ill. by H. A. Rey. HarperCollins, 1941. Subj: Animals – dogs.

Spotty ill. by H. A. Rey. Houghton, 1997. ISBN 978-0-395-83736-8 Subj: Animals – rabbits. Character traits – being different.

Reyher, Rebecca. *My mother is the most beautiful woman in the world* ill. by Ruth S. Gannett. Lothrop, 1945. Subj: Caldecott award honor books. Family life – mothers.

Reynolds, Aaron. *Back of the bus* ill. by Floyd Cooper. Penguin, 2010. ISBN 978-0-399-25091-0 Subj: Character traits – bravery. Ethnic groups in the U.S. – African Americans. Prejudice. U.S. history.

Buffalo wings ill. by Paulette Bogan. Bloomsbury, 2007. ISBN 978-1-59990-062-9 Subj: Activities – baking, cooking. Animals. Birds – chickens, roosters. Food. Sports – football.

Carnivores ill. by Dan Santat. Chronicle, 2013. ISBN 978-0-8118-6690-3 Subj: Animals – lions. Animals – wolves. Ecology. Fish – sharks. Food. Nature. Science.

Chicks and salsa ill. by Paulette Bogan. Bloomsbury, 2005. ISBN 978-1-58234-972-5 Subj: Activities – baking, cooking. Birds – chickens, roosters. Farms. Food.

Creepy carrots! ill. by Peter Brown. Simon & Schuster, 2012. ISBN 978-1-4424-0297-3 Subj: Animals – rabbits. Caldecott award honor books. Emotions – fear. Food.

Creepy pair of underwear! ill. by Peter Brown. Simon & Schuster, 2017. ISBN 978-144240298-0 Subj: Animals – rabbits. Clothing – underwear. Emotions – fear.

Here comes Destructosaurus! ill. by Jeremy Tankard. Chronicle, 2014. ISBN 978-145212454-4 Subj: Behavior – messy. Emotions – anger. Monsters.

Metal man ill. by Paul Hoppe. Charlesbridge, 2008. ISBN 978-1-58089-150-9 Subj: Art. Ethnic groups in the U.S. – African Americans.

Nerdy birdy ill. by Matt Davies. Roaring Brook/Neal Porter, 2015. ISBN 978-162672127-2 Subj: Birds. Character traits – kindness. Friendship.

Pirates vs. cowboys ill. by David Barneda. Knopf, 2013. ISBN 978-0-375-85874-1 Subj: Communication. Cowboys, cowgirls. Pirates. U.S. history – frontier & pioneer life.

President Squid ill. by Sara Varon. Chronicle, 2016. ISBN 978-145213647-9 Subj: Behavior – bossy. Character traits – conceit. Character traits – helpfulness. Squid.

Sea Monkey and Bob ill. by Debbie Ridpath Ohi. Simon & Schuster, 2017. ISBN 978-148140676-5 Subj: Crustaceans – shrimp. Emotions – fear. Fish.

Snowbots ill. by David Barneda. Random House, 2010. ISBN 978-0-375-85873-4 Subj: Rhyming text. Robots. Weather – snow.

Superhero School ill. by Andy Rash. Bloomsbury, 2009. ISBN 978-1-59990-166-4 Subj: Counting, numbers. School.

Reynolds, Adrian. *Pete and Polo's farmyard adventure* ill. by author. Orchard, 2002. ISBN 978-0-439-30913-4 Subj: Birds – ducks. Counting, numbers. Family life – grandfathers. Farms. Toys – bears.

Reynolds, Jan. *Amazon* photos by author. Harcourt, 1993. ISBN 978-0-15-202832-9 Subj: Foreign lands – South America. Indians of South America. Rivers.

Celebrate! connections among cultures photos by author. Lee & Low, 2006. ISBN 978-1-58430-253-7 Subj: Fairs, festivals. Foreign lands. Holidays. World.

Down under photos by author. Harcourt, 1992. ISBN 978-0-15-224182-7 Subj: Foreign lands – Australia.

Far north photos by author. Harcourt, 1992. ISBN 978-0-15-227178-7 Subj: Foreign lands – Arctic. Foreign lands – Lapland. Foreign lands – Norway.

Himalaya photos by author. Harcourt, 1991. ISBN 978-0-15-234465-8 Subj: Foreign lands – Nepal.

Sahara photos by author. Harcourt, 1991. ISBN 978-0-15-269959-8 Subj: Desert. Foreign lands – Sahara Desert.

Reynolds, Luke. *Bedtime blastoff!* ill. by Mike Yamada. Scholastic/Orchard, 2016. ISBN 978-

054577855-8 Subj: Activities – playing. Bedtime. Family life – fathers. Imagination. Transportation.

If my love were a fire truck: a daddy's love song ill. by Jeff Mack. Doubleday, 2017. ISBN 978-110193740-2 Subj: Bedtime. Emotions – love. Family life – fathers. Rhyming text.

Reynolds, Marilynn. *The magnificent piano recital* ill. by Laura Fernandez and Rick Jacobson. Orca, 2001. ISBN 978-1-55143-180-2 Subj: Careers – teachers. Family life – mothers. Musical instruments – pianos.

The name of the child ill. by Don Kilby. Orca, 2002. ISBN 978-1-55143-221-2 Subj: Babies, toddlers. Character traits – bravery. Emotions – fear. Foreign lands – Canada. Illness – influenza. Names.

The new land: a first year on the prairie ill. by Stephen McCallum. Orca, 1997. ISBN 978-1-55143-069-0 Subj: Family life. Farms. Immigrants, immigration. U.S. history – frontier & pioneer life.

The prairie fire ill. by Don Kilby. Orca, 1999. ISBN 978-1-55143-137-6 Subj: Farms. Fire. U.S. history – frontier & pioneer life.

A present for Mrs. Kazinski ill. by Lynn Smith-Ary. Orca, 2001. ISBN 978-1-55143-196-3 Subj: Animals – cats. Birthdays. Old age. Pets.

Reynolds, Michael. *The big question* (Erlbruch, Wolf)

Reynolds, Paul A. *Going places* (Reynolds, Peter H.)

Reynolds, Peter H. *The best kid in the world: a Sugar-Loaf book* ill. by author. Simon & Schuster, 2006. ISBN 978-0-689-87624-0 Subj: Emotions – envy, jealousy. Family life – brothers & sisters. Sibling rivalry.

The dot ill. by author. Candlewick, 2003. ISBN 978-0-7636-1961-9 Subj: Art. Character traits – confidence. Self-concept.

Going places by Peter H. Reynolds and Paul A. Reynolds; ill. by Peter H. Reynolds. Atheneum, 2014. ISBN 978-144246608-1 Subj: Behavior – resourcefulness. Character traits – cleverness. Character traits – cooperation. Contests. Inventions. Sports – racing.

Happy dreamer ill. by Peter H. Reynolds. Scholastic/Orchard, 2017. ISBN 978-054586501-2 Subj: Character traits – individuality. Character traits – patience, impatience. Self-concept.

I'm here ill. by author. Simon & Schuster, 2011. ISBN 978-1-4169-9649-4 Subj: Airplanes, airports. Character traits – being different. Disabilities – autism. Friendship. Paper.

Ish ill. by author. Candlewick, 2004. ISBN 978-0-7636-2344-9 Subj: Art. Family life – brothers & sisters. Self-concept.

My very big little world: a SugarLoaf book ill. by author. Simon & Schuster, 2006. ISBN 978-0-689-87621-9 Subj: Family life. Self-concept.

Rose's garden ill. by author. Candlewick, 2009. ISBN 978-0-7636-4641-7 Subj: Cities, towns. Flowers. Gardens, gardening.

Sky color ill. by author. Candlewick, 2012. ISBN 978-0-7636-2345-6 Subj: Activities – painting. Careers – artists. Concepts – color. School. Sky.

The smallest gift of Christmas ill. by author. Candlewick, 2013. ISBN 978-0-7636-6103-8 Subj: Behavior – dissatisfaction. Behavior – wishing. Family life. Gifts. Holidays – Christmas.

Sydney's star ill. by author. Simon & Schuster, 2001. ISBN 978-0-689-83184-3 Subj: Animals – mice. Boats, ships. Careers – inventors. Contests. Stars. Weather – storms.

Rheingrover, Jean Sasso. *Veronica's first year* ill. by Kay Life. Albert Whitman, 1996. ISBN 978-0-8075-8474-3 Subj: Babies, toddlers. Disabilities – Down syndrome. Family life – new sibling. Family life – sisters.

Rhodes-Pitts, Sharifa. *Jake makes a world: Jacob Lawrence, a young artist in Harlem* ill. by Christopher Myers. Museum of Modern Art, 2015. ISBN 978-087070965-4 Subj: Activities – painting. Art. Careers – artists. Ethnic groups in the U.S. – African Americans. U.S. history.

Ribke, Simone T. *The shapes we eat* ill. with photos. Children's Press, 2004. ISBN 978-0-516-24431-0 Subj: Concepts – shape. Counting, numbers. Food.

Rice, Eve. *At Grammy's house* ill. by Nancy Winslow Parker. Greenwillow, 1990. ISBN 978-0-688-08875-0 Subj: Family life – grandparents.

Benny bakes a cake ill. by author. Greenwillow, 1993. ISBN 978-0-688-11580-7 Subj: Activities – baking, cooking. Animals – dogs. Behavior – misbehavior. Birthdays.

Goodnight, goodnight ill. by author. Greenwillow, 1980. ISBN 978-0-688-84254-3 Subj: Bedtime. Night.

Peter's pockets ill. by Nancy Winslow Parker. Greenwillow, 1989. ISBN 978-0-688-07242-1 Subj: Clothing – pants. Clothing – pockets. Problem solving.

Sam who never forgets ill. by author. Greenwillow, 1977. ISBN 978-0-688-84088-4 Subj: Animals. Food. Zoos.

Swim! ill. by Marisabina Russo. Greenwillow, 1996. ISBN 978-0-688-14275-9 Subj: Family life – fathers. Sports – swimming.

Richards, Barnaby. *Blip!* ill. by author. TOON, 2016. ISBN 978-193517998-6 Subj: Format, unusual – graphic novels. Friendship. Robots. Space & space ships.

Richards, Beah E. *Keep climbing, girls* ill. by R. Gregory Christie. Simon & Schuster, 2006. ISBN 978-1-4169-0264-5 Subj: Ethnic groups in the U.S. – African Americans. Poetry. Self-concept.

Richards, Dan. *Can one balloon make an elephant fly?* ill. by Jeff Newman. Simon & Schuster, 2016. ISBN 978-144245215-2 Subj: Animals. Character traits – curiosity. Ethnic groups in the U.S. – African Americans. Family life – mothers. Zoos.

The problem with not being scared of monsters ill. by Robert Neubecker. Boyds Mills, 2014. ISBN 978-162091024-5 Subj: Behavior – misbehavior. Friendship. Monsters.

Richards, Doyin. *I wonder: celebrating daddies doin' work* ill. with photos. Feiwel & Friends, 2016. ISBN 978-125007895-7 Subj: Activities – working. Family life – fathers.

What's the difference? being different is amazing. Feiwel & Friends, 2017. ISBN 978-125010709-1 Subj: Behavior – seeking better things. Character traits – being different. Character traits – individuality. Ethnic groups in the U.S.

Richards, Jean. *The first Olympic games: a gruesome Greek myth with a happy ending* ill. by Kat Thacker. Millbrook, 2000. ISBN 978-0-7613-1311-3 Subj: Mythical creatures. Sports – Olympics.

Richards, Keith. *Gus and me: the story of my granddad and my first guitar* ill. by Theodora Richards. Little, Brown, 2014. ISBN 978-031632065-8 Subj: Careers – musicians. Family life – grandfathers. Musical instruments – guitars.

Richards, Kitty. *It's about time, Max!* ill. by Gioia Fiammenghi. Kane/Miller, 2000. ISBN 978-1-57565-088-3 Subj: Clocks, watches. Time.

Richards, Laura Elizabeth Howe. *Jiggle joggle jee* ill. by Sam Williams. Greenwillow, 2001. ISBN 978-0-688-17833-8 Subj: Babies, toddlers. Poetry. Toys – trains.

Richardson, Bill. *The alphabet thief* ill. by Roxanna Bikadoroff. Groundwood, 2017. ISBN 978-155498877-8 Subj: ABC books. Crime. Language. Rhyming text.

But if they do ill. by Marc Mongeau. Firefly, 2003. ISBN 978-1-55037-787-3 Subj: Bedtime. Humorous stories. Rhyming text.

Sally Dog Little ill. by Céline Malépart. Annick, 2003. ISBN 978-1-55037-759-0 Subj: Animals – dogs. Ghosts. Pirates.

Richardson, John. *Grunt* ill. by author. Clarion, 2001. ISBN 978-0-618-15974-1 Subj: Animals – pigs. Character traits – individuality. Family life. Self-concept. Sibling rivalry.

Richardson, Justin. *And Tango makes three* by Justin Richardson and Peter Parnell ill. by Henry Cole. Simon & Schuster, 2005. ISBN 978-0-689-87845-9 Subj: Birds – penguins. Family life – same-sex parents. LGBTQ. Zoos.

Christian, the hugging lion by Justin Richardson and Peter Parnell ill. by Amy Bates. Simon & Schuster, 2010. ISBN 978-1-4169-8662-1 Subj: Animals – lions. Foreign lands – England. Foreign lands – Kenya.

Richmond, Lori. *Pax and Blue* ill. by author. Simon & Schuster/Paula Wiseman, 2017. ISBN 978-148145132-1 Subj: Birds – pigeons. Cities, towns. Friendship.

Richmond, Marianne. *Big girls go potty* ill. by author. Sourcebooks, 2012. ISBN 978-1-4022-6662-1 Subj: Toilet training.

I'm not tired yet! ill. by author. Sourcebooks/Jabberwocky, 2012. ISBN 978-1-4022-6878-6 Subj: Bedtime. Family life – mothers.

Oh, the things my mom will do . . . ill. by author. Sourcebooks/Jabberwocky, 2013. ISBN 978-1-4022-8233-1 Subj: Family life – mothers.

Rickards, Lynne. *Jacob O'Reilly wants a pet* ill. by Lee Wildish. Barron's, 2010. ISBN 978-0-7641-6311-1 Subj: Pets. Rhyming text.

Pink! ill. by Margaret Chamberlain. Scholastic, 2009. ISBN 978-0-545-08608-0 Subj: Behavior – bullying, teasing. Birds – penguins. Character traits – appearance. Character traits – being different. Concepts – color.

Rickert, Janet Elizabeth. *Russ and the almost perfect day* photos by Pete McGahan. Woodbine, 2000. ISBN 978-1-890627-18-8 Subj: Behavior – lost & found possessions. Disabilities – Down syndrome. Disabilities – mental disabilities. School.

Riddell, Chris. *Platypus* ill. by author. Harcourt, 2001. ISBN 978-0-15-216493-5 Subj: Animals – platypuses. Crustaceans – crabs. Sea & seashore.

Platypus and the lucky day ill. by author. Harcourt, 2002. ISBN 978-0-15-216723-3 Subj: Animals – platypuses. Behavior – bad day, bad mood. Character traits – luck.

Wendel's workshop ill. by author. HarperCollins, 2010. ISBN 978-0-06-144930-7 Subj: Animals –

mice. Character traits – cleanliness. Inventions. Robots.

Riecherter, Daryn. *The Cambodian dancer: Sophany's gift of hope* ill. by Christy Hale. Tuttle, 2015. ISBN 978-080484516-8 Subj: Activities – dancing. Ethnic groups in the U.S. – Cambodian Americans. Foreign lands – Cambodia.

Riehle, Mary Ann McCabe. *A is for airplane: an aviation alphabet* ill. by David Craig. Sleeping Bear, 2009. ISBN 978-1-58536-358-2 Subj: ABC books. Airplanes, airports.

The little kids' table ill. by Mary Reaves. Sleeping Bear, 2015. ISBN 978-158536913-3 Subj: Etiquette. Food. Rhyming text.

Ries, Lori. *Aggie and Ben: three stories* ill. by Frank W. Dormer. Charlesbridge, 2006. ISBN 978-1-57091-594-9 Subj: Animals – dogs. Pets.

Fix it, Sam ill. by Sue Ramá. Charlesbridge, 2007. ISBN 978-1-57091-598-7 Subj: Character traits – helpfulness. Family life – brothers & sisters.

Punk wig ill. by Erin Eitter Kono. Boyds Mills, 2008. ISBN 978-1-59078-486-0 Subj: Family life. Hair. Illness – cancer.

Riggio, Anita. *Beware the Brindlebeast* ill. by author. Caroline House, 1994. ISBN 978-1-56397-133-4 Subj: Folk & fairy tales. Foreign lands – England. Holidays – Halloween. Monsters.

Secret signs: along the Underground Railroad ill. by author. Boyds Mills, 1997. ISBN 978-1-56397-555-4 Subj: Behavior – secrets. Ethnic groups in the U.S. – African Americans. Slavery. U.S. history.

Riggs, Kate. *Time to build* ill. by Laszlo Kubinyi. Creative Editions, 2015. ISBN 978-156846271-4 Subj: Format, unusual – board books. Tools.

Riggs, Shannon. *Not in Room 204* ill. by Jaime Zollars. Albert Whitman, 2007. ISBN 978-0-8075-5764-8 Subj: Child abuse. Emotions – fear. Family life.

Riley, Linda Capus. *Elephants swim* ill. by Steve Jenkins. Houghton, 1995. ISBN 978-0-395-73654-8 Subj: Animals. Sports – swimming. Water.

Riley, Linnea Asplind. *Mouse mess* ill. by author. Blue Sky, 1997. ISBN 978-0-590-10048-9 Subj: Animals – mice. Behavior – messy. Food. Night.

Rim, Sujean. *Birdie's big-girl dress* ill. by author. Little, Brown, 2011. ISBN 978-0-316-13287-9 Subj: Birthdays. Clothing – dresses. Parties.

Birdie's big-girl hair ill. by author. Little, Brown, 2014. ISBN 978-031622791-9 Subj: Character traits – individuality. Family life – mothers. Hair.

Birdie's big-girl shoes ill. by author. Little, Brown, 2009. ISBN 978-0-316-04470-7 Subj: Activities – playing. Clothing – shoes.

Birdie's first day of school ill. by author. Little, Brown, 2015. ISBN 978-031640745-8 Subj: Emotions – fear. School – first day.

Birdie's happiest Halloween ill. by author. Little, Brown, 2016. ISBN 978-031640746-5 Subj: Clothing – costumes. Holidays – Halloween. Museums. Seasons – fall.

Chee-Kee: a panda in Bearland ill. by author. Little, Brown, 2017. ISBN 978-031640744-1 Subj: Animals – bears. Animals – pandas. Character traits – being different. Character traits – individuality. Moving.

Rinck, Maranke. *I feel a foot!* ill. by Martijn van der Linden. Boyds Mills, 2008. ISBN 978-1-59078-638-3 Subj: Animals. Imagination.

Ringgold, Faith. *Cassie's word quilt* ill. by author. Knopf, 2002. ISBN 978-0-375-91200-9 Subj: Ethnic groups in the U.S. – African Americans. Language. Picture puzzles. Quilts.

Dinner at Aunt Connie's house ill. by author. Hyperion, 1993. ISBN 978-1-56282-426-6 Subj: Art. Ethnic groups in the U.S. – African Americans. Family life. Food. U.S. history.

Harlem Renaissance party ill. by author. Amistad, 2015. ISBN 978-006057911-1 Subj: Careers – musicians. Careers – writers. Ethnic groups in the U.S. – African Americans. U.S. history.

Henry Ossawa Tanner: his boyhood dream comes true ill. by author. Bunker Hill, 2011. ISBN 978-1-59373-092-5 Subj: Careers – artists. Ethnic groups in the U.S. – African Americans. U.S. history.

If a bus could talk ill. by author. Simon & Schuster, 1999. ISBN 978-0-689-81892-9 Subj: Ethnic groups in the U.S. – African Americans. Prejudice. Transportation. U.S. history.

The invisible princesses ill. by author. Crown, 1999. ISBN 978-0-517-80025-6 Subj: Ethnic groups in the U.S. – African Americans. Family life. Folk & fairy tales. Royalty – princesses. Slavery.

My dream of Martin Luther King ill. by author. Crown, 1995. ISBN 978-0-517-59977-8 Subj: Dreams. Ethnic groups in the U.S. – African Americans. Holidays – Martin Luther King, Jr. Day. U.S. history. Violence, nonviolence.

Tar Beach ill. by author. Crown, 1991. ISBN 978-0-517-58031-8 Subj: Activities – flying. Caldecott award honor books. Cities, towns. Dreams. Ethnic groups in the U.S. – African Americans. Quilts.

We came to America ill. by author. Knopf, 2016. ISBN 978-051770947-4 Subj: Immigrants, immigration. U.S. history.

Ringtved, Glenn. *Cry, heart, but never break* ill. by Charlotte Pardi. Enchanted Lion, 2016. ISBN 978-159270187-2 Subj: Death. Emotions – grief.

Rinker, Sherri Duskey. *Big machines: the story of Virginia Lee Burton* ill. by John Rocco. Houghton Mifflin Harcourt, 2017. ISBN 978-054471557-8 Subj: Activities – storytelling. Activities – writing. Careers – illustrators. Careers – writers.

Goodnight, goodnight, construction site ill. by Tom Lichtenheld. Chronicle, 2011. ISBN 978-0-8118-7782-4 Subj: Bedtime. Careers – construction workers. Machines. Rhyming text. Trucks.

Mighty, mighty construction site ill. by Tom Lichtenheld. Chronicle, 2017. ISBN 978-145215216-5 Subj: Careers – construction workers. Character traits – cooperation. Machines. Rhyming text. Trucks.

Silly wonderful you ill. by Patrick McDonnell. HarperCollins/Balzer+Bray, 2016. ISBN 978-006227105-1 Subj: Babies, toddlers. Family life – mothers.

Steam train, dream train ill. by Tom Lichtenheld. Chronicle, 2013. ISBN 978-1-4521-0920-6 Subj: Animals. Night. Rhyming text. Trains.

The twelve sleighs of Christmas ill. by Jake Parker. Chronicle, 2017. ISBN 978-145214514-3 Subj: Activities – making things. Holidays – Christmas. Mythical creatures – elves. Rhyming text. Santa Claus.

Riphagen, Loes. *Animals home alone.* Seven Footer, 2011. ISBN 978-1-934734-55-1 Subj: Animals. Wordless.

Rissi, Anica Mrose. *The teacher's pet* ill. by Zachariah OHora. Disney/Hyperion, 2017. ISBN 978-148474364-5 Subj: Animals – hippopotamuses. Careers – teachers. Pets. School.

Ritchie, Alison. *Duck says don't!* ill. by Hannah George. Good Books, 2012. ISBN 978-1-56148-745-5 Subj: Behavior – bossy. Birds – ducks. Birds – geese. Lakes, ponds.

Me and my dad! ill. by Alison Edgson. Good Books, 2007. ISBN 978-1-56148-565-9 Subj: Animals – bears. Emotions – love. Family life – fathers. Rhyming text.

Me and my mom! ill. by Alison Edgson. Good Books, 2009. ISBN 978-1-56148-657-1 Subj: Animals – bears. Emotions – love. Family life – mothers. Rhyming text.

What Bear likes best! ill. by Dubravka Kolanovic. Good Books, 2005. ISBN 978-1-56148-473-7 Subj: Activities – playing. Animals – bears. Friendship.

Ritchie, Scot. *Look where we live!* ill. by author. Kids Can, 2015. ISBN 978-177138102-4 Subj: Communities, neighborhoods.

My house is alive! the weird and wonderful sounds your house makes ill. by author. OwlKids, 2016. ISBN 978-177147136-7 Subj: Homes, houses. Night. Noise, sounds.

Ritz, Karen. *Windows with birds* ill. by author. Boyds Mills, 2010. ISBN 978-1-59078-656-7 Subj: Animals – cats. Friendship. Homes, houses. Moving.

Rives. *If I were a polar bear* ill. by author. Piggy Toes, 2001. ISBN 978-1-58117-046-7 Subj: Animals – polar bears. Foreign lands – Arctic. Format, unusual – toy & movable books. Rhyming text.

Robart, Rose. *The cake that Mack ate* ill. by Maryann Kovalski. Little, 1987. ISBN 978-0-87113-121-8 Subj: Cumulative tales. Farms. Food.

Robb, Diane Burton. *The alphabet war* ill. by Gail Piazza. Albert Whitman, 2004. ISBN 978-0-8075-0302-7 Subj: Books, reading. Disabilities – dyslexia. School.

Robberecht, Thierry. *Back into Mommy's tummy* ill. by Philippe Goossens. Houghton, 2005. ISBN 978-0-618-58106-1 Subj: Babies, toddlers. Emotions – envy, jealousy. Family life – mothers. Family life – new sibling. Sibling rivalry.

I can't do anything! ill. by Annick Masson. Magination, 2013. ISBN 978-1-4338-1309-2 Subj: Animals. Behavior – misbehavior. Etiquette. Family life.

Sam is never scared ill. by Philippe Goossens. Houghton, 2006. ISBN 978-0-618-73278-4 Subj: Emotions – fear.

Sam is not a loser ill. by Philippe Goossens. Clarion, 2008. ISBN 978-0-618-99210-2 Subj: Games. Sportsmanship.

Sam tells stories ill. by Philippe Goossens. Houghton, 2007. ISBN 978-0-618-73280-7 Subj: Activities – storytelling. Behavior – lying. Character traits – honesty. Friendship. School.

Sam's new friend ill. by Philippe Goossens. Clarion, 2008. ISBN 978-0-618-91448-7 Subj: Animals. Character traits – kindness. Friendship. Sleepovers.

Sarah's little ghosts ill. by Philippe Goossens. Houghton, 2007. ISBN 978-0-618-89210-5 Subj: Behavior – lying. Ghosts.

Stolen smile ill. by Philippe Goossens. Random House, 2002. ISBN 978-0-385-90850-4 Subj: Behavior – bullying, teasing. Emotions.

The wolf who fell out of a book ill. by Gregoire Mabire. Gibbs Smith, 2017. ISBN 978-142364797-3 Subj: Animals – wolves. Books, reading. Folk & fairy tales.

Robbins, Beth. *Tom, Ally, and the baby-sitter* ill. by Jon Stuart. DK, 2001. ISBN 978-0-7894-7426-1 Subj: Activities – babysitting. Animals – cats. Animals – rabbits. Emotions – fear.

Tom, Ally, and the new baby ill. by Jon Stuart. DK, 2001. ISBN 978-0-7894-7431-5 Subj: Animals – cats. Babies, toddlers. Family life – brothers & sisters. Family life – new sibling.

Tom and Ally visit the doctor ill. by Jon Stuart. DK, 2001. ISBN 978-0-7894-7429-2 Subj: Animals – cats. Careers – doctors. Emotions – fear. Family life – brothers & sisters.

Tom's afraid of the dark ill. by Jon Stuart. DK, 2001. ISBN 978-0-7894-7421-6 Subj: Animals – cats. Bedtime. Emotions – fear. Imagination. Night.

Tom's first day at school ill. by Jon Stuart. DK, 2001. ISBN 978-0-7894-7423-0 Subj: Animals. Animals – cats. School – first day.

Tom's new haircut ill. by Jon Stuart. DK, 2001. ISBN 978-0-7894-7425-4 Subj: Animals. Animals – cats. Careers – barbers. Emotions – fear. Hair.

Robbins, Dean. *Margaret and the moon: how Margaret Hamilton saved the first lunar landing* ill. by Lucy Knisley. Knopf, 2017. ISBN 978-039955185-7 Subj: Careers – scientists. Computers. Gender roles. Moon. Space & space ships.

Two friends: Susan B. Anthony and Frederick Douglass ill. by Sean Qualls. Scholastic/Orchard, 2016. ISBN 978-054539996-8 Subj: Ethnic groups in the U.S. – African Americans. Gender roles. Slavery. U.S. history.

Robbins, Jacqui. *The new girl . . . and me* ill. by Matt Phelan. Simon & Schuster, 2006. ISBN 978-0-689-86468-1 Subj: Ethnic groups in the U.S. – African Americans. Friendship. Pets. Reptiles – iguanas. School.

Two of a kind ill. by Matt Phelan. Atheneum, 2009. ISBN 978-1-4169-2437-1 Subj: Behavior – bullying, teasing. Character traits – individuality. Friendship. School.

Robbins, Ken. *Apples* photos by author. Atheneum, 2002. ISBN 978-0-689-83024-2 Subj: Activities – baking, cooking. Farms. Food. Trees.

Autumn leaves ill. by author. Scholastic, 1998. ISBN 978-0-590-29879-7 Subj: Plants. Seasons – fall. Trees.

Pumpkins photos by author. Macmillan, 2006. ISBN 978-1-59643-184-3 Subj: Gardens, gardening. Seasons – fall.

Seeds ill. by author. Atheneum, 2005. ISBN 978-0-689-85041-7 Subj: Plants. Seeds.

Trucks, giants of the highway photos by author. Atheneum, 1999. ISBN 978-0-689-82664-1 Subj: Traffic, traffic signs. Transportation. Trucks.

Robbins, Maria Polushkin. *Mother, Mother, I want another* ill. by Jon Goodell. Random House, 2005. ISBN 978-0-375-92588-7 Subj: Bedtime. Family life – mothers. Kissing. Sleep.

Robbins, Ruth. *Baboushka and the three kings* ill. by Nicolas Sidjakov. Adapt. from a Russian folk tale; verse by Edith R. Thomas; music by Mary Clement Sanks. Parnassus, 1960. ISBN 978-0-395-27672-3 Subj: Caldecott award books. Folk & fairy tales. Foreign lands – Russia. Holidays – Christmas. Music. Rhyming text. Songs.

Robert, Na'ima B. *Ramadan Moon* ill. by Shirin Adl. Frances Lincoln, 2009. ISBN 978-1-84507-922-2 Subj: Holidays – Ramadan. Moon. Religion – Islam.

Robert, Nadine. *Toshi's little treasures* ill. by Aki. Kids Can, 2016. ISBN 978-177138573-2 Subj: Activities – walking. Behavior – collecting things. Family life – grandmothers. Nature.

Roberton, Fiona. *Cuckoo!* ill. by author. Putnam, 2014. ISBN 978-039916497-2 Subj: Birds – cuckoos. Communication. Language.

The perfect present ill. by author. Putnam, 2012. ISBN 978-0-399-25773-5 Subj: Animals – dogs. Birds – ducks. Birthdays. Gifts. Pets.

Wanted: the perfect pet ill. by author. Penguin, 2010. ISBN 978-0-399-25461-1 Subj: Birds – ducks. Disguises. Pets.

Roberts, Bethany. *Birthday mice* ill. by Doug Cushman. Clarion, 2002. ISBN 978-0-618-07772-4 Subj: Animals. Animals – mice. Birthdays. Cowboys, cowgirls. Parties. Rhyming text.

Christmas mice ill. by Doug Cushman. Clarion, 2000. ISBN 978-0-395-91204-1 Subj: Animals – cats. Animals – mice. Holidays – Christmas. Rhyming text.

Cookie angel ill. by Vladimir Vagin. Henry Holt, 2007. ISBN 978-0-8050-6974-7 Subj: Activities – baking, cooking. Angels. Holidays – Christmas. Toys.

Double trouble Groundhog Day ill. by Lorinda Bryan Cauley. Henry Holt, 2008. ISBN 978-0-8050-8280-7 Subj: Animals – groundhogs. Character traits – cooperation. Family life – brothers & sisters. Holidays – Groundhog Day. Multiple births – twins.

Easter mice ill. by Doug Cushman. Clarion, 2003. ISBN 978-0-618-16455-4 Subj: Animals – mice. Eggs. Holidays – Easter. Rhyming text.

Fourth of July mice ill. by Doug Cushman. Clarion, 2004. ISBN 978-0-618-31367-9 Subj: Activities. Animals – mice. Holidays – Fourth of July. Rhyming text.

Gramps and the fire dragon ill. by Melissa Iwai. Clarion, 1997. ISBN 978-0-395-69849-5 Subj: Activities – storytelling. Bedtime. Family life – grandfathers. Fire. Imagination.

Rosie to the rescue ill. by Kay Chorao. Henry Holt, 2003. ISBN 978-0-8050-6486-5 Subj: Animals – squirrels. Family life – aunts, uncles. Family life – parents. Imagination.

Valentine mice! ill. by Doug Cushman. Clarion, 1997. ISBN 978-0-395-77518-9 Subj: Animals. Animals – mice. Holidays – Valentine's Day. Rhyming text.

The wind's garden ill. by Melanie Hope Greenberg. Henry Holt, 2001. ISBN 978-0-8050-6367-7 Subj: Gardens, gardening. Weather – wind.

Roberts, Cynthia. *Tow trucks* ill. with photos. Child's World, 2007. ISBN 978-1-59296-836-7 Subj: Trucks.

Roberts, David. *Dirty Bertie* ill. by author. Abrams, 2003. ISBN 978-0-8109-4259-2 Subj: Behavior. Character traits – cleanliness.

Roberts, Jillian. *What happens when a loved one dies? : our first talk about death* ill. by Cindy Revell. Orca, 2016. ISBN 978-145980945-1 Subj: Death. Emotions – grief.

Where do babies come from? our first talk about birth ill. by Cindy Revell. Orca, 2015. ISBN 978-145980942-0 Subj: Babies, toddlers. Birth. Sex instruction.

Roberts, Justin. *The smallest girl in the smallest grade* ill. by Christian Robinson. Putnam, 2014. ISBN 978-039925743-8 Subj: Behavior – bullying, teasing. Character traits – kindness. Character traits – smallness. Concepts – size. Rhyming text.

Roberts, Lynn. *Cinderella, an Art Deco love story* ill. by David Roberts. Abrams, 2001. ISBN 978-0-8109-4168-7 Subj: Family life – stepfamilies. Folk & fairy tales. Royalty – princes. Sibling rivalry.

Rapunzel, a groovy fairy tale ill. by David Roberts. Abrams, 2003. ISBN 978-0-8109-4242-4 Subj: Character traits – meanness. Family life – aunts, uncles. Folk & fairy tales. Hair.

Roberts, Victoria. *The best pet ever* ill. by Deborah Allwright. Tiger Tales, 2010. ISBN 978-1-58925-089-5 Subj: Imagination. Pets.

Robertson, David A. *When we were alone* ill. by Julie Flett. HighWater, 2017. ISBN 978-155379673-2 Subj: Character traits – bravery. Character traits – individuality. Character traits – perseverance. Family life – grandmothers. Indians of North America – Cree. Prejudice. School.

Robertson, M. P. *The dragon snatcher* ill. by author. Penguin, 2005. ISBN 978-0-8037-3103-5 Subj: Dragons. Eggs. Wizards.

The egg ill. by author. Fogelman, 2001. ISBN 978-0-8037-2546-1 Subj: Behavior – needing someone. Dragons. Eggs.

Hieronymous Betts and his unusual pets ill. by author. Frances Lincoln, 2005. ISBN 978-1-84507-289-6 Subj: Family life – brothers & sisters. Pets.

The sandcastle ill. by author. Rising Moon, 2001. ISBN 978-0-87358-782-2 Subj: Behavior – wishing. Sand. Sea & seashore – beaches.

Robertson, Patrisha Grainger. *Cirque du Soleil* photos by Al Seib. Abrams, 2003. ISBN 978-0-8109-4515-9 Subj: Circus. Concepts – color. Rhyming text.

Robey, Katharine Crawford. *Where's the party?* ill. by Kate Endle. Charlesbridge, 2011. ISBN 978-1-58089-268-1 Subj: Birds. Nature.

Robins, Arthur. *The teeny tiny woman: a traditional tale* ill. by author. Candlewick, 1998. ISBN 978-0-7636-0444-8 Subj: Folk & fairy tales. Foreign lands – England. Ghosts.

Robinson, Bruce. *The obvious elephant* ill. by Sophie Windham. Bloomsbury, 2002. ISBN 978-1-58234-769-1 Subj: Animals – elephants. Humorous stories.

Robinson, Fiona. *Whale shines: an artistic tale* ill. by author. Abrams, 2013. ISBN 978-1-4197-0848-0 Subj: Animals – whales. Art. Careers – artists. Character traits – confidence. Self-concept.

What animals really like: a new song composed & conducted by Mr. Herbert Timberteeth ill. by author. Abrams, 2011. ISBN 978-0-8109-8976-4 Subj: Animals. Careers – composers. Careers – conductors (music). Humorous stories. Songs.

Robinson, Michelle. *And the robot went . . .* ill. by Sergio Ruzzier. Clarion, 2017. ISBN 978-054458652-9 Subj: Animals. Cumulative tales. Rhyming text. Robots.

A beginner's guide to bear spotting ill. by David Roberts. Bloomsbury, 2016. ISBN 978-168119026-6 Subj: Animals – bears. Behavior – resourcefulness. Humorous stories.

Ding dong! Gorilla! ill. by Leonie Lord. Peachtree, 2013. ISBN 978-1-56145-730-4 Subj: Animals – gorillas. Behavior – messy. Behavior – misbehavior.

The forgetful knight ill. by Fred Blunt. Dial, 2016. ISBN 978-080374067-9 Subj: Dragons. Humorous stories. Knights. Memories, memory. Rhyming text.

How to wash a woolly mammoth ill. by Kate Hindley. Henry Holt, 2014. ISBN 978-080509966-9 Subj: Activities – bathing. Animals – woolly mammoths. Humorous stories.

Odd socks ill. by Rebecca Ashdown. Holiday, 2016. ISBN 978-082343659-0 Subj: Behavior – lost & found possessions. Clothing – socks. Emotions – love. Puppets.

There's a lion in my cornflakes ill. by Jim Field. Bloomsbury, 2015. ISBN 978-080273836-3 Subj: Animals. Food. Humorous stories.

What to do if an elephant stands on your foot ill. by Peter H. Reynolds. Dial, 2012. ISBN 978-0-8037-3398-5 Subj: Animals. Humorous stories. Jungle.

Robinson, Sharon. *Testing the ice: a true story about Jackie Robinson* ill. by Kadir Nelson. Scholastic, 2009. ISBN 978-0-545-05251-1 Subj: Character traits – bravery. Ethnic groups in the U.S. – African Americans. Family life – fathers. Sports – baseball.

Under the same sun ill. by A. G. Ford. Scholastic, 2014. ISBN 978-054516672-0 Subj: Birthdays. Family life. Family life – grandmothers. Foreign lands – Tanzania.

Robinson, Sue. *I want to play* ill. by Andy Beckett. Barron's, 2002. ISBN 978-0-7641-5486-7 Subj: Animals – babies. Animals – cats. Family life – mothers. Friendship.

Robinson, Tim. *Tobias, the quig, and the rumplenut tree* ill. by author. Winslow, 2000. ISBN 978-1-890817-20-6 Subj: Birds. Ecology. Rhyming text. Trees.

Robledo, Honorio. *Nico visits the moon* ill. by author. Cinco Puntos, 2001. ISBN 978-0-938317-57-9 Subj: Animals – cats. Family life – parents. Moon. Toys – balloons.

Rocco, John. *Blackout* ill. by author. Hyperion/Disney, 2011. ISBN 978-1-4231-2190-9 Subj: Caldecott award honor books. Family life. Light, lights. Night.

Blizzard ill. by author. Hyperion, 2014. ISBN 978-142317865-1 Subj: Character traits – helpfulness. Weather – blizzards. Weather – snow.

Super Hair-o and the barber of doom ill. by author. Disney/Hyperion, 2013. ISBN 978-1-4231-2189-3 Subj: Careers – barbers. Hair.

Wolf! wolf! ill. by author. Hyperion, 2007. ISBN 978-1-4231-0012-6 Subj: Animals – wolves. Behavior – lying. Behavior – trickery. Folk & fairy tales. Foreign lands – China.

Roche, Denis. *The best class picture ever* ill. by author. Scholastic, 2003. ISBN 978-0-439-26983-4 Subj: Activities – photographing. Careers – teachers. School.

Little Pig is capable ill. by author. Houghton, 2002. ISBN 978-0-395-91368-0 Subj: Animals – pigs. Animals – wolves. Behavior – worrying. Safety.

Mim, gym, and June ill. by author. Houghton, 2003. ISBN 978-0-618-15254-4 Subj: Behavior – bullying, teasing. Friendship. School. Sports – gymnastics.

Rochelle, Belinda. *Jewels* ill. by Cornelius Van Wright and Ying-Hwa Hu. Lodestar, 1998. ISBN 978-0-525-67502-0 Subj: Activities – storytelling. Ethnic groups in the U.S. – African Americans. Family life – great-grandparents. Memories, memory. Slavery. U.S. history.

Rock, Brian. *The deductive detective* ill. by Sherry Rogers. Sylvan Dell, 2013. ISBN 978-1-60718-613-7 Subj: Animals. Birds – ducks. Crime. Problem solving.

With all my heart ill. by Samantha Chaffey. Tiger Tales, 2012. ISBN 978-1-58925-648-4 Subj: Animals – bears. Emotions – love. Family life – mothers.

Rock, Lois. *A child's book of graces* ill. by Alison Jay. Good Books, 2006. ISBN 978-1-56148-514-7 Subj: Religion.

God bless me, God bless you ill. by John Bendall-Brunello. Baker, 2001. ISBN 978-0-8010-4488-5 Subj: Bedtime. Religion. Rhyming text.

I wish tonight ill. by Anne Wilson. Good Books, 2000. ISBN 978-1-56148-315-0 Subj: Behavior – wishing. Dreams. Rhyming text.

I wonder why? ill. by Christopher Corr. Chronicle, 2001. ISBN 978-0-8118-3169-7 Subj: Religion. Rhyming text.

Learning about prayer ill. by Maureen Galvani. Little, 2003. ISBN 978-0-316-60557-1 Subj: Religion.

The Lord's prayer ill. by Debbie Lush. Paulist, 1999. ISBN 978-0-8091-6679-4 Subj: Religion.

Now we have a baby ill. by Jane Massey. Good Books, 2004. ISBN 978-1-56148-451-5 Subj: Babies, toddlers. Emotions – love. Family life. Family life – new sibling. Format, unusual – board books.

Rockhill, Dennis. *Polar slumber / Sueño polar* ill. by author. Raven Tree, 2004. ISBN 978-0-9724973-1-2 Subj: Animals – polar bears. Dreams. Wordless.

Rockliff, Mara. *Chik chak Shabbat* ill. by Kyrsten Brooker. Candlewick, 2014. ISBN 978-076365528-

0 Subj: Behavior – sharing. Communities, neighborhoods. Food. Illness. Jewish culture.

The Grudge Keeper ill. by Eliza Wheeler. Peachtree, 2014. ISBN 978-156145729-8 Subj: Behavior. Behavior – forgiving. Emotions.

Me and Momma and Big John ill. by William Low. Candlewick, 2012. ISBN 978-0-7636-4359-1 Subj: Buildings. Careers. Character traits – persistence. Ethnic groups in the U.S. – African Americans. Family life – mothers. U.S. history.

My heart will not sit down ill. by Ann Tanksley. Knopf, 2012. ISBN 978-0-375-84569-7 Subj: Behavior – sharing. Character traits – generosity. Foreign lands – Cameroon. U.S. history.

Rocklin, Joanne. *This book is haunted* ill. by JoAnn Adinolfi. HarperCollins, 2001. ISBN 978-0-06-028457-2 Subj: Ghosts. Holidays – Halloween. Homes, houses.

Rockwell, Anne. *Apples and pumpkins* ill. by Lizzy Rockwell. Simon & Schuster, 2011. ISBN 978-1-4424-0350-5 Subj: Food. Holidays – Halloween.

At the beach ill. by Harlow Rockwell. Macmillan, 1987. ISBN 978-0-02-777940-0 Subj: Activities – playing. Sea & seashore – beaches.

At the firehouse ill. by author. HarperCollins, 2003. ISBN 978-0-06-029816-6 Subj: Careers – firefighters. Trucks.

At the supermarket ill. by author. Henry Holt, 2010. ISBN 978-0-8050-7662-2 Subj: Shopping. Stores.

Backyard bear ill. by Megan Halsey. Walker, 2006. ISBN 978-0-8027-9573-1 Subj: Animals – bears. Communities, neighborhoods.

Becoming butterflies ill. by Megan Halsey. Walker, 2002. ISBN 978-0-8027-8798-9 Subj: Insects – butterflies, caterpillars. Metamorphosis. School.

Big George: how a shy boy became President Washington ill. by Matt Phelan. Houghton, 2009. ISBN 978-0-15-216583-3 Subj: Character traits – bravery. Character traits – shyness. U.S. history.

Boats ill. by author. Dutton, 1982. ISBN 978-0-525-44004-8 Subj: Animals – bears. Boats, ships.

The boy who wouldn't obey: a Mayan legend ill. by author. Greenwillow, 2000. ISBN 978-0-688-14881-2 Subj: Behavior – misbehavior. Folk & fairy tales. Indians of Central America – Maya.

Brendan and Belinda and the slam dunk! ill. by Paul Meisel. HarperCollins, 2007. ISBN 978-0-06-028443-5 Subj: Animals – pigs. Family life – brothers & sisters. Multiple births – twins. Sports – basketball. Sportsmanship.

Bugs are insects ill. by Steve Jenkins. HarperCollins, 2001. ISBN 978-0-06-028569-2 Subj: Insects.

Bumblebee, bumblebee, do you know me? a garden guessing game ill. by author. HarperCollins, 1999.

ISBN 978-0-06-028212-7 Subj: Flowers. Insects. Insects – bees.

Career day ill. by Lizzy Rockwell. HarperCollins, 2000. ISBN 978-0-06-027566-2 Subj: Careers. School.

Cars ill. by author. Dutton, 1984. ISBN 978-0-525-44079-6 Subj: Automobiles.

Chip and the karate kick ill. by Paul Meisel. HarperCollins, 2004. ISBN 978-0-06-028446-6 Subj: Animals. Animals – rabbits. Character traits – patience, impatience. Sports – karate.

Clouds ill. by Frané Lessac. Collins, 2008. ISBN 978-0-06-445220-5 Subj: Science. Weather – clouds.

Ducklings and pollywogs ill. by Lizzy Rockwell. Macmillan, 1994. ISBN 978-0-02-777452-8 Subj: Family life – fathers. Lakes, ponds. Seasons.

Father's Day ill. by Lizzy Rockwell. HarperCollins, 2005. ISBN 978-0-06-051378-8 Subj: Activities – writing. Books, reading. Family life – fathers. Holidays – Father's Day. School.

Ferryboat ride! ill. by Maggie Smith. Crown, 1999. ISBN 978-0-517-70959-7 Subj: Boats, ships. Islands. Sea & seashore. Transportation.

Fire engines ill. by author. Dutton, 1986. ISBN 978-0-525-44259-2 Subj: Animals – dogs. Careers – firefighters. Trucks.

First comes spring ill. by author. Crowell, 1985. ISBN 978-0-690-04455-3 Subj: Animals – bears. Seasons.

First day of school ill. by Lizzy Rockwell. HarperCollins, 2011. ISBN 978-0-06-050191-4 Subj: School – first day.

The first snowfall by Anne Rockwell and Harlow Rockwell; ill. by authors. Macmillan, 1987. ISBN 978-0-02-777770-3 Subj: Seasons – winter. Weather – snow.

Good morning, Digger ill. by Melanie Hope Greenberg. Penguin, 2005. ISBN 978-0-670-05959-1 Subj: Machines. Trucks.

Growing like me ill. by Holly Keller. Harcourt, 2001. ISBN 978-0-15-202202-0 Subj: Behavior – growing up.

Halloween Day ill. by Lizzy Rockwell. HarperCollins, 1997. ISBN 978-0-06-027568-6 Subj: Clothing – costumes. Holidays – Halloween. School.

Here comes the night ill. by author. Henry Holt, 2006. ISBN 978-0-8050-7663-9 Subj: Bedtime. Night.

Honey in a hive ill. by S. D. Schindler. HarperCollins, 2005. ISBN 978-0-06-028567-8 Subj: Food. Insects – bees.

Katie Catz makes a splash ill. by Paul Meisel. HarperCollins, 2003. ISBN 978-0-06-028445-9 Subj:

Animals. Animals – cats. Emotions – fear. Sports – swimming.

Let's go to the hardware store ill. by Melissa Iwai. Henry Holt, 2016. ISBN 978-080508738-3 Subj: Careers – handymen. Shopping. Stores. Tools.

Library day ill. by Lizzy Rockwell. Aladdin, 2016. ISBN 978-148142731-9 Subj: Books, reading. Libraries.

Little shark ill. by Megan Halsey. Walker, 2005. ISBN 978-0-8027-8955-6 Subj: Fish – sharks.

Long ago yesterday ill. by author. Greenwillow, 1999. ISBN 978-0-688-14411-1 Subj: Babies, toddlers. Family life.

Morgan plays soccer ill. by Paul Meisel. HarperCollins, 2001. ISBN 978-0-06-028444-2 Subj: Animals. Animals – bears. Sports – soccer.

Mother's Day ill. by Lizzy Rockwell. HarperCollins, 2004. ISBN 978-0-06-051375-7 Subj: Holidays – Mother's Day. School.

My pet hamster ill. by Bernice Lum. HarperCollins, 2002. ISBN 978-0-06-028565-4 Subj: Animals – hamsters. Pets.

My preschool ill. by author. Henry Holt, 2008. ISBN 978-0-8050-7955-5 Subj: School – nursery.

My spring robin ill. by Harlow Rockwell and Lizzy Rockwell. Simon & Schuster, 2015. ISBN 978-148141137-0 Subj: Birds – robins. Flowers. Seasons – spring.

No! no! no! ill. by author. Macmillan, 1995. ISBN 978-0-02-777782-6 Subj: Behavior – bad day, bad mood. Family life.

Once upon a time this morning ill. by Suçie Stevenson. Greenwillow, 1997. ISBN 978-0-688-14707-5 Subj: Babies, toddlers. Family life.

One bean ill. by Megan Halsey. Walker, 1998. ISBN 978-0-8027-8649-4 Subj: Plants. Science. Seeds.

100 school days ill. by Lizzy Rockwell. HarperCollins, 2002. ISBN 978-0-06-029145-7 Subj: Counting, numbers. School.

Our yard is full of birds ill. by Lizzy Rockwell. Macmillan, 1992. ISBN 978-0-02-777273-9 Subj: Birds.

Planes by Anne Rockwell and Harlow Rockwell; ill. by authors. Dutton, 1985. ISBN 978-0-525-44159-5 Subj: Airplanes, airports. Transportation.

President's Day ill. by Lizzy Rockwell. HarperCollins, 2008. ISBN 978-0-06-050194-5 Subj: Holidays. School – nursery. Theater.

St. Patrick's Day ill. by Lizzy Rockwell. HarperCollins, 2010. ISBN 978-0-06-050197-6 Subj: Holidays – St. Patrick's Day. School.

Show and tell day ill. by Lizzy Rockwell. HarperCollins, 1997. ISBN 978-0-06-027301-9 Subj: Character traits – individuality. School.

Space vehicles by Anne Rockwell and David Brion; ill. by authors. Dutton, 1994. ISBN 978-0-525-45270-6 Subj: Animals – cats. Space & space ships.

Thanksgiving Day ill. by Lizzy Rockwell. HarperCollins, 1999. ISBN 978-0-06-027795-6 Subj: Holidays – Thanksgiving. School. Theater.

Things that go ill. by author. Dutton, 1986. ISBN 978-0-525-44266-0 Subj: Transportation.

Trains ill. by author. Dutton, 1988. ISBN 978-0-525-44377-3 Subj: Trains. Transportation.

Truck stop ill. by Melissa Iwai. Viking, 2013. ISBN 978-0-670-06261-4 Subj: Restaurants. Trucks.

Trucks ill. by author. Dutton, 1984. ISBN 978-0-525-44147-2 Subj: Trucks.

Two blue jays ill. by Megan Halsey. Walker, 2003. ISBN 978-0-8027-8841-2 Subj: Birds – bluejays. Family life – parents.

Valentine's Day ill. by Lizzy Rockwell. HarperCollins, 2001. ISBN 978-0-06-028515-9 Subj: Holidays – Valentine's Day. Letters, cards. School.

Welcome to kindergarten ill. by author. Walker, 2001. ISBN 978-0-8027-8746-0 Subj: Emotions – fear. School – first day.

What we like ill. by author. Macmillan, 1992. ISBN 978-0-02-777274-6 Subj: Activities – making things. Concepts. Language.

What's so bad about gasoline? fossil fuels and what they do ill. by Paul Meisel. Collins, 2009. ISBN 978-0-06-157528-0 Subj: Earth. Ecology. Science.

Whoo! whoo! goes the train ill. by author and Vanessa van der Baan. HarperCollins, 2009. ISBN 978-0-06-056227-4 Subj: Activities – traveling. Trains.

Willy can count ill. by author. Little, 1989. ISBN 978-1-55970-013-9 Subj: Activities – walking. Counting, numbers. Country. Family life – mothers.

Zoo day ill. by Lizzy Rockwell. Aladdin, 2017. ISBN 978-148142734-0 Subj: Family life. Zoos.

Rockwell, Harlow. *The first snowfall* (Rockwell, Anne)

My dentist ill. by author. Greenwillow, 1975. ISBN 978-0-688-84004-4 Subj: Careers – dentists. Teeth.

My doctor ill. by author. Macmillan, 1973. ISBN 978-0-02-777480-1 Subj: Careers – doctors. Health & fitness.

Planes (Rockwell, Anne)

Rockwell, Lizzy. *The busy body book* ill. by author. Crown, 2004. ISBN 978-0-375-92203-9 Subj: Health & fitness – exercise.

Hello baby! ill. by author. Crown, 1999. ISBN 978-0-517-80012-6 Subj: Babies, toddlers. Birth. Family life – brothers & sisters. Family life – new sibling.

Plants feed me ill. by author. Holiday House, 2014. ISBN 978-082342526-6 Subj: Food. Plants.

Rodanas, Kristina. *The dragonfly's tale* ill. by author. Houghton, 1992. ISBN 978-0-395-57003-6 Subj: Folk & fairy tales. Indians of North America – Zuni. Insects – dragonflies.

Follow the stars ill. by reteller. Little, 1998. ISBN 978-0-7614-5029-0 Subj: Creation. Folk & fairy tales. Indians of North America – Ojibwa.

The little drummer boy ill. by author. Words & music by Katherine Davis, Henry Onorati & Harry Simeonne. Clarion, 2001. ISBN 978-0-395-97015-7 Subj: Gifts. Holidays – Christmas. Music. Musical instruments – drums. Religion – Nativity. Songs.

Roddie, Shen. *Not now, Mrs. Wolf* ill. by Selina Young. DK, 2000. ISBN 978-0-7894-5613-7 Subj: Animals – babies. Animals – wolves. Birds – ducks. Family life – mothers.

Sandbear ill. by Jenny Jones. Bloomsbury, 2002. ISBN 978-1-58234-758-5 Subj: Animals – bears. Animals – rabbits. Friendship. Sand.

Toes are to tickle ill. by Kady MacDonald Denton. Tricycle, 1997. ISBN 978-1-883672-49-2 Subj: Activities – playing. Babies, toddlers. Family life – brothers & sisters. Games.

Roderick, Stacey. *Dinosaurs from head to tail* ill. by Kwanchai Moriya. Kids Can, 2015. ISBN 978-177138044-7 Subj: Dinosaurs. Picture puzzles.

Ocean animals from head to tail ill. by Kwanchai Moriya. Kids Can, 2016. ISBN 978-177138345-5 Subj: Animals. Character traits – questioning. Fish. Sea & seashore.

Rodgers, Richard. *My favorite things* by Richard Rodgers and Oscar Hammerstein ill. by Renée Graef. HarperCollins, 2001. ISBN 978-0-06-029233-1 Subj: Songs.

Rodman, Mary Ann. *First grade stinks!* ill. by Beth Spiegel. Peachtree, 2006. ISBN 978-1-56145-377-1 Subj: Behavior – bad day, bad mood. School – first day.

My best friend ill. by E. B. Lewis. Penguin, 2005. ISBN 978-0-670-05989-8 Subj: Activities – playing. Ethnic groups in the U.S. – African Americans. Friendship.

Surprise soup ill. by G. Brian Karas. Viking, 2009. ISBN 978-0-670-06274-4 Subj: Activities – baking, cooking. Animals – bears. Family life – brothers. Family life – new sibling. Food.

A tree for Emmy ill. by Tatjana Mai-Wyss. Peachtree, 2009. ISBN 978-1-56145-475-4 Subj: Birthdays. Trees.

Rodriguez, Alex. *Out of the ballpark* ill. by Frank Morrison. HarperCollins, 2007. ISBN 978-0-06-115194-1 Subj: Character traits – persistence. Sports – baseball.

Rodriguez, Béatrice. *The chicken thief* ill. by author. Enchanted Lion, 2010. ISBN 978-1-59270-092-9 Subj: Animals – foxes. Birds – chickens, roosters. Wordless.

Fox and hen together ill. by author. Enchanted Lion, 2011. ISBN 978-1-59270-109-4 Subj: Animals – foxes. Birds – chickens, roosters. Friendship. Wordless.

The gingerbread man (The gingerbread boy)

Rodriguez, Bobbie. *Sarah's sleepover* ill. by Mark Graham. Viking, 2000. ISBN 978-0-670-87750-8 Subj: Disabilities – blindness. Family life – cousins. Games. Night. Power failures. Sleepovers.

Rodriguez, Edel. *Sergio makes a splash* ill. by author. Little, Brown, 2008. ISBN 978-0-316-06616-7 Subj: Birds – penguins. Emotions – fear. Sports – swimming.

Sergio saves the game! ill. by author. Little, Brown, 2009. ISBN 978-0-316-06617-4 Subj: Birds – penguins. Character traits – clumsiness. Sports – soccer.

Rodríguez, Rachel Victoria. *Through Georgia's eyes* ill. by Julie Paschkis. Henry Holt, 2006. ISBN 978-0-8050-7740-7 Subj: Art. Careers – artists.

Rodriguez, Sonia. *T is for tutu: a ballet alphabet* by Sonia Rodriguez and Kurt Browning ill. by Wilson Ong. Sleeping Bear, 2011. ISBN 978-1-58536-312-4 Subj: ABC books. Ballet.

Roe, Eileen. *With my brother / Con mi hermano* ill. by Robert Casilla. Bradbury, 1991. ISBN 978-0-02-777373-6 Subj: Ethnic groups in the U.S. – Mexican Americans. Family life – brothers. Foreign languages.

Roehrig, Artemis. *Are pirates polite?* (Demas, Corinne)

Roemer, Heidi Bee. *What kind of seeds are these?* ill. by Olena Kassian. NorthWord, 2006. ISBN 978-1-55971-955-1 Subj: Rhyming text. Seeds.

Roeser, Matt. *Oh no, Astro!* ill. by Brad Woodard. Simon & Schuster, 2016. ISBN 978-148143976-3 Subj: Space & space ships.

Rofé, Jennifer. *Piggies in the pumpkin patch* (Peterson, Mary)

Rogalski, Mark. *Tickets to ride: an alphabetic amusement* ill. by author. Running Press, 2006. ISBN 978-0-7624-2782-6 Subj: ABC books. Parks – amusement.

Rogers, Emma. *Ruby's dinnertime* (Rogers, Paul)

Ruby's potty (Rogers, Paul)

Rogers, Fred. *Adoption* photos by Jim Judkis. Putnam, 1994. ISBN 978-0-399-22432-4 Subj: Adoption. Emotions. Family life.

Divorce photos by Jim Judkis. Putnam, 1998. ISBN 978-0-399-22449-2 Subj: Divorce. Family life.

Extraordinary friends photos by Jim Judkis. Putnam, 2000. ISBN 978-0-399-23146-9 Subj: Disabilities. Friendship.

Going on an airplane photos by Jim Judkis. Putnam, 1989. ISBN 978-0-399-21635-0 Subj: Activities – traveling. Airplanes, airports.

Going to day care photos by Jim Judkis. Putnam, 1985. ISBN 978-0-399-21235-2 Subj: School – nursery.

Going to the doctor photos by Jim Judkis. Putnam, 1986. ISBN 978-0-399-21298-7 Subj: Careers – doctors.

Going to the hospital photos by Jim Judkis. Putnam, 1988. ISBN 978-0-399-21503-2 Subj: Hospitals. Illness.

Going to the potty photos by Jim Judkis. Putnam, 1986. ISBN 978-0-399-21296-3 Subj: Behavior – growing up. Toilet training.

If we were all the same ill. by Pat Sustendal. Random House, 1988. ISBN 978-0-394-98778-1 Subj: Character traits – individuality.

Making friends photos by Jim Judkis. Putnam, 1987. ISBN 978-0-399-21382-3 Subj: Activities – playing. Emotions. Friendship.

Moving photos by Jim Judkis. Putnam, 1987. ISBN 978-0-399-21383-0 Subj: Communities, neighborhoods. Emotions. Family life. Friendship. Moving.

The new baby photos by Jim Judkis. Putnam, 1985. ISBN 978-0-399-21236-9 Subj: Babies, toddlers. Family life – new sibling. Sibling rivalry.

When a pet dies photos by Jim Judkis. Putnam, 1988. ISBN 978-0-399-21504-9 Subj: Death. Emotions – grief. Pets.

Rogers, Gregory. *The boy, the bear, the baron, the bard* ill. by author. Macmillan, 2004. ISBN 978-1-59643-009-9 Subj: Animals – bears. Foreign lands – England. Knights. Wordless.

The hero of Little Street ill. by author. Roaring Brook, 2012. ISBN 978-1-59643-729-6 Subj: Art. Foreign lands. Imagination. Museums. Wordless.

Midsummer knight ill. by author. Macmillan, 2007. ISBN 978-1-56943-183-6 Subj: Animals – bears. Foreign lands – England. Knights. Wordless.

Rogers, Jacqueline. *Kindergarten ABC* ill. by author. Scholastic, 2002. ISBN 978-0-439-36837-7 Subj: ABC books. Books, reading. School.

Tiptoe into kindergarten ill. by author. Scholastic, 1999. ISBN 978-0-590-46653-0 Subj: Family life – brothers & sisters. School.

Rogers, Paul. *Ruby's dinnertime* by Paul Rogers and Emma Rogers ill. by Emma Rogers. Dutton, 2002. ISBN 978-0-525-46847-9 Subj: Animals – mice. Behavior – growing up. Family life. Food. Rhyming text.

Ruby's potty by Paul Rogers and Emma Rogers ill. by Emma Rogers. Dutton, 2001. ISBN 978-0-525-46816-5 Subj: Animals – mice. Behavior – growing up. Rhyming text. Toilet training.

Tiny by Paul Rogers and Korky Paul ill. by Korky Paul. Dutton, 2002. ISBN 978-1-929132-26-3 Subj: Insects – fleas.

What will the weather be like today? ill. by Kazuko. Greenwillow, 1990. ISBN 978-0-688-08951-1 Subj: Rhyming text. Weather.

Rohmann, Eric. *Bone dog* ill. by author. Roaring Brook, 2011. ISBN 978-1-59643-150-8 Subj: Anatomy – skeletons. Animals – dogs. Death. Holidays – Halloween.

The cinder-eyed cats ill. by author. Crown, 1997. ISBN 978-0-517-70897-2 Subj: Animals – cats. Bedtime. Boats, ships. Dreams. Islands. Night.

Clara and Asha ill. by author. Macmillan, 2005. ISBN 978-1-59643-031-0 Subj: Bedtime. Fish. Imagination – imaginary friends.

My friend Rabbit ill. by author. Roaring Brook, 2002. ISBN 978-0-7613-2420-1 Subj: Animals – mice. Animals – rabbits. Caldecott award books. Friendship.

Pumpkinhead ill. by author. Knopf, 2003. ISBN 978-0-375-92416-3 Subj: Activities – traveling. Character traits – being different. Character traits – individuality.

Time flies ill. by author. Crown, 1994. ISBN 978-0-517-59599-2 Subj: Birds. Caldecott award honor books. Dinosaurs. Museums. Time. Wordless.

Rohmer, Harriet. *Atariba and Niguayona: a story from the Taino people of Puerto Rico* ill. by Consuelo Mendez. Adapt. by Harriet Rohmer and Jesus Guerrero Rea. Children's Book Press, 1988. ISBN 978-0-89239-026-7 Subj: Character traits – kindness. Foreign lands – Puerto Rico. Illness.

How we came to the fifth world: a creation story from Ancient Mexico ill. by Graciela Carrillo. Adapt. by Harriet Rohmer and Mary Anchondo. Children's Book Press, 1988. ISBN 978-0-89239-024-3 Subj: Creation. Folk & fairy tales. Foreign lands – Mexico.

Mother scorpion country by Harriet Rohmer and Dorminster Wilson ill. by Virginia Stearns. Children's Book Press, 1987. ISBN 978-0-89239-032-8 Subj: Emotions – love. Folk & fairy tales. Foreign lands – Nicaragua.

Rohmer, Harriet, et al. *The invisible hunters* ill. by Joe Sam. Children's Book Press, 1987. ISBN 978-0-89239-031-1 Subj: Behavior – greed. Folk & fairy tales. Foreign lands – Nicaragua. Sports – hunting.

Rolli, Jennifer Hansen. *Claudia and Moth* ill. by author. Viking, 2017. ISBN 978-042528833-7 Subj: Activities – painting. Insects – butterflies, caterpillars. Insects – moths. Seasons – winter.

Just one more ill. by author. Viking, 2014. ISBN 978-067001563-4 Subj: Behavior – greed. Character traits – selfishness.

Rollings, Susan. *New shoes, red shoes* ill. by author. Orchard, 2000. ISBN 978-0-531-30268-2 Subj: Birthdays. Clothing – shoes. Parties. Rhyming text.

Rollins, Jack. *Frosty the snowman* (Nelson, Steve)

Romain, Trevor. *Jemma's journey* ill. by Pat Lopez. Boyds Mills, 2002. ISBN 978-1-56397-937-8 Subj: Ethnic groups in the U.S. – African Americans. Family life – grandmothers. Trees. U.S. history.

Rong, Yu. *A lovely day for Amelia Goose* ill. by author. Candlewick, 2004. ISBN 978-0-7636-2309-8 Subj: Birds – geese. Day. Frogs & toads.

Roode, Daniel. *Little Bea and the snowy day* ill. by author. HarperCollins, 2011. ISBN 978-0-06-199395-4 Subj: Activities – playing. Insects – bees. Rhyming text. Weather – snow.

Roop, Connie. *Down east in the ocean: a Maine counting book* (Roop, Peter)

Let's celebrate Earth Day by Connie Roop and Peter Roop ill. by Gwen Connelly. Millbrook, 2001. ISBN 978-0-7613-1812-5 Subj: Ecology. Holidays – Earth Day.

Roop, Peter. *Down east in the ocean: a Maine counting book* by Peter Roop and Connie Roop ill. by Nicole Fazio. Down East, 2011. ISBN 978-0-89272-709-4 Subj: Counting, numbers. Sea & seashore.

Let's celebrate Earth Day (Roop, Connie)

Roosa, Karen. *Beach day* ill. by Maggie Smith. Clarion, 2001. ISBN 978-0-618-02923-5 Subj: Rhyming text. Sea & seashore – beaches.

Pippa at the parade ill. by Julie Fortenberry. Boyds Mills, 2009. ISBN 978-1-59078-567-6 Subj: Holidays – Fourth of July. Parades. Rhyming text.

Root, Andrew. *Hamsters don't fight fires!* ill. by Jessica Olien. HarperCollins, 2017. ISBN 978-006245294-8 Subj: Animals – hamsters. Careers – firefighters. Character traits – perseverance. Character traits – smallness.

Root, Barry. *Gumbrella* ill. by author. Putnam, 2002. ISBN 978-0-399-23347-0 Subj: Animals. Animals – elephants. Character traits – kindness to animals.

Root, Phyllis. *All for the newborn baby* ill. by Nicola Bayley. Candlewick, 2000. ISBN 978-0-7636-0093-8 Subj: Holidays – Christmas. Lullabies. Religion – Nativity.

Anywhere farm ill. by G. Brian Karas. Candlewick, 2017. ISBN 978-076367499-1 Subj: Cities, towns. Farms. Gardens, gardening. Rhyming text.

Aunt Nancy and Cousin Lazybones ill. by David Parkins. Candlewick, 1998. ISBN 978-1-56402-425-1 Subj: Character traits – laziness. Family life – cousins.

Aunt Nancy and Old Man Trouble ill. by David Parkins. Candlewick, 1996. ISBN 978-1-56402-347-6 Subj: Behavior – trickery. Folk & fairy tales.

Big belching bog ill. by Betsy Bowen. Univ. of Minnesota, 2010. ISBN 978-0-8166-3359-3 Subj: Ecology. Swamps.

Big Momma makes the world ill. by Helen Oxenbury. Candlewick, 2002. ISBN 978-0-7636-1132-3 Subj: Creation.

Contrary bear ill. by Laura Cornell. HarperCollins, 1996. ISBN 978-0-06-025086-7 Subj: Behavior – mistakes. Family life – fathers. Toys – bears.

Creak! said the bed ill. by Regan Dunnick. Candlewick, 2010. ISBN 978-0-7636-2004-2 Subj: Cumulative tales. Family life. Furniture – beds. Rhyming text. Sleep. Weather – storms.

Flip, flap, fly! ill. by David Walker. Candlewick, 2009. ISBN 978-0-7636-3109-3 Subj: Animals – babies. Rhyming text.

Grandmother Winter ill. by Beth Krommes. Houghton, 1999. ISBN 978-0-395-88399-0 Subj:

Birds – geese. Folk & fairy tales. Foreign lands – Germany. Seasons – winter. Weather – snow.

If you want to see a caribou ill. by Jim Meyer. Houghton, 2004. ISBN 978-0-618-39314-5 Subj: Animals – reindeer. Nature.

Kiss the cow ill. by Will Hillenbrand. Candlewick, 2000. ISBN 978-0-7636-0298-7 Subj: Animals – bulls, cows. Kissing. Tall tales.

Looking for a moose ill. by Randy Cecil. Candlewick, 2006. ISBN 978-0-7636-2005-9 Subj: Animals – moose. Games.

Lucia and the light ill. by Mary GrandPré. Candlewick, 2006. ISBN 978-0-7636-2296-1 Subj: Animals – cats. Mythical creatures – trolls. Seasons – winter. Sun.

Mrs. Potter's pig ill. by Russell Ayto. Candlewick, 1996. ISBN 978-1-56402-924-9 Subj: Animals – pigs. Babies, toddlers. Character traits – cleanliness. Character traits – orderliness.

The name quilt ill. by Margot Apple. Farrar, 2003. ISBN 978-0-374-35484-8 Subj: Family life – grandmothers. Names. Quilts.

Oliver finds his way ill. by Christopher Denise. Candlewick, 2002. ISBN 978-0-7636-1383-9 Subj: Animals – babies. Animals – bears. Behavior – lost. Family life – parents.

One duck stuck ill. by Jane Chapman. Candlewick, 1998. ISBN 978-0-7636-1566-6 Subj: Animals. Birds – ducks. Counting, numbers. Rhyming text.

Paula Bunyan ill. by Kevin O'Malley. Farrar, 2009. ISBN 978-0-374-35759-7 Subj: Tall tales. U.S. history – frontier & pioneer life.

Plant a pocket of prairie ill. by Betsy Bowen. Univ. of Minnesota, 2014. ISBN 978-081667980-5 Subj: Nature. Plants.

Rattletrap car ill. by Jill Barton. Candlewick, 2001. ISBN 978-0-7636-0919-1 Subj: Automobiles. Family life. Humorous stories. Lakes, ponds. Problem solving. Rhyming text.

Rosie's fiddle ill. by Kevin O'Malley. Lothrop, 1997. ISBN 978-0-688-12853-1 Subj: Contests. Devil. Music. Musical instruments – violins. Tall tales.

Scrawny cat ill. by Alison Friend. Candlewick, 2011. ISBN 978-0-7636-4164-1 Subj: Animals – cats. Behavior – lost. Emotions – loneliness.

Ten sleepy sheep ill. by Susan Gaber. Candlewick, 2004. ISBN 978-0-7636-1545-1 Subj: Animals – sheep. Bedtime. Rhyming text. Sleep.

Toot toot zoom! ill. by Matthew Cordell. Candlewick, 2009. ISBN 978-0-7636-3452-0 Subj: Animals. Animals – foxes. Automobiles. Friendship.

What Baby wants ill. by Jill Barton. Candlewick, 1998. ISBN 978-0-7636-0207-9 Subj: Babies, toddlers. Family life. Farms. Lullabies.

What's that noise? (Edwards, Michelle)

Roper, Janice M. *Dancing on the moon* ill. by Lauren Grimm. SIDS Ed. Services, 2001. ISBN 978-0-9641218-6-7 Subj: Babies, toddlers. Death. Dreams. Emotions – envy, jealousy. Emotions – grief. Family life – brothers & sisters. Moon.

Roques, Dominique. *Sleep tight, Anna Banana!* ill. by Alexis Dormal. First Second, 2014. ISBN 978-162672019-0 Subj: Bedtime. Noise, sounds. Toys.

Rosa-Mendoza, Gladys. *What time is it? / Qué hora es?* ill. by Susan Chapman Calitri. Me & Mi, 2001. ISBN 978-0-9679748-9-7 Subj: Foreign languages. Format, unusual – board books. Time.

Rosales, Melodye Benson. *Leola and the honeybears* ill. by author. An African-American retelling of Goldilocks and the Three Bears. Scholastic, 1999. ISBN 978-0-590-38358-5 Subj: Animals – bears. Ethnic groups in the U.S. – African Americans. Folk & fairy tales.

'Twas the night b'fore Christmas: an African-American version ill. by author. Based on the original poem, A visit from St. Nicholas, by Clement C. Moore. Scholastic, 1996. ISBN 978-0-590-73944-3 Subj: Ethnic groups in the U.S. – African Americans. Holidays – Christmas. Poetry. Santa Claus.

Roscoe, Charlie. *The red prince* ill. by Tom Clohosy Cole. Candlewick/Templar, 2016. ISBN 978-076368912-4 Subj: Character traits – bravery. Character traits – cooperation. Royalty – princes.

Roscoe, Lily. *The night parade* ill. by David Walker. Orchard, 2014. ISBN 978-054539623-3 Subj: Bedtime. Night. Parades. Rhyming text.

Rose, Caroline Starr. *Over in the wetlands: a hurricane-on-the-bayou story* ill. by Rob Dunlavey. Random House, 2015. ISBN 978-044981016-3 Subj: Animals. Birds. Swamps. Weather – hurricanes.

Rose, Deborah Lee. *All the seasons of the year* ill. by Kay Chorao. Abrams, 2010. ISBN 978-0-8109-8395-3 Subj: Animals – cats. Emotions – love. Family life – mothers. Rhyming text. Seasons.

Birthday zoo ill. by Lynn Munsinger. Albert Whitman, 2002. ISBN 978-0-8075-0776-6 Subj: Animals. Birthdays. Parties. Rhyming text. Toys. Zoos.

Into the A, B, sea ill. by Steve Jenkins. Scholastic, 2000. ISBN 978-0-439-09696-6 Subj: ABC books. Animals. Sea & seashore.

Ocean babies ill. by Hiroe Nakata. National Geographic, 2005. ISBN 978-0-7922-8312-6 Subj: Animals – babies. Sea & seashore.

Someone's sleepy ill. by Dan Andreasen. Abrams, 2013. ISBN 978-1-4197-0539-7 Subj: Bedtime. Family life – mothers. Rhyming text.

The spelling bee before recess ill. by Carey Armstrong-Ellis. Abrams, 2013. ISBN 978-1-4197-0847-3 Subj: Contests. Rhyming text. School. Sportsmanship.

The twelve days of kindergarten ill. by Carey Armstrong-Ellis. Abrams, 2003. ISBN 978-0-8109-4512-8 Subj: Counting, numbers. Cumulative tales. Poetry. School.

The twelve days of springtime: a school counting book ill. by Carey Armstrong-Ellis. Abrams, 2008. ISBN 978-0-8109-8330-4 Subj: Counting, numbers. Cumulative tales. School. Seasons – spring.

The twelve days of winter: a school counting book ill. by Carey Armstrong-Ellis. Abrams, 2006. ISBN 978-0-8109-5472-4 Subj: Counting, numbers. Seasons – winter.

Rose, Marion. *The Christmas tree fairy* ill. by Jason Cockcroft. Bloomsbury, 2005. ISBN 978-1-58234-668-7 Subj: Behavior – wishing. Fairies. Holidays – Christmas.

Rose, Nancy. *Merry Christmas, squirrels!* photos by author. Little, Brown, 2015. ISBN 978-031630257-9 Subj: Animals – squirrels. Family life – cousins. Holidays – Christmas.

The secret life of squirrels photos by author. Little, Brown, 2014. ISBN 978-031637027-1 Subj: Animals – squirrels. Family life – cousins.

Rose, Naomi C. *Tashi and the Tibetan flower cure* ill. by author. Lee & Low, 2011. ISBN 978-1-60060-425-6 Subj: Communities, neighborhoods. Ethnic groups in the U.S. – Tibetan Americans. Family life – grandfathers. Illness.

Rosen, Michael. *Bear flies high* ill. by Adrian Reynolds. Bloomsbury, 2009. ISBN 978-1-59990-386-6 Subj: Activities – flying. Animals – bears. Fairs, festivals.

Bear's day out ill. by Adrian Reynolds. Bloomsbury, 2007. ISBN 978-1-59990-007-0 Subj: Animals – bears. Friendship.

The bus is for us! ill. by Gillian Tyler. Candlewick, 2015. ISBN 978-076366983-6 Subj: Buses. Rhyming text. Transportation.

Crow and Hawk ill. by John Clementson. Harcourt, 1995. ISBN 978-0-15-200257-2 Subj: Behavior – running away. Birds – crows. Birds – hawks. Folk & fairy tales. Indians of North America – Pueblo.

How the animals got their colors ill. by John Clementson. Harcourt, 1992. ISBN 978-0-15-236783-

1 Subj: Animals. Concepts – color. Folk & fairy tales – pourquoi tales. Poetry.

Howler ill. by Neal Layton. Bloomsbury, 2004. ISBN 978-1-58234-851-3 Subj: Animals – dogs. Babies, toddlers. Emotions – envy, jealousy. Humorous stories.

Poems for the very young ill. by Bob Graham. Kingfisher, 2004. ISBN 978-0-7534-5816-7 Subj: Children as authors. Poetry.

Red Ted and the lost things ill. by Joel Stewart. Candlewick, 2009. ISBN 978-0-7636-4537-3 Subj: Behavior – lost & found possessions. Toys – bears.

Send for a superhero! ill. by Katharine McEwen. Candlewick, 2014. ISBN 978-076366438-1 Subj: Bedtime. Books, reading. Imagination.

A Thanksgiving wish ill. by John Thompson. Blue Sky, 1999. ISBN 978-0-590-25563-9 Subj: Communities, neighborhoods. Death. Family life – grandparents. Holidays – Thanksgiving.

This is our house ill. by Bob Graham. Candlewick, 1996. ISBN 978-1-56402-870-9 Subj: Behavior – sharing. Character traits – selfishness. Homes, houses. Prejudice.

Tiny little fly ill. by Kevin Waldron. Candlewick, 2010. ISBN 978-0-7636-4681-3 Subj: Animals. Insects – flies. Jungle.

Totally wonderful Miss Plumberry ill. by Chinlun Lee. Candlewick, 2006. ISBN 978-0-7636-2744-7 Subj: Behavior – bad day, bad mood. Careers – teachers. School.

We're going on a bear hunt ill. by Helen Oxenbury. Aladdin, 1992. ISBN 978-0-689-71653-9 Subj: Animals – bears. Games. Participation. Sports – hunting.

Rosen, Michael J. *Avalanche* ill. by David Butler. Candlewick, 1998. ISBN 978-0-7636-0589-6 Subj: ABC books. Animals – dogs. Rhyming text. Weather – snow.

Chanukah lights ill. by Robert Sabuda. Candlewick, 2011. ISBN 978-0-7636-5533-4 Subj: Format, unusual – toy & movable books. Holidays – Hanukkah.

Chanukah lights everywhere ill. by Melissa Iwai. Harcourt, 2001. ISBN 978-0-15-202447-5 Subj: Counting, numbers. Holidays – Hanukkah. Jewish culture. Religion.

The dog who walked with God ill. by Stan Fellows. Candlewick, 1998. ISBN 978-0-7636-0470-7 Subj: Animals – dogs. Creation. Indians of North America – Kato. Weather – floods.

A drive in the country ill. by Marc Burckhardt. Candlewick, 2007. ISBN 978-0-7636-2140-7 Subj: Activities – traveling. Family life.

Elijah's angel ill. by Aminah Brenda Lynn Robinson. Harcourt, 1992. ISBN 978-0-15-225394-3 Subj: Careers – woodcarvers. Ethnic groups in the U.S. – African Americans. Friendship. Holidays – Christmas. Holidays – Hanukkah. Jewish culture.

Night of the pumpkinheads ill. by Hugh McMahon. Penguin, 2011. ISBN 978-0-8037-3452-4 Subj: Contests. Holidays – Halloween.

Our eight nights of Hanukkah ill. by DyAnne DiSalvo. Holiday, 2000. ISBN 978-0-8234-1476-5 Subj: Holidays – Hanukkah. Jewish culture.

With a dog like that, a kid like me . . . ill. by Ted Rand. Dial, 2000. ISBN 978-0-8037-2059-6 Subj: Animals. Animals – dogs. Imagination.

Rosenbaum, Andria Warmflash. *Trains don't sleep* ill. by Deirdre Gill. Houghton Mifflin Harcourt, 2017. ISBN 978-054438074-5 Subj: Rhyming text. Trains.

Rosenberg, Liz. *A big and little alphabet* ill. by Vera Rosenberry. Orchard, 1997. ISBN 978-0-531-33050-0 Subj: ABC books. Animals.

The carousel ill. by Jim LaMarche. Harcourt, 1995. ISBN 978-0-15-200853-6 Subj: Animals – horses, ponies. Death. Emotions – grief. Family life – mothers. Family life – sisters. Imagination. Merry-go-rounds.

Eli's night-light ill. by Joanna Yardley. Orchard, 2001. ISBN 978-0-531-33316-7 Subj: Bedtime. Light, lights. Night. Rhyming text.

Nobody ill. by Julie Downing. Roaring Brook, 2010. ISBN 978-1-59643-120-1 Subj: Family life – parents. Imagination – imaginary friends. Morning.

On Christmas eve ill. by John Clapp. Roaring Brook, 2002. ISBN 978-0-7613-2707-3 Subj: Family life. Holidays – Christmas. Santa Claus. Weather – snow. Weather – storms.

Tyrannosaurus dad ill. by Matthew Myers. Roaring Brook, 2011. ISBN 978-1-59643-531-5 Subj: Dinosaurs. Family life – fathers.

We wanted you ill. by Peter Catalanotto. Roaring Brook, 2002. ISBN 978-0-7613-2661-8 Subj: Adoption. Family life – parents.

What James said ill. by Matthew Myers. Roaring Brook, 2015. ISBN 978-159643908-5 Subj: Behavior – gossip, rumors. Behavior – misunderstanding. Friendship.

Rosenberg, Madelyn. *Happy birthday, tree! a Tu B'Shevat story* ill. by Jana Christy. Albert Whitman, 2012. ISBN 978-0-8075-3151-8 Subj: Ecology. Holidays – Tu B'Shevat. Jewish culture. Trees.

The Schmutzy Family ill. by Paul Meisel. Holiday House, 2012. ISBN 978-0-8234-2371-2 Subj: Days of the week, months of the year. Humorous stories. Jewish culture.

Rosenberg, Maxine B. *Mommy's in the hospital having a baby* photos by Robert Maass. Clarion, 1997. ISBN 978-0-395-71813-1 Subj: Babies, toddlers. Birth. Family life – new sibling. Hospitals.

Rosenberry, Vera. *Run, jump, whiz, splash* ill. by author. Holiday, 1999. ISBN 978-0-8234-1378-2 Subj: Activities. Seasons.

Vera goes to the dentist ill. by author. Henry Holt, 2002. ISBN 978-0-8050-6668-5 Subj: Careers – dentists. Health & fitness. Teeth.

Vera runs away ill. by author. Henry Holt, 2000. ISBN 978-0-8050-6267-0 Subj: Behavior – running away. Family life.

Vera's baby sister ill. by author. Henry Holt, 2005. ISBN 978-0-8050-7126-9 Subj: Family life – grandfathers. Family life – new sibling. Sibling rivalry.

Vera's first day of school ill. by author. Henry Holt, 1999. ISBN 978-0-8050-5936-6 Subj: Character traits – shyness. Emotions – fear. School – first day.

Vera's Halloween ill. by author. Henry Holt, 2008. ISBN 978-0-8050-8144-2 Subj: Behavior – lost. Holidays – Halloween.

When Vera was sick ill. by author. Henry Holt, 1998. ISBN 978-0-8050-5405-7 Subj: Illness – chicken pox.

Who is in the garden? ill. by author. Holiday, 2001. ISBN 978-0-8234-1529-8 Subj: Animals. Gardens, gardening.

Rosenfeld, Dina Herman. *Five alive: my Yom Tov five senses* ill. by Tova Leff. Hachai, 2003. ISBN 978-1-929628-09-4 Subj: Holidays. Jewish culture. Senses.

Get well soon ill. by Rina Lyampe. Hachai, 2001. ISBN 978-1-929628-05-6 Subj: Illness. Jewish culture.

How in the world does bread come from the earth? ill. by Rina Lyampe. Hachai, 2002. ISBN 978-1-929628-06-3 Subj: Food. Religion. Rhyming text.

Rosenstock, Barb. *The camping trip that changed America: Theodore Roosevelt, John Muir, and our national parks* ill. by Mordicai Gerstein. Dial, 2012. ISBN 978-0-8037-3710-5 Subj: Camps, camping. Careers – naturalists. Ecology. Parks. U.S. history.

Dorothea's eyes: Dorothea Lange photographs the truth ill. by Gerard DuBois. Boyds Mills, 2016. ISBN 978-162979208-8 Subj: Activities – photographing. Careers – photographers. Gender roles.

The noisy paint box: the color and sounds of Kandinsky's abstract art ill. by Mary GrandPré. Knopf, 2014. ISBN 978-0307978-48-6 Subj: Art. Caldecott award honor books. Careers – artists.

The streak: how Joe DiMaggio became America's hero ill. by Terry Widener. Boyds Mills, 2014. ISBN 978-159078992-6 Subj: Sports – baseball.

Thomas Jefferson builds a library ill. by John O'Brien. Boyds Mills, 2013. ISBN 978-1-59078-932-2 Subj: Books, reading. Libraries. U.S. history.

Vincent can't sleep: Van Gogh paints the night sky ill. by Mary GrandPré. Knopf, 2017. ISBN 978-110193710-5 Subj: Art. Careers – artists. Foreign lands – Holland. Stars.

Rosenthal, Amy Krouse. *Al Pha's bet* ill. by Delphine Durand. Penguin, 2011. ISBN 978-0-399-24601-2 Subj: ABC books. Language. Royalty – kings.

Awake beautiful child ill. by Gracia Lam. McSweeneys/McMullens, 2015. ISBN 978-193807392-2 Subj: ABC books. Day.

Bedtime for Mommy ill. by LeUyen Pham. Bloomsbury, 2010. ISBN 978-1-59990-341-5 Subj: Bedtime. Family life – mothers.

Chopsticks ill. by Scott Magoon. Hyperion, 2012. ISBN 978-1-4231-0796-5 Subj: Friendship. Humorous stories.

Christmas cookies: bite-size holiday lessons ill. by Jane Dyer. HarperCollins, 2008. ISBN 978-0-06-058024-7 Subj: Behavior. Character traits. Holidays – Christmas.

Cookies: bite-size life lessons ill. by Jane Dyer. HarperCollins, 2006. ISBN 978-0-06-058081-0 Subj: Activities – baking, cooking. Behavior. Character traits. Etiquette. Food.

Dear Girl, by Amy Krouse Rosenthal and Paris Rosenthal ill. by Holly Hatam. HarperCollins, 2018. ISBN 978-006242250-7 Subj: Character traits – confidence. Gender roles. Self-concept.

Duck! Rabbit! ill. by Tom Lichtenheld. Chronicle, 2009. ISBN 978-0-8118-6865-5 Subj: Animals – rabbits. Birds – ducks. Optical illusions.

Exclamation mark ill. by Tom Lichtenheld. Scholastic, 2013. ISBN 978-0-545-43679-3 Subj: Character traits – being different. Character traits – individuality. Language. Self-concept.

Friendshape ill. by Tom Lichtenheld. Scholastic, 2015. ISBN 978-054543682-3 Subj: Concepts – shape. Friendship.

I scream, ice cream! a book of wordles ill. by Serge Bloch. Chronicle, 2013. ISBN 978-1-4521-0004-3 Subj: Language.

I wish you more ill. by Tom Lichtenheld. Chronicle, 2015. ISBN 978-145212699-9 Subj: Behavior – wishing.

It's not fair! ill. by Tom Lichtenheld. HarperCollins, 2008. ISBN 978-0-06-115257-3 Subj: Behavior – dissatisfaction. Character traits – questioning. Rhyming text.

Little Hoot ill. by Jen Corace. Chronicle, 2008. ISBN 978-0-8118-6023-9 Subj: Bedtime. Birds – owls.

Little Miss, big sis ill. by Peter H. Reynolds. HarperCollins, 2015. ISBN 978-006230203-8 Subj: Babies, toddlers. Family life – new sibling. Family life – sisters. Rhyming text.

Little Oink ill. by Jen Corace. Chronicle, 2009. ISBN 978-0-8118-6655-2 Subj: Animals – pigs. Character traits – cleanliness.

Little Pea ill. by Jen Corace. Chronicle, 2005. ISBN 978-0-8118-4658-5 Subj: Food.

The OK book ill. by Tom Lichtenheld. HarperCollins, 2007. ISBN 978-0-06-115255-9 Subj: Self-concept.

One of those days ill. by Rebecca Doughty. Penguin, 2006. ISBN 978-0-399-24365-3 Subj: Behavior – bad day, bad mood.

One smart cookie: bite-size lessons for the school years and beyond ill. by Jane Dyer and Brooke Dyer. HarperCollins, 2010. ISBN 978-0-06-142970-5 Subj: Activities – baking, cooking. Behavior. Character traits. Food. Self-concept.

Plant a kiss ill. by Peter H. Reynolds. HarperCollins, 2011. ISBN 978-0-06-198675-8 Subj: Behavior – sharing. Emotions – love. Kissing.

Spoon ill. by Scott Magoon. Hyperion, 2009. ISBN 978-1-4231-0685-2 Subj: Character traits – individuality.

That's me loving you ill. by Teagan White. Random House, 2016. ISBN 978-110193238-4 Subj: Family life. Foster children, foster homes.

This plus that: life's little equations ill. by Jen Corace. HarperCollins, 2011. ISBN 978-0-06-172655-2 Subj: Behavior. Concepts. Counting, numbers.

Uni the unicorn ill. by Brigette Barrager. Random House, 2014. ISBN 978-038537555-9 Subj: Friendship. Mythical creatures – unicorns.

Uni the unicorn and the dream come true ill. by Brigette Barrager. Random House, 2017. ISBN 978-110193659-7 Subj: Magic. Mythical creatures – unicorns. Weather – rain.

Wumbers: it's a word cr8ed with a number! ill. by Tom Lichtenheld. Chronicle, 2012. ISBN 978-1-4521-1022-6 Subj: Counting, numbers. Language.

Yes Day! ill. by Tom Lichtenheld. HarperCollins, 2009. ISBN 978-0-06-115259-7 Subj: Behavior –

resourcefulness. Behavior – wishing. Character traits – questioning. Holidays.

Rosenthal, Betsy R. *An ambush of tigers: a wild gathering of collective nouns* ill. by Jago. Lerner/Millbrook, 2015. ISBN 978-146771464-8 Subj: Animals. Language. Rhyming text.

Which shoes would you choose? ill. by Nancy Cote. Penguin, 2010. ISBN 978-0-399-25013-2 Subj: Clothing – shoes. Rhyming text.

Rosenthal, Eileen. *Bobo the sailor man!* ill. by Marc Rosenthal. Atheneum, 2013. ISBN 978-1-4424-4443-0 Subj: Animals – cats. Behavior – lost & found possessions. Sailors. Toys.

I must have Bobo! ill. by Marc Rosenthal. Simon & Schuster, 2011. ISBN 978-1-4424-0377-2 Subj: Animals – cats. Behavior – lost & found possessions. Toys.

I'll save you Bobo! ill. by Marc Rosenthal. Atheneum, 2012. ISBN 978-1-4424-0378-9 Subj: Activities – storytelling. Animals – cats. Toys.

Rosenthal, Marc. *Archie and the pirates* ill. by author. HarperCollins, 2009. ISBN 978-0-06-144164-6 Subj: Animals – monkeys. Friendship. Pirates.

Big bot, small bot: a book of robot opposites ill. by author. POW!, 2015. ISBN 978-157687750-0 Subj: Concepts – opposites. Format, unusual – toy & movable books. Robots.

Phooey! ill. by author. HarperCollins, 2007. ISBN 978-0-06-075248-4 Subj: Behavior – boredom. Cumulative tales. Humorous stories.

Rosenthal, Paris. *Dear Girl,* (Rosenthal, Amy Krouse)

Roslonek, Steve. *The shape song swingalong* ill. by David Sim. Barefoot, 2011. ISBN 978-1-84686-671-5 Subj: Activities – drawing. Concepts – shape. Songs.

Rosoff, Meg. *Jumpy Jack and Googily* ill. by Sophie Blackall. Henry Holt, 2008. ISBN 978-0-8050-8066-7 Subj: Animals – snails. Emotions – fear. Friendship. Humorous stories. Monsters.

Wild boars cook ill. by Sophie Blackall. Henry Holt, 2008. ISBN 978-0-8050-7523-6 Subj: Activities – baking, cooking. Animals. Behavior – misbehavior. Food. Humorous stories.

Ross, Dave. *A book of hugs* ill. by Laura Rader. HarperCollins, 1999. ISBN 978-0-06-028147-2 Subj: Emotions.

A book of kisses ill. by Laura Rader. HarperCollins, 2000. ISBN 978-0-06-028453-4 Subj: Emotions.

Ross, Eileen. *The Halloween showdown* ill. by Lynn Rowe Reed. Holiday, 1999. ISBN 978-0-8234-1395-9 Subj: Animals. Animals – cats. Holidays – Halloween. Witches.

Ross, Fiona. *Chilly Milly Moo* ill. by author. Candlewick, 2011. ISBN 978-0-7636-5693-5 Subj: Animals – bulls, cows. Character traits – being different.

Ross, Gayle. *How Turtle's back was cracked* ill. by Murv Jacob. Dial, 1995. ISBN 978-0-8037-1729-9 Subj: Animals – wolves. Behavior – boasting, showing off. Folk & fairy tales. Indians of North America – Cherokee. Reptiles – turtles, tortoises.

The legend of the Windigo: a tale from native North America ill. by Murv Jacob. Dial, 1996. ISBN 978-0-8037-1898-2 Subj: Folk & fairy tales. Indians of North America – Algonquin. Indians of North America – Windigos. Insects – mosquitoes. Monsters.

Ross, Michael Elsohn. *Earth cycles* ill. by Gustav Moore. Millbrook, 2001. ISBN 978-0-7613-1815-6 Subj: Concepts. Day. Earth. Night. Seasons.

Mama's milk ill. by Ashley Wolff. Ten Speed, 2007. ISBN 978-1-58246-181-6 Subj: Animals. Babies, toddlers. Family life – mothers. Rhyming text.

Mexican Christmas photos by Felix Rigau. Carolrhoda, 2002. ISBN 978-0-87614-601-9 Subj: Foreign lands – Mexico. Holidays – Christmas.

Play with me ill. by Julie Downing. Tricycle, 2009. ISBN 978-1-58246-255-4 Subj: Activities – playing. Animals. Family life – parents. Rhyming text.

Ross, Tom. *Eggbert, the slightly cracked egg* ill. by Rex Barron. Putnam, 1994. ISBN 978-0-399-22416-4 Subj: Careers – artists. Character traits – individuality. Eggs.

Ross, Tony. *The boy who cried wolf* ill. by author. Dial, 1991. ISBN 978-0-8037-0193-9 Subj: Animals – wolves. Behavior – lying. Behavior – trickery. Folk & fairy tales.

Centipede's 100 shoes ill. by author. Henry Holt, 2003. ISBN 978-0-8050-7298-3 Subj: Clothing – shoes. Crustaceans – centipedes, millipedes.

I didn't do it! ill. by author. Andersen, 2016. ISBN 978-151240598-9 Subj: Behavior – misbehavior. Behavior – misunderstanding. Royalty – princesses.

I don't want to go to the hospital! ill. by author. Andersen, 2013. ISBN 978-1-46771-155-5 Subj: Hospitals. Royalty – princesses.

I feel sick! ill. by author. Lerner, 2015. ISBN 978-146775797-3 Subj: Illness. Royalty – princesses.

I want a friend! ill. by author. Andersen, 2017. ISBN 978-151240555-2 Subj: Friendship. Royalty – princesses.

I want a party! ill. by author. Andersen, 2011. ISBN 978-0-7613-8089-4 Subj: Parties. Royalty – princesses.

I want my light on! ill. by author. Andersen, 2010. ISBN 978-0-7613-6443-6 Subj: Bedtime. Emotions – fear. Ghosts. Royalty – princesses.

I want my tooth ill. by author. Kane/Miller, 2005. ISBN 978-1-929132-85-0 Subj: Royalty – princesses. Teeth.

I want snow! ill. by author. Andersen, 2017. ISBN 978-151248125-9 Subj: Character traits – patience, impatience. Royalty – princesses. Weather – snow.

I want to do it myself! ill. by author. Andersen, 2011. ISBN 978-0-7613-7412-1 Subj: Camps, camping. Royalty – princesses.

I want to win! ill. by author. Andersen, 2012. ISBN 978-0-7613-8993-4 Subj: Contests. Royalty – princesses.

I want two birthdays! ill. by author. Andersen, 2010. ISBN 978-0-7613-5495-6 Subj: Birthdays. Royalty – princesses.

Our Kid ill. by author. Andersen, 2017. ISBN 978-151248127-3 Subj: Animals – goats. Behavior – promptness, tardiness. School.

Rita's rhino ill. by author. Lerner, 2015. ISBN 978-146776315-8 Subj: Animals – rhinoceros. Behavior – hiding things. Pets.

Rossell, Judith. *Oliver* ill. by author. HarperCollins, 2012. ISBN 978-0-06-202210-3 Subj: Character traits – questioning. Imagination.

Ruby and Leonard and the great big surprise ill. by author. IPG/Little Hare, 2010. ISBN 978-1-921272-96-7 Subj: Activities – baking, cooking. Animals – mice. Birthdays. Family life – brothers & sisters.

Rossetti-Shustak, Bernadette. *I love you through and through* ill. by Caroline Jayne Church. Scholastic, 2005. ISBN 978-0-439-67363-1 Subj: Emotions – love. Format, unusual – board books. Rhyming text. Self-concept.

Rossiter, Nan Parson. *Sugar on snow* ill. by author. Dutton, 2002. ISBN 978-0-525-46910-0 Subj: Family life – brothers. Farms. Food.

Rostoker-Gruber, Karen. *Bandit* ill. by Vincent Nguyen. Marshall Cavendish, 2008. ISBN 978-0-7614-5382-6 Subj: Animals – cats. Behavior – running away. Moving.

Bandit's surprise ill. by Vincent Nguyen. Marshall Cavendish, 2010. ISBN 978-0-7614-5623-0 Subj: Animals – babies. Animals – cats. Behavior – sharing.

Ferret fun ill. by Paul Ratz de Tagyos. Marshall Cavendish, 2011. ISBN 978-0-7614-5817-3 Subj: Animals – cats. Animals – ferrets. Pets.

Roth, Carol. *All aboard to work — choo-choo!* ill. by Steve Lavis. Albert Whitman, 2009. ISBN 978-0-8075-0271-6 Subj: Animals. Careers. Rhyming text. Trains.

Little Bunny's sleepless night ill. by Valeri Gorbachev. NorthSouth, 1999. ISBN 978-0-7358-1070-9 Subj: Animals – rabbits. Behavior – dissatisfaction. Friendship. Sleep.

The little school bus ill. by Pamela Paparone. NorthSouth, 2002. ISBN 978-0-7358-1647-3 Subj: Animals. Buses. Rhyming text. School.

Ten dirty pigs / Ten clean pigs ill. by Pamela Paparone. NorthSouth, 1999. ISBN 978-0-7358-1090-7 Subj: Animals – pigs. Bedtime. Counting, numbers. Format, unusual.

Where's my mommy? ill. by Sean Julian. NorthSouth, 2012. ISBN 978-0-7358-4032-4 Subj: Animals – cats. Family life – mothers. Farms.

Will you still love me? ill. by Daniel Howarth. Albert Whitman, 2010. ISBN 978-0-8075-9114-7 Subj: Animals. Emotions – love. Family life – mothers. Family life – new sibling. Rhyming text.

Roth, Judith L. *Goodnight, dragons* ill. by Pascal Lemaître. Hyperion, 2012. ISBN 978-1-4231-4190-7 Subj: Dragons. Sleep.

Roth, Roger. *Fishing for Methuselah* ill. by author. HarperCollins, 1998. ISBN 978-0-06-027592-1 Subj: Friendship. Sports – fishing. Tall tales.

Roth, Ruby. *V is for vegan: the ABCs of being kind* ill. by author. North Atlantic Books, 2013. ISBN 978-1-58394-649-7 Subj: ABC books. Character traits – kindness to animals. Food. Health & fitness. Rhyming text.

Roth, Susan L. *Babies can't eat kimchee!* (Patz, Nancy)

The biggest frog in Australia ill. by author. Simon & Schuster, 1996. ISBN 978-0-689-80490-8 Subj: Foreign lands – Australia. Frogs & toads. Tall tales.

Cinnamon's day out: a gerbil adventure ill. by author. Dial, 1998. ISBN 978-0-8037-2323-8 Subj: Animals – gerbils. Behavior – running away.

Do re mi: if you can read music, thank Guido d'Arezzo ill. by author. Houghton, 2007. ISBN 978-0-618-46572-9 Subj: Music.

Great big guinea pigs ill. by author. Bloomsbury, 2006. ISBN 978-1-58234-724-0 Subj: Animals – guinea pigs. Prehistory.

Hands around the library: protecting Egypt's treasured books by Susan L. Roth and Karen Leggett Abouraya ill. by Susan L. Roth. Dial, 2012. ISBN 978-0-8037-3747-1 Subj: Books, reading. Foreign lands – Egypt. Libraries. Violence, nonviolence.

Happy birthday Mr. Kang ill. by author. National Geographic, 2001. ISBN 978-0-7922-7723-1 Subj: Behavior – wishing. Birds. Character traits – freedom. Cities, towns. Ethnic groups in the U.S. – Chinese Americans. Family life – grandfathers.

Kanahena: a Cherokee story ill. by reteller. St. Martin's, 1988. ISBN 978-0-312-01722-4 Subj: Animals – wolves. Folk & fairy tales. Indians of North America – Cherokee.

Listen to the wind: the story of Dr. Greg and three cups of tea (Mortenson, Greg)

Night-time numbers: a scary counting book ill. by author. Barefoot, 1999. ISBN 978-1-84148-001-5 Subj: Bedtime. Counting, numbers. Night. Rhyming text.

Parrots over Puerto Rico by Susan L. Roth and Cindy Trumbore ill. by Susan L. Roth. Lee & Low, 2013. ISBN 978-1-62014-004-8 Subj: Birds – parakeets, parrots. Ecology. Foreign lands – Puerto Rico.

Rothenberg, Joan Keller. *Inside-out grandma* ill. by author. Hyperion, 1995. ISBN 978-0-7868-2092-4 Subj: Clothing. Family life – grandmothers. Folk & fairy tales. Holidays – Hanukkah. Jewish culture. Religion.

Matzah ball soup ill. by author. Hyperion, 1999. ISBN 978-0-7868-2170-9 Subj: Family life – sisters. Food. Holidays – Passover. Jewish culture.

Rothstein, Gloria. *Sheep asleep* ill. by Lizzy Rockwell. HarperCollins, 2003. ISBN 978-0-06-029106-8 Subj: Animals – sheep. Bedtime. Counting, numbers. Rhyming text.

Rotner, Shelley. *The A.D.D. book for kids* by Shelley Rotner and Sheila M. Kelly; photos by Shelley Rotner. Millbrook, 2000. ISBN 978-0-7613-1722-7 Subj: Behavior. Disabilities – ADD.

All kinds of friends by Shelley Rotner and Sheila M. Kelly; photos by Shelley Rotner. Lerner/Millbrook, 2017. ISBN 978-151243105-6 Subj: Friendship.

Boats afloat photos by author. Orchard, 1998. ISBN 978-0-531-33112-5 Subj: Boats, ships. Transportation.

The body book by Shelley Rotner and Steve Calcagnino; photos by Shelley Rotner. Orchard, 2000. ISBN 978-0-531-33256-6 Subj: Anatomy.

The buzz on bees: why are they disappearing? by Shelley Rotner and Anne Love Woodhull; photos by Shelley Rotner. Holiday House, 2010. ISBN 978-0-8234-2247-0 Subj: Ecology. Insects – bees.

Citybook photos by Ken Kreisler. Orchard, 1994. ISBN 978-0-531-06837-3 Subj: Cities, towns. Rhyming text.

Every season by Shelley Rotner and Anne Love Woodhull; photos by Shelley Rotner. Macmillan, 2007. ISBN 978-1-59643-136-2 Subj: Nature. Seasons.

Everybody works by Shelley Rotner and Ken Kreisler; photos by Shelley Rotner. Millbrook, 2003. ISBN 978-0-7613-1751-7 Subj: Activities – working. Careers.

Faces photos by Ken Kreisler. Macmillan, 1994. ISBN 978-0-02-777887-8 Subj: Anatomy – faces. Character traits – individuality.

Families by Shelley Rotner and Sheila M. Kelly; photos by Shelley Rotner. Holiday House, 2015. ISBN 978-082343053-6 Subj: Family life. Family life – same-sex parents. Family life – single-parent families. Family life – stepfamilies.

Feeling thankful by Shelley Rotner and Sheila M. Kelly; photos by Shelley Rotner. Millbrook, 2000. ISBN 978-0-7613-1918-4 Subj: Emotions.

Grow! raise! catch! how we get our food ill. by author. ill. with photos by the author. Holiday, 2016. ISBN 978-082343643-9 Subj: Careers – farmers. Careers – fishermen. Food. Gardens, gardening.

Hello autumn! photos by author. Holiday, 2017. ISBN 978-082343869-3 Subj: Seasons – fall.

Hello spring! photos by author. Holiday, 2017. ISBN 978-082343752-8 Subj: Seasons – spring.

Hold the anchovies! by Shelley Rotner and Julia Pemberton Hellums; photos by Shelley Rotner. Orchard, 1996. ISBN 978-0-531-08857-9 Subj: Activities – baking, cooking. Food.

Homer (deGroat, Diane)

I'm adopted! by Shelley Rotner and Sheila M. Kelly; photos by Shelley Rotner. Holiday House, 2011. ISBN 978-0-8234-2294-4 Subj: Adoption.

Lots of grandparents by Shelley Rotner and Sheila M. Kelly; photos by Shelley Rotner. Millbrook, 2001. ISBN 978-0-7613-2313-6 Subj: Emotions – love. Family life – grandparents.

Lots of moms by Shelley Rotner and Sheila M. Kelly; photos by Shelley Rotner. Dial, 1996. ISBN 978-0-8037-1892-0 Subj: Ethnic groups in the U.S. Family life – mothers.

Parts photos by author. Walker, 2001. ISBN 978-0-8027-8754-5 Subj: Concepts. Picture puzzles. Rhyming text.

Pick a pet by Shelley Rotner and Cheo García; photos by Shelley Rotner. Orchard, 1999. ISBN 978-0-531-33147-7 Subj: Animals. Pets.

Senses at the seashore photos by author. Lerner, 2006. ISBN 978-0-7613-2897-1 Subj: Sea & seashore – beaches. Senses.

Senses in the city photos by author. Lerner, 2008. ISBN 978-0-8225-7502-3 Subj: Cities, towns. Senses.

Shades of people by Shelley Rotner and Sheila M. Kelly; photos by Shelley Rotner. Holiday, 2009. ISBN 978-0-8234-2191-6 Subj: Anatomy – skin. Concepts – color. Ethnic groups in the U.S.

What can you do? by Shelley Rotner and Sheila M. Kelly; photos by Shelley Rotner. Millbrook, 2001. ISBN 978-0-7613-2119-4 Subj: Activities. Character traits – individuality. Self-concept.

What's love? by Shelley Rotner and Deborah Carlin; photos by Shelley Rotner. Roaring Brook, 2009. ISBN 978-1-59643-362-5 Subj: Emotions – love.

Wheels around photos by author. Houghton, 1995. ISBN 978-0-395-71815-5 Subj: Wheels.

Where does food come from? by Shelley Rotner and Gary Goss; photos by Shelley Rotner. Lerner, 2006. ISBN 978-0-7613-2935-0 Subj: Food.

Whose eye am I? ill. by author. Holiday, 2016. ISBN 978-082343558-6 Subj: Anatomy – eyes. Animals.

Rotter, Charles. *Seals* ill. with photos. Child's World, 2001. ISBN 978-1-56766-891-9 Subj: Animals – seals. Science.

Walruses ill. with photos. Child's World, 2001. ISBN 978-1-56766-894-0 Subj: Animals – walruses. Science.

Rouillard, Wendy. *Barnaby's bunny* ill. by author. Scholastic, 2003. ISBN 978-0-439-33307-8 Subj: Animals. Animals – bears. Eggs. Pets. School.

Rounds, Glen. *Cowboys* ill. by author. Holiday, 1991. ISBN 978-0-8234-0867-2 Subj: Cowboys, cowgirls. U.S. history – frontier & pioneer life.

Once we had a horse ill. by author. Holiday, 1996. ISBN 978-0-8234-1241-9 Subj: Animals – horses, ponies.

Sod houses on the Great Plains ill. by author. Holiday, 1995. ISBN 978-0-8234-1162-7 Subj: Family life. Homes, houses. U.S. history – frontier & pioneer life.

Rouss, Sylvia A. *The littlest frog* ill. by Holly Hannon. Pitspopany, 2001. ISBN 978-1-930143-12-8 Subj: Foreign lands – Egypt. Frogs & toads. Jewish culture.

The littlest pair ill. by Holly Hannon. Pitspopany, 2001. ISBN 978-1-930143-17-3 Subj: Character traits – cooperation. Insects – termites. Religion – Noah.

Sammy Spider's first day of school ill. by Katherine Janus Kahn. Lerner, 2009. ISBN 978-0-8225-8583-1 Subj: Jewish culture. School – first day. Spiders.

Sammy Spider's first Passover ill. by Katherine Janus Kahn. Kar-Ben, 1995. ISBN 978-0-929371-81-8 Subj: Holidays – Passover. Jewish culture. Religion. Spiders.

Sammy Spider's first Shabbat ill. by Katherine Janus Kahn. Kar-Ben, 1997. ISBN 978-1-58013-007-3 Subj: Jewish culture. Religion. Spiders.

Sammy Spider's first Shavuot ill. by Katherine Janus Kahn. Lerner, 2008. ISBN 978-0-8225-7224-4 Subj: Holidays – Shavuot. Jewish culture. Religion.

Sammy Spider's first Tu B'Shevat ill. by Katherine Janus Kahn. Kar-Ben, 2000. ISBN 978-1-58013-065-3 Subj: Holidays – Tu B'Shevat. Jewish culture. Spiders. Trees.

Sammy Spider's first Yom Kippur ill. by Katherine Janus Kahn. Kar-Ben, 2013. ISBN 978-0-7613-9195-1 Subj: Holidays – Yom Kippur. Jewish culture. Religion. Spiders.

Roussen, Jean. *Beautiful birds* ill. by Emmanuelle Walker. Flying Eye, 2015. ISBN 978-190926329-1 Subj: ABC books. Birds.

Rovetch, Lissa. *Ook the book* ill. by Shannon McNeill. Chronicle, 2001. ISBN 978-0-8118-2660-0 Subj: Humorous stories. Language. Poetry. Tongue twisters.

Rowand, Phyllis. *It is night* ill. by Laura Dronzek. HarperCollins/Greenwillow, 2014. ISBN 978-006225024-7 Subj: Animals. Bedtime. Toys.

Rowe, Jeannette. *Whose ears?* ill. by author. Little, 1998. ISBN 978-0-316-75932-8 Subj: Anatomy – ears. Animals. Format, unusual – toy & movable books.

Whose feet? ill. by author. Little, 1998. ISBN 978-0-316-75934-2 Subj: Anatomy – feet. Animals. Format, unusual – toy & movable books.

Whose nose? ill. by author. Little, 1998. ISBN 978-0-316-75933-5 Subj: Anatomy – noses. Animals. Format, unusual – toy & movable books.

Rowe, John A. *I want a hug* ill. by author. Minedition, 2007. ISBN 978-0-698-40064-1 Subj: Animals – porcupines. Emotions – loneliness. Hugging. Reptiles – alligators, crocodiles.

Moondog ill. by author. Minedition, 2005. ISBN 978-0-698-40031-3 Subj: Animals – dogs. Ecology. Moon. Space & space ships.

Rox, John. *I want a hippopotamus for Christmas* ill. by Bruce Whatley. HarperCollins, 2005. ISBN

978-0-06-058549-5 Subj: Animals – hippopotamuses. Holidays – Christmas. Songs.

Royer, Danielle. *All my stripes: a story for children with autism* (Rudolph, Shaina)

Rozen, Anna. *The merchant of noises* ill. by Francois Avril. Godine, 2006. ISBN 978-1-56792-321-6 Subj: Careers – salespeople. Character traits – cleverness. Noise, sounds.

Rozier, Lucy Margaret. *Jackrabbit McCabe and the electric telegraph* ill. by Leo Espinosa. Random House, 2015. ISBN 978-038537843-7 Subj: Concepts – speed. Contests. Tall tales.

Rubel, Nicole. *A cowboy named Ernestine* ill. by author. Dial, 2001. ISBN 978-0-8037-2152-4 Subj: Cowboys, cowgirls. Tall tales.

Ham and Pickles: first day of school ill. by author. Harcourt, 2006. ISBN 978-0-15-205039-9 Subj: Animals – hamsters. Family life – brothers & sisters. School – first day.

No more vegetables! ill. by author. Farrar, 2002. ISBN 978-0-374-36362-8 Subj: Family life – mothers. Food. Gardens, gardening. Plants.

Rubin, Adam. *Big bad bubble* ill. by Daniel Salmieri. Clarion, 2014. ISBN 978-054404549-1 Subj: Bubbles. Emotions – fear. Humorous stories. Monsters.

Dragons love tacos ill. by Daniel Salmieri. Dial, 2012. ISBN 978-0-8037-3680-1 Subj: Dragons. Food.

Dragons love tacos 2: the sequel ill. by Daniel Salmieri. Dial, 2017. ISBN 978-052542888-6 Subj: Dragons. Food.

Robo-Sauce ill. by Daniel Salmieri. Dial, 2015. ISBN 978-052542887-9 Subj: Format, unusual – toy & movable books. Magic. Robots.

Secret pizza party ill. by Daniel Salmieri. Dial, 2013. ISBN 978-0-8037-3947-5 Subj: Animals – raccoons. Crime. Food. Parties.

Those darn squirrels! ill. by Daniel Salmieri. Clarion, 2008. ISBN 978-0-547-00703-8 Subj: Animals – squirrels. Birds. Old age.

Those darn squirrels and the cat next door ill. by Daniel Salmieri. Clarion, 2011. ISBN 978-0-547-42922-9 Subj: Animals – cats. Animals – squirrels. Birds. Old age.

Those darn squirrels fly south ill. by Daniel Salmieri. Clarion, 2012. ISBN 978-0-547-67823-8 Subj: Activities – traveling. Animals – squirrels. Birds. Old age.

Rubin, C. M. *Eleanor, Ellatony, Ellencake, and me* ill. by Christopher Fowler. Gingham Dog, 2003.

ISBN 978-1-57768-412-1 Subj: Family life. Names. Rhyming text. Self-concept.

Rubin, Susan Goldman. *Jean Laffite: the pirate who saved America* ill. by Jeff Himmelman. Abrams, 2012. ISBN 978-0-8109-9733-2 Subj: Pirates. U.S. history.

Matisse dance for joy ill. by author. Chronicle, 2008. ISBN 978-0-8118-6288-2 Subj: Activities – dancing. Art. Format, unusual – board books.

The yellow house: Vincent van Gogh and Paul Gauguin side by side ill. by Joseph A. Smith. Abrams, 2001. ISBN 978-0-8109-4588-3 Subj: Art. Careers – artists. Foreign lands – France.

Rubinger, Ami. *Dog number 1 dog number 10* ill. by author. Abbeville, 2011. ISBN 978-0-7892-1066-1 Subj: Animals – dogs. Counting, numbers. Rhyming text.

I dream of an elephant ill. by author. Abbeville, 2010. ISBN 978-0-7892-1058-6 Subj: Animals – elephants. Concepts – color. Rhyming text.

Rubinstein, Gary. *The girl who never made mistakes* (Pett, Mark)

Ruddell, Deborah. *The popcorn astronauts: and other biteable rhymes* ill. by Joan Rankin. Simon & Schuster/Margaret K. McElderry, 2015. ISBN 978-144246555-8 Subj: Food. Poetry. Seasons.

Today at the Bluebird Cafe: a branchful of birds ill. by Joan Rankin. Simon & Schuster, 2007. ISBN 978-0-689-87153-5 Subj: Birds. Poetry.

A whiff of pine, a hint of skunk: a forest of poems ill. by Joan Rankin. Simon & Schuster, 2009. ISBN 978-1-4169-4211-5 Subj: Animals. Nature. Poetry.

Who said coo? ill. by Robin Luebs. Simon & Schuster, 2010. ISBN 978-1-4169-8510-5 Subj: Animals – pigs. Bedtime. Birds – owls. Birds – pigeons. Character traits – cooperation.

Rudge, Leila. *Gary* ill. by author. Candlewick, 2016. ISBN 978-076368954-4 Subj: Behavior – resourcefulness. Birds – pigeons. Character traits – being different. Cities, towns. Sports – racing.

A perfect place for Ted ill. by author. Candlewick, 2014. ISBN 978-076366781-8 Subj: Animals – dogs. Behavior – needing someone. Behavior – unnoticed, unseen. Character traits – individuality.

Rudolph, Shaina. *All my stripes: a story for children with autism* by Shaina Rudolph and Danielle Royer ill. by Jennifer Zivoin. Magination, 2015. ISBN 978-143381917-9 Subj: Animals – zebras. Disabilities – autism. Family life – mothers. Self-concept.

Rudy, Maggie. *City mouse, country mouse* ill. by author. Henry Holt, 2017. ISBN 978-162779616-3

Subj: Animals – mice. Character traits – compromising. Cities, towns. Country. Friendship.

I wish I had a pet ill. by author. Simon & Schuster/Beach Lane, 2014. ISBN 978-144245332-6 Subj: Animals – mice. Character traits – responsibility. Pets.

Rueda, Claudia. *Bunny slopes* ill. by author. Chronicle, 2016. ISBN 978-145214197-8 Subj: Animals – rabbits. Format, unusual – toy & movable books. Sports – skiing.

Huff and puff: can you blow down the houses of the three little pigs? ill. by author. Abrams, 2012. ISBN 978-1-4197-0170-2 Subj: Animals – pigs. Animals – wolves. Character traits – cleverness. Format, unusual – toy & movable books. Participation.

Is it big or is it little? ill. by author. Eerdmans, 2013. ISBN 978-0-8028-5423-0 Subj: Animals – cats. Animals – mice. Concepts – opposites. Concepts – size.

Let's play in the forest while the wolf is not around ill. by author. Scholastic, 2006. ISBN 978-0-439-82323-4 Subj: Animals. Animals – wolves. Games. Songs.

My little polar bear ill. by author. Scholastic, 2009. ISBN 978-0-545-14600-5 Subj: Animals – polar bears. Behavior – growing up. Emotions – love. Family life – mothers. Foreign lands – Arctic.

No ill. by author. Groundwood, 2010. ISBN 978-0-88899-991-7 Subj: Animals – bears. Bedtime. Hibernation.

Ruelle, Karen Gray. *Bark park* ill. by author. Peachtree, 2008. ISBN 978-1-56145-434-1 Subj: Animals – dogs. Parks.

Ruiz-Flores, Lupe. *Alicia's fruity drinks / Las aguas frescas de Alicia* ill. by Laura Lacámara. Arte Publico/Piñata, 2012. ISBN 978-1-55885-705-6 Subj: Ethnic groups in the U.S. – Mexican Americans. Family life – mothers. Foreign languages. Health & fitness. Illness – diabetes.

Rule, Rebecca. *The iciest, diciest, scariest sled ride ever!* ill. by Jennifer Thermes. Islandport, 2012. ISBN 978-1-934031-88-9 Subj: Seasons – winter. Sports – sledding.

Rumford, James. *Chee-lin: a giraffe's journey* ill. by author. Houghton, 2008. ISBN 978-0-618-71720-0 Subj: Activities – traveling. Animals – giraffes. Foreign lands – China.

Dog-of-the-Sea-Waves ill. by author. Houghton, 2004. ISBN 978-0-618-35611-9 Subj: Animals – seals. Character traits – kindness to animals. Family life – brothers. Foreign languages. Friendship. Hawaii.

Don't touch my hat! ill. by author. Random House, 2007. ISBN 978-0-375-93782-1 Subj: Careers – sheriffs. Clothing – hats. Superstition. U.S. history – frontier & pioneer life.

The Island-below-the-star ill. by author. Houghton, 1998. ISBN 978-0-395-85159-3 Subj: Activities – traveling. Boats, ships. Family life – brothers. Hawaii. Islands.

Max and the dumb flower picture (Alexander, Martha G.)

Nine animals and the well ill. by author. Houghton, 2003. ISBN 978-0-618-30915-3 Subj: Animals. Character traits – pride. Character traits – vanity. Counting, numbers. Folk & fairy tales. Foreign lands – India. Gifts. Parties.

Rain school ill. by author. Harcourt, 2010. ISBN 978-0-547-24307-8 Subj: Foreign lands – Chad. School. Weather – rain.

Sequoyah ill. by author. Houghton, 2004. ISBN 978-0-618-36947-8 Subj: ABC books. Foreign languages. Indians of North America – Cherokee.

Silent music: a story of Baghdad ill. by author. Roaring Brook, 2008. ISBN 978-1-59643-276-5 Subj: Activities – writing. Foreign lands – Iraq. War.

There's a monster in the alphabet ill. by author. Houghton, 2002. ISBN 978-0-618-22140-0 Subj: ABC books. Foreign lands – Greece. Foreign languages. Language.

Tiger and turtle ill. by author. Roaring Brook, 2010. ISBN 978-1-59643-416-5 Subj: Animals – tigers. Behavior – fighting, arguing. Friendship. Reptiles – turtles, tortoises.

Runton, Andy. *Owly and Wormy: bright lights and starry nights!* ill. by author. Simon & Schuster, 2012. ISBN 978-1-4169-5775-1 Subj: Animals – worms. Birds – owls. Emotions – fear. Friendship. Night. Wordless.

Owly and Wormy: friends all aflutter! ill. by author. Simon & Schuster, 2011. ISBN 978-1-4169-5774-4 Subj: Animals – worms. Birds. Friendship. Insects – butterflies, caterpillars. Metamorphosis. Wordless.

Rusackas, Francesca. *Daddy all day long* ill. by Priscilla Burris. HarperCollins, 2004. ISBN 978-0-06-050285-0 Subj: Animals – pigs. Bedtime. Counting, numbers. Emotions – love. Family life – fathers. Family life – sons.

I love you all day long ill. by Priscilla Burris. HarperCollins, 2003. ISBN 978-0-06-050277-5 Subj: Animals – pigs. Family life – mothers. School – first day.

Rusch, Elizabeth. *A day with no crayons* ill. by Chad Cameron. Rising Moon, 2007. ISBN 978-0-87358-910-9 Subj: Careers – artists. Concepts – color.

Ready, set . . . baby! ill. by Qin Leng. Houghton Mifflin Harcourt, 2017. ISBN 978-054447272-3 Subj: Family life – brothers & sisters. Family life – new sibling.

Russell, Joan Plummer. *Aero and Officer Mike* photos by Kris Turner Sinnenberg. Boyds Mills, 2001. ISBN 978-1-56397-931-6 Subj: Animals – dogs. Animals – service animals. Careers – police officers.

Russell, Natalie. *Brown Rabbit in the city* ill. by author. Penguin, 2010. ISBN 978-0-670-01234-3 Subj: Animals – rabbits. Cities, towns. Friendship.

Lost for words ill. by author. Peachtree, 2014. ISBN 978-156145739-7 Subj: Activities – drawing. Animals – tapirs. Character traits – individuality.

Moon rabbit ill. by author. Viking, 2009. ISBN 978-0-670-01170-4 Subj: Animals – rabbits. Cities, towns. Friendship.

Russell-Brown, Katheryn. *Little Melba and her big trombone* ill. by Frank Morrison. Lee & Low, 2014. ISBN 978-160060898-8 Subj: Ethnic groups in the U.S. – African Americans. Gender roles. Music. Musical instruments – trombones.

Russo, Brian. *Yoga Bunny* ill. by author. HarperCollins, 2016. ISBN 978-006242952-0 Subj: Animals – rabbits. Character traits – patience, impatience. Health & fitness – exercise.

Russo, Marisabina. *The big brown box* ill. by author. Greenwillow, 2000. ISBN 978-0-688-17097-4 Subj: Activities – playing. Behavior – sharing. Family life – brothers. Games. Imagination. Sibling rivalry.

The bunnies are not in their beds ill. by author. Random House, 2007. ISBN 978-0-375-93961-7 Subj: Animals – rabbits. Bedtime. Behavior – misbehavior.

Come back, Hannah ill. by author. Greenwillow, 2001. ISBN 978-0-688-17384-5 Subj: Babies, toddlers. Family life – mothers.

Grandpa Abe ill. by author. Greenwillow, 1996. ISBN 978-0-688-14098-4 Subj: Death. Emotions – grief. Family life – grandfathers.

Hannah's baby sister ill. by author. Greenwillow, 1998. ISBN 978-0-688-15832-3 Subj: Babies, toddlers. Family life – brothers & sisters. Family life – new sibling.

I will come back for you: a family in hiding during World War II ill. by author. Random House, 2011. ISBN 978-0-375-86695-1 Subj: Family life – grandmothers. Foreign lands – Italy. Holocaust. Jewish culture. War.

Little Bird takes a bath ill. by author. Random House, 2015. ISBN 978-038537014-1 Subj: Activities – bathing. Birds. Cities, towns. Weather – rain.

Mama talks too much ill. by author. Greenwillow, 1999. ISBN 978-0-688-16412-6 Subj: Cities, towns. Communities, neighborhoods. Family life – mothers. Shopping.

Peter is just a baby ill. by author. Eerdmans, 2012. ISBN 978-0-8028-5384-4 Subj: Animals – bears. Babies, toddlers. Family life – brothers & sisters. Foreign languages.

Sophie sleeps over ill. by author. Roaring Brook, 2014. ISBN 978-159643933-7 Subj: Animals – rabbits. Friendship. Sleepovers.

The trouble with baby ill. by author. Greenwillow, 2003. ISBN 978-0-06-008925-2 Subj: Emotions – envy, jealousy. Family life – brothers & sisters. Toys – dolls.

Under the table ill. by author. Greenwillow, 1997. ISBN 978-0-688-14603-0 Subj: Activities – drawing. Behavior – misbehavior. Family life.

A very big bunny ill. by author. Random House, 2010. ISBN 978-0-375-84463-8 Subj: Animals – rabbits. Character traits – being different. Concepts – size. Friendship. School. Self-concept.

When mama gets home ill. by author. Greenwillow, 1998. ISBN 978-0-688-14986-4 Subj: Family life. Family life – mothers.

Ruth, Greg. *Coming home* ill. by author. Feiwel & Friends, 2014. ISBN 978-125005547-7 Subj: Careers – military. Family life – mothers. War.

Ruurs, Margriet. *In my backyard* ill. by Ron Broda. Tundra, 2007. ISBN 978-0-88776-775-3 Subj: Animals. Nature.

My librarian is a camel: how books are brought to children around the world ill. with photos. Boyds Mills, 2005. ISBN 978-1-59078-093-0 Subj: Careers – librarians. Libraries. World.

My school in the rain forest: how children attend school around the world ill. with photos. Boyds Mills, 2009. ISBN 978-1-59078-601-7 Subj: School. World.

Wake up, Henry Rooster! ill. by Sean Cassidy. Fitzhenry & Whiteside, 2006. ISBN 978-1-55041-952-8 Subj: Birds – chickens, roosters.

When we go camping ill. by Andrew Kiss. Tundra, 2001. ISBN 978-0-88776-476-9 Subj: Camps, camping. Family life. Nature.

Ruzzier, Sergio. *Amandina* ill. by author. Roaring Brook, 2008. ISBN 978-1-59643-236-9 Subj: Animals – dogs. Character traits – perseverance. Character traits – shyness. Theater.

Bear and Bee ill. by author. Disney/Hyperion, 2013. ISBN 978-1-4231-5957-5 Subj: Animals –

bears. Behavior – sharing. Insects – bees. Prejudice.

Hey, Rabbit! ill. by author. Roaring Brook, 2010. ISBN 978-1-59643-502-5 Subj: Animals – rabbits. Friendship. Imagination.

A letter for Leo ill. by author. Clarion, 2014. ISBN 978-054422360-8 Subj: Animals – weasels. Birds. Careers – postal workers. Emotions – loneliness. Friendship. Letters, cards.

The little giant ill. by author. Geringer, 2004. ISBN 978-0-06-052952-9 Subj: Concepts – size. Dwarfs, midgets. Friendship. Giants.

The room of wonders ill. by author. Farrar, 2006. ISBN 978-0-374-36343-7 Subj: Animals – pack rats. Behavior – collecting things. Museums.

This is not a picture book ill. by author. Chronicle, 2016. ISBN 978-145212907-5 Subj: Birds – ducks. Books, reading.

Too busy ill. by author. Disney/Hyperion, 2014. ISBN 978-142315961-2 Subj: Animals – bears. Friendship. Insects – bees.

Two mice ill. by author. Clarion, 2015. ISBN 978-054430209-9 Subj: Animals – mice. Boats, ships.

Ryan, Candace. *Ewe and Aye* ill. by Stephanie Ruble. Hyperion, 2014. ISBN 978-142317591-9 Subj: Activities – flying. Animals – lemurs. Animals – sheep. Character traits – cooperation.

Ribbit rabbit ill. by Mike Lowery. Walker, 2011. ISBN 978-0-8027-2180-8 Subj: Animals – rabbits. Friendship. Frogs & toads.

Zoo zoom! ill. by Macky Pamintuan. Bloomsbury, 2015. ISBN 978-161963357-5 Subj: Animals. Rhyming text. Space & space ships. Zoos.

Ryan, Cheli Durán. *Hildilid's night* ill. by Arnold Lobel. Macmillan, 1986, ©1971. ISBN 978-0-02-777260-9 Subj: Caldecott award honor books. Night.

Ryan, Cheryl. *Red are the apples* (Harshman, Marc)

Ryan, Pam Muñoz. *Amelia and Eleanor go for a ride* ill. by Brian Selznick. Scholastic, 1999. ISBN 978-0-590-96075-5 Subj: Activities – flying. Airplanes, airports. U.S. history.

Armadillos sleep in dugouts: and other places animals live ill. by Diane deGroat. Hyperion, 1997. ISBN 978-0-7868-2222-5 Subj: Animals. Homes, houses. Rhyming text.

The crayon counting book by Pam Muñoz Ryan and Jerry Pallotta ill. by Frank Mazzola. Charlesbridge, 1996. ISBN 978-0-88106-955-6 Subj: Concepts – color. Counting, numbers. Rhyming text.

The flag we love ill. by Ralph Masiello. Charlesbridge, 1996. ISBN 978-0-88106-846-7 Subj: Poetry. U.S. history.

Hello, Ocean! ill. by Mark Astrella. Charlesbridge, 2001. ISBN 978-0-88106-987-7 Subj: Rhyming text. Sea & seashore – beaches. Senses.

Hello Ocean / Hola mar ill. by Mark Astrella. Charlesbridge, 2003. ISBN 978-1-57091-372-3 Subj: Foreign languages. Rhyming text. Sea & seashore – beaches. Senses.

How do you raise a raisin? ill. by Craig Brown. Charlesbridge, 2003. ISBN 978-0-613-82657-0 Subj: Food. Science.

Mice and beans ill. by Joe Cepeda. Scholastic, 2001. ISBN 978-0-439-18303-1 Subj: Animals – mice. Birthdays. Family life – grandmothers. Foreign lands – Mexico. Foreign languages.

Mud is cake ill. by David McPhail. Hyperion, 2002. ISBN 978-0-7868-0501-3 Subj: Activities – playing. Family life – brothers & sisters. Imagination. Rhyming text.

Nacho and Lolita ill. by Claudia Rueda. Scholastic, 2005. ISBN 978-0-439-26968-1 Subj: Birds – swallows. Folk & fairy tales. Missions.

There was no snow on Christmas Eve ill. by Dennis Nolan. Hyperion, 2005. ISBN 978-0-7868-5492-9 Subj: Holidays – Christmas. Religion – Nativity. Rhyming text. Weather.

Tony Baloney ill. by Edwin Fotheringham. Scholastic, 2011. ISBN 978-0-545-23135-0 Subj: Birds – penguins. Family life – brothers & sisters.

Tony Baloney: buddy trouble ill. by Edwin Fotheringham. Scholastic, 2014. ISBN 978-054548169-4 Subj: Birds – penguins. Character traits – responsibility. Family life – brothers & sisters.

When Marian sang: the true recital of Marian Anderson, the voice of a century ill. by Brian Selznick. Scholastic, 2002. ISBN 978-0-439-26967-4 Subj: Careers – singers. Ethnic groups in the U.S. – African Americans. Prejudice. U.S. history.

Ryder, Joanne. *Bear of my heart* ill. by Margie Moore. Simon & Schuster, 2007. ISBN 978-0-689-85947-2 Subj: Animals – bears. Emotions – love. Family life – mothers. Rhyming text.

Big bear ball ill. by Steven Kellogg. HarperCollins, 2002. ISBN 978-0-06-027956-1 Subj: Activities – dancing. Animals. Animals – bears. Rhyming text.

Chipmunk song ill. by Lynne Cherry. Dutton, 1987. ISBN 978-0-525-67191-6 Subj: Animals – chipmunks. Nature. Rhyming text.

Dance by the light of the moon ill. by Guy Francis. Hyperion, 2007. ISBN 978-0-7868-1820-4 Subj: Activities – dancing. Animals. Farms. Rhyming text. Songs.

Each living thing ill. by Ashley Wolff. Harcourt, 2000. ISBN 978-0-15-201898-6 Subj: Animals.

Character traits – kindness to animals. Rhyming text.

A fawn in the grass ill. by Keiko Narahashi. Henry Holt, 2001. ISBN 978-0-8050-6236-6 Subj: Animals. Rhyming text.

Jaguar in the rain forest ill. by Michael Rothman. Morrow, 1996. ISBN 978-0-688-12991-0 Subj: Animals – jaguars. Foreign lands – French Guiana. Jungle.

Little panda ill. with photos. Aladdin, 2001. ISBN 978-0-689-84310-5 Subj: Animals – babies. Animals – pandas. Zoos.

Mouse tail moon ill. by Maggie Kneen. Henry Holt, 2002. ISBN 978-0-8050-6404-9 Subj: Animals – mice. Poetry.

My father's hands ill. by Mark Graham. Morrow, 1994. ISBN 978-0-688-09190-3 Subj: Anatomy – hands. Family life – fathers. Gardens, gardening. Insects.

A pair of polar bears: twin cubs find a home at the San Diego Zoo ill. with photos. Simon & Schuster, 2006. ISBN 978-0-689-85871-0 Subj: Animals – polar bears. Multiple births – twins. Zoos.

Panda kindergarten ill. by Katherine Feng. HarperCollins, 2009. ISBN 978-0-06-057850-3 Subj: Animals – pandas. Foreign lands – China. School.

Rainbow wings ill. by Victor Lee. Morrow, 2000. ISBN 978-0-688-14129-5 Subj: Activities – flying. Science.

Step into the night ill. by Dennis Nolan. Four Winds, 1988. ISBN 978-0-02-777951-6 Subj: Nature. Night. Poetry.

Toad by the road: a year in the life of these amazing amphibians ill. by Maggie Kneen. Henry Holt, 2007. ISBN 978-0-8050-7354-6 Subj: Frogs & toads. Poetry. Seasons.

Tyrannosaurus time ill. by Michael Rothman. Morrow, 1999. ISBN 978-0-688-13683-3 Subj: Dinosaurs. Imagination.

The waterfall's gift ill. by Richard Jesse Watson. Sierra Club, 2001. ISBN 978-0-87156-579-2 Subj: Ecology. Forest, woods. Nature. Water.

Where butterflies grow ill. by Lynne Cherry. Dutton, 1989. ISBN 978-0-525-67284-5 Subj: Insects – butterflies, caterpillars. Metamorphosis. Nature. Science.

White bear, ice bear ill. by Michael Rothman. Morrow, 1989. ISBN 978-0-688-07175-2 Subj: Animals – polar bears. Foreign lands – Arctic. Nature.

Wild birds ill. by Susan Estelle Kwas. HarperCollins, 2003. ISBN 978-0-06-027739-0 Subj: Birds.

Won't you be my hugaroo? ill. by Melissa Sweet. Harcourt, 2006. ISBN 978-0-15-205778-7 Subj: Hugging. Rhyming text.

Rylant, Cynthia. *All I see* ill. by Peter Catalanotto. Watts, 1988. ISBN 978-0-531-08377-2 Subj: Activities – painting. Art. Friendship.

All in a day ill. by Nikki McClure. Abrams, 2009. ISBN 978-0-8109-8321-2 Subj: Day. Rhyming text.

Alligator boy ill. by Diane Goode. Harcourt, 2007. ISBN 978-0-15-206092-3 Subj: Reptiles – alligators, crocodiles. Rhyming text.

Appalachia: the voices of sleeping birds ill. by Barry Moser. Harcourt, 1991. ISBN 978-0-15-201605-0 Subj: Country.

Baby face: a book of love for baby ill. by Diane Goode. Simon & Schuster, 2008. ISBN 978-1-4169-4909-1 Subj: Babies, toddlers. Emotions – love. Poetry.

Bear day ill. by Jennifer Selby. Harcourt, 1998. ISBN 978-0-15-201090-4 Subj: Animals – bears. Rhyming text.

Best wishes photos by Carlo Ontal. R.C. Owen, 1992. ISBN 978-1-878450-20-3 Subj: Activities – writing. Careers – writers. Family life.

The bird house ill. by Barry Moser. Blue Sky, 1998. ISBN 978-0-590-47345-3 Subj: Birds. Homes, houses. Orphans.

Birthday presents ill. by Suçie Stevenson. Watts, 1987. ISBN 978-0-531-08305-5 Subj: Behavior – sharing. Birthdays. Family life. Gifts.

Bless us all: a child's yearbook of blessings ill. by author. Simon & Schuster, 1998. ISBN 978-0-689-82370-1 Subj: Days of the week, months of the year. Religion. Rhyming text.

The bookshop dog ill. by author. Blue Sky, 1996. ISBN 978-0-590-54331-6 Subj: Animals – dogs. Character traits – kindness to animals. Friendship. Weddings.

Brownie and Pearl get dolled up ill. by Brian Biggs. Simon & Schuster, 2010. ISBN 978-1-4169-8631-7 Subj: Activities – playing. Animals – cats. Character traits – appearance.

Brownie and Pearl go for a spin ill. by Brian Biggs. Simon & Schuster, 2012. ISBN 978-1-4169-8633-1 Subj: Animals – cats. Automobiles.

Brownie and Pearl grab a bite ill. by Brian Biggs. Simon & Schuster, 2011. ISBN 978-1-4169-8634-8 Subj: Animals – cats. Food.

Brownie and Pearl hit the hay ill. by Brian Biggs. Simon & Schuster, 2011. ISBN 978-1-4169-8635-5 Subj: Animals – cats. Bedtime.

Brownie and Pearl make good ill. by Brian Biggs. Simon & Schuster, 2012. ISBN 978-1-4169-8636-2 Subj: Animals – cats. Behavior – mistakcs.

Brownie and Pearl see the sights ill. by Brian Biggs. Simon & Schuster, 2010. ISBN 978-1-4169-8637-9 Subj: Animals – cats. Seasons – winter. Shopping.

Brownie and Pearl take a dip ill. by Brian Biggs. Simon & Schuster, 2011. ISBN 978-1-4169-8638-6 Subj: Animals – cats. Sports – swimming.

Bunny bungalow ill. by author. Harcourt, 1999. ISBN 978-0-15-201092-8 Subj: Animals – rabbits. Family life. Homes, houses. Rhyming text.

Christmas in the country ill. by Diane Goode. Blue Sky, 2002. ISBN 978-0-439-07334-9 Subj: Country. Family life – grandparents. Holidays – Christmas.

The cookie-store cat ill. by author. Blue Sky, 1999. ISBN 978-0-590-54329-3 Subj: Activities – baking, cooking. Animals – cats. Careers – bakers.

Creation ill. by author. Simon & Schuster/Beach Lane, 2016. ISBN 978-148147039-1 Subj: Creation. Religion.

Dog Heaven ill. by author. Blue Sky, 1995. ISBN 978-0-590-41701-3 Subj: Angels. Animals – dogs. Death.

Give me grace: a child's daybook of prayers ill. by author. Simon & Schuster, 1999. ISBN 978-0-689-82293-3 Subj: Days of the week, months of the year. Religion. Rhyming text.

The great Gracie chase ill. by Mark Teague. Blue Sky, 2001. ISBN 978-0-590-10041-0 Subj: Animals – dogs. Cumulative tales.

Henny, Penny, Lenny, Denny, and Mike ill. by Mike Austin. Simon & Schuster/Beach Lane, 2017. ISBN 978-148144523-8 Subj: Activities – playing. Aquariums. Fish. Pets.

Herbert's first Halloween ill. by Steven Henry. Chronicle, 2017. ISBN 978-145212533-6 Subj: Animals – pigs. Behavior – worrying. Character traits – confidence. Family life – fathers. Holidays – Halloween.

If you'll be my Valentine ill. by Fumi Kosaka. HarperCollins, 2005. ISBN 978-0-06-009270-2 Subj: Activities – making things. Character traits – kindness. Emotions – love. Holidays – Valentine's Day. Letters, cards. Rhyming text.

In November ill. by Jill Kastner. Harcourt, 2000. ISBN 978-0-15-201076-8 Subj: Activities. Seasons – fall.

Life ill. by Brendan Wenzel. Simon & Schuster/Beach Lane, 2017. ISBN 978-148145162-8 Subj: Animals. Nature.

Little penguins ill. by Christian Robinson. Random House, 2016. ISBN 978-055350770-6 Subj: Activities – playing. Birds – penguins. Seasons – winter. Weather – snow.

Little Whistle ill. by Tim Bowers. Harcourt, 2001. ISBN 978-0-15-201087-4 Subj: Animals – guinea pigs. Stores. Toys.

Little Whistle's Christmas ill. by Tim Bowers. Harcourt, 2003. ISBN 978-0-15-204590-6 Subj: Animals – guinea pigs. Holidays – Christmas. Letters, cards. Santa Claus. Stores. Toys.

Little Whistle's dinner party ill. by Tim Bowers. Harcourt, 2001. ISBN 978-0-15-201079-9 Subj: Animals – guinea pigs. Parties. Stores. Toys.

Little Whistle's medicine ill. by Tim Bowers. Harcourt, 2002. ISBN 978-0-15-201086-7 Subj: Animals – guinea pigs. Illness. Stores. Toys. Toys – soldiers.

Miss Maggie ill. by Thomas di Grazia. Dutton, 1983. ISBN 978-0-525-44048-2 Subj: Character traits – curiosity. Friendship.

Moonlight, the Halloween cat ill. by Melissa Sweet. HarperCollins, 2003. ISBN 978-0-06-029712-1 Subj: Animals – cats. Holidays – Halloween.

Mr. Griggs' work ill. by Julie Downing. Watts, 1989. ISBN 978-0-531-08369-7 Subj: Activities – working. Careers – postal workers. Character traits – pride. Post office.

Nativity ill. by author. Simon & Schuster/Beach Lane, 2017. ISBN 978-148147041-4 Subj: Religion – Nativity.

Night in the country ill. by Mary Szilagyi. Bradbury, 1986. ISBN 978-0-02-777210-4 Subj: Animals. Country. Night.

Puppies and piggies ill. by Ivan Bates. Harcourt, 2008. ISBN 978-0-15-202321-8 Subj: Animals. Bedtime. Emotions – love. Rhyming text.

The relatives came ill. by Stephen Gammell. Bradbury, 1985. ISBN 978-0-02-777220-3 Subj: Activities – traveling. Caldecott award honor books. Family life.

Scarecrow ill. by Lauren Stringer. Harcourt, 1998. ISBN 978-0-15-201084-3 Subj: Country. Farms. Scarecrows.

Silver packages: an Appalachian Christmas story ill. by Chris Soentpiet. Orchard, 1997. ISBN 978-0-531-33051-7 Subj: Accidents. Careers – doctors. Character traits – generosity. Holidays – Christmas. Illness. Trains. Transportation.

Snow ill. by Lauren Stringer. Harcourt, 2008. ISBN 978-0-15-205303-1 Subj: Nature. Weather – snow.

The stars will still shine ill. by Tiphanie Beeke. HarperCollins, 2005. ISBN 978-0-06-054640-3 Subj: Nature. Rhyming text. World.

This year's garden ill. by Mary Szilagyi. Bradbury, 1984. ISBN 978-0-02-777970-7 Subj: Gardens, gardening.

The ticky-tacky doll ill. by Harvey Stevenson. Harcourt, 2002. ISBN 978-0-15-201078-2 Subj: Family life – grandmothers. School.

Tulip sees America ill. by Lisa Desimini. Blue Sky, 1998. ISBN 978-0-590-84744-5 Subj: Activities – traveling. Animals – dogs. Automobiles.

We love you, Rosie! ill. by Linda Davick. Simon & Schuster/Beach Lane, 2017. ISBN 978-144246511-4 Subj: Animals – dogs. Concepts – opposites.

The whales ill. by author. Blue Sky, 1996. ISBN 978-0-590-58285-8 Subj: Animals – whales. Sea & seashore.

When I was young in the mountains ill. by Diane Goode. Dutton, 1982. ISBN 978-0-525-42525-0 Subj: Caldecott award honor books. Family life.

The wonderful happens ill. by Coco Dowley. Simon & Schuster, 2000. ISBN 978-0-689-83177-5 Subj: Emotions – happiness.

Rymond, Lynda Gene. *Oscar and the mooncats* ill. by Nicoletta Ceccoli. Houghton, 2007. ISBN 978-0-618-56316-6 Subj: Animals – cats. Imagination. Moon.

Saab, Julie. *Little Lola* ill. by David Gothard. Greenwillow, 2014. ISBN 978-006227457-1 Subj: Animals – cats. School.

Little Lola saves the show ill. by David Gothard. Greenwillow, 2016. ISBN 978-006227453-3 Subj: Activities – dancing. Animals – cats. Ballet.

Saaf, Donald. *The ABC animal orchestra* ill. by author. Holt/Christy Ottaviano, 2015. ISBN 978-080509072-7 Subj: ABC books. Animals. Musical instruments. Musical instruments – orchestras.

Sabuda, Robert. *Beauty and the beast: a pop-up book of the classic fairy tale* ill. by author. Simon & Schuster, 2010. ISBN 978-1-4169-6079-9 Subj: Animals. Character traits – appearance. Character traits – loyalty. Emotions – love. Folk & fairy tales. Format, unusual – toy & movable books. Magic.

The Blizzard's robe ill. by author. Atheneum, 1999. ISBN 978-0-689-31988-4 Subj: Activities – sewing. Foreign lands – Arctic. Mythical creatures. Northern lights. Sky.

The Christmas alphabet ill. by author. Orchard, 1994. ISBN 978-0-531-06857-1 Subj: ABC books.

Format, unusual – toy & movable books. Holidays – Christmas.

The dragon and the knight: a pop-up misadventure ill. by author. Simon & Schuster, 2014. ISBN 978-141696081-2 Subj: Dragons. Folk & fairy tales. Format, unusual – toy & movable books. Knights.

Encyclopedia prehistorica: dinosaurs by Robert Sabuda and Matthew Reinhart; ill. by authors. Candlewick, 2005. ISBN 978-0-7636-2228-2 Subj: Dinosaurs. Format, unusual – toy & movable books. Prehistory.

Encyclopedia prehistorica: mega-beasts by Robert Sabuda and Matthew Reinhart; ill. by authors. Candlewick, 2007. ISBN 978-0-7636-2230-5 Subj: Format, unusual – toy & movable books. Fossils. Prehistory. Science.

Encyclopedia prehistorica: sharks and other seamonsters by Robert Sabuda and Matthew Reinhart; ill. by authors. Candlewick, 2006. ISBN 978-0-7636-2229-9 Subj: Fish – sharks. Format, unusual – toy & movable books. Fossils. Prehistory. Science. Sea & seashore.

Fairies and magical creatures (Reinhart, Matthew)

Gods and heroes (Reinhart, Matthew)

The movable Mother Goose by Robert Sabuda and Mother Goose; ill. by Robert Sabuda. Simon & Schuster, 1999. ISBN 978-0-689-81192-0 Subj: Animals. Format, unusual – toy & movable books. Insects. Nursery rhymes.

Peter Pan: a pop-up adaptation of J.M. Barrie's original tale ill. by author. Simon & Schuster, 2008. ISBN 978-0-689-85364-7 Subj: Fairies. Folk & fairy tales. Format, unusual – toy & movable books. Imagination.

St. Valentine ill. by author. Macmillan, 1993. ISBN 978-0-689-31762-0 Subj: Holidays – Valentine's Day. Religion.

Tutankhamen's gift ill. by author. Atheneum, 1994. ISBN 978-0-689-31818-4 Subj: Foreign lands – Egypt. Gifts. Royalty – pharaohs.

Winter in white: a mini pop-up treat ill. by author. Simon & Schuster, 2007. ISBN 978-0-689-85365-4 Subj: Format, unusual – toy & movable books. Rhyming text. Seasons – winter.

Winter's tale: an original pop-up journey ill. by author. Simon & Schuster, 2005. ISBN 978-0-689-85363-0 Subj: Format, unusual – toy & movable books. Seasons – winter. Weather – snow.

Sacre, Antonio. *La Noche Buena: a Christmas story* ill. by Angela Dominguez. Abrams, 2010. ISBN 978-0-8109-8967-2 Subj: Ethnic groups in the U.S. – Cuban Americans. Family life – grandmothers. Holidays – Christmas.

A mango in the hand: a story told through proverbs ill. by Sebastià Serra. Abrams, 2011. ISBN 978-0-

8109-9734-9 Subj: Character traits – generosity. Family life. Foreign lands – Cuba. Foreign languages.

Sadler, Judy Ann. *Sandwiches for Duke* ill. by Lorna Bennett. Stoddart, 2001. ISBN 978-0-7737-3313-8 Subj: Animals – dogs. Clothing – hats. Farms. Pets. Weather – storms.

Sadler, Marilyn. *Alice from Dallas* ill. by Ard Hoyt. Abrams, 2014. ISBN 978-141970790-2 Subj: Cowboys, cowgirls. Friendship.

Alistair in outer space ill. by Roger Bollen. Prentice-Hall, 1984. ISBN 978-0-13-022369-2 Subj: Libraries. Space & space ships.

Alistair's time machine ill. by Roger Bollen. Prentice-Hall, 1986. ISBN 978-0-317-39621-8 Subj: Machines. School. Science. Space & space ships. Time.

Tony Baroni loves macaroni ill. by Lucie Crovatto. Blue Apple, 2014. ISBN 978-160905293-5 Subj: Family life – grandmothers. Food. Rhyming text.

Sadu, Itah. *Christopher changes his name* ill. by Roy Candy. Firefly, 1998. ISBN 978-1-55209-216-3 Subj: Ethnic groups in the U.S. – African Americans. Names.

Sáenz, Benjamin Alire. *A gift from papá Diego / Un regalo de papá Diego* ill. by Geronimo Garcia. Cinco Puntos, 1998. ISBN 978-0-938317-33-3 Subj: Birthdays. Ethnic groups in the U.S. – Mexican Americans. Family life – grandfathers. Foreign languages.

Grandma Fina and her wonderful umbrellas / La abuelita Fina y sus sombrillas maravillosas ill. by Geronimo Garcia. Cinco Puntos, 1999. ISBN 978-0-938317-46-3 Subj: Birthdays. Ethnic groups in the U.S. – Mexican Americans. Family life – grandmothers. Foreign languages. Umbrellas.

Safran, Sheri. *All kinds of families: a lift-the-flap book* ill. by Rachel Fuller. IPG/Trafalgar Square, 2011. ISBN 978-1-85707-756-8 Subj: Family life. Format, unusual – toy & movable books.

Sage, Alison. *Teddy bears cure a cold* (Gretz, Susanna)

Sage, Angie. *Molly and the birthday party* ill. by author. Peachtree, 2001. ISBN 978-1-56145-248-4 Subj: Birthdays. Format, unusual – toy & movable books. Gifts. Parties.

Monkeys in the jungle ill. by author. Dutton, 1989. ISBN 978-0-525-44466-4 Subj: Animals. Jungle. Rhyming text.

Sage, James. *Farmer Smart's fat cat* ill. by Russell Ayto. Chronicle, 2002. ISBN 978-0-8118-3502-2 Subj: Animals – cats. Animals – mice. Contests. Farms. Plants.

Mr. Beast: a monster fright in the night! ill. by Russell Ayto. Henry Holt, 2005. ISBN 978-0-8050-7730-8 Subj: Food. Monsters.

Sahagun, Bernardino de. *Spirit child: a story of the Nativity* ill. by Barbara Cooney. Morrow, 1984. ISBN 978-0-688-02610-3 Subj: Folk & fairy tales. Foreign lands – Mexico. Holidays – Christmas. Religion – Nativity.

St. George, Judith. *So you want to be an explorer?* ill. by David Small. Penguin, 2005. ISBN 978-0-399-23868-0 Subj: Careers – explorers.

So you want to be president? ill. by David Small. Philomel, 2000. ISBN 978-0-399-23407-1 Subj: Caldecott award books. U.S. history.

Zarafa: the giraffe who walked to the king ill. by Britt Spencer. Philomel, 2009. ISBN 978-0-399-25049-1 Subj: Animals – giraffes. Foreign lands – Egypt. Foreign lands – France. Royalty – kings.

Saint James, Synthia. *The gifts of Kwanzaa* ill. by author. Albert Whitman, 1994. ISBN 978-0-8075-2907-2 Subj: Ethnic groups in the U.S. – African Americans. Gifts. Holidays – Kwanzaa.

St. Pierre, Stephanie. *What the sea saw* ill. by Beverly Doyle. Peachtree, 2006. ISBN 978-1-56145-359-7 Subj: Animals. Ecology. Sea & seashore.

Sakai, Komako. *Emily's balloon* ill. by author. Chronicle, 2006. ISBN 978-0-8118-5219-7 Subj: Activities – ballooning. Friendship.

Mad at Mommy ill. by author. Scholastic, 2010. ISBN 978-0-545-21209-0 Subj: Animals – rabbits. Emotions – anger. Family life – mothers.

The snow day ill. by author. Scholastic, 2009. ISBN 978-0-545-01321-5 Subj: Animals – rabbits. Family life – mothers. Seasons – winter. Weather – snow.

Salariya, David. *All about me! a baby's guide to babies* photos by author. Random House, 2008. ISBN 978-0-375-84529-1 Subj: Babies, toddlers. Format, unusual – board books.

Salas, Laura Purdie. *A leaf can be . . .* ill. by Violeta Dabija. Millbrook, 2012. ISBN 978-0-7613-6203-6 Subj: Imagination. Rhyming text. Trees.

Water can be . . . ill. by Violeta Dabija. Millbrook, 2014. ISBN 978-146770591-2 Subj: Rhyming text. Water.

Salat, Cristina. *Peanut's emergency* ill. by Tammie Lyon. Whispering Coyote, 2002. ISBN 978-1-57091-440-9 Subj: Behavior – lost. Ethnic groups in the U.S. – African Americans. Problem solving. Safety.

Salerno, Steven. *Wild child* ill. by author. Abrams, 2015. ISBN 978-141971662-1 Subj: Babies, toddlers. Jungle.

Salley, Coleen. *Epossumondas* ill. by Janet Stevens. Harcourt, 2002. ISBN 978-0-15-216748-6 Subj: Animals. Animals – possums. Behavior – misunderstanding. Clowns, jesters. Family life. Folk & fairy tales. Humorous stories.

Epossumondas plays possum ill. by Janet Stevens. Harcourt, 2009. ISBN 978-0-15-206420-4 Subj: Animals – possums. Emotions – fear. Mythical creatures – werewolves. Swamps.

Epossumondas saves the day ill. by Janet Stevens. Harcourt, 2006. ISBN 978-0-15-205701-5 Subj: Animals. Animals – possums. Folk & fairy tales. Humorous stories.

Who's that tripping over my bridge? (Asbjørnsen, P. C)

Saltz, Gail. *Amazing you: getting smart about your private parts* ill. by Lynne Cravath. Button, 2005. ISBN 978-0-525-47389-3 Subj: Anatomy. Birth. Sex instruction.

Saltzberg, Barney. *All around the seasons* ill. by author. Candlewick, 2010. ISBN 978-0-7636-3694-4 Subj: Rhyming text. Seasons.

Andrew drew and drew ill. by author. Abrams, 2012. ISBN 978-1-4197-0377-5 Subj: Activities – drawing. Format, unusual – toy & movable books. Imagination.

Baby animal kisses ill. by author. Harcourt, 2001. ISBN 978-0-15-202635-6 Subj: Animals – babies. Format, unusual – toy & movable books. Kissing.

Chengdu could not, would not, fall asleep ill. by author. Disney/Hyperion, 2014. ISBN 978-142316721-1 Subj: Animals – pandas. Bedtime. Sleep.

Cornelius P. Mud, are you ready for baby? ill. by author. Candlewick, 2009. ISBN 978-0-7636-3596-1 Subj: Animals – pigs. Babies, toddlers. Family life – brothers.

Cornelius P. Mud, are you ready for bed? ill. by author. Candlewick, 2005. ISBN 978-0-7636-2399-9 Subj: Animals – pigs. Bedtime. Hugging.

Cornelius P. Mud, are you ready for school? ill. by author. Candlewick, 2007. ISBN 978-0-7636-2913-7 Subj: Animals – pigs. Kissing. School.

Crazy hair day ill. by author. Candlewick, 2003. ISBN 978-0-7636-1954-1 Subj: Animals – hamsters. Behavior – mistakes. Hair. School.

Hi, Blueberry! ill. by author. Harcourt, 2007. ISBN 978-0-15-205984-2 Subj: Animals – rabbits. Birthdays. Format, unusual – toy & movable books.

Hip, hip, hooray day! ill. by author. Harcourt, 2002. ISBN 978-0-15-202495-6 Subj: Animals – hippopotamuses. Animals – rabbits. Birthdays. Friendship. Sports – roller skating.

Hug this book! ill. by Fred Benaglia. Phaidon, 2016. ISBN 978-071487284-1 Subj: Books, reading. Rhyming text.

I love cats ill. by author. Candlewick, 2005. ISBN 978-0-7636-2588-7 Subj: Animals – cats. Rhyming text.

I love dogs ill. by author. Candlewick, 2005. ISBN 978-0-7636-2587-0 Subj: Animals – dogs. Format, unusual – board books. Rhyming text.

Inside this book (are three books) ill. by author. Abrams/Appleseed, 2015. ISBN 978-141971487-0 Subj: Activities – writing. Books, reading. Children as authors. Family life – brothers & sisters.

Kisses: a pull, touch, lift, squeak, and smooch book! ill. by author. Harcourt, 2010. ISBN 978-0-15-206534-8 Subj: Emotions – love. Format, unusual – toy & movable books. Kissing. Rhyming text.

The problem with pumpkins ill. by author. Harcourt, 2001. ISBN 978-0-15-202489-5 Subj: Animals – hippopotamuses. Animals – rabbits. Clothing – costumes. Friendship. Holidays – Halloween.

Soccer mom from outer space ill. by author. Crown, 2000. ISBN 978-0-517-80064-5 Subj: Clothing – costumes. Family life – mothers. Sports – soccer.

Star of the week ill. by author. Candlewick, 2006. ISBN 978-0-7636-2914-4 Subj: Character traits – being different. Character traits – individuality. School. Self-concept.

Tea with Grandpa ill. by author. Roaring Brook, 2014. ISBN 978-159643894-1 Subj: Computers. Family life – grandfathers. Parties. Rhyming text. Technology.

Salzano, Tammi. *I love you just the way you are* ill. by Ada Grey. Tiger Tales, 2014. ISBN 978-158925161-8 Subj: Emotions – love. Family life – mothers. Rhyming text.

One little blueberry ill. by Kat Whelan. Tiger Tales, 2011. ISBN 978-1-58925-859-4 Subj: Counting, numbers. Food. Insects.

One rainy day ill. by Hannah Wood. ME Media/Tiger Tales, 2011. ISBN 978-1-58925-860-0 Subj: Birds – ducks. Concepts – color. Format, unusual – board books. Weather – rain.

One windy day ill. by Hannah Wood. Tiger Tales, 2012. ISBN 978-1-58925-875-4 Subj: Animals – foxes. Careers – postal workers. Concepts – opposites. Weather – wind.

Sampson, Michael R. *Adam, Adam, what do you see?* (Martin, Bill, Jr.)

Caddie, the golf dog ill. by Floyd Cooper. Tommy Nelson, 1999. ISBN 978-0-8499-5823-6 Subj: Animals – dogs. Character traits – kindness to animals. Weather – storms.

I love our Earth (Martin, Bill, Jr.)

Kitty Cat, Kitty Cat, are you going to school? (Martin, Bill, Jr.)

Kitty Cat, Kitty Cat, are you going to sleep? (Martin, Bill, Jr.)

Kitty Cat, Kitty Cat, are you waking up? (Martin, Bill, Jr.)

Listen to our world (Martin, Bill, Jr.)

Little granny quarterback (Martin, Bill, Jr.)

The little squeegy bug (Martin, Bill, Jr.)

Rock it, sock it, number line (Martin, Bill, Jr.)

Spunky Little Monkey (Martin, Bill, Jr.)

Swish! (Martin, Bill, Jr.)

Trick or treat? (Martin, Bill, Jr.)

Samuels, Barbara. *Aloha, Dolores* ill. by author. DK, 2000. ISBN 978-0-7894-2508-9 Subj: Activities – vacationing. Animals – cats. Contests. Family life – sisters. Hawaii.

Dolores meets her match ill. by author. Farrar, 2007. ISBN 978-0-374-31758-4 Subj: Animals – cats. Family life – brothers & sisters. Humorous stories. Pets.

Duncan and Dolores ill. by author. Bradbury, 1986. ISBN 978-0-02-778210-3 Subj: Activities. Animals – cats. Family life – sisters. Humorous stories.

Faye and Dolores ill. by author. Bradbury, 1985. ISBN 978-0-02-778120-5 Subj: Emotions – love. Sibling rivalry.

Fred's beds ill. by author. Farrar, 2014. ISBN 978-037131813-0 Subj: Animals – dogs. Birthdays. Furniture – beds. Parties. Sleep.

Happy birthday, Dolores ill. by author. Watts, 1989. ISBN 978-0-531-08391-8 Subj: Birthdays. Parties.

Happy Valentine's Day, Dolores ill. by author. Farrar, 2006. ISBN 978-0-374-32844-3 Subj: Animals – cats. Family life – brothers & sisters. Holidays – Valentine's Day. Humorous stories.

The trucker ill. by author. Farrar, 2010. ISBN 978-0-374-37804-2 Subj: Animals – cats. Toys. Trucks.

What's so great about Cindy Snappleby? ill. by author. Watts, 1992. ISBN 978-0-531-08579-0 Subj: Family life – sisters. Frogs & toads. Sibling rivalry.

Samuels, Jenny. *A nose like a hose* ill. by author. Scholastic, 2003. ISBN 978-0-439-37303-6 Subj: Anatomy – noses. Animals – elephants.

SanAngelo, Ryan. *Eddie spaghetti* ill. by Jackie Urbanovic. Boyds Mills, 2002. ISBN 978-1-56397-974-3 Subj: Communities, neighborhoods. Crime. Food. Imagination. Problem solving.

Sánchez, Enrique O. *Saturday market* (Grossman, Patricia)

Sandall, Ellie. *Everybunny dance!* ill. by author. Simon & Schuster, 2017. ISBN 978-148149822-7 Subj: Activities – dancing. Animals – rabbits. Rhyming text.

Follow me! ill. by author. Simon & Schuster/Margaret K. McElderry, 2016. ISBN 978-148147147-3 Subj: Animals – lemurs. Reptiles – alligators, crocodiles. Rhyming text.

Sandburg, Carl. *From daybreak to good night* ill. by Lynn Smith-Ary. Annick, 2001. ISBN 978-1-55037-681-4 Subj: Farms. Poetry.

The Huckabuck family and how they raised popcorn in Nebraska and quit and came back ill. by David Small. The text was originally published in 1923 by Harcourt, Brace & Company in the book Rootabaga stories by Carl Sandburg. Farrar, 1999. ISBN 978-0-374-33511-3 Subj: Careers – farmers. Family life. Farms. Fire. Humorous stories.

Sanders, Nancy. *D is for drinking gourd: an African American alphabet* ill. by E. B. Lewis. Sleeping Bear, 2007. ISBN 978-1-58536-293-6 Subj: ABC books. Ethnic groups in the U.S. – African Americans. Slavery. U.S. history.

Sanders, Rob. *Cowboy Christmas* ill. by John Manders. Random House, 2012. ISBN 978-0-375-86985-3 Subj: Activities – baking, cooking. Cowboys, cowgirls. Holidays – Christmas. Santa Claus.

Outer space bedtime race ill. by Brian Won. Random House, 2015. ISBN 978-038538647-0 Subj: Aliens. Bedtime. Planets. Rhyming text.

Rodzilla ill. by Dan Santat. Simon & Schuster/Margaret K. McElderry, 2017. ISBN 978-148145779-8 Subj: Activities – playing. Babies, toddlers. Behavior – misbehavior. Humorous stories. Imagination.

Ruby Rose: off to school she goes ill. by Debbie Ridpath Ohi. HarperCollins, 2016. ISBN 978-006223569-5 Subj: Activities – dancing. School – first day.

Sanders, Scott R. *Crawdad Creek* ill. by Robert Hynes. National Geographic, 1999. ISBN 978-0-7922-7097-3 Subj: Ecology. Family life – brothers & sisters. Rivers.

A place called Freedom ill. by Thomas B. Allen. Atheneum, 1997. ISBN 978-0-689-80470-0 Subj: Character traits – freedom. Ethnic groups in the

U.S. – African Americans. Slavery. U.S. history – frontier & pioneer life.

Warm as wool ill. by Helen Cogancherry. Bradbury, 1992. ISBN 978-0-02-778139-7 Subj: Animals – sheep. Clothing. U.S. history – frontier & pioneer life.

Sanders-Wells, Linda. *Maggie's monkeys* ill. by Abby Carter. Candlewick, 2009. ISBN 978-0-7636-3326-4 Subj: Family life – brothers & sisters. Imagination.

Sanderson, Ruth. *A castle full of cats* ill. by author. Random House, 2015. ISBN 978-044981307-2 Subj: Animals – cats. Rhyming text. Royalty.

Cinderella ill. by reteller. Little, 2002. ISBN 978-0-316-77965-4 Subj: Family life – stepfamilies. Folk & fairy tales. Royalty – princes. Sibling rivalry.

The enchanted wood ill. by author. Little, 1991. ISBN 978-0-316-77018-7 Subj: Folk & fairy tales. Royalty – princes.

The golden mare, the firebird, and the magic ring ill. by reteller. Little, 2001. ISBN 978-0-316-76906-8 Subj: Animals – horses, ponies. Folk & fairy tales. Foreign lands – Russia. Magic. Royalty – tsars.

Goldilocks (The three bears)

Papa Gatto ill. by author. Little, 1995. ISBN 978-0-316-77073-6 Subj: Animals – cats. Behavior – greed. Folk & fairy tales. Foreign lands – Italy. Royalty – princes.

Sandman, Rochel. *Perfect porridge* ill. by Chana Zakashansky-Zverev. Hachai, 2000. ISBN 978-0-922613-92-2 Subj: Character traits – generosity. Food. Foreign lands – Uzbekistan. Immigrants, immigration. War.

Sandu, Anca. *Churchill's tale of tails* ill. by author. Peachtree, 2014. ISBN 978-156145738-0 Subj: Anatomy – tails. Animals – pigs. Friendship.

Sandved, Kjell Bloch. *The butterfly alphabet* ill. by author. Scholastic, 1996. ISBN 978-0-590-48003-1 Subj: ABC books. Insects – butterflies, caterpillars. Insects – moths.

Sanfield, Steve. *Snow* ill. by Jeanette Winter. Philomel, 1995. ISBN 978-0-399-22751-6 Subj: Rhyming text. Weather – snow.

Sanger, Amy Wilson. *First book of sushi* ill. by author. Tricycle, 2001. ISBN 978-1-58246-050-5 Subj: Activities – baking, cooking. Ethnic groups in the U.S. – Japanese Americans. Food. Format, unusual – board books. Rhyming text.

Sanna, Francesca. *The journey* ill. by author. Flying Eye, 2016. ISBN 978-190926399-4 Subj: Behavior – seeking better things. Character traits – bravery. Death. Emotions – fear. Immigrants, immigration. Refugees. War.

Sanromán, Susana. *Señora Reganoña* ill. by author. Douglas & McIntyre, 1998. ISBN 978-0-88899-320-5 Subj: Bedtime. Emotions – fear. Foreign lands – Mexico. Friendship. Night.

Sansone, Adele. *The little green goose* ill. by Alan Marks. NorthSouth, 1999. ISBN 978-0-7358-1072-3 Subj: Birds – geese. Character traits – being different. Dinosaurs. Family life.

San Souci, Daniel. *The Mighty Pigeon Club* ill. by author. Ten Speed, 2007. ISBN 978-1-58246-213-4 Subj: Birds – pigeons. Clubs, gangs.

The rabbit and the dragon king ill. by Eujin Kim Neilan. Boyds Mills, 2002. ISBN 978-1-56397-880-7 Subj: Animals – rabbits. Dragons. Folk & fairy tales. Foreign lands – Korea. Reptiles – turtles, tortoises. Sea & seashore.

San Souci, Robert D. *The birds of Killingworth* ill. by Kimberly Bulcken Root. Based on a poem by Henry Wadsworth Longfellow. Dial, 2002. ISBN 978-0-8037-2111-1 Subj: Birds. Ecology. Nature.

The boy and the ghost ill. by Brian Pinkney. Simon & Schuster, 1989. ISBN 978-0-671-67176-1 Subj: Ethnic groups in the U.S. – African Americans. Ghosts. Homes, houses.

Brave Margaret: an Irish adventure ill. by Sally Wern Comport. Simon & Schuster, 1999. ISBN 978-0-689-81072-5 Subj: Boats, ships. Folk & fairy tales. Foreign lands – Ireland. Gender roles. Giants. Sea & seashore.

Callie Ann and Mistah Bear ill. by Don Daily. Dial, 1999. ISBN 978-0-8037-1768-8 Subj: Character traits – cleverness. Ethnic groups in the U.S. – African Americans. Folk & fairy tales.

Cendrillon: a Caribbean Cinderella ill. by Brian Pinkney. Simon & Schuster, 1998. ISBN 978-0-689-80668-1 Subj: Folk & fairy tales. Foreign lands – Caribbean Islands.

Cinderella Skeleton ill. by David Catrow. Harcourt, 2000. ISBN 978-0-15-202003-3 Subj: Anatomy – skeletons. Family life – stepfamilies. Folk & fairy tales. Holidays – Halloween. Rhyming text. Royalty – princes. Sibling rivalry.

The enchanted tapestry ill. by László Gál. Dial, 1987. ISBN 978-0-8037-0306-3 Subj: Activities – weaving. Behavior – greed. Character traits – bravery. Family life – brothers. Folk & fairy tales. Foreign lands – China.

The faithful friend ill. by Brian Pinkney. Simon & Schuster, 1995. ISBN 978-0-02-786131-0 Subj: Caldecott award honor books. Folk & fairy tales. Foreign lands – Caribbean Islands. Foreign lands – Martinique.

Feathertop: based on the tale by Nathaniel Hawthorne ill. by Daniel San Souci. Doubleday, 1992. ISBN 978-0-385-42045-7 Subj: Behavior – trickery. Magic. Scarecrows. Witches.

The hired hand: an African-American folktale ill. by Jerry Pinkney. Dial, 1997. ISBN 978-0-8037-1297-3 Subj: Activities – working. Character traits – laziness. Ethnic groups in the U.S. – African Americans. Folk & fairy tales. Magic.

The Hobyahs ill. by Alexi Natchev. Doubleday, 1994. ISBN 978-0-385-30934-9 Subj: Animals – dogs. Folk & fairy tales. Foreign lands – England. Monsters. Rhyming text.

The house in the sky ill. by Wil Clay. Dial, 1996. ISBN 978-0-8037-1285-0 Subj: Folk & fairy tales. Foreign lands – Caribbean Islands. Homes, houses.

The legend of Scarface ill. by Daniel San Souci. Doubleday, 1987. ISBN 978-0-385-15874-9 Subj: Folk & fairy tales. Indians of North America – Blackfoot. Indians of North America – Siksika.

Little gold star ill. by Sergio Martinez. Morrow, 2000. ISBN 978-0-688-14781-5 Subj: Ethnic groups in the U.S. – Hispanic Americans. Family life – stepfamilies. Folk & fairy tales. Foreign languages. Religion. Sibling rivalry.

Little Pierre ill. by David Catrow. Harcourt, 2003. ISBN 978-0-15-202482-6 Subj: Character traits – cleverness. Concepts – size. Family life – brothers. Folk & fairy tales. Little people. Mythical creatures – ogres. Swamps.

Nicholas Pipe ill. by David Shannon. Dial, 1997. ISBN 978-0-8037-1765-7 Subj: Careers – fishermen. Emotions – love. Folk & fairy tales. Mythical creatures – mermaids, mermen. Sea & seashore.

Pedro and the monkey ill. by Michael Hays. Morrow, 1996. ISBN 978-0-688-13743-4 Subj: Animals – monkeys. Folk & fairy tales. Foreign lands – Philippines. Monsters.

Peter and the blue witch baby ill. by Alexi Natchev. Doubleday, 2000. ISBN 978-0-385-32269-0 Subj: Emotions – envy, jealousy. Folk & fairy tales. Foreign lands – Russia. Giants. Royalty – tsars. Sun. Witches.

The red heels ill. by Gary Kelley. Dial, 1995. ISBN 978-0-8037-1134-1 Subj: Careers – shoemakers. Folk & fairy tales. Magic. Witches.

Robin Hood and the golden arrow ill. by E. B. Lewis. Scholastic, 2010. ISBN 978-0-439-62538-8 Subj: Folk & fairy tales. Foreign lands – England. Sports – archery.

The samurai's daughter ill. by Stephen T. Johnson. Dial, 1992. ISBN 978-0-8037-1136-5 Subj: Character traits – bravery. Family life – fathers. Folk & fairy tales. Foreign lands – Japan.

The secret of the stones ill. by James Ransome. Fogelman, 2000. ISBN 978-0-8037-1640-7 Subj: Ethnic groups in the U.S. – African Americans. Folk & fairy tales. Foreign lands – Africa. Magic. Orphans.

The silver charm ill. by Yoriko Ito. Doubleday, 2002. ISBN 978-0-385-32159-4 Subj: Animals – dogs. Animals – foxes. Animals – mice. Folk & fairy tales. Foreign lands – Japan. Magic. Mythical creatures – ogres. Pets.

Six foolish fishermen ill. by Doug Kennedy. Hyperion, 2000. ISBN 978-0-7868-2335-2 Subj: Character traits – foolishness. Sports – fishing.

The snow wife ill. by Stephen T. Johnson. Dial, 1993. ISBN 978-0-8037-1410-6 Subj: Behavior – secrets. Folk & fairy tales. Foreign lands – Japan.

Song of Sedna ill. by Daniel San Souci. Doubleday, 1981. ISBN 978-0-385-15866-4 Subj: Eskimos. Folk & fairy tales.

Sootface: an Ojibwa Cinderella story ill. by Daniel San Souci. Delacorte, 1994. ISBN 978-0-385-31202-8 Subj: Character traits – meanness. Family life – sisters. Folk & fairy tales. Indians of North America – Ojibwa.

Sukey and the mermaid ill. by Brian Pinkney. Four Winds, 1992. ISBN 978-0-02-778141-0 Subj: Ethnic groups in the U.S. – African Americans. Folk & fairy tales. Mythical creatures – mermaids, mermen.

The talking eggs ill. by Jerry Pinkney. Dial, 1989. ISBN 978-0-8037-0619-4 Subj: Caldecott award honor books. Character traits – kindness. Eggs. Folk & fairy tales. Magic.

Two bear cubs: a Miwok legend from California's Yosemite Valley ill. by Daniel San Souci. Yosemite Assoc., 1997. ISBN 978-0-939666-87-4 Subj: Animals. Animals – bears. Animals – worms. Folk & fairy tales. Indians of North America – Miwok.

A weave of words ill. by Raúl Colón. Orchard, 1997. ISBN 978-0-531-33053-1 Subj: Activities – weaving. Folk & fairy tales. Foreign lands – Armenia. Gender roles. Royalty – kings. Royalty – queens.

The white cat ill. by Gennady Spirin. Watts, 1990. ISBN 978-0-531-08409-0 Subj: Animals – cats. Folk & fairy tales. Magic. Royalty.

Santa Claus is coming to town ill. by Laura Blankenmerer. HarperCollins, 2001. ISBN 978-0-694-01559-7 Subj: Format, unusual – toy & movable books. Holidays – Christmas. Music. Santa Claus. Songs.

Santangelo, Colony Elliott. *Brother Wolf of Gubbio* ill. by author. Handprint, 2000. ISBN 978-1-929766-07-9 Subj: Animals – wolves. Cities, towns. Religion.

Santat, Dan. *The adventures of Beekle: the unimaginary friend* ill. by author. Little, Brown, 2014. ISBN 978-031619998-8 Subj: Caldecott award books. Friendship. Imagination – imaginary friends.

After the fall (how Humpty Dumpty got back up again) ill. by author. Roaring Brook, 2017. ISBN 978-162672682-6 Subj: Character traits – perseverance. Eggs. Emotions – fear. Emotions – sadness. Nursery rhymes.

Are we there yet? ill. by author. Little, Brown, 2016. ISBN 978-031619999-5 Subj: Activities – traveling. Behavior – boredom. Imagination.

Santiago, Esmeralda. *A doll for Navidades* ill. by Enrique O. Sánchez. Scholastic, 2005. ISBN 978-0-439-55398-8 Subj: Family life. Foreign lands – Puerto Rico. Gifts. Holidays – Christmas. Toys – dolls.

Santore, Charles. *A stowaway on Noah's Ark* ill. by author. Random House, 2000. ISBN 978-0-679-98820-5 Subj: Animals. Animals – mice. Behavior – hiding. Boats, ships. Religion – Noah.

Three hungry pigs and the wolf who came to dinner ill. by author. Random House, 2005. ISBN 978-0-375-92946-5 Subj: Animals – pigs. Animals – wolves. Food.

Santoro, Lucio. *Wild oceans: a pop-up book with revolutionary technology* by Lucio Santoro and Meera Santoro; ill. by Lucio Santoro. Simon & Schuster, 2010. ISBN 978-1-4169-8467-2 Subj: Format, unusual – toy & movable books. Sea & seashore.

Santoro, Meera. *Wild oceans: a pop-up book with revolutionary technology* (Santoro, Lucio)

Santoro, Scott. *Farm-fresh cats* ill. by author. HarperCollins, 2006. ISBN 978-0-06-078179-8 Subj: Animals – cats. Farms.

Isaac the Ice Cream Truck ill. by author. Henry Holt, 1999. ISBN 978-0-8050-5296-1 Subj: Careers – firefighters. Trucks.

Which way to witch school? ill. by author. HarperCollins, 2010. ISBN 978-0-06-078181-1 Subj: Rhyming text. School. Witches.

Santos, Rosa. *Play date* ill. by Gioia Fiammenghi. Kane, 2001. ISBN 978-1-57565-105-7 Subj: Days of the week, months of the year. Family life.

Santucci, Barbara. *Anna's corn* ill. by Lloyd Bloom. Eerdmans, 2002. ISBN 978-0-8028-5119-2 Subj: Death. Emotions – grief. Family life – grandfathers. Memories, memory. Plants. Seeds.

Loon summer ill. by Andrea Shine. Eerdmans, 2001. ISBN 978-0-8028-5182-6 Subj: Birds – loons. Divorce. Family life – daughters. Family life – fathers.

Sarah, Linda. *Big friends* ill. by Benji Davies. Henry Holt, 2016. ISBN 978-162779330-8 Subj: Activities – playing. Friendship. Imagination.

Sarcone-Roach, Julia. *The bear ate your sandwich* ill. by author. Knopf, 2015. ISBN 978-037585860-4 Subj: Animals – bears. Animals – dogs. Cities, towns. Food.

The secret plan ill. by author. Knopf, 2009. ISBN 978-0-375-85858-1 Subj: Activities – playing. Animals – cats. Animals – elephants. Bedtime.

Subway story ill. by author. Random House, 2011. ISBN 978-0-375-85859-8 Subj: Sea & seashore. Trains.

Sartell, Debra. *Time for bed, Baby Ted* ill. by Kay Chorao. Holiday House, 2010. ISBN 978-0-8234-1968-5 Subj: Babies, toddlers. Bedtime. Rhyming text.

Sassi, Laura. *Goodnight, Ark* ill. by Jane Chapman. Zondervan, 2014. ISBN 978-031073784-1 Subj: Animals. Bedtime. Religion – Noah. Rhyming text.

Sasso, Sandy Eisenberg. *Butterflies under our hats* ill. by Joan Keller Rothenberg. Paraclete, 2006. ISBN 978-1-55725-474-0 Subj: Character traits – hopefulness. Character traits – luck. Foreign lands – Poland. Jewish culture.

Cain and Abel: finding the fruits of peace ill. by Joan Keller Rothenberg. Jewish Lights, 2001. ISBN 978-1-58023-123-7 Subj: Emotions – anger. Family life – brothers. Religion.

For heaven's sake ill. by Kathryn Kunz Finney. Jewish Lights, 1999. ISBN 978-1-58023-054-4 Subj: Family life – grandmothers. Friendship. Religion.

God said amen ill. by Avi Katz. Jewish Lights, 2000. ISBN 978-1-58023-080-3 Subj: Behavior – sharing. Character traits – pride. Character traits – vanity.

God's paintbrush ill. by Annette C. Compton. Jewish Lights, 1992. ISBN 978-1-879045-22-4 Subj: Religion.

In God's name ill. by Phoebe Stone. Jewish Lights, 1994. ISBN 978-1-879045-26-2 Subj: Names. Religion.

Naamah, Noah's wife ill. by Bethanne Andersen. Skylight Paths, 2002. ISBN 978-1-893361-56-0 Subj: Family life. Format, unusual – board books. Plants. Religion – Noah. Seeds.

Satoshi, Kako. *Little Daruma and little Tengu* ill. by author. Tuttle, 2002. ISBN 978-0-8048-3347-9 Subj: Emotions – envy, jealousy. Foreign lands – Japan. Friendship.

Sattler, Jennifer. *Chick 'n' Pug* ill. by author. Bloomsbury, 2010. ISBN 978-1-59990-534-1 Subj: Animals – dogs. Birds – chickens, roosters.

Chick 'n' Pug: the love pug ill. by author. Bloomsbury, 2015. ISBN 978-161963672-9 Subj: Animals – dogs. Birds – chickens, roosters. Humorous stories.

A Chick 'n' Pug Christmas ill. by author. Bloomsbury, 2014. ISBN 978-159990602-7 Subj: Animals – dogs. Birds – chickens, roosters. Holidays – Christmas.

Chick 'n' Pug meet the Dude ill. by author. Bloomsbury, 2013. ISBN 978-1-59990-600-3 Subj: Animals – dogs. Birds – chickens, roosters.

Frankie the blankie ill. by author. Bloomsbury, 2016. ISBN 978-161963675-0 Subj: Animals – gorillas. Behavior – growing up.

Pig kahuna ill. by author. Bloomsbury, 2011. ISBN 978-1-59990-635-5 Subj: Animals – pigs. Emotions – fear. Sports – surfing.

Pig kahuna: who's that pig? ill. by author. Bloomsbury, 2015. ISBN 978-161963632-3 Subj: Animals – pigs. Character traits – shyness. Sea & seashore – beaches.

Pig kahuna pirates! ill. by author. Bloomsbury, 2014. ISBN 978-161963200-4 Subj: Activities – playing. Animals – pigs. Behavior – bad day, bad mood. Family life – brothers. Pirates. Sea & seashore – beaches.

Sylvie ill. by author. Random House, 2009. ISBN 978-0-375-85708-9 Subj: Birds – flamingos. Food.

Uh-oh, Dodo! ill. by author. Boyds Mills, 2013. ISBN 978-1-59078-929-2 Subj: Activities – walking. Behavior – misbehavior. Birds – dodos. Family life – mothers.

Saudo, Coralie. *My dad at the zoo* ill. by Kris Di-Giacomo. Enchanted Lion, 2016. ISBN 978-159270190-2 Subj: Family life – fathers. Zoos.

My dad is big and strong, but . . .: a bedtime story ill. by Kris DiGiacomo. Enchanted Lion, 2012. ISBN 978-1-59270-122-3 Subj: Bedtime. Family life – fathers.

Sauer, Tammi. *Bawk and roll* ill. by Dan Santat. Sterling, 2012. ISBN 978-1-4027-7837-7 Subj: Activities – dancing. Birds – chickens, roosters. Music.

Chicken dance ill. by Dan Santat. Sterling, 2009. ISBN 978-1-4027-5366-4 Subj: Activities – dancing. Birds – chickens, roosters. Contests. Humorous stories.

Cowboy camp ill. by Mike Reed. Sterling, 2005. ISBN 978-1-4027-2224-0 Subj: Behavior – bullying, teasing. Camps, camping. Character traits – individuality. Cowboys, cowgirls.

Ginny Louise and the school showdown ill. by Lynn Munsinger. Disney/Hyperion, 2015. ISBN 978-142316853-9 Subj: Animals. Animals – hedgehogs. Behavior – bullying, teasing. Character traits – kindness. Character traits – meanness. Character traits – optimism. School.

I love cake! : starring Rabbit, Porcupine, and Moose ill. by Angie Rozelaar. HarperCollins/Katherine Tegen, 2016. ISBN 978-006227894-4 Subj: Animals. Behavior – greed. Behavior – mistakes. Birthdays. Food. Friendship. Parties.

Mary had a little glam ill. by Vanessa Brantley-Newton. Sterling, 2016. ISBN 978-145491393-1 Subj: Character traits – appearance. Character traits – confidence. Clothing. Ethnic groups in the U.S. – African Americans.

Me want pet! ill. by Bob Shea. Simon & Schuster, 2012. ISBN 978-1-4424-0810-4 Subj: Animals. Cave dwellers. Pets.

Mostly monsterly ill. by Scott Magoon. Simon & Schuster, 2010. ISBN 978-1-4169-6110-9 Subj: Character traits – being different. Character traits – individuality. Monsters. School.

Mr. Duck means business ill. by Jeff Mack. Simon & Schuster, 2011. ISBN 978-1-4169-8522-8 Subj: Animals. Birds – ducks. Character traits – compromising.

Nugget and Fang: friends forever—or snack time? ill. by Michael H. Slack. Harcourt, 2013. ISBN 978-0-547-85285-0 Subj: Behavior – resourcefulness. Character traits – helpfulness. Fish. Fish – sharks. Prejudice.

Oh, nuts! ill. by Dan Krall. Bloomsbury, 2012. ISBN 978-1-59990-466-5 Subj: Animals – chipmunks. Character traits – conceit. Zoos.

Princess in training ill. by Joe Berger. Harcourt, 2012. ISBN 978-0-15-206599-7 Subj: Camps, camping. Character traits – individuality. Royalty – princesses.

Your alien ill. by Goro Fujita. Sterling, 2015. ISBN 978-145491129-6 Subj: Aliens. Family life. Friendship.

Your alien returns ill. by Goro Fujita. Sterling, 2016. ISBN 978-145491130-2 Subj: Aliens. Friendship. Space & space ships.

Saul, Carol P. *Barn cat* ill. by Mary Azarian. Little, 1998. ISBN 978-0-316-76113-0 Subj: Animals – cats. Counting, numbers. Rhyming text.

Saunders, Dave. *So slow!* by Dave Saunders and Julie Saunders; ill. by Dave Saunders. Marshall Cavendish, 2001. ISBN 978-0-7614-5080-1 Subj: Animals. Animals – snails. Character traits – perseverance. Concepts – speed.

Saunders, Julie. *So slow!* (Saunders, Dave)

Saunders, Karen. *Baby Badger's wonderful night* ill. by Dubravka Kolanovic. Egmont, 2011. ISBN 978-1-60684-172-3 Subj: Animals – badgers. Emotions – fear. Family life – fathers. Night.

Sava, Donna Lynn. *Teddy bear dreams* ill. by Scott Sava. Ipicturebooks, 2002. ISBN 978-1-59019-128-6 Subj: Careers. Dreams. Imagination. Rhyming text. Toys – bears.

Savadier, Elivia. *No haircut today!* ill. by author. Macmillan, 2005. ISBN 978-1-59643-046-4 Subj: Emotions – fear. Hair.

Time to get dressed! ill. by author. Macmillan, 2006. ISBN 978-1-59643-161-4 Subj: Babies, toddlers. Character traits – individuality. Clothing. Family life – fathers.

Will Sheila share? ill. by author. Roaring Brook, 2008. ISBN 978-1-59643-289-5 Subj: Behavior – sharing. Family life – grandmothers.

Savage, Stephen. *Little Plane learns to write* ill. by author. Roaring Brook, 2017. ISBN 978-162672436-5 Subj: Activities – writing. Airplanes, airports. Character traits – persistence.

Little Tug ill. by author. Roaring Brook, 2012. ISBN 978-1-59643-648-0 Subj: Boats, ships. Character traits – helpfulness.

The mixed-up truck ill. by author. Roaring Brook/Neal Porter, 2016. ISBN 978-162672153-1 Subj: Behavior – mistakes. Character traits – perseverance. Humorous stories. Trucks.

Seven orange pumpkins ill. by author. Dial, 2015. ISBN 978-080374138-6 Subj: Counting, numbers. Format, unusual – board books. Holidays – Halloween.

Supertruck ill. by author. Roaring Brook/Neal Porter, 2015. ISBN 978-159643821-7 Subj: Careers – sanitation workers. Machines. Trucks. Weather – snow.

Ten orange pumpkins ill. by author. Dial, 2013. ISBN 978-0-8037-3938-3 Subj: Counting, numbers. Holidays – Halloween. Rhyming text.

Where's Walrus? ill. by author. Scholastic, 2011. ISBN 978-0-439-70049-8 Subj: Animals – walruses. Behavior – running away. Careers – zookeepers. Clothing – hats. Disguises. Wordless. Zoos.

Where's Walrus? and Penguin? ill. by author. Scholastic, 2015. ISBN 978-054540295-8 Subj: Animals – walruses. Behavior – running away. Birds – penguins. Careers – zookeepers. Wordless. Zoos.

Savitz, Harriet May. *The story blanket* (Wolff, Ferida)

Sawyer, Ruth. *Journey cake, ho!* ill. by Robert McCloskey. Viking, 1953. ISBN 978-0-670-40943-3

Subj: Caldecott award honor books. Cumulative tales. Folk & fairy tales. Poverty.

The remarkable Christmas of the cobbler's sons ill. by Barbara Cooney. Viking, 1994. ISBN 978-0-670-84922-2 Subj: Behavior – sharing. Folk & fairy tales. Foreign lands – Tyrol. Holidays – Christmas. Royalty – kings.

Say, Allen. *Allison* ill. by author. Houghton, 1997. ISBN 978-0-395-85895-0 Subj: Adoption. Animals – cats. Behavior – misbehavior. Emotions. Family life.

The bicycle man ill. by author. Houghton, 1982. ISBN 978-0-395-32254-3 Subj: Foreign lands – Japan. Sports – bicycling.

The boy in the garden ill. by author. Harcourt, 2010. ISBN 978-0-547-21410-8 Subj: Birds – cranes. Character traits – kindness. Foreign lands – Japan. Gardens, gardening.

Emma's rug ill. by author. Houghton, 1996. ISBN 978-0-395-74294-5 Subj: Activities – drawing. Ethnic groups in the U.S. – Japanese Americans. Imagination.

Erika-San ill. by author. Houghton, 2009. ISBN 978-0-618-88933-4 Subj: Foreign lands – Japan.

The favorite daughter ill. by author. Scholastic, 2013. ISBN 978-0-545-17662-0 Subj: Character traits – being different. Ethnic groups in the U.S. – Japanese Americans. Family life – daughters. Prejudice. School.

Grandfather's journey ill. by author. Houghton, 1993. ISBN 978-0-395-57035-7 Subj: Activities – traveling. Caldecott award books. Ethnic groups in the U.S. – Japanese Americans. Family life. Family life – grandfathers. Foreign lands – Japan.

Kamishibai man ill. by author. Houghton, 2005. ISBN 978-0-618-47954-2 Subj: Activities – storytelling. Foreign lands – Japan. Theater.

Once under the cherry blossom tree: an old Japanese tale ill. by author. HarperCollins, 1974. ISBN 978-0-06-025217-5 Subj: Folk & fairy tales. Foreign lands – Japan.

A river dream ill. by author. Houghton, 1988. ISBN 978-0-395-48294-0 Subj: Dreams. Family life. Illness. Sports – fishing.

Tea with milk ill. by author. Houghton, 1999. ISBN 978-0-395-90495-4 Subj: Ethnic groups in the U.S. – Japanese Americans. Foreign lands – Japan.

Tree of cranes ill. by author. Houghton, 1991. ISBN 978-0-395-52024-6 Subj: Family life – mothers. Foreign lands – Japan. Holidays – Christmas.

Sayer, Ann Marie Mulhearn. *Caps for sale and the mindful monkeys* (Slobodkina, Esphyr)

More caps for sale: another tale of mischievous monkeys (Slobodkina, Esphyr)

Sayles, Elizabeth. *The goldfish yawned* ill. by author. Henry Holt, 2005. ISBN 978-0-8050-7624-0 Subj: Bedtime. Dreams. Rhyming text.

Sayre, April Pulley. *Army ant parade* ill. by Rick Chrustowski. Henry Holt, 2002. ISBN 978-0-8050-6353-0 Subj: Foreign lands – Panama. Forest, woods. Insects – ants. Science.

Best in snow ill. by author. ill. with photos by the author. Simon & Schuster/Beach Lane, 2016. ISBN 978-148145916-7 Subj: Nature. Seasons – winter. Weather – snow.

The bumblebee queen ill. by Patricia J. Wynne. Charlesbridge, 2005. ISBN 978-1-57091-362-4 Subj: Insects – bees.

Dig, wait, listen ill. by Barbara Bash. Greenwillow, 2001. ISBN 978-0-688-16615-1 Subj: Animals. Desert. Frogs & toads. Science.

Eat like a bear ill. by Steve Jenkins. Henry Holt, 2013. ISBN 978-0-8050-9039-0 Subj: Animals – bears. Days of the week, months of the year. Hibernation. Nature. Seasons.

Full of fall. Simon & Schuster/Beach Lane, 2017. ISBN 978-148147984-4 Subj: Rhyming text. Seasons – fall.

Go, go, grapes! a fruit chant ill. by author. Simon & Schuster, 2012. ISBN 978-1-4424-3390-8 Subj: Food. Rhyming text.

Here come the humpbacks! ill. by Jamie Hogan. Charlesbridge, 2013. ISBN 978-1-58089-405-0 Subj: Animals – whales. Family life – mothers. Migration.

Home at last: a song of migration ill. by Alix Berenzy. Henry Holt, 1998. ISBN 978-0-8050-5154-4 Subj: Animals. Migration.

Honk, honk, goose! Canada geese start a family ill. by Huy Voun Lee. Henry Holt, 2009. ISBN 978-0-8050-7103-0 Subj: Birds – geese. Nature.

The hungry hummingbird ill. by Gay W. Holland. Millbrook, 2001. ISBN 978-0-7613-1951-1 Subj: Birds – hummingbirds. Food. Science.

Hush, little puppy ill. by Susan Winter. Henry Holt, 2007. ISBN 978-0-8050-7102-3 Subj: Animals – dogs. Bedtime. Rhyming text.

If you should hear a honey guide ill. by S. D. Schindler. Houghton, 1995. ISBN 978-0-395-71545-1 Subj: Animals. Birds. Foreign lands – Africa. Insects – bees.

If you're hoppy ill. by Jackie Urbanovic. HarperCollins, 2011. ISBN 978-0-06-156634-9 Subj: Animals. Rhyming text.

It's my city ill. by Denis Roche. Greenwillow, 2001. ISBN 978-0-688-16916-9 Subj: Birthdays. Cities, towns. Family life – brothers & sisters. Rhyming text.

Let's go nuts! seeds we eat ill. by author. Simon & Schuster, 2013. ISBN 978-1-4424-6728-6 Subj: Food. Rhyming text.

Meet the howlers! ill. by Woody Miller. Charlesbridge, 2010. ISBN 978-1-57091-733-2 Subj: Animals – monkeys.

Noodle Man ill. by Stephen Costanza. Orchard, 2002. ISBN 978-0-439-29307-5 Subj: Food. Humorous stories.

Rah, rah, radishes! a vegetable chant photos by author. Simon & Schuster, 2011. ISBN 978-1-4424-2141-7 Subj: Food. Rhyming text.

Raindrops roll photos by author. Simon & Schuster/Beach Lane, 2015. ISBN 978-148142064-8 Subj: Water. Weather – rain.

The shape of Betts Meadow ill. by Joanne Friar. Millbrook, 2002. ISBN 978-0-7613-2115-6 Subj: Ecology. Nature.

Splish! splash! animal baths ill. by author. Millbrook, 2000. ISBN 978-0-7613-1821-7 Subj: Activities – bathing. Animals.

Squirrels leap, squirrels sleep ill. by Steve Jenkins. Henry Holt, 2016. ISBN 978-080509251-6 Subj: Animals – squirrels. Nature. Rhyming text.

Stars beneath your bed: the surprising story of dust ill. by Ann Jonas. HarperCollins, 2005. ISBN 978-0-06-057189-4 Subj: Character traits – cleanliness.

Trout are made of trees ill. by Kate Endle. Charlesbridge, 2008. ISBN 978-1-58089-137-0 Subj: Ecology. Fish. Trees.

Trout, trout, trout ill. by Trip Park. NorthWord, 2004. ISBN 978-1-55971-889-9 Subj: Fish. Rhyming text.

Turtle, turtle, watch out! ill. by Lee Christiansen. Orchard, 2000. ISBN 978-0-531-33285-6 Subj: Character traits – kindness to animals. Migration. Reptiles – turtles, tortoises.

Turtle, turtle, watch out! ill. by Annie Patterson. Charlesbridge, 2010. ISBN 978-1-58089-148-6 Subj: Character traits – kindness to animals. Migration. Reptiles – turtles, tortoises.

Vulture view ill. by Steve Jenkins. Henry Holt, 2007. ISBN 978-0-8050-7557-1 Subj: Birds – vultures. Rhyming text.

Woodpecker wham! ill. by Steve Jenkins. Henry Holt, 2015. ISBN 978-080508842-7 Subj: Birds – woodpeckers. Nature. Rhyming text.

Sayres, Brianna Caplan. *Tiara Saurus Rex* ill. by Mike Boldt. Bloomsbury, 2015. ISBN 978-161963263-9 Subj: Contests. Dinosaurs. Rhyming text.

Where do diggers sleep at night? ill. by Christian Slade. Random House, 2012. ISBN 978-0-375-86848-1 Subj: Bedtime. Machines. Rhyming text. Trucks.

Sazaklis, John. *Fowl play* ill. by Steven E. Gordon. HarperFestival, 2013. ISBN 978-0-06-188536-5 Subj: Birds. Character traits – bravery. Crime. Ecology. Format, unusual – graphic novels.

Scanlon, Elizabeth Garton. *All the world* ill. by Marla Frazee. Simon & Schuster, 2009. ISBN 978-1-4169-8580-8 Subj: Activities. Caldecott award honor books. Family life. Seasons – summer. World.

Another way to climb a tree ill. by Hadley Hooper. Roaring Brook/Neal Porter, 2017. ISBN 978-162672352-8 Subj: Imagination. Trees.

Bob, not Bob! by Elizabeth Garton Scanlon and Audrey Vernick ill. by Matthew Cordell. Disney/Hyperion, 2017. ISBN 978-148472302-9 Subj: Family life – mothers. Illness – cold (disease).

The good-pie party ill. by Kady MacDonald Denton. Scholastic, 2014. ISBN 978-054544870-3 Subj: Food. Friendship. Moving. Parties.

Happy birthday, Bunny! ill. by Stephanie Graegin. Simon & Schuster, 2013. ISBN 978-1-4424-0287-4 Subj: Animals – rabbits. Birthdays. Parties. Rhyming text.

Noodle and Lou ill. by Arthur Howard. Simon & Schuster, 2011. ISBN 978-1-4424-0288-1 Subj: Animals – worms. Birds. Friendship. Self-concept.

A sock is a pocket for your toes ill. by Robin Preiss-Glasser. HarperCollins, 2004. ISBN 978-0-06-029527-1 Subj: Clothing – pockets. Poetry. Rhyming text.

Think big! ill. by Vanessa Brantley Newton. Bloomsbury, 2012. ISBN 978-1-59990-611-9 Subj: Art. Rhyming text. Theater.

Scarry, Huck. *Looking into the Middle Ages* ill. by author. HarperCollins, 1985. ISBN 978-0-06-025224-3 Subj: Format, unusual – toy & movable books. Knights. Middle Ages.

Scarry, Richard. *Richard Scarry's best Christmas book ever!* ill. by author. Random House, 1981. ISBN 978-0-394-94936-9 Subj: Holidays – Christmas.

Richard Scarry's best first book ever! ill. by author. Random House, 1979. ISBN 978-0-394-94250-6 Subj: Concepts. Days of the week, months of the year.

Richard Scarry's please and thank you book ill. by author. Random House, 1973. ISBN 978-0-394-92681-0 Subj: Etiquette.

Schachner, Judith Byron. *Bits and pieces* ill. by author. Dial, 2013. ISBN 978-0-8037-3788-4 Subj: Animals – cats. Behavior – lost & found possessions.

Dewey Bob ill. by author. Dial, 2015. ISBN 978-080374120-1 Subj: Animals – raccoons. Behavior – collecting things. Friendship. Homes, houses.

The Grannyman ill. by author. Dutton, 1999. ISBN 978-0-525-46122-7 Subj: Animals – cats. Character traits – responsibility. Old age.

Sarabella's thinking cap ill. by author. Dial, 2017. ISBN 978-052542918-0 Subj: Character traits – individuality. Character traits – patience, impatience. School. Self-concept.

Skippyjon Jones and the big bones ill. by author. Penguin, 2007. ISBN 978-0-525-47884-3 Subj: Animals – cats. Animals – dogs. Dinosaurs.

Skippyjon Jones Cirque de Olé ill. by author. Dial, 2012. ISBN 978-0-8037-3782-2 Subj: Animals – cats. Animals – dogs. Careers – acrobats. Circus.

Skippyjon Jones class action ill. by author. Penguin, 2011. ISBN 978-0-525-42228-0 Subj: Animals – cats. Animals – dogs. School.

Skippyjon Jones in mummy trouble ill. by author. Penguin, 2006. ISBN 978-0-525-47754-9 Subj: Animals – cats. Animals – dogs. Mummies.

Skippyjon Jones, lost in spice ill. by author. Dutton, 2009. ISBN 978-0-525-47965-9 Subj: Animals – cats. Animals – dogs. Space & space ships.

Yo, Vikings ill. by author. Dutton, 2002. ISBN 978-0-525-46889-9 Subj: Birthdays. Boats, ships. Careers – explorers. Character traits – persistence. Vikings.

Schaefer, Carole Lexa. *ABCers* ill. by Pierr Morgan. Viking, 2012. ISBN 978-0-670-01231-2 Subj: ABC books. Activities – playing. Language. Parks.

Big Little Monkey ill. by Pierre Pratt. Candlewick, 2008. ISBN 978-0-7636-2006-6 Subj: Animals. Animals – monkeys. Jungle.

The Bora-Bora dress ill. by Catherine Stock. Candlewick, 2005. ISBN 978-0-7636-1234-4 Subj: Clothing – dresses. Parties.

The children's garden: growing food in the city ill. by Pierr Morgan. Little Bigfoot, 2017. ISBN 978-157061984-7 Subj: Cities, towns. Gardens, gardening.

Cool time song ill. by Pierr Morgan. Penguin, 2005. ISBN 978-0-670-05928-7 Subj: Animals. Foreign lands – Africa.

Down in the woods at sleepytime ill. by Vanessa Cabban. Candlewick, 2000. ISBN 978-0-7636-0843-9 Subj: Activities – storytelling. Animals. Bedtime. Dreams. Family life – mothers. Forest, woods.

Dragon dancing ill. by Pierr Morgan. Penguin, 2007. ISBN 978-0-670-06084-9 Subj: Activities – dancing. Dragons. Imagination.

Kids like us ill. by Pierr Morgan. Viking, 2008. ISBN 978-0-670-06290-4 Subj: Activities – playing. Imagination. School.

The little French whistle ill. by Emilie Chollat. Knopf, 2002. ISBN 978-0-375-91569-7 Subj: Family life – cousins. Family life – grandfathers. Whistles.

Snow pumpkin ill. by Pierr Morgan. Crown, 2000. ISBN 978-0-517-80016-4 Subj: Activities – playing. Ethnic groups in the U.S. Snowmen. Weather – snow.

Someone says ill. by Pierr Morgan. Viking, 2003. ISBN 978-0-670-03664-6 Subj: Bedtime. Day. Imagination. School – nursery.

Two scarlet songbirds ill. by Elizabeth Rosen. Knopf, 2001. ISBN 978-0-375-91022-7 Subj: Birds. Careers – composers. Music.

Who's there? ill. by Pierr Morgan. Penguin, 2011. ISBN 978-0-670-01241-1 Subj: Bedtime. Emotions – fear.

Schaefer, Lola M. *Airport* ill. with photos. Heinemann, 2000. ISBN 978-1-57572-515-4 Subj: Airplanes, airports. Careers.

Apartment ill. with photos. Heinemann, 2002. ISBN 978-1-4034-0258-5 Subj: Homes, houses.

Chinese New Year ill. with photos. Pebble, 2001. ISBN 978-0-7368-0660-2 Subj: Ethnic groups in the U.S. – Chinese Americans. Foreign lands – China. Holidays – Chinese New Year.

Cinco de Mayo ill. with photos. Pebble, 2001. ISBN 978-0-7368-0661-9 Subj: Ethnic groups in the U.S. – Mexican Americans. Foreign lands – Mexico. Holidays – Cinco de Mayo.

Construction site ill. with photos. Heinemann, 2000. ISBN 978-1-57572-516-1 Subj: Careers – construction workers.

Dental office ill. with photos. Heinemann, 2000. ISBN 978-1-57572-517-8 Subj: Careers – dentists. Teeth.

Frankie Stein ill. by Kevan Atteberry. Marshall Cavendish, 2007. ISBN 978-0-7614-5358-1 Subj: Character traits – being different. Family life. Monsters.

Frankie Stein starts school ill. by Kevan Atteberry. Marshall Cavendish, 2010. ISBN 978-0-7614-5656-8 Subj: Behavior – bullying, teasing. Character traits – being different. Friendship. Monsters. School – first day.

Hanukkah ill. with photos. Pebble, 2001. ISBN 978-0-7368-0662-6 Subj: Holidays – Hanukkah. Jewish culture. Religion.

Homes ABC ill. with photos. Heinemann, 2003. ISBN 978-1-4034-0260-8 Subj: ABC books. Homes, houses.

Homes 123 ill. with photos. Heinemann, 2003. ISBN 978-1-4034-0259-2 Subj: Counting, numbers. Homes, houses.

Hospital ill. with photos. Heinemann, 2000. ISBN 978-1-57572-519-2 Subj: Careers – doctors. Careers – nurses. Hospitals.

House ill. with photos. Heinemann, 2003. ISBN 978-1-4034-0261-5 Subj: Homes, houses.

An island grows ill. by Cathie Felstead. HarperCollins, 2006. ISBN 978-0-06-623930-9 Subj: Islands. Rhyming text. Volcanoes.

Just one bite: 11 animals and their bites at life size! ill. by Geoff Waring. Chronicle, 2010. ISBN 978-0-8118-6473-2 Subj: Animals. Food.

Kwanzaa ill. with photos. Pebble, 2001. ISBN 978-0-7368-0663-3 Subj: Ethnic groups in the U.S. – African Americans. Holidays – Kwanzaa.

Lifetime: the amazing numbers in animal lives ill. by Christopher Silas Neal. Chronicle, 2013. ISBN 978-1-4521-0714-1 Subj: Animals. Counting, numbers. Science.

Loose tooth ill. by Sylvie Wickstrom. HarperCollins, 2004. ISBN 978-0-06-052777-8 Subj: Family life. Rhyming text. Teeth.

Mobile home ill. with photos. Heinemann, 2003. ISBN 978-1-4034-0263-9 Subj: Homes, houses.

One busy day: a story for big brothers and sisters ill. by Jessica Meserve. Disney/Hyperion, 2014. ISBN 978-142317112-6 Subj: Activities – playing. Family life – brothers & sisters. Imagination.

One special day: a story for big brothers and sisters ill. by Jessica Meserve. Hyperion, 2012. ISBN 978-1-4231-3760-3 Subj: Babies, toddlers. Family life – brothers. Family life – new sibling.

Police station ill. with photos. Heinemann, 2000. ISBN 978-1-57572-520-8 Subj: Careers – detectives. Careers – police officers.

Supermarket ill. with photos. Heinemann, 2000. ISBN 978-1-57572-518-5 Subj: Careers – storekeepers. Food. Stores.

This is the sunflower ill. by Donald Crews. Greenwillow, 2000. ISBN 978-0-688-16414-0 Subj: Cumulative tales. Flowers. Nature. Plants. Rhyming text. Seeds.

Toolbox twins ill. by Melissa Iwai. Henry Holt, 2006. ISBN 978-0-8050-7733-9 Subj: Family life – fathers. Rhyming text. Tools.

Tugboats ill. with photos. Heinemann, 2003. ISBN 978-1-4034-0262-2 Subj: Boats, ships. Homes, houses.

The Wright brothers ill. with photos. Pebble, 2000. ISBN 978-0-7368-0549-0 Subj: Airplanes, airports. Careers – inventors. U.S. history.

Schafer, Kevin. *Penguins A B C* ill. with photos. NorthWord, 2002. ISBN 978-1-55971-831-8 Subj: ABC books. Birds – penguins.

Penguins 1 2 3 ill. with photos. NorthWord, 2002. ISBN 978-1-55971-830-1 Subj: Birds – penguins. Counting, numbers.

Schafer, Milton. *That crazy Barb'ra* ill. by G. Brian Karas. Dial, 2003. ISBN 978-0-8037-2584-3 Subj: Behavior – bullying, teasing. Rhyming text. School.

Schanzer, Rosalyn. *How Ben Franklin stole the lightning* ill. by author. HarperCollins, 2003. ISBN 978-0-688-16994-7 Subj: Careers – inventors. Careers – scientists. Science. Tall tales. U.S. history.

The Old Chisholm Trail ill. by author. National Geographic, 2001. ISBN 978-0-7922-7559-6 Subj: Cowboys, cowgirls. Music. Songs. U.S. history.

Scharschmidt, Sherry. *Tuck me in!* (Hacohen, Dean)

Schatell, Brian. *Owl boy* ill. by author. Holiday House, 2015. ISBN 978-082343208-0 Subj: Birds – owls. Camps, camping.

Schaub, Michelle. *Fresh-picked poetry: a day at the farmers' market* ill. by Amy Huntington. Charlesbridge, 2017. ISBN 978-158089547-7 Subj: Careers – farmers. Poetry. Stores.

Scheer, Julian. *By the light of the captured moon* ill. by Ronald Himler. Holiday, 2001. ISBN 978-0-8234-1624-0 Subj: Friendship. Moon. Seasons – summer.

Rain makes applesauce by Julian Scheer and Marvin Bileck ill. by Marvin Bileck. Holiday, 1964. ISBN 978-0-8234-0091-1 Subj: Caldecott award honor books. Humorous stories. Weather – rain.

Scheffler, Axel. *Axel Scheffler's Flip flap safari* ill. by author. Candlewick, 2015. ISBN 978-076367605-6 Subj: Animals. Format, unusual – toy & movable books. Rhyming text.

Pip and Posy: the bedtime frog ill. by author. Candlewick, 2014. ISBN 978-076367068-9 Subj: Animals – mice. Animals – rabbits. Bedtime. Toys.

Pip and Posy: the big balloon ill. by author. Candlewick, 2013. ISBN 978-0-7636-6372-8 Subj: Animals – mice. Animals – rabbits. Toys – balloons.

Pip and Posy: the little puddle ill. by author. Candlewick, 2011. ISBN 978-0-7636-5878-6 Subj: Animals – mice. Animals – rabbits. Behavior – mistakes. Toilet training.

Pip and Posy: the new friend ill. by author. Nosy Crow, 2017. ISBN 978-076369339-8 Subj: Animals – mice. Animals – rabbits. Friendship. Sea & seashore – beaches.

Pip and Posy: the scary monster ill. by author. Candlewick, 2012. ISBN 978-0-7636-5918-9 Subj: Animals – mice. Animals – rabbits. Clothing – costumes. Friendship. Monsters.

Pip and Posy: the snowy day ill. by author. Candlewick, 2013. ISBN 978-0-7636-6607-1 Subj: Animals – mice. Animals – rabbits. Character traits – cooperation. Friendship. Snowmen. Weather – snow.

Pip and Posy: the super scooter ill. by author. Candlewick, 2011. ISBN 978-0-7636-5877-9 Subj: Activities – playing. Animals – mice. Animals – rabbits. Friendship.

Scheffler, Ursel. *Taking care of Sister Bear* ill. by Ulises Wensell. Doubleday, 1999. ISBN 978-0-385-32660-5 Subj: Animals – bears. Babies, toddlers. Behavior – lost. Family life – brothers & sisters.

Who has time for Little Bear? ill. by Ulises Wensell. Doubleday, 1998. ISBN 978-0-385-32536-3 Subj: Animals – bears. Family life. Friendship.

Schembri, Pamela. *The secret lunch special* (Catalanotto, Peter)

Schertle, Alice. *The adventures of old Bo Bear* ill. by David Parkins. Chronicle, 2006. ISBN 978-0-8118-3476-6 Subj: Activities – playing. Character traits – cleanliness. Toys – bears.

Advice for a frog and other poems ill. by Norman Green. Lothrop, 1995. ISBN 978-0-688-13487-7 Subj: Animals. Animals – endangered animals. Frogs & toads. Poetry.

Button up! ill. by Petra Mathers. Harcourt, 2009. ISBN 978-0-15-205050-4 Subj: Animals. Clothing. Poetry.

Down the road ill. by E. B. Lewis. Browndeer, 1995. ISBN 978-0-15-276622-1 Subj: Country. Eggs. Ethnic groups in the U.S. – African Americans. Family life.

Goodnight, Hattie, my dearie, my dove ill. by Ted Rand. HarperCollins, 2002. ISBN 978-0-688-16023-4 Subj: Bedtime. Counting, numbers. Toys.

How now, brown cow? ill. by Amanda Schaffer. Browndeer, 1994. ISBN 978-0-15-276648-1 Subj: Animals – bulls, cows. Poetry.

I am the cat ill. by Mark Buehner. Lothrop, 1999. ISBN 978-0-688-13154-8 Subj: Animals – cats. Poetry.

Jeremy Bean's St. Patrick's Day ill. by Linda Shute. Lothrop, 1987. ISBN 978-0-688-04814-3 Subj: Behavior – hiding. Character traits – being different. Holidays – St. Patrick's Day. Parties. School.

Little Blue Truck ill. by Jill McElmurry. Harcourt, 2008. ISBN 978-0-15-205661-2 Subj: Friendship. Rhyming text. Trucks.

Little Blue Truck leads the way ill. by Jill McElmurry. Harcourt, 2009. ISBN 978-0-15-206389-4 Subj: Cities, towns. Rhyming text. Traffic, traffic signs. Trucks.

Little Frog's song ill. by Leonard Everett Fisher. HarperCollins, 1992. ISBN 978-0-06-020060-2 Subj: Behavior – lost. Frogs & toads.

The skeleton in the closet ill. by Curtis Jobling. HarperCollins, 2003. ISBN 978-0-688-17739-3 Subj: Anatomy – skeletons. Clothing. Rhyming text.

Such a little mouse ill. by Stephanie Yue. Scholastic/Orchard, 2015. ISBN 978-054564929-2 Subj: Animals – mice. Seasons.

Very hairy bear ill. by Matt Phelan. Harcourt, 2007. ISBN 978-0-15-216568-0 Subj: Animals – bears. Hibernation. Seasons.

We ill. by Kenneth Addison. Lee & Low, 2007. ISBN 978-1-58430-060-1 Subj: Poetry. World.

Witch Hazel ill. by Margot Tomes. HarperCollins, 1991. ISBN 978-0-06-025141-3 Subj: Family life – brothers. Moon. Plants. Scarecrows.

Schick, Eleanor. *Mama* ill. by author. Marshall Cavendish, 2000. ISBN 978-0-7614-5060-3 Subj: Death. Emotions – grief. Family life – mothers. Illness. Memories, memory.

My Navajo sister ill. by author. Simon & Schuster, 1996. ISBN 978-0-02-781155-1 Subj: Friendship. Indians of North America – Navajo.

Navajo ABC (Tapahonso, Luci)

Schiffer, Miriam B. *Stella brings the family* ill. by Holly Clifton-Brown. Chronicle, 2015. ISBN 978-145211190-2 Subj: Family life – same-sex parents. Holidays – Mother's Day. LGBTQ.

Schiller, Abbie. *When Lyla got lost (and found)* by Abbie Schiller and Samantha Kurtzman Counter ill. by Kaori Onishi. Mother Company, 2015. ISBN 978-098940712-0 Subj: Behavior – lost. Behavior – worrying. Stores.

Schindel, John. *The babies and doggies book* by John Schindel and Molly Woodward ill. with photos. Houghton Mifflin Harcourt, 2015. ISBN 978-054444477-5 Subj: Animals – dogs. Babies, toddlers. Format, unusual – board books.

Busy penguins by John Schindel and Jonathan Chester ill. with photos. Tricycle, 2000. ISBN 978-1-58246-016-1 Subj: Activities. Birds – penguins. Format, unusual – board books. Rhyming text.

Frog face, my little sister and me photos by Janet Delaney. Henry Holt, 1998. ISBN 978-0-8050-5546-7 Subj: Family life – new sibling. Family life – sisters.

What did they see? ill. by Doug Cushman. Henry Holt, 2003. ISBN 978-0-8050-6167-3 Subj: Animals. Format, unusual – toy & movable books. Mirrors.

Schindler, S. D. *Spike and Ike take a hike* ill. by author. Penguin/Nancy Paulsen, 2013. ISBN 978-0-399-24495-7 Subj: Activities – walking. Animals. Animals – coatis. Animals – hedgehogs.

Schlessinger, Laura. *But I waaannt it!* ill. by Daniel McFeeley. HarperCollins, 2000. ISBN 978-0-06-028775-7 Subj: Behavior – greed.

Dr. Laura Schlessinger's Growing up is hard ill. by Daniel McFeeley. HarperCollins, 2001. ISBN 978-0-06-029201-0 Subj: Behavior – growing up. Family life – fathers. Family life – sons.

Dr. Laura Schlessinger's Where's God? ill. by Daniel McFeeley. HarperCollins, 2003. ISBN 978-0-06-051909-4 Subj: Family life – grandfathers. Religion.

Why do you love me? by Laura Schlessinger and Martha Lewis Lambert ill. by Daniel McFeeley. HarperCollins, 1999. ISBN 978-0-06-027866-3 Subj: Emotions – love. Family life – mothers. Family life – sons.

Schmid, Eleonore. *Hare's Christmas gift* ill. by author. NorthSouth, 2000. ISBN 978-0-7358-1377-9 Subj: Animals – rabbits. Character traits – bravery. Religion – Nativity.

Schmid, Paul. *Hugs from Pearl* ill. by author. HarperCollins, 2011. ISBN 978-0-06-180434-2 Subj: Animals – porcupines. Hugging. Problem solving. School.

Oliver and his alligator ill. by author. Disney/Hyperion, 2013. ISBN 978-1-4231-7437-0 Subj: Character traits – shyness. Emotions – fear. Reptiles – alligators, crocodiles. School – first day.

Oliver and his egg ill. by author. Disney/Hyperion, 2014. ISBN 978-142317573-5 Subj: Eggs. Friendship. Imagination.

Peanut and Fifi have a ball ill. by Randall De Sève. Dial, 2013. ISBN 978-0-8037-3578-1 Subj: Behavior – fighting, arguing. Behavior – sharing. Family life – sisters. Toys – balls.

Perfectly Percy ill. by author. HarperCollins, 2013. ISBN 978-0-06-180436-6 Subj: Animals – porcupines. Problem solving. Toys – balloons.

A pet for Petunia ill. by author. HarperCollins, 2011. ISBN 978-0-06-196331-5 Subj: Animals – skunks. Pets. Toys.

Petunia goes wild ill. by author. HarperCollins, 2012. ISBN 978-0-06-196334-6 Subj: Behavior – misbehavior. Family life – parents. Imagination.

Schmidt, Gary D., reteller. *The Great Stone Face* a tale by Nathaniel Hawthorne; ill. by Bill Farnsworth. Eerdmans, 2002. ISBN 978-0-8028-5194-9 Subj: Folk & fairy tales.

Schmidt, Karen Lee. *Carl's nose* ill. by author. Harcourt, 2006. ISBN 978-0-15-205049-8 Subj: Animals – dogs. Careers – meteorologists. Mountains. Weather.

Schneider, Christine M. *Horace P. Tuttle, magician extraordinaire* ill. by author. Walker, 2001. ISBN 978-0-8027-8789-7 Subj: Behavior – needing someone. Careers – magicians. Humorous stories.

I'm bored! ill. by Herve Pinel. Houghton, 2006. ISBN 978-0-618-65760-5 Subj: Animals – dogs. Behavior – boredom. Toys – bears.

Picky Mrs. Pickle ill. by author. Walker, 1999. ISBN 978-0-8027-8703-3 Subj: Food. Rhyming text. Self-concept.

Saxophone Sam and his snazzy jazz band ill. by author. Walker, 2002. ISBN 978-0-8027-8809-2 Subj: Activities – dancing. Family life – brothers & sisters. Music. Radios. Rhyming text.

Schneider, Howie. *Chewy Louie* ill. by author. Rising Moon, 2000. ISBN 978-0-87358-765-5 Subj: Animals – babies. Animals – dogs. Pets.

Fast 'n Snappy ill. by Jane Manning. Carolrhoda, 2004. ISBN 978-1-57505-539-8 Subj: Careers – postal workers. Crime. Frogs & toads. Humorous stories. Post office. Reptiles – alligators, crocodiles. U.S. history.

Wilky the White House cockroach ill. by author. Penguin, 2006. ISBN 978-0-399-24388-2 Subj: Insects – cockroaches.

Schneider, Josh. *Bedtime monsters* ill. by author. Clarion, 2013. ISBN 978-0-544-00270-8 Subj: Bedtime. Emotions – fear. Monsters.

Everybody sleeps (but not Fred) ill. by author. Clarion, 2015. ISBN 978-054433924-8 Subj: Animals. Bedtime. Behavior – misbehavior. Rhyming text.

Kid Amazing vs. the Blob ill. by author. Clarion, 2017. ISBN 978-054480125-7 Subj: Babies, toddlers. Character traits – helpfulness. Family life – brothers & sisters. Imagination.

Princess Sparkle-Heart gets a makeover ill. by author. Clarion, 2014. ISBN 978-054414228-2 Subj: Animals – dogs. Emotions – envy, jealousy. Friendship. Toys – dolls.

You'll be sorry ill. by author. Houghton, 2007. ISBN 978-0-618-81932-4 Subj: Behavior – misbehavior. Family life – brothers & sisters. Weather – floods.

Schnitzlein, Danny. *The monster who ate my peas* ill. by Matt Faulkner. Peachtree, 2001. ISBN 978-1-56145-216-3 Subj: Food. Monsters. Rhyming text.

Schnitzler, Pattie L. *Widdermaker* ill. by Rick Sealock. Carolrhoda, 2002. ISBN 978-0-87614-647-7 Subj: Animals – bulls, cows. Animals – horses, ponies. Cowboys, cowgirls. Humorous stories. Tall tales. U.S. history – frontier & pioneer life.

Schnur, Steven. *Autumn* ill. by Leslie Evans. Clarion, 1997. ISBN 978-0-395-77043-6 Subj: ABC books. Poetry. Seasons – fall.

Night lights ill. by Stacey Schuett. Farrar, 2000. ISBN 978-0-374-35522-7 Subj: Counting, numbers. Light, lights. Night. Rhyming text.

Spring ill. by Leslie Evans. Clarion, 1999. ISBN 978-0-395-82269-2 Subj: ABC books. Poetry. Seasons – spring.

Spring thaw ill. by Stacey Schuett. Viking, 2000. ISBN 978-0-670-87961-8 Subj: Farms. Nature. Seasons – spring.

Summer ill. by Leslie Evans. Clarion, 2001. ISBN 978-0-618-02372-1 Subj: ABC books. Poetry. Seasons – summer.

The tie man's miracle ill. by Stephen T. Johnson. Morrow, 1995. ISBN 978-0-688-13463-1 Subj: Character traits – kindness. Clothing. Holidays – Hanukkah. Holocaust. Jewish culture.

Winter ill. by Leslie Evans. Clarion, 2002. ISBN 978-0-618-02374-5 Subj: ABC books. Poetry. Seasons – winter.

Schnur, Susan. *Tashlich at Turtle Rock* by Susan Schnur and Anna Schnur Fishman ill. by Alex Steele-Morgan. Lerner/Kar-Ben, 2010. ISBN 978-0-7613-4509-1 Subj: Holidays – Rosh Hashanah. Jewish culture.

Schoebinger, Chris. *Snow angels* (Randall, Angel)

Schoenherr, Ian. *Cat and mouse* ill. by author. HarperCollins, 2008. ISBN 978-0-06-136313-9 Subj: Activities – playing. Animals – cats. Animals – mice. Nursery rhymes. Rhyming text.

Don't spill the beans! ill. by author. HarperCollins, 2010. ISBN 978-0-06-172457-2 Subj: Animals – bears. Behavior – secrets. Birthdays. Rhyming text.

Pip and Squeak ill. by author. HarperCollins, 2007. ISBN 978-0-06-087253-3 Subj: Animals – mice. Animals – rabbits. Birthdays. Weather – snow.

Read it, don't eat it! ill. by author. HarperCollins, 2009. ISBN 978-0-06-172455-8 Subj: Animals. Books, reading. Libraries. Rhyming text.

Schoenherr, John. *Bear* ill. by author. Putnam, 1991. ISBN 978-0-399-22177-4 Subj: Alaska. Animals – bears. Nature.

Rebel ill. by author. Putnam, 1995. ISBN 978-0-399-22727-1 Subj: Birds – geese. Character traits – curiosity. Family life. Lakes, ponds.

Schofield, Jennifer. *Animal babies in grasslands* ill. with photos. Kingfisher, 2004. ISBN 978-0-7534-5789-4 Subj: Animals. Animals – babies.

Animal babies in polar lands ill. with photos. Kingfisher, 2004. ISBN 978-0-7534-5755-9 Subj: Animals. Animals – babies. Foreign lands – Antarctic. Foreign lands – Arctic.

Animal babies in ponds and rivers ill. with photos. Kingfisher, 2004. ISBN 978-0-7534-5790-0 Subj: Animals. Animals – babies. Lakes, ponds. Rivers.

Animal babies in rain forests ill. with photos. Kingfisher, 2004. ISBN 978-0-7534-5788-7 Subj: Animals. Animals – babies. Forest, woods.

Schofield-Morrison, Connie. *I got the rhythm* ill. by Frank Morrison. Bloomsbury, 2014. ISBN 978-161963178-6 Subj: Activities – dancing. Ethnic groups in the U.S. – African Americans. Noise, sounds.

Schoonmaker, Elizabeth. *Square cat* ill. by author. Simon & Schuster, 2011. ISBN 978-1-4424-0619-3 Subj: Animals – cats. Character traits – individuality. Concepts – shape. Self-concept.

Square cat ABC ill. by author. Aladdin, 2014. ISBN 978-144249895-2 Subj: ABC books. Animals – cats. Animals – mice. Gardens, gardening.

Schories, Pat. *Jack and the night visitors* ill. by author. Boyds Mills, 2006. ISBN 978-1-932425-33-8 Subj: Aliens. Animals – dogs. Space & space ships. Wordless.

Jack wants a snack ill. by author. Front Street, 2008. ISBN 978-1-59078-546-1 Subj: Animals – dogs. Wordless.

When Jack goes out ill. by author. Boyds Mills, 2010. ISBN 978-1-59078-652-9 Subj: Aliens. Animals – dogs. Wordless.

Schotter, Roni. *All about grandmas* ill. by Janice Nadeau. Dial, 2012. ISBN 978-0-8037-3714-3 Subj: Character traits – individuality. Family life – grandmothers. Foreign languages. Rhyming text.

The boy who loved words ill. by Giselle Potter. Random House, 2006. ISBN 978-0-375-93601-2 Subj: Language. Self-concept.

Captain Bob sets sail ill. by Joe Cepeda. Atheneum, 2000. ISBN 978-0-689-82081-6 Subj: Activities – bathing. Imagination. Pirates.

Captain Bob takes flight ill. by Joe Cepeda. Atheneum, 2003. ISBN 978-0-689-83388-5 Subj: Activities – flying. Character traits – orderliness. Imagination.

Captain Snap and the children of Vinegar Lane ill. by Marcia Sewall. Watts, 1989. ISBN 978-0-531-08397-0 Subj: Character traits – being different. Character traits – generosity. Character traits – kindness.

Doo-Wop Pop ill. by Bryan Collier. HarperCollins, 2008. ISBN 978-0-06-057968-5 Subj: Activities – singing. Careers – custodians, janitors. Character traits – confidence. Rhyming text. Self-concept.

Go, Little Green Truck! ill. by Julia Kuo. Farrar, 2016. ISBN 978-037430070-8 Subj: Careers – farmers. Farms. Trucks.

Hanukkah! ill. by Marylin Hafner. Little, 1990. ISBN 978-0-316-77466-6 Subj: Holidays – Hanukkah. Jewish culture. Religion.

In the piney woods ill. by Kimberly Bulcken Root. Farrar, 2003. ISBN 978-0-374-33623-3 Subj: Death. Family life – grandfathers. Forest, woods. Trees.

Mama, I'll give you the world ill. by S. Saelig Gallagher. Random House, 2006. ISBN 978-0-375-93612-8 Subj: Beauty shops. Birthdays. Family life – mothers. Family life – single-parent families. Parties.

Passover! ill. by Erin Eitter Kono. Little, Brown, 2006. ISBN 978-0-316-93991-1 Subj: Holidays – Passover. Jewish culture. Religion.

Passover magic ill. by Marylin Hafner. Little, 1995. ISBN 978-0-316-77468-0 Subj: Holidays – Passover. Jewish culture. Religion.

Purim play ill. by Marylin Hafner. Little, 1998. ISBN 978-0-316-77518-2 Subj: Holidays – Purim. Jewish culture. Religion. Theater.

Room for Rabbit ill. by Cyd Moore. Clarion, 2003. ISBN 978-0-618-18183-4 Subj: Divorce. Family life – fathers. Family life – stepfamilies. Toys.

When the Wizzy Foot goes walking ill. by Mike Wohnoutka. Penguin, 2007. ISBN 978-0-525-47791-4 Subj: Behavior – misbehavior. Concepts – size. Giants. Rhyming text.

Schreck, Karen Halvorsen. *Lucy's family tree* ill. by Stephen Gassler. Tilbury, 2001. ISBN 978-0-88448-225-3 Subj: Adoption. Ethnic groups in the U.S. – Mexican Americans. Family life. Genealogy. School. Self-concept.

Schreiber, Georges. *Bambino the clown* ill. by author. Viking, 1947. Subj: Animals – sea lions. Caldecott award honor books. Clowns, jesters.

Schrey, Sophie. *Where's the penguin?* ill. by Chuck Whelon. Simon & Schuster, 2017. ISBN 978-148145999-0 Subj: Birds – penguins. Picture puzzles.

Schrock, Jan West. *Give a goat* ill. by Aileen Darragh. Tilbury, 2008. ISBN 978-0-88448-301-4 Subj: Animals – goats. Behavior – seeking better things. Character traits – generosity. Foreign lands – Uganda. School.

Schroeder, Alan. *Baby Flo: Florence Mills lights up the stage* ill. by Cornelius Van Wright. Lee & Low, 2012. ISBN 978-1-60060-410-2 Subj: Careers – singers. Ethnic groups in the U.S. – African Americans. U.S. history.

Minty: a story of young Harriet Tubman ill. by Jerry Pinkney. Dial, 1996. ISBN 978-0-8037-1888-3 Subj: Ethnic groups in the U.S. – African Americans. Prejudice. Slavery. U.S. history.

Ragtime Tumpie ill. by Bernie Fuchs. Little, 1989. ISBN 978-0-316-77497-0 Subj: Activities – dancing. Ethnic groups in the U.S. – African Americans.

Smoky Mountain Rose: an Appalachian Cinderella ill. by Brad Sneed. Dial, 1997. ISBN 978-0-8037-1734-3 Subj: Animals – pigs. Family life – stepfamilies. Folk & fairy tales.

The stone lion ill. by Todd L. W. Doney. Scribners, 1994. ISBN 978-0-684-19578-0 Subj: Behavior – greed. Character traits – honesty. Character traits – kindness. Character traits – selfishness. Folk & fairy tales. Foreign lands – Tibet.

Schroeder, Lisa. *Baby can't sleep* ill. by Viviana Garofoli. Sterling, 2005. ISBN 978-1-4027-2171-7 Subj: Animals – sheep. Babies, toddlers. Bedtime. Counting, numbers. Rhyming text.

Schubert, Dieter. *Bear's eggs* (Schubert, Ingrid)

There's always room for one more (Schubert, Ingrid)

The umbrella (Schubert, Ingrid)

Schubert, Ingrid. *Bear's eggs* by Ingrid Schubert and Dieter Schubert; ill. by authors. Front Street, 1999. ISBN 978-1-886910-46-1 Subj: Animals – bears. Animals – hedgehogs. Birds – geese. Eggs.

There is a crocodile under my bed ill. by Dieter Schubert. Lemniscaat, 2015. ISBN 978-193595408-8 Subj: Bedtime. Reptiles – alligators, crocodiles.

There's always room for one more by Ingrid Schubert and Dieter Schubert; ill. by authors. Front Street, 2002. ISBN 978-1-886910-77-5 Subj: Animals. Animals – beavers. Friendship. Insects – butterflies, caterpillars. Sports – sailing.

The umbrella by Ingrid Schubert and Dieter Schubert; ill. by authors. Lemniscaat, 2011. ISBN 978-1-9359-5400-2 Subj: Animals – dogs. Umbrellas. Wordless. World.

Schubert, Leda. *Ballet of the elephants* ill. by Robert Andrew Parker. Macmillan, 2006. ISBN 978-1-59643-075-4 Subj: Animals – elephants. Ballet.

Feeding the sheep ill. by Andrea U'Ren. Farrar, 2010. ISBN 978-0-374-32296-0 Subj: Activities – weaving. Animals – sheep. Family life – mothers. Farms. Rhyming text.

Here comes Darrell ill. by Mary Azarian. Houghton, 2005. ISBN 978-0-618-41605-9 Subj: Barns. Character traits – helpfulness. Communities, neighborhoods. Machines. Seasons. Tractors. Trucks.

Monsieur Marceau ill. by Gerard DuBois. Roaring Brook, 2012. ISBN 978-1-59643-529-2 Subj: Clowns, jesters. Foreign lands – France.

The Princess of Borscht ill. by Bonnie Christensen. Roaring Brook, 2011. ISBN 978-1-59643-515-5 Subj: Activities – baking, cooking. Family life – grandmothers. Illness. Jewish culture.

Reading to Peanut ill. by Amanda Haley. Holiday House, 2011. ISBN 978-0-8234-2339-2 Subj: Activities – writing. Animals – dogs. Books, reading. Character traits – perseverance.

Winnie all day long ill. by William Benedict. Candlewick, 2000. ISBN 978-0-7636-1041-8 Subj: Animals – dogs. Sleep.

Winnie plays ball ill. by William Benedict. Candlewick, 2000. ISBN 978-0-7636-1040-1 Subj: Animals – dogs. Birthdays. Toys – balls.

Schuch, Steve. *A symphony of whales* ill. by Peter Sylvada. Harcourt, 1999. ISBN 978-0-15-201670-8 Subj: Animals – whales. Character traits – helpfulness. Dreams. Foreign lands – Russia. Music.

Schuett, Stacey. *Somewhere in the world right now* ill. by author. Knopf, 1995. ISBN 978-0-679-96537-4 Subj: Geography. Time. World.

Schuh, Mari C. *Chickens on the farm* ill. with photos. Pebble, 2002. ISBN 978-0-7368-0991-7 Subj: Birds – chickens, roosters. Farms.

Cows on the farm ill. with photos. Pebble, 2002. ISBN 978-0-7368-0992-4 Subj: Animals – bulls, cows. Farms.

Pigs on the farm ill. with photos. Pebble, 2002. ISBN 978-0-7368-0993-1 Subj: Animals – pigs. Farms.

Sheep on the farm ill. with photos. Pebble, 2002. ISBN 978-0-7368-0994-8 Subj: Animals – sheep. Farms.

Schulman, Janet. *A bunny for all seasons* ill. by Meilo So. Knopf, 2003. ISBN 978-0-375-92256-5 Subj: Animals – rabbits. Gardens, gardening. Seasons.

Countdown to spring ill. by Meilo So. Knopf, 2002. ISBN 978-0-375-81364-1 Subj: Animals. Counting, numbers. Seasons – spring.

Pale Male: citizen hawk of New York City ill. by Meilo So. Knopf, 2008. ISBN 978-0-375-84558-1 Subj: Birds – hawks. Cities, towns.

Ten Easter egg hunters: a holiday counting book ill. by Linda Davick. Random House, 2011. ISBN 978-0-375-86787-3 Subj: Counting, numbers. Eggs. Holidays – Easter. Rhyming text.

10 trick-or-treaters: a Halloween counting book ill. by Linda Davick. Random House, 2005. ISBN 978-0-375-95225-8 Subj: Counting, numbers. Holidays – Halloween. Rhyming text.

10 Valentine friends: a holiday counting book ill. by Linda Davick. Random House, 2011. ISBN 978-0-375-86967-9 Subj: Counting, numbers. Holidays – Valentine's Day. Rhyming text.

Schultz, Sam. *Animal antics: the beast jokes ever* ill. by Brian Gable. Carolrhoda, 2004. ISBN 978-1-57505-640-1 Subj: Animals. Riddles & jokes.

Monster mayhem ill. by Brian Gable. Carolrhoda, 2004. ISBN 978-0-8225-1169-4 Subj: Monsters. Riddles & jokes.

Schulz, Heidi. *Giraffes ruin everything* ill. by Chris Robertson. Bloomsbury, 2016. ISBN 978-161963475-6 Subj: Animals – giraffes. Character traits – being different. Friendship.

Schumaker, Ward. *Dance!* ill. by author. Harcourt, 1996. ISBN 978-0-15-200046-2 Subj: Activities – dancing. Animals. Rhyming text.

In my garden ill. by author. Chronicle, 2000. ISBN 978-0-8118-2689-1 Subj: Counting, numbers. Gardens, gardening.

Schur, Maxine Rose. *Day of delight* ill. by Brian Pinkney. Dial, 1994. ISBN 978-0-8037-1414-4 Subj: Foreign lands – Ethiopia. Jewish culture. Religion.

Schuurmans, Hilde. *Sydney won't swim* ill. by author. Whispering Coyote, 2001. ISBN 978-1-57091-476-8 Subj: Animals – badgers. Emotions – fear. Sports – swimming.

Schwab, Eva. *Robert and the Robot* ill. by author. Front Street, 2001. ISBN 978-1-886910-59-1 Subj: Character traits – orderliness. Robots.

Schwartz, Amy. *Annabelle Swift, kindergartner* ill. by author. Orchard, 1988. ISBN 978-0-531-08337-6 Subj: Character traits – pride. School – first day. Sibling rivalry.

Bea and Mr. Jones ill. by author. Bradbury, 1982. ISBN 978-0-87888-202-1 Subj: Behavior – imitation. Family life – fathers.

A beautiful girl ill. by author. Macmillan, 2006. ISBN 978-1-59643-165-2 Subj: Anatomy. Animals. Animals – elephants. Birds – robins. Character traits – appearance. Fish. Insects – flies.

Begin at the beginning: a little artist learns about life ill. by author. HarperCollins, 2005. ISBN 978-0-06-000112-4 Subj: Behavior – growing up.

The boys teams ill. by author. Atheneum, 2001. ISBN 978-0-689-84138-5 Subj: Activities. School – nursery.

Dee Dee and me ill. by author. Holiday House, 2013. ISBN 978-0-8234-2524-2 Subj: Family life – sisters. Self-concept.

How to catch an elephant ill. by author. DK, 1999. ISBN 978-0-7894-2579-9 Subj: Animals – elephants.

I can't wait! ill. by author. Simon & Schuster/Beach Lane, 2015. ISBN 978-144248231-9 Subj: Character traits – patience, impatience. Family life. Friendship.

Lucy can't sleep ill. by author. Roaring Brook, 2012. ISBN 978-1-59643-543-8 Subj: Bedtime. Rhyming text. Sleep.

Oma and Bobo ill. by author. Bradbury, 1987. ISBN 978-0-02-781500-9 Subj: Animals – dogs. Family life – grandmothers.

100 things I love to do with you ill. by author. Abrams, 2017. ISBN 978-141972288-2 Subj: Friendship. Rhyming text.

One hundred things that make me happy ill. by author. Abrams/Appleseed, 2014. ISBN 978-141970518-2 Subj: Emotions – happiness. Language. Rhyming text.

Oscar: the big adventures of a little sock monkey by Amy Schwartz and Leonard S. Marcus; ill. by Amy Schwartz. HarperCollins, 2006. ISBN 978-0-06-072622-5 Subj: Animals – monkeys. Animals – rabbits. Pets. School. Toys.

Polka dots for Poppy ill. by author. Holiday House, 2016. ISBN 978-082343431-2 Subj: Character traits – appearance. Clothing. Family life – sisters. School – first day.

Some babies ill. by author. Orchard, 2000. ISBN 978-0-531-33287-0 Subj: Activities – storytelling. Bedtime. Family life.

Starring Miss Darlene ill. by author. Macmillan, 2007. ISBN 978-1-59643-230-7 Subj: Animals. Animals – hippopotamuses. Behavior – mistakes. Careers – actors. Self-concept. Theater.

Things I learned in second grade ill. by author. Tegen, 2004. ISBN 978-0-06-050937-8 Subj: Behavior – growing up. School.

Tiny and Hercules ill. by author. Roaring Brook, 2009. ISBN 978-1-59643-253-6 Subj: Animals – elephants. Animals – mice. Friendship.

Willie and Uncle Bill ill. by author. Holiday House, 2012. ISBN 978-0-8234-2203-6 Subj: Activities – babysitting. Family life – aunts, uncles.

Schwartz, Corey Rosen. *Hensel and Gretel: ninja chicks* by Corey Rosen Schwartz and Rebecca J. Gomez ill. by Dan Santat. Putnam, 2016. ISBN 978-039917626-5 Subj: Birds – chickens, roosters. Folk & fairy tales. Rhyming text. Sports – martial arts.

Hop! Plop! by Corey Rosen Schwartz and Tali Klein ill. by Olivier Dunrea. Walker, 2006. ISBN 978-0-8027-8056-0 Subj: Activities – playing. Animals – elephants. Animals – mice. Friendship. Noise, sounds.

Ninja Red Riding Hood ill. by Dan Santat. Putnam, 2014. ISBN 978-039916354-8 Subj: Animals – wolves. Behavior – talking to strangers. Folk & fairy tales. Rhyming text. Sports – martial arts. Sports – martial arts.

The three ninja pigs ill. by Dan Santat. Putnam, 2012. ISBN 978-0-399-25514-4 Subj: Animals – pigs. Folk & fairy tales. Rhyming text. Sports – karate. Sports – martial arts.

Schwartz, David M. *How much is a million?* ill. by Steven Kellogg. Lothrop, 1985. ISBN 978-0-688-04050-5 Subj: Concepts – size. Counting, numbers.

If you hopped like a frog ill. by James Warhola. Scholastic, 1999. ISBN 978-0-590-09857-1 Subj: Animals. Concepts. Counting, numbers. Picture puzzles. Science.

Ready! set! measure! ill. by Steven Kellogg. HarperCollins, 2002. ISBN 978-0-06-623784-8 Subj: Concepts – measurement. Concepts – weight. Counting, numbers.

Where else in the wild? more camouflaged creatures concealed — and revealed by David M. Schwartz and Yael Schy; photos by Dwight Kuhn. Tricycle, 2009. ISBN 978-1-58246-283-7 Subj: Animals. Disguises. Format, unusual – toy & movable books. Poetry.

Where in the wild: camouflaged animals concealed and revealed: ear-tickling poems by David M. Schwartz and Yael Schy; photos by Dwight Kuhn. Ten Speed, 2007. ISBN 978-1-58246-207-3 Subj: Animals. Disguises. Format, unusual – toy & movable books. Poetry.

Schwartz, Henry. *How I captured a dinosaur* ill. by Amy Schwartz. Watts, 1989. ISBN 978-0-531-08370-3 Subj: Camps, camping. Dinosaurs. Pets. Prehistory.

Schwartz, Howard. *Gathering sparks* ill. by Kristina Swarner. Roaring Brook, 2010. ISBN 978-1-59643-280-2 Subj: Character traits – kindness. Character traits – responsibility. Family life – grandfathers. Jewish culture. Religion.

Schwartz, Joanne. *Our corner grocery store* ill. by Laura Beingessner. Tundra, 2009. ISBN 978-0-88776-868-2 Subj: Family life – grandparents. Stores.

Town is by the sea ill. by Sydney Smith. Groundwood, 2017. ISBN 978-155498871-6 Subj: Careers – miners. Cities, towns. Family life – fathers.

Schwartz, Roslyn. *The mole sisters and the cool breeze* ill. by author. Annick, 2002. ISBN 978-1-55037-771-2 Subj: Animals. Animals – moles. Concepts – cold & heat. Family life – sisters.

The mole sisters and the fairy ring ill. by author. Annick, 2003. ISBN 978-1-55037-819-1 Subj: Activities – playing. Animals – moles. Family life – sisters.

The mole sisters and the piece of moss ill. by author. Annick, 1999. ISBN 978-1-55037-583-1 Subj: Animals – moles. Character traits – helpfulness. Character traits – optimism. Family life – sisters.

The mole sisters and the question ill. by author. Annick, 2002. ISBN 978-1-55037-769-9 Subj: Animals. Animals – moles. Family life – sisters.

The mole sisters and the rainy day ill. by author. Annick, 1999. ISBN 978-1-55037-611-1 Subj: Animals – moles. Family life – sisters. Sports – swimming. Weather – rain.

Tales from Parc la Fontaine ill. by author. Firefly, 2006. ISBN 978-1-55451-044-3 Subj: Animals. Nature. Parks.

The Vole brothers ill. by author. OwlKids, 2011. ISBN 978-1-926818-83-2 Subj: Animals – voles. Family life – brothers. Food.

Schwarz, Viviane. *The adventures of a nose* ill. by Joel Stewart. Candlewick, 2002. ISBN 978-0-7636-1674-8 Subj: Anatomy – noses. Emotions – happiness. Self-concept.

How to find gold ill. by author. Candlewick, 2016. ISBN 978-076368104-3 Subj: Friendship. Imagination. Reptiles – alligators, crocodiles.

Is there a dog in this book? ill. by author. Candlewick, 2014. ISBN 978-076366991-1 Subj: Animals – cats. Animals – dogs. Format, unusual – toy & movable books.

Shark and Lobster's amazing undersea adventure ill. by author. Candlewick, 2006. ISBN 978-0-7636-2910-6 Subj: Crustaceans – lobsters. Emotions – fear. Fish – sharks. Sea & seashore.

There are cats in this book ill. by author. Candlewick, 2008. ISBN 978-0-7636-3923-5 Subj: Activities – playing. Animals – cats. Format, unusual – toy & movable books.

There are no cats in this book ill. by author. Candlewick, 2010. ISBN 978-0-7636-4954-8   Subj: Animals – cats. Format, unusual – toy & movable books.

Timothy and the strong pajamas: a superhero adventure ill. by author. Scholastic, 2008. ISBN 978-0-545-03329-9 Subj: Character traits – bravery. Character traits – smallness. Clothing – pajamas.

Schweninger, Ann. *Autumn days* ill. by author. Viking, 1991. ISBN 978-0-670-82758-9 Subj: Animals – dogs. Seasons – fall.

Halloween surprises ill. by author. Viking, 1984. ISBN 978-0-670-35935-6 Subj: Animals – rabbits. Holidays – Halloween.

Valentine friends ill. by author. Viking, 1988. ISBN 978-0-670-81448-0 Subj: Animals – rabbits. Family life. Holidays – Valentine's Day.

Schy, Yael. *Where else in the wild? more camouflaged creatures concealed — and revealed* (Schwartz, David M.)

Where in the wild: camouflaged animals concealed and revealed: ear-tickling poems (Schwartz, David M.)

Scieszka, Jon. *Baloney, Henry P.* ill. by Lane Smith. Viking, 2001. ISBN 978-0-670-89248-8   Subj: Aliens. School. Space & space ships.

Battle Bunny by Jon Scieszka and Mac Barnett ill. by Matthew Myers. Simon & Schuster, 2013. ISBN 978-1-4424-4673-1 Subj: Activities – writing. Animals. Animals – rabbits. Birthdays. Books, reading.

The book that Jack wrote ill. by Daniel Adel. Viking, 1994. ISBN 978-0-670-84330-5 Subj: Cumulative tales. Nursery rhymes.

Cowboy and Octopus ill. by Lane Smith. Penguin, 2007. ISBN 978-0-670-91058-8 Subj: Cowboys, cowgirls. Friendship. Octopuses.

The frog prince, continued ill. by Steve Johnson. Viking, 1991. ISBN 978-0-670-83421-1 Subj: Folk & fairy tales. Frogs & toads. Royalty – princes. Royalty – princesses. Witches.

Melvin might? ill. by David Shannon and Loren Long, et al. Simon & Schuster, 2008. ISBN 978-1-4169-4134-7 Subj: Behavior – worrying. Character traits – bravery. Character traits – helpfulness. Trucks.

Race from A to Z ill. by David Shannon and Loren Long, et al. Simon & Schuster, 2014. ISBN 978-141694136-1 Subj: ABC books. Sports – racing. Trucks.

Robot Zot! ill. by David Shannon. Simon & Schuster, 2009. ISBN 978-1-4169-6394-3 Subj: Humorous stories. Robots. Space & space ships.

Smash! crash! ill. by David Shannon and Loren Long, et al. Simon & Schuster, 2008. ISBN 978-1-4169-4133-0 Subj: Friendship. Trucks.

The Stinky Cheese Man and other fairly stupid tales by Jon Scieszka and Lane Smith ill. by Lane Smith. Viking, 1992. ISBN 978-0-670-84487-6   Subj: Caldecott award honor books. Folk & fairy tales.

Truckery rhymes ill. by David Shannon and Loren Long, et al. Simon & Schuster, 2009. ISBN 978-1-4169-4135-4 Subj: Nursery rhymes. Trucks.

The true story of the three little pigs by A. Wolf, as told to Jon Scieszka ill. by Lane Smith. Viking, 1989. ISBN 978-0-670-82759-6 Subj: Animals – pigs. Animals – wolves. Folk & fairy tales.

Walt Disney's Alice in Wonderland ill. by Mary Blair. Disney, 2008. ISBN 978-1-4231-0728-6 Subj: Behavior – running away. Imagination.

Scillian, Devin. *Brewster the rooster* ill. by Lee White. Little, Brown, 2007. ISBN 978-1-58536-311-7 Subj: Birds – chickens, roosters. Glasses. Rhyming text.

Memoirs of a hamster ill. by Tim Bowers. Sleeping Bear, 2013. ISBN 978-1-58536-831-0 Subj: Animals – cats. Animals – hamsters. Pets.

Sciurba, Katie. *Oye, Celia! a song for Celia Cruz* ill. by Edel Rodriguez. Henry Holt, 2007. ISBN 978-0-8050-7468-0 Subj: Careers – singers. Foreign lands – Cuba. Music.

Scott, Ann Herbert. *Hi!* ill. by Glo Coalson. Philomel, 1994. ISBN 978-0-399-21964-1 Subj: Behavior – unnoticed, unseen. Post office.

On mother's lap ill. by Glo Coalson. Rev. ed. Houghton, 1992. ISBN 978-0-395-58920-5 Subj: Behavior – needing someone. Emotions – love. Eskimos. Family life. Family life – mothers. Sibling rivalry.

Scott, Elaine. *Friends!* photos by Margaret Miller. Atheneum, 2000. ISBN 978-0-689-82105-9 Subj: Friendship.

Scott, Nathan Kumar. *Mangoes and bananas* ill. by T. Balaji. Tara, 2006. ISBN 978-81-86211-06-9 Subj: Animals – deer. Animals – monkeys. Behavior – greed. Behavior – trickery. Folk & fairy tales. Foreign lands – Indonesia.

The sacred banana leaf: an Indonesian trickster tale ill. by Radhashyam Raut. Tara, 2008. ISBN 978-81-86211-28-1 Subj: Animals – deer. Behavior – trickery. Folk & fairy tales. Foreign lands – Indonesia.

Scotton, Rob. *Love, Splat* ill. by author. HarperCollins, 2008. ISBN 978-0-06-083157-8 Subj: Animals – cats. Holidays – Valentine's Day. School.

Merry Christmas, Splat ill. by author. HarperCollins, 2009. ISBN 978-0-06-083160-8 Subj: Animals – cats. Behavior – misbehavior. Holidays – Christmas.

Russell and the lost treasure ill. by author. HarperCollins, 2006. ISBN 978-0-06-059851-8 Subj: Activities – photographing. Animals – sheep.

Russell the sheep ill. by author. HarperCollins, 2005. ISBN 978-0-06-059848-8 Subj: Animals – sheep. Bedtime. Counting, numbers. Sleep.

Russell's Christmas magic ill. by author. HarperCollins, 2007. ISBN 978-0-06-059854-9 Subj: Animals – sheep. Character traits – helpfulness. Holidays – Christmas. Santa Claus.

Scaredy-cat, Splat! ill. by author. HarperCollins, 2015. ISBN 978-006236897-3 Subj: Animals – cats. Clothing – costumes. Holidays – Halloween.

Secret Agent Splat! ill. by author. HarperCollins, 2012. ISBN 978-0-06-197871-5 Subj: Animals – cats. Behavior – lost & found possessions. Careers – detectives.

Splat and the cool school trip ill. by author. HarperCollins, 2013. ISBN 978-0-06-213386-1 Subj: Animals – cats. School – field trips. Zoos.

Splat says thank you! ill. by author. HarperCollins, 2012. ISBN 978-0-06-197874-6 Subj: Animals – cats. Animals – mice. Character traits – kindness. Friendship. Illness.

Splat the cat ill. by author. HarperCollins, 2008. ISBN 978-0-06-083154-7 Subj: Animals – cats. Animals – mice. Humorous stories. School – first day.

Splat the cat: on with the show by Rob Scotton and Annie Auerbach; ill. by Rob Scotton. HarperCollins, 2013. ISBN 978-0-06-209010-2 Subj: Animals – cats. School. Theater.

Splish, splash, splat! ill. by author. HarperCollins, 2011. ISBN 978-0-06-197868-5 Subj: Animals – cats. Emotions – fear. Friendship. Sports – swimming.

Scrimger, Richard. *Eugene's story* ill. by Gillian Johnson. Tundra, 2003. ISBN 978-0-88776-544-5 Subj: Activities – storytelling. Family life – brothers & sisters. Sibling rivalry.

Princess Bun Bun ill. by Johnson, Gillian. Tundra, 2002. ISBN 978-0-88776-543-8 Subj: Family life – aunts, uncles. Family life – brothers & sisters. Monsters. Royalty – princesses.

The scrubbly-bubbly car wash ill. by Cynthia Jabar. HarperCollins, 2003. ISBN 978-0-06-029486-1 Subj: Automobiles. Family life – fathers. Rhyming text.

Scruggs, Afi. *Jump rope magic* ill. by David Diaz. Blue Sky, 2000. ISBN 978-0-590-69327-1 Subj:

Activities – jumping. Ethnic groups in the U.S. – African Americans. Games. Noise, sounds. Rhyming text.

Seabrooke, Brenda. *'Twas the day before Christmas: the story of Clement Clarke Moore's beloved poem* ill. by Delana Bettoli. Dutton, 2008. ISBN 978-0-525-47816-4 Subj: Activities – writing. Holidays – Christmas. Poetry.

Sears, William, M.D. *Baby on the way* ill. by Renée Williams-Andriani. Little, 2001. ISBN 978-0-316-78767-3 Subj: Babies, toddlers. Birth.

Sears, William, M.D., et al. *Eat healthy, feel great* ill. by Renée Williams-Andriani. Little, 2002. ISBN 978-0-316-78708-6 Subj: Food. Health & fitness.

What baby needs ill. by Renée Williams-Andriani. Little, 2001. ISBN 978-0-316-78828-1 Subj: Babies, toddlers. Family life – new sibling.

You can go to the potty ill. by Renée Williams-Andriani. Little, 2002. ISBN 978-0-316-78888-5 Subj: Behavior – growing up. Toilet training.

Seattle, Chief. *Brother eagle, sister sky* ill. by Susan Jeffers. Puffin, 2002. ISBN 978-0-14-230132-6 Subj: Ecology. Indians of North America – Suquamish.

Sebe, Masayuki. *Let's count to one hundred!* ill. by author. Kids Can, 2011. ISBN 978-1-55453-661-0 Subj: Counting, numbers.

One hundred animals on parade! ill. by author. Kids Can, 2013. ISBN 978-1-55453-871-3 Subj: Animals. Counting, numbers. Parades.

One hundred hungry monkeys! ill. by author. Kids Can, 2014. ISBN 978-177138045-4 Subj: Animals – monkeys. Counting, numbers. Food.

Sebra, Richard. *It's Diwali!* ill. with photos. Lerner/Bumba, 2017. ISBN 978-151242563-5 Subj: Ethnic groups in the U.S. – East Indian Americans. Foreign lands – India. Holidays – Diwali. Religion – Hinduism.

Sedaka, Marc. *Dinosaur pet* ill. by Tim Bowers. Imagine, 2012. ISBN 978-1-936140-36-7 Subj: Dinosaurs. Music.

Sedaka, Neil. *Waking up is hard to do* by Neil Sedaka and Howard Greenfield ill. by Daniel Miyares. Imagine, 2010. ISBN 978-1-936140-13-8 Subj: Morning. Reptiles – alligators, crocodiles. Songs.

Seder, Rufus Butler. *Waddle!* ill. by author. Workman, 2009. ISBN 978-0-7611-5112-8 Subj: Animals. Concepts – motion. Format, unusual – toy & movable books.

The Wizard of Oz: a Scanimation book ill. by author. Workman, 2011. ISBN 978-0-7611-6373-2 Subj: Format, unusual – toy & movable books. Wizards.

Seeber, Dorothea P. *A pup just for me . . . A boy just for me* ill. by Ed Young. Philomel, 2000. ISBN 978-0-399-23403-3 Subj: Animals – dogs. Behavior – needing someone. Format, unusual – toy & movable books. Pets. Rhyming text.

Seeger, Laura Vaccaro. *Black? white! day? night! a book of opposites* ill. by author. Macmillan, 2006. ISBN 978-1-59643-185-0 Subj: Concepts – opposites. Format, unusual – toy & movable books.

Bully ill. by author. Roaring Brook, 2013. ISBN 978-1-59643-630-5 Subj: Animals. Animals – bulls, cows. Behavior – bullying, teasing. Emotions – anger.

Dog and Bear: three to get ready ill. by author. Roaring Brook, 2009. ISBN 978-1-59643-396-0 Subj: Animals – dogs. Friendship. Toys – bears.

Dog and Bear: tricks and treats ill. by author. Roaring Brook/Neal Porter, 2014. ISBN 978-159643632-9 Subj: Animals – dogs. Friendship. Holidays – Halloween. Toys – bears.

Dog and Bear: two friends, three stories ill. by author. Macmillan, 2007. ISBN 978-1-59643-053-2 Subj: Animals – dogs. Friendship. Toys – bears.

Dog and Bear: two's company ill. by author. Roaring Brook, 2008. ISBN 978-1-59643-273-4 Subj: Animals – dogs. Friendship. Toys – bears.

First the egg ill. by author. Macmillan, 2007. ISBN 978-1-59643-272-7 Subj: Caldecott award honor books. Concepts – change. Format, unusual – toy & movable books.

Green ill. by author. Roaring Brook, 2012. ISBN 978-1-59643-397-7 Subj: Caldecott award honor books. Concepts – color. Nature.

The hidden alphabet ill. by author. Roaring Brook, 2003. ISBN 978-0-7613-1941-2 Subj: ABC books. Format, unusual – toy & movable books. Picture puzzles.

I had a rooster: a traditional folk song ill. by author. Viking, 2001. ISBN 978-0-670-03521-2 Subj: Animals. Noise, sounds. Songs.

I used to be afraid ill. by author. Roaring Brook/Neal Porter, 2015. ISBN 978-159643631-2 Subj: Behavior – worrying. Emotions – fear.

Lemons are not red ill. by author. Macmillan, 2004. ISBN 978-1-59643-008-2 Subj: Concepts – color. Format, unusual – toy & movable books.

One boy ill. by author. Roaring Brook, 2008. ISBN 978-1-59643-274-1 Subj: Activities – painting. Counting, numbers. Format, unusual. Language.

Walter was worried ill. by author. Macmillan, 2005. ISBN 978-1-59643-068-6 Subj: ABC books. Emotions. Language. Weather – storms.

What if? ill. by author. Roaring Brook, 2010. ISBN 978-1-59643-398-4 Subj: Animals – seals. Behavior – sharing. Friendship. Toys – balls.

Seeger, Pete. *Abiyoyo* ill. by Michael Hays. Macmillan, 1986. ISBN 978-0-02-781490-3 Subj: Folk & fairy tales. Magic. Monsters.

Abiyoyo returns by Pete Seeger and Paul DuBois Jacobs ill. by Michael Hays. Simon & Schuster, 2001. ISBN 978-0-689-83271-0 Subj: Careers – magicians. Folk & fairy tales. Foreign lands – South Africa. Giants. Magic.

The deaf musicians by Pete Seeger and Paul DuBois Jacobs ill. by R. Gregory Christie. Penguin, 2006. ISBN 978-0-399-24316-5 Subj: Careers – musicians. Disabilities – deafness. Music.

Some friends to feed: the story of Stone Soup by Pete Seeger and Paul DuBois Jacobs ill. by Michael Hays. Penguin, 2005. ISBN 978-0-399-24017-1 Subj: Careers – military. Character traits – cleverness. Folk & fairy tales. Food. Foreign lands – Germany.

Segal, John. *Alistair and Kip's great adventure* ill. by author. Simon & Schuster, 2008. ISBN 978-1-4169-0280-5 Subj: Activities – traveling. Animals – cats. Animals – dogs. Boats, ships.

Carrot soup ill. by author. Simon & Schuster, 2006. ISBN 978-0-689-87702-5 Subj: Animals – rabbits. Food. Gardens, gardening.

Far far away! ill. by author. Philomel, 2009. ISBN 978-0-399-25007-1 Subj: Animals – pigs. Behavior – running away. Family life – mothers.

The lonely moose ill. by author. Hyperion, 2007. ISBN 978-1-4231-0173-4 Subj: Animals – moose. Birds. Emotions – loneliness. Friendship.

Pirates don't take baths ill. by author. Penguin, 2011. ISBN 978-0-399-25425-3 Subj: Activities – bathing. Animals – pigs. Imagination.

Segal, Lore Groszmann. *Morris the artist* ill. by Boris Kulikov. Farrar, 2003. ISBN 978-0-374-35063-5 Subj: Activities – painting. Birthdays. Careers – artists. Gifts.

Sehgal, Kabir. *A bucket of blessings* by Kabir Sehgal and Surishtha Sehgal ill. by Jing Jing Tsong. Simon & Schuster/Beach Lane, 2014. ISBN 978-144245870-3 Subj: Animals – monkeys. Birds – peacocks, peahens. Folk & fairy tales. Foreign lands – India. Weather – rain.

The wheels on the tuk tuk by Kabir Sehgal and Surishtha Sehgal ill. by Jess Golden. Simon & Schuster/Beach Lane, 2015. ISBN 978-148144831-4

Subj: Automobiles. Foreign lands – India. Songs. Taxis.

Sehgal, Surishtha. *A bucket of blessings* (Sehgal, Kabir)

The wheels on the tuk tuk (Sehgal, Kabir)

Seibert, Patricia. *Mush! across Alaska in the world's longest sled-dog race* ill. by Jan Davey Ellis. Millbrook, 1992. ISBN 978-1-56294-705-7 Subj: Alaska. Animals – dogs. Sports – racing. Sports – sledding.

Seibold, J. Otto. *Lost sloth* ill. by author. McSweeney's McMullens, 2013. ISBN 978-1-938073-35-9 Subj: Animals – sloths. Character traits – luck. Shopping. Stores.

Penguin dreams by J. Otto Seibold and Vivian Walsh; ill. by J. Otto Seibold. Chronicle, 1999. ISBN 978-0-8118-2558-0 Subj: Activities – flying. Birds – penguins. Dreams. Foreign lands – Antarctic. Rhyming text.

Vunce upon a time by J. Otto Seibold and Siobhan Vivian; ill. by J. Otto Seibold. Chronicle, 2008. ISBN 978-0-8118-6271-4 Subj: Holidays – Halloween. Monsters.

Seim, Donna Marie. *Where is Simon, Sandy? the story of a little donkey that wouldn't quit* ill. by Susan Spellman. PublishingWorks, 2008. ISBN 978-1-933002-73-6 Subj: Animals – donkeys. Character traits – perseverance. Foreign lands. Water.

Seinfeld, Jerry. *Halloween* ill. by James Bennett. Little, 2002. ISBN 978-0-316-13454-5 Subj: Holidays – Halloween. Memories, memory.

Seki, Sunny. *The tale of the lucky cat* ill. by author. East West, 2007. ISBN 978-0-9669437-5-7 Subj: Animals – cats. Character traits – luck. Folk & fairy tales. Foreign lands – Japan.

Selick, Henry. *Moongirl* ill. by Peter Chan. Candlewick, 2006. ISBN 978-0-7636-3068-3 Subj: Merry-go-rounds. Monsters. Moon. Sports – fishing.

Selig, Josh. *Red and Yellow's noisy night* ill. by Little Airplane Productions. Sterling, 2012. ISBN 978-1-4027-9070-6 Subj: Bedtime. Behavior – fighting, arguing. Concepts – color. Lullabies. Noise, sounds.

Selkowe, Valrie M. *Happy birthday to me!* ill. by John Sandford. HarperCollins, 2001. ISBN 978-0-688-16680-9 Subj: Animals. Animals – rabbits. Birthdays. Gardens, gardening.

Selsam, Millicent E. *How to be a nature detective* ill. by Marlene Hill Donnelly. HarperCollins, 1995. ISBN 978-0-06-023448-5 Subj: Animals. Nature.

Keep looking! by Millicent E. Selsam and Joyce Hunt ill. by Normand Chartier. Macmillan, 1988. ISBN 978-0-02-781840-6 Subj: Animals. Farms. Seasons – winter.

Selznick, Brian. *The invention of Hugo Cabret: a novel in words and pictures* ill. by author. Scholastic, 2007. ISBN 978-0-439-81378-5 Subj: Caldecott award books. Foreign lands – France. Mystery stories. Orphans. Robots.

Sendak, Maurice. *Alligators all around: an alphabet* ill. by author. HarperCollins, 1962. ISBN 978-0-06-025530-5 Subj: ABC books. Reptiles – alligators, crocodiles.

Bumble-ardy ill. by author. HarperCollins, 2011. ISBN 978-0-06-205198-1 Subj: Animals – pigs. Birthdays. Parties. Rhyming text.

Chicken soup with rice ill. by author. HarperCollins, 1962. ISBN 978-0-06-025535-0 Subj: Days of the week, months of the year.

Hector Protector, and As I went over the water ill. by author. HarperCollins, 1993. ISBN 978-0-06-028643-9 Subj: Nursery rhymes.

In the night kitchen ill. by author. HarperCollins, 1970. ISBN 978-0-06-026669-1 Subj: Caldecott award honor books. Dreams. Imagination.

Mommy? ill. by author. Paper engineering by Matthew Reinhart. Scholastic, 2006. ISBN 978-0-439-88050-3 Subj: Format, unusual – toy & movable books. Monsters.

One was Johnny: a counting book ill. by author. HarperCollins, 1962. ISBN 978-0-06-025540-4 Subj: Counting, numbers.

Outside over there ill. by author. HarperCollins, 1981. ISBN 978-0-06-025524-4 Subj: Activities – babysitting. Babies, toddlers. Caldecott award honor books. Mythical creatures – goblins.

Pierre: a cautionary tale in five chapters and a prologue ill. by author. HarperCollins, 1962. ISBN 978-0-06-118009-5 Subj: Behavior – indifference. Character traits – individuality. Humorous stories. Rhyming text.

Seven little monsters ill. by author. HarperCollins, 1977. ISBN 978-0-06-025478-0 Subj: Counting, numbers. Monsters. Rhyming text.

The sign on Rosie's door ill. by author. HarperCollins, 1960. ISBN 978-0-06-025506-0 Subj: Activities – playing. Imagination.

Very far away ill. by author. HarperCollins, 1957. ISBN 978-0-06-025515-2 Subj: Animals. Behavior – needing someone. Behavior – running away.

Where the wild things are ill. by author. HarperCollins, 1963. ISBN 978-0-06-025521-3 Subj: Behavior – misbehavior. Caldecott award books. Imagination. Monsters.

Sendelbach, Brian. *The underpants zoo* ill. by author. Scholastic, 2011. ISBN 978-0-545-24935-5 Subj: Clothing – underwear. Rhyming text. Zoos.

Senior, Olive. *Birthday suit* ill. by Eugenie Fernandes. Annick, 2012. ISBN 978-1-55451-369-7 Subj: Behavior – growing up. Clothing.

Senisi, Ellen B. *All kinds of friends, even green* photos by Ellen B Senisi. Woodbine, 2002. ISBN 978-1-890627-35-5 Subj: Disabilities – physical disabilities. Reptiles – iguanas. School.

For my family, love, Allie photos by Ellen B Senisi. Albert Whitman, 1998. ISBN 978-0-8075-2539-5 Subj: Family life. Food. Marriage, interracial.

Hurray for pre-K! photos by Ellen B Senisi. HarperCollins, 2000. ISBN 978-0-06-028897-6 Subj: Activities. Emotions. School – nursery.

Just kids: visiting a class for children with special needs photos by Ellen B Senisi. Dutton, 1998. ISBN 978-0-525-45646-9 Subj: Disabilities. School.

Senning, Cindy Post. *Emily's everyday manners* (Post, Peggy)

Emily's out and about book by Cindy Post Senning and Peggy Post ill. by Leo Landry. Collins, 2009. ISBN 978-0-06-111700-8 Subj: Etiquette. Family life – mothers.

Sensel, Joni. *Bears barge in* ill. by Christopher L. Bivins. Dream Factory, 2000. ISBN 978-0-9701195-0-6 Subj: Animals. Ecology. Rhyming text.

Senshu, Noriko. *Sonny's dream* ill. by author. Roads, 2000. ISBN 978-1-57174-215-5 Subj: Alaska. Animals – bears. Behavior – growing up. Dreams. Emotions – fear. Hibernation.

Serafini, Frank. *Looking closely across the desert* photos by author. Kids Can, 2008. ISBN 978-1-55453-211-7 Subj: Desert.

Looking closely along the shore photos by author. Kids Can, 2008. ISBN 978-1-55453-141-7 Subj: Participation. Picture puzzles. Sea & seashore. Senses – sight.

Looking closely around the pond photos by author. Kids Can, 2009. ISBN 978-1-55337-395-7 Subj: Lakes, ponds.

Looking closely inside the garden photos by author. Kids Can, 2008. ISBN 978-1-55453-210-0 Subj: Gardens, gardening. Plants.

Looking closely through the forest photos by author. Kids Can, 2008. ISBN 978-1-55453-212-4 Subj: Forest, woods.

Serfozo, Mary. *Rain talk* ill. by Keiko Narahashi. Macmillan, 1990. ISBN 978-0-689-50496-9 Subj: Noise, sounds. Weather – rain.

There's a square ill. by David A. Carter. Scholastic, 1996. ISBN 978-0-590-54426-9 Subj: Concepts – shape. Rhyming text.

What's what? a guessing game ill. by Keiko Narahashi. Margaret K. McElderry, 1996. ISBN 978-0-689-80653-7 Subj: Animals – dogs. Concepts – opposites. Ethnic groups in the U.S. – African Americans. Language.

Who said red? ill. by Keiko Narahashi. Macmillan, 1988. ISBN 978-0-689-50455-6 Subj: Concepts – color.

Who wants one? ill. by Keiko Narahashi. Macmillan, 1989. ISBN 978-0-689-50474-7 Subj: Counting, numbers. Rhyming text.

Whooo's there? ill. by Jeffrey Scherer. Random House, 2007. ISBN 978-0-375-84050-0 Subj: Animals. Birds – owls. Forest, woods. Night. Rhyming text.

Seskin, Steve. *A chance to shine* by Steve Seskin and Allen Shamblin ill. by R. Gregory Christie. Ten Speed, 2006. ISBN 978-1-58246-167-0 Subj: Ethnic groups in the U.S. – African Americans. Homeless. Songs.

Don't laugh at me by Steve Seskin and Allen Shamblin ill. by Glin Dibley. Tricycle, 2002. ISBN 978-1-58246-058-1 Subj: Character traits – individuality. Music. Songs.

Seto, Loretta. *Mooncakes* ill. by Renné Benoit. Orca, 2013. ISBN 978-1-45980-107-3 Subj: Ethnic groups in the U.S. – Chinese Americans. Fairs, festivals. Family life. Folk & fairy tales.

Seuling, Barbara. *Drip! drop!* ill. by Nancy Tobin. Holiday, 2000. ISBN 978-0-8234-1459-8 Subj: Water.

Flick a switch ill. by Nancy Tobin. Holiday, 2003. ISBN 978-0-8234-1729-2 Subj: Science.

From head to toe ill. by Edward Miller. Holiday, 2002. ISBN 978-0-8234-1699-8 Subj: Anatomy. Science.

Spring song ill. by Greg Newbold. Harcourt, 2001. ISBN 978-0-15-202317-1 Subj: Animals. Rhyming text. Seasons – spring.

Winter lullaby ill. by Greg Newbold. Browndeer, 1997. ISBN 978-0-15-201403-2 Subj: Animals. Seasons – winter.

Seuss, Dr. *And to think that I saw it on Mulberry Street* ill. by author. Random House, 1989, ©1937. ISBN 978-0-394-94494-4 Subj: Humorous stories. Imagination. Rhyming text.

Bartholomew and the Oobleck ill. by author. Random House, 1949. ISBN 978-0-394-90075-9 Subj: Caldecott award honor books. Humorous stories. Royalty.

The butter battle book ill. by author. Random House, 1984. ISBN 978-0-394-96580-2 Subj: Rhyming text. War.

Did I ever tell you how lucky you are? ill. by Richard Erdoes. Random House, 1973. ISBN 978-0-394-92719-0 Subj: Character traits – luck. Humorous stories. Problem solving. Rhyming text.

Gerald McBoing Boing ed. by Kate Klimo; ill. by author. Random House, 2000. ISBN 978-0-679-99140-3 Subj: Communication. Concepts. Humorous stories. Noise, sounds. Rhyming text. Senses.

Gerald McBoing Boing sound book ill. by author. Random House, 2003. ISBN 978-0-375-82443-2 Subj: Communication. Concepts. Format, unusual. Humorous stories. Noise, sounds. Participation. Rhyming text.

Happy birthday to you! ill. by author. Random House, 1959. ISBN 978-0-394-90076-6 Subj: Birthdays. Humorous stories. Rhyming text.

Horton and the Kwuggerbug and more lost stories ill. by Dr. Seuss. Random House, 2014. ISBN 978-038538298-4 Subj: Humorous stories. Rhyming text.

Horton hatches the egg ill. by author. Random House, 1940. ISBN 978-0-394-90077-3 Subj: Animals – elephants. Birds. Character traits – helpfulness. Eggs. Humorous stories. Rhyming text.

Horton hears a Who! ill. by author. Random House, 1954. ISBN 978-0-394-90078-0 Subj: Animals – elephants. Character traits – kindness. Humorous stories. Rhyming text.

How the Grinch stole Christmas ill. by author. Random House, 1957. ISBN 978-0-394-90079-7 Subj: Character traits – meanness. Holidays – Christmas. Humorous stories. Rhyming text.

Hunches in bunches ill. by author. Random House, 1982. ISBN 978-0-394-95502-5 Subj: Problem solving. Rhyming text.

I can lick 30 tigers today and other stories ill. by author. Random House, 1969. ISBN 978-0-394-90094-0 Subj: Animals – tigers. Humorous stories. Rhyming text.

I had trouble getting to Solla Sollew ill. by author. Random House, 1965. Subj: Activities – traveling. Humorous stories. Rhyming text.

If I ran the circus ill. by author. Random House, 1956. ISBN 978-0-394-90080-3 Subj: Circus. Humorous stories. Rhyming text.

If I ran the zoo ill. by author. Random House, 1950. ISBN 978-0-394-90081-0 Subj: Caldecott award honor books. Humorous stories. Rhyming text. Zoos.

The king's stilts ill. by author. Random House, 1939. ISBN 978-0-394-90082-7 Subj: Humorous stories. Rhyming text. Royalty – kings. Toys.

The Lorax ill. by author. Random House, 1971. ISBN 978-0-394-92337-6 Subj: Ecology. Humorous stories.

McElligot's pool ill. by author. Random House, 1947. ISBN 978-0-394-90083-4 Subj: Caldecott award honor books. Fish. Humorous stories. Imagination. Rhyming text.

Oh, the places you'll go! ill. by author. Random House, 1990. ISBN 978-0-679-90527-1 Subj: Self-concept.

On beyond zebra ill. by author. Random House, 1955. ISBN 978-0-394-90084-1 Subj: Humorous stories. Letters, cards. Rhyming text.

Scrambled eggs super! ill. by author. Random House, 1953. ISBN 978-0-394-90085-8 Subj: Food. Humorous stories. Rhyming text.

The Sneetches, and other stories ill. by author. Random House, 1961. ISBN 978-0-394-90089-6 Subj: Emotions – fear. Humorous stories. Rhyming text.

Thidwick, the big-hearted moose ill. by author. Random House, 1948. ISBN 978-0-394-90086-5 Subj: Animals – moose. Birds. Humorous stories. Rhyming text.

What pet should I get? ill. by Dr. Seuss. Random House, 2015. ISBN 978-055352426-0 Subj: Behavior – indecision. Pets. Rhyming text.

Seven, John. *The ocean story* ill. by Jana Christy. Picture Window, 2011. ISBN 978-1-4048-6785-7 Subj: Ecology. Sea & seashore. Water.

A year with friends ill. by Jana Christy. Abrams, 2013. ISBN 978-1-4197-0443-7 Subj: Days of the week, months of the year. Friendship. Seasons.

Seven spunky monkeys ill. by Lynn Munsinger. Harcourt, 2005. ISBN 978-0-15-202519-9 Subj: Activities. Animals – monkeys. Counting, numbers. Day. Rhyming text.

Sexton, Colleen A. *Let's meet Martin Luther King, Jr* ill. with photos. Chelsea, 2004. ISBN 978-0-7910-7322-3 Subj: Careers – clergy. Ethnic groups in the U.S. – African Americans. Holidays – Martin Luther King, Jr. Day. U.S. history.

Seymour, Dorothy Z. *Ann likes red* ill. by Nancy Meyerhoff. Purple House, 2001. ISBN 978-1-930900-12-7 Subj: Clothing – dresses. Concepts – color.

Shafer, Dana. *Mud Pie Annie: God's recipe for doing your best* (Buchanan, Sue)

Shaffer, Jody Jensen. *Prudence the part-time cow* ill. by Stephanie Laberis. Henry Holt, 2017. ISBN 978-162779615-6 Subj: Animals – bulls, cows. Careers – scientists. Character traits – being different. Character traits – individuality.

Shah, Idries. *The boy without a name* ill. by Mona Caron. Hoopoe, 2000. ISBN 978-1-883536-20-6 Subj: Dreams. Folk & fairy tales. Foreign lands – Middle East. Magic. Names.

The clever boy and the terrible, dangerous animal ill. by Rose Mary Santiago. Hoopoe, 2000. ISBN 978-1-883536-18-3 Subj: Character traits – helpfulness. Emotions – fear. Folk & fairy tales. Foreign lands – Middle East.

Fatima the spinner and the tent ill. by Natasha Delmar. Hoopoe, 2006. ISBN 978-1-883536-42-8 Subj: Activities – weaving. Folk & fairy tales. Foreign lands.

The silly chicken ill. by Jeff Jackson. Hoopoe, 2000. ISBN 978-1-883536-19-0 Subj: Birds – chickens, roosters. Folk & fairy tales. Foreign lands – Middle East.

Shahan, Sherry. *Cool cats counting* ill. by Paula Barragán. August House, 2005. ISBN 978-0-87483-757-5 Subj: Animals. Counting, numbers.

Fiesta! a celebration of Latino festivals ill. by Paula Barragán. August House, 2009. ISBN 978-0-87483-861-9 Subj: Days of the week, months of the year. Foreign lands – Latin America. Holidays.

The jazzy alphabet ill. by Mary Thelen. Philomel, 2002. ISBN 978-0-399-23453-8 Subj: ABC books. Musical instruments. Rhyming text.

That's not how you play soccer, Daddy ill. by Tatjana Mai-Wyss. Peachtree, 2007. ISBN 978-1-56145-416-7 Subj: Family life – fathers. Sports – soccer.

Shakespeare, William. *To sleep, perchance to dream* ill. by James Mayhew. Scholastic, 2001. ISBN 978-0-439-29655-7 Subj: Poetry.

Shamblin, Allen. *A chance to shine* (Seskin, Steve)

Don't laugh at me (Seskin, Steve)

Shange, Ntozake. *Coretta Scott* ill. by Kadir Nelson. Amistad, 2009. ISBN 978-0-06-125364-5 Subj: Ethnic groups in the U.S. – African Americans. Poetry. Prejudice. U.S. history.

Ellington was not a street ill. by Kadir Nelson. Simon & Schuster, 2004. ISBN 978-0-689-82884-3 Subj: Ethnic groups in the U.S. – African Americans. Poetry.

Freedom's a-callin me ill. by Rod Brown. Amistad, 2012. ISBN 978-0-06-133741-3 Subj: Character traits – freedom. Ethnic groups in the U.S. – African Americans. Poetry. Slavery. U.S. history.

Whitewash ill. by Michael Sporn. Walker, 1997. ISBN 978-0-8027-8491-9 Subj: Ethnic groups in the U.S. – African Americans. Prejudice.

Shannon, David. *The amazing Christmas extravaganza* ill. by author. Blue Sky, 1995. ISBN 978-0-590-48090-1 Subj: Emotions – anger. Holidays – Christmas.

A bad case of stripes ill. by author. Blue Sky, 1998. ISBN 978-0-590-92997-4 Subj: Behavior. Character traits – individuality.

Bizzy Mizz Lizzie ill. by author. Scholastic, 2017. ISBN 978-054561943-1 Subj: Character traits – ambition. Contests. Insects – bees.

Bugs in my hair! ill. by author. Scholastic, 2013. ISBN 978-0-545-14313-4 Subj: Hair. Insects – lice.

David gets in trouble ill. by author. Blue Sky, 2002. ISBN 978-0-439-05022-7 Subj: Bedtime. Behavior – misbehavior.

David goes to school ill. by author. Blue Sky, 1999. ISBN 978-0-590-48087-1 Subj: Behavior – misbehavior. School.

David smells: a diaper David book ill. by author. Scholastic, 2005. ISBN 978-0-439-69138-3 Subj: Babies, toddlers. Format, unusual – board books. Senses.

Demasiados juguetes / too many toys ill. by author. Scholastic, 2008. ISBN 978-0-545-07918-1 Subj: Family life. Foreign languages. Toys.

Duck on a bike ill. by author. Blue Sky, 2002. ISBN 978-0-439-05023-4 Subj: Animals. Birds – ducks. Sports – bicycling.

Duck on a tractor ill. by author. Scholastic/Blue Sky, 2016. ISBN 978-054561941-7 Subj: Animals. Birds – ducks. Tractors.

Good boy, Fergus! ill. by author. Scholastic, 2006. ISBN 978-0-439-49027-6 Subj: Animals – dogs. Behavior – misbehavior.

Jangles: a big fish story ill. by author. Scholastic, 2012. ISBN 978-0-545-14312-7 Subj: Activities – storytelling. Family life – fathers. Fish. Sports – fishing. Tall tales.

No, David! ill. by author. Blue Sky, 1998. ISBN 978-0-590-93002-4 Subj: Behavior – misbehavior. Caldecott award honor books.

Oh, David! a diaper David book ill. by author. Scholastic, 2005. ISBN 978-0-439-68881-9 Subj: Babies, toddlers. Behavior – misbehavior. Format, unusual – board books.

Oops! a diaper David book ill. by author. Scholastic, 2005. ISBN 978-0-439-68882-6 Subj: Babies, toddlers. Format, unusual – board books. Language.

The rain came down ill. by author. Blue Sky, 2000. ISBN 978-0-439-05021-0 Subj: Behavior. Behavior – misunderstanding. Weather – rain. Weather – rainbows.

Too many toys ill. by author. Scholastic, 2008. ISBN 978-0-439-49029-0 Subj: Family life. Toys.

Shannon, George. *April showers* ill. by José Aruego and Ariane Dewey. Greenwillow, 1995. ISBN 978-0-688-13122-7 Subj: Activities – dancing. Frogs & toads. Weather – rain.

Busy in the garden ill. by Sam Williams. Harper-Collins, 2006. ISBN 978-0-06-000464-4 Subj: Gardens, gardening. Poetry.

Frog legs: a picture book of action verse ill. by Amit Trynan. Greenwillow, 2000. ISBN 978-0-688-17047-9 Subj: Frogs & toads. Poetry.

Hands say love ill. by Taeeun Yoo. Little, Brown, 2014. ISBN 978-031608479-6 Subj: Anatomy – hands. Emotions – love. Rhyming text.

Heart to heart ill. by Steve Björkman. Houghton, 1995. ISBN 978-0-395-72773-7 Subj: Animals – moles. Animals – squirrels. Friendship. Holidays – Valentine's Day.

Lizard's home ill. by José Aruego and Ariane Dewey. Greenwillow, 1999. ISBN 978-0-688-16003-6 Subj: Character traits – cleverness. Homes, houses. Reptiles – lizards. Reptiles – snakes.

Lizard's song ill. by José Aruego and Ariane Dewey. Greenwillow, 1981. ISBN 978-0-688-84310-6 Subj: Animals – bears. Reptiles – lizards. Songs.

One family ill. by Blanca Gomez. Farrar, 2015. ISBN 978-037430003-6 Subj: Counting, numbers. Ethnic groups in the U.S. Family life.

Rabbit's gift ill. by Laura Dronzek. Harcourt, 2007. ISBN 978-0-15-206073-2 Subj: Animals. Animals – rabbits. Behavior – sharing. Folk & fairy tales. Friendship.

The Secret Chicken Club ill. by Deborah Zemke. Handprint, 2005. ISBN 978-1-59354-118-7 Subj: Animals – bulls, cows. Birds – chickens, roosters. Clubs, gangs.

Spring: a haiku story ill. by Malcah Zeldis. Greenwillow, 1996. ISBN 978-0-688-13889-9 Subj: Foreign lands – Japan. Poetry. Seasons – spring.

The surprise ill. by José Aruego and Ariane Dewey. Greenwillow, 1983. ISBN 978-0-688-02314-0 Subj: Animals – squirrels. Birthdays.

Tippy-toe chick, go ill. by Laura Dronzek. Greenwillow, 2003. ISBN 978-0-06-029824-1 Subj: Animals – dogs. Birds – chickens, roosters. Character traits – bravery.

Tomorrow's alphabet ill. by Donald Crews. Greenwillow, 1995. ISBN 978-0-688-13505-8 Subj: ABC books. Concepts.

Turkey Tot ill. by Jennifer K Mann. Holiday House, 2013. ISBN 978-0-8234-2379-8 Subj: Animals. Birds – turkeys. Character traits – persistence. Farms. Problem solving.

A very witchy spelling bee ill. by Mark Fearing. Harcourt, 2013. ISBN 978-0-15-206696-3 Subj: Contests. Witches.

White is for blueberry ill. by Laura Dronzek. HarperCollins, 2005. ISBN 978-0-06-029275-1 Subj: Concepts – color. Nature. Senses – sight.

Who put the cookies in the cookie jar? ill. by Julie Paschkis. Henry Holt, 2013. ISBN 978-0-8050-9197-7 Subj: Activities – baking, cooking. Food. Rhyming text.

Shannon, Margaret. *Gullible's troubles* ill. by author. Houghton, 1998. ISBN 978-0-395-83933-1 Subj: Animals – guinea pigs. Behavior – trickery. Family life. Monsters.

The red wolf ill. by author. Houghton, 2002. ISBN 978-0-618-05544-9 Subj: Activities – knitting. Folk & fairy tales. Royalty – princesses.

Shannon, Molly. *Tilly the trickster* ill. by Ard Hoyt. Abrams, 2011. ISBN 978-1-4197-0030-9 Subj: Behavior – misbehavior.

Shannon, Terry Miller. *Tub toys* by Terry Miller Shannon and Timothy Warner ill. by Lee Calderon. Tricycle, 2002. ISBN 978-1-58246-066-6 Subj: Activities – bathing. Rhyming text. Toys.

Shapes ill. by Virginie Graire. little bee, 2016. ISBN 978-149980294-8 Subj: Concepts – shape. Format, unusual – board books.

Shapiro, Esmé. *Ooko* ill. by author. Tundra, 2016. ISBN 978-110191844-9 Subj: Animals – foxes. Emotions – loneliness. Self-concept.

Shapiro, J. H. *Magic trash: a story of Tyree Guyton and his art* ill. by Vanessa Brantley Newton. Charlesbridge, 2011. ISBN 978-1-58089-385-5 Subj: Art. Careers – artists. Cities, towns. Ethnic groups in the U.S. – African Americans.

Shapiro, Jody Fickes. *Family lullaby* ill. by Cathie Felstead. HarperCollins, 2007. ISBN 978-0-06-051482-2 Subj: Babies, toddlers. Emotions – love. Family life.

Up, up, up! It's apple-picking time ill. by Kitty Harvill. Holiday, 2003. ISBN 978-0-8234-1610-3 Subj: Family life – grandparents. Farms. Food. Seasons – fall.

Shapiro, Lawrence E. *It's time to give up your pacifier* ill. by Hideko Takahashi. New Harbinger, 2008. ISBN 978-1-57224-585-3 Subj: Babies, toddlers. Behavior – growing up.

Shapiro, Zachary. *We're all in the same boat* ill. by Jack E. Davis. Putnam, 2009. ISBN 978-0-399-24393-6 Subj: ABC books. Animals. Boats, ships.

Religion – Noah. Weather – floods. Weather – rain.

Sharkey, Niamh. *The gigantic turnip* (Tolstoy, Aleksey Nikolayevich)

Santasaurus ill. by author. Candlewick, 2005. ISBN 978-0-7636-2671-6 Subj: Dinosaurs. Holidays – Christmas. Santa Claus.

Sharmat, Marjorie Weinman. *The best Valentine in the world* ill. by Lilian Obligado. Holiday, 1982. ISBN 978-0-8234-0440-7 Subj: Animals – foxes. Holidays – Valentine's Day.

Gila monsters meet you at the airport ill. by Byron Barton. Macmillan, 1980. ISBN 978-0-02-782450-6 Subj: Behavior – misunderstanding. Moving.

Hooray for Father's Day! ill. by John Wallner. Holiday, 1987. ISBN 978-0-8234-0637-1 Subj: Animals – mules. Holidays – Father's Day.

Hooray for Mother's Day! ill. by John Wallner. Holiday, 1986. ISBN 978-0-8234-0588-6 Subj: Birds – chickens, roosters. Holidays – Mother's Day.

I'm terrific ill. by Kay Chorao. Holiday, 1977. ISBN 978-0-8234-0282-3 Subj: Animals – bears. Character traits – conceit. Character traits – pride. Self-concept.

I'm the best ill. by Will Hillenbrand. Holiday, 1991. ISBN 978-0-8234-0859-7 Subj: Animals – dogs. Pets.

The 329th friend ill. by Cyndy Szekeres. Four Winds, 1992. ISBN 978-0-02-782259-5 Subj: Animals. Animals – raccoons. Counting, numbers. Friendship. Self-concept.

Sharmat, Mitchell. *Gregory, the terrible eater* ill. by José Aruego and Ariane Dewey. Four Winds, 1980. ISBN 978-0-590-07586-2 Subj: Animals – goats. Food.

Sharratt, Nick. *The foggy, foggy forest* ill. by author. Candlewick, 2008. ISBN 978-0-7636-3921-1 Subj: Forest, woods. Format, unusual. Humorous stories. Rhyming text.

Pants (Andreae, Giles)

Shark in the park ill. by author. Candlewick, 2002. ISBN 978-0-385-75008-0 Subj: Animals. Birds. Fish – sharks. Format, unusual – toy & movable books. Parks. Rhyming text.

What's in the witch's kitchen? ill. by author. Candlewick, 2011. ISBN 978-0-7636-5224-1 Subj: Format, unusual – toy & movable books. Rhyming text. Witches.

Shaskan, Stephen. *A dog is a dog* ill. by author. Chronicle, 2011. ISBN 978-0-8118-7896-8 Subj: Animals. Animals – dogs. Circular tales. Disguises. Rhyming text.

Toad on the road: a cautionary tale ill. by author. HarperCollins, 2017. ISBN 978-006239347-0 Subj: Frogs & toads. Safety.

Shaskan, Trisha Speed. *Punk skunks* ill. by Stephen Shaskan. HarperCollins, 2016. ISBN 978-006236396-1 Subj: Animals – skunks. Behavior – fighting, arguing. Friendship. Music.

Seriously, Cinderella is so annoying! the story of Cinderella as told by the wicked stepmother ill. by Gerald Guerlais. Picture Window, 2011. ISBN 978-1-4048-6674-4 Subj: Family life – stepfamilies. Folk & fairy tales. Humorous stories.

Shavick, Andrea. *You'll grow soon, Alex* ill. by Russell Ayto. Walker, 2000. ISBN 978-0-8027-8736-1 Subj: Behavior – growing up.

Shaw, Charles Green. *It looked like spilt milk* ill. by author. HarperCollins, 1947. ISBN 978-0-06-025565-7 Subj: Concepts – shape. Games. Imagination. Participation. Sky. Weather – clouds.

Shaw, Greg. *Wake up, sleepy bear!* (Morton-Shaw, Christine)

Shaw, Hannah. *School for bandits* ill. by author. Random House, 2011. ISBN 978-0-375-86768-2 Subj: Animals – raccoons. Behavior – misbehavior. Character traits – helpfulness. Etiquette. School.

Sneaky Weasel ill. by author. Knopf, 2009. ISBN 978-0-375-85625-9 Subj: Animals – weasels. Behavior – bullying, teasing. Friendship.

Shaw, Nancy. *Raccoon tune* ill. by Howard Fine. Henry Holt, 2003. ISBN 978-0-8050-6544-2 Subj: Animals – raccoons. Noise, sounds. Rhyming text.

Sheep blast off! ill. by Margot Apple. Houghton, 2008. ISBN 978-0-618-13168-6 Subj: Animals – sheep. Rhyming text. Space & space ships.

Sheep go to sleep ill. by Margot Apple. Houghton Mifflin Harcourt, 2015. ISBN 978-054430989-0 Subj: Animals – dogs. Animals – sheep. Bedtime. Sleep.

Sheep in a jeep ill. by Margot Apple. Houghton, 1986. ISBN 978-0-395-41105-6 Subj: Animals – sheep. Rhyming text.

Sheep in a shop ill. by Margot Apple. Houghton, 1991. ISBN 978-0-395-53681-0 Subj: Animals – sheep. Rhyming text. Shopping.

Sheep on a ship ill. by Margot Apple. Houghton, 1989. ISBN 978-0-395-48160-8 Subj: Animals – sheep. Boats, ships. Rhyming text.

Sheep out to eat ill. by Margot Apple. Houghton, 1992. ISBN 978-0-395-61128-9 Subj: Animals – sheep. Food. Rhyming text.

Sheep take a hike ill. by Margot Apple. Houghton, 1994. ISBN 978-0-395-68394-1 Subj: Activities – hiking. Animals – sheep. Rhyming text.

Sheep trick or treat ill. by Margot Apple. Houghton, 1997. ISBN 978-0-395-84168-6 Subj: Animals – sheep. Holidays – Halloween. Rhyming text.

Shaw, Natalie, adapt. *Olivia plans a tea party* ill. by Patrick Spaziante. Simon & Schuster, 2011. ISBN 978-1-4423-3962-0 Subj: Animals – pigs. Parties.

Shaw, Stephanie. *A cookie for Santa* ill. by Bruno Robert. Sleeping Bear, 2014. ISBN 978-158536883-9 Subj: Food. Holidays – Christmas. Rhyming text. Santa Claus.

Shea, Bob. *Big plans* ill. by Lane Smith. Hyperion, 2008. ISBN 978-1-4231-1100-9 Subj: Behavior – misbehavior. Humorous stories. Imagination. School.

Cheetah can't lose ill. by author. HarperCollins, 2013. ISBN 978-0-06-173083-2 Subj: Animals – cats. Animals – cheetahs. Behavior – boasting, showing off. Behavior – trickery. Character traits – cleverness. Contests.

Dinosaur vs. bedtime ill. by author. Hyperion, 2008. ISBN 978-1-4231-1335-5 Subj: Bedtime. Dinosaurs.

Dinosaur vs. Mommy ill. by author. Disney/Hyperion, 2015. ISBN 978-142316086-1 Subj: Behavior – misbehavior. Dinosaurs. Family life – mothers.

Dinosaur vs. Santa ill. by author. Disney/Hyperion, 2012. ISBN 978-1-4231-6806-5 Subj: Dinosaurs. Holidays – Christmas.

Dinosaur vs. school ill. by author. Disney/Hyperion, 2014. ISBN 978-142316087-8 Subj: Dinosaurs. School – nursery.

Dinosaur vs. the library ill. by author. Hyperion/Disney, 2011. ISBN 978-1-4231-3338-4 Subj: Dinosaurs. Libraries.

Dinosaur vs. the potty ill. by author. Hyperion/Disney, 2010. ISBN 978-1-4231-3339-1 Subj: Dinosaurs. Toilet training.

The happiest book ever ill. by author. Disney/Hyperion, 2016. ISBN 978-148473045-4 Subj: Behavior – bad day, bad mood. Behavior – dissatisfaction. Emotions – happiness. Frogs & toads.

I'm a shark ill. by author. HarperCollins, 2011. ISBN 978-0-06-199846-1 Subj: Emotions – fear. Fish – sharks.

Kid Sheriff and the terrible Toads ill. by Lane Smith. Roaring Brook, 2014. ISBN 978-159643975-7 Subj: Careers – sheriffs. Crime. Dinosaurs. Frogs & toads. U.S. history – frontier & pioneer life.

New socks ill. by author. Little, Brown, 2007. ISBN 978-0-316-01357-4 Subj: Behavior – growing up. Birds – chickens, roosters. Character traits – confidence. Clothing – socks. Self-concept.

Oh, Daddy! ill. by author. HarperCollins, 2010. ISBN 978-0-06-173080-1 Subj: Animals – hippopotamuses. Family life – fathers.

Race you to bed ill. by author. HarperCollins, 2010. ISBN 978-0-06-170417-8 Subj: Bedtime. Rhyming text.

The scariest book ever ill. by author. Disney/Hyperion, 2017. ISBN 978-148473046-1 Subj: Emotions – fear. Ghosts. Holidays – Halloween. Parties.

Unicorn thinks he's pretty great ill. by author. Disney/Hyperion, 2013. ISBN 978-1-4231-5952-0 Subj: Animals – goats. Emotions – envy, jealousy. Friendship. Mythical creatures – unicorns. Self-concept.

Shea, Kitty. *Out and about at the newspaper* ill. by Zachary Trover. Picture Window, 2006. ISBN 978-1-4048-1149-2 Subj: Careers – journalists.

Out and about at the post office ill. by Becky Shipe. Picture Window, 2004. ISBN 978-1-4048-0294-0 Subj: Careers – postal workers. Post office. School – field trips.

Out and about at the public library ill. by Zachary Trover. Picture Window, 2005. ISBN 978-1-4048-1150-8 Subj: Careers – librarians. Libraries.

Out and about at the science center ill. by Becky Shipe. Picture Window, 2004. ISBN 978-1-4048-0297-1 Subj: Museums. School – field trips. Science.

Out and about at the supermarket ill. by Becky Shipe. Picture Window, 2004. ISBN 978-1-4048-0295-7 Subj: Careers – storekeepers. Food. School – field trips. Stores.

Out and about at the vet clinic ill. by Becky Shipe. Picture Window, 2004. ISBN 978-1-4048-0296-4 Subj: Animals. Careers – veterinarians. Pets. School – field trips.

Shea, Pegi Deitz. *The boy and the spell* ill. by Serena Riglietti. Pumpkin House, 2007. ISBN 978-0-9646010-4-8 Subj: Emotions – anger. Music.

I see me! ill. by Lucia Washburn. HarperCollins, 2000. ISBN 978-0-694-01278-7 Subj: Babies, toddlers. Family life. Format, unusual – board books. Rhyming text.

New moon ill. by Cathryn Falwell. Boyds Mills, 1996. ISBN 978-1-56397-410-6 Subj: Ethnic groups in the U.S. – Hispanic Americans. Family life – brothers & sisters. Moon.

The whispering cloth ill. by Anita Riggio. Stitched by You Yang. Caroline House, 1995. ISBN 978-1-56397-134-1 Subj: Activities – sewing. Ethnic groups in the U.S. – Hmong Americans. Family life – grandmothers. Foreign lands – Thailand. War.

Shea, Susan A. *Do you know which one will grow?* ill. by Tom Slaughter. Blue Apple, 2011. ISBN 978-1-60905-062-7 Subj: Behavior – growing up. Concepts – change. Format, unusual – toy & movable books. Rhyming text.

Sheather, Allan. *Neptune's nursery* (Toft, Kim Michelle)

One less fish (Toft, Kim Michelle)

Sheehan, Kevin. *The dandelion's tale* ill. by Rob Dunlavey. Random House, 2014. ISBN 978-037587032-3 Subj: Birds – sparrows. Friendship. Memories, memory. Plants.

Sheehan, Monica. *Love is you and me* ill. by author. Simon & Schuster, 2013. ISBN 978-1-442436-07-7 Subj: Emotions – love. Rhyming text.

Sheehy, Shawn. *Welcome to the neighborwood* ill. by author. Candlewick, 2015. ISBN 978-076366594-4 Subj: Animals. Format, unusual – toy & movable books. Homes, houses.

Shelby, Anne. *Homeplace* ill. by Wendy Anderson Halperin. Orchard, 1995. ISBN 978-0-531-08732-9 Subj: Family life. Family life – grandmothers.

The man who lived in a hollow tree ill. by Cor Hazelaar. Atheneum, 2009. ISBN 978-0-689-86169-7 Subj: Old age. Trees.

Potluck ill. by Irene Trivas. Watts, 1991. ISBN 978-0-531-08519-6 Subj: ABC books. Ethnic groups in the U.S. Food.

Sheldon, Annette. *Big sister now: a story about me and our new baby* ill. by Karen Maizel. Magination, 2006. ISBN 978-1-59147-243-8 Subj: Babies, toddlers. Family life – brothers & sisters. Family life – new sibling.

Sheldon, Dyan. *Under the moon* ill. by Gary Blythe. Dial, 1994. ISBN 978-0-8037-1670-4 Subj: Dreams. Indians of North America – Sioux.

Unicorn dreams ill. by Neil Reed. Dial, 1997. ISBN 978-0-8037-2284-2 Subj: Imagination. Mythical creatures – unicorns. School.

Shelton, Paula Young. *Child of the civil rights movement* ill. by Raul Colón. Random House, 2009. ISBN 978-0-375-84314-3 Subj: Ethnic groups in the U.S. – African Americans. Prejudice. U.S. history.

Sheneman, Drew. *Nope!* ill. by author. Viking, 2017. ISBN 978-110199731-4 Subj: Animals – babies. Behavior – growing up. Birds. Character traits – stubbornness.

Shepard, Aaron. *The baker's dozen* ill. by Wendy Edelson. Atheneum, 1995. ISBN 978-0-689-80298-0 Subj: Careers – bakers. Character traits – generosity. Folk & fairy tales.

The crystal heart: a Vietnamese legend ill. by Joseph Daniel Fiedler. Atheneum, 1998. ISBN 978-0-689-81551-5 Subj: Folk & fairy tales. Foreign lands – Vietnam.

Forty fortunes: a tale of Iran ill. by Alisher Dianov. Clarion, 1999. ISBN 978-0-395-81133-7 Subj: Careers – fortune tellers. Folk & fairy tales. Foreign lands – Iran.

The gifts of Wali Dad ill. by Daniel San Souci. Atheneum, 1995. ISBN 978-0-684-19445-5 Subj: Behavior – wishing. Folk & fairy tales. Foreign lands – India. Foreign lands – Pakistan. Gifts.

Master man ill. by David Wisniewski. Lothrop, 2000. ISBN 978-0-688-13784-7 Subj: Folk & fairy tales – pourquoi tales. Foreign lands – Nigeria. Tall tales. Weather – lightning, thunder.

One-eye! Two-eyes! Three-eyes! a very Grimm fairy tale ill. by Gary Clement. Simon & Schuster, 2006. ISBN 978-0-689-86740-8 Subj: Animals – goats. Folk & fairy tales. Magic. Royalty – princes.

The princess mouse ill. by Leonid Gore. Atheneum, 2003. ISBN 978-0-689-82912-3 Subj: Animals – mice. Folk & fairy tales. Foreign lands – Finland. Royalty – princesses. Songs.

The sea king's daughter ill. by Gennady Spirin. Atheneum, 1997. ISBN 978-0-689-80759-6 Subj: Careers – musicians. Folk & fairy tales. Foreign lands – Russia. Mythical creatures. Sea & seashore.

Shepherd, Jessica. *Grandma* ill. by author. Child's Play, 2014. ISBN 978-184643602-4 Subj: Behavior – forgetfulness. Family life – grandmothers. Old age.

Sher, Emil. *Away* ill. by Qin Leng. Groundwood, 2017. ISBN 978-155498483-1 Subj: Activities – writing. Behavior – worrying. Camps, camping. Family life – mothers. Letters, cards.

Sheridan, Sara. *I'm me!* ill. by Margaret Chamberlain. Scholastic, 2011. ISBN 978-0-545-28222-2 Subj: Activities – playing. Family life – aunts, uncles. Imagination.

Sherman, Joanne. *Because it's my body* ill. by John Steven Gurney. S.A.F.E. for Children, 2002. ISBN 978-0-9711735-0-7 Subj: Child abuse. Communication. Senses – touch.

Sherman, Pat. *The sun's daughter* ill. by R. Gregory Christie. Clarion, 2005. ISBN 978-0-618-32430-9 Subj: Folk & fairy tales – pourquoi tales. Indians of North America – Iroquois. Sun.

Sherry, Kevin. *Acorns everywhere!* ill. by author. Dial, 2009. ISBN 978-0-8037-3256-8 Subj: Animals – bears. Animals – squirrels. Behavior – forgetfulness.

I'm the best artist in the ocean ill. by author. Dial, 2008. ISBN 978-0-8037-3255-1 Subj: Art. Careers – artists. Sea & seashore. Squid.

I'm the biggest thing in the ocean ill. by author. Penguin, 2007. ISBN 978-0-8037-3192-9 Subj: Concepts – size. Sea & seashore. Squid.

Turtle Island ill. by author. Dial, 2014. ISBN 978-080373391-6 Subj: Animals. Emotions – loneliness. Friendship. Islands. Reptiles – turtles, tortoises.

Sheth, Kashmira. *Monsoon afternoon* ill. by Yoshiko Jaeggi. Peachtree, 2008. ISBN 978-1-56145-455-6 Subj: Family life – grandfathers. Foreign lands – India. Weather – rain.

My Dadima wears a sari ill. by Yoshiko Jaeggi. Peachtree, 2007. ISBN 978-1-56145-392-4 Subj: Clothing. Ethnic groups in the U.S. – East Indian Americans. Family life – grandmothers.

Tiger in my soup ill. by Jeffrey Ebbeler. Peachtree, 2013. ISBN 978-1-56145-696-3 Subj: Animals – tigers. Books, reading. Family life – brothers & sisters. Imagination.

Shewchuk, Pat. *In Lucia's neighborhood* ill. by Marek Colek. Kids Can, 2013. ISBN 978-1-55453-420-3 Subj: Cities, towns. Communities, neighborhoods.

Shields, Carol Diggory. *Baby's got the blues* ill. by Lauren Tobia. Candlewick, 2014. ISBN 978-076363260-1 Subj: Babies, toddlers. Music. Rhyming text.

The bugliest bug ill. by Scott Nash. Candlewick, 2002. ISBN 978-0-7636-0784-5 Subj: Contests. Insects. Poetry. Spiders.

Day by day a week goes round ill. by True Kelley. Dutton, 1998. ISBN 978-0-525-45457-1 Subj: Activities. Days of the week, months of the year. Rhyming text.

I am really a princess ill. by Paul Meisel. Dutton, 1993. ISBN 978-0-525-45138-9 Subj: Behavior – imitation. Character traits – vanity. Family life. Imagination. Royalty – princesses. Self-concept.

I wish my brother was a dog ill. by Paul Meisel. Dutton, 1997. ISBN 978-0-525-45464-9 Subj: Animals – dogs. Babies, toddlers. Behavior – wishing. Emotions – anger. Family life – brothers. Family life – new sibling. Sibling rivalry.

Lucky pennies and hot chocolate ill. by Hiroe Nakata. Dutton, 2000. ISBN 978-0-525-46450-1 Subj: Family life – grandfathers.

Lunch money and other poems about school ill. by Paul Meisel. Dutton, 1995. ISBN 978-0-525-45345-1 Subj: Poetry. School.

Martian rock ill. by Scott Nash. Candlewick, 2000. ISBN 978-0-7636-0598-8 Subj: Aliens. Birds – penguins. Plants. Rhyming text. Space & space ships.

Month by month a year goes round ill. by True Kelley. Dutton, 1998. ISBN 978-0-525-45458-8 Subj: Days of the week, months of the year. Rhyming text. Seasons.

Saturday night at the dinosaur stomp ill. by Scott Nash. Candlewick, 1997. ISBN 978-1-56402-693-4 Subj: Activities – dancing. Dinosaurs. Prehistory. Rhyming text.

Wombat walkabout ill. by Sophie Blackall. Dutton, 2009. ISBN 978-0-525-47865-2 Subj: Animals – wombats. Counting, numbers. Foreign lands – Australia. Rhyming text.

Shields, Gillian. *Dogfish* ill. by Dan Taylor. Atheneum, 2008. ISBN 978-1-4169-7127-6 Subj: Fish. Pets.

Elephantantrum! ill. by Cally Johnson-Isaacs. Tiger Tales, 2013. ISBN 978-1-58925-126-7 Subj: Animals – elephants. Behavior – misbehavior. Emotions – anger.

Library Lily ill. by Francesca Chessa. Eerdmans, 2011. ISBN 978-0-8028-5401-8 Subj: Activities – playing. Books, reading. Friendship. Libraries.

When the world was waiting for you ill. by Anna Currey. Bloomsbury, 2011. ISBN 978-1-59990-531-0 Subj: Animals – rabbits. Family life – new sibling. Rhyming text.

Shindler, Ramon. *Found alphabet* by Ramon Shindler and Wojciech Graniczewski ill. by Anita Andrzejewska and Andrzej Pilichowski-Ragno. Houghton, 2005. ISBN 978-0-618-44232-4 Subj: ABC books. Rhyming text.

Shingu, Susumu. *Traveling butterflies* ill. by author. OwlKids, 2015. ISBN 978-177147148-0 Subj: Insects – butterflies, caterpillars. Metamorphosis. Migration.

Shipton, Jonathan. *Baby baby blah blah blah!* ill. by Francesca Chessa. Holiday, 2009. ISBN 978-0-8234-2213-5 Subj: Activities – writing. Babies, toddlers. Family life – new sibling.

How to be a happy hippo ill. by Sally Percy. Little Tiger, 1999. ISBN 978-1-888444-61-2 Subj: Animals – hippopotamuses. Family life – fathers.

No biting, horrible crocodile! ill. by Claudio Muñoz. Western, 1995. ISBN 978-0-307-17521-2 Subj: Behavior – bullying, teasing. Reptiles – alligators, crocodiles. School.

What if? ill. by Barbara Nascimbeni. Dial, 1999. ISBN 978-0-8037-2390-0 Subj: Imagination. Self-concept.

Shireen, Nadia. *Good little wolf* ill. by author. Random House, 2011. ISBN 978-0-375-86904-4 Subj: Animals – wolves. Character traits – individuality. Self-concept.

Hey, Presto! ill. by author. Knopf, 2012. ISBN 978-0-375-86905-1 Subj: Animals – cats. Animals – dogs. Fairs, festivals. Friendship. Magic.

Shirotani, Hideo. *Let's eat / Vamos a comer* ill. by author. Simon & Schuster, 1992. ISBN 978-0-671-76927-7 Subj: Food. Foreign languages. Format, unusual – board books.

Let's play ill. by author. Little & Woods, 1991. ISBN 978-1-56180-044-5 Subj: Activities – playing. Format, unusual – board books.

Let's take a walk / Vamos a caminar ill. by author. Simon & Schuster, 1992. ISBN 978-0-671-76929-1 Subj: Activities – walking. Foreign languages. Format, unusual – board books.

What color? / Qué color? ill. by author. Simon & Schuster, 1992. ISBN 978-0-671-76930-7 Subj: Concepts – color. Foreign languages. Format, unusual – board books.

Shoemaker, Marla K. *Art museum opposites* (Friedland, Katy)

Shollar, Leah. *A thread of kindness* ill. by Shoshana Mekibel. Hachai, 2000. ISBN 978-1-929628-01-8 Subj: Character traits – generosity. Jewish culture. Religion.

Shore, Diane Z. *Look both ways: a cautionary tale* by Diane Z. Shore and Jessica Alexander ill. by Teri Weidner. Bloomsbury, 2005. ISBN 978-1-58234-968-8 Subj: Animals – squirrels. Rhyming text. Safety.

This is the dream by Diane Z. Shore and Jessica Alexander ill. by James Ransome. HarperCollins, 2006. ISBN 978-0-06-055520-7 Subj: Ethnic groups in the U.S. – African Americans. Prejudice. Rhyming text. U.S. history.

This is the Earth by Diane Z. Shore and Jessica Alexander ill. by Wendell Minor. HarperCollins, 2016. ISBN 978-006055526-9 Subj: Earth. Ecology. Nature.

This is the feast ill. by Megan Lloyd. HarperCollins, 2008. ISBN 978-0-06-623794-7 Subj: Holidays – Thanksgiving. Indians of North America – Wampanoag. Poetry.

Shoulders, Debbie. *D is for drum: a Native American alphabet* (Shoulders, Michael)

Shoulders, Michael. *The ABC book of American homes* ill. by Sarah S. Brannen. Charlesbridge, 2008. ISBN 978-1-57091-565-9 Subj: ABC books. Homes, houses.

D is for drum: a Native American alphabet by Michael Shoulders and Debbie Shoulders ill. by Irving Toddy. Sleeping Bear, 2006. ISBN 978-1-58536-274-5 Subj: ABC books. Indians of North America.

D is for dump truck: a construction alphabet ill. by Kent Culotta. Sleeping Bear, 2016. ISBN 978-158536975-1 Subj: ABC books. Careers – construction workers. Rhyming text. Trucks.

Goodnight Baby Bear ill. by Teri Weidner. Sleeping Bear, 2010. ISBN 978-1-58536-471-8 Subj: Animals – bears. Bedtime. Books, reading. Family life.

Say Daddy! ill. by Teri Weidner. Sleeping Bear, 2008. ISBN 978-1-58536-354-4 Subj: Animals – babies. Animals – bears. Books, reading.

Showers, Paul. *A drop of blood* ill. by Don Madden. Rev. ed. HarperCollins, 1989. ISBN 978-0-690-04717-2 Subj: Anatomy. Science.

Ears are for hearing ill. by Holly Keller. HarperCollins, 1990. ISBN 978-0-690-04720-2 Subj: Anatomy – ears. Science. Senses – hearing.

Hear your heart ill. by Holly Keller. HarperCollins, 2001. ISBN 978-0-06-025411-7 Subj: Anatomy. Noise, sounds. Science.

How you talk ill. by Megan Lloyd. Rev. ed. HarperCollins, 1992. ISBN 978-0-06-022768-5 Subj: Anatomy. Communication. Language.

The listening walk ill. by Aliki. Rev. ed. HarperCollins, 1991. ISBN 978-0-06-021638-2 Subj: Activities – walking. Noise, sounds. Senses – hearing.

Look at your eyes ill. by True Kelley. Rev. ed. HarperCollins, 1992. ISBN 978-0-06-020188-3 Subj: Anatomy – eyes. Ethnic groups in the U.S. – African Americans. Science. Senses – sight.

Sleep is for everyone ill. by Wendy Watson. HarperCollins, 1997. ISBN 978-0-06-025393-6 Subj: Animals. Bedtime. Dreams. Health & fitness. Science. Sleep.

Where does the garbage go? ill. by Randy Chewning. Rev. ed. HarperCollins, 1994. ISBN 978-0-06-021057-1 Subj: Careers – sanitation workers. Ecology. Science.

Your skin and mine ill. by Kathleen Kuchera. Rev. ed. HarperCollins, 1991. ISBN 978-0-06-022523-0 Subj: Anatomy – skin. Ethnic groups in the U.S. – African Americans.

Shreeve, Elizabeth. *Oliver at the window* ill. by Candice Hartsough McDonald. Front Street, 2009. ISBN 978-1-59078-548-5 Subj: Divorce. Moving. School.

Shriver, Maria. *What's wrong with Timmy?* ill. by Sandra Speidel. Little, 2001. ISBN 978-0-316-

23337-8 Subj: Disabilities – mental disabilities. Friendship.

Shulevitz, Uri. *Dawn* ill. by author. Farrar, 1974. ISBN 978-0-374-31707-2 Subj: Camps, camping. Family life – grandfathers. Morning. Sun.

Dusk ill. by author. Farrar, 2013. ISBN 978-0-374-31903-8 Subj: Cities, towns. Family life – grandfathers. Light, lights. Night. Twilight.

How I learned geography ill. by author. Farrar, 2008. ISBN 978-0-374-33499-4 Subj: Behavior – seeking better things. Caldecott award honor books. Geography. Imagination. Maps. Poverty.

The magician by Uri Shulevitz and Isaac Loeb Peretz ill. by adapter. Adapted from the Yiddish of Isaac Loeb Peretz. Macmillan, 1985, ©1973. ISBN 978-0-02-782770-5 Subj: Holidays – Passover. Jewish culture. Magic. Religion.

One Monday morning ill. by author. Aladdin, 1986, ©1967. ISBN 978-0-684-13195-5 Subj: Cities, towns. Days of the week, months of the year. Imagination. Royalty.

Rain rain rivers ill. by author. Farrar, 1969. ISBN 978-0-374-36171-6 Subj: Rhyming text. Weather – rain.

Snow ill. by author. Farrar, 1998. ISBN 978-0-374-37092-3 Subj: Caldecott award honor books. Cities, towns. Nature. Weather – snow.

So sleepy story ill. by author. Farrar, 2006. ISBN 978-0-374-37031-2 Subj: Imagination. Music. Night. Sleep.

The treasure ill. by author. Farrar, 1978. ISBN 978-0-374-37740-3 Subj: Caldecott award honor books. Dreams. Folk & fairy tales.

Troto and the trucks ill. by author. Farrar, 2015. ISBN 978-037430080-7 Subj: Automobiles. Behavior – bullying, teasing. Character traits – smallness. Contests. Sports – racing. Trucks.

What is a wise bird like you doing in a silly tale like this? ill. by author. Farrar, 2000. ISBN 978-0-374-38300-8 Subj: Birds. Character traits – freedom. Royalty – emperors. Tall tales.

When I wore my sailor suit ill. by author. Farrar, 2009. ISBN 978-0-374-34749-9 Subj: Imagination. Sailors.

Shulimson, Sarene. *Lights out Shabbat* ill. by Jeffrey Ebbeler. Lerner/Kar-Ben, 2012. ISBN 978-0-7613-7565-4 Subj: Family life – grandparents. Holidays. Jewish culture. Religion.

Shulman, Goldie. *Way too much challah dough* ill. by Vitaliy Romanenko. Hachai, 2006. ISBN 978-1-929628-23-0 Subj: Behavior – running away. Food. Jewish culture.

Shulman, Lisa. *The moon might be milk* ill. by Will Hillenbrand. Penguin, 2007. ISBN 978-0-525-47647-4 Subj: Activities – baking, cooking. Animals. Family life – grandmothers. Food. Moon.

Over in the meadow at the big ballet ill. by Sarah Massini. Penguin, 2007. ISBN 978-0-399-24289-2 Subj: Ballet. Birds – swans. Rhyming text.

Shulman, Mark. *A is for zebra* ill. by Tamara Petrosino. Sterling, 2006. ISBN 978-1-4027-3494-6 Subj: ABC books.

Aa is for Aardvark ill. by author. Sterling, 2005. ISBN 978-1-4027-2871-6 Subj: ABC books.

Gorilla Garage ill. by Vincent Nguyen. Marshall Cavendish, 2009. ISBN 978-0-7614-5461-8 Subj: Animals – gorillas. Automobiles. Careers – mechanics. Rhyming text.

Shum, Benson. *Holly's day at the pool* ill. by author. Disney/Hyperion, 2017. ISBN 978-148470938-2 Subj: Animals – hippopotamuses. Emotions – fear. Sports – swimming.

Shute, Linda. *Clever Tom and the leprechaun* ill. by author. Lothrop, 1988. ISBN 978-0-688-07489-0 Subj: Folk & fairy tales. Mythical creatures – leprechauns.

Halloween party ill. by author. Lothrop, 1994. ISBN 978-0-688-11715-3 Subj: Holidays – Halloween. Parties. Rhyming text. Witches.

Shuttlewood, Craig. *Through the town* ill. by author. little bee, 2015. ISBN 978-149980076-0 Subj: Cities, towns. Format, unusual – board books. Reptiles – snakes.

Who's in the tree? ill. by author. Sterling, 2014. ISBN 978-145491193-7 Subj: Animals. Format, unusual – toy & movable books. Rhyming text.

Shyba, Jessica. *Bathtime with Theo and Beau* photos by author. Feiwel & Friends, 2016. ISBN 978-125005907-9 Subj: Activities – bathing. Animals – dogs. Pets.

Naptime with Theo and Beau photos by author. Feiwel & Friends, 2015. ISBN 978-125005906-2 Subj: Animals – dogs. Pets. Sleep.

Siberell, Anne. *Whale in the sky* ill. by author. Dutton, 1982. ISBN 978-0-525-44021-5 Subj: Animals – whales. Folk & fairy tales. Indians of North America.

Siddals, Mary McKenna. *Bringing the outside in* ill. by Patrice Barton. Random House, 2016. ISBN 978-044981430-7 Subj: Nature. Rhyming text. Seasons.

Compost stew: an A to Z recipe for the earth ill. by Ashley Wolff. Tricycle, 2010. ISBN 978-1-58246-316-2 Subj: ABC books. Ecology. Rhyming text.

I'll play with you ill. by David Wisniewski. Clarion, 2000. ISBN 978-0-395-90373-5 Subj: Activities – playing. Nature.

Millions of snowflakes ill. by Elizabeth Sayles. Clarion, 1998. ISBN 978-0-395-71531-4 Subj: Rhyming text. Weather – snow.

Morning song ill. by Elizabeth Sayles. Henry Holt, 2001. ISBN 978-0-8050-6369-1 Subj: Morning.

Shivery shades of Halloween: a spooky book of colors ill. by Jimmy Pickering. Random House, 2014. ISBN 978-038536999-2 Subj: Concepts – color. Holidays – Halloween. Rhyming text.

Tell me a season ill. by Petra Mathers. Clarion, 1997. ISBN 978-0-395-71021-0 Subj: Concepts – color. Rhyming text. Seasons.

Sidjanski, Brigitte. *Little Chicken and Little Duck* ill. by author. Minedition, 2007. ISBN 978-0-698-40055-9 Subj: Birds – chickens, roosters. Birds – ducks. Friendship. Prejudice.

Sidman, Joyce. *Before morning* ill. by Beth Krommes. Houghton Mifflin Harcourt, 2016. ISBN 978-054797917-5 Subj: Careers – airplane pilots. Family life. Rhyming text. Weather – snow.

Butterfly eyes and other secrets of the meadow ill. by Beth Krommes. Houghton, 2006. ISBN 978-0-618-56313-5 Subj: Nature. Poetry. Riddles & jokes.

Just us two ill. by Susan Swan. Millbrook, 2000. ISBN 978-0-7613-1563-6 Subj: Animals. Animals – babies. Family life – fathers.

Meow ruff: a story in concrete poetry ill. by Michelle Berg. Houghton, 2006. ISBN 978-0-618-44894-4 Subj: Animals – cats. Animals – dogs. Poetry. Weather – storms.

Red sings from treetops: a year in colors ill. by Pamela Zagarenski. Houghton, 2009. ISBN 978-0-547-01494-4 Subj: Caldecott award honor books. Concepts – color. Poetry. Seasons.

Round ill. by Taeeun Yoo. Houghton Mifflin Harcourt, 2017. ISBN 978-054438761-4 Subj: Concepts – shape. Nature.

Song of the water boatman: and other pond poems ill. by Beckie Prange. Houghton, 2005. ISBN 978-0-618-13547-9 Subj: Caldecott award honor books. Lakes, ponds. Nature. Poetry.

Swirl by swirl: spirals in nature ill. by Beth Krommes. Harcourt, 2011. ISBN 978-0-547-31583-6 Subj: Concepts – shape. Nature.

Ubiquitous: celebrating nature's survivors ill. by Beckie Prange. Houghton Mifflin, 2010. ISBN 978-0-618-71719-4 Subj: Nature. Poetry.

Winter bees and other poems of the cold ill. by Rick Allen. Harcourt, 2014. ISBN 978-054790650-8 Subj: Animals. Nature. Poetry. Seasons – winter.

Siebert, Diane. *Cave* ill. by Wayne McLoughlin. HarperCollins, 2000. ISBN 978-0-688-16448-5 Subj: Caves. Rhyming text.

Heartland ill. by Wendell Minor. HarperCollins, 1989. ISBN 978-0-690-04732-5 Subj: Poetry. U.S. history.

Mojave ill. by Wendell Minor. HarperCollins, 1988. ISBN 978-0-690-04569-7 Subj: Desert. Poetry.

Plane song ill. by Vincent Nasta. HarperCollins, 1993. ISBN 978-0-06-021467-8 Subj: Airplanes, airports. Rhyming text.

Sierra ill. by Wendell Minor. HarperCollins, 1991. ISBN 978-0-06-021640-5 Subj: Nature. Poetry.

Train song ill. by Mike Wimmer. HarperCollins, 1990. ISBN 978-0-690-04728-8 Subj: Rhyming text. Trains.

Truck song ill. by Byron Barton. Crowell, 1984. ISBN 978-0-690-04411-9 Subj: Rhyming text. Trucks.

Siegel, Mark. *Moving house* ill. by author. Roaring Brook, 2011. ISBN 978-1-59643-635-0 Subj: Homes, houses. Moving.

Siegel, Randy. *Grandma's smile* ill. by DyAnne DiSalvo. Roaring Brook, 2010. ISBN 978-1-59643-438-7 Subj: Activities – traveling. Anatomy – faces. Behavior – lost & found possessions. Family life – grandmothers.

My snake Blake ill. by Serge Bloch. Roaring Brook, 2012. ISBN 978-1-59643-584-1 Subj: Pets. Reptiles – snakes.

One proud penny ill. by Serge Bloch. Roaring Brook/Neal Porter, 2017. ISBN 978-162672235-4 Subj: Money. U.S. history.

Siegelson, Kim L. *In the time of the drums* ill. by Brian Pinkney. Hyperion, 1999. ISBN 978-0-7868-2386-4 Subj: Character traits – freedom. Ethnic groups in the U.S. – African Americans. Slavery.

Sierra, Judy. *Ballyhoo Bay* ill. by Derek Anderson. Simon & Schuster, 2009. ISBN 978-1-4169-5888-8 Subj: Art. Careers – artists. Ecology. Rhyming text. Sea & seashore – beaches.

The beautiful butterfly ill. by Victoria Chess. Clarion, 2000. ISBN 978-0-395-90015-4 Subj: Animals – mice. Folk & fairy tales. Foreign lands – Spain. Insects – butterflies, caterpillars. Royalty – kings. Weddings.

Born to read ill. by Marc Brown. Knopf, 2008. ISBN 978-0-375-84687-8 Subj: Books, reading. Rhyming text.

Counting crocodiles ill. by Will Hillenbrand. Harcourt, 1997. ISBN 978-0-15-200192-6 Subj: Animals – monkeys. Counting, numbers. Foreign lands – Asia. Reptiles – alligators, crocodiles.

E-I-E-I-O: how Old MacDonald got his farm ill. by Matthew Myers. Candlewick, 2014. ISBN 978-076366043-7 Subj: Animals. Farms. Gardens, gardening. Rhyming text.

The gift of the crocodile: a Cinderella story ill. by Reynold Ruffins. Simon & Schuster, 2000. ISBN 978-0-689-82188-2 Subj: Fairies. Family life – stepfamilies. Folk & fairy tales. Foreign lands – Indonesia. Reptiles – alligators, crocodiles.

The house that Drac built ill. by Will Hillenbrand. Harcourt, 1995. ISBN 978-0-15-200015-8 Subj: Cumulative tales. Holidays – Halloween. Homes, houses. Monsters. Rhyming text.

Imagine that! how Dr. Seuss wrote The Cat in the Hat ill. by Kevin Hawkes. Random House, 2017. ISBN 978-055351097-3 Subj: Activities – drawing. Activities – writing. Books, reading. Careers – illustrators. Careers – writers.

Make way for readers ill. by G. Brian Karas. Simon & Schuster/Paula Wiseman, 2016. ISBN 978-148141851-5 Subj: Animals. Books, reading. Rhyming text.

Mind your manners, B. B. Wolf ill. by J. Otto Seibold. Random House, 2007. ISBN 978-0-375-83532-2 Subj: Animals – wolves. Etiquette. Folk & fairy tales. Humorous stories. Libraries.

Monster Goose ill. by Jack E. Davis. Harcourt, 2001. ISBN 978-0-15-202034-7 Subj: Monsters. Nursery rhymes.

Preschool to the rescue ill. by Will Hillenbrand. Harcourt, 2001. ISBN 978-0-15-202035-4 Subj: Animals. Character traits – helpfulness. School – nursery.

The secret science project that almost ate school ill. by Stephen Gammell. Simon & Schuster, 2006. ISBN 978-1-4169-1175-3 Subj: Rhyming text. School. Science.

Sleepy little alphabet: a bedtime story from Alphabet Town ill. by Melissa Sweet. Knopf, 2009. ISBN 978-0-375-84002-9 Subj: ABC books. Bedtime. Rhyming text.

Suppose you meet a dinosaur: a first book of manners ill. by Tim Bowers. Knopf, 2012. ISBN 978-0-375-86720-0 Subj: Dinosaurs. Etiquette. Rhyming text. Shopping. Stores.

Tasty baby belly buttons ill. by Meilo So. Knopf, 1998. ISBN 978-0-679-99369-8 Subj: Folk & fairy tales. Foreign lands – Japan. Gender roles. Mythical creatures – ogres.

Tell the truth, B. B. Wolf ill. by J. Otto Seibold. Random House, 2010. ISBN 978-0-375-85620-4 Subj: Activities – storytelling. Animals – wolves. Character traits – honesty. Folk & fairy tales. Humorous stories.

Thelonius Monster's sky-high fly pie: a revolting rhyme ill. by Edward Koren. Random House, 2006. ISBN 978-0-375-93218-2 Subj: Food. Insects – flies. Monsters. Rhyming text.

There's a zoo in room 22 ill. by Barney Saltzberg. Harcourt, 2000. ISBN 978-0-15-202033-0 Subj: ABC books. Animals. Pets. Rhyming text. School.

'Twas the fright before Christmas ill. by Will Hillenbrand. Harcourt, 2002. ISBN 978-0-15-201805-4 Subj: Animals – mice. Cumulative tales. Dragons. Holidays – Christmas. Homes, houses. Monsters. Mythical creatures. Rhyming text.

We love our school! a read-together rebus story. Random House, 2011. ISBN 978-0-375-86728-6 Subj: Animals. Rebuses. Rhyming text. School – first day.

Wild about books ill. by Marc Brown. Knopf, 2004. ISBN 978-0-375-92538-2 Subj: Animals. Books, reading. Careers – librarians. Libraries. Rhyming text. Zoos.

Wild about you! ill. by Marc Brown. Knopf, 2012. ISBN 978-0-307-93178-8 Subj: Animals – babies. Rhyming text. Zoos.

Wiley and the Hairy Man ill. by Brian Pinkney. Lodestar, 1996. ISBN 978-0-525-67477-1 Subj: Character traits – cleverness. Ethnic groups in the U.S. – African Americans. Folk & fairy tales. Monsters.

Zoozical ill. by Marc Brown. Random House, 2011. ISBN 978-0-375-86847-4 Subj: Animals. Rhyming text. Theater. Zoos.

Sif, Birgitta. *Frances Dean who loved to dance and dance* ill. by author. Candlewick, 2014. ISBN 978-076367306-2 Subj: Activities – dancing. Character traits – confidence.

Oliver ill. by author. Candlewick, 2012. ISBN 978-0-7636-6247-9 Subj: Behavior – solitude. Character traits – being different. Friendship. Imagination. Toys.

Swish and Squeak's noisy day ill. by author. Knopf, 2017. ISBN 978-039955622-7 Subj: Animals – mice. Family life – brothers & sisters. Imagination. Noise, sounds.

Where my feet go ill. by author. Knopf, 2016. ISBN 978-055351164-2 Subj: Activities. Animals – pandas. Imagination.

Silbaugh, Elizabeth. *Raggedy Ann's birthday party book* ill. by Laura Francesca Filippucci. Simon & Schuster, 2001. ISBN 978-0-689-82850-8 Subj: Activities. Birthdays. Parties. Toys – dolls.

Sill, Cathryn. *Wetlands* ill. by John Sill. Peachtree, 2008. ISBN 978-1-56145-432-7 Subj: Nature. Science.

Sillifant, Alec. *Farmer Ham* ill. by Mike Spoor. NorthSouth, 2007. ISBN 978-0-7358-2134-7 Subj: Animals – pigs. Birds – crows. Careers – farmers. Farms.

Silvano, Wendi. *Counting coconuts / Contando cocos* ill. by Marty Granius. Raven Tree, 2004. ISBN 978-0-9720192-6-2 Subj: Animals – monkeys. Counting, numbers. Foreign languages.

Just one more ill. by Ricardo Gamboa. All About Kids, 2002. ISBN 978-0-9700863-7-2 Subj: Activities – traveling. Buses. Foreign lands – South America. Mountains.

Turkey Claus ill. by Lee Harper. Amazon, 2012. ISBN 978-0-7614-6239-2 Subj: Birds – turkeys. Clothing – costumes. Holidays – Christmas. Santa Claus.

Turkey trouble ill. by Lee Harper. Marshall Cavendish, 2009. ISBN 978-0-7614-5529-5 Subj: Birds – turkeys. Clothing – costumes. Farms. Holidays – Thanksgiving.

What does the wind say? ill. by Joan M. Delehanty. NorthWord, 2006. ISBN 978-1-55971-954-4 Subj: Poetry. Rhyming text.

Silverhardt, Lauryn. *Happy Chinese New Year, Kai-lan!* ill. by Jason Fruchter and Aka Chikasawa. Simon & Schuster, 2009. ISBN 978-1-4169-8505-1 Subj: Ethnic groups in the U.S. – Chinese Americans. Friendship. Holidays – Chinese New Year.

Silverman, Erica. *Follow the leader* ill. by G. Brian Karas. Farrar, 2000. ISBN 978-0-374-32423-0 Subj: Activities – playing. Bedtime. Family life – brothers. Rhyming text.

Gittel's hands ill. by Deborah Nourse Lattimore. BridgeWater, 1996. ISBN 978-0-8167-3798-7 Subj: Character traits – kindness. Character traits – meanness. Holidays – Passover. Jewish culture. Religion.

The Halloween house ill. by Jon Agee. Farrar, 1997. ISBN 978-0-374-16768-4 Subj: Counting, numbers. Ghosts. Holidays – Halloween. Monsters. Rhyming text. Witches.

The Hanukkah hop! ill. by Steven D'Amico. Simon & Schuster, 2011. ISBN 978-1-4424-0604-9 Subj: Activities – dancing. Holidays – Hanukkah. Jewish culture. Rhyming text.

There was a wee woman . . . ill. by Rosanne Litzinger. Farrar, 2008. ISBN 978-0-374-38253-7 Subj: Character traits – smallness. Clothing – shoes. Homes, houses. Rhyming text.

Wake up, city! ill. by Laure Fournier. little bee, 2016. ISBN 978-149980173-6 Subj: Activities – walking. Cities, towns. Family life – fathers. Morning. Rhyming text.

Silverstein, Shel. *A giraffe and a half* ill. by author. HarperCollins, 1964. ISBN 978-0-06-025656-2 Subj: Cumulative tales. Humorous stories. Rhyming text.

The giving tree ill. by author. HarperCollins, 2003. ISBN 978-0-06-025666-1 Subj: Character traits – generosity. Rhyming text. Trees.

The missing piece ill. by author. HarperCollins, 1976. ISBN 978-0-06-025672-2 Subj: Character traits – individuality. Concepts – shape.

Silvestro, Annie. *Bunny's book club* ill. by Tatjana Mai-Wyss. Doubleday, 2017. ISBN 978-055353758-1 Subj: Animals. Animals – rabbits. Books, reading. Careers – librarians. Libraries.

Mice skating ill. by Teagan White. Sterling, 2017. ISBN 978-145491632-1 Subj: Animals – mice. Seasons – winter. Sports – ice skating.

Sima, Jessie. *Not quite narwhal* ill. by author. Simon & Schuster, 2017. ISBN 978-148146909-8 Subj: Animals – narwhals. Mythical creatures – unicorns. Self-concept.

Simard, Rémy. *Hocus Pocus* (Desrosiers, Sylvie)

Simeon, Jean-Pierre. *This is a poem that heals fish* ill. by Olivier Tallec. Enchanted Lion, 2007. ISBN 978-1-59270-067-7 Subj: Fish. Pets. Poetry.

Simhaee, Rebeka. *Sara finds a mitzva* ill. by Michael Weber. Hachai, 2010. ISBN 978-1-929628-46-9 Subj: Behavior – lost & found possessions. Family life – grandmothers. Jewish culture.

Siminovich, Lorena. *Alex and Lulu: two of a kind* ill. by author. Candlewick, 2009. ISBN 978-0-7636-4423-9 Subj: Animals – cats. Animals – dogs. Character traits – being different. Friendship.

I like bugs ill. by author. Candlewick, 2010. ISBN 978-0-7636-4802-2 Subj: Counting, numbers. Format, unusual – board books. Insects.

I like vegetables ill. by author. Candlewick, 2011. ISBN 978-0-7636-5283-8 Subj: Concepts – opposites. Food. Format, unusual. Gardens, gardening.

Monkey see, look at me! ill. by author. Dial, 2012. ISBN 978-0-8037-3737-2 Subj: Animals. Animals – monkeys. Behavior – imitation.

Simler, Isabelle. *The blue hour* ill. by author. Eerdmans, 2017. ISBN 978-080285488-9 Subj: Concepts – color. Nature. Twilight.

Plume ill. by author. Eerdmans, 2017. ISBN 978-080285492-6 Subj: Animals – cats. Birds. Feathers.

Simmonds, Posy. *Baker cat* ill. by author. Red Fox, 2006. ISBN 978-0-09-945596-7 Subj: Activities –

baking, cooking. Animals – cats. Animals – mice. Careers – bakers.

Simmons, Jane. *Bouncy bouncy Daisy* ill. by author. Little, 2003. ISBN 978-0-316-79570-8 Subj: Birds – ducks. Format, unusual – toy & movable books.

Come along, Daisy! ill. by author. Little, 1998. ISBN 978-0-316-79790-0 Subj: Behavior – lost. Birds – ducks. Family life. Nature.

Daisy and the Beastie ill. by author. Little, 2000. ISBN 978-0-316-79785-6 Subj: Animals. Birds – ducks. Family life – brothers & sisters. Farms.

Daisy and the egg ill. by author. Little, 1998. ISBN 978-0-316-79747-4 Subj: Birds – ducks. Eggs. Family life – brothers & sisters. Family life – new sibling.

Daisy says coo! ill. by author. Little, 2000. ISBN 978-0-316-79764-1 Subj: Animals. Birds – ducks. Format, unusual – board books. Noise, sounds.

Daisy says, "Here we go round the mulberry bush" ill. by author. Little, 2002. ISBN 978-0-316-79811-2 Subj: Activities. Birds – ducks. Format, unusual – board books. Participation. Songs.

Daisy says, "If you're happy and you know it" ill. by author. Little, 2002. ISBN 978-0-316-79940-9 Subj: Birds – ducks. Format, unusual – board books. Noise, sounds. Participation. Songs.

Daisy, the little duck with big feet ill. by author. Little, 2001. ISBN 978-0-316-79454-1 Subj: Birds – ducks. Format, unusual. Noise, sounds.

Daisy's day out ill. by author. Little, 2000. ISBN 978-0-316-79763-4 Subj: Birds – ducks. Format, unusual – board books. Noise, sounds.

Daisy's favorite things ill. by author. Little, 1999. ISBN 978-0-316-79762-7 Subj: Animals. Birds – ducks. Format, unusual – board books. Night. Rhyming text.

Daisy's hide-and-seek ill. by author. Little, 2001. ISBN 978-0-316-79616-3 Subj: Animals. Birds – ducks. Format, unusual – toy & movable books. Games. Noise, sounds.

The dreamtime fairies ill. by author. Little, 2002. ISBN 978-0-316-79523-4 Subj: Bedtime. Fairies. Sleep. Toys.

Ebb and Flo and the greedy gulls ill. by author. Margaret K. McElderry, 2000. ISBN 978-0-689-82484-5 Subj: Animals – dogs. Behavior – misunderstanding. Birds – seagulls. Sea & seashore.

Ebb and Flo and the new friend ill. by author. Little, 1999. ISBN 978-0-689-82483-8 Subj: Animals – dogs. Behavior – sharing. Birds – geese.

Go to sleep, Daisy ill. by author. Little, 1999. ISBN 978-0-316-79761-0 Subj: Bedtime. Birds – ducks. Dreams. Noise, sounds. Sleep.

Little Fern's first winter ill. by author. Little, 2001. ISBN 978-0-316-79667-5 Subj: Activities – playing. Animals. Animals – rabbits. Family life – brothers & sisters. Games. Weather – snow.

Quack, Daisy, quack! ill. by author. Little, 2002. ISBN 978-0-316-79587-6 Subj: Behavior – lost. Birds – ducks. Noise, sounds.

Splish splash Daisy ill. by author. Little, 2003. ISBN 978-0-316-79560-9 Subj: Birds – ducks. Format, unusual – board books. Puzzles.

Together ill. by author. Random House, 2007. ISBN 978-0-375-84339-6 Subj: Animals – dogs. Friendship.

Simmons, Steven J. *Alice and Greta: a tale of two witches* ill. by Cyd Moore. Charlesbridge, 1997. ISBN 978-0-88106-974-7 Subj: Character traits – kindness. Character traits – meanness. Magic. Witches.

Alice and Greta's color magic ill. by Cyd Moore. Knopf, 2001. ISBN 978-0-375-81245-3 Subj: Behavior – misbehavior. Concepts – color. Magic. Witches.

Greta's revenge ill. by Cyd Moore. Crown, 1999. ISBN 978-0-517-80051-5 Subj: Behavior – misbehavior. Magic. Witches.

Simms, Laura. *Rotten teeth* ill. by David Catrow. Houghton, 1998. ISBN 978-0-395-82850-2 Subj: Activities – storytelling. School. Teeth.

Simon, Annette. *Robot zombie Frankenstein!* ill. by author. Candlewick, 2012. ISBN 978-0-7636-5124-4 Subj: Concepts – shape. Monsters. Robots.

Simon, Charnan. *Big bad Buzz* ill. by Len Epstein. Child's World, 2006. ISBN 978-1-59296-617-2 Subj: Animals – dogs. Behavior – animals, dislike of. Character traits – bravery. Emotions – fear.

A greedy little pig ill. by Marcy Ramsey. Child's World, 2006. ISBN 978-1-59296-622-6 Subj: Animals – pigs. Behavior – greed.

Jeremy Jones, clumsy guy ill. by Cari Pillo. Child's World, 2006. ISBN 978-1-59296-619-6 Subj: Character traits – clumsiness.

Messy Molly ill. by Mernie Gallagher-Cole. Child's World, 2006. ISBN 978-1-59296-625-7 Subj: Behavior – lost & found possessions. Behavior – messy. Character traits – orderliness. Toys – bears.

Simon, Francesca. *Calling all toddlers* ill. by Susan Winter. Orchard, 1999. ISBN 978-0-531-30120-3 Subj: Activities – playing. Rhyming text.

Hello, Moon! ill. by Ben Cort. Scholastic, 2014. ISBN 978-054564795-3 Subj: Bedtime. Moon.

Toddler time ill. by Susan Winter. Orchard, 2000. ISBN 978-0-531-30251-4 Subj: Activities. Poetry.

Simon, Norma. *All families are special* ill. by Teresa Flavin. Albert Whitman, 2003. ISBN 978-0-8075-2175-5 Subj: Family life. School.

All kinds of children ill. by Diane Paterson. Albert Whitman, 1999. ISBN 978-0-8075-0281-5 Subj: Character traits – individuality. Self-concept.

All kinds of families ill. by Joe Lasker. Albert Whitman, 1976. ISBN 978-0-8075-0282-2 Subj: Family life.

How do I feel? ill. by Joe Lasker. Albert Whitman, 1970. ISBN 978-0-8075-3414-4 Subj: Emotions. Family life. Multiple births – twins.

The saddest time ill. by Jacqueline Rogers. Albert Whitman, 1986. ISBN 978-0-8075-7203-0 Subj: Death. Emotions – grief.

The story of Hanukkah ill. by Leonid Gore. HarperCollins, 1997. ISBN 978-0-06-027420-7 Subj: Holidays – Hanukkah. Jewish culture. Religion.

The story of Passover ill. by Erika Weihs. HarperCollins, 1997. ISBN 978-0-06-027063-6 Subj: Holidays – Passover. Jewish culture. Religion.

Why am I different? ill. by Dora Leder. Albert Whitman, 1976. ISBN 978-0-8075-9075-1 Subj: Character traits – being different. Character traits – individuality. Self-concept.

Simon, Richard. *Oskar and the eight blessings* by Richard Simon and Tanya Simon ill. by Mark Siegel. Roaring Brook, 2015. ISBN 978-159643949-8 Subj: Character traits – kindness. Holidays – Hanukkah. Holocaust. Jewish culture.

Simon, Tanya. *Oskar and the eight blessings* (Simon, Richard)

Simont, Marc. *The goose that almost got cooked* ill. by author. Scholastic, 1997. ISBN 978-0-590-69075-1 Subj: Activities – flying. Birds – geese. Character traits – individuality. Farms.

The stray dog ill. by author. HarperCollins, 2001. ISBN 978-0-06-028934-8 Subj: Animals – dogs. Caldecott award honor books. Character traits – kindness to animals.

Simple gifts: a Shaker hymn ill. by Chris Raschka. Henry Holt, 1998. ISBN 978-0-8050-5143-8 Subj: Animals. Birds. Forest, woods. Music. Songs.

Simple Simon. *The adventures of Simple Simon* ill. by Chris Conover. Farrar, 1987. ISBN 978-0-374-36921-7 Subj: Nursery rhymes.

Simpson, Lesley. *The Purim surprise* ill. by Peter Church. Kar-Ben, 2003. ISBN 978-1-58013-090-5 Subj: Birthdays. Family life – daughters. Family life – mothers. Holidays – Purim. Jewish culture. Moving.

Simpson-Enock, Sarah. *Mommy, Mommy, what's in your tummy? a lift-the-flap book* ill. by Linzi West. Frances Lincoln, 2009. ISBN 978-1-84507-931-4 Subj: Birth. Character traits – questioning. Family life. Format, unusual – toy & movable books.

Sims, Nat. *Peekaboo barn* ill. by Nathan Tabor. Candlewick, 2014. ISBN 978-076367557-8 Subj: Farms. Format, unusual – board books. Format, unusual – toy & movable books. Noise, sounds.

Singer, Isaac Bashevis. *The parakeet named Dreidel* ill. by Suzanne Raphael Berkson. Farrar, 2015. ISBN 978-037430094-4 Subj: Behavior – lost & found possessions. Birds – parakeets, parrots. Holidays – Hanukkah. Jewish culture.

Why Noah chose the dove ill. by Eric Carle. Farrar, 1974. ISBN 978-0-374-38420-3 Subj: Animals. Birds – doves. Boats, ships. Religion – Noah. Weather – floods. Weather – rain. Weather – rainbows.

Singer, Marilyn. *Boo hoo boo-boo* ill. by Elivia Savadier. HarperCollins, 2002. ISBN 978-0-694-01566-5 Subj: Accidents. Illness. Rhyming text.

The boy who cried alien ill. by Brian Biggs. Hyperion, 2012. ISBN 978-0-7868-3825-7 Subj: Aliens. Behavior – lying. Character traits – honesty. Rhyming text.

Caterpillars. Illus. EarlyLight, 2011. ISBN 978-0-9797455-7-7 Subj: Insects – butterflies, caterpillars.

City lullaby ill. by Carll Cneut. Houghton, 2007. ISBN 978-0-618-60703-7 Subj: Babies, toddlers. Cities, towns. Counting, numbers. Noise, sounds. Rhyming text.

The company of crows ill. by Linda Saport. Clarion, 2002. ISBN 978-0-618-08340-4 Subj: Birds – crows. Poetry.

Creature carnival ill. by Gris Grimly. Hyperion, 2004. ISBN 978-0-7868-1877-8 Subj: Animals. Humorous stories. Mythical creatures. Poetry.

Didi and Daddy on the Promenade ill. by Marie-Louise Gay. Clarion, 2001. ISBN 978-0-618-04640-9 Subj: Activities – walking. Family life – daughters. Family life – fathers. Parks.

Eggs ill. by Emma Stevenson. Holiday House, 2008. ISBN 978-0-8234-1727-8 Subj: Eggs.

Every day's a dog's day: a year in poems ill. by Miki Sakamoto. Dial, 2012. ISBN 978-0-8037-3715-0 Subj: Animals – dogs. Holidays. Poetry.

Feel the beat: dance poems that zing from salsa to swing ill. by Kristi Valiant. Dial, 2017. ISBN 978-080374021-1 Subj: Activities – dancing. Poetry.

First food fight this fall and other school poems ill. by Sachiko Yoshikawa. Sterling, 2008. ISBN 978-1-4027-4145-6 Subj: Poetry. School.

Fred's bed ill. by JoAnn Adinolfi. HarperCollins, 2001. ISBN 978-0-694-01451-4   Subj: Animals. Furniture – beds. Rhyming text.

I'm getting a checkup ill. by David Milgrim. Clarion, 2009. ISBN 978-0-618-99000-9 Subj: Careers – doctors. Health & fitness.

I'm gonna climb a mountain in my patent leather shoes ill. by Lynne Avril. Abrams, 2014. ISBN 978-141970336-2 Subj: Camps, camping. Family life – brothers & sisters. Rhyming text. Self-concept.

I'm your bus ill. by Evan Polenghi. Scholastic, 2009. ISBN 978-0-545-08918-0   Subj: Buses. Rhyming text. School.

Let's build a clubhouse ill. by Timothy Bush. Houghton, 2006. ISBN 978-0-618-30670-1 Subj: Character traits – cooperation. Clubs, gangs. Rhyming text. Tools.

Nine o'clock lullaby ill. by Frané Lessac. HarperCollins, 1991. ISBN 978-0-06-025648-7 Subj: Foreign lands. Time.

On the same day in March ill. by Frané Lessac. HarperCollins, 2000. ISBN 978-0-06-443528-4 Subj: Maps. Weather. World.

The one and only me ill. by Nicole Rubel. HarperCollins, 2000. ISBN 978-0-694-01279-4 Subj: Anatomy. Character traits – individuality. Family life.

Quiet night ill. by John Manders. Clarion, 2002. ISBN 978-0-618-12044-4 Subj: Animals. Camps, camping. Counting, numbers. Night. Noise, sounds.

Shoe bop! ill. by Hiroe Nakata. Dutton, 2008. ISBN 978-0-525-47939-0 Subj: Clothing – shoes. Rhyming text. Shopping.

Solomon sneezes ill. by Brian Floca. HarperCollins, 1999. ISBN 978-0-694-01748-5 Subj: Humorous stories. Rhyming text.

A stick is an excellent thing: poems celebrating outdoor play ill. by LeUyen Pham. Clarion, 2012. ISBN 978-0-547-12493-3 Subj: Activities – playing. Poetry.

Tallulah's Nutcracker ill. by Alexandra Boiger. Clarion, 2013. ISBN 978-0-547-84557-9 Subj: Ballet. Behavior – mistakes. Emotions – embarrassment. Holidays – Christmas.

Tallulah's solo ill. by Alexandra Boiger. Clarion, 2012. ISBN 978-0-547-33004-4 Subj: Ballet. Family life – brothers & sisters.

Tallulah's tap shoes ill. by Alexandra Boiger. Clarion, 2015. ISBN 978-054423687-5 Subj: Activities – dancing. Ballet. Character traits – cooperation. Character traits – perseverance.

Tallulah's toe shoes ill. by Alexandra Boiger. Clarion, 2013. ISBN 978-0-547-48223-1 Subj: Activities – dancing. Ballet. Character traits – perseverance. Clothing – shoes.

Tallulah's tutu ill. by Alexandra Boiger. Clarion, 2011. ISBN 978-0-547-17353-5 Subj: Ballet. Character traits – perseverance.

Turtle in July ill. by Jerry Pinkney. Macmillan, 1989. ISBN 978-0-02-782881-8 Subj: Animals. Days of the week, months of the year. Nature. Poetry.

What is your dog doing? ill. by Kathleen Habbley. Simon & Schuster, 2011. ISBN 978-1-4169-7931-9 Subj: Animals – dogs. Rhyming text.

Singh, Rina. *My first book of Hindi words: an ABC rhyming book of Hindi language and Indian culture* ill. by Farida Zaman. Tuttle, 2016. ISBN 978-080484562-5 Subj: ABC books. Foreign languages. Rhyming text.

Singleton, Debbie. *The king who wouldn't sleep* ill. by Holly Swain. Andersen, 2012. ISBN 978-0-7613-8997-2 Subj: Behavior – trickery. Character traits – cleverness. Counting, numbers. Royalty – kings.

Singleton, Linda Joy. *A cat is better* ill. by Jorge Martin. little bee, 2017. ISBN 978-149980278-8 Subj: Animals – cats. Animals – dogs. Behavior – boasting, showing off. Pets.

Snow dog, sand dog ill. by Jess Golden. Albert Whitman, 2014. ISBN 978-080757536-9 Subj: Animals – dogs. Behavior – resourcefulness. Character traits – cleverness. Illness – allergies. Seasons.

Sinykin, Sheri. *Zayde comes to live* ill. by Kristina Swarner. Peachtree, 2012. ISBN 978-1-56145-631-4 Subj: Death. Family life – grandfathers. Jewish culture. Religion.

Siomades, Lorianne. *Cuckoo can't find you* ill. by author. Boyds Mills, 2002. ISBN 978-1-56397-778-7 Subj: Animals. Behavior – lost & found possessions. Rhyming text.

The itsy bitsy spider ill. by author. Boyds Mills, 1999. ISBN 978-1-56397-727-5 Subj: Character traits – persistence. Nursery rhymes. Spiders.

Kangaroo and cricket ill. by author. Boyds Mills, 1999. ISBN 978-1-56397-780-0 Subj: Activities. Animals. Rhyming text.

Katy did it! ill. by author. Boyds Mills, 2009. ISBN 978-1-59078-602-4 Subj: Insects.

My box of color ill. by author. Boyds Mills, 1998. ISBN 978-1-56397-711-4 Subj: Animals. Concepts – color.

A place to bloom ill. by author. Boyds Mills, 1997. ISBN 978-1-56397-656-8 Subj: Behavior – sharing. Earth. Ecology. Rhyming text.

Three little kittens by Lorianne Siomades and Mother Goose ill. by reteller. Boyds Mills, 2000. ISBN 978-1-56397-845-6 Subj: Animals – cats. Animals – mice. Behavior – lost & found possessions. Clothing – gloves, mittens. Nursery rhymes.

Sirett, Dawn. *Happy birthday Sophie!* ill. by Polly Appleton. DK, 2015. ISBN 978-146543256-8 Subj: Animals – giraffes. Birthdays. Format, unusual – toy & movable books.

Love your world: how to take care of the plants, the animals, and the planet ill. by Rachael Parfitt; photos by Howard Shooter, et al. DK, 2009. ISBN 978-0-7566-4590-8 Subj: Ecology. World.

Sirotich, Erica. *Found dogs* ill. by author. Dial, 2017. ISBN 978-039918641-7 Subj: Animals – dogs. Character traits – kindness to animals. Counting, numbers. Rhyming text.

Sís, Peter. *Ballerina* ill. by author. Greenwillow, 2001. ISBN 978-0-688-17944-1 Subj: Activities – dancing. Ballet. Careers – dancers. Imagination.

Beach ball ill. by author. Greenwillow, 1990. ISBN 978-0-688-09182-8 Subj: Concepts. Sea & seashore – beaches.

Dinosaur! ill. by author. Greenwillow, 2000. ISBN 978-0-688-17049-3 Subj: Dinosaurs. Imagination. Prehistory. Wordless.

Fire truck ill. by author. Greenwillow, 1998. ISBN 978-0-688-15878-1 Subj: Careers – firefighters. Counting, numbers. Format, unusual – toy & movable books. Trucks.

Follow the dream ill. by author. Knopf, 1991. ISBN 978-0-679-90628-5 Subj: Careers – explorers.

Ice cream summer ill. by author. Scholastic, 2015. ISBN 978-054573161-4 Subj: Activities – writing. Family life – grandfathers. Food. Letters, cards. Seasons – summer.

Madlenka ill. by author. Farrar, 2000. ISBN 978-0-374-39969-6 Subj: Behavior – growing up. Foreign lands. Imagination. Teeth.

Madlenka, soccer star ill. by author. Farrar, 2010. ISBN 978-0-374-34702-4 Subj: Communities, neighborhoods. Imagination. Sports – soccer.

An ocean world ill. by author. Greenwillow, 1992. ISBN 978-0-688-09068-5 Subj: Animals – whales. Sea & seashore. Wordless.

The pilot and the Little Prince: the life of Antoine de Saint-Exupery ill. by author. Farrar, 2014. ISBN 978-037438069-4 Subj: Careers – airplane pilots. Careers – writers. Foreign lands – France.

Play, Mozart, play ill. by author. HarperCollins, 2006. ISBN 978-0-06-112182-1 Subj: Careers – musicians. Music.

Robinson ill. by author. Scholastic, 2017. ISBN 978-054573166-9 Subj: Activities – traveling. Character traits – individuality. Clothing – costumes. Dreams. Imagination. Pirates. Self-concept.

Ship ahoy! ill. by author. Greenwillow, 1999. ISBN 978-0-688-16644-1 Subj: Boats, ships. Imagination. Monsters. Sea & seashore. Wordless.

A small tall tale from the far Far North ill. by author. Farrar, 2001. ISBN 978-0-374-37075-6 Subj: Eskimos. Foreign lands – Arctic. Indians of North America – Inuit. Tall tales.

Starry messenger ill. by author. Farrar, 1996. ISBN 978-0-374-37191-3 Subj: Astronomy. Caldecott award honor books. Careers – astronomers. Space & space ships. Stars.

Tibet through the red box ill. by author. Farrar, 1998. ISBN 978-0-374-37552-2 Subj: Activities – traveling. Caldecott award honor books. Foreign lands – Tibet.

Train of states ill. by author. Greenwillow, 2004. ISBN 978-0-06-057838-1 Subj: Trains. U.S. history.

Trucks, trucks, trucks ill. by author. Greenwillow, 1999. ISBN 978-0-688-16276-4 Subj: Format, unusual – toy & movable books. Trucks.

The wall: growing up behind the Iron Curtain ill. by author. Farrar, 2007. ISBN 978-0-374-34701-7 Subj: Caldecott award honor books. Careers – artists. Foreign lands – Czechoslovakia.

Waving ill. by author. Greenwillow, 1988. ISBN 978-0-688-07160-8 Subj: Counting, numbers.

Sisson, Stephanie Roth. *Star stuff: Carl Sagan and the mysteries of the cosmos* ill. by author. Roaring Brook, 2014. ISBN 978-159643960-3 Subj: Astronomy. Careers – astronomers.

Sitomer, Alan Lawrence. *Daddies do it different* ill. by Abby Carter. Hyperion, 2012. ISBN 978-1-4231-3315-5 Subj: Family life – fathers.

Siy, Alexandra. *One tractor: a counting book* ill. by Jacqueline Rogers. Holiday, 2008. ISBN 978-0-8234-1923-4 Subj: Counting, numbers. Pirates. Rhyming text. Tractors.

Skalak, Barbara Anne. *Waddle, waddle, quack, quack, quack* ill. by Sylvia Long. Chronicle, 2005. ISBN 978-0-8118-4342-3 Subj: Behavior – lost. Birds – ducks. Rhyming text.

Skead, Robert. *Something to prove: the great Satchel Paige vs. rookie Joe DiMaggio* ill. by Floyd Cooper. Carolrhoda, 2013. ISBN 978-0-7613-6619-5 Subj: Ethnic groups in the U.S. – African Americans. Prejudice. Sports – baseball. U.S. history.

Skeers, Linda. *Tutus aren't my style* ill. by Anne Wilsdorf. Penguin, 2010. ISBN 978-0-8037-3212-4 Subj: Ballet. Character traits – appearance. Character traits – individuality.

Skinner, Daphne. *Albert keeps score* ill. by Deborah Melmon. Kane, 2012. ISBN 978-1-57565-449-2 Subj: Animals – mice. Counting, numbers.

All aboard! ill. by Jerry Smath. Kane, 2007. ISBN 978-1-57565-239-9 Subj: Activities – traveling. Time. Trains.

Henry keeps score ill. by Page Eastburn O'Rourke. Kane, 2001. ISBN 978-1-57565-102-6 Subj: Counting, numbers. Family life – brothers & sisters. Sibling rivalry.

The right place for Albert ill. by Deborah Melmon. Kane, 2012. ISBN 978-1-57565-446-1 Subj: Animals – cats. Animals – mice. Counting, numbers.

Tightwad Tod ill. by John Nez. Kane, 2001. ISBN 978-1-57565-109-5 Subj: Counting, numbers. Money.

Sklansky, Amy E. *The duck who played the kazoo* ill. by Tiphanie Beeke. Clarion, 2008. ISBN 978-0-618-42854-0 Subj: Birds – ducks. Friendship. Musical instruments.

Out of this world: poems and facts about space ill. by Stacey Schuett. Knopf, 2012. ISBN 978-0-375-86459-9 Subj: Poetry. Space & space ships.

Where do chicks come from? ill. by Pamela Paparone. HarperCollins, 2005. ISBN 978-0-06-028893-8 Subj: Birds – chickens, roosters. Eggs. Science.

Skofield, James. *Bear and Bird* ill. by Jennifer Thermes. Sleeping Bear, 2014. ISBN 978-158536835-8 Subj: Animals – bears. Birds. Death. Emotions – grief.

Skolsky, Mindy Warshaw. *Hannah and the whistling tea kettle* ill. by Diane Palmisciano. DK, 2000. ISBN 978-0-7894-2602-4 Subj: Crime. Family life – grandparents. Gifts. Noise, sounds. Stores.

Skrypuch, Marsha Forchuk. *Enough* ill. by Michael Martchenko. Fitzhenry & Whiteside, 2000. ISBN 978-1-55041-509-4 Subj: Careers – farmers. Folk & fairy tales. Foreign lands – Ukraine.

Skultety, Nancy. *From here to there* ill. by Tammie Lyon. Boyds Mills, 2005. ISBN 978-1-59078-092-3 Subj: Careers – construction workers. Roads. Trucks.

Slack, Michael. *Elecopter* ill. by Michael H. Slack. Henry Holt, 2013. ISBN 978-0-8050-9304-9 Subj: Animals – elephants. Helicopters. Rhyming text.

Monkey Truck ill. by Michael H. Slack. Henry Holt, 2011. ISBN 978-0-8050-8878-6 Subj: Animals. Animals – monkeys. Character traits – helpfulness. Jungle. Rhyming text.

Shorty and Clem ill. by Michael H. Slack. HarperCollins, 2017. ISBN 978-006242158-6 Subj: Birds. Character traits – curiosity. Character traits – patience, impatience. Dinosaurs. Friendship.

Turtle Tug to the rescue ill. by Michael H. Slack. Holt/Christy Ottaviano, 2017. ISBN 978-162779194-6 Subj: Boats, ships. Character traits – bravery. Reptiles – turtles, tortoises. Rhyming text.

Wazdot? ill. by Michael H. Slack. Disney/Hyperion, 2014. ISBN 978-142318347-1 Subj: Aliens. Farms.

Slade, Suzanne. *Climbing Lincoln's steps: the African American journey* ill. by Colin Bootman. Albert Whitman, 2010. ISBN 978-0-8075-1204-3 Subj: Ethnic groups in the U.S. – African Americans. Prejudice. U.S. history.

Dangerous Jane ill. by Alice Ratterree. Peachtree, 2017. ISBN 978-156145913-1 Subj: Behavior – seeking better things. Character traits – helpfulness. Gender roles. Poverty.

Friends for freedom: the story of Susan B. Anthony and Frederick Douglass ill. by Nicole Tadgell. Charlesbridge, 2014. ISBN 978-158089568-2 Subj: Ethnic groups in the U.S. – African Americans. Friendship. Gender roles. U.S. history.

The house that George built ill. by Rebecca Bond. Charlesbridge, 2012. ISBN 978-1-58089-262-9 Subj: Buildings. Homes, houses. U.S. history.

What's new at the zoo?: an animal adding adventure ill. by Joan Waites. Sylvan Dell, 2009. ISBN 978-1-934359-93-8 Subj: Counting, numbers. Zoos.

What's the difference? an endangered animal subtraction story ill. by Joan Waites. Sylvan Dell, 2010. ISBN 978-1-60718-070-8 Subj: Animals – endangered animals. Counting, numbers.

With books and bricks: how Booker T. Washington built a school ill. by Nicole Tadgell. Albert Whitman, 2014. ISBN 978-080750897-8 Subj: Books, reading. Character traits – perseverance. Ethnic groups in the U.S. – African Americans. Prejudice. School.

Slade-Robinson, Nikki. *Muddle and Mo's worm surprise* ill. by author. Starfish Bay, 2017. ISBN 978-176036030-6 Subj: Activities – picnicking. Animals – goats. Animals – worms. Birds – ducks.

Muddle and Mo ill. by author. Clarion, 2017. ISBN 978-054471612-4 Subj: Animals – goats. Birds – ducks. Self-concept.

Slangerup, Erik Jon. *Dirt Boy* ill. by John Manders. Albert Whitman, 2000. ISBN 978-0-8075-4424-2

Subj: Activities – bathing. Behavior – running away. Family life – mothers. Health & fitness.

Slate, Jenny. *Marcel the shell with shoes on: things about me* by Jenny Slate and Dean Fleischer-Camp ill. by Amy Lind. Penguin, 2011. ISBN 978-1-59514-455-3 Subj: Imagination. Sea & seashore.

Slate, Joseph. *The great big wagon that rang* ill. by Craig Spearing. Marshall Cavendish, 2002. ISBN 978-0-7614-5108-2 Subj: Careers – farmers. Rhyming text. U.S. history.

I want to be free ill. by E. B. Lewis. Putnam, 2009. ISBN 978-0-399-24342-4 Subj: Ethnic groups in the U.S. – African Americans. Rhyming text. Slavery.

Little Porcupine's Christmas ill. by Felicia Bond. Geringer, 2001. ISBN 978-0-06-029533-2 Subj: Animals. Animals – porcupines. Holidays – Christmas.

Miss Bindergarten celebrates the last day of kindergarten ill. by Ashley Wolff. Penguin, 2006. ISBN 978-0-525-47744-0 Subj: ABC books. Animals. Careers – teachers. Rhyming text. School.

Miss Bindergarten celebrates the 100th day of kindergarten ill. by Ashley Wolff. Dutton, 1998. ISBN 978-0-525-46000-8 Subj: Animals. Careers – teachers. Counting, numbers. Rhyming text. School.

Miss Bindergarten gets ready for kindergarten ill. by Ashley Wolff. Dutton, 1996. ISBN 978-0-525-45446-5 Subj: ABC books. Animals. Careers – teachers. School – first day.

Miss Bindergarten has a wild day in kindergarten ill. by Ashley Wolff. Penguin, 2005. ISBN 978-0-525-47084-7 Subj: ABC books. Animals. Behavior – bad day, bad mood. Careers – teachers. Rhyming text. School.

Miss Bindergarten stays home from kindergarten ill. by Ashley Wolff. Dutton, 2000. ISBN 978-0-525-46396-2 Subj: ABC books. Animals. Careers – teachers. Illness – cold (disease). Rhyming text. School.

Miss Bindergarten takes a field trip with kindergarten ill. by Ashley Wolff. Dutton, 2001. ISBN 978-0-525-46710-6 Subj: ABC books. Animals. Careers – teachers. Rhyming text. School. School – field trips.

Story time for Little Porcupine ill. by Jacqueline Rogers. Marshall Cavendish, 2001. ISBN 978-0-7614-5073-3 Subj: Activities – storytelling. Animals – porcupines. Creation. Family life – fathers. Folk & fairy tales. Sun.

What star is this? ill. by Alison Jay. Penguin, 2005. ISBN 978-0-399-24014-0 Subj: Religion – Nativity. Rhyming text.

Who is coming to our house? ill. by Ashley Wolff. Putnam, 1988. ISBN 978-0-399-21537-7 Subj: Animals. Animals – mice. Religion. Rhyming text.

Slater, Dashka. *The antlered ship* ill. by Terry Fan. Simon & Schuster/Beach Lane, 2017. ISBN 978-148145160-4 Subj: Activities – traveling. Animals – deer. Animals – foxes. Boats, ships. Character traits – curiosity. Character traits – questioning.

Baby shoes ill. by Hiroe Nakata. Bloomsbury, 2006. ISBN 978-1-58234-684-7 Subj: Babies, toddlers. Clothing – shoes. Concepts – color. Rhyming text.

Escargot ill. by Sydney Hanson. Farrar, 2017. ISBN 978-037430281-8 Subj: Animals – snails. Humorous stories.

Firefighters in the dark ill. by Nicoletta Ceccoli. Houghton, 2006. ISBN 978-0-618-55459-1 Subj: Bedtime. Careers – firefighters. Dreams.

The sea serpent and me ill. by Catia Chien. Houghton, 2008. ISBN 978-0-618-72394-2 Subj: Behavior – growing up. Mythical creatures.

Slater, Teddy. *Smooch your pooch* ill. by Arthur Howard. Scholastic, 2010. ISBN 978-0-545-16736-9 Subj: Animals – dogs. Rhyming text.

Slawson, Michele Benoit. *Signs for sale* ill. by Bagram Ibatoulline. Viking, 2002. ISBN 978-0-670-03568-7 Subj: Family life – daughters. Family life – fathers. Signs.

Slayton, Fran Cannon. *Snowball moon* ill. by Tracy Bishop. little bee, 2017. ISBN 978-149980495-9 Subj: Family life. Rhyming text. Seasons – winter. Sports – sledding. Weather – snow.

Sleator, William. *The angry moon* ill. by Blair Lent. Little, 1970. ISBN 978-0-316-78737-6 Subj: Caldecott award honor books. Folk & fairy tales. Indians of North America – Tlingit. Moon.

Slegers, Liesbet. *Chefs and what they do* ill. by author. Clavis, 2014. ISBN 978-160537179-5 Subj: Careers – chefs, cooks. Restaurants.

The child in the manger ill. by author. Clavis, 2010. ISBN 978-1-60537-084-2 Subj: Holidays – Christmas. Religion.

Fall leaves ill. by author. Clavis, 2012. ISBN 978-1-60537-122-1 Subj: Format, unusual – board books. Seasons – fall.

Funny ears ill. by author. Clavis, 2011. ISBN 978-1-60537-088-0 Subj: Anatomy – ears. Animals. Format, unusual – board books.

Funny feet ill. by author. Clavis, 2011. ISBN 978-1-60537-089-7 Subj: Anatomy – feet. Animals. Format, unusual – board books.

Funny tails ill. by author. Clavis, 2011. ISBN 978-1-60537-090-3 Subj: Anatomy – tails. Animals. Format, unusual – board books.

Happy Easter! ill. by author. Clavis, 2012. ISBN 978-1-60537-114-6 Subj: Animals – rabbits. Eggs. Holidays – Easter.

Katie goes to the doctor ill. by author. Clavis, 2011. ISBN 978-1-60537-076-7 Subj: Careers – doctors.

Kevin goes to the library ill. by author. Clavis, 2011. ISBN 978-1-60537-075-0 Subj: Libraries.

Playing ill. by author. Clavis, 2011. ISBN 978-1-60537-091-0 Subj: Activities – playing. Format, unusual – board books.

Winter snow ill. by author. Clavis, 2012. ISBN 978-1-60537-123-8 Subj: Format, unusual – board books. Seasons – winter.

Slingsby, Janet. *Hetty's 100 hats* ill. by Emma Dodd. Good Books, 2005. ISBN 978-1-56148-456-0 Subj: Behavior – collecting things. Birthdays. Clothing – hats. Counting, numbers.

Hush-a-bye babies ill. by Andy Beckett. Barron's, 2001. ISBN 978-0-7641-5410-2 Subj: Animals. Bedtime. Noise, sounds. Sleep.

Sliwerski, Jessica Reid. *Cancer hates kisses* ill. by Mika Song. Dial, 2017. ISBN 978-073522781-1 Subj: Character traits – bravery. Character traits – perseverance. Family life. Family life – mothers. Illness – cancer.

Sloat, Robert. *Rib-ticklers* (Sloat, Teri)

Sloat, Teri. *Farmer Brown goes round and round* ill. by Nadine Bernard Westcott. DK, 1999. ISBN 978-0-7894-2512-6 Subj: Animals. Farms. Noise, sounds. Rhyming text. Weather – tornadoes.

Farmer Brown shears his sheep: a yarn about wool ill. by Nadine Bernard Westcott. DK, 2000. ISBN 978-0-7894-2637-6 Subj: Animals – sheep. Farms. Rhyming text.

Hark! The aardvark angels sing ill. by author. Putnam, 2001. ISBN 978-0-399-23371-5 Subj: Angels. Animals – aardvarks. Holidays – Christmas. Music. Songs.

I'm a duck! ill. by author. Penguin, 2006. ISBN 978-0-399-24274-8 Subj: Behavior – growing up. Birds – ducks.

Pablo in the snow ill. by Rosalinde Bonnet. Holt/Christy Ottaviano, 2017. ISBN 978-162779412-1 Subj: Activities – playing. Animals – sheep. Behavior – lost. Weather – snow.

Patty's pumpkin patch ill. by author. Putnam, 1999. ISBN 978-0-399-23010-3 Subj: ABC books. Rhyming text.

Pieces of Christmas ill. by author. Henry Holt, 2002. ISBN 978-0-8050-6355-4 Subj: Animals.

Holidays – Christmas. Letters, cards. Rhyming text. Santa Claus.

Rib-ticklers by Teri Sloat and Robert Sloat; ill. by authors. Lothrop, 1995. ISBN 978-0-688-12520-2 Subj: Animals. Riddles & jokes.

There was an old lady who swallowed a trout ill. by Reynold Ruffins. Henry Holt, 1998. ISBN 978-0-8050-4294-8 Subj: Animals. Cumulative tales. Fish. Folk & fairy tales. Humorous stories. Rhyming text.

The thing that bothered Farmer Brown ill. by Nadine Bernard Westcott. Orchard, 1995. ISBN 978-0-531-08733-6 Subj: Animals. Careers – farmers. Insects – mosquitoes. Night. Noise, sounds. Rhyming text. Sleep.

This is the house that was tidy and neat ill. by R. W. Alley. Henry Holt, 2005. ISBN 978-0-8050-6921-1 Subj: Character traits – cleanliness. Rhyming text.

Zip! zoom! on a broom ill. by Rosalinde Bonnet. Little, Brown, 2017. ISBN 978-031625673-5 Subj: Counting, numbers. Holidays – Halloween. Rhyming text. Witches.

Slobodkina, Esphyr. *Caps for sale* ill. by author. Addison-Wesley, 1940. ISBN 978-0-06-025778-1 Subj: Animals – monkeys. Behavior – imitation. Careers – peddlers. Clothing – hats. Humorous stories. Participation.

Caps for sale and the mindful monkeys by Esphyr Slobodkina and Ann Marie Mulhearn Sayer; ill. by Esphyr Slobodkina. HarperCollins, 2017. ISBN 978-006249988-2 Subj: Animals – monkeys. Behavior – imitation. Careers – peddlers. Character traits – helpfulness. Clothing – hats. Humorous stories.

Circus caps for sale ill. by author. HarperCollins, 2002. ISBN 978-0-06-029656-8 Subj: Animals – elephants. Careers – peddlers. Circus. Clothing – hats. Crime. Humorous stories. Participation.

More caps for sale: another tale of mischievous monkeys by Esphyr Slobodkina and Anne Marie Mulhearn Sayer; ill. by Esphyr Slobodkina. HarperCollins, 2015. ISBN 978-006240545-6 Subj: Animals – monkeys. Behavior – imitation. Careers – peddlers. Clothing – hats. Humorous stories. Participation.

Slonim, David. *He came with the couch* ill. by author. Chronicle, 2005. ISBN 978-0-8118-4430-7 Subj: Friendship. Furniture.

I loathe you ill. by author. Simon & Schuster, 2012. ISBN 978-1-4424-2244-5 Subj: Emotions – love. Family life – mothers. Monsters. Rhyming text.

Oh, Ducky ill. by author. Chronicle, 2003. ISBN 978-0-8118-3562-6 Subj: Behavior – lost & found possessions. Food. Toys.

Patch ill. by author. Roaring Brook, 2013. ISBN 978-1-59643-643-5 Subj: Animals – dogs. Pets.

Slovenz-Low, Madeline. *Lion dancer: Ernie Wan's Chinese New Year* (Waters, Kate)

Small, David. *George Washington's cows* ill. by author. Farrar, 1994. ISBN 978-0-374-32535-0 Subj: Animals. Rhyming text. U.S. history.

Imogene's antlers ill. by author. Crown, 1985. ISBN 978-0-517-55564-4 Subj: Animals. Character traits – appearance.

Smallcomb, Pam. *Earth to Clunk* ill. by Joe Berger. Penguin, 2011. ISBN 978-0-8037-3439-5 Subj: Aliens. Family life – brothers & sisters. Pen pals. School. Space & space ships.

I'm not ill. by Robert Weinstock. Random House, 2011. ISBN 978-0-375-86115-4 Subj: Character traits – individuality. Friendship. Self-concept.

Smalley, Elisa. *Zoe Sophia in New York: the mystery of the Pink Phoenix papers* (Mauner, Claudia)

Zoe Sophia's scrapbook (Mauner, Claudia)

Smallman, Steve. *Dragon stew* ill. by Lee Wildish. Good Books, 2010. ISBN 978-1-56148-695-3 Subj: Dragons. Rhyming text. Vikings.

Hiccupotamus ill. by Ada Grey. Tiger Tales, 2015. ISBN 978-158925171-7 Subj: Animals. Animals – hippopotamuses. Jungle. Music. Noise, sounds. Rhyming text.

The lamb who came for dinner ill. by Joelle Dreidemy. Tiger Tales, 2007. ISBN 978-1-58925-067-3 Subj: Animals – sheep. Animals – wolves. Friendship.

My dad! ill. by Sean Julian. Good Books, 2012. ISBN 978-1-56148-744-8 Subj: Animals – bears. Family life – fathers. Rhyming text.

Scowl ill. by Richard Watson. Tiger Tales, 2014. ISBN 978-158925155-7 Subj: Behavior – bad day, bad mood. Birds – owls. Character traits – being different.

The very greedy bee ill. by Jack Tickle. Tiger Tales, 2007. ISBN 978-1-58925-065-9 Subj: Behavior – greed. Behavior – sharing. Insects – bees.

Smalls, Irene. *Don't say ain't* ill. by Colin Bootman. Charlesbridge, 2003. ISBN 978-1-57091-381-5 Subj: Books, reading. Ethnic groups in the U.S. – African Americans. Family life. Prejudice. School.

My Nana and me ill. by Cathy Ann Johnson. Little, Brown, 2005. ISBN 978-0-316-16821-2 Subj: Activities – playing. Ethnic groups in the U.S. – African Americans. Family life – grandmothers.

My Pop Pop and me ill. by Cathy Ann Johnson. Little, Brown, 2006. ISBN 978-0-316-73422-6

Subj: Activities – baking, cooking. Ethnic groups in the U.S. – African Americans. Family life – grandfathers. Rhyming text.

Smalls-Hector, Irene. *Because you're lucky* ill. by Michael Hays. Little, 1997. ISBN 978-0-316-79867-9 Subj: Behavior – sharing. Emotions – envy, jealousy. Ethnic groups in the U.S. – African Americans. Family life – cousins. Friendship.

Beginning school ill. by Toni Goffe. Silver, 1996. ISBN 978-0-382-39328-0 Subj: Ethnic groups in the U.S. – African Americans. School – first day.

Jenny Reen and the Jack Muh Lantern ill. by Keinyo White. Atheneum, 1996. ISBN 978-0-689-31875-7 Subj: Ethnic groups in the U.S. – African Americans. Holidays – Halloween. Slavery. U.S. history.

Jonathan and his mommy ill. by Michael Hays. Little, 1992. ISBN 978-0-316-79870-9 Subj: Activities – walking. Cities, towns. Communities, neighborhoods. Ethnic groups in the U.S. – African Americans. Family life – mothers.

Kevin and his dad ill. by Michael Hays. Little, 1999. ISBN 978-0-316-79899-0 Subj: Ethnic groups in the U.S. – African Americans. Family life – fathers. Rhyming text.

Smath, Jerry. *The animals' Christmas carol* by Jerry Smath and Charles Dickens; ill. by Jerry Smath. An adaption of Charles Dickens' A Christmas Carol. BridgeWater, 2000. ISBN 978-0-8167-6940-7 Subj: Animals. Behavior – greed. Holidays – Christmas.

Sammy Salami ill. by author. Abrams, 2007. ISBN 978-0-8109-9350-1 Subj: Activities – traveling. Activities – vacationing. Animals – cats. Behavior – lost. Pets.

Smee, Nicola. *Clip-clop* ill. by author. Boxer, 2006. ISBN 978-1-905417-09-4 Subj: Animals. Concepts – speed.

Jingle-jingle ill. by author. Boxer, 2008. ISBN 978-1-906250-08-9 Subj: Animals. Seasons – winter. Sports – sledding.

No bed without Ted ill. by author. Bloomsbury, 2005. ISBN 978-1-58234-963-3 Subj: Bedtime. Behavior – lost & found possessions. Format, unusual – toy & movable books. Toys – bears.

What's the matter, Bunny Blue? ill. by author. Boxer, 2010. ISBN 978-1-906250-91-1 Subj: Animals – rabbits. Behavior – lost. Family life – grandmothers. Rhyming text.

Smet, Marian De. *I have two homes* ill. by Nynke Mare Talsma. Clavis, 2012. ISBN 978-1-60537-102-3 Subj: Divorce. Family life.

Smiley, Jane. *Twenty yawns* ill. by Lauren Castillo. Amazon/Two Lions, 2016. ISBN 978-147782635-5 Subj: Bedtime.

Smiley, Norene. *That stripy cat* ill. by Tara Anderson. Fitzhenry & Whiteside, 2007. ISBN 978-1-55005-164-3 Subj: Animals – cats.

Smith, A. J. *Even monsters* ill. by A. J. Smith. Sourcebooks/Jabberwocky, 2014. ISBN 978-140228652-0 Subj: Emotions. Monsters.

Smith, Alex T. *Foxy and Egg* ill. by author. Holiday House, 2011. ISBN 978-0-8234-2330-9 Subj: Animals – foxes. Behavior – trickery. Eggs. Humorous stories.

Little Red and the very hungry lion ill. by Alex T. Smith. Scholastic, 2016. ISBN 978-054591438-3 Subj: Animals – lions. Folk & fairy tales. Foreign lands – Africa.

Smith, Ben Bailey. *I am Bear* ill. by Sav Akyüz. Candlewick, 2016. ISBN 978-076367743-5 Subj: Animals – bears. Behavior – misbehavior. Humorous stories.

Smith, Charles R. *Brick by brick* ill. by Floyd Cooper. Amistad, 2013. ISBN 978-0-06-192082-0 Subj: Buildings. Ethnic groups in the U.S. – African Americans. Slavery. U.S. history.

Dance with me ill. by Noah Jones. Candlewick, 2008. ISBN 978-0-7636-2246-6 Subj: Activities – dancing. Rhyming text.

I am the world ill. by Charles R. Smith. Simon & Schuster, 2013. ISBN 978-1-4424-2302-2 Subj: Ethnic groups in the U.S. Rhyming text. World.

I'll be there photos by Charles R Smith. Composed by Hal Davis, Berry Gordy, Jr., Bob West, & Willie Hutchinson;. Hyperion, 2001. ISBN 978-0-7868-0785-7 Subj: Babies, toddlers. Format, unusual – board books. Music. Songs.

Loki and Alex photos by Charles R Smith. Dutton, 2001. ISBN 978-0-525-46700-7 Subj: Animals – dogs. Ethnic groups in the U.S. – African Americans.

My gal photos by Charles R Smith. Hyperion, 2001. ISBN 978-0-7868-0782-6 Subj: Babies, toddlers. Format, unusual – board books. Music. Songs.

Twenty-eight days: moments in black history that changed the world ill. by Shane W. Evans. Roaring Brook/Neal Porter, 2015. ISBN 978-159643820-0 Subj: Ethnic groups in the U.S. – African Americans. Poetry. U.S. history. Violence, nonviolence.

Smith, Cynthia Leitich. *Holler Loudly* ill. by Barry Gott. Penguin, 2010. ISBN 978-0-525-42256-3 Subj: Character traits – being different. Tall tales.

Jingle dancer ill. by Cornelius Van Wright and Ying-Hwa Hu. Morrow, 2000. ISBN 978-0-688-16242-9 Subj: Activities – dancing. Family life. Indians of North America.

Santa knows by Cynthia Leitich Smith and Greg Leitich Smith ill. by Steve Björkman. Penguin, 2006. ISBN 978-0-525-47757-0 Subj: Holidays – Christmas. Santa Claus.

Smith, Dana Kessimakis. *A brave spaceboy* ill. by Laura Freeman. Hyperion, 2005. ISBN 978-0-7868-0933-2 Subj: Imagination. Moving.

Smith, Danna. *Arctic white* ill. by Lee White. Henry Holt, 2016. ISBN 978-162779104-5 Subj: Concepts – color. Family life – grandfathers. Foreign lands – Arctic. Northern lights. Seasons – winter.

Balloon trees ill. by Laurie Allen Klein. Sylvan Dell, 2013. ISBN 978-1-60718-612-0 Subj: Activities – making things. Toys – balloons. Trees.

Mother Goose's pajama party ill. by Virginia Allyn. Doubleday, 2015. ISBN 978-055349756-4 Subj: Bedtime. Nursery rhymes. Sleepovers.

Pirate nap: a book of colors ill. by Valeria Petrone. Clarion, 2011. ISBN 978-0-574-57531-5 Subj: Concepts – color. Pirates. Rhyming text.

Swallow the leader: a counting book ill. by Kevin Sherry. Clarion, 2016. ISBN 978-054410518-8 Subj: Counting, numbers. Fish. Rhyming text.

Smith, David J. *If America were a village: a book about the people of the United States* ill. by Shelagh Armstrong. Kids Can, 2009. ISBN 978-1-55453-344-2 Subj: Counting, numbers. U.S. history.

This child, every child: a book about the world's children ill. by Shelagh Armstrong. Kids Can, 2011. ISBN 978-1-55453-466-1 Subj: World.

Smith, Dian G. *Hanukkah lights* ill. by JoAnn E. Kitchel. Chronicle, 2001. ISBN 978-0-8118-3257-1 Subj: Holidays – Hanukkah. Jewish culture.

Smith, Greg Leitich. *Santa knows* (Smith, Cynthia Leitich)

Smith, Hope Anita. *My daddy rules the world: poems about dads* ill. by author. Holt/Christy Ottaviano, 2017. ISBN 978-080509189-2 Subj: Family life – fathers. Poetry.

Smith, Jada Pinkett. *Girls hold up this world* ill. by Donyell Kennedy-McCullough. Scholastic, 2005. ISBN 978-0-439-08793-3 Subj: Gender roles. Rhyming text. Self-concept.

Smith, Janice Lee. *Jess and the stinky cowboys* ill. by Lisa Thiesing. Dial, 2004. ISBN 978-0-8037-2641-3 Subj: Activities – bathing. Animals – dogs. Careers – police officers. Character traits – cleanliness. Cowboys, cowgirls. Tall tales. U.S. history – frontier & pioneer life.

Smith, Joseph A. *Circus train* ill. by author. Abrams, 2001. ISBN 978-0-8109-4148-9 Subj: Circus. Moving. Trains.

Smith, Kathryn. *Little Donkey's Christmas story* ill. by Amanda Wood. Candle Books, 2002. ISBN 978-1-85985-441-9 Subj: Animals – donkeys. Format, unusual – toy & movable books. Holidays – Christmas. Participation. Religion – Nativity.

Little Lamb's Christmas story ill. by Amanda Wood. Candle Books, 2002. ISBN 978-1-85985-442-6 Subj: Animals – sheep. Format, unusual – toy & movable books. Holidays – Christmas. Participation. Religion – Nativity.

Smith, Lane. *Abe Lincoln's dream* ill. by author. Roaring Brook, 2012. ISBN 978-1-59643-608-4 Subj: Ghosts. U.S. history.

Glasses . . . who needs 'em? ill. by author. Viking, 1991. ISBN 978-0-670-84160-8 Subj: Glasses. Senses – sight.

Grandpa Green ill. by author. Roaring Brook, 2011. ISBN 978-1-59643-607-7 Subj: Caldecott award honor books. Family life – great-grandparents. Gardens, gardening. Memories, memory. Old age.

It's a book ill. by author. Roaring Brook, 2010. ISBN 978-1-59643-606-0 Subj: Animals. Books, reading. Humorous stories.

John, Paul, George and Ben ill. by author. Hyperion, 2006. ISBN 978-0-7868-4893-5 Subj: Humorous stories. U.S. history.

Madam President ill. by author. Hyperion, 2008. ISBN 978-1-4231-0846-7 Subj: Behavior – seeking better things. Character traits – ambition. Gender roles. Humorous stories.

A perfect day ill. by author. Roaring Brook, 2017. ISBN 978-162672536-2 Subj: Animals. Animals – bears.

Pinocchio, the boy ill. by author. Viking, 2002. ISBN 978-0-670-03585-4 Subj: Fairies. Folk & fairy tales. Humorous stories. Puppets. Self-concept.

The Stinky Cheese Man and other fairly stupid tales (Scieszka, Jon)

There is a tribe of kids ill. by author. Roaring Brook, 2016. ISBN 978-162672056-5 Subj: Animals. Language.

Smith, Linda. *The inside tree* ill. by David Parkins. HarperCollins, 2010. ISBN 978-0-06-028241-7 Subj: Animals – dogs. Homes, houses. Humorous stories. Trees.

Mrs. Biddlebox ill. by Marla Frazee. HarperCollins, 2002. ISBN 978-0-06-028690-3 Subj: Activities – baking, cooking. Emotions. Food. Rhyming text.

Sir Cassie to the rescue ill. by Karen Patkau. Orca, 2003. ISBN 978-1-55143-243-4 Subj: Family life – brothers & sisters. Imagination. Knights.

When Moon fell down ill. by Kathryn Brown. HarperCollins, 2001. ISBN 978-0-06-029497-7 Subj: Animals – bulls, cows. Moon. Rhyming text.

Smith, Lois T. *Carrie and Carl play* ill. by author. Candlewick, 2007. ISBN 978-0-7636-1690-8 Subj: Activities – playing. Format, unusual – toy & movable books.

Smith, Maggie. *Counting our way to Maine* ill. by author. Orchard, 1995. ISBN 978-0-531-08734-3 Subj: Activities – traveling. Counting, numbers.

Dear Daisy, get well soon ill. by author. Crown, 2000. ISBN 978-0-517-80073-7 Subj: Counting, numbers. Days of the week, months of the year. Family life – mothers. Friendship. Illness – chicken pox. Toys.

Desser, the best ever cat ill. by author. Knopf, 2001. ISBN 978-0-375-91056-2 Subj: Animals – cats. Death. Emotions. Pets.

One naked baby: counting to ten and back again ill. by author. Random House, 2007. ISBN 978-0-375-83329-8 Subj: Babies, toddlers. Counting, numbers. Rhyming text.

Paisley ill. by author. Knopf, 2004. ISBN 978-0-375-92164-3 Subj: Animals – elephants. Behavior – needing someone. Toys.

Pigs in pajamas ill. by author. Knopf, 2012. ISBN 978-0-375-84817-9 Subj: Animals – pigs. Rhyming text. Sleepovers.

This is your garden ill. by author. Crown, 1998. ISBN 978-0-517-70993-1 Subj: Gardens, gardening.

Smith, Marie. *N is for our nation's capital: a Washington, DC alphabet* by Marie Smith and Roland Smith ill. by Barbara L. Gibson. Sleeping Bear, 2005. ISBN 978-1-58556-148-3 Subj: ABC books. Cities, towns. U.S. history.

S is for Smithsonian: America's museum alphabet by Marie Smith and Roland Smith ill. by Gijsbert van Frankenhuyzen. Sleeping Bear, 2010. ISBN 978-1-58536-314-8 Subj: ABC books. Museums. U.S. history.

Z is for zookeeper: a zoo alphabet by Marie Smith and Roland Smith ill. by Henry Cole. Sleeping Bear, 2005. ISBN 978-1-58536-158-8 Subj: ABC books. Zoos.

Smith, Matthew Clark. *Lighter than air: Sophie Blanchard, the first woman pilot* ill. by Matt Tavares. Candlewick, 2017. ISBN 978-076367732-9 Subj: Activities – ballooning. Foreign lands – France. Gender roles.

Small wonders: Jean-Henri Fabre and his world of insects ill. by Giuliano Ferri. Amazon/Two Lions, 2015. ISBN 978-147782632-4 Subj: Careers – naturalists. Foreign lands – France. Insects. Nature.

Smith, Mavis. *'Twas the day after Thanksgiving* ill. by author. Simon & Schuster, 2002. ISBN 978-0-689-85234-3 Subj: Animals – mice. Format, unusual – toy & movable books. Holidays – Thanksgiving. Rhyming text.

Smith, Monique Gray. *You hold me up* ill. by Danielle Daniel. Orca, 2017. ISBN 978-145981447-9 Subj: Behavior – sharing. Character traits – generosity. Character traits – kindness. Family life. Friendship.

Smith, Nikkolas. *The golden girls of Rio* ill. by author. Skyhorse/Sky Pony, 2016. ISBN 978-151072247-7 Subj: Gender roles. Sports. Sports – Olympics.

Smith, Roland. *N is for our nation's capital: a Washington, DC alphabet* (Smith, Marie)

S is for Smithsonian: America's museum alphabet (Smith, Marie)

Z is for zookeeper: a zoo alphabet (Smith, Marie)

Smith, Rosie. *Captain Pajamas* (Whatley, Bruce)

Smith, Shoham. *An after bedtime story* ill. by Einat Tsarfati. Abrams, 2016. ISBN 978-141971873-1 Subj: Bedtime. Behavior – misbehavior. Family life. Rhyming text.

Smith, Stu. *The bubble gum kid* ill. by Julia Woolf. Running Press, 2006. ISBN 978-0-7624-2046-9 Subj: Behavior – bullying, teasing. Rhyming text.

Smith, Will. *Just the two of us* ill. by Kadir Nelson. Scholastic, 2001. ISBN 978-0-439-08792-6 Subj: Family life – fathers. Family life – sons. Music. Songs.

Smothers, Ethel Footman. *Auntee Edna* ill. by Wil Clay. Eerdmans, 2001. ISBN 978-0-8028-5154-3 Subj: Activities – baking, cooking. Ethnic groups in the U.S. – African Americans. Food.

Smucker, Anna Egan. *Golden delicious: a Cinderella apple story* ill. by Kathleen Kemly. Albert Whitman, 2008. ISBN 978-0-8075-2987-4 Subj: Food. U.S. history.

Smythe, Theresa. *Chester's colorful Easter eggs* ill. by author. Henry Holt, 2013. ISBN 978-0-8050-9326-1 Subj: Animals – rabbits. Concepts – color. Eggs. Holidays – Easter.

Sneed, Brad. *Deputy Harvey and the ant cow caper* ill. by author. Penguin, 2005. ISBN 978-0-8037-3023-6 Subj: Careers – sheriffs. Crime. Insects – ants. Mystery stories. U.S. history – frontier & pioneer life.

Picture a letter ill. by author. Fogelman, 2002. ISBN 978-0-8037-2613-0 Subj: ABC books. Wordless.

Sneed, Dani. *My even day* (Fisher, Doris)

One odd day (Fisher, Doris)

Snell, Gordon. *'Twas the day after Christmas* ill. by Sean DeLonas. HarperCollins, 2003. ISBN 978-0-06-028952-2 Subj: Animals – mice. Holidays – Christmas. Humorous stories. Rhyming text.

Twelve days, a Christmas countdown ill. by Kevin O'Malley. HarperCollins, 2002. ISBN 978-0-06-028955-3 Subj: Cumulative tales. Holidays – Christmas. Music. Songs.

Snicket, Lemony. *The bad mood and the stick* ill. by Matthew Forsythe. Little, Brown, 2017. ISBN 978-031639278-5 Subj: Behavior – bad day, bad mood. Behavior – misbehavior.

The composer is dead ill. by Carson Ellis. HarperCollins, 2009. ISBN 978-0-06-123627-3 Subj: Musical instruments – orchestras. Mystery stories.

The dark ill. by Jon Klassen. Little, Brown, 2013. ISBN 978-0-316-18748-0 Subj: Emotions – fear. Light, lights. Night.

Goldfish Ghost ill. by Lisa Brown. Roaring Brook/Neal Porter, 2017. ISBN 978-162672507-2 Subj: Emotions – loneliness. Fish. Ghosts.

Thirteen words ill. by Maira Kalman. HarperCollins, 2010. ISBN 978-0-06-166465-6 Subj: Animals – dogs. Birds. Language.

Twenty-nine myths on the Swinster Pharmacy ill. by Lisa Brown. McSweeney's, 2014. ISBN 978-193807378-6 Subj: Family life – brothers & sisters. Mystery stories.

Snitselaar, Nicole. *Little Fox, lost* ill. by Alicia Padron. Pajama, 2016. ISBN 978-177278004-8 Subj: Animals – foxes. Behavior – lost. Family life – mothers.

Snyder, Betsy E. *I can dance* ill. by author. Chronicle, 2015. ISBN 978-145212929-7 Subj: Activities – dancing. Format, unusual – toy & movable books. Format, unusual – toy & movable books.

I can play ill. by author. Chronicle, 2015. ISBN 978-145212905-1 Subj: Activities – playing. Format, unusual – toy & movable books. Format, unusual – toy & movable books. Sports.

I haiku you ill. by author. Random House, 2012. ISBN 978-0-375-86750-7 Subj: Emotions – love. Poetry.

Sweet dreams lullaby ill. by author. Random House, 2010. ISBN 978-0-375-85852-9 Subj: Bedtime. Lullabies. Nature. Rhyming text.

Snyder, Carol. *We're painting* ill. by Lisa Jahn-Clough. HarperCollins, 2002. ISBN 978-0-694-01445-3 Subj: Activities – painting. Concepts – color. Concepts – shape.

Snyder, Dianne. *The boy of the three-year nap* ill. by Allen Say. Houghton, 1988. ISBN 978-0-395-44090-2 Subj: Behavior – trickery. Caldecott award honor books. Character traits – laziness. Folk & fairy tales.

Snyder, Laurel. *Baxter, the pig who wanted to be kosher* ill. by David Goldin. Tricycle, 2010. ISBN 978-1-58246-315-5 Subj: Animals – pigs. Jewish culture.

The forever garden ill. by Samantha Cotterill. Random House, 2017. ISBN 978-055351273-1 Subj: Character traits – helpfulness. Gardens, gardening. Moving.

Good night, laila tov ill. by Jui Ishida. Random House, 2012. ISBN 978-0-375-96868-9 Subj: Camps, camping. Family life. Jewish culture. Rhyming text.

Swan: the life and dance of Anna Pavlova ill. by Julie Morstad. Chronicle, 2015. ISBN 978-145211890-1 Subj: Ballet. Careers – dancers.

So, Meilo. *Gobble, gobble, slip, slop* ill. by author. Knopf, 2004. ISBN 978-0-375-92504-7 Subj: Animals – cats. Behavior – greed. Folk & fairy tales. Foreign lands – India.

So, Sungwan. *Shanyi goes to China* ill. with photos. Frances Lincoln, 2006. ISBN 978-1-84507-470-8 Subj: Foreign lands – China.

Sobat, Vera. *Little Bear and the big fight* (Langreuter, Jutta)

Little Bear brushes his teeth (Langreuter, Jutta)

Little Bear goes to kindergarten (Langreuter, Jutta)

Sobel, June. *The goodnight train* ill. by Laura Huliska-Beith. Harcourt, 2006. ISBN 978-0-15-205436-6 Subj: Bedtime. Rhyming text. Trains.

Shiver me letters: a pirate ABC ill. by Henry Cole. Harcourt, 2006. ISBN 978-0-15-216732-5 Subj: ABC books. Pirates. Rhyming text.

Sobol, Richard. *Adelina's whales* photos by author. Dutton, 2003. ISBN 978-0-525-47110-3 Subj: Animals – whales. Family life. Foreign lands – Mexico.

Sockabasin, Allen. *Thanks to the animals* ill. by Rebekah Raye. Tilbury, 2005. ISBN 978-0-88448-270-3 Subj: Animals. Babies, toddlers. Behavior – lost. Family life – fathers. Indians of North America – Passamaquoddy.

Soffer, Gilad. *Duck's vacation* ill. by author. Feiwel & Friends, 2015. ISBN 978-125005647-4 Subj: Activities – vacationing. Birds – ducks.

Sohn, Tania. *Socks!* ill. by author. Kane/Miller, 2014. ISBN 978-161067244-3 Subj: Clothing – socks. Imagination.

Sokol, Edward. *Meet Stinky Magee* ill. by author. HarperCollins, 2000. ISBN 978-0-688-17416-3 Subj: Food. Magic. Toys – rocking horses.

Solheim, James. *Born yesterday: the diary of a young journalist* ill. by Simon James. Penguin, 2010. ISBN 978-0-399-25155-9 Subj: Activities – writing. Babies, toddlers. Humorous stories.

Santa's secrets revealed ill. by Barry Gott. Carolrhoda, 2004. ISBN 978-1-57505-600-5 Subj: Holidays – Christmas. Santa Claus.

Soltis, Sue. *Nothing like a puffin* ill. by Bob Kolar. Candlewick, 2011. ISBN 978-0-7636-3617-3 Subj: Birds – puffins.

Soman, David. *The amazing adventures of Bumblebee Boy* by David Soman and Jacky Davis; ill. by David Soman. Penguin, 2011. ISBN 978-0-8037-3418-0 Subj: Activities – playing. Family life – brothers. Imagination.

Ladybug Girl by David Soman and Jacky Davis; ill. by David Soman. Dial, 2008. ISBN 978-0-8037-3195-0 Subj: Activities – playing. Imagination.

Ladybug Girl and Bingo by David Soman and Jacky Davis; ill. by David Soman. Dial, 2012. ISBN 978-0-8037-3582-8 Subj: Animals – dogs. Behavior – lost & found possessions. Camps, camping. Imagination.

Ladybug Girl and Bumblebee Boy by David Soman and Jacky Davis; ill. by David Soman. Dial, 2009. ISBN 978-0-8037-3339-8 Subj: Activities – playing. Friendship. Imagination.

Ladybug Girl and the best ever playdate by David Soman and Jacky Davis; ill. by David Soman. Dial, 2015. ISBN 978-080374030-3 Subj: Activities – playing. Friendship. Imagination. Toys.

Ladybug Girl and the big snow by David Soman and Jacky Davis; ill. by David Soman. Dial, 2013. ISBN 978-0-8037-3583-5 Subj: Activities – playing. Imagination. Weather – snow.

Ladybug Girl and the Bug Squad by David Soman and Jacky Davis; ill. by David Soman. Penguin, 2011. ISBN 978-0-8037-3419-7 Subj: Activities – playing. Character traits – cooperation. Friendship. Imagination.

Ladybug Girl and the dress-up dilemma by David Soman and Jacky Davis; ill. by David Soman. Dial, 2014. ISBN 978-080373584-2 Subj: Clothing – costumes. Holidays – Halloween.

Ladybug Girl at the beach by David Soman and Jacky Davis; ill. by David Soman. Penguin, 2010. ISBN 978-0-8037-3416-6 Subj: Emotions – fear. Sea & seashore – beaches.

Ladybug Girl's day out with Grandpa by David Soman and Jacky Davis; ill. by David Soman. Dial, 2017. ISBN 978-080374032-7 Subj: Family life – grandfathers. Museums.

The monster next door ill. by author. Dial, 2016. ISBN 978-052542783-4 Subj: Behavior – fighting, arguing. Friendship. Monsters.

Three bears in a boat ill. by author. Dial, 2014. ISBN 978-080373993-2 Subj: Animals – bears. Behavior – misbehavior. Boats, ships.

Somary, Wolfgang. *Night and the candlemaker* ill. by Simon Bartram. Barefoot, 2000. ISBN 978-1-84148-137-1 Subj: Night. Sleep.

Somers, Kevin. *Meaner than meanest* ill. by Diana Cain Bluthenthal. Hyperion, 2001. ISBN 978-0-7868-2498-4 Subj: Character traits – meanness. Magic. Witches.

Sones, Sonya. *Violet and Winston* by Sonya Sones and Bennett Tramer ill. by Chris Raschka. Dial, 2009. ISBN 978-0-8037-3234-6 Subj: Birds – ducks. Birds – swans. Friendship.

Song, Mika. *Tea with Oliver* ill. by author. HarperCollins, 2017. ISBN 978-006242948-3 Subj: Animals – cats. Animals – mice. Character traits – shyness. Emotions – loneliness. Friendship.

Sookocheff, Carey. *Solutions for cold feet and other little problems* ill. by author. Tundra, 2016. ISBN 978-177049873-0 Subj: Animals – dogs. Problem solving.

Wet ill. by author. Henry Holt, 2017. ISBN 978-1-62779775-7 Subj: Water.

Sorel, Edward. *The Saturday kid* in collab. with Cheryl Carlesimo; ill. by author. Margaret K. McElderry, 1999. ISBN 978-0-689-82399-2 Subj: Behavior – bullying, teasing. Music. Musical instruments – violins.

Sorensen, Henri. *New Hope* ill. by author. Lothrop, 1995. ISBN 978-0-688-13926-1 Subj: Activities – traveling. Family life. U.S. history – frontier & pioneer life.

Sorenson, Ashley. *The very cold, freezing, no-numbers day* ill. by David Miles. Familius, 2016. ISBN 978-194293434-9 Subj: Counting, numbers. Participation.

Soros, Barbara. *Tenzin's deer* ill. by Danuta Maya. Barefoot, 2003. ISBN 978-1-84148-811-0 Subj: Animals – deer. Character traits – kindness to animals. Foreign lands – Tibet. Illness.

Soto, Gary. *Chato and the party animals* ill. by Susan Guevara. Putnam, 2000. ISBN 978-0-399-23159-9 Subj: Animals – cats. Birthdays. Parties.

Chato goes cruisin' ill. by Susan Guevara. Penguin, 2005. ISBN 978-0-399-23974-8 Subj: Animals – cats. Animals – dogs. Boats, ships. Ethnic groups in the U.S. – Mexican Americans. Foreign languages. Illness.

Chato's kitchen ill. by Susan Guevara. Putnam, 1995. ISBN 978-0-399-22658-8 Subj: Animals – cats. Animals – dogs. Animals – mice. Cities, towns. Food. Foreign languages.

Lucky Luis ill. by Rhode Montijo. Putnam, 2012. ISBN 978-0-399-24504-6 Subj: Animals – rabbits. Character traits – luck. Ethnic groups in the U.S. – Mexican Americans. Sports – baseball. Superstition.

My little car / Mi carrito ill. by Pamela Paparone. Penguin, 2006. ISBN 978-0-399-23220-6 Subj: Automobiles. Ethnic groups in the U.S. – Mexican Americans. Family life – grandfathers. Foreign languages. Toys.

The old man and his door ill. by Joe Cepeda. Putnam, 1996. ISBN 978-0-399-22700-4 Subj: Character traits – helpfulness. Ethnic groups in the U.S. – Mexican Americans. Food. Foreign lands. Parties. Senses – hearing.

Snapshots from the wedding ill. by Stephanie Garcia. Putnam, 1997. ISBN 978-0-399-22808-7 Subj: Ethnic groups in the U.S. – Mexican Americans. Family life. Weddings.

Too many tamales ill. by Ed Martinez. Putnam, 1993. ISBN 978-0-399-22146-0 Subj: Ethnic groups in the U.S. – Mexican Americans. Food. Foreign languages. Holidays – Christmas.

Souders, Taryn. *Whole-y cow! fractions are fun* ill. by Tatjana Mai-Wyss. Sleeping Bear, 2010. ISBN 978-1-58536-460-2 Subj: Animals – bulls, cows. Counting, numbers. Rhyming text.

Souhami, Jessica. *Foxy!* ill. by author. Frances Lincoln, 2013. ISBN 978-1-84780-218-7 Subj: Animals. Animals – foxes. Behavior – trickery. Folk & fairy tales.

The leopard's drum: an Asante tale from West Africa ill. by author. Little, 1995. ISBN 978-0-316-80466-0 Subj: Animals – leopards. Folk & fairy tales. Foreign lands – Africa.

The little, little house ill. by author. Frances Lincoln, 2006. ISBN 978-1-84507-108-0 Subj: Folk & fairy tales. Humorous stories. Problem solving.

Mrs. McCool and the giant Cuhullin ill. by author. Henry Holt, 2002. ISBN 978-0-8050-6852-8 Subj: Behavior – fighting, arguing. Character traits – cleverness. Folk & fairy tales. Foreign lands – Ireland. Giants.

No dinner! the story of the old woman and the pumpkin ill. by author. Marshall Cavendish, 2000. ISBN 978-0-7614-5059-7 Subj: Animals. Animals

– wolves. Behavior – trickery. Folk & fairy tales. Foreign lands – India.

Rama and the demon king ill. by reteller. DK, 1997. ISBN 978-0-7894-2450-1 Subj: Animals – monkeys. Folk & fairy tales. Foreign lands – India. Royalty – kings. Royalty – princes.

Sausages ill. by author. Frances Lincoln, 2006. ISBN 978-1-84507-397-8 Subj: Behavior – wishing. Character traits – foolishness. Folk & fairy tales. Food.

Soule, Jean Conder. *Never tease a weasel* ill. by George Booth. Random House, 2007. ISBN 978-0-375-83420-2 Subj: Animals. Behavior – bullying, teasing. Character traits – kindness to animals. Humorous stories. Rhyming text.

Southwell, Jandelyn. *The little country town* ill. by Kay Chorao. Henry Holt, 2000. ISBN 978-0-8050-5711-9 Subj: Country. Night. Noise, sounds. Rhyming text. Senses – smell.

Spafford, Suzy. *Witzy's colors* ill. by author. Lyrick, 2001. ISBN 978-1-58668-055-8 Subj: Animals. Concepts – color. Format, unusual – toy & movable books.

Spalding, Andrea. *It's raining, it's pouring* ill. by Leslie Elizabeth Watts. Orca, 2001. ISBN 978-1-55143-186-4 Subj: Giants. Illness. Imagination. Weather – rain.

Solomon's tree ill. by Janet Wilson. Mask & Tsimshian designs by Victor Reece. Orca, 2002. ISBN 978-1-55143-217-5 Subj: Activities – storytelling. Indians of North America – Tsimshian. Masks. Trees.

Spang, Günter. *The ox and the Donkey* ill. by Loek Koopmans. NorthSouth, 2001. ISBN 978-0-7358-1516-2 Subj: Animals – donkeys. Animals – oxen. Holidays – Christmas. Religion – Nativity.

Spanyol, Jessica. *Carlo likes counting* ill. by author. Candlewick, 2002. ISBN 978-0-7636-1774-5 Subj: Animals – giraffes. Counting, numbers.

Spector, Todd. *How to pee: potty training for boys* ill. by Arree Chung. Henry Holt, 2015. ISBN 978-080509773-3 Subj: Hygiene. Toilet training.

How to pee: potty training for girls ill. by Arree Chung. Henry Holt, 2016. ISBN 978-162779297-4 Subj: Hygiene. Toilet training.

Speed, Toby. *Brave potatoes* ill. by Barry Root. Putnam, 2000. ISBN 978-0-399-23158-2 Subj: Activities – baking, cooking. Fairs, festivals. Plants.

Two cool cows ill. by Barry Root. Putnam, 1995. ISBN 978-0-399-22647-2 Subj: Animals – bulls, cows. Moon. Rhyming text.

Speirs, John. *The little boy's Christmas gift* ill. by author. Abrams, 2001. ISBN 978-0-8109-4399-5 Subj: Gifts. Holidays – Christmas. Religion – Nativity. Trees.

Spelman, Cornelia Maude. *Mama and Daddy Bear's divorce* ill. by Kathy Parkinson. Albert Whitman, 1998. ISBN 978-0-8075-5221-6 Subj: Animals – bears. Divorce. Emotions. Emotions – love.

When I care about others ill. by Kathy Parkinson. Albert Whitman, 2002. ISBN 978-0-8075-8889-5 Subj: Animals – bears. Behavior – sharing. Character traits – kindness. Emotions.

When I feel angry ill. by Nancy Cote. Albert Whitman, 2000. ISBN 978-0-8075-8888-8 Subj: Animals – rabbits. Behavior. Emotions – anger.

When I feel sad ill. by Kathy Parkinson. Albert Whitman, 2002. ISBN 978-0-8075-8891-8 Subj: Animals – guinea pigs. Emotions – sadness.

When I feel scared ill. by Kathy Parkinson. Albert Whitman, 2002. ISBN 978-0-8075-8890-1 Subj: Animals – bears. Emotions – fear.

When I feel worried ill. by Kathy Parkinson. Albert Whitman, 2013. ISBN 978-0-8075-8893-2 Subj: Animals – guinea pigs. Behavior – worrying.

When I miss you ill. by Kathy Parkinson. Albert Whitman, 2004. ISBN 978-0-8075-8910-6 Subj: Animals – guinea pigs. Emotions – loneliness. Family life – parents.

Your body belongs to you ill. by Teri Weidner. Albert Whitman, 1997. ISBN 978-0-8075-9474-2 Subj: Child abuse. Health & fitness. Safety.

Spence, Robert, III. *Clickety clack* ill. by Margaret Spengler. Viking, 1999. ISBN 978-0-670-87946-5 Subj: Animals. Noise, sounds. Rhyming text. Trains.

Sper, Emily. *Hanukkah: a counting book in English, Hebrew, and Yiddish* ill. by author. Scholastic, 2001. ISBN 978-0-439-28291-8 Subj: Counting, numbers. Foreign languages. Holidays – Hanukkah. Jewish culture. Religion.

The Passover seder ill. by author. Scholastic, 2003. ISBN 978-0-439-44312-8 Subj: Format, unusual – toy & movable books. Holidays – Passover. Jewish culture. Language. Religion.

Sperring, Mark. *The fairytale cake* ill. by Jonathan Langley. Scholastic, 2005. ISBN 978-0-439-68329-6 Subj: Birthdays. Books, reading. Food. Rhyming text.

How many sleeps 'til my birthday? ill. by Sébastien Braun. Tiger Tales, 2016. ISBN 978-168010009-9 Subj: Animals – bears. Birthdays. Character traits – patience, impatience. Family life – fathers.

I'll catch you if you fall ill. by Layn Marlow. Simon & Schuster, 2016. ISBN 978-148145206-9 Subj:

Behavior – needing someone. Character traits – questioning. Emotions.

Max and the won't go to bed show ill. by Sarah Warburton. Scholastic, 2014. ISBN 978-054570822-7 Subj: Bedtime. Magic.

Mermaid dreams ill. by The Pope Twins. Scholastic, 2006. ISBN 978-0-439-79610-1 Subj: Bedtime. Mythical creatures – mermaids, mermen. Sea & seashore.

The shape of my heart ill. by Alys Paterson. Bloomsbury, 2013. ISBN 978-1-59990-962-2 Subj: Concepts – shape. Family life – mothers. Rhyming text.

The sunflower sword ill. by Miriam Latimer. Andersen, 2011. ISBN 978-0-7613-7486-2 Subj: Dragons. Friendship. Knights.

Spetter, Jung-Hee. *Lily and Trooper's fall* ill. by author. Front Street, 1998. ISBN 978-1-886910-38-6 Subj: Activities – playing. Animals – dogs. Seasons – fall.

Lily and Trooper's spring ill. by author. Front Street, 1998. ISBN 978-1-886910-36-2 Subj: Activities – picnicking. Activities – playing. Animals – dogs. Seasons – spring.

Lily and Trooper's summer ill. by author. Front Street, 1998. ISBN 978-1-886910-37-9 Subj: Activities – playing. Animals – dogs. Seasons – summer.

Lily and Trooper's winter ill. by author. Front Street, 1998. ISBN 978-1-886910-39-3 Subj: Activities. Animals – dogs. Seasons – winter. Weather – rain. Weather – snow.

Spier, Peter. *Bored — nothing to do!* ill. by author. Doubleday, 1978. ISBN 978-0-385-13178-0 Subj: Airplanes, airports. Behavior – boredom. Humorous stories.

Gobble, growl, grunt ill. by author. Doubleday, 1971. ISBN 978-0-385-24094-9 Subj: Animals. Noise, sounds. Participation.

Noah's ark ill. by author. Doubleday, 1977. ISBN 978-0-385-12730-1 Subj: Animals. Boats, ships. Caldecott award books. Religion – Noah. Rhyming text. Weather – floods. Weather – rain. Wordless.

Oh, were they ever happy! ill. by author. Doubleday, 1978. ISBN 978-0-385-13176-6 Subj: Activities – painting. Concepts – color. Humorous stories.

People ill. by author. Doubleday, 1980. ISBN 978-0-385-13182-7 Subj: World.

Peter Spier's Christmas! ill. by author. Doubleday, 1983. ISBN 978-0-385-13183-4 Subj: Holidays – Christmas.

Peter Spier's circus! ill. by author. Doubleday, 1992. ISBN 978-0-385-41970-3 Subj: Circus.

Peter Spier's rain ill. by author. Doubleday, 1982. ISBN 978-0-385-15485-7 Subj: Weather – rain. Wordless.

We the people: the Constitution of the United States of America ill. by author. Doubleday, 1987. ISBN 978-0-385-23789-5 Subj: U.S. history.

Spinelli, Eileen. *The best story* ill. by Anne Wilsdorf. Dial, 2008. ISBN 978-0-8037-3055-7 Subj: Activities – writing. Contests. Libraries.

A big boy now ill. by Megan Lloyd. HarperCollins, 2012. ISBN 978-0-06-008673-2 Subj: Animals – rabbits. Behavior – growing up. Family life – fathers. Sports – bicycling.

Buzz ill. by Vincent Nguyen. Simon & Schuster, 2010. ISBN 978-1-4169-4925-1 Subj: Activities – flying. Insects – bees.

Callie Cat, ice skater ill. by Anne Kennedy. Albert Whitman, 2007. ISBN 978-0-8075-1042-1 Subj: Animals – cats. Contests. Sports – ice skating.

City angel ill. by Kyrsten Brooker. Penguin, 2005. ISBN 978-0-8037-2821-9 Subj: Angels. Cities, towns. Rhyming text.

Cold snap ill. by Marjorie Priceman. Knopf, 2012. ISBN 978-0-375-85700-3 Subj: Communities, neighborhoods. Seasons – winter. Weather – cold. Weather – snow.

Coming through the blizzard ill. by Jenny Tylden-Wright. Simon & Schuster, 1999. ISBN 978-0-689-81490-7 Subj: Holidays – Christmas. Weather – blizzards.

Do you have a cat? ill. by Geraldo Valério. Eerdmans, 2010. ISBN 978-0-8028-5351-6 Subj: Animals – cats. Rhyming text.

Do you have a dog? ill. by Geraldo Valério. Eerdmans, 2011. ISBN 978-0-8028-5387-5 Subj: Animals – dogs. Rhyming text.

Heat wave ill. by Betsy Lewin. Harcourt, 2007. ISBN 978-0-15-216779-0 Subj: Days of the week, months of the year. Weather.

Here comes the year ill. by Keiko Narahashi. Henry Holt, 2002. ISBN 978-0-8050-6685-2 Subj: Days of the week, months of the year. Rhyming text.

Hero cat ill. by Jo Ellen McAllister Stammen. Marshall Cavendish, 2006. ISBN 978-0-7614-5223-2 Subj: Animals – cats. Character traits – bravery. Fire.

Hug a bug ill. by Dan Andreasen. HarperCollins, 2008. ISBN 978-0-06-051832-5 Subj: Hugging. Rhyming text.

I know it's autumn ill. by Nancy Hayashi. HarperCollins, 2004. ISBN 978-0-06-029423-6 Subj: Rhyming text. Seasons – fall.

In my new yellow shirt ill. by Hideko Takahashi. Henry Holt, 2001. ISBN 978-0-8050-6242-7 Subj:

Birthdays. Clothing – shirts. Concepts – color. Gifts. Imagination.

Jonah's whale ill. by Giuliano Ferri. Eerdmans, 2012. ISBN 978-0-8028-5382-0 Subj: Animals – whales. Religion – Jonah.

Miss Fox's class earns a field trip ill. by Anne Kennedy. Albert Whitman, 2010. ISBN 978-0-8075-5169-1 Subj: Animals – foxes. Counting, numbers. School – field trips.

Miss Fox's class gets it wrong ill. by Anne Kennedy. Albert Whitman, 2012. ISBN 978-0-8075-5165-3 Subj: Animals – foxes. Behavior – gossip, rumors. Careers – teachers. School.

Miss Fox's class goes green ill. by Anne Kennedy. Albert Whitman, 2009. ISBN 978-0-8075-5166-0 Subj: Animals – foxes. Ecology. School.

Miss Fox's class shapes up ill. by Anne Kennedy. Albert Whitman, 2011. ISBN 978-0-8075-5171-4 Subj: Animals – foxes. Careers – teachers. Health & fitness – exercise. School.

Night shift daddy ill. by Melissa Iwai. Hyperion, 2000. ISBN 978-0-7868-2424-3 Subj: Activities – working. Family life – fathers. Night.

Now it is summer ill. by Mary Newell DePalma. Eerdmans, 2011. ISBN 978-0-8028-5340-0 Subj: Animals – mice. Family life. Seasons – fall. Seasons – summer.

Peace Week in Miss Fox's class ill. by Anne Kennedy. Albert Whitman, 2009. ISBN 978-0-8075-6379-3 Subj: Animals. Animals – foxes. Behavior – seeking better things. School.

The perfect Christmas ill. by JoAnn Adinolfi. Henry Holt, 2011. ISBN 978-0-8050-9702-4 Subj: Family life. Holidays – Christmas. Rhyming text.

Polar bear, arctic hare: poems of the frozen North ill. by Eugenie Fernandes. Boyds Mills, 2007. ISBN 978-1-59078-344-3 Subj: Animals. Foreign lands – Arctic. Poetry.

Princess Pig ill. by Tim Bowers. Knopf, 2009. ISBN 978-0-375-84571-0 Subj: Animals – pigs. Farms. Royalty – princesses. Self-concept.

Rise the moon ill. by Raúl Colón. Dial, 2003. ISBN 978-0-8037-2601-7 Subj: Moon. Night. Rhyming text.

A safe place called home ill. by Christy Hale. Marshall Cavendish, 2001. ISBN 978-0-7614-5085-6 Subj: Emotions – fear. Homes, houses. Rhyming text. Safety.

Silly Tilly ill. by David Slonim. Marshall Cavendish, 2009. ISBN 978-0-7614-5525-7 Subj: Animals. Birds – geese. Character traits – foolishness. Farms. Rhyming text.

Six hogs on a scooter ill. by Scott Nash. Orchard, 2000. ISBN 978-0-531-33212-2 Subj: Animals –

pigs. Family life. Humorous stories. Theater. Transportation.

Somebody loves you, Mr. Hatch ill. by Paul Yalowitz. Aladdin, 1994. ISBN 978-0-689-71872-4 Subj: Behavior – mistakes. Careers – postal workers. Communities, neighborhoods. Emotions – loneliness. Friendship. Holidays – Valentine's Day.

Someday ill. by Rosie Winstead. Penguin, 2007. ISBN 978-0-8037-2941-4 Subj: Imagination.

Sophie's masterpiece ill. by Jane Dyer. Simon & Schuster, 1998. ISBN 978-0-689-80112-9 Subj: Art. Character traits – perseverance. Homes, houses. Spiders.

Summerbath, winterbath ill. by Elsa Warnick. Eerdmans, 2001. ISBN 978-0-8028-5179-6 Subj: Activities – bathing. Family life. Poetry. Seasons.

Thankful ill. by Archie Preston. HarperCollins Zonderkidz, 2015. ISBN 978-031000088-4 Subj: Character traits – generosity. Character traits – kindness. Rhyming text.

Thanksgiving at the Tappletons' ill. by Maryann Cocca-Leffler. Addison-Wesley, 1982. ISBN 978-0-201-15892-2 Subj: Animals – wolves. Behavior – sharing. Family life. Holidays – Thanksgiving. Humorous stories.

Together at Christmas ill. by Bin Lee. Albert Whitman, 2012. ISBN 978-0-8075-8010-3 Subj: Animals – mice. Counting, numbers. Holidays – Christmas. Rhyming text. Weather – cold.

Wanda's monster ill. by Nancy Hayashi. Albert Whitman, 2002. ISBN 978-0-8075-8656-3 Subj: Emotions – fear. Family life – grandmothers. Monsters. Problem solving.

What do angels wear? ill. by Emily Arnold McCully. HarperCollins, 2003. ISBN 978-0-06-028887-7 Subj: Activities. Angels. Rhyming text.

When Mama comes home tonight ill. by Jane Dyer. Simon & Schuster, 1998. ISBN 978-0-689-81065-7 Subj: Bedtime. Family life – mothers. Rhyming text.

When no one is watching ill. by David Johnson. Eerdmans, 2013. ISBN 978-0-8028-5303-5 Subj: Character traits – shyness. Friendship. Rhyming text. Self-concept.

When Papa comes home tonight ill. by David McPhail. Simon & Schuster, 2009. ISBN 978-1-4169-1028-2 Subj: Bedtime. Family life – fathers. Rhyming text.

When you are happy ill. by Geraldo Valério. Simon & Schuster, 2006. ISBN 978-0-689-86251-9 Subj: Emotions. Family life.

Spinelli, Jerry. *I can be anything!* ill. by Jimmy Liao. Little, Brown, 2010. ISBN 978-0-316-16226-5 Subj: Careers. Rhyming text.

Mama Seeton's whistle ill. by LeUyen Pham. Little, Brown, 2015. ISBN 978-031612217-7 Subj: Activities – whistling. Family life. Family life – mothers.

My daddy and me ill. by Seymour Chwast. Knopf, 2003. ISBN 978-0-375-90606-0 Subj: Activities. Family life – fathers. Family life – sons.

Spink, Matt. *Some birds* ill. by author. Abrams, 2016. ISBN 978-141972070-3 Subj: Birds. Rhyming text.

Spinner, Stephanie. *It's a miracle* ill. by Jill McElmurry. Atheneum, 2003. ISBN 978-0-689-84493-5 Subj: Family life – grandmothers. Holidays – Hanukkah. Jewish culture.

Spires, Ashley. *Larf* ill. by author. Kids Can, 2012. ISBN 978-1-55453-701-3 Subj: Character traits – being different. Friendship. Mythical creatures.

The most magnificent thing ill. by author. Kids Can, 2014. ISBN 978-155453704-4 Subj: Animals – dogs. Behavior – resourcefulness. Character traits – ambition. Character traits – persistence. Emotions – anger.

Small Saul ill. by author. Kids Can, 2011. ISBN 978-1-55453-503-3 Subj: Character traits – being different. Character traits – smallness. Pirates.

The thing Lou couldn't do ill. by author. Kids Can, 2017. ISBN 978-177138727-9 Subj: Character traits – persistence.

Spires, Elizabeth. *The big meow* ill. by Cynthia Jabar. Candlewick, 2002. ISBN 978-0-7636-0679-4 Subj: Animals – cats. Animals – dogs. Noise, sounds.

Spirin, Gennady. *A apple pie* ill. by author. Penguin, 2005. ISBN 978-0-399-23981-6 Subj: ABC books. Nursery rhymes.

Martha ill. by author. Penguin, 2005. ISBN 978-0-399-23980-9 Subj: Birds – crows. Foreign lands – Russia.

Philipok retold by Ann Keay Beneduce; ill. by author. Philomel, 2000. ISBN 978-0-399-23482-8 Subj: Character traits – ambition. Foreign lands – Russia. School.

The twelve days of Christmas (The twelve days of Christmas. English folk song)

We three kings ill. by author. Simon & Schuster, 2007. ISBN 978-0-689-82114-1 Subj: Holidays – Christmas. Religion – Nativity. Songs.

Spohn, Kate. *By word of mouse* ill. by author. Bloomsbury, 2004. ISBN 978-1-58234-867-4 Subj: Animals – mice. Careers – artists. Family life – sisters.

Snow play ill. by author. Scholastic, 2001. ISBN 978-0-439-26713-7 Subj: Animals – bears. Family life – grandmothers. Format, unusual – board books. Rhyming text. Weather – snow.

The wet dry book ill. by author. Random House, 2002. ISBN 978-0-375-82186-8 Subj: Concepts. Rhyming text.

Spradlin, Michael P. *Baseball from A to Z* ill. by Macky Pamintuan. HarperCollins, 2010. ISBN 978-0-06-124081-2 Subj: ABC books. Sports – baseball.

Off like the wind! the first ride of the Pony Express ill. by Layne Johnson. Walker, 2010. ISBN 978-0-8027-9652-3 Subj: Careers – postal workers. U.S. history – frontier & pioneer life.

Springett, Martin. *Kate and Pippin* ill. by Isobel Springett. Henry Holt, 2012. ISBN 978-0-8050-9487-9 Subj: Animals – deer. Animals – dogs.

Springman, I. C. *More* ill. by Brian Lies. Houghton Mifflin, 2012. ISBN 978-0-547-61083-2 Subj: Animals – mice. Behavior – collecting things. Birds – magpies.

Springstubb, Tricia. *Phoebe and Digger* ill. by Jeff Newman. Candlewick, 2013. ISBN 978-0-7636-5281-4 Subj: Babies, toddlers. Behavior – bullying, teasing. Behavior – lost & found possessions. Family life – new sibling. Parks. Toys.

Sproule, Gail. *Singing the dark* ill. by Sheena Lott. Fitzhenry & Whiteside, 2001. ISBN 978-1-55041-648-0 Subj: Activities – singing. Bedtime. Night.

Spurling, Margaret. *Bilby moon* ill. by Danny Snell. Kane/Miller, 2001. ISBN 978-1-929132-06-5 Subj: Animals. Animals – mice. Desert. Foreign lands – Australia. Moon.

Spurr, Elizabeth. *In the garden* ill. by Manelle Oliphant. Peachtree, 2012. ISBN 978-1-56145-581-2 Subj: Format, unusual – board books. Gardens, gardening. Rhyming text.

A pig named Perrier ill. by Martin Matje. Hyperion, 2002. ISBN 978-0-7868-0302-6 Subj: Animals – pigs. Pets.

Pumpkin hill ill. by Whitney Martin. Holiday House, 2006. ISBN 978-0-8234-1869-5 Subj: Holidays – Halloween.

Two bears beneath the stairs ill. by Nadine Bernard Westcott. Simon & Schuster, 2002. ISBN 978-0-689-84759-2 Subj: Animals. Counting, numbers. Format, unusual – toy & movable books. Rhyming text.

Srinivasan, Divya. *Little Owl's day* ill. by author. Viking, 2014. ISBN 978-067001650-1 Subj: Birds – owls. Day. Forest, woods.

Little Owl's night ill. by author. Penguin, 2011. ISBN 978-0-670-01295-4 Subj: Animals. Birds – owls. Night.

Octopus alone ill. by author. Viking, 2013. ISBN 978-0-670-78515-5 Subj: Character traits – shyness. Friendship. Octopuses.

Staake, Bob. *Beachy and me* ill. by author. Random House, 2016. ISBN 978-038537314-2 Subj: Animals – whales. Behavior – boredom. Character traits – kindness to animals. Friendship. Rhyming text.

Bluebird ill. by author. Random House, 2013. ISBN 978-0-375-87037-8 Subj: Behavior – bullying, teasing. Birds – bluebirds. Death. Emotions – loneliness. Friendship. Wordless.

The Book of Gold ill. by author. Random House, 2017. ISBN 978-055351077-5 Subj: Activities – traveling. Books, reading. Character traits – questioning. Libraries.

The donut chef ill. by author. Random House, 2008. ISBN 978-0-375-84403-4 Subj: Activities – baking, cooking. Careers – chefs, cooks. Rhyming text.

The first pup: the real story of how Bo got to the White House ill. by author. Feiwel & Friends, 2010. ISBN 978-0-312-61346-4 Subj: Animals – dogs. Pets.

Look! a book! ill. by author. Little, Brown, 2011. ISBN 978-0-316-11862-0 Subj: Books, reading. Picture puzzles. Rhyming text.

Look! another book! ill. by author. Little, Brown, 2012. ISBN 978-0-316-20459-0 Subj: Books, reading. Picture puzzles. Rhyming text.

My little ABC book ill. by author. Simon & Schuster, 1998. ISBN 978-0-689-81659-8 Subj: ABC books. Format, unusual – board books.

My little color book ill. by author. Simon & Schuster, 2001. ISBN 978-0-689-83486-8 Subj: Concepts – color. Format, unusual – board books.

My little 1 2 3 book ill. by author. Simon & Schuster, 1998. ISBN 978-0-689-81660-4 Subj: Counting, numbers. Format, unusual – board books.

My little opposites book ill. by author. Simon & Schuster, 2001. ISBN 978-0-689-83487-5 Subj: Animals. Concepts – opposites. Format, unusual – board books.

My pet book ill. by author. Random House, 2014. ISBN 978-038537312-8 Subj: Books, reading. Pets. Rhyming text.

Stadler, Alexander. *Beverly Billingsly borrows a book* ill. by author. Harcourt, 2000. ISBN 978-0-15-202510-6 Subj: Behavior – worrying. Books, reading. Careers – librarians. Libraries. Nightmares.

Beverly Billingsly takes a bow ill. by author. Harcourt, 2003. ISBN 978-0-15-216816-2 Subj: Music. School. Theater.

Beverly Billingsly takes the cake ill. by author. Harcourt, 2005. ISBN 978-0-15-205357-4 Subj: Activities – baking, cooking. Food. Imagination. Parties.

Stadler, John. *Catilda* ill. by author. Atheneum, 2003. ISBN 978-0-689-84728-8 Subj: Animals – cats. Behavior – lost & found possessions. Toys – bears.

The cats of Mrs. Calamari ill. by author. Orchard, 1997. ISBN 978-0-531-33020-3 Subj: Animals – cats. Animals – dogs. Cities, towns. Glasses. Weddings.

Take me out to the ball game: a pop-up book ill. by author. Simon & Schuster, 2005. ISBN 978-0-689-85917-5 Subj: Format, unusual – toy & movable books. Songs. Sports – baseball.

What's so scary? ill. by author. Orchard, 2001. ISBN 978-0-531-33301-3 Subj: Animals. Books, reading. Careers – artists.

Wilson and Miss Lovely: a back-to-school mystery ill. by author. Random House, 2009. ISBN 978-0-375-84478-2 Subj: Animals – rabbits. Careers – teachers. Monsters. School.

Stafford, Liliana. *Just dragon* ill. by Margaret Power. Cygnet, 2000. ISBN 978-1-876268-02-2 Subj: Boats, ships. Death. Emotions – grief. Family life – grandfathers. Kites.

The snow bear ill. by Lambert Davis. Scholastic, 2000. ISBN 978-0-439-26977-3 Subj: Animals – polar bears. Friendship. Indians of North America – Inuit. Weather – snow.

Staines, Bill. *All God's critters* ill. by Kadir Nelson. Simon & Schuster, 2009. ISBN 978-0-689-86959-4 Subj: Animals. Farms. Music. Songs.

Stainton, Sue. *The chocolate cat* ill. by Anne Mortimer. HarperCollins, 2007. ISBN 978-0-06-057245-7 Subj: Animals – cats. Food. Magic.

I love cats! ill. by Bob Staake. HarperCollins/Katherine Tegen, 2017. ISBN 978-006243882-9 Subj: Animals – cats.

I love dogs! ill. by Bob Staake. HarperCollins/Katherine Tegen, 2014. ISBN 978-006117057-7 Subj: Animals – dogs. Rhyming text.

The lighthouse cat ill. by Anne Mortimer. Tegen, 2004. ISBN 978-0-06-009605-2 Subj: Animals – cats. Lighthouses. Weather – storms.

Santa's snow cat ill. by Anne Mortimer. HarperCollins, 2001. ISBN 978-0-06-623828-9 Subj: Animals – cats. Behavior – lost & found possessions. Cities, towns. Holidays – Christmas. Santa Claus.

Stalder, Päivi. *Ernest's first Easter* ill. by Frauke Weldin. NorthSouth, 2010. ISBN 978-0-7358-2241-2 Subj: Animals – rabbits. Eggs. Holidays – Easter.

Stampler, Ann Redisch. *Go home, Mrs. Beekman!* ill. by Marsha Gray Carrington. Dutton, 2008. ISBN 978-0-525-46933-9 Subj: Family life – mothers. Humorous stories. School – first day.

The rooster prince of Breslov ill. by Eugene Yelchin. Clarion, 2010. ISBN 978-0-618-98974-4 Subj: Birds – chickens, roosters. Folk & fairy tales. Jewish culture. Royalty – princes.

Shlemazel and the remarkable spoon of Pohost ill. by Jacqueline M. Cohen. Houghton, 2006. ISBN 978-0-618-36959-1 Subj: Character traits – laziness. Character traits – luck. Folk & fairy tales. Jewish culture.

The wooden sword: A Jewish Folktale from Afghanistan ill. by Carol Liddiment. Albert Whitman, 2012. ISBN 978-0-8075-9201-4 Subj: Careers – shoemakers. Folk & fairy tales. Foreign lands – Afghanistan. Jewish culture.

Stangl, Katrin. *Strong as a bear* ill. by author. Enchanted Lion, 2016. ISBN 978-159270198-8 Subj: Language.

Staniszewski, Anna. *Dogosaurus Rex* ill. by Kevin Hawkes. Henry Holt, 2017. ISBN 978-080509706-1 Subj: Character traits – helpfulness. Dinosaurs. Pets.

Power down, Little Robot ill. by Tim Zeltner. Henry Holt, 2015. ISBN 978-162779125-0 Subj: Bedtime. Robots.

Stanley, Diane. *The Giant and the beanstalk* ill. by author. HarperCollins, 2004. ISBN 978-0-06-000011-0 Subj: Folk & fairy tales. Giants. Humorous stories. Nursery rhymes.

Goldie and the three bears ill. by author. HarperCollins, 2003. ISBN 978-0-06-000009-7 Subj: Animals – bears. Friendship. Homes, houses. Humorous stories.

Joining the Boston Tea Party ill. by Holly Berry. HarperCollins, 2001. ISBN 978-0-06-027068-1 Subj: Activities – traveling. Time. U.S. history.

Raising Sweetness ill. by G. Brian Karas. Putnam, 1999. ISBN 978-0-399-23225-1 Subj: Books, reading. Letters, cards. Orphans.

Rumpelstiltskin's daughter ill. by author. Morrow, 1997. ISBN 978-0-688-14328-2 Subj: Behavior – greed. Folk & fairy tales. Humorous stories.

Thanksgiving on Plymouth Plantation ill. by Holly Berry. Cotler, 2004. ISBN 978-0-06-027076-6 Subj: Activities – traveling. Holidays – Thanksgiving. Multiple births – twins. U.S. history.

The trouble with wishes ill. by author. HarperCollins, 2007. ISBN 978-0-06-055451-4 Subj: Behavior – wishing. Careers – sculptors.

Stanley, Fay. *The last princess* ill. by Diane Stanley. HarperCollins, 2001. ISBN 978-0-06-029215-7 Subj: Hawaii. Royalty – princes. Royalty – princesses. U.S. history.

Stanley, Malaika Rose. *Baby Ruby bawled* ill. by Ken Wilson-Max. Tamarind, 2011. ISBN 978-1-84-853017-1 Subj: Babies, toddlers. Bedtime. Emotions. Family life.

Stanley, Mandy. *At the pool* ill. by author. Kingfisher, 2004. ISBN 978-0-7534-5747-4 Subj: Format, unusual – board books. Language. Sports – swimming.

Bloomer, the dog you can play with ill. by author. Orchard, 2001. ISBN 978-0-531-30311-5 Subj: Activities. Animals – dogs. Format, unusual – toy & movable books.

First word book ill. by author. Kingfisher, 2000. ISBN 978-0-7534-5272-1 Subj: Dictionaries. Language.

In the park ill. by author. Kingfisher, 2004. ISBN 978-0-7534-5750-4 Subj: Format, unusual – board books. Language. Pets.

Lettice the dancing rabbit ill. by author. Simon & Schuster, 2002. ISBN 978-0-689-84797-4 Subj: Activities – dancing. Animals – rabbits. Ballet.

Lettice the flower girl ill. by author. Simon & Schuster, 2006. ISBN 978-1-4169-1157-9 Subj: Animals – rabbits. Weddings.

Lettice the flying rabbit ill. by author. Simon & Schuster, 2004. ISBN 978-0-689-86234-2 Subj: Activities – flying. Airplanes, airports. Animals – rabbits.

On the move ill. by author. Kingfisher, 2004. ISBN 978-0-7534-5749-8 Subj: Automobiles. Format, unusual – board books. Transportation.

Perfect pets ill. by author. Kingfisher, 2004. ISBN 978-0-7534-5748-1 Subj: Format, unusual – board books. Pets.

Stanton, Andy. *Danny McGee drinks the sea* ill. by Neal Layton. Random House, 2017. ISBN 978-152471736-0 Subj: Family life – brothers & sisters. Humorous stories. Rhyming text. Tall tales.

Stanton, Elizabeth Rose. *Henny* ill. by author. Simon & Schuster/Paula Wiseman, 2014. ISBN 978-144248436-8 Subj: Birds – chickens, roosters. Character traits – being different. Character traits – individuality. Self-concept.

Peddles ill. by author. Simon & Schuster/Paula Wiseman, 2016. ISBN 978-148141691-7 Subj: Activities – dancing. Animals – pigs. Character traits – being different. Character traits – persistence. Imagination.

Stanton, Karen. *Monday, Wednesday, and every other weekend* ill. by author. Feiwel & Friends, 2014. ISBN 978-125003489-2 Subj: Animals – dogs. Divorce. Homes, houses.

Papi's gift ill. by René King Moreno. Boyds Mills, 2007. ISBN 978-1-59078-422-8 Subj: Birthdays. Careers – migrant workers. Family life – fathers. Foreign lands – Latin America. Gifts.

Stanton, Melissa. *My pen pal, Santa* ill. by Jennifer A. Bell. Random House, 2013. ISBN 978-0-375-86992-1 Subj: Activities – writing. Holidays – Christmas. Letters, cards. Santa Claus.

Starin, Liz. *Splashdance* ill. by author. Farrar, 2016. ISBN 978-037430098-2 Subj: Animals – bears. Character traits – being different. Character traits – cooperation. Sports – swimming.

Starishevsky, Jill. *My body belongs to me* ill. by Angela Padron. Free Spirit, 2014. ISBN 978-157542461-3 Subj: Child abuse. Health & fitness. Safety. Self-concept. Senses – touch.

Stark, Dan. *Izzy and Oscar* (Estes, Allison)

Starkoff, Vanina. *Along the river* ill. by author. Groundwood, 2017. ISBN 978-155498977-5 Subj: Boats, ships. Rivers.

Starr, Meg. *Alicia's happy day* ill. by Ying-Hwa Hu and Cornelius Van Wright. Star Bright, 2002. ISBN 978-1-887734-85-1 Subj: Birthdays. Emotions – happiness. Ethnic groups in the U.S. – Hispanic Americans. Parties.

Staub, Leslie. *Bless this house* ill. by author. Harcourt, 2000. ISBN 978-0-15-201984-6 Subj: Animals. Bedtime. Earth. Ecology. Lullabies.

Time for (Earth) school, Dewey Dew ill. by Jeff Mack. Boyds Mills, 2016. ISBN 978-159078958-2 Subj: Aliens. Emotions – fear. School – first day.

Stauffacher, Sue. *Nothing but trouble: the story of Althea Gibson* ill. by Greg Couch. Knopf, 2007. ISBN 978-0-375-83408-0 Subj: Ethnic groups in the U.S. – African Americans. Sports. U.S. history.

Stead, Philip C. *Bear has a story to tell* ill. by Erin E. Stead. Roaring Brook, 2012. ISBN 978-1-59643-745-6 Subj: Activities – storytelling. Animals. Animals – bears. Character traits – helpfulness. Hibernation. Seasons.

Hello, my name is Ruby ill. by author. Roaring Brook, 2013. ISBN 978-1-59643-809-5 Subj: Birds. Character traits – smallness. Friendship.

A home for Bird ill. by author. Roaring Brook, 2012. ISBN 978-1-59643-711-1 Subj: Birds. Clocks, watches. Frogs & toads.

Ideas are all around ill. by Philip C. Stead. Roaring Brook, 2016. ISBN 978-162672181-4 Subj: Activities – walking. Activities – writing. Careers – writers. Communities, neighborhoods. Imagination.

Jonathan and the big blue boat ill. by author. Roaring Brook, 2011. ISBN 978-1-59643-562-9 Subj: Activities – traveling. Behavior – lost. Boats, ships. Toys – bears.

Lenny and Lucy ill. by Erin E Stead. Roaring Brook/Neal Porter, 2015. ISBN 978-159643932-0 Subj: Friendship. Moving.

The only fish in the sea ill. by Matthew Cordell. Roaring Brook/Neal Porter, 2017. ISBN 978-162672282-8 Subj: Character traits – kindness to animals. Fish. Pets.

Samson in the snow ill. by Philip C. Stead. Roaring Brook/Neal Porter, 2016. ISBN 978-162672182-1 Subj: Animals – woolly mammoths. Behavior – worrying. Birds. Friendship. Weather – snow.

Sebastian and the balloon ill. by author. Roaring Brook, 2014. ISBN 978-159643930-6 Subj: Activities – ballooning. Activities – traveling.

A sick day for Amos McGee ill. by Erin E. Stead. Roaring Brook, 2010. ISBN 978-1-59643-402-8 Subj: Animals. Caldecott award books. Illness. Old age. Zoos.

Special delivery ill. by Matthew Cordell. Roaring Brook, 2015. ISBN 978-159643931-3 Subj: Activities – traveling. Animals – elephants.

Steedman, Judith. *Windy* (Mitchell, Robin)

Steele, Philip. *A knight's city.* Simon & Schuster, 2008. ISBN 978-1-4169-6124-6 Subj: Format, unusual – toy & movable books. Knights.

Trains: the slide-out, see-through story of world-famous trains and railroads ill. by Sebastian Quigley and Nicholas Forder. Kingfisher, 2010. ISBN 978-0-7534-6465-6 Subj: Format, unusual – toy & movable books. Trains.

Steen, Sandra. *Car wash* by Sandra Steen and Susan Steen ill. by G. Brian Karas. Putnam, 2001. ISBN 978-0-399-23369-2 Subj: Automobiles. Family life – fathers.

Steen, Susan. *Car wash* (Steen, Sandra)

Steffensmeier, Alexander. *Millie and the big rescue* ill. by author. Walker, 2013. ISBN 978-0-8027-3402-0 Subj: Animals – bulls, cows. Behavior – hiding. Farms. Games.

Millie in the snow ill. by author. Walker, 2008. ISBN 978-0-8027-9800-8 Subj: Animals – bulls,

---

cows. Character traits – helpfulness. Holidays – Christmas. Weather – snow.

Millie waits for the mail ill. by author. Walker, 2007. ISBN 978-0-8027-9662-2 Subj: Animals – bulls, cows. Careers – postal workers. Farms. Letters, cards.

Steggall, Susan. *Busy boats* ill. by author. Frances Lincoln, 2011. ISBN 978-1-84780-074-9 Subj: Boats, ships.

Colors ill. by author. Frances Lincoln, 2015. ISBN 978-184780742-7 Subj: Concepts – color. Machines. Trucks.

The diggers are coming! ill. by author. Frances Lincoln, 2013. ISBN 978-1-84780-288-0 Subj: Careers – construction workers. Machines. Rhyming text. Trucks.

The life of a car ill. by author. Henry Holt, 2008. ISBN 978-0-8050-8747-5 Subj: Automobiles.

Rattle and rap ill. by author. Frances Lincoln, 2009. ISBN 978-1-84507-703-7 Subj: Activities – traveling. Ethnic groups in the U.S. – African Americans. Trains. Transportation.

Red car, red bus ill. by author. Frances Lincoln, 2012. ISBN 978-1-84780-184-5 Subj: Concepts – color. Transportation.

Steig, Jeanne. *Fleas!* ill. by Britt Spencer. Philomel, 2008. ISBN 978-0-399-24756-9 Subj: Activities – trading. Cumulative tales. Humorous stories. Insects – fleas.

Steig, William. *The amazing bone* ill. by author. Farrar, 1976. ISBN 978-0-374-30248-1 Subj: Animals – pigs. Caldecott award honor books. Magic.

Brave Irene ill. by author. Farrar, 1986. ISBN 978-0-374-30947-3 Subj: Character traits – bravery. Character traits – perseverance. Seasons – winter. Weather – snow. Weather – storms.

Caleb and Kate ill. by author. Farrar, 1977. ISBN 978-0-374-31016-5 Subj: Animals – dogs. Magic. Witches.

Doctor De Soto ill. by author. Farrar, 1982. ISBN 978-0-374-31803-1 Subj: Animals – foxes. Animals – mice. Character traits – cleverness.

Doctor De Soto goes to Africa ill. by author. HarperCollins, 1992. ISBN 978-0-06-205003-8 Subj: Animals – elephants. Animals – mice. Careers – dentists. Foreign lands – Africa.

Farmer Palmer's wagon ride ill. by author. Farrar, 1974. ISBN 978-0-374-32288-5 Subj: Animals – donkeys. Animals – pigs. Humorous stories.

Gorky rises ill. by author. Farrar, 1980. ISBN 978-0-374-31752-2 Subj: Frogs & toads. Magic.

Pete's a pizza ill. by author. HarperCollins, 1998. ISBN 978-0-06-205157-8 Subj: Activities – playing. Family life – fathers. Food. Games. Imagination.

Potch and Polly ill. by Jon Agee. Farrar, 2002. ISBN 978-0-374-36090-0 Subj: Emotions – love.

Roland, the minstrel pig ill. by author. Simon & Schuster, 1988, ©1968. ISBN 978-0-671-66841-9 Subj: Animals – foxes. Animals – pigs. Music. Musical instruments – lutes. Royalty.

Solomon the rusty nail ill. by author. Farrar, 1985. ISBN 978-0-374-37131-9 Subj: Animals – cats. Animals – rabbits. Behavior – trickery. Magic.

Spinky sulks ill. by author. Farrar, 1988. ISBN 978-0-374-38321-3 Subj: Character traits – stubbornness. Emotions – happiness. Family life.

Sylvester and the magic pebble ill. by author. Simon & Schuster, 1995, ©1969. ISBN 978-0-689-80417-5 Subj: Animals. Animals – donkeys. Caldecott award books. Family life. Magic.

Tiffky Doofky ill. by author. Farrar, 1987. ISBN 978-0-374-37542-3 Subj: Animals – dogs. Careers – sanitation workers. Emotions – love. Magic.

Toby, what are you? ill. by Teryl Euvremer. HarperCollins, 2001. ISBN 978-0-06-205170-7 Subj: Activities – playing. Animals. Behavior – imitation. Family life. Games.

Toby, where are you? ill. by Teryl Euvremer. HarperCollins, 1997. ISBN 978-0-06-205082-3 Subj: Activities – playing. Animals. Behavior – hiding. Family life.

Toby, who are you? ill. by Teryl Euvremer. Cotler, 2004. ISBN 978-0-06-000706-5 Subj: Activities – picnicking. Animals. Family life – parents. Imagination.

The toy brother ill. by author. HarperCollins, 1996. ISBN 978-0-06-205079-3 Subj: Family life – brothers. Middle Ages. Science. Sibling rivalry.

When everybody wore a hat ill. by author. Cotler, 2003. ISBN 978-0-06-009701-1 Subj: Careers – illustrators. Careers – writers. Clothing – hats. Immigrants, immigration. Memories, memory.

Which would you rather be? ill. by Harry Bliss. Cotler, 2002. ISBN 978-0-06-029654-4 Subj: Animals – rabbits. Clothing – hats.

Wizzil ill. by author. Farrar, 2000. ISBN 978-0-374-38466-1 Subj: Birds – parakeets, parrots. Careers – farmers. Character traits – kindness. Witches.

Yellow and pink ill. by author. Farrar, 1984. ISBN 978-0-374-38670-2 Subj: Toys – dolls.

The Zabajaba Jungle ill. by author. Farrar, 1987. ISBN 978-0-374-38790-7 Subj: Dreams. Jungle.

Zeke Pippin ill. by author. HarperCollins, 1994. ISBN 978-0-06-205076-2 Subj: Animals – pigs.

Behavior – running away. Magic. Music. Musical instruments – harmonicas.

Stein, David Ezra. *Because Amelia smiled* ill. by author. Candlewick, 2012. ISBN 978-0-7636-4169-6 Subj: Character traits – kindness. Emotions – happiness. Foreign lands.

Cowboy Ned and Andy ill. by author. Simon & Schuster, 2006. ISBN 978-1-4169-0041-2 Subj: Animals – horses, ponies. Cowboys, cowgirls. Friendship. U.S. history – frontier & pioneer life.

Dinosaur kisses ill. by author. Candlewick, 2013. ISBN 978-0-7636-6104-5 Subj: Dinosaurs. Kissing.

Ice boy ill. by author. Candlewick, 2017. ISBN 978-076368203-3 Subj: Character traits – individuality. Humorous stories. Sea & seashore – beaches. Water.

I'm my own dog ill. by author. Candlewick, 2014. ISBN 978-076366139-7 Subj: Animals – dogs. Character traits – individuality. Pets.

Interrupting chicken ill. by author. Candlewick, 2010. ISBN 978-0-7636-4168-9 Subj: Bedtime. Birds – chickens, roosters. Caldecott award honor books. Humorous stories.

Leaves ill. by author. Penguin, 2007. ISBN 978-0-399-24636-4 Subj: Animals – bears. Hibernation. Seasons. Trees.

Love, Mouserella ill. by author. Penguin, 2011. ISBN 978-0-399-25410-9 Subj: Activities – writing. Animals – mice. Family life – grandmothers. Letters, cards.

Monster hug! ill. by author. Penguin, 2007. ISBN 978-0-399-24637-1 Subj: Activities – playing. Hugging. Monsters.

Ned's new friend ill. by author. Simon & Schuster, 2007. ISBN 978-1-4169-2490-6 Subj: Animals – horses, ponies. Cowboys, cowgirls. Emotions – envy, jealousy. Friendship. U.S. history – frontier & pioneer life.

The nice book ill. by author. Putnam, 2008. ISBN 978-0-399-25050-7 Subj: Animals. Etiquette.

Ol' Mama Squirrel ill. by author. Penguin/Nancy Paulsen, 2013. ISBN 978-0-399-25672-1 Subj: Animals – bears. Animals – squirrels. Character traits – assertiveness.

Pouch! ill. by author. Putnam, 2009. ISBN 978-0-399-25051-4 Subj: Animals – kangaroos. Behavior – growing up. Self-concept.

Tad and Dad ill. by author. Penguin/Nancy Paulsen, 2015. ISBN 978-039925671-4 Subj: Bedtime. Family life – fathers. Frogs & toads.

Stein, Eric. *Granddaddy's turn: a journey to the ballot box* (Bandy, Michael S.)

White water (Bandy, Michael S.)

Stein, Garth. *Enzo's very scary Halloween* ill. by R. W. Alley. HarperCollins, 2016. ISBN 978-006238061-6 Subj: Animals – dogs. Behavior – worrying. Holidays – Halloween.

Stein, Janet. *This little bunny can bake* ill. by author. Random House, 2009. ISBN 978-0-375-84313-6 Subj: Animals – rabbits. Behavior – messy. Careers – chefs, cooks. School.

Stein, Joel Edward. *A Hanukkah with Mazel* ill. by Elisa Vavouri. Kar-Ben, 2016. ISBN 978-146778171-8 Subj: Animals – cats. Careers – artists. Holidays – Hanukkah. Poverty.

Stein, Mathilde. *Brave Ben* ill. by Mies van Hout. Boyds Mills, 2006. ISBN 978-1-932425-64-2 Subj: Character traits – bravery. Emotions – fear.

The child cruncher ill. by Mies van Hout. Boyds Mills, 2008. ISBN 978-1-59078-635-2 Subj: Family life. Imagination. Monsters.

Mine! ill. by Mies van Hout. Boyds Mills, 2007. ISBN 978-1-59078-506-5 Subj: Behavior – sharing. Character traits – selfishness. Ghosts.

Monstersong ill. by Gerdien van der Linden. Boyds Mills, 2007. ISBN 978-1-932425-90-1 Subj: Animals – pigs. Bedtime. Monsters. Rhyming text.

Stein, Peter. *Bugs galore* ill. by Bob Staake. Candlewick, 2012. ISBN 978-0-7636-4754-4 Subj: Insects. Rhyming text.

Cars galore ill. by Bob Staake. Candlewick, 2011. ISBN 978-0-7636-4743-8 Subj: Automobiles. Rhyming text.

Little Red's riding 'hood ill. by Chris Gall. Scholastic/Orchard, 2015. ISBN 978-054560969-2 Subj: Character traits – bravery. Folk & fairy tales. Machines. Trucks.

Trucks galore ill. by Bob Staake. Candlewick, 2017. ISBN 978-076368978-0 Subj: Rhyming text. Trucks.

Stem, J. David. *Kay Thompson's Eloise in Hollywood* by J. David Stem and David Weiss ill. by Hilary Knight. Simon & Schuster, 2005. ISBN 978-0-689-84289-4 Subj: Activities – traveling. Behavior. Hotels.

Stemple, Heidi E. Y. *Not all princesses dress in pink* (Yolen, Jane)

Sleep, black bear, sleep (Yolen, Jane)

You nest here with me (Yolen, Jane)

Stephens, Ann Marie. *Cy makes a friend* ill. by Tracy Subisak. Boyds Mills, 2017. ISBN 978-162979578-2 Subj: Character traits – bravery. Character traits – shyness. Friendship. Monsters.

Stephens, Helen. *Ahoyty-toyty* ill. by author. Fickling, 2004. ISBN 978-0-385-75040-0 Subj: Activities – vacationing. Boats, ships. Etiquette. Friendship.

The big adventure of the Smalls ill. by author. Aladdin, 2012. ISBN 978-1-4424-5058-5 Subj: Behavior – lost & found possessions. Toys – bears.

Fleabag ill. by author. Henry Holt, 2010. ISBN 978-0-8050-7975-2 Subj: Animals – dogs. Moving.

How to hide a lion ill. by author. Henry Holt, 2013. ISBN 978-0-8050-9834-1 Subj: Animals – lions. Behavior – hiding things. Clothing – hats. Crime. Friendship.

I'm too busy ill. by author. DK, 1999. ISBN 978-0-7894-2606-2 Subj: Animals – cats. Format, unusual – board books.

Poochie-poo ill. by author. Fickling, 2003. ISBN 978-0-385-75018-9 Subj: Animals – dogs. Behavior – misbehavior.

Ruby and the muddy dog ill. by author. Kingfisher, 2000. ISBN 978-0-7534-5225-7 Subj: Animals – dogs. Character traits – cleanliness. Character traits – honesty. Character traits – responsibility.

Ruby and the noisy hippo ill. by author. Kingfisher, 2000. ISBN 978-0-7534-5226-4 Subj: Animals – hippopotamuses. Monsters. Noise, sounds.

What about me? ill. by author. DK, 1999. ISBN 978-0-7894-4840-8 Subj: Animals – cats. Emotions – envy, jealousy. Ethnic groups in the U.S. – African Americans. Friendship.

Stephens, J. Moria. *Persephone, the ladybug* ill. by author. Little, 2001. ISBN 978-0-316-81544-4 Subj: Family life – daughters. Family life – mothers. Flowers. Insects – ladybugs.

Steptoe, Javaka. *The Jones family express* ill. by author. Lee & Low, 2003. ISBN 978-1-58430-047-2 Subj: Activities – traveling. Ethnic groups in the U.S. – African Americans. Family life – aunts, uncles. Gifts. Letters, cards. Parties.

Radiant child: the story of young artist Jean-Michel Basquiat ill. by author. Little, Brown, 2016. ISBN 978-031621388-2 Subj: Art. Caldecott award books. Careers – artists. Ethnic groups in the U.S. – Haitian Americans. Ethnic groups in the U.S. – Puerto Rican Americans.

Steptoe, John. *Baby says* ill. by author. Lothrop, 1988. ISBN 978-0-688-07424-1 Subj: Activities – playing. Babies, toddlers. Sibling rivalry.

Creativity ill. by E. B. Lewis. Clarion, 1997. ISBN 978-0-395-68706-2 Subj: Ethnic groups in the U.S. – African Americans. Ethnic groups in the U.S. – Puerto Rican Americans. Friendship. School.

Mufaro's beautiful daughters: an African tale ill. by author. Lothrop, 1987. ISBN 978-0-688-04046-8 Subj: Caldecott award honor books. Character traits – kindness. Character traits – meanness. Folk & fairy tales. Foreign lands – Africa. Royalty – kings.

Stevie ill. by author. HarperCollins, 1969. ISBN 978-0-06-025764-4 Subj: Ethnic groups in the U.S. – African Americans. Friendship.

The story of jumping mouse: a Native American legend ill. by author. Lothrop, 1984. ISBN 978-0-688-01903-7 Subj: Animals – mice. Caldecott award honor books. Folk & fairy tales. Frogs & toads. Magic.

Sterer, Gideon. *Skyfishing* ill. by Poly Bernatene. Abrams, 2017. ISBN 978-141971911-0 Subj: Family life – grandfathers. Imagination. Sports – fishing.

Sterling, Cheryl. *Some bunny to talk to: a story about going to therapy* ill. by Tiphanie Beeke. Magination, 2014. ISBN 978-143381649-9 Subj: Animals – rabbits. Behavior – needing someone. Behavior – worrying. Emotions. Illness – mental illness.

Sterling, Holly. *Hiccups!* ill. by author. Frances Lincoln, 2016. ISBN 978-184780786-1 Subj: Animals – dogs. Hiccups.

Stern, Ellen. *I saw a bullfrog* ill. by author. Random House, 2003. ISBN 978-0-375-92173-5 Subj: Animals. Character traits – appearance. Imagination. Rhyming text.

Sternberg, Julie. *Bedtime at Bessie and Lil's* ill. by Adam Gudeon. Boyds Mills, 2015. ISBN 978-159078934-6 Subj: Animals – rabbits. Bedtime. Behavior – misbehavior.

Puppy, puppy, puppy ill. by Fred Koehler. Boyds Mills, 2017. ISBN 978-162979466-2 Subj: Animals – dogs. Babies, toddlers. Pets.

Steven, Kenneth. *The biggest thing in the world* ill. by Melanie Mitchell. IPG/Lion, 2010. ISBN 978-0-7459-6204-7 Subj: Animals – polar bears. Character traits – questioning. Emotions – love. Family life – mothers.

Stevens, April. *Edwin speaks up* ill. by Sophie Blackall. Random House, 2011. ISBN 978-0-375-85337-1 Subj: Babies, toddlers. Birthdays. Shopping.

Waking up Wendell ill. by Tad Hills. Random House, 2007. ISBN 978-0-375-83621-3 Subj: Communities, neighborhoods. Counting, numbers. Morning. Noise, sounds.

Stevens, Jan Romero. *Carlos and the skunk / Carlos y el zorrillo* ill. by Jeanne Arnold. Rising Moon,

1997. ISBN 978-0-87358-591-0 Subj: Animals – skunks. Farms. Foreign languages.

Carlos digs to China / Carlos excava hasta la China ill. by Jeanne Arnold. Rising Moon, 2001. ISBN 978-0-87358-764-8 Subj: Activities – baking, cooking. Activities – digging. Foreign lands – China. Foreign languages. Hotels.

Twelve lizards leaping: a new Twelve days of Christmas ill. by Christine Mau. Rising Moon, 1999. ISBN 978-0-87358-744-0 Subj: Cumulative tales. Holidays – Christmas. Music. Religion. Songs.

Stevens, Janet. *And the dish ran away with the spoon* by Janet Stevens and Susan Stevens Crummel; ill. by Janet Stevens. Harcourt, 2001. ISBN 978-0-15-202298-3 Subj: Animals. Behavior – running away. Humorous stories. Nursery rhymes.

Cook-a-doodle-doo! by Janet Stevens and Susan Stevens Crummel; ill. by Janet Stevens. Harcourt, 1999. ISBN 978-0-15-201924-2 Subj: Activities – baking, cooking. Animals. Birds – chickens, roosters. Food.

Find a cow now! by Janet Stevens and Susan Stevens Crummel; ill. by Janet Stevens. Holiday House, 2012. ISBN 978-0-8234-2218-0 Subj: Animals – bulls, cows. Animals – dogs. Birds. Farms.

The great fuzz frenzy by Janet Stevens and Susan Stevens Crummel; ill. by Janet Stevens. Harcourt, 2005. ISBN 978-0-15-204626-2 Subj: Animals – prairie dogs. Behavior – greed. Toys – balls.

Help me, Mr. Mutt! expert answers for dogs with people problems by Janet Stevens and Susan Stevens Crummel; ill. by Janet Stevens. Harcourt, 2008. ISBN 978-0-15-204628-6 Subj: Activities – writing. Animals – dogs. Humorous stories. Letters, cards.

The little red pen by Janet Stevens and Susan Stevens Crummel; ill. by Janet Stevens. Harcourt, 2011. ISBN 978-0-15-206432-7 Subj: Character traits – cooperation. Humorous stories. School.

My big dog by Janet Stevens and Susan Stevens Crummel; ill. by Janet Stevens. Golden, 1999. ISBN 978-0-307-10220-1 Subj: Animals – cats. Animals – dogs. Behavior – running away. Friendship.

Old bag of bones ill. by author. Holiday, 1996. ISBN 978-0-8234-1215-0 Subj: Animals. Animals – coyotes. Folk & fairy tales. Indians of North America – Shoshone. Old age.

Tops and bottoms ill. by author. Harcourt, 1995. ISBN 978-0-15-292851-3 Subj: Animals – bears. Animals – rabbits. Behavior – trickery. Caldecott award honor books. Character traits – cleverness. Folk & fairy tales. Gardens, gardening.

Stevenson, Emma. *Hide-and-seek science: animal camouflage* ill. by author. Holiday House, 2013.

ISBN 978-0-8234-2293-7 Subj: Animals. Disguises. Picture puzzles.

Stevenson, Harvey. *Big scary wolf* ill. by author. Clarion, 1997. ISBN 978-0-395-74213-6 Subj: Animals – wolves. Bedtime. Emotions – fear. Noise, sounds.

Looking at liberty ill. by author. HarperCollins, 2003. ISBN 978-0-06-000101-8 Subj: Careers – sculptors. Foreign lands – France. Immigrants, immigration. U.S. history.

Stevenson, James. *All aboard!* ill. by author. Greenwillow, 1995. ISBN 978-0-688-12439-7 Subj: Activities – traveling. Animals – mice. Fairs, festivals. Trains.

Brr! ill. by author. Greenwillow, 1991. ISBN 978-0-688-09211-5 Subj: Family life – grandfathers. Seasons – winter.

The castaway ill. by author. Greenwillow, 2002. ISBN 978-0-688-16966-4 Subj: Activities – flying. Activities – vacationing. Animals – mice. Animals – porcupines. Islands.

Christmas at Mud Flat ill. by author. Greenwillow, 2000. ISBN 978-0-688-17301-2 Subj: Animals. Holidays – Christmas.

"Could be worse!" ill. by author. Greenwillow, 1977. ISBN 978-0-688-84075-4 Subj: Family life. Family life – grandfathers. Farms. Monsters.

Don't make me laugh ill. by author. Farrar, 1999. ISBN 978-0-374-31827-7 Subj: Animals. Behavior. Humorous stories.

Emma ill. by author. Greenwillow, 1985. ISBN 978-0-688-04021-5 Subj: Behavior – trickery. Witches.

Fried feathers for Thanksgiving ill. by author. Greenwillow, 1986. ISBN 978-0-688-06676-5 Subj: Behavior – trickery. Character traits – meanness. Witches.

Fun, no fun ill. by author. Greenwillow, 1994. ISBN 978-0-688-11674-3 Subj: Careers – artists. Careers – writers. Concepts – opposites. Emotions.

Grandpa's great city tour: an alphabet book ill. by author. Greenwillow, 1983. ISBN 978-0-688-02324-9 Subj: ABC books. Activities – flying. Cities, towns. Family life – grandfathers. Wordless.

Grandpa's too-good garden ill. by author. Greenwillow, 1989. ISBN 978-0-688-08486-8 Subj: Family life – grandfathers. Gardens, gardening.

The great big especially beautiful Easter egg ill. by author. Greenwillow, 1983. ISBN 978-0-688-01791-0 Subj: Eggs. Family life – grandfathers.

Happy Valentine's Day, Emma! ill. by author. Greenwillow, 1987. ISBN 978-0-688-07358-9 Subj:

Animals. Character traits – meanness. Holidays – Valentine's Day. Humorous stories. Witches.

Heat wave at Mud Flat ill. by author. Greenwillow, 1997. ISBN 978-0-688-14206-3 Subj: Animals. Weather. Weather – rain.

Higher on the door ill. by author. Greenwillow, 1987. ISBN 978-0-688-06637-6 Subj: Behavior – growing up. Family life – grandparents.

Howard ill. by author. Greenwillow, 1980. ISBN 978-0-688-84255-0 Subj: Behavior – lost. Birds – ducks. Friendship.

I meant to tell you ill. by author. Greenwillow, 1996. ISBN 978-0-688-14178-3 Subj: Behavior – growing up. Careers – artists. Careers – writers. Family life – daughters. Family life – fathers.

July ill. by author. Greenwillow, 1990. ISBN 978-0-688-08823-1 Subj: Family life – grandparents. Sea & seashore. Seasons – summer.

Monty ill. by author. Greenwillow, 1992. ISBN 978-0-688-11241-7 Subj: Animals – rabbits. Birds – ducks. Frogs & toads. Reptiles – alligators, crocodiles.

The most amazing dinosaur ill. by author. Greenwillow, 2000. ISBN 978-0-688-16433-1 Subj: Anatomy – skeletons. Animals. Animals – rats. Dinosaurs. Museums. Prehistory.

Mr. Hacker ill. by author. Greenwillow, 1990. ISBN 978-0-688-09217-7 Subj: Animals. Emotions – loneliness. Pets.

National worm day ill. by author. Greenwillow, 1990. ISBN 978-0-688-08772-2 Subj: Animals. Friendship.

No friends ill. by author. Greenwillow, 1986. ISBN 978-0-688-06507-2 Subj: Family life – grandfathers. Friendship. Moving.

No need for Monty ill. by author. Greenwillow, 1987. ISBN 978-0-688-07084-7 Subj: Animals. Reptiles – alligators, crocodiles. Transportation.

Quick! turn the page! ill. by author. Greenwillow, 1990. ISBN 978-0-688-09309-9 Subj: Problem solving.

Rolling Rose ill. by author. Greenwillow, 1992. ISBN 978-0-688-10675-1 Subj: Activities. Activities – walking. Babies, toddlers.

Sam the Zamboni man ill. by Harvey Stevenson. Greenwillow, 1998. ISBN 978-0-688-14485-2 Subj: Careers. Family life – fathers. Machines. Sports – hockey. Sports – ice skating.

The Sea View Hotel ill. by author. Greenwillow, 1978. ISBN 978-0-688-84168-3 Subj: Activities – vacationing. Animals – mice. Hotels.

The stowaway ill. by author. Greenwillow, 1990. ISBN 978-0-688-08620-6 Subj: Animals – mice. Boats, ships. Friendship.

That dreadful day ill. by author. Greenwillow, 1985. ISBN 978-0-688-04036-9 Subj: Family life – grandfathers. School – first day.

That terrible Halloween night ill. by author. Greenwillow, 1980. ISBN 978-0-688-94281-6 Subj: Family life – grandfathers. Holidays – Halloween.

That's exactly the way it wasn't ill. by author. Greenwillow, 1991. ISBN 978-0-688-09869-8 Subj: Family life – brothers. Family life – grandfathers. Sibling rivalry.

There's nothing to do! ill. by author. Greenwillow, 1986. ISBN 978-0-688-04699-6 Subj: Behavior – boredom. Family life – grandfathers.

A village full of valentines ill. by author. Greenwillow, 1995. ISBN 978-0-688-13603-1 Subj: Animals. Holidays – Valentine's Day.

We can't sleep ill. by author. Greenwillow, 1982. ISBN 978-0-688-01214-4 Subj: Animals. Bedtime. Family life – grandfathers. Sleep.

What's under my bed? ill. by author. Greenwillow, 1983. ISBN 978-0-688-02327-0 Subj: Bedtime. Emotions – fear. Family life – grandfathers. Furniture – beds.

When I was nine ill. by author. Greenwillow, 1986. ISBN 978-0-688-05943-9 Subj: Family life.

Which one is Whitney? ill. by author. Greenwillow, 1990. ISBN 978-0-688-09062-3 Subj: Animals. Fish. Sea & seashore.

Wilfred the rat ill. by author. Greenwillow, 1977. ISBN 978-0-688-84103-4 Subj: Animals – chipmunks. Animals – rats. Animals – squirrels. Friendship.

Will you please feed our cat? ill. by author. Greenwillow, 1987. ISBN 978-0-688-06848-6 Subj: Character traits – helpfulness. Family life – grandfathers. Pets.

The wish card ran out! ill. by author. Greenwillow, 1981. ISBN 978-0-688-84305-2 Subj: Behavior – wishing.

Worse than the worst ill. by author. Greenwillow, 1994. ISBN 978-0-688-12250-8 Subj: Animals – dogs. Behavior – misbehavior. Family life – aunts, uncles.

Worse than Willy! ill. by author. Greenwillow, 1984. ISBN 978-0-688-02597-7 Subj: Babies, toddlers. Family life – grandfathers. Family life – new sibling. Imagination. Sibling rivalry.

The worst person in the world ill. by author. Greenwillow, 1978. ISBN 978-0-688-84127-0 Subj: Friendship.

The worst person in the world at Crab Beach ill. by author. Greenwillow, 1988. ISBN 978-0-688-07299-5 Subj: Friendship. Humorous stories. Sea & seashore – beaches.

The worst person's Christmas ill. by author. Greenwillow, 1991. ISBN 978-0-688-10211-1 Subj: Character traits – meanness. Holidays – Christmas.

Yard sale ill. by author. Greenwillow, 1996. ISBN 978-0-688-14127-1 Subj: Animals. Garage sales, rummage sales.

Yuck! ill. by author. Greenwillow, 1984. ISBN 978-0-688-03830-4 Subj: Magic. Witches.

Stevenson, Robert Louis. *Block city* ill. by Daniel Kirk. Simon & Schuster, 2005. ISBN 978-0-689-86964-8 Subj: Imagination. Poetry. Sea & seashore. Toys.

Block city ill. by Ashley Wolff. Dutton, 1988. ISBN 978-0-525-44399-5 Subj: Imagination. Poetry. Sea & seashore. Toys.

A child's garden of verses sel. by Cooper Edens; ill. by selector. DK, 1997. ISBN 978-0-7894-2068-8 Subj: Poetry.

A child's garden of verses ill. by Diane Goode. Morrow, 1998. ISBN 978-0-688-14584-2 Subj: Poetry.

A child's garden of verses ill. by Jessie Willcox Smith. Children's Classics, 1995. ISBN 978-0-517-12397-3 Subj: Poetry.

A child's garden of verses ill. by Tasha Tudor. Simon & Schuster, 1999. ISBN 978-0-689-81882-0 Subj: Poetry.

The little land ill. by Kim Fernandes. Kids Can, 2002. ISBN 978-1-55337-385-8 Subj: Imagination. Poetry.

The moon ill. by Tracey Campbell Pearson. Farrar, 2006. ISBN 978-0-374-35046-8 Subj: Moon. Poetry.

The moon ill. by Denise Saldutti. HarperCollins, 1984. ISBN 978-0-06-025789-7 Subj: Family life. Moon. Night. Poetry. Sports – fishing.

Where go the boats? ill. by Max Grover. Browndeer, 1998. ISBN 978-0-15-201711-8 Subj: Activities – playing. Poetry.

Stewart, Amber. *Bedtime for Button* ill. by Layn Marlow. Scholastic, 2009. ISBN 978-0-545-12991-6 Subj: Animals – bears. Bedtime. Dreams. Family life – fathers.

I'm big enough ill. by Layn Marlow. Scholastic, 2007. ISBN 978-0-439-90666-1 Subj: Animals – rabbits. Behavior – growing up.

Little by little ill. by Layn Marlow. Scholastic, 2008. ISBN 978-0-545-06163-6 Subj: Animals – otters. Character traits – perseverance. Family life – brothers & sisters. Self-concept. Sports – swimming.

No babysitters allowed ill. by Laura Rankin. Bloomsbury, 2008. ISBN 978-1-59990-154-1 Subj: Activities – babysitting. Animals – rabbits. Emotions – fear.

Puddle's new school ill. by Layn Marlow. Barron's, 2011. ISBN 978-0-7641-4683-1 Subj: Birds – ducks. School – first day.

Rabbit ears ill. by Laura Rankin. Bloomsbury, 2006. ISBN 978-1-58234-959-6 Subj: Animals – rabbits. Character traits – cleanliness.

Too small for my big bed ill. by Layn Marlow. Barron's, 2013. ISBN 978-0-7641-6587-0 Subj: Animals – tigers. Bedtime. Character traits – smallness.

Stewart, Joel. *Addis Berner Bear forgets* ill. by author. Farrar, 2008. ISBN 978-0-374-30036-4 Subj: Animals – bears. Cities, towns. Homeless. Memories, memory. Music. Musical instruments – trumpets.

Dexter Bexley and the big blue beastie ill. by author. Holiday House, 2007. ISBN 978-0-8234-2068-1 Subj: Character traits – cleverness. Friendship. Monsters.

Stewart, Melissa. *Beneath the sun* ill. by Constance R. Bergum. Peachtree, 2014. ISBN 978-156145733-5 Subj: Animals. Concepts – cold & heat. Sun.

Can an aardvark bark? ill. by Steve Jenkins. Simon & Schuster/Beach Lane, 2017. ISBN 978-148145852-8 Subj: Animals. Character traits – questioning. Communication. Noise, sounds.

Feathers: not just for flying ill. by Sarah S. Brannen. Charlesbridge, 2014. ISBN 978-158089430-2 Subj: Birds. Feathers.

A place for birds ill. by Higgins Bond. Peachtree, 2009. ISBN 978-1-56145-474-7 Subj: Birds. Ecology.

A place for frogs ill. by Higgins Bond. Peachtree, 2010. ISBN 978-1-56145-521-8 Subj: Ecology. Frogs & toads.

Under the snow ill. by Constance R. Bergum. Peachtree, 2009. ISBN 978-1-56145-493-8 Subj: Animals. Seasons – winter. Weather – snow.

When rain falls ill. by Constance R. Bergum. Peachtree, 2008. ISBN 978-1-56145-438-9 Subj: Animals. Weather – rain.

Stewart, Paul. *The birthday presents* ill. by Chris Riddell. HarperCollins, 2000. ISBN 978-0-06-028279-0 Subj: Animals – hedgehogs. Animals – rabbits. Behavior – sharing. Birthdays. Gifts.

A little bit of winter ill. by Chris Riddell. HarperCollins, 1999. ISBN 978-0-06-028278-3 Subj: Animals – hedgehogs. Animals – rabbits. Friendship. Hibernation. Seasons – winter.

Rabbit's wish ill. by Chris Riddell. HarperCollins, 2001. ISBN 978-0-06-029518-9 Subj: Animals – hedgehogs. Animals – rabbits. Friendship. Weather – floods.

Stewart, Sarah. *The gardener* ill. by David Small. Farrar, 1997. ISBN 978-0-374-32517-6 Subj: Caldecott award honor books. Careers – bakers. Family life – aunts, uncles. Gardens, gardening. Letters, cards. U.S. history.

The journey ill. by David Small. Farrar, 2001. ISBN 978-0-374-33905-0 Subj: Activities – writing. Birthdays. Cities, towns. Ethnic groups in the U.S. – Amish.

The library ill. by David Small. Farrar, 1995. ISBN 978-0-374-34388-0 Subj: Books, reading. Libraries. Rhyming text.

The money tree ill. by David Small. Farrar, 1991. ISBN 978-0-374-35014-7 Subj: Money. Seasons. Trees.

The quiet place ill. by David Small. Farrar, 2012. ISBN 978-0-374-32565-7 Subj: Ethnic groups in the U.S. – Mexican Americans. Family life – aunts, uncles. Immigrants, immigration. Letters, cards.

Stewart, Shannon. *Sea crow* ill. by Liz Milkau. Orca, 2004. ISBN 978-1-55143-288-5 Subj: Disabilities – physical disabilities. Emotions – fear. Family life – brothers & sisters. Moving.

Stewart, Whitney. *A catfish tale: a bayou story of the fisherman and his wife* ill. by Gerald Guerlais. Albert Whitman, 2014. ISBN 978-080751098-8 Subj: Behavior – greed. Folk & fairy tales. Swamps.

Meditation is an open sky: mindfulness for kids ill. by Sally Rippin. Albert Whitman, 2015. ISBN 978-080754908-7 Subj: Animals. Character traits – patience, impatience. Emotions. Health & fitness. Self-concept.

Stewig, John Warren. *The animals watched: an alphabet book* ill. by Rosanne Litzinger. Holiday House, 2007. ISBN 978-0-8234-1906-7 Subj: ABC books. Animals. Boats, ships. Religion – Noah. Weather – floods. Weather – rain.

Clever Gretchen ill. by Patricia Wittmann. Marshall Cavendish, 2000. ISBN 978-0-7614-5066-5 Subj: Character traits – cleverness. Devil. Folk & fairy tales. Magic.

King Midas ill. by Omar Rayyan. Holiday, 1999. ISBN 978-0-8234-1423-9 Subj: Behavior – greed. Folk & fairy tales. Foreign lands – Greece. Royalty – kings.

Making plum jam ill. by Kevin O'Malley. Hyperion, 2002. ISBN 978-0-7868-2402-1 Subj: Activities – baking, cooking. Family life – aunts, uncles. Farms. Food.

Mother Holly: a retelling from the Brothers Grimm ill. by Johanna Westerman. NorthSouth, 2001. ISBN 978-1-55858-926-1 Subj: Family life – sisters. Family life – stepfamilies. Folk & fairy tales. Foreign lands – Germany.

Stone soup ill. by Margot Tomes. Holiday, 1991. ISBN 978-0-8234-0863-4 Subj: Character traits – cleverness. Folk & fairy tales. Food.

Stickland, Henrietta. *Dinosaur roar!* (Stickland, Paul)

A number of dinosaurs: a pop-up counting book (Stickland, Paul)

Stickland, Paul. *Bears* ill. by author. Ragged Bears, 2001. ISBN 978-1-929927-34-0 Subj: Animals – bears. Animals – sheep. Bedtime. Parties. Rhyming text. Toys.

Dinosaur roar! by Paul Stickland and Henrietta Stickland; ill. by Paul Stickland. Dutton, 1994. ISBN 978-0-525-45276-8 Subj: Concepts – opposites. Dinosaurs. Prehistory. Rhyming text.

Dinosaur stomp! ill. by author. Dutton, 1996. ISBN 978-0-525-45591-2 Subj: Activities – dancing. Dinosaurs. Format, unusual – toy & movable books. Prehistory. Rhyming text.

A number of dinosaurs: a pop-up counting book by Paul Stickland and Henrietta Stickland. Illus. Sterling, 2010. ISBN 978-1-4027-6479-0 Subj: Counting, numbers. Dinosaurs. Format, unusual – toy & movable books.

Ten terrible dinosaurs ill. by author. Dutton, 1997. ISBN 978-0-525-45905-7 Subj: Counting, numbers. Dinosaurs. Prehistory. Rhyming text.

Truck jam ill. by author. Ragged Bears, 2000. ISBN 978-1-929927-03-6 Subj: Format, unusual – toy & movable books. Transportation. Trucks.

Stiegemeyer, Julie. *Gobble gobble crash! a barnyard counting bash* ill. by Valeri Gorbachev. Dutton, 2008. ISBN 978-0-525-47959-8 Subj: Birds – turkeys. Counting, numbers. Farms. Rhyming text.

Seven little bunnies ill. by Laura J. Bryant. Marshall Cavendish, 2010. ISBN 978-0-7614-5600-1 Subj: Animals – rabbits. Bedtime. Counting, numbers. Rhyming text.

Under the baobab tree ill. by E. B. Lewis. Zonderkidz, 2012. ISBN 978-0-310-72561-9 Subj: Family life – brothers & sisters. Foreign lands – Africa. Religion. Trees.

Stier, Catherine. *Bugs in my hair?!* ill. by Tammie Lyon. Albert Whitman, 2008. ISBN 978-0-8075-0908-1 Subj: Insects – lice. School.

Stihler, Chérie B. *The giant cabbage turnip* ill. by Jeremiah Trammell. Sasquatch, 2003. ISBN 978-1-57061-357-9 Subj: Alaska. Animals. Animals – moose. Character traits – cooperation. Cumulative tales. Fairs, festivals. Friendship. Plants.

Stileman, Kali. *Roly-poly egg* ill. by author. ME Media/Tiger Tales, 2011. ISBN 978-1-58925-852-5

Subj: Birds. Eggs. Format, unusual – toy & movable books.

Snack time for Confetti ill. by author. ME Media/Tiger Tales, 2013. ISBN 978-1-58925-127-4 Subj: Birds. Food.

Stiles, Martha Bennett. *Island magic* ill. by Daniel San Souci. Atheneum, 1999. ISBN 978-0-689-80588-2 Subj: Family life – grandfathers. Islands. Nature.

Stille, Ljuba. *Mia's thumb* ill. by author. Holiday House, 2014. ISBN 978-082343067-3 Subj: Family life. Thumb sucking.

Stills, Caroline. *The house of twelve bunnies* by Caroline Stills and Sarcia Stills-Blott ill. by Judith Rossell. Holiday House, 2012. ISBN 978-0-8234-2422-1 Subj: Animals – rabbits. Bedtime. Counting, numbers.

Mice mischief: math facts in action ill. by Judith Rossell. Holiday House, 2014. ISBN 978-082342947-9 Subj: Animals – mice. Circus. Counting, numbers.

Stills-Blott, Sarcia. *The house of twelve bunnies* (Stills, Caroline)

Stillwell, Fred. *The airplane alphabet book* (Pallotta, Jerry)

Stimpson, Colin. *Jack and the baked beanstalk* ill. by author. Candlewick, 2012. ISBN 978-0-7636-5563-1 Subj: Careers – chefs, cooks. Folk & fairy tales. Food. Giants. Magic. Plants.

Stine, R. L. *The Little Shop of Monsters* ill. by Marc Brown. Little, Brown, 2015. ISBN 978-031636983-1 Subj: Monsters. Pets.

Mary McScary ill. by Marc Brown. Scholastic, 2017. ISBN 978-133803856-9 Subj: Character traits – cleverness. Emotions – fear. Family life – cousins.

Sting [Musician]. *Rock steady* ill. by Hugh Whyte. HarperCollins, 2001. ISBN 978-0-06-029231-7 Subj: Animals. Boats, ships. Religion – Noah. Rhyming text. Weather – floods. Weather – rain. Weather – rainbows.

Stinson, Kathy. *The dance of the violin* ill. by Dusan Petricic. Annick, 2017. ISBN 978-155451900-2 Subj: Careers – musicians. Character traits – confidence. Contests. Music. Musical instruments – violins.

The man with the violin ill. by Dusan Petricic. Annick, 2013. ISBN 978-1-55451-565-3 Subj: Careers – musicians. Family life – mothers. Music. Musical instruments – violins.

A pocket can have a treasure in it ill. by Deirdre Betteridge. Annick, 2008. ISBN 978-1-55451-126-6 Subj: Family life – new sibling. Farms.

Stock, Catherine. *Alexander's midnight snack: a little elephant's ABC* ill. by author. Clarion, 1988. ISBN 978-0-89919-512-4 Subj: ABC books. Animals – elephants. Bedtime. Food.

The birthday present ill. by author. Bradbury, 1991. ISBN 978-0-02-788401-2 Subj: Birthdays. Parties.

Christmas time ill. by author. Bradbury, 1990. ISBN 978-0-02-788403-6 Subj: Family life – fathers. Holidays – Christmas.

Easter surprise ill. by author. Bradbury, 1991. ISBN 978-0-02-788371-8 Subj: Family life – mothers. Holidays – Easter.

Gugu's house ill. by author. Clarion, 2001. ISBN 978-0-618-00389-1 Subj: Careers – artists. Family life – grandmothers. Foreign lands – Zimbabwe. Weather – rain.

Halloween monster ill. by author. Bradbury, 1990. ISBN 978-0-02-788404-3 Subj: Activities. Emotions – fear. Holidays – Halloween.

A porc in New York ill. by author. Holiday House, 2007. ISBN 978-0-8234-1994-4 Subj: Activities – vacationing. Animals. Careers – farmers.

Secret Valentine ill. by author. Bradbury, 1991. ISBN 978-0-02-788372-5 Subj: Character traits – kindness. Holidays – Valentine's Day.

Thanksgiving treat ill. by author. Bradbury, 1990. ISBN 978-0-02-788402-9 Subj: Family life – grandfathers. Holidays – Thanksgiving.

Stockdale, Sean. *Max the champion* by Sean Stockdale and Alexandra Strick ill. by Ros Asquith. Frances Lincoln, 2014. ISBN 978-184780388-7 Subj: Disabilities. Sports.

Stockdale, Susan. *Bring on the birds* ill. by author. Peachtree, 2011. ISBN 978-1-56145-560-7 Subj: Birds. Rhyming text.

Fabulous Fishes ill. by author. Peachtree, 2008. ISBN 978-1-56145-429-7 Subj: Fish. Rhyming text.

Spectacular spots ill. by author. Peachtree, 2015. ISBN 978-156145817-2 Subj: Animals. Disguises. Rhyming text.

Stripes of all types ill. by author. Peachtree, 2013. ISBN 978-1-56145-695-6 Subj: Concepts – patterns.

Stockland, Patricia M. *In the horse stall* ill. by Todd Ouren. Abdo, 2008. ISBN 978-1-60270-024-6 Subj: Animals – horses, ponies. Farms.

In the pig pen ill. by Todd Ouren. Abdo, 2008. ISBN 978-1-60270-025-3 Subj: Animals – pigs. Farms.

In the sheep pasture ill. by Todd Ouren. Abdo, 2008. ISBN 978-1-60270-026-0 Subj: Animals – sheep. Farms.

Stoeke, Janet Morgan. *The bus stop* ill. by author. Penguin, 2007. ISBN 978-0-525-47805-8 Subj: Buses. Rhyming text. School.

A friend for Minerva Louise ill. by author. Dutton, 1997. ISBN 978-0-525-45869-2 Subj: Babies, toddlers. Behavior – mistakes. Birds – chickens, roosters.

A hat for Minerva Louise ill. by author. Dutton, 1994. ISBN 978-0-525-45328-4 Subj: Behavior – misunderstanding. Birds – chickens, roosters. Clothing.

Hide and seek ill. by author. Dutton, 1999. ISBN 978-0-525-46189-0 Subj: Animals. Behavior – hiding. Birds – chickens, roosters. Farms. Format, unusual – board books. Games.

It's library day ill. by author. Dutton, 2008. ISBN 978-0-525-47944-4 Subj: Libraries. Rhyming text. School.

The Loopy Coop hens ill. by author. Penguin, 2011. ISBN 978-0-525-42190-0 Subj: Birds – chickens, roosters. Farms.

The Loopy Coop hens: letting go ill. by author. Dial, 2013. ISBN 978-0-8037-3768-6 Subj: Birds – chickens, roosters. Humorous stories. Trees.

Minerva Louise ill. by author. Dutton, 1988. ISBN 978-0-525-44374-2 Subj: Behavior – misunderstanding. Birds – chickens, roosters.

Minerva Louise and the colorful eggs ill. by author. Penguin, 2006. ISBN 978-0-525-47633-7 Subj: Birds – chickens, roosters. Eggs. Holidays – Easter.

Minerva Louise and the red truck ill. by author. Dutton, 2002. ISBN 978-0-525-46909-4 Subj: Birds – chickens, roosters. Careers – construction workers. Trucks.

Minerva Louise at school ill. by author. Dutton, 1996. ISBN 978-0-525-45494-6 Subj: Behavior – misunderstanding. Birds – chickens, roosters. School.

Minerva Louise at the fair ill. by author. Dutton, 2000. ISBN 978-0-525-46439-6 Subj: Behavior – mistakes. Birds – chickens, roosters. Fairs, festivals.

Minerva Louise on Christmas Eve ill. by author. Penguin, 2007. ISBN 978-0-525-47857-7 Subj: Birds – chickens, roosters. Holidays – Christmas. Santa Claus.

Minerva Louise on Halloween ill. by author. Dutton, 2009. ISBN 978-0-525-42149-8 Subj: Birds – chickens, roosters. Holidays – Halloween.

Oh no! a fox! ill. by author. Dial, 2014. ISBN 978-080373952-9 Subj: Animals – foxes. Birds – chickens, roosters.

Pip's trip ill. by author. Dial, 2012. ISBN 978-0-8037-3708-2 Subj: Birds – chickens, roosters. Character traits – bravery. Farms.

Waiting for May ill. by author. Penguin, 2005. ISBN 978-0-525-47098-4 Subj: Adoption. Family life – brothers & sisters. Foreign lands – China.

Stohner, Anu. *Brave Charlotte* ill. by Henrike Wilson. Bloomsbury, 2005. ISBN 978-1-58234-690-8 Subj: Animals – dogs. Animals – sheep. Behavior – resourcefulness. Character traits – bravery.

Brave Charlotte and the wolves ill. by Henrike Wilson. Bloomsbury, 2009. ISBN 978-1-59990-424-5 Subj: Animals – sheep. Animals – wolves. Character traits – bravery. Clubs, gangs.

Stohs, Anita. *An Easter alleluia* ill. by Joel Snyder. Concordia, 2003. ISBN 978-0-7586-0116-2 Subj: Holidays – Easter. Music. Religion. Rhyming text. Songs.

Stojic, Manya. *Rain* ill. by author. Crown, 2000. ISBN 978-0-517-80086-7 Subj: Animals. Cumulative tales. Foreign lands – Africa. Weather – rain.

Snow ill. by author. Knopf, 2002. ISBN 978-0-375-92348-7 Subj: Animals. Forest, woods. Seasons – winter. Weather – snow.

Wet pebbles under our feet ill. by author. Knopf, 2002. ISBN 978-0-375-91519-2 Subj: Family life – grandparents. Islands. Sea & seashore – beaches.

Stolz, Mary. *Emmett's pig* ill. by Garth Williams and Rosemary Wells. HarperCollins, 2003. ISBN 978-0-06-028746-7 Subj: Animals – pigs. Birthdays. Cities, towns.

Storm in the night ill. by Pat Cummings. HarperCollins, 1988. ISBN 978-0-06-025912-9 Subj: Ethnic groups in the U.S. – African Americans. Family life – grandfathers. Night. Weather – storms.

Zekmet, the stone carver ill. by Deborah Nourse Lattimore. Harcourt, 1988. ISBN 978-0-15-299961-2 Subj: Activities – working. Foreign lands – Egypt.

Stone, Tanya Lee. *D is for dreidel* ill. by Dawn Apperley. Price Stern Sloan, 2002. ISBN 978-0-8431-4576-2 Subj: ABC books. Holidays – Hanukkah. Jewish culture. Rhyming text.

Elizabeth leads the way: Elizabeth Cady Stanton and the right to vote ill. by Rebecca Gibbon. Henry Holt, 2008. ISBN 978-0-8050-7903-6 Subj: Behavior – seeking better things. Character traits – assertiveness. Character traits – bravery. Gender roles. U.S. history.

The house that Jane built: a story about Jane Addams ill. by Kathryn Brown. Holt/Christy Ottaviano, 2015. ISBN 978-080509049-9 Subj: Behavior – seeking better things. Character traits – helpfulness. Gender roles. Poverty.

Sandy's circus: a story about Alexander Calder ill. by Boris Kulikov. Viking, 2008. ISBN 978-0-670-06268-3 Subj: Art. Careers – artists. Circus.

Who says women can't be doctors? the story of Elizabeth Blackwell ill. by Marjorie Priceman. Henry Holt, 2013. ISBN 978-0-8050-9048-2 Subj: Careers – doctors. Character traits – assertiveness. Character traits – perseverance. Gender roles. Self-concept. U.S. history.

Stoop, Naoko. *Red Knit Cap Girl* ill. by author. Little, Brown, 2012. ISBN 978-0-316-12946-6 Subj: Animals. Clothing – hats. Forest, woods. Moon.

Red Knit Cap Girl and the reading tree ill. by author. Little, Brown, 2014. ISBN 978-031622886-2 Subj: Animals. Behavior – sharing. Books, reading. Libraries.

Red Knit Cap Girl to the rescue ill. by author. Little, Brown, 2013. ISBN 978-0-316-22885-5 Subj: Activities – traveling. Animals – polar bears. Behavior – lost. Character traits – helpfulness.

Sing with me! ill. by author. Henry Holt, 2016. ISBN 978-080509904-1 Subj: Nursery rhymes. Songs.

Stott, Ann. *Always* ill. by Matt Phelan. Candlewick, 2008. ISBN 978-0-7636-3232-8 Subj: Character traits – questioning. Emotions – love. Family life – mothers.

I'll be there ill. by Matt Phelan. Candlewick, 2010. ISBN 978-0-7636-4711-7 Subj: Behavior – growing up. Emotions – love. Family life – mothers.

Stowell, Penelope. *The greatest potatoes* ill. by Sharon Watts. Hyperion, 2005. ISBN 978-0-7868-5113-3 Subj: Activities – baking, cooking. Careers – chefs, cooks. Ethnic groups in the U.S. Food. Restaurants.

Stower, Adam. *Naughty kitty!* ill. by author. Scholastic/Orchard, 2014. ISBN 978-054557604-8 Subj: Animals – cats. Animals – tigers. Pets.

Silly doggy ill. by author. Scholastic, 2012. ISBN 978-0-545-37323-4 Subj: Animals – bears. Pets.

Slam! a tale of consequences ill. by author. OwlKids, 2014. ISBN 978-177147007-0 Subj: Accidents.

Two left feet ill. by author. Bloomsbury, 2004. ISBN 978-1-58234-884-1 Subj: Activities – dancing. Character traits – clumsiness. Contests. Monsters.

Straaten, Harmen van. *Duck's tale* ill. by author. NorthSouth, 2007. ISBN 978-0-7358-2133-0 Subj: Animals. Birds – ducks. Books, reading. Friendship. Frogs & toads.

For me? ill. by author. NorthSouth, 2004. ISBN 978-0-7358-2163-7 Subj: Animals. Birds – ducks. Friendship. Frogs & toads. Letters, cards.

Strand, Keith. *Grandfather's Christmas tree* ill. by Thomas Locker. Silver Whistle, 1999. ISBN 978-0-15-201821-4 Subj: Birds – geese. Character traits – kindness to animals. Holidays – Christmas. U.S. history – frontier & pioneer life.

Strauss, Anna. *Hush, Mama loves you* ill. by Alice Priestley. Walker, 2002. ISBN 978-0-8027-8806-1 Subj: Character traits – helpfulness. Emotions. Family life – mothers.

Strauss, Linda Leopold. *The Elijah door: a Passover tale* ill. by Alexi Natchev. Holiday House, 2012. ISBN 978-0-8234-1911-1 Subj: Behavior – fighting, arguing. Friendship. Holidays – Passover. Jewish culture. Religion.

The princess gown ill. by Malene Laugesen. Houghton, 2008. ISBN 978-0-618-86259-7 Subj: Activities – sewing. Clothing – dresses. Royalty – princesses.

Strauss, Rochelle. *One well: the story of water on Earth* ill. by Rosemary Woods. Kids Can, 2007. ISBN 978-1-55337-954-6 Subj: Ecology. Water.

Strauss, Susan. *When woman became the sea: a Costa Rican creation myth* ill. by Cristina Acosta. Beyond Words, 1998. ISBN 978-1-885223-85-2 Subj: Creation. Folk & fairy tales. Foreign lands – Costa Rica. Sea & seashore.

Street, Pat. *There's a frog in my throat: 312 animal sayings from the horse's mouth* (Leedy, Loreen)

Strete, Craig Kee. *How the Indians bought the farm* by Craig Kee Strete and Michelle Netten Chacon ill. by Francisco X. Mora. Greenwillow, 1996. ISBN 978-0-688-14131-8 Subj: Animals. Behavior – trickery. Farms. Indians of North America.

They thought they saw him ill. by José Aruego and Ariane Dewey. Greenwillow, 1996. ISBN 978-0-688-14195-0 Subj: Concepts – color. Reptiles – lizards.

Strick, Alexandra. *Max the champion* (Stockdale, Sean)

Stringer, Lauren. *Winter is the warmest season* ill. by author. Harcourt, 2006. ISBN 978-0-15-204967-6 Subj: Seasons – winter.

Yellow time ill. by author. Simon & Schuster/Beach Lane, 2016. ISBN 978-148143156-9 Subj: Concepts – color. Seasons – fall. Trees.

Stroud, Bettye. *Belle, the last mule at Gee's Bend: a civil rights story* (Ramsey, Calvin Alexander)

Dance y'all ill. by Cornelius Van Wright and Ying-Hwa Hu. Marshall Cavendish, 2001. ISBN 978-0-7614-5065-8 Subj: Activities – dancing. Emotions – fear. Ethnic groups in the U.S. – African Americans. Farms. Reptiles – snakes.

Down home at Miss Dessa's ill. by Felicia Marshall. Lee & Low, 1996. ISBN 978-1-880000-39-7 Subj: Character traits – kindness. Ethnic groups in the U.S. – African Americans. Family life – sisters. Illness. Old age. Seasons – summer.

The leaving ill. by Cedric Lucas. Marshall Cavendish, 2001. ISBN 978-0-7614-5067-2 Subj: Ethnic groups in the U.S. – African Americans. Slavery.

The patchwork path ill. by Erin Susanne Bennett. Candlewick, 2005. ISBN 978-0-7636-2423-1 Subj: Character traits – freedom. Ethnic groups in the U.S. – African Americans. Maps. Quilts. Slavery.

Stryer, Andrea Stenn. *Kami and the yaks* ill. by Bert Dodson. Bay Otter, 2007. ISBN 978-0-9778961-0-3 Subj: Animals – yaks. Character traits – bravery. Disabilities – deafness. Foreign lands – Nepal.

Stubbs, Lisa. *Lily and Bear* ill. by author. Simon & Schuster, 2015. ISBN 978-148144416-3 Subj: Activities – drawing. Animals – bears. Imagination.

Lily and Bear: grumpy feet ill. by author. Simon & Schuster/Paula Wiseman, 2017. ISBN 978-148147167-1 Subj: Activities – drawing. Animals – bears. Behavior – bad day, bad mood. Imagination.

Stuchner, Joan Betty. *Can hens give milk?* ill. by Joe Weissmann. Orca, 2011. ISBN 978-1-55469-319-1 Subj: Birds – chickens, roosters. Farms. Humorous stories. Jewish culture.

The Kugel Valley Klezmer Band ill. by Richard Row. Crocodile, 2001. ISBN 978-1-56656-430-4 Subj: Foreign lands – Canada. Jewish culture. Musical instruments – bands.

Sturges, Philemon. *How do you make a baby smile?* ill. by Bridget Strevens-Marzo. HarperCollins, 2007. ISBN 978-0-06-076072-4 Subj: Animals – babies. Rhyming text.

I love bugs ill. by Shari Halpern. HarperCollins, 2005. ISBN 978-0-06-056169-7 Subj: Insects. Rhyming text.

I love planes ill. by Shari Halpern. HarperCollins, 2003. ISBN 978-0-06-028899-0 Subj: Airplanes, airports.

I love school ill. by Shari Halpern. HarperCollins, 2004. ISBN 978-0-06-009285-6 Subj: Family life – brothers & sisters. Rhyming text. School – nursery.

I love tools! ill. by Shari Halpern. HarperCollins, 2006. ISBN 978-0-06-009288-7 Subj: Activities – making things. Homes, houses. Rhyming text. Tools.

I love trains ill. by Shari Halpern. HarperCollins, 2001. ISBN 978-0-06-028901-0 Subj: Rhyming text. Trains.

I love trucks! ill. by Shari Halpern. HarperCollins, 1999. ISBN 978-0-06-027819-9 Subj: Careers – truck drivers. Rhyming text. Trucks.

Ten flashing fireflies ill. by Anna Vojtech. North-South, 1995. ISBN 978-1-55858-421-1 Subj: Counting, numbers. Insects – fireflies. Night. Rhyming text.

This little pirate ill. by Amy Walrod. Penguin, 2005. ISBN 978-0-525-46440-2 Subj: Animals – pigs. Parties. Pirates. Rhyming text.

Waggers ill. by Jim Ishikawa. Penguin, 2005. ISBN 978-0-525-47116-5 Subj: Animals – cats. Animals – dogs. Rhyming text.

What's that sound, Woolly Bear? ill. by Joan Paley. Little, 1996. ISBN 978-0-316-82021-9 Subj: Insects. Insects – butterflies, caterpillars. Insects – moths. Metamorphosis. Noise, sounds.

Who took the cookies from the cookie jar? (Lass, Bonnie)

Sturgis, Brenda Reeves. *Ten turkeys in the road* ill. by David Slonim. Marshall Cavendish, 2011. ISBN 978-0-7614-5847-0 Subj: Birds – turkeys. Careers – farmers. Circus. Counting, numbers. Rhyming text.

Sturm, James. *Birdsong: a story in pictures* ill. by author. TOON, 2016. ISBN 978-193517994-8 Subj: Animals – monkeys. Character traits – meanness. Format, unusual – graphic novels. Wordless.

Gryphons aren't so great by James Sturm and Andrew Arnold; ill. by authors; photos by Alexis Frederick-Frost. Ill. by authors. First Second, 2015. ISBN 978-159643652-7 Subj: Activities – drawing. Animals – horses, ponies. Format, unusual – graphic novels. Knights. Mythical creatures – griffins, gryphons.

Ogres awake! by James Sturm and Andrew Arnold; ill. by authors; photos by Alexis Frederick-Frost. Ill. by authors. First Second, 2016. ISBN 978-159643653-4 Subj: Activities – drawing. Format, unusual – graphic novels. Knights. Mythical creatures – ogres. Royalty – kings.

Sleepless knight by James Sturm and Andrew Arnold; ill. by authors; photos by Alexis Frederick-Frost. Ill. by authors. First Second, 2015. ISBN 978-159643651-0 Subj: Activities – drawing. Animals. Behavior – lost & found possessions. Camps, camping. Format, unusual – graphic novels. Knights.

Stutson, Caroline. *By the light of the Halloween moon* ill. by Kevin Hawkes. Lothrop, 1993. ISBN

978-0-688-12046-7 Subj: Cumulative tales. Holidays – Halloween. Rhyming text.

Cats' night out ill. by Jon Klassen. Simon & Schuster, 2010. ISBN 978-1-4169-4005-0 Subj: Activities – dancing. Animals – cats. Cities, towns. Night. Rhyming text.

Cowpokes ill. by Daniel San Souci. Lee & Shepard, 1999. ISBN 978-0-688-13974-2 Subj: Cowboys, cowgirls. Rhyming text.

Night train ill. by Katherine Tillotson. Roaring Brook, 2002. ISBN 978-0-7613-1598-8 Subj: Rhyming text. Trains.

Prairie primer A to Z ill. by Susan Condie Lamb. Dutton, 1996. ISBN 978-0-525-45163-1 Subj: ABC books. Family life. Farms. Rhyming text. U.S. history – frontier & pioneer life.

Stuve-Bodeen, Stephanie. *Elizabeti's doll* ill. by Christy Hale. Lee & Low, 1998. ISBN 978-1-880000-70-0 Subj: Emotions – love. Foreign lands – Tanzania. Imagination. Rocks. Toys – dolls.

Elizabeti's school ill. by Christy Hale. Lee & Low, 2002. ISBN 978-1-58430-043-4 Subj: Family life. Foreign lands – Tanzania. School – first day.

Mama Elizabeti ill. by Christy Hale. Lee & Low, 2000. ISBN 978-1-58430-002-1 Subj: Babies, toddlers. Family life – brothers. Family life – new sibling. Foreign lands – Tanzania.

A small brown dog with a wet pink nose ill. by Linzie Hunter. Little, Brown, 2010. ISBN 978-0-316-05830-8 Subj: Animals – dogs. Behavior – resourcefulness. Pets.

We'll paint the octopus red ill. by Pam DeVito. Woodbine, 1998. ISBN 978-1-890627-06-5 Subj: Disabilities – Down syndrome. Family life – brothers & sisters.

Subramaniam, Manasi, reteller. *The fox and the crow* ill. by Culpeo Fox. Karadi Tales, 2014. ISBN 978-818190303-7 Subj: Animals – foxes. Behavior – trickery. Birds – crows. Folk & fairy tales.

Suen, Anastasia. *Air show* ill. by Cecco Mariniello. Henry Holt, 2001. ISBN 978-0-8050-4952-7 Subj: Airplanes, airports.

Baby born ill. by Chih-wei Chang. Lee & Low, 1998. ISBN 978-1-880000-68-7 Subj: Babies, toddlers. Behavior – growing up. Rhyming text.

Delivery ill. by Wade Zahares. Viking, 1999. ISBN 978-0-670-88455-1 Subj: Rhyming text. Transportation.

Man on the moon ill. by Benrei Huang. Viking, 1997. ISBN 978-0-670-87393-7 Subj: Moon. Space & space ships. U.S. history.

Raise the roof ill. by Elwood H. Smith. Viking, 2003. ISBN 978-0-670-89282-2 Subj: Buildings.

Careers – construction workers. Family life. Homes, houses. Rhyming text.

Red light, green light ill. by Ken Wilson-Max. Harcourt, 2005. ISBN 978-0-15-202582-3 Subj: Automobiles. Rhyming text. Traffic, traffic signs. Transportation. Trucks.

Road work ahead ill. by Jannie Ho. Penguin, 2011. ISBN 978-0-670-01288-6 Subj: Activities – traveling. Rhyming text. Roads.

Subway ill. by Karen Katz. Viking, 2004. ISBN 978-0-670-03622-6 Subj: Rhyming text. Trains. Transportation.

Up! up! up! skyscraper ill. by Ryan O'Rourke. Charlesbridge, 2017. ISBN 978-158089710-5 Subj: Buildings. Careers – construction workers. Machines.

Window music ill. by Wade Zahares. Viking, 1998. ISBN 978-0-670-87287-9 Subj: Activities – trading. Family life – mothers. Rhyming text. Trains.

Sugarman, Brynn Olenberg. *Rebecca's journey home* ill. by Michelle Shapiro. Lerner, 2006. ISBN 978-1-58013-157-5 Subj: Adoption. Family life. Foreign lands – Vietnam. Jewish culture.

Sullivan, Deirdre. *Ming goes to school* ill. by Maja Löfdahl. Sky Pony, 2016. ISBN 978-151070050-5 Subj: Activities – playing. Character traits – bravery. Ethnic groups in the U.S. – Asian Americans. School.

Sullivan, Kathy. *To the stars! : the first American woman to walk in space* (Van Vleet, Carmella)

Sullivan, Mary. *Ball* ill. by author. Houghton Mifflin, 2013. ISBN 978-0-547-75936-4 Subj: Activities – playing. Animals – dogs. Toys – balls.

Frankie ill. by author. Houghton Mifflin Harcourt, 2017. ISBN 978-054461113-9 Subj: Animals – dogs. Behavior – sharing.

Treat ill. by author. Houghton Mifflin Harcourt, 2016. ISBN 978-054447270-9 Subj: Animals – dogs. Food.

Sullivan, Paula. *Todd's box* ill. by Nadine Bernard Westcott. Harcourt, 2004. ISBN 978-0-15-205093-1 Subj: Activities – walking. Behavior – collecting things. Family life – mothers. Family life – sons.

Sullivan, Sarah. *Dear Baby: letters from your big brother* ill. by Paul Meisel. Candlewick, 2005. ISBN 978-0-7636-2126-1 Subj: Babies, toddlers. Family life – brothers & sisters. Letters, cards.

Once upon a baby brother ill. by Tricia Tusa. Farrar, 2010. ISBN 978-0-374-34635-5 Subj: Activities – storytelling. Activities – writing. Family life – new sibling. Sibling rivalry.

Sullivan, Tom. *Blue vs. Yellow* ill. by author. HarperCollins, 2017. ISBN 978-006245295-5 Subj: Concepts – color. Contests.

I used to be a fish ill. by author. HarperCollins/Balzer+Bray, 2016. ISBN 978-006245198-9 Subj: Evolution.

Summers, Kate. *Milly and Tilly: the story of a town mouse and a country mouse* (Aesop)

Milly's wedding ill. by Maggie Kneen. Dutton, 1999. ISBN 978-0-525-46046-6 Subj: Animals – mice. Emotions – love. Weddings.

Summers, Susan. *The fourth wise man* ill. by Jackie Morris. Based on the story by Henry Van Dyke. Dial, 1998. ISBN 978-0-8037-2312-2 Subj: Religion – Nativity.

The sun, the moon, and the stars ill. by Nancy Elizabeth Wallace. Houghton, 2003. ISBN 978-0-618-26353-0 Subj: Moon. Poetry. Stars. Sun.

Sunami, Kitoba. *How the fisherman tricked the genie* ill. by Amiko Hirao. Atheneum, 2002. ISBN 978-0-689-83399-1 Subj: Behavior – trickery. Careers – fishermen. Emotions – anger. Folk & fairy tales. Mythical creatures – genies.

Sundgaard, Arnold. *The lamb and the butterfly* ill. by Eric Carle. Watts, 1988. ISBN 978-0-531-08379-6 Subj: Animals – sheep. Character traits – freedom. Insects – butterflies, caterpillars.

Supree, Burton. *"Mother, mother I feel sick"* (Charlip, Remy)

Surat, Michele Maria. *Angel child, dragon child* ill. by Vo-Dinh Mai. Raintree, 1983. ISBN 978-0-940742-12-3 Subj: Ethnic groups in the U.S. – Vietnamese Americans. School.

Surovec, Yasmine. *I see Kitty* ill. by author. Roaring Brook, 2013. ISBN 978-1-59643-862-0 Subj: Animals – cats. Imagination.

Surplice, Holly. *Guinea pig party* ill. by author. Candlewick, 2012. ISBN 978-0-7636-6269-1 Subj: Animals – guinea pigs. Counting, numbers. Parties. Rhyming text.

Peek-a-boo Bunny ill. by author. HarperCollins, 2014. ISBN 978-006224265-5 Subj: Animals. Animals – rabbits. Behavior – hiding. Games. Rhyming text.

Sussman, Joni Kibort. *My first Yiddish word book* ill. by Pépi Marzel. Lerner, 2009. ISBN 978-0-8225-8755-2 Subj: Jewish culture. Language.

Sutherland, Marc. *MacMurtrey's wall* ill. by author. Abrams, 2001. ISBN 978-0-8109-4494-7 Subj: Communities, neighborhoods. Sea & seashore. Weather – storms.

Sutton, Benn. *Hedgehug: a sharp lesson in love.* HarperCollins, 2011. ISBN 978-0-06-196101-4 Subj: Animals – hedgehogs. Holidays – Valentine's Day. Hugging.

Sutton, Jane. *Don't call me Sidney* ill. by Renata Gallio. Penguin, 2010. ISBN 978-0-8037-2753-3 Subj: Activities – writing. Animals. Animals – pigs. Names.

The trouble with cauliflower ill. by Jim Harris. Penguin, 2006. ISBN 978-0-8037-2707-6 Subj: Animals – koalas. Character traits – luck. Food. Friendship. Superstition.

Sutton, Sally. *Construction* ill. by Brian Lovelock. Candlewick, 2014. ISBN 978-076367325-3 Subj: Careers – construction workers. Libraries. Machines.

Demolition ill. by Brian Lovelock. Candlewick, 2012. ISBN 978-0-7636-5830-4 Subj: Careers – construction workers. Machines. Trucks.

Roadwork ill. by Brian Lovelock. Candlewick, 2008. ISBN 978-0-7636-3912-9 Subj: Careers – construction workers. Roads. Trucks.

Suzuki, David. *Salmon forest* by David Suzuki and Sarah Ellis ill. by Sheena Lott. Greystone, 2003. ISBN 978-1-55054-937-9 Subj: Ecology. Fish. Nature.

Swaim, Jessica. *The hound from the pound* ill. by Jill McElmurry. Candlewick, 2007. ISBN 978-0-7636-2330-2 Subj: Animals – dogs. Emotions – loneliness. Pets. Rhyming text.

Swain, Gwenyth. *I wonder as I wander* ill. by Ronald Himler. Eerdmans, 2003. ISBN 978-0-8028-5214-4 Subj: Careers – clergy. Careers – composers. Religion. Songs. U.S. history.

Johnny Appleseed ill. by Janice Lee Porter. Carolrhoda, 2001. ISBN 978-1-57505-519-0 Subj: Activities – traveling. Gardens, gardening. Tall tales. Trees. U.S. history – frontier & pioneer life.

Riding to Washington ill. by David Geister. Sleeping Bear, 2008. ISBN 978-1-58536-324-7 Subj: Ethnic groups in the U.S. – African Americans. U.S. history.

Swain, Ruth Freeman. *How sweet it is (and was)* ill. by John O'Brien. Holiday, 2003. ISBN 978-0-8234-1712-4 Subj: Food.

Underwear: what we wear under there ill. by John O'Brien. Holiday, 2008. ISBN 978-0-8234-1920-3 Subj: Clothing – underwear.

Swallow, Pamela Curtis. *Groundhog gets a say* ill. by Denise Brunkus. Penguin, 2005. ISBN 978-0-399-23876-5 Subj: Animals – groundhogs. Holidays – Groundhog Day.

Swamp, Jake. *Giving thanks* ill. by Erwin Printup, Jr. Lee & Low, 1995. ISBN 978-1-880000-15-1 Subj: Ecology. Indians of North America – Mohawk. Nature. Religion.

Swann, Brian. *The house with no door: African riddle-poems* ill. by Ashley Bryan. Harcourt, 1998. ISBN 978-0-15-200805-5 Subj: Folk & fairy tales. Foreign lands – Africa. Poetry. Riddles & jokes.

Swann, Rick. *Our school garden!* ill. by Christy Hale. Readers to Eaters, 2012. ISBN 978-0-9836615-0-4 Subj: Character traits – cooperation. Emotions – loneliness. Gardens, gardening. School.

Swanson, Diane. *The dentist and you* ill. with photos. Firefly, 2002. ISBN 978-1-55037-729-3 Subj: Careers – dentists. Health & fitness. Teeth.

The doctor and you ill. with photos. Firefly, 2001. ISBN 978-1-55037-673-9 Subj: Careers – doctors. Health & fitness.

Headgear that hides and plays ill. by Rose Cowles. Greystone, 2001. ISBN 978-1-55054-819-8 Subj: Anatomy – heads. Animals.

Noses that plow and poke ill. with photos. Greystone, 1999. ISBN 978-1-55054-715-3 Subj: Anatomy – noses. Animals.

Skin that slimes and scares ill. with photos. Greystone, 2001. ISBN 978-1-55054-817-4 Subj: Anatomy – skin. Animals.

Swanson, Matthew. *Babies ruin everything* ill. by Robbi Behr. Imprint, 2016. ISBN 978-125008057-8 Subj: Babies, toddlers. Family life – new sibling.

Everywhere, wonder ill. by Robbi Behr. Imprint, 2017. ISBN 978-125008795-9 Subj: Activities – traveling. Character traits – curiosity. Imagination. World.

Swanson, Susan Marie. *The first thing my mama told me* ill. by Christine Davenier. Harcourt, 2002. ISBN 978-0-15-201075-1 Subj: Birthdays. Family life – mothers. Names. Self-concept.

The house in the night ill. by Beth Krommes. Houghton, 2008. ISBN 978-0-618-86244-3 Subj: Caldecott award books. Homes, houses. Light, lights. Night.

To be like the sun ill. by Margaret Chodos-Irvine. Harcourt, 2008. ISBN 978-0-15-205796-1 Subj: Flowers. Nature. Seeds.

Sweeney, Jacqueline. *What about Bettie?* ill. by Blind Mice Studio; photos by G. K. Hart, et al. Benchmark, 2001. ISBN 978-0-7614-1118-5 Subj: Animals. Birds – ducks. Character traits – being different. Family life – brothers & sisters.

Sweeney, Joan. *Me and my family tree* ill. by Annette Cable. Crown, 1999. ISBN 978-0-517-70966-5 Subj: Family life. Genealogy.

Me and my senses ill. by Annette Cable. Crown, 2003. ISBN 978-0-375-91102-6 Subj: Senses.

Me and the measure of things ill. by Annette Cable. Crown, 2001. ISBN 978-0-375-91101-9 Subj: Concepts – measurement. Concepts – weight.

Me counting time ill. by Annette Cable. Crown, 2000. ISBN 978-0-517-80056-0 Subj: Concepts – measurement. Time.

Suzette and the puppy ill. by Jennifer Heyd Wharton. Barron's, 2000. ISBN 978-0-7641-5294-8 Subj: Animals – dogs. Careers – artists. Foreign lands – France. Parks.

Sweeney, Linda Booth. *When the snow falls* ill. by Jana Christy. Putnam, 2017. ISBN 978-039954720-1 Subj: Cities, towns. Country. Family life. Rhyming text. Weather – snow.

When the wind blows ill. by Jana Christy. Putnam, 2015. ISBN 978-039916015-8 Subj: Family life. Rhyming text. Weather – storms. Weather – wind.

Sweet, Melissa. *Balloons over Broadway: the true story of the puppeteer of Macy's Parade* ill. by author. Harcourt, 2011. ISBN 978-0-547-19945-0 Subj: Parades. Puppets. Toys – balloons.

Carmine: a little more red ill. by author. Houghton, 2005. ISBN 978-0-618-38794-6 Subj: ABC books. Activities – painting. Animals – dogs. Animals – wolves. Concepts – color. Family life – grandmothers. Folk & fairy tales.

Fiddle-i-fee ill. by adapter. Little, 1992. ISBN 978-0-316-82516-0 Subj: Animals. Cumulative tales. Farms. Music. Songs.

Tupelo rides the rails ill. by author. Houghton, 2008. ISBN 978-0-618-71714-9 Subj: Animals – dogs. Character traits – bravery. Homeless.

Sweetland, Nancy Rose. *If I could / Si yo pudiera* ill. by Robert Sweetland. Raven Tree, 2002. ISBN 978-0-9701107-7-0 Subj: Foreign languages. Imagination.

Yelly Kelly ill. by Robert Sweetland. Raven Tree, 2003. ISBN 978-0-9720192-0-0 Subj: Behavior. Etiquette.

Swender, Jennifer. *Count on the subway* (Jacobs, Paul DuBois)

Fire drill (Jacobs, Paul DuBois)

Swenson, Jamie A. *Big rig* ill. by Ned Young. Hyperion/Disney, 2014. ISBN 978-142316330-5 Subj: Tractors. Trucks.

Boom! boom! boom! ill. by David Walker. Farrar, 2013. ISBN 978-0-374-30868-1 Subj: Animals. Bedtime. Rhyming text. Weather – lightning, thunder. Weather – storms.

If you were a dog ill. by Chris Raschka. Farrar, 2014. ISBN 978-037433530-4 Subj: Animals. Imagination.

Swift, Hildegarde Hoyt. *The little red lighthouse and the great gray bridge* by Hildegarde Hoyt Swift and Lynd Ward ill. by Lynd Ward. Harcourt, 1942. Subj: Boats, ships. Bridges. Lighthouses.

Swinburne, Stephen R. *Armadillo trail* ill. by Bruce Hiscock. Boyds Mills, 2009. ISBN 978-1-59078-463-1 Subj: Animals – armadillos.

Guess whose shadow? ill. by author. Boyds Mills, 1999. ISBN 978-1-56397-724-4 Subj: Activities – photographing. Light, lights. Shadows.

Lots and lots of zebra stripes photos by Stephen R Swinburne. Boyds Mills, 1998. ISBN 978-1-56397-707-7 Subj: Animals. Concepts – color. Concepts – patterns. Disguises. Nature.

Safe, warm, and snug ill. by José Aruego and Ariane Dewey. Harcourt, 1999. ISBN 978-0-15-201734-7 Subj: Animals. Animals – babies. Family life – parents.

Swallows in the birdhouse ill. by Robin Brickman. Millbrook, 1996. ISBN 978-1-56294-182-6 Subj: Activities – making things. Birds – swallows. Homes, houses.

Turtle tide: the ways of sea turtles ill. by Bruce Hiscock. Boyds Mills, 2005. ISBN 978-1-59078-081-7 Subj: Reptiles – turtles, tortoises.

Water for one, water for everyone ill. by Melinda Levine. Millbrook, 1998. ISBN 978-0-7613-0269-8 Subj: Animals. Counting, numbers. Foreign lands – Africa.

What color is nature? photos by Stephen R Swinburne. Boyds Mills, 2002. ISBN 978-1-56397-967-5 Subj: Concepts – color. Nature.

What's a pair? What's a dozen? ill. by author. Boyds Mills, 2000. ISBN 978-1-56397-827-2 Subj: Concepts. Counting, numbers.

What's opposite? ill. by author. Boyds Mills, 2000. ISBN 978-1-56397-881-4 Subj: Concepts – opposites.

Whose shoes? a shoe for every job ill. by author. Boyds Mills, 2010. ISBN 978-1-59078-569-0 Subj: Careers. Clothing – shoes.

Swope, Sam. *Gotta go! Gotta go!* ill. by Sue Riddle. Farrar, 2000. ISBN 978-0-374-32757-6 Subj: Foreign lands – Mexico. Insects – butterflies, caterpillars. Migration.

Sykes, Julie. *Careful, Santa* ill. by Tim Warnes. Tiger Tales, 2002. ISBN 978-1-58925-023-9 Subj: Accidents. Animals. Holidays – Christmas. Santa Claus.

Dora's chicks ill. by Jane Chapman. Tiger Tales, 2002. ISBN 978-1-58925-015-4 Subj: Animals. Behavior – lost. Birds – chickens, roosters. Counting, numbers.

Dora's eggs ill. by Jane Chapman. Little Tiger, 1997. ISBN 978-1-888444-09-4 Subj: Animals. Birds – chickens, roosters. Birth. Eggs. Farms.

Hurry, Santa! ill. by Tim Warnes. Little Tiger, 1998. ISBN 978-1-888444-37-7 Subj: Behavior – promptness, tardiness. Holidays – Christmas. Santa Claus.

I don't want to take a bath! ill. by Tim Warnes. Little Tiger, 1997. ISBN 978-1-888444-20-9 Subj: Activities – bathing. Animals. Animals – tigers. Behavior – running away. Family life – mothers.

Little Rocket's special star ill. by Jack Tickle. Dutton, 2000. ISBN 978-0-525-46494-5 Subj: Astronomy. Birthdays. Science. Stars.

Little Tiger's big surprise ill. by Tim Warnes. Little Tiger, 1999. ISBN 978-1-888444-52-0 Subj: Animals – tigers. Emotions – anger. Emotions – envy, jealousy. Family life – new sibling.

Smudge ill. by Jane Chapman. Little Tiger, 1998. ISBN 978-1-888444-44-5 Subj: Animals. Animals – dogs. Weather – rain.

This and that ill. by Tanya Linch. Farrar, 1996. ISBN 978-0-374-37492-1 Subj: Animals – cats. Birth. Farms.

Wait for me, Little Tiger ill. by Tim Warnes. Tiger Tales, 2001. ISBN 978-1-58925-009-3 Subj: Activities – playing. Animals – tigers. Family life – brothers & sisters. Jungle.

Sylver, Adrienne. *Hot diggity dog: the history of the hot dog* ill. by Elwood H. Smith. Penguin, 2010. ISBN 978-0-525-47897-3 Subj: Activities – baking, cooking. Food.

Sylvester, Kevin. *Splinters* ill. by author. Tundra, 2010. ISBN 978-0-88776-944-3 Subj: Folk & fairy tales. Sports – hockey.

Symes, Ruth. *Harriet dancing* ill. by Caroline Jayne Church. Scholastic, 2008. ISBN 978-0-545-03204-9 Subj: Activities – dancing. Animals – hedgehogs. Insects – butterflies, caterpillars.

Little Rex, big brother ill. by Sean Julian. Albert Whitman, 2010. ISBN 978-0-8075-4636-9 Subj: Character traits – smallness. Dinosaurs. Family life – brothers.

Symes, Sally. *Yawn* ill. by Nick Sharratt. Candlewick, 2011. ISBN 978-0-7636-5725-3 Subj: Animals. Bedtime.

Szekeres, Cyndy. *I can count 100 bunnies, and so can you!* ill. by author. Scholastic, 1998. ISBN 978-0-

590-38361-5 Subj: Animals – rabbits. Counting, numbers.

The mouse that Jack built ill. by author. Scholastic, 1997. ISBN 978-0-590-69197-0 Subj: Animals – mice. Clothing. Cumulative tales. Seasons – winter.

Toby! ill. by author. Simon & Schuster, 2000. ISBN 978-0-689-82645-0 Subj: Animals – mice. Behavior – boredom.

Toby's please and thank you ill. by author. Simon & Schuster, 2001. ISBN 978-0-689-84275-7 Subj: Animals – mice. Etiquette. Format, unusual – board books. Rhyming text.

Taback, Simms. *I miss you every day* ill. by author. Penguin, 2007. ISBN 978-0-670-06192-1 Subj: Emotions – loneliness. Emotions – love. Letters, cards. Rhyming text.

Joseph had a little overcoat ill. by author. Viking, 1999. ISBN 978-0-670-87855-0 Subj: Caldecott award books. Clothing – coats.

Kibitzers and fools: tales my zayda told me ill. by author. Penguin, 2005. ISBN 978-0-670-05955-3 Subj: Activities – storytelling. Folk & fairy tales. Jewish culture.

Postcards from camp ill. by author. Penguin, 2011. ISBN 978-0-399-23973-3 Subj: Activities – writing. Camps, camping. Format, unusual. Letters, cards.

Simms Taback's city animals ill. by author. Blue Apple, 2009. ISBN 978-1-934706-52-7 Subj: Animals. Cities, towns. Format, unusual – toy & movable books.

Simms Taback's farm animals ill. by author. Blue Apple, 2011. ISBN 978-1-60905-078-8 Subj: Animals. Farms. Format, unusual – toy & movable books.

Simms Taback's safari animals ill. by author. Blue Apple, 2008. ISBN 978-1-934706-19-0 Subj: Animals. Format, unusual – toy & movable books.

Tabby, Abigail. *Baby face* ill. by Dan Yaccarino. HarperCollins, 2001. ISBN 978-0-694-01530-6 Subj: Babies, toddlers. Emotions. Format, unusual – toy & movable books.

Taber, Norman. *Rufus at work* (Taber, Tory)

Taber, Tory. *Rufus at work* by Tory Taber and Norman Taber; ill. by authors. Walker, 2005. ISBN 978-0-8027-8984-6 Subj: Activities – working. Animals – cats.

Tabor, Corey R. *Fox and the jumping contest* ill. by Corey R. Tabor. HarperCollins/Balzer+Bray, 2016. ISBN 978-006239874-1 Subj: Activities – jumping. Animals – foxes. Behavior – cheating. Contests. Jumping rope.

Tada, Joni Eareckson. *Forever friends* by Joni Eareckson Tada and Melody Carlson ill. by Melody Carlson. Crossway, 2000. ISBN 978-1-58134-216-1 Subj: Friendship. Toys. Toys – dolls.

The incredible discovery of Lindsey Renee ill. by Irena Roman. Crossway, 2001. ISBN 978-1-58134-195-9 Subj: Character traits – generosity. Money. Religion.

Tada, Satoshi. *Mr. Beetle* ill. by author. Carolrhoda, 2001. ISBN 978-1-57505-561-9 Subj: Character traits – kindness to animals. Friendship. Insects – beetles.

Tafolla, Carmen. *Baby Coyote and the old woman / El coyotito y la viejita* ill. by Matt Novak. New ed. designed & ed. by Bryce Milligan. Wings, 2000. ISBN 978-0-930324-48-3 Subj: Animals – babies. Animals – coyotes. Ecology. Foreign languages. Format, unusual – board books. Old age.

Fiesta babies ill. by Amy Córdova. Tricycle, 2010. ISBN 978-1-58246-319-3 Subj: Babies, toddlers. Ethnic groups in the U.S. – Mexican Americans. Fairs, festivals. Rhyming text.

What can you do with a paleta? ill. by Magaly Morales. Tricycle, 2009. ISBN 978-1-58246-221-9 Subj: Cities, towns. Ethnic groups in the U.S. – Mexican Americans. Food.

What can you do with a rebozo? ill. by Amy Córdova. Ten Speed, 2007. ISBN 978-1-58246-220-2 Subj: Clothing. Ethnic groups in the U.S. – Mexican Americans. Foreign lands – Mexico.

Tafuri, Nancy. *All kinds of kisses* ill. by author. Little, Brown, 2012. ISBN 978-0-316-12235-1 Subj: Animals. Family life – mothers. Kissing.

The ball bounced ill. by author. Greenwillow, 1989. ISBN 978-0-688-07871-3 Subj: Babies, toddlers. Toys – balls.

The barn party ill. by author. Greenwillow, 1995. ISBN 978-0-688-04617-0 Subj: Animals. Barns. Birthdays. Parties.

The big storm: a very soggy counting book ill. by author. Simon & Schuster, 2009. ISBN 978-1-4169-6795-8 Subj: Animals. Counting, numbers. Weather – storms.

Blue goose ill. by author. Simon & Schuster, 2008. ISBN 978-1-4169-2834-8 Subj: Activities – painting. Concepts – color. Farms.

The brass ring ill. by author. Greenwillow, 1996. ISBN 978-0-688-14169-1 Subj: Activities – vacationing. Concepts – shape. Concepts – size.

The busy little squirrel ill. by author. Simon & Schuster, 2007. ISBN 978-0-689-87341-6 Subj: Animals – squirrels. Seasons – fall.

Counting to Christmas ill. by author. Scholastic, 1998. ISBN 978-0-590-27143-1 Subj: Activities – making things. Animals. Counting, numbers. Holidays – Christmas.

Daddy hugs ill. by author. Little, Brown, 2014. ISBN 978-031622923-4 Subj: Animals. Family life – fathers. Hugging.

Do not disturb ill. by author. Greenwillow, 1987. ISBN 978-0-688-06542-3 Subj: Activities. Animals. Camps, camping. Family life. Night. Noise, sounds. Wordless.

The donkey's Christmas song ill. by author. Scholastic, 2002. ISBN 978-0-439-27313-8 Subj: Animals. Animals – donkeys. Holidays – Christmas. Noise, sounds. Religion – Nativity.

Early morning in the barn ill. by author. Greenwillow, 1983. ISBN 978-0-688-02329-4 Subj: Farms. Morning. Wordless.

Five little chicks ill. by author. Simon & Schuster, 2006. ISBN 978-0-689-87342-3 Subj: Animals – babies. Birds – chickens, roosters.

Follow me! ill. by author. Greenwillow, 1990. ISBN 978-0-688-08774-6 Subj: Animals – sea lions. Crustaceans – crabs.

Goodnight, my duckling ill. by author. Scholastic, 2005. ISBN 978-0-439-39881-7 Subj: Bedtime. Behavior – lost. Birds – ducks.

Have you seen my duckling? ill. by author. Greenwillow, 1984. ISBN 978-0-688-02798-8 Subj: Birds – ducks. Caldecott award honor books. Character traits – individuality.

I love you, little one ill. by author. Scholastic, 1997. ISBN 978-0-590-92159-6 Subj: Animals. Animals – babies. Emotions – love. Family life – mothers.

Junglewalk ill. by author. Greenwillow, 1988. ISBN 978-0-688-07183-7 Subj: Animals. Dreams. Imagination. Jungle. Wordless.

Mama's little bears ill. by author. Scholastic, 2002. ISBN 978-0-439-27311-4 Subj: Animals – bears. Family life – mothers.

Rabbit's morning ill. by author. Greenwillow, 1985. ISBN 978-0-688-04064-2 Subj: Animals. Animals – rabbits. Wordless.

Silly little goose! ill. by author. Scholastic, 2001. ISBN 978-0-439-06304-3 Subj: Animals. Birds – geese. Clothing – hats. Homes, houses.

Snowy flowy blowy ill. by author. Scholastic, 1999. ISBN 978-0-590-18973-6 Subj: Days of the week, months of the year. Rhyming text. Seasons.

This is the farmer ill. by author. Greenwillow, 1994. ISBN 978-0-688-09469-0 Subj: Animals. Careers – farmers. Cumulative tales. Farms.

What the sun sees / What the moon sees ill. by author. Greenwillow, 1997. ISBN 978-0-688-14493-7 Subj: Bedtime. Dreams. Format, unusual. Moon. Nature. Night. Sun.

Where did Bunny go? ill. by author. Scholastic, 2001. ISBN 978-0-439-16959-2 Subj: Animals – rabbits. Behavior – hiding. Birds. Friendship. Games.

Where we sleep ill. by author. Greenwillow, 1987. ISBN 978-0-688-07189-9 Subj: Animals. Format, unusual – board books. Sleep.

Who's counting? ill. by author. Greenwillow, 1986. ISBN 978-0-688-06131-9 Subj: Animals. Animals – dogs. Counting, numbers. Farms.

Whose chick are you? ill. by author. HarperCollins, 2007. ISBN 978-0-06-082515-7 Subj: Birds. Birds – swans. Eggs. Family life – mothers.

Will you be my friend? ill. by author. Scholastic, 2000. ISBN 978-0-590-63782-4 Subj: Animals – rabbits. Birds. Friendship. Weather – storms.

Tagholm, Sally. *The frog* ill. by Bert Kitchen. Kingfisher, 2000. ISBN 978-0-7534-5215-8 Subj: Frogs & toads. Science.

Taibah, Nadia Jameel. *How many donkeys? an Arabic counting tale* (MacDonald, Margaret Read)

Takabayashi, Mari. *I live in Brooklyn* ill. by author. Houghton, 2004. ISBN 978-0-618-30899-6 Subj: Cities, towns. Family life. Seasons.

I live in Tokyo ill. by author. Houghton, 2001. ISBN 978-0-618-07702-1 Subj: Cities, towns. Family life. Foreign lands – Japan.

Talbott, Hudson. *From wolf to woof: the story of dogs* ill. by author. Penguin/Nancy Paulsen, 2016. ISBN 978-039925404-8 Subj: Animals – dogs. Animals – wolves.

It's all about me-ow: a young cat's guide to the good life ill. by author. Penguin, 2012. ISBN 978-0-399-25403-1 Subj: Animals – babies. Animals – cats. Pets.

Tallec, Olivier. *Who done it?* ill. by author. Chronicle, 2015. ISBN 978-145214198-5 Subj: Picture puzzles.

Who what where? ill. by author. Chronicle, 2016. ISBN 978-145215693-4 Subj: Character traits – questioning. Picture puzzles.

Tamaki, Mariko. *This one summer* ill. by Jillian Tamaki. First Second, 2014. ISBN 978-162672094-7 Subj: Caldecott award honor books. Format, unusual – graphic novels.

Tamar, Erika. *The garden of happiness* ill. by Barbara Lambase. Harcourt, 1996. ISBN 978-0-15-230582-6 Subj: Activities – painting. Cities, towns. Communities, neighborhoods. Flowers. Gardens, gardening.

Tan, Amy. *The Chinese Siamese cat* ill. by Gretchen Schields. Macmillan, 1994. ISBN 978-0-02-788835-5 Subj: Animals – cats. Foreign lands – China.

The moon lady ill. by Gretchen Schields. Macmillan, 1992. ISBN 978-0-02-788830-0 Subj: Behavior – wishing. Family life – grandmothers. Folk & fairy tales. Foreign lands – China. Moon.

Tanaka, Shinsuke. *Wings* ill. by author. Purple Bear, 2006. ISBN 978-1-933327-19-8 Subj: Anatomy – wings. Animals – dogs. Imagination. Wordless.

Tang, Greg. *Math appeal* ill. by Harry Briggs. Scholastic, 2003. ISBN 978-0-439-21046-1 Subj: Counting, numbers. Rhyming text.

Math fables: lessons that count ill. by Heather Cahoon. Scholastic, 2004. ISBN 978-0-439-45399-8 Subj: Counting, numbers. Rhyming text.

Math fables too: making science count ill. by Taia Morley. Scholastic, 2007. ISBN 978-0-439-78351-4 Subj: Animals. Counting, numbers. Rhyming text. Science.

Tankard, Jeremy. *Boo hoo Bird* ill. by author. Scholastic, 2009. ISBN 978-0-545-06570-2 Subj: Animals. Birds. Illness.

Grumpy Bird ill. by author. Scholastic, 2007. ISBN 978-0-439-85147-3 Subj: Animals. Behavior – bad day, bad mood. Birds. Emotions.

Hungry Bird ill. by author. Scholastic, 2016. ISBN 978-054586417-6 Subj: Behavior – sharing. Birds. Food.

Me hungry! ill. by author. Candlewick, 2008. ISBN 978-0-7636-3360-8 Subj: Animals. Food. Humorous stories. Prehistory. Sports – hunting.

Tanner, Suzy-Jane. *Tinyflock Nursery School* ill. by author. HarperCollins, 2004. ISBN 978-0-06-055723-2 Subj: Animals – babies. Animals – sheep. School – first day. School – nursery.

Tapahonso, Luci. *Navajo ABC* by Luci Tapahonso and Eleanor Schick ill. by Eleanor Schick. Macmillan, 1995. ISBN 978-0-689-80316-1 Subj: ABC books. Indians of North America – Navajo. Language.

Tarbescu, Edith. *Annushka's voyage* ill. by Lydia Dabcovich. Clarion, 1998. ISBN 978-0-395-64366-2 Subj: Ethnic groups in the U.S. – Russian Americans. Family life – fathers. Family life – sisters. Immigrants, immigration. Jewish culture. Religion.

The boy who stuck out his tongue: a Yiddish folk tale ill. by Judith Christine Mills. Barefoot, 2000. ISBN 978-1-84148-067-1 Subj: Character traits – stubbornness. Folk & fairy tales. Jewish culture.

Tarlow, Ellen. *Pinwheel days* ill. by Gretel Parker. Star Bright, 2007. ISBN 978-1-59572-059-7 Subj: Animals. Animals – donkeys. Friendship.

Tarpley, Natasha Anastasia. *Bippity Bop barbershop* ill. by E. B. Lewis. Little, 2002. ISBN 978-0-316-52284-7 Subj: Careers – barbers. Ethnic groups in the U.S. – African Americans. Family life – fathers. Family life – sons. Hair.

I love my hair! ill. by E. B. Lewis. Little, 1997. ISBN 978-0-316-52275-5 Subj: Ethnic groups in the U.S. – African Americans. Family life – mothers. Hair.

Joe-Joe's first flight ill. by E. B. Lewis. Knopf, 2003. ISBN 978-0-375-91053-1 Subj: Activities – flying. Careers – airplane pilots. Ethnic groups in the U.S. – African Americans. Imagination. Moon. Prejudice.

Tarpley, Todd. *Beep! beep! go to sleep!* ill. by John Rocco. Little, Brown, 2015. ISBN 978-031625443-4 Subj: Bedtime. Rhyming text. Robots.

How about a kiss for me? ill. by Liza Woodruff. Penguin, 2010. ISBN 978-0-525-42235-8 Subj: Kissing. Rhyming text.

My grandma's a ninja ill. by Danny Chatzikonstantinou. NorthSouth, 2015. ISBN 978-073584199-4 Subj: Character traits – being different. Character traits – individuality. Family life – grandmothers. Sports – martial arts.

Ten tiny toes ill. by Marc Brown. Little, Brown, 2012. ISBN 978-0-316-12921-3 Subj: Anatomy – toes. Babies, toddlers. Behavior – growing up. Rhyming text.

Tarsky, Sue. *The busy building book* ill. by Alex Ayliffe. Putnam, 1998. ISBN 978-0-399-23137-7 Subj: Buildings.

Tashiro, Chisato. *Five nice mice* adapt. by Kate Westerlund; ill. by author. Minedition, 2007. ISBN 978-0-698-40058-0 Subj: Animals – mice. Frogs & toads. Music.

Tatcheva, Eva. *Witch Zelda's birthday cake* ill. by author. Abrams, 2001. ISBN 978-0-8109-4567-8 Subj: Birthdays. Food. Format, unusual – toy & movable books. Holidays – Halloween. Witches.

Tate, Don. *It jes' happened: when Bill Traylor started to draw* ill. by R. Gregory Christie. Lee & Low, 2012. ISBN 978-1-60060-260-3 Subj: Activities – drawing. Art. Ethnic groups in the U.S. – African Americans. Slavery. U.S. history.

Tatham, Betty. *Baby Sea Otter* ill. by Joan Paley. Henry Holt, 2005. ISBN 978-0-8050-7504-5 Subj: Animals – babies. Animals – otters.

Penguin chick ill. by Helen Davie. HarperCollins, 2002. ISBN 978-0-06-028595-1 Subj: Animals – babies. Birds – penguins.

Taulbert, Clifton L. *Little Cliff and the cold place* ill. by E. B. Lewis. Dial, 2002. ISBN 978-0-8037-2558-4 Subj: Concepts – cold & heat. Foreign lands – Arctic.

Little Cliff and the porch people ill. by E. B. Lewis. Dial, 1999. ISBN 978-0-8037-2175-3 Subj: Communities, neighborhoods. Ethnic groups in the U.S. – African Americans. Family life. Food. Friendship. Magic.

Little Cliff's first day of school ill. by E. B. Lewis. Dial, 2001. ISBN 978-0-8037-2557-7 Subj: Emotions – fear. Ethnic groups in the U.S. – African Americans. Family life – great-grandparents. School – first day.

Tauss, Marc. *Superhero* ill. by author. Scholastic, 2005. ISBN 978-0-439-62734-4 Subj: Cities, towns. Ethnic groups in the U.S. – African Americans. Problem solving. Robots.

Tavares, Matt. *Becoming Babe Ruth* ill. by author. Candlewick, 2013. ISBN 978-0-7636-5646-1 Subj: Behavior – growing up. School. Sports – baseball.

Growing up Pedro ill. by author. Candlewick, 2015. ISBN 978-076366824-2 Subj: Foreign lands – Dominican Republic. Sports – baseball.

Henry Aaron's dream ill. by author. Candlewick, 2010. ISBN 978-0-7636-3224-3 Subj: Ethnic groups in the U.S. – African Americans. Prejudice. Sports – baseball. U.S. history.

Mudball ill. by author. Candlewick, 2005. ISBN 978-0-7636-2387-6 Subj: Sports – baseball.

Oliver's game ill. by author. Candlewick, 2004. ISBN 978-0-7636-1852-0 Subj: Family life – grandfathers. Sports – baseball.

Red and Lulu ill. by author. Candlewick, 2017. ISBN 978-076367733-6 Subj: Birds – cardinals. Holidays – Christmas. Trees.

There goes Ted Williams: the greatest hitter who ever lived ill. by author. Candlewick, 2012. ISBN 978-0-7636-2789-8 Subj: Sports – baseball. U.S. history.

Zachary's ball ill. by author. Candlewick, 2000. ISBN 978-0-7636-0730-2 Subj: Sports – baseball.

Taxali, Gary. *This is silly!* ill. by author. Scholastic, 2010. ISBN 978-0-439-71836-3 Subj: Humorous stories. Rhyming text.

Taylor, Alastair. *Swollobog* ill. by author. Houghton, 2001. ISBN 978-0-618-04348-4 Subj: Animals – dogs. Humorous stories. Toys – balloons.

Taylor, Alice. *A child's treasury of Irish rhymes* ill. by Nicola Emoe. Barefoot, 1999. ISBN 978-1-902283-18-0 Subj: Foreign lands – Ireland. Nursery rhymes.

Taylor, Ann. *Baby dance* ill. by Marjorie van Heerden. HarperCollins, 1999. ISBN 978-0-694-01206-0 Subj: Activities – dancing. Activities – singing. Babies, toddlers. Ethnic groups in the U.S. – African Americans. Family life – fathers. Format, unusual – board books.

Taylor, Barbara. *I wonder why zippers have teeth and other questions about inventions.* Kingfisher, 1995. ISBN 978-1-85697-670-1 Subj: Careers – inventors. Character traits – questioning. Inventions.

Taylor, Eleanor. *Beep, beep, let's go!* ill. by author. Bloomsbury, 2005. ISBN 978-1-58234-973-2 Subj: Animals. Animals – dogs. Sea & seashore.

Taylor, Harriet Peck. *Coyote and the laughing butterflies* ill. by author. Macmillan, 1995. ISBN 978-0-02-788846-1 Subj: Animals – coyotes. Indians of North America. Insects – butterflies, caterpillars. Lakes, ponds.

Secrets of the stone ill. by author. Farrar, 2000. ISBN 978-0-374-36648-3 Subj: Animals. Art. Caves. Indians of North America – Southwest. Petroglyphs.

Ulaq and the northern lights ill. by author. Farrar, 1998. ISBN 978-0-374-38063-2 Subj: Animals. Animals – foxes. Foreign lands – Arctic. Northern lights. Sky.

Taylor, Jane. *Twinkle, twinkle, little star* ill. by Heather Collins. Kids Can, 2000. ISBN 978-1-55074-566-5 Subj: Fairies. Format, unusual – board books. Nursery rhymes. Sky. Songs. Stars.

Twinkle, twinkle, little star ill. by Michael Hague. Morrow, 1992. ISBN 978-0-688-11169-4 Subj: Fairies. Nursery rhymes. Sky. Songs. Stars.

Twinkle, twinkle, little star ill. by Julia Noonan. Scholastic, 1992. ISBN 978-0-590-45566-4 Subj: Holidays – Christmas. Nursery rhymes. Santa Claus. Sky. Songs. Stars.

Twinkle, twinkle, little star ill. by Jerry Pinkney. Little, Brown, 2011. ISBN 978-0-316-05696-0 Subj: Animals – chipmunks. Nursery rhymes. Sky. Songs. Stars.

Taylor, Joanne. *Full moon rising* ill. by Susan Tooke. Tundra, 2002. ISBN 978-0-88776-548-3 Subj: Careers – farmers. Days of the week, months of the year. Moon.

Taylor, Sean. *Boing!* ill. by Bruce Ingman. Candlewick, 2004. ISBN 978-0-7636-2475-0 Subj: Health & fitness. Sports – gymnastics.

A brave bear ill. by Emily Hughes. Candlewick, 2016. ISBN 978-076368224-8 Subj: Animals – bears. Family life – fathers.

Crocodiles are the best animals of all ill. by Hannah Shaw. Frances Lincoln, 2009. ISBN 978-1-84507-904-8 Subj: Animals – donkeys. Behavior – boasting, showing off. Reptiles – alligators, crocodiles. Rhyming text.

The grizzly bear with the frizzly hair ill. by Hannah Shaw. Frances Lincoln, 2011. ISBN 978-1-84780-085-5 Subj: Animals – bears. Animals – rabbits. Behavior – trickery. Character traits – cleverness.

Hoot owl, master of disguise ill. by Jean Jullien. Candlewick, 2015. ISBN 978-076367578-3 Subj: Birds – owls. Disguises.

Huck runs amuck! ill. by Peter H. Reynolds. Penguin, 2011. ISBN 978-0-8037-3261-2 Subj: Animals – goats. Flowers.

I want to be in a scary story ill. by Jean Jullien. Candlewick, 2017. ISBN 978-076368953-7 Subj: Emotions – fear. Monsters.

The ring went zing! a story that ends with a kiss ill. by Jill Barton. Penguin, 2010. ISBN 978-0-8037-3311-4 Subj: Cumulative tales. Humorous stories.

Robomop ill. by Edel Rodriguez. Dial, 2013. ISBN 978-0-8037-3411-1 Subj: Character traits – cleanliness. Humorous stories. Robots.

The snowbear ill. by Claire Alexander. Quarto/words & pictures, 2017. ISBN 978-191027743-0 Subj: Animals – bears. Family life – brothers & sisters. Imagination. Seasons – winter. Snowmen.

When a monster is born ill. by Nick Sharratt. Macmillan, 2007. ISBN 978-1-59643-254-3 Subj: Babies, toddlers. Behavior – growing up. Monsters.

The world champion of staying awake ill. by Jimmy Liao. Candlewick, 2011. ISBN 978-0-7636-4957-9 Subj: Bedtime. Toys.

Taylor, Shirley. *The cross in the egg* ill. by Wendell E. Hall. August House, 1999. ISBN 978-0-87483-549-6 Subj: Animals – rabbits. Eggs. Holidays – Easter. Religion.

Taylor, Theodore. *Hello, Arctic!* ill. by Margaret Chodos-Irvine. Harcourt, 2002. ISBN 978-0-15-201577-0 Subj: Animals. Foreign lands – Arctic. Seasons.

Taylor, Thomas. *Little Mouse and the big cupcake* ill. by Jill Barton. Boxer, 2010. ISBN 978-1-907152-47-4 Subj: Animals – mice. Behavior – sharing. Food.

Taylor-Butler, Christine. *Lamb's Easter surprise* ill. by Cathy Ann Johnson. Sterling, 2012. ISBN 978-1-4027-8622-8 Subj: Animals – sheep. Holidays – Easter. Rhyming text.

Tazewell, Charles. *The littlest angel* ill. by Deborah Lanino. Children's Press, 1998. ISBN 978-0-516-20433-8 Subj: Angels. Gifts. Holidays – Christmas. Religion – Nativity. Stars.

The littlest angel ill. by Paul Micich. Ideals, 1991. ISBN 978-0-8249-8516-5 Subj: Angels. Gifts. Holidays – Christmas. Religion – Nativity. Stars.

The littlest angel ill. by Rebecca Thornburgh. CandyCane, 2002. ISBN 978-0-8249-4224-3 Subj: Angels. Gifts. Holidays – Christmas. Religion – Nativity. Stars.

Tchana, Katrin. *Sense Pass King* ill. by Trina Schart Hyman. Holiday, 2002. ISBN 978-0-8234-1577-9 Subj: Character traits – cleverness. Folk & fairy tales. Foreign lands – Cameroon. Royalty – kings.

Teague, David. *Franklin's big dreams* ill. by Boris Kulikov. Hyperion/Disney, 2010. ISBN 978-1-4231-1919-7 Subj: Bedtime. Dreams. Night.

The red hat ill. by Antoinette Portis. Disney/Hyperion, 2015. ISBN 978-142313411-4 Subj: Character traits – persistence. Friendship. Weather – wind.

Teague, Mark. *Baby tamer* ill. by author. Scholastic, 1997. ISBN 978-0-590-67712-7 Subj: Activities – babysitting. Behavior. Circus. Ethnic groups in the U.S. – African Americans.

Dear Mrs. LaRue ill. by author. Scholastic, 2002. ISBN 978-0-439-20663-1 Subj: Activities – writing. Animals – dogs. Humorous stories. Letters, cards. Pets.

Detective LaRue ill. by author. Scholastic, 2004. ISBN 978-0-439-45868-9 Subj: Activities – writing. Animals – cats. Animals – dogs. Careers – detectives. Letters, cards.

Firehouse! ill. by author. Scholastic, 2010. ISBN 978-0-439-91500-7 Subj: Animals – dogs. Careers – firefighters.

Funny farm ill. by author. Orchard, 2009. ISBN 978-0-439-91499-4 Subj: Animals – dogs. Farms. Humorous stories.

Jack and the beanstalk and the french fries (Jack and the beanstalk)

LaRue across America: postcards from the vacation ill. by author. Scholastic, 2011. ISBN 978-0-439-91502-1 Subj: Activities – vacationing. Activities – writing. Animals – cats. Animals – dogs. Letters, cards.

LaRue for mayor: letters from the campaign trail ill. by author. Blue Sky, 2008. ISBN 978-0-439-78315-6 Subj: Animals – dogs. Character traits – ambition. Letters, cards. Pets.

The lost and found ill. by author. Scholastic, 1998. ISBN 978-0-590-84619-6 Subj: Behavior – lost & found possessions. Imagination. School.

One Halloween night ill. by author. Scholastic, 1999. ISBN 978-0-590-63803-6 Subj: Holidays – Halloween. Magic.

Pigsty ill. by author. Scholastic, 1994. ISBN 978-0-590-45915-0 Subj: Animals – pigs. Character traits – cleanliness. Character traits – orderliness.

The pirate jamboree ill. by author. Scholastic/Orchard, 2016. ISBN 978-054563221-8 Subj: Activities – playing. Imagination. Pirates. Rhyming text.

The secret shortcut ill. by author. Scholastic, 1996. ISBN 978-0-590-67714-1 Subj: Behavior – promptness, tardiness. School.

The sky is falling! ill. by author. Scholastic/Orchard, 2015. ISBN 978-054563217-1 Subj: Activities – dancing. Animals. Behavior – trickery. Birds – chickens, roosters. Folk & fairy tales.

The three little pigs and the somewhat bad wolf ill. by author. Scholastic, 2013. ISBN 978-0-439-91501-4 Subj: Animals – pigs. Animals – wolves. Folk & fairy tales. Friendship.

Tebbs, Victoria. *Noah's Ark story* ill. by Melanie Mitchell. Lion, 2010. ISBN 978-0-7459-4901-7 Subj: Animals. Boats, ships. Religion – Noah. Weather – floods. Weather – rain.

Teckentrup, Britta. *Bee: a peek-through picture book* ill. by author. Doubleday, 2017. ISBN 978-152471526-7 Subj: Format, unusual – toy & movable books. Insects – bees.

Big smelly bear ill. by author. Boxer, 2007. ISBN 978-1-905417-37-7 Subj: Activities – bathing. Animals – bears. Character traits – cleanliness.

Busy bunny days: in the town, on the farm, and at the port ill. by author. Chronicle, 2014. ISBN 978-145211700-3 Subj: Animals. Animals – rabbits. Cities, towns. Family life. Farms.

Get out of my bath! ill. by author. Candlewick/Nosy Crow, 2015. ISBN 978-076368006-0 Subj: Activities – bathing. Animals. Animals – elephants. Format, unusual – toy & movable books.

Grumpy cat ill. by author. Boxer, 2008. ISBN 978-1-905417-69-8 Subj: Animals – cats. Emotions – loneliness.

Little Wolf's song ill. by author. Boxer, 2010. ISBN 978-1-907152-33-7 Subj: Animals – wolves. Behavior – bullying, teasing. Behavior – growing up. Noise, sounds.

The odd one out: a spotting book ill. by author. Candlewick/Big Picture, 2014. ISBN 978-076367127-3 Subj: Animals. Picture puzzles. Rhyming text.

One is not a pair: a spotting book ill. by author. Candlewick/Big Picture, 2017. ISBN 978-076369319-0 Subj: Picture puzzles. Rhyming text.

Tree: a peek-through picture book ill. by author. Doubleday, 2016. ISBN 978-110193242-1 Subj: Format, unusual – toy & movable books. Rhyming text. Seasons. Trees.

Where's the pair? ill. by author. Candlewick, 2015. ISBN 978-076367772-5 Subj: Animals. Picture puzzles. Rhyming text.

Teevin, Toni. *What to do? What to do?* ill. by Janet Pedersen. Houghton, 2006. ISBN 978-0-618-44632-2 Subj: Activities – baking, cooking. Birds. Emotions – loneliness.

Tegen, Katherine Brown. *Dracula and Frankenstein are friends* ill. by Doug Cushman. HarperCollins, 2003. ISBN 978-0-06-000116-2 Subj: Friendship. Holidays – Halloween. Monsters. Parties.

Pink cupcake magic ill. by Kristin Varner. Henry Holt, 2014. ISBN 978-080509611-8 Subj: Activities – baking, cooking. Food. Magic.

Snowman magic ill. by Brandon Dorman. HarperCollins, 2012. ISBN 978-0-06-201445-0 Subj: Magic. Seasons – winter. Snowmen. Weather – snow.

The story of the Easter Bunny ill. by Sally Anne Lambert. HarperCollins, 2005. ISBN 978-0-06-050712-1 Subj: Animals – rabbits. Holidays – Easter.

The story of the leprechaun ill. by Sally Anne Lambert. HarperCollins, 2011. ISBN 978-0-06-143086-2 Subj: Careers – shoemakers. Mythical creatures – leprechauns.

Tekavec, Heather. *Manners are not for monkeys* ill. by David Huyck. Kids Can, 2016. ISBN 978-177138051-5 Subj: Animals – monkeys. Etiquette. Zoos.

Telchin, Eric. *The Black and White Factory* ill. by Diego Funck. little bee, 2016. ISBN 978-149980277-1 Subj: Animals – pandas. Animals – zebras. Behavior – messy. Birds – penguins. Concepts – color.

Tellis, Annabel. *If my dad were a dog* ill. by author; photos by Tracy Morgan. Scholastic, 2007. ISBN

978-0-439-91387-4 Subj: Animals – dogs. Family life – fathers. Humorous stories. Rhyming text.

Temple, Charles A. *Train* ill. by Larry Johnson. Houghton, 1996. ISBN 978-0-395-69826-6 Subj: Ethnic groups in the U.S. – African Americans. Rhyming text. Trains. Transportation.

Temple, Frances. *Tiger soup* ill. by author. Orchard, 1994. ISBN 978-0-531-08709-1 Subj: Animals – monkeys. Animals – tigers. Behavior – trickery. Folk & fairy tales. Foreign lands – Jamaica. Spiders.

ten Cate, Marijke. *The very best door of all* (Linders, Clara)

Terasaki, Stanley Todd. *Ghosts for breakfast* ill. by Shelly Shinjo. Lee & Low, 2002. ISBN 978-1-58430-046-5 Subj: Ethnic groups in the U.S. – Japanese Americans. Farms. Ghosts. Humorous stories.

Terry, Michael. *Rhino's horns* ill. by author. Bloomsbury, 2001. ISBN 978-0-7475-5051-8 Subj: Animals. Animals – rhinoceros. Self-concept.

Tessler, Manya. *Yuki's ride home* ill. by author. Bloomsbury, 2008. ISBN 978-1-59990-023-0 Subj: Character traits – bravery. Emotions – fear. Family life – grandmothers. Sports – bicycling.

Teyssèdre, Fabienne. *Joseph wants to read* ill. by author. Dutton, 2001. ISBN 978-0-525-46692-5 Subj: ABC books. Animals. Animals – monkeys. Careers – teachers. Jungle. School.

Thach, James Otis. *A child's guide to common household monsters* ill. by David Udovic. Boyds Mills, 2007. ISBN 978-1-932425-58-1 Subj: Emotions – fear. Monsters. Rhyming text.

Thaler, Mike. *Pig Little* ill. by Paige Miglio. Henry Holt, 2006. ISBN 978-0-8050-6977-8 Subj: Animals – pigs. Sea & seashore – beaches.

Thayer, Ernest Lawrence. *Casey at the bat* ill. by Gerald Fitzgerald. Atheneum, 1995. ISBN 978-0-689-31945-7 Subj: Poetry. Sports – baseball.

Casey at the bat: a ballad of the Republic, sung in the year 1888 ill. by Christopher Bing. Handprint, 2000. ISBN 978-1-929766-00-0 Subj: Caldecott award honor books. Poetry. Sports – baseball.

Casey at the bat: a ballad of the Republic, sung in the year 1888 ill. by Patricia Polacco. Putnam, 1988. ISBN 978-0-399-21585-8 Subj: Poetry. Sports – baseball.

Thayer, Jane. *Part-time dog* ill. by Lisa McCue. HarperCollins, 2004. ISBN 978-0-06-029692-6 Subj: Animals – dogs. Behavior – sharing. Char-

acter traits – kindness to animals. Communities, neighborhoods.

The popcorn dragon ill. by Lisa McCue. Morrow, 1989. ISBN 978-0-688-08876-7 Subj: Dragons. Food. Friendship.

The puppy who wanted a boy ill. by Lisa McCue. Morrow, 1986. ISBN 978-0-688-05945-3 Subj: Animals – dogs. Holidays – Christmas.

Thermes, Jennifer. *Sam Bennett's new shoes* ill. by author. Carolrhoda, 2006. ISBN 978-1-57505-822-1 Subj: Behavior – growing up. Clothing – shoes. Family life. Farms. U.S. history.

When I was built ill. by author. Henry Holt, 2001. ISBN 978-0-8050-6532-9 Subj: Family life. Homes, houses.

Thiele, Bob. *What a wonderful world* (Weiss, George)

What a wonderful world (Weiss, George)

Thien, Madeleine. *The Chinese violin* ill. by Joe Chang. Whitecap, 2001. ISBN 978-1-55285-205-7 Subj: Foreign lands – Canada. Music. Musical instruments – violins.

Thiesing, Lisa. *Me and you: a mother-daughter album* ill. by author. Hyperion, 1998. ISBN 978-0-7868-2338-3 Subj: Family life – daughters. Family life – mothers.

Thimmesh, Catherine. *Friends: true stories of extraordinary animal friendships.* Harcourt, 2011. ISBN 978-0-547-39010-9 Subj: Animals. Friendship.

This little light of mine ill. by E. B. Lewis. Simon & Schuster, 2005. ISBN 978-0-689-83179-9 Subj: Ethnic groups in the U.S. – African Americans. Songs.

Thisdale, François. *Nini* ill. by author. Tundra, 2011. ISBN 978-1-77049-270-7 Subj: Adoption. Foreign lands – China.

Thomas, Eliza. *The red blanket* ill. by Joe Cepeda. Scholastic, 2004. ISBN 978-0-439-32253-9 Subj: Adoption. Emotions – love. Ethnic groups in the U.S. – Chinese Americans. Family life – single-parent families.

Thomas, Frances. *One day, Daddy* ill. by Ross Collins. Hyperion, 2001. ISBN 978-0-7868-0732-1 Subj: Careers – explorers. Family life – parents. Monsters. Space & space ships.

Thomas, Jan. *A birthday for Cow!* ill. by author. Harcourt, 2008. ISBN 978-0-15-206072-5 Subj: Animals. Animals – bulls, cows. Birthdays. Food. Friendship.

Can you make a scary face? ill. by author. Simon & Schuster, 2009. ISBN 978-1-4169-8581-5 Subj: Frogs & toads. Imagination. Insects – ladybugs.

The doghouse ill. by author. Harcourt, 2008. ISBN 978-0-15-206533-1 Subj: Animals. Animals – dogs. Emotions – fear.

The Easter Bunny's assistant ill. by author. Harper-Collins, 2012. ISBN 978-0-06-169286-4 Subj: Animals – rabbits. Eggs. Holidays – Easter.

Here comes the big, mean dust bunny! ill. by author. Simon & Schuster, 2009. ISBN 978-1-4169-9150-2 Subj: Activities – playing. Animals – cats. Humorous stories. Rhyming text.

Is everyone ready for fun? ill. by author. Simon & Schuster, 2011. ISBN 978-1-4424-2364-1 Subj: Animals – bulls, cows. Birds – chickens, roosters. Humorous stories.

Is that wise, Pig? ill. by author. Simon & Schuster, 2016. ISBN 978-141698582-2 Subj: Activities – baking, cooking. Animals. Animals – pigs. Counting, numbers. Humorous stories.

Let's sing a lullaby with the Brave Cowboy ill. by author. Simon & Schuster, 2012. ISBN 978-1-4424-4276-4 Subj: Bedtime. Cowboys, cowgirls. Emotions – fear. Lullabies.

Pumpkin trouble ill. by author. HarperCollins, 2011. ISBN 978-0-06-169284-0 Subj: Animals – mice. Animals – pigs. Birds – ducks. Holidays – Halloween.

Rhyming dust bunnies ill. by author. Atheneum, 2009. ISBN 978-1-4169-7976-0 Subj: Humorous stories. Rhyming text.

Thomas, Jane Resh. *Celebration!* ill. by Raúl Colón. Hyperion, 1997. ISBN 978-0-7868-2160-0 Subj: Activities – picnicking. Ethnic groups in the U.S. – African Americans. Family life. Holidays – Fourth of July.

Lights on the river ill. by Michael Dooling. Hyperion, 1994. ISBN 978-0-7868-2003-0 Subj: Careers – migrant workers. Emotions. Ethnic groups in the U.S. – Mexican Americans. Family life. Farms. Poverty.

Saying good-bye to grandma ill. by Marcia Sewall. Clarion, 1988. ISBN 978-0-89919-645-9 Subj: Death. Emotions – grief. Family life – grandmothers.

Scaredy dog ill. by Marilyn Mets. Hyperion, 1996. ISBN 978-0-7868-0278-4 Subj: Animals – dogs. Character traits – kindness to animals. Character traits – perseverance. Family life – mothers. Pets.

Thomas, Joan G. *If Jesus came to my house* ill. by Lori McElrath-Eslick. HarperCollins, 2008. ISBN 978-0-06-083942-0 Subj: Behavior. Character traits. Religion.

Thomas, Joyce Carol. *The blacker the berry: poems* ill. by Floyd Cooper. HarperCollins, 2008. ISBN 978-0-06-025375-2 Subj: Ethnic groups in the U.S. – African Americans. Poetry.

Brown honey in broomwheat tea ill. by Floyd Cooper. HarperCollins, 1993. ISBN 978-0-06-021088-5 Subj: Ethnic groups in the U.S. – African Americans. Poetry.

Cherish me ill. by Nneka Bennett. HarperCollins, 1998. ISBN 978-0-694-01097-4 Subj: Character traits – individuality. Ethnic groups in the U.S. – African Americans. Poetry.

Crowning glory ill. by Brenda Joysmith. Cotler, 2002. ISBN 978-0-06-023474-4 Subj: Ethnic groups in the U.S. – African Americans. Family life. Hair. Poetry.

Gingerbread days ill. by Floyd Cooper. HarperCollins, 1995. ISBN 978-0-06-023472-0 Subj: Days of the week, months of the year. Ethnic groups in the U.S. – African Americans. Folk & fairy tales. Poetry.

The gospel Cinderella ill. by David Diaz. Amistad, 2004. ISBN 978-0-06-025388-2 Subj: Ethnic groups in the U.S. – African Americans. Family life – stepfamilies. Folk & fairy tales. Music. Swamps.

In the land of milk and honey ill. by Floyd Cooper. Amistad, 2012. ISBN 978-0-06-025383-7 Subj: Activities – traveling. Ethnic groups in the U.S. – African Americans. Trains. U.S. history.

Joy ill. by Pamela Johnson. Hyperion, 2001. ISBN 978-0-7868-0750-5 Subj: Emotions – happiness. Ethnic groups in the U.S. – African Americans. Family life – mothers. Family life – sons. Format, unusual – board books.

Shouting ill. by Annie Lee. Hyperion, 2007. ISBN 978-0-7868-0664-5 Subj: Activities – dancing. Religion.

You are my perfect baby ill. by Nneka Bennett. HarperCollins, 1999. ISBN 978-0-694-01096-7 Subj: Babies, toddlers. Ethnic groups in the U.S. – African Americans. Family life – new sibling.

Thomas, Louis. *Hug it out!* ill. by author. Farrar, 2017. ISBN 978-037430314-3 Subj: Behavior – fighting, arguing. Family life – brothers & sisters. Hugging.

Thomas, Naturi. *Uh-oh! It's Mama's birthday!* ill. by Keinyo White. Albert Whitman, 1997. ISBN 978-0-8075-8268-8 Subj: Birthdays. Ethnic groups in the U.S. – African Americans. Family life – mothers. Gifts.

Thomas, Pat. *My family's changing* ill. by Lesley Harker. Barron's, 1999. ISBN 978-0-7641-0995-9 Subj: Divorce. Family life.

Why is it so hard to breathe? a first look at asthma ill. by Lesley Harker. Barron's, 2008. ISBN 978-0-7641-3898-0 Subj: Illness – asthma.

Thomas, Patricia. *Firefly mountain* ill. by Peter Sylvada. Peachtree, 2007. ISBN 978-1-56145-360-3 Subj: Insects – fireflies. Night. Seasons – summer.

Red sled ill. by Chris L. Demarest. Boyds Mills, 2008. ISBN 978-1-59078-559-1 Subj: Night. Rhyming text. Seasons – winter. Sports – sledding.

Thomas, Peggy. *Snow dance* ill. by Paul Facklam. Pelican, 2008. ISBN 978-1-58980-478-4 Subj: Activities – dancing. Seasons – winter. Weather – snow.

Thomas, Shelley Moore. *A baby's coming to your house* photos by Eric Futran. Albert Whitman, 2001. ISBN 978-0-8075-0502-1 Subj: Babies, toddlers. Family life – new sibling.

A cold winter's Good Knight ill. by Jennifer Plecas. Dutton, 2008. ISBN 978-0-525-47964-2 Subj: Dragons. Etiquette. Knights. Seasons – winter.

A Good Knight's rest ill. by Jennifer Plecas. Penguin, 2011. ISBN 978-0-525-42195-5 Subj: Activities – vacationing. Dragons. Friendship. Knights.

Good night, Good Knight ill. by Jennifer Plecas. Dutton, 2000. ISBN 978-0-525-46326-9 Subj: Bedtime. Dragons. Knights. Magic. Royalty.

No, no, kitten! ill. by Lori Nichols. Boyds Mills, 2015. ISBN 978-162091631-5 Subj: Activities – playing. Animals – cats.

Putting the world to sleep ill. by Bonnie Christensen. Houghton, 1995. ISBN 978-0-395-71283-2 Subj: Bedtime. Cumulative tales. Night. Rhyming text.

Take care, Good Knight ill. by Paul Meisel. Penguin, 2006. ISBN 978-0-525-47695-5 Subj: Animals – cats. Books, reading. Character traits – helpfulness. Dragons. Knights.

Thomas, Valerie. *Winnie the witch* ill. by Korky Paul. HarperCollins, 2007. ISBN 978-0-06-117312-7 Subj: Animals – cats. Concepts – color. Witches.

Winnie's midnight dragon ill. by Korky Paul. HarperCollins, 2008. ISBN 978-0-06-117314-1 Subj: Animals – cats. Dragons. Magic. Witches.

Thomassie, Tynia. *Cajun through and through* ill. by Andrew Glass. Little, 2000. ISBN 978-0-316-84189-4 Subj: Family life – cousins.

Thompson, Colin. *Falling angels* ill. by author. Hutchinson, 2001. ISBN 978-0-09-176817-1 Subj: Activities – flying. Family life. Family life – grandmothers. Imagination.

Unknown ill. by Anna Pignataro. Walker, 2000. ISBN 978-0-8027-8731-6 Subj: Animals – dogs. Behavior – needing someone. Fire.

Thompson, Emma. *The further tale of Peter Rabbit* ill. by Eleanor Taylor. Warne, 2012. ISBN 978-0-7232-6910-6 Subj: Activities – traveling. Animals – rabbits. Foreign lands – Scotland.

Thompson, Jolene. *Faraway fox* ill. by Justin K Thompson. Houghton Mifflin Harcourt, 2016. ISBN 978-054470711-5 Subj: Animals – foxes. Ecology.

Thompson, Kay. *Here comes Eloise!* (Cheshire, Marc)

Kay Thompson's Eloise ill. by Hilary Knight. 50th anniversary ed. Simon & Schuster, 2005. ISBN 978-0-689-82795-2 Subj: Behavior. Hotels.

Kay Thompson's Eloise at Christmastime ill. by Hilary Knight. Simon & Schuster, 1999. ISBN 978-0-689-83039-6 Subj: Holidays – Christmas. Hotels.

Kay Thompson's Eloise in Moscow ill. by Hilary Knight. 40th anniversary ed. Simon & Schuster, 2000. ISBN 978-0-689-83211-6 Subj: Activities – traveling. Foreign lands – Russia. Hotels.

Kay Thompson's Eloise takes a bawth ill. by Hilary Knight and Mart Crowley. Simon & Schuster, 2002. ISBN 978-0-689-84288-7 Subj: Activities – bathing. Hotels. Parties.

Kay Thompson's Eloise's what I absolutely love love love ill. by Hilary Knight. Simon & Schuster, 2005. ISBN 978-0-689-84965-7 Subj: Emotions – love. Hotels. Self-concept.

Thompson, Lauren. *The apple pie that Papa baked* ill. by Jonathan Bean. Simon & Schuster, 2007. ISBN 978-1-4169-1240-8 Subj: Cumulative tales. Food. Trees.

Ballerina dreams: a true story photos by James Estrin. Feiwel & Friends, 2007. ISBN 978-0-312-37029-9 Subj: Activities – dancing. Ballet. Disabilities – cerebral palsy.

Chew, chew, gulp! ill. by Jarrett J. Krosoczka. Simon & Schuster, 2011. ISBN 978-1-4169-9744-3 Subj: Food. Rhyming text.

The Christmas magic ill. by Jon J Muth. Scholastic, 2009. ISBN 978-0-439-77497-0 Subj: Holidays – Christmas. Magic. Santa Claus.

The forgiveness garden ill. by Christy Hale. Feiwel & Friends, 2012. ISBN 978-0-312-62599-3 Subj: Behavior – forgiving. Emotions – hate. Gardens, gardening. Violence, nonviolence.

Hop, hop, jump! ill. by Jarrett J. Krosoczka. Simon & Schuster, 2012. ISBN 978-1-4169-9745-0 Subj: Health & fitness – exercise. Rhyming text.

How many cats? ill. by Robin Eley. Hyperion, 2009. ISBN 978-1-4231-0801-6 Subj: Animals – cats. Counting, numbers. Rhyming text.

Leap back home to me ill. by Matthew Cordell. Simon & Schuster, 2011. ISBN 978-1-4169-0664-3 Subj: Family life – mothers. Frogs & toads. Rhyming text.

Little Quack ill. by Derek Anderson. Simon & Schuster, 2003. ISBN 978-0-689-84723-3 Subj: Animals – babies. Birds – ducks. Character traits – bravery. Counting, numbers.

Little Quack: dial-a-duck ill. by Derek Anderson. Simon & Schuster, 2006. ISBN 978-1-4169-0932-3 Subj: Birds – ducks. Counting, numbers. Format, unusual – board books. Format, unusual – toy & movable books.

Little Quack's bedtime ill. by Derek Anderson. Simon & Schuster, 2005. ISBN 978-0-689-86894-8 Subj: Bedtime. Birds – ducks. Family life – mothers. Night.

Little Quack's hide and seek ill. by Derek Anderson. Simon & Schuster, 2004. ISBN 978-0-689-85722-5 Subj: Birds – ducks. Counting, numbers. Family life – mothers. Games.

Little Quack's new friend ill. by Derek Anderson. Simon & Schuster, 2006. ISBN 978-0-689-86893-1 Subj: Activities – playing. Birds – ducks. Friendship. Frogs & toads. Lakes, ponds.

Love one another ill. by Elizabeth Uyehara. Scholastic, 2000. ISBN 978-0-590-31830-3 Subj: Holidays – Easter. Religion.

Mouse's first Christmas ill. by Buket Erdogan. Simon & Schuster, 1999. ISBN 978-0-689-82325-1 Subj: Animals – mice. Holidays – Christmas. Santa Claus.

Mouse's first fall ill. by Buket Erdogan. Simon & Schuster, 2006. ISBN 978-0-689-85837-6 Subj: Animals – mice. Seasons – fall.

Mouse's first Halloween ill. by author. Simon & Schuster, 2000. ISBN 978-0-689-83176-8 Subj: Animals – mice. Holidays – Halloween.

Mouse's first snow ill. by Buket Erdogan. Simon & Schuster, 2005. ISBN 978-0-689-85836-9 Subj: Animals – mice. Family life – fathers. Seasons – winter. Weather – snow.

Mouse's first spring ill. by Buket Erdogan. Simon & Schuster, 2005. ISBN 978-0-689-85838-3 Subj: Animals – mice. Family life – mothers. Seasons – spring. Weather – wind.

One riddle, one answer ill. by Linda S. Wingerter. Scholastic, 2001. ISBN 978-0-590-31335-3 Subj: Counting, numbers. Riddles & jokes. Royalty – princesses.

One starry night ill. by Jonathan Bean. Simon & Schuster, 2011. ISBN 978-0-689-82851-5 Subj: Animals. Holidays – Christmas. Religion – Nativity.

Polar bear morning ill. by Stephen Savage. Scholastic, 2013. ISBN 978-0-439-69885-6 Subj: Animals – polar bears. Foreign lands – Arctic. Friendship.

Wee little bunny ill. by John Butler. Simon & Schuster, 2010. ISBN 978-1-4169-7937-1 Subj: Animals – babies. Animals – rabbits.

Wee little chick ill. by John Butler. Simon & Schuster, 2008. ISBN 978-1-4169-3468-4 Subj: Birds – chickens, roosters. Character traits – confidence. Character traits – smallness. Farms. Self-concept.

Wee little lamb ill. by John Butler. Simon & Schuster, 2009. ISBN 978-1-4169-3469-1 Subj: Animals. Animals – mice. Animals – sheep. Character traits – shyness.

Thompson, Laurie Ann. *Emmanuel's dream: the true story of Emmanuel Ofosu Yeboah* ill. by Sean Qualls. Random House, 2015. ISBN 978-044981744-5 Subj: Disabilities – physical disabilities. Foreign lands – Ghana. Prejudice. Sports – bicycling.

My dog is the best ill. by Paul Schmid. Farrar, 2015. ISBN 978-037430051-7 Subj: Animals – dogs.

Thompson, Richard. *The follower* ill. by Martin Springett. Fitzhenry & Whiteside, 2000. ISBN 978-1-55041-532-2 Subj: Cumulative tales. Days of the week, months of the year. Mystery stories. Rhyming text. Witches.

The night walker ill. by Martin Springett. Fitzhenry & Whiteside, 2003. ISBN 978-1-55041-672-5 Subj: Behavior – collecting things. Emotions – fear. Imagination. Night. Noise, sounds.

Thoms, Susan Collins. *Cesar takes a break* ill. by Rogé. Sterling, 2008. ISBN 978-1-4027-3653-7 Subj: Pets. Reptiles – iguanas. School.

Thomson, Bill. *Chalk* ill. by author. Marshall Cavendish, 2010. ISBN 978-0-7614-5526-4 Subj: Activities – drawing. Magic. Wordless.

Fossil ill. by author. Amazon/Two Lions, 2013. ISBN 978-1-4778-4700-8 Subj: Animals – dogs. Fossils. Wordless.

The typewriter ill. by author. Amazon/Two Lions, 2016. ISBN 978-147784975-0 Subj: Activities – playing. Activities – writing. Imagination. Language. Magic. Sea & seashore.

Thomson, Pat. *The squeaky, creaky bed* ill. by Niki Daly. Random House, 2003. ISBN 978-0-385-90856-6 Subj: Animals. Cumulative tales. Family life – grandparents. Furniture – beds. Noise, sounds.

Thomson, Sarah L. *Amazing whales* ill. with photos. HarperCollins, 2005. ISBN 978-0-06-054466-9 Subj: Animals – whales.

Around the neighborhood: a counting lullaby ill. by Jana Christy. Amazon Children's, 2012. ISBN 978-0-7614-6164-7 Subj: Animals. Communities, neighborhoods. Counting, numbers. Lullabies. Nursery rhymes.

Cub's big world ill. by Joe Cepeda. Harcourt, 2013. ISBN 978-0-544-05739-5 Subj: Animals – polar bears. Family life – mothers.

Pirates, ho! ill. by Stephen Gilpin. Marshall Cavendish, 2008. ISBN 978-0-7614-5435-9 Subj: Pirates. Rhyming text.

Quick, Little Monkey! ill. by Lita Judge. Boyds Mills, 2016. ISBN 978-162979100-5 Subj: Animals – monkeys. Family life – fathers. Jungle.

Stars and stripes ill. by Bob Dacey and Debra Bandelin. HarperCollins, 2003. ISBN 978-0-06-050417-5 Subj: U.S. history.

Tigers ill. with photos. HarperCollins, 2004. ISBN 978-0-06-054451-5 Subj: Animals – endangered animals. Animals – tigers.

What Lincoln said ill. by James Ransome. Collins, 2009. ISBN 978-0-06-084820-0 Subj: U.S. history.

Where do polar bears live? ill. by Jason Chin. HarperCollins, 2010. ISBN 978-0-06-157518-1 Subj: Animals – polar bears. Foreign lands – Arctic.

Thong, Roseanne. *Día de los muertos* ill. by Carles Ballesteros. Albert Whitman, 2015. ISBN 978-080751566-2 Subj: Foreign lands – Latin America. Foreign languages. Holidays – Day of the Dead.

Fly free! ill. by Eujin Kim Neilan. Boyds Mills, 2010. ISBN 978-1-59078-550-8 Subj: Birds. Character traits – kindness. Foreign lands – Vietnam. Religion.

Gai see: what you can see in Chinatown ill. by Yangsook Choi. Abrams, 2007. ISBN 978-0-8109-9337-2 Subj: Ethnic groups in the U.S. – Chinese Americans. Rhyming text. Seasons. Stores.

Green is a chile pepper: a book of colors ill. by John Parra. Chronicle, 2014. ISBN 978-145210203-0 Subj: Concepts – color. Ethnic groups in the U.S. – Hispanic Americans. Rhyming text.

Round is a mooncake ill. by Grace Lin. Chronicle, 2000. ISBN 978-0-8118-2676-1 Subj: Concepts – shape. Ethnic groups in the U.S. – Chinese Americans.

Round is a tortilla ill. by John Parra. Chronicle, 2013. ISBN 978-1-4521-0616-8 Subj: Concepts – shape. Ethnic groups in the U.S. – Hispanic Americans. Rhyming text.

Tummy girl ill. by Sam Williams. Henry Holt, 2007. ISBN 978-0-8050-7609-7 Subj: Babies, toddlers. Behavior – growing up. Rhyming text.

'Twas nochebuena ill. by Sara Palacios. Viking, 2014. ISBN 978-067001634-1 Subj: Foreign lands – Latin America. Foreign languages. Holidays – Christmas. Rhyming text.

Wish: wishing traditions around the world ill. by Elisa Kleven. Chronicle, 2008. ISBN 978-0-8118-5716-1 Subj: Behavior – wishing.

Thornhill, Jan. *I am Josephine (and I am a living thing)* ill. by Jacqui Lee. OwlKids, 2016. ISBN 978-177147156-5 Subj: Animals. Character traits – individuality. Science. Self-concept.

Is this Panama? a migration story ill. by Soyeon Kim. OwlKids, 2013. ISBN 978-1-926973-88-3 Subj: Birds. Migration. Nature.

The rumor ill. by reteller. Maple Tree, 2002. ISBN 978-1-894379-39-7 Subj: Animals. Animals – rabbits. Behavior – misunderstanding. Cumulative tales. Emotions – fear. Folk & fairy tales. Foreign lands – India.

Wild in the city ill. by author. Sierra Club, 1996. ISBN 978-0-87156-910-3 Subj: Animals. Animals – cats. Birds. Cities, towns. Ecology. Night.

Winter's coming: a story of seasonal change ill. by Josée Bisaillon. OwlKids, 2014. ISBN 978-177147002-5 Subj: Animals. Animals – rabbits. Seasons – winter.

Thorpe, Kiki. *A comfy, cozy Thanksgiving* ill. by Tom Brannon. Based on the TV series Bear in the Big Blue House. Simon & Schuster, 2002. ISBN 978-0-689-85012-7 Subj: Animals. Animals – bears. Character traits – helpfulness. Holidays – Thanksgiving.

Lots of bots ill. by Ben Butcher. Disney, 2008. ISBN 978-1-4231-1052-1 Subj: Rhyming text. Robots.

Time to cha-cha-cha! ill. by Barry Goldberg. Simon & Schuster, 2000. ISBN 978-0-689-83431-8 Subj: Activities – dancing. Animals. Animals – bears. Musical instruments.

The three bears. *Goatilocks and the three bears* by Erica S. Perl; ill. by Arthur Howard. Simon & Schuster/Beach Lane, 2014. ISBN 978-144240168-6 Subj: Animals – bears. Animals – goats. Folk & fairy tales.

Goldilocks by Ruth Sanderson; ill. by author. Little, Brown, 2009. ISBN 978-0-316-77885-5 Subj: Animals – bears. Folk & fairy tales.

Goldilocks and the three bears retold by Jan Brett; ill. by reteller. Dodd, 1987. ISBN 978-0-396-08925-4 Subj: Animals – bears. Folk & fairy tales.

Goldilocks and the three bears retold by Caralyn Buehner; ill. by Mark Buehner. Penguin, 2007.

ISBN 978-0-8037-2939-1 Subj: Animals – bears. Folk & fairy tales.

Goldilocks and the three bears adapt. by Lorinda Bryan Cauley; ill. by adapter. Putnam, 1981. ISBN 978-0-399-20794-5 Subj: Animals – bears. Folk & fairy tales.

Goldilocks and the three bears by Emma Chichester Clark; ill. by author. Candlewick, 2010. ISBN 978-0-7636-4680-6 Subj: Animals – bears. Folk & fairy tales.

Goldilocks and the three bears retold by Valeri Gorbachev; ill. by reteller. NorthSouth, 2001. ISBN 978-0-7358-1438-7 Subj: Animals – bears. Folk & fairy tales.

Goldilocks and the three bears retold by Steven Guarnaccia; ill. by reteller. Abrams, 2000. ISBN 978-0-8109-4139-7 Subj: Animals – bears. Folk & fairy tales.

Goldilocks and the three bears retold by David McPhail; ill. by reteller. Scholastic, 1995. ISBN 978-0-590-48117-5 Subj: Animals – bears. Folk & fairy tales.

Goldilocks and the three bears adapt. by James Marshall; ill. by adapter. Dial, 1988. ISBN 978-0-8037-0543-2 Subj: Animals – bears. Caldecott award honor books. Folk & fairy tales.

Goldilocks and the three bears retold by Gerda Muller; ill. by reteller. Floris, 2011. ISBN 978-0-86315-795-0 Subj: Animals – bears. Folk & fairy tales.

Goldilocks and the three bears retold by Gennady Spirin; ill. by reteller. Marshall Cavendish, 2009. ISBN 978-0-7614-5596-7 Subj: Animals – bears. Folk & fairy tales.

Goldilocks and the three bears retold by Janet Stevens; ill. by reteller. Holiday, 1985. ISBN 978-0-8234-0608-1 Subj: Animals – bears. Folk & fairy tales.

The three bears adapt. by Byron Barton; ill. by adapter. HarperCollins, 1991. ISBN 978-0-06-020424-2 Subj: Animals – bears. Folk & fairy tales.

The three bears ill. by Paul Galdone. Seabury Pr., 1972. Subj: Animals – bears. Folk & fairy tales.

The 3 bears and Goldilocks by Margaret Willey; ill. by Heather Solomon. Atheneum, 2008. ISBN 978-1-4169-2494-4 Subj: Animals – bears. Behavior – misbehavior. Folk & fairy tales.

The three little pigs. *The three little pigs* retold by Gavin Bishop; ill. by reteller. Scholastic, 1990. ISBN 978-0-590-43358-7 Subj: Animals – pigs. Animals – wolves. Character traits – cleverness. Folk & fairy tales.

The three little pigs ill. by Paul Galdone. Seabury Pr., 1970. Subj: Animals – pigs. Animals – wolves. Character traits – cleverness. Folk & fairy tales.

The three little pigs by Maggie Moore; ill. by Rob Hefferan. Picture Window, 2003. ISBN 978-1-4048-0071-7 Subj: Animals – pigs. Animals – wolves. Character traits – cleverness. Folk & fairy tales.

The three little pigs retold by Steven Kellogg; ill. by reteller. Morrow, 1997. ISBN 978-0-688-08732-6 Subj: Animals – pigs. Animals – wolves. Character traits – cleverness. Family life – mothers. Folk & fairy tales.

The three little pigs retold by David McPhail; ill. by reteller. Scholastic, 1995. ISBN 978-0-590-48118-2 Subj: Animals – pigs. Animals – wolves. Character traits – cleverness. Folk & fairy tales.

The three little pigs retold by James Marshall; ill. by reteller. Dial, 1989. ISBN 978-0-8037-0594-4 Subj: Animals – pigs. Animals – wolves. Character traits – cleverness. Folk & fairy tales.

The three little pigs ill. by Bernadette Watts. NorthSouth, 2012. ISBN 978-0-7358-4058-4 Subj: Animals – pigs. Animals – wolves. Character traits – cleverness. Folk & fairy tales.

The three little pigs ill. by Margot Zemach. Farrar, 1988. ISBN 978-0-374-37527-0 Subj: Animals – pigs. Animals – wolves. Character traits – cleverness. Folk & fairy tales.

The three little pigs / Los tres cerditos adapt. by Merce Escardo i. Bas; ill. by Pere Joan. Chronicle, 2006. ISBN 978-0-8118-5063-6 Subj: Animals – pigs. Animals – wolves. Character traits – cleverness. Folk & fairy tales. Foreign languages.

The three little pigs and the big bad wolf retold by Glen Rounds; ill. by reteller. Holiday, 1992. ISBN 978-0-8234-0923-5 Subj: Animals – pigs. Animals – wolves. Character traits – cleverness. Folk & fairy tales. Rhyming text.

The three little pigs and the fox adapt. by William H. Hooks; ill. by S. D. Schindler. Macmillan, 1989. ISBN 978-0-02-744431-5 Subj: Animals – foxes. Animals – pigs. Birds – chickens, roosters. Character traits – cleverness. Folk & fairy tales.

Thurber, James. *The great Quillow* ill. by Steven Kellogg. Harcourt, 1994. ISBN 978-0-15-232544-2 Subj: Careers – toy makers. Character traits – being different. Character traits – cleverness. Giants. Toys.

Many moons ill. by Marc Simont. Harcourt, 1990. ISBN 978-0-15-251872-1 Subj: Clowns, jesters. Illness. Moon. Royalty – princesses.

Many moons ill. by Louis Slobodkin. Harcourt, 1943. ISBN 978-0-15-251873-8 Subj: Caldecott award books. Clowns, jesters. Illness. Moon. Royalty – princesses.

Thurlby, Paul. *Paul Thurlby's alphabet* ill. by author. Candlewick, 2011. ISBN 978-0-7636-5565-5 Subj: ABC books.

Paul Thurlby's wildlife ill. by author. Candlewick, 2013. ISBN 978-0-7636-6563-0 Subj: Animals.

Thurman, Kathryn K. *A garden for Pig* ill. by Lindsay Ward. Kane/Miller, 2010. ISBN 978-1-935279-24-2 Subj: Animals – pigs. Food. Gardens, gardening.

Thury, Frederick. *The last straw* ill. by Vlasta Van Kampen. Charlesbridge, 1999. ISBN 978-0-88106-152-9 Subj: Animals – camels. Gifts. Holidays – Christmas. Religion – Nativity.

Tibi, Marie. *The bear who didn't want to miss Christmas* ill. by Fabian O Lampert. Book House Scribblers, 2017. ISBN 978-191200685-4 Subj: Animals. Animals – bears. Friendship. Hibernation. Holidays – Christmas.

Tibo, Gilles. *The cowboy kid* ill. by Tom Kapas. Tundra, 2000. ISBN 978-0-88776-473-8 Subj: Activities – flying. Animals – horses, ponies. Cowboys, cowgirls. Homeless. Imagination. Magic.

The grand journey of Mr. Man ill. by Luc Melanson. Dominique & Friends, 2001. ISBN 978-1-894363-78-5 Subj: Activities – traveling. Behavior – needing someone. Death. Emotions – grief. Toys – bears. War.

Tierney, Fiona. *Lion's lunch?* ill. by Margaret Chamberlain. Scholastic, 2010. ISBN 978-0-545-17691-0 Subj: Activities – drawing. Animals – lions. Behavior – bullying, teasing. Jungle.

Tildes, Phyllis Limbacher. *Animals in camouflage* ill. by author. Charlesbridge, 2000. ISBN 978-0-88106-120-8 Subj: Animals. Disguises. Picture puzzles.

Baby's first book of birds and colors ill. by author. Charlesbridge, 2017. ISBN 978-158089742-6 Subj: Birds. Concepts – color. Format, unusual – board books.

Billy's big-boy bed ill. by author. Whispering Coyote, 2002. ISBN 978-1-57091-475-1 Subj: Behavior – growing up. Toys – bears.

Eye guess: a fold-out guessing game ill. by author. Charlesbridge, 2005. ISBN 978-1-57091-650-2 Subj: Animals. Format, unusual – toy & movable books.

Tillman, Nancy. *The crown on your head* ill. by author. Feiwel & Friends, 2011. ISBN 978-0-312-64521-2 Subj: Animals. Character traits – individuality. Rhyming text. Self-concept.

On the night you were born ill. by author. Feiwel & Friends, 2006. ISBN 978-0-312-34606-5 Subj: Birth. Night.

The spirit of Christmas ill. by author. Feiwel & Friends, 2009. ISBN 978-0-312-54965-7 Subj: Holidays – Christmas. Rhyming text.

Tumford the terrible ill. by author. Feiwel & Friends, 2011. ISBN 978-0-312-36840-1 Subj: Animals – cats. Behavior – misbehavior. Rhyming text.

Tumford's rude noises ill. by author. Feiwel & Friends, 2012. ISBN 978-0-312-36841-8 Subj: Animals – cats. Behavior – misbehavior. Etiquette. Noise, sounds. Rhyming text.

Wherever you are: my love will find you ill. by author. Feiwel & Friends, 2010. ISBN 978-0-312-54966-4 Subj: Emotions – love. Rhyming text.

You're all kinds of wonderful ill. by author. Henry Holt, 2017. ISBN 978-125011376-4 Subj: Rhyming text. Self-concept.

You're here for a reason ill. by author. Feiwel & Friends, 2015. ISBN 978-125005626-9 Subj: Character traits – individuality. Rhyming text. Self-concept.

Timmers, Leo. *Bang* ill. by author. Gecko, 2013. ISBN 978-1-877579-18-9 Subj: Accidents. Animals. Transportation.

Crow ill. by author. Clavis, 2010. ISBN 978-1-60537-071-2 Subj: Birds. Birds – crows. Character traits – being different. Self-concept.

Franky ill. by author. Gecko, 2016. ISBN 978-192727193-3 Subj: Activities – making things. Friendship. Imagination. Robots. Space & space ships.

Gus's garage ill. by author. Gecko, 2017. ISBN 978-177657092-8 Subj: Animals. Animals – pigs. Careers – mechanics.

Who is driving? ill. by author. Bloomsbury, 2007. ISBN 978-1-59990-021-6 Subj: Activities – driving. Animals. Automobiles. Trucks.

Tingle, Tim. *When Turtle grew feathers: a folktale from the Choctaw nation* ill. by Stacey Schuett. August House, 2007. ISBN 978-0-87483-777-3 Subj: Animals – rabbits. Behavior – trickery. Folk & fairy tales. Indians of North America – Choctaw. Reptiles – turtles, tortoises. Sports – racing.

Tinkham, Kelly A. *Hair for Mama* ill. by Amy Bates. Penguin, 2007. ISBN 978-0-8037-2955-1 Subj: Emotions – love. Ethnic groups in the U.S. – African Americans. Hair. Illness – cancer.

Tirabosco, Tom. *At the same time* ill. by author. Kane/Miller, 2001. ISBN 978-1-929132-17-1 Subj: Activities. Books, reading.

Titcomb, Gordon. *The last train* ill. by Wendell Minor. Roaring Brook, 2010. ISBN 978-1-59643-164-5 Subj: Music. Songs. Trains.

Titherington, Jeanne. *Baby's boat* ill. by author. Greenwillow, 1992. ISBN 978-0-688-08556-8 Subj: Babies, toddlers. Bedtime. Boats, ships. Lullabies. Sea & seashore.

A place for Ben ill. by author. Greenwillow, 1987. ISBN 978-0-688-06494-5 Subj: Babies, toddlers. Emotions – loneliness. Family life – brothers. Family life – new sibling.

Pumpkin pumpkin ill. by author. Greenwillow, 1985. ISBN 978-0-688-50696-4 Subj: Gardens, gardening. Holidays – Halloween.

Where are you going, Emma? ill. by author. Greenwillow, 1988. ISBN 978-0-688-07082-3 Subj: Behavior – lost. Family life – grandfathers.

Titus, Eve. *Anatole* ill. by Paul Galdone. McGraw-Hill, 1957. Subj: Animals – mice. Caldecott award honor books. Foreign lands – France.

Anatole and the cat ill. by Paul Galdone. McGraw-Hill, 1957. Subj: Animals – cats. Animals – mice. Caldecott award honor books. Character traits – bravery. Foreign lands – France. Problem solving.

Tobias, Tobi. *Wishes for you* ill. by Henri Sorensen. HarperCollins, 2003. ISBN 978-0-688-10839-7 Subj: Behavior – wishing. Family life – parents.

Tobin, Jim. *Sue MacDonald had a book* ill. by Dave Coverly. Henry Holt, 2009. ISBN 978-0-8050-8766-6 Subj: Books, reading. Language. Rhyming text. Songs.

The very inappropriate word ill. by Dave Coverly. Henry Holt, 2013. ISBN 978-0-8050-9474-9 Subj: Behavior – misbehavior. Language. School.

Tobola, Deborah. *The big buck adventure* (Gill, Shelley)

Todd, Barbara. *The rainmaker* ill. by Rogé. Annick, 2003. ISBN 978-1-55037-775-0 Subj: Mythical creatures. Umbrellas. Weather – rain.

Todd, Mark. *Food trucks!* ill. by author. Houghton, 2014. ISBN 978-054415784-2 Subj: Food. Rhyming text. Trucks.

Monster trucks ill. by author. Houghton, 2003. ISBN 978-0-618-18208-4 Subj: Rhyming text. Trucks.

Start your engines ill. by author. Callaway, 2000. ISBN 978-0-935112-48-1 Subj: Animals. Automobiles. Counting, numbers. Sports – racing.

What will you be for Halloween? ill. by author. Houghton, 2001. ISBN 978-0-618-08803-4 Subj: Clothing – costumes. Holidays – Halloween. Monsters. Rhyming text.

Todd, Traci. *T is for tugboat: navigating the seas from A to Z* ill. by Sara Gillingham. Chronicle, 2008.

ISBN 978-0-8118-6094-9 Subj: ABC books. Boats, ships.

Toft, Kim Michelle. *Neptune's nursery* by Kim Michelle Toft and Allan Sheather; ill. by Kim Michelle Toft. Charlesbridge, 2000. ISBN 978-1-57091-391-4 Subj: Animals. Picture puzzles. Rhyming text. Science. Sea & seashore.

One less fish by Kim Michelle Toft and Allan Sheather; ill. by Kim Michelle Toft. Charlesbridge, 1998. ISBN 978-0-88106-322-6 Subj: Counting, numbers. Fish. Picture puzzles. Rhyming text.

The world that we want ill. by author. Charlesbridge, 2005. ISBN 978-1-58089-114-1 Subj: Animals. Ecology. Format, unusual.

Toht, Patricia. *Pick a pine tree* ill. by Peter Jarvis. Candlewick, 2017. ISBN 978-076369571-2 Subj: Holidays – Christmas. Rhyming text. Trees.

Tokuda, Wendy. *Humphrey the lost whale* by Wendy Tokuda and Richard Hall ill. by Hanako Wakiyama. Heian Intl, 1986. ISBN 978-0-89346-270-3 Subj: Animals – whales. Behavior – lost. Behavior – needing someone. Sea & seashore.

Tokuda, Yukihisa. *I'm a pill bug* ill. by Kiyoshi Takahashi. Kane/Miller, 2006. ISBN 978-1-929132-95-9 Subj: Crustaceans.

Tokuda-Hall, Maggie. *Also an octopus* ill. by Benji Davies. Candlewick, 2016. ISBN 978-076367084-9 Subj: Activities – storytelling. Books, reading. Imagination. Octopuses. Space & space ships.

Tokunbo, Dimitrea. *The sound of Kwanzaa* ill. by Lisa Cohen. Scholastic, 2009. ISBN 978-0-545-01865-4 Subj: Ethnic groups in the U.S. – African Americans. Holidays – Kwanzaa.

Tolan, Stephanie S. *Bartholomew's blessing* ill. by Margie Moore. HarperCollins, 2004. ISBN 978-0-06-001198-7 Subj: Angels. Animals – foxes. Animals – mice. Holidays – Christmas. Religion – Nativity.

Tolhurst, Marilyn. *Somebody and the three Blairs* ill. by Simone Abel. Watts, 1991. ISBN 978-0-531-08478-6 Subj: Animals – bears. Folk & fairy tales.

Tolman, Marije. *The tree house* by Marije Tolman and Ronald Tolman; ill. by authors. Boyds Mills, 2010. ISBN 978-1-59078-806-6 Subj: Animals. Homes, houses. Trees. Wordless.

Tolman, Ronald. *The tree house* (Tolman, Marije)

Tolstoy, Aleksey Nikolayevich. *The enormous turnip* ill. by Scott Goto. Harcourt, 2002. ISBN 978-0-15-204585-2 Subj: Animals. Character traits – cooperation. Cumulative tales. Farms. Folk &

fairy tales. Foreign lands – Russia. Plants. Problem solving.

The gigantic turnip by Aleksey Nikolayevich Tolstoy and Niamh Sharkey ill. by Niamh Sharkey. Barefoot, 1999. ISBN 978-1-902283-12-8 Subj: Character traits – cooperation. Cumulative tales. Farms. Folk & fairy tales. Foreign lands – Russia. Plants. Problem solving.

Tom Thumb. *The adventures of Tom Thumb* adapt. by Marianna Mayer; ill. by Kinuko Y. Craft. SeaStar, 2001. ISBN 978-1-58717-065-2 Subj: Folk & fairy tales. Giants. Little people. Royalty – kings. Wizards.

Tom Thumb: a tale adapt. by Lidia Postma; ill. by adapter. Based on a tale by Charles Perrault. Schocken, 1983. ISBN 978-0-8052-3855-6 Subj: Folk & fairy tales. Little people.

Tom Tit Tot. *Tom Tit Tot: an English folk tale* ill. by Evaline Ness. Scribners, 1965. Subj: Caldecott award honor books. Folk & fairy tales. Magic. Names.

Tomecek, Steve. *Dirt* ill. by Nancy Woodman. National Geographic, 2002. ISBN 978-0-7922-8204-4 Subj: Nature. Science.

Stars ill. by Sachiko Yoshikawa. National Geographic, 2003. ISBN 978-0-7922-6955-7 Subj: Astronomy. Stars.

Tomlinson, Jill. *The owl who was afraid of the dark* ill. by Paul Howard. Candlewick, 2000. ISBN 978-0-7636-1562-8 Subj: Animals. Birds – owls. Emotions – fear. Night.

Tomp, Sarah Wones. *Red, white, and blue goodbye* ill. by Ann Barrow. Walker, 2005. ISBN 978-0-8027-8962-4 Subj: Careers – military. Family life – fathers.

Tompert, Ann. *A carol for Christmas* ill. by Laura Kelly. Macmillan, 1994. ISBN 978-0-02-789402-8 Subj: Animals – mice. Foreign lands – Austria. Holidays – Christmas. Songs.

Grandfather Tang's story ill. by Robert Andrew Parker. Crown, 1990. ISBN 978-0-517-57272-6 Subj: Animals – foxes. Family life – grandfathers. Foreign lands – China.

Just a little bit ill. by Lynn Munsinger. Houghton, 1993. ISBN 978-0-395-51527-3 Subj: Activities – playing. Animals – elephants. Animals – mice. Concepts. Cumulative tales.

Little Fox goes to the end of the world ill. by Laura J. Bryant. Marshall Cavendish, 2010. ISBN 978-0-7614-5703-9 Subj: Animals – foxes. Family life – mothers. Imagination.

Nothing sticks like a shadow ill. by Lynn Munsinger. Houghton, 1984. ISBN 978-0-395-35391-2 Subj: Animals – groundhogs. Animals – rabbits. Holidays – Groundhog Day. Shadows.

The pied piper of Peru ill. by Kestutis Kasparavicius. Boyds Mills, 2002. ISBN 978-1-56397-949-1 Subj: Animals – mice. Character traits – kindness to animals. Foreign lands – Peru. Religion.

Saint Nicholas ill. by Michael Garland. Boyds Mills, 2000. ISBN 978-1-56397-844-9 Subj: Folk & fairy tales. Religion. Santa Claus.

Saint Patrick ill. by Michael Garland. Boyds Mills, 1998. ISBN 978-1-56397-659-9 Subj: Foreign lands – Ireland. Religion.

Tonatiuh, Duncan. *Dear Primo: a letter to my cousin* ill. by author. Abrams, 2010. ISBN 978-0-8109-3872-4 Subj: Activities – writing. Ethnic groups in the U.S. – Mexican Americans. Family life – cousins. Foreign lands – Mexico. Letters, cards.

Diego Rivera: his world and ours ill. by author. Abrams, 2011. ISBN 978-0-8109-9731-8 Subj: Art. Careers – artists. Foreign lands – Mexico.

Pancho Rabbit and the coyote: a migrant's tale ill. by author. Abrams, 2013. ISBN 978-1-4197-0583-0 Subj: Activities – traveling. Animals – coyotes. Animals – rabbits. Careers – migrant workers. Family life – fathers.

The princess and the warrior: a tale of two volcanoes ill. by author. Abrams, 2016. ISBN 978-141972130-4 Subj: Character traits – loyalty. Emotions – love. Folk & fairy tales. Indians of North America – Aztec. Royalty – princesses. Volcanoes.

Separate is never equal: Sylvia Mendez and her family's fight for desegregation ill. by author. Abrams, 2014. ISBN 978-141971054-4 Subj: Character traits – bravery. Ethnic groups in the U.S. – Mexican Americans. Prejudice. School. U.S. history.

Tone, Satoe. *The very big carrot* ill. by author. Eerdmans, 2013. ISBN 978-0-8028-5426-1 Subj: Animals – rabbits. Food. Imagination.

Topek, Susan Remick. *Ten good rules* photos by Tod Cohen. Lerner, 2007. ISBN 978-1-58013-209-1 Subj: Religion – Moses.

Torres, Leyla. *Liliana's grandmothers* ill. by author. Farrar, 1998. ISBN 978-0-374-35105-2 Subj: Family life – grandmothers. Foreign lands – Latin America. Quilts.

Saturday sancocho ill. by author. Farrar, 1995. ISBN 978-0-374-36418-2 Subj: Activities – baking, cooking. Activities – trading. Family life – grandmothers. Food. Foreign lands – Colombia.

Torres, Melissa A. *The great Christmas tree celebration* ill. by Barbara Lanza. Scholastic, 2001. ISBN 978-0-439-28200-0 Subj: Format, unusual – toy & movable books. Holidays – Christmas. Trees.

Torrey, Richard. *Ally-Saurus and the first day of school* ill. by author. Sterling, 2015. ISBN 978-145491179-1 Subj: Character traits – willfulness. School – first day.

Almost ill. by author. HarperCollins, 2009. ISBN 978-0-06-156166-5 Subj: Behavior – growing up.

The almost terrible playdate ill. by author. Doubleday, 2016. ISBN 978-055351099-7 Subj: Activities – playing. Character traits – compromising. Imagination.

Because ill. by author. HarperCollins, 2011. ISBN 978-0-06-156173-3 Subj: Behavior.

My dog, Bob ill. by author. Holiday House, 2015. ISBN 978-082343386-5 Subj: Animals – dogs. Humorous stories. Pets.

Why? ill. by author. HarperCollins, 2010. ISBN 978-0-06-156170-2 Subj: Character traits – curiosity. Character traits – questioning.

Tortillas and lullabies / Tortillas y cancioncitas ill. by Corazones Valientes. Greenwillow, 1998. ISBN 978-0-688-14629-0 Subj: Family life. Foreign lands – Central America. Foreign languages.

Toscano, Charles. *Papa's pastries* ill. by Sonja Lamut. Zonderkidz, 2010. ISBN 978-0-310-71602-0 Subj: Behavior – sharing. Character traits – generosity. Character traits – kindness. Food. Poverty.

Toten, Teresa. *Bright red kisses* ill. by Deirdre Betteridge. Annick, 2005. ISBN 978-1-55037-909-9 Subj: Character traits – helpfulness. Family life – mothers.

Tougas, Chris. *Art's supplies* ill. by author. Orca, 2008. ISBN 978-1-55143-920-4 Subj: Art. Humorous stories. Imagination.

Dojo Daycare ill. by author. OwlKids, 2014. ISBN 978-177147057-5 Subj: Behavior – misbehavior. Rhyming text. School – nursery. Sports – martial arts.

Dojo daytrip ill. by author. OwlKids, 2015. ISBN 978-177147142-8 Subj: Farms. Rhyming text. School – field trips. Sports – martial arts.

Dojo surprise ill. by author. OwlKids, 2016. ISBN 978-177147143-5 Subj: Birthdays. Rhyming text. School – nursery. Sports – martial arts.

Tourville, Amanda Doering. *A crocodile grows up* ill. by Michael Denman and William J. Huiett. Picture Window, 2006. ISBN 978-1-4048-3157-5 Subj: Reptiles – alligators, crocodiles.

A giraffe grows up ill. by Michael Denman and William J. Huiett. Picture Window, 2006. ISBN 978-1-4048-3158-2 Subj: Animals – giraffes.

A jaguar grows up ill. by Michael Denman and William J. Huiett. Picture Window, 2006. ISBN 978-1-4048-6159-9 Subj: Animals – jaguars.

Townsend, Emily Rose. *Arctic foxes* ill. with photos. Capstone, 2004. ISBN 978-0-7368-2356-2 Subj: Animals – foxes. Foreign lands – Arctic.

Deer ill. with photos. Capstone, 2004. ISBN 978-0-7368-2067-7 Subj: Animals – deer.

Owls ill. with photos. Capstone, 2004. ISBN 978-0-7368-2068-4 Subj: Birds – owls.

Penguins ill. with photos. Capstone, 2004. ISBN 978-0-7368-2357-9 Subj: Birds – penguins. Foreign lands – Antarctic.

Polar bears ill. with photos. Capstone, 2004. ISBN 978-0-7368-2358-6 Subj: Animals – polar bears. Foreign lands – Arctic.

Seals ill. with photos. Capstone, 2004. ISBN 978-0-7368-2359-3 Subj: Animals – seals. Sea & seashore.

Squirrels ill. with photos. Capstone, 2004. ISBN 978-0-7368-2069-1 Subj: Animals – squirrels.

Woodpeckers ill. with photos. Capstone, 2004. ISBN 978-0-7368-2070-7 Subj: Birds – woodpeckers.

Townsend, Michael. *Cute and cuter* ill. by author. Knopf, 2013. ISBN 978-0-375-85718-8 Subj: Animals – cats. Animals – dogs. Emotions – envy, jealousy. Pets.

Train, Mary. *Time for the fair* ill. by Karel Hayes. Down East, 2005. ISBN 978-0-89272-694-3 Subj: Character traits – patience, impatience. Fairs, festivals. Seasons.

Tramer, Bennett. *Violet and Winston* (Sones, Sonya)

Trapani, Iza. *Baa baa black sheep* by Iza Trapani and Mother Goose; ill. by Iza Trapani. Whispering Coyote, 2001. ISBN 978-1-58089-070-0 Subj: Animals. Animals – sheep. Friendship. Humorous stories. Nursery rhymes.

The bear went over the mountain ill. by author. Sky Pony, 2012. ISBN 978-1-61608-510-0 Subj: Animals – bears. Seasons. Senses. Songs.

Haunted party ill. by author. Charlesbridge, 2009. ISBN 978-1-58089-246-9 Subj: Counting, numbers. Ghosts. Holidays – Halloween. Parties.

Here we go 'round the mulberry bush ill. by author. Charlesbridge, 2006. ISBN 978-1-57091-663-2 Subj: Gardens, gardening. Songs.

How much is that doggie in the window? words & music by Bob Merrill; ill. by author. G. Stevens, 1999. ISBN 978-0-8368-2486-5 Subj: Animals – dogs. Family life. Format, unusual – board books. Pets. Songs.

I'm a little teapot ill. by author. Whispering Coyote, 1996. ISBN 978-1-879085-99-2 Subj: Foreign lands. Imagination. Music. Participation. Songs.

The itsy bitsy spider ill. by author. G. Stevens, 1996. ISBN 978-0-8368-1550-4 Subj: Character traits – persistence. Music. Nursery rhymes. Songs. Spiders.

Jingle bells ill. by author. Charlesbridge, 2005. ISBN 978-1-58089-095-3 Subj: Holidays – Christmas. Music. Songs.

Old King Cole ill. by reteller. Charlesbridge, 2015. ISBN 978-158089632-0 Subj: Nursery rhymes.

Row, row, row your boat ill. by author. Whispering Coyote, 1999. ISBN 978-1-58089-022-9 Subj: Animals. Animals – bears. Boats, ships. Family life. Pets. Rhyming text. Weather – storms.

Rufus and friends: school days ill. by author. Charlesbridge, 2010. ISBN 978-1-58089-248-3 Subj: Nursery rhymes. Picture puzzles.

Shoo fly! ill. by author. Whispering Coyote, 2000. ISBN 978-1-58089-052-6 Subj: Animals – mice. Family life. Insects – flies. Music. Songs.

What am I? ill. by author. Whispering Coyote, 1992. ISBN 978-1-879085-76-3 Subj: Animals. Games. Rhyming text.

Trasler, Janee. *Mimi and Bear in the snow* ill. by author. Farrar, 2014. ISBN 978-037434971-4 Subj: Animals – rabbits. Behavior – lost & found possessions. Seasons – winter. Toys – bears. Weather – snow.

Trenc, Milan. *Another night at the museum* ill. by author. Henry Holt, 2013. ISBN 978-0-8050-8948-6 Subj: Animals. Humorous stories. Museums. Water.

Trent, Shanda. *Farmers' market day* ill. by Jane Dippold. ME Media/Tiger Tales, 2013. ISBN 978-1-58925-115-1 Subj: Careers – farmers. Rhyming text. Shopping. Stores.

Trent, Tereai. *The girl who buried her dreams in a can* ill. by Jan Spivey Gilchrist. Viking, 2015. ISBN 978-067001654-9 Subj: Careers – teachers. Foreign lands – Zimbabwe. Gender roles. School.

Tresselt, Alvin R. *Autumn harvest* ill. by Roger Antoine Duvoisin. Lothrop, 1951. ISBN 978-0-688-51155-5 Subj: Holidays – Thanksgiving. Seasons – fall.

The gift of the tree ill. by Henri Sorensen. Original title: The dead tree. Lothrop, 1992. ISBN 978-0-688-10685-0 Subj: Ecology. Forest, woods. Trees.

Hide and seek fog ill. by Roger Antoine Duvoisin. Lothrop, 1965. ISBN 978-0-688-51169-2 Subj: Caldecott award honor books. Sea & seashore. Weather – fog.

The mitten: an old Ukrainian folktale ill. by Yaroslava. Adapt. from the version by E. Rachev. Lothrop, 1989, ©1964. ISBN 978-0-606-04277-2 Subj: Animals. Folk & fairy tales. Foreign lands – Ukraine.

Rain drop splash ill. by Leonard Weisgard. Lothrop, 1946. ISBN 978-0-688-51165-4 Subj: Caldecott award honor books. Cumulative tales. Science. Weather – rain.

Sun up ill. by Henri Sorensen. Lothrop, 1991. ISBN 978-0-688-08657-2 Subj: Farms. Sun. Weather.

Wake up, farm! ill. by Carolyn Ewing. Lothrop, 1991. ISBN 978-0-688-08655-8 Subj: Animals. Farms. Morning. Noise, sounds.

White snow, bright snow ill. by Roger Antoine Duvoisin. Lothrop, 1988, ©1947. ISBN 978-0-688-51161-6 Subj: Caldecott award books. Weather – snow.

Trewin, Trudie. *I lost my kisses* ill. by Nick Bland. Scholastic, 2008. ISBN 978-0-545-05557-4 Subj: Behavior – lost & found possessions. Family life. Kissing.

Tricarico, Christine. *Cock-a-doodle dance!* ill. by Rich Deas. Feiwel & Friends, 2012. ISBN 978-0-312-38251-3 Subj: Activities – dancing. Animals. Farms.

Trice, Linda. *Kenya's art* ill. by Hazel Mitchell. Charlesbridge, 2016. ISBN 978-157091848-3 Subj: Activities – making things. Art. Ecology. Ethnic groups in the U.S. – African Americans.

Kenya's word ill. by Pamela Johnson. Charlesbridge, 2006. ISBN 978-1-57091-887-2 Subj: Ethnic groups in the U.S. – African Americans. Language.

Trimble, Marcia. *Flower Green* ill. by Jill Dubin. Images, 2002. ISBN 978-1-891577-67-3 Subj: Concepts – color. Flowers. Seasons.

Hello sun ill. by Susan Arciero. Images, 2000. ISBN 978-1-891577-50-5 Subj: Activities – photographing. Activities – traveling. Animals – lions. Foreign lands – Africa.

Moonbeams for Santa ill. by Sid Bingham. Images, 2001. ISBN 978-1-891577-89-5 Subj: Holidays – Christmas. Moon. Rhyming text. Santa Claus.

Peppy's shadow ill. by Will Pellegrini. Images, 2003. ISBN 978-1-891577-70-3 Subj: Animals – dogs. Puppets. Theater.

Trimmer, Christian. *Simon's new bed* ill. by Melissa Van der Paardt. Atheneum, 2015. ISBN 978-148143019-7 Subj: Animals – cats. Animals – dogs. Behavior – sharing. Character traits – compromising.

Tripp, Paul. *Tubby the tuba* ill. by Henry Cole. Penguin, 2006. ISBN 978-0-525-47717-4 Subj: Frogs & toads. Musical instruments – orchestras. Musical instruments – tubas.

Trivizas, Eugenios. *The three little wolves and the big bad pig* ill. by Helen Oxenbury. Margaret K. McElderry, 1993. ISBN 978-0-689-50569-0 Subj: Animals – pigs. Animals – wolves. Behavior – misbehavior. Folk & fairy tales. Homes, houses.

Troll, Ray. *Sharkabet* ill. by author. WestWinds, 2002. ISBN 978-1-55868-518-5 Subj: ABC books. Fish – sharks.

Trollinger, Patsi B. *Perfect timing: how Isaac Murphy became one of the world's greatest jockeys* ill. by Jerome Lagarrigue. Penguin, 2006. ISBN 978-0-670-06083-2 Subj: Animals – horses, ponies. Careers – jockeys. Ethnic groups in the U.S. – African Americans. Sports – racing.

Trotter, Deborah W. *How do you know?* ill. by Julie Downing. Houghton, 2006. ISBN 978-0-618-46343-5 Subj: Emotions – love. Family life – mothers. Weather – fog.

Trottier, Maxine. *A safe place* ill. by Judith Friedman. Albert Whitman, 1997. ISBN 978-0-8075-7212-2 Subj: Child abuse. Family life – fathers. Family life – mothers. Safety.

Troupe, Quincy. *Little Stevie Wonder* ill. by Lisa Cohen. Houghton, 2005. ISBN 978-0-618-34060-6 Subj: Careers – musicians. Disabilities – blindness. Ethnic groups in the U.S. – African Americans. Poetry.

Troyer, Andrea. *Dear Santa, Love Rachel Rosenstein* (Peet, Amanda)

Trukhan, Ekaterina. *Apples for little Fox* ill. by author. Random House, 2017. ISBN 978-039955562-6 Subj: Animals – foxes. Food. Mystery stories. Parties.

Me and my cat ill. by author. Sterling, 2015. ISBN 978-145491612-3 Subj: Animals – cats. Friendship.

Patrick wants a dog! ill. by author. Sterling, 2015. ISBN 978-145491613-0 Subj: Animals – dogs. Pets.

Trumbauer, Lisa. *The great reindeer rebellion* ill. by Jannie Ho. Sterling, 2009. ISBN 978-1-4027-4462-4 Subj: Animals. Animals – reindeer. Holidays – Christmas. Rhyming text. Santa Claus.

Trumbore, Cindy. *Parrots over Puerto Rico* (Roth, Susan L.)

Truss, Lynne. *Eats, shoots and leaves: why, commas really do make a diffeerence!* ill. by Bonnie Timmons.

Penguin, 2006. ISBN 978-0-399-24491-9 Subj: Language.

Tryon, Leslie. *Albert's alphabet* ill. by author. Atheneum, 1991. ISBN 978-0-689-31642-5 Subj: ABC books. Activities – making things. Birds – ducks. School.

Albert's birthday ill. by author. Atheneum, 1999. ISBN 978-0-689-82296-4 Subj: Animals. Birds – ducks. Birthdays. Parties.

Albert's Christmas ill. by author. Atheneum, 1997. ISBN 978-0-689-81034-3 Subj: Animals. Birds – ducks. Holidays – Christmas. Rhyming text. Santa Claus.

Albert's Halloween: the case of the stolen pumpkins ill. by author. Atheneum, 1998. ISBN 978-0-689-81136-4 Subj: Animals. Birds – ducks. Careers – detectives. Holidays – Halloween. Mystery stories.

Albert's play ill. by author. Atheneum, 1992. ISBN 978-0-689-31525-1 Subj: Animals. Rhyming text. Theater.

Patsy says ill. by author. Atheneum, 2001. ISBN 978-0-689-82297-1 Subj: Animals. Animals – pigs. Etiquette. School.

The thumbtack dancer ill. by Jan Spivey Gilchrist. Alazar, 2017. ISBN 978-099777200-5 Subj: Activities – dancing. Character traits – persistence. Ethnic groups in the U.S. – African Americans.

Ts'o, Pauline. *Whispers of the wolf* ill. by author. Wisdom Tales, 2015. ISBN 978-193778645-8 Subj: Animals – wolves. Character traits – kindness to animals. Friendship. Indians of North America – Pueblo.

Tschiegg, Anne-Sophie. *Mommy time* (Brami, Elisbeth)

Tseng, Grace. *White tiger, blue serpent* ill. by Jean Tseng and Mou-Sien Tseng. Lothrop, 1999. ISBN 978-0-688-12516-5 Subj: Activities – weaving. Animals – tigers. Folk & fairy tales. Foreign lands – China. Magic. Reptiles – snakes.

Tsubakiyama, Margaret. *Mei-Mei loves the morning* ill. by Cornelius Van Wright and Ying-Hwa Hu. Albert Whitman, 1999. ISBN 978-0-8075-5039-7 Subj: Family life – grandparents. Foreign lands – China. Health & fitness – exercise.

Tsurumi, Andrea. *Accident!* ill. by author. Houghton Mifflin Harcourt, 2017. ISBN 978-054494480-0 Subj: Accidents. Animals. Behavior – forgiving. Behavior – mistakes. Behavior – running away. Emotions – fear.

Tuck, Justin. *Home-field advantage* ill. by Leonardo Rodriguez. Simon & Schuster, 2011. ISBN 978-1-

4424-0369-7 Subj: Family life – sisters. Hair. Multiple births – twins.

Tucker, Kathy. *Do cowboys ride bikes?* ill. by Nadine Bernard Westcott. Albert Whitman, 1997. ISBN 978-0-8075-1693-5 Subj: Character traits – questioning. Country. Cowboys, cowgirls. Rhyming text.

Do knights take naps? ill. by Nick Sharratt. Albert Whitman, 2000. ISBN 978-0-8075-1695-9 Subj: Knights. Middle Ages. Rhyming text. Sleep.

Do pirates take baths? ill. by Nadine Bernard Westcott. Albert Whitman, 1994. ISBN 978-0-8075-1696-6 Subj: Pirates. Rhyming text. Sea & seashore.

The leprechaun in the basement ill. by John Sandford. Albert Whitman, 1999. ISBN 978-0-8075-4450-1 Subj: Clothing – shoes. Holidays – St. Patrick's Day. Mythical creatures – leprechauns.

The seven Chinese sisters ill. by Grace Lin. Albert Whitman, 2003. ISBN 978-0-8075-7309-9 Subj: Dragons. Family life – sisters. Foreign lands – China.

Tucker, Lindy. *Porkelia: a pig's tale* ill. by author. Charlesbridge, 2011. ISBN 978-1-934133-28-6 Subj: Activities – dancing. Animals – pigs. Character traits – ambition. Rhyming text.

Tudor, Tasha. *The doll's Christmas* ill. by author. Simon & Schuster, 1999. ISBN 978-0-689-82809-6 Subj: Holidays – Christmas. Parties. Toys – dolls.

1 is one ill. by author. Walck, 1956. ISBN 978-0-02-688535-5 Subj: Caldecott award honor books. Counting, numbers.

Pumpkin moonshine ill. by author. Simon & Schuster, 2000. ISBN 978-0-689-82846-1 Subj: Farms. Food. Holidays – Halloween.

A tale for Easter ill. by author. Simon & Schuster, 2001, ©1941. ISBN 978-0-689-82844-7 Subj: Animals. Dreams. Eggs. Holidays – Easter.

Tuell, Todd. *Ninja, ninja, never stop!* ill. by Tad Carpenter. Abrams/Appleseed, 2014. ISBN 978-141971027-8 Subj: Family life. Rhyming text. Sports – martial arts.

Tullet, Herve. *Let's play* ill. by author. Chronicle, 2016. ISBN 978-145215477-0 Subj: Activities – playing. Concepts – color. Imagination. Participation.

The book with a hole. Abrams, 2011. ISBN 978-1-85437-946-7 Subj: Format, unusual. Imagination. Participation.

Help! we need a title! ill. by author. Candlewick, 2014. ISBN 978-076367021-4 Subj: Activities – writing. Books, reading. Careers – writers.

Mix it up! ill. by author. Chronicle, 2014. ISBN 978-145213735-3 Subj: Concepts – color. Format, unusual. Imagination. Participation.

Press here ill. by author. Chronicle, 2011. ISBN 978-0-8118-7954-5 Subj: Format, unusual. Imagination. Participation.

Say zoop! ill. by author. Chronicle, 2017. ISBN 978-145216473-1 Subj: Imagination. Noise, sounds. Participation.

Tulloch, Shirley. *Who made me?* ill. by Cathie Felstead. Augsburg Fortress, 2000. ISBN 978-0-8066-4045-7 Subj: Animals. Foreign lands – Africa. Religion.

Tuma, Refe. *What the dinosaurs did at school* by Refe Tuma and Susan Tuma; ill. by Refe Tuma. Little, Brown, 2017. ISBN 978-031655289-9 Subj: Behavior – messy. Dinosaurs. School.

Tuma, Susan. *What the dinosaurs did at school* (Tuma, Refe)

Tunnell, Michael O. *Halloween pie* ill. by Kevin O'Malley. Lothrop, 1999. ISBN 978-0-688-16805-6 Subj: Food. Holidays. Magic. Monsters. Witches.

The joke's on George ill. by Kathy Osborn. Boyds Mills, 2001. ISBN 978-1-56397-970-5 Subj: Careers – artists. Friendship. Museums.

Mailing May ill. by Ted Rand. Greenwillow, 1997. ISBN 978-0-688-12879-1 Subj: Careers – postal workers. Family life – grandparents. Trains. Transportation. U.S. history.

Tupera, Tupera. *Polar Bear's underwear* ill. by author. Chronicle, 2015. ISBN 978-145214199-2 Subj: Animals – mice. Animals – polar bears. Behavior – lost & found possessions. Clothing – underwear. Format, unusual – toy & movable books.

Tupper Ling, Nancy. *My sister, Alicia May* ill. by Shennen Bersani. Pleasant St, 2009. ISBN 978-0-9792035-9-6 Subj: Disabilities – Down syndrome. Family life – sisters.

The story I'll tell ill. by Jessica Lanan. Lee & Low, 2015. ISBN 978-162014160-1 Subj: Adoption. Emotions – love. Family life – mothers. Foreign lands. Imagination.

Turhan, Sedat. *Monkey business: fun with idioms* (Hambleton, Laura)

Turk, Evan. *The storyteller* ill. by author. Atheneum, 2016. ISBN 978-148143518-5 Subj: Activities – storytelling. Foreign lands – Morocco. Mythical creatures – genies. Water. Weather – droughts.

Turkle, Brinton. *Deep in the forest* ill. by author. Dutton, 1976. ISBN 978-0-525-28617-2 Subj: Animals – bears. Folk & fairy tales. Wordless.

Do not open ill. by author. Dutton, 1981. ISBN 978-0-525-28785-8 Subj: Animals – cats. Behavior – trickery. Behavior – wishing. Monsters. Sea & seashore.

Thy friend, Obadiah ill. by author. Viking, 1969. ISBN 978-0-670-71229-8 Subj: Birds – seagulls. Caldecott award honor books. Character traits – kindness to animals. Ethnic groups in the U.S. – Amish. Seasons – winter. U.S. history.

Turnbull, Victoria. *Kings of the castle* ill. by author. Candlewick/Templar, 2017. ISBN 978-076369295-7 Subj: Friendship. Monsters. Sea & seashore – beaches.

Pandora ill. by author. Clarion, 2017. ISBN 978-054494733-7 Subj: Animals – foxes. Behavior – needing someone. Birds. Emotions – loneliness. Friendship.

The sea tiger ill. by author. Candlewick/Templar, 2015. ISBN 978-076367986-6 Subj: Animals – tigers. Character traits – shyness. Friendship. Mythical creatures – mermaids, mermen. Sea & seashore.

Turner, Ann Warren. *Abe Lincoln remembers* ill. by Wendell Minor. HarperCollins, 2001. ISBN 978-0-06-027578-5 Subj: Memories, memory. U.S. history.

Angel hide and seek ill. by Lois Ehlert. HarperCollins, 1998. ISBN 978-0-06-027086-5 Subj: Angels. Picture puzzles. Religion. Rhyming text.

The Christmas house ill. by Nancy Edwards Calder. HarperCollins, 1994. ISBN 978-0-06-023429-4 Subj: Family life. Holidays – Christmas. Homes, houses. Poetry.

Dakota dugout ill. by Ronald Himler. Macmillan, 1985. ISBN 978-0-02-789700-5 Subj: Farms. U.S. history – frontier & pioneer life.

In the heart ill. by Salley Mavor. HarperCollins, 2001. ISBN 978-0-06-023731-8 Subj: Day. Poetry.

Nettie's trip south ill. by Ronald Himler. Macmillan, 1987. ISBN 978-0-02-789240-6 Subj: Activities – traveling. Behavior – disbelief. Ethnic groups in the U.S. – African Americans. Family life.

Pumpkin cat ill. by Amy Bates. Hyperion, 2004. ISBN 978-0-7868-0494-8 Subj: Animals – cats. Holidays – Halloween. Libraries.

Secrets from the dollhouse ill. by Raúl Colón. HarperCollins, 2000. ISBN 978-0-06-024567-2 Subj: Poetry. Toys – dolls.

Shaker hearts ill. by Wendell Minor. HarperCollins, 1997. ISBN 978-0-06-025370-7 Subj: Religion. Rhyming text. U.S. history.

Through moon and stars and night skies ill. by James Graham Hale. HarperCollins, 1990. ISBN 978-0-06-026190-0 Subj: Adoption.

When Mr. Jefferson came to Philadelphia ill. by Mark Hess. HarperCollins, 2003. ISBN 978-0-06-027580-8 Subj: U.S. history. War.

Turner, Barbara J. *Out and about at the orchestra* ill. by Anne McMullen. Picture Window, 2003. ISBN 978-1-4048-0040-3 Subj: Careers – musicians. Music. Musical instruments – orchestras.

Turner, Glennette Tilley. *An apple for Harriet Tubman* ill. by Susan Keeter. Albert Whitman, 2006. ISBN 978-0-8075-0395-9 Subj: Ethnic groups in the U.S. – African Americans. Slavery. U.S. history.

Turner, Pamela S. *Hachiko* ill. by Yan Nascimbene. Houghton, 2004. ISBN 978-0-618-14094-7 Subj: Animals – dogs. Death. Foreign lands – Japan. Pets.

Turner, Sandy. *Grow up* ill. by author. Cotler, 2003. ISBN 978-0-06-000954-0 Subj: Behavior – growing up. Careers. Imagination.

Otto's trunk ill. by author. Cotler, 2003. ISBN 978-0-06-000957-1 Subj: Animals – elephants. Concepts – size. Self-concept.

Silent night ill. by author. Atheneum, 2001. ISBN 978-0-689-84156-9 Subj: Animals – dogs. Holidays – Christmas. Noise, sounds. Santa Claus.

Turner-Denstaedt, Melanie. *The hat that wore Clara B.* ill. by Frank Morrison. Farrar, 2009. ISBN 978-0-374-32794-1 Subj: Clothing – hats. Ethnic groups in the U.S. – African Americans. Family life – grandmothers.

Tusa, Tricia. *Bunnies in my head* ill. by author and young patients at the M.D. Anderson Cancer Center in Houston, Texas. Anderson Cancer Center, 1998. ISBN 978-0-9664551-8-2 Subj: Art. Children as illustrators. Illness – cancer. Imagination.

Follow me ill. by author. Harcourt, 2011. ISBN 978-0-547-27201-6 Subj: Activities – swinging. Concepts – color. Imagination.

Stay away from the junkyard! ill. by author. Macmillan, 1988. ISBN 978-0-02-789541-4 Subj: Art. Behavior – collecting things.

Tutu, Archbishop Desmond. *Desmond and the very mean word: a story of forgiveness* by Archbishop Desmond Tutu and Douglas Carlton Abrams ill. by A. G. Ford. Candlewick, 2013. ISBN 978-0-7636-5229-6 Subj: Behavior – forgiving. Emotions – anger. Foreign lands – South Africa. Prejudice. Sports – bicycling.

God's dream by Archbishop Desmond Tutu and Douglas Carlton Abrams ill. by LeUyen Pham. Candlewick, 2008. ISBN 978-0-7636-3388-2 Subj: Character traits – generosity. Character traits – helpfulness. Religion.

Let there be light (Bible. Old Testament. Genesis)

Tweet, Jonathan. *Grandmother Fish: a child's first book of evolution* ill. by Karen Lewis. Feiwel & Friends, 2016. ISBN 978-125011323-8 Subj: Animals. Evolution.

The twelve days of Christmas. English folk song.
The twelve days of Christmas ill. by Jan Brett. Dodd, 1986. ISBN 978-0-396-08821-9 Subj: Cumulative tales. Holidays – Christmas. Music. Songs.

The twelve days of Christmas adapt. by Jane Cabrera; ill. by adapter. Holiday House, 2013. ISBN 978-0-8234-2870-0 Subj: Cumulative tales. Holidays – Christmas. Music. Songs.

The twelve days of Christmas ill. by Rachel Griffin. Barefoot, 2015. ISBN 978-1-782-85221-6 Subj: Cumulative tales. Holidays – Christmas. Music. Songs.

Twelve days of Christmas by Rachel Isadora; ill. by author. Penguin, 2010. ISBN 978-0-399-25073-6 Subj: Cumulative tales. Holidays – Christmas. Music. Songs.

The twelve days of Christmas ill. by Laurel Long. Penguin, 2011. ISBN 978-0-8037-3357-2 Subj: Cumulative tales. Holidays – Christmas. Music. Songs.

The 12 days of Christmas Greg Pizzoli; ill. by Greg Pizzoli. Disney/Hyperion, 2017. ISBN 978-148475031-5 Subj: Cumulative tales. Holidays – Christmas. Music. Songs.

The twelve days of Christmas ill. by Emma Randall. Penguin Workshop, 2017. ISBN 978-051515763-5 Subj: Cumulative tales. Holidays – Christmas. Music. Songs.

The twelve days of Christmas ill. by Jane Ray. Candlewick, 2011. ISBN 978-0-7636-5735-2 Subj: Cumulative tales. Holidays – Christmas. Music. Songs.

The twelve days of Christmas by Gennady Spirin; ill. by author. Marshall Cavendish, 2009. ISBN 978-0-7614-5551-6 Subj: Cumulative tales. Holidays – Christmas. Music. Songs.

Twohy, Mike. *Mouse and Hippo* ill. by author. Simon & Schuster, 2017. ISBN 978-148145124-6 Subj: Activities – painting. Animals – hippopotamuses. Animals – mice. Friendship.

Oops, pounce, quick, run! an alphabet caper ill. by author. HarperCollins/Balzer+Bray, 2016. ISBN 978-006237700-5 Subj: ABC books. Animals – dogs. Animals – mice.

Outfoxed ill. by author. Simon & Schuster, 2013. ISBN 978-1-4424-7392-8 Subj: Animals – foxes. Behavior – trickery. Birds – ducks. Character traits – cleverness.

Poindexter makes a friend ill. by author. Simon & Schuster, 2011. ISBN 978-1-4424-0965-1 Subj: Animals – pigs. Books, reading. Character traits – shyness. Friendship. Libraries.

Wake up, Rupert! ill. by author. Simon & Schuster, 2014. ISBN 978-144245998-4 Subj: Animals – sheep. Birds – chickens, roosters. Character traits – responsibility. Farms.

Tyger, Rory. *Newton* ill. by author. Barron's, 2001. ISBN 978-0-7641-5390-7 Subj: Emotions – fear. Noise, sounds. Toys – bears.

Tyler, Anne. *Timothy Tugbottom says no!* ill. by Mitra Modarressi. Penguin, 2005. ISBN 978-0-399-24255-7 Subj: Character traits – stubbornness. Sleepovers.

Tyler, Jenny. *Big Pig on a dig* ill. by author. Usborne, 1999. ISBN 978-1-58086-182-3 Subj: Activities – digging. Animals – pigs. Maps.

Tyler, Michael. *The skin you live in* ill. by David Lee Csicsko. Chicago Children's Museum, 2005. ISBN 978-0-9759580-0-1 Subj: Anatomy – skin. Rhyming text. Self-concept.

Uchida, Yoshiko. *The bracelet* ill. by Joanna Yardley. Philomel, 1993. ISBN 978-0-399-22503-1 Subj: Ethnic groups in the U.S. – Japanese Americans. Friendship. Slavery. U.S. history.

The magic purse ill. by Keiko Narahashi. Margaret K. McElderry, 1993. ISBN 978-0-689-50559-1 Subj: Character traits – bravery. Clothing – handbags, purses. Folk & fairy tales. Foreign lands – Japan.

The two foolish cats ill. by Margot Zemach. Macmillan, 1987. ISBN 978-0-689-50397-9 Subj: Animals – cats. Folk & fairy tales. Food.

The wise old woman ill. by Martin Springett. Margaret K. McElderry, 1994. ISBN 978-0-689-50582-9 Subj: Character traits – wisdom. Folk & fairy tales. Foreign lands – Japan. Old age.

Udry, Janice May. *Let's be enemies* ill. by Maurice Sendak. HarperCollins, 1961. ISBN 978-0-06-026131-3 Subj: Behavior – fighting, arguing. Emotions – hate. Friendship.

The moon jumpers ill. by Maurice Sendak. HarperCollins, 1959. ISBN 978-0-06-026145-0 Subj: Caldecott award honor books. Moon. Twilight.

A tree is nice ill. by Marc Simont. HarperCollins, 1956. ISBN 978-0-06-026156-6 Subj: Caldecott award books. Poetry. Seasons. Trees.

What Mary Jo shared ill. by Eleanor Mill. Albert Whitman, 1966. ISBN 978-0-8075-8842-0 Subj: Character traits – shyness. Ethnic groups in the U.S. Ethnic groups in the U.S. – African Americans. Family life – fathers. School.

Uegaki, Chieri. *Hana Hashimoto, sixth violin* ill. by Qin Leng. Kids Can, 2014. ISBN 978-189478633-1 Subj: Character traits – persistence. Ethnic groups in the U.S. – Japanese Americans. Family life – grandfathers. Musical instruments – violins. Theater.

Suki's kimono ill. by Stéphane Jorisch. Kids Can, 2003. ISBN 978-1-55337-084-0 Subj: Character traits – being different. Clothing – kimonos. Ethnic groups in the U.S. – Japanese Americans. Family life – grandmothers. School – first day.

Uff, Caroline. *Happy birthday, Lulu* ill. by author. Walker, 2000. ISBN 978-0-8027-8751-4 Subj: Birthdays. Gifts. Parties.

Hello, Lulu ill. by author. Walker, 1999. ISBN 978-0-8027-8712-5 Subj: Clothing – shoes. Family life. Friendship. Pets.

Lulu's busy day ill. by author. Walker, 2000. ISBN 978-0-8027-8716-3 Subj: Activities. Family life.

Uhlberg, Myron. *Dad, Jackie, and me* ill. by Colin Bootman. Peachtree, 2005. ISBN 978-1-56145-329-0 Subj: Disabilities – deafness. Ethnic groups in the U.S. – African Americans. Family life – fathers. Sports – baseball.

Lemuel, the fool ill. by Sonja Lamut. Peachtree, 2001. ISBN 978-1-56145-220-0 Subj: Activities – traveling. Character traits – foolishness. Cities, towns. Sports – sailing.

Mad Dog McGraw ill. by Lydia Monks. Putnam, 2000. ISBN 978-0-399-23308-1 Subj: Animals – dogs. Problem solving.

The printer ill. by Henri Sorensen. Peachtree, 2003. ISBN 978-1-56145-483-9 Subj: Disabilities – deafness. Family life – fathers. Fire. Sign language.

The sound of all things ill. by Ted Papoulas. Peachtree, 2016. ISBN 978-156145833-2 Subj: Disabilities – deafness. Noise, sounds.

A storm called Katrina ill. by Colin Bootman. Peachtree, 2011. ISBN 978-1-56145-591-1 Subj: Behavior – lost. Ethnic groups in the U.S. – African Americans. Musical instruments. Weather – floods. Weather – hurricanes.

Ulmer, Wendy. *A isn't for fox: an isn't alphabet* ill. by Laura Knorr. Sleeping Bear, 2008. ISBN 978-1-58536-319-3 Subj: ABC books. Rhyming text.

Umansky, Kaye. *I don't like Gloria!* ill. by Margaret Chamberlain. Candlewick, 2007. ISBN 978-0-7636-3202-1 Subj: Animals – cats. Animals – dogs. Emotions – envy, jealousy. Pets.

Underwood, Deborah. *Bad bye, good bye* ill. by Jonathan Bean. Houghton, 2014. ISBN 978-054792852-4 Subj: Friendship. Moving. Rhyming text.

A balloon for Isabel ill. by Laura Rankin. HarperCollins, 2010. ISBN 978-0-06-177987-9 Subj: Animals – porcupines. Character traits – being different. School.

The Christmas quiet book ill. by Renata Liwska. Houghton Mifflin, 2012. ISBN 978-0-547-55863-9 Subj: Holidays – Christmas. Noise, sounds.

Good night, baddies ill. by Juli Kangas. Simon & Schuster/Beach Lane, 2016. ISBN 978-148140984-1 Subj: Bedtime. Folk & fairy tales.

Here comes Santa Cat ill. by Claudia Rueda. Dial, 2014. ISBN 978-080374100-3 Subj: Animals – cats. Behavior – misbehavior. Character traits – generosity. Gifts. Holidays – Christmas. Santa Claus.

Here comes teacher cat ill. by Claudia Rueda. Dial, 2017. ISBN 978-039953905-3 Subj: Animals – cats. Careers – teachers. School.

Here comes the Easter Cat ill. by Claudia Rueda. Dial, 2014. ISBN 978-080373939-0 Subj: Animals – cats. Holidays – Easter. Humorous stories.

Here comes the Tooth Fairy Cat ill. by Claudia Rueda. Dial, 2015. ISBN 978-052542774-2 Subj: Animals – cats. Animals – mice. Fairies. Teeth.

Here comes Valentine Cat ill. by Claudia Rueda. Dial, 2015. ISBN 978-052542915-9 Subj: Animals – cats. Animals – dogs. Holidays – Valentine's Day.

Interstellar Cinderella ill. by Meg Hunt. Chronicle, 2015. ISBN 978-145212532-9 Subj: Careers – engineers. Family life – stepfamilies. Folk & fairy tales. Rhyming text. Royalty – princes. Space & space ships.

The loud book! ill. by Renata Liwska. Houghton Mifflin, 2011. ISBN 978-0-547-39008-6 Subj: Day. Noise, sounds.

Part-time princess ill. by Cambria Evans. Disney/Hyperion, 2013. ISBN 978-1-4231-2485-6 Subj:

Bedtime. Family life. Imagination. Royalty – princesses.

The quiet book ill. by Renata Liwska. Houghton Mifflin, 2010. ISBN 978-0-547-21567-9 Subj: Animals. Behavior – solitude. Noise, sounds.

Super Saurus saves kindergarten ill. by Ned Young. Disney/Hyperion, 2017. ISBN 978-142317568-1 Subj: Dinosaurs. Imagination. School – first day.

Ungar, Richard. *Rachel captures the moon* ill. by author. Adapt. from a story by Samuel Tenenbaum. Tundra, 2001. ISBN 978-0-88776-505-6 Subj: Folk & fairy tales. Jewish culture. Moon.

Rachel's gift ill. by author. Tundra, 2003. ISBN 978-0-88776-616-9 Subj: Activities – baking, cooking. Character traits – kindness. Holidays – Passover. Jewish culture. Religion.

Rachel's library ill. by author. Tundra, 2004. ISBN 978-0-88776-678-7 Subj: Cities, towns. Foreign lands – Poland. Jewish culture. Libraries.

Yitzi and the giant menorah ill. by author. Tundra, 2016. ISBN 978-177049812-9 Subj: Gifts. Holidays – Hanukkah.

Ungerer, Tomi. *Crictor* ill. by author. HarperCollins, 1958. ISBN 978-0-06-026181-8 Subj: Humorous stories. Reptiles – snakes.

Flix ill. by author. Roberts Rinehart, 1998. ISBN 978-1-57098-161-6 Subj: Animals – cats. Animals – dogs. Prejudice.

Moon man ill. by author. Phaidon, 2009. ISBN 978-0-7148-5598-1 Subj: Moon. Space & space ships.

Otto: the autobiography of a teddy bear ill. by author. Phaidon, 2010. ISBN 978-0-7148-5766-4 Subj: Foreign lands – Germany. Holocaust. Jewish culture. Toys – bears. War.

The three robbers ill. by author. Phaidon, 2008. ISBN 978-0-7148-4877-8 Subj: Crime. Orphans.

Unobagha, Uzoamaka Chinyelu. *Off to the sweet shores of Africa and other talking drum rhymes* ill. by Julia Cairns. Chronicle, 2000. ISBN 978-0-8118-2378-4 Subj: Foreign lands – Africa. Poetry.

Upton, Elizabeth. *Maxi the little taxi* ill. by Henry Cole. Scholastic, 2016. ISBN 978-054579860-0 Subj: Character traits – cleanliness. Rhyming text. Taxis.

Urban, Linda. *Little Red Henry* ill. by Madeline Valentine. Candlewick, 2015. ISBN 978-076366176-2 Subj: Behavior – growing up. Family life. Self-concept.

Mouse was mad ill. by Henry Cole. Harcourt, 2009. ISBN 978-0-15-205337-6 Subj: Animals. Animals – mice. Emotions – anger.

Urbanovic, Jackie. *Duck and cover* ill. by author. HarperCollins, 2009. ISBN 978-0-06-121444-8 Subj: Behavior – running away. Birds – ducks. Pets. Reptiles – alligators, crocodiles.

Duck at the door ill. by author. HarperCollins, 2007. ISBN 978-0-06-121438-7 Subj: Birds – ducks. Character traits – individuality. Pets.

Duck soup ill. by author. HarperCollins, 2008. ISBN 978-0-06-121441-7 Subj: Activities – baking, cooking. Animals. Birds – ducks. Friendship. Humorous stories.

Sitting duck ill. by author. HarperCollins, 2010. ISBN 978-0-06-176583-4 Subj: Activities – babysitting. Animals – dogs. Birds – ducks.

Urbigkit, Cat. *A young shepherd* photos by author. Boyds Mills, 2006. ISBN 978-1-59078-364-1 Subj: Animals – sheep. Careers – ranchers. Careers – shepherds.

Urdahl, Catherine. *Emma's question* ill. by Janine Dawson. Charlesbridge, 2009. ISBN 978-1-58089-145-5 Subj: Behavior – worrying. Family life – grandmothers. Hospitals. Illness. Old age.

Polka-dot fixes kindergarten ill. by Mai S. Kemble. Charlesbridge, 2011. ISBN 978-1-57091-737-0 Subj: Behavior – misbehavior. Character traits – assertiveness. Friendship. School. Self-concept.

U'Ren, Andrea. *Pugdog* ill. by author. Farrar, 2001. ISBN 978-0-374-36149-5 Subj: Animals – dogs. Gender roles.

Uribe, Verónica. *Buzz buzz buzz* ill. by Gloria Calderón. Douglas & McIntyre, 2001. ISBN 978-0-88899-430-1 Subj: Animals. Insects – mosquitoes. Sleep.

Ursone, Adele. *The Christmas tugboat: how the Rockefeller Center Christmas tree came to New York City* (Matteson, George)

Usher, Sam. *Rain* ill. by author. Candlewick/Templar, 2017. ISBN 978-076369296-4 Subj: Character traits – patience, impatience. Family life – grandfathers. Imagination. Weather – rain.

Snow ill. by author. Candlewick, 2015. ISBN 978-076367958-3 Subj: Character traits – patience, impatience. Family life – grandfathers. Imagination. Weather – snow.

Uslander, Arlene. *That's what grandparents are for* ill. by Freddie Levin. Peel Productions, 2002. ISBN 978-0-939217-60-1 Subj: Family life – grandparents. Poetry.

Vaës, Alain. *The princess and the pea* (Andersen, Hans Christian)

Vagin, Vladimir, reteller. *The enormous carrot* ill. by reteller. Scholastic, 1998. ISBN 978-0-590-45491-9 Subj: Animals. Cumulative tales. Farms. Folk & fairy tales. Foreign lands – Russia. Plants. Problem solving.

Here comes the cat by Vladimir Vagin and Frank Asch; ill. by authors. Scholastic, 1989. ISBN 978-0-590-41859-1 Subj: Animals – cats. Animals – mice. Foreign languages.

Vail, Rachel. *Flabbersmashed about you* ill. by Yumi Heo. Feiwel & Friends, 2012. ISBN 978-0-312-61345-7 Subj: Emotions – anger. Emotions – loneliness. Friendship. School.

Jibberwillies at night ill. by Yumi Heo. Scholastic, 2008. ISBN 978-0-439-42070-9 Subj: Bedtime. Emotions – fear.

Over the moon ill. by Scott Nash. Orchard, 1998. ISBN 978-0-531-33068-5 Subj: Animals. Moon. Nursery rhymes. Theater.

Piggy Bunny ill. by Jeremy Tankard. Feiwel & Friends, 2012. ISBN 978-0-312-64988-3 Subj: Animals – pigs. Character traits – individuality. Holidays – Easter. Self-concept.

Righty and Lefty: a tale of two feet ill. by Matthew Cordell. Scholastic, 2007. ISBN 978-0-439-63629-2 Subj: Anatomy – feet. Character traits – cooperation.

Sometimes I'm Bombaloo ill. by Yumi Heo. Scholastic, 2002. ISBN 978-0-439-08755-1 Subj: Emotions – anger. Family life – brothers & sisters.

Vainio, Pirkko. *The best of friends* ill. by author. NorthSouth, 2000. ISBN 978-0-7358-1151-5 Subj: Animals – bears. Animals – rabbits. Friendship.

The Christmas angel ill. by author. NorthSouth, 1995. ISBN 978-1-55858-500-3 Subj: Angels. Holidays – Christmas. Homeless. Music. Poverty.

Who hid the Easter eggs? ill. by author. NorthSouth, 2011. ISBN 978-0-7358-2304-4 Subj: Animals – squirrels. Behavior – hiding things. Eggs. Holidays – Easter.

Valckx, Catharina. *Lizette's green sock* ill. by author. Houghton, 2005. ISBN 978-0-618-45298-9 Subj: Birds. Clothing – socks.

Valdivia, Paloma. *Up above and down below* ill. by author. OwlKids, 2012. ISBN 978-1-926973-39-5 Subj: Character traits – being different. Character traits – individuality. World.

Valentina, Marina. *Lost in the roses* ill. by author. Red Cygnet, 2007. ISBN 978-1-60108-014-1 Subj: Birds – chickens, roosters. Flowers – roses.

Valentine, Madeline. *I want that nut!* ill. by author. Knopf, 2017. ISBN 978-110194037-2 Subj: Animals – chipmunks. Animals – mice. Behavior – fighting, arguing. Behavior – sharing.

Valério, Geraldo. *Turn on the night* ill. by author. Groundwood, 2016. ISBN 978-155498841-9 Subj: Imagination. Night. Wordless.

Vallverdu, Josep. *Aladdin and the magic lamp / Aldino y la lampara maravillosa* ill. by Pep Montserrat. Chronicle, 2006. ISBN 978-0-8118-5061-2 Subj: Folk & fairy tales. Foreign lands – Arabia. Foreign languages. Magic.

Vamos, Samantha R. *Alphabet trains* ill. by Ryan O'Rourke. Charlesbridge, 2015. ISBN 978-158089592-7 Subj: ABC books. Rhyming text. Trains.

Alphabet trucks ill. by Ryan O'Rourke. Charlesbridge, 2013. ISBN 978-1-58089-428-9 Subj: ABC books. Rhyming text. Trucks.

Before you were here, mi amor ill. by Santiago Cohen. Viking, 2009. ISBN 978-0-670-06301-7 Subj: Babies, toddlers. Family life. Foreign languages.

The cazuela that the farm maiden stirred ill. by Rafael López. Charlesbridge, 2011. ISBN 978-1-58089-242-1 Subj: Activities – baking, cooking. Animals. Cumulative tales. Farms. Food. Foreign languages.

Van, Muon. *In a village by the sea* ill. by April Chu. Creston, 2015. ISBN 978-193954715-6 Subj: Careers – fishermen. Family life. Foreign lands – Vietnam. Homes, houses.

Van Allsburg, Chris. *Bad day at Riverbend* ill. by author. Houghton, 1995. ISBN 978-0-395-67347-8 Subj: Activities – drawing. Imagination.

The garden of Abdul Gasazi ill. by author. Houghton, 1979. ISBN 978-0-395-27804-8 Subj: Animals – dogs. Behavior – misbehavior. Caldecott award honor books. Imagination. Magic.

Jumanji ill. by author. Houghton, 1981. ISBN 978-0-395-30448-8 Subj: Caldecott award books. Games. Imagination. Jungle.

The misadventures of Sweetie Pie ill. by author. Harcourt, 2014. ISBN 978-054731582-9 Subj: Animals – hamsters. Character traits – kindness to animals. Pets.

The mysteries of Harris Burdick ill. by author. Houghton, 1984. ISBN 978-0-395-35393-6 Subj: Imagination.

The polar express ill. by author. Houghton, 1985. ISBN 978-0-395-38949-2 Subj: Caldecott award books. Holidays – Christmas. Imagination. Night. Santa Claus. Trains.

Probuditi! ill. by author. Houghton, 2006. ISBN 978-0-618-75502-8 Subj: Imagination. Magic.

Queen of the falls ill. by author. Harcourt, 2011. ISBN 978-0-547-31581-2 Subj: Character traits – bravery. Character traits – persistence. U.S. history.

The stranger ill. by author. Houghton, 1986. ISBN 978-0-395-42331-8 Subj: Behavior – forgetfulness. Country. Seasons – fall.

Two bad ants ill. by author. Houghton, 1988. ISBN 978-0-395-48668-9 Subj: Homes, houses. Insects – ants.

The widow's broom ill. by author. Houghton, 1992. ISBN 978-0-395-64051-7 Subj: Magic. Prejudice. Witches.

The wreck of the Zephyr ill. by author. Houghton, 1983. ISBN 978-0-395-33075-3 Subj: Boats, ships. Sailors. Weather – storms.

The Z was zapped ill. by author. Houghton, 1987. ISBN 978-0-395-44612-6 Subj: ABC books.

Zathura ill. by author. Houghton, 2002. ISBN 978-0-618-25396-8 Subj: Activities – playing. Family life – brothers. Games. Space & space ships.

Van Biesen, Koen. *Roger is reading a book* ill. by author. Eerdmans, 2015. ISBN 978-080285442-1 Subj: Books, reading. Noise, sounds.

Van Buren, David. *I love you as big as the world* ill. by Tim Warnes. Good Books, 2008. ISBN 978-1-56148-618-2 Subj: Animals – bears. Emotions – love. Family life. Rhyming text.

Van Camp, Katie. *CookieBot! a Harry and Horsie adventure* ill. by Lincoln Agnew. HarperCollins, 2011. ISBN 978-0-06-197445-8 Subj: Food. Imagination. Robots. Toys.

Harry and Horsie ill. by Lincoln Agnew. HarperCollins, 2009. ISBN 978-0-06-175598-9 Subj: Bubbles. Imagination. Space & space ships. Toys.

Vande Griek, Susan. *The art room* ill. by Pascal Milelli. Douglas & McIntyre, 2002. ISBN 978-0-88899-449-3 Subj: Art. Careers – artists.

Loon ill. by Karen Reczuch. Groundwood, 2011. ISBN 978-1-55498-077-2 Subj: Behavior – growing up. Birds – loons.

Van der Meer, Mara. *Can we play?* ill. by author. Abrams, 2002. ISBN 978-0-8109-0379-1 Subj: Activities – playing. Days of the week, months of the year. Family life. Format, unusual – toy & movable books.

Vander Zee, Ruth. *Always with you* ill. by Ronald Himler. Eerdmans, 2008. ISBN 978-0-8028-5295-3 Subj: Foreign lands – Vietnam. Orphans. War.

Vanderwater, Amy Ludwig. *Every day birds* ill. by Dylan Metrano. Orchard, 2016. ISBN 978-054569980-8 Subj: Birds. Nature.

Van Dusen, Chris. *The circus ship* ill. by author. Candlewick, 2009. ISBN 978-0-7636-3090-4 Subj: Boats, ships. Circus. Rhyming text.

Down to the sea with Mr. Magee ill. by author. Chronicle, 2000. ISBN 978-0-8118-2499-6 Subj: Animals – dogs. Animals – whales. Boats, ships. Rhyming text. Sea & seashore. Sports – sailing.

Hattie and Hudson ill. by author. Candlewick, 2017. ISBN 978-076366545-6 Subj: Activities – singing. Character traits – kindness. Friendship. Lakes, ponds. Monsters. Prejudice.

King Hugo's huge ego ill. by author. Candlewick, 2011. ISBN 978-0-7636-5004-9 Subj: Behavior – boasting, showing off. Magic. Rhyming text. Royalty – kings. Self-concept.

Learning to ski with Mr. Magee ill. by author. Chronicle, 2010. ISBN 978-0-8118-7495-3 Subj: Animals – dogs. Rhyming text. Sports – skiing.

Randy Riley's really big hit ill. by author. Candlewick, 2012. ISBN 978-0-7636-4946-3 Subj: Behavior – resourcefulness. Character traits – cleverness. Rhyming text. Robots. Sports – baseball.

Van Fleet, Matthew. *Fuzzy yellow ducklings* ill. by author. Dial, 1995. ISBN 978-0-8037-1759-6 Subj: Animals. Birds. Concepts – color. Concepts – shape. Format, unusual – toy & movable books.

Heads ill. by author. Simon & Schuster, 2010. ISBN 978-1-4424-0379-6 Subj: Animals. Format, unusual – toy & movable books.

Moo photos by Brian Stanton. Simon & Schuster, 2011. ISBN 978-1-4424-3503-2 Subj: Animals. Farms. Format, unusual – toy & movable books.

One yellow lion ill. by author. Dial, 1992. ISBN 978-0-8037-1099-3 Subj: Animals. Concepts – color. Counting, numbers. Format, unusual – toy & movable books.

Spotted yellow frogs ill. by author. Dial, 1998. ISBN 978-0-8037-2350-4 Subj: Animals. Concepts – color. Concepts – shape. Format, unusual – toy & movable books.

VanHecke, Susan. *An apple pie for dinner* ill. by Carol Baicker-McKee. Marshall Cavendish, 2009. ISBN 978-0-7614-5452-6 Subj: Activities – baking, cooking. Activities – trading. Family life – grandmothers. Food.

Van Kampen, Vlasta. *Bear tales* ill. by author. Annick, 2000. ISBN 978-1-55037-619-7 Subj: Animals – bears. Creation. Folk & fairy tales. Foreign lands – Czechoslovakia. Foreign lands – Russia.

It couldn't be worse ill. by author. Annick, 2003. ISBN 978-1-55037-783-5 Subj: Animals. Behavior – fighting, arguing. Family life. Folk & fairy tales. Humorous stories. Problem solving.

Van Laan, Nancy. *Forget me not* ill. by Stephanie Graegin. Random House, 2014. ISBN 978-044981543-4 Subj: Family life – grandmothers. Illness – Alzheimer's. Memories, memory. Old age.

La boda: a Mexican wedding celebration ill. by Andrea Arroyo. Little, 1996. ISBN 978-0-316-89626-9 Subj: Foreign lands – Mexico. Foreign languages. Indians of North America – Zapotec. Weddings.

Little baby Bobby ill. by Laura Cornell. Knopf, 1997. ISBN 978-0-679-94922-0 Subj: Behavior – running away. Humorous stories. Rhyming text. Toys – bears.

Little Fish lost ill. by Jane Conteh-Morgan. Atheneum, 1998. ISBN 978-0-689-81331-3 Subj: Animals. Family life – mothers. Fish. Foreign lands – Africa. Rhyming text.

The magic bean tree ill. by Beatriz A. Vidal. Houghton, 1998. ISBN 978-0-395-82746-8 Subj: Folk & fairy tales. Foreign lands – Argentina. Indians of South America – Quechua.

Mama rocks, Papa sings ill. by Roberta Smith. Knopf, 1995. ISBN 978-0-679-94016-6 Subj: Activities – babysitting. Babies, toddlers. Counting, numbers. Cumulative tales. Foreign lands – Haiti. Rhyming text.

Moose tales ill. by Amy Rusch. Houghton, 1999. ISBN 978-0-395-90863-1 Subj: Animals. Animals – beavers. Animals – moose. Friendship. Weather – snow.

Nit-pickin' ill. by George Booth. Atheneum, 2008. ISBN 978-0-689-83898-9 Subj: Insects – lice. Rhyming text.

Possum come a-knocking ill. by George Booth. Knopf, 1990. ISBN 978-0-394-92206-5 Subj: Animals – possums. Cumulative tales. Family life. Rhyming text.

Rainbow crow ill. by Beatriz A. Vidal. Knopf, 1989. ISBN 978-0-394-99577-9 Subj: Birds – crows. Concepts – color. Creation. Fire. Folk & fairy tales. Indians of North America – Lenape.

Shingebiss: an Ojibwe legend ill. by Betsy Bowen. Houghton, 1997. ISBN 978-0-316-89627-6 Subj: Birds – ducks. Folk & fairy tales. Indians of North America – Ojibwa. Seasons – winter.

Sleep, sleep, sleep ill. by Holly Meade. Little, 1995. ISBN 978-0-316-89732-7 Subj: Animals. Foreign lands. Foreign languages. Lullabies. Sleep.

So say the little monkeys ill. by Yumi Heo. Atheneum, 1998. ISBN 978-0-689-81038-1 Subj: Animals – monkeys. Folk & fairy tales. Foreign lands – Brazil. Rhyming text.

This is the hat ill. by Holly Meade. Hyperion, 1995. ISBN 978-0-7868-1030-7 Subj: Animals. Circular tales. Clothing – hats. Rhyming text.

Tickle tum ill. by Bernadette Pons. Atheneum, 2001. ISBN 978-0-689-83143-0 Subj: Family life – mothers. Food. Games.

A tree for me ill. by Sheila White Samton. Knopf, 2000. ISBN 978-0-679-99384-1 Subj: Animals. Counting, numbers. Rhyming text. Trees.

When winter comes: a lullaby ill. by Susan Gaber. Atheneum, 2000. ISBN 978-0-689-81778-6 Subj: Animals. Lullabies. Seasons – winter.

Van Leeuwen, Jean. *Across the wide dark sea: the Mayflower journey* ill. by Thomas B. Allen. Dial, 1995. ISBN 978-0-8037-1167-9 Subj: Activities – traveling. Boats, ships. Pilgrims. Religion. U.S. history.

Benny and beautiful baby Delilah ill. by LeUyen Pham. Penguin, 2006. ISBN 978-0-8037-2891-2 Subj: Babies, toddlers. Family life – new sibling.

Chicken soup ill. by David Gavril. Abrams, 2009. ISBN 978-0-8109-8326-7 Subj: Behavior – hiding. Birds – chickens, roosters. Farms. Food. Illness – cold (disease).

Five funny bunnies: three bouncing tales ill. by Anne Wilsdorf. Marshall Cavendish, 2012. ISBN 978-0-7614-6114-2 Subj: Animals – rabbits. Family life – brothers & sisters.

Going west ill. by Thomas B. Allen. Dial, 1992. ISBN 978-0-8037-1028-3 Subj: Family life. Moving. U.S. history – frontier & pioneer life.

Nothing here but trees ill. by Phil Boatwright. Dial, 1998. ISBN 978-0-8037-2180-7 Subj: Careers – farmers. Trees. U.S. history – frontier & pioneer life.

Papa and the pioneer quilt ill. by Rebecca Bond. Penguin, 2007. ISBN 978-0-8037-3028-1 Subj: Family life. Quilts. U.S. history – frontier & pioneer life.

Sorry ill. by Brad Sneed. Fogelman, 2001. ISBN 978-0-8037-2261-3 Subj: Behavior – fighting, arguing. Careers – farmers. Character traits – persistence. Family life – brothers.

The strange adventures of Blue Dog ill. by Marco Ventura. Dial, 1999. ISBN 978-0-8037-1878-4 Subj: Animals – dogs. Farms. Toys.

The tickle stories ill. by Mary Whyte. Dial, 1998. ISBN 978-0-8037-2049-7 Subj: Activities – storytelling. Bedtime. Family life. Family life – grandfathers.

Touch the sky summer ill. by Dan Andreasen. Dial, 1997. ISBN 978-0-8037-1820-3 Subj: Activities – vacationing. Family life. Family life – grandparents. Lakes, ponds. Seasons – summer.

"Wait for me!" said Maggie McGee ill. by Jacqueline Rogers. Fogelman, 2001. ISBN 978-0-8037-2357-3 Subj: Behavior – growing up. Concepts – size. Family life – brothers & sisters.

van Lieshout, Elle. *The wish* by Elle van Lieshout and Erik van Os ill. by Paula Gerritsen. Boyds Mills, 2007. ISBN 978-1-932425-91-8 Subj: Behavior – solitude. Behavior – wishing. Emotions – love. Tractors.

van Lieshout, Maria. *Backseat A-B-see* ill. by author. Chronicle, 2012. ISBN 978-1-4521-0664-9 Subj: ABC books. Activities – traveling. Automobiles. Signs.

Flight 1-2-3 ill. by author. Chronicle, 2013. ISBN 978-1-4521-1662-4 Subj: Airplanes, airports. Counting, numbers.

Hopper and Wilson ill. by author. Penguin, 2011. ISBN 978-0-399-25184-9 Subj: Animals – elephants. Animals – mice. Friendship. Sports – sailing.

Hopper and Wilson fetch a star ill. by author. Philomel, 2014. ISBN 978-039925772-8 Subj: Animals – elephants. Animals – mice. Friendship. Stars.

Peep! a little book about taking a leap ill. by author. Feiwel & Friends, 2009. ISBN 978-0-312-36915-6 Subj: Birds – chickens, roosters. Emotions – fear. Self-concept.

Splash: a little book about bouncing back ill. by author. Feiwel & Friends, 2008. ISBN 978-0-312-36914-9 Subj: Animals – seals. Behavior – bad day, bad mood.

Tumble! a little book about having it all ill. by author. Feiwel & Friends, 2010. ISBN 978-0-312-54859-9 Subj: Animals – bears. Behavior – sharing.

Van Nutt, Julia. *The monster in the shadows* ill. by Robert Van Nutt. Doubleday, 2000. ISBN 978-0-385-32565-3 Subj: Crime. Monsters. Shadows.

The mystery of Mineral Gorge ill. by Robert Van Nutt. Doubleday, 1998. ISBN 978-0-385-32562-2 Subj: Animals – pigs. Mystery stories.

Pignapped! ill. by Robert Van Nutt. Doubleday, 2000. ISBN 978-0-385-32559-2 Subj: Animals – pigs. Character traits – foolishness. Museums.

Pumpkins from the sky? ill. by Robert Van Nutt. Doubleday, 1999. ISBN 978-0-385-32568-4 Subj: Animals – pigs. Fairs, festivals. Weather – storms.

Skyrockets and snickerdoodles ill. by Robert Van Nutt. Doubleday, 2001. ISBN 978-0-385-32553-0 Subj: Activities – writing. Cities, towns. Holidays – Fourth of July. Sports – baseball.

van Os, Erik. *The wish* (van Lieshout, Elle)

VanSickle, Vikki. *If I had a gryphon* ill. by Cale Atkinson. Tundra, 2016. ISBN 978-177049809-9 Subj: Behavior – dissatisfaction. Pets.

Van Slyke, Rebecca. *Dad school* ill. by Priscilla Burris. Knopf, 2016. ISBN 978-038538895-5 Subj: Family life – fathers. School.

Lexie the word wrangler ill. by Jessie Hartland. Penguin/Nancy Paulsen, 2017. ISBN 978-039916957-1 Subj: Cowboys, cowgirls. Language.

Mom school ill. by Priscilla Burris. Doubleday, 2015. ISBN 978-038538892-4 Subj: Family life – mothers. School.

Van Steenwyk, Elizabeth. *First dog Fala* ill. by Michael G. Montgomery. Peachtree, 2008. ISBN 978-1-56145-411-2 Subj: Animals – dogs. U.S. history.

Prairie Christmas ill. by Ronald Himler. Eerdmans, 2006. ISBN 978-0-8028-5280-9 Subj: Birth. Family life. Holidays – Christmas. U.S. history – frontier & pioneer life.

Van Vleet, Carmella. *To the stars! : the first American woman to walk in space* by Carmella Van Vleet and Kathy Sullivan ill. by Nicole Wong. Charlesbridge, 2016. ISBN 978-158089644-3 Subj: Careers – astronauts. Gender roles. Space & space ships.

Van Woerkom, Dorothy. *Abu Ali counts his donkeys* ill. by Harry Horse. Candlewick, 2000. ISBN 978-0-7636-0956-6 Subj: Animals – donkeys. Counting, numbers.

Becky and the bear ill. by Margot Tomes. Putnam, 1975. ISBN 978-0-399-60924-4 Subj: Animals – bears. Character traits – bravery. U.S. history – frontier & pioneer life.

Donkey Ysabel ill. by Normand Chartier. Macmillan, 1978. ISBN 978-0-02-791280-7 Subj: Animals – donkeys. Humorous stories.

Harry and Shelburt ill. by Erick Ingraham. Macmillan, 1977. ISBN 978-0-02-791290-6 Subj: Animals – rabbits. Friendship. Reptiles – turtles, tortoises. Sports – racing.

Hidden messages ill. by Lynne Cherry. Crown, 1980. ISBN 978-0-517-53520-2 Subj: Communication. Insects. Science.

The rat, the ox and the zodiac: a Chinese legend ill. by Errol Le Cain. Crown, 1976. ISBN 978-0-517-51849-6 Subj: Animals. Animals – rats. Character traits – cleverness. Folk & fairy tales. Foreign lands – China. Zodiac.

Van Wright, Cornelius. *When an alien meets a swamp monster* ill. by author. Penguin/Nancy Paulsen, 2014. ISBN 978-039925623-3 Subj: Friendship. Imagination. Reptiles – alligators, crocodiles.

Varela, Barry. *Gizmo* ill. by Ed Briant. Macmillan, 2007. ISBN 978-1-59643-115-7 Subj: Inventions. Machines. Rhyming text.

Varley, Susan. *Badger's parting gifts* ill. by author. Lothrop, 1984. ISBN 978-0-688-02703-2 Subj: Animals – badgers. Death. Friendship. Gifts.

Varon, Sara. *Chicken and Cat* ill. by author. Scholastic, 2006. ISBN 978-0-439-63406-9 Subj: Animals – cats. Birds – chickens, roosters. Friendship. Wordless.

Chicken and Cat clean up ill. by author. Scholastic, 2009. ISBN 978-0-439-63408-3 Subj: Animals – cats. Birds – chickens, roosters. Character traits – cleanliness. Wordless.

Vasilovich, Guy. *The thirteen nights of Halloween* ill. by author. HarperCollins, 2011. ISBN 978-0-06-180445-8 Subj: Cumulative tales. Holidays – Halloween. Rhyming text. Songs.

Vaughan, Marcia Kapok. *Snap!* ill. by Sascha Hutchinson. Scholastic, 1996. ISBN 978-0-590-60377-5 Subj: Animals. Animals – kangaroos. Reptiles – alligators, crocodiles.

We're going on a ghost hunt ill. by Ann Schweninger. Harcourt, 2001. ISBN 978-0-15-202353-9 Subj: Ghosts. Holidays – Halloween. Imagination. Rhyming text.

Whistling Dixie ill. by Barry Moser. HarperCollins, 1995. ISBN 978-0-06-021029-8 Subj: Animals. Pets. Swamps.

Vaughan, Richard Lee. *Eagle boy* ill. by Lee Christiansen. Sasquatch, 2000. ISBN 978-1-57061-171-1 Subj: Birds – eagles. Folk & fairy tales. Indians of North America.

Vega, Denise. *Build a burrito: a counting book in English and Spanish* ill. by David Diaz. Scholastic, 2008. ISBN 978-0-439-44155-1 Subj: Counting, numbers. Food. Foreign languages.

Grandmother, have the angels come? ill. by Erin Eitter Kono. Little, Brown, 2009. ISBN 978-0-316-10663-4 Subj: Character traits – questioning.

Family life – grandmothers. Foreign languages. Old age.

If your monster won't go to bed ill. by Zachariah OHora. Knopf, 2017. ISBN 978-055349655-0 Subj: Bedtime. Monsters.

Veit, Barbara. *Who stole my house?* ill. by AnnaLaura Cantone. NorthSouth, 2007. ISBN 978-0-7358-2122-4 Subj: Animals – snails. Homes, houses.

Velasquez, Eric. *Grandma's gift* ill. by author. Walker, 2010. ISBN 978-0-8027-2082-5 Subj: Art. Ethnic groups in the U.S. – Puerto Rican Americans. Family life – grandmothers. Foreign languages. Gifts. Holidays – Christmas.

Grandma's records ill. by author. Walker, 2001. ISBN 978-0-8027-8760-6 Subj: Activities – storytelling. Ethnic groups in the U.S. – Puerto Rican Americans. Family life – grandmothers. Music.

Looking for Bongo ill. by author. Holiday, 2016. ISBN 978-082343565-4 Subj: Behavior – lost & found possessions. Ethnic groups in the U.S. – Hispanic Americans. Toys.

Venter, Liezl. *Understanding Sam and Asperger syndrome* (Niekerk, Clarabelle van)

Verboven, Agnes. *Ducks like to swim* ill. by Anne Westerduin. Orchard, 1997. ISBN 978-0-531-30054-1 Subj: Animals. Birds – ducks. Farms. Noise, sounds. Water. Weather – rain.

Verburg, Bonnie. *The kiss box* ill. by Henry Cole. Orchard, 2011. ISBN 978-0-545-11284-0 Subj: Activities – traveling. Animals – bears. Emotions – love. Family life – mothers. Kissing.

The tree house that Jack built ill. by Mark Teague. Scholastic/Orchard, 2014. ISBN 978-043985338-5 Subj: Cumulative tales. Homes, houses. Nursery rhymes.

Verde, Susan. *I am yoga* ill. by Peter H. Reynolds. Abrams, 2015. ISBN 978-141971664-5 Subj: Character traits – patience, impatience. Health & fitness – exercise. Imagination.

The museum ill. by Peter H. Reynolds. Abrams, 2013. ISBN 978-1-4197-0594-6 Subj: Art. Museums. Rhyming text.

The water princess by Susan Verde and Georgie Badiel ill. by Peter H. Reynolds. Putnam, 2016. ISBN 978-039917258-8 Subj: Character traits – perseverance. Foreign lands – Africa. Royalty – princesses. Water.

You and me ill. by Peter H. Reynolds. Abrams, 2015. ISBN 978-141971197-8 Subj: Animals – cats. Friendship. Rhyming text.

Verdet, Andre. *All about time* ill. by Celine Bour-Chollet, et al. Scholastic, 1995. ISBN 978-0-590-42795-1 Subj: Clocks, watches. Days of the week, months of the year. Format, unusual – toy & movable books. Seasons. Time.

Verdick, Elizabeth. *On-the-go time* ill. by Marieka Heinlen. Free Spirit, 2011. ISBN 978-1-57542-379-1 Subj: Character traits – helpfulness. Format, unusual – board books. Shopping.

Peep leap ill. by John Bendall-Brunello. Amazon/ Two Lions, 2013. ISBN 978-1-4778-1640-0 Subj: Birds – ducks. Counting, numbers. Rhyming text.

Small Walt ill. by Marc Rosenthal. Simon & Schuster/Paula Wiseman, 2017. ISBN 978-148144845-1 Subj: Character traits – persistence. Character traits – smallness. Concepts – size. Machines. Rhyming text. Weather – snow.

Tails are not for pulling ill. by Marieka Heinlen. Free Spirit, 2005. ISBN 978-1-57542-180-3 Subj: Format, unusual – board books. Pets.

Vere, Ed. *Banana!* ill. by author. Henry Holt, 2010. ISBN 978-0-8050-9214-1 Subj: Animals – monkeys. Behavior – sharing.

Bedtime for monsters ill. by author. Henry Holt, 2012. ISBN 978-0-8050-9509-8 Subj: Bedtime. Monsters.

Chick ill. by author. Henry Holt, 2010. ISBN 978-0-8050-9168-7 Subj: Birds – chickens, roosters.

Everyone's little ill. by author. Orchard, 2001. ISBN 978-0-531-30336-8 Subj: Animals – elephants. Concepts – size. Format, unusual – toy & movable books.

The getaway ill. by author. Simon & Schuster, 2007. ISBN 978-1-4169-4789-9 Subj: Animals – elephants. Animals – mice. Behavior – stealing.

Max and Bird ill. by author. Sourcebooks, 2017. ISBN 978-149263558-1 Subj: Activities – flying. Animals – cats. Birds. Friendship.

Max the brave ill. by author. Sourcebooks/Jabberwocky, 2015. ISBN 978-149261651-1 Subj: Animals – cats. Character traits – bravery.

Verma, Jatinder Nath. *The story of Divaali* ill. by Nilesh Mistry. Barefoot, 2002. ISBN 978-1-84148-936-0 Subj: Folk & fairy tales. Foreign lands – India. Holidays – Diwali. Religion – Hinduism. Royalty – princes.

Vern, Alex. *Where do frogs come from?* ill. with photos. Harcourt, 2001. ISBN 978-0-15-216304-4 Subj: Frogs & toads. Science.

Vernick, Audrey. *Bob, not Bob!* (Scanlon, Elizabeth Garton)

Brothers at bat: the true story of an amazing all-brother baseball team ill. by Steven Salerno. Clarion, 2012. ISBN 978-0-547-38557-0 Subj: Family life – brothers. Sports – baseball. U.S. history.

First grade dropout ill. by Matthew Cordell. Clarion, 2015. ISBN 978-054412985-6 Subj: Emotions – embarrassment. School.

I won a what? ill. by Robert Neubecker. Knopf, 2016. ISBN 978-055350993-9 Subj: Animals – whales. Character traits – helpfulness. Pets.

Is your buffalo ready for kindergarten? ill. by Daniel Jennewein. HarperCollins, 2010. ISBN 978-0-06-176275-8 Subj: Animals – buffaloes. School – first day.

Second grade holdout ill. by Matthew Cordell. Houghton Mifflin Harcourt, 2017. ISBN 978-054487681-1 Subj: Behavior – worrying. School – first day.

She loved baseball: the Effa Manley story ill. by Don Tate. HarperCollins, 2010. ISBN 978-0-06-134920-1 Subj: Ethnic groups in the U.S. – African Americans. Gender roles. Prejudice. Sports – baseball. U.S. history.

Teach your buffalo to play drums ill. by Daniel Jennewein. HarperCollins, 2011. ISBN 978-0-06-176253-6 Subj: Animals – buffaloes. Musical instruments – drums. Noise, sounds.

Verstraete, Larry. *S is for scientists: a discovery alphabet* ill. by David Geister. Sleeping Bear, 2010. ISBN 978-1-58536-470-1 Subj: ABC books. Careers – scientists. Science.

Vestergaard, Hope. *Digger, dozer, dumper* ill. by David Slonim. Candlewick, 2013. ISBN 978-0-7636-5078-0 Subj: Machines. Poetry. Trucks.

Hillside lullaby ill. by Margie Moore. Penguin, 2006. ISBN 978-0-525-47215-5 Subj: Animals. Bedtime. Rhyming text.

Potty animals: what to know when you've gotta go! ill. by Valeria Petrone. Sterling, 2010. ISBN 978-1-4027-5996-3 Subj: Animals. Etiquette. Hygiene. Rhyming text. Toilet training.

What do you do when a monster says boo? ill. by Maggie Smith. Penguin, 2006. ISBN 978-0-525-47737-2 Subj: Monsters. Rhyming text.

Vetter, Jennifer Riggs. *Down by the station* ill. by Frank Remkiewicz. Ten Speed, 2009. ISBN 978-1-58246-243-1 Subj: Songs. Transportation.

Viano, Hannah. *B is for bear: a natural alphabet* ill. by author. Sasquatch, 2015. ISBN 978-163217039-2 Subj: ABC books. Animals. Nature.

Viau, Nancy. *Storm song* ill. by Gynux. Amazon, 2013. ISBN 978-1-4778-1646-2 Subj: Family life. Rhyming text. Weather – storms.

Vidal, Beatriz A. *Federico and the Magi's gift* ill. by author. Knopf, 2004. ISBN 978-0-375-92518-4 Subj: Behavior – misbehavior. Foreign lands

– Latin America. Foreign languages. Holidays – Christmas.

Vidrine, Beverly Barras. *Easter Day alphabet* ill. by Alison Davis Lyne. Pelican, 2003. ISBN 978-1-58980-076-2 Subj: ABC books. Holidays – Easter. Religion.

Vigil-Piñón, Evangelina. *Marina's muumuu / El muumuu de Marina* ill. by Pablo Torrecilla. Piñata, 2001. ISBN 978-1-55885-350-8 Subj: Clothing. Ethnic groups in the U.S. Family life – grandmothers. Foreign languages. Hawaii.

Vigna, Judith. *Boot weather* ed. by Ann Fay; ill. by author. Albert Whitman, 1988. ISBN 978-0-8075-0837-4 Subj: Activities – playing. Clothing – shoes. Imagination. Seasons – winter. Weather.

I wish my daddy didn't drink so much ed. by Ann Fay; ill. by author. Albert Whitman, 1988. ISBN 978-0-8075-3523-3 Subj: Behavior – wishing. Family life – fathers. Illness.

My two uncles ill. by author. Albert Whitman, 1995. ISBN 978-0-8075-5507-1 Subj: Birthdays. Family life – aunts, uncles. Family life – grandfathers. LGBTQ.

Saying goodbye to daddy ill. by author. Albert Whitman, 1990. ISBN 978-0-8075-7253-5 Subj: Death. Emotions. Emotions – grief. Family life – fathers.

Vila, Laura. *Building Manhattan* ill. by author. Viking, 2008. ISBN 978-0-670-06284-3 Subj: Buildings. Cities, towns. U.S. history.

Villa, Alvaro F. *Flood* ill. by author. Capstone, 2013. ISBN 978-1-62370-001-0 Subj: Family life. Weather – floods. Wordless.

Villeneuve, Anne. *Loula is leaving for Africa* ill. by author. Kids Can, 2013. ISBN 978-1-55453-941-3 Subj: Behavior – running away. Careers – chauffeurs. Imagination.

The red scarf ill. by author. Tundra, 2010. ISBN 978-0-88776-989-4 Subj: Animals – moles. Behavior – lost & found possessions. Careers – magicians. Circus. Clothing – scarves.

Villnave, Erica Pelton. *Sophie's lovely locks* ill. by author. Marshall Cavendish, 2011. ISBN 978-0-7614-5820-3 Subj: Character traits – generosity. Hair.

Vincent, Gabrielle. *Ernest and Celestine at the circus* ill. by author. Greenwillow, 1989. ISBN 978-0-688-08685-5 Subj: Animals – bears. Animals – mice. Circus.

Ernest and Celestine's picnic ill. by author. Morrow, 1988, 1982. ISBN 978-0-688-07809-6 Subj: Activities – picnicking. Animals – bears. Animals – mice. Weather – rain.

Merry Christmas, Ernest and Celestine ill. by author. Greenwillow, 1984. ISBN 978-0-688-02606-6 Subj: Animals – bears. Animals – mice. Friendship. Holidays – Christmas. Parties.

Viorst, Judith. *Alexander and the terrible, horrible, no good, very bad day* ill. by Ray Cruz. Aladdin, 1987, ©1972. ISBN 978-0-689-71173-2 Subj: Behavior – bad day, bad mood. Family life.

Alexander, who used to be rich last Sunday ill. by Ray Cruz. Atheneum, 1978. ISBN 978-0-689-30602-0 Subj: Money.

Alexander, who's not (do you hear me? I mean it!) going to move ill. by Robin Preiss-Glasser. Atheneum, 1995. ISBN 978-0-689-31958-7 Subj: Character traits – stubbornness. Family life. Moving.

Alexander, who's trying his best to be the best boy ever ill. by Isidre Monés. Atheneum, 2014. ISBN 978-148142353-3 Subj: Behavior – misbehavior. Family life.

The alphabet from Z to A: (with much confusion on the way) ill. by Richard Hull. Atheneum, 1994. ISBN 978-0-689-31768-2 Subj: ABC books. Games. Language. Poetry.

And two boys booed ill. by Sophie Blackall. Farrar/Margaret Ferguson, 2014. ISBN 978-037430302-0 Subj: Character traits – confidence. Emotions – fear. Format, unusual – toy & movable books. Self-concept. Theater.

The good-bye book ill. by Kay Chorao. Atheneum, 1988. ISBN 978-0-689-31308-0 Subj: Activities – babysitting. Books, reading. Imagination.

I'll fix Anthony ill. by Arnold Lobel. HarperCollins, 1988, ©1969. ISBN 978-0-689-71202-9 Subj: Family life. Sibling rivalry.

Just in case ill. by Diana Cain Bluthenthal. Simon & Schuster, 2006. ISBN 978-0-689-87164-1 Subj: Behavior – worrying.

My mama says there aren't any zombies, ghosts, vampires, creatures, demons, monsters, fiends, goblins, or things ill. by Kay Chorao. Atheneum, 1973. ISBN 978-0-689-30102-5 Subj: Bedtime. Emotions – fear. Family life – mothers. Imagination. Monsters.

Nobody here but me ill. by Christine Davenier. Farrar, 2008. ISBN 978-0-374-35540-1 Subj: Behavior – misbehavior. Behavior – needing someone. Emotions – loneliness. Family life.

Rosie and Michael ill. by Lorna Tomei. Atheneum, 1974. ISBN 978-0-689-30418-7 Subj: Friendship.

Super-completely and totally the messiest ill. by Robin Preiss-Glasser. Atheneum, 2001. ISBN 978-0-689-82941-3 Subj: Character traits – cleanliness. Character traits – orderliness. Family life – sisters.

The tenth good thing about Barney ill. by Erik Blegvad. Atheneum, 1987, ©1971. ISBN 978-0-

689-71203-6 Subj: Animals – cats. Careers – doctors. Death. Emotions – grief. Pets.

Virján, Emma J. *What this story needs is a munch and a crunch* ill. by Emma J. Virján. HarperCollins, 2016. ISBN 978-006241529-5 Subj: Activities – picnicking. Animals – pigs. Humorous stories. Rhyming text.

What this story needs is a pig in a wig ill. by author. HarperCollins, 2015. ISBN 978-006232724-6 Subj: Activities – storytelling. Animals. Boats, ships. Circular tales. Rhyming text.

Vischer, Frans. *Fuddles* ill. by author. Simon & Schuster, 2011. ISBN 978-1-4169-9155-7 Subj: Animals – cats. Behavior – lost.

Fuddles and Puddles ill. by author. Simon & Schuster, 2016. ISBN 978-148143839-1 Subj: Animals – cats. Animals – dogs.

A very Fuddles Christmas ill. by author. Aladdin, 2013. ISBN 978-1-4169-9156-4 Subj: Animals – cats. Holidays – Christmas.

Vischer, Phil. *Sidney and Norman: a tale of two pigs* ill. by Justin Gerard. Thomas Nelson, 2006. ISBN 978-1-4003-0834-7 Subj: Animals – pigs. Emotions – love. Religion.

Viva, Frank. *Along a long road* ill. by author. Little, Brown, 2011. ISBN 978-0-316-12925-1 Subj: Sports – bicycling.

A long way away ill. by author. Little, Brown, 2013. ISBN 978-0-316-22196-2 Subj: Aliens. Format, unusual. Sea & seashore. Space & space ships. Squid.

Outstanding in the rain ill. by author. Little, Brown, 2015. ISBN 978-031636627-4 Subj: Birthdays. Format, unusual – toy & movable books. Language. Parks – amusement. Rhyming text.

A trip to the bottom of the world with Mouse ill. by author. TOON, 2012. ISBN 978-1-93517-919-1 Subj: Animals – mice. Foreign lands – Antarctic. Format, unusual – graphic novels.

Vivian, Siobhan. *Vunce upon a time* (Seibold, J. Otto)

Voake, Charlotte. *Ginger* ill. by author. Candlewick, 1997. ISBN 978-0-7636-0108-9 Subj: Animals – cats. Behavior – running away. Emotions – envy, jealousy.

Ginger and the mystery visitor ill. by author. Candlewick, 2010. ISBN 978-0-7636-4865-7 Subj: Animals – cats.

Hello twins ill. by author. Candlewick, 2006. ISBN 978-0-7636-3003-4 Subj: Family life – brothers & sisters. Multiple births – twins.

Here comes the train ill. by author. Candlewick, 1998. ISBN 978-0-7636-0438-7 Subj: Family life. Trains.

Melissa's octopus and other unsuitable pets ill. by author. Candlewick, 2015. ISBN 978-076367481-6 Subj: Pets.

Pizza kittens ill. by author. Candlewick, 2002. ISBN 978-0-7636-1622-9 Subj: Animals – cats. Family life. Food.

Tweedle - dee - dee ill. by author. Candlewick, 2008. ISBN 978-0-7636-3797-2 Subj: Music. Seasons – spring. Songs.

Voake, Steve. *Insect detective* ill. by Charlotte Voake. Candlewick, 2010. ISBN 978-0-7636-4447-5 Subj: Gardens, gardening. Insects. Science.

Voce, Louise. *Over in the meadow* ill. by author. Candlewick, 1994. ISBN 978-1-56402-428-2 Subj: Animals. Counting, numbers. Nursery rhymes.

Vogel, Vin. *Bedtime for Yeti* ill. by author. Dial, 2016. ISBN 978-110199431-3 Subj: Bedtime. Behavior – lost & found possessions. Emotions – fear. Monsters. Toys.

The thing about yetis ill. by author. Dial, 2015. ISBN 978-080374170-6 Subj: Activities. Monsters. Seasons – summer. Seasons – winter.

Vojtech, Anna. *Surprise in the meadow* ill. by author. Holiday House, 2016. ISBN 978-082343556-2 Subj: Animals – chipmunks. Plants. Seeds.

Volkmann, Roy. *Curious kittens* ill. by author. Random House, 2001. ISBN 978-0-385-32778-7 Subj: Animals – babies. Animals – cats. Sports – swimming.

Volkmer, Jane Anne, adapt. *Song of Chirimia / La Musica de la Chirimia* ill. by adapter. Carolrhoda, 1990. ISBN 978-0-87614-423-7 Subj: Folk & fairy tales. Foreign lands – Mexico. Foreign languages. Indians of Central America – Maya. Religion.

von Olfers, Sibylle. *Mother Earth and her children: a quilted fairy tale* ill. by Sieglinde Schoen Smith. Breckling, 2007. ISBN 978-1-933308-18-0 Subj: Nature. Quilts. Rhyming text. Seasons – spring.

von Roehl, Angela. *Snail started it!* (Reider, Katja)

Vorst, Rochel Groner. *The sukkah that I built* ill. by Elizabeth Victor-Elsby. Hachai, 2002. ISBN 978-1-929628-07-0 Subj: Holidays – Sukkot. Jewish culture. Religion.

Votaw, Carol. *Good morning, little polar bear* ill. by Susan Banta. NorthWord, 2005. ISBN 978-1-55971-932-2 Subj: Animals. Foreign lands – Arctic. Morning.

Waking up down under ill. by Susan Banta. North-Word, 2007. ISBN 978-1-55971-976-6 Subj: Animals. Foreign lands – Australia. Rhyming text.

Votry, Kim. *Baby's first signs* (Waller, Curt)

More baby's first signs (Waller, Curt)

Vozar, David. *Yo, hungry wolf! a nursery rap* ill. by Betsy Lewin. Doubleday, 1993. ISBN 978-0-385-30452-8 Subj: Animals – wolves. Folk & fairy tales. Rhyming text.

Vrombaut, An. *Clarabella's teeth* ill. by author. Clarion, 2003. ISBN 978-0-618-33379-0 Subj: Animals. Friendship. Reptiles – alligators, crocodiles. Teeth.

Vulliamy, Clara. *Ellen and Penguin and the new baby* ill. by author. Candlewick, 1996. ISBN 978-1-56402-697-2 Subj: Babies, toddlers. Family life – brothers. Family life – mothers. Family life – new sibling. Toys.

Small ill. by author. Clarion, 2001. ISBN 978-0-618-19459-9 Subj: Animals – mice. Family life – grandmothers. Sleepovers. Toys.

Vyner, Tim. *World team* ill. by author. Roaring Brook, 2002. ISBN 978-0-7613-2409-6 Subj: Geography. Sports – soccer. Time.

Waber, Bernard. *An anteater named Arthur* ill. by author. Houghton, 1967. ISBN 978-0-395-20336-1 Subj: ABC books. Animals – anteaters.

Ask me ill. by Suzy Lee. Houghton Mifflin Harcourt, 2015. ISBN 978-054773394-4 Subj: Character traits – questioning. Family life – daughters. Family life – fathers.

Bearsie Bear and the surprise sleepover party ill. by author. Houghton, 1997. ISBN 978-0-395-86450-0 Subj: Animals. Bedtime. Seasons – winter. Sleepovers.

Courage ill. by author. Houghton, 2002. ISBN 978-0-618-23855-2 Subj: Character traits – bravery.

Do you see a mouse? ill. by author. Houghton, 1995. ISBN 978-0-395-72292-3 Subj: Animals – mice. Behavior – disbelief. Hotels. Puzzles.

Evie and Margie ill. by author. Houghton, 2003. ISBN 978-0-618-34124-5 Subj: Animals – hippopotamuses. Careers – actors. Emotions – envy, jealousy. Friendship. School. Theater.

Fast food! gulp! gulp! ill. by author. Houghton, 2001. ISBN 978-0-618-14189-0 Subj: Animals. Food. Restaurants. Rhyming text.

Funny, funny Lyle ill. by author. Houghton, 1987. ISBN 978-0-395-43619-6 Subj: Behavior – misunderstanding. Family life. Reptiles – alligators, crocodiles.

Gina ill. by author. Houghton, 1995. ISBN 978-0-395-74279-2 Subj: Emotions – loneliness. Friendship. Moving. Rhyming text. Sports – baseball.

Ira says goodbye ill. by author. Houghton, 1988. ISBN 978-0-395-48315-2 Subj: Emotions. Friendship. Moving.

Ira sleeps over ill. by author. Houghton, 1972. ISBN 978-0-395-13893-9 Subj: Activities – playing. Bedtime. Friendship. Sleep. Toys – bears.

A lion named Shirley Williamson ill. by author. Houghton, 1996. ISBN 978-0-395-80979-2 Subj: Animals – lions. Behavior – running away. Flowers. Names. Zoos.

Lorenzo ill. by author. Houghton, 1961. Subj: Character traits – curiosity. Fish.

Lovable Lyle ill. by author. Houghton, 1969. ISBN 978-0-395-25378-6 Subj: Friendship. Reptiles – alligators, crocodiles.

Lyle and the birthday party ill. by author. Houghton, 1966. ISBN 978-0-395-15080-1 Subj: Birthdays. Emotions – envy, jealousy. Reptiles – alligators, crocodiles.

Lyle at Christmas ill. by author. Houghton, 1998. ISBN 978-0-395-91304-8 Subj: Animals – cats. Holidays – Christmas. Reptiles – alligators, crocodiles.

Lyle at the office ill. by author. Houghton, 1994. ISBN 978-0-395-70563-6 Subj: Activities – working. Reptiles – alligators, crocodiles.

Lyle finds his mother ill. by author. Houghton, 1974. ISBN 978-0-395-19489-8 Subj: Family life – mothers. Reptiles – alligators, crocodiles.

Lyle, Lyle Crocodile ill. by author. Houghton, 1965. ISBN 978-0-395-13720-8 Subj: Character traits – helpfulness. Reptiles – alligators, crocodiles.

Lyle walks the dogs: a counting book ill. by Paulis Waber. Harcourt, 2010. ISBN 978-0-547-22323-0 Subj: Activities – walking. Animals – dogs. Counting, numbers. Reptiles – alligators, crocodiles.

The mouse that snored ill. by author. Houghton, 2000. ISBN 978-0-395-97518-3 Subj: Animals – mice. Noise, sounds. Rhyming text. Sleep – snoring.

Waboose, Jan Bourdeau. *Firedancers* ill. by C. J. Taylor. Stoddart, 2000. ISBN 978-0-7737-3138-7 Subj: Activities – dancing. Family life – grandmothers. Indians of North America – Ojibwa. Night.

Morning on the lake ill. by Karen Reczuch. Kids Can, 1998. ISBN 978-1-55074-373-9 Subj: Family life – fathers. Indians of North America – Ojibwa. Nature.

SkySisters ill. by Brian Deines. Kids Can, 2000. ISBN 978-1-55074-697-6 Subj: Family life – sisters. Indians of North America – Ojibwa. Night. Northern lights. Sky.

Waddell, Martin. *Bee frog* ill. by Barbara Firth. Candlewick, 2007. ISBN 978-0-7636-3310-3 Subj: Behavior – running away. Frogs & toads. Imagination. Self-concept.

The big big sea ill. by Jennifer Eachus. Candlewick, 1994. ISBN 978-1-56402-066-6 Subj: Family life – mothers. Night. Sea & seashore.

Can't you sleep, Little Bear? ill. by Barbara Firth. Candlewick, 1992. ISBN 978-1-56402-007-9 Subj: Animals – bears. Bedtime. Emotions – fear. Family life – fathers. Night. Sleep.

Captain Small Pig ill. by Susan Varley. Peachtree, 2010. ISBN 978-1-56145-519-5 Subj: Animals – goats. Animals – pigs. Birds – turkeys. Boats, ships.

Farmer Duck ill. by Helen Oxenbury. Candlewick, 1992. ISBN 978-1-56402-009-3 Subj: Animals. Birds – ducks. Careers – farmers. Character traits – helpfulness. Farms.

Good job, Little Bear! ill. by Barbara Firth. Candlewick, 1999. ISBN 978-0-7636-0736-4 Subj: Animals – bears. Character traits – confidence. Character traits – helpfulness.

It's quacking time ill. by Jill Barton. Candlewick, 2005. ISBN 978-0-7636-2738-6 Subj: Animals – babies. Birds – ducks. Eggs.

A kitten called Moonlight ill. by Christian Birmingham. Candlewick, 2001. ISBN 978-0-7636-1176-7 Subj: Animals – cats. Behavior – lost. Family life – mothers.

Let's go home, Little Bear ill. by Barbara Firth. Candlewick, 1993. ISBN 978-1-56402-131-1 Subj: Animals – bears. Emotions – fear. Family life – fathers. Forest, woods. Noise, sounds.

Mimi's Christmas ill. by Leo Hartas. Candlewick, 1997. ISBN 978-0-7636-0413-4 Subj: Animals – mice. Behavior – worrying. Family life. Holidays – Christmas.

Night night Cuddly Bear ill. by Penny Dale. Candlewick, 2000. ISBN 978-0-7636-1195-8 Subj: Animals – bears. Bedtime. Family life. Toys – bears.

Owl babies ill. by Patrick Benson. Candlewick, 1992. ISBN 978-1-56402-101-4 Subj: Birds – owls. Emotions – fear. Family life – mothers. Night.

The pig in the pond ill. by Jill Barton. Candlewick, 1992. ISBN 978-1-56402-050-5 Subj: Animals. Animals – pigs. Careers – farmers. Cumulative tales. Lakes, ponds. Sports – swimming.

Rosie's babies ill. by Penny Dale. Candlewick, 1999. ISBN 978-0-7636-0718-0 Subj: Family life – mothers. Family life – new sibling. Toys.

Sailor Bear ill. by Virginia Austin. Candlewick, 1992. ISBN 978-1-56402-040-6 Subj: Behavior – lost. Boats, ships. Sailors. Sea & seashore. Toys – bears.

Sam Vole and his brothers ill. by Barbara Firth. Candlewick, 1992. ISBN 978-1-56402-082-6 Subj: Animals – mice. Emotions – loneliness. Family life – brothers. Sibling rivalry.

Sleep tight, Little Bear ill. by Barbara Firth. Candlewick, 2005. ISBN 978-0-7636-2439-2 Subj: Animals – bears. Bedtime. Emotions – loneliness. Night. Sleep.

Small Bear lost ill. by Virginia Austin. Candlewick, 1996. ISBN 978-1-56402-871-6 Subj: Activities – traveling. Behavior – lost. Toys – bears.

Snow bears ill. by Sarah Fox-Davies. Candlewick, 2002. ISBN 978-0-7636-1906-0 Subj: Activities – playing. Animals – bears. Family life – mothers. Weather – snow.

Squeak-a-lot ill. by Virginia Miller. Greenwillow, 1991. ISBN 978-0-688-10245-6 Subj: Activities – playing. Animals – mice. Noise, sounds.

The Super Hungry Dinosaur ill. by Leonie Lord. Dial, 2009. ISBN 978-0-8037-3446-3 Subj: Animals – dogs. Dinosaurs. Emotions – anger.

Tom Rabbit ill. by Barbara Firth. Candlewick, 2001. ISBN 978-0-7636-1089-0 Subj: Activities – playing. Animals – rabbits. Bedtime. Emotions – fear. Farms. Toys.

We love them ill. by Barbara Firth. Lothrop, 1990. ISBN 978-0-688-09332-7 Subj: Animals – dogs. Animals – rabbits. Friendship.

Webster J. Duck ill. by David Parkins. Candlewick, 2001. ISBN 978-0-7636-1506-2 Subj: Animals. Behavior – lost. Birds – ducks. Family life – mothers.

When the teddy bears came ill. by Penny Dale. Candlewick, 1995. ISBN 978-1-56402-529-6 Subj: Babies, toddlers. Family life – brothers & sisters. Family life – new sibling. Toys – bears.

Who do you love? ill. by Camilla Ashforth. Candlewick, 1999. ISBN 978-0-7636-0586-5 Subj: Animals – cats. Bedtime. Emotions – love.

Yum, yum, yummy ill. by John Bendall-Brunello. Candlewick, 1998. ISBN 978-0-7636-0477-6 Subj: Animals – bears. Behavior – bullying, teasing. Behavior – greed. Family life – mothers. Food.

Wade, Mary Dodson. *Cinco de Mayo* ill. with photos. Children's Press, 2003. ISBN 978-0-516-22664-4 Subj: Foreign lands – Mexico. Holidays – Cinco de Mayo. War.

No year of the cat ill. by Nicole Wong. Sleeping Bear, 2012. ISBN 978-1-58536-785-6 Subj: Animals – cats. Animals – rats. Folk & fairy tales. Foreign lands – China. Royalty – emperors. Zodiac.

Wadham, Tim. *The queen of France* ill. by Kady MacDonald Denton. Candlewick, 2011. ISBN 978-0-7636-4102-3 Subj: Family life – parents. Imagination. Royalty – queens.

Wadsworth, Ginger. *One tiger growls: a counting book of animal sounds* ill. by James M. Needham. Charlesbridge, 1999. ISBN 978-0-88106-273-1 Subj: Animals. Counting, numbers. Noise, sounds.

Waechter, Phillip. *Rosie and the nightmares* ill. by author. Handprint, 2005. ISBN 978-1-59354-130-9 Subj: Animals – rabbits. Emotions – fear. Monsters. Nightmares.

Wagner, Anke. *Tim's big move!* ill. by Eva Eriksson. NorthSouth, 2012. ISBN 978-0-7358-4090-4 Subj: Behavior – worrying. Concepts – change. Friendship. Moving. School. Toys.

Wagner, Karen. *Bravo, Mildred and Ed!* ill. by Janet Pedersen. Walker, 2000. ISBN 978-0-8027-8735-4 Subj: Animals – mice. Character traits – confidence. Friendship.

A friend like Ed ill. by Janet Pedersen. Walker, 1998. ISBN 978-0-8027-8663-0 Subj: Animals – mice. Concepts – opposites. Friendship.

Wagner, Michael. *Bear make den* (Godwin, Jane)

Wagner, Rachel. *A friend for Einstein: the smallest stallion* (Cantrell, Charlie)

Wahl, Jan. *The art collector* ill. by Rosalinde Bonnet. Charlesbridge, 2011. ISBN 978-1-58089-270-4 Subj: Art. Behavior – collecting things.

Elf night ill. by Peter Weevers. Carolrhoda, 2002. ISBN 978-1-57505-512-1 Subj: Bedtime. Dreams. Mythical creatures – elves. Rhyming text.

The field mouse and the dinosaur named Sue ill. by Bob Doucet. Scholastic, 2000. ISBN 978-0-439-09984-4 Subj: Animals – mice. Dinosaurs. Museums. Prehistory.

I met a dinosaur ill. by Chris Sheban. Harcourt, 1997. ISBN 978-0-15-201644-9 Subj: Dinosaurs. Imagination. Museums. Prehistory. Rhyming text.

Little Johnny Buttermilk ill. by Jennifer Mazzucco. August House, 1999. ISBN 978-0-87483-559-5 Subj: Behavior. Character traits – cleverness. Folk & fairy tales. Foreign lands – England. Witches.

Mabel ran away with the toys ill. by Liza Woodruff. Whispering Coyote, 2000. ISBN 978-1-58089-059-5 Subj: Babies, toddlers. Behavior – running away. Emotions – envy, jealousy. Family life – new sibling. Sibling rivalry.

Wahl, Phoebe. *Sonya's chickens* ill. by author. Tundra, 2015. ISBN 978-17704978-9-4 Subj: Animals – foxes. Birds – chickens, roosters. Death. Farms. Nature.

Wahman, Joe. *Snowboy 1, 2, 3* ill. by Wendy Wahman. Henry Holt, 2012. ISBN 978-0-8050-8732-1 Subj: Counting, numbers. Rhyming text. Seasons – winter. Snowmen. Weather – snow.

Wahman, Wendy. *A cat like that* ill. by author. Henry Holt, 2011. ISBN 978-0-8050-8942-4 Subj: Animals – cats.

Don't lick the dog: making friends with dogs ill. by author. Henry Holt, 2009. ISBN 978-0-8050-8733-8 Subj: Animals – dogs. Pets.

Waite, Judy. *Mouse, look out!* ill. by Norma Burgin. Dutton, 1998. ISBN 978-0-525-42031-6 Subj: Animals – cats. Animals – dogs. Animals – mice. Homes, houses. Rhyming text.

The stray kitten ill. by Gavin Rowe. Crocodile, 2000. ISBN 978-1-56656-356-7 Subj: Animals – cats. Behavior – growing up. Behavior – lost.

Waite, Michael P. *Jojofu* ill. by Yoriko Ito. Lothrop, 1996. ISBN 978-0-688-13661-1 Subj: Animals – dogs. Character traits – loyalty. Folk & fairy tales. Foreign lands – Japan.

Waiting for baby ill. by Rachel Fuller. Child's Play, 2010. ISBN 978-1-84643-275-0 Subj: Babies, toddlers. Birth. Format, unusual – board books.

Wakeman, Daniel. *Ben's bunny trouble* ill. by Dirk van Stralen. Orca, 2007. ISBN 978-1-55143-611-1 Subj: Animals – rabbits. Space & space ships. Wordless.

Walburg, Lori. *The legend of the candy cane* ill. by James Bernardin. Zondervan, 2002. ISBN 978-0-310-70447-8 Subj: Folk & fairy tales. Food. Holidays – Christmas. Religion – Nativity.

Waldherr, Kris. *Harvest* ill. by author. Walker, 2001. ISBN 978-0-8027-8792-7 Subj: Gardens, gardening.

Waldman, Debby. *Room enough for Daisy* by Debby Waldman and Rita Feutl ill. by Cindy Revell. Orca, 2011. ISBN 978-1-55469-255-2 Subj: Behavior – messy. Behavior – sharing. Jewish culture.

A sack full of feathers ill. by Cindy Revell. Orca, 2006. ISBN 978-1-55143-332-5 Subj: Behavior – gossip, rumors. Folk & fairy tales. Jewish culture.

Waldman, Neil. *The starry night* ill. by author. Boyds Mills, 1999. ISBN 978-1-56397-736-7 Subj: Art. Careers – artists. Imagination.

They came from the Bronx ill. by author. Boyds Mills, 2001. ISBN 978-1-56397-891-3 Subj: Animals – buffaloes. Ecology. Family life – grandmothers. Indians of North America – Comanche. U.S. history. Zoos.

Waldron, Jan L. *Angel Pig and the hidden Christmas* ill. by David McPhail. Dutton, 2000. ISBN 978-0-525-45744-2 Subj: Animals – pigs. Holidays – Christmas. Rhyming text.

John Pig's Halloween ill. by David McPhail. Dutton, 1998. ISBN 978-0-525-45941-5 Subj: Animals – pigs. Emotions – fear. Holidays – Halloween. Monsters. Parties. Rhyming text.

Waldron, Kevin. *Mr. Peek and the misunderstanding at the zoo* ill. by author. Candlewick, 2010. ISBN 978-0-7636-4549-6 Subj: Animals. Behavior – misunderstanding. Behavior – worrying. Self-concept. Zoos.

Panda-monium at Peek Zoo ill. by author. Candlewick/Templar, 2014. ISBN 978-076366658-3 Subj: Animals. Careers – zookeepers. Parades. Zoos.

Walker, Alice. *Finding the green stone* ill. by Catherine Deeter. Harcourt, 1991. ISBN 978-0-15-227538-9 Subj: Behavior. Character traits. Ethnic groups in the U.S. – African Americans. Rocks.

To hell with dying ill. by Catherine Deeter. Harcourt, 1987. ISBN 978-0-15-289075-9 Subj: Death. Ethnic groups in the U.S. – African Americans. Friendship.

Walker, Anna. *I love birthdays* ill. by author. Simon & Schuster, 2010. ISBN 978-1-4169-8320-0 Subj: Animals – zebras. Birthdays. Parties. Rhyming text.

I love my dad ill. by author. Simon & Schuster, 2010. ISBN 978-1-4169-8319-4 Subj: Animals – zebras. Family life – fathers. Rhyming text.

I love my mom ill. by author. Simon & Schuster, 2010. ISBN 978-1-4169-8318-7 Subj: Animals – zebras. Family life – mothers. Rhyming text.

Peggy: a brave chicken on a big adventure ill. by author. Clarion, 2014. ISBN 978-054425900-3 Subj: Birds – chickens, roosters. Cities, towns.

Walker, Rob D. *Mama says: a book of love for mothers and sons* ill. by Leo and Diane Dillon. Scholastic, 2009. ISBN 978-0-439-93208-0 Subj: Family life. Foreign languages. Poetry. Religion. World.

Walker, Sally M. *Druscilla's Halloween* ill. by Lee White. Carolrhoda, 2009. ISBN 978-0-8225-8941-9 Subj: Holidays – Halloween. Old age. Transportation. Witches.

Freedom song: the story of Henry "Box" Brown ill. by Sean Qualls. HarperCollins, 2012. ISBN 978-0-06-058310-1 Subj: Character traits – freedom. Ethnic groups in the U.S. – African Americans. Slavery. U.S. history.

The Vowel family: a tale of lost letters ill. by Kevin Luthardt. Carolrhoda, 2008. ISBN 978-0-8225-7982-3 Subj: Humorous stories. Language.

Winnie: the true story of the bear who inspired Winnie-the-Pooh ill. by Jonathon D. Voss. Henry Holt, 2015. ISBN 978-080509715-3 Subj: Animals – bears. Books, reading. Careers – military. Foreign lands – Canada. Zoos.

Walker, Sarah. *Birds* (Gray, Samantha)

Wall, Laura. *Goose* ill. by author. HarperCollins, 2015. ISBN 978-006232435-1 Subj: Birds – geese. Emotions – loneliness. Friendship.

Goose goes to school ill. by author. HarperCollins, 2015. ISBN 978-006232437-5 Subj: Birds – geese. School.

Goose goes to the zoo ill. by author. HarperCollins, 2016. ISBN 978-006232441-2 Subj: Birds – geese. Friendship. Zoos.

Goose on the farm ill. by author. HarperCollins, 2016. ISBN 978-006232439-9 Subj: Birds – geese. Farms. Friendship.

Wallace, Ian. *Chin Chiang and the dragon's dance* ill. by author. Atheneum, 1984. ISBN 978-0-689-50299-6 Subj: Emotions – fear. Ethnic groups in the U.S. – Chinese Americans. Family life – grandfathers. Holidays – Chinese New Year.

Wallace, Ivy. *Pookie* ill. by author. Collins, 2000. ISBN 978-0-00-198377-9 Subj: Activities – traveling. Animals. Animals – rabbits. Character traits – being different. Fairies.

Pookie believes in Santa Claus ill. by author. Collins, 2000. ISBN 978-0-00-198380-9 Subj: Animals. Animals – rabbits. Holidays – Christmas. Santa Claus.

Pookie puts the world right ill. by author. Collins, 2001. ISBN 978-0-00-664735-5 Subj: Animals. Animals – rabbits. Behavior – wishing. Seasons – winter.

Wallace, John. *Anything for you* ill. by Harry Horse. HarperCollins, 2004. ISBN 978-0-06-058129-9 Subj: Animals – bears. Bedtime. Family life – mothers.

Tiny Rabbit goes to a birthday party ill. by author. Holiday, 2000. ISBN 978-0-8234-1489-5 Subj: Animals – rabbits. Birthdays. Gifts. Parties.

Wallace, Joseph E. *Big and noisy Simon* ill. by Kevin O'Malley. Hyperion, 2001. ISBN 978-0-7868-2450-2 Subj: Animals – elephants. Behavior. Foreign lands – Africa. Noise, sounds.

Wallace, Karen. *I am an ankylosaurus* ill. by Mike Bostock. Simon & Schuster, 2005. ISBN 978-0-689-87318-8 Subj: Dinosaurs.

Scarlette Beane ill. by Jon Berkeley. Dial, 2000. ISBN 978-0-8037-2475-4 Subj: Food. Gardens, gardening. Magic. Nature. Plants.

Wallace, Mary. *I is for Inuksuk: an Arctic celebration* ill. by author. Maple Tree, 2009. ISBN 978-1-897349-57-1 Subj: Foreign lands – Arctic. Foreign languages.

Wallace, Nancy Elizabeth. *Alphabet house* ill. by author. Marshall Cavendish, 2005. ISBN 978-0-7614-5192-1 Subj: ABC books. Animals – rabbits.

Apples, apples, apples ill. by author. Winslow, 2000. ISBN 978-1-890817-19-0 Subj: Activities – baking, cooking. Animals – rabbits. Family life. Farms. Music. Songs.

Count down to clean up ill. by author. Houghton, 2001. ISBN 978-0-618-10130-6 Subj: Animals – rabbits. Character traits – cleanliness. Counting, numbers.

Fly, monarch! fly! ill. by author. Marshall Cavendish, 2008. ISBN 978-0-7614-5425-0 Subj: Animals – rabbits. Insects – butterflies, caterpillars.

The kindness quilt ill. by author. Marshall Cavendish, 2006. ISBN 978-0-7614-5313-0 Subj: Character traits – kindness. Quilts.

Look! look! look! by Nancy Elizabeth Wallace and Linda K. Friedlaender; ill. by Nancy Elizabeth Wallace. Marshall Cavendish, 2006. ISBN 978-0-7614-5282-9 Subj: Animals – mice. Art. Letters, cards.

Look! look! look! at sculpture ill. by author. Marshall Cavendish, 2012. ISBN 978-0-7614-6132-6 Subj: Animals – mice. Art. Letters, cards.

Paperwhite ill. by author. Houghton, 2000. ISBN 978-0-618-04283-8 Subj: Animals – rabbits. Flowers. Friendship. Gardens, gardening. Plants. Seasons – spring.

Planting seeds ill. by author. Marshall Cavendish, 2010. ISBN 978-0-7614-5643-8 Subj: Animals – rabbits. Counting, numbers. Gardens, gardening. Seeds.

Pond walk ill. by author. Marshall Cavendish, 2011. ISBN 978-0-7614-5816-6 Subj: Animals – bears. Lakes, ponds. Science.

Pumpkin day ill. by author. Marshall Cavendish, 2002. ISBN 978-0-7614-5128-0 Subj: Animals – rabbits. Farms. Food. Plants.

Rabbit's bedtime ill. by author. Houghton, 1999. ISBN 978-0-395-98266-2 Subj: Animals – rabbits. Bedtime. Rhyming text.

Ready, set, 100th day! ill. by author. Marshall Cavendish, 2011. ISBN 978-0-7614-5956-9 Subj: Animals – rabbits. Character traits – cooperation. Counting, numbers. Family life. School.

Recycle every day! ill. by author. Marshall Cavendish, 2003. ISBN 978-0-7614-5149-5 Subj: Animals – rabbits. Contests. Ecology. School.

Rocks! rocks! rocks! ill. by author. Marshall Cavendish, 2009. ISBN 978-0-7614-5528-8 Subj: Animals – bears. Rocks. Science.

Seeds! seeds! seeds! ill. by author. Marshall Cavendish, 2004. ISBN 978-0-7614-5159-4 Subj: Animals – bears. Family life – grandfathers. Seeds.

Shells! shells! shells! ill. by author. Marshall Cavendish, 2007. ISBN 978-0-7614-5332-1 Subj: Animals – bears. Sea & seashore – beaches.

Snow ill. by author. Western, 1995. ISBN 978-0-307-17562-5 Subj: Animals – rabbits. Family life – grandfathers. Weather – snow.

Stars! stars! stars! ill. by author. Marshall Cavendish, 2009. ISBN 978-0-7614-5612-4 Subj: Animals – rabbits. Space & space ships. Stars.

Tell-a-bunny ill. by author. Winslow, 2000. ISBN 978-1-890817-29-9 Subj: Animals – rabbits. Birthdays. Parties.

The Valentine Express ill. by author. Marshall Cavendish, 2004. ISBN 978-0-7614-5183-9 Subj: Animals – rabbits. Holidays – Valentine's Day. School.

Water! water! water! ill. by author. Amazon/Two Lions, 2014. ISBN 978-147784730-5 Subj: Animals – warthogs. Ecology. Friendship. Water.

Wallen, Ila. *The moon in my room* ill. by Robert Sauber. Bent Willow, 2002. ISBN 978-0-9710627-0-2 Subj: Activities – storytelling. Animals. Animals – bears. Bedtime. Emotions – fear. Forest, woods. Problem solving. Rhyming text.

Waller, Curt. *Baby's first signs* by Curt Waller and Kim Votry ill. by Kim Votry. Gallaudet Univ., 2001. ISBN 978-1-56368-114-1 Subj: Books, reading. Disabilities – deafness. Format, unusual – board books. Sign language.

More baby's first signs by Curt Waller and Kim Votry ill. by Kim Votry. Gallaudet Univ., 2001. ISBN 978-1-56368-115-8 Subj: Books, reading. Disabilities – deafness. Format, unusual – board books. Sign language.

Wallis, Quvenzhané. *A night out with Mama* ill. by Vanessa Brantley-Newton. Simon & Schuster, 2017. ISBN 978-148145880-1 Subj: Careers – actors. Ethnic groups in the U.S. – African Americans. Family life – mothers. Self-concept.

Wallmark, Laurie. *Ada Byron Lovelace and the thinking machine* ill. by April Chu. Creston, 2015. ISBN 978-193954720-0 Subj: Computers. Counting, numbers. Gender roles.

Wallner, Alexandra. *Beatrix Potter* ill. by author. Holiday, 1995. ISBN 978-0-8234-1181-8 Subj: Activities – drawing. Animals. Art. Careers – writers. Emotions – loneliness. Imagination.

Betsy Ross ill. by author. Holiday, 1994. ISBN 978-0-8234-1071-2 Subj: Activities – sewing. U.S. history.

Lucy Maud Montgomery: the author of Anne of Green Gables ill. by author. Holiday House, 2006. ISBN 978-0-8234-1549-6 Subj: Activities – writing. Books, reading.

Susan B. Anthony ill. by author. Holiday House, 2012. ISBN 978-0-8234-1953-1 Subj: Gender roles. U.S. history.

Walsh, Ellen Stoll. *Balancing act* ill. by author. Simon & Schuster, 2010. ISBN 978-1-4424-0757-2 Subj: Animals – mice. Concepts.

Dot and Jabber and the great acorn mystery ill. by author. Harcourt, 2001. ISBN 978-0-15-202602-8 Subj: Animals – mice. Animals – squirrels. Seeds. Trees.

Dot and Jabber and the mystery of the missing stream ill. by author. Harcourt, 2002. ISBN 978-0-15-216512-3 Subj: Animals – mice. Rivers.

For Pete's sake ill. by author. Harcourt, 1998. ISBN 978-0-15-200324-1 Subj: Birds – flamingos. Character traits – being different. Character traits – individuality. Reptiles – alligators, crocodiles.

Hamsters to the rescue ill. by author. Harcourt, 2005. ISBN 978-0-15-205202-7 Subj: Animals – hamsters. Behavior – lost & found possessions. Birds – seagulls. Crustaceans – crabs. Friendship. Sea & seashore – beaches.

Mouse count ill. by author. Harcourt, 1991. ISBN 978-0-15-256023-2 Subj: Animals – mice. Counting, numbers. Reptiles – snakes.

Mouse magic ill. by author. Harcourt, 2000. ISBN 978-0-15-200326-5 Subj: Animals – mice. Concepts – color. Magic. Wizards.

Mouse paint ill. by author. Harcourt, 1989. ISBN 978-0-15-256025-6 Subj: Activities – painting. Animals – mice. Behavior – hiding. Concepts – color.

Mouse shapes ill. by author. Harcourt, 2007. ISBN 978-0-15-206091-6 Subj: Animals – mice. Concepts – shape.

Pip's magic ill. by author. Harcourt, 1994. ISBN 978-0-15-292850-6 Subj: Animals. Emotions – fear. Magic. Night. Reptiles – salamanders.

Where is Jumper? ill. by author. Beach Lane, 2015. ISBN 978-148144508-5 Subj: Animals – mice. Behavior – hiding. Games.

You silly goose ill. by author. Harcourt, 1992. ISBN 978-0-15-299865-3 Subj: Animals – foxes. Animals – mice. Birds – geese.

Walsh, Joanna. *The biggest kiss* ill. by Judi Abbot. Simon & Schuster, 2011. ISBN 978-1-4424-2769-3 Subj: Kissing. Rhyming text.

I love Mom ill. by Judi Abbot. Simon & Schuster/ Paula Wiseman, 2014. ISBN 978-148142808-8 Subj: Animals. Family life – mothers. Rhyming text.

The perfect hug ill. by Judi Abbot. Simon & Schuster, 2012. ISBN 978-1-4424-6606-7 Subj: Animals. Hugging. Rhyming text.

Walsh, Liam Francis. *Fish* ill. by author. Roaring Brook/Neal Porter, 2016. ISBN 978-162672333-7 Subj: Language. Sports – fishing. Wordless.

Walsh, Melanie. *Do donkeys dance?* ill. by author. Houghton, 2000. ISBN 978-0-618-00330-3 Subj: Activities. Animals. Nature.

Do lions live on lily pads? ill. by author. Houghton, 2006. ISBN 978-0-618-47300-7 Subj: Animals. Character traits – questioning. Homes, houses. Nature.

Do monkeys tweet? ill. by author. Houghton, 1997. ISBN 978-0-395-85081-7 Subj: Animals. Noise, sounds.

Hide and sleep ill. by author. DK, 1999. ISBN 978-0-7894-4820-0 Subj: Bedtime. Behavior – hiding. Games.

Isaac and his amazing Asperger superpowers ill. by author. Candlewick, 2016. ISBN 978-076368121-0 Subj: Character traits – being different. Disabilities – Asperger's. Disabilities – autism.

Living with Mom and living with Dad ill. by author. Candlewick, 2012. ISBN 978-0-7636-5869-4 Subj: Divorce. Family life – parents. Format, unusual – toy & movable books.

Monster, monster ill. by author. Candlewick, 2002. ISBN 978-0-7636-1669-4 Subj: Format, unusual – toy & movable books. Monsters.

Ned's rainbow ill. by author. DK, 2000. ISBN 978-0-7894-5623-6 Subj: Activities – painting. Weather – rainbows.

10 things I can do to help my world: fun and easy eco-tips ill. by author. Candlewick, 2008. ISBN 978-0-7636-4144-3 Subj: Ecology.

Walsh, Vivian. *Penguin dreams* (Seibold, J. Otto)

Walter, Mildred Pitts. *Brother to the wind* ill. by Leo and Diane Dillon. Lothrop, 1985. ISBN 978-0-688-03811-3 Subj: Activities – flying. Foreign lands – Africa.

Darkness ill. by Marcia Jameson. Simon & Schuster, 1995. ISBN 978-0-689-80305-5 Subj: Night. Shadows.

My mama needs me ill. by Pat Cummings. Lothrop, 1983. ISBN 978-0-688-01671-5 Subj: Emotions – loneliness. Ethnic groups in the U.S. – African Americans. Family life.

Two too much ill. by Pat Cummings. Bradbury, 1990. ISBN 978-0-02-792290-5 Subj: Emotions. Ethnic groups in the U.S. – African Americans. Family life – brothers & sisters.

Ty's one-man band ill. by Margot Tomes. Four Winds, 1980. ISBN 978-0-02-792300-1 Subj: Folk & fairy tales. Music. Musical instruments – bands.

Walter, Virginia. *"Hi, pizza man!"* ill. by Ponder Goembel. Orchard, 1995. ISBN 978-0-531-08735-0 Subj: Animals. Noise, sounds.

Walters, Catherine. *Are you there, Baby Bear?* ill. by author. Dutton, 1999. ISBN 978-0-525-46161-6 Subj: Animals – babies. Animals – bears. Family life – new sibling. Multiple births – twins.

The magical snowman ill. by Alison Edgson. Good Books, 2009. ISBN 978-1-56148-671-7 Subj: Animals – rabbits. Magic. Seasons – winter. Snowmen.

Play gently, Alfie Bear ill. by author. Dutton, 2002. ISBN 978-0-525-46885-1 Subj: Animals – bears. Family life – brothers & sisters. Family life – mothers.

When will it be spring? ill. by author. Dutton, 1998. ISBN 978-0-525-45881-4 Subj: Animals – bears. Character traits – patience, impatience. Family life – mothers. Hibernation. Nature. Seasons – spring. Seasons – winter.

Walters, Eric. *An African alphabet* ill. by Sue Todd. Orca, 2017. ISBN 978-145981070-9 Subj: ABC books. Foreign lands – Africa. Format, unusual – board books.

The matatu ill. by Eva Campbell. Orca, 2012. ISBN 978-1-55469-301-6 Subj: Animals. Buses. Family life – grandfathers. Folk & fairy tales. Foreign lands – Kenya.

Walters, Virginia. *Are we there yet, Daddy?* ill. by S. D. Schindler. Viking, 1999. ISBN 978-0-670-87402-6 Subj: Activities – traveling. Automobiles. Family life – fathers. Maps. Rhyming text.

Walton, Jessica. *Introducing Teddy* ill. by Dougal MacPherson. Bloomsbury, 2016. ISBN 978-168119210-9 Subj: Friendship. Gender identity. Self-concept. Toys – bears.

Walton, Rick. *Baby's first year!* ill. by Caroline Jayne Church. Penguin, 2011. ISBN 978-0-399-25025-5 Subj: Babies, toddlers. Rhyming text.

The bear came over to my house ill. by James Warhola. Putnam, 2001. ISBN 978-0-399-23415-6 Subj: Animals – bears. Rhyming text.

Bertie was a watchdog ill. by Arthur Robins. Candlewick, 2002. ISBN 978-0-7636-1385-3 Subj: Animals – dogs. Concepts – size. Crime.

Bunny school: a learning fun-for-all ill. by Paige Miglio. HarperCollins, 2005. ISBN 978-0-06-057509-0 Subj: Animals – rabbits. Rhyming text. School.

Frankenstein: a monstrous parody ill. by Nathan Hale. Feiwel & Friends, 2012. ISBN 978-0-312-55366-1 Subj: Monsters. Rhyming text.

Frankenstein's fright before Christmas ill. by Nathan Hale. Feiwel & Friends, 2014. ISBN 978-031255367-8 Subj: Holidays – Christmas. Monsters. Rhyming text.

Girl and Gorilla: out and about ill. by Joe Berger. HarperCollins, 2016. ISBN 978-006227891-3 Subj: Activities – walking. Animals – gorillas. Friendship. Parks.

How can you dance? ill. by Ana López-Escrivá. Putnam, 2001. ISBN 978-0-399-23229-9 Subj: Activities – dancing. Rhyming text.

I need my own country! ill. by Wes Hargis. Bloomsbury, 2012. ISBN 978-1-59990-559-4 Subj: Behavior – misbehavior. Imagination.

Just me and 6,000 rats: a tale of conjunctions ill. by Mike Gordon and Carl Gordon. Gibbs Smith, 2007. ISBN 978-1-4236-0219-4 Subj: Animals – rats. Humorous stories. Language.

Little dogs say "Rough!" ill. by Henry Cole. Putnam, 2000. ISBN 978-0-399-23228-2 Subj: Animals. Noise, sounds. Rhyming text.

My two hands, my two feet ill. by Julia Gorton. Putnam, 2000. ISBN 978-0-399-23338-8 Subj: Anatomy – feet. Anatomy – hands. Communication.

Noah's square dance ill. by Thor Wickstrom. Lothrop, 1995. ISBN 978-0-688-11187-8 Subj: Activities – dancing. Animals. Boats, ships. Religion – Noah. Rhyming text. Weather – floods. Weather – rain.

One more bunny ill. by Paige Miglio. Lothrop, 2000. ISBN 978-0-688-16848-3 Subj: Animals – rabbits. Counting, numbers.

Pig, pigger, piggest ill. by Jimmy Holder. Gibbs Smith, 1997. ISBN 978-0-87905-806-7 Subj: Animals – pigs. Castles. Witches.

The remarkable friendship of Mr. Cat and Mr. Rat ill. by Lisa McCue. Penguin, 2006. ISBN 978-0-399-23899-4 Subj: Animals – cats. Animals – rats. Friendship. Gifts.

So many bunnies ill. by Paige Miglio. Lothrop, 1998. ISBN 978-0-688-13657-4 Subj: ABC books. Counting, numbers. Rhyming text. Sleep.

What do we do with the baby? ill. by Paige Miglio. HarperCollins, 2008. ISBN 978-0-06-008419-6 Subj: Animals – rabbits. Babies, toddlers. Emotions – love.

Walty, Margaret. *Rock-a-bye baby: lullabies for bedtime* ill. by author. Barefoot, 1998. ISBN 978-1-902283-03-6 Subj: Bedtime. Lullabies. Music.

Wan, Joyce. *Hug you, kiss you, love you* ill. by author. Scholastic, 2013. ISBN 978-0-545-54045-2 Subj: Animals. Emotions – love. Family life. Format, unusual – board books.

Wang, Andrea. *The Nian Monster* ill. by Alina Chau. Albert Whitman, 2016. ISBN 978-080755642-9 Subj: Foreign lands – China. Holidays – Chinese New Year. Monsters.

Wang, Gabrielle. *The race for the Chinese zodiac* ill. by Sally Rippin. Candlewick, 2013. ISBN 978-0-7636-6778-8 Subj: Animals. Folk & fairy tales. Foreign lands – China. Royalty – emperors. Zodiac.

Wang, Xiaohong. *One year in Beijing* ill. by Grace Lin. China Sprout, 2006. ISBN 978-0-9747302-5-7 Subj: Days of the week, months of the year. Foreign lands – China.

Wangerin, Walter. *Angels and all children* ill. by Tim Ladwig. Augsburg Fortress, 2002. ISBN 978-0-8066-3712-9 Subj: Holidays – Christmas. Music. Religion.

Probity Jones and the Fear Not Angel ill. by Tim Ladwig. Paraclete, 2005. ISBN 978-1-55725-457-3 Subj: Angels. Ethnic groups in the U.S. – African Americans. Holidays – Christmas. Religion – Nativity.

Water come down ill. by Gerardo Suzán. Augsburg Fortress, 1999. ISBN 978-0-8066-3711-2 Subj: Babies, toddlers. Family life. Religion.

Warburton, Tom. *1000 times no* ill. by author. HarperCollins, 2009. ISBN 978-0-06-154263-3 Subj: Behavior – misbehavior. Foreign languages.

Ward, B. J. *Farty Marty* ill. by Steven Kellogg. Simon & Schuster, 2013. ISBN 978-1-4424-3901-6 Subj: Animals – cats. Music. Rhyming text. Senses – smell.

Ward, Cindy. *Cookie's week* ill. by Tomie dePaola. Putnam, 1988. ISBN 978-0-399-21498-1 Subj: Animals – cats. Behavior – misbehavior. Days of the week, months of the year.

Ward, D. J. *What happens to our trash?* ill. by Paul Meisel. Collins, 2012. ISBN 978-0-06-168756-3 Subj: Careers – sanitation workers. Ecology.

Ward, Helen. *The dragon machine* ill. by Wayne Anderson. Dutton, 2003. ISBN 978-0-525-47114-1 Subj: Activities – flying. Dragons. Emotions – loneliness. Imagination.

The king of the birds ill. by author. Millbrook, 1997. ISBN 978-0-7613-0288-9 Subj: Activities – flying. Birds. Character traits – cleverness. Royalty – kings.

Little Moon Dog ill. by Wayne Anderson. Penguin, 2007. ISBN 978-0-525-47727-3 Subj: Animals – dogs. Fairies. Friendship. Moon.

Old shell, new shell ill. by author. Millbrook, 2002. ISBN 978-0-7613-2708-0 Subj: Animals. Crustaceans – crabs. Foreign lands – Australia. Sea & seashore.

The rooster and the fox ill. by author. Millbrook, 2003. ISBN 978-0-7613-2920-6 Subj: Animals – foxes. Birds – chickens, roosters. Character traits – cleverness. Character traits – pride. Character traits – vanity. Farms.

Spots in a box ill. by author. Candlewick, 2015. ISBN 978-076367597-4 Subj: Birds – guinea fowl. Character traits – being different. Character traits – individuality. Concepts. Rhyming text.

The tin forest ill. by Wayne Anderson. Dutton, 2001. ISBN 978-0-525-46787-8 Subj: Animals. Dreams. Ecology. Forest, woods. Jungle. Trees.

Ward, Jennifer. *Feathers and hair, what animals wear* ill. by Jing Jing Tsong. Simon & Schuster/Beach Lane, 2017. ISBN 978-148143081-4 Subj: Anatomy. Animals. Feathers. Hair. Rhyming text.

Forest bright, forest night ill. by Jamichael Henterly. Dawn, 2005. ISBN 978-1-58469-066-5 Subj: Animals. Forest, woods.

Mama built a little nest ill. by Steve Jenkins. Simon & Schuster/Beach Lane, 2014. ISBN 978-144242116-5 Subj: Birds. Homes, houses. Nature. Rhyming text.

Over in the garden ill. by Kenneth J. Spengler. Rising Moon, 2002. ISBN 978-0-87358-793-8 Subj: Counting, numbers. Gardens, gardening. Insects. Music. Rhyming text. Songs.

Somewhere in the ocean by Jennifer Ward and T. J. Marsh ill. by Kenneth J. Spengler. Rising Moon, 2000. ISBN 978-0-87358-748-8 Subj: Animals – babies. Counting, numbers. Rhyming text. Sea & seashore.

There was an old monkey who swallowed a frog (Little old lady who swallowed a fly)

There was an old mummy who swallowed a spider (Little old lady who swallowed a fly)

There was an old pirate who swallowed a fish (Little old lady who swallowed a fly)

Way up in the Arctic ill. by Kenneth J. Spengler. Rising Moon, 2007. ISBN 978-0-87358-928-4 Subj: Animals. Counting, numbers. Foreign lands – Arctic. Rhyming text.

What will grow? ill. by Susie Ghahremani. Bloomsbury, 2017. ISBN 978-168119030-3 Subj: Gardens, gardening. Plants. Science. Seeds.

What will hatch? ill. by Susie Ghahremani. Walker, 2013. ISBN 978-080272311-6 Subj: Eggs. Nature. Science.

Ward, Lindsay. *Brobarians* ill. by author. Amazon/Two Lions, 2017. ISBN 978-150394167-0 Subj: Behavior – fighting, arguing. Family life – brothers. Humorous stories.

Henry finds his word ill. by author. Dial, 2015. ISBN 978-080373990-1 Subj: Babies, toddlers. Language.

The importance of being 3 ill. by author. Dial, 2016. ISBN 978-052542869-5 Subj: Babies, toddlers. Rhyming text.

Please bring balloons ill. by author. Dial, 2013. ISBN 978-0-8037-3878-2 Subj: Animals – polar bears. Foreign lands – Arctic. Merry-go-rounds. Toys – balloons.

Rosco vs. the baby ill. by author. Simon & Schuster, 2016. ISBN 978-148143657-1 Subj: Animals – dogs. Babies, toddlers.

When Blue met Egg ill. by author. Dial, 2012. ISBN 978-0-8037-3718-1 Subj: Birds. Eggs. Seasons – winter. Weather – snow.

Ward, Lynd. *The biggest bear* ill. by author. Houghton, 1952. Subj: Animals – bears. Caldecott award books. Character traits – kindness to animals. Foreign lands – Canada. Pets.

The little red lighthouse and the great gray bridge (Swift, Hildegarde Hoyt)

Ward, Nick. *Come on Baby Duck* ill. by author. Good Books, 2004. ISBN 978-1-56148-447-8 Subj: Birds – ducks. Emotions – fear. Sports – swimming.

Don't eat the babysitter! ill. by author. Random House, 2006. ISBN 978-0-385-75062-2 Subj: Activities – babysitting. Family life – brothers & sisters. Fish – sharks.

Wardlaw, Lee. *The chair where bear sits* ill. by Russell Benfanti. Winslow, 2001. ISBN 978-1-890817-85-5 Subj: Accidents. Animals. Animals – bears.

Babies, toddlers. Character traits – clumsiness. Cumulative tales. Food. Rhyming text.

Red, white, and boom! ill. by Huy Voun Lee. Henry Holt, 2012. ISBN 978-0-8050-9065-9 Subj: Activities – picnicking. Holidays – Fourth of July. Parades. Rhyming text.

Saturday night jamboree ill. by Barry Root. Dial, 2000. ISBN 978-0-8037-2189-0 Subj: Activities – babysitting. Activities – dancing. Family life.

Won Ton: a cat tale told in haiku ill. by Eugene Yelchin. Henry Holt, 2011. ISBN 978-0-8050-8995-0 Subj: Animals – cats. Character traits – kindness to animals. Poetry.

Won Ton and Chopstick: a cat and dog tale told in haiku ill. by Eugene Yelchin. Henry Holt, 2015. ISBN 978-080509987-4 Subj: Animals – cats. Animals – dogs. Poetry.

Wargin, Kathy-jo. *Scare a bear* ill. by John Bendall-Brunello. Sleeping Bear, 2010. ISBN 978-1-58536-430-5 Subj: Animals – bears. Rhyming text.

Warhola, James. *If you're happy and you know it: jungle edition* ill. by author. Scholastic, 2007. ISBN 978-0-439-72766-2 Subj: Animals. Emotions – happiness. Jungle. Songs.

Uncle Andy's ill. by author. Putnam, 2003. ISBN 978-0-399-23869-7 Subj: Careers – artists. Family life. Family life – aunts, uncles.

Uncle Andy's cats ill. by author. Putnam, 2009. ISBN 978-0-399-25180-1 Subj: Animals – cats. Careers – artists.

Waring, Geoff. *Oscar and the bat: a book about sound* ill. by author. Candlewick, 2008. ISBN 978-0-7636-4025-5 Subj: Animals – bats. Animals – cats. Noise, sounds.

Oscar and the cricket: a book about moving and rolling ill. by author. Candlewick, 2008. ISBN 978-0-7636-4029-3 Subj: Animals – cats. Concepts – motion. Insects – crickets.

Oscar and the moth: a book about light and dark ill. by author. Candlewick, 2007. ISBN 978-0-7636-3559-6 Subj: Animals – cats. Day. Light, lights. Night. Shadows.

Waring, Richard. *Alberto the dancing alligator* ill. by Holly Swain. Candlewick, 2002. ISBN 978-0-7636-1953-4 Subj: Behavior – lost. Pets. Reptiles – alligators, crocodiles.

Hungry hen ill. by Caroline Jayne Church. HarperCollins, 2001. ISBN 978-0-06-623880-7 Subj: Animals – foxes. Birds – chickens, roosters.

Waring, Zoe. *No hugs for Porcupine* ill. by author. Running Press, 2017. ISBN 978-076246225-4 Subj: Animals – armadillos. Animals – porcupines. Hugging. Kissing.

Warner, Sunny. *The moon quilt* ill. by author. Houghton, 2001. ISBN 978-0-618-05583-8 Subj: Animals – cats. Death. Family life. Memories, memory. Quilts.

Warner, Timothy. *Tub toys* (Shannon, Terry Miller)

Warnes, Tim. *Daddy hug* ill. by Jane Chapman. HarperCollins, 2008. ISBN 978-0-06-058950-9 Subj: Animals. Family life – fathers. Hugging. Rhyming text.

The great cheese robbery ill. by author. Tiger Tales, 2015. ISBN 978-158925174-8 Subj: Animals – elephants. Animals – mice. Crime. Emotions – fear.

Who's that? (Gamble, Isobel)

Warnick, Elsa. *Bedtime* ill. by author. Browndeer, 1998. ISBN 978-0-15-201471-1 Subj: Activities. Bedtime.

Warren, Rick, commentary. *The Lord's prayer* ill. by Richard Jesse Watson. Zonderkidz, 2011. ISBN 978-0-310-71086-8 Subj: Religion.

Warren, Sarah. *Dolores Huerta: a hero to migrant workers* ill. by Robert Casilla. Marshall Cavendish, 2012. ISBN 978-0-7614-6107-4 Subj: Behavior – seeking better things. Careers – migrant workers. Ethnic groups in the U.S. – Mexican Americans. U.S. history.

Warrick, Karen Clemens. *If I had a tail* ill. by Sherry Neidigh. Rising Moon, 2001. ISBN 978-0-87358-781-5 Subj: Anatomy – tails. Animals. Riddles & jokes.

Who needs that nose? ill. by Sherry Neidigh. North-Word, 2004. ISBN 978-1-55971-887-5 Subj: Anatomy – noses. Animals. Riddles & jokes.

Warwick, Dionne. *Little Man* by Dionne Warwick and David Freeman Wooley ill. by Fred Willingham. Charlesbridge, 2011. ISBN 978-1-57091-731-8 Subj: Activities – working. Character traits – perseverance. Ethnic groups in the U.S. – African Americans. Money. Musical instruments – drums.

Washington, Donna L. *A big, spooky house* ill. by Jacqueline Rogers. Hyperion, 2000. ISBN 978-0-7868-0349-1 Subj: Animals – cats. Mythical creatures.

Li'l Rabbit's Kwanzaa ill. by Shane W. Evans. HarperCollins, 2010. ISBN 978-0-06-072816-8 Subj: Animals – rabbits. Holidays – Kwanzaa.

The story of Kwanzaa ill. by Stephen Taylor. HarperCollins, 1996. ISBN 978-0-06-024819-2 Subj: Ethnic groups in the U.S. – African Americans. Holidays – Kwanzaa. U.S. history.

Washington, Kathy Gates. *Three colors of Katie* ill. by Kathy Farina. College of Dupage, 2010. ISBN 978-1-932514-18-6 Subj: Ethnic groups in the U.S. Family life.

Washington, Ned. *When you wish upon a star* by Ned Washington and Leigh Harline ill. by Eric Puybaret. Imagine, 2011. ISBN 978-1-936140-35-0 Subj: Behavior – wishing. Dreams. Songs. Stars.

Watanabe, Shigeo. *Ice cream is falling!* ill. by Yasuo Ohtomo. Putnam, 1989. ISBN 978-0-399-21550-6 Subj: Animals – bears. Seasons – winter. Weather – snow.

Let's go swimming ill. by Yasuo Ohtomo. Putnam, 1990. ISBN 978-0-399-21896-5 Subj: Animals – bears. Family life – fathers. Sports – swimming.

Where's my daddy? ill. by Yasuo Ohtomo. Philomel, 1982. ISBN 978-0-399-20899-7 Subj: Animals – bears. Behavior – lost. Character traits – perseverance. Family life – fathers.

Waterhouse, Stephen. *Engines, engines* (Bruce, Lisa)

Waters, John F. *Sharks have six senses* ill. by Bob Barner. HarperCollins, 2015. ISBN 978-006028140-3 Subj: Fish – sharks. Senses.

Waters, Kate. *Lion dancer: Ernie Wan's Chinese New Year* by Kate Waters and Madeline Slovenz-Low; photos by Martha Cooper. Scholastic, 1990. ISBN 978-0-590-43046-3 Subj: Activities – dancing. Ethnic groups in the U.S. – Chinese Americans. Holidays – Chinese New Year.

Waterton, Betty. *A bumblebee sweater* ill. by Kim LaFave. Fitzhenry & Whiteside, 2007. ISBN 978-1-55455-028-9 Subj: Activities – knitting. Clothing – sweaters. Theater.

Watkins, Adam F. *R is for robot: a noisy alphabet* ill. by Adam F. Watkins. Price Stern Sloan, 2014. ISBN 978-084317237-9 Subj: ABC books. Robots.

Watkins, Angela Farris. *Love will see you through: Martin Luther King Jr.'s six guiding beliefs* ill. by Sally Wern Comport. Simon & Schuster, 2015. ISBN 978-141698693-5 Subj: Ethnic groups in the U.S. – African Americans. Holidays – Martin Luther King, Jr. Day. Prejudice. U.S. history. Violence, nonviolence.

My Uncle Martin's big heart ill. by Eric Velasquez. Abrams, 2010. ISBN 978-0-8109-8975-7 Subj: Ethnic groups in the U.S. – African Americans. Family life – aunts, uncles. Holidays – Martin Luther King, Jr. Day. U.S. history. Violence, nonviolence.

My Uncle Martin's words for America: Martin Luther King Jr.'s niece tells how he made a difference ill. by Eric Velasquez. Abrams, 2011. ISBN 978-1-4197-0022-4 Subj: Ethnic groups in the U.S. – African Americans. Holidays – Martin Luther King, Jr.

Day. Prejudice. U.S. history. Violence, nonviolence.

Watkins, Rowboat. *Pete with no pants* ill. by author. Chronicle, 2017. ISBN 978-145214401-6 Subj: Animals – elephants. Clothing – pants. Imagination.

Rude cakes ill. by author. Chronicle, 2015. ISBN 978-145213851-0 Subj: Behavior – bossy. Character traits – kindness. Character traits – selfishness. Etiquette. Food.

Watson, Clyde. *Applebet: an ABC* ill. by Wendy Watson. Farrar, 1982. ISBN 978-0-374-30384-6 Subj: ABC books. Fairs, festivals. Rhyming text.

Valentine foxes ill. by Wendy Watson. Watts, 1988. ISBN 978-0-531-08400-7 Subj: Animals – foxes. Family life. Food. Holidays – Valentine's Day.

Watson, Jesse Joshua. *Hope for Haiti* ill. by author. Penguin, 2010. ISBN 978-0-399-25547-2 Subj: Character traits – hopefulness. Earthquakes. Foreign lands – Haiti. Sports – soccer.

Watson, Renée. *Harlem's little blackbird: the story of Florence Mills* ill. by Christian Robinson. Random House, 2012. ISBN 978-0-375-86973-0 Subj: Careers – singers. Ethnic groups in the U.S. – African Americans. U.S. history.

A place where hurricanes happen ill. by Shadra Strickland. Random House, 2010. ISBN 978-0-375-85609-9 Subj: Cities, towns. Communities, neighborhoods. Weather – hurricanes.

Watson, Richard Jesse. *The boy who went ape* ill. by Benjamin James Watson. Scholastic, 2008. ISBN 978-0-590-47966-0 Subj: Animals – chimpanzees. Behavior – misbehavior. School – field trips.

Watson, Wendy. *Bedtime bunnies* ill. by author. Clarion, 2010. ISBN 978-0-547-22312-4 Subj: Animals – rabbits. Bedtime. Seasons – fall.

Boo! it's Halloween ill. by author. Clarion, 1992. ISBN 978-0-395-53628-5 Subj: Family life. Holidays – Halloween.

Happy Easter day! ill. by author. Clarion, 1993. ISBN 978-0-395-53629-2 Subj: Animals – cats. Family life. Holidays – Easter.

Holly's Christmas eve ill. by author. HarperCollins, 2002. ISBN 978-0-688-17653-2 Subj: Character traits – helpfulness. Friendship. Holidays – Christmas. Machines. Santa Claus.

Hurray for the Fourth of July ill. by author. Houghton, 1992. ISBN 978-0-395-53627-8 Subj: Family life. Holidays – Fourth of July. Poetry.

Thanksgiving at our house ill. by author. Houghton, 1991. ISBN 978-0-395-53626-1 Subj: Family life. Holidays – Thanksgiving. Nursery rhymes.

A Valentine for you ill. by author. Houghton, 1991. ISBN 978-0-395-53625-4 Subj: Emotions – love. Holidays – Valentine's Day. Poetry.

Watt, Mélanie. *Bug in a vacuum* ill. by author. Tundra, 2015. ISBN 978-177049645-3 Subj: Character traits – cleanliness. Insects.

Chester ill. by author. Kids Can, 2007. ISBN 978-1-55453-140-0 Subj: Activities – drawing. Activities – writing. Animals – cats.

Chester's back! ill. by author. Kids Can, 2008. ISBN 978-1-55453-287-2 Subj: Activities – drawing. Activities – writing. Animals – cats.

Chester's masterpiece ill. by author. Kids Can, 2010. ISBN 978-1-55453-566-8 Subj: Activities – drawing. Activities – writing. Animals – cats.

Have I got a book for you! ill. by author. Kids Can, 2009. ISBN 978-1-55453-289-6 Subj: Animals – foxes. Books, reading. Careers – salespeople.

Leon the chameleon ill. by author. Kids Can, 2001. ISBN 978-1-55074-867-3 Subj: Character traits – being different. Concepts – color. Reptiles – chameleons.

Scaredy Squirrel ill. by author. Kids Can, 2006. ISBN 978-1-55337-959-1 Subj: Animals – squirrels. Character traits – bravery. Emotions – fear.

Scaredy Squirrel at night ill. by author. Kids Can, 2009. ISBN 978-1-55453-288-9 Subj: Animals – squirrels. Dreams. Emotions – fear. Night. Sleep.

Scaredy Squirrel at the beach ill. by author. Kids Can, 2008. ISBN 978-1-55453-225-4 Subj: Animals – squirrels. Emotions – fear. Sea & seashore – beaches.

Scaredy Squirrel goes camping ill. by author. Kids Can, 2013. ISBN 978-1-89478-686-7 Subj: Animals – squirrels. Camps, camping. Emotions – fear.

Scaredy Squirrel has a birthday party ill. by author. Kids Can, 2011. ISBN 978-1-55453-468-5 Subj: Animals – squirrels. Birthdays. Emotions – fear. Parties.

Scaredy Squirrel makes a friend ill. by author. Kids Can, 2007. ISBN 978-1-55453-181-3 Subj: Animals – dogs. Animals – squirrels. Emotions – fear. Emotions – loneliness. Friendship.

Scaredy Squirrel prepares for Christmas: a safety guide for scaredies ill. by author. Kids Can, 2012. ISBN 978-1-55453-469-2 Subj: Animals – squirrels. Emotions – fear. Holidays – Christmas.

Scaredy Squirrel prepares for Halloween: a safety guide for scaredies ill. by author. Kids Can, 2013. ISBN 978-1-89478-687-4 Subj: Animals – squirrels. Emotions – fear. Holidays – Halloween.

You're finally here! ill. by author. Hyperion/Disney, 2011. ISBN 978-1-4231-3486-2 Subj: Animals

– rabbits. Behavior – misbehavior. Books, reading. Etiquette.

Watters, Debbie, et al. *Where's Mom's hair? a family journey through cancer* photos by Sophie Hogan. Second Story, 2005. ISBN 978-1-896764-94-8 Subj: Family life – mothers. Hair. Illness – cancer.

Watterson, Carol. *An edible alphabet: 26 reasons to love the farm* ill. by Michela Sorrentino. Tricycle, 2011. ISBN 978-1-58246-421-3 Subj: ABC books. Farms.

Watts, Bernadette. *The golden plate* ill. by author. NorthSouth, 2014. ISBN 978-073584175-8 Subj: Behavior – stealing. Character traits – responsibility. Emotions.

The smallest snowflake ill. by author. NorthSouth, 2009. ISBN 978-0-7358-2258-0 Subj: Character traits – smallness. Seasons – winter. Weather – snow.

Watts, Frances. *Kisses for Daddy* ill. by David Legge. Trafalgar, 2008. ISBN 978-1-921272-43-1 Subj: Animals – bears. Bedtime. Family life – fathers. Kissing.

Watts, Jeri. *A piece of home* ill. by Hyewon Yum. Candlewick, 2016. ISBN 978-076366971-3 Subj: Ethnic groups in the U.S. – Korean Americans. Family life – grandmothers. Flowers. Immigrants, immigration. Moving. School.

Watts, Leslie Elizabeth. *The Baabaasheep Quartet* ill. by author. Fitzhenry & Whiteside, 2005. ISBN 978-1-55041-890-3 Subj: Activities – singing. Animals – sheep. Cities, towns. Music.

You can't rush a cat (Bradford, Karleen)

Waugh, Peter. *The great cannon beach mouse caper* ill. by Don Sunderland. Educare, 2002. ISBN 978-0-944638-38-5 Subj: Activities – traveling. Animals – mice. Birds – seagulls. Family life. Sea & seashore – beaches.

Wax, Naomi. *Even firefighters go to the potty: a potty training lift-the-flap story* (Wax, Wendy)

Wax, Wendy. *Even firefighters go to the potty: a potty training lift-the-flap story* by Wendy Wax and Naomi Wax ill. by Stephen Gilpin. Simon & Schuster, 2008. ISBN 978-1-4169-2720-4 Subj: Careers. Format, unusual – toy & movable books. Toilet training.

A very mice Christmas photos by Jon Holderer. HarperCollins, 2003. ISBN 978-0-06-052321-3 Subj: Animals – mice. Format, unusual – board books. Holidays – Christmas. Rhyming text.

Wayland, April Halprin. *More than enough: a Passover story* ill. by Katie Kath. Dial, 2016. ISBN 978-

080374126-3 Subj: Holidays – Passover. Holidays – Seder. Jewish culture.

New Year at the pier: a Rosh Hashanah story ill. by Stéphane Jorisch. Dial, 2009. ISBN 978-0-8037-3279-7 Subj: Holidays – Rosh Hashanah.

Wayne-von Königslöw, Andrea. *How do you read to a rabbit?* ill. by author. Annick, 2010. ISBN 978-1-55451-232-4 Subj: Animals. Books, reading.

We wish you a merry Christmas: a traditional Christmas carol ill. by Tracey Campbell Pearson. Dial, 1983. ISBN 978-0-8037-9400-9 Subj: Behavior – misbehavior. Holidays – Christmas. Songs.

Weatherford, Carole Boston. *Be a King: Dr. Martin Luther King Jr.'s dream and you* ill. by James Ransome. Bloomsbury, 2018. ISBN 978-080272368-0 Subj: Behavior – seeking better things. Character traits – confidence. Character traits – generosity. Character traits – helpfulness. Character traits – kindness. Character traits – perseverance. Ethnic groups in the U.S. – African Americans. Holidays – Martin Luther King, Jr. Day. Violence, nonviolence.

The Beatitudes: from slavery to civil rights ill. by Tim Ladwig. Eerdmans, 2010. ISBN 978-0-8028-5352-3 Subj: Ethnic groups in the U.S. – African Americans. Prejudice. Religion. Slavery. U.S. history.

Before John was a jazz giant: a song of John Coltrane ill. by Sean Qualls. Henry Holt, 2008. ISBN 978-0-8050-7994-4 Subj: Careers – musicians. Ethnic groups in the U.S. – African Americans. Music. U.S. history.

Champions on the bench: the Cannon Street YMCA All Stars ill. by Leonard Jenkins. Penguin, 2007. ISBN 978-0-8037-2987-2 Subj: Ethnic groups in the U.S. – African Americans. Prejudice. Sports – baseball. U.S. history.

Freedom in Congo Square ill. by R. Gregory Christie. little bee, 2016. ISBN 978-149980103-3 Subj: Caldecott award honor books. Ethnic groups in the U.S. – African Americans. Slavery. U.S. history.

Freedom on the menu: the Greensboro sit-ins ill. by Jerome Lagarrigue. Penguin, 2005. ISBN 978-0-8037-2860-8 Subj: Ethnic groups in the U.S. – African Americans. Prejudice. Restaurants. U.S. history.

Gordon Parks: how the photographer captured black and white America ill. by Jamey Christoph. Albert Whitman, 2015. ISBN 978-080753017-7 Subj: Careers – photographers. Ethnic groups in the U.S. – African Americans. Prejudice. U.S. history.

I, Matthew Henson: polar explorer ill. by Eric Velasquez. Walker, 2008. ISBN 978-0-8027-9688-2 Subj: Careers – explorers. Ethnic groups in the

U.S. – African Americans. Foreign lands – Arctic. U.S. history.

In your hands ill. by Brian Pinkney. Atheneum, 2017. ISBN 978-148146293-8 Subj: Behavior – worrying. Character traits – hopefulness. Ethnic groups in the U.S. – African Americans. Family life – mothers. Family life – sons. Religion.

Jazz baby ill. by Laura Freeman. Lee & Low, 2002. ISBN 978-1-58430-039-7 Subj: Activities – playing. Music. Rhyming text.

Juneteenth jamboree ill. by Yvonne Buchanan. Lee & Low, 1995. ISBN 978-1-880000-18-2 Subj: Ethnic groups in the U.S. – African Americans. Holidays – Juneteenth. Slavery. U.S. history.

Leontyne Price: voice of a century ill. by Raúl Colón. Knopf, 2014. ISBN 978-037585606-8 Subj: Careers – singers. Ethnic groups in the U.S. – African Americans. Music.

Moses: when Harriet Tubman led her people to freedom ill. by Kadir Nelson. Hyperion, 2006. ISBN 978-0-7868-5175-1 Subj: Caldecott award honor books. Ethnic groups in the U.S. – African Americans. Slavery. U.S. history.

Sugar Hill: Harlem's historic neighborhood ill. by R. Gregory Christie. Albert Whitman, 2014. ISBN 978-080757650-2 Subj: Ethnic groups in the U.S. – African Americans. Rhyming text. U.S. history.

Voice of freedom: Fannie Lou Hamer, spirit of the civil rights movement ill. by Ekua Holmes. Candlewick, 2015. ISBN 978-076366531-9 Subj: Caldecott award honor books. Ethnic groups in the U.S. – African Americans. Poetry. Prejudice. Violence, nonviolence.

Weaver, Jo. *Little One* ill. by author. Peachtree, 2016. ISBN 978-156145924-7 Subj: Animals – bears. Seasons.

Weaver, Tess. *Cat jumped in!* ill. by Emily Arnold McCully. Houghton, 2007. ISBN 978-0-618-61488-2 Subj: Animals – cats. Behavior – misbehavior.

Frederick Finch, loudmouth ill. by Debbie Tilley. Clarion, 2008. ISBN 978-0-618-45239-2 Subj: Character traits – individuality. Contests. Fairs, festivals. Humorous stories. Noise, sounds.

Opera cat ill. by Andréa Wesson. Clarion, 2002. ISBN 978-0-618-09635-0 Subj: Activities – singing. Animals – cats. Careers – singers. Foreign lands – Italy.

Webb, Holly. *Little puppy lost* ill. by Rebecca Harry. Tiger Tales, 2015. ISBN 978-158925170-0 Subj: Animals – cats. Animals – dogs. Behavior – lost. Friendship.

Weber, Elka. *The Yankee at the seder* ill. by Adam Gustavson. Tricycle, 2009. ISBN 978-1-58246-256-

1 Subj: Holidays – Passover. Holidays – Seder. U.S. history. War.

Weber, Linda Kay. *Louie Larkey and the bad dream patrol* ill. by Nora Hilb. Moon Mt, 2001. ISBN 978-0-9677929-3-4 Subj: Dreams. Toys. Toys – bears.

Webster, Christine. *Otter everywhere* ill. by Tim Nihoff. Candlewick, 2007. ISBN 978-0-7636-2921-2 Subj: Activities – picnicking. Animals – otters. Sports – swimming.

Webster, Sheryl. *Noodle's knitting* ill. by Caroline Pedler. Good Books, 2010. ISBN 978-1-56148-694-6 Subj: Activities – knitting. Animals – mice.

Wechterowicz, Przemyslaw. *Hug me, please!* ill. by Emilia Dziubak. Words & Pictures, 2017. ISBN 978-168297142-0 Subj: Animals – bears. Family life – fathers. Hugging.

Wedeven, Carol. *The Easter cave* ill. by Len Ebert. Concordia, 2001. ISBN 978-0-570-07135-8 Subj: Holidays – Easter. Religion.

Weeks, Sarah. *Be mine, be mine, sweet valentine* ill. by Fumi Kosaka. HarperCollins, 2005. ISBN 978-0-694-01514-6 Subj: Format, unusual – toy & movable books. Gifts. Holidays – Valentine's Day. Rhyming text.

Bite me, I'm a book ill. by Jef Kaminsky. Random House, 2002. ISBN 978-0-375-81261-3 Subj: Babies, toddlers. Books, reading. Format, unusual – board books. Humorous stories. Rhyming text.

Bite me, I'm a shape ill. by Jef Kaminsky. Random House, 2002. ISBN 978-0-375-81262-0 Subj: Babies, toddlers. Concepts – shape. Format, unusual – board books. Rhyming text.

Bunny fun ill. by Sam Williams. Harcourt, 2008. ISBN 978-0-15-205838-8 Subj: Activities – playing. Animals – rabbits. Rhyming text.

Catfish Kate and the sweet swamp band ill. by Elwood H. Smith. Atheneum, 2009. ISBN 978-1-4169-4026-5 Subj: Animals. Books, reading. Character traits – compromising. Fish. Music. Musical instruments – bands. Swamps.

Counting Ovejas ill. by David Diaz. Simon & Schuster, 2006. ISBN 978-0-689-86750-7 Subj: Animals – sheep. Bedtime. Concepts – color. Counting, numbers. Foreign languages.

Crocodile smile ill. by Lois Ehlert. HarperCollins, 1994. ISBN 978-0-06-022867-5 Subj: Animals. Animals – endangered animals. Music. Songs.

Ella, of course! ill. by Doug Cushman. Harcourt, 2007. ISBN 978-0-15-204943-0 Subj: Animals – pigs. Ballet. Problem solving. Umbrellas.

Glamourpuss ill. by David Small. Scholastic, 2015. ISBN 978-054560954-8 Subj: Animals – cats. Animals – dogs. Character traits – vanity. Emotions – envy, jealousy.

I'm a pig ill. by Holly Berry. HarperCollins, 2005. ISBN 978-0-06-074344-4 Subj: Animals – pigs. Rhyming text. Self-concept.

Mrs. McNosh and the great big squash ill. by Nadine Bernard Westcott. Geringer, 2000. ISBN 978-0-694-01202-2 Subj: Gardens, gardening. Homes, houses. Plants. Rhyming text.

Mrs. McNosh hangs up her wash ill. by Nadine Bernard Westcott. Geringer, 1998. ISBN 978-0-694-01076-9 Subj: Humorous stories. Laundry.

My somebody special ill. by Ashley Wolff. Harcourt, 2002. ISBN 978-0-15-202561-8 Subj: Animals. Character traits – questioning. Emotions. Family life – parents. Rhyming text. School – nursery.

Oh my gosh, Mrs. McNosh! ill. by Nadine Bernard Westcott. Geringer, 2002. ISBN 978-0-06-008858-3 Subj: Animals – dogs. Behavior – running away. Humorous stories. Parks. Rhyming text.

Overboard! ill. by Sam Williams. Harcourt, 2006. ISBN 978-0-15-205046-7 Subj: Activities – playing. Animals – rabbits. Babies, toddlers. Rhyming text.

Sophie Peterman tells the truth! ill. by Robert Neubecker. Simon & Schuster, 2009. ISBN 978-1-4169-8686-7 Subj: Babies, toddlers. Family life – new sibling. Sibling rivalry.

Without you ill. by Suzanne Duranceau. Geringer, 2003. ISBN 978-0-06-027816-8 Subj: Birds – penguins. Family life – parents.

Woof: a love story ill. by Holly Berry. HarperCollins, 2009. ISBN 978-0-06-025007-2 Subj: Animals – cats. Animals – dogs. Emotions – love. Music. Musical instruments – trombones. Rhyming text.

Wegerif, Gay. *Up close* ill. by author. Abrams, 2013. ISBN 978-1-4197-0391-1 Subj: Animals. Format, unusual – board books. Picture puzzles.

Wegman, William. *Flo and Wendell explore* ill. by author. Dial, 2014. ISBN 978-080373930-7 Subj: Animals – dogs. Camps, camping. Family life – brothers & sisters.

Weigel, Jeff. *Atomic Ace (he's just my dad)* ill. by author. Albert Whitman, 2004. ISBN 978-0-8075-3216-4 Subj: Family life – fathers. Rhyming text.

Weigelt, Udo. *Bear's last journey* ill. by Sibylle Kazeroid. NorthSouth, 2003. ISBN 978-0-7358-1800-2 Subj: Animals. Animals – bears. Death. Emotions – grief.

The Easter Bunny's baby ill. by Rolf Siegenthaler. NorthSouth, 2001. ISBN 978-0-7358-1442-4 Subj: Animals – rabbits. Behavior – mistakes. Birds –

ostriches. Eggs. Family life – parents. Holidays – Easter.

It wasn't me ill. by Julia Gukova. NorthSouth, 2001. ISBN 978-0-7358-1524-7 Subj: Animals – ferrets. Animals – mice. Behavior – stealing. Birds – ravens. Crime.

Old Beaver ill. by Bernadette Watts. NorthSouth, 2002. ISBN 978-0-7358-1565-0 Subj: Animals. Animals – beavers. Old age. Self-concept.

Super Guinea Pig to the rescue ill. by Nina Spranger. Walker, 2007. ISBN 978-0-8027-9705-6 Subj: Animals – guinea pigs. Disguises. Pets. Television.

Who stole the gold? ill. by Julia Gukova. NorthSouth, 2000. ISBN 978-0-7358-1373-1 Subj: Animals. Animals – hamsters. Behavior – stealing. Friendship.

Weil, Lisl. *The candy egg bunny* ill. by author. Holiday, 1975. ISBN 978-0-8234-0250-2 Subj: Animals – rabbits. Holidays – Easter. Witches.

Weill, Cynthia. *Animal talk: Mexican folk art animal sounds in English and Spanish* ill. by Rubí Fuentes and Efraín Broa. Cinco Puntos, 2016. ISBN 978-194102632-8 Subj: Animals. Art. Foreign lands – Mexico. Foreign languages. Noise, sounds.

Weinberg, Larry. *The Forgetful Bears help Santa* ill. by Jason Wolff. Random House, 2002. ISBN 978-0-375-92291-6 Subj: Animals – bears. Behavior – forgetfulness. Holidays – Christmas. Humorous stories. Santa Claus.

Weinberg, Steven. *Rex finds an egg! egg! egg!* ill. by author. Simon & Schuster, 2015. ISBN 978-148140308-5 Subj: Dinosaurs. Eggs.

Weinert, Matthias. *No bath, no cake! Polly's pirate party* ill. by author. NorthSouth, 2013. ISBN 978-0-7358-4112-3 Subj: Activities – bathing. Character traits – cleanliness. Hygiene. Parties. Pirates.

Weingarten, Gene. *Me and dog* ill. by Eric Shansby. Simon & Schuster, 2014. ISBN 978-144249413-8 Subj: Animals – dogs. Rhyming text.

Weinstein, Ellen Slusky. *Everywhere the cow says "Moo!"* ill. by Kenneth Andersson. Boyds Mills, 2008. ISBN 978-1-59078-458-7 Subj: Animals. Foreign languages. Noise, sounds.

Weinstock, Robert. *Food hates you, too, and other poems* ill. by author. Hyperion, 2009. ISBN 978-1-4231-1391-1 Subj: Food. Poetry.

Weinstone, David. *Music class today!* ill. by Vin Vogel. Farrar, 2015. ISBN 978-037435131-1 Subj: Babies, toddlers. Character traits – shyness. Music. Musical instruments. Rhyming text.

Weis, Carol. *When the cows got loose* ill. by Ard Hoyt. Simon & Schuster, 2006. ISBN 978-0-689-85166-7 Subj: Animals – bulls, cows. Behavior – misbehavior. Circus.

Weisburd, Stefi. *Barefoot: poems for naked feet* ill. by Lori McElrath-Eslick. Boyds Mills, 2008. ISBN 978-1-59078-306-1 Subj: Poetry. Seasons – summer.

Weiss, David. *Kay Thompson's Eloise in Hollywood* (Stem, J. David)

Weiss, Ellen. *I love you, Little Monster* ill. by Alli Arnold. Simon & Schuster, 2012. ISBN 978-1-4424-2850-8 Subj: Emotions – love. Family life – mothers.

Kitten castle (Friedman, Mel)

Playtime for twins ill. by Sam Williams. Simon & Schuster, 2012. ISBN 978-1-4424-3027-3 Subj: Activities – playing. Format, unusual – board books. Multiple births – twins.

The taming of Lola: a shrew story ill. by Jerry Smath. Abrams, 2010. ISBN 978-0-8109-4066-6 Subj: Animals – shrews. Behavior – misbehavior. Emotions – anger. Family life – cousins. Family life – grandmothers.

Weiss, George. *What a wonderful world* by George Weiss and Bob Thiele ill. by Ashley Bryan. Atheneum, 1995. ISBN 978-0-689-80087-0 Subj: Nature. Poetry. Puppets. Songs. World.

What a wonderful world by George Weiss and Bob Thiele ill. by Tim Hopgood. Henry Holt, 2015. ISBN 978-1-627-79254-7 Subj: Nature. Songs. World.

Weiss, Mitch. *The ghost catcher: a Bengali folktale* (Hamilton, Martha)

The hidden feast: a folktale from the American South (Hamilton, Martha)

Priceless gifts: a folktale from Italy (Hamilton, Martha)

Weiss, Nicki. *Where does the brown bear go?* ill. by author. Greenwillow, 1989. ISBN 978-0-688-07863-8 Subj: Animals. Bedtime. Night. Sleep. Toys.

The world turns round and round ill. by author. Greenwillow, 2000. ISBN 978-0-688-17214-5 Subj: Clothing. Ethnic groups in the U.S. Rhyming text. World.

Weitekamp, Margaret A. *Pluto's secret: an icy world's tale of discovery* by Margaret A. Weitekamp and David DeVorkin ill. by Diane Kidd. Abrams, 2013. ISBN 978-1-4197-0423-9 Subj: Planets. Space & space ships.

Weitzman, Elizabeth. *Let's talk about when a parent dies* ill. by author. Rosen, 1996. ISBN 978-0-8239-

2309-0 Subj: Death. Emotions – grief. Family life.

Weitzman, Jacqueline Preiss. *Superhero Joe* ill. by Ron Barrett. Simon & Schuster, 2011. ISBN 978-1-4169-9157-1 Subj: Character traits – bravery. Emotions – fear. Imagination.

Superhero Joe and the creature next door ill. by Ron Barrett. Simon & Schuster, 2013. ISBN 978-1-4424-1268-2 Subj: Emotions – fear. Friendship. Imagination.

You can't take a balloon into the Metropolitan Museum ill. by Robin Preiss-Glasser. Dial, 1998. ISBN 978-0-8037-2302-3 Subj: Art. Cities, towns. Family life – grandmothers. Museums. Toys – balloons. Wordless.

You can't take a balloon into the National Gallery ill. by Robin Preiss-Glasser. Dial, 2000. ISBN 978-0-8037-2303-0 Subj: Art. Cities, towns. Family life – grandmothers. Museums. Picture puzzles. Toys – balloons. Wordless.

Welch, Willy. *Dancing with Daddy* ill. by Liza Woodruff. Whispering Coyote, 1999. ISBN 978-1-58089-020-5 Subj: Activities – dancing. Animals. Family life – fathers. Rhyming text. Trees.

Grumpy Bunnies ill. by Tammie Lyon. Charlesbridge, 2000. ISBN 978-1-58089-053-3 Subj: Animals – rabbits. Rhyming text. School.

Playing right field ill. by Marc Simont. Scholastic, 1995. ISBN 978-0-590-48298-1 Subj: Songs. Sports – baseball.

Weller, Frances Ward. *The angel of Mill Street* ill. by Robert J. Blake. Philomel, 1998. ISBN 978-0-399-23133-9 Subj: Accidents. Angels. Animals – dogs. Careers – musicians. Ethnic groups in the U.S. – Irish Americans. Holidays – Christmas. Weather – snow.

Welling, Peter J. *Andrew McGroundhog and his shady shadow* ill. by author. Pelican, 2001. ISBN 978-1-56554-711-7 Subj: Animals – groundhogs. Hibernation. Holidays – Groundhog Day. Shadows.

Shawn O'Hisser, the last snake in Ireland ill. by author. Pelican, 2002. ISBN 978-1-58980-014-4 Subj: Animals. Foreign lands – Ireland. Humorous stories. Mythical creatures – leprechauns. Reptiles – snakes.

Wellington, Monica. *Apple farmer Annie* ill. by author. Dutton, 2001. ISBN 978-0-525-46727-4 Subj: Careers – farmers. Farms. Food. Stores.

Bunny's first snowflake ill. by author. Dutton, 2000. ISBN 978-0-525-46464-8 Subj: Animals. Animals – rabbits. Format, unusual – board books. Seasons – winter. Weather – snow.

Colors for Zena ill. by author. Dial, 2013. ISBN 978-0-8037-3743-3 Subj: Concepts – color.

Mr. Cookie Baker ill. by author. Penguin, 2006. ISBN 978-0-525-47763-1 Subj: Activities – baking, cooking. Careers – bakers. Food.

My leaf book ill. by author. Dial, 2015. ISBN 978-080374141-6 Subj: Behavior – collecting things. Seasons – fall. Trees.

Night rabbits ill. by author. Dutton, 1995. ISBN 978-0-525-45335-2 Subj: Animals – rabbits. Night. Weather – storms.

Pizza at Sally's ill. by author. Penguin, 2006. ISBN 978-0-525-47715-0 Subj: Activities – baking, cooking. Careers – chefs, cooks. Food. Restaurants.

Riki's birdhouse ill. by author. Dutton, 2009. ISBN 978-0-525-42079-8 Subj: Activities – making things. Birds. Homes, houses.

Squeaking of art, the mice go to the museum ill. by author. Dutton, 2000. ISBN 978-0-525-46165-4 Subj: Animals – cats. Animals – mice. Art. Museums.

Truck driver Tom ill. by author. Penguin, 2007. ISBN 978-0-525-47831-7 Subj: Careers – truck drivers. Transportation. Trucks.

Zinnia's flower garden ill. by author. Penguin, 2005. ISBN 978-0-525-47368-8 Subj: Flowers. Gardens, gardening.

Wells, Robert E. *Did a dinosaur drink this water?* ill. by author. Albert Whitman, 2006. ISBN 978-0-8075-8839-0 Subj: Science. Water.

What's so special about planet Earth? ill. by author. Albert Whitman, 2009. ISBN 978-0-8075-8815-4 Subj: Earth. Space & space ships.

Why do elephants need the sun? ill. by author. Albert Whitman, 2010. ISBN 978-0-8075-9081-2 Subj: Animals – elephants. Science. Sun.

Wells, Rosemary. *The bear went over the mountain* ill. by author. Scholastic, 1998. ISBN 978-0-590-02910-0 Subj: Animals – bears. Mountains. Songs.

Bingo ill. by author. Scholastic, 1999. ISBN 978-0-590-02913-1 Subj: Animals – dogs. Format, unusual – board books. Music. Songs.

Bunny cakes ill. by author. Dial, 1997. ISBN 978-0-8037-2144-9 Subj: Activities – baking, cooking. Animals – rabbits. Family life – brothers & sisters. Family life – grandmothers.

Bunny mail ill. by author. Viking, 2004. ISBN 978-0-670-03630-1 Subj: Activities – picnicking. Animals – rabbits. Family life – brothers & sisters. Family life – grandmothers. Letters, cards.

Bunny money ill. by author. HarperCollins, 1997. ISBN 978-0-06-027258-6 Subj: Animals – rabbits. Family life – brothers & sisters. Family life – grandmothers. Money.

Bunny party ill. by author. Viking, 2001. ISBN 978-0-670-03501-4 Subj: Animals – rabbits. Birthdays. Family life – brothers & sisters. Family life – grandmothers. Parties. Toys.

Carry me! ill. by author. Hyperion, 2006. ISBN 978-0-7868-0396-5 Subj: Animals – rabbits. Emotions – love. Family life. Poetry.

Clean-up time ill. by author. Viking, 2009. ISBN 978-0-670-01171-1 Subj: Animals – rabbits. Bedtime. Character traits – cleanliness. Family life – brothers & sisters. Format, unusual – board books. Rhyming text.

Emily's first 100 days of school ill. by author. Hyperion, 2000. ISBN 978-0-7868-2443-4 Subj: Animals – rabbits. Counting, numbers. School – first day.

Felix stands tall ill. by author. Candlewick, 2015. ISBN 978-076366111-3 Subj: Animals – guinea pigs. Behavior – bullying, teasing. Character traits – assertiveness. Friendship. Theater.

Fiona's little lie ill. by author. Candlewick, 2016. ISBN 978-076367312-3 Subj: Behavior – lying. Birthdays. Friendship. School.

First tomato ill. by author. Dial, 1992. ISBN 978-0-8037-1175-4 Subj: Animals – rabbits. Gardens, gardening. Rhyming text. School.

Forest of dreams by Rosemary Wells and Susan Jeffers ill. by Susan Jeffers. Dial, 1988. ISBN 978-0-8037-0570-8 Subj: Nature. Seasons – spring. Seasons – winter.

Fritz and the mess fairy ill. by author. Dial, 1991. ISBN 978-0-8037-0983-6 Subj: Animals – skunks. Behavior – misbehavior. Character traits – cleanliness. Fairies.

Goodnight Max ill. by author. Viking, 2000. ISBN 978-0-670-88707-1 Subj: Animals – rabbits. Bedtime. Family life – brothers & sisters. Format, unusual – toy & movable books.

The gulps ill. by Marc Brown. Little, Brown, 2007. ISBN 978-0-316-01460-1 Subj: Health & fitness. Health & fitness – exercise. Self-concept.

Hand in hand ill. by author. Henry Holt, 2016. ISBN 978-162779434-3 Subj: Babies, toddlers. Family life – mothers. Rhyming text.

Hands off, Harry! ill. by author. HarperCollins, 2011. ISBN 978-0-06-192112-4 Subj: Behavior – misbehavior. Problem solving. Reptiles – alligators, crocodiles. School.

Hazel's amazing mother ill. by author. Dial, 1985. ISBN 978-0-8037-0210-3 Subj: Animals. Animals – badgers. Behavior – misbehavior. Family life – mothers.

The house in the mail ill. by Dan Andreasen. Viking, 2002. ISBN 978-0-7894-2603-1 Subj: Family life. Homes, houses. U.S. history.

How many? How much? ill. by Michael Koelsch. Viking, 2001. ISBN 978-0-670-89652-3 Subj: Concepts. Counting, numbers. School – first day.

The island light ill. by author. Dial, 1992. ISBN 978-0-8037-1178-5 Subj: Animals – rabbits. Family life – fathers. Illness. Lighthouses.

The itsy-bitsy spider ill. by author. Scholastic, 1998. ISBN 978-0-590-02911-7 Subj: Birds – ducks. Format, unusual – board books. Songs. Spiders.

The language of doves ill. by Greg Shed. Dial, 1996. ISBN 978-0-8037-1471-7 Subj: Birds – doves. Birds – pigeons. Death. Family life – grandfathers. War.

Letters and sounds ill. by Michael Koelsch. Viking, 2001. ISBN 978-0-670-89651-6 Subj: ABC books. Communication. Language. School.

A lion for Lewis ill. by author. Dial, 1982. ISBN 978-0-8037-4686-2 Subj: Activities – playing. Imagination.

The little lame prince ill. by author. Dial, 1990. ISBN 978-0-8037-0789-4 Subj: Animals – pigs. Behavior – greed. Disabilities – physical disabilities. Folk & fairy tales. Royalty – princes.

Love waves ill. by author. Candlewick, 2011. ISBN 978-0-7636-4989-0 Subj: Activities – working. Animals – rabbits. Emotions – love. Family life – parents. Rhyming text.

Lucy comes to stay ill. by Mark Graham. Dial, 1994. ISBN 978-0-8037-1214-0 Subj: Animals – dogs. Pets.

McDuff and the baby ill. by Susan Jeffers. Hyperion, 1997. ISBN 978-0-7868-2258-4 Subj: Animals – dogs. Babies, toddlers. Family life.

McDuff comes home ill. by Susan Jeffers. Hyperion, 1997. ISBN 978-0-7868-2259-1 Subj: Animals – dogs. Behavior – lost.

McDuff goes to school ill. by Susan Jeffers. Hyperion, 2001. ISBN 978-0-7868-2432-8 Subj: Animals – dogs. Communities, neighborhoods. Foreign languages. School.

McDuff moves in ill. by Susan Jeffers. Hyperion, 1997. ISBN 978-0-7868-2257-7 Subj: Animals – dogs. Behavior – needing someone.

McDuff saves the day ill. by Susan Jeffers. Hyperion, 2002. ISBN 978-0-7868-2311-6 Subj: Activities – picnicking. Animals – dogs. Family life. Food. Holidays – Fourth of July. Insects – ants.

McDuff's hide-and-seek ill. by Susan Jeffers. Hyperion, 2004. ISBN 978-0-7868-1935-5 Subj: Animals – dogs. Animals – rabbits. Format, unusual – toy & movable books. Games.

McDuff's new friend ill. by Susan Jeffers. Hyperion, 1998. ISBN 978-0-7868-2337-6 Subj: Animals – dogs. Holidays – Christmas. Santa Claus.

McDuff's wild romp ill. by Susan Jeffers. Hyperion, 2005. ISBN 978-0-7868-1930-0 Subj: Animals – cats. Animals – dogs.

Max and Ruby at the Warthogs' wedding ill. by author. Viking, 2014. ISBN 978-067078461-5 Subj: Animals – rabbits. Behavior – lost & found possessions. Format, unusual – toy & movable books. Weddings.

Max and Ruby's bedtime book ill. by author. Penguin, 2010. ISBN 978-0-670-01141-4 Subj: Animals – rabbits. Family life – brothers & sisters. Family life – grandmothers.

Max and Ruby's Midas ill. by author. Dial, 1995. ISBN 978-0-8037-1783-1 Subj: Animals – rabbits. Behavior – greed. Family life – brothers & sisters. Food.

Max and Ruby's treasure hunt ill. by author. Viking, 2012. ISBN 978-0-670-06317-8 Subj: Animals – rabbits. Family life – brothers & sisters. Family life – grandmothers. Format, unusual – toy & movable books. Nursery rhymes. Participation.

Max cleans up ill. by author. Viking, 2000. ISBN 978-0-670-89218-1 Subj: Animals – rabbits. Babies, toddlers. Character traits – cleanliness. Family life – brothers & sisters.

Max counts his chickens ill. by author. Penguin, 2007. ISBN 978-0-670-06222-5 Subj: Animals – rabbits. Counting, numbers. Holidays – Easter. Sibling rivalry.

Max's ABC ill. by author. Penguin, 2006. ISBN 978-0-670-06074-0 Subj: ABC books. Animals – rabbits.

Max's apples ill. by author. Grosset, 2009. ISBN 978-0-448-45262-3 Subj: Activities – baking, cooking. Animals – rabbits. Family life – brothers & sisters. Food.

Max's bath ill. by author. Dial, 1985. ISBN 978-0-8037-0162-5 Subj: Activities – bathing. Animals – rabbits. Format, unusual – board books.

Max's bedtime ill. by author. Dial, 1985. ISBN 978-0-8037-0160-1 Subj: Animals – rabbits. Bedtime. Format, unusual – board books. Sibling rivalry. Toys.

Max's birthday ill. by author. Dial, 1985. ISBN 978-0-8037-0163-2 Subj: Animals – rabbits. Birthdays. Format, unusual – board books. Toys.

Max's breakfast ill. by author. Dial, 1998. ISBN 978-0-8037-2273-6 Subj: Animals – rabbits. Character traits – patience, impatience. Format, unusual – board books. Sibling rivalry.

Max's bunny business ill. by author. Viking, 2008. ISBN 978-0-670-01105-6 Subj: Animals – rabbits. Family life – brothers & sisters. Money. Shopping.

Max's chocolate chicken ill. by author. Dial, 1999. ISBN 978-0-8037-2351-1 Subj: Animals – rabbits.

Holidays – Easter. Seasons – spring. Sibling rivalry.

Max's Christmas ill. by author. Dial, 1986. ISBN 978-0-8037-0290-5 Subj: Animals – rabbits. Holidays – Christmas. Santa Claus.

Max's dragon shirt ill. by author. Dial, 1991. ISBN 978-0-8037-0945-4 Subj: Activities – babysitting. Animals – rabbits. Behavior – lost. Clothing. Family life – brothers & sisters. Stores.

Max's Easter surprise ill. by author. Grosset, 2008. ISBN 978-0-448-44783-4 Subj: Animals – rabbits. Family life – brothers & sisters. Holidays – Easter.

Max's first word ill. by author. Dial, 1979. ISBN 978-0-8037-6066-0 Subj: Animals – rabbits. Format, unusual – board books. Language.

Max's new suit ill. by author. Dial, 1979. ISBN 978-0-8037-6065-3 Subj: Animals – rabbits. Clothing. Format, unusual – board books.

Max's ride ill. by author. Dial, 1979. ISBN 978-0-8037-6069-1 Subj: Animals – rabbits. Format, unusual – board books. Language.

Max's toys: a counting book ill. by author. Dial, 1979. ISBN 978-0-8037-6068-4 Subj: Animals – rabbits. Counting, numbers. Format, unusual – board books. Toys.

Max's worm cake ill. by author. Grosset, 2009. ISBN 978-0-448-45086-5 Subj: Animals – rabbits. Animals – worms. Family life – brothers & sisters. Gardens, gardening.

Miracle melts down ill. by author. HarperCollins, 2012. ISBN 978-0-06-192115-5 Subj: Animals. Emotions – anger. School.

The miraculous tale of the two Maries ill. by Petra Mathers. Penguin, 2006. ISBN 978-0-670-05960-7 Subj: Foreign lands – France. Religion.

Morris's disappearing bag ill. by author. Viking, 1999. ISBN 978-0-670-88721-7 Subj: Animals – rabbits. Gifts. Holidays – Christmas.

Moss pillows ill. by author. Dial, 1992. ISBN 978-0-8037-1177-8 Subj: Animals – rabbits. Family life. Forest, woods. Rhyming text.

My kindergarten ill. by author. Hyperion, 2004. ISBN 978-0-7868-0833-5 Subj: Animals. Animals – rabbits. Days of the week, months of the year. Rhyming text. School.

Night sounds, morning colors ill. by David McPhail. Dial, 1994. ISBN 978-0-8037-1302-4 Subj: Activities. Family life. Seasons. Senses.

Noisy Nora ill. by author. Dial, 1997. ISBN 978-0-8037-1835-7 Subj: Animals – mice. Behavior – needing someone. Rhyming text.

Otto runs for President ill. by author. Scholastic, 2008. ISBN 978-0-545-03722-8 Subj: Animals – dogs. Behavior – seeking better things. Charac-

ter traits – ambition. Character traits – practicality. School.

Otto se presenta para presidente / Otto runs for President ill. by author. Scholastic, 2008. ISBN 978-0-545-04182-9 Subj: Animals – dogs. Behavior – seeking better things. Character traits – ambition. Character traits – practicality. Foreign languages. School.

Peabody ill. by author. Dial, 1983. ISBN 978-0-8037-0005-5 Subj: Sibling rivalry. Toys – dolls.

Peek-a-boo ill. by author. Viking, 2009. ISBN 978-0-670-01167-4 Subj: Animals – rabbits. Family life – brothers & sisters. Format, unusual – board books. Games.

Read to your bunny ill. by author. Scholastic, 1998. ISBN 978-0-590-30284-5 Subj: Animals – rabbits. Books, reading. Rhyming text.

Red boots ill. by author. Viking, 2009. ISBN 978-0-670-01169-8 Subj: Animals – rabbits. Clothing – boots. Family life – brothers & sisters. Format, unusual – board books. Rhyming text. Weather – snow.

Ruby's beauty shop ill. by author. Viking, 2002. ISBN 978-0-670-03553-3 Subj: Animals – rabbits. Beauty shops. Family life – brothers & sisters. Family life – grandmothers.

Say hello, Sophie! ill. by author. Viking, 2017. ISBN 978-110199925-7 Subj: Animals – mice. Character traits – shyness. Communication. Etiquette.

Shopping ill. by author. Viking, 2009. ISBN 978-0-670-01168-1 Subj: Animals – rabbits. Family life – brothers & sisters. Format, unusual – board books. Shopping.

Shy Charles ill. by author. Dial, 1988. ISBN 978-0-8037-0564-7 Subj: Activities – babysitting. Animals – mice. Character traits – individuality. Family life. Rhyming text.

Small world of Binky Braverman ill. by Richard Egielski. Viking, 2003. ISBN 978-0-670-03636-3 Subj: Emotions – loneliness. Family life – aunts, uncles. Imagination.

Sophie's terrible twos ill. by author. Viking, 2014. ISBN 978-067078512-4 Subj: Animals – mice. Behavior – bad day, bad mood. Behavior – misbehavior. Birthdays. Family life.

Stanley and Rhoda ill. by author. Dial, 1978. ISBN 978-0-8037-8249-5 Subj: Activities – babysitting. Animals – mice. Sibling rivalry.

Stella's Starliner ill. by author. Candlewick, 2014. ISBN 978-076361495-9 Subj: Animals. Behavior – bullying, teasing. Family life. Friendship. Homes, houses.

Ten kisses for Sophie! ill. by author. Viking, 2016. ISBN 978-067001665-5 Subj: Animals – mice. Behavior – worrying.

Time-out for Sophie ill. by author. Viking, 2013. ISBN 978-0-670-78511-7 Subj: Animals – mice. Behavior – misbehavior. Family life.

Timothy goes to school ill. by author. Viking, 2000. ISBN 978-0-670-89182-5 Subj: Animals – raccoons. Behavior – growing up. School – first day.

Use your words, Sophie! ill. by author. Viking, 2015. ISBN 978-067001663-1 Subj: Animals – mice. Communication. Family life – new sibling. Family life – sisters. Language.

A visit to Dr. Duck ill. by author. Candlewick, 2014. ISBN 978-076367229-4 Subj: Birds – ducks. Careers – doctors. Emotions – fear. Format, unusual – board books. Illness.

Yoko ill. by author. Hyperion, 1998. ISBN 978-0-7868-2345-1 Subj: Animals – cats. Animals – raccoons. Ethnic groups in the U.S. – Japanese Americans. Food. Prejudice. School.

Yoko finds her way ill. by author. Disney/Hyperion, 2013. ISBN 978-1-4231-6512-5 Subj: Airplanes, airports. Animals – cats. Ethnic groups in the U.S. – Japanese Americans. Foreign lands – Japan. Signs.

Yoko learns to read ill. by author. Hyperion/Disney, 2012. ISBN 978-1-4231-3823-5 Subj: Animals – cats. Books, reading. Ethnic groups in the U.S. – Japanese Americans. Family life – mothers.

Yoko writes her name ill. by author. Hyperion, 2008. ISBN 978-0-7868-0371-2 Subj: Activities – writing. Animals – cats. Behavior – bullying, teasing. Ethnic groups in the U.S. – Japanese Americans. School.

Yoko's paper cranes ill. by author. Hyperion, 2001. ISBN 978-0-7868-2602-5 Subj: Animals – cats. Birds – cranes. Birthdays. Ethnic groups in the U.S. – Japanese Americans. Family life – grandmothers. Foreign lands – Japan.

Yoko's show-and-tell ill. by author. Hyperion/Disney, 2010. ISBN 978-1-4231-1955-5 Subj: Animals – cats. Behavior – misbehavior. Ethnic groups in the U.S. – Japanese Americans. Gifts. School. Toys – dolls.

Weninger, Brigitte. *Bye-bye, Binky* ill. by Yusuke Yonezu. Minedition, 2007. ISBN 978-0-698-40048-1 Subj: Animals. Behavior – growing up.

Davy in the middle ill. by Eve Tharlet. NorthSouth, 2004. ISBN 978-0-7358-1934-4 Subj: Activities – babysitting. Animals – rabbits. Behavior – growing up. Character traits – helpfulness. Family life. Family life – brothers & sisters.

Davy loves his mommy ill. by Eve Tharlet. NorthSouth, 2014. ISBN 978-073584164-2 Subj: Animals – rabbits. Etiquette. Family life – mothers. Holidays – Mother's Day.

Davy, soccer star! ill. by Eve Tharlet. NorthSouth, 2008. ISBN 978-0-7358-2196-5 Subj: Animals – badgers. Animals – rabbits. Behavior – bullying, teasing. Contests. Sports – soccer.

Double birthday ill. by Stephanie Roehe. Minedition, 2005. ISBN 978-0-698-40015-3 Subj: Animals – mice. Birthdays. Gifts. Toys.

The elf's hat ill. by John A. Rowe. NorthSouth, 2000. ISBN 978-0-7358-1255-0 Subj: Animals. Clothing – hats. Cumulative tales. Fairies. Insects – fleas. Rhyming text.

Good-bye, Daddy! ill. by Alan Marks. NorthSouth, 1995. ISBN 978-1-55858-383-2 Subj: Divorce. Emotions. Family life – fathers. Toys – bears.

Good night, Nori ill. by Yusuke Yonezu. Minedition, 2007. ISBN 978-0-698-40065-8 Subj: Animals – cats. Bedtime.

Happy birthday, Davy ill. by Eve Tharlet. NorthSouth, 2000. ISBN 978-0-7358-1346-5 Subj: Animals – rabbits. Birthdays. Parties.

Happy Easter, Davy ill. by Eve Tharlet. NorthSouth, 2001. ISBN 978-0-7358-1436-3 Subj: Animals – rabbits. Gifts. Holidays – Easter.

Happy Easter, Davy! ill. by Eve Tharlet. NorthSouth, 2014. ISBN 978-073584161-1 Subj: Animals – rabbits. Gifts. Holidays – Easter.

A letter to Santa Claus ill. by Anne Möller. NorthSouth, 2000. ISBN 978-0-7358-1360-1 Subj: Holidays – Christmas. Letters, cards. Santa Claus.

Little apple ill. by Anne Möller. NorthSouth, 2001. ISBN 978-0-7358-1426-4 Subj: Food. Trees.

Merry Christmas, Davy! ill. by Eve Tharlet. NorthSouth, 1998. ISBN 978-1-55858-981-0 Subj: Animals. Animals – rabbits. Behavior – sharing. Holidays – Christmas.

Miko goes on vacation ill. by Stephanie Roehe. Penguin, 2006. ISBN 978-0-698-40017-7 Subj: Animals – mice. Friendship. Sea & seashore – beaches. Sports – swimming. Toys.

Miko wants a dog ill. by Stephanie Roehe. Minedition, 2006. ISBN 978-0-698-40016-0 Subj: Animals – mice. Pets.

"Mom, wake up and play!" ill. by Stephanie Roehe. Minedition, 2005. ISBN 978-0-689-40012-4 Subj: Animals – mice. Family life – mothers. Morning.

"No bath! No way!" ill. by Stephanie Roehe. Minedition, 2005. ISBN 978-0-689-40013-1 Subj: Activities – bathing. Animals – mice. Bedtime. Family life – mothers.

Precious water ill. by Anne Möller. NorthSouth, 2002. ISBN 978-0-7358-1514-8 Subj: Ecology. Nature. Water.

Special delivery ill. by Alexander Reichstein. NorthSouth, 2000. ISBN 978-0-7358-1318-2 Subj:

Family life – mothers. Format, unusual – toy & movable books. Games.

What's the matter, Davy? ill. by Eve Tharlet. North-South, 1998. ISBN 978-1-55858-900-1 Subj: Animals – rabbits. Behavior – lost & found possessions. Toys.

Why are you fighting, Davy? ill. by Eve Tharlet. NorthSouth, 1999. ISBN 978-0-7358-1074-7 Subj: Animals – rabbits. Behavior – fighting, arguing. Character traits – individuality. Friendship.

Will you mind the baby, Davy? ill. by Eve Tharlet. NorthSouth, 1997. ISBN 978-1-55858-732-8 Subj: Activities – babysitting. Animals – rabbits. Babies, toddlers. Family life – new sibling.

Wensink, Patrick. *Go go gorillas: a romping bedtime tale* ill. by Nate Wragg. HarperCollins, 2017. ISBN 978-006238118-7 Subj: Activities – dancing. Animals – gorillas. Bedtime. Rhyming text. Zoos.

Wenxuan, Cao. *Feather* ill. by Roger Mello. Steerforth, 2017. ISBN 978-091467185-5 Subj: Behavior – needing someone. Birds. Feathers.

Wenzel, Brendan. *They all saw a cat* ill. by author. Chronicle, 2016. ISBN 978-145215013-0 Subj: Animals. Animals – cats. Caldecott award honor books. Senses – sight.

Werber, Yael. *Spring for Sophie* ill. by Jen Hill. Simon & Schuster/Paula Wiseman, 2017. ISBN 978-148145134-5 Subj: Seasons – spring. Senses.

Werner, Sharon. *Alphasaurs and other prehistoric types* by Sharon Werner and Sarah Forss; ill. by Sharon Werner. Blue Apple, 2012. ISBN 978-1-60905-193-8 Subj: ABC books. Dinosaurs.

West, Colin. *One day in the jungle* ill. by author. Candlewick, 1995. ISBN 978-1-56402-646-0 Subj: Animals. Cumulative tales. Jungle. Noise, sounds.

West, Judy. *Have you got my purr?* ill. by Tim Warnes. Dutton, 2000. ISBN 978-0-525-46390-0 Subj: Animals. Animals – cats. Behavior – lost & found possessions. Noise, sounds.

Westaway, Kylie. *A whale in the bathtub* ill. by Tom Jellett. Clarion, 2016. ISBN 978-054453535-0 Subj: Activities – bathing. Animals – whales. Character traits – cleanliness.

Westcott, Nadine Bernard. *The lady with the alligator purse* ill. by author. Little, 1988. ISBN 978-0-316-93135-9 Subj: Clothing – handbags, purses. Games. Humorous stories. Poetry.

Peanut butter and jelly: a play rhyme ill. by author. Dutton, 1987. ISBN 978-0-525-44317-9 Subj: Animals – elephants. Careers – bakers. Family life. Food. Rhyming text.

Skip to my Lou ill. by adapter. Little, 1989. ISBN 978-0-316-93137-3 Subj: Farms. Folk & fairy tales. Music. Songs.

There's a hole in the bucket ill. by adapter. HarperCollins, 1990. ISBN 978-0-06-026423-9 Subj: Animals. Farms. Music. Songs.

Weston, Carrie. *If a chicken stayed for supper* ill. by Sophie Fatus. Holiday House, 2007. ISBN 978-0-8234-2067-4 Subj: Animals – foxes. Behavior – misbehavior. Birds – chickens, roosters. Counting, numbers. Night.

The new bear at school ill. by Tim Warnes. Scholastic, 2008. ISBN 978-0-545-05783-7 Subj: Animals – bears. School.

Weston, Mark. *Honda: the boy who dreamed of cars* ill. by Katie Yamasaki. Lee & Low, 2008. ISBN 978-1-60060-246-7 Subj: Automobiles. Careers – inventors. Foreign lands – Japan.

Weston, Martha. *Tuck in the pool* ill. by author. Clarion, 1995. ISBN 978-0-395-65479-8 Subj: Animals – pigs. Emotions – fear. Sports – swimming.

Tuck's haunted house ill. by author. Clarion, 2002. ISBN 978-0-618-15966-6 Subj: Animals – pigs. Family life – brothers & sisters. Holidays – Halloween. Homes, houses. Monsters.

Wethered, Peggy. *Touchdown Mars! an ABC adventure* by Peggy Wethered and Ken Edgett ill. by Michael Chesworth. Putnam, 2000. ISBN 978-0-399-23214-5 Subj: ABC books. Animals – cats. Planets. Space & space ships.

Weulersse, Odile. *Nasreddine* ill. by Rebecca Dautremer. Eerdmans, 2013. ISBN 978-0-8028-5416-2 Subj: Behavior – bullying, teasing. Family life – fathers. Folk & fairy tales. Foreign lands – Middle East.

Wewer, Iris. *My wild sister and me* ill. by author. NorthSouth, 2011. ISBN 978-0-7358-4003-4 Subj: Activities – playing. Emotions – envy, jealousy. Family life – brothers & sisters.

Wharnsby-Ali, Dawud. *A picnic of poems in Allah's green garden* ill. by Shireen Adams. Islamic Foundation, 2011. ISBN 978-0-8603-7444-2 Subj: Poetry. Religion – Islam.

Whatley, Bruce. *Captain Pajamas* by Bruce Whatley and Rosie Smith; ill. by Bruce Whatley. HarperCollins, 1999. ISBN 978-0-06-026614-1 Subj: Aliens. Animals – dogs. Imagination. Night. Sleep.

Clinton Gregory's secret ill. by author. Abrams, 2008. ISBN 978-0-8109-9364-8 Subj: Bedtime. Imagination.

Wait! no paint! ill. by author. HarperCollins, 2001. ISBN 978-0-06-028271-4 Subj: Animals –

pigs. Animals – wolves. Behavior – carelessness. Careers – illustrators.

Wheatley, Nadia. *Luke's way of looking* ill. by Matt Ottley. Kane/Miller, 2001. ISBN 978-1-929132-18-8 Subj: Art. Careers – artists. Careers – teachers. Character traits – individuality. Imagination. Museums.

Wheeler, Eliza. *Miss Maple's seeds* ill. by author. Penguin/Nancy Paulsen, 2013. ISBN 978-0-399-25792-6 Subj: Character traits – kindness. Seeds.

Wheeler, Lisa. *Babies can sleep anywhere* ill. by Carolina Buzio. Abrams, 2017. ISBN 978-141972536-4 Subj: Animals. Babies, toddlers. Rhyming text. Sleep.

Boogie knights ill. by Mark Siegel. Atheneum, 2008. ISBN 978-0-689-87639-4 Subj: Knights. Monsters. Parties. Rhyming text.

Castaway cats ill. by Ponder Goembel. Simon & Schuster, 2006. ISBN 978-0-689-86232-8 Subj: Animals – cats. Behavior – lost. Rhyming text.

The Christmas boot ill. by Jerry Pinkney. Dial, 2016. ISBN 978-080374134-8 Subj: Animals – dogs. Behavior – wishing. Clothing – boots. Emotions – loneliness. Holidays – Christmas. Santa Claus.

Dino-baseball ill. by Barry Gott. Carolrhoda, 2010. ISBN 978-0-7613-4429-2 Subj: Dinosaurs. Rhyming text. Sports – baseball.

Dino-basketball ill. by Barry Gott. Carolrhoda, 2011. ISBN 978-0-7613-6393-4 Subj: Dinosaurs. Rhyming text. Sports – basketball.

Dino-boarding ill. by Barry Gott. Carolrhoda, 2014. ISBN 978-146770213-3 Subj: Dinosaurs. Rhyming text. Sports.

Dino-football ill. by Barry Gott. Carolrhoda, 2012. ISBN 978-0-7613-6394-1 Subj: Dinosaurs. Rhyming text. Sports – football.

Dino-hockey ill. by Barry Gott. Carolrhoda, 2007. ISBN 978-0-8225-6191-0 Subj: Dinosaurs. Rhyming text. Sports – hockey.

Dino-racing ill. by Barry Gott. Carolrhoda, 2016. ISBN 978-151240314-5 Subj: Automobiles. Dinosaurs. Rhyming text. Sports – racing.

Dino-soccer ill. by Barry Gott. Carolrhoda, 2009. ISBN 978-0-8225-9028-6 Subj: Dinosaurs. Rhyming text. Sports – soccer.

Dino-swimming ill. by Barry Gott. Lerner, 2015. ISBN 978-146770214-0 Subj: Dinosaurs. Rhyming text. Sports – swimming.

Dino-wrestling ill. by Barry Gott. Carolrhoda, 2013. ISBN 978-1-46770-212-6 Subj: Dinosaurs. Rhyming text. Sports – wrestling.

Even monsters need to sleep ill. by Chris Van Dusen. HarperCollins/Balzer+Bray, 2017. ISBN 978-006236640-5 Subj: Bedtime. Monsters. Rhyming text. Sleep.

Hokey pokey: another prickly love story ill. by Janie Bynum. Little, Brown, 2006. ISBN 978-0-316-00090-1 Subj: Activities – dancing. Animals – hedgehogs. Animals – porcupines. Friendship.

Jam and jelly by Holly and Nellie ill. by Gijsbert van Frankenhuyzen. Sleeping Bear, 2002. ISBN 978-1-58536-109-0 Subj: Activities – working. Clothing – coats. Family life – mothers. Food. Plants.

Jazz baby ill. by R. Gregory Christie. Harcourt, 2004. ISBN 978-0-15-202522-9 Subj: Babies, toddlers. Music. Rhyming text.

Mammoths on the move ill. by Kurt Cyrus. Harcourt, 2006. ISBN 978-0-15-204700-9 Subj: Animals – woolly mammoths. Rhyming text.

Old Cricket ill. by Ponder Goembel. Atheneum, 2003. ISBN 978-0-689-84510-9 Subj: Behavior. Birds – crows. Character traits – helpfulness. Insects – crickets.

The pet project: cute and cuddly vicious verses ill. by Zachariah OHora. Atheneum, 2013. ISBN 978-1-4169-7595-3 Subj: Animals. Pets. Rhyming text.

Porcupining ill. by Janie Bynum. Little, 2002. ISBN 978-0-316-98912-1 Subj: Animals – hedgehogs. Animals – porcupines. Behavior – needing someone. Emotions – loneliness.

Sixteen cows ill. by Kurt Cyrus. Harcourt, 2002. ISBN 978-0-15-202676-9 Subj: Animals – bulls, cows. Cowboys, cowgirls. Rhyming text.

Turk and Runt ill. by Frank Ansley. Atheneum, 2002. ISBN 978-0-689-84761-5 Subj: Birds – turkeys. Character traits – cleverness. Concepts – size. Family life – brothers. Food. Holidays – Thanksgiving.

Ugly pie ill. by Heather Solomon. Harcourt, 2010. ISBN 978-0-15-216754-7 Subj: Activities – baking, cooking. Animals – bears. Food.

Wool gathering ill. by Frank Ansley. Atheneum, 2001. ISBN 978-0-689-84369-3 Subj: Animals – sheep. Family life. Poetry.

Wheeler, Opal. *Sing in praise: a collection of the best loved hymns* ill. by Marjorie Torrey. Dutton, 1946. Subj: Caldecott award honor books. Music. Religion. Songs.

Sing Mother Goose ill. by Marjorie Torrey. Music by Opal Wheeler. Dutton, 1945. Subj: Caldecott award honor books. Music. Nursery rhymes. Songs.

Wheeler, Valerie. *Yes, please! no, thank you!* ill. by Glin Dibley. Sterling, 2006. ISBN 978-1-4027-3929-3 Subj: Character traits – questioning. Etiquette. Format, unusual – board books.

Whelan, Gloria. *The boy who wanted to cook* ill. by Steve Adams. Sleeping Bear, 2011. ISBN 978-1-58536-534-0 Subj: Activities – baking, cooking. Careers – chefs, cooks. Family life. Foreign lands – France. Restaurants.

Queen Victoria's bathing machine ill. by Nancy Carpenter. Simon & Schuster/Paula Wiseman, 2014. ISBN 978-141692753-2 Subj: Foreign lands – England. Rhyming text. Royalty – queens. Sports – swimming.

Whippo, Walt. *Little white duck* ill. by Joan Paley. Lyrics by Walt Whippo; music by Bernard Zaritzky. Little, 2000. ISBN 978-0-316-03227-8 Subj: Animals. Birds – ducks. Music. Songs. Theater.

Whitaker, Suzanne George. *The daring Miss Quimby* ill. by Catherine Stock. Holiday, 2009. ISBN 978-0-8234-1996-8 Subj: Activities – flying. Careers – airplane pilots. Gender roles. U.S. history.

White, Alexina B. *Frisky brisky hippity hop* adapt. by Susan Lurie; photos by Murray Head. Holiday House, 2012. ISBN 978-0-8234-2410-8 Subj: Animals – squirrels. Rhyming text.

White, Becky. *Betsy Ross* ill. by Megan Lloyd. Holiday House, 2011. ISBN 978-0-8234-1908-1 Subj: Activities – sewing. Flags. Rhyming text. U.S. history.

White, Dianne. *Blue on blue* ill. by Beth Krommes. Simon & Schuster/Beach Lane, 2014. ISBN 978-144241267-5 Subj: Rhyming text. Weather – rain. Weather – storms.

White, Ellen Emerson. *Santa paws* ill. by Robert J. Blake. Scholastic, 2003. ISBN 978-0-439-32438-0 Subj: Animals – dogs. Character traits – helpfulness. Holidays – Christmas.

White, Kathryn. *Ruby's school walk* ill. by Miriam Latimer. Barefoot, 2010. ISBN 978-1-84686-275-5 Subj: Activities – walking. Family life – mothers. Imagination. Rhyming text. School.

The tickle test ill. by Adrian Reynolds. Andersen, 2017. ISBN 978-151248126-6 Subj: Activities – playing. Animals. Games.

When they fight ill. by Cliff Wright. Winslow, 2000. ISBN 978-1-890817-46-6 Subj: Behavior – fighting, arguing. Family life.

White, Linda. *Comes a wind* ill. by Tom Curry. DK, 2000. ISBN 978-0-7894-2601-7 Subj: Birthdays. Contests. Family life – brothers. Family life – mothers. Tall tales. Weather – wind.

Too many pumpkins ill. by Megan Lloyd. Holiday, 1996. ISBN 978-0-8234-1245-7 Subj: Behavior – dissatisfaction. Food. Friendship.

Too many turkeys ill. by Megan Lloyd. Holiday House, 2010. ISBN 978-0-8234-2084-1 Subj: Birds – turkeys. Farms. Gardens, gardening.

White, Marsha. *Hooper has lost his owner* ill. by author. Little, 2002. ISBN 978-0-316-06561-0 Subj: Animals – dogs. Behavior – lost & found possessions. Format, unusual – toy & movable books.

White, Teagan. *Adventures with barefoot critters* ill. by author. Tundra, 2014. ISBN 978-177049624-8 Subj: ABC books. Animals. Seasons.

Whitehead, Jenny. *Lunch box mail and other poems* ill. by author. Henry Holt, 2001. ISBN 978-0-8050-6259-5 Subj: Poetry. School.

Whitehead, Kathy. *Looking for Uncle Louie on the Fourth of July* ill. by Pablo Torrecilla. Boyds Mills, 2005. ISBN 978-1-59078-061-9 Subj: Careers – police officers. Family life – aunts, uncles. Holidays – Fourth of July. Motorcycles. Parades.

Whiteley, Opal Stanley. *Only Opal: the diary of a young girl* sel. & adapt. by Jane Boulton; ill. by Barbara Cooney. An adapt. of The story of Opal. Philomel, 1994. ISBN 978-0-399-21990-0 Subj: Family life. Poetry. U.S. history – frontier & pioneer life.

Whitfield, Susan. *The animals of the Chinese zodiac* ill. by Philippa-Alys Browne. Crocodile, 1998. ISBN 978-1-56656-236-2 Subj: Animals. Foreign lands – China. Zodiac.

Whitford, Rebecca. *Little yoga: a toddler's first book of yoga* ill. by Martina Selway. Henry Holt, 2005. ISBN 978-0-8050-7879-4 Subj: Character traits – patience, impatience. Health & fitness – exercise.

Sleepy little yoga: a toddler's sleepy book of yoga ill. by Martina Selway. Henry Holt, 2007. ISBN 978-0-8050-8193-0 Subj: Character traits – patience, impatience. Health & fitness – exercise.

Whiting, Sue. *The firefighters* ill. by Donna Rawlins. Candlewick, 2008. ISBN 978-0-7636-4019-4 Subj: Careers – firefighters. Imagination. School.

Whitman, Candace. *Lines that wiggle* ill. by Steve Wilson. Blue Apple, 2009. ISBN 978-1-934706-54-1 Subj: Art. Monsters. Rhyming text.

Whitman, Sylvia. *Under the Ramadan moon* ill. by Sue Williams. Albert Whitman, 2008. ISBN 978-0-8075-8304-3 Subj: Holidays – Ramadan. Religion – Islam.

Who took the cookie? ill. by Tom Brannon. Random House, 2002. ISBN 978-0-375-81606-2 Subj: Food. Format, unusual – board books. Puppets.

Why did the chicken cross the road? ill. by Jon Agee. Penguin, 2006. ISBN 978-0-8037-3094-6 Subj: Birds – chickens, roosters. Humorous stories.

Whybrow, Ian. *A baby for Grace* ill. by Christian Birmingham. Kingfisher, 1998. ISBN 978-0-7534-5142-7 Subj: Babies, toddlers. Family life – new sibling. Family life – sisters.

Badness for beginners: a Little Wolf and Smellybreff adventure ill. by Tony Ross. Carolrhoda, 2005. ISBN 978-1-57505-861-0 Subj: Animals – wolves. Behavior – misbehavior. Family life – brothers & sisters.

Bella gets her skates on ill. by Rosie Reeve. Abrams, 2007. ISBN 978-0-8109-9416-4 Subj: Animals – rabbits. Behavior – worrying. Seasons – winter. Sports – ice skating.

Faraway farm ill. by Alex Ayliffe. Carolrhoda, 2006. ISBN 978-1-57505-938-9 Subj: Farms. Picture puzzles. Rhyming text.

Good night, monster ill. by Ken Wilson-Max. Knopf, 2001. ISBN 978-0-375-81579-9 Subj: Animals. Format, unusual – toy & movable books. Monsters.

Harry and the bucketful of dinosaurs ill. by Adrian Reynolds. First pub. in the U.S. by Orchard Books under the title Sammy and the dinosaurs in 1999. Random House, 2003. ISBN 978-0-375-82541-5 Subj: Activities – playing. Dinosaurs. Imagination. Names. Toys.

Harry and the dinosaurs at the museum ill. by Adrian Reynolds. Penguin, 2005. ISBN 978-0-375-83338-0 Subj: Behavior – lost. Dinosaurs. Museums. Toys.

Harry and the dinosaurs go to school ill. by Adrian Reynolds. Random House, 2007. ISBN 978-0-375-84180-4 Subj: Dinosaurs. School – first day. Toys.

Harry and the dinosaurs say "Raahh" ill. by Adrian Reynolds. Random House, 2004. ISBN 978-0-375-82542-2 Subj: Careers – dentists. Dinosaurs. Emotions – fear. Toys.

Harry and the snow king ill. by Adrian Reynolds. Levinson Books, 1997. ISBN 978-1-899607-85-3 Subj: Family life. Seasons – winter. Snowmen. Weather – snow.

Hello! Is this grandma? ill. by Deborah Allwright. Tiger Tales, 2008. ISBN 978-1-58925-072-7 Subj: Animals. Format, unusual – toy & movable books. Reptiles – alligators, crocodiles. Telephone, cell phone.

Sammy and the robots ill. by Adrian Reynolds. Orchard, 2001. ISBN 978-0-531-30327-6 Subj: Family life – grandmothers. Format, unusual – toy & movable books. Hospitals. Illness. Robots. Toys.

Wish, change, friend ill. by Tiphanie Beeke. Margaret K. McElderry, 2002. ISBN 978-0-689-84930-5 Subj: Animals – pigs. Behavior – wishing. Birds – penguins. Books, reading. Snowmen.

Wick, Walter. *Can you see what I see? Christmas* photos by author. Scholastic, 2015. ISBN 978-054583183-3 Subj: Format, unusual – board books. Holidays – Christmas. Picture puzzles. Rhyming text.

Can you see what I see? cool collections photos by author. Scholastic, 2004. ISBN 978-0-439-61772-7 Subj: Animals. Dinosaurs. Games. Picture puzzles. Rhyming text. Seasons.

Can you see what I see? dream machine photos by author. Scholastic, 2003. ISBN 978-0-439-39950-0 Subj: Bedtime. Dreams. Morning. Picture puzzles. Rhyming text.

Can you see what I see? once upon a time photos by author. Scholastic, 2006. ISBN 978-0-439-61777-2 Subj: Folk & fairy tales. Picture puzzles. Rhyming text.

Can you see what I see? out of this world photos by author. Scholastic, 2013. ISBN 978-0-545-24468-8 Subj: Picture puzzles. Rhyming text. Space & space ships.

Can you see what I see? picture puzzles to search and solve photos by author. Scholastic, 2002. ISBN 978-0-439-16391-0 Subj: Picture puzzles. Rhyming text.

Can you see what I see? Seymour and the juice box boat photos by author. Scholastic, 2004. ISBN 978-0-439-61778-9 Subj: Animals. Boats, ships. Picture puzzles. Rhyming text.

Can you see what I see? Seymour makes new friends photos by author. Scholastic, 2006. ISBN 978-0-439-61780-2 Subj: Friendship. Picture puzzles. Rhyming text.

Can you see what I see? the night before Christmas photos by author. Scholastic, 2005. ISBN 978-0-439-76927-3 Subj: Holidays – Christmas. Picture puzzles. Poetry. Santa Claus.

Can you see what I see? toyland express photos by author. Scholastic, 2011. ISBN 978-0-545-24483-1 Subj: Picture puzzles. Toys.

Can you see what I see? treasure ship photos by author. Scholastic, 2010. ISBN 978-0-439-02643-7 Subj: Boats, ships. Picture puzzles. Rhyming text. Riddles & jokes.

Hey, Seymour! a search and find fold-out adventure photos by author. Scholastic, 2015. ISBN 978-054550216-0 Subj: Format, unusual – toy & movable books. Picture puzzles. Rhyming text.

Wickberg, Susan. *Hey Mr. Choo-Choo, where are you going?* ill. by Yumi Heo. Putnam, 2008. ISBN 978-0-399-23993-9 Subj: Rhyming text. Trains.

Wickstrom, Sylvie. *I love you, Mister Bear* ill. by author. HarperCollins, 2003. ISBN 978-0-06-029332-1 Subj: Family life. Toys – bears.

Wiebe, Rudy. *Hidden buffalo* ill. by Michael Lonechild. Red Deer, 2003. ISBN 978-0-88995-285-0 Subj: Animals – buffaloes. Dreams. Foreign lands – Canada. Indians of North America – Cree.

Wiener, Lori S., et al, compiler. *Be a friend: children who live with HIV speak* ill. by Lori S. Wiener. Albert Whitman, 1994. ISBN 978-0-8075-0590-8 Subj: Children as authors. Children as illustrators. Illness – AIDS.

Wiese, Kurt. *Fish in the air* ill. by author. Viking, 1948. Subj: Caldecott award honor books. Foreign lands – China. Humorous stories. Kites.

The five Chinese brothers (Bishop, Claire Huchet)

The story about Ping (Flack, Marjorie)

You can write Chinese ill. by author. Viking, 1945. Subj: Caldecott award honor books. Foreign languages.

Wiesmüller, Dieter. *The adventures of Marco and Polo* ill. by author. Walker, 2000. ISBN 978-0-8027-8729-3 Subj: Activities – traveling. Animals – monkeys. Birds – penguins.

In the blink of an eye ill. by author. Walker, 2002. ISBN 978-0-8027-8855-9 Subj: Anatomy – eyes. Animals. Picture puzzles.

Wiesner, David. *Art and Max* ill. by author. Clarion, 2010. ISBN 978-0-618-75663-6 Subj: Activities – painting. Art. Careers – artists. Reptiles – lizards. Self-concept.

Flotsam ill. by author. Houghton, 2006. ISBN 978-0-618-19457-5 Subj: Caldecott award books. Imagination. Sea & seashore – beaches.

Free fall ill. by author. Lothrop, 1988. ISBN 978-0-688-05584-4 Subj: Bedtime. Books, reading. Caldecott award honor books. Dragons. Dreams. Wordless.

Hurricane ill. by author. Houghton, 1990. ISBN 978-0-395-54382-5 Subj: Family life – brothers & sisters. Imagination. Weather – storms.

The loathsome dragon by David Wiesner and Kim Kahng; ill. by David Wiesner. Clarion, 2005. ISBN 978-0-618-54359-5 Subj: Dragons. Folk & fairy tales. Magic. Royalty.

Mr. Wuffles! ill. by author. Clarion, 2013. ISBN 978-0-618-75661-2 Subj: Aliens. Animals – cats. Caldecott award honor books. Petroglyphs. Space & space ships. Wordless.

Sector 7 ill. by author. Clarion, 1999. ISBN 978-0-395-74656-1 Subj: Caldecott award honor books. School. Weather – clouds. Wordless.

The three pigs ill. by author. Clarion, 2001. ISBN 978-0-618-00701-1 Subj: Animals – pigs. Animals – wolves. Books, reading. Caldecott award books. Character traits – cleverness. Folk & fairy tales.

Tuesday ill. by author. Houghton, 1991. ISBN 978-0-395-55113-4 Subj: Activities – flying. Caldecott award books. Frogs & toads. Magic. Night.

Wigersma, Tanneke. *Baby brother* ill. by Nynke Mare Talsma. Boyds Mills, 2005. ISBN 978-1-932425-55-0 Subj: Babies, toddlers. Family life – grandmothers. Family life – new sibling. Letters, cards.

Wigger, J. Bradley. *Thank you, God* ill. by Jago. Eerdmans, 2014. ISBN 978-080285424-7 Subj: Nature. Religion.

Wight, Tamra. *The three grumpies* ill. by Ross Collins. Bloomsbury, 2003. ISBN 978-1-58234-840-7 Subj: Behavior – bad day, bad mood. Emotions.

Wilbur, Helen L. *Z is for Zeus: a Greek mythology alphabet* ill. by Victor Juhasz. Sleeping Bear, 2008. ISBN 978-1-58536-341-4 Subj: ABC books. Mythical creatures.

Wilbur, Richard. *The disappearing alphabet* ill. by David Diaz. Harcourt, 1998. ISBN 978-0-15-201470-4 Subj: ABC books. Poetry.

Wilcox, Brad. *Hip, hip, hooray for Annie McRae!* ill. by Julie Olson. Gibbs Smith, 2001. ISBN 978-1-58685-058-6 Subj: Emotions – happiness.

Wilcox, Brian. *Full moon* by Brian Wilcox and Lawrence David; ill. by Brian Wilcox. Random House, 2001. ISBN 978-0-385-32792-3 Subj: Birthdays. Cities, towns. Family life – grandmothers. Moon.

Wilcox, Leah. *Waking Beauty* ill. by Lydia Monks. Putnam, 2008. ISBN 978-0-399-24615-9 Subj: Folk & fairy tales. Humorous stories. Rhyming text.

Wild, Margaret. *Bobbie Dazzler* ill. by Janine Dawson. Kane/Miller, 2007. ISBN 978-1-933605-46-3 Subj: Animals – wallabies. Character traits – perseverance. Foreign lands – Australia.

Fox by Margaret Wild and Ron Brooks ill. by Ron Brooks. Kane/Miller, 2001. ISBN 978-1-929132-16-4 Subj: Animals – dogs. Animals – foxes. Birds – magpies. Emotions – envy, jealousy. Emotions – loneliness. Friendship.

Going home ill. by Wayne Harris. Scholastic, 1994. ISBN 978-0-590-47958-5 Subj: Activities – traveling. Dreams. Hospitals.

Harry and Hopper ill. by Freya Blackwood. Feiwel & Friends, 2011. ISBN 978-0-312-64261-7 Subj: Animals – dogs. Death. Emotions – grief.

Hush, hush! ill. by Bridget Strevens-Marzo. Little Hare, 2010. ISBN 978-1-921272-86-8 Subj: Animals – hippopotamuses. Bedtime.

Itsy-bitsy babies ill. by Jan Ormerod. Little Hare, 2010. ISBN 978-1-921541-36-0 Subj: Babies, toddlers. Rhyming text.

Lucy Goosey ill. by Ann James. Little Hare, 2009. ISBN 978-1-921049-87-3 Subj: Birds – geese. Family life – mothers. Migration.

Midnight babies ill. by Ann James. Clarion, 1999. ISBN 978-0-618-10412-3 Subj: Activities – dancing. Babies, toddlers. Night.

Mr. Nick's knitting ill. by Dee Huxley. Harcourt, 1989. ISBN 978-0-15-200518-4 Subj: Activities – knitting. Friendship. Hospitals. Illness.

Nighty night ill. by Kerry Argent. Peachtree, 2001. ISBN 978-1-56145-246-0 Subj: Animals. Bedtime.

Old Pig ill. by Ron Brooks. Dial, 1996. ISBN 978-0-8037-1917-0 Subj: Animals – pigs. Death. Family life – grandmothers. Old age.

Our granny ill. by Julie Vivas. Ticknor & Fields, 1994. ISBN 978-0-395-67023-1 Subj: Family life – grandmothers.

Piglet and Granny ill. by Stephen Michael King. Abrams, 2009. ISBN 978-0-8109-4063-5 Subj: Animals – pigs. Family life – grandmothers. Farms.

Piglet and Mama ill. by Stephen Michael King. Abrams, 2005. ISBN 978-0-8109-5869-2 Subj: Animals – pigs. Emotions – love. Family life – mothers. Farms.

Piglet and Papa ill. by Stephen Michael King. Abrams, 2007. ISBN 978-0-8109-1476-6 Subj: Animals – pigs. Emotions – love. Family life – fathers. Farms.

The pocket dogs ill. by Stephen Michael King. Scholastic, 2001. ISBN 978-0-439-23973-8 Subj: Accidents. Animals – dogs. Behavior – lost. Clothing.

Puffling ill. by Julie Vivas. Feiwel & Friends, 2009. ISBN 978-0-312-56570-1 Subj: Behavior – growing up. Birds – puffins. Family life – parents.

Rosie and Tortoise ill. by Ron Brooks. DK, 1999. ISBN 978-0-7894-2630-7 Subj: Animals – rabbits. Family life – new sibling.

Thank you, Santa ill. by Kerry Argent. Scholastic, 1992. ISBN 978-0-590-45805-4 Subj: Animals – polar bears. Foreign lands – Arctic. Foreign lands – Australia. Holidays – Christmas. Letters, cards.

Tom goes to kindergarten ill. by David Legge. Albert Whitman, 2000. ISBN 978-0-8075-8012-7 Subj: Animals – pandas. Family life. School – first day.

The treasure box ill. by Freya Blackwood. Candlewick, 2017. ISBN 978-076369084-7 Subj: Books, reading. Refugees. War.

Wilde, Oscar. *The happy prince* ill. by Jane Ray. Dutton, 1995. ISBN 978-0-525-45367-3 Subj: Cities, towns. Folk & fairy tales. Poverty. Royalty – kings.

The selfish giant ill. by S. Saelig Gallagher. Putnam, 1995. ISBN 978-0-399-22448-5 Subj: Character traits – kindness. Character traits – selfishness. Folk & fairy tales. Gardens, gardening. Giants. Seasons – spring.

The selfish giant retold by Fiona Waters; ill. by Fabian Negrin. Knopf, 2000. ISBN 978-0-375-90319-9 Subj: Character traits – kindness. Character traits – selfishness. Folk & fairy tales. Gardens, gardening. Giants. Seasons – spring.

The selfish giant ill. by Lisbeth Zwerger. Alphabet, 1984. ISBN 978-0-907234-30-2 Subj: Character traits – kindness. Character traits – selfishness. Folk & fairy tales. Gardens, gardening. Giants. Seasons – spring.

Wilder, Laura Ingalls. *Going to town* ill. by Renée Graef. HarperCollins, 1994. ISBN 978-0-06-023013-5 Subj: Cities, towns. Family life – sisters. U.S. history – frontier & pioneer life.

My little house songbook ill. by Holly Jones. HarperCollins, 1995. ISBN 978-0-06-024295-4 Subj: Music. Songs. U.S. history – frontier & pioneer life.

Santa comes to little house ill. by Renée Graef. HarperCollins, 2001. ISBN 978-0-06-025939-6 Subj: Family life. Holidays – Christmas. Santa Claus. U.S. history – frontier & pioneer life.

Wildsmith, Brian. *Brian Wildsmith 1 2 3* ill. by author. Millbrook, 1995. ISBN 978-1-56294-905-1 Subj: Concepts – shape. Counting, numbers.

Brian Wildsmith's puzzles ill. by author. Millbrook, 1996. ISBN 978-0-7613-0052-6 Subj: Games.

A Christmas story ill. by author. Eerdmans, 1998. ISBN 978-0-8028-5173-4 Subj: Animals – donkeys. Holidays – Christmas. Religion – Nativity.

The Easter story ill. by author. Eerdmans, 2000, ©1993. ISBN 978-0-8028-5189-5 Subj: Animals – donkeys. Holidays – Easter. Religion.

Give a dog a bone ill. by author. Pantheon, 1985. ISBN 978-0-394-97709-6 Subj: Animals – dogs. Format, unusual.

Goat's trail ill. by author. Knopf, 1986. ISBN 978-0-394-98276-2 Subj: Animals. Animals – goats. Cumulative tales. Format, unusual. Noise, sounds.

Joseph ill. by author. Eerdmans, 1997. ISBN 978-0-8028-5161-1 Subj: Religion.

Jungle party ill. by author. Star Bright, 2006. ISBN 978-1-59572-052-8 Subj: Animals. Jungle. Reptiles – snakes.

The little wood duck ill. by author. Star Bright, 2006. ISBN 978-1-59572-042-9 Subj: Birds – ducks.

Mary ill. by author. Eerdmans, 2002. ISBN 978-0-8028-5231-1 Subj: Religion.

Wiles, Debbie. *Freedom summer* ill. by Jerome Lagarrigue. Atheneum, 2001. ISBN 978-0-689-82380-0 Subj: Ethnic groups in the U.S. – African Americans. Friendship. Prejudice.

Wiley, Thom. *One sheep, blue sheep* ill. by Ben Mantle. Scholastic, 2012. ISBN 978-0-545-40284-2 Subj: Animals – sheep. Concepts – color. Counting, numbers. Farms. Format, unusual – board books.

Wilhelm, Hans. *Bunny trouble* ill. by author. Scholastic, 1991. ISBN 978-0-590-63153-2 Subj: Animals – rabbits.

A hole in the wall ill. by author. Holiday House, 2016. ISBN 978-082343535-7 Subj: Animals. Mirrors.

I'll always love you ill. by author. Crown, 1985. ISBN 978-0-517-55648-1 Subj: Animals – dogs. Death. Emotions – grief. Pets.

More bunny trouble ill. by author. Scholastic, 1989. ISBN 978-0-590-41589-7 Subj: Animals – foxes. Animals – rabbits. Eggs. Family life – brothers. Family life – sisters. Holidays – Easter.

Quacky Ducky's Easter egg ill. by author. Harper-Collins, 2004. ISBN 978-0-06-053430-1 Subj: Birds – ducks. Eggs. Format, unusual – board books. Friendship. Holidays – Easter.

Quacky Ducky's Easter fun ill. by author. HarperCollins, 2004. ISBN 978-0-06-053431-8 Subj: Activities – painting. Birds – ducks. Format, unusual – board books. Holidays – Easter.

Schnitzel's first Christmas ill. by author. Simon & Schuster, 1991. ISBN 978-0-671-74494-6 Subj: Animals – dogs. Behavior – needing someone. Holidays – Christmas. Santa Claus.

Willard, Nancy. *The flying bed* ill. by John Thompson. Scholastic, 2007. ISBN 978-0-590-25610-0 Subj: Activities – flying. Behavior – greed. Careers – bakers. Foreign lands – Italy. Furniture – beds. Magic.

Gum ill. by Jeff Newman. Candlewick, 2017. ISBN 978-076367774-9 Subj: Behavior – mistakes. Character traits – persistence.

The Moon and Riddles Diner and the Sunnyside Café ill. by Chris Butler. Harcourt, 2001. ISBN 978-0-15-201941-9 Subj: Food. Poetry. Restaurants.

The mouse, the cat and Grandmother's hat ill. by Jenny Mattheson. Little, 2003. ISBN 978-0-316-94006-1 Subj: Animals – cats. Animals – mice. Birthdays. Family life – grandmothers. Parties. Rhyming text.

Pish posh, said Hieronymous Bosch ill. by Leo and Diane Dillon. Harcourt, 1991. ISBN 978-0-15-262210-7 Subj: Careers – artists. Poetry.

Shadow story ill. by David Diaz. Harcourt, 1999. ISBN 978-0-15-201638-8 Subj: Folk & fairy tales. Mythical creatures – ogres. Orphans. Shadows.

A visit to William Blake's inn: poems for innocent and experienced travelers ill. by Alice Provensen and Martin Provensen. Harcourt, 1981. ISBN 978-0-15-293822-2 Subj: Caldecott award honor books. Imagination. Poetry.

Willems, Mo. *Big Frog can't fit in: a pop out book* ill. by author. Hyperion, 2009. ISBN 978-1-4231-1436-9 Subj: Concepts – size. Format, unusual – toy & movable books. Frogs & toads.

City dog, country frog ill. by Jon J Muth. Hyperion, 2010. ISBN 978-1-4231-0300-4 Subj: Animals – dogs. Friendship. Frogs & toads. Seasons.

Don't let the pigeon drive the bus ill. by author. Hyperion, 2003. ISBN 978-0-7868-1988-1 Subj: Birds – pigeons. Caldecott award honor books. Careers – bus drivers. Humorous stories.

Don't let the pigeon stay up late! ill. by author. Hyperion, 2006. ISBN 978-0-7868-3746-5 Subj: Bedtime. Birds – pigeons. Humorous stories.

The duckling gets a cookie!? ill. by author. Hyperion, 2012. ISBN 978-1-4231-5128-9 Subj: Behavior – sharing. Birds – ducks. Birds – pigeons. Etiquette. Food. Humorous stories.

Edwina, the dinosaur who didn't know she was extinct ill. by author. Hyperion, 2006. ISBN 978-0-7868-3748-9 Subj: Dinosaurs. Self-concept.

Goldilocks and the three dinosaurs ill. by author. HarperCollins, 2012. ISBN 978-0-06-210418-2 Subj: Behavior – misbehavior. Dinosaurs. Folk & fairy tales. Humorous stories.

Knuffle Bunny: a cautionary tale ill. by author. Hyperion, 2004. ISBN 978-0-7868-1870-9 Subj: Animals – rabbits. Behavior – lost & found possessions. Caldecott award honor books. Laundry. Toys.

Knuffle Bunny free: an unexpected diversion ill. by author. HarperCollins, 2010. ISBN 978-0-0619-2957-1 Subj: Activities – traveling. Animals – rabbits. Behavior – lost & found possessions. Character traits – bravery. Toys.

Knuffle Bunny too: a case of mistaken identity ill. by author. Hyperion, 2007. ISBN 978-1-4231-0299-1 Subj: Animals – rabbits. Caldecott award honor books. School – nursery. Toys.

Leonardo the terrible monster ill. by author. Hyperion, 2005. ISBN 978-0-7868-5294-9 Subj: Friendship. Imagination. Monsters.

Naked mole rat gets dressed ill. by author. Disney, 2009. ISBN 978-1-4231-1437-6 Subj: Animals. Character traits – individuality. Clothing.

Nanette's baguette ill. by author. Hyperion, 2016. ISBN 978-148472286-2 Subj: Behavior – mistakes. Food. Foreign lands – France. Frogs & toads. Rhyming text.

The pigeon finds a hot dog! ill. by author. Hyperion, 2005. ISBN 978-0-7868-5248-2 Subj: Birds – ducks. Birds – pigeons. Food. Humorous stories.

The pigeon has feelings, too! a smidgeon of pigeon ill. by author. Hyperion, 2005. ISBN 978-0-7868-3650-5 Subj: Birds – pigeons. Emotions. Format, unusual – board books. Humorous stories.

The pigeon loves things that go! a smidgeon of pigeon ill. by author. Hyperion, 2005. ISBN 978-0-7868-3651-2 Subj: Birds – pigeons. Format, unusual – board books. Transportation.

The pigeon needs a bath ill. by author. Disney/Hyperion, 2014. ISBN 978-142319087-5 Subj: Activities – bathing. Birds – pigeons.

The pigeon wants a puppy! ill. by author. Hyperion, 2008. ISBN 978-1-4231-0960-0 Subj: Animals – dogs. Birds – pigeons. Pets.

Sam the most scaredy-cat kid in the whole world ill. by author. Hyperion, 2017. ISBN 978-136800214-1 Subj: Emotions – fear. Friendship. Monsters.

That is not a good idea! ill. by author. HarperCollins, 2013. ISBN 978-0-06-220309-0 Subj: Animals – foxes. Behavior – trickery. Birds – geese.

Time to pee ill. by author. Hyperion, 2003. ISBN 978-0-7868-1868-6 Subj: Animals – mice. Toilet training.

Time to say "please"! ill. by author. Hyperion, 2005. ISBN 978-0-7868-5293-2 Subj: Animals – mice. Etiquette. Format, unusual – toy & movable books.

Welcome: a Mo Willems guide for new arrivals ill. by author. Hyperion, 2017. ISBN 978-148476746-7 Subj: Babies, toddlers. Family life – parents. Format, unusual – board books.

Willey, Margaret. *Clever Beatrice, an Upper Peninsula conte* ill. by Heather Solomon. Atheneum, 2001. ISBN 978-0-689-83254-3 Subj: Character traits – cleverness. Folk & fairy tales. Giants. Tall tales.

Clever Beatrice and the best little pony ill. by Heather Solomon. Atheneum, 2004. ISBN 978-0-689-85339-5 Subj: Animals. Animals – horses, ponies. Careers – bakers. Character traits – cleverness. Folk & fairy tales. Mythical creatures – lutins.

Clever Beatrice Christmas ill. by Heather Solomon. Atheneum, 2006. ISBN 978-0-689-87017-0 Subj: Character traits – cleverness. Holidays – Christmas. Santa Claus.

Thanksgiving with me ill. by Lloyd Bloom. Geringer, 1998. ISBN 978-0-06-027114-5 Subj: Family life – aunts, uncles. Holidays – Thanksgiving. Rhyming text.

The 3 bears and Goldilocks (The three bears)

Willhoite, Michael. *Daddy's roommate* ill. by author. Wonderland, 1990. ISBN 978-1-55583-178-3 Subj: Divorce. Family life – fathers. Family life – same-sex parents. LGBTQ.

Williams, Barbara. *Albert's gift for grandmother* ill. by Doug Cushman. Candlewick, 2006. ISBN 978-0-7636-2097-4 Subj: Birthdays. Family life – grandmothers. Gifts. Reptiles – turtles, tortoises.

Chester Chipmunk's Thanksgiving ill. by Kay Chorao. Dutton, 1974. ISBN 978-0-525-27655-5 Subj: Animals – chipmunks. Holidays – Thanksgiving.

Williams, Brenda. *Home for a tiger, home for a bear* ill. by Rosamund Fowler. Barefoot, 2007. ISBN 978-1-905236-81-7 Subj: Animals. Homes, houses. Rhyming text. Spiders.

Outdoor opposites ill. by Rachel Oldfield. Barefoot, 2015. ISBN 978-178285094-6 Subj: Camps, camping. Concepts – opposites. Songs.

The real princess: a mathemagical tale ill. by Sophie Fatus. Barefoot, 2008. ISBN 978-1-905236-88-6 Subj: Counting, numbers. Folk & fairy tales. Royalty. Royalty – princesses.

Williams, Carol Ann. *Booming Bella* ill. by Tatjana Mai-Wyss. Putnam, 2008. ISBN 978-0-399-24277-9 Subj: Noise, sounds. School – field trips. Self-concept.

Williams, Garth. *Benjamin's treasure* ill. by author and Rosemary Wells. HarperCollins, 2001. ISBN 978-0-06-028741-2 Subj: Animals – rabbits. Islands. Sea & seashore. Sports – fishing. Weather – storms.

Williams, Karen Lynn. *A beach tail* ill. by Floyd Cooper. Boyds Mills, 2010. ISBN 978-1-59078-712-0 Subj: Activities – drawing. Ethnic groups in the U.S. – African Americans. Sea & seashore – beaches.

Beatrice's dream: a story of Kibera slum. Frances Lincoln, 2011. ISBN 978-1-84780-019-0 Subj: Cities, towns. Foreign lands – Kenya. Poverty. School.

Four feet, two sandals by Karen Lynn Williams and Khadra Mohammed ill. by Doug Chayka. Eerdmans, 2007. ISBN 978-080285296-0 Subj: Behavior – sharing. Clothing – shoes. Foreign lands – Afghanistan. Foreign lands – Pakistan. Refugees.

Galimoto ill. by Catherine Stock. Lothrop, 1990. ISBN 978-0-688-08790-6 Subj: Foreign lands – Africa. Toys.

My name is Sangoel by Karen Lynn Williams and Khadra Mohammed ill. by Catherine Stock. Eerdmans, 2009. ISBN 978-0-8028-5307-3 Subj: Communication. Ethnic groups in the U.S. – Sudanese Americans. Immigrants, immigration. Names. Refugees.

Painted dreams ill. by Catherine Stock. Lothrop, 1998. ISBN 978-0-688-13902-5 Subj: Activities – painting. Foreign lands – Haiti. Problem solving.

Tap-tap ill. by Catherine Stock. Clarion, 1994. ISBN 978-0-395-65617-4 Subj: Clothing – hats. Family life – mothers. Foreign lands – Haiti. Stores. Trucks.

When Africa was home ill. by Floyd Cooper. Watts, 1991. ISBN 978-0-531-08525-7 Subj: Family life. Foreign lands – Africa. Friendship.

Williams, Laura E. *ABC kids* ill. by author. Philomel, 2000. ISBN 978-0-399-23370-8 Subj: ABC books.

The best winds ill. by Eujin Kim Neilan. Boyds Mills, 2006. ISBN 978-1-59078-274-3 Subj: Ethnic groups in the U.S. – Korean Americans. Family life – grandfathers. Kites.

The can man ill. by Craig Orback. Lee & Low, 2010. ISBN 978-1-60060-266-5 Subj: Character traits – generosity. Homeless.

Williams, Linda. *Horse in the pigpen* ill. by Megan Lloyd. HarperCollins, 2002. ISBN 978-0-06-028548-7 Subj: Animals. Family life – mothers. Farms. Rhyming text.

The little old lady who was not afraid of anything ill. by Megan Lloyd. Crowell, 1986. ISBN 978-0-690-04586-4 Subj: Cumulative tales. Emotions – fear. Scarecrows.

Williams, Pharrell. *Happy!* ill. by Kristin Smith. Putnam, 2015. ISBN 978-039917643-2 Subj: Emotions – happiness. Songs.

Williams, Rozanne Lanczak. *The coin counting book* ill. by author. Charlesbridge, 2001. ISBN 978-0-88106-325-7 Subj: Counting, numbers. Money. Rhyming text.

Williams, Sam. *Angel's Christmas cookies* ill. by author. HarperCollins, 2002. ISBN 978-0-06-029651-3 Subj: Angels. Animals – bears. Food. Holidays – Christmas. Mythical creatures – elves. Trees.

Snowy magic ill. by author. HarperCollins, 2002. ISBN 978-0-06-029652-0 Subj: Angels. Holidays – Christmas. Magic. Mythical creatures – elves. Weather – snow.

That's love ill. by Mique Moriuchi. Holiday House, 2007. ISBN 978-0-8234-2028-5 Subj: Emotions – love. Rhyming text.

Williams, Sherley Anne. *Girls together* ill. by Synthia Saint James. Harcourt, 1999. ISBN 978-0-15-230982-4 Subj: Activities – playing. Cities, towns. Ethnic groups in the U.S. – African Americans. Friendship.

Working cotton ill. by Carole M. Byard. Harcourt, 1992. ISBN 978-0-15-299624-6 Subj: Activities – working. Caldecott award honor books. Careers – migrant workers. Ethnic groups in the U.S. – African Americans. Family life.

Williams, Sue. *Dinnertime* ill. by Kerry Argent. Harcourt, 2001. ISBN 978-0-15-216471-3 Subj: Animals – foxes. Animals – rabbits. Counting, numbers. Rhyming text.

I went walking ill. by Julie Vivas. Harcourt, 1990. ISBN 978-0-15-200471-2 Subj: Activities – walking. Animals. Concepts – color. Rhyming text.

Let's go visiting ill. by Julie Vivas. Harcourt, 1998. ISBN 978-0-15-201823-8 Subj: Animals. Counting, numbers. Pets. Rhyming text.

Williams, Suzanne. *Library Lil* ill. by Steven Kellogg. Dial, 1997. ISBN 978-0-8037-1698-8 Subj: Books, reading. Careers – librarians. Tall tales.

My dog never says please ill. by Tedd Arnold. Dial, 1997. ISBN 978-0-8037-1681-0 Subj: Animals – dogs. Behavior – wishing. Family life.

Old MacDonald in the city ill. by Thor Wickstrom. Golden, 2002. ISBN 978-0-307-10685-8 Subj: Animals. Cities, towns. Counting, numbers. Insects. Rhyming text.

Ten naughty little monkeys ill. by Suzanne Watts. HarperCollins, 2007. ISBN 978-0-06-059904-1 Subj: Animals – monkeys. Counting, numbers. Rhyming text.

The witch casts a spell ill. by Barbara Olsen. Dial, 2002. ISBN 978-0-8037-2646-8 Subj: Holidays – Halloween. Music. Mythical creatures. Songs. Witches.

Williams, Treat. *Air show!* ill. by Robert Neubecker. Hyperion/Disney, 2010. ISBN 978-1-4231-1185-6 Subj: Airplanes, airports.

Williams, Vera B. *A chair for always* ill. by author. HarperCollins, 2009. ISBN 978-0-06-172279-0 Subj: Babies, toddlers. Family life. Furniture – chairs.

A chair for my mother ill. by author. Greenwillow, 1982. ISBN 978-0-688-00915-1 Subj: Behavior –

seeking better things. Caldecott award honor books. Family life. Furniture – chairs.

Cherries and cherry pits ill. by author. Greenwillow, 1986. ISBN 978-0-688-05146-4 Subj: Art. Ethnic groups in the U.S. – African Americans. Imagination.

Home at last ill. by Chris Raschka. Greenwillow, 2016. ISBN 978-006134973-7 Subj: Adoption. Bedtime. Behavior – needing someone. Behavior – worrying. Family life – same-sex parents.

"More more more," said the baby ill. by author. Greenwillow, 1991. ISBN 978-0-688-09174-3 Subj: Babies, toddlers. Caldecott award honor books. Ethnic groups in the U.S. Family life.

Music, music for everyone ill. by author. Greenwillow, 1984. ISBN 978-0-688-20604-8 Subj: Family life. Family life – grandmothers. Illness. Music. Musical instruments – accordions.

Something special for me ill. by author. Greenwillow, 1983. ISBN 978-0-688-01807-8 Subj: Birthdays. Family life. Gifts.

Three days on a river in a red canoe ill. by author. Greenwillow, 1981. ISBN 978-0-688-84307-6 Subj: Boats, ships. Camps, camping.

Williams-Garcia, Rita. *Catching the wild waiyuuzee* ill. by Mike Reed. Simon & Schuster, 2000. ISBN 978-0-689-82601-6 Subj: Ethnic groups in the U.S. – African Americans. Hair. Imagination.

Williamson, Sarah. *Where are you?* ill. by author. Knopf, 2017. ISBN 978-152470063-8 Subj: Behavior – hiding. Language. Reptiles – snakes.

Willis, Jeanne. *Boa's bad birthday* ill. by Tony Ross. Andersen, 2014. ISBN 978-146773450-9 Subj: Animals. Birthdays. Gifts. Reptiles – snakes.

The boy who lost his bellybutton ill. by Tony Ross. DK, 2000. ISBN 978-0-7894-6164-3 Subj: Anatomy – navels. Animals. Animals – dogs. Jungle. Reptiles – alligators, crocodiles.

Cottonball Colin ill. by Tony Ross. Eerdmans, 2008. ISBN 978-0-8028-5331-8 Subj: Animals – mice. Behavior – growing up. Family life – mothers.

Delilah D. at the library ill. by Rosie Reeve. Houghton, 2007. ISBN 978-0-618-78195-9 Subj: Imagination. Libraries.

Do little mermaids wet their beds ill. by Penelope Jossen. Albert Whitman, 2001. ISBN 978-0-8075-1668-3 Subj: Behavior. Behavior – bedwetting. Mythical creatures – mermaids, mermen. Rhyming text.

Fly, chick, fly! ill. by Tony Ross. Andersen, 2012. ISBN 978-1-46770314-7 Subj: Activities – flying. Behavior – growing up. Birds – owls. Emotions – fear.

Gorilla! Gorilla! ill. by Tony Ross. Simon & Schuster, 2006. ISBN 978-1-4169-1490-7 Subj: Animals – gorillas. Animals – mice. Behavior – misunderstanding. World.

Hippospotamus ill. by Tony Ross. Andersen, 2012. ISBN 978-1-4677-0316-1 Subj: Animals. Animals – hippopotamuses. Humorous stories. Rhyming text.

I'm sure I saw a dinosaur ill. by Adrian Reynolds. Andersen, 2011. ISBN 978-0-7613-8093-1 Subj: Dinosaurs. Rhyming text. Sea & seashore – beaches.

Misery Moo ill. by Tony Ross. Henry Holt, 2005. ISBN 978-0-8050-7672-1 Subj: Animals – bulls, cows. Animals – sheep. Emotions – happiness. Emotions – sadness. Friendship.

Mommy do you love me? ill. by Jan Fearnley. Candlewick, 2008. ISBN 978-0-7636-3470-4 Subj: Birds – chickens, roosters. Emotions – love.

Poles apart ill. by Peter Jarvis. Candlewick/Nosy Crow, 2016. ISBN 978-076368944-5 Subj: Activities – traveling. Animals – polar bears. Birds – penguins. Friendship.

Slug needs a hug! ill. by Tony Ross. Andersen, 2015. ISBN 978-146779309-4 Subj: Animals – slugs. Character traits – appearance. Family life – mothers. Hugging. Rhyming text.

Susan laughs ill. by Tony Ross. Henry Holt, 2000. ISBN 978-0-8050-6501-5 Subj: Activities. Disabilities – physical disabilities. Emotions. Rhyming text.

Tadpole's promise ill. by Tony Ross. Simon & Schuster, 2005. ISBN 978-0-689-86524-4 Subj: Frogs & toads. Insects – butterflies, caterpillars. Metamorphosis.

That's not funny! ill. by Adrian Reynolds. Andersen, 2010. ISBN 978-0-7613-6445-0 Subj: Animals. Animals – hyenas. Humorous stories.

Troll stinks ill. by Tony Ross. Andersen, 2017. ISBN 978-151243948-9 Subj: Animals – goats. Behavior – bullying, teasing. Mythical creatures – trolls. Rhyming text. Technology. Telephone, cell phone.

What did I look like when I was a baby? ill. by Tony Ross. Putnam, 2000. ISBN 978-0-399-23595-5 Subj: Babies, toddlers. Behavior – growing up. Character traits – appearance.

The wheels on the bus: a read-along sing-along trip to the zoo ill. by Adam Stower. Barrons, 2012. ISBN 978-0-7641-6491-0 Subj: Animals. Buses. Music. Songs. Zoos.

Willis, Nancy Carol. *Red knot: a shorebird's incredible journey* ill. by author. Birdsong, 2006. ISBN 978-0-9662761-5-2 Subj: Birds – sandpipers. Migration.

Wilner, Isabel. *The baby's game book* ill. by Sam Williams. Greenwillow, 2000. ISBN 978-0-688-15916-0 Subj: Babies, toddlers. Family life. Games.

A garden alphabet ill. by Ashley Wolff. Dutton, 1991. ISBN 978-0-525-44731-3 Subj: ABC books. Animals. Gardens, gardening. Rhyming text.

Wilson, Anna. *Over in the grasslands* ill. by Alison Bartlett. Little, 2000. ISBN 978-0-316-93910-2 Subj: Animals. Counting, numbers. Foreign lands – Africa. Poetry.

Wilson, Anne. *Masha and the firebird* (Bateson-Hill, Margaret)

Noah's ark ill. by author. Chronicle, 2002. ISBN 978-0-8118-3563-3 Subj: Animals. Boats, ships. Religion – Noah. Weather – floods. Weather – rain. Weather – rainbows.

Wilson, April. *April Wilson's magpie magic* ill. by author. Dial, 1999. ISBN 978-0-8037-2354-2 Subj: Activities – drawing. Birds – magpies. Concepts – color. Concepts – shape. Concepts – size. Wordless.

Wilson, Dorminster. *Mother scorpion country* (Rohmer, Harriet)

Wilson, Gina. *Ignis* ill. by P. J. Lynch. Candlewick, 2001. ISBN 978-0-7636-1623-6 Subj: Behavior – growing up. Dragons. Fire. Self-concept.

Wilson, Karma. *Animal strike at the zoo, it's true!* ill. by Margaret Spengler. HarperCollins, 2006. ISBN 978-0-06-057503-8 Subj: Animals. Rhyming text. Zoos.

Bear counts ill. by Jane Chapman. Simon & Schuster/Margaret K. McElderry, 2015. ISBN 978-144248092-6 Subj: Animals – bears. Animals – mice. Counting, numbers. Rhyming text.

Bear feels scared ill. by Jane Chapman. Simon & Schuster, 2008. ISBN 978-0-689-85986-1 Subj: Animals. Animals – bears. Behavior – lost. Emotions – fear. Friendship.

Bear feels sick ill. by Jane Chapman. Simon & Schuster, 2007. ISBN 978-0-689-85985-4 Subj: Animals. Animals – bears. Friendship. Illness.

Bear says thanks ill. by Jane Chapman. Simon & Schuster, 2012. ISBN 978-1-4169-5856-7 Subj: Animals. Animals – bears. Behavior – sharing. Etiquette. Rhyming text.

Bear sees colors ill. by Jane Chapman. Simon & Schuster/Margaret K. McElderry, 2014. ISBN 978-144246536-7 Subj: Animals. Animals – bears. Concepts – color. Rhyming text.

Bear stays up for Christmas ill. by Jane Chapman. Margaret K. McElderry, 2004. ISBN 978-0-689-85278-7 Subj: Animals. Animals – bears. Forest, woods. Hibernation. Holidays – Christmas. Rhyming text.

Bear's loose tooth ill. by Jane Chapman. Simon & Schuster, 2011. ISBN 978-1-4169-5855-0 Subj: Animals – bears. Rhyming text. Teeth.

Big bear, small mouse ill. by Jane Chapman. Simon & Schuster, 2016. ISBN 978-148145971-6 Subj: Animals. Concepts – opposites. Rhyming text.

The cow loves cookies ill. by Marcellus Hall. Simon & Schuster, 2010. ISBN 978-1-4169-4206-1 Subj: Animals – bulls, cows. Farms. Food. Rhyming text.

Dinos in the snow! ill. by Laura Rader. Little, Brown, 2005. ISBN 978-0-316-00948-5 Subj: Dinosaurs. Rhyming text. Seasons – winter. Weather – snow.

Don't be afraid, Little Pip ill. by Jane Chapman. Simon & Schuster, 2009. ISBN 978-0-689-85987-8 Subj: Birds – penguins. Emotions – fear. Sports – swimming.

Duddle Puck: the puddle duck ill. by Marcellus Hall. Margaret K. McElderry, 2015. ISBN 978-144244927-5 Subj: Birds – ducks. Character traits – being different. Farms. Noise, sounds. Rhyming text.

Hello, Calico! ill. by Buket Erdogan. Simon & Schuster, 2007. ISBN 978-1-4169-1356-6 Subj: Animals – cats. Format, unusual – board books.

Hogwash! ill. by Jim McMullan. Little, Brown, 2011. ISBN 978-0-316-98840-7 Subj: Activities – bathing. Animals – pigs. Character traits – cleanliness. Farms. Rhyming text.

Horseplay ill. by Jim McMullan. Little, Brown, 2012. ISBN 978-0-316-93842-6 Subj: Activities – playing. Animals – horses, ponies. Careers – farmers. Farms. Rhyming text.

How to bake an American pie ill. by Raúl Colón. Simon & Schuster, 2007. ISBN 978-0-689-86506-0 Subj: Rhyming text. U.S. history.

Mama always comes home ill. by Brooke Dyer. HarperCollins, 2005. ISBN 978-0-06-057506-9 Subj: Animals. Family life – mothers. Rhyming text.

Mama, why? ill. by Simon Mendez. Simon & Schuster, 2011. ISBN 978-1-4169-4205-4 Subj: Animals – polar bears. Bedtime. Character traits – questioning. Rhyming text. Sky.

Moose tracks! ill. by Jack E. Davis. Simon & Schuster, 2006. ISBN 978-0-689-83437-0 Subj: Animals. Animals – moose. Rhyming text.

Mortimer's Christmas manger ill. by Jane Chapman. Simon & Schuster, 2005. ISBN 978-0-689-85511-5 Subj: Animals – mice. Holidays – Christmas. Religion – Nativity.

Mortimer's first garden ill. by Dan Andreasen. Simon & Schuster, 2009. ISBN 978-1-4169-4203-0 Subj: Animals – mice. Gardens, gardening. Religion.

Princess me ill. by Christa Unzner. Simon & Schuster, 2007. ISBN 978-1-4169-4098-2 Subj: Imagination. Rhyming text. Royalty – princesses. Toys.

Sakes alive! a cattle drive ill. by Karla Firehammer. Little, Brown, 2005. ISBN 978-0-316-98841-4 Subj: Activities – driving. Animals – bulls, cows. Rhyming text.

Sleepyhead ill. by John Segal. Simon & Schuster, 2006. ISBN 978-1-4169-1241-5 Subj: Animals – cats. Bedtime. Rhyming text. Toys – bears.

Sweet Briar goes to camp ill. by LeUyen Pham. Penguin, 2005. ISBN 978-0-8037-2971-1 Subj: Animals – porcupines. Animals – skunks. Camps, camping. Emotions – loneliness.

What's in the egg, Little Pip? ill. by Jane Chapman. Simon & Schuster, 2010. ISBN 978-1-4169-4204-7 Subj: Animals – babies. Birds – penguins. Eggs. Family life – new sibling.

Where is home, Little Pip? ill. by Jane Chapman. Simon & Schuster, 2008. ISBN 978-0-689-85983-0 Subj: Animals – babies. Behavior – lost. Birds – penguins. Foreign lands – Antarctic.

Who goes there? ill. by Anna Currey. Simon & Schuster, 2013. ISBN 978-1-4169-8002-5 Subj: Animals – mice. Emotions – fear. Noise, sounds.

Whopper cake ill. by Will Hillenbrand. Simon & Schuster, 2007. ISBN 978-0-689-83844-6 Subj: Activities – baking, cooking. Birthdays. Food. Rhyming text. Tall tales.

Wilson, N. D. *Ninja boy goes to school* ill. by J. J. Harrison. Random House, 2014. ISBN 978-037586584-8 Subj: Imagination. School. Sports – martial arts.

Wilson, Sarah. *Friends and pals and brothers, too* ill. by Leo Landry. Henry Holt, 2008. ISBN 978-0-8050-7643-1 Subj: Family life – brothers. Friendship. Rhyming text. Seasons.

Love and kisses ill. by Melissa Sweet. Candlewick, 1999. ISBN 978-1-56402-792-4 Subj: Animals. Emotions – love. Rhyming text.

Wilson, Steve. *Hedgehugs* ill. by Lucy Tapper. Holt Metropolitan, 2015. ISBN 978-162779404-6 Subj: Animals – hedgehogs. Friendship. Hugging.

Hedgehugs: autumn hide-and-squeak ill. by Lucy Tapper. Henry Holt, 2017. ISBN 978-125011248-4 Subj: Animals – bats. Animals – hedgehogs. Behavior – hiding. Seasons – fall.

Hedgehugs and the Hattiepillar ill. by Lucy Tapper. Henry Holt, 2016. ISBN 978-162779414-5 Subj: Animals – hedgehogs. Insects – butterflies, caterpillars. Metamorphosis.

Wilson, Tony. *The princess and the packet of frozen peas* ill. by Sue deGennaro. Peachtree, 2012. ISBN 978-1-56145-635-2 Subj: Folk & fairy tales. Royalty – princes. Royalty – princesses.

Wilson, Troy. *Liam takes a stand* ill. by Josh Holinaty. OwlKids, 2017. ISBN 978-177147161-9 Subj: Behavior – resourcefulness. Family life – brothers. Money. Multiple births – twins. Sibling rivalry.

Wilson-Max, Ken. *Fuhara means happy: a book of Swahili words* ill. by author. Hyperion, 2000. ISBN 978-0-7868-2480-9 Subj: Foreign lands – Kenya. Foreign languages.

Halala means welcome: a book of Zulu words ill. by author. Hyperion, 1998. ISBN 978-0-7868-0414-6 Subj: Foreign lands – South Africa. Foreign languages.

Max's starry night ill. by author. Hyperion, 2001. ISBN 978-0-7868-0553-2 Subj: Animals – elephants. Emotions – fear. Ethnic groups in the U.S. – African Americans. Stars.

Wimmer, Sonja. *The word collector* ill. by author. IPG/Cuento de Luz, 2012. ISBN 978-8-41524-134-8 Subj: Behavior – collecting things. Language.

Winans, CeCe, et al. *Colorful world* ill. by Melodee Strong. Maren Green, 2008. ISBN 978-1-934277-13-3 Subj: Character traits – individuality. Songs.

Winch, John. *Keeping up with Grandma* ill. by author. Holiday, 2000. ISBN 978-0-8234-1563-2 Subj: Activities. Family life – grandfathers. Family life – grandmothers.

Winer, Yvonne. *Birds build nests* ill. by Tony Oliver. Charlesbridge, 2002. ISBN 978-1-57091-500-0 Subj: Birds. Homes, houses.

Butterflies fly ill. by Karen Lloyd-Jones. Charlesbridge, 2001. ISBN 978-1-57091-446-1 Subj: Activities – flying. Insects – butterflies, caterpillars.

Frogs sing songs ill. by Tony Oliver. Charlesbridge, 2003. ISBN 978-1-57091-548-2 Subj: Behavior. Ecology. Frogs & toads. Noise, sounds.

Wing, Natasha. *Go to bed, monster!* ill. by Sylvie Kantorovitz. Harcourt, 2007. ISBN 978-0-15-205775-6 Subj: Activities – drawing. Bedtime. Imagination. Monsters.

How to raise a dinosaur ill. by Pablo Bernasconi. Running Press, 2010. ISBN 978-0-7624-3342-1 Subj: Dinosaurs. Format, unusual – toy & movable books. Pets.

Jalapeño bagels ill. by Robert Casilla. Atheneum, 1996. ISBN 978-0-02-793077-1 Subj: Ethnic groups in the U.S. Family life. Food. School.

The night before the night before Christmas ill. by Mike Lester. Grosset, 2002. ISBN 978-0-448-42872-7 Subj: Holidays – Christmas. Rhyming text.

Winget, Susan. *Sam the Snowman* ill. by author. HarperCollins, 2008. ISBN 978-0-06-114475-2 Subj: Character traits – generosity. Seasons – winter. Snowmen. Weather – snow.

Tucker's four-carrot school day ill. by author. HarperCollins, 2005. ISBN 978-0-06-054643-4 Subj: Animals – rabbits. Friendship. School – first day.

Winkelman, Barbara Gaines. *Puffer's surprise* ill. by Steven James Petruccio. Soundprints, 2003. ISBN 978-1-59249-032-5 Subj: Fish. Foreign lands – Galapagos Islands. Sea & seashore.

Sockeye's journey home ill. by Joanie Popeo. Soundprints, 2000. ISBN 978-1-56899-829-9 Subj: Ecology. Fish. Migration.

Winne, Joanne. *Blue in my world* ill. with photos. Children's Press, 2000. ISBN 978-0-516-23123-5 Subj: Concepts – color.

Green in my world ill. with photos. Children's Press, 2000. ISBN 978-0-516-23124-2 Subj: Concepts – color.

Let's get ready for Kwanzaa ill. with photos. Children's Press, 2001. ISBN 978-0-516-23175-4 Subj: Ethnic groups in the U.S. – African Americans. Holidays – Kwanzaa.

Red in my world Ill. with photos. Children's Press, 2001. ISBN 978-0-516-23126-6 Subj: Concepts – color.

Winnick, Karen B. *Barn sneeze* ill. by author. Children's Press, 2000. ISBN 978-1-56397-948-4 Subj: Animals. Noise, sounds.

Sybil's night ride ill. by author. Boyds Mills, 2000. ISBN 978-1-56397-697-1 Subj: Animals – horses, ponies. Night. U.S. history. War.

A year goes round ill. by author. Boyds Mills, 2001. ISBN 978-1-56397-898-2 Subj: Days of the week, months of the year. Poetry.

Winnie-the-Pooh's A B C ill. by Ernest H. Shepard. Inspired by A. A. Milne; created with Gallaudet University Pr.; sign language ill. by Lois A. Lehman; sign language consultant Lvey Pittle Wallace. Dutton, 2001. ISBN 978-0-525-46714-4 Subj: ABC books. Disabilities – deafness. Language. Senses – hearing. Sign language.

Winstead, Rosie. *Ruby and Bubbles* ill. by author. Penguin, 2006. ISBN 978-0-8037-3024-3 Subj:

Behavior – bullying, teasing. Birds. Friendship. Pets.

Sprout helps out ill. by author. Dial, 2014. ISBN 978-080373072-4 Subj: Behavior – messy. Character traits – helpfulness. Family life.

Winston, Sam. *A child of books* (Jeffers, Oliver)

Winter, Jeanette. *Angelina's island* ill. by author. Farrar, 2007. ISBN 978-0-374-30349-5 Subj: Emotions – loneliness. Ethnic groups in the U.S. – Jamaican Americans. Immigrants, immigration.

Biblioburro: a true story from Colombia ill. by author. Simon & Schuster, 2010. ISBN 978-1-4169-9778-8 Subj: Animals – donkeys. Books, reading. Foreign lands – Colombia. Libraries.

The Christmas tree ship ill. by author. Philomel, 1994. ISBN 978-0-399-22693-9 Subj: Boats, ships. Holidays – Christmas. Trees. U.S. history.

Cowboy Charlie ill. by author. Harcourt, 1995. ISBN 978-0-15-200857-4 Subj: Activities – playing. Art. Careers – artists. Cowboys, cowgirls. U.S. history – frontier & pioneer life.

Follow the drinking gourd ill. by author. Dragonfly, 1992. ISBN 978-0-679-81997-4 Subj: Ethnic groups in the U.S. – African Americans. Sailors. Slavery. Stars. U.S. history.

Henri's scissors ill. by author. Simon & Schuster, 2013. ISBN 978-1-4424-6484-1 Subj: Art. Careers – artists. Foreign lands – France. Illness. Old age.

Kali's song ill. by author. Random House, 2012. ISBN 978-0-375-87022-4 Subj: Cave dwellers. Character traits – individuality. Music. Sports – hunting.

The librarian of Basra: a true story from Iraq ill. by author. Harcourt, 2005. ISBN 978-0-15-205445-8 Subj: Careers – librarians. Foreign lands – Iraq. Libraries. War.

Malala, a brave girl from Pakistan / Iqbal, a brave boy from Pakistan ill. by author. Simon & Schuster/Beach Lane, 2014. ISBN 978-148142294-9 Subj: Behavior – seeking better things. Character traits – bravery. Character traits – freedom. Foreign lands – Pakistan. School. Violence, nonviolence.

Mama: a true story, in which a baby hippo loses his mama during a tsunami, but finds a new home ill. by author. Harcourt, 2006. ISBN 978-0-15-205495-3 Subj: Animals – hippopotamuses. Family life – mothers. Reptiles – turtles, tortoises. Tsunamis.

Mr. Cornell's dream boxes ill. by author. Simon & Schuster/Beach Lane, 2014. ISBN 978-144249902-7 Subj: Art. Careers – artists. Character traits – shyness. Dreams. Memories, memory.

My baby ill. by author. Farrar, 2001. ISBN 978-0-374-35103-8 Subj: Art. Babies, toddlers. Behavior – growing up. Clothing. Foreign lands – Africa.

Nanuk the ice bear ill. by author. Simon & Schuster/Beach Lane, 2016. ISBN 978-148144667-9 Subj: Animals – polar bears. Ecology. Foreign lands – Arctic.

Nasreen's secret school: a true story from Afghanistan ill. by author. Beach Lane Books, 2009. ISBN 978-1-4169-9437-4 Subj: Behavior – secrets. Foreign lands – Afghanistan. Gender roles. School.

Niño's mask ill. by author. Dial, 2003. ISBN 978-0-8037-2807-3 Subj: Clothing – costumes. Fairs, festivals. Foreign lands – Mexico.

Once upon a time in Chicago ill. by author. Hyperion, 2000. ISBN 978-0-7868-2404-5 Subj: Careers – musicians. Music. Musical instruments – bands.

The tale of Pale Male: a true story ill. by author. Harcourt, 2007. ISBN 978-0-15-205972-9 Subj: Birds – hawks.

Wangari's trees of peace: a true story from Africa ill. by author. Harcourt, 2008. ISBN 978-0-15-206545-4 Subj: Character traits – responsibility. Ecology. Foreign lands – Kenya. Trees.

The watcher: Jane Goodall's life with the chimps ill. by author. Random House, 2011. ISBN 978-0-375-86774-3 Subj: Animals – chimpanzees. Careers – scientists. Foreign lands – Tanzania. Nature.

The world is not a rectangle: a portrait of architect Zaha Hadid ill. by author. Simon & Schuster/Beach Lane, 2017. ISBN 978-148144669-3 Subj: Careers – architects. Foreign lands – Iraq. Gender roles.

Winter, Jonah. *Barack* ill. by A. G. Ford. HarperCollins, 2008. ISBN 978-0-06-170392-8 Subj: Ethnic groups in the U.S. – African Americans. U.S. history.

Diego ill. by Jeanette Winter. Knopf, 1991. ISBN 978-0-679-91987-2 Subj: Art. Careers – artists. Foreign languages.

Dizzy ill. by Sean Qualls. Scholastic, 2006. ISBN 978-0-439-50737-0 Subj: Careers – musicians. Ethnic groups in the U.S. – African Americans. Music.

Here comes the garbage barge! ill. by Red Nose Studio. Random House, 2010. ISBN 978-0-375-95218-0 Subj: Boats, ships. Careers – sanitation workers.

Hillary ill. by Raúl Colón. Random House, 2016. ISBN 978-055353388-0 Subj: Gender roles. U.S. history.

How Jelly Roll Morton invented jazz ill. by Keith Mallett. Roaring Brook, 2015. ISBN 978-159643963-4 Subj: Careers – musicians. Ethnic groups in the U.S. – African Americans. Music. Musical instruments – pianos.

Joltin' Joe DiMaggio ill. by James Ransome. Atheneum, 2014. ISBN 978-141694080-7 Subj: Sports – baseball.

Just behave, Pablo Picasso! ill. by Kevin Hawkes. Scholastic, 2012. ISBN 978-0-545-13291-6 Subj: Activities – painting. Art. Careers – artists.

Lillian's right to vote: a celebration of the Voting Rights Act of 1965 ill. by Shane W. Evans. Random House, 2015. ISBN 978-038539028-6 Subj: Ethnic groups in the U.S. – African Americans. Prejudice. U.S. history.

Muhammad Ali: champion of the world ill. by François Roca. Random House, 2008. ISBN 978-0-375-83622-0 Subj: Ethnic groups in the U.S. – African Americans. Sports – boxing. U.S. history.

Sonia Sotomayor: a judge grows in the Bronx / la juez que creció en el Bronx ill. by Edel Rodriguez. Atheneum, 2009. ISBN 978-1-4424-0303-1 Subj: Careers – judges. Ethnic groups in the U.S. – Hispanic Americans. Foreign languages.

Winters, Kari-Lynn. *Bad pirate* ill. by Dean Griffiths. Pajama, 2015. ISBN 978-192748571-2 Subj: Animals – dogs. Character traits – helpfulness. Character traits – selfishness. Family life – daughters. Family life – fathers. Pirates.

Gift days ill. by Stephen Taylor. Fitzhenry & Whiteside, 2012. ISBN 978-1-55455-192-7 Subj: Character traits – perseverance. Family life – brothers & sisters. Foreign lands – Uganda. School.

Good pirate ill. by Dean Griffiths. Pajama Pr., 2016. ISBN 978-192748580-4 Subj: Animals – dogs. Boats, ships. Character traits – appearance. Pirates.

Winters, Kay. *Abe Lincoln, the boy who loved books* ill. by Nancy Carpenter. Simon & Schuster, 2003. ISBN 978-0-689-82554-5 Subj: Books, reading. U.S. history.

The bears go to school ill. by Katherine Kirkland. Albert Whitman, 2013. ISBN 978-0-8075-0592-2 Subj: Animals – bears. School.

The teeny tiny ghost ill. by Lynn Munsinger. HarperCollins, 1997. ISBN 978-0-06-025684-5 Subj: Emotions – fear. Ghosts. Holidays – Halloween.

The teeny tiny ghost and the monster ill. by Lynn Munsinger. HarperCollins, 2004. ISBN 978-0-06-028885-3 Subj: Contests. Ghosts. Monsters. School.

This school year will be the best! ill. by Renée Williams-Andriani. Penguin, 2010. ISBN 978-0-525-42775-4 Subj: School – first day.

Tiger trail ill. by Laura Regan. Simon & Schuster, 2000. ISBN 978-0-689-82323-7 Subj: Animals – tigers. Behavior – growing up. Nature.

Whooo's haunting the teeny tiny ghost? ill. by Lynn Munsinger. HarperCollins, 1999. ISBN 978-0-06-

027359-0 Subj: Emotions – fear. Ghosts. Holidays – Halloween.

Wolf watch ill. by Laura Regan. Simon & Schuster, 1997. ISBN 978-0-689-80218-8 Subj: Animals. Animals – wolves. Behavior – growing up. Nature. Rhyming text.

Winthrop, Elizabeth. *As the crow flies* ill. by Joan Sandin. Clarion, 1998. ISBN 978-0-395-77612-4 Subj: Divorce. Family life – fathers.

Bear and Mrs. Duck ill. by Patience Brewster. Holiday, 1988. ISBN 978-0-8234-0687-6 Subj: Activities – babysitting. Animals – bears. Birds – ducks.

Bear's Christmas surprise ill. by Patience Brewster. Holiday, 1991. ISBN 978-0-8234-0888-7 Subj: Activities – babysitting. Animals – bears. Birds – ducks. Holidays – Christmas.

A child is born: the Christmas story ill. by Charles Mikolaycak. Holiday, 1983. ISBN 978-0-8234-0472-8 Subj: Holidays – Christmas. Religion – Nativity.

Halloween hats ill. by Sue Truesdell. Henry Holt, 2002. ISBN 978-0-8050-6386-8 Subj: Clothing – hats. Holidays – Halloween. Parades. Rhyming text.

He is risen: the Easter story ill. by Charles Mikolaycak. Holiday, 1985. ISBN 978-0-8234-0547-3 Subj: Holidays – Easter. Religion.

I'm the Boss! ill. by Mary Morgan. Holiday, 1994. ISBN 978-0-8234-1113-9 Subj: Animals – dogs. Character traits – assertiveness. Family life.

Lucy and Henry are twins ill. by Jane Massey. Amazon/Two Lions, 2015. ISBN 978-147782629-4 Subj: Family life – brothers & sisters. Multiple births – twins. Rhyming text.

Promises ill. by Betsy Lewin. Clarion, 2000. ISBN 978-0-395-82272-2 Subj: Emotions. Family life – daughters. Family life – mothers. Illness – cancer.

Shoes ill. by William Joyce. HarperCollins, 1986. ISBN 978-0-06-026592-2 Subj: Clothing – shoes. Rhyming text.

Sledding ill. by Sarah Wilson. HarperCollins, 1989. ISBN 978-0-06-026566-3 Subj: Rhyming text. Sports – sledding.

Squashed in the middle ill. by Pat Cummings. Henry Holt, 2005. ISBN 978-0-8050-6497-1 Subj: Ethnic groups in the U.S. – African Americans. Family life. Self-concept. Sleepovers.

Vasilissa the beautiful ill. by Alexander Koshkin. HarperCollins, 1991. ISBN 978-0-06-021663-4 Subj: Family life – stepfamilies. Folk & fairy tales. Foreign lands – Russia. Royalty – tsars. Toys – dolls. Witches.

Winton, Tim. *The deep* ill. by Karen Louise. Tricycle, 2000. ISBN 978-1-58246-024-6 Subj: Animals – dolphins. Emotions – fear. Nature. Sea & seashore. Sports – swimming.

Wisdom, Jude. *Whatever Wanda wanted* ill. by author. Fogelman, 2002. ISBN 978-0-8037-2693-2 Subj: Behavior. Character traits – selfishness. Islands. Kites.

Wise, Bill. *Silent star: the story of deaf major leaguer William Hoy* ill. by Adam Gustavson. Lee & Low, 2012. ISBN 978-1-60060-411-9 Subj: Disabilities – deafness. Sports – baseball. U.S. history.

Wise, William. *Dinosaurs forever* ill. by Lynn Munsinger. Dial, 2000. ISBN 978-0-8037-2114-2 Subj: Dinosaurs. Humorous stories. Poetry.

Zany zoo ill. by Lynn Munsinger. Houghton, 2006. ISBN 978-0-618-18891-8 Subj: Animals. Language. Zoos.

Wishinsky, Frieda. *Please, Louise!* ill. by Marie-Louise Gay. Groundwood, 2007. ISBN 978-0-88899-796-8 Subj: Animals – dogs. Behavior – wishing. Family life – brothers & sisters.

What's up, bear? a book about opposites ill. by Sean L. Moore. OwlKids, 2012. ISBN 978-1-926973-41-8 Subj: Activities – traveling. Concepts – opposites. Language. Toys – bears.

Where are you, Bear? a Canadian alphabet adventure ill. by Sean L. Moore. OwlKids, 2010. ISBN 978-1-897349-91-5 Subj: ABC books. Foreign lands – Canada.

You're mean, Lily Jean! ill. by Kady MacDonald Denton. Albert Whitman, 2011. ISBN 978-0-8075-9476-6 Subj: Activities – playing. Family life – sisters. Friendship.

Wisnewski, Andrea. *Trio: the tale of a three-legged cat* ill. by author. Godine, 2017. ISBN 978-156792608-8 Subj: Animals – cats. Birds – chickens, roosters. Character traits – perseverance. Disabilities – physical disabilities.

Wisniewski, David. *Elfwyn's saga* ill. by author. Lothrop, 1990. ISBN 978-0-688-09590-1 Subj: Disabilities – blindness. Folk & fairy tales. Foreign lands – Iceland. Magic.

Golem ill. by author. Clarion, 1996. ISBN 978-0-395-72618-1 Subj: Caldecott award books. Folk & fairy tales. Foreign lands – Czechoslovakia. Jewish culture. Mythical creatures.

Rain player ill. by author. Houghton, 1991. ISBN 978-0-395-55112-7 Subj: Foreign lands – Central America. Foreign lands – Mexico. Games. Indians of Central America – Maya.

Sumo Mouse ill. by author. Chronicle, 2002. ISBN 978-0-8118-3492-6 Subj: Animals – mice. Careers – storekeepers. Crime. Foreign lands – Japan. Toys.

Sundiata: lion king of Mali ill. by author. Clarion, 1992. ISBN 978-0-395-61302-3 Subj: Disabilities. Folk & fairy tales. Foreign lands – Mali. Royalty – kings.

Tough cookie ill. by author. Lothrop, 1999. ISBN 978-0-688-15338-0 Subj: Food. Humorous stories.

The warrior and the wise man ill. by author. Lothrop, 1989. ISBN 978-0-688-07890-4 Subj: Character traits – wisdom. Folk & fairy tales. Foreign lands – Japan. Multiple births – twins. Royalty.

Withrow, Sarah. *Be a baby* ill. by Manuel Monroy. Groundwood, 2007. ISBN 978-0-88899-776-0 Subj: Babies, toddlers. Bedtime. Lullabies.

Witte, Anna. *Lola's fandango* ill. by Micha Archer. Barefoot, 2011. ISBN 978-1-84686-174-1 Subj: Activities – dancing. Birthdays. Ethnic groups in the U.S. – Hispanic Americans. Family life – mothers.

The parrot Tico Tango ill. by author. Barefoot, 2004. ISBN 978-1-84148-243-9 Subj: Animals. Behavior – greed. Birds – parakeets, parrots. Cumulative tales. Jungle. Rhyming text.

Wittenstein, Barry. *Waiting for Pumpsie* ill. by London Ladd. Charlesbridge, 2017. ISBN 978-158089545-3 Subj: Ethnic groups in the U.S. – African Americans. Prejudice. Sports – baseball. U.S. history.

Witter, Bret. *Dewey: there's a cat in the library!* (Myron, Vicki)

Tuesday tucks me in: the loyal bond between a soldier and his service dog (Montalván, Luis Carlos)

Wiviott, Meg. *Benno and the night of broken glass* ill. by Josée Bisaillon. Lerner/Kar-Ben, 2010. ISBN 978-0-8225-9929-6 Subj: Animals – cats. Foreign lands – Germany. Holocaust. Jewish culture.

Woelfle, Gretchen. *Katje the windmill cat* ill. by Nicola Bayley. Candlewick, 2001. ISBN 978-0-7636-1347-1 Subj: Animals – cats. Foreign lands – Holland. Weather – floods.

Mumbet's Declaration of Independence ill. by Alix Delinois. Carolrhoda, 2014. ISBN 978-076136589-1 Subj: Character traits – freedom. Ethnic groups in the U.S. – African Americans. Slavery. U.S. history.

Wohl, Lauren L. *Matzoh mouse* ill. by Pamela Keavney. HarperCollins, 1991. ISBN 978-0-06-026581-6 Subj: Family life. Holidays – Passover. Jewish culture. Religion.

A teeny tiny Halloween ill. by Henry Cole. Persnickety, 2016. ISBN 978-1943978-02-1 Subj: Character

traits – smallness. Holidays – Halloween. Seasons – fall.

Wohlrabe, Sarah C. *Helping you heal, a book about nurses* ill. by Eric Thomas. Picture Window, 2004. ISBN 978-1-4048-0086-1 Subj: Careers – nurses.

Helping you learn, a book about teachers ill. by Eric Thomas. Picture Window, 2004. ISBN 978-1-4048-0084-7 Subj: Careers – teachers.

Wohnoutka, Mike. *Dad's first day* ill. by author. Bloomsbury, 2015. ISBN 978-161963473-2 Subj: Family life – fathers. School – first day.

Little puppy and the big green monster ill. by author. Holiday House, 2014. ISBN 978-082343064-2 Subj: Activities – playing. Animals – dogs. Monsters.

Wojciechowski, Susan. *The best Halloween of all* ill. by Susan Meddaugh. 2nd ed. Candlewick, 1998. ISBN 978-0-7636-0458-5 Subj: Clothing – costumes. Holidays – Halloween.

The Christmas miracle of Jonathan Toomey ill. by P. J. Lynch. Candlewick, 1995. ISBN 978-1-56402-320-9 Subj: Careers – woodcarvers. Friendship. Holidays – Christmas. Religion.

A fine St. Patrick's Day ill. by Tom Curry. Random House, 2004. ISBN 978-0-375-92386-9 Subj: Character traits – kindness. Contests. Holidays – St. Patrick's Day.

Wojtowycz, David. *Animal antics from 1 to 10* ill. by author. Holiday, 2000. ISBN 978-0-8234-1552-6 Subj: Animals. Counting, numbers. Hotels.

A cuddle for Claude ill. by author. Dutton, 2001. ISBN 978-0-525-46691-8 Subj: Animals – polar bears. Behavior – running away. Family life – grandmothers.

Elephant Joe, Brave Knight! a tale of knightly chivalrousness ill. by author. Random House, 2012. ISBN 978-0-307-93087-3 Subj: Animals – elephants. Dragons. Knights.

Wojtusik, Elizabeth. *Kitty up!* ill. by Sachiko Yoshikawa. Dial, 2008. ISBN 978-0-8037-3278-0 Subj: Animals – cats. Animals – dogs. Rhyming text.

Wolf, Jake. *Daddy, could I have an elephant?* ill. by Marylin Hafner. Greenwillow, 1996. ISBN 978-0-688-13295-8 Subj: Animals. Family life – fathers. Pets.

Wolf, Karina. *The Insomniacs* ill. by Sean Hilts and Ben Hilts. Putnam, 2012. ISBN 978-0-399-25665-3 Subj: Night. Sleep.

Wolf, Sallie. *Truck stuck* ill. by Andy Robert Davies. Charlesbridge, 2008. ISBN 978-1-58089-119-6 Subj: Rhyming text. Trucks.

Wolf, Winfried. *The Easter bunny* ill. by Agnès Mathieu. Dial, 1986. ISBN 978-0-8037-0239-4 Subj: Animals – rabbits. Holidays – Easter.

Wolfe, Myra. *Charlotte Jane battles bedtime* ill. by Maria Monescillo. Houghton, 2011. ISBN 978-0-15-206150-0 Subj: Bedtime. Pirates.

Wolff, Ashley. *Baby Bear counts one* ill. by author. Simon & Schuster, 2013. ISBN 978-1-4424-4158-3 Subj: Animals – bears. Counting, numbers. Hibernation. Seasons – winter.

Baby Bear sees blue ill. by author. Simon & Schuster, 2012. ISBN 978-1-4424-1306-1 Subj: Animals – bears. Concepts – color. Nature.

I call my grandma Nana ill. by author. Tricycle, 2009. ISBN 978-1-58246-251-6 Subj: Family life – grandmothers. Foreign languages. Names. Rhyming text.

I call my grandpa Papa ill. by author. Tricycle, 2009. ISBN 978-1-58246-252-3 Subj: Family life – grandfathers. Foreign languages. Names. Rhyming text.

Stella and Roy go camping ill. by author. Dutton, 1999. ISBN 978-0-525-45864-7 Subj: Camps, camping. Family life. Sibling rivalry.

When Lucy goes out walking: a puppy's first year ill. by author. Henry Holt, 2009. ISBN 978-0-8050-8168-8 Subj: Animals – dogs. Days of the week, months of the year. Rhyming text.

Where, oh where, is Baby Bear? ill. by author. Simon & Schuster, 2017. ISBN 978-148149916-3 Subj: Animals – bears. Family life – mothers.

Wolff, Ferida. *It is the wind* ill. by James Ransome. HarperCollins, 2005. ISBN 978-0-06-028192-2 Subj: Animals. Bedtime. Noise, sounds. Sleep.

On Halloween night by Ferida Wolff and Dolores Kozielski ill. by Dolores Avendaño. Tambourine, 1994. ISBN 978-0-688-12973-6 Subj: Clothing – costumes. Counting, numbers. Cumulative tales. Holidays – Halloween. Rhyming text. Witches.

The story blanket by Ferida Wolff and Harriet May Savitz ill. by Elena Odriozola. Peachtree, 2008. ISBN 978-1-56145-466-2 Subj: Behavior – sharing. Friendship.

Wolff, Kathy. *What George forgot* ill. by Richard Byrne. Bloomsbury, 2017. ISBN 978-161963871-6 Subj: Behavior – forgetfulness.

Wolff, Nancy. *It's time for school with Tallulah* ill. by author. Henry Holt, 2007. ISBN 978-0-8050-7962-3 Subj: Activities – playing. Animals – cats. School.

Tallulah in the kitchen ill. by author. Henry Holt, 2005. ISBN 978-0-8050-7463-5 Subj: Activities – baking, cooking. Animals – cats. Food.

Wolff, Patricia Rae. *A new, improved Santa* ill. by Lynne Cravath. Orchard, 2002. ISBN 978-0-439-35249-9 Subj: Holidays – Christmas. Santa Claus. Self-concept.

The toll-bridge troll ill. by Kimberly Bulcken Root. Browndeer, 1998. ISBN 978-0-15-277665-7 Subj: Mythical creatures – trolls. Riddles & jokes. School.

Wolkstein, Diane. *The banza: a Haitian story* ill. by Marc Brown. Dial, 1981. ISBN 978-0-8037-0429-9 Subj: Animals – goats. Animals – tigers. Character traits – bravery. Folk & fairy tales. Music. Musical instruments – banjos.

The day Ocean came to visit ill. by Steve Johnson and Lou Fancher. Harcourt, 2001. ISBN 978-0-15-201774-3 Subj: Folk & fairy tales – pourquoi tales. Foreign lands – Africa. Moon. Sea & seashore. Sun.

Little Mouse's painting ill. by Mary Jane Begin. Morrow, 1992. ISBN 978-0-688-07610-8 Subj: Animals. Animals – mice. Careers – artists. Friendship.

Step by step ill. by Joseph A. Smith. Morrow, 1994. ISBN 978-0-688-10316-3 Subj: Friendship. Insects – ants. Insects – grasshoppers.

Sun Mother wakes the world ill. by Bronwyn Bancroft. HarperCollins, 2004. ISBN 978-0-688-13916-2 Subj: Australian aborigines. Creation. Folk & fairy tales. Foreign lands – Australia.

Won, Brian. *Hooray for hat!* ill. by author. Houghton, 2014. ISBN 978-054415903-7 Subj: Animals. Animals – elephants. Behavior – bad day, bad mood. Clothing – hats.

Hooray for today! ill. by author. Houghton Mifflin Harcourt, 2016. ISBN 978-054474803-3 Subj: Activities – playing. Bedtime. Birds – owls. Night.

Wong, Benedict Norbert. *Lo and behold* ill. by author. Taiji, 2003. ISBN 978-0-9728192-0-6 Subj: Dragons. Ethnic groups in the U.S. – Chinese Americans. Family life. Food. Self-concept.

Lo and behold, good enough to eat ill. by author. Taiji, 2003. ISBN 978-0-9728192-1-3 Subj: Dragons. Ethnic groups in the U.S. – Chinese Americans. Family life. Food. Self-concept.

Wong, Janet S. *Buzz* ill. by Margaret Chodos-Irvine. Harcourt, 2000. ISBN 978-0-15-201923-5 Subj: Family life. Insects – bees. Noise, sounds.

The dumpster diver ill. by David Roberts. Candlewick, 2007. ISBN 978-0-7636-2380-7 Subj: Communities, neighborhoods. Ecology.

Grump ill. by John Wallace. Margaret K. McElderry, 2001. ISBN 978-0-689-83485-1 Subj: Babies, toddlers. Family life – mothers. Rhyming text. Sleep.

Hide and seek ill. by Margaret Chodos-Irvine. Harcourt, 2005. ISBN 978-0-15-204934-8 Subj: Behavior – hiding. Counting, numbers. Rhyming text.

Homegrown house ill. by E. B. Lewis. Simon & Schuster, 2009. ISBN 978-0-689-84718-9 Subj: Homes, houses. Moving. Poetry.

This next New Year ill. by Yangsook Choi. Farrar, 2000. ISBN 978-0-374-35503-6 Subj: Ethnic groups in the U.S. Family life. Holidays – Chinese New Year.

The trip back home ill. by Bo Jia. Harcourt, 2000. ISBN 978-0-15-200784-3 Subj: Activities – traveling. Ethnic groups in the U.S. – Korean Americans. Family life. Foreign lands – Korea.

Wong, Liz. *Quackers* ill. by author. Knopf, 2016. ISBN 978-055351154-3 Subj: Animals – cats. Birds – ducks. Character traits – being different. Friendship. Self-concept.

Woo, Alan. *Maggie's chopsticks* ill. by Isabelle Malenfant. Kids Can, 2012. ISBN 978-1-55453-619-1 Subj: Character traits – individuality. Character traits – persistence. Ethnic groups in the U.S. – Chinese Americans. Family life. Food.

Wood, Audrey. *Alphabet adventure* ill. by Bruce Wood. Blue Sky, 2001. ISBN 978-0-439-08069-9 Subj: ABC books. Behavior – lost & found possessions.

Alphabet rescue ill. by Bruce Wood. Scholastic, 2006. ISBN 978-0-439-85316-3 Subj: ABC books. Careers – firefighters. Trucks.

Birdsong ill. by Robert Florczak. Harcourt, 1997. ISBN 978-0-15-200014-1 Subj: Birds. Flowers. Songs.

The Birthday Queen ill. by Don Wood. Scholastic, 2013. ISBN 978-0-545-41474-6 Subj: Birthdays. Family life – mothers. Parties.

Blue sky ill. by author. Scholastic, 2012. ISBN 978-0-545-31610-1 Subj: Nature. Sky.

The Bunyans ill. by David Shannon. Blue Sky, 1996. ISBN 978-0-590-48089-5 Subj: Mythical creatures. Nature. Tall tales. U.S. history – frontier & pioneer life.

The Christmas adventure of Space Elf Sam ill. by Bruce Wood. Blue Sky, 1998. ISBN 978-0-590-03143-1 Subj: Aliens. Holidays – Christmas. Santa Claus. Space & space ships.

A cowboy Christmas ill. by Robert Florczak. Simon & Schuster, 2000. ISBN 978-0-689-82190-5 Subj: Accidents. Cowboys, cowgirls. Family life. Holidays – Christmas.

The deep blue sea: a book of colors ill. by Bruce Wood. Scholastic, 2005. ISBN 978-0-439-75382-1 Subj: Concepts – color. Sea & seashore.

A dog needs a bone ill. by author. Scholastic, 2007. ISBN 978-0-545-00005-5 Subj: Animals – dogs. Rhyming text.

Elbert's bad word ill. by author. Harcourt, 1988. ISBN 978-0-15-225320-2 Subj: Behavior – misbehavior. Family life. Language.

The flying dragon room ill. by Mark Teague. Blue Sky, 1996. ISBN 978-0-590-48193-9 Subj: Activities – making things. Imagination. Magic.

The full moon at the napping house ill. by Don Wood. Houghton, 2015. ISBN 978-054430832-9 Subj: Animals. Cumulative tales. Family life – grandmothers. Sleep.

Heckedy Peg ill. by Don Wood. Harcourt, 1987. ISBN 978-0-15-233678-3 Subj: Behavior – talking to strangers. Character traits – cleverness. Days of the week, months of the year. Folk & fairy tales. Food. Witches.

It's Duffy time! ill. by Don Wood. Scholastic, 2012. ISBN 978-0-545-22089-7 Subj: Animals – dogs. Clocks, watches. Sleep. Time.

Jubal's wish ill. by Don Wood. Blue Sky, 2000. ISBN 978-0-439-16964-6 Subj: Behavior – wishing. Friendship. Frogs & toads. Reptiles – lizards.

King Bidgood's in the bathtub ill. by Don Wood. Harcourt, 1985. ISBN 978-0-15-242730-6 Subj: Activities. Activities – bathing. Caldecott award honor books. Humorous stories. Royalty – kings.

Little Penguin's tale ill. by author. Harcourt, 1989. ISBN 978-0-15-246475-2 Subj: Activities – dancing. Animals. Animals – whales. Birds. Birds – penguins. Foreign lands – Antarctic.

Merry Christmas, big hungry bear (Wood, Don)

Moonflute ill. by Don Wood. Harcourt, 1986. ISBN 978-0-15-255337-1 Subj: Bedtime. Moon. Night. Sleep.

The napping house ill. by Don Wood. Harcourt, 1984. ISBN 978-0-15-256708-8 Subj: Animals. Cumulative tales. Family life – grandmothers. Rhyming text. Sleep.

The napping house wakes up ill. by Don Wood. Harcourt, 1994. ISBN 978-0-15-200890-1 Subj: Animals. Family life – grandmothers. Format, unusual – toy & movable books. Insects – fleas. Rhyming text. Sleep.

Oh my baby bear! ill. by author. Harcourt, 1990. ISBN 978-0-15-257698-1 Subj: Animals – bears. Bedtime. Behavior – growing up.

Piggies (Wood, Don)

Piggy Pie Po ill. by Don Wood. Harcourt, 2010. ISBN 978-0-15-202494-9 Subj: Animals – pigs. Rhyming text.

The rainbow bridge ill. by Robert Florczak. Harcourt, 1995. ISBN 978-0-15-265475-7 Subj: Animals – dolphins. Creation. Folk & fairy tales. Indians of North America – Chumash.

Silly Sally ill. by author. Harcourt, 1992. ISBN 978-0-15-274428-1 Subj: Activities – traveling. Animals. Cumulative tales. Rhyming text.

Sweet dream pie ill. by Mark Teague. Blue Sky, 1998. ISBN 978-0-590-96204-9 Subj: Bedtime. Dreams.

Ten little fish ill. by Bruce Wood. Blue Sky, 2004. ISBN 978-0-439-63569-1 Subj: Counting, numbers. Fish. Foreign lands – South Sea Islands. Rhyming text.

The Tickleoctopus ill. by Don Wood. Harcourt, 1994. ISBN 978-0-15-287000-3 Subj: Activities – playing. Cave dwellers. Family life. Mythical creatures.

Weird parents ill. by author. Dial, 1990. ISBN 978-0-8037-0649-1 Subj: Character traits – being different. Emotions – embarrassment. Family life.

When the root children wake up by Audrey Wood and Sibylle Von Olfers ill. by Ned Bittinger. Scholastic, 2002. ISBN 978-0-590-42517-9 Subj: Flowers. Insects. Nature. Seasons – spring. Songs.

Wood, Don. *Merry Christmas, big hungry bear* by Don Wood and Audrey Wood; ill. by Don Wood. Blue Sky, 2002. ISBN 978-0-439-32092-4 Subj: Animals – mice. Behavior – sharing. Gifts. Holidays – Christmas. Shopping.

Piggies by Don Wood and Audrey Wood; ill. by Don Wood. Harcourt, 1991. ISBN 978-0-15-256341-7 Subj: Animals – pigs. Games.

Wood, Douglas. *Aunt Mary's rose* ill. by LeUyen Pham. Candlewick, 2010. ISBN 978-0-7636-1090-6 Subj: Death. Family life – aunts, uncles. Flowers – roses. Gardens, gardening.

Grandad's prayers of the earth ill. by P. J Lynch. Candlewick, 1999. ISBN 978-0-7636-0660-2 Subj: Death. Emotions – grief. Family life – grandfathers. Nature.

No one but you ill. by P. J. Lynch. Candlewick, 2011. ISBN 978-0-7636-3848-1 Subj: Nature. Senses.

Nothing to do ill. by Wendy Anderson Halperin. Penguin, 2006. ISBN 978-0-525-47656-6 Subj: Activities – playing.

Old Turtle ill. by Cheng-Khee Chee. Pfeifer-Hamilton, 1991. ISBN 978-0-938586-48-7 Subj: Animals. Ecology. Religion.

The secret of saying thanks ill. by Greg Shed. Simon & Schuster, 2005. ISBN 978-0-689-85410-1 Subj: Emotions – happiness. Nature.

What dads can't do ill. by Doug Cushman. Simon & Schuster, 2000. ISBN 978-0-689-82620-7 Subj: Family life – fathers.

What grandmas can't do ill. by Doug Cushman. Simon & Schuster, 2005. ISBN 978-0-689-84647-2 Subj: Family life – grandmothers.

What moms can't do ill. by Doug Cushman. Simon & Schuster, 2000. ISBN 978-0-689-83358-8 Subj: Family life – mothers.

What teachers can't do ill. by Doug Cushman. Simon & Schuster, 2002. ISBN 978-0-689-84644-1 Subj: Careers – teachers. Dinosaurs. School.

When a dad says "I love you" ill. by Jennifer A. Bell. Simon & Schuster, 2013. ISBN 978-0-689-87532-8 Subj: Animals. Emotions – love. Family life – fathers.

When a grandpa says "I love you" ill. by Jennifer A. Bell. Simon & Schuster, 2014. ISBN 978-068981512-6 Subj: Emotions – love. Family life – grandfathers.

Where the sunrise begins ill. by Wendy Popp. Simon & Schuster, 2010. ISBN 978-0-689-86172-7 Subj: Nature. Sun.

Wood, Jakki. *A hole in the road* ill. by author. Frances Lincoln, 2008. ISBN 978-1-84507-286-5 Subj: Careers – construction workers. Machines.

Moo moo, brown cow ill. by Rog Bonner. Harcourt, 1992. ISBN 978-0-15-200533-7 Subj: Animals. Animals – cats. Concepts – color. Counting, numbers. Farms.

Never say boo to a goose! ill. by Clare Beaton. Barefoot, 2002. ISBN 978-1-84148-255-2 Subj: Animals. Animals – cats. Birds – geese. Farms.

Wood, Michele. *Going back home* ill. by author. Children's Book Press, 1996. ISBN 978-0-89239-137-0 Subj: Art. Careers – artists. Ethnic groups in the U.S. – African Americans.

Wood, Muriel. *Old bird* (Morck, Irene)

Wood, Nancy C. *Mr. and Mrs. God in the creation kitchen* ill. by Timothy Basil Ering. Candlewick, 2006. ISBN 978-0-7636-1258-0 Subj: Creation. Religion.

Woodcock, Fiona. *Hiding Heidi* ill. by author. little bee, 2016. ISBN 978-149980350-1 Subj: Activities – playing. Behavior – hiding. Friendship.

Woodhull, Anne Love. *The buzz on bees: why are they disappearing?* (Rotner, Shelley)

Every season (Rotner, Shelley)

Woodruff, Elvira. *Can you guess where we're going?* ill. by Cynthia Fisher. Holiday, 1998. ISBN 978-0-8234-1387-4 Subj: Family life – grandfathers. Libraries.

The memory coat ill. by Michael Dooling. Scholastic, 1999. ISBN 978-0-590-67717-2 Subj: Clothing – coats. Ethnic groups in the U.S. – Russian Americans. Immigrants, immigration. Jewish culture. Memories, memory.

Small beauties: the journey of Darcy Heart O'Hara ill. by Adam Rex. Random House, 2006. ISBN 978-0-375-92686-0 Subj: Family life. Foreign lands – Ireland. Immigrants, immigration. U.S. history.

Woodruff, Liza. *Emerson barks* ill. by author. Holt/Christy Ottaviano, 2016. ISBN 978-162779167-0 Subj: Animals – dogs. Noise, sounds.

Woodson, Jacqueline. *Coming on home soon* ill. by E. B. Lewis. Putnam, 2004. ISBN 978-0-399-23748-5 Subj: Caldecott award honor books. Ethnic groups in the U.S. – African Americans. Family life – grandmothers. Family life – mothers. U.S. history. War.

Each kindness ill. by E. B. Lewis. Penguin, 2012. ISBN 978-0-399-24652-4 Subj: Behavior – bullying, teasing. Careers – teachers. Character traits – being different. Ethnic groups in the U.S. – African Americans. Poverty. School.

The other side ill. by E. B. Lewis. Putnam, 2001. ISBN 978-0-399-23116-2 Subj: Cities, towns. Ethnic groups in the U.S. – African Americans. Prejudice. Seasons – summer.

Pecan pie baby ill. by Sophie Blackall. Penguin, 2010. ISBN 978-0-399-23987-8 Subj: Babies, toddlers. Ethnic groups in the U.S. – African Americans. Family life – new sibling. Family life – single-parent families.

Show way ill. by Hudson Talbott. Penguin, 2005. ISBN 978-0-399-23749-2 Subj: Ethnic groups in the U.S. – African Americans. Family life – mothers. Quilts. Slavery. U.S. history.

Sweet, sweet memory ill. by E. B. Lewis. Hyperion, 2000. ISBN 978-0-7868-2191-4 Subj: Death. Emotions – grief. Ethnic groups in the U.S. – African Americans. Family life – grandparents. Memories, memory.

This is the rope: a story from the Great Migration ill. by James Ransome. Penguin/Nancy Paulsen, 2013. ISBN 978-0-399-23986-1 Subj: Ethnic groups in the U.S. – African Americans. Family life. Migration. U.S. history.

We had a picnic this Sunday past ill. by Diane Greenseid. Hyperion, 1997. ISBN 978-0-7868-2192-1 Subj: Activities – picnicking. Ethnic groups in the U.S. – African Americans. Family life.

Woodward, Molly. *The babies and doggies book* (Schindel, John)

Wooldridge, Connie Nordhielm. *The legend of Strap Buckner* ill. by Andrew Glass. Holiday, 2001. ISBN 978-0-8234-1536-6 Subj: Devil. Folk & fairy tales. Tall tales.

When Esther Morris headed west ill. by Jacqueline Rogers. Holiday, 2001. ISBN 978-0-8234-1597-7 Subj: Gender roles. U.S. history.

Wicked Jack ill. by Will Hillenbrand. Holiday, 1995. ISBN 978-0-8234-1101-6 Subj: Behavior – wishing. Character traits – meanness. Devil. Folk & fairy tales.

Wooley, David Freeman. *Little Man* (Warwick, Dionne)

Woollard, Elli. *The giant of Jum* ill. by Benji Davies. Henry Holt, 2017. ISBN 978-162779515-9 Subj: Character traits – helpfulness. Giants. Rhyming text.

Woolley, Catherine *see* Thayer, Jane

Woollvin, Bethan. *Little Red* ill. by author. Peachtree, 2016. ISBN 978-156145917-9 Subj: Animals – wolves. Behavior – resourcefulness. Behavior – talking to strangers. Character traits – assertiveness. Folk & fairy tales.

Rapunzel ill. by author. Peachtree, 2017. ISBN 978-168263003-7 Subj: Folk & fairy tales. Hair. Witches.

Wormell, Christopher. *Blue Rabbit and friends* ill. by author. Fogelman, 2000. ISBN 978-0-8037-2499-0 Subj: Animals. Animals – rabbits. Friendship. Homes, houses.

Blue Rabbit and the runaway wheel ill. by author. Fogelman, 2001. ISBN 978-0-8037-2508-9 Subj: Animals. Animals – rabbits. Sports – bicycling.

Henry and the fox ill. by author. Trafalgar, 2008. ISBN 978-0-224-07044-7 Subj: Birds – chickens, roosters. Character traits – confidence. Emotions – fear. Self-concept.

The new alphabet of animals ill. by author. Running Press, 2002. ISBN 978-0-7624-1347-8 Subj: ABC books. Animals.

Puff, puff, chugga-chugga ill. by author. Margaret K. McElderry, 2001. ISBN 978-0-689-83986-3 Subj: Animals. Trains.

Wormell, Mary. *Bernard the angry rooster* ill. by author. Farrar, 2001. ISBN 978-0-374-30670-0 Subj: Animals. Behavior – bad day, bad mood. Birds – chickens, roosters. Emotions – anger.

Hilda Hen's happy birthday ill. by author. Harcourt, 1995. ISBN 978-0-15-200299-2 Subj:

Animals. Birds – chickens, roosters. Birthdays. Farms.

Hilda Hen's search ill. by author. Harcourt, 1994. ISBN 978-0-15-200069-1 Subj: Birds – chickens, roosters. Eggs. Farms.

Why not? ill. by author. Farrar, 2000. ISBN 978-0-374-38422-7 Subj: Animals. Animals – babies. Animals – cats. Character traits – questioning. Farms.

Wortche, Allison. *Rosie Sprout's time to shine* ill. by Patrice Barton. Random House, 2011. ISBN 978-0-375-86721-7 Subj: Behavior – boasting, showing off. Emotions – envy, jealousy. Gardens, gardening. Plants. School.

Worth, Valerie. *Pug and other animal poems* ill. by Steve Jenkins. Farrar, 2013. ISBN 978-0-374-35024-6 Subj: Animals. Poetry.

Wright, Betty Ren. *The blizzard* ill. by Ronald Himler. Holiday, 2003. ISBN 978-0-8234-1656-1 Subj: Birthdays. School. Weather – blizzards.

Wright, Catherine. *Steamboat Annie and the thousand-pound catfish* ill. by Howard Fine. Philomel, 2001. ISBN 978-0-399-23331-9 Subj: Activities – singing. Fish. Tall tales.

Wright, Cliff. *Bear and ball* ill. by author. Chronicle, 2005. ISBN 978-0-8118-4819-0 Subj: Animals – bears. Format, unusual – board books. Rhyming text. Toys – balls.

Bear and kite ill. by author. Chronicle, 2005. ISBN 978-0-8118-4820-6 Subj: Animals – bears. Format, unusual – board books. Kites. Rhyming text.

Wright, Courtni Crump. *Journey to freedom* ill. by Gershom Griffith. Holiday, 1994. ISBN 978-0-8234-1096-5 Subj: Character traits – freedom. Ethnic groups in the U.S. – African Americans. Slavery. U.S. history.

Jumping the broom ill. by Gershom Griffith. Holiday, 1994. ISBN 978-0-8234-1042-2 Subj: Ethnic groups in the U.S. – African Americans. Slavery. U.S. history. Weddings.

Wagon train: a family goes west in 1865 ill. by Gershom Griffith. Holiday, 1995. ISBN 978-0-8234-1152-8 Subj: Activities – traveling. Ethnic groups in the U.S. – African Americans. U.S. history – frontier & pioneer life.

Wright, Danielle. *Japanese nursery rhymes: Carp streamers, Falling rain, and other traditional favorites* ill. by Helen Acraman. Tuttle, 2012. ISBN 978-4-80531-188-2 Subj: Foreign lands – Japan. Nursery rhymes.

Wright, Dare. *A gift from the lonely doll* ill. by author. Houghton, 2001. ISBN 978-0-618-07181-4

Subj: Clothing – scarves. Emotions – loneliness. Gifts. Holidays – Christmas. Toys – bears. Toys – dolls.

The lonely doll photos by author. Houghton, 1998. ISBN 978-0-395-90112-0 Subj: Emotions – loneliness. Toys – bears. Toys – dolls.

Wright, Joan Richards. *Bugs* (Parker, Nancy Winslow)

Wright, Joanna. *Bunnies on ice* ill. by author. Roaring Brook, 2013. ISBN 978-1-59643-404-2 Subj: Animals – rabbits. Character traits – confidence. Seasons. Self-concept. Sports – ice skating.

The orchestra pit ill. by author. Roaring Brook/Neal Porter, 2014. ISBN 978-159643769-2 Subj: Musical instruments – orchestras. Reptiles – snakes.

Wright, Maureen. *Barnyard fun* ill. by Paul Ratz de Tagyos. Amazon/Two Lions, 2013. ISBN 978-1-4778-1643-1 Subj: Animals. Animals – sheep. Farms. Holidays – April Fools' Day. Riddles & jokes.

Earth Day, birthday! ill. by Violet Kim. Marshall Cavendish, 2012. ISBN 978-0-7614-6109-8 Subj: Animals. Animals – monkeys. Birthdays. Ecology. Holidays – Earth Day. Rhyming text.

Sleep, Big Bear, sleep! ill. by Will Hillenbrand. Marshall Cavendish, 2009. ISBN 978-0-7614-5560-8 Subj: Animals – bears. Hibernation. Rhyming text. Seasons – winter.

Sneeze, Big Bear, sneeze ill. by Will Hillenbrand. Marshall Cavendish, 2011. ISBN 978-0-7614-5959-0 Subj: Animals – bears. Rhyming text. Seasons – fall. Weather – wind.

Sneezy the snowman ill. by Stephen Gilpin. Marshall Cavendish, 2010. ISBN 978-0-7614-5711-4 Subj: Clothing. Snowmen.

Wright, Michael. *Jake goes peanuts* ill. by author. Feiwel & Friends, 2010. ISBN 978-0-312-54967-1 Subj: Food. Rhyming text.

Jake starts school ill. by author. Feiwel & Friends, 2008. ISBN 978-0-312-36798-5 Subj: Emotions – fear. Rhyming text. School – first day.

Jake stays awake ill. by author. Feiwel & Friends, 2007. ISBN 978-0-312-36797-8 Subj: Bedtime. Rhyming text. Sleep.

Wu, Faye-Lynn. *Chinese and English nursery rhymes: share and sing in two languages* ill. by Kieren Dutcher. Tuttle, 2010. ISBN 978-0-8048-4094-1 Subj: Foreign languages. Nursery rhymes.

Wunderli, Stephen. *Little Boo* ill. by Tim Zeltner. Henry Holt, 2014. ISBN 978-080509708-5 Subj: Gardens, gardening. Holidays – Halloween. Plants. Seeds.

Wyart, Peter. *The shepherds' tale* (Dowley, Tim)

The wise men's tale (Dowley, Tim)

Wyeth, Sharon Dennis. *Always my dad* ill. by Raúl Colón. Knopf, 1995. ISBN 978-0-679-93447-9 Subj: Behavior – needing someone. Country. Ethnic groups in the U.S. – African Americans. Family life – fathers. Family life – grandparents.

The granddaughter necklace ill. by Bagram Ibatoulline. Scholastic, 2013. ISBN 978-0-545-08125-2 Subj: Activities – storytelling. Ethnic groups in the U.S. – African Americans. Family life – mothers. Genealogy. Jewelry. Memories, memory.

Something beautiful ill. by Chris Soentpiet. Doubleday, 1998. ISBN 978-0-385-32239-3 Subj: Cities, towns. Communities, neighborhoods. Ethnic groups in the U.S. – African Americans.

Wyndham, Robert. *The Chinese Mother Goose rhymes* (Mother Goose)

Wynne-Jones, Tim. *The boat in the tree* ill. by John Shelley. Boyds Mills, 2007. ISBN 978-1-932425-49-9 Subj: Adoption. Boats, ships. Family life – brothers & sisters. Sibling rivalry.

Secret Agent Man goes shopping for shoes ill. by Brian Won. Candlewick, 2016. ISBN 978-076367119-8 Subj: Clothing – shoes. Imagination. Shopping.

Xinran, Xue. *Motherbridge of love* ill. by Josée Masse. Barefoot, 2007. ISBN 978-1-84686-047-8 Subj: Adoption. Emotions – love. Family life – mothers. Poetry.

Xiong, Blia. *Nine-in-one Grr! Grr!* adapt. by Cathy Spagnoli; ill. by Nancy Hom. Children's Press, 1989. ISBN 978-0-89239-048-9 Subj: Animals – tigers. Folk & fairy tales. Foreign lands – Laos.

Yaccarino, Dan. *All the way to America: the story of a big Italian family and a little shovel* ill. by author. Random House, 2011. ISBN 978-0-375-86642-5 Subj: Careers – writers. Ethnic groups in the U.S. – Italian Americans. Immigrants, immigration. U.S. history.

Billy and Goat at the state fair ill. by author. Knopf, 2015. ISBN 978-038575325-8 Subj: Animals – goats. Fairs, festivals. Friendship.

The birthday fish ill. by author. Henry Holt, 2005. ISBN 978-0-8050-7493-2 Subj: Birthdays. Fish. Pets.

Deep in the jungle ill. by author. Atheneum, 2000. ISBN 978-0-689-82235-3 Subj: Animals. Animals – lions. Behavior – dissatisfaction. Circus.

Doug unplugged ill. by author. Knopf, 2013. ISBN 978-0-375-86643-2 Subj: Cities, towns. Robots. Technology.

Doug unplugs on the farm ill. by author. Knopf, 2014. ISBN 978-038575328-9 Subj: Farms. Robots. Technology.

Every Friday ill. by author. Henry Holt, 2007. ISBN 978-0-8050-7724-7 Subj: Family life – fathers.

The fantastic undersea life of Jacques Cousteau ill. by author. Knopf, 2009. ISBN 978-0-375-85573-3 Subj: Careers – oceanographers. Sea & seashore.

First day on a strange new planet ill. by author. Hyperion, 2000. ISBN 978-0-7868-2499-1 Subj: Aliens. Planets. School. Space & space ships.

Five little ducks ill. by author. HarperCollins, 2005. ISBN 978-0-06-073465-7 Subj: Animals. Birds – ducks. Format, unusual – board books. Rhyming text. Songs.

Good night, Mr. Night ill. by author. Harcourt, 1997. ISBN 978-0-15-201319-6 Subj: Bedtime. Dreams. Night.

Happyland: big berry: a little moral story about gratitude ill. by author. Workman, 2016. ISBN 978-076118736-3 Subj: Character traits – generosity. Character traits – selfishness. Format, unusual – board books. Friendship.

Happyland: birthday cake: a little moral story about sharing ill. by author. Workman, 2016. ISBN 978-076118734-9 Subj: Behavior – sharing. Birthdays. Format, unusual – board books.

Happyland: rainy day: a little moral story about worry ill. by author. Workman, 2016. ISBN 978-076118735-6 Subj: Activities – playing. Behavior – worrying. Format, unusual – board books. Friendship. Weather – rain.

I am a story ill. by author. HarperCollins, 2016. ISBN 978-006241106-8 Subj: Activities – storytelling. Books, reading. Communication.

If I had a robot ill. by author. Viking, 1996. ISBN 978-0-670-86936-7 Subj: Behavior. Family life. Robots.

Lawn to lawn ill. by author. Random House, 2010. ISBN 978-0-375-85574-0 Subj: Animals. Moving.

The lima bean monster ill. by Adam McCauley. Walker, 2001. ISBN 978-0-8027-8777-4 Subj: Food. Monsters.

Morris Mole ill. by author. HarperCollins, 2017. ISBN 978-006241107-5 Subj: Animals – moles. Family life – brothers. Food. Self-concept.

New pet ill. by author. Hyperion, 2001. ISBN 978-0-7868-2500-4 Subj: Aliens. Pets. Planets. Space & space ships.

An octopus followed me home ill. by author. Viking, 1997. ISBN 978-0-670-87401-9 Subj: Animals. Octopuses. Pets.

Oswald ill. by author. Atheneum, 2001. ISBN 978-0-689-84252-8 Subj: Animals – dogs. Moving. Octopuses. Pets.

So big ill. by author. HarperCollins, 2001. ISBN 978-0-694-01509-2 Subj: Animals. Concepts – size. Format, unusual – toy & movable books. Games.

Unlovable ill. by author. Henry Holt, 2001. ISBN 978-0-8050-6321-9 Subj: Animals – dogs. Friendship. Self-concept.

Zoom! zoom! zoom! I'm off to the moon! ill. by author. Scholastic, 1997. ISBN 978-0-590-95610-9 Subj: Moon. Rhyming text. Space & space ships.

Yacowitz, Caryn. *Pumpkin fiesta* ill. by Joe Cepeda. HarperCollins, 1998. ISBN 978-0-06-027659-1 Subj: Fairs, festivals. Foreign lands – Mexico. Gardens, gardening. Plants.

Yagawa, Sumiko. *The crane wife* ill. by Suekichi Akaba. Morrow, 1982. ISBN 978-0-688-00496-5 Subj: Activities – weaving. Birds – cranes. Character traits – kindness to animals. Folk & fairy tales. Foreign lands – Japan.

Yahgulanaas, Michael Nicoll. *The little hummingbird* ill. by author. Greystone, 2010. ISBN 978-1-55365-533-6 Subj: Birds – hummingbirds. Character traits. Ecology. Folk & fairy tales. Foreign lands – South America.

Yamada, Kobi. *What do you do with a problem?* ill. by Mae Besom. Compendium, 2016. ISBN 978-194320000-9 Subj: Behavior – worrying. Problem solving.

Yamada, Utako. *The story of Cherry the pig* ill. by author. Kane/Miller, 2007. ISBN 978-1-933605-25-8 Subj: Activities – baking, cooking. Animals – pigs. Contests. Foreign lands – Japan.

Yamaguchi, Kristi. *Dream big, little pig!* ill. by Tim Bowers. Sourcebooks, 2011. ISBN 978-1-4022-5275-4 Subj: Animals – pigs. Character traits – ambition. Character traits – persistence. Sports – ice skating.

It's a big world, little pig! ill. by Tim Bowers. Sourcebooks, 2012. ISBN 978-1-4022-6644-7 Subj: Animals. Animals – pigs. Contests. Sports – ice skating.

Yamasaki, Katie. *Fish for Jimmy: inspired by one family's experience in a Japanese American internment camp* ill. by author. Holiday House, 2013. ISBN 978-0-8234-2375-0 Subj: Ethnic groups in the U.S. – Japanese Americans. U.S. history. War.

Yamashita, Haruo. *Seven little mice go to school* ill. by Kazuo Iwamura. NorthSouth, 2011. ISBN 978-0-7358-4012-6 Subj: Animals – mice. Character traits – cleverness. Family life – mothers. School – first day.

Seven little mice have fun on the ice ill. by Kazuo Iwamura. NorthSouth, 2011. ISBN 978-0-7358-4048-5 Subj: Animals – mice. Family life – mothers. Seasons – winter. Sports – fishing.

Yamawaki, Yuriko. *Guri and Gura* (Nakagawa, Rieko)

Guri and Gura's special gift (Nakagawa, Rieko)

Yang, Belle. *Always come home to me* ill. by author. Candlewick, 2007. ISBN 978-0-7636-2899-4 Subj: Birds – doves. Family life – mothers. Foreign lands – China. Multiple births – twins.

Yankey, Lindsey. *Bluebird* ill. by author. Simply Read, 2014. ISBN 978-192701833-0 Subj: Birds – bluebirds. Character traits – confidence. Weather – wind.

Sun and Moon ill. by author. Simply Read, 2015. ISBN 978-192701860-6 Subj: Emotions – envy, jealousy. Moon. Self-concept. Sun.

Yankovic, Al. *My new teacher and me!* ill. by Wes Hargis. HarperCollins, 2013. ISBN 978-0-06-219203-5 Subj: Careers – teachers. Humorous stories. Rhyming text. School – first day.

When I grow up ill. by Wes Hargis. HarperCollins, 2011. ISBN 978-0-06-192691-4 Subj: Careers. Rhyming text. School.

Yarlett, Emma. *Orion and the Dark* ill. by author. Candlewick/Templar, 2015. ISBN 978-076367595-0 Subj: Bedtime. Emotions – fear.

Yarrow, Peter. *Day is done* ill. by Melissa Sweet. Sterling, 2009. ISBN 978-1-4027-4806-6 Subj: Animals. Bedtime. Songs.

Let's sing together! ill. by Terry Widener. Sterling, 2009. ISBN 978-1-4027-5963-5 Subj: Songs.

Puff, the magic dragon by Peter Yarrow and Leonard Lipton ill. by Eric Puybaret. Sterling, 2007. ISBN 978-1-4027-4782-3 Subj: Dragons. Music. Songs.

Yashima, Taro. *Crow boy* ill. by author. Viking, 1955. ISBN 978-0-670-24931-2 Subj: Caldecott award honor books. Character traits – shyness. Emotions – loneliness. Foreign lands – Japan. School.

Umbrella ill. by author. Viking, 1958. ISBN 978-0-670-73858-8 Subj: Birthdays. Caldecott award honor books. Cities, towns. Ethnic groups in the U.S. – Japanese Americans. Umbrellas. Weather – rain.

Yates, Louise. *Dog loves books* ill. by author. Random House, 2010. ISBN 978-0-375-86449-0 Subj: Animals – dogs. Books, reading.

Dog loves counting ill. by author. Knopf, 2013. ISBN 978-0-449-81342-3 Subj: Animals – dogs. Bedtime. Books, reading. Counting, numbers.

Dog loves drawing ill. by author. Knopf, 2012. ISBN 978-0-375-87067-5 Subj: Activities – drawing. Animals – dogs.

Yates, Philip. *Ten little mummies* ill. by G. Brian Karas. Viking, 2003. ISBN 978-0-670-03641-7 Subj: Counting, numbers. Foreign lands – Egypt. Mummies. Rhyming text.

Yee, Brenda Shannon. *Sand castle* ill. by Thea Kliros. Greenwillow, 1999. ISBN 978-0-688-16194-1 Subj: Castles. Cumulative tales. Sand. Sea & seashore.

Yee, Kristina. *Miss Todd and her wonderful flying machine* (Poletti, Frances)

Yee, Paul. *Bamboo* ill. by Shaoli Wang. Simply Read, 2006. ISBN 978-1-894965-53-8 Subj: Folk & fairy tales. Foreign lands – China.

Yee, Wong Herbert. *Big black bear* ill. by author. Houghton, 1993. ISBN 978-0-395-66359-2 Subj: Animals – bears. Behavior – misbehavior. Etiquette. Rhyming text.

Detective Small in the amazing banana caper ill. by author. Houghton, 2007. ISBN 978-0-618-47285-7 Subj: Animals. Careers – detectives. Crime. Rhyming text.

Eek! There's a mouse in the house ill. by author. Houghton, 1992. ISBN 978-0-395-62303-9 Subj: Animals. Cumulative tales. Homes, houses. Rhyming text.

Fireman Small ill. by author. Houghton, 1994. ISBN 978-0-395-68987-5 Subj: Animals. Animals – pigs. Careers – firefighters. Fire. Rhyming text.

Fireman Small, fire down below ill. by author. Houghton, 2001. ISBN 978-0-618-00707-3 Subj: Animals. Animals – pigs. Careers – firefighters. Fire. Hotels. Rhyming text.

Fireman Small to the rescue ill. by author. Houghton, 1998. ISBN 978-0-395-88122-4 Subj: Animals. Animals – pigs. Careers – farmers. Careers – firefighters. Fire. Rhyming text.

Hamburger Heaven ill. by author. Houghton, 1999. ISBN 978-0-395-87548-3 Subj: Activities – working. Animals. Animals – pigs. Food. Restaurants.

Mrs. Brown went to town ill. by author. Houghton, 1996. ISBN 978-0-395-75282-1 Subj: Animals. Homes, houses. Rhyming text.

My autumn book ill. by author. Henry Holt, 2015. ISBN 978-080509922-5 Subj: Nature. Rhyming text. Seasons – fall.

The Officers' Ball ill. by author. Houghton, 1997. ISBN 978-0-395-81182-5 Subj: Activities – dancing. Animals. Animals – hippopotamuses. Careers – police officers. Crime. Rhyming text.

A small Christmas ill. by author. Houghton, 2004. ISBN 978-0-618-32612-9 Subj: Animals. Careers – firefighters. Holidays – Christmas. Rhyming text. Santa Claus.

Summer days and nights ill. by author. Henry Holt, 2012. ISBN 978-0-8050-9078-9 Subj: Day. Ethnic groups in the U.S. – Asian Americans. Night. Rhyming text. Seasons – summer.

Tracks in the snow ill. by author. Henry Holt, 2003. ISBN 978-0-8050-6771-2 Subj: Animals. Nature. Rhyming text. Seasons – winter.

Who likes rain? ill. by author. Henry Holt, 2007. ISBN 978-0-8050-7734-6 Subj: Ethnic groups in the U.S. – Asian Americans. Games. Rhyming text. Seasons – spring. Weather – rain.

Yeh, Kat. *The friend ship* ill. by Chuck Groenink. Disney/Hyperion, 2016. ISBN 978-148470726-5 Subj: Animals – hedgehogs. Boats, ships. Emotions – loneliness. Friendship.

The magic brush: a story of love, family, and Chinese characters ill. by Huy Voun Lee. Walker, 2011. ISBN 978-0-8027-2178-5 Subj: Activities – storytelling. Activities – writing. Death. Ethnic groups in the U.S. – Chinese Americans. Family life – grandfathers. Foreign languages.

Yektai, Niki. *Bears at the beach* ill. by author. Millbrook, 1996. ISBN 978-0-7613-0022-9 Subj: Animals – bears. Counting, numbers. Sea & seashore – beaches.

Bears in pairs ill. by Diane deGroat. Bradbury, 1987. ISBN 978-0-02-793691-9 Subj: Animals – bears. Concepts. Rhyming text.

Hi bears, bye bears ill. by Diane deGroat. Watts, 1990. ISBN 978-0-531-08458-8 Subj: Rhyming text. Toys – bears.

Yelchin, Eugene. *Spring hare* ill. by author. Henry Holt, 2017. ISBN 978-162779392-6 Subj: Activities

– jumping. Animals – rabbits. Imagination. Seasons – spring. Wordless.

Yeoman, John. *Three little owls* (Luzzati, Emanuele)

Yep, Laurence. *Auntie Tiger* ill. by Insu Lee. HarperCollins, 2009. ISBN 978-0-06-029551-6 Subj: Animals – tigers. Disguises. Family life – sisters. Folk & fairy tales. Foreign lands – China.

Dragon prince ill. by Kam Mak. HarperCollins, 1997. ISBN 978-0-06-024393-7 Subj: Dragons. Emotions – envy, jealousy. Family life – sisters. Folk & fairy tales. Foreign lands – China. Sibling rivalry.

The Khan's daughter ill. by Jean Tseng and Mou-Sien Tseng. Scholastic, 1997. ISBN 978-0-590-48389-6 Subj: Folk & fairy tales. Foreign lands – Mongolia. Monsters. Royalty – khans. Weddings.

The man who tricked a ghost ill. by Isadore Seltzer. BridgeWater, 1993. ISBN 978-0-8167-3030-8 Subj: Behavior – trickery. Foreign lands – China. Ghosts. Middle Ages.

The shell woman and the king ill. by Ming-Yi Yang. Dial, 1993. ISBN 978-0-8037-1394-9 Subj: Folk & fairy tales. Foreign lands – China. Magic. Royalty – kings.

Yerkes, Jennifer. *A funny little bird* ill. by author. Sourcebooks/Jabberwocky, 2013. ISBN 978-1-4022-8013-9 Subj: Animals – foxes. Birds. Character traits – appearance. Emotions – loneliness. Self-concept.

Yezerski, Thomas. *Meadowlands: a wetlands survival story* ill. by author. Farrar, 2011. ISBN 978-0-374-34913-4 Subj: Ecology. Nature.

Queen of the world ill. by author. Farrar, 2000. ISBN 978-0-374-36165-5 Subj: Birthdays. Family life – mothers. Family life – sisters. Sibling rivalry.

Yi, Hu Yong. *Good morning China* ill. by author. Macmillan, 2007. ISBN 978-1-59643-240-6 Subj: Foreign lands – China. Morning.

Yim, Natasha. *Goldy Luck and the three pandas* ill. by Grace Zong. Charlesbridge, 2014. ISBN 978-158089652-8 Subj: Animals – pandas. Behavior – sharing. Folk & fairy tales. Holidays – Chinese New Year.

Yin. *Brothers* ill. by Chris Soentpiet. Penguin, 2006. ISBN 978-0-399-23406-4 Subj: Ethnic groups in the U.S. – Chinese Americans. Family life – brothers & sisters. Friendship. Immigrants, immigration. Stores. U.S. history.

Coolies ill. by Chris Soentpiet. Philomel, 2001. ISBN 978-0-399-23227-5 Subj: Ethnic groups in the U.S. – Chinese Americans. Family life – brothers. Immigrants, immigration. Prejudice. Trains. U.S. history.

Dear Santa, please come to the 19th floor ill. by Chris Soentpiet. Philomel, 2002. ISBN 978-0-399-23636-5 Subj: Behavior – worrying. Disabilities – physical disabilities. Ethnic groups in the U.S. – Hispanic Americans. Holidays – Christmas. Homes, houses. Santa Claus.

Ying, Jonathan. *Not quite black and white* ill. by Victoria Ying. HarperCollins, 2016. ISBN 978-006238066-1 Subj: Animals. Concepts – color. Rhyming text.

Yokococo. *Matilda and Hans* ill. by author. Candlewick, 2013. ISBN 978-0-7636-6434-3 Subj: Animals – cats. Behavior – misbehavior.

Yolen, Jane. *All in the woodland early: an ABC book* ill. by Jane Breskin Zalben. Music & lyrics by author. Collins-World, 1980. ISBN 978-0-529-05509-5 Subj: ABC books. Forest, woods.

All star! Honus Wagner and the most famous baseball card ever ill. by Jim Burke. Penguin, 2010. ISBN 978-0-399-24661-6 Subj: Sports – baseball.

All those secrets of the world ill. by Leslie A. Baker. Little, 1991. ISBN 978-0-316-96891-1 Subj: Concepts – perspective. Family life – fathers. War.

Baby Bear's big dreams ill. by Melissa Sweet. Harcourt, 2007. ISBN 978-0-15-205291-1 Subj: Animals – bears. Behavior – growing up. Rhyming text.

Baby Bear's books ill. by Melissa Sweet. Harcourt, 2006. ISBN 978-0-15-205290-4 Subj: Animals – bears. Books, reading. Rhyming text.

Baby Bear's chairs ill. by Melissa Sweet. Harcourt, 2005. ISBN 978-0-15-205114-3 Subj: Animals – bears. Bedtime. Family life – fathers. Rhyming text.

Before the storm ill. by Georgia Pugh. Boyds Mills, 1995. ISBN 978-1-56397-240-9 Subj: Activities – playing. Seasons – summer. Weather – storms.

Beneath the ghost moon ill. by Laurel Molk. Little, 1994. ISBN 978-0-316-96892-8 Subj: Animals – mice. Character traits – bravery. Holidays – Halloween. Rhyming text.

Come to the fairies' ball ill. by Gary A. Lippincott. Boyds Mills, 2009. ISBN 978-1-59078-464-8 Subj: Clothing – dresses. Fairies. Parties. Rhyming text.

Creepy monsters, sleepy monsters: a lullaby ill. by Kelly Murphy. Candlewick, 2011. ISBN 978-0-7636-4201-3 Subj: Bedtime. Monsters. Rhyming text.

The day Tiger Rose said goodbye ill. by Jim LaMarche. Random House, 2011. ISBN 978-0-375-86663-0 Subj: Animals – cats. Death.

Dimity Duck ill. by Sebastien Braun. Penguin, 2006. ISBN 978-0-399-24632-6 Subj: Activities

– playing. Birds – ducks. Friendship. Frogs & toads. Rhyming text.

An egret's day: poems photos by Jason Stemple. Boyds Mills, 2010. ISBN 978-1-59078-650-5 Subj: Birds – herons. Poetry.

Elsie's bird ill. by David Small. Penguin, 2010. ISBN 978-0-399-25292-1 Subj: Birds – canaries. Emotions – loneliness. Moving. U.S. history – frontier & pioneer life.

The emperor and the kite ill. by Ed Young. Philomel, 1988, ©1967. ISBN 978-0-399-21499-8 Subj: Caldecott award honor books. Character traits – smallness. Family life – fathers. Foreign lands – China. Kites. Royalty – emperors.

The firebird ill. by Vladimir Vagin. HarperCollins, 2002. ISBN 978-0-06-028539-5 Subj: Ballet. Folk & fairy tales. Foreign lands – Russia. Magic. Mythical creatures. Royalty – princes. Wizards.

The flying witch ill. by Vladimir Vagin. HarperCollins, 2003. ISBN 978-0-06-028537-1 Subj: Careers – farmers. Character traits – cleverness. Folk & fairy tales. Foreign lands – Russia. Witches.

The girl in the golden bower ill. by Jane Dyer. Little, 1994. ISBN 978-0-316-96894-2 Subj: Folk & fairy tales. Orphans. Witches.

Grandma's hurrying child ill. by Kay Chorao. Harcourt, 2005. ISBN 978-0-15-201813-9 Subj: Babies, toddlers. Birth. Family life – grandmothers.

Harvest home ill. by Greg Shed. Harcourt, 2000. ISBN 978-0-15-201819-1 Subj: Careers – farmers. Farms. Rhyming text.

How do dinosaurs clean their rooms? ill. by Mark Teague. Blue Sky, 2004. ISBN 978-0-439-64950-6 Subj: Character traits – orderliness. Dinosaurs. Format, unusual – board books. Rhyming text.

How do dinosaurs count to ten? ill. by Mark Teague. Blue Sky, 2004. ISBN 978-0-439-64949-0 Subj: Counting, numbers. Dinosaurs. Format, unusual – board books. Rhyming text.

How do dinosaurs eat their food? ill. by Mark Teague. Scholastic, 2005. ISBN 978-0-439-24102-1 Subj: Dinosaurs. Etiquette. Food. Rhyming text.

How do dinosaurs get well soon? ill. by Mark Teague. Blue Sky, 2003. ISBN 978-0-439-24100-7 Subj: Dinosaurs. Illness. Rhyming text.

How do dinosaurs go to school? ill. by Mark Teague. Scholastic, 2007. ISBN 978-0-439-02081-7 Subj: Dinosaurs. Rhyming text. School.

How do dinosaurs go to sleep? ill. by Mark Teague. Scholastic, 2016. ISBN 978-054594120-4 Subj: Bedtime. Dinosaurs. Format, unusual – board books. Rhyming text.

How do dinosaurs learn their colors? ill. by Mark Teague. Scholastic, 2006. ISBN 978-0-439-85653-9 Subj: Concepts – color. Dinosaurs. Rhyming text.

How do dinosaurs play with their friends? ill. by Mark Teague. Scholastic, 2006. ISBN 978-0-439-85654-6 Subj: Behavior. Dinosaurs. Friendship. Rhyming text.

How do dinosaurs say good night? ill. by Mark Teague. Blue Sky, 2000. ISBN 978-0-590-31681-1 Subj: Bedtime. Behavior. Dinosaurs. Rhyming text.

How do dinosaurs say Happy Chanukah? ill. by Mark Teague. Scholastic, 2012. ISBN 978-0-545-41677-1 Subj: Dinosaurs. Holidays – Hanukkah. Rhyming text.

How do dinosaurs say I love you? ill. by Mark Teague. Scholastic, 2009. ISBN 978-0-545-14314-1 Subj: Dinosaurs. Emotions – love. Rhyming text.

How do dinosaurs say I'm mad? ill. by Mark Teague. Scholastic, 2013. ISBN 978-0-545-14315-8 Subj: Dinosaurs. Emotions – anger. Rhyming text.

How do dinosaurs say Merry Christmas? ill. by Mark Teague. Scholastic, 2012. ISBN 978-0-545-41678-8 Subj: Dinosaurs. Holidays – Christmas. Rhyming text.

How do dinosaurs stay friends? ill. by Mark Teague. Scholastic/Blue Sky, 2016. ISBN 978-054582934-2 Subj: Dinosaurs. Friendship. Rhyming text.

How do dinosaurs stay safe? ill. by Mark Teague. Scholastic, 2015. ISBN 978-043924104-5 Subj: Dinosaurs. Rhyming text. Safety.

Hush, little horsie ill. by Ruth Sanderson. Random House, 2010. ISBN 978-0-375-85853-6 Subj: Animals – horses, ponies. Bedtime. Rhyming text.

Jane Yolen's Old MacDonald songbook musical arrangements by Adam Stemple; ill. by Rosekrans Hoffman. Boyds Mills, 1994. ISBN 978-1-56397-281-2 Subj: Animals. Cumulative tales. Farms. Music. Songs.

Johnny Appleseed: the legend and the truth ill. by Jim Burke. HarperCollins, 2008. ISBN 978-0-06-059135-9 Subj: Activities – traveling. Gardens, gardening. Tall tales. Trees. U.S. history – frontier & pioneer life.

King Long Shanks ill. by Victoria Chess. Harcourt, 1998. ISBN 978-0-15-200013-4 Subj: Character traits – pride. Character traits – vanity. Clothing. Folk & fairy tales. Frogs & toads. Imagination. Royalty – kings.

Letting Swift River go ill. by Barbara Cooney. Little, 1992. ISBN 978-0-316-96899-7 Subj: Country. U.S. history. Water.

Mama's kiss ill. by Daniel Baxter. Chronicle, 2008. ISBN 978-0-8118-6683-5 Subj: Family life – mothers. Kissing. Rhyming text.

A mirror to nature: poems about reflection ill. by Jason Stemple. Boyds Mills, 2009. ISBN 978-1-59078-624-6 Subj: Nature. Poetry. Water.

Miz Berlin walks ill. by Floyd Cooper. Philomel, 1997. ISBN 978-0-399-22938-1 Subj: Activities – storytelling. Activities – walking. Ethnic groups in the U.S. – African Americans. Old age.

Moon ball ill. by Greg Couch. Simon & Schuster, 1999. ISBN 978-0-689-81095-4 Subj: Bedtime. Dreams. Space & space ships. Sports – baseball.

My brothers' flying machine ill. by Jim Burke. Little, 2003. ISBN 978-0-316-97159-1 Subj: Airplanes, airports. Careers – airplane pilots. Careers – inventors. Family life – brothers. U.S. history.

My father knows the names of things ill. by Stéphane Jorisch. Simon & Schuster, 2010. ISBN 978-1-4169-4895-7 Subj: Family life – fathers. Rhyming text.

My Uncle Emily ill. by Nancy Carpenter. Philomel, 2009. ISBN 978-0-399-24005-8 Subj: Careers – poets. Family life – aunts, uncles. U.S. history.

Naming Liberty ill. by Jim Burke. Philomel, 2008. ISBN 978-0-399-24250-2 Subj: Behavior – seeking better things. Ethnic groups in the U.S. – Russian Americans. Immigrants, immigration. Jewish culture. U.S. history.

Not all princesses dress in pink by Jane Yolen and Heidi E. Y. Stemple ill. by Anne-Sophie Lanquetin. Simon & Schuster, 2010. ISBN 978-1-4169-8018-6 Subj: Character traits – individuality. Gender roles. Rhyming text. Royalty – princesses.

Off we go! ill. by Laurel Molk. Little, 2000. ISBN 978-0-316-90228-1 Subj: Animals – babies. Family life – grandparents. Rhyming text.

On Bird Hill ill. by Bob Marstall. Cornell Lab, 2016. ISBN 978-194364502-2 Subj: Birds. Nature. Rhyming text.

On Duck Pond ill. by Bob Marstall. Cornell Lab, 2017. ISBN 978-194364522-0 Subj: Lakes, ponds. Nature. Noise, sounds. Rhyming text.

Owl moon ill. by John Schoenherr. Philomel, 1987. ISBN 978-0-399-21457-8 Subj: Birds – owls. Caldecott award books. Family life – fathers. Forest, woods. Night.

Pegasus, the flying horse ill. by Ming Li. Dutton, 1998. ISBN 978-0-525-65244-1 Subj: Character traits – vanity. Folk & fairy tales. Mythical creatures. Mythical creatures – Pegasus.

Picnic with Piggins ill. by Jane Dyer. Harcourt, 1988. ISBN 978-0-15-261534-5 Subj: Activities – picnicking. Animals. Animals – pigs. Birthdays.

Piggins ill. by Jane Dyer. Harcourt, 1987. ISBN 978-0-15-261685-4 Subj: Animals. Animals – pigs. Behavior – stealing. Parties. Problem solving.

Raising Yoder's barn ill. by Bernie Fuchs. Little, 1998. ISBN 978-0-316-96887-4 Subj: Barns. Communities, neighborhoods. Ethnic groups in the U.S. – Amish. Farms.

Romping monsters, stomping monsters ill. by Kelly Murphy. Candlewick, 2013. ISBN 978-0-7636-5727-7 Subj: Activities – playing. Monsters. Rhyming text.

Sing a season song ill. by Lisel Jane Ashlock. Creative Editions, 2015. ISBN 978-156846255-4 Subj: Rhyming text. Seasons.

Sister Bear: a Norse tale ill. by Linda Graves. Marshall Cavendish, 2011. ISBN 978-0-7614-5958-3 Subj: Animals – bears. Folk & fairy tales. Holidays – Christmas. Mythical creatures – trolls.

Sky dogs ill. by Barry Moser. Harcourt, 1990. ISBN 978-0-15-275480-8 Subj: Animals – horses, ponies. Folk & fairy tales. Indians of North America – Blackfoot. Indians of North America – Siksika.

Sleep, black bear, sleep by Jane Yolen and Heidi E. Y. Stemple ill. by Brooke Dyer. HarperCollins, 2007. ISBN 978-0-06-081560-8 Subj: Animals. Bedtime. Hibernation. Lullabies. Seasons – winter.

Soft house ill. by Wendy Anderson Halperin. Candlewick, 2005. ISBN 978-0-7636-1697-7 Subj: Activities – playing. Animals – cats. Behavior – boredom. Family life – brothers & sisters.

The stranded whale ill. by Melanie Cataldo. Candlewick, 2015. ISBN 978-076366953-9 Subj: Animals – whales. Death. Emotions – sadness.

The three bears holiday rhyme book ill. by Jane Dyer. Harcourt, 1995. ISBN 978-0-15-200932-8 Subj: Animals – bears. Holidays. Poetry.

Thunder underground ill. by Josée Masse. Boyds Mills, 2017. ISBN 978-159078936-0 Subj: Nature. Poetry.

Waking dragons ill. by Derek Anderson. Simon & Schuster, 2012. ISBN 978-1-4169-9032-1 Subj: Dragons. Rhyming text.

Welcome to the icehouse ill. by Laura Regan. Putnam, 1998. ISBN 978-0-399-23011-0 Subj: Animals. Foreign lands – Arctic. Nature. Science. Seasons.

Welcome to the river of grass ill. by Laura Regan. Putnam, 2001. ISBN 978-0-399-23221-3 Subj: Animals. Birds. Ecology. Swamps.

Welcome to the sea of sand ill. by Laura Regan. Putnam, 1996. ISBN 978-0-399-22765-3 Subj: Animals. Desert. Ecology. Plants. Poetry.

What to do with a box ill. by Chris Sheban. Creative Editions, 2016. ISBN 978-156846289-9 Subj: Activities – playing. Imagination. Rhyming text.

Where have the unicorns gone? ill. by Ruth Sanderson. Simon & Schuster, 2000. ISBN 978-0-689-82465-4 Subj: Ecology. Mythical creatures – unicorns. Rhyming text.

Wings ill. by Dennis Nolan. Harcourt, 1992. ISBN 978-0-15-297850-1 Subj: Activities – flying. Mythical creatures. Royalty – princes.

You nest here with me by Jane Yolen and Heidi E. Y. Stemple ill. by Melissa Sweet. Boyds Mills, 2015. ISBN 978-159078923-0 Subj: Bedtime. Birds. Rhyming text.

Yolleck, Joan. *Paris in the spring with Picasso* ill. by Marjorie Priceman. Random House, 2010. ISBN 978-0-375-83756-2 Subj: Art. Foreign lands – France. Parties.

Yoo, Paula. *Sixteen years in sixteen seconds: the Sammy Lee story* ill. by Dom Lee. Lee & Low, 2005. ISBN 978-1-58430-247-6 Subj: Ethnic groups in the U.S. – Asian Americans. Sports – Olympics.

Yoo, Taeeun. *The little red fish* ill. by author. Penguin, 2007. ISBN 978-0-8037-3145-5 Subj: Fish. Libraries. Magic.

You are a lion! and other fun yoga poses ill. by author. Penguin, 2012. ISBN 978-0-399-25602-8 Subj: Health & fitness. Imagination.

Yoon, Salina. *At the beach* ill. by author. Feiwel & Friends, 2011. ISBN 978-0-312-66303-2 Subj: Format, unusual – board books. Sea & seashore – beaches.

Be a friend ill. by author. Bloomsbury, 2016. ISBN 978-161963951-5 Subj: Character traits – being different. Character traits – individuality. Emotions – loneliness. Friendship.

Bear's big day ill. by author. Bloomsbury, 2016. ISBN 978-080273832-5 Subj: Animals – bears. School – first day. Toys.

Do cows meow? ill. by author. Sterling, 2012. ISBN 978-1-4027-8956-4 Subj: Animals. Farms. Format, unusual – toy & movable books. Noise, sounds.

Do crocs kiss? ill. by author. Sterling, 2012. ISBN 978-1-4027-8955-7 Subj: Animals. Format, unusual – toy & movable books. Noise, sounds.

Found ill. by author. Bloomsbury, 2014. ISBN 978-080273559-1 Subj: Animals – bears. Behavior – lost & found possessions. Character traits – responsibility. Emotions.

Opposnakes: a lift-the-flap book about opposites ill. by author. Simon & Schuster, 2009. ISBN 978-1-4169-7875-6 Subj: Concepts – opposites. Format, unusual – toy & movable books. Reptiles – snakes.

Penguin and Pinecone: a friendship story ill. by author. Walker, 2012. ISBN 978-0-8027-2843-2 Subj: Birds – penguins. Friendship.

Penguin and Pumpkin ill. by author. Walker, 2014. ISBN 978-080273732-8 Subj: Birds – penguins. Family life – brothers. Farms. Seasons – fall.

Penguin in love ill. by author. Walker, 2013. ISBN 978-0-8027-3600-0 Subj: Activities – knitting. Behavior – lost & found possessions. Birds – penguins. Clothing – gloves, mittens. Emotions – love.

Penguin on vacation ill. by author. Walker, 2013. ISBN 978-0-8027-3397-9 Subj: Activities – vacationing. Birds – penguins. Friendship. Sea & seashore.

Penguin's big adventure ill. by author. Bloomsbury, 2015. ISBN 978-080273828-8 Subj: Activities – traveling. Animals – polar bears. Birds – penguins. Foreign lands – Arctic.

Penguin's Christmas wish ill. by author. Bloomsbury, 2016. ISBN 978-168119155-3 Subj: Behavior – resourcefulness. Birds – penguins. Friendship. Gifts. Holidays – Christmas.

Stormy night ill. by author. Bloomsbury, 2015. ISBN 978-080273780-9 Subj: Animals – bears. Bedtime. Emotions – fear. Family life. Weather – storms.

Tap to play! ill. by author. HarperCollins/Balzer+Bray, 2014. ISBN 978-006228684-0 Subj: Games. Imagination. Participation.

Yorinks, Arthur. *Christmas in July* ill. by Richard Egielski. HarperCollins, 1991. ISBN 978-0-06-020257-6 Subj: Behavior – lost & found possessions. Clothing. Holidays – Christmas. Santa Claus.

Company's coming ill. by David Small. Crown, 1988. ISBN 978-0-517-56751-7 Subj: Behavior – misunderstanding. Humorous stories. Space & space ships.

Company's going ill. by David Small. Hyperion, 2001. ISBN 978-0-7868-0415-3 Subj: Activities – baking, cooking. Aliens. Humorous stories. Planets. Space & space ships. Weddings.

Harry and Lulu ill. by Martin Matje. Hyperion, 1999. ISBN 978-0-7868-2276-8 Subj: Animals – dogs. Emotions – anger. Emotions – love. Foreign lands – France. Imagination. Toys.

Hey, Al ill. by Richard Egielski. Farrar, 1986. ISBN 978-0-374-33060-6 Subj: Animals – dogs. Behavior – running away. Caldecott award books. Dreams. Imagination.

Homework ill. by Richard Egielski. Walker, 2009. ISBN 978-0-8027-9585-4 Subj: Activities – writing. Homework.

The invisible man ill. by Doug Cushman. HarperCollins, 2011. ISBN 978-0-06-156148-1 Subj: Careers – storekeepers. Character traits – being different.

Louis the fish ill. by Richard Egielski. Farrar, 1980. ISBN 978-0-374-34658-4   Subj: Careers – butchers. Fish. Imagination.

The Miami giant ill. by Maurice Sendak. Harper-Collins, 1995. ISBN 978-0-06-205069-4   Subj: Careers – explorers. Foreign lands – Italy. Giants. Jewish culture.

Quack! ill. by Adrienne Yorinks. Abrams, 2003. ISBN 978-0-8109-3548-8   Subj: Animals. Birds – ducks. Quilts. Space & space ships.

What a trip! ill. by Richard Egielski. Scholastic, 2008. ISBN 978-0-545-03611-5   Subj: Humorous stories. Imagination.

Whitefish Will rides again ill. by Mort Drucker. HarperCollins, 1994. ISBN 978-0-06-205037-3   Subj: Careers – sheriffs. U.S. history – frontier & pioneer life.

Yoshitake, Shinsuke. *Still stuck* ill. by author. Abrams, 2017. ISBN 978-141972699-6   Subj: Activities – bathing. Babies, toddlers. Bedtime. Character traits – confidence. Family life – mothers.

You and me ill. by Rachel Fuller. Child's Play, 2010. ISBN 978-1-84643-277-4   Subj: Family life – new sibling. Format, unusual – board books.

Youme. *Mali under the night sky: a Lao story of home* ill. by author. Cinco Puntos, 2010. ISBN 978-1-933693-68-2   Subj: Foreign lands – Laos. War.

Young, Amy. *Belinda and the glass slipper* ill. by author. Penguin, 2006. ISBN 978-0-670-06082-5   Subj: Activities – dancing. Anatomy – feet. Ballet.

Belinda begins ballet ill. by author. Penguin, 2007. ISBN 978-0-670-06244-7   Subj: Activities – dancing. Anatomy – feet. Ballet.

Belinda in Paris ill. by author. Penguin, 2005. ISBN 978-0-670-03693-6   Subj: Activities – dancing. Anatomy – feet. Ballet. Clothing – shoes. Foreign lands – France.

Belinda, the ballerina ill. by author. Viking, 2002. ISBN 978-0-670-03549-6   Subj: Activities – dancing. Anatomy – feet. Ballet.

Don't eat the baby! ill. by author. Viking, 2013. ISBN 978-0-670-78513-1   Subj: Babies, toddlers. Family life – new sibling.

The mud fairy ill. by author. Bloomsbury, 2010. ISBN 978-1-59990-104-6   Subj: Character traits – being different. Fairies. Frogs & toads.

A new friend for Sparkle ill. by author. Farrar, 2017. ISBN 978-037430553-6   Subj: Animals – goats. Emotions – envy, jealousy. Friendship. Mythical creatures – unicorns.

A unicorn named Sparkle ill. by author. Farrar, 2016. ISBN 978-037430185-9   Subj: Animals – goats. Mythical creatures – unicorns. Pets.

Young, Cybèle. *A few bites* ill. by author. Groundwood, 2012. ISBN 978-1-55498-295-0   Subj: Family life – brothers & sisters. Food.

A few blocks ill. by author. Groundwood, 2011. ISBN 978-0-88899-995-5   Subj: Behavior – resourcefulness. Family life – brothers & sisters. Imagination.

Nancy knows ill. by author. Tundra, 2014. ISBN 978-177049482-4   Subj: Animals – elephants. Behavior – forgetfulness. Memories, memory.

Some things I've lost ill. by author. Groundwood, 2015. ISBN 978-155498339-1   Subj: Art. Behavior – lost & found possessions. Behavior – resourcefulness. Concepts – change. Format, unusual – toy & movable books. Imagination.

Ten birds ill. by author. Kids Can, 2011. ISBN 978-1-55453-568-2   Subj: Birds. Counting, numbers. Problem solving.

Ten birds meet a monster ill. by author. Kids Can, 2013. ISBN 978-1-55453-955-0   Subj: Birds. Counting, numbers.

Young, Ed. *Cat and Rat* ill. by author. Henry Holt, 1995. ISBN 978-0-8050-2977-2   Subj: Animals – cats. Animals – rats. Folk & fairy tales. Foreign lands – China. Royalty – emperors. Zodiac.

The cat from Hunger Mountain ill. by author. Philomel, 2016. ISBN 978-039917278-6   Subj: Animals – cats. Behavior – dissatisfaction. Behavior – sharing. Character traits – generosity. Weather – droughts.

Donkey trouble ill. by author. Atheneum, 1995. ISBN 978-0-689-31854-2   Subj: Animals – donkeys. Behavior – misunderstanding. Desert. Folk & fairy tales. Stores.

Hook ill. by author. Roaring Brook, 2009. ISBN 978-1-59643-363-2   Subj: Activities – flying. Birds – chickens, roosters. Birds – eagles. Character traits – being different. Character traits – persistence.

Little Plum ill. by author. Philomel, 1994. ISBN 978-0-399-22683-0   Subj: Character traits – cleverness. Character traits – smallness. Folk & fairy tales. Foreign lands – China.

Lon Po Po: a Red Riding Hood story from China ill. by author. Putnam, 1989. ISBN 978-0-399-21619-0   Subj: Animals – wolves. Caldecott award books. Folk & fairy tales. Foreign lands – China.

The lost horse ill. by author. Silver Whistle, 1998. ISBN 978-0-15-201016-4   Subj: Animals – horses, ponies. Folk & fairy tales. Foreign lands – China. Weather – storms.

Monkey King ill. by author. HarperCollins, 2001. ISBN 978-0-06-027950-9   Subj: Animals – monkeys. Behavior – trickery. Foreign lands – China.

Mouse match ill. by author. Silver Whistle, 1997. ISBN 978-0-15-201453-7 Subj: Animals – mice. Family life – fathers. Foreign lands – China. Format, unusual. Weddings.

My Mei Mei ill. by author. Penguin, 2006. ISBN 978-0-399-24339-4 Subj: Adoption. Emotions – love. Ethnic groups in the U.S. – Chinese Americans. Family life – brothers & sisters. Sibling rivalry.

Night visitors ill. by author. Philomel, 1995. ISBN 978-0-399-22731-8 Subj: Dreams. Folk & fairy tales. Foreign lands – China. Insects – ants.

Seven blind mice ill. by author. Putnam, 1992. ISBN 978-0-399-22261-0 Subj: Animals – elephants. Animals – mice. Caldecott award honor books. Days of the week, months of the year. Disabilities – blindness. Foreign lands – India. Senses – sight.

What about me? ill. by author. Philomel, 2002. ISBN 978-0-399-23624-2 Subj: Cumulative tales. Folk & fairy tales. Foreign lands – Middle East. Religion.

Young, Jessica. *My blue is happy* ill. by Catia Chien. Candlewick, 2013. ISBN 978-0-7636-5125-1 Subj: Concepts – color. Emotions.

Spy Guy: the not-so-secret agent ill. by Charles Santoso. Houghton Mifflin Harcourt, 2015. ISBN 978-054420859-9 Subj: Careers – detectives. Character traits – perseverance. Crime. Family life – fathers.

Young, Judy. *H is for hook: a fishing alphabet* ill. by Gary Palmer. Sleeping Bear, 2008. ISBN 978-1-58536-347-6 Subj: ABC books. Sports – fishing.

Young, Ned. *Zoomer* ill. by author. HarperCollins, 2010. ISBN 978-0-06-170088-0 Subj: Activities – playing. Animals – dogs. Imagination.

Zoomer's out-of-this-world Christmas ill. by author. HarperCollins, 2013. ISBN 978-0-06-199959-8 Subj: Aliens. Animals – dogs. Character traits – generosity. Holidays – Christmas. Space & space ships.

Zoomer's summer snowstorm ill. by author. HarperCollins, 2011. ISBN 978-0-06-170092-7 Subj: Animals – dogs. Imagination. Weather – snow.

Young, Rebecca. *Teacup* ill. by Matt Ottley. Dial, 2016. ISBN 978-073522777-4 Subj: Activities – traveling. Character traits – hopefulness. Emotions – loneliness. Immigrants, immigration. Memories, memory.

Young, Ruth. *Golden Bear* ill. by Rachel Isadora. Viking, 1992. ISBN 978-0-670-82577-6 Subj: Ethnic groups in the U.S. – African Americans. Friendship. Imagination. Rhyming text. Toys – bears.

Who says moo? ill. by Lisa Campbell Ernst. Viking, 1994. ISBN 978-0-670-85162-1 Subj: Animals. Character traits – questioning. Noise, sounds. Riddles & jokes.

Youngquist, Cathrene Valente. *The three Billygoats Gruff and Mean Calypso Joe* (Asbjørnsen, P. C)

Yousafzai, Malala. *Malala's magic pencil* ill. by Kerascoët. Little, Brown, 2017. ISBN 978-031631957-7 Subj: Behavior – seeking better things. Character traits – bravery. Character traits – freedom. Foreign lands – Pakistan. School. Violence, nonviolence.

Yu, Li-Qiong. *A New Year's reunion* ill. by Cheng-Liang Zhu. Candlewick, 2011. ISBN 978-0-7636-5881-6 Subj: Activities – working. Family life – fathers. Foreign lands – China. Holidays – Chinese New Year.

Yuly, Toni. *Cat nap* ill. by author. Feiwel & Friends, 2016. ISBN 978-125005458-6 Subj: Activities – playing. Animals – cats. Sleep.

Early bird ill. by author. Feiwel & Friends, 2014. ISBN 978-125004327-6 Subj: Birds.

The Jelly Bean tree ill. by author. Feiwel & Friends, 2017. ISBN 978-125009406-3 Subj: Animals – giraffes. Birds. Character traits – kindness to animals. Character traits – patience, impatience.

Night owl ill. by author. Feiwel & Friends, 2015. ISBN 978-125005457-9 Subj: Animals – babies. Birds – owls. Noise, sounds.

Thank you, bees ill. by author. Candlewick, 2017. ISBN 978-076369261-2 Subj: Ecology. Nature.

Yum, Hyewon. *Last night* ill. by author. Farrar, 2008. ISBN 978-0-374-34358-3 Subj: Dreams. Emotions. Toys – bears. Wordless.

Mom, it's my first day of kindergarten! ill. by author. Farrar, 2012. ISBN 978-0-374-35004-8 Subj: Behavior – worrying. Family life – mothers. School – first day.

Puddle ill. by author. Farrar, 2016. ISBN 978-037431695-2 Subj: Activities – playing. Behavior – boredom. Family life – mothers. Weather – rain.

There are no scary wolves ill. by author. Farrar, 2010. ISBN 978-0-374-38060-1 Subj: Animals – wolves. Emotions – fear. Imagination.

This is our house ill. by author. Farrar, 2013. ISBN 978-0-374-37487-7 Subj: Family life. Homes, houses.

The twins' blanket ill. by author. Farrar, 2011. ISBN 978-0-374-37972-8 Subj: Behavior – sharing. Character traits – individuality. Family life – sisters. Multiple births – twins.

The twins' little sister ill. by author. Farrar, 2014. ISBN 978-037437973-5 Subj: Babies, toddlers. Family life – sisters. Multiple births – twins.

Zacharias, Ravi. *The merchant and the thief: a folktale from India* ill. by Laure Fournier. Zonderkidz, 2012. ISBN 978-0-310-71636-5 Subj: Folk & fairy tales. Foreign lands – India. Religion.

Zagarenski, Pamela. *Henry and Leo* ill. by author. Houghton Mifflin Harcourt, 2016. ISBN 978-054464811-1 Subj: Behavior – lost & found possessions. Magic. Toys.

The whisper ill. by author. Houghton Mifflin Harcourt, 2015. ISBN 978-054441686-4 Subj: Activities – storytelling. Books, reading. Imagination. Magic.

Zagwÿn, Deborah Turney. *Apple batter* ill. by author. Tricycle, 1999. ISBN 978-1-883672-92-8 Subj: Character traits – persistence. Family life. Food. Gardens, gardening. Sports – baseball. Trees.

The pumpkin blanket ill. by author. Celestial Arts, 1990. ISBN 978-0-89087-637-4 Subj: Behavior – growing up. Foreign lands – Canada. Gardens, gardening. Quilts.

The sea house ill. by author. Tricycle, 2002. ISBN 978-1-58246-030-7 Subj: Boats, ships. Family life – aunts, uncles. Seasons – summer.

Turtle spring ill. by author. Tricycle, 1998. ISBN 978-1-883672-53-9 Subj: Family life – new sibling. Hibernation. Reptiles – turtles, tortoises. Seasons.

The winter gift ill. by author. Tricycle, 2000. ISBN 978-1-883672-93-5 Subj: Family life – grandmothers. Holidays – Christmas. Memories, memory. Moving.

Zahares, Wade, compiler. *Big, bad, and a little bit scary: poems that bite back* ill. by compiler. Viking, 2001. ISBN 978-0-670-03513-7 Subj: Animals. Poetry.

Zalben, Jane Breskin. *Baby Babka* ill. by Victoria Chess. Clarion, 2004. ISBN 978-0-618-23489-9 Subj: Babies, toddlers. Family life. Family life – aunts, uncles. Family life – brothers & sisters.

Baby shower ill. by author. Roaring Brook, 2010. ISBN 978-1-59643-465-3 Subj: Dreams. Parties. Pets.

Beni's first Chanukah ill. by author. Henry Holt, 1988. ISBN 978-0-8050-0479-3 Subj: Animals – bears. Family life. Friendship. Holidays – Hanukkah. Jewish culture.

Beni's first wedding ill. by author. Henry Holt, 1998. ISBN 978-0-8050-4846-9 Subj: Animals – bears. Family life. Jewish culture. Weddings.

Hey, Mama Goose ill. by Emilie Chollat. Penguin, 2005. ISBN 978-0-525-47097-7 Subj: Homes, houses. Nursery rhymes. Rhyming text.

Mousterpiece ill. by author. Roaring Brook, 2012. ISBN 978-1-59643-549-0 Subj: Animals – mice. Art. Careers – artists. Imagination. Museums.

Pearl's eight days of Chanukah ill. by author. Simon & Schuster, 1998. ISBN 978-0-689-81488-4 Subj: Animals – sheep. Holidays – Hanukkah. Jewish culture. Religion.

Pearl's marigolds for grandpa ill. by author. Simon & Schuster, 1997. ISBN 978-0-689-80448-9 Subj: Animals – sheep. Death. Emotions – grief. Family life – grandfathers. Memories, memory.

Pearl's Passover ill. by author. Simon & Schuster, 2002. ISBN 978-0-689-81487-7 Subj: Family life. Holidays – Passover. Jewish culture.

Saturday night at the Beastro by Jane Breskin Zalben and Steven Zalben; ill. by authors. HarperCollins, 2004. ISBN 978-0-06-029228-7 Subj: Food. Monsters. Parties. Rhyming text.

Zalben, Steven. *Saturday night at the Beastro* (Zalben, Jane Breskin)

Zamorano, Ana. *Let's eat!* ill. by Julie Vivas. Scholastic, 1997. ISBN 978-0-590-13444-6 Subj: Family life. Food. Foreign lands – Spain. Health & fitness.

Zane, Alexander. *The wheels on the race car* ill. by James Warhola. Scholastic, 2005. ISBN 978-0-439-59080-8 Subj: Animals. Automobiles. Songs. Sports – racing.

Zapf, Marlena. *Underpants dance* ill. by Lynne Avril. Dial, 2014. ISBN 978-080373539-2 Subj: Activities – dancing. Behavior – resourcefulness. Clothing – underwear. Family life – sisters.

Zappa, Ahmet. *Because I'm your dad* ill. by Dan Santat. Hyperion/Disney, 2013. ISBN 978-1-4231-4774-9 Subj: Family life – fathers.

Zarins, Kim. *The helpful puppy* ill. by Emily Arnold McCully. Holiday House, 2012. ISBN 978-0-8234-2318-7 Subj: Animals – dogs. Farms.

Zecca, Katherine. *A puffin's year* ill. by author. Down East, 2007. ISBN 978-0-89272-742-1 Subj: Birds – puffins.

Zehler, Antonia. *Two fine ladies: tea for three* ill. by author. Random House, 2002. ISBN 978-0-613-84579-3 Subj: Activities – playing. Animals – bears. Family life – sisters. Friendship. Multiple births – twins.

Two fine ladies have a tiff ill. by author. Random House, 2001. ISBN 978-0-375-91104-0 Subj: Activities – playing. Behavior – fighting, arguing. Family life – sisters. Friendship. Multiple births – twins.

Zekauskas, Felicia. *Belly button boy* (Maloney, Peter)

His mother's nose (Maloney, Peter)

One foot two feet: an exceptional counting book (Maloney, Peter)

Zelch, Patti R. *Ready, set . . . wait! what animals do before a hurricane* ill. by Connie McLennan. Sylvan Dell, 2010. ISBN 978-1-60718-072-2 Subj: Animals. Weather – hurricanes.

Zelinsky, Paul O. *The maid and the mouse and the odd-shaped house* ill. by author. Dodd, 1981. ISBN 978-0-396-07938-5 Subj: Animals – mice. Folk & fairy tales. Homes, houses.

The wheels on the bus ill. by adapter. Paper engineering by Roger Smith. Dutton, 1990. ISBN 978-0-525-46506-5 Subj: Buses. Family life – grandmothers. Format, unusual – toy & movable books. Music. Songs.

Zeltser, David. *Ninja baby* ill. by Diane Goode. Chronicle, 2015. ISBN 978-145213542-7 Subj: Babies, toddlers. Family life – new sibling. Sports – martial arts.

Zemach, Harve. *Duffy and the devil: a Cornish tale* ill. by Margot Zemach. Farrar, 1973. ISBN 978-0-374-31887-1 Subj: Caldecott award books. Devil. Folk & fairy tales. Foreign lands – England.

The judge: an untrue tale ill. by Margot Zemach. Farrar, 1969. ISBN 978-0-374-33960-9 Subj: Caldecott award honor books. Careers – judges. Monsters. Rhyming text.

Zemach, Kaethe. *Ms. McCaw learns to draw* ill. by author. Scholastic, 2008. ISBN 978-0-439-82914-4 Subj: Activities – drawing. Careers – teachers. Disabilities. School.

Zemach, Margot. *Eating up Gladys* ill. by Kaethe Zemach. Scholastic, 2005. ISBN 978-0-439-66490-5 Subj: Behavior – bossy. Family life – brothers & sisters.

It could always be worse: a Yiddish folk tale ill. by author. Farrar, 1976. ISBN 978-0-374-33650-9 Subj: Caldecott award honor books. Folk & fairy tales. Humorous stories. Jewish culture. Problem solving.

Some from the moon, some from the sun ill. by author. Farrar, 2001. ISBN 978-0-374-39960-3 Subj: Nursery rhymes. Songs.

The three wishes: an old story ill. by adapter. Farrar, 1986. ISBN 978-0-374-37529-4 Subj: Behavior – wishing. Character traits – foolishness. Folk & fairy tales.

Zeman, Ludmila. *Sindbad: from the tales of the Thousand and one nights* ill. by author. Tundra, 1999. ISBN 978-0-88776-460-8 Subj: Folk & fairy tales. Foreign lands – Arabia. Sailors. Sea & seashore.

Zenz, Aaron. *Chuckling ducklings and baby animal friends* ill. by author. Walker, 2011. ISBN 978-0-8027-2191-4 Subj: Animals – babies.

Monsters go night-night ill. by Aaron Zena. Abrams/Appleseed, 2016. ISBN 978-141971653-9 Subj: Bedtime. Monsters.

Zepeda, Gwendolyn. *Growing up with tamales / Los tamales de Ana* ill. by April Ward. Piñata, 2008. ISBN 978-1-55885-493-2 Subj: Activities – baking, cooking. Ethnic groups in the U.S. – Hispanic Americans. Food. Foreign languages. Holidays – Christmas.

Zhang, Song Nan. *The ballad of Mulan* ill. by author. Pan Asian, 1998. ISBN 978-1-57227-056-5 Subj: Foreign lands – China. Gender roles. War.

Zia, F. *Hot, hot roti for Dada-ji* ill. by Ken Min. Lee & Low, 2011. ISBN 978-1-60060-443-0 Subj: Activities – baking, cooking. Ethnic groups in the U.S. – East Indian Americans. Family life – grandfathers. Food.

Ziarnik, Natalie. *Madeleine's light: a story of Camille Claudel* ill. by Robert Dunn. Boyds Mills, 2012. ISBN 978-1-59078-855-4 Subj: Art. Careers – sculptors. Foreign lands – France. Gender roles.

Ziefert, Harriet. *ABC dentist* ill. by Liz Murphy. Blue Apple, 2008. ISBN 978-1-934706-31-2 Subj: ABC books. Careers – dentists.

Animal music ill. by Donald Saaf. Houghton, 1999. ISBN 978-0-395-95294-8 Subj: Animals. Music. Musical instruments – bands. Rhyming text.

Be fair, share! ill. by Pete Whitehead. Sterling, 2007. ISBN 978-1-4027-3422-9 Subj: Animals. Behavior – sharing.

Beach party! ill. by Simms Taback. Blue Apple, 2005. ISBN 978-1-59354-067-8 Subj: Animals.

Concepts – motion. Format, unusual – board books. Rhyming text. Sea & seashore.

Bigger than Daddy ill. by Elliot Kreloff. Blue Apple, 2006. ISBN 978-1-59354-147-7 Subj: Concepts – size. Ethnic groups in the U.S. – African Americans. Family life – fathers.

The biggest job of all ill. by Lauren Browne. Blue Apple, 2005. ISBN 978-1-59354-100-2 Subj: Careers. Family life – mothers.

Birdhouse for rent ill. by Donald Dreifuss. Houghton, 2001. ISBN 978-0-618-04881-6 Subj: Birds – chickadees. Family life. Homes, houses.

A bunny is funny by Harriet Ziefert and Fred Ehrlich ill. by Todd McKie. Blue Apple, 2008. ISBN 978-1-934706-03-9 Subj: Animals. Poetry.

Bunny's lessons ill. by Barroux. Blue Apple, 2011. ISBN 978-1-60905-028-3 Subj: Animals – rabbits. Behavior. Emotions. Friendship. Toys.

Buzzy had a little lamb ill. by Emily Bolam. Blue Apple, 2005. ISBN 978-1-59354-068-5 Subj: Animals – donkeys. School. Toys.

By the light of the harvest moon ill. by Mark Jones. Blue Apple, 2009. ISBN 978-1-934706-69-5 Subj: Seasons – fall.

Circus parade ill. by Tanya Roitman. Blue Apple, 2005. ISBN 978-1-59354-088-3 Subj: Circus. Parades.

Clara Ann Cookie ill. by Emily Bolam. Houghton, 1999. ISBN 978-0-395-92324-5 Subj: Clothing. Family life – mothers. Rhyming text.

Clara Ann Cookie go to bed! ill. by Emily Bolam. Houghton, 2000. ISBN 978-0-395-97381-3 Subj: Bedtime. Rhyming text. Toys – bears.

Counting chickens ill. by Flensted. Blue Apple, 2010. ISBN 978-1-60905-033-7 Subj: Counting, numbers. Format, unusual.

A dozen ducklings lost and found ill. by Donald Dreifuss. Houghton, 2003. ISBN 978-0-618-14175-3 Subj: Animals – babies. Birds – ducks. Counting, numbers.

Families have together ill. by Deborah Zemke. Blue Apple, 2005. ISBN 978-1-59354-071-5 Subj: Family life. Rhyming text.

First He made the sun ill. by Todd McKie. Putnam, 2000. ISBN 978-0-399-23199-5 Subj: Creation. Religion. Rhyming text.

First Night ill. by S. D. Schindler. Putnam, 1999. ISBN 978-0-399-23120-9 Subj: Holidays – New Year's. Parades. Rhyming text.

From Kalamazoo to Timbuktu! ill. by Tanya Roitman. Blue Apple, 2005. ISBN 978-1-59354-091-3 Subj: Activities – traveling. Rhyming text. Transportation.

Fun Land fun! ill. by Yukiko Kido. Sterling, 2007. ISBN 978-1-4027-3416-8 Subj: Friendship. Parks – amusement.

Grandma, it's for you! ill. by Lauren Browne. Blue Apple, 2006. ISBN 978-1-59354-109-5 Subj: Activities – making things. Clothing – hats. Family life – grandmothers. Gifts.

Grandma's wedding album ill. by Karla Gudeon. Blue Apple, 2011. ISBN 978-1-60905-058-0 Subj: Family life – grandparents. Weddings.

Hanukkah haiku ill. by Karla Gudeon. Blue Apple, 2008. ISBN 978-1-934706-33-6 Subj: Format, unusual. Holidays – Hanukkah. Poetry.

Hats off for the Fourth of July! ill. by Gustaf Miller. Viking, 2000. ISBN 978-0-670-89118-4 Subj: Clothing – hats. Holidays – Fourth of July. Rhyming text.

Home for Navidad ill. by Santiago Cohen. Houghton, 2003. ISBN 978-0-618-34976-0 Subj: Family life – mothers. Foreign lands – Mexico. Foreign languages. Holidays – Christmas.

I swapped my dog ill. by Emily Bolam. Houghton, 1998. ISBN 978-0-395-89159-9 Subj: Animals. Animals – dogs. Cumulative tales. Farms. Rhyming text.

It's time to go to sleep ill. by Barroux. Blue Apple, 2016. ISBN 978-160905601-8 Subj: Bedtime. Format, unusual – board books. Sleep.

It's time to take a nap ill. by Barroux. Blue Apple, 2016. ISBN 978-160905600-1 Subj: Format, unusual – board books. Sleep.

Knick-knack paddywhack ill. by Emily Bolam. Sterling, 2005. ISBN 978-1-4027-2292-9 Subj: Activities – making things. Animals – dogs. Counting, numbers. Cumulative tales. Format, unusual – board books. Songs.

Lights on Broadway: a theatrical tour from A to Z by Harriet Ziefert and Brian Stokes Mitchell ill. by Elliot Kreloff. Blue Apple, 2009. ISBN 978-1-934706-68-8 Subj: ABC books. Theater.

Lucy rescued ill. by Barroux. Blue Apple, 2012. ISBN 978-1-60905-187-7 Subj: Animals – dogs. Toys.

Lunchtime for a purple snake ill. by Todd McKie. Houghton, 2003. ISBN 978-0-618-31133-0 Subj: Activities – painting. Careers – artists. Concepts – color. Family life – grandfathers.

Messy Bessie: where's my homework ill. by Roger De Muth. Blue Apple, 2007. ISBN 978-1-59354-181-1 Subj: Animals – mice. Behavior – messy. Format, unusual. Picture puzzles. Rhyming text. School.

Mighty Max ill. by Elliot Kreloff. Blue Apple, 2008. ISBN 978-1-934706-36-7 Subj: Activities – playing. Imagination. Sea & seashore – beaches.

Mommies are for counting stars ill. by Cynthia Jabar. Putnam, 1999. ISBN 978-0-14-056552-2 Subj: Family life – mothers. Format, unusual – toy & movable books.

Mommy, I want to sleep in your bed! ill. by Elliot Kreloff. Blue Apple, 2005. ISBN 978-1-59354-103-3 Subj: Animals – dogs. Bedtime. Family life – mothers. Sleep.

Mother Goose manners ill. by Pascale Constantin. Blue Apple, 2008. ISBN 978-1-934706-02-2 Subj: Etiquette. Nursery rhymes.

Murphy jumps a hurdle ill. by Emily Bolam. Blue Apple, 2006. ISBN 978-1-59354-174-3 Subj: Animals – dogs. Character traits – perseverance. Sports.

Murphy meets the treadmill ill. by Emily Bolam. Houghton, 2001. ISBN 978-0-618-11357-6 Subj: Health & fitness – exercise. Pets.

My dog thinks I'm a genius ill. by Barroux. Blue Apple, 2011. ISBN 978-1-60905-059-7 Subj: Activities – painting. Animals – dogs.

My forever dress ill. by Liz Murphy. Blue Apple, 2009. ISBN 978-1-934706-45-9 Subj: Activities – sewing. Clothing – dresses. Ecology. Family life – grandmothers.

A new coat for Anna ill. by Anita Lobel. Knopf, 1988. ISBN 978-0-394-97426-2 Subj: Clothing – coats. Family life. War.

No kiss for Grandpa! ill. by Emilie Boon. Orchard, 2001. ISBN 978-0-531-30328-3 Subj: Animals – cats. Family life – grandfathers.

Ode to Humpty Dumpty ill. by Seymour Chwast. Houghton, 2001. ISBN 978-0-618-05047-5 Subj: Character traits – helpfulness. Emotions – grief. Nursery rhymes.

One red apple ill. by Karla Gudeon. Blue Apple, 2009. ISBN 978-1-934706-67-1 Subj: Nature. Trees.

A polar bear can swim: what animals can and cannot do ill. by Emily Bolam. Viking, 1998. ISBN 978-0-670-88056-0 Subj: Activities. Animals. Circular tales.

The princess and the peas and carrots ill. by Travis Foster. Blue Apple, 2012. ISBN 978-1-60905-250-8 Subj: Behavior – misbehavior. Character traits – perfectionism. Family life.

Pumpkin Pie ill. by Donald Dreifuss. Houghton, 2000. ISBN 978-0-618-04883-0 Subj: Animals – goats. Fairs, festivals. Farms.

Pushkin meets the bundle ill. by Donald Saaf. Atheneum, 1998. ISBN 978-0-689-81413-6 Subj: Animals – dogs. Babies, toddlers. Family life.

Pushkin minds the bundle ill. by Donald Saaf. Atheneum, 2000. ISBN 978-0-689-83216-1 Subj: Activities – vacationing. Animals – dogs. Babies, toddlers. Family life.

Robin, where are you? ill. by Noah Woods. Blue Apple, 2012. ISBN 978-1-60905-192-1 Subj: Activities. Birds. Character traits – patience, impatience. Family life – grandfathers. Format, unusual – toy & movable books.

Rockheads ill. by Todd McKie. Houghton, 2004. ISBN 978-0-618-34574-8 Subj: Activities. Counting, numbers. Rhyming text.

Someday we'll have very good manners ill. by Chris L. Demarest. Putnam, 2001. ISBN 978-0-399-23558-0 Subj: Etiquette.

Squarehead ill. by Todd McKie. Houghton, 2001. ISBN 978-0-618-08378-7 Subj: Concepts – shape. Dreams. Self-concept.

Surprise! ill. by Richard Brown. Sterling, 2007. ISBN 978-1-4027-3410-6 Subj: Character traits – generosity. Family life – mothers.

Talk, baby! ill. by Emily Bolam. Henry Holt, 1999. ISBN 978-0-8050-6144-4 Subj: Activities – talking. Babies, toddlers. Family life – new sibling. Format, unusual – toy & movable books.

That's what grandmas are for ill. by Amanda Haley. Blue Apple, 2006. ISBN 978-1-59354-098-2 Subj: Family life – grandmothers.

That's what grandpas are for ill. by Deborah Zemke. Blue Apple, 2006. ISBN 978-1-59354-097-5 Subj: Family life – grandfathers.

There was a little girl who had a little curl ill. by Elliot Kreloff. Blue Apple, 2006. ISBN 978-1-59354-161-3 Subj: Behavior – misbehavior. Character traits – appearance. Hair.

39 uses for a friend ill. by Rebecca Doughty. Putnam, 2001. ISBN 978-0-399-23616-7 Subj: Friendship.

Toes have wiggles, kids have giggles ill. by Rebecca Doughty. Putnam, 2002. ISBN 978-0-399-23617-4 Subj: Activities. Rhyming text.

Train song ill. by Donald Saaf. Orchard, 2000. ISBN 978-0-531-30204-0 Subj: Rhyming text. Trains.

Two little witches ill. by Simms Taback. Candlewick, 1996. ISBN 978-1-56402-621-7 Subj: Counting, numbers. Holidays – Halloween. Witches.

Waiting for baby ill. by Emily Bolam. Henry Holt, 1998. ISBN 978-0-8050-5929-8 Subj: Babies, toddlers. Family life – new sibling.

What do ducks dream? ill. by Donald Saaf. Putnam, 2001. ISBN 978-0-399-23358-6 Subj: Animals. Bedtime. Dreams. Farms. Rhyming text. Sleep.

What is part this, part that? ill. by Tom Slaughter. Blue Apple, 2013. ISBN 978-1-60905-309-3 Subj: Rhyming text. Riddles & jokes.

When I first came to this land ill. by Simms Taback. Putnam, 1998. ISBN 978-0-399-23044-8 Subj: Cumulative tales. Folk & fairy tales. Immigrants, immigration. Poverty. Songs.

Wiggle like an octopus ill. by Simms Taback. Blue Apple, 2011. ISBN 978-1-60905-072-6 Subj: Animals. Format, unusual – board books. Participation. Rhyming text. Sea & seashore.

William and the dragon ill. by Richard Brown. Blue Apple, 2005. ISBN 978-1-59354-089-0 Subj: Dragons. Rhyming text.

You and me: we're opposites ill. by Ethan Long. Blue Apple, 2009. ISBN 978-1-934706-48-0 Subj: Animals. Concepts – opposites. Zoos.

You can't buy a dinosaur with a dime ill. by Amanda Haley. Blue Apple, 2003. ISBN 978-1-929766-81-9 Subj: Counting, numbers. Money. Problem solving.

You can't taste a pickle with your ear ill. by Amanda Haley. Blue Apple, 2002. ISBN 978-1-929766-68-0 Subj: Senses.

Zimmerman, Andrea Griffing. *Fire engine man* ill. by David Clemesha. Henry Holt, 2007. ISBN 978-0-8050-7905-0 Subj: Careers – firefighters. Family life – brothers & sisters.

My dog Toby by Andrea Griffing Zimmerman and David Clemesha ill. by True Kelley. Harcourt, 2000. ISBN 978-0-15-202014-9 Subj: Animals – dogs. Pets.

Train man ill. by David Clemesha. Henry Holt, 2012. ISBN 978-0-8050-7991-3 Subj: Family life – brothers. Imagination. Trains.

Trashy town by Andrea Griffing Zimmerman and David Clemesha ill. by Dan Yaccarino. HarperCollins, 1999. ISBN 978-0-06-027140-4 Subj: Careers – sanitation workers. Cities, towns.

Zimmett, Debbie. *Eddie enough* ill. by Charlotte Murray Fremaux. Woodbine, 2001. ISBN 978-1-890627-25-6 Subj: Behavior. Disabilities – ADD. School.

Zion, Gene. *Harry, the dirty dog* ill. by Margaret Bloy Graham. HarperCollins, 1956. Subj: Activities – bathing. Animals – dogs. Behavior – running away.

No roses for Harry ill. by Margaret Bloy Graham. HarperCollins, 1958. ISBN 978-0-06-026891-6 Subj: Animals – dogs. Clothing.

Zoboli, Giovanna. *The big book of slumber* ill. by Simona Mulazzani. Eerdmans, 2014. ISBN 978-080285439-1 Subj: Animals. Bedtime. Lullabies. Rhyming text.

I wish I had . . . ill. by Simona Mulazzani. Eerdmans, 2013. ISBN 978-0-8028-5415-5 Subj: Anatomy. Animals. Behavior – wishing. Imagination.

Zoehfeld, Kathleen Weidner. *Apples, apples* ill. by Christopher Santoro. HarperCollins, 2004. ISBN 978-0-06-053787-6 Subj: Animals – bears. Food. Format, unusual – board books. Seasons – fall. Trees.

Did dinosaurs have feathers? ill. by Lucia Washburn. HarperCollins, 2004. ISBN 978-0-06-029027-6 Subj: Birds. Dinosaurs.

Dinosaur tracks ill. by Lucia Washburn. HarperCollins, 2007. ISBN 978-0-06-029024-5 Subj: Dinosaurs. Fossils.

Dinosaurs big and small ill. by Lucia Washburn. HarperCollins, 2002. ISBN 978-0-06-027936-3 Subj: Concepts – size. Dinosaurs.

How mountains are made ill. by James Graham Hale. HarperCollins, 1995. ISBN 978-0-06-024510-8 Subj: Earth. Mountains. Science.

Secrets of the garden: food chains and the food web in our backyard ill. by Priscilla Lamont. Random House, 2012. ISBN 978-0-517-70990-0 Subj: Ecology. Food. Gardens, gardening. Science.

Secrets of the seasons: orbiting the sun in our backyard ill. by Priscilla Lamont. Knopf, 2014. ISBN 978-051770994-8 Subj: Seasons. Sun.

What lives in a shell? ill. by Helen Davie. HarperCollins, 1994. ISBN 978-0-06-022999-3 Subj: Animals. Science. Sea & seashore.

What's alive? ill. by Nadine Bernard Westcott. HarperCollins, 1995. ISBN 978-0-06-023444-7 Subj: Animals. Plants. Science.

Where did dinosaurs come from? ill. by Lucia Washburn. HarperCollins, 2011. ISBN 978-0-06-029022-1 Subj: Dinosaurs.

Zolkower, Edie Stoltz. *Too many cooks* ill. by Shauna Mooney Kawasaki. Kar-Ben, 2000. ISBN 978-1-58013-063-9 Subj: Activities – baking, cooking. Holidays – Passover. Jewish culture.

Zolotow, Charlotte. *The beautiful Christmas tree* ill. by Yan Nacimbene. Houghton, 1999. ISBN 978-0-395-91365-9 Subj: Holidays – Christmas. Trees.

The bunny who found Easter ill. by Helen Craig. Houghton, 1998. ISBN 978-0-395-86265-0 Subj: Animals – rabbits. Emotions – loneliness. Holidays – Easter.

Do you know what I'll do? ill. by Javaka Steptoe. HarperCollins, 2000. ISBN 978-0-06-027880-9 Subj: Babies, toddlers. Behavior – growing up. Emotions – love. Ethnic groups in the U.S. – African Americans. Family life.

A father like that ill. by LeUyen Pham. HarperCollins, 2007. ISBN 978-0-06-027864-9 Subj: Ethnic groups in the U.S. – African Americans. Family life – fathers. Family life – single-parent families.

The hating book ill. by Ben Shecter. HarperCollins, 1969. ISBN 978-0-06-443197-2 Subj: Behavior – gossip, rumors. Emotions – hate. Friendship.

I know a lady ill. by James Stevenson. Greenwillow, 1984. ISBN 978-0-688-03837-3 Subj: Character traits – kindness. Old age.

I like to be little ill. by Erik Blegvad. HarperCollins, 1987. ISBN 978-0-690-04674-8 Subj: Behavior – growing up. Family life – mothers.

If it weren't for you ill. by G. Brian Karas. HarperCollins, 2006. ISBN 978-0-06-027875-5 Subj: Family life. Sibling rivalry.

The moon was the best ill. by Tana Hoban. Greenwillow, 1993. ISBN 978-0-688-09941-1 Subj: Moon.

Mr. Rabbit and the lovely present ill. by Maurice Sendak. HarperCollins, 1962. ISBN 978-0-06-026946-3 Subj: Animals – rabbits. Birthdays. Caldecott award honor books. Concepts – color. Family life – mothers. Holidays – Easter.

My friend John ill. by Amanda Harvey. Doubleday, 2000. ISBN 978-0-385-32651-3 Subj: Friendship.

My grandson Lew ill. by William Pène Du Bois. HarperCollins, 1974. ISBN 978-0-06-026961-6 Subj: Death. Emotions – grief. Family life. Family life – grandfathers.

The old dog ill. by James Ransome. HarperCollins, 1995. ISBN 978-0-06-024412-5 Subj: Animals – dogs. Death. Emotions – grief. Ethnic groups in the U.S. – African Americans. Pets.

The poodle who barked at the wind ill. by Valerie Coursen. Henry Holt, 2002. ISBN 978-0-8050-6306-6 Subj: Animals – dogs. Noise, sounds. Pets.

The quarreling book ill. by Arnold Lobel. HarperCollins, 1963. ISBN 978-0-06-026976-0 Subj: Behavior – fighting, arguing. Cumulative tales. Emotions – anger. Weather – rain.

Say it! ill. by James Stevenson. Greenwillow, 1980. Subj: Activities – walking. Emotions – love. Family life – mothers. Nature. Seasons – fall.

Sleepy book ill. by Ilse Plume. Rev. ed. HarperCollins, 1988. ISBN 978-0-06-026968-5 Subj: Animals. Bedtime. Sleep.

Sleepy book ill. by Stefano Vitale. HarperCollins, 2001. ISBN 978-0-06-027873-1 Subj: Animals. Bedtime. Sleep.

Some things go together ill. by Ashley Wolff. Newly illustrated ed. HarperCollins, 1999. ISBN 978-0-694-01197-1 Subj: Emotions – love. Family life. Poetry.

Something is going to happen ill. by Catherine Stock. HarperCollins, 1988. ISBN 978-0-06-027029-2 Subj: Morning. Weather – snow.

The storm book ill. by Margaret Bloy Graham. HarperCollins, 1952. ISBN 978-0-06-027026-1 Subj: Caldecott award honor books. Emotions – fear. Weather. Weather – rain. Weather – rainbows.

Summer is . . . ill. by Ruth Lercher Bornstein. Crowell, 1983. ISBN 978-0-690-04304-4 Subj: Rhyming text. Seasons – summer.

This quiet lady ill. by Anita Lobel. Greenwillow, 1992. ISBN 978-0-688-09306-8 Subj: Family life – mothers.

A tiger called Thomas ill. by Diana Cain Bluthenthal. Hyperion, 2003. ISBN 978-0-7868-0517-4 Subj: Character traits – shyness. Emotions – loneliness. Holidays – Halloween.

A tiger called Thomas ill. by Catherine Stock. Lothrop, 1988. ISBN 978-0-688-06697-0 Subj: Character traits – shyness. Emotions – loneliness. Holidays – Halloween.

When the wind stops ill. by Stefano Vitale. HarperCollins, 1995. ISBN 978-0-06-026972-2 Subj: Bedtime. Nature. Night. Weather – wind.

William's doll ill. by William Pène Du Bois. HarperCollins, 1972. ISBN 978-0-06-027048-3 Subj: Family life. Family life – grandmothers. Toys – dolls.

Zommer, Yuval. *The big blue thing on the hill* ill. by author. Candlewick/Templar, 2015. ISBN 978-076367403-8 Subj: Animals. Character traits – cooperation.

One hundred bones ill. by author. Candlewick/Templar, 2016. ISBN 978-076368183-8 Subj: Animals – dogs. Dinosaurs. Fossils. Pets.

One hundred sausages ill. by author. Candlewick/Templar, 2017. ISBN 978-076369297-1 Subj: Animals – dogs. Crime. Food.

Zonta, Pat. *Jessica's x-ray* ill. by Clive Dobson. Firefly, 2002. ISBN 978-1-55297-578-7 Subj: Hospitals. Illness.

Zucker, Bonnie. *Something very sad happened: a toddler's guide to understanding death* ill. by Kim Fleming. Magination, 2016. ISBN 978-143382266-7 Subj: Death. Emotions – grief. Emotions – sadness.

Zucker, Jonny. *Apples and honey* ill. by Jan Barger Cohen. Barron's, 2002. ISBN 978-0-7641-2265-1 Subj: Holidays – Rosh Hashanah. Jewish culture.

Four special questions ill. by Jan Barger Cohen. Barron's, 2003. ISBN 978-0-7641-2267-5 Subj: Holidays – Passover. Jewish culture.

It's party time ill. by Jan Barger Cohen. Barron's, 2003. ISBN 978-0-7641-2268-2 Subj: Holidays – Purim. Jewish culture.

Zuckerberg, Randi. *Dot* ill. by Joe Berger. HarperCollins, 2013. ISBN 978-0-06-228751-9 Subj: Activities. Computers.

Zuckerman, Andrew. *Creature abc* photos by author. Chronicle, 2009. ISBN 978-0-8118-6978-2 Subj: ABC books. Animals.

Zuckerman, Linda. *I will hold you 'til you sleep* ill. by Jon J Muth. Scholastic, 2006. ISBN 978-0-439-43420-1 Subj: Emotions – love. Family life.

Zuffi, Stefano. *Art 123: count from 1 to 12 with great works of art.* Abrams, 2011. ISBN 978-1-4197-0100-9 Subj: Art. Counting, numbers. Rhyming text.

Zuill, Andrea. *Dance is for everyone* ill. by author. Sterling, 2017. ISBN 978-145492114-1 Subj: Activities – dancing. Ballet. Humorous stories. Reptiles – alligators, crocodiles.

Wolf camp ill. by author. Random House, 2016. ISBN 978-055350912-0 Subj: Animals – dogs. Animals – wolves. Camps, camping.

Zullo, Germano. *Line 135* ill. by Albertine. Chronicle, 2013. ISBN 978-1-4521-1934-2 Subj: Activities – traveling. Cities, towns. Country. Trains.

Little bird ill. by Albertine. Enchanted Lion, 2012. ISBN 978-1-59270-118-6 Subj: Activities – flying. Birds.

Zuniga, Elisabeth. *A friend for Bo* ill. by author. Random House, 2016. ISBN 978-055350998-4 Subj: Animals – rabbits. Eggs. Emotions – loneliness. Friendship.

Zuppardi, Sam. *Jack's worry* ill. by author. Candlewick, 2016. ISBN 978-076367845-6 Subj: Behavior – worrying. Musical instruments – trumpets.

Things to do with Dad ill. by author. Candlewick, 2017. ISBN 978-076368146-3 Subj: Character traits – responsibility. Family life – fathers. Imagination.

Zweibel, Alan. *Our tree named Steve* ill. by David Catrow. Penguin, 2005. ISBN 978-0-399-23722-5 Subj: Family life. Letters, cards. Trees.

Zwillich, Julie. *Phoebe sounds it out* ill. by Denise Holmes. OwlKids, 2017. ISBN 978-177147164-0 Subj: Activities – writing. Names. School.

Title Index

Titles appear in alphabetical sequence with the author's name in parentheses, followed by the page number of the full listing in the Bibliographic Guide. For identical title listings, the illustrator's name is given to further identify the version. In the case of variant titles, both the original and differing titles are listed.

A

B

C

D

E

F

H

I

J

K

M

N

O

P

Pumpkin circle (Levenson, George), 910
Pumpkin countdown (Holub, Joan), 832
Pumpkin day (Wallace, Nancy Elizabeth), 1201
The pumpkin fair (Bunting, Eve), 643
Pumpkin fiesta (Yacowitz, Caryn), 1238
Pumpkin heads (Minor, Wendell), 979
Pumpkin hill (Spurr, Elizabeth), 1147
Pumpkin Jack (Hubbell, Will), 840
The pumpkin man (Moffatt, Judith), 982
Pumpkin moon (Preston, Tim), 1052
Pumpkin moonshine (Tudor, Tasha), 1184
Pumpkin Pie (Ziefert, Harriet), 1249
Pumpkin pumpkin (Titherington, Jeanne), 1179
Pumpkin shivaree (Agran, Rick), 558
Pumpkin smile (Chetkowski, Emily), 665
Pumpkin time! (Deak, Erzsi), 703
Pumpkin town! (McKy, Katie), 947
Pumpkin trouble (Thomas, Jan), 1173
Pumpkinhead (Kimmel, Eric A.), 881
Pumpkinhead (Rohmann, Eric), 1079
Pumpkins (Robbins, Ken), 1073
Pumpkins from the sky? (Van Nutt, Julia), 1192
Punctuation celebration (Bruno, Elsa Knight), 640
Punctuation takes a vacation (Pulver, Robin), 1056
Punk Farm (Krosoczka, Jarrett J.), 894
Punk Farm on tour (Krosoczka, Jarrett J.), 894
Punk skunks (Shaskan, Trisha Speed), 1122
Punk wig (Ries, Lori), 1071
Punxsutawney Phyllis (Hill, Susanna Leonard), 823
Pup and bear (Banks, Kate), 590
A pup just for me . . . A boy just for me (Seeber, Dorothea P.), 1116
The pup speaks up (Hays, Anna Jane), 812
Pup the sea otter (London, Jonathan), 925
Puppies and piggies (Rylant, Cynthia), 1094
Puppies! puppies! puppies! (Meyers, Susan), 974
Puppy finds a friend / Cachorrito encuentra un amigo (Bruzzone, Catherine), 640
Puppy finds a friend / Le petit chien se trouve un ami (Bruzzone, Catherine), 640
A puppy for Annie (Lewis, Kim), 913
Puppy pool party! (Casteel, Seth), 660
Puppy, puppy, puppy (Sternberg, Julie), 1153
The puppy who wanted a boy (Thayer, Jane), 1172
Purim play (Schotter, Roni), 1110
The Purim surprise (Simpson, Lesley), 1132
The purple balloon (Raschka, Chris), 1061
The purple coat (Hest, Amy), 820
Purple, green and yellow (Munsch, Robert N.), 995
The purple hat (Pearson, Tracey Campbell), 1031
The purple kangaroo (Black, Michael Ian), 615
Purple Little Bird (Foley, Greg), 752
Purplicious (Kann, Victoria), 870
Purrfect! (Nash, Sarah), 1002
Push button (Aliki), 563
Push! dig! scoop! (Greene, Rhonda Gowler), 789
Pushkin meets the bundle (Ziefert, Harriet), 1249
Pushkin minds the bundle (Ziefert, Harriet), 1249
Puss and boots (Imai, Ayano), 846
Puss in boots, ill. by Marcia Brown (Perrault, Charles), 1036
Puss in boots, ill. by Lorinda Bryan Cauley (Perrault, Charles), 1036

Puss in boots, ill. by Paul Galdone (Perrault, Charles), 1036
Puss in boots, ill. by Steve Light (Perrault, Charles), 1036
Puss in boots, ill. by Giuliano Lunelli (Perrault, Charles), 1036
Puss in boots, ill. by Fred Marcellino (Perrault, Charles), 1036
Puss in boots, ill. by Bernhard Oberdieck (Perrault, Charles), 1036
Puss in boots, ill. by Jerry Pinkney (Perrault, Charles), 1036
Puss in boots, ill. by Alain Vaës (Perrault, Charles), 1036
Puss in boots: the adventures of that most enterprising feline (Pullman, Philip), 1055
Puss in cowboy boots (Huling, Jan), 842
Pussycat, pussycat and other rhymes (Mother Goose), 993
Pussycats everywhere (McGraw, Sheila), 944
Put it on the list! (Darbyshire, Kristen), 699
Putting the monkeys to bed (Choldenko, Gennifer), 668
Putting the world to sleep (Thomas, Shelley Moore), 1174
Puzzled by pink (Hardy, Sarah Frances), 803
Python (Cheng, Christopher), 665

Q

Quack! (Yorinks, Arthur), 1244
Quack, Daisy, quack! (Simmons, Jane), 1131
Quackers (Wong, Liz), 1233
Quacky baseball (Abrahams, Peter), 552
Quacky Ducky's Easter egg (Wilhelm, Hans), 1222
Quacky Ducky's Easter fun (Wilhelm, Hans), 1222
The Quangle Wangle's hat (Lear, Edward), 903
The quarreling book (Zolotow, Charlotte), 1251
Queen Dog (Heos, Bridget), 818
Queen of Christmas (Engelbreit, Mary), 736
The queen of Eene (Prelutsky, Jack), 1052
The queen of France (Wadham, Tim), 1199
Queen of Halloween (Engelbreit, Mary), 736
The queen of style (Buehner, Caralyn), 641
Queen of the class (Engelbreit, Mary), 736
Queen of the diamond (McCully, Emily Arnold), 938
Queen of the falls (Van Allsburg, Chris), 1190
Queen of the scene (Latifah, Queen), 901
Queen of the track (Lang, Heather), 899
Queen of the world (Yezerski, Thomas), 1240
The queen, the bear and the bumblebee (Petty, Dini), 1038
Queen Victoria's bathing machine (Whelan, Gloria), 1218
Queenie Farmer had fifteen daughters (Campbell, Ann-Jeanette), 651
The queen's feet (Ellis, Sarah), 732
The queen's handbag (Antony, Steve), 574
The Queen's hat (Antony, Steve), 574
Quentin Fenton Herter three (MacDonald, Amy), 939
Quest (Becker, Aaron), 602

R

S

U

V

W

Illustrator Index

Illustrators appear alphabetically in boldface followed by their titles. Names in parentheses are authors of the titles when different from the illustrator. Page numbers refer to the full listing in the Bibliographic Guide.

B

C

D

E

G

H

M

N

W

About the Author

REBECCA L. THOMAS has a PhD in Early and Middle Childhood Education from the Ohio State University. She retired in 2011 after 35 years as an elementary school librarian in the Shaker Heights (Ohio) City Schools. She has also been a university teacher and author in the field of children's literature.